WHO WAS WHO

VOLUME IV

1941–1950

WHO'S WHO

An annual biographical dictionary
first published in 1849

WHO WAS WHO

WHO WAS WHO

1941–1950

A COMPANION TO

WHO'S WHO

CONTAINING THE BIOGRAPHIES
OF THOSE WHO DIED DURING
THE DECADE 1941–1950

A & C BLACK
LONDON

FIRST PUBLISHED 1952
SECOND EDITION 1958
THIRD EDITION 1964
FOURTH EDITION 1967
FIFTH EDITION 1980
REPRINTED 1985, 2007
SIXTH EDITION, 2012

BY A&C BLACK PUBLISHERS LTD
50 BEDFORD SQUARE, LONDON WC1B 3DP

COPYRIGHT © 1952, 1958, 1964, 1967, 1980, 1985, 2007, 2012 A&C BLACK PUBLISHERS LTD

ISBN 978-1-408-15496-0

Printed in the UK by
MPG Books Ltd, Bodmin

PREFACE

This, the fourth volume of biographies removed from *Who's Who* on account of death, contains the entries of those who died between 1941 and 1950. Those whose deaths were not notified until after this volume went to press are listed as Addenda at the beginning of the biographical section.

The entries are as they last appeared in *Who's Who*, with the date of death added and in some cases further information, such as posthumous publications. It has not always been possible to ascertain the exact date of death, and the editors will welcome such information for inclusion in the next edition of this volume.

CONTENTS

ABBREVIATIONS USED IN THIS BOOK

Some of the designatory letters in this list are used merely for economy of space
and do not necessarily imply any professional or other qualification.

A

AA	Anti-aircraft; Automobile Association; Architectural Association; Augustinians of the Assumption
AAA	Amateur Athletic Association
AA & QMG	Assistant Adjutant and Quartermaster General
AAAS	American Association for the Advancement of Science
AAC	Amateur Athletic Club
AACCA	Associate, Association of Certified and Corporate Accountants
AAF	Auxiliary Air Force (*now see* RAuxAF)
AAG	Assistant Adjutant-General
AAMC	Australian Army Medical Corps
AB	Bachelor of Arts (US); able-bodied seaman
ABCFM	American Board of Commissioners for Foreign Missions
Aber.	Aberdeen
Abp	Archbishop
AC	*Ante Christum* (before Christ)
ACA	Associate, Institute of Chartered Accountants
Acad.	Academy
ACAS	Assistant Chief of the Air Staff
ACF	Army Cadet Force
ACG	Assistant Chaplain-General
ACGI	Associate, City and Guilds of London Institute
ACIS	Associate, Chartered Institute of Secretaries
ACP	Associate, College of Preceptors
ACS	Additional Curates Society
ACT	Australian Capital Territory
AD	*Anno Domini* (in the year of the Lord)
ADC	Aide-de-camp
AD Corps	Army Dental Corps
Ad eund.	*Ad eundem gradum* (admitted to the same degree)
ADFW	Assistant Director of Fortifications and Works
ADGB	Air Defence of Great Britain
ADGMS	Assistant Director-General of Medical Services
ADH	Assistant Director of Hygiene
ADJAG	Assistant Deputy Judge Advocate General
Adjt	Adjutant
Adm.	Admiral
ADMS	Assistant Director of Medical Services
ADOS	Assistant Director of Ordnance Services
ADS & T	Assistant Director of Supplies and Transport
Adv.	Advocate
ADVS	Assistant Director of Veterinary Services
Advt	Advertisement
AEA	Air Efficiency Award
AEAF	Allied Expeditionary Air Force
AEC	Army Educational Corps
AEF	American Expeditionary Forces
AEM	Air Efficiency Medal
Æt. or Ætat.	*Ætatis* (aged)
AEU	Amalgamated Engineering Union
AFC	Air Force Cross
AFHQ	Allied Force Headquarters
AFIA	Associate, Federal Institute of Accountants (Aust.)
AFIAeS	Associate Fellow, Institute of Aeronautical Sciences (US)
AFRAeS	Associate Fellow, Royal Aeronautical Society
AFV	Armoured Fighting Vehicles
AG	Attorney-General; Adjutant-General
AGH	Australian General Hospital
AGI	Associate, Institute of Certificated Grocers
AHQ	Army Headquarters
AHWC	Associate, Heriot-Watt College, Edinburgh
AIA	Associate, Institute of Actuaries; American Institute of Architects
AIAE	Associate, Institute of Automobile Engineers
AIBD	Associate, Institute of British Decorators
AIBP	Associate, Institute of British Photographers
AICA	Associate Member, Commonwealth Institute of Accountants
AICE	Associate, Institution of Civil Engineers
AIEE	Associate, Institution of Electrical Engineers
AIF	Australian Imperial Forces
AIG	Adjutant-Inspector-General
AIIA	Associate, Insurance Institute of America
AIL	Associate, Institute of Linguists
AILocoE	Associate, Institute of Locomotive Engineers
AIMarE	Associate, Institute of Marine Engineers
AInstPI	Associate, Institute of Patentees
AISA	Associate, Incorporated Secretaries' Association
AIStructE	Associate, Institution of Structural Engineers
AJAG	Assistant Judge Advocate General
AKC	Associate, King's College London
ALA	Associate, Library Association
Ala	Alabama (US)
ALAA	Associate, London Association of Certified Accountants (*now see* AACCA)
ALCM	Associate, London College of Music
ALFSEA	Allied Land Forces South-East Asia
ALI	Argyll Light Infantry
ALS	Associate, Linnaean Society
Alta	Alberta
AM	Master of Arts (US); Alpes Maritimes; Albert Medal
Amb.	Ambulance
AMF	Australian Military Forces
AMGOT	Allied Military Government of Occupied Territory
AMIAE	Associated Member, Institute of Automobile Engineers
AMICE	Associate Member, Institution of Civil Engineers
AMIEA	Associate Member, Institute of Engineers, Australia
AMIEE	Associate Member, Institution of Electrical Engineers
AMIE (Ind.)	Associate Member, Institution of Engineers, India
AMIMechE	Associate Member, Institution of Mechanical Engineers
AMIMinE	Associate Member, Institution of Mining Engineers

AMINA	Associate Member, Institution of Naval Architects	**AssocMCT**	Associateship of Manchester College of Technology
AMInstBE	Associate Member, Institution of British Engineers	**AssocMIAeE**	Associate Member, Institution of Aeronautical Engineers
AMInstCE	Associate Member, Institution of Civil Engineers	**AssocSc**	Associate in Science
AMInstT	Associate Member, Institute of Transport	**Asst**	Assistant
AMIStructE	Associate Member, Institution of Structural Engineers	**Astr.**	Astronomy
		ASW	Association of Scientific Workers
AMS	Assistant Military Secretary; Army Medical Service	**ATA**	Air Transport Auxiliary
		ATC	Air Training Corps
AMTPI	Associate, Town Planning Institute	**ATCL**	Associate, Trinity College of Music, London
ANA	Associate National Academician (US)		
Anat.	Anatomy; Anatomical	**Ath**	Athabasca (Canada)
ANECInst	Associate, NE Coast Institution of Engineers and Shipbuilders	**ATS**	Auxiliary Territorial Service
		Av.	Avenue
Anon.	Anonymously	**AVD**	Army Veterinary Department
Anzac	Australian and New Zealand Army Corps	**Ave**	Avenue
AOA	Air Officer in charge of Administration		
AOC	Air Officer Commanding		
AOC-in-C	Air Officer Commanding-in-Chief		

B

AOD	Army Ordnance Department	**b**	born; brother
AOER	Army Officers Emergency Reserve	**BA**	Bachelor of Arts
APD	Army Pay Department	**BAFO**	British Air Forces of Occupation
APM	Assistant Provost Marshal	**BAI**	Bachelor of Engineering (*Baccalarius in Arte Ingeniaria*)
APS	Aborigines Protection Society		
AQMG	Assistant Quartermaster-General	**BAO**	Bachelor of Obstetrics
ARA	Associate, Royal Academy	**BAOR**	British Army of the Rhine
ARAeS	Associate, Royal Aeronautical Society	**Barr.**	Barrister
ARAM	Associate, Royal Academy of Music	**Bart or Bt**	Baronet
ARBA	Associate, Royal Society of British Artists	**BAS**	Bachelor in Agricultural Science
ARBC	Associate, Royal British Colonial Society of Artists	**BASc**	Bachelor of Applied Science
		Batt.	Battery
ARBS	Associate, Royal Society of British Sculptors	**BB & CI Rly**	Bombay, Baroda and Central India Railway
ARC	Architects' Registration Council		
ARCA	Associate, Royal Cambrian Academy; Associate, Royal Canadian Academy	**BBC**	British Broadcasting Corporation
		BC	Before Christ; British Columbia
ARCA (Lond.)	Associate, Royal College of Art	**BCE**	Bachelor of Civil Engineering
ARCE	Academical Rank of Civil Engineers	**BCh or BChir**	Bachelor of Surgery
ARCM	Associate, Royal College of Music	**BCL**	Bachelor of Civil Law
ARCO	Associate, Royal College of Organists	**BCMS**	Bible Churchmen's Missionary Society
ARCS	Associate, Royal College of Science	**BCOF**	British Commonwealth Occupation Force
ARE	Associate, Royal Society of Painter-Etchers	**BCom**	Bachelor of Commerce
ARIBA	Associate, Royal Institute of British Architects	**BCS**	Bengal Civil Service
		BD	Bachelor of Divinity
ARIC	Associate, Royal Institute of Chemistry	**Bd**	Board
ARICS	Professional Associate, Royal Institution of Chartered Surveyors	**BDA**	British Dental Association
		Bde	Brigade
Ark	Arkansas (US)	**BE**	Bachelor of Engineering; British Element
ARMS	Associate, Royal Society of Miniature Painters	**BEA**	British East Africa; British European Airways
ARP	Air Raid Precautions		
ARPS	Associate, Royal Photographic Society	**Beds**	Bedfordshire
ARRC	Associate, Royal Red Cross	**BEF**	British Expeditionary Force
ARSA	Associate, Royal Scottish Academy	**BEM**	British Empire Medal
ARSM	Associate, Royal School of Mines	**Berks**	Berkshire
ARTC	Associate, Royal Technical College (Glasgow)	**BGS**	Brigadier General Staff
		BL	Bachelor of Law
ARVIA	Associate, Royal Victorian Institute of Architects	**BLA**	British Liberation Army
		BLE	Brotherhood of Locomotive Engineers
ARWA	Associate, Royal West of England Academy	**BLitt**	Bachelor of Letters
ARWS	Associate, Royal Society of Painters in Water-Colours	**BMA**	British Medical Association
		BMJ	British Medical Journal
AS	Anglo-Saxon	**Bn**	Battalion
ASAA	Associate, Society of Incorporated Accountants and Auditors	**BNAF**	British North Africa Force
		BNC	Brasenose College
ASAM	Associate, Society of Art Masters	**BNOC**	British National Opera Company
ASC	Army Service Corps	**BOAC**	British Overseas Airways Corporation
ASE	Amalgamated Society of Engineers	**Bom. CS**	Bombay Civil Service
AssocINA	Associate, Institution of Naval Architects	**Bom. SC**	Bombay Staff Corps
		Bot.	Botany; Botanical
AssocISI	Associate, Iron and Steel Institute	**BOU**	British Ornithologists' Union

Bp	Bishop
BR	British Railways
BRA	Brigadier Royal Artillery
BRCS	British Red Cross Society
Brig.	Brigadier
BS	Bachelor of Surgery; Bachelor of Science
BSA	Bachelor of Scientific Agriculture; Birmingham Small Arms
BSAA	British South American Airways
BSAP	British South Africa Police
BSC	Bengal Staff Corps
BSc	Bachelor of Science
BSc (Dent.)	Bachelor of Science in Dentistry
BSF	British Salonica Force
BT	Bachelor of Teaching
Bt	Baronet; Brevet
BTA	British Troops in Austria
BTC	British Transport Commission
BTE	British Troops in Egypt
BTh	Bachelor of Theology
BVM	Blessed Virgin Mary
Bucks	Buckinghamshire
BWI	British West Indies
BWM	British War Medal

C

C	Conservative; 100
c	Child; cousin
CA	Central America; County Alderman; Chartered Accountant (Scotland)
Cal.	Calcutta
Calif	California (US)
Camb.	Cambridge
Cambs	Cambridgeshire
CAMC	Canadian Army Medical Corps
CAMW	Central Association for Mental Welfare
Cantab	*Cantabrigiensis* (of Cambridge)
Cantuar	*Cantuariensis* (of Canterbury)
Capt.	Captain
CAS	Chief of the Air Staff
Cav.	Cavalry
CB	Companion, Order of the Bath
CBE	Commander, Order of the British Empire
CBSA	Clay Bird Shooting Association
CC	County Council; Cricket Club; Cycling Club; County Court
CCC	Corpus Christi College; Central Criminal Court
CCG	Control Commission Germany
CCRA	Commander Corps Royal Artillery
CCS	Casualty Clearing Station; Ceylon Civil Service
CD	Canada Forces Decoration
Cdre	Commodore
CE	Civil Engineer
CEF	Canadian Expeditionary Force
CEMA	Council for the Encouragement of Music and Arts
CEMS	Church of England Men's Society
CETS	Church of England Temperance Society
CF	Chaplain to the Forces
CFA	Canadian Field Artillery
CFS	Central Flying School
CGS	Chief of General Staff
CH	Companion of Honour
Chanc.	Chancellor; Chancery
Chap.	Chaplain
Chap. St J	Chaplain, Order of St John of Jerusalem
ChB	Bachelor of Surgery

Ch Ch	Christ Church
Ch Coll.	Christ's College
ChM	Master of Surgery
Chm.	Chairman
CI	Imperial Order of the Crown of India; Channel Islands
CIAD	Central Institute of Art and Design
CID	Criminal Investigation Department
CIE	Companion, Order of the Indian Empire
CIGS	Chief of the Imperial General Staff
CIMarE	Companion, Institute of Marine Engineers
CIMechE	Companion, Institution of Mechanical Engineers
C-in-C	Commander-in-Chief
Cir.	Circus
CIV	City Imperial Volunteers
CJ	Chief Justice
CJM	Congregation of Jesus and Mary (Eudist Fathers)
CL	Commander, Order of Leopold
Cl.	Class
CM	Congregation of the Mission (Vincentians); Master in Surgery; Certificated Master; Canadian Militia
CMB	Central Midwives' Board
CMF	Commonwealth Military Forces; Central Mediterranean Force
CMG	Companion, Order of St Michael and St George
CMO	Chief Medical Officer
CMS	Church Missionary Society
CNR	Canadian National Railways
CO	Commanding Officer; Colonial Office
Co.	County; Company
C of E	Church of England
Co. L or Coal. L	Coalition Liberal
Col.	Colony; Colonel
Coll.	College; Collegiate
Colo	Colorado (US)
Col.-Sergt	Colour-Sergeant
Com.	Communist
Comdg	Commanding
Comdr	Commander
Comdt	Commandant
Commn	Commission
CompIEE	Companion, Institution of Electrical Engineers
Comr	Commissioner
Comy-Gen.	Commissary-General
Conn	Connecticut (US)
Co-op.	Co-operative
Corp.	Corporation; Corporal
Corr. Mem. or Fell.	Corresponding Member or Fellow
COS	Charity Organisation Society
COTC	Canadian Officers' Training Corps
Co. U or Coal. U	Coalition Unionist
CP	Central Provinces; Cape Province
CPAS	Church Pastoral Aid Society
CPR	Canadian Pacific Railway
CPRE	Council for the Preservation of Rural England
CPSU	Communist Party of the Soviet Union
CR	Community of the Resurrection
Cr.	Crown
cr	created or creation
CRA	Commander, Royal Artillery
CRASC	Commander, Royal Army Service Corps
CRE	Commander, Royal Engineers
Cres.	Crescent
CRO	Chief Recruiting Officer
CS	Civil Service

CSC	Conspicuous Service Cross
CSI	Companion, Order of the Star of India
CSIR	Commonwealth Council for Scientific and Industrial Research
CSO	Chief Signal Officer
CSP	Chartered Society of Physiotherapists
CSSR	Congregation of the Most Holy Redeemer (Redemptorist Order)
CStJ	Commander, Order of St John of Jerusalem
CTC	Cyclists' Touring Club
CU	Cambridge University
CUAC	Cambridge University Athletic Club
CUAFC	Cambridge University Association Football Club
CUBC	Cambridge University Boat Club
CUCC	Cambridge University Cricket Club
CURFC	Cambridge University Rugby Football Club
CVO	Commander, Royal Victorian Order

D

D	Duke
d	Died; daughter
DA	Diploma in Anaesthesia
DA (Edin.)	Diploma of Edinburgh College of Art
DAA & QMG	Deputy Assistant Adjutant and Quartermaster-General
DAAG	Deputy Assistant Adjutant-General
DA & QMG	Deputy Adjutant and Quartermaster-General
DACG	Deputy Assistant Chaplain-General
DAD	Deputy Assistant Director
DADMS	Deputy Assistant Director of Medical Services
DADOS	Deputy Assistant Director of Ordnance Services
DADQ	Deputy Assistant Director of Quartering
DADST	Deputy Assistant Director of Supplies and Transport
DAG	Deputy Adjutant-General
DAQMG	Deputy Assistant Quartermaster-General
DASc	Doctor in Agricultural Sciences
DBE	Dame Commander, Order of the British Empire
DC	District of Columbia (US)
DCAS	Deputy Chief of the Air Staff
DCG	Deputy Chaplain-General
DCGS	Deputy Chief of the General Staff (on the Field)
DCh	Doctor of Surgery
DCH	Diploma in Child Health
DCIGS	Deputy Chief of the Imperial General Staff
DCL	Doctor of Civil Law
DCLI	Duke of Cornwall's Light Infantry
DCM	Distinguished Conduct Medal
DCnL	Doctor of Canon Law
DCS or DSc	Doctor of Commercial Sciences
DCT	Doctor of Christian Theology
DCVO	Dame Commander, Royal Victorian Order
DD	Doctor of Divinity
DDL	Deputy Director of Labour
DDMI	Deputy Director of Military Intelligence
DDMS	Deputy Director of Medical Services
DDNI	Deputy Director of Naval Intelligence
DDPS	Deputy Director of Personal Services (Naval)
DDRA	Deputy Director Royal Artillery
DDS	Doctor of Dental Surgery; Director of Dental Services
DDSc	Doctor of Dental Science (Melbourne)

DDSD	Deputy Director Staff Duties
DDST	Deputy Director of Supplies and Transport
Decd	Deceased
deg.	Degree
Del	Delaware (US)
Deleg.	Delegate
DEng	Doctor of Engineering
DEOVR	Duke of Edinburgh's Own Volunteer Rifles
Dep.	Deputy
Dept	Department
D ès L	Docteur ès lettres
DFC	Distinguished Flying Cross
DG	Dragoon Guards
DGAMS	Director-General Army Medical Services
DGMS	Director-General of Medical Services
DGMW	Director-General of Military Works
DGP	Director-General of Personnel
DGStJ	Dame of Grace, Order of St John of Jerusalem
DHL	Doctor of Hebrew Literature
DHQ	District Headquarters
DIC	Diploma of the Imperial College
DIG	Deputy Inspector-General
DIH	Diploma in Industrial Health
Dio.	Diocese; Diocesan
DipEd	Diploma in Education
Div.	Division; Divorced
DJAG	Deputy Judge Advocate General
DJStJ	Dame of Justice, Order of St John of Jerusalem
DL	Deputy Lieutenant
DLC	Diploma Loughborough College
DLI	Durham Light Infantry
DLitt or DLit	Doctor of Literature; Doctor of Letters
DLO	Diploma in Laryngology and Otology
DM	Doctor of Medicine
DMet	Doctor of Metallurgy
DMI	Director of Military Intelligence
DMR	Diploma in Medical Radiology
DMRE	Diploma in Medical Radiology and Electrology
DMS	Director of Medical Services
DMus	Doctor of Music
DMT	Director of Military Training
DN	Diploma in Nursing
DNB	Dictionary of National Biography
DNE	Director of Naval Equipment
DNI	Director of Naval Intelligence
DO	Diploma in Ophthalmology
DOC	District Officer Commanding
Doc. Eng.	Doctor of Engineering
DOL	Doctor of Oriental Learning
Dom.	Dominus (Lord)
DOS	Director of Ordnance Services
Dow.	Dowager
DPA	Diploma in Public Administration; Discharged Prisoners' Aid
DPH	Diploma in Public Health
DPh or DPhil	Doctor of Philosophy
DPM	Diploma in Psychological Medicine
DPP	Director of Public Prosecutions
DPS	Director of Personal Services (Naval); Director of Postal Services
DQMG	Deputy Quartermaster-General
Dr	Doctor
DRAC	Director Royal Armoured Corps
Dr (Œc. Pol.)	Doctor (Œconomiae Politicae)
DSC	Distinguished Service Cross
DSc	Doctor of Science
DScA	Docteur en sciences agricoles
DSD	Director Staff Duties

DSIR	Department of Scientific and Industrial Research
DSM	Distinguished Service Medal
DSO	Companion of the Distinguished Service Order
DSP	Director of Selection of Personnel
dsp	*decessit sine prole* (died without issue)
DSS	Doctor of Sacred Scripture
DST	Director of Supplies and Transport
DStJ	Dame, Order of St John of Jerusalem
DTD	Dekoratie voor Trouwe Dienst (Decoration for Devoted Service)
DTH	Diploma in Tropical Hygiene
DTh or DTheol	Doctor of Theology
DThPT	Diploma in Theory and Practice of Teaching (Durham University)
DTM	Diploma in Tropical Medicine
DTM & H	Diploma in Tropical Medicine and Hygiene
Dunelm	*Dunelmensis* (of Durham)
DUP	Docteur de l'Universite de Paris
DVH	Diploma in Veterinary Hygiene
DVSc	Doctor of Veterinary Science
DVSM	Diploma in Veterinary State Medicine

E

E	East; Earl
e	eldest
EAP	East Africa Protectorate
Ebor	(*Eboracensis*) of York
EC	East Central (postal district)
ECA	Economic Co-operation Administration
Eccl	Ecclesiastical
ECU	English Church Union
Ed.	Editor
ED	Efficiency Decoration
Edin.	Edinburgh
Edn	Edition
Educ.	Educated
Educn	Education
Edw.	Edward
EE	Early English
EEF	Egyptian Expeditionary Force
eh	ehrenhalber (honorary)
EI	East Indian; East Indies
EICS	East India Company's Service
E-in-C	Engineer-in-Chief
EM	Edward Medal
EMS	Emergency Medical Service
Ency. Brit.	Encyclopaedia Britannica
Eng.	England; engineering
Engr	Engineer
ENSA	Entertainments National Service Association
ER	Eastern Region (BR); East Riding
er	elder
esp.	especially
Ext	Extinct; external

F

FA	Football Association
FAAS	Fellow, American Academy of Arts and Sciences
FACCA	Fellow, Association of Certified and Corporate Accountants
FACD	Fellow, American College of Dentistry
FACI	Fellow, Australian Chemical Institute
FACP	Fellow, American College of Physicians

FACS	Fellow, American College of Surgeons
FAGS	Fellow, American Geographical Society
Fahr.	Fahrenheit
FAI	Fellow, Auctioneers' Institute
FANY	First Aid Nursing Yeomanry
FAO	Food and Agricultural Organisation
FAPHA	Fellow, American Public Health Association
Far ELF	Far East Land Forces
Fasc.	Fascicule
FBA	Fellow, British Academy
FBHI	Fellow, British Horological Institute
FBI	Federation of British Industries
FBOA	Fellow, British Optical Association
FBOU	Fellow, British Ornithologists Union
FBritIRE	Fellow, British Institution of Radio Engineers
FBPsS	Fellow, British Psychological Society
FBS	Fellow, Building Societies Institute
FBSI	Fellow, Boot and Shoe Industry
FBSM	Fellow, Birmingham School of Music
FC	Football Club
FCA	Fellow, Institute of Chartered Accountants
FCGI	Fellow, City and Guilds of London Institute
FCH	Fellow, Coopers Hill College
FChS	Fellow, Society of Chiropodists
FCIC	Fellow, Canadian Institute of Chemistry
FCII	Fellow, Chartered Insurance Institute
FCIPA	Fellow, Chartered Institute of Patent Agents
FCIS	Fellow, Institute of Chartered Secretaries and Administrators (*formerly* Chartered Institute of Secretaries)
FCP	Fellow, College of Preceptors
FCPS	Fellow, College of Physicians and Surgeons
FCS	Fellow, Chemical Society
FCST	Fellow, College of Speech Therapists
FCT	Federal Capital Territory
FCTB	Fellow, College of Teachers of the Blind
FCWA	Fellow, Institute of Cost and Works Accountants
FDS	Fellow in Dental Surgery
FDSRCS	Fellow in Dental Surgery, Royal College of Surgeons of England
FEIS	Fellow, Educational Institute of Scotland
FES	Fellow, Entomological Society; Fellow, Ethnological Society
FF	Field Force
FFA	Fellow, Faculty of Actuaries (in Scotland)
FFARCS	Fellow, Faculty of Anaesthetists, Royal College of Surgeons
FFAS	Fellow, Faculty of Architects and Surveyors, London
FFF	French Fighting Forces
FFHom	Fellow, Faculty of Homeopathy
FFI	French Forces of the Interior
FFPS	Fellow, Royal Faculty of Physicians and Surgeons, Glasgow
FFR	Fellow, Faculty of Radiologists
FFSc	Fellow, Faculty of Sciences
FGA	Fellow, Gemmological Association
FGI	Fellow, Institute of Certificated Grocers
FGS	Fellow, Geological Society
FGSM	Fellow, Guildhall School of Music
FHAS	Fellow, Highland and Agricultural Society of Scotland
FIA	Fellow, Institute of Actuaries
FIAA & S	Fellow, Incorporated Association of Architects and Surveyors
FIAeS	Fellow, Institute of Aeronautical Sciences
FIArb	Fellow, Institute of Arbitrators
FIAS	Fellow, Institute of Aeronautical Sciences (America)

FIB	Fellow, Institute of Bankers
FIBD	Fellow, Institute of British Decorators
FIBP	Fellow, Institute of British Photographers
FIC	Fellow, Institute of Chemistry (now see FRIC)
FICI	Fellow, International Colonial Institute
FICS	Fellow, Institute of Chartered Shipbrokers
FID	Fellow, Institute of Directors
FIES	Fellow, Illuminating Engineering Society
FIGCM	Fellow, Incorporated Guild of Church Musicians
FIIA	Fellow, Institute of Industrial Administration
FIInst	Fellow, Imperial Institute
FIL	Fellow, Institute of Linguists
FILA	Fellow, Institute of Landscape Architects
FIM	Fellow, Institution of Metallurgists
FIMI	Fellow, Institute of the Motor Industry
FIMT	Fellow, Institute of Motor Trade
FIN	Fellow, Institute of Navigation
FInstF	Fellow, Institute of Fuel
FInstMet	Fellow, Institute of Metals
FInstP	Fellow, Institute of Physics
FInstPet	Fellow, Institute of Petroleum
FInstPI	Fellow, Institute of Patentees (Incorporated)
FInstW	Fellow, Institute of Welding
FIO	Fellow, Institute of Ophthalmic Opticians
FIOB	Fellow, Institute of Bankers
FIRA(Ind.)	Fellow, Institute of Railway Auditors and Accountants (India)
FIRE	Fellow, Institution of Radio Engineers
FIRI	Fellow, Institution of the Rubber Industry
FISA	Fellow, Incorporated Secretaries' Association
FISE	Fellow, Institution of Sanitary Engineers
FIWM	Fellow, Institution of Works Managers
FJI	Fellow, Institute of Journalists
FKC	Fellow, King's College (London)
FLA	Fellow, Library Association
Fla	Florida (US)
FLAA	Fellow, London Association of Certified Accountants (now see FACCA)
FLAS	Fellow, Land Agents Society
FLCM	Fellow, London College of Music
FLHS	Fellow, London Historical Society
FLS	Fellow, Linnæan Society
Flt	Flight
FM	Field-Marshal
FMS	Federated Malay States
FNI	Fellow, National Institute of Sciences in India
FO	Foreign Office; Field Officer
FOIC	Flag Officer in charge
FPhS	Fellow, Philosophical Society of England
FPhysS	Fellow, Physical Society
FRACP	Fellow, Royal Australasian College of Physicians
FRACS	Fellow, Royal Australasian College of Surgeons
FRAeS	Fellow, Royal Aeronautical Society
FRAgS	Fellow, Royal Agricultural Societies (ie of England, Scotland and Wales)
FRAHS	Fellow, Royal Australian Historical Society
FRAI	Fellow, Royal Anthropological Institute
FRAIA	Fellow, Royal Australian Institute of Architects
FRAM	Fellow, Royal Academy of Music
FRAS	Fellow, Royal Astronomical Society; Fellow, Royal Asiatic Society
FRASB	Fellow, Royal Asiatic Society of Bengal
FRBS	Fellow, Royal Society of British Sculptors; Fellow, Royal Botanic Society

FRCM	Fellow, Royal College of Music
FRCO	Fellow, Royal College of Organists
FRCO (CHM)	Fellow, Royal College of Organists with Diploma in Choir Training
FRCOG	Fellow, Royal College of Obstetricians and Gynaecologists
FRCP	Fellow, Royal College of Physicians, London
FRCPE or FRCPEd	Fellow, Royal College of Physicians, Edinburgh
FRCPI	Fellow, Royal College of Physicians of Ireland
FRCS	Fellow, Royal College of Surgeons of England
FRCSE	Fellow, Royal College of Surgeons of Edinburgh
FRCSI	Fellow, Royal College of Surgeons in Ireland
FRCVS	Fellow, Royal College of Veterinary Surgeons
FREconS	Fellow, Royal Economic Society
FRES	Fellow, Royal Empire Society; Fellow, Royal Entomological Society of London
FRFPS(G)	Fellow, Royal Faculty of Physicians and Surgeons (of Glasgow)
FRGS	Fellow, Royal Geographical Society
FRHistS	Fellow, Royal Historical Society
FRHortS or FRHS	Fellow, Royal Horticultural Society
FRI	Fellow, Royal Institution
FRIAS	Fellow, Royal Incorporation of Architects of Scotland
FRIBA	Fellow, Royal Institute of British Architects
FRIC	Fellow, Royal Institute of Chemistry (formerly FIC)
FRICS	Fellow, Royal Institution of Chartered Surveyors
FRIPHH	Fellow, Royal Institute of Public Health and Hygiene
FRMCM	Fellow, Royal Manchester College of Music
FRMS	Fellow, Royal Microscopical Society
FRMetS	Fellow, Royal Meteorological Society
FRNS	Fellow, Royal Numismatic Society
FRNSA	Fellow, Royal School Naval Architecture
FRPS	Fellow, Royal Photographic Society
FRPSL	Fellow, Royal Philatelic Society, London
FRS	Fellow, Royal Society
FRSA	Fellow, Royal Society of Arts
FRSAI	Fellow, Royal Society of Antiquaries of Ireland
FRSanI	Fellow, Royal Sanitary Institute
FRSC	Fellow, Royal Society of Canada
FRSE	Fellow, Royal Society of Edinburgh
FRSGS	Fellow, Royal Scottish Geographical Society
FRSL	Fellow, Royal Society of Literature
FRSM or FRSocMed	Fellow, Royal Society of Medicine
FRSNZ	Fellow, Royal Society of New Zealand
FRSSA	Fellow, Royal Society of South Africa
FRST	Fellow, Royal Society of Teachers
FRSTM & H	Fellow, Royal Society of Tropical Medicine and Hygiene
FRVIA	Fellow, Royal Victorian Institute of Architects
FRZSScot	Fellow, Royal Zoological Society of Scotland
fs	Graduate, Royal Air Force Staff College
FSA	Fellow, Society of Antiquaries
FSAA	Fellow, Society of Incorporated Accountants and Auditors
FSAM	Fellow, Society of Art Masters
FSArc	Fellow, Society of Architects
FSAScot	Fellow, Society of Antiquaries of Scotland

FSASM	Fellow, South Australian School of Mines
FSE	Fellow, Society of Engineers
FSG	Fellow, Society of Genealogists
FSGT	Fellow, Society of Glass Technology
FSI	Fellow, Royal Institution of Chartered Surveyors (*now see* FRICS)
FSIA	Fellow, Society of Industrial Artists
FSMA	Fellow, Incorporated Sales Managers' Association
FSMC	Fellow, Spectacle-Makers' Company
FSS	Fellow, Royal Statistical Society
FTCD	Fellow, Trinity College, Dublin
FTCL	Fellow, Trinity College of Music, London
FTI	Fellow, Textile Institute
FZS	Fellow, Zoological Society

G

Ga	Georgia (US)
GBA	Governing Bodies Association
GBE	Knight or Dame Grand Cross, Order of the British Empire
GC	George Cross
GCB	Knight Grand Cross, Order of the Bath
GCH	Knight Grand Cross, Order of Hanover
GCIE	Knight Grand Commander, Order of the Indian Empire
GCMG	Knight Grand Cross, Order of St Michael and St George
GCSI	Knight Grand Commander, Order of the Star of India
GCStJ	Bailiff or Dame Grand Cross, Order of St John of Jerusalem
GCVO	Knight Grand Cross, Royal Victorian Order
Gdns	Gardens
Gen.	General
Ges.	Gesellschaft
GFS	Girls' Friendly Society
g g s	Great Grandson
GHQ	General Headquarters
Gib.	Gibraltar
GIMechE	Graduate Institution of Mechanical Engineers
GL	Grand Lodge
Glas.	Glasgow
Glos	Gloucestershire
GM	George Medal
GMIE	Grand Master, Order of the Indian Empire
GMMG	Grand Master, Order of St Michael and St George
GMSI	Grand Master, Order of the Star of India
GOC	General Officer Commanding
GOC-in-C	General Officer Commanding-in-Chief
Gov.	Governor
Govt	Government
GP	General Practitioner
GPDST	Girls' Public Day School Trust
GPO	General Post Office
GQG	Grand Quartier Général (French GHQ)
Gr.	Greek
Gram. Sch.	Grammar School
GS	General Staff
g s	Grandson
GSO	General Staff Officer
GWR	Great Western Railway (*see* BR)

H

HAA	Heavy Anti-Aircraft
HAC	Honourable Artillery Company
Hants	Hampshire
Harv.	Harvard
HBM	His Britannic Majesty (Majesty's)
hc	*honoris causa* (honorary)
HCF	Honorary Chaplain to the Forces
HDD	Higher Dental Diploma
HE	His Excellency
HEH	His Exalted Highness
HEIC	Honourable East India Company
HEICS	Honourable East India Company's Service
Heir-pres.	Heir-presumptive
Herts	Hertfordshire
HFARA	Honorary Foreign Associate, Royal Academy
HFRA	Honorary Foreign Member, Royal Academy
HG	Home Guard
HH	His (or Her) Highness; His Holiness
HIH	His (or Her) Imperial Highness
HIM	His (or Her) Imperial Majesty
HLI	Highland Light Infantry
HM	His (or Her) Majesty, or Majesty's
HMAS	His Majesty's Australian Ship
HMC	Headmasters' Conference
HMCS	His Majesty's Canadian Ship
HMHS	His Majesty's Hospital Ship
HMI	His Majesty's Inspector
HMS	His Majesty's Ship
Hon.	Honourable; Honorary; Honour
How.	Howitzer
h-p	Half-pay
HP	House Physician
HQ	Headquarters
(HR)	Home Ruler
HRCA	Honorary Royal Cambrian Academician
HRH	His (or Her) Royal Highness
HRHA	Honorary Member, Royal Hibernian Society
HRI	Honorary Member, Royal Institute of Painters in Water Colours
HROI	Honorary Member, Royal Institute of Oil Painters
HRSA	Honorary Member, Royal Scottish Academy
HRSW	Honorary Member, Royal Scottish Water Colour Society
HS	House Surgeon
HSH	His (or Her) Serene Highness
Hum.	Humanity (Latin)
Hunts	Huntingdonshire
Hy	Heavy

I

I	Island; Ireland
Ia	Iowa (US)
IA	Indian Army
IAE	Institute of Automobile Engineers
IAHM	Incorporated Association of Headmasters
IAOC	Indian Army Ordnance Corps
IARO	Indian Army Reserve of Officers
Ib. or Ibid.	*Ibidem* (in the same place)
i/c	In charge
ICAA	Invalid Children's Aid Association
ICAO	International Civil Aviation Organization
ICE	Institution of Civil Engineers

Icel.	Icelandic
IChemE	Institution of Chemical Engineers
ICI	Imperial Chemical Industries
ICRC	International Committee of the Red Cross
ICS	Indian Civil Service
Id	Idaho (US)
idc	Completed a course at, or served for a year on the Staff of, the Imperial Defence College
IEE	Institution of Electrical Engineers
IES	Indian Educational Service
IFS	Irish Free State
IG	Instructor in Gunnery
IHS	*Iesus Hominum Salvator* (Jesus the Saviour of Mankind)
Ill	Illinois (US)
ILO	International Labour Office
ILP	Independent Labour Party
IM	Individual Merit
IME	Institute of Medical Ethics
IME	Institute of Mining Engineers
IMEA	Incorporated Municipal Electrical Association
IMechE	Institution of Mechanical Engineers
IMM	Institution of Mining and Metallurgy
IMMTS	Indian Mercantile Marine Trading Ship
Imp.	Imperial
IMS	Indian Medical Service
IN	Indian Navy
INA	Institution of Naval Architects
Inc.	Incorporated
Incog.	*Incognito* (in secret)
Ind	Independent; Indiana (US)
Inf.	Infantry
Insp.	Inspector
Inst.	Institute; Institution
Instn	Institution
InstCE	Institution of Civil Engineers
InstMM	Institution of Mining and Metallurgy
Internat.	International
I of M	Isle of Man
IOGT	International Order of Good Templars
IOM	Isle of Man; Indian Order of Merit
IOOF	Independent Order of Odd-fellows
IOP	Institute of Painters in Oil Colours
IoW	Isle of Wight
IPS	Indian Police Service
IRA	Irish Republican Army
IRO	International Refugee Organisation
Is	Island(s)
IS	International Society of Sculptors, Painters and Gravers
ISC	Indian Staff Corps
ISE	Indian Service of Engineers
ISM	Incorporated Society of Musicians
ISO	Imperial Service Order
IT	Indian Territory (US)
Ital. or It.	Italian
ITO	International Trade Organisation
IW	Isle of Wight
IY	Imperial Yeomanry
IZ	I Zingari

J

JA	Judge Advocate
JAG	Judge Advocate General
Jas	James
JCD	*Juris Canonici Doctor* (Doctor of Canon Law)
JCR	Junior Common Room

JCS	Journal of the Chemical Society
JD	Doctor of Jurisprudence
Jes.	Jesus
Jl	Journal
Joh. or Jno.	John
JP	Justice of the Peace
Jr	Junior
jsc	Qualified at a Junior Staff Course, or the equivalent, 1942-1946
jssc	Joint Services Staff Course
JUD	*Juris Utriusque Doctor* (Doctor of Both Laws (Canon and Civil))
Jun.	Junior
Jun. Opt.	Junior Optime

K

Kans	Kansas (US)
KAR	King's African Rifles
KBE	Knight Commander, Order of the British Empire
KC	King's Counsel
KCB	Knight Commander, Order of the Bath
KCC	Commander, Order of Crown, Belgian and Congo Free State
KCH	King's College Hospital; Knight Commander, Order of Hanover
KCIE	Knight Commander, Order of the Indian Empire
KCL	King's College, London
KCMG	Knight Commander, Order of St Michael and St George
KCSG	Knight Commander, Order of St Gregory the Great
KCSI	Knight Commander, Order of the Star of India
KCSS	Knight Commander, Order of St Silvester
KCVO	Knight Commander, Royal Victorian Order
KDG	King's Dragoon Guards
Keb.	Keble College, Oxford
KEH	King Edward's Horse
KEO	King Edward's Own
KG	Knight, Order of the Garter
KGStJ	Knight of Grace, Order of St John of Jerusalem
KH	Knight, Order of Hanover
KHC	Honorary Chaplain to the King
KHDS	Honorary Dental Surgeon to the King
KHNS	Honorary Nursing Sister to the King
KHP	Honorary Physician to the King
KHS	Honorary Surgeon to the King; Knight, Order of the Holy Sepulchre
K-I-H	Kaisar-i-Hind
KJStJ	Knight of Justice, Order of St John of Jerusalem
KM	Knight of Malta
KORR	King's Own Royal Regiment
KOSB	King's Own Scottish Borderers
KOYLI	King's Own Yorkshire Light Infantry
KP	Knight, Order of St Patrick
KRRC	King's Royal Rifle Corps
KS	King's Scholar
KSG	Knight, Order of St Gregory the Great
KSLI	King's Shropshire Light Infantry
KStJ	Knight, Most Venerable Order of the Hospital of St John of Jerusalem
KT	Knight, Order of the Thistle
Kt or Knt	Knight
Ky	Kentucky (US)

L

(L)	Liberal
LA	Literate in Arts; Liverpool Academy
La	Louisiana (US)
LAA	Light Anti-Aircraft
(Lab)	Labour
LAC	London Athletic Club
L-Corp. or Lance-Corp.	Lance-Corporal
Lancs	Lancashire
LC	Cross of Leo
LCC	London County Council
LCh	Licentiate in Surgery
LCJ	Lord Chief Justice
LCP	Licentiate, College of Preceptors
LD or LDiv	Licentiate in Divinity
Ldr	Leader
LDS	Licentiate in Dental Surgery
LDV	Local Defence Volunteers
L ès L	Licencié ès Lettres
LH	Light Horse
LHD	(*Literarum Humaniorum Doctor*) Doctor of Literature
LI	Light Infantry; Long Island
Lic. Med.	Licentiate in Medicine
Lieut	Lieutenant
Lincs	Lincolnshire
Lit.	Literature; Literary
LitD	Doctor of Literature; Doctor of Letters
Lit.Hum.	*Literae Humaniores* (Classics)
LittD	Doctor of Literature; Doctor of Letters
Liv.	Liverpool
LJ	Lord Justice
LL	Lord-Lieutenant
LLA	Lady Literate in Arts
LLB	Bachelor of Laws
LLCM	Licentiate, London College of Music
LLD	Doctor of Laws
LLL	Licentiate in Laws
LLM	Master of Laws
LM	Licentiate in Midwifery
LMBB	Lady Margaret Boat Club
LMCC	Licentiate, Medical Council of Canada
LMS	London, Midland and Scottish Railway (*see* BR); London Missionary Society
LMSSA	Licentiate in Medicine and Surgery, Society of Apothecaries
LNat	Liberal National
LNER	London and North Eastern Railway (*see* BR)
L of C	Lines of Communication
Lond.	London
LPh	Licentiate in Philosophy
LPTB	London Passenger Transport Board
LRAM	Licentiate, Royal Academy of Music
LRCP	Licentiate, Royal College of Physicians
LRCPE	Licentiate, Royal College of Physicians, Edinburgh
LRCPI	Licentiate, Royal College of Physicians of Ireland
LRCS	Licentiate, Royal College of Surgeons
LRCSE	Licentiate, Royal College of Surgeons, Edinburgh
LRCSI	Licentiate, Royal College of Surgeons in Ireland
LRFPS	Licentiate, Royal Faculty of Physicians and Surgeons
LRIBA	Licentiate, Royal Institute of British Architects
LSA	Licentiate, Society of Apothecaries
LSE	London School of Economics
Lt	Light (*e.g.* Light Infantry)
Lt or Lieut	Lieutenant
LT	Licentiate in Teaching
LTCL	Licentiate, Trinity College of Music, London
Lt-Col	Lieutenant-Colonel
Lt-Gen.	Lieutenant-General
LTh	Licentiate in Theology
(LU)	Liberal Unionist
LUOTC	London University Officers' Training Corps
LXX	Septuagint

M

M	Marquess; Member; Monsieur
m	married
MA	Master of Arts
MAAF	Mediterranean Allied Air Forces
MAAS	Member of the American Academy of Arts and Sciences
MAEE	Marine Aircraft Experimental Establishment
Mag.	Magnetism or Magazine
Magd.	Magdalen; Magdalene
MAI	Master of Engineering (*Magister in Arte Ingeniaria*)
Maj.-Gen.	Major-General
MAmSocCE	Member, American Society of Civil Engineers
MAmSocME	Member, American Society of Mechanical Engineers
Man	Manitoba (Canada)
MAO	Master of Obstetric Art
MAOU	Member, American Ornithologists' Union
MAP	Ministry of Aircraft Production
MArch	Master of Architecture
Marq.	Marquess
MASME	Member, American Society of Mechanical Engineers
Mass	Massachusetts (US)
Math.	Mathematics; Mathematical
MB	Bachelor of Medicine
MBE	Member, Order of the British Empire
MBOU	Member, British Ornithologists' Union
MBritIRE	Member, British Institute of Radio Engineers
MC	Military Cross
MCC	Marylebone Cricket Club
MCE (Melb.)	Master of Civil Engineering (Melbourne University)
MCh or MChir	Master in Surgery
MChOrth	Master of Orthopaedic Surgery
MCMES	Member, Civil and Mechanical Engineers' Society
MCom	Master of Commerce
MConsE	Member, Association of Consulting Engineers
MCS	Madras Civil Service; Malayan Civil Service
MD	Doctor of Medicine; Military District
Md	Maryland (US)
MDS	Master of Dental Surgery
Me	Maine (US)
ME	Mining Engineer
MEC	Member of Executive Council
Mech.	Mechanics; Mechanical
MEd	Master of Education
Med.	Medical
MEF	Middle East Force
MEIC	Member, Engineering Institute of Canada
Melb.	Melbourne
MELF	Middle East Land Forces

MEng	Master of Engineering	MLS	Member, Linnæan Society
MetR	Metropolitan Railway	MM	Military Medal
MFGB	Miners' Federation of Great Britain	Mme	Madame
MFH	Master of Foxhounds	MMet	Master of Metallurgy
MGA	Major-General in charge of Administration	MMSA	Master of Midwifery, Society of Apothecaries
MGC	Machine Gun Corps		
MGI	Member, Institute of Certificated Grocers	MN	Merchant Navy
Mgr	Monsignore	MNAS	Member, National Academy of Sciences (US)
MHA	Member of the House of Assembly		
MHR	Member of the House of Representatives	MO	Medical Officer
MI	Military Intelligence	Mo	Missouri (US)
MIAE	Member, Institution of Automobile Engineers	Mods	Moderations (Oxford)
		MOH	Master of Otter Hounds; Medical Officer(s) of Health
MIAeE	Member, Institute of Aeronautical Engineers		
		MOI	Ministry of Information
MIBF	Member, Institute of British Foundrymen	Mon	Monmouthshire; Montana (US)
MICE	Member, Institution of Civil Engineers	Mont	Montgomeryshire
MICEI	Member, Institution of Civil Engineers of Ireland	Most Rev.	Most Reverend
		MP	Member of Parliament
Mich	Michigan (US)	MPP	Member, Provincial Parliament
MIChemE	Member, Institution of Chemical Engineers	MPS	Member, Pharmaceutical Society
MIEA	Member, Institution of Engineers, Australia	MR	Master of the Rolls; Municipal Reform
MIEE	Member, Institution of Electrical Engineers	MRAC	Member, Royal Agricultural College
MIEI	Member, Institution of Engineering Inspection	MRAS	Member, Royal Asiatic Society
		MRC	Medical Research Council
MIE (Ind.)	Member, Institution of Engineers, India	MRCOG	Member, Royal College of Obstetricians and Gynaecologists
MIESS	Member, Institution of Engineers and Shipbuilders, Scotland	MRCP	Member, Royal College of Physicians
		MRCPE	Member, Royal College of Physicians, Edinburgh
MIEx	Member, Institute of Export		
Mil.	Military	MRCS	Member, Royal College of Surgeons
MILocoE	Member, Institution of Locomotive Engineers	MRCSE	Member, Royal College of Surgeons, Edinburgh
MIMarE	Member, Institute of Marine Engineers	MRCVS	Member, Royal College of Veterinary Surgeons
MIMechE	Member, Institution of Mechanical Engineers		
		MREmpS	Member, Royal Empire Society
MIMinE	Member, Institution of Mining Engineers	MRI	Member, Royal Institution
MIMM	Member, Institution of Mining and Metallurgy	MRIA	Member, Royal Irish Academy
		MRIAI	Member, Royal Institute of the Architects of Ireland
MIMunE	Member, Institution of Municipal Engineers		
Min.	Minister; Ministry	MRSanI	Member, Royal Sanitary Institute
MIN	Member, Institute of Navigation	MRST	Member, Royal Society of Teachers
MINA	Member, Institution of Naval Architects	MRUSI	Member, Royal United Service Institution
Minn	Minnesota (US)	MS	Master of Surgery; Master of Science (US)
MInstCE	Member, Institution of Civil Engineers (now see MICE)	MS, MSS	Manuscript, Manuscripts
		MSA	Member, Society of Apothecaries
MInstGasE	Member, Institution of Gas Engineers	MSAE	Member, Society of Automotive Engineers (US)
MInstME	Member, Institution of Mining Engineers		
MInstMet	Member, Institute of Metals	MS & R	Merchant Shipbuilding and Repairs
MInstPet	Member, Institute of Petroleum	MSAutE	Member, Society of Automobile Engineers
MInstPI	Member, Institute of Patentees (Incorporated)	MSC	Madras Staff Corps
		MSc	Master of Science
MInstRA	Member, Institute of Registered Architects	MSH	Master of Stag-Hounds
MInstT	Member, Institute of Transport	MSIA	Member, Society of Industrial Artists
MInstW	Member, Institute of Welding	MSR	Member, Society of Radiographers
MInstWE	Member, Institution of Water Engineers	Mt	Mountain
MIPE	Member, Institution of Production Engineers	MT	Mechanical Transport
		MTPI	Member, Town Planning Institute
MIRTE	Member, Institute of Road Transport Engineers	MusB	Bachelor of Music
		MusD	Doctor of Music
MISI	Member, Iron and Steel Institute	MusM	Master of Music
Miss	Mississippi (US)	MVO	Member, Royal Victorian Order
MIStructE	Member, Institution of Structural Engineers		
MJI	Member, Institute of Journalists		
MJIE	Member, Junior Institute of Engineers		
MJS	Member, Japan Society		**N**
ML	Licentiate in Medicine; Master of Laws		
MLA	Member of Legislative Assembly	(N)	Nationalist
MLC	Member of Legislative Council	N	Navigating Duties; North
MLitt	Master of Letters	n	Nephew
Mlle	Mademoiselle	NA	National Academician (America)
MLO	Military Liaison Officer	NAAFI	Navy, Army and Air Force Institutes

NABC	National Association of Boys' Clubs	**OBE**	Officer, Order of the British Empire
NAPT	National Association for the Prevention of Tuberculosis	**OBI**	Order of British India
		o c	only child
Nat. Sci.	Natural Sciences	**OC**	Officer Commanding
NB	New Brunswick	**OCF**	Officiating Chaplain to the Forces
NBA	North British Academy	**OCTU**	Officer Cadet Training Unit
NBC	National Book Council; National Broadcasting Company (of America)	**OEEC**	Organisation for European Economic Co-operation
NC	North Carolina (US)	**OFM**	Order of Friars Minor (Franciscans)
NCB	National Coal Board	**OFS**	Orange Free State
NCLC	National Council of Labour Colleges	**OHMS**	On His Majesty's Service
NCU	National Cyclists' Union	**OL**	Officer, Order of Leopold
NDA	National Diploma in Agriculture	**OM**	Order of Merit
N Dak	North Dakota (US)	**OMI**	Oblate of Mary Immaculate
NDD	National Diploma in Dairying	**Ont**	Ontario
NE	North-east	**OP**	*Ordinis Praedicatorum* (of the Order of Preachers (Dominican Ecclesiastical Title))
NEAC	New English Art Club		
Neb	Nebraska (US)		
NECInst	North-East Coast Institution of Engineers and Shipbuilders	**ORC**	Orange River Colony
		Ore	Oregon (US)
Nev	Nevada (US)	**OS**	Old Style in the Calendar (in Great Britain before 1752)
New M.	New Mexico (US)		
NFS	National Fire Service	**o s**	only son
NFU	National Farmers' Union	**OSA**	Ontario Society of Artists
NH	New Hampshire (US)	**OSB**	Order of St Benedict (Benedictine)
NI	Northern Ireland; Native Infantry	**OSFC**	Franciscan (Capuchin) Order
NID	Naval Intelligence Division; National Institute for the Deaf	**OSNC**	Orient Steam Navigation Company
		OSRD	Office of Scientific Research and Development
NJ	New Jersey (US)		
NL	National Liberal	**OStJ**	Officer, Most Venerable Order of the Hospital of St John of Jerusalem
NLF	National Liberal Federation		
Northants	Northamptonshire	**OT**	Old Testament
Notts	Nottinghamshire	**OTC**	Officers' Training Corps
NP	Notary Public	**OU**	Oxford University
NRA	National Rifle Association; National Recovery Administration (US)	**OUAC**	Oxford University Athletic Club
		OUAFC	Oxford University Association Football Club
NRD	National Registered Designer		
NRMA	National Roads and Motorists' Association	**OUBC**	Oxford University Boat Club
NS	Nova Scotia; New Style in the Calendar (in Great Britain since 1752); National Society	**OUCC**	Oxford University Cricket Club
		OUDS	Oxford University Dramatic Society
		OURFC	Oxford University Rugby Football Club
ns	Graduate of Royal Naval Staff College, Greenwich	**Oxf.**	Oxford
		Oxon	Oxfordshire; *Oxoniensis* (of Oxford)
NSA	National Skating Association		
NSPCC	National Society for Prevention of Cruelty to Children		

P

NSW	New South Wales		
NT	New Testament; Northern Territory of South Australia	**PA**	Pakistan Army
		Pa	Pennsylvania (US)
NUI	National University of Ireland	**pac**	passed the final examination of the Advanced Class, The Military College of Science
NUR	National Union of Railwaymen		
NUT	National Union of Teachers		
NUTN	National Union of Trained Nurses	**PASI**	Professional Associate, Chartered Surveyors' Institution *now see* ARICS)
NUWW	National Union of Women Workers		
NW	North-west	**PC**	Privy Councillor; Police Constable; Perpetual Curate; Peace Commissioner (Irish Free State)
NWFP	North-West Frontier Province		
NWP	North-Western Provinces		
NWT	North-Western Territories	**pc**	*per centum* (by the hundred)
NY	New York - City or State	**PCMO**	Principal Colonial Medical Officer
NYC	New York City	**PdD**	Doctor of Pedagogy (US)
NZ	New Zealand	**PEI**	Prince Edward Island
NZEF	New Zealand Expeditionary Force	**PEN**	Poets, Playwrights, Editors, Essayists, Novelists (Club)
		Penn	Pennsylvania (US)

O

		PEP	Political and Economic Planning
		PF	Procurator-Fiscal
O	Ohio (US)	**PhB**	Bachelor of Philosophy
o	only	**PhC**	Pharmaceutical Chemist
OAS	On Active Service	**PhD**	Doctor of Philosophy
O & O	Oriental and Occidental (Steamship Company)	**Phil.**	Philology; Philological; Philosophy; Philosophical
ob.	died	**PhL**	Licentiate in Philosophy

Phys.	Physical
PICAO	Provisional International Civil Aviation Organization
pinx.	(He) painted it
Pl.	Place; Plural
Plen.	Plenipotentiary
PMG	Postmaster-General
PMO	Principal Medical Officer
PMRAFNS	Princess Mary's Royal Air Force Nursing Service
PMS	President, Miniature Society
P&O	Peninsular and Oriental Steamship Company
P&OSNCCo	Peninsular and Oriental Steam Navigation Company
PO	Post Office
Pop.	Population
POW	Prisoner of War; Prince of Wales's
PP	Parish Priest; Past President
Pp	Pages
PPCLI	Princess Patricia's Canadian Light Infantry
PPE	Philosophy, Politics and Economics (Oxford University)
PPRA	Past President, Royal Academy
PPRIBA	Past President, Royal Institute of British Architects
PPS	Parliamentary Private Secretary
PQ	Province of Quebec
PRA	President, Royal Academy
PRCA	President, Royal College of Art
PRE	President, Royal Society of Painter-Etchers
Preb.	Prebendary
Prep.	Preparatory
Pres.	President
PRHA	President, Royal Hibernian Academy
PRI	President, Royal Institute of Painters in Water Colours
PRIA	President, Royal Irish Academy
Prin.	Principal
Proc.	Proctor; Proceedings
Prof.	Professor
Pro tem.	*Pro tempore* (for the time being)
Prov.	Provost
Prox.	*Proximo* (next)
Prox. acc.	*Proxime accessit* (next in order of merit to the winner, or a very close second)
PRS	President, Royal Society
PRSA	President, Royal Scottish Academy
PRWS	President, Royal Society of Painters in Water Colours
PS	Pastel Society
ps	passed School of Instruction (of Officers)
psa	Graduate of RAF Staff College
psc	passed Staff College
PSNC	Pacific Steam Navigation Company
Pte	Private (soldier)
Pty	Proprietary
PWD	Public Works Department (roads, buildings, Govt. railways, telegraphs, etc)
PWO	Prince of Wales's Own

Q

Q	Queen
QAIMNS	Queen Alexandra's Imperial Military Nursing Service
QALAS	Qualified Associate Land Agents' Society
QARANC	Queen Alexandra's Royal Army Nursing Corps
QARNNS	Queen Alexandra's Royal Naval Nursing Service

QC	Queen's Counsel
QHP	Queen's Honorary Physician
Qld	Queensland
Qly	Quarterly
QMAAC	Queen Mary's Army Auxiliary Corps
QMG	Quartermaster-General
QMO	Queen Mary's Own
QO	Qualified Officer
Q(ops)	Quartering (operations)
Qr	Quarter
qs	RAF graduates of the Military or Naval Staff College
QUB	Queen's University, Belfast
QUI	Queen's University in Ireland
qv	*quod vide* (which see)

R

(R)	Radical; Reserve
r	right
RA	Royal Academician; Royal Artillery
RAAF	Royal Australian Air Force
RAAMF	Royal Australian Army Medical Corps
RAC	Royal Automobile Club; Royal Agricultural College; Royal Armoured Corps
RACP	Royal Australasian College of Physicians
RACS	Royal Australasian College of Surgeons
RADA	Royal Academy of Dramatic Art
RAE	Royal Australian Engineers; Royal Aircraft Establishment
RAeS	Royal Aeronautical Society
RAF	Royal Air Force
RAFO	Reserve of Air Force Officers (*now see* RAFRO)
RAFRO	Royal Air Force Reserve of Officers
RAFVR	Royal Air Force Volunteer Reserve
RAI	Royal Anthropological Institute of Great Britain & Ireland
RAIA	Royal Australian Institute of Architects
RAM	Member, Royal Academy of Music
RAMC	Royal Army Medical Corps
RAN	Royal Australian Navy
RANVR	Royal Australian Naval Volunteer Reserve
RAOC	Royal Army Ordnance Corps
RAPC	Royal Army Pay Corps
RARO	Regular Army Reserve of Officers
RAS	Royal Astronomical Society; Royal Asiatic Society
RASC	Royal Army Service Corps
RASE	Royal Agricultural Society of England
RAuxAF	Royal Auxiliary Air Force
RAVC	Royal Army Veterinary Corps
RB	Rifle Brigade
RBA	Member, Royal Society of British Artists
RBC	Royal British Colonial Society of Artists
RBS	Royal Society of British Sculptors
RBSA	Royal Birmingham Society of Artists
RC	Roman Catholic
RCA	Member, Royal Cambrian Academy; Member, Royal Canadian Academy of Arts; Royal College of Art
RCAF	Royal Canadian Air Force
RCamA	Member, Royal Cambrian Academy
RCM	Royal College of Music
RCN	Royal Canadian Navy
RCNC	Royal Corps of Naval Constructors
RCNVR	Royal Canadian Naval Volunteer Reserve
RCO	Royal College of Organists

RCOG	Royal College of Obstetricians and Gynaecologists
RCP	Royal College of Physicians, London
RCPE	Royal College of Physicians, Edinburgh
RCPI	Royal College of Physicians of Ireland
RCS	Royal College of Surgeons of England; Royal Corps of Signals; Royal College of Science
RCS(I)	Royal College of Surgeons (of Ireland)
RCVS	Royal College of Veterinary Surgeons
RD	Rural Dean; Royal Naval Reserve Decoration
Rd	Road
RDC	Rural District Council
RDF	Royal Dublin Fusiliers
RDI	Royal Designer for Industry (Royal Society of Arts)
RE	Royal Engineers; Fellow, Royal Society of Painter-Etchers
Rear-Adm.	Rear-Admiral
REconS	Royal Economic Society
Rect.	Rector
Reg. Prof.	Regius Professor
Regt	Regiment
REME	Royal Electrical and Mechanical Engineers
RERO	Royal Engineers Reserve of Officers
RES	Royal Empire Society
Res.	Resigned; Reserve; Resident
Rev.	Reverend
RFA	Royal Field Artillery
RFC	Royal Flying Corps (now RAF)
RGA	Royal Garrison Artillery
RGS	Royal Geographical Society
RHA	Royal Hibernian Academy; Royal Horse Artillery
RHG	Royal Horse Guards
RHortS	Royal Horticultural Society
RHR	Royal Highland Regiment
RHS	Royal Horticultural Society; Royal Humane Society
RI	Member, Royal Institute of Painters in Water Colours; Rhode Island
RIA	Royal Irish Academy
RIAM	Royal Irish Academy of Music
RIASC	Royal Indian Army Service Corps
RIBA	Royal Institute of British Architects
RIBI	Rotary International in Great Britain and Ireland
RIE	Royal Indian Engineering (College)
RIF	Royal Irish Fusiliers
RIIA	Royal Institute of International Affairs
RIM	Royal Indian Marine
RIN	Royal Indian Navy
RM	Royal Marines; Resident Magistrate
RMA	Royal Marine Artillery; Royal Military Academy, Sandhurst (now incorporating Royal Military Academy, Woolwich)
RMC	Royal Military College, Sandhurst (*now see* RMA)
RMetS	Royal Meteorological Society
RMLI	Royal Marine Light Infantry
RMO	Resident Medical Officer(s)
RMPA	Royal Medico-Psychological Association
RMS	Royal Microscopical Society; Royal Mail Steamer; Royal Society of Miniature Painters
RN	Royal Navy; Royal Naval
RNAS	Royal Naval Air Service
RNC	Royal Naval College
RNEC	Royal Naval Engineering College
RNLBI	Royal National Life-boat Institution
RNR	Royal Naval Reserve

RNVR	Royal Naval Volunteer Reserve
ROC	Royal Observer Corps
R of O	Reserve of Officers
ROI	Royal Institute of Oil Painters
(Rot.)	Rotunda Hospital, Dublin (after degree)
Roy.	Royal
RP	Member, Royal Society of Portrait Painters
RPS	Royal Photographic Society
RRC	Royal Red Cross
RSA	Royal Scottish Academician; Royal Society of Arts
RSAI	Royal Society of Antiquaries of Ireland
RSanI	Royal Sanitary Institute
RSC	Royal Society of Canada
RSE	Royal Society of Edinburgh
RSF	Royal Scots Fusiliers
RSGS	Royal Scottish Geographical Society
RSL	Royal Society of Literature
RSM	Royal Society of Medicine; Royal School of Mines
RSO	Rural Sub-Office; Railway Sub-Office
RSPB	Royal Society for Protection of Birds
RSPCA	Royal Society for Prevention of Cruelty to Animals
RSSAILA	Returned Sailors, Soldiers and Airmen's Imperial League of Australia
RSW	Member, Royal Scottish Water Colour Society
Rt Hon.	Right Honourable
RTO	Railway Transport Officer
RTR	Royal Tank Regiment
Rt Rev.	Right Reverend
RTS	Religious Tract Society; Royal Toxophilite Society
RU	Rugby Union
RUI	Royal University of Ireland
RUSI	Royal United Service Institution
RVC	Royal Veterinary College
RWA	Member, Royal West of England Academy
RWAFF	Royal West African Frontier Force
RWF	Royal Welch Fusiliers
RWS	Member, Royal Society of Painters in Water Colours
RYS	Royal Yacht Squadron

S

(S)	(in Navy) Paymaster
S	Succeeded; South; Saint
s	Son
SA	South Australia; South Africa
SAAF	South African Air Force
SACSEA	Supreme Allied Command, South-East Asia
SADG	Société des Architectes Diplômés par le Gouvernement
Salop	Shropshire
SAMC	South African Medical Corps
Sarum	Salisbury
SAS	Special Air Service
Sask	Saskatchewan
SASO	Senior Air Staff Officer
SATB	Soprano, Alto, Tenor, Bass
SB	Bachelor of Science (US)
SC	Senior Counsel (Eire); South Carolina (US)
sc	Student at the Staff College
SCAO	Senior Civil Affairs Officer
SCAPA	Society for Checking the Abuses of Public Advertising
ScD	Doctor of Science
SCF	Senior Chaplain to the Forces

Sch.	Scholar; School
Scot.	Scotland
SCL	Student in Civil Law
SCM	State Certified Midwife
Sculpt.	Sculptor
SD	Doctor of Science
S Dak	South Dakota (US)
SDF	Sudan Defence Force; Social Democratic Federation
SE	South-east
SEAC	South-East Asia Command
SEALF	South-East Asia Land Forces
Sec.	Secretary
Selw.	Selwyn College, Cambridge
SESO	Senior Equipment Staff Officer
SF	Sinn Féin
SG	Solicitor-General
SGA	Member, Society of Graphic Art
Sgt	Sergeant
SHAEF	Supreme Headquarters, Allied Expeditionary Force
SJ	Society of Jesus (Jesuits)
SJD	Doctor of Juristic Science
SL	Serjeant-at-Law
SM	Master of Science
SMA	Society of Marine Artists
SME	School of Military Engineering
SMIRE	Senior Member, Institution of Radio Engineers (New York)
SMO	Senior Medical Officer
SO	Staff Officer
Soc.	Society
sp	*sine prole* (without issue)
SPCK	Society for Promoting Christian Knowledge
SPG	Society for the Propagation of the Gospel
SPRC	Society for Prevention and Relief of Cancer
Sq.	Square
Sqdn or Sqn	Squadron
SR	Special Reserve; Southern Railway; Southern Region (BR)
SRMC	Southern Rhodesia Medical Corps
SRN	State Registered Nurse
SS	Saints; Straits Settlements; Steamship
SS & AFA	Soldiers, Sailors and Airmen's Families Association
SSC	Solicitor before Supreme Court (Scotland); Sculptors Society of Canada
SSJE	Society of St John the Evangelist
SSM	Society of the Sacred Mission
SSO	Senior Supply Officer
St	Street; Saint
STB	*Sacrae Theologiae Baccalaureus* (Bachelor of Sacred Theology)
STC	Senior Training Corps
STD	*Sacrae Theologiae Doctor* (Doctor of Sacred Theology)
Stip.	Stipend; Stipendiary
STL	*Sacrae Theologiae Lector* (Reader or a Professor of Sacred Theology)
STM	*Sacrae Theologiae Magister* (Master of Sacred Theology)
STP	*Sacrae Theologiae Professor* (Professor of Divinity, old form of DD)
STSO	Senior Technical Staff Officer
Supp. Res.	Supplementary Reserve (of Officers)
Supt	Superintendent
Surg.	Surgeon
Surv.	Surviving
SW	South-west
Syd.	Sydney

T

T	Telephone; Territorial
TA	Telegraphic Address; Territorial Army
TAA	Territorial Army Association
TAF	Tactical Air Force
T & AFA	Territorial and Auxiliary Forces Association
TARO	Territorial Army Reserve of Officers
Tasm.	Tasmania
TCD	Trinity College, Dublin
TCF	Temporary Chaplain to the Forces
TD	Territorial Decoration; (Teachta Dala) Member of the Dáil, Eire
Temp.	Temperature; Temporary
Tenn	Tennessee (US)
Ter. or Terr.	Terrace
Tex	Texas (US)
TF	Territorial Forces
TFR	Territorial Force Reserve
ThL	Theological Licentiate
TP	Transvaal Province
TPI	Town Planning Institute
Trans.	Translation; Translated
TRC	Thames Rowing Club
TRH	Their Royal Highnesses
Trin.	Trinity
TSD	Tertiary of St Dominick
TUC	Trades Union Congress
TYC	Thames Yacht Club

U

(U)	Unionist
u	Uncle
UC	University College
UCH	University College Hospital (London)
UCW	University College of Wales
UDC	Urban District Council
UDF	Union Defence Force
UF	United Free Church
UK	United Kingdom
UN	United Nations
UNA	United Nations Association
UNCIO	United Nations Conference on International Organization
UNESCO	United Nations Educational, Scientific and Cultural Organization
Univ.	University
UNO	United Nations Organization
UNRRA	United Nations Relief and Rehabilitation Administration
UP	United Provinces; United Presbyterian
US	United States
USA	United States of America
USMA	United States Military Academy
USNR	United States Naval Reserve
USS	United States Ship
USSR	Union of Soviet Socialist Republics
UTC	University Training Corps
(UU)	Ulster Unionist

V

V	Five (Roman numerals); Version; Vicar; Viscount; *Vice*
v	*Versus* (against)
v or vid	*Vide* (see)
VA	Victoria and Albert
Va	Virginia (US)

VAD	Voluntary Aid Detachment
VC	Victoria Cross
VCAS	Vice-Chief of the Air Staff
VD	Royal Naval Volunteer Reserve Officers' Decoration (now VRD); Volunteer Officers' Decoration; Victorian Decoration
VDC	Volunteer Defence Corps
Ven.	Venerable (of an Archdeacon)
Very Rev.	Very Reverend (of a Dean)
Vet.	Veterinary
VHS	Honorary Surgeon to Viceroy of India
Vic.	Victoria
Vice-Adm.	Vice-Admiral
Vict.	Victoria
Visc.	Viscount
VL	Vice-Lieutenant
VM	Victory Medal
VMH	Victoria Medal of Honour (Royal Horticultural Society)
Vol.	Volume; Volunteers
VP	Vice-President
VQMG	Vice-Quartermaster-General
VR	*Victoria Regina* (Queen Victoria)
VRD	Royal Naval Volunteer Reserve Officers' Decoration
Vt	Vermont (US)

W

W	West
WA	West Australia
WAAF	Women's Auxiliary Air Force (*now see* WRAF)
Wadh.	Wadham
Wash	Washington State (US)
W/Cdr	Wing Commander

WEA	Workers' Educational Association; Royal West of England Academy
WhSc	Whitworth Scholar
WI	West Indies
Wilts	Wiltshire
Wis	Wisconsin (US)
WLF	Women's Liberal Federation
Wm	William
WO	War Office
WOSB	War Office Selection Board
Worcs	Worcestershire
WR	West Riding; Western Region (BR)
WRAC	Women's Royal Army Corps
WRAF	Women's Royal Air Force (formerly WAAF)
WRNS	Women's Royal Naval Service
WS	Writer to the Signet
WSPU	Women's Social and Political Union
W Va	West Virginia (US)
WVS	Women's Voluntary Services
Wyo	Wyoming (US)

X

X	Ten (Roman numerals)

Y

y	youngest
Yeo.	Yeomanry
YHA	Youth Hostels Association
YMCA	Young Men's Christian Association
Yorks	Yorkshire
yr	younger
yrs	years
YWCA	Young Women's Christian Association

ADDENDA

The following biographies are of those whose deaths occurred between 1941 and 1950 but were not reported until after the main part of this volume had gone to press.

ACLAND, F. A.; *b* Bridgwater, England, 1861; *m* 1888, Elizabeth Adair, Toronto; one *s* one *d*. *Educ:* Bridgwater. Engaged in journalism, various cities England, United States, Canada, 1880–90; Assistant Editor Globe, Toronto, Ont, 1890–1902; various literary work, London, Philadelphia, and Western Canada, 1902–07; Secretary Dept of Labour, 1907; Deputy Minister of Labour for Canada, 1908–23; King's Printer, 1921; retired 1933; was also charged as registrar with administration of Industrial Disputes Investigation Act 1907, commonly known as Lemieux Act; represented Government of Canada at meetings in Paris and London, 1920, Copenhagen and Stockholm, 1921, and Geneva, 1924, of Governing Body of International Labour Office. *Address:* c/o Bank of Montreal, Ottawa, Canada.

Died 1 Sept. 1950.

AICKIN, Thomas Reginald, CBE 1939; Second Secretary, New Zealand Legation, Washington, since 1942; *b* 2 June 1886; *s* of late George Gordon and Margaret Aickin; *m* 1923, Rhoda Elizabeth Young; no *c*. *Educ:* New Plymouth; Wellington, NZ. Civil Service. *Recreation:* tennis. *Address:* 3130 Wisconsin Avenue, Washington DC, USA.

Died 27 Nov. 1948.

AKBAR, Hon. M. T., KC 1925; *b* 15 June 1880; *s* of late M. S. J. Akbar, MMC, merchant and planter; *m* 1917; no *c*. *Educ:* Royal Coll., Colombo; Emmanuel Coll., Cambridge (Scholar). Barrister-at-Law, 1904; Crown Counsel, 1909; Solicitor-General and member Legislative Council, 1924–29; acting Puisne Judge Supreme Court, 1925; Acting Attorney-General, 1927; Puisne Judge of Supreme Court of Ceylon, 1929–37; Member, Executive Council, Ceylon, 1927–29; Chairman and Founder of the Prevention of Crime Assoc. of Ceylon. *Publications:* Asst Editor in Roman-Dutch Law, Burges' Colonial Laws, Vol. IV. *Address:* Colombo, Ceylon.

Died 22 April 1944.

ALI-RAJPUR, Chief, HH Raja Sir Pratap Singhji, Raja of, KCIE 1933 (CIE 1915); *b* 1881; *S* 1891. State covers 836 square miles and has a population of 89,364. The Raja receives a hereditary salute of eleven guns. *Heir: g s* Surendra Sinhji. *Address:* Ali-rajpur (*via* Dohad, BB and CI), Southern States, Central India.

Died 1948.

ANNETT, Henry Edward, MBE; MD, DPH; retired; Turner Research Fellow (Cancer), 1931–38; Hon. Lecturer Pathology of Meat, etc., University of Liverpool, 1922–25; Lecturer in Animal Pathology, University of Liverpool, 1922–28; Cancer Researcher, University of Liverpool, 1923–30; Superintendent, Research Laboratories, Higher Runcorn, 1911–22; Professor of Comparative Pathology, University of Liverpool, 1906–11; *b* 5 June 1871; *m* 1906, E. L., *d* of George Bell. *Educ:* University College, Liverpool; Victoria University, Manchester. Graduated with honours, 1894. Lecturer on Comparative Pathology, University, Liverpool, 1903; Superintendent, Incorporated Liverpool Institute of Comparative Pathology since 1902; member of first expedition sent out by Liverpool School of Tropical Medicine to West Africa, 1891; directed second expedition, 1900; Director Animal Diseases Expedition to Uruguay, 1905, and of Colonial Office Expedition to W Indies, 1906–07; MOH Runcorn Urban District, 1913–23; Acting MOH Widnes Borough District, 1915–19; MO in command Runcorn Vicarage Military Hospital; Joint Author— Report of Malaria Expedition to Sierra Leone, 1899; Report of Expedition to Nigeria (Malaria), 1900; Report of Expedition to Nigeria (Filariasis), 1900. *Address:* 143 Highfield Road, Rock Ferry, Cheshire. *T:* Rock Ferry 518.

Died 10 April 1945.

ANWYL, Rev. John Bodvan; *b* Chester, 1875; 4th *s* of John and Elen Anwyl; *brother* of late Sir Edward Anwyl. Minister of Elim Welsh Congregational Church, Carmarthen, 1899–1901; Superintendent of the Glamorgan Mission to the Deaf and Dumb, 1904–19; Cataloguer at the National Library of Wales, Aberystwyth, 1919–21; Dictionary Secretary to the Board of Celtic Studies of the Univ. of Wales, 1921–35; winner of prize offered by Mr William George for best rendering of National Insurance Act terms into Welsh. *Publications:* Spurrell's Welsh-English Dictionary, editions 1914, 1915, 1918, 1920, 1925, 1930, 1934, 1937; Spurrell's English-Welsh Dictionary, editions 1916, 1922, 1926, 1932, 1937; Spurrell's Pocket Dictionary, Welsh-English and English-Welsh, 1919, 1929, 1930, 1937, 1948; Y Pulpud Bach, 1924; Y Bardd Cwsg (rev. edn), 1927; Drych y Prif Oesoedd (rev. edn), 1932; Englynion, 1933; Fy Hanes i fy Hunan, 1933; Yr Arian Mawr, 1934; has translated about a dozen volumes into Welsh; has written numerous articles, stories, essays, and poems, chiefly in Welsh. *Recreations:* gardening, etc. *Address:* Bryn Bodfan, Llangwnadl, Pwllheli, Caernarvonshire.

Died 22 July 1949.

ARDILL, Rev. John Roche, LLD; *m* 1887, Blanche Annie Morrison (*d* 1929); four *s* three *d*. *Educ:* Trinity College, Dublin. Ordained 1884; Curate of St Mary Athlone, 1884–86; North Derryvullen, 1886–87; St Andrew's, Dublin, 1887–89; Incumbent of Drumcliffe, 1889–99; Rector of Calry, 1899–1944; Dean of Elphin Cathedral, 1933–44; Canon of Elphin Cathedral, 1902. *Publications:* Forgotten Facts of Irish History, 1905; The Closing of the Irish Parliament, 1907; St Patrick, AD 180, 1931. *Address:* Rosses Point, Co. Sligo.

Died 19 Jan. 1947.

ASKURAN, Sir Shantidas, Kt 1942; Chairman and Director of several Mills and Concerns; ex-Member Council of State; *b* 1882; *m* Manibal; one *s* two *d*. *Educ:* at Cutch. Sheriff of Bombay, 1944. Has visited Europe nine times. *Recreations:* racing, cards, billiards. *Address:* Mahendra Bhuvan, Nepean Sea Road, Bombay 6. *TA:* Ravishant, Bombay. *T:* Bombay 40288. *Clubs:* Royal Western Indian Turf, Willingdon, Orient, Cricket Club of India, Bombay Flying (Bombay); Roshanara, Chelmsford (Delhi).

Died 21 Dec. 1950.

BACHELLER, Irving; author; *b* Pierpont, NY, 26 Sept. 1859; *s* of Sanford Paul Bacheller and Achsah Ann Buckland; *m* 1883, Anna Detmar Schultz. *Educ:* Canton, NY, Academy; St Lawrence University; BS, 1882, MS, 1892; AB, 1901; AM, 1903; DHL, 1911; Middlebury College, LittD, 1910; LLD Rollins Coll., 1941. *Publications:* The Master of Silence, 1890; The Still House of O'Darrow, 1894; Eben Holden, 1900; D'ri and I, 1901; Darrell of the Blessed Isles, 1903; Vergilius, 1904; Silas Strong, 1906; Cricket Heron, 1909; The Master, 1910; Keeping up with Lizzie, 1911; Charge It, 1912; The Turning of Griggsby, 1913; The Marryers, 1915; The Light in the Clearing, 1917; Keeping up with William, 1918; Man for the Ages, 1919; The Prodigal Village, 1920; In the Days of Poor Richard, 1921; The Scudders, 1923; Father Abraham, 1925; Dawn, 1927; Coming up the Road, 1928; The House of the Three Ganders, 1929; A Candle in the Wilderness, 1930; The Master of Chaos, 1932; Uncle Peel, 1933; The Harvesting, 1935; The Oxen of the Sun, 1936; A Boy for the Ages, 1938; From Stores of Memory, 1938; Winds of God, 1941. *Clubs:* Century, Authors' (New York).

Died 24 Feb. 1950.

BANSWARA, Maharawal of, HH Rayan Rai Maharadhiraj Maharawalji Sahib Shree Sir Pirthi Singhji Bahadur, KCIE 1933; *b* 15 July 1888; *S* 1914; *m*; two *s*. Area, including Patta Kushalgarh, 1946 square miles, and population 260,670. *Heir:* Maharaj Raj Kumar Sahib Shree Chandra-Veer Singhji. *Address:* Banswara, Rajputana, India.

Died 28 July 1944.

BANTA, Arthur Mangun, BS, MA, PhD; Zoologist; Professor of Experimental Zoology, 1929–30, Research Professor of Biology, 1930–45, Professor Emeritus since 1945, Brown University, USA; *b* 31 Dec. 1877; *s* of J. H. Banta and Mary Mangun; *m* 1906, Mary Charlotte Slack; one *s* two *d*. *Educ:* Indiana University and Harvard University. Resident Investigator Carnegie Experimental Evolution Station, 1909–30. Associate Carnegie Inst. of Washington, 1930–32 and 1936–37. *Publications:* The Fauna of Mayfield's Cave, 1907; Selection in Cladocera on the Basis of a Physiological Character, 1921; Physiology, Genetics and Evolution of some Cladocera, 1939; contrib. to biol. journals. *Address:* 168 Medway Street, Providence, RI, USA.

Died 1 July 1946.

BARLOW, John, MD Edin.; FRCS, FRFPS(G); Ex-President of Royal Faculty of Physicians and Surgeons of Glasgow; Hon. Consulting (formerly Senior) Surgeon, Glasgow Royal Infirmary; Medical Referee under Workman's Compensation Act for Lanarkshire; Surgeon with rank of Lieutenant-Colonel; 4th Scottish General Hospital Examiner in Surgery of Candidates for Scotch Triple Qualification; *b* Leigh, Lancs, 29 Jan. 1853; *m* 1st, 1881, Annie, *d* of late James Smithells, General Manager, Caledonian Railway Co.; 2nd, 1890, Annie, *d* of late John M'Intyre, builder, Glasgow; two *s* three *d*; 3rd, 1938, Agnes MacRoberts, *d* of P. M. Strachan, Colliery Manager. *Educ:* Leigh Grammar Sch.; Anderson's Coll., Glasgow; Univs of Glasgow and Edinburgh. For twenty years was the Notman Professor of Physiology, St Mungo's Coll., Glasgow; a member of the Board of Examiners of Candidates for the Fellowship of the Royal College of Surgeons of England; Examiner in Clinical Surgery, Univ. of Edinburgh; Lecturer, Examiner in Surgery, Univ. of Glasgow. *Publications:* Statistics of Surgical Operations; Abdominal Section in Cases of Intussusception; Physiological Action of Ozonised Air. *Recreation:* fishing. *Address:* Broomfield, Callander, Perthshire. *Clubs:* Liberal (Glasgow).

Died 27 Dec. 1943.

BARNES, Howard Turner, FRS 1911; MA Sc, DSc; FAA; FRS Canada; FRMetS; FAGS; Professor of Physics and former Director of the Macdonald Physics Building, McGill University, Montreal; *b* Woburn, Mass, 21 July 1873; *e s* of Rev. William S. Barnes, LLD; *m* Ann Kershaw (*d* 1912), *y d* of Thomas Cunliffe, Bolton, Lancs. *Educ:* Montreal Acad.; McGill Univ. Joule Studentship, 1900; Sec., Physics Section, Internat. Electricity Congress, 1904; Pres., Section 3, Royal Soc. of Canada, 1909; Pres., Canadian Cttee., Internat. Electrotechnical Commn, 1925, 1926; Tyndall Lecturer, Royal Instn, 1912; Research ice expert power development and navigation. *Publications:* Ice Engineering; many papers dealing with electrical measurements, specific heats, ice formation and radioactivity, which have appeared in various scientific publications in Canada, England and the US. *Recreations:* canoeing, swimming. *Address:* McGill University, Montreal. *TA:* McGill University. *T:* Marquette 9181. *Clubs:* Canadian, Faculty (Montreal); Chemists (New York).

Died 4 Oct. 1950.

BHALJA, Govardhan Shankerlal, CIE 1943; BA (Bom.), BA (Cantab); ICS; Additional Secretary, War Department, Government of India, New Delhi, since Nov. 1944; *b* Umreth, Bombay Presidency, 8 Aug. 1895; *s* of late Shankerlal Motichand Bhalja; *m* 1929, Ushadevi, *d* of Sir Harilal Gosalia; one *s*. *Educ:* Jubilee High School, Umreth; Gujarat College, Ahmedabad; Fergusson College, Poona; Gonville and Caius College, Cambridge. Joined ICS, 1920, and posted to CP and Berar. Director of Industries and Registrar of Co-operative Societies, 1933–37; Member, CP Legislative Council, 1933–37; Sec. to Govt, Local Self-Govt, Medical and Public Health Depts, 1937; Financial Sec. and Secretary PWD in addition, 1939–44; Commissioner, Berar Division, Oct. 1944. *Recreation:* bridge. *Address:* 8a Ratendon Road, New Delhi. *T:* Residence 2064, Office 2480.

Died 30 Dec. 1948.

BHANDARKAR, Devadatta Ramkrishna, MA, PhD (Hon.), FRASB; *b* 19 Nov. 1875; *y s* of late Sir Ramkrishna Gopal Bhandarkar, KCIE. *Educ:* High School and Deccan College, Poona. Bhugwandass Purshotumdass Sanskrit Scholar, 1900 and Pandit Bhagwanlal Indraji Lecturer, Bombay University, 1903 and 1917; Sir William Meyer Lecturer, University of Madras, 1938–39; Carmichael Professor of Ancient Indian History and Culture, Calcutta University, 1917–36; Manindra Chandra Nandy Lecturer, Benares Hindu University, 1925; Superintendent, Archæological Survey, Western Circle, 1911–17; Officer-in-charge, Archæological Section, Indian Museum, Calcutta, 1917–20; Honorary Correspondent of the Archæological Department of the Government of India; Corresponding Member of the Indian Historical Records Commission; Sir James Campbell Gold Medallist (Bombay Asiatic Society), 1911; Vice-Chairman (1925–27) and Member of Board of Trustees, Indian Museum, since 1917; Fellow since 1918 and Philological Secretary (1920–25) of Royal Asiatic Society, Bengal; joint Editor of the Indian Antiquary, 1911–20, and 1928–33; Editor of Indian Culture, since 1934. *Publications:* Reports of Archæol Survey, Western Circle; Carmichael Lectures, 1918 and 1921; Asoka, Some Aspects of Ancient Hindu Polity, Origin of the Saka Era, Gurjaras, Lakulisa Guhilots, Foreign Elements in the Hindu Population, and numerous other contribs. on Indian history and archæology; edited Pt II of Vol. CXLV on India of the Annals of the Amer. Acad. Pol Science, Philadelphia, 1929. *Recreation:* music. *Address:* 2/1 Lovelock St, Calcutta.

Died 30 May 1950.

BLOW, Very Rev. Norman John, MA; Dean of Newcastle, NSW, since 1949; *b* 1915; *s* of F. J. Blow, Stevenage. *Educ:* Queens' College, Cambridge; Westcott House, Cambridge. BA 1935; MA 1939. Deacon, 1939; priest, 1940; Curate of St Martin, Epsom, 1939–42; Priest Vicar of Wells Cathedral and Assistant Organising Secretary, Society for the Propagation of the Gospel, South-Western Area, 1942–44; then Candidates Secretary for SPG, 1944–45; Permission to Officiate, Diocese of Rochester, 1944; Vicar of St Saviour's, Oxton, 1945–49; Dean of Christ Church Cathedral, Newcastle, NSW, 1949–50. *Address:* The Deanery, Newcastle, NSW, Australia.

Died 26 June 1950.

BOWER, Lt-Col George Haddon, CB 1939; TD; *b* 12 Oct. 1871; *s* of James Haddon Bower, Pitmurchie, Torphins, Aberdeenshire; *m* 1916, Amy, d of Robert Davidson Garden, New York, USA; no *c. Educ:* Aberdeen Grammar School; Aberdeen University (MA). Qualified as Law Agent, 1895; assistant, Legal Department, Caledonian Railway, till 1900; in practice in Aberdeen since 1900; member, Society of Advocates, Aberdeen; Proprietor of Estate of Pitmurchie, Aberdeenshire; Private 1st Aberdeen Volunteer Artillery, 1888; 2nd Lieut 5th V. Batt. Gordon Highlanders, 1891, afterwards 7th Batt. Gordon Highlanders TA; Lieut-Col 1914; served European War from Aug. 1914 and went to France, 1915, in command of Battalion; invalided, 1916 (despatches); afterwards commanded 2/7th Black Watch; Member, Territorial Associations of Aberdeenshire and Kincardineshire, 1908–38. *Recreation:* shooting. *Address:* Pitmurchie, Torphins, Aberdeenshire. *T:* Torphins 18. *Club:* University (Aberdeen).

Died 8 Feb. 1950.

BOYCE, Austin Alexander Rodney, CBE 1925; FRAS; FRGS; *b* Hobart Town, Tasmania, 29 Dec. 1870; *s* of J. A. Boyce, ex-Civil Servant, Queensland, Australia; *m* M. A. Muller, *widow* of C. Muller, Magistrate; one *s. Educ:* Toowoomba Grammar School, Queensland. Lands and Survey Office, Brisbane, Queensland, since 1890; Gold Coast Survey, 1902–06 and Sudan Survey Dept, 1906–27; awarded Gill Memorial by Royal Geographical Society, 1922, for triangulations in the Sudan; Chief Commissioner in the Anglo-French Sudan Boundary Commission, 1923; Director of Surveys, Sudan Government, Khartoum; retired, 1927. *Recreations:* sketching landscapes, golf. *Address:* Bona Vista, Rangeville PO, Toowoomba, Queensland, Australia.

Died 2 Oct. 1948.

BREMNER, Brig.-Gen. Arthur Grant, CMG 1916; RE; *b* 13 June 1867; *s* of late Lt-Col J. J. Bremner, Halifax, NS; unmarried. *Educ:* Royal Military College of Canada. Served Dongola, 1896 (two medals); European War, 1914–18 (despatches, CMG, Bt.-Col); retired with hon. rank of Brig.-General, 1920. *Address:* Clementsvale, Nova Scotia, Canada. *Club:* United Service.

Died 31 March 1950.

BRIGDEN, James Bristock; *b* Maldon, Victoria, Australia, 20 July 1887; *s* of James and Mary Brigden; *m* 1920, Dorothy, 3rd d of Daniel James, Camden Square, London; no *c. Educ:* Oriel College, Oxford (Hon. Fellow since 1941). Served with Australian Imperial Force in France, 1916–17 (wounded); Kitchener Memorial Scholarship to Oxford; graduated 1920; Lecturer to 1924, and Prof. of Economics to 1929, Univ. of Tasmania; Economist, Oversea Shipping, Sydney, 1929–30; Director, Queensland Bureau of Industry to 1938; Chm., Nat. Insurance Commission, Canberra, 1938–39; Sec. Depts of Supply and Munitions, Melbourne, 1939–42; Economic Counsellor, Aust. Legation and Embassy, Washington DC, 1942–47. Served on various Govt Commissions in Australia, 1924–40. Represented Australia on numerous United Nations Conferences, 1943–47 (UNRRA, Bretton Woods, etc) and otherwise (member United Nations Assembly expert Cttee on Contributions, 1946–48). Returned to Australia end of 1947. *Address:* Mitcham, Victoria, Australia.

Died 12 Oct. 1950.

BUCK, Edward Clarke, MInstCE, MIMechE, FRGS; MIStructE; Consulting Engineer and Petroleum Mining Expert; JP for Trinidad, Tobago, and British Guiana; *b* 1873; *s* of James Buck of Bristol and Minchinhampton; *m* 1st, 1903, Lilian, d of late Professor Stokoe, MD; one *s* one d; 2nd, 1925, Amelia, d of late Samuel James Kirton, late Manager of Barclays Bank, Port of Spain. *Educ:* Whitgift Grammar School, Croydon. Engaged on extensive engineering works, explorations and surveys in Australia, New Zealand and S Africa; attached to Royal Engineers during the Boer War (Queen's with five bars and King's with two bars); Waterworks, Deputy and Acting City Engr, Pretoria, Transvaal, 1903–08; consulting engineer in London and Trinidad, 1908–13; one of the pioneers of the Trinidad Oilfields; Director of Public Works, British Guiana; further explorations to the sources of the Rivers Orinoco and Amazon, etc.; Member of the Legislature and Executive Council, 1913–21; on special service in BWI, 1915–17; retired, 1921; Governing Director and Founder of the British Engineering Manufacturers' Alliance Ltd; First Chairman of Caribbean Branch of Institution of Mechanical Engineers, 1938, and Member of Council; inventor and patentee, 1902, of an improved method of electrical railway safety signalling, Buck's Patent Astronomical Abney Level, Incendiary and Armour Piercing shells, and other inventions. *Publications:* various official reports and contributions to scientific journals; Oil Fuels and their Values as compared to Coal (1916 and 1920); An Alternative Railway Route to the Hinterland of British Guiana; The Atomic Bomb (pamphlet). *Recreation:* electronics. *Address:* Port of Spain, Trinidad. *TA:* Sulituan, Trinidad. *T:* 21836.

Died 20 Nov. 1950.

BURNE, Col Newdigate Halford Marriot, CMG 1919; DSO 1916; *b* 21 July 1872; *γ s* of late Felix Neeld Burne, of Gritelton, Wilts; *m* 1905, Hillian Ross Blakeway. Joined Cape Mounted Riflemen, 1890; served with that regiment until its amalgamation with the Permanent Forces, Union of South Africa, on staff of which held various appointments; Imperial Service Commissions in 11th SAI; 60th Rifles (KRRC); commanded 7th Batt. KSLI in France and with Army of Occupation, Germany; served Matabele Campaign, 1893–94; Langeberg Campaign, 1896–97; South Africa, 1899–1902; European War, 1914–19 (despatches thrice, DSO, French Croix de Guerre, CMG); commanded 1st Special Service (Reserve) Bn S African (Union) Forces, 1939–40; SA Staff Corps (V) 1940–42, when retired under age limit. *Address:* c/o Barclays (D. C. & O.) Bank, Umkomaas, S Coast, Natal.

Died 5 July 1950.

CALRY, 6th Count de; Count Magawly de Calry; Count Cerati in Bavaria; Count Magawly de Calry in Italy; Count of the Holy Roman Empire; Grandee of Spain; Irish family; *b* Dublin, 19 Jan. 1854; *S* father, 1860; *m* 1880, Ellen Falkenburg (d 1929), d of Redman Abbott, Philadelphia; one *s* one d. *Educ:* Stonyhurst Coll. *Heir: s* Robert Louis [*b* 11 July 1898. Eton; Trinity College, Cambridge; MA. St James']. *Clubs:* (President) British and American (Lausanne); Unione, Florence (Florence); Unione (Parma).

Died 27 April 1950.

CARPENTER, Rev. James Nelson; *b* Mafira Mafira, Australia; *m* Edith Marion Bateman, London. *Educ:* MA Cambridge; DD London. Missionary under the CMS to India, 1890–1911; Principal of Emmanuel Coll.; Saskatoon, Canada, 1916; returned to India, 1918; Sec.

of UP Mission CMS, 1919–23; Missionary and Chaplain, Meerut, 1923–27; Anglican Representative of North India United Theological Coll., Saharanpur. N India, 1929–33; retired. *Address:* CMS, Salisbury Square, EC4.

Died 4 March 1949.

CHAPEL, Sir William, Kt 1933; *b* 24 Nov. 1870; *s* of David Chapel and Mary A. Corsar; *m* 1902, Laura, *d* of Andrew Gilruth of Seaton, Auchmithie; three *s* one *d*. *Educ:* Arbroath High School; Royal High School, Edinburgh; Edinburgh University. Admitted Lawyer, 1892; Hon. Sheriff-Substitute of Angus; President of the Arbroath and District Branch of the British Legion; Senior Partner of D. & W. Chapel, Solicitors, Arbroath. *Recreations:* cricket, golf, fishing, shooting. *Address:* Caenlochan, Arbroath, Angus. *T:* Arbroath 3188.

Died 5 Oct. 1950.

CLARKE, Col John Thomas, CBE 1919; MC (Czechoslovak); *b* Foxboro, Ontario, 27 Feb. 1870; *s* of Thomas and Elizabeth Clarke, both born in England; *m* 1903, Jessie J. Malcolm; two *s* two *d*. *Educ:* Trinity Univ., Toronto; McGill Univ., Montreal. General Practice of Medicine in Toronto, 1897–1906; Associate Coroner for City of Toronto; Permanent Force of Canada, 1906–14 and 1919–33; Director-General of Medical Services for Canada, 1929–33; served in France, Belgium, England and Siberia (despatches twice, CBE, War Cross Czecho-Slovakia); in Permanent Force served in Toronto, Petawawa, Ottawa, Montreal, Quebec and Halifax; Director-General, St John Ambulance (Canadian Branch); retired 1935; Commander, Order of St John of Jerusalem. *Recreations:* golf, badminton, tennis and curling. *Address:* 90 Park Road, Rockcliffe Park, Ottawa, Canada. *T:* 36992. *Clubs:* Rideau, Royal Ottawa Golf, Rideau Curling (Ottawa).

Died 28 Nov. 1947.

CLELAND, Edward Erskine; KC 1912; LLB; **Hon. Mr Justice Cleland;** Judge of the Supreme Court of South Australia, since 1936; *b* 7 April 1869; *s* of John Fullerton Cleland and Elizabeth Glen; *m* 1893, Edith Mary Auld (decd); one *s* two *d*. *Educ:* Prince Alfred College; University of Adelaide (LLB). Practised as a barrister at the Bar of South Australia and High Court of Australia; appeared before Privy Council on three occasions, in two of which represented Govt of South Australia. *Recreations:* pastoralist, vigneron. *Address:* Supreme Court of South Australia, Adelaide.

Died 1 July 1943.

COLQUHOUN, Ethel M., (Mrs Tawse Jollie), OBE 1930; *d* of S. Cookson, MD, Stafford; *m* 1st, 1900, Archibald Colquhoun, writer and explorer (*d* 1914); 2nd, 1915, John Tawse Jollie, of Rhodesia. Travelled in the Far East, Africa, North and South America with her first husband; member Executive Committee, Women's Unionist Association and British Women's Emigration Association; has spoken for these societies, and for National Service League; organised free buffet for soldiers and sailors (under War Office) at Paddington Station, 1915; on death of first husband edited the journal of Royal Colonial Institute; member Legislative Council, Southern Rhodesia; first woman elected for any Colonial Legislature; organiser Rhodesian Responsible Government Association. *Publications:* Two on their Travels (illustrated by author), 1902; The Whirlpool of Europe (jointly), 1906; The Vocation of Woman, 1913; The Real Rhodesia, 1923; contrib. to Quarterly, Nineteenth Century, National, etc.

Died 21 Sept. 1950.

CONNER, Lewis Atterbury, MD; Professor of Medicine, Emeritus, Cornell University Medical College; *b* 17 Jan. 1867; *s* of Charles Horace and Catherine Atterbury Conner; *m* 1st, 1900, Emma Witt Harris (*d* 1921); 2nd, 1923, Laila Ann Coston, MD; one *s* four *d*. *Educ:* Yale Univ., PhB 1887; College of Physicians and Surgeons, Columbia University, MD 1890. Professor of Medicine and Head of Department, Cornell University Medical College, 1916–32; Physician to New York Hospital, 1905–32, Consulting Phys. to New York Hospital since 1932; Editor American Heart Journal, 1925–38; Colonel USA Medical Corps, 1917–19; Brig. General USA Medical Officer Reserve Corps. *Address:* 25 East 67th St, New York 19, NY, USA. *Club:* University (NY City).

Died 3 Dec. 1950.

CONNOLLY, Thomas James D.; *see* Doüll-Connolly.

CONWAY, Arthur William, FRS 1915; R. S. Council, 1935–36; Hon. Fellow, Corpus Christi College, Oxford; *b* Wexford, 2 Oct. 1875; *s* of Myles Conway; *m* Daphne Bingham (decd), Dublin; one *s* three *d*. *Educ:* University Coll., Dublin; Corpus Christi Coll., Oxford. MA (RUI and Oxon). Hon. DSc (RUI) 1908; Hon. ScD (Dub.) 1938; Hon. LLD (St Andrews), 1938; Pontifical Academy of Sciences, 1938; Registrar and Professor of Mathematical Physics, University College, Dublin, 1909–40; President, University Coll., Dublin, 1940–47; ex-Fellow of RUI; Senator National University of Ireland, 1909–47; member Governing Body of Univ. Coll., Dublin, 1909–48; late President Royal Dublin Society; late President RIA; Chairman, Board of Theoretical Physics, Dublin Institute of Higher Studies; Vice-Chancellor Nat. Univ. of Ireland, 1942–45. *Publications:* Various Memoirs on Mathematical Physics; editor of the Mathematical Works of Sir William Rowan Hamilton. *Address:* Colamore Lodge, Dalkey, Co. Dublin. *T:* Dalkey 62. *Clubs:* University of London; National University (Dublin).

Died 11 July 1950.

COURCHESNE, Most Rev. Georges, DD; Archbishop of Rimouski, (RC), since 1946; *b* Pierreville, Qué., 13 Sept. 1880; *s* of Alexandre Courchesne, farmer, and Celina Bazin. *Educ:* Nicolet Seminary, Rome. Ordained to priesthood, 1904; Professor of Rhetoric in Nicolet till 1908; completed his theological studies in Rome, where he obtained his grade of Doctor after three years, 1908–11; spent six months at the University of Friburg; again Professor in Nicolet at the Seminary, 1911–19; Principal of the Normal School of Nicolet, and Professor of Pedagogy at Laval University of Quebec, 1920–28; Catholic Bishop of Rimouski, 1928–46. *Publication:* Nos Humanités, 1927. *Address:* Rimouski, Qué., Canada.

Died 14 Nov. 1950.

COWAN, William Christie, CBE 1939; BL; Solicitor; Senior Partner of Honeyman, Henderson and Christie Cowan, 103 Bath Street, Glasgow, C2; *b* Ardrossan, Ayrshire, 20 May 1878; *s* of Adam Cowan, JP and Jessie Christie; *m* 1907, Jane, *d* of George Herriot, JP; one *s* one *d*. *Educ:* Hutchesons' Grammar School, Glasgow; Glasgow University. Member of Scottish Law Agents' Society, Incorporation of Maltmen, Deacons' Association and Grand Antiquity Society; Hon. Sec., Glasgow Dickens Society; Hon. Vice-Pres., Scottish Liberal National Association. Member of Council of the Faculty of Procurators in Glasgow. *Recreations:* golf, bowling, swimming. *Address:* 20 Corrour Road, Glasgow S3. *T:* Langside 208. *Clubs:* Scottish Liberal (Edinburgh); Literary (Glasgow).

Died 16 Nov. 1950.

COYAJEE, Sir Jahangir Cooverjee, Kt 1928; *b* 11 Sept. 1875; *s* of late Coverjee Coyajee, Rajkot. *Educ:* Caius Coll., Cambridge. Lately member Royal Commissions on the Indian Tariff and Indian Currency; Professor of Political Economy, Presidency College, Calcutta; Member of the Council of State, 1930; Delegate to Assembly of League of Nations, Geneva, 1930–32;

Principal, Presidency College, 1930–31; retired 1931; Correspondent, Royal Economic Society; Member, Indian Coal Mining Committee, 1936–37. *Publications:* The Indian Fiscal Problem, 1923; Indian Currency and Exchange; The Indian Currency System; India and the League of Nations; The Economic Depression; Cults and Legends of Ancient Iran and China; Studies in Shahnameh. *Address:* 29 Ridge Road, Bombay, 6, India.

Died July 1943.

CUMING, Col Helier Brohier, CB 1900; late Commanding Kaffrarian Rifles; Chief Inspecting Officer Cape Colonial Forces, 1901–24; partner in Howard, Farrer, Robinson Co. Ltd, Engineers, Cape Colony; *b* East London, Cape Colony, 19 Feb. 1867; *e s* of late Hugh Cuming, JP; *m* 1899, Marian Blanche, 2nd *d* of John Bardwell Ebden. *Educ:* Public school, East London, Cape Colony. Rowed for Leander (Cape Colony), 1888–96; joined Kaffrarian Rifles, 1884; lieutenant, 1888; captain, 1891; major, 1899; lieutenant-colonel, 1900; colonel, 1901; commanded Northern Column, Bechuanaland Campaign, 1897 (despatches, medal with clasp); served South African War, 1889–1902 (medal, four clasps, despatches, CB). Decorated in recognition of services during the operations under F.-M. Lord Roberts in South Africa. *Recreations:* formerly rowing, gymnastics, football, golf, riding and hunting.

Died 24 July 1950.

DAGA, Raja Rai Bahadur Sir Seth Bisesardass, KCIE 1934; Kt 1921; Rai Bahadur 1901; Raja 1938; banker, mill owner and mine owner; *b* 1877; *s* of late Dewan Bahadur Sir Kasturchand Daga, KCIE; *m* Lady Krishnabai; one *s*. *Educ:* private. Chairman Nagpur Electric Light and Power Co. Ltd; Director Model Mills, Nagpur, Ltd; Director Berar Manufacturing Co. Ltd, Badnera; Director Bank of India, Ltd, Nagpur Branch; Life Member, Countess of Dufferin Fund Committee; Holds First Class Tazim of Bikaner State; Member of Legislative Assembly, Bikaner State. *Publication:* Kasturchand Memorial Dufferin Hospital for Women at Nagpur, CP. *Address:* Nagpur, CP, India. *TA:* Lucky. *Clubs:* Willingdon (Bombay); Gondewana (Nagpur).

Died 18 Aug. 1941.

DAIN, Charles Kenneth, CBE 1927; *b* 1879; *m* 1907, Hilda, *d* of late F. T. Tayler, MD. Assistant Treasurer, Uganda Protectorate, 1904; Deputy Treasurer, 1918; Treasurer, 1922–29; Member of the Executive and Legislative Councils; President of the Government Tender Board; Chairman of the Local Currency Advisory Board, and Currency Officer; Chairman of the Asiatic Widows and Orphans Pension Fund. *Address:* Top Hill House, West Malling, Kent.

Died 7 Sept. 1950.

DAVID, Rev. Richard; Vicar of Llantwit Major, 1912, and Rural Dean of Groneath Lower-Western Division, 1918; Canon of Fairwell in Llandaff Cathedral, 1923; formerly Vicar of Treharris. *Educ:* Cowbridge School; St David's College, Lampeter. *Address:* The Vicarage, Llantwit Major, Glamorgan.

Died 1 Sept. 1947.

DAVIES, Henry Meirion; *b* 29 March 1875; *s* of William and Anne Davies; *m* 1902, Margaret J., *d* of Capt. John Lewis, Borth; one *s* one *d*. *Educ:* Tynyberth Council School, Corris; Old Bank School, Aberystwyth; UCW Aberystwyth; Didsbury College. Travelled Bagillt Circuit (2 terms) Abergele: Rhyl, Pwllheli, Holyhead, Llanrwst, Barmouth, Coedpoeth, Towyn, Caernarvon, Llanrhaedr (2 terms), Liverpool (Oakfield Road); District Chapel Secretary (1st N Wales) Overseas Missions; General Secretary of Overseas Missions for Wales; Journal Secretary of Welsh Methodist Assembly; Assistant Secretary; Secretary of Welsh Methodist Assembly 1921–33; President of Welsh Methodist Assembly 1934–35. *Publications:* articles in Connexional Periodical (Eurgrawn). *Address:* Bronwylfa, Tregeiriog, Wrexham.

Died 28 Jan. 1950.

DAVISON, Charles Stewart, BA, MA, LLB; Hon. Fellow Magdalene College, Cambridge; *b* 14 April 1855; *s* of Edward Francis and Charlotte Sewall (White) Davison; unmarried. *Educ:* on the Continent with tutor; Fay School, Newport, RI; Harvard; Columbia; Cambridge; Inner Temple. Counselor-at-law in New York City since 1877; Specialist in constitutional and commercial law; formerly Chm. Exec. Committee Assoc. of the Bar of the City of New York, etc.; Chevalier Legion of Honor, 1920; devised the Mystery Ships (Q-Boats) for British and French Navies, 1915; Drew the Fisheries Law of the Province of Quebec. *Publications:* Letters to Hiram Freeborn (1915–1918); Reprisal in War; Dealers in Money; Maritime and Belligerent Rights; Treason, etc.; Selling the Bear's Hide, 1902; Freedom of the Seas, 1918; The Alien in Our Midst, 1930; also (with Madison Grant) The Passing of the Great Race, 1916 and The Conquest of a Continent, 1933. *Recreations:* Salmon angling, yachting, golf, large game shooting, breeding domestic animals, etc. *Address:* 25 Broad Street, New York City; Green River Farm, South Williamstown, Mass. *TA:* Cedilla, New York. *T:* Hanover 2–1557, Lackawanna 4–0883. *Clubs:* United University; Down-town Asstn., Harvard, Century (New York); Pitt, Amateur Dramatic (Cambridge).

Died 25 Nov. 1942.

DAY, Frank Parker, MA, LLD, DLitt; *b* Shubenacadie, Nova Scotia, 9 May 1881; *s* of Reverend George Day and Keziah Hardwick; *m* 1910, Mabel Killam, Yarmouth, Nova Scotia; one *s*. *Educ:* Lunenburg and Pictou Academies; Mount Allison University, Sackville, NB; Oxford; University of Berlin. Professor of English, University of New Brunswick, Fredericton, NB, 1909–12; Professor of English and Dean of Freshmen, Carnegie Institute of Technology, Pittsburgh, Pa, 1912–14; European War, 1914–19; raised and commanded 185th Cape Breton Highlanders; in France commanded 25th Infantry Bn (First Nova Scotia Battalion, Fifth Brigade, Second Division); promoted to Colonel on field in battle of Amiens; Director of Academic Studies and Dean of Freshmen, Carnegie Institute of Technology, Pittsburgh Pa, 1919–26; President Union College and Chancellor of University, Schenectady, New York, 1928–33; Professor of English, Swarthmore College, Swarthmore, Pennsylvania. Engaged in various forms of war work in War of 1939–45. *Publications:* River of Strangers; Autobiography of a Fisherman; Rockbound; John Paul's Rock. *Recreations:* fishing, hunting, farming. *Address:* Lake Annis, Nova Scotia. *T:* 4–7402, 47942. *Clubs:* Twenty (Oxford); Century Association (New York City).

Died 31 July 1950.

DEANE, Sir George Campbell, Kt 1930; *b* 7 July 1873; 2nd *s* of John C. Deane, of Barbados, and Laura Robinson; *m* 1904, Maude, *d* of R. A. Swan, formerly 1st Puisne Judge, Trinidad; one *d*. *Educ:* Harrison College, Barbados; St John's College, Oxford. Called to Bar, Inner Temple, 1898; practised at the Bar of British Guiana, 1898–1903, and at Trinidad Bar, 1903–10; Magistrate Arima, Trinidad, 1910–13, when appointed Magistrate of Port of Spain, Trinidad; 2nd Puisne Judge, Trinidad, 1920; Chief Justice of the Leeward Islands, 1923–24; Puisne Judge Supreme Court, Straits Settlements, 1924–29; Chief Justice of the Gold Coast, 1929–35, and President of the West African Court of Appeal; served in the Trinidad Light Horse from 1912, and was Adjutant of the regiment, 1914–18; retired 1935. *Recreations:* riding, racing, swimming.

Died 31 Dec. 1948.

DE GLANVILLE, Sir Oscar James Lardner, Kt 1931; CIE, 1925; OBE, 1918; Officer of St John of Jerusalem. Barrister; member Burma Legislative Council from 1923, President 1932–35; late member of the Senate, Burma Legislature.

Died 1942.

DOULL-CONNOLLY, Thomas James; KC (Scot.) 1946; BL, MA, LLB (Edin.); *b* 21 July 1878; *s* of James Connolly, railway contractor, and Mary Murtha; *m* 1912, Ella Steedman Dickson; two *s* one *d*. *Educ:* privately and at Edinburgh University. Solicitor, 1905; Advocate, 1929. Chm. Scot. Board of Licenses and Gen. Insurance Co. Ltd and of Prudential Investment Building Soc. *Publications:* Handbook on Workmen's Compensation Acts, 1925; Workmen's Compensation Acts, 1930; Select Scots Law Maxims, 1934. *Recreations:* motoring, walking, swimming, brambling. *Address:* Dundrum, Liberton, Edinburgh. *T:* Edinburgh 79261.

Died 16 Oct. 1949.

DREVER, James, MA (Edin.), BSc (Lond.), DPhil. (Edin); FRSE; Emeritus Professor of Psychology, University of Edinburgh; Knight of Royal Norwegian Order of St Olav; Chairman, Royal Blind Asylum and School, Edinburgh, and Scottish National Institute for Blinded Soldiers, etc., 1941–44; Chairman, Executive Committee, Scottish National Institute; Member, Advisory Committee, S. P. Branch, War Office, since 1941; President, Scottish Child Guidance Council, since 1935; President, XIIth International Congress of Psychology, Edinburgh, 1948; Editor, British Journal of Psychology Monographs, and Assistant Editor of British Journal of Psychology; *b* Shapinsay, Orkney Islands, 8 April 1873; *m* Annie May, *e d* of Samuel Watson, Stromness; two *s* one *d*. *Educ:* Stromnness H. G. School; Heriot-Watt College and University, Edinburgh. Studied medicine for two years, taught at Tain, Stronsay, George Watson's College, Edinburgh; Assistant to Professor of Education, Edinburgh, 1906; BSc (First Class, Psychology), London, 1909; organised the Pedagogical Laboratory at Moray House, 1912; Lecturer on Education, Univ. of Edinburgh; Combe Lecturer in Psychology, Univ. of Edinburgh, 1919–31; Professor of Psychology, Univ. of Edinburgh, 1931–45; Pres., British Psychological Society, 1935–38. *Publications:* Greek Education: its Principles and Practice, 1912; Instinct in Man: a Contribution to the Psychology of Education, 1917; The Psychology of Everyday Life, 1921; The Psychology of Industry, 1921; Introduction to the Psychology of Education, 1922; English Editions of Stilling's Psuedo-isochromatishce Tafeln, 1936 and 1939; (with Dr M. Collins) An Introduction to Experimental Psychology, 1926; A First Laboratory Guide in Psychology, 1926; Performance Tests of Intelligence, 1928; A Group Test for Colour Blindness, 1932; Psychology and Practical Life, 1936; (with Miss M. Drummond) The Pre-School Child, 1928; Articles on Psychology in scientific and educl jls. *Address:* 2A Dick Place, Edinburgh.

Died 11 Aug. 1950.

EDWARDS, Lt-Col Ivo Arthyr Exley, CMG 1919; Squadron Leader RAFVR; *b* Singlewell, Kent, 1 Jan. 1881; *s* of Henry Exley Edwards and Clara Edwards, of Parkstone, Dorset; *m* 1st, 1906, Olive Maud Amy Donaldson of Hatton Hall, Windlesham, Surrey; one *d*; 2nd, 1922, Evelyn Marion Stuart; three *s*. *Educ:* Malvern College; Durham University. 2nd Lt RGA 1901; 1st Lt 1904; Capt. 1914; Major, 1916; transferred to RFC 1916; Lt-Col RFC 1917; served in England until 1910; India until 1914; Dardanelles, 1915–16; France, 1916–17, 1917–18; Staff Officer Air Ministry, 1918–19 (despatches thrice, CMG, Chevalier Légion d'Honneur, 1915–16 Star); retired from RAF and RA, 1919; Deputy Director Air Transport Department of Civil Aviation, Air Ministry, 1922. *Publication:* (with F. Tymms)

Commercial Air Transport, 1927. *Recreations:* golf, shooting. *Address:* Cronks Foot, Meadvale, Reigate, Surrey. *T:* Reigate 3072.

Died 19 Aug. 1947.

ELDER, William Alexander, CBE 1941; Principal Veterinary and Agricultural Officer, Swaziland Government; *b* 31 March 1881; *s* of late John and Elizabeth Elder, Wokingham, Berks; *m* 1908, Valerie Estcourt Eady; two *s* one *d*. *Educ:* Kendrick School, Reading, Berks; New Veterinary College, Edinburgh. MRCVS 1902; FRCVS 1914. Went to South Africa as Civil Veterinary Surgeon attached to Army Veterinary Corps in 1902; joined Swaziland Government Service, 1903; pensioned 1941; returned to duty for duration of war, 1941. *Recreations:* football, tennis. *Address:* Mbabane, Swaziland, South Africa. *Clubs:* Royal Empire Society; English (Lourenco Marques); Transvaal Automobile (Johannesburg).

Died 16 April 1946.

ELIOT, Rev. Samuel Atkins, DD, LLD; Minister Emeritus of the Arlington St Church, Boston, Mass; *b* Cambridge, Mass, 24 Aug. 1862; *s* of late Dr C. W. Eliot; *m* 1889, Frances S. Hopkinson, Cambridge. *Educ:* Harvard. Minister, Unity Church, Denver, 1889–93; Church of the Saviour, Brooklyn, 1893–98; Pres. American Unitarian Association, 1898–1927; Pres. Federation of Churches. *Address:* 25 Reservoir St, Cambridge, Mass, USA. *Clubs:* Faculty (Cambridge, Mass); City, Rotary (Boston); Harvard (New York).

Died 11 Oct. 1950.

FELS, Willi, CMG 1936; Managing Director Hallenstein Bros Ltd; *b* Halle, Germany, 1858; *m* 1881, Sara, *d* of Bendix Hallenstein; one *s* three *d*. Chairman Council Otago Museum; presented his collection of ethnographical material to the Museum. *Address:* Manono, London St, Dunedin, New Zealand. *Club:* Dunedin (Dunedin).

Died 29 June 1946.

FLETCHER, John Gould; *b* Little Rock, Arkansas, 3 Jan. 1886; *o s* of John Gould and Adolphine Krause Fletcher; *m* 1st, Florence Emily Arbuthnot (divorced 1936); 2nd, 1936, Charlie May Hogue. *Educ:* Phillips Academy, Andover, Massachusetts; Harvard College; LLD University of Arkansas, 1933. Travelled extensively in Europe, 1908–14; in America 1914–16, visiting California, Arizona, and going down Mississippi River in a steamboat; resident in London, 1916; revisited America 1920, 1923, 1926–27, 1929, 1931; resident in America since 1933. *Publications:* Fire and Wine, 1913; The Dominant City, 1913; Irradiations, 1915; Goblins and Pagodas, 1916; The Tree of Life, 1918; Japanese Prints, 1918; Some Contemporary American Poets (pamphlet), 1920; Breakers and Granite, 1921; Paul Gauguin, His Life and Art, 1921; Parables, 1925; Branches of Adam, 1926; The Dance over Fire and Water, translated from the French of Elie Faure, 1926; The Reveries of a Solitary, translated (with introduction) from the French of J. J. Rousseau, 1927; Captain John Smith, 1928; The Black Rock, 1928; Europe's Two Frontiers, 1930; XXIV Elegies, 1935; Life is my Song, 1937; Selected Poems, 1938 (Pulitzer Prize in Poetry, 1939); South Star, 1941; The Burning Mountain, 1946; Arkansas, 1947. *Recreations:* gipsying and gardening. *Address:* Johnswood, Route 5 Box 435, Little Rock, Arkansas, USA.

Died 10 May 1950.

FORSON, A. J.; *b* Glasgow, 1872; *m* 1896. *Educ:* Glasgow University. First charge, Dundee, 1893; Govan, 1904; Minister (Congregational) Motherwell, 1924–32; Editor of Scottish Congregationalist, 1922–32; President of the Congregational Union of Scotland, 1931–32; introduced Institutional work at Govan with Brotherhood of over 1000 members and Sisterhood of over 800; many other agencies; was mainly instrumental in ending a lock-out in Dundee involving 40,000 workers; was made an Hon. Member of the Boilermakers' Society in recognition of similar service rendered in a big shipyard lock-out; lectured on Economics at the Congregational College, Edinburgh; created theological controversy by his teaching, concerning the Problem of Future Destiny, 1927. *Publications:* The Law of Love; Faith and Ideals; Brochure on Keir Hardie; The Story of Our Union, 1929; contributed articles to various magazines and weekly articles to different papers. *Recreations:* bowling and fishing. *Address:* Gowanlea, Crawford Street, Motherwell, Lanarkshire.

Died 2 Oct. 1950.

FRAZER, Col George Stanley, CMG 1916; late 110th Mahratta Light Infantry; *b* 9 Feb. 1865; *s* of Col W. M. Frazer, Indian Police; *m* Geraldine, *y d* of W. F. Parsons, Risley Hall, Derbyshire. *Educ:* Wellington. Entered East Yorks Regt 1885; Capt. Indian Army, 1896; Major, 1903; Lieut-Col 1910; Col 1916; served Burma, 1887–88 (medal, two clasps); European War, Mesopotamia, 1914–17 (CMG); retired, 1919. *Address:* Heathfield, Ootacamund, South India.

Died 15 Dec. 1950.

GOVINDAN NAIR, Diwan Bahadur Chettur, CIE 1939; Endowments Commissioner (on leave) and Secretary to Orissa Legislative Assembly; *b* 23 Dec. 1881; *s* of U. Raman Menon and C. Narayani Amma; *m* 1911, K. Lakshmi; two *s* four *d. Educ:* Madras Christian College. BA and BL Madras Univ. and Barrister-at-Law (Cert. of Hons) Gray's Inn. Advocate, Madras High Court for some years; joined Madras Judicial Service and rose to position of District and Sessions Judge; was Asst Sec., Under Sec., and Joint Sec. in Law Dept of Madras Secretariat; attached Officer and Deputy Sec. in Legislative Dept of Govt of India; Joint Sec. in Reforms Dept of Govt of Bihar and Orissa and Judicial Sec. and Legal Remembrancer to Govt of Orissa; was nominated Member of Madras Legislative Council and Council of State and Central Assembly in New Delhi; was Sec. to Council of State and Sec. to Advisory Council and Legislative Assembly of Orissa; was a member of Senate of Madras Univ. and Examiner of Master of Law Examination of that Univ. and for Govt Examinations of Madras and Orissa. *Publication:* A Commentary on the Malabar Tenancy Act. *Recreation:* tennis. *Address:* Cuttack, Orissa, India.

Died Nov. 1945.

GRAHAM, Robert James Douglas, FRSE; Professor of Botany, University of St Andrews. *Educ:* MA St Andrews 1904; BSc St Andrews 1906; DSc St Andrews 1917. Indian Agricultural Service, 1907–21; Economic Botanist, Central Provinces, 1908–17; served European War, Mesopotamia, 1917–20 (Lt-Col); Director of Agriculture, Mesopotamia, 1920–21; Lecturer in Botany, University of Edinburgh, 1921–34.

Died 3 Sept. 1950.

GREENFIELD, Herbert; *b* Winchester, 1869; *m* 1st, 1900, Elizabeth Harris (*d* 1922), Strathroy, Ontario; two *s*; 2nd, 1926, Marjorie Greenwood, *widow* of Shibley Cormack, Edmonton, Alberta. *Educ:* Wesleyan School, Dalston, England. Migrated to Ontario, Canada, 1892; farmed there; moved west to Alberta, 1905; active in municipal work; President Alberta Association of Municipalities several years; active in Farmers' Movement; served on Canadian Council of Agriculture; Vice-President, United Farmers of Alberta, 1919–21; Premier of Alberta, 1921–25; Commissioner of Colonisation, Alberta, 1926; Agent-General for Alberta, 1927–31. *Address:* Toronto General Trust Building, Calgary, Alberta.

Died 23 Aug. 1949.

GROOM, Gladys Laurence, (Mrs M. Cordellis); *d* of Rev. Arthur Butt, MA, Balliol, Oxford, and Dora Annette Nolan; *m* 1st, 1913, Arthur Groom; one *s* one *d*; 2nd, 1943, Mavrikios Cordellis. *Educ:* C. D. S., Clifton; abroad. Poet, essayist, short-story writer, journalist, literary, dramatic and art critic, lecturer on English and French literature; did considerable Anglo-French Entente propaganda work after European war; served as voluntary worker with International Red Cross in Greece, 1941–44; Member, Committee of Anglo-Hellenic League (Athens Branch); Hon. Lecturer for the League in Athens on Modern English Literature; has contributed poems, articles, essays, stories, criticisms to The Morning Post, Observer, The Bookman, Sphere, Country Life, Anglo French Review, New World, New York Herald Tribune, La Renaissance, Les Nouvelles Littéraires and most of the popular magazines and reviews. *Publications: poems:* The Ship of Destiny, 1926; The Singing Sword, 1927; François and Katherine, 1929, American edn 1929; Grecian Nocturne, 1933; Poems, 1936–46, 1948; The Magic Country, 1951 (posthumous); *prose:* A Sentimental Journey Through Greece, 1935. *Recreations:* reading, travelling, swimming, walking, play-writing. *Address:* 65A Eressou Street, Athens, Greece. *TA:* c/o Amexco, Athens, Greece.

Died 25 July 1948.

GUPTA, J. N., CIE 1927; MBE; ICS; retired as Member Board of Revenue, Bengal; *b* 1870; *s* of late Ghanashyama Gupta, retired subordinate Judge under Government; *m* 1894, 4th *d* of late Romesh Chandra Dutt, CIE, ICS; four *s* one *d. Educ:* Presidency College, Calcutta; Balliol College, Oxford. Entered the Indian Civil Service, 1892; held successively post of District Magistrate and Commissioner of a division; on special duty on several occasions, notably in 1903, when he was deputed to the Delhi Durbar held under Lord Curzon and was placed in charge of the Indian section of the Press Camp; Secretary of Lord Sinha when the latter went to England, 1918; Represented the Government of India at the Labour Branch of the League of Nations Conference, 1921. *Publications:* Life of Romesh Chandra Dutt, CIE, ICS, 1910; Foundations of National Progress, with an introduction by the Rt Hon. Lord Sinha, 1927; Social Drama in Bengali Monisha and Kasti Pathar. *Recreations:* fond of shooting, plays golf, rides, etc. *Clubs:* National Liberal; Darjiling (Darjiling); South (Calcutta).

Died 1947.

HALSTEAD, Albert; *b* Cincinnatti, 19 Sept. 1867; *s* of Murat Halstead and Mary Banks Halstead; *m* 1896, Aline Wilcox; one *s* two *d. Educ:* Princeton Univ. AB 1889. Student of Law, Cincinnatti Law School, 1889–91; newspaper correspondent, Washington, 1891–96; Col and ADC to Governor William McKinley of Ohio, 1892–96; Editor, Springfield (Mass) Union, 1896–99; Washington Correspondent, 1900–06; contributor to magazines of economic and political matters, 1889–1906; Consul at Birmingham, 1906–15; Consul-General at Vienna, 1915–17; detailed Dept of State, 1917; assigned to Stockholm as Consul-General and Commercial Adviser to US Legation, 1917–18; American Commissioner in Austria, 1919–20; American Consul-General, Montreal, 1920–28; Consul-General of the United States in London, 1928–32; Foreign Service Officer, Class 1, 1924; retired. *Publications:* as publicist wrote many magazine and newspaper articles. *Recreation:* motoring.

Died 21 May 1949.

HARVEY, James Graham; QC 1907; BA, LLB; practising Barrister-at-Law in the City of Winnipeg; Solicitor and Counsel for Greater Winnipeg Water District; *b* Lanark Co., Ontario, 3 June 1869; *s* of J. G. Harvey and Catherine Ferguson; *m* 1897, Ida Mills, Omeemee, Ontario; two *s* one *d. Educ:* Winnipeg Public Schools; Manitoba University, BA 1887; LLB 1890. Barrister and Attorney, 1891; practised law in Winnipeg till 1896; moved to Dauphin, Manitoba, and practised law there until 1913, when returned to Winnipeg; elected to represent the Provincial Constituency of Dauphin in the Manitoba Legislature, 1910; Presbyterian. *Club:* St Charles Country (Winnipeg).

Died 12 Nov. 1950.

HOGARTH, Maj.-Gen. Donald Macdonald, CMG 1918, DSO 1917; *b* 1879; *m* Madge, *d* of H. R. Patterson, Winnipeg; two *s* one *d.* Canadian Army Service Corps; served European War, 1915–18 (despatches, DSO). *Address:* Glen Edyth Place, Toronto, Ont; 3100 Bank of Commerce Building, Toronto, Canada.

Died 2 June 1950.

HOLT, Very Rev. Edward John, MBE 1938; Rector of Holy Trinity and Dean of Trinidad, Port of Spain, 1914–46; resigned on grounds of ill-health, after 57 years' work, 1947; *b* Grantham, Lincs, 29 Sept. 1867; *e s* of late Rev. T. E. Holt, Diocesan Missioner, Winchester; *m* 1895, Mary Jane, 5th *d* of D. S. Osment, Colonial Engineer, St Vincent. *Educ:* St Augustine's College, Canterbury. Ordained, 1890; Curate of St George's Cathedral, Windward Islands, 1890–93; All Saints, Port of Spain, 1893–95; Cathedral, 1895–1914; Chaplain to the Local Forces, 1918. *Recreations:* music (organ), campanology (Member of Soc. College Youths), photography, Freemasonry (PM, Kt 30 deg.), wood-carving. *Address:* Long Circular Road, Port of Spain, Trinidad.

Died 6 Nov. 1948.

HUGHES, Col Edward Talfourd, CB 1904; VD; *b* 29 Dec. 1855; *o s* of Col Sir Edwin Hughes, late MP for Woolwich; *m* 1883, Annie Sarah Gooch (*d* 1922), *d* of late William Smith; two *d. Educ:* Greenwich Proprietary School; King's College School. Articled to his father, 1872; admitted a Solicitor, 1878; retired from business, 1924; member of Woolwich Local Board, 1882; Plumstead Vestry and District Board of Works; Baths Commissioner for Plumstead; elected an Alderman of first Woolwich Borough Council; Commissioner for Oaths, and a Land Tax Commissioner; 2nd Lieutenant in the 2nd Kent Volunteer Artillery, 1873; Lieut-Col and Officer Commanding, 1888; holds VD and rank of Colonel, 1893; Coronation medal, 1902; SA medal (CIV) and Order of League of Mercy; Freeman of the City of London, and on Court of the Worshipful Company of Bakers. *Address:* 58 Leysdown Road, Eltham, SE9.

Died 15 Dec. 1943.

HUNTER, William George, CBE 1926; *b* 1869; *m*; three *s* one *d.* Entered Civil Service (Post Office), 1887; Accountant, National Health Insurance Commission, 1912; Deputy Accountant-General, Ministry of Health, 1920–30; retired, 1930. *Address:* 44 Offington Drive, Worthing.

Died 10 Sept. 1950.

JAISALMER, Maharajahdhiraj of, HH Maharawal Sir Jawahir Singhji Bahadur, KCSI 1918; *b* 18 Nov. 1882; *S,* 1914; *m*; two *s. Educ:* Mayo College, Ajmer. *Address:* Jaisalmer, Rajputana.

Died Jan. 1949.

JECKELL, George Allen; Controller, Yukon Territory, from 1913; Agent, Department of Public Works; Inspector of Income Tax, Yukon Territory; *b* 25 July 1880; *s* of William Jeckell and Essy Case; *m* 2nd, Anna Theresa Boyle; three *s. Educ:* Public and High Schools, Province of Ontario. Teacher, Public and High Schools, Province of Ontario, North West Territories, and Yukon Territory; the position of Gold Commissioner of

Yukon Territory was abolished, and the duties of Office merged with that of Controller, 1932. *Address:* Dawson, Yukon Territory, Canada.

Died 30 May 1950.

KAY, Col William Martin, CMG 1916; CBE 1941; DL; *b* 18 Aug. 1871; *s* of James Cunninghame Kay, Solicitor, Hamilton, Co. Lanark, and Elizabeth Stevenson Crawford; *m* 1903, Christina Russell (*d* 1917), *d* of James Smart, Coalmaster, Hamilton; one *s* one *d. Educ:* Glasgow Academy and Univ. of Glasgow. Joined 2nd VB Scottish Rifles, 1889; TD 1910; commanded 6th Scottish Rifles, TF, 1912–19; served European War, 1914–19 (despatches, CMG, wounded); Colonel, 1918; Hon. Sheriff Substitute of Lanarkshire.

Died 27 Jan. 1948.

KEELAN, Percival Stanley, CIE 1924; Chief Mining Engineer, Bengal Coal Co.; *b* 1875; *m* 1899, H. E. Rooke, Bengal. *Address:* c/o Andrew Yule & Co. Ltd, 8 Clive Row, Calcutta, India.

Died 15 Aug. 1950.

KHALIL, Mohammed Bey, MD (Egypt), PhD (London), MD `(Brussels), MRCP (Lond.), DPH (Oxon), DTM&H (Eng.); Under-Secretary of State, Ministry of Health, Egypt, 1950; *b* 23 May 1895; *s* of Khalil Eff. Abdel Khalik; *m* 1935, (Sit) Farida Hamdy; two *s* one *d. Educ:* Cairo; England; and Belgium. Cairo School of Medicine, 1913–18 (Golden Sultan's Gift). Clinical Assistant at the Kasr-el-Aini Hospital, 1918; House Surgeon for one year; the Egyptian Government sent him to England to specialise in Tropical Medicine at the London School of Tropical Medicine, 1920; Sub-Director of the Parasitic Diseases Research Department of the Public Health Laboratories, 1922–25; lecturer for Parasitology at the Cairo School of Medicine, 1924–25; External Professor of Veterinary Parasitology at the School of Veterinary Medicine, Cairo, since 1924; Professor of Parasitology, Faculty of Medicine, Cairo, 1925, and Director, Research Institute and Endemic Diseases Hospital, PHD, Cairo, 1932; Controller-General of Endemic Diseases, Min. of Public Health, 1939; Member of the Medical Research Committee for the investigation of Ankylostomiasis in the Cornish Mine, 1920; Member of the Filariasis Expedition of the Colonial Office for the West Indies, 1922. Recipient of several Egyptian and foreign Decorations. *Publications:* The Bibliography of Schistosomiasis (Bilharziasis), 1931; The Specific Treatment of Human Schistosomiasis (Bilharziasis), 1931; Dermal Leishmaniasis, a study of an endemic focus in Egypt, 1934. *Address:* Ministry of Public Health, Cairo, Egypt. *T:* 190 Maadi.

Died 7 Oct. 1950.

KIDD, Rt Rev. John Thomas, DD, LLD; Bishop of London, Ont (RC), since 1931; *b* Athlone, Ont, 28 Aug. 1868. *Educ:* Common School; De La Salle High School; St Michael's College, Toronto; Univ. of Propaganda and Univ. of Gregorian, Univ. of Rome. Priest, 1902; returning to native diocese of Toronto, was appointed Assistant, Pastor, Episcopal Secretary and Chancellor, Administrator of Diocese during vacancy of the See, 1911–12; President of St Augustine's Seminary, Toronto, 1913; Bishop of Calgary, 1925–31; LLD (Hon.) University of Ottawa, 1923; University of Western Ontario, 1934. *Address:* 90 Central Ave, London, Ontario, Canada.

Died 2 June 1950.

KNIGHT, Rt Rev. Leslie Albert; *b* York, West Australia, 4 Aug. 1890; *s* of George Edward and Clara Knight, Wandering, WA; *m* 1919, Mary Bertha Moore, Timaru, New Zealand; no *c. Educ:* Boys' High School, Christchurch; University of New Zealand, BA 1913, MA 1914; Univ. of London (Inter. Divinity 1921). Deacon, 1914; priest, 1915; Curate of Fendalton, Christchurch, 1915–16; Vicar of Hororata, West

Malvern, 1916–17; Chaplain to NZEF in France, 1917–19; Vicar of Leithfield, 1919–21; Vicar of Kaiapoi, 1921–23; Rector and Chaplain of St Saviour's Boys' Orphanage, Timaru, 1923–28 (all in NZ); Warden of St Barnabas Theological College, and special preacher St Peter's Cathedral, Adelaide, 1928–38; Bishop of Bunbury from 1938. *Recreations:* golf; painting in oils and water-colour, photography (pictorial). *Address:* Bishopscourt, Bunbury, Western Australia. *TA:* Bunbury, WA. *T:* Bunbury 163. *Clubs:* South Western (Bunbury, WA); Weld (Perth, WA).

Died 31 Dec. 1950.

KOTVAL, Peshotan Sohrabji, CBE 1928; Barrister-at-law; Dean of the Faculty of Law, Nagpur University, since 1927; *b* 10 March 1868; *s* of Sohrabji D. Kotval and Navajbai Dadabhoy Patel; *m* 1905, Shirin, *d* of Dastur Jamshed Dastur Hormuzdiar; three *s* two *d*. *Educ:* St Xavier's College, Bombay; Balliol College, Oxford. Additional Judicial Commissioner, 1919–28; Judicial Commissioner, 1926. *Publications:* Cotton Manufacture in Western India, 1890; Maneckji Limji Gold Medal Essay, Bombay University. *Address:* Civil Lines, Nagpur, CP India. *Club:* Gondwana, Nagpur.

Died 22 Jan. 1949.

LALIQUE, René; artiste décorateur; maître de verrerier; Commandeur de la Légion d'Honneur; Membre du Conseil Supérieur des Beaux Arts; *b* Ay, Marne, 6 avril 1860; *m* Alice Lysiane Ledru. *Œuvres:* Objets d'art. *Recreation:* escrime. *Address:* 40 Cours Albert-Ier, Paris. *T:* Élysées 77–51.

Died 5 May 1945.

LEASK, George Alfred, MA; journalist and author; *b* 29 May 1878; *e s* of late George Leask of Paddington. *Educ:* Aberdeen Univ. MA 1900 (with Classical Hons). Engaged in tutorial work then entered journalism, joining staff of Examiner, 1901; contributor of many articles and stories to various periodicals; literary staff of Amalgamated Press on Universal Encyclopedia, etc; acted as their War Correspondent in France, Sept. and Oct. 1914; founded and edited The World Scout; has contributed Changing London and numerous other articles to Daily Mail Year Book, since 1913; has specialised in interviewing; contributed for years, with hardly a break, a weekly interview to one paper; has specialized and written on hymnology; also lectures on it and other subjects. *Publications:* VC Heroes of the War; Hymns in Time of War; The Story of Our Hymns; Stories of Famous Hymns; Hymn-writers of the Nineteenth Century; Life of Peter Thompson; Life of Sir William Robertson; A Little Book of Success; Golden Deeds of Heroism; Drawing-room Dramas; In Search of Truth; Queen Mab (a 4-act play); The Circus of Europe. *Address:* 28 Northwick Avenue, Harrow.

Died 31 March 1950.

LEMPRIERE, Rev. Philip Charles; *b* 12 April 1890; *s* of late Rev. Philip Alfred Lempriere and of Janet Lempriere; *m* 1915, Kate McKenzie (decd); no *c*. *Educ:* George Watson's College, Edinburgh; Edinburgh University; Edinburgh Theological College. Assistant-Curate St Mary's, Hamilton, 1913–20; Rector, All Saints, Bearsden, 1920–23; St James', Glasgow, 1923–27; St Bride's, Glasgow, 1927–35; St John's, Girvan, 1935–41; St Mary's, Hamilton, 1941–46. In Diocese of Glasgow and Galloway; Examining Chaplain from 1921; Synod Clerk, 1938–43; Dean, 1943–46; Principal of Edinburgh Theological College, and Pantonian Professor of Theology, 1946–48; Canon of St Mary's Cathedral, Edinburgh, 1946–48; Examining Chaplain to the Bishop of Edinburgh, 1947–48; retired 1948. TCF 1917–18. *Recreation:* chess. *Address:* 45 Falcon Gardens, Edinburgh 10.

Died 26 Feb. 1949.

LIVINGSTONE, William P., FRSGS; *b* North Queensferry, Fife; *m* Jeanie Small, Dunfermline; three *s*. Editor, Daily Gleaner, Jamaica; Chief Sub-Editor, Evening Standard and St James's Gazette; Chief Sub-Editor, Evening News, London; Editor, Life and Work, the Record of the Church of Scotland, and Other Lands, the magazine of overseas work, 1912–34; Press Agent, Church of Scotland, 1937–39. *Publications:* Black Jamaica, 1899; The Race Conflict, a Study of Conditions in America, 1911; Mary Slessor of Calabar, 1915; The White Queen of Okoyong, 1916; The New Outlook, 1917; Christina Forsyth, 1918; Dr Laws of Livingstonia, 1921; A Galilee Doctor, 1923; The Master Life, 1925; The Story of David Livingstone, 1929; A Prince of Missionaries, Rev. Alexander Hetherwick, CBE, DD, 1931; The Hero of the Lake, 1933; Empire Church Souvenir, 1938; Church Publicity, 1939; Shetland and the Shetlanders, 1947. *Address:* 121 George Street, Edinburgh.

Died 28 Aug. 1950.

LYLE, Col (Hon. Brig.-Gen.) George Samuel Bateson, CB 1917; RA; *b* 23 July 1865; *m* Grace Adelaide, 2nd *d* of William Lysaght, Beechmount, Mallow. Lt RA 1884; Capt. 1898; Major 1903; Lt-Col 1912; Col 1917; Adjutant, Volunteers, 1888–93; Instructor, School of Gunnery, 1896–1900; RMA, 1900–04; Commandant Gen., Siege School, Lydd, 1916–19. *Address:* Moss End, Pikes Hill Avenue, Lyndhurst.

Died 10 March 1943.

MACINTOSH, Douglas Clyde, MA, PhD, DD, LLD; *b* 18 Feb. 1877; *s* of Peter Macintosh and Elizabeth C. Everett; *m* 1st, 1921, Emily Powell (*d* 1922); 2nd, 1925, Hope G. Conklin; no *c*. *Educ:* McMaster University, Toronto; University of Chicago. Instructor, Philosophy, McMaster University, 1903–04; Professor of Theology, Brandon College, Brandon, Manitoba, 1907–09; Assistant Professor of Theology, Yale Divinity School, 1909–16; Dwight Professor of Theology and the Philosophy of Religion, Yale University, 1916–33, Prof. of Theology and Philosophy of Religion, 1933; Chm. of the Department of Religion in the Graduate School, Yale University, 1920–38. Chaplain CEF, England and France, 1916; YMCA, Secretary AEF France, 1918. *Publications:* God in a World at War, 1918; The Problem of Knowledge, 1915; Theology as an Empirical Science, 1919; The Reasonableness of Christianity, 1925; The Pilgrimage of Faith (Ghosh Lectures) 1931; Religious Realism, 1931; Is There a God?, 1932; Social Religion, 1939; The Problem of Religious Knowledge, 1940; Personal Religion, 1942; Thinking about God, 1942. *Recreation:* gardening. *Address:* 25 Woodlawn Street, Hamden, Conn, USA; c/o Yale Divinity School, 409 Prospect Street, New Haven, Conn, USA.

Died 7 July 1948.

MACKNIGHT, Dodge; artist, painter; *b* Providence, RI, USA, 1 Oct. 1860; *m* 1892, Louise Queyrel. Studied with F. Cormon, Paris, 1884–86; then launched into a painting career, living in France and Spain until 1897, when he returned to America; has since travelled and painted extensively in the Far West, Mexico, Newfoundland, etc. There are many large collections of his water-colour paintings in Boston, Mass at the Museum of Fine Arts, Fogg Museum, Fenway Court and other places; also in Worcester Museum, Brooklyn Museum, New York, etc. *Recreation:* gardening. *Address:* East Sandwich, Mass, USA. *TA:* Sandwich, Mass.

Died 23 May 1950.

McMASTER, Sir Fergus, Kt 1941; Chairman of Directors of Qantas Empire Airways, Ltd and of Queensland and Northern Territory Aerial Service, Ltd; Managing Director McMaster Bros, graziers and woolscourers; *b* 3 May 1879; *m* 1st, 1911, Edith May (*d*

1913), *d* of W. E. R. Scougall; one *d*; 2nd, 1922, Edna, *d* of Alfred Faulkner; three *s*. *Address:* Tamilu, Rees Avenue, Clavfield, Brisbane, Queensland, Australia.

Died 8 Aug. 1950.

M'MEANS, Lt-Col Hon. Lendrum; QC (Can.) 1909; *b* Brantford, Ont, 30 July 1859; *m* 1884; three *s* one *d*. *Educ:* Brantford; Toronto. Called to Bar of Ontario, 1881; Manitoba Bar, 1882; called to the Senate of Canada, 1917; President Autofinance, Limited; MPP South Winnipeg, 1910–14; Lt-Col CEF, Feb. 23, 1916; recruited the 221st Batt. CEF. *Recreations:* golf, motoring, shooting, fishing. *Clubs:* Manitoba, St Charles Country (Winnipeg).

Died 13 Sept. 1941.

MacNEIL, Hermon Atkins, NA; National Academy of Design; sculptor; *b* Everett, Massachusetts, 1866; *s* of Mary Lash Pratt and John Clinton MacNeil; *m* 1895, Carol Brooks; two *s* one *d*; *m* 1946, Cecilia W. Muench. *Educ:* Boston, Massachusetts; Paris; Rome. Many monuments, memorials and busts in New York, Massachusetts, Pennsylvania, etc; works in: Metropolitan Museum, NYC; Art Museum, St Louis, Mo; Art Institute, Chicago; Corcoran Art Gallery, Washington. Medals: Pan-American Expo, Buffalo; Poppenhusen Inst., NYC; Medal of Honour, Arch. League, NYC; medals awarded for busts, reliefs, etc: Paris Expo, 1900 (Silver); Pan-American Expo (Gold); St Louis Expo (Commemorative); San Francisco Expo (Gold); Medal of Numismatic Society of America; Medal commemorating 300th anniversary, NYC; Saltus Medal, 1923; Medal of Paris Salon, 1931. *Recreations:* tennis, boating, motoring, golf. *Address:* College Point, Long Island, New York. *T:* Flushing 0047. *Clubs:* Century, American Academy of Arts and Letters, National Arts (New York).

Died 2 Oct. 1947.

MAHON, Ralph Bodkin, MD, MCh; FRCS Eng.; Emeritus Professor, late Professor of Practice of Medicine, University College, Galway, NUI; Surgeon to Galway Central Hospital; Fellow of the Royal Society of Medicine, London; Fellow of the Royal Academy of Medicine, Ireland; Temp. Captain RAMC; Surgical Specialist to the Dartford War Hospital, 1915; *b* Galway, April 1862; *s* of late Nicholas Mahon, LAHD, and Mary, *d* of late Thomas Bodkin of Brierfort, Co. Galway; *m* 1899, Frances, *y d* of late Captain Charles Philip Roche of Ballygran, Co. Limerick; three *s*. *Educ:* Galway, Dublin, London, Berlin, Munich, Berne. Demonstrator of Anatomy, Queen's College, Galway, 1886; Demonstrator of Anatomy and Assistant to Professor of Physiology, Queen's College, Cork, 1888–89; travelled to South America (Brazil), Canada and United States, Norway, etc. *Publications:* several contributions to medical and scientific journals. *Recreations:* shooting, fishing, golf. *Address:* Merlyn, Merrion, Dublin. *Club:* County (Galway).

Died 21 Aug. 1943.

MARSHALL, Patrick, FRS (NZ); *b* Sapiston, Suffolk, 1869; *m* 1900; one *s* one *d*. *Educ:* Bury St Edmunds; Wanganui College, New Zealand; Otago Univ., New Zealand; Exhibitioner in Natural Science, Canterbury University College, 1889, 1890,1891; BA, BSc 1892; Senior Scholar, 1892, in Geology, NZ Univ.; MA 1st Class Hons Geology, 1893; DSc 1900; Hon. DSc 1949. Lecturer, Natural Sciences, Lincoln College, 1893; Science Master, Auckland College and Grammar School, 1896; Lecturer on Geology, Otago Univ., 1901; Fellow, New Zealand Univ., 1912; Original Fellow, Royal Society of New Zealand, 1919; Professor of Geology and Mineralogy, Otago Univ., 1908–16; Headmaster, Wanganui College, 1916; Geologist and Petrologist, Public Works Department, NZ, 1924; Pres., NZ Inst., 1925; elected Pres., Australian and NZ Assoc. for

Advancement of Science, Canberra, 1939; Pres., Geology Section, Brisbane, 1911; Pres., Geography Section, Sydney, 1932; Pres., Australian and NZ Assoc. for Advancement of Science, Adelaide, 1946; Pres., Royal Society of New Zealand, 1925, Vice-Pres., 1943. Correspondant de l'Académie des Sciences Coloniales, Paris, 1938. Pres., NZ Alpine Club, 1942, 1943. *Publications:* Geography of New Zealand, 1905 and 1912; Geology of New Zealand, 1910; Geology of Mangaia, 1927; Geology of Rarotonga and Atiu, 1930; Scientific Memoirs, in Transactions NZ Institute, Qly Journal Geological Society, London, Royal Geographical Journal, London, Transactions Australian Association Advancement of Science, Mineralogical Society, London, etc. *Recreations:* Rugby football (played for Canterbury Coll. and Province and Otago Univ.), tennis, cricket. *Address:* 50 Ludlam Crescent, Lower Hutt, New Zealand. *Club:* Wellington (NZ).

Died 10 Nov. 1950.

MATTHIESSEN, Francis Otto; writer and teacher; Professor of History and Literature, Harvard University, since 1942; *b* Pasadena, California, 19 Feb. 1902; *s* of Frederic William Matthiessen and Lucy Orne Pratt; unmarried. *Educ:* Hackley School, Tarrytown, New York; Yale University; New College, Oxford; Harvard University. BA (Yale), 1923; Rhodes Scholar, New Coll., Oxford, 1923–25 (BLitt); MA (Harvard), 1926, PhD 1927; DLitt (Princeton), 1947. Cadet for Pilot, RAF, Toronto, Sept.–Dec. 1918; Instructor in English, Yale Univ., 1927–29; Instructor and Tutor in History and Literature, Harvard University, 1929–30, Asst Prof. 1930–34, Associate Prof. 1934–42; Alexander Lecturer, Univ. of Toronto, fall 1944; Lecturer at Salzburg Seminär of American Studies, 1947; Visiting Lecturer, Charles Univ., Prague, fall 1947; Senior Fellow, Kenyon School of English, 1947–; member of Psi Upsilon, Skull and Bones, Phi Beta Kappa, Elizabethan Club, Yale, Signet Society, Teachers Union (AF of L), Harvard, Massachusetts Civil Liberties Union; Vice-Chm. Progressive Party, Mass. *Publications:* Sarah Orne Jewett: A Critical Biography, 1929; Translation: An Elizabethan Art, 1931; The Achievement of T. S. Eliot, 1935 (enlarged ed. 1947); American Renaissance: Art and Expression in the Age of Emerson and Whitman, 1941; Henry James: The Major Phase, 1944; Russell Cheney: A Record of his Work, 1946; The James Family, 1947; From the Heart of Europe, 1948; editor, Selected Poems of Herman Melville, 1944; Stories of Writers and Artists by Henry James, 1944; The American Novels and Stories of Henry James, 1947; Editor (with Kenneth B. Murdock), The Notebooks of Henry James, 1947. *Address:* 87 Pinckney Street, Boston, Massachusetts, USA; Kittery, Maine, USA.

Died 1 April 1950.

MAXWELL, Perriton; editor, author, artist; *b* New York; *s* of Alfred Chester Maxwell and Mary Louise Perriton; *m* Myra Sydney Schuyler. *Educ:* public schools and private tutors, Brooklyn; Brooklyn Art Institute. Consecutively Art Editor, New York Recorder, editorial staff, New York Sun, World Journal, Cosmopolitan Magazine, Philadelphia Saturday Evening Post, Vogue; Editor: Metropolitan Magazine, 1900–06; Cosmopolitan Magazine, 1906–10; Nash's Magazine, London, 1910–15; Leslie's Weekly, 1915–20; Arts and Decoration, 1921–23; Suniland: the magazine of Florida, 1925–26; Theatre Magazine, 1927–29; Editor of first all-spoken daily magazine via wireless; has written many dramas broadcast throughout the USA and Canada. *Publications:* Masterpieces of Art and Nature, 1895; American Art and Artists, 1896; Business Block (play), 1932; A Third of Life (novel), 1935; Aftermath (play), 1935; Famous Story-Teller's Club (radio program series), 1939; Silhouette in Action (novel), 1940; All for the Love of a Lady (fictional diary), 1940; Man with a Mirror (novel), 1946; many contributions to periodicals. *Recreation:* book-collecting. *Address:* 246 West 44th Street, New York, USA.

Died 2 May 1947.

MEENAN, James Nahor, MD, BCh; BAO, RUI 1903; DPH 1905; LM Rotunda Hospital, Dublin, 1902; MD, NUI, 1934; Physician St Vincent's Hospital, Dublin; Consulting Physician St Patrick's College; Maynooth; Professor of Systematic Medicine, University College, Dublin; Member of Governing Body, University College, Dublin; Member of the Medical Registration Council of Saorstat Eireann; *b* Corhally House, Fintona, Co. Tyrone, 6 Sept. 1879; *m* 1909, Mary E. Cleary, BA; three *s* one *d. Educ:* St Macartan's Seminary, Monaghan; Clongowes Wood College; Catholic University Medical School, Cecilia Street. House Physician and Surgeon St Vincent's Hospital; Assistant Medical Supt Cork Street Fever Hospital, Dublin; Chancellor's gold medal Cecilia Street Medical School; gold medal Clinical Medicine St Vincent's Hospital; medallist in Hygiene, Anatomy, Physiology, Materia Medica, and Chemistry Medical School, Cecilia Street. *Recreation:* golf. *Address:* 28 Fitzwilliam Square S, Dublin. *T:* 62066.

Died 20 Nov. 1950.

MENZIES, Tom Alexander, MA, LLB; Sheriff-Substitute of Inverness at Portree, 1925–29, of Argyll at Oban, 1929–33, of Ayrshire at Ayr, 1933–40; retired, 1940, now Hon. Sheriff Substitute at Ayr; *b* Hull, 1877; *s* of late John Menzies, art master, Hull; unmarried. *Educ:* Robert Gordon's College, Aberdeen; Edinburgh University. Advocate, Scotland, 1904; sometime Lieutenant, RGA (T) and Hong Kong and Singapore RGA. *Clubs:* Scottish Conservative (Edinburgh); County (Ayr).

Died 9 Dec. 1950.

MEREZHKOVSKI, Dmitri Sergeievich; Russian novelist and critic; *b* St Petersburg, 14 Aug. 1865. *Publications:* The Death of the Gods, 1901; The Birth of the Gods, 1926; Akhnaton, King of Egypt; December the Fourteenth; The Life of Napoleon; The Secret of the West, 1928 (and later publications in different countries); Napoleon, a Study, 1929; Michael Angelo and other sketches, 1930; The Romance of Leonardo da Vinci, 1931; Jesus the Unknown, 1934; Jesus Manifest, 1935, etc.

Died 9 Dec. 1941.

MIRAJ, (Junior), Chief of; Sir Shrimant Madhavrao Harihar, *alias* **Baba Saheb Patwardhan,** KCIE 1936. *Address:* Miraj, Deccan States Agency, India.
Died 6 May 1950.

MONTAGUE, Major Furry Ferguson, CMG 1918; barrister; *b* 1884; 2nd *s* of late Hon. W. H. Montague; *m* 1923, Margaret, *d* of G. V. Hastings; three *s. Educ:* Upper Canada College; University of Toronto; University of Manitoba (BA). ADC to Lt-Gen. Sir Richard Turner, VC, 1915; General Staff, 2nd Canadian Div., 1916; Assistant Military Secretary, Canadian Headquarters, 1917–18; Department of Personal Propaganda, Ministry of Information, 1918; Manager, Winnipeg Branch, London and Western Trust Co.; Hon. Lt-Col, 1st Regt, Manitoba Mounted Rifles. President: Prairie Thoroughbred Breeders and Racing Assoc.; Manitoba Federation of Game and Fish Associations; Member, Advisory Council, Western Canada and Yukon Game and Fish Associations. Hon. Secretary Manitoba Jockey Club. *Recreation:* racing. *Club:* Manitoba (Winnipeg).

Died 7 June 1950.

MOOR, Samuel Albert, MA. *Educ:* Grammar School, Manchester; Sidney Sussex College, Cambridge (Natural Science Scholar). 1st Class Nat. Sci. Tripos, 1886. Lecturer in Botany University College of Wales,

Aberystwyth; Principal, Grasia College, Gondal, Kathiawar, India; Headmaster, Nantwich Grammar School; Headmaster, Grammar School, Kendal, 1908–24; Westmorland County Council Education Committee; Maternity and Child Welfare Committee, Westmorland County Nursing Association. *Publication:* Translation of Detmer, Das Pflanzenphysiologische Praktikum. *Address:* Vicarage Terrace, Kendal. *T:* Kendal 424.

Died 13 July 1944.

MURRAY, John Pears, CBE 1925; *b* 1866; *s* of late Alfred Everitt Murray, Govt Land Surveyor, East London, SA; *m* 1900, Florence, *d* of late D. R. Trollip, farmer, Aliwal North; three *s* one *d. Educ:* Muller's Private School, East London. Served in the Bechuanaland Border Police, 1885–87; Mercantile and Banking experience in Johannesburg, 1887–94; Accounting clerk Basutoland Administration, 1894; Sub-Inspector Basutoland Mounted Police, 1895; Inspector, 1902; Financial Secretary, 1904; Assistant Commissioner, 1913; Govt Secretary, 1918; Deputy Resident Commissioner, 1920; acted as Resident Commissioner, 1923, 1924, and 1926; retired, 1927. *Recreations:* fishing, shooting, ornithology. *Address:* 13 Nelson Avenue, Cambridge; East London, South Africa. *T:* 3825.

Died 20 April 1947.

NOEL, Andre Espitalier-, CMG 1944; Controller of Supplies, Mauritius, since 1943; *b* 20 June 1898; 4th *s* of late Louis Espitalier-Noel, elected Member Mauritius Legislative Council; *m* 1919, Laurence Leclezio, *g d* of late Sir Henry Leclezio, KCMG; one *s* two *d. Educ:* Paris; privately. Asst Food Controller, 1939; Food Commodity Controller, 1942. *Address:* Clos Gentil, Curepipe, Mauritius.

Died 7 Aug. 1950.

O'CONNOR, Arthur John; Chairman, Army Pensions Board, Ireland, since 1949; Circuit Court Judge for Cork City, 1947; *b* 1888. Qualified, first as a Civil Engineer, then as a Barrister. MP (SF) South Kildare, Dec. 1918–22. *Address:* Elm Hall, Celbridge, Co. Kildare, Ireland.

Died 2 May 1950.

O'CONNOR, Charles Gerald; KC 1939; Puisne Judge, Exchequer Court, Ottawa, since 1945; *b* 3 Dec. 1890; *s* of Frederick Shepherd and Maria Isabella O'Connor; *m* 1920, Victoria Mary Smith; one *s* one *d. Educ:* Alberta Law Society; Osgoode Hall, Toronto. Lieut, Canadian Machine Gun Corps. Alderman, City of Edmonton. Member, Legislative Assembly of Alberta, 1935–40; President, Edmonton Chamber of Commerce. *Address:* Exchequer Court, Ottawa, Canada.

Died 16 Nov. 1949.

O'SULLIVAN, Col Daniel, CMG 1918; CBE 1919; FRCSI; Army Medical Service (retired); *b* 1853; *s* of J. F. O'Sullivan; *m* Georgina Rose (d 1942), *d* of Col A. F. Battye. Served European War, 1914–18 (despatches, CMG, CBE). *Address:* 68 Kensington Park Road, W11.

Died 10 Dec. 1946.

PARKES, Major Harry Reeves, CB 1919; DL; late TF Res; *b* 4 Dec. 1873; *s* of late F. W. Parkes, one of HM Inspectors of Schools; *m* 1900, Lucy, *e d* of R. H. Parker, pottery manufacturer, Stoke-on-Trent; no *c. Educ:* High School, Newcastle-under-Lyme; Univ. of Wales, Aberystwyth. Assistant Master at various Public Schools, 1898–1908; Volunteer Commission, 1900; Assistant Secretary, West Lancashire TF Association, 1909; Secretary, West Lancashire TA and AF Association, 1915–38; various Hon. Secretaryships, including CEMS Federation, Liverpool. *Publication:* Essay on Recruiting for the Territorial Force. *Recreation:* outdoor sports. *Address:* Allandale, Aughton, Lancashire. *T:* Aughton Green 2386. *Club:* Liverpool Press.

Died 1 Jan. 1949.

PARSON, Col George, CBE 1934; DSO 1917; *b* 8 Oct. 1879; *s* of Dr F. J. Parson and E. M. Hall; *m* 1910, Madeline Fynn; two *s*. *Educ:* Bilton Grange; Rugby; RIEC, Coopers Hill. *Recreation:* golf. *Address:* Landstrip, Hillcrest, Natal. *Clubs:* Salisbury; Bulawayo.

Died 22 Nov. 1950.

PASCHALIS, Neoptolemus, OBE 1937; QC 1931; Solicitor-General, Cyprus, 1927–40; Chairman of the Debt Settlement Board, Cyprus, 1940; *b* 17 Feb. 1880; *s* of Paschalis Constantinides, Advocate, and Helen Hava; *m* Catherine Papadopoulos; one *s*. *Educ:* Pancypriot Gymnasium, Nicosia; University of Athens; Middle Temple. Called English Bar, Middle Temple, 1902; journalist and Special Correspondent of the Athenian daily Hestia in London, 1899–1902; private practice as an advocate in Cyprus, 1903–27; Member of the Greek-Christian Board of Education, 1914–29; Member of the Legislative Council of Cyprus, 1916–21; Member of the Cyprus Deputations to England in 1918–19 and 1920; Acting Attorney-General on twelve occasions, 1927–38; Official Member of the Legislative Council on two occasions, 1928–29; Official Member of the Executive Council on eleven occasions, 1927–38. *Publication:* pamphlet entitled Facts and Figures about Cyprus. *Recreations:* golf, bridge. *Address:* PO Box 409, Nicosia, Cyprus. *TA:* Paschalis, Nicosia. *Club:* Nicosia (Nicosia).

Died 28 Nov. 1946.

PERITZ, Rev. Ismar J., AM, PhD; LittD; STD; Editor of Journal of Bible and Religion; Emeritus, since 1938; Professor of Semitic Languages and Biblical Literature, Syracuse University, 1896–1933; Professor Emeritus since 1933; Willard Ives Professor of the English Bible since 1904; *b* Breslau, Germany, 8 Jan. 1863; *s* of Adolph Peritz and Sarah Wieluner; *m* 1885, Caroline Louisa Irwin Cooper, of London. *Educ:* Friederich's Gymnasium, Breslau; Drew Theological Seminary, Madison, NJ; Harvard Univ. At the age of seventeen, while in Berlin, experienced a change in faith from Judaism to Christianity; moved to London; was called to New York City, 1883, to engage in mission work; studied theology in preparation for entering the ministry, 1884–87; ordained deacon, 1889; elder of the Methodist Episcopal Church, 1891; pastor of various churches of this denomination, 1887–95; pursued advanced studies in Semitic Languages and Literature at Harvard University, 1892–95; AM, 1893; PhD, 1898; resident lecturer at the Newman Biblical Institute, Jerusalem, 1913. *Publications:* Woman in the Ancient Hebrew Cult, in the Journal of Biblical Literature, 1898, pt ii; Critical and Exegetical Notes upon the International Sunday School Lessons in the Illustrative Lesson Notes for 1907 and 1908; contributor to the Encyclopædia Biblica and the Abingdon Bible Commentary; Old Testament History, 1915. *Address:* Lake Bluff, Wolcott, NY, USA (May-Sept.); 1121 Washington Avenue, Winter Park, Florida (Oct.-April).

Died 16 July 1950.

PLEDGE, Henry, CBE 1918; late Assistant Director of Naval Construction, Admiralty. *Address:* 9 Prior Avenue, Sutton, Surrey.

Died 16 Oct. 1949.

POOLE, Ernest; writer; *b* Chicago, 1880; American parents; *m* 1907; two *s* one *d*. *Educ:* Princeton. Magazine writer of articles and short stories; often abroad as correspondent for magazines; twice in England, 1940, 1941; had three plays produced, two in New York. *Publications:* The Harbor; His Family (First Pulitzer

Prize); His Second Wife; The Dark People; The Village; Blind, 1920; Beggar's Gold, 1921; Millions, 1922; Danger, 1923; The Avalanche, 1924; The Little Dark Man, 1925; The Hunters' Moon, 1925; With Eastern Eyes, 1926; Silent Storms, 1927; The Car of Crœsus, 1930; The Destroyer, 1931; Nurses on Horseback, 1932; Great Winds, 1933; One of Us, 1934; The Bridge (autobiography), 1940; Giants Gone, 1943; The Great White Hills, 1946; The Nancy Flyer, 1949. *Recreations:* horseback, tennis, mountain tramping. *Address:* Franconia, New Hampshire, USA; 139 E 66th St, New York, NY, USA. *Club:* Century (New York).

Died 10 Jan. 1950.

PORTER, Frederick, MB, CM; *b* Jedburgh, Roxburghshire, 1871; *s* of Alexander Porter, Chief Constable, Roxburgh Selkirk and Berwickshire, and Janet Hay Adie; *m* 1899, Annie Margaret Peploe; one *d*. *Educ:* The Nest Academy, Jedburgh; Edinburgh University. Practising as a physician in Edinburgh; Secretary of the Scottish Medical Guild; Vice-President of National Medical Union; Member of Edinburgh Medico-Chirurgical, Obstetrical and Harveian Societies; Member of the Caledonian Medical Society. *Publications:* Strike; Freedom, and several Plays; various articles in medical journals. *Recreations:* fishing and painting. *Address:* Flodden Lodge, 65 Morningside Road, Edinburgh. *T:* Edinburgh 53024.

Died 12 Feb. 1949.

POWER, Ven. George Edmund; retired; late Archdeacon of Ardfert and Aghadoe; Prebendary of Effin in St Mary's Cathedral, Limerick, 1924–41; Canon of St Patrick's Cathedral, Dublin, 1929–41. *Address:* 97 Upper Leeson Street, Dublin.

Died 6 Jan. 1950.

PRITCHARD, Ivor Mervyn, RCA; lately a Civil Servant; sometime Inspecting Officer Royal Commission on Welsh Historic Constructions; *b* Beaumaris, Isle of Anglesey; *m* 1922, Olwen, *d* of W. Stanley-Jones, Stow Park, Newport. *Educ:* Beaumaris Grammar School; University College of North Wales; London Architectural Association; Royal Academy School; Central School of Arts and Crafts, London. Served European War, with Royal Artillery (Territorial Force) Egyptian Expeditionary Force; Member of Council for the Preservation of Rural Wales; also the Society of Graphic Arts; Works and Engravings exhibited at: Kunsterhaus, Vienna International Exhibition, Los Angeles, Czechoslovakia, Royal Academy, London, Salon, Paris, etc. The Pritchard Collection of Antique Atlases in 80 Folio volumes has been acquired by National Library of Wales. ARIBA until 1941. *Recreations:* art, travel, bibliopolism. *Address:* 12 Calais Gate, Myatts Park, SE5.

Died 10 Feb. 1948.

PROCTOR, Alexander Phimister; sculptor; *b* Canada, 27 Sept. 1862; *m* 1893, Margaret Gerow; four *s* four *d*. *Educ:* New York; London; Paris under Puech and Ingalbert. *Principal Works:* Heroic figure, Pioneer, University of Oregon, Eugene, Ore; Equestrian, The Circuit Rider, Salem, Ore; Indian Fountain Figure, Fort George, NY; The Princeton Tigers, Princeton University; Equestrian, On the War Trail and Bronco Buster, Denver Colo Civic Center, Theodore Roosevelt, Portland, Ore; Colossal 4 Buffaloes on Bridge and 4 Tigers, Washington, DC; Pioneer Mother—Kansas City; Buffalo Reliefs; Artington Bridge, Washington; many portraits in bas relief and many smaller groups of figures and animals. *Address:* 39 West 67th Street, New York. *Club:* Century (New York).

Died 4 Sept. 1950.

PURDON, Lt-Col David William, CMG 1917; late IA; *b* 17 July 1853. Entered army, 1878; US List, 1908; served Burma, 1887–88 (medal with clasp); European War, 1914–17 (CMG); JP Co. Meath. *Address:* Ardrums, Agher, Enfield, Co. Meath, Eire. *Club:* United Service (Dublin).

Died 3 Jan. 1948.

RADIN, Max, LLB, PhD, LLD; Professor of Law, 1919–40; John H. Boalt Professor of Law, University of California, 1940–48; Emeritus since 1948; *b* Kempen, Poland, 29 March 1880; *s* of Adolph M. Radin and Johanna Theodor; brought to United States, 1884; *m* 1st, Rose Jaffe (*d* 1919); one *d*; 2nd, 1922, Dorothea Prall (*d* 1948). *Educ:* College of the City of New York; New York University; Columbia University. Instructor in Classics, High Schools, New York City, 1901; Lecturer in Roman and Civil Law, College of the City of New York, 1919; Instructor in History, Columbia University, 1918–19; Professor of Law, Stanford University Summer Session, 1931; Northwestern University Summer Session, 1936; Storrs Lecturer in Jurisprudence, Yale University, 1940; Hillman Lecturer, Pacific University, 1946; Visiting Prof. of Law, Columbia Univ., 1947; Member Institute for Advanced Study, Princeton, NJ, 1949, 1950; Visiting Prof. of Law, Duke Univ., Durham, N Carolina, 1949. Member of New York and California Bars; Bar of US Supreme Court; Member of American National Committee of International Congress of Comparative Law, 1932–37; American Council Institute of Pacific Relations, 1933; Vice-Pres. Social Science Research Conference of the Pacific Coast, 1932–33; President's Commission for Inter-American University, 1939; Chairman, American Bar Association Committee on Comparative Legal Philosophy; Chairman California Commission on Uniform State Laws; Draftsman Code of Administrative Ethics, State Bar of California, 1946; Member Societé d'Histoire du Droit, Paris; Stair Society, Edinburgh. *Publications:* The Legislation of the Greeks and Romans on Corporations, 1909; The Jews Among the Greeks and Romans, 1916; The Life of the People in Biblical Times, 1929; Handbook of Roman Law, 1927; The Lawful Pursuit of Gain, 1931; The Trial of Jesus of Nazareth, 1931; Handbook of Anglo-American Legal History, 1935; The Law and Mr Smith, 1938; Marcus Brutus, 1939; Manners and Morals of Business, 1939; Law as Logic and Experience, 1940; The Day of Reckoning, 1943; The Law and You, 1948; Epicurus, My Master, 1949; various legal and classical articles. *Address:* 2683 Buena Vista Way, Berkeley, California, USA. *T:* Ashbery 3–2614. *Clubs:* Faculty (Berkeley); Commonwealth, Press (San Francisco).

Died 22 June 1950.

RAHMAN, Sir Ahmed Fazlur, Kt 1942; LLD. Professor of History, MAO College, Aligarh, and later Muslim University, Aligarh, 1914–21; Provost, Muslim Hall, University of Dacca, 1921–27; Vice-Chancellor, University of Dacca, 1934–36; Member, Federal Public Service Commission, India, 1937.

Died 25 March 1945.

RICE, Cale Young; poet, dramatist, novelist; *b* Dixon, Kentucky, USA, 7 Dec. 1872; *s* of Laban M. and Martha Rice; *m* Alice Caldwell Hegan (*d* 1942). *Educ:* AB Cumberland University, 1893; AB Harvard; 1895; AM 1896; LLD University of Kentucky, 1927; LittD, Rollins College, 1928; LittD University of Louisville, 1937. Professor of English Literature, Cumberland University, 1896–97; has since devoted himself to writing, extensive travels, occasional lectures and readings; a founder and first President of the Arts Club of Louisville; Member of Board of Governors of J. B. Speed Memorial Art Museum; Member Advisory Council, Univ. of Louisville. *Publications:* (*poems*): From Dusk to Dusk, 1898; With Omar, 1900; Song-Surf, 1900; Nirvana Days, 1908; Many Gods, 1910; Far Quests, 1912; At the World's Heart, 1914; Collected Plays and Poems, 1915;

Earth and New Earth (including Gerhard of Ryle, a drama), 1916; Trails Sunward, 1917; Wraiths and Realities, 1918; Songs to AHR, 1918; Shadowy Thresholds, 1919; Sea Poems, 1921; Mihrima (a drama) and other Poems, 1922; A Pilgrim's Scrip, 1924; A Sea Lover's Scrip, 1925; Bitter Brew, 1925; Selected Plays and Poems, definitive edition, 1926; Stygian Freight, 1927; Seed of The Moon, 1929; High Perils, 1933; (*poetic dramas*): Charles di Tocca, 1903; David, 1904; Yolanda of Cyprus, included in Plays and Lyrics, 1906, and produced as grand opera, music by Clarence Loomis, 1929; A Night in Avignon, 1907; The Immortal Lure (four one-act dramas), 1911; Porzia, 1913; (*short stories*): Turn About Tales (with Alice Hegan Rice), 1920; Winners and Losers (with Alice Hegan Rice) 1925; Passionate Follies (with Alice Hegan Rice), 1936; Youth's Way (novel), 1923; Early Reaping (novel), 1929; The Swamp-Bird (prose play), 1931; Love and Lord Byron (prose play), 1936; Bridging the Years, autobiography, including Poetry's Genii (criticism), 1939; Quadric Realism, a New Approach to Philosophy. *Recreations:* travel and golf. *Clubs:* Authors'; Arts (Louisville).

Died 23 Jan. 1943.

RICHARDS, Hon. Mr Justice Stephen Elswood; Puisne Judge of the Court of Appeal for Manitoba, since 1932; Chief Commissioner for Manitoba under Farmer's Creditors Arrangement Act, 1939–42; Chairman, Royal Commission (appointed by Dominion Government to report on building of War-time Merchant Ships in BC Shipyards), 1942–43; *b* 28 Aug. 1878; *s* of late Albert Elswood Richards, Judge of the Court of Appeal for Manitoba, and Harriet Edith, *d* of James Henderson; *m* 1st, 1905, late Kathleen Carlotta Bryan; 2nd, 1929, Kathleen Louise Macleod; three *d*. *Educ:* Winnipeg. Admitted to bar of Manitoba, 1900; Practised in Winnipeg, senior member firm Richards, Sweatman, Fillmore, Riley and Watson; KC 1918. *Recreations:* shooting, fishing, golf. *Club:* Manitoba (Winnipeg).

Died 1950.

ROBERTS, Lancelot, RCA (the lettering later became RCamA); Member of the Pastel Society, London. *Address:* Little Meadows, Eglwys Bach, Tal y Cafn, N Wales; c/o The Royal Cambrian Academy of Art, Plas Mawr, High Street, Conway, North Wales.

Died 4 April 1950.

ROCHE, Most Rev. Edward Patrick; *b* 1874. *Educ:* St Bonaventure's College, St John's, All Hallows, Dublin. Priest, 1897. Domestic Prelate to the Pope, 1914. Archbishop of St John's (Newfoundland), (RC), from 1915. *Address:* The Palace, St John's, Newfoundland.

Died 23 Sept. 1950.

SABATIER, Prof. Paul; *b* 1854. Professor of Chemistry, Toulouse University; Nobel Prize, 1912; Royal Society's Davy Medal, 1915; Membre Institut de France (Acad. Sc.), 1913; Foreign Member Royal Society, 1918. *Address:* Allée des Zéphyrs, 11, Toulouse.

Died 14 Aug. 1941.

SAKLATVALA, Sir Sorabji Dorabji, Kt 1941. Member Bombay Legislative Assembly; Director Tata Sons, Ltd, Bombay. *Address:* Tata Sons, Ltd, Bombay.

Died 18 Oct. 1948.

SAPELLNIKOFF, Wassily; concert pianist; has been a regular visitor to England for thirty years; *b* Odessa, 2 Nov. 1868; *e s* of Leon Sapellnikoff, violinist and conductor at Odessa and other parts of Russia. *Educ:* Odessa; St Petersburg. Conservatoire de Musique de la Société Imperiale at St Petersburg; studied the violin, and subsequently the piano, with Louis Brassin and Sophie Menter, and theory and composition with various teachers; a great friend of Tschaikovsky, who brought him to England, where he played in London the

Concerto for pianoforte and orchestra No. 1 in B flat minor in 1889; is an honorary member of the Royal Philharmonic Society, for whom he has played on fifteen occasions. *Publications:* over thirty works for piano. *Recreations:* chess, reading, and visiting beautiful places.

Died 17 March 1941.

SCOTT, Col Wallace Arthur, CMG 1918; BA; MD (Tor.); FRCS; CAMC; *s* of Wm Scott, BA, Principal, Toronto Normal School; *m* Evelyn (*d* 1940), *d* of late Hugh Byron Ronan, Ottawa; no *c. Educ:* Ottawa Collegiate Institute; Toronto University; King's College, London. Served European War (CMG). *Address:* 627 Sherbourne Street, Toronto, Canada.

Died 4 Jan. 1949.

SEXTON, Thomas Miles; JP Co. Durham; *b* 1879; *s* of William Sexton, Wingate, Co. Durham; *m* 1902, Edith Longstaff; one *s. Educ:* Bede College, Durham. Headmaster of Stanhope Council School, Co. Durham, 1909–35; MP (Lab) Barnard Castle Division of Durham, 1935–45. *Address:* Dales Terrace, Stanhope, Co. Durham. *TA:* Sexton, Stanhope. *T:* Stanhope 294; Waverley Hotel, Southampton Row, WC1. *T:* Terminus 6292.

Died July 1946.

SHAHUB-UD-DIN, Khan Bahadur Sir Chaudhri, Kt 1930; formerly: Advocate, High Court; President, Legislative Council, Punjab; Speaker, Punjab Legislative Assembly. *Educ:* Government College; Law College, Lahore (BA, LLB). Member, Lahore Municipal Cttee, 1913; Pres., 1922–24; Minister of Education, Punjab Govt, 1936–37. *Publications:* The Criminal Law Journal of India: Indian Case and two Punjabi poems; founder and proprietor, Indian Cases, and Criminal Law Journal.

Died Aug. 1949.

SIMPSON, Col Robert Mills, CBE 1919; DSO 1918; *b* 1865; *s* of Robert Simpson; *m* 1920, Mona Doreen English. Served European War, 1914–19 (despatches, DSO, CBE).

Died 2 Feb. 1945.

SINHA, Sir Rajivaranjan Prashad, Kt 1942; President, Bihar Legislative Council; *b* 1893; *s* of late Raja Rajrajeshwari Prasad Sinha, Surajpura, Bihar; *m* 1912, Shrimati Keshavanandani, *y d* of late R. B. Jaiprakash Lal, CIE. *Educ:* St Xavier's School, Calcutta; Agra College; Patna College; Muir Central College, Allahabad. MA 1916. MLC Bihar and Orissa, 1920–; President, 1937–; MLA India, 1927–30. *Address:* Surajpura, Patna, Bihar, India.

Died 8 July 1948.

SOLBERG, Thorvald; United States Register of Copyrights, 1897–1930; *b* Manitowoc, Wisconsin, 22 April 1852; *s* of Charles Solberg, Larvik, Norway; *m* 1880, Mary Adelaide Nourse (*d* 1920); no *c. Educ:* Common School, Manitowoc. Library of Congress, 1876–89, 1897–1930; Boston Book Company, 1889–97; Hon. Life Fellow of American Library Institute; Hon. Member of Association Littéraire et Artistique Internationale, Paris; United States Official Delegate to International Copyright Conferences, Paris, 1900; Berlin, 1908; Rome, 1928. *Publications:* various works on copyright, and contributions to periodicals, including The Nation, New York for 25 years, and Le Droit d'Auteur, Berne, up to 1940; also some bibliographical works, including Literary Property, 1886; Bibliography of the Balearic Islands, 1929, and Text editions of the Icelandic Eddas; The Development of International Copyright Relations between the United States and Foreign Countries, 1933; Present Copyright Situation; Copyright and Librarians, 1934; Copyright Miscellanies (limited edition), 1939; The Present International Copyright Situation, 1934; Les récentes mesures prises à Washington pour la Revision de la

Législation pour le Droit d'Auteur (Berne), 1935; The Long Struggle for Honourable International Copyright Relations, contributed to Geistiges Eigentum, Leiden (Holland), 1937; International Copyright in Congress, 1837–1891; History of the Legal Deposit of Books throughout the British Empire, with Bibliography, Library Quarterly, Oct. 1938; Copyright Reform: Legislation and International Copyright; A Chapter in the Unwritten History of the Library of Congress from January 17 to April 5, 1899: The Appointment of Herbert Putnam as Librarian, Library Quarterly, July 1939; Copyright Reform, Notre Dame Lawyer, May 1939; The New Copyright Bill (S.3043), Notre Dame Lawyer, January 1940; Criticism of the new Copyright Bill (S.3043), Nation, 24 February 1940; The Copyright Bill (S.3043), Saturday Review of Literature, 24 February 1940; The Cathedral at Palma, Majorca, Balearic Islands, with description and Bibliography, 1940. *Recreations:* formerly walking; now auto-driving and foreign travel. *Clubs:* Cosmos (Washington, DC).

Died 15 July 1949.

SOLLOWAY, Rev. John, DD Oxford, 1905; Canon of York and Prebendary of Ampleforth, 1918–41, Canon Emeritus since 1941; *b* 16 May 1860; *m*; three *d. Educ:* Oxford Univ. Ordained, 1886; Curate of Thornaby and Scarborough; Rector of Holy Trinity in Mickelgate, York, 1895–1910; Vicar of Selby Abbey, 1910–41; Proctor in Convocation, 1918–22. *Publications:* The Alien Benedictines of York, 1910; Selby Abbey, Past and Present, 1925. *Address:* 6 Sandybed Lane, Scarborough. *T:* 394.

Died 7 Oct. 1946.

STANFIELD, Richard, ARSM, MInstCE, MIMechE, FRSE; Professor of Mechanical Engineering, Heriot-Watt College, Edinburgh, 1889–1929; *b* 23 June 1863; *m*; one *s. Educ:* Manchester Grammar School; Royal School of Mines, London; Whitworth Scholarship, 1884; National Science Scholarship, 1886. Associate Royal School of Mines, 1889; Consulting Engineer to the Highland and Agricultural Society of Scotland; Fellow and Ex-President, Royal Scottish Society of Arts; Engineer and Secretary, Board of Management, SE of Scotland Munitions Committee, 1915–19. *Publications:* Communications and Papers on Technical Subjects to Scientific Societies, etc.; Reports on Trials of Agricultural Machinery, Motors, etc. *Recreations:* angling, bowling. *Address:* 24 Mayfield Gardens, Edinburgh.

Died 10 Oct. 1950.

STEWART, William; Secretary, Scottish Divisional Council of the Independent Labour Party, 1912–33; retired; *b* Dunfermline, 8 July 1856, of working-class parents; unmarried. *Educ:* Elementary Schools. Worked as yarn dresser in linen factories; as a young man began to write to local papers on literary and political subjects; was elected to the first Paris Council of his native city; conducted a local monthly Socialist paper, The Worker, which ceased to exist in 1899, when he went to Glasgow and joined the staff of the Labour Leader, under Keir Hardie; contributed also for six years a weekly article to The Clarion; was for some years a member of the ILP National Administrative Council; regular contrib. to Forward. *Publications:* Fighters for Freedom, 2 eds; The Nativity of Adam, 2 eds; Robert Burns and the Common People, 3 eds; Keir Hardie: a Biography, 2 eds; War Time and Other Times Impression, 1933; various pamphlets. *Recreations:* reading, smoking, walking, and the theatre and concert room occasionally. *Address:* 136 Crail Street, Glasgow, E.

Died 27 Aug. 1947.

STODDARD, Lothrop, AM, PhD; author and traveller; *b* Brookline, Mass, USA, 29 June 1883; *s* of John Lawson Stoddard and Mary Hammond Brown; *m* 1926, Elizabeth Guilford Bates; one *s* one *d; m* 1944, Zoya K.

Dickins. *Educ:* Harvard (AB 1905; AM 1910; PhD 1914). Member various learned societies. *Publications:* The French Revolution in San Domingo, 1914; Present-Day Europe: its National States of Mind, 1917; The Stakes of the War, 1918; The Rising Tide of Colour against White World-Supremacy, 1920; The New World of Islam, 1921; The Revolt against Civilization, 1922; Racial Realities in Europe, 1924; Social Classes in Post-War Europe, 1925; Scientific Humanism, 1926; Re-Forging America, 1927; The Story of Youth, 1928; Luck: Our Silent Partner, 1929; Master of Manhattan: The Life of Richard Croker, 1931; Europe and Our Money, 1932; Lonely America, 1932; Clashing Tides of Colour, 1934; Into the Darkness: Nazi Germany To-day, 1940. *Recreations:* golf, motoring. *Address:* 3148 O. Street, NW Washington, DC, USA. *Clubs:* Harvard, Authors', Cosmos (Washington).

Died 1 May 1950.

TAYLOR, Lt-Col Arthur James, CMG 1918; DSO 1917; MC; Lieut-Col retd; South African Staff Corps; Past Member of Legislative Assembly, Southern Rhodesia; *b* 1876; *γ s* of R. Taylor; *m* Edith Ruby, *e d* of C. Klemsmith, MLA, Midlands, S Rhodesia. Served Boer War, 1899–1902; European War, 1914–19 in German South-West and East Africa (despatches twice, MC, DSO, CMG).

Died 26 March 1949.

TEHRI-GARHWAL, Lt-Col HH Sir Narendra Shah Sahab Bahadur, Retired Maharaja of, KCSI 1932 (CSI 1922); LLD Benares; *b* 3 Aug. 1898; *s* of late Raja HH Sir Kirti Shah Bahadur, KCSI, and *e d* of HH General Rana Padam Jung, Saheb Bahadur of Nepal; *m*; three *s* three *d*. Succeeded to the throne, 1913; abdicated, for health reasons, in favour of his son, 1946. *Educ:* Mayo College, Ajmere, Rajputana. *Address:* Narendranagar, Tehri-Garhwal State, UP Agra and Oudh, India. *TA:* Vishalesh, Narendauagar.

Died 22 Sept. 1950.

THOROLD, William James; Director British and General Debenture Trust, Ltd; Federal Debenture Company Incorporated; Federated Capital Corporation; *b* Toronto, 7 Oct. 1871; *s* of W. H. Thorold, of Thorold, Canada, and Toronto; *m* 1906, Muriel (*d* 1931), *twin d* of Joseph C. Mappin, of London, SW. *Educ:* Parkdale Collegiate Institute, Toronto; McMaster Univ. of Toronto (BA). *Address:* 60 Wall Street Tower (54th floor), New York. *Clubs:* Royal Automobile; Bankers (New York); Royal Canadian Yacht (Toronto); Lido Country, Long Beach (NY).

Died 1942.

TRAHAN, Hon. Arthur, BSc, QC, formerly MLA, PQ, Canada; *b* Nicolet, PQ, 26 May 1877; *s* of Narcisse Trahan, Collector of Customs, JP, and Rebecca Rousseau, both French-Canadians; *m* 1st, 1902, Josephine R., *d* of H. R. Dufresne, NP of Nicolet; four *s* two *d*; 2nd, 1924, Diane, *d* of Charles Le Duc, Hull; one *s*. *Educ:* The Nicolet Seminary. Admitted to Bar, 1901; KC 1912; Secretary of the Commission charged with the revision, consolidation, and modification of the Municipal Code of the Province of Quebec, 1910–12; Alderman of town of Nicolet, 1911–19; MLA, Nicolet, 1913–17, MP, 1917–23. Judge of the Superior Court for Province of Quebec from 1923. Batonnier of the Bar, Dist of Trois Rivières, 1916–17. Chm. of Mobilisation Bd, Montreal, 1941–46. Roman Catholic.

Died 23 Sept. 1950.

VESNIN, Victor; Deputy of the Supreme Soviet of the USSR; Member of the Collegium of the USSR Government Committee on Architecture; President of the Academy of Architecture of the USSR since 1937; Member of the Academy of Sciences of the USSR since 1943; PhD in Architecture; Secretary of the Union of Soviet Architects; *b* 28 March 1882; *s* of Alexander Vesnin and Elizaveta Ermolaeva; *m* 1915, Natalia Bágranovskaia; no *c*. *Educ:* St Petersburg (Leningrad) Institute of Civil Engineers (graduated 1911). Started architectural career in 1904, jointly with brothers Leonid and Alexander Vesnin. Works with his brothers include: The Sirotkin Mansion in Nizhni Novgorod (now the Gorki Regional Lore Museum); the Burnaev-Kurochkin Mansion in Kineshma; the Mantashev Hippodrome Centre in Moscow; the Moscow GPO; the Kuznetsov House in Moscow, etc. After European War 1914–18 took active part in the State reconstruction of plants, settlements, sanatoria, clubs, in the replanning of Baku, etc. Since 1923, Professor at the Moscow Higher Technical College; built the Raw Materials Institute in Moscow, 1924–27; Chief Architect of the Dnieper Hydro-Electric Construction, Dnieprostroy, 1927–32 (Order of the Red Banner of Labour); in 1930–34, with his brothers, built the Palace of Culture of the Stalin Automobile Works in Moscow. During this period also built a cinema theatre on Vorovsky Street in Moscow. Chief Architect of the People's Commissariat of the Heavy Industry, 1933–37; in 1940, with his brother Alexander, designed one of the biggest structures in Moscow, Second House of the Sovnarkom; subsequently participated jointly with his brothers, and on his own, in various architectural contests. Has won more than 25 prizes. Won a diplôme d'honneur at Paris Exhibition in 1925. At the International contest for construction of a grand theatre in Kharkov the design submitted by the Vesnin brothers won the highest prize. Royal Gold Medal for Architecture, 1945. Order of Lenin, 1945. *Address:* Moscow Ulitsa Schukina 8/a, flat 25. *TA:* Academy Architecture, Moscow. *T:* G 6-70-69. *Clubs:* Architects, Scientists (Moscow).

Died 1950.

VIBART, Captain John Fleming, CBE 1919; retired from Royal Indian Navy; *b* 10 Aug. 1877; *o s* of Captain John Vibart, late RA; *m* 1911, Edyth Gladys, *o d* of Col H. J. Bremner, Indian Army, retired; no *c*. *Educ:* Bath; HMS Worcester. Went to sea in the sailing ship Hesperus, 1893, where served his time; did two voyages to Australia as second mate; appointed to the Royal Indian Marine, 1899; took part in S African War (Queen's medal); China, 1900 (medal); Somaliland, 1902–04 (medal); European War, 1914–19 (despatches, CBE, Order of the Nile and Greek Military Cross); retired, 1929. War of 1939–45, rejoined for active service, 1940 (1939–45 Star, Burma Star, Defence Medal, War Medal). *Recreations:* shooting, fishing, golf, tennis. *Address:* c/o Grindlay's Bank Ltd, 54 Parliament St, SW1. *Club:* Naval and Military.

Died 9 Dec. 1948.

WAZIR HASAN, Hon. Sir Saiyid, Kt 1932; BA, LLB; *b* 14 May 1874. Joined the Lucknow Bar, 1903; Secretary, All India Moslem League, 1912–19; was instrumental in bringing about Hindu-Moslem Pact of 1916; Additional Judicial Commissioner of Oudh, 1920; Judge of the Chief Court of Oudh, 1925; Chief Judge, 1930; retired 1934. *Address:* Wazir Hasan Road, Lucknow, India. *Club:* United Service (Lucknow).

Died 31 Aug. 1947.

WIJAYASINGHE SIRIWARDENA, N. D. A. Silva-, The Padikara Mudaliyar, of Ceylon; Knight Commander of the Order of Leopold II 1925; Knight Grand Cross of the Order of St Silvester 1925; Knight Grand Cross of the Order of the Holy Sepulchre 1926; Knight Grand Officer of the Order of the Crown of Italy; Knight Commander of the Order of the Black Eagle; Reconciliation Medal from the Pope, etc; *b* 12 Nov. 1888; *m* 1910, Clarice Maud Matilda, *d* of Wasala Mudaliyar J. E. De S. Surya Bandara (Chief). Received title and gold sword from the British Government, 1913; visited England in 1919; received in Private Audience by the King; Belgium in 1920; Rome in 1925, 1926 and 1930; Germany and Paris, 1928; lectured before the

Belgian Court on the Antiquities of Ceylon, 1926; special Envoy of the Pontifical Knights of the East to the International Eucharist Congress, Dublin, 1932; special Envoy of the Oriental Catholics to Rome in connection with the commemoration of the 19th centenary of the Crucifixion, 1933; President of the Association of the Chiefs of Ceylon (1921–28) and of the Papal Knights of India, Burma and Ceylon; attended Silver Jubilee Celebrations, 1935; attended the Coronation celebrations of King George VI, London, 1937; Oriental Envoy to Coronation of Pope Pius XII, 1939, Rome; mediated with Viceroy of India and Indian National Congress for settlement of outstanding differences; Grand Cross of the Order of St John the Lateran; Jubilee Medal, 1935; Gold Cross of Merit of Society of Arts, Sciences and Letters of France. *Publications:* The Indian Evolution, 1932; The Government of the Island of Ceylon; The Holy See and its Place in International Life, Report on Ceylon, base of the South-East Asia Command, etc. *Address:* Richmond Castle, Ceylon. *Club:* Overseas League.

Died 1949.

WILSON, Archibald Wayet, MA (Oxon); MusDoc (Oxon); FRCO; Organist Emeritus of Manchester Cathedral; 5th *s* of Rev. P. S. Wilson, late Vicar of Horbling, Lincolnshire. *Educ:* Rossall School; Royal College of Music; Keble College, Oxford (Organ Scholar). Organist, St John's, Upper St Leonard's, and St Asaph Cathedral; Organist and Magister Choristarum of Ely Cathedral. *Publications:* Morning, Communion, and Evening Service in E for SATB; Evening Service in E flat for Men's Voices; Communion Service in D for Parish Church Choirs; Anthems and Part-Songs; Ballad for Chorus and Orchestra; The Organs and Organists of Ely Cathedral; The Chorales: their Origin and Influence. *Address:* S Audrey, Sedgley Park Road, Prestwich, Manchester.

Died 1950.

WOOD, William Charles Henry; Canadian author; Lt-Colonel, Retired List, Canadian Army. Comd 8th Regt (Royal Rifles), 1907; R of O, 1910; co-ordinating Officer of the Canadian Special Mission at the Naval and Military Fronts, 1917. Retired, 1924. A student of Imperial History and Defence. *Publications:* The Fight for Canada, 1904; The Logs of the Conquest of Canada, 1909; Select British Documents of the Canadian War of 1812, 3 vols, 1924; six Chronicles of Canada—Louisbourg, Wolfe, Montcalm, Carleton, '1812', and All Afloat, 1914–17; The King's Book of Quebec, 2 vols, 1911; Animal Sanctuaries in Labrador, 1911–12–13; In the Heart of Old Canada, 1913; two Chronicles of America: Elizabethan Sea-Dogs, 1918, and Captains of the Civil War, 1921; a British Naval History for Boys: Flag and Fleet, 1919; The Naval and Military Volumes (vi and vii) of the Pageant of America, 1926; Editor of and contributor to The Storied Province of Quebec, 4 vols, 1930.

Died 2 Sept. 1947.

YEN, W. W.; *b* Shanghai, 1877. *Educ:* BA University of Virginia, 1900; Phi Beta Kappa, 1909. Professor of English, St John's University, Shanghai; Doctor of Literature, Peking, 1906; Secretary, Chinese Legation, Washington, 1908; Hanlin Scholar, Junior Counsellor, Foreign Office, Peking, 1911; Vice-Minister Foreign Affairs, 1912; Minister to Germany, Sweden, and Denmark, 1913–20; Minister Foreign Affairs, 1920–22; Minister Agriculture and Commerce, Prime Minister, Minister Interior, 1924; ex-President Red Cross of China; President, China Internat. Famine Relief Commission; Minister to USA, 1931; 1st Delegate to Ord. and Extraord. Assemblies (Manchurian Conflict), Delegate on Council, Ambassador to Soviet Union, 1932–36; delegate to London Mon. and Econ. Conference; 1st class of all Chinese Orders, also Grand Cross of Dannebrog, Légion d'Honneur, Christ, Le Sol, Polar Star, Pius IX; Mason. *Address:* 955 Chungcheng Road (Central), Shanghai.

Died 25 May 1950.

A

ABBAY, Col Bryan Norman, CB 1931; retired to East Africa; *b* 6 June 1881; *s* of Canon Richard Abbay of Earl Soham and Janet, *d* of Canon Norman, Mistley; one *d*. *Educ:* Felsted; Sandhurst. Joined Pompadours, 2nd Essex Regt; served S African War (medal and four clasps); Exploration Upper Irrawaddy 1908–12 (King's Police Medal and Macgregor Medal and thanks of Burma Govt); served in France, 1914–16, Sialkot Cavalry Bde and Public School Bn; 20th Royal Fusiliers (1914 Star, Victory Medal and GS Medal); Commanded 27th Light Cavalry, Afghan War, commanded column that destroyed Drazinda; operations against Mahsuds, operations against Wazirs (Brevet Lt-Colonel, despatches thrice, medal, 4 clasps); commanded 18th KEO Cavalry. *Publications:* pamphlets and articles on Machine Gunnery, and Natural History. *Recreations:* big game shooting, fishing. *Address:* Nanyuki, Kenya.

Died 19 Jan. 1947.

ABBEY, Lt-Col Walter Bulmer Tate, CBE 1919; Indian Army, retired; *b* 8 Aug. 1872; surv. *s* of late Walter Abbey of Wellingborough Grange, Northants. *Educ:* Monkton Combe; Sandhurst. Joined 2nd Durham Light Infantry, 1892; 7th Bombay Lancers, 1893; 32nd Lancers, 1896; Burma Commission, 1902; Deputy Commissioner, 1915; operations against Kara rebels, 1898; NE Frontier, India (despatches, 1914–15 star); Commanding Chin Hills Operations, 1917–18 (despatches, CBE). *Publications:* Echoes of the East, 1899; Manual of the Maru Language, 1901; Tangier under British Rule, 1940; The Dreamland Garden, 1948. *Address:* c/o Lloyds Bank, 16 St James's Street, SW1. *Clubs:* East India and Sports, Naval and Military; Union (Sydney).

Died 29 March 1949.

ABBEY, William Henry; President of Horsham and Worthing Division of Conservative Association; *b* 1864; *s* of H. Abbey, Brighton; *m* 1888, Florence, *d* of H. Belcher, Hove; one *s* (one *s* killed in war). High Sheriff of Sussex, 1935. Owns over 20,000 acres. Lord of the Manors of Hughenden, Condover, Bayston and Great Lyth, and patron of two livings. *Address:* Sedgwick Park, Horsham, Sussex. *T:* Lower Beeding 4. *Clubs:* Marlborough, Travellers', Carlton.

Died 23 Dec. 1943.

ABBOT, Lt-Col Frederick William, CBE 1934; MICE, FRGS, MAmSoc CE; Chevalier Légion d'Honneur; Commandeur Couronne de la Roumanie, Commandeur Croix de Polonia Restituta, Commandeur de l'Aigle Blanc de Yugoslavia, Commandeur de l'ordre Militaire St Benoit D'aviz Portugal; Chevalier de la Couronne de l'Italie; Chairman, British Legion, Paris Branch: Hon. President Federation Interalliée des anciens combattants; Member of Committee, British Charity Board, Paris; Hertford British Hospital, Paris; *b* 23 Dec. 1862; *s* of Rev. Frederick James Abbot, MA, Chaplain to the Guards, and Harriet, *d* of William Rothery, Head of Doctors Commons; *m* Minnie, *d* of Dr D. C. Gamble. *Educ:* Wellington College. Civil and Executive Engineer with large experience in USA, Canada, Mexico and Spain; constructed about 500,000 Hydro Electric Horse Power and about 1000 miles of High Tension Electric Transmission Lines; when war was declared was engaged in Hydro Electric work in Spain for the electrification of Barcelona; joined Old Boys Corps, Sept. 1914; 2nd Lieut, 1916; member Anglo-Russian Sub-Committee, USA, 1916; Lieut-Colonel, 1917; Deputy Director of Inspection in the USA for the Ministry of Munitions, 1917; retired, 1919; received the thanks of the Russian Ambassador in the USA and of the Minister of Munitions for services rendered. *Recreations:* tennis, squash, swimming. *Address:* Villa St Vallier, Boulevard Franck Pilatte, Nice, France. *Clubs:* Junior United Service, Boodle's, St James's, Royal Thames Yacht, Royal Automobile; Travellers', Paris.

Died 18 Aug. 1942.

ABBOTT, Albert, CBE 1926; MA; *b* 7 March 1872; *s* of George Abbott; *m* Nancy, *d* of Edwin Hargreaves; (one *s* died on active service, 1944) one *d*. *Educ:* Rivington Grammar School; Oxford Univ. HM Inspector of Schools, 1902–18; Secretary Provisional Committees on Research for the Cotton Industry and for the Woollen and Worsted Industries, 1916–18; Assistant Secretary Dept of Scientific and Industrial Research, 1918–21; Chief Inspector Technological Branch, Board of Education, 1921–32; reported to Government of India on vocational education in India, 1937; Adviser on technical education to Government of Hyderabad and Government of Baroda, 1937–38; Medallist and Hon. Life Member Textile Institute; Hon. Member (late Hon. Sec.) Brit. Assoc. for Commercial and Industrial Education; lately Vice-President Bureau International de l'Enseignement Technique. *Publications:* Education for Industry and Commerce in England; Day Continuation Schools (joint author), 1935. *Address:* Woodburnes, Sampford Brett, Williton, Taunton. *T:* Williton 141. *Club:* Athenæum.

Died 19 June 1950.

ABBOTT, Edwin, CBE 1933; former Comptroller General of Customs, Australia; *b* 21 Nov. 1878; *s* of Edwin Abbott and Barbara McKay; *m* 1904, Sarah Jane Walker; five *d*. *Educ:* Fort Street School, Sydney. Entered Customs Dept, 1893; Secretary and Adviser to Australian Delegation to Imperial Conference, London, 1930; Adviser to Australian Delegation, Ottawa, 1932, London, 1938. Retired, 1944. *Recreations:* motoring, swimming, golf. *Address:* 22 Etham Ave, Darling Pt, Sydney, NSW. *T:* FM 6610.

Died 1 Sept. 1947.

ABBOTT, Evelyn Robins, CIE 1921; ICS, retired; *b* 9 May 1873; *s* of late Sam Abbott, MICE; *m* 1909, Lillian, *d* of late Sir William Ovens Clark; two *s* three *d*. *Educ:* Bath College; Balliol College, Oxford. Entered ICS as Assistant Commissioner, Punjab, 1893; Deputy Commissioner, 1903; Senior Secretary to Financial Commissioner, Punjab, 1907; Commissioner Multan Division, 1919; Financial Commissioner, Punjab, 1921; Chief Commissioner, Delhi, 1924; retired, 1928; Chm. Wallingford RDC since 1939; Berks County Council, 1939–46. *Address:* The Old Vicarage, Moulsford, Berks. *T:* Cholsey 43.

Died 7 May 1950.

ABBOTT, Rt Rev. Henry Pryor Almon, MA, DD, LLD; Bishop of Lexington, Kentucky, since 1929; *b* 11 July 1881; *s* of Rev. John Abbott, MA, Rector St Luke's Cathedral, Halifax, NS, and Ella, *d* of Hon. M. B. Almon, Halifax, NS; *m* 1907, Rachel, *d* of Lieut-Col Gwyn, Dundas, Ontario; two *s* three *d*. *Educ:* Rothesay Collegiate School, Rothesay, New Brunswick; University of King's College, Windsor, Nova Scotia; St Stephen's House, Oxford. Ordained, 1904; Curate St Luke's Cathedral, Halifax, NS, 1904–06; Assistant Rector St James the Apostle, Montreal, PQ, 1906; Rector of Christ Church Cathedral, and Dean of Niagara, Hamilton, Ontario, Canada, 1906–10; Dean of Trinity Cathedral Cleveland, Ohio, 1914–19; Rector of Grace and St Peter's Church, Baltimore, 1919–28; Rector of St Chrysostom's Church, Chicago, Ill,

1928–29; Delegate to General Convention, 1922, 1925 and 1928. *Publications:* The Man Outside the Church, and other volumes of sermons. *Recreations:* motoring, yachting. *Address:* Lexington, Ky, USA.

Died 4 April 1945.

ABBOTT, Brig.-Gen. Leonard Henry, CMG 1916; JP; Indian Army, retired; *b* 10 Sept. 1875; *s* of L. C. Abbott, ICS; *m* 1899, Elsie Graham Peddie; one *d. Educ:* Dulwich College; RMC, Sandhurst; Staff College, Quetta. 2nd Lieut Norfolk Regt, 1896; Lieut 11th Rajputs, 1898; Capt. 1905; Major, 1914; Lt-Col 1918, 8th Rajputs; Colonel, 1920. Served European War, 1914–18; Afghanistan, 1919; Arab Rising, Iraq, 1920 (despatches six times, CMG, Officier Legion of Honour, Croix de Guerre avec palmes, Bt Lt-Col, Bt Col); Honorary Colonel 4/7th Rajput Regt, 1932–45. *Address:* The Ride, Little Bealings, Woodbridge, Suffolk. *T:* Kesgrave 40. *Club:* MCC.

Died 5 March 1949.

ABDOOL RAOOF, Khan Bahadur Sir Muhammad, Kt 1926; Judge Punjab High Court, 1920–25.

Died 1947.

ABDUSSAMAD KHAN, Sahibzada Sir, Kt 1934; CIE 1915; *b* 27 Sept. 1874; *s* of Sahibzada Abdussalan Khan; *m*; three *s* three *d. Educ:* In India. Retired from the post of Chief Minister Rampur State after serving in that capacity for 34 years; Attended Round Table Conference in London 1931, Ottawa Conference in Canada 1932, and League of Nations, Geneva 1933. *Address:* Rampur State, UP, India. *Club:* Royal Automobile.

Died 27 Jan. 1943.

à BECKETT, Ada Mary, (Mrs T. A. à Beckett), CBE 1935; MSc; President of Australian Association for Pre-School Child Development, 1938–47, Life Vice-President since 1947; *b* 18 May 1872; *d* of Rev. Henry John Lambert, Presbyterian Minister, Victoria, and Helen, *d* of Rev. James Garrett, AM, Tasmania; *m* 1903, Thomas Archibald à Beckett, BA, LLB (*d* 1930); three *s. Educ:* Advanced School for Girls, Adelaide; University of Melbourne (Annie Grice Scholar, University Exhibitioner and Prizeman, Wyselaskie Scholar). BSc 1895; MSc 1897. First Woman lecturer in University of Melbourne, 1901; Senior Lecturer in Biology, Scotch College, Melbourne, 1917–37; President of Free Kindergarten Union of Victoria, 1918–39; President of Kindergarten Training College Council, 1926–39; President, Lyceum Club, 1926–28; Chm. of Fishermen's Bend (Port Melbourne) Community Centre, 1941–47; Vice-Pres., Playgrounds Assoc. of Victoria, 1944–47. *Publication:* The Land Leeches of Australia (Biological Research). *Address:* Penleigh, 14 Lansdowne Road, East St Kilda, Melbourne, S2. *Club:* Lyceum (Melbourne).

Died 20 May 1948.

ABEL, Henry George; *b* 22 Aug. 1875; *m* E. M., *d* of Rev. Richard England Long, Liverpool. *Educ:* St Olave's; Christ's College, Cambridge. First Class Classical Tripos, 1897; MA 1909. Senior Classical Master, Wakefield Grammar School, 1899–1910; Headmaster, Barnstaple Grammar School, 1910–17; Central Foundation Boys' School, 1918–22; St Olave's School, Tower Bridge, SE1, 1922–37. *Recreations:* walking, music. *Address:* Heath Cottage, Crosthwaite, Kendal. *T:* Crosthwaite 238.

Died 21 Jan. 1945.

ABEL-SMITH, Brig.-Gen. Lionel, DSO 1918; *b* Nov. 1870; *s* of Rev. A. Smith, Wendover, Bucks; *m* 1923, Genevieve, *d* of Robert Walsh, Armagh; two *s. Educ:* Haileybury; RMA. Joined Royal Artillery, 1890; retired, 1925; served European War, 1914–18 (despatches, DSO). *Address:* 10 Durward Ho., Kensington Court, W8. *T:* Western 4654. *Club:* Naval and Military.

Died 20 Dec. 1946.

ABELL, George Foster; JP Glos; Director Lloyds Bank, Ltd; Member of Council, Charing Cross Hospital and Cheltenham College; Member of Financial Commission of Church Assembly; *b* 31 July 1875; *s* of late George Edmund Abell of Grafton Manor, Bromgrove; *m* Jessie Elizabeth, *d* of Rev. E. B. Brackenbury; two *s* two *d. Educ:* Repton. *Address:* Foxcote Manor, Andoversford, Glos. *T:* Andoversford 210.

Died 17 March 1946.

ABERCROMBIE, Peter Henderson, MB, CM, 1890; MD, 1895, Glasgow Univ.; FRSM; retired; consulting Surgeon Royal National Throat, Nose, and Ear Hospital; late Hon. Aural Surgeon, Royal Caledonian Schools; Hon. Consulting Physician (throat, nose, and ear) Royal Infant Asylum, Wanstead; *b* Paisley, 2 Aug. 1867; *s* of late William Abercrombie, banker, Paisley; *m* 1895, Jessie Deans (*d* 1933), *d* of late Cunison Deans Rankin, Glasgow. *Educ:* John Neilson Institution, Paisley; Glasgow University; London and Vienna. Late Resident Medical Assistant to late Professor Sir Wm Gairdner, and Resident Surgical Assistant to late Professor Sir George Macleod, Western Infirmary, Glasgow; Hon. Secretary British Laryngological Association; Assistant Surgeon, Registrar, Clinical Assistant and Anæsthetist, Central London Throat, Nose, and Ear Hospital. *Publications:* MD Thesis: Turbinotomy in Nasal Stenosis; various contributions on Throat, Nose, and Ear Affections in Journal of Laryngology, Transactions of British Laryngological Association, Reports, Central London Throat, Nose, and Ear Hospital, etc. *Recreations:* motoring, travel. *Address:* 24 Balliol House, Manor Fields, Putney Hill, SW15. *T:* Putney 4230. *Club:* Royal Automobile.

Died 30 Sept. 1950.

ABERHART, Hon. William, BA; Premier of Alberta since 1935; Minister of Education and Attorney General for the Province; *b* 30 Dec. 1878; *s* of William Aberhart and Louise Pepper; *m* 1902, Jessie M. Flatt; two *d. Educ:* Queen's University. Principal of Crescent Heights High School, Calgary, Alberta, 1915–35; Organized Calgary Prophetic Bible Institute after many years of public broadcasting; Dean of the Institute; Leader of Social Credit Party; Elected to Legislative Assembly by acclamation, 1935. *Publications:* Social Credit Manual and other pamphlets. *Address:* Macdonald Hotel, Edmonton, Alberta. *T:* 916203.

Died 22 May 1943.

ABINGER, 7th Baron *cr* 1835; **Hugh Richard Scarlett,** DSO 1916; late RA; DL Inverness; *b* 25 Nov. 1878; *s* of late Lieut-Col L. J. Y. C. Scarlett, *g s* of 1st Baron Abinger, and Bessie Florence, *d* of Edward Gibson of Spring Vale, Isle of Wight, *niece* and adopted *d* of Sir Percy F. Shelley, 3rd Bart, and Lady Shelley; *S* brother, 1927; *m* 1913, Marjorie, 2nd *d* of John McPhillamy, Blair Athol, Bathurst, NSW; three *s.* Served S African War (Queen's and King's medals 5 clasps); European War, 1914–18 (despatches, DSO, Bt Lieut-Col, Jan. 1919); Lt-Col 1927; retired pay, 1927; JP Inverness-shire. *Heir:* *s* Hon. James Richard Scarlett, Lieut, RA, *b* 28 Sept. 1914. *Address:* Inverlochy Castle, Inverness-shire. *Clubs:* Carlton, Arts, Royal Automobile.

Died 21 July 1943.

ABLETT, Thomas Robert, HRI; FRGS, FZS, FGS. Founder of the Royal Drawing Society; artist and school-master; exhibitor at the RA, RI, ROI, RBA, and Walker Art Gallery, Liverpool; painter in oil, water-colour and pastel; nominated by the Foreign Office as delegate to the Conference of Artists at the Beaux Arts, Paris, 1900; Hon. Member of the Royal Institute of Painters in Water Colours; Ex-President of the Old Bradfordians Club; Member of the Court (Master, 1936–37) of the Needlemakers Company; Vice-President of the Froebel Society; Headquarters Commissioner in the Boy Scouts Association; originator of a method of enabling the Blind to draw. *Address:* 12

Cromwell Place, SW7. *T:* Kensington 2667; Pembroke Lodge, Outram Road, Addiscombe. *Clubs:* Arts, City Livery, Savage.

Died 5 June 1945.

ABRAHAM, Rt Rev. C. T.; *b* 13 April 1857; *s* of Rt Rev. Charles John Abraham and Caroline Harriet, *d* of Sir C. T. Palmer of Wanlip Hall, Leicester; *m* 1883, Mary Theresa, *d* of Ven. C. W. Furse, Archdeacon of Westminster; of Halsdon House, North Devon; four *s* five *d. Educ:* Eton; Keble College, Oxford. Vicar of All Saints, Shrewsbury, 1885–89; Christ Church, Lichfield, 1889–97; Vicar of Bakewell, Derbyshire, 1897–1918; Prebendary of Southwell Minster, 1905; Bishop Suffragan of Derby, 1909–27; Rector of Astbury, Cheshire, 1927–36. *Address:* The Manor, Upton Noble, Bath, Somerset.

Died 27 Jan. 1945.

ABRAHAM, Sir John Bradley, KBE 1942; CB 1933; Deputy Under Secretary of State, Air Ministry, since 1940; *b* 5 Sept. 1881; *s* of John Abraham; *m* 1914, Gladys Elizabeth Grindy Kirk; two *d. Educ:* King Edward VI School, Macclesfield. Admiralty Second Division Clerk, 1900, Clerk, Class 1, 1912; Acting Assistant Principal Clerk, 1912; Acting Principal Clerk, 1917; Air Ministry Assistant Principal, 1918; Principal, 1919; Assistant Secretary, 1920; Principal Assistant Secretary, 1936; Secretary, South Wales Divisional Committee, Coalfields Distress Funds, 1929; Chairman of the Miscellaneous Trades Joint Council for Government Departments, 1926–38. *Address:* 58 Wildwood Road, NW11.

Died 27 March 1945.

ABRAHAMS, Major Sir Arthur Cecil, Kt 1942; CBE 1920; OBE 1918; Member of Stock Exchange; Chairman, Stores Department and Vice-Chairman, Finance Committee, Red Cross and St John War Organisation; *b* 1878; *s* of Louis Abrahams, 47 Bryanston Square, London W1; *m* 1904, Evaline, *d* of late Sir Joseph Duveen. *Educ:* University College School; abroad. Was Deputy-Director of Stores, Boulogne, and British Red Cross Commissioner in France during European War (despatches twice); Order of St John of Jerusalem. *Address:* Flat 33, Eaton House, 39 Upper Grosvenor Street, W1.

Died 8 Dec. 1944.

ABRAMSON, Major Albert, CBE 1927; OBE 1919; *b* 1 May 1876; *m* Mabel Jessie Harrison (*d* 1941); one *s* one *d. Educ:* privately. BEF Intelligence Officer; Capt., 1918; Major, 1918 (despatches twice); Military Governor, Hebron, 1918; Chief British Representative Trans-Jordan, 1921; District Commissioner Southern District, Palestine, 1922; District Commissioner Northern District, Palestine, 1925; Commissioner of Lands, Palestine, 1927; Rural Property Tax Commissioner, 1935; Member of Palestine Advisory Council; retired 1935. *Address:* 30 Spencer Hill, Wimbledon, SW19.

Died 1 Nov. 1944.

ACHESON, Captain Albert Edward, CBE 1919; OBE 1918; Royal Navy (retired); *b* 2 May 1862; *s* of William Acheson, Dublin; *m* 1883; two *s* one *d. Educ:* Exeter; Taunton. Cadet HMS Conway, 1877–79; apprentice and officer in sailing ships and steamers, 1879–95; Lieutenant, RNR, 1893; Lieut, Royal Navy, 1895; Lieut-Commander, 1903; Commander (retired), 1907; Transport Service, 1914–19. *Address:* c/o Midland Bank, Stretford, Lancs.

Died 22 June 1945.

ACKLAND, William Alfred; journalist; *b* Plymouth, 1875; *s* of Edward Andrew Ackland; *m* Mabel Frederica, *d* of John F. Lethbridge, Plymouth; two *d. Educ:* Plymouth. Junior Reporter and Sub-Editor, Western Daily Mercury, Plymouth, 1890–96; Sub-Editor, Manchester Courier, to 1900; Daily Dispatch, Manchester, to 1905, as Chief Sub-Editor and Acting

Editor; London Office, Birmingham Daily Mail, to 1906; Night Editor, The Tribune, to 1907; Managing Editor, The Daily Graphic, 1907–12; Director and Editor, The Manchester Courier, 1913; Managing Editor, The Times Weekly Edition, 1914–22; Art Editor The Times and subsidiary publications; Night Manager, The Times, 1923; Correspondent of The Times with the Allied Fleets during European War (Hon. Lieut RNVR), 1918; contributor to The Times History of the War, etc.; Director of Publicity Safety First (NSFA), 1924–29; Persian Art Exhibition, Royal Academy, 1931; French Art Exhibition, Royal Academy, 1932; the Royal Academy of Arts, Burlington House, London W1, 1933; travelled Europe, The East, United States of America, Canada and British Columbia.

Died Dec. 1940.

ACKLAND, Major William Robert, MDS, MRCS, LDS, RAMC (T); Consulting Dental Surgeon, Bristol Royal Infirmary and Minehead and West Somerset Hospital; late Member of Dental Board of United Kingdom and General Medical Council; *b* 1863; *s* of late Robert Ackland, Exeter; *m* Georgina (*d* 1943), *widow* of late H. Buckle, Burma Commission. *Educ:* Torquay; Charing Cross Hospital; Royal Dental Hosp. (Saunders Scholar). Demonstrator of Physiology, Charing Cross Hospital, 1895; Demonstrator Royal Dental Hospital, 1896; late Lecturer and Examiner in Dental Surgery, University of Bristol; Pres. Bath and Bristol Branch British Medical Association, 1914–15 and 1933–34; Pres. Odontological Society (Royal Society of Medicine), 1922; Dental Board Examiner (1921 Act); served European War as Major with the 2nd Southern General Hospital. *Publications:* various papers contributed to Medical and Dental journals. *Recreations:* hunting, swimming, motoring. *Address:* 5 Rodney Place, Clifton, Bristol 8.

Died 26 July 1949.

ACKROYD, Thomas Raven, JP; MA (Hon.) Manchester University; Alderman of Manchester City Council; retired bank manager; *b* Aug. 1861; *s* of William and Elizabeth Ackroyd; *m* 1893. *Educ:* Chancery Lane Wesleyan; Manchester Mechanics Institution; Evening Student, Manchester Univ. Entered the service as junior clerk of the Union Bank of Manchester, Ltd, 1878; MP (L) Moss Side Division of Manchester, 1923–24; has taken a very active part in the religious and social life of the city; Chairman of the Manchester and Salford Ragged School Union and Chairman (for 1924) of the Shaftesbury Society and London Ragged School Union; a prominent member of the Wesleyan Methodist Church and local preacher. *Recreations:* walking and golfing. *Address:* 17 Berkley Avenue, Levenshulme, Manchester. *Clubs:* Reform, Manchester.

Died 26 April 1946.

ACLAND, Captain Frank E. Dyke, late RA; *b* 12 May 1857; 6th *s* of Sir Henry W. Acland, 1st Bart, KCB, FRS; *m* Marion (*d* 1937), *e d* of Right Rev. William Kenneth Macrorie, DD, 1st Bishop of Maritzburg, Natal; two *s* two *d. Educ:* Harrow. Lieut Royal Artillery and RHA 1877; retired, 1889; Member of Institution Civil and Mechanical Engineers; FRSA; Naval Institute, USA; Military Institute, USA. *Address:* Walwood, Banstead. *T:* Burgh Heath 115. *Clubs:* Junior United Service, Royal Automobile.

Died 14 March 1943.

ACLAND, Henry Dyke; Barrister and Solicitor; partner Wilding and Acland, Solicitors; *b* 1867; *s* of Hon. J. B. A. Acland, MLC, and Emily, *e d* of Most Rev. H. J. C. Harper; *m* 1906, Elizabeth Grace (*d* 1942), *d* of Hon. James Watson, MLC, Sydney; two *d. Educ:* Christ's College, Christchurch, NZ; Christ Church, Oxford (BA). Called to Bar, Inner Temple, 1891; Member Board of Governors of Canterbury University College since 1909, Chairman, 1918–28; Member Senate University of New Zealand since 1923; Dominion

President, Workers Educational Association; Member New Zealand Meat Producers Board since 1926; President New Zealand Sheepowners' Federation, 1910; Consul for Denmark for South Island of NZ. *Address:* 42 Park Terrace, Christchurch, C1, NZ. *Clubs:* Christchurch; Wellington.

Died 12 Dec. 1942.

ACTON, Hon. Sir Edward, Kt 1925, Bencher, Inner Temple; Hon. Fellow Wadham College, Oxford; *b* 6 Nov. 1865; *s* of Henry Morell Acton; *m* 1903, Edith Nina, *d* of Conrad Tulloch, London. *Educ:* Uppingham (Exhibitioner); Wadham College, Oxford (Classical Scholar and Hody Greek Exhibition). 1st Class in Classical Moderations, 1886; Second Lit. Hum. 1888; Foundation Scholar in Common Law, Inner Temple, 1890. Called to Bar, 1891; Northern Circuit; Lecturer in Law to University of Manchester; Judge of County Courts (Circuit 18), Nottingham, 1918–20; Judge of King's Bench Division, High Court of Justice, 1920–34; retired. *Address:* The Hatch, Churt. *Club:* Athenæum.

Died 17 Nov. 1945.

ADAIR, Brig.-Gen. Hugh Robert, CBE, retired list RA; *b* 8 Sept. 1863; *y s* of late General Sir C. W. Adair, KCB; *m* Sibyl, *y d* of late T. Cayzer, Aigburth. *Educ:* Cheltenham College; RMA, Woolwich. Entered Royal Artillery, 1882; retired, 1920; CRA, Humber Garrison, 1914–16; Thames and Medway Garrison, 1916–20 (despatches, CBE). *Recreation:* reading. *Address:* c/o Lloyds Bank, Cox and King's Branch, 6 Pall Mall, SW1.

Died 14 Nov. 1946.

ADAIR, Sir (R.) Shafto, 5th Bt *cr* 1838; DL Co. Antrim; JP Norfolk and Suffolk; Barrister-at-law; a director of Royal Academy of Music; *b* 18 Aug. 1862; *S* brother, 1915; *s* of 3rd Bt and Harriet Camilla, *d* of Alexander Adair; *m* 1890, Mary, *d* of Henry Anstey Bosanquet; one *s* one *d. Educ:* abroad; Christ Church, Oxford, BA. *Heir: s* Maj.-Gen. Allan (Henry Shafto), CB. *Address:* Flixton Hall, Bungay.

Died 9 Oct. 1949.

ADAM, J. Millen, FRSA; sole partner of the firm J. M. Adam & Co. engineers; *b* Glasgow, 1853; *s* of John Adam, bleacher; *m* 1st, 1885, Isabel, *d* of William Angus, Fellow of the Educational Institute of Scotland, and sometime Secretary of the Institute; no *c*; 2nd, 1913, Annie, *d* of John Kelso, merchant; two *s* one *d. Educ:* Glasgow, by private tuition. A shipbuilding manager in 1881; specialised in engineering costings; subsequently engaged in boiler making; started steel pipe making in 1888; patentee in that year of Adam's Patent Air Pipes of Prismatic Section; since 1893 specialised in scientific ventilation in factories and industrial dust controls; patentee in 1895 of vanes of a conic surface approximating to the wings of birds—the geometric basis of which he studied for air impulsion, ship propulsion, etc., and a year or two later a vortex air purifier known as Adam's Patent Dust Baffle; practises as consultant in all matters relating to the utilization and purification of air and other gaseous fluids at all temperatures. *Publications:* sundry papers in the transactions of the Institute of Engineers and Shipbuilders in Scotland and of the Institute of Naval Architects on Tubular Bends and Junctions, on Geometrical Analysis of Ship Propeller reactions, etc. *Address:* Highbury, Kirklee Place, Glasgow, W2.

Died 17 May 1941.

ADAM, Sir James, Kt 1922; CBE 1918; KC Scot.; King's and Lord Treasurer's Remembrancer, 1921; retired, 1926; *b* 6 Jan. 1870; *o s* of late Hon. Lord Adam, one of the Senators, College of Justice, Scotland; *m* 1896, Edith, *d* of Right Hon. George Young, PC; one *s* three *d. Educ:* Eton; Oxford. Sheriff of Essex, 1938. *Address:* Colne Park, Earls Colne, Essex.

Died 26 Sept. 1949.

ADAMS, Charles Edward, DSc (NZ), FRAS; Deputy Chairman, Carter Observatory Board, Wellington; Hon. Fellow, NZ Institute of Architects; *b* Lawrence, NZ, 1 Oct. 1870; *s* of late C. W. Adams, Chief Surveyor and Commissioner of Crown Lands, NZ; *m* 1896, Eleanor Robina (*d* 1940), *d* of Howard Charles Jacobson, Journalist, Akaroa, NZ; three *s* three *d. Educ:* Wellington College; Otago Boys' High School; Canterbury University College (University of New Zealand). Engineering Scholar and Engineering Exhibitioner, Canterbury University College; Senior University Scholar in Physical Science; Honours in Mathematics and Mathematical Physics, Optics and Astronomy, University of New Zealand; Martin Kellogg Fellow in Astronomy, Lick Observatory, Mount Hamilton, University of California; Government Astronomer and Seismologist for the Dominion of New Zealand; retired, 1936; Associate in Astronomy of the Yale University Observatory. *Publications:* mathematical, geophysical, and astronomical publications in scientific periodicals in Europe, New Zealand and Australia. *Recreations:* walking, bowling. *Address:* 7 Telford Terrace, Oriental Bay, Wellington, E1. *TA:* Astronomer, Wellington. *T:* 50527.

Died 31 Oct. 1945.

ADAMS, David; JP; MP (Lab) Consett division of Durham since 1935; member of D. Adams & Co., Ltd, shipowners, Newcastle, and Anglo-Scottish Trading Co., Ltd, Newcastle-upon-Tyne; *b* 27 June 1871; *s* of John Adams, Newcastle-upon-Tyne; *m* 1897, Elizabeth Havelock, *d* of Captain John Patterson; two *s* one *d. Educ:* Science and Art School and Armstrong College, Newcastle-upon-Tyne. Sheriff of Newcastle, 1922–23; MP (Lab) West Newcastle, 1922–23; Lord Mayor of Newcastle, 1930–31; engineering member of NE Coast Institution of Engineers and Shipbuilders. *Address:* Jesmond Cottage, Newcastle. *T:* Jesmond 428. *TA:* Canute, Newcastle-upon-Tyne.

Died 16 Aug. 1943.

ADAMS, David Morgan; MP (Lab) South Poplar since 1931; *b* 23 Feb. 1875; *s* of late David Morgan Adams, Llwynbrian, Ystradowen, Glamorgan and late Bessie Dent, Poplar; *m* 1900, Ada (*d* 1941); four *s* one *d. Educ:* Ystradowen, nr Cowbridge, South Wales. Worked in coal mines as a boy; seafaring as AB; served in The Welch Regt, 69th Bn, 3 years 130 days in India; seaman in the Light Ships, Trinity House Service (London); docker, Port of London Authority; Trade Union Official, Transport and General Workers Union since 1920; Popular Board of Guardians, 1913–30; Borough Council since 1919; Mayor of the Borough, 1934–35; London County Council, 1930–37; Metropolitan Asylums Board, 1928–30. *Address:* 8 Southill Street, Poplar, E14. *T:* East 3147.

Died 19 May 1942.

ADAMS, Miss E. Proby, SGA; portrait and animal painter; does mural decoration and book illustrations, and exhibits flower-paintings, landscapes and interiors; *b* St Luke's Day, Sudbury, Suffolk, of Irish extraction. *Educ:* Bedford. Trained at Slade School; gained there, Slade Scholarship, British Institution Scholarship of £100, and highest award painting. Exhibitor at Royal Academy, RI, New English Art Club, Walker Art Gallery, Liverpool, Leeds, Los Angeles, Hull, Brighton, etc.; Lecturer on Crafts. *Publication:* Art Critic and Reviewer. *Recreation:* gardening. *Address:* Carysfort, Vine Avenue, Sevenoaks. *TA:* Carysfort, Sevenoaks.

Died 18 Dec. 1945.

ADAMS, Col Francis, DSO 1918; Indian Army, retired; *b* 17 April 1874; *o s* of late Francis Adams, Clifton; *m* 1909, Helen Maude, *er d* of late J. G. Howes of King's Cliffe and 48 Porchester Terrace, W2; no *c. Educ:* Cheltenham College. Joined 3rd Batt. Royal West Kent Regiment, 1891; Indian Army, 1894; Captain 3rd Madras Lancers, 1903; Major, 1912; Lt-Colonel, 1916;

Colonel, 1920; Inspecting Officer Imperial Service Troops, 1906–10; served European War, France, 1914–18 (DSO, despatches, Officier de l'ordre de la Couronne, 1914 Star); EEF Palestine and Syria, 1918–20 (despatches, War Medal, Victory Medal, Belgian Croix de Guerre, Officier de l'Ordre du Mérite Agricole); commanded 20th Royal Deccan Horse, 1916–20. *Recreations:* before the war: hunting and sailing. *Address:* Cliff Close, Highcliffe, Hants. *Clubs:* Cavalry, Royal Automobile; Royal Lymington Yacht.

Died 4 Dec. 1945.

ADAMS, Frank Dawson, FRS, London and Canada; PhD, DSc, LLD, FGS; Emeritus Dean of the Faculty of Applied Science, Vice-Principal and Logan Professor of Geology, McGill University, Montreal; *b* Montreal, 17 Sept. 1859; *m* 1892, Marie Stuart (*d* 1937), *e d* of Samuel Finley. *Educ:* Montreal High School; McGill University; Yale University; Heidelberg University. On Staff of Geological Survey of Canada, 1880; Lecturer in Geology at McGill University, 1889; President, Canadian Institute of Mining and Metallurgy, 1910–11; President, International Congress of Geologists (Canada), 1913; President, Royal Society of Canada, 1913; President, Geological Society of America, 1918; Hon. Member, Institution of Mining and Metallurgy of Great Britain; Hon. Member, American Institute of Mining and Metallurgical Engineers; Hon. Member, Engineering Institute of Canada; Foreign Associate, National Academy of Sciences, USA; Member American Philosophical Society of Philadelphia; Cor. Member, Geological Society of Stockholm; Hon. Member, Royal Swedish Academy of Science; Hon. Member, Geological Society of Edinburgh; Member of the Honorary Advisory Council for Scientific and Industrial Research in Canada. *Publications:* History of the Birth and Development of the Geological Sciences; History of Christ Church Cathedral, Montreal; many papers dealing more especially with problems of metamorphism and the older crystalline rocks of the earth's crust, which have appeared in various scientific publications in Canada, England, and United States; Researches on Experimental Geology; also papers on the National Domain in Canada and its Conservation. *Recreations:* canoeing, camping, and exploration. *Address:* 1173 Mountain Street, Montreal, Canada. *T:* Marquette 8572. *Clubs:* Mount Royal, University, Montreal.

Died 26 Dec. 1942.

ADAMS, Harry William, RBA 1912; Member Royal British Colonial Society of Artists; Member Royal Cambrian Academy, retired; Member Royal Birmingham Society of Artists; President, Malvern Art Club; *b* Worcester, 3 Nov. 1868; *s* of William Henry Adams; *m*; no *c*. *Educ:* private school; School of Art, Worcester. Was for 8 years at the Worcester Royal Porcelain Works; after leaving there studied out of doors, and in 1895–96 went to Paris; first picture at the RA on the line Dec.'s Royal Robe, 1896; 1900, Winter's Sleep, purchased under the Chantrey bequest; Pres. of Birmingham Art Circle, 1935–38. *Publications:* Pictures reproduced, Winter's Sleep; The Valley of the Teme, engraved by Fred Sedcole. *Recreations:* fishing, canoeing. *Address:* The Cottage, Kingswood, Martley, Worcester.

Died 1 May 1947.

ADAMS, Ven. Henry Joseph, MA; Canon Residentiary and Rector of St Paul's Cathedral, Bunbury, West Australia, since 1910; Archdeacon of Bunbury since 1926; *b* Manchester, 1 April 1870; *s* of Rev. Richard Adams, MA, then Rector of St Stephen's, Hulme, Manchester, and Frances L. H. Adams, *d* of Captain H. E. W. Lane, sometime Governor of Manchester City Gaol; *m* 1902, Anne Wright (*d* 1926), *d* of late Dr Thomas Shaw, of Kirkham, Lancs; no *c*. *Educ:* Manchester and Bolton Grammar Schools; Selwyn Coll., Camb. Assist Master Bolton Grammar School, 1891–93; Assist Curate St Michael's, Kirkham, 1893–98; Vicar of Lever Bridge, Bolton, 1898–1910; Rural Dean of

Bunbury, 1910–18; Hon. Chaplain to Bishop of Bunbury, 1918–27. Frequent writer for newspapers and magazines on pastoral and missionary subjects. *Recreations:* bowls, philately. *Address:* The Rectory, Bunbury, W Australia. *Clubs:* Commercial, Bunbury.

Died 14 Dec. 1946.

ADAMS, Herbert; sculptor; President, Saint-Gaudens Museum; Trustee, American Academy in Rome; Trustee, Hispanic Society of America; *b* Concord, Vt, 1858; *s* of Samuel M. Adams and Nancy Powers; *m* 1889, Adeline Valentine Pond, of Auburndale, Mass. *Educ:* Fitchburg, Mass; Inst. of Technology, Worcester, Mass; Mass Normal Art School; Paris, under Mercié. Awards at Chicago, Paris, St Louis and other Expositions. Member and former President National Sculpture Society and Nat. Academy Design; Member Nat. Academy Arts and Letters, etc. *Address:* 131 W 11th St, New York. *Clubs:* Century, New York.

Died 21 May 1945.

ADAMS, James Truslow, MA, LLD, LittD, LHD, FRSL; *b* 18 Oct. 1878; *s* of William Newton Adams and Elizabeth Harper Truslow; *m* 1927, Kathryn M. Seely; no *c*. *Educ:* Brooklyn Polytechnic; Yale University. Banker until 1912; served European War as Captain, US Army, Intelligence Division, Gen. Staff; attached to American Commission to negotiate peace, Paris, 1918–19; Pulitzer Prize 1922 for best book on American History that year; Chancellor of American Academy of Arts and Letters; Fellow Royal Society of Literature, etc.; historian and writer since war. *Publications:* Memorials of Old Bridgehampton; History of Town of Southampton (NY); Founding of New England; New England in the Revolution; New England in the Republic; Provincial Society, 1690–1763; Hamiltonian Principles; Jeffersonian Principles; The Adams Family; The Epic of America; The Tempo of Modern Life; A Searchlight on America; A History of the American People; Henry Adams; America's Tragedy; The Record of America; The Living Jefferson; Building the British Empire; Empire on the Seven Seas; The American, 1943; Frontiers of American Culture, 1944; Big Business in a Democracy; editor-in-chief of The Dictionary of American History, 6 vols, 1940; of the Atlas of American History, 1943; and of Album of American History (4 vols); contributor to leading American magazines and reviews, The Encyclopædia Britannica, The Dictionary of American Biography, etc.; works translated into French, German, Swedish, Hungarian, Italian, Danish, Rumanian, Spanish, Portuguese. Norwegian and Finnish. *Recreations:* books and travel. *Address:* Southport, Conn, USA. *Clubs:* Century (New York); Pequot Yacht (Conn).

Died 18 May 1949.

ADAMS, John, MA; Assistant Dominion Botanist, Canada, retired; *b* nr Ballymena, Co. Antrim, 20 Jan. 1872; *s* of Thomas H. Adams, linen manufacturer; *m* Augusta Eveleen, *d* of Alexander M'Gaffin, Belfast; one *s* one *d*. *Educ:* Royal Academical Instn, Belfast; Queen's Coll., Belfast; St John's Coll., Cambridge. Formerly Lecturer in Botany in City of Dublin Municipal Technical Schs; Asst Prof. of Botany in Royal Coll. of Sci. for Ireland; late Prof. of Botany in Royal Veterinary Coll. of Ireland. *Publications:* Guide to the Principal Families of Flowering Plants; Studies in Plant Life; A Survey of Canadian Plants in Relation to their Environment; A Short Guide to Canadian Genera of Seed Plants; A Student's Illustrated Irish Flora; A Bibliography of Canadian Plant Geography; The Flora of Canada. *Address:* 68 Fairmont Avenue, Ottawa, Canada.

Died 18 May 1950.

ADAMS, Philip Edward Homer, MA, MB, DO Oxon; FRCS; *b* 20 April 1879; *s* of late G. E. D'Arcy Adams, MD; *m* 1st, 1908, Marjorie (*d* 1924), *d* of late Rev. A. C. Smith, Vicar of St Michael's, Oxford; one *s* two *d*; 2nd, 1929, Helon Stewart, *o c* of late Frederick W. Weller-

Poley. *Educ:* Lancing College; Exeter College, Oxford; London Hospital. Worked at the Eye Hospital as Clinical Assistant, Assistant to Surgical Staff, and temporary Assistant Surgeon; Hon. Surgeon to Oxford Eye Hospital and Margaret Ogilvie Reader in Ophthalmology, Oxford University, 1913–41; Consulting Surgeon to Oxford Eye Hospital, 1941; Consulting Ophthalmic Surgeon to Radcliffe Infirmary, 1912; retired from practice in Oxford, 1946; Master Oxford Ophthalmological Congress, 1926–28; Deputy Master, 1929–42. *Publications:* various papers in ophthalmic journals. *Recreations:* fencing, motoring. *Address:* The Old Rectory, Therberton, nr Leiston, Suffolk. *T:* Leiston 82. *Club:* Oxford and Cambridge.

Died 9 Feb. 1948.

ADAMS, William Thomas; MP (Lab) S Hammersmith, since 1945; JP (London); clerk; *b* 10 Sept. 1884; *s* of John Adams and Annie Mary Otway; *m* Florence Nightingale; three *s*. *Educ:* SBL Central Street, St Luke's. Occupationally: many jobs of a clerical nature, starting at the age of 12½ as messenger. Politically: Labour Party, Trade Union and Co-operative Movement, having held many executive offices in all. Public Life: first elected to Hammersmith Borough Council, 1934, after three unsuccessful contests; Alderman Hammersmith Borough Council, 1938–45. Leader of the Council, 1944–45. Contested South Hammersmith, 1935. *Address:* 155 Percy Road, Shepherd's Bush, W12.

Died 9 Jan. 1949.

ADAMSON, Sir Harvey, KCSI 1910; Kt 1906; CSI 1903; MA, LLD; *b* 7 Oct. 1854; *s* of Rev. Alexander Adamson of Kinnermit; *m* 1892, Jane Charlotte, *d* of John Leslie, Corsie, Nairn; one *s* one *d*. *Educ:* Gymnasium, Old Aberdeen; Aberdeen University. MA, 1873; Fullerton Scholar in Mathematics, 1873; Ferguson Scholar in Mathematics, 1874; passed competitive examination for Indian Civil Service, 1875. Joined Burma Commission, 1877; Assistant Commissioner, 1877–79; Settlement Officer, 1880–85; Deputy Commissioner, 1886–93; Commissioner, 1894–99, chiefly of Mandalay Division; Judicial Commissioner, Upper Burma, 1900–05; Lieut-Colonel commanding Upper Burma Volunteer Rifles, 1897–1900 (Burma medal); additional Member of the Council of Governor-General of India, 1903–05; Chief Judge, Chief Court of Lower Burma, 1905–06; Lieut-Governor of Burma, 1910–15; Ordinary Member of Council of Governor-General of India, 1906–10. *Recreation:* golf. *Address:* 92 Bouverie Road, W; Folkestone, Kent.

Died 28 March 1941.

ADAMSON, Sir John Ernest, Kt 1924; CMG 1923; MA and DLit London University; Master of Rhodes University College, Grahamstown, 1925–30; Director of Education for Transvaal, 1905–24; Vice-Chancellor, University of S Africa, 1922–26; *b* Wakefield, Yorkshire, 1867; *m* Gwendolyn Mary, *y d* of late John Howell Thomas of Starling Park, Carmarthenshire. *Educ:* London. On the staff of the Practising School attached to the St Mark's Training College, Chelsea, 1889–90; Tutor and Lecturer in the Theory and Practice of Teaching and Education at the South Wales Training College, Carmarthen, 1891–1902; Principal of the Normal College, Pretoria, 1902–05. *Publications:* The Theory of Education in Plato's Republic; The Teacher's Logic; Songs from the South, 1915; The Individual and the Environment, 1920; Externals and Essentials, 1933; various Educational papers. *Recreations:* golf and tennis. *Address:* 3 Sunrise Mansions, Muizenberg, Cape, SA. *Clubs:* Authors'; Country (Pretoria); Civil Service (Cape Town).

Died 24 April 1950.

ADAMSON, John William, DLit; Fellow King's College, London; Emeritus Professor of Education, University of London, 1924; *b* 22 April 1857; *m* Caroline Amanda Knapman (*d* 1942); one *s* two *d*. *Educ:*
Cheltenham Training College; King's College, London; University, London. Head of the Training Department and Master of Method, King's Coll. London, 1890; Lecturer in Education, 1901; Professor, 1903; Lecturer on the History of Education to the Teachers' Training Syndicate, University of Cambridge, 1919–35; Chairman (1907–09, 1921–24), Secretary (1901–06), Board of Studies in Pedagogy; Chairman, Military Education Committee, University of London, 1926–37; President of Teachers' Training Association, 1909–10; formerly Examiner in Education, Universities of Cambridge, London, Durham, Wales, Liverpool, and Leeds. *Publications:* Our Defective System of Training Teachers, 1904; Pioneers of Modern Education, 1600–1700, 1905; The Practice of Instruction (editor and chief contributor), 1907; The Educational Writings of John Locke, 1912: Education in Cambridge History of English Literature, vols ix and xiv, in Mediaeval Contributions to Modern Civilisation (1921), and in The Legacy of the Middle Ages (1926); A Short History of Education, 1919; A Guide to the History of Education, 1920; English Education, 1789–1902, 1930; Education, in Cambridge Bibliography of English Literature: Education, 1714–1789, in Bibliography of Modern British History (R. Hist. Soc.); The Illiterate Anglo-Saxon, 1946. *Address:* 12 Glebe Court, Highfield, Southampton.

Died 12 March 1947.

ADAMSON, William Murdoch; National Officer of the Transport and General Workers' Union; *b* 12 April 1881; *m* 1902, Jennie L. Adamson, MP. MP (Lab) Cannock Division of Staffs, 1922–31, and 1935–45; a Lord Commissioner of HM Treasury, 1941–44. *Address:* 20 Woodcombe Crescent, Forest Hill, SE23.

Died 25 Oct. 1945.

ADDAMS WILLIAMS, Christopher, CIE 1916; *b* 2 April 1877. Joined PWD 1897; Executive Engineer, 1907; Superintending Engineer, 1914; Chief Engineer, Irrigation Bengal, 1920; retired 1932. *Address:* Llysbrechfa, Llanfrechfa, Mon. *T:* Cwmbran 7626.

Died 16 April 1944.

ADDERLEY, Hon. and Rev. James (Granville), MA, Prebendary of St Paul's since 1935; *b* 1 July 1861; 5th *s* of 1st Baron Norton. *Educ:* Eton; Christ Church, Oxford. Head of Oxford House, Bethnal Green, 1885–86; Deacon, 1887; Priest, 1888; Head of Christ Church Oxford Mission, 1887–93; Curate of Allhallows' Barking, 1893–94; St Andrew's, Plaistow E, 1894–97; Minister of Berkeley Chapel, Mayfair, 1897–1901; Vicar of St Mark's, Marylebone, 1901–04; of Saltley, Birmingham, 1904–11; of St Gabriel's, Birmingham, 1911–18; Rector of St Paul's, Covent Garden, 1918–23; Vicar of St Anne's Highgate, 1923–29; Rector of St Edmund's, EC, 1929–37; Hon. Canon, Birmingham, 1914; Hon. Chaplain to Bishop of Birmingham, 1918; Select Preacher, Oxford University, 1917–19; Cambridge University, 1919. *Publications:* Stephen Remarx, 1893; Francis of Assisi, 1901; In Slums and Society, 1916; Old Seed on New Ground, 1920. *Address:* 1 Priory Mansions, Drayton Gardens, SW10. *Club:* National Liberal.

Died 1 June 1942.

ADDIS, Sir Charles (Stewart), KCMG 1921; Kt 1913; LLD (Hon.) Edinburgh, Hongkong, and Kingston (Ont); Lieutenant of the City of London; late Crown Member Court of University of London; *b* Edinburgh, 23 Nov. 1861; *s* of Rev. Thomas Addis, DD, of Morningside, Edinburgh; *m* 1894, Eba, *d* of James McIsaac of Parkend, Saltcoats; four *s* seven *d*. *Educ:* Edinburgh Academy. Peter Dowie & Co. Leith, 1876–80; Hongkong and Shanghai Bank, London, India, Burma, China and Straits Settlements, 1880–1904; Manager, London, 1905–21; Chairman, London Committee, 1922–33; Director, Bank of England, 1918–32; President of the Institute of Bankers, 1921–23;

Vice-Chairman, Bank for International Settlements, 1929–32; Cunliffe Currency Committee, 1918–19; Indian Currency Committee, 1920; British Alternate Genoa Conference, 1922; Chairman, Exchange Committee Imperial Economic Conference, 1923; Brazilian Financial Commission, 1923–24; National Debt Committee, 1924–26; British Representative on General Council of Reichsbank, 1924–30; China Advisory Committee Boxer Indemnity, 1925; British Delegate on Committee of Experts for Reparations, Paris, 1929; Royal Commission on Canadian Banking, 1933; Order of Sacred Treasure of Japan, 2nd Class; Order of Chiao Ho of China, 2nd Class. *Address:* 9 Gracechurch Street, EC3. *T:* Mansion House 8541; Woodside, Frant, Sussex. *T:* Frant 2. *Clubs:* Athenæum, Albemarle.

Died 14 Dec. 1945.

ADDISON, Sir James, Kt 1935; *b* 13 Nov. 1879; *s* of James Addison, JP, Whitehills, Boyndie, Banff; *m* 1908, Vera Mary Delphine, *d* of James Alfred Cones; one *s* one *d. Educ:* Banff Academy; Aberdeen University (MA, BSc); Simpson Prizeman in Mathematics; Greig Prizeman in Physics; David Rennet Gold Medallist, and Fullarton Mathematical Scholar: passed into Indian Civil Service, 1902; passed year of probation at University College, London. District Judge, Delhi, 1909; Special Land Acquisition Officer, New Delhi 1912; Judge, Small Cause Court, Simla, 1917; District and Sessions Judge, Rawalpindi, 1920; Additional Judge High Court, Lahore, 1925; Puisne Judge, High Court, Lahore, 1927; Acting Chief Justice, High Court, Lahore, 1935, 1938 and 1939; retired, 1939. *Address:* c/o Lloyds Bank, Ltd, 6 Pall Mall, SW1; c/o Standard Bank of South Africa, Adderley St, Cape Town. *Club:* East India and Sports.

Died 17 Sept. 1949.

ADDISON, Margaret E. T., CBE 1934; LLD; Dean of Women Emerita (Victoria College); *b* 21 Oct. 1868; *d* of Peter and Mary Ann Campbell Addison. *Educ:* Victoria University. Teacher Ontario Ladies' College 1889–91; Collegiate Institute Stratford, 1892–1900; Collegiate Institute Lindsay, 1901–03; Dean of Women, Victoria College, 1903–31; Member or Officer of: University Women's Club (Pres. one year), Women's Canadian Club, Local Council of Women, Victoria Women's Association, National Council YWCA, Ontario Educational Association, Association Deans of Women, Woman's Missionary Society United Church of Canada, Board of Christian Education and others. *Recreation:* detective stories. *Address:* 431 Broadview Avenue, Toronto, Canada. *Clubs:* University Women's, Toronto.

Died 18 Dec. 1940.

ADDISON, Oswald Lacy; Emeritus Surgeon, West London Hospital; Consulting Surgeon, Hospital for Sick Children, Great Ormond Street, Infants' Hospital and Princess Louise Kensington Hospital for Children; *b* 1874; *s* of Joseph Addison. *Educ:* Marlborough; University College Hospital. *Publications:* medical papers.

Died 8 Jan. 1942.

ADEANE, Charles Robert Whorwood, CB 1917; JP, Lord-Lieutenant of Cambridgeshire; Hon. LLD Cambridge; *b* 1863; *o s* of late Henry John Adeane, MP, and Lady Elizabeth Philippa, *e d* of 4th Earl of Hardwicke (she; *m* 2nd, 1877, Michael Biddulph, MP); *m* 1888, Madeline Pamela Constance Blanche, CBE 1937 (*d* 1941), *d* of late Hon. Percy Seawen Wyndham; one *s* five *d. Educ:* Eton; Christ-Church, Oxford. Patron of one living; late Lieut 4th Batt Suffolk Regt. *Address:* Babraham Hall, Cambridge. *Club:* Brooks's.

Died 11 Feb. 1943.

ADLAM, George Henry Joseph, OBE 1934; MA, BSc Oxon; Editor School Science Review since 1919; *b* 19 Jan. 1876; *s* of George and Mary Ann Emily Adlam, Wells, Somerset; *m* 1st, Alice Smith, Bristol; 2nd, Florence Lavinia Chun, Marlborough. *Educ:* Wells

Cathedral Grammar School; Wadham College, Oxford. 1st Class Nat. Science (Chem.), 1905. *Address:* Austen, Ash Lane, Wells, Somerset. *T:* Wells (Som.) 398.

Died 30 July 1946.

ADLER, Elkan Nathan, MA, DHL, International Lawyer, Traveller, Book Collector, Hebraist and Historian; Senior Partner in Adler and Perowne, Solicitors, London and Paris; *b* London, 24 July 1861; 3rd *s* of Very Rev. Dr Nathan Marcus Adler, Chief Rabbi. *Educ:* City of London School; University College, London. Vice-President of International Jewish Conferences at Berlin in 1891 and 1903; delegate and advocate of the Jewish cause in many European countries; is a Corresponding Member of the Royal Academy of History of Spain and the American Jewish Historical Society, and was President of the Jewish Historical Society of England and the Union of Jewish Literary Societies. *Publications:* Hebrew Elegies on English Monarchs, 1895; An Eleventh Century Introduction to the Hebrew Bible, 1897; The Persian Jews: Their Books and Ritual, 1898; Une Nouvelle Chronique Samaritaine, 1903; The Inquisition in Peru, 1904; Jews in Many Lands, 1905 (translated into Hebrew, Hungarian, and German, the last under the title of Von Ghetto zu Ghetto); About Hebrew Manuscripts, 1905; Auto-de-fé and Jew, 1908; A Gazetteer of Hebrew Printing, 1917; Catalogue of Hebrew Manuscripts in the Collection of E. N. Adler, 1921; A History of Jews in London, 1930; Jewish Travellers, 1930; The Adler Papyri, 1937; articles to many magazines and newspapers, to the Encyclopaedia of Religion and Ethics, the Jewish Encyclopaedia, to Aspects of the Hebrew Genius, 1910, Judaism and the Beginnings of Christianity, 1923, to various Jubilee and Memorial Volumes and to the Transactions of the Jewish Historical Society and the American Jewish Historical Society. *Address:* 20 Porchester Square, W2. *TA:* Tutissimus London. *T:* Bayswater 1002. *Clubs:* Athenæum, National Liberal.

Died 15 Sept. 1946.

ADLER, Rev. Michael, DSO 1917; BA; Chairman of West Central Jewish Lads' Club; Chaplain Maccabean Branch, British Legion; *b* London, 27 July 1868; *m*; one *s* two *d. Educ:* Jews' College and University College, London. Minister, Hammersmith Synagogue, 1890–1903; Senior Hebrew Master, Jews Free School, E, 1893–1903; Minister of the Central Synagogue, W, 1903–34; Emeritus Minister since 1934; Commission as Chaplain, TF, 1909–26; served as Senior Jewish Chaplain in France, 1915–18 (DSO, despatches twice); Vice-President and Editor of Publications, of Jewish Historical Society of England. *Publications:* First Steps in Hebrew Grammar; Students' Hebrew Grammar; The Jews of the Empire and the Great War; Experiences of a Jewish Chaplain on the Western Front; Soldiers' Prayer Book; British Jewry Book of Honour; Jews of Medieval England. *Address:* c/o 1 Linden Gardens, W2.

Died 30 Sept. 1944.

ADLER, Miss N., CBE 1934; JP attached to Juvenile Courts; *d* of late Chief Rabbi, Dr H. Adler. *Educ:* private school and classes. Began social work as a school manager under the London School Board; co-opted member of the London Education Committee, 1905–10; Member LCC for Central Hackney, 1910–25, and 1928–31; Deputy Chairman, 1922–23; Co-opted member of LCC Public Health Committee, 1931–34; joint Hon. Sec. of the Committee on Wage Earning Children, 1899–1946; Member of the Governing Bodies of the Dalston County School, of the Hackney Downs School and the Hackney Technical Institute; Member of the Departmental Committee on Charity Collections, 1925–27; Member of Council of the Anglo-Jewish Association. *Publications:* articles on Children as Wage Earners, on Women's Work during and after the War, The Early Treatment of Young Offenders, and Boy and Girl Labour since the War, in the Contemporary Review, chapter on Jewish

Life and Labour in East London in New Survey of London Life and Labour, vol. vi, and has written for other journals; article on Juvenile Courts in Encyclopædia Britannica. *Recreations:* week-ends in the country before the war, reading. *Address:* 121a Sinclair Road, Addison Gardens, W14. *T:* Shepherd's Bush 2479.

Died 15 April 1950.

ADSHEAD, Prof. Stanley Davenport, MA, MArch, FRIBA; Architect, London; *b* 1868. Professor of Town-Planning in Liverpool University, 1909–14; Professor of Town-Planning, London University, 1914–35, Emeritus Professor since 1935; late Member Fine Art Commission; executed works, Ramsgate Pavilion, Carnegie Library, Ramsgate; Repertory Theatre, Liverpool; rebuilding of the Duchy of Cornwall Estate, Kennington; Worthing Pavilion and Band Enclosure. *Publications:* Town-Planning and Town Development, 1923; A New England, 1942. Regional Planning Schemes, Chesterfield, South Essex, West Essex, 1923–1933. Town Plans; Southampton, Scarborough, York. *Address:* 94 Regent's Park Road, NW1.

Died 11 April 1946.

ADYE, Frederick James, CBE 1928; Secretary, Pacific Cable Board, since 1913; *b* 17 Feb. 1874; 4th *s* of late Edward Adye; *m* 1906, Mary Amelia Fraser (*d* 1914); no *c*. *Educ:* privately. Entered the firm of Deloitte, Dever, Griffiths & Co., chartered accountants, 1889; remained with them until 1902; joined the Pacific Cable Board as Accountant, 1902. *Recreation:* interested in all sport. *Address:* Senang, 16 Waterside Road, Paignton, Devon.

Died 2 Aug. 1945.

AFFLECK, John Barr, CBE 1929; *b* 26 Oct. 1878; *s* of late John Affleck, MA, DSc; *m* 1928, Anne Bell (formerly Proctor); one *s*. Student Interpreter, China, 1902; 1st Assistant, 1915; served with China Labour Corps, 1917; one of HM Vice-Consuls in China, 1919; one of HM Consuls, 1925; HBM Consul, Tsingtao, China, 1930–34; one of HM Consuls-General in China, 1934; Consul General Tientsin, 1935–38; retired 1938; Silver Jubilee Medal, 1935; Coronation Medal 1937. *Club:* Constitutional.

Died 16 March 1941.

AGAR, Sir Arthur Kirwan, Kt 1939; *b* 31 Aug. 1877; *s* of late Edward Larpent Agar, Milford House, Milford-on-Sea, Hants; *m* 1st, 1905, Winifred Milbourne, *d* of late John George Raynes; two *d*; 2nd, 1930, Josephine, *d* of Hugh Houston Hutchings. *Educ:* Brighton College. Barrister-at-Law, Gray's Inn; served European War, 1915–19; entered Colonial Legal Service, 1920; Chief Justice, British Honduras, 1936–40. *Recreations:* tennis, golf. *Club:* Royal Empire Society.

Died July 1942.

AGATE, James Evershed; author and dramatic critic; dramatic critic to the Sunday Times since 1923; also film critic to The Tatler; also literary critic to The Daily Express; *b* Manchester, 9 Sept. 1877; *e s* of late Charles James Agate, Horsham and Manchester; *m* 1918, Sidonie Joséphine Edmée Mourret-Castillon. *Educ:* Giggleswick; Manchester Grammar School. Dramatic critic to the Daily Dispatch, 1905–06; to the Manchester Guardian, 1907–14; to Saturday Review, 1921–23; to BBC, 1925–32; an exhibitor of show harness ponies; accepted commission in ASC, 1915; served France, 1916–18. *Publications:* L of C (Lines of Communication), 1917; Buzz, Buzz! (Essays of the Theatre), 1918; Alarums and Excursions (Essays), 1919; Responsibility, a novel, 1919; At Half-past Eight (Essays of the Theatre), 1921–1922; The Contemporary Theatre for 1923, 1924, 1925, and 1926; Fantasies and Impromptus, 1922; Blessed are the Rich, 1924; White Horse and Red Lion, 1924; On an English Screen, 1925; The Common Touch, 1926; Agate's Folly, 1927; Rachel: a Biography, 1928; Gemel in London, 1928: Their Hour upon the Stage, 1930; The English Dramatic Critics: an Anthology, 1932; My Theatre Talks, 1932; First Nights, 1934; Ego: An Autobiography, 1935; Ego 2, 1936; More First Nights, 1937; Kingdoms for Horses, 1937; Ego 3, 1938; Bad Manners, 1938; The Amazing Theatre, 1939; Speak for England: an Anthology for the Forces, 1940; Ego 4, 1940; Express and Admirable, 1941; Thursdays and Fridays, 1942; Here's Richness: an Anthology of and by James Agate, 1942; Ego 5, 1942; Brief Chronicles, 1943; These were Actors, 1944; Ego 6, 1944; Red Letter Nights, 1944; Noblesse Oblige, 1945; Immoment Toys, 1945; Ego 7, 1945; Ego 8, 1947; Ego 9, 1948 (posthumous). *Address:* Queen Alexandra Mansions, WC2. *T:* Temple Bar 8965.

Died 6 June 1947.

AGNEW, Sir George (William), 2nd Bt *cr* 1895; JP cos. Lancaster and Suffolk; *b* 19 Jan. 1852; *e s* of 1st Bt and Mary, *d* of G. P. Kenworthy, Peel Hall, Astley; *S* father, 1910; *m* 1878, Fanny (*d* 1937), *y d* of late John Stuart Bolton of Oulton Hall, Aylsham, Norfolk; two *s* four *d*. *Educ:* Rugby; St John's College, Cambridge. BA 1874; MA 1878. Was partner in firm of Thomas Agnew & Sons, art publishers' of London, Manchester, and Liverpool; formerly President of Printsellers' Association; member of Court of Governors of Victoria University, Manchester; Pres. of Manchester Children's Hospital; MP (L) West Salford, 1906–18; High Sheriff of Suffolk, 1922. *Heir: s* John Stuart [*b* 16 Sept. 1879; *m* 1910, Kathleen, 3rd *d* of late T. W. White of Meanwood, Leeds; three *s*]. *Address:* Rougham Hall, Bury St Edmunds. *Club:* Reform.

Died 19 Dec. 1941.

AHERNE, Rev. David, CSSR, DSO 1917; CF; Redemptorist Missioner; *b* 1871; *s* of Daniel Aherne, Ballyhooly, Co. Cork. *Educ:* Paris and Rome. Ordained a priest of the Catholic Church, 1895; became a member of the Missionary Order in that Church, called Redemptorists, 1900; served as CF in France, 1914–19 (despatches twice). *Address:* St Mary's, Kinnoull, Perth.

Died 9 Nov. 1941.

AHLEFELDT-LAURVIG, Count Preben Ferdinand, GCVO; SKD; *b* 27 Oct. 1872; *s* of Count C. Ahlefeldt-Laurvig and Johanne, Baroness Wedell-Wedellsborg, Mistress of the Robes to late Queen Louise of Denmark; *m* 1899, Baroness Marie (Mary) Emilie de Gohr; one *s* one *d*. Entered Foreign Office service in 1901; held various consular posts in Hull, New York and London; Secretary of Legation in Peking, 1908; Envoy Extraordinary and Minister Plenipotentiary to Peking and Tokio in 1912, Warsaw, 1920; London, 1921–37. *Recreations:* tennis, swimming and mountaineering. *Address:* Quinta Achada, Funchal, Madeira; Brolykke, Nordenbro, Langeland, Denmark. *Clubs:* Beefsteak, Travellers, Naval and Military.

Died 22 May 1946.

AHMAD, Sir Zia-Uddin, Kt 1938; CIE 1915; DSc; PhD; Vice-Chancellor Aligarh Muslim University; *b* 1879. *Educ:* Mahomedan Anglo-Oriental College, Aligarh; Trinity College, Cambridge (BA, 1903, MA, 1908); Göttingen University (PhD 1905). *Address:* Aligarh, United Provinces, India.

Died 23 Nov. 1947.

AHMED, Kabeerud-Din, MLA; Bar-at-Law and Senior Advocate, Calcutta High Court and Delhi Federal Court; Member High Court Bar, Calcutta; *b* 1888; *s* of late Muhammad Sabkat-Ullah, landholder; unmarried. *Educ:* Malda Government High English School; Magdalene College, Cambridge. Called to Bar, 1910; Member of Bengal Legislative Council, 1919–20; Member Indian Legislative Assembly, 1921–23, 1924–26, 1927–30, 1931–34, and since 1936 a sitting member; Member Democratic Party in the Indian Legislature, 1921–24; Founder of the Parliamentary Muslim-party in the Indian Legislative Assembly and its

Chief Whip, 1924–26; Member Royal Commission on Labour, 1929–31; Member Central National Mahomedan Association, Calcutta; Member University Court, Dacca; Founder of the Bengal Joatdars and Raiyat's Association; takes great interest in Agriculture and was President, Bengal Agricultural Conference, 1917; Organiser, Founder and President, Indian Seamen's Union, Calcutta, 1921–27. *Publication:* Handbook of Equity, Roman Law, etc. *Recreations:* tennis, riding, etc. *Address:* Biswanathpur, Kansat PO Malda, Bengal. *Clubs:* India, Calcutta; Chelmsford, Simla.

Died 9 March 1939.

AIKMAN, Col Thomas S. G. H. Robertson-, of Ross and Broomhilton, Lanarkshire, and of Grandborough, Warwickshire; CB 1923; JP, DL Co. Lanark; late commanding 4th Highland Light Infantry (Special Reserve); *b* 25 Feb. 1860; *e s* of late Hugh Henry Robertson-Aikman of Ross and Broomhilton and Mary Joyce Stokes of New Parks, Leicestershire; *m* 1899, Constance Henrietta (*d* 1932), *o d* of late Capt. J. A. Middleton, late Royal Dragoons; two *s* one *d*. *Educ:* Eton; BNC Oxford. Joined 1st Royal Lanark Militia, 1880; commanded (4th HLI), 1900–12; commanded Royal Defence Corps No. 1 District, 1915–16; Hon. Lieut-Colonel in the Army since 1900; Master of the Lanarkshire and Renfrewshire foxhounds, 1896–1901; Master of his own barriers 1888–1901 in Lanarkshire, 1901–10 in Derbyshire, 1910–12 in Staffordshire; other favourite pursuits: coaching, cricket, curling, etc.; Captain of the Scottish Curling Teams that visited Canada and the United States 1912 and 1923, and of the winning British team Olympic Games at Chamonix, 1924. *Address:* The Ross, Hamilton. *T:* Hamilton 55. *Clubs:* New, Edinburgh.

Died 18 April 1948.

AILSA, 4th Marquess of, *cr* 1831; **Archibald Kennedy;** Baron Kennedy, 1452; Earl of Casillis, 1509; Baron Ailsa (UK), 1806; JP, DL Ayrshire; Advocate, Edinburgh; Fellow of the Royal Scottish Geographical Society; *b* 22 May 1872; *e s* of 3rd Marquess and Evelyn Stuart (*d* 1888), *d* of 12th Lord Blantyre; *S* father, 1938; *m* 1903, Frances (Lady of Justice, Order of St John of Jerusalem; Order of Mercy), 3rd *d* of Sir Mark MacTaggart Stewart, 1st Bart. *Educ:* Eton; Trinity College, Cambridge; Edinburgh University. Late Major 3rd Batt. Royal Scots Fusiliers; Hon. Col 4/5th Batt. RS Fusiliers (T); served South African War, 1900–02 (2 medals 5 clasps); with British Expeditionary Force, Dec. 1914–May 1919 (despatches); member of Royal Company of Archers, HM Bodyguard for Scotland. *Heir: b* Lord Charles Kennedy. *Address:* Culzean Castle, Maybole, Ayrshire. *T:* Maybole 2102; 6 Carlton Terrace, Edinburgh, 7. *Clubs:* Caledonian; New, Edinburgh.

Died 27 Feb. 1943.

AINLEY, Henry Hinchliffe; actor-manager; *b* Leeds, 21 Aug. 1879; *s* of Richard Ainley; *m* 1st, 1903, Suzanne (*d* 1924), *d* of late Charles H. Sheldon, New York; 2nd, Elaine Fearon; one *s* one *d*. First appeared in London at Lyceum, 1900; Lt RGA 1916–19.

Died 31 Oct. 1945.

AINSLIE, Grant Duff Douglas, MA Oxon; *b* British Embassy, Paris, 1865; family name originally Grant Duff, changed by father. *Educ:* Eton; Balliol and Exeter Colleges, Oxford. BA 1887. Attaché to HM Legation at Athens, 1891; transferred to the Hague, 1892; to Paris, 1893. *Publications:* Escarlamonde and other Poems, 1893; John of Damascus, an Epic of the Meeting of the Creeds, 1901; Moments, lyrical poems, 1905; the Song of the Stewarts, Prelude, 1909; Mirage, Poems, 1911; Adventures Social and Literary, 1922; Chosen Poems, 1928; The Conquest of Pleasure (poems), 1942 (Amer. ed., 1943); translation of Philosophy of the Spirit (four vols) and other translations from the Italian of Benedetto

Croce. *Recreation:* conversation. *Address:* c/o Security Bank, Cahuenga Boulevard, Hollywood (28), California, USA. *Club:* Athenæum.

Died 27 March 1948.

AINSLIE, Lt-Col Henry Sandys, CMG 1915; late Northumberland Fusiliers; *b* 1 Aug. 1869; *m* 1899, Lilian Elizabeth, *d* of late James Lyall; no *c*. Entered army, 1890; Captain, 1896; Major, 1903; Lt-Col 1912; ADC to Governor Straits Settlements, 1897–98; employed with Malay States Guides, 1898–1902; served European War, 1914–15 (CMG, despatches, temp. Brig.-Gen. May–Nov. 1915); retired pay, 1919. *Address:* 28 Clifton Road, Brighton.

Died 19 April 1948.

AINSWORTH, John, CMG 1900; CBE 1919; DSO 1918; FRGS; *b* Manchester, 16 June 1864; *m* 1897, Ina Cameron, MBE, *d* of late John Scott, Brooklyn, USA. *Educ:* privately. Employed on West Coast, Africa, 1884–89; in Imperial Brit. East Africa Company's service, 1889–95; organised Company's transport to Uganda, etc., 1890–91; HM's Sub-Commissioner in charge Ukamba Province, East Africa Protectorate, under Sir Arthur Hardinge, 1895; Vice-Consul, BEA, 1896–1907; Acting Deputy-Commissioner, East Africa Protectorate, 1904–05; Member of Executive and Legislative Councils, East Africa Protectorate; Provincial Commissioner; Local Colonel, 1917 (DSO); seconded as Military Commissioner for Labour East Africa Expeditionary Force, March 1917–June 1918, with local rank of Colonel (despatches); Chief Native Commissioner, EAP, 1918; retired, 1921; during 1924 on special service in Mandated Territory of New Guinea on behalf of the Government of the Commonwealth of Australia; Mayor of Somerset West, 1928–30. *Address:* Nyanza, Lourensford Road, Somerset, West, CP, South Africa.

Died 31 March 1946.

AINSWORTH, Lt-Col William John, CBE 1919; DSO 1900; late Durham Light Infantry; Secretary, Jockey Club of Egypt since 1923; *b* Jhansi, India, 11 Aug. 1873; *e s* of late Captain Ainsworth, late 106th Light Infantry, of Spotland, Rochdale, Lancashire, and Trentham House, Twickenham Park, SW. *Educ:* St Paul's School. Entered RMC, Sandhurst, 1892; 2nd Lieut Durham Light Infantry, 1893; Lieut 1896; Adjutant, 2nd Batt., 1901; Staff-Captain No. 5 District 1911; served S African War, 1899–1900 (DSO medal with four clasps); DAAG, 1914–15; AAG 1915. Decorated for conspicuous gallantry in the affair at Sanna's Post, 31 March 1901; European War, 1914–17 (Bt Lt-Col, CBE, despatches); retired pay, 1923. *Address:* 78 Buckingham Gate, SW. *Clubs:* Army and Navy, Junior United Service.

Died 28 March 1945.

AIREDALE, 2nd Baron *cr* 1907, of Gledhow; **Albert Ernest Kitson;** Bt *cr* 1886; Iron and Steel Manufacturer; Director Midland Bank; *b* 7 Oct. 1863; *e s* of 1st Baron and Emily, *d* of Joseph Cliff, Wortley, Leeds; *S* father 1911; *m* 1890, Florence (*d* 1942), *e d* of late Edward Schunck of Gledhow Wood, Leeds; seven *d*. *Educ:* Trinity College, Cambridge (BA). *Recreations:* shooting, golf, gardening. *Heir: half-brother* Capt. Hon. Roland Dudley Kitson, DSO. *Clubs:* Reform, Bath, Garrick.

Died 11 March 1944.

AITCHISON, Rt Hon. Lord; Craigie Mason Aitchison, PC 1929; KC 1923; MA, LLB; Lord Justice Clerk since 1933; *b* 26 Jan. 1882; *s* of Rev. James Aitchison, Falkirk, and Elizabeth Craigie; *m* 1919, Charlotte, *d* of James Jones of Torwoodhall, Larbert, Stirlingshire; two *s*. *Educ:* Falkirk High School; University of Edinburgh. Van Dunlop Scholar, Mental Philosophy; Muirhead Prizeman, Civil Law. Called to Scottish Bar, 1907; Commissioner of Northern Lights; one of the Lords of the Committee of Privy Council on

Scottish Education; Lord Advocate for Scotland, 1929–33; MP (Lab) Kilmarnock bye-election, 1929–31 (Nat. Lab) 1931–33; contested (Lab) Central Glasgow, 1929. *Address:* 12 India Street, Edinburgh. *T:* 22978.

Died 2 May 1941.

AITCHISON, Patrick Edward, CIE 1934; *b* 17 March 1881; *m* 1908, Margaret Duncan Blair, *d* of late Major John Lyons. *Educ:* Malvern; Cooper's Hill. Joined Indian Forest Service, 1903; Chief Conservator of Forests, Bombay, 1933–35; Retired, 1935. *Address:* Brieryhill, Hawick, Roxburghshire. *T:* Hawick 286.

Died 5 Aug. 1945.

AITCHISON, Sir Stephen, 1st Bt *cr* 1938; Kt 1928; landowner in Northumberland; Joint Governing Director of Walter Willson, Ltd; JP City and Co. of Newcastle-upon-Tyne; JP Co. Northumberland; *b* Devizes, 1863; *m* Alice Mary (*d* 1932), *d* of Walter de Lancey Willson, JP, of Gateshead and Kirklinton Park, Cumberland; four *s* one *d*. *Educ:* privately. *Recreations:* gardening, arboriculture, public work (hospitals and philanthropic), collecting Chinese art, foreign travel, motoring. *Heir:* *s* W. de Lancey Aitchison, *b* 1892. *Address:* Lemmington Hall, Alnwick, Northumberland. *TA:* Aitchison, Lemmington, Alnwick. *Clubs:* Union, Conservative, Newcastle-upon-Tyne.

Died 26 Aug. 1942.

AITKEN, George (Benjamin Johnston), DMus, Cantuar, 1931; ARAM; ARCO; Member, Royal Society of Teachers; Fellow, Professor of pianoforte, and Lecturer, Guildhall School of Music; pianist, organist, composer, and critic; *b* London; *e s* of George Aitken and Cecilia Jane Drinkwater. *Educ:* Choir School, St Andrew's, Wells Street, W; Royal Academy of Music. Organist and Choirmaster Hampstead Parish Church since 1895; has appeared as pianist and composer at principal concert halls in London and the provinces. *Publications:* Church services, Communion service, and anthems; violin and organ music; numerous pianoforte pieces, solo and duet; and many songs; author of Tobias Matthay and his Teachings. *Address:* c/o Barclay's Bank, 28 Hampstead High Street, NW3.

Died 11 May 1942.

AITKEN, Sir James, Kt 1941; District Registrar of the High Court and Group Registrar of County Courts; *b* 1880; *m* Lucy Berry; one *s* two *d*. *Educ:* Rydal School, Colwyn Bay. Member of Nelson Town Council, 1931–32; Mayor of Nelson, 1925–27; Member of Lancashire County Council since 1921, Chairman of the Council; Chairman Lancashire Education Committee; JP Lancs. *Address:* Parrock House, Barrowford, Nelson, Lancashire. *T:* Nelson 623.

Died 5 March 1948.

AITKEN, Col John James, CMG 1919; DSO 1916; OBE 1924; late RAVC; *b* 7 July 1878; *m* 1927, Constance Marion, *d* of Brig.-Gen. B. F. Drake, CB; one *d*. Served S African War, 1900–02 (Queen's medal three clasps, King's medal two clasps); Sikkim and Tibet Mission Force, 1903–04 (medal and clasp); European War, 1914–18 (DSO, CMG, despatches); Waziristan, 1922–23 (OBE); Commandant Royal Army Veterinary School, 1925–28; ADVS Southern Command, 1928; retired pay, 1933.

Died 15 April 1946.

AITKEN, Rev. Canon Robert Aubrey; Vicar of Great Yarmouth since 1920; Rural Dean of Flegg since 1921; Hon. Canon of Norwich Cathedral; Proctor in Convocation for Norwich Diocese since 1931; *b* 15 Aug. 1870; *s* of Canon W. Hay M. H. Aitken, and *g s* of Rev. Robert Aitken of Pendeen; *m* Evelyn Reine, 4th *d* of late Reuben T. Preston of Hayes Court, Kent; three *s* one *d*. *Educ:* Bedford School; Merton College, Oxford. Hons in Mod. Hist. 1893; BA 1893; MA 1896. Ordained, 1894; Curate of the Parish Church, Gateshead, 1894–98; Diocesan Missioner, Hereford, 1898–1903; Vicar of

Holy Trinity, Hereford, 1903–09; North Walsham, 1909–20; Rural Dean of Tunstead, 1911–20. *Recreations:* fishing, motoring, travelling. *Address:* The Vicarage, Great Yarmouth. *T:* Great Yarmouth 2334. *Clubs:* Leander, Overseas League.

Died 14 Dec. 1941.

AITKEN, Stephen Rowan, BA; Barrister-at-law; President Civil Courts in Iraq, 1936–42; *b* 18 Feb. 1883; *o s* of Stephen Rowan Aitken, Camnethan, Ceylon, and of Janet Georgina Robertson (who *m* 2nd, Surg.-Gen. Wm Maxwell Craig, CB, RN); *m* 1918, Ethel Augusta, *d* of John Henrik Reuterdahl, Stockholm; one *s*. *Educ:* privately; Balliol College, Oxford. Law and Mod. History—Honours 1906. Called to Bar (Inner Temple) 1912; Chancery Division, 1912–15; Secretary Anglo-American Unit, British Red Cross, 1915; Secretary to HM Minister in Sweden, 1916–18; Foreign Office, London, 1918–20, Ministry of Blockade and Allied Blockade Committee, Dept of Overseas Trade (Russian and Scandinavian Section); in Macedonia, 1925–28, as President of Sub-Commission of Greco-Bulgar Mixed Commission (Exchange of Populations); in Baroda State, India, 1928–31; Judge in Courts of First Instance and Appeal; Secretary to HH the Maharaja Gaekwar (London Round Table Conference, 1930). *Publications:* Notes on Constitutional Law, 1930; Modern Democracy and Federalism, 1931 (for private circulation in Baroda State). *Recreations:* lawn tennis, golf, music. *Address:* Ministry of Justice, Baghdad.

Died 20 April 1943.

AITON, Sir (John) Arthur, Kt 1937; CBE 1918; JP Derbyshire; Governing Director of Aiton & Co., Ltd, Derby, and of other companies; *b* India, 1864; *s* of John Aiton, Civil Engineer; *m* 1895, Mina, *d* of A. Stoop, Dordrecht, Holland; one *s* two *d*. *Address:* Duffield Park, Derbyshire. *T:* Duffield, Derby, 2393. *Clubs:* Derbyshire, County (Derby).

Died 24 Jan. 1950.

AIYER, Sir Pazhamarneri Sundaram Sivaswamy, KCSI 1915; CSI 1912; CIE 1908; BA, BL; *b* 7 Feb. 1864; *s* of P. Sundaram Aiyer, a pleader of the District Court of Tanjore; *m* Kalyani Ammal (*d* 1939); no *c*. *Educ:* SPG Coll., Tanjore; Government Coll., Kumbhakonam; Presidency Coll., Madras. Enrolled as a Vakil of the High Court, 1885; Assist Prof. of Law, Madras Law College, 1893–99; Examiner in Sanskrit and Law to the University of Madras; a Joint-Editor of the Madras Law Journal, 1893–1907; Fellow of the University of Madras, 1898; represented the University in the Madras Legislative Council, 1904–07; served on the Syndicate of the University for several years; Acting Advocate-General, 1907; Advocate-General, 1908–12; Member of the Executive Council, Madras, 1912–17; Vice-Chancellor of the University of Madras, 1916–18; organised the Indian Defence Force in the Madras Presidency as President of the Recruitment Committee in 1917; Vice-Chancellor of the Hindu University, Benares, 1918–19; President 2nd session of Indian National Liberal Federation at Calcutta in Dec. 1919; President 9th session of INL Federation at Akola, Dec. 1926; Member of the Indian Legislative Assembly for Districts of Tanjore and Trichinopoly, 1920–23; Member of the Indian Military Requirements Committee, 1921; Indian delegate in the third session of the Assembly of the League of Nations at Geneva, 1922; nominated nonofficial Member of the Indian Legislative Assembly, 1924–26; Member of the Indian Territorial and Auxiliary Forces Committee, 1924, and of the Indian Constitutional Reforms Committee, 1924; Member of Indian Military College Committee, 1931; LLD (Hon.) Madras University, 1932, and Benares Hindu University, 1933. *Publications:* Indian Constitutional Problems, 1928; Evolution of Hindu Moral Ideals (Kamala Lectures). *Recreations:* tennis and golf. *Address:* Mylapore, Madras.

Died 5 Nov. 1946.

AKED, Charles Frederic, DD, LLD; DLit; preacher; author; lecturer; Minister of All Souls' Church; *b* Nottingham, 27 Aug. 1864; *s* of Charles Aked, Nottingham; *m* 1886, Anne (*d* 1934), *d* of James Hithersay, Ilkeston, Derbyshire. *Educ:* Mr J. Lee's Commercial School, Midland Baptist Coll., and University Coll., Nottingham. Articled to firm of auctioneers in Nottingham; afterward auctioneer to the Sheriff of Derbyshire; then to Midland College as above; first pastorate, Syston, Leicestershire, 1886; St Helens and Earlestown, 1888; made annual trips preaching and lecturing in the United States since 1893; Vice-President of United Kingdom Alliance; one of the founders of the Passive Resistance League; Warden-Elect of Midland Baptist College; Minister of Pembroke Chapel, Liverpool, 1890–1907; Minister of Fifth Avenue Baptist Church, New York, 1907–11; DD, Temple University, USA, 1901; Minister of First Congregational Church, San Francisco, 1911–15; Minister of First Congregational Church, Kansas City, Missouri, 1919–24; visited Norway, Sweden, Denmark, Holland, and Germany, on Peace Mission, 1915 and 1916; DD Brown University, USA, 1907; LLD, Nevada, 1914; Hon. Member Students' Association of Norway, 1915; LLD Drury College, 1923; DLit, University of Southern California, 1929. *Publications:* The Lord's Prayer: Its Meaning and Message for To-day; Changing Creeds and Social Struggles; The Courage of the Coward; Wells and Palm-trees; Old Events and Modern Meanings; A Ministry of Reconciliation; Mercies New Every Morning; The Divine Drama of Job; numerous pamphlets. *Recreations:* fishing (gold medallist of the Tuna Club, for Yellowtail, 1914); cycling; made many tours on the wheel, France, Germany, Italy, Austria, etc.; horse-riding. *Address:* 3355 Wilshire Boulevard, Los Angeles, California, USA.

Died Aug. 1941.

AKERMAN, John Camille; Director United Newspapers Ltd, and Provincial Newspapers Ltd; Vice-Chairman Illustrated Newspapers Ltd and Deputy Chairman Argus Press Ltd. *Educ:* privately. *Address:* Througham Place, Beaulieu, Hants. *T:* Eastend 239. *Club:* Reform.

Died 30 Oct. 1950.

AKRILL-JONES, Rev. Canon David; Treasurer of Llandaff Cathedral; Canon of Llandaff and late Chief Diocesan Missioner; *b* 1868; *s* of Rector of Glyntaff, Glam; *m* Ellen May, *d* of R. W. Tolfree; (two *s* fell in War, 1914–18) one *d. Educ:* Christ College, Brecon; Merton College, Oxford. Curate of St John's Cardiff; Senior Curate of St Mark's, Newport, and St Philip's, Kensington; Rector of Prendergast, Pemb.; Vicar of Sketty, Glam.; Vicar of Bolsover, Chesterfield; Rural Dean of Bolsover; Vicar of Llandaff, 1925–41. *Publications:* articles on Church and Labour. *Address:* Brookend, Burnham-on-Sea, Somerset.

Died 22 Feb. 1945.

ALBEMARLE, 8th Earl of, *cr* 1696; **Arnold Allan Cecil Keppel,** GCVO 1931; KCVO 1909; CB 1900; MVO 1901; TD; Baron Ashford, 1696; Viscount Bury, 1696; a Lord-in-Waiting to the King, 1922–24. Served with CIV South Africa, as Lieut-Colonel in command of Infantry Battalion, 1900 (despatches, medal and 4 clasps); was Col-Com. 5th Batt KR Rifles (Civil Service); is Hon. Lt-Col in the army; was Hon. Col 4th Batt. Norfolk Regt (Mil.) and of 2nd Vol. Batt. Norfolk Regt; Hon. Col 5th Battalion Norfolk Regiment; was Brig.-Gen. commanding Norfolk Vol. Brigade; *b* London, 1 June 1858; *e s* of 7th Earl and Sophia Mary, 2nd *d* of Hon. Sir Alan Napier M'Nab, 1st and last Bt, Premier of Upper Canada; *S* father 1894; *m* 1881, Lady Gertrude Lucia Egerton, *o c* of 1st Earl Egerton of Tatton; three *s* one *d. Educ:* Eton. Conservative and Churchman; late Dorset Militia; late Scots Guards; MP Birkenhead, 1892–94; has the Grand Cross of the White Lion of Czechoslovakia; Grand Cross of Orange-Nassau.

Recreations: yachting, painting, shooting. *Heir: s* Viscount Bury. *Address:* 7 Cadogan Square, SW1. *T:* Sloane 5674; Quidenham, Norfolk; Eccles Hall, Norfolk. *Clubs:* Brooks', Carlton, Turf; Royal Yacht Squadron, Cowes.

Died 12 April 1942.

ALBERTINI, Luigi; Italian Senator since 1914; Managing Director of the Corriere della Sera, 1900–25; *b* Ancona, 19 Oct. 1871. *Educ:* LLD, Turin, 1893; studied Economical and Political Sciences in London. Joined the Corriere della Sera, 1896; made it the most important Italian paper; was one of the chief promoters of Italy's intervention in the great war; neutralist senators fiercely contested his nomination, but their opposition was defeated; was also one of the chief promoters of the Congress held in Rome of the nationalities oppressed by the Hapsburg Monarchy, and after the victory, of a compromise between the Italian and the Yougoslavs' aspirations on the Adriatic; was one of the Italian Delegates at Washington Conference; was a strenuous defender of law, order and property when Communists seized the factories, 1920; was opposed from the beginning to excesses and abuses of Fascist rulers and followers, and is considered one of the leaders of the movement for the restoring of normal conditions of government, of full political freedom, and the empire of common law in Italy; on account of his opposition to Fascism was obliged to leave Corriere della Sera in 1925. *Address:* via xxiv Maggio 14, Rome 3.

Died 29 Dec. 1941.

ALBERTS, Col Johannes Joachim, CMG 1918; DTD; farmer; *b* 8 June 1872; *m* C. S. G. Wessels; one *s* two *d. Educ:* Standerton. Commandant, Standerton Command, Anglo-Boer War; Delegate at Vereniging when peace was declared; member of first Union Parliament for Standerton; served European War, 1914–18; OC Standerton, Bethal, and Heidelberg Commandos during 1914 rebellion; OC of the 2nd Mounted Brigade with the German West Campaigns; thereafter Inspector of Remounts and Transport for the Union; Senior Sheep Inspector for Eastern Transvaal until 1924. *Address:* Uooitgedacht, PO Davel, District Ermelo, SA.

Died 23 April 1947.

ALBRIGHT, George Stacey, CBE, MA, JP; *b* 15 June 1855; *m* Isabella Margaret (*d* 1927), *d* of Smith Harrison of South Woodford, Essex. *Educ:* Tottenham; Trinity College, Cambridge. *Address:* Bromsberrow Place, Ledbury. *Club:* United University.

Died 28 Dec. 1945.

ALCHIN, His Honour Judge Gordon; Judge of County Courts on Circuit No. 40 (Bow) since 1945; No. 38 (Edmonton, etc.), 1940–45; Hon. Treasurer, Kinsmen Trust; *s* of Alfred Head Alchin, MINA, Rust Hall-Kent; *m* 1924, Sylvia (*d* 1939), *y d* of late T. H. Wrensted; one *s* one *d. Educ:* Tonbridge School; Brasenose College, Oxford. Junior Hulme Scholar, BNC 1913; 2nd Lt RFA, Aug. 1914; RFA Flanders, 1914–15; RFC Flanders, 1915–17 (AFC); demobilised 1919 and returned to Oxford; Senior Hulme Scholar, 1920, BCL, MA, Eldon Scholar. Called to bar, Middle Temple, 1922; practised at Common Law and Commercial Bar till 1940; rejoined RAF (VR, 1940). *Publications:* Verse and short stories; Legal manuals. *Recreations:* walking, yachting, painting and modelling. *Address:* Duffields, Medmenham, Bucks. *Clubs:* RAF; Bar Yacht.

Died 14 May 1947.

ALCOCK, Henry, MA; McCaughey Professor of History and Economics, University of Queensland, Brisbane, since 1922; *b* 14 Oct. 1886; *o s* of late Henry Alcock, of Tunstall, Staffs, and Lucilla, *y d* of James Davis, late of Bitton, Gloucestershire; *m* 1918, Olga Marie Thérèse, *y d* of mile de Tuetey, late of Farnham; three *d. Educ:* King Edward VI School, Bath; Magdalen College, Oxford. Secondary School teaching in England,

1910–13; Lecturer in charge of Dept of History and Social Science, Univ. of Queensland, 1914–22; Chm., Joint Bd of Commercial Studies, 1921–22; Dean of the Faculty of Arts, 1922–28; Dean of the Faculty of Commerce, 1923–32 and since 1939; Member Senate, Univ. of Queensland, 1929–44; President Professional Board, 1932–38; Fellow A & NZAAS; Member, Federal Talks Advisory Committee of the Australian Broadcasting Commission since 1932; Chairman Queensland Council for Social Education, 1938–45, and of Queensland Council of Social Agencies, 1946–; President, Historical Soc. of Queensland, 1945–. *Publications:* various pamphlets, articles, etc. *Recreations:* motoring, photography. *Address:* Kincraig, Sefton Road, Clayfield, N2, Brisbane, Queensland. *T:* M 1541.

Died 26 April 1948.

ALCOCK, Reginald, CBE 1919; FRCSE, JP; Honorary Surgeon to the North Staffordshire Infirmary, Stoke-on-Trent; *b* 1868; *s* of John Alcock, JP, of Portland House, Burslem; *m* 1916, Elizabeth Colebrooke, *d* of Rev. James Cowan, Crawfordjohn; one *s* one *d*. *Educ:* Victoria University, Manchester. Late Surgeon to the Stoke-on-Trent War Hospital. *Recreation:* golf. *Address:* Crawford, Oulton Cross, Stone, Staffs. *T:* 283.

Died 1 Feb. 1944.

ALCOCK, Sir Walter Galpin, Kt 1933; MVO; Mus. Doc., Dunelm; FRCM, FRCO; *b* 29 Dec. 1861; *s* of W. W. Alcock; *m* 1893, Naomi Blanche, *d* of late Rev. Charles Halford Lucas, Rector of Edith Western, Stamford; one *s* five *d*. *Educ:* privately. Society of Arts Scholar at late National Training School for Music, 1876–81. Organist, Parish Church, Twickenham, 1881–87; Quebec Chapel, 1887–95; Holy Trinity, Sloane Street, 1895–1902; Organist and Composer to HM's Chapels Royal, 1902–16; Assistant Organist of Westminster Abbey, 1896–1916; Organist of Salisbury Cathedral, 1916–47; Professor of Organ RCM since 1893; Examiner to the Associated Board Royal Schools of Music, to the RC Orgn and RCM; Examiner in Music, Durham University, 1914, 1915, 1916, 1930, and 1931; Organist at the Coronation of King Edward and Queen Alexandra, and that of King George and Queen Mary; also assisted at Coronation of King George VI and Queen Elizabeth; composed the music to the 'Sanctus' at the Coronation service of 1911; President Royal College of Organists, 1925–26; Member of Livery Company of Musicians, 1919; Chairman of Council of Royal School of Church Music, 1937–47; a Governor of the Foundling Hospital. *Publications:* Treatise on Organ Playing, 1936; Articles in Musical Times, Lectures, Church and Organ Music, etc. *Recreations:* engineering, motoring, astronomy, photography. *Address:* The Close, Salisbury. *T:* 3474. *Club:* Athenæum.

Died 11 Sept. 1947.

ALDEN, Sir Percy, Kt 1933; MA; Bursar of the Sir Richard Stapley Educational Trust; Chairman of Sir Halley Stewart Trust; Hon. Treasurer and Hon. Secretary of Sulgrave Manor Board; *b* Oxford, 6 June 1865; *m* 1899, Dr Margaret Pearse; four *d*. *Educ:* Balliol College, Oxford. Councillor of Borough of West Ham, 1892–1901; Deputy–Mayor, 1898; co-opted Member of the London School Board, 1903. Warden of Mansfield House University Settlement, 1891–1901; Hon. Warden, 1901; Vice-President, 1902; Editor of the Echo, 1901–02; MP (R) Tottenham Division of Middlesex, 1906–18; (Lab) South Tottenham, 1923–24; was Commissioner to Board of Agriculture for Cultivation of Vacant Lands; lectured in the United States, New Zealand, and Australia on social and labour problems. *Publications:* The Unemployed—A National Question; The Unemployable; Housing; Democratic England; Hungary of To-Day; Aspects of a changing Social Structure (Halley Stewart Lectures), etc.

Recreations: yachting, golf. *Address:* Lane End, Sandy Lodge Road, Moor Park, Rickmansworth. *T:* Rickmansworth 2622. *Club:* Reform.

Died 30 June 1944.

ALDERSON, Vice-Adm. William John Standly, CB 1922. Served Egyptian War, 1882 (Egyptian medal, Khedive's Bronze Star); Dongola Expedition, 1896 (Khedive's medal); Flag Captain to Vice-Adm. commanding 4th Battle Squadron, 1914 (British War medal, Victory medal, 1914–15 Star); Commanded Pitot (Brig) at King Edward's Coronation Review (Coronation medal); commanded Isis at King George's Coronation Review (Coronation medal); Officier de la Légion d'honneur, 1918; commanded Reserve Fleet at Nore, 1921–22; retired list, 1923; Vice-Adm., 1925. *Address:* Ovingham House, Cardigan.

Died 30 May 1946.

ALDRED-BROWN, George Ronald Pym, MA, MD, BCh (Oxf.); physician; specialist in rheumatism and gout; Senior Physician to Royal National Hospital for Rheumatic Diseases, Bath; late Physician, Pathologist and Bacteriologist to the Dorset County Hospital; *b* 1896; *o s* of late Richard Aldred-Brown, Controller General of Education, Egyptian Civil Service; *m* 1925, Doreen Mary, *o d* of Col P. B. Crowe; one *d*. *Educ:* Harrow School; Oxford University; London Hospital. Fellow of the Royal Society of Medicine (Member of Council. Section of Physical Medicine); Member of the International Society of Hydrology (Treasurer for Great Britain) and of the Ligue contre le Rheumatisme; served European War in France, 1915–18, Capt. RFA. *Publications:* numerous contributions to various medical journals chiefly in connection with rheumatism and gout. *Recreations:* golf and tennis. *Address:* 24 The Circus, Bath. *T:* Bath 3565. *Clubs:* Bath and County, Bath.

Died 26 July 1946.

ALDRIDGE, Lt-Col Arthur Russell, CB 1918; CSI, 1911; CMG 1917; MB, CM Edin., DPH; *b* 3 Sept. 1864; *s* of late J. H. Aldridge, MD, JP of Southampton; unmarried. RAMC (retired 1914 and rejoined same year from reserve); served with Tibet Expedition, 1904 (despatches, medal); ADMS Gallipoli Force, 1915; Egypt and Salonika, 1916–17; Comdr Order of Redeemer, Greece; Médaille d'or des épidémies, France. *Address:* Penne, Tekel's Avenue, Camberley.

Died 1 June 1947.

ALEKHINE, (Aljechin) Alexander; Chess Champion of the world; writer, Doctor of Law of Paris University; *b* Moscow, 1 Nov. 1892; *s* of A. Alekhine, Marechal de Noblesse of Voronej's Government Nobility, and Member of the Douma, and A. Prokhoroff, *d* of the Moscow Industrial Magnate; *m* Grace Wishaar, *widow* of Captain Archibald Freeman. *Educ:* the Imperial High Law School for Noblemen, the Pravovedenie, Petrograd. After taking his law degree in 1914, entered the Foreign Office; his career was interrupted by the Revolution, when he emigrated to France; served voluntarily in the Great War as Red Cross representative at the front (Sign of the Red Cross, the Military Cross of St Stanislas, and the St George's Cross); as chess player he got the title of Master at the age of sixteen, 1909, and the title of Great Master in 1914; has to his credit more than twenty international Tournaments, and has established world's records for Blindfold Chess (New York 1924, Paris 1925, and Chicago 1933); won the world's Title from J. R. Capablanca in 1927; defended it successfully in 1928 and 1934; lost it against Dr Euwe in 1935 and regained it from him in 1937; produced a World's record score in San Remo Tournament, 1930; on visiting Iceland, made Knight of the Order of Falcon; on visiting French Africa was made Commandeur of the Nichum Iftikar and Knight of the Ouissan Alaouit. *Publications:* Chess in Soviet Russia, 1921; New York Tournament Book, 1924; Hastings Tournament Book, 1922; My Best Hundred Games, 1908–1923; NY Tournament Book,

1927; My Best Games of Chess, 1927; On the Way to the World Championship, 1932; London Tournament Book, 1932; Zürich Tournament Book, 1934; Nottingham Tournament Book, 1936; Deux Cents Parties d'Échecs, 1937; publications in French and foreign periodicals. *Recreations:* bridge, riding, canoeing, tennis, ping pong. *Address:* Le Château, St Aubin-le-Cauf, Seine Inférieure, France. *T:* 7.

Died 24 March 1946.

ALEXANDER, Rev. Archibald, DD (Edin.); Minister of St John's Wood Presbyterian Church, London, since 1921; *b* West Linton, Peeblesshire, 8 March 1874; *e s* of late Archibald Alexander, merchant, West Linton; unmarried. *Educ:* George Heriot's, Edinburgh; Edinburgh University. Ordained at Waterbeck, 1900; Minister of Ayr Trinity UF Church, 1907–21; served as Chaplain in France, 1915–17; Moderator of the General Assembly of Presbyterian Church of England, 1934. *Publications:* The Glory in the Grey; A Day at a Time; The Stuff of Life; By Sun and Candle-light; Turn But a Stone; Feathers on the Moor; Sparrows in the Organ. *Recreation:* golf. *Address:* 67 Apsley House, NW8. *T:* Primrose 3144.

Died 3 June 1942.

ALEXANDER, Brig.-Gen. Charles Henry, CBE 1919; RA retired; *b* 2 June 1856; *s* of John Alexander, Milford, Carlow; *m* 1891, Isabel Annie, *d* of late Sir Campbell Ross, KCB; one *s*. *Educ:* Uppingham, RM Academy, Woolwich. Served in Royal Artillery, 1876–1908; Colonel, 1908; rejoined from retired list in European War, 10 Oct. 1914; formed 19th Divisional Artillery, 1914; formed 21st Divisional Artillery and commanded it with rank of Brigadier-General until after the battle of Loos, 1915; subsequently commanded 69th Divisional Artillery, No. 6 Reserve Brigade, RFA (T.) and No. 5–C. Reserve Brigade, RFA; mentioned for valuable Services during the War; Brig.-General, 1918. *Address:* 54 Dorset Road, Bexhill. *T:* Bexhill 409.

Died 28 April 1946.

ALEXANDER, Sir Claud, 2nd Bt *cr* 1886; *b* 24 Feb. 1867; *s* of 1st Bart and Eliza, *d* of Alexander Speirs of Elderslie; *S* father 1899; *m* 1st, 1889, Lady Diana Montgomerie, *d* of 14th Earl of Eglinton and Winton; 2nd, 1896, Rachel (*d* 1944), *d* of late Rev. Henry Holden, DD; two *s*. one *d*. *Educ:* Eton; New Coll. Oxon. Late Lieut 3rd Batt Royal Scots Fusiliers. *Heir: g s* Claud, *b* 6 Jan. 1927. *Address:* Fay Gate Wood, Sussex.

Died 18 March 1945.

ALEXANDER, Cyril Wilson, CMG 1928; *b* 12 Oct. 1879; *s* of late William Alexander, formerly Local Director Barclays Bank, Limited, Ipswich; *m* 1946, Mrs Annita Mary Simpson. *Educ:* Shrewsbury School; Trinity College, Cambridge. Appointed to Colonial Service as Administrative Officer in Nigeria, 1906; Commissioner or Lands, 1908; Resident of Province, 1919; Lieutenant-Governor of Southern Provinces, 1929–30; Lieutenant-Governor of the Northern Provinces of Nigeria, 1930–32; retired, 1932. *Recreations:* lawn tennis, golf, and fishing. *Address:* The Chart House, East Dean, Sussex.

Died 26 May 1947.

ALEXANDER, David, CMG 1923; LRCS and LRCP Ed.; DPH; DTM and H; late Director of Medical and Sanitary Services, Nigeria; *m* 1913. *Educ:* Glasgow University; Anderson's College of Medicine, Glasgow. Joined West African Medical Staff, 1903. *Address:* 176 Southbrae Drive, Glasgow, W3.

Died 3 April 1944.

ALEXANDER, Sir Douglas, 1st Bt *cr* 1921; *b* Halifax, Yorks, 4 July 1864; *s* of Andrew Alexander, formerly of Errol, Perthshire, afterwards Hamilton, Ont, Canada; *m* 1892, Helen Hamilton (*d* 1923), *d* of George Hamilton Gillespie, Hamilton; two *s*. one *d*. *Educ:* Collegiate Institute, Hamilton; Law Society of Upper Canada. Went to Canada at an early age and settled in the City of

Hamilton, Ontario; called to the bar and admitted as a Solicitor, 1886; after a short practice entered the service of The Singer Manufacturing Co., became a Director in 1896, made Vice-President the same year; Pres. since 1905. Order of the Crown of Belgium; Légion d'Honneur, France; LLD MacMaster University, Canada. *Recreations:* riding, tennis, golf, photography, music. *Heir: s* Douglas Hamilton Alexander, BA, *b* 6 June 1900. *Address:* 1 W 72nd Street, New York; Edgehill, Stamford, Conn. *TA:* Azzecco, New York. *Clubs:* Woodway Country, Hubbard Heights Golf, Stamford; Mendelssohn Glee, New York.

Died 22 May 1949.

ALEXANDER, Ernest Edward; Member, Essex Territorial Army and Air Force Association; *b* 28 June 1872; *e s* of late Edward Reuben Alexander of Leytonstone; *m* 1896, Emmeline Marian, *y d* of late Joseph Conquest, of Bow; one *s*. two *d*. *Educ:* The Stationers' Company's Foundation School. Was an Alderman Essex County Council; Member Metropolitan Water Board, Lee Conservancy, Leyton Urban District Council and its Education Committee; contested East Leyton, 1918–23, and 1929; MP (U) East Leyton, 1922–23, and 1924–29; many years Chairman of the Conservative Party in East and West Leyton; was actively associated with his father in the furtherance of technical education for printers at the Polytechnic, Regent Street. *Address:* Anglefield, Little Clacton, Essex.

Died 29 Sept. 1946.

ALEXANDER, Harold Vincent, CBE 1943; Solicitor of Supreme Court of Jamaica, since 1911 (member firm Livingston Alexander & Levy); Notary Public for Jamaica; Privy Councillor; President, Jockey Club of Jamaica; President, Jamaica Lawn Tennis Association; *b* 19 Nov. 1886; *y s* of M. M. Alexander, JP, merchant; *m* 1912, Marjorie de Saumarez Bell; one *s*. one *d*. *Educ:* St Paul's Prep. School, London; secondary schools in Jamaica. Clerk, Legislative Council, Jamaica, 1925–37; acted Crown Solicitor for six months in 1927. *Recreations:* lawn tennis, golf, horse racing. *Address:* 20 Duke Street, Kingston, Jamaica. *Clubs:* Jamaica, Liguanea, St Andrew, Kingston Cricket, Kingston Polo, Jockey Club of Jamaica (Kingston); Manchester (Mandeville).

Died 11 Oct. 1950.

ALEXANDER, Lt-Col Heber Maitland, DSO 1915; OBE 1919; Indian Army retired; *b* 1 Feb. 1881; 2nd *s* of Major C. A. Alexander, The Spinney, Cooden Beach; *m* 1st, 1909, Mary Brenda (*d* 1914), *d* of late J. H. B. Walch of Hobart, Tasmania; no *c*; 2nd, 1920, Violet Lilian, *d* of late Lt-Col S. L. Aplin, CSI, and *widow* of Major H. M. Hogg, 32nd Lancers; one *d*. *Educ:* Clifton; Sandhurst. Joined Somerset Light Infantry, 1900; transferred to Indian Army, 1911; Lt-Col 1926; served European War in command of 9th Mule Corps, Indian Army, France, Sept. 1914–April 1915, with Lahore Division, and Gallipoli, April to Nov. 1915, with Australian and New Zealand Army Corps; present at first landing in Gallipoli and at battle of Suvla Bay (despatches twice, DSO, OBE); Army Headquarters India, 1917–18; Indian Munitions Board, 1918–20; Deputy Secretary, Government of India, 1921; Director of Purchases, Government of India, 1922–31; retired 1931. *Publication:* On Two Fronts, 1917. *Address:* Summerfield, Alverstoke, Hants.

Died 9 Dec. 1942.

ALEXANDER, Maj.-Gen. Henry Lethbridge, CB 1919; CMG 1919; DSO 1915; (retired pay); late Dorsetshire Regt; *b* 9 March 1878; *m* 1933, Lina, *d* of Hamon Le Strange, Hunstanton Hall, Norfolk, and *widow* of Major Charles Harcourt Wood, 15th Hussars. Entered army, 1897; Captain, 1904; Major, 1914; DA and QMG (temporary Maj.-Gen.), GHQ Italy, 1918; Director of Quartering War Office (tempy. Maj.-Gen.), 1919–20; Colonel on Staff in charge Administration,

Northern Command; Brigade Commander, 150th (York and Durham) Infantry Brigade, 1924–27; served South Africa, 1901–02 (Queen's medal 5 clasps); European War, 1914–18 (despatches, DSO, Bt Lt-Col and Col CB, CMG, Order of St Maurice and Lazarus, Italy, Croix de Guerre, France, Croce di Guerra, Italy); retired pay, 1927. *Address:* Lloyds Bank Ltd, Beaminster, Dorset. *Club:* United Service.

Died 20 June 1944.

ALEXANDER, Herbert, RWS; FRGS; *b* London, 8 Dec. 1874; 3rd *s* of late Lt-Col Boyd Francis Alexander; *m* 1911, Edith Julia, *d* of late Charles Eugene Gunther; one *d. Educ:* Cranbrook School. Painter; enlisted in the 5th Buffs, Aug. 1914; served in India and Mesopotamia; came home Feb. 1919. *Publications:* Boyd Alexander's Last Journey; and articles on painters. *Address:* Old Wilsley, Cranbrook. *T:* Cranbrook 2202. *Club:* Bath.

Died 7 Jan. 1946.

ALEXANDER, Hon. John, CMG 1927; Chevalier of the Legion of Honour; MLC, New Zealand, since 1934; Barrister and Solicitor of the Supreme Court of New Zealand, and Notary Public; senior partner in the firm of Alexander, Bennett, Warnock; *b* 19 April 1876; *s* of Robert Alexander, Belfast; *m* 1905, Amy Constance Evelyn, *d* of late John Watson Walker; one *s. Educ:* Methodist College, Belfast; Prince Albert College, Auckland. Admitted a Solicitor of the Supreme Court of New Zealand, 1899; Barrister of same Court, 1901; President, Auckland Law Society, 1923–24 and 1924–25; appointed Notary Public, 1921; has been Official Visitor to Mental Hospital, Auckland, since 1920; Member of New Zealand Prisons Board since 1926; Past President, and now a trustee, of the Auckland Club; Past President of the Auckland Branch of Navy League Past President Auckland Branch Overseas League; President of the Auckland Savings Bank, 1929–30 and 1930–31; Director at Auckland of the Insurance Office of Australia Ltd; a Member of Te Awamutu Masonic Lodge; Member of Auckland Automobile Association. *Recreations:* yachting for many years; football, cricket, now motoring and tennis. *Address:* 192 Remuera Road, Auckland, SE2, New Zealand. *TA:* Alebensu, Auckland. *Clubs:* Northern, Auckland, Auckland.

Died 15 July 1941.

ALEXANDER, Lt-Col Maurice, CMG 1917; KC 1922; BA, BCL; *b* 24 Dec. 1889; *s* of L. G. Alexander, JP. *Educ:* McGill University (Gold Medallist, Literary Society). Called to Quebec Bar, 1910; member of the firm of Davidson, Wainwright, Alexander & Elder, Barristers, Montreal; commission, Lieutenant, 1st Regiment Grenadier Guards, Canada, 1911; Capt. 1913; Major, 1914; Lt-Col 1916; served European War, 1914–17, with Expeditionary Force; Deputy-Judge Advocate-General, 1916; Judge Advocate-General, 1917 (despatches, CMG); entered the service of Overseas Department, Foreign Office, 1918; Secretary, British Embassy, Washington, 1919–20; called to English Bar, Middle Temple, 1920; appointed to N-E Circuit; MP (NL) Southwark South-East, 1922–23; Director, Elkington Co., Ltd, of Birmingham and London.

Died 16 July 1945.

ALEXANDER, Robert Edward, CMG 1934; *b* April 1874; *s* of Joseph Alexander and Frances Mary O'Donel Long; *m* 1906, Alice McCrea McKinley, Co. Donegal; two *s* two *d. Educ:* Royal Academical Institution, Belfast; Royal College of Science, Dublin. Farming 5 years; Agricultural Instructor, Co. Londonderry, 1903–05; Lecturer in Agriculture, Albert Agricultural College, Dublin, 1905–09; Professor of Agricultural NZ University, 1928–36; Director of Canterbury Agricultural College, Lincoln, New Zealand, 1909–36. *Address:* Holmbank, Macmillan Avenue, Cashmere Hills, Christchurch, S2, NZ.

Died 21 Nov. 1946.

ALEXANDER, Maj.-Gen. Ronald Okeden, CB 1944; DSO 1917; *b* Kandy, Ceylon, 7 Aug. 1888; *e s* of late J. A. Alexander, Ceylon Civil Service; *m* 1917, Gertrude, *y d* of Right Rev. Lennox Williams, DD; two *s* one *d. Educ:* Bedford. Entered Canadian Militia, 1908; the Royal Canadian Regt 1910; served European War, France and Belgium, 1915–18, as 24th Canadian Infantry Battalion and General Staff (DSO, despatches three times, Brevet Lieut-Col); psc 1919; War of 1939–45 (CB). *Clubs:* Union (Victoria, BC, Canada).

Died 28 July 1949.

ALEXANDER, Rev. Sidney Arthur, CMG 1934; CVO 1930; Hon. ARIBA; MA; Canon and Treasurer of St Paul's Cathedral since 1909; Chapter Treasurer, 1911–47; *b* 1866; *m* 1891, Lily (*d* 1937), *d* of late John Redfern. *Educ:* St Paul's School; Trinity Coll., Oxford (Scholar). 1st class in Classical Moderations, 1887; 1st class in Lit. Hum. 1889; Newdigate Prize for English Verse, 1887; Hall Houghton Septuagint Prizes (Junior) 1886, and (Senior) 1891; Hall Houghton Greek Testament Prizes (Junior) 1888, and (Senior) 1891; Denyer and Johnson University Scholarship for Theology, 1890. Curate of St Michael's, Oxford, 1889–92; Lecturer at Keble College, 1890–92; Tutor of Keble, 1892–93; Reader of the Temple, 1893–1902; Canon-Missioner of Gloucester, 1902–09; Select Preacher at Oxford, 1901–03; Select Preacher at Cambridge, 1904 and 1909; Examining Chaplain to Bishop of Hereford, 1895–1913; Member of the Central (Unemployed) Body for London, 1914; Member of the Mansion House War Relief Committee, 1914; President of St Paul's Lecture Society since 1930; completed in June 1930 the scheme for the preservation of St Paul's Cathedral which he started in 1913, and for which he raised in three public appeals a total sum of £400,000; from 1930 to 1935 engaged on his plan (which ultimately formed the basis of a Bill introduced into Parliament by the Corporation of London, and passed in June 1935) for protecting the Cathedral foundations by a sacred area drawn round the building. *Publications:* Buddha (Newdigate Poem), 1887; Christ and Scepticism, 1894; The Christianity of St Paul, 1899; The Mind of Christ, 1903; Progressive Revelation (Lectures to Clergy at St Asaph), 1910; The Saints' Appeal, 1912; The Safety of St Paul's, 1927, 2nd ed. 1930; The Cross and the Dome, 1930; A Cathedral Calendar, 1932; This England (a poem), 1939; Notes for Visitors to St Paul's, 1944; The Survival of St Paul's, 1945, 2nd ed. (making 25,000 copies), 1946. *Address:* 2 Amen Court, St Paul's, EC4. *T:* City 3747.

Died 4 Feb. 1948.

ALEXANDER, Thomas Hood Wilson, MB, ChB, FRCS; JP Morayshire; Senior Surgeon Grays Hospital, Elgin; Consulting Surgeon, Dufftown Hospital; Chairman, Caledonian Associated cinema companies; Director, Century Insurance, Ltd and other companies; Vice-Chairman, National Service Committee, Morayshire; *b* 21 March 1878; *s* of late Thomas Alexander and Elizabeth Hood Wilson; *m* 1901, Agnes Grainger Stewart Kilpatrick; one *s* two *d. Educ:* Perth Academy; Edinburgh University. House Surgeon, E Suffolk Hospital, 1900–01; Clinical Assistant Charité Hospital, Berlin, 1901; medical and surgical practice, Elgin, since 1901; County Director, Red Cross, Morayshire, 1913–16; Capt. RAMC (T) 1st Scottish General Hospital; Major incharge surgical division, Salonica; late chairman Banff, Moray and Nairn British Medical Association and chairman Northern Counties of Scotland British Medical Association; late chairman Moray Education Authority; president Moray and Nairn Liberal Association. *Recreations:* fishing, shooting, golf. *Address:* Woodpark, Lhanbryd, Elgin; 28 Institution Road, Elgin. *T:* Lhanbryd 220, Elgin 600. *Clubs:* Caledonian; Royal Scottish Automobile, Glasgow.

Died 29 April 1941.

ALEXANDER-SINCLAIR, Adm. Sir Edwyn Sinclair, GCB 1930; KCB 1919; CB 1916; MVO 1908; JP, DL; *b* 1865; 2nd *s* of Capt. John Hobhouse Inglis Alexander, Royal Navy, CB (*d* 1875), and Isabella Barbara (*d* 1884), *o d* of late T. C. Hume; *m* 1st, 1892, Julia Margaret (*d* 1930), 3rd *d* of late Colonel Charles Vereker Hamilton Campbell of Netherplace, Ayrshire; two *s* one *d*; 2nd, 1933, Maud Kathleen, *yr d* of late Capt. S. Y. H. Davenport, and *widow* of Major W. R. Campbell, DSO, 14th Hussars. [Assumed additional surname of Sinclair, 1894]. Entered Navy, 1879; in command of Osborne Naval College, 1905–08; of Third Light Cruiser Squadron, 1917–20; Adm.-Superintendent Portsmouth Dockyard, 1920–22; commanded First Battle Squadron Atlantic Fleet, 1922–24; C-in-C, China Station, 1925–26; The Nore, 1927–30; served European War, battle of Jutland Bank, 1916 (despatches twice KCB, CB, Croix de Guerre, 3rd Class Order of St Vladimir, with swords, Russia); Vice-Adm., 1922; Adm., 1926; First and Principal Naval ADC to the King, 1930; retd list 1930. *Address:* Dunbeath Castle, Caithness.

Died 13 Nov. 1945.

ALI, Khan Bahadur Nawab Sir Chaudri Fazal, Kt 1942; OBE 1928; Landlord. Member Legislative Assembly. *Address:* Gujrat, Punjab.

Died 30 Oct. 1942.

ALI, Sir Syed R.; *see* Raza Ali.

ALINGTON, Vice-Adm. Argentine Hugh; JP for Soke of Peterborough; retired; *b* 10 July 1876; 2nd *s* of Admiral Arthur Hildebrand Alington, Swinhope, Binbrook, Lincolnshire; *m* 1904, Janet Marchant, *o d* of Howard H. Tooth, CMG, CB; one *d*. *Educ:* Kelly College, Tavistock; HMS Britannia, Dartmouth. Entered Royal Navy, 1890; 1st sea-going ship, Royal Arthur, as Midshipman; Lieut, 1899; Commander, 1910; Captain, 1916; in action against Zeppelin in N Sea; Commanded HMS Dragon, present at surrender of German submarines at Harwich, Dragon sent to Hamburg to support Allied Commission; after Armistice Flag Captain to Admiral Hon. Victor Stanley, HMS Resolution, present at scuttling of German Fleet, Scapa Flow; in charge of Naval Personnel, Cambridge University, 1921; Flag Captain and Chief of Staff to Adm. Sir Arthur Leveson, HMS Hawkins, China Station, 1922. *Recreation:* motoring. *Address:* Bainton House, Stamford, Lincs. *TA:* and *T:* Bainton Stamford 227. *Club:* Naval and Military.

Died 25 March 1945.

ALLAN, Albert, CBE 1944; MInstT; *b* 30 March 1893; *s* of J. J. Allan; *m* 1920, Margherita, *d* of J. T. Miles; one *d*. *Educ:* High School, South Shields. Traffic apprentice, NER, 1912–14; BEF France, 1914–20; Traffic Inspector, FMS, 1920; Asst Sec. to General Manager, 1921–32; Divisional Supt, 1932; General Manager, Sierra Leone Govt Railway, 1938–44. *Recreations:* Rugby, Association, hockey, tennis, golf. *Address:* Adstock Cottage, Adstock, Bucks. *Club:* Royal Empire Society.

Died 21 Jan. 1948.

ALLAN, Robert W., RWS, RSW, RBC; marine and landscape painter; *b* Glasgow; *y s* of late David Allan. *Educ:* Glasgow; Paris. Exhibited at RA, RSA, and Paris Salon since age of 23; represented in the Permanent Galleries of Glasgow, Aberdeen, Birmingham, Manchester, Liverpool, Leeds, Hull, Venice, Sydney, Auckland, Dunedin, and Santiago, Chile; received silver medal in 1889 and bronze medal in 1900 at International Exposition, Paris; Hors Concours of the Paris Salon; European Juror to International Exhibition, Carnegie Institute, Pittsburg, 1900; sketching tour around the world, 1907; published life and works in Studio Magazines of Sept. 1901 and March 1909. *Recreations:* his

professional work and golf. *Address:* 62 Buckingham Gate, SW1. *T:* Victoria 4058. *Club:* English-Speaking Union.

Died May 1942.

ALLANSON, Col Cecil John Lyons, CMG 1919; CIE 1916; DSO 1915; Croix de Guerre, 1918; late 6th Gurkha Rifles, Indian Army; *b* 2 April 1877; *s* of late J. B. Allanson of Talskiddy, Cornwall; *m* 1925, Marquesa Vda. de Mos y Valladares, Grandee of Spain, *d* of Beresford Whyte, Newton Manor, Co. Sligo. *Educ:* Bedford; RMA, Woolwich. Joined RA, 1897; ADC to Governor of Bengal, 1899–1902; psc, 1907; Private Secretary to Governor of Bengal, 1908–11; Military Secretary to Governor of Madras, 1912–15; commanding 6th Gurkhas, Gallipoli, 1915 (three times wounded); GSOI, France, and War Office, 1916–19; Comdg 6th Gurkhas (wounded) and 9th Infantry Brigade, Waziristan operations, 1920–22; retired, 1922; Vice-Consul Monte Carlo, 1937; Consul, 1938; Croix de Guerre, France. *Address:* c/o Coutts & Co., 440 Strand, WC2. *Club:* International Sportsmen's.

Died 21 Aug. 1943.

ALLARD, Hon. Jules; Advocate; *b* St François du Lac, County of Yamaska, 21 Jan. 1859; *m* 1885, Berthe, *d* of Adolphe Toupin, Montreal; three *s* seven *d*. *Educ:* Nicolet College. Mayor, School Commissioner of the parish of St François du Lac during six years; Registrar of the county during seven years; Member Legislative Assembly, County of Yamaska, 1897–1905; of Drummond, 1910; Minister of Agriculture, 1905–09; Minister of Lands and Forests, Province of Quebec, 1909–19; a Legislative Councillor, 1905–10, and 1916–19; Prothonotary of the Superior Court of Montreal, 1919. *Address:* St François du Lac, Canada. *T:* Pierreville 1. *Club:* Montreal Reform.

Died 3 Jan. 1945.

ALLARDYCE, Brig. John Grahame Buchanan, CMG 1919; DSO 1917; Lord Lieutenant of Nairnshire since 1947; *b* 27 June 1878; 3rd *s* of late Col James Allardyce of Culquoich, Aberdeenshire; *m* 1923, Flora McNeill, 3rd *d* of late A. P. Cameron of Ardsheal, Argyll. *Educ:* RM Academy, Woolwich. 2nd Lieut RA, 1897; Lieut, 1900; Capt., 1905; Major, 1914; Lt-Col 1918; Col, 1922; served SA War, 1899–1902; European War, 1914–18 (CMG, DSO and bar; brevet Lt-Col); retired, 1932. *Address:* Caskieben, Nairn.

Died 21 Sept. 1949.

ALLBERRY, Albert Spenser; Assistant Editor, The Field, April 1946, and Advisory Editor Golf Illustrated; Publicity Officer to Air Ministry and Head of Branch for RAF Exhibitions in liberated countries until April 1946; Editor of Citizen Service (incorporating Rising Strength); Assistant Editor The Navy; Editor-in-Chief Red Cross and St John Emergency Committee, 1939; Pilot Officer RAFVR, 1940, resigned owing to health; in 1942 flew Atlantic in bomber on special mission to USA for the Air Ministry; Free Lance Journalist; Press Liaison Officer, Sea Power, Empire Art and other important Art Exhibitions; Editor-in-Chief Holiday Travel; Editor of This Homeland of Ours, 3 vols; Editor of Piccadilly, 1929–30; late Editor-in-Chief of the Bystander; Acting Editor, 1916; Assistant Editor and Art Editor, 1909; *b* 1880; *m* 1902, Agnes May, *d* of late Thomas E. Rendell, of Chiswick; one *s*. *Educ:* United Westminster Schools. Art Editor of The Car and The Car Magazine, 1902–09; commanded a company in 5th Vol. Batt. Essex Regiment during the war of 1914–18; Major in Command 3rd Batt. Essex Cadet Regiment, 1919–24; Freedom of the City of London, 1913. *Publications:* Booklets and special articles on RAF for Air Ministry; articles on National Defence, travel and gardening and photographs, Editorials and light articles and skits in the Bystander, Graphic and motoring papers, etc. *Recreations:* amateur theatricals, golf, motoring, alpine climbing, fives, lawn-tennis, painting, photography, and gardening. *Address:* Chandos Cottage, Court Road, Ickenham, Mx. *T:* Ruislip 2536.

Died 14 Sept. 1949.

ALLDEN, John Eric, CBE 1923; *b* 1886; *e s* of late John Horatio Allden, Northgate House, Beccles. *Educ:* Charterhouse; Trinity College, Cambridge. Member of War Refugees Committee, 1914–15; European War (Intelligence Officer), 1915–17, Private Secretary to Right Hon. Sir Laming Worthington-Evans, Bart, MP, when Minister without Portfolio, 1920–21, and when Secretary of State for War, 1921–22; attended International Conferences of Paris, Cannes, and Genoa; Hon. Attaché Diplomatic Service and Private Secretary to Sir Ronald Macleay, KCMG, HM Minister in Peking, 1923; Foreign Relations Department, British Red Cross, 1941–46. *Address:* 7 Elvaston Place, SW7. *T:* Western 3023. *Clubs:* Carlton, Hurlingham.

Died 25 Feb. 1949.

ALLEN, Edgar Johnson, CBE 1935; FRS 1914; DSc (Lond.); Hon. LLD (Edin.); Foreign Member, Royal Academy of Denmark; *b* 1866; *s* of late Rev. Richard Allen. *Educ:* Kingswood School; Yorkshire College, Leeds; University of Berlin; University College, London. Sherbrooke Scholarship, 1900; Fellow of Univ. College, University of London, 1938. Secretary Marine Biological Association of the United Kingdom and Director Plymouth Laboratory 1895–1936; Department of Scientific and Industrial Research, Tees and Mersey Survey Committees, 1929–37; Water Pollution Research Board, 1933–37; President, Devonshire Association, 1916; Hansen Memorial Medal and Prize, Copenhagen, 1923; Linean Gold Medal, 1926; Darwin Medal Royal Society, 1936; Agassiz Medal for Oceanography, National Academy of Sciences, Washington, USA, 1938. *Publications:* various memoirs on marine biology in Proceedings Royal Society, Quarterly Journal Microscopical Science, and Journal Marine Biological Association, of which he was editor, 1895–1936. *Address:* Reservoir House, Skardon Place, Plymouth.

Died 7 Dec. 1942.

ALLEN, Edward H.; *see* Heron-Allen.

ALLEN, Engr Rear-Adm. George Bennett; Superintendent Royal Naval Torpedo Factory; *b* 10 Feb. 1888; *s* of Samuel Wesley Allen, Consulting Engineer, Cardiff; *m* 1917, Jessie Josephine Challinor, Leek. *Educ:* privately. Entered Royal Naval Engineering College, 1904; served HM Ships, RN College, Greenwich, Admiralty and HM Dockyards; Engineer Captain, 1934; ADC to the King, 1940; Engr.-Rear-Admiral, 1941. *Recreations:* cricket, golf. *Address:* HMS Ferret.

Died 8 Feb. 1948.

ALLEN, Harold Tuckwell, CMG 1936; *b* 6 Jan. 1879; *s* of late Joshua Allen and late Elizabeth Tuckwell; *m* 1st, 1905, Annie (*d* 1946), *d* of Nicholas Fairley; 2nd, 1946, Augusta Sophia, *widow* of Harry Bevis. *Educ:* Cavendish School, Matlock. Entered Colonial Office, 1898; Assistant Sec., 1931; retired 1936.

Died 19 March 1950.

ALLEN, Rev. Canon Herbert William; Canon of Winterbourne Earls and of Uffculme in Salisbury Cathedral since 1925; Succentor since 1938; Secretary Friends of Salisbury Cathedral since 1938; *s* of J. Allen, Plymouth; *m* Amy, *d* of Capt. T. Gordon, Inniskilling Dragoons, of Cluden Bank, Northam, N Devon; one *d*. *Educ:* The Old Plymouth Grammar School; Trinity College, Dublin. Associate of the Royal College of Organists, 1891; BA; TCD, 1894; MA 1938; Student of Wycliffe Hall, Oxford, 1894–95; Deacon, 1895; Priest, 1896; Curate of Northam, N Devon, 1895–98; St James's Poole, Dorset, 1898–1901; Curate-in-Charge, of Broadstone, Dorset, 1901–04; Rector of S Perrott-cum-Mosterton, 1904–17; Rector of St Paul's, Salisbury,

1917–30; Rector of Breamore, Hants, 1930–36; Vicar of Alderbury, 1936–38; Diocesan Inspector of Schools, 1917; officiating Chaplain to the Forces, Salisbury, 1918; Rural Dean of Wilton, 1929–30 and in 1940; Hon. Chaplain to Bishop of Salisbury, 1940. *Recreation:* photography. *Address:* 25 The Close, Salisbury. *T:* 2121.

Died 4 Dec. 1944.

ALLEN, Hervey, BSc, LittD, FRSA; author; Editor Rivers of America series, since 1943; *b* Pittsburgh, Pennsylvania, USA, 8 Dec. 1889; *s* of William H. Allen and Helen Eby Myers Allen; *m* 1927, Ann Hyde Andrews, Syracuse, NY, USA; one *s* two *d*. *Educ:* United States Naval Academy; University of Pittsburgh; Harvard University. Midshipman, United States Navy; First Lieut, United States Army (European War). *Publications:* Prose; Israfel; The Life and Times of Edgar Allan Poe, 1926; Poe's brother (with Thomas Ollive Mabbott), 1926; Toward the Flame, A War Diary, 1926; Anthony Adverse, 1933; Action at Aquila, 1938; The Forest and the Fort, 1943; Bedford Village, 1945; The City in the Dawn, 1947. Poetry: Wampun and Old Gold; Carolina Chansons (with DuBose Heyward); The Bride of Huitzil, an Aztec Legend; The Blindman; Earth Moods and other Poems; Songs for Annette; Sarah Simon; New Legends. *Recreation:* yachting. *Address:* The Glades Estate, Miami, Florida. *Clubs:* Surf (Miami Beach Fla); Biscayne Bay Yacht; Hamilton Street (Baltimore, Md).

Died 28 Dec. 1949.

ALLEN, Sir Hugh Percy, GCVO 1935; KCVO 1928; Kt 1920; CVO 1926; MA, MusDoc Oxon; Hon. DMus, Camb.; Hon. DLitt, Sheffield and Reading; DPhil Berlin; FRCM; Hon. RAM; Hon. Fellow Christ's College, Cambridge; Fellow of New College, Oxford; Professor of Music in University of Oxford since 1918; President Royal College of Organists; Chairman Mus. Advisory Committee of BBC; President ISM 1930; Conducted at Leeds Festival, 1913, 1922, 1925–28; late Conductor of London Bach Choir and Oxford Bach Choir; *b* 1869; *m* 1902, Winifred, *d* of Oliver Hall of Dedham; one *s* one *d*. *Educ:* Kendrick School, Reading; Christ's College, Cambridge. Organist, St Asaph Cathedral, 1897; Ely Cathedral, 1898; Organist of New College, Oxford, 1901–18; Director of Royal College of Music, 1919–37; Director of Music, University College, Reading, 1908; Subwarden of New College, 1916; Junior Proctor, 1917; Master Worshipful Co. of Musicians, 1937. *Address:* New College, Oxford. *Club:* Athenæum.

Died 20 Feb. 1946.

ALLEN, Inglis, BA; writer and tutor; *b* London, 1879; 2nd *s* of Philip F. Allen and Amy Mayhew; *m* 1907, Rosine, *d* of late Emile Godard; one *s* one *d*. *Educ:* Merchant Taylors' School; Oriel College, Oxford. Wrote series of Varsity Stories in The Idler, 1899–1900; series Highways and Byways in Punch, and similar sketches in The Westminster Gazette, 1902–04; sketches in the Bystander, Punch, Westminster Gazette, Pall Mall Magazine, London Magazine, etc.; 2nd Lieut Royal Flying Corps, 1916; Capt. RAF 1919; demobilised Sept. 1919; series of sketches in the Passing Show, 1919; Sketches in Punch, 1919–28; Verse in Punch, 1931–32. *Publications:* A 'Varsity Man, 1901; A Graduate in Love, 1902; Highways and By-ways, 1903; Sir 'Arry, 1913; The Dear Unfair Sex (Comedy), 1906; Stryver's Nerves (Comedy), 1909; If We Had Only Known (Comedy), 1912; A Wife in the House (one act Comedy), 1927; The Colonel's Manœuvre (one act Comedy), 1927; Stories in The 20 Story Magazine, 1929; Occasional Verse and Prose in Punch, 1930–1937. *Address:* Northgate House, Rottingdean, Sussex.

Died 2 March 1943.

ALLEN, Col Hon. Sir James, GCMG 1926; KCB 1917; TD; *b* S Australia, 10 Feb. 1855; *m* 1877, Mary Hill (*d* 1939), *d* of John Richards, Alford, Somerset; one *s* three *d*. *Educ:* Clifton; St John's College, Cambridge (MA);

Royal School of Mines. MP Dunedin East, 1887–90; Bruce, 1891–1920; Minister of Defence, New Zealand, 1912–20; Minister of Finance and Education, 1912–15; Min. of External Affairs and Finance, 1919–20; High Commissioner in London for NZ, 1920–26; Member of Legislative Council, N Zealand, 1927–41; Legion of Honour; Order of the Crown (Belgium). *Publications:* New Zealand and Federation, the Financial Aspect, 1899; New Zealand's possessions in the South Seas; Notes of Parliamentary Cruise, 1903; New Zealand and Naval Defence, 1930. *Address:* Arana, 110 Clyde Street, Dunedin, N1, NZ. *Club:* Dunedin.

Died 28 July 1942.

ALLEN, John Edsall, ARCA (Lond.); *b* London, 9 Dec. 1861; *s* of David Davis Allen and Elizabeth Allen; *m* 1893, Sara Abrahams; no *c*. *Educ:* private school. Studied at Charterhouse School of Art; gained Scholarship at Royal College of Art. Assistant Master, Charterhouse School of Art, and Assistant Master, Camden School of Art, 1887–90; Birkbeck School of Art, 1891; Visiting Art Master, St Martin's Middle School for Girls, Charing Cross Road, 1887–92; Principal of St Martin's School of Art, 1892–1927; Visiting Art Master, Archbishop Tenison's Grammar School, Leicester Square, 1888–1914; Exhibitor, RA, etc. *Address:* 18 Clarence Square, Brighton.

Died 3 Feb. 1944.

ALLEN, Col John Sandeman, OBE 1938; MC, TD, MP (C) Birkenhead West, 1931–45; *b* 30 May 1892; *s* of late Sir John Sandeman Allen and 1st wife, Amy Spencer; *m* 1916, Eudora Mary, *d* of late A. H. Heal, Birkenhead; one *s* two *d*. *Educ:* Birkenhead School; Germany; France. Formerly with Booth SS Co., Ltd; Underwriting Member of Lloyd's; formerly Consul for Belgium in Liverpool; commanded Lancashire and Cheshire Hy Regt RA and 106th (Lancashire Yeomanry) Field Regt RA, TA; Brevet Col, 1937; served 1914–19, France and Belgium (MC); Beach defence and Lt AA Regts, 1940–42; at sea Staff Officer Movements, 1942–45. Late member Walton-on-Thames UDC; member Birkenhead Chamber of Commerce; Chairman Parliamentary Road Group, British Group Inter-Parliamentary Union, 1935–39, and Stage and Drama Group; contested S Norfolk, 1945. *Recreations:* philately, bridge. *Club:* Constitutional.

Died 29 Sept. 1949.

ALLEN, Col John Woolley, CMG 1916; late 4th Batt. The King's (SR); *b* 6 March 1865; *s* of late Sir Wigram Allen, KCMG; *m* 1893, Elfrida Margaret Frances (*d* 1935), *o d* of late C. G. Hayward, Needham Market, Suffolk; two *d*. *Educ:* Trinity Hall, Cambridge University (BA Hons 1886). Called to Bar, Inner Temple, 1890; served S Africa, 1901–02 (Queen's medal 3 clasps); European War, 1914–18 (despatches, CMG); Army of Occupation, 1919, and with Rhineland High Commission as Kreis officer, Cologne, 1920–21. *Clubs:* Conservative, Royal Automobile, MCC.

Died 19 Feb. 1942.

ALLEN, Lt-Col Robert Candlish, DSO 1917; *b* 1881; *s* of late William Shepherd Allen, Woodhead Hall, Cheadle, Staffs; *m* 1911, Ida Tyrrell (*d* 1929), *d* of Herbert Laidlaw Thompson. Served European War, 1915–19 (despatches thrice, DSO with bar); Hon. ADC to Governor-General of New Zealand, 1920–24.

Died 19 Jan. 1942.

ALLEN, Sir Thomas, Kt 1919; Chairman Anglo-Baltic Produce Co. Ltd and New Zealand Produce Association Ltd; formerly Vice-Chairman Co-operative Wholesale Society and International Co-operative Alliance; Chairman, Co-operative Insurance Society; President Co-operative Congress; President Newport (Mon) Chamber of Commerce; *b* Abertillery, Monmouth, 6

Feb. 1864. Served as Member Macmillan Committee on Finance and Industry and Royal Commission on Trading in Arms. *Recreation:* golf. *Club:* National Liberal.

Died 24 Nov. 1943.

ALLEN, Sir Walter Macarthur, KBE 1926; CBE 1920; OBE 1918; *b* 1870; *s* of late Sir Wigram Allen, KCMG; *m* 1896, Pearl, *d* of Edward Lamb, formerly Minister for Lands, Queensland; one *s* one *d*. *Educ:* Trinity Hall, Cambridge, (BA). Bar, Inner Temple, 1896; Assistant Staff Officer Metropolitan Special Constabulary, 1914; Director of Supplies, 1915–17; Staff Officer, 1918–24; Commandant-in-Chief Metropolitan Special Constabulary, 1925–43; Commander of Order of St John of Jerusalem. *Recreations:* cricket, tennis, and golf. *Club:* Conservative.

Died 27 Nov. 1943.

ALLEN, William; KC 1930; JP Staffs; Barrister-at-law, Oxford Circuit; Recorder of Newcastle-under-Lyme since 1932; *b* 1870; *m* 1st, 1893, Jeannette, *d* of John Hall; one *s*; 2nd, 1929, Mrs Oliver Riley. *Educ:* Emmanuel College, Cambridge. MP (R) Newcastle-under-Lyme, 1892–1900; Member of Royal Commission on Licensing; served in South Africa, March 1900 to Sept. 1901, as Captain with South Australian Mounted Rifles; Military Representative Islington, Jan. 1916–March 1917; Food Campaign, first National War Savings Committee, March 1917–Aug. 1918; Head of Agricultural Branch Ministry of National Service, Nov. 1917–Jan. 1919; Recorder of Ludlow, 1928–32; MP (U) Burslem Division, Stoke-on-Trent, 1931–35; Charity Commissioner, 1935–36; Tithe Commission 1937; Master of the Bench Inner Temple, 1937. *Address:* 68 Berkeley Court, Baker Street, NW1; 3 Paper Buildings, Temple, EC4. *T:* Welbeck 1240, Central 4488. *Club:* East India and Sports.

Died 11 Sept. 1945.

ALLEN, William; Agricultural Commissioner for Canada since 1938; *b* Pucklechurch, nr Bristol, Glos, 9 May 1892; *s* of Charles Allen and Eliza Jane Hallett; *m* 1926, Gwendolen Maude Woodward. *Educ:* Merchant Venturers Technical College, Bristol; Univ. of Saskatchewan (BSA); Cornell (PhD); Harvard (Graduate School). Civil Service, London, Patent Office, 1907; Exchange Telegraph Co. Ltd, 1908–11; emigrated to homestead at Dewar Lake, Saskatchewan, 1911; enlisted 65th Bn Canadian Expeditionary Force (wounded); discharged, 1917; University of Saskatchewan, 1917–22, Univ. Graduation Schol.; Travelling Fellowship in Agriculture; graduate work, Cornell and Harvard, in Agricultural Economics and Economic Theory; Instructor Dept Agric. Econ. Cornell, 1924–25, PhD Cornell, 1925; started Dept of Farm Management, Univ. of Sask, 1925, Professor; Member Canadian Pioneer Problems, Committee, 1930–33; Royal Commissioner, Sask. Milk Inquiry Commission, 1933; Member Milk Control Board of Sask, 1935–37; Land Utilization Board; Member of Council and Delegate to International Conference of Agric. Econ., 1929, 1930, 1934; Member W Canada Wheat Problems Committee; Macmillan Banking Commission, W Provs. Committee; Sask Crop Insurance Committee; Agric. Advisory Committee for Sask, etc. *Publications:* Agricultural Progress on the Prairie Frontier (with Dr R. W. Murchie), 1933; University Extension Bulletins; contributions to technical journals. *Recreation:* general. *Address:* Canada House, Trafalgar Square, SW1. *TA:* Agricult, Lessquare, London. *T:* Whitehall 9741. *Clubs:* Over-Seas League; Canadian, Canadian Institute of International Affairs, Saskatoon.

Died 1 May 1941.

ALLEN, Lt-Col Sir William (James), KBE 1921; DSO 1918; 16th Royal Irish Rifles; MP (U) North Armagh, 1917–22, Co. Armagh since 1922; *b* Oct. 1866; *s* of Joseph and Catherine Allen; *m* 1st, 1892, Maria (*d* 1937), *e d* of late John Ross; one *d*; 2nd, 1938, Lillah Ierne, *d* of late R. Hill and Mrs Forsythe, Lurgan. *Educ:* Lurgan College. DL and JP Co. Armagh. DGM and Grand Secretary, Grand Orange Lodge, Ireland; joined army, 14 Nov. 1914; Major, Sept. 1916; served in France, 1 Oct. 1915 (despatches four times, Chevalier Legion of Honour, DSO). *Address:* 6 Cleaver Park, Belfast.

Died 20 Dec. 1947.

ALLEN-WILLIAMS, Brig.-Gen. Sir Arthur John, KBE 1920; CMG 1918; MICE; JP; Alderman, West Sussex County Council; Member of Littlehampton Harbour Board and of Arun Catchment Board; *b* 1869; *m* 1913, Ursula Mary, *d* of late Francis Allen, JP, of Cockley Cley Hall, Swaffham, Norfolk; one *s* two *d*. *Educ:* Haverfordwest Grammar School; Royal Indian Engineering College, Coopers Hill. Officier de la Légion d'Honneur, 1920. *Address:* Beach Lodge, Littlehampton.

Died 27 Nov. 1949.

ALLFREY, Captain Maurice Charles, DSO 1940; Kent Yeomanry; *b* 13 April 1916; 3rd *s* of Charles M. Allfrey, Beresfords, Boughton Monchelsea, Kent. *Educ:* Harrow; Trinity Hall, Cambridge. *Address:* Beresfords, Boughton Monchelsea, Maidstone, Kent.

Died 1 July 1942.

ALLOM, Sir Charles Carrick, Kt 1913; Founder of White, Allom & Co., London, Montreal, New York, decorative artists and contractors, Contractors to Admiralty and War Office for High Explosive Shells, architectural contractors, London and New York; Past President Faculty Architects and Surveyors; Registered Architect; Vice-President Incorporated Association Architects; Architects Registration Council; Founder of Gosport Aircraft Company; Member of Board of Education's Advisory Committee on Art Education; Local Government Board Buildings Committee and Reconstruction Council; Royal Commissioner, Brussels, Turin and Rome International Exhibitions 1911 and 1912; Council Empire Exhibition, 1923; Council Yacht Racing Association; Ex-Commodore Royal London Yacht Club; *b* 16 June 1865; *s* of Arthur Allom, architect; *g s* of two painters, Thomas Allom and Thomas Carrick; *m* Laura, *d* of Albert Tatham, Warwick; two *d*. *Educ:* Isleworth; Royal College of Art; France; Italy. President Boat-racing Association; Fellow Royal Society of Arts; Member of Royal Agricultural Society of Great Britain and Ireland; Chairman Executive Council Industrial Peace Union of British Empire; Chairman Faculty of Arts; Vice-President Middlesex Rugby Union; Chairman Board of Control World's Sculling Championship; owner of racing yacht White Heather. *Recreations:* all-round athlete; yachting, golf, rugby 3/4, rowing, shooting, chess. *Address:* Westbury Court, Westbury-on-Severn. *T:* Mayfairr 1217. *Clubs:* Royal London Yacht, Royal Thames Yacht, International Sportsmen's; Royal Dorset Yacht; Royal Victoria Yacht; British Sportsman's; Royal Mid-Surrey Golf; Walton Heath Golf; Stinchcombe Hill Golf; Gloucester Golf.

Died 1 June 1947.

ALLPORT, Alfred, MRCS Eng., LRCP Lond.; Hon. Consulting Surgeon to St Paul's Hospital for Skin and Genito-urinary Diseases; Major RAMCV; *b* Brixton, 1867; 3rd *s* of late Franklin Thomas Allport; *m* 1st, Edith Blanche Eicke, *d* of late R. H. Fry; one *s* two *d*; 2nd, Madeline Annie, *d* of late Charles Price; one *s* two *d*. *Educ:* London International College, Isleworth; Guy's Hospital. Attached RAMC Military Hospital, Rochester Row, during War. *Publications:* articles to the medical journals. *Recreations:* rowing, boxing, football (Rugby International, 1891–92–1893). *Address:* 31 Fitzroy Road, NW1. *T:* Primrose 4366. *Club:* Royal Automobile.

Died 2 May 1949.

ALMA-TADEMA, Miss Anna; artist; *d* of late Sir Lawrence Alma-Tadema, OM, RA, and *d* of G. Napoleon Epps, MRCS. *Educ:* 2nd medal Paris Exhibition, 1889. *Address:* c/o Barclay's Bank, St John's Wood Branch, NW.

Died 5 July 1943.

ALMOND, Hon. Col Ven. John Macpherson, CMG 1916; CBE 1919; MA, DCL, Archdeacon of Montreal, 1932; Rector of Holy Trinity Memorial Church, Montreal, 1904; Director of Chaplain Services, Canadian Local Forces; *b* 1872; *m* 1901, Nellie Estella Beemer. *Educ:* Bishop's University, Lennoxville. Ordained, 1896; SPG Missionary, Labrador, 1896–98; Travelling Missionary, Quebec, 1898–99; Chaplain with 1st Canadian Contingent to S Africa, 1899–1901 (Queen's medal 3 clasps); Curate of Quebec Cathedral, 1901–02; Missionary at Grande Mère, 1901–04; with Canadian Contingent in France during European War, 1914–18 (CMG); Long Service Medal, VD, 1935; King's Silver Jubilee Medal, 1935. *Address:* 3825 Marlowe Avenue, Montreal.

Died 17 Sept. 1939.

ALSOP, Ralph, CBE 1941. Director, Consett Iron Co. Ltd, National Benzole Co. Ltd, Consett Spanish Ore Co. Ltd. *Address:* 45 Milbank Road, Darlington, Co. Durham.

Died 6 Oct. 1950.

ALSTEAD, Robert, OBE 1939; JP; *b* Wigan, 1873; *m* 1896; six *s* one *d*. *Educ:* Wigan Elementary School and Wigan Mining Technical College. Founder of Robert Alstead, Ltd, woollen manufacturers and clothing manufacturers, Wigan; Member Wigan Town Council, 1913–29; Mayor of Wigan, 1926–27; Governor, Wigan Grammar School, since 1913; Governor, Wigan Mining Tech. Coll. 1913–32; contested (L) Wigan, 1918; Altrincham, 1922, 1923, 1924, and 1929; MP (L) Altrincham, 1923–24; on list of prospective Liberal parliamentary candidates. *Recreation:* reading. *Address:* Greenhill, Gathurst, Wigan.

Died 9 Sept. 1946.

ALSTON, Alexander Rowland; *b* 2 July 1863; *e s* of late Sir Francis B. Alston, KCMG, Foreign Office, and Emily, *e d* of late Bridges Taylor, of HM's Diplomatic Service; *g s* of Rowland Alston of Pishobury, Herts, MP for Herts, 1835; *m* Muriel (*d* 1941), *e d* of Rev. Canon Blundell, Rector of Halsall, Lancs, and Adelaide, *d* of Sir Francis Astley, Bart; one *s* two *d*. *Educ:* Eton; abroad. Has travelled extensively; Patron of two livings; JP Bedfordshire, 1903; High Sheriff of Bedfordshire, 1917–18; Red Cross, 1917–18; member of the Bedfordshire Standing Joint Committee; on the Licensing Committee, Bedford; member of County Probation Committee, Bedfordshire; Visitor Reformatory, Turvey; Visitor of Licensed Houses under Lunacy Act 1890, and Institutions under Mental Deficiency Act 1913; FRGS; Past Master No 6 Lodge of Friendship; a Past Grand Steward of England; Donor of Colours to 5th Batt. Bedfordshire Regiment, 1912; Patron of livings of Sharnbrook, Souldrop cum Knotting, Beds. *Recreations:* hunting, shooting, fishing and farming. *Heir:* Major Edward Rowland Milles Alston, Scots Guards, *b* 1902. *Address:* 1 Granville Chambers, Portman Square, W1. *Clubs:* MCC; County, Bedford.

Died 9 July 1945.

ALSTON, Lady Hilda, CBE 1920; *d* of late Maj. Gen. Robert Gream; *m* 1900, Rt Hon. Sir Beilby Francis Alston, PC, GBE, KCMG, CB (*d* 1929); one *s* one *d*. *Address:* Forest House, Annesley, Notts. *T:* East Kirkby 2268.

Died 18 March 1945.

ALTHAM, Captain Edward, CB 1919; RN retd; Secretary, Editor and Chief Executive Officer, Royal United Service Institution; *b* 7 Jan. 1882; *e s* of Lt.-Gen. Sir E. A. Altham, KCB, KCIE; *m* 1922, Joyce E. M., *o d* of Louis H. M and Edith A. Dick. Served European War; commanded HMS Wildfire in Belgian coast operations, 1918; commanded HMS General Craufurd at Zeebrugge-Ostend operations; commanded HMS Attentive at bombardment and capture of forts on Modyuski Island, North Russia; Senior Naval Officer Archangel River Expeditions, 1918–19; naval despatches seven times, military despatches three times, CB, Officier of Legion d'Honneur, Order of St Vladimir of Russia. Staff of Naval War College, 1920–21; retired list, 1922; recalled to active service, 1939–44, as Chief of Naval Postal and Telegraph Censorship on Naval Staff, Admiralty. *Publications:* Jellicoe (Order of Merit Series), 1938; Naval Editor of Encyclopaedia Britannica; numerous articles on Imperial Defence, Naval Strategy and Tactics. *Recreation:* sailing. *Address:* 41 Bloomfield Terrace, SW1. *T:* Sloane 3170. *Clubs:* United Service, Little Ship (hon.); (hon.) Royal Yacht Squadron (Cowes); Emsworth Sailing (Emsworth).

Died 16 Oct. 1950.

ALTHAM, Lt.-Gen. Sir Edward Altham, KCB 1916; KCIE 1919; CB 1904; CMG 1901; Colonel, The Royal Scots, 1918–34; retired pay; Member of Winchester Diocesan Board of Finance; *b* Wilton, Somerset, 13 April 1856; 2nd *s* of Major W. S. Altham, late 83rd Foot, of Timbercombe, Bridgwater, and Henrietta, *d* of Mr Moulton-Barrett of Hope End, Herefordshire; *m* 1880, Georgina Emily, *d* of W. Macpherson Nicol of Inverness; two *s* one *d. Educ:* Winchester; Christ Church, Oxford. Entered Army, 1876 (The Royal Scots); passed Staff College, 1900; Intelligence Division, War Office, 1897–99 and 1900–04; General Staff, South Africa, 1906–08; served Bechuanaland Expedition, 1884–85; S Africa, 1899–1900, as AAG for Intelligence (despatches twice, medal with four clasps, promoted Lieut-Col); European War in charge Administration Southern Command, 1914; IGC Dardanelles, 1915; IGC Egyptian Expeditionary Force, 1916; QMG in India, 1917–19 (despatches seven times, KCB, KCIE, prom. Lt.-Gen., Grand Cross, White Eagle, Serbia, Grand Cross, Sacred Treasure, Japan). *Publication:* The Principles of War, 1914. *Address:* 7 Kingsgate Street, Winchester.

Died 27 Sept. 1943.

AMARJIT SINGH, Lt.-Col Maharajkumar, CIE 1935; MA (Oxon); Indian Army (4/11th Sikh Regt); Commandant State Forces; *b* 5 Aug. 1893; *s* of Brig. H. H. the Maharaja of Kapurthala, GCSI. *Educ:* Military Theresianum Academy, Vienna; Christ Church, Oxford. Served in France during European War as 2nd Lieutenant in Indian Army; Recruiting Officer, Kapurthala State, 1917–18; (Hony Captain in Indian Army, 1914–15 Star, British War Medal, Allied Victory Medal); King's Indian Recruiting Medal; Hony ADC to Commander-in-Chief in India, 1926–30; British Staff Officer to General Gouraud, Military Governor, Paris, during his tour in India, 1928–29; Hony Major in Indian Army 1930; Hon. Lieut-Colonel, 1942; King's Silver Jubilee Medal, having attended Silver Jubilee, 1935; Coronation Medal, having attended Coronation, 1937; Commander Legion of Honour, 1938. *Recreations:* riding and swimming. *Address:* Kapurthala State, India. *TA:* Comforkap, Kapurthala. *Clubs:* Marlborough; Imperial Gymkhana, Delhi; Royal Western India Turf, Willingdon Sports, Bombay; Calcutta, Calcutta; Cercle Interallié, Paris.

Died Sept. 1944.

AMES, John Richard Woodland, FSMA; General Works Manager and Sales Manager and Business Organiser; *b* Rochester, Kent, 13 Nov. 1872; *e s* of Richard Ames. *Educ:* privately. Factory organisation (fatigue and scientific research), 1901–08; special educational extension work, 1908–18; Founder Industrial League and Council, 1915, Hon. Sec., 1915–18; Secretary and General Manager, 1918–24; Founder and Managing Director, WM Publicity Service, 1924–26; Secretary and General Manager Red Triangle Cement Organisation, 1927–31; Senior Partner, John Ames & Partners Ltd, Business Consultants and Organisers, 1932–41; Trustee King's Fund, 1918 to close of fund, 1928; Fellow and Past Chairman Incorporated Sales Managers' Association; Member Executive British Peace Award, 1924; Member Ministry of Labour Appointments Committee, 1919–28; Member Executive International Chamber of Commerce, 1931–33; Member Council (British) International Scientific Management Congress. *Publications:* Editor Current Opinion, 1918–1924; Editor Modern Building Construction, 1927–1931; also economic and industrial articles, various magazines and journals. *Recreations:* golf, bowls, reading and conversation. *Address:* 20 Ridgmont Road, St Albans, Herts. *T:* St Albans 4875.

Died 14 March 1947.

AMIGO, Most Rev. Peter E.; Archbishop-Bishop of Southwark (RC), since 1904 (Archbishop, 1937); *b* Gibraltar, May 1864. *Educ:* St Edmund's College; Old Hall, Ware; St Thomas's Seminary, Hammersmith. Rector of St Mary and St Michael's, Commercial Road E, 1899; English Martyrs', Walworth, 1901. Assistant at the Pontifical Throne and Count of the Holy Roman Empire, 1929. *Address:* Bishop's House, St George's Road, Southwark, SE1. *T:* Waterloo 5592.

Died 1 Oct. 1949.

AMOD, Thakor of, Sardar Nawab Sir Naharsinhji Ishwarsinhji, Kt 1938. *Address:* Palace, Amod, India.

Died 16 April 1945.

AMSHEWITZ, J. H., RBA 1914; member of the London Society of Portrait Painters; portrait painter and mural decorator; *b* Ramsgate, 19 Dec. 1882; *s* of Rev. A. Amshewitz, Ramsgate; *m* 1918, Sarah Briana Judes, Johannesburg; one *s. Educ:* Central Foundation School; Royal Academy Schools (prize-winner, Mural Decoration). Awarded first and second places and commission in Liverpool Pageant Memorial Competition, 1908, whereby executed series of mural paintings in Liverpool Town Hall. Executed Historical Panel, Royal Exchange, London, 1910; worked in S Africa, 1916–22; three Historical panels, South Africa House, Trafalgar Square, 1934; Historical Panel for University of Witwatersrand, Johannesburgh, 1936; Historical Panel in City Hall, Pretoria, 1937; Cartoonist on Rand Daily Mail and Sunday Times; painted many portraits of South African notabilities, and executed a series of wall paintings as a war memorial in Church of St Michael and All Angels, Boksburg, Transvaal; paintings placed permanently in principal galleries in South Africa, in South Kensington Museum and the Ferens Gallery, Hull; Leighton House and Metropolitan Museum, New York; Municipal Art Gallery, Brighton; mention Honorable Paris Salon, 1929; first exhibitor in RA, 1904; works in private collections of Prince George, Princess Alice, Countess of Athlone, Gaikwar of Baroda; exhibited at the RBA, Royal Oil Institute, New English Art Club, the International Society of Painters, and at the Royal Portrait Painters' Society at their Royal Academy Winter Exhibitions. *Publications:* Illustrations to Everyman; Myths and Legends of Ancient Israel; The Hagadah; and to Zangwill's Ghetto Tragedies and Ghetto Comedies. *Address:* The Dome Studio, Cuthberts Buildings, Eloff Street, Johannesburg, S Africa.

Died 6 Dec. 1942.

AMULREE, 1st Baron *cr* 1929; **William Warrender Mackenzie,** PC 1930; GBE 1926; KBE 1918; CBE 1917; KC 1914; Hon. LLD (Edin.); *b* 1860; *m* 1897, Lilian (*d* 1916), *e d* of late W. H. Bradbury; one *s* one *d. Educ:* Perth Academy; Edinburgh University (MA 1885);

University College, London. Called to Bar, Lincoln's Inn, 1886; Northern Circuit; received hon. freedom of the city of Perth, 1938; Secretary of State for Air and President of Air Council, 1930–31; Chairman of Committee to Enquire into Manchester Engineering Piece Rates, 1917; Chairman of Commission of Enquiry into Industrial Unrest, South West District, 1917; Member of Lord Atkin's War Cabinet Committee of Inquiry on Women in Industry, 1918–19; Chairman of Government Inquiry on Night Baking, 1919; sole member of Court of Inquiry concerning Engineering Trades Disputes, 1922; Chairman of Committee to enquire into claims of men dismissed from police and prison services on account of 1919 strike, 1924; one of the Chairmen of the Committee on Production, 1917–18; Chairman of Special Arbitration Tribunal under Munitions of War Act, 1917; a Chairman of Interim Court of Arbitration under The Wages (Temporary Regulation) Acts 1918–19; President of Industrial Court, 1919–26; Chairman of the Railway National Wages Board, 1920–26; Government referee under Electricity (Supply) Act 1919; Chairman of Tramway Tribunal for Great Britain since 1924; Chairman of British Government Industrial Delegation to Canada and United States of America, 1926–27; Chairman of Departmental Committee on Shops Hours Acts, 1927; President of Building Industry Council of Review, 1928–33; Chairman of Royal Commission on Licensing Laws, 1929–31; Chairman of Committee of Inquiry into London Motor Coach Services, 1932; Chairman of Royal Commission on Newfoundland, 1933; Chairman of Joint Committee of both Houses on Consolidation of Bills, 1934–39; Chairman of Court of Inquiry into Panel Doctors' Fees, 1937; Chairman of Committee on Holidays with Pay, 1937–38; Chairman of Committee on Highway Law Consolidation, 1938–41; Vice-President of Association of Municipal Corporations, Works Management Association and Institute of Sociology; Chairman of Council of Royal Society of Arts (Chairman of Examinations Committee), 1937–39; Commissioner under Trade Board Acts; Chairman of Tribunal of the Retail Standards Association, 1935; has acted as Arbitrator and Conciliator in industrial differences for the Board of Trade and Minister of Labour; Royal Society of Arts Medal, 1923; Chairman of National Building Council, 1934–35 and National Housing Committee; Member of Council of Royal Empire Society, 1934–39; Chairman of Committee on Workers' Holidays, 1939–41. Hon. Member Incorporated Association of Rating and Valuation Officers; King's Jubilee Medal, 1935. *Publications:* Pratt and Mackenzie's Law of Highways (16 editions); 10th to 21st editions of Paterson's Licensing Acts; one of the Editors of Lord Halsbury's Laws of England; Elementary Education Acts; Arnold's Municipal Corporations (4th and 5th editions), with Sir S. G. Johnson, G. R. Hill; Overseers' Handbook (8 editions); Poor Law Guardian (4 eds); Model Byelaws under Public Health and other Acts, with Mr P. Handford; Practice of the Industrial Court; Industrial Arbitration in Great Britain, 1930; articles in various magazines, etc. *Recreations:* golf, fishing. *Heir:* s Hon. Basil William Sholto Mackenzie, MD. *Address:* 42 Queen Anne's Gate, SW1. *T:* Whitehall 7578; Northfield House, St Abbs, Berwickshire. *T:* Coldingham 20. *Club:* Reform.

Died 5 May 1942.

ANDERSON, Andrew Newton, OBE 1934; Permanent Secretary to the Supreme Court of Judicature of Northern Ireland since 1921; Clerk of the Crown for Northern Ireland since 1923; b 6 Sept. 1880; s of John Anderson, Land Agent of Lurgan and Belfast and Sarah Darley Newton; m 1918, Lilian Dunlop, o c of late John Dunlop Costine, Liverpool and London Civil Servant; one s. *Educ:* Drogheda Grammar School; Campbell College, Belfast. Admitted a solicitor, 1902; Assistant Secretary, Ulster Unionist Council and Unionist

Associations of Ireland, 1906–14; Secretary to late Lieut-Colonel James Craig (Viscount Craigavon), AA and QMG, 36th (Ulster) Division, 1914–15; Royal Irish Rifles, 1915–19; Secretary, Ulster Volunteer Force Patriotic Fund and Secretary of the Mid-Down Unionist Association, 1919–21; Silver Jubilee Medal, 1935; Coronation Medal, 1937. *Recreations:* gardening, stamp collecting. *Address:* Gezina, Downshire Road, Cregagh, Belfast. *T:* Belfast 41288.

Died 10 May 1950.

ANDERSON, Brig.-Gen. Austin Thomas, CMG 1918; late RA; s of late W. M. Anderson (Managing Director of the Oriental Bank, sometime Member of the Legislative Council, and acting Governor of Mauritius) and late M. A., d of Capt. W. Neilly, 40th Regt; m 1904, Ethel Louise, d of late C. C. Mason, Rangamatty, New South Wales; one d. *Educ:* Summer Fields; Eton College; RMA, Woolwich. Commissioned Royal Artillery, 1888; served Tochi Field Force, 1897; Tirah Expeditionary Force, 1897–98 (medal with two clasps); European War, France, 1914–18; Brig.-General CRA 62nd Division, 1916 (once wounded, despatches six times, Brevet of Colonel, CMG, Officier Légion d'Honneur, French Croix de Guerre); retired pay, 1924; Comptroller and Assistant Military Officer to Governor-General of Australia, 1939–44; Private Secretary to the Governor, New South Wales, 1927–36; Private Secretary to Governor-General of Australia, 1936–39; Hon. ADC to the Duke of Gloucester, 1945–46; Silver Medal RA Institution, 1912. *Publications:* Field Gunners' Catechism; A Short History of Lucknow; War Services 62nd Divisional Artillery. *Address:* Ball Green, Turramurra, NSW, Australia. *T:* JW 2292.

Died 22 Feb. 1949.

ANDERSON, Charles, MA, DSc; b Stenness, Orkney, Scotland, 1876; s of John Anderson, crofter, and Margaret Smith; m 1902, Elsie Robertson; one s two d. *Educ:* Stenness Public School; Kirkwall Burgh School; Edinburgh University. Graduated MA, 1898; BSc, 1900; Hope Prize Scholar in Chemistry, DSc, 1908. Observer at Ben Nevis Observatory, 1900–01; Mineralogist to the Australian Museum, Sydney, 1901; Director, Australian Museum, 1921–40. *Publications:* papers on Crystallography and Chemistry of Australian Minerals, and on Australian fossil vertebrates. *Recreations:* shooting, fishing, swimming. *Address:* 17 Towns Road, Rose Bay, Sydney, NS Wales.

Died 30 Oct. 1944.

ANDERSON, Rev. Edward Erskine, MA (Aber.), DD (Aber.); b 28 Dec. 1872; 5th s of late Rev. Alexander Anderson, MA, DD, Minister of the UF Church, Edenkillie, Morayshire; m 1918; no c. *Educ:* University of Aberdeen (First-class Honours in Classics, the Town Council Gold Medal for the most distinguished graduate of the year, the Seafield Gold Medal for Latin, was bracketed equal for the Post-graduate Fullerton Scholarship in Classics); Queens' College, Cambridge; Edinburgh and Berlin; New College, Edinburgh. Ordained to the Ministry of the United Free Church of Scotland, and called to pastorate at East Kilbride, 1899; called to Newton-on-Ayr, 1911; Principal of St Andrew's College, University of Sydney, 1920–37; Hunter-Baillie Professor of Oriental and Polynesian Languages in St Andrew's College 1924–37. *Publications:* Commentary on the Gospel of St Matthew; magazine articles. *Recreations:* golf, tennis. *Address:* Oakham, Sla Strathaven Rd, East Kilbride, Glasgow. *T:* East Kilbride 323.

Died 28 Feb. 1950.

ANDERSON, Rt Rev. Ernest Augustus, DD; b Milton Damerel Rectory, Devons, 24 March 1859; m 1883, Amelia Constance Isabel, 2nd d of Col W. A. Ross, RA; one s four d. *Educ:* Bedford Grammar School; Queens' Coll., Camb. (MA). Ordained 1882; Rector of Mackay, Queensland, 1883–86; Hughenden, 1886–90;

Hon. Canon of Townsville and Rector of St Paul's, West Maitland, NSW, 1890–95; Bishop of Riverina, 1895–1925; retired, 1925. *Address:* Courtville, Auckland, NZ.

Died 5 April 1945.

ANDERSON, Sir Francis, Kt 1936; MA; LLD (Glas.); Emeritus Professor of Philosophy, University of Sydney; *b* Glasgow, 3 Sept. 1858; *s* of Francis Anderson; *m* 1st, 1899, Maybanke Selfe Wolstenholme, Sydney (author of Australian Songs for Children and Mother Lore); 2nd, 1928, Josephine Wight, Sydney. *Educ:* Glasgow University. (Clark) Fellow and Assistant to the Professor of Moral Philosophy, Glasgow University, 1884–86; Assistant Minister of the Australian Church, Melbourne, 1886–88; Lecturer in Philosophy at Sydney University, 1888–90; Professor of Logic and Mental Philosophy, 1890–1922; President of the Mental Science Section of the Australasian Association for the Advancement of Science, Brisbane, 1897; President of the Social Science Section, Adelaide, 1907; Editor of the Australasian Journal of Psychology and Philosophy, 1923–27; President of League of Nations Union (NSW), 1931–41. *Publications:* various articles, lectures and reports on philosophy and education. *Address:* Dunsinane, Woollahra, Sydney, NSW. *Clubs:* University, Sydney.

Died 24 June 1941.

ANDERSON, Sir George, Kt 1924; CSI 1932; CIE 1920; *b* 15 May 1876; *s* of late Edward John Anderson; *m* Gladys Alice Morony; one *d*. *Educ:* Winchester College; University College, Oxford. Transvaal Education Department; Professor of History, Elphinstone College, Bombay; Assist Secretary, Education Department, Government of India; Secretary to the Calcutta Univ. Commission; member of the Auxiliary Committee of the Indian Statutory Commission; Director of Public Instruction, Punjab, 1920; Educational Commissioner with the Government of India; retired, 1936. *Publications:* Expansion of India; British Administration in India; Christian Education in India. *Address:* Spyways, Hartfield, Sussex. *Club:* Athenæum.

Died 15 May 1943.

ANDERSON, Dr George Cranston, CBE 1942; MD, LLD (Hon.); FRCP; Secretary, British Medical Association, since 1932; *b* 14 Nov. 1879; *s* of Rev. K. C. Anderson and Robina Fisher; *m* Elizabeth Alexa Gray; no *c*. *Educ:* Edinburgh University. Engaged in general practice in Denbeath, Methil, Fife, 1906–19; War service in Egypt and Palestine during 1917, 1918, and 1919; Deputy Medical Secretary of the British Medical Association, 1919. *Publications:* several publications in medical journals on medico-political and medico-sociological subjects. *Recreation:* golf. *Address:* BMA House, Tavistock Square, WC1. *TA:* Medisecra, Westcent, London. *T:* Euston 2111. *Clubs:* Savile, Sandy Lodge Golf.

Died 1 Jan. 1944.

ANDERSON, George Knox; JP, DL, Kent; *b* 1854; *m* 1883, Mary Ada, *d* of John T. Prall, Rochester; one *s* one *d*. MP (U) Canterbury in 1918; member of Church Assembly, Diocese of Canterbury, and member of Central Board Church Finance, 1920–30; Hon. Treasurer Canterbury Diocesan Board of Finance, 1915–38. *Address:* Bridge Hill House, near Canterbury. *T:* Bridge 206.

Died 19 March 1941.

ANDERSON, Lt-Col Guy Willoughby, CIE 1936; *b* 3 April 1885. *Educ:* Clifton College; RMC Sandhurst. Commissioned 1904; entered Indian Army, 1905; Capt. 1913; Major, 1919; Lt-Col 1930; retired, 1936; re-employed 1940 and served 1940–44, as Comdt POW Camp, India; retired, 1944, on appointment Chief Inspector Customs, Baluchistan; resigned post 1946. *Club:* Naval and Military.

Died 20 May 1949.

ANDERSON, Col James Dalgliesh, CBE 1919; DSO 1916; AG (Section 2) DHQ Union Defence Force; *b* Dumfriesshire, Scotland, 1877; *m* Sybil Grey Celliers, Pretoria; two *s* one *d*. 2nd Lieut 4th Bn Scottish Rifles, 1899–1901; Lieut acting SO Transport to General Walter Kitchener's Force, 1901–02; Capt. (Reserve of Officers) ADT Repatriation, Transvaal, 1902–08; Major ADT German South-West Africa, 1914–15 (despatches, DSO); Supervisory Board. Remounts DHQ, Pretoria, 1916; Lieut-Col, OC Cape Auxiliary Transport, France, 1917; Assistant Director of Transport, GHQ, France, 1918–19 (despatches, CBE); Supervisory Board Remounts, GHQ, UDF, 1940; President Permanent Court Martial, GHQ, 1941; Comptroller of the Household, Government House, Pretoria, 1942. *Address:* Byanston Drive, Byanston, Johannesburg. *Clubs:* Rand, Turf, Inanda Polo, Johannesburg; Pretoria, Pretoria.

Died 21 Nov. 1947.

ANDERSON, Hon. James Thomas Milton; acting Superintendent, School for the Deaf, Saskatoon, Sask; *b* Fairbank, Ontario, 23 July 1878; *s* of James and Mary Anderson; *m* 1911, Edith Redgwick, Grenfell, Saskatchewan; one *s* one *d*. *Educ:* Fairbank, Ontario, Public School; Humberside Collegiate, West Toronto, Ont BA (1911, Silver Medallist Classics, Manitoba University); MA (Man); LLD (Man); D. Pæd. (Toronto). Taught public schools in Ontario and Manitoba; Principal, Grenfell (Sask) continuation school, 1910–11; school inspector, Saskatchewan, 1911; supt education among non-English in Sask, 1918–24; resigned and was leader Conservative party, 1924–36; elected to Legislature, 1925 and 1929; Premier of Saskatchewan, Minister of Education and Minister of Natural Resources, 1929–34. *Publications:* Canadian Immigration and its Problems; The Education of the New Canadian; also educational and political treatises. *Recreation:* golf. *Address:* 847 Temperance Street, Saskatoon, Saskatchewan, Canada. *Clubs:* Masonic, Orangeman, Saskatoon.

Died 29 Dec. 1946.

ANDERSON, Most Rev. John George, Hon. DD; Archbishop of Moosonee and Metropolitan of Ontario since 1940; *b* Orkney, 23 March 1866; *s* of William and Nancy Anderson; *m* 1889, Annie Violetta, *d* of John Kirkland, FEIS; five *s* two *d*. *Educ:* St Andrews School; St John's College, Winnipeg; BA, LLD Manitoba University. Ordained, 1889; CMS Missionary, Long Sault, 1888; Lac Seul, 1889; Incumbent of St Peter's, Manitoba, 1890–1909; Rural Dean of Lisgar, 1899–1909; Bishop of Moosonee, 1909–40; Member of Revision Committee of McKay Memorial Cree Dictionary, 1938. *Address:* Cochrane, Ontario, Canada.

Died 15 June 1943.

ANDERSON, John Hubback, CMG 1919; CBE 1918; ED; MD; FRACP; JP; Physician, Ruthin Castle; *b* Urana, NSW, 20 Aug. 1883; *s* of late Dr J. F. Anderson, Maloa, Woodend, Victoria; *m* 1919, Ruby Clare (*d* 1937), 2nd *d* of late H. C. Moffatt, of Goodrich Court, Ross, and Hamptworth Lodge, Salisbury; one *s* one *d*. *Educ:* Longford Gram. Sch., Tasmania; Ormond Coll., Univ. of Melbourne. MB, BS, 1908; MD 1910. Senior Demonstrator in Anatomy, Univ. of Melbourne, 1909–11 and 1920–23; Hon. Out-Patient Physician, St Vincent's Hospital, Melbourne, 1911; in private practice Benalla, Victoria, 1914; enlisted AIF Sept. 1914; served Gallipoli, Egypt, France, in various positions (despatches twice). Colonel AAMC and ADGMS, Australian Army Staff, London, 1940–46. *Publications:* various papers to scientific journals. *Recreation:* gardening. *Address:* Bryncelyn, Ruthin, N Wales. *Club:* Naval and Military.

Died 4 Nov. 1950.

ANDERSON, Sir Kenneth (Skelton), 1st Bt *cr* 1919; KCMG 1909; a Manager of Orient Steam Navigation Company; Director of Anderson, Green & Co., shipowners; *b* 21 Dec. 1866; *s* of late James Anderson,

Hilton, Aberdeen; *m* 1894, Louisa Mary, *d* of late J. C. Stevenson, Eltham Court, Kent. *Educ:* Harrow; New Coll., Oxford. Was a representative of British Shipowners at Imperial Navigation Conference, 1907; member of Departmental Committee on Royal College of Art, 1910, of Advisory Committee for Education in Art, and of Departmental Committee on Inshore Fisheries, 1913; Chairman General Shipowners Society, 1913; President Chamber of Shipping of the United Kingdom, 1915; member of Committee on Detention of Neutral Ships, 1916, of Committee on National Scheme of Training for Sea Service, 1918, of Food Investigation Board, 1918, of Shipping Control Committee during the War, and of Imperial Shipping Committee. *Heir:* none. *Address:* The Yair, by Galashiels, Selkirkshire. *T:* Clovenfords 12. *Club:* City of London.

Died 9 Dec. 1942.

ANDERSON, Maj.-Gen. Louis Edward, CB 1913; retired; *b* 27 March 1861; *e s* of late Louis John Anderson, DI, Royal Irish Constabulary, and *g s* of late Louis Anderson, CI, Royal Irish Constabulary; *m* 1888, Emily, *o d* of Henry Fisher, Liverpool; two *s* one *d*. *Educ:* Dundal. Entered army, 1884; Major, 1896; Lt-Col 1900; Colonel, 1908; Major-General, 1912; retired, 1920; served in Nile Expedition, 1884–85, also Suakim, 1885 (medal with 2 clasps, Khedive's star); North-West Frontier, India, 1897–98 (medal with clasp); South African War, Defence of Mafeking (in Protectorate Regt), etc. (Despatches, promoted Lt-Col, Queen's medal 2 clasps; King's medal with 2 clasps, CB); European War (medal). *Recreations:* shooting and fishing. *Address:* 33 De Vere Gardens, Kensington, W8. *Club:* Junior Army and Navy.

Died 30 Dec. 1941.

ANDERSON, Louisa Garrett, CBE 1917; MD, BS London; Fellow Royal Society of Medicine; *b* 28 July 1873; *d* of late James George Skelton Anderson, Shipowner, and late Elizabeth Garrett Anderson, MD; unmarried. *Educ:* St Leonard's School, St Andrews; The London (Royal Free Hospital) School of Medicine for Women. Engaged in private practice and hospital work until the outbreak of war; in Sept. 1914 went to France as Joint-Organiser of and Chief Surgeon to the Women's Hospital Corps, Voluntary Unit; Chief Surgeon Military Hosp., Endell Street, London WC, 1915–18; JP Bucks. *Publications:* Elizabeth Garrett Anderson, 1939; contributions to medical literature. *Address:* Paul End, Penn, Bucks.

Died 15 Nov. 1943.

ANDERSON, Maj.-Gen. Nelson Graham, CB 1918; CMG 1916; DSO 1900; late RASC; psc; late Royal Sussex Regiment; *b* 14 Sept. 1875; *y s* of late Maj.-Gen. R. P. Anderson; *m* 1914, Fanny, *y d* of late William Scott of Hampden House, Ibrox, NB, and *widow* of H. Herbert Harley. Entered Army, 1896; Captain, 1901; Major, 1912; Lt-Col 1917; Col 1917; Maj.-Gen. 1924; served South Africa (DSO, despatches, Queen's medal five clasps, King's medal two clasps); served in Zakka Khel Expedition, 1908 (medal and clasp); on special service in Somaliland, 1908–10, as Assistant Director of Supplies, Transport, and Ordnance (despatches thrice, general service medal and clasp); European War, 1914–18, as DAA and QMG, AA and QMG, AQMG and DA and QMG (temp. Brig.-Gen. Aug. 1916) (despatches eight times, Bt Lt-Col and Col, CMG, CB, Officer Legion of Honour, Commander Crown of Roumania); Assistant Director of Supplies and Transport, 1921–24; ADC to the King, 1922–24; DQMG Staff College, 1919–21; retired pay, 1927.

Died 4 July 1945.

ANDERSON, Air Vice-Marshal Norman Russel, CB 1944. Royal Canadian Air Force; late Deputy AOC-in-C, RCAF Oversea.

Died 31 July 1948.

ANDERSON, Sir Robert Albert, Kt 1934; CMG 1930; Chairman of Nestle and Anglo-Swiss Condensed Milk Co. (Australasia) Ltd since 1934; Chairman of New Zealand Milk Products, Ltd; Managing Director of J. G. Ward & Co., Ltd; a Director of New Zealand Shipping Co. (Chairman since 1941), and New Zealand Insurance Co. Ltd; *b* Queenstown, New Zealand, 26 Sept. 1866; *s* of Robert Anderson, Glasgow; *m* 1888, Elizabeth Maria, *d* of Peter Walker, Invercargill, New Zealand; two *s* two *d*. *Address:* Victoria Park, Waikiwi, via Invercargill, New Zealand.

Died 14 Oct. 1942.

ANDERSON, Maj. Robert Grenville G.; *see* Gayer-Anderson.

ANDERSON, Brig.-Gen. Sir Robert Murray McCheyne, KCMG 1917; CMG 1917; *b* Sydney, 6 Aug. 1867; *m* 1892, Jean Cairns (*d* 1928), *d* of R. Amos, Sydney; three *s* four *d*. *Educ:* Sydney Grammar School. Served in Bank of New Zealand, 1882–97; City Treasurer and afterwards Town Clerk, Sydney, 1897–1900; Timber and Shipping, 1901–14; Royal Commissioner—Australian Sugar Industry, Australian Postal Services, New Zealand War Expenditure; War Service Australian Imperial Force, Egypt (Order of the Nile, 2nd Class) and Europe. *Address:* 181 Clarence Street, Sydney, NSW. *Clubs:* Union, Sydney.

Died 30 Dec. 1940.

ANDERSON, Rt Hon. Sir Robert (Newton), PC (NI) 1927; Kt 1918; *b* 8 Dec. 1871; *s* of late James Anderson, Gortecar House, Co. Fermanagh; *m* 1903, Lydia Elizabeth Smith, *d* of Henry Elliott Smith and Isobel Smith, Fitzwilliam Street, Dublin; two *s* two *d*. *Educ:* privately. Hosiery manufacturer, City of Derry; Mayor of Londonderry, 1915–19; Deputy Lieutenant for City of Derry; MP for County and City of Derry, Northern Parliament, 1921–29; Member Irish Convention; Member Derry Bridge Commissioners, and other local Boards. *Recreations:* fishing and shooting. *Address:* Deanfield House, Londonderry. *TA:* Sir Robert Anderson, Londonderry. *T:* 2405. *Clubs:* Northern Counties, Derry; Ulster Reform, Belfast.

Died 23 May 1948.

ANDERSON, Col Rowland James Percy, CMG 1918; DSO 1900; late 11th Hussars; *b* 12 July 1873; *s* of late Sir H. Percy Anderson, KCB, KCMG, and Fanny, *d* of William Cuthbert, Beaufront Castle, Hexham; *m* 1st, 1914, Phyllis, *o d* of T. Stanley Chappell, Chadshunt, Warwick; one *d*; 2nd, 1924, Kathleen Crawshay-Williams (*d* 1949), *d* of William Rome. Served North-West Frontier, 1897–98 (medal with clasp); Uganda, 1898–1900 (medal with clasp); S Africa, 1900–02 (despatches twice, two medals, DSO); European War, 1914–18 (wounded, despatches twice, CMG); Commander of the Crown of Roumania, 1920; retired pay, 1922. *Address:* Edgehill, Hadleigh, Suffolk. *T:* Hadleigh 29. *Club:* Cavalry.

Died 20 March 1950.

ANDERSON, Rupert Darnley, OBE 1918; DL Surrey; JP Surrey and Staffordshire; *b* 1859; *s* of Thomas Darnley Anderson, JP, and Dorothy Anderson; *m* 1889, Amy Douglas Knyveton Harland, OBE, *d* of Rev. Edward Harland, Bishton Hall, Colwich, Prebendary of Lichfield and Vicar of Colwich, Staffs; one *s* four *d*. *Educ:* Eton; Cambridge. Served as Major, 1914–19, Territorial Army and RAF. *Address:* Waverley Abbey, Farnham, Surrey. *T:* Farnham 5138. *Club:* MCC.

Died 23 Dec. 1944.

ANDERSON, Sherwood; novelist; two *s* one *d*. *Publications:* Windy McPherson's Son; Marching Men; Winesburg Ohio; Mid-American Chants; Poor White; Triumph of the Egg; Many Marriages; Horses and Men; Story Teller's Story; Dark Laughter; Sherwood Anderson's Notebook; A New Testament; Hello Towns; Perhaps Women; The Modern Writer; Beyond

Desire; Death in the Woods; No Swank; Puzzled America; Kit Brandon, a novel; Plays—by Sherwood Anderson. *Address:* Troutdale, Va, USA.

Died 8 March 1941.

ANDERSON, Col William, CB 1936; DSO 1917; MC; DL; JP; member of the firm of Anderson & Garland, valuers, Newcastle-upon-Tyne; President Auctioneers and Estate Agents' Institute, 1933; *b* 11 April 1886; *s* of James Verty Anderson, of Whorlton Hall, Newcastle, and Bridge End, Hexham, and Ann Elizabeth Oubridge; *m* 1914, Elizabeth Gladys, *d* of James T. Robb, JP, Hexham; two *s* two *d. Educ:* Royal Grammar School, Newcastle-upon-Tyne; Clarence School, Somerset. Served European War, 1914–18 (wounded, despatches, DSO, MC, Bt-Major; commanded the 149th (Northumberland) Infantry Brigade (TA), 1931–35; ADC (Additional) to the King, 1935. *Address:* Causey House, Gosforth, Northumberland.

Died 2 Jan. 1944.

ANDERSON, Brig.-Gen. William Christian, CMG 1916; late 1/1st King George's Own Gurkha Rifles (the Malaun Regt), Indian Army; *b* 20 Feb. 1867; 2nd *s* of late Lt-Gen. George G. Anderson; *m* 1906, Beryl Gertrude, *d* of late Col Alfred Borton. Entered Army (2nd Batt. HLI), 1888; 2nd Batt. 1st Gurkha Rifles, 1891; served Mohmand and Tirah, 1897–98 (medal with two clasps); S Africa, 1901–02 (Queen's medal 5 clasps); Somaliland, 1903–04 (medal); European War, 1914–17 (despatches twice, CMG, Bt-Col; Brigade Comdr; dangerously wounded; Russian medal of St Anne's); retired, 1920; JP Worcestershire. *Recreations:* shooting, etc. *Address:* Newcourt, Tenbury Wells, Worcestershire. *Club:* United Service.

Died 13 Sept. 1942.

ANDERSON, Lt-Col William Maurice, CIE 1919; MD, BS (London), DTM&H (Cantab); IMS, retired; *b* 1873; *s* of Rev. J. H. Anderson; *m* 1901, Mabel Elizabeth, *d* of J. Kale, Loughton, Essex; one *s. Educ:* Whitgift School; London Hospital. Entered IMS, 1901; served European War, 1914–19 (despatches twice, CIE); Chief Medical Officer, NW Frontier Province, 1920; Residency Surgeon, Hyderabad, 1924; retired, 1928. *Address:* Fenton, Fleet, Hants. *T:* Fleet 132.

Died 8 July 1946.

ANDERSON, William Thomas, CBE 1920; Director, Anglo-French Exploration Co., Apex (Trinidad) Oil Co., Messina (Transvaal) Development Co., and Tati Co., Ltd; *b* Shildon, Co. Durham, 26 Feb. 1872; *m* Sarah, *d* of late Robert Hornsey, Darlington; no *c. Educ:* Grammar School, Darlington. Mine manager, Transvaal; consulting engineer, Rand Mines group; superintending engineer, East Rand Proprietary Mines, 1911–17; during war Controller of Iron Ore Mines of Cumberland and Lancashire; Chief Labour Adviser Ministry of Munitions, 1919. *Address:* Glenrose, Box Hill, Dorking, Surrey. *T:* Dorking 2845.

Died 28 May 1948.

ANDERSSON, Lt-Col Sir C. Llewellyn, Kt 1922; OBE 1920; *b* 3 Aug. 1861; *e s* of Charles John Andersson, explorer, naturalist, and author of works on South-West Africa; *m* 1st, 1891; one *s*; 2nd, 1900, Josephine Eily (*d* 1939), *d* of John Curran; two *s*. Cape Civil Service, 1875–87; assisted Construction Telegraph Line Pietermaritzburg to Pretoria during Zulu War, 1879; Secretary to Special Commissioner to Damaraland, 1880; Pioneer Johannesburg Witwatersrand, 1887; one of original Founders Wanderers' Club, Johannesburg; took active part in all South African sport and big-game shooting; Member Reform Committee, Jameson Raid, 1895–96; sentenced two years' imprisonment, commuted later to fine, £2000, etc.; served in DEOVR 1876–80; enlisted Basuto War, 1878; served South African War, 1899–1902; raised South African Light Horse; Captain, 1899; Lieut-Col 1902 (Queen's medal,

3 bars); served European War; commanded 8th North Staffords in France; wounded and prisoner of war, 1916–18; organised and commanded Civic Guards, Johannesburg, 1913–40; raised and commanded two Battalions Special Constables and appointed Acting Deputy Commissioner of Police. Revolution, Johannesburg, 1922. *Address:* Dolobran, Victoria Avenue, Parktown, Johannesburg. *Clubs:* Rand, Johannesburg.

Died 3 June 1948.

ANDERTON, Sir Francis Robert Ince, Kt 1923; *b* 1859; 2nd *s* of William Ince Anderton, JP, DL, of Euxton, Co. Lancaster, and Lady Emma Plunkett, *d* of 9th Earl of Fingall. *Educ:* Oratory School, Edgbaston; University of London, MA. Barrister-at-law, Lincoln's Inn, 1882; practised on the Northern Circuit; Alderman LCC 1910 and 1925–31; represented Hammersmith on the LCC, 1913–19, and South Hammersmith, 1919–25; Chairman, 1922–23; formerly JP County of London. *Address:* Castle Mead, Windsor. *Club:* Carlton.

Died 4 Jan. 1950.

ANDREW, Brig.-Gen. Albert William, CMG 1918; Indian Army, retired; *b* 29 March 1866; *s* of late John Richards Andrew, Christchurch, New Zealand. Joined Essex Regiment, 1886; ICS 1889; Captain Indian Army, 1897; Major, 1904; Lieut-Col 1912; served South Africa, 1901–02 (despatches, Bt-Major, Queen's medal 5 clasps); European War, 1914–18 (CMG, despatches); retired, 1920; Hon. Chief Commissioner, New Zealand Boy Scouts Association, 1922–29. *Address:* 6 Kidson Terrace, Cashmere Hills, Christchurch, S2, New Zealand.

Died 19 April 1941.

ANDREW, Alistair Hugh; Headmaster of Felsted School since 1943; *b* 9 Feb. 1908; 2nd *s* of Henry John Andrew; *m* 1939, Mary Winn, *d* of Rev. C. W. Wordsworth; two *d. Educ:* Marlborough; Trinity College, Cambridge. BA 1929; MA 1935. Asst Master and Housemaster, Felsted School, 1932–41; Flight-Lieutenant RAF, 1941–43. *Recreations:* travel, gardening. *Address:* Felsted School, Essex. *Club:* United University.

Died 15 Feb. 1947.

ANDREW, Engr Captain George Edward, CB 1916; RN, retired; *b* 3 Nov. 1869; *s* of Donald McDonald Andrew, of Swindon; *m* 1908, Evelyn Elizabeth (*d* 1927), *e d* of late J. M. Spink; two *s* one *d. Educ:* Swindon; Kaiser Friedrich Wilhelm Universität, Berlin. Trained as Mech. Engineer at the GWR Works, Swindon, and the Earles Shipbuilding Co., Hull; entered Navy as Assist Engineer, 1892; served in HM ships Pembroke, Trafalgar, Victorious, Pelorus, Resolution, Formidable, Chelmer; Admiralty Engineer-Overseer, Glasgow; HMS London; Admiralty Overseer Marine Turbine Works, Newcastle; Assist to Manager Engineering Dept, Devonport Dockyard; special service in Germany; HMS Boadicea, HMS Kent; 1st Assistant to Engineer-Manager and Acting Engineer-Manager, HM dockyard, Chatham, 1916–19; retired, 1919; served Falkland Islands Battle and at the destruction of SMS Dresden off Juan Fernandez (despatches, CB); MIMechE; MIStructE; FRSA. *Address:* Iona, Mitten Rd, Bembridge, IOW. *Clubs:* Malta Union; Mediterranean, Gibraltar.

Died 12 Nov. 1945.

ANDREWES, Rev. Canon Gerrard Thomas, MA Oxon; Hon. Canon of Winchester Cathedral; *b* 1855; *s* of Rev. W. G. Andrewes, Master of St Cross, Winchester; *m* Helen L. (*d* 1936), *d* of T. F. Kirby, Bursar of Winchester College; two *s* one *d. Educ:* Eton; Merton College, Oxford. Curate, Holy Trinity, Gray's Inn Road, Isleworth, Highfield, Southampton; Rector of Chilcomb, Winchester, 1891–1931. *Address:* 1 Beaufort Road, Winchester. *T:* Winchester 442.

Died 6 Feb. 1941.

ANDREWS, Charles M'Lean, AM, PhD, LHD (Trinity, 1905), LLD (Lehigh, 1934, Johns Hopkins University, 1939), LittD (Yale, 1935, Harvard, 1936); Farnam Professor of American History, Emeritus, Yale University; *b* Wethersfield, Connecticut, 22 Feb. 1863; *s* of Rev. W. W. Andrews and Elizabeth Williams, both of New England (Puritan) stock; *m* 1895, Evangeline Holcombe Walker of Washington, DC; one *s* one *d*. *Educ:* Trinity College, Hartford, Conn; Johns Hopkins University. Associate, Associate Professor, and Professor of History, Bryn Mawr College, 1889–1907; Professor of History, Johns Hopkins University, 1907–10; Farnam Professor of American History, Yale University, 1910–31; Director of Historical Publications, Yale University, 1931–33; Member, American Academy, 1937, National Institute of Arts and Letters (gold medallist, 1937); American Historical Association (on Executive Council, 1905–08; Acting President, 1924; Pres., 1925); Member numerous American and foreign historical societies; Member Public Archives Commission, 1901–15; Member Committee on Documentary Publications, US Government, 1907–08 and 1922–29; Member Department of Historical Records, Connecticut, since 1918; Chairman, Committee on Transcripts from Foreign Archives, Library of Congress, 1905–28; Special Lecturer, University of Helsingfors, 1911, Universities of Chicago, Iowa, Michigan, Wisconsin, 1921, New York Univ., 1933, William and Mary College, 1938; Editor Yale Historical Publications, 1912–33. *Publications:* Old English Manor, 1892; Historical Development of Modern Europe, 1896–1898; Contemporary Europe, Asia, and Africa, 1902; History of England for Schools and Colleges, 1903; Colonial Self-Government (American Nation Series, V), 1904; British Committees, Commissions, and Councils, 1622–1675, 1908; Short History of England, 1912; The Colonial Period of American History, 1912; Guide to American Materials in British Archives, three vols, 1908–1914; Fathers of New England and Colonial Folkways in Chronicles of America Series, 1919; The Colonial Background of the American Revolution, 1924, 2nd ed. 1931; contributions to Cambridge History of British Empire, 1929; Our Earliest Colonial Settlements, 1933; The Colonial Period of American History, I, 1934 (Pulitzer Prize), II, 1936; III, 1937; IV, 1938; editor (in collaboration), Journal of a Lady of Quality, 1921, 3rd ed., 1939; Old Houses of Connecticut, 1923; Jonathan Dickinson, God's Protecting Providence, 1944. *Recreations:* travel, tramping, country life. *Address:* 424 St Ronan Street, New Haven, Conn; (Jan.-April), Jupiter, Fla; (June-Sept.), East Dover, Vermont, USA. *Clubs:* Authors'; Graduates, Elizabethan, New Haven.
Died 9 Sept. 1943.

ANDREWS, Ernest Clayton; Associate Editor, Economic Geology; *b* 18 Oct. 1870; *m* 1st 1909, Florence A. Wynne Byron (decd); *m* 2nd 1929, Mabel Agnes Smith. *Educ:* Sydney Univ., BA (Mathematics). Government Geologist, New South Wales, 1920–31; retired 1931; Silliman Lecturer, Yale, 1927; Hon. Member: Washington Academy of Sciences; Royal Society, New Zealand; Sierra Club, California. Pres. Aust. and NZ Assoc. for Advancement of Science, Brisbane meeting, 1929–30; Pres. Australasian Inst. Mining and Metallurgy, 1929; President Royal Society, NS Wales, 1921; President Linnean Society, NS Wales, 1937; Leader Commonwealth Delegation to Pacific Science Congresses, Java, 1929, Canada, 1933, California, 1939; Trustee, Australian Museum, 1924–48; David Syme Prize and Medal for Scientific Research Melbourne, 1915; Clarke Memorial Medal Royal Soc., NSW, 1928; Lyell Medal Geol. Soc., London, 1931; Mueller Memorial Medal, Aust. and NZ, Association for Advancement of Science, 1946. *Publications:* Carrasion by Gravity Streams, 1909; Geol. graphic Unity of Eastern Australia, 1911; Evolution of the Australian Flowering Plants, 1916 Broken Hill Memoir, and

Supplement, 1922–1923; Some Major Problems of Structural Geology, 1938; The Increasing Purpose, 1939; Origin of floras of Inner Pacific, 1939; The Eternal Goodness, 1948. *Recreations:* mountain climbing (first ascent Mount Darwin (13,900 ft), Californian Sierra, August 1908); music. *Address:* 4 Kuring-gai, 241 Old South Head Road, Bondi, Sydney, NSW. *T:* FW 3154.
Died 1 July 1948.

ANDREWS, Captain Francis Arthur Lavington, CBE 1918; RN, retired; *b* 1869. King's Harbourmaster, Malta, 1912–19; retired list, 1923. *Club:* United Service.
Died 30 Dec. 1944.

ANDREWS, Henry Russell, MD, BS Lond., FRCP, FRCOG; Consulting Obstetric Physician, London Hospital; Consulting Gynæcologist to the Ilford Emergency Hospital and Bushey Heath Cottage Hospital; late Vice-President British College of Obstetricians and Gynæcologists; late President of the Obstetric and Gynæcological Section of the Royal Society of Medicine; late Examiner in Obstetric Medicine to Cambridge University; late Examiner in Obstetric Medicine to the London University, Oxford University, the Conjoint Board, Durham University, and the Society of Apothecaries; *b* 13 Sept. 1871; *s* of Rev. John Marshall Andrews, late Vicar of Highgate; *m* 1914, Margaret Dorothea, 2nd *d* of Walter Reynolds, Hawk's Wick, St Albans, Herts. *Educ:* Merchant Taylors' School; London Hospital; Berlin and Vienna. *Publications:* Midwifery for Nurses, 1906; (joint) Midwifery, 1916, and Diseases of Women, 1919; contributions to medical journals. *Recreations:* fishing, shooting. *Address:* The Manor House, Iford, near Lewes, Sussex. *T:* Lewes 388.
Died 7 May 1942.

ANGELL, James Rowland, LittD University Vermont; Hon. PhD Rensselaer Polytechnic Institute; LLD Yale, Harvard, Princeton, Columbia, Chicago, Union, Cincinnati, McGill, Brown, Middlebury, Illinois College, Wesleyan (Conn), Michigan, Wabash, California, New York University, Dartmouth College, Williams, Rutgers, Pennsylvania, Pennsylvania Military College; *b* Burlington, Vt, 8 May 1869; *s* of Dr James Burrill Angell, Pres. of the University of Michigan, and Sarah S., *d* of President Caswell, of Brown University; *m* 1st, 1894, Marion Isabel Watrous (*d* 1931), Des Moines, Iowa; one *s* one *d*; 2nd, 1932, Mrs Katharine Cramer Woodman. *Educ:* AB, 1890; AM, 1891, University of Mich; AM, Harvard, 1892; University of Berlin and University of Halle, 1893; studied Vienna, Paris, Leipzig. Instructor in Philosophy, University of Minnesota, 1893; Assistant Professor Psychology and Director Psychological Laboratory, 1894–1901; Associate Professor, 1901–05; Professor and Head of Department, 1905–19; Senior Dean, 1908–11; Dean of University Faculties, 1911–19; acting President, 1918–19, University of Chicago; Exchange Professor The Sorbonne, Paris, 1914; Member Psychology Committee of National Research Council; Member Committee of the Adjutant-General's office on Classification of Personnel in the Army, 1917–18; Advisory Member Committee on Education and Special Training, 1918; Chairman, National Research Council, 1919–20; President, Carnegie Corporation, 1920–21; President Yale University, 1921–37; Ex-President, University of Chicago Settlement; member American Philosophical Society; member National Academy of Sciences; member American Psychological Association (Pres. 1906); FAAS; Officier de l'Ordre National de la Légion d'Honneur, France; Grand Officer of the Order of the Crown of Italy; Blue Grand Cordon of the Order of the Jade, China; Conn Society of the Cincinnati (Hon.); Vice-President National Committee for Mental Hygiene and Vice-President International Committee; Director New York Life Insurance Co.; Public Service Counsellor of the National Broadcasting Company since 1937, and Member of Board of Directors; Member

Board of Trustees American Museum Natural History, 1937; Gold Medal of National Institute of Social Sciences, 1937; Member Board of Trustees, Museum of Science and Industry, 1940; Pres. English-Speaking Union of the USA; Curator of Stephens College; Director Hall of Fame. *Publications:* Psychology, 1904; 4th ed., revised, 1908; Chapters from Modern Psychology, 1911; Introduction to Psychology, 1913; American Education, 1937; Editor, Psychological Monographs, 1912–1922; and numerous scientific articles. *Address:* 155 Blake Road, New Haven, Conn. *T:* 5–1556. *Clubs:* Cosmos (Washington); Century, Yale (New York); University (Chicago); Yale, University (Boston); Graduates (New Haven).

Died 4 March 1949.

ANGLESEY, 6th Marquess of, *cr* 1815; **Charles Henry Alexander Paget,** GCVO 1928; Baron Paget, of Beau Desert, 1549; Earl of Uxbridge, 1784; Bt 1730; late Capt. Royal Horse Guards; Lord Chamberlain to Queen Mary since 1922; HM Lieut for County of Anglesey since 1942; *b* 14 April 1885; *e s* of late Lord Alexander Victor Paget, DL, and late Hon. Hester Alice Stapleton-Cotton, 2nd *d* of 2nd Viscount Combermere; *S* cousin, 1905; *m* 1912, Lady Victoria Marjorie Harriet Manners, *d* of 8th Duke of Rutland; one *s* five *d. Educ:* Eton; RMC, Sandhurst. Commander of St John of Jerusalem; Order of the Nile, 4th Class; Grand Cross of Star of Italy and of Roumania; Grand Cross of Order of Ismail; Grand Cordon of Star of Ethiopia; Grand Cross of Star of Afghanistan; Commander of Legion of Honour. *Heir: s* Earl of Uxbridge. *Address:* Plâs-Newydd, Llanfair-Pwllgwyngyll, Anglesey. *Clubs:* Turf, Bachelors'; Royal Yacht Squadron, Cowes.

Died 21 Feb. 1947.

ANGUS, J. Mortimer, MA (Cantab), LLD Hon. (Wales); late Registrar, University of Wales; *b* 1850; 2nd *s* of Rev. Joseph Angus, DD; *m* 1882, Mabel Septima (*d* 1942), *d* of Henry M. Harris, Plymouth; four *s* two *d. Educ:* City of London School; Clare College, Cambridge; MA, 1876. Prof. of Latin and Comparative Philology, Univ. Coll. of Wales, Aberystwyth, 1873–1905. *Address:* 67 Hawthorn Rd, Kettering.

Died 23 Feb. 1945.

ANGUS, Rev. Samuel, MA, DD, DLit Queen's University, Belfast, 1923; DD Glasgow, 1924; DD Queen's University, 1929; PhD Princeton; Professor of New Testament and Historical Theology in St Andrew's College, New South Wales; *b* Ireland, 27 Aug. 1881; *m* 1907, Katharine Walker Duryea (*d* 1934), New York; no *c. Educ:* University College, Galway; R. University of Ireland; Princeton University and Theological Seminary; University, Marburg; University, Berlin; and University, Edinburgh; First Classical Honours, RUI. Lecturer on Hellenistic Greek, Hartford Theological Seminary, 1906–10; Gay Lecturer, S Baptist Theological Seminary, Louisville, 1912; Norton Lecturer, 1920; Classical Lecturer, Chatauqua College, New York, 1906; Chaplain Scotch Church, Algiers, 1912–13; Acting-Professor of NT Interpretation, and Elliot Lecturer, Western Theological Seminary, Pittsburgh, USA, 1920; Earle Lecturer, Pacific School of Religion, Berkeley, California, 1925–29; Visiting Professor of Education, Columbia University, New York, 1929–31; member of Berliner Neutestamentliche Gesellschaft, and Society of Biblical Literature (US). *Publications:* Sources of first ten books of Augustine's De Civitate Dei, 1906; The Environment of Early Christianity, 1914; The Mystery-Religions and Christianity, 1925; The Religious Quests of the Graeco-Roman World, 1929; Jesus in the Lives of Men, 1933; Christianity and Dogma, 1933; Religion in National Life, 1933; Truth and Tradition, 1934; The Auld Sinner, 1938; Essential Christianity, 1939; Man and

the New Order, 1941; Alms for Oblivion: Chapters from a Heretic's Life, 1943; articles in Temple Dictionary of the Bible, New International Encyclopædia, Hastings' Encyclopædia of Religion, etc. *Recreation:* golf. *Address:* St Andrew's College, Sydney, NSW. *Clubs:* Royal Societies; Canterbury, Princeton.

Died 17 Nov. 1943.

ANGWIN, Hugh Thomas Moffitt, CMG 1944; BE; MInstCE; MIEAust; FSASM; Engineer-in-Chief, Engineering and Water Supply Department, since 1936; Commissioner, South Australian Harbours Board, since 1935; Chairman, Electricity Trust of South Australia, since 1946; *b* 8 Oct. 1888; *s* of Rev. Thomas Britton Angwin, MA; *m* 1928, Edna, *d* of J. S. Turnbull, Renmark, S Australia; two *d. Educ:* Prince Alfred College, Adelaide; Adelaide University. 15 years associated with construction of Locks, Weirs, and Storages on the River Murray. Engineer for Water Supply, 1929; Chief Engineer SA Harbour Board, 1930–35. *Address:* 5 Lebanon Avenue, Glenunga, South Australia.

Died 12 Sept. 1949.

ANGWIN, Hon. William Charles, CMG 1933; JP; Chairman, Trustees Rural Relief Fund, WA, since 1936; *b* St Just, Cornwall, 8 May 1863; *s* of Benjamin Angwin, grocer, and Mary Angwin; *m* 1884, Sarah Ann, *d* of Jacob Sumpton, Hensingham, Cumberland; one *s* one *d. Educ:* Wesleyan School, St Just. Migrated to Victoria, Australia, 1886; Western Australia, 1892; resided continuously at East Fremantle; Member in the first Municipal Council of that town, 1897–1927; Mayor three years, and Treasurer twenty years; representative of the East Fremantle District to the Legislative Assembly, 1904; Hon. Minister and Member Executive Council, 1904–05; Hon. Minister controlling Health, Charities and Migration, and Member Executive Council, 1911–14; Minister for Public Works and Industries, 1914–16; Minister for Lands, Industries and Migration, 1924–27; Agent-General for Western Australia, 1927–33; Deputy Premier, 1925; Member of the Fremantle Municipal District Tramway and Electric Lighting Board, 1910–26; Member, Fremantle Harbour Trust, 1934–36. *Address:* East Fremantle, Western Australia.

Died 9 June 1944.

ANLEY, Col Henry Augustus, CB 1917; late RAOC; *b* 20 Nov. 1864; *e s* of late Capt. H. T. Anley, The Buffs; *m* 1891, Agnes Pauline, *d* of late Capt. W. P. Bridson, King's Own Regt; three *d.* Joined E Surrey Regt 1885; Capt. 1894; Major, 1904; Lt-Col 1905; Col 1913; served East Africa, 1903 (medal with clasp); Assistant Director War Office, 1911–18; retired pay, 1919. *Address:* Green Gates, Totland Bay, IW.

Died 16 Nov. 1942.

ANSELL, John; musical director; *b* 26 March 1874. *Educ:* Guildhall School of Music. Studied composition under the late Hamish McCunn. Was Musical Director at the Alhambra Theatre, 1913–20, at the Playhouse with Mr Cyril Maude; composed the incidental music to all his productions during that period; was at the Winter Garden Theatre for nearly seven years and afterwards four and a half years at the BBC, Savoy Hill, which he resigned in 1930; has composed several Comic Operas, including Violette, 1918; orchestral works, songs, etc. *Publications:* Overtures: Plymouth Hoe, Overture to an Irish Comedy, John and Sam, etc.; Suites: Danses Miniatures de Ballet, Three Irish Dances, Three Irish Pictures, etc. *Address:* St Elmo, Dedmere Rise, Marlow, Bucks. *Club:* Savage.

Died 14 Dec. 1948.

ANSON, Captain Hon. Alfred; *b* 1876; *y s* of 2nd Earl of Lichfield; *m* 1912, Lela, *widow* of John J. Emery of New York. *Educ:* Harrow. Late Captain Sussex Yeomanry. Served European War, 1914–19. *Address:* 5 East 68th Street, New York. *Clubs:* Turf, White's, Marlborough; Jockey, Paris; Knickerbocker, New York.

Died March 1944.

ANSON, Hon. Claud; JP, DL; *b* 11 Jan. 1864; 5th *s* of 2nd Earl of Lichfield and Lady Harriet Georgiana Louisa, *e d* of 1st Duke of Abercorn, KG; *m* 1901, Lady Clodagh De La Poer Beresford, *y d* of 6th Marquis of Waterford, KP; two *s* one *d*. *Educ:* Harrow. Vice-Lieutenant of County Waterford. *Address:* Ballyin, Lismore, Co. Waterford.

Died 25 Dec. 1947.

ANSON, Lt-Col Hon. Sir George Augustus, KCB 1937; CBE 1925; MVO 1907; DL; *b* 22 Dec. 1857; 2nd *s* of 2nd Earl of Lichfield; *m* 1884, Blanche (*d* 1941), *d* of late G. Miller of Brentry, Gloucester; one *s*. *Educ:* Harrow; RM Academy, Woolwich. Late RA; Chief Constable Staffordshire, 1888–1929; Lt-Col 3rd North Mid. Field Artillery Brigade, 1915–16; Chairman Staffordshire Territorial Force Association, 1922–37. *Club:* Naval and Military.

Died 25 May 1947.

ANTHONY, Henry Montesquieu, CBE 1926; *b* 1873; *m* 1914, Dorothy, 3rd *d* of late Sir Francis Elliot, GCMG, GCVO; one *d*. *Educ:* Clifton College; Lincoln College, Oxford. Entered the service of the Egyptian Government, 1896; Director General, Egyptian State Domains Administration 1916–32; retired 1932; 2nd Class Order of Medjidieh, 1912; 2nd Class Order of the Nile, 1917; Grand Officer, Order of Ismail, 1933; was for many years Member of Council of Royal Egyptian Agricultural Society, and one of the Egyptian Representatives on the International Cotton Committee. *Recreations:* sailing and motoring. *Address:* Matarieh, nr Cairo, Egypt. *Clubs:* Turf (Cairo); Union (Alexandria).

Died 8 May 1949.

ANTHONY, Philip Arnold, CMG 1918; MInstCE; Consulting Civil Engineer; *b* 1873; *m*; two *d*. *Educ:* Mill Hill School. Engineering Department, Great Western Railway, 1894–1910; General Manager and Chief Engineer, Federated Malay States Railways, 1910–24; services lent by FMS Government to Ministry of Munitions, May 1915–Nov. 1916; appointed Royal Commission Enquiry Working and Management South Australian Railways, 1918; reported on Palestine railways, 1925. *Address:* Millmead, Oxford, Kent.

Died 16 July 1949.

ANTHONY, Maj.-Gen. William Samuel, CB 1930; CMG 1919; Colonel Comdt RAVC since 1934; *b* 1874; *m* 1919, Adelaide, *widow* of Lieut Douglas Cooper, RN; one *s* one *d*. Served NW Frontier of India, 1897–98 (medal and clasp); European War, 1914–19 (despatches, CMG, Bt Lt-Col); Director-General, Army Veterinary Services, 1929–33; retired pay, 1933. *Address:* 24 Rivermead Court, Hurlingham, SW6.

Died 15 Nov. 1943.

ANTROBUS, Dame Edith Marion, DBE 1927; Order of Elizabeth of Belgium, 1918; *b* 1862; *d* of John Park Robinson, Liverpool; *m* 1894, Sir Reginald Laurence Antrobus, KCMG, CB (*d* 1942); two *s* two *d*. *Educ:* privately; Germany. Hon. Sec. Overseas Nursing Assoc., 1919–41. *Address:* c/o National Provincial Bank, Ltd, 88 Cromwell Road, SW7.

Died 9 Sept. 1944.

ANTROBUS, Sir Reginald (Laurence), KCMG 1911; CB 1898; *b* St John's Withyham, Sussex, 5 Sept. 1853; *e s* of Rev. George Antrobus and Henrietta, *d* of Rev. Robert Gream; *m* 1st, 1880, Selina Jane (*d* 1890), *d* of Rev. A. Leighton Irwin; two *d*; *m* 2nd, 1894, Edith

Marion Robinson (Dame Edith Antrobus, DBE); two *s* two *d*. *Educ:* Winchester; New College, Oxford (Scholar, 1872); 1st class Moderations, Classics, 1874; 2nd class Final Classical School, 1876; BA 1876. Appointed, after the first open competitive exam., to be a clerk in Colonial Office, 1877. Asst private secretary to Earl of Kimberley, 1880–82; private secretary to 15th Earl of Derby, 1882–85; to Col Rt Hon. F. A. Stanley, MP (afterwards 16th Earl of Derby), 1885–86; to Earl Granville, 1886; acted as Governor of St Helena, 1889–90; Assistant Under-Secretary of State for the Colonies, 1898–1909; Senior Crown Agent for the Colonies, 1909–18. Created CB for services in connection with the negotiations with France relating to West Africa; Member of National Assembly of Church of England, 1920–25, and of Central Board of Finance, 1925–35; Gentleman Usher of the Blue Rod in the Order of St Michael and St George, 1920–35. *Address:* The Roman Villa, Twyford, Winchester.

Died 29 July 1942.

APPLETON, Prof. Arthur Beeny, MA, MD (Cantab); MRCS, LRCP, FZS; Emeritus Professor, University of London; Professor of Anatomy, Royal Academy of Arts; Hunterian Professor, Royal College of Surgeons, 1944; President, Anatomical Society of Great Britain and Ireland, 1947–49; University Representative on Gov. Body, Chelsea School of Physical Education, Eastbourne; Editorial Board, Acta Anatomica, Basel; *s* of Arthur John Appleton and Emily Amelia Beeny; *m* 1918, Eva Gertrude, *d* of Edward George Plewman and Martha Booth; one *s* one *d*. *Educ:* City of London School; Downing College, Cambridge; St Bartholomew's Hospital (Scholar). University Lecturer, Cambridge, 1926; Horton Smith MD Prize, Cambridge, 1922; Symington Prize Anatomical Research, 1923; Lieutenant and Captain, RAMC, 1914–19; Examiner to University of London; late Examiner in Universities of Liverpool, Manchester, Cardiff, and Cambridge; Fellow of Downing College, Cambridge, 1930. *Publications:* Guide to Vertebrate Dissection for Students of Anatomy, 1929; Surface and Radiological Anatomy, 1938, 3rd ed., 1949; Ductless Glands, in Cunningham's Text-Book of Anatomy, 1949; Physique, Body Build and Posture, in British Surgical Practice; papers on the locomotor apparatus, posture, the lungs, etc., in the Journal of Anatomy, Lancet, etc. *Recreation:* painting. *Address:* Institute of Animal Physiology, c/o ARC, 6A Dean's Yard, Westminster. *T:* Primrose 3333.

Died 22 April 1950.

APPLEYARD, Rollo, OBE; MInstCE, MInstEE; JP; Consulting Engineer; *b* 1 Jan. 1867; 2nd *s* of late Septimus Appleyard; *m* 1901, Mabel Laming, *d* of late Worthington Evans. *Educ:* Dulwich (old college); privately. Medal of Science and Art Dept, 1888; Telford Premium, Inst. CE 1903 and 1920. Royal Indian Engineering College Staff, 1885–92; technical adviser and writer on The Times, 1905–14; served in RNVR 1914–20; lent to Air Service to advise on aeronautical instruments, Feb. 1917; appointed to War Staff for Convoy Section, Sept. 1917; founded and directed the Technical History Section of the Admiralty, 1918; edited Convoy Instructions; invented the Conductometer for the measurement of electrical conductivity, and various aeronautical and other instruments; research work on dielectrics, alloys, thermometry, and surface-tension; discovered and tabulated the length-function for the solution of catenary problems. *Publications:* The Conductometer and Electrical Conductivity; Measurement of Air-Speed; Height Measurements by Barometer and Thermometer; The Elements of Convoy Defence in Submarine Warfare; Pioneers of Electrical Communication (awarded Hans Christian Oersted Medal of Copenhagen University, which was presented to him in 1927); A Tribute to Michael Faraday; Charles Parsons—his Life and Work; The History of the Institution of Electrical Engineers, 1871–1931;

contributions to the Fortnightly Review and The Times on naval and other subjects, and numerous papers in the Proceedings of the Physical Society. *Recreation:* golf. *Address:* 80 St Mary's Mansions, Paddington, W2. *T:* Paddington 0642. *Club:* Athenæum.

Died 1 March 1943.

APPLIN, Captain Arthur; novelist and dramatic author; (Hon.) Captain Royal Air Force; *y s* of Capt. V. J. Applin (late HM Legation, Japan, and RMT at Chelstone Manor, Torquay) and Agnes S. I. Ferriera of Chudleigh, Devonshire; *m* 1900, Edyth Olive, actress; no *c. Educ:* Torquay Public College, Newton Abbot. Read for the law, but at the age of twenty-two went on the stage, working under Ben Greet; afterwards played with George Alexander in John Chilcott, MP, and The Man of the Moment; with Charles Wyndham in Cyrano and Cyril Maude in the Black Tulip at Wyndham's and the Haymarket Theatre; with Fred Terry and Julia Neilson in Sweet Nell of Old Drury, etc.; produced Hauptmann's Hannele Scala Theatre for the Playactors' Society, and several other plays; in 1913 wrote the comedy Rags, produced by Louis Calvert at Court Theatre, The Masked Girl; and L'Amour et Le Mort, Ballet, Winter Garden Theatre, 1921; in 1914 war served in Royal Naval Air Service and Royal Flying Corps, and was the first aeronaut to do night flights in free balloons over England (Zeppelin raids); served with Fleet and in Egypt, 1915–16; was among the first hundred aeronauts to be granted the RA Club and FAI Certificate. *Publications:* A Life of Admiral Jellicoe; The Chorus Girl; The Butcher of Bruton Street; Le Collier de Perles; Stories of the Russian Ballet; Shop Girls; The Actress; Luxury Unlimited; The Death Mask, 1931; The Black Nail, 1932; Cold Cream, 1935; Picked Up; Sweeter than Honey; The Gay Adventure, 1939; She Asked for Adventure, 1940; Escape to Romance, 1941; Philandering Angler, 1948; produced Reading Historical Pageant, Torquay Historical Pageant, 1924; Brighton Pageant, 1925. *Recreation:* fishing. *Address:* 18 Addison Av., W11.

Died 10 Sept. 1949.

APPS, Engr Captain William Richard, MVO 1906; *b* 16 April 1862; *s* of late Charles Apps, Chichester; *m* 1885, Florence (*d* 1935), *d* of late T. Lidiard, Bath; two *d.* Assistant Engineer, 1883; Chief Engineer, 1895; Staff Engineer, 1899; Engineer Commander, 1899; Engineer Captain; retired, 1912; served West Coast Africa, 1894; South African War, 1899–1900 (medal); West Coast of Africa, 1901; Cape Colony, 1902; Eng. Comdr HMS Renown, visit of Prince and Princess of Wales to India, 1905–06 (MVO); Chief Engineer HM Naval Yard, Cape of Good Hope, 1908–11; Coronation Medal, 1911; served European War, 1916–17 (medal); formerly Member of Institution of Naval Architects. *Recreations:* archæology, horticulture. *Address:* Branksome, Chandler's Ford, Hants. *Clubs:* Royal Naval, Portsmouth.

Died 4 March 1947.

AP RHYS PRYCE, Gen. Sir Henry Edward, KCB 1932 (CB 1925); CMG 1915; DSO 1917; Indian Army, retired; Hon. Col 499th (London Welsh) Heavy AA Regt; *b* 30 Nov. 1874; *e s* of late Lieut-Col D. D. Pryce, Indian Army, of Penns Rocks, Withyham, Sussex; *m* Alice Louisa, *d* of R. F. H. Pughe, Assist Inspector General, Bengal Police; one *s* (and one killed in France, 1940). *Educ:* Trinity College, Glenalmond; RMC, Sandhurst. Entered Army, 1895; Captain, 1902; Major, 1913; Lt-Col 1916; Colonel, 1919; Major-Gen. 1925; Lieut-Gen. 1931; General, 1936; served Thibet, 1903–04 (medal); European War, 1914–18 (despatches seven times, CMG, Bt Lt-Col, Bt Col, DSO, Croix de Guerre Belge); Commandant, Senior Officers' School, Belgaum, 1920–24; Director Supplies and Transport, AHQ, India, 1925–29; GOC Presidency and Assam District, 1929–30; Deccan District, 1930–32; Master General of the Ordnance, India, 1934–38; ADC General

to the King, 1936–38; retired 1938; Col Comdt RIASC 1938–45. *Publication:* Transport Training Notes. *Recreations:* yachting, big game shooting, golf, tennis. *Address:* c/o Grindlay's Bank Ltd, 54 Parliament St, SW1. *Clubs:* United Service, Royal Empire Society, Overseas League.

Died 21 June 1950.

APSLEY, Lord; Allen Algernon Bathurst, DSO 1918; MC; TD; DL and JP County of Glos; MP (NC) Bristol Central since 1931; Lt-Col commanding 1st Royal Glos Hussars Royal Armoured Corps; President United Kingdom Pilots' Association since 1925; Director Western Airways; *b* 3 Aug. 1895; *e s* of 7th Earl Bathurst; *m* 1924, Viola (author with Lady Diana Shedden of To Whom the Goddess, 1932, and Bridleways through History, 1936), *er d* of late Capt. Bertram Meeking, 10th Hussars, and late Mrs Herbert Johnson, MBE, of Marsh Court, Stockbridge, Hants; two *s. Educ:* Eton; Christ Church, Oxford. Served European War, 1915–19 (DSO, MC); MP (U) Southampton, 1922–29; was Parliamentary Private Sec. (unpaid) to Parliamentary Sec. Overseas Trade Dept, Board of Trade, Dec. 1922–Jan. 1924; a Unionist; Parliamentary Private Sec. to Minister of Transport, Nov. 1925; Parliamentary Private Sec., Ministry for Co-ordination of Defence, 1936–39; JP, County of Gloucester; late Director, Morning Post. *Publication:* The Amateur Settlers, 1926. *Address:* Petty France, Badminton, Glos. *Club:* Bath.

Died 17 Dec. 1942.

ARBUTHNOT, Brig.-Gen. Sir Dalrymple, 5th Bt *cr* 1823; CMG 1915; DSO 1918; late RA; *b* 1 April 1867; 2nd *s* of 3rd Bt and Alice Margaret, *d* of Rev. M. C. Tompson, Vicar of Alderminster; *S brother* 1916; *m* 1918, Alice Maude, *d* of Hugh Arbuthnot; two *s.* Entered Army, 1886; Capt., 1896; Major, 1901; Lt-Col 1913; Staff Officer, S Africa, 1900; Assistant Staff Officer for Colonial Forces, 1902; served Chitral, 1895 (medal with clasp); S Africa, 1899–1902 (Queen's medal 3 clasps, King's medal 2 clasps); served European War, 1914–18 (despatches, Bt-Col, CMG, DSO); temp. Brig.-Gen. 1915; retired pay, 1920. *Heir: s* Robert Dalrymple, *b* 4 July 1919. *Address:* Nash Court, Ludlow, Salop. *Club:* Army and Navy.

Died 31 March 1941.

ARBUTHNOT, Captain Ernest Kennaway, DSO 1917; *b* 3 Sept. 1876; 2nd *s* of Major A. E. Arbuthnot, Madras Cavalry; *m* 1st, Evie Greene (*d* 1917); 2nd, Gladys, 2nd *d* of W. B. Mann, of Downe, Broadhempston, S Devon; two *s. Educ:* HMS Britannia. Joined Royal Navy as Cadet, 1890; awarded Bronze Medal Royal Humane Society, 1897; Lieut 1898; retired, 1911; joined Devon Constabulary, 1914; rejoined Navy, 1914; took part in Battle of Heligoland (despatches); air-raid on Cuxhaven, Battle of the Dogger Bank, operations in North Sea (despatches, Order of St Maurice and St Lazarus); Capture of Bagdad (despatches, DSO); Commodore of Convoys, 1918–19; Chief Constable, Oxfordshire, 1921; retired, 1940. *Recreation:* all outdoor sports. *Address:* 42 Homefield Rd, Worthing.

Died 14 June 1945.

ARBUTHNOT, Major John Bernard, MVO 1902; Scots Guards; Knight of Justice, Order of St John of Jerusalem; *b* 1875; *e s* of late Col George Arbuthnot of Norton Court, Gloucester; *m* 1903, Olive, *o d* of late Sir Henry A. Blake, GCMG; three *s* (and one died on active service, 1943) two *d. Educ:* Eton; Sandhurst. Entered Army, 1896; served South Africa, 1900; ADC and Private Secretary to the Governor and Commander-in-Chief of Hongkong, 1902–03; ADC to the Governor of Ceylon, 1907; retired, 1913; rejoined Scots Guards, 1914; appointed Brigade-Major Brigade of Guards, 1914; ADC to Gen. Sir A. J. Murray, 1916; acting Military Secretary, EEF, 1917 (despatches); employed special Intelligence Department, War Office; Mission to Rome; British Mission to United States, 1918 (despatches); HQ Staff Home Guard, 1940–45; owns about 1000 acres of land in Cumberland; assistant editor Daily Express, 1919. *Publications:* (pen names Beachcomber and Sassenach) Arms and the Irishman; Hands across the Sea; The Bunny Book; Irish Sketches. *Recreations:* golf, fishing, painting. *Address:* 47 Cadogan Square, SW1; Myrtle Grove, Youghal, Co. Cork; Dormansteads, Cumberland. *Clubs:* Carlton, Beefsteak; Royal Cork Yacht (Queenstown); Cork County (Cork).

Died 16 Sept. 1950.

ARBUTHNOT, Major Sir Robert Dalrymple, 6th Bt *cr* 1823; 24th Lancers; *b* 4 July 1919; *e s* of Brig.-Gen. Sir Dalrymple Arbuthnot, 5th Bt, CMG, DSO, and Alice Maude, *d* of Hugh Arbuthnot; *S* father 1941; unmarried. *Educ:* Eton; Magdalene College, Cambridge. 2nd Lieut in 9th Queen's Royal Lancers, April 1940; posted to 24th Lancers, Dec. 1940; Lieutenant, 1941; Temp. Captain, 1942. *Recreations:* hunting, shooting, lawn tennis. *Heir: b* Hugh Fitzgerald, *b* 2 Jan. 1922. *Address:* Nash Court, Ludlow, Shropshire. *TA:* and *T:* Tenbury Wells 19. *Club:* Carlton.

Died 30 June 1944.

ARCHBOLD, William Arthur Jobson, MA, LLB; *b* 5 May 1865; 2nd *s* of Alfred Jobson, late of Darlington; *nephew* of late J. A. P. Archbold; *m* Alphonsine Louise Douilly (*d* 1936). *Educ:* Taunton; Peterhouse, Cambridge (scholar and prizeman); 1st Class Law Tripos; Whewell Scholar and Prince Consort Prizeman in the University of Cambridge. Examiner in the Historical Tripos; Secretary of the Board of India Civil Service Studies; Secretary of the Appointments Association; Assistant Secretary of the Local Examinations and Lectures Syndicate in the University; Acting Superintendent of the Rand Schools; Principal of the Mohammedan Anglo-Oriental College, Aligarh, and Government College, Dacca; Principal of Muir Central College, Allahabad, 1918–20. *Publications:* The Romantic Movement in English Literature, 1921; Recent Essays, 1923; Outlines of Indian Constitutional History, 1926; Twentieth Century Essays, 1927; Bengal Haggis, 1928. *Address:* 39 Grange Road, Cambridge. *T:* Cambridge 4772.

Died 1 June 1947.

ARCHDALE, Brig. Arthur Somerville, DSO 1917; *b* 8 Sept. 1882; *s* of late F. Archdale, Baldock, Herts; *m* 1907, Mildred Barbara Funnell. *Educ:* Repton. Entered RA, 1901; Capt. 1914; Major, 1916; Lt-Col 1931; Col 1935; served European War, 1914–18 (despatches four times, DSO, Croix de Guerre); commanded 9th Field Brigade RA, Bulford, 1931–35; Commander RA, 42nd (East Lancs) Division TA, 1935; retired pay, 1939. *Address:* c/o Lloyds Bank Ltd, 6 Pall Mall, W1.

Died 30 March 1948.

ARCHDALE, Rt Hon. Sir Edward Mervyn, PC Ireland, 1920; 1st Bt *cr* 1928; JP, DL; Hon. LLD Queen's University, Belfast, 1926; engaged in farming; Commodore Enniskillen Yacht Club; President Enniskillen Golf Club; *b* 26 Jan. 1853; *m* 1880, Alicia Bland (*d* 1924), *y d* of late Quintin Fleming, of Chapelville, Liverpool; four *s* (and one killed in war) one *d. Educ:* Naval School, Portsmouth. Entered Royal Navy, 1866, Lieut 1875; retired, 1880; served China Station in Juno; Mediterranean Station in Invincible and Helicon; Sultan when commanded by late Duke of Edinburgh; Cape and West Coast of Africa in Dwarf; High Sheriff, Co. Fermanagh, 1884; Minister of Agriculture and Commerce, Northern Ireland, 1921–25, of Agriculture, 1925–33; MP (C) North Fermanagh, 1898–1903 and 1916–21, Fermanagh and Tyrone, Northern Ireland, 1921–29, Enniskillen Division, 1929–37. *Heir: s* Vice-Adm. N. E. Archdale. *Address:* Riversdale, Ballinamallard, Co. Fermanagh. *T:* Ballinamallard 2. *Club:* Fermanagh County.

Died 2 Nov. 1943.

ARCHDALE, Helen Alexander; journalist; *b* 1876; *d* of late Alexander Russel of the Scotsman and Helen De Lacy Evans; *widow* of Theodore Montgomery Archdale, DSO, Lt-Col Royal Artillery; two *s* one *d. Educ:* St Leonards School, St Andrews; St Andrews University. Co-opted Member of Liaison Committee of Women's International Organisations; Member of Women's Social and Political Union; twice imprisoned during militant suffrage movement; worked on Britannia, organ of WSPU; Editorial Director Time and Tide Publishing Co. since 1920; Editor, 1921–26. *Address:* c/o National Provincial Bank, Westminster Branch, 61–63 Victoria St, SW1; Stilestone, Crouch, Sevenoaks.

Died 8 Dec. 1949.

ARCHER, Lt-Col Charles, CSI 1911; CIE 1906; *b* Perth, Scotland, 18 Aug. 1861; *s* of Thomas Archer, CMG, late Agent-General for Queensland; *m* 1900, Alice (*d* 1928), *d* of Henry G. Hayes of Washington, USA. *Educ:* Rockhampton Grammar School; Edinburgh Institution. Lieut 2nd Batt. Dorsetshire Regt 1882; joined Indian Staff Corps, 1885, and appointed to 2nd Punjab Infantry; entered Political Department as Assistant to Agent to the Governor-General in Baluchistan, 1887; Assistant Secretary in Foreign Department, Government of India, 1891; Political Agent in Zhob, 1894–98; Thal Chotiali, 1899–1900; Malakand, 1901–02; Officiating Revenue Commissioner in Baluchistan and Political Agent, Quetta-Pishin, 1904–08; Revenue Commissioner, 1909; Officiating Agent to the Governor-General in Baluchistan, 1911 and 1914; Revenue Commissioner in Baluchistan, 1911–16; retired, 1916; GSO 3, 1916–19. *Publications:* William Archer: Life, Work, and Friendships, 1931; translation of Ibsen's Peer Gynt, Lady Inger of Ostraat, Rosmersholm (with brother William Archer), of Mantzius History of Theatrical Art, vol. vi, of Sigrid Undset's Kristin Lavransdatter (with J. S. Scott), 1925–1930, etc. *Address:* c/o Lloyds Bank, Ltd, 6 Pall Mall, SW1. *Clubs:* East India and Sports, English-Speaking Union.

Died 20 Nov. 1941.

ARCHER, Sir Gilbert, Kt 1942; JP; *b* 6 Jan. 1882; *s* of late John Mark Archer, Leith; *m* 1907, Isabella Bald, *d* of late James Purves, Leith; one *s. Educ:* Leith High School; George Heriot's School. Civil Defence Commissioner for SE District of Scotland, 1941–44; Master of The Company of Merchants of the City of Edinburgh, 1930–32; President Edinburgh Chamber of Commerce and Manufactures, 1939–40; Chairman, Leith Harbour and Dock Commissioners; Chairman, Leith General Hospital; Director, Commercial Bank of Scotland, Ltd. *Recreations:* motoring, fishing. *Address:* St Ola, Park Road, Leith, Edinburgh, 6. *Clubs:* Northern, Scottish Liberal, Edinburgh.

Died 25 Jan. 1948.

ARCHER, (Henry) Allan (Fairfax Best), OBE 1924; *b* 5 Aug. 1887; *e s* of late Major H. F. B. Archer, 3rd Bn Hampshire Regt, and Catherine Maria, *d* of Lt-Col A. N. Scott, Madras Artillery; *m* 1928, Ruth Isabel, *e d* of A. H. Taylor; two *s. Educ:* Rugby. Student Interpreter in HM Consular Service in China, 1912; attached to Tsinan Consulate for service with Chinese Labour Corps, 1917–19; Vice-Consul at Tsingtao, 1919–21; employed in Foreign Office, 1922; Acting Consul at Chungking, 1923–26; Vice-Consul at Shanghai, 1926; Asst Chinese Secretary at British Legation, Peking, 1928; Senior District Officer at Weihaiwei, 1929; Consul at Weihaiwei, 1 Oct. 1930, on the rendition of the Leased Territory; Consul at Changsha, 1932; at Hankow, 1933, and Acting Consul-General there, Jan.–April 1935; Consul at Peking, 1937–39, with rank of 1st Secretary; Consul at Weihaiwei, 1940; Consul-General, 1940; Consul-General, Harbin, Manchuria, 1941; retired,

1946. Is a Freeman of City of London and member of the Grocers' Company. *Recreation:* golf. *Address:* Peking, Lady Anne Av., Newlands, CP, S Africa.

Died 19 Sept. 1950.

ARCHER, Col James Henry L.; *see* Lawrence-Archer.

ARCHER, Sir John; KBK 1918; JP; Vice-President, Boy Scouts Association; President, Richmond Boy Scouts Association and Royal Hospital, Richmond; Chairman of Advisory Committee (Customs and Excise) on Wines and Spirits, 1916–19; late Chairman Bulloch, Lade & Co., Ltd, Glasgow, London, etc; *b* 13 June 1860; *e s* of late John Archer of Lenzie, Dumbartonshire; *m* 1901, Ella Beatrice, 2nd *d* of late J. C. Sharpe of Goslings and Sharpe, Bankers, Fleet Street, and of Longhope, Gloucestershire, also of Richmond, Surrey, and Byfleet, Surrey; no *c. Educ:* privately. Freedom of Borough of Richmond, 1940. Fellow, Royal Empire Society. *Recreation:* golf. *Address:* Devonshire Lodge Richmond, Surrey. *T:* Richmond 0541. *Clubs:* Junior Carlton, Constitutional, Royal Automobile; Richmond Golf (Richmond).

Died 1 June 1949.

ARCHER, John Beville, CMG 1947; retired Civil Servant; *b* 22 Jan. 1893; 2nd *s* of Herbert Ray Archer, MD, and *o s* of Rosita Evelyn Elizabeth Beville; *m* 1941, Dayang Jami-ah, 3rd *d* of Abang Bagap, Sarawak. *Educ:* Victoria College, Jersey; HMS Worcester. Cadet Sarawak Civil Service, 1912; District Officer, 1922; Divisional Resident, 1930; Sec. for Internal Affairs, 1939; Chief Sec. of Sarawak, 1939–41; several times officer administering the Govt; retired, 1941. Temp. duty as Information Officer, etc., Sarawak, 1941; captured by Japanese, 1941; released, 1945; on release, Political Adviser to British Military Administration, Sarawak; on resumption of Civil Govt appointed Chief Sec. of Sarawak again, and finally officer administering the Govt; handed over the country to HM's Govt, July 1946; retired again, 1946; 1st Class Star of Sarawak, 1941. *Publications:* Lintang Camp; Sarawak. *Recreations:* hunting, riding and writing. *Address:* Kuching, Sarawak. *TA:* Archer Sarawak.

Died 17 July 1948.

ARCHER, Col Samuel Arthur, CMG 1919; MRCSEng., LRCPLond.; late Army Medical Service; *b* 22 April 1871; *s* of Colonel S. Archer, AMS, and M. E. Webster, of Upton Hall, Cheshire; *m* 1899, Violet Marguerite, *d* of Lt-Colonel E. Fairland, AMS; no *c. Educ:* Merchant Taylors' School, Crosby; Victoria University, Liverpool. Qualified, 1894; entered the Army Medical Service as Surgeon Lieutenant, 1896; served Egyptian Campaign, 1898 (Queen's medal and Khedive's medal); Captain, 1899; Major, 1908; mobilised with the 7th Division 15 Sept. 1914, as Officer Commanding 22nd Field Ambulance; landed in Belgium 5 Oct. 1914; present at first battle of Ypres and the battles of Festubert and Neuve Chapelle; Lieut-Colonel, 1915; appointed to command No. 6 General Hospital, Oct. 1915 (despatches); ADMS Abbeville and Amiens Areas, April 1917; ADMS 7th Division with the rank of Colonel, Oct. 1917; accompanied the Division to Italy and was present at the battle of Papudopole and the crossing of the River Piave (despatches, CMG, Croce di Guerra); Substantive Colonel, Oct. 1918; joined the Scottish Command, March 1919 (despatches); retired AMS, 1921. *Recreation:* gardening. *Address:* Homefield, Summerhouse Road, Godalming, Surrey. *T:* Godalming 333.

Died 9 Jan. 1943.

ARCHIBALD, Col (temp. Brig.) Gordon King, DSO 1917; RASC; *m*; two *s*. Served European War, 1914–17 (despatches, DSO, Bt Major); Major, 1924; Bt Lt-Col, 1931; Lt-Col, 1933; Col 1937; Deputy Assistant

Director of Transport, War Office, 1928–32; Assistant Director of Supplies and Transport, Eastern Command, 1938–39. *Address:* c/o National Provincial Bank Ltd, 66 Trafalgar Square, WC2.

Died 28 Dec. 1942.

ARCHIBALD, James; *b* 1863; *s* of James Archibald, Buckie, and Margaret Reid; unmarried. *Educ:* Buckie Public School; Elgin Educational Institute; Edinburgh University. Served successively in five banks, City of Glasgow Bank, Aberdeen Town and County Bank, Glyn Mills Currie & Co., London, Caledonian Bank, and Bank of Scotland; engaged in business in USA in North Carolina, Georgia, and New York; Provost of Buckie, 1906–15; Member of Fishery Board for Scotland, 1911–21; Lord Lieutenant of Banffshire, 1930. *Recreation:* community work. *Address:* Rathburn, Buckie, Banffshire. *T:* Buckie 35.

Died 8 Sept. 1946.

ARGYLL, 10th Duke of, *cr* 1701; **Niall Diarmid Campbell;** Marquis of Lorne and Kintyre; Earl Campbell and Cowal; Viscount of Lochow and Glenisla; Baron Inveraray, Mull, Morvern and Tiry, 1701; Baron Campbell, 1445; Earl of Argyll, 1457; Baron of Lorne, 1470; Baron Kintyre, 1633 (Scotland); Baron Sundridge, 1766; Baron Hamilton, 1776; 34th Baron and 44th Knight of Lochow; Celtic title, Mac Cailean Mhor, Chief of Clan Campbell (from Sir Colin Campbell, knighted 1286); Hereditary Master of the Royal Household, Scotland; Hereditary High Sheriff of the County of Argyll; Admiral of the Western Coast and Isles; Keeper of the Great Seal of Scotland and of the Castles of Dunstaffnage, Dunoon, and Carrick and Tarbert; Lord-Lieutenant of Argyll; late Hon. Colonel of 8th Argyll and Sutherland Highlanders; Hon. Col of 15th (Canadian) Argyll Light Infantry; *b* 16 Feb. 1872; *s* of Lord Archibald Campbell, 2nd *s* of 8th Duke and Janey Sevilla, *d* of James Henry Callander, of Ardkinglass, Argyll, and Craigforth, Co. Stirling; *S* uncle, 1914. *Educ:* St George's, Ascot; Charterhouse; Christ Church, Oxford (BA 1896). *Heir: cousin* Ian Douglas Campbell. *Address:* Inveraray Castle, Argyll; 63 Pall Mall, SW1. *Clubs:* Bath, Carlton; New (Edinburgh).

Died 20 Aug. 1949.

ARKWRIGHT, Rev. Ernest Henry, MVO 1911; MA Oxon; *b* 23 March 1868; 4th *s* of late Rev. George Arkwright, Rector of Pencombe, Co. Hereford; *m* 1912, Bertha Elais (*d* 1943), *d* of late Rev. Canon Scarth, vicar of Bearsted, Kent. *Educ:* Haileybury. Assistant Chaplain of Clifton College, 1900–03; Royal Naval College, Osborne, 1903–05; Royal Naval College, Dartmouth, 1905–19; Harrow School, 1919–20; Rector of Binfield, 1920–27; Chaplain of St Stephen's Hospital, SW10, 1927–30; Vicar of Hollingbourne, Kent, 1930–36. *Address:* Palace Corner, Charing, Kent.

Died 16 Sept. 1950.

ARKWRIGHT, Sir Joseph Arthur, Kt 1937; FRS, 1926; MA, MD, FRCP; Hon. Member of Staff, Lister Institute for Preventive Medicine, Chelsea, SW1; *b* 22 March 1864; *s* of late Arthur William Arkwright, of Broughton Astley, Leicestershire; *m* 1893, Ruth, *d* of late Joseph W. Wilson, civil engineer; three *d. Educ:* Wellington College; Trinity College, Cambridge; St Bartholomew's Hospital. General practice, chiefly at Hales Owen, Worcestershire, 1893–1904; Capt. RAMC temp., 1915–17; Member of Agricultural Research Council, 1931–40. *Publications:* The Carrier Problem in Infectious Disease (with J. C. G. Ledingham); various papers in scientific journals on Bacteriology and Pathology. *Recreations:* field natural history, gardening. *Address:* Cloister Garth, 8 Furze Hill, Purley, Surrey. *T:* Uplands 5002.

Died 22 Nov. 1944.

ARLISS, George; *b* London, 10 April 1868; *m* 1899, Florence Montgomery. *Educ:* London. First appearance at Elephant and Castle Theatre, 1887; first appearance New York, 1901, with Mrs Patrick Campbell; created part of Zakkuri in The Darling of the Gods, under David Belasco management; reappeared in England after twenty-two years in US; played St James' Theatre, in Green Goddess, 1923; ran one year; returned to US to play Sylvanus Heythorp in Old English, Shylock in The Merchant of Venice; commenced Film career, US, 1920; appeared in The Devil; Disraeli; The Green Goddess; Old English; The Millionaire; The Silent Voice; A Successful Calamity; The King's Vacation; The Working Man; The House of Rothschild; The Last Gentleman; Cardinal Richelieu, etc. English Films: The Iron Duke; The Guv'nor; East Meets West; His Lordship; Dr Syn. Hon. MA Columbia University, 1919; Fellow of the Royal Society of Arts. *Publications:* Autobiography, Up the Years from Bloomsbury; George Arliss by Himself, 1940; My Ten Years in the Studio; The Wild Rabbit; There and Back; (joint) The West End; Widow Weeds: Hamilton; What Shall it, Profit? *Address:* 1 Clifton Villas, Maida Hill, W9. *Clubs:* Garrick, Green Room, Curzon House; Phyllis Court, Henley; Players', Coffee House, New York.

Died 5 Feb. 1946.

ARMES, Col Reginald John, CMG 1919; psc; *b* 17 March 1876; *s* of late W. L. Armes, JP, King's Lynn, Norfolk; *m* 1st, 1906, Eleanor, *d* of late Rev. Canon W. R. Bedford, Sutton Coldfield, Warwickshire; two *d*; 2nd, 1927, Margaret, *widow* of Ronald Holmes; one *s*. 4th Suffolk (Militia) Regt 1897; North Staffordshire Regt 1899; served South African War, 1902; European War, 1914–18; RFC and RAF 1915–19 (despatches, Bt Lt-Col, CMG, Chevalier Legion of Honour); retired, 1919. OC 10th Suffolk Home Guard, 1940–43. *Address:* Sudbury, Suffolk. *Club:* United Service.

Died 15 April 1948.

ARMFIELD, Mrs Maxwell; *see* Smedley, Constance.

ARMITAGE, Captain Albert Borlase, RD, RNR (retd); Voluntary ARP Warden since 1938; Resident Governor Royal Merchant Seaman's Orphanage, Bear Wood, Wokingham, 1926–32; *b* Balquhidder, Perthshire, 2 July 1864; *s* of S. H. Tatham Armitage, MD, and Alice, *d* of Edward Lees, Ashton-under-Lyne; *m* 1st, Beatrice Laetitia, *d* of H. Whitehead; one *d*; 2nd, Dorothy Lilian Joyce, *d* of Charles Crigan. *Educ:* privately; TNTC, HMS Worcester. Apprentice and officer in sailing ships, 1880–86; joined P. & O. S. N. Co.'s service as 5th officer, 1886, rising through various grades; awarded Murchison Grant by RGS, 1898; Sub.-Lieut RNR, 1892; lent to Jackson-Harmworth N Polar Expedition as 2nd in Command and Observer, 1894–1907; promoted Lieut RNR 1901; lent to British National Antarctic Expedition, 1901–04; 2nd in Command, Navigator of Discovery, and Magnetic Observer at Sea; first to penetrate Antarctic continent at ice-caps of Victoria Land; received King's and RGS medals; promoted Commdr RNR; received RD decoration, 1907. At sea throughout War, 1914–18; carrying mails, troops and food; in action with enemy, 1917; torpedoed, ship sunk. Captain P. & O., 1907; Commodore P. & O., 1923; Captain (retired) RNR, 1923; retired from P. & O., 1924; Seamanship Examiner TNTC, HMS Worcester, since 1927. *Publications:* Two Years in the Antarctic, 1905; Cadet to Commodore, 1925; Cold Lands, 1931. *Address:* 18 Tattenham Way, Burgh Heath, Tadworth.

Died 31 Oct. 1943.

ARMITAGE, Brig.-Gen. Edward Hume, CB 1912; *b* 28 Jan. 1859; *s* of Rev. E. Armitage; *m* 1908, Mrs Glanville, *widow* of Lt-Col A. Glanville, RA; one *s*. *Educ:* Clifton College; Woolwich. Entered Royal Artillery, 1878; served Burmese Expedition, 1886–89 (despatches, medal with two clasps); S African War, 1899–1901

(despatches, Bt Lt-Col, medal with 5 clasps); European War, 1914–18, Commanding RA 9th (Scottish) Division, 1914–15; RA 66th Division, 1916; Area Commandant and Liaison, 1917–18. *Address:* 5 Empire House, Thurloe Place, SW7. *Clubs:* Army and Navy, MCC.

Died 15 Feb. 1949.

ARMITAGE, Rev. George; *b* Southport, 1856; *m* Annie, *d* of Isaac Kelsall, JP, Ashton-under-Lyne; one *s*. *Educ:* Private School, Liverpool. Entered Primitive Methodist ministry, 1881; ministry spent in Lancashire and London; secretary of Hartley Victoria Theological College for eleven years and secretary of the Denomination, 1919–24; President of the Primitive Methodist Church, 1927–28. *Recreation:* golf. *Address:* Branksome, Ripon Road, Ansdell, Lytham St Annes.

Died 8 April 1948.

ARMITAGE, Robert; *b* 22 Feb. 1866; *s* of William James Armitage of Farnley, Leeds; *m* 1st, 1891, Caroline Katharine (*d* 1933), *d* of Dudley H. Ryder of Westbrook-Hay, Hemel-Hempstead; three *s* four *d*; 2nd, 1936, Mary Dorothea, *widow* of Rev. E. Bacheler Russell. *Educ:* Westminster; Trinity College, Cambridge. Manager and Director of various Companies; MP (L) Central Leeds, 1906–22; Lord Mayor of Leeds, 1904–05; Deputy Lord Mayor, 1905–06, 1906–07, and 1908–09. *Address:* Farnley Hall, Leeds. *T:* Leeds 38432. *Clubs:* National, Bath.

Died 10 Feb. 1944.

ARMITSTEAD, Ven. John Hornby; Vicar of Sandbach since 1919; Archdeacon of Macclesfield since 1932; *b* 1868; *e s* of Canon J. R. Armitstead, Vicar of Sandbach and Hon. Canon of Chester. *Educ:* Westminster; Christ Church, Oxford. Curate of Sandbach, Cheshire, 1892–99; Vicar of Holmes Chapel, 1899–1919; Rural Dean of Congleton, 1918; Hon. Canon of Chester, 1925; JP County of Chester, 1890; Alderman of Cheshire County Council, 1929. *Recreations:* hunting, cricket. *Address:* The Vicarage, Sandbach, Cheshire. *T:* Sandbach 88. *Club:* Oxford and Cambridge.

Died 26 Oct. 1941.

ARMOUR, George Denholm, OBE; *b* Scotland, 30 Jan. 1864; 3rd *s* of Robert Armour and Marion Paterson; *m* 1st, 1898, Mary Emma (*d* 1924), *d* of John Robb, JP, Busby House, Busby; two *s*; 2nd, 1926, Violet, *d* of late Capt. J. P. M. Burton of Brasted House, Kent, and Taverham, Norfolk; one *d*. *Educ:* St Andrews. Studied Art at the Edinburgh School of Art and Royal Scot. Academy from 1880 to about 1888, during which time exhibited in most of chief galleries; afterwards went to London. Working as painter and illustrator; commanded Remount Squadron, 1915; transferred to Salonica, 1917; promoted to Lt-Col to command Remount Depot, BSF, 1917, and to DAD Remounts; exhibits in RA and other galleries. *Works:* equestrian portraits of Dowager Duchess of Beaufort, Sir Lionel Darell, Miss Esmé Jenner, MHH, J. E. Lewis, etc. *Publications:* Humour in the Hunting Field, 1928; Sport and There's the Humour of it, 1935; Bridle and Brush, 1937; illustrator of works of Surtees, etc.; many drawings in the Graphic, Sporting and Dramatic News, Punch, Country Life, etc. *Recreations:* hunting, shooting, fishing, and all field sports. *Address:* Liddington Manor, Liddington, near Swindon, Wilts. *T:* Wanborough 3. *Club:* Savage.

Died 17 Feb. 1949.

ARMOUR, Margaret; *see* MacDougall, Margaret.

ARMSTRONG, 1st Baron *cr* 1903, of Bamburgh and Cragside; **William Henry Armstrong Fitzpatrick Watson-Armstrong;** JP, DL; Major, Northumberland Hussars I. Y., ret.; TD; County Alderman, Northumberland CC, D. C. Rothbury Rural and Urban Councils, Chairman Rothbury Guardians; President for Northumberland of the League of Mercy; Hon. Freeman of Newcastle-upon-Tyne; *b* 3 May 1863; *s* of late John William Watson of Adderstone Hall, Belford; and *grandnephew* of 1st Baron Armstrong (*d* 1900, Barony extinct); *m* 1st, 1889, Winifreda (*d* 1914), *d* of late Sir John Adye, GCB; one *s*; 2nd, 1916, Beatrice Elizabeth (*d* 1934), Lady Pres. of League of Mercy for Northumberland, Order of Mercy, *e d* of late Jonathan Cowx, Tudhoe; 3rd, 1935, Kathleen, *d* of late Rev. C. T. England. *Educ:* Eton; Trinity College, Cambridge. MA; Hon. DCL Durham. *Heir: s* Hon. W. J. Montagu Watson-Armstrong. *Address:* Cragside, Rothbury, Morpeth. *T:* Rothbury 3; Bamburgh Castle, Northumberland. *T:* Bamburgh 5. *Clubs:* Carlton, Constitutional; Northern Counties, Newcastle.

Died 15 Oct. 1941.

ARMSTRONG, Col Bertie Harold Olivier, CB 1919; CMG 1918; late RE; *b* 18 Dec. 1873; 2nd *s* of Charles Newhouse Armstrong, of Montreal, Canada, and Amelia Frances, *d* of J. E. Johnstone; *m* 1914, Dorothy Maud, *d* of James Padgett Cooper, Strawberry Hill, Middlesex; one *d*. *Educ:* Royal Military College, Kingston, Canada. Entered Royal Engineers, 1893; served Sierra Leone Expedition, 1898–99; CRE West Coast of Africa, 1899–1900; South African War, 1900–02; Director of Relief Works, Orange River Colony Government, 1902–05; Member of Industrial Commission ORC, 1903–04; Member of Intercolonial Irrigation Commission, South Africa, 1904–05; Commanding Royal Engineer, Natal and Harrismith, 1906–10; Member of Conciliation Commission, Natal Government Railways, 1909; lent to Colonial Office for Survey of Gambia, 1910; Staff-Captain, War Office, 1911; at War Office till 1918, when transferred as Director of Inland Works to Air Ministry, 1918; retired Nov. 1919. *Publication:* Military Handbook of Natal. *Address:* Yeald House, Overton Hants. *T:* Overton (Hants) 212.

Died 24 Feb. 1950.

ARMSTRONG, Sir Charles Herbert, Kt 1913; Chairman Great Indian Peninsula Railway Co. Annuity Branch; *b* 24 Nov. 1862; 2nd *s* of Thomas Armstrong, Bowdon, Cheshire; *m* 1896, Marie Louise Therese (*d* 1937), *e d* of M. C. C. Magrath, Liverpool. *Educ:* King's School, Canterbury. Went out to India, 1885. Chairman of the Bombay Chamber of Commerce, 1904–05, 1907, 1909, 1911, 1912, 1913; additional Member of Imperial Legislative Council, India, 1909, 1911, 1912, 1913; additional Member of Bombay Legislative Council, 1904, 1905, 1907; President Bank of Bombay, 1908, 1911, 1913; Chairman of the Great Indian Peninsula Railway Co., 1917–25; and for ten years a Trustee of the Port of Bombay. *Address:* Elmhyrst, Guildford.

Died 9 Sept. 1949.

ARMSTRONG, Edmund La Touche, MA, LLB; *b* Herne Hill, Geelong, 1864; *s* of John Simpson Armstrong of the Irish and Victorian Bars, and Alice, *d* of Major O'Dell. *Educ:* Scotch College, Melbourne; University of Melbourne. Assistant in the Public Library, 1881; read law with the intention of practising at the Bar, and graduated in the Law School, 1893; Principal Assistant in the Reference Library, 1895; Chief Librarian and Secretary, Public Library, Museums, and National Gallery of Victoria, 1896–1925. *Publications:* editor of and contributor to the Library Journal of Australasia, 1901–1902; Book of the Public Library, Museums, and National Gallery of Victoria, 1856–1906; continued in conjunction with R. D. Boys, 1906–1931. *Address:* 9 Bates St, East Malvern, Melbourne, SE5, Victoria.

Died 15 Oct. 1946.

ARMSTRONG, Edward Frankland, FRS 1920 (Vice-Pres. 1942–43); DSc, PhD, LLD, Hon. ACTC (Birm.); FRIC; MIChemE; FCGI; Hon. Fellow Imperial College of Science, 1939; JP, Cheshire; Scientific Adviser Ministry of Home Security; Member of Civil Defence Research Committee; Member Ministry of Works

Scientific Advisory Committee; *b* 1878; *s* of late Henry Edward Armstrong, FRS; *m* 1907, Ethel, *d* of C. K. Turpin, Woolwich; one *s* one *d*. President of the Society of Chemical Industry, 1922–24; Chairman Association of British Chemical Manufacturers, 1930–33; Chairman British Association of Chemists, 1926; Chairman British Standards Institution, 1934–35 and 1937–38; Managing Director Joseph Crosfield & Sons, Warrington, 1915–25; Wm Gossage & Son, Widnes, 1915–20; British Dye Stuffs Corporation, Manchester, 1925–28; Director South Metropolitan, South Suburban and Commercial Gas Cos.; Chairman Soap Manufacturers Employers' Federation and of the Joint Industrial Council for the Soap Trade, 1920–25; Governor Imperial College of Science; Governor St Dunstan's College, Catford; Chairman Organising Committee International Congress of Scientific Management, 1935; Vice-Chairman, British Management Council, 1937–39; Treasurer Royal Society of Arts, 1938–43, Pres. 1943–45, and Chairman of Council since 1943; Treasurer Lawes Agricultural Trust Committee; Member Building Research Board, 1944; Chairman Science Commission, Conference of the Allied Ministers of Education, 1943; Chairman War Memorials Advisory Council. *Publications:* The Simple Carbohydrates, 1910; Chemistry in the Twentieth Century, 1924; The Glycosides, 1931; The Sea as a Storehouse, 1945; contributed a large number of original papers to the Royal Society, the Chemical Society, and elsewhere; author of articles in Thorpe's Dictionary and other technical journals. *Address:* 69 Barkston Gardens, SW5. *T:* Frobisher 1798. *Clubs:* Athenæum, Chemical, Gargoyle.

Died 14 Dec. 1945.

ARMSTRONG, Sir Francis Philip, 3rd Bt *cr* 1892; OBE 1918; Barrister, Inner Temple; late Commander RNVR; late Secretary and General Manager, Royal Automobile Club; *b* 16 Oct. 1871; *S* brother, 1940; *m* 1896, Pulcheria Margaret, *d* of late George Fox, Elmhurst Hall, Lichfield. *Address:* Oxleys, Beaulieu, Hants. *T:* Beaulieu 216. *Club:* Royal Automobile.

Died 7 Jan. 1944.

ARMSTRONG, George Gilbert; author and retired journalist; *b* Nottingham, 1870; *e s* of late Rev. Richard Acland Armstrong of Nottingham and Liverpool; *m* 1894, Katharine (*d* 1941), *d* of late William Clark of Nottingham. *Educ:* private schools; University College, Liverpool. Served successively on editorial staffs of Liverpool Mercury, Nottingham Express, North-Eastern Gazette, Bradford Observer, Bolton Evening News, and Morning Leader; editor Northern Echo, Newcastle and Darlington, 1904–08; managing editor northern edition (Manchester) of the Daily News, 1908–21; assistant editor of the Daily News, 1921–23; Director, 1919–22; free lance, 1924–30 (editor of The Inquirer, 1928–30; Chairman, 1934–41); President General Assembly of Unitarian and Free Christian Churches, 1935–36; President Provincial Assembly of Presbyterian and Unitarian Ministers and Congregations of Lancashire and Cheshire, 1916–17; President London District and South-Eastern Provincial Assembly of Unitarian and Free Christian Churches, 1938–40. *Publications:* Why Another World War?; How We Missed Collective Security, 1941; Our Ultimate Aim in the War, 1916; Richard Acland Armstrong; a Memoir, 1906; Memories: Apologia pro Vita Sua, 1944; and pamphlets. *Address:* 133 North End Road, Golders Green, NW11. *T:* Speedwell 7597.

Died 24 Feb. 1945.

ARMSTRONG, Captain Harold Courtenay, OBE; BA (Oxon); Bronze Medal of Royal Humane Society; *b* 20 Oct. 1892; *s* of William Frederick Armstrong and Frances Carnsew. *Educ:* King's School, Worcester; Oxford. Indian Army, 67th Punjabis; to Mesopotamia with Expeditionary Force; captured at Kut-al-Amarah; War Office in MI2 (b); Assistant and Acting Military

Attaché to the British High Commissioner, Constantinople; on staff of GOC in C, Allied Forces of Occupation in Turkey; Supervision of the Turkish Gendarmerie; on staff of Commission for the Assessment of Damages suffered in Turkey, in Paris; British Delegate, Syrian Sub-Commission of above commission. *Publications:* Grey Wolf (Mustafa Kemal of Turkey); Lord of Arabia (King Ibn Saud); Grey Steel (General J. C. Smuts); Unending Battle; Tales of Hazard; On the Run (Escaping Tales); Turkey in Travail; Turkey and Syria Reborn; Hidden. *Recreations:* riding, travel and exploration. *Address:* Burghclere, Newbury.

Died 25 Aug. 1943.

ARMSTRONG, Rt Hon. Henry Bruce, Hon. LLD, Queen's University, Belfast, 1937; Privy Councillor for N Ireland, 1932; *b* Hull House, Shoulden, Kent, 27 July 1844; 2nd *surv. s* of Wm Jones Wright Armstrong, JP, DL, Co. Armagh, High Sheriff, 1840, and Frances Elizabeth, *widow* of Sir Michael McCreagh, KCH, and *d* of late Major Christopher Wilson, 22nd Regt; *m* 1883, Margaret (*d* 1936), *d* of Wm Leader, Rosnalea, Co. Cork; five *s* three *d*. *Educ:* Armagh Royal School; Trinity College, Cambridge. Took Degree 2nd Class Law Tripos, MA, 1870. Barrister-at-law, 1868; JP, DL, Co. Armagh; High Sheriff, Armagh, 1875; Longford, 1894; Vice-Lieut, Co. Armagh, 1920; HM Lieut Co. Armagh, 1924–39; Senator, Queen's University, Belfast, 1920–37; Member of Irish Convention, 1917–18; County Councillor, Armagh, 1899–1920; Chairman, 1909–20; Senator Northern Ireland, 1921–37; returned unopposed to Imperial House of Commons for Mid-Armagh, 1921; 25 years member of Representative Body of Church of Ireland; Chairman, County Armagh Education Committee, 1925–31; President, Association of Education Committees of N Ireland; a Justice for the Government of Northern Ireland in the absence of the Governor, 1938. *Recreations:* travelled extensively in East and Far East for several years; no special recreation, but joins in any available. *Address:* Deans Hill, Armagh. *Clubs:* Ulster, Belfast.

Died 4 Dec. 1943.

ARMSTRONG, Vice-Adm. John Garnet; retired; *b* 19 July 1870; *s* of Surgeon-General W. N. Armstrong; *m* 1893, Ethel Mary (*d* 1923), *d* of Comdr G. P. Heath, RN, OBE; two *s*. *Educ:* Burneys; HMS Britannia. Served in China during the China-Jap. War 1894, also in Boxer War 1899; in European War in command of HMS London in the Channel and Dardanelles and afterwards in HMS King Alfred, and after the war as Superintendent of Pembroke Dockyard; retired 1920; at present doing voluntary work for the SOS Society and others. *Address:* 23 Gordon Square, WC1. *T:* Euston 3980. *Club:* United Service.

Died 30 April 1949.

ARMSTRONG, Sir Richard (Harold), Kt 1948; senior partner in firm of Alsop Stevens & Co., solicitors, Liverpool; *b* 1874; 3rd *s* of Rev. Richard Acland Armstrong, Unitarian Minister, and Clara Wicksteed; unmarried. *Educ:* privately. Hon. Sec. Liverpool Soc. for Prevention of Cruelty to Children, 1906–12; Hon. Sec. to Liverpool Infirmary for Children (later named Royal Liverpool Children's Hosp.), 1913–26; member Council Univ. of Liverpool from 1924, holding successively following offices: Dep. Treas., Treas., Pres. of Council and Pro-Chancellor until Nov. 1948. Hon. LLD Univ. of Liverpool, 1945; Chm. Royal Liverpool United Hosp., 1938–48; Chairman, United Liverpool Hospitals, since 1948. Chm. Ullet Road Church, Liverpool (Unitarian), 1941–. *Recreation:* walking. *Address:* 19 Ullet Road, Liverpool 17. *T:* Liverpool: Sefton Park 1011. *Clubs:* Reform; University, Exchange (Liverpool).

Died 30 March 1950.

ARMSTRONG, Rev. Simon Carter, BA (Resp.); retired; *b* Aug. 1856; *s* of Alan Armstrong, late of Lakeview, Manorhamilton, Co. Leitrim; *m* 1878, Eliza, *d* of John Martin, Solicitor, Dublin; four *s* five *d*. *Educ:* Bournemouth Preparatory College (Wanklyn's); Rathmines School; Trinity College, Dublin. Deacon, 1885; Priest, 1886; Curate of Drumcannon, Tramore, 1885–86; Curate of Drumcannon, Tramore, 1885–86; Rector of Shrule, Ballymahon, 1886–91; Tubbercurry, 1891–92; Curate of Portadown, 1892–94; Rector of Templederry, 1894–1911; Canon of Lockeen (Killaloe), 1909; Rector of Kilrush, 1911–23; Chancellor of St Flannan's Cathedral (Killaloe), 1917; Curate-in-charge of the Light Duty parish of Finglas, 1923–28. *Publication:* The Cooneyites or Dippers: being a Plain Refutation of their Errors. *Recreations:* angling, chess. *Address:* Ard Lorcan, Bray, Co. Wicklow.

Died 31 July 1942.

ARMSTRONG, Rev. Walter H.; Methodist Minister; Moderator, Federal Council of Free Churches of England; *b* 14 Sept. 1873; *m* 1903, Ada White, Lydd, Kent; one *d*. *Educ:* Didsbury College, Manchester. Missionary to Ceylon; held pastorates since return in Manchester, Sunderland, East Ham, John Wesley's Chapel, London and Bradford; President, National Free Church Council of England and Wales, 1940–41; President Methodist Conference, 1941–42. *Publications:* Life of Dr J. Alfred Sharp, 1932; various pamphlets on Christianity and Social Questions. *Recreation:* golf. *Address:* 26 Rokesby Avenue, N8. *T:* Mountview 2910. *Club:* National Liberal.

Died 25 Oct. 1949.

ARMSTRONG, William George, BA, MB, ChM, 1888, Sydney University; DPH Cambridge, 1895; Fellow, Royal Sanitary Institute; Member, New South Wales Board of Health; Member, City of Sydney Building Advisory Committee; Major, AAMC (retired list); late Director-General of Public Health, New South Wales, and President of the Board of Health; late Lecturer and Examiner in Public Health, University of Sydney; *b* Leigh, Essex, 29 May 1859; *s* of Richard R. Armstrong, Commander, RN; *m* 1888, Elizabeth *d* of Rev. C. F. Garnsey of Christ Church, Sydney; one *s* one *d*. *Educ:* The King's School, Canterbury; University of Sydney; London Hospital. Was member City of Sydney Improvement Board and NSW Medical Board, and was President of the Section of Public Health, Australasian Medical Congress, Adelaide, 1905; Dep. Chm. Metropolitan Meat Industry Board, 1924–25. *Publications:* Epidemic Smallpox in New South Wales, Proceedings Royal Society of Medicine, 1914; Preventive Medicine in Australia, Journal Royal Sanitary Institute, 1923; article Public Health in Australian Encyclopædia; other articles on public health and epidemiological subjects. *Address:* 49 Wentworth Road, Vaucluse, Sydney, NSW.

Died 27 Dec. 1941.

ARMSTRONG, Sir William Herbert Fletcher, Kt 1946; CIE 1943; MA (Cantab); FCS (Lond.); IES (retd); *b* 25 April 1892; *s* of Fletcher Armstrong, journalist; *m* 1915, Dorothy Lottie Hornell; one *s* (*yr s* killed in Italy, 1944) one *d*. *Educ:* Carlisle School; Downing College, Cambridge. Professor of Chemistry, Madras Christian College, Madras, 1913–17; IES 1917–47; Director of Public Instruction, Punjab, and Secretary to Govt of the Punjab, Education Dept, 1936–47. *Recreations:* tennis and reading.

Died 9 Feb. 1950.

ARMSTRONG-JONES, Sir Robert; *see* Jones.

ARNAVON, Jacques, Hon. KBE 1938; Officier de la Légion d'Honneur; Grand Officier Order St Olaf, Norway; Commandeur: Ordre Léopold de Belgique, Danebrog (Denmark); Golden Ear (China), etc.; Minister Plenipotentiary; Hon. Secretary of Association

France-Grande Bretagne, 1 rue d'Astorg, Paris VIIIe, since 1929; *b* Marseilles, 16 July 1877; 3rd *s* of L. A. Arnavon; *m* 1904 (marr. diss. 1930); one *s. Educ:* Lycée de Marseille; University of Aixand University of Paris (awards corresponding 1st cl. Hon.). Entered French Diplomatic Service, 1904; Secretary, French Embassy, Switzerland, 1907–08; French Foreign Office, 1909–10; French Embassy in Russia, 1911–12; French Foreign Office, 1913; Xth Army, 1914–15; Chief Assistant to Secretary General, Peace Conference, 1919; Minister Plenipotentiary, 1920; retired. Lectured in French, English, Danish, in England, Scotland, Wales, Belgium, Holland, Denmark, Sweden, Norway, Czechoslovakia, Brazil, Greece, 1920–28; lectures in French towns; organized numerous Franco-British festivities. Secretary's office of France-Grande Bretagne seized by Germans June 1940, home plundered 1942. Summoned by Gestapo May 1944. Association restored after liberation Aug. 1944. Retired 1946. Docteur ès Lettres (Sorbonne), 1948. *Publications:* Nine books on the staging of Molière's plays (four of these awarded prizes of the Académie Française); short biography of Winston Churchill, 1944; La morale de Molière, 1946; Le Don Juan de Molière, 1948. Translation of School for Scandal; four other books, e.g. translation of Tyrrell's Christianity at the Cross Roads; articles in reviews. *Recreations:* golf, travels. *Address:* 42 Rue Cortambert, Paris XVIe.

Died 12 Oct. 1949.

ARNELL, Charles Christopher, CBE 1944; *b* 1881; *s* of late John Christopher Arnell and Mary Anne Kingstone; *m* 1916, Dorothy Winifred Edye; two *s. Educ:* privately. Founded Charles C. Arnell & Company, London, Ship-Managers, Ship-Brokers; Member of Baltic Exchange since 1904; served on Merchant Ship Reserve Advisory Committee, 1939; Hon. Adviser to Minister of Shipping on Matters Relative to the Purchase of Ships; FICS; AINA; ANECInst. *Recreations:* golf, fishing, gardening. *Address:* Pinhaye, Heronsgate, Herts. *Club:* Devonshire.

Died 11 April 1948.

ARNOLD, 1st Baron *cr* 1924, of Hale; **Sydney Arnold;** *b* 13 Jan. 1878; *s* of W. A. Arnold, stockbroker, Manchester. *Educ:* Manchester Grammar School; privately. Before entering the firm of W. A. Arnold & Sons, was articled to a Chartered Accountant and passed Preliminary Examination, 2nd in England; Intermediate Examination, 3rd in England; Member of Manchester Stock Exchange, 1904–22; contested Holderness Division, Dec. 1910; MP (L) Holmfirth Division of West Riding, later Penistone Division, 1912–21; resigned seat owing to ill-health, 1921; Parliamentary Private Secretary to President of Board of Education, and to Financial Secretary to the Treasury, 1914; joined the Labour Party, 1922; Under-Secretary for the Colonies, Jan.–Nov. 1924; Paymaster-General, 1929–31; resigned from Labour Party, 1938, on account of disagreement with its Foreign Policy. *Heir:* none. *Address:* Marley Corner, near Haslemere, Surrey. *Club:* Reform.

Died 3 Aug. 1945.

ARNOLD, Edward Augustus, BA; *b* 15 July 1857; *o s* of Rev. Edward Penrose Arnold and Caroline, daughter of Richard Orlebar of Hinwick, Beds; grandson of Dr Arnold of Rugby and nephew of Matthew Arnold; *m* 1st, Minnie Margaret, *d* of W. H. Wakefield, Sedgwick House, Kendal; 2nd, Christina, *d* of John Burland, Taunton; two *d. Educ:* Eton; Oxford. President of the Publishers Association, 1928–29. *Recreations:* travelling, fishing. *Address:* Lilybrook, Budleigh Salterton.

Died 6 Nov. 1942.

ARNOLD, Edward Carleton, MA; *s* of G. B. Arnold, Mus. Doc. (Oxon), of Winchester. *Educ:* Merchant Taylors' School; Emmanuel College, Cambridge (Scholar). First Class in Classical Tripos, 1890; Senior Classical Master, Elizabeth College, Guernsey, 1891; Senior Classical Master, Eastbourne College, 1899–1924.

Headmaster of Eastbourne College, 1924–29. *Publications:* A Bird Collector's Medley; British Waders; Birds of Eastbourne; Bird Reserves; Memories of Cley. *Address:* 32a Furness Road, Eastbourne.

Died 20 Oct. 1949.

ARNOLD, General of the Army Henry H., Hon. GCB 1945; late Chief of Staff US Army Air Force; *b* Gladwyne, Pa, 25 June 1886; *s* of H. A. Arnold and Louise Harley; *m* 1913, Eleanor Pool; three *s* one *d. Educ:* US Military Academy; Army Industrial College, 1925; Command and General Staff School, 1929. 2nd Lt Infantry, 1907; promoted through grades to General of the Army, 1944. Signal Corps Aviation Section, 1916–17; Commanding Officer 7th Aero Squadron Panama, 1917–18; Dept Air Service Officer, San Francisco, 1919–22; Commanding Officer various air fields, 1922–36; Flight Commander, US Alaska Flight, 1934; Assistant Chief Air Corps, 1936–38; Chief of Army Air Corps, 1938; Deputy Chief of Staff, 1940; Comdg. Gen., Army Air Forces, 1942; retired 1946; DFC, 1934; Clarence H. Mackay Trophy, 1912 and 1935; Collier Trophy, 1943 DSM, 1942; Air Medal, 1943. *Publications:* Bill Bruce Series, 1928; Air Men and Aircraft, 1929. With General Ira C. Eaker: This Flying Game, 1936; Winged Warfare, 1941; Army Flyer, 1942. *Recreations:* hunting, golf, fishing, woodworking, gardening. *Address:* Ft Myer, Virginia; War Department, Washington, DC. *T:* Republic 6700, Extension 2766. *Clubs:* Army and Navy, Columbia Golf and Country (Washington, DC).

Died 15 Jan. 1950.

ARNOLD, Lt-Col Herbert Tollemache, CBE 1919; DSO 1916; late RAPC; *b* 5 April 1867; *s* of late Rev. E. G. and Lady Charlotte Arnold; *m* 1897, Eleanor Josephine, *d* of late H. F. à Beckett Chambers; one *s.* Entered Wilts. Regt 1889; transferred to Army Pay Dept 1901; Lt-Col 1920; retired, 1924; served European War, 1914–18 (despatches, DSO, CBE, Bt Lt-Col). *Club:* United Service.

Died 23 Sept. 1943.

ARNOLD, Thomas George; JP (London County), 1915; *b* 11 March 1866; *s* of John and Harriette Arnold; *m* 1890, Ellen Maria, *d* of John and Keturah Ross; no *c. Educ:* Presbyterian School, Woolwich. Assistant Secretary, Royal Arsenal Co-operative Society, Ltd, Woolwich, 1888–1902; Secretary, 1902–16; member of Central Committee of the International Co-operative Alliance, the Board of Trade Census of Production (1926) Advisory Committee and reappointed for the 1931 Census Committee, and the Royal Commission on Licensing (England and Wales); Director Co-operative Wholesale Society, Ltd, 1916–34. *Recreation:* bowling. *Address:* The Cot, 99 Woolwich Road, Abbey Wood, SE2. *T:* Erith 2909.

Died 9 Nov. 1944.

ARNOLD, Thomas James, CBE 1925; Controller of Pension Issue Office, Ministry of Pensions, since 1928; *b* 10 April 1879; *s* of late H. T. Arnold; *m* 1905, Minnie Linnell; two *d. Educ:* Owen's School, Islington. Entered Civil Service, 1897; Local Government Board, 1897–1916; Military service in European War, 1916–19; Assistant Private Secretary to the Rt Hon. Walter Long (Viscount Long of Wraxall) 1916; appointed to Ministry of Pensions, 1919; Private Secretary to Minister of Pensions, 1920–28. *Recreations:* various. *Address:* 15 Rookfield Close, Muswell Hill, N10.

Died 17 Feb. 1945.

ARNOTT, John; Councillor; *b* Kincardine-on-Forth, 21 Dec. 1871; *s* of Henry and Mary Arnott; *m* 1910, Jane Ellen Parkinson, Preston; no *c. Educ:* Elementary, Gartconner School near Kirkintilloch; Ruskin College, Oxford, 1905 and 1906. To work in shipyard at 13, Thornaby-on-Tees; worked as blacksmith; active in politics before 21; joined ILP 1892 and Trade Union,

ASE, about same time; accepted post as organiser at Preston, Lancs, ILP, later at King's Lynn, Glasgow, Bermondsey; Divisional Organiser, ILP, Leeds, 1911; Leeds City Council, 1913; Leader of Labour Group, 1917–25; contested West Leeds, 1918; SW Hull, 1922, 1923, 1924; MP (Lab) South-West Hull, 1929–31; Lord Mayor of Leeds, 1925–26; Alderman, 1926; Chairman Tramway Committee. *Publications:* a few pamphlets and newspaper articles. *Recreations:* music, walking. *Address:* 40 Harlech Terrace, Leeds, 11.

Died 20 Feb. 1942.

ARNOTT, Col John Maclean, CMG 1918; VD; Retired List, Australian Commonwealth Military Forces; *b* Newcastle, NS Wales, 22 Jan. 1869; *m* 1895, Adeline, *d* of John Hardy, of Strathfield, NS Wales; seven *s. Educ:* Maitland School, NSW. Civilian life, manufacturer; entered Australian Military Forces, 1899; Brigade-Major, Australian Light Horse, 1910; CO 11th LH 1913; Lt-Col Australian Expeditionary Force, 1914, Egypt, Gallipoli; Colonel, 1916; Commandant, Australian and New Zealand Training Centre in Egypt, 1916–19. *Address:* Castlefield, Edgecliff Road, Edgecliff, NS Wales. *Clubs:* Australian, RSGC, Sydney.

Died 31 July 1945.

ARNOTT, Leonard; Director Agence Belge Berner & Nielsen, SA, Brussels; Agence Française Berner & Nielsen, SA, Paris; Canadian & American Wood Agency, Ltd; Lenar Trust Ltd; Pharaoh Gane & Co. Ltd; Pharaohs (Distributors) Ltd; Timber and General Finance Ltd; Associated Pitwood Agents Ltd; Pitwood Export Ltd, Moncton, Canada; Past President Timber Trade Federation of the UK; Treasurer Comité Internationale du Bois; Underwriting Member of Lloyd's; *b* London, 17 July 1887; *s* of James Barocliffe Arnott and Annie Holland; *m* 1940, Edith Grace Daniels; no *c. Educ:* privately, abroad. Served European War, 1914–18. Travelled extensively. *Recreations:* farming, sailing, swimming, and golf. *Address:* Grosvenor House, Park Lane, W1; Larkfield Estate, Itchenor, Sussex. *TA:* Arnott, Grovhows, Audley, London. *T:* Grosvenor 6363. *Clubs:* Royal Thames Yacht, British Russia, Royal Automobile.

Died 19 Sept. 1943.

ARNOULD, Francis Graham, CIE 1928; VD 1924; ACGI; *b* 5 Jan. 1875; 4th *s* of late Alfred Henry Arnould, DCL, of Whitecross, near Wallingford, Berks; *m* 1913, Barbarina Helen Seton, *e d* of late T. S. Dury (Master of the Supreme Court of Judicature); three *d. Educ:* St Paul's School; the City and Guilds Institute. Joined the engineering staff of the BB and CI Railway as an Assistant Engineer, 1895; Chief Engineer, 1920–30; officiated as Director of Civil Engineering, Railway Board, India, April–Sept. 1928. *Address:* Old Court House, Battle, Sussex. *T:* Battle 163.

Died 18 Jan. 1941.

ARROW, Gilbert John, FZS, FRES; late Deputy Keeper, Department of Entomology, British Museum (Natural History); *b* 20 Dec. 1873; *s* of late John Garner Arrow, Streatham; *m* Rachel Katharine Davis. Spent 5 years in an architect's office and afterwards, in 1896, entered the Natural History Museum by competitive examination. *Publications:* 5 volumes on Indian Beetles, in Fauna of India Series, and over one hundred contributions to transactions of learned societies, etc. *Recreations:* music, photography, gardening. *Address:* 9 Rossdale Road, Putney, SW.

Died 5 Oct. 1948.

ARTHUR, Major Christopher Geoffrey, DSO 1915; Reserve of Officers, Canadian Forces; Overseas Representative Canadian Government Department of Pensions and National Health, Canada House, Trafalgar Square; *b* 27 Jan. 1882; *m* 1917, Eirene Primrose Dodd, The Grange, Buxton; one *s* one *d. Educ:* King's College,

London. Served European War, 1914–18 (despatches, DSO). *Address:* Kingsmere, Watford Road, Northwood, Middlesex. *T:* Northwood 1147. *Club:* British Empire.

Died 23 April 1943.

ARTHUR, Sir George (Compton Archibald), 3rd Bt *cr* 1841; MVO 1909; *b* 30 April 1860; *S* father, 1878; *m* 1898, Kate Harriet, *widow* of Arthur Raymond Yates, and *d* of late Horatio Brandon. *Educ:* Eton; Christ Church, Oxford. Lieut 2nd Life Guards, 1880–86; Egyptian Campaign, 1882; Nile Expedition, 1884–85; S Africa (Herts Yeomanry Cav.), and on Staff, 1900; Private Secretary to Earl Kitchener, 1914–16; with Intelligence Department in France, 1917–18; Chevalier Legion of Honour; Order of the Crown of Belgium; Chesney Gold Medal. *Publications:* Story of the Household Cavalry, 1909; The Life of Lord Kitchener of Khartoum, 1920; concerning Winston Spencer Churchill, 1941; edited Letters of Lord and Lady Wolseley, 1922; Sarah Bernhardt, 1923; (with Sir F. Maurice) The Life of Lord Wolseley, 1924; Lord Haig, 1928; General Sir John Maxwell, 1932; A Septuaginarian's Scrap Book, 1933; Queen Alexandra, 1934; Queen Mary, 1935; Phelps to Gielgud, 1936; Seven Heirs Apparent, 1937; Not Worth Reading, 1938; Wellington to Wavell, 1942; Concerning Queen Victoria and Her Son, 1943; Translation of Memoirs of Raymond Poincaré. *Heir:* cousin George Malcolm Arthur, *b* 1908. *Address:* 23 The Boltons, SW10. *T:* Flaxman 9040. *Clubs:* Marlborough, Carlton.

Died 14 Jan. 1946.

ARTHUR, Sir George Malcolm, 4th Bt *cr* 1841; *b* 26 March 1908; *s* of late Edward Malcolm Arthur; *S* cousin 1946; *m* 1928, Doris Fay, *d* of Joseph Wooding, JP, Woodland Grange, Woodbury, and Geraldine, S Canterbury, NZ; one *s* four *d. Heir: s* Basil Malcolm, *b* 1928. *Address:* Kinnoull, Wai-iti Road, Timaru, S Canterbury, NZ. *Club:* Carlton.
[Succession not proved.] *Died 27 July 1949.*

ARUNDALE, Dr George Sydney, MA, LLB, DLitt; President The Theosophical Society (1934); President New India League (1939); Fellow of the Royal Historical Society, London; Freeman of the City of London; Member of the Worshipful Company of Pewterers; *b* Surrey, 1 Dec. 1878; *s* of Rev. John Kay; *m* 1920, Rukmini, *d* of N. K. Sastri, engineer, South India. *Educ:* St John's College, Cambridge. Principal, Central Hindu College, Benares, 1909; Examiner to the University of Allahabad and to the Government, United Provinces, India; Principal of National University of Madras, 1917; Minister of Education to the Government of the Maharaja Holkar, 1923; late Regionary Bishop of the Liberal Catholic Church in India; late Deputy Chief Scout of Indian Boy Scout Association; late Provincial Commissioner of Hindustan Scout Association in Madras Presidency; Editor of The Theosophist, The Theosophical Worker, and Conscience, Madras. *Publications:* many pamphlets and books on Education, Politics, Theosophy: Nirvana, Mount Everest, You, Freedom and Friendship Gods in the Becoming, Kundalini, The Lotus Fire (A Study in Symbolic Yoga). *Recreations:* lawn tennis, chess, detective stories. *Address:* The Theosophical Society, Adyar, Madras, India. *Clubs:* Queen's, Royal Societies.

Died 12 Aug. 1945.

ARUNDELL OF WARDOUR, 16th Baron *cr* 1605; John Francis Arundell; Count of the Holy Roman Empire, 1595; JP for Tisbury, Wilts.; TD; *b* 18 June 1907; *s* of 15th Baron and Ivy, *o d* of late Capt. W. F. Segrave; *S* father, 1939; unmarried. *Educ:* Stonyhurst College; New College, Oxford. BA. Capt. 2nd Bn The Wiltshire Regt; member of the London Stock Exchange; served 1939–40, Capt. (prisoner but repatriated). *Heir:* none. *Address:* Wardour Castle, Tisbury, Wiltshire. *T:* Tisbury 252. *Club:* White's.

Died 25 Sept. 1944.

ASHBEE, C. R.; *b* Isleworth, 17 May 1863; *s* of Henry Spencer Ashbee; *m* 1899, Janet Elizabeth Forbes; four *d*. *Educ:* Wellington; King's College, Cambridge. Architect, now retired, designer and town planner; Master of the Art Workers Guild, 1929; Founder and for twenty-five years Director of the Guild of Handicraft which ended during the war; Founder of the London Survey Committee, and Editor of its earlier publications; the builder of many houses in London, the country, and abroad; extensive church restoration and repair work; Designer in metal-work, jewellery, and various crafts; Founder of the Essex House Press, which he conducted for twelve years, and for which he designed the Prayer Book for King Edward VII; Civic Adviser to the Palestine Administration, first Military, then Civil, 1918–22. *Publications:* Various works on architecture and the crafts in their social aspects; principal writings— Chapters on Workshop Reconstruction and Citizenship; Craftsmanship in Competitive Industry; Modern Silverwork; The Treatises of Benvenuto Cellini; Book of Cottages and Little Houses; also poetry and belles lettres; The Building of Thelema; Echoes from the City of the Sun; The Masque of the Edwards; Lyrics of the Nile; Should We Stop Teaching Art? The Hamptonshire Experiment in Education; Where the Great City Stands; The Private Press—A Study in Idealism; The American League to enforce peace, 1917; Jerusalem, 1918–1920; A Palestine Notebook, 1918–1923; Jerusalem, 1921–1922; Caricature, 1927; Peckover—the Abbotscourt papers, 1932; Kingfisher out of Egypt, 1934; Kings of Minzaman, 1937; Grannie, 1939. *Address:* Godden Green, Sevenoaks, Kent. *T:* Seal 109. *Club:* Overseas League.

Died 23 May 1942.

ASHBOURNE, 2nd Baron *cr* 1885; **William Gibson;** JP; Ex-President of the Gaelic League; *b* 16 Dec. 1868; *s* of 1st Baron Ashbourne and Frances Maria Adelaide, *d* of H. C. Colles; *S* father, 1913; *m* 1896, Marianne, *d* of late M. de Monbrison. *Educ:* Harrow; Dublin University; Merton College, Oxford. Ex-President Gaelic League of London. *Publications:* The Abbé Lamennais and the Liberal Catholic Movement in France, 1896; L'Eglise Libre dans l'Etat Libre, 1907; Gregoire and the French Revolution, a Study, 1932; contributions to reviews. *Heir: nephew* Comdr Edward Russell Gibson, RN [*b* 1 June 1901; *m* 1929, Reta, *d* of E. M. Hazeland, Hong Kong; one *s* one *d*]. *Address:* 17 rue des Domeliers, Compiègne, Oise, France. *Clubs:* Athenæum; St Stephen's Green, Dublin.

Died 21 Jan. 1942.

ASHBURNHAM, Sir Reginald, 10th Bt *cr* 1661; *b* 26 Aug. 1865; *s* of 8th Bt and Isabella, *e d* of late Capt. G. B. Martin, CB, RN; *S* brother, 1935; *m* 1921, Mildred (*d* 1942), *widow* of Walter Cheesman, of Hill House, Crowhurst, Sussex. *Heir: b* Fleetwood Ashburnham [*b* 1869; *m* 1908, Elfrida, *d* of late James Kirkley; one *s* one *d*]. *Address:* Broomham, Guestling, near Hastings. *T:* Pett 56.

Died 29 Jan. 1944.

ASHCOMBE, 2nd Baron *cr* 1892; **Henry Cubitt,** CB 1911; TD; MA; *b* 14 March 1867; *s* of 1st Lord Ashcombe and Laura, *d* of Rev. James Joyce; *S* father, 1917; *m* 1890, Maud (*d* 1945), *d* of late Col Calvert, Ockley Court; three *s*. *Educ:* Eton; Trinity College, Cambridge. Lieut-Col and Hon. Col commanding The Surrey (Queen Mary's Regt) Yeomanry, 1901–12; MP (C) Reigate Division of Surrey; 1892–1906; HM Lieut Surrey, 1905–39. *Heir: s* Hon. Roland Calvert Cubitt. *Address:* Denbies, Dorking. *Club:* Carlton.

Died 27 Oct. 1947.

ASHFIELD, 1st Baron *cr* 1920, of Southwell; **Albert (Henry) Stanley;** PC 1916; Kt, 1914; TD; Member of British Transport Commission since 1947; Hon. Col 84th (LT) AA Regt, RA, 1939; Colonel Engineer and Railway Staff Corps; *b* Derby, 8 Nov. 1874; *s* of late

Henry Stanley, Detroit; *m* 1904, Grace Lowrey Woodruff; two *d*. *Educ:* American Colleges and Technical Schools. Prior to 1907 General Manager of American Electric Railways for 12 years, chiefly the Detroit United Railways and the Public Service Railways of New Jersey; General Manager of Metropolitan District Railway and Tube Railways in London, 1907; Managing Director of the Underground Group of Companies, 1912; Director General of Mechanical Transport, 1916; President Board of Trade, 1916–19; MP (CU) Ashton-under-Lyne, 1916–20; Chairman and Managing Directory of the Underground Group of Companies, 1916–33; Chairman London Passenger Transport Board, 1933–47; Director Midland Bank, Ltd, Imperial Chemical Industries, Ltd; Member Royal Commission on Railways and Transportation in Canada, 1931. *Recreation:* golf. *Address:* The Crossways, Sunningdale. *T:* Ascot 259. *Clubs:* Carlton, Royal Automobile.

Died 4 Nov. 1948 (ext).

ASHFIELD, Percy John, CBE 1927; JP; *b* 1870; *s* of William Ashfield, Stratford-on-Avon; *m* Guendoline, *d* of Captain E. W. Keatinge, JP; one *s* one *d*. *Educ:* King Edward VI School, Stratford-on-Avon. Sheriff of Flintshire, 1943. *Address:* Den Haag, Rhyl. *TA:* Ashfield, Rhyl. *T:* Rhyl 948.

Died 4 June 1946.

ASHLEY, Lord; Anthony Ashley-Cooper; JP, DL, County of Dorset; Major, Royal Wiltshire Yeomanry; *b* 4 Oct. 1900; *e s* and *heir* of 9th Earl of Shaftesbury, KP; *m* 1937, Françoise, *e d* of Georges Soulier, Rouen; one *s* one *d*. *Educ:* Eton; Royal Military College, Sandhurst; Caius College, Cambridge University. ADC to the Governor of Bombay, 1929–30; ADC to the Commander-in-Chief in India, 1930–31; 10th Hussars, 1941; served NW Europe, 1944–45. *Address:* Mainsail Haul, Wimborne-St Giles, Dorset. *Clubs:* Carlton, Buck's, Cavalry, Royal Automobile.

Died 8 March 1947.

ASHLEY, Henry V., FRIBA; Architect in Private Practice; *b* 1872; *y s* of John Ashley; *m* 1900, M. F. Brunton; one *d*. *Educ:* Merchant Taylor's School. Commenced practice in 1896 and since 1907 in partnership with F. Winton Newman. *Principal Works:* Council House Extension and Art Galleries, Birmingham; Masonic Peace Memorial, London, French Bank, London; Glyn Mills Bank, Oxford; Technical College and Colleges of Art and Commerce, Birmingham; Technical College, Cheltenham; housing schemes, hospitals, and domestic work in London and the country. *Recreations:* travel, motoring, and gardening. *Address:* 20 Frognal Gardens, Hampstead, NW3; 27 Thurlow Road, NW3. *T:* Hampstead 3825, Hampstead 2879. *Club:* Arts.

Died 29 July 1945.

ASHLEY, Sir Percy (Walter Llewellyn), KBE 1933; CB 1919; Vice-President, British Standards Institution; Chairman of British Rayon Federation and of Central Rayon Office; *b* 1876; *y s* of James Ashley; *m* 1906, Doris Hayman (*d* 1941); one *s* one *d*. *Educ:* St Olave's School, Southwark; Lincoln College, Oxford (Scholar); MA (First-class Honours Modern History). Formerly Lecturer in History and Public Administration, London School of Economics (University of London). Staff-Officer, Commercial Department, Board of Trade, 1907; Joint-Secretary, Commercial Intelligence Committee; Joint-Secretary, Committee on Commercial and Industrial Policy, 1916–17; Assistant Secretary Board of Trade, 1918–23; Principal Assistant Secretary, Department of Industries and Manufactures, Board of Trade, 1923–32; Secretary to Import Duties Advisory Committee, 1932–39, and member, 1939–42; Cotton Controller, 1939–41. *Publications:* Modern Tariff History; English Local Government; Local and Central

Government; Twice Fifty Years of Europe. *Address:* The British Rayon Federation, 58 Whitworth Street, Manchester. *Club:* Reform.

Died 13 Sept. 1945.

ASHMALL, Rev. Francis James; *b* Hammerwich, Staffs, 17 Dec. 1856; *s* of Elias Ashmole Ashmall and Mary Glover; *m* Anne Mary, *d* of George and Elizabeth Davies Postlethwaite, of Waterloo, Liverpool, and later of Oakleigh, East Grinstead; no *c. Educ:* Cannock Grammar School; Queen's College, Cambridge. Deacon, 1881; Priest, 1882; Curate of Fareham, Hants, 1881–86; Vicar of Holy Trinity, Southampton, 1886–96; Rector of Bishopstoke, 1896–1905; of Hickling, 1905–28; Rural Dean of S Bingham, 1906–28; Hon. Canon of Southwell, 1918–28; retired. *Recreations:* cricket till 1910, football till 1886, golf 1896–1940, cycling 1884–1940. *Address:* (temp.): Hickling, Melton Mowbray.

Died 5 May 1948.

ASHTON, Baroness; Florence Maude, CBE 1937; *b* York, 19 March 1856; *d* of Rev. R. Daniel, BD, Vicar of Osbaldwick, near York; *m* 1st, 1881, Col Joseph Lawson Whalley, JP (*d* 1908) of Richmond House, Lancaster; one *d*; 2nd, 1909, 1st Baron Ashton (*d* 1930). President Lancaster Parliamentary Division Conservative and Unionist Assoc. (Women's Branch); County Pres. NW Lancs Girl Guides Assoc.; Pres. Morecambe Musical Festival; Chairman RSPCA, Westmorland; Vice-President Lancashire Branch, CPRE; Area Vice-President, NW Area, British Legion; President Lancaster Agricultural Soc., 1934–36; Pres. Royal Lancaster Agricultural Soc., 1939–43; Pres. S Lonsdale, Lancaster, and Morecambe Branch of Soldiers', Sailors' and Airmen's Families' Association; Vice-Pres. Lancaster Branch of British Red Cross Society; Freedom of City of Lancaster, 1932, and of Borough of Morecambe and Heysham, 1938. *Address:* Heaves, nr Kendal, Westmorland. *Club:* Ladies' Carlton.

Died 25 July 1944.

ASHTON, Julian Rossi, CBE 1930; Principal, Sydney Art School; *b* 27 Jan. 1851; *s* of Thomas Briggs Ashton and Henrietta Spencer; *m* 1876; two *s* one *d. Educ:* Grammar School, Totnes, Devon. In London until 1878; in Australia (Sydney and Melbourne) since 1878. *Recreation:* gardening. *Address:* The Glen, Bondi, Sydney, NSW, Australia.

Died 27 April 1942.

ASHTON-GWATKIN, Rev. Walter Henry Trelawney; *see* Gwatkin.

ASHTOWN, 3rd Baron *cr* 1800; **Frederick Oliver Trench;** JP, DL; *b* 2 Feb. 1868; *e s* of Hon. Frederick Sydney Charles Trench and Lady Anne Le Poer Trench, *d* of 3rd Earl of Clancarty; *S* grandfather, 1880; *m* 1894, Violet (*d* 1945), *d* of late Col R. G. Cosby; two *s* one *d. Educ:* Eton; Magdalen College, Oxford. Owns 22,000 acres. *Recreations:* shooting, fishing. *Heir: s* Hon. Robert Power Trench. *Address:* Woodlawn House, Co. Galway; Glenahiry Lodge, Waterford.

Died 20 March 1946.

ASHWANDEN, Col Sydney William Louis, CBE 1944; DSO 1917; TD 1918; DL County of London and Berks; JP Bucks; ADC to the King since 1931; *b* 5 Nov. 1878; *s* of W. L. Ashwanden, Bushey, Herts; *m* 1903, Ann Florence, *e d* of late W. T. Robertson, JP, The Grange, Aldershot, Hants; one *s. Educ:* privately. Royal Artillery (Vols), 1899; France and Germany, 1915–19; raised Brigade, RATA 1920, commanded 1920–27. Vice-Chairman, British Legion, 1934–39, National Chairman, 1939–43. *Recreations:* fishing, golf. *Address:* Gore Cottage, Burnham, Bucks. *T:* Burnham (Bucks) 509. *Club:* Junior United Service.

Died 2 June 1947.

ASKEW ROBERTSON, William Haggerston; JP; *b* 1868; *s* of late Watson Askew Robertson and Hon. Sarah, *e d* of first and last Baron Marjoribanks; *m* 1903, Katherine Marjorie Strathearn (*d* 1932), *e d* of late Hon. John Edward Gordon, MP; one *s* one *d. Educ:* Eton; Christ Church, Oxford. Member of Stock Exchange for over 30 years. *Recreation:* country gentleman. *Address:* Castle Hills, Berwick-upon-Tweed. *T:* 376. *Clubs:* New, Edinburgh; Northern Counties, Newcastle-upon-Tyne.

Died 4 March 1942.

ASKWITH, 1st Baron *cr* 1919; **George Ranken Askwith;** of St Ives in the Co. of Hunts, KCB 1911; CB 1909; *b* 17 Feb. 1861; *s* of late Gen. W. H. Askwith, Col-Com. RA; *m* 1908, Ellen, CBE 1918, *widow* of Maj. Henry Graham, 20th Hussars, and *d* of Archibald Peel of Westlea, Broxbourne; one *d. Educ:* Marlborough (Member of Council and Chairman Finance (Committee); Brasenose College, Oxford (Scholar, Hulmeian Exhibitioner, 1st class History, Hon. Fellow, 1919), MA, Hon. DCL 1912, Hon. LLD, Leeds University, 1938; Hon. Doc. Université de Lille, 1938. Barrister Inner and Middle Temple, 1886; Counsel on the Venezuelan Arbitration, to HM's Commissioners of Works, and for the Crown in Peerage Claims; Steward of HM's Manor of the Savoy; Arbitrator and conciliator in many trade disputes; Assistant Secretary Board of Trade (Railways), 1907; British Plenipotentiary to International Congress on Copyright at Berlin, 1908; KC 1908; Comptroller General Commercial Labour and Statistical Depts, Board of Trade, 1909; Chief Industrial Commissioner, 1911–19; Chairman Industrial Council, 1911, and of Fair Wages Advisory Committee, 1909–19; made special report for Government on labour laws of Canada, 1912; Umpire Scottish Coal Conciliation Board, 1913–15; Chairman Government Arbitration Committee under Munitions of War Acts, 1915–17; Chairman of Council Institut Français since 1913; Commander of the Legion of Honour and of the Belgian Order of the Crown, 1919; received hon. freedom of Weaver's Company (Upper Bailiff, 1925 and 1939) and City of London, 1911; Mayor of St Ives, Hunts, 1913; President Middle Classes Union (now National Citizens' Union), 1921–29; Member Royal Commission on Cattle Importation, 1921; Chairman, Malta Royal Commission, 1931; and member of Joint Committees on Consolidation Acts and Guardianship of Infants' Bills and Lords' Committees on Claims to Peerages, and Chairman or Member of other Joint or Select Committees; Chairman Parliamentary delegation to Bermuda, 1932; Member of panel for commissions of inquiry under Art. 412 of the Treaty of Versailles, 1934; Chairman of Council Royal Society of Arts, 1922–24; Treasurer 1925–27, and Vice-President 1927–41; President of British Science Guild, 1922–25; Pres. Inst. of Patentees, 1925–41; Pres. National Assoc. of Trade Protection Societies, 1924–27 and 1928–29; Vice-Pres. Federation of British Industries; Hon. Treasurer YMCA, 1920–33, and Vice-President; late Chairman Governors of Royal Holloway College; late Chairman of Council of Cheltenham Ladies' College, and late Member of Council of St Hilda's College, Oxford; President of the National Greyhound Racing Society of Great Britain; President Institute of Arbitrators, 1933–41; Director of Monotype Corporation and County of London Electric Supply Corporation, and other companies. *Publications:* Industrial Problems and Disputes, 1920; British Taverns, their History and Laws, 1928; Lord James of Hereford, 1930. *Recreation:* travelling. *Heir:* none. *Address:* 5 Cadogan Gardens, SW3. *T:* Sloane 1062. *Clubs:* United University, Athenæum.

Died 2 June 1942.

ASKWITH, Rev. Edward Harrison, DD (Cambridge); *b* 8 Sept. 1864; *s* of late Thomas Askwith of Ripon; *m* 1889, Mary Douglas Fox, *d* of late Sir Douglas Fox; two *d. Educ:* Christ's Hospital; Trinity College, Cambridge

(Scholar); bracketed 10th Wrangler, 1886. Assistant-Master Westminster School, 1888; Headmaster of South-Eastern College, Ramsgate, 1889–91; ordained Deacon, 1888; Priest, 1889; Vicar of St Michael's, Cambridge, 1893–96; Chaplain of Trinity College, Cambridge, 1894–1909; Norrisian prizeman, 1898; Vicar of Kirkby Lonsdale. Westmorland, 1909–17; Hon. Canon of Carlisle, 1917; Rector of Dickleburgh, Norfolk, 1917–24. *Publications:* Papers on Groups of Substitutions in Quarterly Journal of Pure and Applied Mathematics, 1889, etc.; The Epistle to the Galatians—an essay on its Destination and Date, 1899; The Christian Conception of Holiness, 1900; An Introduction to the Thessalonian Epistles, 1902; Pure Geometry, 1903; Essay on Sin and the Need of Atonement, 1905; The Analytical Geometry of the Conic Sections, 1908; The Historical Value of the Fourth Gospel, 1910; The Psalms (Books iv and v), A Rhythmical Translation, 1925. *Recreations:* golf and gardening. *Address:* 29 Storey's Way, Cambridge. *T:* 4605.

Died 21 Dec. 1946.

ASMAN, Rev. Harry Newbitt, MA, BD; *b* Hull, 1877; *s* of Charles Arden and Martha Clark Asman. *Educ:* Hull Grammar School; London University. BA, Double Honours, 1900; MA, 1903; Durham University, BD, 1907. Deacon, 1903; Priest, 1904; Assistant Master, Hull Grammar School, to 1899; Assistant Master, Owen's School, 1899; Second Master, 1907; Curate, St Andrew's, Alexandra Park, 1903–10; Chaplain to the Manor House, Brondesbury, 1910–29; Headmaster of Owen's School, EC1, 1929–39. *Publications:* A Junior Latin Prose; An Introduction to the History of Rome; Selections from English Literature, 1700–1900. *Recreations:* walking, music. *Address:* Beenham Vicarage, Berks. *T:* Woolwich.

Died 22 Oct. 1950.

ASPINALL, Major John Ralph; JP; *b* 1878; *s* of late Col Ralph John Aspinall and Mabel Federica Frances, *y d* of late Robert Lloyd Jones-Parry of Aberdunant, Carnarvonshire, and of Plâs Tregayan, Anglesey; *m* 1st, 1901, Florence Augusta (*d* 1923), 3rd *d* of late Col George Blucher Heneage Marton; 2nd, 1926, Muriel, *y d* of late John Lawson Johnston; one *s. Educ:* Eton; Trinity Hall, Cambridge. Major in 1/1 Lancashire Hussars; Patron of two livings. *Address:* Standen Hall, Clitheroe. *Club:* Cavalry.

Died 16 March 1946.

ASQUITH, Hon. Herbert; *b* 11 March 1881; *e surv. s* of 1st Earl of Oxford and Asquith; *uncle* and *heir-pres.* to 2nd Earl; *m* 1910, Lady Cynthia Charteris *e d* of 11th Earl of Wemyss and March; two *s. Educ:* Winchester; Balliol College, Oxford. President of Oxford Union Society, 1903; called to Bar, Lincoln's Inn, 1907; Captain (late) RFA; active service in France and Flanders, European War, 1914–18; Volunteer in Sussex Home Guard 1940, and later 2nd in command of a Company. *Publications: Poems*—The Volunteer; A Village Sermon; Pillicock Hill; Poems, 1912–1933; Youth in the Skies, 1940. *Novels*—Wind's End; Young Orland; Roon; Mary Dallon; *Memoir*—Moments of Memory. *Recreations:* shooting and golf. *Address:* 8 Sussex Place, Regent's Park, NW1. *T:* Paddington 0914; Claverton Lodge, Bathwick Hill, Bath. *Club:* Brooks's.

Died 5 Aug. 1947.

ASSER, Gen. Sir (Joseph) John, KCB 1924 (CB 1915); KCMG 1918; KCVO 1917; late Dorset Regt; *b* 31 Aug. 1867; *s* of late S. B. V. Asser, Windlesham, Surrey; *m* 1901, Leila, *d* of James Wotherspoon of New York; one *d*. Entered Army, 1887; Captain, 1893; Major, 1907; Lt-Col 1907; Col 1911; retired July 1914; restored to active list 1916 as Maj.-Gen.; Gen. 1926; ADC to GOC Egypt, 1892; AG Egyptian Army, 1907–14; served Nile Expedition, 1897 (medal and clasp); Nile Expedition, 1898 (Bt-Major, medal and two clasps); Nile Expedition, 1899 (clasp); Expedition Southern Kordofan (in command), 1910 (medal and clasp); European War, 1914–18 (despatches, Base Comdt, GOCL of C area, GOC British Troops, France and Flanders, 1919, KCMG, CB, prom. Lt-Gen., 1914 Star, British and Victory medals, Order St Anne (crossed swords), Belgian Order de la Couronne); Governor and Commander-in-Chief, Bermuda, 1922–27; 2nd class Osmanieh; 2nd class Mejidie Sacred Treasure, Aviz, Grand Officier Legion of Honour, Croix de Guerre (France and Belgium); ADC General to the King, 1929–30; retired pay, 1930; for some years a member of Sudan Govt Council; a Pasha in Egypt; Hon. Member Phi, Beta, Kappa, William and Mary College, Virginia. *Recreations:* shooting, fishing, and golf. *Address:* The Old Vicarage, Hambledon, Hants. *T:* Hambledon 132. *Club:* Army and Navy.

Died 4 Feb. 1949.

ASSER, Brig.-Gen. Verney, CB 1931; CMG 1919; DSO 1902; *b* Beadonwell, Kent, 28 Dec. 1873; 3rd *s* of late S. B. V. Asser, JP, Windlesham, Surrey; *m* 1911, Hyacinth, *d* of late Henry Irwin, CIE, Madras; (one *s* killed in action, 1940) one *d. Educ:* Uppingham School. Joined Yorkshire Artillery, 1893; served with British SA Police in Matabele War, 1896 (medal); commissioned to Royal Artillery, 1899; on service in Anglo-Boer War, 1900–02 (Queen's medal three clasps, King's medal and clasps, despatches, DSO); operations on Blue Nile, 1908 (medal); Adjutant, 11th Brigade, 1905–08; attached Egyptian Army, 1908–12; Adjt RMA 1913–14; served European War, 1914–18, Staff Capt. RA, Brigade Major RA, GSO2, CRA (despatches, Bt Lt-Col, CMG, Greek Military Cross); CRA 44th (Home Counties) Division; AAG War Office, 1925–27; commanded RA, 4th Division, 1927–30; retired pay, 1930. *Address:* Upperlands, Lodsworth, Sussex. *T:* Lodsworth 49. *Club:* Army and Navy.

Died 13 Jan. 1944.

ASTLEY, Reginald Basil; *b* 8 Jan. 1862; 3rd *s* of late Lt-Col Francis L'Estrange Astley and Rosalind Alicia Frankland-Russell-Astley, of Chequers Court, Bucks; *m* 1st, 1913, Caroline Douglas (*d* 1921), *o c* of late James Affleck Stewart, 11th Hussars, and *widow* of Sir Walter Orlando Corbet, 4th Bart; 2nd, 1931, Kathleen Mary, CBE, *d* of late T. M. C. Vigors of Burgage, Co. Carlow, and *widow* of Hon. Wilfred Gilbert Thesiger, DSO. *Educ:* Eton. Served in Metropolitan Special Constabulary, 1914–19; Sub-Inspector in Metropolitan Special Constabulary Reserve, 1919–22. *Address:* The Milebrook, Bucknell, Shropshire. *T:* Knighton 34. *Club:* Carlton.

Died 6 Oct. 1942.

ASTLEY-CORBETT, Sir (Francis) Henry (Rivers), 5th Bt *cr* 1821; 2nd Lieut Scots Guards; *b* 29 Dec. 1915; *s* of John Dugdale Pelham Astley-Corbett and Marcia Georgina Ruth Pitt Rivers; *S* grandfather, 1939. *Educ:* Stowe. *Recreations:* riding, motoring, and outdoor games. *Heir: kinsman* Francis Jacob Dugdale Astley, *b* 26 Oct. 1908. *Club:* Bachelors'.

Died 10 Sept. 1943.

ASTON, Francis William, FRS 1921; MA, ScD, DSc, FIC; Fellow of Trinity College, Cambridge, since 1920; Chairman of the International Committee on Atoms, since 1935; *b* 1 Sept. 1877; 2nd *s* of William Aston, Harborne, Birmingham. *Educ:* Malvern College; Mason College (Forster Research Scholar); Birmingham University (University Research Scholar); Cambridge University. Assistant-Lecturer in Physics, Birmingham University, 1909; entered Trinity College and Cavendish Laboratory, Cambridge, 1910; BA research degree, 1912; Clerk-Maxwell Studentship, 1913; DSc Birmingham, 1914; Technical Assist, RAE, Farnborough, 1914–19; MA Cambridge, 1919; Mackenzie Davidson Medal of the Röntgen Society, 1920; Hughes Medal of the Royal Society, 1922; Nobel Prize for Chemistry, 1922; John Scott Medal, Philadelphia, 1923; Paterno Medal, Rome, 1923; Hon.

LLD Birmingham, 1923; ScD Cambridge, 1924; Corr. Mem. Acad. Sci. Russia, 1925; Foreign Member R Accad. Lincei, Rome, 1926; Bakerian Lecturer Royal Society, 1927; Hon. DSc Dublin, 1929; Hon. PhD Freiburg, 1930; Pres. of Section A British Association, 1935; Hon. DSc, Benares, 1937; Hon. Silver Jubilee Member Indian Science Congress Association, 1938; Joykissen Mookherjee Medal Calcutta, 1938; Hon. DL Calcutta, 1938; Royal Medal of Royal Society, 1938; Duddell Medal of Physical Society, 1944. *Publications:* Isotopes, 1922; Mass-spectra and Isotopes, 1933. 2nd Edition, 1942; numerous papers in the Proceedings of the Royal Society, Philosophical Magazine, and other scientific periodicals on electric discharge in gases, mass-spectra, isotopes, and other physical and chemical subjects. *Recreations:* music, golf, and travel. *Address:* Trinity College, Cambridge. *T:* Cambridge 3441. *Club:* Athenæum.

Died 20 Nov. 1945.

ATHERTON, Gertrude Franklin; author; *b* San Francisco, California, on Rincon Hill; *o d* of Thomas L. Horn and Gertrude Franklin, *great-grandniece* of Benjamin Franklin; *m* George H. Bowen Atherton, Menlo Park, California (decd); one *d. Educ:* St Mary's Hall, Benicia, California; Sayre Inst., Lexington, Kentucky; private tutors. Doctor of Letters, Mills College; Doctor of Laws, University of California. President of North California PEN. *Publications:* The Dooms-woman, 1892; A Whirl Asunder, 1895; Patience Sparhawk and Her Times, 1897; His Fortunate Grace, 1897; American Wives and English Husbands, 1898; The Californians, 1898; A Daughter of the Vine, 1899; The Valiant Runaways, 1899; Senator North, 1900; The Aristocrats, 1901; The Conqueror, 1902; The Splendid Idle Forties, 1902; A Few of Hamilton's Letters, 1903; Mrs Pendleton's Four-in-Hand, 1903; Rulers of Kings, 1904; The Bell in the Fog, 1905; The Travelling Thirds, 1905; Rezánov, 1906; Ancestors, 1907; The Gorgeous Isle, 1908; Tower of Ivory, 1910; Julia France and Her Times, 1912; Perch of the Devil, 1914; California, 1914; Mrs Balfame, 1916; The Living Present, 1917; The White Morning, 1918; The Avalanche, 1919; Sisters in Law, 1921; Dormant Fires, 1922; Black Oxen, 1923; The Crystal Cup, 1925; The Immortal Marriage, 1927; Vengeful Gods, 1928; Dido: Queen of Hearts, 1929; The Sophisticates, 1931; Adventures of a Novelist, 1932; The Foghorn, 1935; Golden Peacock, 1936; Can Women Be Gentlemen?, 1938; The House of Lee, 1940; The Horn of Life, 1942; Golden Gate Country, My San Francisco, A Wayward Biography, 1945. *Address:* 2280 Green Street, San Francisco, USA.

Died 14 June 1948.

ATHOLL, 8th Duke of, *cr* 1703; **John George Stewart-Murray,** KT 1918; GCVO 1923; CB 1917; DSO 1898; MVO 1902; Lord Murray of Tullibardine, 1604; Earl of Tullibardine, Lord Gask and Balquhidder, 1606; Earl of Atholl, 1629; Marquess of Atholl, Viscount Balquhidder, Lord Balvenie, 1676; Marquess of Tullibardine, Earl of Strathtay, Earl of Strathardle, Viscount Glenalmond, Viscount Glenlyon, 1703—all in the Peerage of Scotland. Lord Strange of Knockyn (England), 1628; Lord Percy (by writ), 1722; Earl Strange and Lord Murray of Stanley, 1786—all in the Peerage of Great Britain. Lord Glenlyon of Glenlyon (UK), 1821; Lord-Lieutenant and Hereditary Sheriff county of Perth; Brevet Major Army, retired pay; Lt-Col and Hon. Col RATA; late Hon. Col 3rd Bn Black Watch and Liverpool Scottish; MP (U) West Perthshire, 1910–17; Lord High Commissioner to the Church of Scotland, 1918–20; *b* 15 Dec. 1871; *s* of 7th Duke of Atholl and Louisa (*d* 1902), *d* of Sir Thos Moncreiffe, 7th Bt; *S* father, 1917; *m* 1899, Katharine Marjory, DBE, LLD, *d* of Sir James Henry Ramsay, 10th Bt; no *c. Educ:* Eton. Lord Chamberlain, 1922; Lt 3rd Bt Royal Highlanders (Black Watch), 1890–92; Lt Royal Horse Guards, 1892; Capt., 1900; served with Egyptian Cavalry as Staff

Officer to Col Broadwood during Nile Expedition, 1898; present at Reconnaissance on the Atbara, battles of Atbara and Khartoum (medals, two clasps and DSO, despatches twice); served South Africa 1899–1902, first attached Royal Dragoons, later as Lieut-Col commanding 1st and 2nd Scottish Horse (despatches 3 times, Queen's medal 6 clasps, King's medal 2 clasps); Commandant Scottish Horse and Brig.-General, European War (despatches Gallipoli and Egypt, CB, Servian Order of White Eagle of Serbia with crossed swords, 3rd Class). *Heir: b* Major Lord James Stewart-Murray. *Address:* Blair Castle, Blair-Atholl, Perthshire; Eastwood, Dunkeld. *Clubs:* Carlton, Naval and Military, Royal Aero (Chairman); New, Edinburgh.

Died 15 March 1942.

ATKEY, Sir Albert (Reuben), Kt 1935; JP, Member of Nottingham City Council since 1908; Sheriff, 1911; Alderman, 1928; Lord Mayor, 1929; Chairman of Water Committee since 1909; *b* Nottingham, 1 July 1867; *m* 1st, 1890, Euphemia Althea (*d* 1941), *d* of Robert Hawksley; one *s* two *d*; 2nd, 1942, Mrs Lilian M. Stembridge, Chapel Allerton, Leeds. *Educ:* Huntingdon St Board School; Univ. Coll. Nottingham. Started in Water Engineers Dept Nottingham Corp 1880; Articled pupil, 1884; Assist Engineer, 1888–92; MP (CU), Central Division of Nottingham, 1918–22; motor engineering since 1897; Founder Member, Advisory Committee on Water to Ministry of Health, 1922; Chairman Derwent Valley Water Board; President Nottingham Mechanics Institution; Member Central Water Advisory Committee to Ministry of Health, 1937; President British Waterworks Association 1919–21, 1939; Hon. Treasurer, Freshwater Biological Association of the British Empire; President Motor and Cycle Trades Benevolent Fund, 1938–39; Pres. Nottingham Operatic Society. *Recreations:* gardening and golf. *Address:* 30 Burleigh Mansions, St Martin's Lane, WC2. *T:* Temple Bar 7939; The Park, Nottingham. *T:* 44496. *Club:* Royal Automobile.

Died 9 Nov. 1947.

ATKIN, Baron *cr* 1928 (Life Peer), of Aberdovey; **James Richard Atkin,** PC 1919; Kt 1913; FBA; Lord of Appeal in Ordinary since 1928; *b* 1867; *e s* of late Robert Travers Atkin, Fernhill, Co. Cork, MLA, Queensland; *m* Lucy Elizabeth (*d* 1939), *e d* of William Hemmant, Bulimba, Sevenoaks, formerly Colonial Treasurer, Queensland; one *s* [Hon. William Robert Atkin, *m* 1st Constance Emilia Bourchier (*d* 1930); one *s*; 2nd 1935, Mary McMurtrie] six *d. Educ:* Christ College, Brecon; Magdalen College, Oxford (Demy, Hon. Fellow, 1924). Barrister, Gray's Inn, 1891; Bencher, 1906; KC 1906; South Wales and Chester Circuit; Judge of the High Court, 1913–19; Lord Justice of Appeal, 1919–28; Judge of Munitions Tribunals Appeals Court, 1916–19; President of Naturalisation of Aliens (Revocation) Committee, 1918–19; Chairman of War Cabinet Committee on Women in Industry, 1918–19; Chairman of Termination of the War Committee, 1918; Member of Committee on British and Foreign Legal Procedure, 1918–19; Chairman of Irish Deportees Compensation Tribunal, 1924; Chairman of Committee on Crime and Insanity, 1924; President of Medico-Legal Society, 1923–27; Member of Councils of University College of Wales, Aberystwyth, Christ College, Brecon; Governor of Charterhouse; Chairman of Council of Legal Education, 1919–34. *Address:* 74 Ashley Gardens, SW1; Craigydon, Aberdovey, N Wales. *T:* Victoria 7075.

Died 25 June 1944.

ATKINS, Prof. Henry Gibson, MA (Cantab), DLit (Lond.), Emeritus Professor of German in the University of London; *b* 3 Jan. 1871; *e s* of J. Atkins and Mary Gibson; *m* 1903, Lilian Walford; two *s* two *d. Educ:* Queen Elisabeth Grammar School, Atherstone; private study France and Germany; Trinity College, Cambridge. Professor of German, King's College, 1900–37; Fellow, 1912; Assistant Principal, 1919–23 and 1925–37;

Member University Senate, 1918–33, and of University Court, 1929–33. *Publications:* A Short History of French Literature (with Prof. L. E. Kastner); Goethe's Poems, a selection (with Prof. Kastner); Goethe (Oxford Biographies); The Teaching of Modern Foreign Languages (with H. L. Hutton); A History of German Versification; The Farmer in Purgatory (translated from Hans Sachs); Heine (in The Republic of Letters); The Poems of Annette von Droste-Hülshoff; German Literature through Nazi Eyes, etc.; Articles and Reviews; Joint Editor of the Modern Language Review. *Address:* Timber Hill Lodge, Caterham Valley.

Died 13 Aug. 1942.

ATKINSON, Brig.-Gen. Ben, CB 1918; CMG 1916; late RA; *b* 9 Jan. 1872; *m* 1903, Laetitia Janet Emily Norman, *o d* of late E. K. Norman of Mistley Lodge, Manningtree; two *s* one *d*. Served S Africa, 1899–1902 (despatches, Queen's medal 6 clasps, King's medal 2 clasps); European War, 1914–18 (despatches, CMG, CB, Bt Col, Officer de l'Ordre de Leopold); retired, 1920. *Address:* Mistley Hall, Manningtree, Essex.

Died 31 March 1942.

ATKINSON, Ven. Charles Frederic; Archdeacon Emeritus; *b* Stratford-on-Avon, 19 July 1855; *s* of John Atkinson, Second Master, King Edward's Grammar School, Stratford-on-Avon; *m* 1st, 1881, Agnes Helen, *e d* of James Fichat, Civil Commissioner and Resident Magistrate, Queenstown, Cape of Good Hope; two *s*; 2nd, 1939, Daisy Elizabeth Leonard. *Educ:* Grammar School, Stratford-on-Avon. In commercial life, 1869–75; entered S Augustine's College, Canterbury, 1875; ordained, 1878; proceeded at once to the Cape, Deacon and Priest-in-Charge S John Baptist in Wilderness, Schoonberg, 1878–80; Assistant Curate of George, and Principal St Mark's Coll., 1880–83; Incumbent of Uniondale, Dio. Capetown, 1883, 1885; Rector of Caledon, 1885–92; Rector of Woodstock, Capetown, 1893–1902; Rector of Oudtshoorn, 1902–28; Archdeacon of Oudtshoorn, 1912–28; retired, 1928; Vicar-General, Diocese of George, 1920. *Publications:* various sermons, lectures, etc. *Recreations:* science, literature, walking, etc. *Address:* van der Riet Street, Oudtshoorn, CP, South Africa.

Died 27 July 1942.

ATKINSON, Lt-Gen. Sir Edwin Henry de Vere, KCB 1929; KBE 1921; CB 1918; CMG 1917; CIE 1913; *b* 19 Feb. 1867; *s* of late E. F. T. Atkinson, CIE, Indian Civil Service; *m* 1896, Etheldred, *d* of E. Steward, Winton House, Richmond, Surrey; one *s* three *d*. *Educ:* Charterhouse; Royal Military Academy, Woolwich. Commission in the Royal Engineers, 1885; Capt., 1895; Major, 1903; Lt-Col 1910; Col 1914; Brig.-Gen. 1916; Maj.-Gen. 1919; Lt-Gen. 1927; served in Lushai Expedition, 1888–89; Chin-Lushai Expedition, 1889–90; Zhob Valley Expedition, 1890–91; European War, 1915–19 (CB); Mesopotamia, 1919–21 (KBE); Instructor in Fortification at the Roy. Military Academy, Woolwich, 1895–99; Director of Military Works, India, 1921–23; Engineer-in-Chief, AHQ, India, 1923–24; Master General Supply, India, 1924–29; Master General of the Ordnance in India, 1929–30; retired, 1930; Col Comdt RE, 1930–37. *Address:* 52 Courtfield Gardens, SW5. *T:* Frobisher 7235.

Died 1 April 1947.

ATKINSON, Brig.-Gen. Francis Garnett, CB 1908; *b* 10 Nov. 1857; *s* of late Rev. T. Atkinson; *m* 1883, Eliza (*d* 1941), *d* of Franklin Prestage; one *s*. *Educ:* Mr Burney's School, Gosport. Entered army, 1876 Capt. ISC, 1887; Major, 1896; Bt Lieut-Col 1898; Lieut-Col Indian Army, 1902; Brevet Col, 1904; served Egypt, 1882 (medal with clasp, bronze star); NW Frontier, India, 1897 (despatches, Brevet Lt-Col); Mohmand Expedition (medal and clasp), commanded 17th Cavalry; Brig.-Comdr, Bangalore Cavalry Brigade, 1906–09;

retired, 1914; Special Service under War Office, 1915–19. *Address:* 2 Hatfield Road, Northallerton, Yorks. *Club:* United Service.

Died 25 July 1941.

ATKINSON, George, RHA; ARCA. Director, National College of Art, Kildare St, Dublin. *Address:* 13 Fitzwilliam Place, Dublin.

Died 24 March 1941.

ATKINSON, Lt-Col John, DSO 1917; OBE; *s* of late James Atkinson, Blakeney, Gloster; *m* 1928, Eileen Cynthia Marjorie, MBE, *d* of Robert U. Morgan, MBE, Beaconsfield; three *d*. *Educ:* Crypt School, Gloucester; King's College, London. Barrister-at-law; Bacon Prizeman in Constitutional Law and Legal History; served European War, 1914–19 (despatches thrice, DSO, OBE); commanded 27th Reserve Park, Canadian Training Depôt and New Zealand ASC. *Publications:* Humour among the Clergy; Humour among the Lawyers; Humour among the Doctors; Humour in the Army; ABC of the Army; many military, scouting, and humorous works. *Recreations:* writing, lecturing, and looking on. *Address:* Fieldcote, Prestbury, Cheltenham. *T:* Cheltenham 7308.

Died 5 July 1945.

ATKINSON, Thomas Dinham, (FRIBA retired); Architect in general practice and to the Dean and Chapter of Winchester Cathedral and formerly to the Warden and Fellows of Winchester College; *b* 9 April 1864; *s* of Rev. George Barnes Atkinson, MA, Rector of Swanington, Norfolk; *m* Annie Gertrude, *d* of Rev. J. Chataway, MA, Rector of Rotherwick Hants. *Educ:* Rossall; University College, London. Pupil of Sir Arthur Blomfield, ARA; practice at Winchester; formerly architect to the Dean and Chapter of Ely Cathedral and hon. consulting architect to Inc. Church Building Society; student of the British School at Athens; Hon. Sec. Cambridge Antiquarian Soc. *Principal works:* University Buildings (Observatory and Library), Cambridge, work at Ely Cathedral, ecclesiastical and domestic buildings. *Publications:* Old Cambridge Plate, 1896 (joint editor); Cambridge Described and Illustrated, 1897; English Architecture, 1904 (12th ed. 1946); Phylakopi, Melos 1904 (Soc. Hellen. Stud., Suppl. Pap. No. 4, Sec. Architecture); Glossary of English Architecture, 1906 (6th ed. 1946); English and Welsh Cathedrals, 1912; An Architectural History of the Benedictine Monastery of St Etheldreda at Ely (with Dedication to the King), 1933; Survey of the Street Architecture of Winchester, 1934; Key to English Architecture, 1936; Local Style in English Architecture, 1948; County Architecture in England; articles on antiquarian subjects. *Address:* 7 Christ Church Road, Winchester. *T:* Winchester 2409 and 2695.

Died 29 Dec. 1948.

ATKINSON, Thomas John Day, OBE 1919; KC N Ireland, 1924; DL Co. Donegal, 1921; Registrar, Railway Rates Tribunal, 1922–44; *b* 4 March 1882; *o s* of late Thomas J. Atkinson, JP, DL, Cavangarden, Ballyshannon, Ireland; *m* 1918, Cicely Helen Burrington (JP Co. Devon, 1949), *o c* of late Capt. H. B. Hawkshaw, RN; one *d*. *Educ:* Trinity College, Dublin (Mod.). Medallist in Legal Science; Hon. MA, conferred for special service to University, 1927. Called to Irish Bar, 1904; NW Circuit; President University Philosophical Society, TCD, 1905; JP Co. Donegal, 1905; one of founders of Dublin University Contingent, OTC, 1909; Captain (TF), 1911; Captain 5th Bn R Irish Fusiliers, 10th (Irish) Division, 1914; Staff-Captain, 31st Infantry Brigade, 1915; severely wounded Suvla Bay, Gallipoli, Aug. 1915; Staff-Captain, General Headquarters, Ireland, 1917–19; Joint Secretary, Irish Charity Commissioners, 1917–21; Chairman Caterham and Warlingham UDC 1938–39. *Publication:* Lipsett and Atkinson, Law of Carriage by Railway in Great Britain and Ireland, 1928. *Recreations:* fishing and shooting.

Address: 38 Three Beaches, Paignton, Devon. *T:* Paignton 57282; Cavangarden, Ballyshannon, Co. Donegal, Eire. *Club:* Univ. (Dublin).

Died 11 Dec. 1949.

ATTA, Nana Sir Ofori, KBE 1927; CBE 1918; Omanhene (Paramount Chief) of Akyem Abuakwa; an Unofficial Member, Executive Council of Gold Coast, since 1942; Provincial Member of the Legislative Council, Gold Coast Colony; President of the Provincial Council of Chiefs, Eastern Province, Gold Coast Colony; Member of the Board of Education, Gold Coast Colony; Director of Akim, Limited; Member of District Agricultural Committee, Akim Abuakwa; *b* 11 Oct. 1881; *m* 1903. *Educ:* Basel Mission Elementary School at Anum; Kyebi and Abetifi; Senior School at Begoro; Theological Seminary, Akropong. CBE for services to the Government of the Gold Coast Colony. *Recreations:* reading and walking. *Address:* Ofori Panin Fie, and Ahenfie, Akyem Abuakwa, Gold Coast.

Died 24 Aug. 1943.

AUCKLAND, 6th Baron *cr* Irish barony, 1789, British, 1793; **Frederick Colvin George Eden**; Associate Institution of Naval Architects; RAF, VR since Sept. 1939; *b* 21 Feb. 1895; *s* of 5th Baron and Sybil, *d* of late Col G. M. Hutton, CB; *S* father, 1917; *m* 1st, 1917, Susan Hartridge (marr. diss. 1925) of Jacksonville, Florida; one *d*; 2nd, 1939, Constance Caroline, *d* of Benno Hart, San Francisco. *Educ:* Malvern College; Camborne School of Mines. Instructor of Flying throughout the War; Assistant to Air Attaché, Paris, 1940. *Recreations:* golf, riding, flying, shooting, fishing, and yachting, etc. *Heir: cousin* Capt. Geoffrey Morton Eden, MBE, *b* 17 Feb. 1891. *Address:* SY Lantana, c/o Royal Thames Yacht Club, 60 Knightsbridge, SW1. *Clubs:* Carlton, Royal Thames Yacht.

Died 16 April 1941.

AUDETTE, Hon. Louis Arthur; *b* Quebec, 14 Dec. 1856; *s* of George S. Audette, merchant, and Leocadie R. Marcou; *m* Mary Grace, *d* of late Sir Andrew Stuart, Chief Justice of Superior Court, PQ, and Elmire C. Aubert de Gaspé; four *s* one *d*. *Educ:* Quebec Seminary; Laval University; LLB. Called to Bar, 1880; practised in Quebec; Deputy Prothonotary, District of Quebec; Registrar Exchequer Court, 1887; was Secretary to Board of Arbitration, 1893, to determine disputed matters of account between Canada and the Provinces of Ontario and Quebec; was given jurisdiction of Judge in chambers, 1908; KC 1908; Assistant Judge, 1912; Puisne Judge, Exchequer Court of Canada, 1919–31; retired, 1931; DCL Laval University, 1909; University of Ottawa, 1911; Commissioner to investigate the claims of Pelagic Sealers under both the Washington Treaty, 7 July 1911, and Paris Award Regulations, 1893, 1913. *Publications:* The Practice of the Exchequer Court of Canada, 1895; second edition, 1909. *Recreation:* yachting. *Address:* 161 Daly Avenue, Ottawa. *T:* R 6.0040.

Died 19 Jan. 1942.

AUDLEY, Baroness, Eng. *cr* 1312–1313; **Mary Thicknesse-Tuchet;** *b* 13 Aug. 1858; *er d* of George Edward, 21st Baron; *S* father on death of younger sister in 1937. *Heir: kinsman* Thomas Percy Henry Touchet Tuchet-Jesson, *b* 15 Sept. 1913. *Address:* c/o Westminster Bank Ltd, 1 Connaught Street, W2.

Died 27 May 1942.

AULT, Norman, Hon. MA (Oxon); author and artist; *b* 17 Dec. 1880; *s* of John K. Ault, West Bromwich; *m* 1st, Lena Marian, *e d* of Lt-Col T. Lockhart, Newbury; two *d*; 2nd, Ethel Marion, *e d* of J. S. Streeter, Croydon. *Educ:* King Edward VI Grammar School, Birmingham. Studied art and architecture at West Bromwich, Birmingham and London. Wrote and illustrated, with first wife books for children, 1903–07, including The Podgy Book of Tales, 1907; and illustrated many books, 1906–18. Specialised in the study of English literature,

particularly English lyric poetry and its bibliography, and the life and works of Alexander Pope, for which the University of Oxford conferred on him the hon. degree of MA in 1941. *Publications:* Life in Ancient Britain, 1920; Dreamland Shores (poems and pictures), 1920; The Poets' Life of Christ, 1922; Elizabethan Lyrics, 1925, revised 1949; Seventeenth Century Lyrics, 1928, revised 1950; Pope's Own Miscellany, 1935; The Prose Works of Alexander Pope, Vol. I, 1936; A Treasury of Unfamiliar Lyrics, 1938; New Light on Pope, 1949; contributor to The Cambridge Bibliography of English Literature, 1940, and to various learned journals. *Recreations:* study of prehistoric life and times; experimental shadow shows. *Address:* 255 Cowley Road, Oxford.

Died 6 Feb. 1950.

AUROBINDO, Sri; (having dropped use of family name of Ghose); *b* Calcutta, Bengal, 15 Aug. 1872. *Educ:* Cambridge. Civil and educational Service, Baroda; leader Nationalist movement; Yogi. *Publications:* Essays on the Gita, 1st series; 5th ed.; 2nd series; 4th ed.; Speeches; A System of National Education, 4th ed.; Ideals and Progress, 3rd ed.; Superman, 4th ed.; Evolution, 5th ed.; Thoughts and Glimpses, 6th ed.; Ishopanishad, text translation and commentary, 4th ed.; Renaissance in India, 3rd ed.; The Ideal of the Karmayogin, 7th ed.; Bankin-Tilak Dayanand; Yoga and its Objects, 5th ed.; Uttarpara Speech, 5th ed.; Brain of India, 5th ed.; Kalidasa, 2nd ed.; The Mother, 5th ed.; The Riddle of this World, 3rd ed.; Lights on Yoga, 4th ed.; Bases of Yoga, 5th ed.; The Life Divine; Heraclitus; Views and Reviews, 2nd ed.; The National Value of Art, 3rd ed.; Poems: Collected Poems and Plays, 2 vols; Six Poems; Poems Past and Present; Dharma O Jatiyata, 3rd ed.; Gitar Bhumika; Sri Aurobinder Patra; Hymns to the Mystic Fire (Agni Hymns from the Rig Veda, trans in their esoteric sense, with Text); Significance of Indian Art; The Spirit and Form of Indian Polity; Letters of Sri Aurobindo; also 2nd series; Savitri: An Epic Poem, Part I (Books I-III); Synthesis of Yoga, Part I, More Lights on Yoga; Messages; Letters (literary), 3rd series; The Human Cycle; The Ideal of Human Unity, 2nd Rev. Ed. *Address:* Sri Aurobindo Ashram, Pondicherry. *TA:* Aurobindo, Pondicherry.

Died 5 Dec. 1950.

AUSTEN, Harold William Colmer, MD, BS Lond., MRCS, LDS Eng.; late Lieut RNVR; Surgeon (retired); *b* 1868; *s* of late Josiah Austen, Staff Surgeon, RN; *m* 1917, Juliette Mazet. *Educ:* Tonbridge School; St Bartholomew's and Royal Dental Hospitals. Consulting Dental Surgeon St Bartholomew's Hospital; late Dental Surgeon Royal Dental Hospital; late Lecturer on Materia Medica to the London School of Dental Surgery; Member Amateur Chamber Music, Psychical Research and other Societies. *Publications:* Materia Medica, Pharmacology and Therapeutics for Dental Students and Practitioners (joint-author); papers to various medical journals. *Recreations:* music, painting, garden. *Address:* Dormy Pool, Aldeburgh, Suffolk.

Died 22 Jan. 1943.

AUSTIN, 1st Baron *cr* 1936, of Longbridge; **Herbert Austin**, KBE 1917; LLD; JP; MIME; Chairman of Austin Motor Co., Ltd; President of Institution of Automobile Engineers, 1930, and President of Society of Motor Manufacturers and Traders, 1934; Master of Company of Coachmakers and Coach Harness Makers of London, 1934; *b* Little Missenden, Bucks, 8 Nov. 1866; *m* 1887, Helen, *d* of James Dron, merchant; two *d*. *Educ:* Rotherham Grammar School; Brampton College. Served apprenticeship to engineering at Langlands Foundry, Melbourne; managed several small works in Melbourne; came over to England in 1890 to control manufacture of the Wolseley Sheep Shearing Machine; made a Director, 1900; was manager of the Wolseley Tool and Motor Car Co., Ltd, Birmingham, 1900–05; commenced manufacture of motor cars on own account at Longbridge Works, Northfield, Birmingham, 1905; MP (U) King's Norton, Birmingham, 1919–24; Commandeur de l'Ordre de Leopold II. *Address:* Lickey Grange, nr Bromsgrove. *T:* Hillside 1066. *Clubs:* Carlton, Royal Automobile, 1900; Conservative, Birmingham.

Died 23 May 1941.

AUSTIN, Frederick Britten; author and playwright; *b* 8 May 1885; *s* of Frederick James Austin; *m* 1st, 1908, Edith Constance, *d* of William and Caroline Abbott of Westcliff; one *s* two *d*; 2nd, 1919, Ethel Mildred *d* of James Frederick and Frances Mary King of Dawlish; one *s*. *Educ:* Grocers' Company School, Hackney Downs. Enlisted LRB 4 Aug. 1914; served overseas with BEF two and a half years; first Commission 8 Sept. 1914; exchanged RASC 11 April 1915; demobilised with rank of Captain, 19 Jan. 1919. *Publications:* The Shaping of Lavinia, 1911; In Action, 1913; Battlewrack, 1917; According to Orders, 1918; On the Borderland, 1922; Under the Lens, 1924; Thirteen, 1925; The War-God Walks Again, 1926; When Mankind was Young, 1927; A Saga of the Sword, 1928; A Saga of the Sea, 1929; Tomorrow? 1930; The Red Flag, 1932; Told in the Market Place, 1935; The Road to Glory, 1935; Forty Centuries Look Down, 1936. Contributor chiefly to Strand Magazine, Sunday Pictorial, and Saturday Evening Post. *Play:* The Thing that Matters, 1921. *Recreations:* travel, book-collecting. *Address:* 3bis Avenue Franco-Russe, Paris, 7. *T:* Inv. 19–96. *Club:* Savage.

Died 12 March 1941.

AUSTIN, Sir Harold (Bruce Gardiner), Kt 1935; OBE; Knight Commander of Order of Vasa; Speaker of House of Assembly, Barbados, since 1934; Member since 1915; *b* 15 July 1877; *s* of John Gardiner Austin and Dorothy Frere Grant; *m* Marie Lilian, *d* of late Dr Charles Dennehy, PMO of St Lucia, BWI; two *d*. *Educ:* Harrison College, Barbados. Member Executive Committee, Barbados, 1919–34; President Board of Education, 1925–35. *Recreations:* cricket, lawn-tennis, golf. *Address:* Enmore, Barbados, BWI. *Clubs:* Junior Carlton, MCC, IZ; Royal Mid-Surrey Golf.

Died 27 July 1943.

AUSTIN, Reginald McPherson, CBE 1941; *b* 20 Oct. 1887; *m* 1917, Aileen Tierney Graves (*née* Hansell); no *c*. *Educ:* Mercers' School. Consul-General at Houston, Texas, USA, in 1946. Retired from Foreign Service, Aug. 1946. *Recreations:* billiards, golf. *Address:* Yamano Cottage, 30 Boulevard de Belgique, Monaco (via France). *Club:* Thatched House.

Died 2 July 1950.

AVELING, Claude, MA; *b* 1869; 2nd *s* of late Stephen Aveling, Restoration House, Rochester; *m* 1903, Theodora, *o d* of late Canon W. H. Robins; one *d*. *Educ:* King's School, Rochester (scholar); Westminster (scholar); Christ Church, Oxford (exhibitioner). Assistant to Director of Royal College of Music, 1894; Assistant Registrar, then Registrar, 1913–35; sang in choir at Coronation of King Edward VII (1902) and King George V (1911) in Westminster Abbey; late Representative Governor of Vice-Wells Foundation. *Publications:* Princess Zara, 1900; King Thrushbeard, 1901; Triumph of Alcestis, 1902; Adaptations of Gluck's Alcestis, 1904; Armida, 1906; Saint Agnes, 1905; Bach's Matthew Passion, 1908; Der Geist hilft, 1907; Wachet, betet, 1908; Germania, 1907; Tess, 1909; Lakmé, 1910; Häuslicher Krieg, 1910; Suzanne's Secret, 1911; Don Quixote, 1912; Jewels of the Madonna, 1912; St Francis, Colonel Chabert, Monna Vanna, Thérèse, L'Amore Medico, 1913; Parsifal, Trouvères and Troubadours, 1914; Goldsmith of Toledo, 1922; The Fulfilment, 1926; The Sower, 1929; If Marchand had Come, 1935. *Recreation:* bridge. *Address:* Vines Cottage, Rochester. *T:* Chatham 3556.

Died 28 Dec. 1943.

AVELING, Francis Arthur Powell, PhD (Louvain), DSc (London), DLit (London), DD (Rome), Agrégé de l'Université de Louvain; Fellow of King's College; Carpenter Medallist (London); Professor of Psychology in the University of London King's College; late Assistant Professor of Psychology, University of London University College; late Examiner in Psychology, University of Reading; Examiner in Philosophy, National University of Ireland; in Psychology, University of Manchester, University of Edinburgh; served as Chaplain during the war (despatches, MC; Commander of the Order of Christ); *b* St Catherine's, Ontario, Canada, 28 Dec. 1875; *m* 1925, Ethel Mary, *d* of Stephen Good Dancy of Steyning, Sussex. *Educ:* Bishop Ridley College; McGill University, Montreal; Keble College, Oxon; Canadian College, Rome; University of Louvain; Univ. College, London. 1st Class Honours PhL, PhD, and Fellowship, Louvain, where he began a series of researches on the Higher Thought Processes which he is still prosecuting. Council (President, 1927–30) British Psychological Society; Council, British Association for the Advancement of Science (President Psychological Section, 1933); Council, International Congress of Psychology, National Institute of Industrial Psychology, and Child Guidance Council; Member (representing University of Bishop's College) Universities Bureau of the British Empire; Aristotelian Society. *Publications:* On the Consciousness of the Universal and the Individual—a contribution to the Phenomenology of the Thought Processes; Confirmations expérimentales d'une théorie du processus cognitif; Arnoul the Englishman; The Immortality of the Soul; Science and Faith; The God of Philosophy; Modernism; The Philosophers of the Smoking-Room; The Spectrum of Truth (with Rev. A. B. Sharpe); Directing Mental Energy; The Psychological Approach to Reality; Personality and Will; An Introduction to Psychology; Psychology: The Changing Outlook; editor of Westminster Lectures, Expository Essays in Christian Philosophy; Contemporary Library of Psychology; contributor to numerous periodicals, magazines. *Address:* 12 Weymouth Mews, W1. *T:* Langham 3639. *Club:* Union.

Died 6 March 1941.

AVERY, Charles Harold; novelist and writer of books, serials, etc, for young people, since 1894; *b* Headless Cross, Worcestershire, 1867; *s* of late William Avery, JP; *m* 1898, Winifred, *d* of late Rev. G. L. Allen; one *s*. *Educ:* New College, Eastbourne. Army Service, 1914–18. *Publications:* An Armchair Adventurer, 1903; Highway Pirates, 1904; Out of the Running, 1904; Play the Game, 1906; Firelock and Steel, 1906; Captain Swing, 1907; The Wizard's Wand, 1908; In Days of Danger, 1909; A Week at the Sea, 1910; Off the Wicket, 1910; Every Dog his Day, 1911; Head of the School, 1912; The Chartered Company, 1915; Line UP! 1918; Caught Out, 1919; The Runaway, 1920; Schoolboy Pluck, 1921; The Prefects' Patrol, 1922; Between Two Schools, 1923; Thumbs Up, 1925; Who Goes There? 1926; Day Boy Colours, 1928; No Surrender, 1933; The Marlcot Mystery, 1935; Through Thick and Thin, 1938; The Side Line, 1939; A Girl at the Helm, 1941, etc. *Address:* 87 Elm Road, Evesham, Worc.

Died 25 Sept. 1943.

AXFORD, Surg. Rear-Adm. Walter Godfrey, CB 1919; FLS; *b* 1861; *s* of William Axford; *m* Emily, 2nd *d* of late E. A. Appelbe, Kildarra House, Bandon, Co. Cork; two *d*. *Educ:* LRCP, LRCS Edin., 1885. Retired from Royal Navy, 1919. *Address:* 4 St George's Court, Gloucester Road, SW7.

Died 23 Feb. 1942.

AYKROYD, Sir Frederic Alfred, 1st Bt *cr* 1929; JP; Chairman of F. A. Aykroyd & Co. Ltd, Belwarp Limited; The Midland Combing Co. Ltd, and Aspinalls (Paints) Ltd; President, Bradford Chamber of Commerce, 1923; *b* 25 June 1873; 2nd *s* of late William

Edward Aykroyd, of Ashdown, Apperley Bridge, Yorkshire; m Lily May, e d of Sir James Roberts, 1st Bart, LLD, of Strathallan Castle, Perthshire, and Fairlight Hall, near Hastings; three s one d. Member of Advisory Committee, Board of Trade, 1926–29; Chairman, Animal Fibres Committee Imperial Institute, 1927–31; President of Institute of Bankers (Bradford Centre), 1935–36; Member of the Appointments Board. University of Cambridge, 1928–34; Local Director (Bradford) the National Provincial Bank; Sheriff of Yorkshire, 1941. Recreations: shooting, fishing. Heir: e s Cecil William Aykroyd. Address: Birstwith Hall, near Harrogate. T: Birstwith 50. Club: Constitutional.

Died 31 Dec. 1949.

AYKROYD, Sir William Henry, 1st Bt cr 1920; JP; Life Director of T. F. Firth & Sons, Ltd, carpet manufacturers, of Brighouse, Heckmondwike; b 8 May 1865; s of Alfred Aykroyd of Oakwood, Manningham, and Ellen, d of Henry Milnes of Nearcliffe, Bradford; m 1890, Emma Louisa (d 1946); three s one d. Educ: Thorparch Grange, under Dr Hiley. Commenced business with father and uncle, Bradford; Managing Director of Bradford Dyers' Association for twelve years; High Sheriff of Yorkshire, 1926. Recreations: shooting, motoring. Heir: e s Major Alfred Hammond Aykroyd [b 3 June 1894; m 1919, Sylvia, d of late Francis Walker, Huddersfield, and widow of Lt-Col Foster Newton Thorne; one s one d Charterhouse. Linton Spring, Wetherby]. Address: Grantley Hall, Ripon. T: Ripon 19. TA: Aykroyd, Grantley, Ripon.

Died 3 April 1947.

AYLESFORD, 9th Earl of, cr 1714; Heneage Michael Charles Finch; Baron of Guernsey, 1703, Captain, RA; b 31 Oct. 1908; g s of 8th Earl and e s of late Lord Guernsey, Capt. 1st Batt. Irish Guards, killed at the Battle of the Aisne, 14 Sept. 1914, and the Hon. Gladys Fellowes, 2nd d of 2nd Baron de Ramsey; S grandfather, 1924; m 1940, Mrs Pamela Elizabeth Dugdale, er d of late Col Hon. Charles Coventry and of Mrs Coventry, 50 Charles Street, W. Owns about 9000 acres. Heir: uncle Hon. Charles Daniel Finch-Knightley. Address: Packington Hall, Coventry; Diddington Hall, Coventry; The Friars, Aylesford.

Died 28 May 1940.

AYLIFF, Henry Kiell; actor and producer; b Grahamstown, South Africa; s of late Hon. Jonathan Ayliff, MLA, and Susanah, d of late Hon. George Wood, MLC; m 1906, Gertrude Homewood, d of Charles Stephenson Homewood; one s two d. Educ: St Andrew's College, South Africa. Studied painting at Royal Academy Schools and Julian's, Paris; Studied for stage under late Hermann Vezin and Mrs Emil Behnke. After acting for some years, joined Sir Barry Jackson as Producer to the Birmingham Repertory Theatre in 1922; since then has directed many productions in Birmingham, London and New York, including Heartbreak House, Back to Methuselah, The Applecart, Too True to be Good, The Farmer's Wife, Yellow Sands, many Shakespearean productions including the ones in Modern Dress of Hamlet (afterwards done in Vienna with Alexander Moissi), and The Taming of the Shrew, in London and New York, the Barretts of Wimpole Street, A Sleeping Clergyman, The Black Eye, Spring Tide, Cure for Love, etc.; Produced all the plays for the Malvern Festival from its inauguration in 1929 till 1933, and again in 1938 and 1939, during which seasons he did the first productions of Shaw's Geneva and In Good King Charles' Golden Days, James Bridie's The Last Trump and What Say They, J. B. Priestley's Music at Night, &c., as well as a revival of S Joan with Elizabeth Bergner in the name part; went back to Birmingham to assist Sir Barry Jackson in difficulties or war years, reviving plays by Shakespeare, Shaw, Barrie, etc. Returned to London to revive Yellow Sands with Sir Cedric Hardwicke and to produce A Cure for Love for Robert Donat at Westminster Theatre, and afterwards

do an interesting revival of James Bridie's A Sleeping Clergyman at Criterion Theatre. Recreation: gardening. Address: 4 Holford Road, Hampstead, NW3. T: Hampstead 5664. Club: Garrick.

Died 25 May 1949.

AYLING, Sir William Bock, Kt 1915; b 30 Aug. 1867; s of Frederick William Ayling; m 1894, Emma Annie Graham (d 1912); two s one d. Educ: Weymouth College; Magdaiene College, Cambridge. Entered Indian Civil Service as probationer, 1886; went to India, 1889; served as Assistant Collector, Sub-Collector and Joint-Magistrate, Collector and District Magistrate, District and Sessions Judge, Judge of the High Court of Judicature, Madras, 1912–24; retired 1924. Address: Graeme Lodge, Berkhamsted. Club: East India and Sports.

Died 25 Sept. 1946.

AYLWARD, Florence; b 10 March 1862; d of Rev. Augustus Aylward, Rector of Brede, Sussex, and Mary, e d of Thomas Frewen of Brickwall, Sussex; m 1881, Harold A. Kinder (d 1940); one s. Educ: chiefly at home. First song Day Dawn, 1888. Publications: about 150 songs, or more. Address: Bvways, Baldslow, St Leonards-on-Sea.

Died 14 Oct. 1950.

AYSCOUGH, Florence, LittD; writer and translator of Chinese literature; d of Thomas Reed Wheelock and Edith H. Clarke, Shanghai, China and Boston, USA (father a Canadian); m 1st, Francis Ayscough (d 1933), Leicestershire and Shanghai, China; no c, 2nd, 1935, Prof. Harley Farnsworth MacNair. Educ: Shaw School, Boston. For many years Hon. Librarian, North China Branch Royal Asiatic Society, Shanghai; Student of Chinese Art, Literature, and Sociology; contributor of articles to various proceedings of learned societies, etc.; Lecturer on China, her art, literature and sociology in London, Paris, Berlin, New York, etc. Publications: Friendly Books on Far Cathay; Fir-Flower Tablets, poems (with Amy Lowell) translated from the Chinese; A Chinese Mirror; The Autobiography of a Chinese Dog; Tu Fu, the Autobiography of a Chinese Poet; Fire-cracker Land, 1932; Travels of a Chinese Poet, Vol. II, 1934; Chinese Women Yesterday and To-day, 1937; articles in Encyclopædia Sinica. Recreations: enjoys games, sailing, swimming, and riding, interested in theatre and music. Address: House of the Wutung Trees, 5533 Woodlawn Avenue, Chicago, Ill, USA. Clubs: English Speaking Union; Chicago.

Died 24 April 1942.

AYSON, Judge Hugh Fraser, CMG 1929; b Clutha, New Zealand, 1884; m; two d. Educ: Wellington College and Victoria University College of New Zealand. In practice as Barrister and Solicitor, Wellington, New Zealand, 1906–16; Judge of High Court and Land Court of Cook Islands, 1916; Judge of New Zealand Native Land Court, 1919; seconded as Resident Commissioner of Cook Islands, Chief Judge of High Court of Cook Islands, and Chief Judge of Native Land Court, 1922–37, and 1938–44. Retired 1944, and returned to NZ. Address: 1 Tui Road, Days Bay, Wellington, NZ.

Died 1 Feb. 1948.

AYTOUN, Col Andrew, CMG 1917; CBE 1919; DSO 1900; b 2 July 1860; s of late Robert Aytoun, WS, of Capeldrae, Fife; m 1st, 1889, Helen Lilias (d 1920), 4th d of late Robert Graham of Fintry; 2nd, 1925, Dagmar, o d of late E. A. and Mrs Helena Lindh, Karlstad, Sweden. Joined Argyll and Sutherland Highlanders, 1881; Captain, 1890; Major, 1902; served South Africa, 1900–01; in command of 4th Queensland Imperial Bushmen; retired, 1908; served European War as Embarkation Commandant at Liverpool, Ostend, and Folkestone, 1914–19. Club: Caledonian.

Died March 1945.

AZARIAH, Rt Rev. Vedanayakam Samuel; Bishop of Dornakal since 1912 (1st native bishop in India); *b* 17 Aug. 1874; *s* of Rev. T. Vedanayakam, CMS Vellalanvillai, Mengnanapuram, Tinnevelly, S India (*d* 1889), and Ellen Vedanayakam (*d* 1909); *m* Anbu Mariammal Samuel of Tinnevelly; four *s* two *d*. *Educ:* CMS High School, Mengnanapuram; CMS College, Tinnevelly; Madras Christian College. Travelling Secretary in South India for the Young Men's Christian Association, 1896; Associate General Secretary, 1903–09; one of the founders of the Indian Missionary Society of Tinnevelly, 1903; Hon. Secretary, 1903–09; Hon. Gen. Secretary of the National Missionary Society of India, 1906–09; visited Japan as a Delegate of the World Student Christian Federation, 1907, and its Vice-President, 1909–11; Deacon, 1909; Priest, 1909; visited England as a Delegate to the World's Missionary Conference, 1910; Head of the Dornakal Mission, 1909–12; Hon. LLD Cambridge, 1920. *Publications:* English: India and the Christian Movement; (with Bishop Whitehead) Christ in Indian Villages. Tamil and Telugu; Holy Baptism; Confirmation; Studies in First Corinthians; India and the Christian Movement; Evangelism, South India Union; Christian Giving; Studies in the Book of Job; A Commentary on Second Corinthians. *Address:* Dornakal, Kothagudium, PO, Deccan. *TA:* Dornakal N.

Died Jan. 1945.

AZIZUL HUQUE, Khan Bahadur Sir M., KCSI 1946; Kt 1941; CIE 1937; BL, DLitt (Calcutta); Commerce Member, Governor-General's Executive Council, India, 1943–46; *b* 1892; *s* of late Moniruddin Ahmed; *m*. Minister for Education (excluding European Education) Wakf and Registration to Government of Bengal, 1934–37; Speaker Bengal Legislative Assembly, 1937–42; Vice-Chancellor Calcutta University, 1938–42; Head of Dept of Islamic History and Culture, Calcutta University, 1940–42; High Commissioner for India in UK, 1942–43. *Publications:* Man Behind the Plough; History and Problems of Muslim Education in Bengal; Education and Retrenchment; Separate Electorate in Bengal. *Address:* New Delhi, India.

Died 22 March 1947.

B

BABINGTON, Captain Gervase, MC, MFH; retired pay; *b* 6 Feb. 1890; *e s* of Charles H. and late Grace Babington, of Croan, Wadebridge, Cornwall; *m* 1921, Mary B. Blew Jones. *Educ:* Eton. Served European War in Flanders, N Somerset Yeomanry and 6th Cavalry Brigade (MC, despatches, wounded Loos, Sept. 1915). Re-employed, 1941, Officers Emergency Reserve General List; served Adjutant 3rd Bn Cornwall HG, Launceston, 1941–43; Sector Adjutant Mid Devon Section, 1943–45; attached USA March–June 1944; discharged, 1945. *Recreations:* hunting, shooting. *Address:* Townley, Lew Down, Devon. *T:* Lew Down 6. *Club:* Carlton.

Died 4 May 1948.

BABONAU, Col Alexander Frederick, CIE 1920; OBE 1919; Indian Medical Service, retired; *b* 15 Oct. 1882. *Educ:* Edinburgh University, MB, ChB. Served Afghan War, 1919 (CIE); retired, 1939. *Address:* Ruapuna, Songhor, Kenya.

Died 9 May 1949.

BACKHOUSE, Sir Edmund Trelawny, 2nd Bt *cr* 1901; FRGS; FRSA; Member, Standing Council Baronetage; Member Académie Diplomatique Internationale, Paris; *b* 20 Oct. 1873; *e s* of Sir J. E. Backhouse, 1st Bt, and Florence (*d* 1902), *d* of Sir John S. Trelawny, 9th Bt; *S* father, 1918. *Educ:* Winchester (Scholar); Merton College, Oxford (Postmaster). Present in siege of Legations at Peking (medal with clasp); Professor at Peking University, 1903; head of school for Chinese Studies at King's College, London, 1913; presented 27,000 Chinese books and MSS to the Bodleian Library; thanked by special decrees of Convocation of Oxford University, 1913 and 1921. *Publications:* (with J. O. Bland) China under the Empress Dowager, 1910; The Court of Peking, 1914; an Anglo-Chinese Dictionary by Hillier, Barton, and Backhouse; translated the secret Russo-Chinese agreement of 1901, Anglo-Tibetan treaty of 1904, and many Chinese state-papers for The Times; translations of agreements, treaties, and state papers for British Govt; A Documentary Course of Chinese for Student Interpreters of the British Legation, compiled by request of the latter in 1922; The Encyclical Letter of the Lambeth Conference translated into Chinese, 1923; honorary translator to HM Embassy, Peiping, in Japanese; honorary adviser to British Municipal Council's schools for Chinese nationals in Tientsin, N China. *Heir:* nephew Maj. John Edmund Backhouse, MC. *Address:* British Embassy Compound, Peking, China. *Club:* Carlton.

Died 8 Jan. 1944.

BACKHOUSE, Major Sir John Edmund, 3rd Bt *cr* 1901; MC 1944; RA; *b* 30 April 1909; *s* of Adm. of the Fleet Sir Roger Roland Charles Backhouse, GCB, GCVO, CMG (4th *s* of 1st Bt), and Dora Louisa, *d* of John Ritchie Findlay, Aberlour, Banffshire; *S* uncle 1944; *m* 1937, Jean Marie Frances, *d* of Lt-Col G. R. V. Hume Gore, MC, The Gordon Highlanders; two *s* three *d*. *Educ:* Harrow; RMA, Woolwich. 2nd Lt RA, 1929, Lt, 1932, Capt., 1938, Temp. Major, 1939. *Heir: s* Jonathan Roger, *b* 1939. *Club:* United Service.

Died 29 Aug. 1944.

BACKHOUSE, Adm. Oliver, CB 1915; *b* 5 June 1876; 2nd *s* of late Sir J. E. Backhouse, 1st Bt; *m* 1920, Margaret Susan, *er d* of Dyson Perrins, Ardross, Rossshire, and Davenham, Malvern. *Educ:* HMS Britannia. Lieut 1898; served Somaliland Expedition, present at capture of Illig, 1904 (despatches, medal);

Com. 1908; Capt., 1914; Rear-Adm., 1925; Vice-Adm., 1929; Commodore in command of 2nd RN Brigade, 1914; served at siege of Antwerp, 1914 (despatches); Dardanelles Expedition, 1915 (despatches twice, CB, Croix d'Officier Legion of Honour and Croix de Guerre); Commanded HMS Orion at Battle of Jutland (despatches, Italian Silver Medal for Valour); Commanded HMS Royal Sovereign at Allied occupation of Constantinople, 1920; Naval Member of Ordnance Committee, 1920–23; Captain Superintendent of Sheerness Dockyard, 1923–25; Admiral Superintendent of Devonport Dockyard, 1927–31; retired list, 1929; Adm., retired, 1934. *Club:* United Service.

Died 25 March 1943.

BACON, Frederic, MA (Cantab), AMInstCE, MIMechE, MIEE; Professor of Engineering, University College, Swansea, since 1920; Past Chairman IMechE (SW Branch); Past-President SWIE; *b* 28 Dec. 1880; *s* of Rev. J. M. Bacon, MA, FRAS, of Coldash, Newbury; *m* 1911. *Educ:* Trinity College, Cambridge; First Class Honours, Mechanical Sciences Tripos, 1902. Served in various engineering works, including Messrs Yarrow of Poplar, and the British Westinghouse and Manufacturing Co., Trafford Park, Manchester, 1902–05; Demonstrator and Lecturer in Applied Mechanics and Electrical Design at the Royal Naval College, Greenwich, 1905–13; Lecturer in Photo-Microstructure of Metals, University College, London, 1910–12; Professor of Engineering, University College, Cardiff, 1913; served as Lieut RNVR in Paravane Dept HM Dockyard, Portsmouth and Anti-Submarine Division, Admiralty as technical expert in experimental development of anti-mine and anti-submarine devices, 1916–19; President, South Wales Institute of Engineers, 1937. *Publications:* various papers on scientific and technical subjects. *Address:* University College, Singleton Park, Swansea. *T:* 5059. *Club:* Royal Societies.

Died 23 Aug. 1943.

BACON, Gertrude, (Mrs T. J. Foggitt); lecturer, writer; *b* 19 April 1874; *d* of late Rev. J. M. Bacon, Coldash, Newbury, scientific aeronaut; *m* 1929, County Alderman Thomas J. Foggitt (*d* 1934), Stoneybrough, Thirsk. *Educ:* home. Assisted and accompanied her father in his aeronautical and scientific work, and in three Eclipse Expeditions, Lapland, India, America; the first woman to make a 'right away' voyage in an airship, and among the first Englishwomen to ascend in an aeroplane. *Publications:* Balloons, Airships, and Flying Machines; The Record of an Aeronaut (Life of John M. Bacon); How Men Fly; All about Flying; Memories of Land and Sky. *Recreation:* hunting wild flowers. *Address:* at Boundway Top, Sway, Hants.

Died 22 Dec. 1949.

BACON, Sir Hickman Beckett, 11th Bt of Redgrave, 1611, and 12th Bt of Mildenhall, 1627; Premier Baronet of England; late Lieutenant Grenadier Guards; *b* 14 April 1855; *S* father, 1872; unmarried. *Educ:* Eton. High Sheriff of Lincolnshire, 1887; County Alderman of Lindsey (Lincs) Council; Chairman, 1914–24. Owns about 9000 acres. *Heir: b* Nicholas Henry. *Address:* Thonock Hall, Gainsborough, Lincs. *TA:* Gainsborough.

Died 13 April 1945.

BACON, Sir Nicholas Henry, 12th Bt of Redgrave, 1611, and 13th Bt of Mildenhall, 1627; Premier Baronet of England; *b* 22 Oct. 1857; 2nd *s* of Sir Henry Hickman Bacon, 10th and 11th Bt; *S* brother, 1945; *m* 1893,

Constance Alice, CBE, *y d* of late A. S. Leslie Melville; one *s* five *d. Educ:* Eton. Late Capt. 4th Dragoon Guards; served Egyptian Campaign, 1882 (medal and clasp, and Kedive's star); High Sheriff, Norfolk, 1895; JP. *Heir: s* Edmund Castell, OBE; TD [*b* 1903; *m* 1936, Priscilla Dora, *d* of Col Charles Edward Ponsonby, MP; two *d*]. *Address:* Raveningham Hall, Norwich. *T:* Raveningham, Norfolk 232. *Club:* Carlton.

Died 1 Jan. 1947.

BACON, Adm. Sir Reginald (Hugh Spencer), KCB 1916, KCVO 1916; CVO 1907; DSO 1897; retired; *b* 1863; *s* of Rev. T. Bacon and Emma, *d* of George Shaw; *m* 1894, Cicely, *d* of Henry Surtees of Redworth; one *d*. *Educ:* HMS Britannia. Entered Britannia, 1877; silver medal Italian Government for saving life at wreck of Utopia, 1891; commander HMS Theseus; chief of intelligence dept, Benin expedition, 1897 (DSO, medal and clasp, despatches); started the submarine boat service in the Royal Navy; Naval Assistant to First Sea Lord of the Admiralty, 1905; Captain of HMS Dreadnought during her first commission; ADC, 1909; Director of Naval Ordnance and Torpedoes, 1907–09; retired Nov. 1909 to take post of Managing Director of the Coventry Ordnance Works, 1910–15; resigned the appointment and gazetted Colonel 2nd Commandant RMA, 1915; commanded Heavy Howitzer Brigade RMA with Expeditionary Force in France; commanded the Dover Patrols, 1915–18; Controller Munitions Inventions, Jan. 1918–April 1919; Company Commander, Home Guard, up to April 1941; Grand Officer Legion of Honour; Grand Officer of Leopold of Belgium; Croix de Guerre Belge; United States Gold Medal for distinguished service; DL County of Southampton; JP. *Publications:* Benin, the City of Blood; The Dover Patrol 1915, 1916, 1917; The Jutland Scandal, 1925; A Naval Scrap Book, First Part, 1877–1900, 1924; The Motor Car and How it Works, 1927; A Social Sinner, 1928; The Life of Lord Fisher of Kilverstone, 1929; The Concise Story of the Dover Patrol, 1932; The Life of John Rushworth, Earl Jellicoe, 1936; From 1900 Onward, 1939; Modern Naval Strategy (with Francis E. M'Murtrie), 1940, etc. *Recreation:* shooting. *Address:* Braishfield Lodge, Romsey, Hants. *TA:* Bacon Braishfield. *T:* Romsey 332.

Died 9 June 1947.

BACON, Comdr Sidney Kendrick, DSO 1915, RD, RNR; *b* 29 March 1871; *s* of Capt. K. V. Bacon, JP, late 29th Regt (now Worcestershire Regt). Joined RNR 1901; Lieut 1903; Lt-Comdr 1913; Comdr, 1917; joined Egyptian Government Service, 1912, retired 1924; served S African War, 1901–02; served on patrol duty European War, in Royal Navy, 1914–19 (despatches, DSO). *Address:* Hale, Farnham, Surrey. *Club:* East India and Sports.

Died 29 April 1950.

BADCOCK, Paymaster Captain Kenneth Edgar, DSO 1919; DSC, RN; *b* 13 Feb. 1886; *m* Frances Pinsent; two *s*. Served European War, 1914–19 (despatches twice, DSC, DSO); Secretary to Admiral of the Fleet Sir R. Tyrwhitt, 1913–33. *Address:* RN Hospital, Haslar, Gosport, Hants.

Died 22 Jan. 1947.

BADEN-POWELL, 1st Baron *cr* 1929, of Gilwell; **Robert Stephenson Smyth Baden-Powell,** Bt *cr* 1922; GCMG 1927; GCVO 1923; KCB 1909; OM 1937; KCVO 1909; Kt 1909; CB 1900; CVO 1909; LLD, FRGS; Chevalier Order of Christ of Portugal; Grand Cross Alfonso XII; Grand Cross Order of Dannebrog; Order of Merit Chile; Grand Cross of the Order of the Redeemer of Greece; Order of the Crown of Belgium; Cross of Commander of Legion of Honour; Knight of Grace, St John Order; Order of Polonia Restituta (Poland); 1st Class Order of Merit (Hungary); Order of White Lion (Czecho-Slovakia); Order of Phoenix (Greece); Grand Cross Order of Merit (Austria); Grand Cross of Gediminas (Lithuania); Grand Cross of

Orange of Nassau (Holland); Grand Cross of Order of the Sword (Sweden); Grand Cross of Three Stars (Latvia); *b* 22 Feb. 1857; 6th *s* of Rev. Prof. Baden-Powell, of Oxford and Langton Manor, and Henrietta Grace, *d* of Adm. W. H. Smyth, KSF; *m* 1912, Olave (GBE 1932), *d* of Harold Soames, Lilliput, Dorset; one *s* two *d. Educ:* Charterhouse. Joined 13th Hussars, 1876; Adjutant, served with that regiment in India, Afghanistan, and South Africa; served on the Staff as Assist Mil. Sec. South Africa, 1887–89; operations in Zululand, 1888 (despatches); Assist Mil. Sec. Malta, 1890–93; special service, Ashanti, in command of Native Levies, 1895 (star, brevet Lieut-Col); Chief Staff Officer, campaign in Matabeleland, 1896–97 (despatches, brevet Col); Colonel of Irregular Horse, South Africa; promoted from 13th Hussars to command of 5th Dragoon Guards, 1897; Lieut-Col commanding 5th Dragoon Guards, 1897–99; defence of Mafeking, 1899–1900 (promoted Maj.-Gen.; despatches); operations Transvaal, 1900–01 (despatches, CB); organised S African Constabulary; Inspector-General of S African Constabulary; 1900–03; Inspector-General of Cavalry, 1903–07; Lieut-Gen. commanding Northumbrian Territorial Division, 1908; retired, 1910; late Colonel-in-Chief 13/18th Hussars; founded the organisation of Boy Scouts and Girl Guides to promote good citizenship in rising generation, 1908; exhibited Sculpture in Royal Academy, 1907. *Publications:* Pig-sticking or Hog-hunting, 1889; Reconnaissance and Scouting, 1890; Vedette, 1890, Cavalry Instruction, 1895; The Downfall of Prempeh, 1896; The Matabele Campaign, 1896; Aids to Scouting, 1899; Sport in War, 1900; Sketches in Mafeking and East Africa, 1907; Scouting for Boys, 1908; Quick Training for War, 1914; My Adventures as a Spy, 1915; Indian Memories, 1915; The Wolf Cubs Handbook, 1916; Girl Guiding, 1917; Aids to Scoutmastership, 1920; Old Wolf's Favourites, 1921; What Scouts can do, 1921; Rovering to Success, 1922; Pig-sticking (revised edition), 1924; Life's Snags, 1927; Scouting and Youth Movements, 1929; Lessons from the 'Varsity of Life, 1933; Adventures and Accidents, 1934; African Adventure, 1936; Birds and Beasts in Africa, 1938; Paddle your Own Canoe, 1939; More Sketches of Kenya, 1940. *Recreations:* pig-sticking (winner of Kadir Cup), fishing, polo, big-game shooting. *Heir: s* Hon. Arthur Robert Peter Baden-Powell, *b* 30 Oct. 1913. *Address:* Paxtu, Nyeri, Kenya. *Clubs:* Cavalry, Beefsteak.

Died 8 Jan. 1941.

BADEN-POWELL, Agnes; National Vice-President of the Girl Guides, Author of Girl Guides Handbook; on Council and Executive of Duty and DisciplineSociety; Vice-President of Westminster Division, British Red Cross, since 1912; Local President, League of Mercy; Vice-President, Sunlight League; a President of Queen Mary's Needlework Guild; on Executive of The Dante Society; certificated steel engraving; medallist metal repoussé work; *b* 1858; *d* of Professor Baden-Powell, Langton Manor, Kent. *Recreations:* organ music, bicycle polo, bee-keeping. *Address:* 15 Lombard Street, EC.

Died 2 June 1945.

BADGER, Rev. Canon George Edwin; Hon. Canon of Birmingham, 1929; *b* 1868; *s* of S. T. Badger, surgeon, Birmingham; *m* 1924, Hermione, *d* of F. Doughty, Leicester; one *s. Educ:* Solihull Grammar School; King Edward's School, Birmingham; Oxford University, BA, 1893; Wycliffe Hall, Oxford, MA, 1897. Curate of Holy Trinity, Bordesley, 1893–95; S Aldate's, Oxford; Aston, 1897–1900; Vicar of Bishop Ryder's Church, Birmingham, 1900–33; Rural Dean of Birmingham Central, 1925–33; Vicar of Cofton Hackett near Birmingham, 1933–39; member of Birmingham Board of Guardians, 1916; Chairman of Board, 1922–23; member of the Board of Governors of the Nerve Hospital since its foundation; Chairman of Board, 1940–46; Chairman of Birmingham Branch of CETS

Prison Gate Mission and Free Night Shelter; President, Birmingham Clerical Society, 1928–30; Member of Local Pensions Committee and Public Assistance Committee; President of the Birmingham Library, 1930, Treasurer, 1936–38. *Address:* 40 Portland Road, Birmingham 16. *T:* Edgbaston 2389.

Died 20 May 1948.

BADHAM, Edward Leslie, RCA; RI; RBA; ROI; Member of Society of Sussex Painters; *s* of late Major R. Leslie S. Badham; *m* R. J. Gillett; one *d. Educ:* Clapham School of Art; South Kensington; Slade School. Official Purchaser, Brighton, Eastbourne, Worthing and Hastings Art Galleries and University of Hull; Water Colours in Water Transport Section of South Kensington Museum. *Recreations:* knots, bends, splices, rigging model ships. *Address:* Isleworth, 22 Priory Road, Hastings, Sussex.

Died March 1944.

BADOCK, Sir Stanley Hugh, Kt 1943; LLD; JP; *b* 27 April 1867; *s* of William Frederick and Miriam Badock; *m* 1894, Edna Haycroft Pethick; three *d. Educ:* Clifton College. Chairman of Directors, 1905–36 now a Director, Capper, Pass & Son, Ltd, Metal Refiners; Chairman of Bristol Civic League of Social Service, 1908–36; Sheriff of Bristol, 1908–09; Pro-Chancellor and Chairman of Council, University of Bristol; Treasurer, 1918–39; commanded 6th Gloster (Vol.) Bn 1916–18, retired with rank of Major. *Recreations:* fishing, golf. *Address:* The Oak, Knoll Hill, Sneyd Park, Bristol. *TA:* Badock, Knoll Hill, Bristol 9. *Clubs:* Constitutional, Bristol.

Died 12 Dec. 1945.

BAEKELAND, Leo Hendrik; Hon. Professor, Columbia University NY since 1917; *b* Ghent, Belgium, 14 Nov. 1863; *s* of Karel L. Baekeland and Rosalie Merchie; *m* 1889, Celine, *d* of Professor T. Swarts, Ghent; one *s* one *d. Educ:* University of Ghent, BS 1882; DNatSc, Maxima cum lauda, 1884; Laureate of the four Belgian Universities, 1887; Hon. DCh Univ. of Pittsburgh, 1916; Hon. DSc, Columbia Univ. 1929; Hon. DApSc., Univ. of Brussels, 1934, Hon. LLD, Univ. of Edinburgh, 1937. President, Bakelite Corporation, New York, 1910–29; Pres. or member of many chemical and scientific societies and committees; recipient of numerous awards by scientific societies; many patents, USA and abroad on the subject of organic chemistry, electrical insulation, synthetic resins, plastics, etc.; Officer of Crown of Belgium, 1919; Officer of Legion of Honour, France, 1923; Commander of Order of Leopold of Belgium, 1924. *Publications:* Relating to research in theoretical and applied chemistry covering— physical chemistry, photochemistry, electrochemistry, and organic chemistry; Patent Reform. *Recreation:* yacht cruising. *Address:* 30 East 42nd Street, New York, NY; Coconut Grove, Florida; Yonkers, New York. *TA:* Bakelite-New York. *T:* Murray Hill, 2–6800. *Clubs:* Chemists (Hon. Member), University, Columbia Faculty, Cruising Club of America, New York; Cosmos, Washington; Biscayne Bay Yacht, Florida; Engineers, Dayton, Ohio (Hon. Member).

Died 23 Feb. 1944.

BAGCHI, Satischandra, MA, LLD; Barrister-at-law; Reader in Natural Philosophy, Calcutta University since 1938; *b* Jan. 1882; *s* of Ramgopal Bagchi; *m* Charubala, 2nd *d* of Kedarnath Roy, Krishnagar; two *d* two *s. Educ:* Santipur Municipal School; GAI Calcutta; St John's College, Cambridge. BA Calcutta University, 1901; BA Mathematical Tripos, Cambridge, 1904; Law Tripos, Part II, in 1906; LLB Cambridge and Dublin; LLD Trinity College, Dublin, 1907 (First in the list). Principal, University Law College, Calcutta, 1909–38; Fellow of the Calcutta University, 1909–34; Tagore Professor of Law, 1914; Asutosh Mookerjii Lecturer, 1931; Head of Law Department and Dean of the Faculty of Law, Allahabad University, 1931–32; Member of the

Faculty of Law, Dacca University; called to Bar, Gray's Inn, 1907; Vice-President, Calcutta Mathematical Society, 1926–36. *Publications:* Mathematical papers in the Educational Times, English Mechanic, Bulletin of Calcutta Mathematical Society, Nature; Translations from French Stories into Bengali; Text-books and papers on law, mathematics, physics, history, etc. *Recreations:* angling, walking, billiards, and tennis. *Address:* University Law College, Darbhanga Buildings, Calcutta; Bellevue, West End Madhupur (SP), India.

Died 1 April 1939.

BAGGE, Stephen Salisbury, CMG 1907; FRGS; FZS; *b* 22 Sept. 1859; *s* of Rev. P. S. Bagge of Walpole, Norfolk, and Caroline, *e d* of Stephen Creyke, Archdeacon of York; unmarried. *Educ:* St Peter's, York. Served in Imperial British East Africa Company, 1890–93; District Officer, Uganda Protectorate, 1894–1902; Provincial Commissioner, East Africa Protectorate, 1902–10; retired, 1910; served as Political Officer, Mafia Island, 1915, during naval operations against Konigsberg GEA, and in 1916–17 as Political Officer on mainland, GEA. Decorated for services as Chief Political Officer, Nandi Field Force. *Recreations:* fishing, shooting, walking. *Address:* 69 Eaton Terrace, SW1.

Died 10 Oct. 1950.

BAGNOLD, Col Arthur Henry, CB 1907; CMG 1918; FRAS, MIEE; *b* 18 March 1854; *s* of Major-General M. E. Bagnold, HEI Co's Service; *m* 1888, Ethel (*d* 1931), *d* of W. H. Alger; one *s* one *d. Educ:* Cheltenham College; RM Academy, Woolwich. Entered RE, 1872; Captain, 1884; Major, 1891; Lieut-Col 1899; Colonel, 1903; Instructor School of Military Engineering, 1891–96; Superintendent Building Works, Royal Arsenal, Woolwich, 1903–11; Military Assistant to Chief Superintendent Ordnance Factories, 1914–16; Chief Experimental Officer, Signals Exp. Estab., 1916–17. Served South Africa, 1881; Soudan, 1884–85 (despatches, medal with clasp, bronze star, brevet-major); retired, 1911; European War, 1914–18 (CMG). *Address:* Warren Wood, Shooters Hill, SE18. *T:* Woolwich 0233. *Club:* Junior United Service.

Died 9 Dec. 1943.

BAGOT, 5th Baron *cr* 1780; **Gerald William Bagot;** Bt 1627; *b* 13 May 1866; *s* of Admiral Henry Bagot and Eleanor, *d* of Edward Sacheverell Chandos-Pole; *S cousin,* 1932. *Educ:* Haileybury College. *Recreations:* hunting, shooting. *Heir: cousin* Caryl Ernest Bagot, *b* 9 March, 1877. *Address:* Blithfield, Rugeley, Staffs.

Died 5 April 1946.

BAGSHAWE, Sir Arthur William Garrard, Kt 1933; CMG 1915; MB; retired; *b* 29 July 1871; 2nd *s* of late Rev. Alfred Drake Bagshawe, Rector of Wormhill, nr Buxton; *m* 1910, Alice Mary (*d* 1944), *d* of late Joseph Harry Thornber; two *s. Educ:* Marlborough; Caius College, Cambridge. Medical Officer Uganda Protectorate, 1900; served Lango Expedition, 1901; with Anglo-German Boundary Commission, 1902–04; employed in investigations, Uganda, 1906–07; Director of Sleeping Sickness Bureau, 1908–12; Director, Bureau of Hygiene and Tropical Diseases, London, 1912–35. *Address:* Upper Tylecrwn, Llanvillo, Talgarth, S Wales.

Died 24 March 1950.

BAGSHAWE, Col Frederick William, CIE 1918; *b* 1868; *s* of Col S. L. Bagshawe, Indian Army; *m* 1894, Catherine Sinclair, *d* of Col A. S. Grove. Colonel Indian Army, 1920; retired, 1922; served South African War, 1899–1901; European War, 1914–19 (CIE). *Address:* 34 Manor Park, Redland, Bristol.

Died 25 July 1945.

BAGWELL, John; JP, DL, Co. Tipperary; *b* 1874; *o s* of Richard Bagwell of Marlfield, Clonmel; *m* 1901, Louise, *d* of Maj.-Gen. George Shaw, CB; two *s* one *d. Educ:* Harrow; Trinity College, Oxford. Assistant

Superintendent of Line Midland Railway, 1905–09; Superintendent of Passenger Service, 1910–11; General Manager Great Northern Railway of Ireland, 1911–26; Senator, The Irish Free State, 1922–36. *Recreations:* hunting, mountaineering, etc. *Address:* Marlfield, Clonmel. *T:* Clonmel 105. *Clubs:* Travellers', Alpine; Kildare Street, Dublin.

Died 22 Aug. 1946.

BAGWELL, Lt-Col John, MVO 1909; MC; late Norfolk Regt; *b* 3 March 1884; *o s* of W. Bagwell, JP; *m* 1914, Mary Ethel, *y d* of late Samuel Kingan, DL, of Co. Down; one *s* one *d. Educ:* Harrow; Sandhurst. Joined Norfolk Regt 1903; Capt. 1912; served Somaliland Expedition, 1908–10 (medal and clasp); retired, 1914; served European War, 1914–18 (Bt Major, MC, Légion d'Honneur, Serbian White Eagle, despatches four times). Commanded 1 Down Bn Ulster Home Guard, 1940–44. *Recreations:* hunting, polo. *Address:* Eastgrove, Queenstown, Ireland. *Clubs:* United Service; Kildare Street (Dublin).

Died 4 July 1949.

BAHRAIN, Ruler of; HH Shaikh Sir Hamed bin Isa Al Khalifah, KCIE Hon. 1935; CSI Hon. 1921; *b* 1875; *e s* of Shaikh Sir Isa bin Ali Al Khalifah, KCIE; *m*; eight *s.* Acceded 1932. *Recreations:* hawking, shooting. *Address:* The Palace, Manama, Bahrain. *TA:* Bahrstate.

Died 20 Feb. 1942.

BAIKIE, Alfred, CB 1941; JP; *b* 1861; *y s* of William Layman Cowan and Deborah Hodgson, *d* of late Captain Joseph Dover of Causewayfort, Cumberland; *m* 1st, 1888, Annie Traill (*d* 1896), *d* of Ralph Fotheringhame of Lynnfield, Kirkwall; 2nd, 1902, Mary Ann Stewart, *y d* of late Thomas Traill, of Holland, Orkney; one *s* one *d.* Assumed surname Baikie, 1898; Lord-Lieutenant of Orkney and Shetland since 1930; a Consulting Engineer. *Address:* Hall of Tankerness, near Kirkwall.

Died 21 Oct. 1947.

BAILEY, Gertrude Mary, CBE 1918; JP; Médaille de la Reine Elisabeth of Belgium; *b* 1870; *d* of James Buchanan, Sunderland; *m* 1895, Charles Henry Bailey (*d* 1907). *Address:* 23 Skinner Street, Newport, Mon.

Died 14 Nov. 1941.

BAILEY, Horace Thomas; JP County of Monmouth, and Borough of Monmouth; *b* 1852; *s* of William Bailey, Weston-super-Mare; *m* 1st, Charlotte Josephine Elizabeth (*d* 1897), *o d* of late William Johnson Whichelo; 2nd, Mary Aphra, *widow* of Captain R. E. Hamilton, Royal Engineers, *d* of late S. Stackpoole Furnell, of Victoria, Australia, and *niece* of late Surgeon-General Furnell, MD, FRCS, CIE, of Madras; two *s. Educ:* Monmouth School. Foundation Manager Monmouth Church Schools; a Vice-President and ex-Chairman of Monmouth Unionist Association; member of Monmouth Diocesan Conference and other public bodies. *Address:* The Willows, Monmouth. *T:* Monmouth 117. *Clubs:* Monmouth and County, Monmouth.

Died 18 Jan. 1945.

BAILEY, Sir John Milner, 2nd Bt *cr* 1919; *b* 15 June 1900; *e s* of Sir Abe Bailey, 1st Bt, KCMG; *S* father 1940; *m* 1st, 1932, Diana (who obtained a divorce, 1935), *e d* of Rt Hon. Winston Churchill, OM; 2nd, 1939, Mrs Muriel Mullins (marr. diss. 1945); 3rd, 1945, Stella Mary, *d* of late Charles Chiappini, 2 Stephen Street, Cape Town.

Died 13 Feb. 1946.

BAILEY, Adm. Sir Sidney Robert, KBE 1938; CB 1933; CBE 1927; DSO 1919; *b* Aug. 1882; *s* of late Sir James Bailey; *m* 1922, Mildred, *d* of late Col Charles Bromwell, US Army; one *s* one *d.* Joined HMS Britannia, 1896; served in Seymour's Expedition for the Relief of Pekin, 1900 (despatches, special promotion to

Lieutenant); Commander, 1914; served on Staff of C-in-C Grand Fleet, 1916–19 (despatches); Captain, 1918; ADC 1930–31; Rear-Adm. 1931; Vice-Adm. 1935; Admiral, 1939; retired list, 1939. *Club:* Carlton.

Died 27 March 1942.

BAILEY, Sir William (Thomas), Kt 1946; Director: Westminster Press Provincial Newspapers Ltd; Oxford Times Ltd; Garden City Press Ltd; Loxley Bros Ltd; Newsprint Supply Co. Ltd; Pachesham and Barberrys Steamship Companies; *b* Bedale, Yorkshire, 1 Feb. 1873; two *s* one *d. Educ:* Christ Church Schools, West Hartlepool. District representative Northern Daily Gazette, Middlesbrough; in turn: Sales, Advt, and Asst Manager, Northern Echo, Darlington; Sales Manager, General Manager and Director, Sheffield Independent; General Manager Westminster Gazette when morning paper. President The Newspaper Society, 1939–46; Member of Reuters Trust. *Recreations:* model-making, reading. *Address:* 70 Woodfield Avenue, Streatham, SW16. *T:* Streatham 4771.

Died 15 June 1949.

BAILLET-LATOUR, Comte de; Henry; Président du Comité International Olympique; *b* 1 March 1876; *m* 1904, Comtesse Élisalex Clary et Aldringen; one *d. Educ:* Université de Louvain, Belgium. Attaché à la Légation du Belgique à La Haye, 1914–20; Président du Jockey Club de Belgique; Commandeur de l'Ordre de la Couronne de Belgique; Officier de l'Ordre de Léopold. *Recreations:* racing and hunting. *Address:* 23 rue du Trône, Bruxelles, Belgique; Comité International Olympique, Mon Repos, Lausanne, Suisse. *Clubs:* Jockey, Newmarket (Hon.).

Died 6 Jan. 1942.

BAILLIE, Sir Adrian William Maxwell, 6th Bt of Polkemmet; 1823; DL Linlithgow; JP; late Lieutenant Royal Scots Greys and Second Secretary in the Diplomatic Service; *b* 5 May 1898; *s* of 4th Bt and Isabel (*d* 1945), *d* of D. E. Wilkie, Rathobyres, Midlothian; *S* brother, 1914. *Educ:* Eton; RMC, Sandhurst. MP (U) Linlithgow, 1931–35; MP (C) Tonbridge Division of Kent, 1937–45; contested (C) Linlithgowshire, 1929 and 1935. *Heir: s* Gawaine George Hope, *b* 8 March 1934. *Address:* 54 Porchester Gate, W2; Polkemmet, Whitburn, Linlithgowshire. *Clubs:* Beefsteak, Turf, Carlton, Cavalry, Buck's.

Died 8 Jan. 1947.

BAILLIE, Hon. (George) Evan (Michael), MC; TD; *b* 19 Dec. 1894; *e s* of late Col James E. B. Baillie, MVO, and Baroness Burton; *m* 1923, Lady Maud Mackintosh, *e d* of 9th Duke of Devonshire and *widow* of Captain Angus Mackintosh, *o c* of late The Mackintosh; two *s* one *d. Educ:* Eton. Director, Bass, Ratcliff & Gretton, Ltd, Lt-Col commanding 4th Batt. (Territorial) Queen's Own Cameron Highlanders since 1937. *Heir: s* Michael Evan Victor, *b* 27 June 1924. *Address:* Ballindarroch, Scaniport, Inverness. *T:* Scaniport 8. *Clubs:* Bachelors', Carlton.

Died 6 June 1941.

BAILLIE, Col Hugh Frederick, DSO 1915; late Seaforth Highlanders (Ross-shire Buffs, the Duke of Albany's); *b* 30 March 1879; *s* of late Gen. Duncan J. Baillie of Loch Loy, and Anna, *d* of Rev. G. A. Burnaby, Somerby Hall, Leicester. Entered Army, 1898; Captain, 1904; Major, 1915; Lt-Col 1921; DAA and QMG Highland Division, 1909–13; served S Africa, 1899–1902 (Queen's medal 5 clasps, King's medal 2 clasps); N Nigeria, 1903–04 (medal and clasp); European War, 1914–18; served on General Staff, GSO2, Jan. 1910–May 1917; GSO1, May 1917–July 1918; Assistant Director Staff Duties, GHQ, France, July 1918 to end of war (DSO, Bt Lt-Col); retired pay, 1925. *Address:* Loch Loy, Nairn.

Died 15 April 1941.

BAILLIE, Ronald Hugh, OBE 1920; JP, DL, Nairn; *b* 1 June 1863; *e s* of late Lieut-General Duncan Baillie of Loch Loy, Nairn (Royal Horse Guards); *m* 1897, Elizabeth Margaret, MBE (*d* 1933), *y d* of late Major Rose of Kilravock; two *d. Educ:* Wellington College. Called to Scottish Bar, 1887; Sheriff-Substitute of Roxburgh, Berwick, and Selkirk, 1897; retired. *Address:* Jedbank, Jedburgh.

Died 14 Dec. 1948.

BAILLIE-SAUNDERS, Margaret; novelist; *b* Scarborough, 1873; *d* of G. O. Crowther, solicitor; *m* 1901, Rev. Frederick Baillie-Saunders (*d* 1941), Rector of Shepperton. *Educ:* private tuition; Haddo House School, Scarborough. *Publications:* (novels): Saints in Society; London Lovers; A Shepherd of Kensington; The Mayoress's Wooing; The Bride's Mirror; Litany Lane; Lady Q; The Prince's Shadow; The Belfry; Captain the Curé; The Distaff Dreamers; Young Madam at Clapp's; Black Sheep Chapel; Michael Good-News; Becky and Co.; McBride's First Wife; John o'Chimes; Makeshifts; Madge Hinton's Husbands; Scarlet Sails; Dimity Hall; Rooftops; Mr Churchwarden and Lady; Herself, MP; The Lighted Caravan; Mary Simnel's Marrying; Upstarts; Green Sanctuary; Under the Fanlight; The Gilded Widower, 1933; Featuring Eliza, 1934; Jill o' the Wisp, 1935; Answer that Bell, 1935; Widdowson's Wives, 1936; The Candle Virgins, 1937; The Sign of the Swan, 1938; Stained Glass Wives, 1939; The Trinket Shop, 1940; Dear Devotee, 1941; Lonesome Lover, 1942; Shadow City, 1944; Lost Landladies, 1946; Quality Fair, 1948. *Address:* 17 Carisbrooke Road, St Leonards-on-Sea.

Died 24 April 1949.

BAILY, Francis Gibson, MA, FRSE, MIEE; Professor of Electrical Engineering, Heriot-Watt College, Edinburgh, 1896–1933, Emeritus Professor since 1933; *b* 18 March 1868; *s* of Walter Baily, MA, and Mary Ann Gibson; *m* 1899, Margaret Naismith Osborne Pagan; one *s. Educ:* University College School, London; Kön. Bergakademie, Clausthal; St John's College, Cambridge (First class Nat. Sci. Tripos, 1888 and 1889). Engineering pupilage, James Simpson and Co., 1889–90; on the staff of Siemens Bros and Co., 1890–92; Lecturer on Electro-technology, University College, Liverpool, 1892–95; has acted as examiner in Science and Engineering for the Civil Service, Cambridge, London, Edinburgh, and other Universities; has practised as Consulting Engineer for various lunacy boards, school boards, colleges, schools, trusts, and companies; war work, inventions for War Department; Vice-Chairman of Cockburn Association; Vice-President of Scottish Anglers' Association; Treasurer of Association for Preservation of Rural Scotland; Member of Council of National Trust for Scotland, Zoological Soc. of Scotland, Scottish Nature Reserve Committee, and of Advisory Committee for the Argyllshire National Park; Vice-President of Scottish Council for National Parks; Chairman of Scottish Rivers Protection Council. *Publications:* papers in the Philosophical Transactions, Jl Institution Electrical Engineers, Proc. Roy. Soc. Edinburgh, etc. *Recreations:* golf, angling, horticulture, handicraft. *Address:* Newbury, Juniper Green, Midlothian. *T:* Edinburgh 87022. *Clubs:* Scottish Arts, University Union, Edinburgh; Baberton Golf.

Died 23 Feb. 1945.

BAIN, Sir Frederick, Kt 1945; MC; Hon. LLD (Aberdeen), 1950; Deputy Chairman, Imperial Chemical Industries, Ltd; Director: Royal Insurance Co., Liverpool & London & Globe Insurance Co. Ltd; *b* 22 March 1889; *s* of late James Bain, Macduff, Banffshire; *m* 1921, Isabel (*d* 1945), *d* of late J. George Adami, CBE, FRS, MD, Vice-Chancellor of University of Liverpool; one *s. Educ:* Macduff; Banff Academy; Aberdeen Univ. Served European War, 1914–18, Capt. 4th Gordon Highlanders (MC, twice wounded, despatches twice;

Deputy Director Chemical Warfare Supply, Ministry of Munitions, 1916–18; Chairman, Chemical Control Board, Ministry of Supply, 1941–44; Chairman, Chemical Planning Committee, Ministry of Production, 1942–44; Pres. Federation of British Industries, 1947–49; Vice-Pres. British Employers' Confederation, 1945–49; Vice-Chairman Assoc. British Chemical Manufactures; Member: Ministry of Pensions Artificial Limbs Committee, 1945; Board of Trade Committee on Management, 1945; Nat. Production Advisory Council on Industry; Cttee on Civil Service Remuneration, 1948; Joint Chairman, Anglo-American Council on Productivity, UK Section, 1948. Commander of Order of the Dannebrog (2nd Class). *Address:* 29 Palace Court, W2. *T:* Bayswater 1421. *Clubs:* Brooks's, Garrick, Caledonian; University, Racquet (Liverpool).

Died 23 Nov. 1950.

BAIN-MARAIS, Colin; Minister for Union of South Africa to Royal Netherlands and Belgian Governments since 1941; *b* 8 March 1893; *s* of late S. T. Bain and Margaret Elizabeth Fraser and stepson of late P. J. Marais; *m* 1920, Anne, *d* of late Sir Thomas Cullinan; one *s* one *d. Educ:* Diocesan College, Rondebosch, Cape; School of Agriculture, Potchefstroom. (Captained College 1st Rugby XV and winner of Rhodes Cup). Winner S African Maize Championship Natal, 1914. European War, served Natal Light Horse, 1914, Rebellion; SAMR Field Artillery, 1915, S West Africa; Coldstream Guards, 1916–19, France and Flanders, Captain (despatches, French Croix de Guerre). A member of South African Parliament, 1933–39; Minister for Union of South Africa to France, 1939–42; Member of Empire Parliamentary Delegation to United Kingdom, 1935; Coronation, 1937. *Recreations:* tennis and golf. *Address:* c/o South Africa House, WC2. *Clubs:* Rand, Country, Johannesburg.

Died 14 Aug. 1942.

BAINBRIDGE, Maj.-Gen. Sir (Edmund) Guy (Tulloch), KCB 1918; CB 1913; *b* 11 Nov. 1867; *e s* of late Colonel Sir Edmond Bainbridge, KCB, RA; *m* 1904, Alice May, *d* of Colonel M. Goldie, RE; two *d. Educ:* Marlborough College; Sandhurst. Joined The Buffs, 1888; Captain, 1897; Brevet Major, 1898; Brevet Lt-Col 1901; Major, 1905; Brevet-Col 1905; Colonel, 1912; Maj.-Gen., 1917; served Dongola Expedition, 1896 (despatches); Nile Expedition, 1897 (despatches); Nile Expedition, 1898 (despatches twice); South African War, 1899–1900; present at Paardeberg, Poplar Grove, Hout-Nek, Zand River, Relief of Kimberley, Johannesburg, Pretoria, Diamond Hill, Wittenbergen, and Lady Brand (despatches twice); British Sudan Medal; Khedive's medal with 3 clasps; Queen's South African medal with 5 clasps; 3rd Class Order of Medijidie); European War, 1914–18; commanded 110th Infantry Brigade and afterwards 25th Division (despatches seven times, prom. Maj.-Gen., KCB, Commandeur Légion d'Honneur, Croix de Guerre avec Palm); GOC 1st Division, Aldershot, 1919–23; retired 1923. *Recreations:* hunting, shooting, fishing. *Address:* Leigh, Newtown, Newbury.

Died 27 Sept. 1943.

BAINBRIDGE, Rev. Howard Gurney D.; *see* Daniell-Bainbridge.

BAIRD, Sir David, 4th Bt *cr* 1809, of Newbyth; MVO 1909; DL East Lothian; *b* 6 May 1865; *s* of Sir David Baird, 3rd Bt and Ellen Stuart, *d* of 12th Baron Blantyre; S father, 1913; *m* 1901, Lilian Gertrude, widow of Colonel Maxwell Willshire, Black Watch; one *d.* Served in 42nd Royal Highlanders, 1887–1902, also 1914–18; was ADC to Governor of Malta, 1890, also to GOC Scottish Command; is an administrator of the Seafield Estates. Heir: *nephew* David Charles Baird, *b* 6 July 1912. *Clubs:* Carlton; New, Edinburgh.

Died 6 Jan. 1941.

BAIRD, John Logie; inventor of the Televisor, the first practical television apparatus for the instantaneous transmission of scenes or objects over a distance by wire or wireless; also invented the Noctovisor, an apparatus for seeing in the dark by invisible rays; consulting technical adviser to Cable and Wireless Ltd since 1941; also Director John Logie Baird Ltd, and Capital and Provincial Cinemas Ltd; *b* 13 Aug. 1888; father, Minister of the West Parish Church, Helensburgh, Scotland; *m* 1931, Margaret Albu; one *s* one *d*. *Educ:* Larchfield; Royal Technical College and Glasgow Univ. Hon. FRSE; Fellow of the Physical Society. Associate of the Royal Technical College. First demonstration of true Television ever given, Royal Institution, 27 Jan. 1926; German Post Office commenced Television Broadcasting using the Baird System, July 1929; the BBC commenced a television broadcasting service with the Baird System, Sept. 1929; demonstrated his invention of Noctovision in 1926, and television in colour in 1928; transmission of television across the Atlantic, 1928; showed finish of the Derby by television in the Metropole Cinema, London, 1932; showed for the first time television in relief and full natural colour, Dec. 1941. *Address:* 3 Crescent Wood Road, Sydenham, SE26. *T:* Forest Hill 4678. *Club:* Caledonian.

Died 14 June 1946.

BAIRD, Sir William MacDonald, Kt 1936; JP; FSI; FRSE; Chartered Surveyor, Sir William Baird and Partners, Edinburgh and London; *b* Edinburgh, 10 April 1881; *m* 1908, Marjorie Barron; two *s* one *d*. Former Lord Dean of Guild, City of Edinburgh; Past President, Faculty of Surveyors of Scotland. *Address:* 23 Belgrave Crescent, Edinburgh. *T:* Edinburgh 27897. *Clubs:* Scottish Liberal, Edinburgh.

Died 29 Dec. 1946.

BAIRNSFATHER, Captain George Edward Beckwith, CBE 1918; Divisional Naval Transport Officer, Dover, 1914–18; *b* 16 Sept. 1855; *s* of Peter Bairnsfather, DL, of Dumbarrow, Forfarshire; *m* Charlotte Emily, *d* of H. Roberts of Cambridge. *Educ:* St Andrews. Joined HMS Britannia, 1869.

Died 10 Feb. 1945.

BAIRSTOW, His Honour Arthur William; KC 1908; *b* 24 Sept. 1855; *e s* of J. Bairstow, Halifax; *m* 1st, Henriette (*d* 1919), *d* of J. Stacey, Farrington; three *d*; 2nd, 1920, Annie, *d* of late Samuel Simpson, Wolstanton, Staffs. *Educ:* Trinity Hall, Cambridge. Barrister Inner Temple, 1878; Bencher of the Inner Temple, 1915, Treasurer, 1937; North-Eastern Circuit; Solicitor-General of County Palatine, Durham, 1915; Recorder of Scarborough, 1917–18; Judge of County Courts, Circuit 12, 1918–24; Metropolitan Courts, 1924–26; Clerkenwell, 1926–28. *Address:* 30 Farm Avenue, NW2. *T:* Gladstone 3520. *Club:* Reform.

Died 28 March 1943.

BAIRSTOW, Sir Edward C., Kt 1932; Hon. DLitt (Leeds); MusD (Dunelm); FRCO; Organist and Master of the Choir of York Minster since 1913; Professor of Music, Durham University, since 1929; *b* Huddersfield, 1874; *s* of James O. Bairstow, clothing manufacturer; *m* 1902, Edith, *d* of late Dr J. T. Hobson, Government analyst; two *s* one *d*. *Educ:* privately. Pupil of and Assistant to Sir F. Bridge, 1893–99; Organist of All Saints, Norfolk Square, W, 1893; Parish Church, Wigan, 1899; Parish Church, Leeds, 1906; Conductor of Wigan Philharmonic Society, 1901–06; Blackburn S Cecilia Society, 1903–13; Preston Choral Society, 1907–13; York Musical Society, 1913–39; York Symphony Orchestra, 1913–14; Leeds Philharmonic Society, 1917. *Publications:* Music for Piano and Violin; Songs, Part-songs, Church and Organ Music; Text-books, Counterpoint and Harmony, The Evolution of Musical Form; Singing learned from Speech. *Address:* 1 Minster Court, York. *T:* York 2743.

Died 1 May 1946.

BAJPAI, Sir Seetla Prasad, Rai Bahadur, Kt 1939; CIE 1933; Chief Justice and Judicial Member of Council, Jaipur, Rajputana; *b* 19 April 1865; *o s* of Pandit Sham Manohar Bajpai, Governor, Wards Institution, Oudh; *m* Rukmini, *d* of Pandit Uma Charan Shukla; two *s* one *d*. *Educ:* Canning College, Lucknow. Temporary Professor of Sanskrit, Canning College, Lucknow; after studying law, joined the UP Judicial Service 1890; and retired from post of District and Sessions Judge in 1923; appointed to revise laws in Jaipur State, 1923. *Recreation:* gardening. *Address:* Jaipur, Rajputana, India. *T:* Jaipur 26.

Died 1 Feb. 1947.

BAKER, Alfred, MA, LLD; Emeritus Professor of Mathematics since 1919; Professor of Mathematics, University of Toronto, 1887–1919; Dean of the Faculty of Arts, 1912–19; *b* Toronto, of Yorkshire parents; *m* Norah Kathleen, 2nd *d* of late John M'Cormack of Wilmette, Illinois, 1894. *Educ:* Grammar School, and University of Toronto, BA with gold medal in mathematics. After being principal of several high schools in Ontario he was appointed mathematical master in Upper Canada College, and became mathematical tutor in University College, Toronto, 1875; registrar, 1880; dean of residence, 1884; a Member of Senate of University of Toronto, 1887–1906; ex-officio, 1906–19, and since 1920; retired from Queen's Own Rifles, 1883, with rank of captain; FRS Canada; a member of the Société Mathématique de France, and of the American Mathematical Society; President of the Ontario Educational Association, 1895; President of the Royal Society of Canada, 1915–16, having been President of Section III, 1905–06; Member of Brit. Empire League: in conjunction with Dr John Seath reorganised geometrical teaching in schools of Ontario, 1904. *Publications:* Articles relating to Quaternions, Geometry of Position and Foundations of Geometry (translated into Japanese), in the Proceedings of the Royal Society of Canada; also elementary treatises on synthetic and analytical geometry: has edited elementary treatises on Trigonometry and on Mechanics. *Recreations:* walking and boating. *Address:* 81 Madison Avenue, Toronto.

Died 27 Oct. 1942.

BAKER, Sir Alfred, Kt 1931; DL County of London; JP; Solicitor, admitted 1899; *b* 25 Sept. 1870; *s* of James Baker, Exeter; *m* Edith Ellen, *d* of George Baines; one *d*. *Educ:* Exeter. Legal adviser to the National Labour Party, London Labour Party, Miners' Federation of Gt Britain, etc. 1912; member of London County Council since 1919; Deputy Chairman, 1930; Chairman, 1943; JP for County of Middlesex, 1922; Vice-Chairman Gore Division of the County of Middlesex; Representative of Minister of Agriculture on Thames Conservancy and previously, since 1928, represented London County Council as member of Thames Board of Conservators; Member Port of London Authority and representative of Territorial Army and Air Force Association of the County of London; Member Dulwich College Foundation; Governor Regent St Polytechnic and of Holloway School; Life Governor London Hospital. *Recreation:* golf. *Address:* Wyldewood, The Bishop's Avenue, N2. *TA:* Sunrising Estrand London. *T:* Speedwell 1178. *Clubs:* Union, Eighty.

Died 2 April 1943.

BAKER, Brig.-Gen. Arthur Slade, CMG 1915; late RA and Army Ordnance Department; retired, 1920; *b* 13 Dec. 1863; *m* 1895, Caroline Fisher (*d* 1923), *d* of late Gwynne Harris Heap; two *s*. Entered army 1882; Capt., 1891; Major, 1900; Lt-Col 1912; Inspector AOD 1901–05; Deputy Assistant Director War Office, 1908–12; served South Africa, 1900–01 (Queen's Medal 2 clasps); European War, 1914–18 (despatches, CMG, Bt

Col, Hon. Brig.-Gen.). *Address:* Peans Wood, Roberts-bridge, Sussex. *T:* Robertsbridge 36. *Club:* Army and Navy.

Died 3 Sept. 1943.

BAKER, (Charles) Alma, CBE 1919; *b* New Zealand, 1857; *m* 1886, Florence (*d* 1934), *d* of late Sir Frederick Whitaker. Owner of Rubber Estates and Tin Mines (Malaya), Sheep and Cattle Stations (Australia and New Zealand); Founder of Australian and Malayan Battleplane Squadrons, totalling ninety-four battleplanes, European War; Hon. Member of Royal Aeronautical Society. *Publications:* (Brochure) Facts relating to New Scientific Discoveries converning Life-giving Foods, 1918; Australian and Malayan Battleplane Souvenir, 1920; Rough Guide to New Zealand's Big Game Fishing, 1937; The Soil and its Products, 1938; Peace with the Soil, 1939. *Address:* Kinta, Perak, FMS. *Club:* Royal Air Force.

Died 8 April 1941.

BAKER, Lt-Col Sir Dodington George Richard S.; *see* Sherston-Baker.

BAKER, Edward Charles Stuart, CIE 1932; OBE; JP; FLS; FZS; MBOU; HFAOU; HFHOU; Indian Police (retired); *b* 1864; *s* of late Edward B. Baker, Indian Police; *m* 1897, Ethel May Roffey; four *d. Educ:* Trinity College, Stratford-on-Avon. Entered Indian Police, 1883; Assistant Political Officer, North Cachar Hills, 1886; District Superintendent of Police, Dibrugarh, 1900; PA to Inspector General of Police, Assam, 1905; Deputy Inspector General of Police, CID, 1907; officiating Inspector General Police, Assam, 1909; Special Criminal Investigation Duty, 1910; appointed to reorganise Port of London Police, 1912; retired 1925; Member of Advisory Committee to Government Plumage Bills and Protection of Birds; Councillor of Croydon Town Council; Alderman, 1938; Mayor of Croydon, 1937–38 and 1938–39; Deputy Mayor, 1939–42; Hon. Secretary and Treasurer, British Ornithological Union, 1913–36. *Publications:* Birds of N Cachar, 1890; numerous Shooting and Natural History articles, Asian, Indian Field, etc., 1889–1912; Game Birds India, Ducks, 1908; Indian Pigeons and Doves, 1915; Game Birds, two vols, 1921, one vol., 1930; Fauna of India, Birds, vols i-xvii, 1922–1930; Mishi the Man-eater, 1928; numerous-papers in Ibis, proceedings Zoological Society, etc., 1900–1940; Nidification Birds of the Indian Empire, 1932–1934; Cuckoo Problems, 1942. *Recreations:* big game hunting and ornithology. *Address:* 6 Harold Road, Upper Norwood, SE19. *T:* Livingstone 0930. *Club:* Savile.

Died 16 April 1944.

BAKER, Ernest A.; author; *b* Bath, 1869; *s* of B. J. Baker; *m* Louise Gardner (*d* 1932); two *s* two *d. Educ:* BA London, 1892; 1st Class Honours (English), 1896; MA (Classics), 1898; DLit 1908. Sub-Librarian, Bath Royal Literary and Scientific Inst., 1886–92; Librarian, Midland Railway Institute, Derby, 1893–1903; Chief Librarian, Wallasey Public Libraries, 1904–06; Borough Librarian, Woolwich Public Libraries, 1906–12; Librarian, HM Customs and Excise, 1919–20; first Director, University of London School of Librarianship, 1919–34. *Publications:* A Guide to the Best Fiction, 1903; 3rd ed. 1932; Moors, Crags, and Caves of the High Peak, 1903; History in Fiction, a guide to historical romances, novels and tales, 1908; 3rd ed. 1933; Praise of a Simple Life, an anthology; The Netherworld of Mendip (with H. E. Balch, FSA), 1907; Voices of Nature, an anthology, 1908; The Voice of the Mountains, an anthology, 1908; The Voice of the Mountains, an anthology, 1905; editor of Half-forgotten Books, and Library of Early Novelists; Cassell's New English Dictionary, 1919; Cassell's French Dictionary, 1920; The Public Library, 1921; The Highlands with Rope and Rucksack, 1923; History of the English Novel, vols i-x, 1924–1939; Caving, 1932; On Foot in the Highlands, 1932, new edition 1933; The

Highlands of Britain, 1933; editor The Uses of Libraries, 1927; many articles. *Recreations:* mountain-climbing, cave-exploring, fly-fishing. *Address:* St James's Lodge, Kidbrook Park Road, Blackheath, SE3. *T:* Greenwich 1954. *Club:* University of London.

Died 18 Jan. 1941.

BAKER, Flora May, CBE 1941; JP for Middlesex; County Alderman Middlesex County Council; Chairman Public Health Committee; *b* 19 May 1882; *d* of Rev. Justin Evans; *m* 1900, Charles Baker; one *s. Educ:* private schools. *Address:* Rembrandt Hotel, Thurloe Place, SW7.

Died 16 March 1949.

BAKER, Sir Herbert, KCIE 1930; Kt 1926; RA 1932; ARA 1922; FRIBA; Gold Medallist, 1927; architect, practising in London; *b* 1862; *s* of T. H. Baker, Cobham, Kent; *m* Florence, *d* of late General H. Edmeades, RA, Nurstead Court, Kent; three *s* one *d. Educ:* Tonbridge School. Practised at Cape Town, 1892; built Groote Schuur and other buildings for Cecil Rhodes; transferred to Transvaal, 1902; works include Government House and the Capital Buildings for the South African Government at Pretoria; the Rhodes Memorial on Table Mountain; Cathedrals at Capetown, Johannesburg, Pretoria, and Salisbury, Rhodesia; practised in London and Delhi from 1913; built Secretariat and Legislative Buildings for the New Capital at Delhi; one of the principal Architects for the Imperial War Graves Commission; Government Houses at Nairobi and Mombasa and other buildings in Kenya. Chief works in England: The Bank of England, Winchester College War Memorial; Rhodes House, Oxford; Ninth Church of Christ, Scientist; India House, Aldwych; South Africa House, Trafalgar Square; Martins and Glyn Mills Banks in Lombard Street; Royal Empire Society in Northumberland Avenue; Church House, Westminster. *Publications:* Cecil Rhodes, 1934; Architecture and Personalities, 1944. *Address:* 2 and 3 The Sanctuary, Westminster, SW1. *T:* Abbey 7206; Owletts, Cobham, Kent. *Club:* Athenæum.

Died 4 Feb. 1946.

BAKER, Herbert Arthur, MA (Oxon); JP, DL County of London; Barrister-at-Law; *b* Dec. 1875; 2nd *s* of late Sir John Baker, sometime MP for Portsmouth; *m* 1903, Madeleine, *y d* of late Joseph McGaw, Kooba, New South Wales; one *d. Educ:* Portsmouth Grammar School; Christ Church, Oxford. Called to Bar, Inner Temple, 1902; Member of London County Council, 1919–28 (an Alderman 1922–28), and later a co-opted Member of Central Public Health Committee; a Member of College Committee University College, London; Vice-Pres. and Member of Committee of Management of Royal National Life-boat Institution; Hon. Treas. of National Association for the Prevention of Tuberculosis; several Parliamentary candidatures; High Sheriff of County of London, 1937. *Address:* Weybrook House, Haslemere. *Clubs:* Athenæum, Oxford and Cambridge.

Died 10 Dec. 1946.

BAKER, Ven. Archdeacon John Percy; Rector of Winwick since 1935; Archdeacon Emeritus since 1947; *b* 9 Feb. 1871; *s* of John Lake Baker, CE, and Adelaide Sarah Emma, *d* of Rev. S. V. Edwards; *m* 1901, Alice Maud, *d* of Dr Wilkinson, Archdeacon of Totnes; one *s* one *d. Educ:* Kimbolton Grammar School; King Edward's School. Birmingham; Emmanuel College and Ridley Hall, Cambridge (MA Cantab). Curate of St Aubyn, Devonport, 1894–98; St Andrew's, Plymouth, 1898–1901; Vicar of Ellacombe, Torquay, 1901–09; Charles, Plymouth, and Chaplain HM Prison, 1909–21; Vicar of Mossley Hill, Liverpool, 1921–35; Chaplain TF, 1913–18; Major Cadet Force, Co. Devon, 1918–21; Prebendary of Exeter Cathedral, 1920–34; Rural Dean of Three Towns and Proctor in Convocation, 1921–22; Rural Dean of Child-wall, 1926–32; Chaplain to Lord Mayor of Liverpool, 1923–24; Examining Chaplain to

Bishop of Liverpool, 1928–46, Proctor in Convocation, 1930–34; Archdeacon of Warrington, 1934–47. *Publications:* The Church of Plymouth, called Charles Church; The Story of Mosslake Hill. *Address:* Winwick Rectory, near Warrington. *T:* Warrington 866.

Died 28 Dec. 1947.

BAKER, Ray Stannard; author; *b* Lansing, Mich, USA, 17 April 1870; *s* of Major Joseph Stannard Baker and Alice Potter; *m* 1896, Jessie I., *d* of Professor William James Beal; two *s* two *d. Educ:* BS, Mich State College, 1889; LLD 1917; partial law course and studies in Literature, Univ. of Mich; LittD, Amherst, 1925; Sullivan Medal, Rollins College, 1936; LittD, Duke University, 1938. Reporter and Sub-editor Chicago Record, 1892–97; Managing Editor McClure's Syndicate, 1897–98; Assoc. Editor McClure's Magazine, 1899–1905; one of Editors American Magazine, 1906–15; Special Commissioner, Dept of State in Great Britain, France, and Italy, 1918; Director Press Bureau of American Commission to negotiate Peace at Paris, 1919; Trustee Jones Library of Amherst; Director Woodrow Wilson Foundation; member Nat. Inst. Arts and Letters, Society American Historians, and Phi Beta Kappa. *Publications:* Seen in Germany, 1901; Following the Color Line, 1908; The Spiritual Unrest, 1910; What Wilson did at Paris, 1919; The New Industrial Unrest, 1920; Woodrow Wilson and World Settlement, a History of the Peace Conference (3 vols), 1922; edited (with Prof. W. E. Dodd): The Public Papers of Woodrow Wilson (6 vols), 1925–1926; Woodrow Wilson, Life and Letters (authorized biography), first 2 vols 1927, second 2 vols 1931, fifth vol. 1935, sixth vol. 1937, seventh and eighth vol. 1939 (awarded Pulitzer prize, 1940, for best biography); Native American: The Book of My Youth, 1941; American Chronicle, Autobiography, 1945; also under pseudonym of David Grayson: Adventures in Contentment, 1907; Adventures in Friendship, 1910; The Friendly Road, 1913; Hempfield, 1915; Great Possessions, 1917; Adventures in Understanding, 1925; Adventures in Solitude, 1931; The Countryman's Year, 1936; Under My Elm, 1942; (with J. B. Baker) American Pioneer in Science (Life of William James Beal), 1925. *Recreations:* gardening, bee-keeping, tramping. *Address:* 118 Sunset Avenue, Amherst, Mass, USA. *T:* Amherst 169. *Clubs:* Century, New York.

Died 12 Jan. 1946.

BAKER, Richard Thomas; for 13 years Lecturer on Forestry, Sydney University; *b* Woolwich, 1 Dec. 1854; *s* of Richard Thomas Baker and Sarah Colket, Down, Kent; *m* Ann Dawson; one *d. Educ:* Woolwich; Peterborough; South Kensington (Science). Honorary Member Pharmaceutical Society of Great Britain, Philadelphia College Pharm. and NSW Pharmaceutical Society; 25 years Curator, Technological Museum, Sydney; has carried out scientific researches on the Botany of Australia; Mueller Medal, 1921, by the Australasian Association for the advancement of Science; Clarke Memorial Medal, 1922, Royal Society, NSW; the author of many new species of plants and a new genus. *Publications:* Hard Woods of Australia; Cabinet Timbers of Australia; Australian Flora in Applied Art; Building and Ornamental Stone of Australia; 120 original research papers on Australian Botany and Palæontology. With H. G. Smith: A Research on the Eucalypts and their Essential Oils, 1st and 2nd ed.; A Research on the Pines of Australia; Wood Fibres of some Australian Timbers. *Recreation:* bowls. *Address:* The Crescent, Cheltenham, Sydney, NSW. *T:* Epping 636, NSW. *Clubs:* Old Newingtonians, Sydney.

Died 14 July 1941.

BAKER, Rev. Dr Stanley; Vicar Choral of Salisbury Cathedral since 1897; Vicar of Laverstock, Wilts, since 1938; Canon (non-residentiary) of Salisbury Cathedral since 1947, and Prebendary of Ilfracombe; *b* 14 Oct. 1868; *s* of Rev. John and Caroline Baker; *m* 1907, Ethel

Alice Mary Buller (*d* 1946); one *d. Educ:* Manchester Grammar School; Queen's College, Oxford. Second Master at S Michael's College Tenbury, and ordained to the curacy of the parish 1892; Chaplain of Christ Church, Oxford, 1895; curate of S Mary's Oxford, 1895; Lecturer 1903 and Chaplain of Salisbury Diocesan Training College 1913. *Publications:* Notes on Latin and Greek Syntax; Notes on the Church Catechism; The Faith of the Church; The Rudiments of Christianity; A Catechism on the Teaching of the Church; A Catechism on Christian Faith, Duty, Prayer. *Recreations:* Searching for the lost glass of Salisbury Cathedral, a search which has been partly successful; also the restoration of ancient houses. *Address:* The Close, Salisbury. *T:* Salisbury 2806.

Died 20 April 1950.

BAKER, Ven. William Arthur, MA (Cantab); Archdeacon of Sheffield, 1938–43; Archdeacon Emeritus, 1943; one of the Bishop's Hon. Chaplains since 1943; Hon. Canon of Sheffield, 1934; *b* 23 May 1870; *s* of William and Mary Elizabeth Baker; *m* 1st, 1899, Margaret Sharman (*d* 1907), *d* of Rev. J. Franey, Ely; one *s*; 2nd, 1909, Hilda Mary, *d* of Rev. F. P. Gilbert, South Wootton; one *d. Educ:* Cheltenham College; Christ's College, Cambridge. Chaplain and Assistant Master at King William's College, Isle of Man, 1892–96; Curate of St Mary's, Ely, 1896–98; Vicar of Hapton, Norfolk, 1898–1907; Vicar of Bourn and Rector of Kingston (Cambs), 1907–15; Rector of Handsworth, Yorks, 1915–43; Rural Dean of Handsworth, 1927–38. *Recreations:* cricket, woodcarving. *Address:* 6 Hemper Lane, Bradway, Sheffield.

Died 14 Dec. 1950.

BAKER, Sir William (Thomas Webb), Kt 1934; BA (Oxon); ICS, retired; *b* Abergavenny, 6 Dec. 1873; *e s* of late Henry Lawrence Baker, Pentre Court, Abergavenny, and Caroline Elizabeth, *d* of late Thomas Townsend Webb, Tiddington House, Stratford-on-Avon; *m* 1899, Clare, *d* of late C. W. Priestley, PWD, India; two *d. Educ:* Rugby; Exeter College, Oxford. Entered ICS, Bombay Presidency, 1897; District and Sessions Judge, 1916; Judicial Commissioner, Central Provinces, 1923–25; Western India States Agency, 1926; Additional Judge, High Court, Bombay, 1927; Puisne Judge, High Court, Bombay, 1929–33; Offg. Chief Justice, June–July 1933; retd 1933. *Address:* St Michaels, Bramley, Guildford; c/o Grindlay's Bank, 54 Parliament St, SW1.

Died 17 April 1948.

BAKER-CARR, Brig.-Gen. Christopher D'Arcy Bloomfield Saltern, CMG 1917; DSO 1916; *b* 1878; *s* of late Rev. Robert James Baker-Carr, of Abberton Hall, Worcestershire; *m* 1902, Sara de Witt Quinan (who obtained a divorce, 1932). Entered Rifle Brigade, 1898; served Nile, 1898 (Egyptian medal with clasp, medal); S Africa, 1899–1902 (despatches, King's medal and 2 clasps, Queen's medal and 4 clasps); European War, 1914–18 (despatches, DSO); commanded 1st Brigade Tank Corps, 1917–18; serving in Cairo, 1946; late Member of Council British Electrical Federation. *Publication:* From Chauffeur to Brigadier, 1930.

Died 10 Jan. 1949.

BALASINOR, HH Babi Shri Jamiatkhanji Manawar Khanji, Saheb Bahadur, Nawab of; *b* 10 Nov. 1894; *S* father, 1899. *Educ:* Rajkumar College, Rajkot, Kathiawar, India. Joined the Imperial Cadet Corps, 1913. Salute, nine guns. Area of the State is 189 sq. miles. Population over 52,000. *Address:* Balasinor, Gujarat States, India. *Clubs:* Willingdon Sports, Bombay.

Died Feb. 1945.

BALDWIN OF BEWDLEY, 1st Earl *cr* 1937; **Stanley Baldwin;** Viscount Corvedale, *cr* 1937, of Corvedale, KG 1937; PC 1920; PC Can. 1927; FRS 1927; Hon. DCL (Oxford and Durham); Hon. LLD (Cambridge, St

Andrews, Edinburgh, Birmingham, London, Belfast, Liverpool, Wales, Leeds, Columbia, Toronto, McGill); Elder Brother of Trinity House; Hon. Master of Bench of Inner Temple; High Steward of Tewkesbury; *b* 3 Aug. 1867; *s* of late Alfred Baldwin, MP, and Louisa, *d* of Rev. George Macdonald; *m* 1892, Lucy (GBE 1937) (*d* 1945), *e d* of late E. L. J. Ridsdale, of Rottingdean; two *s* four *d*. *Educ:* Harrow; Trinity College, Cambridge. Contested Kidderminster, 1906; MP (U) Bewdley Division of Worcestershire, 1908–37; Financial Secretary to the Treasury, 1917–21; President of the Board of Trade, 1921–22; Chancellor of the Exchequer, 1922–23; Prime Minister and First Lord of the Treasury, 1923–24, 1924–29 and 1935–37; Lord Privy Seal, 1932–34; Lord President of the Council, 1931–35; Lord Rector of Edinburgh Univ. 1923–26, and Glasgow, 1928–31; Chancellor of St Andrews Univ. since 1929; Chancellor of Cambridge Univ. since 1930; Member of Académie des Sciences Morales et Politiques (Institut de France) since 1930. *Publications:* Peace and Goodwill in Industry, 1925; The Classics and the Plain Man; On England and other Addresses, 1926; Our Inheritance (Speeches), 1928; This Torch of Freedom; Speeches and Addresses, 1935; Service of Our Lives, 1937; An Interpreter of England, 1939. *Heir: s* Viscount Corvedale. *Address:* Astley Hall, Stourport-on-Severn, Worcs. *Clubs:* Carlton, United University, Athenæum, Travellers'.

Died 14 Dec. 1947.

BALDWIN, Rev. Edward Curtis, MA; Hon. Canon of Ely since 1916; *b* 1844; *s* of late Edward Baldwin, proprietor of Standard newspaper; *m* 1875, Caroline Maria (*d* 1927), *d* of late Rev. C. B. Lowe, Rector of Tydd St Mary; one *d*. *Educ:* Rottingdean; Oswestry; Hertford College, Oxford. Sometime Rector and Rural Dean of Queenstown, S Africa; Select Preacher Cambridge, 1895; Proctor in Convocation, 1915–29. *Publications:* sermons, pamphlets, etc. *Recreations:* formerly cricket and lawn-tennis; at present, chess. *Address:* 96 Blinco Grove, Cambridge.

Died 22 Oct. 1941.

BALDWIN, Brig.-Gen. Guy Melfort, DSO 1895; *b* Penang, 22 March 1865; 2nd *s* of late Col A. T. Baldwin, and late Margaret, *d* of late Col J. Johnston; *m* 1898, Christine, *γ d* of late Christopher Sparrow, of Urmston Lodge, Urmston; one *s* one *d*. *Educ:* Royal High School, Edinburgh; Wimbledon College; RMC Sandhurst. Joined 1st Batt. LNL Regiment, 1886; 4th Punjab Infantry, 1888; served with this regiment as Wing Officer in Hazara Expedition, 1888 (action of Kotkni) (medal with clasp); 'QO' Corps of Guides (cavalry), 1890; served with above regiment as Squadron Commander in Chitral Expedition, 1895 (wounded, despatches, medal with clasp, DSO); also NW Frontier Expedition, 1897–98; present at operations at Malakand; Mahmund, and Buneyrwal (severely wounded at Malakand, despatches, 2 clasps, Brev. of Maj.); operations NW Frontier, 1915–17 (despatches, Bt Col); commanded Derajat Brigade and 10th Cavalry Brigade, 1917–19; Afghanistan, 1919 (medal and clasp); retired, 1920. *Address:* Melfort Cottage, Yately, Hants.

Died 22 March 1945.

BALDWIN, John Herbert Lacy; *b* 1863; *e s* of late John Baldwin, Broomfield, Halifax; *m* Mary Beatrice, *d* of late Rev. W. A. Norris, Rector of Flore, North Hants; two *s* two *d*. *Educ:* Rugby. Entered business of J. & J. Baldwin, Halifax, knitting-wool spinners; was Chairman of J. & J. Baldwin & Partners, Ltd, and later of Patons & Baldwins, Ltd; was a Director of Lloyds Bank, Limited. *Address:* Levisham Hall, nr Pickering, Yorks. *T:* Lockton 23; Roxby Manor, Thornton-le-Dale, Yorks. *T:* Thornton-le-Dale 17.

Died 26 Feb. 1945.

BALDWIN, Joseph Mason, MA, DSc, FInstP; Government Astronomer for Victoria, 1920–44; *b* Carlton, Victoria, 9 Sept. 1878; *s* of Joseph Baldwin and Emma Maria Graham; *m* 1st, 1907, Jessie Redmond (*d* 1935); two *s* one *d*; 2nd, 1938, Florette Jessie Bostock. *Educ:* South Melbourne College; University High School; Melbourne University. 1851 Exhibition Scholar, 1906. Volunteer Assistant, Royal Observatory, Cape of Good Hope, 1906; Volunteer Assistant, Potsdam Astrophysical Observatory, 1907–08; Chief Assistant, Melbourne Observatory, 1908; Syme Prizeman (Melbourne University), 1913; Acting Government Astronomer for Victoria, 1915; Pres. Royal Society of Victoria, 1925, 1926; President, Section A, Australasian Association for the Advancement of Science, 1930; Pres. Melbourne Univ. Assoc., 1930–31. *Publications:* papers in Philosophical Magazine, Monthly Notices of the Royal Astronomical Society, Proceedings of the Royal Society of Victoria. *Recreation:* gardening. *Address:* Observatory House, South Yarra, Melbourne SE1, Victoria, Australia.

Died 6 July 1945.

BALFOUR, 2nd Earl of, *cr* 1922, and Viscount Traprain of Whittingehame; **Gerald William Balfour,** PC; Hon. LLD Cambridge; late Fellow of Trinity College, Cambridge; *b* 9 April 1853; 4th *s* of late James Maitland Balfour, Whittingehame, and Lady Blanche Cecil, *d* of 2nd Marquis of Salisbury, KG; *S* brother, 1930; *m* 1887, Lady Betty (*d* 1942), *d* of 1st Earl of Lytton; one *s* five *d*. *Educ:* Eton; Trinity College, Cambridge (1st Class Classical Tripos; MA). Was a member of Commission on Labour, and Private Secretary to his brother Rt Hon. A. J. Balfour, when President of Local Government Board, 1885–86; Chief Secretary for Ireland, 1895–1900; President of Board of Trade, 1900–05; President of Local Government Board, 1905–06; Chairman of Commission on Lighthouse Administration, 1908; Chairman of Cambridge Committee of Commission on Oxford and Cambridge Universities; MP (C) Central Leeds, 1885–1906. *Heir: s* Viscount Traprain. *Address:* Lady Eleanor's Cottage, Whittingehame, Haddington, Scotland.

Died 14 Jan. 1945.

BALFOUR, Lt-Col Frederick Robert Stephen, CVO 1944; FLS; DL, JP, Peeblesshire; Lt-Col 1916; a member of King's Scottish Bodyguard since 1900; Director of Guardian Assurance Company, Cable and Wireless Ltd, London Committee Bank of Montreal, and other companies; *b* Mount Alyn, Denbighshire, 11 March 1873; *e surv. s* of late Alexander Balfour and Mrs Balfour of Dawyck, Tweeddale; *m* 1904, Gertrude, *o d* of late F. H. Norman, DL, of Moor Place, Herts; one *s* one *d*. *Educ:* Loretto; Trinity College, Oxford (MA). Spent the greater part of four years on the Pacific Coast of N America; very much interested in forestry and arboriculture; in 1916 served as member of the Home Grown Timber Committee, and later in that year was sent by the War Office to act as liaison officer to the French Government for Army timber supplies; a Victoria Medallist of Honour of the Royal Horticultural Society. *Publications:* occasional papers on subjects connected with arboriculture and botany. *Address:* Dawyck, Stobo, Tweeddale. *T:* Stobo 2. *Clubs:* Brooks's; New, Edinburgh.

Died 2 Feb. 1945.

BALFOUR, George, JP, MIMechE; MIEE; MP (U) Hampstead since 1918; founder and head of the firm of Balfour, Beatty & Co., London; Chairman of the Power Securities Corporation; *b* Portsmouth, 1872; *m* 1901, Margaret Malloch, *d* of David Mathers, Dundee; four *s* one *d*. *Educ:* Portsmouth; Technical Institute and University College, Dundee. Contested Govan Division of Lanark, 1910–11. *Address:* Elmstead Lodge, Chislehurst, Kent. *T:* Chislehurst 45. *Clubs:* Carlton, City of London.

Died 26 Sept. 1941.

BALFOUR, Margaret Ida, CBE 1924; MBCM Edin., FRCOG, KIH; Women's Medical Service, India; retired; *d* of Robert Balfour, CA, Edinburgh. *Educ:* Edinburgh and London. Medical Officer in charge Zenana Hospital, Ludhiana, India, 1892–95; Medical Supt Women's Hospital, Nahan, India, 1896–1902; Medical Superintendent, Lady Dufferin Hospital, Patiala, 1903–13; Assistant to Inspector-General, Civil Hospitals, Punjab, 1914–16; Joint Secretary, Countess of Dufferin's Fund, Delhi and Simla, 1916–24; Chief Medical Officer, Women's Medical Service, India, 1920–24. *Publications:* First Lessons for Country Mid-wives, 1920; Hukm Dey and her Baby, 1921; The Care of the Baby, 1922; Infant Mortality in India and England, 1923; Maternal Mortality in Childbirth in India, 1927; Anaemia of Pregnancy, 1927; (Joint) The Work of Medical Women in India, 1929; Maternity Conditions of Women Millworkers, Bombay, 1930; Indian Mothercraft, 1932; A Study of the effect on Mother and Child of gainful occupation during pregnancy, 1938; Supplementary Feeding in Pregnancy, 1944. *Recreations:* motoring, walking. *Address:* 146 Burbage Rd, Dulwich, SE21.
Died 1 Dec. 1945.

BALL, Alderman Sir Albert, Kt 1924; JP; *b* 1862; *s* of George Ball, Lenton, Notts; *m* 1st, 1886, Mary (*d* 1931), *d* of Henry Page, Derby; 2nd, 1933, Estelle Dorothy Bella, *e d* of James Dannah, Cheveney Manor, Quorn. Lord of the Manors of Bunny, Bradmore, and Tollerton; Mayor of Nottingham, 1909–10, 1920, and Lord Mayor, 1935–36. *Address:* Stansted House, Wollaton Park, Nottingham.
Died 27 March 1946.

BALL, Sir (Charles) Arthur (Kinahan), 2nd Bt *cr* 1911; MD, MCh, FRCSI; Regius Professor of Surgery, Trinity College, since 1933; *b* 29 March 1877; *s* of 1st Bt and Annie J., *e d* of late D. Kinahan, JP, Roebuck Park, Dublin; *S* father, 1916; *m* 1907, Elizabeth, *d* of Joseph S. Wilson, Berkeley, California; no *c. Educ:* Trinity College, Dublin; Berne; Baltimore. Surgical Travelling Prizeman, University of Dublin; Surgeon, Sir Patrick Dun's Hospital; Consulting Surgeon, Monkstown Hospital, Stewart Institution, Drogheda Cottage Hospital, Rest for the Dying; Member of Council Royal College of Surgeons, Ireland; Member of Council Royal Zoological Society, Ireland; late Assistant Surgeon Sir Patrick Dun's Hospital; Lecturer in Operative Surgery, Royal Medical Services School, Trinity College, Dublin. *Publications:* various medical papers. *Heir: b* Nigel Gresley, *b* 1892. *Address:* 24 Merrion Square, Dublin. *TA:* Sphaira Dublin. *T:* 62049; Cool-na-Greine, Carrickmines, Co. Dublin. *Clubs:* University, Dublin.
Died 21 Dec. 1945.

BALL, E. Bruce, JP; FRSE; Past President and Hon. Life MIMechE; Hon. Life Member American Society of Mech. Engs; Managing Director, Glenfield and Kennedy, Ltd, Kilmarnock; Director, British Pitometer Co. Ltd, London; Chairman, Hydrautomat (1931) Ltd, London; *b* 21 May 1873; *m* 1891; one *s* one *d. Educ:* Thetford, Norfolk; Manchester. Gained two science scholarships, Whitworth Exhibition, and Queen's Prizeman for Science. Chief designer to Benj. Goodfellow and Co., Hyde, Manchester; Works Manager to Reavell and Co. Ltd, Ipswich; Works Manager, Clarkson, Ltd, Steam Car Works, Chelmsford; Technical Director to San Giorgio Co., Genoa; Commercial Engineer, Samuel and Co. Ltd, Shanghai and Manchuria; General Works Manager to D. Napier and Son, Ltd, Acton. *Publications:* Improvements in Mechanical Contrivances in Connection with the Storage and Distribution of Water (JMechE); Irrigation Engineering (Cambridge University Engineering and Aeronautical Society); Methods Employed to Remedy Water Hammer Shock in Pumping Systems (American Society of Mechanical Engineers), 1938. *Recreation:*

fishing. *Address:* Eldo House, Monkton, Ayrshire. *T:* Prestwick 7381. *Clubs:* Constitutional, Royal Automobile.
Died 17 June 1944.

BALL, Harry Standish, OBE; MSc, FGS, MInstMM, FInstPet; Principal, School of Metalliferous Mining, Cornwall; *b* 9 Sept. 1888; *s* of late Thomas John Ball, JP, and late Jessie Philipson Stow. *Educ:* St John's College, Johannesburg; Witwatersrand University; McGill University, Montreal. Mining Engineer and Petroleum Technologist; Transvaal Chamber of Mines Research Scholarship and Gold Medal; professional appointments South Africa, Canada, Trinidad, South America; Major (RE) BEF, France, 1915–19 (despatches four times); Commandant First Army Mine School; Assistant Inspector of Mines, GHQ. *Publication:* Economics of Tube Milling and Work of the Miner on the Western Front, Transactions IMM. *Recreations:* swimming, tennis, golf. *Address:* c/o Standard Bank of South Africa, Ltd, Clement's Lane, EC. *Clubs:* Roehampton, Mining and Metallurgical; Country, Johannesburg.
Died 26 Sept. 1941.

BALL, John, OBE 1918; DSc (Lond.), PhD, MInstCE, ARSM, FGS, FRGS; Technical Counsellor, Survey of Egypt; *b* 1872; *e s* of late Ebenezer Ball, Derby; *m* 1918, Kate, *y d* of late James Russell Waite; one *s. Educ:* Royal College of Science and Royal School of Mines, London; Royal Academy of Mines, Freiberg; University of Zurich. Apprenticed to the Phœnix Foundry Co., Derby, where engaged on construction of Battersea Bridge, Liverpool Overhead Railway, and other large works; silver medal and first prize in mechanical engineering, City and Guilds of London, 1892; Senior Whitworth Scholar, 1894; De la Beche Medal, Royal School of Mines, 1894; mining work in Isle of Man, Germany, and Spain, 1895–96; joined the Survey of Egypt, 1897, and has since been chiefly engaged in geographical and geological explorations in Egypt, Sinai, and the Sudan; services lent to the Public Works Dept as engineer in charge of the underpinning of the Temples of Philae, 1901–02, for which work he was decorated with the Mejidie; during European War was attached to military patrols for carrying out reconnaissance-surveys in the Libyan Desert; prepared numerous military maps for the use of the Egyptian Expeditionary Force, and conducted surveys for the British Government in Somaliland and Arabia; in 1921 surveyed the Cairo-Baghdad air-route in conjunction with the Royal Air Force; Victoria gold medal of the Royal Geographical Society for contributions to scientific geography, 1926. *Publications:* The Serpentine and Associated Rocks of Davos, 1897; Topography and Geology of Kharga Oasis, 1900; Baharia Oasis, 1903; Gebel Garra and the Oasis of Kurkur, 1902; A Description of the First or Aswan Cataract of the Nile, 1907; A New Method of Coast Surveying, 1911; Geography and Geology of South-Eastern Egypt, 1912; Topography and Geology of the Phosphate District of Safaga, 1914; Geography and Geology of West-Central Sinai, 1916; Handbook of the Prismatic Astrolabe, 1919; Contributions to the Geography of Egypt, 1939. *Address:* Maadi, Egypt.
Died 12 July 1941.

BALL, Sir William Girling, Kt 1938; FRCS (Eng.); Surgeon to St Bartholomew's Hospital; Consulting Surgeon, City of London Truss Society; Surgeon, Alexandra Hospital for Hip Disease; Surgeon to Royal Masonic Hospital; Surgeon to Harrow and Wealdstone Hospital; Dean, Medical College, St Bartholomew's Hospital; Vice-President, Royal College of Surgeons of England; Member, Council, University of London; Consulting Surgeon, RAF; Sector Hospital Officer, Sector III Emergency Medical Service (Ministry of Health); ex-President Royal Society of Medicine; Joint Lecturer in Surgery, SBH; *s* of late William Ball; *m* 1912, Violet Isobel, *d* of late William Cavander. *Educ:* Merchant Taylors' School; St Bartholomew's Hospital.

Luther-Holden Scholar in Surgery; Jacksonian Prize, Royal College of Surgeons, 1909. Hunterian Professor, RCS, 1911; Warden of the College, SBH, 1913–20; Sub-Dean St Bart.'s Hospital, 1920–25; MO in Charge Military Wing, SBH, 1914–19; Surgeon Special 53rd General Hospital, BEF, 1917–18; MO in Charge, Ven. Dept; Dem. Path., SBH; Clinical Assistant, St Peter's Hospital; Hon. Surgeon to various charity foundations. *Publications:* Diseases of the Kidney (with Dr Geoffrey Evans), 1932; General Surgical Pathology and Bacteriology (Gask and Wilson's Surgery); numerous articles, etc., on Pathological and Genito-urinary subjects. *Address:* (temp.): The Grove, Mill Hill Village, NW7. *T:* Mill Hill 1006 and 3640. *Club:* Athenæum.

Died 16 July 1945.

BALLANTINE-DYKES, Col Frescheville Hubert; see Dykes, Col F. H. B.

BALLANTYNE, Sir Henry, Kt 1906; JP, DL; *b* 1855; *s* of late David Ballantyne of Sunnybrae, Walkerburn, Peeblesshire; *m*. Provost of Peebles nine years; with his father started March Street Tweed Mill in Peebles, 1884; Chairman of the Liberal Committee; acted as Chairman of the Royal Commission on Housing (Scotland). *Address:* Monkrigg, Haddington.

Died 15 July 1941.

BALLARD, Brig.-Gen. Colin Robert, CB 1916; CMG 1918; *b* 20 July 1868; *y s* of Lieut-Gen. J. A. Ballard, CB, RE; *m* L. E. A., *d* of Gen. Jenkin Jones, RE; no *c. Educ:* US College, Westward Ho! Joined Norfolk Regt, 1888; served in Burma, 1891–92 (medal with clasp); Chitral, 1895 (medal with clasp); Tirah, 1897–98 (despatches); S Africa, 1899–1902 (despatches, Bt-Major, Queen's medal 6 clasps, King's medal 2 clasps); Somaliland, 1903–04 (despatches, medal with clasp); Commanded 1st Norfolk Regt and afterwards 7th and 95th Brigades, European War (despatches thrice, Bt-Col, CB); wounded on the Somme; later commanded 57th Brigade; Military Attaché in Rumania 1917–18 and Member of Military Mission (Order of Star of Rumania, Order of the Carol); President Allied Police Commission, Constantinople 1920–23; retired pay, 1923. *Publications:* Russia in Rule and Miss Rule, 1920; Napoleon, an Outline, 1924; Military Genius of Abraham Lincoln, 1926; The Great Earl of Peterborough, 1929; Smith-Dorrien, 1931. *Clubs:* United Service, Badminton.

Died 17 June 1941.

BALLARD, Adm. George Alexander, CB 1913; retired list, 1921; *b* India, 7 March 1862; *s* of late General J. A. Ballard, CB, LLD, Royal Engineers; *m* 1898, Mary Frances, *d* of late J. Paterson of Whitelee, Selkirk; two *s* one *d. Educ:* HMS Britannia. Entered RN 1875; present as sub-lieutenant of HMS Hecla at operations round Suakim, 1884, including the battle of Tamai (special promotion); served as naval ADC to General Prendergast, Burmah, 1885–86, present at all the engagements fought on the river, and at the personal surrender of King Theebaw and occupation of his palace; served as Commander in HMS Isis during the Boxer rising in China in 1900; served during European War as Admiral of Patrols on East Coast of England and Admiral Commanding at Malta; Naval ADC to King George V; late Director of Operations Division Admiralty War Staff; Admiral retired, 1924; Vice-Pres. of Society for Nautical Research; a member of the Victory Restoration Committee; Commander Legion of Honour; Commander of St Maurice and St Lazarus; Grand Cordon of the Sacred Treasure of Japan. *Publications:* Rulers of the Indian Ocean, 1927; America and the Atlantic; Gold Medal Prize Essays of the Royal United Service Institution for 1897 and 1899. *Recreations:* shooting, fishing, and natural history. *Address:* Hill House, Downton, Wilts. *Clubs:* Naval and Military; Union (Malta).

Died 16 Sept. 1948.

BALLARD, Philip Boswood, MA, DLit (Lond.); *b* Maesteg, Glamorgan, 13 Feb. 1865; *s* of Evan Ballard, Maesteg; *m* 1st, Florence Lucy Stone; 2nd, Freda Mary, *d* of F. W. Bartlett; one *d. Educ:* Maesteg; Borough Road College. Taught in London Schools, 1886–98; Headmaster of Pupil Teachers' School, Tondu, Glamorgan, 1898–1903; Inspector of Schools to the Glamorgan Education Committee, 1903–05; Inspector, Education Department of LCC 1906–30; gold medallist MA (Lond.); Carpenter medal DLit; twice President of the Association of Inspectors and Educational Organisers; former President of the Child Study Society; of Chiswick Group of Artists; of London Branch Mathematical Association, 1935–36; for some years Chairman of Borough Road College Committee. *Publications:* Obliviscence and Reminiscence, 1913; Mental Tests, 1920; Group Tests of Intelligence, 1922; The New Examiner, 1923; The Changing School, 1925; Teaching the Mother Tongue, 1921; Teaching the Essentials of Arithmetic, 1928; Handwork as an Educational Medium, 1910; Fundamental Arithmetic; Fundamental English; The Bargerys, 1934; Thought and Language, 1934; Things I cannot Forget, 1937; The ABC of Algebra; Teaching and Testing English, 1939; (ed. of Eng. edn) Thorndike Junior Dictionary, 1947; (ed. of Eng. edn) Thorndike English Dictionary, 1948; etc. *Recreation:* water colour painting. *Address:* Hazel Cottage, Chute Forest, nr Andover, Hants. *T:* Chute Standen 232.

Died 1 Nov. 1950.

BALME, Archibald Hamilton, CBE 1921; OBE 1918. Was Technical Expert in Wool, Ministry of Munitions, during European War.

Died 6 April 1942.

BALY, Edward Charles Cyril, CBE 1918; FRS 1909; Grant Professor of In-organic Chemistry, University of Liverpool, 1910–37; *b* 9 Feb. 1871; *s* of late Edward Ely Baly, of Bank of England, London; *m* 1902, Ellen Agnes, *d* of T. Jago; four *s. Educ:* Temple Grove School; Aldenham; University College, London. Assistant Professor of Chemistry and Lecturer in Spectroscopy at University College, London, 1903–10; Deputy Inspector of High Explosives, Liverpool Area, 1915–21; Fellow Institute of Chemistry. *Publications:* Spectroscopy, 1929; Photosynthesis, 1940; many papers. *Recreation:* climbing. *Address:* Redgable, Coombe Avenue, Wendover, Aylesbury, Bucks. *T:* Wendover 2267.

Died 3 Jan. 1948.

BAMBER, Col Charles James, MVO 1911; DPH Cant., MRCSE, LRCPL; Indian Medical Service (retired); *b* 14 July 1855; *s* of Henry J. Bamber; *m* Claudine Oclanis, *e d* of Edward O'Brien, ICS, *g d* of Hon. Henry O'Brien; two *s* one *d. Educ:* Bedford Grammar School. Entered Indian Medical Service, 1878; served in the Mahsud Waziri Expedition, 1881; Burma War, 1886–87 (medal and clasp); Civil Surgeon of Rawalpindi, 1893–98; served in north-west frontier, Malakand, 1897 (medal); Sanitary Commissioner to the Punjab Government, 1900–10; Inspector-General of Civil Hospitals, Punjab, 1910–15; Administrative Medical and Sanitary Officer, Delhi Durbar, 1902–03 (medal); Administrative Medical and Sanitary Officer, Coronation Durbar, 1911 (medal); member of Coronation Durbar Committee. *Publication:* Plants of the Punjab. *Address:* c/o Thos Cook and Son (Bankers), Ltd, 45 Berkeley Street, W1.

Died 9 Jan. 1941.

BAMFORD, Rt Rev. Thomas Ambrose, OSB, Abbot; Rector of the Church of Our Lady of St Wilfrid, Blyth, Northumberland; *b* Coventry, 17 Aug. 1861. *Educ:* Douai College, France. Monk, English Benedictine Congregation, 1880; Priest, 1887; Professor for seven years, then appointed to the English Mission, where served for ten years; Abbot of Woolhampton, 1903; resigned, 1905. *Address:* St Wilfrid's, Blyth, Northumberland.

Died 23 Jan. 1945.

BANDARANAIKE, Sir Solomon Dias, KCMG 1925; Kt 1907; CMG 1902; Maha Mudaliyar and JP for the Island of Ceylon; *b* 22 May 1862; *o s* of late D. C. H. Dias Bandaranaike, JP for the Island Mudaliyar of the Governor's Gate, etc. etc., and *g s* of late Don Solomon Dias Bandaranaike, referred to in Sir Emerson Tennant's History of Ceylon; *m* Daisy Ezline, *e d* of late Hon. Sir S. C. Obeyesekere; one *s* two *d. Educ:* St Thomas Coll., Colombo. Created Mohandirum of the Governor's Gate, and invested by late Duke of Clarence, 1882; visited England, 1895, 1897, 1902, 1910, 1914, 1919, 1920, 1924, 1928, and 1938; received Diamond Jubilee Gold Medal, 1897, having been sent as a delegate from Ceylon; presented with a gold medal by the inhabitants of Siyane Korle East, 1896, in recognition of services rendered to that district while administering its affairs as Mudaliyar; presented with a Gold Sword of Honour, 1901, by public subscription; acted in capacity of extra ADC to Duke of York during visit of Duke and Duchess to Ceylon, 1901; one of Ceylon's representatives at the Coronation; Coronation gold medal, 1902; Royal Order of Merit, Cambodia, 1907; received in private audience by The King at Buckingham Palace, Nov. 1914 and 1920. *Publication:* Remembered Yesterdays, 1929. *Recreations:* riding, driving, shooting, horse-breeding, country life; retired, 1927, on pension after 43 years' public service. *Address:* Horagolla Veyangoda, Ceylon. *TA:* Maha, Veyangoda. *Club:* East India and Sports.

Died 1 Aug. 1946.

BANDON, Georgina, Countess of; Georgina Dorothea Harriet, CBE 1920; *b* 1853; *d* of 7th Baron Carbery; *m* 1876, 4th Earl of Bandon (*d* 1924). *Address:* Coolkelure, Dunmannay, Co. Cork; Laxton Park House, Stamford; 23 Princes Gardens, SW7.

Died 29 June 1942.

BANERJI, Sir Albion Rajkumar, Kt 1925; Rajamantra Dhurina, 1924; CSI 1921; CIE 1911; late ICS; *b* Bristol, 10 Oct. 1871; *s* of Mr Sasipada Banerji of Barnagore, near Calcutta, and Mrs Raj Kumari Banerji, the first Indian lady of high caste to visit England; *m* 1898, *d* of late Sir Krishna Gupta, KCSI; one *d. Educ:* Calcutta University, scholar and medallist; Balliol College, Oxford; MA 1892. Entered Indian Civil Service as Assistant Magistrate and Collector, 1895; served as district officer in the Madras Presidency; sent on Foreign Service as Diwan (Prime Minister) to HH the Maharaja of Cochin, 1907–14; reverted to British service, Jan. 1915; Collector and District Magistrate, Cuddupah; Member of the Executive Council of HH the Maharaja of Mysore, 1916; Acting Diwan of Mysore, 1918; Senior Member of Executive Council until March 1922; retired from ICS, 1922; Diwan of Mysore, 1922–26; Foreign and Political Minister Kashmir State, 1926–29. *Publications:* The Indian Tangle, 1933; An Indian Pathfinder, 1934; The Rhythm of Living, 1940; What is wrong with India, 1945; Through an Indian Camera, Vol. I and Vol. II, 1946. *Address:* c/o Imperial Bank of India, Bangalore, India.

Died 25 Feb. 1950.

BANFIELD, John William; JP; MP (Lab) Wednesbury since 1932. General Sec. of the Amalgamated Union of Operative Bakers and Confectioners until 1940; Government Adviser at Geneva, 1924–25; contested Aston division of Birmingham Dec. 1918 and West Fulham, 1930 and Oct. 1931. *Address:* 3 Rosedew Road, W6.

Died 25 May 1945.

BANGOR, 6th Viscount *cr* 1781; **Maxwell Richard Crosbie Ward;** Baron, 1775, Irish Representative Peer, 1913; PC Northern Ireland 1931; OBE 1919; RA, retired; Speaker of Senate of Northern Ireland since 1930; *b* 4 May 1868; *e surv. s* of 5th Viscount and Mary, *d* of Rev. Henry King, Ballylin, King's Co.; *S* father, 1911; *m* 1905, Agnes Elizabeth, 3rd *d* of late Dacre Hamilton of Cornacassa, Monaghan; one *s* three *d. Educ:* Harrow; RMA, Woolwich. Entered army, 1887; Captain, 1898; Major, 1906; retired, 1912; served European War, 1914–19; Lt-Col (OBE); member of the Church of Ireland; Conservative. *Recreations:* yachting, shooting, fishing. *Heir: s* Hon. Edward Henry Harold Ward [*b* 5 Nov. 1905; *m* 1st, 1933, Elizabeth (who obtained a divorce 1937), *e d* of T. Balfour, Wrockwardine Hall, Wellington, Shropshire; 2nd, 1937, Mary Kathleen, *d* of W. Middleton, Shanghai; 3rd, 1947, Leila Mary, *d* of David R. Heaton, Brookfield, Crownhill, S Devon; one *s* (*b* 9 Aug. 1948)]. *Address:* Castle Ward, Downpatrick, Co. Down. *Clubs:* Army and Navy; Royal Yacht Squadron (Cowes); Royal Ulster Yacht (Bangor, Co. Down).

Died 17 Nov. 1950.

BANKART, Surg. Rear-Adm. Sir Arthur Reginald, KCVO 1923; CVO 1911; MVO 1898; KHP, MB, MCh Edinburgh, 1892; Diploma in Public Health (London), 1905; RN; one of HM's Honorary Physicians, 1910; *b* 19 Dec. 1868. Member Royal Medical Society of Scotland; Fellow Royal Society of Medicine, London; late Surgeon of HM Yacht Osborne and Surgeon-Captain, HM Yacht Victoria and Albert; 4th class Osmanieh; Order of St Stanislaus of Russia, Class II (Chevalier); Order of The Redeemer, of Greece, Class IV; Hon. Physician to King Edward VII, 1905; Order of the Danebrog (Denmark) IV class; The Gilbert Blane Gold Medal, 1910; promoted to Staff-Surgeon, 1903, for distinguished service; present at Battle of Jutland Bank, 1916, and noted for early promotion; Retired List, 1924. *Clubs:* Royal Societies; Royal Naval, Portsmouth.

Died 19 June 1943.

BANKES, Rt Hon. Sir John Eldon, PC 1915; CCB 1927; Kt 1910; *b* 17 April 1854; *e s* of John Scott Bankes, Soughton Hall, Flintshire; *m* 1882, Edith (*d* 1931), *e d* of Robert Peel Ethelston; one *s* one *d. Educ:* Eton; Univ. College, Oxford. Called to Bar, Inner Temple, 1878; Chancellor St Asaph, 1908–10; Judge of King's Bench Division, High Court, 1910–15; Lord Justice of Appeal, 1915–27; retired, Lord Justice of Appeal, 1915–27; retired, 1927. *Address:* Soughton Hall, Northop, Flintshire. *T:* Northop 207. *Club:* Carlton.

Died 31 Dec. 1946.

BANKES, Ralph George Scott; Chancellor of Diocese of Blackburn since 1935, of Manchester since 1935, of Coventry since 1937, and of Durham since 1940; *b* 24 Oct. 1900; *er s* of late R. V. Bankes, KC, and of Ethel G. Bankes. *Educ:* Winchester College; Magdalen College, Oxford (Demy). BA 1923; MA 1927. Barrister, Inner Temple, 1924; Deputy Chairman of Flintshire Quarter Sessions, 1940–43; Chairman, 1943; Temporary Principal Ministry of Labour and National Service, 1941–46; Member of Executive of Working Men's College since 1926; Hon. Secretary Butterflies CC 1924–31; Hon. Secretary Old Wykehamist Football Club, 1921–31; Member of Church Assembly, 1945; Member of Bishop of London's Commission on City Churches, 1941. *Recreations:* cricket, lawn tennis. *Address:* 39 St George's Square, SW1. *T:* Victoria 2134. *Club:* MCC United University.

Died 22 May 1948.

BANKS, Rev. Samuel John Sherbrooke; Canon of S Edmundsbury and Ipswich since 1931; *b* 14 Jan. 1861; *s* of Rev. Samuel Banks, late Rector of Cottenham, Cambs; *m* Gratiana Lucy, *d* of late Sir Alfred Hughes, Bart of East Bergholt, Suffolk; one *s* one *d. Educ:* Bury St Edmunds; Clare College, Cambridge. Deacon, 1888;

priest, 1889; curate of S Marks, Lakenham, Norwich, 1888–92; curate in charge of Littleport, Isle of Ely, 1892–94; Charterhouse Mission, Southwark, 1894–96; Rector of Trimley S Martin, Suffolk, 1896–1939; Rural Dean of Colneys, 1925–32. *Address:* Linden House, Tomline Road, Felixstowe.

Died 10 Jan. 1941.

BANNER, Maj. Sir Harmood H.; *see* Harmood-Banner.

BANNERMAN, Charles Edward Woolhouse, OBE 1924; Puisne Judge, Supreme Court, Gold Coast, since 1935; Member of the West African Court of Appeal since 1935; Acting Chief Justice, Supreme Court, on various occasions; *b* Accra, Gold Coast, 12 Oct. 1884; *s* of late Samuel Bannerman; *m* 1918, Esther Theresa, *d* of late C. J. Bannerman, Barrister-at-Law, Accra; one *d.* *Educ:* privately. Called to Bar, Middle Temple, 1913; Police Magistrate, Gold Coast, 1919; Acting Puisne Judge, Supreme Court, on various occasions, 1925–31; Acting Circuit Judge, Ashanti and Northern Territories Judiciary, 1933–34; Circuit Judge, Ashanti and the Northern Territories, 1934; Silver Jubilee Medal, 1935; Coronation Medal, 1937. *Recreation:* walking. *Address:* The Supreme Court, Accra, Gold Coast. *Club:* Royal Empire Society.

Died 10 Nov. 1943.

BANON, Brig.-Gen. Frederick Lionel, CB 1916; King's Shropshire Light Infantry; *b* 2 June 1862; *s* of Richard Davys Banon, Inspector-General, AMS; *m* 1890, Helen, *d* of R. M'Ilwraith. *Educ:* Downside; Sandhurst; passed Staff College. Entered Army, 1882; Captain, 1890; Major, 1900; Lt-Col 1905; Col 1909; served Egyptian campaign, 1885 (Suakin medal and clasp and bronze star); S African War, 1899–1902 (despatches, Queen's medal 4 clasps, King's medal 2 clasps); European War, 1914–16 (despatches, CB); Assistant to Military Governor of Johannesburg, 1901–02; commanded 17th Batt. Imperial Yeomanry and Mobile Column; DAQMG Dublin, 1902; Headquarter Staff, 3rd Army Corps, Dublin, 1903–05; General Staff Officer 2nd Grade, Staff College, 1905; 1st Grade, 1908–09; AAG War Office, 1910–15; commanded 50th and 197th Infantry Brigades, British Expeditionary Force; retired pay, 1919; a Commissioner, Royal Hospital, Chelsea, since 1920; Member Special Grants Committee Ministry of Pensions, 1921–26. *Recreations:* fishing, travelling. *Address:* 45 Rivermead Court, Hurlingham, SW6. *T:* Renown 1644. *Clubs:* Army and Navy, Fly-fishers', Hurlingham.

Died 14 Aug. 1950.

BANTING, Sir Frederick Grant, KBE 1934; MC; FRS 1935; Hon. FRCS 1930; Hon. FRCP 1936; DSc (McGill), 1939; Maj. RCAMC; Professor Medical Research University of Toronto since 1923; *b* Alliston, Ont, 1891; *m*; obtained divorce 1932; one *s.* *Educ:* Alliston Public and High Schools; University of Toronto. Served in Canada, England, and France, 1915–19 (wounded at Cambrai, MC); Membership in Royal College of Surgeons, England, 1918; Resident Surgeon, Hospital for Sick Children, Toronto, 1919–20; practised medicine till May 1921, at London, Ontario; part-time Assistant in Physiology, Western University, London, Ontario, 1920–21; commenced research on the internal secretion of pancreas in University of Toronto, 16 May 1921; Lecturer in Pharmacology, University of Toronto, 1921–22; awarded Starr Gold Medal for Doctorate, University of Toronto, 1922; Senior Demonstrator, Dept of Medicine, University of Toronto; Nobel Prize, 1923; Scott Medal, 1924; DSc Toronto, 1923; ScD Yale, 1924; LLD University of Western Ontario, 1924; LLD Queen's, 1923; Fellow, Royal Society, Canada, 1926; Cameron Prize (Edinburgh), 1927; Flavelle Medal of the Royal Society of Canada, 1931; Apothecaries' Medal (London), 1934;

FNG Starr Gold Medal (Can. Med. Assoc.), 1936. *Publications:* articles in medical magazines. *Address:* University of Toronto, Toronto, Canada. *Clubs:* Canadian, Toronto.

Died 21 Feb. 1941.

BANTOCK, Sir Granville, Kt 1930; MA; DMus (Edinburgh); FRCM; Professor of Music, Birmingham University, 1908–34, now Emeritus Professor; *b* London, 7 Aug. 1868; *e s* of late Dr George Granville Bantock; *m* 1898, Helen, *d* of Hermann von Schweitzer; three *s* one *d.* *Educ:* London for Indian Civil Service. First holder of the Macfarren scholarship for composition at the Royal Academy of Music, London, 1889. Round the world in 1894–95 as conductor of the Gaiety Company in America and Australia; Musical Director at the Tower, New Brighton, 1896–1900; conductor and adjudicator at Festivals in Great Britain, and also in Canada, 1923. *Publications: published compositions*— Helena Variations, produced Liverpool, 1898; The Witch of Atlas, produced Worcester Festival, 1902; Sappho Songs; Sapphic Poem and Celtic Poem, for 'cello and orchestra; music to Sophocles' Electra; The Time-Spirit, and Sea Wanderers, for choir and orchestra; Omar Khayyam, Part I, produced Birmingham Festival, 1906; Part II, Cardiff Festival, 1907; Part III, Birmingham Festival, 1909; Orchestral Poems, Fifine at the Fair; Dante and Beatrice, produced Queen's Hall, 1911; The Pierrot of the Minute, produced Worcester Festival, 1908; Overture to a Greek Tragedy; Hebridean Symphony, produced Glasgow, 1916; Pan in Arcady, produced Glasgow, 1919; Judith, Orchestral Suite, 1919; Pagan Chants, Orchestra and Tenor, Birmingham, 1926; various songs and part-songs for female, male voice and mixed choir; Atalanta in Calydon, Manchester Hallé Choir, 1912, Cincinnati, USA, 1935; Vanity of Vanities, for unaccompanied choir; Scenes from the Scottish Highlands; Pageant of Human Life, (Thomas More) Choral Symphony, 1914; Violin Sonata; Viola Sonata; Violoncello Sonata; The Seal-Woman (opera); The Song of Songs, produced Manchester, 1927; The Burden of Babylon, Gloucester Festival, 1928; Incidental Music, Macbeth; The Pilgrim's Progress, Queen's Hall, Chorus and Orchestra, 1928; The Bacchae of Euripides, Five Choral Songs and Dances, 1930; Prometheus Unbound, Incidental Music, Shelley's Drama, Symphonic Prelude brass instruments' test-piece, Crystal Palace, 1933; Orchestral Suites; Lalla Rookh, 1917; Arabian Nights, 1920; Comedy Overture, The Frogs, 1935 (Aristophanes); Pagan Symphony BBC 1936; King Solomon. BBC (commemorating coronation of George VI), 1937; music for children's play, Fairy Gold, 1938, etc. *Address:* Sheriff Cottage, Barnt Green, Worcestershire.

Died 16 Oct. 1946.

BARBER, Rev. Benjamin Aquila; Hon. CF; *b* 12 May 1876; *s* of George Calvert Barber and Hannah Carter; *m* 1903, Helen Nicholson Yorke; one *s* one *d.* *Educ:* Leeds High Sch.; Hartley College, Manchester. Entered Primitive Methodist Ministry, 1899; Tunstall, Spennymoor, Bishop Auckland, Leeds; served as Chaplain to HM Forces in France, 1916–17, Italy, 1917–18; Education Officer, Lines of Communication, Italy, 1919; Minister, Newcastle-on-Tyne, 1920; Dragon Parade Church, Harrogate, 1921–31; Pres. of Harrogate Literary Society, 1926–28; Connexional Editor, The Primitive Methodist Publishing House, 1931; Connexional Editor, The Methodist Publishing House, 1932–35; Minister, Moor Lane Methodist Church, Lancaster. *Publications:* Robert Louis Stevenson, a Critical Appreciation; A Methodist Pageant; joint author of The Methodist Church, its Origin, Division, and Reunion; The Art of Frank O. Salisbury; pamphlets, articles, reviews. *Recreations:* reading and climbing.

Died 4 Oct. 1946.

BARBER, Sir George William, Kt 1927; Solicitor; JP Middlesex; Clerk to Worshipful Company of Broderers; Alderman Middlesex County Council; *b* 16 Oct. 1858; *s* of George Henley Barber and Julia Sophia Shoolbred. *Educ:* Uppingham. High Sheriff, Middlesex, 1916–17; late Chairman Brentford Petty Sessional Division of Middlesex. *Recreations:* shooting and fishing. *Address:* Park House, Englefield Green. *T:* Egham 14. *Clubs:* Junior Carlton, St Stephen's, Gresham.

Died 20 Feb. 1945.

BARBER, Rev. William Theodore Aquila, DD; *b* Jaffna, Ceylon, 4 Jan. 1858; *e s* of Rev. William Barber, Wesleyan minister; *m* 1st, Alice, *d* of late John Dingley; 2nd, Emma (*d* 1923), *d* of late John Clapham. *Educ:* Gymnasium, Stellenbosch, Cape Colony; New Kingswood School, Bath; Caius College, Cambridge; exhibitioner, first-class Honourman, Prizeman, BA London University; Foundation Scholar, Wrangler, MA, Caius College, Cambridge; DD Trinity College, Dublin. Assistant Master, The Leys School, 1877, and Dunheved College, 1880; Wesleyan Minister, 1882; Assistant Tutor, Theological College, Richmond, 1882; Principal, Wuchang Missionary High School, Central China, 1884; Secretary, General Missionary Conference, Shanghai, 1890; Leeds (Brunswick) Circuit, 1893; General Secretary, Wesleyan Missionary Society, 1896; Headmaster, The Leys School, Cambridge, 1898–1919; Principal, Theological College, Richmond, 1920–29; retired 1929; Fernley Lecturer, 1917; President of the Wesleyan Conference, 1919. *Publications:* editor, Proceedings of the Shanghai Missionary Conference; David Hill, Missionary and Saint; Raymond Lull, The Illuminated Doctor; The Morning of Life; The Unfolding of Life; Contributor E. R. E. *Recreation:* golf. *Address:* The Porch, Grantchester Street, Cambridge. *T:* Cambridge 3162.

Died 18 Oct. 1945.

BARBIER, Paul, MA (Lond.), BèsL (Paris), member of the Guild of Graduates of the University of Wales; Professor of French Language and Literature and of Romance Philology in the University of Leeds, 1903–38; examiner in French, the Universities of London, Birmingham, Sheffield; *b* Manchester, 6 Aug. 1873; *s* of late Prof. Paul Barbier and *g s* of Pastor Georges Barbier of London; *m* 1906, Cécile Delaloie. *Educ:* Manchester Grammar School; University College, Cardiff, open scholarship; BA (Lond.); first in first class French honours, exhibitioner in both intermediate, 1891, and final, 1893. Clerk to French Consulate for several short periods, 1893–95; private in the 26th Horse Artillery at Le Mans (Sarthe), 1895–96; student in Welsh department at Univ. Coll., Cardiff, 1896–97; awarded chief essay prize of £50 at National Eisteddfod at Newport for work on Welsh history in the 12th century, 1897; second Master at the Gainsborough Grammar School, 1897–99; assistant lecturer in French Language and Literature in the Yorkshire College and lecturer to Victoria University, 1899; lecturer in Romance Philology in the Victoria University, 1901. *Publications:* The Age of Owain Gwynedd: an historical essay on Wales in the middle of the 12th century; philological and literary articles. *Address:* University of Leeds.

Died 11 Aug. 1947.

BARBOUR, George Freeland, DPhil, JP; *b* Free Church Manse, Cults, Aberdeenshire, 15 Feb. 1882; *s* of late Rev. Robert W. Barbour of Bonskeid and Charlotte Rachel, 2nd *d* of late Sir Robert N. Fowler, Bart, MP, of Gastard, Wilts; *m* 1919, Helen Victoria, *e d* of 7th Baron Polwarth; two *s* three *d*. *Educ:* private; Morrison's Academy, Crieff; Edinburgh University; MA 1905; DPhil 1910. Joint Hon. Secretary Scottish Temperance Legislation Board, 1904–13; contested West Perthshire (L), Dec. 1910 and May 1929; member Royal Commission on Housing (Scotland), 1913–17. Worked for League of Nations Union, 1919–39; Member, Perth and Kinross CC, 1942–45, and Education Committee,

1919–45; Member British Council of Churches and Provisional Committee, World Council of Churches. *Publications:* The Old Quadrangle (joint-author), 1907; A Philosophical Study of Christian Ethics, 1911; The Ethical Approach to Theism, 1913; The Unity of the Spirit, 1921; Life of Alexander Whyte, DD, 1923; Addresses in a Highland Chapel, 1924; Katherine Scott—a Memoir, 1929; Pringle-Pattison's Realism (ed. with Memoir), 1933. *Recreations:* travel, walking. *Address:* Fincastle, Pitlochry, Perthshire. *T:* Killiecrankie 9.

Died 18 Nov. 1946.

BARCLAY, Alfred Ernest, OBE, MA, MD (Cantab), DM (Oxon), DSc (Hon. Causa, Oxon), DMRE (Cantab); FRCP, MRCS; Hon. Radiologist to the Nuffield Institute for Medical Research, Oxford (Acting Director, 1947–48); Consultant adviser in Radiology to Minister of Health, 1939; Consulting Radiologist to Radcliffe Infirmary, Oxford; late lecturer in Medical Radiology, University of Cambridge; *b* 30 Sept. 1876; *s* of late Robert Barclay and late M. A. Noton; *m* 1906, Mary McFarlane; no *c*. *Educ:* Leys, Cambridge; Christ's Coll., Cambridge; Manchester Royal Infirmary; London Hosp. Various appointments at London Hosp.; Hon. Medical Officer to X-ray Dept, Ancoats Hosp., Manchester, Manchester Royal Infirmary; lecturer in Radiology, Victoria University of Manchester; President of Elect. Therap. Sect. Roy. Soc. Med., 1919–20; Brit. Med. Assoc., 1920 and 1930; Röntgen Society, 1924–25; British Inst. of Radiology, 1931–32; Chm. British X-Ray and Radium Protection Cttee; Hon. Member Liverpool Med. Inst., Soc. of Radiographers, Chartered Soc. of Massage; Hon. Fellow of the American College of Radiology; Hon. Member of the Radiology Society of North America and of the American Röntgen Ray Society; Hon. Member of the Australian and New Zealand Association of Radiology and various foreign Radiological Societies; late Captain RAMC (T) and ACD of the BRC. *Publications:* books and publications in English and foreign medical journals, on the digestive tract, the lungs, foetal circulation and renal circulation. *Address:* Nuffield Institute for Medical Research, Oxford; The Cottage, Southfield House, Oxford. *Clubs:* Athenæum; Clarendon (Manchester).

Died 26 April 1949.

BARCLAY, Edward Exton, MA; JP; Master of the Puckeridge Foxhounds; *b* 16 Feb. 1860; *s* of late Joseph Gurney Barclay, of Leyton, Essex; *m* 1st, 1883, Elizabeth Mary (*d* 1927), *e d* of William Fowler, MP; one *s* one *d*; 2nd, 1927, Elizabeth Mary (*d* 1929), *widow* of Harry Fordham, and *d* of late Marlborough Pryor, of Weston Park, Herts. *Educ:* Cambridge (MA). Lord of the Manor. *Recreations:* hunting, shooting, fishing. *Address:* Brent Pelham Hall, Buntingford, Herts. *Clubs:* Boodle's, City of London, Farmers.

Died 4 March 1948.

BARCLAY, Col Henry Albert, CVO 1906; MVO 1901; TD; late Comdg King's Own Royal Regt Norfolk Y., which he raised; JP, DL Norfolk and Surrey; *b* 19 April 1858; *s* of late Joseph Gurney Barclay of Knotts Green House, Essex, Higham, Suffolk, and Cromer, Norfolk; *m* 1st, 1881, Marion Louisa (*d* 1938) *o d* of Francis Hoare; two *s* two *d*; 2nd, 1938, Mrs I. A. Hawkins, Great Bookham, Surrey. ADC to King Edward VII, 1906–10; to King George V, 1910–25; holds Royal Order of Commander of St Olaf of Norway. *Recreations:* riding, shooting. *Address:* Hanworth Hall, Norfolk. *TA:* Hanworth Norfolk. *T:* Hanworth, Norfolk 203.

Died 19 Aug. 1947.

BARCLAY, Col Reginald, CB 1911; late commanding 3rd Batt. Duke of Edinburgh's Wiltshire Regt; *b* 24 Dec. 1861; 3rd *s* of late Hedworth David Barclay, of Eastwick Park Leatherhead. *Educ:* Eton. Commandant prisoners of war, St Helena, 1901–02. *Recreations:* shooting, fishing. *Address:* Balkail Glenluce, Wigtownshire. *Clubs:* Windham Orleans, White's.

Died 12 Dec. 1945.

BARCLAY, Robert Francis, CBE 1939; MA, LLB, LLD; Solicitor in Glasgow; *b* 15 Jan. 1867; *s* of Robert Barclay. Manufacturer, Glasgow, and Susan Campbell, *d* of James White, Overtoun Dumbartonshire; *m* 1905, Grace Cook, *d* of James David Hedderwick, DL, LLD, Stock-broker, Glasgow; three *s* one *d*. *Educ:* Glasgow High School; Glasgow University. Chairman of various Investment Trust and other Companies. *Recreations:* shooting, fishing, riding, motoring, photography. *Address:* 21 Park Terrace, Glasgow. *T:* Douglas, Glasgow, 4544. *Clubs:* Western, Royal Scottish Automobile, Glasgow.

Died 6 April 1948.

BARCLAY, Sir Thomas, Kt 1904; LLB, PhD; barrister; member of honour, Institute of International Law; vice-president, International Law Association; member, Royal Academy of Jurisprudence of Spain; member, Académie Diplomatique Internationale; examiner in international public and private law to University of Oxford, 1900; president d'honneur des Amis de la Paix, Paris; Chairman of Council, Persia Society; President, British Chamber of Commerce in Paris, 1899–1900; Commander of the Legion of Honour; Knight of the Order of Leopold, Grand Officer of Order of the Lion and the Sun; *b* Dunfermline, 1853; *e s* of late George Barclay, LLD, of Bonvil, Cupar, Fife; *m* Marie-Thérèse, *d* of R. Teuscher, MD, Rio de Janeiro and Jena (authoress of a translation into English of Villiers de l'Isle Adam's La Révolte, etc.); two *d*; *s* killed in the War, 1918. *Educ:* University College, London; Univ. of London; Univ. of Paris; Univ. of Jena. Went to Paris as a correspondent of The Times, 1876; resigned, 1882, to devote himself exclusively to French law practice; founded the Franco-Scottish Society, 1895; since 1900 identified with agitation for and preservation of good understanding with France; visited United States in 1903 and 1904, and there stirred up agitation for an Anglo-American treaty of arbitration and conciliation. Founded the International Brotherhood Alliance, 1905; in Feb. 1905, at invitation of Associated Chambers of Commerce of Germany, visited Berlin and delivered addresses in favour of improving Anglo-German relations; Member of the Mosely Educational Commission, 1903; MP (L) Blackburn, 1910; Gold Medal of the Société d'Economie Politique, 1927. *Publications:* Problems of International Practice and Diplomacy, 1907; International Law and Practice, 1917; the Turco-Italian War and its Problems, 1912; the articles on International Law in the Encyclopedia of the Law of England and the Encyclopedia Britannica, 11th, 12th, and 13th editions; Thirty Years Anglo-French Reminiscences, 1914; Law and Usage of War, 1914; Sands of Fate, Dramatised Study of an Imperial Conscience, 1917; New Methods for Adjustment of International Disputes, 1918; Le Président Wilson et l'évolution de la politique étrangère des États Unis, 1918; Collapse and Reconstruction, 1919; Wisdom of Lang-Sin, 1927. *Address:* 71 rue de Montreuil, Versailles, France. *Club:* Athenæum.

Died 20 Jan. 1941.

BARCLAY, William Singer, FRGS; General Secretary to Tower Hill Improvement Trust, since 1934; *b* 15 June 1871; *s* of Livingstone Barclay and Emily Wyatt; *m* 1924, Doris (*d* 1942), *d* of W. A. Heap. *Educ:* Bedford Grammar School. Engaged in ranching, railway construction in River Plate, later travel in most of the Latin-American Republics as well as in United States, and Canada, 1890–1910; awarded Royal Geographical Society Back Bequest, 1913; Commercial Secretary to British (de Bunsen) Mission to South America, 1918; Commissioner for Federation of British Industries with Brazilian Commercial Delegation to England, 1919;

General Secretary British Empire Trade Exhibition, held in Buenos Aires, 1929–31; Gen. Manager of Argentine Chamber of Commerce in London, 1931; work (hon.) at Ministry of Economic Warfare, 1940–41. *Publications:* From Buenos Aires to the Iguazu, 1903; Magellanes: the Ona and other Indians, 1904; The River Parana, 1908; The Geography of South American Railways, 1917; The Land of Magellan, 1926; The Basin of the R. Parana, 1931; editor Philip's Library and Commercial Map of S America, 1922. *Recreations:* reading, travel. *Address:* 2 St Mark's Square, Regent's Park, NW1. *T:* Primrose 0424.

Died 15 March 1947.

BARCLAY-SMITH, Edward, MA, MD, BCh (Cantab); late Professor of Anatomy, University of London; Emeritus Professor, 1927; Fellow, and Member of the Council, King's College, London; late Chairman of the Board of Intermediate Medical Studies, and of the Board of Human Anatomy and Morphology, University of London; late Representative of the Council of King's College on Committee of Management, King's College Hospital; late Hon. Secretary of Anatomical Society of Great Britain and Ireland; member Association des Anatomistes; one of the Editors of the Journal of Anatomy, of Buchanan's Manual of Anatomy, and of Buchanan's Dissection Guide; Fellow of the Cambridge University, Philosophical Society, etc; *s* of Captain W. E. Smith, Royal Sherwood Foresters, and Louisa Barclay, *d* of Captain R. Barclay, RN; *m* Ida Mary (*d* 1944), *d* of G. Porter Rogers, JP; one *s* three *d*. *Educ:* Brighton College; Downing College, Cambridge; London Hospital. Late Lecturer on Advanced Human Anatomy, University of Cambridge, Dean of the Medical Faculty, King's College, London, etc.; Examiner in the Universities of Cambridge, London, Durham, Manchester, Birmingham, Royal College of Physicians, London, etc. *Publications:* various papers in Journal of Anatomy and Physiology; Journal of Anatomy; Journal of Physiology; Nature; Transactions of Cambridge Philosophical Society; Dendy's Problems of Science; St Thomas's Hospital and King's College Hospital Gazettes, etc. *Recreations:* golf, philately. *Address:* Barclays Bank, 448 Strand, WC2. *Club:* Athenæum.

Died 5 July 1945.

BARCROFT, Sir Joseph, Kt 1935; CBE 1918; FRS 1910; Hon. FRSE; Hon. FRCOG; MA Camb., BSc Lond.; Hon. Degrees: MD Sofia, Louvain; DSc Queen's Univ., Belfast; DSc National Univ. of Ireland; DSc Harvard; ScD Trinity College, Dublin; Director of Unit of Animal Physiology (Agricultural Research Council), since 1941; Fellow and formerly Lecturer, King's College, Cambridge; Member, Chemical Warfare Committee of the War Office, 1917, and formerly of the Ministry of Munitions; Member, Chemical Board, Ministry of Supply, 1939; Member, Army Medical Directorate Consultative Committee, 1928–43, RAF Medical Advisory Board and Agricultural Research Council, 1938–43; Chairman, Food Investigation Board; Member, Advisory Council of Department, Scientific and Industrial Research, 1939–44; Foreign Member, Société Royale des Sciences Medicales et Naturelles de Bruxelles; Konigle Danske Videnskabernes Selskub; K. Akademie Halle; Société de Chemie Biologique, Paris; Chinese Physiological Society; American Physiological Society; Corr. Member, Société de Biologie, Paris, Czeckoslovak Society of Physicians, Bratislav, Czeck Society of Physicians, Prague; and Des Moines Academy of Medicine; Hon. Member, National Academy of Buenos Aires, Biological Society of Argentina, Kungl Fysiografiska Sällekapets i Lund, National Academy of Medicine of Mexico and American Academy of Arts and Sciences; Foreign Associate Member, National Academy of Sciences; Foreign Associate Member, National Academy of Sciences, USA; *b* 26 July 1872; *s* of the late Henry Barcroft, DL, and Anna Richardson Barcroft of Newry, Co. Down; *m* 1903, Mary Agnetta, *d* of late Sir Robert S. Ball; two *s*. *Educ:* Bootham School, York; the

Leys School, Cambridge; King's College, Cambridge; Prizeman and Exhibitioner, 1894; Natural Science Tripos Class I, in Parts I and II, degree 1896; 2nd Walsingham medal, 1899; Gedge Prize, 1900. Proctor, 1910–11; Oliver-Sharpey lecturer, Royal College of Physicians, 1915; Lowell Lecturer, 1922; Fullerian Professor of Physiology, Royal Institution, 1923–26; Professor of Physiology, Cambridge University, 1926–37; Dunham lecturer (Harvard), 1929; Croonian Lecturer (Royal Society); Purser Lecturer (Trinity College, Dublin, 1935 and 1946); Huxley Lecturer (Birmingham), 1935; Terry Lecturer, Yale; Sharpey-Schafer Lecturer, Edinburgh; Linacre Lecturer, Cambridge, 1942; President of the Physiological Section of the British Association, 1920; Vice-President of Marine Biological Association, 1940; President of Nutrition Society; Royal medal, 1922; Baly medal, 1923; Copley medal, 1944. *Publications:* The Records of original researches on physiological subjects, chiefly in the Journal of Physiology; The Respiratory Function of the Blood; Features in the Architecture of Physiological Function; The Brain and its Environment; Editor of the Sixth Edition of Huxley's Physiology; Joint Editor of the Cambridge Comparative Physiology; Departmental (Physiology) Editor of the 14th edition of the Encyclopædia Britannica. *Recreations:* gardening and sailing. *Address:* 13 Grange Road, Cambridge. *T:* Cambridge 5159. *Club:* Athenæum.

Died 21 March 1947.

BARDSLEY, Rev. Canon Ernest John, MA; Canon Emeritus of Southwell; *b* 15 Oct. 1868; *s* of Canon James Wareing Bardsley and Jane Ann Bardsley; *m* 1903; one *s* two *d*. *Educ:* Merchant Taylors', Charterhouse Square; Marlborough College; Worcester College, Oxford. Curate of Sandal Magna, Wakefield, 1891; St Paul's, Kersal Manchester, 1897; Vicar of St Silas, Blackburn, 1900; St Andrew's, Nottingham, 1911; Rector of Barton-in-Fabis, 1929–40. *Address:* Charnwood, Buckhurst Hill, Essex. *T:* Buckhurst 5356.

Died 17 Sept. 1948.

BARIA, Raja of, Lt-Col HH Maharawal Sir Shri Ranjitsinhji, KCSI 1922; *b* 10 July 1886; one *s* one *d*. *Educ:* Rajkumar College, Rajkot; Imperial Cadet Corps, Dehradoon. Ascended the throne 1908; State has area of 813 square miles, and population of 159,429; receives salute of eleven guns; served European War, 1914–15, and in the Afghan War, 1919. *Recreations:* has won the Salmon, Sir Pertap and Gujarat Cups in the Gujarat Pig-sticking Meets; polo. *Address:* Devgad-Baria, India.

Died 7 Sept. 1949.

BARING, Hon. Hugo, OBE; *b* 6 Oct. 1876; 6th *s* of 1st Lord Revelstoke; *m* 1905, Lady Evelyn Harriet Ashley (*d* 1931), 2nd *d* of 8th Earl of Shaftesbury, and *widow* of 2nd Lord Magheramorne. Late Lieut 4th Hussars; served Tirah Campaign, 1897; S Africa (wounded); Captain 10th Hussars, Sept. 1914; General Staff, Dec. 1915; wounded at Ypres; served with British Mission in Siberia, 1918–19. *Address:* 16 South Lodge, Grove End Road, NW8.

Died 20 Aug. 1949.

BARING, Wing-Comdr Hon. Maurice, OBE 1918; journalist and author; Member of the Academic Committee and Fellow of the Royal Society of Literature; *b* 27 April 1874; 4th *s* of 1st Lord Revelstoke. *Educ:* Eton; Trinity College, Cambridge. Entered Diplomatic Service, 1898; Attaché to British Embassy in Paris, 1898; transferred to Copenhagen, 1900; 3rd secretary, 1900; transferred to Rome, 1902; employed in Foreign Office, 1903–04; resigned, 1904; acted as war correspondent for Morning Post in Manchuria, 1904; acted as special correspondent for Morning Post in Russia, 1905–08; special corresp. for Morning Post in Constantinople, 1909; special corresp. for the Times in the Balkans, 1912; European War (despatches); gazetted

temporary Lieut Intelligence Corps, attached to RFC, British Expeditionary Force, 1914; promoted Staff Lieut 1915; Assistant Equipment Officer Royal Flying Corps, and promoted from temporary Lieut to Lieut (SR), Sept. 1915; Capt. Oct. 1915; Staff-Capt. May 1916; Major, 1917; SO2 Royal Air Force, 1918; Personal Secretary to Gen. Sir Hugh Trenchard. Jan.–April 1918; Staff Officer Independent Air Force, May–Dec. 1918; demobilised, 1919; Officer, Legion of Honour, 1935; granted an hon. commission as Wing Commander in Reserve of Air-Force Officers, 1925. *Publications:* Hildesheim, Quatre Pastiches (Paris), 1899; The Black Prince, 1902; Gaston de Foix, 1903; With the Russians in Manchuria, 1905; Mahasena, 1905; Desiderio, 1906; Sonnets and Short Poems, 1906; Thoughts on Art and Life of Leonardo da Vinci, translated, 1906; A Year in Russia, 1907; Proserpine, 1908; Russian Essays and Stories, 1909; Orpheus in Mayfair, 1909; The Story of Forget Me Not and Lily of the Valley 1909; Landmarks in Russian Literature, 1910; Dead Letters, 1910; The Glass Mender, 1910; Diminutive Dramas, 1910; Collected Poems, 1911; The Russian People, 1911; The Grey Stocking and other Plays, 1912; Letters from the Near East, 1913; Palamon and Arcite, 1913; What I Saw in Russia, 1913; Lost Diaries, 1913; The Main-springs of Russia, 1914; An Outline of Russian Literature, 1914; Round the World in any Number of Days (Boston), 1914; English Landscape: an anthology, 1916; Translations by SC 1916; Poems, 1914–1917, 1918; Translations Ancient and Modern, 1919; Diminutive Dramas, 1919; Round the World in any Number of Ways, 1919; RFCHQ 1914–1918, 1920; Poems, 1914–1919, 1921; Passing By, 1921; The Puppet Show of Memory, 1922; Overlooked, 1922; His Majesty's Embassy, 1923; A Triangle, 1923; C, 1924; Punch and Judy and other Essays, 1924; Hildesheim Quatre Pastiches, 1924; Half a Minute's Silence, 1925; Collected Poems, 1925; Translations, with Originals, 1925; Cat's Cradle, 1925; Daphne Adeane, 1926; Last Days at Tsarkoe Selo (translated) 1926; Tinker's Leave, 1927; Comfortless Memory, 1928; Algæ, 1928; The Coat without Seam, 1929; Fantasio (translated), 1929; Robert Peckham, 1930; In the End is my Beginning, 1931; Lost Lectures, 1932; Friday's Business, 1932; Sarah Bernhardt, 1933; The Lonely Lady of Dulwich, 1934; Unreliable History, 1935; Darby and Joan, 1935; Have you anything to declare? 1936; Russian Lyrics, 1943. *Clubs:* White's, Athenæum, Turf, Buck's, Beefsteak.

Died 14 Dec. 1945.

BARKER; *see* Granville-Barker.

BARKER, Captain Sir David W., Kt 1920; RD; RNR; FRSE; *b* 1 Oct. 1858; *s* of David W. Barker, Welsh Mill House, Frome, Somerset. *Educ:* Lord Weymouth's Grammar School, Warminster; HMS Worcester. On completing nautical studies joined R. & H. Greens, Blackwall Line; later joined Silvertown Telegraph Works, commanding the ss Dacia; Captain-Superintendent, Nautical Training College, HMS Worcester, 1892–1919; President Royal Meteorological Society, 1903–05; Member Council of Royal Geographical Society, 1903–07; Member of Side Lights Committee, 1895; Vice-President International Pollok Prize Committee at Havre for Life-Saving at Sea, 1901; Chairman of British Section of Marseilles International Fisheries Exhibition, 1906; Arbitrator in Trattles Eyesight Test, 1909; sent to Gambia by Colonial Office, summer of 1922, on a special mission; a Director of the Nitrates Railway Co.; Member (and on Council) Royal United Service Institution. *Publications:* Elementary Seamanship (10th edition); Mercantile Marine in War Time (Lectures at Royal Naval College, Greenwich); (with W. Allingham) Navigation; (with Captain A. Carpenter, DSO, RN), Nature Notes for Ocean Voyagers; Things a Sailor Needs to Know; numerous papers on clouds, wind, etc., to Royal Meteorological

Society. *Recreations:* meteorology, photography, and natural history. *Address:* c/o Royal United Service Institution, Whitehall, SW1.

Died 15 June 1941.

BARKER, George; JP; *b* Hanley, Stoke-on-Trent, 13 March 1858; *s* of William and Elizabeth Barker; *m* 1883, Margaret, *d* of Edward and Sarah Sadler. Served seven years in the Buffs; Zulu War, 1879 (medal and clasp); MP (Lab) Abertillery, 1920–29. *Recreations:* microscopy and photography.

Died 28 Oct. 1936.

BARKER, Sir Henry Edward, KCMG 1942; Kt 1927; Grand Cordon of the Order of the Nile; Commander of the Order of St Olaf; *b* Alexandria, 18 March 1872; *s* of late Henry Barker; *m* 1896, Emmiline Mary, *d* of late J. E. Cornish, CMG; one *s* one *d*. *Educ:* Fettes College, Edinburgh. Past President of the British Chamber of Commerce in Egypt, and of the British Community in Alexandria. *Address:* 8 Rue Abassides, Alexandria, Egypt.

Died 20 July 1942.

BARKER, Henry James, MA; *b* 1 Feb. 1852; *s* of William Barker of Ecclesall, nr Sheffield; *m* Elizabeth Mary (*d* 1909), *y d* of late J. Langham; three *s* two *d*. *Educ:* Westfield School, Sheffield; St John's Coll., SW; Trinity College, Dublin. *Publications:* books on Humour at school—e.g., Merry Moments with Scholars: Comic School Tales; Our Boys and Girls at School; Comic Side of School Life; Little Humorists at School. In fiction—A Nice Pair; Scarlet Feather; The Wonder Seekers. In poetry—Lays and Ballads; King Edmund the Martyr, and other Poems: also, Practical Aid in Composition, and numerous educational articles in the magazines; contributed to Punch, Weekly Graphic, Illustrated London News, and London daily press. Gives occasional readings or tells stories from his humorous books; has studied the manners and Customs of English Gypsies. Founded the present Society of Yorkshiremen in London, 1899, and became its first Hon. Secretary; Barrister at the Middle Temple. *Recreations:* golf and travel; country walks and studying nature. *Club:* Wimbledon Park Golf.

Died 5 Jan. 1934.

BARKER, Sir Herbert Atkinson, Kt 1922; specialist in manipulative surgery, rendering unnecessary many cutting operations and orthopædic appliances; *b* Southport, 21 April 1869; *s* of late Thos Wildman Barker, lawyer and coroner for SW Lancashire, and Agnes Atkinson; *m* 1907, Jane Ethel, *d* of late Wilson Walker, JP. *Educ:* Kirkby Lonsdale Grammar School; private tutors. Intended for legal profession, and educated to that end; showed marked ability at an early age for manipulative surgery; placed at the age of 20 under the tutorship of Mr J. Atkinson, who succeeded the late Mr Robert Hutton; took Atkinson's practice at his death in 1904. Principal operations: the cure or alleviation of derangements of knee cartilages without surgical interference; the correction of flat-foot, tennis elbow, recurrent dislocation of shoulder, hallux rigidus, metatarsalgia, sacro-iliac displacements, and other kinds of abnormalities of the joints by manipulation; gave demonstration of his methods before British Orthopædic Assoc. on their invitation at St Thomas's Hospital at instigation of Lord Moynihan in 1936, and made series of films at same hospital in 1939 for perpetuation of his technique; unanimously elected Manipulative Surgeon to Noble's Hospital, Isle of Man, in 1941. *Publications:* Leaves from my Life, an Autobiography, 1927; articles in Nineteenth Century, Fortnightly and other Reviews, urging the Faculty to give closer attention to the bloodless methods of operating, maintaining that they have been almost entirely neglected by the surgical schools; paper on Manipulative Surgery, Encyclopædia Britannica, 1926. *Recreations:* billiards, walking,

swimming, and listening to music. *Address:* Noble's Hospital, Douglas, Isle of Man; Merchiston Lodge, St Brelade, Jersey, CI.

Died 21 July 1950.

BARKER, J. Ellis; author; editor of Heal Thyself, the Homœopathic World; *b* Cologne, 9 May 1870; *s* of physician; *m* 1947, Eileen Homer, Shrewsbury. *Educ:* Cologne. Devoted his literary career, from 1900, to warning England of the danger of a war with Germany and to urging military, naval and economic preparation, co-operating with Lord Roberts, Mr Joseph Chamberlain and others; one of the founders of the New Health Society, acting as Hon. Sec. from its beginning. *Publications:* The Rise and Decline of the Netherlands; British Socialism; Modern Germany; Great and Greater Britain—The Problems of Motherland and Empire; The Foundations of Germany; The Great Problems of British Statesmanship; Economic Statesmanship—The Great Industrial and Financial Problems arising through the War; America's Secret: the Causes of her Economic Success, 1927; Cancer: How it is Caused, how it can be Prevented; Good Health and Happiness—A New Science of Health; Chronic Constipation—The Most Deadly and the Most Insidious of Diseases; Cancer, The Surgeon and the Researcher; Miracles of Healing and How They are Done—A New Path to Health; New Lives for Old—How to Cure the Incurable; My Testament of Healing; 101 Points against Free Trade; 200 Points for Tariff Reform; contributions to reviews, etc. *Recreations:* walking, swimming, cycling, riding. *Address:* 26 Park Crescent, Portland Place, W1. *T:* Welbeck 9642.

Died 16 July 1948.

BARKER, Lewellys F., MD; Emeritus Professor of Medicine, Johns Hopkins University and visiting Physician, Johns Hopkins Hospital; *b* Norwich, Ontario, Canada, 16 Sept. 1867; *s* of James F. Barker and Sarah Jane Taylor; *m* 1903, Lilian H. Halsey; two *s* one *d*. *Educ:* Pickering College; University of Toronto; University of Munich; and University of Berlin. Professor of Medicine Johns Hopkins University and physician-in-Chief, Johns Hopkins Hospital, 1905–13. *Publications:* The Nervous System and Its Constituent Neurones, 1899; Translation of Werner Spalteholz's Hand Atlas of Human Anatomy, 1900; Laboratory Manual of Human Anatomy (with Dean DeWitt Lewis and D. G. Revell), 1904; The Clinical Diagnosis of Internal Diseases, 1916; Tuesday Clinics at Johns Hopkins Hospital, 1922; Blood Pressure (with N. B. Cole), 1924; The Young Man and Medicine, 1927; Co-Editor, Endocrinology and Metabolism, 1922; numerous medical papers and addresses. *Recreations:* bridge and crossword puzzles; reading. *Address:* 1035 North Calvert Street, Baltimore, USA; 208 Stratford Road, Baltimore, USA. *T:* Vernon 5301, University 0797. *Clubs:* Maryland, Baltimore; Century, New York.

Died 13 July 1943.

BARKER, Sir Rayner Childe, Kt 1923; CIE 1889; engineer; late Director-in-Chief-Indo-European Telegraph Department; formerly Director of Persian section of Indo-European Telegraph Department, 1898–1910; *b* 1858; *m* 1894, Ella (*d* 1930), *d* of late Lieut-Col S. Guise-Moores; one *s*. Served Burma, 1886–88; Hazara, 1888 and 1891. *Address:* Oakhurst, Netley Abbey, Hants.

Died 14 May 1945.

BARKER, Dr Sydney George, OBE 1934; Scientific Adviser Indian Jute Mills Association, Calcutta, since 1934; *b* York, 29 March 1887; *m* 1915, Irene Leonora Knight; no *c*. *Educ:* Archbishop Holgate's Grammar School, York; Imperial College of Science, London; Berlin University. Vice-Principal, The Maharajah's College, Trivandrum, S India, University of Madras; Director of Industries to the Government of Travancore; Director of Research, Wool Industries Research

Association; King Edward VII Research Scholar; Diploma of the Imperial College of Science, London; Medallist, Society of Dyers and Colourists, 1934; Fellow of the Physical Society; the Zoological Society; of Textile Institute; of Royal Society of Edinburgh and Institute of Physics; of Royal Society of Arts, London, 1837; Member of the Institute of Chemical Engineers and of the Faraday Society; formerly member of Imperial Institute Committee on Vegetable Fibres, 1938; former Member, Wool Breeding Council, Board of Agriculture, Scotland; Imperial Institute Advisory Committee on Animal Fibres; Member, National Illumination Committee on Colorimetry; formerly Member, Publications Committee of Textile Institute; formerly Vice-Chairman, Society of Chemical Industry Chemical Engineering Group Committee; Member General Committee, British Association for Advancement of Science; Inspector, Sandbag Proofings, Ministry of Home Security, 1940–41, and Ministry of Supply to date. *Publications:* Wool, a study of the fibre; Wool Quality; Sisal; Coir, Industrial Survey of Travancore; Survey of the Indian Jute Industries, Bengal, 1935; Jute Research in 1935–1936; The Moisture Relationships of Jute, 1939; numerous papers to learned Societies. *Recreation:* work. *Address:* 191 Coombe Lane, SW20. *T:* Wimbledon 1520; Imperial Institute, SW7. *T:* Kensington 3264 and 5626. *Club:* Royal Societies.

Died 28 Aug. 1942.

BARKER, Wright, RBA. *Address:* Thorn Lea, 16 Duchy Road, Harrogate.

Died 10 March 1941.

BARKLA, Charles Glover, FRS 1912; MA (Cantab); DSc, LLD (Liverpool); MSc (Victoria); FRSE; Professor of Natural Philosophy, University of Edinburgh, since 1913; *b* 7 June 1877; *s* of John Martin Barkla, late Secretary Atlas Chemical Co., Widnes; *m* Mary Esther, *e d* of John T. Cowell, JP, Receiver-General, IOM; two *s* one *d*. *Educ:* Liverpool Institute; University College, Liverpool; Trinity and King's Colleges, Cambridge. Oliver Lodge Fellow University of Liverpool, 1902. Demonstrator and Assistant Lecturer in Physics, 1905; Lecturer in Advanced Electricity, 1907; Wheatstone Prof. of Physics, University of London (King's College), 1909–13; Bakerian Lecturer, Royal Society, 1916; Hughes Medallist, Royal Society, 1917; received Nobel Prize for Physics, 1917; discovered (1) characteristic X-rays of elements—X-ray spectra; (2) polarisation of X-rays; (3) X-ray scattering and laws of scattering; (4) X-ray fluorescence; (5) X-ray absorption edges (with C. A. Sadler) and photographic edges (with G. H. Martyn); (6) laws governing transmission of X-rays through matter and the excitation of secondary rays. *Publications:* various papers on Electric Waves, X-Rays and Secondary Rays in Transactions and Proceedings of Royal Society, Philosophical Magazine, Jahrbuch der Radioaktivität, Proceedings of Camb. Phil. Soc., etc. *Recreations:* golf, singing (King's College Chapel Choir, 1901–02). *Address:* Braidwood, Edinburgh 10.

Died 23 Oct. 1944.

BARKLEY, William Henry, CBE 1924; *b* Albury, NSW, 2 March 1869; *s* of late George Barkley; *m* Edith, *o d* of R. Bryant, Newcastle, NSW. *Educ:* Albury, NSW. Entered NSW Customs Department, 1883; Chief Clerk in the Central Administration at Melbourne, 1902; Inspector at Sydney, 1906–10; first Commonwealth Customs representative, London, 1910–12; Chief Surveyor, Central Administration, March 1912; Collector of Customs, Queensland, 1912; Collector of Customs, New South Wales, 1914–33; retired, 1933; represented the Commonwealth at the Empire Customs Conference in London, 1921, and made a second official visit to USA. *Recreations:* golf and gardening.

Died 14 March 1942.

BARLOW, Sir Hilaro (William Wellesley), 5th Bt *cr* 1803; CB 1913; CMG 1918; Colonel; retired; *b* 19 June 1861; *s* of 4th Bt and Annie Catherine, *d* of Rev. Dr Whiteside, Vicar of Scarboro'; *S* father, 1904; *m* 1891, Victoria Katherine, *e d* of Col Hugh Hibbert of Birtles Hall, Cheshire; two *s* three *d*. *Educ:* Eton; RMA, Woolwich. *Heir: s* Richard Hugh, AFC, Wing-Commander RAF [*b* 30 June 1904; *m* 1928, Rosamund Sylvia, *d* of late F. S. Anderton and late Lady Temple, wife of Lt-Col Sir R. D. Temple, 3rd Bt; three *s*]. *Address:* The Cottage, Thruxton, Andover.

Died 16 Oct. 1941.

BARLOW, Sir Richard Hugh, 6th Bt *cr* 1803; AFC 1940; Wing Commander late RAF; *b* 30 June 1904; *s* of Sir Hilaro Barlow, 5th Bt; *S* father, 1941; *m* 1928, Rosamund Sylvia, *d* of late F. S. Anderton; three *s* one *d*. *Educ:* RN Colleges, Osborne and Dartmouth; RAF College, Cranwell. Entered Osborne, 1918; Dartmouth, 1919; left RN, 1921; entered RAF College, 1922; commissioned, 1924; retired as Flight Lieutenant, 1935; re-employed, 1940; S/Ldr, 1940; W/Cdr, 1941; retired, 1946. *Heir: s* Christopher Hilaro, *b* 1 Dec. 1929. *Address:* The Cottage, Thruxton, Andover.

Died 3 Dec. 1946.

BARLOW, Sir Thomas, 1st Bt *cr* 1900; KCVO 1901; FRS 1909; FRCP, MD (Lond.); BSc (Lond.); LLD (Hon.), Aberdeen, St Andrews, Durham, Harvard, Montreal, Toronto, and Edinburgh; DSc (Hon.), London and Victoria; MD (Hon.) Christiania; MD (Hon.) Dublin; Consulting Physician to University College Hospital; late Holme Professor of Clinical Medicine to the Medical School; Consulting Physician to the Hospital for Sick Children, Great Ormond Street; President Royal College of Physicians, London, 1910–15; President of International Medical Congress, London, 1913; formerly Physician to Queen Victoria's Household, Physician; Extraordinary to Queen Victoria, King Edward VII and King George V; *b* 4 Sept. 1845; *m* 1880, Ada Helen (*d* 1928), *d* of Patrick Dalmahoy, WS; two *s* one *d*. *Heir: s* Sir James Alan Noel Barlow, KCB. *Address:* 10 Wimpole Street, W1; Boswells, Wendover. *T:* Langham 1242. *Club:* Athenæum.

Died 12 Jan. 1945.

BARLOW, Walter Sydney L.; *see* Lazarus-Barlow.

BARNARD, George Henry; KC 1907; represents Victoria, BC, in the Senate since 1917; *b* Victoria, BC, 9 Oct. 1868; *m* Ethel Burnham, *e d* of Col H. C. Rogers, Peterborough, Ont. *Educ:* Trinity College School, Port Hope, Ontario. Called to Bar, 1891; Alderman, Victoria, 1902–03; Mayor, 1904–05; elected House of Commons for Victoria, 1908 and 1911. *Address:* Duvals, Victoria, BC. *Clubs:* Union (Victoria); Rideau (Ottawa); Vancouver (Vancouver).

Died 2 Feb. 1948.

BARNARD, Joseph Edwin, FRS; FInstP, formerly Hon. Director of Department of Applied Optics, National Institute for Medical Research, Hampstead; President R Microscopical Society; *m*; one *s* one *d*. *Address:* 19 Grimwade Avenue, Addiscombe, Surrey. *T:* Addiscombe 5236. *Club:* Athenæum.

Died 25 Oct. 1949.

BARNARD, Rev. Percy Mordaunt, BD; *b* 1868; *s* of Rev. Mordaunt Barnard, MA; *m* 1900, Alice Mary, *d* of late Rev. F. Taunton, MA, of Kingswood Vicarage, Epsom; two *s* one *d*. *Educ:* Christ's College, Cambridge. Assistant Master, St John's Foundation School, Leatherhead, 1892–97; Rector of Headley, near Epsom, 1898–1905; Examiner for Theological Tripos, Cambridge, 1899–1900, 1904–05, etc.; President of the Antiquarian Booksellers Association (International), 1928. *Publications:* Jezebel: a Drama, 1904; Clement of

Alexandria: Quis Dives Salvetur, 1897; Biblical Text of 1899; etc. *Recreation:* book-hunting. *Address:* 17 Church Road, Tunbridge Wells. *T:* 755.

Died 2 April 1941.

BARNATO, Woolf; *b* 1895; *s* of B. I. Barnato; *m* 1st, 1915, Dorothy Maitland (marr. diss. 1922), *d* of H. V. Falk, New York, USA; two *d*; 2nd, 1932, Jack Claridge (marr. diss. 1940), *d* of Mrs J. A. Quealy, San Francisco; two *s.* Served European War, 1914–18, also 1940–45. *Address:* Ridgemead, Englefield Green, Surrey. *T:* Egham 690.

Died 27 July 1948.

BARNEBY, William Theodore; JP, DL; *b* 1873; *e s* of William Barneby (*d* 1895), and Katharine Anne, *y d* of late William Lutley Sclater, of Hoddington, Hants; *m* 1912, Verena, *y d* of late Algernon Turnor; (*o s* killed in action in Burma, March 1944); one *d. Educ:* Eton; Trinity College, Cambridge (MA 1898). Called to Bar, Inner Temple, 1898; High Sheriff, Herefordshire, 1904; Patron of two livings. *Address:* Saltmarshe Castle, Bromyard, Herefordshire. *TA:* Tedstone-Wafre. *Club:* Junior Carlton.

Died 23 May 1946.

BARNES, Alfred Schwartz, FRAI, MSc Tech. (Manch.), MIEE; *b* 4 Oct. 1868; 3rd *s* of John Schwartz of Sevenoaks; *m* 1902, Maria Alexandra, 2nd *d* of Charles Lavers Lavers-Smith of Ditton Hill, Surrey; two *d. Educ:* Eastbourne; King's College, London. For five years Assistant to Professor Henry Robinson of Westminster in design and erection of electrical power stations for St Pancras, Norwich, Leyton, etc.; Acting Head of Electrical Department, Chelsea Polytechnic, 1895; Chair of Physics and Electrical Engineering, School of Technology, Manchester, 1901; Prof. of Electrical Engineering, Manchester University, 1905; Staff Inspector Engineering, Board of Education, Whitehall, 1912–28; Science Secretary to the Advisory Council on Scientific and Industrial Research, 1915–18. *Publications:* Original Researches; Low Tension Thermal Cut-Outs; Flexibles; Fuse Phenomena; The Testing of Rubber for Electrical Work; Mechanical Hysteresis; Some Physical Properties of Ruber; The Corrugation of Rails. *Recreation:* archæology. *Address:* Dormers, Holwood Park Avenue, Farnborough, Kent. *T:* Farnborough, Kent 311.

Died 5 Nov. 1949.

BARNES, Bernard, CB 1947; MC; Under Secretary (since 1946) and Accountant-General (since 1942), Ministry of Fuel and Power; *b* 24 June 1890; *s* of late Frederick Barnes, The Glen, Saxmundham, Suffolk; *m* Margaret Julia, 2nd *d* of late Peter King, District Inspector, Royal Irish Constabulary; one *s. Educ:* King Edward VII School, Kings Lynn; Strand School, King's College, London Univ. Incorporated Accountant, 1926; entered Exchequer and Audit Dept, 1910; Ministry of Labour, 1919; ARP Dept Home Office, Asst Sec., 1939. Served European War, 1914–18 (France and Palestine), Civil Service Rifles and Machine-Gun Corps; Lt-Col (MC, despatches thrice). *Recreation:* golf. *Address:* 29 Birch Grove, Acton Hill, W3. *T:* Acorn 2410; Cromwell House, Dean Stanley Street, Millbank, SW1.

Died 17 Oct. 1950.

BARNES, Edwin Clay, CBE 1920; DL, JP; *b* 6 April 1864; *s* of Alfred Barnes, JP, DL (formerly MP for Chesterfield Division of Derbyshire), of Ashgate Lodge, Chesterfield; unmarried. *Educ:* Wellington College; Trinity College, Cambridge; BA 1885. Called to the Bar, Inner Temple, 1890; Chairman of Derbyshire County Council, 1920–37; High Sheriff of Derbyshire, 1923–24. *Recreations:* shooting, fishing, golf. *Address:* Ashgate Lodge, Chesterfield. *Clubs:* Boodle's, Reform.

Died 22 Jan. 1941.

BARNES, Sir George Stapylton, KCB 1915; KCSI 1920; CB 1909; *b* Umballa, India, 8 Feb. 1858; *e s* of George Carnac Barnes, CB, formerly Foreign Secretary in India, and Margaret Diana, *d* of Major Henry Chetwynd-Stapylton; *m* 1887, Sybil de Gournay, *d* of late Charles Buxton; MP, of Foxwarren, Cobham, Surrey; two *s. Educ:* Eton; University College, Oxford. Barr Inner Temple, 1883; assisted the late Lord Russell of Killowen in his work at the Bar, 1883–93; Counsel to Board of Trade in Bankruptcy Matters, 1886; Official Receiver in Companies Liquidation, 1893; Senior Official Receiver, 1896; Comptroller of the Companies Department of the Board of Trade, 1904–11; Comptroller General of the Labour Department of the Board of Trade, 1911–13; Second Secretary Board of Trade, 1913; Joint Permanent Secretary, 1915; Member of Committee on Amendment of the Company Laws, 1906; of Committee for remodelling the Statutory Forms of Railway Accounts and Statistics, 1909; of Royal Commission on Sugar Supplies during the war, 1914; of Treasury Committee on New Issues of Capital during the war, 1915; Member of the Council of the Viceroy of India, 1916–21. *Publication:* Handbook to the Death Duties (with Sydney Buxton, MP). *Address:* Foxholm, Cobham, Surrey. *T:* Byfleet 183.

Died 9 Dec. 1946.

BARNES, Maj.-Gen. Sir Reginald Walter Ralph, KCB 1919; CB 1916; DSO 1900; DL, JP; late 10th Hussars; *b* 18 April 1871; *s* of Preb. R. H. Barnes of Stoke Canon, near Exeter; *m* 1919, Gunilla, *widow* of C. J. Wijk; one *s. Educ:* Westminster. Served with Spanish Army in Cuban Insurrection, 1895 (medal); served S Africa as Adjt Imperial Light Horse, 1899–1900, and as Lt-Col 2nd IY, 1901–02 (severely wounded, despatches, Queen's medal six clasps, King's medal two clasps, DSO); European War, 1914–18 (wounded twice, despatches seven times, CB, prom. Maj.-Gen., KCB, Croix de Guerre); retired pay, 1921. *Address:* Glenside, Sidmouth, Devon. *Club:* Cavalry.

Died 19 Dec. 1946.

BARNES, Walter Mayhew, ARCA (Lond.); FSAM; *b* 10 Jan. 1871; *s* of Thomas Turner Barnes; *m* 1900, Lilian Emma Hough; three *s* one *d. Educ:* Private School; Royal College of Art. Design Master, Blackburn School of Art, 1895–1918; Head Master, Loughborough School of Art, 1918–20; West Ham School of Art, 1920–32; President of National Society of Art Masters, 1929–30; Examiner for Board of Education, 1929–31; Member of Examination Board City and Guilds of London Institute, 1928–31; Member of Burnham Committee, 1931–34. *Publication:* section on Schools of Art in The Education Year Book 1932. *Recreations:* gardening, walking. *Address:* The Old Cooperage, Debenham, Suffolk.

Died 31 Dec. 1950.

BARNETT, Alfred John, MVO 1912; Senior Pilot, Portsmouth Dockyard; retired, 1920; *b* 1857. *Address:* Kenilworth, 43 St Andrews Road, Southsea.

Died April 1943.

BARNETT, Rev. Arthur Thomas, MA Camb.; Canon of Gibraltar since 1903; Board of Church Army since 1911; *b* 21 Oct. 1858; *e s* of late Thomas Barnett, of Knighton Grange, Chichester; *m* 1884, Amy, *d* of late George Rosher, The Knowle, Higham, near Rochester. *Educ:* Brighton College; St John's College, Cambridge (Moral Science Tripos); Cambridge Clergy Training School. Curate of Holy Trinity, Clapham, 1881–83; Falmouth, 1883–85; Secretary White Cross League, 1886–89; Chaplain at Bordighera, Italy, 1889–1911; Hon. Sec. Mediterranean Mission to Seamen, 1900–11; Vicar of Hatham, 1911–12; Vicar, Stoke Poges, Bucks, 1912–26; Chaplain to the Bishop of Gibraltar, 1904–13. *Publications:* The Shadow of Heaven; The Purpose of Life. *Recreations:* motoring, fishing. *Address:* Westover, Guildford. *T:* Guildford 1384.

Died 2 Sept. 1941.

BARNETT, Col George Henry, CMG 1919; DSO 1917; King's Royal Rifles; retired, 1920; one of HM's Bodyguard of Hon. Corps of Gentlemen-at-Arms since 1926; *b* 12 Nov. 1880; *s* of late Frank Henry Barnett of Glympton Park, Woodstock; *m* 1904, Mary Dorothea, *d* of late Rev. R. Lowbridge-Baker, Ramsden, Oxon; one *s* three *d. Educ:* Radley; RMC, Sandhurst. Joined King's Royal Rifles, 1899; served S African War (severely wounded, Queen's medal with 5 clasps); Somaliland, 1902–03 (medal and clasp); succeeded to Glympton estates in 1907; Adjutant Queen Victoria's Rifles, 1910–13; served European War, 1914–18 (DSO, CMG); Capt. 1907; Major, 1915; Bt Lt-Colonel, 1918; Bt Col 1924; Col 1924; Commanding 4th Bn Oxford and Bucks Light Inf., 1921–25; Lord of the Manor of Glympton; Patron of one Living; JP, DL Oxon. *Recreations:* hunting, shooting, fishing. *Address:* Glympton Park, Woodstock, Oxon. *T:* Woodstock 11. *Clubs:* Boodle's, Royal Automobile; Oxford and County, Oxford.

Died 8 Oct. 1942.

BARNETT, Sir Louis Edward, Kt 1927; CMG 1918; MB, CM, FRCS; Emeritus Professor of Surgery, University of Otago, New Zealand, since 1925; *b* 24 March 1865; *s* of late Alfred A. Barnett, JP, of Wellington, NZ; *m* Mabel Violet, *d* of late Hon. James Fulton, MLC, of Ravenscliffe, Otago, NZ; three *s* one *d. Educ:* Wellington State School and College; Otago University; Edinburgh University; Middlesex Hospital, MB, CM Edin., 1888 (1st class honours); FRCS Eng., 1890. House Surgeon Middlesex Hospital, 1889–90; Hon. Surgeon Dunedin Hospital for thirty years (to 1925); Lecturer and Professor of Surgery, Univ. of Otago, for thirty years (to 1925); War Service, 1915–17, with RAMC and NZMC; Consulting Surgeon, NZMC, with rank Lieut-Col; President of Australasian Medical Congress, 1927; Past President of NZ Branch BMA; one of Founders of Royal Australasian College of Surgeons; President, 1937–39; Hon. Fellow American College of Surgeons, 1926; Knight of Grace Order of St John of Jerusalem; Chairman of Otago and Southland Division of British Empire Cancer Campaign, 1928–38; Chairman NZ Hydatid Research Committee. *Publications:* numerous contributions to the literature of Hydatid Disease. *Address:* Hampden, North Otago, New Zealand. *Clubs:* Fernhill and Otago University, Dunedin, NZ.

Died 28 Oct. 1946.

BARNETT, Percy Arthur, MA; *b* 1858; *m* Annie (*d* 1941), 2nd *d* of J. P. G. Beeching. *Educ:* City of London School; Trinity Coll., Oxford. Professor of English in Firth (University) Coll. Sheffield, 1882–88; Principal of the British and Foreign School Society's Central Training College for Teachers (Borough Road and Isleworth), 1889–93; HM Inspector of Schools, 1893–1918; Assistant Inspector of Training Colleges, 1894; Seconded from the Imperial Service as Superintendent of Education, Natal, 1902–04; Member of Civil Service Board of Natal, and of Council of University of Cape of Good Hope, 1902–04; Chief Inspector for Training of Teachers, 1905–12; Civil Adviser to War Office on Army Education, 1919–21. *Publications:* Teaching and Organisation (editor and contributor), 1897; Common Sense in Education, 1899; Natal: the State and the Citizen (with G. W. Sweeney), 1904; The Story of Robinson Crusoe in Latin, 1906; Common Sense Grammar, 1923; various smaller publications and magazine articles. *Address:* 593 Park West, Marble Arch, W2.

Died 26 Oct. 1941.

BARNETT, Rev. T. Ratcliffe, PhD (Edin.); FSAScot; Minister of Greenbank Church of Scotland, Edinburgh, since 1914; *b* Burnbrae, Kilbarchan, Renfrewshire, 23 Dec. 1868; *m* 1900, Maggie Muirhead, *e d* of William Forrest, Glasgow; two *d. Educ:* Paisley; Glasgow University; Edinburgh Theological Hall. Ordained to

first charge at Fala, Blackshiels, Midlothian, 1899–1905; St Andrew's Church, Bo'ness, 1905–13; Chaplain to Forces, 1916–18. *Publications:* The Dame of the Fine Green Kirtle, 1902; The Finest Baby in the World, 1904; The Blessed Ministry of Childhood, 1906; Fairshiels: Memories of a Lammermoor Parish, 1906; Reminiscences of Old Scots Folk, 1913; The Winds of Dawn: Parables from Nature, 1914; The Makers of the Kirk, 1915; The Road to Rannoch and the Summer Isles, 1924; Border Byways and Lothian Lore, 1925; Margaret of Scotland—Queen and Saint, 1926; The Land of Lochiel and the Magic West, 1927; The Story of the Covenant: Fifty Years of Fighting Faith, 1928; Autumns in Skye, Ross and Sutherland, 1930; The Land of Lorne—and the Isles of Rest, 1933; The Cradle of Christianity: A Pilgrimage to the Holy Places, 1936; Highland Harvest, 1937; Scottish Pilgrimage, 1943. *Recreations:* walking, climbing, writing. *Address:* 7 Corrennie Gardens, Edinburgh. *Clubs:* University, Edinburgh.

Died 20 Feb. 1946.

BARNISH, Captain Geoffrey Howard, DSO 1918; RD, RNR, retired; Marine Superintendent and Harbour Master, London Midland and Scottish Railway Co., Heysham Harbour; *b* 13 Jan. 1887; *y s* of late Dr W. Croudson Barnish, of Wigan; *m* 1922, Margery Helen, *o d* of Alfred Renfree, of 11 Portland Avenue, Exmouth; two *s* one *d. Educ:* School Ship Conway. Served seven years in sailing ships; twenty-one years in Cunard SS Co. from Junior Officer to Staff Captain; served European War, 1914–18 (DSO); JP Morecambe and Heysham. *Address:* Seamore, Heysham Harbour. *TA:* Heysham. *T:* Heysham 73.

Died 27 Nov. 1941.

BARON-SUCKLING, Rev. Charles William, MA Oxon; Rector of Barsham since 1921; *b* 1862; 2nd *s* of late Rev. Wm Joseph Baron, MA; assumed name of Baron-Suckling, by Royal Warrant, 1924; *m* 1895, Hilda Madeleine Hancock; two *s* (and one killed in last war) two *d. Educ:* Christ's Hospital, London; Christ Church, Oxford (Exhibitioner). Ordained, 1886; Curate of St Mary-le-Wigford, Lincoln, 1886–89; Vice-Principal of St Paul's Missionary College, Burgh, Lincs, 1889–91; Domestic Chaplain to Bishop King of Lincoln, 1891–94; worked in Colonial Church at Allora and Brisbane, Queensland, 1894–1903; Vicar of Alford, Lincs, 1903–21; Prebendary in Lincoln Cathedral, 1915; Rural Dean of South Calcewaith, 1916–21; Lord of Manor of Barsham and Shipmeadow, Suffolk, since 1923. *Recreations:* fishing, carpentry. *Address:* The Rectory, Barsham, Beccles, Suffolk. *TA:* Barsham, Beccles. *T:* Beccles 2162.

Died 6 Jan. 1944.

BARR, Alexander Wallace, CBE 1943; MIMarE; Chief Engineer Officer, Merchant Navy; *b* 13 Dec. 1886; *s* of Robert Barr and Janet Wallace; *m* 1910, Marion Britten McGowan; two *s* one *d. Educ:* Kilmarnock. *Address:* 5 Norma Road, Waterloo, Liverpool 22. *T:* Waterloo 2605.

Died 9 Nov. 1949.

BARR, Rev. James, MA (Glasgow), BD (Glasgow); *b* Beanscroft, 26 July 1862; *s* of late Allan Barr, of Beanscroft, Fenwick, Ayrshire; *m* 1890, Martha Wilson, *d* of A. H. Stephen, Hosier, Kilmarnock; two *s* one *d. Educ:* Kilmarnock Academy (Gold Medallist in Mathematics); Glasgow Univ. (Gartmore Gold Medal for an Essay on Political Economy); MA, with first-class honours in Mental Philosophy; Glasgow Free Church College. Minister at Johnstone and Wamphray Free Church, 1889–96; Dennistoun Free Church (afterwards Rutherford United Free Church) Glasgow, 1896–1907; St Mary's United Free Church, Govan, Glasgow 1907–20; Home Mission Secretary of United Free Church of Scotland, 1920–25; Moderator of the United Free Church of Scotland, 1929, and again in 1943; was

11 years on School Board of Glasgow; a member of the Royal Commission on the Housing of the Industrial Population of Scotland; Temperance Advocate; formerly a Scottish Liberal, he is now a member of the Scottish Labour Party; MP (Lab) Motherwell, 1924–31; MP (Lab) Coatbridge division of Lanarkshire, 1935–45; Chairman of the Select Committee on Capital Punishment which reported in Dec. 1930; Chairman of the Consultative Committee of the Parliamentary Labour Party, 1931. *Publications:* Christianity and War, 1903; the Scottish Church Question, 1920; The Church and War, 1932; The United Free Church of Scotland, 1934; Religious Liberty in the Totalitarian States, 1938; The Scottish Covenanters, 1946. *Address:* 75 Clouston Street, Glasgow, NW. *T:* Glasgow, Maryhill 965.

Died 24 Feb. 1949.

BARR, Mark, FCGI, MIEE; *b* Pennsylvania, USA (but born a British subject), 18 May 1871; *s* of Charles B. Barr, MA, and Ann M'Ginnis; *m* 1897, Mabel Mary Richie; two *s*. *Educ:* Belfield Public School. Worked with Nikola Tesla in America, and in laboratory of Dr Pupin at Columbia University, New York; studied chemistry with Dr Elliott, at New York; Assistant Editor, Electrical World, New York, 1891; graduated in Physics and Mathematics at Central College (London University), 1895; Institution of Electrical Engineers Premium Prize, 1895–96; Gold Medal, Paris, 1900; elected member of Committee on Screw Threads, British Association, 1903; Committee of Standards, 1905; new methods for computing roots of equations and theory of new calculating mechanisms, 1918–24; contributed papers on Physics and Mechanics to technical journals, England and America. *Recreations:* mathematics and swimming. *Address:* 1125 Grand Concourse, New York City, USA. *Clubs:* Athenæum, Savile; Century (New York).

Died 15 Dec. 1950.

BARR, Venie, CBE 1920; Hon. Treasurer of Ulster Gift Fund for War Hospital Supplies and Serving Forces; *d* of James Moyles, Queen's County; *m* 1901, Ainsworth Barr. Hon. Secretary Women's Gift Fund for Prisoners of War, British Red Cross. Ulster, during European War. For many years Hon. Treasurer of Ulster Women's Unionist Council and of Girl Guides, Province of Ulster and Pres. of Toc H Women Helpers (Belfast Branch). *Address:* Ravenna, Malone Park, Belfast.

Died 1 Nov. 1947.

BARRAN, Sir Rowland (Hirst), Kt 1917; *b* 1858; 6th *s* of Sir John Barran, 1st Bt, and Ann, *d* of M. Hirst of Leeds; *m* 1st, 1887, Rose Cardew, *d* of Rev. Gilbert Bradley; one *s* two *d*; 2nd, 1909, Louise (*d* 1947), *d* of J. Stevenson Brown, Montreal. MP (L), North Leeds, 1902–18, when retired. *Address:* The Bridge House, West Overcliff Drive, Bournemouth. *T:* Westbourne 63247. *Club:* Bournemouth (Bournemouth).

Died 6 Aug. 1949.

BARRAND, Arthur Rhys; interested in Insurance; *b* Stoke Newington, 28 Oct. 1861; *m* Emily Brydon, *d* of Henry Fletcher Schofield, Manchester. *Educ:* Birkbeck School, Kingsland, Finsbury Technical College. Actuary, 1895; Bar, Middle Temple, 1906; MP (CL) Pudsey and Otley Division of Yorks, Dec. 1918–22; joint Editor of last edition of Bunyan's Law of Life Assurance. *Address:* Trenance, Dunbar Road, Bournemouth. *Club:* National Liberal.

Died 3 Aug. 1941.

BARRATT, Sir Albert, Kt 1922; JP; Chairman of Barratt & Co. Ltd, 1912–21; *b* 22 Nov. 1860; *y s* of late George Osborne Barratt of Stroud House, Hornsey, Middlesex, and Sarah, *d* of John William Peterson of Lee, Kent; *m* 1894, Milly (*d* 1930), *e d* of late Samuel Reeves, London; one *s*. *Educ:* privately. Governor of the Prince

of Wales's General Hospital since 1921, Chairman, 1931–35. *Recreations:* golf, croquet. *Address:* Totteridge Park, Hertfordshire. *T:* Mill Hill 1262.

Died 28 Nov. 1941.

BARRATT, John Arthur, KC 1923, LLB; Barrister, Inner Temple, 1901; VP International Law Association; VP The Pilgrims; *b* 15 Nov. 1857; *s* of late J. A. Barratt; *m* 1894, Edith M. (*d* 1942), *d* of late Sir Richard Wyatt, DL; no *c*. *Educ:* College of City of New York, MA; Vice-President (London Chapter) Phi Beta Kappa; Columbia Law School, LLB, 1880. Read law 1878–81 with Hon. James C. Carter of New York, Counsel for US Behring Sea Arbitration; at New York Bar, 1880–98; US Supreme Court Bar; English Bar since 1901; expert on American Law before House of Lords (Committees); Member American Bar Association; Comité Juridique International d'Aviation; VP International Law Conference, The Hague, 1921; Vienna, 1926; a founder of The Pilgrims; donor of Sailing of the Mayflower; Croix d'Officier de l'ordre de la Couronne, Belgium; President Emeritus Columbia Alumni (London); Columbia Medals (1933). *Publications:* English Law for Americans; American Company Law; Jurisdiction in Divorce; Monroe Doctrine; papers at Law Conferences in Berlin, Portland, Me; Buda Pesth, London, Paris, Madrid, Oxford; articles in Encyclopædia Britannica, American Law Review, Law Quarterly, etc. *Recreations:* travel, rowing. *Address:* c/o Pilgrims, Savoy Hotel, WC2. *Clubs:* Pilgrims; Bar Association, New York.

Died 1 March 1944.

BARRET, Rt Rev. John Patrick, DD, BA; Bishop of Plymouth, (RC), since 1929; *b* Liverpool, 31 Oct. 1878; *s* of late Robert and Jane Barrett. *Educ:* St Edward's College, Liverpool; St Joseph's College, Upholland; Beda College, Rome. BA London Univ., 1899; DD Gregorian University, Rome, 1910. Priest, 1906; Professor of Moral Theology at Upholland College, 1913–18; at Oscott College, Birmingham, 1919–26; Vice-Rector of Upholland College, 1926; Titular Bishop of Assus and Auxiliary to the Archbishop of Birmingham, 1926–29. *Address:* (temp.): Stoodley Knowle, Torquay.

Died 2 Nov. 1946.

BARRETT, Col Dacre Lennard, CBE 1919; RMLI, retired; *b* 11 Sept. 1858; *s* of late Henry Alfred Barrett, Rector of Chedgrave, Vicar of Langley, Norfolk; *m* 1884, Maud Mary, *y d* of late Henry Charles Hast, 31 Russell Road, Kensington; four *d*. *Educ:* Marlborough. Entered Royal Marines, 1878; distinguished Military Law and Fortification, 1st Class Gunnery; Army Gymnastics and Physical Training Gunnery Instructor; also Superintendent Gymnasia; served General Staff Royal Marines, RN Division, Dunkirk, as Chief Paymaster to both services; head of postal service during operations round Antwerp; then Command Paymaster for short time; then Brigade Paymaster, RM, Walmer, Shillingstone, Chatham, Blandford, and Aldershot, 1914–19 (mentioned for useful work by Admiralty and War Office); retired District Commissioner Boy Scouts. *Recreations:* fishing, shooting, motoring. *Address:* Vigers Hall, Tavistock. *T:* Tavistock 128. *Clubs:* Fly-Fishers, Public Schools.

Died 11 Nov. 1941.

BARRETT, Edward Ivo Medhurst, CIE 1916; Captain (retired); *b* 22 June 1879; *s* of late Edward Barrett, Farnham, Surrey; *m* 1st, Winifred Wall (decd), Southampton; one *s* one *d*; 2nd, 1928, Katherine Isabel Brown (*née* Craven). *Educ:* Cheltenham Coll.; Sandhurst. Lancs Fusiliers, 1900; served South African War, Malay States Guides, 1903; Municipal Police, Shanghai, 1907; Commissioner of Police, Shanghai, 1925–29. *Recreations:* English Rugby International, 1903,

Hampshire County XI, 1895–1925; amateur golf champion, Japan, 1917. *Address:* 25 Talbot Hill Road, Bournemouth. *Clubs:* MCC, Senior Golfers.

Died 10 July 1950.

BARRETT, Lady Florence Elizabeth, CH 1929; CBE 1917; MD, MS, BSc Lond. University; Consulting Obstetric and Gynæcological Surgeon, Royal Free Hospital; Consulting Obstetric Surgeon, Mothers' Hospital, Clapton; Hon. Surgeon Marie Curie Hospital; President (late Dean) of the London (RFH) School of Medicine for Women; Fellow Royal Society of Medicine; late President Medical Women's International Association; *b* Compton Greenfield, Gloucestershire; *d* of late Benjamin Perry of Avonleigh, Stoke Bishop; *m* 1916, Sir William Fletcher Barrett, FRS (*d* 1925). *Educ:* private tuition; University College, Bristol; London (RFH) School of Medicine for Women. Matriculated (London University) 1893 (1st Div.); BSc 1895 (1st Div.); qualified and registered as Medical Practitioner, 1900 (MB Lond. with honours in Obstetrics, BSc 1901, MS 1904, MD 1906). Held posts at the Royal Free Hospital successively as Assistant Anæsthetist, Ophthalmic Assistant, House Surgeon, Clinical Pathologist and Assistant Pathologist, Surgical and Gynæcological Registrar with charge of X-ray Department, Clinical Gynæcological Assistant and Anæsthetist till 1908; in 1908 appointed to position on the Honorary Staff of the Royal Free Hospital as Assistant Physician for Diseases of Women; Lecturer in Midwifery, 1913–21. *Publications:* Notes on the Smaller Fibromyomata, Trans. Roy. Soc. Med., 1909; Menstruation and Menorrhagia, Journal Obst. and Gyn., 1909; Amenorrhœa, Dysmenorrhœa, Leucorrhœa, Sexual function and derangements (Ency. Mid. and Dis. Women); A Plea for the Feeding of Nursing Mothers as a Means of preventing the Waste and Maiming of Child Life; Diseases of Women, a Handbook for Nurses, 1912; Conception Control, 1922; Personality survives Death, 1937. *Recreations:* riding, walking, reading. *Address:* Hill House Cottage, Cookham Dean, Berks. *T:* Marlow 99. *Club:* Cowdray.

Died 7 Aug. 1945.

BARRETT, Col Henry Walter, CB 1917; (retired pay), A. Ord. Department; *b* 27 Jan. 1857; *m* M. K. Melvill (*d* 1947); one *d.* Entered Army, 1876; Col 1902; retired, 1909; served S Africa, 1879 (medal with clasp), and 1900–01 (Queen's medal 4 clasps). *Club:* Junior United Service.

Died 3 Feb. 1949.

BARRETT, Herbert Roper; solicitor (sole partner in firm of Joseph Barrett & Son, 1 Leadenhall Street, EC3); *b* 24 Nov. 1873; *e s* of late Joseph and Louisa Barrett, Upton, Essex; *m* 1926, Helen, *widow* of John Glenny, Hawick and Ipswich. *Educ:* Merchant Taylors School. Vestry Clerk of St Peter-upon-Cornhill-City, 1907; elected a member of the Corporation of London (Lime Street Ward), 1910; Chairman of the following Committees: Law and City Courts, 1913; Billingsgate and Leadenhall Markets, 1915; Streets, 1918; Music, 1920 and 1940 and 1941; City of London Schools, 1922 and 1923; City Lands, 1924 (Chief Commoner); American and Canadian Bar Council Reception, 1924; West Ham Park, 1925; Epping Forest, 1932; Port of London Health, 1943; Past-Master of the Worshipful Company of Farriers, London, 1921 and 1933; Chairman of the Board of Income Tax Commissioners (City of London Schedule E), 1942; one of HM Lieutenants for the City of London; Commander of the Crown of Italy; Commander of the Star of Roumania. *Recreations:* lawn tennis. Won Doubles Championship thrice and many other championships and prizes; presented with Jubilee Commemoration medal at Wimbledon, June 1926; Chairman of the Lawn Tennis Association, 1934; played football for Casuals,

Corinthians, Surrey. *Address:* 1 New Cottages, Barns Green, Horsham, Sussex. *T:* Mansion House 2393, Southwater 221. *Clubs:* Guildhall, City Livery, Roehampton.

Died 27 July 1943.

BARRETT, Lt-Col Sir James William, KBE 1918; CB 1918; CMG 1911; MD, MS, FRCS; FRACS; LLD (Hon.); CMZS; late RAMC and AAMC; Consulting Surgeon to Victorian Eye and Ear Hospital; Consulting Oculist, Royal Australian Navy; Oculist, Royal Victorian Institute for the Blind; Oculist, Marine Board of Victoria; *b* Victoria, 27 Feb. 1862; *s* of James Barrett, physician, and Catherine Edkins; *m* 1st, 1888, Marian (*d* 1939), *d* of Charles Rennick and *widow* of Frederick Joy Pirani; one *s* (and one *s* killed in action) three *d;* 2nd, 1940, Monica Heinze, *sister* of Prof. Bernard Heinze. *Educ:* Melbourne University; King's College, London. Consulting Oculist and Aurist to HM Forces in Egypt; Registrar to the First Australian Hosp., 1915; ADMS Aust. Forces in Egypt, 1918; Lt-Col AAMC, 1915; Lt-Colonel RAMC, 1916; Consulting Aurist, EEF, 1916–18; Vice-Chancellor of Melbourne University, 1931–34; Chancellor, 1935–39; Member of Council, Melbourne University; President British Medical Association, 1935–36; Chairman National Parks Committee; Pres. Town Planning Association, Playgrounds Association, and Proportional Representation Society; Hon. Sec. Victorian Bush Nursing Assoc.; holds Order of the Nile, 3rd Class. *Publications:* (with Lieut Deane) The Australian Medical Corps in Egypt, 1919; The Twin Ideals, 1918; The YMCA in Egypt, 1919; A Vision of the Possible, 1919; The Diary of an Australian Soldier, 1921; Save Australia, 1925. *Address:* 105 Collins Street, Melbourne, C1, Australia. *Clubs:* Melbourne, Melbourne.

Died 6 April 1945.

BARRETT, Gp Captain John Francis Tufnell, DSO 1928; DFC, RAF; *b* 3 May 1898. *Educ:* Haileybury College. Joined RFC 1916; served Aden Protectorate, 1938 (Bar to DSO). *Club:* Royal Air Force.

Died Sept. 1941.

BARRETT, Robert John; *b* 31 Dec. 1861; *m;* one *s* one *d.* After a varied newspaper training in the provinces, came to London and specialised in financial journalism, with which he has been identified for many years; has travelled extensively, and has done work as a special correspondent in Canada, the United States, Russia, Siberia, Germany, Austria, Hungary, Mexico, Turkey, and the Balkan States; Member of the Royal Colonial Institute; Member of the Council of the Empire Economic Union. *Publications:* Canada's Century; Russia's New Era; etc. *Recreations:* yachting, golf. *Clubs:* Royal Thames Yacht; Royal Corinthian Yacht.

Died 21 Aug. 1942.

BARRINGER, Paul Brandon; *b* Concord, NC, 13 Feb. 1857; *s* of Gen. Rufus Barringer and Eugenia Morrison; *m* Nannie I. Hannah of Virginia, 1882; five *s* four *d. Educ:* Bingham's School, NC; Kenmore Univ. School, Va.; University of Virginia; MD, 1877; afterwards pursued education in Europe; MD of University of city of NY, 1878; honorary LLD of Davidson Coll. NC and University of South Carolina. For six years practitioner of Medicine, then principal of Preparatory Medical School at Davidson Coll. NC; for eighteen years professor and eight years chairman of Faculty of University of Va.; President, Virginia Polytechnic Institute, 1907–13. *Publications:* Brochure on Venomous Serpents of US 1890; Text-Book of Physiology, 1892–1893. The American Negro, and other papers on the race problem. *Recreation:* American Paleontology. *Address:* University, Virginia, USA.

Died 9 Jan. 1941.

BARRINGTON, Sir Charles (Burton), 5th Bt *cr* 1831; MBE; *b* 1848; *S* father, 1890; *m* 1895, Mary Rose (*d* 1943), *d* of Sir Henry Hickman Bacon, 10th and 11th Bt; two *s. Educ:* Rugby; Trin. Coll., Dublin (MA). JP, DL Co. Limerick; High Sheriff, 1877; Hon. Col City Artillery Militia; Provincial Grand Master of Freemasons of North Munster; served with the French at the front in European War, 1915. *Heir: s* Charles Bacon [*b* 6 June 1902; *m* 1930, Constance Doris, *d* of E. J. Elkington; one *d.* Eton]. *Address:* Fairthorne Manor, Botley, Hants. *Clubs:* Kildare Street, Dublin.

Died 12 Aug. 1943.

BARRINGTON-WARD, John Grosvenor; Student and Classical Tutor, Christ Church, Oxford; *b* Worcester, 26 Dec. 1894; 5th *s* of late Rev. Canon Barrington-Ward, DD; *m* 1924, Diana Beatrice Eleanor, *o d* of late J. E. Macfarlane, Ardquin, Hindhead; one *s* one *d. Educ:* Westminster; Christ Church, Oxford. Chancellor's Latin Verse Prize, 1913; Hertford Scholar, 1914. Served with R. Marine Artillery (Captain) in Dardanelles, Egypt, France, 1914–18; attached Head Quarters RA VIth Army Corps from March 1918; Student of Christ Church, 1919; Librarian, 1928–38; AK Fellow, 1929; Governor of Westminster School since 1920; GBA Representative, 1942; Supervisor of ICS Probationers and Secretary to ICS Delegacy, 1937; Deputy for the Public Orator, 1940–45; Member of Conservative Sub-Committee on Education, 1942, and of Lord Fleming's Committee on the Public Schools, 1943–44. *Publications:* contributions to The Mind of Rome, 1926. *Recreation:* golf (Hon. Treas. OUGC since 1920). *Address:* Christ Church, Oxford.

Died 6 June 1946.

BARRINGTON-WARD, Robert M'Gowan, DSO 1918; MC; Editor, The Times, since 1941; Barrister atlaw, Lincoln's Inn; *b* 1891; 4th *s* of late Rev. M. J. Barrington-Ward, DD; *m* 1926, Margaret Adele, *o d* of late E. H. Radice, CIE, ICS; two *s* one *d. Educ:* Westminster; Balliol College, Oxford; MA Tancred Student, Lincoln's Inn, 1911; President Oxford Union Society, 1912; Hon. Fellow of Balliol, 1947. Editorial Secretary The Times, 1913; joined Duke of Cornwall's LI Aug. 1914; served in France and Belgium, 1915–19 (despatches three times, DSO, MC); Assistant Editor: The Observer, 1919–27; The Times, 1927–41. *Address:* 2 Welbeck House, W1. *Clubs:* Marlborough-Windham, Beefsteak, Athenæum.

Died 29 Feb. 1948.

BARRON, Claud Alexander, CSI 1921; CIE 1911; CVO 1922; FRGS; *b* 22 Dec. 1871; *s* of Col W. Barron, BSC; *m* 1912, Ida Mary, *e d* of late Major-General Sir R. H. Ewart, KCMG, CB; one *s. Educ:* Grammar School and University, Aberdeen; Clare College, Cambridge. Entered ICS (Punjab), 1892; Settlement Officer, Kohat (NWFP) 1900–06; Secretary to Committee Survey of India, 1904–05; Chief Secretary Punjab Government, 1912–16; Chief Commissioner, Delhi Province, 1918–24; Member, Council of State, India, 1921–24; Financial Commissioner, Punjab, 1924–27; retired from ICS, 1928; Revenue Minister, Bahawalpur State, 1927–31; Lt-Col 5th Punjab LH (IDF), 1918–21. *Address:* Ensham, Newbury, Berks. *Club:* East India and Sports.

Died 29 Dec. 1948.

BARRON, Brig.-Gen. Netterville Guy, CMG 1919; CBE 1922; DSO 1918; JP; late RA; *b* 1867; *s* of Netterville John Barron; *m* 1899, Esme, *d* of R. B. Lloyd. *Educ:* Haileybury; RM Academy, Woolwich. Entered RA 1887; Lieut-Col, 1914; Brig.-Gen. 1916; served European War, 1914–18 in France and Belgium (wounded, despatches, DSO, CMG); retired, 1920; Divisional Commissioner, Munster, 1921–22 (CBE). *Address:* 18 Richmond Mansions, SW5. *Clubs:* Naval and Military, Army and Navy.

Died 21 April 1945.

BARROW, Sir Francis Laurence John, 4th Bt *cr* 1835; *b* 11 Aug. 1862; *s* of 3rd Bt and Emily, *d* of Nathaniel Merriman, MD; *S* father, 1900; *m* 1st, 1890, Winifred Sarah (*d* 1932), 2nd *d* of William C. Steward of Whitehaven; three *s* one *d*; 2nd, 1932, Edith, *d* of Wm Townsend, Somerton. *Heir: s* Capt. Wilfrid John Wilson Croker [late Royal Fusiliers; *b* 28 Dec. 1897; *m* 1926, Patricia, *o surv. d* of late R. G. FitzGerald Uniacke, FSA, FRSA; one *s* three *d*]. *Address:* 3 Claremont Road, Folkestone, Kent.

Died 9 June 1950.

BARRY, Brig. Arthur Gordon, CBE 1941; DSO 1919; MC; MA, BSc; late Royal Tank Corps; *b* 6 Sept. 1885; *e s* of late Commander A. Barry, RN; *m* 1925, Doreen, *o d* of late G. Barbour-Turnbull; one *s. Educ:* Pembroke College, Cambridge; Oriel College, Oxford. Graduate Royal Staff College, 1923. Amateur Golf Champion, 1905; Army Golf Champion, 1922 and 1925; Lt-Col 1935; Col 1938. *Clubs:* Windham; Royal and Ancient, St Andrews.

Died 21 Aug. 1942.

BARRY, Lt-Col Arthur John, CBE 1919; TD, Knight of Grace of Order of St John; Officer Légion d'Honneur; Croix de Guerre; Lt-Col late Engineer and Railway Staff Corps, RE (TA); Member of the Institution of Civil Engineers; senior partner in firm of A. J. Barry & Partners, 23 Palace Street, SW1; Consulting Engineer to the British and Chinese Corporation, to the Trustees of the Port of Bombay, to the Trustees of the Port of Aden; *b* 1859; *s* of Charles Barry, FRIBA; *m* 1st, Mabel Maude Josephine, *d* of late Col I. Ostrehan; 2nd, Theresa Laura Marjorie, *d* of late Colonel W. Terry. *Educ:* Uppingham. Has been responsible for the construction of many important public works, railways, docks, bridges, etc. in Great Britain, India, China and other places abroad; served as Inspector-General in Command of British Red Cross and other Ambulance Convoys attached to French Army, 1914–18. *Address:* Hunnersley, Burley, Ringwood, Hants. *T:* Burley 64. *Clubs:* Athenæum, Royal Automobile; Royal Bombay Yacht.

Died 10 Sept. 1944.

BARRY, Sir Edward (Arthur), 2nd Bt *cr* 1899; Lt-Col, formerly commanding Berks Yeo.; JP, DL, Berks; High Sheriff, 1907; *b* 25 April 1858; *e s* of 1st Bt and Sarah Douglas, *d* of Arthur Herron of Northiam, Sussex; *S* father, 1907; *m* 1st, 1883, Kathleen Ellen (*d* 1885), *d* of Percy Bicknell; one *s*; 2nd, 1891, Eleanor Margaret (*d* 1916), *d* of Col C. H. S. Scott; one *s* three *d. Educ:* Harrow; Cambridge. Served European War, 1914–16. *Heir: s* Claude Francis [*b* 16 Dec. 1883; *m* 1st, 1908, Angela Doris Manners, *e d* of Herbert C. Hume-Spry of Nunney, Frome, Somerset; one *s* two *d*; 2nd, 1927, Violet, *yr d* of late Alfred Darby, of Brentwood, Essex]. *Address:* Ockwells Manor, Bray, Berks. *Club:* Berkshire.

Died 23 July 1949.

BARRY, Major James D.; *e s* of late Rt Hon. C. R. Barry (O'Barrymore of the Galtees) and Kate, *yr sister* of Lord Fitzgerald of Kilmarnock; *m* 1895, Hon. Florence Madeleine, *d* of 4th Baron Clanmorris, and *widow* of John Pollok, Lismany, Ballinasloe. Served with Royal Horse Artillery, 1876–80; ADC to Lords-Lieut of Ireland, 1880–84; rejoined army for South African Campaign, 1899 (medal with three clasps, despatches, promoted Major); embarked with 1st Expeditionary Force, Aug. 1914, as Major 5th Royal Irish Lancers (despatches), and served with regiment at the front until appointed to Headquarters Staff, 55th Division, in France, Jan. 1916; JP County and City of Dublin; Local Director, General Accident Assurance Association, Ireland. *Address:* Ongar, Clonsilla, Co. Dublin. *T:* Clonsilla 12. *Clubs:* St James's; Kildare Street, Dublin; Royal St George Yacht, Kingstown.

Died 12 Jan. 1941.

BARRY, Hon. Jeremiah Hayes, LLD; Chief Justice of the Supreme Court, King's Bench Division, Province of New Brunswick; *b* Maugerville, Sunbury Co., NB, 21 May 1858; *s* of Patrick Barry and Julia Hayes, Cork, Ireland; *m* 1891, Isabella E., *d* of John Owens and Isabella Rossiter; two *s* two *d. Educ:* Public Schools; private tuition. Admitted to the Bar, 1882; Clerk of the York County Court, 1885; Judge of Probate, county of York, 1897; KC, 1899; is a member of the Senate of the University of New Brunswick, and has for many years a member of the Provincial Board of Health of NB; one of the Trustees and President of the Board in 1912 of the Victoria Public Hospital, Fredericton; a Roman Catholic; a Liberal. *Address:* Fredericton, NB Canada. *T:* 421–11.

Died 23 March 1946.

BARRY, Col Stanley Leonard, CMG 1915; CBE 1919; DSO 1900; MVO 1915; Chevalier Legion of Honour, 1915; HM Bodyguard of Hon. Corps of Gentlemen-at-Arms, 1923; late Major 10th Royal Hussars, and Major and Bt-Col (Col TA) Reserve of Officers; JP Northamptonshire, 1914, and Buckinghamshire, 1927; *b* 31 Dec. 1873; *γ s* of Sir F. T. Barry, 1st Bt; *m* 1st, 1906, Hannah Mary (*d* 1924), *e d* of James Hainsworth; one *d*; 2nd, 1927, Laline, *widow* of Lt-Col Arthur Hohler, DSO, *d* of late W. Astell, Woodbury Hall. *Educ:* Harrow. Berkshire Militia, 1891–94; 10th Hussars, 1894–1907; Commanded 4th Batt. Northamptonshire Regt, 1914; served South Africa, 1899–1902 (despatches, Bt Maj., DSO); European War, 1914–18 (despatches, CMG, CBE, MVO, Bt Col); High Sheriff of Bucks, 1935; Lord of the Manors of Hampton Gay, Oxon, and Long Crendon, Bucks. *Address:* Long Crendon Manor, Aylesbury, Bucks. *T:* Long Crendon 246. *Club:* Turf.

Died 22 Dec. 1943.

BARRY, Col Thomas David Collis, CBE 1919; MRCS, LRCP, DPH (RCP and S), FRSE, FIC; IMS and RAF, retired. Served European War, 1914–19 (despatches, CBE).

Died 26 March 1943.

BARRYMORE, John; actor; *b* 15 Feb. 1882; *s* of late Maurice Barrymore and Georgie Drew; *m* 1st, Katherine Corri Harris; 2nd, Mrs Leonard M. Thomas (Blanche Oelrichs); 3rd, Dolores Costello; 4th, Elaine Barrie. First appearance on stage, Chicago, 1903; produced and played Hamlet at the Haymarket, London, 1925, subsequently in motion pictures and radio programmes in America. *Clubs:* Garrick; Lambs, New York.

Died 30 May 1942.

BARSTOW, Maj.-Gen. Arthur Edward, CIE 1941; MC; Indian Army; *b* 17 March 1888; *m* 1927, Nancy Lewkenor, *d* of late Brig.-Gen. Henry Lewkenor Knight, CMG, DSO. *Educ:* Bradfield; RMC, Sandhurst. 2nd Lieut Indian Army, 1909; Capt. 1915; Major, 1923; Bt Lt-Col 1931; Lt-Col 1932; Col 1935; Maj.-Gen. 1941; served European War, 1914–19 (wounded, despatches, MC); Afghanistan, 1919; Iraq, 1920 (despatches); Kurdistan, 1923 (despatches); NW Frontier, 1930 (despatches); Waziristan, 1940 (despatches, CIE). *Address:* Le Court, Liss, Hants.

Died Jan. 1942.

BARTER, Rev. Herbert Francis Treseder; Canon Emeritus since 1940; *b* Plymouth, 21 Oct. 1869; *s* of Rev. Herbert John Edward Barter and Betsy Maria Bragg Treseder; *m* 1895, Gertrude Isobel Harrison; one *s* three *d. Educ:* Trinity College, Dublin; MA, 1892. Deacon, 1892; Priest, 1893; Assistant Curate of St Saviour's, Pimlico; of Oakham and Chapelries; of West Kirby; Vicar of Honley, 1904–17; Vicar of Meltham, 1917–40; Rural Dean of Huddersfield, 1935–40; Hon. Canon of Wakefield Cathedral, 1927–40. *Address:* 8 Halland Road, Cheltenham, Glos. *T:* Cheltenham 3714.

Died 28 Jan. 1949.

BARTH, Lt-Col Sir Jacob William, Kt 1922; CBE 1919; *b* 23 July 1871; *s* of late William Wright Barth; *m* Ida Russell, 2nd *d* of late Harry Burnand; four *d. Educ:* Wadham Coll., Oxford; Heidelberg. Barrister-at-law, Middle Temple, 1900; Registrar of High Court of East Africa, 1902; Crown Advocate, 1902; Judge of High Court, 1905; Member of Land Commission, East Africa Protectorate, 1905; Attorney-General, 1914; Chairman of Labour Commission, 1912; Chairman of Soldier Settlement Commission, 1918; Chairman of Education Commission, 1919; Chairman of Commissioners on Punishment of Natives and Divorce, 1921; served in Forces in E Africa, 1914–19; Temp. Lt-Col 1914–19; retains rank; Chief Justice of Supreme Court of Kenya, 1920–34; retired 1934. *Recreations:* shooting, sailing. *Address:* Talgai, Albury, Surrey. *Clubs:* East India and Sports, Oxford and Cambridge.

Died 30 May 1941.

BARTHOLOMEW, Maj.-Gen. Arthur Wollaston, CB 1933; CMG 1918; CBE 1919; DSO 1915; Col Comdt RA since 1942; *b* 5 May 1878; *s* of late A. C. Bartholomew; *m* 1906, Helen May Ethel, *e d* of late Gen. W. W. Anderson. *Educ:* Marlborough; Trinity College, Oxford. Entered RA, 1900; Captain, 1911; Major, 1914; Lt-Col, 1927; Col, 1929; Maj.-Gen., 1932; served European War, 1914–18 (despatches six times, CMG, CBE, DSO, Bt Lt-Col); Instructor, Senior Officers' School, Sheerness, 1929–30; Commanding RA 4th Div., 1930–32; ADC to the King 1931–32; Inspector of Royal Artillery, War Office, 1933–35; GOC British Troops in China, 1935–38, retired pay, 1938; Lieutenant of the Tower of London, 1939–42. *Address:* The Manor House, Ottery St Mary. *T:* 229. *Club:* Army and Navy.

Died 29 Jan. 1945.

BARTHOLOMEW, Sir Clarence Edward, Kt 1939; OBE; Officer Order of St John of Jerusalem; Hon. Col 62nd Anti-Tank Regiment, RA; Chairman and Managing Director of Bryant and May Ltd, and of British Match Corporation Ltd; *b* 1879; *s* of late Gilbert Bartholomew; *m* 1910, Dorothy Cottam Perry, Melbourne, Australia; one *s* two *d. Educ:* Clifton; Germany and Switzerland. Entered match business (Bryant and May Ltd), 1901; Hon. Secretary Match Control Board, 1918–19; Chairman Administrative Committee Matches Control since 1940; Member of Board of Referees (Finance Acts) since 1928; Member of Home Office Committee on Employment of Prisoners, 1932; Member of London Diocesan Board of Finance, 1915–24; a Member of the Court of the Skinners' Company (Master, 1934–35); a Governor of Tonbridge School; Treasurer Philanthropic Society's School, Redhill since 1924; Commandant London Church Lads' Brigade, 1919–24; Treasurer Seaside Camps for London Boys since 1923; President Royal Commercial Travellers' Schools, 1938; President Old Cliftonian Society, 1937–39; Deputy President Industrial Co. Partnership Assoc. 1945. Past Grand Deacon, United Grand Lodge of Freemasons of England. *Recreation:* gardening. *Address:* Margery Wood, Lower Kingswood, Surrey. *T:* Reigate 2069. *Clubs:* Constitutional, Royal Automobile; Walton Heath.

Died 31 March 1946.

BARTHORPE, Major Sir Frederick James, Kt 1925; one of HM's Lieutenants, City of London; late Alderman City of London; Sheriff, 1924–25; Officer, Legion of Honour; Knight Commander St Gregory the Great; Chairman Marconi International Code Co. Ltd; late Chief Joint General Manager, London County and Westminster Bank, Limited; *s* of William John Barthorpe, North Willingham, Lincs; *m* 1910, Marie Evelyn (*d* 1931), *o c* of T. G. Cuyper, OBE, Calcutta; one *s. Educ:* privately. Secretary London and County Banking Co., 1903; Deputy Head Office Manager, 1907; Head Office Manager, 1909; Joint General Manager of the London County and Westminster Bank, and General Manager London County and Westminster

Bank (Paris), Ltd, 1915; Fellow and former President of Chartered Institute of Secretaries; Fellow of Institute of Bankers; retired with the rank of Major from 4th (City of London) Battalion of the London Regiment (Royal Fusiliers), 1911; assisted in raising the 26th (Service) Battalion of the Royal Fusiliers (Bankers' Battalion) and also the National Guard Volunteer Corps. *Publications:* Consols and the Sinking Fund; Indian Currency—its first and second lines of defence. *Recreations:* at present golf, formerly cricket. *Address:* 16 Leigham Court Road, Streatham Hill, SW. *T:* Streatham 3766. *Clubs:* Bath, National Liberal.

Died 28 Feb. 1942.

BARTLEET, Rev. Edwin Berry, DD; Prebendary of Hereford; *b* 1872; *s* of late T. H. Bartleet, FRCS, Birmingham; *m* Sophie Demuth, Edgbaston; two *s* two *d*. *Educ:* Clifton; New College, Oxford. Curate of Doncaster Parish Church and of Rushall; Rector of Hope; Vicar of Much Wenlock and Lydbury North; Rector of Wistanstow, 1926–33; Archdeacon of Ludlow, 1928–32; temporary Chaplain during the War; DACG. *Publications:* pamphlets on Army Work. *Recreation:* golf. *Address:* Hope Cottage, Rushbury, Salop.

Died 17 Dec. 1946.

BARTLETT, Cdre Charles Alfred, CB 1916; CBE 1920; RD 1907; RNR (retired); late Senior Marine Superintendent to the White Star and Associated Lines; *b* London, 21 Aug. 1868; 3rd *s* of late S. W. Bartlett, Brixham; *m* 1898, Edith Kate, 2nd *d* of J. R. Ellis of Hillcrest, Gorleston, Suffolk; one *d*. *Educ:* Cowper Street School, London. Apprenticed to D. Bruce clippers of Dundee, 1882; served in British India Company, 1888–94; joined White Star Line, and in command of Atlantic Liners, 1903–12; Marine Superintendent of the Line, 1912; was called to service (RNR) Nov. 1914; served twelve months on patrol work in North Sea (CB); in command of HM Hospital Ship Britannic from Dec. 1915 to Nov. 1916; served as ADC to HM from 1919–21; elected Younger Brother of the Trinity House, 1916; a member of the RNR Advisory Committee, 1921; Mariner Warden of the Honourable Company of Master Mariners, 1931; Vice-President, King George's Fund for Sailors. *Recreations:* yachting and fishing. *Clubs:* Constitutional, Liverpool.

Died 15 Feb. 1945.

BARTLETT, George Bertram, BA, MRCS; *b* Shapwick, Blandford, 9 April 1880; 2nd *s* of Arthur Bartlett of Wimborne Minister; *m* 1916, Annie Sinclair, *d* of Alexander Jenkinson; five *s*. *Educ:* Weymouth College; Sydney Sussex College, Cambridge; London Hospital, E. Natural Science Tripos at Cambridge. Assistant Director Pathological Institute, London Hospital, 1908–20; Lecturer on Pathological Histology, London Hospital Medical College, 1912–20; Professor of Pathology, The University, Cape Town, 1920–24; enlisted in Royal Fusiliers, 1914; Infantry Commission, 1915; RAMC Commission, 1915–19; Pathologist to No. 21 General Hospital, Alexandria, and to No. 27 General Hospital, Cairo; Malaria Laboratory 4th London General Hospital, 1917; 4th Mobile Laboratory, E Africa, 1918; researches on arterial disease, tuberculosis, cancer, dysentery, and malaria. *Recreations:* hound work and hunting on foot, tramping, fresh-water fishing, modern literature. *Address:* 30 Reynolds Road, Hove, Sussex.

Died 3 June 1944.

BARTÓK, Béla; composer and pianist; *b* 25 March 1881; *s* of Béla Bartók and Paula Voit; *m* 1923, Edith Pásztory; two *s*. *Educ:* High School of Music, Budapest. *Compositions:* 17 orchestral works; 6 string quartets; 2 sonatas and 2 rhapsodies for violin and piano; Ballet: The Wooden Prince; Opera: Bluebeard's Castle; Pantomime: The Wonderful Mandarin—many pianoforte pieces,

songs and choral works. *Publication:* Hungarian Folk Music (London 1931). *Address:* 11 Csalán Ut, 29, Budapest.

Died 27 Sept. 1945.

BARTOLOMÉ, Adm. Sir Charles Martin de, KCMG 1919; CB 1913; RN; *b* 26 Nov. 1871; *s* of Mariano Martin de Bartolomé and Mary Emily, *d* of J. Jackson; *m* 1916, Gladys Constance, *d* of late J. K. Wilson of Snaithing Brook, Sheffield; two *s* one *d*. *Educ:* HMS Britannia. Joined RN 1885; Capt. 1907; Rear-Admiral, 1919; 3rd Sea Lord and Controller of the Navy, 1918–19; retired from Royal Navy, 1919; Vice-Admiral retired, 1925; Admiral retired, 1929; Director General of Development, Ministry of Transport, 1919–22. *Address:* Glen Kin, West Malvern.

Died 25 May 1941.

BARTON, Lt-Col Baptist Johnston, DSO 1915; DL, JP Co. Donegal; High Sheriff, 1922; late The Duke of Wellington's (West Riding Regiment) KOYLI and Royal Newfoundland Regt; *b* 21 Oct. 1876; *e s* of late Col Baptist Barton, DL, ADC, of Greenfort; *m* 1908, Kathleen Maude, *d* of late Egbert de Hamel, Middleton Hall, Warwicks; one *d*. *Educ:* Foyle College; Sandhurst. Entered Army, 1896; Captain, 1902; retired 1911; served European War, 1914–18 (DSO and bar, brevet, despatches thrice). *Address:* The Grey Bungalow, Powick, Worcester.

Died 18 Dec. 1944.

BARTON, Lt-Col Charles Walter, CMG 1915; DSO 1900; late Northamptonshire Regt; *b* 15 Aug. 1876; *s* of Walthew C. Barton, MICE. *Educ:* Harrow. Entered Army, 1897; served South Africa, 1899–1902 (wounded, despatches, DSO); Somaliland, 1903–04; Nyasaland, German East Africa, and Portuguese East Africa, 1914–18 (wounded, despatches, CMG, bar to DSO); employed with King's African Rifles, 1903–08 and 1913–18; commanded Nyasaland Field Force, 1914; retired, 1925. *Address:* Kenistone, Mersham, Ashford, Kent.

Died 21 Sept. 1950.

BARTON, Captain Francis Rickman, CMG 1906; *b* 4 Jan. 1865; *s* of late Rev. Gerard Barton of Fundenhall, Norfolk; *m* 1908, Santa Carla, *d* of Alfred Tofft; one *s* two *d*. *Educ:* Norwich Grammar School; in Germany. After farming in United States for three years, passed into Sandhurst, joined West India regiment, and rose to be Captain; served at Sierra Leone and in Barbados; was Private Sec. and ADC to Sir James Hay, Governor of Barbados; Private Sec. to Sir George Le Hunte, Lieut-Governor of British New Guinea, 1899; Resident Magistrate, Central Division, British New Guinea, 1903; Administrator of Papua, 1904–07; Financial Member Zanzibar Govt, 1908; First Minister, 1908; retired 1913. *Publications:* Some New Letters of Edward FitzGerald, 1924; Translation of With the Migratory Birds to Africa, by Bengt Berg, 1931. *Address:* c/o Westminster Bank Ltd, 34 Henrietta St, WC2.

Died 4 Oct. 1947.

BARTON, Rev. George Aaron, MA, PhD, DD, LLD, FAAS, FSA; Professor Emeritus (Professor 1922–32) of Semitie Languages University of Pennsylvania; Professor Emeritus (Professor 1921–37) of New Testament Literature and Language in the Divinity School of the Protestant Episcopal Church in Philadelphia; *b* East Farnham, Quebec, Canada, 12 Nov. 1859; *s* of Daniel Barton and Mary S. Bull; *m* 1st, 1884, Caroline Brewer Danforth (*d* 1930); 2nd, 1931, Katherine Blye Hagy. *Educ:* Haverford College (AB 1882, AM 1885, LLD 1914); Harvard University (AM 1890, PhD 1891). Teacher of Higher Mathematics and Classics in Friends' School, Providence, 1884–89; Lecturer on Bible Languages, Haverford College, 1891–95; Professor of Biblical Literature and Semitic Languages in Bryn Mawr College, 1891–1922; Minister, Society of Friends,

1879–1918; Deacon, Protestant Episcopal Church, 1918; Priest, 1919; Director of the American School of Oriental Research. Jerusalem, 1902–03; Director of the American School of Oriental Research at Baghdad, 1921–34; Sec. and Treasurer of the American Schools of Oriental Research, 1918–34; President of the Society of Biblical Literature and Exegesis, 1913–14; Pres. of the American Oriental Society, 1916–17. *Publications:* A Sketch of Semitic Origins, Social and Religious, 1902; The Roots of Christian Teaching as found in the Old Testament, 1902; A Year's Wandering in Bible Lands, 1904; The Haverford Library Collection of Cuneiform Tablets, or Documents from the Temple Archives of Telloh, Parts I–III, 1905–1914; A Critical and Exegetical Commentary on Ecclesiastes in International Critical Commentary, 1908; The Heart of the Christian Message, 1910, 2nd ed. 1912; Commentary on Job in Bible for Home and School, 1911; The Origin and Development of Babylonian Writing, 1913; Sumerian Business and Administrative Documents from the Earliest Times to the Dynasty of Agade, 1915; Archæology and the Bible, 1916, 7th ed. 1937; The Religions of the World, 1917, 4th ed. 1937; Sumerian Religious Texts, 1918; The Religion of Israel, 1918, 2nd ed. 1928; Jesus of Nazareth, a Biography, 1922 (Translations into Korean and Japanese, 1938); Royal Inscriptions of Sumer and Akkad, 1929; Hittite Studies, No. 1, 1928, No. 2, 1932; Studies in New Testament Christianity, 1928; A History of the Hebrew People, 1930; A Sketch of Semitic and Hamitic Origins, 1934 (revision of a Sketch of Semitic Origins, 1902); Christ and Evolution, 1934; The Apostolic Age and the New Testament Bohlen lectures, 1936; contributions to Encyclopedias, etc. *Recreation:* walking. *Address:* Weston, Massachusetts, USA; 3610 Royal Palm Avenue, Coconut Grove, Miami, Florida, USA. *Clubs:* Oriental, Clericus, Phi Alpha, Philadelphia.

Died 28 June 1942.

BARTON, Lt-Col Richard Lionel, DSO 1918; late RGA; *b* 1875; *m*; three *s.* Served South African War, 1899–1900 (Queen's medal and three clasps); European War (DSO, Croix de Guerre); retired pay, 1922. *Address:* (temp.): The Little House, Sheringham, Norfolk. *Club:* United Service.

Died 29 June 1942.

BARTON, Sir Sidney, GBE 1936; KCVO 1930; KBE 1926; CMG 1913; *b* 26 Nov. 1876; *y s* of Captain James Barton, late RA, and Mary Barbara, *y d* of Sir David Edward Barclay, 10th Bt of Pierston, Ayrshire; *m* 1904, Mary Ethel Winifred, CBE 1937, OBE 1928 (*d* 1945); *e d* of Alexander Palmer MacEwen; one *s* two *d. Educ:* St Paul's School. Barrister-at-law. Middle Temple, 1910; entered HM Consular Service in China, 1895; Special Service, Weihaiwei, 1899–1901; Vice-Consul, Peking, 1901–02; Tientsin, 1905–06; Shanghai, 1906–10; Chinese Sec. HM Legation, Peking, 1911–22; Consul-General, Shanghai, 1922–29; Envoy Extraordinary and Minister Plenipotentiary to Abyssinia, 1929–37; served as Interpreter and Assistant Political Officer to British Contingent, North China Field Force, June–Aug. 1900 (despatches, medal with clasp); Captain North China British Volunteer Corps, 1915–18. *Address:* c/o National Provincial Bank, Ltd, 88 Cromwell Road, SW7.

Died 20 Jan. 1946.

BARTON, Lt-Col William Hugh, DSO 1917; JP, DL; late Scottish Rifles and RASC; *b* 30 May 1874; *e s* of late Capt. C. R. Barton, JP, DL, The Waterfoot, Co. Fermanagh, and Henrietta Martha, *d* of H. Mervyn Richardson, DL, of Rossfad; *m* 1917, Ardvn Marion, *y d* of late Col H. T. S. Patteson, VD, JP, DL; (*s* killed in action) one *d. Address:* The Waterfoot, Letter, Co. Fermanagh. *Club:* Army and Navy.

Died 1 Feb. 1945.

BARTTELOT, Adm. Sir Brian Herbert Fairbairn, KBE 1927; CB 1917; MVO 1915; Commander, Legion of Honour; 3rd class Rising Sun (Japan); *b* 31 Dec. 1867; 2nd *s* of late Brian Barttelot-Barttelot, JP, Ditton, Torquay; unmarried. *Educ:* Stubbington House, Fareham; HMS Britannia. Joined HM Navy as a Cadet, 1881; Midshipman, 1883; Sub-Lieut, 1887; Lieutenant, 1889; Commander, 1901; Captain, 1906; Rear-Admiral, 1918; Vice-Admiral and Retired List, 1923; Director of Dockyards and Repairs, 1923–28; Admiral, 1927. As Captain served as Flag Captain to Rear-Admiral John Denison in HMS Leviathan, 1908–09; Commanded HMS Blenheim, 1909–10; Captain of the Nore Gunnery School, 1910–12; Commanded HMS Monmouth in China, 1912–14; Captain Supt, and SNO Clyde District, 1914–17; Commanded HMS Resolution, 1917–18; Admiral Supt, Malta Dockyard, 1918–21. *Clubs:* Naval and Military; Royal Western Yacht, Plymouth.

Died 4 Feb. 1942.

BARTTELOT, Lt-Col Sir Walter de Stopham, 4th Bt *cr* 1875; DSO 1944; Coldstream Guards; *b* 27 Oct. 1904; *s* of 3rd Bt and Gladys St Aubyn (she *m* 2nd, 1920, Capt. N. W. Diggle, CMG, RN, retired); *y d* of W. C. Angrove; *S* father, 1918; *m* 1938, Sara Patricia, *d* of Lt-Col H. V. Ravenscroft, The Abbey, Storrington, Sussex; two *s. Educ:* Eton; RMC, Sandhurst. *Heir: s* Brian Walter de Stopham, *b* 17 July 1941. *Address:* Keeper's Cottage, Stopham, Pulborough, Sussex.

Died 16 Aug. 1944.

BASDEN, Rev. George Thomas, OBE 1934; MA, DLitt, FRGS; Rector of Jevington, Sussex; Commissary in England to the Bishop on the Niger; Vice-President of Church Missionary Society; lately Secretary Church Missionary Society Niger Mission; Archdeacon of the Niger; Examining Chaplain to the Bishop on the Niger; Unofficial Member of the Legislative Council for the Ibo Division of Nigeria, 1930; *b* 31 Oct. 1873; *s* of James and Kezia Basden; *m* 1906, Eleanor Emma Scott Lorimer, SRN; four *s. Educ:* CMS College, Islington; University College, Durham. Offered to CMS as a pioneer missionary to open up work in the Ibo Country on the Niger, W Africa; sailed from Liverpool, 6 Sept. 1900; first overland journey Asaba Hinterland, Dec. 1900; subsequent years surveyed Onitsha Province; proceeded to Awka, Jan. 1904; first Principal of the Training College and Superintendent of the Awka and Enugwu Districts; on appointment, statistics stood at nil; on transfer to Onitsha as Secretary of the Mission in 1925, over 130 Churches and Schools established in above Districts, fully self-supporting and governed by two Church Councils; mainly responsible for building and equipping Awka Training College, with accommodation for 100 resident students. *Publications:* Among the Ibos of Nigeria, 1920; Edith Warner of the Niger, 1927; Niger Ibos, 1938. *Address:* Jevington Rectory, Polegate, Sussex. *T:* Polegate 202.

Died 30 Dec. 1944.

BASKERVILLE,   Lt-Col   Charles   Herbert Lethbridge; *b* 17 Oct. 1860; *e s* of late Rev. Canon Baskerville, vicar of Tonbridge; *m* 1887, Mary (*d* 1929), *d* of Henry Duggan of Queenstown, and *widow* of Lt-Col S. Davies Smith, AOD. *Educ:* Marlborough; Sandhurst. Joined 51st Light Infantry, 1879; Army Service Corps, 1884; served Afghanistan, 1880 (medal); Nile, 1885; Adjutant 1st Durham RE (V), 1888–93; Major Royal Irish Regiment, 1894; retired, 1895; commanded Falmouth Division RE (M), 1897–1907; employed with RE, 1900–04; Lt-Col, retired pay, 1902 (for services); Special Reserve Royal Engineers, 1907–20; CRE, Falmouth, 1914–19; Master of the Worshipful Company of Innholders, 1930–31; is interested in travel and touring; Grand Sword-Bearer, Freemasons, England, 1913. *Publications:* various newspaper articles. *Recreations:* cycling, golf, travel. *Address:* 52 Fitzharris Avenue, Bournemouth. *T:* Winton 1211. *Club:* United Service.

Died 20 Nov. 1946.

BASKERVILLE, Geoffrey, MA; FRHistS; *b* 23 Aug. 1870; *s* of Colonel John Baskerville, Crowsley Park, Oxon. *Educ:* Royal Navy; Christ Church, Oxford. *Publications:* English Monks and the Suppression of the Monasteries, 1937; Contributions to Essays in History presented to R Lane Poole; Mediæval England, 1924; various archæological and historical papers. *Recreation:* travel. *Address:* Crowsley Park, Henley on Thames. *T:* Kidmore End 3150.

Died 22 July 1944.

BASKERVILLE, Rev. Canon George Knyfton, MA; licensed to officiate in Diocese of Winchester from 1930; *b* Croscombe, near Wells, 30 Aug. 1867; *s* of late Rev. Canon C. G. Baskerville, and *brother* of Lt-Col C. H. L. Baskerville; *m* 1902, Rosetta Gage, *d* of late John Harvey, of the Educational Department, Indian Civil Service. *Educ:* Marlborough College; Corpus Christi College, Cambridge; Ridley Hall, Cambridge. CMS Missionary, Uganda, 1890; Deacon, 1890; Priest, 1891; Superintending Missionary in Kyagwe, Uganda, 1893–1912; Archdeacon of Uganda, 1912; Secretary of Board of Missions, Diocese of Uganda, 1913; Examining Chaplain to Bishop of Uganda, 1913; Sub-Dean and Chancellor of the Cathedral, 1917, and Canon *ex-officio* of the Cathedral Church, 1917; Chaplain Victoria Nyanza Lodge of Freemasons; Hon. Canon for life of Cathedral Church of St Paul the Apostle, Uganda, 1922, Commissary to Bishop of Uganda, 1922–34; Assistant Chaplain St Paul's, Hyères, 1921–22; Assistant Chaplain (Hon.) of Holy Trinity, Cannes, 1922–25; Chaplain at Tamaris for Toulon and neighbourhood, 1925–30. *Publications:* Edited Reference Bible in Luganda; translated life of Mahomed, Commentary on St Matthew in Cambridge Bible for Schools, Book of Forms in Luganda and English for use in Diocese of Uganda, Lectures to African Clergy on Levitical Sacrifices; and various pamphlets in Luganda language. *Address:* Amblève, St Aubins, Jersey. *Club:* Overseas.

Died April 1941.

BASSET, Arthur Francis; DL; *b* 29 Jan. 1873; *o s* of late Gustavus Lambart Basset and Charlotte Mary, *d* of late William Elmhirst, West Ashby Manor, Co. Lincoln; *m* 1st, 1898, Rebecca Harriet Buller (*d* 1947), 2nd *d* of Sir William Lewis Salusbury-Trelawny, 10th Bart; one *s* one *d*; 2nd, 1950, Kathleen Ann Tabor, *d* of late Rev. Frederick William Floyd. High Sheriff, Cornwall, 1901. *Address:* Norcot Hill, Northchurch, Berkhampstead, Herts. *Club:* Boodle's.

Died 30 May 1950.

BASSETT, Herbert Harry; writer on finance and kindred subjects, and editor of statistical compilations; *b* South Darenth, Kent, 1874; 4th *s* of late R. G. Bassett, founder of Kentish District Times series of Kent papers; *m* 1899, Eleanor, *y d* of late George Dearing, of Beckenham, Kent; two *s*. *Educ:* Stationers Company's School (before its removal from Fleet Street). Financial Times editorial staff, 1895–97; revised Fenn on the Funds (16th edition), 1898; editor Journal of Finance (monthly review), 1899; compiled Men of Note, 1900; Investor's Blue Book, 1903–05; Harmsworth's Encyclopedia (railways and steamships), 1905; Investor's Shilling Year-Book, 1908–13; Editor Financial Review of Reviews, 1905–13; author British Commerce, 1913; City Editor, The Globe, 1914–19; Editor of Bradshaw's Railway Manual, 1904–24; City Editor, Birmingham Post, 1920–30. *Address:* The Lane House, Rotherfield, Sussex.

Died Aug. 1939.

BASTABLE, Charles F., MA, LLD, FBA; *b* Charleville, Co. Cork, 1855; *o s* of Rev. R. Bastable. *Educ:* Fermoy College; Trinity Coll. Dublin. Professor of Political Economy, Dublin Univ., 1882–1932; Prof. of Jurisprudence and PoliticalEconomy, Queen's Coll., Galway, 1883–1903; Prof. of Jurisprudence and International Law, Dublin Univ., 1902; Regius Prof. of

Laws, 1908–32; Examiner, Universities of London, Wales, Ireland, Manchester, Belfast, Cambridge, Liverpool, Sheffield, Birmingham; George Rae Lecturer, University College of North Wales, 1905; Warburton Lecturer, Univ. of Manchester, 1909–10; President of Section F Brit. Assoc. (Oxford), 1894. *Publications:* Theory of International Trade; Commerce of Nations; Public Finance; contributor to Encyclopædia Britannica, articles English Finance, Finance, Money (9th, 10th, and 11th eds). *Address:* 52 Brighton Road, Rathgar, Dublin.

Died Jan. 1945.

BATE, Edward Raoul, CB 1918; *b* 15 Oct. 1859; *s* of late Edwin Bate; *m* 1890, Margaret Grace Buck; one *s*. *Educ:* Royal Naval College, Greenwich. Assistant Constructor, Admiralty; Naval Constructor, Malta, 1900–04; Portsmouth, 1904–05; Chatham, 1905–11; Chief Constructor Hong Kong, 1911–15; Admiralty, 1915–17; Deputy Director of Dockyards and Repairs Admiralty, 1917. *Recreations:* golf, etc.

Died 16 May 1948.

BATE, Francis, OBE; JP; artist, painter; *s* of Henry Francis Bate, MD; *m* 1894, Laura Ellen (*d* 1937), *d* of J. L. Fairless; one *s* one *d*. *Educ:* Christ's Hospital; South Kensington Art Schools; Académie Royal d'Anvers. Scholarship at South Kensington, 1877; exhibitor at the principal art exhibitions. *Publication:* The Naturalistic School of Painting, 1887. *Recreations:* walking, gardening. *Address:* Bucklebury, near Reading, Berks. *Club:* Berkshire (Reading).

Died 28 Nov. 1950.

BATE, Very Rev. Herbert Newell, MA; Hon. DD (Edin.); Dean of York since 1932; *b* 1871; *s* of Rev. George Osborn Bate; *m* 1904, Isobel Dutton, *e d* of Col W. M. Angus, CB; two *s* two *d*. *Educ:* St Paul's School; Trinity College, Oxford. 1st class Moderations, 1891; 1st class Lit. Hum. 1893; Liddon Student, 1894; Hall Senior Greek Testament Prize, 1895. Tutor of Keble College, 1895–97; Fellow and Tutor of Magdalen College, 1897–1904; Dean of Divinity, 1903–04; Examining Chaplain to the Bishop of London, 1901–20; Vicar of St Stephen's, Hampstead, 1904–13; Christ Church, Lancaster Gate, W, 1913–20; Canon of Carlisle, 1920–28; Rector of Hadleigh, Suffolk, and Dean of Bocking, 1928–32; Select Preacher in the University of Oxford. 1912–13 and 1924–25; in the University of Cambridge, 1932–33; Speaker's Lecturer in Biblical Studies, Oxford, 1919; Order of Star of Roumania, 2nd Class. *Publications:* Church History to ad 325; The Healthful Spirit; Sibylline Oracles, III–V; Guide to the Epistles of St Paul, 1926; Faith and Order, 1927. *Address:* The Deanery, York. *T:* York 3608.

Died 18 May 1941.

BATEMAN, Harry, FRS 1928; PhD Johns Hopkins 1913; Professor of Mathematics, Theoretical Physics, and Aeronautics, California Institute of Technology, Pasadena, California; *b* 29 May 1882; *s* of Samuel and Marnie Elizabeth Bateman; *m* 1912, Ethel Horner Dodd; one *d*. *Educ:* Manchester Grammar School; Trinity College, Cambridge (Sen. Wrangler (Bracketed), 1903; Smith's Prizeman, 1905). Fellow of Trinity Coll., Cambridge, 1905–11; Johnston Scholar, Johns Hopkins University, 1912–15. *Publications:* report on integral equations, 1910; Electrical and Optical Wave Motion, 1915; Differential Equations, 1918; Partial Differential Equations of Mathematical Physics, 1932 papers in various Mathematical and Physical journals. *Recreations:* motoring, chess. *Address:* 1107 San Pasqual Street, Pasadena, California, USA. *T:* SY 6–2049.

Died 21 Jan. 1946.

BATEMAN-CHAMPAIN, Rt Rev. John Norman; Chaplain of St Monica Home of Rest, Bristol, since 1948; *b* 14 March 1880; *y s* of late Colonel Sir John Bateman-Champain, KCMG, C-in-C of Indo-European Telegraph Company; *m* 1912, Jeanie Monsell

Maud, *e d* of late Bishop of Kensington; one *s* (and one killed on active service, 1943) two *d*. *Educ:* Cheltenham College; Caius College, Cambridge (choral exhibitioner); Wells Theological College. Deacon, 1903; Priest, 1904; Curate of St Mary Redcliffe, Bristol, 1903–08; Vicar of Germiston, South Africa, 1909–12; Vicar of St Mary Redcliffe, Bristol, 1912–28; Hon. Canon of Bristol Cathedral; Rural Dean of Bedminster, 1927–28; Vicar of the Cathedral Church of St Nicholas, Newcastle upon Tyne and Provost of the Cathedral, 1928–38; Bishop of Knaresborough, 1938–48; resigned, 1948. CF in France, 1917–19, being Church of England chaplain at GHQ, 1918. *Recreations:* cricket, golf. *Address:* St Augustine, Westbury-on-Trym, Bristol. *Clubs:* I Zingari, Free Foresters.

Died 22 Oct. 1950.

BATES, His Hon. Arthur Henry; KC 1919. County Court Judge for Co. Down; Chairman of Quarter Sessions, Co. Down, since 1919; called to Bar, King's Inns, Dublin, 1879. *Address:* Lemnarory, Greenisland, Co. Antrim.

Died 2 April 1947.

BATES, Rt Hon. Sir Dawson; *see* Bates, Rt Hon. Sir R. D.

BATES, Sir Percy Elly, 4th Bt *cr* 1880; GBE 1920; Hon. Captain Royal Naval Reserve; *b* 12 May 1879; *s* of 2nd Bt and Constance, *d* of late S. R. Graves, MP, Liverpool; *S* brother, 1903; *m* 1907, Mary Ann Lefroy, *y d* late Very Rev. W. Lefroy, Dean of Norwich (*o s* killed on active service, 1945). *Educ:* Winchester. Chairman of Cunard Steamship Co., Ltd, of Cunard-White Star Line since 1934. *Heir:* nephew Geoffrey Voltelin Bates, *b* 2 Oct. 1921. *Address:* Hinderton Hall, Neston, Cheshire. *Clubs:* Beefsteak, Oriental, Windham's, Flyfishers', Royal Automobile.

Died 16 Oct. 1946.

BATES, Rt Hon. Sir (Richard) Dawson, PC Ireland, 1921; 1st Bt *cr* 1937; Kt 1921; Solicitor; Vice-President Ulster Unionist Council, and Clerk to the Lieutenancy of Co. Down; DL Belfast; JP Co. Down; MP East Belfast and Victoria Division, 1921–29, and 1929–43; *b* 23 Nov. 1876; *o s* of Richard Dawson Bates, Solicitor, Belfast, and Mary, *d* of Prof. R. F. Dill, MD; *m* 1920, Muriel, *d* of late Sir Chas Cleland, KBE, MVO, LLD; one *s*. Admitted Solicitor, 1900; Mem. of E & RD Bates and Upritchard, Solicitors; Home Sec. under the Govt for N Ireland, 1921–43; one of the founders of Ulster Volunteer Force Hospitals during war, and of Ulster Volunteer Force Patriotic Fund; Hon. Secretary to both. *Recreations:* golf and yachting. *Heir: s* Maj. John Dawson, *b* 21 Sept. 1921. *Address:* Butleigh House, nr Glastonbury, Somerset. *Clubs:* Constitutional; Ulster, Royal Ulster Yacht (Belfast).

Died 10 June 1949.

BATEY, Joseph; *b* 4 March 1867; *s* of Isaac Batey, a coal miner, and Hannah Batey, from coal mining family; *m* 1888, Martha Irving. *Educ:* Colliery School, West Moor. Started work down coal mine first day after reaching 12 years of age; continued to work down coal mine until elected Miners' Secretary and Checkweighman in 1896 at St Hilda Colliery, South Shields; elected to South Shields Board of Guardians, 1894; South Shields Town Council, 1896; President South Shields Co-operative Society, 1906; a Member of the Durham Miners' Executive Committee, 1901; continued to serve on that body until 1915, when elected by Durham miners as Miners' Agent; then removing to Durham City and resigning all official positions in South Shields; a member for three years of the Executive Committee of Miners' Federation of Great Britain, resigning that position and also Durham Miners' Agency when elected MP; MP (Lab) Spennymoor Div. of Durham, 1922–42. *Address:* 32 Morpeth Avenue, South Shields.

Died 21 Feb. 1949.

BATH, 5th Marquess of, *cr* 1789; **Thomas Henry Thynne,** KG 1917; PC 1922; CB 1919; Bt 1641; Viscount Weymouth and Baron Thynne, 1682; Master of the Horse, 1922–24; HM's Lieut for Somerset; *b* 16 July 1862; *e s* of 4th Marquis and Frances Isabella Catherine, *e d* of 3rd Viscount de Vesci; *S* father, 1896; *m* 1890, Violet Caroline (*d* 1928), *d* of Sir Charles Mordaunt, 10th Bt; one *s* three *d* (and one *s* decd). *Educ:* Eton; Balliol College, Oxford; MA 1888. MP (C) Somerset Frome Div. 1886–92, 1895–96; Parliamentary Under-Secretary of State for India, 1905; Chairman, Wilts CC; Lt-Col Wilts Yeomanry; retired, 1911. *Heir: yr s* Viscount Weymouth, *b* 26 Jan. 1905. *Address:* Longleat, Warminster, Wilts.

Died 9 June 1946.

BATHURST, 7th Earl *cr* 1772; **Seymour Henry Bathurst,** CMG 1902; JP; DL; TD; CC Cirencester; Baron Bathurst of Battlesden, Beds, 1712; Baron Apsley of Apsley, Sussex, 1771; Earl Bathurst of Bathurst, Sussex, 1772; Colonel 4th Battalion Gloucester Regt Militia, retd, 1898–1908; late Hon. Colonel 5th Battalion Gloster Regt; *b* 21 July 1864; *e s* of 6th Earl and 1st wife, Hon. Meriel Leicester Warren, *d* of 2nd Baron de Tabley; *S* father, 1892; *m* 1893, Hon. Lilias Margaret Frances Borthwick, *d* of 1st and last Baron Glenesk; two *s* (and one *s* one *d* decd). *Educ:* Eton; Christ Church, Oxford. Master of Vale of White Horse Foxhounds. Owns 10,762 acres in Cirencester; 2000 in Derbyshire; minerals in Derbyshire. Church of England. Conservative. *Publications:* The Breeding of Foxhounds, 1926; A Supplement to the Foxhound Kennel Stud Book, 1928; The Earl Spencer's and Mr John Warde's Hounds, 1932; History of the VWH Country, 1936; The Charlton and Raby Hunts, 1938. *Recreations:* hunting, shooting. *Heir: g s* Lord Apsley. *Address:* Cirencester Park, Cirencester; Bathurst House, Belgrave Square, SW1. *T:* Victoria 4493 and Cirencester 0133. *Club:* Travellers'.

Died 21 Sept. 1943.

BATHURST, Lt-Col Hon. (Allen) Benjamin; DL; *b* 1872; *y s* of 6th Earl Bathurst and 1st wife, Hon. Meriel Leicester Warren, *d* of 2nd Baron de Tabley; *m* 1902, Augusta Ruby, *e d* of late Lord Edward Spencer-Churchill; one *s*. *Educ:* Eton; Royal Agricultural College, Cirencester. MP (C) Cirencester Division, Gloucestershire, 1895–1906, and 1910–18. Major 4th Batt. Gloster Regt Militia, retired 1908; Lt-Col 5th Batt. Gloster Regt, 1908–13, and 2/5th Batt., 1914–16. *Publication:* Letters of Two Queens, 1924. *Recreation:* shooting. *Address:* Queensmead, Windsor.

Died 8 Oct. 1947.

BATSON, Col Herbert, CB 1900; the Devonshire Regt; *b* 22 Oct. 1853; *m* Ella Florence Charlotte, *d* of E. Snow, of Franklyn, Exeter. Entered Army, 1875; Captain, 1883; Major, 1895; served South Africa, 1899–1901 (despatches thrice, Queen's medal 6 clasps, King's medal 2 clasps; CB, Brevet Lt-Col); retired, 1904. *Address:* Crapstone, Yelverton, S Devon.

Died 7 Sept. 1941.

BATTEN, Herbert Ernest, FRCS (Eng.); Consulting Orthopædic Surgeon Charing Cross Hospital and Royal Masonic Hospital; *b* 6 Aug. 1877; *s* of late Henry Batten, Ilminster, Somerset; *m* 1917, Margaret E. Evans; one *s*. *Educ:* Ilminster Grammar School. MRCS, LRCP, 1904; FRCS 1914. *Address:* 17 Ravenscourt Square, W6. *T:* Riverside 6373.

Died 8 Jan. 1950.

BATTERSBY, Henry Francis Prevost; (pen-name Francis Prevost); author; *s* of late Major-General J. Prevost Battersby 60th Rifles, and Louise, *d* of Sir William Dillon, 4th Bt; *m* 1909, Frances Muriel, *d* of H. C. Saunders. *Educ:* Westminster School; RMA Woolwich; RMC, Sandhurst (Honours and Special Mention). Lieutenant 1st Batt. Royal Irish Rifles; was correspondent to Morning Post, South Africa 1899–1900 (wounded); Somaliland, 1902; France and Flanders, 1915–16 (wounded); Reuter's war correspondent, American and British Fronts, 1918 (gassed, Nov. 1918); special correspondent with Prince of Wales in India, 1905–06; has travelled in Russia, Central Asia, India and the East, Africa and Europe. *Publications:* Melilot (poems), 1893; Fires of Greenwood (poems), 1894; Rust of Gold, 1895; Hockey, 1895; On the Verge, 1896; False Dawn, 1897; Entanglements, 1898; Hockey in 'Football, Hockey, and La Crosse', 1899; In the Web of a War, 1900; The Plague of the Heart, 1902; The Avenging Hour, 1906; India under Royal Eyes, 1906; The Last Resort, 1912; The Silence of Men, 1913; Richard Corfield of Somaliland, 1914; The Lure of Romance, 1914; The Edge of Doom, 1919; Ash of Roses (poems), 1920; Psychic Certainties, 1930; Spirit Voices of the Bible, 1933; Man outside himself, 1942; Monographs: London Water, 1899; The Future of Cavalry, 1904; translated, with Vladimir Tchertkoff, L. Tolstoi's Christ's Christianity, 1893; L. Tolstoi's What to Do, 1894; Plays: The Way of War, 1902; The Voice of Duty, 1904; Articles in Edinburgh, New (under W. E. Henley), Nineteenth Century, and National Reviews, etc. *Recreations:* cricket, hunting, big game shooting, football (South), hockey (International), boating, tennis. *Address:* Creek End, Bosham, Sussex. *T:* Bosham 2174. *Clubs:* Savile, Royal Automobile.

Died 20 June 1949.

BATTERSBY, Maj.-Gen. Thomas Preston, CB 1917; *s* of Charles John Battersby of Cromlyn, Westmeath; *m* Agnes Janet, *d* of John Evens of The Haven, St Stephens, Canterbury; one *s*, killed at Ypres, 1914. *Educ:* Royal School, Armagh; Woolwich. Lieutenant, Royal Artillery, 1876; served in the Army Ordnance Department for 36 years, and at the War Office in the appointments of Assistant Director-General of Ordnance, Director of Equipment and Ordnance Stores, Inspector of Army Ordnance Services; retired as Principal Ordnance Officer, 1918. *Publications:* some works under a pseudonym. *Recreations:* chiefly scientific; is a Fellow of the Royal Astronomical Society. *Address:* Trinco, Kingsdown, Deal.

Died 13 Feb. 1941.

BATTINE, Lt-Col Reginald St Clair, DSO 1918; retired Indian Army; *b* Eathorpe Hall, Warwick, 1869; *s* of late Colonel Battine, retired, 16th and 17th Lancers; *m* 1899, Mary Annabella, *d* of late Major Priestley, Plas Hên, Carnarvonshire; one *s*. *Educ:* Charterhouse; RMC Sandhurst. Served Waziristan, 1894; Chitral Relief Force, 1895; Tochi Valley, 1897; European War 1914–18, France, Russia, Central Asia; Afghan War, 1919, commanding 21st Cavalry (DSO, Stanislaus, Russia; Officer's Cross, Franz Joseph, Austria); psc; 1st class Interpreter, French, German, Russian. *Address:* Pauntley Place, Redmarley, Gloucestershire. *T:* Newent 21. *Clubs:* Salcombe Yacht; Royal South-Western Yacht, Plymouth.

Died 12 Oct. 1942.

BATTY, James Henly, FRGS; Chairman, Ashanti Goldfield Co. Ltd; Bibiani Gold Mining Co.; Taquah and Abosso Mining Co.; Trust of Insurance Shares Ltd; Director, Atlas Assurance Co.; Consolidated Goldfields of South Africa; *b* 26 April 1868; *s* of James Campbell Batty and Jane Buckland; *m* 1st, Violet, *d* of late Sir George Paget, Cambridge; 2nd, Mary, *widow* of James Birkmyre, Ingmanthorpe Hall, Wetherby, Yorkshire; no *c. Educ:* privately. Spent over twenty years in West Africa; was a member of the Legislative Council on the Gold Coast; Dutch Consul at Elmina; Member on Council National Institute for the Blind. Spends most of his spare time in the work of the blind. *Recreations:* lawn tennis, golf. *Address:* Chorleywood Court, Chorleywood. *T:* Chorleywood 29. *Clubs:* Reform, City of London, Hurlingham.

Died 9 Jan. 1946.

BATTYE, Lt-Col Walter Rothney, DSO 1916; MS, MB, BSc (Lond.), FRCS (Eng.); FRSM; Lt-Col Indian Medical Service (retired); Medical Superintendent, King George V Merchant Seamens' Memorial Hospital, Malta; late Chief MO Central India; Residency Surgeon, Indore; and Superintendent, King Edward Hospital and Medical School; *b* 20 Jan. 1874; 4th *s* of late Major Legh Richmond Battye, 5th Gurkha Rifles, Frontier Force, and Margaret, *e d* of Major-General Augustus Moffat; *m* 1898, Maud St George, 2nd *d* of late Lieut-Col Anthony Oliver Molesworth, RA; two *s* one *d. Educ:* privately; University College, London (Medical Entrance Exhibition, Gold and Silver Medallist); Army Medical School, Netley. BSc (London), 1893, first-class honours in Zoology, University Scholar; MRCS and LRCP (London) and MB, BS (London), 1897; passed out second from Army Medical School, Netley, with Parkes Memorial Medal; Indian Medical Service, 1898. Served with 10th Bengal Lancers, 12th Bengal Cavalry, accompanied 14th Sikhs to China in 1900, Boxer Rebellion; entered Political Employ of Government of India, 1903; British Vice-Consul at Meshed, 1904; HBM's acting Consul-General in Khorassan and Agent of the Government of India, 1906; Residency Surgeon, Udaipur State, Rajputana, 1910; OC 108th Indian Field Ambulance, 1914; SMO Suez Canal Defences Northern Section, 1914; served for three months at Cape Helles with 29th Division, and four and a half months at Anzac, till the evacuation (DSO, despatches four times, Chevalier of the Legion of Honour); special duty in France with the 5th Army (GHQ) 1917; DADMS at GHQ, Baghdad, 1918; Secretary for Health, and Director, Civil Medical Services, Mesopotamia, 1919–20; Commander Order of St John of Jerusalem. *Publications:* Climate and Health of Meshed, Gazetteer of Persia, 1906; Plague in Ajmer-Merwara, 1910; Spinal Anæsthesia, Indian Medical Gazette, 1913; Treatment of Wounded in Field Ambulances in Reports of Anzac Medical Association, 1916. *Recreation:* travel. *Address:* 22 Sandecotes Road, Parkstone, Dorset.

Died 27 April 1943.

BAUDAINS, Captain George La Croix, DSO 1918; MC; *b* St Heliers, Jersey, 21 April 1892; *yr s* of Ph. A. Baudains, Janvrin Road, Jersey. *Educ:* Jersey Modern School. Civil Service, 1908; Army, Aug. 1914–May 1919, 2nd and 9th London Regts (TF) and 9th Royal Fusiliers (DSO, MC, despatches). *Recreations:* Shakespeare and Amateur Swimming Association, Diving Committee; Olympic, International and English Diving Judge, Coach, Lecturer, Writer, etc. *Address:* 11 Cedars Road, Clapham Common, SW4.

Died 13 Oct. 1942.

BAUDRILLART, Henri Marie Alfred; Archevêque Cardinal; Rector of the Catholic Institute of Paris since 1907; Director of the Comité catholique des amitiés françaises à l'étranger; Member of the French Academy; *b* Paris, 6 Jan. 1859. *Educ:* Lycée Louis le Grand; Ecole normale Supérieure. Doctor of letters and theology. *Principal Publications:* Philippe V et la Cour de France (which was awarded the Gobert Prize); La Renaissance et le Protestantisme; Quatre Cents Ans de Concordat; L'enseignement catholique dans la France contemporaine; La Vie de Mgr d'Hulst; La vocation catholique de la France etc. *Address:* 21 rue d'Assas, Paris, 6°.

Died 19 May 1942.

BAVERSTOCK, Rev. Alban Henry; Warden of the Sisters of the Transfiguration, Wingrave, Bucks; *b* Stratford, Essex, 1871; *s* of Edwin Henry Baverstock of the National Debt Office, and Emily Augusta Foster Kirby; unmarried. *Educ:* Merchant Taylors' School; Keble College, Oxford; 2nd Class Classical Honour School; 3rd Class Lit.Hum. Deacon, 1895; Priest, 1896; Assistant Curate at Evesham, 1895–96; St Michael's, Walthamstow, 1897–99; Rector and Vicar of Hinton Martel, Wimborne, 1899–1930; founder of Catholic

Literature Association, 1907, and Secretary till 1919; Founder of the Homes of the Holy Family, 1915; Co-founder, and Warden since foundation, of the Sisters of the Transfiguration, Wingrave, Bucks; Chaplain-General of the Society of Mary, 1935–43; Editor of Ave, 1936–40; President of the Society for Catholic Publications, 1936; President Society for the Promotion of Catholic Unity, since 1947. *Publications:* Priesthood in Liturgy and Life; Benediction and the Bishops; The Priest as Confessor; When should Children be Confirmed? The Supreme Adventure; The Unscathed Crucifix; The English Agricultural Labourer; The Failure of the Church in the Villages; The Compassion of Saint Mary; The Truth about the Prayer Book; Counsels for Confessors; various pamphlets. *Recreation:* bridge. *Address:* 26 Mansfield Road, Reading. *T:* 4360.

Died 25 April 1950.

BAVIN, Hon. Sir Thomas Rainsford, KCMG 1933; KC 1924; BA; LLB; Order of the Spanish Republic, 2nd Class; Justice of Supreme Court, New South Wales, since 1935; *b* Kaiapoi, New Zealand, 5 May 1874; *s* of Rev. Rainsford Bavin and *d* of Rev. Thomas Buddle; *m* Edyth, *d* of Hon. F. E. Winchcombe, MLC (NSW); one *s* three *d*. *Educ:* Auckland Grammar School; Newington College, Sydney; Sydney University. Called to Bar, NSW, 1897; Professor of Law and Modern History, University of Tasmania, 1900; Private Secretary to Sir E. Barton, first Prime Minister of Australia, 1901–04; Secretary and chief Law Officer of Commonwealth, 1907; elected to Parliament, 1917; Lt-Commander, Royal Australian Navy, 1916–18; Attorney-General of NSW, 1922–25; Leader of the Opposition (National Party), State Parliament of NSW, 1925–27; Premier of New South Wales, 1927–30; Treasurer of NSW, 1927–30; Treasurer of NSW, 1927–29; Lecturer of Opposition, NSW, 1930–32. *Publications:* Observations on Federal System of Government; Reports on Food Supplies of Sydney (Royal Commission), 1911–1913; Life of Sir Henry Parkes. *Recreations:* tennis, fly-fishing, music. *Address:* Supreme Court, Sydney, Australia. *Clubs:* Australian, University, Royal Sydney, Golf, Sydney.

Died 30 Aug. 1941.

BAXTER, John Babington Macaulay, PC; KC 1909; DCL, LLD; Chief Justice of New Brunswick since 1935; *b* 16 Feb. 1868; *s* of William S. and Margaret Baxter; *m* 1924, Grace W. Coster; two *s* two *d*. *Educ:* Public Schools, St John. Attorney, 1890; Barrister, 1891; Alderman, St John, 1892–96, 1900–04, 1905–10; Lieutenant-Colonel 3rd New Brunswick Regt Canadian Artillery, 1907–12; Lecturer King's College Law School, St John; Dean Univ. of New Brunswick Law School, since 1938; MPP St John County, 1911–21 and 1925–31; Attorney-General of New Brunswick, 1914–17; leader of NB Opposition, 1921; Premier and Attorney-General, 1925–31; Minister of Customs, Canada, Sept. to Dec. 1921; MP for City and Counties of St John and Albert, 1921–25; Recorder City of St John, NB, 1910–31; Judge of Appeal Division, Supreme Court, New Brunswick 1931–35; Hon. DCL, King's College, Windsor, NS, 1915; Hon. LLD University of New Brunswick, 1926, and University of St Joseph, 1932. *Publications:* Historical Records, NB Reg. Artillery, 1793–1896; Captain Simon Baxter, the first UE Loyalist to arrive in New Brunswick, 1943. *Address:* 34 Dufferin Row, St John, New Brunswick. *Club:* Cliff St John.

Died Dec. 1946.

BAXTER, Thomas Tennant; artist; *b* Paris, 22 Oct. 1894; *s* of Frank Baxter; *m* 1935, Cordelia Marguerite, *d* of Sir Malcolm Stewart, 1st Bart, OBE. *Educ:* Eton. Member New English Art Club. *Recreations:* walking and riding. *Address:* 59 Drayton Gardens, SW10. *Club:* Athenæum.

Died 4 Nov. 1947.

BAYFORD, Major Edmund Heseltine, DSO; late 18th QMO Royal Hussars; *b* 16 March 1873; *s* of late R. A. Bayford, KC; *m* 1911, Muriel (*d* 1929), *o d* of late John Buller-Colthurst. *Educ:* Eton. Entered Army, 1894; served South Africa, 1899–1902 (wounded, despatches twice, Queen's medal 5 clasps, King's medal 2 clasps, DSO); ADC to Governor of Bombay, 1903–05; General Staff, England and France, World War (2 medals, despatches); retired pay, 1922; Founder and Chairman Spotlights Amateur Dramatic Organisation and Companionship. *Club:* Cavalry.

Died 17 Nov. 1942.

BAYLEY, Col Arthur George, CBE 1916; DSO 1919; Librarian at Staff College, Camberley, since Aug. 1939; Lecturer since 1936, Head of Department of Military Studies, since 1940, University of London; *b* 5 July 1878; *s* of Kennett Bayley, Inchicore, Dublin; *m* 1923, Katherine May Frederica, *d* of late Brig.-Gen. F. A. Fortescue, CB, CMG; one *d*. *Educ:* Shrewsbury; Sandhurst. Gazetted to Oxfordshire and Buckinghamshire Light Infantry, 1898; served with regiment in South African War, 1899–1902; served on General Staff, World War, 1914–18; Chief Instructor Senior Officers School, Woking, 1919–23; commanded 43rd Light Infantry, 1923–27; General Staff Officer, 1st Grade, Peshawar District, 1927–30; AA and QMG 3rd Division, 1931–35; retired, 1935. *Address:* Staff College, Camberley, Surrey.

Died 1 March 1949.

BAYLIFFE, Col Alfred Danvers, CMG 1915; TD; DL; late commanding The Rangers, 12th London Regt (TA); *b* 20 June 1873; *m* 1903, Lucy Mildred, *d* of J. Allen Brown, FRGS. *Educ:* Haileybury. Served European War, 1914–19 (CMG, Military Order of Savoy, despatches twice). *Address:* 7 Kent Gardens, Ealing, W. *Club:* Junior Army and Navy.

Died 8 Oct. 1942.

BAYLY, Hugh Wansey, MC, MA; MRCS, LRCP; retired; *b* 10 May 1873; *s* of late Alfred Bayly, Warminster; *m* 1st, 1910, Edith Margery, *o d* of late Rodolph Fane de Salis; one *d*; 2nd, 1918, Beatrice Sybil, *o d* of A. C. H. Pendlebury; one *d*; 3rd, 1942, Edith Marian, *e d* of late Neale Edwards. *Educ:* Clare College, Cambridge; St George's Hospital, London. Late trooper Imperial Yeomanry and Civil Surgeon, S African War, 1900–01 (Queen's Medal four clasps); hospital appointments and GP, Hoxton, 1902–05; Surgeon, MN, 1906 (thanks of Army Council for successful first operation at sea perf. duodenal ulcer); Organiser and Medical Officer in charge Venereal Dept, St George's Hospital; Pathologist to the London Lock Hospitals; Clinical Pathologist to the National Hospital for Paralysed, 1907–14; Organiser of a London Troop for and Surgeon to the Enniskillen Horse (Ulster Volunteer Force), April to Aug. 1914; late Surgeon RN (temp.), (1914–15 Star); Capt. (acting Lt-Col) RAMC (TF), 1915–19; attached 1st Scots Guards, RFA (twice wounded); 143 Harley Street W, 1919–39; joint founder with late Lord Willoughby de Broke (1919) of Society for Prevention of Venereal Disease; Hon. Secretary, 1919–28; VP, 1928–43; Independent candidate Sutton Division, Plymouth, General Election, 1922; witness before Lord Trevethin's Committee on Prevention of Venereal Disease, 1922; Joint Hon. Secretary to the Joint Committee of Ex-Servicemen; Pres. Ex-Service Men's National Movement, 1923–24; Pres. Workers' Liberty and Employment League, 1924–25; member of Lord Queensborough's Deputation to Home Secretary on amendment of Naturalisation of Aliens Act, 1925; Venereal Specialist, Royal Herbert Hospital, Woolwich, 1933–34; Surgeon to New Zealand Shipping Company, 1937–39; Surgeon, HMT Ettrick, 1939–40 (invalided, 1940) (1939–45 Star). Donor of small collection of English School oil paintings to the Art Gallery, Auckland, NZ, 1940. *Publications:* The Clinical Pathology of Syphilis and Parasyphilis, 1912; Venereal

Disease, its Prevention, Symptoms and Treatment, 1920, 5th rev. ed., 1934; What we Drink (Editor and Contributor), 1930; Triple Challenge (Memoirs), 1934; Air Challenge and the Locusts, 1939; weekly war commentary 'Norfolk Chronicle,' 1941. *Address:* Clevency Cottage, Great Snoring, Fakenham, Norfolk. *T:* Walsingham 227.

Died 6 Feb. 1946.

BAYNE, Charles Gerwien, CSI 1901; Indian Civil Service; retired 1906; *b* 5 Dec. 1860; *s* of late Dr Peter Bayne, LLD; *m* 1890, Alice Augusta (*d* 1941), *d* of late Rev. G. C. Hodgkinson; one *s* two *d*. *Educ:* Uppingham; University College, Oxford. Served in various capacities in the Indian Civil Service in Burma, 1880–1906. *Address:* 14 Foxgrove Road, Beckenham, Kent.

Died 6 Dec. 1947.

BAYNE, Ven. Percy Matheson, MA; Archdeacon Emeritus since 1938; *b* South Weald, nr Brentwood, Essex, 11 June 1865; 2nd *surv. s* of late Rev. George Smith Bayne, MA, Vicar of Bishop Stortford, Herts; *m* 1891, Alice Susannah, *d* of late George Charles Rogers, formerly of Great Parndon, Essex; no *c*. *Educ:* Highgate School (Foundation Scholar); Hertford College, Oxford (Scholar). 1st Class Moderations (Classics), 1886; 3rd Class Lit. Hum., 1888. Private tutor, 1888–89; Deacon, 1889; Priest 1890; held curacies at St Michael and All Angels, Walthamstow, and Holy Trinity, Barking Road, Canning Town; in charge of St Augustine's Mission, Leytonstone; Rector of Little Ilford, 1894–1913; Surrogate, 1906–13; Rural Dean of Barking, 1912–13; Hon. Canon of St Albans, 1913; of Chelmsford, 1914–22; Hon. Chaplain to Bishop of Chelmsford, 1917–22; Clerical Secretary of the London-over-the-Border Church Fund, late Bishop of St Albans Fund, 1913–22; Clerical Secretary of the Diocesan Funds, 1922–30; Archdeacon of Southend, 1922–37. *Address:* 107 St Andrew's Road, Ilford, Essex.

Died 11 Oct. 1942.

BAYNES, Rt Rev. Arthur Hamilton, DD (Oxon); DD (St Andrews); *b* 1854; *s* of late Rev. Joseph Ash Baynes; *m* 1st, 1894, Cecilia (*d* 1919), *d* of late Canon Crompton of Pinetown, Natal; three *s* two *d*; 2nd, 1923, Mary Constance, *d* of G. H. Burnett, Hampstead. *Educ:* Balliol and Oriel Colleges, Oxford; 1st class Lit. Hum.; MA 1882. Ordained, 1881; Vicar St James, Nottingham, 1884–88; domestic chaplain to Archbishop of Canterbury, 1888–92; Six-Preacher in Canterbury Cathedral, 1891–93; Vicar Christ Church, Greenwich, 1892–93; Bishop of Natal, 1893–1901; Vicar of St Mary's, Nottingham, 1901–13; Assistant Bishop in Diocese of Southwell, 1901–13; Hon. Canon of Southwell, 1905–13; Assistant Bishop in Diocese of Birmingham, Provost and Hon. Canon of Birmingham, 1913–37; Proctor in Convocation and Proprolocutor; Hon. Chaplain to S Notts Hussars, IY; Hon. Col S Africa Medal; TD; Hon. Chaplain to High Sheriff of Somerset, 1905. *Publications:* My Diocese during the War, 1900; S Africa (Handbook of Church Expansion), 1908; Two Centuries of Church Life, 1915. *Address:* Little Mead, Goring-on-Thames.

Died 30 June 1942.

BAYNES, Helton Godwin, BA, MB, BC Cantab; MRCS, LRCP; consulting physician; *b* Hampstead, 26 June 1882; *s* of late Helton Arnold Baynes and Ellen Mary Foster; *m* 1st, 1913; 2nd, 1922; 3rd, 1926; 4th, 1931, Agnes Sarah, *d* of Frederick P. Leay; three *s* three *d*. *Educ:* Trinity Coll., Cambridge. Rowed in Cambridge boat against Harvard, 1906, also in Varsity crew against Oxford, 1907; House Physician, St Bartholomew's Hospital, 1909–10; Surgeon i/c Red Crescent Mission to Turkey in Balkan War, 1911–12; Captain RAMC; War Service in France, Mesopotamia, and Persia; Maudesley Hospital Resident Staff, 1919; Assistant to Dr C. G. Jung of Zürich, 1919–22; organised Dr Jung's Expedition to East Africa, 1925–26, for purposes of psychological research among Masai tribes of Mount Elgon, Kenya; specialist in Jung's system of Analytical Psychology. *Publications:* Mythology of the Soul, 1939; Germany Possessed, 1941; editor and translator Jung's Psychological Types, 1921, Jung's Contributions to Analytical Psychology and Two Essays on Analytical Psychology. *Recreations:* golf, tennis. *Address:* 11 Mansfield Street, W1; Reed House, Old Avenue, W Byfleet, Surrey. *T:* Langham 4171. *Club:* Leander.

Died 6 Sept. 1943.

BAZETT, Henry Cuthbert, CBE 1946; MC; MD (Oxon), DSc (West Ontario), MA (Oxon), FRCS (Eng.); Professor Physiology Medical School, University of Pennsylvania, Philadelphia, since 1921; *b* 25 June 1885; *s* of Henry Bazett, MA (Oxon), MRCS, LRCP, and Eliza Ann Cruickshank; *m* 1917, Dorothy Rufford Livesey; one *s* one *d*. *Educ:* Dover College; Wadham College, Oxford; St Thomas's Hospital, London. Demonstrator Physiology St Thomas's Hospital, 1910–11; Graduate work Harvard Med. School, 1912–13; Radcliffe Travelling Fellow, Oxford, 1912–15; Fellow Magdalen College, Oxford, 1912–20. Lt-Capt.-Major, Special Reserve RAMC 1914–35; France, RAMC Aug. 1914–Dec. 1918 (despatches thrice, MC, OBE). Demonstrator Pathology, Oxford, 1913–16; Christopher Welch Lecturer in Clinical Physiol., Oxford, 1919–21; Visiting Prof. of Med. Research, Univ. of Toronto (in charge of Aviation Medical Research after death of Sir Frederick Banting), 1941–43 (on leave of absence from Univ. of Penn.); Member of Exec. Comm. of Aviation, Med. Res., Canada, 1941–45; Member of Sub-Comm. on Clothing of Amer. Committee Av. Med., 1943–45; Consultant to OQMG Amer. Army, Washington, 1943–44; working for Canadians at RAE, Farnborough, 1943; temporary member of staff of Brit. MRC working for Admiralty and visiting India, 1944; Amer. Physiological Soc. (Councillor 1946–50, President 1950–51). *Publications:* Circulation section in Macleod's Physiology in Modern Medicine, 8th and 9th editions; numerous publications in American and English physiological literature particularly on circulation and temperature control. *Recreations:* travel, model building. *Address:* Medical School, Univ. of Pennsylvania, Philadelphia, USA; 629 Haydock Lane, Haverford, Pa, USA. *T:* Ardmore 2036 J. Pennsylvania. *Club:* British Officers' (Philadelphia).

Died 12 July 1950.

BEACH, Rex; author; *b* 1 Sept. 1877; *s* of Henry Walter Beach and Eva Eunice Canfield; *m* 1907, Edith Crater (*d* 1947). *Educ:* Chicago Coll. of Law; Rollins Coll., Winter Park, Fla; Kent College of Law, Chicago. President, Authors' League of America, 1917–21. *Publications:* Pardners, 1905; The Spoilers, 1906; The Barrier, 1907; The Silver Horde, 1909; Going Some, 1910; The Ne'er-do-Well, 1911; The Net, 1912; The Iron Trail, 1913; The Auction Block, 1914; Heart of the Sunset, 1915; Rainbow's End, 1916; The Crimson Gardenia, 1916; Laughing Bill Hyde, 1917; The Winds of Chance, 1918; Oh, Shoot, 1921; Flowing Gold, 1922; Big Brother, 1923; The Goose Woman, 1925; Padlocked, 1926; The Mating Call, 1927; Don Careless, 1928; Son of the Gods, 1929; Money Mad, 1931; Beyond Control, 1932; Masked Women, 1933; Wild Pastures, 1934; Jungle Gold, 1935; Men of the Outer Islands, 1932; Valley of Thunder, 1939; Personal Exposures, 1941; The World in His Arms, 1945. *Plays:* Going Some (with Paul Armstrong); The Spoilers (with James McArthur). *Address:* Sebring, Florida. *Clubs:* Dutch Treat, Coffee House, St Andrews Golf, Explorers (New York).

Died 7 Dec. 1949.

BEACH, Col Thomas Boswall, CMG 1916; CBE 1919; AMS (RP); *b* 28 May 1866; *s* of late Rev. Canon Beach, MA, CF. *Educ:* Bloxham; King's College, London. House Physician, King's College, Hospital, 1889; entered AMS, 1891; Lt-Col 1912; Col 1915;

served S Africa, 1899–1902 (despatches, Queen's medal 7 clasps, King's medal 2 clasps; promoted Major); European War, 1914–19; ADMS Alexandria, Egypt (CMG, despatches, CBE). *Recreations:* golf, shooting. *Address:* 181 King's Road, Reading.

Died 3 April 1941.

BEADLE, James Prinsep Barnes; painter of military and other subjects; *b* Calcutta, 22 Sept. 1863; *s* of Major-General James Pattle Beadle, RE; *m* 1891, Anna M. G., *d* of late J. A. M. Cope of Pembridge Square and Drummilly, Co. Armagh. *Educ:* private schools. Entered studio of Sir Edgar Boehm at age of 13, held scholarship under Legros at the Slade School for 3 years, afterwards studied under Cabanel at the Ecole des Beaux-Arts, Paris, and finally under G. F. Watts in London. Exhibited RA regularly since 1884, also at the New and other Galleries; bronze medal, Paris International Exhibition 1899, for his first serious military picture, Her Majesty's Life Guards. War Memorial pictures for the United Service Club, etc. *Address:* 17b Eldon Road, Kensington, W8.

Died 13 Aug. 1947.

BEADNELL, Surg. Rear-Adm. Charles Marsh, CB 1924; Hon. Physician to the King, 1925; *b* Rawalpindi, India, 17 Feb. 1872; *e s* of late Major C. E. Beadnell, RA, JP, Montgomeryshire; *m* Ellen Louisa, *d* of George Bailey, Gloucester. *Educ:* Cheltenham College; Guy's Hospital. While surgeon of HMS Powerful, 1898–1900, served in American-Filipino war and was landed in action with American troops; served in Naval Brigade, S Africa (despatches three times, awarded eight years special promotion to staff surgeon); served in HMS Renown when conveying the King and Queen of Spain to and from England in 1907; Medical Officer of HMS King Alfred, flagship, China; served as Fleet Surgeon of HMS Shannon, flagship, second Cruiser Squadron, European War, 1914–17; Retired List. 1926; late Naval member of the Medical Consultative Board, Admiralty; Pres. Rationalist Press Assoc., London; MRCS Eng.; LRCP Lond.; LSA Lond.; FZS, FBAS. *Publications:* Physical Measurements of the Sailor; Decline of Scurvy Afloat; Atavistic Mental States; Evolution and Dreams; Circumcision and Clitoridectomy in E Africa; Subtlety in Nature and War; Environmental Factors Afloat; Disposal of Wounded in Naval Actions; Mind and Matter; Evolution and Speech; The Dynamics of Small-bore Projectiles; Bullets in War and Sport; Picture Book of Evolution; Dictionary of Scientific Terms; Encyclopædic Dictionary of Science and War; Origin of the Kiss. *Address:* c/o Nat. Prov. Bank Egham, Surrey.

Died 27 Sept. 1947.

BEADNELL, Hugh John Llewellyn, FGS, FRGS; Major (re-employed, 1940–43); *b* 14 Oct. 1874; 2nd *s* of late Major C. E. Beadnell, RA; *m* 1904, May Grace Thomson (*d* 1942), *g d* of Very Rev. W. R. Pirie, DD, Principal of Aberdeen University; one *d. Educ:* Cheltenham College; King's College, London; Royal School of Mines. Geological Survey of Egypt, 1896–1906; mapped large areas of Nile Valley and Libyan Desert; discovered new extinct fauna in the Fayum desert, including Arsinoitherium and the ancestors of the modern elephants (Moeritherium and Palæomastodon); reclaimed extensive tracts of desert in the Kharga depression by sinking artesian bores, 1906–10; ranching in Canada, 1912–15; enlisted Artists Rifles, 1916; served with EEF 1916–19, Major, Acting Lt-Col, on demobilisation (despatches, Order of the Nile); surveyed Red Sea Coast and Central Sinai for Whitehall Petroleum Co. and Egyptian Government, 1921–25; mapping and sinking deep wells (Bir Sahra and Bir Messaha) in SW Libyan Desert between Darb el Arbain and Oweinat, 1927–29; Resident Engineer on the Qattara Depression hydro-electric project of Egyptian Government, 1930–32; received awards from Geological and Royal Geographical Societies for work in the Egyptian deserts. *Publications:* An Egyptian Oasis,

1910; Wilderness of Sinai, 1926; scientific publications on the sand-dunes, water-supply and geology of the Egyptian deserts and Oases. *Recreations:* shooting, fishing, gemmology. *Address:* BM/GEMS, London, WC1.

Died 2 Jan. 1944.

BEADON, Col Roger Hammet, CBE 1919; late RASC; *b* 16 Jan. 1887; *e surv. s* of late Lt-Col J. Hammet Beadon of Blackerton, East Anstey, Devon; *m* 1913, Eleonora, *y d* of John Lowry Crumley of Ardara, County Donegal; no *c. Educ:* Clifton College. Entered Army Service Corps from Devon Militia, 1907; Captain, 1914; Bt Major, 1917; Bt Lt-Colonel, 1918; served European War in Africa, France, and Italy, at War Office and Supreme War Council, Versailles; subsequently on the British Delegation to the Peace Conference, Paris (CBE, Commander of the Crown of Italy, Officer of the Legion of Honour, Officer of the Order of Leopold I, Distinguished Service medal of the United States, Iraq order of El Rafidain); graduated at the Staff College, 1922; employed under Colonial Office in Iraq, 1925–28; retired, ill health, 1929. *Publications:* History of the Transport and Supply Services of the British Army, vol. II; Some Memoirs of the Peace Conference; Robert Blake; various articles in reviews and Encyclopædia Britannica, etc. *Address:* Gotton House, Taunton. *Club:* Junior United Service.

Died 14 Dec. 1945.

BEAL, Rev. T. Gilbert; *b* 26 July 1865; *e s* of Rev. S. Beal, DCL the Oriental Scholar; *m* Marcia Maziere Uniacke, 3rd *d* of Very Rev. the Dean of Qu'appelle; two *d. Educ:* S Edwards, Oxford; S Augustine's College, Canterbury. Curate Moosomin, NW Canada, 1887–90; Rector of Grenfell, Sask, Canada, 1890–1909; Rural Dean of Eastern Assiniboia, 1898–1909; Senior Canon S Peter's Cathedral, Qu'appelle; Member of Provincial Synod of Rupertsland and General Synod of Canada; Chaplain 16th Light Horse, 1907–10; Deputation for SPG, 1909–10; Commissary to the Bishop of Edmonton, 1914–30; organising secretary Archbishops' Western Canada Fund, 1910–20; Rector of Sandhurst, with Newenden, Kent, 1920–44; Hon. DD Regina, Canada, 1939. *Address:* c/o Mall's Bank, Black Boys, Sussex.

Died 28 July 1948.

BEALL, Lt-Col Edward Metcalfe, CMG 1918; DSO 1915; late 4th Bn The King's Regt (Liverpool); *b* 1877. *Educ:* Beaumont. Served South Africa, 1900–02; European War, 1914–18 (DSO, CMG, despatches five times). *Club:* Junior United Service.

Died 13 March 1950.

BEAMAN, Brevet Lt-Col Ardern Arthur Hulme, DSO 1916; JP; late Royal Gloucestershire Hussars Yeomanry; *b* 18 Aug. 1886; *o s* of Sir Frank Beaman; *m* 1st, 1920, Diana Vernon Constance (*d* 1945), *o d* of Sir William Guise, 5th Bt, Elmore Court, Glos; two *s*; 2nd, 1948, Madeleine, *widow* of F. R. Meath-Baker, Hasfield Court, Glos. *Educ:* Rugby; Sandhurst. S Wales Borderers, 1905; 1st Lancers, 1907; ADC to GOC Derajat, 1910–11; PA to Commissioner, Sind, 1911; Adjutant, 1912; Zakka Khel Expedition, 1908; European War, 1914–18; Mohmand Frontier, 1915; France, 1917–19 (wounded, despatches, Croix de Guerre); retired, 1924. Hon. Treasurer Glos British Legion, 1932–38; County Commissioner Boy Scouts for Glos, 1940–47; High Sheriff of Gloucestershire, 1948–49; Member of Glos Agricultural Exec. Cttee. *Publications:* Stories of the Idler; Travels without Baedeker; The Squadron; At Government House. *Recreations:* cricket, tennis, hunting. *Address:* Hasfield Court, Glos. *Club:* Cavalry.

Died 26 Aug. 1950.

BEAMISH, Wing-Comdr (Acting Gp-Captain) Francis Victor, DSO 1940; DFC 1940; AFC 1938; Royal Air Force; *b* 27 Sept. 1903; *s* of late Francis George Beamish, Dunmanway, Co. Cork, and Mary

Elizabeth Beamish, Coleraine, Co. Derry; unmarried. *Educ:* Coleraine; RAF College, Cranwell. Commissioned in RAF 1923, since served at Home, in Overseas Commands, and also two years lent to the Royal Canadian Air Force; Graduate of RAF Staff College; Commanded Fighter Squadrons and a Fighter Station, War of 1939– (DSO and Bar, DFC); played Rugby for Harlequins, Leicester, Hants, Royal Air Force and Irish Trials for several years. *Recreation:* all sports. *Address:* Royal Air Force, North Weald, Epping, Essex; Kildollagh House, Coleraine, Co. Derry, Northern Ireland. *Club:* Royal Air Force.

Died 28 March 1942.

BEAN, William Jackson, CVO 1936; ISO 1924; late Curator, Royal Botanic Gardens, Kew; *b* Leavening, near Malton, York, 26 May 1863; *s* of George and Lydia Bean; *m* 1901, Frances Ada, *d* of late Charles Ewart; one *s* one *d*. *Educ:* Holgate School, York. Entered Kew, 1883; retired, 1929; Victoria Medal of Honour in Horticulture, 1917; Veitch Memorial Medal, 1922. *Publications:* Royal Botanic Gardens, Kew, an historical and descriptive account, 1908; Trees and Shrubs hardy in the British Isles, 1914; Shrubs for Amateurs, 1924; Ornamental Trees for Amateurs, 1926; Wall Shrubs and Hardy Climbers, 1939. *Recreation:* golf. *Address:* 2 Mortlake Road, Kew. *T:* Richmond 1394. *Club:* Royal Mid Surrey Golf.

Died 19 April 1947.

BEARD, Charles A.; retired; *b* 27 Nov. 1874; *s* of William H. and Mary Payne Beard; *m* 1900, Mary Ritter; one *s* one *d*. *Educ:* De Pauw University; Oxford; Cornell University; Columbia University. Instructor, Associate Professor, and Professor, Columbia University, 1904–17; Adviser of Viscount Goto, Japanese Minister of Home Affairs, 1923; President American Political Science Association, 1926; President American Historical Association, 1933. *Publications:* American Government and Politics; American City Government; Economic Interpretation of the Constitution; Economic Origins of Jeffersonian Democracy; Administration and Politics of Tokyo; Rise of American Civilization (with wife); The Idea of National Interest; The Open Door at Home, 1934; The Discussion of Human Affairs, 1936; America in Midpassage (with wife), 1939. *Recreation:* dairy-farming in Connecticut. *Address:* New Milford, Conn, USA.

Died 1 Sept. 1948.

BEARD, John, CBE 1938; Agricultural Section, Transport and General Workers' Union; Member Wheat Commission, Agricultural Wages Board; Ex-President General Council Trades Union Congress; *b* Ellerdine Heath, Wellington, Salop, 1871. *Educ:* Primitive Methodist Elementary School, Ellerdine Heath. Farm worker; Builders' labourer; Coalminer; Engineering shop labourer; Insurance Agent. *Recreations:* various, none particularly. *Address:* 27 Wyndale Avenue, Kingsbury, NW9.

Died 25 Sept. 1950.

BEARN, Edward Gordon, CB 1942; CBE 1928; Controller of Health Insurance and Pensions, and Under-Secretary Ministry of Health since 1941; *b* 1887; *s* of late James Bearn, Withington, Manchester; *m*; two *s* one *d*. *Educ:* Manchester Grammar School; Manchester University, MA 1908; Shuttleworth Scholarship (Economics) and Dauntesey Legal Scholarship. Entered Civil Service, 1910. *Address:* 29 Cornwall Road, Cheam, Surrey. *T:* Vigilant 0647. *Club:* Reform.

Died 25 July 1945.

BEARSTED, 2nd Viscount *cr* 1925, of Maidstone; **Walter Horace Samuel,** MC; Baron *cr* 1921; Bt *cr* 1903; Director Lloyds Bank, Ltd, Alliance Assur. Co; *b* 13 March 1882; *o s* of 1st Viscount and Fanny Elizabeth (*d* 1927), *o d* of late Benjamin Benjamin; *S* father, 1927; *m* 1908, Dorothea, *e d* of late E. Montefiore Micholls;

three *s. Educ:* Eton; New College, Oxford. Formerly Captain, West Kent (QO) Yeomanry; served European War, 1914–18 (MC, despatches); acting Colonel General List while specially employed, 1939–43; Trustee, Tate Gallery, 1938–42; Trustee of National Gallery, 1936–43, Chairman, 1942–43 and Trustee from 1946. Trustee and Chairman of Whitechapel Art Gallery since 1944. *Heir: s* Major Hon. Marcus Richard Samuel, Warwickshire Yeomanry [*b* 1909; *m* 1947, Elizabeth Heather, *e d* of G. Firmston-Williams; one *d*]. *Address:* H5/6 Albany, Piccadilly, W1. *T:* Regent 5317; Upton House, Banbury. *T:* Edgehill 42; Phones, Newtonmore, Invernesshire; La Séréna, St Jean-Cap-Ferrat, AM. *Clubs:* Carlton, White's, Buck's, Beefsteak.

Died 8 Nov. 1948.

BEASLEY, Rt. Hon. John Albert; PC 1946; High Commissioner for Australia in London since 1946; *b* Werribee, Victoria, 9 Nov. 1895; *s* of John Beasley; *m* 1927, Alma, *d* of Alexander Creighton; two *s* two *d*. Member House of Representatives for West Sydney, 1928–46; Assistant Minister for Industry and External Affairs in Scullin Govt 1929–31; Leader NSW Labour Party, House of Representatives, 1931–36; Leader Non-Communist Labour Party in Federal Parliament, 1940–41; Minister of Supply and Shipping, 1941–45; Vice-Pres. Executive Council, Feb.–July 1945; Minister of Defence, 1945–46; Resident Minister in London Jan.–Aug., 1946. *Address:* Australia House, Strand, WC2.

Died 2 Sept. 1949.

BEATON, Lt-Col Angus John, CMG 1918; MInstCE, VD, FSA Scot; *b* 1858; *e s* of John Beaton or Bethune, Bayfield, Ross-shire; *m* 1908, Florence, *d* of late Charles Bredell, Barberton, Transvaal; two *s* one *d*. *Educ:* Munlochy Public School; Inverness Royal Academy; Owen's College, Manchester. Articled to James Fraser, MInstCE, consulting engineer, Inverness; 18 years on Engineers Staff London and North-Western Railway; final position Resident Engineer New Works; 18 years South African Government Railways; Assistant Engineer-in-Chief, 1910–19; acting Engineer-in-Chief for three separate periods; served in Anglo-Boer War as Captain; in German South West Campaign as Major in Engineer Corps (CMG, despatches twice); East African Campaign with rank of Lieut-Colonel. *Publications:* History of Highlands of Scotland; several Brochures on Railway Engineering Subjects; History of Railway Construction, German SW African Campaign. *Recreations:* golf, shooting. *Clubs:* Rand, Johannesburg.

Died 29 Sept. 1945.

BEATTIE, Francis; MP (C) Cathcart Division of Glasgow since 1942; DL and JP, Glasgow; *b* 26 Oct. 1885; *e s* of late William Beattie, JP, Dineiddwg, Stirlingshire; *m* 1922, Sarah Edith, *d* of late Henry Lewis-Thomas, London; no *c*. *Educ:* Whitehill School, Glasgow; Blairlodge, Stirlingshire; Glasgow University. Chairman of William Beattie Limited and various other Bread Bakeries in Scotland; Deputy Director of Emergency Bread Supplies, and Trade Adviser on Bread Supplies for Scotland, Ministry of Food to 1942; Member of Sea-Fish Commission, 1933–36; of Market Supply Committee (Agricultural Marketing Act, 1933), 1937–39, and other Government Committees; Committee of Enquiry on Rating and Valuation in Scotland, 1943. Deacon Convener of the Trades of Glasgow, 1933–35; Freeman and Liveryman of City of London, a Governor of Royal Technical College, Glasgow; Member Board of Management of Western Infirmary, Glasgow; General Commissioner of Income Tax for Lower Ward of Lanark; Trustee Savings Bank of Glasgow; Director Merchants' House, Glasgow; Member Exec. Committee of Scottish Development Council; Member Territorial Army and Air Force Assoc., Glasgow; Member Board of Trade Local Price-Regulation Committee for the South-Western District of Scotland. Served overseas, 1914–18, with 9th Bn HLI (T) Glasgow Highlanders (Brevet Major, despatches).

Recreations: golf, cricket, gardening. *Address:* Auchans, Dundonald, Ayrshire; 5 Crown Terrace, Glasgow, W2. *Clubs:* Carlton, Caledonian; Western, New, Art, Conservative, Glasgow.

Died 28 Dec. 1945.

BEATTIE, Sir (John) Carruthers, Kt 1920; FRSE; DSc; LLD (Edin., Capetown, and Wits.); *b* Dumfriesshire, 21 Nov. 1866; *m* 1898, Elizabeth, 3rd *d* of W. Paton, Scarborough; two *d. Educ:* Edinburgh (1851 Science Research Scholar, Vans Dunlop Scholar, Physics); Munich; Berlin; Vienna; Glasgow. Medallist of South African Association for Advancement of Science, 1910. President South African Philosophical Society, 1905–06; crossed Africa in 1909 from Capetown to Cairo on a magnetic survey in conjunction with Professor J. T. Morrison; President Section A South African Association for Advancement of Science, 1910; Hon. General Secretary Royal Society of South Africa, 1912; Member University Statutes Commission, 1916; Member of the Scientific and Industrial Research Committee, 1917; Member Industries and Science Board, 1920; Chairman Survey Commission, 1921; Member Mining Industry Board, 1923; President South African Association for the Advancement of Science, 1928; Principal South African College, 1917; Prof. of Physics, South African College, Capetown, 1897–1918; Vice-Chancellor and Principal, University of Capetown, 1918–37. Chairman South African National Gallery. *Publications:* Report of a Magnetic Survey of South Africa, 1909; various papers in physical periodicals. *Clubs:* Civil Service, Capetown.

Died 10 Sept. 1946.

BEATTIE, Hon. Col Rev. William, CMG 1916; VD; DD; ex-Director of Chaplain Services, Canada; *b* 11 April 1873; *s* of late William and Georgina Beattie, Palmerston, Ontario; *m* 1905, Alice Mabel Heath, *e d* of late Robert Heath, JP, of Biddulph Grange, Congleton, Cheshire; three *s* one *d. Educ:* Toronto University; Knox College, Toronto; UF Coll., Glasgow. Lt-Col 1916; Col 1918; retired. *Address:* 232 Central Avenue, London, Ontario, Canada.

Died 19 Aug. 1943.

BEATTY, Sir Edward Wentworth, GBE 1935; KC, LLD; DCL; Chairman, Canadian Pacific Railway, since 1924; Chancellor, McGill University, since 1921; *b* Thorold, Ontario, Oct. 1877; *s* of late Henry Beatty. *Educ:* Toronto Univ. Called to Bar, 1901; joined legal branch of CPR, 1901; Vice-President, 1914; Vice-Chairman, Canadian Pacific Steamships Ltd; Chairman, Consolidated Mining and Smelting Co.; and West Kootenay Power and Light Co.; Director, Bank of Montreal; Royal Trust Co.; Royal Exchange Assurance Co.; Sun Life Assurance Co. of Canada; Minneapolis St Paul and SS Marie Railway; New Brunswick Railway Co.; Canadian Industries, Ltd and Canadian Investment Fund; Henry Gardner Company; Amalgamated Metal; etc. President, Seigniory Club Community Association and Boy Scouts' Association of Canada; President, Canadian Airways; Vice-President and Director Toronto, Hamilton and Buffalo Railway Co.; President and Trustee, Royal Victoria Hospital; Hon. Bencher Middle Temple, 1935; KGStJ 1934; Knight Commander, First Class, Order of St Olaf, Norway, 1924. *Address:* Canadian Pacific Railway Offices, Montreal, Canada; 1266 Pine Avenue West, Montreal. *Clubs:* Marlborough, Mount Royal, St James, University, St George's, Montreal; York, Toronto; Rideau, Ottawa; Century Association, New York.

Died 24 March 1943.

BEATTY, James, MA, MD (Dub.); MB (Lond.); MRCP (Lond.); DPH (RCPSI); Specialist in Dermatology; Consulting Dermatologist Royal Infirmary, Cardiff; *b* 7 July 1870; *s* of James Beatty, Ballymena, Co. Antrim; *m* 1904, Ralphine Jessop, *o c* of late William Saurin, Teignmouth, *g d* of late Lieut-Col Saurin, 31st Regt

Bengal Native Infantry and *g g d* of late Rt Rev. James Saurin, DD, Lord Bishop of Dromore; no *c. Educ:* Coleraine; Trinity College, Dublin (Scholar in Classics, Senior Moderator in History etc. [large Gold Medal], Medical Scholarships, and Travelling Prize); Gold Medallist and Honours, University of London. Assistant Physician and Pathologist Dr Stevens Hospital, Dublin, 1898–1900; Demonstrator in Anatomy, Trinity College, Dublin, 1896–1900; Assistant to Medical Officer of Health, Manchester, 1901–02; Medical Officer of Health, Northampton, 1903–07; Practice in Northampton, 1908–15; Temp. Capt. RAMC, 1915–19; Lecturer in Chemical Physiology, Medical School, Cardiff, 1918–19; Physician Specialist, Ministry of Pensions, 1921–28; Assistant Lecturer in Pharmacology, 1921–35, and Lecturer in Dermatology, Welsh National School of Medicine, 1922–37; Dermatologist, Royal Infirmary, Cardiff, 1922–37; Dermatologist, General Hospital, Weston-super-Mare, 1933–42. *Publications:* Method of Enzyme Action, 1917; Reports on the Health of Northampton, 1903–1907, various papers on Public Health subjects, various papers on Dermatological subjects from 1926. *Recreation:* motoring. *Address:* 84 Cathedral Road, Cardiff. *T:* Cardiff 5282. *Club:* Fortnightly (Cardiff).

Died 16 Oct. 1947.

BEATTY, Wing-Comdr William Dawson, CBE 1919; OBE 1919; AFC; late RAF; Aviation Department, Shell Co. of Egypt, Ltd; *b* 1884; *s* of Thomas Beatty late PWD, Bengal; *m* 1932, Elsie Mary Hutcheson. *Educ:* RMA, Woolwich. RE 1901; RFC 1912; RAF, retd 1919. Was Deputy Controller of Information and Planning, Air Ministry; served European War, 1914–19 (despatches, AFC, OBE, CBE). *Recreations:* squash racquets, lawn tennis. *Address:* PO Box 228, Cairo, Egypt. *Clubs:* Royal Air Force, London Rowing.

Died 18 May 1941.

BEAUBIEN, Hon. Charles Philippe; KC 1909; BA, LLL; Senator for Canada since 1915; *b* Montreal, Quebec, 10 May 1870; *s* of Hon. Louis Beaubien, French Canadian, and Lauretta Stuart, Scotch; *m* 1899, Margaret Rosemary, *d* of N. J. Power, of San Diego, Calif; one *s* two *d. Educ:* St Mary's College; Laval University. To Bar, 1894; Pres. of the Canadian Section of the Inter-Parliamentary Union in 1922; delegate to Conferences of the Inter-Parliamentary Union held at Geneva in 1919 and in Vienna in 1922; represented Canada on Special Missions to France in 1919, 1920, 1922, and 1923; and negotiated for the Canadian Government the Franco-Canadian Trade Treaty of 1921; was Canadian delegate to the League of Nations in Geneva in 1931 and to the Pan-American Postal Congress held in Madrid in 1931; was delegate to the Empire Parliamentary Association Conference held in Bermuda in 1932; President of Canadian Delegation to France attending celebrations of the Jacques Cartier Celebrations, 1934; Director of the following companies: Banque Canadienne Nationale, Canadian Car and Foundry Co. Ltd, Dominion Steel and Coal Co., Credit Foncier Franco Canadien, Beaubien Ltd, Canada Fire Insurance Co., British American Oil Co. *Recreations:* tennis, golf. *Address:* 84 Notre Dame Street, West Montreal; 436 St Catherine Road, Outremont, PQ, Canada. *T:* Calumet 6504, Lancaster 5790. *Clubs:* Rideau (Ottawa); Montreal (Montreal); Laval-sur-le-Lac; Automobile, Union Interallié (Paris).

Died 17 Jan. 1949.

BEAUCHAMP, Col Sir Frank, 1st Bt *cr* 1918; CBE 1919, DL, JP Somerset; *b* 6 Oct. 1866; *s* of late W. Beauchamp of Norton Hall, nr Bath; *m* 1897, Mabel Constance, *e d* of James Norman Bannon, County of Kent; two *s* two *d. Educ:* privately. For eighteen years an officer in the Somerset Volunteer and Territorial Forces, retiring with hon. rank of Major; joined the Army, May 1915; retired with rank of Colonel and sent on special service in America; Member Somerset CC, 1907–46;

contested (U) Northern Division of Somerset, twice 1910. *Recreations:* shooting, fishing, motoring, etc. *Heir: e s* Douglas Clifford [*b* 11 March 1903; *m* 1st 1926, Nancy (who obtained a divorce, 1933), *o d* of Laurence E. Moss, Sydney, New South Wales; 2nd, 1933, Pamela Chandor]. *Address:* c/o Westminster Bank Ltd, Radstock, nr Bath. *Clubs:* Carlton; Bath and County (Bath).

Died 17 June 1950.

BEAUCHAMP, Rt Rev. Mgr Henry, CBE 1945; MC 1916; Principal RC Chaplain, RAF, since 1930; Domestic Prelate, 1939; *b* 8 June 1884; *e s* of Henry Beauchamp, JP, and Margaret Delaney, Queen's County, Eire. *Educ:* Knockbeg College, Carlow; Maynooth. RUI Army Chaplain, 1915–19 (MC). Royal Air Force since 1919, Vicar-General, Royal Air Force. *Recreations:* hunting, shooting, polo, etc. *Address:* Care of Air Ministry, London. *Clubs:* Army and Navy, Royal Automobile.

Died 26 April 1948.

BEAUMONT, Sir Henry Hamond Dawson, KCMG 1926; JP County of Southampton, 1928; *b* 4 Feb. 1867; 3rd *s* of late Rev. T. G. Beaumont, Rector of Chelmondiston, Suffolk; *m* 1908, Henrietta, *d* of late Col Baldwin Wake, 21st Lancers; one *s* one *d*. *Educ:* Winchester; Balliol College, Oxford, BA. Attaché Diplomatic Service, 1892; 3rd Secretary, 1894–98; 2nd Secretary, 1898–1905; Secretary, 1905–09; Counsellor of Embassy, 1909–16; Chargé d'Affaires, Montenegro, 1909–10; British Delegate on International Financial Commission at Athens and Acting 1st Secretary HM Legation, Athens, 1910–14; Counsellor, Constantinople, 1914; Rome, 1915–16; Envoy Extraordinary and Minister Plenipotentiary to Venezuela, 1916–23; British representative on International Plebiscite Commission, W Prussia (Marienwerder), 1919–20. *Address:* Stanswood House, Fawley, Southampton. *Club:* Brooks's.

Died 15 Dec. 1949.

BEAUMONT, Captain Hubert; MP (Lab) Batley and Morley since 1939; Deputy Chairman of Ways and Means, July 1945–48; *b* Birmingham; *m;* one *s. Educ:* Saltley College School; Ruskin and Central Labour Colleges, Oxford. County Councillor (Derbyshire) 1914–25; contested (Lab) Aldershot 1924, Harrow 1929, Peckham 1931, and Colchester 1935. Parly Private Sec. to Parly Sec. Ministry of Agriculture, 1940–45; Member, Luxmoore Commission on Agricultural Education, 1943–44. *Address:* Crows Nest, Frays Avenue, West Drayton. *T:* West Drayton 2177. *Clubs:* Farmers', National Trade Union.

Died 2 Dec. 1948.

BEAUMONT-THOMAS, Col Lionel, MC; JP; late RH and RFA; Director of Richard Thomas & Co. and of other companies; Member of Haberdashers' Company and Freeman of the City of London; *b* Aug. 1893; *e s* of late Richard Beaumont-Thomas, of Alvington Court, Glos; *m* 1st, Pauline Grace (marr. diss. 1934), *o d* of Sidney Frederick Marriott; three *s* one *d*; 2nd, 1934, Iseult Margery Hazlehurst, *d* of Oscar T. Bland. *Educ:* Rugby. Served European War, 1914–18 (MC); contested (C) Llanelly, 1923; Pontypool, 1924; Herefordshire County Council, 1925; MP (C) King's Norton Division of Birmingham, 1929–35. *Recreations:* shooting, yachting, tennis. *Address:* Great Brampton, Herefordshire. *T:* Madley 244. *Clubs:* Carlton, Cavalry, Royal Automobile, Royal Thames Yacht.

Died Dec. 1942.

BEAVEN, Rt Rev. Frederic Hicks, DD; *b* Rodwell, Calne, Wilts, 11 April 1855; *e s* of late Christopher Beaven, Rodwell, Calne, Wilts; *m* 1883, Georgina Braithwaite, *y d* of late Captain Edward Alleyne Dawes, 97th Regiment; no *c. Educ:* Queen Elizabeth's School,

Wimborne; University College, Durham. Curate of St Martin's, Brighton, 1878; Vicar of Newborough, Staffs, 1881–85; of St Chads, Stafford, 1885–87; of St Paul's, Burton-on-Trent, 1887–1901; Acting Chaplain to Forces in S Africa, 1900; Archdeacon of Matabeleland, 1903; Dean of Salisbury (Rhodesia), 1908; Bishop of Southern Rhodesia, 1910–25; Rector of Thelnetham, Suffolk, 1925–26. *Address:* Cranleigh Court Hotel, Worthing, Sussex.

Died 22 Jan. 1941.

BEAZLEY, John Godfrey, CIE 1928; *b* 9 Feb. 1885; *s* of late J. H. Beazley, Noctorum, Cheshire; *m* 1911, Roberta, *d* of late David Mitchell, JP, Polmont, Stirlingshire. *Educ:* Rugby; Trinity College, Oxford, MA. Entered ICS 1908; Under-Sec. for Revenue, Punjab Government, 1915–17; Colonisation Officer, Lower Bari Doab Canal, 1918–20; Additional Deputy-Secretary to Government of India, Department of Commerce, 1920–21; Secretary to Government, Punjab, Transferred Departments, 1924; officiating Chief Secretary to Government, Punjab, 1928–29; retired from ICS 1931. ARP Local Controller, Abingdon Rural District, 1938–45. *Publication:* Municipal Law and Practice in the Punjab. *Address:* Frilford Grange, Frilford, near Abingdon, Berks. *T:* Frilford Heath 243.

Died 1 Feb. 1948.

BECHER, Dame Ethel Hope, GBE 1918; RRC and Bar; Lady of Grace, Order of St John of Jerusalem; *b* 1867; *d* of late Col Arthur W. R. Becher, Bengal Staff Corps (retired), and *g d* of late General Sir Arthur Becher, KCB. *Educ:* privately. Trained London Hospital, 1893–99; served in South African War, 1899–1902 (despatches, awarded RRC and Queen's and King's medals); Principal Matron, QAIMNS Headquarters, War Office, Jan. 1903–10; Matron-in-Chief Queen Alexandra's Imperial Military Nursing Service, War Office, 1910–19.

Died 10 May 1948.

BECK, Arthur Clement, CVO 1936 (MVO 1925); formerly Land Agent to the King at Sandringham; *b* 1865; *s* of Edmund Beck and A. M. Sheringham; *m* 1899, Mary (*d* 1939), *d* of Rev. Dawson Campbell, Vicar of Ware, Herts; five *s. Address:* Heydon, Norwich.

Died 3 July 1949.

BECK, Conrad, CBE 1918; Managing Director R. & J. Beck, Ltd, Scientific Instrument Manufacturers; late President, Royal Microscopical Society; Vice-Chairman British Scientific Instrument Research Association; 1st President of British Optical Instrument Manufacturers Association, 1915–19; *s* of Joseph Beck, LCC, CC; *m* 1895, Annie, *e d* of John Collings, Leighton Buzzard; one *s* one *d. Educ:* Olivers Mount School, Scarborough. *Publications:* Cladocera of the English Lakes; Photographic Lenses (a simple treatise); The Theory of the Microscope (Cantor Lectures); The Microscope, Theory and Practice. *Recreations:* sketching, skating, motoring. *Address:* 34 Upper Addison Gardens, Kensington, W14. *T:* Park 5269. *Club:* Savile.

Died 31 Oct. 1944.

BECK, Egerton, MA; Barrister of Lincoln's Inn; *b* 1858; *e s* of late Decimus Egerton Beck, 10th *s* of James Beck, JP, DL, of Allesley Park, Warwickshire; *m* Jessie, *d* of late Charles Robert Robinson of Teignmouth, and *widow of* Charles Alfred Clifton of Liskeard; one *d. Educ:* Derby School; Sidney Sussex College, Cambridge; later joined Jesus College. Specially employed by the Committee of Imperial Defence July 1916 to Jan. 1917, and then attached to the Cabinet Secretariat till Dec. 1922. Formerly assistant-editor of the Burlington Magazine. *Publications:* articles (chiefly on historical subjects) and reviews in papers and magazines. *Address:* 17 Gleneldon Road, Streatham, SW16.

Died 9 March 1941.

BECK, Harvey Mortimer, MA; *b* 11 May 1868; *s* of Lister Beck; *m* 1st, 1912, Mary Constance (*d* 1919), *d* of Joseph Thomas, Wood Hall, Shenley; no *c*; 2nd, 1921, Emmeline Lucy, *o c* of late George Langford, Shefford Woodlands, Berks. *Educ:* Eton College (KS); King's College, Cambridge (Scholar). First-Class Classical Tripos, 1890. Assistant Master Aldenham School, 1893–1917; Head Master Aldenham School, 1920–33. *Recreation:* golf. *Address:* 65 Wentworth Avenue, Southbourne, Hants. *T:* Southbourne 2266. *Club:* United University.

Died 6 Dec. 1948.

BECK, Captain Oliver Lawrence, CBE 1919; DSO 1920; RN, retired. Served European War, 1914–19. *Address:* Three Corners, West Clandon, Surrey.

Died 28 Sept. 1947.

BECKE, Brig.-Gen. (retired) John Harold Whitworth, CMG 1918; DSO 1917; AFC 1919; late Sherwood Foresters and RAF; *b* 1879; *m* 1915, Annie Peto Adamson; two *s*. *Educ:* Trinity College, Glenalmond. Served South African War, 1899–1902 (Queen's medal 3 clasps, King's medal 2 clasps); European War, 1914–18 (despatches seven times, CMG, DSO, AFC, Officier Legion of Honour, Croix de Guerre, Bt Lt-Col). *Address:* Priestoun, Edzell, Angus. *T:* Edzell 28.

Died 7 Feb. 1949.

BECKETT, Arthur, FRSL; FSA. Chairman and Governing Director, of T. R. Beckett, Ltd, newspaper proprietors; Chairman Sussex Printers, Ltd; Chairman, Sussex Express and County Herald, Ltd; Editor and founder of Sussex County Magazine; Pres. (since 1923) of Society of Sussex Downsmen; Deputy Chairman Princess Alice Memorial Hospital, Eastbourne. *Publications:* Emancipation: A Woman's Question considered in Story, 1907, 8th edn 1908; The Spirit of the Downs, 1909, 6th edn 1923; Sussex at War and Poems of Peace, 1916; Adventures of a Quiet Man, 1933; contributor to The Times, Spectator, Outlook, Morning Post, Daily Mail, Daily News, Country Life, Field, Nation, Westminster Review, and many other publications. *Address:* Anderida, Hartfield Road, Eastbourne. *T:* 988. *Clubs:* Savage, Authors; Sussex, Eastbourne.

Died 8 May 1943.

BECKETT, Captain Walter Napier Thomason, MVO 1925; DSC 1917; RN; Captain of Dockyard, Deputy Superintendent and King's Harbour Master of Devonport Dockyard since 1939; *b* 25 March 1893; *s* of Brigadier-General WTC Beckett, CBE, DSO, and Bessie Drummond, *d* of General C. S. Thomason, RE, Bengal; *m* 1928, Gladys Hemery, *d* of late E. B. Lindon; one *d*. *Educ:* Park House School, Kent; RNC, Osborne. Entered Navy, 1906; midshipman, 1910; Sub-Lieut, 1913; Lieut, 1915; Lt-Comdr, 1923; Comdr 1929; Capt. 1936; served in HMS Legion Harwich Force and Dover Patrol, 1914–16; Heligoland, Dogger Bank, Terschilling, Belgian Coast, Coastal Motor Boats, 1916 (DSC); N Russia, 1919 (Dwina river). *Publications:* The Boatswain's Call: How it is Used, and some Facts about it, 1922; A Few Naval Customs, Expressions, Traditions and Superstitions, 1930. *Recreations:* shooting, fishing, nautical history and research. *Address:* St Regulus, Shirley Warren, Southampton. *T:* Southampton 71801. *Club:* Naval and Military.

Died 10 March 1941.

BECKWITH, Brig.-Gen. Arthur Thackeray, CB 1919, CMG 1918; DSO 1915; late 2nd Battalion Hampshire Regiment; late 2nd Battalion Hampshire Regiment; *b* 28 Oct. 1875; *s* of Rev. G. Beckwith of Winchester Cathedral; *m* 1904, Dorothy, *d* of late J. B. Thomson, ICS; one *s* one *d*. *Educ:* Radley College. Adjutant 7th Battalion Liverpool Regiment, TF, 1907–11; served with S Lancashire Regt in S African

War (despatches twice); as Adjutant 1st Hampshire Regt, Aden Hinterland, 1903; served European War, Dardanelles, in command of 2nd Hampshire Regt, 1915 (wounded thrice, DSO); elsewhere, 1916–18 (CB, CMG); Commanded Brigades in 51st Highland Div., 12th Div., and 5th Div., 1917–18, and 28th Div., 1920; Col on the Staff Ottoman Gendarmerie, 1921; Commanded 85th Brigade Chanak, 1922–23; retired pay, 1924. *Address:* 21 Tryon Street, SW3; The Little House, Berwick, Sussex.

Died 5 Oct. 1942.

BECKWITH-SMITH, Maj.-Gen. Merton, DSO 1914; *b* 11 July 1890; *o s* of late Beckwith Beckwith-Smith of Aberarder; *m* 1918, Honor Dorothy, *o c* of late John Blundell Leigh; two *s* two *d*. *Educ:* Eton; Christ Church, Oxford. Joined Coldstream Guards, 1910; Adjutant, 1st Coldstream Guards, March–Sept. 1915; Brigade Major, 1st Guards Brigade, June 1916 to Aug. 1917; GSO 2; Guards Division, Aug. 1917–Jan. 1918; GHQ France, Jan.–Nov. 1918; served European War, 1914–18 (despatches four times, DSO, MC, Croix de Guerre); transferred to Welsh Guards, 1930; Commanded the Bn and Regimental District, 1932–37; Commander Lahore Brigade Area, India, 1938–39; served war of 1939– (despatches); Commander 1st Gds Bde, 1939–40; Maj.-Gen., 1940; awarded Royal Humane Society's Certificate, 1909; Hon. MA Oxford. *Address:* The Manor House, Stratton Audley, Bicester, Oxon; Aberarder, Strathnairn, Inverness. *Clubs:* Guards', Turf.

Died 11 Nov. 1942.

BEDDY, Brig. Percy Langdon, CB 1927; CMG 1919; DSO 1919; Indian Army, retired. Served NWF India, 1897–98 (medal with 2 clasps); China, 1900 (medal with clasp); European War, 1914–18 (wounded, despatches thrice, Bt Lt-Col, DSO, CMG, 1914–15 Star, British War Medal, Victory Medal); Kurdistan, 1919 (medal with clasp); NW India, 1921–24 (medal with clasp). *Address:* West Hill Lodge, Budleigh Salterton, Devon.

Died 18 July 1945.

BEDELLS, Charles Herbert; *b* London, 26 Feb. 1862; *s* of Charles King Bedells; *m* 1890, Marion Jane, *d* of Randolph Nott, Sydney, NSW; one *s* one *d*. *Educ:* Mill Hill School. Studied architecture and construction, University College, London; Architectural Association, etc. Senior partner firm of Lander, Bedells & Crompton, Architects and Surveyors, 33 John Street, Bedford Row, WC1; past Pres. of College of Estates Management; Member of Council of Chartered Surveyors' Institution since 1916; President of the Surveyors' Institution, 1929–30; Member of Building Industries National Council, 1933–40. *Publications:* contributions to Transactions, etc., of the Surveyors' Institution on subjects relating to building, estate management, and legislation. *Recreations:* music, photography, handicraft, travel. *Address:* 145 Hornsey Lane, N6. *Clubs:* National, Old Millhillians.

Died 24 Nov. 1943.

BEDFORD, Vice-Adm. Arthur Edward Frederick, CB 1934; CSI 1937; *b* 1881; *s* of Admiral Sir Frederick Bedford, GCB, GCMG; *m* 1914, Gladys, *d* of William Edye Mort, Sydney (one *s* killed on active service, 1942). *Educ:* HMS Britannia. Joined RN, 1895; Rear-Adm., 1931; Vice-Adm., 1936; served European War, 1914–18; ADC to the King, 1931; Flag Officer Commanding Royal Indian Navy, 1934–37; retired list, 1937; served 1938–45; reverted to Retired List, May 1945. *Address:* Easthampnett, near Chichester. *Clubs:* United Service, MCC.

Died 5 Dec. 1949.

BEDFORD, Herbert, FGSM; composer, artist, author; The English Member of the Permanent Council for the International Co-operation of Composers; first English composer to be awarded Brahms medal (1935, Hamburg); *b* 1867; *s* of Deputy J. T. Bedford; *m* 1st,

1894, Liza Lehmann, composer (d 1918); one s; 2nd, 1927, Pauline Murray. Educ: City of London School. Musical compositions include Kit Marlowe, an opera in one act; scene from Romeo and Juliet, for voices and orchestra; two ballets Peribanou and a Chinese ballet, The Mask of Gold; two concert overtures; A Pastoral, The Shepherd and his Pipe; A Lyrical Interlude; Ceremonial Fanfare; Shelley's Ode to Music; Chamber music and songs; Portraits in miniature; exhibited London, Paris, New York, etc.; engaged during the 1914 War on the Anti-Aircraft Defences of London, with a RNVR commission (despatches); inventor of the Anti-Aircraft Range adopted by the War Office for the instruction of all Anti-Aircraft Gunnery Officers. Publications: The Heroines of George Meredith, illustrated by twenty of his miniatures; Essay on Modern Unaccompanied Song; Life of Robert Schumann; The Chart of the Arts, including Music, Painting, Poetry, Sculpture and Architecture, from Vth century BC to 1900 AD, 1938. Recreations: tennis, golf. Address: 41 Litchfield Way, Hampstead, NW 11.

Died 13 March 1945.

BEDI, Raja Sir Baba Gurbukhsh Singh, KBE 1921; Kt 1916; CIE 1911; Hon. Extra Assistant Commissioner in the Punjab. Title of Raja was conferred in 1921. Address: Kallar, Punjab.

Died 22 Nov. 1945.

BEDINGFIELD, Sir Henry Edward P.; see Paston-Bedingfield.

BEDSON, Peter Phillips, MA, Hon. DCL (Durham), DSc (London and Durham), BSc (Vict.), FIC, FCS (London); Hon. Member of Institution of Mining Engineers, and of North of England Institute of Mining and Mechanical Engineers; Greenwell Gold Medallist of North of England Institution of Mining and Mechanical Engineers; Hon. Member of Coke Oven Managers Association; President, Section B. British Association, 1919; b Manchester, 2 April 1853; 3rd s of late George Bedson Bradford, Manchester, and Sarah, d of Peter Phillips, Warrington; m 1884, Annie, e d of late Samuel Hodgkinson, JP, Marple, Cheshire; one s one d. Educ: Fairfield School, near Manchester; Manchester Grammar School; Owens College, Manchester; Univ. of Bonn. Scholarship in Chemistry Univ. of London, 1874; Dalton Chemical Scholar of Owens College, 1875. Assistant Lecturer and Demonstrator in Chemistry, Owens College, 1878–82; also Lecturer on Chemistry, Victoria University; Professor of Chemistry Durham College of Science, Newcastle upon Tyne (now King's College, Durham University), 1882; retired, 1921; now Emeritus Professor. Publications: co-translator with late Prof. Carleton Williams of Meyer's Modern Theories of Chemistry, and Outlines of Theoretical Chemistry, and Outlines of Theoretical Chemistry; papers in Journal of Chemical Society, London; papers dealing with the 'gases enclosed in coal dust,' experiments illustrating the inflammability of mixtures of air and coal dust, in the Transactions of the North of England Institute of Mining and Mechanical Engineers. Address: Stony Keld, Purley Hill, Purley, Surrey.

Died 4 April 1943.

BEDWELL, Cyril Edward Alfred; Hon. Secretary of the Society of Comparative Legislation, 1917; b Clapham; o s of Edward Bedwell, Poulton, Wilts; m 1908, Lizzie Maria, d of Gilbert James Scott; three s one d. Educ: Merchant Taylors' School. Honorary Member of the Middle Temple, 1921; in business, 1895–98; Assistant Librarian of Middle Temple, 1898–1909; Examining Officer Military Service (Civil Liabilities) Committee, 1916–19; Keeper of the Library of the Hon. Society of the Middle Temple, 1909–21; House Governor and Secretary to King's College Hospital, 1922–39; Vice-Pres., Medico Legal Society, 1941; Chairman Camberwell Employment Cttee, 1941–48; Chm. Camberwell Hosp. Management Cttee, 1948–.

Publications: Increase of the Episcopate, 1906; A brief History of the Middle Temple, 1909; Catalogue of the printed books in the Library of the Hon. Society of the Middle Temple, 3 vols, 1914; edited Legislation of the Empire, 4 vols, 1909; Australasian Judicial Dictionary, 1920; joint-editor of Journal of Comparative Legislation, 1913–1925; Editor of Hosp. Library Manual, 1947; contributor to Dictionary of National Biography and periodical literature. Address: 8 Sunray Avenue, Herne Hill, SE24. T: Brixton 1782. Club: Royal Empire Society.

Died 24 April 1950.

BEEBY, Sir George Stephenson, KBE 1939; b Sydney, 23 May 1869; m 1892; four c. Educ: State Schools. Started work at age of fourteen years in an iron store, and followed various occupations, including journalism; studied law, and called to New South Wales Bar, 1911; Member of State Parliament for Blayney, Wagga-Wagga and Murray, 1907–20; Minister for Education, 1910–11; and for Labour and Industry, 1910–12; subsequently resigned Education Portfolio; Minister for Lands, and Minister for Labour and Industry, New South Wales, to 1912; Minister of Labour and Industry, 1916–19; Judge of Arbitration Court, NSW, 1920–26, and President of the NSW Board of Trade; Judge of Federal Conciliation and Arbitration Court, 1926–39, Chief Judge, 1939–41. Publications: particularly interested in industrial legislation; was responsible for the present industrial Arbitration Act, the latest experiment in regulation of strikes in Australia; also the author of the new Crown Lands Act now in force in NSW, under which a perpetual lease tenure was created on 2½ per cent rental basis, with various new concessions in favour of small settlers; responsible for a number of educational reforms, particularly establishment of evening continuation schools as part of Public School System. Several plays published in Australia, and a Satirical Comedy in verse, In Quest of Pan; also of a Treatise on Industrial Matters. Recreation: The Drama. Address: Tomal, Manly, New South Wales.

Died 18 July 1942.

BEERY, Wallace; actor; b 1 April 1885; s of Noah Beery; m 1st, Gloria Swanson (divorced); 2nd, Rita Gilman (granted a divorce, 1939). Educ: Chase School, Kansas City. Toured with Ringling Brothers' Circus; in chorus of New York musical comedies; star of the Yankee Tourist; toured as head of stock company; went into motion pictures at Essanay Studios; director in early period of film industry; went to Hollywood with Keystone Comedies; alternated between stage and screen; signed by Metro-Goldwyn-Mayer Studios; appeared in The Big House, Min and Bill, The Champ, Hell Divers, Grand Hotel, Flesh, Secret Six, Viva Villa, Ah Wilderness, Bad Man of Brimstone, and Port of Seven Seas. Recreations: hunting, flying, the theatre. Address: c/o Metro-Goldwyn-Mayer Studios, Culver City, California.

Died 15 April 1949.

BEETON, Alan, ARA 1938; b 1880; o s of late H. R. Beeton; m Geneste, d of Rev. John Penrose; two s one d. Educ: Charterhouse; Trinity College, Cambridge. Address: Checkendon, Reading.

Died 20 Dec. 1942.

BEETON, Sir Mayson, KBE 1920; BA (Oxon); s of late S. O. Beeton, and Isabella Mary Mayson; m Louie Swinley (d 1942), d of Wm Price Jones, MD; three d. Educ: Marlborough (Scholar); Magdalen College, Oxford (Demy). Visited West Indies as Special Commissioner for Daily Mail, 1896; assisted in organising the Anti-Bounty League which took leading part in securing the abolition of the foreign Sugar-Bounty System by international agreement, 1897–1902; President Anglo-Newfoundland Development Company of Grand Falls, Newfoundland, 1903–13; worked in Finance Department of the Ministry of

Munitions, and organised and administered the Newfoundland Forestry Corps, 1915–18. *Recreations:* golf and shooting. *Address:* High Lands, Seven Hills Road, Walton-on-Thames. *Club:* United University.

Died 24 June 1947.

BEEVOR, Comdr Sir Thomas Lubbock, 6th Bt *cr* 1784; RN; *b* 1 June 1897; *s* of Sir Hugh Beevor, 5th Bt, and Emily Georgina, *d* of Sir William Foster, 2nd Bt, of the Grove, Hardingham; *S* father, 1939; *m* 1919, Edith Margaret Agnew; one *s* three *d*. *Educ:* Osborne and Dartmouth. Served European War, 1914–19, Midshipman, Sub-Lieutenant and Lieutenant, 1918; Lieut-Commander, 1926; Commander, 1932. *Heir: s* Thomas Agnew, *b* 6 Jan. 1929. *Address:* Hargham Hall, Norwich. *Club:* United Service.

Died 29 April 1943.

BEGGS, Engr Captain James, CIE 1942. Royal Indian Navy; Director of Shipbuilding, Munitions Production Branch, Department of Supply, India. *Address:* Department of Supply, New Delhi, India.

Died 15 May 1949.

BEHRAM, Sir Jehangir Bomonji B.; *see* Bomon-Behram.

BEHREND, George L., RBA; water-colour painter; *b* 1868; *s* of late George Behrend, Liverpool; pupil of the late Alfred W. Rich. *Address:* 4 Livingstone Drive South, Sefton Park, Liverpool, 17.

Died 30 Dec. 1950.

BEIRNE, Hon. Thomas Charles, KSG 1929; Member of the Legislative Council of Queensland, 1905–22; merchant; Managing Director of T. C. Beirne, Ltd, Brisbane; Director of Beirne (Pty) Ltd, Mackay and Ipswich; *b* Ballymacurly, Roscommon, Ireland, 1860; *m* 1887, Annie, *d* of late Bernard Kavanagh, Dublin; five *d*. *Educ:* Franciscan Monastery, Faraher, Ireland. Apprenticed to the drapery business, 1874; emigrated to Australia, 1884; after spending some time in Victoria, arrived in Queensland, 1885; commenced business on his own account in Brisbane, 1886; Warden of University of Queensland, 1928–40. *Recreations:* croquet, tennis, golf. *Address:* The Valley, Brisbane, Queensland. *TA:* Beirne, Brisbane. *Clubs:* Brisbane (Brisbane, Queensland).

Died 21 April 1949.

BELCHER, Rev. Arthur Hayes; *b* 31 March 1876; *s* of Thomas Hayes Belcher and Annie Neame; *m* 1908, Mildred, *d* of late Col H. T. Howell; no *c*. *Educ:* Brighton College; Queen's College, Oxford. Assistant Master at Victoria College, Jersey, 1899–1902; Assistant Master at Brighton College, 1902–33; Headmaster of Brighton College, 1933–36. *Recreations:* cricket, golf, shooting, fishing, ski-ing. *Address:* Bramley, Ditchling, Sussex.

Died 19 Jan. 1947.

BELCHER, Major Ernest Albert, CBE 1918; Company Director and author; *b* 1871; *o surv. s* of late Albert Belcher. *Educ:* Queen's College, Taunton; Lincoln College, Oxford (History Exhibitioner). BA 1897; MA 1913. Assistant Master, Durban High School, Natal, 1902–08; Clifton, 1908–12; Headmaster of Christ's College, NZ, 1912–14. Served in European War with DCLI and NZ Rifle Brigade. Seconded to the Ministry of Food (Potato Controller), 1917–18. Assistant General Manager, British Empire Exhibition, 1921–25 and Head of Dominion Mission, 1921. Lived in USA 1926. Has travelled extensively in the Dominions and Near East. During War of 1939–45 was Assistant Master at Dover College, Stowe and Eton; retired from Eton, 1945. *Publications:* (with J. Williamson) Migration within the Empire, 1924; A Political Outline of the History of the USA (1783–1865); (with G. W. Knight) A

Pilgrimage in Prose and Verse: The Isles of Scilly, the Chilterns and East Anglia, 1946. *Recreation:* travelling. *Clubs:* Pilgrims, Oxford and Cambridge.

Died 29 April 1949.

BELCHER, George Frederick Arthur, RA 1945; ARA 1931; *b* 19 Sept. 1875; *s* of Joseph Belcher, MD; *m* Joan (*d* 1942), *d* of late Alfred Harvey, Clifton; one *s*. *Educ:* King Edward VI School, Berkhampstead; Studied in Gloucester School of Art. *Publications:* Drawings in Charcoal in The Tatler, Punch, Graphic, etc.; Set of Etchings of Members and Boxers of The National Sporting Club; Portfolio London Types and Characters, Posters, Portraits; Taken from Life; Characters; (with Stacy Aumonier) Odd Fish, 1923; Potted Char and other delicacies; Taken from Life by George Belcher. *Recreation:* fishing. *Address:* Fisher Lane, Chiddingfold. *Club:* Savage.

Died 3 Oct. 1947.

BELFIELD, Lt-Col Sydney, CBE 1919; JP; *b* 1862; 3rd *s* of late John Finney Belfield, of Primley Hill, Paignton, Devon; *m* 1902, Annie (*d* 1944), *er d* of late C. W. Mitchell, of Jesmond Towers, Newcastle-on-Tyne; one *s* one *d*. *Educ:* Cheltenham College; RMA, Woolwich. Served in Royal Horse and Royal Field Artillery, 1881–1905; South African War, 1898–99 (medal with clasp); recalled for duty in Aug. 1914; Embarkation Staff, Southampton; thence transferred to Railway Transport Staff, Horse Guards, until March 1919, when relinquished appointment of Assistant Director. *Address:* Barn Hill, Brampford Speke, Exeter. *Clubs:* Army and Navy; Devon and Exeter.

Died 25 Aug. 1946.

BELFRAGE, Sydney Henning, MD (Lond.); Physician; *b* Lambeth, London, 1871; *m* 1899, Frances Grace, *d* of Canon Powley; three *s*. *Educ:* Merchant Taylors' School; University College, St Thomas' Hospital. Medical practice, London, since 1900. *Publications:* Illness, 1938; Facts about Food, 1938; Some Observations on the Law of Nullity, etc. *Recreation:* gardening. *Address:* Little White House, Penn, Bucks. *T:* Penn 3195.

Died 31 May 1950.

BELHAVEN AND STENTON, 11th Baron *cr* 1647; **Robert Edward Archibald Udny-Hamilton,** CIE 1918; Representative Peer for Scotland, 1922–45; Indian Army (retd); DL, Lanarks; *b* 8 April 1871; *o s* of Lieut Archibald William Hamilton, RN, and Elizabeth Ann, *d* of W. Billyard, Sydney, NSW; *S* uncle, 1920; surname changed to Udny-Hamilton; *m* 1st, 1898, Kathleen Gonville (*d* 1935), *d* of Colonel Sir B. P. Bromhead, 4th Bart, CB; one *s* one *d*; 2nd, 1938, Sheila de Hauteville, *o d* of Major A. G. Pearson, DSO; two *d*. *Educ:* Westminster; RMC, Sandhurst. Joined Royal Scots Fusiliers, 1890; 4th Gurkhas, 1893; in civil employ under the Govt of India, 1898–1923; Major, 1908; Lt-Col, 1916; served Chitral, 1895 (medal with clasp); East Africa, 1896 (medal); Tirah, 1897–98 (two clasps); with Mesopotamian Expeditionary Force, 1915–18 (despatches, CIE); Gold Medal of the Kaiser-i-Hind, 1905. *Heir: s* Master of Belhaven. *Address:* Udny Castle, Aberdeenshire. *T:* Udny Green 9. *Clubs:* United Service; Royal Northern (Aberdeen).

Died 26 Oct. 1950.

BELL; *see* Morrison-Bell.

BELL, Archibald Græme, CMG 1914; MInstCE (retired); *b* London, 15 March 1868; *s* of late Valentine Græme Bell, CMG, and Rebecca, *d* of Alex. Bell Filson, MD; *m* 1899, Katharine Sarah (*d* 1944), *d* of late Walter Ogilvy Ross; one *d*. *Educ:* Felsted; Uppingham. Employed on surveys of Jamaica Railway by Government 1887–88, and by Jamaica Railway Company, after sale of line, 1889–90; Assistant to late Sir William Shelford, KCMG, 1890, and to Hawkshaw and Hayter, 1890–91; Assistant Engineer, PWD British Guiana, 1891; Assistant Colonial Civil Engineer, 1900;

Colonial Civil Engineer, 1901; an official Member of Court of Policy of British Guiana, 1901; Director of Public Works for Trinidad and Tobago, 1907–23; and Member of Executive, 1908–23, and Legislative, 1907–23, Councils; retired, 1923. *Publications:* Various official reports and casual publications in periodicals; a contributor to the 11th edition Encyclopædia Britannica. *Recreations:* yachting, fishing, cricket, tennis, golf. *Address:* 8 Garden Court, NW8. *T:* Maida Vale 4671. *Clubs:* MCC, Incogniti.

Died 8 Feb. 1948.

BELL, Maj.-Gen. Sir Arthur Lynden L.; *see* Lynden-Bell.

BELL, Aubrey FitzGerald; *b* 20 Aug. 1881; *m* 1933, Barbara Lindsay Wilkie, Edinburgh; two *s. Educ:* privately; Keble College, Oxford (classical scholar). Assistant Librarian in the Department of Printed Books, British Museum, 1905–08. *Publications:* The Magic of Spain, 1912; Four Plays of Gil Vicente, 1920; Portuguese Literature and Bibliography, 1922; Spanish Galicia, 1922; A Pilgrim in Spain, 1924; The Oxford Book of Portuguese Verse, 1925; Luis de Leon, 1925; Contemporary Spanish Literature, 1925; Lyrics of Luis de Leon, 1928; Four Dialogues of Hollanda, 1928; Castilian Literature, 1938; Cervantes, 1947; contributions to Revue Hispanique, 1920–1930. *Address:* Crossways, Box 2273, RR4, Victoria, BC.

Died 7 May 1950.

BELL, Bertram Charles, DSO 1917; DSC; grazier; *b* 5 April 1893; *s* of James Thomas Marsh Bell; *m* 1926, Adeline Grace Barnes; one *s* one *d. Educ:* Toowoomba Grammar School. Station manager and grazier, 1920–32; served European War in Royal Naval Air Service and Royal Air Force, 1914–18 (despatches, DSO, DSC, Croix de Guerre). *Recreations:* polo, shooting, tennis, golf. *Address:* Aroo, Boonah, Queensland, Australia. *T:* Boonah 16. *Clubs:* Queensland, Brisbane; Royal Sydney Golf.

Died 15 June 1941.

BELL, Sir Charles (Alfred), KCIE 1922; CMG 1915; CIE 1919; FRGS; Indian Civil Service, retired, 1919; formerly Political Officer for Tibet, Bhutan, and Sikkim; *b* 31 Oct. 1870; *e surv. s* of Henry Bell, ICS, and Anne, *d* of George Dumbell, of Douglas, Isle of Man; *m* 1912, Cashie Kerr (*d* 1935), *d* of David Fernie, of Warrenside, Blundellsands, Lancs; one *s* two *d. Educ:* Winchester (scholar); New College, Oxford. Joined Indian Civil Service, 1891; served in Bengal, Bihar, and Orissa as Assistant Magistrate, District Magistrate, Settlement Officer, and District Judge; conducted exploratory mission in Bhutan in 1904, and political mission to that country in 1910, concluding a Treaty, by which the foreign relations of Bhutan were placed under the British Government; on political duty in Tibet, Bhutan, and Sikkim in 1904–05, 1906, 1908–18, 1920–21; was employed on the Tibet Conference between Great Britain, China, and Tibet, 1913–14; conducted a diplomatic Mission to Lhasa in 1920, remaining there for eleven months. In 1934 and 1935 travelled in Tibet, Mongolia, Manchuria, and Siberia; Lawrence Memorial Medal, Royal Central Asian Society, 1937. *Publications:* Tibet: Past and Present, 1924, second impression, 1926, cheap edition, 1927; The People of Tibet, 1928; The Religion of Tibet, 1931; Portrait of The Dalai Lama, 1946; Grammar of Colloquial Tibetan, third ed. 1939; English-Tibetan Colloquial Dictionary, 1905, second and enlarged editions, 1920. *Recreations:* long travels and short walks. *Address:* c/o The Royal Bank of Canada, Government Street, Victoria, BC, Canada. *Clubs:* Athenæum, East India and Sports; Union, Victoria, BC.

Died 8 March 1945.

BELL, Edward Price, LLD, DLitt, MA; journalist, author, and lecturer on foreign affairs; Political Editor, Saturday Spectator, Terre Haute, Ind, USA, since 1941; *b* Parke County, Indiana, USA, 1 March 1869; *s* of Addison William Bell, farmer; *m* 1897, Mary Alice Mills, Crawfordsville, Indiana; two *s* one *d. Educ:* Wabash College, Indiana. Entered journalism at thirteen; established a weekly in the coal-mining district of Parke County, Indiana; edited several city dailies; joined the reportorial staff of the Chicago Daily News, 1890; exposed widespread political corruption and jury-bribing in Illinois; London correspondent of the Chicago Daily News, 1900–22; first journalist to interview a British Secretary of State for Foreign Affairs; accompanied Hoover on his Latin-American Goodwill tour in 1928–29; arranged the MacDonald-Hoover meeting in Washington, 1929, preliminary to the London Five Power Naval Conference, 1930; toured the world on a political mission for the Literary Digest, 1934; travelled throughout America on Peace Mission, 1935–36. *Publications:* World Chancelleries, 1929; Europe's Economic Sunrise, 1927; Primary Diplomacy, 1933; Let us go Seaward, 1937; Studies of Great Political Personalities, 1938; Seventy Years Deep (autobiography), 1940; The Basic Principles of Journalism, 1940; numerous short stories in Strand Magazine. *Recreations:* driving a motor car, walking, swimming. *Address:* Merrywood, Gulfport, Mississippi, USA. *Clubs:* Pilgrims, American; City, Chicago.

Died 23 Sept. 1943.

BELL, Col Hon. Sir George John, KCMG 1941; CMG 1918; DSO 1902; VD; Member of House of Representatives, Parliament of Commonwealth of Australia, 1919–22 and 1925–43; Speaker, 1934–40; late 10th Australian Light Horse Regiment, Victoria, and 22nd Light Horse Regiment, Tasmania; *b* 29 Nov. 1872; *s* of George Bell, Cambridge, England; *m* 1919, three *s* two *d.* Served South Africa with Victorian contingent (severely wounded, despatches twice, two medals, nine clasps, DSO) European War (Gallipoli, Egypt, Palestine), 1915–18 (CMG); ADC to Governor-General, 1927–30; Chairman of Committees, 1932–34. *Address:* Parklands, Burnie, Tasmania.

Died 5 March 1944.

BELL, Preb. George Milner, MA; Rector of Worthen since 1922; Prebendary of Hereford Cathedral, 1928; Surrogate, 1929; member of Salop Educ. Committee, 1928; *b* 1872; *s* of Canon G. C. Bell, formerly Head of Marlborough College and Rector of St Michael's, Cornhill, EC, and Elizabeth Milner; *m* Lucy Macdonald Quick; one *d. Educ:* Marlborough; New College, Oxford (Scholar). 2nd Class Mods. and Lit. Hum., 1895. Master at Bradfield College, 1895–96; Clifton College, 1897–99; Leeds Clergy School; ordained, 1900, to St Agnes, Bristol, 1900–06; Curate of St Michael's, Cornhill, and Dean of Balliol House, Toynbee Hall, 1906–09; Secretary of Stepney Council of Public Welfare; Rural Dean of Chafford, 1917; Canon of Chelmsford Cathedral, 1922; Vicar of Romford, 1909–22; Rural Dean of Pontesbury, 1923–36. *Publication:* Social Service. *Recreations:* music, mountaineering. *Address:* The Rectory, Worthen, Salop. *T:* Worthen 20. *Club:* Alpine.

Died 9 March 1947.

BELL, Lt-Col Henry Stanley, CMG 1917; DSO 1900; *b* 6 June 1874; *s* of late Thomas Bell, JP, DCL; *m* 1910, Annie, *d* of late George Wilkinson, Newcastle-on-Tyne; one *s* four *d.* Served South Africa (despatches, DSO); European War in France (despatches three times, CMG, TD); DL JP, Northumberland; Sheriff of Northumberland, 1939. *Address:* Bavington Hall, Capheaton, Newcastle-on-Tyne.

Died 18 Dec. 1949.

BELL, Henry Thurburn Montague; Editor of Annual Register until 1947; *b* Colombo, 10 July 1873; *s* of James Leonard Bell, Alexandria and Ceylon; *m* 1903, Eva Muriel Chadwick; three *d. Educ:* St Paul's School (Scholar); Peterhouse, Cambridge (Scholar). First Class Classical Honours; Foreign Correspondent of The Times, 1895–1906, Berlin, Balkans, South Africa; War Correspondent, S African War, 1900–02; Editor, North China Daily News and Herald, Shanghai, 1906–11; Managing Director and Editor-in-Chief The Near East and India, 1916–35; Joint Founder and Editor of The China Year Book; Editor and Proprietor of The Near East Year Book, 1927–31. *Club:* Travellers'.

Died 6 Nov. 1949.

BELL, Sir James, Kt 1921; shipowner; Member of James Bell and Co., Hull; *b* 26 Aug. 1878. *Address:* Fairholme, Anlaby Road, Hull.

Died Feb. 1948.

BELL, Sir John, 2nd Bt *cr* 1895; *b* 19 Aug. 1876; *o s* of Sir James Bell, 1st Bt, CB, and Helen (*d* 1909), *e d* of William Findlay, Hallhill, Lanarkshire; *S* father 1929; *m* 1937, Agnes Molesworth, *y d* of late Captain E. N. M. Kindersley. *Educ:* Uppingham; University College, Oxford. Late Captain Ayrshire Yeomanry; JP Ayrshire and Lanarkshire. *Heir:* none. *Address:* Montgreenan, Kilwinning, Ayrshire. *T:* Kilwinning 6. *Club:* Carlton.

Died 31 Dec. 1943.

BELL, Mrs Mary Taylor Watson, CBE 1929; JP; Bailie of City of Glasgow; *d* of Arthur Watson, Easter Busby, Lanarkshire; *m* Robert Bell, Dumfries; one *s. Address:* Chiselhurst, 19 Newlands Road, Glasgow.

Died 16 Aug. 1943.

BELL, Col Sir Maurice Hugh Lowthian, 3rd Bt *cr* 1885; CMG 1916; TD; DL Yorkshire; JP North Riding, Yorkshire; Director of Horden Collieries Co. Ltd, Dorman, Long and Co. Ltd; Hon. Col 4th Bn Yorks Regt (TF); *b* 29 March 1871; *e s* of Sir Hugh Bell, 2nd Bt, CB, and Mary (*d* 1871), *d* of late John Shield, Newcastle; *S* father, 1931. *Educ:* Eton; Paris; Germany. Commission 1st Vol. Batt. (APWO) Yorkshire Regt 1890; served S African War (Queen's medal and six clasps), Hon. Capt. in Army; served European War, taking the Battalion to Flanders 1915 (despatches twice, CMG); High Sheriff of Durham, 1921. *Recreations:* shooting, fishing, hunting. *Heir:* nephew Hugh Francis, *b* 7 Dec. 1923. *Address:* Mount Grace Priory, Northallerton. *T:* East Harlsey 6. *Club:* Brooks's.

Died 17 Nov. 1944.

BELL, Thomas Reid Davys, CIE 1919. Joined Indian Forest Dept 1884; Deputy-Conservator of Forests and Divisional Forest Officer, Bombay, 1892; Chief Conservator, Bombay Presidency, 1909; retired 1920. *Address:* Karwar, North Kanara District, Bombay Presidency, India; c/o Lloyds Bank Limited, Cox and King's Branch, 6 Pall Mall, SW1.

Died 24 June 1948.

BELL, Walter George, FSA, FRAS; Editorial Staff, The Daily Telegraph, 1899–1936; *b* London; *s* of late Robert George Bell, FGS; *m* Edith Phillippa, *d* of late William Mackenzie Duckworth. After training in art schools entered journalism in North of England. Chairman, London and Middlesex Archæological Society; Member of Council, Newspaper Press Fund. *Publications:* Fleet Street in Seven Centuries; Unknown London; The Great Fire of London in 1666; The Tower of London; More about Unknown London; The Great Plague in London in 1665; Where London Sleeps; Solar Eclipse of 1927; London Rediscoveries; A Short History of the Tylers and Bricklayers Company; London Tells her Story; contributor to History, Encyclopædia Britannica, Fortnightly Review, and other monthlies. *Recreations:* travel in London, fishing. *Address:* 31 Baskerville Road, SW18. *T:* Battersea 1914. *Club:* Press.

Died 24 May 1942.

BELL, William, CIE 1904; MA Edin. 1885; FEIS; Vans Dunlop Scholar, Edinburgh, 1882–85; *b* Arbroath, Angus, 1860; *m* 1887, Isabella (*d* 1930), *d* of S. Maclvor, Edin.; one *s* one *d. Educ:* Moray House Training College, Edinburgh; Edinburgh University. Tutor for LLA diploma; occasional Inspector of Schools; Master of Method, Holy Cross Academy, Edinburgh; Delegate 3rd Congress of Universities of the Empire, 1926. Joined Indian Educational Service, 1885, as Principal, Central Training College; afterwards Principal of Government College, Lahore, and Inspector of European Schools, 1895; Organising Secretary for Khalsa College of the Sikhs; Director of Public Instruction in the Punjab, and Under-Secretary to Government of Punjab Home (Education) Department, 1901–08; Fellow and Syndic of Punjab University since 1886; Inspector of Chiefs' Colleges in India, 1903–07; Inspector-General of Reformatory Schools, Punjab, 1904–07; President Punjab Text-Book Committee, 1901–07; University Registrar at various times; Indian Universities Commission, 1902; Examiner in Philosophy, Allahabad and Punjab Universities; Indian Coronation Decoration, 1903. *Publications:* numerous text-books, school-books, essays, lectures, and reviews. *Address:* 5 Essex Road, Weymouth, Dorset. *T:* Weymouth 1710.

Died 21 March 1946.

BELLEROCHE, Albert de; British painter (lithograph); *b* Swansea, 1864; *m* Emilie Julie Visseaux; two *s* one *d. Educ:* Paris. Pupil of Carolus Duran. Chevalier de l'ordre de Leopold I; Membre Fondateur Salon d'Automne; Hors concours, Paris Salon. Principal pictures: The Artist's Mother, at National Museum of Wales; En Visite, Swansea Art Gallery; Disappointment (Brussels), 1937; Printemps (Luxembourg), 1904; Henri Rochfort, 1895; Ennui, 1900; La Robe verte, 1909; Mention Honorable, 1900; Médaille, 3ème classe, 1905; Médaille 2ème classe, 1908; Médaille d'Or, Amiens, 1909; Exposition Bruxelles, Médaille d'Argent, 1911; private exhibitions of Lithographs: Vienna, 1903; Goupil Gallery, 1903; Graves (London), 1906; Paris, 1908; Estampe (Brussels), 1910; Dowdeswell Galleries, 1913; Kennedy's Gallery (New York), 1914; Colnaghi's Galleries; Lithographs, British Museum, S Kensington, Luxembourg, Bibliothèque Nationale, Dresden Museum, etc.; National Museum of Wales; Ashmolean Museum, Oxford; Retrospective Bibliothèque Royale, Brussels; patentee of process for detecting forged water marks, 1915. *Publication:* Sargent's Lithographs (Print Collector's Quarterly). *Address:* The Old Manor, Rustington, Sussex. *T:* Rustington 42.

Died 14 July 1944.

BELLESSORT, André; Member of the French Academy since 1935, perpetual secretary since 1940; *b* Laval, 1861. *Publications:* Virgile et son Temps, Etudes et figures; La Societè du Second Empire. *Address:* rue Boileau 48, Paris xvie.

Died 26 Jan. 1942.

BELLEW; *see* Grattan-Bellew.

BELLHOUSE, Sir Gerald, Kt 1924; CBE 1918; *b* 1867; *s* of late William Bellhouse, Alderley Edge, Cheshire; *m* 1898, Edith Marion, *e d* of W. R. R. Gemmell, Alderley Edge, Cheshire. *Educ:* Fettes College, Edinburgh; Trinity College, Cambridge (BA 1888). One of HM Inspectors of Factories, 1891; District Inspector, 1895; Superintending Inspector, 1908; Deputy Chief Inspector, 1917–22; Chief Inspector, 1922–32; Member of Committees on the Check-weighing of Piecework Wages in Dock Labour, 1907, and on Partial Exemption from School Attendance, 1908; Chairman of Employment of Van-boys Committee, 1912; Member of Health of Munition Workers Committee, 1916; Chairman of Demobilisation of Civil War Workers Committee under Ministry of Reconstruction, 1917; served (1917) under National Service Depart, first as Commissioner for London and South-Eastern Area, and subsequently as Chief Commissioner; Chairman of Poisons Board, Home Office, 1933; Member of Departmental Committee on Wages and Conditions in Road Transport Industry (Goods), 1936; Chairman Unemployment Assistance Board Advisory Committee for SE London, 1936. *Recreations:* golf, shooting. *Address:* Chawton Lodge, Alton, Hants. *T:* Alton 3193. *Club:* United University.

Died 15 Sept. 1946.

BELLOC, Marie Adelaide, (Mrs Lowndes); *b* 1868; *o d* of Louis Belloc, French barrister, and Bessie Parkes through whom she is descended from Joseph Priestley; *m* Frederic Sawrey Lowndes (*d* 1940); one *s* two *d*. *Publications:* The Heart of Penelope, 1904; Barbara Rebell, 1905; The Pulse of Life, 1907; The Uttermost Farthing, 1908; Studies in Wives, 1909; When no Man Pursueth, 1910; Jane Oglander, 1911; The Chink in the Armour, Mary Pechell, 1912; Studies in Love and in Terror, and The Lodger, 1913; The End of Her Honeymoon, 1914; Good Old Anna, 1915; The Red Cross Barge, and Lilla, a Part of her Life, 1916; Love and Hatred, 1917; The Lonely House, From the Vasty Deep, 1920; What Timmy Did, 1921; The Terriford Mystery, 1924; Bread of Deceit, 1925; What Really Happened, 1926; Thou Shalt not Kill, 1927; The Story of Ivy; Cressida, 1928; One of those Ways, 1929; Duchess Laura, 1929; Letty Lynton, 1930; Jenny Newstead, 1932; Another Man's Wife, 1934; The Chianti Flask, 1935; Who Rides on a Tiger, 1936; The House by the Sea, 1937; The Marriage-Broker, 1937; Motive, 1938; And Call It Accident, 1939; Lizzie Borden, 1940; I, too, have lived in Arcadia, 1941; Where Love and Friendship dwelt, 1943; The Merry Wives of Westminster, 1946; A Passing World, 1947; She Dwelt with Beauty, 1949 (posthumous). *Plays:* With all John's Love, 1932; The Second Key, 1935; What Really Happened, 1936. *Recreation:* reading. *Address:* 1 Barton Street, Westminster, SW1.

Died 14 Nov. 1947.

BELMONT, Perry; *b* New York, 28 Dec. 1851; *e s* of late August Belmont; *m* Jessie Robbins. *Educ:* Harvard: Columbia Law School. Practised law until 1881; Member of Congress, 1880–87; Chairman Com. on Foreign Affairs, 1884–87; US Minister to Spain, 1887–89; Inspector-General with rank of Major, First Division Second Army Corps, USV, 1898; Democrat; delegate to the Democratic National Conventions of 1892, 1896, 1900, 1904, and 1912; Captain Quartermaster Corps, Remount Section, USA, 1917. *Publications:* National Isolation an Illusion, 1925; Survival of the Democratic Principle, 1926; Abolition of Secret Party Funds, 1927; Political Equality, Religious Toleration, from Roger Williams to Jefferson, 1927; An American Democrat, 1940. *Address:* Newport, RI, USA.

Died 25 May 1947.

BELMORE, 5th Earl of, *cr* 1797; **Armar Lowry-Corry;** Baron Belmore, 1781; Viscount Belmore, 1789; JP, DL, Co. Fermanagh, High Sheriff, 1895; JP Co. Tyrone, High Sheriff, 1901; *b* Sydney, 5 May 1870; *e s* of 4th Earl of Belmore and Anne Elizabeth Honoria (*d* 1919), *d* of late Capt. John N. Gladstone, RN, MP and sister of Sir J. E. Gladstone, 4th Bt; *S* father, 1913; unmarried. *Educ:* Winchester; Trinity Hall, Cambridge (MA). Church of Ireland. Is a landowner in Cos Tyrone, Fermanagh, Monaghan, and Kent. Barrister-at-law, Inner Temple, 1897; a Commissioner of Education (Endowed Schools) for Ireland, 1919–24; a County Councillor for Co. Fermanagh (representing Enniskillen Rural District Council, of which he was Chairman, 1899–1939); Chairman Fermanagh Education and Tuberculosis Committees; a member since 1894 of Committee of Management of Omagh District Lunatic Asylum (Chairman since 1944); member of Enniskillen Board of Guardians, of the Representative Body of the Church of Ireland and of its Glebes, Commutation and Parish Boundaries Committee, of the General Synod of Church

of Ireland, and of its Standing Committee and Board of Education; of Clogher, Derry and Raphoe, Kilmore, and Dublin and Glendalough and Kildare Diocesan Synods and Councils, of Armagh Synod, of the Church of Ireland Jubilee Fund and Widows' and Orphans' Fund Boards, and of four Incorporated Diocesan Boards of Education; Life Member of the Court of the University of Reading; a Governor of Rotunda Hospital, Dublin, of Church of Ireland Training College and of Incorporated Society for the Promotion of Protestant Schools in Ireland; Chairman of the Visiting Justices to Londonderry Prison; a Conservator of Fisheries for Enniskillen District; a Trustee of Enniskillen Savings Bank; Captain 3rd Battalion Royal Inniskilling Fusiliers, 1893–96. *Recreations:* theatre-going, visiting cathedrals, watching lawn tennis; Secretary Enniskillen Badminton Club, 1918–43. *Heir: b* Hon. Cecil Lowry-Corry. *Address:* Castlecoole, Enniskillen. *Clubs:* Carlton; University, Dublin; Fermanagh, Enniskillen; Tyrone County, Omagh; Northern Counties, Londonderry; Armagh, Armagh.

Died 12 Feb. 1948.

BELMORE, 6th Earl of, *cr* 1797; **Cecil Lowry-Corry;** Baron Belmore, 1781; Viscount Belmore, 1789; High Sheriff, Co. Tyrone, 1916; High Sheriff, Co. Fermanagh, 1922; DL, Co. Fermanagh; JP, Co. Fermanagh and Co. Tyrone; *b* 20 March 1873; *s* of 4th Earl of Belmore, PC, GCMG; *S* brother 1948; unmarried; Church of Ireland. *Educ:* Wellington College. Studied Farming and Land Agency Work in Kent and Dorset for six years; Grand Juror Counties Fermanagh and Tyrone; a Visiting Justice of Londonderry and Belfast Prisons; Chairman: Fermanagh County Council; Fermanagh County Educ. Cttee; Fermanagh County Finance, Library, and Technical Cttees; Health and Welfare Cttees; Enniskillen Board of Guardians; Enniskillen Rural District Council; Enniskillen Unemployment Assistance Advisory Cttee; Member of the General Synod of Church of Ireland, of Clogher, of Armagh, and of Derry and Raphoe Diocesan Synods and Councils, of the Church of Ireland Trustees, of the Incorporated Society for the Promotion of Protestant Schools in Ireland, of the Executive Cttees, of the Fermanagh Protestant Orphan Soc. and The Lord Enniskillen Memorial Orphan Soc.; Hon. Sec. Fermanagh Club; a Lady Diocesan Sec. for Clogher Diocese; Conservative; a Member of Ulster Unionist Council; a Deputy Grand Master and Grand Treasurer of the Grand Orange Lodge of Ireland; a Deputy Grand Master and Grand Treas. of the Imperial Grand Black Chapter of the British Commonwealth. *Recreations:* walking and riding. *Heir: cousin* Major Galbraith Armar Lowry-Corry, Royal Inniskilling Fusiliers, *b* 14 April 1913. *Address:* Castlecoole, Enniskillen, Northern Ireland. *Clubs:* Fermanagh (Enniskillen); Tyrone County (Omagh); Northern Counties (Londonderry); Ulster (Belfast).

Died 2 March 1949.

BELTON, Leslie James, MA, MSc; Government Official in Germany (Education); *b* Brighton, 31 Jan. 1897; *s* of James Henry Belton and Marion Cecilia Bodle; *m* 1924, Ethel Muriel, *d* of Capt. W. J. Haughton (one *s* killed in action, 1945). *Educ:* High School, Hastings; University of Liverpool; University of Birmingham; Manchester College, Oxford. War service, 1914–18; prisoner of war in Germany, 1915–18; Minister, All Souls Unitarian Church, Wolverhampton, 1924–27; Aberdeen Unitarian Church, 1927–31; All Souls Unitarian Church, Golders Green, 1932–37; Upper Chapel, Sheffield, 1939–46. Lecturer in English Dept, University of Leipzig, 1931–32; Editor, The Inquirer, 1932–39. WEA Lecturer, Sheffield, 1941–46. *Publications:* Psychical Research and Religion, 1932; World Vision, 1937; Creeds in Conflict, 1938; Can we still believe in Man? 1941; Religion and the Scientists,

1945; contributor to various journals and reviews. *Recreations:* walking, painting, amateur theatricals. *Address:* 19 St James's Drive, SW17.

Died 8 July 1949.

BEMONT, Charles, Archiviste paléographe; Docteur ès lettres; LLD Oxford; Corresponding Fellow of the Royal Historical Society, of the British Academy, of the Medieval Academy of America; Membre de l'Institut de France; Directeur de la Revue historique; *b* Paris, 16 Nov. 1848; *m* 1885, Lina Frick, Strasbourg. *Educ:* Paris; élève au lycée Charlemagne, puis à l'école nationale des Chartes. Directeur à l'école des Hautes études, Sorbonne. *Publications:* Simon de Montfort, comte de Leicester; a new edition, translated by C. F. Jacob, 1930; De la condamnation de Jean Sans Terre, 1884; Histoire de l'Europe au moyen âge, de 395 à 1270 (avec G. Monod), 1891, nouv. édit. 1921; Rôles gascons; supplément au tome i, tomes ii et iii (1242–1307); Recueil d'actes relatifs à l'administration des rois d'Angleterre en Guyenne au XIIIe siècle, 1914; Chronique latine sur le premier divorce de Henri VIII, 1917; nombreux articles dans la Revue critique d'histoire et de littérature, la Revue historique, etc. *Address:* La Revue historique, Paris.

Died Dec. 1939.

BENCRAFT, Sir Henry William Russell, Kt 1924; JP; *b* 4 March 1858; *s* of late Dr Henry Bencraft, Southampton; *m* 1889, Kate Margaret (*d* 1942), 2nd *d* of Walter Perkins, JP, Portswood House, Southampton. *Educ:* St Edward's School, Oxford; St George's Hospital, London. Former County Councillor for Southampton; Past Member of Committee of MCC; Past President, Captain, and Hon. Secretary for 25 years of Hampshire County Cricket Club; President Hampshire Rugby Union; Past President of Southern Football League and Hants Football Association. *Recreations:* motoring, golf. *Address:* Cheniston, Compton, nr Winchester. *Clubs:* MCC, I Zingari, Junior Carlton, Free Foresters.

Died 25 Dec. 1943.

BENDA, Wladyslaw Theodor; illustrator, painter; *b* Poznan, Poland, 15 Jan. 1873; *s* of Jan. S. Benda, pianist and composer; *m* 1920, Romola Campfield, New York; two *d. Educ:* School of Technology, and Academy of Fine Arts, Cracow; Art Schools in Vienna, San Francisco, New York. Went to California, 1900, where he taught art; New York, 1902; naturalised, 1911; illustrates for most of the leading American periodical publications, Century Magazine, Scribner's, Collier's Weekly, Cosmopolitan Liberty, Harper's Bazaar, and others; also does mural painting; creator of Benda Masks used on the stage in Europe and America; Member of Society of Illustrators, Architectural League, Society of Mural Painters; Chevalier d'ordre Polonia Restituta. *Publication:* article on Modern Masks in new edition of Encyclopaedia Britannica. *Address:* 27 West 67th Street, New York City. *T:* Susquehanna 7–3750. *Clubs:* Players, Coffee House, Dutch Treat (New York).

Died 30 Nov. 1948.

BENECKE, Paul V. M., MA, Fellow of Magdalen College, Oxford; *b* 7 June 1868; *s* of Charles Victor Benecke and Marie, *e d* of Felix Mendelssohn Bartholdy. *Educ:* Haileybury; Magdalen College, Oxford. Demy of Magdalen, 1886; Fellow, 1891; 1st Class Classical Moderations, 1888; Litteræ Humaniores, 1890; Theology, 1891; Junior Greek Testament Prize, 1890; Senior, 1892; Senior Septuagint Prize, 1893; Denyer and Johnson Scholar, 1891; Ellerton Essay, 1893. Treasurer of Lady Margaret Hall, Oxford; Hon. Sec. Oxford Diocesan Church Building Committee. *Address:* Magdalen College, Oxford. *Club:* Oxford and Cambridge Musical.

Died 25 Sept. 1944.

BENEDICT, Ruth Fulton; Professor of Anthropology, Columbia University, USA; *b* 5 June 1887; *d* of Dr Fred S. Fulton and Bertrice J. Shattuck; *m* 1914, Prof. Stanley R. Benedict (*d* 1936); no *c. Educ:* Vassar College; Columbia University. Department of Anthropology, Columbia University, 1923–; Office of War Information, Washington, DC, 1943–46 (on leave from Columbia Univ.); Pres., American Anthropological Assoc., 1947. *Publications:* Patterns of Culture, 1934; Zuni Mythology, 1935; Race: Science and Politics, 1940; The Chrysanthemum and the Sword: Patterns of Japanese Culture, 1946. *Address:* Dept of Anthropology, Columbia University, NYC 27, USA.

Died 17 Sept. 1948.

BENES, Dr Eduard; late President Czechoslovak Republic; *b* Kozlany, Bohemia, 28 May 1884; *s* of Matthew Beneš, farmer; *m* Anna Vlček. *Educ:* Grammar School, Gymnasium; University, Prague; University, Sorbonne, Paris; University, Berlin; University, London; University, Dijon. Prof. of Political Economy at the Czechoslovak Commercial Acad., Prague, and Professor in Ordinary in Sociology at the Prague University, 1921; during the war in 1915 proceeded to Paris to work as a diplomat and publicist in the cause of the liberation of the Czechoslovak nation, and there, in collaboration with Professor T. G. Masaryk, late President of the Czechoslovak Republic, and the late General Stefanik, laboured for the victory of the Entente and for the renewal of an independent Czechoslovak State; General Secretary of the Czechoslovak National Council at Paris, 1917, the supreme administrative organ for the defence of Czechoslovak interests, and the basis of the subsequent Czechoslovak Government; Minister of Foreign Affairs 1918–35 of the Czechoslovak Republic; Premier 1921–22; President of the Czechoslovak Republic, 1935–38; Prof., Univ. of Chicago, Chicago, Ill, 1939; Rapporteur Général of the Disarmament Conference; one of the members of the Czechoslovak delegation to the Peace Conference at Paris, Dec.; Member of the Council of the League of Nations, 1923–27, and since 1933; President of the Assembly, 1935; one of the drafters of the Geneva Protocol, 1924; one of the leading figures in the Little Entente: member of the Institut de France, Académie des Sciences morales et politiques since 1929. After the decision of Munich left Czechoslovakia, held lectures at the University of Chicago. After the occupation of Czechoslovakia (15 March 1939) became leader of the movement for Czechoslovak freedom in exile; elected in Oct. 1939 President of the Czechoslovak National Committee in London; in July 1940 recognised by the Allied powers as President of the Czechoslovak Republic. In May 1945 returned to the liberated Republic; on 28 Oct. 1945 confirmed in office by the Prov. Nat. Assembly as President of the Republic; re-elected as President for a term of 7 years, 1946; resigned, 1948. *Publications:* Le problème autrichien et la question tchèque, 1908; The History of the Labour Movement in Bohemia and in Austria, 1913; Bohemian case for Independence, 1917; La Boemia contro l'Austria Ungheria, 1917; Détruisez l'Autriche-Hongrie, 1916; Le socialisme autrichien et la guerre, 1914; Political Partisanship, 1912; The War and Culture, 1915; The Spirit of the Czechoslovak Revolution, 1923; Problems of New Europe and the Foreign Policy of Czechoslovakia, 1924; Difficulties of Democracy, 1924; Diplomatic Struggle for the Czechoslovak Independence, 1925; The Problem of Small Nations after the World-War, 1925; Problem of Slavonic Policy, 1926; My War Memoirs, 1928; The Austro-German Customs Union Project, 1931; The Problem of Central Europe and the Austrian Question; Democracy: Today and Tomorrow, 1939; then during 1939–1946: Building a New Europe; My Fears and My Hopes; Nazi Barbarism in Czechoslovakia; Czechoslovakia's Second Struggle for Freedom; Towards a Lasting Peace; The Organisation of Post-War Europe; The Rights of Man and International Law; The

Way to Victory; What would be a good Peace; Czechoslovak Policy for Victory and Peace; Our Fight for the Liberation of the Republic; Our Political Work in the Second and Third Year of the War; The President's Third Message to the State Council; The New Slavonic Policy; On the Way to Victory; Reflections on Slavdom; Six Years of Exile and of the Second World War, 1946. *Address:* Prague.

Died 3 Sept. 1948.

BENÉT, Stephen Vincent; poet and novelist; *b* 22 July 1898; *s* of Colonel James Walker Benét (US Army); *m* 1921, Rosemary, *d* of Thomas Carr, Chicago; one *s* two *d*. *Educ:* Yale University. *Publications:* Five Men and Pompey, 1915; Young Adventure, 1918; Heavens and Earth, 1920; The Beginning of Wisdom, 1921; Young People's Pride, 1922; Jean Huguenot, 1923; Tiger Joy, 1925; Spanish Bayonet, 1926; John Brown's Body, 1928; Ballads and Poems, 1915–1930, 1931; James Shore's Daughter, 1934; Burning City, 1936; The Devil and Daniel Webster, 1937; Thirteen O'Clock, 1937; Johnny Pye and the Fool-Killer, 1938; Tales Before Midnight, 1939. *Recreations:* tennis, swimming. *Address:* c/o Brandt and Brandt, 101 Park Avenue, New York. *Clubs:* Century, New York.

Died 13 March 1943.

BENÉT, William Rose, LittD; author and editor; Associate Editor Saturday Review of Literature, New York; *b* 2 Feb. 1886; *e s* of Col James Walker Benét and Frances Neill Rose; *m* 1st, 1912, Teresa Frances Thompson (decd); one *s* two *d*; 2nd, Elinor Wylie; 3rd, Lora Baxter; 4th, Marjorie Flack. *Educ:* Albany Academy, Albany, NY; Sheffield Scientific School; Yale University European War, 1918. 2nd Lieut US Army Air Service (Ground Officer); as editor associated with Century Magazine, Nation's Business, Literary Review, and Saturday Review of Literature; Sec. Nat. Inst. Arts and Letters; Hon. LittD (Dickinson Coll.). *Publications:* poems: Merchants from Cathay, 1913; The Falconer of God, 1914; The Great White Wall, 1916; The Burglar of the Zodiac, 1918; Perpetual Light (a memorial to T. F. B.), 1919; Moons of Grandeur, 1920; Wild Goslings, 1927; Man Possessed, 1927; Starry Harness, 1933; Golden Fleece, 1935; The Dust Which is God (narrative poem), 1941 (awarded Pulitzer Prize, 1941); Day of Deliverance: A Book of Poems in Wartime, 1944; The Stairway of Surprise, 1947; novels: The First Person Singular, 1922; Rip Tide (novel in verse), 1932; children's books: The Flying King of Kurio, 1926; Adolphus the Adopted Dolphin (with Marjorie Flack), 1941; translation: (jointly with wife) The East I know (by Claudel), 1914; air ballads: With Wings as Eagles, 1940; Editor: Poems for Youth, 1923; Fifty Poets—an Auto-Anthology, 1933; The Reader's Encyclopedia, 1949; Co-editor: Twentieth Century Poetry (with Canby and Drinkwater), 1930; The Oxford Anthology of American Literature (with N. H. Pearson), 1938; The Poetry of Freedom, an Anthology (with Norman Cousins), 1945; Day's End: a fantasia in one act, produced Dock St Theatre, Charleston, SC, 1939 (Nat. Play-wrighting Award). *Recreations:* collecting, second-hand books of forgotten merit. *Address:* Saturday Review of Literature, 25 West 45 Street, New York 19, NY. *Clubs:* Elizabethan (Yale Univ., New Haven, Conn).

Died 4 May 1950.

BENETT, Lt-Col Henry Cleeve, CMG 1918; late RM; *b* 1877; *m* 1912, Eleanor Mabel, *d* of J. W. Murray, Liverpool. Commandant Ascension Island, 1913; Lt-Col, 1927; retired list, 1928. *Address:* c/o Barclay's Bank, Chatham.

Died 10 Jan. 1941.

BENGOUGH, Guy Dunstan, MA (Cantab); DSc (Liv.); FCS; FRS, 1938; Consultant to Department of Scientific and Industrial Research; *b* 1876; *s* of late Major E. B. Bengough, The Grange, Chislehurst, Kent; *m* Constance Helen, *d* of late Lt-Col Jelf-Sharp, Kincarrathie,

Perthshire and Scots Guards; no *c*. *Educ:* Malvern; Cambridge; Royal School of Mines. After acquiring research experience with late Sir William Roberts-Austin at Royal Mint, followed by practical work in handling gold and tin ores in Burma, was appointed to lectureships at Birmingham and Liverpool Universities, and later became Investigator on corrosion to the Institute of Metals; joined RA as subaltern, 1914; Captain and Adjutant, 1915; Seconded at request of Admiralty for research work on Naval problems, 1916; subsequently carried out similar work for RAF; after demobilisation was appointed a Principal Scientific Officer, Department of Scientific and Industrial Research (Chemical Research Laboratory). *Publications:* numerous papers on Metallography and Corrosion of Metals in Proceedings of Royal Society and other Scientific Journals. *Recreations:* golf and gardening. *Address:* Mulberry House, Hampstead Lane, Highgate Village, N6. *T:* Mountview 3445.

Died 20 Jan. 1945.

BENHAM, Sir Gurney; *see* Benham, Sir W. G.

BENHAM, Sir William Blaxland, KBE 1939; FRS; CM; DSc (Lond.), MA (Oxon), Hon. DSc (NZ), FRS (NZ), CM Roy. Soc. Tasmania; Professor Emeritus since 1937; ex-Fellow of University of NZ; *b* Isleworth, Middlesex, 29 March 1860; 3rd *s* of E. Benham, solicitor, London; *m* Beatrice, *d* of John Eadie, London; one *s* one *d*. *Educ:* Marlborough; Univ. Coll., London. Assist to Sir E. Ray Lankester, Univ. Coll. 1886–90; Aldrichian Demonstrator in Morphology, Univ. of Oxford, 1891–98; Lecturer in Biology, Bedford College for Women, London, 1886–98; Professor of Biology, Univ. of Otago, NZ, 1898–1937; President Sect. D Australasian Assoc. Advancement of Science, 1902; Governor New Zealand Institute, 1905–11; President, 1916–17; Hutton Memorial Medal, 1911; Hector Medal, 1935; Coronation Medal, 1937. *Publications:* numerous memoirs on Zoology, especially on Oligochæta, in QJ Mic. Science; Trans. Zool. Soc. Proc. Zool. Soc.; Ann. Mag. Nat. History; Echinoderms and other non-vertebrates of NZ; Trans. NZ Institute; Polychæta, etc., Cambridge Natural History, 1896; Platyhelmia and Nemertines in Lankester's Treatise on Zoology, 1902; Report on Polychaeta in Australian Antarctic Expedition, 1921; Report on Polychæta of Terra Nova Antarctic Expedition, 1927; Extinct Cetacea of NZ 1936–1939; Octopods of NZ, 1942–1943. *Recreation:* gardening. *Address:* 20 Pitcairn Street, Dunedin, W1, New Zealand.

Died 21 Aug. 1950.

BENHAM, Sir (William) Gurney, Kt 1935; FSA; FRHistS; JP; journalist and company director; *b* 16 Feb. 1859; *s* of Edward Benham and Mary Carr; *m* 1st, Maria Louisa Quilter (*d* 1884); 2nd, Ethel Hervey, *d* of Alderman H. H. Elwes; three *s* three *d*. *Educ:* Merchant Taylors' School. Journalism in Wiltshire, Salisbury Journal, etc.; since 1884 proprietor and editor, Essex Co. Standard; Member of Colchester Town Council since 1892; Alderman since 1911; High Steward of Colchester and Hon. Freeman of Borough; Mayor, 1892–93, 1908–09, 1933–34; Member of Essex County Council, 1925–40; Director (Vice-Chairman) of Essex and Suffolk Insurance Society, Ltd, Daniell and Sons Breweries, Ltd (Chairman), Colchester Gas Company (Chairman), and other Companies; Chairman of Colne Oyster Fishery Board; Member of Council of Essex Archæological Society; lecturer, Essex Women's Institutes, etc. *Publications:* Wiltshire Legends (verse), 1881; Red Paper Book of Colchester, 1902; Oath Book of Colchester, 1907; Benham's Book of Quotations, many editions since 1907; Colchester Oyster Feast (illus.), 1902; Amy's Wonderful At Home (verse), 1907, and other children's books; Essex Co. and Borough Arms; Essex Sokens and other local books; History of Playing Cards, 1932, etc.

Recreations: literature, art and archæology. *Address:* Westfields, 14 Lexden Road, Colchester. *T:* Colchester 2643.

Died 13 May 1944.

BENN, Engr Rear-Adm. Edward Piercy St John, CB 1929; *b* Natal, 15 June 1872; *s* of late Edward Piercy Benn, 26th Cameronians; *m* 1904, Ethel Christine, *o d* of late Claude Halsey, Blackheath; one *s* four *d*. *Educ:* privately. RN Engineering College, Devonport. Entered RN, 1889; served China, 1898–1901, Boxer Campaign (medal); 'lent' to Imperial Government, China, 1907–12, and decorated with Order of Double Dragon by Emperor of China, 1911; served European War, 1914–19; Cameroons Expedition, etc.; Engineer Captain, 1921; Staff of C. in C., Western Approaches, 1921–22; Staff of Vice-Admiral commanding 1st Battle Squadron, 1922–24; commanded the Royal Naval Engineering College, Devonport, 1925–28; ADC to the King, 1926; Engineer Rear-Admiral, 1927; Staff of C-in-C The Nore, 1928; retired list, 1931. *Recreations:* cricket, lawn tennis, etc. *Address:* Millfield, Cobham, Kent. *T:* Cobham 3167.

Died 5 May 1947.

BENNETT, 1st Viscount *cr* 1941, of Mickleham, Surrey and of Calgary and Hopewell, Canada; **Richard Bedford Bennett,** PC 1930; PC (Can.), JP, LLB, KC 1907; Hon. LLD Dalhousie Univ.; Queen's Univ. (Kensington); Univ. of Alberta; Queen's Univ. (Belfast); Univ. of Edinburgh; Univ. of Toronto; McGill Univ.; Wesleyan Univ. (Middletown, Conn); Univ. of State of New York; Rensselaer Polytechnic Institute (Troy, NY); Harvard Univ. (Cambridge, Mass); Univ. of Rochester (Rochester, NY); Hon. DCL Mount Allison Univ. (NB), Univ. of New Brunswick, Univ. of Bishop's College, and Syracuse Univ. (NY); FRSC; *b* Hopewell, NB, 3 July 1870; *e s* of Henry J. Bennett and Henrietta Stiles; unmarried. *Educ:* Public and High Schools, New Brunswick; Dalhousie Univ., Halifax, Nova Scotia. Admitted Bar of New Brunswick, 1893; commenced practice Chatham, New Brunswick; Member of Town and Municipal Councils of Northumberland, NB, 1896; removed to Calgary. Alberta, 1897; Member Legislative Assembly of North-West Territories, 1898–1905; Legislative Assembly, Alberta, 1909; resigned, 1911; MP for Calgary in House of Commons of Canada, 1911–17, for Calgary West, 1925–38; Director-General of National Service until passing of Military Service Act, 1917; Minister of Justice and Attorney-General, Canada, 1921; resigned with defeated Meighen Administration; Minister of Finance, July–Sept. 1926 and 1930; Prime Minister and Minister of External Affairs, 1930–35; Leader of the Conservative Party in Canada, 1927–38; Pres. Alberta Division and Member of Executive Committee and Central Council Canadian Red Cross Society, 1914–19; Chairman, Advisory Committee, Canadian Red Cross Society in London since 1939; twice represented Canada at Geneva at meetings League of Red Cross Societies, and International Red Cross Society; Member of Executive Committee of Canadian Patriotic Fund, 1914–19; accompanied Prime Minister to England, France, and Belgium, 1916; represented Canada at the Imperial Conference, London, 1930; settled for Canada amended terms of the Statute of Westminster; Chairman Imperial Economic Conference, Ottawa, 1932; leader of Canadian delegation to World Economic Conference, London, 1933; Chairman of the Wheat Conference, London, 1933; represented Canada at League of Nations Assembly, 1934. Knight of Grace of the Venerable Order of the Hospital of St John of Jerusalem; Past Pres. and Honorary Life President of Canadian Bar Association, 1932; Bencher of the Law Society of Alberta; Hon. Bencher, Lincoln's Inn; Hon. Bencher Law Society of Upper Canada; Hon. Col 10th Battalion Calgary Highlanders and New Brunswick Rangers; Hon. Life Member, Canadian Legion, BESL; Vice-Pres. Royal

Empire Society; Pres. Royal Society of Arts. *Recreation:* reading. *Address:* Juniper Hill, Mickleham, Surrey. *Clubs:* Athenaeum, Carlton; Ranchmen's, Calgary; Rideau, Ottawa.

Died 27 June 1947 (ext).

BENNETT, Sir Albert James, 1st Bt *cr* 1929; JP; Chairman and Director of Companies; *b* 17 Sept. 1872; *s* of Edward Bennett and Elizabeth Chapple; *m* 1st, 1896, Caroline (who obtained a divorce, 1938; she died 1945), *d* of Jacob Backus; two *s* one *d*; 2nd, 1938, Leopoldine, *d* of Leopold Armata; one *s*. *Educ:* privately. MP (L) Mansfield Division 1922–23; (C) Nottingham Central, 1924–30; during war was Member Mechanical Transport Board War Office, and Leather Control Board; Controller of Propaganda South and Central America Ministry of Information; JP Co. Nottingham; MFH the Rufford, seasons 1921–22. *Recreations:* hunting, shooting, golf. *Heir: s* Major Charles Wilfrid [*b* 15 March 1898; *m* 1927, Agnes Marion, *d* of late James Somervell; one *s* one *d*]. *Address:* Oakhurst, West Byfleet, Surrey. *T:* Byfleet 83. *Club:* Brooks's.

Died 14 Dec. 1945.

BENNETT, Alexander John Munro, of Dunloskin; CBE 1922; OBE 1919; TD, MA, Major late 8th (Argyllshire) Batt. Argyll and Sutherland Highlanders; Solicitor; *b* 7 May 1868; *s* of Hugh Christie Bennett and Ellen Munro; *m* 1895, Josephine Katherine, *d* of Archibald Robertson and Caroline Michel Clinkskill; three *d*. *Educ:* Tillicoultry School; Glasgow University. *Address:* Struan Lodge, Dunoon. *TA:* Union Dunoon. *T:* Dunoon 93. *Clubs:* Caledonian; Royal Clyde Yacht.

Died 2 April 1943.

BENNETT, Col Alfred Joshua, CMG 1915; DSO 1901; VD; JP; *b* Brucedale Park, Wagga Wagga, NSW, 10 Jan. 1865; *s* of late B. B. Bennett, JP; *m* 1920, Catherine Josephine, *d* of late John Lawler, Sydney and Springwood, NSW. *Educ:* Wagga Wagga Public School; Fort St College, Sydney. Served with NSW Contingent to Soudan, 1885, advance on Tamai (Egyptian medal with clasp, Suakim and Khedive's star); 2nd Lieut 1st Infantry Regt, NSW, 1886; retired from Australian Military Forces, 1925; South Africa, served with 1st NSW Mounted Rifles, Major, 3rd NSW Mounted Rifles (severely wounded at Driefontein; despatches twice, DSO, Queen's medal and three clasps, King's medal and two clasps). Attended King Edward VII Coronation, representing Australian soldiers in the field (Coronation medal in silver); served throughout European War with AIF; present landing Gallipoli, 1915; Commanded 4th and 1st Batts. AIF; Lone Pine (wounded); Transport Service, 1916–17; France, 1917–18; Commanded 20th Batt. and Australian Corps Reinforcement Camps (wounded; CMG, Dardanelles, 1914–15 Star, Victory Medal with laurels, Allies Victory Medal); Administrator and Chief Magistrate of Norfolk Island, 1929–32. *Address:* Ada Street, Randwick, Sydney, NSW. *Clubs:* Imperial Service, Australian Jockey, Sydney.

Died 1 Aug. 1946.

BENNETT, Andrew Percy, CMG 1912; late HM Diplomatic Service; *b* 30 July 1866; 4th *s* of late Rev. Augustus F. Bennett; *m* 1st, 1896, Winifred May, *e d* of E. C. Youell of Galatz, Roumania; one *d*; 2nd, 1928, Edith Primrose, *widow* of Ambrose Mustard, East Bergholt, Suffolk. *Educ:* Christ's College, Cambridge. Graduated in 1891 with Honours, MA 1897. Vice-Consul at Manila, 1893; transferred to Galatz, 1895; HM's Consul at NY, 1896; Commercial Attaché, Vienna, Rome, Athens, Bucharest, and HM's Consul-General at Zürich, 1899–1918; British Minister to the Republics of Panama, 1919–23, and Costa Rica, 1920–23; Venezuela, 1924–27; retired, 1927; a Royal Commissioner, 1909, for International Exhibitions at

Brussels, Rome, and Turin. *Address:* 27 Ashley Court, SW1. *T:* Victoria 4631; 1 First Avenue, Hove. *T:* Hove 6834. *Clubs:* St James's; Union, Brighton.

Died 3 Nov. 1943.

BENNETT, Sir Charles Alan, Kt 1929; **Hon. Mr Justice Bennett;** Judge of Chancery Division High Court of Justice since 1929; *b* Caterham, Surrey, 9 May 1877; *e s* of Charles Hudson and Elizabeth Bennett; *m* Constance Radeglence, *o d* of Major J. N. Still, KOSB, of Musbury, Devon; two *s* one *d*. *Educ:* Winchester College. Called to the Bar, Lincoln's Inn, 1899; KC 1923; Bencher, 1928. *Recreations:* shooting, golf. *Address:* Middle Meadow, Beaconsfield, Bucks. *T:* Beaconsfield 201; Blue Tile Farm, Brancaster, King's Lynn, Norfolk. *T:* Brancaster 66; Royal Courts of Justice, WC2. *Club:* Reform.

Died 20 Dec. 1943.

BENNETT, Sir Ernest Nathaniel, Kt 1930; late Fellow of Hertford College, Oxford; JP Oxon; MP (Lab) Central Cardiff, 1929–31, and (Nat. Lab), 1931–45; *b* 12 Dec. 1868; *o s* of late Rev. George Bennett, MA, Rector of Rede, Suffolk; *m* 1915, Marguerite, *e d* of H. G. Kleinwort of Wierton, Kent; two *s* one *d*. *Educ:* Durham School; Hertford College, Oxford. 1st Class Classical Mods., 1st Class Lit. Hum., 1st Class Hon. Theol., Senior Hall-Houghton Greek Testament prize; Fellow, 1891. Late Lecturer of Wadham, Pembroke, Lincoln, and Hertford Colleges, and Public Examiner; late Capt. 4th Batt. Oxford and Buckinghamshire Light Infantry; served as War Correspondent during Cretan insurrection, 1897, and with Soudan expedition, 1898, present at battle of Omdurman (medal with clasp), also with Vol. Ambulance Corps in S Africa 1899–1900 (medal), subsequently commanding Oxfordshire Volunteers in Orange River Colony, 1902 (medal with three clasps); Member of Council of Psychical Research Society; explored island of Sokotra with late Theodore Bent, 1896; joined Ottoman Army in Tripoli, 1911; Press Censor on Turkish Staff in Thrace, Balkan War, 1912; MP (L) Woodstock Division, Oxfordshire, 1906–10; Parliamentary Private Secretary to Lord Strachie (Board of Agriculture), 1909; Assistant Postmaster-General, 1932–35; British Red Cross Commissioner in Belgium, France, and Serbia, 1914–15 (3rd Class Order of the White Eagle); later attached HQ Staff, 11th (Reserve) Infantry Brigade; Special Service under Admiralty Intelligence Division; attached HQ IX Army Corps, BEF; Silver Jubilee Medal, 1935; joined the Labour Party, 1916; contested W Wilts, Banbury, and SW St Pancras, 1918–24; Chairman, Near and Middle East Association; Temp. Chairman of Committees, House of Commons; Chairman, Admiralty Committee Entrance RN (Cadets); Member Archbishops' Committee Church and State; Member Indian Franchise Committee, 1932; Member British Delegation, League of Nations Assembly 1934; Select Committee on National Expenditure since 1939; Member Governing Body, Church in Wales. *Publications:* The Downfall of the Dervishes (3 editions); Christianity and Paganism in the 4th and 5th Centuries; With Methuen's Column on an Ambulance Train; With the Turks in Tripoli; Problems of Village Life; The German Army in Belgium; Apollonius, or the Future of Psychical Research; Apparitions and Haunted Houses: A Survey of Evidence. *Recreations:* shooting, fishing, investigating haunted houses. *Address:* 22 Egerton Ter., SW3. Cwmllecoediog, Aberangell, Machynlleth. *T:* Kensington 9178, Aberangell 3. *Clubs:* Bath, Reform, Flyfishers'.

Died 2 Feb. 1947.

BENNETT, Sir (Francis) Noel C.; *see* Curtis-Bennett.

BENNETT, Sir Francis Sowerby, Kt 1912; JP Lincolnshire (Lindsay) and Grimsby; *b* 9 Oct. 1863; *s* of late Joseph Bennett, MP, of The Cedars, Louth, and Maria, *d* of Francis Sowerby of Aylesby, near Grimsby; *m*

1891, Julia Elizabeth, *o d* of late Thomas Ouston of Holmefield, near Pontefract; two *s* two *d*. *Educ:* The Leys, Cambridge; Germany. Entered the office of Bennetts & Co., timber merchants, Grimsby, 1880; retired, 1947; High Sheriff Lincolnshire, 1916–17. *Address:* Fryston, Grimsby. *T:* Grimsby 7147.

Died 31 March 1950.

BENNETT, Very Rev. Frank Selwyn Macaulay; *b* 28 Oct. 1866; *s* of Henry Edward Bennett, of Sparkford, Somerset, and Louisa Birchall, *d* of Sir James Buchanan Macaulay; *m* Ida, *d* of Clegg Livesey of Arden, Bredbury, Cheshire; one *s*. *Educ:* Sherborne; Keble College, Oxford. Private Chaplain to Bishop Jayne of Chester; Vicar of Portwood, Stockport; Vicar of Christ Church, Chester; Rector of Hawarden, 1910–20; Dean of Chester, 1920–37. *Publications:* Coué and his Gospel of Health, 1923; A Soul in the Making, 1924; The Nature of a Cathedral, 1925; Expecto, 1926; Mary Jane and Harry John, 1927; On Cathedrals in the Meantime, 1928; The Resurrection of the Dead, 1929. *Address:* The Orchard, Wilton Hill, Taunton, Somerset.

Died 14 Nov. 1947.

BENNETT, Rt Rev. Frederick Augustus, CMG 1948; Bishop of Aotearoa since 1928; Suffragan to Bishop of Waiapu; *b* Ohinemutu, NZ, 1872. *Educ:* Ohinemutu; St Stephen's College, Auckland; Nelson College, NZ; Bishopdale Theological College. Deacon, 1896; Priest, 1897; Missionary to Maoris in Southern Taranaki, 1899–1905; at Rotorua, 1905–17; Assistant Superintendent to Maori Mission, Hawkes Bay, 1917–28. *Address:* Kohupatiki, Clive, New Zealand.

Died 16 Sept. 1950.

BENNETT, Geoffrey Thomas, ScD, FRS. Fellow and sometime Lecturer in Mathematics of Emmanuel College, formerly Fellow of St John's College, Cambridge. *Address:* Emmanuel College, Cambridge. *Club:* Royal Societies.

Died 11 Oct. 1943.

BENNETT, Rt Rev. George Henry, DD, LLD; *b* Antigua, West Indies, 24 June 1875; *s* of G. W. Bennett, civil engineer. *Educ:* Edinburgh Academy; Abbey School, Fort Augustus; Scots College, Rome. Took Degree of Doctor in Philosophy, Theology and Canon Law. Priest, 1898; returned to Scotland, 1901; Curate at St Patrick's Church, Edinburgh; afterwards for 2 years at North Berwick and 5½ years at Hawick; RC Bishop of Aberdeen, 1918–46. Hon. LLD Aberdeen University, 1931. *Address:* 19 Golden Square, Aberdeen. *T:* 766.

Died 25 Dec. 1946.

BENNETT, Sir John, Kt 1937; *b* 28 Oct. 1876; *s* of Frederick Bennett, Birch Vale, Derbyshire; *m* 1926, Dorothy May, *d* of Rev. Norman Lowndes; one *s* one *d*. *Educ:* Clifton College; New College, Oxford. MA. Called to Bar, Lincoln's Inn, 1900; practised at the Lancashire Palatine Bar; Bench of Lincoln's Inn, 1935; Vice-Chancellor of County Palatine of Lancaster, 1936–48; served European War in France with 21st Battalion Manchester Regt. *Publication:* Practice of the Chancery of the County Palatine of Lancashire, 1914. *Recreations:* shooting, fishing, golf. *Address:* Hill Top, Butley, Macclesfield. *T:* Prestbury 8327. *Clubs:* United University; Union (Manchester).

Died 30 Aug. 1948.

BENNETT, Hon. Sir John R., KBE 1926; *b* St John's, 8 Aug. 1866; *s* of Edward W. and Amelia Goff Bennett; *m* 1st, 1891, Laura *d* of Thomas and Leah Taylor; three *s* one *d*; 2nd, 1936, Beatrice Shannon Greaves, *d* of late George A. Hutchings. *Educ:* Bishop Field College. Started career as clerk with C. F. Bennett and Co., 1881; became proprietor of Aerated Water Works, 1894; organized and became President Bennett Brewing Co. Ltd, 1898; senior municipal councillor for City of St John's, 1902–06; MHA St John's West, 1904; re-elected, 1908, 1909, 1914, 1919 and for Harbour

Grace, 1924; on several occasions was acting Prime Minister; Colonial Secretary of Newfoundland and member of Executive Council, 1913–17; Minister of Militia, 1917; Colonial Sec., Newfoundland, 1924–28; Member of Newfoundland Legislative Council, 1933; District Grand Master of English Freemasonry for Newfoundland, 1923. *Recreations:* fishing, golf, and curling. *Address:* Reading, Monkstown Road, St John's, Newfoundland. *TA:* Bennett, St John's. *T:* 359. *Clubs:* Masonic City, Bally Haley Golf and Country, St John's.

Died 23 Oct. 1941.

BENNETT, Sir John Thorne Masey, KCSI 1947; Kt 1946; CIE 1939; CBE 1933; MC; Chief Constable of the Ministry of Civil Aviation Constabulary since 1948; *b* 7 Oct. 1894; *s* of John Masey Bennett and Adeline Johnston; *m* 1917, Janet Smith Hodge; one *s*. *Educ:* Foyle College, Londonderry. Entered Indian Police, 1914; served in Royal Inniskilling Fusiliers, 1915–20 (MC); Superintendent of Police, Attock, Ambala, and Rawalpindi, 1922–29; Assistant Inspector General of Police, Punjab, 1929–34; Dep. Insp. Gen., CID, 1934–41; Addl Insp. Gen. of Police and Director, Civil Defence, 1941–43; Inspector General of Police and Joint Sec. to Government, Punjab Home Dept, 1943–47. King's Police Medal, 1936; Indian Police Medal, 1940. *Recreation:* tennis. *Address:* West Bank, Northumberland Road, Londonderry.

Died 20 May 1949.

BENNETT, Sir Norman Godfrey, Kt 1930; MA, BCh Cantab; LDS Eng.; Consulting Dental Surgeon St George's Hospital; Consulting Dental Surgeon to the Royal Navy; *b* 16 June 1870; *s* of Thomas and Selina Bennett; *m* 1903, Maida Mabel, *d* of John Henderson; one *s* two *d*. *Educ:* St John's College, Cambridge; St George's Hospital; Royal Dental School. *Publications:* Editor and contributor, Science and Practice of Dental Surgery; article on Dental Disease in Rolleston's Encyclopaedia of Medical Treatment; article on Dental Surgery in Latham and English's System of Treatment; chapter on Teeth, Pye's Surgical Handicraft. *Address:* 57 Harley St, W.

Died 14 Sept. 1947.

BENNETT, Sir Reginald, Kt 1928; Vice-Chancellor, Primrose League; *y s* of late Rev. Henry Bennett, Vicar of St Nicholas at Wade, Isle of Thanet; *m* Nona, *y d* of late Rev. H. Newland. *Publication:* editor, Primrose League Gazette, and Primrose Bud. *Address:* 54 Victoria Street, SW1. *Club:* Authors'.

Died 1 Jan. 1944.

BENNETT, T. C. S.; *see* Sterndale-Bennett.

BENNETT, T. Izod, MD, FRCP, etc; Physician and Medical Tutor, Middlesex Hospital; Physician to Royal National Orthopædic Hospital; Consulting Physician to Hostel of St Luke and to Faversham Hospital; Senior Physician to Stoke Mandeville Hospital, Ministry of Pensions; Examiner in Medicine Royal College of Physicians; *b* 14 July 1887; *o s* of late Arthur William Bennett of Christchurch, NZ; *m* Ruth Iris, *y d* of late N. Weiss, of the Société de l'Histoire du Protestantisme Française, 54 rue des Saints Pères, Paris. *Educ:* Christchurch, New Zealand; Guy's Hospital, London University. MB, BS, 1914–18, MO to 8th Batt. N Staffordshire Regt on Western Front, subsequently Physician to 54 CCS with rank of Major until after the Armistice; Medical Assist and Demonstrator of Physiology (Guy's), 1919; MPCP, 1920; and MD London; Fellow of Royal Society of Medicine; awarded Beit Memorial Fellowship for Medical Research, 1921; Goulstonian Lecturer, Royal College of Physicians, 1928; Dean of Middlesex Hospital Medical School, W, 1929–34; Fellow of Medical Society of London; Member of Association of Physicians. *Publications:* The Stomach in Health and Disease, 1925; Nephritis, 1929;

Treatment of Diabetes, 1931; many contributions to medical journals. *Address:* 39 Hill Street, Mayfair, W1; Middlesex Hospital, W1. *T:* Museum 8333. *Club:* Savile.

Died 10 July 1946.

BENSLY, Rev. William James, DSO 1919; TD, MA; *b* 14 Aug. 1874; *y s* of late Robert L. Bensly, Lord Almoner's Professor of Arabic, Cambridge University. *Educ:* Sherborne School; Emmanuel College, Cambridge. Assistant Master, Giggleswick School, 1899–1904; Deacon, 1902; Priest, 1903; Assistant Master, Uppingham School, 1904–05; Sherborne School, 1905–13 and 1919–34; Lecturer, Christchurch College, Cawnpore, 1913–15; served European War, 1915–19 (Major, DSO, despatches); returned to Sherborne School, 1919; on Staff of Toc H. 1934–36. *Publications:* Editor: Caesar, Civil War, Bk 1 (Bell's Illustrated Classics, Intermediate Series and Elementary Series); Sherborne Register (3rd Edition), 1937. *Recreations:* librarianship, travelling, gardening. *Address:* Nowell Cottage, Sherborne, Dorset. *Club:* Royal Societies'.

Died 28 Nov. 1943.

BENSON, Rev. John Peter; Prebendary of Exeter; JP Devon; *m* Florence Margaret (*d* 1935). Vicar of Witheridge, 1893–1920; Lord of the Manor of Bradford Tracey. *Address:* Bradford Cottage, Witheridge, N Devon.

Died 12 March 1944.

BENSON, Col (Hon. Brig.) Ralph Hawtrey Rohde, CBE 1930; *b* 30 Jan. 1880; 2nd *s* of Sir Ralph Benson, ICS. *Educ:* Clifton College; RM Academy, Woolwich. 2nd Lt Royal Artillery, 1899; Capt. 1904; Major, 1914; Bt Lt-Col 1917; Colonel, 1925; Chief Inspector of Armaments, 1925–29; Member of the Ordnance Committee, 1929–32; Commandant Military College of Science, Woolwich, 1932–36; ADC to the King, 1932–36; retired 1936. *Recreations:* golf and sailing. *Address:* 39 Talgarth Mansions, W14. *Club:* Army and Navy.

Died 19 April 1943.

BENSON, William John, CBE 1918; FRGS; *s* of late John Benson, Leamington; *m* Emma, *d* of late Charles Richardson, Magherafelt, Ireland; one *d*. Sometime in British Consular Service; subsequently associated with banking and mining interests, South Africa; during European War was a Section Director and acted as Deputy Director-General (B Section), Ministry of Munitions; Order of St Stanislas (with star) for special services rendered to Russian Government in early stages of the war; now actively engaged in political work; a voluntary speaker for Conservative and Unionist Central Office; Chairman of Advisory Committee of all affiliated Conservative Clubs in Metropolitan Area; and of Central Southwark Conservative Association; ex-officio member of executive and other political Committees in London; on outbreak of war in 1939 accepted honorary appointment of Reception and Liaison Office in Ministry of Supply. *Address:* 76 Redcliffe Gardens, SW10. *Clubs:* Carlton, Conservative.

Died 21 Aug. 1941.

BENT, Rear-Adm. Eric Ritchie, CB 1941; DSC; retired; *b* 26 Sept. 1888; *s* of late Charles Bent, Royal Artillery; *m* 1918, Eileen Beatrice Hill; two *s*. *Educ:* HMS Britannia. Entered Royal Navy, 1903; Retired with rank of Rear Adm., 1939. *Address:* The Gabled House, Alverstoke, Hants. *Club:* United Service.

Died 9 June 1949.

BENTHALL, Major John Lawrence, CBE 1919; TD, Order of the Rising Sun of Japan, 3rd Class; Director of Vickers Ltd, retired, 1926; *b* 7 Feb. 1868; *o s* of late Lieut-Col John Matthew Benthall (1st King's Dragoon Guards) of Furzewell House, Torquay; *m* 1st, 1895, Emily Maud (*d* 1907), *e d* of late Octavius Bradshaw, JP, of Powderham Castle, South Devon; two *s* one *d*; 2nd,

1919, Henrietta, *d* of late R. Watson Hall, Lowton St Mary, Lancashire. *Educ:* Harrow. Started at Samuda Bros Ltd on the Thames as a ship-builder, 1886; MINA 1890; North Somerset Yeomanry, 1890; Vickers, Sons & Co. Ltd 1892; 2nd in Command North Somerset Yeomanry at outbreak of war, seconded for special service with the Admiralty, 1914–18; Member of the Shell Committee, 1918, and of the Naval Inter-Allied Commission of Control in Germany and Austria, 1920; a Major of T. F. Reserve, 1919, and retired, 1921; Freedom of the Cutlers' Co. Sheffield, 1921; Freedom and Livery of the Worshipful Company of Shipwrights, and Freedom of the City of London, 1924. *Recreations:* shooting, golf, racquets, motoring; searching out the family pedigree and writing a book on the Family History. *Address:* Holly Bowers, Chislehurst, Kent. *TA:* Benthall, Chislehurst, 343. *T:* Chislehurst 343. *Clubs:* Cavalry, MCC.

Died 27 July 1947.

BENTINCK, Frederick Cavendish-; JP; *b* 1856; *s* of late Rt Hon. George Augustus Frederick Cavendish-Bentinck, MP; *m* 1887, Ruth Mary St Maur; two *s* two *d*. *Educ:* Westminster; Trinity College, Cambridge; BA. Bar, Lincoln's Inn, 1879; a family Trustee of British Museum, and a member of the Standing Committee; late director Alliance Assurance Co., Ltd. *Address:* 36 Harley House, Marylebone Road, NW1. *Clubs:* Carlton, Turf, Beefsteak.

Died 13 Nov. 1948.

BENTINCK, Adm. Sir Rudolf (Walter), KCB 1926; KCMG 1919; CB 1916; *b* 20 March 1869; 3rd *s* of late Walter Bentinck (13th Baron), 15th Hussars; *m* Mabel, *o d* of late Timothy and Hon. Mrs Fetherstonhaugh of The College, Kirkoswald, Cumberland; one *s* one *d*. *Educ:* HMS Britannia. Entered RN, 1882; Prom. Lieut (four firsts); 1st Lieut of Sandfly; engaged in operations at Tokar, Eastern Soudan, 1891 (Khedive Bronze Star); Flag-Commander to C-in-C, China, 1904–06; received Order of Sacred Treasure (3rd class) from HIM the Emperor of Japan; Member of Ordnance Board, 1908–10; in command of RN College, Osborne, 1913; Chief of Staff to Vice-Adm. Sir David Beatty, HMS Lion; present at Battle of Jutland (CB); Naval Secretary to First Lord of the Admiralty, 1918–21; Rear-Adm. First Battle Squadron, 1921–22; C-in-C, Africa Station, 1922–24; Vice-Adm. 1924; Vice-Admiral commanding Reserve Fleet, 1926; Commander-in-Chief, Plymouth Station, 1926–29; Admiral, 1928; retired list, 1929; Officer of Legion of Honour; Order of Crown of Italy; Order of St Vladimir (Russia—with swords). *Recreations:* shooting, fishing. *Address:* Winklebury Hill, Basingstoke, Hants. *Clubs:* Junior United Service; Royal Yacht Squadron, Cowes (naval member).

Died 31 March 1947.

BENTLEY, Arthur Owen, PhC; Head of School of Pharmacy, University College, Nottingham, since 1925; Major, TA, Major, HG; 2 i/c 1st Bn Notts (City) HG; OC University College, Nottingham, STC, since 1940; *b* 10 Oct. 1898; *s* of Arthur Mee Bentley and Annie Evangeline Rorke; *m* 1923, Gladys Madeline, *e d* of Robert Limpenny; three *d*. *Educ:* Mundella School and University College, Nottingham. Served in Special Brigade RE's, 1916; N Staffs Regt, 1917; 2nd Lieut RFC, 1917; Lieut RAF France, 1918–19; Pharmacist with Boots, Ltd, 1920; Demonstrator at Univ. Coll., Nottingham, 1920; Lecturer, 1922; Reader, 1937; Examiner for Statutory Examinations of Pharmaceutical Soc. since 1927; Pres. of Nottingham and District Branch of Pharmaceutical Soc., 1930–31; Member of Board of Studies in Pharmacy of University of London since 1931; External Examiner to University of Wales, 1938. *Publications:* Text-book of Pharmaceutics (4th Edn, 1937); Aids to Dispensing (with A. E. Kenyon) (3rd Edn, 1942); Text-book of Pharmaceutical Chemistry (with J. E. Driver), 1925; numerous original papers and articles in Manufacturing Chemist, Pharmaceutical

Journal, etc. *Recreations:* motoring and bridge. *Address:* University College, Nottingham. *TA:* University College, Nottingham. *T:* Beeston 54265, 55222.

Died 26 March 1943.

BENTLEY, Bertram Henry, MA, FLS; Professor of Botany, University of Sheffield, 1931–39, Emeritus Professor since 1939; *b* Manchester, 2 March 1873; *e s* of John Eugene and Caroline Bentley; *m* 1905, Esther Lloyd (*d* 1942), 2nd *d* of David Lloyd Davies, Wyre Court, Bewdley; no *c*. *Educ:* Shrewsbury School (scholar); Keble College, Oxford (scholar). 1st Nat. Science, 1896; Assistant Lecturer in Biology, Firth College, Sheffield, 1896; University Coll., Sheffield, 1897; Lecturer in Botany, University of Sheffield, 1905; Head of Department of Botany, 1908. *Recreations:* natural history, photography, gardening, music. *Address:* Kingsland, Hatherley Court Road, Cheltenham. *T:* Cheltenham 52215.

Died 24 June 1946.

BENTLEY, Charles Albert, CIE 1929; Commandant of the Order of the Nile, 1937; Emeritus Professor of Hygiene in the Egyptian University; Director, London Cinchona Bureau, since 1949; late Director of Public Health with the Government of Bengal; *b* Chipping Norton, Oxfordshire, 25 April 1873; *m* 1916, Gwendoline Mary Harper; two *s* two *d*. *Educ:* privately; University College, Liverpool (Silver medals in Chemistry and Materia Medica and prize for Practical Anatomy); Edinburgh University and Royal Colleges, Edinburgh (Prizeman in Public Health); MB, CM Edinburgh University; took diploma in Public Health, Cambridge, 1905; diploma in Tropical Medicine and Hygiene at Cambridge, 1905. Hon. MD, Calcutta, 1931. Junior Surgeon, Royal Southern Dispensary, Liverpool, 1898; CMO Empire of India and Ceylon Tea Company, Assam, 1900–07; Duar's Blackwater Fever and Malaria Commission, 1907–09; Bombay Malaria Enquiry, 1909–11; Deputy Sanitary Commissioner, Bengal, 1911–15; Kaiser-i-Hind Gold medal, 1916. Discovered that Ground-Itch was caused by larval anchylostomes in infected soil in 1901; discovered first known leucocytozoan, 1903; discovered Leishman-Donovan parasites in cases of Kala-Azar in Assam, 1903. FRSM, FRSTM & H, Fellow of Society of Medical Officers of Health, Member BMA. *Publications:* Malaria in the Duars and Blackwater Fever in the Duars (jointly with Lieut-Colonel Sir S. R. Christophers); Bombay Malaria, 1911; Malaria at Dinajpur, 1912; Report on Malaria in Bengal, 1916; Malaria and Agriculture, Bengal, 1925; numerous Public Health Reports from 1915. *Recreation:* motoring. *Address:* (Office) 10 Princes St., SW1. *T:* Whitehall 8360; 102 Beddington Gardens, Wallington, Surrey.

Died 23 Nov. 1949.

BERESFORD, Denis R. P.; *see* Pack-Beresford.

BERESFORD, John Davys; *b* 7 March 1873; *s* of late Rev. J. J. Beresford, Rector of Castor, near Peterborough; *m* Beatrice, *e d* of late J. W. H. Roskams of Clifton, Bristol; three *s* one *d*. *Educ:* Oundle, Peterborough. Came to London at eighteen, and was articled to Lacey W. Ridge, FRIBA, architect; practised architecture for some years; began to write for publication, 1906. *Publications: novels:* Jacob Stahl, 1911; The Hampdenshire Wonder, 1911; A Candidate for Truth, 1912; Goslings, 1913; The House in Demetrius Road, 1914; The Invisible Event, 1915; The Mountains of the Moon, 1915; These Lynnekers, 1916; House Mates, 1917; Nineteen Impressions, 1918; God's Counterpoint, 1918; The Jervaise Comedy, 1919; An Imperfect Mother, 1920; Revolution, 1921; Signs and Wonders, 1921; The Prisoners of Hartling, 1922; (with E. O. Hoppe), Taken from Life, 1922; Love's Pilgrim, 1923; The Imperturbable Duchess, and other Stories, 1923; Unity, 1924; The Monkey Puzzle 1925; That Kind of Man, 1926; The Tapestry, 1927; All or Nothing, 1928; The Instrument of Destiny, 1928; Writing Aloud,

1928; Real People, 1929; The Meeting Place, 1929; Love's Illusion, 1930; Seven Bobsworth, 1930; An Innocent Criminal, 1931; The Old People, 1931; The Next Generation, 1932; The Middle Generation, 1932; The Young People, 1933; The Inheritor, 1933; The Camberwell Miracle, 1933; The Case for Faith-healing, 1934; Peckover, 1934; On a Huge Hill, 1935; Blackthorn Winter, 1936; The Faithful Lovers, 1936; Cleo, 1937; What I Believe, 1938; The Unfinished Road, 1938; Snell's Folly, 1939; Quiet Corner, 1940; (with Esmé Wynne-Tyson) Strange Rival, 1940; What Dreams May Come, 1941; A Common Enemy, 1942; The Long View, 1942; (with Esmé Wynne Tyson) Men in the Same Boat, 1943; If This were True, 1944; The Prisoner, 1946; (with Esmé Wynne-Tyson) The Riddle of the Tower, 1944, and The Gift, 1947; belles lettres: H. G. Wells, 1915; (with Kenneth Richmond) W. E. Ford, a Biography, 1917; plays (with late Arthur Scott Craven): A Royal Heart; The Compleat Angler; (with Kenneth Richmond) Howard and Son; numerous short stories and critical articles. Recreation: carpentry. Address: c/o Westminster Bank Ltd, Oxford.

Died 2 Feb. 1947.

BERESFORD-PEIRSE, Major Sir Henry Bernard de la Poer, 4th Bt cr 1814; DSO 1901; late Lieut Yorkshire Hussars; 3rd Batt. Imperial Yeomanry; b 9 Jan. 1875; e s of Sir Henry Beresford-Peirse, 3rd Bt, and Lady Adelaide Bernard (d 1884), d of 3rd Earl of Bandon; S father, 1926; m 1904, Lady Mabel M. Campbell, d of 3rd Earl Cawdor; two s. Educ: Eton; Magdalen Coll., Oxford; BA. Served S Africa, 3rd Imperial Yeomanry, 1900–01 (despatches twice, DSO); hon. rank of Major in the army. Heir: s Henry Campbell de la Poer [BA Oxon; b 24 April 1905; m 1932, Margaret, d of Frank Grant, Knockie, Inverness-shire; two s]. Address: St Gregory's, Bedale, Yorkshire.

Died 14 May 1949.

BERGIN, Osborn Joseph, PhD; DLitt; LittD. Emeritus Professor of Early (including Mediæval) Irish Language and Literature, National University of Ireland; Vice-President of Philological Society. Publications: Stories from Keating's History of Ireland; Keating's Three Shafts of Death; (with RI Best) Lebor na Huidre; contributions to Eriu, etc. Address: 19 Grosvenor Place, Dublin.

Died 6 Oct. 1950.

BERGIN, William; Emeritus Professor of Physics, University College, Cork; b Kildare, 1864; s of late Charles Bergin; m 1911, Aileen Grace, d of late Denny Lane, MA, Cork; two d. Educ: Tullabeg, King's Co.; Trinity College, Dublin (Math. Scholar, Gold Medallist, and M'Cullagh Prizeman). Address: St Brandons, Cork. Clubs: County, Cork.

Died 29 Dec. 1942.

BERGIUS, Friedrich Karl Rudolph; Member of the Board of the Deutsche Bergin-Aktiengesellschaft; Chairman of the Board of the Holzhydrolyse Aktiengesellschaft; of the International Sugar and Alcohol Co. Isaco, The Hague; b Goldschmieden, Silesia, 11 Oct. 1884; s of Heinrich Bergius, President of the Chemische Fabrik, Goldschmieden, and Marie, d of Professor Friedrich Haase, of the University of Breslau; m Ottilie Kratzert; two s one d. Educ: Breslau; Leipzig; Karlsruhe; Berlin. Dr phil., Leipzig, 1907; Privatdozent an der Technische Hochschule, Hannover, private research laboratory there; later Director of different stock-holding companies of the chemical-oil and coal industry in Germany and abroad; inventor of process for the transformation of coal into oil and the process for the transformation of wood into sugar; Dr phil.nat. hc, Heidelberg; Dr ing eh Hannover; Hon. Dr of Science, Harvard University; Nobel Prize for Chemistry, 1931; Inhaber der Liebig-Medaille; Melchett-Medaille; Esener Medaille; Hon. Member Institute of Petroleum, Academia de Stiinte din Roumania, Physikalischer Verein, Frankfurt-a-M, Verein zur Beförderung des

Gewerbfleisses, Berlin; member of a number of scientific societies in Germany and abroad. Publications: Die Anwendung hoher Drucke bei chemischen Vorgängen und eine Nachbildung des Entstehungsprozesses der Steinkohle, 1913; Verfahren zur Herstellung von flüssigen oder löslichen organischen Verbindungen aus Steinkohle udgl, 1913; Die Verflüssigung der Kohle, 1925; The Transformation of Coal into Oil by means of Hydrogenation, 1926; Contributions to Knowledge of the Transformation of Cellulose and Lignin into Coal, 1928; Recent Developments in the Realm of Coal, Oil, and the Chemistry of Wood, 1928; Die Herstellung von Zucker aus Holz und ähnlichen Naturstoffen, 1931; Chemische Reaktionen unter hohem Druck, 1932; Conversion of Wood to Carbohydrates and Problems in the Industrial use of Concentrated Hydrochloric Acid, 1937. Recreations: travelling, fine arts, bibliophile, golf, riding, motoring, swimming. Address: Heidelberg, Albert Ueberlestrasse 3, Germany. TA: Bergin, Heidelberg. T: office 6412, private 2971. Clubs: Automobilclub von Deutschland, Deutscher Klub, Berlin.

Died 29 March 1949.

BERGSON, Henri (Louis); Member of the French Academy, 1914; Member of the Institute; Grand Cross Legion of Honour; Officer de l'Instruction Publique; b Paris, 18 Oct. 1859; s of late Michael and Kate Bergson. Educ: Lycée Condorcet; Ecole Normale. Professor of Philosophy, Lycée d'Angers, 1881–83; Lycée de Clermont, 1883–88; Professor at the Collège Rollin, 1888–89; Lycée Henri IV, 1889–97; Professor at the Ecole Normale supérieure, 1897–1900; Professor at the College of France, 1900–21; Gifford Lecturer, Edinburgh, 1912; Nobel Prize for Literature, 1927. Publications: Essai sur les données immédiates de la conscience, 1889; Matière et mémoire, 1896; Le Rire, 1900; L'Evolution créatrice, 1907; L'énergie spirituelle, 1919; Les deux sources de la morale et de la religion, 1932; La Pensée et le Mouvant, 1935, etc. Address: 47 Boulevard Beauséjour, Paris.

Died 5 Jan. 1941.

BERKELEY, 8th Earl of, cr 1679; **Randal Thomas Mowbray Rawdon Berkeley,** FRS; Viscount Dursley, 1679; b 31 Jan. 1865; S father, 1888; m 1st, 1887, Kate (d 1898), d of William Brand, and widow of Arthur Jackson; 2nd, 1924, Mary Emlen Lloyd, d of late John Lowell, of Boston, USA. Late Lieut RN. Heir: none. Address: Berkeley Castle, Gloucestershire. Club: Army and Navy.

Died 15 Jan. 1942.

BERKELEY, Sir Comyns, Kt 1934; MA, MD, MC Cantab, FRCP, FRCS, FRCOG, MMSA (Hon.); Consulting Obstetric and Gynæcological Surgeon, Middlesex Hospital; Consulting Obstetric Surgeon, City of London Lying-in Hospital; Consulting Surgeon to Chelsea Hospital for Women; Consulting Gynæcological Surgeon, Hornsey, Central and Eltham Hospitals; Chairman of the Central Midwives Board; Surgeon in charge of the Middlesex War Hospital, Clacton-on-Sea, 1914–18; b London, 16 Oct. 1865; e s of G. A. Berkeley, Belgrave Rd, SW; m 1895, Ethel (d 1945), y d of E. King Fordham, DL, JP, of Ashwell, Herts. Educ: Marlborough; Caius College, Camb. Entered Middlesex Hospital, 1888; filled offices of Home Surgeon, House Physician, Obstetric House Surgeon, Obstetrical Registrar, Tutor in Obstetrics and Diseases of Women, elected to Staff, 1903; sometime Examiner in Midwifery and Diseases of Women, to the Universities of Oxford, Cambridge, Bristol, Birmingham, London, Liverpool, Manchester, Leeds, St Andrews, Sheffield, Glasgow, and Wales, to the Conjoint Board of England, Society of the Apothecaries, and to Central Midwives' Board; Hon. Treasurer The College of Nursing; also worked as House Physician at the Brompton Consumption Hospital and at the Children's Hospital, Great Ormond St. Publications: The Abnormal in Obstetrics, 1938; A Text-book of Gynæcological

Surgery, 4th edition, 1941; The Difficulties and Emergencies of Obstetric Practice, 3rd edition, 1921; Gynæcology in General Practice, 2nd edition, 1922; A Handbook for Midwives and Obstetric Dressers, 13th edition, 1945; Gynæcology for Nurses and Gynæcological Nursing, 10th edition, 1945; Pictorial Midwifery, 4th Edition, 1941; Editor of The Journal of Obstetrics and Gynæcology of the British Empire; Editor of The Ten Teachers, Midwifery and Diseases of Women; articles on Obstetrics and Gynæcology in Churchill's System of Treatment, the Encyclopædia of Medicine, and in The System of Gynæcology. *Recreations:* travelling, golf. *Address:* 53 Wimpole Street, W1. *T:* Welbeck 5644. *Clubs:* Oxford and Cambridge, Cowdray.

Died 27 Jan. 1946.

BERLYN, Mrs Alfred; journalist and author; one *d.* *Educ:* Queen's College, Harley Street. *Publications:* Vera in Poppyland; Sunrise Land; Rambles in Eastern England, etc. Contributor to Lady's Pictorial, 1886; dramatic critic of The Queen, 1886–1908; contributor to The World (Ambrosia), 1903–1913, and of essays, stories, and descriptive articles to other prominent papers and magazines; is an authority on East Anglia. *Address:* 12 Flanders Road, W4.

Died 11 April 1943.

BERNACCHI, Louis Charles, OBE, FRGS, Chevalier of the Legion of Honour (Lieut-Commander RNVR (Anti-Submarine Division), 1914–19); Special Service Section since 1939; scientist and explorer; *b* 1876; *e s* of A. G. D. Bernacchi, JP, Tasmania; *m* 1906, Winifred Edith, 3rd *d* of Alfred Hellyer Harris, South End, Donnington, Chichester; two *s* two *d*. *Educ:* The Hutchins School, Tasmania; Melbourne University (Observatory Branch). Physicist to Southern Cross Antarctic Expedition, 1898; came to England, 1900; received Cuthbert Peek Grant from Royal Geographical Society; Physicist to the National Antarctic Expedition under Capt. Scott, 1901–04; The King's Antarctic Medal; Royal Geographical Medal; Member of Council, Royal Geographical Soc., 1929–31; travelled in British Namaqualand and German SW Africa, 1905, Primeval Forests of Peru (Upper Amazon Basin) 1906, Central Borneo and other remote parts of the World; contested (L) Widnes Division, Lancashire, 1910; Chatham Borough, Kent, Dec. 1910; 1914–15 Star; USA Navy Cross. *Publications:* To the South Polar Regions, 1901; A Very Gallant Gentleman (No Surrender Oates), 1933; Saga of the 'Discovery,' 1938; various publications of the scientific results of the Southern Cross and the Discovery, on Terrestrial Magnetism, Meteorology, Seismology, Gravity, Atmospheric Electricity, etc. *Recreations:* tennis, fencing. *Address:* 55 Porchester Terrace, W2. *T:* Paddington 0718. *Clubs:* Athenæum, Reform.

Died 24 April 1942.

BERNADOTTE, Count Folke; *b* 2 Jan. 1895; *s* of Oscar, Prince Bernadotte and Ebba Munck af Fulkila; *m* 1928, Estelle Romaine, *d* of H. E. Manville, Pleasantville, New York; two *s*. Lieutenant Royal Horse Guards (Sweden), 1918; Capt. 1930; Army Reserve, 1930; Major, 1941. President Swedish Scouting Association, 1943; President Swedish Red Cross Association, 1946; Leader Swedish Red Cross Delegation to Germany for evacuation of Scandinavian concentration camp prisoners, March–May 1945. UN mediator in Palestine, 1948. *Publications:* Pojkar och scouting (Boys and Scouting), 1940; Slutet (The End), 1945. Instead of Arms, 1949; To Jerusalem, 1951 (posthumous). *Address:* Dragongarden, Stockholm.

Died 17 Sept. 1948.

BERNARD, Col Ronald Playfair St Vincent, DSO 1917–18; MC; special employment general staff; *b* 25 April 1888; *s* of late F. G. Bernard, Singapore; *m* 1st, 1921, Kathleen Mary (*d* 1922), *d* of John H. Cleland,

Eversfield House, Richmond, Surrey; 2nd, 1923, Katharine Etheldreda, *e d* of Rev. Percy Frederick Wigan, Puckrup Hall, Twining, near Tewkesbury; two *s* one *d*. Served European War, 1915–18 (despatches, MC, DSO); retired 1938. *Address:* Lawnwood, Ash Hill, Compton, Wolverhampton. *T:* 20322.

Died 25 Jan. 1943.

BERNAYS, Robert Hamilton; MP (L) Bristol (North) since 1931 (L National since 1936); *b* 6 May 1902; *s* of late Rev. Preb. S. F. L. Bernays, The Rectory, Finchley, N3; *m* 1942, Nancy, *o d* of late G. B. Britton and Mrs Britton, Shortwood Lodge, Pucklechurch, nr Bristol; two *s*. *Educ:* Rossall; Worcester College, Oxford (Major Exhibitioner History). Pres., Oxford Union, 1925; Mem. of Oxford debating team to USA, 1925; contested (L) Rugby, 1929; leader-writer on News-Chronicle, 1925; special correspondent for News-Chronicle in India, 1931, and in Germany and Austria, 1934; Member of Makerere and Sudan Education Commissions, 1937; Parliamentary Private Secretary to Sir Robert Hamilton, Under-Secretary for the Colonies, 1931–32; Parliamentary Secretary, Ministry of Health, 1937–39; Parliamentary Secretary, Ministry of Transport, 1939–40; Deputy Regional Commissioner for Southern Civil Defence Region, 1940–42; resigned Deputy Commissionership and joined Army as a sapper in Royal Engineers, 1942; commissioned RE 1943, Capt. 1944. *Publications:* Naked Fakir, a study of Gandhi; Special Correspondent. *Address:* Allington Court, Allington Street, SW1. *T:* Victoria 2024. *Club:* Beefsteak.

Died Jan. 1945.

BERNERS, 14th Baron *cr* 1455; **Gerald Hugh Tyrwhitt-Wilson;** Bt *cr* 1808; *b* 18 Sept. 1883; *s* of late Commodore Hon. Hugh Tyrwhitt and Julia Mary, *d* of W. Orme Foster, MP (she *m* 2nd, Col W. W. Bennet); *S* uncle, 1918; assumed by Royal licence, 1919, additional surname of Wilson. *Educ:* Eton. Honorary attaché in the Diplomatic Service, 1909–20. Musical works: (Opera) Carrosse du Saint Sacrement, first performed Paris, Theatre des Champs Elysées, 1923; (Ballet) Triumph of Neptune, given by Diaghileff Ballet, London, Paris, Monte Carlo, 1926; (Ballet) Luna Park, Cochran's 1930 Review; (Ballet) A Wedding Bouquet, Sadler's Wells, 1937; (Ballet) Cupid and Psyche, Sadler's Wells, 1939; (Ballet) Les Sirenes, 1946; film music to The Half-Way House, 1944. Held exhibitions of oil paintings, Lefèvre Galleries, 1931 and 1936. *Publications:* First Childhood, 1934; The Camel, 1936; The Girls of Radcliff Hall, 1937; Far from the Madding War, 1941; Percy Wallingford and Mr. Pidger, 1941; Count Omega, 1941; The Romance of a Nose, 1942; A Distant Prospect, 1945. *Recreations:* none. *Address:* Faringdon House, Berkshire; 3 Foro Romano, Rome.

Died 19 April 1950.

BERNERS, Brig.-Gen. Ralph Abercrombie, DSO 1917; retired pay; *b* 1871; 2nd *s* of late Chas. H. Berners of Woolverstone Park, Ipswich, Suffolk, and Mary, 2nd *d* of Sir Ralph Anstruther, 4th Bart; *m* 1898, Laura Gertrude, 2nd *d* of late General Sir Robert Michael Laffan; no *c*. *Educ:* Eton; RM College, Sandhurst. Gazetted to the Royal Welch Fusiliers, 1890; served Hazara Expedition, 1891; International Occupation of Crete, 1897–98; European War, 1914–18; 3rd Afghan War, 1919; commanded a Brigade, 1916–19; late Colonel of the Royal Welch Fusiliers; retired in 1920 with the hon. rank of Brig.-General. *Address:* Chaffeymoor Grange, Bourton, Dorset. *TA:* Bourton, Dorset.

Died 25 Feb. 1949.

BERRIDGE, Harold, CIE 1919; OBE 1914; MInstCE, MIMechE; *b* 1872; *s* of late Henry and Maud Berridge, Leicester; *m* 1st, Alice Harriet (*d* 1933), *d* of late Col W. H. C. Lye, HEICS; two *s*; 2nd, 1934, Phyllis Kathleen, *d* of late Lt-Col Philip Mervyn Doyle, RAMC. *Educ:* City of London School. Civil engineering pupilage, 1890–93;

Resident Engineer, Poole Harbour, 1893–96; Engineer to John Mowlem & Co., City and South London Railway, 1897–98; Agent W. Hill & Co., Plymouth Rock Removal Contracts, 1898–1901; Agent Scott & Middleton, Pallion Shipyard Contracts, 1901–02; Assist-Supt New York approaches Hudson Tunnel, 1902–03; Chief Engineer Aden Port Trust, 1904–24; Assistant Marine Transport Officer, Aden, Aug.–Oct. 1914; Commission as Major and Commandant Aden Volunteers and Aden Rifles IDF, 1917–18; Garrison Engineer and DAD Rys Aden Field Force, 1918–20 (twice despatches, CIE, OBE); Assistant to Administrator of Housing Development Schemes, London County Council, 1925–31. *Publications:* professional papers in Proceedings Institution of Civil Engineers. *Address:* c/o National Bank of India, 26 Bishopsgate, EC.

Died 17 June 1949.

BERRY, Rev. Canon Edward Arthur, MA; Canon and Prebendary of York, 1926–47; Surrogate, 1914–47; Proctor in Convocation, 1921–47; Vicar of Drypool, 1914–47; Chaplain HM Prison, Hull, 1922–40; Chaplain Millitary Detention Barracks, 1940; OCF; *b* 12 Oct. 1871; *s* of Edward Berry; *m* late Annie Rosa Suffolk; one *s. Educ:* Norwich; Hatfield Hall, Durham (Exhibitioner); Ridley Hall, Cambridge. Deacon, 1898; Priest, 1899; Treasurer York House of Convocation, 1922–47; Curate, Langley, Worcs, 1898–1900; Holy Trinity, Nottingham, 1900–09; Vicar of St Barnabas, Mansfield (or Pleasley Hill), 1909–14; Rural Dean of Kingston-upon-Hull, 1932–38; Member Church of England Clergy Pension Board; Central Council Women's Work; Standing Committee of House of Clergy; Standing Committee of Church Assembly; Social and Industrial Commission. *Publication:* article in Voces Clamantium. *Address:* South Lawn Cottage, College Road, Lansdown, Bath. *Clubs:* Church House, Overseas.

Died 11 March 1949.

BERRY, Sir James, Kt 1925; BS London University; FRCS; Hon. DCL Durham; Hon. FRSM; Lauréat de l'Académie française; Officer of Star of Rumania, and Cross Meritul Sanitar of Rumania; Order of St Sava of Serbia and St Anne of Russia; FSA; Consulting Surgeon and Emeritus Lecturer on Clinical Surgery, Royal Free Hospital; Ext. Examiner in Surgery, University of Wales, 1922–24; President Medical Society of London, 1921–22 (Lettsomian Lecturer, 1913, Orator, 1932); President Royal Society of Medicine, 1926–28; Joint-Head of Anglo-Serbian Hospital Unit, Serbia, 1915–16; Head of British Red Cross Unit, Russia and Rumania, 1916–17; *b* 1860; *e s* of late Edward Berry, Solicitor and Shipowner, Kingston, Ont and Croydon, and of Ada, *d* of Ethanan Bicknell, Herne Hill; *m* 1st, 1891, Frances May (*d* 1934), *d* of late S. S. Dickinson, formerly MP for Stroud; 2nd, 1935, Mabel Marian, *d* of late T. Lewis Ingram, The Priory, Wimbledon Common, SW. *Educ:* Whitgift School (Scholar); St Bartholomew's Hospital (Scholar). *Publications:* Diseases of the Thyroid Gland, 1901; Manual of Surgical Diagnosis, 1904; and other books on surgical, and papers on archæological-subjects; A Red Cross Unit in Serbia (with his wife and others), 1916; A Cromwellian Major-General (with Stephen G. Lee), 1938. *Recreations:* archæology, history and travelling. *Address:* Kirby Gate, Westmead, Roehampton, SW15. *T:* Putney 5571. *Clubs:* Athenæum, National Liberal, Roehampton.

Died 17 March 1946.

BERRY, Martha McChesney; Director of Berry Schools, Mount Berry, Ga; *b* 7 Oct. 1866; *d* of Capt. Thomas Berry and Frances Rhea; unmarried. *Educ:* Edgeworth School, Baltimore; European travel; PdD, Univ. of Ga, 1920; LLD, Univ. of NC, 1930. Founded the Berry Schools (for underprivileged mountain boys and girls), 1902; Member of Colonial Dames of America; Member of Daughters of the American Revolution;

voted distinguished citizen by Georgia Legislature, 1924; awarded Roosevelt Medal for services to the nation, 1925; Pictorial Review award of $5000 for outstanding service, 1927; voted one of 12 greatest American women in nation-wide poll, 1931; gold medal of Town Hall Club, New York, for accomplishment of lasting merit, 1931; resolution of appreciation voted by the State Senate, 1933; only woman member of Board of Regents, Georgia University system, 1933; and of Georgia State Planning Commission, 1937; LLD, Bates College, 1933, University of Wisconsin, 1934; Duke University, 1935; Oberlin University, 1936; Eleanor Van Rennsaeller Fairfax Medal by Colonial Dames of America for patriotic service, 1933; LHD Berry College, 1933; DPS Oglethorpe University, 1935; Annual Medal of American Institute of Social Science, 1939; Episcopalian; Vice-Pres. of American Forestry Association. *Publications:* The Southern Highlander; The Mount Berry News. *Address:* Mount Berry, Georgia, USA. *Clubs:* Woman's, Town Hall, Cosmopolitan, New York.

Died 27 Feb. 1942.

BERTEAU, Francis Cyrus; JP; ISO 1914; *b* 12 May 1856; *s* of late F. Berteau, JP, Stipendiary Magistrate, Twillingate; *m* 1883, Margaret (*d* 1938), *d* of late Major Coen, HM 49th Regiment; one *s* three *d. Educ:* Victoria College, Jersey. Entered Newfoundland Civil Service as Clerk in HM Customs, 1878; Clerk in Treasury, 1880; Collector HM Customs, Labrador, 1881; Clerk in Colonial Secretary's Office, 1889; Chief Clerk, 1891; sent on mission to Ottawa to inquire into Canadian financial system with a view of applying same to Newfoundland, 1898; remodelled Newfoundland Government's financial system, 1898; Comptroller and Auditor-General Colony of Newfoundland 1898–1934; Acting Manager Government Savings Bank, 1910–13; Financial Agent of Commissioners Newfoundland Railway, 1923; Member Advisory Board Newfoundland Saving Banks since 1934; Member Overseas League. *Address:* St John's, Newfoundland. *Clubs:* City, Curling, St John's.

Died 21 Sept. 1945.

BERTHON, Henry Edward, MVO 1914; MA Wadham College, Oxford; late Reader in French Literature in the University of Oxford; French Tutor to Prince of Wales, 1912–14 and to Prince Olaf of Norway, 1924–26; Officier d'Académie; *b* Paris, 11 Dec. 1862; *s* of Jean Edouard Berthon, and Lucie Mailand; *m* 1892, Edith Annie Rooker; one *s* two *d. Educ:* College Ste Barbe, Paris; University of Paris. Assistant-Master at King Edward's High School, Birmingham, 1890; Lecturer in and afterwards Professor of French Language and Literature, at University College, Nottingham, 1895. *Publications:* Synoptic Tables of Old French Phonology; Advanced French Composition; French Grammar; Modern French Verse; Modern French Prose; Nine French Poets; critical editions of various French Classics, etc. *Recreations:* music, the drama, travelling. *Address:* 10 Norham Gardens, Oxford. *T:* 3266.

Died 2 March 1948.

BERTIE, Col Hon. Reginald Henry, CB 1900; Royal Welch Fusiliers; *b* 26 May 1856; 6th *s* of 6th Earl of Abingdon; *m* 1892, Lady Amy Evelyn (*d* 1948), *e d* of Lord Courtenay (*d* 1898), and *sister* of 14th Earl of Devon. *Educ:* Eton. Entered Army, 1874; Lieut-Col, 1899; served in command of 2nd Batt. RW Fusiliers in Relief Expedition, Pekin, China, 1900 (medal and clasp, despatches, CB); occupation of Crete, 1897–98. *Address:* Reynell, Newton Abbot, Devon.

Died 15 June 1950.

BERTRAM, Julius; Solicitor; *b* 8 Nov. 1866; *s* of late Julius Alfred Bertram and Martha Janei, *d* of Capt. James Gammell, of Ardiffery, NB; *m* 1907, Marjorie, *d* of late Hon. Sir Henry Sutton; one *s. Educ:* Repton; New

College, Oxford; BA 1889. MP (L) Hitchin Div. Herts, 1906–10. *Address:* Abington Hall, Camb.; Martinhoe Cleave, N Devon; 8 Breams Buildings, EC4.

Died 5 Nov. 1944.

BERTRAND, Louis (Marie Emile); Member of the French Academy since 1925; *b* Spincourt, Meuse, 20 March 1866. *Educ:* Lycée de Bar-le-Duc; Lycée Henri IV; L'Ecole Normale Supérieure. Professor of Rhetoric, Lycée d'Alger, 1891–1900; Chevalier Légion d'Honneur. *Publications:* La Fin du classicisme et le retour à l'antique, 1897; Le Sang des races roman, 1899; La Cina, 1901; Le Rival de don Juan, 1903; Pépète le bien-aimé, 1904; Le Jardin de la Mort, 1905; L'Invasion, 1907; Le mirage oriental, 1909; Mademoiselle de Jessincourt, 1911; Saint Augustin, 1913; Sanguis martyrum, 1917; L'Infante, 1920; Les Villes d'or, 1921; Louis XIV, 1923; etc. *Address:* 183 rue de l'Université, Paris.

Died 6 Dec. 1941.

BERWICK, 8th Baron *cr* 1784; **Thomas Henry Noel-Hill;** *b* 2 June 1877; *s* of Hon. and Rev. Thomas Noel, twin brother of 7th Baron (*d* 1888), and Frederica Sarah (*d* 1883), *d* of late Rev. Wm David Morrice, Hon. Canon of Salisbury Cathedral; *S* uncle, 1897; *m* 1919, Edith Teresa, *d* of late William Hulton, Venice. Late Shropshire Yeomanry. *Educ:* Radley College; Trinity College, Oxford. Hon. Attaché to British Embassy, Paris, 1903–11 and 1915–16. Owns about 4000 acres. *Heir: c* Charles Michael Wentworth Noel-Hill. *Address:* Attingham Park, Shrewsbury. *Clubs:* Carlton, St James's.

Died 12 June 1947.

BERWICK, William Edward Hodgson, ScD, FCPS; Professor of Mathematics, University College of North Wales, Bangor, 1926–41, Emeritus since 1942; *b* Bradford, 1888; *m* 1923, Daisy May, *y d* of Dr W. R. Thomas, Sheffield. *Educ:* Bradford Grammar School; Clare College, Cambridge (Scholar), Fourth Wrangler, 1909; 1st Class, Part II Math. Tripos, 1910; Smith's University Prize, 1911; Fellow of Clare College, 1921–24. Assistant Lecturer University of Bristol, 1911–13; Lecturer in Mathematics, University College, Bangor, 1913–20; Reader in Mathematical Analysis in Leeds University, 1921–26; Lecturer there, 1920–26; during European War of 1914–18 rendered valuable service on Technical Staff of Anti-Aircraft Experimental Section of the Munitions Inventions Dept at Portsmouth. *Publications:* various papers on mathematical subjects (chiefly arithmetical). *Address:* Ceinwen Villa, Bangor, Carnarvonshire.

Died 13 May 1944.

BESIER, Rudolf; dramatist; *b* July 1878; of Dutch extraction; *m* Charlotte, *d* of Rev. J. P. S. Woodward, Plumpton, Sussex. *Educ:* Elizabeth College, Guernsey; Heidelberg. Worked for several years in various journalistic capacities, especially for the firm of C. Arthur Pearson, Limited; since 1908 has devoted himself chiefly to the theatre. *Plays:* The Virgin Goddess; Olive Latimer's Husband; Don; Lady Patricia; Kipps (with H. G. Wells); Kings and Queens; Buxell; Robin's Father (with Hugh Walpole) The Prude's Fall; The Ninth Earl; Secrets (with May Edginton); The Barretts of Wimpole Street; and several translations and adaptations from the French. *Address:* c/o Curtis Brown Ltd, 6 Henrietta Street, Covent Garden, WC2.

Died June 1942.

BESLY, Maurice, MA Oxon, BA Cantab; conductor, composer, solicitor and Notary Public; also Director of Performing Rights Society Ltd; *b* 28 Jan. 1888; *e s* of Rev. E. F. S. Besly, Rural Dean of Cleveland, Yorks, and Evelyn Georgina Moore, Brighton; *m* 1st, Kathleen Eleanor Mary Bullen; one *s*; 2nd, 1930, Marceline d'Alroy, Lecturer and author of d'Alroy's Diary. *Educ:* Tonbridge; Caius College (classical scholar of both), Cambridge. Leipsic conservatorium under Teichmuller,

Schreck, and Krehl; assistant music master at Tonbridge till the war; commissioned, 1914; served in France till 1918 (wounded, prisoner at Mainz); Organist of Queen's College, Oxford, and Conductor of Oxford Orchestra, 1919–26; with the Scottish Orchestra, 1919–26; with the Scottish Orchestra, 1924. *Publications:* numerous songs, part-songs, and orchestral suites. *Address:* c/o Boosey and Hawkes, 295 Regent Street, W1.

Died 20 March 1945.

BESSELL-BROWNE, Brig. Gen. Alfred Joseph; *see* Browne.

BEST, Hon. Margaret, CBE 1938; OBE 1929; Hon. Secretary School Empire-Tour Committee since 1927; *b* 6 Oct. 1872; *e d* of 5th Baron Wynford. *Educ:* privately. Served on local and County Committees in connection with Cottage Hospital, Red Cross, Arts and Crafts, etc., in Dorset; Clerk in the War Office, 1915–18. *Recreations:* walking, cruising, travelling. *Address:* 14 Avenue Court, Chelsea, SW3. *T:* Kensington 8514. *Club:* Royal Empire Society.

Died 30 Nov. 1941.

BEST, Hon. Sir Robert Wallace, KCMG 1908; *b* Fitzroy, Victoria, 18 June 1856; *s* of Robert Best, Custom Department; *m* 1st, Jane (decd), *d* of Hon. G. D. Langridge, sometime Chief Secretary of Victoria; 2nd, Maude Evelyn, *d* of George Crocker Smith, of St Kilda; three *s* six *d. Educ:* Fitzroy. Called to Bar, 1881; Mayor of Fitzroy, 1888–89; MLA Fitzroy, 1889–1901; President of Board of Land and Works, Minister for Lands, and Commissioner for Trade and Customs, 1894–99; was Chairman of Royal Commission on Constitutional Reform; Chairman of Committees in the Senate of the first Federal Parliament, 1901–03; Vice-President of Executive Council of Commonwealth of Australia and Leader of Government in Senate 1907–08; Minister of Trade and Customs, 3rd Deakin Administration, 1909–10; Member House of Representatives, Federal Parliament, 1910–22. *Recreations:* horse-riding, tennis, golf. *Address:* 54 Berkeley Street, Hawthorn, E2, Victoria, Australia.

Died 27 March 1946.

BEST, Sir Thomas Alexander Vans, KCMG 1932; KBE 1926; CMG 1916; CBE 1918; *s* of Robert; *s* of late Alexander Vans Best, FRCP and S; *m* 1904, Lady Helena, *y d* of late Admiral the Hon. V. A. Montagu, and *sister* of 9th Earl of Sandwich, FSA; one *s. Educ:* Cheltenham; Magdalen College, Oxford; BA 1894. Gold medallist French Ministry of Public Instruction. Taylorian Scholar, Oxford; in British Central Africa under Foreign Office, and Colonial Office; Colonial Secretary Trinidad, 1919–25; Lieut-Governor on Malta, 1925–30; Governor and Commander-in-Chief of the Windward Islands, 1930–33; retired 1933; has administered the Governments of the Falkland Islands, Leeward Islands, Trinidad, and Malta. *Recreations:* music, languages. *Club:* St James's.

Died 24 Nov. 1941.

BETHELL, 1st Baron of Romford, UK, 1922; **John Henry Bethell;** Bt *cr* 1911, Kt 1906; JP Essex; *b* 23 Sept. 1861; *s* of late George Bethell, S Woodford; *m* 1895, Florence, *d* of James W. Wyles; two *s* three *d.* Was first Mayor of East Ham; MP (L) Romford Division, Essex, 1906–18, and East Ham (North) Dec. 1918–22; Director of Barclays Bank, Ltd, Royal Exchange Assurance; Chairman, Frederick Hotels Ltd and British Land Co., Ltd. *Heir: s* Hon. John Raymond Bethell. *Address:* Bushey House, Bushey, Herts. *Clubs:* National Liberal, Reform.

Died 27 May 1945.

BETHELL, Captain Adrian; late 2nd Life Guards; MFH the Holderness Hunt since 1927; *b* 11 Sept. 1890; *s* of late William Bethell; *m* 1st, 1915, Hon. Clarissa Tennant (whom he divorced 1918), *o d* of 1st Lord Glenconner (she *m* 2nd, 3rd Baron Tennyson); one *d*; 2nd, 1921,

Cicely, d of Sir John Cotterell, 4th Bt; three s. Address: Rise Park, near Hull; Watton Abbey, Driffield. Clubs: Guards, Buck's, Bachelors'.

Died 16 July 1941.

BETHELL, Maj.-Gen. Sir (Hugh) Keppel, KBE 1935; CB 1919; CMG 1918; CVO 1919; DSO 1917; late 7th (Queen's Own) Hussars; b 24 Sept. 1882; s of late Col E. H. Bethell, CMG, DSO; m 1928, Henriette Pauline Ella, widow of Herman Schiele, of Cincinnati, Ohio. Educ: Charterhouse; RMA, Woolwich; Staff College (psc). Served European War; commanded 1st Northamptonshire Regiment (48th Foot), 1st Division, BEF, 1915–16; 74th Brigade, 25th Division, BEF, 1916–18; 66th Division, 4th British Army, 1918–19 (American Distinguished Service Medal, Croix de Guerre avec palmes, Croce di Guerra, Belgian Croix de Guerre); Military Attaché to Washington, 1919–23; commanding 2nd Rhine Brigade, 1924–28; Brigadier, Northern Command, India, 1928–30; commanded Presidency and Assam District, India, 1930–34; retired pay, 1935. Recreations: hunting, shooting, polo. Clubs: Cavalry, Hurlingham, Royal Automobile.

Died 3 March 1947.

BETHUNE, Lt Col Henry Alexander; DL, JP, County of Fife; b 12 July 1866; e s of late Major Robert Bethune, late 92nd Highlanders, Nydie, Co. Fife, JP; heir-pres. to Baronetcy; m 1902, Elinor Mary, y d of late John Brown Watt, Sydney, NS Wales; one d. Educ: Glenalmond. Served S African War, 1899–1902 (despatches twice, brevet Major); retired pay, Gordon Highlanders 1905; Major 7th Bn Black Watch, 1905–10; Lt Col Comdg Depôt Gordon Highlanders, 1914–19; Capt. Royal and Ancient Golf Club of St Andrews, 1919. Recreations: shooting, golf. Address: Mountquhanie, Cupar, Fife. T: Gauldry 252. Clubs: Naval and Military; New, Edinburgh.

Died 16 Jan. 1946.

BETT, Surg. Rear-Adm. William, CB 1922; MVO 1911; MRCS, LRCP, late RN; b 1863; m 1903, Rosellen Gretchen, y d of John James Torre, of Snydale Hall, Yorkshire; five s two d. Entered Naval Medical Department, 1886; Deputy Surgeon-General, 1917; Surgeon Rear-Admiral, 1920; retired list, 1923. Address: The Staithe, Mudeford, nr Christchurch.

Died 3 March 1946.

BETTANY, Frederick George; b 1868; e s of J. Bettany; m 1913, Marie Catherine, d of Frederic Cox. Educ: The Grammar School, Leeds; Christ Church, Oxford (Scholar). First Class, Classical Moderations, 1888; First Class Classical Finals, 1890; First Class History, 1891. Senior Demy of Magdalen College, Oxford, 1891–93; joined the staff of the London Echo, 1893, and acted as Literary Reviewer and Dramatic Critic for several years; subsequently Dramatic Critic and Reviewer of Athenæum and Dramatic Critic of the Illustrated London News; Literary Editor of Sunday Times, 1901–17; on the staff of Morning Post, 1918–30; contributed to other newspapers, magazines, and reviews. Publication: Stewart Headlam, a Biography, 1926. Address: 3 Porchester Sq., W2. T: Paddington 2269. Club: Savage.

Died 27 Feb. 1942.

BETTINGTON, Gp Captain (Arthur) Vere, CMG 1919; late RAF; JP Beds; b 12 June 1881; 2nd s of late Col R. A. A. Bettington; m 1921, Florence Evelyn, o d of late Sir William Wright, of The Holt, Scalby, Yorks; no c. Served in South African War, 1899–1902; Zulu War (Natal), 1906; World War, 1914–18 (Legion on Honour); Air Adviser, New Zealand Govt, 1919; commanded RAF in Ireland, 1922; Air Attaché, S America, 1923–28, British Embassies, Buenos Aires, Rio

de Janeiro, British Legations, Santiago, and Montevideo; Order of Merit, Chile (2 class), 1925; retired list, 1931; recalled to Active List Aug. 1939 for special duties; reverted to retired list, 1945. Recreations: golf, shooting, fishing. Club: United Service.

Died 2 Aug. 1950.

BETTS, William Andrew, CMG 1917; MD; b 1866; s of late Rev. H. J. Betts, St Anne's, Birkenhead; m 1893, Adelaide Maria (d 1928), d of Jonathan Burnett, Newcastle and S Kensington. Educ: Clergy Orphan School, Canterbury; Edinburgh Univ. MD Cape Univ.; MD Edinburgh; MB, CM, FRCS, Edinburgh. House Surgeon, Borough Hospital, Birkenhead, and Royal Southern Hospital, Liverpool, 1889–93; Assist Surgeon, Provincial Hosp., Port Elizabeth, 1895–96; Civil Surgeon, attached RAMC, Egypt, 1899–1904; Inspector Public Health Dept 1904–12; Director Municipal Section, Ministry of Interior, Egypt, 1912. Publication: Egyptian Arabic Primer. Address: The Old House, Crowborough, Sussex.

Died 9 March 1945.

BETTY, Lt-Col Paget K.; see Kemmis Betty.

BEUTTLER, Brig. V. O., CBE 1940; DSO 1917; late RASC; b 14 Feb. 1886; s of James Oakley Beuttler, MA; m Eileen, d of C. B. Beddoe; one s one d. Educ: Elizabeth College, Guernsey. Joined the Army, 1907; served European War (Brevet Major, DSO); Lieut-Colonel 1933; Colonel 1937; Assistant Director of Supplies and Transport, Southern Command, 1938–39; retired pay, 1941. Address: Deepdene, Dawlish Road, Teignmouth, S Devon.

Died 2 Feb. 1948.

BEVAN, Edwyn Robert, OBE, FBA 1942; MA; Hon. Fellow of New College, Oxford; Hon. DLitt (Oxford); Hon. LLD (St Andrews); Lecturer on Hellenistic History and Literature at King's College, London, 1922–33; Gifford Lecturer for the University of Edinburgh, 1932–34; b London, Feb. 1870; s of Robert Cooper Lee Bevan; m 1896, Mary (d 1935), d of 3rd Baron Radstock; two d. Educ: Cheam, Surrey; Monkton Combe, Bath; New College, Oxford. Travelled in India, 1893; worked at the British School of Archæology in Athens, 1894; co-operated in excavations at Alexandria, Egypt, 1895; worked in Propaganda Department, 1914–17; in Department of Information, 1917–18; in Foreign Office, Political Intelligence Department, 1918–19. Publications: The Prometheus Bound of Æschylus, rendered into English Verse, 1902; The House of Seleucus, 1902; Jerusalem under the High Priests, 1904; Indian Nationalism, 1913; Stoics and Sceptics, 1913; The Method in the Madness, 1917; The Seven against Thebes of Æschylus rendered into English Verse, 1912; The Land of the Two Rivers, 1917; German Social Democracy during the War, 1918; A Memoir of Leslie Johnston, 1921; Hellenism and Christianity, 1921; two chapters in the Cambridge History of India, vol. i, 1922; joint-editor of The Legacy of Israel, 1927; Later Greek Religion, 1927; A History of Egypt under the Ptolemaic Dynasty, 1927; Sibyls and Seers, 1928; Thoughts on Indian Discontents, 1929; Chapters in Cambridge Ancient History, vols viii and ix; The Poems of Leonidas of Tarentum translated into English verse, 1931; Christianity (Home University Library), 1932; Symbolism and Belief (Gifford Lectures), 1938; Holy Images (Gifford Lectures), 1940; Christians in a World at War, 1940; The Hope of the Dawn and other poems, 1942; articles in the Encyclopædia Britannica (11th ed.), Hastings's Encyclopædia of Religion and Ethics, etc. Address: 38 Winchester Court, W8. Club: Athenæum.

Died 18 Oct. 1943.

BEVAN, Hon. Dame Maud Elizabeth, DBE 1918; *b* 18 Aug. 1856; *d* of 1st Viscount Hampden and 23rd Baron Dacre (Speaker of the House of Commons); *m* 1885, David Augustus Bevan (*d* 1937); two *s* one *d. Educ:* home. JP, 1920. *Address:* Ponters, Letty Green, Hertford, Herts. *Club:* Guards'.

Died 8 Jan. 1944.

BEVERIDGE, Rev. John, MBE 1920; Knight of St Olaf (Norway), 1938; MA; BD (Glas.); FBEA; FSA Scot.; Minister Emeritus of Gartmore, Perthshire; *b* 29 June 1857; *s* of Robert Morris Beveridge, Ayr; *m* 1884, Alice Alexandra, *d* of James Henderson, Sydney, NSW; two *d. Educ:* Ayr Academy; Glasgow University; United Presbyterian College, Edinburgh. Ministerial charges at Stow, Midlothian, 1882; Wolverhampton, 1893; Dundee, 1900; Fossoway, Kinross-shire, 1913; Gartmore, Perthshire, 1919. A pioneer of cycling in Norway he became a close student of Norwegian affairs, and received the Centenary medal of Oslo University, 1911; was the first president of the Scottish Esperanto Federation; President of the Scottish Beekeepers' Association; Grand Chaplain, IOGT (Scotland); Chaplain 1st Kinross-shire Volunteer Regt; Hon. Commissioner, Scottish War Savings Committee; one of the translators of the New Testament into Esperanto. *Publications:* History of Stow United Presbyterian Church, 1888; Dahle's Life after Death, 1896, and Konow's Sketches of Child Life, 1897, both translated from the Norse; The Covenanters, 1905; Give Me Thine Hand, 1908; La Prediko sur la Monto (Esperanto), 1910; Everyman's Library; The Olaf Sagas, 1914; The Norse King Sagas, 1930; The Scottish Expedition in Norway in 1612, 1933; Two Scottish XIII Century Songs, 1939; Petter Dass, Scoto-Norwegian Poet-Preacher, 1940; many reviews and articles on Norse, apicultural and travel subjects. *Recreations:* angling, apiculture, and travel in Norway. *Address:* 38 Broomhouse Road, Edinburgh, 12. *T:* Edinburgh 66422.

Died 29 Aug. 1943.

BEWES, Wyndham Austis, LLB Lond.; formerly Honorary Secreta of the Grotius Society and of International Law Association; *b* Dublin, Aug. 1857; *e s* of Col Wyndham Bewes, 73rd Regiment; *m* 1890, Ellen Elizabeth (*d* 1928), *d* of William C. Muller, Hillside, Shenley, Herts, *widow* of Edward Wyld, The Tile House, Denham, Bucks. *Educ:* Repton; University of London. Called to the Bar, Lincoln's Inn, 1880. *Publications:* Several books and articles, including the Law of Waste; The Romance of the Law Merchant, 1923; was editor and chief author of the last volume of Burge's Colonial and Foreign Law, 1928; for the Commercial Laws of the World, translated into English the Codes of Commerce of the chief Spanish-speaking countries. *Recreations:* travelling and reading. *Address:* 2 Priory Walk, SW10; Odsey, Ashwell, Baldock, Herts (for war's duration). *T:* Kensington 6416.

Died 28 July 1942.

BEWLEY, Henry, MD, FRCPI; physician; Consulting Physician to Adelaide Hospital and late Lecturer on Forensic Medicine and Hygiene in Trinity College, Dublin; Visiting Physician to Bloomfield Private Lunatic Asylum, Dublin; *b* Booterstown, Co. Dublin, 1860; *m* 1887; four *s. Educ:* Trinity College, Dublin; Vienna. *Publications:* various articles in medical journals. *Address:* 27 Pembroke Road, Dublin. *T:* Dublin 62033.

Died 8 Jan. 1945.

BEWLEY, Thomas Kenneth, CMG 1939; Principal Assistant Secretary in HM Treasury; *b* 3 July 1890; *s* of H. T. Bewley, MD, and E. E. Pim, Dublin; *m* 1919, Phyllis Mary Malden; two *s. Educ:* Winchester; New College, Oxford. Entered Civil Service (Treasury), 1913; served European War (RASC), 1914–18;

seconded to Irish Free State Ministry of Finance, 1922–23; Financial Adviser to HM Embassy in Washington, 1933–39. *Address:* 11 Hampstead Hill Gardens, NW3. *T:* Hampstead 3164. *Club:* Athenæum.

Died 23 June 1943.

BEWOOR, Sir Gurunath Venkatesh, KCIE 1946 (CIE 1932); Kt 1939; ICS (retired); Director, Tata Industries Ltd, Bombay; Director-in-charge Air-India and Air-India International; *m* 1912; two *s* three *d. Educ:* Deccan College, Poona; Sydney Sussex College, Cambridge. Indian Civil Service, 1912; Under-Secretary to Government of Central Provinces, Nagpur; Director-Gen. Posts and Telegraphs, India, 1934–41; Addl Sec. to Govt Defence Dept, 1941–42. Indian Delegate to Air Mail Conference, Hague, 1927, Universal Postal Congress, London, 1929, Imperial Telecommunications Conference, London, 1937, Canberra, 1942, and London, 1945, and International Civil Aviation Conference, Chicago, 1944. Secretary to Govt of India, Posts and Air Department, 1942–46; Member for Commerce and Commonwealth Relations, 1946. *Recreations:* tennis, scouting. *Address:* Shri Krishna Niwas, Poona 4, India. *TA:* Airindia, Bombay. *T:* Bombay 32871. *Clubs:* Cricket Club of India (Bombay); Poona Gymkhana (Poona); Imperial Gymkhana (New Delhi).

Died 29 Nov. 1950.

BEWSHER, Brig. Frederick William, CBE 1942 (OBE 1923); DSO 1919; MC 1916; BA, FRGS, FZS; Vice-Chairman, The Egyptian Hotels, Ltd; Bursar Victoria College, Cairo; *b* Headley, Hants, 6 Aug. 1886; *s* of S. Bewsher, Bursar, St Paul's School; *m* 1st, 1913, Eira Margaret (decd), *d* of W. Evans, CB, Board of Trade; one *s*; 2nd, 1922, Uarda, *d* of Lt-Col G. Gray Donald; one *d. Educ:* St Paul's School (Foundation Scholar); Merton College, Oxford. Assist Master, St Paul's School, 1909; Bursar, 1913–14; ADC to GOC 1st Lond. Div., 1914; Bde Major 175th Infantry Bde, 1915; Bde Major 152nd Infantry Bde, 1916 (despatches); Commandant 5th Army Musketry School, 1917 (despatches); GSO 2nd grade, 51st Highland Division, 1917; GSO 2nd grade, IVth Army Corps, 1918 (despatches); Secretary War Office Committee Status of Infantry, 1919; Bde Major 234th Inf. Bde 1919; DAAG 3rd Lahore Div. 1920; Assist Director Public Security, Director of Prisons, Palestine, 1920; raised the Palestine Gendarmerie and commanded it, 1921; granted regular commission in the Royal Fusiliers, 1921; transferred to Devon Regt, 1923; appointed to raise and command the Transjordan Frontier Force, 1926; Brevet Major and Major, 1929; Bt Lt-Col 1931; attached to Egyptian Army for Training duties with rank of Miralai, 1934; Lt-Col 1937; Col 1939; Brig. 1940; despatches, 1942 and 1943; commanded 1st Bn Royal Fusiliers, 1937–39; commanded Alexandria Area, Nov. 1939–Nov. 1945; formerly in London Rifle Brigade; Order of the Nile 3rd Class, 1936. *Publications:* Aids to the Writing of English Composition; Reformation and Renaissance; part author Rivington's British History and Rivington's Junior British History; History of 51st Highland Division. *Recreations:* shooting, fishing. *Address:* Grenville House, Sharia Gezira, Cairo. *Clubs:* Army and Navy, MCC.

Died 26 Sept. 1950.

BEWSHER, Lt-Col William Dent, DSO 1917; *b* 1868; *s* of William Blackett Bewsher; *g s* of Rev. J. Bewsher of Boulogne; unmarried. *Educ:* Clifton College; Sandhurst. Joined 2nd Hampshire Regt 1888; Adjutant 1st Hampshire Regt; served India and Aden Hinterland Expedition; retired as Major, 1909; Temp. Lt-Col, Oct. 1914, to command 10th (S) Hampshire Regt; served in Gallipoli and France (despatches); promoted Lt-Col on retirement. *Recreations:* golf, fishing, shooting. *Address:* Southwick, Sussex.

Died 9 April 1942.

BEYNON, Brig.-Gen. Henry Lawrence Norman, CMG 1916; late RA; *b* 22 June 1868. Served NW Frontier, India, 1897–98 (medal with clasp); Tirah 1897–98; capture of Sampagha and Arhanga Passes (clasp); European War, 1914–17 (CMG, Bt Col); retired pay, 1920. *Address:* Talfan, Cellan, Lampeter, Cardiganshire, West Wales.

Died 30 April 1950.

BEYNON, Sir John Wyndham, 1st Bt *cr* 1920; CBE; Sub-Prior of the Priory for Wales Order of St John of Jerusalem, since 1943; *b* 1864; *o s* of late Thomas Beynon, JP, DL, High Sheriff of County of Monmouth, 1890; *m* 1931, Lilian, *widow* of Jens E. A. Müller. *Educ:* Clifton College; abroad. JP, DL; High Sheriff of County of Monmouth, 1917–18. *Address:* The Coldra, near Newport, Mon; 9 Oakwood Court, W14. *Clubs:* Carlton, Royal Automobile.

Died 13 Oct. 1944.

BHABHA, H. J., CIE 1926; MA; Hon. DLitt; retired Inspector-General of Education in Mysore; *b* 27 June 1852; *m* 1873, Jerbai Edalji Batiwala; one *s* one *d. Educ:* Elphinstone Coll., Bombay; University College, London. Senior Fellow and Lecturer, Elphinstone College, 1874; Assistant Professor, 1875–76; Fellow of the Bombay University, 1876; Vice-Principal Professor of Logic and Moral Philosophy, Central College, Bangalore, 1876; Principal, Maharaja's College, Mysore, 1884; Education Secretary to Government of Mysore, 1890; Fellow of the Madras University, 1893; Inspector-General of Education in Mysore, 1895; retired from the Mysore service, 1910; Member of Council, Indian Institute of Science, 1928; delegate to the Congress of Imperial Universities, 1926, by the Universities of Bombay and Mysore; DLitt, Mysore University, 1926. *Publications:* Special Report on Manual Instruction in Schools of General Education, 1909; Report on the Education of Parsi Youth, 1913; A Visit to British Universities, 1926; Parsees and Modern Cremation, etc. *Recreations:* golf, riding. *Address:* Malabar Hill, Bombay 6, India. *Clubs:* National Liberal; Willingdon Sports, Bombay.

Died 23 April 1941.

BHANOT, Harnam Dass, CSI 1946; CIE 1942; ICS; Chief Secretary to Government, Punjab, since 1945; *b* 6 Jan. 1897; *s* of Pandit Bishen Dass Bhanot; *m* 1924, Santosh Swift; two *d. Educ:* St Stephen's College, Delhi; Punjab University; Sidney Sussex College, Cambridge. Served European War in Poona, Persia, and Mesopotamia, 1917–19, and in Waziristan, 1919. Joined ICS, 1921; Colonisation Officer, Nili Bar Colony, 1931–34; Senior Secretary to the Financial Commissioner, Punjab, 1934–37; Finance Secretary to Govt, Punjab, 1937–42; Commissioner, Multan, 1942–45. *Recreations:* riding and swimming. *Address:* Punjab Civil Secretariat, Lahore, Punjab. *TA:* Punjab, Lahore. *T:* Lahore 5086, 4534.

Died 24 Oct. 1948.

BICKERTON, Reginald Ernest, DSO 1917; TD; MB, ChB; Ophthalmic Surgeon; Vice-President, Seamen's (Dreadnought) Hospital Society Greenwich, 1948; *b* 1870; 4th *s* of Thomas Bickerton, FRCS Edin., Liverpool; *m* Constance, *d* of W. H. Livesey; one *s* one *d. Educ:* King Edward VI School, Berkhampstead; Univ. College, Liverpool; Vienna, Berlin, Zurich. Late House Physician and House Surgeon, Ophthalmic Assistant and Senior Resident Medical Officer, Royal Infirmary, Liverpool; late Surgeon, Pacific Steam Navigation Co.; Ophthalmic Assistant, Eye Department, General Hospital, Vienna, also Berlin and Zurich; Chief Clinical Assistant, Royal London Ophthalmic Hospital, Moorfields, and Central London Ophthalmic Hospital; Clinical Assistant, Royal Westminster Ophthalmic Hospital; Lecturer on Ophthalmology, Medical Graduates' College and Polyclinic, Chenies Street; Ophthalmic Surgeon, Seamen's Hospital, Greenwich;

Lieutenant RAMC (T) 1909; Captain, 1912; mobilised 4 Aug. 1914; served British Ex. Force, Belgium and France; Mediterranean Ex. Force, Alexandria; British Salonika Force, Salonika, and Army of the Black Sea, Turkey and Asia Minor (despatches twice, DSO); Lieut-Colonel in command 84th (1/2nd London) Field Ambulance from Aug. 1916. and attached to 28th Division throughout; Ophthalmic Specialist, BSF, and Acting ADMS to Army of the Black Sea, 1919; Hon. Surgeon to the King, 1927–32. Ophthalmic Surgeon, Seamen's Hospital, Greenwich (Dreadnought); Consulting Ophthalmic Surgeon, Evelina Hosp. for Sick Children, Southwark, Royal Waterloo Hosp. for Women and Children, and St Dunstan's Hostel for Blinded Sailors and Soldiers; Ophthalmic Consultant to Ministry of Pensions; Consulting Ophthalmic Surgeon, Hornsey Cottage Hospital; late Visiting Oculist to Min. of Pensions Special Surgical Neurological Hospital, Richmond Park; Member: BMA and Ophthalmological and RS of M, London; City of London Territorial Association; Medical Referee for Ophthalmic cases under WC Act, Home Office; Chairman and Visiting Ophthalmic Surgeon, Royal School for Blind, Leatherhead. Honorary Colonel 56th (1st London) Div. TA, 1932–40. *Publications:* Notes on Opthalmology, British Medical Journal, 1898; Blindness resulting from Mustard Gas burns during the War, British Medical Journal, 1934. *Recreations:* motoring, yachting. *Address:* 33 Portland Place, W1. *Club:* Royal Automobile.

Died 13 Sept. 1949.

BICKFORD, Brig.-Gen. Edward, CMG 1918; late RA; *b* 1861. Served Burma Expedition, 1885–87; Sikkim Expedition, 1888 (despatches); retired pay, 1918.

Died 1 Feb. 1949.

BICKFORD, Rev. William Pennington, MA, Rector of St Clement Danes since 1910; *b* Plymouth, 28 Sept. 1874; *s* of late Rear-Admiral James Edward Bickford and Sophia Jane Bickford; *m* 1907, Louie, *d* of Rev. J. J. H. Septimus Pennington, MA, Rector of St Clement Danes. *Educ:* Ashburton Grammar School, S Devon; Clare College, Cambridge. BA in Theology and Music, 1904; MA 1905. Assistant Organist and Secretary of Clare College Musical Society; Founder of the Clare College Orchestra; Curate and Churchwarden of St Clement Danes, 1905; Chaplain and Major of the Holborn Batn London Diocesan Church Lads' Brigade, 1905–10; Member of Strand Board of Guardians and Chaplain to the Bear-Yard Institution; Member for many years of the Westminster Board of Guardians; Chaplain to the Order of St John of Jerusalem; Chaplain to the London County Association of Change-Ringers; Chaplain and Founder of St Clement's Youths; Assistant Chaplain to the Royal Society of St George; Chaplain and Almoner of the London Devonian Association; Chaplain to the Staffordshire Society; Chaplain to the English County Societies; Chaplain-in-Chief to the Legion of Frontiersmen; Vice-President and Chaplain to the London DCM League; Hon. Member of the London Society of Organists; Hon. Member and Chaplain to the West London District of Oddfellows; Member and Past Master (1922) of the St Clement Danes Lodge of Freemasons; Assistant Grand Chaplain of English Freemasons, 1932; restored the Bells of St Clement's, 1919; instituted Annual Children's Festival of Oranges and Lemons, 1919; revived the Churchwarden's Box Supper and the Beating of the Bounds; Founder and Chairman of the Johnson Society of London, 1928; Founder and Conductor of the St Clement Danes Choral and Orchestral Society, 1920; Trustee of the Holborn Estate Charity, Craven Charity, Langford Charity, Nevill Charity, Ducketts Charity, and other Charities; Governor of the Holborn Estate Grammar School; President and Treasurer of the Housekeepers and Caretakers Society, 1910; President and Founder of the St Clement Danes Social and Benevolent Society; secured the Roman Bath in Strand Lane, 1922.

Publications: The Notes of St Clement Danes, 1921; St Clement Danes Guide Book, 1925; Composer (with his wife as Author) of the St Clement Danes Hymns. *Recreations:* music, rowing, tennis, philately. *Address:* The Anchorage, St Clement Danes, Strand, WC1. *T:* Holborn 0620.

Died 12 June 1941.

BIDDLE, A. J. Drexel, FRGS; Col US Marine Corps Reserve; Instructor of Individual Combat, US Marine Corps, Federal Bureau of Investigation, USA Department of Justice and the Philadelphia Police Force; author, explorer, and lecturer; *b* Philadelphia, 1874; *s* of Edward Biddle and Emily Drexel; *m* 1895, Cordelia Rundell Bradley, of Pittsburg; two *s* one *d. Educ:* Heidelberg. Lived in Madeira Islands, studying conditions there; returned to native country, 1891; joined staff of Philadelphia Public Ledger; revived Philadelphia Sunday Graphic, 1895, and became its editor; head of publishing house of Drexel Biddle, in New York, Philadelphia, and San Francisco, 1895–1904; Founder, Drexel Biddle Citizens' Military Corps under US Government; Founder and President, Drexel Biddle Bible Classes, USA, Great Britain, West Indies, and Canada; as Marine Corps Captain, Reserve, in France, 1918; Commanded the Hand-to-hand Combat Team of the US Marine Corps that exhibited in 1926 during the Philadelphia Sesqui-Centennial Exposition. *Publications:* A Dual Rôle, 1894; All Round Athletics, 1894; An Allegory and Three Essays, 1894; The Froggy Fairy Book, 1896; The Second Froggy Fairy Book, 1897; Shantytown Sketches, 1898; Word for Word and Letter for Letter, 1898; The Flowers of Life, 1898; The Madeira Islands, 2 vols, 1900; The Land of the Wine, 2 vols, 1901; De or Die, a Manual issued by the United States Marine Corps as a guide for training in individual combat, 1937. *Recreations:* church work, rehabilitation of churches, and boxing (amateur boxing champion). *Address:* 112 Drexel Building, Philadelphia, USA. *Clubs:* Philadelphia, Rittenhouse, Philadelphia.

Died 27 May 1948.

BIDDLECOMBE, Rev. Stuart Holman, LTh; Hon. CF, Rector of Blendworth since 1942; Officiating CF in the Whippingham and East Cowes Area, 1939–42 and Horndean area since 1942; Officiating Minister to the RNAH, Idsworth, since 1943; *b* 31 Dec. 1879; *s* of Thomas Ewens Biddlecombe; *m* Florence May Brooks; two *s* two *d. Educ:* Stockton and Middlesboro' High Schools; CM College, Islington (University of Durham, LTh., 1917). CMS Missionary at Isfahan, Persia, 1904–26; Deacon and Priest, 1911; Chaplain to the Forces Western Front, 1915–16; India, Mesopotamia, and Caspian Sea Front, 1917–18; Hon. CF, 1919; Hon. Chaplain to the Bishop in Persia, 1920; Archdeacon of Isfahan, 1921; Vicar of Kew, 1926–37; Rector of Whippingham, 1937–42; Hon. Chaplain to King Edward VII's Convalescent Home for Officers, Osborne, 1937–42; Examiner in Persian, Indian Civil Service Exams, 1924. *Publications:* articles: Times Trades Supplement, CMS Review, Church of England Newspaper, The Church Overseas. *Recreations:* golf and tennis. *Address:* The Rectory, Blendworth, Horndean, Hants.

Died 5 Aug. 1944.

BIDDULPH, 2nd Baron *cr* 1903; **John Michael Gordon Biddulph;** JP, DL; Director of Martins Bank, Ltd; *b* 19 Nov. 1869; *e s* of 1st Baron and Adelaide Georgiana (*d* 1872), *y d* of Rt Hon. Gen. Peel; *S* father, 1923; *m* 1896, Marjorie Caroline Susan, *d* of late Col W. Mure of Caldwell; two *s* two *d. Educ:* Eton; Christ Church, Oxford. *Recreations:* shooting, fishing, golf. *Heir: s* Hon. Michael William John Biddulph. *Address:* Ledbury, Herefordshire; Kemble House, Cirencester. *Club:* Brooks's.

Died 7 Dec. 1949.

BIDDULPH, Sir Theophilus George, 8th Bt *cr* 1664; *b* 3 April 1874; *s* of 7th Bt and Mary, *d* of 17th Lord Somerville; *S* father, 1883; *m* 1907, Eleanor, OBE 1920, *y d* of late Samuel Thompson of Muckamore Abbey, Co. Antrim. *Heir: kinsman* William Hugh [Col lately Commanding Ceylon Planters' Rifle Corps; *b* 2 June 1869; *m* 1st, 1892, Annette Louisa, *d* of late Lt-Col H. Master; 2nd, 1915, Kathleen Anna Herring, *d* of late Harman Herring-Cooper, Shrule Castle, Carlow. Major, 8th Batt. Rifle Brigade, Sept. 1914; Lt-Col Commanding 7th Batt. Dorset Regt, Feb. 1915; 8th Batt. Loyal North Lancs, July 1915; JP Warwickshire and Ceylon. *Address:* 33 Kenilworth Rd, Leamington Spa. *T:* 938]. *Address:* The Pavilion, Melrose, Roxburghshire. *Clubs:* Travellers'; New, Edinburgh.

Died 31 Jan. 1948 (ext).

BIDWELL, Rt Rev. Edward John, MA, DD, DCL; Canon Emeritus of Canterbury Cathedral since 1941; *b* 26 Nov. 1866; 4th *s* of late Rev. George Bidwell, Rector of Sympson, Bucks; *m* 1894, Frances Mary, *e d* of late Joseph Morris of Leamington Spa; one *s* five *d. Educ:* Bradfield College (Foundation Scholar); Wadham College, Oxford (Open Classical Scholar); BA (2nd class Mod. and Lit. Hum.), 1889; MA 1893. Chaplain, Leamington College, 1891; Deacon, 1891; Priest, 1892; Headmaster, Preparatory School, Leamington College, 1894–97; Cathedral Grammar School, Peterborough, 1897–1903; Bishop's College School, Lennoxville, Canada, 1903–09; Dean of Ontario and Rector of St George's Cathedral, Kingston, Ontario, 1909–13; DCL (hon.), 1907, and DD (jure dignitatis), Lennoxville University, 1909; DD (hon. causa), Trinity University, Toronto, 1909, and Queen's University, Kingston, 1912; DD Oxford University (Hon.), 1919; Secretary to the Prayer-book Reversion Committee, General Synod of Canadian Church, 1911–13; Prolocutor of Lower House, Provincial Synod of Ontario, 1912–13; Coadjutor Bishop of Ontario and Bishop of Kingston (Canada), 1913–17; Secretary, House of Bishops, 1917; Bishop of Ontario, 1917–26; Vicar of Sellindge, nr Ashford, Kent, 1930–41; Assistant Bishop of Diocese of Canterbury, 1935–41; Hon. Canon of Canterbury Cathedral, 1936–41. *Publications:* Private Prayers for Boys; Pulpit and Platform. *Address:* c/o Lloyd's Bank, Thetford, Norfolk.

Died 11 Aug. 1941.

BIERMANS, Rt Rev. John Henry Mary; Titular Bishop of Gargara; Superior-General of St Joseph's Foreign Missionary Society, 1924–34; *b* Westerhoven, Holland, 8 Nov. 1871. *Educ:* Gymnasium Gemert; Episcopal Seminary of Bois-le-Duc; philosophical studies, Mission House, Roosendaal, Holland; theological studies, Mill Hill, NW. Priest, 1896; left for Mission in Uganda, 1896; Titular Bishop of Gargara and Vicar Apostolic of the Upper Nile, 1912. *Address:* Mission House, Roosendaal, Holland.

Died 24 Jan. 1941.

BIERNACKI, Roderick Korneli, CIE 1918; ISO 1911. late Locomotive Superintendent Indian State Railways. *Address:* c/o Lloyds Bank, Ltd, 6 Pall Mall, SW1.

Died 24 Jan. 1943.

BIFFEN, Prof. Sir Rowland, Kt 1925; FRS 1914; MA; DSc; Professor Agricultural Botany, Cambridge University, 1908–31; Professor Emeritus, since 1931; *b* 28 May 1874. *Educ:* Emmanuel College, Cambridge. *Address:* c/o School of Agriculture, Cambridge.

Died 12 July 1949.

BIGGAR, Oliver Mowat, CMG 1943; BA, KC (Alberta 1913, Canada 1920); Commander Legion of Merit (US) 1946; *b* Toronto, 11 Oct. 1876; *s* of Charles Robert Webster Biggar, MAKC; *m* 1908, Muriel Elizabeth Whitney; one *d. Educ:* Upper Canada College and University College, Toronto. Admitted to Ontario Bar, 1901; practised in Toronto, 1901–02; went to

Edmonton and was admitted to Alberta Bar, 1903; Bencher Law Society of Alberta, 1907–19; Member Board of Governors, University of Alberta, 1911–17; member Edmonton Hospital Board, 1913–16; Lt 101st Regt EF, 1916; Assist Judge Advocate General, MD 13 (Major), 1916–17; member Military Service Council to assist in administration of Military Service Act, 1917–18; Judge Advocate General, Canada (Lt-Col 1918, Col 1919); member of Militia Council, 1918; member Canadian Delegation to Peace Conference, acting there as British Secretary to Commission on the Responsibility of the Authors of the War and on Penalties, and as Assistant Secretary of British Delegation; Vice-Chairman, Air Board (Canada), 1919–22; Chief Electoral Officer for Canada, 1920–27; Chairman, Canadian Section Permanent Joint Board on Defence (Canada-United States), 1940–45; Director of Censorship, Canada, 1942–44; member War-time Information Board, 1943–44. *Publication:* Canadian Patent Law and Practice. *Address:* 197 Clemow Avenue, Ottawa, Canada. *T:* 2–5541. *Clubs:* Ridean, Country (Ottawa).

Died 4 Sept. 1948.

BIGGART, Sir Thomas, Kt 1936. Solicitor; Senior Partner of Biggart, Lumsden & Co., Solicitors, Glasgow; Chairman or Director of various Industrial and Commercial Companies; first Secretary and Solicitor of Engineering Employers' Federation, 1896–1909; Secretary of Shipbuilding Employers' Federation, 1898–1917 and Consultant and Hon. Vice-President, 1917–42; Hon. President of Foremen and Staff Mutual Benefit Society; Member of Board of Referees, Finance Acts, 1915–41. *Address:* 105 West George Street, Glasgow, C2. *T:* Glasgow Central 9961: Rossarden. Kilmacolm, Renfrewshire *T:* Kilmacolm 16. *Club:* New (Glasgow).

Died 20 May 1949.

BIGGER, Sir Edward Coey, Kt 1921; MD, DPH, etc.; late Medical Commissioner, Local Government Board, Ireland; Chairman of Irish Public Health Council; Chairman of the Central Midwives Board, Ireland; Chairman of the General Nursing Council for Ireland; late Crown Representative for Ireland on the General Medical Council; *b* Belfast, 1861; 6th *s* of Joseph Bigger, Airdrie, Belfast; *m* 1886, Maude Coulter (*d* 1926), *d* of William Warwick, MD, Belfast; one *s* one *d*. *Educ:* Liverpool Institute; Queen's College, Belfast; London Hosp. Formerly Visiting Physician, Ulster Hospital for Women and Children, Belfast; Visiting Physician, Belfast Infectious Diseases Hospital; Supt Medical Officer of Health, Belfast Rural District; Medical Inspector, Local Government Board, Ireland; Senator Irish Free State, 1925–36. *Publication:* Irish Report on the Physical Welfare of Mothers and Children, for Carnegie Trust. *Recreation:* golf. *Address:* Lisnacran, Glenageary, Co. Dublin. *T:* Kingston 99. *Clubs:* Royal Societies; Royal Irish Automobile, Dublin; Royal St George Yacht, Kingstown.

Died 1 June 1942.

BIGGS, Leonard Vivian; *b* Hackney, London, N, 29 March 1873; *s* of James and Mary Biggs, Enfield, Middlesex; *m* 1902, Marion, *d* of Charles J. and Eleanor Row; one *s* three *d*. *Educ:* Enfield Grammar School. Trained as journalist on Middlesex Gazette (Enfield); sub-editor African Critic and Critic (London), 1895–98, after free lance work in London went Australia, 1898; Age staff, Melbourne, 1899–1920; Melbourne correspondent Daily Chronicle and Manchester Guardian, 1900–14; Chief of Staff, Age, 1914–20; Organising Secretary National Union, 1920–25; rejoined Age, 1925; Editor of Age, 1926–39; prominent in Anglican Church work prior to editorship, representing Melbourne Diocese in General and Provincial Synods for many years; re-elected to General Synod, 1942; Lay Canon St Paul's Cathedral Melb., 1917–26 and since 1943; Pres. or Vice-Pres. Diocesan

CEMS, 1914–26; City Councillor of Hawthorn, 1911–13; Pres. Royal Society of St George (Melbourne), 1924–26; Pres. Melbourne Chess Club, 1926–29, 1934–35 and 1937–39; Pres. VCA, 1938–43. *Publications:* South Africa: Its Peoples, Progress, and Problems (with W. F. Purvis), 1895; Great Melbourne, 1901; Christian Socialism, 1904; Housing Reform, 1905; Ancient and Modern Editing, 1938. *Recreations:* walking, golf, chess, debating. *Address:* Enfield, Fordholm Road, Hawthorn, Melbourne, E2, Victoria, Australia. *T:* Hawthorn 1347. *Clubs:* Savage, Melbourne.

Died 30 Jan. 1944.

BIGLAND, Rt Rev. Monsignor John; HCF; Parish Priest, St Mary's, Boston, Lincs; *b* 17 May 1871; *s* of John Bigland and Catherine Emma Haynes. *Educ:* Wallasey Grammar School; Liverpool College. Received into the Catholic Church, 1889; Theological studies at St Joseph's Seminary, Leeds. Ordained priest of the Diocese of Middlesbrough, 1916; CF, Egypt and Palestine, European War; Private Secretary to Archbishop Goodier of Bombay, Chaplain to British Troops, and Parish Priest of Colaba, Bombay 1920–27, and of Holy Name, Bombay, 1927–29; Domestic Prelate to the Pope, 1926; Parish Priest at Louth, Lincs, 1930–33; Administrator St Barnabas' Cathedral, Nottingham, 1933–38. *Recreation:* motoring. *Address:* The Presbytery, Horncastle Road, Boston, Lincs. *T:* Boston 2056.

Died Nov. 1945.

BIGSBY, Sydney Herbert, CIE 1934; *b* 26 July 1885; *s* of Sydney Herbert Bigsby and Sarah Lehrs; *m* 1912, Evelyn Marjorie Baker; one *s* one *d*. *Educ:* Tonbridge School; Royal Indian Engineering College, Cooper's Hill. Assistant Engineer, PWD, Punjab, 1907; Executive Engineer, 1915; employed in the construction of the Upper Jhelum and Upper Swat Canals in the Punjab and NWFP; Under Secretary to Government for two years and for nine years Superintending Engineer; Public Works Member of the State Council, Jaipur State, Jaipur, Rajputana; Chief Engineer and Secretary to Government, Punjab, PWD, Irrigation Branch, 1936. *Recreations:* golf, shooting. *Clubs:* East India and Sports; Punjab, Lahore.

Died 6 June 1946.

BIGWOOD, Sir Cecil, Kt 1938; Chairman London Standing Joint Committee; Chairman Finsbury Bench; DL and JP County London; *b* 1863; *s* of James Bigwood, Twickenham; *m* 1908, Maud (*d* 1942), *d* of Robert Porter; no *c*. *Educ:* Westminster; Trinity Hall, Cambridge, MA 1885. *Address:* 11 Kings Bench Walk, Temple, EC. *Club:* United University.

Died 4 July 1947.

BIJAWAR STATE, HH Bharat Dharm-indu Maharajah Sawai Sir Sawant Singh Bahadur, KCIE 1911; *b* 25 Nov. 1877; 2nd *s* of late Maharaja of Orchha and Bundela Rajput; ascended Gaddi, 1900; *m* 1st, in Ponwar family; 2nd, in Karahya family; one *s* two *d*. Area of state 973 square miles, population 115,852. *Recreations:* big-game shooting; one of the finest shots in India. *Address:* Bijawar State, Bundel Khund, India.

Died 30 Oct. 1940.

BIKANER, Maharajah of, Gen. HH Maharajadhiraj Raj Rajeshwar Narendra Shiromani Maharajah Sri Ganga Singbji Bahadur, GCSI 1911; GCIE 1907; GCVO 1919; GBE 1921; KCB 1918; KCSI 1904; KCIE 1901; Hon. LLD, Cambridge, Edinburgh, Benares, and Osmania University, Hyderabad; Hon. DCL, Oxford; *b* 13 Oct. 1880; *S* 1887; *m* Maharani Sri Bhatiyaniji Sahib, CI, 1908; one *s* one *d*. *Educ:* Mayo College, Ajmer. Assumed full ruling powers, 1898; granted hon. commission of Major in the British Army, 1900, and attached to 2nd Bengal Lancers, now 2nd Royal Lancers; Lt-Col 1909; Col 1910; Maj.-Gen. 1917; Lt-Gen. 1930; Gen. 1937; Hon. Col 2nd Royal Lancers (Gardner's Horse) since 1919; served with British Army in China in command of Bikaner Camel Corps (1901 medal, despatches, KCIE); served European War, 1914–15 (despatches twice, KCB, Maj.-Gen., 1914 Bronze Star, Grand Cordon of the Order of the Nile); awarded First Class (gold) Kaiser-i-Hind Medal for public service in India during great famine of 1899–1900; attended the Coronation of King Edward VII, 1902, King George V, 1911 and King George VI, 1937; attended their Majesties Silver Jubilee celebrations, 1935; Hon. ADC to King George V, when Prince of Wales, 1902–10, and 1910–36; Hon. ADC (extra) to King Edward VIII in 1936 and to King George VI since 1937; one of the three Representatives of India at the Imperial War Cabinet and Conference, 1917, and one of the two Representatives at the Imperial War Cabinet and Peace Conference, 1919; received the freedom of the cities of London, Edinburgh, Manchester, and Bristol; Donat of the Order of St John of Jerusalem; represented the Ruling Princes of India at the Assembly of the League of Nations, 1924; Leader of the Indian Delegation to the Assembly of the League of Nations, 1930; one of the three Representatives of India at the Imperial Conference, 1930; Member of the Indian States Delegation to the Indian Round Table Conference in London, 1930–31 and 1931; Hon. Gen. Secretary to the Indian Princes Conference, 1916–21, and first Chancellor of the Chamber of Princes, 1921–26; Pro-Chancellor of the Benares Hindu University, 1923–29, and Chancellor since 1929; Life Member of the American Museum of Natural History, New York; is a Patron and President of many institutions and associations. Salute, 19 guns, granted 1918. *Recreations:* polo, racquets, tennis, motoring, big-game shooting. *Address:* Bikaner, Rajputana, India. *Clubs:* Marlborough; Western India Turf, Willington Sports, Bombay; Rajputana, Abu.

Died 2 Feb. 1943.

BIKANER, Maharaja of, 1943–1950; **Lt-Gen. HH Maharajadhiraj Raj Rajeshwar Narendra Shiromani (Sri Sadul Singhji Bahadur),** GCSI 1947; GCIE 1946; CVO 1922; *b* 7 Sept. 1902; *S* 1943; *m* 1922, Rewa Princess, aunt of Maharaja of Rewa; two *s* one *d*. Hon. Commission of Lieut in British Army, 1918; Capt. 1921; Lt-Col 1943; Maj.-Gen. 1945; Lt-Gen. 1946; Hon. Col 2nd Royal Lancers, 1947; attended Coronation of King George V in London in 1911, and Page to His Majesty at Coronation Durbar, Delhi, 1911; visited Europe several times; accompanied his father when he represented the Princes of India at the Peace Conference, 1919; and at League of Nations, Geneva, 1924; attached to the Staff of the Prince of Wales during his Indian Tour, 1921–22. Served Middle East War Front with his younger son in Nov. 1943 and the Burma Front in Nov. 1944. Hon. Life Member of American Museum of Natural History, New York; Vice-Patron, Bombay Natural History Society; Life Member, Society for the Preservation of the Fauna of the Empire; Associate Knight of Venerable Order of St John of Jerusalem, 1945. *Recreations:* polo, golf, tennis, motoring, pig-sticking, big-game shooting, etc. *Address:* Lallgarh, Bikaner, Rajputana, India. *Clubs:* Cricket Club of India, Willingdon Sports (Bombay); Rajputana (Abu).

Died 25 Sept. 1950.

BILBROUGH, Rt Rev. Harold Ernest, DD Oxon 1916; *b* Twickenham, 22 Feb. 1867; *s* of Arthur Bilbrough, JP, Camden Court, Chislehurst; unmarried. *Educ:* Winchester College; New College, Oxford. Deacon, 1890; Priest, 1891; Curate of St Mary's, South Shields, 1890–97; Vicar of St John E, Darlington, 1897–1904; Vicar of St Hilda's, South Shields, and Rural Dean of Jarrow, 1904–10; Hon. Chaplain to Bishop of Durham, 1901–16; Rector of Liverpool, Sub-Dean of Liverpool Cathedral; Rural Dean of Liverpool North, 1910–16; Suffragan Bishop of Dover, 1916–27; Bishop of Newcastle, 1927–41; Hon. Commissary of the Bishop of Madagascar; Hon. Canon of Durham Cathedral, 1909–11; of Liverpool 1911–16; of Canterbury,

1916–27; House of Lords, 1936–41. *Recreations:* formerly football, now fishing, etc. *Address:* Nizels, Chislehurst, Kent.

Died 15 Nov. 1950.

BILGRAMI, Sayyid Sir Mehdi Husain, Nawab Mahdi Yar Jang Bahadur, Kt 1944. Judicial and Education Member, His Exalted Highness the Nizam's Executive Council. *Address:* Hyderabad, Deccan.

Died 8 April 1948.

BILGRAMI, Syed Akeel, Nawab Sir Akeel Jung Bahadur, Kt 1938; Member and Vice-President Executive Council, HEH the Nizam's Government (India), in charge of Commerce and Industries Departments; *b* Bilgram (Oudh), 2 Oct. 1874; *s* of late Nawab Imad-ul-Mulk Bahadur, Syed Hosain Bilgrami, once Member of India Council; *m* 1902; three *s* three *d*. *Educ:* Nizam College, Hyderabad. Served HEH the Nizam's Government for 47 years as District Collector, Army Secretary, Minister of Paigahs, Minister for Commerce, Industries and Co-operative Departments, Minister for Public Works Department, Minister for Army, Medical, Aviation, Wireless and General Departments. *Recreations:* tennis and other light out-door games. *Address:* Khairatabad, Hyderabad, Deccan, India.

Died April 1945.

BILLETT, Rev. Canon Frederick, MA; Vicar of Maisemore, Gloucester, since 1916; Hon. Canon of Gloucester, 1910; *m* Maria (*d* 1932). *Educ:* Hertford College, Oxford; Wycliffe Hall. Ordained 1884; Curate of Holy Trinity, Bristol, 1884–86; Vicar of Christ Church, Barton Hill, Bristol, 1886–95; Vicar of St James's, Gloucester, 1895–1916. *Address:* Maisemore Vicarage, Gloucester.

Died 27 Nov. 1941.

BILLING, N. Pemberton; *b* Hampstead, 1880; *s* of Charles Eardley Billing, Birmingham, iron founder, and Annie Emilia Claridge, Coventry; *m* 1903, Lilian Maud (*d* 1923), *d* of Theodore Henry Schweitzer, Bristol. Fought in Boer War, 1899–1901; Royal Naval Air Service, 1914–16; retired Squadron Commander; contested Mile End, 1916, in support of strong Air Policy; MP (Ind) East Herts, 1916–21; play produced, High Treason, 1928. *Publications:* Endowment by Increment; contributor to Nineteenth Century, Fortnightly and other reviews on industrial and social problems. Founder and Editor of Aerocraft, 1908–1910. *Club:* Royal Aero.

Died 11 Nov. 1948.

BINDLOSS, Harold; author; *b* Liverpool, 1866. Spent several years at sea and in various colonies; returned to this country 1896; became contributor to magazines and newspapers author of books dealing with colonial life. *Publications:* In the Niger Country; A Wide Dominion; Ainslie's Ju-Ju; A Sower of Wheat, 1902; The Concession Hunters, 1903; The Mistress of Bonaventure, The League of the Leopard, and Daventry's Daughter, 1904; Alton of Somasco, Misty Seas, The Impostor, 1905. Beneath her Station, The Cattle Baron's Daughter, 1906; A Damaged Reputation, 1906; The Dust of Conflict; His Lady's Pleasure, 1907; By Right of Purchase; The Liberationist, Thrice Armed, 1908; The Greater Power, 1909; The Gold Trail, Rancher Carteret, 1910; Alison's Adventure, 1911; The Pioneer, 1912; The Wastrel, 1913; The Allinson Honour, Blake's Burden, 1914; The Secret of the Reef, The Intruder, 1915; the Borderer, 1916; His One Talent, 1916; Carmen's Messenger, Sadie's Conquest, 1917; Agatha's Fortune, Askew's Victory, 1918; Wyndham's Partner; Dearham's Inheritance, 1919; Stayward's Vindication, 1920; The Head of the House, 1920; Musgrave's Luck, 1921; The Man from the Wilds, 1922; The Keystone Block, 1923; Andrew's Folly, 1924; A Debt of Honour, 1925; Helen the Conqueror, 1925; The Broken Net, 1926; Footsteps; The Dark Road,

1927; The Firm Hand; Halford's Adventure, 1928; Frontiersmen, 1929; The Harder Way; A Moorside Feud, 1930; Carter's Triumph, 1931; Right of Way, 1932; The Loser Pays; The Stain of the Forge, 1933; Sonalta Gold, 1934; The Lady of the Plain, 1935; The Forbidden River, 1936; Fellside Folk, 1937; Posted Missing, 1938; Valeria goes West, 1939; What's Mine I Hold, 1940; The Call of the Soil, 1941; The Secret of the Scree, 1942; Caverhills, 1943; The Laird o'Borrane, 1945. *Address:* Vallum, Burgh-by-Sands, Carlisle.

Died 30 Dec. 1945.

BINGHAM, Col Sir Albert (Edward), 2nd Bt *cr* 1903; OBE, VD; TD; *b* 23 Nov. 1868; *o s* of Sir John Edward Bingham, 1st Bt of West Lea, Sheffield, and Maria, *d* of late William Fawcett; *S* father, 1915; *m* 1893, Lucy, *d* of late Duncan L. McAllum, Gosforth; one *d. Educ:* Blairlodge. Master Cutler of Cutlers' Company, Sheffield, 1918; High Sheriff, County of Notts, 1926–27; Joint Master, The Grove Hunt, 1926–27 to 1931–32; Hon. Col West Riding Division RE (T); Governing Director of Walker and Hall, Ltd, Sheffield (silver, cutlery and electro-plate manufactures). *Heir:* none. *Address:* Ranby House, nr Retford, Notts. *T:* Retford 138. *Clubs:* Boodle's, Royal Automobile; The Club, Sheffield.

Died 25 Feb. 1945.

BINGHAM, Brig.-Gen. Oswald Buckley Bingham Smith-, CMG 1916; DSO 1901; late 3rd Dragoon Guards; late commanding 3rd Cavalry Brigade and Inspector-General of Cavalry; *b* 7 Oct. 1868; 2nd *s* of late O. Smith-Bingham; *m* 1903, Edythe Mary (*d* 1945), 2nd *d* of late R. Tunstall-Moore of Stedalt Co. Meath, Ireland; three *s. Educ:* Winchester. Entered Army, 1889; Captain, 1898; Major, 1903. Lt-Col 1912; Col 1916; Brig.-Gen. 1917; served India, 1889–92; S Africa, 1892–95, 1900–02 (despatches, DSO); European War, 1914–15 (twice wounded, despatches, CMG). *Recreations:* hunting, shooting, etc.; hunted Dundalk hounds, 1899–1900. *Address:* Mickleton Manor, Chipping Campden, Glos. *Clubs:* Army and Navy, Cavalry, White's; Kildare Street (Dublin).

Died 27 March 1949.

BINGHAM, Lt-Col Samuel, DSO 1918; late Liverpool Regt; *m.* Served European War, 1914–18 (despatches twice, DSO, Belgian Croix de Guerre).

Died 9 Dec. 1941.

BINGLEY, 1st Baron *cr* 1933, of Bramham; **George Richard Lane-Fox;** PC 1926; JP, DL; Barrister; CC and Alderman, West Riding CC, 1898–1928; late Col Yorks Hussars; *b* 15 Dec. 1870; *e s* of J. T. R. Lane-Fox of Bramham, Yorks; *m* 1903, Hon. Mary Agnes Emily Wood, *d* of 2nd Viscount Halifax; four *d. Educ:* Eton; New College, Oxford. MP (U) Barkston Ash Division, WR Yorks, 1906–31; Secretary for Mines, 1922–24 and Nov. 1924–Jan. 1928; Member, Indian Statutory Commission, 1928–29; Chairman, Pig Products Commission, 1932, Fat Stock Reorganisation Commission, 1933; served European War, 1914–17 (wounded). *Recreations:* hunting, cricket, shooting, fishing. *Address:* Bramham Park, Boston Spa SO, Yorks. *TA:* Bramham. *T:* Boston Spa 2114. *Clubs:* Carlton, Turf.

Died 11 Dec. 1947 (ext).

BINGLEY, Lt-Gen. Sir Alfred Horsford, KCIE 1918; CB 1915; CIE 1909; Knight of Grace, Order of St John of Jerusalem, 1925; Colonel 3/7th Rajput Regiment (DCO), 1934; *b* 28 May 1865; *s* of late Peregrine Taylor Bingley; *m* 1893, Mabel, *e d* of late Col G. A. Way, CB; one *d. Educ:* St Edward's School, Oxford; RMC, Sandhurst. Lieut Leinster Regiment, 1885; Indian Staff Corps, 1887; Captain Indian Army, 1896; Major, 1903; Lieut-Col 1906; Bt-Col 1910; Col 1911; Maj.-Gen. 1915; Lt-Gen. 1920; employed on plague duty, Bombay, 1897–98 (thanks of Government, Kaiser-i-Hind medal,

1st class); DAAG Headquarters Staff, India, 1901–06; Deputy Sec. Army Dept Govt of India, 1906–09; Commandant 7th DCO Rajputs, 1909–11; General Staff Officer, 1st Grade, Headquarters Staff, India, 1911–14; Deputy Adjutant-General, Headquarters Staff, India, 1914; Brig.-Gen. for Administration, 1914; Brigade Commander, 1915; Sec. Army Dept Govt of India, 1916–21; retired, 1921; served Burma, 1891–92 (medal with clasp); China, 1900 (despatches, Brevet-Major, medal with clasp); War of 1914–16 (despatches, promoted Major-General, Japanese Order of Rising Sun); Gold Medal United Service Institution of India, 1896. *Publications:* series of Handbooks on the races recruited in the Indian Army. *Address:* The Causey, Cranleigh, Surrey. *T:* Cranleigh 396. *Club:* United Service.

Died 20 April 1944.

BINNEY, Lt-Col Edward Victor, DSO 1917; RE; *b* 1885; 2nd *s* of Thomas Godfrey Binney, late of Guisnes Court, Tolleshunt D'Arcy, Essex; *m* 1923, Marjorie Blanche, *yr d* of late Brooke Mockett, Prescott House, Ealing, and of Mysore, India; one *s* one *d. Educ:* Rugby School. Served Mesopotamia, 1916–17 (despatches, DSO); Afghanistan, 1919; Commandant Royal Bombay Sappers and Miners, 1930–33; retired, 1933. *Club:* United Service.

Died 14 July 1942.

BINNEY, Captain Ralph Douglas, CBE 1942; RN (retd); Chief of Staff to Flag Officer, London, since 1943; *b* 14 Oct. 1888; 4th *s* of T. G. Binney, late of Guisnes Court, Tolleshunt D'Arcy, Essex; *m* 1918, Ruth Frances Livingstone Learmonth; (one *s* killed in action, 1943) one *d. Educ:* Cordwalles, Maidenhead. Joined HMS Britannia, 1903; retired with rank of Captain 1934, having served throughout European War; served in navy of Colombia, South America, 1934–39; resumed service in RN, 1939; staff of Rear-Admiral, Alexandria, till Nov. 1942. *Club:* United Service.

Died 8 Dec. 1944.

BINNIE, William James Eames, MA; MInstCE, FGS; Consulting Engineer, Senior Partner of firm of Binnie, Deacon and Gourley; *b* 10 Oct. 1867; *s* of Sir Alexander Richardson Binnie, formerly Chief Engineer to LCC; *m* Ethel, (*d* 1947), *d* of Remy Morse, Lounde Hall, Suffolk; two *s. Educ:* Rugby; Trinity College, Cambridge. Graduated, 1888. Employed on Birmingham Water-works, Welsh Scheme, 1893–95; joined staff of late Sir Benjamin Baker, FRS, as Resident Engineer on Central London railway, 1896–1900; went to Alexandria, Egypt in 1900 as Resident Engineer on Khedival Graving Dock; returned to England, 1902, and joined his father in practice as a Consulting Engineer; President of Institution of Civil Engineers 1938–39; Past President of Institution of Water Engineers and of Institution of Sanitary Engineers; acted as a member of or Technical Adviser to six Government Commissions, viz. three British and three International. Chevalier de Légion d'Honneur (France). *Publications:* several papers in Technical Journals. *Recreation:* golf. *Address:* Apple Tree Cottage, Church End Lane, Tilehurst, Berkshire.

Died 4 Oct. 1949.

BINNS, Asa, MInstCE, MIMechE; Past President IMechE; Consultant, Rendel Palmer and Tritton, Consulting Engineers, Westminster; Lt-Col, RE, TA, Engineer and Railway Staff Corps; *b* 3 Oct. 1873; 4th *s* of Thomas Binns and Ann Riley, Keighley, Yorks; *m* 1st, 1899, Annie Ogden; one *s* two *d*; 2nd, *m* 1918, widow of Charles Lord, *née* Lonsdale. *Educ:* Keighley Grammar School; Leeds University. Engineering works in Leeds and Bradford; drawing office experience in Ipswich and at Hull Docks; Asst Engr Admiralty and over thirty years in the Port of London from which service retired as Chief Engineer in 1938 to join Rendel Palmer and Tritton as Consultant. *Publications:* papers on Dock Construction to InstCE and IMechE and in technical press. *Address:* Rendel Palmer and Tritton, 55 Broadway, SW1. *TA:* Rendels, Sowest, London. *T:* Whitehall 4455, Kensington 8789. *Clubs:* Reform, City Livery.

Died 2 July 1946.

BINYON, (Robert) Laurence, CH 1932; author; Hon. DLitt Oxford; Hon. LLD Glasgow; Officer de l'Instruction Publique; Chevalier de la Légion d'Honneur; Fellow of the Royal Society of Literature; *b* Lancaster, 10 Aug. 1869; 2nd *s* of Rev. F. Binyon and Mary, *d* of R. B. Dockray; *m* 1904, Cicely Margaret, *e d* of Henry Pryor Powell; three *d. Educ:* St Paul's School; Trinity College, Oxford (Newdigate Prize, 1890, Hon. Fellow, 1933). Entered British Museum, Department of Printed Books, 1893; transferred to Dept of Prints and Drawings, 1895; Assistant Keeper, 1909; Deputy Keeper in charge of sub-department of Oriental Prints and Drawings, 1913–32; Keeper of Prints and Drawings, 1932–33; lectured in USA 1912 (Lowell Lecturer), 1914, 1926; lectured in Japan, 1929; Charles Eliot Norton Professor of Poetry, Harvard University, 1933–34; President of the English Association, 1933–34; President, English Verse-Speaking Association, 1934–35; Byron Professor, University of Athens, 1940. *Publications:* Lyric Poems, 1894; Poems, 1895; edited Shilling Garland, 1895–1898; London Visions, Book I, 1895; Book II, 1898; The Praise of Life, 1896; Porphyrion and other Poems, 1898; Western Flanders, 1898; Odes, 1900; The Death of Adam, 1903; Penthesilea, 1905; Paris and Oenone, 1906; Catalogue of English Drawings in the BM, Vol. I, 1898; Vol. II, 1900; Vol. III, 1902; Vol. IV, 1907; William Blake, Vol. I, 1906; Attila, 1907. Painting in the Far East, 1908; London Visions (collected ed.), 1908; England and other Poems, 1909; The Flight of the Dragon, 1911; Botticelli, 1913; Auguries (poems), 1913; The Winnowing Fan, 1915; Bombastes in the Shades, 1915; The Anvil, 1916; The Cause, 1917; Catalogue of Japanese Woodcuts in British Museum, 1917; For Dauntless France (Britain's Aid to the French Wounded), 1918; The New World (poems), 1918; The Four Years, 1919; Sakuntala (from Kalidasa), 1920; The Secret, 1920; Court Painters of the Grand Mogul, 1921; Drawings and Engravings of W. Blake, 1922; Arthur, a Tragedy, 1923; Japanese Colour-Prints (with J. J. O'Brien Sexton), 1923; Ayuli (play); The Sirens, an Ode, 1924; edited The Letters of Maurice Hewlett, 1926; Oriental Art in the British Museum; The Followers of William Blake; The Golden Treasury of Modern Lyrics, 1925; Chinese Painters in English Collections; Blake's Engraved Designs, 1926; Chinese Frescoes in the Eumorfopoulos Collection; Boadicea; Sophro the Wise, 1927; Versions from Dante; Paintings in the Eumorfopoulos Collection; The Idols, 1928; Poems of Nizami, 1928; Landscape in English Painting and Poetry, 1929; Three Short Plays, 1930; Collected Poems, 1931; Persian Miniatures (joint author), 1933; Akbar, 1932; Dante's Inferno (verse translation), 1933; English Water-Colours, 1933; Painting in the Far East, 1934; The Spirit of Man in Asian Art, 1935; The Young King, 1935; Dante's Purgatorio (verse translation); Brief Candles (Play), 1938; Art and Freedom (Romanes Lecture), 1939; The North Star and other poems, 1941. *Plays produced:* Paris and Oenone, 1906; Attila, 1907; Sakuntala, 1920; Arthur, 1923; The Young King, 1924; Boadicea, 1925. *Address:* Westridge Farm House, Streatley, Berks. *Club:* Athenæum.

Died 10 March 1943.

BION, Frederick Fleetwood, CIE 1924; *b* 1870; *m* 1896, Rhoda Salter (*d* 1939), *d* of Wilfred Kemp; one *s* one *d. Educ:* St Paul's School, Darjeeling; Civil Engineering College, Calcutta. Entered Public Works Dept, India 1892; Executive Engineer, 1903; Superintending Engineer, 1916; Chief Engineer and Joint Secretary to Govt, United Provinces, 1921; retired 1925. *Address:* c/o Grindlay & Co., 54 Parliament Street, SW1.

Died 15 Feb. 1949.

BIRCH, John Henry Stopford; *e s* of John Arden Birch and the late Viscountess Barrington of Beckett, Shrivenham, Berks; *m* 1927, Rannfrid, *d* of General Holtfodt, late Commander-in-Chief of Norwegian Army; one *s. Educ:* Eton; Magdalen College, Oxford. Entered Diplomatic Service, 1908; served at Vienna, Cairo, Rio de Janeiro, Madrid, Prague, Tokio, Oslo, Rio de Janeiro. Helsingfors, Copenhagen; Minister to Central America, 1933–38; retired 1940. *Publication:* Denmark in History, 1938. *Recreations:* tennis, golf, music. *Clubs:* Carlton, Marlborough-Windham.

Died 20 July 1949.

BIRCH, Wyndham Lindsay, DSO 1919; MBE; *b* 22 March 1879; *s* of Sir Arthur Birch; *m* 1920, Lady Susan Yorke, *d* of 7th Earl of Hardwicke; one *s. Educ:* Marlborough. Prime Warden of Fishmongers' Company, 1919–20; served as Private in London Scottish; as Subaltern in the West Yorkshire Regiment; as an Observer and Pilot in the RFC and RAF in France, Salonica, Palestine, Syria, and Somaliland (despatches twice, DSO, MBE, Croix de Guerre); Brigade Major of Palestine Brigade; Gold Staff Officer at Coronation of George VI; High Sheriff of County of Essex, 1940; DL Essex; Lt-Col 9th Bn Essex Home Guard, retired 1943. *Address:* 22 Albert Road, NW1; Beaumont Hall, Beaumont, Essex. *Clubs:* Travellers', Turf, Royal Automobile.

Died 16 April 1950.

BIRCHALL, Sir John Dearman, Kt 1929; TD; DL; *b* 26 Sept. 1875; *m* 1900, Adela, *d* of P. J. Digby Wykeham, Tythrop House, Oxfordshire. *Educ:* Eton; New College, Oxford (history honours). Contested North Leeds (U), 1906 and 1910; MP (U) North-East Leeds, 1918–40; was a Major in the Gloucestershire Yeomanry; served European War in France; late Alderman Gloucester CC; 2nd Church Estates Commissioner, 1923–24, and 1925–29; Member National Assembly. *Address:* Cotswold Farm, Cirencester.

Died 6 Jan. 1941.

BIRCHAM, Sir Bernard Edward H.; *see* Halsey-Bircham.

BIRD, Sir Charles Hayward, Kt 1929; CBE 1924; chemical manufacturer; *b* 1862; *s* of late Robert Bird, Cardiff; *m* 1886, Lilian, *d* of late Benjamin Waite, Ben Rhydding, Yorkshire; two *s. Educ:* Taunton School. JP and Alderman for the City of Cardiff; Lord Mayor, 1910–11; Honorary Freeman, 1923; Past President of the British Waterworks Association, 1923; Member of Court of Governors and of Council of University College of South Wales and Monmouthshire; has been Chairman of Cardiff Waterworks Committee since 1911, of Local Employment Committee since 1917, and of Licensing Committee, 1922–43; Member of Inland Water Survey Committee, 1935. *Address:* Seys Dene, Cyncoed Road, Cardiff. *Club:* National Liberal.

Died 5 Sept. 1944.

BIRD, Elliott Beverley S.; *see* Steeds-Bird.

BIRD, Sir Ernest Edward, Kt 1944; Solicitor; Partner in firm of Bird & Bird, Solicitors, 5 Gray's Inn Square, WC1; *b* 1 Sept. 1877; *y s* of George Adam Bird, Worcester, and Margaret Harvey, *o d* of William Brinton, Kidderminster; *m* 1910, Gertrude Hannah, *y d* of Charles Florance Young, 22 Cranley Gardens, SW, and Wandsworth; one *s* two *d. Educ:* King's School, Worcester. Admitted a Solicitor 1900; Member of Council of Law Society since 1923, President, 1943–44; Member of Disciplinary Committee since 1938; Director of Legal and General Assurance Society Ltd (Chairman since 1936); Director of Gresham Life Assurance Society, Ltd, Gresham Fire and Accident Society Ltd, Staveley Coal and Iron Co. Ltd, Park Gate Iron and Steel Co. Ltd, Williams Deacon's Bank Ltd, and other companies; Member of Court of Assistants of

Salters Co. (Master, 1939–40 and 1940–41), and of Makers of Playing Cards Co. (twice Master); Director and Hon. Treasurer of Solicitors Benevolent Association. *Clubs:* Reform, Garrick, Hurlingham.

Died 6 Feb. 1945.

BIRD, Sir Harry, Kt 1922; JP, CC; *b* 6 April 1862; *m* 1st, 1885, Marian (*d* 1937), *e d* or George Frith, Coventry; two *s* one *d*; 2nd, 1938, Susan, *d* of Enoch Williams, Bridgnorth. *Educ:* Grammar School, Coventry. Member of Court of Common Council since 1895; Deputy Alderman of City of London, 1917; one of HM Lieutenants for City of London; Governor and Past Almoner of St Bartholomew's Hospital; Chief Commoner of Corporation of the City of London, 1920; JP Essex. *Address:* 158 Lauderdale Mansions, W9. *Club:* Constitutional.

Died 10 April 1944.

BIRD, Squadron Comdr Sir James, Kt 1945; OBE 1916; FRAeS; MINA; RNAS (retired); Special Director of Vickers-Armstrongs Ltd; Chairman of Director of various industrial companies; Member Southampton Harbour Board; *b* 19 March 1883; 2nd *s* of late Samuel Bird, Slatwoods, East Cowes, Isle of Wight, and Bird & Co., Calcutta; *m* 1937, Pamela, *yr d* of late Arthur Ramsden; one *s* by previous marriage. *Educ:* Marlborough. Various appts with Armstrong Whitworth & Co., and as a Consulting Naval Architect, 1902–14; served European War in RN and RNAS, 1914–18; successively Director, Managing Director, and Proprietor of Supermarine Aviation Co., 1918–28; various appts with Vickers Aviation Ltd and Vickers-Armstrongs Ltd, 1928–41. *Recreations:* yachting, shooting, golf. *Address:* Park Place, Wickham, Hants. *T:* Wickham 2147. *Clubs:* Royal Thames Yacht, Royal Aero, Buck's.

Died 13 Aug. 1946.

BIRD, Maj.-Gen. Sir Wilkinson Dent, KBE 1923; CB 1916; CMG 1918; DSO 1900; *b* 4 May 1869; *s* of late Capt. J. D. Bird, 20th Hussars; *m* 1902, Winifred Editha, *d* of Major J. B. Barker; two *d*. *Educ:* Wellington; RMC, Sandhurst. Entered The Queen's Royal Regiment, 1888; Captain and Brevet Major, 1897; Brevet Lieut-Colonel, 1909; Lieut-Colonel, 2nd Royal Irish Rifles, 1913; Col 1913; Maj.-Gen. 1921; Chief Instructor and Staff Officer, School of Musketry, Hythe, 1903–05; Professor, Staff College, India, 1905–09; General Staff Officer, 2nd Grade, War Office, 1910–13; 1st Grade, 1915; Director of Staff Duties, 1916–17; Lt-Governor Royal Hospital, Chelsea, 1918–23; retired pay, 1923; served Niger Expedition, 1897 (despatches, medal with clasp, Brevet Major); NW Frontier of India, 1897–98 (medal with two clasps); South Africa, 1899–1900, present at relief of Mafeking (severely wounded, despatches, DSO); European War, 1914–18 (severely wounded, leg amputated, despatches, ADC to King, Officer Legion of Honour, CB, CMG, Croix de Guerre); Colonel of Queen's Royal Regiment, 1929–39; has Royal Geographical Society's Diploma. *Publications:* Lectures on the Strategy of the Franco-German and Russo-Japanese Wars; Direction of War; A Chapter of Misfortunes in Mesopotamia, 1915. *Address:* Glenturf, Camberley, Surrey.

Died 6 Jan. 1943.

BIRD, Sir William Barrott Montfort, Kt 1920; JP; *b* 11 July 1855; 2nd *s* of Wm Frederic Wratislaw Bird of Wilmington, Kent, and Gray's Inn, solicitor, and Fanny, *d* of Wm Bateman; *m* 1895, Martha Elizabeth (*d* 1933), *widow* of J. H. Murray; no *c*. *Educ:* Bruce Castle, under the late Dr Birkbeck Hill, DCL, of Pembroke College, Oxford. Solicitor, 1880; retired; travelled round the world in 1901; has shot big game in Nepal, East Africa, and the Sudan; was Master and is on the Court of Assistants of the Salters' Company (Master, 1919–20) and the Makers of Playing Cards (past Master); High Sheriff of Sussex, 1912–13; MP (U) Chichester Division of

West Sussex, 1921–23. *Address:* Eartham, nr Chichester, Sussex. *TA:* Bird, Eartham, Slindon. *T:* Slindon 236. *Clubs:* Carlton, Marlborough-Windham.

Died 13 Nov. 1950.

BIRDWOOD, Lt-Col George Christopher McDowall, CBE 1919; Indian Army, retired; *b* 1863. Served Burma, 1885–89 (medal and two clasps); retired, 1909; European War, 1914–19 (despatches, CBE). *Address:* 16 Gloucester Road, Redhill.

Died 4 Oct. 1944.

BIRKETT, Brig.-Gen. Herbert Stanley, CB 1917; VD; CAMC; MD, CM, LLD (McGill); Professor of Laryngology and Otology, 1895; Emeritus Professor since 1931; Dean of the Medical Faculty, McGill University, Montreal, 1914–22; Consulting Laryngologist and Otologist to Royal Victoria Hospital and Alexandra Hospital; Hon. Physician and Hon. ADC to Governor-General of Canada; *b* Hamilton, Canada, 17 July 1864; *s* of late William Birkett, merchant, and late Caroline Amelia, *d* of Jacob Ball of Grantham, Ontario; *m* 1899. *Educ:* Forest House School, Chester, Eng. MD, McGill University, 1886. Senior House Surgeon Montreal General Hospital, 1886–87; Assistant Physician Montreal Dispensary, 1887–89; Laryngologist to Montreal Dispensary, 1889–91; to Montreal General Hosp., 1891–99; Junior Demonstrator of Anatomy, McGill University, 1889–90; Demonstrator, 1890–96; for some years General Secretary Dominion Medical Association, and Montreal Medico-Chirurgical Society; Governor Montreal General Hospital; President Montreal Medico-Chirurgical Society; Vice-Pres. Section of Laryngology and Otology, British Medical Association, 1897, 1906, 1930 and 1932; Pres. American Laryngological Association, 1907–08; Fellow of the Royal Society of Medicine; President American Otological Society, 1921; organized and commanded for 3½ years No. 3 Canadian General Hospital (McGill) for Overseas service (despatches); Consultant in Oto-Laryngology (Boulogne); Colonial Officers' Auxiliary Decoration; Assistant Director-General, Medical Services Overseas, Military Forces of Canada; President American Laryngological, Rhinological, and Otological Society, 1918–19; Hon. President, Clinical Congress of Laryngology, London, 1919; Semon Lecturer (University of Lond.), 1922; Hon. Member Scottish Otological and Laryngological Society, 1924; American Academy of Ophthalmology and Oto-Laryngology; The Italian Society of Laryngology; German Ear, Nose and Throat Society, 1938; Hon. Fellow American Laryngological Assoc., 1939; Hon. President, The Mackay Institute for the Deaf. *Publications:* Hemiatrophy of the Tongue; Empyæma of the Antrum; Thyrotomy for Sub-cordal Sarcoma; Dermoid Cyst of the Nose; Anomalous Cases of Primary Nasal Diphtheria; Carcinoma of the Larynx; Diphtheria, its Treatment and Nursing; Syphilis of the Larynx, Trachea, and Bronchi; Diseases of the Oro- and Naso-pharynx (Posey and Wright); Rhinoliths; Salivary Calculi; Lupus of the Oro-pharynx and Naso-pharynx; Diphtheria (Hare's System of Therapeutics), with Dr J. C. Cameron; Perichondritis of the Larynx, from an unusual cause; Foreign Body in the Naso-pharynx Oidium Albicans; Address to the Graduating Class of the Medical Faculty (McGill University); Otomycosis due to the Aspergillus Glaucus; Seventh Lecture of the Somerville Course, before the Montreal Natural History Society; Diseases of the Larynx (Osler's Modern Medicine); Early History of Medicine of the Province of Quebec; The Transatlantic Development of Rhino-laryngology (Semon Lecture, University of London, 1922); Diseases of the Tonsil and their Treatment (Jackson and Coates' book). *Recreation:* golf. *Address:* 71 The Linton, 1509 Sherbrooke Street, Montreal, Canada. *Clubs:* (Hon. Mem.) Mount-Royal, St Lawrence Yacht, University, Montreal.

Died 19 July 1942.

BIRKETT, Brig. Richard Maule, DSO 1918; Colonel Royal Sussex Regiment since 1941; *b* 2 Jan. 1882; *s* of late D. M. Birkett, MA, JP; *m* 1916, Mary Hilda Verrall (Croix de Guerre), Manor House, Lewes; one *s* one *d*. *Educ*: Rugby; RMC, Sandhurst. Served S Africa, 1902; India with 1st Bn Royal Sussex Regt, 1903–13; Adjutant, 1910–13; served in France and Italy between 1914–18, with 7th Bn Royal Sussex Regt, and commanded 17th London Regt, 2nd Bn Queen's Royal Regt, and 7th Bn Machine Gun Corps (wounded twice, despatches four times, DSO, Bt Lt-Col); served with 1st Bn in Ireland and Eng., 1920–31; commanded 2nd Bn The Royal Sussex Regiment in India, 1931–34; Commander 133rd (Sussex and Kent) Infantry Brigade TA, 1934–38; retired pay, 1938; re-employed from Sept. 1939 to June 1941. *Recreations*: Member of Rugby School XV, 1900, and Sandhurst XV and XI, 1901, hockey, squash, etc. *Address*: White Mill, Fontwell, nr Arundel, Sussex.

Died 30 Nov. 1942.

BIRKIN, Sir Alexander Russell, 4th Bt *cr* 1905; *b* 9 Sept. 1861; *s* of 1st Bt and Harriet, *y d* of Matthew Tebbutt; *S* nephew, 1933. *Heir*: *b* Philip Austen Birkin, OBE, *b* 1869.

Died 5 May 1942.

BIRLEY, Lt-Col Bevil Langton, DSO 1917; Commanding 5th Bn Wiltshire Home Guard since 1940; late The King's Own Royal Regiment; *b* 19 Sept. 1884; *s* of H. A. Birley and Amy Chichester of Woodside, Knutsford; *m* 1914, Eleanor Mary Cordeaux; two *s* two *d*. *Educ*: Winchester. Militia Rifle Brigade; received Commission in 4th Foot—King's Own Royal Regt; Adjt of 6th (S) Battalion of Regiment, 1914; served European War, Gallipoli and Mesopotamia, 1915–19 (Acting Lt-Col, Brevet Major, DSO, despatches twice); retired pay, 1924. *Recreation*: hunting. *Address*: Kingsdown House, Swindon. *T*: Stratton St Margaret 42.

Died 24 Sept. 1943.

BIRLEY, Rt Rev. Thomas Howard; Chaplain to St Giles Homes and Community of Sacred Passion, East Hanningfield, since 1944; *b* 1864; unmarried. *Educ*: Radley; Christ Church, Oxford; Cuddesdon. Deacon, 1888; Priest, 1889; Curate of St Saviour, Roath, 1888–96; Vicar of St Thomas the Martyr, Oxford, 1896–1908; UMCA Mission at Korogwe, Zanzibar, 1908; Archdeacon on Korogwe ond Zigualand and Canon of Zanzibar, 1911–25; Bishop of Zanzibar, 1925–43. *Address*: St Giles Lodge, East Hanningfield, Chelmsford, Essex.

Died 31 March 1949.

BIRMINGHAM, George A.; *see* Hannay, Rev. James O.

BIRNIE, Captain Harry Charles, DSO 1918; RNR, retired list; at present on active service as Commodore RNR; Elder Brother of Trinity House since 1926; Member of Committee of Management, Seamen's Hospital Society, since 1927; Member of Southampton Harbour Board, 1936; *b* 1 Oct. 1882; *er s* of late Rev. Charles Birnie, MA, of Aberdour, Aberdeenshire. *Educ*: New Aberdour Public School; privately. Junior Officer, Cunard Line, 1905; commanded various steamships for the Cunard Line, 1919–26; commanded HM Torpedo Boat 82, 1915; HMS Fairy, N Sea, 1916–17; HMS P57, 1917–18, North Sea and Dover Patrol (DSO, despatches). *Address*: Trinity House, Tower Hill, EC3.

Died 9 March 1943.

BIRRELL, Col Edwin Thomas Fairweather, CB 1917; CMG 1915; MB; late RAMC; *b* 28 Feb. 1874; 5th *s* of late James Birrell, JP, formerly of Uttershill, Penicuik; *m* 1907, Kate Davida, 3rd *d* of late David Gibson of Jonsered, Sweden; one *s* one *d*. *Educ*: Trinity

College, Glenalmond; Edinburgh University. MB 1895. Entered army, 1896; Captain, 1899; Major, 1907; Lt-Col 1915; Col 1917; DADG, AMS, 1908–12; served Balkan War, 1912–13, as BRCS Commissioner for Bulgaria; and European War, 1914–19, as DADMS 1st Cavalry Division, ADMS General Headquarters, British Expeditionary Force, ADMS General Headquarters, British Salonika Force, DDMS 16th Army Corps, British Salonika Force, and DDMS British Military Mission, South Russia (despatches, CB, CMG, 1914 Star with clasp, medal, victory medal with emblem, Serbian White Eagle, 4th class, with swords; Officer, Greek Order of Redeemer; Russian St Anne, 2nd Class; Greek Military Merit, 3rd Class); retired pay, 1923. Home Guard, Company Commander 1940, Major, 1941. *Address*: Redgables, Penicuik, Midlothian. *T*: Penicuik 85. *Club*: Army and Navy.

Died 29 May 1944.

BISCOE, Rev. Cecil Earle T.; *see* Tyndale-Biscoe.

BISSCHOP, Willem Roosegaarde, LLD; Knight Officer, Order of Orange Nassau; *b* 31 Dec. 1866; 2nd *s* of late Rt Hon. P. J. Roosegaarde Bisschop, LLD, Vice-President of the Supreme Court of Judicature of the Netherlands Indies, and Elisabeth, *g d* of Field Marshal Daendels, Governor-General of the Netherlands Indies, 1806–10; *m* May Cowen; two *d*. *Educ*: Arnhem Gymnasium; Leiden University (LLD 1896). Advocate of the Court of Appeal at Amsterdam, 1897; Standing Counsel to the Dutch Legation, 1897–1941; Hon. Sec. of the Netherlands Chamber of Commerce in London, 1897–1913; Barrister-at-Law, Lincoln's Inn and Middle Temple, 1901; Lecturer and Examiner in Roman Dutch Law to the Inns of Court, 1907–10; Examiner in Roman Dutch Law to the Inns of Court, 1925–26, and to the University of London; Member of the Society of Dutch Literature, 1904; Member Utrechtsch Historisch Genootschap, 1921; Hon. Sec. General International Law Association, 1939; Hon. Sec. Grotius Society, 1940; one of Managers of Royal Institution of Great Britain, 1940–42. *Publications*: De Opkomst der Londensche Geldmarkt (1640–1826), 1896; The Mining Law of the Netherlands East Indies, 1899; The Rise of the London Money Market, 1910; Roman Dutch Law part of Burge's Colonial and Foreign Laws, new edition; Received for Shipment Bills of Lading, 1923; The Saar Controversy, 1924; General Average, York-Antwerp Rules, 1924, 1925; Limitation of Shipowners' Liability and Compulsory Insurance of Passengers, 1927; A Commonwealth of European States, 1939; The Altmark, 1940; reviews and articles. *Address*: 2 Dr Johnson's Buildings, EC4. *T*: Central 1696; 35 York Terrace, Regent's Park, London NW1. *T*: Welbeck 6231. *TA*: Bisschop, 3 Temple, London. *Club*: Athenæum.

Died 22 Feb. 1944.

BISWAS, Rt Rev. Dr Nirod Kumar; Bishop of Assam since 1946; Licentiate of State Medical Faculty (Cal.); *b* 26 Dec. 1905; *s* of late Rev. R. C. Biswas, Putimari, Nadia, Bengal, India; *m* 1937, Violet Downey; one *s* three *d*. *Educ*: St Paul's School, St Paul's Cathedral College, University College of Science and Campbell Medical School and finally, for theological studies, Bishop's College—all at Calcutta. Medical Missionary with Church Missionary Society, Bengal, 1929–30; Oxford University Mission, Bengal, 1930–31; Bible Churchmen's Missionary Society at Bina, Central Provinces, 1932–37; Palace Surgeon and Asst Palace Surgeon to Nawab of Kurwai, Central India, and Maharaja Scindia of Gwalior, Central India, respectively, 1937–41; Bishop's Coll., Calcutta, 1941–43; Deacon, 1943; Priest, 1944; in charge of SS. Philip and James' Church, Katni, Central Provinces, 1943–46. *Recreations*: music, gardening. *Address*: Bishop's House, Dibrugarh, Assam, India. *TA*: Bishop Assam.

Died 17 Nov. 1948.

BLACK, Sir Alec, 1st Bt *cr* 1918; JP for the Parts of Lindsey; steamship owner; *b* 23 Dec. 1872; *s* of William Black, Great Grimsby, and Charlotte, *d* of John Charles Fox, Barton-on-Humber, Lincs; *m* 1902, Florence Mary (who obtained a divorce, 1927), *d* of David Smith, Great Grimsby; no *c. Educ:* privately. *Recreations:* angling, shooting, motoring. *Heir:* none. *Address:* Field House, Great Grimsby. *T:* Great Grimsby 2329. *Clubs:* Royal Automobile; County, Great Grimsby.

Died 28 June 1942.

BLACK, Sir Arthur William, Kt 1916; *b* 28 Feb. 1863; *s* of late William Edward Black and Annie Hatton; *m* 1887, Helena, *y d* of late John Spence, Paisley; one *d. Educ:* Nottingham. Lace manufacturer; started in business, 1888. Entered City Council of Nottingham, 1895; Sheriff of Nottingham, 1898–99; Mayor, 1902–03; MP (L) North Beds, 1906–18; contested the Doncaster Division, 1900, Mid Bedford Division, 1918. *Recreations:* motoring, gardening. *Address:* 3 South Road, The Park, Nottingham. *TA:* Black 43202, Nottingham.

Died 13 July 1947.

BLACK, Lt-Col Claud Hamilton Griffith, DSO 1917; late 12th Royal Lancers; re-employed at War Office, Oct. 1939; Liaison Officer with Free French and Allied Forces since 1941; *s* of Rev. John Black, Canon of St Mary the Virgin, Elphin, and Francis, *d* of Henry Griffith, DL, JP, of Castle Nenoe, Co. Sligo; *m* 1913, Augusta Sarah, *d* of T. J. Shipton Green; two *s. Educ:* Cheltenham College; Sandhurst. Joined Indian Cavalry, 1901; Captain, 1909; Major, 1923; served on Staff of Army Headquarters, India; passed Staff College, 1912; transferred to 12th Royal Lancers, 1914; served with regiment in France, 1914 and part of 1915; afterwards on General Staff of 2nd Cavalry Division, 1st Division (DSO, Bt Major), 6th Army Corps and 40th Division (Bt Lt-Col, Officier de la Légion d'Honneur, Croix de Guerre); after the Armistice served in the Army of Occupation in Germany, on the Allied Military Committee of Versailles and British Delegation to Peace Conference in Paris; Staff Highland Area, 1922–26; retired pay, 1927; recalled to active list in Oct. 1939 for Welfare and Liaison Duties with Fighting French Forces. *Address:* Orchard House, Sheen Common, SW14. *T:* Prospect 2189. *Clubs:* United Service, Hurlingham.

Died 25 June 1946.

BLACK, Colin Mackenzie, CVO 1937; partner of the firm of Mackenzie & Black, Writers to the Signet, Edinburgh; *b* 7 Oct. 1877; *o s* of late A. D. M. Black, WS, Edinburgh; *m* 1911, Rose Emily, *d* of late Canon W. J. Knox Little, and *widow* of Fred Usher. *Educ:* Eton (rowed in the Eight, 1896). Chairman of Royal Edinburgh Hospital for Sick Children; Secretary of the King's Bodyguard for Scotland, Royal Company of Archers; Director of the Scottish Union and National Insurance Company and the National Bank of Scotland; served European War. *Recreations:* shooting, fishing. *Address:* 2 Randolph Cliff, Edinburgh. *Clubs:* Boodle's; New, Edinburgh.

Died 5 Oct. 1943.

BLACK, Rev. Canon Gibson (James Hunter Monahan); Vicar of Coxwold since 1927; Canon of York since 1948, and Prebendary of Bugthorpe; *b* 1867; *s* of Rev. John Black and Anna Maria Black, *d* of Francis Macdonogh, KC; unmarried. *Educ:* privately. Deacon, 1900; priest, 1901; Curacies; St Mark, Dalston; St Andrew, Dublin; St Mary, Walthamstow; Vicar of; St Thomas, Barnsbury; St Barnabas, Hull. *Recreations:* reading, gardening. *Address:* The Vicarage, Coxwold, York.

Died 8 Feb. 1950.

BLACK, Very Rev. James Macdougall, MA; DD (Edin.); Chaplain to the King in Scotland since 1942; Minister of St George's West, Church of Scotland, Edinburgh, since 1921; *b* Rothesay, Isle of Bute, 25 Jan. 1879; *s* of late Hugh Black, Rothesay; *m* 1909, Sarah Florence Bain, Inverness; one *s* two *d. Educ:* Rothesay Academy; Glasgow University; United Free Church Coll., Glasgow; Marburg University. Ordained Castlehill Church, Forres, 1903; Broughton Place Church, Edinburgh, 1907–21; Moderator of the General Assembly of the Church of Scotland, 1938–39; served as Chaplain in France with 15th and 16th Royal Scots and 2nd Seaforths, 1915–18, rank, Major (despatches); Warrack Lecturer on Preaching, 1922–23; James Sprunt Lectureship. Union Seminary, Richmond, Virginia, 1923; Turnbull Lectureship, Melbourne, 1928; Baird Lecturer, 1914. *Publications:* The Pilgrim Ship; The Burthen of the Weeks; Around the Guns; The Mystery of Preaching; The Dilemmas of Jesus; The Unlocked Door; An Apology for Rogues; The Man on the other Cross; A World Without Christmas; His Glorious Shame; The Boys Play Soldiers: New Forms of the Old Faith (Baird Lectures). *Recreations:* golf and gardening. *Address:* 35 Coates Gardens, Edinburgh 12. *T:* 62196. *Club:* United Service.

Died 18 Oct. 1949.

BLACK, Col John Campbell Lamont, CMG 1917; *b* 23 Aug. 1869; *m* 1894, Zoë (*d* 1942), *d* of E. W. Tichener; one *s. Educ:* Harrow School. Entered Army, E Kent Regt (The Buffs), 1889; Capt. ASC 1897; Major, 1903; Lt-Col 1912; Col 1916; Deputy Assist Director Supplies and Transport, Aldershot, 1909–12; served S Africa, 1899–1900 (Queen's medal 2 clasps); retired pay, 1922.

Died 9 Feb. 1950.

BLACK, William John; *b* Dufferin County, Ontario Province, 29 Nov. 1872; *s* of William Black and Mary Jane McMahon; *m* 1904, Ida M. Day, Creemore, Ontario. *Educ:* Agricultural College, Guelph, Ontario. Graduated Toronto University, 1902. Associate Editor, Farmers' Advocate, London, Ontario; Editor, Farmers' Advocate, Winnipeg, 1902–04; Deputy Minister of Agriculture and Immigration, Manitoba, 1904–05; organised Manitoba Agricultural College, 1905; President, 1905–15; Secretary, Federal Economic and Development Commission, 1915–16; Commissioner of Agriculture for Canada, 1916–18; Chairman, Soldier Settlement Board of Canada, 1918–20; Deputy Minister of Immigration and Colonisation, 1921–23; European Manager Colonization and Development Canadian National Railways, London, 1924; Director, Department of Colonization and Agriculture, Canadian National Railways, Montreal, Canada, 1925–39; Hon. LLD, Manitoba University, 1932; Hon. DScA, University of Montreal, 1934. *Recreation:* golf. *Address:* 625 Murray Hills, Westmount, Montreal, Que., Canada. *Clubs:* Mount Stephen, Montreal.

Died 22 Dec. 1941.

BLACKBURN, Hon. Lord; Robert Francis Leslie Blackburn; *b* 27 April 1864; *s* of late Robert Blackburn; *m* 1893, Lady Constance Bowes-Lyon, *d* of 13th Earl of Strathmore; three *d.* KC Scot 1906; Judge of Court of Session, Scotland, 1918–35, with title of Lord Blackburn; contested Forfar (C), 1909 and 1910. *Address:* 125 Grange Loan, Edinburgh; Merklands, Blairgowrie. *Clubs:* Caledonian; New, Edinburgh.

Died 21 March 1944.

BLACKBURN, Maurice McCrae; Member for Bourke Federal House of Representatives, 1934–43; *b* 19 Nov. 1880; *s* of Maurice Blackburn and Thomas Ann Cole McCrae; *m* 1914, Doris Amelia Hordern; two *s* one *d. Educ:* Church of England Grammar School, Melbourne; University of Melbourne, BA, LLB. Practising Barrister and Solicitor in Melbourne since 1910; Member of the Legislative Assembly of the State of Victoria, 1914–17 and 1925–34; Speaker of the Legislative Assembly,

1933–34; now President of Australian Council for Civil Liberties. *Recreation:* walking. *Address:* Louisville Avenue, Pascoe Vale South near Melbourne, Australia.

Died 31 March 1944.

BLACKER, Col Frederick St John, DSO 1917; *b* 1881; *o surv. s* of late William Blacker of Castle Martin and 1st wife, late Hon. Mary, 4th *d* of 3rd Baron Cloncurry; *m* 1910, Sheela Maude, *d* of late John Pollok of Lismany, Ballinasloe, Co. Galway; two *s. Educ:* Harrow. Joined Rifle Brigade, 1899; served South African War; Capt. Rifle Brigade, 1905–10; Special reserve, 1910–14; rejoined, 1914–19 (DSO); retired, 1918. *Address:* Castle Martin, Newbridge, Co. Kildare. *TA:* Kilcullen. *T:* Kilcullen 7. *Clubs:* Naval and Military; Kildare Street, Dublin.

Died 29 March 1942.

BLACKER, Sir George, Kt 1923; CBE 1920; MD (Lond.) Honours, BS (Lond.) First-Class Honours, FRCP, FRCS; Consulting Obstetric Physician, University College Hospital and Royal Northern Hospital; Fellow of University College, London; late President Radium Institute; Director, Clerical Medical and General Life Assurance Society; late Chairman, Farnham Division, and Hon. Life Member, British Red Cross Society; President, Old Cheltonian Society, 1928–29; late Dean and Lecturer on Obstetric Medicine, University College Hospital Medical School; Member, University College Hospital Committee, Royal Northern Hospital Committee, and Vice-President, Mt Vernon Hospital; Fellow, Royal Society of Medicine and late President, Obstetrical Section; late Captain RAMC, 1915–18 (despatches twice); *b* Dublin, 1865; 3rd *s* of Major-General Latham Blacker and Harriet De Maine *d* of Captain Bagot Smith; *m* 1904, Shirley Elvina, 2nd *d* of late Canon T. J. Bowen of Bristol; one *s. Educ:* Cheltenham College; University College, London. Scholar and Exhibitioner, London University. Examiner in Midwifery to Royal College of Surgeons England, Universities of London, Liverpool and New Zealand. *Publications:* editor 7th edition Galabin's Practice of Midwifery; Contributions on Medical Subjects to Lancet and other medical journals. *Address:* Oak Hill Cottage, Frensham, Surrey. *T:* Frensham 276. *Club:* Royal Automobile.

Died 21 May 1948.

BLACKER, Harold Alfred Cecil; Mr Justice Blacker; Puisne Judge, HM High Court of Judicature at Lahore since 1937; *b* 15 Aug. 1889; *yr s* of late Major L. C. M. Blacker, Royal Artillery; *m* 1922, Barbara Helen Lyne Graeme, *d* of Dr J. Leask, Colonial Civil Service, late of Singapore; one *d. Educ:* Charterhouse; Bedford Grammar School; Queens' College, Cambridge. Entered ICS, 1914; served Indian Army, 1917–18, with rank of Captain, President Punjab Conspiracy Case Tribunal, 1930–33; Additional Judge, Lahore High Court, 1934–35; Acting Judge, June and July, 1936, April–July, 1937, and Nov.–Dec., 1937. *Recreation:* golf. *Address:* 4 Mayfair Court, Lahore, Punjab, India. *TA:* Lahore. *T:* Lahore 2897. *Club:* East India and Sports.

Died 18 July 1944.

BLACKFORD, 1st Baron *cr* 1935, of Compton Pauncefoot; **William James Peake Mason;** 1st Bt *cr* 1918; JP; *b* 1862; *m* 1885, Edith, *d* of late Alexander Murray Affleck of Dumfries; one *s.* Barrister Middle, Temple; North-Eastern Circuit; Hull Sessions; contested South Somerset (C), 1900; North Somerset, 1906; and East Finsbury, twice in 1910; High Sheriff of Somersetshire, 1928–29. *Recreations:* hunting and shooting. *Heir: s* Col Hon. G. K. M. Mason, DSO. *Address:* Compton Castle, Compton-Pauncefoot, Somerset. *Club:* Carlton.

Died 21 July 1947.

BLACKIE, Rt Rev. Ernest Morell; Dean of Rochester since 1937; *b* 19 Aug. 1867; *s* of late Rev. J. M. Blackie, LLB; *m* 1903, Caroline Sophia Campbell, *d* of late Rev. J. Haldane Stewart, MA, Rector of Brightwell, Berks; two *s* two *d. Educ:* Cheltenham Grammar School; London University (BA, 1889). Deacon, 1891; Priest, 1892; Senior Assistant Master, King's School Gloucester, and Curate of St Mark's, Gloucester, and Assistant Diocesan Missioner, 1891–92; Minor Canon, Rochester Cathedral, 1892–1900; Curate, St John's, Chatham, 1894–99; Rector of Limpsfield, 1900–06; Rector of St Paul's, York Place, Edinburgh, 1906–13; Canon of St Mary's Cathedral, Edinburgh, 1912–13; Vicar of Windsor, 1913–21; Hon. Chaplain to the King, 1914–18; Chaplain to the King, 1918–30; Canon and Precentor of Lincoln, and Archdeacon of Stow, 1921–37; Bishop of Grantham, 1930–35; Bishop of Grimsby, 1935–37; Select Preacher, Cambridge, 1928. *Publications:* The Pylgrimage of Robert Langton (London 1522), edited, with Introduction and Notes 1924; A Friendly Farewell to Sir Francis Drake (London, 1585), edited, with Introduction, 1924; Church Councils at Work, 1928; article on Reginald Peacock, in English Historical Review, 1911; articles to Dictionary of English Church History. *Recreation:* travelling. *Address:* The Deanery, Rochester. *Club:* Authors'.

Died 5 March 1943.

BLACKMAN, Frederick Frost, FRS 1906; MA, DSc (Lond.); Fellow of St John's College, Cambridge, and formerly Reader in Botany in the University; retired 1936; *b* 1866; *m* 1917, Elsie, *d* of Samuel Chick, Chestergate, Ealing; one *s. Address:* Upper-cross, 34 Storey's Way, Cambridge. *T:* Cambridge 4964. *Club:* Athenæum.

Died 30 Jan. 1947.

BLACKMAN, Winifred Susan; Diploma in Anthropology, Oxford; Fellow of the Royal Anthropological Institute; Member of the Royal Asiatic Society; Research Student to the Committee for Anthropology, Oxford; *e d* of late Rev. J. H. Blackman, Vicar of St Paul's, Norwich, and Anne Mary, *y d* of the late Rev. G. A. Jacob, DD (Oxon), Headmaster of Christ's Hospital. *Educ:* privately; University of Oxford. Engaged in anthropological research among the Fellāhīn since the winter, 1920–21; in charge of the Percy Sladen Expedition to Egypt, 1922–26, and of the Wellcome Expedition to Egypt, 1927–31. *Publications:* The Fellāhīn of Upper Egypt, 1927; numerous articles in the Journal of Egyptian Archæology, Man, The Journal of the Royal Anthropological Institute, Discovery, and other periodicals and newspapers. *Recreations:* travelling and lecturing. *Address:* c/o National Provincial Bank, Abergele, N Wales.

Died 12 Dec. 1950.

BLACKSHAW, J. F., OBE 1918; *b* 22 May 1875; *m* 1899, Winifred Mary, *d* of William Trimmer, solicitor, Alton, Hants; one *s* two *d. Educ:* University of Wales. Late Commissioner of Dairying, Ministry of Agriculture and Fisheries; HMI Board of Education; Principal of the Midland Agricultural College; Assistant Professor of Agriculture, West of Scotland Agricultural College. *Publications:* many Reports on Agricultural Experiments. *Address:* The Elms, Whitchurch, Shropshire. *T:* Whitchurch, 281. *Club:* Farmers'.

Died 17 Dec. 1943.

BLACKTON, James Stuart; Chairman and Managing Director of J. Stuart Blackton Photoplays; Director of Vitagraph Company of America; *b* Sheffield, 1875; *m* 1908, Paula Hunt Hilburn of Atlanta, Georgia; two *s* two *d. Educ:* Eton House Collegiate School, Sheffield; College of the City of New York. Left England for America, 1886; as journalist and artist met Thomas A. Edison, who interested him in early motion pictures; became a pioneer in cinematography; produced film plays and news pictorials, beginning 1897; with Albert E.

Smith founded the Vitagraph Company of America, the first company organised to make screen plays, 1900; produced the first one-, two-, three-, five- and seven-reel film plays; organised the Motion Picture Board of Trade of America, becoming its first President; founded the first magazine devoted to films; opened first cinema for artistic presentation of pictures with orchestra accompaniment; first put literature and Bible stories on the screen; trained many of the leading actors and film producers of to-day; resumed residence in England, 1921, and produced first screen play in natural colours. *Recreations:* yachting, motor-boat racing, golf; Commodore Atlantic Yacht Club, NY, and Motor-boat Club of America. *Clubs:* Aero of America; Automobile of America; Salmagundi, NY Athletic, National Arts, New York.

Died 13 Aug. 1941.

BLACKWELL, Sir (Cecil) Patrick, MBE 1919; **Hon. Mr Justice Blackwell;** High Court Judge, Bombay, 1926–44; acted as Chief Justice during parts of 1935, 1937, 1938, and 1941; *b* 8 Nov. 1881; *o s* of Patrick Thomas Blackwell, Barrister-at-law (Inner Temple), and Cecilia Tudor, *y d* of late Capt. G. F. Westbrook, RN; *m* 1910, Marguérite Frances (Kaisar-i-Hind Gold Medal, 1935), *d* of late J. A. Tilleard, MVO. *Educ:* Blackheath Proprietary School; City of London School; University College, London (Hollier Greek Scholar); Wadham College, Oxford (Classical Exhibitioner). 1st Class Classical Hon. Mods., 2nd Class Lit.Hum. (BA 1905). Secretary Oxford Union Society, 1904; called to Bar, Inner Temple, 1907; joined the Northern Circuit; was Lieut TF Reserve, and on Recruiting Staff and in Ministry of National Service during the war; contested (L) Kingswinford Division of Staffordshire. *Recreations:* lawn tennis and golf. *Clubs:* Devonshire; Royal Bombay Yacht, Byculla, Willingdon, Bombay.

Died 7 Nov. 1944.

BLACKWELL, Sir Ernley Robertson Hay, KCB 1916; CB 1911; *b* St Andrews, 6 June 1868; *s* of late James Hay Blackwell, St Andrews; *m* 1936, Kathleen Mabel Maurice. *Educ:* Glenalmond. Called to Bar, Inner Temple, 1892; Assistant Under-Secretary of State, 1906, and Legal Assistant Under-Secretary of State, Home Department, 1913–33; Chm. of Statutory Committee of the Pharmaceutical Society, 1934–39; Capt. Royal and Ancient Golf Club, 1933–34. *Address:* 7 Hay Hill, W1. *T:* Regent 7160. *Clubs:* Windham; Royal and Ancient Golf, St Andrews.

Died 21 Sept. 1941.

BLACKWELL, Sir Patrick; *see* Blackwell, Sir C. P.

BLACKWELL, Thomas Geoffrey, OBE; Deputy-Chairman Crosse & Blackwell, Ltd; *b* Harrow Weald, 28 July 1884; *s* of Thomas Francis Blackwell, JP, DL, of Harrow Weald, Middlesex; *m* 1909, Shirley Maud, *d* of late John Lawson-Johnston; two *s* two *d. Educ:* Harrow; New College, Oxford. Director of Crosse & Blackwell, Ltd, since 1905; Chairman of Board, 1924–28; during European War served on Admiralty War Staff and in Ministry of Blockade, 1914–19 (OBE); Treasurer of Royal Commercial Travellers' Schools, 1915–21; is a Governor of St Thomas's Hospital and of London Lock Hospital; Local Representative National Arts Collections Fund. *Recreations:* shooting, golf, cricket. *Address:* Norcott Hill, Berkhamsted, Herts. *T:* Berkhamsted 76. *Clubs:* Carlton, Conservative. Boodle's, MCC; Royal and Ancient Golf, St Andrew's.

Died 22 May 1943.

BLACKWELL, Maj.-Gen. William Richard, CB 1931; CMG 1918; *b* Dublin, 25 Jan. 1877; *s* of Captain T. S. Blackwell, *m* 1906, Mary Ethel (*d* 1942), *d* of late A. L. and Hon. Mrs Aylmer; two *d. Educ:* St Francis College, Richmond, Canada; private; Royal College of Surgeons, Ireland. Joined RAMC, 1899; served South Africa, 1899–1902 (despatches); European War,

1914–19 (despatches thrice, CMG, Brevet Colonel Legion of Honour); NW Frontier, India and Afghanistan, 1919–20; DADG War Office, 1914; ADGMS, GHQ, France, 1918; ADMS, AHQ, India, 1919–23; ADMS, Baluchistan District, 1925–27; DDMS, AHQ, India, 1927–29; Deputy Director-General Army Medical Services. War Office, 1929–33; Hon. Surgeon to the King, 1930–33; retired pay, 1933. *Recreations:* cricket, golf, tennis, etc. *Club:* Army and Navy.

Died 9 July 1946.

BLACKWOOD, George William; Editor of Blackwood's Magazine; publisher and printer; *b* Murree, India, 12 July 1876; *e s* of Major George F. Blackwood, RHA (killed in action at Maiwand, 1880); *g g s* of William Blackwood, founder of the publishing house of William Blackwood & Sons, Edinburgh and London; *m* 1921, Nina Amelia, 2nd *d* of late E. F. Dudgeon, Gogar Bank, Midlothian; two *s. Educ:* Repton. *Address:* 45 George Street, Edinburgh; Gogar Mount, Corstorphine, Edinburgh; 37 Paternoster Row, EC. *T:* Edinburgh 22491. *Clubs:* Carlton, Royal Automobile; New, Edinburgh; The Hon. Company of Edinburgh Golfers, Muirfield.

Died 26 April 1942.

BLACKWOOD, Sir Henry Palmer Temple, 5th Bt *cr* 1814; *b* 12 May 1896; *s* of late Henry Robert Temple Blackwood (*e s* of 4th Bt) and Rebecca Paffard (she *m* 2nd, 1930, Walter G. C. Stevenson), *d* of J. Scullard; *S* grandfather, 1924; *m* 1926, Ethel Edith Mary, *d* of Humphrey Grenfell Ratcliffe. *Heir: b* Francis Elliot Temple [*b* 11 March 1901; *m* 1921, Lilian, *d* of H. F. MacGuigan].

Died 1 Sept. 1948.

BLACKWOOD, Captain Maurice Baldwin Raymond, DSO 1917; RN, retired; *b* 1882; *s* of Sir Francis Blackwood, 4th Bt and second wife, Dorothy Frances, *d* of Rev. E. H. Quicke; *m* 1915, Dorothea, *d* of late Hon. G. Bertrand Edwards, of Hurn Park, Sydney, NSW; three *s* one *d.* Served World War, 1914–17 (DSO); retired list, 1922.

Died 26 Aug. 1941.

BLADES, Major Walter William, DSO 1915; late Royal Army Ordnance Corps; *b* 14 April 1863; *s* of late Lieut-Colonel Joel Blades, Royal Artillery; *m* 1914, Janet Stoddart. Served South Africa, 1899–1901 (despatches, Queen's medal 2 clasps); European War, 1914–18 (DSO, despatches). *Address:* Tigh Na Mara, Marine Drive West, Barton-on-Sea, New Milton, Hants.

Died 28 Feb. 1943.

BLAGDEN, Charles Otto, MA, DLitt, MRAS, FRAI; Corresponding Member of the Burma Research Society and several other societies; *b* 30 Sept. 1864; *e s* of William George Blagden; *m* 1896, Sophie, *e d* of Robert Martin; one *s* one *d. Educ:* Dulwich College; Corpus Christi College, Oxford (Scholar, 1883; BA, First Class Lit. Hum., 1887; MA 1894). Appointed to Straits Settlements Civil Service, 1888; held various administrative and judicial posts in Malacca and Singapore; a Magistrate and JP for Singapore, Penang, and Malacca; retired on ground of ill-health, 1897; Holt Scholar, Gray's Inn, 1898; called to the Bar, 1900; Joint-Assistant Editor of Encyclopædia of Forms and Precedents, 1902–06; Member of Council Royal Asiatic Society, 1910–14, 1915–19, 1920–24, 1925–29, 1933, and of the Royal Anthropological Institute, 1916–18, 1922–24, 1929; Examiner in Malay at the University of London since 1910; Lecturer in Malay at the School of Oriental Studies and Reader in Malay in the Univ. of London, 1917–35; Secretary of the Board of Oriental Studies (University of London), 1919–25; Dean of the School of Oriental Studies, 1922–35; DLitt (hon.), Rangoon, 1923; a Vice-President of the Royal Anthropological Institute, 1926–28, 1931, and of the

Royal Asiatic Soc., 1929–33, 1935–38; Hon. Secretary of the Royal Anthropological Institute, 1932–35; Hon. Vice-Pres. Royal Asiatic Society, 1938. *Publications:* various papers on the Languages, Folklore, and History of the Malay Peninsula, etc. (principally in the Journal of the Straits Asiatic Society and the Journal of the Royal Asiatic Society of Great Britain and Ireland), since 1894; (with W. W. Skeat) Pagan Races of the Malay Peninsula, 1906; Catalogue of Manuscripts in European Languages belonging to the Library of the India Office, vol. i part i; (with R. O. Winstedt), A Malay Reader, 1917; (in Epigraphia Birmanica) Môn Inscriptions, 1920, 1923, 1928, 1935; first two sections in One Hundred Years of Singapore; introductions to various books on Malavan subjects; An English-Malay Phrase Book, 1934. *Address:* 40 Wychwood Avenue, Whitchurch Lane, Edgware, Middlesex.

Died 25 Aug. 1949.

BLAIKLOCK, George; Barrister-at-law; Recorder of Grantham since 1915; *b* London, 11 April 1856; *s* of John Musgrave Blaiklock, who was born on estate belonging to his parents on Lake Simcoe; *m* 1st, Lavinia Dudley (*d* 1930); three *s* five *d*; 2nd, 1931, Mrs Minnie Willard. *Educ:* mainly self-educated; studied at various evening colleges; took first-class certificates in science; specially studied literature and elocution. Became public speaker, lecturer and writer at 25 years of age; has travelled and lectured in Australia, New Zealand, South Africa, United States, and Canada; interviewed President Kruger in Pretoria; passed preliminary exam. for the Bar, 1892; entered Gray's Inn; called to Bar 1895; been in large number of leading cases; contested (L) Hammersmith, 1906, Jan. 1910, and Dec. 1910; takes a keen interest in Temperance and Social Reform, and is a member of the Board of Management and Hon. Secretary of the National Temperance Hospital; JP Kent; twice Chairman of Herne Bay Council; President Herne Bay League of Nations' Union; President of Herne Bay Fortnightly Club. *Publications:* The People's Handbook of Licensing Law; The Alcohol Factor in Social Conditions; a large number of pamphlets. *Recreations:* boating, fishing, and gardening. *Address:* Filstone, Beacon Road, Herne Bay, Kent. *T:* Herne Bay 676.

Died 10 Jan. 1943.

BLAIN, Sir Herbert Edwin, Kt 1925; CBE 1921; MInstT; Under-writing Member of Lloyd's and Director of Public Companies; *b* Liverpool, 14 May 1870; *s* of Arbuthnot Harrisson Blain, Freeman of Great Grimsby, and Elizabeth Stalker, Carlisle. *Educ:* privately; Liverpool Technical School. With Liverpool Corporation up to 1903, latterly as Principal Traffic Assistant, Liverpool Corporation Tramways; Tramways Manager, West Ham Corporation, 1903–13; 1913 to 1924 with the London Underground Railways and London General Omnibus Company group, as Purchasing Agent, 1913, Operating Manager, 1914, and Assistant Managing Director, 1921–24; Principal Agent, Conservative and Unionist Party, 1924–27; President of the Municipal Tramways Association (inc.), 1910–11; Founder and ex-Chairman National Association of Local Government Officers; Founder and Vice-President London Safety First Council; Founder and Past President, Royal Society for the Prevention of Accidents; Hon. Life Member, Institute of Transport; ex-member of the Technical Committee on London Traffic. *Publications:* Dicksee and Blain's Office Organisation; Pitman's Secretary's Handbook, etc. *Address:* Hammond's Place, Burgess Hill, Sussex. *T:* Burgess Hill 3238. *Club:* Constitutional.

Died 16 Dec. 1942.

BLAIR, Alexander, CBE 1927; FSI; *b* 1864; *e s* of late James Blair; *m* Maggie Gibb, *e d* of late William Clark; three *s* (*e s* killed in action, 1915). *Educ:* Highlanders' Academy, Greenock; Technical College, Glasgow. Served tutelage to Land Surveying and Estate Agency; entered the Valuation Department, 1909; Chief Valuer to the Board of Inland Revenue in Scotland, 1913–29.

Recreations: shooting, golf, curling, and motoring. *Address:* 44 Queen Square, Glasgow, S1. *T:* Pollok 0846. *Clubs:* Royal Scottish Automobile, Glasgow.

Died 2 Oct. 1944.

BLAIR, Brig.-Gen. Arthur, DSO 1900; late KOSB; *b* 2 Sept. 1869; *s* of late Capt. J. Blair, Central Indian Horse; *m* 1st, 1909, Mary Beryl (*d* 1912), *d* of late General Buchanan, CB; 2nd, 1914, Elizabeth Mary, *y d* of late Col Sir C. Hoskyns, Bt; two *s* one *d. Educ:* Cheltenham College; Sandhurst. Gazetted KOSB 1890; passed Staff College, 1897; General Staff Officer, Egypt; Lt-Col, April 1915; retired pay, 1920; served Soudan campaign with Egyptian army, 1898, including Atbara (medal, Egyptian medal with clasp); South African campaign on Staff (severely wounded, despatches five times, Queen's medal six clasps, King's medal two clasps, DSO); European War, 1914–18 (despatches twice, promoted Bt Col). *Address:* Drumdelnies, Nairn. *Clubs:* Naval and Military; New, Edinburgh.

Died 4 Feb. 1947.

BLAIR, Duncan MacCallum, DSc (Lond.), MB, ChB (Glas.), FRFPSG; Regius Professor of Anatomy, Glasgow University, since 1936; *b* 22 July 1896; *s* of late Dr Alexander Blair, Ashington, Northumberland and Crinan, Argyll; *m* 1928, Leonie Elspet, *er d* of James Stewart, Aberdeen; two *d. Educ:* Woodside School, Glasgow; University of Glasgow. Surgeon Sub-Lieut, RNVR 1915–17; MB, ChB (with Honours) 1919; Demonstrator of Anatomy 1919–22; Lecturer in Regional Anatomy, 1922–27, University of Glasgow; Symington Prize 1923; Professor of Anatomy, and sometime Dean of Medical Faculty, King's College, University of London, 1927–35; John Hunter Lecturer in Applied Anatomy, St George's Hospital Medical School, 1931–35; sometime Examiner in Anatomy, Royal College of Physicians, London, Universities of St Andrews, Sheffield, Aberdeen; Fellow, Royal Microscopical Society; Fellow, Royal Society of Edinburgh; Member Anatomical Society of Great Britain and Ireland and American Association of Anatomists. *Publications:* article: Arthrology, Cunningham's Text-Book of Anatomy, 6th, 7th, and 8th Editions; papers in Journal of Anatomy, British Journal of Surgery, British Medical Journal, etc. *Recreations:* sailing, living in Argyll. *Address:* 2, The University, Glasgow, W2. *T:* Western 3986.

Died 10 Nov. 1944.

BLAIR, Captain Sir Edward H.; *see* Hunter-Blair.

BLAIR, Eric; *see* Orwell, George.

BLAIR, Col Frederick Gordon, CB 1900; CMG 1918; TD, JP, DL Co. Ayr; JP Rutland; late Capt. 16th Lancers, and Col 4th Battalion Imperial Yeomanry; Hon. Colonel, Leicestershire Yeomanry, 1906–38; ADC to the King, 1914–20; Order of St Anne (2nd Class) of Russia, 1916; *b* 11 Nov. 1852; *s* of late Captain William Fordyce Blair, RN, of Blair; *m* 1880, Mary Elizabeth, *d* of William Baird of Elie, Fife; one *d.* Served South Africa, 1900–02; commanded Mounted Troops, 8th Division (wounded, despatches, CB, medal four clasps); served European War, Staff, 1914–18 (despatches); High Sheriff, Rutland, 1886; Chairman Rutland and Leicester Territorial Assoc.; Asst Military Sec., 1914–18. *Address:* Ashwell Hall, Oakham; Blair, Dalry, Ayrshire. *Club:* Turf.

Died 2 Oct. 1943.

BLAIR, Hon. Sir James William, KCMG 1935; Kt 1930; Lieutenant-Governor of Queensland since 1933; Chancellor of University of Queensland since 1927; President, Queensland National Art Gallery, Queensland Art Trustees, and Free Library; *b* Ipswich, 16 May 1871; *m* 1912, M. C. Gibson. *Educ:* primary schools; Ipswich Grammar School. Called to Queensland Bar, 1894; Member (Ipswich) of the Legislative Assembly of Queensland, 1902–15; Attorney-General and Sec. for

Mines, 1903–08; Sec. for Public Instruction, 1912–15; Judge Supreme Court, Queensland, 1922–25; Chief Justice, Supreme Court of Queensland, 1925–40; accomplished a pioneering motor trip of 3000 miles through the remote parts of Queensland, 1908; Pres. of the Queensland Scottish Union, 1909–14; Pres. Queensland Branch Royal Geographical Society, Australia, 1914; declined appointment of Supreme Court Judge, 1908; Member of University Senate, 1914–16. *Publications:* Blair on the Workers' Compensation Act; Queensland Police Guide (Ranking and Blair). *Recreations:* fishing, motoring, shooting, cricket, golf, and music; President Queensland Cricket Association. *Address:* Crescent Road, Hamilton, Brisbane, Queensland. *Clubs:* Tattersall's; Johnsonian, Queensland, Queensland Irish Association, Queensland Scottish Union, Garrick, Australian Natives' Association, Queensland Turf, Townsville Turf, and North Queensland.

Died 18 Nov. 1944.

BLAIR, Robert Kerr; WS; partner of Blair and Cadell, Writers to the Signet, Edinburgh; *b* 1 Nov. 1876; 2nd *s* of late Alexander Blair, Sheriff of the Lothians and Peebles; *m* May (*d* 1939), *d* of late James Craik, WS, Edinburgh; one *s* one *d*. *Educ:* Sedbergh. Director National Bank of Scotland Ltd, Lloyds Bank Ltd, Scottish Equitable Life Assurance Society; Trustee of the National Galleries of Scotland; served South African War, 1900–01. *Address:* 19 Ainslie Place, Edinburgh. *Clubs:* Conservative; New, Edinburgh; Western, Glasgow.

Died 14 Jan. 1942.

BLAKE, Sir (Francis) Edward (Colquhoun), 2nd Bt *cr* 1907; Captain late TA Reserve of Officers; *b* 11 Aug. 1893; *s* of Sir Francis Blake, 1st Bt, and Selina Colquhoun (*d* 1915), *d* of James Cleland Burns; S father, 1940; *m* 1924, Olive Mary (*d* 1946), *d* of Charles Liddell Simpson; one *s* one *d*; 2nd 1947, Doreen Maud, *d* of James Bertram Sample, Garden Ho., Bothal, Northumberland; one *d*. *Educ:* Bradfield; Trinity Hall, Cambridge. Served European War, 1914–18; War of 1939–45, in RA. *Recreation:* shooting. *Heir: s* Francis Michael, *b* 11 July 1943. *Address:* The Dower House, Tillmouth Park, Cornhill-on-Tweed. *TA:* and *T:* Coldstream 43. *Clubs:* Royal Automobile, Boodle's.

Died 24 Nov. 1950.

BLAKE, Lt-Col Sir (George) Reginald, Kt 1934; TD; DL Wilts.; JP; *b* 1882; *s* of late John Heritage Blake, JP, Beechfield, Melksham; *m* 1912, Norah Frances, *e d* of late Rev. Francis E. Thomas; three *d*. *Educ:* Clifton. Served European War, 1914–19. *Address:* Beechfield, Melksham, Wilts. *T:* Melksham 41.

Died 5 Feb. 1949.

BLAKE, Herbert Frederick, MA; *b* 1866. *Educ:* St Paul's School; Pembroke College, Cambridge. Master of the Supreme Court (Taxing Office), 1929–35; retired 1935. *Address:* 9 Avereng Road, Folkestone, Kent.

Died 8 July 1946.

BLAKE, Jack Percy; *e s* of John and Mary Blake; *m* 1909, Maud Ethel Priestley; one *s* one *d*. *Educ:* Whitfield School, EC. Chairman of London County Council, 1942–43; Member of London County Council for 23 years (sometime Chairman Entertainments and Fire Brigade Committees); Member Port of London Authority for 18 years; DL, JP County of London; Commissioner of Income Tax for City of London since 1926; Member Hambledon Committee on Advanced Art Education; Governor The Old Vic and Sadlers Wells, Dulwich College Foundation, Imperial Coll. of Science, Regent Street Polytechnic; Member Council Royal Albert Hall; Trustee National Theatre, City Parochial Foundation, Dickens House. In charge Priority Section High Explosives Dept, Ministry of Munitions, 1915–18. *Publications:* novels: A Lady's Honour, The

Money God; various short stories; also; Chippendale and his School; Little Books about Old Furniture (part author); Old Furniture for the Small Collector (part author). *Recreations:* formerly water polo (played for London), boxing, and fencing (Amateur Epée Champion, 1911, Runner-up, 1920); represented Great Britain in three Olympiads; London, 1908, Stockholm, 1912, Antwerp, 1920; Member First British International Fencing Team to visit USA, 1922; Vice-Pres. Epée Club. *Address:* 12 Lansdowne Road, W11. *Clubs:* Athenæum, Reform, Savage.

Died 19 Dec. 1950.

BLAKE, Lt-Col Sir Reginald; *see* Blake, Lt-Col Sir G. R.

BLAKEMAN, John, MA (Camb.); MSc (Manchester); Principal of Northampton College of Technology, 1911–41; *b* Oldham, 28 Jan. 1881; *s* of John Thomas Blakeman, Oldham; *m* 1908, Hannah, *d* of William Lees, Oldham; two *s*. *Educ:* Owens College, Manchester (Dalton Scholar); Trinity College, Cambridge (Major Scholar); Derby Scholar, Manchester University, 1901 and 1902. Assistant to Professor Karl Pearson at University College, London, 1904–06; Head of Mathematics Department, Leicester College of Technology, 1906–11; first Director of the British Boot, Shoe and Allied Trades Research Association, 1919–22. *Publications:* Study of English Brain Weights (Biometrika); Tests for Linearity of Regression in Frequency Distributions (Biometrika); (with Karl Pearson) On the Probable Error of the Co-efficient of Mean Square Contingency (Biometrika) and a Mathematical Theory of Random Migration (Biometric Series); Caster Shapes (Boot and Shoe Research Assoc.); Text Book in Applied Science for Boot and Shoe Manufacture; (with Miss G. P. Rumming) Text Book on Commerce and Business Economics. *Recreations:* motoring and tennis. *Address:* 72 Birchfield Road, Northampton. *TA:* College of Technology, Northampton. *T:* Northampton 1005, Extension 5.

Died 14 June 1942.

BLAKENEY, Col Herbert Norwood, CMG 1918; DSO 1900; *b* 26 April 1871; *s* of late Col Henry Blakeney. Entered Army, 1890; Capt. 1900; Major, 1905; Lt-Col 1916; served South Africa, 1900–02 (despatches, DSO, Queen's medal 5 clasps, King's medal 2 clasps); European War, 1914–16 (despatches, wounded, CMG); retired pay, 1920.

Died 20 Dec. 1946.

BLAKENEY, Rev. Richard, MA; Canon Residentiary of Peterborough Cathedral, 1923–44, non-residentiary Canon since 1944; *b* 14 Oct. 1857; *e s* of Rev. R. P. Blakeney, DD, LLD, Canon of York, Rector of Bridlington and Rural Dean; *m* 1884, Alice, *e d* of Henry Unwin, JP, Broom Cross, Sheffield. *Educ:* Merton College, Oxford. BA 1880; MA 1884. Deacon, 1881; Priest, 1882; Curate of Parish Church, Sheffield, 1881; Priory Church, Bridlington, 1882; Vicar of Bishopthorpe, York, 1884; Acaster Malbis cum Bishopthorpe, 1889–91; Vicar of Melton Mowbray, 1891–1924; Proctor for Diocese of Peterborough, 1921; Canon of St Martin's Collegiate Church, Leicester, 1922–24; Hon. Canon of Peterborough Cathedral, 1904–24; Rural Dean of Framland II, 1901; Chap. 5th Bt Leicestershire Regt 1891; offered more than once Colonial Bishoprics and other appointments. *Publications:* various sermons on special subjects. *Recreations:* tennis, golf, bicycling. *Address:* The Precincts, Peterborough. *T:* Peterborough 2592. *Club:* Junior Carlton.

Died 28 Feb. 1946.

BLAKENEY, Rev. Robert Bibby, MA; Rector of Southport, Lancashire, since 1905; Rural Dean of North Meols 1917–29; Hon. Canon of Liverpool Cathedral since 1917; Surrogate for Diocese of Liverpool since 1906; *b* 1 Feb. 1865; *s* of Richard Paul Blakeney, DD; *m*

Constance Eleanor (*d* 1937), *d* of Col Henry Zouch Darrah, ISC; no *c*. *Educ:* St Peter's College, Cambridge; St Stephen's House, Oxford. Deacon, 1891; Priest, 1892; Curate Parish Church, Malew, IOM, 1891–93; Incumbent of St Iudes Andreas, IOM, 1893–94; Rector of Wombwell, Yorks, 1894–1905; Vice-Chairman, Wombwell School Board, 1896–1905; Organising Secretary SPG Archdeaconry of Sheffield, 1901–05; Secretary for Deanery of North Meols, 1908–17; Chaplain to Forces in Southport, 1915–18; Chaplain Southport Batt. National Reserve, 1914–18; Lieutenant Cambridge University Rifles, 1885–86; Lieutenant 4th Batt. West Yorkshire Regt, 1886–88; Chairman man Meols Hall Auxiliary Military Hospital, 1915–19. *Recreations:* golf, tennis, motoring. *Address:* The Rectory, Southport. *T:* 8325.

Died 31 May 1948.

BLAKENEY, Col William Edward Albemarle, CBE 1919; retired; *er s* of late Edward Blakeney and Mary Parker; *m* 1894, Mary Emily, 2nd *d* of late Colonel Long, CMG, JP, of Newton House, Clevedon; one *d*. *Educ:* Jersey; Sandhurst. 1st King's Shrop. LI 1882; Egyptian Campaign (medal and star); KOSB India, 1883–86; Cureton's Multanis, 1886–87; 3rd Skinner's Horse, 1887–1913; Commandant, 1908–13; served Tirah Campaign, 1897–98 (medal 3 clasps); with IVth Corps Belgium and France as Camp Commandant, 1914–15 (two medals and 1914 Star); In command of 1st Garrison Bn Bedfordshire and Hertfordshire Regiment, 1916–20. *Recreation:* bridge. *Address:* Abbert, Camberley, Surrey. *T:* Camberley 599.

Died 7 March 1942.

BLAKISTON, Sir Charles Edward, 6th Bt *cr* 1763; *b* 28 Dec. 1862; 2nd *s* of late Rev. Horace Mann Blakiston, BD; *S* brother, 1936; *m* 1887, Harriett Eleanor, *d* of Robert Wills, Highbury; no *c*. *Educ:* Tonbridge School; Bishops Stortford High School. Medical profession, but health prevented, did not qualify. *Recreation:* walking. *Heir: nephew* Arthur Frederick (*o s* of late Frederick Turnley Blakiston), *b* 1892. *Address:* Crindledyke, 12 Coombe Road, Croydon, Surrey.

Died 12 Aug. 1941.

BLAKISTON, Cuthbert Harold; JP Sussex; *b* 12 May 1879; *s* of Rev. C. D. Blakiston, late of Exwick and Sidbury, Devon; unmarried. *Educ:* Malvern College; Exeter School; Christ Church, Oxford (Scholar). Craven Fellow in Univ. of Oxford, 1901–03. Assistant Master at Sherborne School, 1903; at Eton College, 1904–25; Housemaster, 1920–25; Headmaster of SS Mary and Nicolas College (Lancing College) 1925–34. *Publication:* Elementary Civics. *Recreations:* travel, gardening. *Address:* Charlton House, Steyning, Sussex. *T:* Steyning 2285. *Club:* Athenæum.

Died 24 Jan. 1949.

BLAKISTON, Rev. Cyril Ralph Noel, MA; *b* 23 Dec. 1880; *s* of Very Rev. R. M. Blakiston, Dean of Bocking. *Educ:* Felsted; Pembroke College, Cambridge (Scholar). Assistant Master, Wellington College, 1907–09; Cambridge Mission to Delhi, 1911–13; Headmaster, St Michael's College, Tenbury, 1923–25; Warden, St Deinol's Library, Hawarden, 1925–30; Headmaster, St George's School, Jerusalem, 1930–33; Chaplain, Málaga, Spain, 1933–34; Vicar of Westbury, Bucks, 1937–39. *Address:* The Flat, Ludgrove, Wokingham, Berks.

Died 2 Jan. 1941.

BLAKISTON, Rev. Herbert Edward Douglas, MA, DD; President of Trinity College, Oxford, 1907–38; formerly (from 1887) Fellow and (from 1898 to 1907) Senior Tutor and Junior Bursar and from 1915–38 acting Estates Bursar; *b* St Leonards, 5 Sept. 1862; *e* and *o surv. s* of late Rev. Douglas Yeoman Blakiston, MA, Vicar of East Grinstead, and Sophia, *d* of Rev. William Dent, MA, Crosby Cote, Yorkshire, NR. *Educ:* Tonbridge School; Trinity College, Oxford (Scholar, 1881–85). 1st

class in Class. Hon. Mods, 1882; 1st class in Lit. Hum., 1885; Classical Honour Moderator, 1895–97 and 1905–06. Junior Proctor, 1899–1900; University Auditor, 1903–17; Vice-Chancellor, 1917–20; one of the Clerks of the Market since 1932. *Publications:* Select Speeches of Cicero translated (1894); Some Durham College Rolls (Oxf. Hist. Soc., 1896); History of Trinity College (1898); various articles in the Dictionary of National Biography, etc. *Address:* Orchard Lea, Boars Hill, Oxford.

Died 29 July 1942.

BLANCHE, Jaques Emile; painter and Man of Letters; art critic; novelist; Member of Institute of France; Member of the International Society of Sculptors, Printers, and Gravers; *b* Paris, 1 Feb. 1862; *s* of Dr Emily Antoine Blanche; *m* John Lemoinne. *Educ:* Paris and England. Exhibited, Arthur Tooth & Son, Bond Street, 1937, One Man Show; Works in Tate Gallery, National Portrait Gallery, Manchester City Art Gallery, Sheffield, Leeds, Dublin National Gallery and in private collections. *Publication:* (in English), Portraits of a Lifetime, vol. i, 1937, vol. ii, 1938. *Address:* 19 rue de Docteur Blanche, Paris, 16; Offzamville, Seine Inférieure, Normandy.

Died 30 Sept. 1942.

BLANCO, Alfredo Ernesto; Director The Anti-Opium Information Bureau, Geneva; Hon. Adviser Chinese Permanent Delegation to the League of Nations; *b* 31 June 1877; *s* of Pedro Blanco and Martha Kendal; *m* 1917, Roma Gallon. *Educ:* Lycée de Pau; Southport Grammar School; The World. Chinese Maritime Customs, 1897–1922; founded the Anti-Opium Information Bureau, Geneva, 1928; Freelanced for limitation of manufacture of narcotics; devised the Scheme of Stipulated Supply which eventually led to drafting and adoption of the Convention for Limiting the Manufacture and Regulating the Distribution of Narcotic Drugs signed at Geneva July 13, 1931. *Publications:* Piece Goods Manual, 1917; Communiques on the Opium and Narcotic Drugs problems; Press Notes, Special Documents; and Reference Documents series on the same subject since 1928. *Recreations:* Fighting the non-medical use of opium and narcotics, spreading information concerning narcotic problems. *Address:* The Anti-Opium Information Bureau, 33 Avenue de Champel, Geneva, Switzerland. *TA:* Antiopium.

Died 18 Sept. 1945.

BLAND, Brig.-Gen. Edward Humphry, CB 1916; CMG 1919; late RE; *b* 3 May 1866; *s* of Major-Gen. E. L. Bland, RE, of White Abbey, Co. Antrim; *m* 1894, Bertha Mary, *d* of J. Fletcher Moore, DL, Manor, Kilbridge; two *d*. Served Miranzai 2nd Expedition, 1891 (medal, and clasp); Isazai Expedition, 1892; European War (CB, CMG); retired pay, 1923; White Eagle of Serbia, 3rd class, 1916. *Address:* c/o Lloyd's Bank 6 Pall Mall, SW1.

Died 15 Feb. 1945.

BLAND, Edward Maltby, CMG 1927; MInstT; *b* Ingersoll, Ont, 17 June 1878; *s* of Rev. Edward M. Bland; *m* 1913, Frances Mary Middleton, 2nd *d* of John Harding, Stone, Staffs; one *d*. *Educ:* Trinity College School, Port Hope, Ont; Royal Military College, Kingston, Canada. Employed with Canadian Pacific and Canadian Northern Railways, 1897–1900; served in Boer War with Strathcona's Horse (medal and three clasps); Assistant Engineer Imperial Military Railways, South Africa, 1901–02; Central South African Railways, 1902–08; Executive Engineer Baro Kano Railway, Northern Nigeria, 1908; acted as Director of Railways, Northern Nigeria, during 1912; Assistant Chief Engineer, Nigerian Railways, 1913; special mission to British Guiana to report railway development, 1913; Engineer-in-Chief onm construction of Nigerian Eastern Railway, 1914; General Manager Gold Coast

Railways, 1917; General Manager of the Nigerian Railway, 1918–33; Reported on Barbados, British Honduras and Jamaica Railways, 1937. *Recreations:* golf and tennis. *Address:* Matfield Gate, Matfield, Kent. *T:* Brenchley 111.

Died 3 Dec. 1946.

BLAND, Francis Lawrence, FRMetS; FZS; JP Isle of Ely, 1900–38, Suffolk from 1926; Chairman of the County Councils Association, 1941; Chairman of East Suffolk County Council since 1940; County Alderman East Suffolk; Chairman Mental Hospital Committee East and West Suffolk; Chairman Joint Valuation Committee E and W Suffolk; Treasurer East Suffolk and Ipswich Hospital; Director of Barclays Bank Limited and of British Linen Bank; Chairman of the Ipswich Board Alliance Assurance Co. Ltd; President of Institute of Bankers 1933–35; *b* 7 Sept. 1873; *s* of Francis Maltby Bland and Edith Richenda Barclay; *m* 1899, Mabel Barbara Gooch; two *s* two *d*. *Educ:* Eton College (Captain of the School and Captain of the Shooting Eight). Entered Gurney and Co's Bank, 1894, at Wisbech; Local Director of Barclay and Company Limited Ipswich, 1901; Treasurer of County Borough of Ipswich, 1905–30; President of East Suffolk and Ipswich Hospital, 1928–30; President of Suffolk Agricultural Association, 1932; President of Suffolk County Rifle Association, 1933–34 and 1938; Chairman of Ministry of Labour Employment Committee for Ipswich and District, 1926–30; Sheriff of Suffolk, 1940; Member of East Suffolk County Council, 1919; Alderman, 1926; Representative of East Suffolk County Council on County Councils Association since 1927; Vice-Chairman of the Highways Committee of the Association Committee for England and Wales since 1934, and of London School of Hygiene and Tropical Medicine; a Governor of City of London College since 1934. *Publications:* sundry pamphlets on Banking, Agriculture and Sociology. *Address:* Rookwood, Copdock, Ipswich. *TA:* Bland Copdock. *T:* Copdock 66, Ipswich 2121. *Clubs:* Royal Automobile; County Ipswich; Royal Harwich Yacht.

Died 26 Aug. 1941.

BLAND, John Otway Percy; author and journalist; *b* 15 Nov. 1863; 2nd *s* of Major-General E. L. Bland, RE, of Whiteabbey, Co. Antrim; *m* 1889, Louise, *d* of late Captain H. C. Dearborn, USA. *Educ:* Switzerland; Victoria College, Jersey; Trinity College, Dublin. Joined the Chinese Imperial Maritime Customs, 1883; was for two years Private Secretary to Sir Robert Hart; resigned in 1896 to become Secretary to the Municipality for the Foreign Settlements at Shanghai; Representative in China of the British and Chinese Corporation, Ltd, 1906; negotiated four railway loans with the Chinese Govt; resigned and left China in 1910; holds Orders of the Double Dragon, Pao Hsing (China) and Rising Sun (Japan); Times Correspondent at Shanghai, 1897–1907; Peking, 1907–10; after returning to England, engaged chiefly in journalism; invited to lecture on the Far East at the Lowell Institute of Boston, USA, 1912, and again in 1934; revisited China, 1920. *Publications:* Lays of Far Cathay, 1890; Verse and Worse, 1902; Houseboat Days in China, 1909; Recent Events and Present Policies in China, 1912; (with Edmund Backhouse) China under the Empress Dowager, 1910, and Annals and Memoirs of the Court of Peking, 1913; Germany's Violations of the Laws of War, 1915; Li Hung-Chang, 1917; Men, Manners, and Morals in South America, 1920; China, Japan, and Korea, 1921; Something Lighter, 1924; China: the Pity of It, 1932. *Recreations:* fishing, shooting, and farming. *Address:* Brudenell House, Aldeburgh, Suffolk. *T:* Aldeburgh 113. *Clubs:* Thatched House: Country, Shanghai.

Died 23 June 1945.

BLAND, Robert Norman, CMG 1910; *b* 8 Oct. 1859; *s* of Maj.-Gen. E. L. Bland, RE, of White Abbey, Co. Antrim; *m* 1895, Laura, *d* of late Thomas Shelford, CMG; one *d*. *Educ:* Cheltenham; Trinity College, Dublin. Entered Civil Service, Straits Settlements, 1882; retired, 1910. Captain Singapore Volunteer Infantry. Served in the Ministry of Pensions (Soldiers' Award Branch), 1917–20; worked for Fulham Cttee, Charity Organisation Soc., 1920–30. *Publications:* The Historical Tombstones of Malacca; various notes and articles in the Journal of the Straits branch of the Royal Asiatic Society. *Address:* Brown Gable, Crawley Down, Crawley, Sussex.

Died 30 March 1948.

BLAND, Col (Brig.-Gen.) William St Colum, CB 1917; CMG 1919; RA; *b* 6 June 1868; *s* of Major-General E. L. Bland of Woodbank, Whiteabbey, Co. Antrim; *m* 1903, Ellen Kathleen, *d* of Edward Ogilvie of Yulgilbar, NSW; two *d*. Entered RA 1887; Capt. 1897; Major, 1906; Bt Lt-Col 1913; Lt-Col 1914; Bt Col 1916; Col 1919; retired with hon. rank Brig.-Gen. 1920; Instructor School of Gunnery, 1906–09; Superintendent of Experiments, 1909–13; Member Ordnance Board, 1914; Temp. Brig.-Gen. 1915–19; President, Ordnance Committee, 1916–19; Controller of Munitions Design, 1919; Commandant Ordnance College, 1919–20; served Burma, 1891–92; Waziristan Expedition, 1894–95 (medal with clasp); China, 1900 (medal with clasp, despatches, American Order of the Dragon); European War, 1914–18 (despatches, CB, CMG, 1914 Star with clasp, British War medal and Victory medal). *Address:* Warden Hill, Weeke, Winchester. *T:* Winchester 2095.

Died 9 Feb. 1950.

BLANDFORD, Laurence James, CBE 1919; TD, MD; BS, DPh; Colonel Army Medical Service, TAR; Principal Medical Officer, Ministry of Pensions for Midlands Région, retired; *b* 1876; *s* of J. W. Blandford, Colonel KHP; *m* Clara, *d* of H. Hobson; one *s*. *Educ:* Repton, Durham. Late Hon. Surgeon, Stockton and Thornaby Hospital; late Assistant, MOH, Stockton-on-Tees; served with 50th Division in BEF. *Address:* 60 Battenhall Road, Worcester. *T:* Worcester 3911. *Club:* Junior Army and Navy.

Died 29 Feb. 1944.

BLANDY, Beatrice Charlotte, CBE 1918; *y d* of late Henry Henty, Victoria, Australia; *m* 1927, Graham Frederic Blandy. *Educ:* St John's, Preston, England; Ruyton, Kew, Victoria, Australia. Hon. Superintendent of Voluntary Workers Australian Comforts Fund, Victorian Division, 1915–20 (CBE), also 1939–46. *Address:* Toorak, SE2, Victoria, Australia. *Club:* Alexandra (Melbourne).

Died 5 March 1950.

BLANDY, Sir Edmond Nicolas, KCIE 1942; CSI 1939; CIE 1933; Indian Civil Service; Chairman Bengal Public Service Commission; *s* of Adam Fettiplace Blandy, Abingdon, Berks; *m* 1st, 1917, Helen Elisabeth, 2nd, 1922, Dorothy Kathleen, both *d* of W. Newbold Marshall, Aberdeen; one *s* one *d*. *Educ:* Clifton; Balliol College, Oxford. 2nd class Class. Mods, 2nd Class Lit. Hum.; Boden Scholar of Sanskrit; ICS, 1900. Assistant Magistrate, East Bengal and Assam, 1910; Under-Secretary to Government of Bengal Finance Dept, 1914; in addition Custodian of Enemy Property and Liquidator Hostile Firms, 1916; Secretary Provincial Recruiting Board, 1917; Under-Secretary Government of India Finance Dept, 1919; Collector of Income Tax Calcutta, 1921; Commissioner of Income Tax, Bengal, 1922; Collector and Magistrate, Bakarganj, 1924; 24 Parganas, 1928; Deputy-Commissioner, Darjeeling, 1928; Secretary to Government of Bengal Finance Dept, April 1930–33; Commissioner Chittagong, 1933–34; Chief Secretary to the Govt of Bengal, 1934–35; Commissioner Chittagong, 1935–36; Finance Secretary to Government of Bengal, Feb.–Aug., Chief Secretary, Aug.–Dec., 1936 and Feb.–Oct. 1939; Member Board of Revenue, 1939–40; Chief Secretary, Bengal, 1941. *Clubs:* East India and Sports; Bengal, Calcutta; United Service, Simla.

Died 8 Sept. 1942.

BLANESBURGH, Baron (Life Peer) of Alloa; **Robert Younger,** PC 1919; GBE 1917; *b* 12 Sept. 1861; *γ s* of late James Younger, Alloa, Co. Clackmannan; unmarried. *Educ:* Edinburgh Academy; Balliol College, Oxford (Visitor, 1934; Hon. Fellow, 1916; BA 1883; MA 1909). Called to Bar, 1884; QC 1900; Bencher, Lincoln's Inn, 1907; Treasurer, 1932; Hon. DCL Oxford, 1928; Hon. LLD Edinburgh, 1919; St Andrews, 1929; Fellow and Chairman of the Delegacy of King's College; a Vice-President and Fellow of the Royal College of Music; Hon. RWS; Prime Warden Goldsmiths' Company, 1931–32; Judge High Court of Justice, 1915–19; a Lord Justice of Appeal, 1919–23; a Lord of Appeal in Ordinary, 1923–37; Principal British Delegate on the Reparation Commission, Paris, 1925–31. *Address:* 73 South Audley Street, W; The Grey Friars, Winchelsea, Sussex. *T:* Winchelsea 94. *Clubs:* Athenæum; New, Edinburgh.

Died 17 Aug. 1946.

BLATCHFORD, Robert; journalist; late editor of The Clarion; *b* Maidstone, 17 March 1851; parents, actors; *m* 1880, Sarah Crossley of Halifax; one *s* two *d*. *Educ:* nowhere. Served time brushmaking, but did not follow it; joined 103rd Regt, Dublin Fusiliers; left 1878 (as sergeant); became clerk, Northwich; joined Bell's Life Staff, London, 1884; Sunday Chronicle, 1885; left Chronicle and started Clarion, 1891. *Publications:* Merrie England; Tommy Atkins; Julie; Dismal England; A Son of the Forge; My Favourite Books; A Bohemian Girl; Tales for the Marines; Britain for the British, 1902; A Book about Books, 1902; God and My Neighbour, 1903; Not Guilty, a Plea for the Bottom Dog, 1905; Sorcery Shop, an Impossible Romance, 1907; As I lay A-thinking, 1926; My Eighty Years, 1931.

Died 17 Dec. 1943.

BLATHERWICK, Col Sir Thomas, KCB 1949 (CB 1935); DSO 1919; MC, TD, JP, DL County Palatine of Lancaster, 1935; ADC 1941; *b* 31 Aug. 1887; *s* of late Thomas Blatherwick, of Bramley, Knutsford, Cheshire; unmarried. *Educ:* Rugby School. Gazetted to 6th Bn The Manchester Regiment TA 1909; Captain, 1915; Major, 1917; A/Lieut-Colonel, 1918; to command 5th Bn The Manchester Regt 1918; appointed to command 6th Bn the Manchester Regt, 1918; served European War 4 Aug. 1914 to 8 April 1919, Egypt, Gallipoli, Sinai, and France; Lieut-Colonel commanding 6th Bn The Manchester Regt, 1920–28; Bt Colonel, 1924; Substantive Colonel TA, 1928; Commander 127th Manchester Infantry Brigade, 1930–34; Deputy Regional Commissioner and Military Liaison Officer for NW Civil Defence Region, 1939–42; Chairman East Lancs Territorial Army and Air Force Association, 1945; Chairman East Lancs Army Cadet Force Committee, 1943; Chairman Bucklow Petty Sessional Bench, 1941; Chairman Humphrey Chethams Hospital School, Manchester, 1944; Chairman Hospital Management Cttee North and Mid-Cheshire, 1948. Jubilee Medal, 1935; Coronation Medal, 1937. *Address:* Bramley, Knutsford, Cheshire. *T:* Knutsford 4. *Clubs:* Naval and Military; Union (Manchester).

Died 12 June 1950.

BLEACKLEY, Engr Rear-Adm. Hubert, CBE 1942; MVO 1922; *b* 18 June 1886; *o s* of late J. Bleackley, Grassendale Park, Aigburth, Liverpool; one *s* two *d*. *Educ:* Grammar School, Douglas, IOM Engr. Lt-Cdr of HMS Renown during tour of Prince of Wales to India and Japan, 1921–22. Retired Dec. 1945. *Address:* Westwynds, Bridgewood, Maidstone Road, Rochester. *T:* Blue Bell Hill 317.

Died 19 June 1950.

BLENKINSOP, Maj.-Gen. Sir Layton John, KCB 1921; CB 1919; DSO 1898; JP Cambs; FRGS; *b* 27 June 1862; 3rd *s* of Lt-Col William Blenkinsop and Elizabeth, *d* of William Sandford; *m* 1905, Ethel Alice, *d* of John Wells, JP, Booth Ferry House, Goole. *Educ:* King's School, Canterbury; Royal Veterinary College, London. Coleman Medallist, 1883. Entered AV Department, 1883; Advising Veterinary Surgeon to Punjab Government, and Professor Lahore Veterinary College, 1891–93; SVO for British Troops, Soudan Expedition, 1898 (despatches, Egyptian medal with clasp, English medal, DSO); senior Veterinary officer in Egypt, 1896–99; served South Africa, 1899–1902 as SVO Cavalry Division under Lieut-Gen. Sir J. D. P. French until Sept. 1901, and SVO Remounts in South Africa to Dec. 1902 (despatches, SA medal with six clasps, King's medal with two clasps, promoted Maj.); principal veterinary officer, Irish Command, 1904–06; South Africa, 1906–09; Northern Command, 1910; Southern Command, 1910–12; Aldershot Command, 1913; Director Vet. Services, India, 1916–17; Director-General Army Veterinary Service, War Office, 1917–21; Colonel Commandant Royal Army Veterinary Corps, 1921–32; retired pay, 1921. *Publications:* Co-Editor of the Official History of the War: Veterinary Services; various professional papers and addresses. *Address:* Melstead, Melbourn, near Royston, Herts. *T:* Melbourn 207. *Clubs:* Junior United Service; Cambridge County.

Died 28 April 1942.

BLISS, Col Thomas Gordon, CBE 1919; *b* 30 Aug. 1869; *s* of late T. Bliss, Bengal; *m* 1891; one *s*. *Educ:* St Charles College; privately. Joined 3rd Lancashire Fusiliers, 1889; first commission in Lancashire Fusiliers, 1893; transferred to the Army Pay Dept as Captain, 1899; continued service in the same until retired with hon. rank of Colonel, 1922; re-employed as cashier of the Southern Command, 1927–34. *Recreations:* chess, golf and gardening. *Address:* Westgarth, Parkstone, Dorset.

Died 24 Oct. 1949.

BLOCH, Olaf F., Hon. LLD, FIC, Hon. FRPS; FIBP; research chemist; *b* London, of Danish parents; *m* 1899, Emmeline Powell; no *c*. *Educ:* City of London School; Finsbury Technical College. Research in conjunction with Sir Wyndham Dunstan, FRS; subsequently with Dr W. J. Russell, FRS; Consulting Chemist, Ilford, Ltd; also to J. V. Rushton (London) Ltd. *Publications:* numerous relating to the chemistry and physics of photography. *Address:* 9 Broughton Gardens, Shepherds Hill, N6. *T:* Mountview 8765; Cudworth Copse, Newdigate, Surrey. *Club:* Alpine.

Died 19 Oct. 1944.

BLOCK, Sir Adam Samuel James, KCMG 1907; CMG 1895; *b* Lucknow, 25 June 1856; *e s* of Adam H. G. Block, Indian Civil Service; *m* 1885, Louisa Constance (*d* 1922), *d* of Robert Cumberbatch; one *s* one *d*. *Educ:* Clifton College. Passed a competitive exam. and appointed a student interpreter at HM Embassy, Constantinople, 1877; Interpreter at HM Embassy, 1880; Vice-Consul, Beyrout, 1882; Damascus, 1883; Constantinople, 1885; Consul, 1890; 1st Dragoman, 1894; Secretary of Legation, 1902; appointed by the Council of Foreign Bondholders to represent British Bondholders on the Council of Administration of the Ottoman Public Debt, Constantinople, 1903; also represented the Dutch Bondholders, and was alternative President of the Council; resigned 1929; President of British Chamber of Commerce, Constantinople, 1907–18; on the outbreak of the War was for some time Chairman of the Admiralty Sub-Committee at the War Trade Department, and Head of the Finance Section of the Foreign Trade Department; later appointed Controller of the Finance Section of the Ministry of Blockade (despatches for services rendered to Army of Black Sea); Vice-Chairman of Constantinople Telephone Co.; granted Grand Cordon of the Order of

Osmania in brilliants by the Sultan of Turkey for services rendered, and Gold Medal of the Imtiaz; received the Grand Cordon of the Order of St Anne for services rendered to Russia in connection with the War. *Address:* Corner Cottage, Shiplake on Thames.

Died 16 April 1941.

BLOFELD, Rev. Stuart, BA, BSc, FCS; Vicar of Edgbaston, Birmingham, 1923–49; Examining Chaplain to Bishop of Birmingham since 1914; Hon. Canon, Birmingham, 1915; Rural Dean of Edgbaston since 1940; Chaplain 5th Royal Warwickshire Regiment since 1910; *b* Cullompton, Devonshire, 28 April 1872; 3rd *s* of Robert George Blofeld, of HM Civil Service; *m* Berta, *d* of late James Hardie, MA, of Linton House School, W; two *s* two *d*. *Educ:* privately, Reading and London; King Edward VI School, Nuneaton; University of London (BA 1891; BSc 1898); Post-graduate Research Royal College of Science, 1899. Deacon, 1901; Priest, 1902; Assistant Master Swindon High School, Teignmouth Grammar School, Linton House School, W, 1891–1900; Tutor and Assistant Chaplain St Mark's College, Chelsea, 1900; Vice-Principal St John's College, Battersea, 1903; Principal Saltley College, Birmingham, 1909–23; Rural Dean of East Birmingham, 1918–23; Lieut 1st Vol. Batt. Devonshire Regiment, 1894–96; President Training College Association of England and Wales, 1920 and 1922 (part); Governor, King Edward's High School, Birmingham; Life Governor, University of Birmingham; Vice-President SPG. *Publications:* Small Text Books; various Educational, Theological, and Literary Papers. *Recreations:* golf, tennis, fishing, etc. *Address:* Edgbaston Vicarage, Birmingham. *T:* Edgbaston 0070, Birmingham.

Died 19 Aug. 1950.

BLOIS, Sir Ralph Barrett Macnaghten, 9th Bt *cr* 1686; Capt. late Scots Guards; *b* 21 Nov. 1866; *S* father, 1888; *m* 1898, Freda, *y d* of late Col E. Hegan Kennard; one *s* three *d*. *Educ:* Wellington Coll. Owns about 7000 acres. *Heir:* *s* Gervase Ralph Edmund, Capt. Scots Guards [*b* 6 June 1901; *m* 1938, Audrey Winifred, *o d* of Col Harry Johnson, DSO; two *s* one *d*]. *Address:* Cockfield Hall, Yoxford, Suffolk. *Club:* Guards' Conservative.

Died 18 March 1950.

BLOMFIELD, Joseph, OBE 1919; MD, BC, BA Cantab; Consulting Anæsthetist St George's Hospital; late Chairman Anæsthetics Committee (Medical Research Council and Royal Society of Medicine); Editor, British Journal of Anæsthesia; late President Association of Anæsthetists; late Anæsthetist, King Edward VII Hospital for Officers, etc.; Fellow Royal Society of Medicine; *b* London, 1 March 1870; *s* of Louis and Salie Blumfeld; *m* 1st, 1912, Sheila Lehmann; one *s*; 2nd, 1933, Dorothy Kathleen Bell (Secretary to Society of Genealogists). *Educ:* University College School, London; Gonville and Caius College, Cambridge; St George's Hospital. Nat. Science Tripos, Cambridge, Class II, 1891. Was Anæsthetist to various London hospitals, including St Mary's and the National Dental, 1897–1912; Member Anæsthetics Committee British Association 1910; late President Anæsthetics Section, Royal Society of Medicine. Served War of 1939–45, EMS. *Publications:* book on anæsthetics (4th edition, 1917); Anæsthetics in Practice and Theory, 1922; St George's Hospital, 1733–1933; various contributions on anæsthetics to medical journals and to surgical Systems. *Address:* 57 Church Street, Old Isleworth, Middlesex. *T:* Hounslow 0391. *Club:* United University.

Died 9 Nov. 1948.

BLOMFIELD, Sir Reginald, Kt 1919; RA 1914; ARA 1905; MA, FSA; Hon. Fellow of Exeter College, Oxford; LittD Liverpool; Past President, Gold Medallist, Royal Institute of British Architects; late Member, Royal Commission of Fine Art; Member of Board of Ancient Monuments and of Advisory Council Victoria and

Albert Museum; a Principal Architect of Imperial War Graves Commission; Hon. Member, American Academy of Arts and Letters; Officer de l'instruction publique and Hon. Corresponding Member of Societé des Architectes Diplomés de France and of Society of Architects of Argentine; Hon. Member of Royal Academy of Belgium; Hon. Member of National Academy of Design of America; a Vice-President, Royal Historical Society; Chevalier of the Legion of Honour; Officer of the Orders of the Crown and Leopold I, Leopold II of Belgium; Architect; *b* 20 Dec. 1856; 3rd *s* of Rev. George John Blomfield, MA, late Rector of Aldington, Kent, and Isabella, *d* of C. J. Blomfield, late Bishop of London; *m* 1886, Frances, *d* of late Henry Burra of Playden, Sussex; two *s*. *Educ:* Haileybury (Exhibitioner); Exeter College, Oxford (Scholar, 1875); 2nd in Classical Mods, 1st Classical Greats, 1879. President RIBA, 1912–14. Principal works—Domestic and civil architecture and garden designs including; Brocklesby Park; Moundsmere, Hants; Wyphurst, Surrey; Wretham, Norfolk; completion of Quadrant, County Fire Office; Swan & Edgar; Pinchin Johnson, Carlton Gardens; Barclay's Bank, Leeds; United University Club; Carlton Club; Headrow, Leeds; Lambeth Bridge; Gardens, Godinton and Mellerstáin; The Menin Gate, Ypres, and War Cemeteries in France and Belgium. *Publications:* The Formal Garden in England, 1892, 3rd ed., 1901; A History of Renaissance Architecture in England, 1897; A Short History of Renaissance Architecture in England, 1900; Studies in Architecture, 1906; The Mistress Art, 1908; a History of French Architecture, 1494–1661, 1911; Architectural Drawing and Draughtsmen, 1912; History of French Architecture, 1661–1774, 1920; The Touchstone of Architecture, 1925; Byways, Leaves from an architect's note-book, 1929; Memoirs of an Architect, 1932; Modernismus, 1934; Six Architects, 1935; Sebastien le Prestre de Vauban, 1938; Life of R. Norman Shaw, 1940. *Address:* 1 New Court, Temple, EC4; 51 Frognal, Hampstead, NW3; Point Hill, Playden, Sussex. *T:* Central 5888. *Club:* Athenæum.

Died 27 Dec. 1942.

BLONDIN, Lt-Col Hon. Pierre Edouard; PC (Can.); NP (Champlain); *b* Saint Francois du Lac, County of Yamaska, 14 Dec. 1874; *s* of Louis M. Blondin, French Canadian, and Elodie Barnard, English Canadian; *m* 1901, Marie Rose Buisson; one *d*. *Educ:* Seminaire de Nicolet; St Michel's College, Toronto; Laval University, Montreal. Clerk of Circuit Court, county of Champlain; Alderman for the town of Grand 'Mère; elected to House of Commons for Champlain, 1908 and 1911; Deputy Speaker at first session of the 12th Parliament, 1911; Sworn of the Privy Council and appointed Minister of Inland Revenue, 1914; re-elected by acclamation after assuming office; Secretary of State, 1915; enlisted in 1917 and was given command of the 158th Battalion CEF; went overseas Oct. 1917 (Commander of the Legion of Honour); Conservative MP for county of Champlain, 1917; called to the Senate in 1918; Speaker of Senate of Canada, 1930–35; late Postmaster-Gen., Canada. *Recreation:* outdoor sports. *Address:* St Francois-du-Lac, Quebec, Canada.

Died 29 Oct. 1943.

BLOOD-SMYTH, Rev. William A., MA; *b* 24 April 1853; *s* of late M. Blood-Smyth, Barrister-at-law, 80 Merrion Square, Dublin; *m* 1887, Amy M., *d* of Rev. Canon S. R. Wills, MA, Rector of Rathkeale; one *s* two *d*. *Educ:* Marlborough; Trinity College, Dublin. Curate of Kenmare, 1877–79; Incumbent of Kilgarvan, 1879–81; of Waterville, 1882–83; Curate of St Thomas', Oldham, 1883–85; Curate of St Paul's, Lisson Grove, NW, 1885–86; Incumbent of Ballingarry, 1886–88; Incumbent of Kilkieragh, Kilkee, 1888; Curate-in-Charge of Killard, 1908; Incumbent of Kilnasoolagh,

Newmarket-on-Fergus, 1922–38; Archdeacon of Killaloe, 1927–38; Prebendary of St Patrick's Cathedral, Dublin, 1920–31.

Died 12 Sept. 1940.

BLOSSE, Sir Robert Lynch, 12th Bt *cr* 1622; DL, JP, High Sheriff for Co. Mayo, 1921; *b* 14 Feb. 1861; *s* of 10th Bt and Lady Harriet Browne, *d* of 2nd Marquis of Sligo; *S* brother, 1918; *m* 1893, Alice Gertrude Nina, *d* of E. P. Knox-Gore of Cooleronan House, Co. Mayo; one *d*. Late Capt. King's Own Scottish Borderers; served as Staff Officer Burmese Expedition, 1889–90; retired pay, 1897; temporary Major Service Batt. 7th Royal Inniskilling Fusiliers and Reserve Garrison Batt. Royal Irish Fusiliers. *Heir: cousin* Robert Cyril Lynch Blosse [*b* 16 Jan. 1887; *m* 1st, 1911, Dorothy Mary (*d* 1926), *d* of late Edward Cunliffe-Owen, CMG; one *s* one *d*; 2nd, 1932. Frances Dorothy, *e d* of Charles Edward Banks].

Died 23 June 1942.

BLOUNT, Edward Francis Riddell-; JP Northumberland; Bailiff Grand Cross Sov. Order of Malta; *b* 6 July 1865; *e s* of Francis Riddell of Cheeseburn Grange and Ellen, *d* of Michael Blount of Mapledurham; *m* 1912, Caroline Elisabeth, *d* of F. de Bille, late Danish Minister at Court of Saint James; three *d*. *Educ:* Woburn Park; Corpus Christi College, Oxford. Late Major Northumberland Yeomanry (retired, 1902); assumed by Royal Licence the additional name of Blount on succeeding to the Mapledurhan estate on the death of his uncle J. Darell Blount, 1908. *Address:* Cheeseburn Grange Newcastle-on-Tyne; Mapledurham, Oxon. *Club:* Brooks's.

Died 14 Oct. 1943.

BLUM, Léon; Député de L'Aude; President of Socialist Party of France; director of Le Populaire since 1921; *b* Paris, 9 April 1872. *Educ:* Lycées Charlemagne and Henri IV Ecole Normale. Maître des Requêtes aú Conseil d'Etat; Chef de Cabinet of Minister of Public Works, 1914; Deputy for Paris, 1919 Prime Minister, 1936–37; Vice-President of Cabinet, 1937–38; Prime Minister and Finance Minister, March–April 1938; Ambassador Extraordinary of France, 1946; Prime Minister and Foreign Minister, Provisional Government, Dec. 1946–Jan. 1947. *Publications:* De Mariage, 1907; Stendhal et le Beylisme Nouvelles Conversations avec Eckermann; At Théâtre; En Lisant; Les Problèmes de la Paix; La Réforme Gouvernmentale; L' Exercice du Pouvoir. *Recreation:* Littérature.

Died 30 March 1950.

BLUMENFELD, Ralph David; Chairman, Daily Express; *b* USA, 7 April 1864; *s* of David Blumenfeld, American editor; *m* 1892, Daisie *d* of Louis Blumfeld; two *s* one *d*. Reporter Chicago Herald, 1884; Editor, Music and Drama, 1885; Correspondent, United Press, Europe, 1887; Editor, Evening Telegram, New York; London Correspondent, New York Herald, until 1893; Superintendent, New York Herald, 1894; News Editor, Daily Mail, 1900–02; Editor Daily Express, 1902–32; travelled extensively as a special correspondent Founder and Member Executive Committee The Anti-Socialist Union; President Institute of Journalists, 1928; Master, Company of Newspaper Makers, 1931–33; Deputy Master Worshipful Company of Stationers and Newspaper Makers, 1934–35; Chairman Essex Rural Community Council, 1934–37; Director, Book Society Ltd. *Publications:* The Pick-Axe Club, 1885; Exiled in England, 1896; What is a Journalist, 1930; R. D. B's Diary, 1887, 1914, 1930; All in a Lifetime, 1931; The Press in My Time, 1933; RDB's Procession 1935; Home Town, 1944. *Address:* c/o Daily Express, Fleet Street, EC4.

Died 17 July 1948.

BLUMENTHAL, George; President The Metropolitan Museum of Art; President Emeritus Mount Sinai Hospital; Director, Continental Insurance Company, Fifth Avenue Bank, Niagara Fire Insurance Co; *b* 7 April 1858; *m* 1935, Mary Ann Payne. *Educ:* High School, Germany. Banker 1882–1925, since then retired from business. *Address:* 50 East 70th Street, New York. *TA:* Geblum, New York. *Clubs:* Lotos, River, Turf and Field, New York City; Travellers, Paris.

Died 26 June 1941.

BLUNDELL, Henry Seymour Moss-, CBE 1917; LLD; Barrister-at-law; lately Deputy Chairman Herring Industry Board and previously Chief Inspector of Fisheries; *b* 6 Dec. 1871; *s* of late J. Seymour Moss-Blundell; *m* Elizabeth Hilda, *d* of late A. E. Cumberbatch of Great Sarratt Hall, Herts; one *s* one *d*. *Educ:* Rugby; St John's College, Cambridge. *Address:* Callipers Hall, Chipperfield, Herts. *T:* King's Langley 7383. *Club:* Oxford and Cambridge.

Died 29 March 1947.

BLUNT, Arthur Powlett, CMG 1923; *b* 1883; *s* of late Maj.-Gen. Grant Blunt, RE; *m* 1919, Winifred Grace (who obtained a divorce, 1937), *d* of Dr W. H. Fawcett; two *s*. *Educ:* Bradfield. Entered HM Consular Service, China, 1905; 2nd Class Assistant, 1911; 1st Class Assistant, 1918; Vice-Consul, 1922; Consul, 1928; Consul General, 1935; Acting Vice-Consul, Ningpo, 1912; Local Vice-Consul, Shanghai, 1912–17; served with Chinese Labour Corps in France, 1917–18; seconded for service with Wei-hai-wei Government, 1919–23; Senior District Officer, 1919–21; Acting Commissioner, Wei-hai-wei, 1921–23; Acting Consul, Ichang, 1925–26; Acting Consul-General, Chungking, 1927–28; HM Consul, Peking, 1929; Shanghai, 1930; Swatow, 1931–32; Nanking, 1933; acting Consul-General Nanking, 1934; Consul-General for Philippine Islands at Manila, 1935–37; Canton, 1937–41; retired, 1943; British Red Cross and St John Commissioner in China, 1943–44. *Recreations:* golf, tennis. *Club:* Thatched House.

Died 15 April 1946.

BLUNT, Col Conrad Edward Grant, CBE 1919; DSO 1917; late Director of Supplies, Egyptian Army; *b* 1868; *e s* of late Maj.-Gen. Grant Blunt, RE; *m* 1st, 1900, Aimée (*d* 1918), *d* of Col Abel Straghan, CB; one *s* one *d*; 2nd, 1920, Beatrice (*d* 1946), *widow* of Frank Fullagar. *Educ:* Bradfield; Sandhurst. Leinster Regiment, 1889; ASC 1893; attached Egyptian Army, 1894; served Dongola Expedition, 1896 (despatches, 4th Class Medjidie); Nile Expedition, 1898 (despatches, Bt Major); European War, 1915–19 (despatches, CBE, DSO); 3rd Class Osmanieh; 2nd Class Order of the Nile. *Club:* Junior United Service.

Died 26 Dec. 1948.

BLUNT, Sir Edward Arthur Henry, KCIE 1934; CIE 1922; OBE; ICS (retired); *b* 14 March 1877; *s* of late Captain F. E. Blunt, Chief Commissioner, Seychelles Islands, and late Mrs Blunt of Littlehampton, Sussex; *m* 1901, Ada, *d* of C. H. Stone, RN; one *s* two *d*. *Educ:* Marlborough College; Corpus Christi College, Oxford. ICS 1901; Under-Secretary to Government UP 1905–07; Superintendent Census Operations, UP, 1910–12; Settlement Officer, Basti District, 1915–18; Director of Civil Supplies UP 1918–19; Revenue Secretary to Government UP 1919; Financial Secretary to Government of United Provinces, 1920–31; Member of Governor's Executive Council, UP 1931–35. *Publications:* Christian Tombs and Monuments of Historical interest in the UP 1911; Financial Administration under the Reforms Scheme, 1921; The Caste System of Northern India, 1932; The ICS, 1937; (Editor) Social Service in India, 1939. *Recreations:* tennis, golf. *Address:* Heathfield, Reading Road, Fleet, Hants.

Died 29 May 1941.

BLUNT, John Silvester, RBA 1912; painter in oil, water colour, pastel, etc; *b* Alderton, Northants, Jan. 1874; *o s* of John Edward Blunt; *m* 1900, Edith, *e d* of Alfred Allen, metallurgist, London; one *d. Educ:* privately; Denstone College, Staffs. Studied Ecclesiastical Architecture under H. M. Townsend, ARIBA. Diocesan surveyor, Peterborough; afterwards studying art chiefly under private tuition. *Principal Works:* street scenes and landscapes; Exhibition, London and Provincial Galleries. *Recreations:* motoring and cricket. *Address:* Aldrington, The Avenue, Potters Bar, Middlesex. *T:* Potters Bar 4274. *Club:* Chelsea Arts.

Died 30 Dec. 1943.

BLUNT, Reginald, CBE 1933; AKC; Hon. Freeman of Chelsea, 1934; *b* 1857; 2nd *s* of Rev. Gerald Blunt, Rector of Chelsea; *m* Victoria de Guérard (*d* 1925); one *s. Educ:* Haileybury; King's College, London. Engineering work, LSW Rly, Sir W. G. Armstrong and Sir A. M. Rendel, 1879–87; Sec. Cheyne Hospital, Chelsea, 1887–1902; Manager to William De Morgan, 1897–99; General Superintendent to Managers of the Stock Exchange, 1902–19; Trustee, Carlyle's House, 1895; Chairman, Chelsea Park Dwellings Co. Ltd; Chairman, Cheyne Hospital for Children, Finance Committee; Founder and Hon. Secretary, The Chelsea Society, 1927. *Publications:* The Carlyles' Chelsea Home, 1895; A Handbook to Chelsea, 1900; Paradise Row, 1906; Memorials of Gerald Blunt of Chelsea, 1911; In Cheyne Walk and Thereabout, 1914; The Wonderful Village, 1918; By Chelsea Reach; some riverside records, 1921; The Lure of Old Chelsea, 1922; Elizabeth Montagu, Letters and Memoir, 1923; The Cheyne Book, 1924; Crown and Anchor (editor), 1925; Red Anchor Pieces, 1928; Chelsea Old Church, (editor), 1932; Thomas, Lord Lyttelton, 1936; Random Rhymes, 1940. *Recreations:* fishing and books. *Address:* 60 Glebe Place, SW3. *T:* Flaxman 0230. *Club:* Chelsea Arts.

Died 25 Oct. 1944.

BLYTH, 2nd Baron *cr* 1907; **Herbert William Blyth;** Bt *cr* 1895; *b* 1 March 1868; *e s* of 1st Baron Blyth and Eliza (*d* 1894), *d* of William Mooney, Clontarf, Co. Dublin; *S* father, 1925; *m* 1927, Sylvia Mary Cole, *o d* of late Edwin E. Dennis. *Heir: nephew* Ian Audley James Blyth, *b* 28 Oct. 1905. *Address:* 14 Chester Terrace, Regent's Park, NW1. *Clubs:* Devonshire, Hurlingham, Baldwin.

Died 27 Feb. 1943.

BLYTH, Lt-Col Charles Frederick Tolmé, CMG 1916; solicitor; *b* 20 April 1868; *s* of late Edmund Kell Blyth, Hampstead; *m* 1896, Agatha, *d* of late Philip Henry Lawrence, Barrister; one *s* one *d. Educ:* University, College School and University College, London; LLD, BSc (London). Artists Rifles, 1887–1908; served RASC, European War, 1914–17 (CMG). *Address:* Windy Sayles, Felden, Hemel Hempstead, Herts.

Died 12 July 1950.

BLYTH, Ormond Alfred; *b* 15 Oct. 1879; *y s* of Henry Arthur Blyth, Stansted House; Essex; unmarried. *Educ:* Harrow School. Treasurer, London Assoc. of the Blind; Chairman, National Hospital, Queen Square, WC; Member of Committee: Homes for Little Boys, Farningham and Swanley, Royal Dental Hospital, Corporation of the Sons of Clergy, St Mary's Home, Maplestead, London Over the Border Church Fund, Given-Wilson Institute, Plaistow, E13. Council of Royal Academy of Dancing and of Anglo-Danish Soc. Life Governor of Society of St George; Member of Company of Wheelwrights; PGD Grand Lodge of England. *Recreations:* interested in all sports. Member of Goodwood, Newmarket, and Epsom. *Clubs:* Devonshire (Chairman), Arts, Public Schools, Thatched House.

Died 16 June 1947.

BOARD, Peter, CMG 1916; MA; Director of Education, and Under-Secretary, Department of Public Instruction, New South Wales, 1905–22 (retired); *b* 27 March 1858; *m* Jessie Allan Bowes (*d* 1932); one *d. Educ:* Sydney University, MA (graduated 1888), Hons Mathematics. Entered the service as pupil teacher, 1873; and Training College, Fort Street, Sydney, 1876; Inspector, 1893; visited Great Britain and Continent, 1903; America, 1909, to study the educational systems; attended Imperial Education Conference, 1911. *Publications:* various Educational Reports. *Address:* Morven Road, Leura, Blue Mountains, NSW.

Died 12 Feb. 1945.

BOARD, Sir William John, Kt 1935; OBE; JP Notts; Solicitor; *b* 12 May 1869; *s* of John Board, formerly of Weston-super-Mare; *m* Ada, 2nd *d* of late Alderman Henry Parfitt, JP, Pontnewydd, Monmouthshire; two *s* (eldest son killed in European War, 1918), one *d. Educ:* Cardiff, privately. Deputy Town Clerk, Cardiff, 1897–1904; Deputy Clerk of the Peace, Cardiff, 1901–04; Town Clerk and Clerk of the Peace, Rotherham, 1904–12; Town Clerk 1912–36 and Clerk of the Peace, 1921–36, Nottingham; Life Governor, Nottingham University College, Hon. Secretary, 1912–36; President, Society of City and Borough Clerks of the Peace, 1929–30; Chairman, Law Committee, Association of Municipal Corporations, 1929–31; President, Society of Town Clerks, 1933–34, 1934–35, 1935–36; an Hon. Freeman of City of Nottingham, 1934. *Recreations:* golf, gardening. *Address:* The Spinney, Oxton Hill, nr Southwell, Notts. *T:* Oxton, Notts 206.

Died 2 Nov. 1946.

BOARDMAN, Paymaster Captain John Cogswell, CMG 1919; RN, retired; *s* of late Admiral F. R. Boardman, CB; *m* 1921, Margaret (*d* 1928), *o d* of late Henry P. Spottiswoode; one *s. Educ:* Cordwalles, Maidenhead; Tonbridge School. Entered Royal Navy as Assistant Clerk, 1900; served as Additional Secretary to Commander-in-Chief, Grand Fleet, Aug. 1917–April 1919 (CMG); retired list, 1937. *Address:* Bothorpe, Guildford Road, Woking. *T:* Woking 1303. *Club:* Naval and Military.

Died 28 Nov. 1942.

BOAS, Franz, PhD, LLD, ScD (Oxon, Columbia, Clark); MD (Kiel); Professor of Anthropology, Columbia University, 1899–1936; emeritus 1936; *b* Minden, Westphalia, 9 July 1858; *m* 1887, Marie A. E. Krackowizer, New York; one *s* two *d. Educ:* University, Heidelberg; University, Bonn; and University, Kiel. Explored Baffin Land, 1883–84. *Publications:* Baffin Land, 1885; Chinook Texts, 1894; Indianische Sagen von der Nordwestküste Amerikas, 1895; The Growth of Children, 1896; Social Organisation and Secret Societies of the Kwakiutl-Indians, 1898; Kathlamet Texts, 1900; The Eskimo of Baffin Land and Hudson Bay, 1901, 1907; Handbook of American-Indian Languages, vol. i 1911, vol. ii, 1923, vol. iii, 1938, vol. iv, 1941; The Mind of Primitive Man, 1911–1937; Changes in Bodily Form of Descendants of Immigrants, 1912; Kultur und Rasse, 1914; Tsimshian Mythology, 1917; Kutenai Tales, 1918; Tlingit Grammar, 1917; Ethnology of the Kwakiutl, 1921; Primitive Art, 1927; Keresan Texts, 1928; Anthropology and Modern Life, 1929–1932; Religion of the Kwakiutl Indians, 1930; Kwakiutl Culture as reflected in Mythology, 1935; (with others) Anthropology, 1938; Race, Language and Culture, 1939; Dakota Grammar (with others) Anthropology, 1938; Race, Language and Culture, 1939; Dakota Grammar (with Ella Deloria), 1941; also volumes of Kwakiutl and Tsimshian Texts, numerous scientific reports, etc. *Address:* Grantwood, Bergen County, New Jersey.

Died 21 Dec. 1942.

BODDAM-WHETHAM, Rear-Adm. Edye Kington, CBE 1942; DSO 1917; *b* 4 Feb. 1887; *s* of late J. W. Boddam-Whetham of Kirklington Hall, Notts; *m* 1915, Elizabeth Margaret, *widow* of Gordon Ayers. *Educ:* Sandroyd; HMS Britannia. Served European War; DSO for services in command of a destroyer off the Belgian coast, June 1917; retired list, 1939. *Recreations:* golf, shooting. *Address:* Hyde Gate, Long Sutton, Basingstoke, Hants. *T:* Long Sutton 14.

Died 27 March 1944.

BODENSTEIN, Helgard Dewald Johannes, LLD (Leyden); Barrister, Middle Temple; Secretary for External Affairs and Secretary to Prime Minister, Union of South Africa, since 1927; *b* 31 July 1881; 2nd *s* of Dewald Johannes Bodenstein, Potchefstroom, Transvaal; *m* 1910, Margaretta Elisabeth van der Veen; one *s* one *d.* *Educ:* Leyden; London (Council of Legal Education). Transvaal Civil Service, 1909–12; Professor of Roman-Dutch Law at University of Amsterdam, 1912; returned to South Africa, 1919; Assistant Chief Editor of Die Burger, 1919–21; Professor of Roman-Dutch Law at Stellenbosch University, 1922. *Publications:* Treatise on Contract of Letting and Hiring; and numerous articles. *Recreations:* riding, chess, and mountaineering. *Address:* Pretoria or Cape Town.

Died 21 Jan. 1943.

BOGERT, Clarence Atkinson; Chairman of Board of Directors, 1934, President, 1933, Vice-President, 1925, General Manager, 1906, Dominion Bank; retd 1948; *b* Napanee, Ont, 7 July 1864; *s* of late Ven. Archdeacon James John Bogert and late Elizabeth Grant Bogert; unmarried. *Educ:* Trinity College School, Port Hope. Entered the service of the Dominion Bank, Toronto, 1881; Assistant Inspector 1893; Assistant Manager, Toronto, 1895; Manager, Montreal, 1898. *Recreation:* golf. *Address:* Room 719, Dominion Bank Building, Toronto, Canada. *T:* Elgin 3750. *Clubs:* York, Toronto, Toronto Golf, Toronto Hunt, Toronto Cricket, Ontario Jockey, Empire (Toronto); Mount Royal, Royal Montreal Golf (Montreal).

Died 17 Dec. 1949.

BOILEAU, Col Etienne Ronald Partridge, CB 1923; CIE 1919; CBE 1920; *b* 8 April 1870; *s* of late Colonel F. W. Boileau, CB, Elstowe, Camberley; *m* Dorothy Lucy, 2nd *d* of late Morris Richardson, Hurley House, Hurley, Marlow; no *c.* *Educ:* Cheltenham College. East Lancashire Regiment, 1890–95; then Indian Army; General Staff AHQ India, 1909–13; Commandant 2/2 Gurkhas, 1916–20; temp. Commandant Quetta Cadet College, 1917–19; Deputy Military Secretary, AHQ India, 1919–21; served Chitral, 1895 (medal with clasp); Samana, 1897 (clasp); Tirah, 1897–98 (2 clasps); Tibet, 1903–04 (medal); European War, 1914–18 (despatches, Bt Lt-Col, 3 medals, CIE); Afghan War, 1919 (despatches, CBE, medal); commanded 11th Infantry Brigade India, 1921–23; retired, 1923. *Address:* Wechvlstone, Speldhurst, Kent. *Club:* United Service.

Died 5 Nov. 1947.

BOILEAU, Sir Francis James, 5th Bt *cr* 1838; JP; *b* 6 Nov. 1871; *s* of late E. W. P. Boileau, 3rd *s* of 1st Bt; *S* cousin, 1942; *m* 1895, Wilhelmina, *d* of late George Lyon, Beechworth, Victoria, Australia; three *s* one *d.* *Heir: s* Gilbert George Benson, MB, BS [*b* 1898; *m* 1924, Chica Patricia, *d* of J. L. Edgworth-Somers, LRCSI; two *d*]. *Address:* St Croix, Stanhope Street, Melbourne, Victoria, Australia.

Died 20 Feb. 1945.

BOILEAU, Sir Raymond Frederic, 4th Bt *cr* 1838; DL and JP, Norfolk; *b* 6 Oct. 1868; *s* of Sir Francis G. M. Boileau, 2nd Bt and Lucy Henrietta, *e d* of Sir George Nugent, Bt; *S* brother 1937; *m* 1905, Ethel Mary (*d* 1942), *d* of Rev. James Foster Young; no *c.* *Educ:* Eton; Sandhurst. 2nd Bn Northamptonshire Regt, 1888–93,

Lieut; PWO Norfolk Artillery (Militia) 1897–1908, Capt. and Hon. Major and Instructor of Artillery; served European War, France, 10th (Service) Bn Royal Fusiliers, 1914–16, Major 2nd, in Command; 135 Heavy Battery RA, 1916–17, Major Commanding; Labour Corps, 1917–19, Lt-Col 1919, Commanding at Rouen (despatches); Provincial Grand Master of Freemasons for Norfolk from 1926. *Recreations:* formerly; hunting, shooting, fishing, cricket, golf, billiards, etc. *Heir: cousin* Francis James [*b* 6 Nov. 1871; *m* 1895, Wilhelmina, *d* of late George Lyon, Beech-worth, Victoria, Australia; one *s*]. *Address:* Ketteringham Park, Wymondham, Norfolk. *T:* Hetherset 35. *Club:* Travellers'.

Died 23 June 1942.

BOIS, Col John, DSO, MC; *b* 24 Oct. 1881; *s* of John Charles Bois and F. M. Phillips; *m* 1912, Edith Norah Beardsley. *Educ:* Marlborough College. 2nd Lieut The King's own Royal Regt 1901; served South Africa, 1902; Kisii Expeditionary Force, 1908; Somaliland, 1909–10; European War, 1914–19; Commanded 2nd Bn The King's Own Royal Regt, 1916–19 and 1931–35; Officer i/c Records, Preston, 1935–38; retired pay, 1938. *Address:* Beechfield, Yealand Conyers, Carnforth, Lancs. *Club:* Junior United Service.

Died 26 Dec. 1941.

BOLES, Sir Gerald Fortescue, 2nd Bt *cr* 1922; Capt. 17th/21st Lancers; *b* 19 June 1900; *o surv. s* of Sir Dennis Fortescue Boles, 1st Bt, and late Beatrice Ringrose, *y d* of late John Lysaght, of Hengrave Hall, Suffolk; *S* father, 1935; *m* 1927, Violet Blanche, *er d* of late Major Hall Parlby, Manadon, Crown Hill, S Devon; one *s.* *Educ:* Eton; RMC Sandhurst. Joined 17th Lancers, 1920; ADC to Governor and Commander-in-Chief, Bermuda, 1927–29; retired, 1930. *Recreations:* hunting, fishing, shooting. *Heir: s* Jeremy John Fortescue, *b* 9 Jan. 1932. *Address:* Watts House, Bishops Lydeard, Taunton. *T:* 202. *Club:* Cavalry.

Died 9 April 1945.

BOLST, Captain Clifford Charles Alan Lawrence E.; *see* Erskine-Bolst.

BOLSTER, Francis, CMG 1919; MD; Surgeon-Captain RN, retired; *b* Mallow, Co. Cork; *s* of Chas B. Bolster; *m* 1913, Violet, *d* of Ven. Archdeacon Adams; one *s* one *d.* *Educ:* Midleton College; Trinity College, Dublin. Joined HM Navy as surgeon, 1907; served in China during Boxer rebellion (medal); served during European War; in charge of hospital ship, China, for nine months; in HMS Warrior, sunk Jutland 1916; lent to Army for duty in France, Aug. 1918; awarded the West London Medico-Chirurigical Society's gold medal, 1916, for treatment of wounded in action. *Recreation:* fishing. *Address:* Monkton, Biggleswade, Beds.

Died 11 Feb. 1941.

BOLT, Rev. G. H., MA, LTh Durham; DCL University of King's College, Windsor, Nova Scotia; *b* 15 Sept. 1863; *s* of William and Elizabeth A. Bolt; *m* Elizabeth M. Morris; one *s* two *d.* *Educ:* St John's, Newfoundland; Durham University; Hatfield College, Durham, BA 1889; LTh 1890; MA 1892. Deacon, 1890; Priest, 1891; Episcopal Commissary, 1922; Examining Chaplain to Bishop of Newfoundland, 1909; Diocesan Registrar, 1898; Canon of St David in Newfoundland Cathedral, 1911; Curate of Bonavista, 1890–91; SPG, Missionary Lamaline, 1891–93; Bay de Verde, 1893–95; Brigus, 1895–97; Curate of St Mary's, St John's, 1897–1900; Sec.-Treas. Executive Committee of Diocesan Synod, 1897–1900; Rector of St Mary's, St John's, Newfoundland, 1900–02; Secretary-Treasurer Diocesan Synod of Newfoundland, 1902–34; member of Council of Higher Education; Grand Chaplain of District Grand Lodge of Newfoundland of AF and A. Masons, RE; Life Governor Canadian Bible Society, 1924; Vice-President Colonial and Continental Church Society, 1924; Hon.

Governor of the British and Foreign Bible Society, London, 1931. *Address:* Synod House, St John's Newfoundland.

Died 25 May 1947.

BOLTON, 5th Baron *cr* 1797; **William George Algar Orde-Powlett;** Lord-Lieutenant North Riding, Yorks, 1935; *b* 21 Aug. 1869; *e s* of 4th Baron Bolton and Lady Algitha Frederica Mary Lumley (*d* 1919), *d* of 9th Earl of Scarbrough; *S* father, 1922; *m* 1893, Hon. Elizabeth Mary Gibson (*d* 1943), *d* of 1st Baron Ashbourne; one *s* one *d.* MP (U), Richmond Div., Yorks, 1910–18; formerly Lieut KRRC; late Lieut Yorkshire Hussars Yeomanry Cavalry. *Heir: s* Hon. Nigel Amyas Orde-Powlett. *Address:* Bolton Hall, Leyburn, Yorks. *Club:* Carlton.

Died 11 Dec. 1944.

BOLTON, Arthur Thomas, FSA, FRIBA; Soane Medalist, 1893; Architect; Curator of Sir John Soane's House and Museum since 1917; *b* 14 April 1864; 2nd *s* of Thos Bolton of the Sanctuary and Emily Wildman of Chilham Castle; *m* 1897, Harriet Barnes (*d* 1944), *d* of Samuel Fall, Carolina; three *s* two *d. Educ:* Haileybury; Univ. College, London. Articled pupil Sir R. W. Edis, Fitzroy Square; in charge of work for Ewan Christian, PRIBA at Folkestone; student with R. Phené Spiers, FSA; travelled in Greece, Italy, France, and Spain, and later on in Egypt; 1st Master AA School of Architecture, 1901–03; Architectural work of a varied character; St Stephen's Schools, Bayswater; Ingram House, Stockwell; P & O, Cockspur Street; houses, etc., in the country; restoration and additions to Chandos House, etc. *Publications:* Essay, Medal RIBA, 1895; Influence of Literature on Architecture; The Architecture of R. and J. Adam, 1922; Gardens of Italy, 1919; The Works of Sir John Soane, 1924; The Portrait of Sir John Soane, 1928; Editor for the Wren Society, 20 volumes, 1924–1944; Cantor Lectures, 1920, Arch. and Decor. of R. Adam and Sir J. Soane; Lectures on Architecture at the Royal Academy by Sir John Soane, 1809–1837, 1929. *Recreation:* travel. *Address:* 13 Lincoln's Inn Fields, WC2; 14 Westbourne Park Road, W2. *T:* Museum 2107, Park 1719.

Died 17 Jan. 1945.

BOLTON, Charles, CBE 1920; FRS 1918; MD, DSc, FRCP; Consulting Physician; late Physician to University College Hospital, and Lecturer in Clinical Medicine, University College Hospital Medical School; late Director of Pathological Studies and Research, and Lecturer on General Pathology, University College Hospital Medical School; late Physician to Queen's Hospital for Children; *b* Whitby, Yorkshire; *m* 1911, Ethel Mary, *d* of late Henry George. *Educ:* University College. *Publications:* papers on medical and scientific subjects in Proceedings Royal Society, in Transactions of Medical Societies, and in medical and scientific journals. *Address:* 11 De Walden Court, 85 New Cavendish Street, W1. *Club:* Athenæum.

Died 6 Dec. 1947.

BOLTON, Joseph Shaw; Emeritus Professor of Mental Diseases, University of Leeds; Hon. Consulting Physician, Bucks Mental Hospital; Medical Director, W Riding Mental Hospital, Wakefield, 1910–33; *b* Whitby, Yorks, 1867; *m* 1906; two *s* one *d. Educ:* University College and Hospital, London. MD, DSc, BS (Lond.); Hon. DSc (Leeds); Fellow of the Royal College of Physicians of London; Fellow of University College, London. Goulstonian Lecturer (RCP), 1910; Lumleian Lecturer (RCP), 1935; Member and ex-President Royal Medico-Psychological Association, Maudsley Lecturer, 1925; Lecturer, Henderson Trust, 1933; Foreign Member Société Medico-Psychologique de Paris, Nederlandsche Vereeniging voor Psychiatrie en Neurologie; alienist and neurologist; late Examiner in Mental Diseases and Neurology, University of Manchester; late Hon. Academic Consulting Physician,

Leeds General Infirmary. *Publications:* The Brain in Health and Disease, 1914; articles in scientific and medical journals. *Recreation:* gardening. *Address:* Merevale, Brownswood Road, Beaconsfield, Bucks. *T:* Beaconsfield 399. *Club:* University of London.

Died 12 Nov. 1946.

BOLTON, Brig.-Gen. William Kinsey, CBE 1918; VD; *b* 1861; *s* of John Hammersley Bolton; *m* 1st, 1881, Jean Morpeth Gillies; 2nd, 1894, Margaret Ford. *Educ:* State Schools, Victoria. Served European War, 1914–15; member of Senate, Commonwealth of Australia, 1917–23; Past President, Returned Sailors' and Soldiers' Imperial League, Victoria. *Address:* Gralem, 108 South Road, Brighton Beach, Victoria, Australia.

Died 8 Sept. 1941.

BOMON-BEHRAM, Sir Jehangir Bomonji, Kt 1934; Trustee of The Parsi Panchayet Funds and Properties; JP; BA, LLB; *b* July 1868; *s* of Bomonji Rastamji Bomon-Behram of Bombay; *m* Jerbai (*d* 1889), *d* of Merwanji Mulla; no *c. Educ:* Fort High School; St Xavier's and Elphinstone Colleges. A Solicitor; Jurisprudence Prizeman, Narayan Vasudeo Scholar and Fellow of the Elphinstone Coll.; Member Bombay Municipal Corporation for about 20 years; First Mayor of Bombay; on Board of Bombay Port Trust 3 years; Member Advisory Board of GIP Railway Co. 4 years; Pres. Hosp. Maintenance Fund Cttee; Chm. Advisory Board, JJ and Allied Hosps; Vice-Pres. Soc. for the Protection of Children in Western India, etc.; inaugurator and President of Conciliation Committee to prevent inter-communal trouble in the City; inaugurated Welfare of India League to promote co-operation between Indians and the British people; Director of several Joint Stock Companies, etc. *Address:* Merwan Mansion, Nepean Sea Road, Bombay 6, India. *T:* 42806. *Club:* Ripon (Bombay).

Died 29 Dec. 1949.

BONAR, James, MA Glas. and Oxford; LittD Cambridge, 1935; LLD Glas. 1886; retired Civil Servant; Fellow of British Academy, 1930; Foreign Member of Reale Accademia dei Lincei, 1932; *b* Collace, Perthshire, 27 Sept. 1852; *s* of Rev. Dr Andrew A. Bonar and Isabella Dickson, both of Edinburgh; *m* 1883, Mary Mewburn Miller of Liverpool (*d* 1908); one *s* two *d. Educ:* Glasgow Academy and University; Leipzig; Tübingen; Balliol Coll., Oxford; Second in Mods, 1875; First in Greats, 1877; Terminal Prize Foils. Lecturer in East London, 1877–80; Junior Examiner in HM Civil Service Commission, 1881; Senior Examiner, 1895; Deputy Master of Canadian Branch of Royal Mint, 1907–19; President of Section F of British Association, 1898; Vice-Pres., Royal Statistical Society, 1920, and of Royal Economic Society, 1930; Newmarch Lecturer, University College, London, 1929. *Publications:* Beck's Biblical Psychology (tr.), 1877; Parson Malthus, 1881; Malthus and his Work, 1885, 2nd ed., 1924; (Japanese translation, 1930); Ricardo's Letters to Malthus, 1887 (Magyar trans., 1913); Philosophy and Political Economy, 1893, 4th imp. 1927 (Japanese translation, 1921); Moral Sense, 1930; Catalogue of Adam Smith's Library, 1894, 2nd ed. 1932; Ricardo's Letters to Trower (with Prof. Hollander), 1899; Elements of Political Economy, 1903; Disturbing Elements in Political Economy, 1911; translation (with Mrs Lucas) of Knapp on Money, 1924; The Tables Turned, 1926; the same with other Dialogues, 1931; Theories of Population from Raleigh to Arthur Young, 1931; contributions to Seth and Haldane's Philosophical Criticism, 1882, Craik's Prose Authors, Palgrave's Dictionary of Pol Econ., Conrad's Handwörterbuch der Staatswissenschaften, Encyclopædia Britannica. *Recreations:* various. *Address:* 13 Redington Road, Hampstead. *Clubs:* Savile; University, Ottawa; Canadian Alpine, Vancouver.

Died 18 Jan. 1941.

BOND, Carrie Jacobs-; composer; *b* Janesville, Wis, 11 Aug. 1862; *m*; one *s*. *Educ:* Janesville. Hon. Member of Sorosis Club of San Francisco, Women's Athletic Club of Los Angeles, Hollywood Women's Club, Musicians' Club of Chicago, etc. *Publications:* A Perfect Day; Just Awearyin' For You; I Love You Truly; A Cottage in God's Garden; A Little Bit o' Honey; The Soul of You; To-day; Do You Remember; Shadows; Tales of Little Cats; Tales of Little Dogs; Book of Poems; Roads of Melody (autobiography); Remember to Forget, etc. *Recreation:* automobiling. *Address:* 2042 Pinehurst Road, Hollywood, California, USA. *Clubs:* Chicago Musical, Woman's Association of Commerce, Chicago.
Died 28 Dec. 1946.

BOND, Lt-Col Chetwynd Rokeby Alfred, CIE 1920; CBE 1919; Indian Army, retired; *b* 1863. Served Isazai Expedition, 1892; Dongola Expedition, 1896 (Egyptian medal); NW Frontier of India, 1897–98 (medal with clasp); Commander of Order of Aviz of Portugal; Chevalier Legion of Honour.
Died 22 Jan. 1944.

BOND, Engr Captain Edmund Edward, CMG 1913; DSO 1898; *b* 1865; *m* 1922, Eveleen (*d* 1924), *d* of late Judge W. Bowen-Rowlands, KC, MP. Entered Navy, 1887; specially promoted to Chief Engineer, 1900; Engineer Commander, 1904; retired, 1907; in charge of Egyptian War Department Steamers and Director of Sudan Government Steamers, 1899–1914; 3rd class Osmanieh, 1907; served Nile, 1898–99 (medals and 2 clasps, Medjidie 4th class, DSO); 2nd class Medjidie, 1914; East Coast and Dover Patrol 1914–15; Special Service, 1915–19 (1914–15 Star, War and Victory medals); Engineer Captain on retired list, 1919.
Died 20 Dec. 1943.

BOND, Frederick Bligh, MInst RA; FRIBA; ecclesiastical architect and author; *b* at the Royal Free Grammar School, Marlborough, Wilts, 30 June 1864; 3rd *s* of Rev. Frederick H. Bond, MA, and Mary Isabella, *d* of Major Dela Fosse, CB; *m* 1894; one *d*. *Educ:* Bath College. Hon. Architect to the Bath and Wells Diocesan Societies, 1909; Consulting Architect to Malvern Priory Church, 1909–14; specialist in mediaeval woodwork; prominent in psychical research; editor of Psychic Science, 1921–26; Editor of the Journal of the American SPR, 1930–35; was first in applying psychical research methods to archæological work; discovered the Edgar and Loretto Chapel sites at Glastonbury Abbey by this means; Director of Excavations at Glastonbury Abbey, 1908–21. *Publications:* Roodscreens and Roodlofts, 1909; An Architectural Handbook of Glastonbury Abbey, 1910; The Gate of Remembrance, 1918; The Hill of Vision, 1919; The Company of Avalon, 1924; The Rose Miraculous, 1924; The Gospel of Philip the Deacon, 1926; The Secret of Immortality, 1934; The Mystery of Glaston, 1938; numerous pamphlets in the Proceedings of the Somerset, Devon, and Cambs Archæological Societies. *Recreations:* antiquities, science of form. *Address:* Brithdir, Dolgelley N Wales.
Died 8 March 1945.

BOND, Sir Hubert, KBE 1929; CBE 1920; DSc, MD Edin., LLB Lond.; FRCP; Senior Commissioner Board of Control, 1930–45; *b* Ogbourne St George, Wilts, 1870; *er s* of late Rev. Alfred Bond of Powick, Worcester, and Chipping, Lancs and late Frances Elizabeth, *d* of late Charles Smallridge, Clerk of Peace of Gloucester; *m* 1900, Janet Constance, *o d* of late Fred. R. Laurie, Worcester; one *d*. *Educ:* Univ. Edinburgh; King's College, London, and privately. MB 1892, BSc (Pub. Health) 1893; Gaskell Gold Medallist in Mental Disorders, 1898. Consultant in Neurol. and Mental Disorders Royal Navy, since 1925; Mem. Central Med. War Cttee since 1939; President, Assoc. Occupational Therapists since 1937; Vice-Pres. Lebanon Hosp. since 1937; Governor St Mary's Hall School, Brighton, since

1931; member of Court of Assistants of Corp. of Sons of Clergy since 1942 Emeritus Lecturer in Psychiatry, Middlesex Hospital; Lecturer in Mental Disorders at Maudsley Hospital, 1919–39; William Withering Lecturer, University of Birmingham, 1931; Maudsley Lecturer, 1931; Examiner (1920–24) in Neurology and Psychology, Med. Conjt Bd in England; Do. (1925–28) in Psychol. and Mental Disorders, Univ. Lond.; Do. (1925–29) for DPM Univ. of Leeds; Associate Member of the Society Medico-Psychologique of Paris since 1927; Fellow (President, 1922–23, Section of Psychiatry) Royal Society of Medicine; President, 1921–22, Hon. Gen. Sec. 1906–12, and Hon. Member since 1928 of Royal Medico-Psychological Association; Chairman of Departmental Committee on Nursing in County and Borough Mental Hospitals, 1922–24; member of the Shell-Shock Committee (War Office), 1920–22; formerly member of the medical staffs of Morningside, Wakefield, and Banstead Mental Hospital; first Dep. Supt Bexley Mental Hospital, 1898–1903; First Med. Supt Ewell Colony for Epileptics, 1903–07; First Med. Supt London County Mental Hospital, Long-Grove, 1907–12; Commissioner in Lunacy, 1912–14; Commissioner of Board of Control, 1914–30. *Publications:* article on Epileptic Insanity in Ency. Medica and on Lunacy Statistics, Hospital Treatment of the Insane, Asylum Construction and Management, etc., in various medical journals. *Recreations:* genealogical research and fell walking in Lancs. *Club:* Union.
Died 18 April 1945.

BOND, Col James Henry Robinson, CBE 1919; DSO 1917; MRCS, LRCP Lond.; late RAMC; *b* 21 July 1871. Entered army, 1899; Lieutenant-Colonel, 1915; served S Africa, 1899–1902 (Queen's medal with six clasps, King's medal with two clasps); Mesopotamia, 1915–18 (despatches, DSO, CBE); retired pay, 1924. *Address:* Kenelm, Eldorado Crescent, Cheltenham.
Died 14 Jan. 1943.

BOND, John Wentworth Garneys, CB 1926; JP, DL Dorset; on County Council of Dorset; *b* 12 Sept. 1865; *s* of Nathaniel Bond of Grange, Dorset, and Lady Selina Jane Scott, *d* of 2nd Earl of Eldon; *m* Helen Violet, *d* of Frederic Fane; no *c*. *Educ:* Eton; Oriel College, Oxford. Called to Bar, Inner Temple, 1893; Clerk in House of Commons, 1890–1926; Clerk of the Journals, 1921–26. *Address:* Grange, Wareham, Dorset. *TA:* Creech. *T:* Wareham 259. *Club:* Travellers'.
Died 8 Oct. 1948.

BOND, Richard Warwick, MA (Oxon), FRSL; Professor (Emeritus) of English Language and Literature in University College, Nottingham; *b* 30 Sept. 1857; *s* of Rev. R. S. Bond, MA (Oxon); unmarried. *Educ:* Bromsgrove School; Queen's College, Oxford. Classical and Philosophical Honours; BA 1880; MA 1887. Lecturer to the Oxford Extension Delegacy since 1886. *Publications:* The Immortals and other Poems, 1890; Ode to the Sun, 1892; Ed. Poetical Works of William Basse, 1893; At Stratford Festival (poem), 1896; Another Sheaf, 1898; Zenobia, a Drama, 1899; Ed. Complete Works of John Lyly, 3 vols, 1902; Bercher's Nobylytye of Wymen, 2 vols 1904–1905; Part Ed. Variorum, Beaumont and Fletcher, 1904–1906–1907; Taming, Two Gentlemen (Arden Shakespeare), 1904, 1906; Montaigne, a Study, 1906; Early Plays from the Italian, 1911; Ed. The Birth of Hercules (Malone Society), 1911; The Pedlar, Part I (narrative poem), 1922; Part II, 1924; The Marlay Letters, 1778–1820, 1937; Studia Otiosa, 1938; contributor to Quarterly, 19th Century, Dublin, Contemporary, Fortnightly, and other reviews; for some time joint-editor of the Ruskin quarterly Saint George. *Recreations:* travelling, golf, croquet, bicycling, etc. *Address:* Lynwood, Tattershall Drive, The Park, Nottingham.
Died 2 May 1943.

BOND, Stanley Shaw; Chairman and Governing Director of Butterworth & Co. (Publishers) Ltd, London and Associated Companies in Africa, Australia, Canada, and India; Hon. Treasurer Royal Association in aid of the Deaf and Dumb; Governor Queen Alexandra's Hospital Home for Soldiers; Vice-Chairman Central Board of Finance of the Church of England; *b* 8 July 1877; 2nd *s* of late Charles Bond, The Downs, Wimbledon; *m* 1938, Myrtle, *er d* of Lt-Col A. F. Fletcher, DSO; two *s. Educ:* privately. *Recreations:* shooting, stalking, golf, travel. *Address:* Dycheham Park, nr Petersfield; Braemar Castle, Aberdeenshire. *TA:* Inhopetter, London. *Clubs:* Carlton, Bachelors; Royal Northern, Aberdeen.

Died 14 Feb. 1943.

BOND, Sir Walter Adrian M.; *see* Macgeough Bond.

BOND, Hon. Mr Chief Justice William Langley, KC 1911; BA, DCL; VD; of the Superior Court (Montreal) of the Province of Quebec, Canada, since 1942; *b* Montreal, 20 Jan. 1873; *s* of Lt-Col Frank Bond and Mary S. Scott; *g s* of late Primate of all Canada; *m* Beatrice, *d* of William Hanson; one *d. Educ:* Montreal. Called to Bar, 1898; Judge of the Superior Court, 1927–29; Judge of the Court of King's Bench, 1929–42; Major in 245th Overseas Battalion (Canadian Grenadier Guards), CEF; Chancellor of the Diocese of Montreal; Member of the Council of Education of the Province of Quebec. *Address:* 484 Mount Pleasant Avenue, Westmount, PQ, Canada. *T:* Fl. 1871. *Clubs:* St James's, Mount Royal, Forest and Stream, Royal Montreal Golf, Polo and Country, Lake Placid, Montreal.

Died 3 Oct. 1947.

BOND, William Linskill; HM Consul-General, Marseilles, 1948; *b* 24 Nov. 1892; *s* of Francis and Ada Bond; *m* 1934, Garth Winifred Faith Lindrea Boissevain. *Educ:* Whitgift School. Entered Consular Service in 1913; was attached to Residency in Cairo in 1915 and 1916 and to Legation in Athens in 1917; served as Vice Consul in Crete, Turkey and Morocco; Agent and Consul in Jedda 1929; Consul, Athens 1930; Addis Ababa, 1932, Casablanca, 1937–40; Foreign Office, 1940–42; Consul-Gen. Casablanca, 1942–43; Counsellor of Embassy and Consul-General, Cairo, 1943–48. *Recreations:* shooting, polo, golf, tennis. *Address:* c/o Foreign Office, SW1.

Died 12 Oct. 1950.

BONE, John Wardle, MB, CM Edin. (1st Class Honours) 1891; BSc Edin. 1895; Hon. LLD Edin. 1946; President and Consulting Surgeon Luton and Dunstable Hospital, Luton; Treasurer of General Medical Council; Treasurer and Member of Council British Medical Association; Member of Poisons Board, Home Office; *b* 1869; *e s* of late Jacob Rowell Bone, Newcastle-on-Tyne; *m* 1900, Alice (*d* 1932), *e d* of late Henry Durler, Luton; two *s* one *d. Educ:* School of Science (now Rutherford College) Newcastle-on-Tyne; Edinburgh University. In general medical practice 1896–1933; Hon. Medical Officer Bute Hospital, Luton, 1898–1933; Hon. Medical Superintendent Children's Hospital, Luton, 1911–33; Member of Departmental Committee on Morphine and Heroin Addiction, Ministry of Health; Member of Departmental Committee on Training of Midwives, Ministry of Health. *Address:* Rookwood, 76 New Bedford Road, Luton. *TA:* and *T:* Luton 286. *Clubs:* Royal Thames Yacht, Savile.

Died 14 April 1949.

BONHAM, Lt-Col Charles Barnard, DSO 1918; late RE; *b* 1871; *s* of late Admiral C. W. Bonham, RN; *m* 1900, Camille Claire, *sister* of 6th Marquess Testaferrata-Olivier; two *s* two *d. Educ:* Wellington College. Served European War, 1914–19 (DSO, despatches twice, Italian Croix de Guerre); retired pay, 1923. *Address:* Chapel St Claire, Penzance.

Died 7 April 1943.

BONN, Sir Max J., KBE 1926; CBE 1923; *b* New York, 1877; *s* of late William B. Bonn. *Educ:* New York; University of Munich (1st in Economics and Statistics). Partner in Bonn & Co. (merchant bankers); 1921 Amalgamated with Helbert Wagg & Co., Ltd; Director of the Bank of London and South America, Ltd; and of the Helbert Wagg Holdings Ltd; Chairman of the United Glass Bottle Manufacturers, Ltd; Hon. Lieutenant RNVR, 1917–19; Chairman London Regional Advisory Council for Juvenile Employment; Member of Forster Committee of Enquiry on Recruitment of Juvenile Labour in the Coal Mining Industry, 1942; Treasurer, Inoculation Department, St Mary's Hospital; Trustee, Camperdown House, Aldgate, E1; Chairman of Council, Jewish Lads' Brigade; Silver Jubilee Medal, 1935; Coronation Medal, 1937. *Address:* Upper Ifold, Dunsfold, Surrey; 18 Bryanston Court, George Street, W1. *T:* Paddington 3121.

Died 25 March 1943.

BONNER-SMITH, David; *see* Smith, D. B.

BONNEY, Rev. Edwin; Professor of Sacred Eloquence and Senior English Master, Ushaw College; *b* Blackburn, 1873. *Educ:* Ushaw College, Durham. Priest, 1901; Choirmaster at Ushaw, 1899–1918; Editor of Ushaw Magazine, 1903–15; Librarian at Ushaw 1902–27. *Publications:* Life and Letters of John Lingard, 1912; many articles in Catholic Encyclopædia, Ushaw Magazine, and other periodicals. *Address:* St Cuthbert's College, Ushaw, Durham.

Died 27 June 1946.

BONUS, Col William John, DSO 1900; *b* 9 July 1862; *s* of late General Bonus, JP. *Educ:* Harrow; Sandhurst. Joined Dorset Regt, 1883; commanded 1906–10; served in India and Egypt; ADC, 1895; DAAG Scottish District to 1899; served with Dorset Regt in Natal till relief of Ladysmith, afterwards as DAAG 4th Division (Queen's medal 5 clasps, King's medal 2 clasps, despatches); European War, served as AQMG 4 Aug. 1914–July 1916, and subsequently in other capacities till Peace proclaimed, 1919. *Club:* Naval and Military.

Died 21 Oct. 1943.

BONWICK, Alfred James; JP; *b* London, 1 Nov. 1883; *o s* of James Bonwick and Elizabeth Fowler; *m* 1909, Florence Elizabeth, *y d* of late Major W. Robinson; one *d. Educ:* Chippenham Division of Wiltshire, 1922–24; a Liberal Whip, 1924; Member of the Committee of Enquiry into Government Printing Establishments, 1923–27. *Address:* Lingmell, Parsonage Road, Horsham, Sussex.

Died 4 Sept. 1949.

BOOME, Brig.-Gen. Edward Herbert, CB 1918; CMG 1917; late 102nd (King Edward's Own) Grenadiers, Indian Army; *b* 1865; *m* Margaret May Wharton; one *s* one *d.* Served Chin-Lushai Expedition, 1889–90; China, 1900; Tibet, 1902–03; European War (Mesopotamia), 1915–18 (despatches, CB, CMG); brevet Colonecy, 1916; retired, 1920.

Died 17 Jan. 1945.

BOOT, Sir Horace, Kt 1942; MInstCE; MIMechE; MIEE; chartered civil, mechanical and electrical engineer; Chairman and Founder of the Eastwood Group of Companies; *b* 1873; *m* 1915, Mabel Jane (*d* 1941), *d* of late Charles Baker, Holt. *Educ:* City of London School. Sheriff of City of London, 1940–41; Master of Cutlers Company, 1936–37; Liveryman of Loriners Company; a Governor of Sheffield University; Life Member of National Trust; Member (retired) of Lloyd's; President of National Federation of Clay Industries, 1939–41; President of Institute of Arbitrators, 1923–24; President, Institute of Clayworkers, 1935–37; President, Institution of Municipal Engineers, 1913; President, Royal East Berks Agricultural Assoc., 1938; Chairman since 1933 of Bisham and Hurley Branch of Conservative and Unionist Assoc., Windsor Division.

Recreations: work, yachting and hunting, motoring. *Address:* Clarefield Court, Pinkney's Green, Maidenhead. *T:* Maidenhead 1221 and 243. *Clubs:* Carlton, City Livery, United Wards, etc.

Died 31 March 1943.

BOOTH, Sir Alfred (Allen), 1st Bt *cr* 1916; sometime Chairman of Cunard Steamship Ltd; Director of Alfred Booth & Co., Ltd; *b* 17 Sept. 1872; *y s* of late Alfred Booth, JP, of Liverpool; *m* 1st, 1903, Mary, Blake (*d* 1924), *d* of Edmund Dwight, of New York; two *s* one *d*; 2nd, 1925, Margaret Lucy (*d* 1943), *d* of late Charles Edward Brightwen. *Educ:* Harrow; King's College, Cambridge (Wrangler, 1894). Hon. LLD Liverpool; Member of the Royal Commission on the Civil Service, 1911–14; Chairman of the Board of Trade Committee on the shipping and Shipbuilding Industries, and Member of Lord Balfour of Burleigh's Committee on Commercial and Industrial Policy, 1916; Chairman of the Liverpool Committee for the Co-ordination of the Naval, Military and Civil Requirements of the Port, 1915–19. *Heir: s* Philip [*b* 8 Feb. 1907; *m* 1935, Stella Fenton Wood, *d* of late I. J. Gerr]. *Address:* Barton Hatch, Limpsfield, Surrey. *T:* Limpsfield Chart 2138. *Club:* Alpine.

Died 13 March 1948.

BOOTH, Evangeline Cory, General of the Salvation Army (retired); DSM; MA; LLD; Order of the Founder SA; Fairfax medal for Eminent Patriotic Service, 1928; Vasa Gold Medal (Sweden); Gold Medal National Institute of Social Science (USA) (1933); 7th *c* of late General William Booth. Had charge of the work successively in Great Britain, Canada, and Newfoundland, and 1904–34 National Commander in the United States; General of the Salvation Army, 1934–39; retired from active service, 1939. Orator, musician, poet, and composer of many songs. *Publications:* Love is All; Songs of the Evangel, 1927; Towards a Better World, a volume of Sermons, 1929; Woman, 1930; numerous contributions to principal magazines and newspapers. *Address:* c/o 120 West 14th Street, New York, NY.

Died 17 July 1950.

BOOTH, Frederick Handel; retired Ironmaster; *b* near Manchester, 1867; *m* Alice Lockwood Ellis. *Educ:* Bolton le Moor High School. Contested King's Lynn, 1900; Wentworth, 1918; MP (L) Pontefract, 1910–18. *Recreations:* bowls, chess. *Address:* Hampden, Fernden Lane, Haslemere. *Clubs:* Windlesham, Hove.

Died 24 Feb. 1947.

BOOTH, Sir Josslyn (Augustus Richard) Gore-, 6th Bt *cr* 1760; *b* 25 Feb. 1869; *s* of 5th Bt and Georgina, *o d* of late Col C. J. Hill of Tickhill Castle, Yorks; *S* father, 1900; *m* 1907, Mary, *d* of Rev. S. L'E. Malone; three *s* four *d*. Owns property in Salford, Manchester. *Recreation:* horticulture. *Heir: s* Michael Savile, *b* 24 July 1908. *Address:* Lissadel, Sligo.

Died 14 March 1944.

BOOTHBY, Comdr Hubert Basil, DSO, 1915; RNR; Life Governor of the Royal National Lifeboat Institution; *b* 1863; *m* 1912, Frances Ann, *d* of late John Carr Good, Grimsby. Served European War, 1914–15 (despatches, DSO). *Publication:* Spunyarn, 1935. *Address:* Summerlea, 37 South Terrace, Littlehampton. *T:* Littlehampton 298.

Died 10 Nov. 1941.

BOOTHBY, Sir Robert Tuite, KBE 1929; CA; Manager of the Scottish Provident Institution, and a Director of the Bank of Scotland; *b* 1871; *s* of late Col R. T. Boothby, St Andrews, Fife; *m* 1898, Mabel, *d* of late Henry H. Lancaster, Advocate; one *s. Educ:* St Andrews. A member of the Royal Company of Archers (HM Bodyguard for Scotland). *Recreations:* golf (Captain of the

Royal and Ancient Golf Club of St Andrews, 1921); shooting. *Address:* Beechwood, Murrayfield, Edinburgh. *Clubs:* Windham; New, Edinburgh.

Died 7 Feb. 1941.

BOOTY, Vice-Adm. Edward Leonard, CB 1916; MVO 1911; Officer, Légion d'Honneur, 1918; *b* 19 May 1871; *s* of late Edward Booty, of St Leonards-on-Sea; *m* 1911. Training ship Worcester, 1884; Naval Cadet, RN, 1886; Sub-Lieutenant, 1890; Lieutenant, 1892; Commander, 1903; Captain, 1908; Commodore, 1915–17; Rear-Adm. 1920; served in Brass River (1895), M'weli (1895), and Benin (1897) Expeditions (General Africa medal and clasps); Master of the Fleet for the Coronation Naval Review at Spithead, 1911; Ariadne; Dryad (Navigation School), 1912–14; Otway, 10th Cruiser Squadron, 1914–17 (1914–15 Star, General Service and Victory Medals); Admiralty 1917–20; retired, 1921; Vice-Admiral retired, 1925. *Address:* 1 Chepstow Crescent, W11.

Died 8 March 1949.

BOREEL, Sir Francis William Robert, 11th Bt *cr* 1645; *b* 19 March 1882; *s* of late Robert Eugene Boreel; *S* kinsman 1937. *Heir: b* Alfred [*b* 1883; *m* 1st, 1911, Countess Aletta Cornelia Anna (*d* 1913), *d* of Count Francis David Schimmelpenninck; 2nd, 1919, Countess Reiniera Adriana, *d* of Count Francis David Schimmelpenninck; one *s* one *d*]. *Address:* 225 East 51st Street, Los Angeles, California.

Died 1 June 1941.

BORENIUS, Tancred, Grand Cross of the Order of St Sava, of the Order of Charles III, and of the Order of St Anne; Knight Commander of the Order of the White Rose of Finland, of the Order of Our Lady of the Conception of Villa Viçosa, of the Order of St Gregory the Great and of the Order of Polonia Restituta; Grand Officer of the Order of the Grand Duke Gediminas of Lithuania; Officer of the Legion of Honour; Knight of the Order of the Fleur-de-Lis and the Order of SS Mauritius and Lazarus; Officer d'Académie; Associate Officer of the Order of St John of Jerusalem; PhD, DLit; FSA; Professor of History of Art, University College, London, 1922–47; Lecturer since 1914; Secretary to the Diplomatic Mission notifying the independence of Finland to Great Britain, France, Belgium, Spain, Italy, and the Holy See, 1918; Temporary Diplomatic Representative of Finland in England, 1919; Secretary, Finnish Delegation to Economic Conference, London, 1933; Member of the Finska Vetenskaps Societeten, Helsingfors; Conseiller d'honneur of the Chambre Internationale des Experts d'art, Paris; Managing Director and Hon. Acting Editor, 1940–45, of The Burlington Magazine, Ltd; took the initiative to, and directed excavations of Clarendon Palace, near Salisbury, 1933; Commissioner for England, Leonardo da Vinci Exhibition, Milan, 1939; Hon. Secretary-General, Polish Relief Fund, 1939; Hon. Appeal Director, Finland Fund, 1940; *b* Wiborg, Finland, 1885; *s* of late Carl Borenius, Conseiller de Commerce and sometime member of Finnish Diet; *m* 1909, Anne-Marie Runeberg, *g d* of J. L. Runeberg, the poet; one *s* two *d. Educ:* Svenska Klassiska Lyceum, Wiborg; Helsingfors University. *Publications:* The Painters of Vicenza, 1909; Italian Trans, 1912; new edition of Crowe and Cavalcaselle's History of Painting in North Italy, 1912; Catalogue of the Collection of Sir Frederick Cook, vol. i (Italian Schools), 1913; vols v and vi of authorised new edition of Crowe and Cavalcaselle's History of Painting in Italy, 1914; Pictures by Old Masters, Library of Christ Church, Oxford, 1916; The Picture Gallery of Andrea Vendramin; Catalogue of Viscount Lee of Fareham's Collection, vols I and II; Four Early Italian Engravers, 1923; English Primitives, 1924; Forty London Statues, 1926; English Mediæval Painting, 1927 (with Prof. E. W. Tristram; also in German); Memorial Volume on Flemish Exhibition, Burlington House, 1927 (Section Pictures); The Iconography of St Thomas of Canterbury, 1929; Florentine Frescoes, 1930;

The Leverton Harris Collection, 1931; St Thomas Becket in Art, 1932; Catalogue of the Pictures and Drawings in the Collection of the Earl of Harewood, 1936; Catalogue of the Collection of Drawings of Sir Robert Mond, 1937 (with Dr R. Wittkower); English Painting in the XVIIIth Century, 1938 (also in French); Field-Marshal Mannerheim, 1940; on Art and Connoisseurship (translation from Max J. Friedlander), 1941; Rembrandt, 1942; Italian Painting and later Italian Painting, 1945; Dutch Indoor Subjects, 1946; Sieuese Paintings, 1946, etc.; Editor of University College (London) Monographs on English Mediaeval Art. *Recreation:* growing of trees. *Address:* Stocks Bridge Cottage, Coombe Bissett, Wiltshire. *T:* Coombe Bissett 257. *Clubs:* St James's, Sette of Odd Volumes.

Died 2 Sept. 1948.

BORLAND, Captain John MacInnes, CB 1923; DSO 1917; RD, RNR; retired Commander, Peninsular and Oriental Company; *b* 1869; *s* of Andrew Borland, merchant, Glasgow, and Helen Hunter; *m* 1901, Christian (*d* 1938), *e d* of Rev. George Gladstone. *Educ:* private schools. At sea in Australian clippers, 1884–94; in the service of the Peninsular and Oriental Company, 1894–1929; Sub-Lt RNR, 1894; as Acting-Lt RNR, served on HMS Goliath during China War, 1900, and with landing party at Shanhai Kwan (medal); Lieutenant, 1901; Commander, 1914; on patrol services, North Sea, 1914–17; Commander-in-Charge of Grand Fleet Armed Boarding Steamers; Commodore of Scandinavian Convoys, 1918; Captain RNR, 1919 (Chevalier Legion of Honour, DSO, CB); Younger Brother of Trinity House. *Address:* Ballantrae, Ayrshire.

Died 15 May 1946.

BORLAND, Kenneth Alexander; Sheriff Substitute of Argyll at Campbeltown since 1942; *s* of William Borland, Writer, Glasgow; *m* Ethel Margaret Russell; one *s* two *d. Educ:* Glasgow Academy; Glasgow University. *Address:* Rosemount, Campbeltown, Argyll.

Died 23 March 1948.

BORLAND, Rev. William, MA, DD; Minister Emeritus of the Scots Church, Melbourne; Minister, 1913–35; *b* Dumfriesshire, 3 Aug. 1867; *s* of late William Borland, farmer at Townfoot, Dumfriesshire, and North Balloch, Ayrshire; *m* 1898, Sophie Frances, *d* of late Thomas Wilson, Glasgow; three *s* three *d. Educ:* Ayr Academy; Wallacehall Academy, Closeburn; Edinburgh University (MA, DD); University of Jena and University of Berlin. Asst Minister of Glasgow Cathedral, 1893–95; Minister of Rosemount Parish, Aberdeen, 1895–1901; Dunbar, East Lothian, 1901–13; President of the Melbourne College of Divinity, 1935–36; Chairman of Council of Ormond Coll., Melbourne Univ., 1926–42; Moderator of the Presbyterian Church of Victoria (1930–31). *Publication:* formerly editor of In Far Fields, the foreign mission magazine of the Church of Scotland. *Recreations:* reading and bowls. *Address:* Glenard, Wellesley Road, Hawthorn E2, Victoria, Australia. *T:* Hawthorn 6853.

Died 15 Aug. 1945.

BORRADAILE, Brig.-Gen. Harry Benn, DSO 1895; late IA; *b* 4 Oct. 1860; *e s* of A. A. Borradaile, late Bombay Civil Service; *m* 1890, Florence (*d* 1935), *o c* of H. Soden; one *s* three *d. Educ:* Charterhouse. Entered army, 1880; Captain, 1891; Brevet-Major, 1895; Major, 1900; Lt-Colonel, 1904; Brevet-Colonel, 1907; Substantive Col 1912; Commanded the 34th Sikh Pioneers, 1902–09; served Burmah, 1885–89 (medal with two clasps); with Sikkim Expeditionary Force, 1889; Chitral, 1895 (despatches, Bt-Maj., DSO, medal with clasp); retired, 1913; served European War, 1915 (wounded); hon. rank of Brig.-Gen. 1919. *Address:* 18 Egerton Gardens, SW3; The Beeches, Barcombe, Sussex. *Club:* Naval and Military.

Died 21 Aug. 1948.

BORRADAILE, Lancelot Alexander, ScD; Fellow since 1913 of Selwyn College, Cambridge; *b* 26 Sept. 1872; *s* of J. O. Borradaile; unmarried. *Educ:* Felsted School; Selwyn College, Cambridge. Nat. Sci. Tripos Part I Class I, 1893; BA, 1893; Scholar, 1893; Nat. Sci. Tripos Part II Class I, 1894. Lecturer at Selwyn College, 1895–1937; Demonstrator in Animal Morphology in the University, 1909–10; Lecturer in Zoology in the University, 1910–37; Dean of Selwyn College, 1912–20; Tutor of Selwyn College, 1920–37. *Publications:* A Manual of Zoology, 1912; The Animal and its Environment, 1923; The Invertebrata (with other authors), 1932; numerous memoirs on zoological subjects. *Address:* 31 Grange Road, Cambridge.

Died 20 Oct. 1945.

BORRETT, Lt-Gen. Sir Oswald Cuthbert, KCB 1937 (CB 1923); CMG 1918; CBE 1922; DSO 1915; *b* 4 March 1878; 5th *s* of late Major-General H. C. Borrett, CB; *m* Blanche, *d* of Col A. Murray. *Educ:* Wellington College. Entered Army, King's Own Royal Regt, 1898; Capt. 1902; Adjt 1905–08; Maj. 1914; Col 1923; Maj.-Gen. 1930; Adjt Indian Volunteers, 1911–14; served S Africa, 1899–1902 (Queen's medal 3 clasps, King's medal 2 clasps); European War, 1914–19 (DSO and bar, Bt Lt-Col, Bt Col, ADC to the King, 1915 Star, CMG, Chevalier Légion d'Honneur); NW Frontier, India, 1920–21 (medal and bar, Waziristan, CBE, CB); Col Comdt 7th Indian Infantry Bde, 1923–27; ADC to the King, 1919–30; commanded British Troops, Shanghai Area, 1927–31; Commander 46th (North Midland) Division TA, 1931–32; GOC British Troops in China, 1932–35; Lieutenant Tower of London, 1936–39; retired pay, 1938; Colonel the King's Own Royal Regiment (Lancaster), 1926–45. *Address:* c/o Cox & Co., 6 Pall Mall, SW1. *Club:* United Service.

Died 28 July 1950.

BORWICK, 2nd Baron *cr* 1922; **George Borwick;** Bt *cr* 1916; *b* 22 May 1880; *e s* of 1st Baron; *S* father 1936; *m* 1st, 1908, Mary Mason, *d* of Lewis Cruger Hasell of New York (marr. diss. 1913); 2nd, Dorothea Gertrude (from whom he obtained a divorce, 1938; she *m* 2nd, 1939, Sir H. Gordon Ley), *d* of late Charles Grey of Anerley. *Educ:* Eton; New College, Oxford (BA Jurisprudence). Barrister-at-Law, Middle Temple, 1905; contested (Liberal Unionist) Barnstaple Division, Jan. 1910; (Unionist) Eye Division, Dec. 1910; served European War, Bedfordshire Regt, 1914–16, and RAF, 1916–18. *Recreations:* fishing, tennis, golf. *Heir: b* Hon. (Robert) Geoffrey Borwick. *Address:* 1 Albert Court, SW7. *T:* Kensington 9854. *Club:* Bath.

Died 27 Jan. 1941.

BOSANQUET, Vivian Henry Courthope; Hon. Life Member of Royal Institute of Public Health, 1931; received Freedom of University of Frankfort-on-Main, May 1931; *b* 13 April 1872; *y s* of late S. Courthope Bosanquet of Dingestow Court, Monmouth; *m* 1912, Dorothy Mary Cautley, *o d* of late Charles Moule, Senior Fellow and President of Corpus Christi College, Cambridge; one *s* one *d. Educ:* Eton; Trinity College, Cambridge. Vice-Consul at Odessa, 1901; transferred to Nicolaieff, 1905; to Drama and Serres, Turkey, 1906; to Rio de Janeiro, 1908; and to Moscow, 1910; HM Consul at Riga, 1911; Political Adviser to British Admiral Commanding in the Baltic, 1918–19; Representative of HM Government at Reval, with local rank of Consul-General, April to Nov. 1919; Assistant Commissioner on S Baltic Commission, 1919; Consul at Nantes, 1920; HBM Consul-General at Frankfort-on-Main, 1924–32. *Recreations:* travel, Oriental ceramics and antiques. *Address:* Beechingstoke Manor, Marlborough. *Club:* Athenæum.

Died 25 Dec. 1943.

BOSANQUET, William Cecil, MD, FRCP; Consulting Physician to Charing Cross Hospital and to Brompton Hospital for Consumption; Physician to London Lock Hospital; *s* of late Admiral G. S. Bosanquet. *Educ:* Eton; New College, Oxford (Fellow, 1890–97). *Publications:* Meditatio Medici, 1937; various books on pathology. *Address:* 59 Springfield Road, NW8. *T:* Maida Vale 8841.

Died 24 Jan. 1941.

BOSCAWEN, Rt Hon. Sir Arthur Sackville Trevor G.; *see* Griffith-Boscawen.

BOSTOCK, Rev. Charles; Master of St Cross Hospital and Minister of St Faith's Parish, Winchester since 1936; *b* 10 Feb. 1869; *s* of John Stileman and Emily Bostock; *m* 1902, Olive Marian Palmer; one *s* three *d*. *Educ:* Highgate School; Selwyn College, Cambridge; Leeds Clergy School. Curate Aldmondbury, Huddersfield, 1892–97; Orgn Sec. SPG dio. Winchester, 1898–1902; Rector of N Waltham, 1902–06; Vicar of Lymington, Hants, 1906–22; Rural Dean of Lyndhurst, 1917–22; Vicar of St Ambrose Bournemouth, 1922–36; Rural Dean of Bournemouth, 1933–36. *Publication:* History of Lymington Church. *Recreation:* motoring. *Address:* Master's Lodge, St Cross Hospital, Winchester. *T:* Winchester 888.

Died 9 Jan. 1943.

BOSTON, 6th Baron *cr* 1761; **George Florance Irby;** Bt 1704, DL, MA, FGS, FSA; LLD (Hon.) Wales; *b* 6 Sept. 1860; *s* of 5th Baron and Hon. Augusta Caroline, 2nd *d* of 3rd Lord de Saumarez (who married, 2nd, late Sir H. P. Anderson); *S* father, 1877; *m* 1890, Cecilia (*d* 1938), *d* of Hon. Augustus A. F. Irby, Hillingdon Grove, near Uxbridge. Anglican. *Educ:* Eton; Christ Church, Oxford. Lord-in-Waiting to HM, 1885–86. *Heir: nephew* Greville Northey Irby, *b* 24 Aug. 1889. *Address:* Monkshatch, Compton, Guildford; Lligwy, Moelfre, Anglesey; 266a St James's Court, SW1.

Died 16 Sept. 1941.

BOSWORTH SMITH, Reginald Montagu, CBE 1929; *b* 1872; 3rd *s* of late R. Bosworth Smith of Binghams Melcombe, Dorset; *m* 1st, Agnes Val Davies; 2nd, Kate Evelyn Radclyffe; two *s* three *d*. *Educ:* Harrow. Four years farming in Florida till 1893; Central SA Railways, 1894; Sub-Inspector Basutoland Military Police, 1895; Inspector, 1905; Assistant Commissioner, 1909; Acting Deputy Resident Commissioner various periods, 1920–28; Government Secretary, Basutoland Administration, 1920–30. *Recreations:* golf, tennis, shooting. *Address:* The Knoll, Kowie West, Cape, SA. *Clubs:* Basutoland; Port Alfred Golf.

Died 18 Oct. 1944.

BOTTOMLEY, Albert Ernest, RBA, ARCA; *b* Leeds, 1 March 1873; *e s* of Samuel and Alexandrina Bottomley, Leeds; *m* Emily Frances, *d* of late John Frederick Green, Stoke-on-Trent and Rhyl; one *d*. *Educ:* Leeds Middle Class Schools. Intended for commercial career, but love for paint and brushes proved too strong. Exhibited New English Art Club. Royal Academy (some 32 paintings), Royal Institute of Oils and Water Colours, Goupil Gallery Salon, in British Japanese Exhibition, 1911, Venice International, 1924; Worthing and Leeds Corporation Galleries, 1923, and most Provincial Galleries; works purchased by Leeds, Bolton, and Worthing Corporations. *Recreations:* reading, gardening. *Address:* Westbury, Dovers Green, Reigate, Surrey. *T:* Reigate 4410.

Died 25 Aug. 1950.

BOTTOMLEY, Gordon; author; *b* Keighley, 20 Feb. 1874; *m* 1905, Emily (*d* 1947), *y d* of Matthew Burton, of Arnside. *Educ:* Keighley Grammar School. President, Scottish Community Drama Assoc.; Vice-Pres., British Drama League; awarded Femina Prize, Paris, 1923; Benson Medal of Royal Soc. of Literature, 1925; FRSL, 1926; LLD Aberdeen, 1930; DLitt Durham, 1940; LittD

Leeds, 1944. *Publications:* The Gate of Smaragdus, 1904; Chambers of Imagery—two series, 1907, 1912; A Vision of Giorgione, 1910; King Lear's Wife and other plays (King Lear's Wife, 1915; The Crier by Night, 1902: The Riding to Lithend, 1909; Midsummer Eve, 1905; Laodice and Danaë, 1909), 1920; Gruach and Britain's Daughter, 1921; Poems of Thirty Years, 1925; Scenes and Plays, 1929; Festival Preludes, 1930; Lyric Plays, 1932; The Acts of St Peter (Exeter Cathedral Festival Play), 1933; The White Widow (Scottish One-Act Plays, 1936); The Falconer's Lassie (25 One-Act Plays, 1937); Choric Plays, 1939; Ealasaid (Fifty One-Act Plays, 2nd Ser., 1940); Before Daybreak (for music), 1941; Deirdire (play in English and Gaelic), 1944; Kate Kennedy; comedy in three acts, 1945; Maids of Athers (1 Act) (Private issue, 1946); Crookback's Crown (Private issue, 1947); A Stage for Poetry, 1948; Contributions to Georgian Poetry, 1912–1919, and an Annual of New Poetry, 1917. *Recreations:* literature and music. *Address:* The Sheiling, Silverdale, near Carnforth. *TA:* Sheiling, Silverdale, Lancs. *T:* Silverdale 211.

Died 25 Aug. 1948.

BOUGHTON, Rev. Canon Charles Henry Knowler, BD; Vicar of St John the Baptist, Knighton, since 1928; Canon Theologian of Leicester since 1932; Canon Residentiary of Leicester Cathedral since 1937; Proctor in Convocation, 1937; Rural Dean of Christianity, 1938; Examining Chaplain to the Bishop of Leicester, 1929; *b* Leicester, 6 Jan. 1883; *s* of late Rev. Thomas Boughton, MA; *m* 1912, Evelyn Mabel, *d* of late Francis Michael Cotton, MInstCE, formerly Engineer of Holyhead Harbour; three *d*. *Educ:* Faversham Grammar School; Wadham College, Oxford. (2nd Class Classical Mod.; 2nd Class Mathemat. Mod.; 1st Class Lit. Hum.; 1st Class Theology; Abbott Scholar; Aubrey Moore Student; Senior Greek Testament Prize). Ordained 1907; Chaplain and Vice-Principal of Wycliffe Hall, Oxford, 1907–12; Lecturer of Parish Church, Bolton, 1912; Principal of Ripon Clergy College, 1912–15; Vicar of Calverly, 1915–22; Diocesan Inspector of Schools, Bradford, 1915–22; Secretary Bradford Diocesan Board of Finance, 1920–22; Secretary, British and Foreign Bible Society, 1922–28; Hon. Canon of Bradford, 1921–22; Commissary to the Bishop of Gippsland, 1917–42. *Publications:* Talks to Teachers in Sunday Schools, 1918; The Faith of a Churchman, 1919; The Meaning of Holy Baptism, 1920; The Quest for Happiness, 1935. *Address:* St John's Vicarage, St Mary's Road, Leicester. *T:* Leicester 7531.

Died 30 Dec. 1943.

BOUGHTON-KNIGHT, Charles Andrew R.; *see* Rouse-Boughton-Knight.

BOULENGER, Edward George; Director Zoological Society's Aquarium, 1923–43; Curator of Reptiles and Lower Vertebrates in the Society's Gardens, 1911–23 and 1937–43; *b* 8 May 1888; *s* of late G. A. Boulenger, FRS; *m* 1914, Margaret, *d* of late Rev. A. A. Carre; one *d*. *Educ:* St Paul's School. Balloon observer in 1914–18 war; General Staff, War Office, 1939. Part designer of Zoological Society's Aquarium. *Publications:* Reptiles and Batrachians, Queer Fish, The Aquarium Book; A Naturalist at the Zoo; A Naturalist at the Dinner-Table; Animal Mysteries; The Under-Water World, Animals in the Wild and in Captivity; Animal Ways; The Zoo Cavalcade; Infants at the Zoo; A Natural History of the Seas; Apes and Monkeys; Searchlight on Animals; The London Zoo; World Natural History, etc.; numerous articles of a natural history nature; a regular contributor to the Proceedings of the Zoological Society. *Address:* Nursling House, Nursling, Hants. *Club:* Savile.

Died 30 April 1946.

BOULTON, A. C. Forster; JP Surrey; barrister; *b* Port Hope, Ontario, Canada, 1862; *o s* of late James Forster Boulton, barrister, Ottawa, Canada, and Moulton, Lincs, and Jane, *d* of Col Graham, 75th Regiment, and *g d* of late General Graham, Governor of Stirling Castle; *m* 1891, Florence (*d* 1903), *o c* of late Henry Harms; one *d*. *Educ:* Trinity College School and Trinity College, Toronto. Sometime Lieut Royal Grenadiers, Canadian Militia; called to Canadian Bar, 1888; Inner Temple, 1896; South-eastern Circuit; Counsel to the Post Office at the Central Criminal Court, 1906–31 Commissioner to the Local Government Board under Military Service Act, Lancashire, 1916; and Arbitrator, Ministry Munitions; has travelled extensively through United States, Canada and Europe; Canadian Pacific Land Explorers, Rocky Mountains, 1885; MP (L) Ramsey Division Hunts, 1906–10; contested same division, 1910, and New Forest and Christchurch Div. of Hants, 1923. Joint founder with the late Sir Walter Besant of the Atlantic Union, now English-speaking Union. *Publications:* Adventures, Travels and Politics; The Law and Practice of a Case Stated, the Law of Criminal Appeal, Grant's Law of Banking, and various Canadian editions of English textbooks; Liberalism and the Empire. *Recreations:* cycling, travelling, motoring. *Address:* Shirley Holmes, Newdigate, Surrey. *T:* Newdigate 220. *Club:* English-Speaking Union.

Died 12 March 1949.

BOULTON, Sir William Whytehead, 1st Bt *cr* 1944; DL Essex; *b* 10 Jan. 1873; *s* of William Whytehead Boulton, JP Beverley, E Yorks, and Mary Hudleston, *d* of John Gibson, RN; *m* 1905, Rosalind Mary, *d* of Sir John Milburn, 1st Bt of Guyzance, Northumberland; three *s*. *Educ:* privately. MP (U) Central Sheffield, 1931–45; Lord Commissioner of the Treasury and Assistant Government Whip, 1940–42; Vice-Chamberlain, HM Household, 1942–44; late Lt Household Cavalry RHG Res. Regt, late Major 7th Batt. Essex Vol. Regt; Lord of Manors Great Braxted and Kelvedon Hall. *Heir: s* Major Edward John, *b* 11 April 1907. *Address:* Alresford Hall, nr Colchester, Essex. *T:* Wivenhoe 450. *Club:* Carlton.

Died 9 Jan. 1949.

BOURDILLON, Sir Bernard Henry, GCMG 1937; KCMG 1934; KBE 1931; CMG 1924; Knight of Grace of the Order of St John of Jerusalem, 1933; JP, MA (Oxon); Hon. Fellow of St John's College, Oxford; Member of Colonial Economic and Development Council; Member of Councils of Zoological and Royal Africa Societies; Chm. British Empire Leprosy Relief Assoc.; MBOU; Director of Barclay's Bank (DC & O) and of Barclay's Overseas Development Corp.; Chairman, Orion Property Trust; *b* Emu Bay, Tasmania, 3 Dec. 1883; *e s* of late Rev. B. K. Bourdillon; *m* 1909, Violet Grace, *e d* of late Rev. H. G. Billinghurst of Lynch, Sussex; two *s* (and one killed on duty in Jerusalem, 1946). *Educ:* Tonbridge; St John's College, Oxford. Joined Indian Civil Service, 1908; Under-Sec. to Government, United Provinces, 1913; Registrar, High Court, Allahabad, 1915; Temp. 2nd Lieut IARO, 1917; proceeded Mesopotamia, 1918; Temp. Captain, 1918; Major, 1919; despatches, Iraq Insurrection; Political Secretary to High Commissioner, 1921; Secretary, 1922; Counsellor, 1924–29; Acting High Commissioner, 1925–26, with powers plenipotentiary for negotiation of 1925 Anglo-Iraq Treaty; Colonial and Chief Secretary, Ceylon, 1929–32; Acting Governor in 1930 and 1931; Governor and Commander-in-Chief of Uganda, 1932–35; Governor and Commander-in-Chief of Nigeria, 1935–43. *Publication:* The Future of the Colonial Empire, 1945. *Recreations:* photography, ornithology. *Address:* Sandpits, Bepton, Midhurst, Sussex. *T:* Midhurst 184. *Club:* East India and Sports.

Died 6 Feb. 1948.

BOURDILLON, Lancelot Gerard, DSO 1916; MC; MB, BS; DPH; *b* 1888; *s* of late Rev. B. K. Bourdillon, Cape Town; *m* 1922, Sylvia Caroline, *d* of late Charles A. Reiss and Mrs Reiss, Hill House, Streatley; one *s* two *d*. Served European War, 1914–18 (despatches 6 times,

DSO, MC and bar, Brevet Major, Croix de Guerre). Served War of 1939–45, Col Army Medical Staff. *Address:* Stow House, Goring, Oxon.

Died 4 Jan. 1950.

BOURKE, Gp Captain Ulick John Deane, CMG 1918; retired; *b* April 1884; *o s* of Sir George Bourke, KCMG, CB; *m* 1917, Irene (from whom he obtained a divorce in 1934), *y surv. d* of Lewis Ashhurst, Norwich; one *d*. *Educ:* Cheltenham College; Sandhurst. Oxfordshire Light Infantry, 1903; RFC, 1913; served European War with RFC and RAF (CMG, despatches twice); retired, 1930. *Recreations:* hunting, golf, fishing, etc. *Address:* 30 Frenchgate, Richmond, Yorks. *Club:* Junior United Service.

Died 4 March 1948.

BOURNE, Thomas Johnstone, CBE 1919; MInstCE; *b* 4 June 1864; *s* of late Rev. S. W. Bourne, BA, and Mary Caroline, *d* of late Henry Cassin, MD; *m* Edith Mary, *y d* of H. W. Bridges; two *s* one *d*. *Educ:* St Edmond's School. Canterbury; King's Coll. School. Whitworth Exhib., 1888; Associated with Chinese Government Railways from 1889 and later with S. Pearson & Son, Ltd; Engineer-in-Chief Pu Sin Railway, 1913; Chia Huo decoration, China, 1913; War Office Representative for the Recruitment of the Chinese Labour Corps at Wei-hai-wei and Tsingtao, 1916–18; Deputy Agent, Makwar Dam, Sudan, 1923.

Died 27 Jan. 1947.

BOUSFIELD, William Robert, KC; FRS 1916; *b* 1854; *s* of E. T. Bousfield, Bedford; *m* 1879, Florence (*d* 1919), *d* of George Kelly, Shanklin, IW. *Educ:* Bedford Modern School; Caius College, Cambridge. College scholarship, 1873; Whitworth Scholar, 1873; 16th Wrangler, 1876; MA, 1879. Barrister, 1880; QC, 1891; Bencher, Inner Temple, 1897; contested Mid-Lanark (C), 1885, 1888; MP (C) Hackney N, 1892–1906. *Publications:* A Neglected Complex; The Basis of Memory; The Mind and its Mechanism. *Address:* St Swithin's, West Hill, Ottery St Mary, S Devon.

Died 16 July 1943.

BOUSTEAD, Rev. Canon Harry Wilson, DD; *b* 25 Oct. 1858; *s* of John Boustead and Augusta Twentyman; *m* 1909, Kathleen Louisa Nash. *Educ:* Eagle House, Wimbledon; Harrow; Magdalen College, Oxford; Ely Theological College. Curate of St Mark's, Swindon, 1882–91; Vicar of All Saints with All Hallows, Bristol, 1891–1905; Vicar of Basingstoke, 1905–36. *Recreations:* association football, rowed in college boat, Head of River, 1880, violinist. *Address:* 4 Berkeley Place, Wimbledon, SW19.

Died 6 Sept. 1942.

BOUTENS, Dr Peter Cornelis; Man of Letters; President, Society of Dutch Authors; Hon. President, Literary Club (Dutch PEN Club), etc; *b* Middleburg, Isle of Walcheren, 20 Feb. 1870. *Educ:* Utrecht University. *Publications:* Verzen, 1898; Præludiën, 1902; Sonnetten, 1907; Stemmen, 1907; Beatrys, 1908; Vergeten Liedjes, 1910; Carmina, 1912; Lentemaan, 1916; Liederen van Isoude, 1921; Zomerwolken, 1922; Louise Labé, 1925; Oud-Perzische Kwatrynen, 1927; Egidius; Alexis; Bezonnen Liedjes, 1929; Aan W. A. van Konynenburg; Morgengedachten, 1930; Bezonnen Verzen, 1931; Andries de Hoghe, 1932; Hollandsche Kwatrynen, 1933; Oudere Verzen, 1936; Homeros' Odyssee, 1937; Christus in Scheveningen, 1939; Translations from Homer, Æschylus, Sophocles, Plato, Sappho, Omar Khayyam, Goethe, Rossetti, Wilde, etc. *Address:* 49 Laan Copes van Cattenburch, The Hague, Holland. *T:* 112267. *Clubs:* Witte, The Hague.

Died 14 March 1943.

BOUTFLOWER, Rt Rev. Cecil Henry, DD; *b* Brathay, Windermere, 1863; *s* of Ven. S. P. Boutflower, formerly Archdeacon of Carlisle, and Margaret, *d* of Giles Redmayne of Brathay Hall; *m* 1933, Joyce, *d* of late

Rev. Halsall Segar. *Educ:* Uppingham, 1875–82; Christ Church, Oxford (Scholar, 2nd Class Mods, 2nd Class Lit. Hum., and Theol. Final Schools); MA 1889 and of Durham, 1895; Newdigate Prize Poem, 1884. Ordained, 1887; Curate of St Mary, South Shields, 1887–90; Domestic Chaplain to Bishop Westcott of Durham, 1890–1901; Vicar of St George's, Barrow-in-Furness, and Archdeacon of Furness; Examining Chaplain to the Bishop of Carlisle, 1901–05; Bishop of Dorking, 1905–09; Bishop of South Tokyo, 1909–21; Bishop of Southampton, 1921–33; Residentiary Canon of Winchester, 1925–33. *Address:* Paddock Brow, Boars Hill, Oxford.

Died 19 March 1942.

BOUVERIE, Col Hon. Stuart P.; *see* Pleydell-Bouverie.

BOVILL, Major Anthony Charles Stevens, MC; Master North Shropshire Hunt since 1934; *b* 17 Oct. 1888; *s* of late C. A. and late Hon. Mrs Bovill; *m* 1918, Eleanor Victoria Monins, Ringwould House, Kent; one *s* three *d*. *Educ:* Eton; RMC, Sandhurst. Joined 9th QR Lancers in 1909; served in France, 1914–18 (despatches, MC, Russian Order of St Anne); retired, 1919, with rank of Major; High Sheriff for Shropshire, 1942; Master of Isle of Wight Foxhounds, 1924–33. *Recreations:* hunting and fishing. *Address:* Mytton Hall, Montford, Bridge, Shrewsbury. *Club:* Cavalry.

Died 13 Oct. 1943.

BOVILLE, Thomas Cooper, CMG, 1912; Deputy Minister of Finance, 1906–20; *b* Grange, Co. Antrim, 14 March 1860; *m* 1905, Margaret Caroline Tapling, *d* of W. N. Silver, Halifax, NS. *Educ:* Toronto University. Went to Canada, 1874; entered Public Service, 1883. *Address:* Chester, Lunenburg Co., Nova Scotia.

Died 24 Aug. 1948.

BOWATER, Major Sir Frank H., 1st Bt *cr* 1939; Kt 1930; TD; Alderman of City of London, Bridge Without Ward; one of HM's Lieutenants of City of London; *b* Manchester, 3 April 1866; *s* of late William Vansittart Bowater of Bury Hall, Lower Edmonton; *m* 1891, Ethel Anita (*d* 1943), *d* of late Mark Fryar, Burmah; two *s* two *d*. *Educ:* Broughton College, Manchester. Major, 4th London Howitzer Brigade RFA TF; during period of war commanded battery in France, etc.; Sheriff of London, 1929–30; member LCC 1934–37 Lord Mayor of London, 1938–39; PGT of England (Masonic); Commander of Order of St John of Jerusalem; Chevalier of the Legion of Honour; Knight Grand Cross Order of the Crown of Roumania; Order Third Class Sacred Treasure of Japan. *Recreations:* golf, tennis, etc. *Heir: s* Noël Vansittart, MC. *Address:* The Warren, Friston, Suffolk. *Clubs:* Constitutional, Aldeburgh, etc.

Died 10 Nov. 1947.

BOWATER, Sir Rainald Vansittart, 2nd Bt *cr* 1914; *b* 27 Jan. 1888; *e s* of Sir T. Vansittart Bowater, 1st Bt, MP; *S* father 1938; *m* 1914, Ethel Maud Keeler-Grix; two *d*. *Educ:* Whitgift Grammar School; abroad. Joined father's business, 1905, and with same Company, originally W. V. Bowater and Sons, Ltd, now Bowaters and Lloyds Sales Co. Ltd until 1941. *Recreations:* cricket, hockey, golf. *Heir: b* Thomas Dudley Blennerhassett [*b* 29 Sept. 1889; *m* 1916, Kathleen Mary (*d* 1921), *d* of Albert A. Frost, Bayfield, Rugby; one *d*]. *Address:* The Summer House, Tongdean Avenue, Hove, Sussex. *T:* Preston 2501.

Died 2 March 1945.

BOWDEN, Lt-Col John, CVO 1944; OBE; MInstCE, MIMechE; Consulting Engineer, Privy Purse Office; *m* Constance (*d* 1945), *d* of Robert J. O. Hudson, Newcastle-on-Tyne. *Address:* St Margaret's Lodge, Merryhill Road, Bushey, Herts.

Died 20 Dec. 1948.

BOWDEN, Vivian Gordon, CBE 1941; Australian representative in Singapore, 1941; *b* Sydney, Australia, 28 May 1884; *s* of Vivian Rothwell Bowden and Marion Harrison Cazaly; *m* 1917, Dorothy Dennis; one *s* two *d*. *Educ:* Bedford School, England. In Australia till age of 12, then 2½ years in Yokohama, Japan, followed by nearly 3 years in England, 1½ years Germany, 2 years France (Lyons), 3 years, 1905–07, as silk inspector in Canton, China, 1908–14, in Japan (business); business trip round world, 1911; 1915–18, with BEF France (despatches); Deputy Asst Director of Docks, at Boulogne; demobilised, 1919, as Temp. Major RE; trading expedition to Black Sea, 1919; Japan, 1920–21; Shanghai, 1921; Australian Government Trade Commissioner in China, 1935–41. *Publications:* under nom-de-plume Vivian Gordon: The Skipper, 1929; Rumfy, 1930. *Recreations:* golf, walking. *[Interned Singapore, escaped, re-captured, killed 1942.]*

Died 17 Feb. 1942.

BOWDEN, William Douglas, CBE 1928; *b* 22 June 1875; *s* of Rev. J. Davis Bowden; unmarried. *Educ:* privately in Edinburgh and Dresden; MA (Edin.), 1901. Assistant Engineer, Sierra Leone Railway Construction, 1901–05; Assistant District Commissioner, 1905; District Commissioner, 1915; Provincial Commissioner, Sierra Leone, 1920–32; Acting Colonial Secretary, 1921–22; Acting Governor, Aug. 1928. *Recreations:* tennis, fishing, gardening. *Address:* Hobsburn, Hawick, Roxburghshire. *TA:* Bowden, Bonchester Bridge. *T:* Bonchester Bridge 12.

Died 24 April 1944.

BOWEN, David; KC 1938; Bencher of Lincoln's Inn; *b* 13 Feb. 1885; *s* of John and Eliza Bowen, Pentre, Rhondda; *m* 1912, Mabel Staniland Cobb. *Educ:* privately; University College, Cardiff. Lecturer in Geology, Mining and Mine Surveying, School of Mines, Camborne, Cornwall, 1908–09; Assistant Professor of Mining, University of Leeds, 1909–10; Head of the Mining Department, University of Leeds, 1911–13; Consulting Mining and Civil Engineer, 1911–14; served European War, Capt. 8th West Yorks Regt (TF); Seconded as Capt. RE (Tunnelling Companies), 1915–16, and Assistant Commanding Royal Engineers, Cannock Chase, 1917–19; admitted as student to Lincoln's Inn, 1919; Called to Bar, Lincoln's Inn, 1920; contested Aberdare Div. (Liberal) Oct. 1924, Neath (National), 1945. *Publications:* Mines and Quarries Acts, 1923; Vendors and Purchasers, 1922, 2nd ed. 1929; Law relating to Fixtures, 1923, 2nd ed. 1931, 3rd ed., 1947; Mines, Minerals and Quarries in Halsbury's Laws of England (Hailsham Edition); The Coal Act, 1938; Sections on Mines, Minerals and Quarries, and Trade Marks and Trade Names in Atkin's Court Forms and Precedents; Mining Statutes in Halsbury's Statutes of England (2nd ed.); numerous papers on mining matters in The Colliery Guardian, 1919–1938. *Recreations:* riding, golf, tennis. *Address:* 1 New Square, Lincoln's Inn, WC2. *T:* Holborn 0616.

Died 27 Nov. 1950.

BOWEN, Col Herbert Walter, CIE 1919; DSO 1918; late RA; *b* 19 Sept. 1870. Entered army, 1890; Col 1921; served Mesopotamia, 1914–18 (despatches, DSO); retired, 1924; Col Comdt Indian Army Ordnance Corps, 1931.

Died 8 Oct. 1944.

BOWER, Sir Alfred (Louis), 1st Bt *cr* 1925; Kt 1913; JP Alderman of the Langbourn Ward, 1918–41; one of HM Lieutenants for the City of London; late Trustee of Mordern College; *b* 8 Oct. 1858; *s* of Edward Thomas Bower and Hannah, *d* of William Tavernor, JP, Essex; *m* 1901, Dorcas Mona (*d* 1946), Dame of Grace of St John of Jerusalem, *d* of Captain Edward Algernon Blackett, RN, JP, DL, of Wylam, Northumberland and King's County, Ireland; one *d*. Sheriff of London, 1912–13; Lord Mayor of London, 1924–25; Governor of St

Thomas's, Christ's, St Bartholomew's, Bethlem, Queen Mary's, Royal Dental Hospitals; a Vice-President of the Alexandra Orphanage and Working School; received Freedom of Verdun, 1925, being the first Englishman to receive the life freedom of any French city; has been Chairman of the Corporation of London Improvements and Finance Committee, the Cattle Markets Committee, and Chairman of a Special Reception Committee; also Chairman of the Guildhall School of Music; Past Master Vintners' Company; Liveryman of the Spectacle Makers' Co. and of the Loriners Co.; Grand Officer of the Legion of Honour; Kt Comdr of the Order of St Gregory the Great; Comdr of the Second Class of the Order of the Dannebrog. *Heir:* none. *Address:* Manor Place, Chislehurst. *T:* Imperial 129; 1 Hare Place, EC4. *T:* Central 5384. *Club:* Royal Automobile.

Died 16 Nov. 1948 (ext).

BOWER, Frederick Orpen, FRS, FRSE, FLS, ScD (Camb.), DSc (Dublin, Sydney, and Leeds), LLD (Aberdeen, Glasgow, and Bristol); Emeritus Professor of Botany, University of Glasgow; appointed, 1885, retired, 1925; formerly Lecturer in Botany at Imperial College of Science; Ex-President, Royal Society of Edinburgh; thrice President of Botanical section of British Association; President of British Association for 1930; *b* Ripon, 4 Nov. 1855. *Educ:* Repton; Trinity College, Cambridge; Würzburg and Strasbourg; Royal Gold Medal; Darwin Medal; Linnæan Gold Medal; Neill Prize, RSE. *Publications:* A Course of Practical Instruction in Botany, 3rd ed. 1891; Practical Botany for Beginners, 1894; The Origin of a Land Flora, 1908; Plant Life on Land, 1911; Botany of the Living Plant, 1919; 3rd edition, 1939; The Ferns, vol. i, 1923; vol. ii, 1926; vol. iii, 1928; Plants and Man, 1925; Size and Form in Plants, 1930; Primitive Land-Plants, 1935; Sixty Years of Botany in Britain, 1938; also numerous memoirs presented to learned societies, Annals of Botany, etc. *Address:* The Old Deanery Hotel, Ripon, Yorks. *Club:* United University.

Died 11 April 1948.

BOWER, Alderman Sir Percival, Kt 1927; MBE 1920; JP, City of Birmingham; Member Central Electricity Board; Chairman (Local Board of Directors) Phoenix Assurance Co. Ltd; *b* 1880; *s* of William Henry Bower, Hythe, Kent; *m* 1st, 1904, Alice Edith (*d* 1933), *d*, of John Hare, Canterbury; 2nd, 1941, Mildred, *d* of late George Henry Ogden, Dronfield, Derbyshire. *Educ:* Hythe Church School. Lord Mayor of Birmingham, 1924–26. *Address:* Bythorn, Gravelly Hill, Erdington, Birmingham.

Died 7 May 1948.

BOWERMAN, Rt Hon. Charles William; PC 1916; JP; ex-President of the National Printing and Kindred Trades Employees Federation; *b* 22 Jan. 1851; *m* 1876, Louisa, *d* of W. Peach. Alderman of LCC, 1901–07; General Secretary London Society of Compositors, 1892–1906; MP (Lab) Deptford, 1906–31; Pres. Trades Union Congress, 1901; Secretary, 1911–23; Chairman, Ruskin College, Executive Committee. *Address:* 4 Battledean Road, N5.

Died 11 June 1947.

BOWERS, Col Percy Lloyd, CIE 1919; MC; AMInstCE; *b* 1879; *o s* of late Ven. Percy Harris Bowers, Archdeacon of Loughborough; *m* 1931, Dorothy, *widow* of Lieut Cecil Bowers, RN, and *d* of late R. Hudson Crabtree, St Anne's-on-Sea, Lancs. *Educ:* Rugby; Central Technical College, S Kensington. Joined PWD Bombay Presidency, 1903; retired 1934; served European War, 1914–19 (CIE, MC, despatches 5 times) and Afghan War, 1919, in Indian Army Reserve of Officers, attached 3rd R Bombay Sappers and Miners; retired with rank of Colonel, 1934; Hon. Secretary, Poona and Kirkee Hounds, 1925–26; Huntsman, 1927; Joint Master, 1934; Member of Committee and Steward

West of India Turf Club, 1932–34. *Recreations:* hunting, racing, cricket, shooting. *Address:* The Bowery, Mandelieu, AM, France. *Clubs:* East India and Sports, Hurlingham, Royal Automobile, Incognito; Royal Bombay Yacht, Western India and Sind.

Died 8 June 1943.

BOWES-LYON, Hon. Francis; JP, DL; *b* 23 Feb. 1856; 2nd *s* of 13th Earl of Strathmore and Frances Dora, 3rd *d* of late Oswald Smith, of Blendon Hall, Kent, and *grandnephew* of late Viscountess Barrington, of Hetton Hall; *m* 1883, Lady Anne Catherine Sybil Lindsay (*d* 1936), 5th *d* of 25th Earl of Crawford; two *s* (and one *s* killed in European War) three *d*. Late Lieut-Col Comdg 2nd Vol. Batt. the Black Watch (Royal Highlanders); Member of the King's Bodyguard for Scotland since 1881. *Heir: s* Capt. Geoffrey Francis Bowes-Lyon. *Address:* Ridley Hall, Bardon Mill, Northumberland. *Clubs:* Carlton, Bachelors'.

Died 17 Feb. 1948.

BOWIE, James Alexander, MA, DLitt; Principal, School of Economics, Dundee; *b* 1888; 3rd *s* of William Bowie, Aberdeen; *m* Rosa Tatham, Manchester; one *s* one *d*. *Educ:* Aberdeen University; Double Honours in Philosophy and in Economic Science, Hutton Prizeman 1914; Carnegie Research Scholar in Economics at Aberdeen University. Lieutenant, Royal Artillery, active service in Palestine and Balkans; Assistant in and later Director of the Department of Industrial Administration, College of Technology, Manchester; Special Lecturer at University of Pennsylvania, USA, 1931; Secretary of Economic Section of the British Association, 1928–33; Food Executive Officer for Dundee, 1939–43. *Publications:* Sharing Profits with Employees, 1922; Education for Business Management, 1930; Rationalisation, 1931; American Schools of Business, 1932; The Future of Scotland, 1939; The Basis of Reconstruction, 1941; numerous papers on industrial administration subjects. *Recreations:* gardening, fishing. *Address:* School of Economics, Dundee.

Died 1 Sept. 1949.

BOWIE, John; portrait painter; Member of the Royal Scottish Academy and Société Nationale des Beaux-Arts, Paris; *b* Edinburgh; *s* of John Bowie, MD. *Educ:* Began education in art at School of Art, Mound, Edinburgh; afterwards entering the Life School of Royal Scottish Academy there; studied also in Paris at L'Academie Julien under Mess. Bouguereau and Robert Fleury; visiting afterwards Amsterdam to study Franz Hals and Madrid to study Velasquez. Principal portraits: Principal Rainy, Bishop Dowden, Sir Alexander Kinloch, Bart, Gilmerton, Drem, Sir George Reid, PRSA, Sir Edward Letchworth, FSA, Hon. Macdougal Hawkes, USA; Large group life size portraits of Queen Victoria's Chaplains, Rev. Jas Macgregor, Right Hon. Lord Salvesen, Very Rev. Dr Norman Maclean, Very Rev. Marshall B. Lang, etc. *Address:* 14 Drummond Place, Edinburgh 3.

Died 8 Oct. 1941.

BOWIE, Sir William Tait, Kt 1941; OBE; General Manager in Africa of Blantyre & East Africa, Ltd, and member of Board of Directors; *b* Scotland, 16 May 1876; *s* of Andrew Ferguson Bowie, Edinburgh; *m* 1906, Agnes Anna Brown de l'Hoste, *d* of D. F. de l'Hoste Ranking, MA (Oxon), LLD; three *s*. *Educ:* George Watson's College, Edinburgh; Edinburgh University. Articled to Horatius Stuart, SSC, Edinburgh; Nyasaland, 1899–1902; Malaya, engaged in planting, 1903–13; returned to Nyasaland, 1913, engaged in planting operations; served as volunteer in Nyasaland Volunteer Reserve, 1914–19 (African General Service Medal). *Address:* Michiru House, Blantyre, Nyasaland. *TA:* Blantyre, Nyasaland. *T:* Blantyre 38. *Club:* Overseas.

Died 30 April 1949.

BOWLE-EVANS, Maj.-Gen. Charles Harford, CMG 1915; CBE 1920; MB, Indian Medical Service, retired; *b* 19 Oct. 1867; *s* of late John Bowle-Evans of Byletts; *m* 1902, Ellen, *d* of late Major-Gen. W. Flack Stevenson, CB. Captain IMS, 1895; Major, 1905; Lt-Col, 1913; Col, 1921; Major-Gen., 1923; served Waziristan, 1894–95 (medal with clasp); Chitral, 1895 (medal with clasp); NW Frontier, 1897–98 (clasp); China, 1900 (medal); European War, 1914–15 (CMG); Director of Medical Services, HM Forces, India, 1923; retired, 1923. *Address:* Applegarth, Queen's Road, Cheltenham.

Died 23 Aug. 1942.

BOWLES, Brig.-Gen. Frederick Gilbert, late RE; 3rd *s* of late John Samuel Bowles of Milton Hill, Steventon, Berks; *m* Grace Mary, *d* of late John Howlett Harvey of Halifax, Nova Scotia; one *d. Educ:* Radley; Woolwich. Joined Royal Engineers, 1876; served Suakin Expedition, 1885. *Address:* 9 Northwick House, St John's Wood Road, NW8. *Club:* Naval and Military.

Died 26 April 1947.

BOWLES, Sir Henry Ferryman, 1st Bt *cr* 1926; JP, DL; *b* 19 Dec. 1858; *s* of late H. C. B. Bowles, of Myddleton House, Enfield; *m* 1889, Florence (*d* 1935), 3rd *d* of J. L. Broughton of Almington Hall, Market Drayton, Salop. *Educ:* Harrow; Jesus College, Cambridge (MA). Late Hon. Colonel 7th Batt. Middlesex Regiment; County Councillor, 1889–1908, Alderman from 1903; MP (C) Enfield Division of Middlesex, 1889–1906 and 1918–22; High Sheriff, Middlesex, 1928–29; Barr (Inner Temple); late Major and Hon. Col 7th Batt. Rifle Brigade. *Recreations:* shooting, botany. *Heir:* none. *Address:* Forty Hall, Enfield. *T:* Enfield 0099. *Clubs:* Carlton, Conservative.

Died 14 Oct. 1943.

BOWMAN, Alexander, DSc, FRSE. Superintendent of Scientific Investigations under the Fishery Board for Scotland, 1923; retired, 1934. *Address:* 29 St Swithin Street, Aberdeen.

Died 14 Jan. 1941.

BOWMAN, Herbert Lister, MA, DSc; Waynflete Professor of Mineralogy and Crystallography, 1909–41, now Emeritus Professor, Fellow of Magdalen College, Oxford, 1909; *b* 1874; *s* of J. Herbert Bowman; *m* Pleasance Edith, *d* of James Walker of Kempsey, Worcester. *Educ:* Eton; New College, Oxford. Demonstrator in Mineralogy at the University Museum, Oxford, 1898–1909. *Publications:* various papers on mineralogical and crystallographic subjects. *Address:* 8 Fyfield Road, Oxford.

Died 22 April 1942.

BOWMAN, Isaiah; President Emeritus, Johns Hopkins University (President, 1935–49); *b* Waterloo, Ontario, Canada, 26 Dec. 1878; *s* of Samuel Cressman Bowman and Emily Shantz; *m* 1909, Cora Olive Goldthwait; two *s* one *d. Educ:* Harvard University, BS; Yale University, PhD; Hon. MA Yale University, 1921; Hon. MEd, Mich State Normal College, 1927; Hon. DSc, Bowdoin, 1931; Hon. LLD, 1935, Charleston, Dartmouth, and Dickinson Colleges, University of of Pennsylvania and Harvard; Wisconsin 1936; Queen's Univ., 1937; Univ. Western Ontario, 1937; Washington Coll. 1940; Hon. ScD Arequipa and Cuzco, Peru, 1941; Hon. DSc Oxford Univ., 1948; Hon. LittD Marietta Coll., 1947. Member of the Faculty of Yale Univ. as Instructor and Asst Prof. of Geography 1905–15; Director of the American Geographical Soc., New York, 1915–35; Leader, First Yale South American Expedition, 1907; Geographer-Geologist, Yale Peruvian Expedition, 1911; Leader, American Geog. Society's Expedition to the Central Andes, 1913; gold medals of several societies, including Patron's Gold Medal, Royal Geographical Soc. (London), 1940, David Livingstone Gold Medal of Royal Scottish Geog. Soc., 1928 and Amer. Geog. Soc. of New York, 1945; Chief Territorial Adviser, American Commission to Negotiate Peace, Paris, 1918–19; hon. corresponding member of various geographical societies including Chili, Peru, Colombia, Paris, Rome, Finland, etc.; Pres., Association of American Geographers, 1931; Vice-Pres. Explorers' Club, 1923; Director, Council on Foreign Relations; Pres. International Geographical Union, 1931–34; Chairman, National Research Council, 1933–35; Director Science Advisory Board, 1933–35; National Commissioner, International Commission US and China, 1939; Member of American delegation, Dumbarton Oaks Conference, 1944; Adviser to The Secretary of State, San Francisco Conference of United Nations, 1945; Consultant, Economic Co-operation Administration, 1949–. Member National Academy of Sciences (Vice-Pres., 1940–45); President American Association Adv. of Science, 1943–44. Member of many scientific societies. *Publications:* Andes of Southern Peru, 1916; S America, 1915; Forest Physiography, 1911; Human Geography, 1920; The New World-Problems in Political Geography, 1921; Desert Trails of Atacama, 1924; The Pioneer Fringe, 1931; Geography in Relation to the Social Sciences, 1934; A Design for Scholarship, 1936; Editor and contributor, Limits of Land Settlement, 1937; The Graduate School in American Democracy, 1939. *Address:* The Johns Hopkins University, Baltimore 18, Md, USA. *T:* (home) Belmont 2398, Baltimore. *Clubs:* Century (New York); Cosmos (Washington).

Died 6 Jan. 1950.

BOWMAN, Laurence George, MA, BSc, MRST; *b* 16 March 1866; *m* 1893, Fanny (*d* 1942), *d* of Rev. M. L. Cohen; one *d* (only son killed, 1917). *Educ:* Jews Free School; University College, London. Assistant Master at Jews' Free School, 1880–98; Vice-Master, 1898–1907; Headmaster, 1908–30; Chairman of the Education Committee of the Jewish Religious Education Board. London University degrees: BA (Hons in Mental and Moral Science), MA (Philosophy, etc.) and BSc; Teachers' Diploma (University of London); Representative on Appeal Tribunal of Unemployment Assistance Board; Vice-Chairman of Central School Employment Committee; Member of various educational and political bodies; Lecturer and Speaker on Educational and Political Subjects; Parliamentary Liberal Candidate for SE St Pancras; Pres. South Hendon Div. Liberal Assoc. *Recreation:* golf. *Address:* 25 Strawberry Hill Road, Twickenham, Mddx. *T:* Popesgrove 6969. *Club:* National Liberal.

Died 21 Nov. 1950.

BOWMAN, Thomas, MA. *Educ:* Wadham College, Oxford. 1st class Math. Mods, 1873; 1st class Mods, 1874; 1st class Math. Finals, 1875; senior Math. Scholar, 1878. Formerly Fellow, Principal of the Postmasters, Tutor and Dean of Merton College; Warden of Merton College, Oxford, 1903–36. *Address:* Merton College, Oxford.

Died 1 May 1945.

BOWRA, Cecil Arthur Verner; late London Secretary, Inspectorate-General of Chinese Maritime Customs; retired, 1927; Chief Secretary, Pekin, 1910–23; officiating Inspector-General of Chinese Customs, 1913, 1918–19, 1920, and 1923; *b* 22 Aug. 1869; *s* of late E. C. Bowra, Commissioner of Chinese Customs, Canton; *m* 1896, Ethel Fleay, *d* of late V. L. Lovibond of the Hermitage, Fulham, SW; two *s* two *d. Educ:* Park House School, Gravesend; St Paul's; Inns of Court. Joined the Chinese Customs Service, 1886; Commissioner of Customs, 1903; Commandant of the Newchwang Volunteer Force at Newchwang, S Manchuria, during the Boxer uprising of 1900; Seconded from the Chinese Customs Service, May 1905, for appointment as Chief Commissioner of the Royal Korean Customs, Seoul, Korea, but unable to take up the appointment owing to the result of the Russo-Japanese War; Barrister-at-Law of the Inner Temple, 1904; Civil Rank of the Third Class (Blue Button), China, 1904; Double Dragon,

Third Division, First Class, China, 1904; Officier de l'Ordre Royal du Cambodge, 1907; Civil Rank of the Second Class (Red Button), China, 1910; Order of the Chia Ho, Third Class, China, 1914; Second Class, 1918; China Expedition Medal, 1900; Great Britain, 1904; Rising Sun, Third Class, Japan, 1915; Yuan Shih-kai medal, 1915; Knight of the First Class of the Order of St Olaf, Norway, 1919; Order of the Chia Ho, Second Class with Sash, China, 1920; Order of the Chia Ho, Second Class with Sash and Jewels, China, 1923; Order of the Wen Hu, Second Class, China, 1923. *Address:* The Bower House, Ightham, Sevenoaks. *Club:* Royal Societies.

Died 23 April 1947.

BOWRAN, Rev. John George; (pseudonym, Ramsay Guthrie); retired Methodist Minister; ex-Connexional Editor; *b* Gateshead-on-Tyne, 25 June 1869; 3rd *s* of William Bowran; *m* 1st, 1893, Elizabeth Batey Robson, Oxford Villa, Gateshead; 2nd, 1911, Eleanor Hedley Davison, Oakhurst, Chester-le-Street; three *s* three *d*. *Educ:* Wesleyan School, Gateshead; Hartley College, Manchester. Ministered at Hyde, Cheshire, 1889–93; Cockermouth, 1893–96; Brandon, Durham, 1896–1900; Middlesbrough, 1900–06; Hexham-on-Tyne, 1906–11; Stockton-on-Tees, 1911–16; editor of Primitive Methodist Magazines, 1916–21; Surrey Chapel, London, 1921–25; Newcastle on Tyne, 1925–31; Harrogate, 1931–35; President of Primitive Methodist Conference, 1928. *Publications:* On God's Lines; Kitty Fagan; Black Dyke; A Son of the Silence; Neddy Jacques; The Maddisons of Moorlea; Brotherhood Stories; The Canny Folks o'Coal-Vale; Elsie Macgregor; With Signals Clear; The Old Folks at Home; Bessie Binney; Davie Graham, Pitman; Idylls of Rosehill; The Doctor's Daughter; The Cranstons; The Hartley Lecture for 1923, Christianity and Culture; Life of Arthur T. Guttery, DD, etc. *Address:* 76 Osborne Avenue, Newcastle-upon-Tyne. *T:* Jesmond 1981.

Died 8 Dec. 1946.

BOWRING, Sir Charles Calvert, KCMG 1925; KBE 1919; CMG 1908; JP for the Borough of Bedford; *b* 20 Nov. 1872; *s* of late J. C. Bowring; *m* 1909, Ethel Dorothy, CBE, *d* of late G. K. Watts, Commissioner of Public Works, East Africa; four *s* three *d*. *Educ:* Clifton. Entered Colonial Audit Branch of Exchequer, 1890; Hong-Kong, 1892; holds gold medal for services in connection with plague epidemic, 1894; local auditor British Central Africa, 1895; East Africa Protectorate, and Uganda Railway, 1899; Treasurer, 1901; member of Executive and Legislative Councils East Africa Protectorate, 1907; Chief Secretary, 1911–24, East Africa Protectorate, now Kenya; acting Governor on various occasions; Governor of Nyasaland, 1924–29. Croix de Commandeur, Order of the Crown of Belgium, 1921. *Address:* 28 St Andrew's Road, Bedford. *T:* 3367. *Club:* East India and Sports.

Died 13 June 1945.

BOWRING, Hon. Sir Edgar Rennie, KCMG 1934; Kt 1915; Chairman C. T. Bowring & Co. Ltd, London and Liverpool; Chairman Bowring Brothers Ltd, St John's, Newfoundland; Director of Bowring & Co., New York; *b* St John's, 17 Aug. 1858; *s* of John Bowring and Mary Rennie; *m* 1888, Flora Munn (*d* 1939), *d* of Hon. James Clift. *Educ:* Bishop Field College, St John's; Liverpool and Scarborough, England. Member of Newfoundland Legislative Council, 1897; Member Dominions Royal Commission, 1912; first High Commissioner for Newfoundland, 1918–22, and again 1933–34. *Recreations:* motoring, golf, riding. *Address:* Hyde Park Hotel, Knightsbridge, SW1; The Bungalow, Topsail, Newfoundland. *Clubs:* City of London, Royal Automobile, Bath.

Died 23 June 1943.

BOWRING, Walter Andrew, CBE 1928; *b* 30 Nov. 1875; 5th *s* of late J. C. Bowring; *m* 1909, Nita Maud, *d* of late Major J. E. W. Howey; one *s* one *d*. *Educ:* Eton. Entered Colonial Audit Branch of Exchequer and Audit Department, 1894; Assistant Auditor, East Africa Protectorate and Uganda Railway, 1899; Local Auditor, Uganda, 1902; Treasurer, Cyprus, 1909; Member of Executive and Legislative Councils, Cyprus, 1909; Chief Refugee Commissioner, Cyprus, from 1915 during War; on special duty, Aden and Somaliland, 1921–22; Treasurer, Gibraltar, 1924–31; Member of Executive Council, Gibraltar, 1924; Chairman, City Council, Gibraltar, 1924–27; Administrator of Dominica, 1931–33; retired, 1933. *Recreations:* shooting, fishing, golf. *Address:* Jama el Mokhra, Tangier. *TA:* Wabowring, Tangier.

Died 3 Nov. 1950.

BOWYER, Sir George Henry, 9th and 5th Bt *cr* 1660 and 1794; late Lieut 4th Batt. Cheshire Regt; *b* 9 Sept. 1870; *o s* of late H. G. Bowyer; *S* uncle, 1893; *m* 1899, Ethel, *d* of late Francis Hawkins (whom he divorced 1900). *Heir:* (to Denham Btcy only) *kinsman* Baron Denham. *Address:* c/o Lloyds Bank Ltd, 6 Pall Mall, SW1.

Died 27 Sept. 1950 (ext as to 5th Btcy).

BOXALL, Col Sir Alleyne Percival, 2nd Bt *cr* 1919; OBE 1923; TD; Hon. Col 57th (Home Counties) Field Brigade, RA (TA), since 1929; *b* 14 Sept. 1882; *s* of 1st Baronet and Mary Elizabeth, *e d* of J. H. Lermitte, JP, of Knightons; *S* father, 1927. *Educ:* Eton; University College, Oxford; MA. Served European War, 1914–18 (wounded, despatches twice); DL Sussex. *Heir:* none. *Address:* 14 Cambridge Square, W2. *Clubs:* Bath, MCC.

Died 29 June 1945.

BOYAGIAN, Henry Samuel Rogers, CIE 1938; Civil Engineer (retd); *b* 1875; *s* of Rev. Thomas Boyagian; *m* 1914, Elizabeth Wilhelmina, *d* of S. E. Salberg; one *s*. *Educ:* University College, London. Joined Assam Bengal Railway, 1904; chief engineer, 1927; retired 1934; reappointed engineer-in-charge Meghna Bridge construction, 1935. AMICE 1903. *Address:* Eastway, Sutton Road, Seaford, Sussex. *Clubs:* Royal Societies, East India and Sports.

Died 16 Aug. 1947.

BOYCE, Arthur Cyril, KC 1908; DCL 1913; *b* Wakefield, 12 Sept. 1867; *s* of late Rev. J. C. Boyce, MA (Oxon), Cornwall, Oxford; *m* 1891, Victoria, *d* of Rev. Canon C. J. Machin, Bac. Mus.; one *s* three *d*. *Educ:* Wakefield; York; Carlisle. Called to Bar, 1890 (Honours and bronze medal); contested (C) Algoma, 1900; MP for Riding of West Algoma, 1904; re-elected, 1908–11; Chancellor of the Diocese of Algoma, 1910–32; Hon. Lt-Col 51st Sault Ste Maria Rifles, 1914; Fellow Royal Colonial Institute, 1914; member Board of Railway Commissioners for Canada, 1917–27. *Address:* Ottawa, Ontario, Canada. *Clubs:* Rideau, Country, Ottawa.

Died 4 Aug. 1942.

BOYD, Alfred Ernest; Consulting Anæsthetist, House of Industry Hospitals, Dublin; Hon. Secretary Royal Medical Benevolent Fund Society of Ireland; late Visiting Physician Alan Ryan Hospital for Consumption, Dublin, and Hon. Secretary of the Dublin Branch of the National Association for the Prevention of Tuberculosis; *y s* of Samuel Boyd, JP, of Illerton, Killiney; unmarried. *Educ:* Rathmines School; Cheltenham College; Trinity College, Dublin; Vienna. Graduated MB, BCh, BAO, 1896; DPH, 1897. Served European War in 83rd (Dublin) General Hospital BEF. *Address:* Sloperton, Kingstown, Co. Dublin. *T:* 81217. *Clubs:* University (Dublin); Royal Irish Yacht (Kingstown).

Died 23 Dec. 1949.

BOYD, Edmund Blaikie, CMG 1935; CVO 1938; Assistant Secretary, Colonial Office, since 1937; *b* 1894; *s* of late David James Boyd; *m* 1st, 1929, Mary Mure Ritchie (marr. diss. 1939); 2nd, 1941, Elsie Olive Percival; one *d. Educ:* Aberdeen Grammar School; Univ. of Aberdeen. MA, 1916 with First Class Honours in Classics (Distinction in Greek History, Liddel Prizeman, and Dr Black (Joint) Prizeman). On military service, 1916–19; 2nd Lieut RGA (Special Reserve), 1917; served in France and Belgium; Lieut, 1919; entered Colonial Office, 1919; Private Secretary to Parliamentary Under-Secretaries of State, 1922–24; Principal, 1925; Secretary to Colonial Office Conference, 1927; Principal Private Secretary to successive Secretaries of State (Lord Passfield, 1930–31; Mr J. H. Thomas, 1931; Sir Philip Cunliffe-Lister, 1931–35; Mr Malcolm MacDonald, 1935; Mr Thomas, 1935; Mr Ormsby-Gore, 1936–37). Member of East African Currency Board, 1937–41, and of Palestine Currency Board, 1941–45. *Recreation:* golf. *Address:* 32 Rossetti Gardens Mansions, Chelsea, SW3. *Club:* Caledonian.

Died 20 April 1946.

BOYD, Edward Charles Percy; *b* 3 Sept. 1871; *s* of late Lt-Col Alexander Boyd. *Educ:* Fettes College, Edinburgh; Trinity College, Cambridge (2nd Class Historical Tripos, BA, 1893). Called to Bar, Inner Temple, 1896; Junior Counsel to the Treasury, Middlesex Sessions, 1912; one of the Junior Counsel to the Treasury Central Criminal Court, 1912–16; Metropolitan Magistrate, Greenwich and Woolwich 1916, West London 1917, Westminster 1924; Great Marlborough Street, 1933; retired 1941. *Address:* 37 De Vere Gardens, W8. *T:* Western 3821. *Clubs:* United University, Marlborough-Windham; Royal and Ancient (St Andrews).

Died 30 May 1949.

BOYD, Ernest; author; Associate Member Irish Academy of Letters, 1933; editor the American Spectator, 1932; *b* Dublin, 28 June 1887; *s* of James Robert Boyd and Rosa Kempston. *Educ:* privately. Studied abroad for British Consular Service and passed competitive examination, 1913. Appointed, Baltimore, Md, 1913; Barcelona, 1916; Copenhagen, 1919; resigned, 1919; settled in New York, 1920; on editorial staff of New York Evening Post, 1920–22; engaged ever since in various forms of independent editorial and critical work. *Publications:* Ireland's Literary Renaissance, 1916, revised edition, 1922; Contemporary Drama of Ireland, 1917; Appreciations and Depreciations, 1917; Portraits: Real and Imaginary, 1924; Studies in Ten Literatures, 1925; H. L. Mencken, 1925; Guy de Maupassant, 1926; (with Madeline Davidson) After the Fireworks: a Comedy, 1932; The Pretty Lady: a Comedy, 1933. Many translations from French and German; edited collected novels and stories of Guy de Maupassant, 18 vols. *Recreations:* cycling, mountaineering, reading, conversation, no games or sports. *Address:* 151 East 19th Street, New York City. *T:* Gramercy 5–4133.

Died 30 Dec. 1946.

BOYD, Frank M.; journalist; *b* Edinburgh, 1863; 2nd *s* of Very Rev. A. K. H. Boyd (*d* 1899), and of Margaret Buchanan, *d* of late Captain Kirk, 77th Regiment. *Educ:* St Andrews; Germany. Tried painting with moderate success; then on Lloyd's for some years; founder and editor of The Pelican, 1889–1917. *Publications:* A Pelican's Tale, 1919; contributed regularly to various journals and magazines. *Recreations:* cycling, yachting, fishing, painting. *Address:* Gresham Lodge, 143 New Church Road, Hove, Brighton. *T:* Portslade 8950.

Died 4 Feb. 1950.

BOYD, Henry, CBE 1921; Chevalier de la Légion d'honneur, 1936; Consulting Engineer and Naval Architect. Was Director of National Shipyards, Ministry of Shipping. *Address:* Bel-Air, St Germain-en-Laye, S. et O., France.

Died 1 Dec. 1942.

BOYD, Lt-Col Henry Alexander, CMG 1918; DSO 1916; late RA; *b* 11 July 1877; *s* of Rt Hon. Sir Walter Boyd, 1st Bart; *m* 1908; one *s* one *d. Educ:* Trinity College, Dublin. Entered Army (RFA), 1900; served S African War, 1901–02 (Queen's medal, 5 clasps); European War, 1914–18 (despatches four times, CMG, Croix de Chevalier, French Legion of Honour, DSO); retired pay, 1928. *Recreations:* hunting, golf, yachting. *Address:* 66 Merrion Square, Dublin.

Died 1 Nov. 1943.

BOYD, Rev. Herbert Buchanan, MA. Canon Emeritus of Rochester, 1934; *s* of late Very Rev. A. K. H. Boyd, DD, LLD; *m* Beatrice Josephine (*d* 1935). *Educ:* Fettes College, Edinburgh; Trinity Hall, Cambridge. Ordained, 1889; Curate of Aylesford, 1889–96; Holy Trinity, Guildford, 1896–97; Cliffe-at-Hoo, 1897–99; Rector and Rural Dean, 1899–1915; Hon. Canon, Rochester, 1914; Vicar of Lamberhurst, 1915–20; of Westerham, 1920–27. *Address:* Quietways, Rodborough Common, Stroud, Gloucestershire. *T:* Amberley 22.

Died 2 Nov. 1941.

BOYD, James; MFH; author; *b* Pennsylvania, 2 July 1888; *s* of John Yeomans Boyd and Eleanor Herr Boyd; *m* 1917, Katherine Lamont, New York; two *s* one *d. Educ:* Princeton; Trinity College, Cambridge. In publishing business (Doubleday Page & Co.) before War; served in France as 1st Lt, AAS, Italian Front, St Mihiel, 1st and 2nd Argonne offensives; on resigning from service returned to family place, Southern Pines, North Carolina, and devoted self to writing. *Publications:* Drums; Marching On; Long Hunt; Roll River; Bitter Creek; stories and poems in magazines. *Recreations:* hunting (for 14 seasons huntsman and joint master, Moore County hounds, NC), tennis, sailing. *Address:* Southern Pines, North Carolina, USA. *Clubs:* Coffee-House, Century, National Institute of Arts and Letters, New York.

Died 25 Feb. 1944.

BOYD, Col Mossom Archibald, CBE 1919; *b* 11 June 1860; *s* of General Brooke Boyd; *m* 1887, Adeline Lea-Smith (*d* 1944), *d* of J. Smith, Woodlands, Chigwell, Essex; one *s* one *d. Educ:* Clifton College; RM Academy, Woolwich. Joined Royal Engineers, 1880; Substantive Col in the Army, 1910; retired, 1911; re-employed, 1914–19. *Address:* Morcote, London Road, Guildford.

Died 19 May 1943.

BOYD, Air Vice-Marshal Owen Tudor, CB 1939; OBE 1919; MC; AFC; *b* 30 Aug. 1889; *s* of A. B. P. Boyd; *m* 1921, Ira Marjorie Tudor; one *s. Educ:* Forest School; RMC Sandhurst. Entered Indian Army, 1909; RAF 1916; served European War, 1914–19; AOC Central Area RAF 1935–36; Director of Personal Services, Air Ministry, 1936–38; Air Officer Commanding Balloon Command, 1938; served War 1939– (prisoner, but escaped 1944). *Address:* Cheyne Cottage, Stanmore. *T:* Stanmore 252. *Clubs:* Army and Navy, Royal Air Force.

Died 5 Aug. 1944.

BOYD, Ven. Sydney Adolphus, BCL, MA; Archdeacon Emeritus; *b* Landour, NW Provinces, India, 7 Jan. 1857; *e s* of General Brooke Boyd, Indian Army; *m* 1881, Rosalie, *d* of John Smith, of Chigwell, Essex; one *s* one *d. Educ:* Clifton College; Worcester College, Oxford; BA 1879; MA and BCL 1882. Called to Bar, Inner Temple, 1880; Curate of Holy Trinity, Hampstead, 1880–85; Vicar of St Giles', Norwich, 1886–93; Vicar of Macclesfield, 1893–1902; Rector of Bath, 1902–38; Archdeacon of Bath, 1924–38; Proctor for the Archdeaconry of Macclesfield, 1895–1902; Chaplain, Royal United Hospital, Bath, 1902–38; Chaplain, Royal Mineral Water Hosp., Bath, 1933–38; Prebendary of Ilton in Wells Cathedral since 1903; Proctor for the Diocese of Bath and Wells, 1907–29 and 1934–38; Rural Dean of Bath, 1902–24. *Address:* 2 Park Place, Bath, Somerset.

Died 17 May 1947.

BOYD, Thomas Herbert, CB 1938; Assistant Director General, General Post Office, since 1936; *b* 1890; *m* 1924, Mary Schofield, *d* of John Nelson, Bury; one *s*. *Educ:* Owen's School, Islington. BA London University. Examiner, Exchequer and Audit Dept, 1909; Asst Surveyor, GPO, 1914; served European War, Pilot, RNAS and RAF; Asst Controller, London Postal Service, 1932; Postmaster Surveyor, Glasgow, 1935; Director of Establishments, GPO, 1936. *Address:* GPO, EC1.

Died 28 May 1941.

BOYD, Sir Walter Herbert, 2nd Bt *cr* 1916; KC 1918; Barrister; *b* 31 March 1867; *s* of 1st Bt and Annie, *d* of M. Anderson, Dublin; *S* father, 1918; *m* 1901, Ruth, *d* of late Sir William Fry; one *d*. *Educ:* Dublin University. Chief Registrar in Bankruptcy (Ireland), 1912–37. *Heir: nephew* Alexander Walter [*b* 1934; *s* of late Cecil Anderson Boyd, MC, MD, and Marjorie Catharine, *e d* of late Francis Kinloch, JP, Shipka Lodge, North Berwick]. *Address:* Balnagowan, Palmerston Park, Dublin; Howth House, Howth, Co. Dublin.

Died 17 April 1948.

BOYD, Rev. William Grenville, MA (Oxon); Vicar of Swinbrook, Oxford; *b* London, 22 May 1867; *s* of Thomas Boyd, of J. and C. Boyd, Friday Street, EC; *m* 1914, Dorothy M. G., *d* of Rev. Wm Clarke, Vicar of Rumburgh, Suffolk; three *s* one *d*. *Educ:* Sherborne School; Hertford College, Oxford; Wells Theological College. Curate at S Mary, Portsea, 1891–94; All Hallows, London Wall, 1894–96; S Dunstan's, Stepney (in charge of S Faith's Mission Church), 1896–1904; Resident Chaplain to the Archbishop of Canterbury, 1905–10; Head of the Edmonton Mission of the Archbishop's Western Canada Fund, 1910–15; Rector of S Faith's, Edmonton, and Canon of the Diocese of Edmonton, Canada, 1915–18; Vicar of Minster, Thanet, 1919–35; Rural Dean of Thanet, 1932; Hon. Canon of Canterbury, 1933. *Recreations:* painting, fishing. *Address:* Swinbrook Vicarage, Oxford.

Died 14 May 1941.

BOYDEN, Rev. A. H., BA, BSc, BD; retired Methodist Minister; *s* of Rev. W. Boyden, ex-President of United Methodist Free Churches; *m* 1st, Mary Gertrude Steel; 2nd, Muriel Harriet Hill; one *d*. *Educ:* Ashville College, Harrogate; Manchester University. Shuttleworth Exhibition and Warburton Scholarship in Political Economy and Lee Prize in Hellenistic Greek at Manchester University; prizeman in Hebrew and Hellenistic Greek at London University. Educational appointments under LCC and Wolsey Hall, Oxford; has had churches at Exeter, Preston, London and Cardiff; formerly a speaker for Headquarters of League of Nations Union, London. *Recreation:* gardening.

Died 19 July 1940.

BOYER, Rear-Adm. (S) George Christopher Aubin, CBE 1919; *b* 28 Feb. 1862; *m* 1894, Gertrude Elizabeth, 3rd *d* of James Allen, of Battenhurst, Ticehurst, Sussex; one *d*. *Educ:* St James' Collegiate School, Jersey. Joined Royal Navy, 1878; served Soudan Campaign, 1884–85 (Egyptian Medal and Khedive's Bronze Star); Silver Dongola Medal, 1896; Boxer Rising, 1900 (China Medal); Commander of the Order of the Crown of Italy, 1911; Chevalier, Legion of Honour, 1918; Naval Base

Agent at Boulogne, 1916–18 (despatches twice); Paymaster Rear-Admiral (retired), 1921. *Address:* Windsor Villa, St Stephen's Road, Saltash.

Died 25 Sept. 1949.

BOYLE, Sir Alexander George, KCMG 1921; CMG 1908; CBE 1919; *b* 6 March 1872; *m* Sibyl Blanche Hodgson (*d* 1941); three *s*. *Educ:* Charterhouse; Clifton; RIEC, Coopers Hill. Assist Treas. Uganda Protectorate, 1895; Acting Sec. to HM Comr, 1896–98; Acting Treasurer, 1899–1900; Deputy Treasurer, 1900; Acting Sec. to Administration, 1901–02; Collector, 1902; Assistant Sec., 1902; Acting Sub-Comr, Eastern Province 1903; Sub-Comr 1905; Acting Deputy Comr, 1907; Acting Chief Secretary, 1909; Provincial Comr Eastern Province, Uganda Protectorate, 1905–10; Acting Governor, 1909–10; Adm. Government of Southern Nigeria, May–Sept. 1911; Colonial Secretary Southern Nigeria, 1910–13; Lieut-Governor of Nigeria, 1913–20; Adm.-Gov. of Nigeria, Nov. 1918. *Address:* High Barn, Limington, Yeovil, Somerset.

Died 18 April 1943.

BOYLE, Adm. Hon. Sir Algernon (Douglas Edward Harry), KCB 1924 (CB 1916); CMG 1918; MVO 1901; RN, retired; *b* 21 Oct. 1871; 6th *s* of 5th Earl of Shannon and Julia Charlotte, *y d* of Sir W. E. Cradock Hartopp, 3rd Bart. Entered Navy, 1884; Lieutenant, 1891; Commander, 1902; Captain, 1907; Rear-Admiral, 1919; Vice-Admiral, 1924; Admiral (retired), 1928; European War, 1914–18 (despatches four times, CB, CMG; Legion of Honour; Russian Order of St Anne, 2nd class, with swords; 3rd class Order of Rising Sun, Japan; French Croix de Guerre; Commander of Order of Crown of Belgium); a Naval ADC to the King, 1918–19; 4th Sea Lord, Admiralty, 1920–24; retired list, 1924; Member of Port of London Authority, 1925–29. *Address:* 11 Cranley Gardens, SW7. *Clubs:* United Service, MCC.

Died 13 Oct. 1949.

BOYLE, Air Cdre Archibald Robert, CMG 1939; OBE 1919; MC and bar; RAFVR; *b* 11 Aug. 1887; *s* of late Rear-Admiral R. H. Boyle; *m* 1913, Edith Mary Constable Curtis; one *s* one *d*. *Educ:* Bradfield; Royal Military College. The Argyll and Sutherland Highlanders, 1907 till retirement; seconded for service with RAF 1918 till retirement from Army; subsequently served in Air Ministry as civil servant. *Address:* White House, Stoke Hill, Guildford. *T:* Guildford 5954. *Club:* Army and Navy.

Died 6 March 1949.

BOYLE, Col Cecil Alexander, CIE, 1937; DSO; late 5th KEO Probyn's Horse, IA; late Secretary and Adviser in Languages to the Board of Examiners, Army Headquarters; *b* 28 March 1888; *s* of Col P. D. Boyle, Grenadier Guards (retired); *m* 1923, Dulcie, *o d* of Lt-Col R. A. E. Benn, CIE; two *d*. NW Frontier Militias, 1911–17; Inspector-General Arab and Kurdish Levies, 1917–21; retired from Indian Army, 1938; Commanding 1st Bn Ayrshire Home Guard since 1940; Degree of Honour, 1st Division, and Gold Medallist in Arabic, Persian, and Urdu. *Address:* The Craig, Fairlie, Ayrshire.

Died 1 July 1941.

BOYLE, Sir Edward, 2nd Bt *cr* 1904; *b* 12 June 1878; *o s* of 1st Bt and Constance (*d* 1944), *d* of William Knight, JP; *S* father, 1909; *m* 1920, Beatrice, *er d* of late Henry Greig of Belvedere House, Kent; two *s* one *d*. *Educ:* Eton; Balliol College, Oxford; MA, Hon. LLD, Sofia. Barrister Inner Temple, 1902; JP Sussex; Chairman, Burwash Bench, 1926; FRGS; High Sheriff of Sussex, 1927; Associate of the Surveyors' Institution; Member of Committee appointed by India Office to promote welfare of Indian students; A Trustee of Johnson House; Chairman Balkan Committee; Hon. Treasurer Serbian Relief Fund, 1914; Vice-Chairman, 1920; Acting British Commissioner for Serbia, 1915; in charge Serbian

Colonies in Corsica, 1916; Order of Civil Merit (Bulgaria) 1st Class; Order of Skanderbeg (Albania) 1st Class; Grand Officier of the Order of St Sava (Serbia); Serbian Red Cross; and Cross of Charity; Director, Richard Thomas & Co., Ltd, and other companies. *Publications:* Biographical Essays, 1790–1890, 1936; Literary and political articles in the monthly Reviews; various songs. *Recreations:* music, gardening, travel. *Heir: s* Edward Charles Gurney, *b* 31 Aug. 1923. *Address:* (temp.): Chesilbourne Manor, Dorchester, Dorset. *T:* Milborne St Andrews 26; 63 Queen's Gate, London SW7; Ockham, Hurst Green, Sussex. *T:* Western 4964, Hurst Green 4. *Clubs:* Athenæum, Garrick, Johnson (President 1934).

Died 31 March 1945.

BOYLE, Henry Edmund Gaskin, OBE 1920; FRCS, MRCS, LRCP; DA; Anæsthetist to St Bartholomew's Hospital; Lecturer on Anæsthetics, St Bartholomew's Hospital Medical School; Captain RAMC (TF), attached to No. 1 City of London Base Hospital; *b* Barbados, West Indies, 2 April 1875; *s* of Henry Eudolphus Boyle and Elizabeth Gaskin; *m* 1910, Mildred Ethel, *d* of J. W. Wildy, and *widow* of Leslie Green, FRIBA. *Educ:* Harrison College, Barbados; St Bartholomew's Hospital. Late Casualty Officer, Royal Infirmary, Bristol; Junior and Senior Resident Anæsthetist, St Bartholomew's Hospital; Hon. Anæsthetist, Paddington Green Children's Hospital; Anæsthetist to St Andrew's Hospital; Fellow Royal Society of Medicine; late President, Section of Anæsthetists; ex-President Abernethian Society; Mem. BMA. *Publications:* Practical Anæsthetics, 3rd edition (with C. Langton Hewer), 1923; articles, Mixtures and Sequences, Nitrous Oxide and Nitrous Oxide and Oxygen, Practitioners' Encyclopædia, 1912; An Apparatus for the Intratracheal Insufflation of Ether, Lancet, 1913; Nitrous Oxide and Oxygen with Regulated Rebreathing in Military Surgery, Lancet, 1917; Boyle's Nitrous Oxide–Oxygen Ether Outfit, Lancet, 1918; Nitrous Oxide and Oxygen in Combination with C. E. for Nose and Throat Operations, 1918; Nitrous Oxide and Oxygen in Midwifery, BMJ, 1929; Nitrous Oxide: History and Development, BMJ, 1934. *Recreation:* golf. *Address:* 77 Gloucester Place, W1. *T:* Welbeck 9191. *Clubs:* West Indian; Stoke Poges.

Died 15 Oct. 1941.

BOYLE, Brig.-Gen. Roger Courtenay, CB 1915; CMG 1918; late Royal Munster Fusiliers; *b* 12 April 1863; *s* of late Maj.-Gen. R. Boyle, CB; *m* 1894, Elizabeth (*d* 1943), *d* of W. L. Martin, Lee Moor, Plympton, Devon. *Educ:* Cheltenham. Entered Army, 1885; Captain, 1893; Major, 1905; Lt-Col 1909; Col 1913; served Burma, 1885–89 (medal 2 clasps); S Africa, 1900–02 (Queen's medal 3 clasps, King's medal 2 clasps); European War, 1914–18 (CB, CMG, 1914 star); retired pay, 1919; Order of the Nile, 3rd class; Coronation medal, 1911; Commander, Legion of Honour, St Maurice and Lazarus, and George I of Greece. *Recreation:* golf. *Address:* Holmfield, Northam, N Devon. *Club:* Army and Navy.

Died 3 April 1944.

BOYNE, 9th Viscount *cr* 1717; **Gustavus William Hamilton-Russell;** JP, DL; Baron Hamilton, 1715; Baron Brancepeth, 1866; *b* 11 Jan. 1864; *s* of 8th Viscount and Lady Katherine Frances Scott, *d* of 2nd Earl of Eldon; *S* father, 1907; *m* 1906, Lady Margaret Lascelles, CBE 1920, *d* of 5th Earl of Harewood; three *s* one *d.* Formerly Captain, 3rd Batt. Northumberland Fusiliers. *Heir: g s* Gustavus Michael George Hamilton-Russell, *b* 10 Dec. 1931. *Address:* Belgrave House, Belgrave Square, SW1; Burwarton, Bridgnorth, Salop. *T:* Sloane 1469. *Clubs:* Carlton, Travellers'.

Died 18 Jan. 1942.

BOYNTON, Captain Thomas Lamplugh W.; *see* Wickham-Boynton.

BOYS, Sir Charles Vernon, Kt 1935; FRS; Hon. FRS Edin.; ARSM; Hon. LLD Edin.; Fellow of the Imperial College; Officier de l'Instruction Publique; Hon. Member New York Academy of Sciences and Physical Society of Moscow; Past President Physical Society of London and Röntgen Society; Vice-President Royal Automobile Club; Gas Referee for 40 years; *b* Wing, Rutland, 15 March 1855; *s* of Rev. Charles Boys; *m* 1892, Marion Amelia, *d* of Heny Pollock (whom he divorced 1910); one *s. Educ:* Marlborough; Royal School of Mines, Cambridge. Invented and made moving lens lightning camera, 1900; with which Schonland in South Africa and MacEachron at Pittsfield, USA, have discovered the gradual development of a lightning flash; Member of the Ordnance Committee; Royal Medal and Rumford Medal of Royal Society; Duddell Medal of Physical Society; Elliott Cresson Gold Medal of Franklin Institute. *Publications:* Soap Bubbles, their Colours and the Forces which Mould Them; the Natural Logarithm, 1935; Weeds, Weeds, Weeds, 1937, and numerous papers published by the Royal and other Societies on Integrating mechanism, Quartz fibres, Radiomicrometer, Heat of the moon and stars, Constant of gravitation, Soap bubbles, Solid dipleidoscope prisms, Gas Calorimetry, Speed of lightning, and other subjects; edited and completed Dynamometers by the late Rev. F. J. Jervis-Smith, FRS. *Address:* St Marybourne, Andover. *Club:* Royal Automobile.

Died 30 March 1944.

BOYS, Geoffrey Vernon, MA; MIMechE; MIEE; Secretary of Institution of Naval Architects since 1936; *b* 1893; *s* of late Sir Charles Vernon Boys; *m* 1933, Helen Florence Mary, *yr d* of Frank Gossling; one *s. Educ:* Marlborough; Trinity College, Cambridge. Served (RE), European War, 1914–18; fourteen years with Kennedy & Donkin, Consulting Engineers, engaged in electricity supply and distribution at home and abroad; Sept. 1939–May 1944, Naval Construction Dept, Admiralty. *Address:* 3 Queen's Rise, Richmond, Surrey. *Club:* United University.

Died 15 March 1945.

BOYS, Guy Ponsonby, BA, LLB; *b* 10 Aug. 1871; *s* of Henry Scott Boys (Indian Civil Service) and Ethel Rigaud Strong; *m* 1906, Maude Mary Beazley; one *s. Educ:* Wellington College; Trinity Hall, Cambridge; Inner Temple. Practised at the Bar until appointed to the Bench; officiating judge, 1924–26; Puisne Judge, 1926–32, Allahabad High Court, India; retired, 1932. *Recreations:* squash rackets, tennis. *Address:* Thornhill, Stockton Avenue, Fleet, Hants.

Died 5 Nov. 1950.

BOYS, Brig.-Gen. Reginald Harvey Henderson, CB 1915; DSO 1901; RE; *b* 17 Oct. 1867; *s* of late Adm. Henry Boys; *m* 1st, 1896, Elizabeth Mary (*d* 1908), *d* of late Kenneth Murray of Geanies, Co. Ross; 2nd, 1912, Dorothy Conyers, *d* of Conyers Baker; two *s* one *d.* Entered Army, 1886; Capt. 1896; Major, 1905; Lt-Col 1913; Col 1917; served South Africa, 1899–1902 (despatches thrice, Queen's medal five clasps, King's medal two clasps, DSO); European War, 1914–18 (despatches twice, CB, wounded, Bt-Col); Brig.-Gen. 1916; War Office, AAG, 1919–23; retired pay, 1923; received thanks of community of Hong Kong and service of plate for services rendered during plague in 1894. *Address:* c/o Lloyds Bank, Cox's Branch, 6 Pall Mall, SW1.

Died 15 Jan. 1945.

BRABNER, Rupert Arnold, DSO 1942; DSC 1943; MP (U) Hythe since 1939; Joint Parliamentary Under-Secretary of State for Air since 1944; Banker; Director of Singer & Friedlander Ltd; Member of LCC for West Lewisham, 1937–45; *b* 29 Oct. 1911; *s* of William

Wilberforce Brabner; *m* 1944, Mrs Phyllis Myfanwy
Berner, *d* of late Walter Everett Molins. *Educ:* Felsted
School; St Catharine's College, Cambridge. Served war
of 1939–45. Sub-Lt RNVR Fleet Air Arm; in Illustrious,
Eagle (when sunk), Victorious, Indomitable, and in
Crete and North Africa; commanded Fighter Squadron
in HMS Eagle during Malta convoys, 1942; Staff of
Vice-Admiral Aircraft Carriers for landings in North
Africa, 1942, and subsequently; Cdr 1943; Technical
Assistant to 5th Sea Lord, 1943. *Recreations:* Rugby,
cricket, squash rackets, music. *Address:* 55 Bishopsgate,
EC2; House of Commons, SW1. *Clubs:* Royal Aero,
Carlton.

Died 27 March 1945.

BRABOURNE, 6th Baron *cr* 1880; **Norton Cecil
Michael Knatchbull;** 15th Bt *cr* 1641; Lieut Grenadier
Guards; *b* 11 Feb. 1922; *s* of 5th Baron and Lady Doreen
Geraldine Browne (Order of the Crown of India; Dame,
St John of Jerusalem), *y d* of 6th Marquess of Sligo; *S*
father, 1939. *Educ:* Eton. *Heir: b* Hon. John Ulick
Knatchbull, Lt Coldstream Guards, *b* 9 Nov. 1924.
Address: Mersham-le-Hatch, nr Ashford, Kent.

Died 15 Sept. 1943.

BRACE, Col Henry Fergusson, DSO 1918; MC; *b* 10
Oct. 1888; *s* of late Frank Addison Brace, JP, of
Doveridge Hall, Derby, and Annie Isobel, *d* of Hickson
Fergusson of The Knowe, Ayr; *m* 1st, 1916, Beatrice Ida
Feilden; 2nd, 1937, Susan Agnes Rhodes, *d* of late
Colonel R. H. Tilney, DSO. *Educ:* Eton; Sandhurst.
Joined 15th The King's Hussars, 1908; served European
War (DSO, MC, wounded twice, despatches twice);
commanded 15th–19th The King's Royal Hussars,
1930–34; Officer Commanding Troops at Canterbury
and in charge of Cavalry Records, 1934–38; Col 1934;
retired pay, 1938; Zone Commander Kesteven Home
Guard, 1940; DL Lincolnshire, 1944. *Address:* Gonerby
House, Hillfoot, Grantham. *T:* Grantham 435. *Club:*
Cavalry.

Died 26 Nov. 1948.

BRACE, Rt Hon. William; PC 1916; *b* 23 Sept. 1865;
m 1890, Nelhe, *d* of William and Harriet Humphreys.
Educ: Risca Board School. Working miner; later,
Miners' Agent and President of the South Wales Miners'
Federation; MP (Lab) Glamorgan, South, 1906–18;
Abertillery Division of Monmouth, 1918–20;
Parliamentary Under-Secretary of State, Home
Department, 1915–18; Chief Labour Adviser to Dept of
Mines, 1920–27. *Publications:* special articles, reviews,
etc., on labour topics. *Recreation:* angling. *Address:* Bryn
Ivor, 60 Allt-yr-yn Avenue, Newport, Mon.

Died 12 Oct. 1947.

BRACKENBURY, Sir Henry Britten, Kt 1932; MD;
LLD; MRCS; LRCP; Vice-President, British Medical
Association (Chairman of Council, 1927–34); Vice-
President, late Chairman of Council, Tavistock Clinic;
Vice-President, Association of Education Committees
(President, 1914–18); Member, General Medical
Council; Member of Advisory Committee to Ministry of
Health; *b* 1866; *s* of Rev. Thomas Brackenbury; *m* 1st,
1892, Catherine Ada (*d* 1892), *d* of D. W. Edwards; 2nd,
1898, Amy Florence, *d* of Henry Sadler; one *s* one *d*.
Educ: Kingswood School, Bath; Westminster Hospital.
In general medical practice, 1892–1927; Borough of
Hornsey: Member of School Board, 1898–1903,
Chairman of Education Committee, 1903–13, Mayor,
1905–06, Alderman till 1930, Freeman, 1930; British
Medical Assoc.: Member of Council since 1914,
Chairman of Insurance Acts Committee, 1915–24,
Chairman of Representative Body, 1924–27, President
of Metro. Counties Branch, 1921; Soc. of Medical
Officers of Health; Member of Council since 1927;
Member of Middlesex County Education Committee,
1904–40; Vice-President Central Assoc. for Mental
Welfare; Chairman of Governors of Stationers'

Company's School for Boys, and of N London
Collegiate School for Girls and Camden School for Girls;
Hon. Freeman and Liveryman of the Company of
Stationers and Newspapers Makers; Fellow of the
Chartered Insurance Institute. *Publications:* Patient and
Doctor, 1935; numerous articles on Social Insurance,
Mental Deficiency, and Educational and Public Health
Administration. *Address:* Old Dairy House, Mudford,
Yeovil, Somerset. *T:* Marston Magna 367.

Died 8 March 1942.

BRACKETT, Oliver; formerly Keeper of Department of
Woodwork, Victoria and Albert Museum (retired,
1935); *b* 1875. *Educ:* Warwick School; Birmingham
School of Art. Joined staff of Victoria and Albert
Museum; member of Committee of Exhibition of Art
Treasures of the West Country, Bristol, 1937, and
Exhibition of Art of the 17th Century, RA, 1938.
Publications: Thomas Chippendale, 1924; An
Encyclopedia of English Furniture, 1927; English
Furniture (Benn's Sixpenny Library); The Interior of the
House, in Johnson's England, 1933; articles in magazines
and catalogues; also reviews of books. *Address:* 5 Earl's
Terrace, Kensington, W8. *T:* Western 7471. *Club:*
Savile.

Died 16 Jan. 1941.

BRACKLEY, Air Cdre Herbert George, CBE 1941;
DSO 1917; DSC; Chief Executive, British South
American Airways Corporation since 1948; *b* 1894; *m*
1922, Frida, *er d* of late Sir Robert Mond, FRS; two *s*
one *d*. Served European War, 1914–18 (despatches,
DSO, DSC, Ordre de la Couronne, Belgium, Croix de
Guerre, France, Order of Rising Sun, Japan). Adviser to
Naval Air Service, Japan; Air Superintendent, Imperial
Airways, 1924–39; recalled to RAF Sept. 1939; Deputy
Air Officer Administration, Coastal Command,
1940–41; Senior Air Staff Officer, 19 Group Coastal
Comd, 1941–42; Senior Air Staff Officer, Transport
Command, 1943–45; relinquished commission, 1945;
late Assistant to Chairman, BOAC. *Address:* The Old
Rectory, Blakeney, Norfolk. *T:* Cley 210. *Clubs:* Royal
Air Force, Royal Aero.

Died 15 Nov. 1948.

BRADBURY, 1st Baron *cr* 1925, of Winsford; **John
Swanwick Bradbury,** GCB 1920 (KCB 1913; CB
1909); Hon. LLD (Camb. and Manch.); Hon. Fellow
Brasenose College, Oxford; *b* 23 Sept. 1872; *m* 1911,
Hilda (*d* 1949), 2nd *d* of W. A. Kirby; two *s* one *d. Educ:*
Manchester Grammar School; Brasenose College,
Oxford. An Insurance Commissioner and a member of
the National Health Insurance Joint Committee,
1911–13; Joint Permanent Secretary to HM Treasury,
1913–19; Principal British Delegate to Reparation
Commission, Paris, 1919–25; Chairman of National
Food Council, 1925–29; Chairman of Bankers' Clearing
House Committee and President of British Bankers'
Association, 1929–30 and 1935–36; Prime Warden of
the Goldsmiths' Company, 1938–39. *Heir: s* Hon. John
Bradbury [*b* 7 Jan. 1914; *m* 1st, 1939; one *s* one *d*; 2nd,
Gwerfyl, *d* of late E. Stanton Roberts, Gellifor, Ruthin,
Denbighshire; one *d*. Westminster; Brasenose College
Oxford]. *Address:* 20 Birchin Lane, EC3. *Club:* United
University.

Died 3 May 1950.

BRADBY, Godfrey Fox, MA; author; *b* 1863; *e s* of
Rev. E. H. Bradby, DD, formerly Headmaster of
Haileybury College; unmarried. *Educ:* Rugby; Balliol
College, Oxford. Assistant Master at Rugby, 1888–1920;
Housemaster, 1908–20; retired, 1920. *Publications:*
history: The Great Days of Versailles; literature: About
Shakespeare and his Plays; About English Poetry; Short
Stories in Shakespeare; Christianity and Common Sense;
The Brontes, 1932, etc.; novels: Dick; Lanchester
Tradition; The Eternal Past; Mrs D.; Little George, etc.;

verse: Broadlands; The Way; Parody and Dust-Shot; The Sage's Note-book, etc. *Address:* 80 Dunchurch Road, Rugby.

Died 20 June 1947.

BRADFIELD, John Job Crew, CMG, 1933; DSc (Eng.); ME, DE, MInstCE, MIEA; member, Dr J. J. C. Bradfield & Son, Consulting Engineers since 1933; Technical Adviser to Hornibrook Highway Ltd, Brisbane; Consulting Engineer for design, fabrication and construction of Brisbane River Bridge and Approaches; Director, Queensland Electric Steel since 1940; Deputy Chancellor, University of Sydney, 1942–43; late Chief Engineer, Sydney Harbour Bridge and Metropolitan Railway Construction; *b* 26 Dec. 1867; *s* of John Edward Bradfield and Marie Crew; *m* Edith, *d* of late John V. Jenkins, Llandaff, Wales; five *s* one *d*. *Educ:* Grammar School, Ipswich, Queensland; University of Sydney. BE, ME and DSc (Eng.) each with first-class Honours and University Medal. Public Works Department, NSW, 1891; Chief Engineer of Sydney Harbour Bridge and City Transit, 1912; designed and supervised the construction of the City Underground Railway and Sydney Harbour Bridge; Member of the Sydney University Senate since 1913; Member of Council of the Women's College within the University; Fellow of Australian and New Zealand National Research Council; Member of Board which established the first Civil Aviation School in Australia, 1916; Member of Patents Investigation Board established during the War; Member of the Town Planning Advisory Board; President, Sydney University Engineering Society; Australian Representative on Council of Institution of Civil Engineers, London, 1936–39; Peter Nicol Russell Medal by the Institution of Engineers, Australia, 1932; Kernot Memorial Medal, by Melbourne University; Telford Gold Medal by the Institution of Civil Engineers, 1934; President RGS of Queensland, 1938; Geog. Soc.'s John Thomson Gold Medal, 1942. *Publications:* Australian Timbers, 1896; Spit and Manly Tramway; Traffic Problems of Greater Sydney, 1917; Town Planning; Report on City and Suburban Electric Railways; Linking of Sydney with North Sydney; various papers on the early history of Sydney and the construction of the Sydney Harbour Bridge and City Underground Railway. *Recreations:* gardening and reading. *Address:* Kholo, 23 Park Avenue, Gordon, Sydney; 16 Barrack Street, Sydney. *Clubs:* University, Sydney.

Died 23 Sept. 1943.

BRADFORD, Rev. E. E., DD, Vicar of Nordelph; *b* 1860; unmarried. *Educ:* Exeter College, Oxford; BA (Hon. Theol.), 1884; MA, 1901; BD 1904; DD 1912; Diplomé (Degré Superieur, Mentionné) Alliance Française, Paris, 1896. Held curacies High Ongar, 1884–86; Walthamstow, 1886–87; English Church, St Petersburg, 1887–89; Paris, 1890–99; Eton, 1889–1905. *Publications:* Sonnets, Songs and Ballads, 1908; Passing the Love of Women, 1913; In Quest of Love, 1914; Lays of Love and Life, 1916; The New Chivalry, 1918; The Romance of Youth, 1920; Ralph Rawdon, 1922; The True Aristocracy, 1923; The Tree of Knowledge, 1925; The Kingdom Within You, 1927; Strangers and Pilgrims, 1929; Boyhood, 1930. *Address:* Nordelph Vicarage, Downham Market, Norfolk.

Died 7 Feb. 1944.

BRADFORD, Samuel Clement, DSc Lond., FLA; physical chemist; bibliographer; *b* London, 10 Jan. 1878; *e s* of late Samuel Joseph Bradford; *m* Cora Mabel, *d* of late Walter Monnery. Assistant, South Kensington Museum, 1899; Science Museum, 1909; Assistant Keeper, 1922; Keeper, 1930–38; Chief Librarian Science Library, 1925–38. Founded, with Prof. A. F. C. Pollard, the British Society for International Bibliography. British National Section of the International Federation for Documentation, in 1927, amalgamated with Assoc. of Special Libraries and Information Bureaux in 1948;

President, 1945–48; Vice-Pres. International Federation for Documentation; Chairman, Internat. Cttee on Classification. *Publications:* various official catalogues including Classification for works on Pure and Applied Science; second edition, 1921; third edition, 1936; Hand-list of short titles of Current Periodicals in the Science Library; 4th edition, 1926; 5th edition, 1938; Books: Romance of Roses, 1946; Documentation, 1948; contributions to scientific and technical journals and works on: Scientific Apparatus; The Kinetic Theory of Gases and Liquids; The Molecular Theory of Solution; Colloid Solutions; The Formation and Structure of Jellies; The Crystallisation of Gelatin; The Liesegang Phenomenon; The Science of Rose Growing; The Classification and Indexing of Scientific Literature; The Principles of Classification; The Organisation of Scientific Bibliography; and Library Cataloguing. *Recreation:* roses. *Address:* Mulberry Cottage, Marryat Road, Wimbledon, SW19. *T:* Wimbledon 2811.

Died 13 Nov. 1948.

BRADLEY, Arthur Granville; *b* 11 Nov. 1850; *s* of late George Granville Bradley, Dean of Westminster and Marian, *d* of Archdeacon Philpot; *m* Florence (*d* 1925), *d* of W. A. Rackham, MRCS; one *d*. *Educ:* Marlborough; Trin. Coll. Cambridge. *Publications:* joint author of History of Marlborough College, 1893; Life of Wolfe, 1895; Sketches from Old Virginia, 1897; Highways and Byways of North Wales, 1898; The Fight with France for North America, 1900; Highways and Byways of the English Lake District, 1901; Owen Glyndwr, 1901; Highways and Byways of South Wales, 1903; Canada in the Twentieth Century, 1903; contributor to Cambridge Modern History, 1903; Captain John Smith; The March and Borderland of Wales, 1905; Round about Wiltshire; Life of Guy Carleton, Lord Dorchester, 1907; The Romance of Northumberland, 1908; The Making of Canada, 1763–1815, 1900; Worcestershire, 1909; Rivers and Streams of England, 1909; Wiltshire and Herefordshire (Cambridge County Geographies), 1909; The Wye, 1910; Shakespeare's Avon, 1910; Britain across the Seas, America, 1911; Canada (Home University Library), 1911; The Gateway of Scotland, 1912; Other Days, 1913; Clear Waters (trout fishing), 1915; An Old Gate of England, 1918; A Book of the Severn, 1919; England's Outpost: The Story of the Kentish Cinque Ports, 1921; Canada, in Nations of To-day; In Praise of N Wales, 1925; Exmoor Memories, 1926; When Squires and Farmers Thrived, 1927; Romance of Wales, 1929; United Empire Loyalists, 1932; articles to the Reviews. *Recreations:* all out-door games and field-sports at different periods. *Address:* West Watch, Rye.

Died 25 Jan. 1943.

BRADSHAW, Harold Chalton, CBE 1935; Hon. MArch (Liverpool), FRIBA; architect; Secretary, Royal Fine Art Commission; Member of Council and Executive Committee, British School at Rome; Member of Council and Board of Education, Architects' Registration Council; for several years Member Council Royal Institute of British Architects, and Council Architectural Association; *b* 15 Feb. 1893; *e s* of late J. H. Bradshaw, Liverpool; *m* 1918, Mary, *e d* of late Professor J. W. Taylor, FRCS, MSc; three *s*. *Educ:* University of Liverpool (Holt Scholar, 1913); awarded First Rome Scholarship in Architecture, 1913; Médaille Paris Salon, 1920. Architect Guards' Memorial, London (with Gilbert Ledward, RA); Memorials to Missing at Cambrai and Ploegsteert Wood for Imperial War Graves Commission, country houses, banks, and other works; during last War served in Belgium, France, and Italy; Captain RE (TF) (Croce de Guerra). *Publications:* Praeneste, A Study for its Restoration in Papers, BSR; various contributions to RIBA Journal and technical press and to 14th ed. Ency. Brit. *Address:* 11 Ornan Road, Hampstead, NW3. *Club:* Athenæum.

Died 15 Oct. 1943.

BRADSHAW, William Graham, CBE 1920; member of firm of R. Bradshaw & Son, solicitors, Moorgate-Station Chambers, Moorfields, EC2; Chairman, Bombay Gas Co. Ltd; Joint Deputy-Chairman, Midland Bank, Ltd; Director, Eagle, Star and British Dominions Insurance Co., Ltd, etc; *b* 1861; *s* of Richard Bradshaw; *m* 1890, Dora Sophia, *d* of Edward Studd. *Address:* Down Park, Crawley Down, Sussex.

Died 16 March 1941.

BRADY, Major Gerald Charles Jervis, DSO 1918; late RA; 3rd *s* of late Captain G. W. Brady, RN; *m* 1924, Florence Ellen, *d* of late Thomas Pattenden, London. Served S Africa, 1900 (Queen's medal three clasps); European War, 1914–18 (DSO). *Address:* Wickhall, Hove, Sussex.

Died 27 Dec. 1941.

BRADY, Patrick Joseph; Past President Incorporated Law Society of Ireland; Director of Great Southern Railways, Ireland; *b* 1868; *e s* of late James Brady; *m* Evelyn (*d* 1931), *y d* of late John Douglas Parminter, Paymaster, RN. *Educ:* St Vincent's College, Castleknock; University College, Dublin. Admitted a Solicitor, 1893; MP (N) St Stephen's Green Division of Dublin, 1910–18. *Address:* Glena, Booterstown, Dublin. *T:* Blackrock 82. *Clubs:* Stephen's Green, Dublin; Royal Irish Yacht.

Died 20 May 1943.

BRAGG, Sir William (Henry), OM 1931; KBE 1920; CBE 1917; FRS, MA, DSc; President of the Royal Society, 1935–40; Hon. Fellow, Trinity College, Cambridge; Director of the Royal Institution of Great Britain; Fullerian Professor of Chemistry, Royal Institution, and Director of Davy-Faraday Research Laboratory, since 1923; Member of Advisory Council for Scientific and Industrial Research since 1937; *b* 2 July 1862; *e s* of R. J. Bragg, Stoneraise Place, Wigton, Cumberland; *m* 1889, Gwendoline (*d* 1929), *d* of late Sir Charles Todd; one *s* one *d*. *Educ:* King William's College, Isle of Man; Trinity College, Cambridge (Major Scholar, 1882). Third Wrangler, 1884; 1st class in Part III of Mathematical Tripos, 1885; Professor at Adelaide University, 1886–1908; Cavendish Professor at Leeds University, 1909–15; Quain Professor of Physics, University of London, 1915–23; Hon. Fellow, Trinity College, Cambridge, 1920; received 1915 Nobel Prize (in conjunction with his son W. L. Bragg), and the Barnard Gold Medal (Columbia University) (with W. L. Bragg), for work on X-rays and crystals; Rumford Medal of Royal Society, 1916; Copley Medal, 1930; Gold Medal of the Societé Italian della Scienze, 1917 (in conjunction with W. L. Bragg); Franklin Gold Medal, Franklin Institute, Philadelphia, 1930; Faraday Medal, Institution of Electrical Engineers, 1936; John Carty Medal of National Academy of Sciences of the United States of America, 1939; Hon. DSc, Manchester, 1914, Brown University, Rhode Island, USA, 1914, Leeds University, 1919, Trinity College, Dublin, 1920; Sheffield University, 1931; University of Pennsylvania, 1924; Hon. DCL Durham, 1924; Hon. LLD St Andrews, 1925; Edinburgh, 1937; Hon. DSc Oxford, 1926; Hon. DSc Bristol, 1927; Hon. LLD Glasgow, 1928; Hon. ScD Cambridge, 1932; Hon. DSc. Univ. of Wales, Bangor, 1934; Hon. DSc. London, 1936, Birmingham, 1939; Mem. Kongl. Danske Vidensk Selskat; Corr. Mem. Reale Accad. Sci. Turin; Corr. Mem. Acad. Sci. Paris; Forr. Mem. Soc. Hollandaise des Sciences. Hon. Mem. Videnskap Akademiet Norvège; Corr. Mem. Academia de Ciencias, Madrid; Foreign Associate, National Academy of Sciences, United States of America; Hon. Member New York Academy of Science; Soc. Sci. Fenn. *Publications:* Studies in Radio-activity; X-rays and Crystal Structure; The World of Sound; Concerning the Nature of Things; Old Trades and New Knowledge; An Introduction to Crystal Analysis; The Universe of Light, 1933; various papers in the Philosophical Magazine, the Transactions of the Royal Society, and elsewhere on scientific subjects. *Recreation:* golf. *Address:* Royal Institution, Albemarle Street, W1. *T:* Regent 0669; Watlands, Chiddingfold, Surrey. *Club:* Athenæum.

Died 12 March 1942.

BRAIDWOOD, Harold Lithgow, CSI 1929; late Indian Civil Service; *b* 12 Aug. 1872; *s* of Lithgow Braidwood, St Margarets, Middlesex; *m* 1st, 1900, Ethel (*d* 1921), *d* of H. R. P. Carter; one *s*; 2nd, 1928, Margery, *d* of Joseph Byers, Chester. *Educ:* St Paul's School; Corpus Christi College, Oxford, MA; University College, London. Entered ICS 1896; Resident, Travancore and Cochin, 1917–20; Member, Board of Revenue, Madras, 1927–29; retired, 1930. *Address:* 28 Pearl Court, Eastbourne, Sussex. *T:* Eastbourne 31.

Died 5 July 1949.

BRAINE, Brig. Herbert Edmund Reginald Rubens, CB 1933; CMG 1919; DSO 1916; late Royal Munster Fusiliers and Royal Scots Fusiliers; *b* Mysore, India, 1876; *s* of late Edmund Francis Braine, Royal Scots Fusiliers, of Leckhampton, Gloucestershire; *m* 1927, Violet Helen, *widow* of Colonel Allan McConaghey, CIE, and *d* of late Col Andrew Barry. *Educ:* Dulwich College. After five wasted years in Burma, Bengal and Siam, gazetted, 1900, to Royal Munster Fusiliers from the Border Regt Militia; Capt. 1910; psc 1910; Major, 1915; Lt-Col 1917; Col 1921; Brigadier, 1930; served South African War, 1900–02 (despatches, Queen's medal five clasps), NW Frontier of India, 1908 (despatches, medal and clasp); European War, 1914–18 (despatches eight times, 3 war medals, Bt Major, Bt Lt-Col, Bt Col, CMG, DSO and Ordre de la Couronne, Belgium); Burma operations, 1931–32 (despatches, medal, CB); held various appointments on the General Staff at War Office and elsewhere, ending with Chief General Staff Officer, Northern Command, York, 1927–28; commanded 2nd Bn Royal Scots Fusiliers in India, 1923–27; 133rd (Sussex and Kent) Infantry Brigade, TA, 1928–30; 12th Infantry Brigade, Secunderabad Area, 4th Division, India, 1930–33; retired, 1933. *Recreations:* polo, hunting, shooting, fishing, golf. *Address:* 11 Zetland House, Marloes Road, W8. *T:* Western 8533. *Clubs:* Army and Navy, White's.

Died 27 April 1942.

BRAITHWAITE, Charles; ARHA 1913; landscape painter and craftsman; *m* 1916. *Educ:* Belfast Government School of Art; Royal Coll. of Art, London. First exhibited at Royal Hibernian Academy, 1912, member of Guild of Irish Art Workers. *Address:* Lisalore, 165 Cliftonpark Avenue, Belfast.

Died 25 Feb. 1941.

BRAITHWAITE, Dame (Florence) Lilian, DBE 1943; actress; *b* 9 March 1873; *d* of late Rev. J. M. Braithwaite, Vicar and Rural Dean of Croydon; *m* Gerald Lawrence (marr. diss.); one *d*. *Educ:* Croydon and Hampstead High Schools; Dresden. Played many Shakespearian parts with Sir Frank Benson; in modern plays with the late Sir George Alexander, Sir Herbert Tree, Lewis Waller, also with Cyril Maude, Fred Terry, Sir Gerald du Maurier and other managements; for a year in Mr Wu with Matheson Lang, 1913–14; General Post, 1916–17; most important parts since the war were in The Bill of Divorcement, The Vortex (both in London and New York), Caroline, The Silver Cord, The Truth Game, Symphony in Two Flats, After All, Flat to Let, Party and Fresh Fields; Family Affairs; Full House; Lady of La Paz; Bats in the Belfry; Elizabeth; A House in the Square, 1940; Ducks and Drakes, 1941; Arsenic and Old Lace, 1942–46; Truant in Park Lane, 1947; Royal Circle, 1948. *Recreations:* swimming, reading, watching other people act. *Address:* 20 Chesham Place, SW1. *Club:* Three Arts.

Died 17 Sept. 1948.

BRAITHWAITE, Gen. Sir Walter Pipon, GCB 1929; KCB 1918; Bath King of Arms since 1933; *b* 11 Nov. 1865; *s* of late Rev. W. Braithwaite and Laura, *d* of late Com.-General Pipon, Seigneur of Noirmont, Jersey; *m* 1895, Jessie Adine, *d* of late Caldwell Ashworth (one *s* killed in action, 1916). *Educ:* Bedford; RMC, Sandhurst. Entered Army, P. A. Somerset Light Infantry 1886; Captain 1894; Major 1906; Lieutenant-Colonel 1906; Colonel, 1909; Brig.-Gen. 1911; Major-Gen. 1915; Lt-Gen. 1919; General, 1926; General Staff Officer, Staff Coll., 1906–09; War Office, 1909–11; Commandant, Staff College, Quetta, 1911–14; Director Staff Duties War Office, 1914–15; Chief of General Staff, Mediterranean Expeditionary Force, March–Oct. 1915; commanded 62nd Division, Dec. 1915–Aug. 1918, and IX Army Corps, 18 Aug. 1918 to 9 Sept. 1919; served Burma, 1886–87 (despatches, medal with clasp); S Africa, 1899–1902 (despatches thrice, brevet Major, Queen's medal 6 clasps, King's medal 2 clasps); European War; Légion d'honneur, Croix de Commandeur, 1915; Grand Officier Ordre de la Couronne, 1919; Croix de Guerre with two palms (French), 1918; Croix de Guerre (Belgian), 1919; promoted Maj.-Gen. and Lt-Gen., KCB; despatches nine times; GOC-in-C Western Command, India, 1920–23; Scottish Command, Edinburgh 1923–26; Eastern Command, 1926–27; ADC General to the King, 1927–31; Adjutant-General to the Forces, 1927–31; retired pay, 1931; Governor of Royal Hospital, Chelsea, 1931–38; Col The Somerset LI (Prince Albert's), 1929–38. *Address:* The Ricks, Rotherwick, Hampshire. *T:* Hook 114. *Club:* Army and Navy.

Died 7 Sept. 1945.

BRAMAH, David, CBE 1920; General Secretary Marine Engineers' Association, Ltd, 1916–43; *b* 1875; *m* 1st, Emilia (*d* 1920), *d* of Charles Henry Hobday; 2nd, 1923, Mrs Lilian Harrison Male (*d* 1931). *Address:* Ashgrove Road, Seven Kings, Essex.

Died 13 Aug. 1947.

BRAMAH, Ernest; author. *Publications:* English Farming, 1894; The Wallet of Kai Lung, 1900; Mirror of Kong Ho, 1905; What Might Have Been, 1907 (as The Secret of the League, 1909); The Transmutation of Ling, 1911; Max Carrados, 1914; Kai Lung's Golden Hours, 1922; The Eyes of Max Carrados, 1923; The Specimen Case, 1924; Max Carrados Mysteries, 1927; Kai Lung Unrolls his Mat, 1928; A Guide to the Varieties and Rarity of English Regal Copper Coins, 1929; Short Stories of To-day and Yesterday, 1929; A Little Flutter, 1930; The Moon of Much Gladness, 1932 (in USA as The Return of Kai Lung); The Bravo of London, 1934; The Kai Lung Omnibus, 1936; Kai Lung Beneath the Mulberry Tree, 1940. *Address:* c/o A. P. Watt & Son, Hastings House, Norfolk Street, WC2.

Died 23 June 1942.

BRAMWELL, Edward George; was Modelling Master at the Westminster School of Art for 25 years (now resigned); *b* 29 July 1865; *m* Hettey Amy Sheen. *Educ:* St Saviour's Grammar School, Southwark, SE School of Art, at Leeds, Tamworth and the City and Guilds of London; many prizes, and City and Guilds Sculpture Studentship of £100 and two years' free tuition and their travelling scholarship. Worked in Sir Geo. Frampton's studio, also the studios of W. S. Frith, RBS, and late Sterling Lee, RBS; was one of the successful Competitors for Sculpture for the New Art Gallery, Glasgow; has exhibited many times at the Royal Academy, also at Liverpool and other Provincial towns; first exhibited at the RA, sketch design for a tomb, 1898. *Principal Works:* The Millenary Monument to Ethelfreda at Tamworth Castle; made the Designs for the Sculpture for the Bristol Art Gallery. *Ideal Works:* Æolus ruling the Four Winds, bronze 1905; Hero mourning over the Body of Leander, 1909; Labor Omnia Vincit, 1912; Mother and Sea Urchins, 1914. *Address:* The Old Bell, Godshill, nr Ventnor, Isle of Wight.

Died 7 Nov. 1944.

BRAND, Col David Ernest, CBE 1944; DSO 1918; TD 1925; DL Lanarkshire, 1942; JP, Glasgow; Hon. Col 5th Bn Highland LI; Chairman, Glasgow TA and AF Association, and of the Glasgow Academicals War Memorial Trust; partner of Carruthers, Gemmill & McKillop, Solicitors, Glasgow; *b* 7 Nov. 1884; *s* of late Adam Brand, Glasgow, and Helen, *d* of John Ferguson, shipbuilder, Glasgow; *m* 1918, Mary Christabel, *y d* of W. B. Billinghurst. Served European War, 1914–18 (despatches, DSO, 1914–15 star, two medals). *Address:* Birkwood, Symington, Lanarkshire. *Clubs:* Caledonian; Western (Glasgow).

Died 16 March 1948.

BRAND, Hon. Roger, CMG 1919; DSO 1916; Honorary Brigadier-General, late Rifle Brigade; *b* 23 Nov. 1880; 5th *s* of 2nd Viscount Hampden; *m* 1913, Muriel H. L., *d* of H. B. Montgomery; one *d*. Served S Africa, 1900–02 (two medals 5 clasps); European War (CMG, DSO and bar, despatches, Chevalier Légion d'Honneur). *Address:* Lindsay Lodge, Devenish Road, Sunningdale, Berks. *Club:* Turf.

Died 23 Oct. 1945.

BRANDEIS, Louis Dembitz; *b* Louisville, Kentucky, 13 Nov. 1856; *s* of Adolph Brandeis and Fredericka Dembitz; *m* 1891, Alice Goldmark; two *d*. *Educ:* Louisville High School (University of Louisville); Annen Real School, Dresden; Harvard Law School. Began the practice of the law at St Louis, Missouri, 1878; practised then in Boston, 1879–1916; Associate Justice of the Supreme Court of the United States, 1916–39. *Publications:* Business a Profession: Other Peoples' Money, 1914; The Curse of Bigness, 1934. *Address:* Washington, DC, USA.

Died 5 Oct. 1941.

BRANDON, Captain Vivian R., CBE 1919; RN; lately Professional Officer, Ministry of War Transport and previously Mercantile Marine Department, Board of Trade, from 1927; *b* 1882; *s* of G. S. Brandon; *m* 1915, Joan Elizabeth Maud, *e d* of Capt. H. V. Simpson, RN; two *s* one *d*. Entered Britannia, 1896; Sub-Lieut 1901; Lt 1902; Commander, 1914; commanded HM ships Bramble, 1914, Odin, 1920, Cyclamen, 1920–23; Acting-Captain and Assistant Director of Naval Intelligence, 1918–19; Mine Clearance Officer in Norwegian waters, 1919 (despatches); Naval Assist to Hydrographer of the Navy, 1923–27; retired list, 1927; Légion d'honneur (officier). *Address:* 33 Argyll Road, W8.

Died 3 Jan. 1944.

BRANSON, William Philip Sutcliffe, CBE 1919; MD Cantab; FRCP London; retired; Consulting Physician, Royal Free Hospital; Consulting Physician to St Andrew's Hospital, Dollis Hill, NW; sometime Medical Officer, Sun Life Office; Medical Attendant to Nursing Staff, St Bartholomew's Hospital; Associate Examiner in Medicine, University of London; Physician, Duchess of Westminster Hospital, BEF, and Temp Col AMS; Consulting Physician 5th Army BEF; *b* 1874; 3rd *s* of late James H. A. Branson, Barrister-at-law. *Educ:* Bedford; Trinity College, Cambridge; St Bartholomew's Hospital. *Publications:* Sober Pieces and Songs; various contributions to medical literature. *Address:* Bradfield Hall, Nr Bury St Edmunds, Suffolk. *Clubs:* United University; West Suffolk County (Bury St Edmunds).

Died 5 March 1950.

BRASSEY, Lt-Col Edgar Hugh, MVO 1909; late comdg 1st Life Guards; *b* 6 April 1878; *s* of late Henry A. Brassey; *m* 1911, Margaret Hepburn-Stuart-Forbes-Trefusis, *y d* of late Col Hon. Walter Rodolph Trefusis,

CB, and *niece* of 6th Duke of Buccleuch; one *s* one *d*. High Sheriff, Wiltshire, 1927. *Address:* Dauntsey Park, Chippenham.

Died 11 April 1946.

BRASSEY, Captain Robert Bingham; JP; *b* 18 Oct. 1875; *o s* of late Albert Brassey and Hon. Matilda Maria Helena Bingham OBE, *d* of 4th Baron Clanmorris; *m* 1st, 1904, Violet (*d* 1919), 2nd *d* of late Armar Henry Lowry-Corry; one *s* three *d*; 2nd, Lady Dalmeny (who obtained a divorce, 1927; she *m* 3rd, 1929, C. Hilton-Green), *y d* of late Lord Henry Grosvenor; 3rd, 1927, Constance Marion, *d* of late Thomas Britten, Johannesburg. MP Banbury Division, Oxfordshire, Jan. to Nov. 1910; late 17th Lancers; Brigade-Major, 1915–16. *Address:* The Node, Codicote, Hitchin, Herts. *Club:* Cavalry.

Died 14 Nov. 1946.

BRATTON, Rt Rev. Theodore Du Bose; Bishop of Mississippi, 1903–38; *b* Winnsboro, SC, 11 Nov. 1862; *s* of General John and Elizabeth Du Bose Bratton; *m* 1st, Lucy Beverley Randolph, Tallahassee, Florida; three *s* three *d*; 2nd, Mrs Ivy Perrin Gass. *Educ:* The University of the South, DD, LLD University of Mississippi. On attaining manhood accepted position as Registrar of his Alma Mater, and later as a Master in her Preparatory School; Rector of the Church of the Advent, Spartanburg, 1888; served as Trustee of the University of the South and of St Mary's, Raleigh, NC; Professor of History in Converse College, 1890–99; Deputy to the General Convention; Member of the Standing Committee and Board of Missions of SC and Examining Chaplain; Rector of St Mary's School for girls, Raleigh, NC, 1899; Pres. of the Province of Sewanee, 1926; Chaplain General, United Confederate Veterans, 1930; Chancellor of the University of the South, Sewanee, Tennessee, 1935. *Publications:* Wanted—Leaders: A Study of Negro development; An Apostle of Reality, The Life and Thought of the Rev. William Porcher Du Bose, STD; Addresses, educational and historical, and sermons from time to time in pamphlet. *Address:* 1541 W Capitol Street, Jackson, Mississippi, USA.

Died 26 June 1944.

BRAUNHOLTZ, Eugen Gustav Wilhelm, MA (Camb.), PhD (Berlin); Reader in Romance, Cambridge University; *b* 21 Jan. 1859. *Educ:* University of Tübingen; University of Berlin; University of Paris. *Publications:* Dissertation on Barlaam and Josaphat, 1884; editions of Molière's Les Précieuses ridicules, 1890; Le Misanthrope, 1894; and L'Avare, 1897; Racine's Les Plaideurs, 1890; Corneille's Polyeucte, 1892; Books of Reference for Students and Teachers of French: a Critical Survey, 1901; contributions to philological and literary reviews. *Recreation:* music. *Address:* King's College, and Adams Road, Cambridge. *T:* 3676.

Died 8 Feb. 1941.

BRAY, Sir Edward Hugh, Kt 1917; CSI 1919; *b* 15 April 1874; *e s* of late Judge Sir E. Bray; *m* 1912, Constance, *d* of Sir John Graham, 1st Bt. *Educ:* Charterhouse; Trinity College, Cambridge. Cambridge University football eleven 1895–97, cricket eleven 1896–97. Partner firms of Ogilvy, Gillanders and Co., and Gillanders, Arbuthnot and Co., retired 1920; President Bengal Chamber of Commerce, 1917; Sheriff of Calcutta, 1916; Controller of Contracts, Army Headquarters, India, with temporary rank of Brigadier-General, 1918. *Address:* Rovindene, Rye, Sussex. *Club:* United University.

Died 27 Nov. 1950.

BRAY, Francis Edmond; KC 1936; Chairman, Board of Referees, 1939; *b* 2 March 1882; *s* of Sir Reginald More Bray and Emily Octavia Barclay; *m* 1919, Hon. Ruth Hester Frances Scarlett (*d* 1943); one *d*. *Educ:* Harrow; Trinity College, Cambridge. President Cambridge Union Society 1904; University Shooting Eight

1902–05; called to Bar, 1906; Territorial Army 1909–26, retired as Lt-Col; served European War (MC, despatches twice); TD; DL for Surrey. *Publications:* British Rights at Sea; Trade Marks Act, 1938. *Address:* Trenchmore, Shere, Surrey. *T:* Shere 138.

Died 8 May 1950.

BRAYBROOKE, 7th Baron *cr* 1788; **Henry Neville,** BA 1876, MA 1880; Hereditary Visitor of Magdalene College, Cambridge; DL and JP Cambs; JP Herts and Essex; *b* 11 July 1855; *s* of 6th Baron and Lucy Frances, *d* of John T. Le Marchant; *S* father, 1904; *m* 1st, 1898, Emilie Pauline (*d* 1912), *y d* of late Antoine Gonin of the Chateau de Condemine, Macon, France; 2nd, 1917, Dorothy, JP Essex, *y d* of late Sir George Lawson, KCB; two *s* one *d*. *Educ:* Eton; Magdalene College, Cambridge. *Recreations:* shooting, golf. *Heir: s* Hon. Richard Henry Cornwallis Neville, *b* 13 July 1918. *Seats:* Audley End, Saffron Walden; Heydon House, Royston. *Address:* Audley End, Saffron Walden. *T:* Saffron Walden 54. *Club:* Travellers'.

Died 9 March 1941.

BRAYBROOKE, 8th Baron *cr* 1788; **Richard Henry Cornwallis Neville;** Lieut Grenadier Guards; Hereditary Visitor of Magdalene College, Cambridge; *b* 13 July 1918; *s* of 7th Baron and Dorothy, *y d* of late Sir George Lawson, KCB; *S* father, 1941. *Educ:* Eton; Magdalene Coll., Cambridge. *Heir: b* Hon. George Robert Latimer Neville, *b* 1920 (missing, 1941). *Address:* Mill House, Littlebury, Saffron Walden. *T:* Saffron Walden 105; Heydon, Royston, Herts.

Died 23 Jan. 1943.

BRAZIER-CREAGH, Col George Washington, CB 1917; CMG 1901; AMS; *b* 20 June 1858; *s* of late George Washington Brazier-Creagh, Woodville, Buttevant, and Creagh Castle, Doneraile, Co. Cork. *Educ:* Trinity College, Dublin. Conducted Missions to SE Persia, 1893–94; to Seistan, Persia, 1896–97, and brought same to a successful issue; making extensive explorations of little-known regions throughout Eastern Persia and Baluchistan, and opening up the Seistan-Nushki trade route; thanked by Government of India; Punjab Frontier Expedition, 1897–98 (medal and clasp); accompanied Pekin Syndicate throughout North China, 1898–99; served South Africa, 1899–1902 (despatches thrice, Queen's medal six clasps, King's medal two clasps, CMG); European War, 1914–19 (despatches four times, 1914 Star, CB); retired, 1911. Royal Humane Society Medal. *Recreations:* steeplechasing, hunting, polo, shooting. *Address:* 27 Carlton Vale, NW6. *Club:* Royal Empire Society.

Died 10 Oct. 1942.

BRAZIL, Angela; *b* Preston, 30 Nov. 1868; of old Irish ancestry. *Educ:* Ellerslie College, Victoria Park, Manchester. Studied Figure Painting at The Heatherley Studio, London, and Landscape Painting in Wales; has travelled much in Italy, Sicily, Tyrol, Southern France, Palestine, Egypt, etc. Member of Incorporated Society of Authors. *Publication:* forty-nine school stories for girls: My own Schooldays: an Autobiography, 1925. *Recreations:* sketching, natural history, botany, archæology, gardening, travelling, music. *Address:* The Quadrant, Coventry. *T:* Coventry 5128; The Haven, Polperro Cornwall.

Died 13 March 1947.

BREADING, Lt-Col George Remington, DSO 1904; late Worcestershire Regiment and King's African Rifles; *b* 2 Oct. 1877. Entered Army, 1900; Captain, 1904; served British East Africa, 1901 (medal with clasp); East Africa, 1902–04 (slightly wounded, despatches, two clasps, DSO); with West African Frontier Force, 1906–10; served Somaliland, 1908–10 (clasp), 1914–15 (despatches), and 1920 (despatches).

Died 9 March 1942.

BREALEY, William Ramsden, ROI 1921; RBA 1929 (ARBA 1923); artist; portrait painter; *b* 29 June 1889; *m* 1916, Katie Mary Le Pla; one *s* one *d. Educ:* College of Art, Sheffield. (Hon. mention) Société des Artistes Français; Exhibitor Société des Artistes Français, Royal Academy, Royal Institute of Oil Painters, Royal Society of British Artists, Liverpool, Hull, etc. *Works:* Arthur and Ruby (mention honorable); The Gipsy; Burmese Dancer; Wife of the Artist; The Lord Mayor of London (Sir Stephen Killik), 1934–35, etc.; Ministry of Information, official purchase for the Crown oil painting, Gas Mask, 1941. *Recreations:* fishing and motoring. *Address:* c/o Westminster Bank Ltd, 100 High St., Brentford. *Club:* Chelsea Arts.

Died 23 Feb. 1949.

BREDIUS, Dr. Abraham; late Director, late Adviser, at the Royal Picture Gallery, Maurits Huis, The Hague; *b* Amsterdam, 18 April 1855; unmarried. Hon. Doctor, Amsterdam, Giessen, and Cracow; large gold medal (litteris et artibus) from the Emperor of Austria, 1883; Grand Croix de l'Ordre d'Orange Nassau; Membre Correspondant de l'Institut; Membre of the Royal Academy of Holland, Belgium, and Poland; Hon. Member Burlington Fine Arts Club, London. *Publications:* Künstler Inventare, 8 vols (Archiv. documents on Art in Dutch and German); Die Meisterwerke des Ryks Museums in Amsterdam; Die Meisterwerke der Königl. Gemäldegallerie im Haag; Rembrandt Exhibition at Leiden; Torrentius; Amsterdam in de XVIIᵉ eeuw (part: de Schilderkunst); die Groszherzogl. Gem. Galerie, Oldenburg; Catalogue Royal Picture Gallery, the Hague; Kunstliefde Utrecht; several for the Ryks-Museum, etc.; Jan Steen, 1925; many articles on Art in Nederl. Spectator, Oud Holland, Gazette des Beaux Arts, Burlington Magazine, Revue de l'Art ancien et moderne, Zeitschrift für bildende Kunst, etc. *Recreation:* music. *Address:* Villa Evelyne Boulevard de Belgique, Monaco.

Died 13 March 1946.

BREESE, Air-Cdre (acting Air Vice-Marshal) Charles Dempster, CB 1933; AFC 1918; AFRAeS; Air Officer Commanding No. 18 (Reconnaissance) Group, RAF since 1938; *b* 23 April 1889; *y s* of late G. C. Breese; *m* 1916, Mary Eleanor, *y d* of late Henry Colpoys Tweedy of Cloonamahon, Collooney, Co. Sligo; two *s.* Entered Royal Navy, 1905; transferred for flying duties, 1913; served European War, 1914–18, France and Flanders; Deputy Director of Training, Air Ministry, 1918; served N Kurdistan, 1932 (CB); Air Commodore, 1932; Air Officer Commanding No. 17 (Training) Group, 1937–38. *Club:* Naval and Military.

Died 6 March 1941.

BREMNER, Alexander, CBE 1943; TD; Hon. Physician Children's Hospital, Sheffield; Lecturer, Diseases of Children, Sheffield University; *b* 9 July 1890; *s* of Robert S. Bremner; *m* 1919, Isabella A. J. Elphinston. *Educ:* Edinburgh Univ. (MB, ChB 1913, MD 1919, DPH, DTM & H). Served European War, 1914–18 (despatches, MC); War of 1939–45 (despatches, CBE). *Address:* 408 Fulwood Road, Sheffield. *T:* 31744.

Died 29 Sept. 1944.

BREND, William A., MA Camb. (1st class Natural Science Tripos), BSc Lond., MD Lond. (Gold Medallist in State Medicine); MRCP; Barrister-at-law, Inner Temple; Lecturer on Forensic Medicine, Charing Cross Hospital; Medical Referee under the Workmen's Compensation Act; Examiner in State Medicine to the University of London; late Neurological Deputy Commissioner of Medical Services (Ministry of Pensions); Member of the British Psycho-Analytic Society; late Vice-President of Medico-Legal Society; Fellow of the Royal Society of Medicine; *b* Kensington, 1873; *s* of William Brend, MRCS; *m* Lillian, *d* of G. B. Clark, MD, late MP for Caithness; one *s. Educ:* St Paul's School; Sidney Sussex College, Cambridge; King's

College Hospital and University College Hospital. Late temp. Major, RAMC; in charge during European War of Special Medical Board for Functional Nerve Disorders. Gave Chadwick Lecture on Nervous Shock in Peace and War, 1942. *Publications:* Handbook of Medical Jurisprudence and Toxicology (8th edition); Inquiry into the Statistics of Deaths from Violence, 1915; Health and the State, 1917; Psychotherapy and War Experience, 1921; Sacrifice to Attis, 1936; Traumatic Mental Disorders in Courts of Law, 1938; Foundations of Human Conflicts, 1944; numerous contributions to Nineteenth Century, Edinburgh Review, New Statesman, and other journals. *Address:* 14 Bolingbroke Grove, SW11. *Clubs:* Savage, Athenæum.

Died 5 Oct. 1944.

BRENNAN, Hon. Frank, LLB; MHR for Batman, Victoria, 1911–31 and 1934–49; *b* Sedgwick, Victoria; *m* 1913, Sheila O'Donnell; one *s* one *d. Educ:* Melbourne University, LLB. Attorney-General, Commonwealth of Australia, 1929–31. *Address:* 3 St Neot's Avenue, Northcote, Melbourne, N.16, Victoria, Australia.

Died 5 Nov. 1950.

BRERETON, Maud Adeline Cloudesley-; Consultant and Editor of publications to the British Commercial Gas Association since its foundation in 1912 (united 1945 in the British Gas Council); retired from Editorial Chair, June 1932; *b* London; *e c* of late Matthew Ford and Ellen Catherine Macdonald of Glencoe; *m* 1st, 1897, Principal John Charles Horobin, MA (*d* 1902); two *s* one *d*; 2nd, 1904, Cloudesley Shovell Henry Brereton (*d* 1937); two *s. Educ:* Hockerill College, Bishop's Stortford (Senior Scholar, Bishop's and Archbishop's Exhibitioner, Divinity First). First Headmistress of Girls' Secondary School, St Andrew's, Willesden, 1893; Headmistress the Baroness Burdett-Coutts School, St Anne's, South Highgate, 1894, 1895; Principal and afterwards Bursar of Homerton Training College, Cambridge; Fellow of the Royal Sanitary Institute; Fellow of the Royal Institute of Public Health and Hygiene; first woman Hon. Fellow of the Institution of Sanitary Engineers; Member of the Institute of Journalists; Vice-President of the Society of Women Journalists; decorated by the French Government for services to International Public Health, Officier d'Académie, 1907; Chairman, 1923–24, Association for Education in Industry and Commerce; President, 1931, re-elected, 1932. The Efficiency Club. *Recreations:* every branch of needlecraft, travel, light literature. *Address:* c/o The British Gas Council, Gas Industries House, 1 Grosvenor Place, SW1.

Died 16 April 1946.

BRERETON, Reginald Hugh, CIE 1910; *b* 12 Nov. 1861; *s* of late E. W. Brereton, Cheltenham; *m* 1885, Edith Margaret (*d* 1940), *y d* of late Dr W. Dunne, Londonderry; one *s. Educ:* Cheltenham; Balliol College, Oxford. Entered ICS 1880; Joint-Magistrate, 1892; Dep.-Comr 1895; Magistrate and Collector, 1896; Inspector-Gen. Police, 1900; retired, 1909; King's Police Medal, 1911. *Address:* Cross Lanes Farm, Woking, Surrey.

Died 26 Feb. 1944.

BRETT, George Sidney, MA (Oxon); Professor of Philosophy, University of Toronto, since 1916; *b* 1879; *s* of George J. Brett; *m* 1911; two *s* one *d. Educ:* Christ Church, Oxford. First-class Lit. Hum. Entered Indian Educational Service (Professor of Philosophy, Government College, Lahore); Professor of Ethics, Trinity College, Toronto Canada, and Lecturer in the University of Toronto, 1908–16; Dean of the School of Graduate Studies; Fellow of the Royal Society of Canada. *Publications:* Philosophy of Gassendi, 1908; History of Psychology (3 vols), 1912–1921; Psychology, Ancient and Modern, 1928; Ency Brit. (14th ed. 1930) Article, Psychology, History of; and others. *Address:* 127 Albany Avenue, Toronto, Canada. *T:* Lakeside 8357.

Died 27 Oct. 1944.

BRETT, William Bailie, CSI 1937; CIE 1933; *b* 27 Nov. 1889; *s* of William Leopold and Julia Brett; *m* 1926, Elizabeth Wynne Vincent Lloyd-Williams; one *d.* *Educ:* Liverpool College; Hertford College, Oxford. Entered ICS 1912; Private Secretary to the Governor of Bihar and Orissa, 1921–22; Magistrate and Collector of Bihar and Orissa, 1922–29; Finance Secretary, 1929–33; Relief Commissioner, 1934; Chief Secretary, Bihar, 1935; retired, 1940. *Address:* Overbury, nr Tewkesbury, Glos.

Died 15 Sept. 1947.

BREWIN, Arthur Winbolt, CMG, 1911; *b* 12 June 1867; *m* Ada Mary (*d* 1943), *d* of late John Russell, Glenview, Limerick. *Educ:* Winchester. Cadet Hong-Kong Civil Service, 1888; JP 1894; Inspector of Schools, 1897; Registrar-General and Member Legislative Council, 1901; retired, 1912. *Address:* Eyrefield, Killiney, Co. Dublin.

Died 12 Aug. 1946.

BREWSTER, Rt Rev. Benjamin; Bishop of Maine since 1916; *b* 25 Nov. 1860; *s* of Rev. Joseph Brewster, Rector of Christ Church, New Haven, Conn, and Sarah Jane Bunce Brewster; *m* 1st, 1891, Stella Yates (*d* 1929); two *s* two *d*; 2nd, 1937, Mary Phillips Hay. *Educ:* Yale College, AB; General Theological Seminary, New York, BD. Assistant minister in Cavalry Parish, NY City, 1886–91; Rector of the Church of the Holy Communion, South Orange, NJ, 1891–95; Grace Church, Colorado Springs, Col, 1895–1906; Dean of St Mark's Cathedral, Salt Lake City, Utah, 1906–09; Missionary Bishop of Western Colorado, 1909–16; Hon. DD, Bowdoin College, 1929; Hon. LHD, Univ. of Maine, 1937. *Publications:* occasional Sermons, in local papers. *Recreation:* walking. *Address:* 143 State Street, Portland, Maine, USA. *T:* 4–1976.

Died 2 Feb. 1941.

BREWSTER, Rt. Rev. Chauncey Bunce, DD; *b* Windham, Conn, 5 Sept. 1848; *s* of Rev. Joseph Brewster and Sarah Jane Bunce; *m* 1st, 1873, Susan Huntington (*d* 1885), *d* of Eli Whitney; 2nd, 1893, Alice Tucker, *d* of George Stephenson; one *d. Educ:* Yale University; Berkeley Divinity School. Deacon, 1872; priest, 1873; Assistant in St Andrew's, Meriden, Conn, 1872–73; Rector of Christ Church, Rye, NY, 1873–81; Christ Church, Detroit, 1881–85; Grace Church, Baltimore, 1885–88; Grace Church, Brooklyn Heights, NY, 1888–97; Bishop Coadjutor of Connecticut, 1897; Bishop of Connecticut, 1899–1928. *Publications:* Key of Life, 1894; Aspects of Revelation; Baldwin Lectures for 1900; The Catholic Ideal of the Church, 1904; The Kingdom of God and American Life, 1912. *Address:* 98 Woodland Street, Hartford, Conn.

Died 9 April 1941.

BRICKDALE; *see* Fortescue-Brickdale.

BRIDGE, Frank; composer and conductor; *b* Brighton, 26 Feb. 1879; *s* of William Henry Bridge and Elizabeth Warbrick; *m* Ethel Elmore Sinclair, Melbourne. *Educ:* Royal College of Music. Has written a good deal of chamber and orchestral music, including string quartet and sextet, for piano and strings, a Trio, quartet and quintet, quartet in E minor gaining *mention d'honneur,* Bologna, 1906, Orchestral works—Isabella, 1907; Dance Rhapsody, 1909; Suite, The Sea, 1912; Dance Poem, 1914; Enter Spring, 1927; Phantasm, Piano and Orch., 1931; Oration, 'Cello and Orchestra, 1936. *Address:* 4 Bedford Gardens, W8. *T:* Park 5521.

Died 10 Jan. 1941.

BRIDGE, John Crosthwaite, CBE 1934; FRCSE; MRCPE, DPH; Barrister-at-law, Middle Temple, 1913; *b* Essex, 5 June 1877; 2nd *s* of Rev. James Henry Bridge; *m* 1st, 1904, Bessie (*d* 1933), *d* of Gateward Coleridge Davis; 2nd, 1935, Joan Phyllis, *d* of James S. Hann, Finchley. *Educ:* Carlisle Grammar School; Middlesex Hospital (Entrance Exhibitioner). Medical Officer of Health, County of Brecon; entered Civil Service, 1914; HM Medical Inspector of Factories; HM Senior Medical Inspector of Factories; retired, 1942; KHP, 1937–41. *Publications:* various medical. *Recreations:* golf, gardening. *Address:* Corfe, Southgate Road, Crawley, Sussex.

Died 27 Sept. 1947.

BRIDGE, Peter Gonzalez, DD; Principal St Paul's Cathedral Mission College, Calcutta since 1923; Fellow, Calcutta University; *b* 1885; *s* of Stephen Gonzalez and Gabriela Puente; *m* 1917; one *s. Educ:* Pontifical University, Burgos. Emeritus scholar in classics; ordained by the Cardinal of Burgos (RC); received in Anglican Church, 1916; Vice-Rector of Pontifical Seminary, Verapoly, India, 1912–16 and Prof. of Theology; Prof. of Philosophy at St Andrew's College, Gorakhpur, UP, India, 1917–22. *Publications:* Ramon Lull; lectures on Plato and Aristotle; contributions to theological and religious magazines. *Address:* St Paul's Cathedral College, 33 Amherst Street, Calcutta, India; 6 Salisbury Square, EC4.

Died 5 March 1942.

BRIDGES, Robert, ('Droch'); literary adviser; *b* Shippenburg, Pa, USA, 13 July 1858; unmarried. *Educ:* Princeton (AB 1879, AM 1882; LittD 1919). Reporter, Rochester Democrat and Chronicle, 1880; assistant news editor, New York Evening Post, 1881–87; literary critic of Life, 1883–1900; assist editor, Scribner's Mag. 1887–1914, editor, 1914–30; Hon. LittD, Columbia, 1924. *Publications:* Overheard in Arcady, 1894; Suppressed Chapters, 1895; Bramble Brae (collected poems), 1902; edited, with Introduction, The Roosevelt Book, 1904. *Address:* c/o Chase National Bank, Trust Dept, 11 Broad Street, New York. *Clubs:* University, Century, Princeton, Coffee House, New York; Nassau, Ivy, Princeton, NJ.

Died 2 Sept. 1941.

BRIDGLAND, Albert Stanford; journalist and fashion expert; *s* of Richard Bridgland and Fanny Stanford; *m* 1916, Eleanor, *e d* of late W. H. Crawford, Ercildun, New Malden; no *c. Educ:* privately. Master Tailor; Teacher of Cutting; Trade Journalist; Director, Tailor and Cutter, editor 1924–36; Member Institute of Journalists; Freeman City of London; Member Worshipful Company Needlemakers; Freemason; Fellow Royal Horticultural Soc. *Publications:* various technical and business works. *Recreations:* walking, reading, research into history of dress. *Address:* 6 Elm Park Gardens, NW4. *T:* Hendon 6628.

Died 26 July 1944.

BRIFFAULT, Robert Stephen, MB, ChB; writer; *b* London, 1876; *s* of Frederic Briffault and Margaret M. Stewart; *m* 1st, Anna Clarke (*d* 1919); one *s* one *d*; 2nd, Herma Hoyt. *Educ:* privately abroad; Florence; London. Went to New Zealand, 1894; practised as surgeon; served European War, Gallipoli, France, Flanders, attached 5th York and Lancaster (twice decorated); retired from medical practice after the war. *Publications:* The Making of Humanity, 1919; Psyche's Lamp, 1921; The Mothers, 1927; Rational Evolution, 1930; Sin and Sex, 1931; Breakdown, 1932; Reasons for Anger, 1936; The Decline and Fall of the British Empire, 1938; Les Troubadours et le Sentiment romanesque, 1945, English edn, 1948. Novels: Europa, 1935; Europa in Limbo, 1937; Fandango, 1940; New Life of Mr Martin, 1946: articles in reviews and journals. *Address:* The Chase Bank, Bush House, WC1.

Died 11 Dec. 1948.

BRIGGS, Lt-Gen. Sir Charles (James), KCB 1917; KCMG 1918; CB 1914; *b* 22 Oct. 1865; *s* of late Col C. J. Briggs, JP, DL, Hylton Castle, Durham; *m* 1921, Rosamund Daphne, 2nd *d* of C. F. Ryder; one *d. Educ:* privately in France and Germany; Sandhurst. Joined King's Dragoon Guards, 1886; Captain, 1893; Major, 1900; Major, Dragoon Guards, 1904; Lt-Col 1902; Col

1908; Maj.-Gen. 1915; ADC extra GOC Egypt, 1892–93; Brigade Adjutant, 4th Cavalry Brigade, 1897–99; Brigade Major, 3rd Cavalry Brigade, S Africa, 1899–1900; in command of 1st Imperial Light Horse, 1901–02; in command of Mobile Column, 1901–02 (Brevet of Major, Brevet of Lt-Colonel, despatches twice, Queen's medal 6 clasps, King's medal 2 clasps); Natal Native Rebellion, 1906 (medal with clasp); European War, 1914–18; Lt-Gen. commanding 16th Corps and afterwards the British Forces at Salonica (despatches 8 times); promoted Maj.-Gen. Feb. 1915, and Lt-Gen. 1 Jan. 1919 for distinguished service in the field; retired pay, 1923; Colonel, King's Dragoon Guards, 1926–39; White Eagle and Star of Serbia, Redeemer and Star of Greece, Greek Croix de Guerre with Palm, Distinguished Service decoration of Greece with Laurels, Commander Legion of Honour; White Eagle Grand Cordon Russia; JP Suffolk. *Address:* The Manor House, Wickhambrook, nr Newmarket. *Club:* Cavalry.

Died 27 Nov. 1941.

BRIGGS, Lt-Col Ernest, CBE 1944; DSO 1917; BSc; MIChemE; Director W. J. Fraser & Co. Ltd, Dagenham; *b* 1881; *e s* of James Burnett Briggs, Claughton, Birkenhead; *m* 1st, 1908, Maud Mary (*d* 1925), *d* of William Martin Horniblow of Watchet, Somerset; two *s* one *d*; 2nd, 1927, Isabel Frances (marr. diss.), *o d* of George Carruthers Thomson, Rockferry, Cheshire; two *s* one *d*. *Educ:* Merchant Taylors' School, Crosby; University College, Liverpool. Territorial Officer Royal Engineers since 1909; served European War, 1914–18, in France and Italy; CRE 48th Division (DSO, Croce di Guerra, brevet Lieut-Colonel, despatches 4 times). *Recreation:* motoring. *Address:* Peyton Hall, Boxford, Suffolk. *T:* Boxford 254. *Club:* East India and Sports.

Died 12 Oct. 1947.

BRIGGS, Captain Harold Douglas, CMG 1919; Royal Navy; *b* 1877; 4th *s* of late Col C. J. Briggs, of Hylton Castle, Co. Durham; *m* Mabel (*d* 1938), *d* of R. Thompson, of West Hall, Whitburn; one *s* one *d*. Entered HMS Britannia, 1892; served in HMS Pigmy during Boxer Rebellion; HMS Fox in Somaliland, and during operations in Persian Gulf; Commander of Bellerophon during European War, and afterwards transferred to Naval Air Service and RAF; retired RAF with rank of Brigadier General, 1919; returned to Navy, 1919; retired list, 1922; rejoined RN on outbreak of war; holds Royal Aero Club Flying Certificate; Commander Legion d'honneur, and Rising Sun of Japan. *Address:* Hill House, Feltwell, Norfolk. *Club:* United Service.

Died 13 Sept. 1944.

BRIGGS, Henry, Hon. LLD Liverpool; MB (Edin.), FRCS (Eng.); Emeritus Professor of Midwifery and Gynæcology, University of Liverpool; Consulting Surgeon to the Hospital for Women, Liverpool, and to the Maternity Hospital, Liverpool; Ex-President, Obstetrics and Gynaecology Section, RSM; Hon. Fellow, Obstetrical Society, Edinburgh; ex-member, Central Midwives Board, London; *b* Pilkington, Lancashire; *s* of James Briggs; *m* Annie Rosalie, *e d* of Egerton F. Hall, MD, of Prescot, Lancashire; two *d*. *Educ:* private schools; Manchester Grammar School; Owens College, Manchester; University of Edinburgh. As a student, senior medallist in anatomy with Sir William Turner, medallist and first prizeman in clinical surgery under Lord Lister; afterwards Demonstrator of Anatomy in the Liverpool Medical School; Senior Resident Medical Officer, Surgical Tutor, and Anæsthetist at the Liverpool Royal Infirmary, and Assist. Lecturer in Surgery, University College, Liverpool; Examiner in Obstetrics University of Edinburgh. *Publications:* papers on subjects in his department. *Recreations:* golf, shooting. *Address:* Sandhurst, Hoylake. *Clubs:* University, Liverpool.

Died 22 Nov. 1944.

BRIGGS, (W. J.) Harold; *b* 26 May 1870; *s* of Wm Briggs, JP; *m* 1893, Jessie, *d* of Ambrose Veevers, Didsbury; one *d*. *Educ:* Seafield, Lytham, and privately. MP (C) Blackley Division of Manchester, 1918–23, and 1924–29; CC, Surrey since 1930; Traffic Commissioner, SE area; a Commissioner of Taxes; a Governor of Holloway Sanatorium; President of the Fly Fishers Club, 1938; travelled in Europe, America, Australia. *Publication:* Confessions of an Unbeliever. *Recreation:* fishing. *Address:* Broadford, Chobham, Surrey. *T:* Chobham 22. *Clubs:* Carlton, Fly Fishers.

Died 6 May 1945.

BRIGHT, Allan Heywood, JP Herefordshire; FSA; *b* Liverpool, 1862; *s* of Henry Arthur Bright; *m* 1st, 1885, Edith, (*d* 1929), *y d* of Alfred Turner, Liverpool; one *d*; 2nd, 1929, Kelburn Milroy, *d* of late James Ramsay of Auchencairn; one *d*. *Educ:* Harrow. Contested Oswestry Division, 1901, 1904, and 1906; twice contested Exeter, and twice Stalybridge; MP (L) Oswestry Division Shropshire, 1904–06. *Publication:* New Light on Piers Plowman. *Address:* Barton Court, Colwall, Herefordshire. *Club:* Athenæum.

Died 3 Aug. 1941.

BRIGHT, Mrs Golding; *see* Egerton, George.

BRIGHT, Brig.-Gen. Reginald Arthur, CB 1918; CBE 1920; RA; *b* 1870; *s* of late Gen. Sir Robert O. Bright, GCB; *m* 1913, Dorothea Margaret, *d* of Major-Gen. Sir George Barker, KCB. Served S African War, 1899–1902 (despatches, Queen's medal with four clasps, King's medal with two clasps); Mesopotamia, 1916–18 (despatches, CB); Afghan War, 1919 (CBE); CRA Peshawar, 1919–21; BGRA Northern Command, India, 1921–23; retired, 1924.

Died 22 May 1942.

BRIGHT, Major Richard George Tyndall, CMG 1901, FRGS; *b* 5 Feb. 1872; *s* of late C. E. Bright, CMG, and Hon. Mrs Bright; *m* 1912, Murielle, *d* of Sir R. L. Lucas-Tooth, 1st Bt; two *s*. Entered Rifle Brig. 1892; Capt. and Bt Maj. 1899; Maj. 1908; served Uganda, 1897–98 (despatches, Bt Maj., medal with clasp); Juba Expedition, 1898–99 (despatches, Star of Zanzibar, 3rd Class); Expedition surveying Sudan and Abyssinian Frontier, 1899–1900; Expedition on the Frontier between Abyssinia and the Sudan and Protectorates of Uganda and British East Africa, 1900–02 (CMG); second British Commissioner on Anglo-German Boundary Commission, Uganda, 1902–04; British East Africa, 1904–06; British Delegate at Conference on Anglo-German Frontiers, 1906; Chief British Commissioner Anglo-Congolese Boundary, 1907–10; served in France, 1918–19; received the Back Grant from Royal Geographical Society, 1906. *Address:* West Thorn, Lymington, Hants. *T:* Lymington 367.

Died 10 July 1944.

BRILL, Abraham Arden; physician; Consulting Psychiatrist Manhattan State Hospital, New York City, etc; *b* Austria, 12 Oct. 1874; *s* of Philip and Esther Brill; *m* 1908, K. Rose Owen, New York; one *s* one *d*. Formerly Assistant Physician Central Islip State Hospital and in Clinic of Psychiatry of Zürich; formerly Chief of Clinic in Psychiatry, Columbia University; Lecturer on Psycho-analysis and Abnormal Psychology, New York University; Assist. Professor Psychiatry, Grad. Med. Sch.; Lecturer on Psycho-analysis and the Psycho-sexual Sciences, Columbia University; Salmon Lecturer of 1943. *Publications:* Psycho-analysis: its Theories and Application, 1914; Fundamental Conceptions of Psycho-analysis, 1922; The Basic Writings of Sigmund Freud, 1938. Translations of Freud, Breuer, Jung, etc.; contributions to Encyclopædia Britannica. *Address:* 88 Central Park West, New York. *T:* Trafalgar 7–8070. *Clubs:* City, Lotos (New York).

Died 2 March 1948.

BRIMS, Charles William, CBE 1920; MC, TD; Lieut-Colonel, late RFA (T.); Hon. Col 64th Anti-Aircraft Regt RA, TA; Chairman of Brims & Co., Ltd, Civil Engineering Contractors, Newcastle-on-Tyne; *b* 1877; *e s* of late David N. Brims, Harbour and Dock Contractor of Newcastle-on-Tyne; *m* 1909, Vera, *d* of late W. S. Vaughan, JP, MInstCE, Gosforth, Northumberland; two *s* one *d.* Lieut in Volunteer Artillery, 1900; Captain, 1905; continued in Northumbrian Division Territorial Force, RFA; retired, 1924; served European War; mobilised 1914, and went to France with the 4th Northumbrian Brigade, 1915, and commanded field batteries until wounded 1917, near Arras (MC, TD, Bt-Lieut-Col); after recovery attached to Admiralty and appointed Director of Extensions to Private Shipyards and Docks, also acted in same capacity for Ministry of Shipping until April 1919 (CBE). *Address:* Almouth, Northumberland; Pandon Buildings, Newcastle. *T:* Alnmouth 21, Newcastle 23538. *Clubs:* Union, Newcastle.

Died 28 Aug. 1944.

BRINDLEY, Harold Hulme, MA, FSA; Associé Correspondant étranger de la Société Nationale des Antiquaires de France; Fellow of St John's, Cambridge, 1931; *b* London, 17 June 1865; *s* of J. B. Brindley of Gray's Inn, Recorder of Hanley, and Mary, *d* of Joshua Brough, JP, Leek; *m* 1st, 1896, Gertrude Roberta Froggatt (*d* 1921), *d* of Robert Brindley of Alstonsfield, Staffs; one *d*; 2nd, 1922, Maud Doria (*d* 1941), *d* of late Rev. F. E. Haviland and late Fellow of Newnham College, Hon. Member BOU; one *d. Educ:* Mill Hill; St John's College, Cambridge. 2nd Lieut, CURV, 1886–87; President of Cambridge Antiquarian Society, 1915–16; Examiner in Zoology, Universities of Glasgow, 1915–18, 1924–29, 1931–34, and Camb., 1913–14, 1917–18, 1922–24; University Demonstrator in Zoology, Camb., 1926–34; Steward of St John's College, 1914–23; Hon. Sec. Camb. Philosophical Soc., 1917–22; a Councillor of Navy Records Society, 1911–21, 1925–29, 1932, 1937–38 (a Vice-President, 1921–25), and of Society for Nautical Research (a Vice-President, 1921–26, 1933–34, and 1938); Head of the Seal Room, National Maritime Museum, Greenwich, 1935; Hon. Keeper of the Water Transport Collections, Museum of Archæology and Ethnology, Cambridge, 1935. *Publications:* article, Mollusca, in Victoria County History of Cambridgeshire, 1937; articles on mural paintings of St Christopher in Clement Ingleby's Supplement to Blomefield's Norfolk, The Antiquaries Journal, etc.; Catalogue of the Seal Room, National Maritime Museum, 1938; also many papers on animal variation and nautical archæology in various journals. *Recreation:* sailing. *Address:* St John's College, Cambridge. *T:* Cambridge 5052. *Clubs:* Athenæum; Cambridge University Cruising.

Died 18 Feb. 1944.

BRISCOE, Arthur John Trevor, RI 1935; marine painter and etcher; *b* 1873; *s* of John Briscoe, Liverpool and St Asaph; *m* Alice Conyers (*d* 1942), *y d* of Commander Robert Baker, RN. *Educ:* Shrewsbury School; Slade School, under Professor Fred Brown; Paris, at Julien's. Exhibited in London and the Provinces since 1896; etching and paintings in various Museums and Galleries; Associate of the Royal Society of Painter Etchers and Engravers, 1930, Fellow, 1933; served as Lieutenant RNVR in the Auxiliary Patrol, 1914–18. *Publications:* Handbook on Sailing (written under the nom-de-plume of Clove Hitch); articles on sailing navigation, and technical matters connected with the sea. *Recreations:* all kinds of sailing, from square-rigged ship to model yachts; shooting, fly-fishing. *Address:* Twizzle, Mill Lane, Walton-on-the-Naze. *Clubs:* Royal Automobile, Chelsea Arts, Seven Seas.

Died 27 April 1943.

BRISE, Col Sir Edward Archibald R.; *see* Ruggles-Brise.

BRISTOW, Frederick George, CBF 1932; FCIS; MInstT; barrister-at-law, Inner Temple; Chief Executive Officer, Commercial Motor Users Association since 1906; Chairman of the Royal Society for the Prevention of Accidents; Member of Ministry of War Transport Statutory Advisory Panel of Experts; Member of Ministry of War Transport Road Safety and Traffic Signs Committees; British Government representative on the Permanent International Commission of Road Congresses; Member of the International Chamber of Commerce Committee on Highway Transport; Hon. Joint Secretary, Road and Rail Central Conference; Westminster City Councillor; Trustee of St Martin-in-the-Fields Almshouses and Pension Charity; Master of Company of Carmen; Liveryman of Company of Founders and Company of Gold and Silver Wyre Drawers; 3rd *s* of John Bristow, Hungerford; *m* 1944, Gillian, *e d* of Robert Porteous, Albemarle, Parkside, Wimbledon. Hon. Secretary, Standing Joint Committee of Mechanical Road Transport Associations, 1912–34; Hon. Secretary, Motor Transport Employers Federation, 1918–42; Hon. Secretary, Joint Industrial Council for the Road Transport Industry, 1919–20; Hon. Secretary, Empire Motor Fuels Committee of the Imperial Motor Transport Council, 1920–30; Hon. Sec. British Road Federation, 1933–36 and 1939–43; member Board of Trade Road Transport Advisory Committee, 1918; Ministry of Transport Advisory Committee on the Registration and Licensing of Motor Vehicles, 1920; Home Office Committee on Traffic Problems, 1925; Ministry of Transport Technical Advisory Committee on Experimental Work, 1929–33; Ministry of Transport Departmental Committee on Traffic Signs, 1931–33; Ministry of Transport Committee on Road Safety, 1934–36; Ministry of Labour Joint Conciliation Board for Road Transport, 1934–39; Ministry of Supply and Ministry of Transport Motor Vehicle Maintenance Advisory Committee, 1941; Ministry of War Transport Committee on Road Safety in War, 1941–44; Hon. British Government Delegate, International Road Congress (Munich), 1934, (Hague), 1938; Vice-Pres. International Safety Conference (Amsterdam), 1937. *Publications:* The Law of Motor Vehicles, 1931; Digest of the Construction and Use of Motor Vehicles Regulations, 1931; Digest of the Motor Vehicles Use and Construction Regulations, 1937; Legal Guide for Commercial Motor Drivers, 1938; Digest of the Construction and Use of Motor Vehicles Regulations, 1941; papers before International Road Congress (Munich), 1934; International Safety Conference (Amsterdam), 1937; many papers, pamphlets, and articles on transport, highway and traffic questions. *Address:* 50 Pall Mall, SW1. *Clubs:* Royal Automobile, City Livery.

Died 2 June 1945.

BRISTOW, Walter Rowley, MB, BS Lond., FRCS Eng.; Croix de Chevalier, Légion d'Honneur; Croix de Guerre avec Palme; Consulting Orthopædic Surgeon to St Thomas's Hospital; to the Army; to King Edward VII Convalescent Home for Officers, Osborne; Surgical Director St Nicholas' and St Martin's Orthopædic Hospital, Pyrford; late Hunterian Professor, Royal College of Surgeons; Hon. Member American, French and Belgian Orthopædic Associations; Associate Member: French Acad. of Surgery, Belgian Surgical Society; late Brig. RAMC; *b* 12 Dec. 1882; *s* of Henry Joseph Bristow, Bexley, Kent; *m* 1910, Florence, *o d* of James White, LLD; one *s* two *d. Educ:* St Thomas's Hospital; London University. Medical Officer, Middlesex Yeomanry, Gallipoli, Suvla Bay (despatches); Egypt, Aug. 1914–June 1916; Surgeon, Military Orthopædic Hospital, Shepherd's Bush, June 1916–Nov. 1919 (despatches, Brev. Maj. RAMC, T); Assistant Inspector Military Orthopædics; Chm., War Office Committee on Electro-Therapy; Consulting Surgeon, Ministry of Pensions Hospital, Shepherd's Bush, 1919–23. *Publications:* The Treatment of Muscle and Joint Injuries, 1917; The Treatment of Fractures in

General Practice, 1923; The Results of Operations on Peripheral Nerves, International Surg. Congress, 1923; Internal Derangement of the Knee Joint (Hunterian Lecture, 1935); The Treatment of Fractures: some principles re-affirmed (Hugh Owen Thomas Memorial Lecture, 1937); Orthopædic Surgery—Retrospect and Forecast (Presidential Address BOA, 1937); Peripheral Nerve Surgery in two world wars (Robert Jones Memorial Lecture) Brit. Jl Surg., 1947. *Address:* 149 Harley Street, W1. *T:* Welbeck 4444; Darenth, West Byfleet. *T:* Byfleet 182. *Clubs:* Bath, Conservative, Thatched House.

Died 10 Nov. 1947.

BRITTAIN, Lady Alida Luisa, DBE 1929; Iquique, Chile, *o d* of late Sir Robert Harvey; *m* 1905, Sir Harry Ernest Brittain, KBE, CMG; one *s* one *d.* President Society Women Journalists, 1929–32; Chairman Women's Section London Municipal Society; Chairman Unionist Women's Parliamentary Council, Southern Area, 1920–23; received presentation from British Press in recognition of her services in connection with First Imperial Press Conference, 1909; in charge London Depôt making War Material, 1914–18; Chairman first Official Delegation of British Women to visit Devastated War Zone, Northern France; winner First Prize International Competition for Harp Composition, Boston, USA, 1921; other work produced Metropolitan Opera House, New York; organised and led the Band of Harps at the Welsh National Eisteddfod, 1922; Adjudicator, 1924; admitted into the Gorsedd Circle under Bardic title of Telynores y Golomen Wen; inaugurated (1927) Choral and Solo Competitions for members of Conservative organisations in London and Greater London; appointed (July 1927) by the Conservative Central Office Honorary Musical Director of the National Conservative Musical Union for the purpose of extending the movement throughout the constituencies of England and Wales, culminating annually in Final Contests known as the National Festival of Song; made a Bard of Cornwall, 1933. *Publications:* harp music, various ballads, and articles for many newspapers. *Address:* 2 Cowley Street, Westminster, SW1; Kirklands, Headley, Hants. *T:* Headley Down 2145. *Club:* Ladies' Carlton.

Died 5 Jan. 1943.

BRITTLEBANK, Lt-Col Joseph William Forster, CMG 1918; late RAVC; Chairman Veterinary Ins Co. Ltd; *b* 1876; *s* of Major J. W. Brittlebank; *m* 1915, Maud Evelyn, *d* of W. R. Davis, Enfield; one *s* three *d.* Late External Examiner, London University and Liverpool University, and late Chief Veterinary Officer, Manchester; President Royal College of Veterinary Surgeons, 1926–28. *Address:* Wimborne House, Sawbridgeworth, Herts.

Died 18 Dec. 1944.

BRITTON, Rev. Canon John, BA (Durham); Vicar of St Paul's, Penzance, since 1945; Hon. Canon of Truro Cathedral, 1945; *b* Dartmouth, 1881; *s* of late Rev. E. C. Britton; *m* 1st, 1910, Anna Adeliza, *d* of late Robert Samuel Jacob, Howth, Dublin; one *d*; 2nd, 1914, Annie Young, *d* of late John Harvey, Indian Education Dept retired; one *s. Educ:* CMS College; University College, Durham. Curate, St George's, Worthing, 1906–07; CMS Missionary to Uganda, 1907–16; TCF, 1914–16; Principal, Maseno School, Kavirondo, Kenya, 1917–26 Secretary of Kenya Mission and Canon of All Saints Cathedral, Nairobi, 1926–29; Member of Executive and Leg. Councils, Kenya, 1927; Dean of Mombasa, 1929–33; Vicar of St Keverne, Cornwall, 1933–36; of Tuckingmill, 1936–45. *Address:* St Paul's Vicarage, Penzance. *T:* Penzance 630.

Died 6 Aug. 1948.

BROAD, William Henry, TD, MD, BS; Regional Consulting Adviser in Physical Medicine, Ministry of Health; Hon. Surgeon in charge Orthopædic Physiotherapy Department, Northern Hospital, Liverpool; Consulting Surgeon, Liverpool Foot Hospital; late Lecturer in Physical Anthropology, Liverpool University; FRAI; late Major, RAMC (TF); Associate Member, British Orthopaedic Association; late Surgeon in charge, Physical Treatment Department, Pensions Hospital, Liverpool; late member, City Council, Liverpool; *b* Manchester, 13 Sept. 1875; *m* Cynthia, *d* of late Henry Morgan-Hawkes, Adelaide, South Australia; one *s. Educ:* Liverpool Institute and privately; Liverpool University; Stockholm. After qualifying in 1900, held various residential surgical posts (hospital), and then acted as Junior Demonstrator of Anatomy, holding the Robert Gee Fellowship in Anatomy; awarded the Holt Fellowship in Physiology at Liverpool University; spent two years travelling, visiting America, Canada, Australia, and the Cape; attended clinics at Stockholm and Berlin for the study of Orthopædic Surgery; member of Medical Advisory Committee, Marine Dept Board of Trade; Ex-President Liverpool Literary and Philosophical Society. *Publications:* articles in medical and scientific journals. *Address:* 17 Rodney St, Liverpool. *TA:* Broad, Liverpool. *T:* Royal 1621. *Clubs:* Royal Automobile; RNR (Liverpool).

Died 1 Dec. 1948.

BROADBENT, Maj.-Gen. Sir Edward Nicholson, KBE 1937; CB 1919; CMG 1918; DSO 1916; Col of KOSB since 1938; *b* Simla, 5 May 1875; *s* of late Col J. E. Broadbent, CB; *m* 1911, Florence Anna, 2nd *d* of late Christopher Kay, JP, DL, of Ravenscroft Hall, Middlewich; no *c. Educ:* Sedbergh; Sandhurst. Joined KOSB in India, 1895; saw active service attached to 3rd Batt. Rifle Brigade in the Tochi Valley Expedition (Indian Frontier medal and clasp); Tirah Expedition, 1897–98 (clasp to Indian Frontier medal inscribed Tirah); S African War (King's and Queen's South African medals with 5 clasps); with the Egyptian Army, 1905; served in Camel Corps and commanded Xth Sudanese Regiment, Tagoi Mountain Expedition (medal and clasp, despatches, Order of the Osmanieh, 4th class); left Egyptian Army, 1911, to command British Camel Corps at Cairo; served European War, DAA and QMG Force in Egypt, Sept. 1914–1 Dec. 1915; Brevet Lt-Col 1915; Lt-Col 1921; Col 1923; Maj.-Gen. 1930; AQMG Force in Egypt, 1915–16; AQMG Lines of Communication, Egyptian Expeditionary Force, March–Oct. 1916; AQMG General Headquarters, EEF, 1916–May 1917, despatches five times, Order of the White Eagle of Serbia, 4th class, DSO, CMG, Officer of the Legion of Honour, 3rd Class of the Order of the Sacred Treasure (Japan), CB, Order of the Nile, 3rd Class); GOC Palestine Lines of Communication, with temp. rank of Brig.-Gen., 1917; Commanded 2nd KOSB, 1921–23; Brigadier i/c Administration, British Army of the Rhine, 1925–27, Scottish Command, 1928–30; ADC to the King, 1929–30; Director of Movements and Quartering, War Office, 1930–34; Lieut Governor of Guernsey and commanding troops in Guernsey District, 1934–39; retired pay, 1939. *Recreations:* shooting, golf. *Address:* Beaufort House, St Cross, Winchester. *T:* Winchester 2563. *Club:* Army and Navy.

Died 18 June 1944.

BROADBENT, Captain Harvey William, RD, RNR; late Captain Cadet Ship Conway; *b* Sealand, Chester, 12 April 1864; *s* of John Harvey Broadbent; *m* 1899, Maud Frances, 5th *d* of Th. Wilson, Preston, Lancs. *Educ:* abroad; Cadet Ship Conway. Went to sea in Merchant Service, 1882; joined Staff of Conway, 1898;

Captain, 1903; retired, 1927. *Recreation:* gardening. *Address:* Nuttree House, Higher Brixham, S Devon. *T:* Brixham 3162.

Died 21 Nov. 1942.

BROADBENT, Sir John, 2nd Bt *cr* 1893; MA, MD, MRCS, FRCP; *b* 16 Oct. 1865; *s* of 1st Bt and Eliza, *d* of John Harpin; *S* father, 1907; *m* 1895, Margaret Elizabeth, *d* of G. P. Field, MRCS; one *s* three *d*. *Educ:* Rugby; Oxford; St Mary's; Paris. Consulting Physician to St Mary's Hospital; Consulting Physician, King Edward VII Sanatorium, Midhurst; Consulting Physician London Fever Hospital; Past President Medical Society of London and the Harveian Society; formerly House Physician and Clinical Assistant, Hospital for Sick Children, Great Ormond St; Medical Registrar, House Phys., etc., St Mary's. *Publications:* Heart Disease; The Establishment of Immunity in Infectious Fevers, etc. *Heir: s* William Francis [*b* 29 Nov. 1904; *m* 1935, Veronica Pearl, twin *d* of late Benjamin F. Eustace]. *Address:* Halefield, Wendover, Bucks. *T:* Wendover 2108. *Clubs:* Athenæum, Leander, MCC.

Died 27 Jan. 1946.

BROADBENT, Joseph Edward, ISO 1932; BA; Parliamentary Counsel and Draftsman of Queensland, 1937–48; Member of Editorial Board and Consultant Editor, Queensland Statutes Reprint, 1937–40; *b* Brisbane, 14 Dec. 1883; *s* of late Kendall Broadbent, of Queensland Museum, Brisbane; *m* 1914, Daisy, *d* of late A. B. Nelson, Queensland Railway Dept; one *d*. *Educ:* Kelvin Grove State School; Brisbane Grammar School; Queensland University (BA). Entered Queensland Public service, 1900; First Clerk, Dept of Justice, and Sec. to Govt Representative in Legislative Council, 1916; Parliamentary Secretary, 1917; Barrister at Law, 1919; Assistant Parliamentary Draftsman, 1925; Parliamentary Draftsman, 1927; member Legal Committee, Canberra Constitutional Convention, 1942; member of State Housing Committee, 1941; of Committee of Investigation of Liquid Fuel, 1942; Certifying Barrister, Friendly Societies Acts, 1921–29; Compiler Friendly Societies Acts and Regulations, 1943. Trustee Brisbane Grammar Schools, 1921–31, and 1939–47. *Publications:* Editor and Compiler of Labour-Laws of Queensland; Land Laws of Queensland; Mining Laws of Queensland; Harbour Laws, Electoral laws and Liquor Laws; Legislative and Administrative Acts of the Government of Queensland; Editor of Queensland Digest of Case Law, 1861–1924; co-editor of Queensland Statutes; Contributor to Journal of Comparative Legislation and International Law (Eng.). *Recreations:* fishing, gardening, and reading. *Address:* Parliamentary Draftsman's Office, Chief Secretary's Dept, Brisbane; Euroa, Jane St, West End, Brisbane.

Died 15 Dec. 1948.

BROADWAY, Sir Alan Brice, Kt 1928; *b* 2 Nov. 1873. Assistant Legal Remembrancer, Punjab, 1909; Administrator-General and Official Trustee, 1916; Additional Judge, Chief Court, 1916; Judge High Court, Punjab, 1919–33; Acting Chief Justice, 1927 and 1932; retired, 1933.

Died 1 June 1948.

BROATCH, Surg. Rear-Adm. George Thomas, CBE 1918 (retired); *b* Kirkcudbright, 1862; *m* 1895, Mary Willis, *d* of G. Willis-Jones, Liverpool. *Educ:* Edinburgh University; King's College, London; MB, CM Edin. 1883. Entered Royal Navy, 1886; served throughout European War ashore and afloat; in charge of RN Hospital, Malta, 1916–19 (despatches, CBE, Officer of Legion of Honour). *Address:* 32 Carew Road, Eastbourne.

Died 11 Jan. 1945.

BROCK, Lt-Col Alec Walter Saumarez, CMG 1919; DSO 1915; late Leicester Regt; *b* 1 Aug. 1878. Entered Army, 1900; Captain, 1907; served S Africa, 1899–1900 (Queen's medal 3 clasps); European War, 1914–18 (DSO, CMG); retired pay, 1927.

Died 25 Feb. 1949.

BROCK, Sir Laurence George, Kt 1935; CB 1919; Chevalier of the Order of the Crown of Italy, 1920; *b* 1879; *o s* of late G. W. F. Brock of Afton, Bromley, Kent; *m* 1917, Margery, *y d* of late John Williams, Carisbrooke, Bromley Common; two *s* one *d*. *Educ:* Dulwich; Corpus Christi College, Oxford. First Class in Classical Moderations, 1900; First Class in Final School of Litteræ Humaniores, 1902. Entered War Office, 1903; transferred to the Admiralty, 1903; Private Secretary to Rt Hon. E. G. Pretyman, MP, Rt Hon. Edmund Robertson, MP, and Rt Hon. T. J. Macnamara, MP; Assistant Secretary, National Health Insurance Commission, 1912; Acting Secretary, 1917–19; Secretary of National Relief Fund, 1914–23; Assistant Secretary, Ministry of Health, 1919–25; Principal Assistant Secretary, 1925–28; Chairman, Board of Control, 1928–45. *Publications:* occasional articles in the monthly reviews. *Recreations:* gardening and photography. *Address:* Brendon, 388 Banbury Road, Oxford. *T:* Oxford 58233.

Died 29 April 1949.

BROCK, Adm. of the Fleet Sir Osmond de Beauvoir, GCB 1929; KCB 1919; KCMG 1918; KCVO 1917; CB 1914; CMG 1916; DCL (Oxon), 1929; JP West Sussex; Trustee of National Maritime Museum since 1936; *b* 5 Jan. 1869; *m* 1917, Irene Catherine (*d* 1939), *d* of late Sir Baldwin W. Walker, Bt, and *widow* of Captain Philip Francklin, RN; one *d*. Assistant Director Naval Mobilisation, 1910; ADC to HM, 1913; Rear-Admiral, 1915; Admiral, 1924; Admiral of the Fleet, 1929. Served Naval Engagements in North Sea, 1914–15 (despatches, CB); battle of Jutland 1916 (CMG, despatches); was Chief of Staff to Commander-in-Chief, Grand Fleet, 1916–19; then Deputy Chief of the Naval Staff and a Lord Commissioner of the Admiralty, 1919–21; Commander-in-Chief, Mediterranean Station, 1922–25; Commander-in-Chief, Portsmouth Command, 1926–29. *Address:* St Ann's, Links Road, Winchester. *Club:* Army and Navy.

Died 14 Oct. 1947.

BROCKLEBANK, Sir (Clement) Edmund (Royds), Kt 1937; *b* 28 Aug. 1882; *y s* of late Thomas Brocklebank, JP, DL, of Wateringbury Place, Kent; *m* 1927, Grace, *e d* of late Arthur John Wise, Wold House, Nafferton, Yorks; one *d*. *Educ:* Eton; Magdalen College, Oxford. MA. Contested Smethwick, 1923; East Birkenhead, 1929; MP (U) East Nottingham, 1924–29; MP (U) Fairfield Division, Liverpool, 1931–45; Parly Priv. Sec. to Parly Under Sec. of State, Home Office, Nov. 1927–May 1931; to Minister of Health, Dec. 1934–June 1935; to Rt Hon. Malcolm Macdonald when Sec. of State for the Colonies, June 1935; for the Dominions, Nov. 1935, for the Colonies May 1938, and when Minister of Health, May 1940–Feb. 1941; to Rt Hon. Sir John Anderson when Lord President of the Council March 1941 and when Chancellor of the Exchequer Sept. 1943–July 1945. *Address:* Winsley, Bradford on Avon. *Clubs:* Athenæum, Carlton.

Died 24 Aug. 1949.

BROCKLEBANK, Major John Jasper, DSO 1900; late Scottish Horse and 1st Dragoon Guards; *b* 5 Sept. 1875; 2nd *s* of late Sir Thomas Brocklebank, 2nd Bt; *m* 1914, Constance Mary, *d* of late Sir R. Leonard Powell; two *s*. *Educ:* Eton; Cambridge. Served with 8th Battalion Imperial Yeomanry and KDG South Africa (despatches, DSO). *Address:* Stratton, Marlow, Bucks. *Clubs:* Orleans, Royal Automobile.

Died 26 Feb. 1942.

BROCKLEHURST, Rev. Canon George, MA; Hon. Canon of Canterbury, 1924–44, Canon Emeritus since 1944; *b* Macclesfield, 1868; *m* Rose Mary, *d* of late H. J. Lawton, Burslem; one *s* one *d*. *Educ:* Macclesfield Grammar School; Trinity College, Dublin. Headmaster of Grammar School, Formby; Secretary of Church Schools, Board of Education, Birmingham; Diocesan Inspector of Schools for the Diocese of Canterbury; Proctor for Canterbury. *Publication:* Tithe and Tithe Rent-charge, a Text-Book for Clergy. *Address:* 65 Gloucester Court, Kew Road, Kew.

Died 10 July 1946.

BROCKLEHURST, Major John Henry Dent-, OBE, JP; *b* 1882; *s* of Henry Dent-Brocklehurst and Marion, *o c* of Hon. Egremont William Lascelles of Middlethorpe Manor, Yorkshire; *m* 1924, Mary Morrison; one *s* three *d*. *Educ:* Eton; Sandhurst. Late Coldstream Guards. Sheriff of Gloucestershire, 1939. *Address:* Sudeley Castle, Winchcombe, Cheltenham. *T:* Winchcombe 8. *Club:* Guards'.

Died 20 July 1949.

BROCKLEHURST, Robert Walter Douglas Phillips; *b* 31 May 1861; *s* of C. D. F. Phillips, MD, LLD, FRS Edin., and Martha, *d* of Thos Brocklehurst, The Fence, Macclesfield; *S* uncle, F. D. Brocklehurst, JP, DL, of Hare Hill, Cheshire, 1905, and assumed additional name of Brocklehurst; *m* 1902, Isabel Edith, CBE, *d* of Sir Patrick Heron Watson, MD, LLD; one *s*. *Educ:* Eton; Trinity College, Cambridge (BA, 1882). JP, 1906; High Sheriff, 1914; DL, 1914; Served in S African War, Hon. Lt in Army; European War, 1914–17; Lt-Col Cheshire Yeomanry (retd); Vice-Chairman Fine Cotton Spinners and Doublers Association Ltd (retd). *Address:* 7 Williamstreet House, Lowndes Square, SW1. *T:* Sloane 7673.

Died 22 Dec. 1948.

BROCKMAN, Maj.-Gen. Hon. Mr Justice Edmund Alfred D.; *see* Drake-Brockman.

BROCKMAN, Sir Edward Lewis, KCMG 1913; CMG 1908; *b* 29 June 1865; *m* 1907, Mrs F. S. B. Gaffney. Cadet Straits Settlements, 1886; Collector Land Revenue, Malacca, 1898; Commissioner Court of Requests, Singapore, 1902; Assist Colonial Secretary, 1904; Acting Colonial Secretary, 1905–06; Federal Secretary, Federated Malay States, 1907; Acting Resident General, Federated Malay States, 1907; Acting British Resident, Perak, 1908; British Resident, Pahang, 1908, and Negri Sembilan, 1910; Colonial Secretary, Straits Settlements, 1911; Chief Secretary Federated Malay States, 1911–20; retired on pension, 1920; in charge of Malay States Information Agency, 1920–25. *Address:* 31 Egerton Terrace, SW3. *T:* Kensington 6169. *Club:* East India and Sports.

Died 10 Jan. 1943.

BRODHURST, Henry William Frederick Cottingham, CMG 1911; *b* 26 Aug. 1856; *e s* of late William Henry Brodhurst, BCS; *m* 1900, Lucy Helen Jane (*d* 1918), *d* of James Weir, Bedford; two *s*. *Educ:* Cheltenham College. Writer Ceylon Civil Service, 1878; District Judge, Kalutara, 1904; Acting Treasurer, 1907 and 1910; Government Agent and Fiscal, Western Province, Ceylon, 1908; retired, 1911. *Address:* Parkstone, Dorset.

Died 21 Dec. 1943.

BRODIE OF BRODIE, Ian, DSO 1902; MC; JP; late Lord-Lieutenant Nairnshire; landed proprietor; *b* 26 Sept. 1868; *e s* of late Hugh Brodie of Brodie and Lady Eleanor Brodie, *sister* of 3rd Earl of Ducie; *m* 1904, Violet, OBE, *d* of late Col Montagu Hope; one *s*. *Educ:* Eton; Cambridge. Served Scots Guards, 1890, for about three years; S Africa (Lord Lovat's Scouts), 1900–02;

European War (Dardanelles, Egypt, and Palestine), 1915 (despatches). *Address:* Brodie Castle, Forres, Morayshire. *TA:* Brodie. *Club:* Guards'.

Died 15 Feb. 1943.

BRODIE, Rt Rev. Matthew Joseph; RC Bishop of Christchurch, New Zealand, since 1916; *b* New Zealand, 1864. *Educ:* St Joseph's College, Sydney; St Patrick's College, Manley. Ordained, 1888; Vicar-General to Bishop Cleary of Auckland, 1908–16; Domestic Prelate to the Pope, 1912. *Address:* Bishop's House, Christchurch, C1, New Zealand.

Died 11 Oct. 1943.

BROMFIELD, William; JP; *b* 24 Jan. 1868. MP (Lab) Leek Division of Stafford, 1918–31 and 1935–45. *Address:* Wilbermar, Ball Haye Road, Leek, Staffs.

Died 3 June 1950.

BROMLEY, John; Member of General Council of T. U. Congress, 1921–36; *b* 1876. General Secretary of Associated Society of Locomotive Engineers and Firemen, 1914–36; contested NE Leeds Dec. 1918; Barrow-in-Furness, 1922–23; MP (Lab) Barrow-in-Furness 1924–31. *Address:* 9 Arkwright Road, Hampstead, NW3.

Died 7 Sept. 1945.

BROMLEY, Lancelot, MA, MCh (Cantab); FRGS Eng. etc.; Surgeon, Consultant; *b* London, 18 Feb. 1885; *s* of Sir John Bromley, Seaford, Sussex; *m* 1914, Dora Ridgway Lee, Dewsbury, Yorks; one *s* one *d*. *Educ:* St Paul's School; Cambridge University; Guy's Hospital. *Address:* Little Thatch, Seaford, Sussex.

Died 17 Dec. 1949.

BROMLEY-DAVENPORT, Brig.-Gen. Sir William, KCB 1924 (CB 1922); CMG 1918; CBE 1919; DSO 1900; JP, DL; Lord Lieutenant of the County of Chester since 1920; *b* 21 Jan. 1862; *e s* of late Lieut-Col W. Bromley-Davenport, MP. *Educ:* Eton; Balliol College, Oxford. Colonel-Commanding Staffs Yeomanry; commanded 4th Batt. Imperial Yeomanry, South Africa, 1900–01 (despatches, Queen's medal 4 clasps, DSO); commanded 1st Staffordshire Yeomanry since outbreak of war, and went with them to Egypt, Nov. 1915; MP (C) Macclesfield Div. Cheshire, 1886–1906; contested same Division, 1910; Financial Secretary, War Office, 1903–05; Brig.-Gen. in Command 22nd Mounted Brigade, Egypt, 1916; Assistant Director of Labour, France, 1917 (CMG); 2nd Army, Italian Expeditionary Force, Nov. 1917–April 1918. *Address:* Capesthorne, Chelford, Cheshire. *Club:* Carlton.

Died 6 Feb. 1949.

BROMLEY-MARTIN, Granville Edward; banker; London Managing Director Martin's Bank, Ltd; *s* of George Edward Martin, of Ham Court, Upton-on-Severn; *m* Olivia Maude, *d* of late Hon. Richard Strutt; two *s* three *d*. *Educ:* Eton; New College, Oxford. *Recreations:* Oxford Cricket XI, 1897, 1898. *Address:* 9 Cheyne Place, Chelsea, SW3. *T:* Flaxman 5622. *Clubs:* White's, Savile.

Died 31 May 1941.

BROODBANK, Sir Joseph Guinness, Kt 1917; JP Essex; late Chairman and Treasurer, Popular Hospital for Accidents; Member of the Lord Lieutenant's Advisory Committee for Essex, 1912–35; Chairman of Employers' Liability Assurance Corporation, 1928–34; Technical Adviser to the Committee of Transport of the League of Nations; British Commercial Adviser, Central Rhine Commission; Member of Dock Rates Advisory Committee of the Ministry of Transport, 1922–34; Chairman of Food Investigation Board, 1928–34; *b* 15 July 1857; *s* of Caleb Broodbank, Folkestone; *m* 1st, 1883, Alice (*d* 1916), *d* of R. W. Reid, Woodford; 2nd, 1917, Maud Mary, *d* of Samuel Barfoot, Wanstead; no *c*. *Educ:* private school. Most of his life in service of London

Dock Companies, or as Member of the Port of London Authority, upon which he was Chairman of the Dock and Warehouse Committee, 1909–20; Member of the Port and Transit Executive Committee, 1915–22; President of Institute of Transport, 1923–24. *Publications:* History of the Port of London; many pamphlets and articles in press on Port questions. *Address:* Writtle Wick, Chelmsford. *T:* Chelmsford 3358.

Died 14 July 1944.

BROOK, Canon Alfred Eyre-; *s* of Rev. A. Brook, Vicar of Mansfield, Woodhouse, rural dean, and Harriet, *niece* of Bishop Blomfield of London; *m* 1st, 1896, Maria (*d* 1905), *d* of Col Eyre, 3rd Bombay Cavalry, of Eyrecourt, Ireland; 2nd, 1905, Norah, *d* of Major Gubbins, Royal Body Guard; two *s* two *d*. *Educ:* Uppingham School; Keble College, Oxford. MA 1881 (2nd class Theological honours); BD 1893. Ordained, 1882; Chaplain, Cuddesdon College, 1885–87; Rector of St Andrew's, Tain, 1890–92; Residentiary Canon of Inverness, 1892–1915. *Publications:* The Creed of the Christian Church; Some Sermons preached in a Highland Cathedral. *Recreations:* football at Uppingham; coxed college eight for several years at Oxford; chess, etching and water colours. *Address:* The Cottage, Portishead, near Bristol.

Died 11 April 1949.

BROOKE OF OAKLEY, 1st Baron *cr* 1939, of Oakley, co. Northampton; **Arthur Richard de Capell-Brooke;** 5th Bt *cr* 1803; DL, JP, BA; *b* 12 Oct. 1869; *s* of 4th Bt and Mary Grace, *d* of Rt Rev. E. Trollope, Bishop of Nottingham; *S* to father's Baronetcy, 1892; *m* 1897, Fanny Cecil Talbot (*d* 1942), *d* of late Capt. Duncan McNeill of Oronsay Priory, Argyllshire. *Educ:* Eton; Christ Church, Oxford. High Sheriff of Rutland, 1899; contested East Northants (C) 1906 and Jan. and Dec. 1910; JP, DL, Co. Northampton; Chairman, Northants County Council; Captain and Hon. Major 3rd Northants Regiment. *Heir:* (to Baronetcy only) *b* Edward Geoffrey de Capell Brooke, CBE. *Address:* Great Oakley Hall, Kettering. *Club:* Carlton.

Died 17 Nov. 1944 (Barony ext.)

BROOKE, Rear-Adm. Sir Basil Vernon, GCVO 1943; KCVO 1933; CVO 1922; Treasurer to the Queen since 1937; Groom-in-Waiting and Extra Equerry to the King since 1937; *b* 9 March 1876; *s* of late Arthur Basil Brooke; *m* 1915, Olave, *o d* of late Commander C. E. F. Cunninghame Graham, RN, MVO. *Educ:* HMS Britannia. Joined RN 1892; retired 1922; Comptroller and Equerry to the Duke of York, 1924–37. *Recreations:* shooting, fishing, golf. *Address:* 3 Oxford Square, W2.

Died 11 Dec. 1945.

BROOKE, Brig.-Gen. Christopher Robert Ingham, CMG 1917; DSO 1915; late KOYLI; *b* 4 July 1869; *o surv. s* of late Ven. Archdeacon Brooke; *m* 1899, Irene Spencer (*d* 1925), *e d* of late Lt-Col A. B. Coddington, RE; one *s* one *d*. *Educ:* Winchester College. Militia 3 KOYLI 1888; entered Army, 1890; Captain, 1899; Brevet Major, 1900; Major, 1908; Lieut-Col 1916; retired, 1920; Col on the retired list, with hon. rank of Brig.-Gen.; Honorary Col of the 5th (T) Battalion, KOYLI, 1924–35; MP (C) West Riding of Yorkshire, Pontefract Division, 1924–29; served South Africa, 1899–1902 (despatches twice, Brevet-Major, Queen's medal 4 clasps, King's medal 2 clasps); European War (despatches 5 times, DSO, CMG). *Address:* The Rath, Heatherlands, George, CP, S Africa. *Clubs:* Naval and Military; Civil Service (Cape Town).

Died 27 Dec. 1948.

BROOKE, Brig.-Gen. Hugh Fenwick, CB 1917; CMG 1915; CBE 1919; *b* 9 June 1871. Entered army, Royal Inniskilling Fusiliers, 1892; Captain, ASC 1899; Major, 1906; Lt-Col 1914; Temp.-Col 1915; Col 1918; Temp. Brig.-Gen., 1920; Deputy Director Supplies and Transport, War Office; Commandant, RASC Training College; Deputy Director of Supplies, General Headquarters, France; served S Africa, 1900–01 (Queen's medal 3 clasps); European War, 1914–18 (CMG, CB, CBE, despatches four times); retired pay, 1924. *Address:* Dyke Cottage, Ferring, Sussex.

Died 13 April 1948.

BROOKE, Major Sir Robert Weston, 2nd Bt *cr* 1919; DSO 1918; MC; late Yorkshire Dragoons Yeomanry; DL Co. Ross and Cromarty; *b* 1885; *s* of 1st Bt and Blanche, *d* of Major Weston of Morvich, Sutherland; *S* father, 1920; *m* 1909, Margery Jean, MBE, *d* of Alex. Geddes, Blairmore, Aberdeen; two *s* two *d*. *Heir: s* John Weston, *b* 1911. *Address:* Fearn Lodge, Ardgay, Ross-shire.

Died 24 Aug. 1942.

BROOKE, Zachary Nugent, LittD; FBA 1940; Professor of Medieval History in the University of Cambridge, and Fellow of Gonville and Caius College; *b* 1 Feb. 1883; *s* of George Brooke, Inland Revenue Dept, Somerset House, Barrister-at-law, Middle Temple, and Alice Elizabeth Nicholas; *m* 1919, Rosa Grace, *d* of Rev. A. H. Stanton, Rector of Hambleden, Bucks; three *s*. *Educ:* Bradfield College; St John's College, Cambridge (Scholar). Fellow and Lecturer in History, Gonville and Caius College, Cambridge, 1908; 2nd Lieut CUOTC, Nov. 1914; Temp. Lieut 11th Batt. East Surrey Regt, Feb. 1915; temp. Capt., Jan. 1916; Intelligence Corps, 1918–19. *Publications:* The English Church and the Papacy, 1066–1210, 1931; A History of Europe, 911–1198, 1938; Editor, Cambridge Medieval History. *Address:* Gonville and Caius College, Cambridge.

Died 7 Oct. 1946.

BROOKER, Brig.-Gen. Edward Part, CB 1918; CMG 1916; late RE; *b* 28 May 1866. Served S Africa, 1900–02 (Queen's medal 3 clasps, King's medal 2 clasps); European War, 1914–18 (CMG, CB); retired pay, 1923. *Club:* United Service.

Died 3 July 1946.

BROOKING, Maj.-Gen. Sir Harry Triscott, KCB 1916; KCSI 1919; KCMG 1917; CB 1914; DL; *b* 13 Jan. 1864; *s* of Lieutenant Arthur Yelverton Brooking, Indian Army; *m* 1889, Amy Agnès (*d* 1934), 2nd *d* of Albert Smith; one *d*. *Educ:* Wellington; Sandhurst. Joined the South Wales Borderers, 1884; Indian Army, 1885; served Burma Campaign, 1885–89 (despatches, medal with 2 clasps); Chin Hills Expedition, 1892–94 (clasp); North-West Frontier Campaign, 1897, and Samana (medal and 2 clasps); Tirah, 1897–98; Actions of Chagru Kotal and Dargai (clasp); China Expedition, 1900–01 on the Staff; Relief of Pekin (despatches, Brev. Major, medal and clasp); Mesopotamia, 1915–18 (despatches, promoted Major-General); retired, 1920. *Address:* Marrick, Lansdowne Road, Bournemouth. *T:* Bournemouth 3906.

Died 17 Jan. 1944.

BROOKS, Captain Arthur William, DSO 1919; RN, retired; *b* 1887; *s* of late William James Brooks, Barrister. Served European War (DSO); winner of Royal Navy Rifle Championship, 1921; retired list, 1933; Member of Council of National Rifle Association, 1933. *Address:* Dundagil, Starrs Green, Battle, Sussex.

Died 18 July 1941.

BROOKS, Sir James Henry, KCB 1920; CB 1909; JP; *b* 15 April 1863; *s* of late Dr J. H. Brooks, Henley Villa, Seychelles; *m* 1901, Charlotte Elizabeth, MBE, *d* of late Rev. W. A. Bathurst. *Educ:* Charterhouse. Joined Admiralty, 1883; Principal Clerk in Secretary's Department, Admiralty, 1906; Director of Navy Victualling, Admiralty, 1911–23; has American DSM. *Address:* Crossways, Wimborne, Dorset. *Club:* MCC.

Died 13 Oct. 1941.

BROOKS, Hon. Marshall (Jones); JP Lancashire and Cheshire; *b* 1855; 2nd *s* of 1st Baron Crawshaw; *m* 1889, Florence, CBE (*d* 1934), *d* of late Frederick Freeman Thomas, and *sister* of 1st Marquis of Willingdon; two *s* two *d*. *Educ:* Brasenose College, Oxford (MA). *Address:* Portal, Tarporley, Cheshire. *Club:* Brooks's.

Died 5 Jan. 1944.

BROOKSBANK, Sir Edward Clitherow, 1st Bt *cr* 1919; DL, JP West Riding; *b* 24 Nov. 1858; *s* of Edward Brooksbank, of Healaugh Manor, and Lucy Mary, *d* of Edward York, of Wighill Park; *m* 1885, Katharine Graham (*d* 1939), *d* of H. M. Lang, of Broadmeadows, Selkirk. *Educ:* Eton; Trinity Hall, Cambridge. Rowed in Eton Eight, 1877; rowed stroke in Cambridge University Eight, 1881; late Major, Yorkshire Artillery (M); retired, 1890; late Major commanding 8th Vol. Batt. PWO West Riding Regt; late Chairman, WR Quarter Sessions. *Recreations:* shooting, fishing. *Heir: g s* Edward William [*b* 1915; *s* of late Edward York Brooksbank and Hazel, *d* of late H. F. Brockholes Thomas]. *Address:* Healaugh Manor, Tadcaster. *TA:* Tadcaster. *T:* Tadcaster 3251. *Clubs:* Oxford and Cambridge; Yorkshire, York.

Died 24 Nov. 1943.

BROSTER, Dorothy Kathleen, MA Oxon; author; *e d* of Thomas Mawdsley Broster and Emilie Kathleen Gething. *Educ:* Cheltenham Ladies' College; St Hilda's College, Oxford. *Publications:* Chantemerle, 1911, The Vision Splendid, 1913, both with Miss G. W. Taylor; Sir Isumbras at the Ford, 1918; The Yellow Poppy, 1920; The Wounded Name, 1922; 'Mr Rowl,' 1924; The Flight of the Heron, 1925; The Gleam in the North, 1927; The Dark Mile, 1929; Ships in the Bay! 1931; A Fire of Driftwood, 1932; Almond, Wild Almond, 1933; World Under Snow (with G. Forester), 1935; Child Royal, 1937; The Sea without a Haven, 1941; Couching at the Door, 1942; The Captain's Lady, 1947. *Address:* Broomhill, Catsfield, Battle, Sussex. *T:* Battle 298. *Clubs:* Forum, University Women's.

Died 7 Feb. 1950.

BROTHERTON, Charles Frederick Ratcliffe, FRGS; FCS; LLD; JP; *b* Gravesend, 17 Jan. 1882; *e s* of Frederick Edwin Ratcliffe and Florence Anne, *d* of Theophilus Brotherton of Ardwick Green; and *nephew* of late Edward Allen, Baron Brotherton of Wakefield; assumed surname of Brotherton in lieu of Ratcliffe by deed poll 1931; *m* 1st, 1909, Dorothy Una Clough; 2nd, 1933, Ethel Isabel (*d* 1935), 2nd *d* of Sir William Worsley, 3rd Bt; 3rd, 1938, Lurline Winifred (Muffy), *o d* of Col Elliot-Pyle, Burchetts Green, Berks; one *s* one *d*. *Educ:* St Francis Xavier's College, Bruges; Paris; Berlin. JP for the City of Leeds, 1924; LLD (Leeds), 1948. Member of Council of University of Leeds; President of Leeds Maternity Hospital, 1917–27; President Grand Yorkshire Flower Show and Gala Association, 1933; established, Feb. 1940, Charles Brotherton Trust £250,000, for the advancement of education, the furtherance of medical and surgical research, and for charitable purposes in certain named places; Aug. 1942 made gift of £50,000 to General Infirmary at Leeds to cover cost of Brotherton Wing for paying patients. *Recreations:* hunting, yachting, golf, foreign travel. *Address:* Kirkham Abbey, York; Greycourt, Roundhay, Leeds; City Chambers, Leeds. *TA:* Brotherton, Leeds. *Clubs:* Carlton; Yorkshire (York).

Died 28 July 1949.

BROTHERTON, John; *b* 7 March 1867; *s* of Francis and Sarah Brotherton; *m* 1897, Haidee Wigglesworth; two *s* six *d*. *Educ:* elementary schools, Dacre Banks and Summer Bridge. At 10 years of age half-timer in a flax mill; at 16½ removed to Leeds and was apprenticed to engineering; at 21 joined the ASE, now AEU, and onward became active Trade Unionist and office-bearer; was 21 years a Branch Secretary; delegate to many National Conferences; before the ILP was formed was advocating Independent Labour Representation; contested seat on Leeds CC as a Socialist; Leeds City Councillor, 1927–30, and since 1932; nominated at party meeting and ran second for Lord Mayoralty of Leeds, 1922 and 1925; MP (Lab) Gateshead, 1922–23; contested Gateshead, 1918. *Publications:* articles and correspondence to the Press at intervals. *Recreations:* none in particular. *Address:* 12 Camden Street, Beeston Hill, Leeds.

Died 8 March 1941.

BROUGHTON, Major Sir (Henry John) Delves, 11th Bt *cr* 1660; DL, JP; late Irish Guards; *b* 10 Sept. 1883; *s* of 10th Bt and Rosamund, *d* of John Lambert Broughton of Almington Hall, Staffs; S father, 1914; *m* 1st, 1913, Vera Edyth (who obtained a divorce, 1940), *d* of Mr Boscawen, Trevalyn Hall, Rossett, N Wales; one *s* one *d*; 2nd, 1940, Diana Motion, *d* of Seymour Caldwell. *Educ:* Eton. Owns about 15,200 acres. *Heir: s* Evelyn Delves, *b* 2 Oct. 1915. *Address:* Doddington Park, Nantwich; Broughton Hall, Eccleshall, Staffs. *Clubs:* Guards', Turf.

Died 5 Dec. 1942.

BROUNGER, Captain Kenneth, DSO 1919; RN, retired; *b* 1881; 2nd *s* of late R. E. Brounger, MInstCE; unmarried. *Educ:* Kensington Grammar School. Served South African War (afloat); European War, North Sea, Coast of Syria (DSO), and Dardanelles; Chevalier Legion of Honour, 1919. *Recreation:* golf. *Address:* Beaconscroft, Churt, Farnham, Surrey. *Club:* Hankley Common Golf.

Died 24 April 1942.

BROWN, A. Curtis; Managing Director International Publishing Bureau, Curtis Brown Ltd London, Paris, New York; *b* 30 Oct. 1866; *s* of Lewis H. Brown and Ellen Curtis; *m* 1890, Caroline Louise Lord; one *s* one *d*. *Educ:* American Public Schools. Editorial Staff Buffalo Express 1884–94; Editor Sunday edition New York Press 1894–98; London Correspondent New York Press 1898–1910; Proprietor Curtis Brown Newspaper Syndicate, London, 1898–1915; established International Publishing Bureau, London, 1900; Managing Director Curtis Brown Ltd 1916. *Publications:* Contacts (memoirs), magazine articles, etc. *Recreations:* golf, fishing. *Address:* 6 Henrietta Street, WC2. *TA:* Browncurt, London. *T:* Temple Bar 1873. *Club:* Devonshire.

Died 22 Sept. 1945.

BROWN, Alfred Barratt, MA (Oxon), BA (Lond.); Educational Adviser, Community Education Trust; *b* 31 Dec. 1887; *o s* of late Alfred Kemp Brown, MA, BD; *m* 1912, Doris Eileen, *d* of late J. J. Cockshott, OBE, of Southport; two *s* two *d*. *Educ:* Bootham School, York; Merton College, Oxford. 2nd Class in Honours School of Literæ Humaniores, 1911. Lecturer at Woodbrooke Settlement, Selly Oak, Birmingham, 1912–21; Vice-Principal of Ruskin Coll., Oxford, 1921–26; Principal of Ruskin Coll., Oxford, 1926–44; Regional Welfare Officer, Ministry of Labour, 1940–47. *Publications:* The Naturalness of Religion (with Professor J. W. Harvey), 1929; The Machine and the Worker, 1934; Great Democrats (editor), 1934; Democratic Leadership, 1938. *Recreation:* gardening. *Address:* The Malt House, South Stoke-Goring-on-Thames.

Died 2 Oct. 1947.

BROWN, Wing-Comdr Arthur James, DSO 1916; Gold Medal, Order of St John of Jerusalem, 1915; MRCS (Eng.); LRCP (London), 1909; RAF, retired; late Capt. RAMC; *b* Westend, Hants, 26 May 1884; *s* of late Arthur John Brown; *m* 1st, Beatrice (*d* 1934), *d* of late James Percy Fitzgerald; no *c*; 2nd, Gwendolyn Ann, *o d* of William Arthur Bloxham. Retired list RAF, 1935. *Address:* 3 Ashburn Place, SW7. *Clubs:* Junior United Service, Royal Automobile.

Died 20 Oct. 1949.

BROWN, Sir Arthur W.; see Whitten-Brown.

BROWN, Cecil Jermyn, MA; b 1886; s of E. Jermyn Brown, Ipswich; m Gladys, d of W. A. Smith, Bradford; three s. Educ: Queen Elizabeth's School, Ipswich; Trinity College, Oxford. Appointed to staff of the Canning College, Lucknow, 1909; Fellow of Allahabad University, 1919–21; Reader in English Literature in Lucknow University, 1921; Member of the Lucknow Improvement Trust, 1920–22; Professor of English Literature, University of Lucknow, 1923–26; bronze medal of Numismatic Society of India, 1920; silver medal 1923. Publications: Catalogue of the Mughal Coins in the Provincial Museum, Lucknow, 2 vols, Oxford, 1920; The Coins of India (Heritage of India Series), 1923; a number of articles on numismatics in various journals, also educational publications. Address: St Mary's School, Melrose, Scotland.

Died 25 Oct. 1945.

BROWN, Rev. Charles, DD; Pastor Emeritus; b of poor parents, Clipston, Northants, 1855; m 1884, Florence E. Harding (d 1934); five c. Educ: Bristol Univ. and Baptist Coll. Began to work on a farm at eight years of age; left home for Birmingham at fifteen; always passionately fond of reading; entered Bristol College, 1879; began ministry at Nailsworth, 1883; Baptist Minister of Ferme Park and Campsbourne Baptist Church, London, N, 1890–1925; President of Baptist Union of Great Britain, 1910; President of National Free Church Council, 1912; Moderator of Federal Council of Evangelical Free Churches, 1930–31. Publications: Talks to Children on Bunyan's Holy War; Light and Life; The Wonderful Journey; Children on the King's Highway; Letters of Christ; Heavenly Visions; Trial and Triumph; The Message of God; Devotional Commentary on James, Ephesians, and Acts, etc. Recreation: gardening. Address: Furzefield, Chorley Wood, Herts. T: Chorley Wood 279.

Died 6 June 1947.

BROWN, Charles Herbert, KC; MA, LLB; Sheriff of the Lothians and Peebles since 1927 and Sheriff of Chancery since 1938; Vice-Dean of the Faculty of Advocates, 1921; b 1868; s of late William Brown of the Clydesdale Bank, Limited; m 1st, 1898, Sarah Sherwin (d 1929), d of late John Maxwell Cunningham; three s one d; 2nd, 1931, Mary Lennox, 2nd d of Lt-Col W. Glen Liston, CIE; one s two d. Educ: Rossall College; Glasgow University. Called to Scotch Bar, 1894; Sheriff of Dumfries and Galloway, 1924–27; FSA Scot., 1925. Recreations: golf, music, fishing. Address: Rosehill, Inveresk. T: Musselburgh, 348.

Died 6 April 1942.

BROWN, Col Charles Turner, DSO 1917; DL; b 1875. Served European War, 1914–17 (despatches, DSO). Address: Thievane, Beach Road, Port St Mary, IOM.

Died 11 Nov. 1939.

BROWN, Christopher Wilson, CBE 1942 (OBE 1934); MC; MInstCE; b 6 July 1891; s of late Samuel Brown, Dumfries; m 1929, Mollie Hilda, o d of Col H. M. Beasley, DSO; one s one d. Educ: Dumfries Academy; Royal Technical College. Associate Royal Technical Coll., 1911; engaged Civil Engineering works, Canada; served European War, 1914–20, Royal Scots Fusiliers, in Belgium, France, Egypt, and Sudan; Drainage Engineer, Gold Coast Colony, 1920; Public Health Engineer, Gold Coast, 1923; Senior Hydraulic Engineer, Gold Coast, 1926; Deputy Director of Public Works, Sierra Leone, 1928; Director of Public Works, Sierra Leone, 1932; Director of Public Works, Palestine, 1938–48; retired from Colonial Engineering Service, 1948. Publication: The Water Supply of Kumasi, Ashanti, 1939 (with late Col C. H. Howard Humphreys, TD, MInstCE).

Recreations: golf, fishing. Address: Hilltops, Burntwood Lane, Caterham, Surrey. T: Caterham 2765. Club: Naval and Military.

Died 16 Jan. 1949.

BROWN, Edward Clifton C.; see Clifton-Brown.

BROWN, Edward Thomas, JP, FLS; agricultural and motoring journalist; b 27 Oct. 1879; m 1904, Anna, e d of late James Carnegie Shee, Ballyreddin, Kilkenny; one d. Educ: University College, London. Motoring-Editor of the Birmingham Daily Mail; late Lecturer to Royal Agricultural College, Cirencester, and to eight county councils; has travelled extensively throughout Europe and America on agricultural work; Governor, Dunford House Association. Publications: Make Your Garden Feed You; Gardening in War-Time; Your Few Acres; A Thousand Agricultural Problems Solved; A Year in my Flower Garden; The Poultry-keeper's Text Book; Farm Tractors; The Owner-Driver's Hand-book; The Complete Motor-Cyclist; Motoring for the Owner-Driver; The Book of the Light Car. Recreations: fishing and motoring. Address: Haywards Grange, Jarvis Brook, Sussex. T: Crowborough 503. Clubs: Authors', Press, Reform.

Died 26 Dec. 1943.

BROWN, Ernest, MSc; MEng; DEng (Toronto); Emeritus Professor of Applied Mechanics and Hydraulics, McGill University, Montreal; Hon. Member, Engineering Institute of Canada; Consulting Engineer, water power development and general practice; in charge of testing of Hydraulic Turbine Models, Shawinigan, Water and Power Co., 1924–45; b St Helens, Lancs, 1878; m Ruby, e d of W. M. Kirkus, Liverpool; two s one d. Educ: Cowley Schools, St Helens; University College, Liverpool; Central Technical College, London. Gamble and Ranger Scholar, University College, Liverpool; 1851 Exhibition Scholar. Assistant lecturer in engineering, Liverpool University College; then lecturer in Applied Mechanics, University of Liverpool; Assistant and Associate Professor in Applied Mechanics, McGill University, 1905; Dean of Faculty of Engineering, 1930–42. Publications: Rise of Temperature in Field Coils of Dynamos (Institution of Electr. Eng.); Tests of reinforced concrete beams (Canadian Soc. Civil Eng.); sundry technical papers and addresses; reinforced concrete ship design; Reports on investigations in connection with Quebec Bridge (with H. M. Mackay, Dominion Govt Report on Quebec Bridge, Dept of Railways and Canals); Appendix F— Experiments on Strength of Ice, Report of Joint Board of Engineers St Lawrence Waterway Project; Tests on Thrust exerted by ice against dams (with G. F. Clarke, Engineering Inst. of Canada, 1932). Address: 1469 Drummond St, Apt 51, Montreal 25. T: Pl. 3636.

Died 24 June 1949.

BROWN, F. Gregory, RBA 1914; ROI 1917; b London, 4 Jan. 1887; s of John Terrell Brown and Clara Louisa, d of John Mahon; m; one s one d. Exhibitor at RA, ROI, RBA, Walker Art Gallery, Liverpool, Royal West of England Academy, Corporation Art Galleries of Hull, Worthing, Brighton, Huddersfield, and Oldham, International Society of Sculptors, Painters, and Gravers; has illustrated most of the leading magazines and periodicals; did much of the pioneer work in Poster designing and one of the first Artists to design posters for the Underground Railway; chief work poster designing for Underground Railway, Southern Railway, and many leading business firms; original designs for many of these posters are in permanent collection at South Kensington Museum, and have been exhibited all over the world; painter in oils and water-colours; received diploma for posters at Monza Palace, Milan (International Exhibition of Decorative Art), 1923; gold medal for textile design, Paris International Exhibition, 1925. Publications: numerous articles in Daily Press on Design. Recreation:

motoring round the English countryside finding new subjects to paint. *Address:* 14 Adamson Road, Hampstead, NW3; Westbury, Dorking, Surrey.
Died 5 March 1941.

BROWN, Francis Y.; *see* Yeats-Brown.

BROWN, Prof. Frederick; Emeritus Professor of the University of London; *b* Chelmsford, March 1851. *Educ:* South Kensington and Paris. Slade Professor of Fine Art, London Univ., 1892–1917; Self portrait and landscape, The Ivy Arch, in Tate Gallery; paintings in Municipal Galleries of Dublin and Liverpool; Member of New English Art Club. *Address:* Ormond House, Richmond, Surrey. *T:* Richmond 3401. *Club:* Chelsea Arts.
Died 8 Jan. 1941.

BROWN, Col Frederick John, CB 1900; *b* 16 May 1857; *s* of late John Brown, JP, of Marlborough Lawn, Cheltenham; *m* 1903, Dorothy, *y d* of late Edmund Ellery Bowden; one *s. Educ:* Cheltenham College. Entered Army, 1875; Captain, 1882; Major, 1891; Lieut-Col commanding 2nd Batt. Essex Regiment (Pompadours), 1902; Bt-Col, 1905; served Nile Expedition, 1884–85 (Egyptian medal with clasp, Khedive's Bronze Star); South Africa, 1899–1902 (despatches, Queen's medal with 6 clasps, King's medal with 2 clasps, CB); retired on retired pay, 1906; rejoined, 1915; commanding 1st Garrison Battalion, The Royal Scots; served with Egypt Expeditionary Force, 1915–19 (despatches, medal, Victory medal, 1915 Star). *Address:* The Moorings, Limmer Lane, Felpham.
Died 26 Sept. 1941.

BROWN, George, MBE; Sheriff Substitute of Caithness, Orkney, and Zetland, at Kirkwall, since 1933; *b* 9 March 1872; *e s* of late William Brown of Dunkinty, Elgin, and Alice Catherine, *e d* of late Admiral Gilbert Brydon Rutherford, RN; *m* Anne, *y d* of late David Bruce, Stirling; no *c. Educ:* Inverness College; University of Edinburgh. Business in London and West Indies; called to Scottish Bar, 1899; Sheriff-Substitute in Orkney of Caithness, Orkney, and Zetland, 1926–32; of Ross, Cromarty, and Sutherland, at Dingwall, 1932–33. *Address:* Berstane, by Kirkwall, Orkney. *T:* Kirkwall 96. *Clubs:* New, Edinburgh.
Died 29 Oct. 1946.

BROWN, George Clifford; *b* 29 May 1879; *s* of Dr George Brown and Lucy Anne Hallett; *m* 1902, Catherine Harvey Robertson Smith (*d* 1930); three *s* one *d. Educ:* Solent College, Lymington. MA University of London. Headmaster of Tollington School, 1906–12; Headmaster of Worcester College for the Blind, 1913–38. *Publications:* How the Blind See; numerous articles on the Higher Education of the Blind. *Recreations:* swimming, golf, chess. *Address:* at Hawford House, nr Worcester.
Died 16 July 1944.

BROWN, Rt Rev George Francis G.; *see* Graham Brown.

BROWN, George Mackenzie; *b* Canada, 1869; *s* of Hon. George Brown of Toronto, many years leader of the Liberal party in Canada; *m* 1901, Mary Elinor, *y d* of late Thomas Nelson, St Leonard's, Edinburgh. *Educ:* Upper Canada College, Toronto; Merchiston Castle School, Edinburgh; King's College, Cambridge. MP (L) Central Edinburgh, 1900–06. *Address:* Ichrachan, Taynuilt, Argyll.
Died 14 July 1946.

BROWN, George Ronald Pym A.; *see* Aldred-Brown.

BROWN, H. Harris; artist; *b* 29 Dec. 1864; *s* of Henry Brown, The Pond House, Duston, Northants. *Educ:* Paris, under Bougereau and Robert Tony-Fleury. First exhibited at the Royal Academy, 1888, and there and at the New Gallery has shown many portraits; for many

years exhibited at the Salon of the Société National des Beaux-Arts, Paris, and in 1902 the French Government purchased his portrait, Mrs Boyd of Glastry, for the National Collection at the Luxembourg Gallery; his portrait of William Alexander, Archbishop of Armagh, was purchased for the National Gallery of Ireland; and his picture of Mrs Hungerford Pollen is included in the Winthrop Collection in the Fogg Museum, Harvard Unive exhibited Mrs Arthur Dugdale at the Société des Artistes Français, 1908 (Mention Honorable); and Mrs Ince Anderton, 1911 (medal); member of Royal Society of Portrait Painters; he has painted many portraits in the United States and in Canada. *Recreations:* riding, walking, gardening. *Address:* Garden House, 20 The Vale, Chelsea, SW3. *T:* Flaxman 5165. *Clubs:* Athenæum, Chelsea Arts: Lotos (New York).
Died 27 Aug. 1948.

BROWN, Harold George, BA, LLB; *b* 24 Dec. 1876; *e s* of Harold Brown; *m* Dorothy, 3rd *d* of late James S. Beale and Mrs Beale of Standen, East Grinstead, Sussex; three *s* three *d. Educ:* Harrow; Trinity College, Cambridge. Member of Cambridge Crew, 1898; served as member of Greene Cttee on Company Law Amendment and Anderson Cttee on Fixed Trusts. *Address:* Copthorne House, Copthorne, Sussex.
Died 12 Nov. 1949.

BROWN, Helen Gilman; *b* New York City, 12 Oct. 1869; *d* of Daniel Rogers Noyes, Old Lyme, Conn, and Helen Gilman, New York City; *m* 1892; William Adams Brown; three *s. Educ:* Miss Porter's School. Has held the following offices: President Society Colonial Dames in the State of New York, Vice-President National Society Colonial Dames of America, President Women's Land Army of America, Vice-President National War Work Council of the YWCA, President and Charter Member Cosmopolitan Club, New York, National Chairman Sulgrave Manor Endowment Fund of the Colonial Dames of America, Hon. Chairman Women's Committee for Washington Cathedral; Chairman Advisory Committee Colonial Dames in the State of New York; member National Advisory Committee of Women of the Federal Council of Churches of Christ in America; is a member of the Order of Colonial Lords of the Manor, Hospitality Committee English-Speaking Union; Church Protestant Episcopal; Republican. *Publication:* The Story of John Adams, a New England Schoolmaster. *Recreations:* golf, bridge. *Address:* 1105 Park Avenue, New York City; The Tree-Tops, Seal Harbour, Maine, USA. *Clubs:* Albemarle; Colony, Cosmopolitan, New York.
Died 12 Dec. 1942.

BROWN, Sir Herbert, KBE 1920; Organiser, British Farmers Red Cross Fund; Knight of Grace, Order of St John of Jerusalem: in charge of Appeal Branch, French Red Cross, 1918 (in England); Chairman Appeal Branch, Officers' Association, 1920 and 1921; Chairman Appeal Branch of the British Legion on its formation in 1921; Governor St Thomas Hospital and Member of Star and Garter Management Committee; President National Association of British and Irish Millers, 1922; President, Croydon Hospital; Chevalier Legion of Honour (France); Officier Ordre Léopold (Belgium); *b* 4 March 1869; *m* 1st, 1890, Anna Flora Monica (*d* 1933), *d* of John Frith, Oaklands, Croydon; two *s*; 2nd, 1934, Margaret Barnett, Little Steading, Upper Warlingham. *Address:* Shepheard's Hurst, Outwood, nr Redhill.
Died 16 May 1946.

BROWN, Herbert Charles, CBE 1933; *b* 17 April 1874; *s* of William Brown and Ann Robinson Gardner; *m* 1906, Alice Ann Schofield; four *s. Educ:* St Philips Church of England Grammar School, Sydney. Joined the postal service, 1891; Finance Member, Commonwealth Shipbuilding Board of Control, 1921; Delegate of the Public Trustee and Controller of the Clearing Office, 1925; Secretary Commonwealth Dept of Markets, 1928;

Secretary, Dept of the Interior, 1932–35; Auditor-General for the Commonwealth of Australia, 1935–38; retired 1938. *Recreation:* golf. *Address:* Neville Court, 119 New South Head Road, Vaucluse, Sydney, NSW.

Died 16 July 1940.

BROWN, Brig.-Gen. Howard Clifton; DL, JP; MP Unionist, Newbury, Division, Berks, 1922–23, and 1924–45; *b* 1868; *e s* of late Col James Clifton Brown, MP; *m* 1903, Mary Eirene, *e d* of late Sir Henry Hodges; three *d. Educ:* Eton; Cambridge. Served S African War, 1899–1902; commanded 12th Lancers, 1908–12; served European War Commanding South Eastern Mounted Bde, 1913–16. *Address:* Holmbush, Faygate, Sussex. *T:* Faygate 203. *Club:* Cavalry.

Died 11 Sept. 1946.

BROWN, Hubert Sydney, MusBac; composer, author, concert director, adjudicator; Principal of Hubert Brown School of Singing and Dramatic Art; *b* 28 Sept. 1898; *s* of Charles Hubert Brown, Principal of the Hubert Brown School of Singing and Dramatic Art; *m* Sylvia Brent. *Educ:* King Edward's School, Aston; Birmingham University; Birmingham and Midland Institute. Studied composition under Sir Granville Bantock; Festival adjudications include the Royal Albert Hall in 1928 and 1930; sole representative of Great Britain at the first competition for singing and violin at Vienna, 1932; Director of Concerts to the Birmingham Sunday Lecture Society. *Publications:* The Principles of Expression in Song; The Art of Song Composition, with foreword by Josef Holbrooke; The Complete Singing Teacher (with Foreword by Norman Allin); Success in Amateur Opera (Foreword by Derek Oldham); upwards of 6 light operas; composer of a large number of published songs and nearly three hundred unpublished songs. *Recreation:* music. *Address:* 68 Grange Road, Erdington, Birmingham. *Club:* MM.

Died 30 March 1949.

BROWN, James, CBE 1918. Managing Director of Scotts' Shipbuilding and Engineering Co., Ltd, Greenock. *Address:* 13 Newark St Greenock.

Died 13 Jan. 1941.

BROWN, Major James Pearson, DSO 1916; TD, MA, MB, FRFPS Glas.; late RAMC; *b* 1868; *s* of late Thomas Brown, Ardmore, Campbeltown. Served South Africa, 1899–1901 (Queen's medal 4 clasps); European War, 1914–19 (despatches, DSO); JP; Argyll. *Address:* Drumfin, Campbeltown, Argyll. *T:* Campbeltown 2045. *Clubs:* Western, Glasgow; Caledonian United Service, Edinburgh; The Club, Campbeltown.

Died 21 Feb. 1942.

BROWN, John Frank, CMG 1912; *b* Bristol, 1856; *s* of Edward Brown of Roscommon; *m* 1885, *d* (*d* 1938) of P. Cooke of New End, Gloucestershire; one *s* four *d. Educ:* Gloucester Grammar School; Malvern. Entered PO service, Gloucester, 1874; Secretary's Office, GPO London, 1883; Assistant Surveyor, Bedford, 1885; Lincoln, 1898; Western District of England; Postmaster-General, Natal, 1900; Transvaal, 1902; was member of first Legislative 1902; was member of Committee and of Executive Committee of Transvaal Provincial 1910–14. *Address:* St Monica, Campbell Road, Parktown West, Johannesburg.

Died 16 Dec. 1941.

BROWN, Captain Sir John Hargreaves P.; *see* Pigott-Brown.

BROWN, Sir John Rankine, KBE 1946; MA; Professor of Classics, Victoria University College, Wellington, 1899–1945. *Educ:* Worcester College, Oxford (Scholar). *Address:* 9 Burnell Avenue, Wellington, New Zealand.

Died 14 Oct. 1946.

BROWN, John Wesley; JP Middlesbrough; *b* 1873. Ex-Mayor of Middlesbrough, a member of Town Council and Chairman of the Finance Committee; Chairman, Education Committee; a member of The Tees Conservancy Commission, The Tees Pilotage Commission; Vice-Consul, Argentine Republic; MP (C) East Middlesbrough, 1922–23. *Recreation:* motoring. *Address:* Riftswood, Cambridge Road, Linthorpe, Middlesbrough. *TA:* Brown, care Lion, Middlesbrough. *T:* Linthorpe 8549. *Clubs:* Cleveland, Middlesbrough.

Died 8 Nov. 1944.

BROWN, Leonard Graham, MC; MA; MD (Oxon), FRCS (Eng.); Ear, Nose and Throat Surgeon (Specialist); War Work; Medical Supt Charing Cross Hospital; *b* Brisbane, 6 Sept. 1888; 2nd *s* of late John Graham Brown, Lurgan, N Ireland; *m* 1915, Margaret Jane Menzies, Edinburgh; two *d. Educ:* Brisbane Grammar School; Balliol College, Oxford (Rhodes Scholar). BA 1912 (Natural Science 2nd Class Honours). Served European War; Lt RAMC 1915, France and Belgium; Capt. 1916; Lt Col 1918 (MC, Despatches); MA and BM (Oxon) 1919; DM (Oxon) 1920; FRCS (England) 1924; Senior Surgeon (Ear, Nose and Throat Dept) Charing Cross Hospital; late Aural Specialist North Middlesex County Hospital; late Examiner for DLO of Royal Coll. of Surgeons, England; Past Pres. Section of Otology RSM; Vice-Pres. Rugby Football Union, 1937–47, Pres., 1948–49. *Publications:* Convalescent Depôts in France during Great War (RAMC Journal, 1919); Affections of the Ear (Hutchison's Index of Treatment); various articles on Ear, Nose and Throat in current medical journals. *Recreations:* golf; Oxford University Rugby Football Team, 1910–11–1912 (Capt. 1912); England Rugby XV, 1910–12–1913–21–1922 (Capt.); rowed Torpids, 1909, College Eight, 1910. *Address:* 82 Portland Place, W1. *T:* Welbeck 5267. *Clubs:* United University; Walton Heath Golf; Manchester Golf.

Died 23 May 1950.

BROWN, Lilian Mabel Alice, (Lady (Richmond) Brown), FLS, FZS, FRGS, FRAI; *e d* of late R. W. Roussel, Rohais, Guernsey, Channel Islands; *m* 1906, Sir Melville Richmond Brown, 3rd Bart (who obtained a divorce, 1931; he died 1944). *Educ:* St Joseph's Convent, Guernsey. Travelled extensively in Central America, in conjunction with F. A. Mitchell-Hedges, 1921–22; explored San Blas Archipelago; penetrated unknown part of Panama, discovering Chucunaque Indians; returned with large ethnological collection, which has been presented to British Museum, 1923; carried out deep-sea research work among the Cayes in the Caribbean Sea off the coast of British Honduras and Guatemala; explored and excavated in the interior of British Honduras (Maya ruins), collection given to the British Museum, 1924–28; explored interior of Spanish Honduras (in the Mosquitia), artifacts and ethnological specimens given to the American Indian Museum, Heye Foundation, New York, 1930–31; member of the Maya Committee; Founder-member of the Pacific Geographical Society, 1931; Fellow, American Geographical Society; Life member of the Royal Scottish Geographical Society. *Publications:* Unknown Tribes; Uncharted Seas; articles in press and magazines on exploring and deep-sea research work. *Recreations:* big-game fishing, yachting. *Address:* The Lodge, Playden, nr Rye, Sussex. *Club:* Forum.

Died 4 Oct. 1946.

BROWN, Sir Melville Richmond, 3rd Bt *cr* 1863; *b* 13 Oct. 1866; *e s* of 2nd Bt of Astrop, Northants, and Emily, *d* of Gen. W. T. B. Mountsteven; *S* father, 1906; *m* 1906, Lilian Mabel Alice, *e d* of Robert Roussel (whom he divorced 1931; she *d* 1946). *Educ:* Eton; Cambridge University. *Heir: nephew* Charles Frederick Richmond, Capt., Welsh Guards [*b* 6 Dec. 1902; *m*

1933, Audrey, 2nd *d* of late Brig.-Gen. Hon. Everard Baring one *s* two *d*. Eton. Stonely Woods, Kirbymoorside, Yorks].

Died 20 Feb. 1944.

BROWN, Sir Peter Boswell, Kt 1945; JP; late Chairman and Managing Director of Hadfields Ltd, Sheffield; *b* Greenock, 1866; *s* of late John Brown, Glasgow; *m* 1894, Mary Jackson, *d* of late John and Elizabeth Willis, Sheffield; two *s* three *d*. *Educ:* Greenock; Woolwich; Sheffield University. Engineering training at Easton and Anderson's, Erith, Kent; Member of the Institution of Civil Engineers; late Vice-Pres., Iron and Steel Institute; Member of Sheffield University Council; Hon. Vice-President of British Iron and Steel Federation; Director of the Lilleshall Company, Ltd, Tinsley Rolling Mills Ltd; Master of the Cutlers' Company of Hallamshire, 1930–31. *Recreations:* golf, gardening, motoring. *Address:* Storth Lodge, Sheffield. *T:* Sheffield 31400. *Clubs:* Reform; Sheffield (Sheffield).

Died 12 Oct. 1948.

BROWN, Richard King, MD, BCh, BA, DPH, RCPS, late Medical Officer of Health, Metropolitan Borough of Bermondsey; late Lecturer in Public Health, Guy's Hospital; Member of the British Medical Association; Fellow of the Royal Institute of Public Health and Hygiene; ex-President of the Metropolitan Branch of the Society of Medical Officers of Health; late Medical Editor of British Journal of Physical Medicine; late Examiner for BA (Architecture) and MD (State Medicine), London University; *b* Athlone, Co. Roscommon, 16 Feb. 1864; *s* of Rev. Samuel Edgar Brown, BA; *m* 1892, Sara Elizabeth, *d* of William Smith, Illinois, USA; one *s* one *d*. *Educ:* Coleraine Academical Institution; University of Belfast. BA (Hon. RUI); MB, BCh, 1891; MD, gold medal, 1903 (Royal University of Ireland); DPH, RCPS (London), 1894. *Publications:* translator (from the German) of Sunlight in Surgery by O. Bernhard (St Moritz); and of Short Wave Therapy by Schliephake (Giessen); editor of English Edition of Bestrahlung mit Quarzlampe (Bach). *Recreations:* German literature, travel (Australia, New Zealand, Italy, France, Germany). *Address:* 2 Nutley Crescent, Goring-by-Sea, Sussex. *T:* Goring-by-Sea 42,432.

Died 28 April 1942.

BROWN, Robert Cunyngham, CBE, MD, MB and BS; Officer of Order of Christ (Portugal); Officer of the Order of St Sava, 4th Class (Serbia); *b* 1867; 2nd *s* of Rev. Robert Brown, Paisley, and Mary Cheyne, *d* of James Hoseason of Aywick and Mossbank, Shetland; *m* 1895, Arabella Halyburton, *d* of late Dr John J. Johnstone, Brampton, Cumberland; two *s* one *d*. *Educ:* Universities of Glasgow. Durham, and Frankfurt. After the usual resident hospital appointments and three years in general practice, worked under Prof. Carl Weigert in his neuro-pathological laboratory at Frankfurt, AM; followed by one and a half years at the National Hospital for Paralysed and Epileptic, London; later was Pathologist to the County Asylum, Chester, and in 1899 entered HM Prison Service as Deputy Medical Officer; transferred in 1911 to Scotland as Deputy Commissioner in Lunacy; was seconded to Army in 1915; Major RAMC and OC Springburn-Woodside Military Hospital, Glasgow, till 1916, when served in Macedonia with the 37th General Hospital attached Royal Serbian Army, and as Mental Specialist. Salonika Command (despatches); recalled England; was lent to Ministry of National Service, and in 1919 officially transferred to the Ministry of Pensions as Deputy Director-General of Medical Services, retiring 1925; a Commissioner of the Board of Control, 1926–32; Commissioned by Sec. of State for Colonies to advise and report on care and treatment of lunatics in Nigeria, Gold Coast, Sierra Leone, Gambia, 1936. *Publications:* papers in medical journals; Report on the Family Care of the Insane Poor

to the Royal Commission on the Care and Control of the Feeble-minded, 1905, etc. *Address:* 3 Quadrille Ct, Lymington, Hants.

Died 7 Oct. 1945.

BROWN, Sidney George, FRS, MIEE; FInstP; Inventor and Electrical Engineer; Fellow of London University College; *b* Chicago, 6 July 1873; *e s* of Sidney Brown, Bournemouth; *m* 1908, Alice, *d* of late Rev. C. J. Stower of Sudbury, and *niece* of late Professor John Perry, FRS. *Educ:* Harrogate Coll.; London Univ. Coll. Late Proprietor of the firm of S. G. Brown, Ltd, Acton; Founder and late Chairman of the Telegraph Condenser Co.; invented the drum cable relay and magnetic shunt which first relayed messages over long submarine cables, 1899; also the cable magnifying relay and thermo-electric relay; in conjunction with late Sir Henry Hozier discovered first practical methods of directing Hertz waves (the first Beam System), 1899; invented the single point iridium microphonic relay, 1908, also the granular carbon microphone relay, an improved Telephone receiver of great sensitiveness of much use in wireless telegraphy (the first Reed Telephone), 1910; the first practical loud speaker for wireless; invented methods used by the Flying Corps by which for the first time airships and aeroplanes could receive wireless messages, 1913; discovered the stimulation of oxidation and other chemical actions by the (cathalytic?) action of alternating currents of high frequency, 1915, and other inventions; invented a Gyroscopic Compass much used on board ship, 1914; a Gyroscopic Compass for Air Service; an Artificial Horizon, Automatic Helmsman, Gun Directional Compass, also Turning Indicator for Aeroplanes, 1929; Aeroplane Speed Indicator, 1930; and numerous other inventions including the Liquid Microphone Sound Devices; Electro-Megaphone for sea, land, and air use, 1931; a special Magnetic Compass for Aeroplanes, Wireless Receiving, 1932–33, and secret devices for the British and foreign Governments; served on the Admiralty Ordnance Council during the last War, and Royal Commission on Awards to Inventors. *Publications:* papers before the Royal Society, British Association, Physical Society, Electrical Engineers, etc. *Address:* Brownlands, Salcombe Regis, Sidmouth. *T:* Sidmouth 53. *Clubs:* Athenæum, Royal Automobile.

Died 7 Aug. 1948.

BROWN, Rev. Canon Sydney Lawrence, DD; Canon Residentiary and Master of the Fabric, Worcester, since 1944; Examining Chaplain to Bishop of Worcester and Director of Religious Studies, 1944; Commissary to Bishop in Jerusalem, 1938; Fellow of King's College, 1943; *b* 16 Feb. 1880; *s* of Wm A. and Laura Brown, Driffield, E Yorks; *m* 1906, Clare, *d* of late Chas. Mitchell of Enthorpe; no *c*. *Educ:* Pocklington School; Wadham College, Oxford (Scholar). Pusey and Ellerton Hebrew Scholar, Hall-Houghton LXX Prize, Liddon Student, Kennicott Hebrew Scholar, Denyer and Johnson Theological Scholar, Houghton Syriac Prize; BA (1st class honours in Theology); MA, 1907, BD and DD, 1924. Deacon, 1904; Priest, 1905; Chaplain and Lecturer, Ripon Theological College, 1904–05; Vice-Principal Bishop Jacob Hostel, Newcastle-on-Tyne; Curate of Benwell, 1905–10; Warden of the Church Hostel, Bangor, 1910–15; Rector of Fryerning, 1915–27; Proctor in Convocation, 1923–45; Rural Dean of Barstable, 1920–37; Vicar of Brentwood, 1927–35; Professor of Hebrew and Old Testament in the University of London, at King's College, 1935–44; Hon. Canon of Chelmsford, 1922; Secretary of the Central Advisory Council of Training for the Ministry, 1924–27; Hon. Sec. 1927–44; Examining Chaplain to the Bishop of Bangor, 1910–24; to the Bishops of Chelmsford, 1919–44; McBride Preacher, 1909, 1924 and 1943; Examiner for Greek Test, LXX and Syriac Prizes, Oxford, 1909; Examiner in Theology, University of London, 1912–14 and 1937–47; in Hebrew, Oxford, 1914 and 1936, London, 1937–44; in Biblical Languages,

London, 1917–20; Public Examiner in Theology, Oxford, 1919–22; Examiner in Denyer and Johnson Theological Scholarship, 1925. *Publication:* Hosea, in Westminster Commentaries, 1932. *Recreations:* has played cricket, football, lawn tennis and golf. *Address:* 10 College Yard, Worcester. *T:* 4874.

Died 18 Jan. 1947.

BROWN, Thomas Brown R.; *see* Rudmose-Brown.

BROWN, Rt Hon. Thomas Watters; PC Ireland, 1921; Northern Ireland, 1922; KC; Judge of the High Court of Northern Ireland since 1922; *b* 17 March 1879; 2nd *s* of James A. Brown, late of Newtownards, Co. Down, merchant; *m* 1913, Mary E. Hadden, Belfast; two *s* one *d*. *Educ:* Campbell College, and Queen's College, Belfast. Called to Irish Bar, 1907; to Inner Bar, 1918; English Bar, Gray's Inn, 1919; MP (U) North Down, Dec. 1918–22; Solicitor-General for Ireland, 1921; Attorney-General, Ireland, Sept. 1921, resigned, Dec. 1921; Chairman of Convocation and Member of Senate, Queen's University, Belfast; DL County Down, 1937. *Address:* Ben Ingan, Donaghadee, Co. Down. *Clubs:* Ulster, Belfast.

Died 7 Oct. 1944.

BROWN, Walter Hugh; lately Trustee of the National Amalgamated Approved Society of Euston Square, NW; Fellow of the Chartered Insurance Institute; formerly Chairman and Managing Director of the London and Manchester Assurance Company, Limited; *b* 1873. Spent his entire business life with the Company; commenced as a junior clerk, 1887; Secretary, 1905; Director, 1908; Managing Director, 1913; Chairman, 1923; retired 1938. *Address:* Little Dene, Bramley, Surrey.

Died 11 April 1950.

BROWN, Sir Walter L.; *see* Langdon-Brown.

BROWN, William, BSc, MIEE; late Professor of Applied Physics, Royal College of Science, Ireland; *b* Dumfries, Dec. 1856. *Educ:* Glasgow University (Scholar and Gold Medalist). *Publications:* (Joint) Text-Books of Physics; Handbook of Electro-Technology; 37 papers, joint author of 7; 6 small books, one conjoint a translation into esperanto. *Address:* 48 Dartmouth Square, Leeson Park, Dublin.

Died 9 Feb. 1945.

BROWN, William Adams, MA, PhD, DD, STD; Theologian; Roosevelt Professor of Systematic Theology in the Union Theological Seminary, New York, 1898–1930; Research Professor in Applied Theology, 1930–36; 1936; *b* New York, 29 Dec. 1865; *s* of John Crosby Brown and Mary E. Adams; *m* 1892, Helen Gilman Brown (*d* 1942) three *s*. *Educ:* St Paul's School, Concord, NH; Yale University (MA 1888, DD 1907, PhD 1901); Union College (DD 1903); University of Berlin; DD University of St Andrews, Scotland, 1922; STD Columbia University, 1937; DD Oxford University, 1937. Instructor in Church History in the Union Theological Seminary, 1892; transferred to systematic theology, 1893, serving successively as instructor, 1892–95; provisional professor, 1895–98; Fellow of Yale University, 1917–34; Acting Provost, 1919–20; director New York Institution for Deaf and Dumb; a founder (1907) and director Grenfell Association; Pres. Universal Christian Council since 1937; Member Executive Committee, World Conference on Faith and Order; Chairman several committees on religious education, etc.; Editor, International Religious Library; Hon. Canon Washington Cathedral, 1937. *Publications:* Musical Instruments and their Homes, 1888; The Essence of Christianity, 1902; Christian Theology in Outline, 1906; Life of Morris K. Jesup, 1910; The Christian Hope, 1912; Modern Theology and the Preaching of the Gospel, 1914; Is Christianity Practicable? 1916; Modern Missions in the Far East, 1917; The Church in America,

1922; The Creative Experience, 1923; Imperialistic Religion and the Religion of Democracy, 1923; The Quiet Hour, 1926; The Life of Prayer in a World of Science, 1926; Beliefs that Matter, 1928; Pathways to Certainty, 1930; God at Work, 1933; The Education of American Ministers, Vol. I, 1934; The Church: Catholic and Protestant; Eng. ed. Your Church and Mine; Finding God in a New World, 1935; Church and State in Contemporary America, 1936; The Minister: His World and His Work, 1937; The Case for Theology in the University; A Teacher and His Times, 1940; The Fellowship of the Free, 1941; The Religions of Democracy, 1941 (with Drs Finkelstein and Ross). *Recreations:* mountain climbing, tennis, golf. *Address:* 1105 Park Avenue, New York City. *T:* Sacramento 2–5960. *Clubs:* Authors'; Century, Authors', American Alpine, Yale, New York; Royal and Ancient, St Andrews.

Died 16 Dec. 1943.

BROWN, Brig.-Gen. William Baker, CB 1917; *b* 27 April 1864; *s* of Isaac Baker Brown, FRCS (Eng.), (*d* 1873), and second wife, Catherine Read, ward of 8th Earl of Denbigh; *m* 1891, Frances Kate, 2nd *d* of Ven. R. J. French, Archdeacon of Mauritius; three *d*. *Educ:* Charterhouse; Woolwich; School of Military Engineering, Chatham. Lieutenant Royal Engineers, 1883; Captain, 1891; Major, 1900; Lieut-Colonel 1907; Colonel, 1911; employed at School of Submarine Mining, Chatham, 1885–88; Assistant Instructor at SM School, Gosport, 1892–96; Chief Instructor at SM School, Chatham, 1896–1901; commanded local companies of RE at Mauritius, 1889–92; and Hong-Kong, 1901–04; employed at War Office as Inspector of Submarine Mines and Electric Light, 1904–08; Commanding Royal Engineer No. II District, Malta, 1908–12; Chief Engineer, South China, 1913–15; Chief Engineer Eastern Command (Brig.-Gen.), 1915–16; Deputy Director of Works, France, 1916–18; Chief Engineer, Ireland, 1918; retired pay, 1921; Member of RE Committee, 1896–1901 and 1904–08; Prize Medal of Royal United Service Institution, 1898; is a member of the Royal US Institution, and the RE Institute. *Publications:* History of Submarine Mining in the British Army (RE Inst., 1910); articles on Coast Defence and Submarine Mines in Encyclopædia Britannica, 1910; various articles in military magazines. *Recreation:* watercolour sketching. *Address:* 75 Mulgrave Road, Sutton, Surrey.

Died 6 May 1947.

BROWN, Sir William (Barrow-clough), KCB 1938; KCMG 1937; CB 1934; CBE 1931; Permanent Under-Secretary of State for Air since 1945; *b* 1893; *s* of G. Lang Brown, Monkseaton, Northumberland; *m* 1923, Elizabeth Mabel (*d* 1942), *d* of late W. Scott, MB, CM, Ruthwell, Dumfriesshire; three *s*. *Educ:* Royal Grammar School, Newcastle-on-Tyne; King's College, Cambridge. Northumberland Fusiliers, 1914 (wounded); invalided, 1917; entered Board of Trade (temporary), 1918; appointed Home Civil Service, 1919; Private Secretary to successive Presidents of the Board of Trade, 1924–34; Principal Assist Sec., Board of Trade, 1934; Deputy to Chief Industrial Adviser to HM Government, 1935; Second Sec., Board of Trade, 1935–37; Permanent Secretary, Board of Trade, 1937–40; Acting Secretary of Ministry of Supply, 1940–42; Secretary, Petroleum Division, Ministry of Fuel and Power, 1942–43; Secretary to Ministry of Home Security, 1943–45. *Address:* Ruthwell, Chesham Bois, Bucks. *Club:* United University.

Died 12 Feb. 1947.

BROWNE, Captain Alexander Crawford; MP (U) West Belfast since 1931; JP. *Address:* 18 Windsor Park, Belfast. *Clubs:* Constitutional; Reform, Belfast.

Died 11 Dec. 1942.

BROWNE, Brig.-Gen. Alfred Joseph Bessell-, CB 1918; CMG 1915; DSO 1902; VD; American DSM; *b* 3 Sept. 1877; *s* of William H. Bessell-Browne of Sydney; *m* 1903, Muriel Maud, *d* of Henry E. Manning. Served S Africa with W Australian contingent; European War, 1914–18 (CMG, CB). Commander Volunteer Defence Corps, W Australia, 1940–42. *Address:* Marri Mia, Anzac Terrace, Bassendean, Western Australia. *Club:* Naval and Military (Perth).

Died 3 Aug. 1947.

BROWNE, Arthur Scott; JP, DL; *b* 1866; 4th *s* of William James Browne; *m* 1894, Mary Frances (*d* 1945), *y d* of Hon. Mark Rolle. *Educ:* Eton; Sandhurst. Served in 16th Lancers, 1886–91; Royal North Devon Hussars as Major, 1892–1905; served in Royal North Devon Hussars 2/1 as Major, 1914–18. *Address:* Buckland Filleigh, Beaworthy, N Devon. *Club:* Naval and Military.

Died 14 Feb. 1946.

BROWNE, Maj.-Gen. Beverley Wood, CB 1944; DSO; MC. Canadian Army.

Died 17 March 1948.

BROWNE, Sir (George) Buckston, Kt 1932; LLD Aberdeen; FRCS, (Eng.); Prel. Scientific 1st MB London University; retired surgeon; a Trustee of the Hunterian Collection, Royal College of Surgeons of England; Life President Harveian Medical Society of London; President Old Owensian Association; Vice-President The Dickens Fellowship; Hon. Fellow Medical Society of London; Donor and Hon. Curator of Down House, Kent, Charles Darwin's home for forty years; Donor of Royal College of Surgeons Research Farm, Kent; Hon. Freeman Worshipful Society of Apothecaries; *b* Manchester, 13 April 1850; *o s* of late Dr Henry Browne, Physician to Manchester Royal Infirmary and lecturer on medicine in the Pine Street School, and Ann, *d* of George Hadfield, twenty-three years MP, Sheffield; *m* 1874, Helen Elizabeth (*d* 1926), *d* of George Vaine, Sparsholt, Hants; one *s* (killed in war) one *d*. *Educ:* Amersham Hall School, Reading; Owens College, Manchester; University College, London. Medallist in Chemistry, Anatomy, Midwifery, and Liston Gold Medallist in Surgery. House Surgeon to Sir John Erichsen; Demonstrator of Anatomy, University College Medical School; associated with Sir Henry Thompson, for fourteen years in private surgical practice in London, and then for thirty years practised alone; in memory of his son has endowed the Harveian Society's biennial surgical prize of £100 and medal, and the annual dinner of the Society; has also endowed the annual Fellows' and Members' dinner of the Royal College of Surgeons; (Honorary Gold Medal, 1931). *Publications:* articles in Heath's Dictionary of Surgery; Harveian Lectures, 1901; many papers in Lancet and British Medical Journal, and in the Transactions of the Medical, Pathological, Clinical, and Harveian Societies of London. *Recreations:* collecting, travelling, walking. *Address:* 80 Wimpole Street, W1.

Died 19 Jan. 1945.

BROWNE, Col George Herbert Stewart, CB 1917; late Suffolk Regiment; *b* 19 July 1866; *e s* of late Bishop G. F. Browne; *m* 1915, Evelyn Bertha *widow* of Col F. J. Lambkin, AMS, and *d* of late Major H. R. Mitford. *Educ:* Marlborough; Pembroke College, Cambridge; Sandhurst. Joined Suffolk Regt 1886; Capt. 1897; Major, 1909; Lt-Col 1914; Col 1915; Adjutant, Volunteers, 1898–1903; Officer, RM College, 1903–06; Experimental Officer, School of Musketry, Hythe, 1908–13; Chief Inspector of Small Arms, 1914–19; Deputy Director at the War Office, 1919; retired pay, 1920; served Hazara Expedition, 1888 (medal with clasp); European War, 1914–18 (CB); JP, Oxfordshire. *Club:* Army and Navy.

Died 27 Dec. 1944.

BROWNE, George Sinclair, CMG 1931; barrister; Board of Trade since 1942; *b* 1880. *Educ:* Malvern College; Hertford College, Oxford, MA. Called to Bar, Gray's Inn, 1905; Assistant Resident, Northern Nigeria 1906; Secretary, Northern Provinces, 1921–25; Senior Resident, Adamawa Province, 1926–29; Secretary, Native Affairs, 1929; Acting Chief Secretary, 1931; Senior Resident, Cameroons Province, 1931–32; Acting Lieutenant-Governor, Northern Provinces, 1930 and 1932–33; Chief Commissioner, Northern Provinces, Nigeria, 1933–36; retired, 1936; Chief Air Raid Warden, Westminster, 1939; Ministry of Food, 1939.

Died 19 May 1946.

BROWNE, Sir Granville St John O.; *see* Orde Brown.

BROWNE, Rev. Henry J., SJ, MA (Oxon); Emeritus Professor of Greek, University College, Dublin; *b* Birkenhead, 7 Aug. 1853; 2nd *s* of J. Wilson Browne, Birmingham, and *g s* of Capt. J. Murray Browne, 48th Foot, who fought at Albuera and throughout the Peninsular War, and joined the Portuguese army, where he became Assistant-Quartermaster-General under Marshal Beresford. *Educ:* King Edward's High School, Birmingham; New College, Oxford. Entered the Irish Province of the Society of Jesus, 1877, where he was engaged in secondary schools and in the Royal (later the National) University of Ireland; made his theological studies and ordained priest at St Beuno's Coll., N Wales; took a leading part in founding the Classical Association of Ireland (President, 1913); was on Council, Society of Hellenic Studies; Chairman of Archæological Aids Committee Assoc. for Reform of Latin Teaching; member of Committee of British Association on Museums in relation to Education, and visited USA to report on same, 1916; also of Prime Minister's Committee on Classical Studies, 1920; has experimented in the melodic rendering of Greek choral rhythms, giving demonstrations before the British Association at the Dublin meeting (1908), and at Columbia and Chicago Universities. *Publications:* Our Renaissance— Essays on the Reform and Revival of Classical Studies, 1917; Handbook of Homeric Study, 1905; Handbooks of Greek and Latin Composition; several pamphlets and articles on theological and devotional subjects; edited The City of Peace, 1903; contributed to History of Religions, 1910; The Catholic Evidence Movement, 1924; Darkness or Light? 1925. *Address:* Manresa, Roehampton, SW.

Died 14 March 1941.

BROWNE, Julius Basil, CBE 1932; BCom; *b* 1892; *y s* of late General Horace Albert Browne and Marie Browne; *m* 1925, Norma Kathryn Smith. *Educ:* Wellington College; Birmingham University. Vice-Consul, Mexico City, 1915–19; Acting Consul, Stockholm, 1919; Acting Consul-General, Gothenburg, 1920–21; Vice-Consul, St Gall, 1921; Vice-Consul, Essen, 1922–23; Consul, Galveston, 1924–25; Consul-General (local rank) Mexico City, 1926–30; Consul, Funchal, Madeira, 1931–38; HBM Consul, Seville, Spain, 1939; retired, 1940. *Recreations:* shooting, fishing. *Address:* British Country Club, Funchal, Madeira.

Died 2 April 1947.

BROWNE, Kathleen A.; ex-Senator, Irish Free State; Peace Commissioner for Co. Wexford; *e d* of late Michael Browne, Rathronan Castle, Wexford, and Mary Eleanor, *d* of John Stafford, Baldwinstown Castle, Wexford. *Educ:* privately at home. Practical farmer; member of the Irish Farmers' Union, their delegate to World's Poultry Congress, London, 1930; expert in dairy management; historian and archæologist; identified with Irish National movements since 1912; supporter of Anglo-Irish Treaty of 1921. *Publications:* History of Wexford; Glimpses into the Past; numerous articles in historical journals. *Recreations:* hunting, gardening, nature study. *Address:* Rathronan Castle, Wexford, Ireland. *TA:* Bridgetown, Wexford.

Died 9 Oct. 1943.

BROWNE, Nassau Blair, RHA 1902; formerly Governor of the National Gallery of Ireland and Secretary of Royal Hibernian Academy; *s* of John Blair Browne; *m* Anna Georgina Wood. *Educ:* privately. *Address:* 86 Marlborough Road, Donnybrook, Dublin.

Died 6 Aug. 1940.

BROWNE, Sir Philip Henry, Kt 1932; CBE 1918 (OBE 1917); *b* 7 March 1877; *s* of late F. P. Browne, Redhill, Surrey; *m* 1911, Margaret Joan Springett, *d* of late Col R. C. Sanders, IMS; three *d. Educ:* Haileybury. Lieutenant-Colonel Special List, and Commander RNVR in Mesopotamia, 1916–19. *Address:* Packways, Petersfield. *Club:* Oriental.

Died 27 May 1950.

BROWNE, Maj.-Gen. Reginald Spencer, CB 1901; VD; FRGS; *b* Oaklands, NSW, 1856; family from Sligo, Ireland; *m* 1889, Katharine Fraser, *d* of late Duncan Munro, Glasgow and Brisbane. *Educ:* Appin, Liverpool, NSW; England. Colonel and Brig. 5th LHB 1907; went to South Africa with 1st Queensland Contingent; served on staff of Major-General Alderson, march to Kimberley relief; Paardeberg, Koodoe's Rand, Poplar Grove, Osfontein, Driefontein, and Abraham's Kraal; joined staff of Lt-Gen. Pilcher again (DAAG), and took part in operations at Kroonstad, Johannesburg, and Pretoria, and battle of Diamond Hill; in operations east and west of Pretoria (despatches twice, CB, South African war medal 5 clasps); organised and commanded in Egypt 4th Light Horse Brigade, 1915; commanded 6th Australian Infantry Brig., Gallipoli; Australian Training Centre at Tel-el-Kebir, and at Salisbury Plain; later commanded AIF at Weymouth and Concentration Camp at Federal Capital, Australia. *Address:* Brisbane, Queensland. *Clubs:* Queensland United Service, Constitutional of Queensland, Brisbane; Australasian Pioneers, Sydney.

Died Nov. 1943.

BROWNE, Col Sherwood Dighton, CB 1915; CBE 1919; RA; *b* 25 May 1862; *s* of late Gen. Sir Samuel Browne, VC; *m* Hilda (*d* 1941), *d* of J. P. Law, Hallfield, Wetherby. *Educ:* Wellington. Entered Army, 1882; Capt., 1890; Major, 1899; Lt-Col, 1908; Colonel, 1911; employed with Bechuanaland Border Police, 1892–94; served Matabili Campaign, 1893–94 (medal); North-West Frontier, India, 1897–98 (despatches, medal, 2 clasps); European War, 1914–15 (CB); retired with hon. rank of Brigadier-General, 1919. *Address:* Sherborne Cowdray, Basingstoke.

Died 3 Sept. 1947.

BROWNE, Dame Sidney Jane, GBE RRC and bar; DN Leeds University Hon.; International Red Cross Gold Medal; First President, The College of Nursing, Henrietta Street, W1; *b* 5 Jan. 1850; *d* of Dr Benjamin Stocks Browne. *Educ:* privately. Served Netley, Woolwich, Aldershot, Curragh Camp, Malta; Egypt, 1884; Suakim, 1885; Boer War, 1899–1902; European War, 1914–19 (despatches). *Publications:* Times History of the War, Nursing Dept; Cassell's History of Nursing. *Address:* Charnes, Tivoli Road, Cheltenham. *T:* Cheltenham 3327. *Clubs:* Cowdray, United Nursing Services.

Died 13 Aug. 1941.

BROWNE-CAVE; *see* Cave-Brown-Cave.

BROWNELL, (Peleg) Franklin, RCA; artist (painter); *b* New Bedford, Mass, USA, 28 July 1857; *s* of Leander Brownell and Annice Willard Snow; *m* 1889, Louise, *d* of John W. Nickerson of New Bedford; one *d. Educ:* Public Schools of Mass. Studied art at School of Boston Museum of Art, and at Paris with Bouguereau and Fleury. Head Master of Ottawa Art Association,

1885–98; present work genre and landscape painting; exhibited at Paris salons and principal exhibitions of US and Canada; bronze medal, Paris Exposition of 1900; representative works at the Canadian National Gallery; Member of Royal Canadian Academy and Canadian Art Club. *Recreations:* rod and gun. *Address:* 177 Stewart Street, Ottawa, Canada. *T:* 3–7244.

Died 13 March 1946.

BROWNING, Mrs Adeline Elizabeth, CBE 1918; *b* 1869; *d* of Capt. John Hubert, Jersey, CI; *m* 1894, Hon. John Browning, MLC Newfoundland. First President of Alliance Française of Newfoundland; gave her house for Hospital Red Cross work, 1914–18; built hospital for tuberculosis among soldiers and sailors, 1916; organised and carried through Receptions for all returning soldiers and sailors, 1916–19. *Address:* c/o Bank of Montreal, Montreal, Canada. *Clubs:* Chautauqua Woman's (Chautauqua, NY); Women's (Keystone Heights, Fla); Women's (Gainsville, Fla).

Died 4 Dec. 1950.

BROWNING, Col George Dansey-, CBE 1919; *b* Nov. 1870; *m* 1907, Lilian Stoddart; one *s* one *d. Educ:* Royal Naval School; Lycée of Lorient, Rennes; Westminster Hospital. MRCS, LRCP, DPH Edinburgh, DTM Liverpool, MRCP London. Joined RAMC 1894; late Medical Officer of Health, Gibraltar; late Med. Director, Enham Village Centre for Disabled Service Men, near Andover, Hants; Assistant Director, Medical Services, UP District, Lucknow, India; retd pay, 1923. *Address:* 97 Iverna Court, W8. *T:* Western 8639.

Died 2 Feb. 1941.

BROWNING, Adm. Sir Montague Edward, GCB 1924; GCMG 1919; GCVO 1933; KCB 1917; CB 1916; MVO 1908; DL, JP Hants; *b* 18 Jan. 1863; *s* of Col M. C. Browning, CB; *m* 1890, Ruth, *d* of Lieut.-Gen. G. N. Boldero; one *d*. Entered Navy, 1876; Commander, 1897; Captain, 1902; Rear-Adm., 1911; Vice-Adm. 1917; served Egyptian War, 1882 (medal, Khedive's bronze star); Secretary to Parliamentary Committee on Water Tube Boilers, 1900; Chief of Staff, Channel Fleet, 1908–09; Inspector of Target Practice, 1911–13; Rear-Adm. 3rd Battle Squadron Grand Fleet, 1913–15; commanding 3rd Cruiser Squadron Grand Fleet, 1915–16; C-in-C N America and W Indies, 1916–17; commanding 4th Battle Squadron Grand Fleet, 1918; President Allied Naval Armistice Commission, 1918–19; Second Sea Lord of Admiralty, 1919–20; C-in-C, Devonport, 1920–23; retired, 1926; Rear-Admiral of the United Kingdom, 1929–39; Vice-Admiral of the United Kingdom and Lieutenant of the Admiralty, 1939–45; ADC to the King, 1910–11; First and Principal Naval ADC to the King, 1925–26. Grand Cordons of Sacred Treasure (Japan), 1918, and of Excellent Crop (China), 1920; Distinguished Service Medal (United States), 1919; Commander Legion of Honour, 1917. *Address:* Sleepers Hill House, Winchester. *T:* Winchester 4309. *Clubs:* Army and Navy; Royal Yacht Squadron (Cowes).

Died 4 Nov. 1947.

BROWNRIGG, Charles Edward; *b* 3 Feb. 1865; 2nd *s* of late T. M. Brownrigg, formerly Assist Insp-Gen. of Royal Irish Constabulary; *m* 1st, 1897, Adolphine Mary (*d* 1904), *e d* of late William Arbuthnot, JP, of Coworth Park, Berks, and of Mrs Arbuthnot of the Ham Manor, Newbury; one *d*; 2nd, 1908, Valerie Margaret Elizabeth (*d* 1929), *e d* of W. S. Akerman; two *s. Educ:* Haileybury College; Magdalen College, Oxford. Classical Exhibition, 1883; 1st class Mods, 1885; 2nd class Lit. Hum., 1887; BA, 1887; MA, 1890. Assistant Master at Eton, Jan.–July 1888; Second Master of Magdalen College School, 1888–1900; Headmaster of Magdalen College School, 1900–30; WM of the Apollo University Lodge of Freemasons, 1900; WM of SM Magdalen Lodge, London, 1901; PSGW Oxfordshire, 1904–05; First Principal Apollo University Chapter, 1906–07; MWS Apollo University Rose Croix, 1908; editor

Oxford University Magazine, 1895–99. *Publications:* A Classical Compendium (3rd ed., 1900); Latin Prose of the Silver Age; Xenophon, Anabasis I; Milton's L'Allegro and Il Penseroso. *Recreations:* golf, croquet. *Address:* Half Acre, Iffley, Oxon. *T:* Oxford 7013. *Clubs:* Royal Automobile, Phyllis Court, Henley; Vincent's, City and County, Oxford.

Died 7 June 1942.

BROWNRIGG, Adm. Sir (Henry John) Studholme, KBE 1937; CB 1933; DSO 1916; serving as Commodore RNR 2nd Class; *b* 1882; *s* of Colonel H. S. Brownrigg, late Rifle Brigade; *m* 1912, Eileen Amy Norah, *d* of G. P. Kinahan. *Educ:* China Medal, 1900. Served at Battle of Jutland, 1916 (despatches, DSO, Order of St Stanislas of Russia); Chief of Staff, Africa Station; Deputy Director of the Gunnery Division, Naval Staff, 1925; Director, 1926–27; Chief of Staff, Plymouth, 1927–29; Capt. HMS Courageous, 1929–30; Dept of Director of Naval Ordnance, 1931; Rear-Adm. Commanding Third Cruiser Squadron, 1933–35; Vice-Adm. (Base) Mediterranean, 1935; Admiral Commanding Reserves 1936–38; Admiral, 1939; Commander-in-Chief, The Nore, 1939; commanded Home Guard, Chatham Area, 1940–41; Director of Greenwich Hospital, 1940–41. *Address:* Anne House, Fishers' Pond, Eastleigh, Hants. *Club:* United Service.

Died 24 Jan. 1943.

BROWNRIGG, Lt-Gen. Sir W. Douglas S., KCB 1939; CB 1936; DSO 1916; Col The Sherwood Foresters since 1941; *b* 21 April 1886; *γ s* of late Gen. J. S. Brownrigg, CB (Grenadier Guards); *m* 1919, Mona, *o d* of Maj.-Gen. H. B. Jeffreys, CB, CMG. *Educ:* Mulgrave Castle; RMC, Sandhurst. Joined 1st Battalion The Sherwood Foresters, 1905; Adjutant, 1910; Maj.-Gen., 1934; Lt-Gen., 1938; served with the 13th Division under Lt-Gen. Sir Frederick Shaw in Gallipoli, 1915; and under Lt-Gen. Sir Stanley Maude in Gallipoli and Mesopotamia, 1915–18 (despatches six times, Brevets of Major and Lt-Col, DSO, the Order of St Vladimir with swords); DAAG War Office, 1919; Staff College, 1920; GSO (2) Royal Military College, 1921; GSO (1) War Office, 1923–27; AA and QMG i/c Administration N China Command, 1928, and of China Command, 1929–31; Commander 159th (Welsh Border) Infantry Brigade, 1931–33; 11th Infantry Brigade, 1933–34; 51st (Highland) Division TA 1935–38; Military Secretary to Secretary of State for War 1938–39; Director-General of Territorial Army, War Office, and Member of Army Council, 1939; Adjutant-General to British Expeditionary Force, 1939–40; retired pay, 1940; Zone and Sector Commander Home Guard since 1941; ADC to the King, 1933–34. *Publications:* Unexpected—a Book of Memories, 1942; regular contributor to Evening News, Christian Science Monitor and Ministry of Information Commentaries. *Address:* 48 Thurloe Square, SW7. *Clubs:* Naval and Military, Kennel, MCC.

Died 7 Feb. 1946.

BRUCE, Vice-Adm. Alan Cameron, CB 1919; DSO 1917; *b* 19 Jan. 1873; 2nd *s* of Commander John Bruce, Royal Navy, and Annie Marie Boyes; *m* 1922, Marion Roseanna Neilson Agnew (*nés* Hedderwick); one *s* one *d*. *Educ:* Cheltenham College (Junior); Burney's Royal Naval Academy, Gosport. Entered Royal Navy, 1886; Midshipman, 1888; Sub.-Lieut, 1892; Lieutenant, 1894; Commander, 1905; Captain, 1913; passed for Interpreter in French, 1911; Captain of Devonport War College, 1913; served in command of Destroyer Flotilla during the World War (DSO, French Croix de Guerre with Palm, despatches); served as Senior Naval Officer, Archangel, 1919, until final evacuation (despatches, CB); served as Commanding Officer North of Scotland Area, 1920–22; Rear-Admiral, 1923; retired, 1923; Vice-Admiral, retired, 1928. *Address:* Sunnybrae, Beech Grove, Moffat. *T:* Moffat 88.

Died 20 Aug. 1947.

BRUCE, Lt-Col Charles Edward, CSI 1929; CIE 1920; CBE 1925 (OBE 1919); late Indian Political Department; late AGG and Chief Commissioner Baluchistan; *b* 23 March 1876; *s* of late R. I. Bruce, CIE; *m* Doris, *d* of J. Wilding, Preston; two *d*. *Educ:* Wellington College; RMC, Sandhurst. Joined 20th Lancashire Fusiliers 1896; 24th Baluchistan Regt, 1897; Indian Political Dept, 1901; served China 1900 (medal); NW Frontier, India, 1902, operations against the Darwesh Khel Wazirs; European War, 1914–19 (despatches twice, OBE); Afghanistan and NWF 1919 (despatches, CIE); Waziristan, 1923 (despatches twice, CBE, CSI); retired 1931. *Publications:* Waziristan, 1936–1937; and others on various tribes along the NW frontier of India. *Address:* Sweet Orchard, Finchampstead, Wokingham. *T:* Eversley 2164. *Club:* United Service.

Died 24 Jan. 1950.

BRUCE, Adm. Sir Henry Harvey, KCB 1920 (CB 1917); MVO 1912; President Metropolitan Area, British Legion; Chairman King's Roll Clerks Association; *b* 1862; *o s* of late Captain Sir Thomas Cuppage Bruce, RN; *m* 1913, Nina Broome (*d* 1915), *e d* of late F. E. Nicholson, Ashfield Balby and Leicester House, Doncaster; one *s*. Captain of HMS Hercules, Grand Fleet, 1914–15; Commodore and Admiral-Superintendent HM Dockyard, Rosyth, 1915–20; Vice-Admiral, 1922; retired list, 1922; retired Admiral, 1926. *Clubs:* United Service; Dormy House (Rye); Royal Naval (Portsmouth).

Died 14 Sept. 1948.

BRUCE, Robert, CB 1942; DSO 1917; MD; JP; DL for County of Aberdeen; Doctor of Medicine; *b* Insch, Aberdeenshire; *s* of late Peter Bruce, JP, Insch; *m* Charlotte A. S. Collie; two *s*. *Educ:* Aberdeen Grammar School; Aberdeen University. MA, MB ChB and MD. Served European War 1914–19 in 7th Bn Gordon Highlanders (Lt-Col 1916, Bt Col 1922, DSO Jan. 1917, Medaille de Reconnaissance, France 2nd class, despatches thrice, TD); Hon. Colonel 5/7 Bn Gordon Highlanders, 1932–45; Chairman Aberdeen County Territorial Association; President, Aberdeen and Kincardine Division of BMA; ex-President of Aberdeen Branch BMA; Vice-Chairman, Aberdeen County Insurance Committee. *Address:* Drumrunie, Braemar, Aberdeenshire. *T:* Braemar 255.

Died 28 April 1949.

BRUCE, Hon. (Robert) Randolph, BSc, CE, FRGS; LLD (Glas.); *b* St Andrews, Lhanbryd, Elgin, 16 July 1863; *s* of Rev. Charles Bruce, MA (Aberdeen), and Margaret Sellar, Woodpark, Elgin; *m* 1st, Lady Elizabeth Northcote (*d* 1915), *γ d* of 2nd Earl of Iddesleigh; no *c*; 2nd, 1932, Edith Badgley, *d* of late W. A. Molson, MD, Montreal, and *widow* of Richard Benedict Van Horne. *Educ:* The Gymnasium, Old Aberdeen; Glasgow University. On the Scientific staff of Wm Denny and Bros, Dumbarton, 1883–87; emigrated to Canada, 1887; on Engineering Staff of Canadian Pacific Railway, 1887–97; engaged in silver-lead mining, 1897–1926, during which time resided at Lake Windermere, British Columbia; Lieut-Governor of the Province of British Columbia, 1926–31; Envoy Extraordinary and Minister Plenipotentiary for Canada to Japan, 1936–38; President of the Mine Owners' Association of the Interior, 1923–25; Director Consolid. Mining and Smelting Co. of Canada. *Recreation:* gardening. *Clubs:* Caledonian; Mount Royal, Montreal.

Died 21 Feb. 1942.

BRUCE, Sir Wallace, Kt 1927; *b* 3 Aug. 1878; *s* of late John Albert Bruce of Kapunda, S Australia; *m* 1905, Winifred Drummond, *d* of John Marshall Reid, Adelaide; one *s* four *d*. *Educ:* Prince Alfred College, Adelaide. Elected to Adelaide City Council as Councillor for MacDonnell Ward, 1916; Lord Mayor of Adelaide, 1925–27; represented City Council on

Municipal Tramways Trust, 1919–25; Trustee of the Savings Bank of South Australia; President of Associated Chambers of Commerce of Australia, 1927–28; President of Adelaide Chamber of Commerce, 1925–27; Chairman of Industrial Peace Conference convened by Commonweath Government, 1928; Chairman, South Australian Harbours Board; Chairman of Committee appointed by the Commonwealth Government of Australia to make a Survey of the Economic Problem, 1932; Director of many Commercial and Industrial Companies. *Address:* Dutton Terrace, Medindie, South Australia. *Clubs:* Stock Exchange, SA Tattersall's, Naval and Military, Adelaide.

Died 16 Nov. 1944.

BRUCE-PORTER, Sir (Harry Edwin) Bruce, KBE 1919; CMG 1917; MD, MRCS, LRCP (Lond.); Knight of Grace and Member of Chapter General of the Order of St John of Jerusalem, England; DL County of London; *b* Woolwich, 5 Feb. 1869; *s* of late Capt. J. Porter, RA; *m* 1896, Essie (*d* 1937), Lady of Grace of the Order of St John of Jerusalem in England, *d* of late Rev. D. Bruce, DD, Auckland, NZ, *widow* of J. H. Honeyman, MD, Auckland NZ; twin *d. Educ:* privately; London Hospital; Brussels; Vienna. Won at London Hospital Medical College—Anatomy-Physiology Scholarship, 1889–90; Practical Anatomy Scholarship, 1891–92; Duckworth Nelson Scholarship in Practical Medicine and Surgery, 1892–93; Scholarship Clinical Medicine, 1892–93. Hon. Certificate Surgery, Prox. Accessit, 1892–93; Hon. Mention Military Medicine and Clinical Medicine and Surgery, Army Medical School, Netley, 1893; late Military Member Council of Territorial Force Association, London; Col AMS (Territorial), retired, late commanding 3rd London General Hospital, 40 British General Hospital, Mesopotamia (despatches, CMG); Past President Hunterian Society; Vice-President Shaftesbury Society and Ragged School Union; late Physician King Edward VII's Hospital for Officers; was member of Home Office Committee to inquire into existing Acts for treatment of Inebriates to suggest amendments; late Surg.-Capt. Army Medical Staff, etc.; Hon. member Smeatonian Society of Civil Engineers. *Publications:* various articles on Medical Subjects and on Motoring. *Address:* 22 Cranmer Court, Sloane Avenue, SW3. *Clubs:* Royal Automobile, Pilgrims, Wentworth, Eccentric.

Died 15 Oct. 1948.

BRUCE-WILLIAMS, Maj-Gen. Sir Hugh Bruce; *see* Williams.

BRUHL, L. Burleigh, RBA 1897, RCA 1929; ARCA 1909; landscape painter; *b* Bagdad, Asia Minor, 29 July 1861; *m* 1st, 1890, Alice, *d* of G. H. With, FRS; 2nd, 1940, Maud May. *Educ:* Vienna. Author of farce, A China Dish, and Landscape Painting (Press Art School) and serials, The Wye and I, and The Other Vagabond; President, Old Dudley Art Society, 1905; Constable Sketching Club, 1912; British Water Colour Society, 1914; Liverpool Academy, 1918; Vice-President Yarmouth Art Society, 1909; two drawings in National Collection (S Kensington), in 18 public galleries, England and Colonies, and in 4 Churches. *Recreation:* golf. *Address:* Glen Rothes, Watford. *T:* Watford 4962. *Club:* Savage.

Died 29 Jan. 1942.

BRUMMER, Rev. Prof. Nicolaas Johannes, MA, BD; *b* Dordrecht, Cape Colony, 1866; *s* of B. J. Brümmer and G. W. Van Zyl; *m* 1st, R. M., *d* of late Rev. G. W. Stegmann of Adelaide, CP; one *s* one *d*; 2nd, H., *d* of late Professor Marais, Stellenbosch; one *s. Educ:* Victoria College, Stellenbosch; Edinburgh; Leipsic. After taking (BA) First-Class Honours) in the University of the Cape of Good Hope, specialised in Philosophy and Economics; entered Theological Seminary, Stellenbosch; licensed as a candidate for the DR Church; BD St Andrews. Served for 3 years in a charge at Jansenville,

then 12 years at 3 Anchor Bay, Cape Town; Professor of Moral and Political Philosophy at the University of Stellenbosch, 1911–41. *Publications:* Spoken; Eerbied; Die Spraaksame Ossewa; Die Unie-Burger; The South African Citizen; numerous pamphlets. *Recreations:* walking, gardening. *Address:* Menslage, Stellenbosch, SA. *TA:* Stellenbosch, SA. *T:* 193.

Died 13 May 1947.

BRUN, Constantin; Chamberlain to HM the King of Denmark; *b* Copenhagen, 5 Oct. 1860. *Educ:* Herlufsholm; University of Copenhagen. Doctor of Laws, 1883; Second Lieutenant in the Hussars of the Guard, 1885; Secretary of Legation in Berlin, 1887–91; Paris, 1891–95; Envoy Extraordinary and Minister Plenipotentiary in Washington, 1895–1908; London, 1908–12; Envoy Extraordinary and Minister Plenipotentiary to United States, 1912–30; First Delegate from Denmark to Peace Conference at the Hague, 1907; retired 1930 with designation as Hon. Counsellor to the Danish Legation; Grand Cross of Dannebrog. *Publication:* Report on the Second Peace Conference at the Hague, 1907. *Recreations:* hunting, shooting. *Address:* 1605 22nd Street, Washington, DC, USA. *TA:* North 3052. *Clubs:* Metropolitan, Washington.

Died 23 Dec. 1945.

BRUNEAU, Hon. Arthur Aimé; *b* 4 March 1864; *m* 1st, 1887, Arzeli (*d* 1903), *d* of Prof. J. B. Cloutier; 2nd, 1904, Lilian, *d* of late W. M. Foy. *Educ:* College of the Sacred Heart, Sorel; Jesuits' Coll., Montreal; Laval University. Advocate, 1887; KC, 1899; MP (L) Richelieu, 1892–1907; Judge Superior Court, Montreal, 1907.

Died 1 Dec. 1940.

BRUNKER, Maj.-Gen. Sir James Milford Sutherland, KCMG 1917; Col Comdt RA, since 1921; *b* 30 May 1854; 2nd *s* of late Maj.-Gen. J. R. Brunker; *m* 1883, Anne Eliza (*d* 1939), *d* of late Maj.-Gen. Hutchinson, CB. *Educ:* Cheltenham College; RM Academy, Woolwich. Entered RA 1873; Captain, 1882; Major, 1890; Lt-Col 1899; Bt Col 1903; Col 1905; Maj.-Gen. 1910; AAG Headquarters of Army, 1905–07; Inspector of Artillery S Army, India, 1907–10; Brigade Comdr, India and France, 1911–15; Inspector RH and RFA at home, 1915–18; served Afghan War, 1880 (medal); European War (1914 Star, British and Victory Medals). *Address:* Fair Oaks, Addlestone, Surrey. *Club:* United Service.

Died 10 March 1942.

BRUNTON, Sir (James) Stopford Lauder, 2nd Bt *cr* 1908; mining geologist; *b* 11 Oct. 1884; *s* of 1st Bt and Louisa Jane (*d* 1909), *d* of late Ven. Edward A. Stopford, Archdeacon of Meath; *S* father, 1916; *m* 1915, Elizabeth, *o d* of Professor J. Bonsall Porter; one *s* one *d. Educ:* Cheltenham College; RMA Woolwich; McGill University; Columbia Univ., New York. Overseas service with Canadian Artillery. *Heir: s* Edward Francis Lauder, *b* 10 Nov. 1916. *Address:* Holydean Hill, Guysborough, Nova Scotia. *Clubs:* Caledonian; University, Montreal; University, Ottawa.

Died 25 July 1943.

BRUNYATE, Sir William (Edwin), KCMG 1916; CMG 1907; Hon. LLD (Hong Kong); *b* 12 Sept. 1867; 2nd *s* of late Rev. W. Brunyate, of Bath; *m* 1896, Bertha Maud Vipond, MBE, 1920 (*d* 1941), *d* of late Andrew Davies, JP, of Varteg, Mon; no *c. Educ:* Kingswood School, Bath; Trinity College, Cambridge. 2nd Wrangler, 1888; 1st division 1st class, 2nd part of Mathematical Tripos, 1889; Smith's Prizeman, 1890; Fellow of Trinity, 1890–96; called to Bar, Lincoln's Inn, 1894; entered Egyptian Government Service, 1898; Khedivial Counsellor, 1903; Grand Officer, Order of the Osmanieh, 1905, Grand Cordon, Order of the Nile, 1918; President of Cambridge Union Debating Society,

1890; Counsel to the Sultan of Egypt, 1914–16, and Legal Adviser to HBM's Residency, Cairo, 1915–16; Judicial Adviser, 1916–19; acting Financial Adviser, Nov. 1917–April 1919 (despatches twice, 1914–19); Vice-Chancellor of Hong-Kong Univ., 1921–24; JP Suffolk and Hong-Kong; County Councillor, West Suffolk, 1928; Alderman, 1939. *Address:* The Old School, Boxford, Suffolk. *Club:* Athenæum.

Died 29 Aug. 1943.

BRYAN, Col Sir Herbert, KBE 1925; CMG 1906; DSO 1918; *b* 13 June 1865; *s* of late Rev. Hugh Bryan of Lyddington House, Rutland; *m* 1901, Agnes Christobel (*d* 1938), *d* of Cecil Algernon Wetenhall of Stanwick, Northants. *Educ:* Oakham School. In ranks, 7th Hussars, 1885–92; 2nd Lieut Lincolnshire Regt 1892; Captain, Manchester Regt, 1899; Brevet Major, 1900; served W Africa, 1897–98; operations on the Niger (despatches, medal with 2 clasps); N Nigeria, 1900 (slightly wounded, despatches, clasp); Ashanti, DAAG, 1900 (despatches twice, medal); Chief Staff Officer, Gambia Expedition, 1901 (despatches, medal with clasp); Staff Officer, West Africa Frontier Force, 1901; employed Colonial Office, 1902–03; Colonial Secretary, Gold Coast, 1904–14; twice thanked by Secretary of State for services; rejoined Army, Jan. 1915; commanding 9th batt. Northumberland Fusiliers, Dec. 1915; ADL Third Army, BEF; AAG, GHQ, BSF (despatches five times, Bt Lt-Col, Bt Col, DSO); French Médaille d'Honneur avec Glaives; Colonial Sec., Jamaica, 1914–25; retd, 1925. *Recreations:* gardening, golf. *Address:* Highfield, Keevil, Wilts.

Died 28 Sept. 1950.

BRYANS, Rev. John Lonsdale; *b* 21 March 1853; *s* of William and Sophia Bryans; *m* 1881, Sibella E. Tomkinson; one *s. Educ:* Radley; Magdalen College, Oxford. Deacon, 1876; Priest, 1877; Rector of New Radnor, 1881; Vicar of St John's, Builth Wells, 1893–1936; Rural Dean of Elwet, 1907; Canon of Brecon Cathedral, 1923; Canon Emeritus, 1934. *Recreations:* such as are suitable to his age. *Address:* St Just, Worcester Road, Malvern. *Club:* Overseas.

Died 16 May 1945.

BRYANT, Frederick, CB 1936; OBE; late Deputy Director of Naval Construction; *b* 1878; *s* of Edward Bryant; *m* 1901, Edith Maud Quinton; one *s* one *d. Educ:* Royal Naval College, Greenwich. *Address:* 9 Queen's Road, Monkseaton, Northumberland. *T:* Whitley Bay 2558.

Died 27 April 1942.

BRYCE, James McKie, CBE 1920; Member of Industrial Court since 1919; *e s* of Thomas Bryce, Saltcoats, Scotland; *m* 1901, Helena, *d* of Hugh Alexander, Birkenhead; one *s* three *d. Educ:* Clifton Park College, Birkenhead. HM Civil Service, 1894–1910; Secretary of the Engineering and National Employers Federations, the National Confederation of Employers Organisations, etc., 1910–19. *Recreation:* golf. *Address:* Green End, Woldingham, Surrey. *T:* Woldingham 2332.

Died 30 Dec. 1946.

BRYCE, Thomas Hastie; Professor of Anatomy, University of Glasgow, 1909–35, now Emeritus Professor; *b* 20 Oct. 1862; *s* of late William Bryce, MD, Edinburgh; *m* 1889, Mary Russell Landale (*d* 1934), *d* of George Wilson of Dalmarnock; one *s. Educ:* Edinburgh Collegiate School; University of Edinburgh; MA, MD, LLD (Glas.). FRS, FRSE. Lecturer on Anatomy, Queen Margaret College, Glasgow, 1890; Lecturer in Anatomy, University of Glasgow, 1892–1909; Keith Prize, Royal Society of Edinburgh, 1906; Member Royal Commission on Ancient Monuments, Scotland, 1908. *Publications:* Quain's Anatomy, 11th edition, vol. i, vol. iv, parts i and ii; The Book of Arran, Prehistoric Sepulchral Remains, 1910; various memoirs and papers on Anatomical, Anthropological, and Archæological subjects. *Recreations:* golf, fishing. *Address:* c/o Bannatyne, Kirkwood, France & Co., Writers, 145 West George Street, Glasgow, C2.

Died 16 May 1946.

BRYCESON, Sir Arthur Benjamin, Kt 1920; *b* 22 Nov. 1861; *s* of George Bryceson and Selina Jesson; *m* Margaret H., 2nd *d* of Major W. McIlroy, RA; two *s* two *d. Educ:* Cowper St School, City. Articled to the late Sir Edwin Hughes, MP; admitted solicitor, 1886; Town Clerk, Metropolitan Borough of Woolwich, 1900–33. *Recreation:* golf. *Address:* Park Side, Eltham Park, SE9.

Died 10 Aug. 1943.

BUCHAN, Anna (O. Douglas); JP for Peeblesshire; *o d* of late Rev. John Buchan and Helen, *d* of John Masterton of Broughton Green, Peeblesshire; unmarried. *Publications:* Olivia in India, 1913; The Setons, 1917; Penny Plain, 1920; Ann and her Mother, 1922; Pink Sugar, 1924; The Proper Place, 1926; Eliza For Common 1928; The Day of Small Things, 1930; Priorsford, 1932; Taken by the Hand, 1934; Jane's Parlour, 1937; The House that is Our Own, 1940; Unforgettable Unforgotten, 1945. *Address:* Bank House, Peebles, Scotland.

Died 24 Nov. 1948.

BUCHAN, Brig. David Adye, DSO 1918; late RA; *b* 7 Sept. 1890; *s* of late W. A. Buchan, MB, Plymouth; *m* 1st, Phyllis Mary, *d* of late Major R. Peters, RMLI (one *s* killed in action, 1941); 2nd, Phyllis Eileen, *e d* of late Col H. Bourke Jordan, DL, Thornhill, Kiltimagh, Co. Mayo, and Bashley, Shandon, Dumbartonshire; one *s. Educ:* Epsom College; RMA, Woolwich. Entered Army, 1910; Capt. 1916; Maj. 1927; Lt-Col 1937; Col 1940; served European War, 1914–18 (wounded, despatches, DSO); NWF India, 1935; War of 1939–45 (1939–43 Star); psc; retired pay, Hon. Brig., 1942. *Address:* Clonmore, Dunleer, Co. Louth, Eire. *Club:* Junior United Service.

Died 12 Oct. 1950.

BUCHANAN, J. Courtney, CBE 1920; *b* 19 Sept. 1877; *s* of Theodore James Buchanan, Richmond, Surrey; *m* 1909, Frances Marjory, 2nd *d* of late George Forbes Bassett, MA, of Bassett Mount, Bassett, near Southampton; one *s* two *d. Educ:* Christ's Hosp. (Grecian); London University (Mitchell Scholar). Lincoln's Inn, Barrister-at-law, 1907; trained in Hospital Secretarial work at St Bartholomew's Hospital, 1897–1906; Secretary, Building Committee, Bolingbroke Hospital, 1906; Secretary, Metropolitan Hospital, London, 1908; Officer-in-charge of Military Section, 1914–19; Hon. Secretary British Hospitals Association, 1915–30; Secretary of The Cancer Hospital, 1920–33; President Hospital Officers' Club, 1923–25. *Publications:* The Function of the Voluntary Hospitals, 1911; The Voluntary Hospitals and the proposed Ministry of Health, 1918. *Recreation:* golf. *Address:* Southwold, Suffolk.

Died 10 May 1949.

BUCHANAN, Rev. John, BA, MD, DD; Missionary of the Presbyterian Church in Canada at Amkhut, India, and Moderator of the General Assembly of the Presbyterian Church in Canada; *b* Glenmorris, Ontario; *m* Mary MacKay, MD, of Riverton, Picton, Nova Scotia; two *d. Educ:* Brantford High School; Queen's University of Theology, Canada; Post Graduate Surgery in New York. Has given fifty years' service in mission work in India; Kaisar-i-Hind gold medal for conspicuous service involving courage and self-sacrifice, 1913; represented the British Government in Southern Rajputana to allay the fears of the Bhils while in revolt, and to report upon conditions; Jubilee Medal, 1935. *Publication:* The Bhils of Central India, 1934. *Address:* Amkhut, Central India.

Died 31 Jan. 1945.

BUCHANAN, Leslie, MD; Hon. Consulting Surgeon to Eye Infirmary, late Surgeon; *b* 5 Sept. 1868; *s* of late Walter Buchanan and late Maria Manning; *m*; one *s*. *Educ:* Glasgow University. MB, CM, 1889. House Physician and Surgeon, the Royal Infirmary, 1890; House Surgeon, the Glasgow Eye Infirmary, 1891–92; successively Pathologist and Assistant Surgeon, the Eye Infirmary, 1900; MD (Commend.), 1900; Member of the Ophthalmological Society of the United Kingdom and other Medical Societies. *Publications:* many papers in Transactions of the Ophthalmological Society in The Ophthalmoscope and other journals. *Recreations:* photomicrography and histology. *Address:* 5 Royal Crescent, Glasgow, C3. *T:* Douglas 5251.
Died 24 June 1943.

BUCHANAN, Rev. Robert M., DD, BD; Librarian in Trinity College, Glasgow; *b* 8 Oct. 1871; *s* of William Buchanan and Marion Hutchisen; *m* 1902, Louisa Kirkwood; one *s*. *Educ:* Glasgow High School; University of Glasgow; University of Marburg; and University of Berlin. Kerr Travelling Scholarship, 1895. Minister of Bank Street Church, Kirriemuir, 1901–12. *Address:* 19 Lilybank Gardens, Glasgow. *T:* W. 766.
Died 15 Feb. 1945.

BUCHANAN-DUNLOP, Col Henry Donald, CMG 1919; DSO 1915; late the Queen's Own Royal West Kent Regiment; *b* 24 July 1878. Entered Army, 1898; Captain, 1904; Major, 1915; Lt-Col, 1921; Col, 1923; served European War, 1914–19 (DSO, Brevet Lieut-Col, CMG, wounded, despatches); commanded 144th (Gloucestershire and Worcestershire) Infantry Brigade, 1927–31; retired pay, 1931. Raised and commanded Home Defence Battalion in War of 1939–45. *Address:* Meadow House, Walmer, Kent. *T:* Deal 888. *Clubs:* Royal Cinque Ports Golf (Deal); Royal St George's Golf (Sandwich).
Died 25 Nov. 1950.

BUCHANAN-SMITH, Sir Walter, Kt 1935; CMG 1930; MC; Hon. Secretary-General Royal Empire Society, 1941; *b* 25 May 1879; *s* of late J. G. Smith, Rhu, Dumbartonshire, and Christina, *d* of late Walter Buchanan of Shandon (MP for Glasgow 1857–65). *Educ:* Bilton Grange, Rugby; Repton. British North Borneo Civil Service, 1903–08; Assistant District Commissioner, S Nigeria, 1909; Acting Commissioner of Lands, 1912, 1914; served with Nigeria Regiment in Cameroons, 1914–15; in German E Africa, 1916–18 (MC, despatches, wounded); 1st class District Officer, 1918; Resident, 1921; Acting Secretary, Southern Provinces, 1923 and 1925; Senior Resident Cameroons, 1926; Acting Lieut-Governor, 1928–29; Lieut-Governor, Southern Provinces of Nigeria 1930; Administered Government of Nigeria, 1930 and 1934; retired 1935; Chairman Colonial Empire Committee, Empire Exhibition, Scotland, 1938; Administered Government of Seychelles 1939; Member of Northern Rhodesian Copperbelt Commission, 1940. *Club:* Constitutional.
Died 27 Nov. 1944.

BUCK, Sir Edward John, Kt 1929; CBE 1918; OBE 1918; *s* of late Henry J. Buck, MD; *m* Annie Margaret, *d* of late General Sir Robert Jennings, KCB. Late Reuter's Agent with Government of India; now adviser to Eastern News Agency, including Associated Press of India and Indian News Agency; a Vice-President of National Association for providing female medical aid to women of India; Chairman Associated Hotels of India, Ltd; Chairman Kalka and Simla Suburbs Electric Supply Coy (India); Hon. Sec. Our Day in India, 1917. *Publication:* Simla Past and Present. *Address:* Simla, India. *Clubs:* Oriental; United Service (Simla); Bengal (Calcutta).
Died 27 April 1948.

BUCK, Sir Percy Carter, Kt 1936; MA, MusDoc, Oxon; Hon. MA Dublin; Hon. Fellow of Worcester College, Oxford; Fellow of the Royal College of Music; King Edward Professor of Music, University of London, 1925–38, Emeritus since 1938; late Musical Adviser to LCC; *b* 1871; *m* 1896, Lucy (*d* 1940), *e d* of Thomas Bond, FRCS, Senior Surgeon to Westminster Hospital; three *s* two *d*. *Educ:* Merchant Taylors' School; Royal College of Music; Worcester College, Oxford. Organist Wells Cathedral, 1896; Bristol Cathedral, 1900; Director of Music in Harrow School, 1901–27; Professor of Music in Dublin University, 1910–20; Cramb Lecturer in Music, Glasgow University, 1923; quondam Examiner in Music to the Universities of Oxford, Cambridge, Dublin, Durham, Edinburgh, and London. *Publications:* various musical books and compositions. *Address:* 78 Buckingham Gate, SW1. *Club:* Athenæum.
Died 3 Oct. 1947.

BUCKERIDGE, Surg. Rear-Adm. Guy Leslie, CB 1937; OBE 1927; late Hon. Surgeon to the King; *b* 2 Dec. 1877; 3rd *s* of Walter Buckeridge, Norfolk House, Angmering, Sussex; *m* 1914, Helen Margaret, 3rd *d* of Thomas Barry Lillis, JP, Carrig, Queenstown, Co. Cork; one *s*. *Educ:* Guy's Hospital. Joined RN as Surgeon, 1903; served RNC Osborne, HMS Bulwark, etc.; during European War in HMS Halcyon, 1914–16. HMS Topaze, 1916–18; Deputy Medical Director General of the Navy as Surgeon Captain, 1929–33, as Surgeon Rear Admiral, 1934–35; in charge of Royal Naval Hospital, Haslar, 1935–37; retired list, 1937. *Publications:* Hygiene in the Royal Navy, Practitioner, July 1926 (with Surgeon Vice-Admiral Sir Joseph Chambers); The Naval Medical Service, in Encyclopædia Britannica. *Recreation:* literature. *Address:* c/o Lloyds Bank, Devonport. *Club:* Army and Navy.
Died 14 July 1944.

BUCKHURST, John William; late Joint-General Manager London County, Westminster, and Parr's Bank, Ltd; *b* Stoke, Rochester, 21 June 1853; *s* of late Benj. John Buckhurst, grazier, New Romney, Kent; *m* Elizabeth, *d* of V. Hills, JP, Rochester; no *c*. *Educ:* King's School, Rochester. Entered the London and County Bank, Dartford Branch, 1872; Manager at Bishop Stortford, 1898; joined Head Office as Assistant Chief Inspector, 1905; Assistant Country Manager, 1909; Country Manager, 1914. *Recreation:* gardening. *Address:* Hendon Hall, Biddenden, Kent.
Died 8 Nov. 1943.

BUCKLAND, Charles Edward, CIE 1895; late Bengal Civil Service; *b* Chittagong, Bengal, 19 Sept. 1847; 2nd *s* of late Charles Thomas Buckland, Bengal Civil Service, and Mary A. L., *d* of late Sir Henry Ricketts, KCSI; *m* 1st, 1873, Laura Anna (*d* 1918), 2nd *d* of late C. R. Lindsay, Bengal Civil Service; four *s* three *d*; 2nd, 1919, Frances Evelyn, 2nd *d* of late J. T. Palmer, of Whinhurst, Seaton, Devon. *Educ:* Eton, 1860–66; Balliol College, Oxford, double 2nd Moderations, 1868. Indian Civil Service, 1868; BA 1869; Barrister-at-Law (Inner Temple), 1885. Joined the Bengal Civil Service, 1870; Assistant Magistrate; Attaché, Foreign Department; Private Secretary to Lieut-Governor of Bengal and Governor of Bombay, Sir R. Temple; acting Under Home Secretary and Press Commissioner with Government of India; Magt. Collr. of Howrah and Gaya, Sec. to Board of Revenue; Revenue-General Sec. to Government of Bengal, and Member of Bengal Legislative Council; Commissioner of Burdwan and Presidency Divisions; Chief Sec. to Government of Bengal; Senior Member of the Bengal Board of Revenue; retired, 1904. Decorated for work as Secretary and Member of Council. *Publications:* a number of official manuals; Bengal under the Lieut-Governors, 2 vols; Dictionary of Indian Biography. *Recreations:*

formerly cricket, rowing, riding, lawn tennis, bicycling. *Address:* 8 Kensington Palace Mansions, De Vere Gardens, W8. *T:* Western 8121. *Club:* Athenæum.

Died 1 Oct. 1941.

BUCKLAND, Sir Thomas, Kt 1935; Chairman, Pitt Son & Badgery Ltd and United Insurance Co. Ltd; Director, Permanent Trustee Co. Ltd; President of the Buckland Convalescent Hospital, Springwood; *b* 1 Aug. 1848; *s* of John Buckland and Martha Smith; *m* 1890, Mary Kirkpatrick (*d* 1937); two *s* four *d. Educ:* Rocky Hill House Academy, Maidstone. Commenced business in Sydney; went to Gympie, Queensland, on discovery of gold, and took up gold mining, 1867; later joined Bank of New South Wales in Sydney as assayer; resigned from bank in 1872 and managed several gold mines; returned to England in 1890 to live, but in 1892 was again back in Australia; was representative and attorney of Cobar Gold Mines; in early '70's bought Cardigan cattle station in North Queensland, St Annes, and Yacamunda stations; President Bank of New South Wales, 1922–37. *Recreation:* golf. *Address:* Lyndhurst, Stanley Road, Hunter's Hill, Sydney, NSW. *T:* Hunter 29. *Clubs:* Australian, Sydney.

Died 12 June 1947.

BUCKLAND, William Warwick, MA; LLD; Hon. LLD Edin. and Harvard; Hon. Dr en Droit, Lyon, Louvain and Paris; Hon. DCL, Oxon; Fellow of the British Academy; Ames Prize, Harvard, 1922; Corresponding Foreign Member of the Academy of the Institute of Bologna, 1928; Associate Member of the Royal Academy of Belgium, 1929; Foreign Hon. Member of the American Academy of Arts and Sciences, 1938; President of Gonville and Caius College, since 1923; Regius Professor of Civil Law, Cambridge University, 1914–45; *b* 1859; *m* Eva (*d* 1934), *d* of C. M. Taylor; one *d. Educ:* Hurstpier-point; Caius College, Cambridge (Scholar); first in Law Tripos, 1884, awarded Chancellor's medal for Legal Studies, 1885; Fellow, 1887. Law Lecturer, 1895; Tutor, 1903; Barrister, Inner Temple. *Publications:* Works on Roman Private Law and Jurisprudence; articles in various publications, etc. *Address:* Gonville and Caius College, Cambridge.

Died 16 Jan. 1946.

BUCKLEY, Ven. Eric Rede, MA; Rector of Polstead, 1921–45; Archdeacon of Ipswich, 1932–45, Archdeacon Emeritus, 1946; *b* 31 Aug. 1868; *s* of Robert Orford Buckley and Anne Cooper Buckley; *m* 1893, Gertrude Haworth; one *s* one *d. Educ:* Merchant Taylors' School; St John's College, Oxford. Vicar of Kirtlington, 1895–1902; Vicar of Burley in Wharfedale, 1902–21; Archdeacon of Sudbury, 1930–32; Proctor in Convocation, 1911–21; Examining Chaplain to the Bishops of Bradford, 1920–31, and St Edmundsbury and Ipswich, 1926–45. *Publications:* An Introduction to the Synoptic Problem; A Lily of Old France; Monsieur Charles; The Prisoner of Vincennes. *Recreation:* mainly literary. *Address:* 209 Mile End Road, Colchester.

Died 6 March 1948.

BUCKLEY, Llewellyn Eddison, CSI 1918; VD; *b* 1866; *s* of J. A. Buckley, Taxing Master in Chancery; *m* 1899, Innes Elphinston, *d* of late Lt-Col Sir Donald Robertson, KCSI; two *s* two *d. Educ:* Clifton; New College, Oxford. Entered ICS 1885; Member of Board of Revenue, Madras; retired, 1922; Lt-Col and Col 10th Southern Provinces Mounted Rifles. *Address:* Graffham, Petworth. *Club:* Leander.

Died 14 June 1944.

BUCKMAN, Rosina, Hon. RAM; operatic and concert artist; Professor of Singing, Royal Academy of Music; *b* Blenheim, NZ, of NZ parentage; *m* 1919, Maurice d'Oisly. *Educ:* privately and at Palmerston North, NZ. Studied singing at the Birmingham School of Music. Went into light opera and musical comedy under J. C. Williamson in Australia; and then was engaged for Dame

Melba's Opera Season there; concert tour followed with John MacCormack; returned to England, 1913; engaged Covent Garden, 1914, making debut in La Bohême; Robert Courtneidge's Opera Season, 1915, when she made huge success as Madame Butterfly; Leading Soprano Sir Thomas Beecham's Opera Co., 1915–20; singing principal dramatic rôles, including Isolde; created soprano rôle in English in Isidore de Lara's Naïl and in Dame Ethel Smyth's The Boatswain's Mate; Principal Soprano Covent Garden Grand Season, 1919–20; world tour, 1922–23. *Recreations:* farming and swimming.

Died 31 Dec. 1948.

BUCKMASTER, Charles A., MA, JP; *b* 16 May 1854; *e s* of late J. C. Buckmaster (Science and Art Department, South Kensington); *m* Lucy Ormerod (*d* 1943), *d* of H. Colley March, MD; three *d. Educ:* Laleham; Ashby de la Zouch Grammar School; Lincoln College, Oxford. Arts degree (Pass Schools), 1874; 1st Class Nat. Sci. Hon. Schs., 1874; Post-graduate course in biology, 1875. Engaged in research work in mineral chemistry with late T. H. G. Wyndham; Assistant Master, Magdalen College School, Oxford, 1874–76; Llandovery College, 1876–80; Examiner in the Science and Art Department, 1880; Inspector, 1882; Senior Inspector, 1890; Chief Inspector, 1900; Assistant Secretary under Board of Education, 1908–14; Life Fellow of the Chemical and Physical Societies. *Publications:* joint-author (with his father) of text-books in chemistry and physics. *Address:* Mill Hill Park, Acton, W3. *T:* Acorn 1044. *Club:* National Liberal.

Died 24 May 1949.

BUCKMASTER, Engr Rear-Adm. Frederick Henry, CBE 1946; retired; *b* Nov. 1883; *er s* of late Frederick Henry Buckmaster; *m* 1910, Margaret, *er d* of late Thomas Somerville Murray, Passage West, Co. Cork; two *d. Educ:* privately; Royal Naval Engineering College, Devonport. Joined Royal Navy, 1900. Served European War, 1914–18; ADC King George VI, 1937; Retired, 1937; Rejoined, 1939–46. *Address:* c/o National Provincial Bank, Weymouth. *Clubs:* Royal Dorset Yacht, Weymouth.

Died 6 April 1947.

BUCKSTON, George Moreton; JP; *b* 1881; *s* of late Rev. Henry Buckston and Eliza Amy, *d* of William John Marrow; *m* 1907, Victoria Alexandrina, *y d* of late H. C. Okeover; two *s* two *d. Educ:* Eton; Trinity College, Cambridge. Lord of the Manor of Ash; patron of one living; High Sheriff of Derbyshire, 1926. *Address:* Sutton-on-the-Hill, Derby; Bradborne Hall, Ashbourne. *Club:* Boodle's.

Died 24 Nov. 1942.

BUDD, Sir Cecil Lindsay, KBE 1919; CBE 1918; Officier de la Légion d'Honneur; Chairman of firm of Vivian Younger & Bond, Ltd; Chairman of the London Metal Exchange, 1902–28; Director of The British Metal Corporation, Ltd; *b* 29 Sept. 1865; 6th *s* of late Edward Budd, Vale Lodge, Leatherhead; *m* 1st, 1892, Bloom, *d* of late Mrs A. H. Tritton; 2nd, 1905, Muriel Edmee, *d* of Mrs W. A. Bevan; four *s* three *d. Educ:* Winchester College; on the Continent. Engaged in the metal trade as merchant and tin smelter; on several Committees of Ministry of Munitions, Board of Trade, and Ministry of Reconstruction. *Recreations:* cricket and all games. *Address:* Burley Hill, Ringwood, Hants. *T:* Burley 82.

Died 27 Dec. 1945.

BUDD, Herbert Ashwin, ARCA 1907; ROI 1921; artist, painter of subject pictures and portraits, and designer; Teacher of Painting, Hornsey School of Art; *b* Ford Green, North Staffs, 10 Jan. 1881; *s* of Thomas Budd and Henrietta Octavia Ashwin; *m* 1915, Helen Margaret, *d* of Hugh J. Mackenzie, CE and architect, Ladyhill, Elgin. *Educ:* privately. Studied Art at Hanley School of Art, Royal College of Art, S Kensington. Exhibitor at Royal Academy; honourable mention

Salon, 1927; exhibited NEAC, Nat. Soc., etc. Portraits painted include: Thomas Graham, 1st Pres. of Chemical Soc., from a contemporary lithograph; W. A. S. Hewins, School of Economics; F. R. Dale, DSO, MC, MA, Headmaster, presented to City of London School, 1948. Official purchases: In Billets, Winter, Rations Up, War Museum, 1930; The Bird Shop, Oldham, 1927; Stripping Lavender, Bradford, 1936. Served with Queen's Westminster Rifles and RE Camouflage Section in France. *Publication:* article on work in The Studio, 1928. *Recreations:* painting, walking. *Address:* 10 Avenue Studios, Sydney Close, SW3. *T:* Kensington 2314. *Club:* Chelsea Arts.

Died 3 June 1950.

BUDDEN, Henry Ebenezer, CBE 1918; President New South Wales Institute of Architects, 1931–32; architect; FRIBA; *b* Rockley, NSW, 11 Aug. 1871. Commissioner of Australian Comforts Fund during European War. *Address:* 79 Pitt Street, Sydney, NSW.

Died 25 Dec. 1944.

BUDGE, Sir Henry Sinclair Campbell, Kt 1935; CMG 1928; *b* Parramatta, 12 Oct. 1874; *s* of late Alec C. Budge, Sydney, New South Wales; *m* Rosa Elise, *d* of late Hon. George Le Fevre, MD, MLC, Melbourne, Victoria; two *s* three *d*. *Educ:* The King School, Parramatta. Entered Premier's Dept, NSW Govt, 1889; transferred to Govt House as Secretary to Governor, 1902–37; Secretary to Executive Council in addition to former office, 1916–37; Hon. Sec. Ben Fuller Trust, 1919; Lay Canon of St Andrew's Cathedral, Sydney, 1930. *Recreations:* cricket and golf. *Address:* Point Piper, Sydney, NSW. *Clubs:* Royal Automobile, Sydney.

Died 5 June 1946.

BUDGEN, Rear-Adm. Douglas Adams, CB, 1942; Royal Navy, retired. Served European War, 1914–19; Flag Officer-in-Charge, Simonstown, until 1942. *Address:* The Manor Farm, Misterton, Somerset.

Died 13 Jan. 1947.

BUELL, Lt-Col William Senkler, CBE 1919; VD; Chevalier Legion of Honour; KC 1936; *b* Brockville, Ontario, 11 Oct. 1868; *s* of Lt Col J. D. Buell and Margaret Sophia Senkler; *m* Sophia Elizabeth Bowie; one *s* two *d*. *Educ:* Brockville Public Schools; Upper Canada College, Toronto. Called to Bar of Ontario, 1891, and of British Columbia, 1893; practised at Brockville, 1894–1914; Mayor of Brockville, 1901; Lt-Col 41st Brockville Rifles, 1910; Lt-Col 4th Canadian Infantry, CEF, Sept. 1914; wounded at 2nd Battle of Ypres, April 1915; commanded 3rd Canadian Reserve Batn in England, 1916–19; has practised law in Vancouver, BC, since 1919, first with firm of Senkler Buell and Van Horne, and since death of both partners in 1926, with firm of Buell, Ellis and Sargent; President, Vancouver Military Institute, 1925–26; DDGM of AF and AM (BC), 1929–30; President, BC Canadian Legion BESL, 1933–38; President United Empire Loyalists Association of Vancouver, 1934–36. *Publications:* legal, military and masonic articles in magazines. *Recreations:* golf, fishing, sailing, etc. *Address:* 202 Pacific Building, Vancouver, BC. *TA:* Senks. *T:* Pacific 9281. *Clubs:* Vancouver, Vancouver.

Died Aug. 1941.

BUER, Mabel Craven, DSc; Independent Lecturer in Economics (in charge of subject), University of Reading, since 1919; Hon. Treasurer, British Federation University Women; *b* 1881; *d* of William Knill Buer and Marian Thornton Craven; unmarried. *Educ:* Streatham Hill High School; Jersey Ladies' College; London School of Economics. Hutchinson Research Studentship, 1912, BSc (Econ.) 1st Cl. Hons 1911; DSc (Econ.) 1927. Assistant London School of Economics, 1912–15; Temp. Lecturer in Economics University College Reading, 1916. *Publications:* Economics for Beginners; Health,

Wealth and Population in the early days of the Industrial Revolution. *Recreations:* reading, drama. *Address:* 55 London Road, Reading.

Died 9 Dec. 1942.

BULKELEY, Sir Richard Henry Williams-, 12th Bt *cr* 1661; KCB 1922; CB 1916; VD; Hon. Commodore, RNR; Lord-Lieutenant Anglesea since 1896; late Lieut commanding Royal Naval Artillery Vols, Liverpool Brigade; late Colonel commanding Royal Anglesea RE Militia; now Lieut-Col in Army; late Commander Mersey Div. RNVR; Hon. Commodore RNR and late Chairman Admiralty Volunteer Committee; appointed to command Royal Naval Depot at Crystal Palace, 1914; Younger Brother, Trinity House; Commodore RNR; First Officer RNR appointed to this rank; Chairman Quarter Sessions, 1889; retired, 1929; *b* London, 4 Dec. 1862; *S* father, 1884; *m* 1885, Lady Magdalene Yorke (*d* 1940), *d* of 5th Earl of Hardwicke; three *d*. *Educ:* Eton. *Recreations:* principally yachting, shooting, fishing; Master Anglesea Harriers for four years; Commodore, Royal Yacht Squadron; Commodore, Royal Angle-sea Yacht Club. *Heir:* *g s* Richard H. D. Williams-Bulkeley. *Address:* 49 Hallam Street, W1. *T:* Langham 3830; Pen-y-Parc, Beaumaris, N Wales. *Clubs:* Turf; Royal Yacht Squadron, Cowes.

Died 7 July 1942.

BULL, A. J., MSc (Lond.); PhD; FInstP, Hon. FRPS; late Principal, LCC School of Photo-engraving; *b* 10 June 1875. *Educ:* private school; Royal College of Science. *Publications:* Photo-engraving, 1934; Scientific papers in Photographic Journal, Transactions of Optical Society, Journal of Scientific Instruments, Geological Magazine, and Proceedings of Geologists' Association. *Recreation:* geology. *Address:* 22 Thanet House, Coombe Road, Croydon, Surrey. *T:* Croydon 4742.

Died 15 April 1950.

BULL, Bartle; Barrister-at-Law; *b* 1 April 1902; *e s* of late William Perkins Bull, KC, LLD; *m* 1931, Rosemary (marr. diss. 1949), *d* of late Jacob Baur, Chicago; one *s* one *d*. *Educ:* Eton; Magdalen College, Oxford (MA). Barrister-at-Law, Inner Temple. MP (C) for Enfield Division of Middlesex, 1935–45; Parliamentary Private Sec. to late Capt. Rt Hon. Euan Wallace, MC, MP, when Financial Sec. to the Treasury, May 1938, and when Minister of Transport, April 1939 to May 1940, and to Major Rt Hon. Gwilym Lloyd George, MP, Minister of Fuel and Power, June 1944; Lt Coldstream Guards, Sept. 1939. *Address:* 1 Paper Buildings, Temple, EC4. *Clubs:* Carlton, Boodle's.

Died 17 Oct. 1950.

BULL, Rev. Paul Bertie; Priest in the Community of the Resurrection, Mirfield; *b* Richmond, Surrey, 1864; *s* of James Burrington Bull, Clerk of the Journals in House of Commons. *Educ:* St John's College, Hurstpierpoint; Worcester College, Oxford. Schoolmaster at Mansfield and Hurstpierpoint; Priest, 1889; a Diocesan Missioner in Chichester and Gloucester and Bristol Diocese, 1892; Curate of S Nicolas, Guildford; joined Community of the Resurrection, 1894; served as Chaplain in Army at Aldershot, and to Guards at Chelsea, 1900; as Chaplain to General French's Cavalry Division rode through many battles in the South African War (medal with 5 bars); preached Missions in many large towns in England; and has given moral instruction in Royal Navy for five years; preaching tours in United States, Canada, and to the Army in India; much work among men and boys in the north of England; Lecturer in Homiletics at General Theological Seminary, New York, for five months, 1924–27; and at Trinity College, Toronto, 1928. *Publications:* God and our Soldiers; The Missioners' Handbook; The Revival of the Religious Life; The Sacramental Principle; Instructions on the Atonement; The Three-Fold Way; Peace and War; Lectures on Preaching and Sermon Construction; The Economics of the Kingdom of God; The Spirit of Wisdom, Love, and

Power; The Way of Conversion; Science and Faith on Life, Death, and Immortality; A Man's Guide to Courtship and Marriage; His Life in Prayer; A Preacher's Note Book; Manuals and Tracts. *Address:* Community of the Resurrection, Mirfield, Yorkshire; The Priory of the Resurrection, 39 Pont Street, SW1.

Died 13 March 1942.

BULL, René; *b* Ireland. War artist for Black and White during South African War, 1900; present at all the big battles in Natal till the relief of Ladysmith; invalided back during the second year of war; war artist Black and White in 1896, during Armenian massacres; also during Turco-Greek War; fell into the hands of the Turks and escaped during the second night from Volo; twice visited India—Indian frontier Tirah campaign, and also for the plague and famine; twice war artist in the Soudan, for the Atbara and Omdurman campaigns; created a record in being through three campaigns in three different continents in ten months; received medals for the Soudan and South African campaigns; studied engineering in Paris, but gave it up for art work in London in 1892; joined HM Forces as Lieut RNVR attached RNAS March 1916; drafted to France for Active Service, July; Lieut-Commander RNVR June 1917; transferred to Royal Air Force, April 1918; Major RAF (despatches); entered service of Air Ministry for technical duties, 1940. *Address:* Darby Green Farm, Blackwater, Hants. *T:* Yateley 3128.

Died 14 March 1942.

BULL, Sir Stephen John, 2nd Bt *cr* 1922; Flt-Lieut, RAFVR; partner in Bull and Bull, solicitors, 3 Stone Buildings, Lincoln's Inn, and Hammersmith; *b* 11 Oct. 1904; *e s* of Rt Hon. Sir William Bull, 1st Bt, and Lilian, 2nd *d* of Mrs Brandon of Oakbrook, Ravenscourt Park, and Heene, Worthing, Sussex; *S* father, 1931. *Educ:* Gresham's School, Holt; New College Oxford (MA). Admitted solicitor, 1928; Vice-Chairman Hammersmith (S) Conservative Association; Liveryman of the Mercers' Company; a Freeman of the City of London; Hon. Solicitor to the League of Mercy, The Royal Life Saving Society and to the Royal Society of St George; Governor of the Upper Latymer Foundation School; Member of the Board of Management of the West London Hospital. *Recreation:* travelling. *Heir:* *b* George [*b* 19 June 1906; *m* 1933, Gabrielle, 2nd *d* of late Bramwell Jackson; one *s*]. *Address:* 2 Ryder Street, St James's, SW1. *Clubs:* Carlton, 1900, Crockfords.

Died 9 March 1942.

BULL, William Perkins, KC; LLD; BA of Victoria University, and LLB of Toronto University; Graduate of Osgoode Hall; *b* Downsview, York County, Ontario, 25 July 1870; *e s* of Bartholomew Hill Bull of Brampton, Ontario, and Sarah Duncan; *m* Maria (*d* 1934), *d* of Michael Brennen, lumberman, Hamilton, Ontario; seven *c.* Founder of the Perkins Bull Hospital for Canadian Officers at Putney Heath, carried on throughout European War, 1914–18; Hon. President of the Canadian Jersey Cattle Club; President of B. H. Bull & Son of Brampton; founder of firm of Bull, Holliss & Wilson, Barristers, Toronto; a Member of the League of Mercy; of the Council of the British American Fellowship; of the Executive Committee and Chairman of the Overseas Dept of the British Empire Union. *Publications:* 13 vols on the history and development of Peel County, Ontario. *Recreation:* travelling among the North American Indians and the Far North. *Address:* National Club, Toronto. *Clubs:* Garrick, Royal Automobile; National, Royal Canadian Yacht (Toronto).

Died 30 June 1948.

BULLARD, Rev. John Vincent, MA Oxon; Rector of Melsonby since 1909; *b* 1869; *yr s* of late Charles Bullard, Rochester; *m* 1897, Alice Maude, *d* of late George Homan, Rochester; three *s* two *d. Educ:* Rochester King's School (King's Scholar); University College,

Oxford (Gunsley Scholar). Curate at Lambeth and Peckham, 1893–97, Vicar of Flamstead, Herts, 1897–1909, during which time he repaired the Church; served on Board of Guardians twelve years, and on various Committees of Diocese and Convocation; Queen Anne's Bounty Tithe Area No. 2 Committee and Committee on relations between Church Assembly and Convocation; Vice-Chairman of House of Clergy; Chairman United Parochial Clergy Group; Proctor for Archdeaconry of Richmond, 1921–41; Rural Dean of Richmond East, 1926–37 and since 1940; Hon. Canon in Ripon Cathedral, 1929. *Publications:* Flamstead, its Church and History, 1904; Lyndwood's Provinciale, joint editor, 1929; The Canons of 1604, Latin, English and Notes, 1934; editor Standing Orders of the Church of England, 1934; The English Parish and Diocese, 1938. *Recreations:* Canon Law, archæology. *Address:* Melsonby Rectory, Richmond, Yorks. *Club:* Authors'.

Died 18 Aug. 1941.

BULLARD, Lt-Gen. Robert Lee; President of the National Security League; *b* 15 Jan. 1861; *s* of Daniel Bullard and Susan Mizell; *m* 1st, 1888, Rose Douglas, *d* of Reece B. Bradson, of Chattanooga, Tenn; three *s* one *d*; 2nd, 1928, Mrs Ella Reiff Wall. *Educ:* US Military Academy. 2nd Lieut 10th Inf., 1885; Brig.-Gen., 1917; Maj.-Gen., 1917; Lieut-Gen., 1918; 3rd Corps, 1918; 2nd American Army, 1918–19; served Cuba, Philippine Islands; Eastern Department and 2nd Corps Area, 1919–21; Distinguished Service Medal; Commandeur Legion of Honour; Croix de Guerre, two palms; Belgian Order of Leopold; Order of St Maurice and St Lazarus (Italian). *Publications:* Personalities and Reminiscences of the World War; American Soldiers also Fought; articles in magazines and military journals. *Recreations:* polo, golf, hunting, riding. *Address:* 2 East 86th Street, New York City, USA. *Clubs:* Union League, Nassau Country, Lotos, St Nicholas, New York Athletic, Military-Naval (New York).

Died 12 Sept. 1947.

BULLER, Arthur Henry Reginald, FRS 1929; BSc London, DSc Birmingham, PhD Leipzig; FRSC; Professor of Botany, University of Manitoba, Winnipeg, 1904–36; Professor Emeritus, 1936; *b* Birmingham, 19 Aug. 1874; *s* of late A. G. Buller, magistrate and county councillor, Birmingham; unmarried. *Educ:* Queen's College, Taunton; Mason College, Birmingham (Heslop gold medal); University of Leipzig and University of Munich. Awarded an 1851 Exhibition Scholarship, 1898; International Marine Biological Station at Naples, 1900–01. Lecturer and Demonstrator in Botany, University of Birmingham, 1901–04; Secretary of Section K of the British Association, Winnipeg, 1909; Pres. British Mycological Society, 1913; Pres. Section IV Royal Society of Canada, 1914–15; Pres. Canadian Phytopathological Society, 1920; Pres. Mycological Section of the American Botanical Society, 1921; Membre Associé de la Société Royale de Botanique de Belgique, 1921; Hon. LLD University of Manitoba, 1924; Norman Wait Harris Foundation lecturer at Northwestern University, 1927; President, Botanical Society of America, 1928; President, Royal Society of Canada, 1927–28; Hon. LLD University of Saskatchewan, 1928; Flavelle Medal of the Royal Society of Canada, 1929; Hon. DSc Univ. of Pennsylvania, 1933; Corresponding Member Netherlands Botanical Society, 1935; President, Section for Mycology and Bacteriology, Sixth International Botanical Congress (Amsterdam), 1935; Vice-President Mycological Society of America, 1936; Medal of Manitoba Natural History Society, 1936; Royal Medal of the Royal Society, 1937; Delegate of British Association, Calcutta, 1937; Hon. DL University of Calcutta, 1937; Visiting Professor of Botany, Louisiana State University, 1941; Hitchcock visiting Professor of Botany, University of California, 1942; Schiff Foundation lecturer, Cornell University, 1942. *Publications:* a number of scientific papers on physiological botany and other biological subjects; Researches on Fungi, Vol. I 1909, Vol. II 1922; Vol. III 1924; Vol. IV 1931; Vol. V 1933; Vol. VI 1934; Essays on Wheat, 1919; Practical Botany, 1929; The Fungi of Manitoba (with G. R. Bisby and J. Dearness), 1929; Editor (with C. L. Shear) of W. B. Grove's English translation of Tulasne's Selecta Fungorum Carpologia, 3 Vols, 1931; collaborator in G. R. Bisby's The Fungi of Manitoba and Saskatchewan, 1938. *Recreations:* billiards, and crossing the Atlantic. *Address:* Manitoba University, Winnipeg, Canada; The Herbarium, The Royal Botanic Gardens, Kew, Surrey, England.

Died 3 July 1944.

BULLER, Rear-Adm. Francis Alexander Waddilove, DSO 1917; late RN; *b* 1879; *s* of late Adm. Sir Alexander Buller, GCB; *m* 1916, Mary Caroline, *d* of late Stephen Hammick. Served European War, 1914–17 (despatches, DSO, promoted); retired list, 1922. *Address:* Park Cottage, Midhurst, Sussex.

Died 14 July 1943.

BULLER, Ralph Buller H.; *see* Hughes-Buller.

BULLOCH, William, MD; FRS 1913; LLD Aber. 1920; Emeritus Professor of Bacteriology University of London; original Member of Medical Research Council under National Insurance Act; *b* Aberdeen, 19 Aug. 1868; *s* of late John Bulloch; *m* 1923, Irene Adelaide, *widow* of Alfred Augustus Baker. *Educ:* Aberdeen University (highest honours); Leipzig; Vienna; Paris; King's College, London. Late Assistant Professor of Pathology, University Coll., London; Bacteriologist, Lister Institute of Preventive Medicine; late Examiner in the Universities of London, Leeds and Liverpool, and the Royal College of Veterinary Surgeons; late Grocers' Co. Research Scholar in Preventive Medicine; President, Pathological Section Royal Society of Medicine; Chairman of the Governing Body, Lister Institute of Preventive Medicine; Tyndall Lecturer, Royal Institution, 1922; Member of Government Foot and Mouth Disease Committee; Hon. Fellow Royal Soc. of Medicine, 1939. *Publications:* numerous contributions on bacteriological and pathological subjects. *Address:* 4 Upper Phillimore Gdns, W8. *Club:* Arts.

Died 11 Feb. 1941.

BULLOCK, Lt-Col Edward George T.; *see* Troyte-Bullock.

BULLOCK, Fred, LLD London; Secretary and Registrar, Royal College of Veterinary Surgeons; *b* 15 Feb. 1878; *m* 1916, Janet H. Lindsay Salmond, MA, LLB; one *s*. *Educ:* Stafford Grammar School; London University (King's College). Called to the Bar, Gray's Inn, 1926; Chevalier de la Légion d'Honneur; Officier de l'Ordre du Nichan Iftikhar (Tunis); Member of the Farriers' Company and Freeman of the City of London; Hon. Fellow of Central Veterinary Society, London (awarded their Victory Medal, 1944); General Secretary of the International Veterinary Congress, London, 1930. *Publications:* La Fondation de la Colonie Française de la Côte d'Ivoire, 1913; Handbook for Veterinary Surgeons, 1927, 3rd edition, 1936; Law relating to Medical, Dental, and Veterinary Practice, 1929; contributor to 14th edition Encyclopædia Britannica; edited Smith's History of Veterinary Literature, Vol. IV, 1933. *Address:* 10 Red Lion Square, WC1.

Died 14 Feb. 1946.

BULLOCK, Ralph, CBE 1920; *b* 1868; *s* of Wm Henry Bullock; unmarried. *Educ:* privately. Retired London Manager of an Eastern Trading Company; served many years in Territorials, 3rd London Brigade, RFA (originally 2nd Mx VA); has specially studied police work; appointed to succeed Sir John Fuller as Commander of N Div. Special Constabulary, 1915; retired, 1939; several times commended by Commissioner of Police; joined Ministry of Food

Eastern II Div., 1940; OBE 1918. *Recreations:* golf, motoring. *Address:* c/o CGTF, 5 Lloyd's Avenue, EC3. *T:* Royal 6564. *Club:* Royal Automobile.

Died 18 Dec. 1946.

BULLOCK, Walter Ll., MA, PhD; Cavaliere della Corona d'Italia; Professor of Italian Studies, University of Manchester since 1935; Chairman of Executive Committee, Regional Committee for Adult Education in HM Forces (Manchester Area), since 1940; *b* 7 March 1890; *e s* of Rev. Ll. C. Watson Bullock, late Rector of Great and Little Wigborough, Essex and Margaret Cecil, *d* of Edmund Robert Spearman, CMG; *m* 1920, Helene Louise, *d* of J. W. Buhlert, Boston, Mass. *Educ:* Liverpool College; Rugby; Harvard University. Went to USA, 1909; spent five years as a metallurgical chemist; after the war, took up post graduate studies in languages and literature (PhD Harvard, 1923), and since 1922 has been almost entirely occupied with Italian studies (Head of Italian Dept at Bryn Mawr College, 1922–27; University of Chicago, 1927–35), and (until 1935), with various activities in the Modern Language Association of America, the Mediæval Academy, the American Association of Teachers of Italian, etc. also as Editor-in-Chief of the Heath-Chicago Italian Series, and editor of Modern Philology. *Publications:* various studies and essays in the field of Italian Literature; General Editor of Italian Studies. *Recreations:* bibliomania, amateur theatricals, tennis. *Address:* Arborfield, Langham Road, Bowdon, Cheshire. *T:* Altrincham 0904.

Died 19 Feb. 1944.

BULLOCK, Ven. William, AKC; Vicar of St Peter's, Wellington; Archdeacon of Wellington since 1940; Vicar General of Wellington Diocese, 1937; Commissary to Bishop of Melanesia; *b* 12 Feb. 1885; *m* 1916; one *s*. CF, 1917; Archdeacon of Wairarapa, 1934–40. *Publication:* The Dominant Design. *Address:* St Peter's Vicarage, Wellington, C2, NZ.

Died 9 Nov. 1944.

BULLOCK, Willoughby; Valuer and Assessor; *b* 1882; *s* of late Francis B. Bullock of St Leonard's, Northumberland, and Ada, *d* of late General M. W. Willoughby, CB; *m* 1921, Anita, *o d* of E. F. Clemente. *Educ:* Haileybury; University of Edinburgh and University of Montpellier. Engaged for some years in secretarial and legal work, London; Fellow and member of Council, Incorporated Secretaries' Association; Barrister-at-law, Gray's Inn and Inner Temple; SE Circuit and Central Criminal Court; Lieut-Col 2nd Cd. Bn Sussex Yeomanry; resigned 1921 and appointed Hon. Colonel; Assistant-Commissioner, St John Ambulance Brigade, and Assistant-Director, British Red Cross Society; Member International Law Association; Marshal to Hon. Mr Justice Greer; Attorney-General and Admiralty Advocate, Bahamas; Chairman, Bahamas Board of Education; President Commission to enquire into administration Police Force; Member Executive and Legislative Councils; acted as Chief Justice Supreme Court, 1921, 1922, and 1924; represented Bahamas at Imperial Education Conference, 1923; Attorney-General of British Honduras, 1925–27; acted as Colonial Secretary, 1925; Deputy Governor on several occasions; Relieving President of District Courts, Palestine, 1927; Chief Justice of St Vincent, 1928–30; Administered the Government, 1928; Master of the Wor. Company of Curriers, 1930; Chairman, Court of Referees, 1931; appointed member of Panel to hear Appeals under Road Traffic Act, 1935; Deputy Chairman of the Traffic Commissioners for the Yorkshire Area, 1936; Divisional Food Officer, Food Defence Plans Dept, 1938; Chairman, Military Service Hardships Committee, 1939; Dept Chm. Furnished Houses Rent Tribunal, 1946; Pres. Valuers Institution, 1947. Order of St John; FRGS. *Publications:* Bahamas Practice; Handbook for Coroners, and various articles on legal subjects. *Recreations:* building and motoring. *Address:* Tangles, Old Bosham, Sussex. *T:* Bosham 2132. *Clubs:* Royal Automobile, Authors', RMY, East India and Sports.

Died 20 April 1950.

BULMER, Edward Frederick, JP; MA; Director of H. P. Bulmer and Co. Ltd, Hereford; *b* 1865; *s* of Charles Henry Bulmer, MA and Mary Grace Cokram; *m* 1899, Sophie F. Rittner; three *s* two *d. Educ:* Shrewsbury School; King's College, Cambridge. Joint Founder with his late brother H. P. Bulmer, of the firm of H. P. Bulmer and Co. Ltd, cider makers, Hereford; has taken an active part in local government; Mayor of Hereford, 1908 and 1925; late Member and Alderman of the Herefordshire CC; late Chairman of the National Health Insurance Committee; Chairman of the Hereford Garden City and Hereford Dwellings Co. Ltd; ran for Cambridge against Oxford in mile, 1889; High Sheriff of Herefordshire, 1934. *Recreations:* work, fishing, shooting, travel. *Address:* Adams Hill, Hereford. *TA:* Bulmerco, Hereford. *T:* 2696.

Died 2 Sept. 1941.

BUNCH, John L., MD, DSc, BS, MRCP; Fellow of the Medical Society of London and of the Royal Society of Medicine; Mem. Corr. de la Soc. Franç. de Dermatologie. *Educ:* University College (gold medallist in medicine and surgery); Vienna and Paris. Consulting Physician to Skin Department, Queen's Hospital; Consulting Physician to Hospital for Diseases of the Skin, Leicester Square; late Assistant Physician to NW London Hospital, and to German Hospital; Research Scholar British Medical Association. *Publications:* papers on medical, dermatological, and scientific subjects in Transactions of medical societies and in medical and scientific journals. *Recreations:* golf and skating. *Address:* 30 Pall Mall, SW1. *T:* Western 3825. *Clubs:* Junior Carlton; Royal Wimbledon Golf.

Died 22 April 1941.

BUNDI, Captain HH Maharao Raja Sir Ishwari Singh Bahadur, Maharao Raja of, GCIE 1937; MC 1946; ADC to the King; *b* 8 March 1893; *S* 1927. *Address:* Bundi, Rajputana, India.

Died 23 April 1945.

BUNNY, Rupert Charles Wolston; Australian artist; *b* St Kilda, Victoria, 29 Sept. 1864; 3rd *s* of late Judge Bunny; *m* 1902, *d* of Col Morel. *Educ:* private school, St Kilda; Melbourne National Gallery under G. F. Folingsby; London in Calderon's atelier; Paris under Jean Paul Laurens. Exhibited Old Paris Salon, 1886; Societaire New Salon. *Works:* Après le Bain and Un Rayon du Soleil (Luxembourg); Descending Angels (Adelaide Gallery); Portrait of Madame Melba, etc.

Died 24 May 1947.

BUNOZ, Rt Rev. Emile Marie, OMI, DD; Bishop of Tentyris and Vicar Apostolic of Yukon and Prince Rupert since 1917; *b* Sales, Savoy, France, 24 Feb. 1864. *Educ:* Rumilly, La Roche, and Rome (Gregorian University). Ordained in Rome, 1891; sent to British Columbia same year; rector of St Louis College, New Westminster, 1898; rector of St Mary's, Dawson, 1892; first Prefect Apostolic of Yukon, 1908. *Address:* Prince Rupert, BC, Canada.

Died 8 Sept. 1945.

BURBIDGE, Sir (Richard) Woodman, 2nd Bt *cr* 1916; CBE 1919; Chairman Harrods Ltd, D. H. Evans, Ltd, and Dickins and Jones, Ltd; Member of Ministry of Munitions Staff Investigation Committee and Stores Purchases Advisory Committee; Treasurer of Tariff Commission, 1917–22; Member of the Empire Marketing Board; Chairman and Managing Director Harrods (Buenos Aires) Ltd and Associate Companies, 1913–44; Member of Board of Trade Advisory Council; *b* 7 Dec. 1872; *s* of 1st Bt and Emily (*d* 1905), *y d* of late J. Woodman of Melksham, Wilts; *S* father, 1917; *m*

1896, Catherine Jemima, *d* of H. Grant, Sodbury House, Great Clacton, Essex; one *s* three *d.* Marie Regina Cross of Roumania; Commandeur de l'Ordre de Leopold II of Belgium. *Heir: s* Richard Grant Woodman. *Address:* Cisswood, Lower Beeding, Horsham. *T:* Lower Beeding 16. *Clubs:* Royal Automobile, Royal Thames Yacht.

Died 3 June 1945.

BURDER, Brig.-Gen. Ernest Sumner, CMG 1916; late Duke of Cornwall's LI; *b* 27 Jan. 1866. *Educ:* Haileybury College. Served NW Frontier, India, 1897–98 (medal 2 clasps); European War, 1914–18 (CMG, Bt Col); Ordre de Leopold; JP Berks. *Address:* Compton House, Compton, Newbury.

Died 2 Jan. 1946.

BURDETT, Sir Henry Aylmer, MC, 10th Bt *cr* 1665; late Essex Regt; *b* 28 Nov. 1881; *s* of late Rev. William Jerome Burdett, 2nd *s* of 6th Bt; *S* kinsman, 1940; *m* 1928, Audrey Grace Chichester, *d* of George Cutcliffe; one *s* two *d. Heir: s* Savile Aylmer, *b* 24 Sept. 1931. *Address:* Ngewe, Ruiru, Kenya Colony.

Died 23 Aug. 1943.

BURDON, Rowland, JP, DL, VD; *b* 19 June 1857; *e s* of late Rev. John Burdon of Castle Eden, and Elizabeth Anne, *d* of Henry Hale; *m* 1887, Mary Arundell (*d* 1930), 2nd *d* of late Wyndham Slade of Montys Court, Taunton; three *d. Educ:* Repton; University College, Oxford. MP (Co. U) Sedgfield Division of Durham, 1918–22; late Col Commanding 1st Vol. Batt. Durham Light Infantry; VD; Lord of the Manors of Little Eden and Castle Eden; Patron of one living. *Address:* Castle Eden, Co. Durham.

Died 1 Aug. 1944.

BURDWAN, Sir Bijay Chand Mahtab, Maharajadhiraja Bahadur of, GCIE 1924 (KCIE 1909); KCSI 1911; IOM 1909; FRGS, FRSA, FRCI, FNBA, MRAS, FZS, FRHortS; Hon. LLD Edinburgh and Cambridge; a Member of 3rd Class in Civil Division of Indian Order of Merit for conspicuous courage displayed by him in the Overtoun Hall, Calcutta, 7 Nov. 1908; *b* 19 Oct. 1881; adopted by late Maharajadhiraja and succeeded, 1887; *m*; two *s* two *d.* Has travelled much in India; made a tour through Central Europe, and visited British Isles in 1906, when he was received by King Edward; a Member of Imperial Legislative Council, 1909–12; Bengal Legislative Council 1907–18; temp. Member of the Bengal Executive Council, 1918; Member of the Bengal Executive Council, 1919–24; Member of the Indian Reforms Enquiry Committee, 1924; Member of the Indian Taxation Enquiry Committee, 1924–25; Trustee of the Indian Museum, 1908; President, Agri-Horticultural Society of India, Calcutta, 1911 and 1912; President of the British Indian Association, Calcutta, 1911–18, 1925–28, and from 1935; Trustee of the Victoria Memorial, Calcutta, since 1914; Chairman, Calcutta Imperial (King-Emperor George V and Queen Empress Mary) Reception Fund Committee, 1911–12; President of the Bengal Volunteer Ambulance Corps and of the Bengalee Regiment Committees during the War; Delegate from India to the Imperial Conference, London, 1926, when he was received by King George V; received the Freedom of the Cities of Manchester, Edinburgh, and Stoke-on-Trent, 1926. *Publications:* Vijaya Gitika, and various other Bengali poetical works and dramas; Studies; Impressions (the Diary of a European Tour); Meditations; The Indian Horizon, 1932, etc. *Recreations:* tennis, golf, rowing. *Heir:* Maharajadhiraja Kumar Uday Chand Mahtab [BA, Dewan-i-Raj of the Burdwan Raj, 1927–29, and since 1937; Hon. Manager, 1930–37; Private Secretary to the Maharajah at Imperial Conference, London 1926; *b* 14 July 1905]. *Address:* The Palace, Burdwan, India; Bijay Manzil, Alipore, Calcutta; The Retreat, Kurseong, Bengal; Rosebank, Darjeeling; Mosapher Manzil, Agra,

UP, etc. *Clubs:* Carlton, Marlborough, Royal Automobile; Aftab, Burdwan; Calcutta, Calcutta; Gymkhana, Darjeeling; Agra, Agra.

Died 20 Aug. 1941.

BURGES, Lt-Col Dan, VC, DSO 1918; *b* 1 July 1873; *e s* of late D. Travers Burges, Town Clerk of Bristol; *m* 1st, 1905, Katharine Blanche (*d* 1931), 2nd *d* of late Captain Edmund Fortescue, Rifle Brigade; no *c*; 2nd, 1932, Mrs Florence Wray Taylor, *d* of late W. G. Cox, Nutgrove, Rathfarnham, Dublin. *Educ:* Winchester; RMC, Camberley. Joined 2nd Gloucestershire Regiment; served South African War (Queen's medal 4 bars, King's medal 2 bars); Adjutant Punjab Vol. Rifles, 1908–13; European War with 2nd Gloucester Regt at second battle of Ypres (despatches, wounded), commanded 10th (S) Bn E Yorks Regt, Dec. 1915–June 1916 Instructor Senior Officers' School, Oct. 1916–March 1917; Commanded 7th (S) Bn SWB Salonica Army, Sept. 1917–Sept. 1918 (VC for operations at Jumeaux, Balkans, 18 Sept. 1918; DSO, Croix de Guerre avec Palme, Greek Mil. Cross (2nd class), despatches twice, mentioned in French General Orders, severely wounded); retired, pay, 1923; Resident Governor and Major of the Tower of London, 1923–33. County Director, British Red Cross, 1943–45. *Address:* Hyde Lodge, Durdham Down, Bristol.

Died 24 Oct. 1946.

BURGESS, Arthur Henry, LLD (Hon.) Manitoba, MB, ChB, MSc (Manch.), FRCS (Eng.), LRCP (Lond.), FACS (Hon.) DL (Lancs); Vice-President, British Medical Association (President, 1929–30); Professor Emeritus of Clinical Surgery, University of Manchester; Hon. Consulting Surgeon, Manchester Royal Infirmary and Manchester Christie Hospital for Cancer; John B. Murphy Orator for 1931, Clinical Congress of American College of Surgeons; Member of Council, Royal College of Surgeons of England; Hunterian Orator, RCS for 1941; formerly Examiner in Surgery, University of Sheffield, and University of Bristol; Consultant Adviser in Surgery to the EMS; Fellow of Royal Society of Medicine; Past President, Association of Surgeons of Great Britain and Ireland; *b* Stretford, Lancs, 2 Feb. 1874; *er s* of John Henry Burgess, Merchant, and Elizabeth Sharrocks; *m* Elspeth (*d* 1941), 2nd *d* of Thos Robinson, Leek, Staffs; five *s* one *d. Educ:* The Owens College, Manchester. Dalton Natural History Prizeman, 1892; Dauntesey Medical Scholar, 1892; Junior and Senior Platt Physiological Exhibitioner, 1893–94; Victoria University Scholar in Medicine, 1894; Turner Medical Scholar, 1896; Dumville Surgical Prizeman, 1896. Formerly House-Surgeon and Resident Surgical Officer to the Manchester Royal Infirmary; Visiting Surgeon, Manchester Children's Hospital and Lecturer in Surgery, University of Manchester; served European War, 1914–19 at home and abroad; Consulting Surgeon to the Mesopotamian Expeditionary Force (despatches). *Publications:* Surgery of the Thyroid Gland, Ency. Medica; many contributions to medical journals. *Recreations:* music, chess, golf. *Address:* Ashlea, Cheadle, Cheshire. *T:* Gatley 2787. *Club:* Union (Manchester).

Died 6 May 1948.

BURGESS, Rev. Francis, FSA Scot; Musical Director of Gregorian Association; Hon. Captain RAF (retired); *b* 1879; *s* of Henry Burgess, formerly of Harleston, Norfolk; *m* Mabel (decd), *e d* of J. B. Thistleton; one *d. Educ:* privately. Secretary of the London Organ School, 1900–01; Organist of St Mary-the-Virgin, Primrose Hill, 1901–02; St Mark's, Marylebone, 1902–04; St Columb's, North Kensington, 1904–14; St Augustine's, Queen's Gate, SW, 1919–23; Professor at Trinity College, London, 1914; Director of the Plainsong and Mediæval Music Society's Choir, 1904, and Director of the Gregorian Festival since 1910. Took Holy Orders, 1944. *Publications:* A Textbook of Gregorian Music, 1906; six volumes in the Nights at the Opera series,

1907; The Organ of Fifty Years Hence, 1908; Textbook of Plainsong, 1912; Two Lectures delivered at the Royal College of Organists, 1912; The Music of the Mass, 1912; A Plainsong Primer, 1925. *Recreations:* music and motoring. *Address:* Villa Vita, New Milton, Hants. *Club:* Royal Air Force.

Died 15 June 1948.

BURGESS, Frederick William, FJI; editor, author, etc; *b* Sandbach, 1855; *m* 1880, Eveline, *d* of late Thomas Hancock; one *d. Educ:* Sandbach Grammar School; Hawthorn Hall, Wilmslow. Editor of London Journals for 50 years; collector of curios and an authority on antiques. *Publications:* Chats on Old Coins; Old Copper and Brass; Household Curios; Antique Furniture; Old Pottery and Porcelain; Antique Jewellery and Trinkets; Silver, Pewter, Sheffield Plate; Old Prints and Engravings, etc.; contributor to Art Magazines and Traders' and Collectors' Journals. *Address:* 16 Darley Road, Darley Park, Manchester 16.

Died 28 Oct. 1945.

BURGESS, Herbert Edward, CBE 1924; *b* 14 March 1863; *s* of late Capt. John Burgess, RN; *m* 1897, Mary Helen, *d* of late J. Fisher Reese, New York; one *s. Educ:* Christ's Hospital. Admitted as Solicitor, 1884; entered the Solicitor's Dept, Board of Trade, 1891; transferred to the Bankruptcy Dept, 1901; Senior Official Receiver in Companies Liquidation, 1921–28. *Address:* Norton Corner, Freshwater, I of W.

Died 20 Feb. 1948.

BURGESS, Robert Nelson; Editor and Managing Director of The Cumberland News and The Cumberland Evening News, Carlisle; *b* 1867; *s* of late John Burgess, editor of The Carlisle Patriot; *m* Jean, *er d* of late George Deans Lawie, Carlisle; one *s* two *d.* Vice-President of the Newspaper Society of Great Britain (President, 1931–32); Director of the Press Association and of Reuters Ltd, 1925–32; Fellow of the Institute of Journalists. *Address:* Evening Hill, Thursby, Carlisle. *T:* Dalston, Carlisle, 235.

Died 26 March 1945.

BURGETT, Rt Rev. Arthur Edward; *b* 1869; *s* of Edward William Burgett and Henrietta Warneford; unmarried. *Educ:* Radley; Trinity Hall, Cambridge; Cuddesdon Theological College. Served eight years in Duke of Wellington's West Riding Regiment; five years Lieut; three years Captain; ordained to Parish, Tottenham, 1897; Missionary, Diocese of Quebec; Chaplain to the Bishop; Rector of St Paul's, Quebec; Secretary of Synod, Diocese of Quebec; General Missionary, Diocese of Qu'Appelle, 1913; Archdeacon of Assiniboia, 1918–24; of Edmonton, N, 1924–31; Bishop of Edmonton, 1932–41; DD (Hon.) Manitoba Univ. 1931; DD Toronto University 1932. *Publications:* Door of Heaven, Holy Communion, Manual; A Service of Preparation for Holy Communion. *Recreations:* sailing, boating, fishing, shooting. *Clubs:* Bembridge Sailing, Bembridge, IW; Edmonton, Golf and Country, Edmonton, Alberta.

Died 13 Dec. 1942.

BURGHARD, Frédéric François, CB 1915; MS and MD (London); FRCS (England); Fellow of King's College, London; Colonel, RAMC (TF) (retired); Consulting Surgeon, King's College Hospital and the Children's Hospital, Paddington Green; *b* 27 Feb. 1864; *m* 1st, 1893, May (*d* 1919), *d* of late A. A. Pollock; 2nd, 1923, Betty, *d* of late Henry Atkins, Bushey, Herts. *Educ:* Christ's College, Finchley; Guy's Hospital (Prizeman and Gold Medallist in Surgery); London University. Formerly Senior Surgeon to and Lecturer on Clinical Surgery at King's College Hospital; Consulting Surgeon to Queen Alexandra's Hospital, Millbank; Member of Council and Court of Examiners, Royal College of Surgeons of England; Member of Senate, London University; Member Medical Advisory Board, Air

Ministry; Examiner in Surgery to the Universities of Cambridge and London. Surgical Registrar, Guy's Hospital, 1888; Assistant Surgeon to King's College Hospital, 1890; served as Colonel AMS, Consultant Surgeon, BEF, European War, 1914–16 (despatches, CB). *Publications:* A Manual of Surgical Treatment (with Sir Watson Cheyne); editor of A System of Operative Surgery; numerous papers in the medical press. *Address:* 7 Causewayside, Cambridge. *T:* Cambridge 3640.

Died 31 Oct. 1947.

BURGIN, Rt Hon. Edward Leslie, PC 1937; LLD; MP (L) Luton Division, 1929–31 (LNat) since 1931; solicitor, member of firm of Denton Hall & Burgin, Gray's Inn and Paris; late Principal and Director of Legal Studies to the Law Society; *b* 13 July 1887; *s* of late Edward Lambert Burgin, solicitor; *m* 1912, Dorothy Theresa, 3rd *d* of Charles H. Cooper; one *s* four *d*. *Educ:* Christ's College, Finchley; Lausanne; Paris. 1st in 1st class Honours LLB with University Scholarship, 1908; 1st in 1st class Honours Solicitors Final of the Law Society with Clement's Inn Daniel Reardon Prizes, 1909; Scott Scholar of the Law Society, 1909; LLD London, in 1913, on Thesis, since published as a text-book. Member of Council of Law Society; Deputy Chairman Beds Quarter Sessions; served as Intelligence Officer in European War (despatches, Italian Croce di Guerra); contested (L) Hornsey, 1921, 1922, 1923, and 1924; East Ham, 1926; Charity Commissioner, 1931–32; Parliamentary Secretary, Board of Trade, 1932–37; Minister of Transport, 1937–39; Minister of Supply, 1939–40; Member of Senate of London Univ.; Member of General Council of League of Nations Union; Member of Lord Chancellor's Committee on Delegated Legislation; Chairman Commercial Arbitration Committee of International Chamber of Commerce; Pres. Institute of Arbitrators; a British delegate to the League of Nations, 1935. *Publications:* Administration of Foreign Estates; The Students Conflict of Laws. *Recreations:* foreign languages, mountaineering, tennis. *Address:* 3 Gray's Inn Place, WC. *TA:* Burginhal. *T:* Chancery 7485; Aplins Close, Harpenden, Herts. *T:* Harpenden 422. *Clubs:* Reform, National Liberal, Royal Automobile, Whitefriars, Eighty.

Died 16 Aug. 1945.

BURGIN, George B., FJI; novelist, critic, and journalist; *b* Croydon, 15 Jan. 1856; *s* of late Joseph Burgin, Barrister; *m* 1893, Georgina Benington (*d* 1940). *Educ:* Totteridge Park Public School. Private Secretary to Baker Pasha, and accompanied him to Asia Minor as Secretary of Reform Commission in Armenia; returned to England, 1885; sub-editor of The Idler to 1899; Secretary Authors' Club, 1905–08; Vice-President, OP Club, 1915–17; Vice-President, After Dinner Club; Vice-President The Dickens Fellowship; Fellow of the Institute of Journalists. *Publications:* over 90 novels, 1894–1938. *Recreation:* gardening. *Address:* 12 Clarence Rd, Harpenden, Herts. *Clubs:* Whitefriars', After Dinner, OP.

Died 20 June 1944.

BURKE, Edmund Tytler, DSO 1917; MB, ChB; Lt-Col RAMC (retd); Member of Executive Committee and of Medical Advisory Board, British Social Hygiene Council; Member Therap. Trials Committee, Medical Research Council; Vice-President, Medical Society Study of VD; Late Director, LCC (Whitechapel) Clinic; Late Consultant Venereologist to Public Health Dept, LCC; Late Lecturer in VD London Hospital Medical School; Commanded 40th British Field Ambulance, 13th Division, 1915–19; *b* Elgin, 18 April 1888; *e s* of W. M. Burke, JP, FSA Scot; *m* 1919, Mina, 3rd *d* of late Charles Stewart, Craigie, Perth; two *s* one *d*. *Educ:* Perth Academy; Glasgow University; St Andrews University. In Special Reserve, 23 Feb. 1913; Adjutant 40th Field Ambulance early in 1915; served Gallipoli, June 1915; promoted Major and given Command of Unit; served to end of Campaign (despatches); Mesopotamia, Feb.

1916–Aug. 1918 (despatches, Lieut-Col, DSO, Serbian Order of White Eagle with Swords); ADMS North Persian Force, 1918; Caucasus, 1918–19; SMO Baku (despatches); Order of St George of Russia; Order of St Vladimir of Russia (with swords); late VD officer for the City of Salford; late VD officer County Borough of Warrington; late Assistant Surgeon, VD Department, Royal Infirmary, Wigan; Assistant Dermatological Department, Royal Infirmary, Manchester; late Assistant MO Northern Hospital for Women and Children, Manchester. *Publications:* The Venereal Problem, 1919; Venereal Disease during War (Quarterly Review, April 1920); The Routine Treatment of Venereal Disease in General Practice, 1926; Scourges of To-day, 1929; As From an Inn (English Review, Sept. 1928); Toll of Secret Disease (Nineteenth Century, Nov. 1927); articles in medical papers; Textbook on Venereal Diseases, 1940; Modern Treatment of Venereal Diseases (Monographs of Modern Medicine Series). *Recreations:* photography, shooting. *Address:* (temp.): Avoca, Old London Road, Sutton, near Macclesfield, Cheshire.

Died 14 June 1941.

BURKE, Harold Arthur, RBA; Master of W. Company of Skinners, 1906–07; Governor of Sir Andrew Judd's Foundation and Skinners' Schools; *b* 28 Jan. 1852; 7th *s* of late James St George Burke, QC, of Auberies, Essex, and Ann Eliza, *d* of John Grubb, JP, of Horsendon, co. Bucks; *m* 1893, Beatrix Mary Clifford, *d* of Stephen Thomas Aveling of The Restoration House, Rochester. *Educ:* Cheltenham College; Liège University. Studied art at South Kensington RA, and the Beaux Arts, Paris, under Gerome and E. Vernet Lecomte. Exhibits at RA. *Recreations:* boat-sailing, billiards, books. *Address:* Vespers, Findon, Sussex. *T:* Findon 46. *Clubs:* Arts, Savage, Royal Canoe.

Died 5 Jan. 1942.

BURKE, Col Herbert Francis Lardner, DSO 1916, MC, VD; Hon. Col Kimberley Retg; Director De Beers Consolidated Mines Ltd, Consolidated Co., Bullfontein Mine Ltd, Griqualand West Diamond Mining Company, Dutoitspan Mine Ltd and the South-West Finance Corporation Ltd; *b* 3 Oct. 1883; 5th *s* of late Henry Lardner Burke, KC, Solicitor-General of the Cape Colony; *m* 1915, Emilie Josephine Cruickshank; two *s* one *d*. *Educ:* St Andrew's College, Grahamstown. Joined the Secretary's Office of De Beers Consolidated Mines Ltd as a junior clerk, 1899; Asst Sec. 1929; Sec. 1931–44; joined Kimberley Regt as 2nd Lt 1910; Capt. 1912; served in German South-West Africa, 1914–15 as Adjt of the Regiment (DSO, despatches); at conclusion of SW Africa campaign joined the 11th SA Infantry as Company Commander and served in German East Africa, 1916–17 (despatches and MC); Major, 1922; Lt-Col Commanding Kimberley Regiment, Union of South Africa Defence Forces, 1929–35, Officer Commanding 12th Bn National Volunteer Brigade, Union Defence Forces, 1940–43; Colonial Auxiliary Forces Officers' Decoration, 1927; King George V Silver Jubilee Medal, 1935. *Recreations:* golf and motoring. *Address:* PO Box 616, Kimberley, S Africa. *Club:* Kimberley.

Died 12 Aug. 1950.

BURKE, John Benjamin Butler, MA (Camb. and Dublin); FInstP; physicist and scientific author; *b* 4 Nov. 1871; *s* of late John Burke, MD, and late Victoria, *o c* of late Benjamin Butler of Manila, and *g s* of late Joseph Burke, JP, of Ower, Co. Galway; *m* 1911, Isabella, *d* of G. H. O'Sullivan. *Educ:* Trinity College, Dublin (Mathematical Scholar, Senior Moderator, and Gold Medallist in Experimental Science, Physics and Chemistry), BA, 1893, MA, 1897; Trinity College, Cambridge (Degree for Research as an advanced student, 1900), MA, 1905. Formerly Lecturer Mason College, Birmingham, and Berkeley Fellow, Owens College, Manchester; lectured extensively throughout the United Kingdom on his own special work on artificial cells.

Publications: The Origin of Life, 1906; The Emergence of Life, 1931; The Mystery of Life, 1931; Symbolic Logic; Papers on Fluorescence, Phosphorescence, and Luminosity, in the Philosophical Transactions, Philosophical Magazine; also numerous articles and Patents. *Recreations:* chess, travelling. *Address:* 35 Dover Street, SW1. *Clubs:* Royal Societies, Authors', English Speaking Union.

Died 14 Jan. 1946.

BURKE, Thomas; author; *b* London, 1886; *m* Winifred Wells (pen-name Clare Cameron; author of Rustle of Spring, Green Fields of England, A Stranger Here, Far From Home, etc.). *Publications:* Verses; Pavements and Pastures; Nights in Town; Limehouse Nights; Twinkletoes; The London Spy; The Wind and the Rain; The Song Book of Quong Lee; The Sun in Splendour; The Book of the Inn; The Ecstasies of Thos de Quincey; The Flower of Life; The Bloomsbury Wonder; The English Inn; The Pleasantries of Old Quong; City of Encounters, 1932; The Real East End, 1932; The Beauty of England, 1933; London in My Time, 1934; Night Pieces, 1935; Murder at Elstree, 1936; Vagabond Minstrel, 1936; The Winsome Wench, 1938; Living in Bloomsbury, 1939; Abduction, 1939; The Streets of London, 1940; English Night-Life, 1941; Victorian Grotesque, 1941; Travel in England, 1943; English Inns, 1944; Dark Nights, 1944; The English Townsman, 1945; Son of London, 1945. *Recreation:* hearing music. *Address:* 66 Queensway, W2. *T:* Bayswater 6931.

Died 22 Sept. 1945.

BURKE, Thomas Michael, CMG 1942; Chairman of Directors T. M. Burke Proprietary Ltd since 1915; Hon. Consul for Poland since 1933; *b* 30 June 1870; *m* 1898, Margaret Duggan, *d* of Patrick Brady; five *s* two *d. Educ:* Ararat, Victoria, High School. Chairman Charities Board, Victoria, 1938–39, 1944–45. *Address:* 340 Collins Street, Melbourne, Australia.

Died 16 Feb. 1949.

BURKHART, Harvey J., DDS; LLD; FACD; DSc; Director Eastman Dental Dispensary; Representative of late George Eastman in the establishment of dental clinics in London, Stockholm, Paris, Brussels, and Rome; *b* Cleveland, Ohio, 14 Aug. 1864; *m* 1st, 1890, Jane Hingston; one *s*; 2nd, 1917, Lou Mercereau Davenport. *Educ:* Cleveland, Ohio; Dansville, NY; Baltimore, Maryland. Past President 8th Dist Dental Society; New York State Dental Society; American Dental Association; Fourth International Dental Congress; Chairman, Dental Council, New York State Board of Health; Trustee, American Dental Association; President, New York State Board of Dental Examiners. *Publications:* Care of Mouth and Teeth; papers and articles in various dental journals. *Recreations:* hunting, fishing, etc. *Address:* PO Box 879, Rochester, NY. *Clubs:* Rochester; Monroe Golf, Rochester.

Died 22 Sept. 1946.

BURKITT, Col Bernard Maynard H.; *see* Humble-Burkitt.

BURKITT, Ven. Robert Scott Bradshaw; Hon. Secretary Board of Missions, 1913; *b* 1857; *y s* of late Ven. Francis Hassard Burkitt, Archdeacon of Clonfert; *m* 1890, Jean, *o c* of late Alexander Stuart of Katesbridge, Co. Down; one *d. Educ:* Trinity College, Dublin. Ordained 1880; Hon. Secretary C. M. S. Lismore, 1913; Curate of Killinane, Clonfert, 1880–81; Cappoquin, 1881–98; Rector of Cappoquin, 1898–1940; Archdeacon of Lismore, 1912; First Archdeacon of Waterford and Lismore, 1939–40; Examining Chaplain to Bishop of Cashel, 1912; Hon. Secretary Diocesan Council and Synod, 1905; Rural Dean, 1908, and Surrogate, 1910. *Address:* Petra, Dunmore East, Waterford. *TA:* Dunmore, Waterford.

Died 24 Dec. 1940.

BURLTON, Lt-Col Philip Sykes Murphy, CIE 1921; Indian Army, retired; *b* 1865. Entered Indian Army, 1886; Assistant Commissioner, Punjab, 1891; District Judge, 1901; Deputy Commissioner, 1906; Commissioner, 1919; retired 1921; served Hazara, 1891 (medal and clasp).

Died 17 Oct. 1950.

BURMAN, Sir John Bedford, Kt 1936; JP; Alderman (Birmingham City Council); *b* 6 Oct. 1867; *s* of William Burman, Edgbaston; *m* 1906, Elizabeth Vernon (*d* 1936), *d* of C. H. Pugh, Penns, Warwickshire; one *s. Educ:* privately. Sometime a journalist on the staff of the Birmingham Gazette, Birmingham Mail, and The Sportsman; subsequently interested in Bicycling News and other journals; has travelled extensively; Chairman of Burman & Sons, Ltd, Burman, Cooper & Co. Ltd; Chairman of C. H. Pugh, Ltd, and Director of Sheffields, Ltd; Member of Birmingham City Council since 1908; MP (U) Duddeston Division of Birmingham, 1923–29; introduced the Moneylenders Act in the House of Commons, 1927; Lord Mayor of Birmingham, 1931–32; High Sheriff of Warwickshire, 1940–41; Life Governor of University of Birmingham; Chairman, Birmingham Unionist Association. *Recreations:* travel and motoring. *Address:* 45 Carpenter Road, Edgbaston, Birmingham. *T:* Edgbaston 1026. *Clubs:* Carlton, Constitutional; Union, Birmingham.

Died 4 March 1941.

BURN, Col Alexander Henderson, CIE 1921; OBE 1919; FSA 1942; Indian Army retd; *b* 5 Feb. 1885; *s* of Lt-Gen. James Burn, Bath. Entered Indian Army, 1905; Capt. 1913; Major, 1919; Lt-Col 1928; Col 1932; served NW Frontier of India, 1908 (medal with clasp); European War, 1914–18 (despatches, OBE); Mesopotamia, 1918–21 (despatches); NW Frontier of India, 1930–31; retired 1934; War of 1939–45, 1940–44. *Club:* United Service.

Died 24 Feb. 1949.

BURN, Sir Joseph, KBE 1920 (CBE 1918); Commander of the Order of the Crown of Belgium; President and Director, Prudential Assurance Co.; Fellow and Past-President Institute of Actuaries; Past-President, London Insurance Institute; Fellow of the Surveyors' Institute; Member, Royal Commission on Decimal Coinage; Vice-President Empire Rheumatism Council; Member Grand Committee St Thomas' Hospital; Member Weekly Board, Management Committee and Finance Committee Royal Free Hospital; Member, General Council of Anglo-Belgian Union; Actuary of a number of Pension Funds; *b* 6 March 1871; *m* 1894, Emily Harriet, *d* of Richard Smith; three *s* two *d. Publications:* Vital Statistics Explained; Stock Exchange Investments in Theory and Practice. *Address:* Rydal Mount, Potters Bar, Middlesex. *T:* Potters Bar 2016.

Died 12 Oct. 1950.

BURN, Sir Richard, Kt 1927; CSI 1917; FRASB 1916; MA (Oxon); *b* Liverpool, 1 Feb. 1871; *m* 1899, Grace Irene Cargill (*d* 1918); two *s* two *d. Educ:* Liverpool Institute; Christ Church, Oxford. Entered Indian Civil Service, 1891; Under-Secretary to Government United Provinces, 1897; Superintendent Census, and subsequently Gazetteer, 1900; Editor Imperial Gazetteer of India, 1905; Kaiser-i-Hind gold medal for famine services, 1907–08; Secretary to Government, 1910; Chief Secretary, 1912; Commissioner, 1918; Member Board of Revenue, United Provinces, 1922; Acting Finance Member, 1926; retired, 1927. *Publications:* Census Report, United Provinces, 1902; Provincial Gazetteer, United Provinces, 1907; Part Editor Imperial Gazetteer of India, 3rd edition; various papers on numismatics in Journals, Royal Asiatic Society, Asiatic Society of Bengal, and Numismatic Chronicle; Editor

Cambridge History of India Vol. IV and four chapters Vol. VI. *Recreation:* numismatics. *Address:* 9 Staverton Road, Oxford. *T:* 5685. *Club:* Royal Empire Society.

Died 26 July 1947.

BURNABY, (George) Davy; *b* 7 April 1881; *s* of Henry Fowke and Louisa Jane Burnaby; *m* 1915, Mabel Grace Woof; three *d*. *Educ:* Haileybury; Pembroke College, Cambridge. Theatrical career, chief successes, Gaiety Theatre; To-night's the Night; Yes, Uncle; Theodore and Co.; The Co-optimists, 1921. Has appeared in innumerable films. *Publications:* Lyric writer; chief success, Lords of the Air. *Recreations:* golf, cricket. *Address:* (temp.): 12 Brighton Road, Cheltenham. *Club:* MCC.

Died 17 April 1949.

BURNAGE, Col Granville John, CB 1915; VD; late 13th (NSW) Inf. Batt. Aust. Imperial Force; *b* 14 Dec. 1858; *s* of Thomas Burnage, merchant; *m* 1915, Helen, 6th *d* of late Rev. Boulby Haslewood, of Oswaldtwistle and Startforth Hall, Barnard Castle; no *c*. 2nd Lieut in 4th Infantry Regt 1883; commanded the Regiment, 1906–07; commanded coast defences, Newcastle, NSW, 1906–13; served S Africa, 1901–02 (despatches, Queen's medal 5 clasps); European War, 1914–16 (despatches, CB, wounded). *Address:* Woorilla, Toronto, Newcastle, New South Wales.

Died 12 July 1945.

BURNE, Lt-Col Lindsay Eliott Lumley, CIE 1929; CBE 1919; Indian Army, retired; late Deputy Commissioner, Burma; *b* 1 July 1877; *s* of late Knightley Grey Burne, of the Burma Commission; *m* 1912, Joan Knightley, *d* of late Gen. Sir James Brind, GCB; one *s* three *d*. *Educ:* Cranleigh, Indian Army and Burma Commission (Political Service). *Address:* 22 Bathwick Hill, Bath.

Died 11 April 1944.

BURNELL-NUGENT, Brig.-Gen. Frank, CB 1933; DSO 1916; OBE 1919; *b* 1880; *y s* of late Albert Nugent, of Beacon Lodge, Christchurch, Hants; *m* 1905, Ellen Coke Burnell (*d* 1941), *o d* of T. Coke Burnell, St Cross Grange, Winchester; one *s*. *Educ:* Horris Hill; Winchester College; Royal Military College, Camberley. Joined Rifle Brigade, 1899; Lieut-Col 1927; Col 1930; served with Mounted Infantry in S Africa, 1901 (dangerously wounded, medal with 4 clasps); European War, 1914–17 (in the retreat from Mons) (wounded); commanded 2nd Batt. Rifle Brigade, 1915–16, and 167th and 182nd Infantry Brigades with temp. rank of Brig.-Gen. (DSO, Bt Lt-Col, despatches); served with 1st Batt. Rifle Brigade, during suppression of Arab rebellion in Mesopotamia, 1920; Instructor, Senior Officers' School at Belgaum, 1925–26; commanded 2nd Bn Rifle Brigade, 1927–30; Commander Tientsin Area, 1930–33; retired pay, 1933; MA Hon. Manchester University, 1914. *Address:* The Old Brewery House, Kingsclere, near Newbury. *Club:* Army and Navy.

Died 12 March 1942.

BURNET, John Rudolph Wardlaw; KC 1934; Sheriff of Fife and Kinross; Vice-Dean of Faculty of Advocates; *b* 31 Dec. 1886; *s* of George Wardlaw Burnet, Advocate, and Mary Crudelius; *m* 1917, Lucy Margaret Wallace; two *s* one *d*. *Educ:* Fettes College, Edinburgh; Cambridge University, BA; Aberdeen University, LLB. Admitted to Faculty of Advocates, 1912; Clerk of Faculty, 1925–37; Junior Counsel to the Admiralty in Scotland, 1926. *Recreation:* fishing. *Address:* 60 Northumberland Street, Edinburgh. *T:* 27709. *Clubs:* Caledonian; University, Edinburgh.

Died 26 Feb. 1941.

BURNETT, Brig.-Gen. Charles Kenyon, CB 1918; CMG 1916; retired; *b* Biggleswade, 1868; *m* 1903, Georgina Violet, *d* of late Col Paley of 77 Onslow Gardens, SW; (one *s* one *d* decd). *Educ:* Rugby; Elstree. Joined 18th Hussars, 1889; served in India till 1898; then

in S Africa till 1902; in Ladysmith during the siege; served throughout the war (despatches twice, two medals 5 clasps, Bt Major); Instructor at Sandhurst, 1903–07; commanded 18th Hussars, 1914; served in France and Flanders from outbreak of war till May 1915 (once wounded, later suffered from effects of gas poisoning, invalided, despatches twice, CMG, Bt Col); on recovery posted to Staff in England; commanded Midland District, Ireland, 1918–19. *Publications:* 18th Hussars in South Africa; Memoirs of 18th Hussars. *Address:* New Grove, Petworth. *T:* Petworth 3147. *Club:* Cavalry.

Died 8 July 1950.

BURNETT, Air Chief Marshal Sir Charles Stuart, KCB 1936; CB 1927; CBE 1919; DSO 1918; Commandant Central Command, ATC, since 1943; *b* 1882; *s* of John Alexander Burnett of Kemnay, Aberdeenshire; *m* 1914, Sybil Bell; four *d*. Served South African War, 1900–01 (medal and three clasps); Northern Nigeria, 1904–07 (wounded, despatches, medal and four clasps); European War, 1914–18 (despatches, CBE, DSO, 3rd Class Order of the Nile), Iraq, 1920, operations Iraq and Persia (despatches, medal and two clasps); Director of Operations and Intelligence, Air Ministry, and Deputy Chief of Air Staff, 1931–33; Air Officer Commanding Iraq Command, 1933–35; Training Command, 1936–39; Inspector-General of RAF, 1939–40; Chief of Air Staff, Royal Australian Air Force, 1940–42; retired list, 1942; Knight Commander of the Sword of Sweden, 1934. *Address:* Small Dean, Wendover, Bucks.

Died 9 April 1945.

BURNETT, Major John Chaplyn, DSO 1900; OBE 1919; late Royal Artillery; *b* 24 Dec. 1863; *s* of late Charles Mountford Burnett, MD, and Emily Jane Chaplyn. Entered Army, 1884; Captain, 1893; Major, 1902; served South Africa, 1900–02 (Queen's medal 3 clasps, King's medal 2 clasps), Reserve of Officers; European War, 1914–18 (OBE). *Publications:* Hyper and Ornate Magic Squares, consecutive and non-consecutive numbers; Easy Methods for the Construction of Magic Squares, 1936. *Address:* Barkston, Grantham, Lincs.

Died 22 Aug. 1943.

BURNETT, Dame Maud, DBE 1918; JP 1920; Councillor, Borough of Tynemouth; retired, 1921, re-elected 1926; retired, 1934; *b* 1863; *d* of Jacob Burnett, JP; spinster. *Educ:* Tynemouth; Vevey. Mayor of Tynemouth, 1928–29 and 1929–30. *Recreations:* reading, walking. *Address:* Collingwood House, Tynemouth, Northumberland. *T:* North Shields 604.

Died 17 Nov. 1950.

BURNHAM, 3rd Baron *cr* 1903; **William Arnold Webster Lawson;** Bt *cr* 1892, DSO 1900; *b* 19 March 1864; *y s* of 1st Baron and Harriette Georgiana, *o d* of B. N. Webster; *S* to Barony of brother 1st Viscount Burnham, 1933; *m* 1887, Sybil Mary (whom he divorced 1912), *e d* of late Sir Frederick Marshall; one *s* two *d*. Scots Guards, 1884; Capt. 1897; Major, 1902; Bt Col 1918; commanded 10th Batt. Imperial Yeomanry, S Africa, 1900–01 (despatches twice, promoted major, Queen's medal 4 clasps, DSO); army reserve; Hon. Lt-Col in the army, 1903; European War (despatches, Bt Col). *Heir: s* Maj.-Gen. Hon. Edward Frederick Lawson, CB. *Address:* Barton Court, Kintbury, Berks. *Clubs:* Turf, Bath.

Died 14 June 1943.

BURNHAM, John Charles, CSI 1911; CBE 1920; FIC, FCS; *b* 9 Dec. 1866; *s* of Charles Burnham, Camberwell, London; *m* Lillian, *d* of Charles Sinclair Cox of Southend, Bromley, Kent; one *s* two *d*. *Educ:* Owens College and Victoria University, Manchester (BSc). Chemist, War Department, Woolwich, 1888–94; served on Sir F. Abel's special committee on explosives, 1888–91; Chemist in charge Experimental Cordite Factory, Kirkee, 1894–99; Manager, Government of

India Explosives Factory, Nilgiris, 1899; and other special services to the Government of India in connection with chemical industries; services loaned by the Government of India to the Ministry of Munitions, 1915–21; Director of Production and Superintendent, HM Factory, Gretna, 1915–21; General Works, Manager, British Dyestuffs Corporation, Manchester, 1922–24. *Address:* Grindlay & Co., Parliament Street, SW1.

Died 28 June 1943.

BURNS, Cecil Delisle, MA (Cantab), DLit (Lond.); *b* 1879; *s* of Agnes Delisle and James Burns, Treasurer of St Christopher-Nevis, and *g s* of Patrick Burns, Auditor-General of the Leeward Islands; *m* 1912, Margaret Hannay; two *s. Educ:* Christ's College, Cambridge; Rome. British Editor of Ethics: an international journal of Social Philosophy; University Extension Lecturer for Oxford, Cambridge, and London Universities, 1908–15; Lecturer in USA Lent Terms, 1911–14; Ministry of Reconstruction, 1917–19; Assistant Secretary International Organising Committee, Labour Office, League of Nations, 1919; Intelligence Division, Ministry of Labour, 1919–20; Assistant Secretary Joint Research Department of Trade Union Congress and Labour Party, 1921–24; Lecturer in Logic and Philosophy, University of London, Birkbeck College; Lecturer in Social Philosophy, London School of Economics, 1925–27; Stevenson Lecturer in Citizenship, University of Glasgow, 1927–36. *Publications:* Political Ideals; Modern Civilization on Trial, 1931; Leisure, 1932; Horizon of Experience, 1933; Challenge to Democracy, 1934; Civilisation, 1938. *Address:* Edgehill, Deepdene Park Road, Dorking, Surrey.

Died 22 Jan. 1942.

BURNS, Rev. James, MA; Ex-Moderator of the Presbyterian Church of England; *b* Haddington, East Lothian, 1865; *m* 1896, Elizabeth Scott; two *s. Educ:* Durham University; Queen's Square, now Westminster College, Cambridge. Pastorates: Cheltenham, Liverpool, Stoke-Newington, London; latterly engaged in work of Church Extension; Art lecturer to War Office and YMCA during war; Art Lecturer to LCC; travelled widely in Europe, Asia and the Dominions. *Publications:* The Christ Face in Art; Sermons in Art; Illustrations from Art; Revivals, their Laws and Leaders; Laws of the Upward Life; Laws of Life and Destiny; Pulpit Manual; New Pulpit Manual; etc. *Recreation:* golf. *Address:* 34 Brockswood Lane, Welwyn Garden City, Herts.

Died 16 Sept. 1948.

BURNS, Rt Hon. John; MP (R) Battersea, 1892–1918; Labour Representative; *b* London, 20 Oct. 1858; 2nd *s* of Alexander Burns; *m* 1881, Charlotte Gale (*d* 1936), also of London. *Educ:* Battersea and night schools, and still learning. 'Came into the world with a struggle; struggling now, and prospects of continuing it'. President of the Local Government Board, 1905–14; President of the Board of Trade, 1914; resigned on declaration of war. *Publications:* pamphlets, articles, speeches. *Recreations:* cricket, skating, rowing, boxing. *Address:* 110 North Side, Battersea, SW.

Died 24 Jan. 1943.

BURNS, John George; advocate; *b* 1880; *s* of late J. H. Burns, Solicitor, Falkirk. *Educ:* George Watson's College; The University, Edinburgh. Solicitor (Scotland), 1908; called to Scottish Bar, 1911; Army, 1914–19, 9th Bn (Highlanders) The Royal Scots; Captain; Sheriff-Substitute of Ross and Cromarty and Sutherland at Stornoway, 1927–34; and of Stirling, Dumbarton and Clackmannan at Dumbarton, 1934–45. *Address:* c/o Bank of Scotland, Shandwick Place, Edinburgh. *Club:* Western (Glasgow).

Died 6 Feb. 1950.

BURNS, Very Rev. Michael John, DD; *b* Baltimore, Co. Cork, Ireland, 17 May 1863; *s* of Michael Burns, late of the Royal Navy and Coastguard Service, and Mary A. McCarthy, of Castletownshend, Co. Cork. *Educ:* Collegiate School, Plymouth; English College, Valladolid. Priest, 1888; retained in his old college as Professor till 1900, teaching successively Humanities, Logic, Philosophy, Ethics, and Dogmatic Theology; recalled to Plymouth, 1900; founded St Boniface's College, Plymouth, Principal for eleven years; Administrator, Plymouth Cathedral installed as Canon in Residence at the Cathedral, 1913; Rural Dean of the Conference of St Boniface (Devonport); Guardian of the Poor for St Peter's Ward; Member of the Board of Management of the National Catholic Benefit and Thrift Society (Liverpool); founded the College Printing Press at Valladolid in 1895; Rector of the English College, Valladolid, Spain, 1915–25; started the Catholic Mission in Wimborne, 1926; in Ensbury, 1927, and consolidated that of West Moors, 1928; Provost of the Plymouth Diocesan Chapter, March 1930; Rural Dean of the Exeter Conference, 1932; Chaplain to the Teignmouth, OSB Abbey, 1938; retired, 1942. *Recreations:* photography and printing, also stamp collecting and astronomy. *Address:* St Scholastica's Abbey, Dawlish Road, Teignmouth, S Devon. *T:* Teignmouth 394.

Died 26 Dec. 1949.

BURNS, Robert, ARSA 1902, resigned 1920; *b* Edinburgh, 9 March 1869. *Educ:* Royal High School, Edinburgh; Dollar Academy. Pictures in public galleries of Melbourne, Munich, Liverpool, Oldham, Edinburgh, Dunfermline, and Perth. *Publications:* The House that Jack Built, 1937; Scots Ballads, 1940. *Address:* Newlandburn, Gorebridge, Midlothian. *Clubs:* Arts, Edinburgh.

Died 30 Jan. 1941.

BURNS-LINDOW, Lt-Col Isaac William, DSO 1915; DL, JP; CC Cumberland, 1934; High Sheriff of Cumberland, 1935; Vice-President, Cumberland Development Council, 1937; *b* 10 June 1868; *e s* of Jonas Lindow Burns-Lindow, JP, DL, of Irton Hall and Ehen Hall, Cumberland (*d* 1893), and Mary (*d* 1904), *e d* of late Mark Hildesley Quayle, of Crogga, Clerk of the Rolls for the Island, Isle of Man; *m* 1896, Madelaine Harriette Mary Theresa, *d* of Col George Wilson Boileau, of Old Catton, Norwich. *Educ:* Christ Church, Oxford. Capt. 8th Hussars, 1898; served South African War, 1900–01 (severely wounded, Queen's Medal, 6 clasps); Major 8th Hussars, 1903; Major South Irish Horse, 1904; Lt-Col 1917; served European War, 1914–17 (despatches four times, DSO, Mons Star and Bar, General Service, Allies' Victory Medals); relinquished commission, 1922; Sheriff of Cumberland, 1935; formerly MFH, South Union; Patron of the Living of Drigg and Lay Rector of Beckermet. *Address:* Ingwell, Moor Row, Cumberland. *TA:* Cleator Moor 278. *Clubs:* Cavalry, Royal Automobile.

Died 19 June 1946.

BURNSIDE, Rev. Walter Fletcher; Hon. Canon of Canterbury, 1921; *b* 1874; *s* of late Canon Burnside, Rector of Hertingfordbury, Hertford; Hon. Canon of St Albans and Chaplain to the Bishop; *m* 1898, Annie (*d* 1949), *e d* of late G. Lawson of Aintree, Liverpool; three *d. Educ:* Bromsgrove School. Pembroke Coll., Cambridge, Scholar; BA, 1895 (1st Cl. Class. Trip. Pt i, 1st Cl. Class. Trip. Pt ii 1896); MA, 1902. Deacon, 1898; Curate of Hucclecote, 1898–99; Asst Master and House Master, Cheltenham Coll., 1897–1908; Headmaster and Chaplain, St Edmund's School, Canterbury, 1908–32; Rector of Bishopsbourne, 1932–45. Member Classical Association. *Publications:* Old Testament History, 1904; Short Lives of Great Men (Joint), 1905; St Luke's Gospel in Greek, 1913; Acts of the Apostles in Greek, 1916. *Address:* Ryecroft, 13 Ethelbert Rd, Canterbury, Kent. *T:* Canterbury 2970. *Club:* East Kent (Canterbury).

Died 12 Oct. 1949.

BURPEE, Lawrence Johnston, LLD, FRGS, FRSC; Laureat de l'Institut; Secretary for Canada, International Joint Commission; *b* Halifax, NS, 5 March 1873; *s* of Lewis Johnston Burpee and Alice De Mille; *m* 1899, Maud, *d* of late Canon Hanington; three *s* two *d*. Private Secretary to three successive Ministers of Justice in the Dominion Government, and for several years Librarian of the Ottawa Public Library; President, Section II, Councillor, and Vice-President, Royal Soc. of Canada, 1935; President, 1936–37; former President, Canadian Historical Association; former National President, Canadian Authors Association; former Chairman, Ottawa Group, Canadian Institute of International Affairs; former Editor of Canadian Geographical Journal; National Chairman, United Polish Relief Fund; Hon. Secretary-Treasurer, Canadian United Allied Relief Fund; Tyrrell Gold Medal of Royal Society of Canada, 1931; Medaille de Vermeil of the Institut de France, 1931; Jubilee Medal, 1935; Coronation Medal, 1937. *Publications:* Bibliography of Canadian Fiction, 1904; Canadian Life in Town and Country, 1905; The Search for the Western Sea, 1908, new and revised edition, 1935; Flowers from a Canadian Garden, 1909; Fragments of Haliburton, 1909; By Canadian Streams, 1909; Songs of French Canada, 1909; A Little Book of Canadian Essays, 1909; Century of Canadian Sonnets, 1910; Canadian Eloquence, 1910; Dictionary of Canadian History, 1911; Scouts of Empire, 1912; Canadian Humour, 1912; Among the Canadian Alps, 1914; Pathfinders of the Great Plains, 1914; Sandford Fleming, Empire Builder, 1915; The Soldiers' Dictionary, 1916; edited new edition, Paul Kane's Wanderings of an Artist, 1926; On the Old Athabaska Trail, 1926; Encyclopædia of Canadian History, 1926; Historical Atlas of Canada, 1927; Journals of La Vérendrye (Champlain Society), 1927; Jungling in Jasper, 1929; Discovery of Canada, 1929, new and enlarged ed., 1945; edited History of Emily Montague for Canada Series, 1931; Good Neighbours, 1940. *Recreations:* golf, chess, curling. *Address:* 22 Rideau Terrace, Ottawa, Canada. *TA:* Ottawa. *T:* 34143, 2-8211. *Clubs:* Rideau, Royal Ottawa Golf, Ottawa Canoe, Rideau Curling, Ottawa; Arts and Letters, Toronto.

Died 13 Oct. 1946.

BURRARD, Col Sir Sidney Gerald, 7th Bt *cr* 1769; KCSI 1911; CSI 1911; FRS 1904; RE; *b* 12 Aug. 1860; *s* of late Sidney Burrard; *S* cousin, 1933; *m* 1887, Gertrude Ellen (*d* 1928), *d* of Maj.-Gen. C. Haig; one *s* one *d*; 2nd, 1935, Alice (*d* 1938), *o d* of late Alfred Simons. Superintendent, Trigonometrical Survey, India, 1899–1910; Surveyor-General of India, 1910–19; Victoria Medal for Science, RGS, 1913. *Publications:* A Sketch of the Geology and Geography of the Himalayan Mountains and Tibet, 1908; On the Origin of the Himalayan Mountains, 1912. *Heir: s* Major G. Burrard, DSO. *Address:* Foxhill, Farnborough, Hants.

Died 16 March 1943.

BURRELL, Harry James, OBE 1937; Research Naturalist; Fellow Royal Zoological Society of New South Wales; Life Member of the American Museum of Natural History, New York; Corresponding Member of the Australian Museum, Sydney; Corresponding Member London Zoological Society; *b* Double Bay, NSW, Australia, 19 Jan. 1873; *s* of late Douglas and Sarah Rose Burrell, English; *m* 1st, 1901, Susan Emily Hill (*d* 1941); 2nd, 1942, Daisy Ellen Brown. *Educ:* Public School. Time devoted to compiling original typescript solely in the interest of science; principal studies are in connection with the natural habits of Australian Mammals, particularly the Monotremes; donated a unique and complete sequence of Monotreme exhibits to Australian Institute of Anatomy, Canberra, ACT. *Publications:* The Platypus, 1927; Co-author of The Wild Animals of Australasia, 1926; contributor of Monotreme articles in the Australian Encyclopædia, 1926. *Address:* Yarrenbool, 141 Darley Road, Randwick, NSW. *T:* FX 5663.

Died 29 July 1945.

BURRIDGE, Frederick Vango, OBE 1926; RE, ARCA Lond.; member of the Art Workers' Guild, London; *b* London, 28 Nov. 1869; 2nd *s* of Alfred Burridge, London; *m* 1897, Eleanor, *e d* of Edward Doughty, London; two *s*. *Educ:* King's College School, London, Studied art at the Royal College of Art, London, gained British Institution Scholarship for Black and White, 1892, and Royal College of Art Travelling Scholarship, 1893. Assistant Master, Royal College of Art, 1895–96; Headmaster, Liverpool School of Art, 1897–1905; Principal, Liverpool City School of Art, 1905–12; Principal, LCC Central School of Arts and Crafts, 1912–30; medal Paris Exhibition (for etching), 1900; a member of the Board of Education's Standing Committee of Advice for Education in Art, 1911–16, and of the Advisory Council of the Victoria and Albert Museum since 1914; a founding member of the Design and Industries Assoc., 1916; Superintended the Design and Production of the King's Scrolls of Honour for all Who Died in the War, 1919–21; a Co-founder and Governor of the British Institute of Industrial Art, 1920–33; member of the Committee for the Fine Arts, University of Oxford, 1919–24; Examiner in Art, University of London, 1922–32; Member of Committees and Judge in Industrial Design Competitions of Royal Society of Arts, 1924–33; Member of Committees of British Empire Exhibition 1924, and Paris 1925; Member of the Postmaster General's Commemorative Postage Stamp Committees, 1924, 1929 and 1937–39; Member of Council, Edwin Austin Abbey Memorial Scholarships, 1926, Chairman since 1933; Member of Board of Trade's Council for Art and Industry, 1934–38; Chairman of Books Committee and member of other Committees of British Exhibit, Paris Exhibition, 1937; Livery of the Goldsmiths' Company, 1936, and Freeman of the City of London, 1936; Coronation Medal, 1937; Chairman E. A. Abbey Mural Decoration Fund since 1938; Member of Council of British School at Rome since 1938. *Publications:* Ministry of Reconstruction Pamphlet No. 17, Art and Industry, 1919; Editor, Little Craft Books since 1930; various articles. *Recreations:* etching and sketching. *Address:* The Chase Hotel, Ingatestone, Essex.

Died 12 July 1945.

BURROUGHS, Edgar Rice; novelist; President Edgar Rice Burroughs, Inc; *b* Chicago, Illinois, 1 Sept. 1875; *s* of Major George Tyler Burroughs and Mary Evaline Zieger; *m* 1st, 1900, Emma Centennia Hulbert, of Chicago; two *s* one *d*. *Educ:* private tutors; Harvard School, Chicago; Phillips Academy, Andover, Mass; Michigan Military Academy, Orchard Lake, Michigan. Served in 7th US Cavalry, Fort Grant, Arizona, short time (discharged by favour); treasurer American Battery Co., Chicago, 1899–1903; Department Manager, Sears, Roebuck & Co., 1906–08; A. W. Shaw Co., publishers of System, 1912–13; in interim was gold miner in Oregon, storekeeper and cowboy in Idaho, policeman in Salt Lake City, etc.; Major 1st Battalion 2nd Infantry Illinois, Reserve Militia, 14 Sept. 1918 to 2 Jan. 1919; United Press Correspondent Sept. 1942 until VJ Day (15 Aug. 1945). Member Loyal Legion. *Publications:* Tarzan of the Apes, 1914; The Return of Tarzan, 1915; The Beasts of Tarzan, 1916; The Son of Tarzan, 1917; A Princess of Mars, 1917; Tarzan and the Jewels of Opar, 1918; The Gods of Mars, 1918; Jungle Tales of Tarzan, 1919; The War Lord of Mars, 1919; Tarzan the Untamed, 1920; Thuvia, Maid of Mars, 1920; Tarzan the Terrible, 1921; The Mucker, 1921; The Man without a Soul (Eng.), 1922; At the Earth's Core, 1922; The Chessmen of Mars, 1922; Tarzan and the Golden Lion, 1923; The Girl from Hollywood, 1923; Pellucidar, 1923; The Land that Time Forgot, 1924; Tarzan and the

Ant Men, 1924; The Cave Girl, 1925; The Bandit of Hell's Bend, 1925; The Eternal Lover, 1925; The Moon Maid, 1926; The Mad King, 1926; The Outlaw of Torn, 1927, The War Chief, 1927; The Tarzan Twins, 1927; The Master Mind of Mars, 1928; Tarzan. Lord of the Jungle, 1928; The Monster Men, 1929; Tarzan and the Lost Empire, 1929; Tanar of Pellucidar, 1930; Tarzan at the Earth's Core, 1930; A Fighting Man of Mars, 1931; Tarzan the Invincible, 1931; Jungle Girl, 1932; Tarzan Triumphant, 1932; Apache Devil, 1933; Tarzan and the City of Gold, 1933; Pirates of Venus, 1934; Tarzan and the Lion Man, 1934; Lost on Venus, 1935; Tarzan and the Leopard Men, 1935; Swords of Mars 1936; Tarzan's Quest, 1936; The Oakdale Affair and the Rider, 1937; Back to the Stone Age, 1937; The Lad and the Lion, 1938; Tarzan and the Forbidden City, 1938; Carson of Venus, 1939; Tarzan the Magnificent, 1939; Synthetic Men of Mars, 1940; The Deputy Sheriff of Comanche County, 1940; Land of Terror, 1944; Escape on Venus, 1946; Tarzan and the Foreign Legion, 1947; Llana of Gathol, 1948. *Recreations:* horses, aviation and motoring. *Address:* Tarzana, California. *T:* Rugby 61222.

Died 19 March 1950.

BURROWES, Brig.-Gen. Arnold Robinson, CMG 1915; DSO 1918; Princess Victoria's (Royal Irish Fusiliers); retired pay; *b* 29 March 1867; *e s* of late Arnold Burrowes; *m* 1893, Lilian Emma (*d* 1936), *d* of late Rev. Randolphe Pigott, JP, Grendon Hall, Aylesbury; one *s*. Entered Army, 1888; Captain, 1897; Major, 1906; DAA and QMG, Bermuda, 1906–07; General Staff Officer, 2nd grade, Bermuda, 1907–10; served Hazara, 1891 (medal with clasp); S African War, 1899–1902 (Queen's medal 4 clasps, King's medal 2 clasps); European War, 1914–18 (despatches four times, CMG, DSO, Croix de Guerre avec Palme); retired 1920; was designer of the service web equipment worn throughout the army. *Address:* Coneycroft, Selborne, Alton, Hants; Stradone, Co. Cavan. *T:* Selborne 224. *Club:* Junior United Service.

Died 9 Feb. 1949.

BURROWES, Thomas Fraser, CBE 1918; JP; Barrister at Law; *m* Lena, *d* of Hugh Sproston; two *s* two *d*. Was Controller of Customs and Receiver of Enemy Estates, Nigeria. *Address:* Antigua, Leeward Islands, BWI.

Died 18 Aug. 1947.

BURROWS, George Thomas; agricultural and sporting journalist; *b* 31 Oct. 1876; *s* of late Robert Burrows, Chester. Edited Agricultural Gazette until 1918; Vinton's hunting and agricultural publications until 1932, including Baily's Magazine of Sports and Pastimes and Baily's Hunting Directory. Editor Live Stock Journal, 1915–33; agricultural correspondent of the Daily Telegraph, 1915–33; Mayor of Wimbledon, 1928–29 and 1929–30; press director of Red Cross Agriculture Fund, 1940–45; received journalistic training on Chester Courant and Cheshire Observer; sub-editor Sporting Chronicle, Manchester, and allied papers, 1899–1906. *Publications:* several books on pedigree farm live stock, old inns, racing, hunting, bowls, and other sports and pastimes. *Recreations:* bowls; won late Lord Rosebery's gold medal for rink play, and eleven championships in Wimbledon area; also many prizes at sprint running and bicycle riding. *Address:* 18 Montana Road, Wimbledon, SW20. *T:* Wimbledon 2825.

Died 21 July 1949.

BURSTALL, Lt-Gen. Sir Henry (Edward), KCB 1918; KCMG 1919; CMG 1917; CB 1915; *b* 26 Aug. 1870; *s* of late John Burstall; *m* 1907, Frances, *d* of J. Denison Mackenzie; three *d. Educ:* Bishop's College School, Lennoxville, PQ; Royal Military College, Kingston, Ont. 1st Commission Royal Canadian Artillery, 1889; passed Staff College, 1906. Served Yukon Force, 1898–99; South Africa, 1st Canadian Contingent, 1899–1900; S African Constabulary, 1901 to end of war (despatches twice, Queen's medal 4 clasps,

King's medal 2 clasps; Bt Major); commanded Royal Canadian Horse Artillery, 1907–11; Inspector of Canadian Artillery, Horse, Field and Heavy, 1911, until commencement of war; Hon. ADC to the Duke of Connaught, 1912; Brig.-Gen. Commanding Artillery, 1st Canadian Division, 1914–15 (despatches, CB); GO Commanding RA, Canadian Corps, 1915–16 (despatches, CMG); GOC 2nd Canadian Division to end of War; Divisional Commander, Canadian Corps, 1916 (despatches, KCB, KCMG); on Staff of Prince of Wales during Canadian Tour, 1919; Quartermaster-General (Canada), 1919–20; Inspector General (Canada), 1920–23; ADC to HM, 1917–21; retired to Reserve of Officers, 1923; DL Hants, 1930; DCL (Hon.) Bishops College; Order of St Stanislas (Russia), 2nd Class; Commander, Legion of Honour. *Recreation:* fishing. *Address:* Headbourne Grange, near Winchester, Hants. *T:* Winchester 54. *Club:* Army and Navy.

Died 8 Feb. 1945.

BURT, Brig.-Gen. Alfred, CB 1920; CMG 1919; DSO 1917; AM 1918; *b* London, 18 April 1875; *s* of late F. J. Burt, Stoke Poges, Bucks. *Educ:* Oundle; Heidelberg. Artist Volunteers, 1894; 3rd Battalion Royal Warwickshire Regt, 1895–96; joined 3rd Dragoon Guards, 1896; attended Turco-Greek War, 1897; served South African War, 1899–1902; Adjt 3rd DG (Bt Major, despatches); attended Prussian Guard Corps Manœuvres, 1907; Austrian Corps Manœuvres, Lemberg, Galicia, 1909; Spanish Morocco War (Riff Country) as War Correspondent, 1910; Brigade Major Welsh Border Mounted Brigade, 1912–14; European War, 1915–19; Comdg 3rd Dragoon Guards till 1918 when commanded 7th Cavalry Brigade (DSO and bar, Brevet Lieut-Colonel, Albert Medal, Legion of Honour, Croix d'officier, CMG, despatches five times); Chief of Military Mission to Lativa and Lithuania operating against Germans under Bermondt, and against Bolshevists, June 1919–Feb. 1920 (CB, despatches); General Staff, War Office, Feb.–March 1920; retired with rank of Brigadier-General, 11 March 1920; Etoile Noire avec Plaque (de Commandeur), 1923; Order of the Three Stars of Latvia, 1st Class; Order of the Eagle of Estonia, 1st Class; Order of the White Rose of Finland, 1st Class. *Recreations:* boxing (runner-up for semi-final of heavy-weight, Army and Navy Meeting, Aldershot), hunting, polo, football. *Club:* Cavalry.

Died 26 Feb. 1949.

BURT, Sir Bryce Chudleigh, Kt 1936; CIE 1930; MBE 1919; Director of Animal Feeding Stuffs, Ministry of Food, since Sept. 1939; *b* Newark-on-Trent, 29 April 1881; *s* of late Isaac Burt, Churcham, Glos; *m* 1906, Beatrice Maud, *e d* of Alfred Geary, Bristol; one *d. Educ:* Merchant Venturers College; University College, London (Clothworker's Exhibitioner in Chemistry 1900). BSc London, 1st class Honours, 1901. Assistant Lecturer, Liverpool University, 1902–04; Assistant Government Chemist and Lecturer on Tropical Agriculture, Trinidad, BWI, 1904–08; appointed to Indian Agricultural Service, 1908; Deputy Director of Agriculture, Cawnpore, 1908–21; Director of Industries, UP, in addition, 1912–15; Secretary, Indian Central Cotton Committee, 1921–28; Director of Agriculture, Bihar and Orissa, 1928–29; Agricultural Expert, Imperial Council of Agricultural Research, 1929–35, Vice-Chairman, 1935–39; Official Adviser to Indian Delegation, Imperial Economic Conference, Ottawa, 1932; Kaisar-i-Hind Medal (silver), 1912; Foundation Fellow, National Institute of Sciences of India. *Publications:* numerous on scientific and agricultural matters in Journal of Chemical Society, Bulletins of the Imperial Department of Agriculture in India and Agricultural Journal of India, etc. *Recreations:* golf and music. *Address:* Bryndene, Allanson Road, Rhos-on-Sea, Denbighshire. *T:* Colwyn Bay, 48059. *Clubs:* Athenæum, Royal Bombay Yacht.

Died 2 Jan. 1943.

BURTON, Sir Bunnell Henry, Kt 1935; JP Suffolk and Ipswich; Chairman of Burton Son and Sanders, Ltd; Chairman of Governing Body of Ipswich School since 1902; Chairman of St Edmundsbury Diocesan Board of Finance since 1915, and of other Committees; Member of Church Assembly; Vice-Chairman of Central Board of Finance, 1923–32; *b* 9 July 1858; *m* 1890, Eveline Mary (*d* 1936), *d* of Rev. S. W. Earnshaw. Mayor of Ipswich, 1907; Chairman of Ipswich Education Committee, 1906–35; Chairman of Prisoners of War Committee, Suffolk. *Address:* Birkfield, Ipswich. *T:* 2160. *Club:* Athenæum.

Died 29 May 1943.

BURTON, Brig. Colin, CBE, 1922; DSO 1917; late RASC; *b* 1883; *m* 1907, Gladys Astley, (*d* 1937), *d* of late Major L. L. Astley Cooper; one *s* two *d. Educ:* Marlborough College. Served South African War, 1901–02 (Queen's medal and four clasps); European War, 1914–18 (despatches, DSO, Bt Lt-Col); retired pay, 1938. *Address:* Essex House, Farnborough, Hants.

Died 4 May 1945.

BURTON, Brig.-Gen. Edmund Boteler, CB 1911; *b* 22 April 1861; *s* of Lieut-Gen. E. F. Burton; *m* 1915, Eileen, *d* of Eaton Travers Cummins. Entered army, 1879; Captain ISC 1890; Major Indian army, 1899; Lieut-Col 1905; Col 1907; Brig.-Gen. 1911; retired 1913; served Mahsud-Waziri Expedition, 1881; Egyptian Expedition, 1882, battle of Tel-el-Kebir (medal with clasp, bronze star), Burma, 1886–87 (despatches, medal with 2 clasps); Chitral, 1895 (despatches, medal with 2 clasps); Chitral, 1895 (despatches, medal with clasp); European War in France and Italy, 1916–18; Commandant 17th Cavalry, Indian Army, 1906–11; Commanded Secunderabad and Meerut Cavalry Brigades, 1911–13; reconnaissance in Persia, 1890–91, 1897; Consul for Muhammarah and Arabistan, 1903–04; FRGS; MacGregor Memorial Medal, 1901. *Address:* Cambridge Lodge, Torquay.

Died 7 June 1942.

BURTON, Eli Franklin, OBE 1943; BA (Cantab), PhD (Toronto), FRSC; Associate Professor of Physics, University of Toronto, 1911–24; Professor, 1924–32; Head of Department of Physics and Director of McLennan Laboratory since 1932; *b* 14 Feb. 1879; *s* of George and Eliza Barclay Burton; *m* 1906, Fannie May, *d* of late Rev. J. W. Wicher; one *s* one *d. Educ:* Toronto; Emmanuel College, Cambridge. Fellow in Mathematics, University of Toronto, 1901–02; 1851. Exhibition Scholar, 1904–06; Advanced Studentship, Emmanuel College, Cambridge, 1904–06; Special Dissertation Prize, 1908. Demonstrator in Physics, University of Toronto, 1906–11; President, Royal Canadian Institute, Toronto, 1931–32; Member of National Research Council of Canada, 1937–46. *Publications:* Physical Properties of Colloidal Solutions, 1st ed. 1916, 3rd ed. 1938; various papers on physical subjects since 1902; Superconductivity, 1934; College Physics (with C. A. Chant), 1933; Phenomena at the Temperature of Liquid Helium (with H. G. Smith and J. O. Wilhelm), 1940; The Electron Microscope (with W. H. Kohl), 1942, 2nd ed. 1946. *Address:* Weston, Ontario. *T:* Toronto, Midway 6611, Weston Zone 4,366. *Clubs:* Faculty Union, University of Toronto, York, Toronto.

Died 6 July 1948.

BURTON, Frank Ernest; Chairman, Joseph Burton and Sons, Ltd; *b* 18 March 1865; *e s* of Joseph Burton, Malvern House, Nottingham; *m* 1902, Fannie Mabel, *d* of John Lambert, Nottingham; one *d. Educ:* Nottingham High School; privately. International football (Association) player; JP County of Notts; FSA; FRNS; High Sheriff of Notts, 1938. *Address:* Orston Hall, Notts. *T:* Whatton 259.

Died 10 Feb. 1948.

BURTON, Rev. Henry Darwin, OBE; *b* 23 May 1858; *m* 1st, Helen Philippa Baumgartner; five *d*; 2nd, Lilian Toulmin. *Educ:* Trinity Hall, Cambridge; Lichfield College. Ordained, 1881; Curate St James, Wednesbury, 1881–83; Chelmsford, 1883–86; Enfield Lock, 1886–88; Carshalton, 1888–92; St Albans Diocesan Missioner, 1892–1910; Acting Chaplain to the Forces, S Africa, 1901; Vicar of St Saviour's, St Albans, 1906–10; Vicar of St Michael's and All Angels, Christchurch, NZ, 1910–15; Hon. Canon of Christchurch, NZ, 1913; C of E Principal Chaplain, NZEF, 1915–19; Vicar of St Martin's, Brighton, 1919–25; Diocesan Missioner in Barbados, 1926–29; Vicar of St John's, Burgess Hill, 1930–36. *Publications:* Paul Nugent, and other novels. *Address:* 182 Tivoli Crescent N, Brighton. *T:* Preston 2301.

Died 17 March 1943.

BURTON, Col Henry Walter, OBE; MP (U) Sudbury Division of West Suffolk, Oct. 1924–July 1945; *b* 1876; *s* of late Rev. W. H. Burton; *m* Constance Mary (*d* 1935), *d* of Edward Desmoulins; two *d. Educ:* Goudhurst. Served Matabele Rebellion, 1896; South African War, 1899–1901; European War, 1915–18 (despatches three times); occupation Cologne, 1918–20; British Representative Inter-Allied Navigation Commission. Commanded 1st Essex Bn Home Guard, 1940–43. *Address:* Church Hill, Wickford, Essex. *Clubs:* Carlton, St Stephen's, Royal Automobile.

Died 23 Nov. 1947.

BURTON, Rt Rev. Lewis William, DD; *b* Cleveland, Ohio, 9 Nov. 1852; *o s* of Rev. Lewis Burton, DD, and Agnes Jane Wallace; *m* 1883, Georgie Hendree Ball (*d* 1931), Decatur, Georgia; two *d. Educ:* Kenyon College; AB 1873; AM 1886; DD 1896; Philadelphia Divinity School; Graduated 1877; DD University of the South; Hon. LLD St John's College, Annapolis and Transylvania College, Lexington, Kentucky. Deacon, 1877; Priest, 1878; Assistant Minister, All Saints', Cleveland, Ohio, 1877–78; Rector of same, 1878–80; Assistant Minister, St Mark's, Cleveland, Ohio, 1881; Rector of same, 1882–84; Rector, St John's, Richmond, Virginia, 1884–93; St Andrew's, Louisville, Kentucky, 1893–96; Bishop of Lexington, 1896–1928; Past President of the Fourth Province of the Protestant Episcopal Church; Member Phi Beta Kappa Society; Member Society of Colonial Wars. *Publications:* printed Sermons, Episcopal Charges and Addresses; Annals of Henrico Parish, Virginia, in Moore's Virginiana, 1904. *Address:* 408 West Sixth Street, Lexington, Kentucky, USA. *T:* 1412.

Died 16 Oct. 1940.

BURTON, Sir Pomeroy, Kt 1923; retired; *b* 1869; *m* 1st, 1894, Mary Helen MacConnell; 2nd, 1925, Barbara Sedley Bramson, 2nd *d* of late Henry Sedley. *Address:* Château La Cröe, Cap D'Antibes, S France.

Died 15 Oct. 1947.

BURTON, Brig.-Gen. St George Edward William; The Royal Highland Regt; *m* Grace Pelham Clinton, *d* of late Rev. C. Stewart Ratcliffe, Downham, Essex. Entered Army, 1879; Captain, 1886; Major, 1895; Lieut-Colonel, 1906; Colonel, 1910; commanded Argyll and Sutherland Brigade, 1911–15; served Soudan, Nile Expedition, 1884–85 (medal with two clasps, Khedival bronze star); South Africa, 1901–02 (Queen's medal with five clasps); served European War (despatches). Claims as 15th Baronet the abeyant Baronetcy of Stockerton, 1622. *Club:* United Service.

Died 12 Dec. 1943.

BURTON, Sir William James Miller, Kt 1925; *b* 29 June 1862; *s* of Rev. W. H. Burton; *m* 1897, Maud, *d* of W. Whiffin, of Stamford Hill; one *s. Educ:* privately. Entered London Rifle Brigade, 1879; Captain for many years of English International Rifle Team at Bisley Meeting; Vice-President National Rifle Association

Council; Chairman London (City and County) and Middlesex Cadet Committee; late Alderman of the City of London for the Ward of Tower; one of HM's Lieutenants of the City of London. *Recreations:* yachting, golf. *Clubs:* Royal Thames Yacht; Royal Wimbledon Golf.

Died 30 Nov. 1946.

BURTON, Sir William Parker, KBE 1921; OBE 1918; JP; *b* 29 Oct. 1864; *s* of late Henry May Burton; *m* 1887, Emily (*d* 1941), 2nd *d* of William Chandler of Sproughton Hall, near Ipswich; one *d. Educ:* Ipswich Grammar School. Master of Staghounds, 1907–14; Joint-Master the Essex and Suffolk Foxhounds, 1912–28; President of the Yacht-Racing Association. *Recreations:* hunting, yachtracing. *Address:* The Cottage, Burstall, Ipswich. *TA:* Burton Copdock 24. *T:* Copdock 24. *Clubs:* Royal Harwich Yacht (Commodore); Royal Thames Yacht; Royal Victoria Yacht, etc.; County, Ipswich, etc.

Died 19 Nov. 1942.

BURY, Judson Sykes, MD (Lond.), FRCP (Lond.), BSc (Vict.); Consulting Physician, Manchester Royal Infirmary; Major, RAMC (T); *m*; one *d. Educ:* Amersham Hall, Reading; Owens College; University College Hospital, London. Resident posts in University College Hospital, 1875–78; Resident Medical Officer, Children's Hospital, Pendlebury, 1878–79; Past President, Manchester Pathological Society and Manchester Medical Society; Bradshaw Lecturer, RCP, 1901; Professor of Clinical Medicine, Manchester University, 1911–12. *Publications:* Manual of Clinical Medicine, 3rd edition, 1913; Diseases of the Nervous System, 1912; Treatise on Peripheral Neuritis (jointly), 1893; many contributions to medical journals. *Recreations:* golf, lawn tennis. *Address:* Pendle, Chinley, Derbyshire. *T:* Chinley 18. *Clubs:* Old Rectory, Manchester.

Died 10 June 1944.

BURY, Oliver R. H., MInstCE. General Manager and Chief Engineer of Entre Rios Railway (Argentine), 1894; General Manager of The Buenos Aires and Rosario Railway, 1900; in 1904 was appointed (with Lord Farrer and Major Le Breton) as Commissioner to inquire into the working management of the Egyptian State Railways; General Manager Great Northern Railway, 1902–12; a Director of the Great Northern (now London & N Eastern) Railway 1913–45; Chairman London Electricity Supply' Corporation and London Power Company. *Address:* 7 The Vale, Chelsea, SW3. *Club:* Conservative.

Died 21 March 1946.

BUSH, Col Harry Stebbing, CB 1917; CMG 1916; late Royal Army Ordnance Corps; *b* 7 Oct. 1871; *s* of J. Bush, Hanworth House, Middlesex; *m* 1903, Helen Ethel, MBE, *d* of late Professor John Van Someren Pope. *Educ:* Dover College. Joined Royal W Kent Regiment, 1894; Adjutant, 1st Batt., 1899–1902; served NW Frontier, India, 1897–98 (medal with clasp); European War, 1914–18 (despatches six times, CMG, CB, Bt-Col Croix de Guerre); retired pay, 1928. *Recreations:* shooting, fishing, cricket, golf. *Club:* Army and Navy.

Died 18 March 1942.

BUSH, Irving T.; President and Director, Bush Terminal Co., and Bush Terminal R. R. Co., New York; *b* Ridgeway, Mich, 12 July 1869; *s* of Rufus T. Bush and Sarah M. Hall; *m* 1st, Belle Barlow; One, Maud Howard, *widow* of Francis D. Beard; one *s*; 3rd, Marian Spore. *Educ:* The Hill School, Pottstown, Pennsylvania. Travelled extensively in youth; entered commerce; created his present company; Congregationalist; President Chamber of Commerce, 1922–24; VP 1924–28; Member, New York Chamber of Commerce. Holland Society, The Pilgrims of the US, Sons of the American Revolution, France-America Society, Inc.,

American Soc. of the French Legion of Honor, (Life) Amer. Museum of National History. Recipient French Legion of Honor. *Publications:* Working with the World, 1926; contributor on Economic subjects, current literature USA. *Recreations:* yachting, golfing. *Address:* 280 Park Avenue, New York; 100 Broad Street, New York. *Clubs:* New York Yacht, India House, National Arts (New York).

Died 21 Oct. 1948.

BUSH, Rear-Adm. James Tobin, CBE 1919; *b* 1874; *s* of late James Charles Tobin Bush, Bromley, Kent; *m* 1904, Antonia Harriet Lander, *d* of John Richard Leonard Cridland, Copenhagen and Exeter; one *s* one *d. Educ:* HMS Britannia. Entered Navy, 1889; Capt. 1913; retired list, 1922; Rear-Adm., retired, 1924; served European War, 1914–19 (CBE). *Address:* 4 Durham Avenue, Bromley, Kent. *T:* Ravensbourne 1402.

Died 31 March 1949.

BUSH, Brig.-Gen. John Ernest, CB 1916; *b* 31 Dec. 1858; *s* of late Major Robert Bush, 96th Regt; *m* 1893, Mabel Katharine, *d* of late Hon. Mr Justice Beverley of the High Court, Calcutta; one *d. Educ:* Clifton College. Entered Army, 1880; Lieut Durham LI, 1881; Adjutant, 1884–89; Capt., 1889; Major, 1900; Lt-Col, 1906; Col, 1910; Inspector and Adjutant, Great Indian Peninsular Railway Volunteer Corps, 1895–98; Adjutant, Militia, 1900–03; served Soudan, 1885–86 (medal, bronze star); S Africa, 1902 (Queen's medal three clasps); European War, 1914–17, commanded York and Durham Brigade (despatches, CB); retired pay, 1917. *Recreations:* cricket, football, Gloucestershire County XV, Rugby International, England *versus* Ireland, 1880–81. *Address:* Gulmarg, Berkhamsted, Herts. *T:* Berkhamsted 296.

Died 28 Oct. 1943.

BUSHBY, Sir Edmund Fleming, Kt 1926; retired cotton merchant; *b* 14 Nov. 1879; *s* of John Cannell Bushby, Liverpool; *m* 1907, Elaine, *e d* of late John Heap Hutchinson; no *c. Educ:* Sedbergh. Eleven years in Southern States of US; founded firm of Bushby Bros, Liverpool, 1910; retired, 1923; firm now dissolved; Director Royal Insurance Co., Ltd and Liverpool and London and Globe Insurance Company Ltd; Chairman Wrexham and East Denbighshire Water Co.; served European War, France, with 1st King's (Liverpool) Regt; contested Wrexham 1923, withdrew 1924 to ensure straight fight against Labour; bought Bronwylfa estate, 1919; contested Wrexham, 1929; High Sheriff of Denbighshire, 1931; Chairman, Liverpool Royal Infirmary. *Recreations:* racing, shooting. *Address:* Bronwylfa Hall, Wrexham. *T:* Wrexham 2475. *Club:* Carlton.

Died 11 July 1943.

BUSHNELL, Frank George, MD, BS (Lond.), DPH (Camb.), MRCS (Eng.), LRCP (Lond.); late Hon. Organising Secretary, Socialist Workers National Health Council; *b* London, 1868; *s* of Robert Bushnell and Laura Dunstan Hale; *m* Eleanor Murton Holmes; no *c. Educ:* St Paul's School; Univ. College and Hospital; External Graduate in Medicine and Surgery, London Univ. Travelled Europe, N Africa, Australasia, N America, and Near and Far East; Councillor, City of Plymouth; Vice-President and Life Governor, Devon and Cornwall Sanatorium; late Tuberculosis MO, Plymouth and Essex CC; Pathologist, Royal Sussex and South Devon and East Cornwall Hospitals; Clinical Assist, University College Hospital and Victoria Park Hospital, Diseases of the Chest; Major RAMC (TF), (retired) (1914–15 Star, General War Service and Victory medals); Member Socialist and British Medical Associations, late Member Society of Medical Officers of Health, and of the Labour and Independent Labour Parties; late Labour candidate, Univ. of London, Moseley and Taunton, Divisions. *Publications:* The

Evolution of our Sanitary Institutions; A Plea for a Ministry of Public Health, etc. *Address:* Nutley Cottage, Mimbridge, Chobham, Surrey.

Died 14 Oct. 1941.

BUSSAU, Hon. Sir (Albert) Louis, Kt 1941; *b* 9 July 1884; *s* of J. A. and M. E. Bussau; *m* 1912, Mary Scott Baird; no *c. Educ:* Warracknabeal College. Held Portfolios of Attorney-General, Solicitor-General and Minister of Transport, 1935–38, in Country Party Ministry of Victoria; Member Victorian Parliament, 1932–38; Agent-General for Victoria, 1938–44; Chief Pres. Australian Natives Assoc., 1924; Chief Pres. Australian Wheatgrowers Federation of Australia, 1932–33; Victorian President Country Party, 1929. *Recreations:* cricket, golf, bowls. *Address:* Evelyn Crescent, Hopetoun, Victoria, Australia.

Died 5 May 1947.

BUSSELL, Rev. Frederick William; *b* 23 April 1862; *s* of Fredk Bussell, Vicar Great Marlow, and Mary, *d* of Captain Yates, RN; *m* Mary Winifred, *d* of Sir Robert Dibdin, Hampstead. *Educ:* Charterhouse; Magdalen College, Oxford; BA 1885; MA 1889; BD and BMus 1892; DD 1897; 1st Class in Class. Moderns, 1882, Lit., Hum. 1885, Hon. Theology 1886; Craven Scholar, 1885. Select Preacher at St Mary's 1895 and 1896; Bampton Lecturer, 1905; Examiner Craven and Ireland Scholarships, 1901, 1902; and Denyer and Johns Theol Schol. 1904; Deacon, 1891; Priest, 1892; Fellow (1886), Tutor (1895), Chaplain (1892), Vice-Principal (1896–1913) of Brasenose College, Oxford (Lecturer in Classics, Philosophy, Theology, Ancient and Modern History); Chaplain and Donor of Shelland Donative, Suffolk, 1896–1938; Sequestrator and Patron of Brushford Perpetual Curacy, Devon, 1909; Rector of Baddesley Clinton, Warwickshire; Vicar and Rector of Northolt, 1917–25; Rector of North Tuddenham, 1932–33; Almoner of Christ's Hospital for University of Oxford, 1895–1910; Coxe Lecturer at Kirtlington, Oxon, and late Morley Lecturer at St Margaret's, Westminster. *Publications:* Itinerarium Rutilianum, 1886; Doctrine of Office and Person of Christ in first four centuries, 1892; School of Plato, 1896; Christian Theology and Social Progress, 1907; Subordinate Dualism (Studia Biblica, vol. iv); The Future of Ethics (in Sturts' Personal Idealism); Marcus Aurelius and the later Stoicism, 1909; Constitutional History of the Roman Empire from Accession of Domitian (81 AD) to the Retirement of Nicephorus III (1081 AD), 2 vols; Social Origins (a study in ethical, social, and political development); Merovingian Land-tenure (Latin poem in 2 books); De Medietate Hominis (on mystical philosophy in 3 books); A Survey of Monarchical Institutions from earliest times, with especial reference to Constitutional Development in recent times, 1909; The Principle of Monarchy, 1918; The National Church and the Social Crisis, 1918; Systems of Land Tenure; Case of Breamore Curacy, 1913; Religious Thought and Heresy in the Middle Ages, 1918. Music: Magnificat (Latin), five voices, strings, wood, and organ (9 numbers); Mass (Latin, for Italian Church, Hatton Garden), voices, strings, and organ; Services and Anthems; an arranger and collector of Baring-Gould's Devon Folksongs. Incidental Music (Full Orchestra), Merchant of Venice, 1895, for OUDS (Oxford); Choral and Incidental Music for Greek play Knights, 1897; 13 Arias or Solo-Anthems for organ and orch., 1913. *Recreations:* none; is interested in the question of Housing. *Address:* Fourteen, Warren Road, Worthing.

Died 29 Feb. 1944.

BUTCHER, Arthur Douglas Deane, CBE 1928; *b* 16 July 1884; *s* of late William Deane Butcher; *m* 1st, Berthe Mildred Wenham (*d* 1940); one *s* two *d*; 2nd, 1942, Maria Bilham. *Educ:* Rugby; Christ's College, Cambridge (Scholar). Mechanical Science Tripos, 1st class. Joined the Egyptian Irrigation Service, 1906; Resident Engineer, Delta Barraga, 1918; Consulting

Engineer (Hydraulics) to the Sudan Government, 1924; Director Hydraulics, Ministry of Public Works, Egypt, 1927–29; Director-General Irrigation, Sudan and Southern Nile, 1929; Order of the Nile, 2nd class; Order of Ismail, 3rd class. *Publications:* upon various hydraulic subjects. *Clubs:* Junior Carlton; Turf, Cairo.

Died 21 Aug. 1944.

BUTE, 4th Marquess of, *cr* 1796; **John Crichton-Stuart,** KT 1922; Viscount Ayr, 1622; Bt 1627; Earl of Dumfries, Lord Crichton of Sanquhar and Cumnock, 1633; Earl of Bute, Viscount Kingarth, Lord Mountstuart, Cumrae, and Inchmarnock, 1703; Baron Mountstuart, 1761; Baron Cardiff, 1776; Earl of Windsor; Viscount Mountjoy; Hereditary Sheriff of Bute; late Lord-Lieutenant of Buteshire; *b* 20 June 1881; *s* of 3rd Marquis and Hon. Gwendoline Mary Anne Fitzalan-Howard (*d* 1932), *e d* of 1st Baron Howard of Glossop; *S* father, 1900; *m* 1905, Augusta Mary Monica, DBE, *d* of Sir H. Bellingham, 4th Bt; five *s* two *d*. Owns about 117,000 acres. *Heir: s* Earl of Dumfries. *Address:* Mount Stuart, Rothesay, Buteshire; 26 Queen Anne's Gate, SW1; Cardiff Castle, Glamorganshire; Dumfries House, Ayrshire; Old Place of Mochrum, Wigtownshire; 5 Charlotte Square Edinburgh.

Died 25 April 1947.

BUTLER, Alfred Trego, MVO 1944; MC, FSA; Windsor Herald since 1931; late Genealogist Order of the Bath and (Hon.) of the Royal Victorian Order; Comdr of Order of St John of Jerusalem; *b* 1880; *e surv. s* of late Robert Frederick Butler, Lyncroft Gardens, Hampstead; *m* 1905, Grace, *d* of J. Hughes Blunt, Huntingdon; two *d*. Served European War, 1915–18, with 8th Batt. Worcs Regt; Captain, 1918; Secretary to Garter King of Arms, 1919–30; Portcullis Pursuivant of Arms, 1926–31. *Publications:* editor of Burke's Peerage, 1922–1926; The Visitation of Worcs 1634. *Address:* College of Arms, EC4; 9 Wellington Place, St John's Wood, NW8. *Club:* Junior Carlton.

Died 22 Dec. 1946.

BUTLER, Col Arthur Graham, DSO 1915; VD; Australian Army Medical Corps (retired); Australian War Memorial Staff; *b* Kilcoy, Queensland, 25 May 1872; *s* of William Butler; *m* Lilian Kate Mills; one *d*. *Educ:* Ipswich Grammar School, Queensland; St John's College, Cambridge; St Mary's Hospital, London. Served European War, Dardanelles, 1914–15 (DSO); France, 1916–19; Editor, Official History of the Australian Army Medical Services, 1914–18. *Publication:* The Digger: a Study in Democracy, 1945. *Recreations:* literature, horticulture, social service. *Address:* Reid, Canberra, ACT.

Died 27 Feb. 1949.

BUTLER, (Arthur) Hugh (Montagu); *b* 23 Nov. 1873; 2nd *s* of late Very Rev. H. Montagu Butler, Master of Trinity; *m* 1900, Margaret Edith, 2nd *d* of F. L. Latham, Gad's Hill Place, Higham by Rochester, formerly Advocate-General of Bombay; one *s* two *d*. *Educ:* Harrow; abroad. A Clerk in House of Lords, 1895–97; Assistant Librarian, 1897–1914; Secretary of Commissions to Lords Chancellors Loreburn and Haldane, 1909–14; Librarian to the House of Lords, 1914–22; Secretary to the Statute Law Revision Committee, 1902–22. *Address:* 8 Palliser Court, W14.

Died 28 May 1943.

BUTLER, Lt-Col Arthur Townley, CMG 1915; late RA; *b* 5 Jan. 1867; *s* of Philip Butler of Tickford Abbey, Newport Pagnell; *m* 1906, Kathleen, 3rd *d* of B. Horace Wood, Claremont, Natal. Entered Army, 1886; Capt., 1896; Major, 1901; Lt-Col 1913; served S African War, 1899–1902 (despatches; Queen's medal 5 clasps; King's medal 2 clasps); European War, 1914–17 (despatches four times, CMG). *Club:* Junior United Service.

Died 15 July 1948.

BUTLER, Lt-Col Charles Henry, DSO 1917; DSO; Pilot Officer, RAFVR; *b* 1881; *m* Gertrude; one *d.* Served European War, 1914–17 (despatches, DSC, DSO and bar); Member of Butler, Holliday and Co., Le Houlme, Seine Inférieure, France.
Died Jan. 1941.

BUTLER, Sir Edwin John, Kt 1939, CMG 1932; CIE 1921; FRS 1926; DSc, LLD, MB; *b* Kilkee, Co. Clare, 13 Aug. 1874; *y s* of Thomas Butler of Suirville, Co. Tipperary; *m* 1901, *d* of A. J. Le Mesurier, Guernsey; one *s* two *d*. *Educ:* Queen's (now University) College, Cork (Senior Scholar, 1896); Royal University, Ireland, MB (Hons), 1898; travelling scholarship in Botany (Exhibition of 1851) in Paris, Antibes, and Freiburg, 1899–1900. Cryptogamic Botanist to Government of India, 1901; Imperial Mycologist, India, 1905; Joint Director, Agricultural Research Institute, Pusa, India, 1919; Agricultural Adviser to Govt of India, 1920; Director Imperial Mycological Institute, Kew, 1920–35; Secretary Agricultural Research Council, 1935–41; President, British Mycological Society, 1927; President, Association of Economic Biologists, 1928–29; Vice-President, Linnean Society of London, 1929. *Publications:* Fungi and Disease in Plants, 1918; The Fungi of India (with Dr G. R. Bisby), 1932; papers in scientific journals. *Recreation:* travel. *Address:* 34 Glazbury Road, Baron's Court, W14. *T:* Fulham 4460. *Club:* Athenæum.
Died 4 April 1943.

BUTLER, Hugh; *see* Butler, A. H. M.

BUTLER, Hugh Myddleton; JP; *b* 3 May 1857; *s* of Ambrose Edmund and Isabella Butler of Kepstorn and Kirkstall Forge, Leeds; *m* 1881, Annette (*d* 1932), *d* of Edward Scofield of Sandringham; three *d*. *Educ:* Grammar School and Yorkshire College, Leeds. Ironmaster and engineer; Member Institute of Mechanical Engineers and Member of Executive of Federation of Iron and Steel Manufacturers; partner in Kirkstall Forge, near Leeds, with his two brothers since 1875; in early life took an active part in support of Church Day Schools and was leader of the Church party in the Leeds School Board; Chairman of the North Leeds Conservative Association since 1902; MP (C) North Leeds, 1922–23. *Address:* St Anns, Burley, Leeds, Yorkshire. *Clubs:* Engineers; Conservative, Leeds.
Died 10 Oct. 1943.

BUTLER, Kathleen Teresa Blake, MA (Cantab); Hon. Fellow of Girton since 1949; *b* Bardsea (Lancs), 26 Sept. 1883; *e d* of late Theobald Fitzwalter Butler, JP, DL, and of Catherine Elizabeth Barraclough. *Educ:* Hanover; Paris; Newnham College, Cambridge. Lecturer in French, Royal Holloway College, 1913–15; Lecturer in Modern Languages, Girton College, 1915–42; Director of Studies in Modern Languages, 1917–38; Associate of Newnham College, 1918–33; Cassel Research Fellow of Girton College, 1926–29; University Lecturer in Italian since 1926; Vice-Mistress of Girton College, 1936–38, 1941–42; Mistress of Girton College, 1942–49. Chairman of the Italian Committee of the Modern Languages Association, 1934–45; Organiser of two Summer Schools of Italian held in Cambridge, 1919 and 1935; Pres. of Cambridge Women's Research Club, 1933–36, and since 1948; Joint Founder and Editor of Italian Studies, 1936; External Expert on Board of Advisers in Italian, Univ. of London, since 1938. *Publications:* A History of French Literature, 2 vols, 1923; Les Premières Lettres de Guez de Balzac. éd. critique (with H. Bibas), 2 vols, Paris, 1933–1934; Tredici novelle moderne (with B. Reynolds), 1946; contributor to: The Year's Work in Modern Language Studies; Rev. d'Hist. litt. de la France, Mod. Lang. Rev.; Italian Studies; Journal of Warburg Institute, etc. *Recreations:* travelling, research, gardening. *Address:* Girton College, Cambridge. *Club:* Sesame.
Died 2 May 1950.

BUTLER, Mildred, RWS 1937; ARWS 1896; Academician, Ulster Academy of Arts, 1930; *y d* of late Henry Butler of Kilmurry, Thomastown. *Educ:* Studied painting with late Paul Naftel, RWS, Frank Calderon, Norman Garstin of Newlyn. A constant exhibitor at Royal Academy and New Gallery; also Member of the Society of Lady Artists; The Morning Bath was exhibited at the Royal Academy, 1896, and selected by the president and council for purchase for the Chantrey Collection; the picture is now at the Tate Gallery; A Cosy Corner and A Sunshine Holiday were purchased for the Municipal Art Gallery, Belfast. *Recreation:* takes a great pleasure and interest in the music of the parish church of Thomastown. *Address:* Kilmurry, Thomastown, Co. Kilkenny.
Died 11 Oct. 1941.

BUTLER, Nicholas Murray, PhD, LLD (Cantab); Jur. D, Hon. DLitt (Oxon); *b* Elizabeth, NJ, 2 April 1862; *s* of Henry Leny Butler and Mary J. Murray; *m* 1st, 1887, Susanna Edwards Schuyler (*d* 1903); (one *d* decd.); 2nd, 1907, Kate La Montagne. *Educ:* Paterson (NJ) High School; Columbia Coll. (AB 1882, AM 1883, PhD 1884); University of Berlin and University of Paris, 1884–85. Fellow of Columbia Coll., 1882–85. Instructor in Philosophy, 1885–89; Adjunct Prof. 1889–90; Prof. of Philosophy and Dean of the Faculty of Philosophy, 1890–1901; Pres., 1901–45, Pres. Emeritus, 1945, and Prof. of Philosophy and Education, 1889–1901, Columbia University; also President Barnard College and Teachers College, 1901–45; College of Pharmacy, 1904–45, New York; President Bard College, 1928–44; President NY Post-Graduate Medical School, 1931–45; Member of New Jersey State Board of Education, 1887–95; Special Commissioner from New Jersey to Paris Exposition, 1889; President of Paterson (NJ) Board of Education, 1892–93, and of National Education Assoc. 1895; first Pres. of Teachers College, 1886–91; Editor Educational Review, 1889–1920; Editor, Great Educators Series, 1892–1901; Teachers' Professional Library, 1894–1929; Chairman, Administrative Board, International Congress of Arts and Sciences, St Louis Exposition, 1904; Chairman Lake Mohonk Conference on International Arbitration, 1907, 1909–12; Watson Professor of American History and Institutions at British Universities, 1923; President American Branch of Conciliation Internationale; Trustee of the Carnegie Foundation since 1905; Trustee of the Carnegie Endowment for International Peace, 1910 (President, 1925–45; Pres. Emeritus, 1945; Carnegie Corporation, 1925–45; Chairman, 1937–45; American-Slav Institute in Prague (Pres. since 1924); Cathedral of St John the Divine since 1914; Columbia University Press; Director of the New York Life Insurance Co., 1915; Hon. Trustee, French Institute in the United States, 1938; some 40 hon. degrees from universities in America and many foreign countries. Grand Croix de la Légion d'Honneur, 1937; many foreign Orders. Nobel Peace Prize, 1931; Goethe Gold Medal, 1932; member American Academy of Arts and Letters since 1911, Chancellor 1924–28. President 1928–41; Pilgrims Society (VP 1913–28, President, 1928–46; Hon. President, 1946); France-America Society (President, 1914–24); Chairman of the National Committee on the reconstruction of the University of Louvain, 1915–25; Member of the Commission on the reorganisation of the State Government of New York, 1925–26; Vice-Chairman of the Mayor's New York City Committee on Plan and Development, 1926–27; Hon. President Citizens Budget Commission of NY (Pres. 1933–46); Hon. Member many foreign learned societies. Member, Bricklayers', Masons', and Plasterers' International Union of America (Union No. 84, City of New York, Stone Setter) since 1923. Member Society of American Historians, 1939; Delegate, Republican National Conventions, 1888, 1904, 1908, 1912, 1916, 1920, 1924, 1928, and 1932; Chairman, New York Republican State Convention, 1912; received

Republican electoral vote for Vice-Pres. of the USA, 1913; New York Acad. of Public Educ. Medal, 1938. Award of City of New York for Distinguished and Exceptional Public Service, 1945; first Alexander Hamilton Medal, 1947. *Publications:* The Meaning of Education; True and False Democracy; The American as He Is; Philosophy; Why Should We Change Our Form of Government? The International Mind; A World in Ferment; Is America Worth Saving? Education in the US (2 vols Edited): Scholarship and Service; Building the American Nation; The Faith of a Liberal; The Path to Peace; Looking Forward; Between Two Worlds, 1934; The Family of Nations, 1938; Across the Busy Years, 1939; Why War?, 1940; Liberty, Equality, Fraternity, 1942; The World Today, 1946. *Recreation:* golf. *Address:* 60 Morningside Drive, New York. *T:* University 4–0060. *Clubs:* Athenæum, (Hon.) Reform; Union, Century, University, (Hon.) Metropolitan, Columbia University, (Hon.) Lotos (Pres. 1923–34), Round Table Dining, (Hon.) Lawyers' (New York); University (Washington); (Hon.) National Golf Links of America (New York); Bohemian (San Francisco); Beach (Southampton); (Hon.) American (Paris); Faculty, Columbia University.

Died 7 Dec. 1947.

BUTLER, Rudolph Maximilian, RHA; FRIBA; MRIA; MArch; MInstCEI; Architect practising in Dublin; Professor of Architecture, National University of Ireland, since 1924; *b* Dublin, 1872. *Educ:* Pupil of late Walter Glynn Doolin, MA, FRIBA. *Principal Works:* Ecclesiastical, Civil, Domestic, Schools, and Commercial; designed University College, Dublin, churches at Newport, Westport, Claremorris, Balla, Castletownberehaven, Holyhead; also hospitals including New County Hospital, Mayo, County Sanatorium, Wicklow, etc., New Maternity Hospital, The Coombe, Dublin, etc. *Publications:* numerous contributions to technical and general press on subjects of Architectural and Archæological interest, etc. *Address:* 82 Merrion Square, Dublin; 73 Ailesbury Road, Dublin. *T:* Dublin 61641. *Clubs:* Devonshire; Kildare Street, Dublin; Royal Irish Yacht, Kingstown.

Died 3 Feb. 1943.

BUTLER, Thomas Harrison, DM, Oxford; FRCS; AINA Ophthalmic Surgeon; *b* Stanhope, Durham, 19 March 1871; *s* of Rev. G. W. Butler, late of Broadmayne with West Knighton, Dorset; *m* Ellen, 2nd *d* of late Dr W. H. Reed of Westbury, Wilts; two *s* three *d*. *Educ:* St Paul's (Exhibitioner); Corpus Christi College, Oxford (Scholar); St Bartholomew's Hospital; Paris; Kiel; Berlin; Dresden; Vienna; Zürich. 1st class Honours Nat. Science, Oxford; Radcliffe Travelling Fellow of Oxford University. Rowed in Corpus Eight; for four years Assistant Surgeon to the British Ophthalmic Hospital, Jerusalem; Plague Medical Officer, Cape Town; now on the Consulting Staff of the Birmingham Eye Hospital, the Coventry and Warwickshire Hospital, the Warneford, Leamington, and South Warwickshire Hosp., Hospital of St Cross, Rugby; President Little Ship Club; Past-President Ophthalmological Society. *Publications:* An Illustrated Guide to the Slit Lamp; many papers in connection with Ophthalmic Surgery, several contributions to the Yachting Journals. *Recreations:* yachting, yacht designing. *Address:* Duclair, Hampton-in-Arden, Warwickshire. *T:* Hampton-in-Arden 134. *Club:* Royal Cruising.

Died 29 Jan. 1945.

BUTLER, Brig.-Gen. William John Chesshyre, CB 1918; retired pay; *b* 1864; *s* of Philip Butler of Tickford Abbey, Bucks; *m* 1895, Charlotte H. (*d* 1942), *d* of William Shepheard, of Erpingham. *Educ:* Charterhouse; Christ Church, Oxford (BA). Col 5th Dragoon Guards, 1907. *Club:* Cavalry.

Died 31 July 1946.

BUTT, Most Rev. Joseph; titular Archbishop of Nicopsis; *b* 27 March 1869; *e s* of Richard Austin Butt, formerly of Slough, Bucks. *Educ:* Baylis House, Slough; St John's Seminary, Wonersh, Guildford. Ordained for diocese of Southwark, 1897; Procurator at St John's Seminary, 1897; Rector, 1901–07; Cameriere Segreto to Leo XIII, 1901; in charge of mission at Surbiton for a few months during 1907; Chancellor of the diocese of Westminster, 1907–08; Vice-Rector of the Collegio Beda, Rome, 1908–11; Domestic Prelate to Pius X, 1909; Bishop, 1911; Auxiliary to the Archbishop of Westminster, 1911–38; Provost of the Cathedral Chapter, 1919–38; Vicar General of Diocese of Westminster, 1932–37; Assist at the Pontifical Throne, 1936. *Address:* Downside Abbey, Stratton-on-the-Fosse, nr Bath.

Died 23 Aug. 1944.

BUTTENSHAW, Hon. Ernest Albert; Managing Director of Farmers and Graziers Co-operative Wool and Grain Company; *b* Young, NSW, 23 May 1876; *m* 1st, 1903; three *s* four *d*; 2nd, 1928, Clare Sugars, Roseville, NSW. *Educ:* Young Superior Public School. Went into Post Office for about twelve months on leaving school, then took up farming and grazing; cultivated up to 2000 acres of wheat during European War; President of the Farmers and Settlers' Association of NSW for two years; President of the Bland Shire for five years; Chairman of Voluntary Wheat Pool for four years; entered Parliament, 1917; leader of the Country Party, 1926–32; joined the Bavin Administration in 1927, and Acting Premier during Mr Bavin's absence in England; Minister for Works and Railways and Deputy Premier, 1927–30; Minister for Lands, NSW, 1932–38; Member of Legislative Assembly, NSW; Deputy Leader of Country Party; 1942, a member of Central Wool Committee to carry out British Wool Purchase Agreement. Councillor of Royal Agricultural Society. Trustee of Sydney Cricket Ground. *Recreations:* has played 1st grade cricket and tennis, all-round athlete. *Address:* Strathfield, Sydney, Australia. *Club:* Royal Automobile.

Died 26 June 1950.

BUTTERFIELD, Sir Frederick William Louis (d'Hilliers Roosevelt Theodore), Kt 1922; JP Borough of Keighley; *b* Paris; *o s* of late Henry Isaac Butterfield of Cliffe Castle, Keighley, and Mary Roosevelt, *d* of late Hon. M. Burke, New York City; *m* 1st, 1888, Jessie Kennedy (*d* 1927), *o d* of Captain Jacob Ridgway, Philadelphia, USA; one *d*; 2nd, 1930, Hilda, *d* of late John Johnston, Banker, Milwaukee, USA. *Educ:* privately in Switzerland; Columbia College Law School, New York City; Balliol College, Oxford, MA. Prospective candidate (U) Shipley, 1912–18; United States Consul, Ghent, 1888–90; Mayor of Keighley, 1916–18. *Publications:* The Battle of Maldon; The Crevasse; My West Riding Experiences; A Visit to the Cape; US Consular Reports, 1888–1890; miscellaneous pieces and articles. *Recreations:* music (graduate of Leipzig Conservatory, 1887), fencing, swimming, Alpine climbing, golf. *Address:* Cliffe Castle, Keighley, Yorks. *T:* 2084. *Clubs:* Junior Carlton, Authors'.

Died 21 July 1943.

BUTTERWORTH, Sir Alexander Kaye, Kt 1914; LLB; *b* 4 Dec. 1854; *s* of Rev. George Butterworth and Frances Maria, *y d* of John Kaye, DD, Bishop of Lincoln; *m* 1st, 1884, Julia (*d* 1911), *d* of George Wigan, MD, of Portishead, Somerset; 2nd, 1916, Dorothea Mavor, *y d* of Luke A. Ionides. *Educ:* Marlborough College; London University. Barrister of the Inner Temple, 1878–83; Solicitor's department of the Great Western Railway, 1883–90; Clerk to the Bedfordshire County Council, 1890–91; Solicitor to the North-Eastern Railway, 1891–1906; General Manager of the North Eastern Railway, 1906–21; Civil Service Arbitration Board, 1917–20, 1921–22; Chm. of the London Chest Hospital, 1916–35, Vice-Chairman, 1936; Director of Welwyn

Garden City, Ltd; Chairman of Pedestrians' Association, 1930–39. *Publications:* Railway Rates and Traffic; Practice of the Railway and Canal Commission; Maximum Rates. *Address:* Compton Leigh, Frognal Gardens, NW3. *T:* Hampstead 2734.

Died 23 Jan. 1946.

BUTTON, Frederick Stephen, CBE 1947; JP County of London (Westminster Bench); late Member Industrial Court; *b* Erith, Kent, 1873. *Educ:* Manor Road Board School, Erith. Engineer Apprentice, Maxim Nordenfeldt Gun Coy, Erith; Member ASE and AEU since 1893; Erith Town Councillor; Hon. Sec. Erith Trades Council; Founder Dartford Central Labour Party; Member Executive Council ASE; Member Arbitration Board London Chamber of Commerce; Member of Whitley Committee; Founder and Hon. Sec. Nat. Trade Union Committee for HM Dockyards; Chairman Great Western Rly Conciliation Boards; Member of Coupar Barrie Committee for Ex-Service Men; Member of Committee on Production; Member of Home Office Commission on Hours of Labour of Juveniles; Member of Council of Industrial Welfare Society and of National Industrial Alliance; Director Contact Publications Ltd, 26 Manchester Square, W1. *Publications:* articles on Welfare in Industry; Joint Industrial Councils; Arbitration; Payment by Results. *Recreations:* motoring, gardening, golf. *Address:* 1 Abbey Garden, Westminster, SW1. *T:* Whitehall 4571. *Club:* National Trade Union.

Died 8 Feb. 1948.

BUTTON, Sir Howard (Stransom), Kt 1936; Alderman, City of London for Ward of Tower; one of HM's Lieutenants and Commissioner of Assize, City of London; DL, JP County Middlesex; Alderman Middlesex County Council; Chairman Central Valuation Committee; Member Cinematograph Advisory Committee; Hon. Col 61st (Middlesex) AA Regt, RA; Military Member Middlesex Territorial Army and Air Force Association and Chairman Buildings Committee; General Commissioner Income Tax; Freeman of City of London; Member Court of Assistants, Guild of Freemen, Renter Warden Worshipful Company of Gardeners; Member of Court Worshipful Companies of Bakers, Broderers and Paviors; Vice-President, United Wards Club and President, City Livery Club; President, National Fire Brigades Association (South Midland District); Member Governing Body, University College School; Chairman Alfred Button & Sons, Ltd, and Associated Companies; Director County Fire Office, Ltd, Uxbridge Maidenhead and Wycombe and District Gas Co. and Ascot Gas Co.; Warden for Middlesex King George's Jubilee Trust; Member King George's National Memorial Fund Committee and King George's Fields Foundation; Member, London Court of Arbitration; Officer of Order of St John of Jerusalem; Life Member, Royal Society of St George; *b* 14 Feb. 1873; *s* of late Alfred Button, Uxbridge; *m;* two *s. Educ:* University College School. MP (U) Wrekin Division Shropshire, 1922–23; Chairman Middlesex County Council, 1933–36; High Sheriff of Middlesex, 1937–38; Senior Sheriff of City of London, 1941–42; Silver Jubilee Medal, 1935; Coronation Medal, 1937. *Recreations:* fishing, motoring. *Address:* The Cedar House, Hillingdon, Middlesex; Fircote, Ibstone, Bucks. *Clubs:* Carlton, St Stephen's, City Livery, Devonshire.

Died 18 Aug. 1943.

BUXTON; *see* Noel-Buxton.

BUXTON, Charles Roden; *b* 27 Nov. 1875; 3rd *s* of Sir T. F. Buxton, 3rd Bart; *m* 1904, Dorothy Frances, *d* of late Arthur Trevor Jebb, and niece of late Sir Richard Jebb, MP for Cambridge University; one *s* one *d. Educ:* Harrow; Trinity College, Cambridge; MA. Private secretary to his father when Governor of South Australia, 1897–98; called to Bar, Inner Temple, 1902; Principal of Morley College (for working men and women),

1902–10; first President of South London Branch of Workers' Educational Association; has had ranching experience in Texas; Editor of the Albany Review (formerly Independent Review), 1906–08; contested East Herts, 1906; Mid Devon, 1908 and Dec. 1910; Accrington, 1918, 1923, and 1924; MP (L) Mid or Ashburton Div., Devon, Jan.–Dec. 1910; MP (Lab) Accrington, Nov. 1922–Dec. 1923; Elland Division of West Riding, Yorks, 1929–31; Hon. Sec. to Land Enquiry Committee, 1912–14; Treasurer of the Independent Labour Party, 1924–27; Parliamentary Adviser to the Labour Party, 1926. During the War (1914–15) went on a political mission with his brother, Lord Noel-Buxton, with the object of securing the neutrality of Bulgaria; in the course of this an attempt was made on their lives by a Turkish assassin (Oct. 1914), and he was shot through the lung. *Publications:* Towards a Social Policy (joint); Electioneering up to Date; Turkey in Revolution; The ABC Home Rule Handbook; Home Rule Problems (joint); The War and the Balkans (with Lord Noel-Buxton), 1915; Towards a Lasting Settlement, 1915 (joint); Shouted Down, 1916; Peace this Winter, 1916; The Secret Agreements, 1918; The World after the War, and In a German Miner's Home (both with Mrs Buxton), 1920; In a Russian Village, 1922; A Politician Plays Truant; Essays on English Literature, 1929; The Race Problem in Africa, 1931; The Alternative to War, 1936; numerous contributions to newspapers and reviews. *Address:* 6 Erskine Hill, Golders Green, NW11. *T:* Speedwell 2149.

Died 16 Dec. 1942.

BUXTON, Henry Fowell; Director Truman, Hanbury, Buxton and Co., Brewers, Spitalfields, E1; *b* 1876; *s* of late John Henry Buxton, Easneye, Herts; *m* 1900, Katharine Tayspel (*d* 1945), *d* of Rt Hon. James Round, PC, MP, Birch Hall, Colchester; five *s;* 1945, Mairi, *widow* of Norman Clark-Neill, Home Close, Hursley, Hants. *Educ:* Harrow; Trinity College, Cambridge. High Sheriff of Herts, 1938. *Address:* Easneye, Ware. *T:* Ware 2; Smoo Lodge, Durness, Sutherland. *T:* Durness 211.

Died 16 Jan. 1949.

BUXTON, Sir Thomas Fowell, 5th Bt *cr* 1840; *b* 8 Nov. 1889; *s* of 4th Bt and Anne Louisa Matilda, 2nd *d* of Rev. H. T. O'Rorke; *S* father, 1919; *m* 1st, 1923, Hon. Dorothy Cochrane (*d* 1927), *yr d* of Lord Cochrane of Cults; one *s* one *d*; 2nd, 1931, Eva, *d* of late Edward Balfour of Balbirnie. *Educ:* Eton; Trinity College, Cambridge. Called to the Bar; Lieut late Essex Yeomanry; served European War; JP, DL, Essex. *Heir: s* Thomas Fowell Victor, *b* 18 Aug. 1925. *Address:* Woodredon, Waltham Abbey, Essex. *Clubs:* Brooks's, Athenæum, Alpine.

Died 28 Oct. 1945.

BUZZARD, Sir E. Farquhar, 1st Bt *cr* 1929; KCVO 1927; MA, MD (Oxon), FRCP, Hon. LLD (Manitoba), Hon. LLD (Belfast); Physician in Ordinary to the King, 1932–36, Extra Physician since 1937; Regius Professor of Medicine, Oxford, 1928–43, now Emeritus Regius Professor; Vice-President of the Radcliffe Infirmary; Consulting Physician St Thomas's Hospital, and to Ministry of Pensions; Hon. Colonel RAMC (TF); Hon. Fellow of Magdalen College since 1928; Hon. Freeman of Society of Apothecaries since 1937; Hon. Student of Christ Church, 1943; Hon. FRSM 1944; *b* London, 20 Dec. 1871; *e s* of late Thomas Buzzard, MD, FRCP; *m* May, *d* of late E. Bliss; two *s* three *d. Educ:* Charterhouse School (Science Exhibitioner); Magdalen College, Oxford; St Thomas's Hospital (Mead Medallist). Member of the Oxford University Association Football XI, 1892–94; of the Old Carthusian XI, winners of Amateur Cup, 1894 and 1897; London Senior Cup, 1895, 1896, 1897; Goulstonian Lecturer on Acute Infective and Toxic Conditions of the Nervous System at the Royal College of Physicians, 1906; late Physician and Lecturer on Medical Pathology at the Royal Free Hospital for Children and National Hospital for

Paralysed and Epileptic; President of Sections of Clinical Medicine, Neurology and Psychiatry, Royal Society of Medicine; President of the British Medical Association, 1936; President of Association of British Neurologists, 1938; President of Association of Physicians, 1941; Osler Memorial Medal, 1940; Harveian Orator, Royal College of Physicians, 1941. *Publications:* Pathology of the Nervous System (Joint); Articles on Diseases of the Nervous System in Allbutt's System of Medicine, Osler's Modern Medicine, French's Index of Differential Diagnosis, and many papers, chiefly Neurological, in Brain, The Lancet, The British Medical Journal, etc. *Recreations:* golf, fishing, shooting. *Heir: s* Capt. Anthony Wass Buzzard, DSO. *Address:* Munstead Grange, Godalming. *T:* Godalming 31. *Club:* United University.

Died 17 Dec. 1945.

BUZZARD, Brig.-Gen. Frank Anstie, DSO 1917; psc, 1912; late RA; *b* 1875; 3rd *s* of late Thomas Buzzard, MD; *m* 1911, John, *y d* of late Hon. John Collier; two *s* one *d. Educ:* St Paul's School; RMA, Woolwich. Commission 1895; served European War (DSO and bar, wounded). *Address:* Haxted House, Edenbridge, Kent. *T:* Edenbridge 2158.

Died 28 Feb. 1950.

BYATT, Edwin, RI 1933; *b* 16 Dec. 1888; *s* of Frederick Charles Byatt and Elizabeth Hockham; *m* 1911, Florence Ethel Islip; three *d.* Apprenticed at the age of 15 to lithographic artist for 7 years; afterwards Commercial Artist to firm of printers; Exhibitor at the RA since 1925; Exhibitor at the RI, Paris Salons, Walker Gallery, and other provincial galleries. *Recreations:* walking and outdoor sketching. *Address:* 14 Ewell House Grove, Ewell, Surrey.

Died 7 Aug. 1948.

BYNG, Hon. Ivo Francis; JP; *b* 20 July 1874; 2nd *s* of 5th and *heir-pres.* to 6th Earl of Strafford; *m* 1901, Agnes Constance, *d* of late S. Smith Travers, Hobart, Tasmania; one *s. Educ:* Radley; Cirencester Royal Agricultural College. *Address:* Well End Lodge, Barnet, Herts. *T:* Elstree 1550.

Died 11 June 1949.

BYNG, L. C.; *see* Cranmer-Byng.

BYRNE, Brig.-Gen. Sir Joseph Aloysius, GCMG 1934; KCMG 1928; KBE 1918; CB 1917; Knight of Grace of the Order of St John of Jerusalem; *b* 2 Oct. 1874; *s* of Dr J. Byrne, DL, Londonderry; *m* 1908, Marjorie, *d* of late Allan F. Joseph, Cairo; one *d. Educ:* St George's College, Weybridge; Maison de Melle, Belgium. Joined the Royal Inniskilling Fusiliers, 1893; served South African War, including the Siege of Ladysmith, where wounded; afterwards employed with the Central Judicial (Claims) Commission in Pretoria; served as Assistant Adjutant-General at the War Office; granted rank of Brevet Lieut-Col 1 April 1915; Deputy Adjutant-General, Irish Command, 27 April 1916, with rank of Brig.-Gen. (despatches, CB); Inspector-Gen., Royal Irish Constabulary, 1916–20; Governor Seychelles, 1922–27; Sierra Leone, 1927–31; Governor and Commander-in-Chief, Kenya, 1931–37. Called to bar, Lincoln's Inn, 1921. *Recreations:* fishing, shooting, golf. *Club:* United Service.

Died 13 Nov. 1942.

BYRNE, Richard; MP (Nat.) Falls Div. of Belfast, Parliament of N Ireland, since 1929. *Address:* Parliament Buildings, Belfast.

Died 28 Aug. 1942.

BYRON, 10th Baron *cr* 1643; **Frederick Ernest Charles Byron,** MA; *b* 26 March 1861; *s* of Frederick Byron, 2nd *s* of 7th Baron, and Mary Jane, *d* of Rev. W. Wescombe, Rector of Langford, Essex; *S* brother, 1917; *m* 1921, Anna, *d* of late Rev. Lord Charles Fitzroy and Lady Charles Fitzroy, The Tannery House, Thetford. *Educ:* Exeter College, Oxford. Ordained, 1888; Curate of Royston, Herts, 1888–90; Rector of Langford, Essex, 1891–1914; Vicar of Thrumpton, Notts, 1914–42; Rector of Barton in-Fabis, 1941–42. *Publication:* The Gorge, 1934. *Heir: kinsman* Rupert Frederick George Byron, farming in Australia [*b* 13 Aug. 1903; *m* 1931, Pauline Augusta, *d* of T. J. Cornwall, Wagin, WA; one *d.* Served War of 1939–45, in Royal Navy]. *Address:* Thrumpton Hall, Nottingham; Langford Grove, Maldon, Essex.

Died 6 June 1949.

BYRON, Brig.-Gen. John, CB 1918; CMG 1919; late Royal Artillery; *b* 1872; *e s* of late Commander R. H. Byron, RN, and *g s* of late Thomas Byron, of Coulsdon Court, Surrey; *m* 1st, Mary (*d* 1915), *d* of late Charles Leathley; two *d*; 2nd, Ethel, (*d* 1940), *d* of late John Phillips. *Educ:* Royal Military Academy, Woolwich. Joined the Royal Artillery, 1892; Lieut-Colonel, 1915; served with the Malakand Field Force, NW Frontier, 1897 (despatches, medal with clasp); South Africa, 1900 (despatches, Queen's medal with 4 clasps); European War, Assistant Superintendent Royal Arsenal, 1914–15; Special Appointment Ministry of Munitions, 1915–16; Deputy-Director of Artillery, War Office, 1916–18; Commanding Divisional Artillery, Italy, 1918–19; Commanded Royal Artillery, Palestine and Egypt, 1920–24; Bt-Col 1917; retired pay, 1925. *Recreations:* shooting, golf. *Address:* East Boldre House, Brockenhurst, Hants. *Club:* Army and Navy.

Died 2 Oct. 1944.

BYRON, Robert; *b* 26 Feb. 1905; *s* of Eric Byron. *Educ:* Eton; Merton College, Oxford. *Publications:* Europe in the Looking Glass, 1927; The Station, 1928; The Byzantine Achievement, 1929; The Birth of Western Painting, 1930; Articles on New Delhi in Architectural Review and Country Life, 1930 and 1931; An Essay on India, 1931; The Appreciation of Architecture, 1932; First Russia, then Tibet, 1933; The Road to Oxiana, 1937. *Address:* Overton House, Marlborough, Wiltshire. *Clubs:* Garrick, Beefsteak.

Died Sept. 1941.

C

CABLE, Boyd; (pseudonym of Lt-Col Ernest Andrew Ewart); author, journalist, publicist, traveller; Editor, The Trident, Magazine of Sea and Travel; *b* India, Scots parentage; *m* 1923, Osca M'Camley. *Educ:* Aberdeen and Banff Grammar Schools. Very mixed career; served South Africa, 1900–01, as Scout, and since then has followed many occupations, from teamster and tramp in Australia and farm hand in New Zealand to business manager and partner in commercial work; has sailed before the mast, and been trimmer, fireman, and greaser in steamships; applied for commission in Aug., 1914, and went to France that year; served there in RFA and RAF until armistice. *Publications:* By Blow and Kiss (Australian novel); Between the Lines (war stories written at the Front); Doing their Bit (description of home munition works); Action Front (more Front stories); Grapes of Wrath, 1917; Front Lines, 1918; Air Men o' War, 1918; The Old Contemptibles, 1919; The Rolling Road (stories of the sea), 1923; A Double Scoop (novel); 1924; Labour and Profits (Economics), 1925; British Battles of Destiny (key battles of our history—Cæsar's Invasion to Waterloo); Stormalong—sailing ship novel; Flying Courier—air-mail novel; A Hundred Year History of P. and O.; film stories, dialogue, etc. *Recreations:* any sort of travel; and research in military, naval and nautical history—of their flags in particular. *Address:* 9 Stone Buildings, Lincoln's Inn, WC.

Died 12 Aug. 1943.

CABOT, Lt-Col Hugh, CMG 1918; Medical Director, White Cross Medical Service Plan of Mass; *b* 1872; *s* of James Elliot Cabot; *m* 1902, Mary Anderson Boit (decd); three *s*; 1938, Elizabeth Cole Amory. *Educ:* Harvard, AB, MD, LLD Queen's Univ., Belfast, 1925. Asst Prof. and Professor of Clinical Surgery, Harvard, 1913–19; Professor of Surgery and Dean of Medical Faculty, University of Michigan, 1920–30; Professor of Surgery, Graduate School, University of Minnesota, Consulting Surgeon, Mayo Clinic, 1930–39; served European War, 1914–19 (despatches four times, CMG). *Publications:* Modern Urology, 3rd ed., 1936; Surgical Nursing (with Mary Dodd Giles), 3rd ed., 1936; The Doctor's Bill, 1935; The Patient's Dilemma, 1940. *Address:* 465 Warren Street, Needham, Massachusetts.

Died 14 Aug. 1945.

CACLAMANOS, Demetrius, Hon. LittD (Univ. of Wales); Fellow of Academy of Athens, 1947; Hon. Greek Minister; *b* Nauplia, 1872. *Educ:* Athens University. Editor of Asty, 1892–1901, and of Neon Asty, 1901–07. Entered Greek Diplomatic Service as Chief of the Press Bureau at the Ministry for Foreign Affairs, 1907; 1st Secretary Greek Legation in Paris, 1910–12; Chargé d'Affaires in Rome, 1912–14; Political Director in the Ministry for Foreign Affairs, 1914–15; Chargé d'Affaires in Petrograd, 1915–16; Councillor Greek Legation in Paris, 1916; Minister at Washington, 1916; resigned his post Dec. 1916, to represent the Provisional Government of M. Venizelos at Petrograd, 1917; Greek Minister in Petrograd, June 1917; accredited also at Stockholm, Oct. 1917; Greek Envoy-Extraordinary and Minister Plenipotentiary to the Court of St James, 1918–35; Delegate of Greece at the Council of the League of Nations, 1919–20; Second Greek Delegate at the First Session of the Assembly of the League of Nations, Geneva, 1920; Second Greek Delegate at the Lausanne Peace Conference, 1922–23; First Greek Delegate at the Assembly of League of Nations, Geneva, 1926; granted on retirement by the Greek Government the title of Envoy Extraordinary and Minister Plenipotentiary of 1st class for life; Vice-President of the Anglo-Hellenic League; Chairman of the Greek Byron Committee; Grand Cross of the Order of George the First of Greece; Grand Officer of the Order of the Redeemer of Greece; Grand Officer of the Order of the Italian Crown, Serbian Order of St Sava, Order of the Roumanian Crown; Officer of the Légion d'honneur, etc. *Publications:* many literary essays in Greek reviews and newspapers; translated Shakespeare's Winter's Tale into modern Greek; Rupert Brooke: an essay, in Greek, 1925; Anthology of a selection from English Poets into modern Greek; Modern Athens in the Greek Encyclopædia; Addresses in England (in English); Memoir on Venizèlos (in Greek), 1937; articles in Contemporary Review, Quarterly Review, etc. Edited Thucydides in Modern Greek; a volume of Essays under title Greece in Peace and War, 1942; Thucydides and Modern Politics, 1943; Greece: A Panorama, 1944. *Address:* Carrington House, Hertford Street, W1. *T:* Maytair 2620.

Died 7 June 1949.

CADBURY, Edward, JP; Hon. LLD, Birmingham University, 1937; Director of Daily News, ltd; Trustee of Bournville Village Trust; Director of British Cocoa and Chocolate Co., Ltd; Life Governor of Birmingham University; Chairman and Treasurer of the Council of Selly Oak Colleges; *b* 20 March 1873; *e s* of George Cadbury and Mary Tylor; *m* 1896, Dorothy, *d* of Francis Howitt, MD, Nottingham; no *c*. *Educ:* Friends' School, Oliver's Mount, Scarborough. *Publications:* Women's Work and Wages (with George Shann), 1906; Sweating (with George Shann), 1907; Experiments in Industrial Organisation, 1912. *Recreations:* golf, fishing, and farming. *Address:* Central House, Selly Oak Colleges, Birmingham 29.

Died 21 Nov. 1948.

CADDELL, Col Henry Mortimer, CMG 1920; DSO 1915; *b* 20 Feb. 1875; *s* of late Col Henry Caddell, Summerview, Fleet, Hants; *m* 1906, Margaret Caroline, *d* of late Rev. Isaac Hughes Jones. *Educ:* Royal School, Armagh; Trinity College, Dublin; BA. Entered Army Service Corps, 1900; Capt., 1905; Adjt, 1911–13; Maj., 1914; Lt-Col, 1922; Col 1922; Deputy Assist Director of Transport, France, 1914; Assist Director of Transport, 1915; Comdt RASC Training College, 1917–18; Assist Director of Transport, War Office, 1918–22; Assist Director of Military Transport, Royal Arsenal, Woolwich, 1926–30; retired pay, 1930; served S Africa, 1899–1902 (despatches; Queen's medal 4 clasps, King's medal and 2 clasps); European War, 1914–18 (despatches thrice, DSO, CMG, Brevet Lt-Col; 1914 Star, British war medal, Victory medal). *Address:* Whitehall, Pembroke, Wales.

Died 10 Sept. 1944.

CADMAN, 1st Baron *cr* 1937, of Silverdale; **John Cadman,** GCMG 1929; KCMG 1918; CMG 1916; FRS 1940; DSc; Hon. LLD Birmingham; Hon. DEng Melbourne; Hon. Associate College of Technology, Manchester University; Hon. DCL Durham; Grand Officier Légion d'Honneur, France; Knight Commander Crown of Italy; Order of the Rafidain Class 1; Pasha 1st Class (Transjordan); Emeritus Professor, Birmingham University; Chairman, Anglo-Iranian Oil Company Ltd and Iraq Petroleum Company Ltd; Director, Suez Canal Company and Great Western Railway; late Member of Advisory Council of Department of Scientific and Industrial Research; Research Committee Prime Minister's Economic Advisory Council, Board of Managers Royal Institution. Member of Government Industrial Transference Board, 1928; Economic Advisory Council, 1930, Committee of Enquiry into the

Post Office, 1932, Television Committee, 1934; late Consulting Petroleum Adviser, HM Government, late Director HM Petroleum Executive; Chairman Inter-Allied Petroleum Council; Technical Adviser, Government of Nigeria; *b* Silverdale, Staffordshire, 7 Sept. 1877; *s* of Jas C. Cadman, MICE; *m* 1907, Lilian, *d* of late John Harragin, Trinidad; two *s* two *d*. *Educ:* Newcastle-under-Lyme; Durham University. Past President Institution of Petroleum Technologists, Institute of Fuel, Society of British Gas Industries, Institution of Mining Engineers. Manager Silverdale Collieries, N Staffs, 1900; Assistant Agent Walter Scott, Ltd, Durham, 1901; HM Inspector of Mines, East Scotland, 1902; Stafford District, 1903; Government Mining Engineer Trinidad, 1904; appointed to conduct special research for Royal Commission on Mines, 1907–08; Prof. Mining and Petroleum Technology, Birmingham University, 1908–20; Consulting Petroleum Adviser to Colonial Office and Govt of Trinidad; Adviser to Coal Mines Dept, Board of Trade; a member of a Royal Commission which reported upon the oilfields of Iran; numerous papers to scientific societies on Coal, Ironstone and Petroleum problems. *Heir:* Hon. John Basil Cope Cadman [*b* 23 March 1909; *m* 1936, Marjorie Elizabeth Bunnis; one *s b* 3 July 1938]. *Address:* 46 Orchard Court, Portman Square, W1. *T:* Welbeck 8813; Shenley Park, Bletchley, Bucks. *T:* Shenley Church End 233. *Clubs:* Athenæum, City of London.

Died 31 May 1941.

CADMAN, James, DSC; DL; JP Borough of Newcastle-under-Lyme; MIME; Director of National Provincial Bank; Chairman of Norton and Biddulph Collieries, Ltd; Director of Parker's Burslem Brewery, Ltd; *b* Silverdale, Staffs, 1878; *s* of late Jas C. Cadman, MICE; *m* 1906, Una Mildred (*d* 1919), *d* of late Simon Tate, MICE, Durham; one *s* two *d*. *Educ:* Newcastle-under-Lyme. Commission RNVR 1914; with Armoured Cars, France (despatches DSC); High Sheriff of Staffordshire, 1933; Member of the Coal Mines National Industrial Board; and of Coal Production Council; Joint Master of North Staffordshire Hunt, 1927–30. *Address:* Walton Hall, Eccleshall, Staffs. *T:* Eccleshall 225. *Club:* Junior Carlton.

Died 8 Sept. 1947.

CADOUX, Cecil John, MA (Lond. and Oxon), DD (Lond. and Edin.); DLitt (Oxon); since 1933 Mackennal Professor of Church History, and Vice-Principal, Mansfield College, Oxford; *b* Smyrna, Turkey in Asia, 24 May 1883; 3rd *s* of late William H. Cadoux, merchant (*s* of Rev. John H. Cadoux, Congregational Minister of Wethersfield, Essex), and Emma Temple, *d* of Josiah Temple, of the Guildhall, London; *m* 1915, Marguerite Mary, *d* of Thomas Asplin, Catford; two *s* two *d*. *Educ:* Stamford House School, Croydon; St Dunstan's College, Catford; Strand School, King's College, London; Mansfield College, Oxford. Served in Victualling Department, Admiralty, London, 1902–11; studied at Mansfield College, Oxford, 1911–14; Isherwood Fellow and Lecturer in Hebrew at Mansfield College, Oxford, 1914–19; Professor of New Testament Criticism, Exegesis, and Theology, and of Christian Sociology, Yorkshire United Independent College, Emm Lane, Bradford, 1919–33. *Publications:* The Early Christian Attitude to War, 1919; The Guidance of Jesus for To-day, 1920; The Christian Crusade, 1924; The Message about the Cross, 1924; The Early Church and the World, 1925; The Resurrection and Second Advent of Jesus, 1927; Catholicism and Christianity, 1928; Deuteronomy (in National Adult School Union's series of books of OT in colloquial speech), 1932; Roman Catholicism and Freedom, 1936; Ancient Smyrna, 1938; The Case for Evangelical Modernism, 1938; Christian Pacifism Re-examined, 1940; The Historic Mission of Jesus, 1941; edited Church-Life and Church-Order (lectures of late J. Vernon Bartlet), 1942; A Pilgrim's Further Progress, 1943; The Congregational Way, 1945;

Philip of Spain and the Netherlands, 1947; The Life of Jesus (Pelican Book), 1947; articles in religious and theological periodicals. *Recreation:* sketching. *Address:* 179 Woodstock Road, Oxford. *T:* Oxford 58381.

Died 16 Aug. 1947.

CAHAN, Hon. Charles Hazlitt, KC; AB; LLB, LLD; Barrister; *b* Yarmouth, NS, 31 Oct. 1861; *s* of Lt-Col Charles and Theresa Flint Cahan; *m* 1st, 1887, Mrs Mary J. Hetherington (*d* 1914); 2nd, 1918, Juliette Hulin, Paris; two *s* one *d*. *Educ:* Yarmouth Seminary; Dalhousie University and Dalhousie Law School, Halifax, Nova Scotia. Leader of Conservative Party in Nova Scotia Legislature, 1890–94; declined portfolio in Dominion Cabinet, 1896; Member of Bar of Nova Scotia and of Quebec; Member of House of Commons for District of St Lawrence-St George, Montreal, 1925–40; Secretary of State, Canada, 1930–35; Associate Member of the Association of the Bar of the City of New York, USA; for some time, during the War, Director of Public Safety, Canada; represented Government of Canada at Berlin, Oct. 1930, in effecting settlement of accounts with German Government arising out of war; one of Canadian delegates at Imperial Conference at Ottawa, July 1932; senior delegate of Government of Canada at Thirteenth Assembly of League of Nations at Geneva, Sept. and Oct. 1932; senior delegate of Government of Canada at Special Assembly of League of Nations at Geneva, Dec. 1932, which dealt with Lytton Report on Sino-Japanese Affairs; represented Government of Canada at Paris, Dec. 1932 and Jan. 1933, in negotiating new Trade Agreement between Canada and France and a Convention concerning the Rights of Nationals and Commercial and Shipping Matters. *Publications:* many pamphlets on Inter-Imperial Relations, Finance, Politics. *Address:* The Château, 1321 Sherbrooke Street West, Montreal. *TA:* Nahac, Montreal. *Clubs:* Mount Royal, Royal Montreal Golf, Montreal, Montreal; Rideau, Ottawa; Halifax, Halifax; Bankers' University, Canadian, New York City.

Died Aug. 1944.

CAHN, Sir Julien, 1st Bt *cr* 1934, Kt 1929; Knight Commander of the Order of George I (Greece); Officier de la Legion d'Honneur; Lord of the Manor of Stanford-on-Soar; JP; *s* of Albert Cahn and Matilda, *d* of late Dr S. Lewes, Liverpool; *m* Phyllis Muriel, *d* of A. Wolfe, Bournemouth; two *s* one *d*. *Educ:* privately. Chairman of the National Birthday Trust Fund; President City of Nottingham Conservative Association; President Nottingham Operatic Society; took and captained a cricket team to Jamaica, 1929; the Argentine, 1930; Denmark and Jutland, 1932; Canada, USA, and Bermuda, 1933; Ceylon and Singapore, 1937; and to New Zealand, 1939; MFH Burton Hunt, 1928–34; MFH Woodland-Pytchley, 1935–37, and of Fernie's Hunt, 1937–39. *Heir: s* Albert Jonas, *b* 27 June 1924. *Address:* Stanford Hall, Loughborough. *T:* East Leake 33. *Clubs:* Carlton, Royal Automobile.

Died 26 Sept. 1944.

CAIE, John Morrison, CB 1943; LLD; MA, BL, BSc; FRSE; Deputy Secretary, Department of Agriculture for Scotland (retired); *b* 20 Aug. 1878; *s* of Rev. W. S. Caie, MA, Minister of Enzie, Banffshire, and Helen Smith, *d* of John Scott, Montrose; *m* 1908, Mary A, 2nd *d* of Rev. Robert MacLeod, Aberdeen; two *d*. *Educ:* Milne's Institution, Fochabers; Aberdeen Univ. County lecturer under Irish Dept of Agriculture, 1905, and thereafter on staffs of the Edinburgh and Aberdeen Colleges of Agriculture and lecturer in Aberdeen University; joined the Dept—then the Board—of Agriculture for Scotland on its formation in 1912; Member of various committees and other bodies; President, Agriculture Section of British Association, 1937. *Publications:* articles on agricultural and other subjects and miscellaneous prose and verse; two vols of poems in Scots and English; The Kindly North, 1934 (2nd ed. 1935), and 'Twixt Hills and

Sea, 1939. *Recreations:* hill-climbing, riding, cycling, music, chess. *Address:* 2 Cobden Road, Edinburgh 9. *T:* Edinburgh 42196. *Club:* Authors'.

Died 22 Dec. 1949.

CAILLAUX, Joseph; Senateur depuis 1925 et Président du Conseil Général de la Sarthe; *s* de Eugene Caillaux, successivement Député, Sénateur, Ministre; *m* 1911, Madame Raynouard (*d* 1943). *Educ:* Lycée Condorcet, Paris. Inspecteur des Finances, 1888–98; Député de l'Arrondissement de Mamers, 1898–1919; Ministre des Finances, 1899–1902, 1906–09, Mars-Juin 1911, 1913–14, 1925–26, 1935; Président du Conseil, Ministre de l'Intérieur, 1911–12; Président de la Commission des Finances depuis 1932. *Publications:* Les Impôts en France (traité technique); Agadir; Mes Prisons; Où va la France? Où va l'Europe?; Ma Doctrine; D'Agadir à la Grande Penitence. *Address:* 11 rue Lesueur, Paris.

Died 21 Nov. 1944.

CAIRNS, 4th Earl *cr* 1878; **Wilfred Dallas Cairns,** CMG 1915; Baron Cairns, 1867; Viscount Garmoyle, 1878; *b* 28 Nov. 1865; *s* of 1st Earl and Mary, *d* of John M'Neile, Parkmount, Co. Antrim; *S brother* 1905; *m* 1894, Olive, *d* of late J. P. Cobbold, MP; one *s* four *d. Educ:* Wellington. Late Captain Rifle Brigade; Lt-Col commanding London Rifle Brigade, 1912; served South African War; European War, 1914–15 (CMG). *Heir: s* Viscount Garmoyle. *Address:* Farleigh House, Bath.

Died 24 Oct. 1946.

CAIRNS, Very Rev. David Smith, OBE 1918; MA (Edin.), DD (Aberdeen, Debrecin (Hungary), and Edinburgh); LLD (St Andrews and Aberdeen); *b* 1862; 2nd *s* of Rev. D. Cairns, Stitchel, and Elizabeth, *d* of Rev. D. Smith, DD, Biggar; *m* 1901, Helen Wilson, *d* of Henry Hewat Craw, West Foulden, Berwickshire; one *s* one *d. Educ:* Ednam Public School; Kelso High School; Edinburgh University; United Presbyterian College, Edinburgh; Marburg University. Minister of United Presbyterian Church, and United Free Church, Ayton, Berwickshire, 1895–1907; Professor of Dogmatics and Apologetics, United Free Church College (now Christ's College), Aberdeen, 1907–37; Principal, 1923–37; Professor of Christian Dogmatics, Aberdeen University, 1935–37; Joint Chairman and Draughtsman of Commission on the Missionary Message, World Missionary Conference, Edinburgh, 1910; joint Chairman of Interdenominational Committee and Draughtsman of Report on The Army and Religion, 1920; Deems Lecturer in New York University and Lafayette College, 1923; Lyman Coleman Lecturer in Theology in Auburn Theological Seminary, New York State, 1923; Moderator of the General Assembly of the United Free Church of Scotland, 1923–24; travelled in Northern China at the invitation of the Chinese Student Christian Movement, 1927; Baird Lecturer, 1932. *Publications:* Christianity in the Modern World; The Reasonableness of the Christian Faith; The Life and Times of A. R. MacEwen, DD; The Faith that Rebels, a re-examination of the Miracles of Jesus, 1928; The Riddle of the World (Baird Lecture), 1937; various theological articles in reviews and periodicals. *Address:* 13 Mayfield Terrace, Edinburgh. *T:* 41994. *Clubs:* University, Edinburgh.

Died 27 July 1946.

CAIRNS, William Murray, CBE 1920; *b* 1866; *s* of William Sproat Cairns; *m* 1892, Eleanor Stephenson, *d* of Rev. James Anderson, Polmont, Stirlingshire. *Educ:* Liverpool Institute; Edinburgh University (MB, CM 1891, Buchanan Scholar, MD, 1914). Commander of Order St John of Jerusalem; Chairman, St John Ambulance Association, Liverpool Centre; County Surgeon, St John Ambulance Brigade. *Address:* Howgate, 60 Seabank Road, Wallasey, Cheshire. *T:* Wallasey 7462.

Died 28 Nov. 1949.

CAITHNESS, 18th Earl of, *cr* 1455; **Norman Macleod Buchan,** CBE 1919; LLD, Aberdeen University; Baron Berriedale, 1455; Bt 1631; DL, Convener of the County of Aberdeen, 1928–42; late Lieut-Colonel 5th Battalion Gordon Highlanders; *b* 4 April 1862; *s* of 16th Earl and Janet, *d* of Roderick M'Leod; *S* brother, 1914; *m* 1893, Lilian (*d* 1933), 2nd *d* of Highford Higford, 23 Eaton Place, SW; four *d. Educ:* Uppingham; Trinity Hall, Cambridge. [Changed his surname from Sinclair to Buchan, 1911]. *Heir: nephew* Brig. James Roderick Sinclair, DSO 1944, The Gordon Highlanders [*b* 1906; *s* of late Rev. Canon Hon. Charles Augustus Sinclair; *m* 1933, Grizel Margaret, *d* of late Sir George Miller-Cunningham, KBE, CB; three *d*]. *Address:* Auchmacoy House, Ellon, Aberdeenshire. *T:* Ellon 229. *Club:* Caledonian.

Died 25 March 1947.

CALDECOTE, 1st Viscount *cr* 1939, of Bristol; **Thomas Walker Hobart Inskip,** PC 1932; Kt 1922; CBE 1920; KC 1914; LLD (Hon.) Bristol University; Lord Chief Justice of England, 1940–46; High Steward of Kingston-on-Thames since 1943; *b* 5 March 1876; 2nd *s* of late James Inskip, of Clifton Park House, Bristol; *m* 1914, Lady Augusta Orr Ewing, *widow* of Charles Orr Ewing, MP for Ayr Burghs, and *e d* of 7th Earl of Glasgow; one *s. Educ:* Clifton; King's College, Cambridge. MA Classical tripos, 1897. Called to Bar, Inner Temple, 1899; Unionist candidate, Berwick-on-Tweed Division, 1906 and Jan. 1910; Naval Intelligence Division, Admiralty, 1915–18; Head of Naval Law Branch Admiralty, 1918; Admiralty Representative on War Crimes Committee, 1918–19; Bencher Inner Temple; JP Wigtownshire; Chancellor of Truro Diocese, 1920–22; MP (U) Central Bristol, Dec. 1918–29; MP (U) Fareham Div. of Hants, 1931–39; Solicitor-General, Nov. 1922 to Jan. 1924, Nov. 1924 to March 1928, and 1931–32; Attorney-General, 1928–29 and 1932–36; Minister for the Co-ordination of Defence, 1936–39; Secretary of State for Dominion Affairs, 1939; Recorder of Kingston-on-Thames, 1928–39; Lord Chancellor, 1939–40; Dominions Secretary, 1940; Leader of the House of Lords, 1940; Chm., Council Westfield College, Univ. of London, 1921–46; Chm. Council of Legal Education; Vice-President Classical Association. *Heir: s* Hon. Robert Andrew Inskip, DSC 1941, Lieut, RNVR [*b* 8 Oct. 1917; *m* 1942, Jean Hamilla, *d* of Rear-Admiral H. D. Hamilton; one *s* one *d*]. *Address:* Greystones, Enton, Godalming. *T:* Godalming 370; Knockinaam, Stranraer, Wigtownshire. *Clubs:* Athenæum, Hurlingham, MCC.

Died 11 Oct. 1947.

CALDER, George Alexander, CB 1922; *b* 11 July 1859; *s* of John Grant Calder of Rothes, Morayshire, Scotland; *m* 1898, Alice (*d* 1935), *d* of Frederick Hannam. *Educ:* privately. Entered the office of the Public Works Loan Board, 1876; Secretary to the Board, 1913. Retired, but remained in an advisory capacity (at the special request of the Board and with the consent of the Treasury) until 1923, finally retiring after nearly forty-seven years' service; JP; Chairman of Joseph Rodgers & Sons, Sheffield 1931; Chairman of Hine, Parker & Co., Gresham Street, EC, 1934. *Recreations:* golf and amateur acting. *Address:* Red Bank, The Drive, Sevenoaks. *T:* Sevenoaks 307.

Died 27 April 1945.

CALDERON, W. Frank; figure and animal painter; *b* 1865; *s* of late Philip H. Calderon, RA; *m* 1892, Ethel, *y d* of late H. H. Armstead, RA; one *s* one *d. Educ:* Slade School of Art under Prof. Le Gros. Founder and Principal, The School of Animal Painting, 1894–1916; regular exhibitor at the RA, etc., 1881–1921; first Royal Academy picture, Feeding the Hungry, purchased by Queen Victoria. *Principal works:* John Hampden, mortally wounded, riding from Chalgrove Field; Flood; Market Day; A Son of the Empire; The Crest of the Hill (National Gallery, Brisbane); Lot 97, A Grey Mare;

Showing His Paces (Schwabe permanent collection, Hamburg); Coursing; Passive Resistance; Orphans; The Coming Shower; Dante in the Valley of Terrors; Gelert; Blue Hussar; Reigate Heath Cattle Fair; The Erl King; On a Sea-Beat Coast where Hardy Thracians Tame the Savage Horse (MacKelvie Trust Gallery, Auckland, New Zealand); Hippolytus; How Four Queens found Sir Launcelot Sleeping, Summer Night, and many portraits. *Publication:* Animal painting and Anatomy, 1936. *Address:* Santillana, Havenview, Seaton, Devon. *Club:* Arts.

Died 21 April 1943.

CALDERWOOD, W. L., ISO 1925; FRSE; Fisheries Adviser to North of Scotland Hydro-Electric Board since 1943; *b* Glasgow, 1865; *o s* of Henry Calderwood, LLD, FRSE, for thirty years Professor of Moral Philosophy in University of Edinburgh; *m* Lily de Courcy, *d* of Capt. T. C. Pullen, RN; one *s* two *d*. *Educ:* Merchiston Castle; Edinburgh University. Specialised first in Zoology; Demonstrator in Edinburgh University; studied in Naples and Germany; appointed Naturalist on Staff of Fishery Board for Scotland; Director of Marine Biological Association's Laboratory, Plymouth, 1889–93; Inspector of Salmon Fisheries for Scotland, 1898–1930; has reported on Salmon Fisheries of Eastern Canada and also of Newfoundland; advised respecting salmon aspects of British Hydro-Electric Schemes. Has also painted many portraits. *Publications:* Mussel Culture and Bait Supply, 1895; Life of Henry Calderwood (joint), 1900; The Life of the Salmon, 1907; Salmon Rivers and Lochs of Scotland, 1909, 2nd edition 1921; Salmon and Sea Trout, 1930; Salmon Hatching, 1931; Salmon! Experiences and Reflections, 1938; numerous Scientific Papers and official reports. *Recreations:* fishing, curling. *Address:* Ardnacoille, Carr Bridge, Invernessshire. *T:* Carr Bridge 236. *Club:* New (Edinburgh).

Died 2 May 1950.

CALDWELL, Maj.-Gen. Frederick Crofton H.; *see* Heath-Caldwell.

CALDWELL, William, MA, DSc, Professor (Emeritus) of Philosophy, McGill University, Montreal; *b* Edinburgh, Nov. 1863; *s* of William Caldwell and Margaret Munro; *m* Atha Haydock, Cincinnati; one *s*. *Educ:* Daniel Stewart's Institution, and University of Edinburgh (1st Class Honours in Philosophy, 1886); Post-graduate study in Germany, Paris, Cambridge, 1887–91; Degree Doctor Mental and Moral Science, Edinburgh; Bruce of Grangehill Scholar and Medallist, Edinburgh, 1886; Sir William Hamilton Fellow, Edinburgh, 1887–90. Assistant Professor Logic and Metaphysics, Edinburgh, 1887–88; Ferguson Scholar in Philosophy, 1887; gained Shaw Fellowship in Mental Philosophy (highest academic distinction in Scotland); Government Examiner in Philosophy, St Andrews, 1889–92; called to Sage School of Philosophy, Cornell University, NY, 1891; to University of Chicago, 1892; Professor of Moral and Social Philosophy, North-Western University, 1894–1903; official and member American Psychological and Philosophical Associations; Vice-President of the Alliance Française—the Montreal Group; Officier d'Académie, 1924; Officer of the Order of the White Lion (Czecho-Slovakia); Officer de l'Instruction Publique, 1922; Knight Commander of the Order of Polonia Restituta, 1927; Order of Merit, Poland, 1933; Knight Commander Order of St Sava (Yugoslavia). *Publications:* Schopenhauer's System in its Philosophical Significance, 1896 (substance—expanded—of Shaw Fellowship Lectures, Edinburgh, 1893); Pragmatism and Idealism, 1913; contributor to leading philosophical and general reviews. *Recreations:* study of contemporary literature, politics, social questions. *Clubs:* McGill Faculty, Montreal.

Died 14 Dec. 1942.

CALLENDER, Sir Geoffrey Arthur Romaine, Kt 1938; MA, FSA, FRHistSoc, AINA, Director National Maritime Museum since 1934; late Professor of History and English, Royal Naval College, Greenwich; Lecturer in History to the RN War College and RN Staff College; *b* Manchester, 1875; *e s* of Arthur W. Callender, JP, and Agnes, *d* of Rev. George Woodgate, and *grand-nephew* of first Viscount Hardinge; unmarried. *Educ:* St Edward's School, Oxford; Merton College, Oxford. Head of the History and English Department, RN College, Osborne, until 1921; head of the History Department, RN College, Dartmouth, 1921–22; Hon. Treasurer, The London Survey Committee; Hon. Secretary and Treasurer of the Society for Nautical Research; Trustee of the Implacable, Trafalgar Ship for Boys and Foudroyant, Training Ship; Hon. Secretary and Treasurer for the Restoration of HMS Victory; on Executive Council of the British Records Association, Hakluyt Society, Wren Society, and Institute of Naval Architects; Vice-President of King George's Fund for Sailors, the Navy Records Society, Historical Association and Liverpool Nautical Research Society; Lecturer on Naval History for Board of Education, 1918, at King's College, London, 1919, and to WRNS Officers, 1939–40; awarded the Chesney Gold Medal by the Royal United Service Institution, 1924; Fellow of the American Geographical Society; Hon. Corresponding Member of Institut Historique et Héraldique de France; Silver Jubilee and Coronation Medals. *Publications:* Sea Kings of Britain, 1907–1911; The Life of Nelson, 1912; The Story of HMS Victory, 1914; Spindrift, 1915; Realms of Melody, 1916; Nelson's Flagship, 1919; The Life of Admiral Sir John Leake, 1920; Southey's Nelson, 1922; Bibliography of Naval History, 1924; The Naval Side of British History, 1924; Nelson Relics, 1928; Marine Art, 1929; The Wooden World; The Queen's House, The Portrait of Peter Pett and the Sovereign of the Seas, 1930; The Caird Collection, 1934; Masters of Maritime Art, 1936, 1937, and 1938; The Model-maker's Plans of HMS Victory, 1937; Catalogue of the National Maritime Museum, 1937; Sea-Passages, an Anthology, 1943; has contributed to Dictionary of National Biography, Encyclopædia Britannica, etc. *Address:* 1 Vanbrugh Park, Blackheath, SE.

Died 6 Nov. 1946.

CALTHORPE, 9th Baron *cr* 1796; **Ronald Arthur Somerset Gough-Calthorpe;** Bt 1728; Flying Officer RAFVR; *b* 22 June 1924; *s* of late Hon. Frederick Somerset Gough-Calthorpe and Rose Mary Dorothy, *d* of late Leveson William Vernon-Harcourt; *S* grandfather, 1940. *Educ:* Stowe; Jesus College, Cambridge. *Recreations:* golf and cricket. *Heir:* *b* Hon. Peter Waldo Somerset Gough-Calthorpe, *b* 13 July 1927. *Address:* Home Green, Worplesdon Hill, Woking. *T:* Brookwood 2149.

Died 9 Oct. 1945.

CALVE, Emma; Chevalier de la Légion d'Honneur; operatic singer; *b* France, 1866. *Educ:* under R. Laborde. Made her début at Brussels (Gounod's Faust), 1882; Covent Garden (Mascagni's Cavalleria Rusticana), 1892. *Principal Parts:* Opéra Comique, Paris; Aben Hamet, Chevalier Jean, Cavalleria, Navarraise, Sapho de Massenet, Pêcheurs de Perles and Carmen de G. Bizet; Au Théâtre, Paris; Damnation de Faust de Berlioz, Hérodiade de Massenet, Messaline de de Lara. *Address:* 9 rue d'Artois, Paris, VIIIe.

Died Jan. 1942.

CALVERT, Albert Frederick; Knight Grand Cross of the Royal Order of Alfonso XII; Corresponding Member of the Royal Spanish Academy; Hon. Member Spanish Chamber of Commerce in London; Member of the Hispanic Society of America; author; *b* 20 July 1872; *e s* of Frederick Calvert; *m* Florence, *d* of late James Holcombe. Has travelled extensively; made four expeditions into interior of North-West Australia; circumnavigated the island continent, 1891–92;

despatched at own expense scientific exploring expedition to traverse unexplored region of Central Australia. *Publications:* Western Australia, its History and Progress; The Aborigines of Western Australia; The Mineral Resources of Western Australia; The Discovery of Australia, 1894; My Fourth Tour in Western Australia 1896; The Exploration of Australia, 1896; History of the Old King's Arms Lodge, 1899; Bacon and Shakespeare, 1902; Impressions of Spain, 1903; The Alhambra, 1904; Life of Cervantes, 1905; Alfonso XIII in England, 1905; Summer in San Sebastian, 1905; Moorish Remains in Spain, 1906; The Spanish Royal Wedding, 1906; Southern Spain, 1908; Spain, 1909; Nigeria and its Tin Fields, 1910; Cook's Handbook to Spain, 1911; Salt in Cheshire, 1914; The German African Empire, 1915; South-West Africa (1884–1914), 1915; Mineral Resources of Minas Geraes, Brazil, 1915; The Cameroons, 1916; German East Africa, 1916; Pearls and Pearl Culture, 1921; General Editor, The Spanish Series. *Recreations:* yachting, motoring, driving, racing. *Address:* Royston, Eton Avenue, NW3. *TA:* Quarterage, London. *T:* Primrose 3102.

Died 27 June 1946.

CALVERT, Lt-Col John Telfer, CIE 1919; IMS retired; late Principal and Professor of Medicine, Medical Hospital and College, Calcutta; *s* of late J. M. Calvert of Rochdale; *m* Ethel B., *o d* of late A. Margetts of Wouldham; three *s* one *d. Educ:* St Thomas's Hospital, MB Lond.; FRCP Lond.; DPH Camb. Late Fellow of and Dean of Faculty of Medicine, Calcutta Univ.; President Board of Health, Calcutta; Vice-Pres. State Medical Faculty of Bengal; Member Bengal Council of Medical Registration; served in NEF Expedition, Manipur (medal with clasp); NWF Expedition (Tirah medal with two clasps). *Publications:* contributions to Indian Medical Gazette. *Address:* Templecombe, Willingdon Road, Eastbourne.

Died 20 Sept. 1944.

CALVERT, William Archibald, JP, CC; *b* 19 Feb. 1868; *s* of late Col A. M. Calvert, Ockley Court, Surrey; *m* Hon. Beatrice Hayward Cubitt, *y d* of 1st Baron Ashcombe, 1891; four *s* one *d. Educ:* Harrow; Trinity Hall, Camb. (MA). *Address:* Ockley Court, Ockley, Surrey. *T:* Capel 35.

Died 26 July 1943.

CALVERT, William Robinson; journalist and author; deputy managing editor Kemsley Newspapers; *b* 30 June 1882; *s* of William Calvert and Elizabeth Robinson; *m* 1907, Lilly, *e d* of Joseph Dalzell, Salmon Hall, nr Workington, Cumberland; one *s* two *d. Educ:* St Bees; College de Blois. Joined reporting staff of Standard, 1905; editor Newnes Publications, 1911; News Editor, Sunday Times, 1918; News Editor, Daily Graphic, 1920. *Publications:* Secret of the Wild, 1927; Just Across the Road, 1929; Sorrowstones, 1930; Just Round the Corner, 1931; Family Holiday, 1932; Watchings, 1933; The Hungry Hills, 1933; The Passions of the Wild, 1936; Wild Life on Moor and Fell, 1937; Nature and the Rambler, 1939; Watchers of the Wild, 1947. *Recreations:* walking, watching wild life, gardening. *Address:* Courtlands, Hooke Road, East Horsley, Surrey.

Died 3 Oct. 1949.

CAMACHO, Sir Maurice Vivian, Kt 1941; KC 1924; Chief Justice, British Guiana, since 1938; *b* 1885; *s* of E. O. Camacho; *m* 1917, Evelyn Helen, *d* of Lewis Punnett; one *s. Educ:* St Edmund's College, Herts. Called to Bar, Middle Temple, 1906; practised at Bar, Rangoon, 1907; Leeward Islands, 1913–20; Attorney-General, Leeward Islands, 1920–26; Solicitor-General, Trinidad, 1927–31; Attorney-General, Jamaica, 1931–38. *Address:* Georgetown, British Guiana.

Died 10 Oct. 1941.

CAMBRIDGE, Elizabeth; *see* Hodges, B. K.

CAMDEN, 4th Marquess *cr* 1812; **John Charles Pratt,** GCVO 1933; JP, TD; Baron Camden, 1765; Earl Camden, Viscount Bayham, 1786; Earl of Brecknock, 1812; *b* 9 Feb. 1872; *s* of 3rd Marquis and Clementine, *y d* of 6th Duke of Marlborough; *S* father, 1872; *m* 1898, Lady Joan Marion Nevill, CBE 1920, *d* of 3rd Marquess of Abergavenny; two *s* two *d. Educ:* Eton; Trinity Coll. Cambridge. Lord-Lieutenant Kent, 1905; late Major West Kent Yeomanry; President Kent Territorial Association, 1908; served European War, 1914–16; a Younger Brother of Trinity House, 1927; Knight of Grace of St John of Jerusalem, 1930; owns about 18,000 acres. *Heir: s* Earl of Brecknock. *Address:* Bayham Abbey, Lamberhurst, Kent. *T:* Tunbridge Wells 9; 128 Mount Street, W1. *Clubs:* Carlton, Turf; Royal Yacht Squadron, Cowes (Commodore).

Died 14 Dec. 1943.

CAMERON, Rev. A. D.; Free Church Minister of Creich since 1912; Moderator of the Free Church of Scotland, 1928; *b* Monar, Ross-shire; *s* of John Cameron and Margaret Mackae; *m* 1919, Euphemia M., *eldest living daughter* of George and Annie Munro, Bonar Bridge, and first cousin of Lord Alness; one *d. Educ:* Grammar School, Old Aberdeen; King's College, Aberdeen; and New College, Edinburgh. Settled as Free Church Minister at Lochfyneside, Argyllshire, 1898. *Publications:* edited his mother's poems in Gaelic with biographical sketch in English. *Recreations:* visiting his flock, and especially the sick. *Address:* Free Church Manse, Creich, Bonar Bridge, Sutherlandshire. *TA:* Cameron, Free Manse, Bonar Bridge.

Died 28 Feb. 1946.

CAMERON, Alexander Gordon; Building Contractor; *b* Oban, 1886. Contested Kirkdale Jan. and July 1910, Jarrow Dec. 1910, West Woolwich 1918; MP (Lab) Widnes Division of Lancs, 1929–31. *Address:* 28 Crowhurst Road, Brixton, SW.

Died 30 May 1944.

CAMERON, Alexander T., CMG 1946; Professor of Biochemistry, Faculty of Medicine, University of Manitoba, Winnipeg, Canada, since 1923; *b* London, 1882; *s* of Alexander Cameron and Jane M. Clapp; *m* 1923, Airdrie Edna, *d* of C. N. Bell, LLD, Winnipeg; one *s* one *d. Educ:* University of Edinburgh; University of London (University College); University of Karlsruhe; and University of Heidelberg. MA (Edin.) 1904; BSc (Edin.) 1906; DSc (Edin.) 1925; FRIC; FRSC. Lecturer in Physiology, 1909; Associate Professor of Biochemistry, 1920, in the University of Manitoba; Biochemist, Winnipeg General Hospital, 1929; President Canadian Institute of Chemistry, 1931–33; Chairman, Fisheries Research Board of Canada, since 1934; Captain RAMC (T); Chemist for examination and purification of water, BEF 1916–19 (despatches). *Publications:* A Text-book of Biochemistry, 1928, 6th edition, 1942; Recent Advances in Endocrinology, 1933; 6th edition, 1947; (with F. D. White) A Course in Practical Biochemistry, 1930; 5th edition, 1946; (with C. R. Gilmour) The Biochemistry of Medicine, 1933; 2nd edition, 1935; numerous papers in scientific journals. *Recreations:* philately, golf. *Address:* Department of Biochemistry, Medical College, Winnipeg, Canada.

Died 25 Sept. 1947.

CAMERON, Gen. Sir Archibald Rice, GBE 1937; KCB 1933; CB 1917; CMG 1915; Col of the Black Watch (Royal Highland Regt), 1929–40; *b* 28 Aug. 1870; *s* of late Ralph Abercrombie Cameron. Entered Army, The Black Watch, 1890; Captain, 1899; Adjutant, 1900–04; Major, 1908; Lieut-Col, 1915; Bt-Col, 1916; Maj.-Gen., 1921; Lt-Gen. 1931; General, 1936; Military Secretary to Governor, Cape of Good Hope, 1904–07; served S African War, 1899–1902 (wounded, despatches, Bt-Maj.; Queen's medal 3 clasps, King's medal 2 clasps); European War, 1914–17 (wounded, despatches, CB, CMG, Bt-Col); Director of Staff Duties, War Office,

1925–27; General Officer Comdg 4th Div., 1927–31; General Officer Commanding-in-Chief, Scottish Command, 1933–37; Governor of Edinburgh Castle, 1936–37; retired pay, 1937. *Clubs:* Naval and Military, Turf, Arthurs; New, Edinburgh.

Died 18 June 1944.

CAMERON, Charlotte, OBE, FRGS; woman traveller; *b* Portsmouth; *d* of Captain Jacob Wales-Almy, RN; *widow* of Major Donald Cameron, 42nd Highlanders. Made extensive journeys in India, South America, Russia, Alaska and the Yukon, the South Seas, and Borneo, visiting many regions hitherto unexplored by white women; lectured during the war all through the United States; presented collection of native handicraft to Liverpool Museum, 1938; and an Oriental collection to the Royal Scottish Museum in Edinburgh, 1945; Fellow of the Royal Empire Society. *Publications:* A Durbar Bride; A Woman's Winter in South America; Zenia—Spy in Togoland; The Winged One; A Cheechako in Alaska; 100,000 Miles in the South Seas; Marriquitta of Monte Carlo; A Passion in Morocco; Two Years in Southern Seas, 1923; Wanderings in South Eastern Seas, 1924; Mexico in Revolution, 1924. *Address:* c/o Lloyds Bank Ltd, 39 Piccadilly, W1.

Died 9 Dec. 1946.

CAMERON, Col Hon. Cyril St Clair, CB 1900; 9th Lancers, retired; late ADC to Governor-General; *b* 5 Dec. 1857; *s* of late Hon. Donald Cameron, MLC; *m* 1887, Margaret Honywood (*d* 1940), *d* of late Sir W. T. Hughes, KCB of Dunley, Bovey Tracy; three *s* one *d*. *Educ:* Church Grammar School, Tasmania; Edinburgh University. Served 9th (Queen's Royal) Lancers, Afghan War, 1878–80, including march Cabul to Kandahar (medal with clasp, bronze star); commanded 1st Tasmanian Mounted Infantry in South Africa, 1900 (twice wounded, despatches, Queen's medal three clasps, CB); commanded Australian Commonwealth Corps at Coronation, 1902; commanded 12th Regt Australian Light Horse; AAG Australian and New Zealand Army Corps Headquarters; present at landing at Gaba Tepe on 25 April 1915; Hon. Colonel 26th AL Horse, 1916; Senator, Australian Commonwealth, 1901–04 and 1907–13; welcomed and given a seat on floor of Senate on return from Gallipoli, Sept. 1915; presented by the President with a copy of Proceedings. *Recreation:* polo. *Address:* Fordon, The Nile, Tasmania. *Clubs:* Army and Navy, United Service, Hurlingham.

Died 22 Dec. 1941.

CAMERON, Sir David Young, Kt 1924; RA 1920; ARA 1911; RSA 1918; RWS, RSW; LLD Glasgow Univ., 1911; LLD Manchester, 1923; LLD Cambridge, 1928; St Andrews, 1936; painter and etcher; HM Painter and Limner in Scotland since 1933; *b* Glasgow, 28 June 1865; *s* of Rev. Robert Cameron; *m* 1896, Jean (*d* 1931), *d* of Robert MacLaurin, Thornville, Glasgow. *Educ:* Glasgow Academy; Edinburgh. Medals, Antwerp, 1893; Chicago, 1893; Brussels (silver), 1895; Dresden (gold), 1897; Paris (gold), 1900; Munich (gold), 1905. Pictures in the public collections of Manchester, Liverpool, Dublin, Glasgow, Edinburgh, Aberdeen, Preston, Abo (Dundee), Perth, Paisley, Greenock, Pittsburg, Fitzwilliam, Cambridge, Oxford, Birmingham, Durban, Adelaide, Budapest, Munich, Melbourne; National Gallery, Ottawa; Contemporary Art Society, Tate Gallery, Victoria and Albert Museum, and British Museum, London, etc.; Trustee of National Gallery of Scotland. *Publications:* The Clyde Set, 1890; North Holland, 1892; North Italy, 1896; The London Set, 1900; Paris Etchings, 1904; Etchings in Belgium, 1907; Illustrations to Sir Herbert Maxwell's Story of the Tweed, 1905; Etchings to illustrate The Compleat Angler, 1902; Illustrations for District of Menteith, by R. B. Cunninghame Graham, edition de luxe, 1930;

Highways and Byways in West Highlands. *Address:* Dun Eaglais, Kippen, Stirlingshire. *T:* Kippen 209. *Clubs:* New, Edinburgh; County, Stirling.

Died 16 Sept. 1945.

CAMERON, Sir Donald Charles, GCMG 1932; KCMG 1926; KBE 1923; CMG 1918; LLD (Hon.) Cantab; Member of Education Advisory Committee, Colonial Office; Vice-Chairman Governing Body, Imperial College of Agriculture; *b* 3 June 1872; *s* of late Donald Charles Cameron of Demerara, British Guiana; *m* 1903, Gertrude, *d* of Duncan Gittens of Oldbury, Barbados. *Educ:* Rathmines School, Dublin. Colonial Civil Service: British Guiana, 1890–1904; Mauritius, Acting-Colonial Secretary, 1904–07; Southern Nigeria, 1908 Acting-Colonial Sec., 1912; Sec. to Central Govt, Nigeria, 1914; Chief Sec. to Govt, 1921–24; administered the government, 1921, 1923, and 1924; Governor and Commander-in-Chief of Tanganyika Territory, 1925–31; Governor and Commander-in-Chief of Nigeria, 1931–35. *Publication:* My Tanganyika Service, 1939. *Address:* Grosvenor Court, Sloane Street, SW1. *T:* Sloane 6951. *Club:* East India and Sports.

Died 8 Jan. 1948.

CAMERON, Sir Edward (John), KCMG 1916; CMG 1905; *b* 14 May 1858; 4th *s* of late John Charles Cameron, MD, Deputy Surgeon-General, and Julia, *d* of late James Mooyaart, Auditor-General of Ceylon; *m* 1887, Eva Selwyn (*d* 1944), *y d* of Robert Mackintosh Isaacs, LLD, NS Wales; one *s* two *d*. *Educ:* Shrewsbury School; Clifton College; Merton College, Oxon. Private Secretary to late Sir Charles Cameron Lees, KCMG, Governor of the Bahamas, 1882; accompanied him in the same capacity to the Leeward Islands, 1884; Assistant Colonial Secretary and Treasurer, Sierra Leone, 1884; acted as Colonial Secretary, 1885–86; President of the Virgin Islands with seat in Leeward Islands Executive and Legislative Councils, 1887–93; Commissioner of the Turks and Caicos Islands, 1893–1901; Administrator, St Vincent, 1901–09; Administrator of St Lucia, 1909–13; acted Gov., Windward Islands, on several occasions; Governor and Commander-in-Chief, Colony of the Gambia, 1913–20; retired, 1920. *Recreation:* sundry. *Address:* c/o G. F. Cameron, Higher Bay Cottage, Northam, N Devon.

Died 20 July 1947.

CAMERON, Lt-Col George Cecil Minett Sorell-, CBE 1926; *b* 9 July 1871; *s* of Henry Wallace Sorel-Cameron; *m* 1906, Marguerite Emily, *d* of late Hon. Hamilton James Tollemache; two *s* two *d*. *Educ:* privately; Royal Military College, Sandhurst. Joined 79th QO Cameron Highlanders, 1893; attached Egyptian Army, 1899–1906 (4th Class Medjidie); commanded 2nd Battalion Queen's Own Cameron Highlanders, 1919–23; served Nile Expedition, 1898 (medal, Egyptian Medal two clasps); European War, 1914–19 (prisoner, 1914 star, two medals); S Kurdistan, 1925–26, commanding combined column Iraq Army and Iraq Levies (despatches, CBE, medal); 1932 GS medal and clasp, Northern Kurdistan; retired pay, 1926; served with Iraq Levies, 1923–32. *Address:* Gorthleck House, Gorthleck, Inverness-shire. *T:* Gorthleck 23. *Clubs:* United Service; Highland, Inverness.

Died 28 June 1947.

CAMERON, Isabella Douglas, MD, DPH, MRCOG; *d* of James Cameron, Stanley, Perthshire. *Educ:* Medical College for Women, Edinburgh. RMO Crichton Royal Institution, Dumfries; RMO Children's Hospital, Sheffield; MO to Carnegie Trust, Dunfermline; MO and Lecturer on Hygiene, Provincial Training Coll., Edinburgh; Senior Medical Officer Ministry of Health; retired 1940. *Publications:* official reports. *Address:* c/o Westminster Bank, Caxton House, Tothill Street, SW1.

Died 10 Jan. 1945.

CAMERON, Col James Black, DSO 1917; TD; DL for County of City of Edinburgh; Member of Edinburgh Town Council; late Chairman City of Edinburgh Territorial Army Association; *b* 1882; *s* of James Cameron, Keeper of HM Register of Deeds, Edinburgh; *m* 1908, Helen Rhenius, *d* of Frederick Coles, antiquarian; two *d*. *Educ:* George Watson's College, Edinburgh; Edinburgh University (MA, LLB). By profession a Writer to His Majesty's Signet and a Notary Public. Served European War, 1914–18 (despatches, DSO); in command of City of Edinburgh Heavy Battery and of various Brigades of RGA; retd from TA, 1940; commanded City of Edinburgh Zone Home Guard, 1940–41; now Secretary TA Association, City of Edinburgh and Counties of West Lothian, East Lothian and Peebles and Secretary Edinburgh, Midlothian, West Lothian, East Lothian and Peebles Cadet Committees. *Recreation:* golf. *Address:* 15 Eglinton Crescent, Edinburgh. *TA:* Frederick, Edinburgh. *T:* Edinburgh 63293. *Clubs:* Caledonian United Service, Edinburgh; Royal and Ancient Golf, St Andrews.

Died 12 Feb. 1946.

CAMERON, Rev. John Kennedy, MA; DD; Professor of Systematic Theology, Free Church College, Edinburgh since 1906; *b* parish of Rosskeen, Ross-shire, 11 May 1860; *s* of Alex. Cameron, Obsdale, Alness, Ross-shire; *m* 1891; one *s* three *d*. *Educ:* Edinburgh University; New College, Edinburgh. Was ordained Free Church Minister, Kilbride, Arran, 1890; Clerk of General Assembly of Free Church, 1900–36; Moderator of General Assembly, 1910. *Publications:* (Joint) Religious Life in Ross; (Joint) The Free Church of Scotland, 1843–1910; A Vindication; The Church in Arran; Peru and its Free Church Mission: The Scottish Church Union of 1900; The Free Church General Assembly Clerkship. *Address:* Free Church Offices, Edinburgh. *TA:* Citadel, Edinburgh.

Died 5 Oct. 1944.

CAMERON, Col John Philip, CSI 1932; CIE 1923; VHS, 1933; FRCPE; IMS, retd; *b* 22 May 1879; *s* of late John Cameron, FLS, Mysore Government Service; *m* 1904, Eleanor Grace (*d* 1947), *e d* of Dr William Mackenzie Barclay, Grantown on Spey; two *d*. *Educ:* private; University of Edinburgh and University of London; Roy. Coll. of Surgeons, Edinburgh. MRCP (Ed.), DTM&H (Camb.), 1912; FRCPE 1929. Military duty in India, 1902–05, including 18 months' Field Service in Somaliland in the 1902–04 Campaign (medal and two clasps); military duty European War, 1914–19, including 17 months' overseas service (1914–15 Star, British War medal, 1914–19, and Victory medal); Superintendent of Prisons, Madras, 1906–12; Medical Superintendent, Central Jail, Coimbatore, 1912–14; Inspector-General of Prisons, Madras Presidency, 1919–31; Inspector-General of Civil Hospitals and Prisons, Assam, 1931–35; Commandant Convalescent Hospital for Head Injuries under the War Organisation of the British Red Cross Society and Order of St John of Jerusalem, 1940–45. *Recreations:* golf and motoring. *Address:* Garth, Park Avenue, Camberley. *Clubs:* St Andrew's; Camberley Heath Golf.

Died 26 May 1950.

CAMERON, Col Kenneth, CMG 1918; surgeon, retired; *b* 1863. *Educ:* Trinity College School, Port Hope, Ont; BA, MD, CM McGill University, Montreal. Served with Canadian AMC, European War, 1914–18 (despatches thrice, CMG); Consulting Staff, Montreal General Hospital. *Publication:* History of No. 1 Canadian General Hospital, 1914–1919. *Address:* Apt. 51, 418 Claremont Avenue, Westmount, Que., Canada. *Clubs:* University, Montreal.

Died 25 Dec. 1939.

CAMERON, Captain Ludovick Charles Richard Duncombe-Jewell; ARP Warden, Folkestone, 1940–45 (Defence Medal); ex-Master of Hounds; *b* Liskeard, Cornwall, 6 Sept. 1866; *e s* of late Richard Jewell; *m* 1st, 1895, Mary Amy (*d* 1904), *e d* of late Lieut-Col Charles Slaughter, RMLI; 2nd, Janet Sarah (*d* 1928), *d* of late General Robert Bruce of Glendouglie; 3rd, Katharine Gertrude, *g d* of late Sir George Findlay. *Educ:* private tutor, and on the Continent. Formerly Lieut Royal Fusiliers; acted as special war correspondent of the Times and Morning Post; served South Africa, 1899–1900 (medal and 2 clasps); Lieut Cameron Highlanders, 1914–16, and Instructor, Northern Command School of Scouting; served with BEF, France, 1915–16 (1914–15 Star, British War and Victory Medal); resumed surname of Cameron by deed-poll, 1904. *Publications:* The Book of the Caravan, 1907; Otters and Otter-hunting, 1908; The Otter-Hunter's Diary and Companion; The Hunting Horn: What to Blow and How to Blow it, 1910; Scarlet and Blue, a hunting novel, 1912; Infantry Scouting, 1916; The Wild Foods of Great Britain, 1917; Minor Field Sports, 1921; Rhymes of Sport in old French verse forms, 1925; Rod, Pole and Perch: Angling and Otter Hunting Sketches, 1927; Love Lies Bleeding: Lyrics, 1929; The Lady of the Leash: A Sporting Novel, 1935; Lonsdale Library: Deer, Hare and Otter Hunting (Otter Hunting Section), 1936; Shooting in the Eastern Counties (in British Sports and Sportsmen), 1938; Otter Hunting (with Lord Coventry), 1938; Yachting: Small Cabin Cruising, 1939; Through Fair and Through Foul: a novel of sport and War, 1940. *Address:* 19 Earls' Avenue, Folkestone, Kent.

Died Feb. 1947.

CAMM, Dom Bede, OSB; MA; FSA; *b* Sunbury Park, 26 Dec. 1864; *e s* of late John B. M. Camm, MA, sometime 12th Lancers, and Caroline, *d* of Richard Edward Arden, of Sunbury Park, Middlesex, and East Burnham House, Bucks. *Educ:* Westminster School; Keble College, Oxford (BA with 2nd Class Theological Honours, 1887); Cuddesdon Theological College. Ordained in Anglican Orders, 1888; Curate, St Agnes', Kennington Park, till 1890; received into Catholic Church at Maredsons Abbey, 1890; became Benedictine monk there same year; studied at Rome for the priesthood; ordained 1895, and until 1912 stationed at Erdington Abbey; summoned to Caldey to arrange the reception of the Anglican Benedictines there into the Catholic Church, 1913; appointed Novice-Master of the Community by the Holy See, 1913; affiliated to the Community of St Gregory's Abbey, Downside, 1913; Chaplain to the Forces, 1915–19, stationed in Egypt; MA (Cantab), 1919; Master of Benet House, Cambridge, the Downside School of Studies, 1919–31. *Publications:* numerous works and articles on English Catholic history: A Benedictine Martyr in England, 1897; A Day in the Cloister, 1900; In the Brave Days of Old, 1900; Lives of the Blessed English Martyrs, 1904; Tyburn Conferences, 1906, 1909; William Cardinal Allen, 1909; Forgotten Shrines, 1910; Pilgrim Paths in Latin Lands, 1923; Joint author with F. Bligh Bond of Roodscreens and Roodlofts, 1909; Some Norfolk Rood-screens—being Parts VII-VIII of the new Supplement to Blomefield's Norfolk (Clement Ingleby), 1929; Nine Martyr Monks, 1931; Life of B. John Wall, the Martyr of Harvington, 1932; Life of the Foundress of Tyburn Convent, 1933. *Address:* Downside Abbey, Stratton-on-the-Fosse, near Bath.

Died 8 Sept. 1942.

CAMPBELL, Lt-Col Alexander, CMG 1919; DSO 1916; *b* 14 March 1881; *y s* of A. D. Campbell, 8 Bellevue Crescent, Edinburgh; unmarried. *Educ:* Edinburgh Academy; RMA, Woolwich. Entered army, 1900; retired 1925; served S African War, 1901–02 (medal and 5 clasps); operations on NW Frontier of India, 1908 (medal and clasp); European War, France, 1914–19 (despatches six times, CMG, DSO); NW

Frontier of India and Afghanistan, 1919 (despatches, clasp). *Recreations:* fishing and shooting. *Address:* c/o Lloyds Bank, Ltd, Cox and Kings Branch, 6 Pall Mall, SW1.

Died 8 Feb. 1941.

CAMPBELL, Very Rev. Andrew James, MA, DD; *b* 30 June 1875; *s* of John Campbell, Ardallie, Aberdeenshire, and Isabella Helen Waters; *m* 1st, 1902, Caroline Cumming Spence, MA; 2nd, 1927, Anna Mary Robertson, MA. *Educ:* Fettes College, Edinburgh; St John's College, Cambridge; Divinity Hall, Edinburgh Univ. Assistant, East Parish Church of St Nicholas', Aberdeen, 1900–02; Minister of Lerwick, Shetland, 1902–09; Minister of St John's, Glasgow, 1909–29; Clerk of the Presbytery of Glasgow, 1929–36; Minister of Evie, Orkney, 1936–48; retired, 1948. BA Cambridge, 1897; DD Glasgow, 1933. Hastie Lecturer, University of Glasgow, 1924; Moderator of General Assembly of the Church of Scotland, 1945. European War, Chaplain attached 52nd Division, 1914–17. *Publications:* Two Centuries of the Church of Scotland, 1929; The Church in Orkney, 1936; The Church (Bible Class Handbook), 1935. *Recreations:* golf, walking. *Address:* 21 Eildon St, Edinburgh, 4. *Club:* Scottish Conservative (Edinburgh).

Died 1 May 1950.

CAMPBELL, Sir Archibald Henry, Kt 1931; *b* 28 May 1870; *e s* of George Augustus Campbell and Hon. Mrs Campbell, *d* of 8th Viscount Barrington; *m* 1905, Hon. Beryl Dawnay, *d* of 8th Viscount Downe; no *chidren*. *Educ:* Eton. Member of the Stock Exchange, 1896; Deputy Chairman, 1918; Chairman, 1923–36; Governor of Guy's Hospital; Member of the London Committee of the Soldiers' and Sailors' Families Association, 1914–19; Chairman of the Shoreditch War Pensions Committee; Member of the London War Pensions Committee, 1925–26; Lieutenant of City of London, 1931; Member Company Law Amendment Committee appointed by Board of Trade. *Recreations:* travelling, reading, gardening. *Address:* Commonwood Lodge, Chipperfield, Herts. *T:* Kings Langley 7283.

Died 10 May 1948.

CAMPBELL, Sir Archibald (Spencer Lindsey), JP, DL; 5th Bt of Succoth, Dumbartonshire; 1808; *b* 27 June 1852; *s* of late George Ramsay Campbell, HEICS, and Lucy, *e d* of Thomas Spencer Lindsey, of Hollymount, Co. Mayo, and *g g s* of Sir Ilay Campbell, 1st Bt; *S* cousin, 1874; *m* 1887, Harriet K. G., (*d* 1940), *d* of Col Reynell-Pack, CB; one *s* one *d*. *Educ:* Harrow; Univ. Coll., Oxford (BA). Formerly Lieut Highland Borderers (Stirling Militia). Barr (Scot.) 1880; President, 1916–22, of National Bible Society of Scotland; a Vice-President CMS. *Heir:* *s* George Ilay [*b* 20 Jan. 1894; *m* 1926, Clematis (marr. diss. by Court of Session, 1935), *e d* of late Walter Waring and Lady Clementine Waring, CBE; one *s*. Captain Argyll and Sutherland Highlanders; retired]. *Address:* Garscube, Bearsden, Glasgow. *TA:* Garscube, Bearsden. *T:* Bearsden 2. *Clubs:* Carlton; New, Edin.; Western, Scottish Automobile, Glasgow.

Died 1 March 1941.

CAMPBELL, Sir Charles Ralph, 12th Bt *cr* 1628; Capt. SR, 2nd Life Guards; *b* 14 Dec. 1881; *s* of 11th Bt and Sara, *d* of Hon. William Robinson, of Cheviot Hills, NZ; *S* father, 1919; *m* 1915, Nancy Sarah, *o d* of late Edward Chapman, Canterbury, New Zealand; one *d*. *Educ:* Eton. Served European War with 2nd Life Guards RR, Tank Corps and on personal staff of Gen. Sir Alex. Godley, etc. *Recreations:* yachting, polo, golf. *Heir:* *b* Norman Dugald Ferrier, *b* 1883. *Address:* Davaar, Bembridge, Isle of Wight. *Clubs:* Naval and Military; Royal Yacht Squadron (Cowes).

Died 19 April 1948.

CAMPBELL, Charles Stewart, CBE; MA; ICS (retired); *b* 14 March 1875; *s* of late Col Frederick Campbell, CB, VD, JP, *s* of Sir John Campbell, Bt of Airds, Argyllshire, and Emilie Guillaumine, *d* of Donald Maclaine of Lochbuie, Isle of Mull; unmarried. *Educ:* Dulwich College; King's College, Cambridge. First Class Classical Tripos; passed into ICS 1898. Arrived in India, 1899; Registrar of Co-operative Credit Societies, Bombay Presidency, 1906–11; served in Indian Army Reserve of Officers, during war, as Recruiting Officer of the Bombay Presidency; from which retired, after war, and granted rank of Lt-Col. *Recreations:* tennis, music. *Address:* c/o Lloyds Bank, Limited, 6 Pall Mall, SW1. *Clubs:* East India and Sports, National.

Died 10 Nov. 1942.

CAMPBELL, Sir Edward (Taswell), 1st Bt *cr* 1939, of Airds Bay and Bromley; Kt 1933; JP; MP (C) Bromley since 1930; *b* 9 April 1879; *s* of late Col F. Campbell, CB; *m* 1904, Edith Jane Warren, a Lady of Grace of Order of St John of Jerusalem, Order of League of Mercy, *d* of A. J. Warren, Epsom, Surrey; one *s* three *d*. *Educ:* Dulwich College (a Governor). Private in the London Scottish Volunteers, 1895–99; worked in James Finlay & Co., London, 1895–99; tobacco planter in Sumatra, 1900; joined Maclaine Watson & Co., Java, 1900; retired as partner, 1921; connected with British Consulate in Java, 1900–20; British Vice-Consul, 1914–20, and Acting French Consul; member of LCC for W Lewisham, 1922–25; contested the Parliamentary Division of NW Camberwell, 1923; MP (C) NW Camberwell, 1924–29; Parliamentary Private Secretary to Sir Kingsley Wood, when Post Master General, 1931–34, when Minister of Health, 1934–38, when Secretary of State for Air, 1938–40, and 1940–43, when Lord Privy Seal and subsequently Chancellor of the Exchequer; to H. U. Willink, Minister of Health, since 1943; KGStJ; Commander on HQ Staff of Metropolitan Special Constabulary; Vice-President National and Kent Associations of Boys' Clubs; on the Council of the Boy Scouts; on Executive of National Playing Fields Association; Chairman of Governors of James Allen's Girls' School; Chairman Royal Normal College for the Blind; Chairman Anglo-Netherlands Society; Captain of Society of London Golf Captains, 1938; Captain of Sundridge Park Golf Club since 1939; President of Club Cricket Conference, 1936. *Recreations:* cricket, lawn tennis, and golf. *Heir:* *s* Charles Duncan Macnair [*b* 12 Sept. 1906; *m* 1941, Gwendolen Olive Mary Gladstone, *y d* of James Martin, Bedfont, Middlesex. Dulwich College; Cambridge University (MA)]. *Address:* Ambleside, 52 Westmoreland Road, Bromley, Kent. *TA:* E. T. Campbell, Bromley, Kent. *T:* Ravensbourne 1776. *Clubs:* Carlton, MCC, I Zingari.

Died 17 July 1945.

CAMPBELL, Gen. Sir Frederick, KCB 1916; DSO 1898; DL; *b* 25 Feb. 1860; *s* of late Capt. L. G. A. Campbell of Fairfield, Ayrshire; *m* 1886, Eleanor Martha, *d* of late J. Cannon; one *d*. *Educ:* Wellington Coll.; RMC Sandhurst. Lieut Royal Ayr and Wigtown Militia, 1877–78; served with HM 40th Foot, 1879–82; QO Corps of Guides, 1882–99; DAAG Musketry 1891–95; comdt 40th Pathans, 1899–1906; AAG Musketry, Army Headquarters, India, 1906–08; commanded a Brigade, 1908–15, and 1st (Peshawar) Division, 1915–19; Hazara Expedition, 1888, Assistant Superintendent Signalling, 3rd Column (medal with clasp); Relief of Chitral, 1895, action of Malakand Pass (despatches, brevet of Major, medal with clasp); North-West Frontier, India, 1897–98, Malakand; operations in Bajaur and the Mamund Country, Utmankheyl (despatches twice); Buner (despatches, DSO, clasp); Tibet, 1903–04, operations at and around Gyantse (wounded); march to Lhassa (medal with clasp, despatches, Brevet Colonel); Colonel 40th Pathans, 1911; European War, 1914–18 (despatches, 1914–15 Star, British War Medal, Victory Medal, KCB;

promoted Lieut-General); General, 1919; retired, 1920; good service pension, 1922; DL Co. Argyll. *Address:* Bothan an Rudha, Ardrishaig, Argyll.

Died 29 Aug. 1943.

CAMPBELL, Vice-Adm. George William McOran, CMG 1920; RN, retired; *b* 1877; *s* of William McOran Campbell, Tullichewan Castle, Alexandria, Dumbartonshire; *m* 1905, Maud Cicely, *d* of late H. Pasley Higginson, MICE, Wellington, NZ; two *s*. Served S Africa; European War, 1914–19 (despatches, promoted); 1st Destroyer Flotilla in Baltic, 1919 (despatches, CMG); Assistant Director of Mobilisation, Admiralty, 1922–24; Naval ADC to the King, 1927–28. *Address:* Monkswell, Sampford Spiney, Horabridge, Devon. *T:* Yelverton 78. *Club:* Naval and Military.

Died 23 Feb. 1948.

CAMPBELL, James Argyll, MD; Research Staff, National Institute for Medical Research, since 1921; *b* Brisbane, 30 March 1884; *s* of late James Colin Campbell, MD, Bute and Brisbane; *m* 1914, A. B., *d* of late T. S. Cowell, London and Brisbane; one *s* three *d*. *Educ:* Brisbane Grammar School; Edinburgh University (nine university medals, Aitken Carlyle Bursar); Vans Dunlop scholar, 1905, and again 1908; Carnegie scholar, 1911; Crichton scholar, 1912; MB, ChB, with Honours, 1909; MD (Thesis highly commended), 1912; DSc (Physiology), Edin. in absentia, 1914. Assist to Professor Schafer, University of Edinburgh, 1911–13; Professor of Physiology, Government School of Medicine, Singapore, 1913–21; Medical Adviser to a Commission on a Malay State, 1918; member Medical Advisory Committee, Food Control, Singapore, 1919. *Publications:* Readable Physiology and Hygiene, 1927; papers on Physiological, Pathological and Medical Subjects; (with Leonard Hill, FRS) Health and Environment, 1925; (with E. P. Poulton) Oxygen and Carbon Dioxide Therapy, 1934. *Recreations:* tennis, golf, fishing; cricket blue, Edin.; interstate cricket, Malaya. *Address:* National Institute for Medical Research, Hampstead, NW.

Died 20 April 1944.

CAMPBELL, Maj.-Gen. John, CB 1918; CMG 1915; DSO 1900; Queen's Own Cameron Highlanders; *b* 7 March 1871; *m* 1902, Amy Leighton, 3rd *d* of Rev. Canon Hopkins. Entered Army, 1892; Captain, 1898; Brevet Major, 1898; Major, 1905; Bt Lt-Col 1914; Brigade Commander, 1915; Lt-Col 1916; Bt Col 1917; temp. Major-General, 1918; served Soudan, 1898, including Atbara and Khartoum (despatches twice, Brevet Major, British medal, Khedive's medal 2 clasps); South Africa, 1900 and 1901 (despatches, medal 5 clasps, DSO); European War, 1914–18 (despatches seven times, CMG, Order of St Stanislas, 3rd Class with Swords, 1915; Bt Col, CB); Colonel, 1919; Commander Belgian Ordre de la Couronne with Croix de Guerre, 1919; Commander Légion d'Honneur, 1919; retired Hon. Maj.-Gen. Jan. 1921. *Address:* Harlyn, Waldron, Sussex.

Died 5 April 1941.

CAMPBELL, Sir John, KCMG 1933; Kt 1925; CSI 1923; OBE 1918; ICS (retired); Chairman of International Tin Committee; *b* 2 Sept. 1874; *s* of John Campbell, of Carcaston, Hamilton, Scotland; *m* 1906, Helen Margaret, *d* of Rev. A. Brooke-Webb, Rector of Dallinghoo, Suffolk; one *s* one *d*. *Educ:* Glasgow University; Christ Church, Oxford. Entered Indian Civil Service, 1897; Under-Secretary to the Government of the United Provinces; Under-Secretary to the Government of India; Chairman of the Cawnpore Municipality; Deputy Commissioner of Kheri; Director of Civil Supplies for the United Provinces; retired, 1922; thereafter Financial Officer of the University of London; Vice-Chairman of the Greek Refugee Settlement Commission, 1923–27, and temporarily 1929; Economic and Financial Adviser to the Colonial Office, 1930–42; Knight Commander of the Order of the Redeemer,

Greece; Grand Cross of the Order of the Phœnix, Greece. *Address:* Holmbury, 33 Aldenham Avenue, Radlett, Herts. *T:* Radlett 6345.

Died 3 Dec. 1944.

CAMPBELL, Lt Col Sir John Bruce Stuart, DSO 1917; of Ardnamurchan, 2nd Bt UK, 1913, with precedence from 1804; Mine owner, Perlis; *b* 3 Jan. 1877; *e s* of 1st Bt and Catherine, *o d* of W. W. Cavie, Harwood House, Plymouth; *S* father, 1915; *m* 1902, Jessie Nicholson, 3rd *d* of John Miller of Parkside, S Australia; one *s* three *d*. Served S Africa (wounded, medal seven clasps); European War, 1914–18, Commanded 11th Batt., Royal Scots, 1916–18 (wounded, DSO and bar). *Heir: s* Bruce Colin Patrick, *b* 2 July 1904. *Address:* Kangar, Perlis.

Died 14 Oct. 1943.

CAMPBELL, John Dermot; DL (Belfast); MP (U) Co. Antrim since 1943; Deputy Flax Controller for Northern Ireland since 1940; *b* 20 Jan. 1898; *s* of R. Garrett Campbell, CBE; *m* 1930, Josephine Patricia, *d* of late Sir Joseph McConnell, 2nd Bart, DL, MP; two *s* one *d*. *Educ:* Lockers Park; Wellington College; RMA Woolwich. Lieut Royal Artillery, Palestine, 1918–19; Managing Director, Henry Campbell & Co. Ltd, Flax Spinners and Linen Thread Manufacturers, 1919–40. *Recreations:* gardening, fishing, walking, ski-ing. *Address:* 59 Somerton Road, Belfast. *T:* Belfast 46803. *Clubs:* Carlton, Constitutional; Ulster, Belfast.

Died Jan. 1945.

CAMPBELL, Lt-Col John Hay, CBE 1919; DSO 1900; late RAMC; *b* Edinburgh, 31 Dec. 1871; *s* of late Maj.-Gen. Thomas Hay Campbell, RA; *m* 1895, Clara Edith (*d* 1933), *d* of late James Hedley, Richmond, Yorks. *Educ:* Linton House School; St Mary's Hospital, London. Matriculated at London University, 1888; became MRCS (Eng.), LRCP (London), 1894. Gazetted to Army Medical Staff, 1895; Captain RAMC 1898; served in Boer War, with 3rd King's Royal Rifle Corps, from Dec. 1899 to Oct. 1900 (severely wounded, Queen's medal three clasps, DSO); Major, 1907. Decorated for meritorious service whilst in medical charge of 3rd King's Royal Rifles. *Address:* c/o Glyn, Mills, Currie, Holt & Co., Kirkland House, Whitehall, SW1.

Died 29 Aug. 1946.

CAMPBELL, Brig.-Gen. John Vaughan, VC 1916; CMG 1918; DSO 1900; member of Hon. Corps of Gentlemen-at-Arms since 1934; *b* 31 Oct. 1876; *s* of late Captain Hon. Ronald Campbell, Coldstream Guards; *m* 1st, 1904, Amy Dorothy (*d* 1927), *d* of late John Penn, MP; one *d*; 2nd, 1937, Margaret Emily Robina, *yr d* of Dr A. Tennyson Smith, Rodborough Grange, Bournemouth. Entered Army, 1896; Adjutant, 1900; Captain, 1903; Major, 1913; Brevet Lieut-Col 1916; Temp. Brig.-General, 1916; Bt Colonel, 1919; Colonel, 1920; served South Africa, 1899–1902 (despatches, Queen's medal six clasps, King's medal two clasps, DSO); European War, 1914–18 (CMG, despatches); commanded Coldstream Guards, 1923–27; ADC to the King, 1919–33; retired pay, 1933. *Address:* Benwell House, Woodchester, Stroud, Glos. *T:* Nailsworth 137. *Club:* Guards.

Died 22 May 1944.

CAMPBELL, Kenneth, OBE; *s* of late Hugh Campbell of Wimpole Street, W, and Eweland Hall, Margaretting; *m* Rosamond, (*d* 1936), *d* of late Col G. Gribbon, AMS, and *g d* of late Sir Hugh Allan of Montreal. *Educ:* Edinburgh; London; Dublin; and Paris. MB University of Edinburgh and FRCS England. Consulting Surgeon to the Western Ophthalmic Hospital and late Ophthalmic surgeon to the Southern Command; served as Lieut, Captain, and Major during European War. *Publication:* Refraction of the Eye. *Address:* Wittersham, Isle of Oxney, Kent.

Died 10 March 1943.

CAMPBELL, Brig.-Gen. Leslie Warner Yule, CMG 1916; *b* 24 Aug. 1867; *s* of Maj.-Gen. A. H. E. Campbell (retired Indian Army); *m* 1st, 1890, F. M. (*d* 1911), *d* of Colonel W. N. Wroughton, IA; two *s* two *d*; 2nd, 1928, *widow* of W. M. Upton; one *s*. *Educ:* Boulogne-sur-Mer; Cheltenham College. Entered KOS Borderers, 1886; Indian Army, 1888; Captain Indian Army, 1897; Major, 1904; Lt-Col 1912; DAAG for Musketry, India, 1902–04; Brigade Major, 1904–07; served Tirah, NW Frontier, 1897–98 (wounded); European War, 1914–18; Commandant 89th Punjabis at taking of Shaik Syed, 1914; Attack on Suez Canal (Kantara), Gallipoli (Helles), France, 1915; Commanded 9th Infantry Brigade in France (Battle of Loos), 1915; Mesopotamia, 1916–18 (battles for Relief of Kut); wounded, taking of Baghdad; action at Jebel Hamrin (wounded, despatches three times, Bt-Col, CMG, Serbian Order of White Eagle with Swords); Brigade Commander in India, 3rd Afghan War, 1919 (despatches); retired, 1921; Hon. Colonel 1/8th Punjab Regt; Jubilee and Coronation medals. *Recreations:* gardening, motoring. *Address:* Badshot House, Farnham, Surrey.

Died 26 July 1946.

CAMPBELL, Lloyd; MP (U) North Belfast, Parliament of Northern Ireland, 1921–29. Formerly Managing Director, Henry Campbell & Co., flax spinners, Mossley, Co. Antrim. *Address:* Glen House, White Abbey, Co. Antrim, Ulster.

Died 20 Feb. 1950.

CAMPBELL, Major Sir Malcolm, Kt 1931; MBE; Member of Lloyds; Director Zürich Insurance Co. Ltd; late Infantry, TA; *b* 11 March 1885; *s* of William Campbell, Chislehurst; *m* 1st, Dorothy (from whom he obtained a divorce, 1940), *d* of Maj. William Whittall; one *s* one *d*; 2nd, 1945, Mrs Betty Nicory *d* of Sir John Humphrey. *Educ:* Uppingham; Germany 18 months; France 1 year. Commenced career as a broker and underwriter; became Member of Lloyds, 1906; joined HM Forces at outbreak of war; Demobilised, 1919; First served in Royal West Kent Regt and transferred to RFC as a pilot, 1916. Joined HM Forces again, April 1939, demobilised Oct. 1945; started flying, 1909; commenced motor racing as a hobby, 1910, although participated in motor cycle racing events first in 1906; first man in the world to reach 300 mph on land; holder of World's Water Speed Record. Has travelled extensively. *Publications:* A Boy's Life of Sir Henry Segrave (with J. Wentworth Day); My Greatest Adventure; Speed, 1931; Salute to the Gods, 1934; My Thirty Years of Speed, 1935; The Romance of Motor-Racing, 1936; Peril from the Air, 1936; The Roads and the Problem of their Safety, 1937; Drifting to War, 1937. *Recreations:* motor racing, fishing, riding, yachting, also dog breeding: Alsatians and Airedale terriers. *Address:* Little Gatton, Reigate, Surrey. *Clubs:* Royal Thames Yacht, White's, Royal Automobile.

Died 31 Dec. 1948.

CAMPBELL, Col Rev. Malcolm Sydenham Clarke, CB 1919; CIE 1907; Albert Medal, 1912; *b* 2 Nov. 1863; *s* of Major-General A. H. E. Campbell, late Madras Cavalry, and *g g s* of William Campbell of Fairfield, Ayrshire; *m* 1889, Jessie (*d* 1933), 3rd *d* of late Rev. John Hay, Edinburgh. *Educ:* Cheltenham College. Commissioned in Royal Artillery, 1883; served Burma, 1885–87 (medal with clasp); China, 1900 (despatches, medal with clasp); Deacon, 1919; Priest, 1920; Vicar of Ivybridge, 1922–46; retired from Holy Orders, 1946. *Address:* Hamtun, Crowthorne, Berks.

Died 22 July 1949.

CAMPBELL, Sir Nigel Leslie, Kt 1937; Director: Helbert Wagg and Co. Ltd; District Bank; Glaxo Laboratories Ltd, Stewarts and Lloyds, Ltd (Deputy Chairman); 2nd *s* of late John Campbell of Stonefield and Adela Harriet, *d* of Lord Charles Pelham Clinton; *m* 1905, Harriette, *d* of Judge Leslie Russell, New York;

three *d*. *Educ:* Eton. Royal Canadian Humane Association and United States Medal of Honour for saving life at sea; partner in Wm A. Read and Co., New York, 1913–19; High Sheriff of Bucks, 1937; Joint MFH Old Berkeley Hunt, 1925–29; Chairman: National Benevolent Society for the Deaf; Trustees of Nuffield Trust for Special Areas; Development Areas Treasury Advisory Cttee. *Recreations:* hunting, shooting. *Address:* Fordcombe Manor, Tunbridge Wells. *Clubs:* Junior Carlton, Lansdowne.

Died 4 March 1948.

CAMPBELL, Norman Robert, ScD; *b* 1880; 3rd *s* of William Middleton Campbell of Colgrain, Dumbartonshire; *m* 1912, Edith (*d* 1948), *e d* of Rev. J. C. Sowerbutts. *Educ:* Eton (KS); Trinity College, Cambridge (Scholar); Fellow, 1904. Hon. Fellow of Leeds University, 1913, On Research Staff of General Electric Co. Ltd, 1919–44. *Publications:* Modern Electrical Theory, 1906, 1913, etc.; Principles of Electricity, 1912; Physics, 1920; What is Science? 1921; Measurement, 1928; Photoelectric Cells (with Dorothy Ritchie), 1929, 1934; numerous scientific papers. *Address:* Bilborough Rectory, Aspley, Nottingham.

Died 18 May 1949.

CAMPBELL, Lt-Col Norman St Clair, CMG 1918; DSO 1916; late RA; *b* 1877; *m* Betty (*d* 1928). Served European War, 1914–18 (despatches, DSO, CMG, Order of St Stanislas of Russia, Bt Lt-Col).

Died 30 June 1949.

CAMPBELL, Lt-Col Hon. Ralph Alexander, CBE; retired pay; *b* 18 Feb. 1877; 3rd *s* of 3rd Earl Cawdor; *m* 1st, Marjorie (*d* 1911), *d* of Sir Arthur Fowler, Bart; one *d*; 2nd, Marjorie, *d* of H. G. Devas; two *s* one *d*. *Educ:* Eton. Fifteen years in the Cameron Highlanders, retiring, 1914; employed in the War Office as DAAG 1914–19 (Bt Lt-Col, CBE); served Soudan, 1908, including Battle of Omdurman and occupation of Khartoum; South Africa, attached Seaforth Highlanders and present at battle of Maagersfontein; ADC to Gen. Sir H. Colville, with MI (Bt Major). *Recreation:* shooting. *Address:* The Manor House, Padworth, Reading.

Died 1 Aug. 1945.

CAMPBELL, Brig. Robert Morris, CBE 1919; late RASC; *b* 3 July 1883; *s* of late Rev. Edward F. Campbell, Sheskburn, Ballycastle; *m* 1907, Louise, *d* of Alexander John Henry, Rathescar, Dunleer. Entered Army from TCD and 4th Bn Royal Inniskilling Fusiliers (Militia), 1903; Capt. 1912; Major, 1914; Bt Lt-Col 1918; Lt-Col 1929; Col 1933; served European War, 1914–19 (despatches thrice, Bt Lt-Col, CBE Order of Crown of Italy); Assistant Director of Supplies and Transport, War Office, 1933–37; retired pay, 1937; in War of 1939–45 DDST Eastern Command, 1939–42. *Address:* Cairn Dhu, Park Road, Sunbury-on-Thames.

Died 9 June 1949.

CAMPBELL, Sir Rollo Frederick G.; *see* Graham-Campbell.

CAMPBELL, Major Roy Neil Boyd, DSO 1921; OBE 1919; Indian Army, retired; *b* Barrackpore, Bengal, India, 24 Sept. 1884; *e s* of late J. Roy Campbell and Harriet, 2nd *d* of late J. P. Boyd, Rose Hill, Buenos Ayres and London; *m* 1911, Effie Muriel, *y d* of late Major Charles Pierce, Indian Medical Service; one *s* one *d*. *Educ:* Bedford School; Norwich School; RMC, Sandhurst. First Commission in Queen's Royal West Surrey Regiment, 1903; Posted to 23rd Sikh Pioneers Indian Army, 1905; served Indian Frontier, Zakka Khel Expedition, 1908 (medal and clasp); European War in EEF and Palestine, 1916–19 (GS and Victory medals, despatches thrice, OBE); with 3/23rd Sikh Infantry in Mesopotamia Rebellion, 1920 (DSO, medal and clasp, despatches); retired from Indian Army and became Assistant Master Mount House School, Plymouth, 1925; Headmaster, Mount House School, 1927–37; re-employed in Pioneer Corps, Sept. 1939 (including BEF France Lines of Communication, 1939–40); relegated on account of age, 1943 (1939–45 Star, Defence Medal, War Medal); Admin. Officer, Home Guard, 1943–45. Church of England. *Address:* 2 Sowden Close, Lympstone, Devon. *Club:* Junior United Service.

Died 9 May 1950.

CAMPBELL, Thomas Joseph; KC 1918; MP (Nat.) Central Belfast, Northern Ireland, since 1934; Bencher of the King's Inns, Dublin, 1924, and of the Inn of Court of Northern Ireland, 1938; Father of the Circuit of Northern Ireland, 1943; *b* Belfast; 2nd *s* of Joseph and Sarah Campbell; *m* 1918, Nora, *d* of Michael Gilfedder, JP, and Hanna Gilfedder, Belfast; four *s* one *d. Educ:* Christian Brothers School and St Malachy's College, Belfast. Editor, Irish News, Belfast, 1895–1906; Chairman, Ulster District Institute of Journalists, 1899; MA (Hons) of the Royal University of Ireland, 1897; Gold Medal for Oratory, Gold Medal for Legal Essay, Silver Medal for Legal Debate, 1900–01; called to Irish Bar, 1900; English Bar, 1904; Revising Barrister, 1910–14; Local Government Election Commissioner, 1921; Irish Parliamentary Party candidate for South Monaghan, 1918; Nationalist Candidate for East Belfast in the election of 1921 in Northern Ireland; First Treasurer of the Bar of Northern Ireland and First Secretary of the Circuit of Northern Ireland, 1922; First Nationalist Senator who signed the Roll in the Senate of Northern Ireland, June 1929; resigned Senatorship, 1934; contested (Nationalist) West Belfast, UK, General Election, 1931; author of Wild Birds Protection Act (Northern Ireland), 1931; Slaughter of Animals Act (Northern Ireland), 1932; and Dogs Protection Act (Northern Ireland), 1934; awarded RSPCA Silver Medal, 1934. *Publications:* Workmen's Compensation; Fifty Years of Ulster: 1890–1940. *Recreation:* walking. *Address:* 27 Old Cavehill Road, Belfast.

Died 3 May 1946.

CAMPBELL, Sir William Andrewes Ava, 5th Bt *cr* 1831; late Capt. Fife and Forfar Yeomanry; *b* 11 Dec. 1880; *s* of 3rd Bt and Henrietta Ellen, *d* of Rev. E. H. Uthwatt; *S* brother, 1916. Served South Africa; European War, 1915–18 (MC). *Heir:* none. *Address:* Malika, PO Sepani, S Africa.

Died 4 Oct. 1949 (ext).

CAMPINCHI, César; Avocat à la Cour de Paris; Député de la Corse, 1932–40; *b* Calcatoggio, Corse, 4 Mai 1882; *m* 1925, Helène Landry. *Educ:* Paris, Lycée Condorcet. Ancien Membre du Conseil de l'Ordre des Avocats de Paris; Ministre de la Marine, 4 fois; Ministre de la Justice, 1 fois. *Recreations:* boxe, escrime.

Died 23 Feb. 1941.

CAMPION, George Goring, LDS Eng.; Hon. MSc Manchester; Consulting Dental Surgeon, Dental Hospital of Manchester; *b* 27 Nov. 1862; *s* of Henry Campion, Manchester; *m* Evelyn Harriet, *d* of Rev. J. Coombes, Stockport; two *s. Educ:* Birkenhead School; St Bartholomew's Hospital. President Odontological Section Royal Society of Medicine, 1918; Pres. British Society for Study of Orthodontics, 1922; President British Dental Association, 1923. *Publications:* various professional papers; (with Sir Arthur Keith) A Contribution to the Mechanism of Growth of the Human Face, 1922; Elements in Thought and Emotion, 1923; The Neural Substrata of Reflective Thought, 1925; The Organic Growth of the Concept as one of the Factors in Intelligence, 1928; Meaning and Error, 1929; The Thalamo-Cortical Circulation of Neural Impulse, 1929; (with Dr Matthew Young) The relative positions of the Cartilagenous and Osseous Transmeatal axes in the Human Head, 1931; The Thalamo-Cortical Circulation of Neural Impulse and the Psycho-Neuroses, 1932; (with the late Sir Grafton Elliot Smith) The Neural Basis of Thought, 1934; Mental Connectedness and Neurology, 1943; Memorandum on Correspondence with the late

Sir Grafton Elliot Smith, 1944. *Recreations:* golf, sailing, and epistemology. *Address:* Inglegarth, Bramhall, Cheshire. *T:* Bramhall 765. *Clubs:* Old Rectory, Manchester.

Died 23 June 1946.

CAMPION, Rev. Canon Herbert Roper, MA; Hon. Canon since 1924 of Ely Cathedral; Minor Canon, 1896–1926; late Hon. Secretary, Ely Diocesan Board of Missions; *b* 17 May 1868; 4th *s* of Henry Campion, MRCS, 264 Oxford Road, Manchester; *m* Mildred Agnes, *y d* of late Rt Rev. Bishop W. K. Macrorie, DD, Bishop of Maritzburg. *Educ:* Charterhouse; Keble College, Oxford; Cuddesdon Theological College. Assistant Curate, Cheadle, Cheshire, 1891–96. *Recreations:* photography, gardening. *Address:* Inver Lodge, Avenue Road, Banstead, Surrey.

Died 19 July 1941.

CANAWAY, Arthur Pitcairn; KC 1911; *b* Hobart, 1857; *s* of Phillip Canaway. *Educ:* Oxford University (BA). Called to New South Wales Bar, 1885. *Publications:* The Misfit Constitution, 1919; Facets of Federalism, 1921; The Failure of Federalism in Australia, 1930; various legal works. *Address:* Denman Chambers, Phillip Street, Sydney, NSW. *Club:* Australian (Sydney).

Died 2 Feb. 1949.

CANHAM, Ven. Thomas Henry, DD; CMS. *Educ:* CM College, Islington. Ordained 1880; Curate of Camerton, Cumberland, winter of 1880–81; Missionary Portage le Prairie, 1881–82; Peel River, 1882–87; Lower Yukon River, 1888–92; Rector, St Andrew's, Fort Selkirk, 1892–1910; Missionary, St Saviour's, Carcross, 1910–22; Secretary, Tukudh Mission, 1888–91; Diocese of Selkirk, 1891–1906; Archdeacon of Yukon, 1892–1924. *Address:* 68 Ravina Crescent, Toronto, E, Canada.

Died 22 Oct. 1947.

CANN, His Honour Sir William Moore, Kt 1929; *b* 6 July 1856; 2nd *s* of Abraham Cann of Nottingham, Solicitor; *m* 1901, Mary Katherine (*d* 1944), *d* of John Burgess, Saddington Hall, Leicestershire; one *s* two *d. Educ:* Nottingham Grammar School; Shrewsbury School; Clare College, Cambridge. Millington Scholarship, Shrewsbury School, 1876; Open Classical Scholarship, Clare College, 1876; Foundation Scholarship, Clare College, 1877; graduated BA Classical Tripos, 1880. Called to Bar, Inner Temple, 1883; Judge of County Courts, Leicester Circuit, 1914–21, Sussex Circuit 1921–31; retired 1931. *Address:* 78 Clarence Road, St Albans, Herts. *T:* St Albans 1720.

Died 18 April 1947.

CANNEY, Maurice Arthur, MA (Oxford and Manchester); Emeritus Professor of Semitic Languages and Literatures, University of Manchester; Member of the Royal Asiatic Society; *b* London, 18 March 1872; *e s* of late Rev. Edward Canney, Rector of St Peter's, Saffron Hill; *m* 1915, Gladys Kittie (*d* 1940), *e d* of R. F. Myddleton, Colne Mead, Rickmansworth. *Educ:* Merchant Taylors' School, London; Oxford University. Junior and Senior Fish Exhibitioner for Hebrew at St John's College, Oxford, 1891–96; Pusey and Ellerton Hebrew Scholar, 1892; 2nd class Honours in Theology, 1894; Junior Kennicott Hebrew Scholar, 1895. Called to Bar, 1908; dramatic critic on Star, 1909–10. *Publications:* Peter Homunculus, 1909; John Christopher (translation), 1910; John Christopher, vols ii and iii, Devious Ways, 1911; Little Brother, 1912; Round the Corner, John Christopher, vol. iv; Four Plays, The Joy of the Theatre, The Yoke of Pity, (translation), 1913; Old Mole, 1914; Young Ernest, Samuel Butler, Windmills (Poems), 1915; Three Pretty Men, Mendel, 1916; Everybody's Husband, 1917; Mummery, 1918; The Stucco House, 1918; The Anatomy of Society, 1919; Pink Roses, 1919; Time and Eternity, 1920; Pugs and Peacocks, 1921; Sembal, 1922; Old Maid's Love,

1922; Annette and Bennett, 1922; Noel, 1922; Seven Plays, 1923; Letters from a Distance, 1923; The House of Prophecy, 1924; A. O. Barnabooth: His Diary (translation), 1924. *Plays:* Miles Dixon, 1910; James and John, 1911; Mary's Wedding, 1912; Wedding Presents, 1912; The Perfect Widow, 1912; The Arbour of Refuge, 1913; The Release of the Soul, 1920. *Recreations:* travelling and journalism. *Address:* c/o A. M. Heath & Co., Ltd, 188 Piccadilly, W1.

Died 16 May 1942.

CANNON, Annie Jump, Astronomer BS Wellesley, 1884; MA 1907; LLD 1925; DSc University of Delaware, 1918; Oxford, 1925; Oglethorpe University, 1935; Mt Holyoke College, 1937; Doctor Astronomy, Groningen University, 1921; Fellow AAAS; Hon. Member R Astronomical Society, 1914; Member of American Philosophical Society, of Wellesley Chapter Phi Beta Kappa and Harvard Chapter of Sigma Xi; Recipient of the Draper Gold Medal for Discoveries in Astronomical Physics from the National Academy of Sciences, 1931; and of the Ellen Richards Research Prize, 1932; Curator of Astronomical Photographs at Harvard College Observatory since 1911; William Cranch Bond Astronomer, 1938; *b* Dover, Delaware, 11 Dec. 1863; *d* of Wilson Lee Cannon and Mary Elizabeth Jump. *Educ:* Wilmington Conference Academy, Dover, Delaware, 1877–80; Wellesley College, Wellesley, Mass, 1880–84; Astronomy Courses at Radcliffe College, Cambridge, Mass, 1895–96. Assistant Harvard College Observatory, 1897–1911. *Publications and work done:* Bibliography of variable stars comprising 500,000 cards; a Catalogue of stellar spectra of which 430,000 have been classified; made regular visual observations of variable stars; discovered 300 variable stars and 5 new stars, and various stars having peculiar spectra. Spectra of 1122 Bright Southern Stars, Second Catalogue of Variable Stars, Maxima and Minima of Variable Stars of Long Period, The Spectrum of Nova Persei, The Spectra of 1477 Stars, The Spectra of 1688 Southern Stars, Spectra of 745 Double Stars, Comparison of Objective Prism and Slit Spectrograms, Spectra having Bright Lines, The Henry Draper Catalogue, and the Extension, all in Harvard Annals. *Recreations:* music, photography. *Address:* Harvard Observatory, Cambridge, Massachusetts. *Clubs:* College, Boston.

Died April 1941.

CANNON, James, DD; *b* Salisbury, Md, 13 Nov. 1864; *s* of James Cannon and Lydia Robertson Primrose; *m* 1st, 1888, Lura Virginia Bennett (*d* 1928); five *s* two *d*; 2nd, Helen Hawley McCallum. *Educ:* Randolph-Macon College; Princeton University; Princeton Theological Seminary. Entered Ministry, 1888; Principal Blackstone Female Institute, 1894–1911; General Superintendent, Southern Assembly, Waynesville, NC, 1911–19; Editor Baltimore and Richmond Christian Advocate and President Advocate Publishing Co., 1904–19; Superintendent Anti-Saloon League of Virginia, 1907–19; Independent Democrat; Chairman Legislative Committee Anti-Saloon League of America since 1913; Member Executive Committee Anti-Saloon League of America since 1902, Chairman Administrative Committee since 1937; Chairman Executive Committee World League against Alcoholism; President Blackstone College for Girls, 1914–18; Chairman Board of Temperance and Social Service of Methodist Episcopal Church South 1918–34; Bishop, in charge of Mission Work, Methodist Episcopal Church South, 1918–34, in Mexico, Belgian-Congo, Cuba, and Brazil; Chairman Near East Advisory Committee, 1922–30; Trustee, Church Peace Union since 1924; Chairman Anti-Smith Democrats Campaign, 1928; Delegate to World Conference on Life and Work, Oxford, 1937, to World Conference on Faith and Order, Edinburgh, 1937, to World Peace Conference, Geneva, 1937. *Address:* 131 B Street, SE, Washington, DC, USA.

Died 6 Sept. 1944.

CANNON, Hon. Lucien, PC; KC 1920; LLD Laval University, 1928; Puisne Judge of Superior Court of Quebec since 1936; *b* Arthabaska, Quebec, 16 Jan. 1887; *s* of Lawrence John Cannon, Judge of the Superior Court of the Province of Quebec, and Aurelie Dumoulin; *m* Edith Pacaud; three *s. Educ:* Quebec Seminary; Laval University. Member of the law firm of Cannon & Cannon, Quebec; Senior Crown Prosecutor for the district of Quebec, 1920; Solicitor-Gen. of Canada, 1925–26 and 1926–30; candidate for the House of Commons in the County of Charlevoix, 1911; elected to Quebec Legislative Assembly for the County of Dorchester, 1913, 1916, and to the House of Commons of Canada, 1917, 1921, 1925, 1926, and 1935. *Address:* 135 Grande Allee, Quebec, PQ, Canada; East Block, Ottawa. *T:* East Block—Queen 6400 Loc. 491; 135 Grande Allée, Quebec—2—5378. *Clubs:* Garrison, Reform (Quebec); Reform (Montreal).

Died 14 Feb. 1950.

CANNON, Walter Bradford, AM, MD, SD, LLD; George Higginson Professor of Physiology, Medical School, Harvard University, 1906, Emeritus, 1942; Visiting Professor of Physiology, Peiping Union Medical College, China, 1935; Hitchcock Professor, California, 1941; *b* 19 Oct. 1871; *s* of Colbert Hanchett Cannon and Wilma Denio; *m* 1901, Cornelia James, St Paul, Minn; one *s* four *d. Educ:* Public Schools (Milwaukee and St Paul); Harvard Coll.; Harvard Medical School. AB 1896; AM 1897; MD 1900 (Harvard); SD (Hon.), Yale, 1923, Harvard, 1937; LLD (Hon.), Wittenberg, 1927, Boston University, 1929, Washington, 1940; Doctor, honoris causa, University of Liège and University of Strasbourg, 1930, Paris, 1931, and Madrid, 1938. Instructor in Zoology, Harvard University, 1899–1900; in Physiology, 1900–02; Assistant Professor, 1902–06; Croonian Lecturer, Royal Society, London, 1918; Harvard Exchange Professor to France, 1929–30; Linacre Lecturer, Cambridge University, 1930; Baly Medallist, Royal College of Physicians, London, 1931; Medallist, National Institute of Social Sciences, 1934, and American Gastro-enterological Society, 1941; Fellow, American Assoc. for the Advancement of Science (President, 1939), American Academy of Arts and Sciences (Vice-President, 1931–40); hon. member many European and South American scientific and medical societies; in British medical military service, May–Nov. 1917; in American service, 1917–19; Lt-Col 1918; CB 1919; Distinguished Service Medal, United States. *Publications:* A Laboratory Course in Physiology, 9th edition, 1936; The Mechanical Factors of Digestion, 1911; Bodily Changes in Pain Hunger, Fear, and Rage, second edition, 1929; Traumatic Shock, 1923; The Wisdom of the Body, 1932, 2nd ed., 1939; Digestion and Health, 1936; Autonomic Neuro-Effector Systems (with A. Rosenblueth), 1937. *Recreations:* gardening, tramping in New Hampshire Hills, modelling in clay. *Address:* Harvard Medical School, Boston, Mass, USA. *Clubs:* Faculty, Cambridge.

Died 2 Oct. 1945.

CANNOT, Brig.-Gen. Fernand Gustave Eugene, CB 1919; CMG 1915, DSO 1918; *b* 1 Feb. 1873; *m* 1897, Mildred Grace (*d* 1934), *d* of late W. Barker, JP; no *c. Educ:* Jesuits College, Canterbury; King's College. Entered army (South Staffs Regiment), 1892; ASC 1895; Captain, 1900; Major, 1907; Lt-Col 1914; DADS and T Aldershot Command, 1913; Chief Instructor, ASC Training, Establishment, 1914; served S African War, 1899–1900 (Queen's medal 3 clasps); European War, 1914–18 (CB, CMG, DSO); retired, 1919; Is an Hon. Associate of St John of Jerusalem, Commander Order of the Redeemer (Greece); Officier Legion of Honour (France); Officier Instruction Publique (France); Officier Order of Leopold (Belgium), Officier St Maurice and St Lazarus (Italy); Officier of Military Merit (Spain); holds

Belgian Croix de Guerre. *Address:* 32 Davies Street, W1; Friar's Walk, Farnborough, Hants. *Clubs:* Savage, Junior Athenæum.

Died 14 April 1941.

CANNY, Col James Clare Macnamara, CBE 1919; DSO 1900; late R Army Service Corps; *b* 6 Dec. 1877; *s* of late John Macnamara Canny; *m*; one *d*. *Educ:* Uppingham; Hertford College, Oxford. Entered Army, 1899; Capt., 1908; Major, 1914; Lt-Col, 1925; Col, 1929; served South Africa, 1899–1902 (despatches, Queen's medal three clasps, King's medal two clasps, DSO); European War, 1914–18 (despatches Bt Lt-Col); Waziristan, 1922–24 (despatches); Assistant Director of Supplies and Transport, Scottish Command, 1930–31, Eastern Command, 1931–34; retired pay, 1934. *Address:* The Outlook, Gong Hill, Farnham, Surrey. *Club:* Army and Navy.

Died 13 Sept. 1942.

CANTERBURY, 6th Viscount *cr* 1835; **Charles Graham Manners-Sutton;** Baron Bottesford, 1835, late Captain Submarine Miners, RE; *b* 23 Jan. 1872; *o surv. s* of late Hon. Graham Manners-Sutton, 2nd *s* of 3rd Viscount Canterbury and Charlotte Laura, *d* of Lt-Col F. L'Estrange Astley, Burgh Hall, Norfolk; *S* cousin, 1918; *m* 1903, Ethelwyn, *d* of late Charles Hindle. Served South African War, 1900–02; European War, 1914–18. DL (retired), JP, Norfolk. *Recreations:* motoring, fishing, shooting. *Heir:* none. *Address:* Lyndhurst, Hants; Bergh-Apton, Norwich.

Died 26 Feb. 1941 (ext).

CANTWELL, Most Rev. John Joseph, DD; RC Archbishop of Los Angeles since 1936; *b* Limerick, Ireland, 1 Dec. 1874; *s* of Patrick Cantwell and Ellen O'Donnell. *Educ:* Jesuit College, Limerick; Patrician Brothers, Fethard, Tipp. Studied for priesthood at St Patrick's Seminary, Thurles, Ireland. Priest, 1899; Assistant Rector, Catholic Church, Berkeley, 1899–1904; Founder of Newman Club, University of California; Secretary to Archbishop of San Francisco, 1904–14; Vicar-General, 1914–17; Bishop of Monterey and Los Angeles, 1917–22; Bishop of Los Angeles and San Diego, 1922–36; active in the foundation and organization of The Legion of Decency, for the improvement of motion pictures; Bishop Assistant to the Papal Throne, 1929; awarded the Golden Rose of Tepeyac by the Bishops of Mexico, 1930; Knight Commander of the Holy Sepulchre, 1931; received the Medal of Honor of the Republic of Lebanon, 1937. JUD, Loyola University; LLD, St Mary's College and Notre Dame University. *Publication:* Pastorals. *Address:* 100 Fremont Place, Los Angeles; Office, Petroleum Building, 714 West Olympic Boulevard, Los Angeles. *T:* Prospect 0203. *Clubs:* Jonathan, University, Newman (Los Angeles).

Died 30 Oct. 1947.

CAPABLANCA, José R.; Chess Champion of the World, 1921–27 inclusive; *b* 19 Nov. 1888; *s* of José M. Capablanca of Bayamos, Oriente, Cuba, and Matilde M. Graupera of Matauzas, Cuba; *m* 1st, 1921, Gloria Simoni Betaucourt of Camagiiey, Cuba; one *s* one *d*; 2nd, 1938, Princess Olga Chagodalf. *Educ:* Cuba; Columbia University, New York City (1910 Science Class). Has been connected with the Cuban State Dept for Foreign Affairs since 1913; made head of information service outside Cuba, of the Cuban State Dept for Foreign Affairs, Sept. 20, 1927; awarded a Gold Medal in special Session of the Havana City Council, 1911; awarded a gold King's Crown by Columbia University, 1928; Order of Carlos Manuel de Cespedes, 1934, Comendador, 1937. *Publications:* Torneo Internacional de la Habana, 1913; Cartilla de Ajedrez, 1913; Havana Championship Match, 1921; My Chess Career; Chess Fundamentals, 1921; A Primer of Chess, 1935.

Recreations: nearly all sports and general reading. *Clubs:* Union, Tennis, Habana; Hon. Member innumerable Chess Clubs throughout the world.

Died 8 March 1942.

CAPE, Thomas, MBE, JP; Miners' Agent; MP (Lab) Workington Division of Cumberland, Dec. 1918–45; *b* Cockermouth, 5 Oct. 1868; *s* of William Cape, miner; *m* 1890; Dinah, *d* of Jonathan and Eleanor G. Hodgson, three *s* three *d*. *Educ:* Gt Broughton Endowed School. Started work in the Buckhill Colliery 13 years of age; was a miner till 38; a representative of the workmen when 23 years of age; then President of Cumberland Miners' Association and Financial Secretary, and since then General Secretary; Honorary Freeman of the Borough of Workington, 1936. *Address:* Argyle House, 91 Harrington Road, Workington.

Died Nov. 1947.

CARBERY, Col Andrew Robert Dillon, CBE 1919; VD; FRCSI; late New Zealand Medical Corps; Medical Officer in charge of Treatment, Pensions Department, New Zealand; *b* 1868; *s* of Andrew T. H. Carbery, formerly Assistant Surgeon, 14th Foot. Served European War, 1914–19 (despatches, CBE); retired, 1932. *Publication:* The New Zealand Medical Services in the Great War, 1914–1918. *Address:* Stratford, NZ.

Died 28 Sept. 1948.

CARBUTT, Lt-Col Clive Lancaster, CMG 1935; JP; Director of Rhodesia Plough and Machinery Manufacturing Co., Ltd, Bulawayo, and of Pelletier Ltd, Ndola, N Rhodesia; *b* 26 March 1876; *s* of Hugh Lancaster Carbutt and Elizabeth Grace Knight; *m* 1st, 1901, Frances Gertrude (*d* 1940), *d* of A. M. Anderson, Pietermaritzburg; two *s* two *d*; 2nd, 1942, Dorothy Marion, *d* of H. G. Field. *Educ:* Pietermaritzburg Coll. Asst Native Commissioner, S Rhodesia, 1897; Native Commissioner, 1899; seconded for war service with Rhodesia Native Regiment in German East Africa with rank of Major, 1916; Lt-Col, commanding Rhod. Nat. Regt, 1917 (despatches twice, Croix de Guerre, Victory and General Service medals); Superintendent of Natives, 1921; Chief Native Commissioner and Permanent Head of Dept of Native Affairs, S Rhodesia, 1930; Secretary of Native Affairs and Director of Native Development, 1935; retired, 1936; King's Jubilee Medal, 1935. *Publication:* The Racial Problems in S Rhodesia, published in the Native Affairs Dept Annual, 1934. *Recreations:* polo and tennis. *Clubs:* Bulawayo (Bulawayo); Salisbury (Salisbury, S Rhodesia).

Died 8 April 1948.

CARDEN, Sir Herbert, Kt 1930; JP; Solicitor; *b* Brighton; *m* 1889, Caroline, *d* of John FitzHugh, Northampton; one *s* two *d*. *Educ:* Brighton Grammar School. Admitted Solicitor, 1889; Alderman, Brighton Corporation, 1903; Mayor of Brighton, 1916–18; Hon. Freeman, 1926. *Address:* 103 Marine Parade, Brighton. *T:* Brighton 4217.

Died 14 Feb. 1941.

CARDEN, Col Louis Peile, CMG 1918; late RA; *b* 1860; *s* of late Capt. Andrew Carden, JP, DL; *m* 1891, Mary Elizabeth (*d* 1933), *d* of late James MacCarthy Morrogh; one *d*. Served European War, 1914–19 (despatches, CMG). *Address:* Cedar Grange, Tupwood Road, Caterham, Surrey.

Died 19 Dec. 1942.

CARDEW, Rev. Prebendary Frederic Anstruther, OBE 1933; AKC; Chevalier de la Légion d'Honneur, 1930; Hon. Chaplain of St George's Church, Paris; Actors Church Union, Paris and British Hospital, Paris; Prebendary of St Paul's Cathedral, London, since 1931; Rural Dean for France, 1923; Founder and Director of the Cardew Theatre Girls' Hostel, Paris; President of the Paris British School; *b* Meanmear, India, 6 March 1866; *s* of Sir Frederic Cardew, KCMG, late Governor of Sierra Leone; *m* 1st, 1894, Norah Kington (*d* 1931); four s; 2nd, 1933, Margaret, e d of late Canon Stokes, Cambridge. *Educ:* Lancing; Dover College. Went to Canada, 1884; fought in North West Indian Rebellion against Louis Riel, in 91st Winnipeg Light Infantry, 1885; led a life of adventure in Mexico and Western Territories of the United States for several years; took theological degree of AKC (1st Class), London University, 1889; Deacon, 1891; Priest, 1892; Curate, St Mary Abbots Kensington, 1891–94; Rector of All Saints, Charleville, Queensland, 1895–98; Rector of All Saints, Brisbane, Queensland, 1898–1901; Rector of Sudborne with Orford, 1901–07; Rural Dean of Orford, 1904–07; Chaplain of St George's Church, Paris, 1907–34. *Address:* 41 Shrewsbury House, Cheyne Walk, SW3.

Died 12 July 1942.

CARDEW, Lt-Col George Ambrose, CMG 1918; DSO 1917; late RFA; s of late Capt. C. B. and late Hon. E. J. Cardew, East Hill, East Liss, Hants; m 1895, L. Shirley; one s one d. *Educ:* Wellington College; RMA, Woolwich. Joined RFA 1885; RHA 1890; Captain, 1895; Major, 1900; Lieut-Col 1912; served European War, 1914–18 (DSO and bar, CMG, Belgian Croix de Guerre); retired pay, 1919. *Recreations:* shooting, fishing. *Address:* 62 Kensington Mansions, SW5. *T:* Frobisher 1769. *Club:* United Service.

Died 21 Feb. 1941.

CARDEW, Col George Hereward, CBE 1919; DSO 1902; b 3 Jan. 1861; e s of Rev. George Cardew of St Minver, East Liss; m 1888, Emma Marian (d 1943), d of J. Bolster Burchell, BA; one s. *Educ:* Haileybury. Entered Army from Militia, 1882; Lieut 18th Hussars, 1882; Capt. 1886; Major ASC 1898; served South Africa, 1900–02 (despatches, Queen's medal with 4 clasps, King's medal with 2 clasps); retired, 1911; AA and QMG 1st Mounted Division, Central Force, 1914–16; Group Comdr Labour Corps for overseas duty, 13 Feb. 1917. *Address:* 16 Church Terrace, Lee, SE13.

Died 22 Jan. 1949.

CAREW-HUNT, Lt-Col Thomas Edward, DSO 1916; OBE; late Royal Berks Regt; b 27 Nov. 1874; s of late Henry Thomas Carew-Hunt; m 1st, 1898, Ethel Emily (d 1931), d of late C. Lindsay Nicholson; one d; 2nd, 1932, Mrs Gladys Mida Dale-Glossop, o c of C. W. Pantin. Joined Royal Berkshire Regt from Militia, 1897; Lieut 1900; Captain, 1904; Major, 1915; Adjutant 1st VB Royal Berkshire Regt 1904–07; Brigade Major, March 1915; GSO3, April 1916; GSO2, Aug. 1916; GSO1, April 1918; served European War, 1914–18 (despatches twice, DSO, OBE, 1914 Star, British War Medal, Victory Medal); GSO2, War Office, Sept. 1919–March 1920; District Commissioner Klagenfurt Plebiscite Commission, April 1920–Dec. 1920; Military Inter-Allied Commission of Control, Berlin, 1921; DAAG, Aug.–Dec. 1921; GSO2, 1922–23; Lt-Colonel (retired), 1924; Senior Assistant Historical Section (Military Branch) Committee of Imperial Defence, 1927–33. *Address:* 12 The Lawns, Lee Terrace, Blackheath, SE3. *Club:* United Service.

Died 15 Dec. 1950.

CAREY, Rev. Albert Darell T.; see Tupper-Carey.

CAREY, Charles William; Keeper of the Picture Gallery and Head of the Art Department at the Royal Holloway College since its foundation in 1887; b London, 21 Aug. 1862; o surv. s of late Francis Carey; m 1886, Clara Dursley, of Bristol; two s one d. *Educ:* private; St Mark's College, Chelsea. Studied art at South Kensington, Heatherley's School of Art, British Museum, St John's Wood Art Schools, and Cola Rossi's Studio in Paris; gained studentship in the Royal Academy, 1881. Restored the whole collection of pictures belonging to Christ's Hospital (Blue Coat School) on its removal to Horsham (this included the 'Charter' picture, 30 ft long, and the great picture by Antonio Verrio, 90 ft long);

established the identity of J. M. W. Turner's four 'Van Tromp' pictures; discovered Turner Relic; Medal gained by J. M. W. Turner in 1793, Connoisseur, Feb. 1923. *Address:* Dursleigh, Egham. *TA:* Egham.

Died 20 May 1943.

CAREY, Maj.-Gen. George Glas Sandeman, CB 1916; CMG 1918; RA; retired; b 13 Feb. 1867; m 1906, Amy C. E. H., (d 1940), o d of C. H. Master of Barrow Green Court, Oxted, Surrey; one s two d. Served S Africa, 1900 (Queen's medal 2 clasps); European War, 1914–18 (despatches thrice, Bt-Col, CB, CMG); Officer commanding troops in Jamaica, 1920–22; retired pay, 1922. JP West Sussex, 1927; DL West Sussex, 1937. *Address:* The Old Rectory, Trotton, near Petersfield. *Club:* Royal Automobile.

Died 5 March 1948.

CAREY, Brig.-Gen. Harold Eustace, CMG 1919; DSO 1917; late RA; b 15 Jan. 1874; 2nd s of late Maj.-Gen. W. D. Carey and Mrs Carey of Drumblade, Southampton; m 1910, Elsie, d of F. Hughes and Mrs Hughes of Wallfield, Reigate; one s three d. *Educ:* United Services College, Westward Ho! Joined Royal Artillery, 1893; served in RFA South Africa, 1899–1902; European War in 3rd Division, France, 1914–15; 28th and 22nd Divisions, 1916–18; Salonika, CRA, 22nd Division, 1916; Brevet Colonel (1919), Croix de Guerre with palms; CRA 55th (West Lancs Division), 1923–27; retired pay, 1927. *Address:* Watergate House, Bulford, Wilts.

Died 27 Feb. 1944.

CAREY, Col Herbert Clement, CMG 1918; b 1865; s of J. Westropp Carey, Victoria, BC; m 1894, Kate, d of Wakefield Moren, Halifax, NS. Entered RE 1884; Col 1912; retired, 1914; served European War, 1914–19 (despatches, CMG). *Club:* United Service.

Died 30 Nov. 1948.

CAREY, Herbert Simon, CB 1911; b 1856; 4th s of John Carey, FLS, The Paragon, Blackheath; m Alice Henrietta, d of Henry Owen Williams, JP and DL, of Tre'-Castell and Tre Arddur, Anglesey. *Educ:* Winchester; Oxford. Joint 2nd Secretary GPO, 1914–19. *Address:* Bury Hill, Woodbridge, Suffolk.

Died 22 Sept. 1947.

CARILL-WORSLEY, Philip Ernest T.; see Tindall-Carill-Worsley.

CARLEBACH, Col Sir Philip, Kt 1938; CMG 1917; CBE 1943; DL Middlesex; one of HM Lieutenants for City of London; late Commandant of City of London Cadet Brigade; b 1873; s of Joseph Carlebach; m 1905; three d. *Educ:* University College School, London. Hon. Colonel Royal Corps of Signals, 1939–48. *Address:* 88 Greencroft Gardens, NW6.

Died 30 May 1949.

CARLETON, Major Guy Audouin, DSO 1902; late The King's Own (Royal Lancaster Regiment); b 23 Nov. 1859. Entered Army, 1880; Captain, 1888; Major, 1899; served S Africa, 1899–1902 (despatches, Queen's medal 3 clasps, King's medal 2 clasps); retired. *Club:* Army and Navy.

Died 10 Feb. 1941.

CARLETON, Brig.-Gen. Montgomery Launcelot, CBE 1919; b 4 June 1861; s of late General Henry Alexander Carleton, CB, of Clare, Co. Tipperary and Greenfields, Co. Cork; m 1908, Marguerite Helen, d of Sir Lionel Edward Darell, 5th Bt. Entered Army, 1881; served Hazara, 1888 and 1891; Uganda, 1898 (despatches, Bt Major, medal); European War, 1914–18 (despatches, CBE); retired pay, 1918. *Club:* Army and Navy.

Died 18 Aug. 1942.

CARLILE, Sir (Edward) Hildred, 1st Bt *cr* 1917; Kt 1911; CBE 1919; *b* 10 July 1852; 2nd *s* of Edward and Maria Louisa Carlile, Richmond Hill, Surrey; *m* 1876, Isabella (*d* 1924), 3rd *d* of Cornelius Hanbury, Manor House, Little Berkhampstead, Herts; three *d. Educ:* privately in England and abroad. Formerly a captain in the 2nd West Yorkshire Yeomanry Cavalry, and subsequently commanded 2nd VB West Riding Regiment (now 43rd (Duke of Wellington's Regiment) AA Battalion), Hon. Col, 1906–39; TD 1912; Chairman Board of Trade Committee on Work of National Importance, 1916–19; MP (U) St Albans Division of Hertfordshire, 1906–19; Member of House of Commons Public Accounts Committee, 1910–19; War Work in connection with the Red Cross, 1914–19 (CBE); High Sheriff of Hertfordshire, 1922; on Councils of Bedford College (First Fellow) and Haileybury and Aldenham Schools; JP and DL Hertfordshire; JP West Riding, Yorkshire. *Heir:* none (*o s* killed in action 22 March 1918). *Address:* Bishop's Down Grange, Tunbridge Wells, Kent. *T:* Tunbridge Wells 412.

Died 26 Sept. 1942 (ext).

CARLILE, Rev. John Charles, CH 1929; CBE, ROB, DD, DLitt (Canada); Minister Folkestone Baptish Church; Editor of the Baptist Times; *b* London; *s* of John C. Carlile of Perthshire and Helen, *d* of A. Hamilton, Glasgow; *m* 1st, Louise H., *d* of George Hay, London; 2nd, S. Muriel, *d* of Rev. G. Moore. *Educ:* Royal Schools of Science; Metropolitan College. Baptist minister in London; became a leader in social reform; with Cardinal Manning in organising Dock Strike Mediation Committee; member of the London School Board, Secondary Education Committee, etc.; Acting Secretary Baptist Union of Great Britain and Ireland, 1924–25; President, 1921, 1922; during the war went five times to France to organise lectures for officers and men; went to America and Canada for promoting good relations with England; received special thanks of the King of the Belgians and ROB distinction for work in relief of refugees. *Publications:* History of the English Baptists, Folkestone during the War, Life of Dr MacLaren, Royal Lives, Vision and Vocation, Talks to Little Folks, Christianity and Labour; A Colony of Heaven; The Greatest Adventure; Christian Union in Social Service; The Challenge, C. H. Spurgeon, 1934; My Life's Little Day, 1936. *Recreation:* golf. *Address:* 13, The Leas, Folkestone; Church House, Southampton Row, WC. *Clubs:* International, Authors'.

Died 16 Aug. 1941.

CARLILE, Sir (William) Walter, 1st Bt *cr* 1928; OBE 1920; DL, JP; KStJ; *b* 15 June 1862; *s* of late J. W. Carlile, Ponsbourne Manor, Herts; *m* 1st, 1885, Blanche (*d* 1939), *d* of Rev. E. Cadogan; 2nd, 1940, Katherine Elizabeth Mary, *o d* of Rev. G. H. Field, Milton Keynes Rectory, Bletchley, Bucks. *Educ:* Harrow; Clare College, Cambridge. Contested N Bucks, 1892; MP (C) Bucks, Buckingham Div., 1895–1906; served in France during European War with General Fabian Ware's unit of the Missing Bureau (1914 Mons Star with clasp and other decorations). *Recreations:* shooting, golf, tennis. *Address:* Gayhurst, Newport Pagnell. *T:* Newport Pagnell 8. *Clubs:* Carlton, Royal Automobile.

Died 3 Jan. 1950 (ext).

CARLILE, Rev. Wilson, CH 1926; Hon. DD (Oxon) 1915, and Toronto, 1926; Preb. of St Paul's Cathedral, 1904; Founder and Hon. Chief Secretary Church Army since 1882; Rector of St Mary-at-Hill, EC, 1892–1926; Hon. Curate of St Mary-at-Hill since 1926; *b* Brixton, 14 Jan. 1847; *s* of a City merchant; *m* Flora Vickers (*d* 1925); five *s. Educ:* London College of Divinity. Entered commercial life, 1862; college, 1878; ordained, 1880; founded Church Army in the slums of Westminster, 1882 (total receipts, inc. War Work, £815,065 for 1940–41); founded Social System of Church Army in Marylebone, 1889. *Publications:* The Church and Conversion, 1882; Spiritual Difficulties, 1885;

Continental Outcast, 1906; Baptism of Fire, 1907. *Recreations:* gardening, open-air preaching. *Address:* Headquarters of Church Army, Marble Arch, W1. *TA:* Battleaxe Wesdo, London.

Died 26 Sept. 1942.

CARLILL, Hildred, MA, MD Cantab; FRCP (Lond.); Consulting Physician; Specialist in Nervous Diseases; *m* 1922, Mildred Constance Godfrey; one *s* two *d. Educ:* Harrow; Cambridge; Guy's Hospital. Late Senior Physician and Lect. to Westminster Hospital; Visitor and Lecturer for King Edward's Hospital Fund since 1928; Consulting Physician to Western Dispensary; Member of Association of Physicians of Great Britain and Ireland; Fellow of Royal Society of Medicine; formerly House Physician and House Surgeon at Guy's Hospital, Resident Medical Officer, East London Children's Hospital, Physician to Miller General Hospital, Belgrave Children's Hosp., Seamen's Hospital, Greenwich, Victoria Park Chest Hosp. and West End Hosp. for Nervous Diseases (15 years); Physician to Ministry of Pensions; Neurologist and Psychiatrist, RN Hospital, Haslar; Hunterian Professor and Arris and Gale Lecturer, RCS England; visited medical schools in America and Japan, 1912; Surgeon-Lieutenant RN, 1914–19; 18 months in battle cruiser New Zealand (battle of Dogger Bank), and 3 years at RN Hospital, Haslar (despatches). *Publications:* Pathology of Amaurotic Family Idiocy (with late Prof. Mott), 1911; Hunterian Lecture on Syphilis of Nervous System, 1918; scientific papers on Hypnotism, Hysteria, Epilepsy and other neurological subjects, etc. *Address:* 146 Harley Street, W1. *T:* Welbeck 2378. *Clubs:* Hawks, Cambridge; Royal St George's, Sandwich.

Died 16 April 1942.

CARLISLE, Rt Rev. Arthur, BA, DD, DCL, LLD; Bishop of Montreal since 1939; *b* Portsmouth, England, 29 Nov. 1881; *s* of Fl. Engr James Carlisle, RN and Mary Agnes Stares; *m* 1919, May Emery; one *s* one *d. Educ:* London Collegiate Institute, London, Ont; Western Ontario University, London, Ont; Huron Theological College, London, Ont. Deacon, 1904; Priest, 1905; Curate, Memorial Church, London, Ont, 1904–07; Rector Holy Trinity Church, Lucan, 1907–10; Rector All Saints Church, Windsor, Ont, 1910–21; Canon of St Paul's Cathedral, London, Ont, 1919; Archdeacon of Perth, 1921; Hon. Capt. and Chaplain IVth Bde BEF, 1914–17; Dean and Rector, of Christ Church Cathedral, Montreal, 1921–39; Hon. Lt-Col and Chaplain, Canadian Grenadier Guards, 1922; elected Bishop of Huron, 1931 (declined); Prolocutor Lower House General Synod, Canada, 1934–39. *Recreation:* golf. *Address:* 1545 McGregor Street, Montreal, Canada. *TA:* Montreal, Canada. *T:* FI 6448 Montreal. *Clubs:* Canadian, University, Montreal.

Died Jan. 1943.

CARLISLE, Engr Rear-Adm. Frank Scott, CBE 1937; *b* Welling, Kent, 8 May 1882; *s* of Frances Sarah Tye and William Carlisle; *m* 1910, Elsie May Cecilia Sacret, Lanscombe, Cockington; two *s* two *d. Educ:* Alleynes School, Dulwich. Joined Royal Navy in 1898; First Eng. Captain in Command of the Mechanical Training Establishment, Chatham; served European War, Battles of Dogger Bank, Jutland, first attempt on Zeebrugge; retired list, 1939; Rugby football, played for Royal Navy, United Services, Devon, Kent, etc. *Recreations:* shooting, fishing, golf. *Address:* Searigs, St Mawes, Cornwall.

Died 9 Sept. 1941.

CARLISLE, R. H.; *b* April 1865; *o surv. s* of late Richard Carlisle, JP, Llanrapley Court, Abergavenny, Mons., and Rosa Maria, *d* of Lewis Mosley of Rolleston Hall, Staffs; *m* 1st, 1893, Gertrude Mary (*d* 1934), *d* of late Count Barretto, Buenos Aires; 2nd, 1935, E. A. Lawrence. *Educ:* Harrow; Royal Military College, Sandhurst. Served in 18th Hussars and 14th (PWO) Yorks Regt,

1885–93; since then has contributed to Field ten years, Land and Water, and other sporting papers in U States. *Publications:* The Racecourse Guide, 1901; Foxhunting, Past and Present, 1908; Romance of the French Turf. Pseudonym (in US) Hawkeye; Racer Stud and Silk, 1934; Facts, Figures and Fancies (Breeding), 1935. *Recreation:* any sport in season. *Address:* 68 Munster Road, Teddington. *Club:* United Sports.

Died 28 March 1941.

CARLOW, Viscount; George Lionel Seymour; Lieut Grenadier Guards (Reserve of Officers); Air Commodore, AAF; *b* 20 Dec. 1907; *o s* of 6th Earl of Portarlington; *m* 1937, Peggy, *yr d* of late Charles Cambie; two *s*. *Address:* 67 Westminster Gardens, SW1; Willards Farm, Dunsfold, Surrey.

Died 17 April 1944.

CARLYLE, Rev. Alexander James, FBA 1936; MA, DLitt; DD Glasgow University; Hon. Fellow of University College, Oxford, 1935; *b* 24 July 1861; *s* of Rev. J. E. Carlyle, Minister of the Free Church of Scotland, Bombay; *m* 1895, Monti (*d* 1941), *d* of late Rev. Walter C. Smith; two *d*. *Educ:* Glasgow University; Exeter College, Oxford. History Exhibitioner, 1883; BA, First Class Honours in History, 1886; Second Class Honours in Theology, 1888. Pres. of the Oxford Union Society, 1888; Ordained, 1888, to Curacy of St Stephen's, Westminster; Sec. for General Purposes to the SPCK, 1890–91; Fellow of University College, Oxford, 1893–95; Rector of St Martin's and All Saints, Oxford, 1895–1919; Canon of Worcester, 1930–34; Examining Chaplain to the Bishop of Worcester, 1897–1901; Select Preacher to the Univ. of Cambridge, 1921 and 1934; Chaplain and Lecturer in Politics and Economics, University College; Lecturer in English Literature, Lincoln College and the Non. Coll. Society; Secretary to the Committee for Economics and Political Science, Oxford; Consultative Member of Executive Committee of Ruskin College, Oxford; Senior Treasurer of the Oxford Union Society; Lowell Lecturer, Boston, 1924; Birkbeck Lecturer in Ecclesiastical History, Trinity College, Cambridge, 1926–28; Preacher to the University of Glasgow, 1922, 1935; Olaus Petri Lecturer, Upsala University, Sweden, 1918; Foreign Member of the Royal Academy of Naples; Hon. President of International Institute for the Philosophy of Law since 1934. *Publications:* Life of Bishop Latimer, with Mrs Carlyle; Essay on the Church in 'Contentio Veritatis'; History of Mediæval Political Theory in the West, vols I II III IV V VI, with late Sir R. W. Carlyle; The Influence of Christianity on Social and Political Ideas; Wages; Christianity in History (with J. V. Bartlet); The Christian Church and Liberty; Political Liberty, 1941. *Address:* 35 Holywell, Oxford.

Died 27 May 1943.

CARMICHAEL, Lady Mary Gertrude, CBE 1919; BA; *d* of C. T. Glover, Shipowner, Aberdeen; *m* Sir George Carmichael, KCSI (*d* 1936); two *s*. *Educ:* Aberdeen High School; North London Collegiate School; Bedford College. *Address:* Elmsleigh, Woodchester, Stroud, Glos.

Died 8 April 1941.

CARNEGIE, Col David, CBE 1920; FRSE; MInstCE; JP; *b* 1868; *s* of David and Margaret Carnegie, Aberdeen; *m* Frances Ellen, *d* of Thomas Howard Lloyd, Leicester; three *s*. *Educ:* Gordon's College, Aberdeen; Royal College of Science, London. Civil and Ordnance Engineer; Hon. Consulting Technical Ordnance Adviser, Canadian Govt; Member and Ordnance Adviser, Shell Committee, Canada, 1915; Member and Ordnance Adviser of Imperial Munitions Board, Canada, 1915–19; Chairman of Commission (Canadian Govt) to inquire into the feasibility of refining zinc and copper in Canada, 1915; Chairman, Inventions Committee,

Canada; Canadian Government Delegate to National Industrial Conference, Ottawa, 1919; Canadian Govt Member ILO, 1922; Member Executive Committee, League of Nations Union, 1925–34; contested (L) Canterbury, 1924, Nov. 1927, and 1929; Hon. Col Canadian Militia; Canadian Member Temporary Mixed Commission for the Reduction of Armaments, League of Nations, 1921–24. *Publications:* Liquid Steel; Can Church and Industry Unite?; The History of Munitions Supply in Canada, 1914–1918, 1924; The Arms Industry, 1936; The Steel Sanction, 1937; World Economics and Peace, 1939; The ILO in World Affairs, 1943; Armaments with Security Explained, 1945; and Scientific papers. *Address:* The Haven, Seasalter, Kent. *T:* Whitstable 2080.

Died 14 March 1949.

CARNEGIE, Sir Francis, Kt 1939; CBE 1925; MICE, MIME; *b* 1874; *s* of David and Margaret Carnegie, Aberdeen; *m* Theodora, *d* of the Rev. E. W. Matthews, late Secretary of British Sailors' Society; two *s* one *d*. Superintendent, Royal Small Arms Factory, Enfield Lock, 1921; Chief Superintendent of Ordnance Factories, Royal Arsenal, Woolwich, 1926–44. *Publications:* scientific paper—Thesis on Vibration of Rifle Barrels, Telford Premium—The Inst. of Civil Engineers, 1912–1913; The Economical Production and Distribution of Steam in Large Factories, The Inst. of Mechanical Engineers, 1930. *Address:* 11 St John's Park, Blackheath, SE3. *T:* Greenwich 1377.

Died 3 Aug. 1946.

CARNEGIE, Lady Helena Mariota; *b* 1865; 6th *d* of 9th Earl of Southesk. *Publications:* Letters from Nigeria of the Hon. D. W. Carnegie, with Biographical Preface, 1902; (with Mrs Arthur Jacob) The Infant Moralist, 1903; Editor of Catalogue of the Southesk Collection of Antique Gems, 1908. *Address:* Rohallion, Murthly, Perthshire. *T:* Dunkeld 343. *Club:* Ladies' Empire.

Died 24 Jan. 1943.

CARNEGIE, Louise, (Mrs Andrew Carnegie); *b* New York, 7 March 1857; *d* of John William and Fannie Davis Whitfield; *m* 1887, Andrew Carnegie (*d* 1919); one *d*. Master of Humane Letters, New York University, June 1921; Doctor of Laws, St Andrews University, June 1935; Freedom of City of Dunfermline, 1907; of City of Edinburgh, 1935; Member National Society of Colonial Dames in the State of New York; Member of Huguenot Society; Member, Daughters of the Cincinnati. Gold Medal of Pennsylvania Society, 1934. *Address:* 2, East 91st Street, New York; Skibo Castle, Sutherland.

Died 24 June 1946.

CARNWATH, 16th Earl of, *cr* 1639; **Arthur Edward Dalzell,** CB 1900; Baron Dalzel and Liberton, 1628 (Scot.); Bt 1666 (Nova Scotia); Representative Peer for Scotland; Brig.-Gen.; Comdr Order of St Bento d'Aviz; *b* 25 Dec. 1851; *S* nephew, 1931; *m* 1902, Muriel Wyndham, *d* of Colonel Norton Knatchbull; one *d*. *Educ:* East Sheen; Cheltenham Coll. Entered Army, 52nd Light Infantry, 1870; Captain, 1882; Major, 1889; Lieut-Colonel, 1899; Col 1903; served throughout Burmah, 1891–92 (medal with clasp); South Africa, 1899–1902, in command of 1st Batt. Oxfordshire Light Infantry (medal with 4 clasps, King's medal with 2 clasps, CB, despatches); was on Staff, Government of India, 1892–96; Colonel in command of No. 6 District, and in charge Records. North Midland District, 1906–08; Colonel Commanding a District, 1908–11; Colonel Commanding 12th Service Batt. Cheshire Regt, 1914–15; Brigadier Commanding 207th Brigade, Jan. 1915–Aug. 1916; served in European War, May 1917–Christmas, 1918. *Heir:* none. *Address:* Sand House, Wedmore, Somerset. *Club:* Army and Navy.

Died 9 March 1941 (ext).

CARPENTER, Brig.-Gen. Charles Murray, CMG 1918; DSO 1916; *b* 18 Aug. 1870; *s* of late C. Wilson Carpenter; *m* 1906, Christelle Hills, *d* of A. J. Nicholson. Served China, 1900 (medal with clasp); European War, 1914–18 (despatches, DSO, Brevet Lieut-Col, CMG). *Address:* 10 Connaught Street, W2. *T:* Paddington 5669.
Died 18 March 1942.

CARPENTER, George Lyndon; General, Salvation Army, 1939–46; *b* 20 June 1872; *s* of late Tristan d'Acunha Carpenter, Newcastle, NSW, Australia; *m* 1899, Minnie Lindsay Rowell; one *s* one *d. Educ:* Public School. Began life on a country newspaper in New South Wales; entered service of Salvation Army 1892, and was trained in the Training College at Melbourne; appointments included 18 years in Australia in Property, Training and Literary Work; 1911–27, served at International Headquarters, for most part with General Bramwell Booth, as Literary Secretary; 1927–33, further service in Australia, including Chief Secretaryship; then 4 years as Territorial Commander in South America, followed by 2 years in similar capacity in Canada. Conducted campaigns many lands, including N and S America and W Indies during war; later Sweden, Finland, Norway, Denmark, Holland, Germany, France, Switzerland, also Australia and New Zealand. *Publications:* Keep the Trumpets Sounding, 1943; Religion with a Punch, 1944; Banners and Adventures, 1945. *Recreation:* walking. *Address:* 101 Queen Victoria Street, EC4. *TA:* Salvation, Cent, London.
Died 9 April 1948.

CARPMAEL, Raymond, OBE; MInstCE; MInstT; *b* 14 Sept. 1875; *s* of late Deanston Carpmael; *m* 1900, Frances Elsie (*d* 1931), *d* of late Sir Francis Colville Ford, Bart. *Educ:* privately; Dulwich College. Entered the Great Western Railway service in the Bridge Department at Paddington, 1900; Chief Engineer Great Western Railway, 1929–39; Fellow of the Permanent Way Institution and of the Royal Horticultural Society; awarded the Institute of Transport Gold Medal (Engineering), 1928; JP County Borough of Reading. *Recreations:* sailing, gardening, carpentry, etc. *Address:* The Chase, Reading, Berks. *T:* Reading 4523. *Club:* Berkshire County (Reading).
Died 8 March 1950.

CARR, Rt Rev. Charles Lisle, MA, DD; Bishop of Hereford, 1931–41; *b* 1871; γ *s* of Robert Carr, of West Ditchburn, Alnwick, Northumberland; *m* 1902, Isabel Wortley, *d* of late Rt Rev. T. W. Drury, DD; one *s. Educ:* Liverpool College; St Catharine's College, Cambridge (Hon. Fellow, 1934); Ridley Hall, Cambridge. Curate of Astonjuxta-Birmingham, 1894–97; Redditch, 1897; Tutor of Ridley Hall, Cambridge, 1897–1902; Vicar of St Sepulchre, Cambridge, 1901–02; Vicar of Blundellsands, Liverpool, 1902–06; Rector of Woolton, Liverpool, 1906–12; Archdeacon of Norfolk, 1916–18; Archdeacon of Norwich, 1918–20; Vicar of Yarmouth, 1912–20; Vicar of Sheffield, 1920–22; Archdeacon of Sheffield, 1920–22; Bishop of Coventry, 1922–31; Hon. Canon of Sheffield Cathedral, 1920; late Examining Chaplain to Bishop of Sheffield. *Club:* National.
Died 2 Feb. 1942.

CARR, Brig.-Gen. Christopher D'Arcy Bloomfield Saltern B.; *see* Baker-Carr.

CARR, Sir Emsley, Kt 1918; FJI; Chairman and Editor, News of the World; Vice-chairman, Western Mail, Cardiff; South Wales, Echo, Evening Express, Cardiff; and Weekly Mail, Cardiff; Director, George Newnes, Limited; President, Press Benefit Society for S Wales and Monmouthshire; Chairman, Walton Heath Golf Club, Ltd, Chairman, Newspaper Press Fund, 1936; Chairman, Printers' Pension Corporation, 1939; President, Artizan Golfers Society; President, National Association of Public Courses; President, Newspapers and Advertisers Golfers Society; Vice-President, Professional Golfers Association; President, British Games (Achilles Gold Medallist); Vice-President, Counties Athletic Union (Gold Medallist), etc.; Founder, Knights of the Road; *b* Leeds, 1 May 1867; *e s* of Thomas Hay Carr, Leeds; *m* 1895, Jenny Lascelles, *e d* of Lascelles Carr, Cardiff; five *s* two *d. Educ:* Leeds. Sheriff of Glamorgan, 1938; Chairman, Press Gallery, House of Commons, 1929–30; President Institute of Journalists, 1932 and 1933; Delegate Imperial Press Conference, Canada, 1925, Australia, 1930. *Recreations:* golf, motoring. *Address:* Wonford, Walton Heath, Surrey. *T:* Tadworth 3271. *Clubs:* Carlton, Constitutional, Savage; Walton Heath Golf; Mid-Surrey Golf; Royal and Ancient Golf, St Andrews.
Died 31 July 1941.

CARR, Frank Arnold; High Sheriff of Cumberland, 1941–42; *b* 4 May 1873; *s* of Henry Carr and Sarah Forster; *m* 1913, Kathleen Mary Pattison; one *d. Educ:* Monkton Combe School, Bath; Oliver's Mount School, Scarborough; Paris. Chairman, Carr's Flour Mills Ltd; Trustee of Carlisle and NW Counties Savings Bank; Cumberland County Council, Chairman of Finance Committee; District Commissioner of Boy Scouts, 1911–28. *Recreations:* golf, ski-ing, tennis. *Address:* Rosebery House, Gorebridge, Midlothian. *T:* Temple 220. *Clubs:* County, Carlisle.
Died 16 Nov. 1942.

CARR, Harry Lascelles; Pilot Officer RAFVR; News Editor, News of the World, since 1926; Director, News of the World, since 1935; *b* 8 Oct. 1907; twin *s* of late Sir Emsley Carr; *m* 1932, Eileen Mary, *d* of Bracewell Smith, MP; two *s* one *d. Educ:* Clifton College; Trinity College, Cambridge (BA, golf and billiards blue). Reporter, Western Mail, 1931–33; Sub-Editor, South Wales Echo, 1933–36; High Sheriff of Glamorgan, 1940. *Recreations:* golf, billiards, contract bridge, shooting. *Address:* Corbar, Beech Hill, Hadley Wood, Middlesex. *Clubs:* MCC; County, Cardiff; Royal and Ancient, St Andrews; Walton Heath, Hamilton and Hadley Wood Golf.
Died 17 Aug. 1943.

CARR, Maj.-Gen. Howard, CB 1915; MD; late AMS; *b* 8 March 1863; *s* of late Lt-Col George Carr; *m* 1903, Constance Harriet (*d* 1936), *d* of late Thomas Kough of Glendine, Kilkenny; two *s* one *d. Educ:* Queen's College, Cork. Served Burma, 1885–87 (medal with clasp); 2nd Miranzai Expedition, 1891; Dongola, 1896; Nile Expedition, 1898 (despatches, Egyptian medal 2 clasps, medal); South Africa, 1900–02 (Queen's medal 3 clasps, King's medal 2 clasps); European War, 1914–18 (despatches, CB, 3 medals); Knight of Grace, Order of St John of Jerusalem; Grand Officer Order of the Avis); retired pay, 1919. *Recreation:* yachting. *Address:* c/o Glyn Mills & Co., Holt's Branch, Kirkland House, Whitehall, SW1.
Died 23 May 1944.

CARR, John Walter, CBE 1920; MD; FRCP (Lond.); FRCS (Eng.); Consulting Physician to Royal Free Hospital and to Victoria Hospital for Children, Chelsea; Emeritus Lecturer in Medicine, London School of Medicine for Women; Fellow, Royal Society of Medicine, and Past President of Clinical Section; Fellow and Past President of Medical Society of London; *b* 1862; *s* of John Carr, JP, London; *m* 1895, Jessie, *d* of Walter Griffith, Streatham Hill; one *s* three *d. Educ:* University Coll. School, College, and Hospital, London. Formerly Censor and Examiner in Medicine to Royal College of Physicians and External Examiner in Medicine, University of Birmingham; Master of the Worshipful Company of Haberdashers, 1929–30. *Publications:* (joint) The Practitioner's Guide; How to

Live Long; numerous papers on medical subjects. *Address:* 10 Ferncroft Avenue, Hampstead, NW3. *T:* Hampstead 5885.

Died 29 Sept. 1942.

CARR, Sir William, Kt 1931; *b* 9 Feb. 1872. *Educ:* Lancaster Grammar School; Christ's College, Cambridge. Entered Indian Civil Service 1893; Judge Small Causes Court, Mandalay, 1905; Judge of High Court, Rangoon, 1924–32; retired, 1932. *Address:* 22 Cottenham Park Road, SW20.

Died 18 Sept. 1949.

CARRARA, Arthur Charles, CMG 1931; KC 1923; JP; Chairman of an Advisory Committee under Defence Regulations since 1940; 3rd *s* of late James Carrara, Gibraltar; *m* 1937, Mrs Lily Ann Reid (*née* Young), Kirkcudbright, Scotland. *Educ:* St Joseph's College, London. Barrister-at-law; called to Bar, Inner Temple, 1899; Member of the Executive Council of Gibraltar, 1922–28 and 1937–40; Chief Censor of Postal and Telegraphic communications, 1939–41; Stipendiary Magistrate and Coroner, Gibraltar, 1941–43; Acting Chief Justice, Jan.–Feb. 1940, May–Aug. 1942; and July–Aug. 1943; Visitor of the Mental Hospital; Member: Board of Visitors of the Cemetery; Medical and Dental Board; Chairman: Board of Visitors of the Colonial Hospital; Military Service Hardship Cttee; Trades Tax (Appeal) Cttee; Hon. Corr. Sec. of R. Empire Soc. Coronation Medal, 1937. *Recreations:* hunting, yachting, and tennis. *Address:* 12 Library Gardens, Gibraltar. *Club:* Royal Empire Society.

Died 9 Nov. 1949.

CARRE, Major Ralph G. Riddell; *b* 1868; *s* of Lt-Col T. A. Riddell-Carre of Cavers Carre; *heir presumtive* to Sir John Charles Buchanan-Riddell, Bt; *m* 1905, Kathleen Sadier Lawe, *d* of Col Stoney, RA, The Downs, Delgany; one *s*. *Educ:* Harrow. Served in Royal Scots Fusiliers, 1888–1905 and 1914–18. *Address:* Cavers Carre, Lillies-leaf, Roxburghshire. *T:* Lilliesleaf 4. *Clubs:* New, Edinburgh.

Died 25 June 1941.

CARREL, Dr Alexis; Staff of the Rockefeller Institute for Medical Research, New York, 1906–12, Member, 1912–39, Member Emeritus, 1939; special war mission for French Ministry of Public Health, Sept. 1939–May 1940; *b* Sainte-Foy-les Lyon, 28 June 1873; *s* of Alexis Carrel and Anne Ricard; *m* 1913, Anne de la Motte. *Educ:* LB, University of Lyon, 1890, ScB., Univ. of Dijon, 1891, MD, University of Lyon, 1900, ScD, Columbia, 1913, Brown, 1920, Princeton, 1920, University of the State of New York, 1937, Manhattan College, 1938; MD, Belfast, 1919; LLD, University of California, 1936; Phi Beta Kappa, Dartmouth College, 1937. Interne des hôpitaux de Lyon, 1896–1900; prosecteur à la faculté de médecine, University of Lyon, 1900–02; went to Canada, 1904; to United States, 1905; winner of Nobel prize, 1912, for success in suturing blood-vessels and transplantation of organs; winner of Nordhoff-Jung Cancer Prize, 1931; Newman Foundation Award, University of Illinois, 1937: Rotary Club of New York Service Medal, 1939; Major FAMC; Commander Legion of Honour; Commander of the Order of Leopold of Belgium; DSM; CMG Northern Star of Sweden, Isabella of Spain; Senior Fellow, American Surgical Association; Fellow American College of Surgeons, etc.; Corresponding Member various American and European Academies and Societies. *Publications:* (with Georges Dehelly) The Treatment of Infected Wounds, 1919; Man, the Unknown, 1935; (with Charles A. Lindbergh) The Culture of Organs, 1938; Contributions on biological and surgical subjects. *Address:* Rockefeller Institute, 66 Street and York Avenue, New York. *Clubs:* Century, New York.

Died 5 Nov. 1944.

CARRINGTON, Brig. Charles Ronald Brownlow, DSO 1916; OBE 1942; late RA; *b* 7 April 1880; *m* Violet M., *d* of H. Herbert Smith; one *s* two *d*. *Educ:* Eton. Served European War, 1914–18 (despatches six times, DSO, Bt Lieut-Col); Commander Royal Artillery, 48th (South Midland) Division, TA 1931–33; Assistant Director of Remounts, War Office, 1933–37; retired pay, 1937.

Died 22 Dec. 1948.

CARRINGTON, Very Rev. Charles Walter; Commissary for the Bishop of Quebec; *b* Bath, 1859; *s* of H. E. Carrington, proprietor and editor of Bath Chronicle; *m* Margaret Constance (*d* 1930), *d* of Rev. E. Pugh, Vicar of Bangor and Rural Dean of Anglesey; three *s* two *d*. *Educ:* Bath; Cambridge. ii Class Theo. Trip., AB 1888, MA 1903. In engineering profession at Crystal Palace College, 1877–85; afterwards with E. Wilson & Co., Westminster, and GER; engaged in railway work; Curate of St Clement's, Notting Hill, 1888–89; Mission Chaplain to Bishop MacLagan at Lichfield, 1890; Vicar Christ Church, W Bromwich, 1894; Principal of Upper Department of Christ's College, Christchurch, 1903; Dean of Christchurch, New Zealand, and Commissary for the Bishop of Christchurch, 1913–27; Hon. Canon of Christchurch Cathedral, 1910; Examining Chaplain, Diocesan Nominator, etc.; resigned, 1927. *Address:* Glenview, Limpley Stoke, Bath.

Died 30 July 1941.

CARROLL, Most Rev. John J., DD; Bishop of Lismore, NSW (RC), since 1910; *b* Ireland, 1865. *Educ:* Mount Melleray Seminary; Carlow Diocesan College. Priest, 1890; went to Sydney, 1890. *Address:* St Carthage's Cathedral, Lismore, NSW.

Died 8 May 1949.

CARRUTHERS, Bt Lt-Col Francis John, CB 1943; HM Lieutenant in the County of Dumfries; Brigadier the Royal Company of Archers (King's Bodyguard for Scotland); *b* 15 March 1868; 2nd and *e surv. s* of William Francis Carruthers, Dormont; *m* 1905, Olive Christian, *d* of Arthur Henry Johnstone Douglas, Lockerbie; six *s*. *Educ:* Charterhouse; RMC Sandhurst. Joined KOS Borderers 1888; served in Egypt 1888–89 (Medal and Star); S Africa 1900–02 (despatches twice, Queen's and King's Medals); Brevet Major; retired 1904; DA Director War Office 1915–19; Brevet Lieut-Col; Hon. Colonel 5th Bn KOS Borderers 1931–36. *Recreation:* all sports. *Address:* Dormont, Lockerbie, Dumfriesshire. *TA:* and *T:* Carrutherstown 213. *Clubs:* New, Edinburgh.

Died 22 May 1945.

CARRUTHERS, Brig.-Gen. Robert Alexander, CB 1908; CMG 1916; DA and QMG of Australian Corps throughout European War; Indian Army, retired 1919; *b* 20 Feb. 1862; *s* of Walter Carruthers, Inverness; *m* 1892, Florence, *d* of Henry Wintle; one *s* one *d*. *Educ:* Fettes College, Edinburgh. Joined Devon Regt 1883; ISC 1885; Probyn's Horse, Captain, 1894; Major, 1901; Lt-Col 1908; Col 1912; Brig.-Gen. 1914; late Offg General Staff, India; late Commandant 59th Scinde Rifles; served Chitral Relief Expedition, 1895; Zakka Khel and Mohmand Expeditions, 1908 (CB); Dardanelles, European War, 1914–18 (CMG, despatches six times, Officer Legion of Honour). *Address:* c/o Cox's Branch, 6 Pall Mall, SW1. *Club:* Junior Army and Navy.

Died 13 Dec. 1945.

CARSON, Sir Charles William Charteris, Kt 1939; CIE 1927; OBE 1919; late Finance Department, Government of India; *b* 21 July 1874; *m* 1st, 1906, Emily Olive (*d* 1935), *d* of late Lt-Col Charles Mountstuart Erskine; one *s* one *d*; 2nd, 1937, Edith Mary, *widow* of G. T. Hutton, and *d* of Lieut-Col Dundas, Tivoli, Cork. Joined service, 1893; Deputy Controller of Currency, Bombay, 1919; Accountant-General, United Provinces, 1922; Accountant-General, Punjab, 1923; officiating

Controller of Civil Accounts, 1927; retired, 1929; re-employed in the service of the Gwalior State, 1930; Finance Minister, Gwalior Government, 1935; retired 1942. *Address:* Midhurst, ABU, Rajputana, India.

Died 10 May 1945.

CARSON, Captain Hon. Walter Seymour; Royal Navy, retired; Cdg Officer Solent Division RNVR since 1939; *b* 1890; *o s* of late Baron Carson, and 1st wife, Sarah Annette Foster, *d* of late H. Persse Kirwan; *m* 1916, Violet Taswell, *d* of Charles Taswell Richardson; one *s* three *d.* Lieut, RN, 1914; Commander, 1927; retired list, 1939.

Died 1 March 1946.

CARSWELL, Catherine Roxburgh; *b* 27 March 1879; *yr d* of late George Gray Macfarlane, merchant, Glasgow; *m* 1st, 1903, late Herbert P. M. Jackson (marriage annulled 1908); 2nd, 1915, Donald Carswell (*d* 1940); one *s. Educ:* Park School, Glasgow; Univ. of Glasgow. Studied music at Frankfurt Conservatorium. Reviewer and Dramatic critic, Glasgow Herald, 1907–11. *Publications:* Open the Door, a novel, 1920; The Camomile, a novel, 1922; The Life of Robert Burns, 1930; The Savage Pilgrimage: a narrative of D. H. Lawrence, 1932; Robert Burns (Great Lives Series), 1933; Contributed the article Proust's Women to Marcel Proust—a Memorial Tribute, edited by C. K. Scott-Moncrieff, 1926; Anthologies with Daniel George: A National Gallery, 1933, and The English in Love, 1934; The Fays at the Abbey (with W. G. Fay), 1935; The Tranquil Heart, A Portrait of Giovanni Boccaccio, 1937. *Recreation:* seeing things. *Address:* 125 Parkway, NW1.

Died 18 Feb. 1946.

CARTE, Rupert D'Oyly; *see* D'Oyly Carte.

CARTE, Col Thomas Elliott, CB 1917; late Royal Artillery (retired); *b* Auckland, New Zealand, 23 Feb. 1861; *s* of late John Elliott Carte, CB, 2/14th Regt and Inspector General of Hospitals; unmarried. *Educ:* Brighton College; Royal Military Academy, Woolwich. Lieut RA 1880; Capt. 1888; Major, 1898; Lieut-Col 1907; Col 1911; was Assistant Inspector of Warlike Stores; Assistant Inspector of Position Finding; Inspector of Position Finding; Chief Instructor Ordnance College; Assistant Director of Artillery, War Office, 1912–18; employed in Design Department, Ministry of Munitions, 1918. *Address:* 4 Ashburn Gardens, SW7. *T:* Frobisher 1390.

Died 26 March 1945.

CARTER, Albert Thomas, CBE 1917; KC 1921; DCL; Hon. Fellow, Queen's College, Oxford; *b* 1861; *e s* of T. A. Carter, MD, FRCP, of Shottery Hall, Stratford-on-Avon. *Educ:* Queen's College, Oxford (Scholar); 1st Class Mods; 1st Class Lit. Hum.; Eldon Scholar; Vinerian Scholar. Barrister, Inner Temple, 1886; Student of Christ Church, Oxford, 1895; Reader in Constitutional Law and Legal History in the Inns of Court, 1898–1910; decorated for services in connection with the Department of HM's Procurator General and Treasury Solicitor, 1917. *Address:* Albany, Piccadilly, W1. *T:* Regent 1458. *Club:* Oxford and Cambridge.

Died 29 July 1946.

CARTER, Ven. Anthony Basil, MA, Hon. CF; Archdeacon of Cleveland since 1938; Rector of Stokesley since 1936; *b* 27 April 1881; *s* of Rev. Charles Clement Carter and Helen Maud Sophia Young; *m* 1917, Hilda Joan Linton (decd); one *s* one *d. Educ:* privately; Trinity College, Dublin. Schoolmaster, 1900–07; BA 1907; MA 1910; Cuddesdon College, 1907–08; Curate, St Michael's, Battersea, 1908–13; Curate-in-charge, St Dunstan's, Armley, 1913–15; TCF, 1916–17; Vicar, Christ Church, Leeds, 1917–22; Vicar, St Margaret's Ilkley, 1922–30; Vicar, and Rural Dean, Scarborough, 1930–36; Rural Dean of Stokesley,

1936–38. *Recreations:* cricket, association football, hockey (played for Berkshire County), tennis. *Address:* The Rectory, Stokesley, Middlesbrough. *TA:* Stokesley. *T:* Stokesley 225.

Died 14 March 1942.

CARTER, Brig.-Gen. Charles Herbert Philip, CB 1913; CMG 1900; CBE 1919; late the Royal Scots; *b* 14 Feb. 1864; *s* of late Capt. Willoughby H. Carter of Annagkeen, Co. Galway; *m* 1st, 1899, Kathleen Maud (*d* 1922), *d* of James Hartley; 2nd, 1923, Ethel Pollock, *d* of late Henry W. Horne. *Educ:* Stubbington, Fareham; Cheltenham College. Naval cadet, 1878; entered Black Watch 1888; Capt. Royal Scots, 1897; served Benin Expedition, 1897 (despatches, promoted Captain, brevet of Major, medal with clasp); commanded force against the Kwo Ibibios, Southern Nigeria, also Benin Territories, 1899 (despatches twice, CMG, clasp); took part with the Ashanti Field Force for the relief of Kumasi, 1900, in command of 3rd West African Frontier Force (severely wounded, medal and clasp); Bt Lt-Col commanded 2nd Bn Scottish Rifles (The Cameronians), 1910–12; Substantive Colonel, 1913; Commandant Nigeria Regiment, West African Frontier Force, 1913–14; Brigade Commander, European War (France), 1915–16 (despatches, CBE). *Address:* Sandecotes Holt, Parkstone, Dorset. *Club:* Naval and Military.

Died 22 Oct. 1943.

CARTER, Col Duncan Campbell, CB 1905; CMG 1917; RA; late Commanding RA Divisional Troops; *b* 15 Aug. 1856. Entered Army, 1876; Capt. 1884; Major, 1893; served Egypt, 1884 (medal with clasp, bronze star); Soudan, 1884–85 (despatches, clasp); S Africa, 1899–1901 (despatches twice, brevet Lieut Col, Queen's medal 5 clasps); retired pay, 1907; served in Remount Department, 1914–19. *Address:* Heighthorne, Park Place, Cheltenham.

Died 12 Jan. 1942.

CARTER, Sir Frank Willington, Kt 1919; CIE 1915; CBE 1918; *b* 16 Jan. 1865; *s* of Rev. W. A. Carter, Fellow and Bursar of Eton College; *m* 1912, Mary, *widow* of Comdr Charles Collins, *e d* of late Rev. Dacres Olivier; no *c. Educ:* Cheltenham College. India, 1891; Member of the Legislative Council of Bengal, Jan. 1917; Sheriff of Calcutta, 1918; Member of the Indian Legislative Assembly. *Recreation:* shooting. *Address:* Chota Hubra, Crazies Hill, Wargrave. *Clubs:* Oriental, Royal Automobile; Bengal, Calcutta.

Died 31 Jan. 1945.

CARTER, Lt-Col Sir Gordon, KCVO 1929; CVO 1919; MVO 1903; for 15 years Adjutant of 1st Life Guards; Secretary to the King's Representative, and Clerk of the Course, Ascot; *b* 1853. Served South African War, 1899–1900; Relief of Kimberley; operations in the Orange Free State, including operations at Paardeberg, actions at Poplar Grove and Dreifontein; actions at Houtnek (Thoba Mountain), Vet River, and Zand River; operations in the Transvaal, including actions near Johannesburg, Pretoria, and Diamond Hill; operations in the Transvaal west of Pretoria, including actions at Elands River; operations in the Orange River Colony, including actions at Bethlehem and Wittebergen; operations in Cape Colony, including actions at Colesberg (despatches, Queen's medal 6 clasps, Bt-Lt-Col); in charge of the King's Hospital and Recruiting Officer at Ascot during European War; accompanied Earl Fitzwilliam in his search for treasure on Cocos Island in the Pacific. *Recreations:* riding, hunting, and travelling. *Address:* Royal Enclosure, Ascot. *T:* Ascot 83 and 127. *TA:* Troops, Ascot. *Clubs:* Naval and Military, Bucks; Berkshire, Reading.

Died 16 Nov. 1941.

CARTER, Herbert James, BA (Camb.); FES; *b* 23 April 1858; *s* of James Carter, Marlborough, Wilts; *m* Antoinette Charlotte Moore, Woodbridge, Suffolk; two *s* two *d*. *Educ:* Aldenham; Jesus College, Cambridge (Mathematical Scholar). 2nd Class Honours (Math. Tripos), 1881. Assistant Master, Sydney Grammar School, 1882–1902; Principal of Ascham School, Sydney, 1902–14; President Linnean Society, NS Wales, 1925–26. *Publications:* Gulliver in the Bush, 1933; Science Editor Angus and Robertson's Encyclopædia of Australia; some seventy papers on Australian Coleoptera, in various Scientific Journals (Proc. Linn. Soc., NSW; Roy. Soc., SA; Roy. Soc., Vict.; Entomol. Soc. Lond., etc.). *Recreations:* formerly cricket and tennis, latterly gardening and entomology. *Address:* Garrawilla, Wahroonga, NS Wales. *T:* Wahroonga 648. *Clubs:* University, Sydney.

Died 16 April 1940.

CARTER, Hester Marion, CBE 1918; *b* 16 Dec. 1867; *d* of late James Rose, Inverness; *m* 1904, Most Rev. William M. Carter, KCMG (*d* 1941), late Archbishop of Capetown. *Address:* Bear Ash, Twyford, Berkshire.

Died 22 March 1944.

CARTER, Huntly; writer, journalist, symposia editor, publicist, traveller, lecturer, and interpreter of National and World creative constructive movements, in particular, sociological and cultural; early medical training in psychiatry and sexual pathology; before the War engaged in sociological and radical reform movements and journalism of ideas; Reconstruction and Recovery movements in Europe and Russia, 1915–41; editor of a unique series of international symposia surveys of momentous tendencies in science, art, drama, economics, industry and new social life to which upward of 700 distinguished representative men and women contributed; Civil List Pension for services to Literature, 1931; additional Civil List Pension, 1939. *Publications:* symposia and formative works on the international theatre, drama, cinema, etc., in their relation to social philosophy; contributor to Manchester Guardian, innumerable constructive articles in the international quality Press. *Address:* The Studio, Windmill Hill, Old Hampstead, NW3. *T:* Hampstead 1702.

Died 29 March 1942.

CARTER, Rev. John, MA; Vicar of Tollesbury since 1941; *b* 7 Nov. 1861; *s* of John Carter, Toronto, Canada. *Educ:* Upper Canada College, and Trinity University, Toronto; Exeter Coll. Oxford (Exhibitioner), 2nd class Lit. Hum. 1887. Curate of Limehouse Parish Church, 1887–89; Resident at Pusey House, 1889–1921; Assistant-Chaplain Exeter Coll., Oxford, 1890–95; Hon. Secretary of the Christian Social Union from its foundation in 1889 till 1910, then Vice-President; Editor of the Economic Review, 1891–1914; University Member, Oxford Town Council, 1901–33; Alderman 1913–32; Mayor, 1925–26; Fellow of the Inst of Public Administration, 1926. *Address:* Tollesbury Vicarage, Maldon, Essex.

Died 18 Sept. 1944.

CARTER, Lt-Col John Fillis Carré, CBE 1925; *b* 11 Jan. 1882; *s* of late Captain Charles Carré Carter, RE; *m* 1915, Gwendolyn Marjorie, *d* of late Colonel W. P. Georges, RA; one *s* one *d*. *Educ:* Wellington; Royal Military College, Sandhurst. Entered Indian Army, 1900; served Waziristan, 1901–02 (medal and clasp); joined Indian Police (Burma), 1905; served European War, 1914–18, on the Imperial General Staff, GSO2 (despatches twice, Brevet Lieut-Col); joined Metropolitan Police, 1919; Deputy Assistant Commissioner, Metropolitan Police, 1922–38; Assistant Commissioner, Metropolitan Police, 1938–40; Order of St Maurice and Lazarus; White Lion of Czechoslovakia; Crown of Italy; Legion of Honour. *Address:* Stoneridge, Tavistock, Devon. *Club:* Royal Thames Yacht.

Died 14 July 1944.

CARTER, John Ridgely, LLD Trinity College, 1911; at present with Morgan, Morgan et Cie., Paris; *b* Baltimore, Maryland, 28 Nov. 1865; *s* of Bernard Carter and Mary Ridgely Carter; *m* 1887, Alice Morgan; one *s* one *d*. *Educ:* Trinity College, Hartford, BA 1883, MA 1885; Leipzig, 1884; LLB Maryland Univ., 1887; Harvard Law School, 1888. Admitted to Maryland Bar, 1889; Secretary to American Ambassador, 1894; 2nd Secretary of Embassy, 1896; Chargé d'Affaires, 1897; Associate Secretary, Alaska Boundary Tribunal, 1903; Councillor of American Embassy, 1905–09; Minister to Roumania, Servia, and Bulgaria, 1909–11; Constantinople, 1910–11. *Recreations:* shooting, tennis, golf. *Address:* 14 Place Vendôme, Paris. *Clubs:* St James's, Prince's, Beefsteak; Knickerbocker, New York; Metropolitan, Washington; Cercle de l'union, Travellers', Paris.

Died 3 June 1944.

CARTER, Hon. Thomas Fortescue; *b* 2 March 1855; *s* of Thomas Fortescue Carter and Ann Holderness of Wood Park, near Neston, Cheshire; *m* Ellen Fannin, *d* of William Robinson Shaw, Natal. *Educ:* Buckfast Abbey, Devon. Journalist until 1886; came to Natal, 1879; acted as war correspondent in first Boer War; joined Natal Bar, 1885; Member for Klip River Division, Natal, in Legislative Assembly; joined Mr Moor's Ministry, 1906; ministerial head of the Mining and Police Departments; Minister of Justice and Minister of Public Works; Attorney-General and KC, 1908–10; Judge of the Supreme Court, Natal, 1910; retired as a Judge, 1931; Union Com. Medal, Colony of Natal. *Publication:* A Narrative of the Boer War (three editions). *Address:* The Hermitage, near Pietermaritzburg. *Clubs:* Victoria, Pietermaritzburg; Country, Durban.

Died 4 April 1945.

CARTER, William Henry, CBE 1928; MINA, RCNC (retired); *b* 1868; *m* Beatrice, *d* of William Phillips; one *d*. *Educ:* RNE College, Keyham; Royal Naval College, Greenwich. Assistant Constructor, 1892; Naval Constructor, Malta, 1906; Admiralty, 1907; Inspecting Officer of Contract-built ships, 1908; Chief Constructor, 1917; Assistant Director of Naval Construction, 1923–28. *Address:* 29 Palmeira Square, Hove, Sussex. *T:* Hove 4641.

Died 27 Dec. 1944.

CARTER, Most Rev. William Marlborough, KCMG 1931; DD; *b* Eton, July 1850; *s* of Rev. W. A. Carter, late Fellow of Eton College; *m* 1904, Hester Marion, CBE, *y d* of late James Rose, Inverness. *Educ:* Eton; Pembroke College, Oxford (MA 1877). Ordained, 1874; Curate Christ Church, W Bromwich, 1874–78; Bakewell, 1878–80; Eton Mission, Hackney, 1880–89 and 1890–91. Bishop of Zululand, 1891–1902; Bishop of Pretoria, 1902–09; Archbishop of Cape Town, 1909–30. *Address:* Bear Ash, Twyford, Berks.

Died 14 Feb. 1941.

CARTIER DE MARCHIENNE, Baron de, GCVO (Hon.) 1934; GBE (Hon.) 1937; Hon. LLD; Belgian Ambassador to the Court of Saint James since 1927; *b* 30 Nov. 1871; *m* 1919, Marie Dow (*d* 1936), New York. Entered Diplomatic Service, 1892; Minister to China, 1910; to the United States of America, 1917; Ambassador to the United States, 1920; Grand Cross of the Order of Leopold II; Grand Officer of the Order of Leopold. *Address:* 36 Belgrave Square, SW1. *T:* Sloane 1752; 103 Eaton Square, SW1. *Clubs:* Athenæum, Turf, Beefsteak, Marlborough; Cercle du Parc, Brussels; Cercle de l'Union, Paris.

Died 10 May 1946.

CARTWRIGHT, Beatrice, CBE 1934; JP, County Alderman; *d* of R. A. and Hon. Mrs Cartwright. *Educ:* home. Has worked politically and in local Government for 50 years; Member of Northants County Council Member of Finance, Education, Public Health

Committees, etc.; Mayor of Brackley, 1934–37 and 1938–41; Alderman of County Council and Borough; Member of Central Council Conservative Association and Chairman of Daventry Division Women's Unionist Association; Vice-President GFS; President Brackley Women's Institute; Chairman Finance Committee County Nursing Association. *Recreation:* bridge. *Address:* Warden House, Brackley, Northants. *TA:* Brackley. *T:* Brackley 33. *Club:* Forum.

Died 24 March 1947.

CARTWRIGHT, Col Charles Marling, CB 1916; CMG 1918; Indian Army; *b* 1862; *s* of H. D. Cartwright; *m* Ida Eleanor, *d* of late Maj.-Gen. H. Coape-Smith; no *c. Educ:* Bradfield; Sandhurst. Lt 2nd Royal Irish Fusiliers, 1881; 20th Bombay Infantry, 1883; 36th Jacob's Horse, 1886; Commanded 36th Jacob's Horse, 1907–12; thanked twice by Bombay Govt for services in Mekran and Lower Sind; served European War, 1914–19 (despatches, CB, CMG); retired, 1920. *Address:* c/o Lloyds Bank (Cox and King's Branch), 6 Pall Mall, SW1.

Died 30 Sept. 1946.

CARTWRIGHT, Lt-Col Henry Aubrey; JP; *b* 1858; *e s* of Col Henry Cartwright, MP (*d* 1890), of Eydon Hall, Northamptonshire, and Jane, *d* of W. Holbech, of Farnborough Hall, Co. Warwick; *m* 1892, Mildred Margaret (*d* 1944), *d* of Charles Joseph Parke, of Henbury, Dorset. *Educ:* Eton. Was Capt. 68th Durham Light Infantry. *Address:* Upwood, Handley, Salisbury.

Died 24 July 1945.

CARTWRIGHT, Lt-Col John Rogers, DSO 1917, late Devonshire Regt; *b* 6 Jan. 1882; *s* of Rev. Arthur Rogers Cartwright, Butcombe, Somerset; *m* 1910, Isabella, *d* of late George Edward Aubert Ross, KC; one *s* one *d. Educ:* Haileybury. Served S Africa, 1902; European War, 1914–18 (despatches thrice, Bt Major, DSO); retired pay, 1931. *Address:* Seafield House, Seaton, Devon. *T:* Seaton 210.

Died July 1942.

CARTWRIGHT, Lt-Col Robert, CMG 1900; fruit farmer, on Okenagon Lake; late Assistant Adjutant-General for Musketry Headquarters, Canada, Commandant Canadian School of Musketry, and AAG Militia Force of Canada; Major and Brevet Lieut-Col Royal Canadian Regt; *b* 4 Nov. 1860; *e s* of late Rt Hon. Sir R. Cartwright; *m* 1885, Ivy Maria Russell, *d* of Benjamin C. Davy; two *d. Educ:* Royal Military College, Kingston, Ont. Served North-West Rebellion, 1885 (medal); South Africa, Canadian Contingent (despatches, medal, four clasps). *Address:* Summerland, British Columbia. *Clubs:* Rideau, Ottawa.

Died 27 Oct. 1942.

CARUANA, Most Rev. Maurus, KBE 1918; OSB; Bishop of Malta and Titular Archbishop, since 1915; *b* 16 Nov. 1867. *Educ:* Fort Augustus Abbey School. Took vows as Benedictine, 1885; ordained priest, 1891. *Address:* Mdina, Malta.

Died 17 Dec. 1943.

CARUS-WILSON, Charles Ashley, MA Cantab; *b* Dec. 1860; *s* of Rev. C. Carus-Wilson, Vicar of Ramsgate, *g s* of Rev. W. Carus-Wilson of Casterton Hall, Westmorland; *m* 1893, Mary Louisa Georgina (*d* 1935), *d* of Col Martin Petrie; one *s* one *d. Educ:* Haileybury; Pembroke College, Cambridge. Royal Indian Engineering Coll., Coopers Hill. Sent out to Bucharest in 1882 to light up the King of Roumania's Palace with electric light; on the Staff of Coopers Hill, 1887–90; Prof. of Electrical Engineering, McGill University, Montreal, 1890–98; has since practised in Westminster as a consulting engineer and lectured on various engineering and scientific subjects at University College and other Institutions. In the last War, on Staff of Royal Naval College, Osborne. *Publications:* Electro-Dynamics, 1898; numerous scientific papers read before

the Royal Society, the Society of Arts, the Physical Society, and the Institutions of Civil, Mechanical, and Electrical Engineers. *Address:* Hanover Lodge, Kensington Park, W11.

Died 7 Aug. 1942.

CARVER, Captain Edmund Clifton, DSO 1917; late RN; *b* 20 Sept. 1873; *s* of Henry Clifton Carver, Manchester; *m* 1st, 1915, Alison, *y d* of Col E. W. Creswell, RE; two *s*; 2nd, 1931, Marcella Mary, *d* of late William Knight, barrister. *Educ:* Royal Navy. Lieut 1894; Comr 1906; retired, Captain, 1912; served European War in RN till Sept. 1917 (despatches twice); joined RFC 1918.

Died 30 Nov. 1942.

CARWARDINE, Thomas, MS, MB (Lond.), FRCS (Eng.); retired; Consulting Surgeon Bristol Royal Infirmary; *e s* of Thomas Carwardine, London; *m* May, *d* of I. Walker Hall, MD. *Educ:* University College, London; Middlesex Hospital. Gold Medallist in Surgery, in Anatomy, and in Diseases of Women, London University. *Publications:* Operative and Practical Surgery; various papers on Abdominal Surgery in Medical Journals. *Address:* Manormead, Hindhead, Surrey.

Died 17 Dec. 1947.

CASE, Robert Hope, BA (London); Emeritus Professor, University of Liverpool; *b* 1857; 4th *s* of Thomas Case, Liverpool, and Oxton, Cheshire; *m* 1902, Hilda, *d* of Thomas Trew of Axbridge; one *s. Educ:* Birkenhead School; University College, Liverpool. Lecturer in Elizabethan Literature, 1906; Lecturer in English Literature and Associate Professor, 1907; Dean of the Faculty of Arts, 1912–16; Andrew Cecil Bradley Professor, 1919–23; Secretary, University Press of Liverpool, 1923; Hon. Secretary, 1928–33; General Editor of the Arden Shakespeare since 1909, and of the Works and Life of Marlowe, 1930–33. *Publications:* English Epithalamies, 1895; ed. Antony and Cleopatra (Arden Shakespeare), 1906; Coriolanus, 1922; The Post-Captain (1805), 1928; Reflections: in Verse by RQ, 1928; Lancashire in Prose and Verse, 1930; reviews in Quarterly Review, Modern Language Review, Review of English Studies, Blackwood's Magazine, etc. *Address:* (temp.: Avalon, Pant, nr Oswestry); 7 Albert Park West, Liverpool, 17. *Clubs:* University, Athenæum, Liverpool.

Died 28 Dec. 1944.

CASELLA, Alfredo; artiste; titulaire depuis 1931 d'une classe de perfectionnement pianistique à l'Académie de Sainte-Cécile à Rome; *b* Turin, 25 Juin 1883; *m* 1921, Yvonne Muller; one *d. Educ:* Turin et Paris (Conservatoires). Pianiste et chef d'orchestre connu dans toute l'Europe et dans les deux Amériques à la suite de nombreuses tournées de concerts; compositeur, auteur d'un grand nombre d'œuvres théâtrales, symphoniques et de musique de chambre; a enseigné durant quatre années au Conservatoire de Paris; Commandeur de l'Ordre de la Couronne d'Italie, et de l'ordre du St Sauveur de Grèce; Chevalier de l'ordre des SS Maurice et Lazare; Chevalier de la Légion d'honneur de France, et de la Couronne de Roumanie; Membre de l'Académie de Sainte-Cécile à Rome; membre honoraire étranger de la American Academy of Arts and Sciences de Boston; Membre Correspondant de l'Académie de France. *Address:* via G. Nicotera, 5, Roma (149). *T:* 30.086. *Clubs:* Automobile, Roma.

Died 5 March 1947.

CASEY, Thomas Worrall; JP; *b* Intake, nr Sheffield, 13 Oct. 1869; *s* of William and Jemima Ann Casey; *m* 1894; two *s* (eldest son lost in War, 1916) three *d. Educ:* Gleadless Church Schools, nr Sheffield. Started work at 12 years of age on farm; at 13 went to work at Birley Colliery, nr Sheffield; remained there until 18 years of age; employed at this time as engineman; left and started at Cadeby Colliery, nr Rotherham, as winding engineman, and remained there 24 years; on leaving was presented with Gold Hunter Watch by workmen and officials; was General Secretary of National Winding and General Engineers Society for 25 years; MP (L) Attercliffe Division of Sheffield, Dec. 1918–22; JP City of Sheffield, 1920. Methodist local preacher for 60 years, now retired. *Recreation:* formerly athlete. *Address:* Leveston House, Bents Road, Ecclesall, Sheffield 11. *T:* Sheffield 70883.

Died 29 Nov. 1949.

CASGRAIN, Alexandre Chase-; Judge of Superior Court for Province of Quebec since 1934; formerly senior member of law firm Casgrain & Weldon; *b* Quebec, 23 April 1879; *s* of Hon. T. Chase-Casgrain, ex-Postmaster General of Canada, and Dame Marie-Louise Lemoine; *m* 1912, Marguerite Pinsonneault; one *s* one *d. Educ:* Quebec Seminary; St Mary's College at Montreal; McGill University, Montreal. Has always practised law as Barrister at Montreal; Ex-Treasurer of Montreal Bar. *Address:* 536 Clarke Avenue, Westmount, Canada. *Clubs:* University of Montreal, Montreal, Amateur and Athletic Association, Montreal Little Saguenay Fish and Game, Cape Tourmente Fish and Game, Montreal; Addington Fish and Game.

Died 27 Oct. 1941.

CASGRAIN, Rev. Philippe Henri Duperron, CMG 1917; *b* Quebec, 31 May 1864. *Educ:* Royal Military Coll., Kingston. Served North-West Territory, Canada, throughout Rebellion, as Adjutant 9th Rifles, 1885 (medal); Lieut RE 1885; Interpreter in Russian, 1893; Captain, 1894; Major, 1902; served Manipur Expedition, 1891 (medal and clasp); Ordnance Survey, Bedford, 1891–95; served S African War (despatches, two medals, and five clasps); retired, 1907; studied for the priesthood in Rome; ordained, 1911; Director Catholic Immigration Association of Canada; at outbreak of war served as Military Chaplain, 1914; and then on General Staff, War Office, London (despatches, London Gazette, CMG, Order of St Stanislas, Russia; decorated by Pope Pius XI with Cross, Pro Pontifice et Ecclesia, 1923). *Publications:* 1913, Examen Conscientiae et interrogationes proponendae in collatione, Examen Baptismi et Matrimonii, Examen Lingua Polonica Editum et Locutioni gallicae phonetice adaptatum; The Catholic Soldiers' and Sailors' Prayer-book, 1915. *Address:* Cardinal's Palace, Quebec, Canada.

Died 4 Oct. 1942.

CASSEL, Gustav; Professor, University Stockholm; *b* 20 Oct. 1866; *s* of Oscar Cassel and Leontine Dahlstrand; *m* 1895, Johanna Björnson-Möller; two *s* two *d. Educ:* Stockholm. Doctor in mathematics, Uppsala, 1895; Professor, Political Economy, Stockholm, 1904; Correspondent for Sweden to the Royal Economic Society; Hon. Doctor of the Universities of Cologne, Munich, Innsbruck and Athens; Hon. Dr of Law, University of Stockholm; Member and former President of the Royal Swedish Academy of Science; Hon. Member of the American Economic Association; Member of the Gold Delegation of the League of Nations, 1929–32; Rhodes Memorial Lecturer, Oxford, 1932; Swedish delegate to the World Monetary and Economic Conference, London, 1933; Lecturer at International Institute in Geneva. *Publications:* Nature and Necessity of Interest, 1902; Theoretische Sozialökonomie, 1918 (5 German, 2 English and American, 1 French, 1 Japanese, 1 Lithuanian ed., revised Swedish ed., 1934 and 1938); The World's Monetary Problems, Two Memoranda to the League of Nations, 1921; Money and Foreign Exchange after 1914, 1922; Fundamental Thoughts in Economics, 1925; Post-War Monetary Stabilisation, 1928; The Crisis in the World's Monetary System, 1932; On Quantitative Thinking in Economics, 1935; The Downfall of the Gold Standard, 1936 German edition, 1937; Autobiography, 2 Vol., 1940–1941 (Swedish). *Address:* Djursholm, Sweden. *T:* 551513.

Died 14 Jan. 1945.

CASSELLS, Hugh Hutchison, CBE 1936; MVO 1930; MA; *b* 1886. *Educ:* St Andrews University. Vice-Consul in the Consular Service, 1911; Consul, 1920; Commercial Secretary, British Legation, Copenhagen, 1928–33; Consul-General, Valparaiso, 1934; retired 1946. *Recreations:* golf, fishing, gardening. *Address:* Little Woolgarston, Corfe Castle, Dorset.

Died 10 Jan. 1950.

CASSELLS, Thomas; Solicitor; Dean of Guild for Burgh of Falkirk; Sheriff-Substitute of Inverness, Elgin and Nairn, at Fort William since 1941; Member of Legal Firm of J. & F. Cassells, Solicitors and Notaries, Hamilton, Kilsyth and Falkirk; Legal Adviser to Trades Union Movement in Scotland since 1926; *b* Hamilton, Lanarkshire, 7 Aug. 1902; *m* 1927; one *s* one *d. Educ:* Hamilton Academy; University, Glasgow and University, Edinburgh. McFarlane Scholar in Law, Glasgow University. MP (Lab) for County of Dumbarton, 1935–41. Travelled extensively in Europe and United States studying social conditions. *Recreations:* tennis, skiing (Swiss Bronze Medal). *Address:* Thornlea, Falkirk. *TA:* Cassells, Falkirk. *T:* Falkirk 858 and 859, Hamilton 194, Kilsyth 47.

Died 16 June 1944.

CASSELS, Brig. George Hamilton, CMG 1919; KC Canada, 1929; member of Blake, Lash, Anglin & Cassels, Toronto; *b* 17 July 1882; *s* of late Sir Walter Cassels; *m* 1909, Cecil Vivian, *d* of late Hon. Senator J. K. Kerr, PC; no *c. Educ:* Trinity Col School. Port Hope, Canada; R. Military College of Canada, Kingston. Called to bar, Province of Ontario, and enrolled as a Solicitor, 1905; served in France with the 58th Canadian Infantry Battalion, and subsequently appointed AAG at Canadian Headquarters in London (despatches, médaille d'honneur). *Address:* 107 Woodlawn Avenue, W, Toronto, Canada. *Clubs:* Toronto, Toronto Golf, Toronto Hunt, Toronto.

Died 11 May 1944.

CASSERLY, Col Gordon; Indian Army (retired); Honorary Commandant of the United Arts Rifles; Life Member of the Société de Géographie d'Alger; *b* Dublin; *s* of James H. Casserly of Eastersnow, Co. Roscommon; unmarried. *Educ:* Dublin University. Joined the Army as 2nd Lieutenant; went with his regiment to India and transferred to the Indian Army; went with the Indian Expeditionary Force to China for the Boxer War, 1900; after the 1914–18 War was invalided from the Army for ill-health contracted on service; British Consul, St Moritz, 1916–17; travelled extensively. *Publications:* The Elephant God; The Jungle Girl; The Red Marshal; The Desert Lovers; The Sands of Death; The Monkey God; Tiger Girl; Love's Lottery (novels); Daughters of Eve (short stories); The Land of the Boxers; Algeria Today; Tripolitania; Life in an Indian Outpost (travel); Dwellers in the Jungle; In the Green Jungle (Nature); Jungle and River Warfare; Training of the Volunteers for War; Tactics for Beginners; Company Training; Trench Warfare (Military); Bubbles and the Don (play); The Idol, The Test, Lady Hamilton, The Fatal Empress, The Lunatic (one-act plays); contributor to English and American magazines. *Recreations:* yachting, big-game shooting. *Address:* 76 Ladies Mile Road, Brighton, 6.

Died 7 April 1947.

CASSIA, Francis Joseph Nicholas Paul S.; see Sant-Cassia.

CASSIDY, Sir Maurice Alan, GCVO 1949 (KCVO 1934); CB 1929; MA, MD, BCh Cantab, FRCP Lond., MRCS Eng.; Médaille du Roi Albert; Physician to the King since 1937; Physician to the Lord Mayor Treloar's Cripples Hospital, Alton; Consulting Physician to: St Thomas's Hospital; King Edward VII Sanatorium, Midhurst; Children's Heart Hospital, West Wickham; Director Clerical, Medical and General Life Assurance Society; *b* 29 Feb. 1880; *e s* of late D. M. Cassidy, CBE,

MD; *m* 1918, Elsie, *y d* of late Frederick Relfe. *Educ:* Clare College, Cambridge (Scholar); St Thomas's Hospital. Hon. Fellow, Clare Coll., Cambridge, 1949. 1st Class Honours in Part I and in Part II of Natural Science Tripos, 1901, 1902. Goulstonian Lecturer, Royal College of Physicians, 1914; Physician to No. 2 Anglo-Belgian Fever Hospital, Calais, 1914–15; BEF 1916; Salter's Company Research Fellow, 1907, 1912, 1913; Physician to HM's Household, 1930; Physician Extraordinary to King George V, 1932–36, and to King Edward VIII, 1936; late Senior Censor of Royal College of Physicians; late Physician and Chief Medical Officer to the Metropolitan Police; late Examiner in Medicine, Universities of London and Cambridge, Manchester, Edinburgh, and to the Conjoint Board; Pres. Royal Society of Medicine, 1946–48. *Publications:* numerous contributions to medical literature. *Recreation:* fishing. *Address:* 42 Montagu Square, W1. *Club:* United University.

Died 22 Oct. 1949.

CASSON, Stanley, MA, FSA, Hon. ARIBA; Fellow of New College, Oxford; Reader in Classical Archæology in the University of Oxford; *b* 7 May 1889; *s* of William A. and Kate Elizabeth Casson; *m* 1924, Joan, *er d* of M. Ruddle, Harewood House, Langham, Rutland; one *d*. *Educ:* Merchant Taylors School; Lincoln College, Oxford. Senior Scholar, St John's College, Oxford, 1912; Student of British School at Athens, 1913. Served European War, Aug. 6, 1914–April 1919 with 1st Bn East Lancashire Regt in Flanders, 1915; British-Salonika Force 1916–18, General Staff, 1918; Constantinople and Turkestan, 1919 (despatches); Assistant Director British School at Athens, 1919–22; Fellow of New College, Oxford, 1920; Conington Prize, 1924; Reader in Archæology, 1927; Junior Proctor, 1928; Director of British Academy Excavations at Constantinople, 1928–29; Special Lecturer in Art at Bristol University, 1931; visiting Professor at Bowdoin College, Maine, USA, 1933–34; second European War Service from Sept. 1939 in Holland and Greece; has excavated and travelled in Macedonia and Thrace; Member of German Archæological Institute and of Bulgarian Archæological Institute; Greek Order of the Redeemer. *Publications:* Catalogue of the Acropolis Museum Vol. II, 1922; Ancient Greece (new edition 1939); Macedonia, Thrace and Illyria, 1926; Some Modern Sculptors, 1928; 20th Century Sculpture, 1930; Technique of Early Greek Sculpture, 1933; Progress of Archæology, 1934; Steady Drummer, 1935; Progress and Catastrophe, 1937; Ancient Cyprus, 1937; Murder by Burial, 1938; The Discovery of Man, 1939; Greece Against the Axis, 1942; Greece (Oxford pamphlet), 1942; Greece and Britain, 1943; articles in archæological journals. *Recreation:* nil. *Address:* New College, Oxford. *Club:* Authors'.

Died 17 April 1944.

CASTILLEJO, José, LLD, PhD (Madrid); Hon. DLitt (Columbia University); Lecturer at The School of Hispanic Studies of Liverpool University; *b* 30 Oct. 1877; *e s* of Daniel Castillejo, barrister; *m* 1922, Irene L. Claremont; two *s* two *d*. *Educ:* Secondary School, Ciudad-Real; University of Madrid; University of Berlin; and University of Halle-a-d-S. Spanish Govt Scholar in Germany, 1904–06; Professor of Law, Univ. of Seville, 1907; Secretary to the Junta para Ampliación de Estudios e Investigaciones científicas, 1907–34; Professor of Law, Univ. of Valladolid, 1909; Professor of Law, Univ. of Madrid, 1920–37; Director of the Fundación Nacional para Investigaciones científicas, Madrid, 1932–36; Visiting Professor at Univ. of Leeds, 1907; Columbia University, New York, 1938; Carleton College, Minn, USA, 1939; Univ. of London Institute of Education, 1940; Member of International Commission on Intellectual Co-operation of the League of Nations, 1932–38. *Publications:* La forma contractual en el Derecho de Sucesiones, 1904; La Educación en Inglaterra, 1919; Historia del Derecho Romano, 1935;

Wars of Ideas in Spain, 1937; Education and Revolution in Spain, 1937; Britain as the Centre of European Reconstruction, 1940; Numerous Reports on Education and articles in Reviews and newspapers of Europe and America. *Recreations:* riding, cycling, walking, travelling. *Address:* 25 The Park, NW11. *T:* Speedwell 2767.

Died 30 May 1945.

CASTLEMAN-SMITH, Col Edward Castleman, CB 1914; late Lt-Colonel Commanding 3rd Dorset Regt; JP Dorset; *e s* of late Edwin A. and Jane Castleman-Smith; *m* Beatrice Mary (*d* 1943), *y d* of John H. Devenish, Weymouth; no *c*. *Educ:* privately. Entered army, 3rd Dorset Regiment, 1882. *Address:* Chevington Croft, Parkstone, Dorset. *T:* Parkstone 275.

Died 8 Dec. 1943.

CATHER, Willa Sibert; author; *b* Winchester, Va, 7 Dec. 1876; *d* of Charles F. Cather and Mary Virginia Boak; unmarried. *Educ:* BA, University of Nebraska, 1895; LittD 1917; University of Michigan, 1922; Columbia University, 1928; Yale University, 1929; Princeton University, 1931; Doctor of Laws, Creighton University, 1928; University of California, 1931. Editor McClure's Magazine, 1906–12. *Publications:* April Twilights, 1903; The Troll Garden, 1905; Alexander's Bridge, 1912; O Pioneers, 1913; The Song of the Lark, 1915; My Antonia, 1918; Youth and the Bright Medusa, 1920; One of Ours (Pulitzer prize novel), 1922; A Lost Lady, 1923; The Professor's House, 1925; My Mortal Enemy, 1926; Death Comes for the Archbishop, 1927; Shadows on the Rock, 1931; Obscure Destinies, 1932; Lucy Gayheart, 1935; Not Under Forty, 1936; Sapphira and the Slave Girl, 1940. *Address:* c/o A. A. Knopf, 501 Madison Avenue, New York, USA.

Died 24 April 1947.

CATLOW, Alderman Sir John William, Kt 1943; JP and High Sheriff of Middlesex, 1943–44; County Alderman, Middlesex; Vice-President National Foundation for Adult Education; Chairman Executive Committee, British Institute of Adult Education; Governor of Mill Hill School and University College School; *e s* of William and Ann Catlow, Darwen, Lancs; *m* May, *o d* of John and Elizabeth Peer, Darlington and Loughborough; no *c*. *Educ:* Darwen Grammar School; Univ. College, Bangor. Treasurer, Central Council for Physical Recreation; Member Willesden Borough Council, 1928–44; Deputy Mayor of Willesden, 1942–43; Chairman Middlesex Education Committee, 1941–46; Member School Broadcasting Council, Reading University Court and Council, etc.; former President Association of Education Committees and Incorporated Sales Managers' Association. *Recreations:* music, reading. *Address:* 148 Anson Road, NW2. *T:* Gladstone 4738.

Died 12 May 1947.

CATON-JONES, Col Frederick William, CB 1915; MB; late RAMC; *b* 24 Aug. 1860; name changed by deed poll to Caton-Jones; *m* 1916, Alice Pownall, 2nd *d* of late Thomas Fielden, Grimston Park, Tadcaster. Major, 1897; Lt-Col 1905; Col 1914. Served Burma, 1886–88 (despatches, medal with 2 clasps); Nile Expedition, 1898 (Queen's medal and Khedive's medal); South African War, 1899–1902 (despatches twice, Queen's medal 4 clasps, King's medal 2 clasps); European War, 1914–17 (despatches, CB); JP Salop. *Address:* Earlsdale, Pontesford, Salop. *T:* Pontesbury 37. *Clubs:* East India and Sports; Shropshire, Shrewsbury.

Died 9 June 1944.

CATOR, John; JP, DL; *b* 24 Sept. 1862; *e s* of late Albemarle Cator and Mary Molesworth Cordelia, 3rd *d* of C. A. Mohun-Harris of Hayne, Devon; *m* 1895, Maud (*d* 1943), 2nd *d* of late Henry J. Adeane of Babraham, Cambs; one *s* one *d*. *Educ:* Eton; Christ

Church, Oxford (BA). MP (U) Huntingdon, 1910–18; High Sheriff of Norfolk, 1920–21. *Address:* Woodbastwick Hall, Norwich. *Clubs:* Carlton, Turf.

Died 27 April 1944.

CATOR, Temp. Lt-Col Philip James, DSO 1940; RE; CRE 7th Indian Division; *b* 14 April 1901; *s* of Gerald Cator, RN (retd), and Lilian Martha Nance; *m* 1933, Nita Ralston (*widow*), née Tisdall, Toronto, Canada; no *c. Educ:* St Paul's; RMA, Woolwich. 2nd Lieut RE, 1920; Captain, 1931; Major, 1938; served in India, 1924–29, and since 1939, and in Malaya, 1935–38; War of 1939–45 (despatches twice). *Recreations:* golf, travelling. *Address:* c/o Lloyds Bank, Rawalpindi, India. *Club:* Junior United Service.

Died Feb. 1944.

CATOR, Sir Ralph Bertie Peter, Kt 1931; *b* 21 Nov. 1861; *e s* of late Bertie Peter Cator, Beckenham, Kent, and Mary Elizabeth, *d* of late Aretas Akers, Malling Abbey, Kent; *m* 1907, Adeh, *d* of Jonkheer O. von Schmidt auf Altenstadt, of the Hague; no *c. Educ:* Radley; Keble College, Oxford. Judge of the British East Africa Protectorate, 1896–1905; Judge of HBM Supreme Court for the Ottoman Dominions, 1905–16; and of HBM Supreme Court for Egypt, 1915–16; President of HBM Prize Court in Egypt, 1914–16; President International Mixed Court of Appeal in Egypt, 1931; retired, 1932. *Address:* Bulkeley, Alexandria, Egypt. *Clubs:* Athenæum, Savile.

Died 29 July 1945.

CATTERALL, Arthur; Professor of Violin, Royal Academy of Music since 1931; *b* Preston, Lancs, 1884; four *d. Educ:* St Bede's College, Manchester; Royal College of Music, Manchester, under Dr Brodsky; studied under Wilby Hess, 1893. Concertmeister of the Queen's Hall Promenade Concerts, 1909–14; appointed leader Hallé Orchestra, 1914; resigned, 1925; solo violin and leader of BBC Symphony Orchestra, 1929–36; Leader of Catterall String Quartet. *Recreations:* gardening, tennis, walking. *Address:* 35 London Road, Stanmore, Middlesex. *T:* Grimsdyke 1389.

Died 28 Nov. 1943.

CATTERSON-SMITH, John Keats, MEng (Liverpool); MIEE; University Professor of Electrical Engineering, King's College, Strand, WC2; *b* 27 Dec. 1882; *e s* of late R. Catterson-Smith, MA; *m* 1918, Rita, *e d* of late G. M. Thom, JP, Dundee; one *s* one *d. Educ:* City of London School; South Western Polytechnic; University of Birmingham. Bowen Research Scholar, 1902–04; Siemens Dynamo Works, Stafford, 1904–07; Assistant Lecturer and Demonstrator in Electrical Engineering, 1907–12; Lecturer in Electrical Machinery, 1909–12, in the University of Liverpool; Chief Assistant to Professor Silvanus P. Thompson, Finsbury Technical College, 1912–15, and to Dr W. H. Eccles, 1919–23; War Service, RNVR abroad, 1915–16; Experimental wireless officer, HMS Vernon and HM Signal School, 1916–19; Lecturer in Electrical Machinery, Faraday House, 1919–22; Professor of Electrical Technology, Indian Institute of Science, Bangalore, 1923–30; Hon. Fellow, Indian Institute of Science, 1930. *Publications:* contributions to technical journals; founded Electrotechnics, India, editor, 1926–1930. *Address:* King's College, WC2. *T:* Temple Bar 5651. *Clubs:* Savile, London Corinthian Sailing.

Died 25 Jan. 1945.

CAULCUTT, Sir John, KCMG 1937; Kt 1931; Chairman, Barclays Bank (Dominion, Colonial, and Overseas) since 1937; Director of Barclays Bank, Ltd; Director of Barclays Bank (France), Ltd; Director of Barclays Bank (Canada); Director of Phœnix Assurance Company, Ltd; Director of The Eastern Bank, Ltd; Director of Agricultural Mortgage Company of Palestine Ltd; Chairman of Export Guarantees Advisory Council of the Board of Trade; Chairman of Executive Committee of Export Credits Guarantee Department; Member of Board of Trade Central Committee of Export Groups; Member of Palestine Currency Board; a Vice-President of Institute of Bankers, President, 1935–37; a Vice-President of Council of Royal Empire Society; Hon. Treasurer Anglo-Egyptian Chamber of Commerce; Chairman Governing Body British Postgraduate Medical School; Chairman Board of Management, Watford and District Peace Memorial Hospital; Finance Chairman, St Dunstan's; Grand Cordon of the Order of the Nile; *b* 1876; *s* of late John Caulcutt of Bedfordshire; *m* 1902, Alice Lillian May; one *s* two *d. Educ:* City of London School. *Recreation:* fishing. *Address:* Oaklands, Watford. *T:* Watford 3523. *Clubs:* Athenæum, Junior Carlton.

Died 29 April 1943.

CAULFEILD, Brig.-Gen. Charles Trevor, CMG 1916; *b* 1863; *s* of late Colonel Robert Caulfeild; *m* 1903, Kathleen Mary (*d* 1946) (author of Ahana, The Cloudy Porch, etc.), *d* of late Rt Hon. Sir John Edge, KC, PC; one *s* one *d. Educ:* RMA, Woolwich. Joined Royal Artillery, 1882; foreign service, India and S Africa; commanded RHA, Ipswich, 1909–13; Home Counties, Divisional Artillery, 1913–14; took command West Riding Divisional Artillery, Jan. 1915; served European War, 1915–16 (despatches, CMG); Commanding Royal Artillery, 2nd (Rawal Pindi) Division, 1918–20; Afghan War, 1919; retired pay, 1920. *Address:* 44 Charles St, Berkeley Sq., W1.

Died 25 Sept. 1947.

CAULFEILD, Vice-Adm. Francis Wade, CBE 1936; *b* 25 Jan. 1872. Joined HMS Britannia, 1885, chief captain of cadets, passed out as a midshipman, 1887; Sub-Lieut 1891; Lieut 1892, gaining five first-class certificates; specialised in Gunnery; Commander, 1903; Naval Intelligence Division, Admiralty, 1903–06; Commander of Implacable, 1906–08, obtained the record for coaling ship, with 394 tons per hour, as against previous best of 319 tons by Duke of Edinburgh; Captain, 1908; Senior Naval Officer, Persian Gulf, 1912–14; served European War, 1914–19, in command of Fox, 1914–15; Venerable, 1916–17; Britannia battleship, 1917–18; and Temeraire, 1919; retired at own request on promotion to Rear-Admiral, Feb. 1920; Vice-Admiral (retired), Aug. 1925; received expression of their lordships' high appreciation of magnificent conduct on the occasion of the loss of the Britannia by torpedo attack from submarine. Founder and President of ARNO (Assoc. of Retired Naval Officers), founded Trafalgar Day, 1925. *Address:* ARNO, Empire House, 175 Piccadilly, W1. *T:* Regent 7130. *Club:* United Service.

Died 7 Nov. 1947.

CAULFEILD, Captain James Montgomerie, CBE 1919; RN, retired; *b* 22 Feb. 1855; *m* 1889, Kathleen Ruth, *d* of late Lt-Col H. A. Crofton. Served Egyptian War, 1882 (Medal, Khedive's bronze star); Soudan, 1883–84 (clasp); Brass River, 1895 (medal and clasp); European War (CBE); on Cameroon Boundary Survey, and in command of Niger Coast Protectorate Yacht, Evangeline, 1894; served as Harbour-master at Mauritius, 1902; commanded HMS Agincourt at Jubilee Review, 1897 (Medal). *Recreations:* tennis, boat sailing, boys' booklets. *Clubs:* United Service; Royal Yacht Squadron, Cowes (Hon. Member).

Died 26 Oct. 1946.

CAUTLEY, 1st Baron *cr* 1936, of Lindfield; **Henry Strother Cautley;** 1st Bt *cr* 1924; KC; JP; *b* 1863; *m* 1902, Alice Bohun (*d* 1943), *e d* of late B. H. C. Fox, JP of Maplewell, Woodhouse Eaves. *Educ:* Charterhouse; King's Coll., Cambridge (1st class Mathematical Tripos). Called to Bar, 1886; contested Dewsbury 1892 and 1895; MP (C) East Leeds, 1900–06; East Grinstead Division, Sussex, 1910–36; Recorder of Sunderland, 1918–35; KC 1919; A Member of Ecclesiastical Committee of House of Lords; Chairman of Quarter

Sessions for East Sussex; a Member of East Sussex County Council. *Recreations:* farming, shooting. *Heir:* none. *Address:* Buxhalls Park, Lindfield, Sussex. *T:* Lindfield 60. *Clubs:* Carlton, Oxford and Cambridge.

Died 21 Sept. 1946 (ext).

CAUTLEY, Edmund, MD, FRCP; retired; Consulting Physician to Belgrave Hospital for Children and to Metropolitan Hospital; *s* of late Henry Cautley, Bramley, Leeds; *m* 1st, Evelyn Grace, *d* of late Lt-Gen. Willes, BSC; 2nd, Louisa, *d* of late George Henry Cumming, Torquay. *Educ:* Charterhouse; King's College, Cambridge. *Publications:* Diseases of Children; The Feeding of Infants. *Address:* Westminster Bank Ltd, Hanover Square, W1.

Died 1 Dec. 1944.

CAVALIERI, Lina; *b* Rome, 1874; *m* Lucien Muratore. First appeared at Royal Theatre, Lisbon, as Nedda in Pagliacci, 1900. Principal rôles in La Vie de Bohème, La Traviata, Rigoletto, Mignon, Fedora.

Died Feb. 1944.

CAVAN, 10th Earl of, *cr* 1647; **Frederic Rudolph Lambart,** KP 1916; GCB 1926; GCMG 1919; GCVO 1922; GBE 1927; KCB 1917; CB 1915; MVO 1910; Baron Cavan, 1618; Baron Lambart, 1618; Viscount Kilcoursie, 1647; Colonel of the Irish Guards since 1925; *b* 16 Oct. 1865; *e s* of 9th Earl and Mary, *o c* of Rev. John Olive, Rector of Ayot St Lawrence, Herts; *S* father, 1900; *m* 1st, 1893, Inez (*d* 1920), *e d* of late George Baden Crawley and Mrs Pringle; 2nd, 1922, Lady Joan Mulholland (DBE 1927), *widow* of Captain Hon. A. E. S. Mulholland, Irish Guards, and *d* of 5th Earl of Strafford; two *d*. *Educ:* Eton; RMC, Sandhurst. ADC to Governor-General (Lord Stanley of Preston) of Canada, 1891–93; served South Africa 1901 (despatches); European War, 1914–18; commanded 14th Corps, BEF; commanded Brigade of Guards, subsequently Guards Division (despatches seven times, CB, prom. Lieut-General, KCB, GCMG); was in charge of operations of the Tenth Italian Army on the Piave front, 1918; ADC to the King, 1920–22; Commander-in-Chief, Aldershot, 1920–22; General, 1921; Chief of Imperial General Staff, 1922–26; Field-Marshal, 1932; head of War Office Section of the British Delegation at the Washington Conference, 1921; Captain of the Gentlemen-at-Arms, 1929–31; Commanded the Troops at Coronation of King George VI; Grand Officer Legion of Honour, Belgian Order de la Couronne, Croix de Guerre. *Recreations:* shooting, fishing, golf. *Heir: b* Ven. Hon. H. E. S. S. Lambart, TD. *Address:* 47 Hyde Park Gate, SW7. *Club:* Turf.

Died 28 Aug. 1946.

CAVAN, 11th Earl of, *cr* 1647; **Horace Edward Samuel Sneade Lambart,** MA; TD; Baron Cavan, 1618; Baron Lambart, 1618; Viscount Kilcoursie, 1647; Archdeacon Emeritus of Salop and Prebendary Emeritus of Lichfield Cathedral; *b* 25 Aug. 1878; *s* of 9th Earl and Mary, *o c* of Rev. John Olive, Rector of Ayot St Lawrence, Herts; *S* brother 1946; *m* 1907, Audrey Kathleen (*d* 1942), *o d* of late A. B. Loder; one *s* two *d*. *Educ:* Charterhouse; Magdalen College, Oxford. Late Lieut 1st Volunteer Batt. Oxfordshire Light Infantry; served S Africa, 1900; Ordained, 1903; Curate of St Dunstan's, Stepney, 1903–08; Vicar of Leaton, 1908–13; Vicar of Market Drayton, 1913–18; Vicar of St Mary the Virgin, Shrewsbury, 1918–25; Provost of Denstone, 1928–48; Chaplain to Shropshire Yeomanry, European War, 1914–17. *Heir: s* Viscount Kilcoursie, TD. *Address:* Plex House, Hadnall, Salop.

Died 9 Dec. 1950.

CAVE, Charles John Philip, MA; JP; FSA; late temp. Capt., RE; *b* 1871; *e s* of Laurence Trent Cave and Lucy, *d* of John Greenwood, QC; *m* 1895, Wilhelmina, OBE (*d* 1944), *d* of late Maj. Francis Kerr, the Rifle Brigade;

four *s* one *d*. *Educ:* The Oratory School. Edgbaston; Trinity College, Cambridge. Fellow Royal Meteorological Society (President, 1913–15; 1924–26), Royal Astronomical Society, Royal Photographic Society; Vice-Pres. of Royal National Lifeboat Institution. *Publications:* The Structure of the Atmosphere in Clear Weather, 1912; Clouds and Weather Phenomena, 1926, new version, 1943; The Roof Bosses in the Cathedral Church of Canterbury, 1934; do., Winchester, 1935; do. Bristol, 1935; Roof Bosses in Medieval Churches, 1948; The Roof Bosses of Lincoln Cathedral, 1949; papers in Journal of Royal Meteorological Society and in Journals of various Archæological Societies. *Recreations:* sailing, photography. *Address:* Stoner Hill, Petersfield. *T:* Petersfield 405. *Clubs:* Athenæum; Royal Yacht Squadron (Cowes).

Died 8 Dec. 1950.

CAVE, Edmund; *b* 1859; *s* of late Thomas Cave, MP of Queensberry House, Richmond, Surrey; *m* Blanche Emily Tankerville Chamberlaine; one *d*. Admitted a solicitor, 1883; a Master of the Supreme Court (Taxing Office), 1923–33; retired, 1933. *Publication:* one of the Editors of Russell on Arbitration and Award, 13th Ed. and of the treatise on Arbitration in the Encyclopædia of the Laws of England, 3rd Ed.

Died 6 April 1946.

CAVE, Sir Edward Charles, 3rd Bt *cr* 1896; *b* 2 Jan. 1893; *e s* of Sir Charles Henry Cave, 2nd Bt, and Beatrice Julia, OBE, 3rd *d* of Sir Frederick Martin Williams, 2nd Bt; *S* father 1932; *m* 1922, Betty (who obtained a divorce, 1942), *o d* of Rennell Coleridge, Salston, Ottery St Mary; one *s* two *d*. *Educ:* Eton, Magdalene College, Cambridge. *Heir: s* Charles Edward Coleridge, *b* 28 Feb. 1927. *Address:* Sidbury Manor, Sidmouth. *Clubs:* United University; Devon and Exeter, Exeter.

Died 4 Oct. 1946.

CAVE, His Honour Edward Watkins; KC 1921; *s* of late Justice Cave; *m* Mary Geraldine, *d* of late Surgeon-General Tyrell Carter Ross, CIE; one *s*. *Educ:* Rugby School (Classical Scholar); King's College School; Oriel College, Oxford (Classical Scholar). Called to bar, Inner Temple, 1897; Master of Bench of Inner Temple, 1928; Recorder of Birmingham, 1932–37; Judge of County Courts Circuit No. 55 (Bournemouth, etc.), 1937–46. *Address:* Dale House, Blandford Dorset. *T:* Blandford 335.

Died 24 April 1948.

CAVE-BROWNE-CAVE, Sir Clement Charles, 15th Bt *cr* 1641; Owner and Manager of Cave & Co. Ltd, 567 Hornby St, Vancouver; *b* 27 Nov. 1896; *o s* of Edward Lambert Cave-Browne-Cave and Rachael Marion Fortin; *S* uncle, 1943; *m* 1923, Dorothea Plewman, *d* of Robert Greene Dwen, Chicago, Ill; one *s*. *Educ:* University School, Victoria, BC. Served overseas with 196th Western Universities Bn, 46th Bn, CEF and RAF in European War, 1914–18. *Recreation:* golf. *Heir: s* Robert Edward, *b* 8 June 1929. *Address:* 1905 West 45th Avenue, Vancouver, BC, Canada. *TA:* Cave-Vancouver. *T:* Kerrisdale 2821, (office) Marine 8341. *Clubs:* Vancouver, Capilano Golf and Country, Vancouver.

Died 21 April 1945.

CAVE-BROWNE-CAVE, Sir Rowland Henry, 14th Bt *cr* 1641; *b* 14 April 1865; 4th *s* of late Ambrose Sneyd Cave-Browne-Cave, 3rd *s* of 10th Bt; *S* brother, 1930; *m* 1895, Honora Phoebe Gertrude (*d* 1924); widow of Edward Seymour Fowler, and *d* of Benjamin Bright, Colwall; one *d*. *Heir: nephew* Clement Charles [*b* 28 Nov. 1896; *m* 1923, Dorothea Plewman, *y d* of Robert Greene Dwen, Chicago; one *s*].

Died 23 Dec. 1943.

CAVENAGH, Prof. Francis Alexander; University Professor of Education, King's College, London, since 1937; *b* 8 March 1884; *s* of Frank and Mary A. Cavenagh; *m* 1911, Susie, *d* of late William Evans, JP, Liverpool; one *s* two *d*. *Educ:* University College, London, BA 1904, MA (Classics, distinction), 1909; Fellow of University College, London, 1910; London Day Training College, 1905; Teacher's Diploma. Assistant Master, Cheltenham Grammar School, 1906–08; King Edward VII School, Lytham, 1910–14; Lecturer, Dept of Education, Manchester University, 1914–21; Professor of Education, University College of Swansea 1921–33; Acting Head of Education Department, King's College, London, 1933–34; Professor of Education, Reading University, 1934–37; served in Artists' Rifles and RGA; Lecturer, War Office School of Education, Oxford, 1919; Member of Council British Inst. of Adult Education; Central Council for Group Listening (BBC); New Education Fellowship; National Froebel Foundation; Member, British Psychological Society; Editor of Adult Education. *Publications:* The Ethical End of Plato's Theory of Ideas, 1909; Editions of Scott's Ivanhoe, Antiquary, and many other English texts; articles and reviews in Journal of Education, Adult Education, Forum of Educ., Year Book of Education, 1932, 1936, etc.; Griffith Jones, 1930; James and J. S. Mill on Education, 1930; Herbert Spencer on Education, 1931. *Address:* 31 Glebe Road, Barnes, SW13. *T:* Prospect 3869. *Clubs:* Savile, University of London.

Died 21 April 1946.

CAVENDISH, Brig.-Gen. Alfred Edward John, CMG 1900; FRGS; *b* 19 June 1859; 2nd *s* of late Francis W. H. Cavendish, Clerk in the Foreign Office; *m* 1886, Alice Isabella, *γ d* of Hon. John Van der Byl of Cape of Good Hope; one *s*. *Educ:* Trinity Coll. Cambridge; RMC, Sandhurst. 2nd Lt 91st Highlanders, 1880; Lt A. and S Highlanders, 1881; Capt. 1886; Major, 1897; Adjt 1st A. and S Highlanders, 1885–87; passed Staff College, 1889; Military Attaché to Chinese Army, 1894, and to British Legation, China, 1895, during China-Japanese War; attached to Korean special mission during Diamond Jubilee, 1897; DAAG Dublin District, 1897–1900; DAAG Aldershot, 1900; DAAG SA Field Force, 1900–02; served on Military Compensation Commission, S Africa, 1903; commanded 2nd Batt. Argyll and Sutherland (Princess Louise's) Highlanders, 1907–11; AAG Southern Command, 1913–14; European War, 1914–18; AAG, GHQ, BEF, 1914; DA and QMG, 1915; AAG Aldershot Command, 1915; AAG, GHQ, Mediterranean Expeditionary Force, and Dardanelles Army, 1915–16; GOC S African Command, 1916–18 (despatches). Decorated for SA Campaign. *Publications:* Korea and the Sacred White Mountain; the 93rd Sutherland Highlanders, 1929. *Address:* Hanover Court, Hanover Square, W. *Club:* Naval and Military.

Died 2 Feb. 1943.

CAVENDISH, Lord Charles A. F.; *b* 5 Aug. 1905; 2nd *s* of 9th Duke of Devonshire and Lady Evelyn Fitzmaurice; *m* Adèle Astaire, New York. *Educ:* Eton; Trinity College, Cambridge. 2nd Lieutenant Reserve Derbyshire Armoured Car Corps; served two years with J. P. Morgan & Co., New York. *Recreations:* shooting, racing. *Address:* Lismore Castle, Lismore, Co. Waterford, IFS. *TA:* Lismore, Waterford. *Clubs:* Brooks's, Pratt's, Buck's.

Died 23 March 1944.

CAVENDISH, Richard Charles Alexander, CBE 1939; Commander of Order of St John of Jerusalem; Commissioner of Police, Kenya Colony; *b* 1885; *s* of Reginald Richard Frederick Cavendish; *m* 1936, Margaret Barbara Duncan Lyon, widow of F. O. Lyon; no *c*. *Educ:* Framlingham College. British South Africa Police, Southern Rhodesia, 1906–11; Nigeria Police,

West Africa, 1912–31; Kenya Police, East Africa, since 1931. *Recreations:* shooting, fishing. *Address:* PO Box 83, Nairobi, Kenya Colony. *Club:* East India and Sports.

Died 28 April 1941.

CAVENDISH, Rt Hon. Lord Richard (Frederick), PC 1912; CB 1919; CMG 1918; Hon. Col 56th (King's Own Regt), ATR; Chairman Development Commission; *b* 31 Jan. 1871; 2nd *s* of late Lord Edward Cavendish; *brother* of 9th Duke of Devonshire; *m* 1895, Lady Moyra de Vere Beauclerk (*d* 1942), 3rd *d* of 10th Duke of St Albans; one *s* four *d*. *Educ:* Eton; Trinity College, Cambridge. MP (LU) N Lonsdale Div. Lancashire, 1895–1906; served European War, 1914–15 (despatches, wounded). *Address:* Holker Hall, Cark-in-Cartmel, Lancashire. *T:* Flookburgh 20. *Clubs:* Brooks's, Turf.

Died 7 Jan. 1946.

CAVENDISH-BENTINCK, Frederick; *see* Bentinck.

CAW, Sir James Lewis, Kt 1931; LLD (Edin.); HRSA; HRSW; FSA Scot; *b* Ayr, 25 Sept. 1864; *m* 1909, Annie (*d* 1949), *e d* of late William M'Taggart, RSA. *Educ:* Ayr Academy; West of Scotland Technical College; Edinburgh University. Trained as an engineer, and was engaged in designing machinery for a number of years; but studied art in Glasgow and Edinburgh; Curator of Scottish National Portrait Gallery, 1895–1907; Director of National Galleries of Scotland, 1907–30; with Stanley Cursiter, RSA, arranged Exhibition of Scottish Art, RA, 1939. Art Critic of The Scotsman, 1916–33. *Publications:* Sir Henry Raeburn (with R. A. M. Stevenson and Sir Walter Armstrong), 1901; Scottish Portraits, 1903; The Scott Gallery, 1903; Scottish Painting Past and Present, 1908; Raeburn (masterpieces in colour), 1909; The National Gallery of Scotland, 1911; William McTaggart, RSA, 1917; Scottish History told by Portraits, 1924 and 1934; The Pictures, and How to Enjoy Them, 1926 and 1931; Hours in the Scottish National Gallery, 1927; Sir James Guthrie, PRSA, 1932; Allan Ramsay (Walpole Society), 1937; Sir D. Y. Cameron, RA, (RSW), 1949; contributions to Dictionary of National Biography, and many articles on the arts. *Recreations:* sketching, reading and a little gardening. *Address:* Edinkerry, Lasswade, Midlothian. *T:* Lasswade 2227. *Clubs:* Scottish Arts (Edinburgh); Pen (Scottish).

Died 5 Dec. 1950.

CAWTHRA-ELLIOT, Maj.-Gen. Harry Macintire, CB 1921; CMG 1918; *b* 1867; *s* of Maj.-Gen. Henry Riversdale Elliot, Cheltenham; *m* 1st, 1899, Blanche A. (*d* 1911), *d* of W. N. Wickwire, Halifax, NS; 2nd, 1921, Grace M. K., *d* of Henry Cawthra, Toronto. Served S Africa, 1899–1900 (Queen's medal with clasp); China, 1900 (medal); Master-General of Ordnance, Canadian Expeditionary Force, 1915–21. *Address:* Cawthra Lotten, Lakeview, Ontario, Canada.

Died 27 June 1949.

CAYLEY, Adm. George Cuthbert, CB 1916; *b* 30 Aug. 1866; 2nd *s* of Digby Cayley, *s* of 7th Bt of Brompton; *m* 1897, Cecil Mildred May (*d* 1937), *d* of Col Price Jones; one *s* one *d*. Naval Cadet of Monarch at bombardment of Alexandria, 1882, and during Egyptian War (medal, bronze star); Lieut, wrecked in Victoria, 27 June 1892; commanded boys' training ship, St Vincent, Portsmouth, 1904–06; served on Staff, RN War College, Portsmouth, 1909; Assist Director of Naval Mobilisation, 1909; Flag Captain, China, 1910–13; in command of Shotley Training Establishment, 1913; Commodore in charge at Harwich, 1914; Rear-Admiral in charge, Harwich, 1917; European War, 1914–17 (CB); retired, 1919; Vice-Admiral retired, 1922; Admiral, 1926. *Address:* c/o Arthur Cayley, Horncliffe House, Berwick-on-Tweed.

Died 21 Dec. 1944.

CAYZER, Sir August Bernard Tellefsen, 1st Bt *cr* 1921; *b* 21 Jan. 1876; 3rd *s* of Sir Charles Cayzer, 1st Bt of Gartmore, Perthshire; *m* 1904, Ina Francis (*d* 1935), 2nd *d* of William Stancomb, Blounts Court, Wiltshire; two *s* one *d*. *Educ:* HMS Britannia. Lieut-Commander, 1906; resigned in 1902 and transferred to Emergency List; Chairman, Cayzer, Irvine & Co., Clan, Houston and Scottish Shire Line of Steamers; Director Suez Canal Co.; JP City of Glasgow. *Recreations:* shooting, golf, fishing, etc. *Heir: s* (William) Nicholas [*b* 21 Jan. 1910; *m* 1935, Betty, *e d* of late Owain Williams; one *d*]. *Address:* Roffey Park, Horsham; Gartmore Perthshire. *T:* Faygate 205. *Clubs:* Bath, City of London, Carlton.

Died 28 Feb. 1943.

CAYZER, Major Harold Stanley; High Sheriff of Warwickshire, 1935; *b* 8 Aug. 1882; *s* of Sir Charles Cayzer, 1st Bt; *m* 1908, Mary Kate Dudgeon (*d* 1946); one *s* one *d*. *Educ:* Rugby; RMC Camberley. Joined XI Hussars, 1901; retired, 1913; served in France with XI Hussars, 1914; DAAG Mediterranean Expeditionary Force, 1915–18; Managing Director Clan Line Steamers; Joint Master, Pytchley Hounds, 1921–23. *Recreations:* hunting, shooting, racing. *Address:* Dunchurch Lodge, Rugby. *T:* Dunchurch 202. *Club:* Cavalry.

Died 27 Feb. 1948.

CAYZER, Sir Nigel John, 4th Bt *cr* 1904; Lieut Scots Guards, 1941; *b* 16 Nov. 1920; *e s* of Sir Charles William Cayzer, 3rd Bt, MP, and Beatrice Eileen, *d* of late James Meakin and the late Countess Sondes; *S* father, 1940. *Educ:* Eton; Christ Church, Oxford (BA 1942). *Heir: b* James Arthur, *b* 1931. *Address:* Kinpurnie Castle, Newtyle, Angus. *T:* Newtyle 7. *Club:* Guards'.

Died Sept. 1943.

CAZALET, Lt-Col Victor Alexander, MC; MP (U) Chippenham, since 1924; Political liaison officer to General Sikorski since 1940; *b* 27 Dec. 1896; *s* of late W. M. Cazalet of Fairlawne, Tonbridge, Kent, and Maud Lucia Heron, *d* of Sir John Heron Maxwell of Springkell, 7th Bt; unmarried. *Educ:* Eton (President of Eton Society); Christ Church, Oxford. Joined West Kent Yeomanry, 1915; 1st Life Guards a Household Batt, 1916; served in trenches, 1916–18; then at Supreme War Conference Versailles; on British Staff in Siberia, 1918–19; contested Chippehham, 1923; Private Secretary (unpaid) to Sir Philip Cunliffe Lister during 1922–23; Parliamentary Private Secretary to President, Board of Trade, 1924–26; Amateur Squash Champion, 1925, 1927, 1929 and 1930; travelled extensively Europe, Africa, Middle, Near, and Far East. *Publications:* articles on travel and politics. *Recreations:* tennis, racquets and squash, travel, Oxford Blue for tennis, lawn tennis and racquets. *Address:* Great Swifts, Cranbrook, Kent. *Clubs:* Brooks's, Bath, MCC.

Died 4 July 1943.

CECIL, Ean Francis; *b* 1880; *s* of late Lieut Lord Francis H. P. Cecil, RN, *s* of 3rd Marquess of Exeter, and Edith, *d* of late Sir William Cunliffe Brooks, 1st Bt (she *m* 2nd, Capt. Philip Francis Tillard, RN); *m* 1901, Hilda (*d* 1939), *y d* of late Col C. Wemyss; one *d*. *Educ:* Eton. Entered F. Army, 1899; served South Africa, 1900; late Lieut 2nd Lincoln Regt. *Recreations:* shooting, fishing, motoring. *Address:* 17 Hyde Park Square, W2; Fasnadarach, Dinnet, Aberdeenshire. *Clubs:* Carlton, Marlborough.

Died 22 Feb. 1942.

CECIL, Lord John (Pakenham), Joicey-; late Lt-Col and Hon. Col 4th Batt Lincolnshire Regiment; *b* 1867; *s* of 3rd Marquess of Exeter; *m* 1896, Isabella Maud, *e d* of late Col John Joicey, MP; two *s* two *d*. MP (U) Stamford Division of Lincolnshire, 1906–10; late Lieut Grenadier Guards; volunteered for service, Sept. 1914; raised and commanded 8th Wilts, and commanded 1st HS Royal Berks. [Assumed by Royal Licence additional surname of Joicey]. *Address:* Highfield, Andover, Hants. *Club:* Junior Carlton.

Died 25 June 1942.

CECIL, Lord William, CVO; FRGS; Extra Gentleman Usher to the King; late Comptroller to Princess Henry of Battenberg; Bailiff Grand Cross, St John of Jerusalem; *b* 2 Nov. 1854; *s* of 3rd Marquess of Exeter; *m* 1st, 1885, Mary Rothes Margaret, Baroness Amherst of Hackney (*d* 1919); three *s*; 2nd, 1924, Violet Maud (Dame of Grace, St John of Jerusalem), *d* of late Percy Freer, and formerly wife of H. O. Collyer, whom she divorced. Formerly Captain Grenadier Guards and Lieut-Col and Hon. Col 4th Batt Lincoln Regt; served in Suakin Expedition, 1885; late Groom-in-Waiting to Queen Victoria. *Address:* 15 Neville Street, Onslow Gardens, SW7. *T:* Kensington 1646.

Died 16 April 1943.

CEDERSTRÖM, Baron Rolf; JP; *m* 1st, 1889, Madame Adelina Patti; 2nd, 1923, Hon. Hermione Frances Fellowes, *d* of 2nd Lord De Ramsey; one *d*. *Educ:* Upsala. *Club:* White's.

Died 24 Feb. 1947.

CENEZ, Rt Rev. Jules Joseph, OMI; Titular Bishop of Nicopolis and Vicar Apostolic of Basutoland, 1909; retired; *b* 1865. *Address:* N. D. de Sion, par Vézelise, Meurthe-et-Moselle, France.

Died 2 March 1944.

CERUTTY, Charles John, CMG 1927; *b* Sale, Victoria, 25 Nov. 1870; 2nd *s* of late John and Elizabeth Cerutty; *m* 1894, Wilhelmina, *y d* of Alexander Mercer, Ballarat; one *d*. Entered the Victorian Public Service as Treasury Clerk, 1888; Secretary, Public Service Reclassification Board, 1897; Sub-Accountant, Commonwealth Treasury, 1901; Accountant, 1910; Assistant Secretary, 1916, whilst Assistant Secretary filled position of Secretary, Finance Council; Director of Note Issue Department, Commonwealth Bank, 1920; Chairman, Gold Mining Conference, 1923, and on numerous occasions acted as Secretary to the Treasury and as Commissioner of Old Age Pensions and Maternity Allowances; Auditor-General for the Commonwealth, 1926–35. *Recreations:* golf, shooting. *Address:* Bonshaw, 112 Dandenong Road, Caulfield North, SE7, Victoria, Australia.

Died 19 Jan. 1941.

CHADBURN, George Haworthe, FRSA; FCIAD; RBA 1902; *b* Yorks, 1870; *s* of Rev. James Chadburn of Sutton, Surrey, and Grace Tetley of Bradford; *m* 1899, Mabel Harwood, illustrator of children's books, of Boston, Lincs; two *s* one *d*. *Educ:* Mill Hill School, Middlesex. Studied at St John's Wood School of Art, Royal Academy schools, Westminster, The Slade. Worked in Paris under Lefèvre and Robert Tony Fleury; Member of the Union Internationale des Beaux-Arts and des Lettres; Member of the Art Workers Guild: Exhibitor at the Salon and Royal Academy. *Recreations:* horticulture (Dykes Medalist, 1934 and 1941; Michael Foster Medal, 1946), chess. *Address:* High Croft, Budleigh Salterton, S Devon.

Died 29 Jan. 1950.

CHADWICK, Hector Munro, MA; Hon. DLitt (Oxf. and Durh.), Hon. LLD (St Andr.), FBA; Hon. Fellow (late Fellow) of Clare College, Cambridge; Elrington and Bosworth Professor of Anglo-Saxon, Cambridge, 1912–41; formerly University Lecturer in Scandinavian; *b* 22 Oct. 1870; *m* Nora [Fellow of Newnham College, Cambridge, 1941–44; formerly lecturer in St Andrews University. *Publications:* Stories and Ballads of the Far Past, transl. from the Norse, 1921; Anglo-Saxon and Norse Poems, 1922; An Early Irish Reader, 1927; Russian Heroic Poetry, 1932; Poetry and Prophecy 1941; The Beginnings of Russian History, 1946], *d* of late James Kershaw. *Educ:* Wakefield Grammar School;

Clare Coll., Cambridge (1st Class Classical Tripos, parts 1 and 2). *Publications:* Studies in Old English, 1899; The Cult of Othin, 1899; Studies in Anglo-Saxon Institutions, 1905; The Origin of The English Nation, 1907; The Heroic Age, 1912; The Study of Anglo-Saxon, 1941; The Nationalities of Europe, 1945; (with wife) The Growth of Literature: Vol. I, 1932; Vol. II, 1936; Vol. III, 1940; Early Scotland: The Picts, The Scots and the Welsh of Southern Scotland, 1949 (posthumous). *Address:* 1 Adams Road, Cambridge.

Died 2 Jan. 1947.

CHADWICK, Roy, CBE 1943; FRSA; FRAeS; MSc; *b* Lancs, 30 April 1893. *Educ:* Manchester Coll. of Technol. Technical Director, A. V. Roe & Company Ltd; Associate of Manchester College of Technology. *Address:* c/o A. V. Roe & Co. Ltd, Greengate, Middleton, Manchester.

Died 23 Aug. 1947.

CHALMERS, Archibald Kerr, LLD (Hon.) Glasgow, 1926; MD, DPH (Cambridge); Fellow (1901) Hon. Fellow (1932) RFPS (Glasgow); VD; TD; Médaille du Roi Albert, Belgium; Lt-Col RAMC (T) (retired). Medical Officer of Health, Glasgow, 1892–1925; Medical Officer of Glasgow Port Local Authority, 1904–25; *b* Greenock, 1856; *s* of William Kerr Chalmers and Margaret Nicoll; *m* Margaret Jessie, *d* of Henry Stewart (Glasgow); two *s. Educ:* Glasgow University. Watsonian Lecturer, RFP & S (G) 1925; Examiner for Diplomas in Public Health, in Hygiene and in Tropical Medicine and Hygiene, Cambridge University, 1923–25, 1929–31; Member Central Midwives Board, Scotland; President Public Health Section BMA Meeting, Glasgow, 1922; Examiner for Fellowship of Roy. Fac. Physicians and Surgeons, Glasgow; Pres. Epidemiological Section, Royal Society of Medicine, 1920–22; one of first members of General Nursing Council of Scotland and of Consultative Council, Medical and Allied Services, Scottish Department of Health, 1920–26, and 1930–36; Member of Belfast Health Commission, 1907; Member of the Medical Research Committee (now Council National Health Insurance Act), 1916–18; formerly Assessor Examiner for Degrees in Medicine, in Medical Jurisprudence, and Public Health, Universities of Aberdeen, St Andrews and Liverpool, and in Public Health, University of Glasgow and Conjoint Board for Scotland; Pres. of Society of Medical Officers of Health, 1913–14, and of Royal Sanitary Association of Scotland, 1898–99; Fellow Royal Society of Medicine, Royal Sanitary Institute, and formerly of Royal Institute of Public Health. *Publications:* A new Life Table for Glasgow, based on the mortality of the ten years 1881–1890; The Epidemic Diseases of the Central Nervous System; National Death Rates in Relation to National Differences in Methods of Housing; Editor Memorial Volume on Public Health Administration of Glasgow by the late Jas B. Russell, MD; The Function of the Isolation Hospital in a General Scheme of Hospital Provision; Progress of Sanitation in Great Britain (Annals of the American Academy of Political and Social Science, March 1905); The Health of Glasgow, 1818–1925; An Outline; and other papers on Public Health subjects. *Address:* at Glasdrum, Fort William, Inverness-shire.

Died 24 Jan. 1942.

CHALMERS, Arthur Morison, CMG 1917; *b* 1 May 1862; *s* of late Rev. John Chalmers, LLD; *m* 1893, Jessie Elder Davidson, OBE; no *c. Educ:* School for Sons of Missionaries, and Grammar School, Aberdeen. Entered Japan Consular Service, 1882; Consul, Shimonoseki, 1903; Tamsui, 1904; Nagasaki, 1909; Consul-General for Corea, 1912–14; at Yokohama, 1914–20; retired on a pension, 1920. *Address:* 28 Morpeth Mansions, SW1.

Died 20 Nov. 1949.

CHALMERS, Lt-Col Frederick Roydon, CMG 1919; DSO 1918; Administrator of Nauru, Central Pacific, since 1938; *b* 1881. Served European War, 1915–18 (despatches, DSO, CMG). *Address:* Nauru, Central Pacific.

Died 29 March 1943.

CHALMERS, Patrick Reginald; banker, author; *e s* of Patrick Chalmers of Aldbar, Forfarshire; *m* Winifred (*d* 1934), *d* of Canon Henry Arnott; no *c. Educ:* Rugby. Director Mercantile Bank of India, Ltd. *Publications:* Green Days and Blue Days; A Peck of Maut; Pipes and Tabors; Pancakes; The Little Pagan Faun; Away to the Maypole; The Frequent Gun; a Dozen Dogs or So; Forty Fine Ladies; At the Sign of the Dog and Gun; Mine Eyes to the Hills (an anthology of the deer forest); Gun-dogs; A Fisherman's Angles; Collected Rhymes of Flood and Field; Where the Spring Salmon Run; The Golden Bee (a novel); At the Tail of the Weir; Dogs of Every Day; Kenneth Grahame, a Memoir; The Cricket in the Cage; Green Fields and Fantasy; Sport and Travel in East Africa, An Account of Two Visits, 1928 and 1930, of the Prince of Wales, 1934; Deerstalking (The Sportsman's Library); The Angler (English View Library); Birds Ashore and Birds Aforeshore; The History of Fox-Hunting (Lonsdale Library); Field Sports of the Highlands (Sportsman's Library); The Shooting Man (English View Library); The Horn, A Lay of the Grassington Fox-Hounds; The Angler's England; The Barrie Inspiration (a critique); Prior's Mead (a novel); A Pipe of Rowan-Wood (a fantasy); Racing England; A Design of Dogs. *Recreations:* field sports and literature. *Address:* Eskmount, Goring-on-Thames, Oxon. *Club:* Fly-fishers'.

Died 12 Sept. 1942.

CHALMERS, Thomas Andrew, CSI 1916; late Superintendent Bazaloni Tea Co., Ltd; late member of Legislative Assembly, India.

Died 7 May 1944.

CHAMBERLAIN, Lady Ivy Muriel, GBE 1925; Lady of Grace St John of Jerusalem; Gold Medal of Merit of Italy; Chevalier Légion d'Honneur; *d* of late Col H. Lawrence Dundas; *m* 1906, Rt Hon. Sir (Joseph) Austen Chamberlain, KG, PC, MP (*d* 1937); two *s* one *d*. *Address:* 24 Egerton Terrace, SW3. *T:* Kensington 7740.

Died 13 Feb. 1941.

CHAMBERLAIN, Col Sir Neville (Francis Fitzgerald), KCB 1903; KCVO 1911; CB 1900; Knight of Grace of the Order of St John of Jerusalem; Lt-Col ISC; retired; *b* 13 Jan. 1856; *s* of late Lieut-Col Charles Chamberlain, CB, Indian Army; *m* 1886, Mary Henrietta (*d* 1936), *e d* of late Maj.-Gen. A. C. Hay. *Educ:* abroad; Brentwood School, Essex. Joined the army, 1873; served in the 11th (Devon) Regt 1873–76; Central India Horse, 1876; on staff of Sir F. Roberts throughout the Afghan War, 1878–80 (wounded, medal and four clasps, bronze star); ADC to Sir F. Roberts, 1881–85; Persian interpreter, 1885–90; Burmah campaign, 1886–87 (medal and clasp); Military Secretary to Kashmir Government, and reorganised Kashmir Army, 1890–97; commanded Khyber Force, 1899; private secretary to Field-Marshal Lord Roberts in South African War, 1899–1900 (despatches, medal and five clasps); Insp.-Gen. Royal Irish Constabulary, 1900–16. *Recreations:* shooting, golf. *Address:* The Wilderness, Ascot, Berks. *Club:* Naval and Military.

Died 28 May 1944.

CHAMBERLAIN, Sir William, Kt 1939; MInstT; Regional Transport Commissioner, North-Western Region, since 1939; *b* 3 Oct. 1877; *m* 1915, Lilian Hood. Served as electrical engineer with Corporations of Lancaster and Wallasey, and with Mersey Docks and Harbour Board; mains superintendent and distributing engineer to Oldham Corporation Electricity Department, 1902; joint borough electrical engineer and manager of the undertaking, 1914; General Manager, Oldham Corporation Tramways, 1918; General Manager, Leeds Corporation Tramways, 1925; General Manager and Engineer, Belfast City Tramways, 1928; Chairman of Traffic Commissioners, North-Western Traffic Area, 1931; Licensing Authority under the Road and Rail Traffic Act 1933, 1934; chief witness on behalf of the municipalities at the inquiry into the Railway Companies' (Road Transport) Bills before the Joint Committee of Lords and Commons in 1928; presented the case of the municipalities before the Royal Commission on Transport; president Municipal Tramways and Transport Assoc., 1928–29. *Address:* Ministry of War Transport, North-Western Region, Arkwright House, Parsonage Gardens, Manchester 3. *TA:* Transco, Manchester. *T:* Blackfriars 6866. *Clubs:* Albion, Oldham.

Died 19 May 1944.

CHAMBERLIN, Frederick, LLB, FRHistS, FSA; historian, lawyer, archæologist; *b* North Abington, Mass, 21 May 1870; *o s* of Edward Chamberlin and Sarah Jane Herrin; *m* 1894, Frances Mansfield Harvey of Charlestown, Boston, Mass, *e d* of Hiram M. Harvey of Canaan, Vermont. *Educ:* Public Schools of North Abington; Phillips Exeter Academy; Harvard University; University of Paris; Harvard Graduate School. Regular Harvard correspondent for Boston Record; special correspondent for Boston Globe from Harvard; regular correspondent in Paris of Boston Herald and New Orleans Picayune, and special correspondent for Boston Globe, New York Sun, Harper's Weekly, etc., on art, the stage, and music, 1894–95; returned to US and admitted Boston Bar, 1895; in active practice of law till 1912 when settled in London; moved to Palma, Majorca, in 1919; enlisted in 5th Mass Regt Inf., 1900, and served four years in ranks and as 1st Lieut, Battalion Adjt, and Inspector of Rifle Practice; for many years a trustee of Lincoln Memorial University; in April 1927 completed survey of monuments of the island of Minorca (212 sites). *Publications:* The Blow from Behind, 1903; In the Shoe String Country, 1906; Around the World in Ninety Days, 1906; The Philippine Problem, 1913; The Private Character of Queen Elizabeth, 1921; The Sayings of Queen Elizabeth, 1923; Wit and Wisdom of Queen Bess, 1925; Chamberlin's Guide to Majorca, 1925; The Balearics and their Peoples, 1927; The Private Character of Henry VIII, 1931; Elizabeth and Leycester, 1939. *Recreations:* mountaineering, hunting. *Address:* 22 Alleyn Road, SE21. *Clubs:* Pilgrims, PEN; Harvard.

Died 20 Sept. 1943.

CHAMBERS, Adm. Bertram Mordaunt, CB 1919; *b* 1866; *s* of Charles Harcourt Chambers, Barrister, and Lucibella Hare; *m* 1901, Nora, *d* of late W. Wickham Bertrand, JP, of Roy Cove, West Falkland Islands; one *s* one *d*. *Educ:* Clifton College; Stubbington; Naval Institutions. Joined Navy 1879; Egyptian War, 1882, present at the Bombardment of Alexandria in HMS Monarch; was on staff of Naval War College, 1906; a member of the first Naval Board of Commonwealth of Australia, 1911–13; Organiser of Australian Naval Training College, 1913–14; in command of Illustrious and Roxburgh in North Sea, 1914–15; Admiralty Port Officer, Scapa (*i.e.* King's Harbour-Master), 1915–17; retired list, 1917; Senior Officer of Escorts and Principal Port Convoy Officer in Canada, 1917–19 (CB); Admiral, retired, 1927; Member of Met. Asylums Board, 1921; is a Younger Brother of Trinity House; awarded the Shadwell Testimonial Prizes for Surveys in the years 1894 and 1895. *Publications:* Salt Junk, a Memoir, 1928; a number of articles and short stories; has also assisted in the preparation of technical works on naval matters. *Recreations:* golf, trout fishing, sketching in water colours. *Address:* Hill Crestm, Chagford, Devon.

Died 27 April 1945.

CHAMBERS, Sir Cornelius, Kt 1933; JP; Chairman Gaskell and Chambers, Ltd, Birmingham, Gaskell and Chambers (London), Ltd, and subsidiary companies; *b* 17 April 1862; *s* of John Chambers and Harriet Worton; *m* 1883 (wife *d* 1941); two *s* one *d*. *Educ:* privately. Articled to Law; entered manufacturing business, 1882; late Chairman, Birmingham Conservative Association; Treasurer, Birmingham Unionist Association, since 1905; late Chairman, Edgbaston Conservative Divisional Association; late Chairman, Moseley, Unionist Divisional Association; Governor of Royal Cripples Hospital, Birmingham; on committees of other public bodies; Liveryman of the Worshipful Company of Pewterers; PPGJD Provincial Grand Lodge of Warwickshire. *Recreation:* golf. *Address:* Monkspath Priory, Shirley, Warwickshire. *TA:* Monkspath, Birmingham. *T:* Shirley 1084. *Clubs:* Constitutional; Conservative, Midland Conservative, Birmingham; Moseley Golf.

Died 6 Aug. 1941.

CHAMBERS, John Ferguson; Consulting Physician; Hon. Physician to in-Patients Alfred Hospital, Hon. Consultant Physician to Austin Hospital, Melbourne; *b* 9 Sept. 1894; *s* of Alfred Henry Chambers, late Gen. Manager Union Bank of Australia, and Mary A. F. Ferguson; *m* 1924, Helen Gordon Craig; two *s*. *Educ:* Tudor House; Sydney Grammar School; Melbourne University. Resident Physician Perth and Royal Melbourne Hospitals after graduation; served European War, 2 years, Captain AAMC, AIF; attached to St Thomas's Hospital, London, 1921–22; served as Major, War of 1939–41. *Publications:* Articles in Medical Journal of Australia; Basal Metabolism, A Clinical Study; Polycythaemia. *Address:* Strathkyle, Toorak, SE2, Victoria; 12 Collins Street, Melbourne. *Clubs:* Melbourne, Royal Melbourne Golf, Victoria Racing, Victorian Amateur Turf.

Died April 1941.

CHAMBERS, Lt-Col Joseph Charles, CB 1916, VD; late Commanding 49th (West Riding) Divisional Train; *b* Stockton-on-Tees, 31 Jan. 1857; *e s* of late John Charles and Marion Chambers; *m* 1881, Dorcas Clementina, *o d* of late William H. Mewburn, West Rounton Grange, Northallerton; one *s* one *d*. *Educ:* private school. Joined 1st Durham Volunteers as bugler, 1868; afterwards became sergeant; joined 3rd Volunteer Battalion, West Riding Volunteers (Leeds Rifles, and now 7th West Yorks) as Lieut; became Capt. and Hon. Major, and was Adjutant, 1900–03; remained till Territorial movement inaugurated, when he raised the new ASC Column for the West Riding Division; served European War with the Division in France, 1915–16 (despatches, CB); was with National Telephone from 1880 until the State took it over on 31 Dec. 1911, when he retired; for several years was Provincial Superintendent (Northern Province). *Recreations:* in early days rowing, later golf. *Address:* 54 St Michael's Road, Headingley, Leeds 6. *T:* Headingley 51114. *Clubs:* Conservative, Leeds.

Died 6 Feb. 1940.

CHAMBERS, Raymond Wilson, FBA 1927; Quain Professor of English Language and Literature, University College, London, 1922–41; Hon. Director of the Early English Text Society; *b* 12 Nov. 1874; *o s* of late Thomas Herbert Chambers and Annie, *d* of William Wilson; unmarried. *Educ:* Grocers' Company School, and University College, London. BA 1894; MA 1902; DLit 1912; Hon. DLitt (Durham), 1932; Leeds, 1936; Quain Student, University College, London, 1899–1904; Librarian of the College, 1901–22; Assistant Professor of English, 1904; Fellow of University College since 1900; Fellow of the Bavarian Academy. *Publications:* Widsith, a Study in Old English Heroic Legend, 1912; Beowulf, an introduction to the study of the poem, with a discussion of the stories of Offa and Finn, 1921 (revised, 1932); England before the Norman Conquest, 1926; Thomas

More, 1935; Bede (Annual lecture of the British Academy on a Master Mind), 1936; The Jacobean Shakespeare and Measure for Measure (Annual Shakespeare lecture of the British Academy), 1937; Man's Unconquerable Mind: Studies of English Writers, from Bede to A. E. Housman and W. P. Ker, 1939; King Lear (the first W. P. Ker Memorial Lecture, University of Glasgow, 1939); Poets and their Critics: Langland and Milton (Annual Warton Lecture on English Poetry, British Academy); The Teaching of English in the Universities of England (English Association Pamphlet), 1922; has edited (with Professor W. P. Ker) The Chronicle of Froissart, translated by Sir John Bourchier, Lord Berners, 6 vols, 1901–1903; (with Dr W. W. Seton) A Fifteenth Century Courtesy Book and two Franciscan Rules (Early English Text Society), 1914; (with Mr A. J. Wyatt) Beowulf and the Finnsburg Fragment, 1914; (with Marjorie Daunt) A Book of London English, 1384–1425, 1931; (with Dr E. V. Hitchcock) Harpsfield's Life of Sir Thomas More (Early English Text Society), 1932; The Continuity of English Prose from Alfred to More and his school, 1932; (with Professor Max Förster and Dr Robin Flower) The Exeter Book in facsimile, 1932; contributions to the Scottish Historical Review, History, the Essays and Studies by members of the English Association and the Huntington Library Bulletin; has also contributed to Mr A. W. Pollard's volume on Shakespeare's Hand in the Play of Sir Thomas More, 1923. *Recreation:* he has learnt from his dog Breslau (now dead) to share 'the characteristic passion of the good and wise for walking'. *Address:* University College, London.

Died 21 April 1942.

CHAMIER, Sir Edward Maynard Des Champs, KCSI 1934; KCIE 1924; Kt 1916; *b* 4 June 1866; *s* of late Maj.-Gen. F. E. A. Chamier, CB, CIE; *m* 1894, Alice Mary (*d* 1940), *d* of late W. H. Cobb of Clifton, York; two *s* one *d*. *Educ:* Haileybury College. Called to Bar, Inner Temple, 1887; Government Advocate to the Government of the North-Western Provinces, 1895; Judicial Commissioner of Oudh, 1901; Puisne Judge of the High Court for the North-Western Provinces of India, 1911–15; Chief-Justice of High Court of Judicature at Patna, 1916–17; Legal Adviser to Secretary of State for India, 1917–33, retired 1933. *Address:* c/o Barclays Bank Ltd, 74 Kensington High Street, W8. *Club:* East India and Sports.

Died 17 Nov. 1945.

CHAMINADE, Cécile; composer; many decorations, including Jubilee Medal, Legion of Honour; *b* Paris; *m* C. Carbonel of Marseilles; no *c*. *Educ:* Le Vésinet, Seine et Oise. Studied Piano with Le Coupey, and Harmony with Augustin Savard. Has given a series of recitals of her compositions in London and the Provinces, as well as in America. *Publications:* plusieurs suites for orchestra, a dramatic symphony and concert-stuck for piano and orchestra, two trios and a large number of works for piano solo, piano and violin, etc., besides many songs. *Address:* Monte Carlo, Monaco.

Died April 1944.

CHAMNEY, Lt-Col Henry, CMG 1900; *b* Shillelagh, Co. Wicklow, Jan. 1861; 2nd *s* of late Rev. J. Chamney, DD, of Ard Ronan, Co. Louth; *m* 1st, 1907, Hon. Cecilia Mary Barnewall (*d* 1908), *sister* of 18th Lord Trimlestown; 2nd, 1913, Alice (*d* 1941), *d* of Col W. E. Bellingham of Castle Bellingham, Co. Louth. *Educ:* Monaghan Diocesan School. Served South Africa, 1899–1902 (despatches thrice, Queen's medal four clasps, King's medal and two clasps); first as Captain and then as Major, 2nd in Command of Lumsden's Horse (despatches twice) and later with South African Constabulary; joined Indian Police, 1909; Principal Police Training College, Surdah, Bengal; retired 1920; previous to going to South Africa was in India, 1881–99; on retirement was granted the rank Lieut-Col by Government; holds the Eastern Frontier medal, India,

one bar; also Volunteer Officer's decoration and the Indian Auxiliary Long Service medal. *Recreation:* sport. *Address:* Avon More Farm, Rustenburg, Transvaal, South Africa. *Club:* Oriental.

Died 8 June 1947.

CHAMPAIN, Rt Rev. John Norman B.; *see* Bateman-Champain.

CHAMPION, Arthur Mortimer, CMG 1935; retired Colonial Civil Servant; *b* 4 April 1885; *s* of John Kenrick Champion and Emma Mortimer; unmarried. *Educ:* Clifton College; RMC Sandhurst. Indian Army, 1905; relinquished commission owing to ill-health, 1907; East African Administrative Service, 1909; District Commissioner, 1918; served European War in Europe in the RFA 1915–19; Provincial Commissioner, Turkana Province, 1931; retired, 1935; now living in Nairobi; re-engaged by Government for cinema propaganda amongst the native tribes of Kenya, 1940; Jubilee Medal, 1935; Order of St John of Jerusalem, 1938; Founder's Gold Medal, Royal Geographical Society 1939. *Publications:* minor contributions to Man, RG Society, etc. *Recreations:* natural history and travel, several pioneer motor trips in South, East and West Africa including Nairobi to Cape Town in 1927, and Cape Verde to Nairobi in 1936–37. *Clubs:* Royal Empire Society, Overseas League; Nairobi (Nairobi).

Died 9 May 1950.

CHAMPION, Pierre; homme de lettres; maire de Nogent-sur-Marne; Conseiller général de la Seine; *né* Paris, 1880; fils d'Honoré Champion, éditeur et frère d'Édouard Champion; *m* Madeleine Smith, artiste peintre; pas d'enfants. *Educ:* Collège Henri IV; École des Chartes. Élève diplômé de l'Ecole des Chartes; archiviste paléographe; disciple de Marcel Schwob dont il a publié les œuvres; ami d'Anatole France dont lequel il collabora pour sa Jeanne d'Arc; deux fois grand prix Gobert à l'Académie. A fait la guerre dans l'infanterie avec les bretons d'où il rapporta le livre, Françoise au Calvaire; a découvert le manuscrit autographe de Charles d'Orléans, reconnu l'écriture de Ronsard et d'Antoine de la Sale. *Publications:* Guillaume de Flavy; La Vie de Charles d'Orléans; François Villon; Ronsard et son temps; Le Procès de Jeanne d'Arc; Le Proësies de Charles d'Orléans; Saintré; Les Cent Nouvelles Nouvelles; Marcel Schwob; Tristan et Iseult; Les Villes du Maroc; Louis XI; Mon vieux quartier; La dauphine mélancolique; Jeanne d'Arc; L'avènement de Paris; Splendeurs et Misères de Paris; la Renaissance et le Moyen âge; l'envers de la Tapisserie; Paris au temps des guerres de Religion; la galerie des Rois; Catherine de Médicis; Charles IX. *Recreation:* voyages. *Address:* 16 rue Charles VII, Nogent-sur-Marne; 4 rue Michelet, Paris.

Died 29 June 1942.

CHAMPION DE CRESPIGNY, Brig.-Gen. Sir Claude Raul, 5th Bt *cr* 1805; CB 1919; CMG 1918; DSO 1916; Grenadier Guards, retired, 1920; *b* 19 Sept. 1878; *s* of Sir Claude Champion de Crespigny, 4th Bt; *S* father, 1935; *m* 1913, Vere (who obtained a divorce, 1927), *d* of late Charles P. Sykes, of West Ella, Yorks. Deputy Lieutenant for Essex. Served S Africa, 1901–02 (Queen's medal 4 clasps); European War, 1914–18 (despatches 7 times, DSO, Montenegrin Cross, CB, CMG). *Heir: cousin* Lt-Col Henry Champion de Crespigny, MC, Indian Army, retired, *b* 11 July 1882. *Clubs:* Guards', White's, Turf, St James's.

Died 15 May 1941.

CHAMPION DE CRESPIGNY, Comdr Sir Frederick Philip, 7th Bt *cr* 1805; RN retd; *b* 30 Dec. 1884; British; 2nd *s* of late Lt Philip Augustus Champion de Crespigny, RN (2nd *s* of 3rd Bt); *S* brother, 1946; *m* 1909, Mabel, *d* of Roland Stagg; no *c*. *Educ:* Durham School. Entered HMS Britannia, 1900; served European War, 1914–18 (despatches); retired, 1920; Comdr (retd), 1924; called up for war appointment in Naval Control

Service in Norway, 1939 (prisoner, 1940, and sent to Germany); later released and served as Naval Control Service Officer at Harwich until 1945. *Recreations:* shooting and fishing. *Heir: cousin* Col Vivian Tyrell Champion de Crespigny [*b* 25 April 1907; *s* of late Brig.-Gen. T. O. W. Champion de Crespigny (3rd *s* of 3rd Bt); *m* 1st, 1930; one *d*; 2nd, 1943 (marriage annulled, 1947)]. *Address:* Cedar House, Ulting, Nr Maldon, Essex. *TA:* and *T:* Hatfield Peverel 83.

Died 12 Aug. 1947.

CHAMPION DE CRESPIGNY, Lt-Col George Harrison, CBE 1919; JP; *b* 1863; *s* of late Col C. B. Champion de Crespigny; *m* 1890, Gwendoline Blanche (*d* 1923), *d* of late W. C. Clarke-Thornhill, Rushton Hall, Northants; CO. 3rd Northamptonshire Regt, 1914–18. *Address:* Instow, N Devon. *T:* Instow 44. *Club:* Junior United Service.

Died 1 Jan. 1945.

CHAMPION DE CRESPIGNY, Sir Henry, 6th Bt *cr* 1805; MC; Sqdn. Ldr late RAF (VR) A & SD; *b* 11 July 1882; British; *s* of late Lt Philip Augustus Champion de Crespigny, RN, 2nd *s* of 3rd Bt; *S* cousin 1941. *Educ:* Durham School; RMC Sandhurst. Commissioned in 1902; served with 13th Frontier Force Rifles (IA); retired, 1934, as Lieut-Colonel. Served European War, 1914–18, Egypt, Gallipoli, France (despatches thrice, MC). *Heir: b* Frederick Philip, Lieut-Comdr RN retd [*b* 1884; *m* 1909, Mabel, *d* of Roland Stagg. Served European War, 1914–18 (despatches)]. *Address:* Champion Lodge, Maldon, Essex. *T:* Wickham Bishops 209.

Died 28 Oct. 1946.

CHANCE, Frederick Selby; JP; *b* 1886; *s* of Sir Frederick William Chance, KBE; *m* 1923, Isabel Mary, *d* of late A. D. Curwen, Workington Hall, Cumberland; two *s*. High Sheriff of Cumberland, 1934. *Address:* Home Acres, Carlisle, Cumberland. *T:* Carlisle 303.

Died 27 May 1946.

CHANCELLOR, Henry George; *b* Walton, near Glastonbury, 3 June 1863; *s* of John Chancellor, Walton, and Louisa, *d* of John Porter, Ashcott; *m* 1885, Mary Dyer Surl (*d* 1942), Newent, Gloucester; one *s* three *d*. *Educ:* Elmfield College, York. Entered business of C. Chancellor & Co. 1883; managing partner and afterwards sole proprietor until formed into Ltd Co. (private), 1910; active worker in Liberal and Progressive interest from about 1885; also in peace and temperance movements; President, North Islington Liberal Association, since 1895; President, English League for Taxation of Land Values, 1910 and 1920; Hon. Sec. International Arbitration League, 1938; contested N Islington (Progressive) for LCC, 1907; MP (L) Haggerston, 1910–18; ran a Progressive newspaper, The Londoner, 1896–99. *Publications:* How to Win, a volume of addresses, and numerous papers and pamphlets. *Recreations:* none. *Address:* Hillsborough, 15 Crescent Road, Hornsey, N8. *T:* Mountview 5666. *Club:* National Liberal.

Died 14 March 1945.

CHANDLER, Frederick George, MA, MD (Cantab), FRCP (Lond.); Physician. St Bartholomew's Hospital; Senior Physician, The London Chest Hospital, Victoria Park; Consultant, King Edward VII Sanatorium, Midhurst; Consulting Physician for Diseases of the Chest, Tropical Disease Hospital; Examiner in Medicine, Oxford University; *s* of George Chandler of Sutton, Surrey; *m* Marjorie, *d* of late Frederick Raimes, JP, Co. Durham; one *s* two *d*. *Educ:* The Leys School, Cambridge; Jesus Coll., Cambridge (Scholar); First Class Hons, Natural Science Tripos; Raymond Horton Smith Prize for MD Thesis. Late Physician with charge of Out-Patients, Medical Tutor and Lecturer on Medicine, Charing Cross Hospital; House Physician and Casualty Physician, St Bartholomew's Hospital. *Publications:* Lipiodol in the Diagnosis of Thoracic Disease; several other contributions to medical literature, especially on diseases of the chest. *Address:* 1 Park Square West, Regent's Park, NW1. *T:* Welbeck 2270.

Died 8 Oct. 1942.

CHANDLER, Pretor Whitty, FSA; FRHS; *b* 1858; 4th *s* of late B. Chandler and Elizabeth, *d* of Dr Richard Worsley, Blandford; *m* Ethel Mary, *yr d* of late Edmund Kendall; one *s* two *d*. *Educ:* Sherborne School. Admitted a Solicitor in 1882; a Master of the Supreme Court (Chancery Division), 1913–38; Examiner in Conveyancing for Finals in Common Law and Equity for Honours, and in Trust Accounts for Law Examinations. *Publications:* Trust Accounts, 6th edition, and other books. *Recreation:* travel. *Address:* Frognal Dene, Hampstead, NW3. *T:* Hampstead 0659. *Club:* Reform.

Died 5 Aug. 1941.

CHANNER, Frederick Francis Ralph, CIE 1930; OBE 1918; *b* 20 June 1875; 3rd *c* of late Rev. E. C. Channer, late Vicar of Ravensthorpe, Northants, and Catherine Bridgman; *m* Edith Janie (*d* 1949), 7th *c* of Gen. G. N. Channer, VC, CB, and Isabella Watson; two *d*. *Educ:* St Paul's School; Royal Indian Engineering College, Coopers Hill. Assistant Conservator of Forests in the Indian Forest Service, 1896; Conservator of Forests, 1919; Chief Conservator of Forests, 1926; retired, 1930. *Address:* 13 Gayton Crescent, NW3.

Died 1 April 1950.

CHAPAIS, Hon. Sir Thomas, Kt 1935; *b* St Denis de la Bouteillerie, Quebec, 23 March 1858; *y s* of late Hon. J. C. Chapais and Henriette Georgina, *d* of late Hon. A. Dionne; *m* 1884, Marie Sophie Justine Hectorine (*d* 1934), *e d* of late Sir H. L. Langevin, KCMG. *Educ:* St Anne's College; Laval University (Licentiate in Law and Doctor in Letters). Called to Bar, 1879; editor of Le Courrier du Canada from 1884 to 1901; member of Legislative Council, 1892; of Taillon Government, 1893; Speaker of the Legislative Council, 1895; President of the Executive Council, 1896; Minister of Colonisation and Mines, 1897; Senator for Grandville Division, 1919; Minister without portfolio, in the Duplessis Cabinet, and leader of the Legislative Council (Province of Quebec); resigned Nov. 1939; again Minister in the second Duplessis Cabinet in 1944, and leader of the Legislative Council; Fellow, Royal Society of Canada; Prof. of History at Laval University; Chevalier de la Légion d'Honneur, France, Commandeur de l'Ordre de Saint-Gregoire le grand; delegated at the League of Nations at Geneva as a representative of Canada, 1930; Roman Catholic. *Publications:* Discours et Conférences i, ii, iii, 1898–1913; Jean Talon, intendant de la Nouvelle, France, 1904; Mélanges de polémique et d'études religieuses, politiques et littéraires, 1905; le Marquis de Montcalm, 1911; le Serment du Roi; Cours d'Histoire du Canada, vols i, ii, iii, iv, v, vi, vii, viii, 1919–1935, etc. *Recreation:* reading. *Address:* 8 Parlor Street, Quebec, Canada.

Died 15 July 1946.

CHAPLIN, 2nd Viscount *cr* 1916, of St Oswalds, Blankney, in the county of Lincoln; **Eric Chaplin;** Vice-Lieutenant, Sutherland; JP Sutherland; *b* 27 Sept. 1877; *o s* of 1st Viscount and Florence, *d* of 3rd Duke of Sutherland; *S* father, 1923; *m* 1905, Hon. Gwladys Alice Gertrude Wilson, 4th *d* of 1st Baron Nunburnholme; two *s*. *Heir: s* Hon. Anthony Freskyn Charles Hamby Chaplin, Flight Lieut, RAFVR [*b* 14 Dec. 1906; *m* 1933, Alvilde, *o d* of late Lt-Gen. Sir Tom Bridges, KCB, KCMG; one *d*]. *Address:* 23 Chelsea Sq., SW3. *Clubs:* Carlton, Turf; Royal Yacht Squadron (Cowes).

Died 12 Sept. 1949.

CHAPLIN, (T. H.) Arnold, BA Cantab, MD Cantab, 1893; FRCP, 1902; Consulting Physician, London Chest Hospital; late Medical Inspector, P. & O., British India, and New Zealand Shipping Companies; Fitzpatrick Lecturer at the Royal College of Physicians on the History of Medicine, 1917 and 1918; Harveian Librarian since 1918, Royal College of Physicians, Harveian Orator Royal College of Physicians, London, 1922; President, Section for History of Medicine, Royal Society of Medicine, 1923–24; Chairman, Board of Trade Committee for the revision of the Scales of Drugs on board ship; President, Section History of Medicine, BMA Meeting at Oxford, 1936; *b* Aug. 1864; *y s* of A. T. Chaplin, of Fulbourn, Cambs; *m* 1909, Margaret Douie (*d* 1938), *widow* of William Dougal. *Educ:* Tettenhall College; St John's College, Cambridge (Natural Science Tripos, 1886); St Bartholomew's Hospital. *Publications:* Fibroid Diseases of the Lung, 1893 (jointly); Science and Art of Prescribing 1901: The Illness and Death of Napoleon (A Medical Criticism), 1913; Thomas Shortt, 1914; The Fatal Illness of Napoleon; a Paper read before the Historical Section of the International Congress of Medicine, 1913; A St Helena Who's Who, 1914 and 1920; Medicine in England during the Reign of George III, 1919; The Engraved Portraits of British Medical Men, in the Print Collector's Quarterly, July, 1930; many papers on Diseases of the Chest in journals. *Recreation:* literature. *Address:* The Old House, Fulbourn, Cambs. *Club:* Athenæum.

Died 18 Oct. 1944.

CHAPMAN, Brig.-Gen. Archibald John, CB 1914; CMG 1916; CBE 1919; *b* 29 Dec. 1862; *s* of John Edward Chapman, of Monkstown, Co. Dublin, and Anna Maria, 3rd *d* of Sir A. Weldon, 4th Bt of Rahinderry and Kilmorony, Athy, Queen's Co.; *m* Annie Evelyn, 2nd *d* of George Orr Wilson, of Dunardagh, Blackrock, Co. Dublin; two *d*. *Educ:* privately. Lt 3rd Royal Inniskilling Fusiliers, 1880–84; joined 2nd Royal Dublin Fusiliers, 1884; commanded 1st Royal Dublin Fusiliers, 1906–10; Commanded Staff Infantry, Brigade TF, 1911–12; General Staff, Northern Command, 1912–14; served in SA campaign, 1898–1902 (despatches thrice, Queen's medal and 6 clasps, King's medal and 2 clasps, Bt Lt-Col, wounded); European War, 1914–19 (despatches, CMG); Officer of the Legion of Honour, 1918. *Address:* Pool Farm, Willersey, Glos. *T:* Broadway 143.

Died 9 June 1950.

CHAPMAN, Charles Williams, MD, MRCP; Consulting Physician to the Hospital for Diseases of the Heart; *b* 1843; *m* 1883, Mary, *d* of David Wedderspoon, Perth; two *s* two *d*. *Educ:* Guy's Hospital. *Publications:* Handbook on the Heart and its Diseases, 1927; Heart Disease in Childhood and Youth. *Address:* Four Weirs, Kings Somborne, Stockbridge, Hants. *T:* Kings Somborne 323.

Died 31 Jan. 1941.

CHAPMAN, Frank M., ScD; Curator Emeritus of Birds, American Museum of Natural History, New York City, Curator 1908–42; *b* 12 June 1864; *s* of Lebbeus Chapman and Mary Parkhurst; *m* 1898, Fannie Bates Embury; one *s*. *Educ:* Academic; ScD, Brown Univ. 1913. Assistant Curator, 1888–1901; Associate Curator, 1901–08; Associate Editor The Auk, 1894–1911; Founder of Bird-Lore, 1898; Editor, 1898–1934; Director Publications American Red Cross, 1917–18; Commissioner to Latin America, 1918–19; NY Linnean Society's medal, 1912; Elliot medal, Nat. Acad., 1918; Roosevelt medal, 1928; Medal Burroughs Memorial Society, 1929; Brewster Medal, Amer. Ornith. Union, 1933; Member Nat. Acad. Sci.; Fellow Amer. Ornith. Union (Pres. 1911); Member Philos. Soc.; Fellow NY Acad. (Vice-President, 1908–09); NY Linnean Soc. (Pres., 1897); Hon. Member NY Zool. Soc., Wash Biol. Soc.; Hon. Member British Ornith. Union; Ornith. Gesell.; Soc. Ornith. La Plata; Club van Nederlandsche Vogelkund; Vice-President Explorers' Club, 1910–18; President, Burroughs Memorial Assoc., 1921–25; geographic distribution; systematic relationships and life histories of birds; popularization of natural history studies. *Publications:* Handbook of Birds of Eastern North America, 1895, rewritten 1912, 1932; Bird-Life: A Guide to the Study of our Common Birds, 1897; Bird Studies with a Camera, 1900; Color Key to North American Birds, 1903; The Warblers of North America, 1907; Camps and Cruises of an Ornithologist, 1908; Color Key to North American Birds, 1912; The Travels of Birds, 1916; Distribution of Bird-Life in Colombia, 1917; Our Winter Birds: How to Know and Attract Them, 1918; What Bird is That? 1920; The Distribution of Bird-Life in the Urubamba Valley of Peru, 1921; The Distribution of Bird-Life in Ecuador, 1926; My Tropical Air Castle, 1929; Autobiography of a Bird-Lover, 1933; Life in an Air Castle, 1938; The Post-Glacial History of Zonotrichia capensis, 1940; Birds and Man, 1943; many papers, bulletins, etc. *Address:* American Museum of Natural History, New York City, NY. *TA:* Museology, New York. *Clubs:* Century, Explorers, New York.

Died 15 Nov. 1945.

CHAPMAN, Frederick, ALS, Hon. FRMS; FGS; Hon. Palæontologist, National Museum, Melbourne and to Victorian Geol. Survey; Hon. Curator, Maranoa Native Garden, Balwyn; *b* Camden Town, London, 13 Feb. 1864; *s* of late Robert Chapman (Assistant to Michael Faraday and John Tyndall) and Eleanor Dinsey; *m* 1890, Helen Mary, *e d* of John Malsbury Dancer, Northamptonshire; one *s* one *d*. *Educ:* Chelsea; Exeter Hall; Private Study. Assistant to Professor Judd, Geological Department Royal College of Science, 1881–1902; Palæontologist to State National Museum, Melbourne, 1902–27; Commonwealth Palæontologist, Australia, 1927–35; Lecturer in Palæontology, University of Melbourne, 1920–32; Fellow Royal Microscopical Society, 1892 and Hon. Fellow 1929; Associate Linnean Society, London, 1896; Awarded Lyell Fund for Research, 1899 and Lyell Medal, 1930, Geological Society, London; President Microscopical Society, Victoria, 1919–20, and to Field Naturalists' Club of Victoria, 1920; President Royal Society of Victoria, 1929–30; Awarded Syme Prize and Medal for Research, 1920; Member of Australian National Research Council since 1922; Hon. Fellow Royal Society of South Australia, 1926; corr. member Palæontological Soc. of America; awarded Clarke medal for Research Royal Society NS Wales 1932, Hon. Member, 1939; Hon. Member of the Royal Society of NZ 1932; Member Internat. Com. Zool. Nomencl., Washington since 1926; Australian Natural History Medallion, 1940. *Publications:* The Foraminifera, 1902; New or Little-Known Victorian Fossils in National Museum, 30 parts, 1902–1927; Australasian Fossils, 1914; Silurian Bivalved Mollusca of Victoria, 1908; Succession and Homotaxial Relationships of the Australian Cainozoic System, 1914; Antarctic Results (Shackleton and Mawson Expeditions, 1907–1909 and 1911–1914), 1917 and 1937; Tertiary and Cretaceous Fish Remains of New Zealand, 1918; Foraminifera and Ostracoda of New Zealand, 1926; The Sorrento Bore, 1928; Open-air Studies in Australia, 1929; Guide to Fossil Collections, National Museum, Melbourne, 1929; The Book of Fossils, 1934; also more than 400 scientific papers in various journals and many popular science articles for the press. *Recreations:* gardening, music, popular science talks. *Address:* Hellas, 50 Stawell Street, Kew, E4, Melbourne, Australia. *T:* Haw. 5159.

Died 10 Dec. 1943.

CHAPMAN, Sir Henry, Kt 1937; CBE 1933. Resident Director and Technical Adviser to the Rhodesia Railways Ltd. *Address:* The Rhodesia Railways, Ltd, Bulawayo, S Rhodesia.

Died 22 June 1947.

CHAPMAN, James Ernest, CB 1913; *m* 1st, Janette, *o d* of late John Le Cronier, MD, Jersey; one *s*; 2nd, Edith Rosa, *o d* of late George Le Cronier. *Educ:* France; Victoria College, Jersey. Secretaries' Office Inland Revenue, 1872; Assistant Secretary, 1902; Secretary for Taxes, 1909; Joint Secretary to Board of Inland Revenue, 1909–16. *Address:* 2 Victoria Crescent, Jersey. *Club:* Authors'.

Died 28 Nov. 1941.

CHAPMAN, Sir Robert William, Kt 1937; CMG 1927; MA, BCE; MIEA; President of S Australian School of Mines since 1939; *b* Stony Stratford, Bucks, 27 Dec. 1866; *m* 1889, Eva Maud Hall; six *s* two *d. Educ:* Wesley College and University, Melbourne. After practical experience on railway and bridge construction, Lecturer at the Adelaide University, 1889; Professor of Engineering, University of Adelaide, 1907–37; President of Australian Institute of Mining and Metallurgy, 1920–21; President of Institution of Engineers, Australia, 1922; President South Australian Institute of Surveyors, 1914–28. *Publications:* Astronomy for Surveyors; Reinforced Concrete; a number of pamphlets dealing with Australian tides, and other papers containing the results of research on South Australian timbers, wire ropes, reinforced concrete and other subjects chiefly relating to structural engineering. *Recreations:* gardening, bowls. *Address:* Burnside, South Australia.

Died 27 Feb. 1942.

CHAPMAN, Sir Samuel, Kt 1920; *b* 1859. MP (U) South Edinburgh, 1922–45; specially identified with the Perth and Perthshire Prisoners of War Fund; contested (U) Perth, 1906 and 1910; Greenock, 1910 and 1918; Director of Public Companies; Member of Perthshire Education Authority; Chairman of Perth Academy School Management Committee; JP County of Perth; visited S America, 1927; Canada, 1928, as Member of Parliamentary Delegation. *Clubs:* Constitutional; Scottish Conservative, Edinburgh.

Died 29 April 1947.

CHAPMAN, Rt Rev. Thomas Alfred, DD (Oxon, Dublin); *b* Hanley, Staffs, 20 Nov. 1867; *m* 1st, 1894, Catharine Mary (*d* 1928), *d* of late C. T. Bewes, Plymouth; one *s* one *d*; 2nd, 1929, Audrey Sybil Eirene, *y d* of Rev. T. Sadgrove. *Educ:* Exeter College, Oxford. Ordained, 1890; Vicar of St John, Carlisle, 1896–99; Holy Trinity, Bristol, and Rural Dean of East Bristol, 1899–1905; Vicar of Charles, Plymouth, and Rural Dean of the Three Towns, 1905–09; Vicar and Rural Dean of Bolton, 1909–22; Bishop and Archdeacon of Colchester, 1922–33; Proctor in Convocation, Hon. Canon of Manchester; Chaplain to Territorial Forces attached to 3rd East Lancashire Royal Field Artillery, 1909–22; Chaplain HM Prison, Plymouth, 1906–09; Chaplain to High Sheriffs of the County Palatine of Lancaster, 1913–15; Vice-Chairman of the Bolton Primary Education Committee, 1909–22. Specially interested in Poor Law work and education; sometime Poor Law Guardian in Bristol and Plymouth, and Member of the Bristol School Board. *Address:* The Old Rectory, Frating, near Colchester. *T:* Great Bentley 251.

Died 31 May 1949.

CHAPPELL, Sir Ernest, Kt 1922, CBE, JP; Director Mosenthal Bros Ltd, General Merchants and Importers, until he retired in 1922; *b* London, 1864; *m* 1897, Florence (*d* 1924), *d* of Peter Roe, Dublin. *Educ:* Woodbridge Grammar School. Went to South Africa, 1890; member Pretoria Town Council, 1904–07; Ex-President Pretoria Chamber of Commerce; Johannesburg Chamber of Commerce and the Associated Chambers of Commerce of South Africa; member of various Government Commissions on matters of Finance and Taxation; member of Government Conference that led to the establishment of the S African Reserve Bank; Director of the Reserve Bank; Chairman of Government Mission to East Africa to promote closer trade relations between the British Colonies there and the Union of South Africa; Adviser to the South African Delegation to the Economic Conference, 1923. *Address:* Glen Dirk, Wynberg, Cape Province, South Africa. *Clubs:* Conservative; Civil Service, Cape Town; Rand, Johannesburg; Pretoria, Pretoria.

Died 3 Aug. 1943.

CHAPPLE, Harold, MC Cantab, FRCS Eng.; FCOG; Senior Obstetric Surgeon and Gynæcologist to Guy's Hospital; Victoria Hospital, Kingston; Gynæcologist to London Jewish Hospital; St John's Hospital, Lewisham; *b* 13 Feb. 1881; *s* of late Frederic Chapple, CMG; *m* 1911, Irene Briscoe Arbuthnot, 2nd *d* of Sir Wm Arbuthnot Lane, 1st Bt, CB; two *s. Educ:* Cambridge University; Guy's Hospital; Berlin. Temp. Captain RAMC, BEF. *Publications:* Joint Author of Midwifery, and Diseases of Women; various articles in the medical journals. *Address:* 149 Harley St, W1. *T:* Welbeck 4444. *Club:* Athenæum.

Died 8 March 1945.

CHARKHARI STATE, HH Maharaja-Dhiraja Sipahdar-ul-Mulk Arimardan Singh Ju Deo Bahadur; *b* 29 Dec. 1903; *S* 1920; *m* 1st, 1928, Maharaj Kumari Sahiba of Banswara, Rajputana; 2nd, 1931, *d* of HH Senior Commanding General Sir Mohan Shamsher Jung Bahadur Rana, KCIE, of Nepal; 3rd, *d* of Thakur Dewan Singh of Almora; one *d. Educ:* Mayo College, Ajmer. Area of state, 880 square miles; entitled salute of 11 guns. *Address:* Charkhari State, Bundelkhand, Central India.

Died 8 Nov. 1941.

CHARLEMONT, 8th Viscount *cr* 1665; **James Edward Caulfeild,** Privy Councillor, N Ireland, 1926; Hon. ARIBA; Hon. LLD Queen's University, Belfast; Baron Caulfeild of Charlemont *cr* 1620; DL Co Tyrone; *b* London, 12 May 1880; *o s* of late Hon. Marcus Caulfield, CB, and Gwyn, 4th *d* of Robert Williams, 2nd *s* of Sir Robert Williams, Bt, Fryars, Anglesea; *S* uncle, 1913; *m* 1st, 1914, Evelyn, *d* of Edmund Charles Pendleton Hull, Park Gate House, Ham Common, Surrey; 2nd, 1940, Hildegarde, *d* of R. Slock-Cottell, Malstapel, Ruiselede, Belgium. *Educ:* Winchester. A Representative Peer; Member of Senate of N Ireland, 1925–37; Minister of Education, 1926–37. *Heir: cousin* Charles Edward St George Caulfeild. *Address:* Newcastle, Co. Down. *T:* Newcastle 2219.

Died 30 Aug. 1949.

CHARLES, Sir Ernest Bruce, Kt 1928; CBE 1919; KC 1913; *b* 1871; *s* of late Rt Hon. Sir Arthur Charles, PC. *Educ:* Clifton; New College, Oxford. Barrister Inner Temple, 1896; Bencher, 1922; late Commissary General of diocese of Canterbury; Chancellor of Wakefield and Hereford, 1912–28, and of Chelmsford, 1922–28; Recorder of Bournemouth, 1915–24, of Southampton, 1924–28; Judge of the King's Bench Division, 1928–47; Kt of Grace of St John of Jerusalem. *Address:* Bruce House, Deal. *Clubs:* Athenæum, Savile.

Died 3 May 1950.

CHARLES, Captain Ulick de Burgh, CBE 1923; General Representative, Rio Tinto Company, Ltd, Spain; *b* 6 Oct. 1884; *s* of John Georges Charles, BCS (*d* 1915), and Lady Edith Hester (*d* 1936), 2nd *d* of 5th Marquess of Sligo; *m* 1928, Maria Ysabel, *d* of Mr de Oliva of Seville, and *widow* of Mr Vidal. *Educ:* Felsted School; Lincoln College, Oxford. In business, Chile, 1907–10; rubber planting, Malay, 1911–14; served World War, 1915–19; Commercial Secretary (Grade 3) to HM Embassy, Madrid, 1919; Commercial Secretary (Grade 1), 1920–27; resigned, 1928. *Recreation:* golf. *Address:* General Castanos 4, Madrid. *TA:* Abono, Madrid. *Clubs:* Travellers', Conservative, Bath.

Died 14 Feb. 1947.

CHARLESWORTH, Rev. Martin Percival, MA, FBA, FSA; Laurence Reader in Ancient History and President and Classical Lecturer of St John's College in the Univ. of Cambridge; Hon. D-ès-L (Bordeaux); Hon. DLitt (Wales), 1947; *b* 18 Jan. 1895; *s* of Rev. Ambrose Charlesworth and Alice Whish. *Educ:* Birkenhead School; Jesus Coll., Cambridge (Sch.); Princeton Univ., New Jersey; Bell Scholar, 1915; Craven Scholar, 1920; Chancellor's Classical Medallist, 1921; Fellow of Jesus College, 1921; Procter Fellow of Princeton University, USA, 1921; Hare Prize, 1922; Fellow of St John's College, 1923. Tutor 1925–31; Martin Lecturer at Oberlin College, Ohio, 1935; ordained Priest, 1940; Joint-editor of the Cambridge Ancient History; Member of the Governing Body of Sedbergh School. *Publications:* Trade Routes and Commerce of the Roman Empire, 1924, 2nd ed., 1926, French ed., 1938; Five Men, 1936; The Lost Province, 1949; Chapters in the Cambridge Ancient History and articles in various periodicals. *Recreations:* music, walking. *Address:* St John's College, Cambridge. *T:* Cambridge 5052.

Died 26 Oct. 1950.

CHARLTON, Matthew; *b* Linton, Victoria, 15 March 1866; *m* 1889, Martha Rollings; one *s* one *d. Educ:* Lambton Public School. Started work in coal mine at age of 14; went to Western Australia, 1896, and worked in various gold mines in and around Kalgoorlie; became foundation member of Australian Workers' Union in West Australia; after 2½ years returned to Lambton, NSW, and worked in Waratah Colliery; became Miners' Delegate on District Board; shortly after, Treasurer to Coal Miners' Federation; MLA for West Waratah, 1904, re-elected for Northumberland; resigned, 1909; Federal Member for Hunter, 1910–28; Leader of Federal Labour Party, 1922–28; temporary Chairman of Committees, 1913–20; Chairman of Joint Committee of Public Accounts, 1914–22; an Australian delegate to League of Nations Assembly, 1924; Alderman of Lambton Municipal Council since 1935. *Recreation:* bowls. *Address:* High Street, Lambton, NSW, Australia.

Died 8 Dec. 1948.

CHARLTON, Captain William Henry, TD; Managing Partner of Purcell and Co., Saltillo, Mexico, and Director of the Mazapil Copper Co., Ltd; *b* 25 May 1876; *e s* of late William Oswald Charlton and Mary Grant, *o d* of Archibald Campbell, Washington, USA; *m* 1914, Bridget A., *d* of W. J. Purcell, late of Saltillo, Mexico; one *d. Educ:* The Oratory School, Edgbaston, Birmingham. Late 12th Royal Lancers and Northumberland Hussars Yeomanry; High Sheriff for Northumberland, 1932–33; JP Northumberland. *Address:* Hesleyside, Bellingham, Northumberland. *Club:* Northern Counties (Newcastle-on-Tyne).

Died 6 Sept. 1950.

CHARNWOOD, 1st Baron *cr* 1911; **Godfrey Rathbone Benson,** MA; *b* 6 Nov. 1864; 4th *s* of William Benson, JP, of Langtons, Alresford, Hants, and Elizabeth, *d* of Thomas Smith of Colebrooke Park, Tonbridge; *m* 1897, Dorothea Mary (author of Call Back Yesterday, 1937; she *d* 1942), *d* of late Roby Thorpe, Nottingham and *g d* of late Rt Hon. A. J. Mundella, MP; one *s* two *d. Educ:* Winchester; Balliol College, Oxford; 1st Class Lit. Hum. 1887. Sometime Lecturer at Balliol. MP (L) Woodstock Division, Oxford, 1892–95; Mayor of Lichfield, 1909–11, Councillor and afterwards Alderman, 1904–38; DL, JP, Staffs, from 1929 to 1939 Chairman of Quarter Sessions. *Publications:* Abraham Lincoln, 1916; Theodore Roosevelt, 1923; According to St John, 1926; Tracks in the Snow, 1927; Prefatory Memoirs to Discourses and Letters of Hubert Murray Burge, and to Essays and Addresses of John Burnet. *Heir:* s Hon. John Roby Benson [*b* 31 Aug. 1901; *m* 1933, Beryl Joan, *e d* of Percy Quilter. *Address:* 108 Eaton Square, SW1. *T:* Sloane 4100]. *Address:* 5 Cadogan Court, Draycott Avenue, SW3. *T:* Kensington 7844. *Club:* Brooks's.

Died 3 Feb. 1945.

CHARTERIS, Brig.-Gen. John, CMG 1919; DSO 1915; late RE; *b* 8 Jan. 1877; *s* of late Prof. Charteris, Glasgow Univ.; *m* Noel, *d* of C. D. Hodgson; two *s* (and one killed in action). Entered Army, 1896; Capt. 1905; Major, 1914; Bt Lt-Col 1915; Bt Col 1917; Col 1921; Staff Capt. HQ, India, 1909–10, General Staff Officer, 2nd Grade, 1910–12; AMS; to General Officer commanding Aldershot, 1912–14; served European War, 1914–18 (despatches, CMG, DSO, Bt Col, Legion of Honour, Commander of Order of the Couronne of Belgium, Rising Sun of Japan, Croix de Guerre, American Distinguished Service Cross); DQMG, India, 1920; DA and QMG, Eastern Command, India, 1921–22, and Temp. Col on Staff; retired 1922; contested (U) Dumfriesshire, 1923; MP (C) Dumfriesshire, 1924–29. *Publications:* Field-Marshal Earl Haig, 1929; At GHQ 1931; Haig, 1933. *Address:* Bourne House, Thorpe, Surrey. *Club:* United Service.

Died 4 Feb. 1946.

CHARTERS, Col Alexander Burnet, CMG 1916; DSO 1918; VD; sometime Headmaster of Lyall Bay School, Wellington, NZ; *b* Christchurch, NZ, 30 June 1876; *s* of late W. W. Charters, Christchurch, NZ; *m* 1903, Eliza Caroline, *e d* of late H. B. Curtis, of Inglewood, NZ; one *s* one *d. Educ:* Opawa and West Christchurch Schools; Christ's College, Canterbury, and Victoria University Colleges, NZ (BA 1903; MA 1908). Twenty-one years service in NZ Volunteers and Territorial Force, beginning in ranks of Canterbury Scottish Rifles, Christchurch, NZ; served in Kelburn Rifles, Wellington, as Lieutenant, giving up commission to enlist, in the ranks, in NZ contingent for service in South Africa (Queen's medal 3 clasps), whence rose to rank of Regtl Sergt.-Major; Lieut in Wellington Engineer Company; thence Captain, Masterton Rifle Vols, 1903; Greytown Rifle Vols, 1908; Major, 1909; Lt-Col 1912; commanding 17th (Ruahine) Regt NZ Territorial Force; enlisted in NZ Expeditionary Force, 1914, reverting to Major to get away; temp. Lieut-Colonel, 1915; Lieut-Colonel, 1915 (despatches four times, CMG, DSO); Col, NZ Territorial Force, 1925; ADC to Governor-General of NZ, 1928–30; Colonel, retired list, 1936; Headmaster of Greytown District High School, 1907–12; Inspector of Schools, 1912–24; Principal of Whangarei High School 1924–31; retired. *Recreations:* when younger, Rugby football, rowing, rifle-shooting, walking, and cycling.

Died 10 May 1948.

CHASE, Lewis, PhD; Co-editor of the TH Chivers Project, Brown University; *b* Sidney, Maine, US, 27 June 1873; *m* 1st, Pearl Rowell Mikesell, New York; 2nd, Emma Service Lester, Augusta, Georgia. *Educ:* University of Rochester; University of Stanford; University of Columbia (MA; PhD); University of Harvard; University of Grenoble. On the Staff Columbia University, 1899–1902; Indiana University, 1903–07; University of Louisville, Ky, 1907–08; University of Bordeaux, 1909–10; Univ. of Wisconsin, 1916–17; University of Rochester, 1917–19; Muhammadan Anglo-Oriental College (transformed 1920 into the Muslim University, Aligarh), 1919–21; Yenching University and National University of Peking, 1921–25; Peking Normal, 1923–25; California Institute of Technology, 1926; University of California (SB Ex. Div.), 1925–27; Riverside Junior College, 1926–27; Union College, 1927–29; Duke, 1929–31; Brown, 1931–33; Asheville Normal, summers since 1933. *Publications:* The English Heroic Play; Introduction to Emerson's Compensation; Bernard Shaw in France; Poe and his Poetry; Intermediate Poetical Selections (with P. A. Rashid); several Western Classics intended for Eastern readers; Thomas Holley Chivers—a Selection; A New Poe Letter. *Recreation:* billiards. *Clubs:* Cosmos, Washington.

Died 23 Sept. 1937.

CHASE-CASGRAIN, Alexandre; *see* Casgrain.

CHASTEL DE BOINVILLE, Rev. Basil William; *m* 1st, 1889, Nancy Millicent (*d* 1932), *d* of Richard Neville Somerville of Roscarbery, Co. Cork; 2nd, 1934, Olive Swalwell, *er d* of William and Ada Frances Sainsbury. *Educ:* Corpus Christi College, Cambridge (MA). Ordained, 1889; Curate of Kirk Braddon, Isle of Man, 1889–91; Rector of Fethard, 1891–1904; Vicar of St Peter, Pietermaritzburg, 1904–14; Rector of Tipperary, 1914–20; Prebendary of Cashel Cathedral and Rural Dean of Tipperary, 1915–20; and Chaplain to the Forces; Vicar of Norton, 1920–25; Rector of Oxwich, 1925–33; Rural Dean of West Gower, 1930–33; Rector of Heyope, 1933–40; retired, 1941. *Address:* Castlebank, Norton, Presteigne, Radnorshire.
Died 22 June 1943.

CHASTENEY, Howard Everson; HM Chief Inspector of Factories since 1946; *b* 9 Aug. 1888; *s* of Frederick Chasteney; *m* 1916, Ellen, *d* of H. J. Bonner; two *d*. *Educ:* Nottingham High School; St John's College, Cambridge. Wrangler, 1910. HM Inspector of Factories, Home Office, 1913; RE and RGA, 1915–19; Deputy Chief Inspector of Factories, 1938. *Address:* Red House, Woodland Way, Purley, Surrey. *T:* Uplands 2154. *Club:* United University.
Died 18 Feb. 1947.

CHATFIELD-TAYLOR, Hobart Chatfield, LittD; FRGS; author; *b* Chicago, 24 March 1865; *s* of late Henry Hobart Taylor and Adelaide, *d* of late Horace Chatfield; *m* 1st, 1890, Rose, (*d* 1918) *d* of late US Senator Charles Benjamin Farwell, Illinois; three *s* one *d*; 2nd, 1920, Estelle, *d* of George Harrison Barbour, Detroit, and widow of George Schley Stillman, New York. *Educ:* private schools in France; Cornell University (BSc 1886). Studied law, but instead of entering the legal profession founded a weekly, literary, and political review called America (1888–90); foreign correspondent of Chicago Daily News, 1891–92; Consul for Spain at Chicago, 1892–94; Chevalier of the Legion of Honour and of Italian, Belgian, Spanish and Ecuadoran orders, etc. *Publications:* With Edge-Tools, 1891; An American Peeress, 1893; Two Women and a Fool, 1895; The Land of the Castanet, Spanish sketches, 1896; The Vice of Fools, 1898; The Idle Born, 1900; The Crimson Wing, 1902; Molière, a Biography, 1906; Fame's Pathway, 1909; Goldoni, a Biography, 1913; Chicago, 1917; Cities of Many Men, 1925; Tawny Spain, 1927; Charmed Circles, 1935. *Recreation:* foreign travel. *Address:* 900, Hot Springs Road, Santa Barbara, California, USA. *Clubs:* Orleans, Authors'; Union, Century, New York.
Died 16 Jan. 1945.

CHATTAWAY, Frederick Daniel, FRS; MA Oxon; DSc Lond., PhD Munich; Fellow of the Queen's College, Oxford. *Educ:* Christ Church, Oxford; University of Birmingham; University of Wales; and University of Munich. Governor and Member of Council of Univ. College of Wales, Aberystwyth; Governor and Member of Council of the Univ. of Birmingham. *Address:* The Queen's College, Oxford. *T:* Oxford 58485.
Died 26 Jan. 1944.

CHATTERJI, Sir Nalini Ranjan, Kt 1920; MA, BL. Judge, Calcutta High Court, 1910–26.
Died 6 Sept. 1942.

CHATTERTON, Edward Keble; late Lt-Com. RNVR; author, journalist; *b* Sheffield, 1878; *o s* of late Jas Isaac Chatterton, Sheffield; unmarried. *Educ:* Oxford (BA). Came to London and entered journalism; wrote on Art and the Drama for several journals; sub-editor of the Art Record, 1902; sub-edited John Ruskin's MSS for the Library Edition of Ruskin, 1902–03; London correspondent of the Sheffield Weekly Independent, 1902; dramatic critic for two journals; sub-editor Daily Mail; editor of The Lady's Realm, 1904–06; dramatic

critic, 1904–08. Temp. Lieut RNVR, Sept. 1914; promoted (Acting) Lieut-Com., 1918; commanded various ships in Auxiliary Patrol Service, 1914–17; on staff of Historical Section Committee of Imperial Defence, 1917–21. *Publications:* T. Sidney Cooper, RA: His Life and Art, 1903; Sailing Ships: The Story of their Development from the Earliest Times to the Present Day, 1909; New Edition, 1923; The Marriages of Mayfair, 1909; Modern Journalism, 1909; Steamships and their Story, 1910; Down Channel in the Vivette, 1910; The Romance of the Ship, 1910; The Boy's Book, 1910; The Story of the British Navy, 1911; Britain's Record: What She has Done for the World, 1911; Fore and Art: the Story of the Fore and Aft Rig, 1911; Royal Love Letters, 1911; Through Holland in the Vivette, 1912; King's Cutters and Smugglers, 1912; Ships and Ways of Other Days, 1913; The Old East Indiamen, 1914; New revised Edition, 1933; The Romance of Piracy, 1914; Q-Ships and their Story, 1922; second edition, 1923; The Mercantile Marine, 1923; The Auxiliary Patrol, 1923; Ship Models, 1923; The Romance of the Sea Rovers, 1923; Seamen All, 1924, new edition, 1928; Steamship Models, 1924; Whalers and Whaling, 1925, new edition 1930; Battles by Sea, 1925; The Ship Under Sail, 1926; Naval Prints, 1926; Windjammers and Shellbacks, 1926; new edition, 1935; The Brotherhood of the Sea, 1927; Captain John Smith, 1927; Old Ship Prints, 1927; Ventures and Voyages, 1928; new edition, 1935; Old Sea Paintings, 1928; On the High Seas, 1929, new edition, 1931; English Seamen and the Colonization of America, 1930 (published in USA as Seed of Liberty); England's Greatest Statesman, William Pitt; The Sea Raiders, 1931; Sailing the Seas, 1931; Gallant Gentlemen, 1931; The Konigsberg Adventure, 1932; The Big Blockade, 1932; The Yachtsman's Pilot, 1933; Third revised edition, 1937; Through Brittany in Charmina, 1933; Below the Surface, 1934; To the Mediterranean in Charmina, 1934; Danger Zone, The Story of the Queenstown Command, 1934; Sailing Models, Ancient and Modern, 1934; Amazing Adventure, 1935; Dardanelles Dilemma, 1935; Seas of Adventures, 1936; Valiant Sailormen, 1936; Sea Spy (Novel), 1937; Charmina on the Riviera, 1937; Severn's Saga, 1938; Secret Ship (Novel), 1939; The Epic of Dunkirk, 1940; The First Fifteen Months of War, 1941; Fighting the U-Boats, 1941; The Commerce Raiders, 1943; Beating the U-Boats, 1943. *Recreations:* yachting, playgoing, picture galleries. *Address:* Hyde Park House, Knightsbridge, SW. *Clubs:* Royal Thames Yacht, Royal Cruising.
Died 31 Dec. 1944.

CHATTERTON, Rt Rev. Eyre, DD, FRGS; Late President of the Indian Church Aid Association; *b* Monkstown, Co. Cork, 22 July 1863; *s* of late A. T. Chatterton; *m* 1st, 1910, Lilian Agnes (*d* 1944), *y d* of late Henry Alexander Haig; 2nd, 1945, Iona, *er d* of late Harold Graham, 9 Watts Avenue, Rochester. *Educ:* Haileybury; Dublin University. Honours in classics and literature; Senior Moderator and Gold Medallist in Ethics and Logic; First Theological Exhibitioner. Ordained by Bishop Lightfoot, 1887; Curate, Holy Trinity, Stockton-on-Tees, 1887–91; Head of the Dublin University Mission to Chhóta Nagpur, Bengal, 1891–1900; Curate, Parish of Richmond, Surrey, 1901–02; on active service with troops (Episcopal visitations) in Mesopotamia in 1916, 1917 (despatches), and 1919; Bishop of Nagpur, 1903–26; Assistant Bishop in Canterbury Diocese, 1926–30; Rector of Merstham, Surrey, 1926–31; Hon. Canon Canterbury, 1927–30. *Publications:* The Story of Fifty Years' Mission Work in Chhóta Nagpur; The Story of Gondwana, 1916; With the Troops in Mesopotamia, 1916; Mesopotamia Revisited, 1917; History of the Church of England in India since the Early Days of the East India Company, 1924; The Church's Youngest Daughter; India Through a Bishop's Diary, 1935; Alex Wood, Bishop of Nagpur,

A Memoir, 1939; The Anglican Church in India, 1946. *Recreation:* golf. *Address:* Queen's Gate House, 206 Kew Road, Richmond, Surrey. *Club:* Royal Empire Society.

Died 8 Dec. 1950.

CHATTISHAM, 1st Baron *cr* 1945, of Clitheroe; **William Brass,** Kt 1929; MP (C) Clitheroe Division of Lancashire, 1922–45; *b* 11 Feb. 1886; *o s* of late William Brass; unmarried. *Educ:* Eton; Trinity College, Cambridge. A Cambridge Athletic Blue in 1905; gazetted to the Surrey Yeomanry, 1912; served European War in France, Egypt, and Italy, in the Royal Flying Corps and Royal Air Force; Parliamentary Private Secretary to Postmaster-General, 1922; to the Minister of Health, 1922 and 1924–29; and to the Chancellor of the Exchequer, 1923; acted as Parliamentary Private Secretary to the Colonial Secretary on his Dominion tour, 1927–28; Parliamentary Private Secretary to the Minister of Transport and the Minister of Aircraft Production, 1941; a Member of Parliamentary Delegations to South Africa in 1924 and to Canada, 1943; Chairman of St John's Hospital, Lewisham, SE13; Chairman of the British Film Institute; a Director of Guardian Assurance Company, Ltd. *Publications:* (Limited gift editions): Westminster Hall, 9 May 1935; Westminster Hall, 7 May 1937. *Recreations:* shooting, golf. *Address:* The Old Rectory, Chattisham, Ipswich, Suffolk. *Clubs:* Carlton, Travellers'.

Died 24 Aug. 1945 (ext).

CHAUNCY, Col Charles Henry Kemble, CB 1928; CBE 1922. Indian Army, retired. *Address:* Rushlands, Shaldon, Teignmouth, Devon.

Died 19 Sept. 1945.

CHAUVEL, Gen. Sir Henry George, GCMG 1919; KCB 1918; KCMG 1917; CB 1916; CMG 1900; JP; Inspector-in-Chief Australian Home Guard; Hon. Col 9th (North Auckland) NZ Mounted Rifles, and 10th and 15th Australian Light Horse Regiments; a Director of the National Bank of Australasia and the Colonial Mutual Life Assurance Society and Chairman of the Australian Board of the General Accident, Fire, and Life Assurance Corporation; *b* NSW, 16 April 1865; *s* of late C. H. E. Chauvel, of Canning Downs South, Queensland and Tabulam, NSW; *m* 1906, Sibyl, OBE 1939, 2nd *d* of G. Keith Jopp of Karaba, Brisbane; two *s* two *d*. *Educ:* Sydney Grammar School; Toowoomba Grammar School. Joined NSW Cavalry Regt as 2nd Lt, 1886; joined Queensland Mounted Infantry Regt, 1890; served Queensland Mounted Police with temporary rank of Sub-Inspector, 1894–95; appointed to Queensland permanent staff, 1896; Hon. ADC to Govnr of Queensland, 1899–1901; Ad.-General to the Military Forces of Australia, 1911–14; Australian Representative, Imperial General Staff, War Office, 1914; Inspector-Gen., Australian Military Forces, 1919–30; Chief of the General Staff, 1923–30; served in South Africa as Adjutant, Qld. Mtd Infantry, and commanded 7th Battalion Australian Commonwealth Horse (despatches, CMG, Queen's medal four clasps, Bt Lt-Col); ADC to Governor-General of Australia, 1904–11; European War, 1914–18; commanded 1st Australian Light Horse Brigade, Egypt and Gallipoli, 1914–15; 1st Australian Div., Gallipoli and Egypt, 1915–16; Australian and New Zealand Mounted Division, Sinai Campaign, 1916–17; The Desert Column, 1917, and The Desert Mounted Corps, 1917–19, in the Palestine and Syrian Campaigns, including the Capture of Damascus (despatches nine times, CB, KCMG, KCB, GCMG, 3rd and 2nd Classes Order of the Nile and Croix de Guerre (France)); led Australian Contingent at Coronation and commanded all Dominion and Colonial Troops at subsequent Parade, 1937. *Recreation:* riding. *Address:* 49 Murphy Street, South Yarra, Melbourne, SE1, Australia. *Clubs:* Cavalry; Melbourne, Navy, Army and Air Force, Melbourne; Brisbane, Queensland, Brisbane.

Died 4 March 1945.

CHAUVEL, Ven. John Henry Allan, MA, ThL; Rector of St Paul's, Carr Street, West Perth, since 1939; *b* 29 April 1895; *s* of Major James Allan Chauvel, OBE, and Susan Isabella Barnes; *m* 1936, Joyce Wynter Linedale. *Educ:* Southport School, Queensland; Sydney Grammar School; St Paul's College, University of Sydney. Deacon 1919; priest 1920; 1st curacy, Cootamundra, NSW, also Curate at Wagga Wagga, NSW; Senior curate, St Mary's, Lewisham, Diocese of Southwark; Incumbent of St Peter's, Broken Hill, and St Philip's, Railway Town, NSW, 1930–39; Archdeacon of Broken Hill, 1933–39. *Recreation:* motoring. *Address:* St Paul's Rectory, Carr Street, West Perth, W Australia.

Died 28 Feb. 1946.

CHAYTOR, Lt-Col Clervaux Alexander, CB 1941; DSO; JP, DL, NR Yorks; landowner; *s* of late C. D. Chaytor of Spennithorne Hall, Leyburn; unmarried. *Educ:* Aysgarth School; Clifton College. Direct Commission, KOYLI, 1901; served in Northern Nigeria, 1904–09 (despatches, medal with 2 clasps, wounded); European War (despatches, DSO, Brevet of Lieut-Col, Croix de Guerre with Palm); retired, 1921. *Recreations:* shooting and fishing. *Address:* Spennithorne Hall, Leyburn, Yorkshire. *TA:* Spennithorne. *T:* Middleham 33. *Clubs:* Yorkshire, York.

Died 22 Sept. 1941.

CHEAPE, James; *b* 1853; *o s* of Alexander Cheape (*d* 1892) and Hon. Anne Charlotte (*d* 1914), *d* of 8th Viscount Arbuthnott; *m* 1897, Lady Griselda Johanna Helen Ogilvy (*d* 1934), *y d* of 7th Earl of Airlie; two *s* one *d*. *Address:* Strathtyrum, St Andrews, Fife.

Died 21 July 1943.

CHEESMAN, Rev. Alfred Hunter, MA; Vicar of Twigworth, Gloucester, 1912; Hon. Canon of Gloucester, 1925; *b* 10 Nov. 1864; 2nd *s* of Alfred Cheesman, Bosham, Sussex, and Elizabeth Amelia Hunter. *Educ:* Chichester; Worcester College, Oxford. Curate of All Saints, Gloucester, 1888–1912; Served in France during 1918. *Publication:* Editor of Gloucester Diocesan Kalendar, 1900–1927. *Recreations:* motoring, botany, and genealogy. *Address:* Twigworth Vicarage, Gloucester.

Died 26 April 1941.

CHERRINGTON, Rt Rev. Cecil Arthur; 1st Bishop of Waikato since 1926; *s* of late Rev. A. O. Cherrington; *m* Mary Selina Addams-William (*d* 1926). *Educ:* St Aidan's College; London University, BA, BD; Hons in New Testament Greek, etc. Curate of St Chad's, Liverpool, 1896; Chaplain of Birkenhead School; Chaplain and Lecturer of Lichfield Theological College; Vicar of Tunstall; Archdeacon of Mauritius, 1922; Examining Chaplain to the Bishop. *Address:* 61 Clarence Street, Hamilton, New Zealand.

Died Aug. 1950.

CHERRY, Sir John Arnold, Kt 1934; CIE 1919; Barrister-at-law, Gray's Inn, 1908; MInstT; *b* 13 Feb. 1879; *s* of late G. W. Cherry, London; *m* 1909, Doreen, *d* of late W. T. Wiley, Cape Town, South Africa; one *s* three *d*. Bombay Port Trust, 1908–20; IARO 1917–20, retired as Lt-Col; Chairman Port Commissioners, Rangoon, 1921–36. *Address:* c/o Barclay's Bank, (Dominion, Colonial and Overseas), Cape Town, S Africa. *Club:* East India and Sports.

Died 4 April 1950.

CHESTER, Sir George, Kt 1948; CBE 1944; FRHS; FBSI; Director of the Bank of England since 1949; General Secretary, National Union of Boot and Shoe Operatives since 1930; *b* 16 Jan. 1886; *s* of Robert and Elizabeth Chester; *m* 1920, Beatrice Annie Becks; one *s* one *d*. *Educ:* Elementary School, Kettering; WEA Classes; Technical Schools. Boot operative, 1899–1915; Asst Sec. Kettering No. 1 Branch, Nat. Union of Boot and Shoe Operatives, 1915–30. Member General Council Trades Union Congress since 1936; Secretary,

Kettering and District Naturalists Soc., 1908–30. *Publications:* chapter on National Union of Boot and Shoe Operatives in British Trades Unionism Today, 1938; numerous articles in Report of the Union; magazine articles on Trade Unionism, 1930–1947; articles on the Flora of Northants, 1916–1930. *Recreations:* natural science, botany, gardening. *Address:* The Limes, Earls Barton, Northampton. *T:* Earls Barton 301.

Died 21 April 1949.

CHESTER-MASTER, Rev. Harold, MA; Chaplain, Wellington School, Som., since 1946; *b* Christchurch Vicarage, Bootle, Liverpool, 11 Sept. 1889; 2nd *surv. s* of late Rev. Francis Charles Chester-Master. *Educ:* Monkton Combe School, near Bath; University College, Durham. Durham University Hebrew Scholar, 1913. Deacon, 1913; Priest, 1914; Assistant Curate of Guisborough, Yorks, 1913–15; Temporary CF, 1915; served in France (wounded, 1916); Chaplain No. 1 Officer Cadet Battalion, 1917; Pilot RAF, 1918; Chaplain to North Russian Relief Force, 1919 (MC); Hon. CF, 1919; Chaplain Moorland House, Heswall, Cheshire, 1920–22; Assistant Master Ashbury College, Ottawa, Canada, 1922–25; Chaplain Moorland House, Heswall, 1925–27; Chaplain and Foundation House Master St Bees School, Cumberland, 1927–28; Headmaster, Bishop's Stortford School, Herts, 1928–29; Chaplain and Assistant Master Malvern College, 1930–34; Second Master, King's College, Taunton, 1935–39; Chaplain, Wellington School Som., 1939–44; Assistant Master, King's College, Taunton, 1944–45. *Recreations:* riding, motoring. *Address:* Wellington School, Som. *Club:* Overseas.

Died 3 July 1948.

CHETTIAR, Hon. Dr Rajah Sir Annamalai Chettiar of Chettinad; Hereditary Rajah, Kt 1923; Hon. LLD University of Madras, 1932; *b* 30 Sept. 1881. Pro-Chancellor of the Annamalai University; a banker and merchant with extensive business in India, Ceylon, Burma, Straits Settlements, Malay States, Cochin-China; was a member of the Council of State and Central Assembly; a Governor of the Imperial Bank of India; Founder of the Annamalai University at Annamalainagar, Chidambaram; also of the Rajah Annamalai Music College, and other educational institutions; has given Chettinad the Lady Pentland Women and Children's Hospital and an aerodrome and Madras, the Willingdon Club, Member of Madras Legislative Council, 1916; is a life member of the Senate of the University of Madras; Rao Bahadur, 1912; Diwan Bahadur, 1922; hereditary Rajaship, 1929. *Address:* Chettinad House, Adyar, Madras.

Died 15 June 1948.

CHETWODE, 1st Baron *cr* 1945, of Chetwode; **Philip Walhouse Chetwode;** 7th Bt *cr* 1700, GCB 1929 (KCB 1918; CB 1915); OM 1936; GCSI 1934; KCMG 1917; DSO 1900; DCL Oxford, late 19th Hussars; Bailiff Grand Cross, Order of St John; Grand Cross Order of St Olaf (Norway); Grand Cross Royal Order of George I (Greece); Knight Grand Cross Order of Orange Nassau (Netherlands); Order of Brilliant Star with Grand Cordon (China); Col of the Royal Scots Greys, 1940–48, of the 8th Light Cavalry, 1935–, of the 15th/19th Hussars, 1940–48; *b* 21 Sept. 1869; *e s* of Lt-Col Sir George Chetwode, 6th Bt, and Alice, *d* of late Michael T. Bass, Rangemore, Staffordshire; *S* father, 1905; *m* 1899, Hester Alice Camilla (*d* 1946), *e d* of late Col Hon. Richard Stapleton-Cotton; one *d* (one *s* decd). *Educ:* Eton. Entered Army, 1889; Capt., 1897; Major, 1901; Lt-Col, 1909; Col, 1912; Brig.-General, 1914; Major-General, 1916; Lieut-General, 1919; General, 1926; Field-Marshal, 1933; served Chin Hills, Burmah, 1892–93 (medal with clasp); South Africa, 1899–1902 (despatches twice, Queen's medal 5 clasps, King's medal 2 clasps, DSO); European War, 1914–18; commanded 5th Cavalry Brigade, 1914–15 (wounded, CB); 2nd

Cavalry Division, 1915–16; commanded Desert Corps, Egypt, 1916–17; commanded East Force, 1917; commanded 20th Army Corps, 1917–18; capture of Jerusalem and campaign in Palestine and Syria (despatches eleven times; 1914 Star, British General Service Medal and Allied Medal, KCB, Commander Legion of Honour, Croix de Guerre, Grand Officer Order of the Nile, 1st Class Order of the Sacred Treasure (Japan); Military Secretary, War Office, 1919–20; Deputy Chief of the Imperial General Staff, 1920–22; Adjutant-General to the Forces, 1922–23; Commander-in-Chief, Aldershot Command, 1923–27; ADC General, 1927–31; Chief of General Staff, India, 1928–30; Commander-in-Chief of the Army in India, 1930–35; Chairman of Executive Committee of Red Cross and St John Joint War Organisation, 1940–47; Constable of the Royal Palace and the Tower of London, 1943–48. *Heir:* *g s* Philip [*b* 26 March 1937; *s* of late Capt. Roger Chetwode and Hon. Patricia Berry, 3rd *d* of 1st Viscount Camrose]. *Address:* Flat 7, The Hall, 23a Grove End Road, St John's Wood, NW8. *T:* Cunningham 8827; Chetwode, Bucks. *Clubs:* Cavalry, Royal Societies, Turf.

Died 6 July 1950.

CHHOTA UDEPUR, Maharawal Shri Natwarsinhji Fatehsinhji, Raja of; *b* 16 Nov. 1906; *S* 1923, invested with full powers, 1928; *m* 1st, 1927, *sister* (*d* 1928) of the Maharaja of Rajpipla; 2nd, 1928, *e d* of Maharaja of Rajpipla; one *s. Educ:* St Xavier's and Rajkumar Colleges. Visited Europe, 1926 and 1937. Is a Chowan Rajput. Area of State, 890.34 square miles; population, 162,145. The Gad Boriad State, with an area of 128 sq. miles and a population of 13,120 souls, has been attached to this State. Is entitled to a permanent salute of 9 guns. *Recreations:* cricket, shooting, and riding. *Address:* Chhota Udepur, Gujarat States, India.

Died 15 Oct. 1946.

CHHOTU RAM, Rao Bahadur Chaudhri Sir, Kt 1937. Member Punjab Legislative Assembly; Minister of Revenue, Punjab Govt. *Address:* Lahore, Punjab.

Died Jan. 1945.

CHIASSON, Rt Rev. Patrice Alexandre, CJM; RC Bishop of Bathurst, NB, since 1938; *b* Grand Etang, CB, 10 Nov. 1867. *Educ:* College Sainte-Anne; Grand Seminary in France. Prof. and Sup.-College Sainte-Anne, NS; former Vicar Apostolic of Gulf of St Lawrence, 1917; Bishop of Chatham, NB, 1920–38. *Address:* Bathurst, NB, Canada.

Died Feb. 1942.

CHICHESTER, 8th Earl *cr* 1801; **John Buxton Pelham;** Bt 1611; Baron Pelham of Stanmer, 1762; Capt. Scots Guards; *b* 1912; 2nd *s* of 6th Earl of Chichester (*d* 1926) and Ruth, *e d* of late F. W. Buxton; *S* brother, 1926; *m* 1940, Ursula, *o d* of Catalina and late Walter de Pannwitz, De Hartekamp, Bennebroek, Holland; one *s* one *d. Educ:* Eton; Trinity College, Oxford. Hon. Attaché at HM Embassy in Warsaw, 1931; Washington, 1933; Hon. Private Secretary to High Commissioner in Canada for HM Government in the United Kingdom, Dec. 1933–July 1934; Press Attaché, British Legation, The Hague, 1939. *Heir:* *s* John Nicholas, *b* 14 April 1944. *Address:* Stanmer, Lewes, Sussex. *T:* Preston 2074; 36 Chesham Place, SW1. *T:* Sloane 4144. *Clubs:* Brooks's, Buck's.

Died 21 Feb. 1944.

CHICHESTER, Lt-Col Alan, OBE 1924; DL Hunts; Chief Constable of Hunts, 1901–27; 2nd *s* of late Hon. Frederick A. H. Chichester; *m* 1st, Hon. Georgina Morgan, *d* of 1st Baron Tredegar; 2nd, Beatrice, *d* of Edmund Snow, of Franklyn, Exeter; no *c. Educ:* Felsted School. Late Lieut-Colonel, 18th Royal Irish Regiment; served as Adjutant; ADC to GOC 1st Brigade, Aldershot; severely wounded at battle of Tel-el-Kebir, 1882 (medal and clasp, 5th class, Order of Medijieh, Khedive's bronze star); served as Provost Marshal to

Natal Army, Boer War, 1900 (despatches, medal and six clasps, Brevet Lt-Colonel). *Recreations:* cricket, hunting, polo, shooting, and fishing. *Address:* 100 Drayton Gardens, SW10. *Clubs:* Army and Navy, MCC.

Died 6 March 1947.

CHICHESTER, Maj.-Gen. Sir Arlington Augustus, KCMG 1919; CB 1915; DSO 1900; *b* 2 July 1863; *s* of late Major-General J. O. Chichester, of Western House, Chudleigh, Devon; *m* 1st 1891, Eva Isabella Maude, 3rd *d* of Major-General H. Justice, formerly ISC, of Riven Hall, Southsea; (divorce 1910) one *s*; 2nd 1923, Kathleen Mary Elizabeth, *d* of Henry Liversidge, Portington Hall, Yorkshire. *Educ:* Cheltenham College; Royal Military College; passed Staff College. Entered Dorsetshire Regt 1884; Captain, 1891; Major, 1902; Lieut-Col, 1910; Col, 1913; Maj.-Gen. 1917. Served South African war, 1899–1901 (on Staff); relief of Ladysmith, and action at Spion Kop, etc. (despatches, Queen's medal with 5 clasps, King's medal with 2 clasps, DSO); DAQMG and DAAG General Staff at Hong-Kong, 1903–07; European War, 1914–19 (despatches 11 times, CB, promoted Major-General for distinguished service, KCMG, 1914 Star, Belgian Order of the Crown and Croix de Guerre, Italian Order of St Maurice and Lazarus, French Legion of Honour and Croix de Guerre); Colonel-in-Chief, Dorsetshire Regt, 1922–33. *Address:* Haighton, Folkestone, Kent. *TA:* Folkestone. *T:* 3200. *Club:* Army and Navy.

Died 1 Sept. 1948.

CHICHESTER-CONSTABLE, Walter George Raleigh; JP, DL; *b* 1863; *e s* of late Lt-Col Charles Raleigh Chichester, and Mary Josephine, *e d* and heir of late James Balfe, of Runnamoat; *S* mother, as heir of entail, 1871; *m* 1888, Edith (*d* 1937), 3rd *d* of J. H. Smyth-Pigott, of Brockley Court, Somerset; three *s* three *d. Educ:* Stonyhurst College. High Sheriff, Roscommon, 1896; Major late 3rd Batt. King's (Liverpool) Regt; Lieut-Colonel (late) 2/5 Yorkshire Regt; 44th Lord Paramount of the Seigniory of Holderness; assumed by Royal Licence additional surname of Constable, 1895. *Heir: e s* Raleigh Charles Joseph Chichester-Constable, DSO. *Address:* Burton Constable, and Wood Hall, Hull.

Died 15 Feb. 1942.

CHIGNELL, Rev. Hugh Scott, BA, Lond. Univ. Curate of Croydon Parish Church, 1901–03; Minor Canon of Worcester, 1903–07; Vicar of Lower Umgeni, Natal, 1908–14; St Peter's, Maritzburg, 1914–20; Yeovil, Johannesburg, 1920–24; Rector of Parktown, Johannesburg, 1929–35; Dean of Kimberley, 1935–41. Rector of St Augustine's Parish, Orange Grove, Johannesburg, 1941–45. *Address:* 11 Taylor Road, Scotsville, Maritzburg, Natal. *T:* Scotsville Maritzburg, Natal 4130.

Died 19 Sept. 1950.

CHILCOTT, Lt-Comdr Sir Warden (Stanley), Kt 1922; JP, DL Hants; *b* 11 March 1871. Served with the Royal Naval Air Service in France; MP (C) Walton Division of Liverpool, 1918–29. *Publication:* Political Salvation, 1930–1932, 1932. *Address:* 36 St James's Street, SW1. *T:* Regent 4868; The Salterns, Warsash, Southampton. *Clubs:* Carlton; principal racing and yachting clubs.

Died 8 March 1942.

CHILD, Harold Hannyngton, FRSL; author and journalist; writer on The Times and The Times Literary Supplement since 1902; *b* Gloucester, 1869; *s* of Rev. Thomas Hannyngton Irving Child and Florence, *d* of Thomas Crossman; *m* 1st, Drusilla Mary Cutler (*d* 1918); 2nd, 1934, Helen Mary, *d* of late Prof. Spenser Wilkinson. *Educ:* Winchester (Scholar); Brasenose, Oxford (Scholar); BA 1892; MA 1931. Sec. of Royal Society of Painter-Etchers and Engravers, 1902–05; Assistant Editor of The Academy, 1905–07; Burlington

Magazine, 1907–10; dramatic critic to The Observer, 1912–20. *Publications:* Phil of the Heath, a novel, 1899; Aucassin and Nicolete, 1911; Thomas Hardy, 1916 (revised, 1925); The Yellow Rock (poems), 1919; Love and Unlove, 1921; libretto of R. Vaughan Williams's opera, Hugh the Drover; A Poor Player, 1939; several translations and editions; contributor to the Cambridge Modern History, the Cambridge History of English Literature, The Dictionary of National Biography, the Quarterly Review, The Review of English Studies, The New Cambridge Shakespeare, publications of the Royal Society of Literature and the Shakespeare Association, the Enciclopedia Italiana, etc. *Club:* Garrick.

Died 8 Nov. 1945.

CHILDERS, Lt-Col Hugh Francis Eardley, CIE 1933; IA retired; Officer i/c Government Stud Farm, Burma, and Commandant, Reserve Battalion, Burma Frontier Force; *b* 17 July 1886; *s* of late Col E. S. E. Childers, CB, RE; *m* 1911, Gladys, *e d* of Col G. M. Porter, RE. *Educ:* Haileybury; RMC Sandhurst. Indian Army, 1905; 32nd Lancers, 1906; Personal Assistant to Resident in Kashmir, 1909; seconded to Burma Military Police, 1910; rejoined 32nd Lancers in Mesopotamia, 1917 (British War and Victory Medals); seconded for re-employment with Burma Military Police, 1919; India General Service Medal with Clasp 'Burma 1930–32'; King's Police Medal, 1939. *Recreations:* riding, polo, shooting. *Address:* Pyawbwe, Upper Burma. *Clubs:* Brooks's, Cavalry.

Died 27 Sept. 1941.

CHILDS, Maj.-Gen. Sir (Borlase Elward) Wyndham, KCMG 1919; KBE 1921; CB 1918; CMG 1916; *b* 15 Dec. 1876; *s* of late Borlase Childs; *m* 1925, Ethel Allanson, *d* of late John Metcalfe Young of Tynemouth, Northumberland. Entered Duke of Cornwall's Light Infantry, 1900; Captain, Royal Irish Regiment, 1910; Brevet Major, 1912; Major Duke of Cornwall's Light Inf., 1915; Brevet Lieut-Col 1916; Brevet Col 1917; Colonel, 1919; Brig.-Gen. 1916; Temp. Major-General, 1917; Staff Capt. War Office, 1911–14; DAAG War Office, 1914; DAAG, GHQ, BEF 1914; AAG, GHQ, BEF 1914–16; AAG, War Office, 1916; Director of Personal Services, War Office, 1916–19; Deputy Adjt-General to the Forces, 1919–21; retired pay, 1922; Assistant Commissioner Metropolitan Police, 1921–28; High Sheriff of Cambs, Hunts, and Isle of Ely, 1932–33; JP; served European War, 1914–18 (despatches thrice, Bt Lt-Col and Col, CMG, CB); Legion of Honour; Crown of Belgium; Crown of Italy. *Publication:* Episodes and Reflections, 1930. *Club:* Marlborough.

Died 27 Nov. 1946.

CHILSTON, 2nd Viscount *cr* 1911, of Boughton Malherbe; **Aretas Akers-Douglas;** Baron Douglas *cr* 1911, PC 1939; GCMG 1935; KCMG 1927; CMG 1918; *b* 17 Feb. 1876; *e s* of 1st Viscount and Adeline, *e d* of H. Austen Smith, Hayes Court, Kent; *S* father, 1926; *m* 1903, Amy, *d* of late J. R. Jennings-Bramly, Royal Horse Artillery; one *s. Educ:* Eton College. Formerly Captain 3rd Battalion Royal Scots; Attaché in Diplomatic Service, 1898; served at Cairo; 3rd Secretary, 1900; served at Madrid, Constantinople, and Athens; 2nd Secretary, 1905; served in the Foreign Office; was Acting Agent and Consul-General at Sofla, 1907; served at Rome, and at Vienna; Chargé d'Affaires in Montenegro in 1911 and 1913, and in Roumania in 1912 and 1914; Secretary of Embassy at Vienna, 1909–14; Diplomatic Secretary to Secretary of State for Foreign Affairs, 1919; British Minister at Vienna, 1921–27, and Consul-General, 1927; at Budapest, 1928–33; British Ambassador in Moscow, 1933–38. *Heir: s* Hon. Eric Akers-Douglas, Flight Lieut RAFVR, *b* 1910. *Address:* Chilston Park, Maidstone. *T:* Lenham 214. *Club:* Carlton.

Died 25 July 1947.

CHILTON, Rev. Arthur, MVO 1930; DD; Rector of Colne Engaine, 1932–45; Prebendary of St Paul's Cathedral, 1923; *b* Manchester, 19 June 1864; *s* of late William Chilton; *m* 1893, Ethel *d* of late Halsall Segar, JP, of Birkenhead; two *s* one *d*. *Educ*: Christ's Hospital; Christ Church, Oxford (Exhibitioner). Master at Christ's Hospital, 1890–94; Head Master and Chaplain of Emanuel School, Wandsworth Common, 1894–1905; Deacon, 1891; Priest, 1892; Curate of Holy Trinity, Sloane Street, 1891–94; Headmaster of the City of London School, 1905–29. *Address*: The Shieling, Earl's Colne, Colchester, Essex. *T*: Earl's Colne 283.

Died 6 April 1947.

CHINNERY-HALDANE, James Brodrick; 25th of Gleneagles; JP; *b* Edinburgh, July 1868; *m* 1902, Katherine Annie, *d* of late W. H. E. Napier; two *s* two *d*. *Educ*: Loretto (head of School and Captain of Rugby XV); Christ Church, Oxford (History Honours), MA. Became possessed of the old Barony of Gleneagles in 1918 in accordance with the entail executed by Robert Haldane of Gleneagles and Airthrey (1766). *Address*: Gleneagles, Auchterarder, Perthshire. *T*: Blackford 49.

Died 2 May 1941.

CHINTAMANI, Sir Chirravoori Yajneswara, Kt 1939; DLitt (Allahabad), LLD (Benares Hindu University); President of National Liberal Federation of India, 1920 and 1931; Chief Editor of the Leader; member of United Provinces Legislative Council, 1916–23 and 1927–36; member of the (Lothian) Indian Franchise Committee, 1932; *b* 11 April 1880; *s* of Chirravoori Ramasomayajulu Garu; *m* Srimati Krishnavenemma; five *s* one *d*. *Educ*: Maharajah's College, Vizianagaram. Minister of Education, United Provinces, 1921–23. *Publications*: Indian Social Reform, 1901; Speeches and Writings of Sir Pherozeshah Mehta, 1905; Indian Politics since the Mutiny, 1937. *Address*: 26 Hamilton Road, Allahabad, India.

Died June 1941.

CHIRNSIDE, Captain John Percy, CMG 1905; OBE 1919; *b* 2 Oct. 1865; *y s* of late Andrew Chirnside of Carranballac and Haprich, Berwickshire; *m* Ethel Mary, *d* of G. O. Ross-Fenner; three *s* one *d*. *Educ*: Grammar School, Geelong, Victoria. Twenty years Victorian Military Forces; served 4½ years with Imperial Army during Great War (despatches twice, CBE); MLA Grant, Victoria, 1894–1904. *Address*: Brandon Park, Oakleigh, Melbourne, SE12, Victoria, Australia. *Club*: Melbourne.

Died 6 Jan. 1944.

CHISHOLM, Col Hugh Alexander, CMG 1919; DSO 1915; MD; *b* 8 Feb. 1883; *s* of Duncan Chisholm, Tynwood, NS; *m* 1910, Mary Eulalia, *d* of Hon. Peter Smyth. *Educ*: McGill University, Montreal. Served European War, 1914–17 (despatches, DSO). *Address*: Halifax, Nova Scotia. *Clubs*: Halifax; Frontenac, Kingston.

Died 25 Sept. 1940.

CHISHOLM, Hon. Sir Joseph (Andrew), Kt 1935; KC 1907; MA, LLD, 1932; DCL, 1939; Chief Justice of Nova Scotia since 1931; *b* St Andrews, NS, 9 Jan. 1863; *s* of William Chisholm, JP, and Flora Mackintosh; *m* 1891, Frances Alice (*d* 1903), *d* of late Captain James Affleck of Halifax; four *d*. *Educ*: St Francis Xavier's University, Antigonish; Dalhousie Law School, Halifax. Admitted to Bar, 1886; contested (C) Antigonish Co. for House of Commons, 1895 and 1896; Mayor of Halifax, 1909, 1910, and 1911; President, Union of Nova Scotia Municipalities 1910; President, Union of Canadian Municipalities, 1910; Chairman, Halifax School Board, 1909; Member, Executive of Strathcona Trust for Military Training in the Schools, 1908; President of Nova Scotia Branch of St John's Ambulance, 1910–31; President, Halifax Anti-Tuberculosis League, 1913; Judge of the Supreme Court of Nova Scotia, 1916–31; President, Nova Scotia Historical Society, 1921–24;

Esquire of Order of St John of Jerusalem, 1915; Chairman of Royal Commission which investigated and settled labour troubles in collieries in Nova Scotia, 1917; Member of the Board of Commissioners of Victoria General Hospital; member of the Board of Trustees of the Public Archives of Nova Scotia since 1931; acted as Administrator of the Province of Nova Scotia on several occasions. *Publications*: Joseph Howe: a Sketch; edited The Speeches and Public Letters of Joseph Howe. *Address*: The Law Courts, Halifax, NS. *TA*: Chisholm, Halifax. *T*: 1917. *Club*: Halifax (Halifax).

Died 22 Jan. 1950.

CHITRAL, Major HH Muhammad Sir Nasir-ul-Mulk, Mehtar of, KCIE 1941; *b* 1898; *S* 1936. *Address*: Chitral, NW Frontier Province, India.

Died 29 July 1943.

CHITTENDEN, Frederick James, OBE 1950; FLS, VMH; Editor, Royal Horticultural Society's Dictionary of Gardening; Secretary, Scientific Committee of RHS, since 1904; *b* West Ham, 25 Oct. 1873; *e s* of William Chittenden; *m* 1901, Esther Ada Farnes. *Educ*: Leyton; Carpenter's Institute, Stratford; Technical Laboratories, Chelmsford. Engaged in teaching, 1892–1900; Lecturer in Botany, Woolwich Polytechnic, 1899–1900; Lecturer in Biology to Essex County Council, 1900–07; Director, RHS Laboratory, 1907–19 and of Experimental Gardens, 1919–31; Editor RHS Journal, 1908–39; Technical Adviser, RHS, and Keeper, Lindley Library, 1931–39. *Publications*: The Garden Doctor; papers on Fungi and Mosses in scientific journals; reports of investigations in plant diseases, pollination in orchards, and other technical matters in the leading horticultural papers. *Recreations*: field natural history, angling, and gardening. *Address*: East Lane House, Dedham, Essex.

Died 31 July 1950.

CHITTENDEN, Russell Henry, PhD, LLD, ScD, MD (Hon.); Professor Physiological Chemistry, 1882; Emeritus, 1922; Director Sheffield Scientific School, Yale University, 1898–1922; *b* 18 Feb. 1856; *s* of Horace H. Chittenden and Emily E. Doane; *m* 1877, Gertrude L. Baldwin; two *d*. *Educ*: Yale University; Heidelberg University. Member National Academy of Sciences; Member American Philosophical Society; American Academy Arts and Sciences; Société des Sciences Medicales et Naturelles de Bruxelles; Corresponding Member Société de Biologie, Paris; Referee Board of Consulting Scientific Experts to the Secretary of Agriculture; United States Representative on Interallied Scientific Food Commission at London, Paris, and Rome, 1918; President American Physiological Society, 1895–1904; President American Society of Biological Chemists, 1907; President, American Society of Naturalists, 1893; Hon. Fellow New York Academy of Medicine; Hon. Fellow, Connecticut State Medical Society. *Publications*: 4 vols Studies in Physiological Chemistry; Digestive Proteolysis; Physiological Economy in Nutrition; The Nutrition of Man; History of the Sheffield Scientific School of Yale University; The Development of Physiological Chemistry in the United States; etc. *Recreation*: fishing. *Address*: New Haven, Connecticut. *Clubs*: Yale, New York; Graduates New Haven.

Died Dec. 1943.

CHITTY, Sir Arthur, KCMG 1910; CMG, 1908; *b* 1864; *s* of late Capt. A. W. Chitty, IN, CIE; unmarried. *Educ*: Clifton Coll. Entered Egyptian Government Service, 1883; Controller of Direct Taxes, Ministry of Finance, 1892–1900; Director-General of Customs, 1900–06; Director-General, Revenue, 1906–08; Adviser to Ministry of Interior, Egypt, 1908; retired, 1910; Osmanieh, 1st class; Medjidieh, 3rd class. *Address*: c/o Royal Empire Society, Northumberland Avenue, WC2.

Died 3 March 1948.

CHITTY, Sir Joseph Henry Pollock, Kt 1933; *b* 11 Jan. 1861; 2nd *s* of late Rt Hon. Sir Joseph William Chitty, a Lord Justice of the Court of Appeal; *m* 1889, Adele Johanna Torry (*d* 1939); two *s. Educ:* Winchester; Trinity College, Oxford (MA); 2nd class honours, Law School, Oxford. Formerly Solicitor and Examiner to Law Society, Honours Common Law, 1901–10; Master of Chancery Division, Supreme Court, 1910–32; Chief Master, 1932–36. *Address:* Torrie Lodge, Esher, Surrey. *Club:* United University.

Died 6 Feb. 1942.

CHOLMELEY, Norman Goodford, CSI 1910; *b* 5 May 1863; *s* of Montague Cholmeley, Indian Army; *m* 1903, Mary Katherine, *d* of late Hallet George Batten; two *s* one *d. Educ:* Charterhouse; Balliol College, Oxford. Joined ICS, 1883; Deputy Commissioner, 1890; Commissioner, 1903; Commissioner of Magwe Division, Burma, 1901–11; retired, 1911; with Anglo-French Red Cross, 1914–17; Ministry of Food, 1917–18. *Address:* c/o Grindlay's Bank, 54 Parliament St, Westminster, SW1.

Died 26 Aug. 1947.

CHOLMELEY, Robert Francis, CBE 1927; MA Oxon; *b* 22 Feb. 1862; *e s* of Rev. John Cholmeley, Rector of Carleton Rode, Norfolk; *m* 1888, Blanche Emily Roberta, *d* of Rev. J. G. Darling, Rector of Eyke, Suffolk; one *d* (*one son* killed in Flanders, 1915). *Educ:* Marlborough; Corpus Christi College, Oxford. Assistant Master, Eton, 1886; St Paul's, 1886–1909; Headmaster, Owen's School, Islington 1909–27; Secretary, Lord Kitchener National Memorial Fund, 1928–41; Chairman, Assistant Masters' Association, 1908; President, Incorporated Association of Headmasters, 1923 and 1927; OBE 1918; Officier de l'instruction publique, 1927. *Publications:* Secondary Education in England; a few school editions of single plays of Shakespeare. *Address:* 11 Archery Fields House, Wharton St, WC1.

Died 31 Dec. 1947.

CHOLMONDELEY, Brig.-Gen. Hugh Cecil, CB 1900; CBE 1919; DL, JP Salop; *b* Sledmere, Yorkshire, Dec. 1852; *e s* of Col the Hon. Thomas Grenville Cholmondeley, and Katherine Lucy, *d* of Sir Tatton Sykes, Bart, of Sledmere; *m* 1st, 1885, Mary Stewart (*d* 1929), *d* of Horace Payne Townshend; one *d*; 2nd, 1931, Violet, *er d* of late Prebendary Hon. Archibald Parker; one *d. Educ:* Rugby. Joined Rifle Brigade, 1873; Adjt 4th Batt. during Afghan War, 1878–79 (medal and clasp); Adjutant 5th Battalion Rifle Brigade, 1882–87; commanded London Rifle Brigade, 1890–1901 commanded CIV Mounted Inf. South Africa, 1900 (despatches twice, medal 6 clasps, CB); Commanded 173rd Infantry Brig., 1916; Staff-Officer for Volunteer Services Western Command, 1917–18 (CBE); Vice-Chairman Shropshire Territorial Force Association; Master North Shropshire Hounds (retired). *Recreation:* all field sports. *Address:* Edstaston, Wem, Salop. *TA:* Cholmondeley, Wem. *T:* Wem 23. *Club:* Bath.

Died 13 Dec. 1941.

CHOMLEY, Charles Henry, BA, LLB; Barrister (Melbourne); Editor since 1908 of the British Australian and New Zealander (formerly the British Australasian); *b* 1868; *s* of late H. B. Chomley, Victoria, Australia; *m* 1891, Ethel Beatrice Ysobel (*d* 1940), *d* of late Hon. W. A. C. à Beckett, Melbourne; one *s* three *d. Educ:* Trinity College; Melbourne University. *Publications:* Protection in Australasia and Canada; Australian Pros and Cons; Law for Laymen; The Flight of the Black Swan; The True Story of the Kelly Gang; Mark Meredith; Money Based on the World's Goods; (with R. L. Outhwaite) The Wisdom of Esau and Land Values Taxation—the Essential Reform; edited new edition of Lord Farrar's Free Trade versus Fair Trade. *Address:* 5 Ladbroke Gardens, W11. *T:* Park 6222.

Died 21 Oct. 1942.

CHOPE, Brig. Arthur John Herbert, DSO 1916; *b* 1884; *m* 1916, Elizabeth Susanna Winifred, *widow* of Major H. C. Nicolay. *Educ:* Sandhurst. Commission in the West Riding Regiment (The Duke of Wellington's); passed into Indian Army, 1906; served Abor Expedition, 1911–12; Adjt of the Regt in this Expedition; European War, 1914–17 (DSO), Order of the Nile, 4th Class; Staff College, 1919–20; Brigade Major 19th Infantry Brigade (Lucknow), 1921; DAAG Eastern Command, 1923–24; Lt-Col, 1927; commanded 2/2nd King Edward's Own Goorkhas (The Sirmoor Rifles) 1927–31; Colonel, 1931; officiated as AAG Army HQ, 1931; AAG Army Headquarters, India, 1931–34; Commanded 5th Infantry Brigade, Quetta, 1934–36; Commanded Sind (Independent) Brigade Area, 1936–38; retired, 1938. *Address:* c/o Cox's Branch, 6 Pall Mall, SW1. *Club:* United Service.

Died 26 Sept. 1942.

CHOQUETTE, Rt Rev. Mgr Charles Philippe, RC, MA, Licès Scs; LLD Hon.; Vice-President of the College of Saint Hyacinthe and Professor of Science; *b* Beloeil, of French parents; *brother* of Senator Choquette and Dr Choquette, Legislative Counsellor and Publicist. *Educ:* College of Saint Hyacinthe. Spent one year in Paris, a student in the Collège de France, Sorbonne, and Institut Catholique, and worked in the laboratories of Collège de France under Berthelot and Mascart; Director of the Provincial Laboratory, 1889–1901; Professor of Physic, Laval University, Montreal; Hon. Commissioner to the Paris Exhibition and Delegate of Canada to the Scientific Congresses, 1900; Member of the Board of Examiners for the Official Chemists of the Dominion; Member of the Board of Visitors to the Royal Military College of Kingston; President of the College of St Hyacinthe, 1904–13; Canon Cathedral of St Hyacinthe and delegate of the Chapter to the Plenary Council of Canada in 1909; Domestic Prelate to the Pope, 1911; Delegate by Laval University to the Congress of the Universities of the Empire, London, 1912, and to the International Congress of Geology, Toronto, 1913; Charter Member of the Société Internationale des Electriciens, Paris; Member of the Commission of Conservation, Canada. *Publications:* Un Siècle—Histoire du Seminaire de Saint-Hyacinthe; A la Poursuite de l'éclipse, 1905; Une Mission Astronomique en Norvège, 1927; Histoire de la Ville de St Hyacinthe, 1932; various scientific papers and lectures. *Recreations:* Microscopy, X-rays, and Wireless. *Address:* College of Saint Hyacinthe, Saint Hyacinthe, PQ, Canada.

Died 15 Feb. 1947.

CHORLTON, Alan Ernest Leofric, CBE 1917; MInstCE; MIMechE, MIEE; *b* nr Manchester, Feb. 1874; *s* of Thomas Chorlton, solicitor; *m* 1907, Louise de Ady (*d* 1932); one *s* two *d*; 1939, Ivy Curling. *Educ:* private; Technical College, Manchester; Manchester Univ. After technical training and full apprenticeship went abroad, principally to Russia; on various engineering works; later to Germany on internal combustion engines; returned to this country to hold various positions; MP (U) Platting Division, Manchester, 1931–35, and Bury, 1935–45; Chairman of several industrial companies. *Publications:* papers on the reorganisation of the water supply of this country, also high speed railway service, etc. *Address:* 55 Lower Belgrave Street, Eaton Square, SW1. *Clubs:* Junior Carlton, St Stephen's.

Died 6 Oct. 1946.

CHRISTIE, Brig.-Gen. Herbert Willie Andrew, CB 1919; CMG 1915; late RFA; *b* 29 Nov. 1868; *s* of late George Christie Bouverie, Sevenoaks; *m* 1st, 1894, Olive Chivelle (decd), *d* of late Edward Anthony; 2nd, Mabel C. (*d* 1931), *d* of J. Walker Wordley, Lancs; 3rd, 1932, Marian, *d* of W. J. Shannon, County Antrim; one *s. Educ:* Dulwich; RMA. Entered army, 1888; Captain, 1898; Major, 1903; Staff Officer, 1902; Lt-Col 1914; Colonel, 1918; retired 1920; served S African War,

1899–1902 (despatches five times, Bt Major, Queen's medal 5 clasps, King's medal 2 clasps); European War, 1914–18 (wounded, despatches five times CMG, CB).
Died 2 Feb. 1946.

CHRISTIE, John Denham; *s* of late Charles John Denham Christie and Alice Christie; *m* Mary, *d* of late Paulin Martin, Abingdon, Berks; one *s* one *d*. *Educ:* Tynemouth; Switzerland. Shipbuilder and Naval Architect; MINA; Fellow of North East Coast Institution of Engineers and Shipbuilders; Member of Worshipful Company of Shipwrights; apprenticed with John Elder and Co., Fairfield Shipbuilding Co., Govan, Glasgow; later partner in firm Wigham Richardson and Co.; Director, Wigham Richardson and Co., Ltd; late Director (formerly Chm.), Swan Hunter and Wigham Richardson, Ltd; late Director Wallsend Slipway and Engineering Co. Ltd; Mem. of the Tyne Improvement Commission; retired 1947. Volunteer officer, 2nd Vol. Bn, Northumberland Fusiliers retiring with hon. rank Lt-Col, VD; Knight of Wasa Order of Sweden. *Address:* Hill House, Melbury Road, Newcastle-on-Tyne 7.
Died 10 Oct. 1950.

CHRISTISON, Sir Robert Alexander, 3rd Bt *cr* 1871; RGA Militia (retired); *b* 23 Feb. 1870; *s* of 2nd Bt and Jemima Anne (*d* 1876), *d* of James Cowley Brown, HCS; *S* father, 1918; *m* 1900, Mary Russell, *d* of A. R. Gilzean. *Educ:* Fettes College. Served with 3rd HLI South African War, 1902; Acting British Vice-Consul, Lima, Peru, 1916–19. *Heir: half-brother* Lt-Gen. Sir Alexander Frank Philip Christison, KBE. *Address:* The Lodge, Lympstone, Devon. *T:* Exmouth 3391.
Died 15 May 1945.

CHRISTOPHER, Col Charles de Lona, CIE 1919; Indian Army, retired; *b* 1885; *s* of late Maj.-Gen. Leonard William Christopher, CB; *m* 1909, May, *d* of Colonel H. J. W. Barrow; two *d*. *Educ:* Wellington College. Served Mesopotamia, 1916–19 (despatches, Bt Major, CIE); Afghanistan, 1919; retired, 1938. *Address:* Cherrolande, Brockenhurst, Hants.
Died 1 Feb. 1942.

CHRISTOPHERSON, Douglas, CBE 1918; *b* 1869; 7th *s* of late Derman Christopherson, Blackheath, Kent; *m* 1910, Alma Gwenllian, *e d* of W. Griffiths, Cardiff; two *s*. *Educ:* Bedford. Served in Matabeleland Rebellion and South African War. *Address:* 49 Moorgate, EC.
Died 5 March 1944.

CHRISTOPHERSON, Stanley; late Chairman, Midland Bank; *b* Blackheath, Kent; *s* of Derman Christopherson and Catherine Christopherson; *m* 1887, Margaret Isabel Leslie; two *d*. *Educ:* Uppingham. Stock Exchange, 1882–99; subsequently Director Public Companies; High Sheriff of Norfolk, 1929; JP for Norfolk; President MCC, 1939–45. *Recreations:* cricket, golf, tennis; played cricket for England *versus* Australia, 1884, and for Gentlemen *versus* Players, 1884, 1885, 1886, and for Kent County; hockey, captained England, 1897–98, 1898–99. *Address:* Hyde Park Hotel, Knightsbridge, SW1. *Club:* Athenæum.
Died 6 April 1949.

CHRYSTAL, Sir George (William), KCB 1922; CB 1920; *b* 28 Aug. 1880; *e s* of late Professor Chrystal, Edinburgh University; unmarried. *Educ:* George Watson's College, Edinburgh; Edinburgh University; Balliol College, Oxford. Entered Admiralty, 1904; Transferred to Home Office, 1906; Joint Secretary Royal Commission Mines and Royal Commission Metalliferous Mines and Quarries; Assistant Private Secretary to Rt Hon. Reginald McKenna, Home Secretary; Private Secretary to Parliamentary and Permanent Under-Secretaries of State; Assistant Secretary, Ministry of National Service, 1917; Secretary of the Ministry of National Service and the Ministry of Reconstruction, also of the Demobilisation Section of the War Cabinet, 1918–19; Secretary of the Ministry of

Pensions, 1919–35; Permanent Sec. Ministry of Health, 1935–40. *Publications:* The Meditations of Marcus Aurelius Antoninus—a new rendering, 1902; Memoirs of Prince Choldwig of Hohenlohe Schillingsfuerst (English Edition), 1906; The Development of Modern Art (from the German of Julius Meier Graefe), 1908 (with Florence Simmonds); The Life of William Robertson Smith (with late Dr J. Sutherland Black); Lectures and Essays of William Robertson Smith, 1912. *Address:* The Manor House, Madingley, Cambridge. *Club:* Athenæum.
Died 1 Nov. 1944.

CHUBB, Sir Lawrence Wensley, Kt 1930; Secretary, Commons, Open Spaces, and Footpaths Preservation Society, 1896–48; Scapa Society for Prevention of Disfigurement of Town and Country since 1915; General Secretary, National Playing Fields Association, 1928–47; *b* Lauraville, Victoria, 1873; *e s* of late L. W. Chubb, JP; *m* 1905, Gertrude Elizabeth Anthony; one *s* one *d*. Formerly Secretary, National Smoke Abatement Society; Joint Founder of Federation of Rambling Clubs; First Secretary, The National Trust, 1895–96; Committee Member CPRE. *Publications:* Rambling Guide Books; brochures on public rights and local government. *Recreations:* rambling, chess, gardening. *Address:* 71 Eccleston Square, SW1; 29 Cator Road, Sydenham, SE26. *Club:* Devonshire.
Died 18 Feb. 1948.

CHUDOBA, František, PhD Prague; Professor of English Literature in the Masaryk University, Brno, Czechoslovakia, 1920–39; *b* Dedice, Moravia, 4 June 1878; *s* of Jan and Marie Chudoba; *m* 1905, Marie Petrová, *d* of F. Petr, Třešt; two *s*. *Educ:* Secondary school (Gymnasium) at Přerov, Moravia; Charles University in Prague; Leipsic University; Oxford Univ.; Berlin Univ. From 1902 teacher and later Professor of Modern Languages and Literatures in Kroměříž, Velké Meziříčí, Brno, and Prague; Lecturer in English Literature, Charles University, Prague, 1913–20; lectured on Czech language and literature at King's College, University of London, 1920–22. *Publications:* Books in Czech: Wordsworth, an essay, 1911; Poets, Prophets, and Fighters, vol. i, 1915; vol. ii, 1920; Under the Greenwood Tree, 1932; William Shakespeare, vols i–ii, 1940; Translations into Czech; P. B. Shelley, Selections from Shelley's Prose, 2 vols 1920; A. F. Pollard, History of England, with notes, 1921; Tea Blossoms, Poems from Old China, 1934; in English: A Short Survey of Czech Literature, 1924; Edited Letters of Slavonic Writers to John Bowring, 1912; Jan Blahoslav's Tract on Sight, 1928; Selections from the Critical Writings of F. X. Šalda, with Introd. and Notes, 1939. Articles, essays, reviews, etc., in Czech periodicals and in Slavonic Review. (Ed. posthumously by his son) collected works in 4 vols. *Address:* Veveří 75, Brno, Czechoslovakia.
Died 7 Jan. 1941.

CHURCH, Samuel Harden; President of the Carnegie Institute, Pittsburgh; *b* Caldwell County, Mo, 24 Jan. 1858; *s* of William Church and Emily, *d* of Walter Scott, who emigrated from Scotland to Pennsylvania in 1819; *m* 1898, Bertha Jean, *d* of James M'H. Reinhart of Pittsburgh, Pa. *Educ:* Pittsburgh public schools and Bethany Preparatory School, in West Virginia. After filling various clerkships with the Pennsylvania Railroad Company, he was made Superintendent of Transportation in Columbus, Ohio, and later Vice-President in Pittsburgh; received the honorary degrees LLD, LittD and MA from Pittsburgh, Yale and Western Pennsylvania Universities; Director Blaw-Knox Co.; trustee Carnegie Corporation of New York; delegate to Republican National Convention in 1904; speaker for Republican National Committee in all Presidential campaigns until 1932; returned to Republican Party, 1936; was Col on staff of Governor Hoadly of Ohio; Legion of Honour. *Publications:* Oliver Cromwell, a

History, 1894; John Marmaduke, a Romance of the English Invasion of Ireland in 1649, 1889; Beowulf, a Poem, 1901; Penruddock of the White Lambs, 1902; The Two Mrs Lorings (a play), 1914; The American Verdict on the War, 1915; other war pamphlets and speeches, 1917–1918; Flames of Faith, 1924. *Recreations:* motoring, golf. *Address:* 4781 Wallingford Street, Pittsburgh, Pa; Carnegie Institute, Pittsburgh, Pa. *Clubs:* Duquesne, University, Pittsburgh Golf, Athletic, Allegheny Country, Rolling Rock, Pittsburgh; Authors', New York; France-Amerique, American, Paris.

Died 10 Nov. 1943.

CHURCHILL, John (Strange Spencer), DSO; Major, TA Reserve (late Oxfordshire Yeomanry); *b* Feb. 1880; *yr s* of late Rt Hon. Lord Randolph Churchill; *m* 1908, Lady Gwendeline Theresa Mary Bertie (*d* 1941), *d* of 7th Earl of Abingdon; two *s* one *d.* Served South African War, 1899–1900 (wounded, despatches, medal); European War, 1914–18 (despatches, Legion of Honour, Croix de Guerre, Order of Avis of Portugal). *Address:* 42 Chester Terrace, Regent's Park, NW1. *T:* Welbeck 1748. *Club:* Bath.

Died 23 Feb. 1947.

CHURCHILL, Winston; writer; *b* St Louis, Mo, USA, 10 Nov. 1871; *o s* of Edward Spalding Churchill of Portland, Maine, and Emma Bell Blaine, of St Louis; *m* 1895, Mabel Harlakenden Hall, of St Louis; two *s* one *d.* *Educ:* Smith Academy, St Louis; graduated from the US Naval Academy, 1894. An editor of the Army and Navy Journal of New York, 1894; managing editor of Cosmopolitan Magazine, 1895; member New Hampshire Legislature, 1903 and 1905; Hon. degrees, MA 1903 LittD 1914; LLD 1915. *Publications:* The Celebrity; Richard Carvel, 1899; The Crisis, 1901; The Crossing, 1903; Coniston, 1906; Mr Crewe's Career, 1908; A Modern Chronicle, 1910; The Inside of the Cup, 1913; A Far Country, 1915; The Dwelling-Place of Light, 1917; The Uncharted Way, 1940. *Address:* Windsor, Vermont, USA.

Died 13 March 1947.

CHURCHMAN, Sir William Alfred, 1st Bt *cr* 1938; Kt 1920; DL Suffolk; *b* 23 Aug. 1863; 2nd *s* of Henry Charles Churchman, Ipswich; *m* 1891, Lois Adelaide (*d* 1934), *d* of Alfred Wrinch, JP, Ipswich. Mayor of Ipswich, 1899–1900; JP, Suffolk; commanded 4th Batt. Suffolk Regiment, 1906–12; rejoined, 1914; commanded the 2/4th Suffolk Regiment to 1917, then entered Ministry of Munitions as Director in the Explosive Department; is a Director of the Imperial Tobacco Company and other Companies. *Address:* The Lodge, Melton, Suffolk. *T:* Woodbridge 93. *Club:* Carlton.

Died 25 Nov. 1947 (ext).

CHURTON, Lt-Col William Arthur Vere, DSO, TD, BA, LLB; Solicitor since 1901; Member of Firm W. H. Churton & Son, solicitors, Chester; *b* 16 Dec. 1876; *e s* of late William Henry Churton, Hillside, Chester; *m* 1921, Katharine Sophia, 2nd *d* of late Rev. T. E. Jones, Rector of Hope, Flintshire, and Mrs Jones, Riverscote, Chester; one *s.* *Educ:* Shrewsbury School; Gonville and Caius Coll., Cambridge. Received Commission in 2nd VB Cheshire Regiment, 1899; served continuously with them and 5th (E of C) Cheshire Regiment throughout the War in France; commanded battalion Feb. 1918 until demobilization, July 1919 (despatches thrice); Mayor of Chester, 1928–29. *Publication:* War Record 1/5 (E of C) Cheshire Regiment. *Recreations:* cricket and golf. *Address:* Spring Hill, Chester.

Died 26 July 1949.

CIANO, Conte di Cortellazzo, Galeazzo; Cavaliere dell' Ordine Supremo della SS Annunziata; Cav. di. Gran Croce dei SS Maurizio e Lazzaro, Cav. di Gran Croce della Corona d'Italia, Cav. di Gran Croce dell' Ordine Coloniale della Stella d'Italia; *b* Livorno, 18

March 1903; *s* of late S. E. Costanzo Ciano, Conte di Cortellazzo, Presidente della Camera dei Fasci e delle Corporazioni, and of Carolina Pini; *m* 1930, Edda, *d* of Benito Mussolini; three *s.* *Educ:* Laureato in Giurisprudenza presso la R. Università di Roma. Entrato nella carriera diplomatica, 1925; prestò servizio come Segretario alle RR. Rappresentanze Diplomatiche di Rio de Janeiro, Buenos Aires, Pechino, Santa Sede; come Console Génerale, incaricato d'Affari con lettere e successivamente Ministro, a Shanghai; Capo Uffico Stampa del Capo Governo; Sottosegretario di Stato per la Stampa e la Propaganda; Ministro per la Stampa e Propaganda; Ministro Segretario di Stato per gli Affari Esteri; Membro del Gran Consiglio del Fascismo; Ambasciatore al Vaticano, 1943; Capitano Pilota di compl. arma aeron.; Volontario in AO; promosso maggiore per merito di guerra; decorato di due medaglie d'argento al valor militare e della croce al merito di guerra; fregiato della medaglia commemorativa della Marcia su Roma. *Recreations:* aviazione, scherma, caccia.

Died 11 Jan. 1944.

CILEA, Francesco; Italian composer; *b* Palmi, Calabria, 26 July 1866; *m* Rosy Lavarello. Was Professor in the Conservatory at Florence; Director Conservatory in Palermo and Naples. *Operas:* Gina (when pupil); Tilde, Arlesiana, Adriana Lecouvreur, Gloria, respectively represented for the first time in 1892, 1897, 1902, 1907; Symphonic Poem, Suite, Sonata, etc. *Address:* Via Ajaccio 14, Rome.

Died 20 Nov. 1950.

CLAPHAM, Sir Alfred William, Kt 1944; CBE 1932; FBA; Secretary, Royal Commission on Historical Monuments, England, 1933–48; Commissioner, 1948; *b* 27 May 1883; *s* of Rev. J. E. Clapham. *Educ:* Dulwich Coll. Technical Editor, Royal Commission on Historical Monuments, England, 1913–33; served in Royal Sussex Regt during European War, 1914–18; Sec. of the Society of Antiquaries, 1929–39, Pres., 1939–44; Pres. Royal Arch. Inst. 1945–48; Trustee London Museum. *Publications:* Lesnes Abbey, 1915; Beeleigh Abbey (part author), 1922; English Romanesque Architecture, 1930, 1934; European Romanesque Architecture, 1936; contributions to Archæologia, Archæological Journal, etc. *Club:* Athenæum.

Died 26 Oct. 1950.

CLAPHAM, Edward William, MRCS, LRCP; Consulting Anæsthetist at the London Hospital; late Honorary Anæsthetist to King Edward VII's Hospital for officers; *s* of late George Dixon Clapham of Great Dunmow, Essex. *Educ:* London Hospital. *Address:* Fishing Lodge, Britford, Salisbury. *Club:* Connaught.

Died 6 Nov. 1943.

CLAPHAM, Sir John (H.), Kt 1943; CBE 1918; LittD; Fellow of the British Academy, President 1940–45; Hon. LittD Leeds and Harvard; Foreign Member of Royal Swedish Academy of Sciences; Professor of Economic History, Cambridge, 1928–38; *b* 1873; *s* of late John Clapham of Prestwich, Manchester; *m* 1905, Mary Margaret, *d* of W. E. Green of Ross, Hereford; one *s* three *d.* *Educ:* Leys School, and King's College, Cambridge. 1st Class Historical Tripos, 1895; Lightfoot Scholar, 1896; Prince Consort Prize, 1897. Fellow of King's College, 1898–1904, and since 1908; Dean, 1908–13; Tutor, 1913–28; Vice-Provost, 1933–43; lecturer on historical and economic subjects at Cambridge, 1898–1902; Professor of Economics, University of Leeds, 1902–08; at the Board of Trade, 1916–18; President, Section F, British Association, 1920; Ford's Lecturer, Oxford, 1926; Creighton Lecturer, London, 1937; Syndic of Cambridge University Press; Chairman, Cambridge Employment Committee. *Publications:* The Causes of the War of 1792, 1899; articles in English Historical Review, Economic Journal, Alpine Journal, Cambridge Historical Journal, etc.; contributor to Cambridge Modern History, vols x and xi

(1907–1908); to Cambridge History of British Foreign Policy, vols i and ii (1922–1923); to Cambridge Mediæval History, vol. vi (1929); to Cambridge History of the British Empire vol. ii (1940); (with M. M. Clapham) to Early Victorian England (1934); The Woollen and Worsted Industries, 1907; The Abbé Sieyès, 1912; The Economic Development of France and Germany, 1815–1914, 1921; An Economic History of Modern Britain (vol. i), 1926; (vol. ii), 1932; (vol. iii), 1938; The Study of Economic History, 1929; The Bank of England, a History, 1944. Editor, Cambridge Studies in Economic History, Cambridge Economic History. *Address:* King's College, and Storey's End, Cambridge. *T:* Cambridge 4046. *Clubs:* Athenæum, Alpine.

Died 29 March 1946.

CLARK, Hon. Mr Justice Adrian, OBE, LLB; Judge of the Supreme Court of the Straits Settlements since 1936; *b* London, 9 April 1889; *s* of M. Clark, Valparaiso, and Blanche Leslie, Fifeshire; *m* 1929, Marguerite Muriel, *d* of J. C. Brooks, of St Anthony, Virginia Water; one *s* one *d*. *Educ:* Westminster (King's Scholar and Goodenough Medallist); London University. Called to Bar. Inner Temple, 1910; served in France, 1915–19 (Lt-Colonel, OBE, Brevet majority, despatches); Junior Counsel to the Treasury, 1917; Magistrate, Trinidad, 1924; Puisne Judge, Jamaica, 1927; DPP Singapore, 1934; Solicitor General SS 1935; interned Singapore, War of 1939–45. *Club:* RAF.

Died 21 March 1944.

CLARK, Alfred; retired; first Chairman and first President, Electric and Musical Industries, Ltd; ex-Chairman, The Gramophone Co., Ltd, and Columbia Graphophone Co., Ltd; first President, Radio Industry Council (until 1947); *e s* of late Walter Lowrie and Mary Rowe Clark, New York; British subject by naturalisation, 1928; *m* 1921, Gertrude Ivy, *y d* of late Haydn and Louisa Arnold Sanders; no *c*. *Educ:* College of the City of New York; Cooper Union School of Art and Science, New York. In 1889 joined organisation then set up by Thomas A. Edison to develop the Phonograph; produced in 1895 at the Edison Laboratory, Orange, New Jersey, the first moving picture films with plot or continuity; in 1896 worked in the Laboratory at Washington, DC, of Emile Berliner, inventor of the Gramophone; joined the Gramophone Co. of London and founded the French Gramophone Co. in Paris 1899; in 1907 founded the Musée de la Voix in the Archives of the National Opera, Paris; Managing Director of The Gramophone Co., Ltd, 1909–31. Patented various inventions in sound reproduction from 1896. Officer of the Legion of Honour (French). *Recreations:* Oriental ceramics and photography. *Address:* Black Firs, Fulmer, Bucks. *T:* Fulmer 33. *Clubs:* City of London, MCC, Oriental.

Died 16 June 1950.

CLARK, Alfred Joseph, FRS 1931; Professor of Materia Medica, University of Edinburgh; Member of Medical Research Council, 1934–38 and since 1939; *b* Glastonbury, Somerset, 19 Aug. 1885; *s* of Francis Joseph Clark of Street, Somerset; *m* 1919, Beatrice Powell, *d* of late Dr Hazell, Cape Town; two *s* two *d*. *Educ:* King's College, Cambridge (Scholar); St Bartholomew's Hospital, London (Scholar). BA Cantab 1907, MB Cantab 1910, MRCP 1912, MD 1914; FRCP 1921; MRCPE 1926; FRSE 1927. Hon. Captain RAMC (Military Cross). *Publications:* Applied Pharmacology; Comparative Physiology of the Heart; Mode of Action of Drugs on Cells; General Pharmacology. *Recreation:* climbing. *Address:* 67 Braid Avenue, Edinburgh. *T:* Edinburgh 52876. *Clubs:* Athenæum, Alpine.

Died 30 July 1941.

CLARK, Lt-Col Charles Watson, CMG 1917; late RA; *e s* of late C. J. Clark, of Oxton, Birkenhead; *m* 1895, Freyda, *d* of late Captain A. S. Creyke, RE; one *d*. *Educ:* Birkenhead School; RM Academy, Woolwich.

Commissioned, 1885; served in India, Malta, and Gibraltar; Lieut-Colonel, 1913; Private Secretary and ADC to Governor of Trinidad, 1893–94; Brigade Major, RA, SE District, 1901–03; served in France and Belgium, Aug. 1915–18 (despatches twice, CMG). *Club:* United Service.

Died 21 Nov. 1944.

CLARK, Christopher, RI 1905; Historical painter (of military subjects especially); *b* London, 1 March 1875. Selftaught. Exhibitor, Royal Acad., Continent and America. *Publications:* contributor to weekly publications magazines, and book illustrator, in colour, and black and white, posters, etc. Served as Lieut RNVR, 1917–1919. *Address:* Studio House, King's Langley, Herts. *T:* King's Langley 7170. *Clubs:* Arts, London Sketch.

Died 9 Feb. 1942.

CLARK, Lt-Col Craufurd Alexander G.; *see* Gordon-Clark.

CLARK, Lt-Col Edwin Kitson, TD; DL; MA, FSA; MInstCE; President, Institution of Mechanical Engineers, 1931–32; President, Institution of Locomotive Engineers, 1921–22; President, Thoresby Society; Director, Kitson & Co. Ltd, Airedale Foundry, Leeds; *b* 1866; *s* of late Dr E. C. Clark, Regius Professor of Civil Law, Cambridge University, Ellenthorp Hall, Aldborough, Yorkshire; *m* 1897, Georgina, *d* of late George Parker Bidder, QC; two *s* one *d*. *Educ:* Shrewsbury (head boy); Trinity College, Cambridge (Exhibitioner, Major Scholar), 1st class Classical Tripos, 1888. Apprenticed Engineer Kitson & Co. 1888; 2nd Lt Leeds Rifles, 1891; raised OTC Leeds University, 1909; OC 8th West Yorks, 1913–15; OC 49th Div. Depot, France, 1915–18. *Publications:* Papers in Journal of Society of Antiquaries, etc.; On Locomotive Development and on Industrial questions; History of Harfleur; History of Leeds Philosophical and Literary Society; Historical Guide to Leeds Parish Church; Kitsons of Leeds, 1837–1937. *Recreations:* archæology, gardening. *Address:* Meanwoodside, Leeds. *T:* Leeds 52200. *Clubs:* Athenæum; Leeds.

Died 15 April 1943.

CLARK, Sir George Ernest, 2nd Bt *cr* 1917; DL; MINA; Deputy Chairman Great Northern Rly of Ireland; Comr of Irish Lights; Belfast Harbour Comr; *b* 25 July 1882; *er s* of Sir George Smith Clark, 1st Bt, and Frances Elizabeth Matier, Belfast; *S* father, 1935; *m* 1910, Norah Anne, *d* of W. G. Wilson, Glasgow; three *s* one *d*. *Educ:* Rugby; Trinity College, Cambridge, MA. *Heir: s* George Anthony Clark. *Address:* Seapark, Greenisland, Co. Antrim. *T:* Whiteabbey 3191 (Belfast). *Clubs:* Royal Thames Yacht; Ulster (Belfast).

Died 10 Nov. 1950.

CLARK, Rev. Henry W., Hon. DD St Andrews; Fellow of the Royal Historical Society; Congregational Minister; *b* London, 8 Feb. 1869; *m* 1897. *Educ:* University College School; private study in Germany; Hackney Theological College. Ministry began at George Square Church, Greenock, 1890–91; several years' illness; Minister of Congregational Church, Woking, 1899–1904; literature and scholastic work since then; Sixth Form Master at St George's School, Harpenden, 1919–26; Head Master of St John's School, Broxbourne, 1930–34. *Publications:* Meanings and Methods of the Spiritual Life, 1901; Echoes from the Heights and Deeps (poems), 1902; The Christ from Without and Within, 1904; The Philosophy of Christian Experience, 1906; The Gospel of St John (Westminster New Testament), 1908; The Christian Method of Ethics, 1908; Laws of the Inner Kingdom, 1909; Studies in the Making of Character, 1910; History of English Nonconformity, 1911 and 1913; The Book of the Seven Ages (an anthology), 1911; Towards a Perfect Man, 1911; Life of John Goodwin, 1913; Liberal Orthodoxy (in Great Christian Theologies series, which he also edited), 1914;

The Watch-Tower (poems), 1920; Pilate, and other Poems, 1922; Short History of the British Empire, 1935; Collected Poems, New and Old, 1942; The Cross and the Eternal Order, 1943; various educational books. *Address:* The Harpes, Broxbourne, Herts. *T:* Hoddesdon 2748.

Died 8 July 1949.

CLARK, James, Hon. Retired RI, Hon. ARCA; late Art Examiner for Board of Education and Cambridge University. *Address:* Chartway New House, Reigate, Surrey. *T:* Reigate 3500.

Died 10 Jan. 1943.

CLARK, Col Sir James (Richardson Andrew), 2nd Bt *cr* 1883; CB 1902; CMG 1916; FRCSE; DPh Cantab; FRIPH; Lieut-Colonel Royal Army Medical Staff Corps, retired; Bailiff Grand Cross of St John of Jerusalem; *b* 24 Aug. 1852; *S* father, 1893; *m* 1893, Lilian Margaret, 2nd *d* of Robert Hopkins, Tidmarsh Manor, Berkshire; one *s*. In charge of Edinburgh Hospital, S Africa, 1900; served European War, 1914–16 (CMG). *Heir:* s Andrew Edmund James Clark, MBE, MC. *Address:* Braywick Grove, Maidenhead. *Club:* Constitutional.

Died 18 Jan. 1948.

CLARK, John Brown, CBE 1935; MA, LLD; FRSE; JP; Headmaster, George Heriot's School, Edinburgh, 1908–26; *b* West Linton, Peeblesshire, 30 April 1861; *e s* of late George Clark, Newbigging, Lanarkshire; *m* 1891, Mary (*d* 1946), *e d* of William Mackay, Edinburgh; three *d*. *Educ:* Edinburgh University. Pupil teacher; student in Established Church Training College, Edinburgh; Assistant Master in St Leonard's Public School, Edinburgh, 1883–85; graduated MA with Honours in Natural Science, 1889; Mathematical and Physics Master in George Heriot's School till 1908; Past President of Edinburgh Univ. Physical Society, of Edinburgh Mathematical Society, and of Association of Teachers in the Secondary Schools of Scotland; Member of University Court of Univ. of Edinburgh, of Scottish Universities Entrance Board, and of Education Committee of Edinburgh Town Council; Chairman of Edinburgh Provincial Committee for the Training of Teachers. *Publications:* (Joint) Arithmetic for Schools and Colleges; Mathematical and Physical Tables. *Recreations:* golf and shooting. *Address:* 146 Craiglea Drive, Edinburgh. *T:* Edinburgh 53390. *Clubs:* Scottish Liberal, Edinburgh.

Died 19 July 1947.

CLARK, Lt-Gen. John George Walters, CB 1941; MC; *b* 12 May 1892; *s* of late George Clark, Paisley; *m* 1915, Jane, *d* of late Buchan Baxter, Greenock. *Educ:* Winchester; RMC, Sandhurst. Joined 16th (the Queen's Lancers, 1911; served in France and Flanders, 1914–18 (wounded, MC and clasp, despatches thrice); commanded 16th/5th Lancers, 1933–36; 12th Inf. Bde and Deputy Constable of Dover Castle, 1938–39; Major-General, 1940; GOC 1st Cavalry Div., 1939–42; GOC Lines of Communication, AF HQ, 1942–43; Chief Administrative Officer, AF HQ, Jan.–Dec. 1944; Head of SHAEF Mission to Netherlands, Jan.–Sept. 1945; Head of British Economic Mission to Greece, 1945–47; retired pay, 1946, with hon. rank of Lt-Gen.; Hon. MA Oxon. Officer and Commander, Legion of Merit, USA; Officer, Legion of Honour, France; Grand Officer, Iftan Niftikar; Grand Officer, Orange Nassau. *Recreations:* yachting, golf. *Address:* c/o Clydesdale Bank, 30 Lombard Street, EC3. *Clubs:* Cavalry; Royal and Ancient Golf (St Andrews); Royal Yacht Squadron (Cowes).

Died 16 May 1948.

CLARK, Col (acting Brig.) Percy William, CBE 1940; DSO 1919; MC; AMICE; RE; *b* Putney, 1888; *s* of Jas Clark, RI, ARBC, Hon. ARCA Lond.; *m* 1920, Dorothy, *e d* of F. T. Foulger; two *s* one *d*. *Educ:* St

Mark's, Chelsea; London University Engineering Course at SW Polytechnic. Articled pupil to H. W. Ravenshaw, MICE, MIME; with Alfred Parsons at Newcastle, and Willians & Robinsons at Rugby. Given an Army Commission, Sept. 1914; served three and a half years in France, the last two years as Major in command of the 61st Divisional Signal Company (despatches, MC, DSO); Northern Kurdistan, 1931–32 (bar to DSO); Chief Engineer under Air Ministry, Iraq, 1937–39; in France as Chief Engineer to Advanced Air Striking Force. *Recreations:* shooting, fishing, tennis. *Address:* Longstanton Vicarage, near Cambridge. *Club:* United Sports.

Died 15 Feb. 1943.

CLARK, Col Robert, CBE 1923; OBE 1919; VD; DL; formerly Lt-Col commanding 5th Bn The Royal Scots (Queen's Edinburgh Rifles); late Chairman of City of Edinburgh Territorial Army and Air Force Association; *b* 1859. *Address:* 4 Cambridge Street, Edinburgh. *Club:* Royal Scots.

Died 23 Dec. 1940.

CLARK, Rev. Canon Stuart Harrington, MA; Vicar of Tonbridge, 1913–36; Canon Emeritus of Rochester since 1936; *b* 2 Sept. 1869; *s* of Rev. Robert Clark, MA, Amritsar, India; *m* 1st, 1904, Minnie L. Collins (*d* 1935); one *s*; 2nd, 1938, Dorothea Vetterli King. *Educ:* St Paul's School; Clare College, Cambridge (Mathematical Scholar). Ordained, 1894; Incumbent of The Old Church, Calcutta, 1900–08; Vicar of Belper, 1909–13; Chaplain of the University and Public School Brigade, 1914; Co. Sec. of the Mansfield College, Oxford, Reunion Conferences, 1917–20; Rural Dean of Tonbridge, 1926–35; Hon. Canon of Rochester Cathedral, 1929–36; Hon. Chairman of the Guild of Health, 1928–31. *Publications:* St Augustine, Catholic and Protestant; God and Life; Editor of Towards Reunion. *Address:* 11 Madeira Park, Tunbridge Wells. *T:* Tunbridge Wells 2705.

Died 18 Aug. 1947.

CLARK, Hon. William George, LLD, DCL; President, J. Clark & Son Limited since 1918; President, Lounsbury Company Limited since 1902; *b* Queensbury, 1865; *m* 1894, Harriet Richardson; one *s* one *d*. Lieutenant-Governor of New Brunswick, 1940–45. Member Canadian Parliament, 1935–40; Mayor, City of Fredericton, 1926–35. *Address:* 82 Waterloo Row, Fredericton, New Brunswick, Canada.

Died 18 Jan. 1948.

CLARKE, Alfred Henry; KC 1902; **Hon. Mr Justice Clarke;** Justice of Appellate Division Supreme Court of Alberta since 1921; *b* 25 Oct. 1860; *m* 1st, 1888, Margaret (*d* 1905), 3rd *d* of D. Z. Gibson, Brantford, Ontario; 2nd, 1912, Margaret Wightman, Windsor, Ont. *Educ:* Manilla Grammar School; Oakwood High School; Toronto University. Barrister, 1882; MP Essex, South, 1904–17. *Address:* Calgary, Alberta.

Died 30 Jan. 1942.

CLARKE, Astley Vavasour, MA, MD (Cantab); DL County of Leicester, 1928; JP City of Leicester, 1921; Alderman City of Leicester, 1941; Vice-President and Chairman of Council, Leicester University College; *b* 7 Feb. 1870; *s* of Julius St T. Clarke, MS, FRCS, Leicester, and Hannah Vawser, March, Cambs; *m* 1899, Ethel Mary, *d* of H. Simpson Gee, Leicester; one *s* two *d*. *Educ:* Oakham School; Caius College, Cambridge; Guy's Hospital and abroad. Hon. Physician Leicester Royal Infirmary, 1896–1930; Hon. Cons. Phys. Min. of Pensions (E Med. Div.), 1920; Member Leic. and Rut. Territorial Assoc. since 1910; Col AMS (TA); ADMS N Mid. Div., 1913; retired, 1925; Deputy Chairman Leicester City Health Committee; Chairman of City General Hospital; Pres. Leicester Lit. and Phil. Soc. 1912; Pres. Leicester Medical Soc. 1911; Sheriff of Rutland, 1942. *Publications:* various contribs to Medical

Journals; History of Lyddington, 1936. *Recreation:* collecting village antiquities. *Address:* 10 University Road, Leicester; Home Close, Lyddington, Rutland.

Died 21 Feb. 1945.

CLARKE, Sir Basil, Kt 1923; journalist; Chairman Editorial Services, Ltd (12 Buckingham Street, Strand, WC2. *T:* Temple Bar 3351); *b* 1879; *s* of James T. Clarke, Winchfield, Bowdon, Cheshire; *m* Alice, *d* of G. Camden, Hale, Cheshire; four *s* one *d*. *Educ:* Manchester Grammar School; Oxford University. After short banking experience travelled Germany, Bohemia, Austria, etc.; began journalism, 1903; Sub-Editor, 1904, and later Special Correspondent Manchester Guardian; joined staff of Daily Mail as Special Correspondent for North of England, 1910; travelled Canada, US, as an emigrant, as Special Commissioner on Emigration; War Correspondent in Flanders, 1914, for Daily Mail; also in Greece, Serbia, Bulgaria, Rumania, Transylvania, Bukovina, Bessarabia, 1915; Special Commissioner Daily Mail, Holland, Denmark, Sweden, Norway, investigating German blockade, 1916; War Correspondent for Reuters and the Press Association at GHQ British Army, France, during the later battles of the Somme; Director Special Intelligence Branch, Ministry of Reconstruction, 1918; Editor Sheffield Independent, 1919; Director Public Information, Ministry of Health, 1920–23; lent for service as Director of Public Information, Irish Government, Dublin Castle, 1920–22. *Publications:* The Cow-Cake Papers (skit); My Round of the War; many newspaper and magazine articles; music; several songs. *Address:* 14 Blandford Close, N2. *Club:* Authors'.

Died 12 Dec. 1947.

CLARKE, Ven. Charles Philip Stewart; Canon Residentiary of Chichester Cathedral since 1936; *b* 1871; *s* of Rev. C. J. Clarke; *m* Madeline Harriet, *d* of J. T. Brooke, Haughton, Shifnal; one *s* two *d*. *Educ:* Clifton; Christ Church, Oxford; Wells. Head of Ch Ch Mission, Poplar, 1901–08; Vicar of Fenton, 1908–11; Vicar of High Wycombe 1911–16; Rector of Donhead St Andrew, 1916–32, of North Stoneham, 1932–34; Rector of Trotton, 1934–36; Archdeacon of Chichester, 1934–46; Prebendary of Salisbury; Examining Chaplain to the Bishop of Salisbury; Proctor in Convocation for Diocese of Salisbury, 1926. *Publications:* Everyman's Book of Saints, 1914; Church History: from Nero to Constantine, 1920; Short History of the Christian Church, 1929; Saints and Heroes, 1931; The Oxford Movement and After, 1932; The Via Media, 1937; Life of Bishop Chandler, 1939. *Address:* The Chantry, Chichester. *T:* Chichester 2902. *Club:* Authors'.

Died 18 Dec. 1947.

CLARKE, Edward Henry Scamander, CSI 1911; CIE 1903; *b* 21 May 1856; *s* of late S. H. Clarke of Blackheath. *Educ:* Blackheath. Entered service of Govt of India, 1875; extra Assistant Commissioner, Punjab; Personal Assistant to Chief Political Officer, Kabul, 1880 (War Medal); Afghan Boundary Commission, Herat, 1884–86; Special Duty, St Petersburg, 1887; Member of Durand Mission to Kabul, 1893 (Gold Afghan Order of Hurmat); entered Indian Political Dept, 1894; served as Assistant, Under-, and Deputy Secretary in the Foreign Department Secretariat of the Govt of India; retd, March 1912. *Address:* Kabul House, Bexhill-on-Sea.

Died 2 Feb. 1947.

CLARKE, Hon. Sir Frederick James, KCMG 1911; CMG 1907; JP; *b* 27 July 1859; *s* of James Samuel Clarke, proprietor of sugar estates in Barbados; *m* 1st, 1882, Sarah Senhouse (*d* 1929), *d* of late Rev. J. W. Greenridge; one *s*; 2nd, 1930, Theresa, widow of Sir C. P. Clarke. *Educ:* Christ Church Middle School, Barbados; Caius College, Cambridge; BA 1879. Sugar planter; entered House of Assembly as one of the

Representatives of Christ Church Parish, 1887; Speaker, 1898–1934. *Address:* Blythswood, Christ Church, Barbados.

Died 28 July 1944.

CLARKE, Sir Geoffrey, Kt 1925; CSI 1921; OBE 1918; ICS (retired); Director, P and O and British India SN Companies; Chairman, Calcutta Tramways; Past President, London Chamber of Commerce; Past President, Associated Chambers of Commerce of Great Britain; Member, Prime Minister's Advisory Panel of Industrialists on Rearmament, 1938–39; *s* of George Richard Clarke; *m* Hilda Geraldine Seymour; two *s*. *Educ:* Trinity Coll., Dublin. Entered the Indian Civil Service, 1895; appointed to act as Postmaster-General, Punjab, 1903; joined Min. of Munitions, 1916, and sent on special deputation to America and Canada; Director General Posts and Telegraphs, India, 1918; represented the Government of India at the International Postal Congress, Madrid, 1920, and Stockholm, 1924, also International Telegraph Congress, Paris, 1925; Servian Order of the Sveti Sava, 1923. *Publications:* The Outcastes, a brief history of the Maghaya Doms; The Post Office of India and its Story. *Recreations:* golf and bowls. *Address:* 7 Grand Avenue, Hove, Sussex. *Clubs:* Oriental, Junior Carlton.

Died 11 Oct. 1950.

CLARKE, George, CIE 1926; *b* 23 Oct. 1878; *s* of George Clarke, Long Sutton, Lincolnshire. *Educ:* University College, Nottingham. Indian Agricultural Service, 1907–33; Director of Agriculture, United Provinces, 1921–33; retired 1933; Official Member of the Legislative Council of the Governor of the United Provinces, 1921–31. *Publications:* numerous papers on Agricultural Chemistry and Indian Agriculture. *Address:* Long Sutton, Lincolnshire. *Club:* East India and Sports.

Died 27 May 1944.

CLARKE, Brig.-Gen. Goland (Vanhalt), CMG 1919; DSO 1902; late Capt. 18th QMO Hussars; retired, 1907; *b* 25 Nov. 1875; 7th *s* of late Stephenson Clarke, Croydon Lodge and Brook House, Sussex; *m* 1918, Yvonne, *o c* of late Albert Defrance, Ambassadeur de France; one *s* two *d*. *Educ:* Winchester. Served South Africa, 1899–1902 (despatches twice, Queen's medal 5 clasps, King's medal 2 clasps); European War, 1914–18; commanded City of London Yeomanry, 1915–17; Brig.-Gen. commanding 7th Mounted Brigade and 14th Cavalry Brigade, 1917–19; on Staff of High Commissioner, Constantinople, 1920 (Bt Lt-Col, CMG). *Address:* Maudlyn House, Steyning, Sussex; 9 Herbert Crescent, SW1. *Club:* Cavalry.

Died 27 Aug. 1944.

CLARKE, Brig.-Gen. Henry Calvert Stanley, CB 1919; CMG 1917; DSO 1915; DL and JP Dorset; late RA; *b* 6 Dec. 1872; *e s* of late Maj.-Gen. Willoughby Charles Stanley Clarke, Indian Army; *m* 1913, Alice, *o d* of Colonel Hervey Morris Stanley Clarke; two *d*. *Educ:* Bedford School. Entered army, 1893; Captain, 1900; Major, 1910; Lt-Col 1915; Bt Col 1918; temp. Brig.-Gen., RA, 1916–19; Colonel, 1920; retired, 1927, with hon. rank of Brig.-General; served European War, 1914–18 (DSO, CMG, CB). *Address:* Ham Gate, Sturminster Newton, Dorset. *Club:* Army and Navy.

Died 27 Feb. 1943.

CLARKE, Adm. Henry James Langford, CBE 1919; *b* 1 Jan. 1866; *s* of late Captain E. F. Clarke, RN, of Kingsgate, Isle of Thanet; *m* 1898, Alice Melliar (*d* 1923), *d* of late S. M. Moens, Indian Civil Service; one *s*. Joined Britannia, 1879; Lieut, 1887; Commdr, 1898; Captain, 1904; Rear-Admiral, 1916; Vice-Admiral, 1919; Admiral, retired, 1924; served Somali Expedition, 1889 (despatches); Benin River Expedition, 1894 (West African medal); Captain Dockyard and Deputy

Superintendent, Devonport, 1913–16; Senior Naval Officer, Dakar French Senegal, 1917–18. *Address:* Hillside, Rottingdean, Sussex. *T:* Rottingdean 9213.

Died 28 March 1944.

CLARKE, J. Jackson, MB Lond., FRCS. Hon. Consulting Surgeon to Hampstead and NW London and Royal National Orthopædic Hospitals; retired. *Publications:* Congenital Dislocation of the Hip; Orthopædic Surgery; The Surgical Affections of the Joints and the Spine; The Urgent Surgery of the Peritoneum and Acute Appendicitis; Protozoa and Disease, etc. *Address:* 1 Park Crescent, W1.

Died 4 Dec. 1940.

CLARKE, Brig.-Gen. John Louis Justice, CMG 1916; *b* 23 Nov. 1870; *o s* of late Lt-Col A. F. S. Clarke, MD, RAMC; *m* 1904, Lilian Georgina (*d* 1932), *d* of late Sir George O'Farrell, MD, JP; no *c. Educ:* Wellington College. 2nd Lt East Yorkshire Regt, 1889; Capt., 1897; Bt-Major, 1900; Major, 1907; Lt-Col, 1915; Col 1919; served South African War, 1899–1902 (despatches, Bt-Major); served on the Staff of the Army DAAG Irish Command, 1903–06; GSO Western Coast Defences, 1907–11; DAA and QMG Eastern Coast Defences, 1913–14; FRGS, 1903; Commanded 1st Batt. East Yorkshire Regiment, European War, in France and Belgium, 1914–16; commanded 52nd Infantry Brigade, March 1916–June 1917 (despatches 3 times, CMG); Commander 43rd Infantry Brigade, Lahore, Sept. 1918–July 1919; GOC Lahore Brigade during the Punjab Disturbances, April–May 1919, and commanded the Tochi Column for the relief of Miranshah, June 1919; Officer i/c Infantry Records, York, 1921–25; retired, 1925; Col The East Yorkshire Regt, 1933–40. *Recreations:* golf, lawn tennis. *Address:* 27a Bramham Gardens, SW5. *T:* Frobisher 5238. *Club:* Naval and Military.

Died 3 Jan. 1944.

CLARKE, Sir Orme Bigland, 4th Bt *cr* 1831; CBE 1920; Barrister-at-law, Inner Temple; *b* 1880; *s* of Frederick Clarke; *S* uncle 1932; *m* 1905, Elfrida, *e d* of Alfred Roosevelt, New York; two *s. Educ:* Eton; Magdalen College, Oxford, BA. Was Legal Adviser to Ottoman Government. *Heir: er s* Humphrey Orme, *b* 6 July 1906. *Address:* Bibury Court, Glos. *T:* Bibury 244. *Clubs:* Brooks's, Oxford and Cambridge.

Died 31 March 1949.

CLARKE, Lt-Col Robert Joyce, CMG 1918; DSO 1916; *b* 1874; *s* of late J. H. Clarke, Abingdon; *m* 1946, Muriel Dorothy, *widow* of Ernest Roland Davies. *Educ:* Charterhouse. Served S Africa, 1899–1902; European War, 1914–19 (despatches, DSO, CMG, Italian Croix de Guerre). *Address:* 50 Belvidere Road, Princes Park, Liverpool 8.

Died 31 Dec. 1949.

CLARKE, Rev. Sidney Lampard; *b* 15 Jan. 1871; *s* of Edward Clarke and Susan Clarke; *m* Emma Caroline Weir (*d* 1938), Horncastle; one *s* two *d. Educ:* Eccles Grammar School, St Andrews University; MA Hon. in Math, BSc Hon. in Chemistry. Ordained, 1899; Curate Horncastle, 1899–1901; Chaplain and Naval Instructor RN, 1901–18; transferred to RAF 1918; RAF Chaplain, Halton Camp, 1919–30; Chaplain-in-Chief, RAF, 1930–33; Hon. Chaplain to the King, 1931–34; retired 1933; Vicar of Cranwell, Lincs, 1934–38. *Recreations:* cricket, football, golf. *Address:* Beaumont Hotel, Princes Square, W2.

Died Nov. 1945.

CLARKE, Stephenson Robert, CB 1911; JP; LLD Leeds; *b* 28 June 1862; *e s* of Stephenson Clarke (*d* 1891), of Croydon Lodge, Croydon, and Brook House, West Hoathly, Sussex, and Agnes Maria Clarke, *d* of Charles Bridger of Ashurst; *m* 1st, 1890, Edith Gertrude (*d* 1941), *d* of Joseph Godman, DL, JP, Park Hatch, Surrey; three *s* one *d*; 2nd, 1943, Constance Gwendoline, *widow* of Lt-

Col Robert Bellamy, DSO, Royal Sussex Regt, and *e d* of late Lt-Col A. J. Borton, Welch Regt. *Educ:* Winchester. Gazetted to Royal Sussex Light Infantry Militia, 1880; served SA War, 1901–02 (Queen's medal 5 clasps, despatches); Hon. Major in Army, 1902; Lt-Col and Honorary Colonel (retired) commanding 3rd Battalion Royal Sussex Regiment, 1906–12; High Sheriff, Sussex, 1915; Master of the Clothworkers' Company, 1924. *Recreations:* horticulture, fishing, stalking, and hunting. *Address:* Borde Hill, Haywards Heath, Sussex. *T:* Haywards Heath 28. *Clubs:* Carlton, Conservative.

Died 3 Nov. 1948.

CLARKE, Col Thomas Henry Matthews, CMG 1903; CBE 1919; DSO 1899; late Army Medical Service; *b* 15 June 1869; *o s* of late Staff Surgeon Thos Matthews Clarke, BA, MB, Trinity College, Dublin, Army Medical Department; *m* Susan Morrell, *d* of P. E. Chapin of Washington and Paris, and *g d* of Hon. D. J. Morrell of Pennsylvania, USA; one *d. Educ:* Trinity College, Dublin (BA, MB, BCh, BAO). Entered Army Medical Service, 1897; served in Kandia, Crete, during the Massacre of Christians by Moslems; Member of the Kandia Provisional British Administration, 1898–99 (despatches); wounded, affair 6 Sept. (despatches). Decorated for gallantry in the attack by Moslems on the British Hospital, Kandia, Crete (wounded); 'seconded' under the Foreign Office; Personal Physician to Prince George of Greece, 1900–03; Physician and Surgeon, Royal Hospital, Kilmainham, 1912; received thanks of the Cretan Chamber of Deputies, 1903; Knight of the Order of the Saviour of Greece. *Publications:* Sanitary Work in Crete; Blue Book, Turkey, No. 1; Prehistoric Sanitation in Crete (Knossus), British Medical Journal, Sept. 1903. *Recreations:* usual. *Clubs:* Army and Navy, Royal Automobile.

Died 4 March 1941.

CLARKSON, Mabel, CBE 1931; JP; Town Councillor, Norwich, 1912–23, and since 1926; *d* of Richard Clarkson, Solicitor, Calne, Wilts; unmarried. *Educ:* Private School, Reading. Poor Law Guardian, 1905–30; Sheriff of Norwich, 1928–29; Lord Mayor of Norwich, 1930–31. *Address:* 5 Mount Pleasant, Norwich. *T:* Norwich 1954.

Died 21 March 1950.

CLARRY, Sir Reginald, Kt 1936; MP (C) Newport Division, 1922–29 and since 1931; consulting engineer, and director of companies; *b* Derby, 24 July 1882; *s* of George Clarry, FCIS, and Helen, *d* of John Duesbury of Derby; *m* 1906, Laura, *d* of Edmund and Marion Sapey; three *d. Educ:* Marling School, Stroud; Technical College. Articled pupil in gas engineering in London works; Engineer Manager and Secretary to the Swansea Gas Co.; Managing Director of the Duffryn Steel and Tin Plate Works, Morriston, Glam.; in honorary advisory capacity to the Ministry of Munitions, 1914–18. *Recreations:* golf and lawn tennis. *Address:* 5 Chandos Court, Westminster, SW1. *T:* Abbey 2303. *Clubs:* Carlton, Royal Automobile.

Died 17 Jan. 1945.

CLAUSE, William Lionel; painter; Honorary Secretary, New English Art Club; *b* Middleton, Lancs, 7 May 1887; *s* of William H. and Minna Clause; *m* Lucy, *e d* of Professor R. A. Sampson, late Astronomer Royal of Scotland; one *d. Educ:* Gresham's School, Holt. Art education, Slade School under Professor Fred. Brown and Professor Henry Tonks; seven drawings acquired by the Contemporary Art Society; represented by three works in Manchester, two in Bradford, one in Leamington, one in Carlisle; several works acquired for the War Artists National Gallery by the Artists' Advisory Committee. *Address:* 16 New End Square, Hampstead, NW3. *Club:* Chelsea Arts.

Died 9 Sept. 1946.

CLAUSEN, Sir George, Kt 1927; RA, 1908; RWS 1898; *b* London, 1852; *s* of a decorative artist; *m* Agnes (*d* 1944), *d* of Geo. Webster, King's Lynn, 1881; three *s* one *d. Educ:* Student at South Kensington Schools, 1867–73. Medals: Paris, 1889; Chicago, 1893; Brussels, 1897; Paris, 1900. For a time in the studio of E. Long, RA, and in Paris, under Bouguereau and Fleury; paints figure and landscape; ARA 1895; sometime Professor of Painting in Royal Academy. *Publications:* Royal Academy Lectures. *Address:* Cold Ash, Newbury, Berks. *Club:* Arts.
Died 22 Nov. 1944.

CLAUSON, 1st Baron *cr* 1942, of Hawkshead; **Albert Charles Clauson,** PC 1938; Kt 1926; CBE 1920; *b* 14 Jan. 1870; *y s* of C. Clauson and Julia, *d* of Rev. J. W. Buckley; *m* 1902, Kate, *d* of J. T. Hopwood, and *widow* of L. Thomasson. *Educ:* Merchant Taylors' School; St John's College, Oxford (1st Cl. Mods 1889, 1st Lit. Hum. 1891, Senior Scholar 1894, Hon. Fellow 1927). Tancred Student, Lincoln's Inn, 1889. Called, 1891; KC 1910; Bencher, 1914; unpaid Assistant Controller's Dept Admiralty, 1917–18; Counsel to Oxford University, 1923–26; Standing Counsel to Royal College of Physicians, 1923–26; Judge of Chancery Division, High Court of Justice, 1926–38; a Lord Justice of Appeal, 1938–42; Treasurer of Lincoln's Inn, 1937; Past Master of Merchant Taylors Company; JP Herts. *Address:* Hawkshead House, North Mymms, Hatfield, Herts. *T:* Potters Bar 2009. *TA:* North Mymms. *Clubs:* Athenæum, United University.
Died 15 March 1946 (ext).

CLAY, Charles Felix, MA; for many years Chairman of R. Clay & Sons, Ltd, printers, London and Bungay; *b* Cambridge, 5 Nov. 1861; *y s* of late C. J. Olay, for many years printer to the University of Cambridge, and Emily Jane, *d* of W. Eady of Campsbourne; *m* 1905, Ethel Alice, *d* of Col C. J. Mead, Bengal Artillery and Indian Staff Corps; two *d. Educ:* Temple Grove, E Sheen; Haileybury; Trinity College, Cambridge. Associated with the Cambridge University Press at Cambridge and in London, 1884–1925; sole Manager of the London publishing house of the Press from 1905; President of the Publishers' Association of Great Britain and Ireland, 1923–25; Chairman of the Publishers' Employment Circle, 1919–20, and of the Book Trade Employers' Federation, 1921–22; Hon. Secretary Amateur Fencing Association, 1900–05, and of the Epée Club, 1901–05; Cambridge Borough Alderman, 1926; Master of the Stationers and Newspaper Makers Company, 1938. *Publication:* Secrets of the Sword, translated from the original French of Baron de Bazancourt, 1900. *Recreations:* fencing, bee-keeping. *Address:* Upton House, 11 Grange Road, Cambridge. *T:* Cambridge 3946.
Died 16 Feb. 1947.

CLAY, Sir Felix, 5th Bt *cr* 1841; BA; FRIBA; Architect; *b* Hatfield, 24 Nov. 1871; 2nd and *o surv. s* of Sir Arthur Clay, 4th Bart, and Margaret, *d* of A. K. Barclay of Bury Hill, Dorking; S father, 1928; *m* 1904, Rachel, *er d* of late Rt Hon. Henry Hobhouse; two *s* three *d. Educ:* Charterhouse; Trinity College, Cambridge. Articled to Basil Champneys, 1893; private practice, 1897; Chief Architect to the Board of Education, 1904–27. *Publications:* Modern School Buildings, 1902; 2nd edition, 1906; 3rd edition, 1929; The Origin of the Sense of Beauty, 1908. *Heir: s* Henry Felix [*b* 8 Feb. 1909; *m* 1933, Phyllis Mary, *yr d* of Dr R. H. Paramore, FRCS; one *s* two *d*]. *Address:* 18 Kensington Park Gardens, W11. *T:* Park 4710. *Club:* Athenæum.
Died 11 Nov. 1941.

CLAY, Col Henry, CBE 1919; OBE 1918; DCM; late East Surrey Regt; *b* 1 Jan. 1872. Served S Africa, 1899–1902 (despatches twice, Queen's medal with five clasps, King's medal with two clasps, DCM); European War, 1914–19 (OBE, CBE); was Deputy Director of Recruiting, Eastern Command; Commandant London Recruiting Zone; retired, 1937; commanding No. 9 Recruiting Centre, 1939–43. *Address:* 26 Revell Road, Kingston-on-Thames. *T:* Kingston 3974.
Died 11 July 1945.

CLAY, Sir Joseph Miles, KCIE 1936 (CIE 1925); CSI 1934; OBE 1918; *b* 1881; *s* of late Arthur Lloyd Clay, ICS, Cambridge; *m* 1906, Edith Marguerite Florence, *d* of E. T. Hall, FRIBA, Dulwich; two *d. Educ:* Winchester; New College, Oxford. Entered ICS 1905; became Under-Secretary to Government, UP, 1911; Deputy-Commissioner, Garhwal, 1913; Magistrate and Collector, Cawnpore, 1921; Deputy Commissioner Naini Tal, 1925; Secretary to Government, UP, 1929; Chief Secretary to Government of United Provinces 1931–35; Finance Member of Governor's Executive Council, United Provinces, 1935–37; Adviser to Secretary of State for India, 1937–42. *Address:* Trowswell, Goudhurst, Kent. *T:* Goudhurst 49.
Died 19 Feb. 1949.

CLAYDEN, Arthur William, MA; *b* Boston, Lincolnshire, 12 Dec. 1855; *e s* of P. W. Clayden and his first wife; *m* 1883, Ethel, 2nd *d* of A. S. Paterson; one *s* one *d. Educ:* Univ. Coll. School; Christ's Coll., Camb. (Scholar, Nat. Sciences Tripos, 1876). Appointed Science Master, Bath Coll., 1878; University Extension Lecturer, 1887; Hon. Sec. BA Committee on Meteorological Photography, 1890; Principal, University College, Exeter, 1894–1920; retired, 1920. *Publications:* Cloud Studies; The History of Devonshire Scenery; various papers on Astronomy, Photography, Meteorology, Physics, and Geology, on A Working Model of Ocean Currents, 1889, and on Black Electric Sparks, 1889; also annual reports to the BA on measurement of cloud altitudes. *Recreations:* meteorological research, painting, gardening. *Address:* Wellwood, Guest Road, Parkstone, Dorset. *T:* Parkstone 768.
Died 21 Feb. 1944.

CLAYTON, Col Forrester; DL Middlesex; Chairman, Brentford Petty Sessions; Chairman, Middlesex Standing Joint Committee; Chairman, Visiting Committee of Wormwood Scrubbs Prison; President, Brentford Conservative Association; Member, London Passenger Transport Board, Thames Conservancy, Lee Conservancy and Home Counties Traffic Advisory Committee; President, National Association of Canal Carriers; *b* 3 Nov. 1878. *Educ:* Hartlebury. High Sheriff of Middlesex, 1934–35; Chairman of Middlesex County Council, 1937–40. *Recreations:* golf, shooting, racing. *Address:* 7 Gunnersbury Avenue, W5. *T:* Acorn 2024. *Clubs:* Carlton, Royal Thames Yacht, Constitutional.
Died 6 Aug. 1942.

CLAYTON, Sir (George) Christopher, Kt 1933; CBE 1919; PhD Heidelberg; JP; *b* 1869; *m* 1896, Mabel, *d* of D. Grainger, Culmore, Liverpool. *Educ:* Harrow; Liverpool University; abroad. MP (U) Widnes Division of Lancs, 1922–29; MP (U) Wirral Division, Cheshire, 1931–35. *Address:* Kilry Lodge, Alyth, Perthshire.
Died 28 July 1945.

CLAYTON, Sir Hugh Byard, Kt 1938; CIE 1924; ICS (retired); *b* Queensland, 1877; *s* of late R. B. B. Clayton; *m* 1915, Annie Blanch Nepean, MBE 1946; one *s* one *d. Educ:* St Paul's School; Wadham College, Oxford; 1st Class Hon. Mods, 1st Class Lit. Hum. Entered ICS, 1901; served in Bombay Presidency; services lent to War Office for duty in Intelligence Dept, 1914–19; Municipal Commissioner for City of Bombay, 1919–28; Chairman Haj Enquiry Committee, 1929–30; Commissioner, Poona, 1931–33; Belgaum, 1934–36; Chairman Bombay Sind Public Services Commission, 1937–42; Chairman Bombay Hospitality Committee, 1942–45; Kaisar-i-

Hind Gold Medal, 1944. *Recreations:* golf, shooting. *Clubs:* East India and Sports; Royal Mid-Surrey Golf (Richmond).

Died 27 Sept. 1947.

CLAYTON, Rev. John Francis; Canon Residentiary of Norwich Cathedral since 1940; *b* 18 April 1883; *s* of late Admiral F. S. Clayton, RN, and late Edith Margaret Clayton; unmarried. *Educ:* Marlborough; Keble College, Oxford. Ordained 1908; Curate of Sudbury (Suffolk), 1908–11; S Paul Clifton, Bristol, 1911–20; CF 1916–19 (MC); Tutor Ordination Test School, Knutsford, 1919–20; Domestic Chaplain to Bishop of Durham, 1921–26; Diocesan Chaplain to Bishop of Salisbury, 1926–29; Warden of S Nicholas Hall, University of Bristol, 1929–33; Reader at the Temple Church, London, 1931–40; Prebendary of Hereford Cathedral, 1937–40; Lecturer Salisbury Theological College, 1926–29; Warminster Theological College since 1926; Ripon Hall, Oxford, 1935–39; Editor of Bristol Diocesan Review, 1930–31; Examining-Chaplain to the Bishop of Winchester since 1931; to Bishop of Hereford since 1937; and to Bishop of Norwich since 1944. Select Preacher, University of Cambridge, 1938. *Recreations:* cycling, rowing, cross-country running. *Address:* 52 The Close, Norwich. *T:* Norwich 24726.

Died 27 Aug. 1947.

CLAYTON, Joseph, FRHistS; *b* London, 28 April 1868; *m* 1898, Margaret Souter; no *c. Educ:* Worcester College, Oxford. Editor and proprietor of the New Age, 1906–07; enlisted London Irish Rifles from National Reserve, Oct. 1914; Garrison duty in Burma, 1915–16; Labour Corps, France, 1917–18; Retired, Jan. 1919. *Publications:* Father Dolling: a Memoir, 1902; Grace Marlow: a Novel, 1903; John Blankset's Business: a Novel, 1904; Bishop Westcott: a Biography, 1906; The Bishops as Legislators, 1906; The Truth about the Lords, 1907; Robert Owen; a critical biography, 1908; Wat Tyler and the Peasant Revolt, 1909; The True Story of Jack Cade, a Vindication, 1910; Leaders of the People; Studies in Democratic History, 1910; The Under-Man: a Novel; The Rise of the Democracy, 1911; Robert Kett and the Norfolk Rising, 1912; Co-operation and Trade Unions (People's Books), 1912–1913; Father Stanton of St Alban's, Holborn: A Memoir, 1913; Economics for Christians, 1923; The Historic Basis of Anglicanism, 1925; The Rise and Decline of Socialism in Great Britain, 1926; Continuity in the Church of England, 1928; St Hugh of Lincoln: a biography, 1931; St Anselm, a biography, 1933; Sir Thomas More: a short study, 1933; The Protestant Reformation in Great Britain: a short history, 1934; Luther and his Work, 1937; Pope Innocent III, 1940. *Address:* Littleworth, Campden, Glos.

Died 19 Nov. 1943.

CLEAVE, John Kyrie Frederick; Barrister-at-Law; Western Circuit; Recorder of Tiverton since 1932; *b* 1861; *o s* of late John Ones Cleave, barrister-at-law, and Matilda Phillott; unmarried. *Educ:* Forest School, Walthamstow, E; Hertford College, Oxford (scholar). Called to bar, Gray's Inn, 1888; Lee and Richards Prizeman; Examined for Inn scholarships; Commissioner to try Municipal Election petitions, 1911; nominated by Local Government Board to hold arbitrations, 1912–14; has sat as deputy judge in many of the Metropolitan County Courts; Registrar of Board of Referees under Finance and Income Tax Acts since 1915; Jubilee Medal, 1935. *Publications:* articles in Halsbury's Laws of England on Juries and Statutes; Occasional articles on legal and social subjects. *Recreations:* foreign travel, walking, music. *Address:* 1 Paper Buildings, Temple, EC4. *TA:* 58 Temple, London. *T:* Central 0165, Holborn 7641, Ext. 181. *Clubs:* Oxford and Cambridge, United.

Died 5 Feb. 1947.

CLEAVER, Col Frederick Holden, CBE 1919; DSO 1917; retired; *b* 1875; 4th *s* of Richard Stuart Cleaver, Haymans Green, West Derby, Liverpool; *m* Janet Nosworthy, 3rd *d* of W. J. Mann, of Highfield, Trowbridge, Wilts. *Educ:* HMS Britannia. Served South African War with Roberts' and Kitchener's Horse, 20th Hussars, 1914; RFC 1915–18; Aeroplane and balloon observer, 1918; Staff Officer and Commandant, RAF Cadet School; Aeronaut's certificate No. 45. *Recreation:* yachting. *Address:* Teg Down House, Weeke, Winchester, Hants.

Died 29 Nov. 1944.

CLEEVE, Lt-Col Herbert, CBE 1919; late South Wales Borderers and RASC; *b* 15 Sept. 1870; *s* of late Col C. K. Cleeve; *m* 1904, Clara, *d* of late John F. Holt. *Educ:* Wellington Coll. Entered army 1892; served S Africa 1899–1901 (despatches twice, Queen's Medal seven clasps); European War, 1914–19 (despatches, CBE). *Club:* Naval and Military.

Died 15 July 1948.

CLEGG, Sir James Travis T.; see Travis-Clegg.

CLEGG, William Henry; *s* of George Clegg, Stanley, Yorkshire; *m* 1916, Elinor, *d* of Rev. E. J. Bowen, Rector of Redhill, Havant; two *s* one *d.* Chief Accountant, Bank of England, 1919; Governor (first) of South African Reserve Bank, 1920–31; Chairman of Hong Kong Currency Commission, 1931; Director of Bank of England, 1932–37; Lieutenant of City of London since 1932. *Address:* Silwood House, Winchester, Hants. *Clubs:* Hampshire, Winchester.

Died 16 March 1945.

CLELAND, Sir Charles, KBE 1917; MVO, DL; JP Lanarkshire; JP, DL, Glasgow; LLD of Glasgow University; Hon. FEIS; *b* 15 April 1867; *e s* of late Charles Cleland, Bonville, Maryhill; *m* 1888, Janet Houston, 2nd *d* of late William Burrell of Elmbank, Bowling; three *d. Educ:* privately; Glasgow Academy. Chairman, Education Authority of Glasgow, 1919–28; Chairman of Hutcheson's Educational Trust, 1928–35; Vice-Consul for the Republic of Panama in Glasgow; Chairman, Income Tax Commissioners for City of Glasgow; Member of Corporation of City of Glasgow, 1891–1907 and 1929–34; Senior Magistrate, City of Glasgow, 1901; Member of Clyde Trust, 1903–07; Chairman, Glasgow Unionist Association, 1914–25; Vice-Chairman, The Central Council for School Broadcasting; Chairman, Licensing Court of Appeal, City of Glasgow. *Address:* Bonville, Maryhill, near Glasgow. *T:* 19 Maryhill. *Clubs:* Scottish Constitutional, Glasgow.

Died 19 Jan. 1941.

CLEMENS, Sir William James, Kt 1937; CMG 1934; ISO; *b* 27 March 1873; *s* of James and Catherine Clemens; *m* 1st, 1899, L. B. White (*d* 1911); two *s* three *d*; 2nd, 1914, B. M. Webster; one *s* one *d. Educ:* Beechworth State School, Victoria. Entered Public Service, Victoria, 1889; transferred Commonwealth of Australia, Public Service, 1901; Postmaster General's Dept 14 years; then Senior Clerk, Registrar, Secretary to Commonwealth Public Service Commissioner, 1903–16; Commonwealth Public Service Inspector of Victoria and Tasmania, 1916–23; Royal Commissioner, investigating and reporting on Public Service of Mandated Territory of New Guinea and Secretary and Chief Inspector, Commonwealth Public Service Board, 1923–28; Secretary Dept Home and Territories, 1928–29; Public Service Commissioner, 1929–33; Chairman Commonwealth Public Service Board of Commissioners, 1933–37; retired 1937. *Recreations:* golf, bowls, horticulture. *Address:* Wickham Crescent, Red Hill, Canberra, ACT.

Died 4 Sept. 1941.

CLEMENT, Ernest Wilson, MA; *b* Dubuque, Iowa, 21 Feb. 1860; *e s* of Jesse Clement and Lucetta Blood; *m* 1887, Nellie Hall; one *s* two *d. Educ:* University of Chicago. Teacher in America, 1881–87 and 1891–94; Teacher, Mito, Japan, 1887–91; Principal, Duncan Baptist Academy, Tokyo, 1895–1911; Professor of English Literature, First National College, Tokyo, 1911–27 (retired); Special Correspondent Chicago Daily News, 1895–1920; Acting-Interpreter US Legation, Tokyo, 1896–97, 1906–07; Librarian, Recording Secretary, Vice-President, Asiatic Society of Japan; Editor, Japan Evangelist, 1899–1909; Editor, Christian Movement in Japan, 1906–09. *Publications:* Handbook of Modern Japan, 1903; Japanese Floral Calendar, 1905; Christianity in Modern Japan, 1905; Hildreth's Japan as It Was and Is, 1906; Japanese Chronology, 1910; A Short History of Japan, 1915; Constitutional Imperialism in Japan, 1916; Fifty Sessions of the Japanese Imperial Diet, 1926 Numerical Categories in Japanese, 1927. *Recreations:* reading and baseball. *Address:* 162 Bellmore Street, Floral Park, NY, USA. *Clubs:* Phi Beta Kappa, Psi Upsilon Fraternity.

Died 11 March 1941.

CLEMENTI, Sir Cecil, GCMG 1931, KCMG 1926; CMG 1916; Knight of Grace of Order of St John of Jerusalem, 1926; MA, FRGS; MRAS; Hon. Fellow Magdalen College, Oxford, 1938; *b* 1 Sept. 1875; *s* of late Colonel Montagu Clementi Judge-Advocate-General in India; *m* 1912, Marie Penelope Rose, MBE, *d* of Admiral C. J. Eyres, DSO, OBE; one *s* two *d. Educ:* St Paul's School; (Demy) Magdalen College Oxford; hon. mention Hertford Schl, 1895; 1st cl mods, 1896; hon. mention Ireland and Craven Schl, 1896; Boden Sanskrit Scholar, 1897; prox. acc. Gaisford (Greek Prose) 1897; 2nd cl. lit. hum., 1898; BA 1898; prox. acc. Chancellor's Latin essay, 1899; MA 1901; Hon. LLD Hong-Kong University, 1925; cadet, Hong-Kong, 1899; passed in Cantonesel, 1900, and in Pekingese 1906. Asst Registrar-General, 1901; Member Board of Examiners in Chinese, 1902; seconded for special service under govt of India, 1902; JP 1902; seconded for famine relief work in Kwang Si, 1903; Member of Land Court; Assistant Land Officer and Police Magistrate, New Territories, Hong-Kong, 1903–06; Asst Colonial Secretary and Clerk of Council, 1907; attended International Opium Conference at Shanghai, 1909; Private Secretary to HE the Administrator, 1910; Acting Colonial Sec. and Member Executive and Legislative Councils, Hong-Kong, 1911–12; received Cuthbert Peek award of Royal Geographical Society, 1912; Colonial Secretary, British Guiana, 1913–22; Colonial Secretary, Ceylon, 1922–25; administered the government of British Guiana, 1916–17, 1919, 1921; administered the government of Ceylon, 1922–23, 1925; Governor of Hong-Kong, 1925–30; Governor and Commander-in-Chief of the Straits Settlements and High Commissioner for Malaya, 1930–34. Master of Mercers' Company, 1940–41. *Publications:* Cantonese Love Songs; Pervigilium Veneris; Summary of Geographical Observations taken during a journey from Kashgar to Kowloon (1907–1908); The Chinese in British Guiana; Elements in Analysis of Thought; A Constitutional History of British Guiana, 1937. *Recreation:* travel. *Address:* Holmer Court, Holmer Green, High Wycombe, Bucks. *Club:* Royal Empire Society.

Died 5 April 1947.

CLEMENTS, Col Robert William, CMG 1918; DSO 1917; BA, MB, BCh, BAO, RUI, DPH Camb.; late RAMC. *Educ:* Queen's College, Galway; Edinburgh; Diploma of Tropical Medicine, Liverpool. Served European War, 1914–18 (despatches five times, DSO, CMG); retired pay, 1922. *Address:* Glyn Mills & Co., Kirkland House, Whitehall, SW1.

Died 22 Jan. 1941.

CLEMENTS, (William Dudley) Bernard, OSB, Benedictine Monk (Anglican); Vicar of All Saints, Margaret Street, W1, since 1934; *b* 8 May 1880; *e s* of Walter Henry Clements and Jeannie Mary Fabricius. *Educ:* St Andrew's School, Eastbourne; Magdalen College School, Oxford; Pembroke College, Cambridge, BA Dublin (Modern Literature). Schoolmaster at St Wilfrid's Bexhill; Dunstable Grammar School and Central Foundation School, London, 1901–08. Ordained (Church of England), Deacon, 1908; Priest, 1909; Assistant Priest St Peter-le-Poer, Friern Barnet, N 1908–11; Chaplain, Royal Navy, 1911–17; Chaplain, Training-Ship Mercury, 1917–18; Vicar of St Michael and All Angels, Portsmouth, 1919–21; since 1921 a member of the Anglican Benedictine Community, Nashdom Abbey, Burnham, Bucks; lent by the community for service in the Diocese of Accra, West Africa, 1926–31, Rector of St Augustine's Theological College, Kumasi, West Africa; Licensed Preacher Diocese of Oxford since 1932; Select Preacher, Cambridge University, 1934–35; Commissary for Bishop of Nassau since 1934, for Bishop of Accra since 1935; Warden of the Guild of Catholic Writers since 1938. *Publications:* How to Pray, 1929; Philip Cometh to Andrew, 1930; Members of Christ, 1932; The Merchantman in Africa, 1933; The Royal Banners, 1934; The Precepts of the Church, 1936; When Ye Pray (Broadcast Addresses), 1936; Learning to be a Christian (Broadcast Addresses), 1938; What Happens When I Die (Broadcast Addresses), 1939; The Weapons of a Christian (Broadcast Addresses), 1940; A Monk in Margaret Street, 1941; 7.55 am (Broadcast Addresses), 1941; The Training of an Apostle (Broadcast Addresses), 1942. *Address:* All SS Vicarage, Margaret Street, W1. *T:* Museum 1788; Nashdom Abbey, Burnham, Bucks. *Club:* Athenæum.

Died 13 Sept. 1942.

CLEMINSON, Frederick John, MA, MChir (Camb.); FRCS; Hon. Director of Research, Ferens Institute of Otology, Middlesex Hospital and Consulting Surgeon, Aural Department, Middlesex Hospital; Consulting Laryngologist to the Heart Hospital; Consulting Aural Surgeon, Evelina Hospital for Children; Ex-President Otological Section Royal Society of Medicine; *b* 1878; *s* of Rev. J. R. Cleminson, Hull; *m* 1906, Sara, *d* of E. M. Smucker, Philadelphia, USA; one *s* two *d. Educ:* Kingswood School, Bath; Gonville and Caius College, Cambridge (Scholar and Shuttleworth Scholar). Demonstrator of Anatomy, Cambridge, 1902–05; served European War, Captain, RAMC (Salonica and France), 1915–18; surgeon to Throat Hospital, Golden Square (retired 1923). *Publications:* articles on various Surgical and Otological subjects in Medical Journals. *Recreations:* sailing, ornithology. *Address:* Spain End, Willingale, Ongar, Essex. *T:* Fyfield 216. *Clubs:* Athenæum, Royal Cruising.

Died 21 Aug. 1943.

CLEMSON, Brig.-Gen. William Fletcher, CMG 1917; DSO 1915; *b* 31 March 1866; *m* 1923, Mona, 2nd *d* of late Captain George Stanley, CB, RN. Entered Army, 1887; Captain, 1899; Adjutant, 1900–04; Major, 1906; Hon. Brig.-Gen. retired 1920; served European War, 1914–18 (wounded, DSO and bar, CMG, Bt Col); Colonel of the York and Lancaster Regiment, 1932–36.

Died 12 Dec. 1946.

CLERK, Sir George James Robert, 9th Bt *cr* 1679; late Capt. The Royal Scots; *b* 4 Oct. 1876; *s* of 8th Bt and Aymée, *d* of late Sir R. M. Napier, 8th Bt; *S* father 1911; *m* 1903, Hon. Mabel Honor, *y d* of late Col Hon. Charles Dutton and sister of 6th Baron Sherborne, DSO; one *s* two *d.* DL Edin.; JP. *Heir: s* John Dutton, Lieut RNVR, *b* 30 Jan. 1917. *Address:* West Bay House, North Berwick, East Lothian. *T:* North Berwick 176; Penicuik House, Midlothian. *T:* Pen. 18. *Clubs:* Bath; New, Edinburgh.

Died 21 Nov. 1943.

CLERK, Hugh Edward, CIE 1914; *b* 11 June 1859; *s* of late Col Alexander Clerk; *m* Edith Elizabeth, *d* of late Willoughby Beauchamp of Hampden, Bucks. *Educ:* Clifton College; Felsted School; RIEC Coopers Hill. Joined the Madras Public Works Dept, 1880; held various appointments in that Presidency, where he directed the design and execution of large irrigation works; was chief engineer and secretary to Government PWD and Fellow of the Madras University; retired, 1914; employed in Ministry of Munitions, 1917–19. *Recreation:* water-colour painting. *Address:* Northgate, Beaconsfield, Bucks. *T:* Beaconsfield 338.

Died 17 Feb. 1942.

CLERKE, Major Augustus Basil Holt, CBE 1918; MIAE; MISI; late RFA; late Deputy Chairman and Managing Director, Hadfields Ltd; *b* 1871; *s* of late Colonel Shadwell H. Clerke; *m* 1893, Mabel (*d* 1923), *d* of J. Seymour Salaman; two *d*; *m* 1941, Mabel Isabel Oliphant, *d* of late Thomas Carruthers, Helensburgh, Scotland. *Educ:* Cheltenham; Royal Military Academy, Woolwich. 2nd Lieut Royal Artillery, 1889; Capt., 1900; Major, 1906; Assistant Inspector of Steel, 1899; Instructor Ordnance College, 1904; Chief Instructor, 1906; Commanded 19th Battery RFA, India, 1907; Inspector Royal Arsenal, 1908; Retired, 1911; Director, Hadfields, Ltd, 1913. *Publications:* professional papers and articles. *Recreations:* various. *Address:* 14 Endcliffe Crescent, Sheffield, 10. *T:* Sheffield 61644; Birdham Holt, Birdham, Sussex. *T:* Birdham 307. *Club:* United Service.

Died 13 May 1949.

CLEWER, Maj.-Gen. Donald, CB 1942; LDS, RCS England 1914; Col Comdt The Army Dental Corps since 1943, and Deputy Senior Dental Officer, Ministry of Health, since 1942; *b* 26 Oct. 1892; *s* of late George John Clewer, Hove, Sussex; *m* 1920, Lilian, o *d* of William Bowes, Rochester, Kent; one *d. Educ:* Taunton House School, Brighton; Guy's Hospital. Dental House Surgeon, Guy's Hospital, 1914; Lieut The Army Dental Corps, 1915; Capt. 1921; Major, 1927; Lt-Col 1934; Col 1935; Maj.-Gen. 1940; Maj.-Gen. RARO 1942; Assist Director of Dental Service, Eastern Command, 1934–36; Inspector of Army Dental Services, India, 1936–37; Director Army Dental Service, War Office, 1937–42; served European War, 1915–19, France and Belgium, 1916–18, Germany, 1919 (despatches); President, Allied Forces Dental Soc., 1942–43. *Publications:* papers in dental and medical journals. *Address:* 27 Park Hill, Ealing, W5. *T:* Perivale 1553. *Club:* Army and Navy.

Died 11 Dec. 1945.

CLIFFORD OF CHUDLEIGH, 10th Baron *cr* 1672; **William Hugh Clifford;** Count of the Holy Roman Empire; *b* 17 Dec. 1858; *s* of 8th Baron and Hon. Agnes Catherine, *γ d* of 11th Baron Petre; *S* brother, 1916; *m* 1st, 1886, Catherine Mary, *d* of R. Bassett; three *s*; 2nd, 1943, Grace Muriel, *d* of late W. St Clair-Munro, Glasgow and London. *Educ:* Beaumont. Left England, 1876; lived in New Zealand until 1890, working on a station; then farmed in Tasmania; returned to England, 1916; discovered the Clifford Colour Rays, 1922; is an authority on Radiology and has made visible the colours of the Ultra-Violet and Infra Red Rays; FGS; FZS; FCI; owns about 8000 acres. *Publications:* The Portal of Evolution, 1922; The Evolution of Civilization and Society; The Theology of Creation; Light Rays; What they are and how they cure; pamphlets and articles in scientific journals on Radiology. *Heir:* s Hon. Charles (Oswald Hugh) Clifford. *Address:* Ugbrooke Park, Chudleigh, Devon; The Hall, Headcorn, Kent.

Died 5 July 1943.

CLIFFORD, Lady Elizabeth Lydia Rosabelle, (Mrs Henry de la Pasture), CBE 1918; novelist and dramatist; *e d* of late Edward Bonham, HM Consul, Calais; *m* 1st, Henry de la Pasture (*d* 1908), JP, of Llandogo Priory, Monmouthshire, 3rd *s* of late 14th Count and 3rd Marquis de la Pasture; two *d*; 2nd, 1910, Sir Hugh Clifford, GCMG, GBE (*d* 1941). *Publications:* The Little Squire (dramatised and played at Lyric Theatre), 1894; A Toy Tragedy; Deborah of Tod's, 1897; Adam Grigson, 1899; Catherine of Calais, 1901; Cornelius, 1903; Peter's Mother, 1905; The Man from America, 1906; The Unlucky Family; The Lonely Lady of Grosvenor Square, 1907; The Grey Knight, 1907; Catherine's Child, 1908; The Tyrant, 1909; Master Christopher, 1911; Erica, 1912; Michael Ferrys, 1913. *Plays:* The Lonely Millionaires, 1906; Peter's Mother, Wyndham's, Apollo, Comedy, Haymarket, and at Sandringham, 1906; revival Haymarket, 1909; Her Grace the Reformer, Haymarket, 1907; Deborah, 1909–1910, Boston, USA. *Address:* Kensington House, 139 Bayswater Road, W2. *Clubs:* Ladies' Empire, Women Writers'.

Died 30 Oct. 1945.

CLIFFORD, Henry Charles; landscape painter, but has also made records of old and disappearing London; *b* 10 Sept. 1861; *e surv. s* of late Henry Clifford, Blackheath; *m* 1899, Ethel Lilian, 2nd *d* of late Horatio Fletcher, Blackheath. *Educ:* Rugby. Studied Art in Paris under Bouguereau Fleury and Benjamin Constant. Exhibitor at Royal Academy; RBA 1912–37. *Recreations:* reading, walking, and collecting Oriental objects of art. *Address:* Rothbury, Storrington, nr Pulborough, Sussex.

Died 17 Sept. 1947.

CLIFFORD, Sir Hugh, GCMG 1921; GBE 1925; KCMG 1909; CMG 1900; FRGS; *b* London, 5 March 1866; *e s* of late Major-Gen. Hon. Sir Henry Clifford, VC, KCMG, CB, and Josephine, *o d* of Joseph Anstice, of King's College and Madeley Wood, Salop; *g s* of 7th Baron Clifford of Chudleigh; *m* 1st, 1896, Minna (*d* 1907), *o d* of late Gilbert à Beckett; one *s* (killed in action, 1916) two *d*; 2nd, 1910, Mrs Henry de la Pasture, CBE 1918. *Educ:* Woburn Park, under the 13th Lord Petre. Passed for Sandhurst with an Hon. Queen's Cadetship in 1883, but instead joined the Malay States Civil Service as a cadet, 1883; passed final examinations in Malay, 1884; sent on special mission to Sultan of Pahang in 1887, obtained promise of Treaty and received thanks of Secretary of State; Governor's Agent, Pahang, 1887–88; Superintendent Ulu Pahang, 1889; Acting Resident, Pahang, at different times from 1890–95; took a leading part in suppression Pahang Rebellion, 1892; Commissioner to the Cocos-Keeling Islands, 1894; led armed expeditions into Native States of Trenggânu and Kelantan in July 1894, and in March–June 1895, received thanks of the Secretary of State; British Resident, Pahang, 1896–99; nominated by Colonial Office to post of Governor North Borneo and Labuan under Chartered Company 1900, but resigned and reappointed Resident, Pahang, 1901; in attendance upon Sultan Idris bin Iskandar of Perak, the Senior Colonial Guest, during Coronation of King Edward VII, 1902; Colonial Secretary, Trinidad and Tobago, 1903–07; Colonial Secretary, Ceylon, 1907–12; administered Government of Trinidad, 1904 and 1906, and Government of Ceylon, 1907, 1909, 1911, and 1912; Governor, Gold Coast, 1912–19; Governor, Nigeria, 1919–25; gazetted Governor of Ceylon, Nov. 1924, but remained in Nigeria till May 1925, in order to entertain the Prince of Wales in April 1925; Governor of Ceylon, 1925–27; Governor of the Straits Settlements, High Commissioner for the Malay States and British Agent for Borneo, 1927 to end of 1929, when he resigned owing to Lady Clifford's serious illness; received the special thanks of the Secretary of State for the Colonies for his work from 1912 to 1925 as a Governor in West Africa; negotiated with the French Colonial Authorities in Aug. 1914 the agreement entered into for the provisional administration of Togoland; as Governor Gold Coast was responsible for the administration of British Sphere of Occupation in Togoland, 1914–19.

Publications: In Court and Kampong, 1897; Studies in Brown Humanity, 1898; Since the Beginning, 1898; In a Corner of Asia, 1899; Bush-Whacking, 1901; A Free-Lance of To-Day, 1903; Further India, 1904; Sally, A Study, 1904; Heroes of Exile, 1906; Saleh: A Sequel, 1908; The Downfall of the Gods, 1911; Malayan Monochromes, 1913; The Further Side of Silence, 1916; The German Colonies, 1918; The Gold Coast Regiment in the East African Campaign, 1920; In Days that are Dead, 1926; A Prince of Malaya, 1926; Some Reflections on the Ceylon Land Question, 1927; Bush-whacking and other Asiatic Tales and Memories, 1929; joint author with Sir Frank Swettenham of a Dictionary of the Malay Language; author of a Malay translation of the Penal Code. *Recreations:* reading, writing, golf, shooting, swimming, flying, tennis. *Address:* 17 Morpeth Mansions, Westminster, SW1. *Clubs:* Athenæum; St George's Hill Golf.

Died 18 Dec. 1941.

CLIFFORD, Rev. Robert Rowntree; Superintendent of the West Ham Central Mission, Barking Road, E13, since 1897; *b* 1 Oct. 1867; *s* of Robert Rowntree Clifford and Anne Sophia Crosley; *m* 1910, Hettie, *d* of Stephen Bannister, Stoke Golding; two *s. Educ:* Regent's Park. Founder West Ham Central Mission, 1897; President London Baptist Association, 1921–22; President Baptist Union of Great Britain and Ireland, 1933–34. *Address:* Marnham House Settlement, 409 Barking Road, E13. *T:* Grangewood 2363.

Died 8 Nov. 1943.

CLIFFORD, Sir Walter Lovelace, 4th Bt *cr* 1887; *b* 20 May 1852; 2nd *s* of Sir Charles Clifford, 1st Bt; *S* nephew, 1938; *m* 1883, Catherine (*d* 1925), *d* of late Edward Bath, Bryn-y-Mor, Swansea; two *d.* Formerly a civil engineer. *Heir: nephew* Rev. Lewis Arthur Joseph, *b* 1896. *Address:* 14 Garden Road, Fendalton, Christchurch, NW1, NZ.

Died 26 May 1944.

CLIFFORD, Brig.-Gen. Walter Rees, CBE 1919; retired pay; *b* April 1866; *s* of late Deputy Surgeon-General F. M. Clifford, IMS; *m* 1899, Nina, *e d* of late R. Fitzmaurice, MD, Cloghers, Tralee, Co. Kerry. *Educ:* Clifton College. Joined Cheshire Regt 1885; commanded 2nd Batt. 1908–12; served in Burma, Karen Expedition, 1889 (medal with clasp); S African War (on Staff), 1900–02 (Queen's medal with 3 clasps, King's medal with 2 clasps, despatches); European War (CBE). *Recreations:* sketching, shooting, and fishing. *Address:* Glendalough, Caragh Lake, Co. Kerry, Eire. *Club:* Army and Navy.

Died 6 Jan. 1947.

CLIFTON, Lt-Col Percy Robert, CMG 1918; DSO 1916; *b* 1872; *s* of Sir H. J. L. Bruce, 4th Bt. [assumed name of Clifton by Royal Licence, 1919]; *m* 1st, 1898, Aletheia Georgina (*d* 1904), *d* of Rt Hon. Sir R. H. Paget, 1st Bt; 2nd, 1909, Evelyn Mary Amelia, *d* of Major Thomas Leith of Petmathen, Aberdeen; one *s* one *d. Educ:* Eton. Served European War, 1914–18 (DSO, CMG); DL, JP Notts; High Sheriff, Nottinghamshire, 1929. *Address:* Clifton Hall, Nottingham. *Club:* Brooks's.

Died 10 Nov. 1944.

CLIFTON-BROWN, Edward Clifton; JP Bucks; partner in the Anglo American banking firm of Brown, Shipley & Co.; *b* 10 Feb. 1870; 2nd *s* of late Col James Clifton Brown, DL, JP, of Holmbush, Fay Gate, Sussex; *m* 1897, Dora Winifred, *y d* of George Hanbury of Blythewood, Maidenhead; two *s* one *d. Educ:* Cheam; Eton. Double name assumed by deed poll, 1923 (enrolled at College of Arms), taking additional name of Clifton; Director of Westminster Bank, Ltd; Standard Bank of South Africa, Ltd, and Deputy Governor Royal Exchange Assurance; also director of Burnham Dorney

& Hitcham Waterworks Co. Ltd; High Sheriff of Buckinghamshire, 1936. *Recreation:* shooting. *Address:* Burnham Grove, Burnham, Bucks. *T:* Burnham Bucks 10. *Clubs:* Brooks's, Farmers', Royal Automobile.

Died 1 Nov. 1944.

CLINTON, Osbert Henry F.; *see* Fynes-Clinton.

CLITHEROW, Dr Richard; MP (Lab) for Edge Hill Division of Liverpool since 1945; *b* Liverpool, 18 Jan. 1902; *e s* of John and Ida Clitherow, Liverpool; *m* 1930, Gladys Florence, *o d* of the late John Arber and Mrs Florence Dix, London; two *s. Educ:* Liverpool Schools and University. Served with Royal North-West Mounted Police, 1919–22; Pharmacist (London), 1927. LMSSA 1945; LRCP, MRCS 1946. Represented Fairfield Ward in Liverpool City Council, 1937–45. *Address:* 79 Underley St, Edgehill, Liverpool 7. *T:* Sefton Park 2974; 8a Maunsel Street, Westminster, SW1.

Died 3 June 1947.

CLIVE, Viscount; Mervyn Horatio Herbert; 17th Baron Darcy de Knayth *cr* 1332; Squadron Leader RAF; *b* 7 May 1904; *o surv. s* and *heir* of 4th Earl of Powis; *S* to mother's barony, 1929; *m* 1934, Vida, *o d* of late Capt. J. Harold Cuthbert, Scots Guards, and Lady Rayleigh; one *d. Educ:* Eton; Trinity College, Cambridge. Called to Bar, Inner Temple, 1929. *Recreation:* flying. *Heir: to Barony: d* Hon. Davina Marcia Herbert, *b* 10 July 1938. *Address:* Powis Castle, Welshpool. *T:* Welshpool 60; 22 Belgrave Square, SW1. *T:* Sloane 7009.

Died 23 March 1943.

CLIVE, Rt Hon. Sir Robert Henry, PC 1934; GCMG 1936; KCMG 1927; CMG 1919; *b* 27 Dec. 1877; 3rd *s* of C. M. B. Clive of Whitfield, Herefordshire, and Lady Katherine, *d* of 8th Earl of Denbigh; *m* 1905, Hon. Magdalen, 3rd *d* of late Lord Muir Mackenzie, GCB; two *s* one *d. Educ:* Haileybury; Magdalen Coll., Oxford. Attaché, 1902; 3rd Secretary, 1904; 2nd Secretary, 1908; 1st Secretary, 1915; Counsellor, 1920; served at Rome, Tokyo, Cairo, Berne, Stockholm, Peking; has been Consul-General at Munich and at Tangier; British Minister at Teheran, 1926–31, and to the Holy See 1933–34; Ambassador to Japan, 1934–37; Ambassador to Belgium and Minister to Luxemburg, 1937–39. *Address:* Cherry Orchard, Forest Row, Sussex. *T:* 242. *Club:* Brooks's Bath.

Died 13 May 1948.

CLOETE, Col Evelyn, CBE 1919; Royal Horse Artillery (retired, 1919); *b* 29 Jan. 1863; *o s* of late General Sir A. J. Cloete, KCB, KH, and Annie Woolcombe, *d* of late Thomas Louis, of Culloden, Barbados; *g d* of Sir Thomas Louis, Bart, KMT, KSF, Admiral of the White; *m* 1882, Selma Mary (*d* 1924), *d* of late Rev. H. W. Bagnell; one *d. Educ:* Wellington College; RMA, Woolwich. Joined Royal Artillery, 1882; served Egyptian Campaign, 1885 (medal with clasp for Suakin, 1885, Khedive's Bronze Star); European War, 1914–19; in France, Oct. 1914–Dec. 1916 (despatches twice); in command of the 111th Brigade, RFA in France, and commanded RHA Brigade at Woolwich, 1917–19; Coronation Medal, 1910. *Recreations:* polo, lawn tennis, golf, billiards. *Address:* 8 West Park, Eltham. *Club:* Naval and Military.

Died 15 Oct. 1943.

CLOSE, Etta, OBE 1918; FRGS, FRHS; *e d* of late Henry Gaskell Close and Ellinor, *d* of Sir Harry Mainwaring, Bt, of Peover Hall, Knutsford, Cheshire. Has travelled extensively in many countries. *Publications:* A Woman Alone in Kenya, Uganda, and the Belgian Congo, 1924; Excursions and Some Adventures, 1926; a play in three acts, The Gates of Paradise, 1928. *Address:* 1 Lombard Street, EC.

Died 13 March 1945.

CLOSE, Brig.-Gen. Geoffrey Dominic, CB 1918; late RE; *b* 1866. Served Burma, 1887 (medal and 2 clasps); Hazara Expedition, 1891 (clasp); Gallipoli, 1915; Chief Engineer, 1916–21; retired pay, 1921.

Died 1 June 1942.

CLOSE, Ralph William, KC 1912; BA, LLB; *b* Cape Town, 27 Oct. 1867; *s* of George and Jane Close; *m* 1897, Florence Agnes Mills; one *d. Educ:* South African College, Cape Town (University of the Cape of Good Hope). Public Service Cape of Good Hope, 1887–94; practised at Cape Town as Advocate of Supreme Court, Cape of Good Hope or Cape Province Division, 1895–1933; Member of Parliament of Union of South Africa, 1915–33; Minister at Washington, of the Union of South Africa 1933–43; President of Convocation, University of Cape Town, 1916–33. *Address:* Heatherton, off Palmyra Road, Newlands, Cape Town. *Clubs:* Chevy Chase, Cosmos, University, Metropolitan, Washington; Civil Service, Owl, University, Cape Town.

Died 21 March 1945.

CLOUDESLEY-BRERETON, Maud Adeline; *see* Brereton.

CLOUGH, Tom; on Council of RCA; *b* 12 July 1867; *m*; one *s* one *d. Educ:* Bolton. Spent first sixpence he possessed on paints; trained for printing, but took every available opportunity of sketching out of doors; as an amateur exhibited first picture on the line at RA, The Gorsy Marsh, also at Walker Art Gallery, Liverpool; took prizes at Royal National Welsh Esteddfod during early career; commenced painting as a profession 43 years ago in Conway Valley, joining a coterie of artists; exhibited many times at RA, RI, etc., mostly large drawings; exhibiting oils also at RA, visited Italy thrice, spending considerable time in Italian Lakes, Amalfi, Ravello, Capri and Venice, also Brittany, Devon, Cornwall, etc.; some of his pictures in permanent collections of Bolton and Blackpool; owes most of his knowledge to an untiring study of Nature. *Recreations:* music and fishing.

Died 3 Feb. 1943.

CLOUSTON, David, CIE 1919; MA, BSc, DSc, FRSE, FRSGS; *b* 13 April 1872. Agricultural Adviser and Director, Agricultural Research Institute, Pusa, 1923–26; retired, 1929. *Publication:* From the Orcades to Ind, 1936. *Address:* Forthview, Boswall Road, Edinburgh.

Died 18 April 1948.

CLOUSTON, J. Storer, OBE, FSA Scot; JP; author; *b* Cumberland, 23 May 1870; *e s* of late Sir T. S. Clouston, MD; *m* 1903, Winifred, *d* of Charles Stewart Clouston, MD; two *s* one *d. Educ:* Merchiston Castle, Edinburgh; Magdalen College, Oxford. Called to Bar, Inner Temple, 1895; Sub-Commissioner National Service Department (Scotland), Agricultural Section, 1917–18; Convener of Orkney since 1930; Chairman of Orkney Harbour Commissioners since 1935. *Publications:* The Lunatic at Large; The Duke; Adventures of M. D'Haricot; Our Lady's Inn; Garmiscath; Count Bunker; A County Family; The Prodigal Father; Tales of King Fido; The Peer's Progress; His First Offence; Two's Two; The Spy in Black; The Man from the Clouds; Simon; Carrington's Cases; The Lunatic at Large Again; The Lunatic still at Large; Two Strange Men; The Lunatic in Charge; Mr Essington in Love; The Jade's Progress, 1928; After the Deed, 1929; Colonel Dam, 1930; The Virtuous Vamp, 1931; The Best Story Ever, 1932; A History of Orkney, 1932; Button Brains, 1933; The Chemical Baby, 1934; Our Member, Mr Muttlebury, 1935; Scots Wha Ha'e, 1936; Scotland Expects, 1936; Not Since Genesis, 1938; The Man in Steel, 1939; Beastmark the Spy, 1941; various short stories, historical papers, etc.; Edited Records of Earldom of Orkney and The Orkney Parishes. *Plays:* The Pocket

Miss Hercules, 1907; The Gilded Pill, 1913; Real Champagne, 1934. *Address:* Smoogro House, Orkney. *Clubs:* New, Edinburgh.

Died 23 June 1944.

CLOWES, Col George Charles Knight, DSO 1916; OBE, TD, JP; Chairman and Managing Director of William Clowes and Sons, Ltd, Printers and Publishers; Hon. Col The London Scottish, 1939; *b* 1882; *s* of late William Charles Knight Clowes; *m* 1911, Winifred Lucy, *d* of late Ven. Archdeacon of Sarum. *Educ:* Winchester; Magdalen College, Oxford. Served European War, 1914–18. *Address:* The Kennels, Wooburn Green, Bucks. *Clubs:* United University, Caledonian.

Died 16 Aug. 1941.

CLUER, His Honour Albert Rowland; *b* 1852; *s* of J. T. T. Cluer; *m* 1881, Julia (*d* 1937), *d* of R. A. Cooper. Barrister, Lincoln's Inn, 1877. Recorder of Deal, 1894–95; Police Magistrate, South-Western District, 1895–96; Worship Street, 1896–1911; Judge of Whitechapel County Court, 1911–34; retired 1934.

Died 12 Jan. 1942.

CLYDE, Rt Hon. Lord; Rt Hon. James Avon Clyde, PC 1916; KC, 1901; LLD (Edinburgh and St Andrews); JP, Lord Lieutenant of Kinross-shire; Chairman of Trustees of National Library of Scotland since 1936; *b* Dollar, 14 Nov. 1863; 2nd *s* of late James Clyde, MA, LLD, and Elizabeth Rigg, Whitehaven; *m* 1895, Anna Margaret M'Diarmid, *d* of late P. W. Latham, MD; two *s. Educ:* Edinburgh Academy and Univ. MA and Gray Scholar, 1884; LLB 1888. Called to Scots Bar, 1889; KC 1901; Solicitor-General, Scotland, 1905–06; contested the united counties of Clackmannan and Kinross (U), 1906; Dean of Faculty of Advocates, 1915–18; Lord Advocate, Scotland, 1916–20; Honorary Bencher, Gray's Inn, 1919; MP (LU) Edinburgh West, 1909–18, Edinburgh North (Co. U), 1918–20; Lord Justice-General of Scotland and Lord President of the Court of Session, 1920–35. *Recreations:* fishing, sketching. *Address:* Briglands, Rumbling Bridge, Kinross-shire. *Clubs:* New, Edinburgh.

Died 16 June 1944.

CLYNES, Rt Hon. John Robert; PC 1918; *b* Oldham, 27 March 1869; *m* 1893, *d* of Owen Harper. MP (Lab) Manchester (Platting Division), 1906–31 and 1935–45; Past President National Union of General and Municipal Workers, and Chairman of the Executive Council; Parliamentary Secretary Minister of Food, 1917–18; Food Controller, 1918–19; DCL Oxford and Durham, 1919; Chairman Parliamentary Labour Party, 1921–22; Lord Privy Seal and Deputy Leader of House of Commons, 1924; Secretary of State for Home Affairs, 1929–31. *Publication:* Memoirs, Vols I and II, 1937. *Address:* 41 St John's Avenue, SW15.

Died 23 Oct. 1949.

COATEN, Arthur Wells; racing correspondent (Watchman) of the Daily Telegraph and Morning Post; Editor of The Polo Monthly since 1919; *b* 4 Aug. 1879. *Educ:* Camden Collegiate School. Assistant Editor of Horse and Hound to 1910; joined the Morning Post as Racing Correspondent; in 1937 went on to the Daily Telegraph and Morning Post; many years associated with the Observer, the Bystander, the Field, etc.; served European War with the Royal Air Force. *Publications:* British Hunting; International Polo; Famous Horses of the British Turf; The Point-to-Point Calendar; contributor to The Encyclopedia of Sport; The Book of the Horse, the Lonsdale Library, etc. *Recreation:* golf. *Clubs:* Constitutional, Press; Royal Wimbledon Golf.

Died Jan. 1939.

COATES, John; tenor; *b* 29 June 1865; *s* of late Richard and Elizabeth Coates, of well known Yorkshire musical family; *m e d* of late John Hammond of Bradford; two *s* two *d. Educ:* Bradford Grammar School. First London appearance, Savoy Theatre, 1894, and for five years sang principally in comic opera and musical comedy, creating leading parts at half a dozen London theatres, and touring twice in America; came into more prominent notice by his singing in The Gay Pretenders at the Globe Theatre, 1900; first appearance at the Royal Opera, Covent Garden, 1901, when he sang Faust and created Claudio in Much Ado; first appearance in Germany at the Gürzenich Concerts in Cologne, 1901, afterwards Gewandhaus Concerts, Leipzig, and other cities; first opera appearances in Germany at Cologne, 1901, afterwards Gewandhaus Concerts, Leipzig, and other cities; first opera appearances in Germany at Cologne, 1901, as Lohengrin, Romeo, and Faust; Berlin Royal Opera House, and Hannover Royal Opera House, 1902; opera and concerts in Dresden, Hamburg, Bremen, Düsseldorf, Barmen, Frankfurt, Mannheim, etc.; Paris, 1906; Cincinnati Festival, 1906; Holland, 1910; first Festival engagement, Leeds, 1901, and has sung at all the musical festivals and principal concerts since; Covent Garden, 1902, Moody-Manners; Carl Rosa season, 1909; Beecham spring and winter seasons, 1910; Moody-Manners season at Lyric Theatre, 1907; His Majesty's production of Dr Ethel Smyth's The Wreckers, 1909; Beecham summer season at His Majesty's, 1910. Toured in opera with Moody-Manners, 1907–08; Denhof Ring performances, both Siegfrieds, 1911; Quinlan tour, United Kingdom, South Africa, and Australia, 1911–13; joined National Reserve, Aug. 1914; London, Univ. OTC Nov. 1914; commissioned April 1915; served in France (Yorkshire Regt), 1916–19 (twelve months at the Front); demobilised with rank of Capt. and resumed professional career, March 1919; developed own recitals (being one of the first to decentralise), establishing them at Chelsea Town Hall and extending them to the provinces, 1919 to end of 1924; withstood Performing Right Society's injunction action, end of 1924, judgment against him; first recitals in America, April and May 1925; second recital tour in America and across Canada, Jan.–March 1926; gave free recitals to Bradford school children, May 1928 on the 50th anniversary of his first concert appearance when 12 years of age. Address: The Coterie, Northwood, Middlesex.

Died 16 Aug. 1941.

COATES, Rt Hon. Joseph Gordon, PC 1926; MC; MP for Kaipara, NZ; Minister without portfolio and member of War Cabinet, 1940; Minister of Armed Forces and War Co-ordination, 1942; b Matakohe, NZ, 1878; e s of late Edward Coates and Eleanor, d of Dr Thomas Aickin, Auckland, NZ; m 1914, Marjorie, d of Dr W. Coles, London; five d. Educ: Matakohe Public School. Elected to House of Representatives for Kaipaira, 1911; Minister of Justice, 1919–20; Postmaster-General and Minister of Telegraphs, 1919–25; Minister of Public Works, 1920–26; Prime Minister of New Zealand, 1925–28; Minister of Railways, 1923–28; Minister of Native Affairs, 1921–28, and of External Affairs, 1928; Leader of HM Opposition, 1928–31; Minister of Public Works, Employment and Transport, Coalition Ministry, 1931–33; Minister of Finance, Customs, and Transport, 1933–35; served with New Zealand Forces in European War in France, 1917–19 (promoted Major, MC and bar). Address: Matakohe, New Zealand. Clubs: Wellington, Wellington, NZ; Northern, Auckland.

Died 27 May 1943.

COATES, Sir Leonard James, Kt 1924; partner in the firm of Blackburns, Coates & Co., chartered accountants, London, Leeds, Bradford, etc; b 30 Oct. 1883; s of George Coates, of Westbury-on-Trym, Bristol, and Elizabeth A. E. Glanfield, of Ilfracombe, Devon; m 1910, Ada Mary, y d of Thomas Newman of Clifton, Bristol; two d. Educ: Clifton College (Scholar and Member of Shooting Eight). Chartered Accountant (Honours), 1907; Chief Accountant, Allan Line, 1911;

Chief Accountant, Canadian Pacific Ocean Services, Ltd, and member of various Shipping Committees, 1915; Controller of Accounts, Ministry of Munitions, 1919; Deputy Accountant-General and Chairman of Liquidation Committee, Ministry of Munitions, 1920; Member of Liquidation Board, Disposal and Liquidation Commission, 1921; Hon. Adviser on Liquidation, 1923; Member of Council and Court of Leeds University, 1932–37; Member Royal Commission on Tithe Rent-Charge, 1934–35; North Eastern Area Meat and Livestock Officer, 1939. Recreations: tennis, golf, motoring. Address: St Mary's, Weetwood, Leeds. T: Leeds 52881 and 29631, London Metro 6913. Clubs: Athenæum; Leeds.

Died 11 July 1944.

COATH, Howell Lang L.; see Lang-Coath.

COATS, Rev. Walter William, DD, JP; Minister of Brechin Cathedral since 1901; Hon. Chaplain, Territorial Force; b Glasgow, 18 June 1856; γ s of John Coats of Dykehead, MD, Glasgow, and Jane, d of John Jackson of Hall Hill, Lanarkshire; m 1888, Margaret Janet (d 1926), d of Dundas Hamilton, Glasgow; one s one d. Educ: Glasgow Academy; Glasgow University. MA 1875; Cleland and Rae Wilson Gold Medals for Theological Essays, BD, 1878. Minister of Girthon, Kirkcudbrightshire, 1880; First Charge of Brechin, 1901; Hon. Freeman of Guildry of Brechin; President, Brechin Infirmary; Pres., Brechin Savings Bank; President, Mechanics Institute, Brechin; Past-Grand Chaplain, Grand Lodge of Freemasons of Scotland; Vice-President Angus Branch, British Red Cross Society; Hon. President, Church Service Society. Publications: A Short History of Brechin Cathedral, 1903; sermons and reviews. Address: The Manse of Brechin, Angus. T: Brechin 33. Clubs: University, Edinburgh.

Died 21 June 1941.

COATSWORTH, Emerson; KC 1907; b Toronto, 9 March 1854; s of Emerson Coatsworth, for thirty years City Commissioner of Toronto; m 1883, Helen, d of late John Robertson, De Cew Falls, Ontario; two s two d. Educ: Toronto Public Schools; Br. Am. Com. College; Upper Canada Law School, and Toronto University. Called to Bar, 1879; MP (Conservative), East Toronto, 1891–96; Alderman for Ward 2, 1904 and 1905; Mayor of Toronto, 1906 and 1907; KC 1908; Junior Judge, 1914–19, Senior Judge, 1919–29, of the County Court of the County of York; retired, 1929; Senior Magistrate for Toronto; retired, 1934 and resumed law practice; United Church Temperance man, Mason. Address: Corner May Street and May Square, Toronto. TA: Coatsworth. T: Randolph 2676, Adelaide 2845. Clubs: Albany, Royal Canadian Yacht, Thornhill Golf and Country, Toronto; Golf and Country, Bala.

Died 11 May 1943.

COBB, Lt-Col (temp. Brig.) Charles, CIE 1946; CBE 1921; OBE 1919; Indian Army, retd; b 20 Aug. 1884. Entered Indian Army, 1905; Capt. 1913; Major, 1919; Lt-Col 1930; served NW Frontier of India, 1908 (medal and clasp); European War, 1914–19 (despatches, OBE); Waziristan, 1920–21 (CBE); retired, 1932. Address: Royal Bombay Yacht Club, Bombay.

Died 10 April 1947.

COBB, Frederick Arthur, MP (Lab) Elland Div. of W Yorks, 1945–50, Brighouse and Spenborough, since 1950; AIEE; Member of Institute of Radio Engineers (USA); radio engineer and industrial manager; b 11 Feb. 1901. Served in Merchant Navy during European War, 1918. Address: House of Commons, SW1.

Died 27 March 1950.

COBB, Henry Venn, CSI 1913; CIE, 1910; CBE 1919; MA, LLM Cantab; ICS (retired); b 1864; 4th s of late Rev. Clement F. Cobb, MA; unmarried. Educ: King's School, Canterbury; Trinity College, Cambridge. Appointed to Indian Civil Service, 1885; arrived India,

1886; served as Assistant Collector, Head Assistant Collector, Sub-Collector, Under-Sec. to Govt, Deputy Director Land Records, Deputy Commissioner, Salt and Abkari under Madras Government till 1895; Assistant Resident, Mysore; Assistant Commissioner and Commissioner, Ajmer, 1895–97; Assistant Resident, Kashmir, 1899–1900; Resident, Jaipur, 1900–03; Gwalior, 1904–07; Jodhpur and Western Rajputana States, 1908; officiating as the Agent to the Governor-General for Central India, 1909; Resident, Baroda, 1909–12; Kashmir, 1914–15; Resident Mysore and Chief Commissioner of Coorg, 1916–20. *Recreations:* shooting, golf, travelling. *Address:* 1 St James's Street, Pall Mall, SW1. *T:* Whitehall 8269. *Clubs:* East India and Sports, Thatched House.

Died 26 Nov. 1949.

COBB, John William, CBE 1919; Hon. DSc; FRIC; Professor Emeritus University of Leeds; Dean of the Technological Faculty, 1920–22; Pro-Vice-Chancellor, 1925–29; Hon. Member Institution of Gas Engineers, Coke Oven Managers' Association, North British Association of Gas Managers; William Young Memorial Lecturer, 1918; Hon. Secretary, Joint Research Committees of the University of Leeds with the Institution of Gas Engineers and the National Benzole Association; *b* Leeds, Yorks, 6 Feb. 1873; *s* of James Cobb; *m* 1920, Alice, *d* of John Eadie, Paisley; two *d*. *Educ:* Modern School, Leeds; University of Leeds. Chemist to Farnley Iron Company, 1892–1901; Technical Assistant to Managing Director (FICo.), 1901–12; Livesey Professor of Coal Gas and Fuel Industries, University of Leeds, 1912–38; Deputy Inspector of High Explosives, Ministry of Munitions, during European War. *Publications:* papers in Trans. Inst. Gas Eng., Jl Chem. Soc., Jl Ceram. Soc., Edinburgh Review, Jl Soc. Chem. Ind, Jl Soc. Glass Tech., etc. *Address:* 7 Ashwood Villas, Headingley, Leeds. *T:* 52037.

Died 25 Nov. 1950.

COBB, Rev. William Frederick G.; *see* Geikie-Cobb.

COBBE, Hon. John George; JP; *b* Ireland; *s* of Richard Cobbe; *m* Frances Amelia (*d* 1935), *d* of Richard Elders, Philipstown, Ireland; two *s* one *d*. MP for Oroua, New Zealand, 1928–38, for Manawatu, 1938–43; Minister of Marine and Minister of Immigration, New Zealand, 1928–30; Minister of Industries and Commerce, 1928–29; Minister of Defence, 1929–35; also of Justice, Police and Prisons, 1930–35; and Minister of Marine, 1931–35. *Address:* 38 West Street, Feilding, New Zealand.

Died 29 Dec. 1944.

COBBETT, Louis, MD (Camb.), FRCS (England); retired; *b* 1862; 3rd *s* of late Arthur Cobbett of Weybridge. *Educ:* Lancing Coll.; Trin. Coll., Camb.; St Thomas's Hospital, London. Demonstrator of Pathology, Cambridge Univ.; John Lucas Walker Student of Pathology; Scientific Investigator to Royal Commission on Tuberculosis; Lecturer on Bacteriology, University of Cambridge, 1907–29; late Professor of Pathology, Sheffield University. *Publication:* The Causes of Tuberculosis, 1917, etc. *Address:* Inch-ma-home, Adams Road, Cambridge. *T:* 2887.

Died 9 March 1947.

COBBOLD, Herbert St George, CBE 1920; JP; member of Ipswich and East Suffolk War Pensions Committees; *m* 1909, Evelyn Anna, *d* of late John Patteson Cobbold. *Address:* The Rookery, Sproughton, Ipswich.

Died 23 Nov. 1944.

COBBOLD, Lt-Col John Murray; DL, JP; rejoined Scots Guards, 1939; Chairman Cobbold & Co. Ltd; Director Liverpool & London & Globe and Central Insurance Cos; *b* 1897; *s* of late John Dupuis Cobbold and of Lady Evelyn Cobbold; *m* 1919, Lady Blanche Cavendish, 2nd *d* of 9th Duke of Devonshire; two *s* two

d. *Educ:* Eton. Sheriff of Suffolk, 1934. *Address:* Glemham Hall, Woodbridge, Suffolk. *Clubs:* Turf, White's.

Died June 1944.

COBDEN, Lt-Col George Gough, CBE 1921 (OBE 1919); late 9th Lancers; *b* 2 Aug. 1878. Entered Army, 1898; Lt-Col 1920; served European War, 1914–19 (despatches, OBE); Sudan, 1920–21 (CBE) retired pay, 1924. *Address:* Grove, Fethard, Co. Tipperary. *Clubs:* Army and Navy; Kildare Street (Dublin).

Died 14 Aug. 1949.

COBHAM, 9th Viscount *cr* 1718; **John Cavendish Lyttelton,** KCB *cr* 1942 (CB 1937); KStJ; Baron Lyttelton, 1756 (renewed 1794); Baron Westcote, 1776; Bt 1618, KCB 1942 (CB 1937); KStJ; MFH; Lord-Lieutenant, County and City of Worcester, since 1923; Chairman of Worcestershire Standing Joint Committee, since 1927; *b* 23 Oct. 1881; *e s* of 8th Viscount and Hon. Mary Susan Caroline Cavendish (*d* 1937), *d* of 2nd Baron Chesham; *S* father, 1922; *m* 1908, Violet, *y d* of Charles Leonard; one *s* three *d*. Lieut Rifle Brig., 1901–08; ADC and Assistant Private Secretary to High Commissioner of South Africa, 1905–08; served South Africa, 1902 (medal with three clasps); MP (U) Droitwich Division Worcestershire, 1910–16; Parliamentary Under-Secretary of State for War, 1939–40; served European War, 1914–17, with Worcestershire Yeomanry, Gallipoli, Egypt, Sinai, Palestine (despatches); Bt Col commanding 100th Field Brigade RA (TA) 1925–31; Hon. Col 53rd Air Landing Light Regt RA (Worcs Yeo.); Chairman of Council of Country Territorial Associations since 1942; Chairman of Malvern College and Bromsgrove School Governors; President MCC, 1935; Treasurer MCC since 1938; Order of the Golden Treasure (Japan). Owns about 6000 acres. Hagley Hall Picture Gallery. Pictures by Vandyck, Mirevelt, Lely, Van Somer, Reynolds, etc. *Heir: s* Acting Lt-Col Hon. Charles John Lyttelton, RA [*b* 8 Aug. 1909; *m* 1942, Elizabeth Alison, *yr d* of J. R. Makeig-Jones, Southern House, near Ottery St Mary, Devon; two *s* one *d*]. *Address:* Hagley Hall, Stourbridge. *Club:* Brooks's.

Died 31 July 1949.

COBORN, Charles, (Colin Whitton McCallum); member of Variety profession and star comedian since 1879; *b* 4 Aug. 1852; *s* of Colin McCallum, shipbroker and Freeman, City of London, and Frances Whitton; *m* 1882, Ellen Stockley (*d* 1941); four *s* three *d*. *Educ:* private school. Commercial life in City, 1866–71; first salaried engagement as music-hall artist, 1872; first pantomime, Sandgate, 1875; after three weeks' busking, started regular tours North of England and Midlands, Scotland and Ireland, 1877; first engagement at the Middlesex, then the Oxford, 1879; first London pantomime, Alexandra Palace, 1879–80; pantomime with Mrs Sarah Lane, at the Britannia, 1881; first efforts on behalf of musichall professionals, federation, co-operation and benevolence, 1880–82; first London Pavilion engagement, 1880; wrote and produced Two Lovely Black Eyes, 1886; Jack and the Beanstalk, Sadler's Wells, 1887; produced Man who broke the Bank at Monte Carlo, 1891; engaged by Sir Augustus Harris for the Palace Theatre, The Sleeper Awakened, 1883; musichall engagement Palace Theatre, break and litigation, 1894; visited Canada and United States, 1900; joined Volunteer Civil Force (VCF) entertained everywhere in huts, hospitals, camps, etc., 1915 onwards; film, The Man who broke the Bank at Monte Carlo, at Monte Carlo, 1919; began first long-distance walk to Land's End, 17 March 1921; 2nd, to Glasgow; 4th, to John o' Groats; fourteen in all; has been music publisher, concert party proprietor, agent, editor newspaper correspondent; once member of Press, Club for nine years; Church sidesman and lay-reader; film actor; BBC artiste; long-distance walker. *Publication:* The Man who broke the Bank (autobiography), 1928. *Recreations:* walking, reading, church service, rummy. *Address:* 27

Elgin Mansions, W9. *TA:* Chascobo, London. *T:* Cunningham 2349. *Club:* Paddington Bowling and Sports.

Died 23 Nov. 1945.

COCHIN, HM Maharaja Sir Sri Rama Varma, Maharaja of, GCIE 1935; LLD; *b* 30 Dec. 1861; *S* 1932. *Address:* Cochin, Madras States, S India.

Died April 1941.

COCHIN, HH Maharaja Sri Sir Kerala Varma, Maharaja of, GCIE 1943. *Address:* Cochin, Madras States, S India.

Died 13 Oct. 1943.

COCHRANE, Alfred; *b* 1865; 2nd *s* of Rev. David C. Cochrane, MA, Master of Etwall Hospital, Derbyshire; *m* 1895, Ethel, MBE, *y d* of Sir Andrew Noble, 1st Bt. *Educ:* Repton School; Hertford College, Oxford (BA 1888, MA 1891). Contested Tyneside division of Northumberland, 1910; a member of the River Tyne Commission, 1912–27; Governor of Repton School, 1921–44. *Publications:* The Kestrel's Nest, 1894; Leviore Plectro, 1896; Told in the Pavilion, 1896; Collected Verses, 1903; The Sweeper of the Leaves, 1908; Later Verses, 1918; Records of the Harlequins, 1930; many verses and articles for newspapers and magazines. *Recreations:* once cricket (Oxford Eleven, 1885, 1886, and 1888), shooting, fishing, and golf. *Address:* Elm Hurst, Batheaston, Somersetshire.

Died 14 Dec. 1948.

COCHRANE, Dame Anne Annette Minnie, DCVO 1938; Lady in Waiting to Princess Beatrice; *d* of late Admiral of the Fleet, Sir Thomas Cochrane. *Address:* Coolrath, Talbot Avenue, Bournemouth. *T:* Winton 2285.

Died 6 Jan. 1943.

COCHRANE, Helen Lavinia, RI; member of Society of Women Artists and of Tempera Society; *b* Bath; *d* of Henry Shaw, lawyer, and Marion Selby Hele; *m* W. Percy Cochrane. *Educ:* Liverpool School of Art; Westminster; Munich. Painter in water-colour, oil, and tempera; Exhibitions, Fine Art Society, Ltd; exhibited RA, RI; WAG, Liverpool; Laing Art Co., Newcastle-upon-Tyne, and under Duveen Scheme and elsewhere; Member of the Lega Artisti Stranieri of Italy; Directrice Hospital Entente Cordiale No. 222, 1915–16; Directrice Military Hospital, Sarzana, 1916–18; gold medal CR Française, Reconnaissance française, etc. *Address:* 9 Hurlingham Court, SW6. *Club:* Albemarle.

Died 17 Nov. 1946.

COCHRANE, Brig.-Gen. James Kilvington, CMG 1918; *b* 2 July 1873; *s* of Thomas Cochrane, Stapleford Abbotts, Romford; *m* 1904, Edith Brandon, *d* of H. W. Poor, 777 Madison Avenue, New York City; one *s* three *d. Educ:* Bedford; RMC Sandhurst. Joined Leinster Regt 1893; took part in the expedition to Bida and Kontagora, Northern Nigeria, 1901; psc, 1908; served European War as GSOI 55th (West Lancashire) Div., and subsequently commanded 61st Light Infantry Bde (despatches five times, Bt Lt-Col 1916, Bt Col 1917, CMG); retired with hon. rank of Brig.-Gen., 1920. *Recreations:* golf, shooting. *Club:* United Service.

Died 29 Dec. 1948.

COCHRANE, Sir Stanley Herbert, 1st Bt *cr* 1915; late 7th Batt. Royal Dublin Fusiliers; *b* 19 Sept. 1877; 4th *s* of Sir Henry Cochrane, 1st Bt, and *brother* of Sir E. C. Cochrane. 2nd Bt, High Sheriff of County Wicklow, 1911; of Co. Dublin, 1912; MA Trinity College, Dublin; DL, JP Co. Dublin; JP Co. Wicklow. *Heir:* none. *Address:* Woodbrook, Bray, Co. Wicklow; Mill House, Uggeshall, Beccles, Suffolk. *Clubs:* Bath; University (Dublin); Royal St George's Yacht (Kingstown).

Died 23 Oct. 1949 (ext).

COCHRANE, Col Thomas Henry, MVO 1904; OBE 1919; *b* 22 Dec. 1867; *m* 1909, Jean, *d* of W. Wilkin Lumb, Meadow House, Whitehaven. Entered RE 1888; Captain, 1898; Major, 1906; Lt-Col 1914; Colonel, 1918; Inspector of Iron Structures, War Office, 1905–09; DCE Scottish Command, 1920; Chief Engineer, London District, 1921; retired, 1923; MIME, MIAE. *Address:* 28 Buckingham Terrace, Edinburgh. *Clubs:* Army and Navy, Royal Automobile.

Died 29 Nov. 1950.

COCK, F. William, MD, MS; Physician and Anæsthetist; retired; *b* 1858; *s* of Frederick Cock, MD, MRCP, London; *m* 1898, Frances L. (*d* 1937), *d* of late Alfred Evans, of Exeter; one *s. Educ:* University College School; University College, London; University, Durham. MRCS 1883; MB and MS Durham; 1st class hons 1884; MD 1886. Late Hon. Anæsthetist to the King George Hosp.; Member and Past Pres., Harveian Soc. of London; Member of Apothecaries Society; FSA; Member of Council of Kent Archæological Society; JP Kent; medallist in Physiology and Chemistry, University College; late anæsthetist, Dental School, Guy's Hospital. *Publications:* various papers on Antiquarian, Medical and General Subjects. *Recreation:* is collecting materials for local history in Kent. *Address:* The Well House, Appledore, Kent. *TA:* Appledore, Kent. *T:* Appledore 32.

Died 9 Oct. 1943.

COCKBURN, Col Charles Douglas L.; *see* Learoyd-Cockburn.

COCKBURN, Sir James Stanhope, 10th Bt of that Ilk, 1671; *b* 11 Nov. 1867; *s* of 8th Bt and Mary Ann Francis, *d* of R. K. Elliot, Harwood and Clifton, Roxburghshire; *S* brother, 1938; *m* 1928, Ethel, *e d* of late Lord Francis Cecil and *widow* of Major E. Hawkshaw. Served S African War; Captain on the Embarkation Staff, 1915–18. *Heir:* *b* Lt-Col John Brydges Cockburn, DSO. *Address:* Pennoxstone Court, Herefordshire.

Died 1 April 1947.

COCKBURN, Lt-Col Sir John Brydges, 11th Bt of that ilk, 1671; DSO 1918; late Royal Welch Fusiliers; *b* 1870; *y s* of Sir Edward Cockburn, 8th Bt; *S* brother, 1947; *m* 1919, Isabel Hunter, *y d* of late James McQueen of Crofts, Stewartry of Kirkcudbright; one *s* one *d. Educ:* Cheltenham College. Served in Lagos Hinterland, 1898 (medal with clasp); Munshi Expedition, 1900 (clasp, despatches); South African War, 1901–02, including operation in Transvaal and ORC (medal 5 clasps); served in Nigeria, 1906; action against Sokoto rebels (medal and clasp); served in Cameroon Campaign, 1914–16 (despatches, Bt of Lt-Col, Officer Légion d'Honneur, 1914–15 Star); served in BEF France, 1916–18 (DSO, despatches twice, twice severely wounded); retired pay, 1923; awarded Silver Medal Royal Humane Society. *Recreations:* shooting, fishing. *Heir:* *s* John Elliot, *b* 7 Dec. 1925. *Address:* Merrivale Place, Ross on Wye, Herefordshire.

Died 2 May 1949.

COCKERAM, William Henry, CBE 1920; OBE 1919; *b* 1857. Principal District Officer, Survey Staff, Board of Trade, Glasgow; retired, 1921. *Address:* Rosebank, Beechgrove, Moffat, Dumfriesshire.

Died 27 Feb. 1946.

COCKERELL, Douglas Bennett, MBE, RDI; Partner Douglas Cockerell and Son, Bookbinders; Teacher, Royal College of Art at Ambleside, retired 1944; *b* 1870; *s* of Sydney John Cockerell, Beckenham, Kent; *m* 1st, 1898, Florence Arundel (*d* 1912); two *s* one *d*; 2nd, 1914, Bessie Marion Gilford, MB. *Educ:* St Paul's School. In Canada, mostly in the Imperial Bank of Canada, 1885–90; working at Bookbinding with T. J. Cobden-Sanderson, 1893–98; set up on own account, 1898, first in London and then in Ewell; Controller of W. H. Smith and Son's binding workshops, 1904;

Ministry of Munitions, 1914, afterwards printing adviser to Imperial War Graves Commission; Teacher for LCC Central School of Arts and Crafts; Lecturer to School of Librarianship, University College, Gower Street; Repaired and bound the Codex Sinaiticus at the British Museum. *Publications:* Bookbinding and the Care of Books, 1901; Some notes of Bookbinding, 1929; Bookbinding as a School Subject. *Recreation:* gardening. *Address:* 298 Norton Way, Letchworth, Herts. *TA:* Letchworth. *T:* Letchworth 35. *Club:* Authors.

Died 25 Nov. 1945.

COCKERLINE, Sir Walter Herbert, Kt 1922; *b* 1856; *m* 1st, Mary Ann Vivian (*d* 1928); one *s* one *d*; 2nd, 1930, Mary Emily, *widow* of Rev. E. J. Carrington. Ex-Sheriff of the City of Hull; member of the Council of the North of England Shipowners' Association. *Address:* Hartford House, Filey Road, Scarborough.

Died 13 Feb. 1941.

COCKRAM, George, RI 1913; RCA; Member of Manchester Academy; *b* 9 March 1861; *s* of William Cockram, coachbuilder, Leicester; *m* 1890, Lucy Mary, *d* of J. H. Cole, RCA; two *d*. *Educ:* Liverpool schools; School of Art, Liverpool Institute. Exhibited first picture at Royal Academy at age of 18; adopted water-colour as his medium, and has been a frequent exhibitor of drawings at the RA, RI, and principal provincial galleries, his subjects being general landscape, mountains as seen above the tree line, shore and sea, and of late Venetian studies; his large water colour Solitude was purchased by the trustees under the terms of the Chantry Bequest, 1892; other works are to be found in the Corporation permanent collections of Liverpool, Oldham, Hull, Birkenhead, Dudley, Stretford, Bournemouth, Wellington, NZ, Hobart. *Address:* Noddfa, Rhosneigr, Anglesey. *Clubs:* Artists, Wayfarers (Liverpool).

Died 27 Sept. 1950.

COCKS, Hon. Sir Arthur Alfred Clement, KBE 1923; Managing Director, Arthur Cocks & Co., Ltd; *b* Victoria, 27 May 1862; *s* of Thomas Cocks; *m* 1886, Elizabeth Agnes (*d* 1936), *d* of Charles Gibb, Richmond, NSW; one *d*. Lord Mayor of Sydney, 1912–13; MLA St Leonards, 1910–20, North Shore, 1920–25; Colonial Treasurer, NS Wales, 1922–25; Agent-General for the State of NSW 1925; President of Sydney YMCA, 1924–34. *Address:* Kulnura, Cross Street, Mosman, NSW. *T:* XM 1130.

Died 24 April 1943.

COCKSHUTT, Col Hon. Henry, LLD; Chairman and Chief Executive, Cockshutt Plow Company, Ltd, Brantford, Ontario, Frost & Wood Co. Ltd, Smith's Falls, Ontario; Chairman Cockshutt Moulded Aircraft Ltd, Brantford; Director of the Bank of Montreal, Canadian Pacific Railway Co., Royal Trust Co.; Lake Erie and Northern Railway Co., Bell Telephone Co. of Canada, Gypsum Lime and Alabastine, Canada, Ltd (Chairman), International Nickel Co. of Canada, Ltd and the Guarantee Company of North America; Member of Canadian Advisory Board of Sun Insurance Co. of London; *b* Brantford, Ont, 8 July 1868; *s* of Ignatius Cockshutt and Elizabeth Foster; *m* Isabelle Rolls (*d* 1944); two *d*. *Educ:* Brantford Public and High Schools. Hon. LLD Toronto Univ. and Univ. of Western Ontario; organised 215th Bn 1916, as Lt-Col in command; retired from active list, 1926, with title of Hon. Col; Past-Pres. Canadian Manufacturers' Association, 1906–07; Lieut-Governor of Ontario, 1921–27; Governor Trinity College, Toronto, Ontario; Chancellor of the University of Western Ontario, London, Ont; Vice-President, Canadian Board of the Dr Barnardo's Homes; Governor, Victorian Order of Nurses for Canada. *Address:* Brantford, Ontario, Canada.

Clubs: Brantford; National, York, Toronto; Mount Royal, Montreal; Rideau, Ottawa; Manitoba, Winnipeg.

Died 26 Nov. 1944.

CODE, Rev. Canon George Brereton; Canon Residentiary of Carlisle Cathedral since 1933; *b* 24 Aug. 1886; *s* of George Code and Phœbe Roberts. *Educ:* Monkton Combe School; Pembroke College, Cambridge; Bishop's Hostel, Bishop Auckland. Deacon, 1910; Priest, 1912; Curate, St Oswald, West Hartlepool, 1910–14; Birmingham Cathedral, 1914–19; Warden, Birmingham Boys' and Girls' Union, 1914–23; Vicar, St Bartholomew, Birmingham, 1919–27; Maryport, 1927–33; Member of Archbishops' Evangelistic Committee from 1936. *Publications:* War and the Citizen, 1917; A Religion for Everyman, 1925; A Cathedral College of Clergy, 1944. *Recreation:* music. *Address:* The Abbey, Carlisle.

Died 21 Sept. 1946.

CODLING, Sir William (Richard), Kt 1935; CB 1926; CVO 1921; CBE 1918; MVO 1914; Controller HM Stationery Office, 1919–42; Member of the Statute Law Committee; Chairman of Advisory Committee of London School of Printing; Member of Advisory Committee of School of Photo-Engraving and Lithography; *b* 5 April 1879; *m*; one *d*. *Educ:* The Grammar School, Enfield; King's College, London. *Club:* Union.

Died 28 March 1947.

CODRINGTON, Lt-Gen. Sir Alfred Edward, GCVO 1936; KCB 1921; KCVO 1911; CB 1904; CVO 1905; Grand Officer of the Legion of Honour; Knight Grand Cross of the Redeemer of Greece; *b* 4 May 1854; 2nd *s* of General Sir Wm J. Codrington; *m* 1885, Adela Harriet, CBE 1920 (*d* 1935), *d* of Melville Portal of Laverstoke and Lady Charlotte, *d* of 2nd Earl of Minto; three *s* one *d*. *Educ:* Harrow. Entered Coldstream Guards, 1873; Lieut-Col 1898; served Egyptian War, 1882, including Kassassin and Tel-el-Kebir (despatches, medal with clasp, 5th class Medjidie, Khedive's star); served S Africa, 1899–1900 and 1901–02 (twice wounded, despatches; Queen's medal 3 clasps, King's medal 2 clasps; Brevet Col); commanded 1st London Division, Territorial Force, 1908–09; General Officer Commanding London District, 1909–13; Military Secretary to Secretary of State for War, Aug. to Oct. 1914; commanded an army, Central Force, Home Defence, 30 Oct. 1914–31 March 1916; Colonel of the Coldstream Guards, 1918. *Publications:* Responsibility in the Army; (with Sir Edward Parry) War Pensions, past and present. *Address:* 110 Eaton Square, SW1. *T:* Sloane 1590; Preston Hall, Uppingham, Rutland. *T:* Uppingham 43; (War Address: The Bay House, Preston, Uppingham, Rutland. *T:* Manton 240).

Died 12 Sept. 1945.

COFFEY, Dr Denis Joseph, MA, MB, BCh; LLD (Hon. Causâ) Dublin and Belfast Univs.; DSc (Hon. Causâ) National Univ. Ireland. *Educ:* Catholic University Coll.; Medical School, Dublin (Honours in Arts and Medicine); University Studentship in Biology, 1889. Formerly Professor of Physiology, Catholic University School of Medicine, Dublin; late Fellow of the Royal Univ.; worked in University Laboratories at Louvain, Marburg, Leipzig, Madrid, etc.; served in the Royal Commission on Trinity College and University of Dublin, 1906; Member of Dublin Commissioners, Irish Universities Act, 1908; Pres. Univ. Coll. Dublin, 1908–40; Representative of the National Univ. of Ireland on the General Medical Council since 1921; Chevalier de la Légion d'honneur; Kt Grand Cross Papal Order of St Silvester. *Address:* 136 Sandford Road, Clonskeagh, Dublin.

Died 3 April 1945.

COFFEY, Rev. Peter, PhD, STLBCL; Professor of Logic and Metaphysics, Maynooth College, Ireland; *b* Rathrone, Co. Meath, 1876. *Educ:* Baconstown National School; Trim Model School; Meath Diocesan Seminary of Navan. Entered Maynooth College for the Diocese of Meath, 1894; priest, 1900; continued theological studies for degrees during two years in the Dunboyne establishment there; Professor of Philosophy, 1902; studied philosophy at the Philosophical Institute in the University of Louvain (PhD 1905); since then occupied exclusively in professional work. *Publications:* Translations of Professor De Wulf's Scholasticism Old and New, 1907, and History of Medieval Philosophy, 1909; The Science of Logic, 2 vols, 1912; Ontology, 1914; Epistemology, 2 vols, 1917; articles on philosophical subjects in the Irish Ecclesiastical Record, the Irish Theological Quarterly, and the Catholic Encyclopedia. *Address:* Maynooth College, Ireland.

Died 7 Jan. 1943.

COFMAN-NICORESTI, Carol Adolph, BèsLettèsSc, MPS, FRSM; Managing-Director of Solidol Chemical Ltd, Director of Société Française du Lysol, Solidol S/A, and Solidol Gmbh; on the Trade Marks Committee, and also Poison Law Committee, British Chemical Manufacturers; on Boycott Council of German goods and services; *b* Nicoresti, Moldavia, Sept. 1881; *s* of Alter Moise Cofman-Nicoresti and Gisella Witling; *m* 1914, Beatrice Winchcombe; four *d*. *Educ:* Lycée Codreanu; London South College; King's College; St Thomas' Medical School. Founded literary paper Aurora at sixteen; came to London 1899; studied chemistry, pharmacy, medicine; while engaged in retail, research, and manufacturing business obtained patents for solidification of Lysol (Lysolats) also solidification of volatile oils, turpentine, etc., and for various medical, chemical, and hygienic appliances, also patent for preservation of mushrooms; contributed to scientific and lay press as book reviewer, translator and original articles; chief subject is the study of energy, constitution of matter, truth in history, trying to teach scientists logic; lawyers, law, and journalists how not to divulge anything they may have discovered during the exercise of thier professional duty; Hannen Swaffer calls him a Modern Galileo; Sir Richard Gregory maintains that he belongs to the times of Lavoisier, Boyle, and Mayow; predicted eight years beforehand that Lord Rutherford will completely change his views on the destruction of the atom as a source of energy, and Lord Rutherford did so. *Publications:* Universal Manufacturer, Energology; Monographies on Combustion; Constitution of Matter; Catalysis; Hidden Corners in Chemistry; Food; Chemistry in the XXth Century; Energology; Stovaine; Roumanian Petroleum; Adsorption Volatile Oils and Fatty Acids; Heat; Telepathy, etc. *Recreations:* enjoys a good meal and good wine, his own jokes, and a long walk. *Club:* London streets.

Died 27 April 1938.

COGHILL, Col Charles Edward, CMG 1917; Royal Field Artillery; *b* 28 Sept. 1861; 4th *s* of late H. Coghill, Brampton Tree House, Newcastle, Staffordshire; *m* 1909, Charlotte Blanche (*d* 1940), *y d* of John Tayleur, Buntingsdale, Market Drayton; two *d* one *s*. *Educ:* Cheltenham College; RMA, Woolwich. Commissioned in Royal Artillery, 1881; served S African War, 1899–1902 (Bt Lt-Col, despatches, two medals and seven clasps); Bt Col 1906; retired, 1911; recalled 5 Aug. 1914; retired, Jan. 1919 (despatches, CMG). *Recreations:* hunting, shooting. *Address:* Tern Hill, Market Drayton. *TA:* Tern Hill Hall. *T:* Tern Hill 208. *Club:* Naval and Military.

Died 11 Nov. 1948.

COGHILL, Rev. Canon Ernest Arthur, MA; Vicar of Holy Trinity, Southwell, since 1890; Hon. Canon of Southwell, since 1929; *b* 1859; *s* of late Harry Coghill, of Brampton Tree House, Newcastle-under-Lyme; *m* Helen Agnes, *e d* of William Henry Chalk, Redhill; two

s four *d*. *Educ:* Cheltenham College; Trinity Hall, Cambridge; read with Dean Vaughan at the Temple and Llandaff, 1882–83. Curate of All Saints, Pontefract, and of Halesowen. *Address:* Holy Trinity Vicarage, Southwell. *T:* 59. *Club:* United University.

Died 4 Feb. 1941.

COHAN, George (Michael); comedian, playwright, and producer; *b* Providence, RI, 4 July 1878; *s* of Jerry John Cohan and Helen Frances Costigan; *m* 1st, Ethel Levy, actress; 2nd, 1908, Agnes Nolan, Boston. First appearance, Haverstraw, NY, at nine years of age, in Daniel Boone; appeared in Peck's Bad Boy, 1890; later in vaudeville, in The Four Cohans; starred in Little Johnny Jones, 1904–06; in George Washington, Jr, 1906–07. *Publications:* (plays) The Wise Guy; The Governor's Son (3–act comedy); Running for Office; Little Johnny Jones, 1904; Forty-five Minutes from Broadway, 1905; George Washington, Jr, 1906; Popularity, 1906; The Talk of New York; Fifty Miles from Boston, 1907; The Man who Owns Broadway, 1908; The Yankee Prince, 1909; Get-Rich-Quick Wallingford, 1910; The Little Millionaire, 1911; Seven Keys to Baldpate, 1913; Hit-the-Trail Holliday, 1915; The Cohan Revue, 1916; The Cohan Revue, 1918; Baby Cyclone, 1928; many popular songs, including Over There. *Address:* George M. Cohan Productions, 227 West 45th Street, New York.

Died 5 Nov. 1942.

COHEN, Sir Benjamin Arthur, Kt 1929; KC 1914; Barrister, Inner Temple; *b* 1862; *e s* of late Rt Hon. Arthur Cohen; *m* 1890, *d* of M. Cohen. *Address:* Champions, Limpsfield, Surrey. *Club:* Oxford and Cambridge.

Died 22 Dec. 1942.

COHEN, Hannah F., OBE; Member of Council of Roedean School, Swanley Horticultural College, Society for Overseas Settlement of British Women; *b* London; *d* of Sir Benjamin Louis Cohen, Bt. *Educ:* Roedean School; Newnham College, Cambridge. *Publications:* Changing Faces, 1937; Let Stephen Speak, 1946. *Address:* Durford Heath, Petersfield, Hants. *Clubs:* University Women's, Lansdowne.

Died 21 Nov. 1946.

COHEN, Brig. Hon. Harold Edward, CMG 1918; CBE 1934; DSO 1917; VD; Australian Artillery; Deputy Adjutant-General, Aust. Mil. Forces, since 1943; solicitor; *b* Melbourne, 25 Nov. 1881; *o s* of late Montagu Cohen. *Educ:* St Xavier's College, Kew, Melbourne; Melbourne University. Served European War (despatches, CMG, DSO); MLC, Victoria, 1929–35; MLA for Caulfield, Victoria, 1935–43; Minister of Public Instruction and Solicitor-General, 1935; Asst Minister of Railways 1932–35; Commissioner in Middle East representing Australian Red Cross Society, 1940–42; Director of Army Amenities, Australian Army, 1942–43; President Melbourne Rotary Club, 1926–27; President Legacy Club, 1924–25; Pres. Constitutional Club, 1926–27; President Boy Scouts Assoc. of Victoria, 1923–45. *Address:* Collins House, Collins Street, Melbourne.

Died Oct. 1946.

COHEN, Hon. Henry Isaac, KC (Victoria, 1920), (Tasmania, 1925); BA, LLB; *b* Melbourne, Victoria, 21 Feb. 1872; *s* of David Cohen and Rachel Marks, both of London; *m* 1901, Ethel Mary, *d* of Philip Tobyn Keon, Launceston, Tasmania; three *s* two *d*. *Educ:* Scotch College, Melbourne (Dux): University of Melbourne, BA 1893; LLB 1895. Admitted to Bar, 1896; Leader of Victorian and Tasmanian Bars; Representative of Melbourne Province in Legislative Council, 1921–37; unofficial Leader of Legislative Council, 1922–23, 1924–28 and 1935–37; Hon. Minister, 1923; Minister of Public Works, Minister of Mines, Attorney-General, Solicitor-General, 1924; Minister of Public Instruction and Leader of Legislative Council, Victoria, Australia, 1928–29; Minister of Water Supply and Minister in charge of Electrical Undertakings, Victoria, 1935. *Recreations:* bowls, golf. *Address:* 64 Selborne Chambers, Chancery Lane, Melbourne, C1, Australia. *Clubs:* Public Schools, Melbourne.

Died 20 Dec. 1942.

COHEN, Col Jacob Waley, CMG 1919; CBE 1926; DSO 1916; late Royal Corps of Signals, TA; *b* 1874; *s* of late Nathaniel Louis Cohen, and *d* of Jacob Waley, MA; *m* 1st, 1897, Katharine, (*d* 1924), 4th *d* of late Rt Hon. Arthur Cohen, KC; one *s* one *d*; 2nd, 1934, Evelyn, *d* of Lt-Col H. M. A. Hales and *widow* of Comdr. N. Grabowsky Atherstone, AFC, RN. *Educ:* Clifton College; Merton College, Oxford. Joined Queen's Westminster Rifle Volunteers, 1893; served South African War, 1900, with City of London Imperial Volunteers (CIV), first as Signal Officer, then as Brigade Signalling Officer, 21st Infantry Brigade (despatches medal, and four clasps); European War with Queen's Westminster Rifles and Army Signals 1914–19 (despatches, CMG, DSO, Croix de Guerre). Army Welfare Officer, Eastern Command, 1940–45. *Address:* Shalford Cottage, Garden Close, Watford. *T:* Watford 4538. *Club:* Junior Army and Navy.

Died 12 July 1948.

COHEN, Sir Samuel Sydney, Kt 1937; JP; Chairman of Directors of David Cohen & Co. Pty Ltd, J. A. Bull & Co. Ltd, Paul & Gray Ltd, Newcastle and Hunter River S. S. Co. Ltd, Commonwealth Investments Pty Ltd; Director of Tooth & Co. Ltd, Central Trading Co. Pty Ltd, Royal Exchange of Sydney; *b* Sydney, 11 March 1869; *e s* of George Judah Cohen, merchant, Sydney, and Rebecca Levy; *m* 1901, Elma (*d* 1946), *d* of Alfred D. Hart, Melbourne; two *s* one *d*. *Educ:* Royston College. Vice-Pres., British Orphans' Adoption Soc., Council of Social Services of NSW; Trustee, Queens' Jubilee Fund; Silver Jubilee Medal, 1935; Coronation Medal, 1937. *Recreation:* reading. *Address:* 89 Ocean St, Woollahra, NSW. *T:* FB1576. *Clubs:* Devonshire; New South Wales, Royal Sydney Yacht Squadron (Sydney); Newcastle (NSW).

Died 27 Aug. 1948.

COIT, Stanton; Minister of the Ethical Church, London; Founder Moral Education League; *b* Columbus, Ohio, 11 Aug. 1857; *s* of Harvey and Elizabeth Greer Coit; *m* 1898, Mrs Fanny Adela Wetzlar (*d* 1932); two *d*. *Educ:* Amherst College, Massachusetts, USA; Columbia College, New York City; Berlin University. Doctor of Philosophy; preaches at the Ethical Church, Queen's Road, Bayswater, W; former head worker and founder (1886) New York University Settlement; Parliamentary Labour Candidate for Wakefield, 1910. *Publications:* National Idealism and a State Church, 1907; National Idealism and the Book of Common Prayer, 1908; The Spiritual Nature of Man, 1910; The Message of Man: a Book of Ethical Scriptures; Compiler and Editor of Social Worship, 1913; The Soul of America, 1914; English translation of N. Hartmann's Ethik, 1932. *Address:* 30 Hyde Park Gate, SW7. *TA:* Coiffames, London. *T:* Western 4993. *Club:* Bath.

Died 15 Feb. 1944.

COKE, Adm. Sir Charles Henry, KCVO 1911; *b* 2 Oct. 1854; *e s* of Rev. J. H. Coke, rector of Ropsley, Lincolnshire, and *g s* of D'Ewes Coke, JP, DL, of Brookhill Hall, Derbyshire; *m* 1883, Anna Marie Madeleine, *o c* of T. Tierney Fergusson, Chefoo, China; one *s* one *d*. *Educ:* Oundle School. Entered HMS Britannia, 1868; Midshipman of HMS Druid during Ashanti war, 1873–74; Lieut from Royal yacht, 1877; Capt., 1899; Admiral, 1917; retired, 1917; Divisional Transport Officer, Thames District, for embarkation of South African Field Force, 1899–1900; Captain of HMS Terpsichore, 1901–04; employed on west coast of Cape Colony during second phase of Boer war and landed at Lambert's Bay; Senior Naval Officer on east coast of Africa during latter part of Ogaden-Somali war and landed at Kismayu; Captain of HMS Cornwallis, Channel Fleet, 1905–07; commanded Sheerness Gunnery School, 1907–08; ADC to King Edward VII, 1907; Rear-Admiral, 1908; Vice-Admiral commanding on the coast of Ireland, 1911–15. *Address:* Hughenden, Exmouth.

Died 23 Feb. 1945.

COKE, Brig.-Gen. Edward Sacheverell D'Ewes, CMG 1915; DSO 1918; late the King's Own Scottish Borderers; *b* 3 Dec. 1872; *s* of late Maj.-Gen. J. Talbot Coke; *m* 1905, Maud, *y d* of late John A'Deane, Alderley, Glos; two *s* two *d*. Entered army, 1894; Captain, 1901; Major, 1913; Bt Lt-Col 1916; temp. Brig.-Gen.; Bt Col 1919; served Chitral, 1895 (severely wounded; medal with clasp); NW Frontier, India, 1897–98 (two clasps); European War, 1914–19 (CMG, DSO, Bt Col); retired pay, 1922. *Address:* Trusley Manor, Sutton-on-the-Hill, Derby. *Club:* United Service.

Died 17 April 1941.

COKER, Ernest George, MA Cantab, Hon. DSc (Sydney and Louvain), DSc (Edin.), FRS, FRSE, MInstCE; Member of Council of the Institution of Mechanical Engineers; Member of Royal Institution, Associate Institute of Naval Architects; Emeritus Professor of Civil and Mechanical Engineering, University of London since 1934; *b* 26 April 1869; *s* of late G. Coker, Wolverton; *m* 1899, Alice Mary (*d* 1941), *e d* of late R. King, Wolverton. Formerly Associate Professor of Civil Engineering, McGill University, Montreal; and later Professor of Civil and Mechanical Engineering in the City and Guilds of London Technical College, Finsbury; President of Section G (Mechanical Science), Australian Meeting of the British Association, 1914; awarded Gold Medal of the Institution of Naval Architects, 1911; Telford Medal InstCE, 1921; Thomas Hawksley Medal Inst. Mech. Eng., 1922; Howard N. Potts Medal Franklin Institute, 1922; Levy Medal, 1926; Howard Quinquennial Medal Inst. CE, 1932; Rumford Medal Royal Society, 1936. *Publications:* A Treatise on Photo-Elasticity (with Prof. Filon, FRS); various papers in the transactions of Royal Societies of London, Edinburgh, and Canada, Institution of Civil Engineers, Institution of Mechanical Engineers, and Institution of Naval Architects. *Recreations:* fishing and golf.

Died 9 April 1946.

COLAM, Robert Frederick; KC 1912; 3rd *s* of late John Colam, Croydon; *m* 1887, Ethel (*d* 1935), *d* of John Addison Russell of West Norwood; one *s* six *d*. Called to Bar, Middle Temple, 1884; Recorder of Croydon, 1900–39; Associate Surveyors' Institution. *Address:* The Dene, Westcott, nr Dorking. *T:* Westcott 21; 4 Essex Court, Temple, EC4. *T:* Central 0541.

Died 3 May 1942.

COLBECK, Edmund Henry, OBE 1920; MD, BC, DPH (Cantab), BA (Cantab); FRCP (London); Emeritus and Consulting Physician to the London Chest Hospital, Victoria Park, E2; Physician to the Metropolitan Dispensary, EC; Consulting Physician Harrow Hospital and to the Northwood Hospital; *b* Batley, Yorks, 1865; *s* of William Henry Colbeck; *m* Susanna Mary, *d* of Henry Winearls of King's Lynn, Norfolk; one *s* one *d*. *Educ:* Tonbridge School; Nelson and Wellington Colleges, NZ; Caius College, Cambridge. Exhibitioner in Natural Science, BA, 1887 (1st Class Honours Natural Science Tripos); University Scholar and House Physician, St Mary's Hospital; General Hospital, Vienna, 1891; Physician to the Marine and General Mutual Life Assurance Society; sometime Physician in London to Royal National Hospital for Consumption, Ventnor; Consulting Physician to the New Zealand Military Hospital, Walton-on-Thames, and to the South African Military Hospital, Richmond. Additional Examiner in

Medicine, University of Cambridge, 1911; Major (temp.) New Zealand Medical Corps. *Publications:* Diseases of the Heart (2nd edition); The Science and Art of Prescribing (2nd edition); papers to the medical journals dealing with diseases of the heart and lungs. *Address:* 55 Upper Berkeley St, Portman Sq., W1. *T:* Paddington 2600.

Died 16 Dec. 1942.

COLBORNE, Surg. Rear-Adm. William John, CB 1919; MRCS; LRCP; RN, retired; *b* 1865; *s* of William Higgs Colborne; *m* 1st, 1893, Isabel Baker (*d* 1929); 2nd, 1930, Evelina Maud Bragg. Served European War, 1914–19 (despatches, CB); Commander of Order of Crown of Italy, 1911. *Address:* 21 Marion Road, Southsea.

Died 21 June 1945.

COLCLOUGH, Rear-Adm. (S) Beauchamp Urquhart, CBE 1918; RN, retired; *b* 18 Feb. 1867; *s* of late Capt. B. Colclough, 19th Foot; *m* 1st, Amabel Mildred (*d* 1911), *d* of late Major C. G. Gooch, 93rd Foot; one *s*; 2nd, Beatrice (*d* 1945), *d* of late R. M. Pearson, Sydney, NSW; 3rd, 1948, Emily Brown. *Educ:* Portsmouth Grammar School. Entered Royal Navy, 1884; retired list, 1923; 1914–15 Star: Victory and Allies medals. *Recreation:* gardening. *Address:* Green Acre, Englefield Green, Surrey. *T:* Egham 437.

Died 5 April 1949.

COLDSTREAM, Col William Menzies, CIE 1923; late RE; retired; *b* 19 Feb. 1869; *e s* of late William Coldstream, ICS, *e d* of Major O. Anson, 9th Lancers; *m* Adèle Margaret Edith, *d* of late Sir John Foster Stevens; one *d*. *Educ:* Edinburgh Academy; Mill Hill; RMA, Woolwich. Served in Samana Expeditions, 1891; Isazai Field Force, 1892; Afghan Boundary Commission, 1894–95; European War, 1915–18 (wounded in France); officiated as Surveyor-General of India, 1920; retired, 1924. *Address:* Oak Avenue, Curdridge, Hants. *Club:* United Service.

Died 10 Nov. 1943.

COLE, Col Sir Edward Hearle, Kt 1937; CB 1916; CMG 1918; *b* 27 July 1863; *s* of William Turney Cole, HEICS; *m* 1893, Annie Violet (*d* 1945), *d* of Colonel Elphinston Shaw; one *d*. Entered Army, 1883; Capt. ISC, 1894; Major Indian Army, 1901; Lt-Col, Commanding XIth KEO Lancers Probyn's Horse, 1909–14; Col, 1914; DAAG, India, 1900–04; served Burma, 1886–87 (medal 2 clasps); Hazara, 1891 (clasp); Chitral, 1895 (medal with clasp); NW Frontier, India, 1897–98 (despatches twice, 2 clasps); China, 1900 (despatches, medal); European War, 1914–18 (CB, CMG, despatches three times, severely wounded). *Address:* Coleyana, Okara, Punjab. *Clubs:* East India and Sports, Royal Automobile.

Died 15 April 1949.

COLE, Percival Pasley, OBE 1947; MB, ChB Birm., FRCS Eng.; LDS, RCS Eng.; Hunterian Professor of Surgery, Royal College of Surgeons, 1918; Consulting Surgeon and Director, VD Dept, Seamen's Hospital, Greenwich; Consulting Surgeon, Royal Cancer Hospital; Consulting Surgeon, Queen Mary's Hospital for the East End; FRSM; Member, British Association of Plastic Surgeons; Hon. Life Member, National Union of Seamen; *b* Weymouth; *m* 1909, Amy Gladys, *γ d* of T. J. Templeman, JP, Weymouth; one *s* one *d*; 1933, Marjorie Pearl Christine, *d* of Francis Ernest Greene, Dublin. *Educ:* Weymouth College; Guy's Hospital. Hunterian Professor Royal College of Surgeons, 1917–18; House Surgeon Guy's Hospital; Demonstrator of Anatomy University of Birmingham and Middlesex Hospital; Sub-Warden Queen's College, University of Birmingham; Surgical Registrar Cancer Hospital; Hon. Surgeon King George Hospital; Operating Surgeon Brook War Hospital; Surgeon EMS.

Publications: various articles on surgical subjects, including cancer, abdominal surgery, plastic surgery of the jaws and face, and hernia. *Address:* 41 Lancaster Grove, NW3. *T:* Primrose 2204.

Died 19 Oct. 1948.

COLE, Gp Captain Robert Arthur Alexander, CBE 1944 (OBE 1941); RAF (retd); *b* 12 Sept. 1901; *s* of late Capt. A. J. Cole, RIM, and of Esther Cole; *m* 1938, Cynthia St George, *d* of Major N. Baker, IA, retd; one *s*. *Educ:* St George's College, Weybridge. Midshipman, 1916–20; transferred to RAF 1922. Served in Egypt, Aden, Soudan, Palestine, Singapore. Served War of 1939–45 (despatches thrice, OBE, CBE); retired 1948. Order of Leopold with Palme and Croix de Guerre 1940 with palme (Belgium) awarded 1947. *Recreations:* fishing, golf, shooting, hockey. *Address:* c/o Grindlay's Bank Ltd, 54 Parliament Street, SW1; Three Ways, Coney Weston, Bury St Edmunds, Suffolk.

Died 18 May 1949.

COLE, Sophie; novelist and writer of sketches on Old London; *b* 15 Nov. 1862; *d* of William and Elizabeth Cole, Clapham, SW; unmarried. *Educ:* private schools. Began to write for recreation, continued to do so as a means of living. *Publications:* novels, amongst the most successful of which are The Toy Maker; Money isn't Everything; Daffodil Alley; Paying the Piper; A Strolling Singer; Primrose Folly; A London Rose; Shade of Old Tuke; Sixpence in Her Shoe; Bill and Patricia; A London Posy; Secret Joy; Cobbler's Corner; The Joyous Pedlar; Bachelor's Banquet; The Valiant Spinster; Actor's Haven; Chairman of the Lanes, 1943; So long as We're together, 1943; M for Maria; two volumes of London Studies—The Lure of Old London; The Lure of London Town. *Recreation:* searching out hidden nooks and corners of Old London. *Address:* Littledown, Kingwood, Henley-on-Thames.

Died 11 Feb. 1947.

COLE, Lt-Col Stanley James, CMG 1940; OBE 1930; *b* Wakefield, Yorks, 1884; *m*; one *d*. *Educ:* Private School in Norfolk. Joined Irish Guards; commissioned in field, Wiltshire Regt; transferred accelerated promotion South Lancashire Regt. Served Royal West African Frontier Force, 1908–20; Adjt 1st Nigeria Regt; Acting Staff Capt. Nigeria Regt; employed Political and Admin. Service, Nigeria. Staff GOC Dublin Dist 1920–21; Adjt 1st Wiltshire Regt 1921–24; Bt Maj. 1924; at Colonial Office as Staff Officer RWAFF (GSO2), 1925–29; Staff Officer RWAFF and KAR 1929–38; AA and QMG Colonial Forces, 1938–42; relinquished military appt 1942 with rank Lt-Col; employed Colonial Office in charge of Prisoners of War and Civilian Internees Dept, 1942–46. *Address:* 276 Milton Road, Cambridge.

Died 2 Jan. 1949.

COLE, Rev. Theodore Edward Fortescue, LLM. *Educ:* Downing College, Cambridge. Curate of St Bartholomew, Charlton next Dover, 1885–86; Thurnham, 1886–88; Wateringbury, 1889–89; Indian Government Chaplain (Bengal), 1889–1911; served Thibet, 1904 (medal with clasp); Canon of Calcutta Cathedral, 1907–11; Rector of Longford, 1911–15; EEF and BEF 1915–20; General Licence Dioceses of London and Guildford. *Address:* c/o Grindlay & Co., 54 Parliament Street, SW.

Died 18 March 1944.

COLE-HAMILTON, Air Vice-Marshal John Beresford, CB 1943; CBE 1941; AOC a group in Fighter Command since 1944; *b* 1 Dec. 1894; *s* of late J. Cole-Hamilton; *m* 1928, Hilda (*d* 1945), *d* of C. Leslie Fox, Rumwell Hall, Taunton; one *d*. *Educ:* RN Colleges Osborne and Dartmouth. Midshipman HMS Princess Royal 1912; Battles of Heligoland and Dogger Bank; transferred to RNAS 1915, RAF 1918; served in India, 1923–26 and 1934–38; RAF Component, BEF, France,

1940; AOC West Africa, 1943. *Recreations:* hunting, fishing. *Address:* Bicknoller, Taunton, Somerset. *Club:* Naval and Military.

Died 22 Aug. 1945.

COLEMAN, Rt Rev. John Aloysius; Bishop of Armidale, (RC), 1932–48; *b* Mount Melleray, Ireland, 1887. Went to Australia 1912; coadjutor Bishop of Armidale, NSW, 1929.

Died 22 Dec. 1947.

COLEMAN, Rev. Canon Noel Dolben, MA, Hon. CF; Secretary for Translations and Librarian of British and Foreign Bible Society since 1944; Examining Chaplain to Bishop of Bradford since 1931; Hon. Canon of St Sitha in Bradford Cathedral since 1936; *b* 12 Dec. 1891; *y s* of late William Frederic and Phoebe Coleman; *m* Dorothy Margaret Charlotte, *o d* of late Matthew H. Bobart; two *d*. *Educ:* Southwell Minster Grammar School; St John's College, Cambridge (Foundation Scholar); Wells Theological College (Organ Scholar). Seven times prizeman of St John's, Cambridge, 1910–14, Mason Prize, Hughes Exhibitioner for Eccles. History; BA 1914; Naden Divinity Student (post graduate). Carus Greek Testament Prize, 1913 deacon, 1915; priest, 1916; Curate of Alfreton, 1915; St Werburgh's, Derby, 1916; Temp. C. F. Palestine and Egypt, 1918–19; curate of Matlock, 1919; MA Cantab 1916, MA Dunelm, by vote of Convocation, 1920; Lecturer in Theology and Hellenistic Greek, University of Durham, 1920–44; Chaplain of Univ. College, Durham, 1924–44; Member of Senate, Durham University, 1938–44; Member of Council of Durham Colleges, 1923–37; Estates Committee, 1927–30; Dean of Faculty of Theology, 1933–35; Chairman of General Board of Faculties, 1934–35; Censor of Non-collegiate Students, 1923–41; assisted at Durham Cathedral, 1932–44; and Acting Precentor, 1939–44; Commissioner of Land Tax and Additional Commissioner of Income Tax for Easington Ward, Co. Durham, 1938–44. *Publications:* contributor to Bishop Gore's New Commentary on Holy Scripture, Journal of Theological Studies, Expository Times. *Recreations:* music, gardening. *Address:* 146 Queen Victoria Street, EC4; 40 Madeley Road, Ealing, W5. *T:* Central 7884, Perivale 3880.

Died 13 May 1948.

COLES, Principal-Emeritus Charles, OBE 1934; BSc; Principal, City of Cardiff Technical College, 1916–37; *b* 2 June 1878; *s* of William and Emily Coles; *m* 1918, Ellen Hardy, *d* of James Massey Sumner, Manchester. *Educ:* University College of S Wales and Monmouthshire. Superintendent of Technical Instruction, Cardiff, 1907–16; Chairman Association of Technical Institutions, 1927–28; President Association of Principals of Technical Institutions, 1928–29; Chairman Association of Navigation Schools, 1924–26; President Cardiff Rotary Club 1927–28. *Publications:* The Place of Technical Education in a National System of Education; The Necessity for close Cooperation between the Technical Colleges and the Universities; Non-Resident Students in Technical Colleges; The Course System in Technical Institutions. *Recreations:* golf, travel, bowling. *Address:* Newlands, Upper Manor Road, Paignton, Devon. *T:* 82080.

Died 3 Feb. 1947.

COLES, Edward Horsman, CB 1922; *b* 26 Sept. 1865; *s* of late T. Horsman Coles; *m* 1897, Marie Louise (*d* 1925), *y d* of late George du Maurier. *Educ:* Winchester College; New College, Oxford. Called to Bar, 1894; Controller of Lands, War Office, 1908–25. *Recreation:* golf. *Address:* 9 Elm Park Road, Chelsea, SW. *T:* Flaxman 1488.

Died 27 Nov. 1948.

COLES, Col Morton Calverley, CMG 1915; the Queen's (Royal West Surrey Regiment); *b* 29 Sept. 1863. Entered Army, 1884; Captain, 1892; Major, 1901; Lt-Col 1912; Col 1916; retired 1920; served European War, 1914–18 (despatches, CMG). *Club:* Junior United Service.

Died 3 March 1943.

COLIJN, Hendrikus; *b* 22 June 1869; *m* 1893, Helena Groenberg; three *s*. Active Service in Dutch East Indies; Captain, 1900; Assistant Resident, 1904–05; Secretary to Government of the Dutch Indies, 1907; member of Second Chamber, 1909–11, 1922–23, 1929–33, and of Upper Chamber, 1914–19 and since 1939; War Minister, 1911–13; Minister of Marine, 1912–13; director of Royal Dutch Shell, 1914–22; editor of De Standaard, 1922–33; Finance Minister, 1923–26; delegate to World Economic Conference, Geneva, 1927; vice-president of Economic Committee, League of Nations, 1928; Prime Minister, 1925–26 and 1933–39; Colonial Minister, 1933–37; Defence Minister, 1935–37; Minister of General Affairs, 1937–39; President of Central Committee of League of Nations, 1940. *Publication:* Saevis Tranquillus in Undis, 1932. *Address:* Stadhouderslaan 151, The Hague.

Died 16 Sept. 1944.

COLLARD, Maj.-Gen. Albert Sydney, CB 1917; CVO 1917; *b* 31 July 1876; *s* of late Albert Collard, Canterbury; *m* 1902, Kathleen, *d* of late Michael Pyne, Cashel, Co. Tipperary; one *s* one *d*. *Educ:* Canterbury. Served S African War (Queen's medal with three clasps); Senior Executive Engineer, Baro Kano Railway, Northern Nigeria, 1908–12; Director of Surveys, Northern Nigeria, 1912–14; Staff Captain. War Office, 1914–15; Deputy Assistant Director of Movements, War Office, 1915–16; Director of Inland Waterways and Docks, with rank of Brig.-Gen., War Office, 1916–17 (CB); Deputy Controller Auxiliary Shipbuilding Admiralty, with rank of Maj.-Gen., 1917–18; Director-General of Administration to Controller-General of Merchant Shipbuilding, 1918–19; received freedom of the City of Canterbury (for services during European War), 1919.

Died 27 Aug. 1938.

COLLARD, Col Alexander Arthur Lysons, CBE 1919; late Hampshire Regt and RAPC; *b* 10 June 1871; *s* of late Canon John Marshall Collard; *m* 1900, Kathleen Louisa, *d* of late W. C. Turner, ICS, one *s* one *d*. Entered Army, 1893; Lt-Col 1916; served S African War 1901, 1902 (Queen's Medal); Somaliland 1903–04 (medal); European War, 1914–19 (despatches, CBE); retired pay, 1928. *Address:* Entonhurst, Godalming, Surrey. *T:* Godalming 668.

Died 28 Feb. 1947.

COLLARD, Major Alfred Stephen, CBE 1918, JP (retired); *b* 1865; *s* of late J. A. Collard, merchant, Liverpool; *m* 1896, Florence (*d* 1937), *o c* of late J. M. Haigh, Ledsham Hall, Cheshire; one *d*. *Educ:* Peel Grammar School; privately. Served Gordon Relief Expedition, 1885; Argentine, 1889–93; Shipowner, Liverpool, 1893–1909; Ex-Chairman of Liverpool Steamship Owners' Association; served European War in France, 1914–19; Commandant Stretcher Bearers British Red Cross, Order of St John of Jerusalem (despatches twice); Knight of Grace of the Order of St John of Jerusalem. *Recreations:* golf, shooting. *Address:* 40 Upper Grosvenor Street, W1. *Clubs:* Carlton, Junior Carlton, Hurlingham.

Died 7 March 1941.

COLLARD, Lt-Col Charles Edwin, CB 1916; RMLI (retired). Served European War, 1914–18, including Jutland Bank (despatches, CB, Order of St Stanislas of Russia).

Died 19 Aug. 1942.

COLLEDGE, Lionel, MB (Cantab); FRCS (Eng.); Consulting Surgeon, Ear and Throat, St George's Hospital, SW1; Consulting Surgeon Royal National Throat and Ear Hospital; Consulting Otologist to the Navy; Aural Surgeon West End Hospital for Nervous Diseases and Freemasons Hospital, Ravenscourt Park; Consulting Laryngologist Royal Cancer Hospital; Surgeon, Ear and Throat, Prince of Wales General Hospital, Tottenham; *b* 5 Oct. 1883; *s* of late Major John Colledge, Lauriston House, Cheltenham; *m* Margaret, *d* of late Admiral J. W. Brackenbury, CB, CMG; one *d*. *Educ:* Cheltenham College; Caius College, Cambridge; St George's Hospital. Late Capt. RAMC (TF); Aural Surgeon to 1st Army BEF in France; Semon Lecturer in Larvngology, University of London for 1927. *Publications:* Diseases of Ear, Larynx and Pharynx, (Rolleston's) British Encyclopaedia of Medical Practice; Guide to Diseases of Nose and Throat (With C. A. Parker); Injuries to Ear in Modern Warfare; Surgical Treatment of Paralysis of Vocal Cords (with C. A. Ballance); Cancer of the Larynx (with St Clair Thomson); Papers on Cancer of the Larynx and on Diseases of the Ear. *Address:* 2 Upper Wimpole Street, W1. *T:* Welbeck 4971. *Club:* Union.

Died 19 Dec. 1948.

COLLEN, Lt-Col Edwin Henry Ethelbert, CMG 1919; DSO 1900; retired; Royal Artillery; *b* 6 May 1875; *s* of late Lt-Gen. Sir E. H. H. Collen, GCIE, CB; *m* 1906, Constance Mary, *e d* of late C. J. Cater Scott; one *s* one *d*. *Educ:* Cheltenham College. Entered Army, 1895; served NW Frontier, India, 1897–98 (despatches, medal with two clasps); South Africa, 1899–1900 (despatches, DSO, medal with four clasps). Staff Coll., Camberley, 1903–04; Mil. Prof., Camb. Univ., 1912–14; European War, 1914–19 (despatches, Bt Lt-Col CMG). *Address:* Brakeys, Hatfield Peverel, Essex. *Club:* Junior Army and Navy.

Died 29 Nov. 1943.

COLLES, Henry Cope, MA, DMus Oxon; FRCM; Hon. RAM; Musical Critic of The Times since 1911; *b* 1879; *e s* of late Abraham Colles, MD, and Emily, *d* of Major Alexander R. Dallas; *m* 1906, Hester Janet, *y d* of late Thomas Matheson. *Educ:* privately; Royal College of Music; Worcester College, Oxford (Organ Scholar); BA 1902; BMus 1903; DMus (Hon.), 1932. Hon. Freeman of Worshipful Company of Musicians 1935; Hon. Fellow of Worcester College, Oxford, 1936; joined staff of RCM as Lecturer in Musical History and Form, 1919; Member of the RCM Board of Professors, 1923, and of the Associated Board of the RAM and RCM, 1924. *Publications:* Brahms, 1908; The Growth of Music, Part I 1912, Part II 1913, Part III 1916; Editor of Third Edition of Grove's Dictionary of Music and Musicians, 1927; Fourth Edition of Grove's Dictionary with Supplement, 1940; Voice and Verse (Cramb Lectures), 1928; The Royal College of Music, 1933; Oxford History of Music, Vol. vii 1934; On Learning Music and Other Essays, 1940; Walford—A Biography, 1942. *Address:* The Times, Printing House Square, EC4. *Club:* Athenæum.

Died 4 March 1943.

COLLET, Clara E., MA; Fellow of University College, London; Governor of Bedford College, London; Member of College Hall, London; *b* 10 Sept. 1860; 2nd *d* of late Collet Dobson Collet and Jane, *d* of John Sloan. *Educ:* N London Collegiate School; University College, London. Assist Mistress, Wyggeston Girls' School, Leicester, 1878–85; student 1885–88; worked for Charles Booth, 1888–92; President of Association of Assistant Mistresses in Public Secondary Schools, 1891; Assistant Commissioner to Royal Labour Commission, 1892; Labour Correspondent, Board of Trade, 1893–1903; Senior Investigator, Board of Trade, 1903–17; Ministry of Labour, 1917–20; Appointed Member of Trade Boards, 1921–32; Member of Council of Royal Statistical Society, 1919–35; Member of Council of Royal Economic Society, 1920–41. *Publications:* Appendix to The Private Letter Books of Joseph Collet, 1933; Colet's Inn at Dublin, 1938. Articles and official Reports on economic position of women; Hon. Member (since 1894) Association of Assistant Mistresses in Secondary Schools. *Address:* Clifton, Cliff Road, Sidmouth.

Died 3 Aug. 1948.

COLLET, Sir Mark (Edlmann), 2nd Bt *cr* 1888; *b* 12 Jan. 1864; *s* of 1st Bt and Antonia Frederica, *d* of Joseph Edlmann of Hawkwood, Kent; *S* father, 1905; *m* 1st, 1888, Nina Emma Caroline (*d* 1922), *d* of late Rev. Canon C. Theobald; 2nd, 1931, Violet Frederica, *e d* of late Frederick J. Edlmann, Hawkwood, Chislehurst, Kent. *Educ:* Eton; Trin. Coll., Cambridge. High Sheriff, Kent, 1912; County Councillor, 1913; Alderman, 1925–36. *Heir:* none. *Address:* Ballamanaugh, Sulby, Isle of Man; Le Bocage, Hyères, France. *Club:* Oxford and Cambridge.

Died 24 Sept. 1944.

COLLETT, Col Hon. Herbert Brayley, CMG 1919; DSO 1917; VD, JP; Senator for Western Australia, 1933–47; for many years Sub-Librarian, Public Library, Museum and Art Gallery of Western Australia; *b* St Peter Port, Guernsey, 12 Nov. 1877; 2nd *s* of late F. A. E. Collett; *m* 1904, Annie, *e d* of T. E. Whitfield, Perth, West Australia; two *s*. *Educ:* privately; Perth Grammar School, West Australia. Emigrated with parents to Western Australia, 1884; entered public service, 1891; joined Volunteer Force, 1894; commanded 11th Australian Infantry Regt (Militia), 1908–15; raised and commanded 28th Battalion, Australian Imperial Force; served in Egypt 1915–16; Gallipoli, 1915, and France, 1916–18 (wounded, despatches, DSO, Bt-Colonel, AMF); commanded Australian troops, Weymouth, 1918–19; commanded 13th Infantry Brigade, AMF, 1922–27; ADC to Governor-General of Australia, 1922–26; Minister without Portfolio, Australia, 1939; Vice-President of Executive Council, 1940; Minister for Repatriation and in charge of War Service Homes, 1940–41; in Freemasonry, an Officer of the Grand Lodge of Western Australia. *Publications:* Infantry in Attack, 1906; The 28th, a Record of War Service, 1922. *Address:* Cobo, Guildford Road, Mt Lawley, Perth, Western Australia. *Clubs:* Naval, Military and Air Force (a founder) (Perth).

Died 15 Aug. 1947.

COLLETT, Col John Henry, CMG 1916; DL; JP; late 5th Gloucesters Regt (TF); Chairman Sharpness Dock Co; *b* 1876; *e s* of late J. M. Collett, JP, of Wynstone Place, nr Gloucester; *m* 1908, Dorothy, *d* of late T. Nelson Foster, JP, Cheltenham; two *s*. *Educ:* Manchester Univ. (MSc). Served European War, 1914–17 (despatches, CMG). *Address:* 7 Pittville Cres., Cheltenham. *Club:* Junior Army and Navy.

Died 8 Nov. 1942.

COLLETT, Rt Rev. Dom Martin; Abbot of Pershore and Nashdom since 1934; *b* 3 Nov. 1879; *s* of Thomas James Collett and Emily H. E. Townsend. *Educ:* Central School, Leeds; Univ. Coll., Sheffield; King's College, London; BSc London, 1905, Sheffield, 1908. Assistant Lecturer in Physics at Birkbeck College, 1903–06; deacon, 1908; priest, 1909; Curate St Philip's, Bethnal Green, 1908–13; St Cyprian's, Dorset Square, 1913–15; St Mark's, Gloucester, 1915–19; TCF 1918–19; Rector of St Augustine's College, Kumasi, W Africa, 1924–26. *Publications:* Accra, 1927; various articles and reviews in Laudate, etc. *Address:* Nashdom Abbey, Burnham, Bucks. *T:* Burnham, Bucks, 176. *Club:* University of London.

Died 12 March 1948.

COLLIE, J. Norman, FRS; DSc, LLD, FRSE, FRGS, etc; *b* 10 Sept. 1859; *s* of John Collie and Selina Mary Winkworth. Professor of Organic Chemistry, University College, Gower Street, 1902–28, and Director of Chemical Laboratory 1912–28; Emeritus Professor since 1928; ex-President of the Alpine Club; ex-Vice-President of the Royal Geographical Society. *Publications:* Climbing on the Himalaya, 1902; Climbs and Exploration in the Canadian Rockies (with H. E. M. Stutfield), 1903. *Address:* Sligachan, Isle of Skye.

Died 1 Nov. 1942.

COLLIER, Charles Saint John, CMG 1933; Comptroller and Auditor General to Ethiopian Government; *b* 1880; *e s* of late William Edward Collier, St John, New Brunswick, and Emily, *d* of Charles Watters. *Educ:* High School, Dundee. *Address:* Addis Ababa, Ethiopia. *Club:* Thatched House.

Died 26 July 1944.

COLLIER, Sir George Herman, Kt 1921; CIE 1918; late Director-General of Stores, India Office, London; *b* 18 Jan. 1856; 3rd *s* of late John Pycroft Collier, Assist Paymaster-Gen.; *m* 1887, Julia Matilda, *d* of late Maj.-Gen. Sir John E. W. Inglis, KCB and Hon. Lady Inglis; two *s* two *d*. *Educ:* Uppingham School. Member of the India Office, 1876; transferred to the Dept of the High Commissioner for India, 1920; retired, 1921. *Address:* Hill Cottage, Forest Row, Sussex. *T:* Forest Row 46.

Died 20 Feb. 1941.

COLLIER, Hon. Philip, MLA Boulder; *b* Woodstock, Victoria, 21 April 1874. Migrated to the goldfields of Western Australia, 1904; was elected to Parliament as Member for Boulder, 1905; Minister for Mines and Railways, State of Western Australia, 1911–14; Minister for Mines and Water Supplies, 1914–16; Leader of Parliamentary Labour Party in Opposition, 1916–24, and 1930–33; Premier, Treasurer, and Minister of Forests, Labour Government, Western Australia, 1924–30; Premier and Treasurer, 1933–36. *Address:* Perth, Western Australia.

Died 18 Oct. 1948.

COLLINGE, Walter E., DSc (St And.), MSc (Birm.); Keeper of the Yorkshire Museum, 1921–41; editor of The Journal of Zoological Research; late Research Fellow and Lecturer in Comparative Embryology, St Andrews; Lecturer on Economic Zoology, University of Birmingham. *Educ:* Huddersfield Coll.; Yorkshire Coll. (Victoria Univ.); St Andrews University. Established the Journal of Malacology, 1890; Demonstrator in Biology, St Andrews, 1891; Lecturer in Zoology and Comparative Anatomy, Birmingham, 1900; Woodall Fisheries Prizeman, 1892; Darwin Gold Medal, 1895; Walker Trust Research Scholar, 1915–17; Carnegie Fellow, 1916–19; for many years President of the Midland Malacological Society, Founder Association Economic Biologists; For. Mem. Assoc. Econ. Entomol. Washington, USA; Hon. FRHS; Corresponding Fellow of the American Ornithologists' Union; Member Wild Bird Protection Advisory (Scotland) Cttee, 1920–44; Pres. Northern Ecological Assoc., 1942–47. *Publications:* A Manual of Injurious Insects; The Food of Some British Wild Birds; papers in scientific journals. *Address:* The Hollies, 141 Fulford Road, York.

Died 24 Nov. 1947.

COLLINGRIDGE, George Rooke; Joint Editor, City Press; *b* 1867; *s* of William Hill Collingridge and Ann Minshaw; *m* 1906, Anne Melicena (*d* 1937). *Educ:* Clewer House, Windsor. Associated with Editorial Department, City Press, since leaving school. *Recreation:* work. *Address:* 35 Canfield Gardens, NW6. *T:* Maida Vale 5908. *Club:* City Livery.

Died 23 May 1944.

COLLINGS, Albert Henry, RBA, RI; artist, portrait painter. Exhibitor, Royal Academy, Paris Salon, Royal Institute of Painters in Water Colours, etc.; gold medal, Paris Salon, for portrait. *Recreations:* music, golf. *Clubs:* Savage, Arts.

Died 6 May 1947.

COLLINGS, Col Godfrey Disney, DSO 1902; *b* 13 Nov. 1855; *s* of late Rev. P. B. Collings, MA; *m* 1891, J. K. (*d* 1936), *d* of late Hon. P. L. van der Byl, MLC, Cape Colony; two *s*. *Educ:* King's School, Canterbury. Joined 91st Highlanders, 1874; joined APD, 1884; Paymaster, 1884; Hon. Major, 1894; Lieutenant-Colonel, 1904; Staff Paymaster, 1899; Colonel and Chief Paymaster, 1908; retired, Nov. 1916; served with 91st Highlanders Zulu War, 1879 (medal with clasp); South Africa, 1900–02 (Queen's medal with 3 clasps, King's medal 2 clasps); European War, 1914–16. *Address:* c/o Lloyds Bank (Cox's Branch), 6 Pall Mall, SW1.

Died 26 June 1941.

COLLINGWOOD, Robin George, Hon. LLD (St Andrews); Fellow of the British Academy; Member of the Archæological Institute of the German Empire; FSA; Waynflete Professor of Metaphysical Philosophy, Oxford University, 1935–41; formerly Fellow, Tutor and Librarian of Pembroke College and University Lecturer in Philosophy and Roman History; *b* 1889; *o s* of late William Gershom Collingwood; *m* 1918, Ethel Winifred, 3rd *d* of late R. C. Graham of Skipness; one *s* one *d*; *m* 1942, Kathleen Frances, 2nd *d* of late F. E. Edwardes, Harrow. *Educ:* Rugby School; University College, Oxford. 1st class Honour Moderations, 1910; 1st class Lit. Hum., 1912. Admiralty ID, 1915–19. *Publications:* Religion and Philosophy, 1916; Ruskin's Philosophy, 1920; Roman Britain, 1921, rewritten 1932; Speculum Mentis, or the Map of Knowledge, 1924; Outlines of a Philosophy of Art, 1925; Archæology of Roman Britain, 1930; Essay on Philosophical Method, 1933; Roman Britain and the English Settlements (Oxford History of England, Vol. I, with J. N. L. Myres), 1936; Human Nature and Human History (British Academy), 1936; Britain (in Tenney Frank's Economic Survey of Rome), 1937; The Principles of Art, 1938; Autobiography, 1939; Essay on Metaphysics, 1940; The First Mate's Log, 1940; The New Leviathan, 1942; translations, including Croce's Vico, 1913; Croce's Autobiography, 1927; Ruggiero's History of European Liberalism, 1927; numerous papers, mostly on history and archæology (especially Roman and pre-historic Britain) and philosophy, in periodicals. *Address:* Magdalen College, Oxford; Lanehead, Coniston, Lancashire.

Died 9 Jan. 1943.

COLLINS, Alfred Tenison; General Manager, 1903–37, and a Director, 1908–39, of the Hibernian Bank, Ltd; *b* 1852. Entered the service of the Hibernian Bank, 1869; Secretary, 1883; President of Institute of Bankers in Ireland, 1929 and 1930; elected a Currency Commissioner, Irish Free State, 1931; retired, 1939. *Address:* c/o Hibernian Bank, College Green, Dublin. *Club:* Royal Societies.

Died 31 Jan. 1945.

COLLINS, Cyril George, CMG 1946; JP; retired; Controller and Auditor-General, NZ; *b* 26 Sept. 1880; *s* of Col Robert Joseph Collins, CMG, ISO, VD, and Anne Matilda Collins; *m* 1912, Mary Teresa, *d* of Maurice O'Connor; two *s* one *d*. *Educ:* St Patrick's College, Wellington, NZ. NZ Govt Service, 1899–1945. *Address:* 76 Waterloo Road, Lower Hutt, NZ. *Clubs:* Wellesley, Wellington, NZ.

Died 30 Jan. 1947.

COLLINS, Patrick; outdoor amusement caterer, theatre and cinema proprietor; *b* 1859; 2nd *s* of John Collins, Chester; *m* 1st, 1880, Flora Ross, Wrexham; one *s*; 2nd, 1935, Clara Mullett. *Educ:* St Werburgh Catholic

School. Farmer; engineering works proprietor; concerned in early development of steam roundabouts and of outdoor amusements generally, also in introducing and popularising cinema industry in this country; nineteen years President Showmen's Guild of Great Britain and Ireland, of which one of founders; Councillor for Walsall, 1918; Alderman from 1930; MP (L) Walsall, 1922–24. *Recreation:* motoring. *Address:* Lime Tree House, Bloxwich. *T:* 6324; Amusement Depot, Bloxwich. *TA:* Gondola, Bloxwich. *T:* Bloxwich 6231/2. *Clubs:* National Liberal, National Sporting.

Died 8 Dec. 1943.

COLLINS, Rev. Percy Herbert; Rector of Lydd, 1910–41; Hon. Canon of Canterbury, 1917; *m* 1883, Augusta Caroline Charlotte (*d* 1927), *e d* of Maj.-Gen. W. Calcott Clarke; two *s* one *d. Educ:* Corpus Christi College, Cambridge; MA. Ordained 1880; Curate of Christ Church, Gipsy Hill, 1880–83; of St John, Bexley, 1883–85; St Thomas, Westbournegrove, 1885–87; Rector of High Halden, 1887–99; Curate of Holy Trinity, Guildford, 1899–1901; Rector of Smarden, 1901–05; Vicar of St Paul, Thornton Heath, 1905–10.

Died 18 Dec. 1941.

COLLINS, Maj.-Gen. Robert John, CB, 1933; CMG 1918; DSO 1916; Editor Army Quarterly since 1942; *b* 22 Aug. 1880; *y s* of late H. Collins, of Leopold House, Reading, and *g s* of Rev. F. Collins, of Betterton, Wantage, Berks; *m* 1912, Violet, *d* of late Alex. Monro, CIE, and *widow* of Capt. S. Hill; one *d. Educ:* Marlborough College. Joined 6th Warwick (Militia), 1897; R. Berks Regt 1899; served through S African War (King's and Queen's medals with 5 clasps); Egyptian Army, 1904–11 (ADC to Sirdar, 1905–06); Somaliland as Private Secretary to GOC during withdrawal, 1910 (despatches); Staff College, 1912–13; served European War successively General Staff Officer, 3rd grade Central Force and 1st Corps BEF; 2nd grade 2nd Army 1st grade 2nd Army, 17th Div. and 5th Army; Chief Instructor Staff School, Cambridge, 1918; commanded 73rd Infantry Brigade 24th Div. BEF, July 1918–March 1919 Bt Major and Lt-Col, CMG, DSO, Chevalier of Legion of Honour and Croix de Guerre, despatches eight times); Instructor, Staff College, Camberley, 1919–23; Bt Colonel, 1923; Substantive Colonel, Director Military Training, India, 1924–26; Col Commandant 9th Infantry Brigade, 1926–27; Col Commandant 7th Infantry Brigade and Experimental Armoured Force, 1927–28; Maj.-Gen. 1932; Commandant Small Arms School, 1929–32; GOC 3rd (Meerut) Indian Division, 1934–38; retired pay, 1938; Appointed GOC 61st Div. Sept. 1939; Comdt Staff College, Camberley, Nov. 1939–41; reverted to retired pay, 1941; Colonel, Royal Berkshire Regt, 1940–46; Deputy Regional Commissioner, Southern Region, 1942–44. DL Berks, 1949. *Publication:* Lord Wavell, 1948. *Address:* Horne Mead House, Donnington, Newbury, Berks. *Club:* United Service.

Died 6 March 1950.

COLLINS, Sir Thomas, Kt 1916; *b* 23 July 1860. Chief Inspector, Board of Inland Revenue, 1914–20. *Address:* Lyndale, West Byfleet, Surrey.

Died 4 Dec. 1944.

COLLINS, Lt-Col William Alexander, CBE 1943; DSO 1918; Chairman and Managing Director, Wm Collins, Sons & Co., Ltd, Glasgow and London, publishers, and Collins, Bros and Co., Ltd, Australia and New Zealand; Chairman and Managing Director, Castell Bros, Ltd, London and Glasgow; Director of Clydesdale Bank, Ltd; Director of the Scottish Board of the Liverpool and London and Globe Insurance Co; *b* 26 March 1873; *e s* of late A. G. Collins of Skelmorlie; *m* 1899, Grace, *d* of William Brander; three *s* one *d. Educ:* Temple Grove; Harrow. Joined RASC Feb. 1915; served in France, May 1915–July 1919; appointed AD S

and T 1918 (despatches, DSO, Ordem Militar de Airs (Portuguese), 1919). *Recreation:* shooting. *Address:* Grey Gables, Monkton, Ayrshire; 144 Cathedral Street, Glasgow. *TA:* Collins, Glasgow. *T:* Troon 53; Glasgow, Bell 4031. *Clubs:* White's; Western, Glasgow; Mudhook.

Died 3 Sept. 1945.

COLLINS, Sir William Henry, Kt 1944; Chairman and Managing Director of Cerebos, Ltd, John Crampton & Co., Ltd, Middlewich Salt Co., Ltd, and Verdin Cooke & Co., Ltd; Chairman Fortnum & Mason, Ltd; Director Carreras Ltd; Chairman of King Edward VII Hospital, Windsor; *m* 1946, Mrs Norah Royce Callingham. Hon. gold medal of Royal College of Surgeons, 1944. *Address:* Wexham Park, Bucks.

Died 30 Nov. 1947.

COLLINS, Sir William Job, Kt 1902; KCVO 1914; DL, JP, MD, MS, BSc (Lond. Univ.), FRCS; Vice-Lieutenant of County of London, 1925–45; *b* London, 9 May 1859; *e s* of Dr W. J. Collins, and Mary Anne Francisca, *e d* of late E. Treacher; member of Huguenot family of Garnault; *m* 1898, Jean (*d* 1936), *d* of late John Wilson, MP (Govan), DL. *Educ:* University Coll. School, London, and St Bartholomew's Hospital. Fellow, Scholar and gold medallist in Sanitary Science and in Obstetrics of London University. Honours in Physiology, Forensic Medicine, and Surgery; Vice-Chancellor London Univ., 1907–09, and 1911–12; Senator, 1893–1927; Demonstrator of Anatomy, 1884–85; Jeaffreson Exhibitioner (1876), St Bartholomew's Hosp.; Doyne Medallist in Ophthalmology, Oxford, 1918; Consulting Surgeon to Royal Eye Hospital and Western Ophthalmic Hosp.; Chm. of London County Council, 1897–98; Vice-Chm., 1896–97; Chairman of London Education Committee, 1904–06; member Council of King's Hospital Fund; Hon. Secretary League of Mercy, 1899–1928; President Sanitary Inspectors Association, 1922–27; President Medico-Legal Society, 1901–05; Chairman of Chadwick Trust; Chairman Sussex Agricultural Wages Committee, 1920–39; Member RC on Vivisection, 1906–12; and of RC on Vaccination, 1889–96; Member of City Churches Commission 1919–20; Chairman of Select Committee on Hop Industry, 1908; a Plenipotentiary for Great Britain at Three International Opium Conferences at The Hague, 1911–12, 1913, and 1914, and received thanks of HM Government; Commissioner for Red Cross in France, Nov. 1914; Independent Chairman of the Cumberland Joint District Board under the Coal Mines (Minimum Wage) Act, 1912; temporary Chairman of Committees of House of Commons, 1910; Chairman Departmental Committee on Accidents to Railway Servants, 1914–19; President of Huguenot Society, 1926–29; received Livery of Turners' Co., *honoris causa,* 1909; Chairman of Conciliation and Arbitration Board for Civil Servants, 1917–18; President of Central Council for District Nursing; MP (L) West St Pancras, 1906–10, Derby, 1917–18; elected LCC (W St Pancras), 1892, 1895, 1898, 1901, and 1904; contested W St Pancras, 1895; University of London, 1900. *Publications:* Specificity and Evolution in Disease, 1884 and 1890; On Cataract, 1897, 1906; Spinoza, 1889; The Man *versus* the Microbe, 1903 and 1929; Physic and Metaphysic, 1905; Sir Samuel Romilly's Life and Work, 1908; The Ætiology of the European Conflagration, 1915; The Ethics and Law of Drug and Alcohol Addiction, 1916; The Life and Doctrine of Sir Edwin Chadwick, 1924. *Address:* 1 Albert Terrace, Regent's Park, NW1. *T:* Primrose Hill 0896. *Club:* Reform.

Died 12 Dec. 1946.

COLLINS, Col Comdt Hon. William Richard, DTD, DSO 1916; Minister of Agriculture and Forestry, South Africa, since 1938; *b* Lydenburg Dist, Transvaal, 31 Dec. 1876; *s* of John Thomas Collins and Magdalena Olivier; *m* 1st, 1902, Elizabeth H. M. Collins; 2nd, 1931, Ada

Frances Meyer; two *s* two *d*. *Educ:* private schools; State Gymnasium, Pretoria. Government Official, 1894; Education Dept, Secretary of State and State Attorney's Dept, 1894–99; took part in Boer War, 1899–1902; practised at Ermelo, Tvl., as Attorney, Notary, etc., 1902–38; Member, Native Affairs Commission, 1936–38; Military record: Anglo-Boer War, 1899–1902; ended as Lieut (DTD); Rebellion, 1914, Major; German South West Campaign, Colonel; Commandant O/C Left Wing, 2nd Mounted Brigade (DSO). *Recreation:* hunting. *Address:* Union Buildings, Pretoria. *Clubs:* Pretoria, Pretoria; United Party, Johannesburg.

Died 28 Feb. 1944.

COLLINSON, Col Harold, CB 1919; CMG 1918; DSO 1916; TD; MB, MS (London), FRCS, RAMC (TF, retired); Chevalier Légion d'Honneur; Honorary Consulting Surgeon, General Infirmary, Leeds; late Professor of Surgery and Dean of Faculty of Medicine, University of Leeds; *b* 19 Aug. 1876; *s* of late J. W. Collinson, Halifax; *m* Alice Maude, *d* of late J. B. Pickford, London. Served European War, 1914–18 (despatches, DSO, CMG, CB). *Publications:* numerous articles in medical journals. *Recreations:* hunting, fishing, golf. *Address:* 27 Park Square, Leeds; Orchard Cottage, Linton, Wetherby, Yorks. *T:* Leeds 25878. *Club:* Leeds.

Died 25 Jan. 1945.

COLLIS, Very Rev. Maurice Henry Fitzgerald; *b* 3 June 1859; 2nd *s* of Maurice Henry Collis, MD, Dublin, and Sarah Marcella Lyster, *d* of William Jameson, MD; *m* 1st, 1889, Constance Mary (decd), *d* of Henry Mitchell of Drumreaske, Co. Monaghan, High Sheriff, Co. Monaghan, 1861; one *s* six *d*; 2nd, 1910, Ida Kathleen, *d* of Wakefield Dixon, Dunowen, Belfast. *Educ:* Trinity College, Stratford-on-Avon; Trinity College, Dublin, 1st of 1st Prizes in English Literature; 1st of 1st Hons in Ethics. BA (Sen. Mod. and Gold Medallist, Ethics and Logics), 1881; Bishop Forster's Divinity Prize (Second), 1881; Divinity Test (2nd Cl.), 1882; BD 1895. Deacon, 1882; Priest, 1883; Curate of Drumcannon, Co. Waterford, 1882–84; St Mary's, Newry, 1885–89; Vicar of Antrim, 1889–1945; Prebendary of Cairncastle, 1919–25; Treasurer of Connor, 1925–32; Dean of Connor, 1932–45; retired 1945; Examining Chaplain to the Bishop of Down, 1919–42; Rural Dean of Ballymena, 1898–1924, of Antrim, 1924. *Publications:* articles in the English Church Quarterly, etc. *Recreations:* motoring, golf, reading. *Address:* Calpe, Muckamore, Co. Antrim, Northern Ireland.

Died 14 Oct. 1947.

COLLIS, Maj.-Gen. Sir (William) James Norman C.; *see* Cooke-Collis.

COLLISTER, Sir Harold (James), Kt 1944; **Hon. Mr Justice Collister;** *b* 14 Jan. 1885; *s* of John George Henry Collister and Henrietta Amelia Dolman; *m* 1920, Dora Elaine Cunningham; one *s*. *Educ:* St Lawrence College (Scholar); Sidney Sussex College, Cambridge (Scholar). Classical Tripos, 1906; Indian Civil Service examination, 1908; acted on High Court, Allahabad, 1933; Additional Judge, 1934. Puisne Judge, Allahabad High Court, 1935–45. *Address:* Wrecclesham Grange, Farnham, Surrey.

Died 22 Feb. 1950.

COLLYER, Maj.-Gen. (retired) John Johnston, CB 1917; CMG 1916; DSO 1916; Officer, Legion of Honour; Commander, St John of Jerusalem; 2nd class, St Anne with swords (Russia); Military Secretary to Minister of Defence, S Africa, since Sept. 1939; JP (Norfolk), 1930; *b* 21 Sept. 1870; *e s* of John Monsey Collyer; *m* 1903, Hilda, *d* of M. H. Quinn, Fort Hare; two *d*. *Educ:* St Paul's School. Served Anglo-Boer War, 1899–1902; European War, 1914–18 (CB, CMG, DSO, despatches). Member of Council of Defence, Union of South Africa. *Publications:* The Campaign in German South-West Africa, 1937; The South Africans with

General Smuts in German East Africa, 1939. *Address:* Eastry, Wynberg, Cape Town. *Clubs:* Civil Service, Cape Town; Pretoria, Pretoria.

Died 2 Aug. 1941.

COLMAN, Sir Jeremiah, 1st Bt *cr* 1907; MA (Cambridge), DL, JP Surrey; President, East Surrey Hospital; Chairman, London Surrey Society, 1926 and 1927; *b* 24 April 1859; *s* of late Jeremiah Colman, Carshalton Park, Surrey; *m* 1885, Mary, *d* of J. Short McMaster; one *s*. *Educ:* King's College School, London; St John's College, Cambridge. High Sheriff of County of Surrey, 1893; one of HM Lieutenants for City of London; Chairman J. and J. Colman Ltd, and Gatton Parish Meeting, 1894–1933; Chairman Reigate Petty Sessions Court, 1902–28; Chairman Commercial Union Assurance Co., Ltd, 1892–93, 1902–03, 1908–09, 1913–14, 1918–19; President Surrey County Cricket Club, 1916–23; Master Skinners' Company, 1899–1900; Chairman of the Governors of Tonbridge School, 1899–1900; Hon. Freeman of Borough of Reigate; built and presented the Colman Institute, Redhill, 1904; a Vice-President Boy Scouts Association; Vice-President of YMCA; Member of Appeal Tribunal, County of Surrey, Military Service Act; Chairman and Organising Member of Emergency Committee under Defence of Realm Act, and Chief Special Constable for Reigate Petty Sessional Area; one of the Board of Referees under the Finance Act, 1915; Knight of Grace of the Ancient Order of St John of Jerusalem; Chevalier of Order of Leopold; presented 1930, the Building for the Surrey Convalescent Home for Children, Bognor. *Publications:* printed for private circulation: Hybridisation of Orchids; Observations of a Magistrate; Reminiscences of the Great War, 1914–1918; The Noble Game of Cricket Illustrated and Described from Pictures, Drawings and Prints in the Collection of Sir Jeremiah Colman, Bt, at Gatton Park, Surrey. *Recreations:* shooting, golf, cricket (captain St John's College, Cambridge XI, 1882), horticulture (VMH), and agriculture. *Heir: s* Jeremiah Colman, JP. *Address:* Gatton Park, Surrey. *TA:* Gatton, Redhill. *T:* Merstham 2. *Clubs:* Reform, Devonshire, National Liberal, Royal Empire Society.

Died 16 Jan. 1942.

COLMAN, Russell James; DL; HM Lieutenant for Norfolk, 1929–44; High Steward of Great Yarmouth; Alderman Norfolk County Council; *b* 5 Sept. 1861; *s* of late J. J. Colman, MP, of Carrow House, Norwich; *m* 1888, Edith M. Davies, Treborth, Bangor, N Wales; two *d*. *Educ:* private school; Switzerland; Germany. Served as Sheriff of Norwich; served as Mayor of Norwich; served as High Sheriff of Norfolk; Hon. Freeman of Norwich and of Great Yarmouth. *Recreations:* shooting, sailing, fishing. *Address:* Crown Point, Norwich. *T:* Norwich 21614. *Clubs:* Norfolk, Norwich; Royal Yacht Squadron, Cowes; Royal Norfolk and Suffolk Yacht, Lowestoft.

Died 22 March 1946.

COLQUHOUN, Sir Iain, 7th Bt of Luss, 1786; KT 1937; DSO 1916; Chief of the Clan; Lord-Lieutenant of Dumbartonshire; Lt-Col, late Scots Guards; Chairman, National Advisory Council for Scotland on Physical Training, since 1937; *b* 1887; *s* of 6th Bt and Justine, *d* of John Kennedy, Underwood, Ayrshire, and Alterton, Lancashire; *S* father, 1910; *m* 1915, Geraldine Bryde (Dinah), *d* of late F. J. Tennant; two *s* three *d*. Served European War, 1914–18 (wounded, DSO and bar, despatches, Bt Major); Member Race-course Betting Control Board, 1928–38; Lord High Commissioner to the General Assembly of the Church of Scotland, 1932, 1940 and 1941; Lord Rector of Glasgow University, 1934–38. *Heir: s* Ivar Iain [*b* 4 Jan. 1916, *m* 1943, Kathleen, 2nd *d* of late W. A. Duncan and of Mrs Duncan, Gorhambury, St Albans; two *s* one *d*]. *Address:* Rossdhu, Luss, Scotland.

Died 12 Nov. 1948.

COLQUHOUN, Col Malcolm Alexander, CMG 1918; DSO 1916; VD; *b* 1870. Served European War, 1914–19 (despatches thrice, DSO, 1914–15 Star, two medals). *Address:* 237 Dalhousie Street, Brantford, Ontario, Canada.

Died 3 Aug. 1950.

COLSON, Francis Henry; *b* 24 April 1857; *s* of Rev. Canon Colson, late Fellow of St John's College, Cambridge, and Emma Mary, *d* of Rev. Dr Taylor, formerly Head Master of Dedham School; *m* Maud (*d* 1940), *d* of Very Rev. Principal Tulloch of St Andrews, Dean of the Order of the Thistle; one *s* one *d.* *Educ:* Haileybury College; St John's College, Cambridge. 4th Classic, University Prizeman in Greek Testament; Fellow of St John's College, Cambridge, 1881–87. Assistant Master at Clifton College, 1881–83; Senior Classical Master at Bradford School, 1883–89; Head Master of Plymouth Coll., 1889–1908; formerly Member of Head Masters' Conference and other educational societies; Member of Plymouth Education Committee, 1903–08; of Cambridgeshire, 1919–39. *Publications:* Quintilian, Book I, Introduction and Commentary; The Week: an essay on the origin and development of the seven-day cycle; Translator originally with G. H. Whitaker of Philo (Loeb series); Editor of Cicero's Pro Milone; Some Selections from Thucydides; Macmillan's Greek Reader; Pope's Iliad Books XXI–XXIV; St Boniface; Sunday Evening Addresses at Plymouth Coll.; many articles in classical and theological journals. *Address:* 23 Grange Road, Cambridge. *T:* Cambridge 3127.

Died 11 June 1943.

COLSON, Lionel Hewitt, CIE 1934; Indian Police, retired; *b* 24 May 1887. Joined Indian Police, 1906; Deputy Inspector-General, 1930; Commissioner of Police, Calcutta, 1931; King's Police Medal, 1916.

Died 15 June 1943.

COLVILE, Lancelot Edward; mine-owner and manufacturer, formerly of Malaga, Spain; *b* Jan. 1876; 3rd *s* of Henry Algernon Colvile of Deansfield, Romsey, Hants; *m* 1st, Katherine Mary, *o d* of William Henry Tudor of Merridale, Staffs; one *d;* 2nd, 1941, Evelyn Dorothy, *d* of Edwin Lester Arnold and Constance Boyce and *g d* of Sir Edwin Arnold. *Educ:* Hurstpierpoint. The first and only British subject to receive the Medalla de Trabajo (Distinguished Industrial Service Order), created by the Spanish Government. *Publication:* owned and edited a newspaper in Spain during the European War for propaganda purposes. *Address:* 16 Belsize Grove, Hampstead, NW3.

Died 2 Aug. 1947.

COLVILE, Comdr Mansel Brabazon Fiennes, DSO 1919; RN (retired); *b* 19 Jan. 1887; *s* of late Rev. G. H. Colvile of Barton House, Leamington, and Mary Elinor Hallowes of Glapwell Hall, Chesterfield; *m* 1st, 1913, Helen Marion (*d* 1923), *d* of J. W. Withers of St John's, Newfoundland; one *s* one *d;* 2nd, 1924, Constance Patricia West-Walker, *d* of A. J. Walker, of Knotmead, Montimer, Berks; one *s.* *Educ:* HMS Britannia. Served European War (DSO); retd list, 1930. *Recreations:* shooting, fishing, sailing. *Address:* Kings Barn, Odiham, Hants.

Died 14 Jan. 1942.

COLVILLE of Culross, 3rd Viscount *cr* 1902; **Charles Alexander Colville;** 13th Baron (Scot.), 1604; 3rd Baron (UK), 1885; *b* 26 May 1888; *s* of 2nd Viscount and Ruby (*d* 1943), *d* of late Col Henry D. Streatfeild, Chiddingstone, Kent; *S* father, 1928; *m* 1931, Kathleen Myrtle, *e d* of late Brig.-Gen. H. R. Gale, RE, CMG, of Bardsey, Saanichton, Vancouver Island; three *s.* Midshipman 1904; Sub-Lt 1908; Lt 1910; Battle of Jutland (despatches) Lieut-Comdr 1918; retired, 1920;

Commander on retired list, 1928. *Heir: s* Master of Colville. *Address:* Fawsyde, Kinneff, Inverbervie, Kincardineshire, Scotland. *Club:* United Service.

Died March 1945.

COLVILLE, Brig.-Gen. Arthur Edward William, CB 1902; late Rifle Brigade; retired; *b* 20 Nov. 1857; *e s* of late Colonel Hon. Sir W. J. Colville, KCVO; *m* 1883, Olivia, *d* of Lord Alfred Spencer Churchill; one *s.* *Educ:* Marlborough. Entered Army, 1875; Capt. 1884; Major, 1898; Lt-Col 1899; Colonel, 1903; served Afghan War, 1878–79 (medal); Mahsood Wuzeeree Expedition, 1881; North-West Frontier, India, 1897 (medal with clasp); South Africa, 1900–02 (Queen's medal six clasps, King's medal two clasps, CB). *Club:* Naval and Military.

Died 26 Feb. 1942.

COLVILLE, Hon. George (Charles), MBE; *b* 1867; *y s* of 1st Viscount Colville of Culross; *m* 1908, Lady (Helen) Cynthia Crewe-Milnes (DCVO 1937), *y d* of 1st Marquess of Crewe, KG; three *s.* *Educ:* Winchester; Trinity Coll. Cambridge (BA). Barrister-at-law, Lincoln's Inn; High Sheriff of County of London, 1930; Younger Brother, Trinity House. *Recreation:* yachting. *Address:* 66 Eccleston Square, SW1. *Clubs:* Turf; Royal Yacht Squadron, Cowes.

Died 19 Sept. 1943.

COLVIN, Sir C. Preston, Kt 1935; OBE 1919; *b* 12 July 1879; *s* of Clement Sneyd Colvin, CSI, and Alice Jane Lethbridge; *m* 1919, Dorothea Mary (*d* 1921), *d* of George Mair, Sydney, NSW; no *c.* *Educ:* Eastman's Academy, Stubbington; Dulwich College. Joined Burma Railways Coy, 1900; Director Traffic of the Indian Railway Board, 1928; Member of the Indian Railway Board in charge of the combined Traffic and Staff portfolios, 1933; Hon. Secretary of Their Majesties' Silver Jubilee Fund, India, 1934; retired, 1936. *Address:* 75 Ashley Gardens, SW1. *T:* Victoria 5889. *Club:* Devonshire.

Died 12 Dec. 1950.

COLVIN, Lt-Col Elliot James Dowell, CIE 1933; *b* 27 July 1885; *s* of late Lieut-Colonel John Russell Colquhoun Colvin; unmarried. *Educ:* Charterhouse; Sandhurst. First Commission, 1904; attached 2nd Batt. R. W. Fusiliers; Central India Horse, 1906; joined Political Dept, 1908; Assistant Resident, Hyderabad till 1910; Secretary to the AGG in CI, 1914, and again 1919; Political Agent, Baghelkhand and Bundelkhand, 1921; Adviser to Maharaja Rewa, 1924–29; Resident Gwalior, 1930; Political Agent, Eastern Rajputana States, 1931–32; Prime Minister, Jammu and Kashmir State, 1932–37; Resident for Baroda and Gujarat States, 1938; served European War, 1914–18 and commanded Bunder Abbas Brigade (South Persia), 1917–18. *Recreations:* shooting, fishing. *Clubs:* Cavalry, Marlborough-Windham.

Died 1 Sept. 1950.

COLVIN, Col J. M. C., VC; retired; *b* 26 Aug. 1870; *e s* of late J. C. Colvin, BCS, and Camilla, *d* of late Rev. E. Morris; *m* 1904, Katharine, *y d* of late Col G. A. Way, CB; two *s* one *d.* *Educ:* Charterhouse; Royal Military Academy, Woolwich (Pollock Gold Medal). Joined Royal Engineers, 1889; served Chitral Relief Expedition, 1895 (medal and clasp); Malakand Field Force, 1897 (despatches, clasp, VC); Buner Field Force, 1898; South Africa, 1901–02 (medal with three clasps, brevet of Major, and qualified for Staff employ); passed Staff College, Camberley, 1909; retired, 1921. *Address:* Catchbells, Stanway, near Colchester. *T:* Marks Tey 28.

Died 7 Dec. 1945.

COLVIN, Thomas, MD, MS; JP, KSG; physician and surgeon; *b* Glasgow, 1863; *s* of late Charles Colvin, Glasgow; *m d* of John Collier, Sefton Park, Liverpool; two *s* one *d.* *Educ:* University of Glasgow. Hon. President of the Catholic Young Men's Societies of Great Britain; a Past Master of St Luke's Catholic

Medical Guild; a writer to the Catholic press on medico-social subjects; Knight of St Gregory, 1923. *Recreations:* walking and golf. *Address:* Marielea, Queen's Drive, Glasgow. *T:* Queen's Park 23.

Died 31 Dec. 1940.

COLVIN, Very Rev. William Evans; Dean of Killala (retired); *m* 1895, Amy, *o d* of Robert Drysdale Turner, Hampstead, NW. *Educ:* Trinity College, Dublin (MA). Ordained 1889; Curate of Killoran, 1889–91; St James's, Didsbury, 1891–93; Wotton, Surrey, 1893–95; Incumbent of Dromard, 1895–1926; Archdeacon of Killala, 1911–28. *Address:* 22 Portland Place, Brighton.

Died 30 Sept. 1949.

COLWELL, Hector Alfred, PhD (Lond.), MB (Lond.); MRCP (Lond.); DPH (Oxon); Late Member of Grand Council and Executive Committee British Empire Cancer Campaign; *b* London, 1875. *Educ:* Tollington Park College; St Bartholomew's Hospital; King's College. Pathological Assistant Middlesex Hospital; served Salonika and Italy, 1916–18; Fellow Royal Society of Medicine; late Vice-President and Examiner Society of Radiographers; Garton Gold Medallist and Prizeman, 1934. *Publications:* Radium X-Rays and the Living Cell (jointly); Practical Biological Chemistry (translation); Essay on the History of Electrotherapy; Introduction to the Study of X-Rays and Radium (jointly); X-Ray and Radium Injuries (with Prof. Russ), 1934; The Mode of Action of Radium and X'Rays on Living Cells (Garton Prize Essay), 1934; Malignant Disease of Gall Bladder, Stomach, and Intestines, etc. (Arch. Middlesex Hosp.); Gideon Harvey (Ann. Med. Hist.); Conversion of Starch to Dextrin by X-Rays (jointly) (Trans. Physical Soc.); Action of repeated Doses of X-Rays upon Developing Chick Embryo (jointly) (Journal Anatomy); Radium Therapy, 1931; The Reducing power of Beta Radialides (Lancet), Radium as a Pharmaceutical Poison (jointly), (Lancet). *Address:* 123 Herne Hill, SE24.

Died 22 July 1946.

COLWYN, 1st Baron *cr* 1917; **Frederick Henry Smith;** Bt *cr* 1912; PC 1924; DL Denbighshire; India rubber and cotton manufacturer; Director of Martin's Bank Ltd; Royal Commission on Income Tax, Bank Amalgamation Committee, Government Contracts Committee, Flax Control Committee, Admiralty Committee on Dockyards, and member of various other Government Committees; JP Denbighshire, Carnarvonshire, Cheshire; *b* 24 Jan. 1859; *s* of late Joshua Smith of Eccles and Elizabeth, *d* of late G. H. Whalley of Trawden; *m* 1882, Elizabeth (*d* 1945), *d* of late Hamilton Savage; one *s* three *d*. High Sheriff Carnarvonshire, 1917–18; Mayor of Colwyn Bay, 1934–35. *Heir: g s* Frederick John Vivian Smith, *b* 26 Nov. 1914. *Address:* Queen's Lodge, Colwyn Bay. *Clubs:* Reform, Devonshire, St James's; Clarendon, Manchester.

Died 26 Jan. 1946.

COMBE, Brig.-Gen. Lionel, CBE (retired); *b* 1861; 2nd *s* of Maj.-General J. J. Combe; *m* 1894, Katherine Louise (*d* 1942), *o d* of W. Shipp, Civil Engineer; one *s*. *Educ:* Charterhouse. Joined the Cameronians, 1883; retired, 1918; in command of Kent Infantry Brigade, 1914, and later the 202nd Infantry Brigade till retired, 1918. *Address:* Dunmow House, Fleet, Hants.

Died 22 April 1950.

COMBE, Sir Ralph Molyneux, Kt 1920; *b* 2 Dec. 1872; *s* of late Major-General J. J. Combe; *m* 1905, Effie Lee, 3rd *d* of James Melville Woodhouse, three *d*. *Educ:* Haileybury College; Exeter College, Oxford. BA 1894. Called to Bar, Inner Temple, 1897; Crown Advocate, East Africa Protectorate, 1905; Attorney-General, 1912; Attorney-General of Nigeria, 1914–18; Chief Justice of Nigeria, 1918–29; retired, 1929. *Address:* Bunce's Shaw, Farley Hill, Berks.

Died 16 Feb. 1946.

COMBRIDGE, Annie, CBE 1935; *b* Sept. 1862; *d* of Mark Barker and Sarah Birch; *m* 1887, Cornelius Combridge (*d* 1934); no *c*. *Educ:* Ladies' Boarding School, Worcester. Vice-Chairman Birmingham Women's Unionist Association. *Recreation:* croquet. *Address:* 7 Westfield Road, Edgbaston, Birmingham. *T:* Edgbaston 1125.

Died 26 Oct. 1949.

COMERFORD, Lt-Col Augustine Ambrose, DSO 1940; TD; MRCVS; OC 1st Defence Regiment RA Home Forces; *b* 30 Jan. 1886; *s* of Major M. H. Comerford, Woodford Green, Essex; *m* 1910, Magdalen Mary van Zeller; two *s* two *d*. *Educ:* St George's, Weybridge; Mount St Mary's, Chesterfield; Royal Veterinary College, London. MRCVS, 1909; attached Remounts Purchasing Comp., 1914–16; Commissioned RAVC, 1916; Balkan Expeditionary Force, 1916; Demobilised, 1919; joined RAVC, TA, 1920; Commanded 418th Battery, RA, 1933–39, when command of the 105th Field Regiment Bedfordshire Yeomanry was assumed; Regt went to France, 1940, as 52nd Heavy Regiment RA. *Recreations:* hunting, was Hon. Sec. to Cambridgeshire Foxhounds, 1929–36. *Address:* The Limes, Potton, Beds. *T:* Potton 218.

Died 25 Feb. 1944.

COMFORT, Mrs J. A.; *see* Marchant, Bessie.

COMMONS, John Rogers; Emeritus Professor of Economics, University of Wisconsin, Madison; *b* 13 Oct. 1862; *s* of John and Clara Rogers Commons; *m* 1890, Ella Downey; one *s* one *d*. *Educ:* Oberlin College; Johns Hopkins University. Instructor, Wesleyan University, 1890; Professor, Oberlin College, 1892; Indiana University, 1893–95; Syracuse University, 1895–99; Expert, Industrial Commission (US), 1901, and National Civic Federation, 1902–04; member Wisconsin Industrial Commission, 1910–13; member US Commission on Industrial Relations, 1913–15; member Wisconsin Minimum Wage Board since 1919; LLD, Oberlin College, University of Wisconsin, 1931. *Publications:* distribution of Wealth, 1894; Proportional Representation, 1896; Races and Immigrants in America, 1906; Trade Unions and Labour Problems, 1905, 1922 (2nd series); Labour and Administration, 1913; Labour Legislation (with J. B. Andrews), 1915, 1919, 1925, 1936; History of Labour in US (with associates), 1915 (2 vols); Documentary History of American Industrial Society (10 vols), 1914; Industrial Goodwill, 1919; Industrial Government, 1920; Legal Foundations of Capitalism, 1924; Institutional Economics, 1934; Myself: An Autobiography, 1934. *Address:* 1315 NE 5th Terrace, Fort Lauderdale, Fla, USA. *Clubs:* Town and Gown, Madison.

Died 11 May 1945.

COMPTON, Col Lord Douglas (James Cecil), CBE 1918; *b* 15 Nov. 1865; 4th *s* of 4th Marquis of Northampton, KG; *m* 1917, Dollie, *d* of late M. Woolf. *Educ:* Eton College; Sandhurst. Joined the 9th Lancers, 1885; served in India and South Africa, 1891–1910; first on the staff of Lord Wenlock when Governor of Madras, afterwards with the 9th Lancers; served throughout the S African war with that regiment (despatches twice; brevet majority) commanded the 9th Lancers, 1908–12; retired, May 1914; commanded an Infantry Base Depot in France, 1915–19 (despatches). *Recreation:* fond of almost all sports and most games. *Address:* Beverley House, Frant Road, Tunbridge Wells, Kent.

Died 23 July 1944.

COMPTON, Henry Francis; JP, DL; Official Verderer of the New Forest since 1936; *b* 16 Jan. 1872; *e s* of late Henry Compton; *m* 1st, 1895, Dorothy, *e d* of Sir Richard Musgrave, 11th Bt; two *d*; 2nd, 1940, Violet-Lindsay de Bathe, *d* of late Nicholas Wood. MP (C), New Forest Division, Hants, 1905; Capt. 4th Vol. Batt. Hants Regt, 1900–02; Capt. Hants RHA 1915–19;

Verderer of the New Forest. *Address:* Blackwater, Lyndhurst; Minstead Manor, Lyndhurst. *Clubs:* Marlborough, Turf.

Died 11 April 1943.

COMPTON-THORNHILL, Sir Anthony John; *see* Thornhill.

COMRIE, Leslie John, MA, PhD; FRS 1950; FRAS; Founder Scientific Computing Service; *b* Pukekohe, NZ, 15 Aug. 1893; *m* 1933, Phyllis Betty, *d* of late H. D. Kitto, Stroud, Glos; one *s*. *Educ:* Auckland Grammar School; Auckland University College (Sir George Grey Scholar, Senior University Scholar); Cambridge University (PhD, Isaac Newton Student). Assist Prof. of Mathematics and Astronomy, Swarthmore College, Pa, USA, 1922; Assistant Professor of Astronomy, Northwestern University, Chicago, 1924; Deputy Superintendent, HM Nautical Almanac Office, Royal Naval College, SE 10, 1926, Superintendent 1930–36. Hon. Member, NZ Astronomical Society, 1933, and Royal Society of NZ, 1945. *Publications:* Third edition of Barlow's Tables 1930; Standard Four-Figure Mathematical Tables, 1931; Four-Figure Tables with the Argument in Time, 1931; Hughes' Tables for Sea and Air Navigation, 1938; The Application of the Brunsviga Twin 13Z Calculating Machine to Survey Problems, 1940; Fourth edition of Barlow's Tables, 1941; The Twin Marchant Calculating Machine and its Application to Survey Problems, 1942; Chambers's Four-Figure Mathematical Tables, 1947; Chambers's Six-Figure Mathematical Tables, 1948; About one hundred papers on astronomical subjects, calculating machines and mathematical tables. *Recreations:* tennis, shooting (Cambridge half-blue), foreign travel. *Address:* 131 Maze Hill, Blackheath, SE3. *T:* Greenwich 1545.

Died 11 Dec. 1950.

COMYN, Lt-Col Edward Walter, CMG 1919, DSO 1918; late RA; *b* 1868; *s* of S. E. Comyn, MD; *m* 1st, Elinor, *d* of J. Fall; 2nd, Margaret, *d* of A. L. French, Ceylon, and *widow* of G. S. Taylor, Lt RASC; no *c*. *Educ:* Oxford Military College; Royal Military Academy, Woolwich. 1st Commission in Royal Artillery, 1887; served in various stations at home and abroad; commanded a field and heavy brigade of artillery on the Western Front, 1915–18 (despatches four times, CMG, DSO, Croix de Guerre); retired, 1920. *Address:* Church Farm House, Rotherwick, Basingstoke.

Died 21 Nov. 1949.

COMYN, Henry Ernest Fitzwilliam, CB 1912; late Assistant Solicitor to the Treasury; *b* 25 Jan. 1854; *s* of late Henry Fitzwilliam Comyn of Staplefield, Sussex; *m* 1884, Marian (*d* 1938), *d* of late C. R. Skinner, Bedwardine House, Worcester. *Educ:* Bedford. *Address:* 56 The Avenue, Surbiton.

Died 27 Jan. 1941.

COMYNS, Henry Joseph, CBE 1933; retired Civil Servant; *b* 24 July 1868; *s* of Patrick Joseph Comyns (Civil Servant) and Grace Mary Allen; *m* 1911, Sylvia Agnes Davenport, *g d* of Sir George Macfarren (Composer); one *s* one *d*. *Educ:* St Charles's College, Notting Hill. Clerk in the Legal Dept of the Local Government Board, 1889; Called to Bar, Gray's Inn, 1897; Assistant Private Secretary and Private Secretary to Rt Hon. John Burns, MP, 1907–12; Secretary of the Disabled Sailors and Soldiers Committee 1915; Member of the Committee on Old Age Pensions, 1918; Assistant Solicitor to the Minister of Health, 1919–33; Member of Viscount Chelmsford's, and Lord Addington's Committees on the consolidation of the Local Government Acts and the Public Health Acts, 1930–36. *Recreations:* formerly cricket, cycling, tennis and golf. *Address:* Mill Road, Angmering, Littlehampton.

Died 21 Dec. 1943.

CONERNEY, Very Rev. John Pirrie, MA; Dean of Raphoe since 1917; Chaplain to Lord Bishop of Derry. *Educ:* Trinity College, Dublin. Ordained 1894; Curate of Donagheady, 1894–97; incumbent of Learmount, 1897–1900; Rector of Templecrone, 1900–02; Burt, 1902–03; Upper Cumber, 1903–05; Dunfanaghy, 1905. *Address:* Dunfanaghy, Co. Donegal, Ireland.

Died 2 Nov. 1940.

CONEYBEER, Hon. Frederick William; *b* Bristol, England, 27 Sept. 1859; *s* of late J. P. Coneybeer; *m* 1886, Margaret Jane, *d* of John Thomas, Merthyr-Tydvil; three *s* one *d*. *Educ:* Orange, NSW. Went to Australia with his parents, 1865; settled at Orange, New South Wales; served apprenticeship with his father in trade of collar-making; arrived in South Australia, 1881; President of first Organising Committee Trades and Labour Council; for twenty years Life Trustee of Adelaide Trades Hall, which he helped to found, also assisted to establish Daily Herald newspaper, of which he was a Director from its inception; Ex-President of Eight Hours' Movement and on original Committee of the Homestead Blocks' League; twenty years Visiting Magistrate to Mental Defectives' Home; MP for East Torrens, 1893–1921, and 1924–30; Secretary and Whip to Parliamentary Labour Party for ten years; Whip to Price-Peake Government, four years; Minister of Education Price-Peake Cabinet 1908–09, and in Verran Govt, 1910–12; Speaker of the House of Assembly, South Australia, 1915–21; First Parliamentary Representative on Adelaide University Council; Member of Board of Governors of Botanic Gardens. *Recreations:* gardening, reading, photography, and collecting public and political records. *Address:* Fourth Avenue, St Peters, South Australia. *T:* Cent. 22.

Died 30 May 1950.

CONGREVE, Comdr Sir Geoffrey, 1st Bt *cr* 1927; DSO 1940; late RN; 2nd *s* of late General Sir Walter Congreve, VC; *m* Madeleine, *d* of late H. Allhusen of Stoke Court, Stoke Poges; three *d*. *Educ:* RN Colleges, Osborne and Dartmouth. Served in Grand Fleet as midshipman, sub-lieutenant and lieutenant during European War; ADC to GOC in command Egypt and Palestine, 1920–21; retired list, 1928; served War of 1939–40 (DSO). Owns about 3000 acres. *Recreations:* steeplechasing and hunting. *Heir:* none. *Address:* Chartley Hall, Stafford; Congreve Manor, Stafford. *Club:* Travellers'.

Died 28 July 1941 (ext).

CONINGHAM, Air Marshal Sir Arthur, KCB 1942; KBE 1946; CB 1941; DSO 1917; MC; DFC; AFC; *b* Brisbane, 1895; *m* 1932, Lady Frank, *widow* of Sir H. G. Frank, Bt, GBE, KCB; one *d*. *Educ:* New Zealand. Served War, 1914–19, with New Zealand Forces, Samoa and Egypt, 1914–16; joined RFC 1916; European War, 1916–19 (despatches, MC, DSO, DFC); Kurdistan, 1923 (despatches); flew from Cairo to Kano, Oct. 1925 (AFC); War of 1939–45, Bomber Command (CB), worked with 8th Army in North Africa (KCB); formed 1st Tactical Air Force, French North Africa, 1943; operations, Sicily and Italy, 1943; AOC-in-C Second Tactical Air Force, 1944–45; Air Marshal, 1946; AOC-in-C, Flying Training Command, 1945–47; retired, 1947. *Recreations:* flying, sailing, golf. *Address:* The Hockett, Cookham Dean. *T:* Marlow 588. *Clubs:* Royal Air Force, Royal Aero, International Sportsmen's; Royal Corinthian Yacht (Burnham-on-Crouch); RAF Yacht (Calshot); Royal Yacht Squadron (Cowes); Travellers' (Paris).

Died 30 Jan. 1948.

CONNAL, Benjamin Michael, MA (Oxford and New Zealand); Emeritus Professor of the University of Leeds; *b* Christchurch, NZ, 27 March 1861; *m* 1909, Clara Winifred Matthews, Headmistress, Dulwich High School for Girls; two *d*. *Educ:* Christ's College, Christchurch, NZ; Canterbury College of the New

Zealand University; Corpus Christi College, Oxford (Exhibitioner), 1st Class Classical Mods., 1883; 1st Class Lit. Hum., 1886. Assistant Lecturer in Classics in the Yorkshire College, Leeds, 1887; Lecturer in Ancient History, 1889; Lecturer in Latin, 1894; Professor of Classics, 1904-23; Professor of Latin, 1923-26; Acting Professor of Latin, 1930; Member of Council of the Classical Association, 1912-15; Member of the Northern Universities Joint Matriculation Board, 1904-26; Vice-Chairman, 1909-26; Member of the Teachers Registration Council, 1913-27; Member of the Secondary School Examinations Council, 1917-27. *Address:* Raupaki, Bramhope, nr Leeds. *TA:* Bramhope, Leeds. *T:* Arthington 46.

Died 28 April 1944.

CONNAL, Col Kenneth Hugh Munro, CB 1935; OBE 1920; TD; DL County of the City of Glasgow; *b* 28 Feb. 1870; *s* of William Connal, Solsgirth, Dollar and Emily Jessie, *d* of Col R. N. Campbell, of Ormidale, Argyllshire; *m* 1901, Kitty MacIndoe, *d* of Alex. Cochran, Glasgow; two *d. Educ:* Cheltenham College. 2nd Lieut Glasgow Highlanders, 1887; transferred to QO Royal Glasgow Yeomanry; served with them in South African War, 1900-01 (Queen's medal, four clasps); commanded QOR Glasgow Yeomanry in European War, 1914-19, served in Gallipoli, Palestine, France and Belgium; commanded V Corps mounted troops, 1916-17 (1914-15 star and medals). *Recreation:* hunting. *Address:* Monktonhead, Monkton, Ayrshire. *T:* Prestwick 7559. *Clubs:* United Service, Cavalry; Western (Glasgow); County (Ayr).

Died 6 Aug. 1949.

CONNAUGHT AND STRATHEARN, 2nd Duke of, *cr* 1874; Earl of Sussex *cr* 1874; **Alastair Arthur Windsor;** Lt R. Scots Greys; *b* 9 Aug. 1914; *o c* of the Duchess of Fife and Prince Arthur of Connaught (*d* 1938); *S* grandfather, 1942.

Died 26 April 1943.

CONNELL, James MacLuckie; Minister, author and lecturer; *b* Perth, 30 March 1867; *s* of James Hamilton Connell and Margaret MacLuckie; *m* Margaret Davidson Cowan; no *c. Educ:* Public School, Kirn, Argyll. Junior Assistant Curator, Kelvingrove Museum and Art Galleries, Glasgow; studied at Glasgow and Edinburgh Universities and Manchester College, Oxford; and Ministered at Newbury, Glasgow, Exeter, Bury St Edmunds, and for 25 years at Westgate Chapel, Lewes; retired 1936; a Trustee of Dr Williams' Library, London, 1920-40; President, Lewes Rotary Club 1933-34. *Publications:* Edited A Book of Devotional Readings from the Literature of Christendom, 1913; The Story of an Old Meeting House, 1916; Problems of Reconstruction, 1919; The New Gate to an Old Meeting House, 1921; Devotional Classics: Upton Lectures delivered at Manchester College, Oxford, 1924; contributed Thomas Paine's Residence in Lewes, to At the Sign of the Bull, Lewes 1924; edited Common Prayer in Nine Services, 1926; Thomas Walker Horsfield, the Historian of Sussex, 1927; The Continuity of Divine Inspiration since New Testament Times: a Plea for an Extended Lectionary, 1928; Lewes: its Religious History, 1931; The Wheel: a Rotary Address, 1933; Thomas Paine, 1939; John Henry Every, 1941; contributor to The Hibbert Journal, The Rotarian, etc. *Recreation:* travel. *Address:* 6 St Anne's Crescent, Lewes. *T:* Lewes 192.

Died 17 June 1947.

CONNELLY, Sir Francis Raymond, Kt 1948; Lord Mayor of Melbourne; *b* Melb., 1 Sept. 1895; *s* of late John Connelly, E St Kilda; *m* 1948, Patricia Annie, *d* of G. Holschier, Womboota, NSW. *Educ:* Xavier Coll., Melb. Mem. Melb. City Cl., 1934; Lord Mayor, 1945-46, 1946-47, 1947-48; Mg. Dir, Moreland Grain and Free Stores Pty Ltd, Latrobe Motors Pty Ltd.

Recreations: golf, tennis, bowls, racing. *Address:* 10 Como Av., South Yarra, Vic., Australia. *Clubs:* MCC; Victoria Amateur Turf, VR (Melbourne); Peninsula Golf, Metropolitan Golf.

Died 4 May 1949.

CONNIBERE, Sir Charles (Wellington), KBE 1936; unmarried. A Founder of the Australian firm of Connibere Grieve & Connibere; a generous donor to philanthropic works; President of Victorian Eye and Ear Hospital; Vice-Pres. of Sunday Christian Observance Council, and of Victorian Institute of Almoners; a Member of Advisory Committee of Melbourne Children's Hospital, of Council of Anglican Diocese of Melbourne, of Australian and Victorian Red Cross Councils, of Executive Committee of Melbourne City Mission. *Address:* Southdean, Irving Road, Toorak, SE2, Melbourne, Australia.

Died 25 June 1941.

CONNOLLY, Martin; Assistant General Secretary Boilermakers and Iron Shipbuilders Society; City Councillor Newcastle-upon-Tyne; *b* 1874; *m* 1st, 1898, Mary (*d* 1926), *d* of William Young; 2nd, 1929, Mrs Hannah Margaret Whitelaw, Byker; one *s.* Contested Middlesborough, 1922 and 1923; MP (Lab) Newcastle East, 1924-29. *Address:* Broomridge House, 40 Broomridge Avenue, Condercum Estate, Newcastle-on-Tyne, 5. *TA:* Executive Newcastle. *T:* Newcastle-on-Tyne 34981.

Died 8 Aug. 1945.

CONNOLLY, Richard Joseph, (in religion, Hugh), OSB; *b* 1873; *s* of Nathaniel Connolly of Werajel, Carcoar, NSW. *Educ:* Downside; Christ's College, Cambridge (BA 1899, 2nd Tyrwhitt Hebrew Scholarship, 1901). Priest, 1899; Head of Benet House, Cambridge, 1904-16; Lecturer in Syriac, Christ's College, 1911; on Board of Oriental Studies, 1911-12. *Publications:* The Liturgical Homilies of Narsai; The So-called Egyptian Church Order; Didascalia Apostolorum; volumes in the Corpus Scriptorum Christianorum Orientalium and Text and Translation Series; The De Sacramentis, a work of St Ambrose (privately printed); articles in Journal of Theological Studies, etc. *Address:* Downside Abbey, Stratton-on-the-Fosse, nr Bath.

Died 16 March 1948.

CONOLLY, Brig. John James Pollock, CIE 1946; retired; *b* 7 June 1896; *s* of W. G. Conolly, MA, LLD, Grantstown House, Waterford, Ireland; *m* 1938, Rona Madge, *d* of Rt Hon. W. A. Watt, PC; one *d. Educ:* Foyle College, Londonderry; RMC, Sandhurst. European War, 1915-18 (wounded, despatches twice); NW Frontier, India, 1930, and 1936-39; War of 1939-45, Comdr Sikh Regt, Lt-Col 1940; Brig. 1942; retired, Jan. 1947. *Address:* National Bank of Australasia, Collins Street, Melbourne, Australia. *Club:* Naval and Military.

Died 7 Dec. 1950.

CONROY, Charles O'Neill, KC, OBE; General Counsel and Director Reid Newfoundland Co., Ltd; *b* Dublin, 24 Jan. 1871; *s* of Judge James G. Conroy and Elizabeth O'Neill; *m* 1899, Mary A. (decd), *d* of George Weathers, MRCS, LRCP London; four *s* three *d. Educ:* St Bede's College, Manchester; University College and School, London; Wren and Gurney's. Admitted Solicitor, 1899; called to Bar, 1900; KC 1913; Master Supreme Court of Newfoundland, 1914; Bencher Law Society of Newfoundland since 1909, Treasurer since 1941; retired from general practice, 1919; resumed, 1931; Lieut-Col commanding Catholic Cadet Corps, 1911-26; Member Executive Committee, Newfoundland Patriotic Association during War; President, Permanent Marine Disasters Fund Committee. *Recreations:* motoring, angling, photography, golf. *Address:* Raheen, Bonaventure Avenue, St John's, Newfoundland. *TA:* Yornoc, Saintjohns. *Clubs:* Knights of Columbus, St John's.

Died 21 Dec. 1946.

CONSETT, Rear-Adm. Montagu William Warcop Peter, CMG 1919; JP, DL, North Riding Yorks; *b* 15 April 1871; *e surv. s* of late William Warcop Peter Consett and Edith, *e d* of Lord Charles Lennox Kerr; *m* 1st, 1908, Ethel Maud (*d* 1933), *d* of Hon. William Wilson, New South Wales; three *s*; 2nd, 1937, Aileen Ada Bann. Entered Navy, 1884; Lieut 1893; Commander, 1904; Captain, 1911; Rear-Adm. 1921; retired, Nov. 1921; Naval Attache, Norway and Sweden, 1912–19; Denmark, 1912–17; Naval Adviser to the Supreme Allied Council in Paris and the Council of Ambassadors, and British Naval Representative on the Inter-Allied Committee of Versailles, April–Dec. 1920; Officer of Legion of Honour; Commander 2nd Class Order of St Olaf (Norway), of 1st Class Order of the Sword (Sweden). *Publication:* The Triumph of Unarmed Forces (1914–1918), 1923. *Address:* Brawith Hall, Thirsk. *T:* Thirsk 2187.

Died 8 March 1945.

CONSTABLE, Walter George Raleigh C.; *see* Chichester-Constable.

CONTI, Italia; actress and Head of large Training School for the Stage; *b* last part of nineteenth century; *d* of Luigi Conti, singer, Italian by birth but later a naturalised Englishman, and Emily Mary, *e d* of James Castle, late Professor Regius of King's College. *Educ:* Warden Court, Haywards Heath; Kensington Academy. Went on the stage at an early age; appeared first with Ada Rehan at Lyceum Theatre, then toured with F. R. Benson, and later with John Hare and the Bancrofts; played in several London seasons with great success; produced Where the Rainbow Ends for Charles Hawtrey, 1911, this started her Stage School and her famous Acting and Dancing Children, now known all over the world; in 1918 asked by President of Board of Education to help him form an Advisory Committee to draw up regulations for licensing of stage children and present Theatrical Licence is direct result of those efforts; among the famous stars who have passed through her hands are Noel Coward, Gertrude Lawrence, Jane Baxter, Brian Aherne, Freddie Bartholomew, Anton Dolin, Margaret Lockwood, Jack Hawkins, Roma Beaumont, Jimmy Hanley, etc.; founder and Hon. Organiser of Rainbow League, which helps British Hospitals and Youth Organisations. *Publications:* has written several plays and reconstructed The Windmill Man. *Recreations:* motoring, and is devoted to children and dogs. *Address:* Rainbow League Ltd Offices, Tavistock Little Theatre, WC1. *TA:* Taliacont, Kincross, London. *T:* Euston 2796. *Club:* Arts Theatre.

Died 8 Feb. 1946.

CONVERSE, Frederick Shepherd, AB, Mus. Doc; *b* 5 Jan. 1871; *s* of Edmund Winchester Converse and Charlotte Augusta Shepherd; *m* 1894, Emma C. Tudor, Boston; five *d*. *Educ:* private school; Harvard University; Königle Academie der Tonkunst, Munich, Germany. Teacher of Musical Composition at New England Conservatory of Music and at Harvard University until 1906; retired to devote entire time to composition; Vice-Pres. and Trustee, Boston Opera Co. until 1914, also Vice-Pres. and Trustee, NE Conservatory; Captain in Massachusetts State Guards, 1917–18; Dean of Faculty, New England Conservatory, 1930–38; Member American Academy of Arts and Letters, NY, 1936. *Publications:* principal musical works: Festival of Pan (tone poem), 1906; Mystic Trumpeter (tone poem), 1907; Job (oratorio), 1910; Ormazd (tone poem), 1910; The Pipe of Desire (opera), 1911; The Sacrifice (opera), 1913; The Peace Pipe (cantata), 1914; The Flight of the Eagle (cantata), 1921; Flivver Ten Million (fantasy for orchestra), 1926; California (festival scenes for orchestra),

1929; American Sketches (symphonic suite), 1933. *Recreations:* formerly golf, polo, fishing; now watching others do these things. *Address:* The Four Winds, Westwood, Mass, USA. *T:* Dedham 0041. *Clubs:* Tavern, St Botolph, Boston.

Died 8 June 1940.

CONWAY, Robert Russ, MA; *b* Rochester, 1863; *s* of late Rev. R. Conway, Vicar of Alconbury, Huntingdon; *m* 1899, Bertha Charlotte Pinwill; one *d*. *Educ:* Haileybury; St Catharine's College, Cambridge. Assistant Master at Chardstock and King's School, Rochester; Perse School, Cambridge, 1887–1902; Bursar and 2nd Master, Weymouth College, 1902–17; Headmaster, 1917–27; represented Cambridge in Athletics and Cross-Country; President CUH and H, 1888–1902; Past Senior Grand Warden of Dorset; Past Assistant GDC England, Past Grand St B England (Royal Arch); Past Grand Mark Deacon, England; Past Provincial Grand Mark Master of Dorset; JP Weymouth. *Publications:* A History of Weymouth College, 1901–1927; a few articles on Athletics. *Recreations:* now confined to watching other people's games, especially cricket. *Address:* 29 Spa Road, Weymouth. *T:* 1866.

Died 16 Nov. 1950.

CONYERS, Dorothea; *b* 1873; *d* of Col J. Blood Smyth, Fedamore, Co. Limerick; *m* 1st, 1892, Col Charles Conyers (*d* 1916), Royal Irish Fusiliers, *s* of Grady Conyers, Castletown Conyers, Co. Limerick; one *s* one *d*; 2nd, 1917, Capt. J. White, Nantenan, Co. Limerick. *Publications:* The Thorn Bit; The Boy, some Horses and a Girl; Peter's Pedigree; The Strayings of Sandy; Conversion of Concregan; For Henry of Navarre; Some Impostors and Tinker; The Arrival of Antony; Sally; Further Strayings of Sandy; Old Andy; Recollections of Sport in Ireland; A Mixed Pack; Meave; The Trading of Gannymeade Bun, 1917; The Blighting of Bartram, 1918; BEN, 1919; Sporting Reminiscences, 1919; Tiranogue, 1919; Treasury Notes, 1926; Bobbie, 1928; Managing Ariadne, 1931; Whoopee, 1932; The Elf, 1936; Phil's Castle, 1937; A Lady of Discretion, 1939; Gulls at Rossnacorey, 1939; The Best People, 1941; Rosalie, 1945; Dark, 1946; Kicking Foxes, 1947. *Recreations:* hunting, skating, tennis, fishing, fond of opera. *Address:* Nantenan, Ballingrane, Co. Limerick.

Died 25 May 1949.

CONYERS, Evelyn Augusta, CBE 1919; RRC; Director, Victorian Trained Nurses' Club, Ltd; Vice-President, Royal Victorian College of Nursing; late Matron-in-Chief Australian Army Nursing Service, AIF; *d* of William Conyers. Served European War, 1914–19 (CBE); RRC with bar Florence Nightingale medal; Silver Jubilee Medal, 1935. *Address:* 130 Wattle Valley Road, East Camberwell, Victoria, Australia.

Died 5 Sept. 1944.

CONYERS, His Hon. Sir James Reginald, Kt 1944; CBE 1936; JP; Speaker of House of Assembly, Bermuda, since 1933; *b* Hamilton, Bermuda, 3 Sept. 1879; *s* of James Adam and Emma Maria Conyers; *m* 1946, Florence Duncan Trott. *Educ:* Saltus Grammar School, Bermuda. Called to Bar, Inner Temple, 1902; Bermuda Bar, 1903; has been acting Attorney-General and Police Magistrate for Central and Western Districts; Justice of Peace; Member of House of Assembly, Bermuda, since 1904; Chairman of Board of Trade, 1925–27; Jubilee medal, 1935; represented Bermuda at Coronation, 1937; Coronation Medal, 1937. *Recreations:* fishing, golf. *Address:* Blue Water, Pembroke, Bermuda. *TA:* Rex. *T:* 1342. *Clubs:* Royal Bermuda Yacht, Mid-Ocean (Bermuda).

Died 26 July 1948.

COOK, Sir Basil (Alfred) Kemball-, KCMG 1925; CB 1918; *b* 21 May 1876; *m* 1st, 1906, Nancy Pavitt (who divorced him 1930); four *s* one *d*; 2nd, 1931, Cécile, *d* of General Olenitch, Imperial Russian Army. *Educ:* Eton;

King's College, Cambridge. Joined Transport Department Admiralty 1900; Director of Naval Sea Transport, Ministry of Shipping, 1917; Director of Admiralty Transports, 1919; Chairman of the Managing Board of the Maritime Service Reparation Commission, 1920; Asst British Delegate Reparation Commission, 1921–26; Managing Director, British Tanker Co., 1927–35; Director British Guiana Consolidated Goldfields, Ltd, 1936–38; Deputy Post Warden, Post 3 ARP Mayfair, 1940–42; Deputy Divisional Food Officer, London, 1942; Divisional Food Officer, London, 1944–48; Commandeur Légion d'Honneur; Cr Order of Leopold; Commendatore San Maurizio e San Lazzaro; Commander Order of St Stanislas (with Star). *Address:* 9 Queen's Gate, SW7.

Died 28 Nov. 1949.

COOK, Sir Edmund Ralph, Kt 1934; CBE 1930; LLD (Hon.) Manchester, 1938; *yr* and *o surv. s* of Edmund Alleyne Cook; *m* Florence Ruth, *yr d* of Arthur Thomas Burton; no *c. Educ:* Fulneck School near Leeds; Königsfeld, Black Forest. Admitted a Solicitor, 1894; Secretary to The Law Society, 1914–39; Hon. Member of the Canadian Bar Association, 1932; Hon. Member of Scottish Law Agents Society, 1932; Hon. Member of the Yorkshire Law Society, 1935. *Recreation:* golf. *Address:* 95 Chiltern Court, Baker Street, NW1. *T:* Welbeck 5544, Extension 95. *Club:* Reform.

Died 13 Feb. 1942.

COOK, Sir Ernest Henry, Kt 1923; DSc London and Bristol (Hon.); Alderman and JP City and County of Bristol; Chairman of Education Committee, 1903–31; Past President, Association of Education Committees of England and Wales; *b* Bristol, 1855; *s* of John and Charlotte Cook of Gloucestershire; *m* 1st, Emily (*d* 1898), *d* of William Lawson of Bristol; 2nd, Margaret Hessie, *d* of S. R. Potter, MD, of Cullompton, Devon; one *s* two *d. Educ:* Bristol Trade and Mining School; Royal College of Science, Dublin; London University. Royal Exhibition, 1872; Associate Royal College of Science, 1875; BSc and Exhibition in Chemistry at Lond. Univ. 1877; DSc 1887; elected Bristol School Board, 1895; Town Council, 1900; JP Bristol, 1905; Alderman, 1909; Lord Mayor of Bristol, 1921–22; One of the founders of Bristol University; Chevalier de la Légion d'honneur, 1927; Past Provincial GM of Freemasons. *Publications:* sundry papers and scientific treatises. *Address:* 40 Alma Road, Clifton, Bristol. *T:* Bristol 36439.

Died 18 Jan. 1945.

COOK, Sir Frederick Charles, Kt 1942; CB 1937; DSO 1919; MC; MInstCE, FSI; Civil Engineer; Partner Howard Humphreys & Sons, Consulting Engineers, Westminster; Vice-President Institution of Civil Engineers; Hon. Member Institution of Royal Engineers and Institution of Municipal and County Engineers; *b* 1875; *s* of late C. C. Cook, Worthing; *m* Amelia May, *d* of late G. F. Bult; three *s.* Articled to late Miles Aspinall, civil engineer, and subsequently held various engineering appointments in local Government Service; Engineering Inspector, Ministry of Transport, 1920; Divisional Road Engineer, 1921; Deputy Chief Engineer, 1929; Chief Engineer, 1935; retired, 1942; but remained on in the Ministry of Transport for three years in an advisory capacity and acted as Chairman of many important Government Committees. Served European War, 1914–19, in Royal Engineers (despatches, MC, DSO, Croix de Guerre). *Address:* The Mount, Ashtead Park, Ashtead, Surrey.

Died 15 May 1947.

COOK, Brig.-Gen. Henry Rex, CIE 1919; *b* 1863; *m* 1914, Frances Helen (*d* 1938), *d* of John O'Sullivan, Cork. Served Burma, 1886; East Africa, 1901 (medal with clasp); European War, 1914–19 (CIE). *Address:* Castle, Lostwithiel, Cornwall.

Died 21 Jan. 1950.

COOK, Hon. James H.; *see* Hume-Cook.

COOK, Rt Hon. Sir Joseph, PC 1914; GCMG 1918; *b* England, Dec. 1860; *m* 1885, Mary (DBE 1925), *d* of George Turner, of Chesterton, Staffs; two *s* two *d.* Went to Australia, 1885; MLA Hartley, 1891–1901; Postmaster-Gen., 1894–98; Minister for Mines and Agriculture, 1898–99; Member of House of Representatives for Parramatta, 1901–21; Minister for Defence, 1909–10; Prime Minister and Minister Home Affairs, Commonwealth of Australia, 1913–14; Minister for the Navy, 1917–20; Commonwealth Treasurer, 1920–21; High Commissioner for Australia, 1921–27; a representative of Australia at Versailles Peace Conference, 1919; Senior Australian Delegate to the 3rd Assembly of the League of Nations, 1922; Australian Delegate to the Genoa International Conference, 1922. Free Trader. *Address:* Silchester, Fairfax Road, Bellevue Hill, Sydney, New South Wales.

Died 30 July 1947.

COOK, Stanley Arthur, LittD; Hon. DLitt (Oxford); Hon. DD (Aberdeen); FBA; Fellow of Gonville and Caius College, Cambridge; *b* King's Lynn, 12 April 1873; *s* of J. T. Cook and Francis Else; *m* Annette (*d* 1942), *d* of W. T. Bell. *Educ:* Wyggeston School, Leicester; Gonville and Caius College, Cambridge. 1st class Semitic Languages Tripos, 1894; 1st class Tyrwhitt Scholar and Mason Hebrew Prize, 1895; Jeremie Septuagint Prize, 1896. Editorial staff of the Encyclopædia Biblica, 1896–1903; Editorial Adviser on Old Testament and Semitic subjects, Ency. Brit. 11th edit., and Department Editor for Biblical Subjects, 14th edition; Editor for the Palestine Exploration Fund 1902–32; College Lecturer in Hebrew, 1904–32, and inn Comparative Religion, 1912–20; Regius Professor of Hebrew, 1932–38; Joint-editor of the Cambridge Ancient History; Pres. of the Society for Old Testament Study, 1925; Hon. Member of the Society of Biblical Literature and Exegesis (USA). *Publications:* Glossary of Aramaic Inscriptions, 1898; completion of Wm Wright's Syriac Catalogue, University Library, Cambridge, 1901; ed. Nash Papyrus; the Laws of Moses and Code of Hammurabi, 1903; Critical Notes on Old Testament History, 1907; Religion of Ancient Palestine, 1908; contributor to Cambridge Biblical Essays (ed. Swete), 1909, to R. H. Charles' ed. of Apocrypha (1 Esdras), 1913, to People and the Book (ed. Peake), to Old Testament Essays (ed. D. C. Simpson), to Hammerton's Universal History; to the Cambridge Ancient History, vols i–iii, vi, and to presentation volumes to Ridgeway, Cumont, T. H. Robinson, and A. Bertholet; The Foundations of Religion (People's Books); The Study of Religions, 1914; new ed. of Prof. Robertson Smith's Kinship and Marriage in Early Arabia (1903), and of his Religion of the Semites (1927); The Religion of Ancient Palestine in the Light of Archæology (Schweich Lectures, 1930); Place of the Old Test in Modern Research; ed. of Essays by late Prof Kennett, 1933; The Old Testament; a Reinterpretation, 1936; The 'Truth' of the Bible, 1938; The Rebirth of Christianity, 1943; An Introduction to the Bible, 1946; The Crisis in Religion; numerous articles on Biblical and Semitic subjects and on comparative religion. *Address:* 26 Lensfield Road, Cambridge.

Died 26 Sept. 1949.

COOKE, Col Alfred Fothergill, CMG 1918; late 2nd KO Yorkshire LI and APD; *b* 1871; *s* of H. R. Cooke, Bombay Civil Service; *m* 1900, Mimi Lucardie Crawford, *d* of Hugh Crawford, of Crummock, Beith, Ayrshire. *Educ:* Sedbergh; RMC Sandhurst. Served NW Frontier of India, 1897–98 (medal and two clasps); served throughout European War; retired pay, 1920. *Address:* 11 Clifton Crescent Folkestone.

Died 5 May 1946.

COOKE, Brig.-Gen. Bertram Hewett Hunter, CMG 1918; CBE 1919; DSO 1916; late Rifle Brigade; *b* 3 July 1874; *s* of late John Edward Cooke, RN; *m* 1903, Mary Henrietta, 2nd *d* of Thomas Hume Cardwell of Newton House, Tetbury, Glos; two *s* one *d*. *Educ*: Eton; Sandhurst. Entered Army, 1895; served with 2nd Batt. Rifle Brigade, Nile Expedition, 1898; battle of Omdurman (Queen's medal and Khedive's medal and clasp); Adjutant 4th batt. 1899–1901; served South African War, 1901–02, with Mounted Infantry (wounded, Queen's medal and 5 clasps); Adjutant London Rifle Brigade, 1903–06; passed Staff College, Quetta, 1910; Staff Captain, War Office, 1911–13; Brigade Major, 2nd Infantry Brigade, Aldershot Command, 1913–14; served European War, 1914–18; was on Staff as Brigade-Major (severely wounded battle of Marne), DAAG, AAG, and DA and QMG (despatches five times, Bt Lt-Col, DSO, CMG, CBE, 1914 Star, Order of St Stanislas, 3rd class with swords (Russia), Belgian Croix de Guerre, Commandeur Ordre du Mérite Agricole (France)); served with Royal Air Force, 1918–19, as Brig.-Gen. in charge of Administration, and in command of Midland Area; served as AAG Inter-allied Military Commission of Control in Austria and Hungary, 1920–22; retired pay, 1923; Acting Comptroller of the Household to Duke of Connaught, 1939–40. *Address*: 86 Osborne Road, Windsor. *Clubs*: Naval and Military, MCC.

Died 20 Sept. 1946.

COOKE, Sir Clement K.; *see* Kinloch-Cooke.

COOKE, Henry Arthur, CMG 1919; *b* 1862. *Educ*: Cambridge University, MA. Commercial attaché, Diplomatic Service, 1907; Consul-General at Odessa, 1919; retired, 1923; Russian Imperial Humane Society's gold medal and British Royal Humane Society's and Lloyd's silver medals for saving life. *Address*: Clare Cottage, Quickley Lane, Chorley Wood.

Died 9 Oct. 1946.

COOKE, Sir (James) Douglas, Kt 1945; *s* of John Cooke, New Zealand; *m* Elsie Muriel, *d* of General James Burston, Melbourne; one *s* three *d*. *Educ*: Melbourne University; London Hospital, MB, BS (Melbourne University), 1901; FRCS 1905. Served European War, RAMC in France, 1915–19 (despatches); Lieut 1915; Capt. 1916; Major, 1918; formerly practised at Stanmore, Middlesex; contested Peckham, 1929; MP (U) Hammersmith, South, 1931–45. *Recreations*: golf, shooting, tennis, etc. *Address*: 48 Kingston House, Princes Gate, SW7. *T*: Kensington 0249. *Club*: Carlton.

Died 13 July 1949.

COOKE, Philip Tatton Davies-; JP, DL; *b* 1863; *e s* of late Philip Bryan Davies-Cooke and Emma Julia, *y d* of Sir Tatton Sykes, 4th Bart; *m* 1894, Doris (*d* 1935), *d* of late Charles Donaldson Hudson, MP, of Cheswardine, Shropshire; two *s*. *Educ*: Eton; Trinity Hall, Cambridge; BA 1885. Formerly Lieut, Yorkshire Dragoons Imp. Yeo., and Major Denbighshire Imp. Yeo. *Address*: Gwysaney, Mold.

Died 10 June 1946.

COOKE, Sir Stenson, Kt 1933; *b* 5 Oct. 1874; *m* May, *d* of Charles Edward Brooke of Baynards Manor, Sussex; one *s* one *d*. *Educ*: privately. Secretary of the Automobile Association since its inception in 1905; served in London Rifle Brigade as Cadet, Subaltern, and Captain, retiring 1903; joined 8th Essex TF on outbreak of war with large contingent of AA staff; appointed Staff Captain at War Office, 1915; Major, 1916; Controller of Supplies, Ministry of National Service, 1917; Vice-President, Alliance Internationale de Tourisme, 1932; Chevalier of the Legion of Honour; Great Silver Badge of Austria; Order of Merit with Star of Hungary; Officer of Order of the Crown of Belgium; Commandeur de l'Ordre de la Couronne de Chêne, Luxembourg. *Publication*: This Motoring, This Pilgrimage, These Stories. *Recreation*: fencing—Amateur Foils Champion, 1923. *Clubs*: Reform, Devonshire, Savage.

Died 19 Nov. 1942.

COOKE, William Ernest; *b* 25 July 1863; *s* of Ebenezer Cooke, late Audit Commissioner of South Australia; *m* 1887, Jessie Greayer; three *s* two *d*. *Educ*: Adelaide. Entered Adelaide Observatory, 1878; MA degree Adelaide University, 1889; First Assistant Adelaide Observatory, 1883; Hon. Secretary University Extension Committee, 1897–1906; Government Astronomer of Western Australia, 1896–1912; Government Astronomer of New South Wales, 1912–26; Prof. of Astronomy at the Sydney University; retired, 1926. *Publications*: Climate of Western Australia; Annual Meteorological Reports of Western Australia; Perth Catalogue of Standard Stars, 31°–41° S; Meridian Observations, vols ii, iii, iv, v; Sydney Catalogue of Intermediate Stars. Also astrographic catalogues; and numerous papers on astronomical and meteorological subjects. *Recreations*: motoring, bridge. *Address*: 69 Halton Terrace, Kensington Park, SA.

Died 7 Nov. 1947.

COOKE-COLLIS, Maj.-Gen. Sir (William) James Norman, KBE 1937; CB 1920; CMG 1919; DSO 1918; late Royal Ulster Rifles; chief organiser of Civil Defence in Northern Ireland since 1940; Ulster Agent in London since 1938; *b* 7 May 1876; *e s* of late Colonel William Cooke-Collis, CMG; *m* Cléonice, *d* of Major George Francis Gamble; one *d*. *Educ*: Cheltenham. Entered Army, 1900; Captain, 1908; Major, 1915; Brevet Lt-Col, 1916; Lt-Col, 1923; Col 1925; Maj.-Gen., 1932; served S African War (despatches, Queen's medal 3 clasps, King's medal 2 clasps); European War (despatches eight times; Officer, Legion of Honour, France; Order St Stanislaus 3rd class with swords, Russia; CMG; CB; 1914–15 Star; British War Medal; Victory Medal); Military Governor, Batoum, 1919; Brig.-Commander 11th Infantry Brigade, 1927–31; ADC to the King, 1930–31; Commander 55th (West Lancs) Division TA 1934–35; GOC N Ireland District, 1935–38; retired pay, 1938. *Clubs*: Army and Navy, Carlton.

Died 14 April 1941.

COOKE-HURLE, John A.; *see* Hurle.

COOKE-YARBOROUGH, Rev. John James; *see* Yarborough.

COOKSON, Christopher, MA; *e s* of Rev. Christopher Cookson of Dallington, Northants, and Harriet, *d* of Robert Onebye Walker, Senior Registrar of the Court of Chancery. *Educ*: Clifton College; Corpus Christi College, Oxford (scholar). 1st class Classical Moderations, 1880, 2nd class Lit. Hum., 1883; Gaisford Greek Verse, 1881. Assistant Master at St Paul's School, 1884–94; Classical Moderator, 1901–02, 1908–09; Fellow and Tutor of Magdalen College, Oxford, 1894–1919; HM Inspector of Schools, 1919–21. *Publications*: (with J. E. King) Principles of Sound and Inflexion as illustrated in the Greek and Latin Languages, 1888; Comparative Grammar of Greek and Latin, 1890. *Address*: 15 Staverton Road, Oxford. *T*: Oxford 5504.

Died 7 May 1948.

COOKSON, Henry Anstey, CBE 1947; MB, ChB (Edin.), FRCS, FRCP (Edin.), DPH (Cantab); FRSE; Director Pathological Laboratories, Royal Infirmary and Children's Hospital, Sunderland; and Darlington Memorial Hospital; Consulting Pathologist, Durham Co. Hospital; Bacteriologist, Sunderland Co. Borough; Pathologist, Durham County and Sunderland Eye Infirmary; Pathologist, Municipal Hospital, Sunderland; Lecturer in Bacteriology, Sunderland Technical College; *b* 1 July 1886; *s* of late Major Henry Cookson, Indian Army; *m* 1915, Elizabeth Mackie, *d* of Rev. G. M. Chedworth, Gloucestershire; two *s*. *Educ*: Clifton

College; Emmanuel College, Cambridge; King's College, London; Edinburgh University. Examiner: FRCS (Ed.), Diploma in Public Health, Royal College of Surgeons, Edinburgh, and Medical Jurisprudence and Public Health, Royal College of Surgeons, Edinburgh Member of Council, British Clinical Pathologist Association; late Major, RAMC (TF); served BEF, France. *Publications:* articles on Bacteriology and Pathology in Medical Journals. *Recreations:* archæology and fishing; University blues: hockey, athletics, cricket; International hockey, athletics (long jump). *Address:* Greatwood, Gainford, Co. Durham. *T:* Gainford 224. *Club:* Flyfishers'.

Died 15 May 1949.

COOMARASWAMY, Ananda K., DSc (London), FLS, FGS, MRAS; Fellow for Research in India, Persian and Muthammadan Art, Museum of Fine Arts, Boston, Mass; Fellow of University College, London; Vice-President, India Society, London; Hon. Correspondent, Archæological Survey of India, Vrienden der aziatische Kunst, The Hague, Gesellschaft für Asiatische Kunst, Berlin, Coïmbra Institute, Hon. Member, Bhandarkar Oriental Research Institute, Poona, etc; *b* 1877; *s* of late Sir Mutu Coomaraswamy, Ceylon; *m* Doña Luisa Runstein; one *s. Educ:* Wycliffe College, Stonehouse, Glos; UC, London. Director Mineralogical Survey of Ceylon, 1903–06; initiated movement for National Education, teaching of vernaculars in all schools, and revival of Indian culture; Pres. Ceylon Social Reform Society with these objects; member Ceylon Univ. Association; assisted to found India Society, 1910; in charge of Art Section at United Provinces Exhibition, 1910–11; writes and lectures on the history of Indian art, and general æsthetic, symbolism, and metaphysics. *Publications:* Reports on the Geology of Ceylon, 1903–1906; Völuspa; Mediæval Sinhalese Art; The Indian Craftsman; Essays in National Idealism; Art and Swadeshi; Burning and Melting (with Y. Daud); Selected Examples of Indian Art; Indian Drawings, 2 vols; Visvakarma; Myths of the Hindus and Buddhists (with Sister Nivedita); Arts and Crafts of India and Ceylon (also French edition); Vidyapati (with A. Sen); The Taking of Toll; Rajput Painting; Buddha and the Gospel of Buddhism; The Mirror of Gesture (with K. G. Duggirala); The Dance of Siva (also French edition); Portfolio of Indian Art (Museum of Fine Arts, Boston); Catalogue of the Indian collections in the Museum of Fine Arts, Boston; an Introduction to Indian Art; Pour comprendre l'art hindoue; History of Indian and Indonesian Art (also German edition); Yaksas; Les miniatures orientales de la Collection Goloubew; A New Approach to the Vedas; The Transformation of Nature in Art; Elements of Buddhist Iconography; La Sculpture de Bodhgayâ; Spiritual Authority and Temporal Power, the early Indian theory of government, 1942; Hinduism and Buddhism, 1943; Why Exhibit Works of Art, 1943; Figures of Speech or Figures of Thought, 1945; Religious Basis of the Forms of Indian Society, 1946; Am I my Brother's Keeper?, 1947; articles in leading art journals and in Encyclopædia Britannica. *Recreations:* gardening, books. *Address:* Museum of Fine Arts, Boston, Mass., USA; 649 South Street, Needham Mass.

Died Sept. 1947.

COOPER, Archibald Samuel, CB 1919; CMG 1916; *b* 1871; *s* of late Horace Cooper, JP, Marlborough, Wilts; *m* Jessie Maud, *d* of late Henry Cooper, Valparaiso; one *s* two *d. Educ:* Marlborough College. Entered Colonial Civil Service, 1897; Uganda Railway, BEA, 1897–1908; Lagos Railway, 1908–12; Acting Financial Commissioner, Southern Nigeria, March–Sept. 1912; General Manager, Nigerian Railway, 1912–16; temp. Brig.-Gen. and Director Inland Waterways and Docks, Royal Engineers, 1917; General Representative of the

Peruvian Corporation, Ltd, in Peru, 1919–31; Director, Peruvian Corporation, 1931. *Address:* Holmwood, Lovelace Road, Long Ditton, Surrey.

Died 15 Oct. 1942.

COOPER, Rev. Arthur Nevile; *b* 22 Feb. 1850; *s* of late W. B. Cooper, of Henley-on-Thames; *m* 1891, Maude, *d* of Walter Nicholson of Burley-in-Wharfedale; two *s* two *d. Educ:* Christ's Hospital; Christ Church, Oxford. Began life in the Inland Revenue, London, and while a clerk there kept his terms at Oxford; BA 1876; MA 1877; was curate of Chester-le-Street, 1876–80, involving much walking exercise; Vicar of Filey, 1880–1935; retired, 1935; Canon of York, 1915, Canon Emeritus, 1941; walked to Rome, 1887; Buda Pesth, 1890; Venice, 1900; Monte Carlo, 1903; Barcelona, 1904; Copenhagen, 1905; Stockholm, 1906; Pompeii, 1907; crossed the Carpathians, 1909; pilgrimage to Lourdes, 1910; through Joan of Arc's country, 1911; through the Hartz and Thuringia to Vienna, 1912; to Berlin, 1913; to Rome (2nd time) 1914; to Madrid, 1920. *Publications:* The Tramps of the Walking Parson; Round the Home of a Yorkshire Parson; Quaint Talks about Long Walks; With Knapsack and Note-book; Across the Broad Acres, 1908; A Tramp's Schooling, 1909; Walking as Education, 1911; Tales of my Tramps, 1913; East Yorkshire, 1913. *Address:* Holbeck House, Scarborough.

Died 20 Aug. 1943.

COOPER, Very Rev. Cecil Henry Hamilton; *b* 1871; *s* of Rev. H. W. Cooper, formerly Vicar of West Norwood, SE; *m* Cecil Hatherley (*d* 1932), *d* of Very Rev. W. R. Wood Stephens, DD, late Dean of Winchester. *Educ:* Pocklington School; Keble College, Oxford. Ordained 1895; Curate of Alverstoke, 1895–1901; St Faith with St Cross Hospital, Winchester, 1901–03; Rector of Compton, 1903–09; St Thomas, Winchester, 1909–13; Vicar of Scarborough, 1913–22; Vicar of St Michael Le Belfrey, York, 1923–26; Archdeacon of York 1923–33; Canon Residentiary of York, 1926–33; Dean of Carlisle, 1933–38; Dean Emeritus since 1938; Prebendary, 1918; Examining Chaplain to Archbishop of York. *Address:* Compton, Winchester.

Died 6 Jan. 1942.

COOPER, Sir Charles Naunton Paston P.; *see* Paston-Cooper.

COOPER, Sir Clive F.; *see* Forster-Cooper.

COOPER, Sir Dhanjishah Bomanjee, Kt 1937. Member of Executive Council of Governor of Bombay, 1934–37; Premier Bombay Presidency, 1937. *Address:* Huntworth, Satara, India.

Died 30 July 1947.

COOPER, Maj.-Gen. Edward Joshua, CB 1904; MVO 1906; DSO 1900; retired pay; late Royal Fusiliers; *b* 21 April 1858; *e s* of late Colonel J. H. Cooper of Dunboden, Westmeath; *m* 1894, Effie, *o d* of J. F. Balmain. *Educ:* Marlborough. Entered Army, 1876; Captain, 1885; Major, 1897; Lieut-Col 1901; Col 1904; served S Africa, 1899–1902; Tibet, 1904 (despatches, CB); commanded troops N China, 1910–14; European War, 1914–18; retired 4th Jan. 1918 with rank of Major-General; DL, Westmeath. *Address:* The Abbey, Abingdon, Berks. *T:* Abingdon 220. *Clubs:* Naval and Military, Royal Automobile.

Died 8 March 1945.

COOPER, Sir Edwin; *see* Cooper, Sir T. E.

COOPER, Sir Francis D'Arcy, 1st Bt *cr* 1941; Chairman of Lever Brothers and Unilever, Ltd, The Niger Co., Ltd, Mac-Fisheries, Ltd; Director of Phoenix Assurance Co., etc.; Member of Industrial Export Council, Board of Trade; Vice-Chairman of Permanent Hops Committee; Member of Royal Commission on the Distribution of the Industrial Population; *b* Nov. 1882; *o s* of late Francis Cooper and Ada Frances, *e d* of late Henry Power, FRCS; *m* 1913, Evelyn Hilda Mary, *e d* of late Arthur Lock Radford; no *c. Educ:* Wellington College; abroad. Partner in firm of Cooper Brothers & Co.; served European War in RFA (wounded); Vice-Chairman of Lever Bros, Ltd, 1923; Chairman on death of late Lord Leverhulme, 1925; Knight of the First Class of the Royal Order of Saint Olaf (Norway); Commander of Order of the Crown of Belgium; Commander's Cross of the Order of St Alexander (Bulgaria). *Recreations:* shooting and golf. *Address:* Westridge, Reigate, Surrey. *Clubs:* Athenæum, Reform.

Died 18 Dec. 1941 (ext).

COOPER, Hon. Frank Arthur; Lieutenant-Governor of State of Queensland, Australia, since 1946; *b* 16 July 1872; *s* of Charles and Mary Cooper; *m* 1924, Maisie Agnes Hardy; one *d. Educ:* Public School, Blayney, NSW. Member for Bremer, Legislative Assembly of Queensland, 1915–46; Minister for Education and Assistant Treasurer, 1932–38; Treasurer, 1938–42; Premier of Queensland, 1942–46; member Senate, University of Queensland, 1946. *Recreations:* golf, bowls. *Address:* Tendring, Sixth Avenue, Kedron, Brisbane, Queensland. *T:* LU. 1349, Brisbane.

Died 30 Nov. 1949.

COOPER, His Honour Frank Shewell; Judge of the Mayor's and City of London Court, 1922–36; *b* Deal, 20 May 1864; *y s* of late Lt-Colonel Henry Fallowfield Cooper, RMLI, and Elizabeth Shewell; *m* 1900, Margaret, *e d* of late Rev. J. M. Blackie, Cheltenham; one *s* one *d. Educ:* Clifton College; Pembroke College, Cambridge; BA (2nd Class Honours in Classics) 1886; MA 1890. Assistant Master at Lancaster Grammar School, 1886–91; Barrister, Inner Temple, 1893; South-Eastern Circuit; Deputy Stipendiary Magistrate for West Ham, 1917–22; Master of Fanmakers Company, 1932. *Publications:* Debentures, 1920; also joint author of the following: The Common Form Draftsman, 1899; Notes on the Companies Acts, 1903; Notes on the Companies Act 1907, 1907; Notes on the Companies (Consolidation) Act 1908, 1909; Secretarial Practice, 1912; 3rd edition, 1926. *Recreations:* literary and rural. *Address:* The Wyke, Marsham Way, Gerrards Cross. *T:* Gerrards Cross 3350.

Died 7 Dec. 1949.

COOPER, Rev. Frederic Wilson, MA; Hon. Canon of Manchester, 1920–40, Canon Emeritus since 1940; Rural Dean; *b* Aug. 1860; *s* of Rev. John Edward Cooper, Rector of Forncett; *m* 1890, Hon. Hilda Mary Sturt (*d* 1905), *e d* of 1st Lord Allington; no *c. Educ:* Norwich Grammar School; Keble College, Oxford. Assistant Curate of Hurstmonceaux, 1884–87; Saint Andrew's Missioner in the Diocese of Salisbury, 1887–90; Vicar of Longbridge Deverill, 1890–97; of S Paul's, King Cross, Halifax, 1898–1900; Rector of Prestwich, 1900–40. *Address:* 17 Ellesmere Road S, Chorlton-cum-Hardy, Manchester.

Died 3 Oct. 1941.

COOPER, Gerald Melbourne, MC; Hon. RAM; musicologist; *b* 13 Sept. 1892; 3rd *s* of Sir William Charles Cooper of Woollahra, 3rd Bt. Served European War; Hon. Secretary of Royal Philharmonic Society, 1929–32; Hon. Secretary Purcell Society; Chairman, London Contemporary Music Centre, 1946; Director, Torch Theatre; Organiser of Gerald Cooper Chamber Concerts from 1942. *Publications:* Popular Edition of Purcell; contributions to Oxford History of Music; various contributions to musical periodicals. *Address:* Chapel Farm, St Leonards, Tring. *Clubs:* Athenæum, Savage.

Died 17 Nov. 1947.

COOPER, Henry, DSO 1918; MA (Cantab); MRCS Eng.; LRCP Lond.; Group Captain RAF Medical Service, retired; late PMO Air Defences of Great Britain (formerly Surgeon Commander, RN); *b* 3 Jan. 1877; 2nd *s* of late John Spyvee Cooper, Kingston-upon-Hull, and Oldfield, Windermere; *m* 1906, Grace Elizabeth, *e d* of late John Shone of Whitchurch, Salop; one *d. Educ:* Denstone College; Emmanuel College, Cambridge; London Hospital. Science Tripos Cambridge, 1899; Freeman of the Cities of London and Hull; joined Royal Navy as Surgeon, 1904; served in HMS Diana in Mediterranean, 1906–08; Staff-Surgeon, 1912; HMS Medea, 1911–13; present at fall of Salonika and in Constantinople during Balkan War; Senior Naval Medical Officer for Port of Dunkerque and district, Nov. 1914–Dec. 1917; Representative of British Red Cross and Order of St John for Dunkerque district, and sole representative abroad for King Albert's Civilian Hospital Fund, 1914–17 (Officer of Order of St John of Jerusalem in England, DSO, 1914 Star, Officer of the Order of the Crown of Belgium); Hon. Surgeon to the King, 1930–32; retired list, 1932; Clerk and Registrar to the Soc. of Apothecaries of London, 1932–39; recalled to Active List as PMO Balloon Command, 1939–41; Acting Air Commodore, 1940; reverted to Retired list, 1941; Assistant Director of Personnel, Emergency Medical Service, Ministry of Health, 1942–45. *Address:* 6 Holly Place, NW3. *T:* Hampstead 3849.

Died 13 Dec. 1947.

COOPER, James; Crown Solicitor for Co. Fermanagh; Solicitor to Fermanagh County Council, Fermanagh Regional Education Committee and Enniskillen Rural District Council; DL; *b* 26 Feb. 1882; 2nd *s* of James Cooper, late of Brook View Lodge, Enniskillen; *m* 1906, *o d* of late Walter W. Hume, St Nessans, Ballsbridge, Dublin; two *s* two *d. Educ:* Portora Royal School, Enniskillen; Wesley College, Dublin. Admitted solicitor, Incorporated Law Society, Ireland, 1905; MP Fermanagh and Tyrone (U), Parliament of Northern Ireland, 1921–29; Chairman Fermanagh County Council, 1924–28; a DGM Grand Orange Lodge of Ireland. Custodian Trustee Enniskillen Savings Bank. *Recreations:* fishing, golf. *Address:* Brook View Lodge, Enniskillen. *TA:* Cooper, Enniskillen. *T:* Enniskillen 2074. *Clubs:* Fermanagh County; Enniskillen Yacht.

Died 21 July 1949.

COOPER, Sir Richard (Ashmole), 2nd Bt *cr* 1905; *b* 11 Aug. 1874; *s* of 1st Bart and *e d* of E. A. Ashmall of Hammerwich, Staffs; *S* father, 1913; *m* 1900, Alice E., *d* of Rev. E. Priestland, of Spondon; three *s. Educ:* Clifton College. Chairman of Cooper, McDougall & Robertson, Ltd, chemical manufacturers; MP (Ind Unionist) Walsall, 1910–22. *Heir: s* William Herbert Cooper. *Address:* Shenstone Court, Berkhamsted, Herts. *T:* Berkhamsted 67. *Clubs:* Carlton, Royal Thames Yacht.

Died 5 March 1946.

COOPER, Sir Robert Elliott-, KCB 1919; MInstCE, VD, FRGS; Civil Engineer; *b* Leeds, 29 Jan. 1845; *s* of late Robert Cooper of York and Leeds; *g s* of Capt. Elliott, RN, of Elliott House, Ripon; *m* 1878, Fanny, *d* of late William Leetham, Hull; one *s* three *d. Educ:* Leeds Grammar School. Commenced engineering career as a pupil of late John Fraser of Leeds; commenced practice on his own account in Westminster, 1876; has constructed many railways and other engineering works in England, the Crown Colonies, and South Africa, and has travelled extensively in connection with his professional work in Europe, Asia Minor, Egypt, India, South Africa, and the West Indies; Past President of the Institute of Civil Engineers; late Col-Commandant of the Engineer and Railway Staff Corps; was Consulting Engineer for Railways in Nigeria and Gold Coast Colonies, 1908–16; Consulting Engineer Regent's Canal and Dock Co., now Grand Union Canal; Chairman of the War Office Committee of Institute of

Civil Engineers, and member of several other Committees during the war. *Clubs:* Athenæum, Hurlingham.

Died 16 Feb. 1942.

COOPER, Robert Higham, CBE 1919; Consulting Radiologist Royal Victoria and West Hants Hospital, Bournemouth; *b* 12 Aug. 1878; *m* 1903, Alice Mary, *d* of James T. Tatlow, Horwich. *Educ:* Macclesfield Grammar School; Owens College, Manchester; Charing Cross and Westminster Hospitals. Assistant to Sir James Mackenzie Davidson, 1900–01; X-ray and Electrical Assistant, Charing Cross Hospital; Physician in charge of X-ray and Electrical Department at Prince of Wales' Hospital, Tottenham; Radiographer to Evelina Hospital and Royal Waterloo Hospital; Medical Officer in charge X-ray and Electrical Departments, West End Hospital; Lecturer on X-rays, Seamen's Hospital, Greenwich; temp. Lieutenant-Colonel, RAMC; Consulting Radiologist to the British Armies in France, 1914–19; X-ray Expert to the London Command, 1919 (despatches twice, CBE); Medical Officer in charge of X-ray, Electrical and Light Departments at University College Hospital, and Lecturer to the Medical School, 1904–19; X-ray Officer to the Royal London Ophthalmic Hospital; Radiologist to the Egyptian Govt, 1919–22; FRSM. *Publications:* Uses of X-rays in General Practice, 1906; various articles in British Medical Journal, Lancet, Practitioner, etc. *Address:* 53 Lansdowne Road, Bournemouth.

Died 25 Sept. 1944.

COOPER, Canon Sydney, MA; Canon emeritus of Truro Cathedral; *b* 1862; *s* of Henry and Catharine Cooper; *m* 1890, Edith Williams (*d* 1942); four *s* four *d*. *Educ:* Charterhouse; New Coll., Oxford (1st Cl. History, 2nd Cl. Modns.); Cuddesdon Theological Coll. Assistant Curate Probus, 1886; Cirencester, 1889; Vicar, Christ Church, Frome, 1894; Rector, Upper Heyford, 1912; Chancellor and Canon Residentiary of Truro Cathedral, 1919–32; Examining Chaplain to Bishop of Truro, 1919–32; Proctor in Convocation, 1924–28. *Publications:* The Sacrifice of Praise; The Days of the Martyrs; A Little Psalter. *Recreation:* general reading. *Address:* Evreham Lodge, Iver, Bucks. *T:* Iver 335.

Died 17 July 1942.

COOPER, Sir (Thomas) Edwin, Kt 1923; RA 1937; ARA 1930; Treas., RA; Hon. Member, Lloyd's; Royal Gold Medallist; Governor of Star and Garter Homes, Richmond and Sandgate; Member of Council, Nations Fund for Nurses, National Trust, London Society; *b* 21 Oct. 1874; *m* Mary E., *d* of late H. Wellburn; one *s* one *d*. Architect for the Port of London Authority Building, Tower Hill; Marylebone Town Hall and Extensions, Hull Guildhall and Law Courts, Star and Garter War Memorials for British Red Cross Society, Roy, Coll. of Nursing and Cowdray Club, University Buildings, Cambridge, The New Lloyd's; Royal Mail Building; Gray's Inn Law Library, National Provincial Bank, Princes and Mansion House Street, EC, St Mary's Medical Schools, Nurses' Home, and Pay Bed Blocks, Paddington; Spillers' Head Offices, Banque Belge, Devonport School of Pathology and Nurses' Home, Greenwich; Cranleigh Schools, Surrey, Additions and Speech Hall; Additions and New Library, St Hilda's College, Oxford; Gatton Park, Surrey; Bryanston School Additions, Dorset; The Riddell Home, St Thomas's Hospital; South London Hospital for Women; St Marylebone Public Library and Health Centre; St Marylebone Crematorium, Grove Road Health Centre No. 2; Peasmarsh Place, Sussex; Tilbury Custom Hall, for the Port of London; and many other public and private buildings. *Address:* 4 Verulam Buildings, Gray's Inn, WC. *T:* Chancery 7988; 46 Lower Belgrave Street, Eaton Square, SW1. *Club:* Athenæum.

Died 24 June 1942.

COOTE, Howard; late HM Lieutenant for Huntingdonshire; *b* Bournemouth, 11 Feb. 1865; *y s* of late Thomas Coote, of Oaklands, Fenstanton, Hunts; *m* 1892, Jean Reith, 2nd *d* of late A. R. Gray, Aberdeen; two *s*. *Educ:* Rugby. High Sheriff of Hunts and Cambs, 1911; JP for Hunts and Cambs; Lord Lieutenant of Hunts, 1916–22. *Address:* Rochester House, Parkfield, Sevenoaks. *T:* Seal 16.

Died 19 April 1943.

COOTE, Sir Ralph (Algernon), 13th Bt *cr* 1621; Premier Bt of Ireland; late Capt. 17th Lancers; *b* 22 Sept. 1874; *s* of 12th Bt, and Jean (*d* 1880), *d* of Capt. Trotter; S father, 1920; *m* 1904, Alice, *y d* of late Thomas Webber of Kellyville, Queen's Co.; two *s*. *Heir: s* John Ralph [Lt-Comdr RN; *b* 1905; *m* 1927, Noreen Una, *o d* of Wilfrid Tighe of Rossanagh, Ashford, Co. Wicklow; two *s*. *Address:* c/o Mrs Tighe, Rossanagh Cottage, Ashford, Co. Wicklow].

Died 2 July 1941.

COPE, 1st Baron *cr* 1945, of St Mellons; **William Cope;** 1st Bart *cr* 1928, KC 1933; TD; *b* 18 Aug. 1870; *o s* of late Matthew Cope, JP, St Mellons, nr Cardiff; *m* 1900, Helen, *y d* of Major Alexander Shuldham, JP, DL, of Flowerfield, Co. Londonderry; one *d*. *Educ:* Repton; Clare College, Cambridge; MA. Barrister, Inner Temple, 1895; MP (U) Llandaff and Barry, 1918–29; a Lord Commissioner of the Treasury, 1923–24, and Nov. 1924–Jan. 1928; Comptroller of HM Household, 1928–29; Civil Commissioner for London and Home Counties, General Strike, 1926; DL, JP County of Glamorgan; High Sheriff, 1932; Vice-Chairman Quarter Sessions, 1933–39; Major (retired), Glamorgan Yeomanry; sometime Director of Albion Colliery Co., Welsh Navigation Colliery Co., S Wales Electrical Power Distribution Co. KStJ and Sub-Prior of the Priory for Wales. *Recreations:* hunting, shooting, golf; formerly Rugby football, Cambridge Univ. XV, 1891; Welsh International XV 1896. *Address:* Quarry Hill, St Mellons, nr Cardiff. *T:* St Mellons 8. *Clubs:* Carlton, Oxford and Cambridge.

Died 15 July 1946 (ext).

COPE, Charles Elvey, ARCO, MRST; author, poet, composer and organist; Organist and Choirmaster at S Mary Magdalen, Bexhill-on-Sea, 1908–42; *s* of an organist and composer; *m* Lilian Poland, niece of late Sir Harry Bodkin Poland, KC; two *s* one *d*. *Educ:* privately. Began writing verse at eight years of age, and has contributed some hundreds of lyrics and poems to various journals; ARCO, 1897; has specialised in the teaching of the pianoforte and theory of music; has composed much church music and two Masses. *Publications:* Songs of a City, 1923; The Golden Art, 1925; Out of the World's Medley, 1928; Thor, an epic, 1930; Downland Echoes, 1937. *Recreation:* gardening. *Address:* 17 Wellington Square, Hastings; Yew Tree Cottage, Guestling, Sussex.

Died 27 Dec. 1943.

COPE, John Hautenville; country gentleman; Member of the Wokingham Rural District Council and Guardians' Committee; Secretary and Editor The Oxfordshire Record Society, 1927–36; formerly Editor Powysland Club and Montgomery Collections; formerly Editor to Hants Field Club; *y s* of Sir William Cope, 12th Bart, of Bramshill Park, Hampshire, and 2nd wife, Harriet Margaret; *m* 1899, Emma Elizabeth, *co-heiress* of Major Thoyts of Sulhamstead Park, and Anne Annabella, *e d* of Sir Richard Pryce Puleston, Bt, of Emral Park, Flintshire. *Educ:* privately. Formerly Hon. Secretary, Westminster Hospital Ladies' Association; Editor on Staff of Victoria County History; Fellow, Royal Historical Society, and member of many Archæological Societies, etc. *Recreation:* gardening. *Address:* Finchampstead Place, Berkshire. *T:* Eversley 3274. *Club:* Berkshire County.

Died 8 Nov. 1942.

COPE, Sir Ralph, Kt 1936; *b* 18 Sept. 1862. Entered service of Great Western Railway Company, 1877; Chief Accountant, 1916–38, when he retired after over 61 years in the service of the Company, a record in British Railway Service. *Address:* 6 Brondesbury Park, NW6.

Died 14 Feb. 1949.

COPEAU, Jacques, Officer de la Légion d'Honneur; Administrateur général interimaire de la Comédie Française depuis Mai 1940; Metteur en scène à la Comédie Française depuis 1936; *b* à Paris, le 4 Février 1879; *m* 1902, Agnès Thomsen; one *s* two *d. Educ:* Lycée Condorcet, Paris. Il founde La Nouvelle Revue Française, 1908; Il fonde le Théâtre du Vieux Colombier, 1913; avec la troupe du Vieux Colombier, il monte 32 spectacles au Garrick Theatre à New York, 1917–19; reconstitution du Vieux Colombier à Paris, 1919–23; en 1923 il se retire en Bourgogne avec ses élèves; il joue dans les villages et les villes de province; ces élèves forment en 1929 La Compagnie des Quinze; Monte à Florence le Mistère de Santa Uliva dans le Cloitre de Santa Croce, 1933; As You Like It, au Théâtre de l'Atelier, 1934; Much Ado About Nothing, au Théâtre de la Madeleine; Napoléon Unique, de Raynal et joué le rôle de Fouché au Théâtre de la Porte St Martin; Le Misanthrope à la Comédie Française, 1936; Le Trompeur de Seville, d'André Obey au Théâtre de la Porte St Martin, 1937; Bajazet de Racine à la Comédie Française, 1937; Asmodée de F. Mauriac à la Comédie Française, 1937; As you like it de Shakespeare à Florence, Palais Pitti, 1938. *Publications:* (avec Jean Croué) Les Frèes Karamazov, Drame en cinq actes d'après Dostoievski, 1911; Les Amis Du Vieux-Colombier (No 1 des Cahiers du Vieux-Colombier) 1920; L'École Du Vieux-Colombier (No 2 des Cahiers du Vieux-Colombier) 1921; La Maison Natale, Drame en trois actes, 1923; Critiques D'Un Autre Temps, 1923; Une Femme Tuée Par La Douceur (Traduction de Thomas Heywood) pièce en cinq actes, 1924; (avec Suzanne Bing) Le Conte D'Hiver, Traduction de Shakespeare, 1924; Œuvres Complètes De Molière, 1930; Souvenirs Du Vieux Colombier, Deux Conférences, 1931; Traduction de 10 Tragédies de Shakespeare; Le Petit Pauvre (François d'Assise), drame en 6 actes. *Address:* Pernand-Vergelesses, Côte-d'Or, France.

Died 21 Oct. 1949.

COPEMAN, Col Charles Edward Fraser, CMG 1917; DL, JP, Norfolk and Isle of Ely; TD, MA; 5th *s* of late Canon Copeman, Norwich; *m* 1899, Ethel Maude (*d* 1933), *d* of Richard Yeo. *Educ:* Norwich School, Selwyn, and King's College, Cambridge. During the War commanded 1/1st Cambs Regt (France, Feb. 1915), and 9th Northants Regt; formerly for 28 years Clerk of the Peace for Isle of Ely, and Clerk of the County Council; Director Wisbech Hotels, Ltd, and Eagle and Star Insurance Co. Ltd (East Anglian Board); Under Sheriff for Cambs and Hunts on several occasions. *Address:* Salisbury Lodge, Salisbury Rd, Hove. *T:* Hove 5086. *Club:* Naval and Military.

Died 16 April 1949.

COPEMAN, Sydney A. Monckton, FRS 1903; MA; MD Cantab; FRCP Lond.; DPH; FZS; Medical Officer, retired, Ministry of Health; ex-Member LCC (Hampstead); formerly Member Hampstead Borough Council (late Chairman Public Health and other Committees); late Senior Medical Inspector HM Local Government Board; Vice-President (late President), Epidemiological Section, Royal Society of Medicine; late Member of Council, Royal College of Physicians, London, and Zoological Society; Member of Faculty of Medicine, and Chairman of Board of Studies in Hygiene, University of London; Emeritus Lecturer on Public Health, Westminster Hospital; Knight of Grace, Order of St John of Jerusalem and Member of Chapter-General of the Order; Lt-Col in charge of Hygiene Department, Royal Army Medical College, 1916–17; late Divisional Sanitary Officer, 2nd London Division, Territorial Force; TD; Chadwick Lecturer in Hygiene, 1914; late Examiner in Public Health and in Forensic Medicine and Toxicology, University of Bristol; Examiner in Public Health, Royal College of Physicians; Examiner in Hygiene and Public Health, University of Leeds; in State Medicine, University of London, and in Public Health, Royal College of Surgeons, England; Milroy Lecturer, 1898, Royal College of Physicians, London; Research Scholar and Special Commissioner, British Medical Association; Government Delegate to Germany, France, Austria, Switzerland, Belgium, and USA in connection with investigations undertaken for Home Office, Board of Trade, Local Government Board, and Ministry of Health; Member of various Departmental Committees; Member of Livery, Apothecaries Company and Freeman of City of London; Joint Founder (1891) of Medical Research Club; Buchanan Gold Medallist, Royal Society of London, 1902; Cameron Prizeman, University of Edinburgh, 1899; Fothergillian Gold Medallist, Medical Society of London, 1899; Jenner Medallist, Royal Society of Medicine, 1925; invented Glycerinated Lymph, officially adopted, 1898, and now in general use in this and other countries for anti-smallpox vaccination; Gold Medallist, International Faculty of Sciences, 1938; Hon. Fellow Hunterian Society, 1938; joint patron of living of Hadleigh, Essex; *b* 21 Feb. 1862; *e s* of late Rev. Canon Copeman of Norwich; *m* Ethel Margaret (*d* 1944), γ *d* of late Sir William Boord, 1st Bt; one *s* two *d. Educ:* King Edward VI School, Norwich; Corpus Christi College, Cambridge (Scholar, Exhibitioner, and Prizeman); St Thomas's Hospital, London. *Publications:* Vaccination, its Natural History and Pathology (Milroy Lectures, 1898); numerous reports dealing with public health matters in official publications; contributions to the Encyclopædia Britannica, the Dictionary of National Biography, to medical and scientific treatises, and to the Proceedings or Transactions of the Royal and other learned and scientific Societies *Address:* Flat 6, 8 King's Gardens, Hove, Sussex. *Club:* Athenæum.

Died 11 April 1947.

COPLESTON, Waters Edward, CSI 1922; late Indian Forest Service. Joined service, 1894; Chief Conservator of Forests, Bombay, 1920; retired, 1927. *Address:* Ireson House, Wincanton, Som.

Died 1 Dec. 1949.

COPLEY, John, RE 1947; RBA 1933; Hon. Foreign Member of the Pulchri Studio, The Hague; Pres. RBA 1947; *b* Manchester, 1875; *s* of late Professor W. Crawford Williamson, FRS, LLD, and Ann, *d* of Edward Heaton; *m* 1913, Ethel Leontine Gabain, RBA ROI; one *s. Educ:* privately; Owens College, Manchester. Studied Art at the Manchester School of Art, at the Studio of Watson Nicol and Cope and at the RA School. Spent two years in Italy; came early under the personal influence of Ford Madox Brown; began lithography in 1907; Hon. Secretary of the Senefelder Club, 1910–16; lithographs acquired by British Museum; Victoria and Albert Museum; Municipal Galleries of Manchester, Liverpool, and Bradford; Academy of Pennsylvania; Public Library, New York; National Gallery of Canada; Galleria Moderna Rome; Galleria Corsini Rome; Uffizi, Florence; private collection of the King of Italy; prints rooms of Stuttgart and Wimar; Municipal Museum, The Hague; A complete collection by Library of the City of Boston, 1946. Chief award and medal in the first International Exhibition of Lithographs at the Art Institute of Chicago, 1930. *Address:* 10 Hampstead Sq., NW3. *T:* Hampstead 3001. *Club:* Arts.

Died 16 July 1950.

COPLEY, Mrs John; *see* Gabain, E. L.

COPPING, Arthur E.; author, journalist, traveller; *b* London, 22 July 1865; *s* of Edward Copping (author of Aspects of Paris, etc.) and Rosa, *d* of J. Skinner Prout, water-colour painter; *b* of Harold Copping, Bible illustrator; *m* Nancy, *d* of Dr H. Guard Knaggs; one *d*. *Educ:* North London Collegiate School. On Daily News, 1884–1906; authorship and travelling followed; visited continental countries, Canada, Scandinavia, and Palestine, 1917–20; was Daily Chronicle correspondent at sea (commission in RNVR), throughout N Russian campaigns, and in Soviet Russia; visited South Africa, Australia, New Zealand, South Sea Islands, and Alaska, 1927–28; travelling 14 months through West, South, East and Central Africa, 1930–31; for many years keenly interested in Salvation Army affairs and a frequent contributor to its publications; ardent advocate of temperance reform; takes part in local government (late Guardian, District Councillor, etc.). *Publications:* Pictures of Poverty, 1905; Gotty and the Guv'nor, 1907; Gotty in Furrin Parts, 1908; Jolly in Germany, 1910; A Journalist in the Holy Land, 1911; The Golden Land, 1911; Canada To-day and To-morrow, 1911; Improved Ontario Farms, 1912; The Canadian Winter, 1913; Smithers, 1913; The Laundress, 1916; Souls in Khaki, 1916; Tommy's Triangle, 1917; Stories of Army Trophies, 1928; Banners in Africa, 1933. *Recreations:* gardening, carpentry. *Address:* 106 Marina, St Leonard's-on-Sea.

Died 13 July 1941.

COPUS, George Frederick, CBE 1924; retired; *b* 10 Sept. 1868; *s* of Cyrus Copus of Kennington; *m* Ellen, *d* of James Welch, Wareham, Dorset; two *s* two *d*. Entered service of New Zealand Government in London, 1886; Accountant, Insurance, Estates and Indents Officer, 1909; Finance Officer and Loan and Stock Agent, 1916; Financial Adviser, 1924; war services connected with NZ Transports, Hospital Ships, Pay and Allowances of Troops, Pensions, distribution of Comforts and Relief Funds, etc.; served on committees in connection with Reparations, Inter-Imperial Exchange, and Taxation of Shipping. *Address:* Keswick Road, Orpington. *T:* Orpington 310.

Died 17 Feb. 1949.

CORBET, Hon. Mrs Katharine, MBE 1918; Lady of Grace, St John of Jerusalem, 1918; *b* 14 Dec. 1861; *γ d* of 23rd Baron de Clifford; *m* Reginald Corbet (*d* 1945); one *d*. *Publications:* Animal Land, 1897; Sybil's Garden of Pleasant Beasts, 1898. *Address:* Devon House, Shropshire Street, Market Drayton, Salop.

Died 6 March 1950.

CORBET, Reginald; JP; *b* 9 Oct. 1857; *s* of late Henry Reginald Corbet of Adderley and Anne Mary Elizabeth, *e d* of Sir Philip Egerton, 13th Bart, of Oulton Park, Cheshire; *m* 1891, Hon. Katharine Russell, *d* of 23rd Baron de Clifford; one *d*. *Educ:* Radley. Maj. Shropshire Vol. Regt and Yeomanry; Master, South Cheshire Hounds, 1900–08. *Publication:* Management of a Pack of Foxhounds. *Address:* Adderley Hall, Market Drayton. *TA* and *T:* Adderley 221. *Club:* Turf.

Died 9 Dec. 1945.

CORBETT, Sir (Francis) Henry (Rivers) A.; *see* Astley-Corbett.

CORBETT, William John, FRCS, LRCP, DPH Camb.; JP County of London; *s* of late Martin Corbett, JP, Bunratty House, Co. Clare; unmarried. *Educ:* Clongowes Wood College; Trinity College, Dublin. Consulting Ophthalmic Surgeon, Walthamstow Education Authority, National Union of Teachers, London Teachers' Assoc.; late Temporary Captain RAMC; Ophthalmic Specialist, Dublin Unit BEF; Member of the Ophthalmological Society; late President Irish Medical Schools and Graduates Association.

Publications: various papers on the Vision of School Children. *Recreations:* travel and the theatre. *Address:* Seamount, Howth, Co. Dublin. *Clubs:* Reform, Bath.

Died 19 Nov. 1941.

CORBETT-SMITH, Arthur, Major RA; retired; MA (Oxon); national publicist; *b* Cheltenham, 1879; *s* of late Sir William Robert Smith, MD; *m* 1921, Tessie, violinist, *d* of Oscar Thomas, Neath, Glamorgan; one *s* one *d*. *Educ:* Winchester; Christ Church, Oxon. Commission in RH and FA 1902; called to Bar, Middle Temple, 1905; Deputy-Secretary Shanghai Municipal Council, 1907–10; Hon. Sec. Gen., the Naval and Military Musical Union; Officier de l'Instruction Publique; served in France first nine months of first German War (wounded twice, despatches); later, much Navy and Air Service; Freeman and Hon. Freeman of City of London; production Mr Wu, Strand Theatre, 1913; in 1912 initiated educational movement in Sexual Disease; and in 1915 similar movement for Englightenment of public in War Facts and Ideas; Director of Publicity, British National Opera, 1921; Director, Cardiff Broadcasting Station, 1923; Artistic Director of British Broadcasting Company, 1924. *Publications:* The Balance, The Evolution of Modern China, 1912; The Chinese Drama Yesterday and To-day, 1913; The Chinese and their Music; The Problem of the Nations (Sexual Disease and the Individual); Prologue for St George's Day, 1914; The Retreat from Mons; Active Service Chats, 1916; The Marne, and After, 1917; The Seafarers; The Soul of France, 1919; The Cinema of To-morrow, 1920; China and her People; The National Opera Handbooks (14 vols), 1922; Riders of the Air, 1923; My Radio Year, 1925; Nelson—The Man; Harry Binns, Seafarer, 1926; English Letters to my American Nephew, 1928; Woman—Theme and Variations, 1932; Self Portrait of a Privateer, 1937; Love Technique—an Introduction, 1938; A People's War (Verse), 1941; China Reborn (poem), 1942. *Photo-plays:* Bats amongst Birds; Love of Women; A Naval Honeymoon. *Radio-drama:* A Commonwealth of Nations; Under the White Ensign. *Musical works:* Song Album, Under the Window (with Kate Greenaway), 1907; two Suites for Orchestra of Irish Folkmelodies, 1909; three Elizabethan Lyrics, voice and orchestra, 1909; Concert Overture, On the Irish Shore, 1911; Elizabeth, an opera to own libretto, 1912 (produced 1923); The Soldier Songs from The Shropshire Lad; The Battle of Jutland Bank; The Irish Guards (with Rudyard Kipling); Peacock Pie (with W. de la Mare); Song of the Home Guard; Canada Ho!; Chamber music, and about 150 songs published in a definitive edition. *Recreation:* change of work. *Address:* Bishopstone, Herne Bay. *Club:* Savage.

Died 17 Jan. 1945.

CORBETT-WINDER, Major William John; JP; Lord Lieutenant of Montgomeryshire since 1944; *b* 1875; *m* 1906, Margery Sophia, 3rd *d* of T. N. F. Bardwell of Bolton Hall, Wilberfoss, York; one *s* three *d*. *Educ:* Eton; Christ Church, Oxford. Major in 7th RWF. *Address:* Vaynor Park, Berriew, Mont. *TA:* Berriew 4.

Died 9 April 1950.

CORCORAN, Rev. Timothy, SJ, DLitt; Professor of Education, National University of Ireland since 1909; Member of Governing Body, University College, Dublin, 1916–44; Senator, NUI, since 1924; *b* 1872; *s* of Thomas Corcoran, first Chairman (1899–1911). County Council of North Tipperary. *Educ:* Clongowes Wood College; Royal University of Ireland; Louvain (Univ. Scholar in Classics; Univ. Gold Medallist in Latin and in English Verse; BA 1st-Cl. History and Economics; Gold Medallist in Education, 1906; DLitt, by thesis, 1912). Assistant Master, Clongowes Wood College, 1894–1901, 1904–06. *Publications:* Studies in the History of Classical Education, 1911; State Policy in Irish Education (1536–1816), 1916; Renovatio Litterarum, 1925; Renatae Litterae, 1926; Plato and Modern

Education, 1927; Education Systems in Ireland, 1928; Newman's Theory of Liberal Education, 1929; Quintilian and Renaissance Education, 1930; Illegal Schools in Ireland, 1931; The Clongowes Record, 1932; The Humanist Teaching Process, 1937; The Louvain Faculties and Ireland, 1939; Irish Jesuit Educators, 1940; The Paris Faculties and Ireland, 1942. *Address:* 35 Lower Leeson Street, Dublin. *Club:* National University.

Died 23 March 1943.

CORDEAUX, Col Edward Kyme, CBE 1919; DL, JP Lincolnshire; Sheriff, 1925; *b* 1866; 2nd *s* of late John Cordeaux, FRGS, JP, of Great Coates House, near Grimsby; *m* 1893, Hilda, MBE, *yr d* of late Sir Henry Bennett, JP, DL, of Grimsby; two *s* one *d*. *Educ:* Oakham School. Joined 4th Batt. Lincolnshire Regt, 1890; retired with rank Lt-Col on disbandment of Battalion, 1908; served South African War with 2nd Batt. Lincolnshire Regt, 1900–01 (despatches, Queen's medal and four clasps); joined 10th (S) Batt. Lincolnshire Regt, Sept. 1914; Lt-Col commanding Battalion, July 1916; transferred to command 12th (L) Batt. Devonshire Regt, Jan. 1917; commanded 57th Labour Group, April 1917; Labour Commandant, 19th Army Corps, with rank of Colonel, 1918–19; Commander Hazebrouck Sub-area, March to Oct., 1919 (despatches twice, Croix de Guerre (Belge), CBE). *Recreation:* field sports. *Address:* Brackenborough Lawn, Louth, Lincolnshire. *TA:* Louth. *T:* Louth 187. *Club:* United Service.

Died 16 July 1946.

CORDEAUX, Major Sir Harry Edward Spiller, KCMG 1921; CB 1904; CMG 1902; *b* 15 Nov. 1870; *s* of late Edward Cordeaux, ICS; *m* 1912, Maud, *d* of late Hon. George Wentworth-Fitzwilliam, and *widow* of the Hon. Cospatrick Thomas Dundas. *Educ:* Cheltenham College; St John's College, Cambridge (BA; graduated in Honours in Classics, 1892). Entered Army, 1894; appointed Lieut in Indian Staff Corps, 1896; entered Bombay Political Department as a probationer, 1898, and was appointed Assistant Resident at Berbera, on the Somali Coast, 1898; HBM's Vice-Consul, Berbera, Somaliland Protectorate, 1898–1906; Sub-Commissioner and Consul, 1902–06; Deputy Commissioner, 1904; Commissioner and Commander-in-Chief, 1906–10; HM's Governor and Commander-in-Chief, Uganda, 1910–11; Governor St Helena, 1912–20; Governor and Commander-in-Chief of the Bahama Islands, 1921–26. *Recreation:* field sports. *Address:* 43 Lowndes Square, SW1. *T:* Sloane 7809. *Club:* United Service.

Died 2 July 1943.

CORDER, Paul Walford, FRAM; Professor of Harmony and Composition at the Royal Academy of Music since 1907; Professor of Composition at Tobias Matthay School; *b* London, 14 Dec. 1879; *s* of late Frederick Corder; unmarried. *Educ:* private school; Royal Academy of Music. Won Goring Thomas Scholarship for composition, 1901; principal works include two operas, violin concerto, a ballet, a wordless music-drama, and other dramatic, choral and orchestral works, also much piano music. *Publications:* Nine Preludes for Piano; Transmutations of an Original Theme; Passacaglia; Dross, Music-Drama without Words; Three Studies; Romantic Study; Heroic Elegy; An Autumn Memory; Four Sea Songs; Spanish Waters. *Recreations:* numerous and varied from time to time; since 1912 furniture making has predominated. *Address:* White Cottage, Netley Heath, W Horsley, Surrey; Looe Island, Cornwall.

Died 6 Aug. 1942.

CORK, Philip Clark, CMG 1904; *b* 1854; *s* of Rev. J. Cork, late Rector of St Anne's, Jamaica; *m* 1881, Mary Druce, *d* of A. Woodburn Heron; two *d*. *Educ:* privately. Clerk, Immigration Department, Jamaica, 1875; Inspector of Immigrants, 1877; Protector of Immigrants, Grenada, 1881; Jamaica, 1884; Commissioner under

Kingston Improvement Laws, 1894; member of Legislative Council, 1896; Assistant Colonial Secretary, 1897; Colonial Secretary, British Honduras, 1901–05, and Acting Governor, 1903–04 and 1905; Administrator of St Lucia, 1905–08; Acting Governor, Windward Islands, 1906 and 1908; Colonial Secretary, Jamaica, 1909–14; Acting Governor, 1909, 1911, 1912, 1913; retired, 1914. *Address:* Barbican, Liguanea PO, Jamaica.

Died April 1936.

CORNER, Edred Moss, BSc (London), MA, MB, MC (Cantab), FRCS (England); Consulting Surgeon to St Thomas's Hospital; late Surgeon to Children's Hospital, Great Ormond Street; to King George Hospital and 5th Territorial Base Hospital; late Consulting Surgeon, Queen Mary Convalescent Auxiliary Hospitals, Wood Green Hospital, the Purley Hospital, to the Waifs and Strays Home, Byfleet, to Epsom College, and to various Red Cross Hospitals; Major, RAMC (T); Member of Board of Advanced Medical Studies, University of London; Vice-President of Harveian Society, of Medical Society; Visitor for King Edward's Hospital Fund; President of the Medical and Physical Society of St Thomas' Hospital; *b* 1873; *s* of late Francis Mead Corner, JP; *m* 1903, Henrietta, *d* of James Henderson of the Gows, Invergowrie, Dundee; one *s* two *d*. *Educ:* Epsom Coll.; Sidney Sussex Coll., Cambridge; St Thomas's Hospital. Scholar and Prizeman at Cambridge and London; the only candidate who has been first in every subject of the MB, BC Cantab. Erasmus Wilson Lecturer, Royal Coll. of Surgeons, 1904; Arris and Gale Lecturer, 1919; Harveian Lecturer, 1919; first scientific paper published in 1895. *Publications:* Clinical and Pathological Observations in Acute Abdominal Disease, 1904; the Surgery of the Diseases of the Appendix, 1904 and 1910; Diseases of the Male Generative Organs, 1907 and 1909; Operations of General Practice, 1907, 1908, and 1910; The Life-history, Function, and Inflammation of the Appendix; and to many scientific journals. *Recreations:* walking, motoring and mountaineering, scientific research and literature. *Address:* Stratton End, Beaconsfield, Bucks. *T:* Beaconsfield 42.

Died 2 May 1950.

CORNER, George, MA, TD; *b* 30 March 1869; *s* of William and Susan Lutley Corner; *m* 1913, Nancy (*d* 1941), *y d* of Captain Sinclair; one *s*. *Educ:* Nottingham; London; Bonn. German Master, Merchant Venturers College, Bristol 1892; Modern Language Master, Hymers College, Hull; Lecturer in French for the East and West Ridings of Yorkshire County Council 1893–99; Headmaster, Wellington School, Somerset, 1899–1938; served in the 2nd Volunteer Battalion Somerset Light Infantry, 1901; Commandant of Wellington School OTC 1902–20; Member of IAHM Committee on Military training; Chairman of Wellington Food Economy Committee during war, engaged in training officers; Member of Incorporated Association of Headmasters since 1899; HMC 1933; developed Wellington School from a small Proprietary School to a fully developed Public School, governed by a scheme under the Charitable Trusts Act; on being challenged in 1897 Jubilee rode a pedal bicycle from King's Cross, London, to Hull in one day. *Recreations:* riding, formerly football, cricket, and tennis. *Address:* Ruggin Court, West Buckland, Wellington, Som. *T:* Blagdon Hill 256.

Died 16 April 1947.

CORNFORD, Francis Macdonald, LittD, Hon. DLitt (Birm.); FBA, 1937; Fellow of Trinity College and Emeritus Professor of Ancient Philosophy since 1939, Cambridge; *b* 27 Feb. 1874; *s* of James Cornford and Mary Emma Macdonald; *m* Frances Crofts, *d* of Sir Francis Darwin; three *s* two *d*. *Educ:* St Paul's; Trinity College, Cambridge. Lecturer in Classics, Trinity College, 1904; War service in Home Forces and Ministry of Munitions, 1914–18. *Publications:* Thucydides Mythistoricus, 1907; Microcosmographia

Academica, 1908; From Religion to Philosophy, 1912; Origin of Attic Comedy, 1914; Greek Religious Thought, 1923; (with P. H. Wicksteed) Aristotle, Physics (Loeb Library), 1929; Laws of Motion in Ancient Thought, 1931; Before and After Socrates, 1932; Plato's Theory of Knowledge, 1935; Plato's Cosmology, 1937; Plato and Parmenides, 1939; Plato's Republic (translated), 1941. *Address:* Conduit Head, Madingley Road, Cambridge. *T:* Cambridge 3097.

Died 3 Jan. 1943.

CORNIL, Georges; *b* Charleroi, 13 May 1863. *Educ:* University of Brussels; University of Göttingen; University of Leipzig. Doctor of Law, Prof. honoraire at the Univ. of Brussels; Correspondant de l'Académie internationale de droit comparé (La Haye); Member of the Royal Academy of Belgium; Président de l'Institut des Hautes-Etudes de Belgique; Membre de l'Institut international de philosophie du droit et de sociologie juridique, Paris; Membre de la Société D'Histoire du Droit, Paris. *Publications:* Etude sur la publicité de la propriété dans le droit romain, 1890; Du louage de services, 1895; L'Assurance municipale contre le chômage involontaire, 1898; Traité de la possession dans le droit romain, 1905; Droit romain, aperçu historique sommaire, 1921; Le Droit privé, essai de sociologie juridique simplifiée, 1924; Mélanges de Droit romain, dédiés à Georges Cornil, 1926; Ancien Droit Romain: le Problème des Origines, 1930; Une Vision allemande de l'Etat à travers l'Histoire et la Philosophie, 1936. *Address:* 40 rue Langeveld, Uccle (near Brussels).

Died 11 Jan. 1944.

CORNISH, Henry Dauncey; Barrister-at-law; *b* 7 Aug. 1877; *s* of Henry Cornish, Barrister-at-law; *m*; one *s* one *d*. *Educ:* Charterhouse; Trinity College, Cambridge. Called to Bar, Inner Temple, 1902; Lieut RGA in European War, 1914–18; Administrator-General and Official Trustee of Madras, 1921–29; Judge, High Court of Judicature, Madras, 1929–37. *Publications:* Handbooks of Hindu Law; Probate Procedure in British India. *Address:* 2 Paper Buildings, Temple, EC4.

Died 6 Oct. 1948.

CORNISH, Herbert, FJI; *b* 1862; *m* 1888, Alice Mary Abbott. *Educ:* Christ's Hospital, Ipswich (scholarship). Pupil 1878–82, to Engineering Director, Ipswich; Private Secretary, 1882–84, to Richard Gowing, journalist author, and Secretary, Cobden Club; Charter Draughtsman, Petitioner and 1st Secretary, Institute Journalists, 1886–1926; Editor, School Government Chronicle, 1894–1928; Proprietor, 1902–21; Chairman School Government Publishing Co., 1921–28; first (now retired) Hon. Warden, Flatford Mill; Executive Councillor National Education Association since 1894; Original Member, 1919–26, London University Journalism Committee; Hon. Member Assoc. Directors of Education; Organiser, 1886–1926, of many British Home and Overseas and International Conferences, etc., of Journalists. *Publications:* SGC, 67 vols, numerous handbooks on Education, Law, Administration; The Constable Country 100 Years after John Constable, RA, 1932, etc. *Address:* Fairmeade, Whitton, Ipswich.

Died 18 Aug. 1945.

CORNISH, Vaughan, DSc (Manchester); FRGS; geographer; *b* 22 Dec. 1862; 3rd and *y s* of late Rev. C. J. Cornish, MA (Oxon); *g s* of C. J. Cornish, JP, DL, of Salcombe Regis, Devon; *m* 1st, 1891, Ellen Agnes (*d* 1911), *e d* of Alfred Provis of Kingston Lisle, Berks; 2nd, 1913, Mary, *d* of late Rev. W. R. Watson and *widow* of E. A. Floyer. *Educ:* St Paul's School; Victoria University, Manchester. Gill Memorial Award, Royal Geographical Society, 1900; Grand Prix, Franco-British Exhibition, 1908, for scientific photography; retired from position of Director of Technical Education, Hampshire County Council, 1895, and since then occupied in geographical research and in the movement for preserving the scenery of Rural England. Dedicated South Combe Farm on Sidmouth Cliffs as an Open Space in perpetuity. On Thorn Farm, Salcombe Regis, has erected a monument beside the historic Thorn Tree upon which the welfare of the parish is traditionally dependent. Pres. Geographical Section, British Association, 1923; Pres. Geographical Association, 1928; Pres. of the Conference of Delegates of Corresponding Societies, British Association, 1928. *Publications:* The Panama Canal and its Makers; Waves of the Sea and other Water Waves; The Travels of Ellen Cornish; Waves of Sand and Snow; A Geography of Imperial Defence; A Strategical Atlas of the Oceans; The Great Capitals; National Parks and the Heritage of Scenery, 1930; The Poetic Impression of Natural Scenery, 1931; The Scenery of England, 1932, 2nd ed. 1937; Ocean Waves and Kindred Geophysical Phenomena, 1934; Scenery and the Sense of Sight, 1935; Borderlands of Language in Europe, 1937; The Scenery of Sidmouth, 1940; Historic Thorn Trees in the British Isles, 1941; A Family of Devon, 1942; The Beauties of Scenery, 1943; The Churchyard Yew, an Emblem of Immortality, 1946; Geographical Essays, 1946; Photography of Scenery, 1946; Wise Saws and Modern Instances, 1946; and original papers in Geographical Journal. *Recreations:* sketching, travel. *Address:* Inglewood, 46 Gordon Road, Camberley, Surrey. *T:* Camberley 582.

Died 1 May 1948.

CORNWALL, Lt-Col John Wolfran, CIE 1927; IMS (retired); *b* 2 Aug. 1870; *s* of W. W. G. Cornwall, ICS; *m* 1st, 1904, Effie Esme (*d* 1928), *d* of Surg.-Gen. D. Sinclair, CSI; one *s* two *d*; 2nd, 1936, Evelyn Mary, widow of J. Gray, ICS. *Educ:* Clifton College; Trinity College, Cambridge; St Thomas's Hospital. Director Pasteur Institute of Southern India, Coonoor, 1906–26. *Address:* Burford Lodge Elstead Godalming.

Died 20 Feb. 1947.

CORSAN, Brig. Reginald Arthur, DSO 1918; MC; TD; Director, Glass Works; Commander RA, TA, since 1939; *b* 3 Sept. 1893; *s* of John Tamset Corsan and Ada Lovering Corsan; *m* 1920, Doris Pears; one *s* one *d*. *Educ:* Dulwich College; Paris; Wiesbaden. Served European War, 1914–18 (despatches, MC, DSO). *Address:* St Julien, Sandy Lane, Cheam.

Died 9 Feb. 1942.

CORTISSOZ, Royal, DHL; art critic New York Herald Tribune since 1891; Literary Editor also 1897–1913; Member of the American Academy of Arts and Letters; Trustee of the American Academy in Rome; Hon. Fellow of the American Institute of Architects; Hon. Member of Architectural League of New York; and of Society of American Etchers; Hon. Fellow of the Metropolitan Museum of Art and of National Sculpture Society; Trustee of Hispanic Society of America; Chevalier of the Order of Leopold of Belgium; *b* Brooklyn, New York, 1869; *m* Ellen Mackay Hutchinson (*d* 1933). *Publications:* Augustus Saint Gaudens, 1907; John La Farge, 1911; Art and Common Sense, 1914; The Life of Whitelaw Reid, 1921; Nine Holes of Golf, 1922; The New York Tribune, 1923; American Artists, 1923; Personalities in Art, 1925; The Painter's Craft, 1930; An Introduction to the Mellon Collection, 1937; edited the Autobiography of Benvenuto Cellini and Don Quixote, with illustrations by Daniel Vierge; Whitelaw Reid's American and English Studies, and other volumes. *Address:* 167 East 82nd Street, New York. *Clubs:* Century. The Players, Coffee House (New York).

Died 17 Oct. 1948.

CORY, Ven. Charles Page; Rural Dean of Wilford since 1924; *b* 16 June 1859; *s* of John Augustus and Emily Anne Cory, Botcherby, Carlisle; *m* 1884, Grace Margaret Gross; two *s* one *d*. *Educ:* Sedbergh School; St John's College, Cambridge (MA). Ordained 1883; Curate of Bexley, 1884; Vice-Principal St Paul's College, Madagascar, 1884–90; Curate of Sedbergh,

1890–91; Chaplain Rangoon Cantonments, 1892–95; Thatyetmyo, 1895–99; Incumbent of Port Blair, 1901–03; Chaplain of Rangoon Cathedral, 1903–04; Rangoon Cantonments, 1904–05; Acting Archdeacon and Commissary, 1906–07; Maymyo, 1906–14; Rector of Campsea Ashe, Wickham Market, 1915–37; Archdeacon of Rangoon, 1907–17. *Recreations:* sketching in water-colours, riding, fishing, shooting; ran for Cambridge in the Inter-University cross-country race, 1880–81. *Address:* Star Cross, Warren Hill, Woodbridge, Suffolk.

Died 7 Nov. 1942.

CORY, Sir Clifford John, 1st Bt *cr* 1907; JP, DL, Chairman of Cory Brothers and Company, Ltd, colliery proprietors, foreign coal and oil depot owners and coal exporters and oil refiners and oil tank storage; *b* Cardiff, 10 April 1859; *s* of late John Cory, JP, DL; *m* 1893, Jane Ann Gordon, *d* of late Albert Arthur Erin Lethbridge. *Educ:* privately and on the Continent. Formerly Captain 3rd Batt. Welsh Regiment; contested South Monmouthshire, 1895; Tonbridge Division of Kent, 1900; MP (L) St Ives Division, 1906–22 and 1923–24; High Sheriff of Monmouthshire, 1905; County Councillor for Glamorganshire, 1892–1910; President of the Monmouthshire and South Wales Coal Owners Association, 1906; Chairman (*pro tem.*) of the Conciliation Board for the Coal Trade of Monmouthshire and South Wales, 1906; also Chairman, Cardiff Liberal Association, 1906–11; President Cardiff Incorporated Chamber of Commerce, 1907 and 1908; Chairman of South Wales and Monmouthshire Schools of Mines; and Governor of University College of South Wales; Commander of the Order of Leopold II. *Recreations:* hunting, shooting, farming, polo. *Heir:* none. *Address:* Llantarnam Abbey, Monmouthshire. *T:* 7634 Cwmbran; 98 Mount Street, W1. *T:* Grosvenor 2032. *Clubs:* Reform, Hurlingham, Roehampton.

Died 3 Feb. 1941 (ext).

CORY, Mrs Theodore; *see* Graham, Winifred.

CORY, Sir Vyvyan Donald, 3rd Bt *cr* 1919; *b* 2 Nov. 1906; *e s* of Sir Herbert George Donald Cory, 2nd Bt, and Gertrude, *d* of Henry Thomas Box; *S* father 1935; unmarried. *Educ:* Harrow; Clare College, Cambridge. *Recreations:* fishing, shooting, gardening. *Heir:* *b* Clinton James [*b* 1 March 1909; *m* 1935, Mary, *o d* of Dr A. Douglas Hunt, Park Grange, Derby]. *Address:* 62 Albert Hall Mansions, SW1. *Club:* Reform.

Died 17 March 1941.

CORY, William Wallace, CMG 1909; *b* Strathroy, Ontario, 16 June 1865; *s* of Thomas Cory, Lostwithiel, Cornwall, and Margaret Johanna Garret, Glasgow; *m* 1888, Laura Watson, Lincolnshire; two *s* one *d*. *Educ:* St John's College. Entered firm of Archibald, Howell, Hough and Campbell as a law student, 1886; Munson and Allan, 1888; joined Civil Service, Province of Manitoba, as clerk in Atorney-General's office, 1889; resigned, 1900; appointed to Interior Department, 1901; Inspector of Yukon Offices, 1901; Assistant Commissioner of Dominion Lands, 1904–05; Deputy Minister of the Department of the Interior, 1905–31; Commissioner of NW Territories, 1919–31. *Address:* Ottawa. *Clubs:* Rideau, Royal Ottawa Golf, Ottawa.

Died Sept. 1943.

COSGRAVE, Mary Josephine, LLA St Andrews; Member of Dublin Corporation; Chairman of the Meath Hospital Committee; Chairman Co. Dublin Libraries Committee; Chairman Irish Women's Citizens Association, 24 S Frederick Street, Dublin; *d* of James and Jane Daly formerly of Naas, Co. Kildare; *m* 1901, Maurice Cosgrave, Barrister-at-Law, journalist, etc. *Educ:* Convent of Mercy, Naas; privately. Professor of History at the Training College of Our Lady of Mercy, Baggot Street, Dublin; Examiner in English under Intermediate Board of Education, Ireland; interested in social work especially maternity and child welfare work. *Recreations:* reading, golfing. *Address:* Woodside, Cowper Gardens, Dublin. *T:* Rathmines 575.

Died 17 Nov. 1941.

COSSAR, George Carter, CBE 1937; MC; MA (Oxon); LRCPE, etc; *b* 16 Sept. 1880; *s* of Dr T. Cossar, East Craigs, Corstorphine. *Educ:* Cargilfield; Rugby; Oxford University. Since 1905, taken interest in various branches of Welfare work, particularly among needy boys; has started several farms, Homes and Boys' Clubs in Scotland and Canada; Chairman Todhill Boys' Farm, Kilwinning; Ex-Chairman National Bible Society of Scotland; took medical degree during the war and served in RAMC in France; has been member of various Government Committees. *Recreations:* motoring, travelling, land work. *Address:* Clydeneuk, Uddingston; Cossar Farm, Lower Gagetown, NB, Canada. *T:* Uddingston 299.

Died 5 Feb. 1942.

COSTE, John Henry, FRIC, FInstP; *b* 8 April 1871; *s* of John Henry and Margaret Coste; *m* 1905, Gertrude E. Galer; two *s* two *d*. *Educ:* Finsbury Technical College. Assistant in Laboratory of Royal Agricultural Society of England, 1889–94; Assistant and Chief Assistant Chemical Department, London County Council, 1894–1913; Chemist-in-Chief to the London County Council, 1913–36. *Publications:* Books, Chemistry of Pigments (with E. J. Parry); Calorific Power of Gas, Examination of Fuel, (with E. R. Andrews); Section on Air in Lunge and Keane (with J. S. Owens); Numerous papers on Analytical Chemistry, Physical Chemistry and on Water Pollution and Sewage Treatment. *Recreations:* sailing, riding, walking. *Address:* Covertside, Smallfield, Burstow, Sy. *T:* Smallfield 128.

Died 3 Jan. 1949.

COSTELLO, Brig.-Gen. Edmund W., VC 1897; CMG 1918; CVO 1920; DSO 1917; DL; Hon. MA Cantab; Indian Army, retired; *b* 7 Aug. 1873; *s* of late Col Costello, IMS; *m* 1902, Elsie Maud, *d* of Chas. Lang Huggins of Hadlow Grange, Buxted; one *d*. *Educ:* Beaumont College; Stonyhurst College; RMC, Sandhurst; Staff College, psc. Joined West Yorks, 1892; joined 22nd Punjab Infantry, 1894; served with Malakand Field Force 1897 (twice wounded, despatches, VC, medal and 2 clasps); operations in the Mohmand country, 1908 (medal and clasp); European War (Mesopotamia), 1914–18 (despatches 6 times, Bt Lieut-Colonel, CMG, DSO, Bt Col, Croix de Guerre); commanded Indian Contingent at Peace Celebration, 1919; retired, 1923; late Director of Military Studies, Cambridge University. *Address:* 2 Derraclare Court, Eastbourne. *T:* 624.

Died 7 June 1949.

COTES, Everard; journalist; *b* 1862; *m* 1st, 1890, Sara Jeannette Duncan (*d* 1922); 2nd, 1923, Phoebe Violet Delaforce; one *s* one *d*. *Educ:* Clifton; Paris; Oxford. On staff of Indian Museum, Calcutta, 1884–94; editor, Indian Daily News, 1895–97; Managing Director, Eastern News Agency, Ltd, including Associated Press of India, and Indian News Agency, 1910–19; accompanied tours of Prince of Wales in Canada, USA, Australasia, and West Indies, as Reuter's agent, 1919–20; on London staff of the Christian Science Monitor, Boston, USA, 1922–39. *Publications:* Signs and Portents in the Far East; Down Under with the Prince; Indian Forest Zoology, and other scientific works. *Address:* Birdshill Cottage, Oxshott, Surrey. *Clubs:* National Liberal; Bengal, Calcutta.

Died 4 Oct. 1944.

COTES-PREEDY, His Honour Judge Digby, KC 1925; MA, LLM (Cantab); MA (Oxon); LSA; JP; Barrister-at-law; Bencher of Inner Temple; Chairman Bucks Quarter Sessions since 1937; Chancellor of Diocese of Worcester since 1935; Chairman the

Worcestershire Association; *b* Fladbury, Worcestershire, 1875; *e s* of late Rev. D. H. Cotes-Preedy, Vicar of King's Norton, and sometime Minor Canon of Worcester Cathedral; *m* 1908, Margaret, *y d* of late S. Bradley, of Blakedown, Worcestershire; one *s*. *Educ:* privately; Emmanuel College, Cambridge. House Physician at St George's Hospital, 1903; called to Bar, Inner Temple, 1904; Secretary to Committee on Administration, etc., of Royal Flying Corps, 1916; to Select Committee on Military Service (Review of Exceptions) Act, 1917–18; Member of Committee on Coroners, 1935; Recorder of Smethwick, 1919–32; Recorder of Oxford, 1932–36; County Court Judge, Circuit No. 36 (Oxford), 1936–41; retired, 1941. *Publications:* The Law relating to Hospital Authorities, their Staffs and Patients; many contributions on medico-legal subjects, and several musical compositions. *Recreations:* music, shooting, fishing, and golf. *Address:* 3 Paper Buildings, Temple, EC; Fladbury Lodge, Gerrard's Cross, Bucks. *Club:* Conservative.

Died 16 Sept. 1942.

COTSWORTH, Moses B., FCA, FSS, FGS; Director and originator of the International Fixed Calendar League; *b* Willitoft, near York, 3 Dec. 1859; *s* of George and Sarah Cotsworth; *m* 1884, Kezia H. Gardiner, Blairendinnie, Aberdeenshire; one *s* four *d*. *Educ:* York Blue Coat School; private tuition. Entered office of the Chief Goods Manager of North Eastern Railway, 1874; Aire and Calder Navigation, 1881; Traffic Manager for Trent Navigation, 1884–86; Manager Manners Colliery, Derbyshire, 1887–91; returned to Chief Goods Manager's Office, NE Railway Co., as expert for railway rates revision and research work, 1892–1907; appointed by British Columbian Government as Chairman of the Commission to reorganise and regrade the Civil Service, 1907; in business as accountant and investigator of the cost of living for Western Canada, 1909–21; Director of the International Fixed Calendar League, and Expert to the League of Nations' Committee on Calendar Reform, 1922–31; Has visited more than 60 countries advocating Calendar-Reform; Secretary to British Association's Research Committee on Geological Evidence of Climatic Change, 1934–37. *Publications:* Railway Maximum Rates and Charges; Direct Calculator, 'O,' etc.; The Rational Almanac; The Evolution of Calendars; Time to Fix the Year; Geology's Interest hinges on Changing Climates; series of more than 50 pamphlets on Calendar Reform. *Recreations:* music, walking, and gardening. *Address:* 4510 Osler, Vancouver, BC, Canada. *Club:* Penn.

Died 4 June 1943.

COTTENHAM, 6th Earl of, *cr* 1850; **Mark Everard Pepys;** Bt 1784 and 1801; Baron Cottenham (UK) 1836; Viscount Crowhurst, 1850; *b* 29 May 1903; *s* of 4th Earl and Lady Rose Nevill (*d* 1913), *d* of 1st Marquess of Abergavenny; *S* brother, 1922; *m* 1927, Venetia (marr. diss. 1939), *o d* of Captain J. V. Taylor, North Aston Manor, Oxfordshire; two *d*. *Educ:* Charterhouse. Vickers Ltd, Aviation Department; Faculty of Engineering, Univ. College, London. Member of the Alvis motor-racing team, 1925–26; Member of the Sunbeam motor-racing team, 1926; Reserve driver also for the Talbot motor-racing team, 1926; Holder of a Royal Aero Club pilot's certificate. Secretary of the Roads and Road Transport Committee of the House of Lords, 1926–27; Lecturer at the Chief Constables' Annual Conference, 1928; Chairman of the Order of the Road, 1928–33; Adviser to Metropolitan Police Motor Driving School, 1937; Adviser to Home Office on Mobile Police Training, 1937–38; Civil Assistant attached General Staff War Office, 1939–40; Lt Leicestershire Yeomanry (retired). Vice-Patron of the Amateur Boxing Association of Great Britain, Vice-President of the Fitzroy Lodge Boxing Club. *Publications:* Motoring without Fears, 1928; Motoring To-day and To-morrow, 1928; All Out, a novel, 1932; Steering-

Wheel Papers, 1932; Sicilian Circuit, a novel, 1933; Mine Host, America, a book of travel, 1937; contributor to many newspapers and journals. *Recreations:* reading, observation and travel. *Heir: b* Hon. John Digby Thomas Pepys [2nd Lieut 10th Royal Hussars (retired), *b* 14 June 1907; *m* 1933, Lady Angela Larnach-Nevill, *d* of 4th Marquess of Abergavenny; two *d*]. *Clubs:* Travellers'; Brooklands Automobile Racing.

Died 19 July 1943.

COTTINGTON-TAYLOR,   Dorothy   Daisy; Director, Good Housekeeping Institute, 1924–40; Associate Editor, Homes and Gardens; Director of Ballachulish Hotel Co., Ltd; Member of Tribunal of the Retail Trades Standards Tribunal; *d* of W. Willis Gale, AMICE, LRIBA, Civil Engineer; *m* 1st, 1919, T. H. Cottington-Taylor (*d* 1929); no *c*; 2nd, 1935, Albert E. Mash. *Educ:* Sutton High School (GPDST); National Training School of Domestic Science; King's College for Women. Qualified as Teacher of Domestic Economy and Sanitary Inspector, Royal Sanitary Institute; Welfare Supervision, Woolwich Arsenal, 1915–17; Lady Superintendent, No. 1 Aeroplane Factory, Waddon, 1917–19; contributor to Household Encyclopædia, Encyclopædia Britannica, Good Housekeeping. *Publications:* Food Wisdom, 1925; The ABC of Cookery, 1929; Menu and Recipe Book, 1926; Housekeeping by Modern Methods, including Catering, 1933; Cake Making, 1933; Sweets and Candies, 1934; Preservation of Fruit and Vegetables, 1935; Pies and Puddings. *Recreation:* gardening. *Address:* The Weald, Betchworth, Surrey. *T:* Betchworth 282.

Died 17 March 1944.

COTTON, Sir George Frederick, Kt 1942; CB 1939; MVO 1924; OBE 1927; Under Secretary, Admiralty, 1939–42; *b* 10 Jan. 1877; *s* of George Cotton, Clapham; *m* 1st, 1906, Edith Mary (*d* 1931), *d* of late Charles Barrell, Ipswich; 2nd, 1933, Ethel, *d* of late Richard Osmond Hearson, Westleigh, N Devon. *Educ:* Stationers' School and King's College, London. Second Division Clerk, Local Government Board, 1898; Admiralty, 1899; Staff Clerk, 1913; 1st Division Clerk, 1914; Principal, Secretary's Dept 1921–31; Director of Victualling of the Navy, 1931–36; Principal Assistant Secretary, Admiralty, 1936–39. *Recreation:* golf. *Club:* East India and Sports.

Died 23 March 1943.

COTTRELL-DORMER, Charles Walter; JP, DL; *b* 1860; *e s* of late Clement Upton-Cottrell-Dormer and Florence Anne, *y d* of late Thomas Upton, of Ingmire Hall, Westmorland, and sister of Sir John Henry Greville Smyth, 1st and only Bart, of Ashton, Somerset; *m* 1889, Ursula, *y d* of Thomas Robert Brook Leslie-Melville-Cartwright, of Newbottle Manor, Northamptonshire; one *s*. *Educ:* Eton. High Sheriff, Oxfordshire, 1902; late Captain Reserve of Officers, and 13th Hussars; was Lieutenant Northampton and Rutland Militia; served in the Remount Department, 1914–18; Patron of two livings. *Address:* Rousham, Steeple Aston, Oxford. *Club:* Naval and Military.

Died 3 Dec. 1945.

COUCH, Sir Arthur Thomas Q.; *see* Quiller-Couch.

COUCHMAN, Sir Francis Dundas, KBE 1919; MInstCE; Indian State Railways, retired; *b* 15 Feb. 1864; *s* of late Thomas Barnes Couchman, Beaudesert Park, Henley in Arden, Warwickshire, and Sarah Whitby-Smith, Aspley Guise, Beds; *m* 1902, (Daisy) Isabella McLean, *d* of late Lt-Col D. E. McMahon; two *d*. *Educ:* Rossall School; Royal Indian Engineering College, Cooper's Hill. Assistant Engineer Indian State Railways, 1886; Railway Survey on NW Frontier and Bengal, 1887–89; Construction and open line work on railways in Baluchistan and Sind, 1889–95; construction of Godaveri Bridge East Coast Railway, 1896–99; Government Inspector of Railways Bombay and

Calcutta, 1899–1900; Under-Secretary to Government of India for Railways, 1901–05; Government Inspector Consulting Engineer and Secretary to Govt for Railways, Burma, 1906–08; Chief Engineer Burma Railways, 1909–12; Agent and General Manager Burma Railways, 1913–15; Member of Indian Railway Board, 1915–20; President Stores Purchase Committee, Dec. 1919–July 1920; Railway Adviser to Jodhpur Durbar, 1921–26; Director Madras and Southern Mahratta Railway, 1927–41. *Recreations:* golf, shooting. *Address:* c/o Standard Bank of South Africa, Grahamstown, CP; 1 Florence Street, Grahamstown, CP, S Africa. *T:* Grahamstown 642. *Club:* East India and Sports.

Died 26 Nov. 1948.

COUCHMAN, Rev. Reginald Henry, MA; Rector of St Lawrence Jewry, EC2, since 1940; *b* 20 June 1874; *s* of Rev. Henry Couchman, Assistant-Master Haileybury College, and Mary Jane Pooley; *m* 1906, Catharine Seton, *d* of Capt. W. P. A. Ogle, RN. *Educ:* Haileybury College; Worcester College, Oxford; Cuddesdon Theological College. Deacon, 1900; priest, 1901; Assistant Curate at Tynemouth, Northumberland, 1900–03; Chaplain at Cuddesdon College, 1903–06; Principal, Diocesan Training College, Exeter, 1906–14; Minor Canon of St Paul's Cathedral, 1914–34; Headmaster of St Paul's Cathedral Choir School, 1914–37; Sub-Dean of St Paul's, 1928–37; Assist Curate St John's, Hampstead, 1939. *Address:* Manor Lodge, Vale of Health, Hampstead, NW3. *T:* Hampstead 5916.

Died 3 Feb. 1948.

COULTON, George Gordon, FBA 1929; LittD Camb.; Hon. DLitt Durham; Hon. LLD Edinburgh; LLD Queen's University; Corresponding Member of Medieval Academy of America; Fellow of St John's College, Cambridge, and Hon. Fellow of St Catharine's College; late University Lecturer in English; *b* 15 Oct. 1858; 3rd *s* of J. J. Coulton, solicitor, of King's Lynn, and Sarah Radley; *m* Rose Dorothy, *d* of Owen Ilbert of Thurlestone; two *d. Educ:* Lynn Grammar School; Lyceé Impérial, St Omer; Felsted School; St Catharine's Coll., Cambridge; Heidelberg University. Assistant Master at Sherborne, Sedbergh, and Dulwich; Birkbeck Lecturer in Ecclesiastical History, Trinity College, Cambridge; Ford's Lecturer in English History, Oxford, 1930–31; Rhind Lecturer at Edinburgh, 1931; temporary Professor of Mediæval History in University of Toronto, 1940–43. *Publications:* Father Rhine, Public Schools and Public Needs, Friar's Lantern, From St Francis to Dante, Chaucer and his England, A Mediæval Garner, Mediæval Studies (2 Series), The Main Illusions of Pacificism, The Case for Compulsory Service, Social Life in Britain from the Conquest to the Reformation; Christ, St Francis, and To-day; Five Centuries of Religion: vol. i (St Bernard), 1923; vol. ii (Tradition), 1927; vol. iii, 1936; vol. v, 1947; A Victorian Schoolmaster, 1923; The Medieval Village, 1925; Art and the Reformation, 1928; Life in the Middle Ages, 4 vols, 1928–1929; Crusades, Commerce and Adventure, 1929; Romanism and Truth, vol. i, 1930, vol. ii, 1931; Reservation and Catholicity, 1930; The Medieval Scene, 1930; Studio Winter Number, 1930; Defence of the Reformation, 1931; Papal Infallibility, 1932; St Bernard and St Francis, 1932; Scottish Abbeys and Social Life, 1933; Fowler and King's English, 1934; Medieval Panorama, Sectarian History, Inquisition and Liberty, 1938; Medieval Thought; Europe's Apprenticeship, 1940; The RC Church in Politics, 1940; Fourscore Years, 1943; Is the Roman Church anti-social, 1945. *Recreation:* vegetating. *Address:* St John's College, Cambridge.

Died 4 March 1947.

COUPER, James Brown; DL, JP County of the City of Glasgow, also for Argyllshire; *s* of late John Stewart Couper, shipowner, Glasgow. *Educ:* Glasgow High School. Shipowner; a member of the Baltic Shipping Exchange, of the Glasgow Royal Exchange, Trades House, Merchants House, and Chamber of Commerce, Glasgow; MP (U) Maryhill Division of Glasgow, 1924–29; a member of the British Delegation attending the Conference of the Inter-Allied Parliamentary Union at Washington and Ottawa, 1925; one of the British delegates of the Empire Parliamentary Association to Australia, 1926; is interested in numerous charitable, benevolent, and philanthropic institutions. *Address:* Tollard House, Toward, Argyll. *Clubs:* Carlton, Royal Automobile, 1900, Unionist; Royal Clyde Yacht; Royal Gourock Yacht; Royal Scottish Automobile, Conservative, Glasgow.

Died 14 Oct. 1946.

COUPER, Sir Ramsay George Henry, 3rd Bt *cr* 1841; *b* 1 Nov. 1855; *e s* of 2nd Bt and Caroline Penelope, *sister* of Sir Henry Every, 10th Bt; *S* father, 1908; *m* 1884, Norah (*d* 1925), *d* of Horatio Willson Scott; one *s* two *d*. Late Lieut 60th Foot; served Afghanistan, 1878 (medal with two clasps and bronze star). *Heir: s* Guy [*b* 12 March 1889. Served European War, 1916–18]. *Address:* Resides abroad.

Died 20 March 1949.

COURAGE, Brig.-Gen. Anthony, DSO 1917; MC; retired pay; Colonel of 15/19th Hussars since 1929; *b* 22 Oct. 1875; *s* of late Henry Courage of Gravenhurst, Bolney, Sussex; *m* May, *e d* of late Sir John P. Hewett, GCSI; two *s* one *d. Educ:* Rugby. Joined 15th Hussars, 1896; Adjutant; served in India and South Africa; Adjutant, Dorset Yeomanry; sailed with 15th Hussars in original Expeditionary Force; wounded, 2nd Battle of Ypres; employed on Staff, General Headquarters, France, 1916; commanded 2nd Tank Brigade Messines, 3rd Ypres, Cambrai, 1917; Commanded 5th Tank Brigade (attached Australian Corps) Hamel, Montdidier, Villers Brittoneux, Amiens, Hindenburg Line; commanded Group of Two Tank Brigades (despatches six times, Bt Lt-Col, Bt Col, DSO, Croix de Guerre avec palme); Chairman Courage & Co., Ltd; a Director of White Horse Distillers, Ltd, Hyderabad (Deccan), Company, Ltd. *Recreations:* hunting, polo, fishing, shooting. *Address:* Williamscote, near Banbury. *Clubs:* Cavalry, Army and Navy.

Died 27 Feb. 1944.

COURTAULD, Major John Sewell, MC; MP (U) Chichester since 1924; *b* 26 Aug. 1880; *s* of Sydney Courtauld; *m* Henrietta Barbara, *d* of late Sir Arthur Holland; one *d. Educ:* Rugby; King's College, Cambridge. *Address:* Burton Park, Petworth, Sussex. *T:* Petworth 2238. *Clubs:* Turf, Carlton; Jockey, Newmarket.

Died 20 April 1942.

COURTAULD, Samuel, DLit; *b* 1876; 2nd *s* of Sydney Courtauld, of Bocking Place, Braintree; *m* Elizabeth Theresa Frances (*d* 1931), *o d* of late Edward Kelsey; one *d. Educ:* Rugby. Chairman of Courtaulds Ltd, 1921–46; a Trustee of the Tate Gallery, 1927–34, and 1935–37; a Trustee of the National Gallery, 1931–38 and 1939–47. *Address:* 12 North Audley Street, W1. *T:* Mayfair 4517. *Clubs:* Athenæum, Burlington Fine Arts.

Died 1 Dec. 1947.

COUSENS, Col Robert Baxter, DSO 1918; *b* 25 March 1880; 8th *s* of late John Cousens, Wanstead; *m* 1903, Esther, *y d* of late Patrick Cummins, ICS (retired); four *s* (and one killed in action, 1941), one *d. Educ:* Epsom College; Clare College, Cambridge. Entered Army, 1900; Bt Lt-Col 1919; Lt-Col 1927; Col 1930; served European War, Gallipoli, Palestine, France (despatches four times); passed Staff College, 1919; Staff Employment, 1920–22 and 1924–27; Commanded 13th Field Brigade, Royal Artillery, 1927–31; AA and QMG i/c of Administration, China, 1931–33; retired pay, 1934; AA and QMG East Lancs Area, 1939; reverted to retired pay, 1941; holds Royal Humane Society testimonial for saving life at sea. *Address:* 16a Inverleith Row, Edinburgh. *Club:* United Service.

Died 27 Jan. 1943.

COUSINS, Arthur George, CBE 1919; Director of Public Companies, including Odhams Press Ltd (Chairman), The Daily Herald (1929) Ltd (Chairman); Member of Reuter Trust; *b* 1882; *s* of Harry Cousins of Braunton, Devon; *m* Kate, *d* of late Robert Riches; one *s* one *d.* Served European War, 1914–18; Assist Quartermaster-General, London District Command, 1918–19 (despatches). *Address:* Bix Manor Farm, near Henley-on-Thames. *Club:* Thatched House.

Died 25 Sept. 1949.

COUSINS, Herbert H., MA (Oxon); *b* 1869; *s* of Rev. W. E. Cousins, MA; *m* Minnie (*d* 1945), *d* of R. J. Hardy; one *s* two *d. Educ:* Merton College, Oxford; Heidelberg University. 1st Class honours Natural Science, Oxford, 1889. Demonstrator, Chemical Department, Oxford University; University Extension Lecturer; Lecturer in Chemistry at SE Agricultural College, Wye, Kent, 1894; Island and Agricultural Chemist, Jamaica, 1900; Director of Agriculture and Island Chemist, Jamaica, 1908–32; Member of the Legislative Council, 1907–23; Chairman of Commission to inquire into Distressed Districts. *Publications:* Chemistry of the Garden; Farm Foods (trans.); History of Hope Farm; Jamaica Herd Book, 1933; many papers and reports on Agric. Chemistry and Tropicall Agriculture. *Address:* 34 Upland Park Road, Oxford.

Died 14 Dec. 1949.

COUTTS, Francis James Henderson, CB 1923; MD, BSc, DPH; *b* Queensland, Australia, 1865; *s* of late Robert Coutts of Windermere; *m* 1899, Elizabeth Efford, *d* of late Charles Godfrey Boullen of Ambleside; two *d. Educ:* Owens College, Manchester University; MB, ChB, MD (Gold Medal), DPH, BSc Fellow of Royal Sanitary Institute and of Chemical Society. Assistant Public Health Department, Victoria University, Manchester, 1899–1901; Medical Officer of Health, Blackpool, 1901–08; Medical Inspector Local Government Board, 1908–19; Senior Medical Officer, Ministry of Health, 1919–30 member, Ministry of Health Committee of Inquiry into anti-Tuberculosis Service in Wales and Monmouthshire, 1937–38. *Publications:* Reports to Local Govt Board on Anthrax due to Infected Shaving Brushes; Condensed Milks, with Special Reference to their Use as Infants' Foods; Use of Proprietary Foods for Infant Feeding; Dried Milks, with Special Reference to Use for Infant Feeding; An Unusual Source of Lead Poisoning (Med. Chronicle, 1895); The Present Position of the Tuberculosis Problem, J. Roy. San. Inst., 1928–1929; Report (with Clement Davies, KC, MP) on anti-tuberculosis service in Wales, 1938; and other papers on Tuberculosis. *Recreation:* gardening. *Address:* Rusland, Spencer Road, Canford Cliffs, Bournemouth.

Died 13 Feb. 1949.

COUZENS, Sir Henry Herbert, KBE 1937. Vice-President and a director of Brazilian Traction, Light and Power Co. Ltd, City of Santos Improvements Co. Ltd, and São Paulo Electric Co. Ltd.

Died 17 Nov. 1944.

COWAN, James; author and journalist; *b* New Zealand, 1870; father pioneer settler from County Down, mother from Isle of Man. Newspaper work; editor of numerous publications for New Zealand Government; specialised in study of Maori-Polynesian history and folk-lore; engaged by Government to write history of the New Zealand Wars. *Publications:* The Maoris of New Zealand; Adventures of Kimble Bent; Fairy Folk-Tales of the Maori; History of the New Zealand Wars (2 vols); Travel in New Zealand (2 vols); History of the Maori

Pioneer Battalion in the Great War; The Old Frontier; Samoa and its Story; The Tongariro National Park; Legends of the Maori (2 vols) (with late Hon. Sir Maui Pomare); The Maori, Yesterday and To-Day; Tales of the Maori Coast; Tales of the Maori Bush; Hero Stories of New Zealand; A Trader in Cannibal Land; Suwarrow Gold, and other Stories of the Great South Sea; Biography of Sir Donald Maclean; The Forest Rangers; Farmers and Frontiersmen, etc.; many short stories, ethnological articles. *Address:* 52 Connaught Terrace, Brooklyn, Wellington, NZ.

Died 6 Sept. 1943.

COWAN, Col James Henry, RE; CB 1917; *b* Chiswick, 28 Sept. 1856; *e s* of William Cowan, LLD, JP, and Selina, *d* of late W. Deeming; *m* 1880, Alice, *d* of late Gen. de Butts, RE; two *s* one *d. Educ:* Edinburgh Academy; Cheltenham College; RMA, Woolwich. Passed first into RE, with various prizes; Pollock Medal, RMA; Fowke Medal, Chatham. Late Instructor in Fortification at RMA Woolwich; served South Africa, Oct. 1899 (despatches); Commissioner Wei Hai Wei, China, 1901; Member Ordnance Committee, 1902–05; commanding Royal Engineer, Chatham, 1905–07; Assistant Director of Fortifications and Works, War Office, SW, 1908–12 and 1914–18; retired, 1912. Owns about 1300 acres. *Recreations:* won Spencer Cup, Wimbledon, 1872; has shot frequently in Scottish and Army Eights, Wimbledon and Bisley; Captain of the Army Eight, 1908–12; bicycling. *Address:* Moffat, Dumfriesshire. *Club:* English Speaking Union.

Died 7 Aug. 1943.

COWAN, John, LLD; DSc Glasgow; MD, BA, Cambridge; FRFPS; Physician to the King in Scotland; Consulting Physician, Royal Infirmary; *b* 1870; *y s* of late John B. Cowan, LLD, MD, Professor of Materia Medica, Glasgow University; *m* Maud Mary (*d* 1936), *d* of late George W. Hamilton, Rhu, Dumbartonshire; two *s* one *d. Educ:* Fettes Coll.; King's Coll., Cambridge; Glasgow Univ. Foulis Memorial Scholar, Research Fellow, Glasgow University. Gibson Lecturer, RCPE, 1926; St Cyres Lecturer, 1930; Physician, Scot. National Red Cross Hospital, South Africa, 1900; Consulting Physician, EEF, 1917–19; Professor of Medicine, Anderson College of Medicine. *Publications:* numerous medical papers. *Recreations:* fishing, golf, etc. *Address:* Shenvalla, Kilmacolm. *Club:* Western (Glasgow).

Died 15 Aug. 1947.

COWARD, Sir Henry, Kt 1926; MA; MusDoc Oxon; Hon. MusDoc Sheffield; FISC, Freeman City of Sheffield, Freeman Cutlers' Company; President of the Tonic Sol-Fa College, London; *b* Liverpool, 26 Nov. 1849; widower; four *s* four *d. Educ:* various schools. Apprenticed to cutlery business; at twenty-two entered scholastic profession; at thirty nine entered musical; retired 1933. *Publications:* numerous cantatas, anthems, glees, part-songs, and songs. *Address:* Dewlyn, 6 Kenwood Road, Sheffield.

Died 10 June 1944.

COWDROY, Joan Alice; writer; 3rd *d* of late Arthur Rathbone Cowdroy. *Publications:* Novels: Brothers-in-Love, 1922; The Inscrutable Secretary, 1924; The Virtuous Fool, 1924; A King of Space, 1925; The Idler, 1926; The Immortal, 1927; Mask, 1928; Tapestry of Dreams, 1929; The Mystery of Sett, 1930; Watch Mr Moh!, 1931; (in USA), Flying Dagger Murder; Murder of Lydia, 1933; Disappearance, 1934; Murder Unsuspected, 1936; Framed Evidence, 1936; Our Miss Flower, 1937; Death Has No Tongue, 1938; Nine Green Bottles, 1939; Merry-go-Round, 1940; Murder out of Court, 1943; various poems, articles, and short stories contributed to the Daily Telegraph, the English Review, etc. *Address:* Hope's Rest, Gt Holland, Essex.

Died 14 Aug. 1946.

COWELL, Philip Herbert, FRS; Hon. DSc Oxon; late Chief Assistant Royal Observatory, Greenwich; Superintendent Nautical Almanac Office, 1910–30; *m* 1901, Phyllis, *d* of late Holroyd Chaplin of 2 Holland Villas Road, W. Senior Wrangler, 1892; formerly Fellow of Trinity College, Cambridge. *Address:* 63 Crag Path, Aldeburgh, Suffolk.

Died 6 June 1949.

COWELL, Sibert Forrest, MA; *b* 24 Sept. 1863; 2nd *s* of Thomas William Cowell, MRCS; unmarried. *Educ:* Westminster School; University College, Oxford. BA 1886, MA 1911. Assistant Secretary of Royal College of Surgeons, 1888–1901; Secretary of the Royal College of Surgeons of England, 1901–34. *Address:* 27 Upper Lattimore Road, St Albans, Herts.

Died 13 Jan. 1949.

COWIE, Maj.-Gen. Charles Henry, CB 1919; CIE 1915; RE; *b* 20 April 1861. Entered RE 1881; Captain, 1889; Major, 1899; Lt-Col 1908; Col 1906; Deputy-Manager Eastern Bengal Railway, 1897; NW Railway, 1899; served Tirah, 1897 (medal 2 clasps); South Africa (despatches, Bt-Lt-Col; Queen's medal 3 clasps, King's medal 2 clasps); Assistant Director of Railways, 1900–02; General Manager Imperial Military Railways, 1902; Manager Eastern Bengal State Railway, 1906; Agent O and R Railway, 1909; North Western State Railway, 1913; Deputy Director of Railway Transport, Eastern Command, 1916; Director-General of Transport, Constantinople with temp. rank of Major-General, 1919; retired with rank of Major-General, 1919. *Address:* Lloyds Bank, Cox & Co., 6 Pall Mall, SW1.

Died 8 Nov. 1941.

COWLAND, Bt Lt-Col Walter Storey, DSO 1919; TD; MA (Oxon); *b* 1888; *o s* of late John Andrew Cowland, Woodlands, Brockenhurst; *m* 1925, Dorothy *o d* of Ernest William Marshall, Yattendon Manor, Berks. *Educ:* Winchester College; University College, Oxford. Served European War, Hampshire Regiment, Gallipoli (Cape Helles), 1915, 2nd Bn; Macedonia, 1916–18, 10th Bn and 12th Bn (2nd in command) (DSO, despatches twice, Croix de Guerre avec Palme); Adjutant, Winchester College OTC, 1919–33; Officer Commanding, 1933–39; Bt Lt-Col, Jan. 1935; Jubilee Medal, 1935; Coronation Medal, 1937. *Address:* Winchester College; The Quarry, Mullion. *T:* Winchester 15, Mullion 251. *Club:* Naval and Military.

Died 31 March 1942.

COWLEY, John Duncan, MA, FLA; Director, University of London School of Librarianship, 1934–44; Goldsmiths' Librarian, University of London, since 1944; *b* 3 Oct. 1897; *s* of Robert Harrild Cowley; *m* 1922, Isobel, *d* of late Matthew Kirsop; two *s. Educ:* Merchant Taylors' School; St John's College, Oxford. Commissioned Machine Gun Corps, 1916; service in France, 1916–17, 1918; Assistant librarian, Middle Temple, 1922–24; County Librarian of Lancashire, 1925–34; visited USA at Invitation of American Library Association, 1933, and as Rockefeller Fellow, 1937; visited Czechoslovakia, Hungary, Austria and Switzerland as surveyor for the Library Association, 1936; examiner, assessor and member of Council of Library Association; Chairman, County Libraries Section, 1931–34; Principal Librarian, Service Libraries and Books Fund, 1940; RAFVR, 1940. *Publications:* A bibliography of the abridgments, digests, dictionaries and indexes of English law, 1932; The use of reference material, 1937; Training for librarianship in the United States, 1938; Bibliographical description and cataloguing, 1939. *Address:* Leadale, Davenham Avenue, Northwood, Middx. *T:* Northwood, Middx 1342.

Died Aug. 1944.

COWLIN, Sir Francis Nicholas, Kt 1935; FRSA; Hon. RWA; Fellow Institute of Builders; Chairman, William Cowlin and Son, Ltd, Bristol; *b* 23 Sept. 1868; *s* of William Henry Cowlin and Annie Scull; unmarried. *Educ:* privately; University College, Bristol. Past President Anchor-Grateful and Colston Research Societies; Trustee of Bishop Monks Horfield Trust; Chairman, Bristol Branch of Playing Fields Association; President, Bristol Rugby Football Club. *Address:* Rodborough House, Sneyd Park, Bristol. *TA:* Construct Bristol. *T:* Bristol, Stoke Bishop 81509. *Clubs:* Clifton; Bristol.

Died 26 July 1945.

COWLING, George H., MA; *b* 29 Dec. 1881; *o s* of late Thomas Cowling, Leeds; *m* 1916, Muriel Margaret, *e d* of Angus McIntosh Wilson, Darlington; three *s* one *d. Educ:* Modern School, Leeds; Leeds University; Hamburg. First Class English L and L, 1912; Gladstone Prize, 1912. Served European War, 1915–19; Lecturer in English Language and Literature, Leeds, 1919; Reader in English, 1925; Prof. of English Language and Literature, University of Melbourne, 1928–42; retired, 1943; Examiner in English to the University of London, 1927; Secretary Yorkshire Dialect Society, 1919–25; President Melbourne Shakespeare Society, 1929–31. *Publications:* Music on the Shakespearean Stage, 1913; The Dialect of Hackness, North-East Yorkshire, 1914; A Preface to Shakespeare, 1925; Chaucer, 1927; An English Bibliography, 1931; The Use of English, 1934; Selections from Chaucer, 1935; Shelley and other Essays, 1936. *Address:* 50 Aroona Road, Melbourne, SE7, Australia.

Died 23 July 1946.

COWPER, Henry Swainson, JP, FSA; *b* 1865; *m* 1902, Amy Mary, *d* of late Maj.-Gen. C. S. Dundas, RA; one *s. Educ:* Harrow. Travelled in Mesopotamia, Egypt, Tripoli (Barbary) and Asia Minor. *Publications:* Through Turkish Arabia, 1894; The Hill of the Graces (Travels in Tripoli), 1897; Hawkshead, its History, Archæology, etc., 1899; editor of the Early Registers of Aldingham and Hawkshead, Lancs; The Development of the Art of Attack, 1906; Loddenden and the Usbornes of Loddenden, 1914. *Recreation:* archæology. *Address:* High House, Hawkshead, Ambleside. *T:* Hawkshead 30. *Club:* Royal Automobile.

Died 7 April 1941.

COWTAN, Air Vice-Marshal Frank Cuninghame, CB 1943; CBE 1946; MRCS, LRCP; *b* 1888; *yr s* of late Frank Cowtan and late Janet Dougall, Campden Hill; *m* 1915, Nora Alice, *d* of late Lieut-Col W. P. Kennedy, CSI, West Byfleet; one *s* one *d. Educ:* Linton House and St Paul's Schools; St Thomas's Hospital. Commissioned RAMC, 1912; served 1914–19, 7th Division and Mesopotamian Expeditionary Force (despatches 4 times, Brevet Major); transferred to RAF Medical Branch, 1920; Wing Comdr 1926; Group Capt. 1934; Air Commodore 1939; temp. Air Vice-Marshal, 1942; subst. 1943; KHS, 1941–45; retired Dec. 1945; despatches, 1940, 1945. *Recreations:* fishing, rifle shooting, ornithology, drawing. *Address:* Sandford, Shortheath, Farnham, Surrey. *T:* Farnham 68134.

Died 5 March 1950.

COX, Adelaide, CBE 1925; Commissioner in Salvation Army; *b* 1860. In command of Women's Social Operations, Great Britain and Ireland, 1912–26. *Publication:* Hotchpotch, 1937, 2nd edition, 1938. *Address:* 28 Rotherwick Road, Golders Green, NW11. *T:* Speedwell 7052.

Died 19 March 1945.

COX, Maj.-Gen. Charles Frederick, CB 1902; CMG 1918; DSO 1918; VD; *b* 2 May 1863; *s* of F. C. Cox of Carlingford; *m* 1894, Minnie, *d* of W. K. Gibbens; one *d.* Served South Africa, 1899–1902 (despatches, Queen's medal with eight clasps, King's medal with two clasps);

European War, 1914–18 (despatches, CMG), commanded 1st Cavalry Division, New South Wales; Federal Senator, 1919–38; Queen's Jubilee medal; King's Coronation medal; King's Jubilee Medal. *Address:* 3 Fitzroy Street, Croydon, New South Wales. *Clubs:* Australian Pioneers', Imperial Service (Sydney).

Died 20 Nov. 1947.

COX, Major Harding, LLB; late Vice-Chairman and Trustee of The Field, Queen, Law Times, Bazaar, and other newspapers and periodicals; late Dramatic Critic, Vanity Fair; *o s* of late Mr Serjeant Cox, and 2nd wife, Rosalinda, *d* of Mr Commissioner de Fonblanque; *m* Hebe Gertrude, *d* of late W. H. Barlow; three *s. Educ:* Harrow (shooting XI); Trinity College, Cambridge, (First Trinity First Boat, and holder of two river records). Late Captain Duke of Cambridge's Hussars; gazetted Captain 5 Dec. 1914; in command of 29th and after of 35th Coy. RDC; seconded 28 Jan. 1916, and posted to 10th (Co. of London) Battalion, The London Regiment, and attached 102nd and 100th Provisional Bns Royal Fusiliers; ARO on Eastern Command Staff, 1917; Ministry of Information, 1918; specially invited by the Austrian Government to inspect and report on the fisheries of Bosnia and Hertzgovina, 1897; author of the scheme for cultivation of freshwater fish (Board of Agriculture), and of the scheme, The better Control of Dogs (Home Office); Founder and Life Member of the Fox-terrier and Cocker Spaniel Clubs; Original Director British Diesel Engine Co. *Publications:* Coursing (Badminton Library), Lyrics and Recitations; Dogs; Chasing and Racing, 1922; A Sportsman at Large, 1923; Dogs and I, 1923; Yarns without Yawns, 1923; The Amateur's Derby, 1924; Fugleman the Foxhound, 1926; Dogs of To-Day, 1931; Fringes of Philosophy; Kennel Editor Illustrated Sporting and Dramatic News 1923; contributor of social, sporting and scientific articles to periodicals. *Recreations:* late master Missenden and Hambleden Vale Harriers, afterwards master of the Old Berkeley Foxhounds; formerly racehorse owner and amateur jockey with special licence from the Jockey Club and NHC to ride on equal terms with professional jockeys; shooting. *Address:* Newick, Sussex. *Clubs:* Garrick (Senior Life), Leander (Life).

Died 18 June 1944.

COX, Rev. James Taylor, MA, BD, DD; *b* 19 May 1865; *s* of Henry William Cox and Margaret Taylor; *m* 1st, 1893, Mary (*d* 1915), 2nd *d* of late James Morrison, Phingask, Fraserburgh, Aberdeenshire; 2nd, 1917, Lilian Gertrude Lees, *o d* of late James Sykes, Sefton Park, Liverpool; one *s* one *d. Educ:* Grammar School, Old Aberdeen; University of Aberdeen. Minister of Dyce, Aberdeenshire, 1888–1936; Clerk to the Presbytery of Aberdeen, 1903–47; Clerk to the Synod of Aberdeen, 1913–48; Depute Clerk of the General Assembly, 1927–28; Principal Clerk of the General Assembly of the Church of Scotland, 1928–46; Vice-Chairman of the General Assembly's Special Commission on the Financial Position of the Church, 1926–29; DD (Aberdeen) 1928; declined Moderatorship of General Assembly of Church of Scotland, 1937; member of various educational bodies. *Publications:* Assisted in Editing 4th edition of Dr William Mair's Digest of Church Laws; Editor of Practice and Procedure in the Church of Scotland. *Recreations:* fishing and walking. *Address:* 87 Anderson Drive S, Aberdeen. *T:* Aberdeen 6511. *Clubs:* Conservative, Overseas (Edinburgh).

Died 5 Nov. 1948.

COX, Rev. Lionel Edgar, MA; *b* 28 March 1868; *s* of Rev. Thomas Cox, Rector of Norton Juxta Twycross, Leicestershire, and of Ideford, Devon, and Laura Eleanor, *d* of William Henry Jones of Brawdy, Pembrokeshire. *Educ:* Somerset College, Bath; Dorchester Theological College; Durham University. Deacon, 1891; Priest, 1894; Curate of St Paul's, Kandy, 1891; Incumbent of St John's, Kalutara, 1895; joined the Madras Ecclesiastical Establishment, 1898; Archdeacon

of Madras and Bishop's Commissary, 1910–22; Chaplain of St George's Cathedral, Madras, 1912–19; Rector of Lyndon, Oakham, 1922–29. *Address:* 10 Apsley Road, Bath.

Died 6 Dec. 1945.

COX, Maj.-Gen. Lionel Howard, CB 1945; CBE 1942; MC 1918; *b* 1 April 1893; *s* of Doctor William Cox, Winchcombe, Gloucestershire; *m* 1940, Sheila, *d* of Eric Athelstane Field; two *d. Educ:* Lancing College; RMC, Sandhurst. 2nd Lt Gloucestershire Regt 1912; served European War, 1914–18 (MC, Brevet of Major, despatches twice); Iraq operations, 1919–20; Lieut-Col commanding 2nd Bn Gloucestershire Regt 1935; Colonel (temp. Brigadier), 1938; Major-Gen. 1943; retired, 1948; UK Delegate UN Special Cttee on the Balkans, 1948. *Clubs:* Army and Navy; Royal Tank Regt.

Died 29 July 1949.

COX, Stephen, CIE 1921; MBE 1918; retired Indian Civilian; *b* Osbaston Hall, Market Bosworth, 23 Dec. 1870; 4th *s* of Alfred Cox, JP; *m* 1913, Nora, *d* of late Sir Alfred Bourne, KCIE, FRS; one *s* two *d. Educ:* Harrow; Cooper's Hill. Entered Indian Forest Service as Assistant Conservator, 1893; retired as Chief Conservator, 1923. *Address:* Barton Lodge, nr Bury St Edmunds. *T:* Bury 287 Y. *Club:* Junior Carlton.

Died 11 April 1943.

COX, Thomas, CBE 1918; JP; *b* 1865. Was Controller, Unionist Party Central Office and Hon. Secretary, National War Aims and National War Savings Committee. *Address:* 7 The Ridgway, Sutton, Surrey.

Died 3 June 1947.

COX-DAVIES, Rachael Annie, CBE 1923; RRC; Member of General Nursing Council; Dame of Grace Order of St John of Jerusalem; *b* 1863; *d* of late Edward Cox-Davies, Crickhowell, Monmouthshire. *Educ:* St Stephen's College, Windsor. Was Civil Matron, Queen Alexandra's Imperial Army Nursing Board; Matron Royal Free Hospital, Gray's Inn Road; Principal Matron Territorial Army Nursing Service; served in South Africa with Portland Hospital. *Address:* 20 Abbey Road, NW8. *Clubs:* Cowdray United, Nursing Services.

Died 30 Oct. 1944.

COXEN, Maj.-Gen. Walter Adams, CB 1919; CMG 1918; DSO 1917; Australian Staff Corps, retired; *b* Egham, Surrey, 22 June 1870; *s* of late Henry William Coxen of Brisbane; *m* Adelaide Rebe, *d* of late F. J. Beor of Beaudesert, Queensland; one *s* four *d. Educ:* Toowoomba and Brisbane Grammar Schools. Served European War, 1914–18 (despatches, DSO, CMG, Belgian Croix de Guerre); Maj.-Gen. 1927; Chief of General Staff, Australian Military Forces, 1930. *Address:* 83 Caroline Street, South Yarra, Melbourne, SE1, Australia.

Died 15 Dec. 1949.

COXEN, Sir William George, 1st Bt *cr* 1941; Kt 1929; *b* 1867; *s* of George Nickel and Fanny Coxen, Hampstead; *m* 1912, Kathleen Alice, *d* of Edward Doncaster of Silk, Willoughby, Lincs and Snettisham, Norfolk. *Educ:* Ongar Grammar School; King's College, London. Alderman of City of London; Sheriff of the City of London, 1928–29; Lord Mayor of London, 1939–40; during the war Commanding Officer 4th Batt. County of London VR (London Volunteer Rifles); Liveryman of the Worshipful Companies of Cordwainers, Basketmakers, Glaziers, Loriners, Spectaclemakers, Carmen and Gold and Silver Wyre Drawers; Member of the Court of Common Council, 1920–31; Mayor of Holborn, 1919–20; Chairman of Joint Industrial Council (Municipal Services, London District), 1920–22; A Director of Trust Houses, Ltd; Treasurer of the Royal National Orthopædic Hospital;

Trustee of the Metropolitan Nursing Association. *Address:* Wildwood, Seal, Kent. *T:* Seal 24. *Clubs:* Junior Carlton, Royal Automobile.

Died 7 April 1946 (ext).

COYLE, James Vincent, CBE 1926; *b* 15 Dec. 1864; *e s* of late Charles Coyle, Rutland Square, Dublin, and Anne M., *o c* of late T. Duggan; *m* 1889, Grettie Mary (*d* 1921), *d* of John O'Sullivan, of Drumcondra, Co. Dublin, and Leap, Co. Cork; five *s. Educ:* Belvedere College, SJ, Dublin; Trinity College, Dublin. Called to the Irish Bar, King's Inns, Dublin, 1896; entered Collector General's Office, Dublin, 1884; First Class Clerk therein, 1892–99; Department of Agriculture and Technical Instruction, Dublin, 1900–21; Principal Staff Officer and Deputy Chief Clerk therein; Chairman of Agricultural Wages Board for Ireland, 1919–21; Assistant Secretary, Ministry of Agriculture, Northern Ireland, 1922–30; retired, 1930; Chairman Committee of Management Peamount Sanatorium, Co. Dublin, 1934–43. *Recreations:* gardening and fishing. *Address:* Glenburn, Castle Grove, Clontarf, Dublin.

Died 5 July 1948.

COZENS-HARDY, Edgar Wrigley, CMG 1926; *b* 1872; *s* of late Theobald Cozens-Hardy of Sprowston. *Educ:* Amersham Hall. Chief Engineer, Gold Coast Government Railways, 1906–19; General Manager, 1919–26. *Recreations:* shooting, golf. *Address:* Oak Lodge, Sprowston, Norwich. *T:* Norwich 1603. *Clubs:* East India and Sports; Norfolk, Norwich.

Died 1 April 1945.

CRACKANTHORPE, Dayrell (Montague), CMG 1918; *e surv. s* of late Montague Crackanthorpe and Blanche, *d* of Rev. Eardley C. Holt; *m* 1898, Ida (*d* 1918), *o d* of General Daniel Sickles, New York; one *d. Educ:* St Paul's; France and Germany; Merton College, Oxford. Attaché Diplomatic Service, 1896; 3rd Secretary, Madrid; passed examination in public law, 1897; 2nd Secretary, Washington, 1900; appointed to Brussels, 1902, where he acted from time to time as Chargé d'Affaires; was in charge of HM Legation at Bucharest, June–Sept. 1906; 1st Secretary, Vienna, 1906; Tokyo, 1910–12; granted an allowance for knowledge of Japanese; 1st Secretary, Belgrade, 1912, where he was in charge of HM Legation during year preceding and at outbreak of the European War; Counsellor of Embassy Jan. 1, 1917, on which date he was appointed to HM Legation at Athens and to British Delegate on the International Financial Commission; was in charge of HM Legation at Athens, June–Oct. 1917; Counsellor of Embassy at Madrid, 1918; in charge at HM Embassy, July–Oct. 1919; Appointed Minister to Central American Republics, Oct. 1919; retired, 1922; High Sheriff of Cumberland, 1928; JP Westmorland, 1915–37; Cumberland, 1921–37; Platoon Commander in LDV, 1940; Lieut Home Guard, 1941. Owns 6000 acres in Westmorland and Cumberland. Lord of the Manors of Newbiggin, Ousby, and Bank. *Recreations:* shooting, golf, skating. *Address:* Newbiggin Hall, Temple Sowerby, Penrith. *T:* Kirkby Thore 210. *Clubs:* St James', International Sportsmen's, Lansdowne.

Died 9 Feb. 1950.

CRADOCK-HARTOPP, Sir George Francis Fleetwood; *see* Hartopp.

CRAFER, Rev. Thomas Wilfrid, DD Cambridge; Vice-President Guild of St Raphael; Examining Chaplain to the Bishop of London; *b* 1870; *m* 1895, Helen Catherine Philbrick; four *d. Educ:* Scholar of Christ's and Jesus Colleges, Cambridge; Classical and Theological honours and Carus Greek Testament Prize. Tutor at St Aidan's College, Birkenhead, 1896; Chaplain and Lecturer at Downing College, Cambridge, 1902–17; Vicar of All Saints', Cambridge, 1903–17; Incumbent of S Germains, Blackheath, 1917–24; Rector of Brampton, Hunts, 1924–25; Rector of Milton, Cambridge,

1925–27; Rector of Tatsfield, Surrey, 1934–37; Dean and Professor of Theology at Queen's College, London, 1918–30; Warden of the Southwark College of Greyladies, 1919–36. *Publications:* Ezra and Nehemiah; Hosea; and Haggai and Zechariah; The Apocriticus of Macarius Magnes; Men of the Passion; Women of the Passion; Scenes in Drama from St Paul's Life; The Atonement and the Eucharist; Studies in Jeremiah; To Lighten the Gentiles; Christ's Healing Miracles; The Church's Help in Sickness; Outline Meditations drawn from the Daily Lessons, etc.; contributor to Hastings' Dictionary of Ethics and Religion, and A New Commentary, 1928; Editor of The Church and the Ministry of Healing, 1934; The Priest's Vade Mecum, 1946. *Address:* c/o Lloyds Bank, Woking. *Club:* Church Imperial.

Died 21 Nov. 1949.

CRAIG, Maj. Sir Algernon Tudor T.; *see* Tudor-Craig.

CRAIG, Edward Hubert Cunningham, BA (Cantab) FRSE, FGS; Consulting Geologist; Geological Adviser to Burmah Oil Co., and many other petroleum companies; Founder-Member and former Member of Council of Institution of Petroleum Technologists; *b* Edinburgh, 1874; *y s* of late Edward Cunningham-Craig; *m* Iona Irene, *d* of late Rev. William Cleaver; no *c. Educ:* Trinity College, Glenalmond; Clare College, Cambridge. Joined Staff of HM Geological Survey, 1896; lent to Colony of Trinidad and Tobago, 1903, as Government Geologist; resigned from Government Service, 1907; conducted Geological Surveys and Investigations in Persia, Burma, India, Baluchistan, Barbados (for Colonial Government), Venezuela, South Africa (for Union Government), Alberta, Manitoba, New Brunswick, 1907–14; Representative of the Director, Trench Warfare Supply Dept at three chemical factories, 1916; Senior Geologist, Petroleum Research Dept under Ministry of Munitions and Admiralty, 1917; Geological Adviser and Chief Officer for Co-ordination of Research and Production, Petroleum Executive, 1917–18; Technical Adviser to Committee on the Production of Oil from Cannel Coal, etc., 1918; conducted Geological Investigations in Egypt, Ecuador, East Indies, Rumania, Jugo-Slavia, Java, and USA, 1920–24. *Publications:* Oil-Finding, an Introduction to the Geological Study of Petroleum; Joint Author of A Treatise on British Mineral Oil; Numerous Scientific Papers. *Recreations:* shooting, fishing, golf. *Address:* The Dutch House, Beaconsfield. *TA:* Naphtology, London. *Club:* West Indian.

Died 24 April 1946.

CRAIG, George, CMG 1928; ISO 1935; LLD; *b* 1873; *s* of James Craig, farmer, Southland, NZ; *m* 1901, Teresa Imelda, *d* of James Moran, surveyor, Auckland; three *d. Educ:* Boys' High School, Dunedin; Victoria University College, Wellington. Joined Customs Department, 1891; Audit Officer, Customs Branch, 1907; Chief Clerk, Customs Department, 1910; Assistant Comptroller, 1913; Comptroller of Customs, Wellington, NZ, 1923–35; retired 1935; Chairman, New Zealand Tariff Commissions, 1927 and 1933. *Recreations:* bowls, golf. *Clubs:* University, Wellington.

Died 9 June 1947.

CRAIG, J. Humbert, RHA; landscape artist; *s* of Alexander Craig and Marie Sabine Metzenen; *m* 1924; no *c. Educ:* Bangor Grammar School; Model School, Belfast. Began career with his father, wholesale tea merchant; left home for the United States and tried his hand at various jobs which were temporary and eventually gave up everything for painting and remains a lover of his profession; exhibitor at mostly all the art shows in England, Scotland and Ireland from time to time. *Recreations:* angler, river and deep sea. *Address:*

Dunedin, Antrim Road, Belfast; Cushenden, Co. Antrim. *Clubs:* Ulster Academy of Arts, Belfast; Royal Hibernian Academy, Dublin.

Died 12 June 1944.

CRAIG, James Alfred; *b* 12 Oct. 1858; *e s* of Adam Hunter Craig of Patrick, Glasgow. Assistant editor of Great Thoughts, 1890–1914; editor, 1914–36; editor of The Christian Age, 1900–17, and of Helping Words, 1891–1907. Has also edited Grace and Truth, Light in the Home, Sunday at Home, and was tracts Editor for the Religious Tracts Society. *Recreation:* reading. *Address:* Selah, Hassocks. *T:* Hassocks 55.

Died 24 Dec. 1942.

CRAIG, James Douglas, CMG 1945; CBE 1930; 3rd Class Order of the Nile; retired; *b* 11 April 1882; *e s* of late James Craig, MD, Beckenham, Kent; *m* 1912, Marjorie, *d* of late Joseph Dobbs, Coolbawn House, Castlecomer, Ireland; one *s* two *d*. *Educ:* Shrewsbury; Hertford College, Oxford. Joined Sudan Political Service, 1906; Governor Kordofan Province, 1922–26; Deputy Civil Secretary 1926–29; retired, 1929. Asst Sec. to UK Representative, Eire, 1939–45. Chairman East Suffolk CC, 1947. *Address:* Broom Heath, Woodbridge, Suffolk. *T:* Woodbridge 576. *Club:* Conservative.

Died 13 May 1950.

CRAIGMYLE, 2nd Baron *cr* 1929, of Craigmyle; **Alexander Shaw;** Hon. Captain Royal Naval Reserve, 1935; Hon. Col RAMC 1940; *b* 28 Feb. 1883; *o s* of 1st Baron and Elsie Stephen (*d* 1939), *d* of George Forrest, Ludquharn, Aberdeenshire; *S* father 1937; *m* 1913, Lady Margaret Cargill Mackay, *e d* of 1st Earl of Inchcape, of Strathnaver; one *s* three *d*. *Educ:* George Watson's College, Edinburgh; Edinburgh University; Trinity College, Oxford (MA). President Oxford Union Society, 1905; called to Bar, Inner Temple, 1908; practised in King's Bench Division and Parliamentary Bar; contested (L) Midlothian by-election, 1912; MP (L) Kilmarnock, 1915–23; Parliamentary Private Secretary to Sir John Simon, MP, Home Secretary, 1915; and to Sir Albert Stanley, MP, President of Board of Trade, 1917–18; High Sheriff of County of London, 1931; a Lieutenant, City of London; DL Selkirkshire; Commission Royal Marine Artillery, 1915; served throughout Battle of the Somme, 1916; Member of Disabled Sailors' and Soldiers' Compensation Committee (Home Office), 1918; Chairman Special Arbitration Tribunal on Wages of Women Munition Workers, 1917–18; Member of Enemy Aliens Repatriation Tribunal, 1919; Member Board of Trade Advisory Council, 1927; President Chamber of Shipping of United Kingdom, 1927; Member Imperial Shipping Committee, 1931; Chairman of P. & O. Steam Navigation Co. and British India Steam Navigation Co. 1932–38; a Director of the Bank of England, 1923–43. *Publications:* various articles and papers on social and economic subjects. *Heir: s* Hon. (Thomas) Donald (Mackay) Shaw, *b* 17 Nov. 1923. *Address:* 122 Leadenhall St, EC3; Fairnilee, by Galashiels, Selkirkshire. *Clubs:* Reform, Royal Automobile, Roehampton.

Died 29 Sept. 1944.

CRAIK, Lt-Col James, DSO, 1916; late Indian Army; *b* 24 Nov. 1871; *e s* of late William Craik; *m* 1908, Sybil Margaret, *widow* of C. F. Balfour, ICS; one *d*. *Educ:* Dover College; Royal Military College, Sandhurst. Joined 1st Hampshire Regt, 1891; transferred to 19th Bengal Lancers (now 19th KGO Lancers), 1896; served China, 1900 (medal); European War, 1914–18 (DSO, despatches); retired, 1911. *Address:* Court Manor, Corfe Mullen, Wimborne, Dorset.

Died 3 July 1942.

CRAM, Ralph Adams; architect and author; *b* Hampton Falls, New Hampshire, 16 Dec. 1863; *s* of Rev. William Augustine Cram and Sarah Elizabeth Blake; *m* 1900, Elizabeth Carrington, *d* of late Capt. Clement

Carrington Read, CSA, of Virginia. *Educ:* LittD Princeton, 1910, Williams, 1928; LLD Yale, 1915; Notre Dame, 1925. Architect, 1889; Mem. Nat. Inst. Arts and Letters; ex-President Boston Society Architects; Fellow Am. Academy Arts and Sciences; American Academy of Arts and Letters; AIA, Royal Geographical Society, Royal Society of Arts, London; Past President Mediæval Academy of America; Hon. Corr. Member Royal Inst. British Architects; ANA; Member Am. Federation of Arts; Phi Beta Kappa, Harvard, 1921. *Publications:* The Decadent; Black Spirits and White; Church Building, 1901; The Ruined Abbeys of Great Britain, 1906, new ed., 1928; Impressions of Japanese Architecture and the Allied Arts, 1906; The Gothic Quest, 1907; Excalibur, 1908; The Ministry of Art, 1914; Heart of Europe, 1915; The Substance of Gothic, 1917; The Nemesis of Mediocrity, 1918; The Great Thousand Years, 1918; The Sins of the Fathers, 1919; Walled Towns, 1919; Gold, Frankincense, and Myrrh, 1919; Towards the Great Peace, 1922; The Catholic Church and Art, 1930; Convictions and Controversies, 1934; My Life in Architecture, 1936; The End of Democracy, 1937. *Address:* 248 Boylston Street, Boston; Whitehall, Sudbury, Mass. *Clubs:* Century, New York.

Died 22 Sept. 1942.

CRAMER, William, PhD, DSc, MRCS, LRCP; Cancer Research Associate, Barnard Skin and Cancer Hospital, St Louis, Mo; Research Associate, Anatomy Department, Washington University, St Louis; *b* 2 June 1878; *m* 1906, Belle Klauber, New York; two *s*. *Educ:* University of Munich; University of Berlin; University of Edinburgh; University College Hospital, London. Lecturer in Chemical Physiology, Edinburgh University, 1905–14; Imperial Cancer Research Fund, 1903–05, 1914–39; Foreign Member, German Society for Investigation of Cancer; Member Leeuvenhoek Vereeniging; Member Am. Assoc. for Cancer Research; Official Delegate International Cancer Congress, Madrid, 1933; International Cancer Conference, Paris, 1934; Atlantic City, 1939; British Delegate to Union Internationale contre le Cancer; delivered Middleton Goldsmith Lecture of New York Pathological Society, 1941. *Publications:* Practical Course in Chemical Physiology, 4th edn, 1920; Fever, Heat Regulation, Climate and the Thyroid Adrenal Apparatus, 1928; Sectional Editor, The Cancer Review; Editor of Acta of the Union Internationale contre le Cancer; numerous papers in scientific reports of Imperial Cancer Research Fund and in scientific journals on cancer, nutrition, physiology, bio-chemistry. *Address:* Barnard Skin and Cancer Hospital, St Louis, Mo, USA.

Died 10 Aug. 1945.

CRAN, Marion, FRSA; author; Founder of the original Garden Club in Mayfair; Vice-President, National Gardens Guild; the original Broadcaster of Garden Talks from the London Station; has also broadcast from Cape Town, New York and Vancouver Stations; *b* South Africa, 1875; *d* of late Rev. H. E. Dudley, Rector of Little Billing, Northants; *m* 1931, Fergus Scott Hurd-Wood (*d* 1936). *Educ:* St Mary's Hall, Brighton. Trained at Rotunda Hosp., Dublin, 1899; Sub-Editor of Connoisseur, 1901; Burlington Magazine, 1903; Art Critic, 1904; Commissioner for the Canadian Government to report on conditions for women in the North-West, 1908; Matron of Whitmead Sanatorium for TB, 1915–16; Assistant-Secretary and Interviewer of the Imperial Association for assisting Disabled Officers, 1916–19; Commissioned through Africa, Rhodesia, Australia, New Zealand and Canada, by the Imperial Association and British Press to report on conditions of Migration within the Empire, 1920; awarded Civil List Pension, 1939, for services to literature. *Publications:* Herbert Beerbohm Tree, 1907; A Woman in Canada, 1909; Song of a Woman (Poems), 1909; Garden of Ignorance, 1913; Garden of Experience, 1921; Story of my Ruin, 1924; Garden Register and Garden Talks,

1925; Gardens of Good Hope, 1926; Joy of the Ground, 1928; Wind Harps and the Lusty Pal, 1929; Gardens in America, 1931; I know a Garden, 1933; The Squabbling Garden, 1934; Making the Dovecot pay, 1935; Pipers Lay, 1936; The Garden beyond, 1937; Gardens of Character, 1939; Hagar's Garden, 1941. *Recreations:* nature-study, travel. *Address:* Coggers, Benenden, Kent.

Died 2 Sept. 1942.

CRANMER-BYNG, L., JP, CA; FRSA; Editor of the Wisdom of the East series; *b* 23 Nov. 1872; *e s* of Lieutenant-Colonel A. M. Cranmer-Byng, JP, DL; *m* 1st, Harriet (*d* 1913), *d* of Isaac Hammersley; 2nd, Daisy, *d* of N. Beach; one *s. Educ:* Wellington; Trinity College, Cambridge. Closely identified with the literary movement of the early 'nineties; lectures on Eastern subjects, especially Chinese poetry; JP and Alderman for Essex and Chairman of the County Records Committee; Member of the Lee Conservancy Board; Member of Board of Visitors, HM Prison, Chelmsford; Chairman of Essex County Library. *Publications:* A Feast of Lanterns; A Lute of Jade; The Odes of Confucius; The Rose Garden of Sa'di; The Vision of Asia; To-morrow's Star. *Recreation:* tree-planting. *Address:* Southill, Great Easton, Dunmow, Essex. *T:* Great Easton 93.

Died 15 Jan. 1945.

CRANSTOUN, Charles Joseph Edmondstoune-, CB 1945; DSO 1919; KSG; TD; JP; Vice-Lieut Lanarkshire; Bt Col, TA; *b* 1877; *e s* of late Charles E. H. Edmondstoune-Cranstoun of Corehouse, and late Edith Mary, *d* of C. W. E. Jerningham of Painswick, Glos. *Educ:* Oratory School; Christ Church, Oxford, BA. Served European War, Lanarkshire Yeomanry and 6th Bn Gordon Highlanders, 1914–19 (despatches twice, DSO, Croix de Guerre avec Palme); Lieut-Col commanded Lanarkshire Yeomanry, 1920–25; Chairman Lanarkshire TAA, 1940–47. *Address:* Corehouse, Lanark. *Club:* New (Edinburgh).

Died 7 July 1950.

CRA'STER, Lt-Col Edmund Henry Bertram, CBE 1919; late RA; *b* 1 Sept. 1869; *s* of late Edmund Craster, Beadnell Hall, Chathill, Northumberland; *m* 1902, Margaret Eleanor Mary, *d* of Col William Craster; one *d.* Entered Army, 1889; Lt-Col 1916; served Isazai Expedition, 1892; European War, 1914–19 (despatches, CBE); retired pay, 1920. *Address:* c/o Lloyd's Bank, 6 Pall Mall, SW1.

Died 7 March 1942.

CRA'STER, Col Shafto Longfield, CB 1918; CIE 1917; RE; *b* 31 July 1862; *s* of late Maj.-Gen. George Ayton Cra'ster, RE; *m* 1888, Elizabeth Maude, *d* of late Charles King, Hampstead; two *d. Educ:* United Services College, Westward Ho!; Royal Military Academy, Woolwich. Lieut RE 1882; Capt 1890; Major, 1899; Lt-Col 1906; Col 1911; employed on railway survey and construction work in India and elsewhere, 1885–1903; in charge of (i) Khyber-Railway Survey, and construction Nowshera-Dargai Railway, 1899, (ii) Berbera-Harar Railway Survey, 1903 (thanks of the Foreign Office); Lahore District NW Railway 1904–05; Deputy Chief Engineer, Central, Northern and Southern Sections, NW Railway, 1905–10; Chief Engineer, Eastern Bengal State Railway, 1912–13; Chief Engineer, North-Western Railway, 1913–15; Agent, NW Railway, 1916–17; President Punjab Engineering Congress, 1915 and 1916; Chief Mechanical Engineer War Office, 1917–19; retired, 1919; served Tirah 1897–98 (despatches, medal 2 clasps); N China, 1901–02, as British Deputy Director British Railway Administration; received thanks of the Chinese Govt for service in bringing the Court into Peking by railway, Jan. 1902; East Africa, 1903 (medal with clasp); European War (despatches, CB). *Publications:* History of the Railways in the SA War; Monographs on Railways (Military and Commercial) in N China, Somaliland,

Abyssinia, Bermuda, and NW India. *Recreations:* big-game shooting, rowing, yachting. *Address:* c/o Lloyds Bank, 6 Pall Mall, SW1.

Died 21 Dec. 1943.

CRAUFURD, Mrs Eleanor Louisa Houison; Principal, Downham School, Hatfield Heath, Bishop's Stortford; *d* of J. F. Dalrymple Hay and Ellen Douglas (*d* of R. H. Johnston Stewart of Physgill), of Dunlop House, Dunlop; *m* 1903, Brig.-General John Archibald Houison Craufurd, CMG, CBE (*d* 1933); two *s. Educ:* at home. Vice-Pres. Girl Guides Assoc. *Address:* Downham, Hatfield Heath, Bishop's Stortford. *TA:* and *T:* 42 Matching. *Club:* Ladies' Empire.

Died 15 Dec. 1950.

CRAUFURD, Col Robert Quentin, DSO 1918; late RSFus; *b* Grove Lodge, Tring, Herts, 9 March 1880; *s* of late H. R. G. Craufurd of Brightwood, Tring, and Alice Jane, *d* of Rev. R. M. Wood, Rector of Aldbury, Tring, Herts; *m* 1st, Mildred Mary (*d* 1929), *d* of late Rt Hon. Mr Justice Kenny of the High Court in Ireland, of Marlfield, Cabinteely, Co. Dublin; four *d*; 2nd, 1931, Muriel Frances, *d* of George E. Darroch, 42 Stanhope Gardens, W2, and Braidley, Canford Cliffs, Bournemouth. *Educ:* Harrow; RMC Sandhurst. Gazetted R. Scots Fusiliers, 1899; Lieut-Col 1927; Col, 1931; passed Staff College, 1914; served South African War, 1899–1902 (Queen's medal and 5 clasps, King's medal and 2 clasps); European War, 1914–18 (despatches three times, DSO, Brevet Lt-Col, Croix de Guerre); AQMG, Western Command, 1931–32; Retired pay, 1932. *Address:* Marlin End, Berkhamstead, Herts. *Club:* Army and Navy.

Died 10 Jan. 1943.

CRAVEN, Comdr Sir Charles (Worthington), 1st Bt *cr* 1942; Kt 1934; OBE 1919; Royal Navy (retired); Industrial Adviser to Minister of Production, since 1943; Deputy Chairman and Managing Director, Vickers Ltd; Chairman and Managing Director, Vickers-Armstrongs, Ltd; World Auxiliary Insurance Corporation, Ltd, Gresham & Craven, Ltd (Chairman), Shipbuilding Corporation, Ltd (Chairman), and other Companies; Chairman, Industrial Welfare Society; Member, Committee of Lloyd's Register; Member, Air Council, 1940; *b* 10 May 1884; *s* of Jonas Craven, Manchester; *m* 1907, Constance (*d* 1944), *e d* of James Clunes; one *s. Educ:* Rossall School; HMS Britannia; Royal Naval College, Greenwich. Served European War, 1914–16; Pres. British Employers' Confederation; Controller-General, Ministry of Aircraft Production, 1941–42. *Heir:* *s* Derek Worthington Clunes. *Address:* The Abbey House, Furness Abbey, Lancs. *T:* Barrow 462/3; Crowherst Place, Crowhurst, near Lingfield, Surrey. *T:* Lingfield 56; Balfour Cottage, 6 Balfour Mews, Mayfair, W1. *Clubs:* Royal Navy, United Service, Garrick.

Died 18 Nov. 1944.

CRAVEN, Sir Derek Worthington Clunes, 2nd Bt *cr* 1942; Director of Gresham, Craven & Heatly (Holdings) Ltd, Gresham & Craven (India) Ltd, and Abbey Sand Co. Ltd; *b* 6 June 1910; *s* of Commander Sir Charles Craven, 1st Bt, OBE, and Constance (*d* 1944), *e d* of James Clunes; *S* father, 1944; *m* 1st, 1935, Nancy Dorothy Gwenllian (marr. diss. 1945), *d* of R. H. Green, Willesborough, Asford, Kent; 2nd, 1945, Mrs Marjorie Kathleen Wallis; one *d. Heir:* none. *Address:* Barkbooth, Windermere, Westmorland; Balfour Cottage, 6 Balfour Mews, Mayfair, W1.

Died 3 Feb. 1946 (ext).

CRAWFORD, His Honour John Dawson; Judge of County Courts, Circuit No. 38 (parts of Middlesex and Essex), 1918–34; *b* 4 Aug. 1861; 2nd *s* of late Joseph Dawson Crawford, MD, FRCSE, of Liverpool; *m* 1909, Harriet (*d* 1942), *widow* of late Arthur Cooper. *Educ:* Trinity College, Cambridge (Honours in Law Tripos, 1882). Called to Bar, Jan. 1884; joined Northern Circuit;

extensive practice in London and on Circuit. *Publications:* A Ministry of Justice; Reflections and Recollections, 1936. *Recreations:* travelling and golf. *Address:* The Orchard, Wellesley Road, Gunnersbury, W4. *T:* Chiswick 0196. *Club:* Oxford and Cambridge.

Died 28 June 1946.

CRAWFORD, Robert; DL, JP. MP (U) Antrim, 1922–29, Mid-Antrim, 1929–38, Parliament of Northern Ireland. *Address:* Ashville, Galgorm Road, Ballymena.

Died 28 July 1946.

CRAWFORD, Sir William S., KBE 1927; Vice-Chairman of the Post Office Publicity Committee; Chairman and Governing Director of W. S. Crawford, Ltd, London; Chairman; Sir William Crawford & Partners Ltd, St James's Restaurant Ltd; Director: Simpson (Piccadilly) Ltd, Poster Services Ltd; Adviser to the Ministry of Agriculture since 1929; *b* 1878; *s* of Robert Crawford, DL, LLD, JP, Glasgow; *m* Marion Stewart, *d* of William Whitelaw, MD, JP, Kirkintilloch, Dumbartonshire; one *s* two *d*. *Educ:* Blair Lodge; Frankfurt a/Main. Member of Empire Marketing Board, 1926–31; Member of Advisory Publicity Committee to the Ministry of Health, 1923; President of the Thirty Club, 1923; Member of Imperial Economic Committee, 1925–26; Chm. of the Buy British Campaign, 1931; President National Advertising Benevolent Society, 1932; Chairman of the Advertising and Marketing Exhibition, 1933; President, Institute of Incorporated Practitioners in Advertising, 1937–40; Member of Industrial Advisory Council, National Savings Committee; Member of Art in Industry Council. *Publication:* The People's Food, 1938. *Address:* 233 High Holborn, WC1. *T:* Holborn 4381; 5 Chesterfield House, South Audley Street, W1. *T:* Mayfair 4400.

Died 19 Nov. 1950.

CRAWLEY, Rev. Canon Arthur Stafford, MA, MC; Canon of St George's Chapel, Windsor, since 1934; Chaplain to the King since 1944; *b* 18 Sept. 1876; *y s* of late George Baden Crawley and Eliza Inez Hulbert; *m* Anstice Katharine, 2nd *d* of Antony and Janet Gibbs, Tyntesfield, Flax Bourton, Somerset; three *s* two *d*. *Educ:* Harrow; Magdalen College, Oxford. Curate Stepney Parish and St Lukes, Chelsea, 1901–05; Vicar of Benenden, Kent, 1905–10; Bishopthorpe, Yorks, 1910–18; Chaplain to the Archbishop of York; Temporary Chaplain to the Forces with the Guards Division, the 8th and the 48th Divisions, 1915–19 (MC with bar); Vicar of East Meon, Hants, 1922–24; Secretary York Diocesan Board of Finance, 1924–28; Chaplain to the Archbishop of York; Hon. Canon of York Minster, 1926; Diocesan Sec., Diocese of St Albans, 1929–34; Hon. Canon of St Albans Abbey, 1930–34. *Recreations:* cricket, tennis, lawn tennis. *Address:* 4 The Cloisters, Windsor Castle. *T:* Windsor 736. *Club:* Oxford and Cambridge.

Died 8 Oct. 1948.

CRAWSHAW, 3rd Baron *cr* 1892; **Gerald Beach Brooks;** Bt 1891; *b* 1 April 1884; *e s* of 2nd Baron and Mary Ethel (*d* 1914), *d* of Sir Michael Hicks Beach, 8th Bart; *S* father, 1929; *m* 1930, Sheila, *o d* of late Lt-Col P. R. Clifton, CMG, DSO; three *s* one *d*. *Educ:* Eton; Christ Church, Oxford (MA). *Heir: s* Hon. William Michael Clifton Brooks, *b* 25 March 1933. *Address:* Whatton, Loughborough, Leicestershire. *TA:* Kegworth.

Died 21 Oct. 1946.

CRAWSHAW, Lionel Townsend, RSW, RBSA, BA, LLM Cantab; *s* of Edward Crawshaw and Mary Ursula Whiting; *m* 1st, 1901, Juliette Menut; one *s*; 2nd, 1931, Frances Hutchinson, *d* of late Canon Robert Fisher, Whitby. *Educ:* St Peter's School, York; Christ's College, Cambridge. Qualified for the Law; then studied art in Düsseldorf and Karlsruhe for a year; afterwards in Paris.

Left France, 1903, and took a studio in Whitby; afterwards lived in Edinburgh and Droitwich. Exhibitor RA, RSW, Glasgow, Leeds, Liverpool, Salon, etc.; *official purchase:* Auckland; Pt works: Bach Concerto at Queen's Hall, Procession in Amiens Cathedral. Silver Medal, Lorient, Brittany. *Publication:* published a colour print of The Endeavour leaving Whitby for the Thames to join Capt. James Cook before his first voyage in 1768 from his oil painting. *Address:* Tucketts, Trusham, nr Newton Abbot, Devon. *Club:* Overseas League.

Died 16 March 1949.

CREAGH, Maj.-Gen. Arthur Gethin, CB 1896; *b* Kingstown, 12 Feb. 1855; *e s* of John B. Creagh of Ballyandrew, Co. Cork, and Matilda, *d* of late Maj. Garnet Wolseley, KO Borderers; *m* 1889, Beatrice Carlota, *d* of late John Grenfell; two *d*. *Educ:* private school; RMA, Woolwich. 1st Commission in RA 1874; served in the Zulu War, 1879; capture of Sekukuni's stronghold, 1879; Egyptian War, 1882; Nile Expedition, 1884–85; Suakim, 1885 (despatches in all three campaigns, also medals and clasps); Brevet Majority, 1883; Brevet Lieut-Colonelcy, 1885; Bronze Star, 5th class Mejidieh; DAAG Western District, 1889–92; served in India and Burma from 1892; commanding 2nd Class District, India, 1901–06; troops in Mauritius, 1906–09; Colonel Commandant RA, 1912–38. *Recreation:* fishing. *T:* 2652. *Club:* Royal Western Yacht of England.

Died 21 Feb. 1941.

CREAGH, Col Arthur Henry Dopping, CMG 1916; MVO 1911; retired Indian Army; *b* 1866; *s* of late Maj.-Gen. Wm Creagh, Indian Army; *g s* of late Maj.-Gen. Sir Michael Creagh (86th Foot and 11th Foot); *m* 1913, Winifred, *d* of late Rev. T. Ruggles Fisher and *widow* of Col A. E. Leslie. *Educ:* Sandhurst. Gazetted 1st Battalion Worcestershire Regiment, 1887; Captain Indian Army, 1898; Major, 1905; Lt-Col 1911; Col 1916; served operations in Mekran, 1898; Egypt and Suez Canal zone, 1914–15; Mesopotamia, 1915–16 (wounded three times, despatches twice, Serbian white eagle with swords).

Died 27 Nov. 1941.

CREAGH-OSBORNE, Captain F.; *see* Osborne.

CREASE, Captain Thomas Evans, CB 1916; CBE 1919; RN; retired; Orders of Merit of Turkey, Rising Sun of Japan, St Maurice and St Lazarus of Italy, Legion of Honour; *b* 24 Feb. 1875; *m* 1898, Louise (*d* 1938), *y d* of late John Johnson, The Abbey, Thetford, Norfolk; two *s* one *d*. Entered RN, 1889; Lieut 1895; Comdr 1905; retired, 1910; Naval Assistant to First Sea Lord, 1914–15; Naval Assistant and Secretary Board of Invention and Research, 1915–16; British Representative Anglo-Russian Supply Committee in United States of America, 1916–17; Naval Assistant to Controller of the Navy, 1917; Private Secretary to First Lord of the Admiralty, 1917–19; Secretary of the Allied Naval Council, 1917–19; Captain, 1918. *Address:* River Cottage, Datchet, Bucks. *Club:* Junior Carlton.

Died 24 Sept. 1942.

CREASEY, Gordon Leonard, CBE 1930; retired Chartered Accountant; *b* 19 Nov. 1873; *s* of late R. G. M. Creasey, Chartered Accountant, Blackheath and late Laura Miriam Creasey; *m* Maud White Parsons; no *c*. *Educ:* Queen Elizabeth Grammar School, Cranbrook, Kent; Eastbourne College. Qualified as a chartered accountant, 1896; practised in London until 1901; Inspecting Auditor in South Africa to the South African Breweries, Ltd; arrived in Launceston, 1904; appointed by Tasmanian Government on numerous enquiries and boards; a Deputy Commissioner for Tasmania at Wembley Exhibition, 1925; appointed by the Government, Hon. Secretary to Tasmanian Flood Relief Fund and was responsible for the distribution of a fund amounting to £116,000, 1929; a Royal Commissioner on Commonwealth Grants Commission, 1937–38; has travelled very extensively. *Address:* 128b Elphin Road, Launceston, Tasmania.

Died 10 Jan. 1943.

CREASY, Harold Thomas, CBE 1927; MInstCE; *b* Galle, Ceylon, 3 May 1873; 2nd *s* of late E. B. Creasy, Sutton, Surrey, and Colombo; and 1st wife, Mary Latham Lloyd, Betley, Cheshire; *m* 1909, Anne Katharine, MBE 1932, 2nd *d* of late W. R. Hands, Stafford Place, Shifnal, and Bremersdorp, S Africa. *Educ:* Bedford School; Crystal Palace School of Engineering. Articled Pupil and Assistant to A. C. Pain, MICE; Consulting Engineer, Westminster, 1893–97; District Engineer Public Works Department, Ceylon, 1897; Provincial Engineer, 1910; Deputy Director, 1917; Acting Director of Public Works and Member of the Legislative Council, Ceylon, 1921 and 1923; Director of Public Works, Hong-Kong, 1923–32; Member of the Executive and Legislative Councils. *Recreations:* tennis, golf. *Address:* 5 St John's Avenue, Putney Hill, SW15. *Club:* Royal Empire Society.

Died 31 Oct. 1950.

CREE, Mrs Douglas; *see* Rorke, Kate.

CREED, Edward ffolliott, DM, FRCP; Director of Pathology, King, College Hospital and Medical School, since 1922; Sector Pathologist, Emergency Medical Service, since 1939; *b* 6 May 1893; 2nd *s* of Rev. C. J. Creed, MA, Vicar of All Saints', Leicester; *m* 1923, Stella, 2nd *d* of Joseph Parker, CSI, Sompting; two *d.* *Educ:* Wyggeston School, Leicester; Trinity College, Oxford (Millard Scholar); King's College Hospital (Burney Yeo Scholar). BA, Final Honour School of Natural Science (Chemistry), 1913; BM, BCh (Oxon), 1916. House Physician, King's Coll. Hosp., 1916–17 and 1920; Lieut RAMC, SR, 1916; Captain, 1918–20; served in West Africa, Officer i/c District Laboratory, Sierra Leone; Bacteriologist, King's College Hospital, 1920–22; MA, 1921; DPH (Oxon), 1922; MRCP (Lond.), 1923; DM (Oxon), 1927; FRCP, 1932; Examiner in Pathology Universities of Cambridge and London, and Conjoint Board. *Publications:* various articles in medical and pathological journals. *Address:* King's College Hospital, SE5; 5 Ashley Court, Epsom. *T:* Brixton 6471/2 Epsom 3648. *Clubs:* United University, Roehampton.

Died 27 Sept. 1947.

CREELMAN, Col John Jennings, DSO 1917; KC 1919; Advocate, Montreal; *b* Toronto, 14 Feb. 1882; *s* of Adam R. Creelman, KC; *m* 1st, 1908, Katharine Mélanie Weekes (*d* 1918), Galveston, Texas; one *s* one *d*; 2nd, 1920, Maud Hamilton Baker, Montreal. *Educ:* Upper Canada College, Toronto; University of Toronto (BA), 1904; McGill University (BCL), 1907; University of Grenoble, France (Diploma). Called to Bar of Province of Quebec, 1907; Lecturer in Railway Economics, McGill Univ., 1913; Lt-Col 6th Montreal Brigade, Canadian Field Artillery, 1912; member of Canadian Coronation Contingent, 1911; Militia Staff Course, Canada, 1913; served European War; OC 2nd Canadian Field Artillery Brigade, BEF, Aug. 1914–March 1917 (wounded, despatches twice, Russian Order of St Stanislas 3rd class with swords, DSO); Colonel Commandant, 2nd Montreal Regiment, now Royal Canadian Artillery, 1920–23 and 1940–46; Hon. Col, 1934–40 and since 1942; President, Canadian Artillery Association, 1921 and 1940–46; Colonial Auxiliary Forces Long Service Medal, 1920; Colonial Officers' Auxiliary Forces Decoration, 1922; Alderman, City of Montreal, 1918–26, and Councillor, City of Montreal, from May 1948 for 3 years; Member of Corporation of McGill University, 1919–22; Member Protestant Board of School Commissioners, 1918–25; Chairman, 1923–25; Member of Metropolitan Commission of Montreal, 1921–26; contested (L) Montreal (St George)

Provincial, 1923, and Montreal (St Antoine) Dominion, 1926; Presbyterian. *Recreations:* curling, fishing. *Address:* 1444 Sherbrooke Street West, Montreal, Canada; Mont Tremblant, PQ. *Clubs:* Mount Royal, University, Thistle Curling (Montreal); Rideau (Ottawa); Toronto (Toronto); Garrison (Quebec).

Died 29 June 1949.

CREES, Dr James Harold Edward; *b* 21 July 1882; *s* of James Stephens and Annie Sophia Crees; *m* 1925, Amy Mary, *d* of the late Edward Martin, of Westcliff-on-Sea. *Educ:* Westminster City School; St John's College, Cambridge. BA London, with 1st Class Honours in Classics, 1902 (University Exhibitioner in Greek, 1900); MA 1903; DLit 1907; Foundation Scholar and Prizeman St John's College, Cambridge; 1st Class (Division 2) Classical Tripos. Part I, 1904; 1st Class Classical Tripos, Part II (Ancient History), 1905; Thirlwall Prizeman and Medallist, 1906; MA 1908; studied music, theory and practice, under Dr Madeley Richardson, St Saviour's Cathedral, Southwark; Dr Cyril Rootham, St John's College, Cambridge; Dr C. H. Kitson, Christ Church Cathedral, Dublin. Assistant Master Wyggeston School, Leicester, 1907–10; Headmaster Crypt Grammar School, Gloucester, 1911–19; Headmaster Cathedral Grammar School, Hereford, 1919–40; has studied and written upon educational problems; Examiner to the University of London in Ancient History, 1911–15; Member of Council of Headmasters' Association and Committee of Headmasters' Conference. *Publications:* Claudian as an Historical Authority, 1908; The Reign of the Emperor Probus, 1912; Didascalus Patiens, a Satire, a Medley, and a Romance, 1915; George Meredith, a study of his personality, 1918; Gloucester, 1911–1919; joint Editor of Apollonius Rhodius, Book III, 1927; Meredith Revisited, 1921; member of the Board of Delegates for the Oxford Local Examinations, 1926. *Recreations:* literary composition, music, chess, cricket, cycling, motoring. *Address:* Wonder View, Much Birch, Hereford. *T:* Wormelow 12.

Died 29 Dec. 1941.

CRESWELL, Col Edmund Fraser, DSO 1916; *b* 17 Dec. 1876; *s* of late Colonel E. W. Creswell, Royal Engineers, of Copse Hill, Ewhurst, Surrey; *m* 1920, Anne Rickards, *d* of C. W. Carver, West Derby, Liverpool. *Educ:* Wellington College; RMA, Woolwich. First Commission Royal Artillery, 1896; Capt. 1901; Major, 1914; Lieut-Col, 1921; Col 1922; served European War, in Belgium and France 1914–18 (DSO, Bt Lt-Col); War Office, 1921–24 (Bt Col); Commandant, Anti-Aircraft School; retired pay, 1925. *Recreations:* cricket, golf, etc. *Clubs:* United Service, MCC; Royal St George's, Sandwich.

Died 5 Nov. 1941.

CRESWELL, Lt-Col Hon. Frederic Hugh Page, DSO 1916; *b* 13 Nov. 1866; *s* of Edmund Creswell, Deputy Postmaster-General and Surveyor of the Mediterranean, and Mary M. W. Fraser; *m* 1920, Margaret P. B., *d* of Rev. H. Boys, formerly Rector of Layer Marney; no *c*. *Educ:* Bruce Castle and Derby School; Royal School of Mines. Engaged in mining in Venezuela, Asia Minor, Rhodesia and Transvaal; managed Durban Deep Mine before Boer war; enrolled as Lieut in Imperial Light Horse on beginning of that War, and on resumption of mining on the Rand was Gen. Manager of Village Main Reef Mine; took prominent part in opposing introduction of Chinese labour to Transvaal and resigned managership at end of 1903; afterwards took prominent part in successful movement for abolition of Chinese labour; member Union Parliament, 1910–38; served as 2nd in command Rand Rifles, SW Africa, 1914–15 campaign, and as 2nd in command, and as Commanding Officer 8th SA Infantry, East Africa, 1916–17; Minister of Defence, 1924–33; Minister of Labour, 1924–25 and 1929–33;

President, 1935, Annual Conference International Labour Organisation, Geneva. *Address:* Kuils River, Cape Province. *Club:* Civil Service (Cape Town).

Died 25 Aug. 1948.

CRESWELL, William Thomas; KC 1933; Captain (retired 1923); of the South-Eastern Circuit; *b* 11 Nov. 1872; *s* of late Henry John and late Margaret Ann Creswell; *m* 1896, Mary Isabel, *d* of late George Carr, Barnsley. *Educ:* privately; King's College, Strand. Barrister (Gray's Inn), 1921; early served as an architectural and engineering assistant, and then on Royal Engineer Staff of War Office on reconstruction schemes at Aldershot, Colchester, and Hong Kong; during South African War, a Division Officer of Royal Engineers; subsequently in private practice as an architect and civil engineer; a Division Officer of Royal Engineers, Salisbury Plain, Assistant commanding Royal Engineer and Staff Officer; Intelligence and Educational Officer and Member of the Military Court of Alexandria, Egypt, 1914–23 (mentioned for services rendered); Hon. ARIBA, etc.; Vice-Pres. RSanI and Chairman of its Council, 1934–35; Chairman RSI and SI Examination Joint Board, 1942–45; Test: IM and Cty E; Hon. Mem. Institute of Arbitrators, RVA and SIA; An Arbitrator under the Electricity (Supply) Acts and Examiner in Law to many technical bodies; Liveryman, Worshipful Company of Plumbers; Freeman and Member of the Court of Common Council, City of London. *Publications:* The Law relating to Building and Engineering Contracts; The Powers of the Architect; The Law relating to Dilapidations and Waste; The Law of Fixtures; The 1939 Form of Building Contract; 'Extras'; Procedure and Evidence in Arbitrations; London Building Acts (Amendment) Act, 1939; contributions to Encyclopædia of the Laws of England and to the Practical Surveyor, Auctioneer and Estate-Agent, and to the Builder and other journals and societies; Legal Editor of Building Encyclopædia, and Encyclopædia of Plumbing, Heating and Sanitary Engineering, etc. *Recreations:* riding, walking. *Address:* New Court, Temple, EC4. *T:* Central 4480; Mervyn, Epsom. *T:* Epsom 9588.

Died 10 Oct. 1946.

CRESWICK, Paul, OBE 1920; *b* 1866; *grand-nephew* of William Creswick, the actor; *m* 1893, Maude Morris; one *s*. *Educ:* privately. Left studies at 16 to enter life assurance business; now in Prudential Assurance Company's Head Office; took up writing, in spare time, in 1890; first book published, 1894; founded and edited The Windmill, 1898; Chief Transport Officer for Kent Voluntary Aid Detachments; Hove Borough Councillor, 1940. *Publications:* At the Sign of the Cross-keys; The Temple of Folly; Bruising Peg; In Alfred's Days; Under the Black Raven; Robin Hood, 1902; Hasting, the Pirate, 1903; Richard the Fearless, 1904; In a Hand of Steel, 1907; Idols of Flesh, 1908; Honesty's Garden, 1910; The Ring of Pleasure, 1911; The Kitty Confidences, 1912; Psyche, 1914; Our Little Kingdom, 1917; The Beaten Path, 1924; King Arthur, 1925; The Turning Wheel, 1928; Providence Square, 1930. *Address:* The Fairway, Hove Park Road, Hove.

Died 13 April 1947.

CREW, Albert, FSA; Barrister-at-Law; Recorder of Sandwich (with Ramsgate) since 1934; *s* of late Edward Crew, Bath; *m* Ellen Elizabeth (*d* 1938), *d* of late William Poulton, Leominster. Called to Bar, Gray's Inn (Lee Prizeman), 1908; Admitted, Middle Temple, 1926; Secretary, Central Criminal Court Bar, Old Bailey, and Member of the General Council of the Bar since 1927; Vice-President of the Medico-Legal Society of London since 1932; Member of Council of Institute for Scientific Treatment of Delinquency since 1937. *Publications:* London Prisons of To-day and Yesterday; The Old

Bailey; Judicial Wisdom of Mr Justice McCardie; Rates and Rating, 10th Edition; The Conduct of and Procedure at Public Company and Local Government Meetings, 17th Edition (with Evelyn Miles); The Law and Practice relating to Meetings of Local Authorities, 2nd Edition; The Law relating to Secret Commissions and Bribes 2nd (American Edition; Joint Stock Companies Guide, 12th Edition; A Dictionary of Medico-Legal Terms (with Dr K. W. Aylwin Gibson); Public Meetings and Processions (with Evelyn Miles); The Profession of a Secretary. *Address:* Kingsdown, Green Lane, St Albans, Herts; Mitre House, 45 Fleet Street, EC4. *T:* Central 1184.

Died 22 July 1942.

CREWE, 1st Marquess of, *cr* 1911; **Robert Offley Ashburton Crewe-Milnes,** KG 1908; PC 1892; MA, FSA; DCL hon. Oxford; LLD hon. Camb.; Baron Houghton of Great Houghton in county of York, 1863; Earl of Crewe *cr* 1895; Earl of Madeley *cr* 1911; HM Lieutenant County of London, 1912–44; Elder Brother of Trinity House; late Chancellor of Sheffield University; *b* 16 Upper Brook Street, 12 Jan. 1858; *s* of 1st Baron Houghton and Annabella Hungerford, *d* of 2nd Baron Crewe; *S* to father's Barony, 1885; *m* 1st, 1880, Sibyl Marcia (*d* 1887), *d* of Sir Frederick Graham, 3rd Bt, Netherby, and Lady Hermione, *d* of 12th Duke of Somerset; three *d*; 2nd, 1899, Lady Margaret Primrose, CI (JP Co. of London), *y d* of 5th Earl of Rosebery; one *d* Church of England; Liberal. *Educ:* Harrow; Trinity College, Cambridge. Assist Priv. Sec. to Sec. for Foreign Affairs (Earl Granville), 1883–84; Lord-in-Waiting to the Queen, 1886; Lord-Lieut of Ireland, 1892–95; Lord President of the Council, 1905–08, and 1915–16; Lord Privy Sea, 1908, and 1912–15; Secretary of State for the Colonies, 1908–10; Secretary of State for India, 1910–15; President Board of Education, 1916; Chairman LCC 1917; HM Ambassador in Paris, 1922–28; Secretary of State for War, 1931. *Publications:* Stray Verses, 1889–1890; Lord Rosebery, 1931. *Recreations:* country pursuits; library and collection of autograph letters. *Heir:* none. *Address:* Argyll House, 211 Kings Road, SW3. *T:* Flaxman 5154; West Horsley Place, Leatherhead, Surrey. *T:* East Horsley 32; Madeley Manor, Crewe, Cheshire. *Clubs:* Brooks's, Athenæum, Reform, Turf.

Died 20 June 1945.

CRICHTON, Sir Robert, Kt 1948; CBE 1939; Chairman West Cumberland Industrial Development Co. Ltd; Jt Vice-Chairman, Lancashire Steel Corporation Ltd; *b* 4 Sept. 1881; *s* of Hugh Crichton, JP, and Elizabeth Walker; *m* 1913, Mary Kennedy Davie; no *c*. *Educ:* Royal Technical College, Glasgow (ARTC); The University, Glasgow (BSc (Engineering)). Director and Vice-Chm. Scottish Iron and Steel Co. Ltd; Director and Gen. Manager, The United Steel Cos. Ltd, Cumberland; President Cumberland Development Council Ltd. *Address:* Derwent Lodge, Cockermouth, Cumberland. *T:* 2293 Cockermouth. *Clubs:* Junior Carlton, Conservative, Royal Scottish Automobile (Glasgow).

Died 8 May 1950.

CRIMMIN, Col John, VC CB 1913; CIE 1901; LRCP, LRCS, and DPH, Ireland; IMS, retired; *b* 19 March 1859; *m*; two *s* three *d*. Entered IMS 1882; Surg.-Maj. 1894; served Burmese Expedition, 1886–89 (despatches, VC, medal with two clasps); Karen Field Force, 1888–89; served North-West Frontier India, 1914–18 (medal); Assistant Director of Medical Services, India, 1913–19; Hon. Physician to the King, 1916–19; retd 1919. *Address:* c/o National Bank of India, 26 Bishopsgate, EC2.

Died 20 Feb. 1945.

CRIPPS, Col Arthur William, CB 1916; *b* 16 Jan. 1862. Entered Army, 1882; Capt. ISC, 1893; Major Indian Army, 1901; Lt-Col, 1908; Col, 1913; served 1st Miranzai Expedition, 1891; Tirah, 1897–98 (medal, 2 clasps); China, 1900 (despatches, medal with clasp); European War, 1914–16 (despatches, CB); retired, 1920.

Died 29 Jan. 1945.

CRIPPS, Hon. Lionel, CMG 1933; Farmer since 1894; Chairman Central African Archives Commission; *b* Simla, 11 Oct. 1863; *s* of General John Matthew Cripps, Bengal Staff Corps, and Agnes Sophia Blackburn; *m* 1893, Mary Constance Lovemore, Port Elizabeth, Cape Province; four *s* one *d. Educ:* Junior Preparatory School, Cheltenham; Queen Elizabeth's School, Wakefield; Reading School. Came to England, 5 years of age; educated for 11 years in England; went to Port Elizabeth at 16 years, 1879; worked in store 5 years; farmed in Somerset East district, Karoo, working on Cranemere with ostriches, goats, horses and cattle, 2 years; prospecting, etc., in Transvaal, 3 years; went to Mashonaland with Pioneer Column, 1890; prospected for gold and mined; farmed, 1891–92; worked in De Beers, Kimberley, for some months; married and returned to Mashonaland, 1893; prospected and mined; Member of Legislative Council, 1914–23; Speaker House of Assembly, Southern Rhodesia, 1924–35. *Recreations:* searching for ancient Rock Paintings in S Rhodesia, tracing, sketching, and colouring same; worked on over 900 separate sites. *Address:* Cloudlands, Umtali, Southern Rhodesia. *TA:* Cripps, Umtali, S Rhodesia. *T:* 90423.

Died 3 Feb. 1950.

CRISP, Sir Harold, Kt 1938; *b* Hobart, Tasmania, 1874; *s* of David Henry Crisp, Barrister, of Hobart; *m* Harriett, *d* of Hon. Alfred Page, MLC, Tasmania; one *s* two *d. Educ:* Christ's College, Hobart. Called to Bar, Tasmania, 1896; raised to Bench, 1914; Senior Puisne Judge, 1915–37; Chief Justice of Supreme Court of Tasmania, 1937–40. *Address:* 17 Elizabeth Bay Road, Sydney, NSW.

Died 12 May 1942.

CRISP, Sir John Wilson, 3rd Bt *cr* 1913; *b* 28 May 1873; *s* of 1st Bt and Catherine, *o d* of George D. Howes; *S* brother, 1938; *m* 1920, Marjorie, *d* of F. R. Shriver; one *s* one *d.* Heir: *s* John Peter, *b* 19 May 1925. *Address:* 17 York House, York Street, Montagu Square, W1.

Died 11 Oct. 1950.

CRITCHETT, Sir (George) Montague, 2nd Bt *cr* 1908; MVO 1932; Lord Chamberlain's Office, St James's Palace, since 1912, and is State Invitation Assistant; *b* 7 June 1884; *s* of 1st Bt and Agnes, *d* of late C. J. Dunphie; *S* father, 1925; *m* 1914, Innes, 3rd *d* of late Col F. G. A. Wiehe, The Durham Light Infantry; one *s. Educ:* Harrow; Clare College, Cambridge. Formerly Lieut 3rd Batt. Oxfordshire and Bucks LI; served European War, 1914–18; Captain, TA Reserve, 1919–34; Officer of the Order of St John of Jerusalem; Order of the Astur of Afghanistan. *Recreation:* golf. *Heir: s* Ian George Lorraine, *b* 9 Dec. 1920. *Address:* 24 Avenue Road, Regent's Park, NW8. *T:* Primrose 2162. *Clubs:* Bath, MCC.

Died 30 May 1941.

CROCKET, James, MD, ChB, DPH, FRCPE; Consulting Physician; *b* Leith, 1878; *m* 1909, Helen King Sandilands, Musselburgh; two *s* two *d. Educ:* University, Edinburgh and University, Glasgow. Formerly Lecturer on Tuberculosis, Glasgow University and St Mungo's College, Glasgow; Medical Superintendent, Consumption Sanatoria of Scotland and Colony of Mercy for Epileptics. *Publications:* The Problem of Epilepsy; The Induction of Artificial Pneumothorax in the Treatment of Pulmonary Tuberculosis; Lectures on Tuberculosis; Tuberculin in Epilepsy; The Physical Examination of the Chest; The Problem of the Tuberculous Child; Ultraviolet Ray Treatment in Tuberculosis; The Physical and Radiological Examination of the Lungs; Pulmonary Tuberculosis and Pregnancy; The Present Position of Compression Therapy. *Address:* 17 Royal Crescent, Glasgow, C3. *T:* Glasgow, Douglas 4175. *Clubs:* Overseas, Glasgow.

Died 6 Nov. 1944.

CROCKET, Oswald Smith, KC, LLD; a Judge of the Supreme Court of Canada, 1932–43; *b* 13 April 1868; *m* 1st, 1893, Birsa (*d* 1903), *d* of late T. Stanger, Fredericton; 2nd, 1905, Clarine, *d* of late Dr Stevenson; two *s* one *d. Educ:* High School, Fredericton; New Brunswick University. Barrister, 1892; MP York, NB, 1904–13; Judge of New Brunswick Supreme Court, 1913–32. *Address:* Ottawa, Canada.

Died 2 March 1945.

CROCKETT, Rev. William Shillinglaw, DD (Edin.); Minister of Tweedsmuir, since 1894; Ex-County Councillor and Member of the Education Authority for Peeblesshire; JP, Peeblesshire; President of Berwickshire Naturalists' Club, 1936; *b* Earlston, Berwickshire, 24 June 1866; *y* and *o surv. s* of William Crockett and Margaret Wood; *m* 1894, Mary (*d* 1944), *e d* of J. Davidson Ross, Edinburgh. *Educ:* Earlston Parish School; Edinburgh University. An apprentice chemist, 1881–85; then student for Church of Scotland ministry; licensed 1893, and ordained 1894; Lecture-Tour in Canada and United States, 1906–07. *Publications:* Minstrelsy of the Merse; The Poets and Poetry of Berwickshire, 1893; A Berwickshire Bard, 1897; Centenary edition of Henry Scott Riddell's Works and Memoir, 1898; In Praise of Tweed, 1899; Biggar: Historical, Traditional, Descriptive, 1900; The Scott Country, 1902; 6th edition, 1930; Sir Walter Scott, 1903; Robert Burns, 1904; The English and Scottish Border ('British Isles'), 1905; Abbotsford, 1905; In the Border Country, 1906; Footsteps of Scott, 1907; The Scott Originals, 1912, 3rd edition 1932; Abbotsford, 1912; The Centenary of Waverley, 1915; Dr Mair of Earlston, 1920; Berwickshire and Roxburghshire (Cambridge Series), 1925; Lays from Leaderside, 1928; The Berwickshire Scene, 1936; Tweedsmuir Church and Churchyard, 1936; General Editor of the new edition of Fasti Ecclesiæ Scoticanæ, vol. i, 1915; vol. ii, 1916; vol. iii, 1920; vol. iv, 1922; vol. v, 1925; vol. vi, 1926; vol. vii, 1928. *Recreations:* local literature and history. *Address:* The Manse, Tweedsmuir, Scotland. *TA:* Tweedsmuir. *T:* Tweedsmuir 205.

Died 25 June 1945.

CROFT, 1st Baron *cr* 1940, of Bournemouth; **Henry Page Croft;** PC 1945; 1st Bart of Knole, Bournemouth *cr* 1924, CMG 1915; TD; DL, County Hertford; *b* 1881; *s* of late Lieut Richard Benyon Croft, RN, JP, DL, of Fanhams Hall, Ware, and *g g s* of Sir Richard Croft, 6th Bart of Croft Castle, Hereford; *m* Hon. Nancy Beatrice Borwick, *y d* of 1st Baron Borwick; one *s* three *d. Educ:* Eton; Shrewsbury; Trinity Hall, Cambridge. Contested city of Lincoln, 1906; MP (C) Bournemouth, 1918–40, previously Christchurch, 1910–18; Member of Speaker's Conference on the Franchise, 1918; Civil List Committee, 1936; Select Committee on the Speaker's Seat, 1939; Committee of Privileges, 1939; Parliamentary Under-Secretary of State for War, 1940–45. Chm. of Organisation Cttee of Tariff Reform League, 1913–17; Chairman of the Executive of the Empire Industries Association; Chancellor Primrose League, 1928–29, Grand Prior, 1946; Colonel late 1st Batt. Herts Regt; served European War, 1914–16 (despatches CMG; promoted temp. Brig.-Gen. Feb. 1916 (despatches); Colonel and Hon. Brigadier-General, 1924; retired, 1924; Military Member Hertfordshire Territorial Association; Lt-Col Commanding 61st (WO) Battalion County of London, HG 1943; Chairman Henry Page & Co. Ltd, Ware; owner of a coffee plantation in Kenya. *Publications:* The Path of Empire, 1912; Twenty-two Months under Fire, 1917; My Life of

Strife, 1949. *Recreations:* rowing; Shrewsbury School VIII (three years), twice won Thames Cup at Henley, and rowed three years for Trinity Hall, Cambridge; shooting. *Heir: s* Hon. Michael Henry Glendower Page Croft, BA, Hon. Capt. RASC [*b* 20 Aug. 1916. Eton; Trinity Hall, Cambridge]. *Address:* 46 Whitehall Court, SW1; Croft Castle, Herefordshire. *Club:* Carlton.

Died 7 Dec. 1947.

CROFT, Sir James Herbert, 11th Bt *cr* 1671; *b* 24 May 1907; *s* of 10th Baronet, and 2nd wife, Katharine Agnes, *d* of late J. Charlton Parr; *S* father 1915. *Educ:* Eton; Brasenose College, Oxford. Master of North Hereford Foxhounds. *Heir: uncle* Hugh Matthew Fiennes [*b* 10 May 1874; *m* Lucy, *e d* of Frederick G. Taylor, Terrible Vale, New South Wales. Salisbury Court, Uralla, NSW]. *Address:* Croft Castle, Kingsland, Herefordshire. *TA:* and *T:* Yarpole 4.

Died 15 Aug. 1941.

CROFTON, 4th Baron *cr* 1797; **Arthur Edward Lowther Crofton;** JP, DL, Co. Roscommon; late 1st Batt. Northumberland Fusiliers; *b* 7 Aug. 1866; *s* of late Hon. Charles St George Crofton, and Theresa Augusta, *d* of Daniel Tighe of Rossana, Co. Wicklow; *S* uncle, 1912; *m* 1893, Jessie (*d* 1923), *d* of James Hewitson, and *widow* of Nevile Paddon; one *s* one *d.* Entered army (Northumberland Fusiliers), 1886; Capt. 1895; Adjt 3rd Vol. Batt. 1896; served European War, 1914 (despatches); Representative Peer for Ireland, 1916. *Heir: g s* Edward Blaise Crofton [*b* 31 May 1926; *o s* of late Hon. Edward Charles Crofton and Cecilia Mabel, *d* of John T. Day, Hayeswood, Streatham Park, and *widow* of Alexander Francis Macdonald]. *Address:* Mote Park, Roscommon, Ireland. *Club:* Naval and Military.

Died 15 June 1942.

CROFTON, Brig.-Gen. Cyril Randell, CBE 1918; retired; *b* 27 March 1867; *e s* of late Rev. William Arthur Crofton-Atkins, formerly of Combe Bank, Kent; reverted to surname of Crofton, only, by Deed Poll, 1936; *m* 1905, M. R. Josephine, *o d* of Arthur Henry Lyne Evans, Haydock, Lancs, and Llanddogett Park, Co. Denbigh; one *s* two *d. Educ:* privately; Sandhurst. Joined XLVth Regt (Sherwood Foresters), 1887; served in Sierra Leone, 1898–99 (medal and clasp); South African War, 1899–1902, Officer on General Staff and DAAG Mounted Infantry Corps (Queen's medal 4 clasps, King's medal 2 clasps, despatches twice, Brevet of Major); European War, Commanded 2nd Bn The Sherwood Foresters, in France, 1914–15; Brig.-Gen. commanding 1st line Forth Defences, 1916–18; commanded 9th Scottish Yeomanry Cavalry Brigade, 1918–19 (wounded, despatches, CBE). *Club:* Army and Navy.

Died 30 Nov. 1941.

CROFTON, Vice-Adm. Edward George L.; *see* Lowther-Crofton.

CROFTON, Col Malby, DSO 1916; *e s* of late Col M. E. Crofton, King's Own Regiment, and *g s* of Sir Malby Crofton, 2nd Bart, of Longford House, Ballysodare, Co. Sligo; *m* 1911, Sarah Dorothy Beatrice, *e d* of late Col W. F. N. Noel of Stardens, Newent, Glos; one *d. Educ:* Rossall; RMA, Woolwich. Commission in RA 1899; served South African War, 1901–02 (Queen's medal with 5 clasps); Captain, 1907; Major, 1914; served European War, 1914–18 (DSO and bar, Brevet Lt-Col, despatches 6 times); Lieut-Col 1921; Col 1926; CRA 42nd (E Lancs) Division, 1927; CRA 44th Home Counties Division, 1928–32; rtd pay, 1932. *Address:* West House, Warminster, Wilts. *T:* 294.

Died 30 Dec. 1948.

CROFTS, Lt-Col Leonard Markham, DSO 1917; retired pay; late The Queen's Royal Regt; *b* 17 Dec. 1867; *s* of late Major Edmund Crofts, Royal Welsh Fusiliers, and Mrs Crofts, of Merrieleas, Eastleigh; *m* 1906, Margaret, *o d* of late Colonel W. A. Spence; (*o s* killed in action in the Battle of Britain in Sept. 1940) one

d. Educ: St Edward's, Oxford; Sandhurst. Joined the Queen's Royal Regt, 1889; served S African War, 1899–1901, with Ladysmith Relief Forces; on Staff, 1901–02 (despatches, Queen's medal with 5 clasps, King's medal with 2 clasps); European War, 1914–18 (despatches twice, wounded thrice, DSO, Chevalier de l'Ordre de Leopold). *Recreations:* cricket, shooting, fishing; in Army Revolver Team, Bisley, 1904. *Address:* Stella's Cottage, Waverley, Farnham, Surrey.

Died 29 Nov. 1942.

CROFTS, Thomas Robert Norman, MA; *b* 16 July 1874; *s* of late John Crofts, Long Lawford Hill, Warwicks; *m* 1903, Emily May (*d* 1939), 3rd *d* of late W. Thomas-Moore; three *s* one *d. Educ:* Rugby; Caius College, Cambridge; 2nd Class Div. I Classical Tripos, and 2nd Class Modern Languages Tripos. Five years a master at Glenalmond; Merchant Taylors' School, 1902–10; Headmaster of Roan School, Greenwich, 1911–15; Headmaster R. Masonic School, Bushey, 1915–38. *Publications:* editor and author of school textbooks. *Recreations:* shooting, tennis, golf, gardening, ornithology. *Address:* Sunset, Wrecclesham, Farnham, Surrey.

Died 2 Oct. 1949.

CROLL, David Gifford, CBE 1919; VD; Medical Practitioner, Brisbane; Colonel CMF; *b* Glasgow, 1885; *s* of Andrew Usher Croll and Mary Gifford; *m* Marian Winifred Payne. *Educ:* Fort St School, Sydney; University of Sydney. Medical Practitioner, Brisbane, 1910–14; Capt. Commonwealth Forces, 1911; Major, 1914; acting PMO 1st Military District; on active service with Australian Imperial Force, 1914–18; Major, 2nd Light Horse Field Amb., Gallipoli Campaign, 1914–15; Lieut-Colonel CO 2nd Light Horse Field Ambulance, Sinai Campaign, 1916–17; Colonel, ADMS Mtd Division Palestine Campaign, 1917–18; DDMS, AIF in Egypt, 1919; CO 112 Aust. General Hospital, 1941–42; CO 101 Convalescent Depot, 1942–44; Hon. Consulting Physician, Hospital for Sick Children, Brisbane. *Recreations:* yachting; Commissioner for Sea Scouts. *Address:* Sherwood, Brisbane, Queensland. *Clubs:* Queensland, United Service, Royal Queensland Yacht.

Died 4 May 1948.

CRONE, John Smyth, LRCPI; L and MSA; Deputy Coroner West Middlesex, 1916–39; *b* Belfast, 25 Nov. 1858; *e s* of John and Isabel Crone; *m* 1st, Mary Hirst (*d* 1897), *d* of Rev. Thos Smyth; 2nd, 1899, Nina Gertrude (*d* 1933), *d* of Peter Roe, Dublin; four *s. Educ:* Royal Academical Institution, Belfast; Queen's University, Belfast; London Hospital. For nearly forty years in medical practice in Willesden; JP 1907; Sheriff of Middlesex 1933–34; Chm. Willesden Petty Sessional Division, 1939–43; contested (L) West Willesden, 1918; President, Irish Literary Society, London, 1918–25; MRIA; FRSAI; Lieut, RAMC (V), and MO 6th Middlesex Vol. Regt, 1914–19; Past President, Willesden Medical Society. *Publications:* Editor, Irish Book Lover, 1909–1925; Concise Dictionary of Irish Biography, 1928; Henry Bradshaw: His Life and Work, 1931. *Recreations:* literature and book-hunting. *Address:* Castlereagh, 34 Cleveland Road, Ealing, W13.

Died 6 Nov. 1945.

CRONIN, Rt Rev. Mgr Michael, MA, DD; Vicar General Archdiocese of Dublin since 1930; *b* Dublin, 19 April 1871. *Educ:* Clonliffe College, Dublin; Propaganda College, Rome; University of Berlin and University of Munich. BA and MA Royal University of Ireland; studied theology at Rome. Ordained, 1895; Doctor of Divinity, 1895; won junior Fellowship in Royal University of Ireland, 1904; Professor of Ethics and Politics, University College, Dublin, National University of Ireland, 1909–25; appointed Canon of Dublin Metropolitan Chapter and Parish Priest of

Rathgar, Dublin, 1925. *Publications:* The Science of Ethics, 1909; Primer of the Principles of Social Science, 1927. *Address:* 50 Rathgar Road, Dublin.

Died 24 Aug. 1943.

CRONWRIGHT, Samuel Cron, Int. BA; (pen-name, S. C. Cronwright-Schreiner); retired; *b* at the farm Gideons Hoek, District of Bedford, Cape of Good Hope, 26 Jan. 1863; *s* of S. C. Cronwright and Zipporah Featherstone; *m* 1st, 1894, Olive Schreiner; 2nd, 1924, Leonora Bush; one *d. Educ:* St Andrew's Coll., Grahamstown (Champion Athlete). Went farming in the Karoo of the Cape of Good Hope, 1884; farmed and lived there until 1919; was 'detained' by the British Military in Hanover (Cape) during most of the Boer war. MP for Colesberg, 1902; Beaufort West (including Prince Albert), 1903–10. *Publications:* Life of Olive Schreiner; Letters of Olive Schreiner (edited); Migratory Springbucks of South Africa; The Ostrich; The Angora Goat; The Land of Free Speech; Her South African Ancestors; Some Arachnids at Hanover; Little Songs for South Africans; The Political Situation (in South Africa in 1895), with Olive Schreiner; Olive Schreiner's posthumous works, with introductions. *Recreation:* walking. *Address:* PO Box 36, Strand, Cape Province, SA. *TA:* Cronwright, Sparta, Cape Town. *T:* Strand 73. *Clubs:* University, Cape Town.

Died 8 Sept. 1936.

CROOK, Thomas Mewburn, Hon. ARCA, HRI, FRBS, Hon. Treasurer; *b* Tonge Moor, Bolton, 4 Dec. 1869; 3rd *s* of late James Crook, cotton waste dealer, Bolton; *m* 1929, Winifred, *d* of E. T. Saunders, Barnes; one *s* four *d. Educ:* Xavierian Collegiate Institute, Manchester; Church Institute, Bolton; Technical School, Manchester; Royal College of Art, South Kensington (medallist and diploma). Assistant Master at the Royal College of Art, 1894–95; and Modelling Master and Anatomy Lecturer at the Municipal School of Art, Manchester, 1896–1905. *Works:* choir stalls, panels, and Lady Altar Church of St Mary's, Wigan; marble statue of Gen. Sir Thomas Picton, Cardiff City Hall; exhibitor of life-size figures at the Royal Academy; Evening Prayer, 1904; Madonna and Child, 1905; Eurydice, 1906; Mysteries, 1910 marble figure, 1911; Youth, 1912; The Lily, 1913; Roses 1914; The Spring, 1915; Tidal Wave, 1916; Ricochet, 1917; Sir Thomas Picton and Belgium, 1918 (Royal Academy); Exhibitor at the RI, the ROI galleries, etc. *Recreations:* golf, swimming. *Address:* 10 Gainsborough Road, W4. *T:* Chiswick 1243. *Club:* Arts.

Died 18 Jan. 1949.

CROOK, William Montgomery, OBE 1918; BA; FRGS, FZS; *b* Sligo, 23 Jan. 1860; *e s* of late Rev. W. Crook, DD, and Maria, *d* of late Rev. Fossey Tackaberry; *m* 1923, Ethel Mary, *widow* of A. H. Spokes, Recorder of Reading. *Educ:* Methodist College, Belfast; Grammar School, Drogheda; Trinity College, Dublin. Classical Sizarship, TCD, 1877; 1st Erasmus Smith Exhibition, 1877; Classical Scholar, 1880; BA; 1st class Honours and Gold Medal in Classics, 1881. Classical Master, Wesley Coll. Dublin. 1879–86; contested (L) Wandsworth, General Election, 1892; on staff of Methodist Times, 1892–98; editor of Echo, 1898–1900; Sec. Home Counties Liberal Federation, 1902–31; Hon. Sec., 1931–40; Hon. Organizer of the Church Collections for the British Red Cross Society, 1914–18. *Publications:* Memoir of Owen Glynne Jones, in his Rock-Climbing in the English Lake District (2nd ed.), 1900; a chapter in Hugh Price Hughes as we Knew Him, 1902; ed. The Ancestry of the Wesleys, by late Rev. W. Crook, DD, 1938. *Recreations:* walking-tours and old books. *Address:* Wyldwood, Coldharbour, Dorking. *T:* Dorking 73269. *Clubs:* National Liberal, Devonshire, Eighty, Climbers', Irish Lit. Soc.

Died 16 May 1945.

CROOKE, Lt-Col Charles Douglas Parry, CMG 1916; JP; late Suffolk Regiment; *b* 12 Jan. 1870; *m* 1906, Dorothy Joan (*d* 1946), *d* of G. W. Deakin; two *d.* Served European War, 1914–18 (despatches, CMG). *Address:* Pakenham, Suffolk. *Club:* Army and Navy.

Died 25 May 1948.

CROOKENDEN, Harry Mitton, MA; solicitor, retired; *b* 29 Jan. 1862; *s* of I. Adolphus Crookenden and Jane Sophia Mitton; *m* 1908, Edith Mary Frank; two *d. Educ:* Marlborough College; Worcester College, Oxford; France. Director of various companies. *Recreations:* shooting, walking, sculling, farming. *Address:* Headley Manor, nr Epsom, Surrey. *T:* Headley 46. *Club:* Oxford and Cambridge.

Died 7 Nov. 1947.

CROOKHAM, Rev. William Thomas Rupert, CBE 1919; TD, AKC; *m* Beatrice (*d* 1938), 2nd *d* of late Archdeacon Emery; three *d. Educ:* King's College, London University. Chaplain to the Forces South African War, 1900; Hon. Freeman of Cambridge, 1901; European War, 1914–19 (despatches, CBE); Vicar of Haddenham, Ely, 1893–1905; of Wisbech, 1905–32; Rural Dean of Wisbech, 1907–14 and 1919–26; Surrogate 1910; Hon. Canon of Ely Cathedral, 1922–40, Canon Emeritus, 1940; Hon. Emeritus, 1940; Hon. Chaplain Forces 1st Class, 1923. *Address:* Gorseland, Milford on Sea, Hants.

Died 20 Dec. 1945.

CROOKSHANK, Maj.-Gen. Sir Sydney D'Aguilar, KCMG 1919; CB 1918; CIE 1912; DSO 1916; MVO 1911; *b* 3 June 1870; 2nd *s* of late Colonel A. C. W. Crookshank, CB, Indian Army; *m* 1919, Beryl Mary, *y d* of late Commander Willoughby Still, RN. Entered RE, 1889; Indian State Railways, 1892; served Chitral, 1895 (medal with clasp); Capt., 1900; Under-Sec., PWD, Gov. United Provinces, 1907; Major, 1909; Supt Works, Royal Durbar, 1911; Supt Eng. Imperial Capital, 1912; Lt-Col (temp.), 1915; Col 1917; served European War, France and Flanders, 1914–19 (despatches seven times, DSO, CB, Bt-Col, KCMG); Sec. to Gov. of India, PW Dept, 1919–23; Member Viceroy's Legislative Council; Consulting Engineer for Government of India 1923; Member Legislative Assembly, 1921–23; Commanding Simla Rifles AFI, 1922–23; Chief Engineer, Southern Command, 1925–27; retired, 1927; Colonel Commandant, RE, 1936–40; General Secretary, Officers' Association, 8 Eaton Square, SW1; Knight of Grace Order of St John of Jerusalem; Commander Légion d'Honneur and Croix de Guerre avec palmes; Commander Ordre de Leopold and Croix de Guerre; Grand Officer Ordre d'Aviz; American DCM. *Address:* Windmill House, Fleet, Hants. *T:* 428. *Club:* United Service.

Died 17 Aug. 1941.

CROSBIE, Brig.-Gen. James Dayrolles, CMG 1919; DSO 1917; DL, JP; *b* 19 Aug. 1865; *s* of late Col J. Crosbie, of Ballyheigue Castle, Co. Kerry, and *d* of Sir John Lister-Kaye, Bart; *m* May, *d* of Major Leith, VC; one *d. Educ:* Harrow; Sandhurst. Joined 2nd Batt. Royal Welch Fusiliers, 1885; resigned, 1893; lived on own estate in Co. Kerry and took an active interest in county work, serving on most county boards and committees and chairman of local railways; rejoined army, Aug. 1914; commanded 11th Batt. Lancashire Fusiliers and took it to France; commanded as Brig.-Gen. 12th Inf. Brigade; came home, 1917; commanded 16th Batt. The Queen's Regt, and in Nov. 1918 went as Base Commandant to Archangel (despatches five times, CMG, DSO). Chairman Fife County Council, 1938–45. *Recreations:* country gentleman's shooting, hunting, etc. *Address:* Ballyheigue, Co. Kerry; Muircambus House, Kilconquhar, Fife. *Clubs:* Naval and Military; Royal and Ancient (St Andrews).

Died 18 Dec. 1947.

CROSBIE, Robert Edward Harold, CMG 1943; OBE 1927; BA; *b* 24 Jan. 1886; *o s* of late Rev. Howard Augustus Crosbie and Ellen Arabella, *d* of late Major-General Edward Scott; *m* 1921, Elsa, *e d* of late Frederick E. G. Muller; two *d. Educ:* Cheltenham College; Pembroke College, Cambridge. Egyptian Civil Service, 1910–19; Seconded for military service with Egyptian Expeditionary Force, 1915–19; Occupied Enemy Territory Administration (South), 1918–20; Palestine Civil Service, 1920; District Commissioner and Member of Advisory Council, 1931; retired, 1944, and re-employed as Chairman of War Economic Advisory Council, 1944–46. *Address:* 16 Barons Keep, W14. *Club:* Oxford and Cambridge University.

Died 4 Aug. 1950.

CROSS, Arthur Lyon, PhD, FRHistS; Corresponding Member, Mass Hist. Society; Hudson Professor of English History, University of Michigan; *b* Portland, Maine, 14 Nov. 1873; *s* of Emerlous D. Cross and Charlotte Noyes; unmarried. *Educ:* Harvard University. AB 1895; AM 1896; PhD 1899; Berlin and Freiburg i/B. Assistant and graduate student at Harvard, 1895–97, 1898–99; Member of History Department at University of Michigan since 1899; non-resident lecturer at Harvard, 1909–10. *Publications:* The Anglican Episcopate and the American Colonies, 1902, 2nd ed. 1924; A History of St Andrew's Church, Ann Arbor, 1906; A History of England and Greater Britain, 1914; A Shorter History of England and Greater Britain, 1920, rev. ed. 1929, 3rd ed. 1939; Selected Documents relating to Forests, the Sheriff and Smugglers, 1928; Editor of Chapter on Great Britain and Ireland in A Guide to Historical Literature, 1931; contributor to Bibliography of British History, Tutor Period, 1933, and to various periodicals. *Recreation:* golf. *Address:* Ann Arbor, Michigan, USA. *T:* 8331. *Clubs:* Royal Societies; Φ BK, ΔΨ, Golf, University, Ann Arbor; Harvard, Boston.

Died 21 June 1940.

CROSS, Francis John Kynaston; JP County of Berks; *b* 14 Nov. 1865; 2nd *s* of late Edward Cross, Bolton; *m* 1895, Eleanor Mary (*d* 1949), *e d* of 1st Baron Phillimore, PC; three *s* one *d. Educ:* Harrow; New College, Oxford. Won mile for Oxford v. Cambridge, 1886–87–1888–89; won ½ mile and 1 mile Amateur Athletic Championships, 1887; held ½ mile record, 1888–1908; called to Bar, Lincoln's Inn, 1893; Managing Director, Mill Hill Spinning Company, Bolton, 1894–99; Member of Bolton School Board; Member of Wallingford Rural District Council, 1902–42; Berkshire County Council, 1906–42. *Address:* Aston-Tirrold Manor, Didcot, Berks. *T:* Blewbury 280. *Clubs:* Bath, East India and Sports, Farmers'.

Died 31 Dec. 1950.

CROSS, Sir William Coats, 2nd Bt *cr* 1921; *b* 28 May 1877; *o s* of 1st Bt and Jessie Mackenzie, 2nd *d* of Sir Peter Coats of Auchendrane, Ayrshire; *S* father, 1914; *m* 1939, Sheila, 2nd *d* of Gilbert Moffit, Gwalia, Western Australia. *Educ:* Rugby. Commanded 2/1st Queen's Own Royal Glasgow Yeomanry. *Heir: b* Alexander Cross, *b* 4 April 1880. *Address:* Scatwell, Rossshire; Ramsay Lodge, Wentworth, Virginia Water, Surrey. *Clubs:* Cavalry, Boodle's, Bath.

Died 5 Dec. 1947.

CROSSE, Rev. Arthur John William, CBE 1918; BA; TD; *b* 22 April 1857; *s* of late Ven. A. B. Crosse and Virginia, *d* of J. J. Winter, Norwich; *m* 1893, Mary Charlotte Sisson (*d* 1935); three *d. Educ:* Dedham Grammar School; University of London; Leeds Clergy School. Curate, St George's, Barrow-in-Furness, 1883–88; Vicar of Rye, Sussex, 1888–1902; St Cyprian's, Durban, Natal, 1902–06; St James', Barrow-in-Furness, 1906–10; Vicar of St Cuthbert's, Carlisle, 1910–15; Senior Chaplain to 32nd Division at the Front, 1915–19 (CBE, despatches thrice); Vicar of Stow Bardolph, and Rector of Wimbotsham, Norfolk,

1919–26; Vicar of S Augustine's, Wisbech, 1926–35; has served as Chaplain to Volunteers and Territorials since 1890, 4th Royal Sussex, 4th King's Own Royal Lancs, and 4th Border Regts; Provincial Grand Chaplain of Freemasons in Sussex, West Lancashire, Natal, and Cambridgeshire; District Grand Senior Warden in Natal; Grand Chaplain to the Sons of England in South Africa; Chaplain to the Guild of Saddlers, 1927 and 1928. Priest in charge of Bexwell, Norfolk. *Publications:* Pow-wows by a Padre at the Front; In the House of My God, a Manual for Parish Clerks and Vergers. *Recreations:* tennis, golf, fishing. *Address:* 12 Bardwell Rood, Oxford.

Died 29 Nov. 1948.

CROSSE, Ven. Edmond Francis, JP, CVF; FSS; *b* 1858; *s* of late Archdeacon A. B. Crosse, Canon Residentiary of Norwich Cathedral; *m* 1894, Margaret (*d* 1932), *d* of Atherton Selby of Atherton Hall, Lancashire; five *s* three *d. Educ:* Dedham; south of France. Took orders, 1889; Curate of Leigh, Lancashire; Vicar, Heyside, 1892; Vicar, St Luke's, Barrow, 1892; Vicar of Chesterfield, 1905–18; Rural Dean, 1906; Archdeacon of Chesterfield, 1910–29; Rector of Whitwell, 1918–29; Select Preacher, Cambridge University, 1925. *Publications:* Sermons Preached at St Paul's Cathedral; Some Phenomena; 18,000 Miles with the Mission of Help in S Africa, etc. *Address:* Swan Lane, Burford, Oxon.

Died 1 Aug. 1941.

CROSSMAN, Hon. Sir (Charles) Stafford, Kt 1934; **Hon. Mr Justice Crossman;** Judge of High Court of Justice, Chancery Division since 1934; *b* 8 Dec. 1870; 3rd *s* of Edward Crossman, MD, Hambrook, near Bristol and Veronica Mathilde Marsh; *m* 1902, Helen Elizabeth, *y d* of late David Howard, Buckhurst Hill, Essex; two *s* three *d. Educ:* Winchester College (scholar); New College Oxford (scholar) 1st Class Mods. 1891, 1st Class Lit. Hum. 1893, Hertford Scholar 1890. Assistant Master Winchester College, 1893–94; Barrister-at-law, Lincoln's Inn, 1897; Bencher, 1927; Junior Counsel to Board of Inland Revenue, 1926–27; Junior Counsel to Treasury, 1927–34; Counsel to Royal College of Physicians, 1927–34. *Address:* Buckhurst Hill House, Buckhurst Hill, Essex. *T:* Buckhurst 0267. *Club:* Athenæum.

Died 1 Jan. 1941.

CROSSMAN, Maj.-Gen. Francis Lindisfarne Morley, CB 1941; DSO 1919; MC; RA; Lord of the Manor of Holy Island; *b* 16 Aug. 1888; *e s* of late L. Morley Crossman of Cheswick House, Berwick-on-Tweed, Northumberland; *m* 1919, Ruth, *y d* of Captain V. Gartside-Tippinge of Berrywell, Duns, Berwickshire; one *s* one *d. Educ:* Wellington College. Royal Military Academy, Woolwich. Second Lieut RFA 1907; Lieut 1910; Captain, 1914; Maj. 1917; Bt Lt-Col 1929; Lt-Col 1935; Col 1936; Maj.-Gen. 1939; served in European War, 1914–18 (despatches five times, DSO, MC); Commander 1st AA Division TA 1939–40; Commander 2nd AA Division, 1940–42; retired pay, 1942; HM Forces War Savings, India, 1942–45. *Address:* Cheswick House, Berwick-on-Tweed, Northumberland. *T:* Ancroft 34. *Club:* Junior United Service.

Died 16 Aug. 1947.

CROSSMAN, Col George Lytton, CMG 1916; DSO 1902; late Northampton Regiment and The West Yorks Regiment; *b* 18 Feb. 1877; *s* of late Edward Crossman, MD; *m* 1914, Julia Mary Anne, *e d* of late Rev. J. J. Tapson, Vicar of Hooe, South Devon. *Educ:* Radley College; Sandhurst. Entered Army, 1897; served South Africa, 1899–1901 (despatches twice, DSO); Captain, May 1904; Adjutant 2nd West Yorkshire Regiment, 1904 (Queen's SA medal and five clasps, King's SA medal and two clasps); European War, 1914–18 (CMG, Bt Lt-Col, despatches six times); Instructor RMC Camberley, 1908–12; Lt-Col, 1925; Col, 1929; Commander 133rd (Sussex and Kent) Infantry Brigade

TA, 1930–34; retired pay, 1934. *Address:* Westbury, Colchester, Essex. *T:* Colchester 2931. *Clubs:* Junior United Service, MCC.

Died 17 Jan. 1947.

CROTCH, William Walter, FRSA; Editor-in-Chief of International Press Bureau at Paris; *b* 17 Oct. 1874; *s* of William Crotch and Martha Mace. *Educ:* Norwich Grammar School. Commenced journalistic career on old Norwich Mercury; Entered London journalism under late T. P. O'Connor on Weekly Sun; Parliamentary Secretary to Sir Thomas Richardson, MP, and subsequently Editor and Manager of Northern Daily Guardian; returned London and after acting as Parliamentary Secretary to Lord Dalziel assisted in founding and became Editor of Week-End; invited by Sir Hall Caine to revive Dickens's old paper Household Words and assumed editorial charge; Originated and assisted in founding the Dickens Fellowship 1902; President 1915–20; Freedom of City of Norwich, 1897, of City of London 1914; Assisted in founding and joined staff of London Daily Herald; Cross of St John Lateran 1906; Edited Advocate of India, 1916; made four lecture tours through America; constant contributor to London daily newspapers and British and American magazines and Reviews; contested (Independent) Richmond, Surrey, 1918; joined staff of International Press Bureau in Paris 1924. Was made prisoner by Germans in 1940 and subsequently acted as accredited SHAEF War Correspondent. After liberation gave series 26 lectures for French Government on French wines to American troops stationed in Paris. Wrote three books during captivity. *Publications:* Cottage Homes of England; Treasure House of Wales; Charles Dickens; Social Reformer; The Pageant of Dickens; The Wine in the Cup; The Soul of Dickens; Industrial Anarchy and the Way Out; The Secret of Dickens; The New World; The Touchstone of Dickens; The Humanism of Hardy; Reticences and Revelations of Biography; The Winepress; Vineland Wanderings in France; A Gay Wine Cavalcade; A Book about Burgundy; dozens of brochures. *Recreations:* motoring and travelling in strange lands. *Address:* 4 Square des Aigles, Chantilly, Oise, France. *TA:* Crotch, Chantilly (Oise). *T:* Chantilly 485.

Died 4 May 1947.

CROUCH, Col Hon. Richard Armstrong, VD; *b* Ballarat, Victoria, 19 June 1869; *s* of George Crouch. *Educ:* Mount Pleasant School; Melbourne University (Bowen Prizeman, Chief Justice's Law Prize). Life Member Australian Natives Association; Member Executive Victorian Historical Society, Australia; Chairman Melbourne Co-operative Trust; Chairman National Provident Life Assurance Company; Chairman Commonwealth Building Society; Commanded Yarra Borderers, 56th Australian Infantry Regiment; Officer Commanding 22nd Batt. Infantry, 6th Brigade Australian Imperial Forces (active service) at Dardanelles; MP Corio, Australian Parliament, 1901–10, for Corangamite 1929–31; Deputy Chairman Committees Federal Parliament; Australian Delegate to International Labour Conference, Oxford, Aug. 1924; and to British Commonwealth Labour Conference, London, Sept. 1924. *Publications:* Australian Finance at the Cross Roads; Australia a Nation; The Labor Party and the War; The World's Crisis and its Remedy, magazine articles. *Recreations:* book and autograph collecting. *Address:* Point Lonsdale, Vic., Australia.

Died April 1949.

CROUDACE, Rev. William Darnell, BA; Hon. Canon of Durham; *b* 1848; *s* of William Croudace, Newcastle-on-Tyne; *m* 1876, Maria Tuke; one *s*. *Educ:* Grange School, Sunderland; University College, Durham. Ordained, 1873; Curate of St Andrew's, Auckland, 1873–76; in charge Castle Eden Colliery, 1876–78; Vicar of St Peter's, Bishop Auckland, 1878–97; of Consett, 1898–1903; Rector of Boldon, 1903–06;

Vicar of Eastgate, 1906–31; Rural Dean of Stanhope, 1912–34. *Address:* Elm-Tree House, Stanhope, Co. Durham.

Died 3 Oct. 1942.

CROW, Douglas Arthur; Ear and Throat Consulting Surgeon, Royal Sussex County Hospital, Brighton; *b* 2 Aug. 1889; *s* of Arthur Crow; *m* 1913, Mary Crabtree; three *d*. *Educ:* Fort William; Edinburgh University. Qualified MB ChB Edinburgh Univ. 1911. House Surgeon Doncaster Royal Infirmary, 1912; Temp. Capt. RAMC; Hon. Surgeon Sussex Throat and Ear Hospital, Brighton, 1920; Hon. Surgeon for Throat and Ear Diseases, Royal Sussex County Hospital, 1925; Consulting Otolaryngologist, Royal Alexandra Hospital for Sick Children, Brighton, 1925; Consulting Otolaryngologist, Haywards Heath Hospital, 1926; Consulting Otolaryngologist, Brighton Infirmary, 1926; Fellow (member Laryngological and Otological section) of Royal Society of Medicine; member Sussex Medico-Chirurgical Society, President, 1938–39. *Publications:* The Ear, Nose and Throat in General Practice, 1927; papers to medical journals; The Pacifist Faith of a Surgeon, 1938; A Blind Man with a Lantern, 1938; Unwitting Crowd, a novel, 1942. *Recreations:* gardening, reading. *Address:* 27 Brunswick Square, Hove, Sussex.

Died 2 Nov. 1945.

CROWDY, Edith Frances, CBE 1919; Hon. Serving Sister of the Order of St John of Jerusalem, 1917; 3rd *d* of late James and Isabel Crowdy; unmarried. *Educ:* home. VAD, 1912–17; Deputy Director, Women's Royal Naval Service, 1917–19; Secretary, Hellenic Travellers' Club, 1926–39. *Recreations:* reading and music. *Address:* 100 Beaufort Street, Chelsea, SW. *Clubs:* University Women's, Ex-Service Women's.

Died 23 July 1947.

CROWE, Brig.-Gen. John Henry Verinder, CB 1917; DL Berkshire; *b* 14 Sept. 1862; *s* of late Edward F. Crowe; *m* Mary Margaret (*d* 1922), *widow* of Wilfred Watts-Russell; one *s* one *d*. *Educ:* Charterhouse; RMA Woolwich. Entered Royal Artillery, 1882; Captain, 1890; Major, 1899; Lieut-Col 1907; Col 1911; psc 1899; Private Secretary to the Lieut-Governor of the Punjab, 1892–97; Staff Captain and DAQMG Intelligence Dept War Office, 1899–1902; Chief Instructor Royal Military Academy, 1904–08; commanding 28th Brig. RFA 1908–09; Comdt of the Royal Military College of Canada, 1909–13; commanding RA, East Africa, 1915–17; General Staff, 1917–18; Head of Missions to and representative of CGS in Italy; retired, 1919; Knight Commander of the Danebrog (Denmark); Order of Merit (Spain); Officer of the Order of S Maurice and S Lazarus (Italy) and of S Bento d'Aviz (Portugal). *Publications:* General Smuts' Campaign in East Africa; Problems in Manœuvre Tactics; Epitome of the Afghan War, 1878–1880; Epitome of the Russo-Turkish War, 1877–1878; Handbook of the Armies of Norway and Sweden; articles to magazines, Encyclopædia Britannica, etc.; translated Drill Regulations of the German Field Artillery; Count Sternberg's Reminiscences of the Boer War. *Club:* Naval and Military.

Died 8 Jan. 1948.

CROWLEY, James, MRCVS. Member Dail Eireann, Kerry and West Limerick, 1921–23; Co. Kerry, 1923–32; MP (SF) North Kerry, Dec. 1918–22. *Address:* Church Street, Listowel, Co. Kerry.

Died 21 Jan. 1946.

CROWLEY, Rt Rev. Timothy, CSC; Bishop of Dacca, since 1929; *b* Limerick, 1880. *Educ:* Limerick; Notre Dame University, Ind, USA; Catholic University, Washington. Missionary in Bengal since 1907. Kaisar-i-Hind Gold Medal, 1944. *Address:* Bishop's House, Ramna PO, Dacca, Bengal, East India.

Died 2 Oct. 1945.

CROWTHER, James Arnold, MA, ScD, FInstP; Professor Emeritus, University of Reading; Hon. Member Faculty of Radiologists; President, British Institute of Radiology, 1936; Vice-Chairman, Parliamentary and Science Committee, 1944–46; *b* Sheffield, 28 Aug. 1883; *s* of Councillor J. W. Crowther; *m* 1912, Florence Maud, 3rd *d* of J. F. Billinger, Cambridge; two *s. Educ:* Royal Grammar School, Sheffield; St John's College, Cambridge (Scholar). Mackinnon Student of the Royal Society; Fellow of St John's College, Cambridge, 1908–12. Demonstrator and Lecturer in Physics in the Cavendish Laboratory, Cambridge, 1912–24; Lecturer in Physics Applied to Medical Radiology in the University of Cambridge, 1921–24; Lecturer in Physics Applied to Medical Radiology in the University of Cambridge, 1921–24; Professor of Physics, University of Reading, 1924–46; Hon. Secretary, Institute of Physics, 1932–46, Vice-Pres. 1946–49. *Publications:* Ions, Electrons, and Ionizing Radiations; Molecular Physics; Manual of Physics; Practical Physics; Principles of Radiology; Life of Michael Faraday; Handbook of Industrial Radiography (Ed.); numerous original papers to scientific journals. *Recreations:* golf, bridge. *Address:* Fairways, Treyarnon Bay, Padstow. *Club:* Athenæum.

Died 25 March 1950.

CROZIER, Major Sir Thomas Henry, Kt 1930; late Royal Field Artillery; *b* Monkstown, Co. Dublin; *e s* of Major-General H. D. Crozier, retired RE; *m* 1898, Ethel Minnie, 2nd *d* of Christopher Lethbridge; one *s. Educ:* United Services College, Westward Ho. 2nd Lieut Royal Artillery, 1888; Capt., 1898; Major, 1903; passed advanced class of Ordnance Coll. 1899; Professor of Artillery, Ordnance College, 1899–1904; Chief Instructor of Artillery, RM Academy, Woolwich, 1906–08; HM Chief Inspector of Explosives, Home Office, 1926–31; retired, 1931. Rejoined Explosives Department, Home Office, 1940; retired, 1944, owing to illness. *Recreations:* fishing and shooting. *Address:* Cylinder, Saltwood, Kent.

Died 26 Sept. 1948.

CROZIER, William Percival; Editor of the Manchester Guardian since May 1932; Director of the Manchester Guardian and Evening News, Ltd since 1921; *b* Stanhope, Durham, 1879; *s* of Rev. Richard Crozier, Wesleyan Methodist Minister; *m* 1906, Gladys, *d* of late G. F. Baker, Maidstone; one *s* two *d. Educ:* Manchester Grammar School; Trinity College, Oxford (Scholar). First class Honour Moderations; first class Lit. Hum. Joined Manchester Guardian, 1903. *Publications:* Letters of Pontius Pilate, 1928; CPS in the Office in J. L. Hammond's Life of C. P. Scott, 1934; The Fates Are Laughing (posthumous), 1945. *Address:* Manchester Guardian.

Died 16 April 1944.

CRU, Robert L.; Director and Secretary, Maison de l'Institut de France à Londres (Fondation Edmond de Rothschild); Officier de la Légion d'Honneur; *b* Maré, Loyalty Islands, New Caledonia, 8 May 1884; 4th *s* of Rev. J. P. L. Cru and Catherine Norton; *m* 1910, Nona, *d* of Rev. A. C. Blake and Martha Fewster of Nailsworth, Gloucestershire; three *s* one *d. Educ:* Tournon; Lyon; Ecole Normale Supérieure, Paris. Agrégé de langue et de littérature anglaises, 1909; PhD Columbia University, New York, 1913. French Instructor, Williams College, Williamstown, Mass, 1907–08; Assistant Professor, Hunter College, New York, 1909–14; Interpreter attached to BEF, 1914–16; London Office of the Maison de la Presse, 1916–19. *Publications:* Diderot as a Disciple of English Thought, 1913; Montesquieu's Lettres Persanes, 1914, and La Rochefoucauld's Maximes, 1927, critical editions; several translations from the English (Les États-Unis, puissance mondiale by A. C. Coolidge, 1908; David Lloyd George, étude biographique, by Harold Spender,

1919). *Address:* 185 Queen's Gate, Kensington, SW7. *T:* Kensington 4010 and 2512; Pierreplane, Bandol (Var), France. *T:* Bandol 98.

Died Feb. 1944.

CRUISE, Sir Richard (Robert), GCVO 1936; KCVO 1922; CVO 1917; FRCS Eng., LRCP London; Surgeon Oculist to Queen Mary; late Surgeon Oculist to King George V; Captain RAMC (T), Aug. 1914; ophthalmic surgeon; *b* Purneah, India; *s* of late Francis Cruise; *m* 1929, Eileen, *d* of late Matthew Greenlees and of Mrs Selby Lowndes, of Whaddon Hall, Bletchley; one *s* two *d. Educ:* Harrow. Pursued medical and ophthalmic studies at St Mary's Hospital, Royal London Ophthalmic Hospital, Royal Westminster Eye Hospital, Royal Eye Hospital (Southwark), Paris. is surgeon on staff of the Royal Westminster Ophthalmic Hospital; Consultant Surgeon, Harrow Cottage Hospital. *Publications:* Clinical Refraction, 1914; contributions to medical papers on ophthalmic subjects. *Recreations:* hunting, shooting, golf. *Address:* 34 Wimpole Street, W1. *T:* Welbeck 7607. *Club:* Bath MCC.

Died 24 Dec. 1946.

CRUM, Walter Ewing, FBA; MA; Hon. PhD Berlin (1910); Hon. DLit Oxf.; Hon. Member American Oriental Society; JP Renfrewshire; *b* 1865; *s* of Alexander Crum and Nina Ewing. *Educ:* Eton (Rev. E. Hale's); Balliol College, Oxford; Paris (Maspero); Berlin (Erman). *Publications:* various, relating to Coptic Egypt (Bibliography 1892–1940 in Jl Egypt. Archaeol. XXV). *Address:* 19 Bathwick Hill, Bath.

Died 18 May 1944.

CRUMP, Basil Woodward; author and journalist; *b* London, ·11 Sept. 1866; *o s* of F. O. Crump, QC, and Isabel Woodward. *Educ:* Jesus College, Cambridge. Barrister Middle Temple and sub-editor Law Times, 1892; began Oriental studies, 1893, joining Tibetan Esoteric School; Editor Law Times and Reports, County Courts Chronicle and Cox's Criminal Cases, 1900; also motor and aero editor Field and Queen; retired, 1912; researches in India, China and Japan since 1918, joining Tashi Lama's Order, 1920. *Publications:* Evolution as Outlined in the Archaic Eastern Records, 1930; with Mrs Leighton Cleather; Wagner's Music-Dramas, 4 vols, 1903–1912; Buddhism, the Science of Life, 1928; Centenary edition of H. P. Blavatsky's Voice of the Silence with notes and comments, 1931. *Recreations:* drama, music, motoring, photography. *Address:* c/o Chartered Bank, Calcutta, India.

Died 30 May 1945.

CRUMP, Sir Henry Ashbrooke, KCIE 1921; CSI, BA (Oxon); *b* 1863; *s* of Charles Crump, Barrister-at-law; *m* Frances Gertrude, 2nd *d* of late E. J. Kennedy-Gleason, Limerick; three *d. Educ:* Balliol College, Oxford. Joined the Indian Civil Service, 1885; served in the Central Provinces as Assistant-Commissioner, Commissioner of Excise, Deputy Commissioner; Chief Secretary to Chief Commissioner, 1901–02 and 1906–07; Officiating Chief Commissioner, 1912; Financial Commissioner, Central Provinces, India, 1913–20; retired, 1920. *Recreations:* shooting, motoring. *Address:* Villa Francesca, Alassio, Italy. *Club:* Royal Automobile.

Died 16 Sept. 1941.

CRUTTWELL, Charles Robert Mowbray Fraser, MA, DLitt; *b* 23 May 1887; *s* of Rev. Canon Cruttwell and Annie Maud, *d* of Rt Hon. Sir John Mowbray, Bt, MP; unmarried. *Educ:* Rugby School; Queen's College, Oxford (Open Scholar in Classics and History); 1st Class, Hon. Mods, 1908, Lit. Hum. 1910, Mod. History, 1911; Fellow of All Souls College, 1911. Lecturer in Modern History, Hertford College, 1912; 2nd Lieut 1/4 R. Berks Regt, Aug. 1914; France and Belgium, 1915–16; invalided home; Captain, G. S. Mil. Intell. War Office, 1918–19; Fellow of Hertford College, 1919; Statutory Commissioner for the University, 1923; Examiner in

Modern History, 1923–25; University Lecturer in Modern History, 1926–30; Principal, Hertford College, Oxford, 1930–39; JP Hampshire. *Publications:* The War Service of the 1/4 R. Berkshire Regt, 1920; A History of the Great War, 1935; Wellington, 1936; The Role of British Strategy in the Great War, 1936; A History of Peaceful Change in the Modern World, 1937; Chapters in the History of the Peace Conference, 1920; and in Cambridge History of British Foreign Policy, 1921; Text-books on English History, 1760–1822, and on European History, 1814–1878. *Recreations:* golf, lawntennis, and country life generally. *Address:* Vinnicks, Highclere, Newbury, Berks. *T:* Oxford 2947 and Highclere 62. *Club:* United University.

Died 14 March 1941.

CUBITT, Sir Bertram (Blakiston), KCB 1920; CB, 1911; DL, JP; Commandeur Legion of Honour; late Assistant Under-Secretary of State, War Office; *b* 20 Aug. 1862; *s* of late Major Frank Astley Cubitt, Thorpe Hall, Norwich and Fritton House, Suffolk; *m* 1897, Leila, *d* of late Captain William Norman Leslie, Gordon Highdrs, and step *d* of late Arthur Raby, Consular Service; two *s. Educ:* Rugby (Scholar and Exhibitioner); Balliol College, Oxford. Acting Assistant Private Secretary to Right Hon. E. Stanhope, Secretary of State for War, 1890–91; Private Secretary to Right Hon. St John Brodrick, 1896–98; Vice-President, Royal Patriotic Fund; Vice-President Imperial War Museum; a Commissioner of the Royal Hospital, Chelsea. *Recreation:* rowing. *Address:* Hillstead, Weston, Bath. *Club:* Union.

Died 23 Sept. 1942.

CUBITT, Thomas, BA Oxon; *b* 1870; *o s* of Capt. Lewis Cubitt, 26th Cameronians, and Charlotte Anne, *d* of R. W. Kennard, MP for Newport, IoW; *m* 1893, Fede Maria, RRC, *o surv. c* of late Count Adolfo Riccardi of Vercelli, Italy; one *s* three *d. Educ:* Eton; Merton College, Oxford. Assumed by royal licence additional name of Riccardi 1904, and in 1905 granted royal licence of King Edward VII to bear the title of Count in this country conferred by the King of Italy but both the title of Count and the additional name of Riccardi discontinued 1940. Served European War, 1914–19, on Transport Staff, BEF. *Club:* Carlton.

Died 30 July 1947.

CULLEN, Hon. Lord; William James Cullen; a Judge of the Supreme Courts of Scotland, 1909; retired, 1925; *b* 9 Sept. 1859; *s* of Thomas Cullen, Inland Revenue, Edinburgh; *m* 1888, Grace Rutherford, *d* of William John Clark, Manchester; one *s* one *d.* Writer to the Signet, 1884; Advocate, 1891; KC 1905; Sheriff of Fife and Kinross, 1906; appointed Judge of Supreme Courts of Scotland, 1909, with judicial title of Lord Cullen. *Address:* 10 Darnaway Street, Edinburgh. *T:* 24023 Edinburgh.

Died 19 June 1941.

CULLEN, William, LLD (University of the Witwatersrand), FRIC, MInstMM, MIChemE, etc; Consulting Chemical and Metallurgical Engineer; Director of Public Companies; Hon. Treasurer, Universities Bureau of British Empire; *b* 18 May 1867; *s* of William Cullen, JP, and Margaret Johnston of Uddingston, Scotland; *m* 1897, Jean Crichton Maclachlan, OBE (*d* 1945); three *s* one *d*; 1946, Agnes Campbell Macmillan (Nan), of Glasgow, and of Staff of Univ. of Witwatersrand. *Educ:* Hutcheson's Grammar School, Glasgow; Andersonian College, Glasgow; School of Mines, Freiberg, Saxony. Trained as a chemist under Prof. Dittmar, 1883–90; entered service of Messrs. Nobels Explosive Co. Ltd, 1890; then of Messrs. Kynoch Ltd, as Technical Adviser, 1898–1901; General Works Manager, Dynamite Factory, Modderfontein, Transvaal, 1901–15; Founder of S African Red Cross Society; Chairman of what is now the University of the Witwatersrand; in command of Imperial Light Horse for

7 years but saw no active service; President of Chemical, Metallurgical & Mining Soc., 1905–06, of Inst. MM, 1929–30, of IChemE, 1937–39, of Society of Chemical Industry, 1941–43; of Science Masters' Assoc., 1944; member of Advisory Council of Imperial Institute (mineral section); associated with many scientific and technical societies and public bodies. *Publications:* contributed many papers during past 40 years to technical and scientific societies. *Recreation:* public work. *Address:* 119 North Gate, Regent's Park, NW8. *T:* Primrose 0633. *Clubs:* Devonshire, Chemical, Mining and Metallurgical, Royal Empire Society.

Died 14 Aug. 1948.

CULLEY, Rev. Arnold Duncan, MA, Mus Bac Cantab, MA (ad eundem), Dunelm, FRCO, ARCM (Theory and Organ); *b* 9 March 1867; *y s* of late Benjamin Culley and Hannah, *e d* of late George Childs; *m* 1906, Eliza, *e d* of late William Granger, MInstCE. *Educ:* Great Yarmouth Grammar School; Royal College of Music, London (Norfolk and Norwich Scholar); Emmanuel College, Cambridge (Organist Scholar). Formerly Curate of the Chapel Royal, Brighton; Deputy Priest Vicar and Sub-Organist of Exeter Cathedral; Minor Canon and Precentor, 1906–32, and Organist and Master of the Choristers, 1907–32, of Durham Cathedral; Rector of Burwarton with Cleobury North, 1932–41; Rural Dean of Stottesdon, 1939–41. *Publication:* Anthems, Part Songs, Songs. *Address:* Pool Cottage, Seifton, Ludlow, Shropshire. *T:* Seifton 233.

Died 3 Dec. 1947.

CULLING, James William Henry, CB 1931; CBE 1920 (OBE 1918); *b* 1870; *s* of James Culling; *m* 1909, Winifred, *d* of Henry Taylor. Entered for service under Victualling Dept of the Admiralty, Royal Clarence Yard, Gosport, 1890; transferred to Admiralty Office, London, 1894; Assistant Director of Victualling, 1905; Director, 1923–31. *Address:* Rostellan, Woodlands Road, Bushey, Herts.

Died 30 Jan. 1949.

CULLIS, Charles Gilbert, DSc (London), MInstMM; Professor of Mining Geology, University of London, Royal School of Mines, Imperial College of Science and Technology, S Kensington, 1930–36, Emeritus Professor, since 1937; Past President, Institute of Mining and Metallurgy; Member, Non-Ferrous Metallic Ores Committee, Ministry of Supply; *b* 1871; *y s* of Frederick John Cullis of Gloucester; *m* 1913, Winifred Jefford, 2nd *d* of late Sir George Jefford Fowler; three *s* two *d. Educ:* King Edward VI School and Mason College, Birmingham; Royal College of Science, London. Demonstrator and Assistant Professor of Geology, Royal College of Science, 1892–1914; Professor of Economic Mineralogy, Imperial College of Science and Technology, 1914–30. *Publications:* Report on World's Production of Silver for Indian Currency Committee, 1919; Report on Copper Deposits of Cyprus for Colonial Office, 1922; Geology and Mineral Resources of Cyprus, 1924. *Address:* 81 Murray Road, Wimbledon Common, SW19. *T:* Wimbledon 1966. *Club:* Athenæum.

Died 27 April 1941.

CULLUM, Ridgwell; novelist; *b* London, 13 Aug. 1867; British subject; *m* 1898, Agnes Winifred Matz; no *c.* Left England at age of seventeen; spent many years travelling through Colonies and foreign countries; joined earlier gold rush in Transvaal, and later passed some years trading in the remoter interior of Africa; saw much service in the Kaffir wars; later on crossed to the United States and travelled through the far north-west of Canada (Yukon and Alaska) fur hunting and trading; ultimately spent many years cattle ranching in the State of Montana and adjoining states; took part in some of the later Indian risings; novelist since 1904, settled in England. *Publications:* The Twins of Suffering Creek; The One Way Trail; The Watchers of the Plains; The Night-

Riders; The Devil's Keg; The Sheriff of Dyke Hole; The Men who Wrought; The Purchase Price; The Luck of the Kid; The Son of his Father; The Wolf Pack; The Law-Breakers; The Compact; The Brooding Wild; The Hound from the North; The Law of the Gun; The Riddle of Three-Way Creek; The Way of the Strong; The Trail of the Axe; The Triumph of John Kars; The Heart of Unaga; The Man in the Twilight; The Mystery of the Barren Lands; The Tiger of Cloud River; The Treasure of Big Waters; The Bull Moose; Sheets in the Wind; The Flaming Wilderness; The Vampire of N'Gobi; One Who Kills, etc. *Recreations:* golf, billiards.

Died 3 Nov. 1943.

CULPIN, Ewart Gladstone, JP, FRIBA; Officier de l'Ordre de la Couronne de la Belgique; Grand Officer of the Crown of Roumania; Commander of Order of the Black Star of Benin; Trustee, Official Czech Refugee Trust Fund; *b* 3 Dec. 1877; *s* of Ben Ephraim Lamartine and Eliza Culpin; *m* 1903, Nora Driver; two *s*. *Educ:* Alleynes Gram. School, Stevenage; Hitchin Gram. Sch. Sec. Garden City Association 1905; Founded International Garden Cities and Town Planning Association 1907; President Société Belge pour la reconstruction de la Belgique; Chairman, Standing Conference on London Regional Planning, 1926–46. Labour candidate North Islington, 1924; Alderman, LCC; Vice-Chm., LCC, 1934–37; Chairman, 1938–39; Pres. Incorporated Assoc. of Architects and Surveyors, 1930; Pres. TPI, 1937–38. *Publications:* a number of booklets on Housing and Town Planning. *Address:* 18 Selwyn House, Manor Fields, Putney Hill, SW15. *T:* Putney 4659. *Club:* Athenæum.

Died 1 Dec. 1946.

CUMING, Sir Arthur Herbert, Kt 1928; *s* of late Williams Cuming, Deputy-Accountant-General of the Navy; *m* 1905, Beryl Christine Austen; one *s*. *Educ:* Westminster School; Oriel College, Oxford. Entered the Indian Civil Service, 1893; came out to India, 1894; served in Bengal (old Province) as Assistant Magistrate and Collector; in Assam as Deputy-Commissioner; in Eastern Bengal and Assam as Magistrate and Collector, and District and Sessions Judge; in Bengal as District and Sessions Judge; Puisne Judge, High Court, Calcutta, 1921–31. *Recreation:* bridge. *Address:* Alipore House, Cheltenham. *Clubs:* United Service; New, Cheltenham; Royal Calcutta Turf, Calcutta.

Died 15 Feb. 1941.

CUMING, Edward William Dirom; author and editor; *b* 4 May 1862; *e surv. s* of the late Col Edward William Cuming, late 79th QO Cameron Highlanders, Ballyjamesduff, Co. Cavan, Ireland; *m* 1892, Ethel Maud, *e d* of late Col H. Locock, CB, RE. *Educ:* private schools. In business in Lower Burma, 1880–87, when he returned to England and adopted literature as a calling; assist editor Land and Water, 1892–96. *Publications:* In the Shadow of the Pagoda, 1893; With the Jungle Folk, 1897; Wonders in Monsterland, 1900; assistant editor Baily's Magazine, 1900–1910; (with J. A. Shepherd) The Arcadian Calendar, 1903; (with late Sir Walter Gilbey) George Morland, His Life and Works, 1907; Three Jovial Puppies, 1908; British Sport, Past and Present, 1909; Bodley Head Natural History, 1913; Rbt S. Surtees, Creator of Jorrocks, 1924; edited Thoughts on Hunting and Other Matters, by R. S. Surtees and John Jorrocks, 1925; edited a Game-Ranger's Note-Book, 1924; rescued Squire Osbaldeston's Autobiography and edited with Commentary; edited A Hunting Diary by Capt. N. W. Apperley; Robert S. Surtees' forgotten and unfinished novel Tom Hall, 1926; edited, with additions, Nimrod's My Life and Times; edited selections of Surtees' Hunting Tours, 1927; edited A Game Ranger on Safari; Nimrod's My Horses, and other Essays; compiled A Fox-Hunting Anthology, 1928; edited selection of Surtees' magazine essays as Town and Country Papers, 1929; edited T. B. Bruce's Missing, 1930; Introduction to N. Cox's Hunting, 1928; to R.

Blome's Hawking, 1929; Sports and Games Chapter for Johnson's England, 1933; Idlings in Arcadia, 1934; planned and compiled Baily's Hunting Directory; editor Sports Department, Victoria History of the Counties of England, 1903–1907; novels: A Vendor of Dreams, 1923; (under pseud. Evelyn Tempest) The McArdle Peerage, 1910; Poor Emma! 1911; The Doubts of Diana, 1911; A Rogue's March, 1912. *Recreations:* angling, gardening, natural history. *Address:* The Orchard House, Appleford, Berks. *T:* Clifton Hampden 55.

Died 3 Dec. 1941.

CUMMING, Col Charles Chevin, CB 1916; MB, late RAMC; *b* 19 Feb. 1875; *s* of late Dr James Simpson Cumming; *m* 1914, Muriel Grace, *y d* of late Dep. Insp.-Gen. RE Biddulph, RN. *Educ:* High School and University, Glasgow. Served S Africa, 1900–02 (Queen's medal 6 clasps, King's medal 2 clasps); European War, 1914–18 (CB); retired pay, 1930. *Publications:* medical papers. *Recreations:* boating, swimming.

Died 3 April 1947.

CUMMING, Rev. James, DD; Ex-Professor of Old Testament Language and Literature, Knox College, Dunedin; *s* of late Rev. Alex. Cumming, Forfar; *m*; two *s* two *d*. *Educ:* Forfar Academy; George Watson's College, University, and New College, Edinburgh. MA (Hons) Edin., BD (Lond.), BD (Hons) Melbourne, DD (by thesis) Melbourne. Presbyterian minister at Cromwell, Invercargill, Wellington; Moderator of Presbyterian Church of New Zealand, 1923. *Address:* 304 York Place, Dunedin, NZ.

Died 13 Feb. 1946.

CUMMINGS, David Charles, CBE 1918; *b* 16 Dec. 1861; *s* of George William Cummings, Greenwich; *m* Lucy Elizabeth Watkins; one *s* two *d*. *Educ:* Roans School, Greenwich. Apprentice to Shipbuilding Trade, 1876; joined the Trade Union, 1880; District Delegate for Yorkshire, 1895; Member of Leeds School Board, 1898; General Secretary of Boilermakers, 1900; JP Newcastle-on-Tyne, 1906; Member of Parliamentary Committee Trades Union Congress, 1902–08; Chairman and President, 1905–06; joined Board of Trade Labour Dept, 1908; transferred to Chief Industrial Commissioner as Assistant Industrial Commission, 1911; transferred to Ministry of Labour, 1916; Member of the Industrial Court, 1919–40; Member of Lewisham Boro Council, 1927; Chairman of Courts of Referees, 1930. *Publication:* History of the United Society of Boilermakers and Ironshipbuilders. *Recreation:* bowls. *Address:* 41 Thornsbeach Road, Catford, SE6.

Died 16 April 1942.

CUMMINS, Herbert Ashley Cunard, CMG 1921; OBE 1918; *b* 1871; *s* of William Travers Cummins; *m* Claire Marie, *d* of late Gustave Mueller, San Antonio, USA. *Educ:* Christ's College, Finchley. Vice-Consul at Gomez Palacio, Mexico, 1911; Consul at Juarez, Mexico, 1916; Commercial Attaché, Mexico, 1916; HM Representative in Mexico, 1917–24; HM Consul at Pernambuco, 1925; HM Consul at Pernambuco, 1925; HM Consul and Chargé d'Affaires in Paraguay, 1925; Special Envoy at inauguration of the President of Paraguay, 1928; retired, 1932. *Address:* Tilcara, Province of Jujuy, Argentina.

Died 21 Nov. 1943.

CUMMINS, Col Stevenson Lyle, CB 1919, CMG 1915; LLD, MD; late AMS David Davies Professor of Tuberculosis, Welsh National School of Medicine, 1921–38; *b* 18 June 1873; *s* of late W. J. Cummins, MD, Cork; *m* 1906, Eleanor Fenton, *d* of late Robert Hall, Rockcliffe, Co. Cork; four *c*. Entered Army, 1897; Captain, 1900; Major, 1909; Lt-Col 1915; Col 1918; served Nile Expedition, 1898 (medal with clasp, despatches); Sudan, 1900–02; Sudan, 1904 (clasp); Osmanieh 4th class, 1907; European War, 1914–18 (CB, CMG, despatches six times, Bt-Col); Legion of Honour (officier), Couronne de Belgique (officier); Col 1918; Croix de Guerre (Belgian), 1918; retired from Army, 1921. *Address:* c/o Glyn Mills & Co., Kirkland House, Whitehall, SW1. *Club:* Athenæum.

Died 26 May 1949.

CUMONT, Franz Valery Marie; Professeur à l'Université de Gand, 1892–1910; Conservateur au Musée du Cinquantenaire, Bruxelles, 1899–1912; *b* Alost, Flandre Orientale, 3 Jan. 1868; célibataire. *Educ:* Athénée de Bruxelles; Université, Gand; Université, Bonn; Université, Berlin; Université, Paris; etc. Member of several European Academies. Chargé de faire des conférences à Oxford (Hibbert Trust) en 1901 et en 1906; DLitt hon. causa, Oxford, 1912; Cambridge, 1928; LittD (hon.) Trinity College, Dublin, 1929; Paris, 1929. *Publications:* Textes et Monuments relatifs aux mystères de Mithra, 2 vols, 1894–1901; The Mysteries of Mithras, translated by MacCormack, Chicago and London, 1903; Catalogus codicum astrologorum graecorum 1898–1945 (en collaboration); Studia Pontica, Exploration archéologique du Pont et de l'Arménie (en collaboration avec M. Anderson d'Oxford), 1901–1911; Les religions orientales dans le paganisme romain, Paris, 1906 (4ᵉ éd.), 1929, traduction anglaise, 1911); Recherches sur le manichéisme, 1908–1912; Astrology and Religion in Antiquity, 1912; Etudes syriennes, 1917; Comment la Belgique fut romanisée, 1914 (2ᵉ éd. 1919); After-life in Roman Paganism, 1922; Iuliani imp. epistulae et fragmenta (avec M. Bidez), 1922; Fouilles de Doura-Europos, 1926; L'Egypte des Astrologues, 1937; Les mages hellénisés, Zoroastre, Ostanes, Hystaspe (avecl M. Bidez), 1938; Recherches sur le Symboisme funéraire des Romains, 1942; etc. *Address:* 19 Corso d'Italia, Rome.

Died 19 Aug. 1947.

CUNINGHAME, Sir Thomas Andrew Alexander Montgomery-, of Corsehill, Ayrshire, and Kirktonholm, Lanarkshire; 10th Bt *cr* 1672; DSO 1900; Col retired pay, 1924; late Major, Rifle Brigade; *b* 30 March 1877; *e s* of 9th Bt and Elizabeth (*d* 1936), *d* of E. B. Hartopp of Dalby Hall, Leicester; *S* father, 1897; *m* 1st, 1904, Alice Frances Denison, *d* of late Sir William Des Voeux, GCMG; one *d*; 2nd, Nancy Macaulay, *e d* of late W. S. Foggo, Aberdeen and Coldstream, British Columbia, Canada; two *s. Educ:* Eton; RMC, Sandhurst. Served Natal Field Force (wounded, Vaal Krantz) and Transvaal; afterwards on staff (despatches, Queen's medal, 5 clasps; King's medal, 2 clasps; DSO); DAQMG 5th Division; Irish Command, 1909–12; served European War, 1914–18 (despatches); Commander Legion of Honour; American Distinguished Service Medal; Czechoslovak Croix de Guerre; Commander Greek Order of the Saviour; Maria Theresa Medal (Vienna); 1914 as General Staff Officer, French General Headquarters; Military Attaché, Athens, 1915; Lt-Col, Gen. Staff, 34th Division, 1917; British Representative American Staff Coll. in France, 1918; British Military Representative in Austria, 1919–20; British Military Attaché, Vienna and Prague, 1920–23. As heir-male, claimant to dormant Earldom of Glencairn. *Publication:* Dusty Measure, 1939. *Heir: s* Andrew Malcolm Martin Oliphant, *b* 1929. *Address:* 1a Queen's Gate, SW7. *T:* Western 6804. *Clubs:* Army and Navy; Ayr County.

Died 5 Jan. 1945.

CUNLIFFE, John William, LittD Columbia University, New York City, 1929; Director Emeritus of the School of Journalism at Columbia University, New York City; Director London Branch of the American University Union in Europe, 1918–19; Secretary of American University Union, New York, 1919–26; *b* Bolton, Lancashire, 1865; *m* 1897, Jane Butler Erskine, of Montreal, Canada. *Educ:* Owens College, now the University of Manchester (Shakespeare Scholar and Berkeley Fellow in English Literature). BA University of London, 1884; MA (Classics), 1886; Modern Languages, 1888; DLit, 1893. Assistant Managing Editor, Montreal

Gazette, 1893–99; Lecturer and Associate Professor of English at McGill University, Montreal, up to 1907; Professor and Chairman of the Department of English at the University of Wisconsin, 1907–12. *Publications:* The Influence of Seneca on Elizabethan Tragedy; Early English Classical Tragedies; The Complete Works of George Gascoigne; English literature during the last Half-Century; (with G. R. Lomer) Writing of To-day; Modern English Playwrights; (with Pierre de Bacourt) French of To-day; French Literature during the Last Half Century; Century Readings in English Literature; Century Readings in the Bible; Century Readings in European Literature; Century Readings in the English Novel; Pictured Story of English Literature; English Literature in the Twentieth Century; Leaders of the Victorian Revolution; edited various Elizabethan plays, and contributed to the Cambridge History of English Literature and numerous learned publications; (with A. H. Thorndike) revised (University) edition of the Warner Library (30 vols); editor in chief, Columbia University Course in Literature; (with Margaret Barnard Pickel) Century Readings in Victorian Prose, England in Picture, Song and Story, Pictured Story of English Literature. *Recreations:* canoeing and chess. *Address:* Columbia University, New York City.

Died 18 March 1946.

CUNLIFFE, Sir Robert Neville Henry, 7th Bt *cr* 1759; *b* 8 Feb. 1884; *s* of 5th Bt and Eleanor (*d* 1898), *o d* of Major Egerton Leigh, West Hall, Cheshire; *S* brother, 1916. *Educ:* Rugby; Hertford Coll., Oxford. *Recreations:* shooting, motoring. *Heir: cousin* Cyril Henley, *b* 3 March, 1901. *Address:* 25 St James' Court, Buckingham Gate, SW1. *Clubs:* Union, Queen's; Vancouver (Vancouver).

Died 1 May 1949.

CUNLIFFE-OWEN, Lt-Col F., CMG 1916; late RA; *m* Ethel Beatrice, *d* of late A. J. Bainbridge, Judge, Indian Civil Service. *Educ:* Clifton College, PSC. Served War Office, Military Secretary's Branch and General Staff; Military Attaché, Constantinople; General Staff during European War on four fronts; Civil Administration, Mesopotamia, 1919–22; Refugee Settlement Commission, Greece, 1923–26; served Somaliland, 1903–04; Balkan Wars (with Greek Forces as Military Attaché), 1912–13; European War, 1914–18 (despatches five times); operations in Irak, 1920 (despatches); Greek and Serbian decorations. *Address:* c/o Lloyds Bank (Cox's and King's Branch), 6 Pall Mall, SW1. *Club:* Army and Navy.

Died 10 Jan. 1946.

CUNLIFFE-OWEN, Sir Hugo, 1st Bt *cr* 1920; President British-American Tobacco Co. Ltd; Chairman Cunliffe-Owen Aircraft Ltd, etc; *b* 16 Aug. 1870; *yr s* of late Sir Philip Cunliffe-Owen, KCMG, KCB; *m* 1st, 1918, Helen Elizabeth (*d* 1934), *d* of James Oliver, New York; one *s* two *d*; 2nd, 1935, Mauricia Martha (separated under deed, 1946), *d* of Herbert Shaw, California. *Educ:* Brighton College; Clifton College. Civil Engineer articled to Sir John Wolf Barry. *Recreations:* racing, shooting. *Heir: s* Dudley Herbert [*b* 1923; *m* 1947, Mary Maud, *e d* of R. R. Redgrave]. *Address:* Sunningdale Park, Ascot. *T:* Ascot 157. *Clubs:* White's, St James'.

Died 14 Dec. 1947.

CUNNING, Joseph, MB BS (Melbourne), FRCS Eng., FRACS, Australia; Member of Dorking and Horley Rural District Council; late Senior Surgeon to the Royal Free Hospital; late Surgeon to the Cancer Hospital; late Surgeon to the Victoria Hospital for Children; Consulting Surgeon to the Thames Ditton Cottage Hospital; late President of the Australian and New Zealand Association of Medical Men in England; *b* 29 March 1872; *s* of James Erskine Cunning; *m* Annie Broomhall, *d* of E. C. Thin; two *s* one *d. Educ:* Ballarat; University of Melbourne; St Bartholomew's Hospital. 1st Class Honours Physiology, University of Melbourne;

final honours in Medicine and Surgery. House Surgeon and House Physician Melbourne Hospital, 1895–96; Senior Resident Medical Officer Royal Free Hospital, 1901–04. *Publications:* Aids to Surgery, 1904, third edition, 1913; numerous contributions to medical journals. *Recreations:* golf, fishing. *Address:* Broome Park, Betchworth, Surrey. *T:* Betchworth 3333. *Clubs:* Ski Club of Great Britain; Walton Heath Golf (Epsom).

Died 29 July 1948.

CUNNINGHAM, Lt-Col Aylmer Basil, CBE 1919; DSO 1916; late RE; *b* 1879. Employed in Ashanti and N Territories, 1908–11; served European War, 1915–18 (despatches, DSO, Brevet Lt-Col, CBE Order of El Nahda of the Hedjaz and of the Nile of Egypt); retired pay, 1928. *Address:* Kitale, Kenya Colony. *Club:* Constitutional.

Died 28 Oct. 1940.

CUNNINGHAM, Rev. Bertram Keir, OBE 1919; *b* 26 March 1871; *y s* of late George Miller-Cunningham, CE, of Leithenhopes, Peeblesshire. *Educ:* Marlborough College; Trinity College, Cambridge. BA 1893. Joined the Staff of the Cambridge University Mission to Delhi, N India, and was made a lay-reader in the Lahore diocese; returned in 1897, and was ordained to the curacy of St Anne's, Wandsworth, SW; Hon. Canon of Winchester Cathedral, 1908; Warden of the Bishops' Hostel, Farnham, 1900–17; TCF, 1917–19; Hon. CF 1919; Principal of the Clergy Training School, Westcott House, Cambridge, 1919–44; Chaplain to the King, 1920–44; Examining Chaplain to the Bishop of Exeter, 1917; and Carlisle, 1920; Commissary to Bishop of Tinnevelly, 1939. *Address:* 112 Comiston Drive, Edinburgh. *Club:* Oxford and Cambridge.

Died 10 Sept. 1944.

CUNNINGHAM, Brysson, DSc, BE, FRSE, MInstCE; chartered civil engineer; prior to retirement in 1940, Consultant to a number of public bodies, including the Kent County Council, Dartford River Wall Commissioners, Dartford and Crayford Navigation Commissioners, Canvey Island Commissioners, Darenth Valley Main Sewerage Board, Gosport Borough Council and Waterford Harbour Commissioners; formerly partner in Case & Cunningham, Consulting Engineers, Westminster; *b* Stoneycroft, Liverpool, 1868; *s* of late John Cunningham; *m* Annie, *d* of late Robert Isaac; one *s* two *d*. *Educ:* Liverpool College. Medallist, City and Guilds of London Institute, 1889; and Institute of Transport, 1923; Exhibitioner, Royal University of Ireland, 1893; BE 1895; DSc Queen's University, Belfast, 1915; engaged on important dock construction works at Liverpool, 1890–1906; Resident Engineer, London and India Docks Company, and Port of London Authority (Headquarters Staff), 1906–21; Lecturer on Waterways, Harbours and Docks at Univ. College, London, 1921–36; Lecturer on Port Planning, Architectural Association's School of Planning and Research for National Development, 1936–38; Member (1909–21) and Vice-Chairman (1917–21) of Advisory Sub-Committee of LCC School of Engineering, Poplar; Co-opted on Awards Committee, Institute of Marine Engineers, 1918–21; and Education and Examinations Committees, Institute of Transport, 1923–38; Examiner for the latter on Ports and Inland Water Transport, 1929–42; Member of Gen. Cttee of Br. Assoc. and of Research Cttee on Inland Water Survey, 1932–35; Member of House of Laymen, Province of Canterbury, and of Representative Church Council, 1919–20. Has lectured to scientific societies at various places in UK, USA, and Canada. *Publications:* Text-book on Building Construction (third edition, 1923); Principles and Practice of Dock Engineering (third edition, 1922); Principles and Practice of Harbour Engineering (third edition, 1927); Dock and Harbour Engineer's Reference Book (second edition, 1923); Cargo Handling at Ports (second edition, 1926); Port Administration and Operation, 1925; Port Economics, 1926; Port Studies,

1928; Revision and enlargement of Coast Erosion and Protection (by late Prof. Matthews), 1934; Editor of The Dock and Harbour Authority, 1920–1926, and 1937–1946; Associate Editor, Engineer's Year Book, 1910–1946; papers to congresses. *Recreation:* extensive travel. *Address:* Alwyn, 17 Jevington Gardens, Eastbourne, Sussex.

Died 31 July 1950.

CUNNINGHAM, George Charles, CBE 1944; *b* 13 Jan. 1883; *s* of late Alexander Cunningham, Edinburgh; *m* 1st, 1908, Sophie, *d* of late Duncan Whyte, Colintraive; one *s* two *d*; 2nd, 1931, Mary Alice, *d* of late Capt. A. G. Bridges, Leith; 3rd, 1942, Margaret Whitelaw Smellie, *d* of late Robert Grant, Edinburgh. *Educ:* in London; Edinburgh Univ. (Prizeman in Scots Law and Conveyancing). Solicitor, 1904; entered Estate Duty Office, Edinburgh, 1906; Asst Principal Clerk, 1920; Principal Clerk, 1922; Registrar of Death Duties for Scotland, 1924–48; retired 1948. *Publications:* articles on Estate and other Death Duties in Encyclopædia of the Laws of Scotland in 1928 and subsequent editions. *Recreations:* golf, literature. *Address:* 81 Grange Loan, Edinburgh. *T:* Edinburgh 43910.

Died 26 Feb. 1950.

CUNNINGHAM, Brig.-Gen. George Glencairn, CB 1900; CBE 1919; DSO 1896; *b* 24 July 1862; 2nd *s* of late Maj. William Cunningham, MSC; *m* 1902, Dorothy L., *d* of late R. Yeo of Drayton House, Ealing; one *s*. *Educ:* Wellington; Sandhurst. Entered (Duke of Cornwall's LI) Army, 1881; Colonel, 1900; served Egyptian War, 1882, including Magfar, Tel-el-Mahuta, Kassassin (twice wounded, despatches, medal, brevet of Major, 5th class Medjidie, and Khedive's star); Nile Expedition, 1884–85 (clasp); Egyptian Army Soudan Frontier Field Force, 1887–89, including Sarras, Arguin, Toski (wounded, despatches, 4th cl. Osmanieh); commanded Unyoro Expedition, 1895 (wounded, despatches, medal); commanded Nandi Expedition, 1895–96 (despatches, DSO); Assistant-Commissioner and Commandant of Troops, Uganda, 1895–96; served Niger-Soudan campaign, 1897, as 2nd in command (despatches, brevet of Lieut-Col, medal); Sierra Leone Rising, 1898–99; in command of Mendiland and Karene columns and Protectorate Expedition; commanded West African Regiment, 1899 (despatches, brevet of Colonel, clasp); Acting AAG Third Division South Africa, and in command of a Brigade, 1900–02 (despatches, CB, 2 medals); Brig.-Gen. Plymouth General Reserve, 1914–16; Special employment BEF France, 1917; Base Commandant, Brest, 1918 (despatches, CBE, Commander, Legion of Honour, 2 medals); Mayor, Hythe, Kent, 1927–29. *Address:* Boyne House, Cannongate Road, Hythe, Kent. *T:* Hythe 67083. *Club:* Junior United Service.

Died 21 July 1943.

CUNNINGHAM, Sir George M.; see Miller-Cunningham.

CUNNINGHAM, Rev. Canon John Manstead; Canon Residentiary of Ripon Cathedral since 1937; Examining Chaplain to Bishop of Ripon since 1937; Chairman of Skellfield School; Hon. Treasurer of Ripon, Wakefield and Bradford Diocesan Training College, etc.; Member Council of Church Training Colleges, and of Consultative Committee of National Society; Member of Education Committee, North Riding CC, 1938; Director of Religious Education for Diocese of Ripon, 1944; *b* 29 Oct. 1879; *s* of Rev. John and Susannah Maltby Cunningham; *m* 1906, Katie Elizabeth Butler; one *d*. *Educ:* Magdalen College Schools, Brackley and Oxford; Lincoln College, Oxford; BA 1901 (Aegrotat, Modern History); MA 1904; Leeds Clergy School. Curate of King's Norton, Birmingham, 1902–09; Vicar of Littleover, Derby, 1909–18; Organising Secretary (CMS) for Dioceses of York and Sheffield, 1918–19; Northern Provincial Secretary

(CMS), 1919–22; Vicar of St Peter's, Harrogate, 1922–37; Hon. Canon of Ripon, 1935; Proctor in Convocation, 1936. *Publications:* Adventure for Christ, 1920; The Story of St Peter's, Harrogate, 1934; The Church, The Children, and The Schools, Nos II and III, 1939; One hundred years ago (The Church in the West Riding 1836–1856). *Recreations:* fishing, gardening, travelling. *Address:* Canons Lodge, Ripon. *T:* Ripon 465.

Died 17 Nov. 1947.

CUNNINGHAM, John Richard, CIE, 1921; MA; LLD; Vidya-bisarad, FSA Scotland; *b* 18 Feb. 1876; *s* of late Dr John Cunningham, of Campbeltown. *Educ:* private; Grammar School, Campbeltown; studied Arts, Science, and Law in University, St Andrews and University, Edinburgh. Qualified as a Solicitor; was Professor of English Language and Literature, Pachiappa's College, Madras; Professor of English and Philosophy, Presidency College, Calcutta; Director of Public Instruction in Assam and for some time Member of Public Service Commission, Delhi and Simla; retired 1931; on special duty, Assam University Enquiry, 1935–36. *Recreations:* golf, gardening, archæology. *Address:* Askomil End, Campbeltown, Argyll. *T:* Campbeltown 2267.

Died 23 May 1942.

CUNNINGHAM, Lt-Col John Sydney, DSO 1917; JP Roxburghshire; retired pay; *b* 6 Dec. 1876; *s* of John Archibald Cunningham and Kate Hitchcock. *Educ:* Highgate School. 2nd Lieut 4th Black Watch, 1898; 2nd Lieut Middlesex Regt, 1900; served South African War, 1902 (Queen's medal); European War, 1914–18 (three medals, DSO, Bt Lt-Col, despatches, Order of the Nile). *Publications:* articles to Regimental Journal and the Field. *Recreations:* public work, Town Council, etc. *Address:* Darnick, Melrose, Scotland. *T:* Melrose 104.

Died 21 Jan. 1943.

CUNNINGHAM, Rt Hon. Samuel; PC 1920; Senator of Northern Ireland; *b* Belfast, 14 Oct. 1862; *s* of Josias Cunningham, of Glencairn, Belfast, and Jane Agnes, *d* of James Davis, solicitor, Belfast; *m* 1898, Janet Muir Knox, (*d* 1941), *d* of Dunlop McCosh, Solicitor, Dalry, Ayrshire; four *s. Educ:* RBAI Belfast Academy; Merchiston Castle, Edinburgh. *Recreation:* gardening. *Address:* Fernhill, Belfast. *T:* Belfast 44177. *Clubs:* Ulster Reform, Union, Belfast.

Died 23 Aug. 1946.

CUNYNGHAM, Major Sir Colin Keith Dick-, 11th Bt *cr* 1707; 9th Bt *cr* 1669; of Prestonfield and Lamburghtoun; Black Watch; *b* 3 March 1908; *s* of late Capt. Robert Henry Dick-Cunyngham, 21st Lancers, *s* of 9th Bt; *S* uncle, 1922. ADC to Commander 4th Division, Colchester, 1935–37 and 1938–39; Capt., 1938. *Heir:* none. *Address:* St Mary's Grange, Easthorpe, Essex. *T:* Marks Tey 103. *Clubs:* Army and Navy; New, Edinburgh.

Died 31 Oct. 1941 (ext).

CUNYNGHAME, Sir Percy, 10th Bt (of Milancraig), 1702; OBE; DL; JP; *b* 21 Feb. 1867; *s* of 9th Bt and Jessica, *d* of Rev. W. H. Bloxsome; *S* father, 1900; *m* 1903, Maud Albinia Margaret, *o d* of late Major Selwyn-Payne, Badgeworth Court, Gloucester; two *s.* A Lt-Col late 5th Bn Duke of Cambridge's Own (Middlesex Regt); formerly on Staff of H. H. Sir Charles Brooke, GCMG, Rajah of Sarawak, as Resident, 1st Div. (acted as officer and administering the Govt); retired, 1909; JP, DL, Co. of London; served European War (despatches twice). *Recreations:* shooting, fishing. *Heir:* s Henry David St Leger Brooke Selwyn, *b* 7 Feb. 1905. *Address:* 55 Onslow Square, SW7. *T:* Kensington 7172. *Club:* Carlton.

Died 7 Jan. 1941.

CURLE, James, Writer to the Signet; JP; LLD; FSA; FSA Scot.; Member of the Archæological Institute of the German Empire; *b* 27 March 1862; *e s* of Alexander Curle and Christian, *o d* of Sir James Anderson, Kt, MP; *m* 1902, Alice Mary Blanchette (*d* 1940), *o d* of Col Herbert A. T. Nepean, Indian Staff Corps; three *d. Educ:* Fettes College. Member of County Council, Roxburghshire, 1889–1929; a trustee for the National Library of Scotland; Member of Royal Commission on Ancient Monuments for Scotland, of Ancient Monuments Board for Scotland, and Royal Company of Archers; a Vice-President of Society for promotion of Roman Studies; Rhind Lecturer in Archæology, 1907; directed the excavation of the Roman Fort, Trimontium, at Newstead, near Melrose, 1905–10. *Publications:* A Roman Frontier Post and its People, 1911; various contributions to archæological literature. *Address:* St Cuthberts, Melrose. *Clubs:* New, Edinburgh.

Died 1 March 1944.

CURLING, Rev. Canon Thomas Higham, MA; Vicar of Halstead, 1912–44; Chaplain to the Bishop of Colchester; Surrogate; Clerk to the Chapter of Chelmsford Cathedral, 1933–44; Hon. Secretary, Diocesan Board of Patronage, 1935; Member of Cathedral Council, 1935; *b* 25 Aug. 1872; *s* of John Harris Curling and Emily Higham of Perry Court, Faversham, Kent; *m* 1907, Dorothy Buckley Elliot; three *s. Educ:* Queen Elizabeth's Grammar School, Faversham; Wadham College, Oxford (Theological School, 3rd Class Honours). Deacon, 1895; Priest, 1897; Assistant Master, Kent House School, Eastbourne, 1894–96; Curate of Eastbourne Parish Church, 1895–99; St Mark, South Norwood, 1899–1901; Rector of Bradwell next Coggeshall, 1901–06; Diocesan Inspector of Schools, 1901–06; Curate of St Mary-at-the-Walls, Colchester, 1906–10; Vicar of St Osyth, 1910–12; Chaplain to High Sheriff of Essex, 1916; Rural Dean of Halstead and Hedingham, 1925–35; Hon. Secretary Essex Archæological Society, 1903–23; Hon. Curator of the Museum, Colchester Castle, since 1918; Hon. Canon of Chelmsford, St Ethelburga Abbess, 1931. *Publications:* Handbook to St Osyth; several articles; The Story of St Andrew's Church, Halstead. *Address:* The Vicarage, Halstead, Essex.

Died 13 Nov. 1944.

CURREY, Henry Latham; Director SA Mutual Life Assurance Society; Cape Portland Cement Company; Local Director Barclays Bank DC & O; *b* 1863; *e s* of John B. Currey; *m* Ethelreda, *d* of C. A. Fairbridge; three *s* two *d. Educ:* King's School, Canterbury. Cape Civil Service, 1880–86; Secretary Consolidated Gold Fields of South Africa, Ltd, Johannesburg, 1887–94; called to Bar, Inner Temple, 1897; Member of the House of Assembly for George in the Cape Parliament, 1902–10; Minister without Portfolio, 1908–10; MLA for George in the Union Parliament of S Africa, 1910–15; Private Secretary to Right Hon. J. X. Merriman, 1883–85, and to Right Hon. C. J. Rhodes, 1891; Member of the Civil Service Commission (Cape), 1904–05. *Recreation:* golf. *Address:* Woodford, Kenilworth, S Africa. *T:* 7.1291. *Clubs:* Civil Service, Capetown.

Died Jan. 1945.

CURRIE, Maj. Hon. Sir Alan; *see* Currie, Maj. Hon. Sir H. A.

CURRIE, Brig.-Gen. Arthur Cecil, CB 1918; CMG 1916; late RA; *s* of late Gen. A. A. Currie, CB; *m* Amy, 4th *d* of late Col T. T. Haggard, RA; one *s* two *d. Educ:* Haileybury; RMA Woolwich. Served Burma, 1885–86; S Africa, 1899–1901 (Queen's medal 3 clasps); European War, 1914–18 (despatches, CMG, CB); retired pay, 1920. *Address:* The Breaches, Westerham, Kent.

Died 20 April 1942.

CURRIE, George Welsh; Member of House of Laity representing London in Church Assembly; Member of Central Board of Finance of C of E, and of Governing Body of Imperial College of Science and Technology; a Church Commissioner since 1948; *b* 1870; *y s* of late Rev. James Currie, MA, LLD, Edinburgh, and Jane Lyall, *y d* of late George Key, Berryfauld, St Vigeans; *m* 1901, Georgina Stuart, *y d* of late Lt-Col Charles Stuart Silver, Halifax, NS. Senior President of the Diagnostic Society and Secretary of the Boat Club at Edinburgh University; President of the Scottish Society of Economists; Treasurer Tariff Reform League, Scotland, 1906; Lay Elector in the Diocese of Edinburgh; MP (U) Leith Burghs, 1914–18; President of Chelsea Labour Party, 1936–39; Central National Service Com., 1917; Wrenbury Committee on Company Acts; Chairman National Health Investigation Committee, 1916; Central War Aims Committee; Munitions Contract Board, 1917; Adviser and Assistant Comptroller Ministry of Munitions, 1918; Government Arsenals Committee, 1918; Central Profiteering Committee, 1920; Government Member Dye Stuffs Advisory Committee, 1921; Chairman Departmental Inquiry Building Workmen's Dwellings in Scotland, 1921; Life Governor Corporation of Sons of Clergy, 1921; Guildford Diocesan Conference; Hon. Treasurer Mothers Union, 1924–46; Chairman, Chelsea Housing Association, 1925; a Commissioner under the Merchandise Marks Act, 1926; Chairman, Poor Clergy Relief Corporation, 1932–39; Chairman, Bishop of London's Housing Committee; Treasurer, Church Patronage Protection Committee, 1931; Chairman Additional Curates Society, 1933–40; Member of Church of England Pensions Board, 1935–; Member (Lab) LCC for Central Wandsworth, 1935–40. *Address:* Pinehurst Heights, Witley, Surrey. *T:* Wormley 45. *Clubs:* Athenæum; University (Edinburgh); Royal and Ancient (St Andrews).

Died 3 June 1950.

CURRIE, Major Hon. Sir (Henry) Alan, Kt 1937; MC; a Director of Equity Trustees Co.; *b* Geelong, 6 June 1868; *s* of late John Lang Currie, Larra, Camperdown, Victoria; *m* 1902, Muriel, *d* of late Albert Miller, Toorak, Victoria. *Educ:* Church of England Grammar School, Melbourne; University of Melbourne. Qualified as a civil engineer; served European War, RFA, BEF, 1915–19 (wounded, MC); MLC Victoria, 1928–40; Chairman Victoria Racing Club since 1936. *Address:* Ercildoune, Burrumbeet, Victoria, Australia.

Died 10 Oct. 1942.

CURRIE, Sir James Thomson, KCB 1919; *b* 23 June 1868; *s* of late James Geddes Currie, Edinburgh; *m* 1895, Mary Emily, *d* of late G. R. Payter, Sontapier, Bengal; one *s* two *d. Educ:* George Watson's College and University, Edinburgh. Assistant Surveyor-General of Supply, War Office, 1917–19; War Office Representative on the American Board, 1917–18, and Chairman of Army Clothing Committee, War Office, 1917–19; Personal Assistant to the Minister of Munitions, 1919–20; formerly Director Hambro's Bank, Ltd, British Mexican Petroleum Co., President Lago Petroleum Corporation. *Recreation:* golf. *Address:* c/o Lloyds Bank, Ltd, 71 Lombard Street, EC. *Clubs:* City of London, Caledonian.

Died 5 Feb. 1943.

CURRIE, Prof. John Ronald, MA, MD, DPH, FRCPE; LLD; Captain RAMC; MOH (retd) County of Bute and Burgh of Rothesay; *b* Ayr; *s* of late Donald Currie, Alloway Place, Ayr; *m* 1901, Sara Jean, *d* of late William Browne of Parton, Kirkcudbrightshire; one *d. Educ:* Ayr Academy; Lincoln College, Oxford. Edinburgh University, MA, 1891; University of Oxford, scholar and exhibitioner, First Class in Classical Honour Moderations, BA, 1896, MA, 1910; University of Glasgow, MB ChB with commendation, 1898, MD

with high commendation 1910, LLD, 1940; University of Birmingham, DPH, 1904; RCP Edinburgh, Member, 1922; Fellow, 1934. Resident House Physician and House Surgeon, Glasgow Royal Infirmary; Assistant Physician, Belvidere Fever Hospital, Glasgow; Physician, Glasgow Smallpox Hospital; Assistant Medical Investigator, Royal Commission on Poor-Laws; MOH City of Chester; MOH County of Fife; Medical Officer, Scottish Insurance Commission, 1912; War Service with BEF, Italy and France; Specialist Sanitary Officer, Taranto and Dunkirk, also Scottish and Southern Commands; Medical Officer, Scottish Board of Health, 1919; Professor of Preventive Medicine, Queen's University, Kingston, Ontario, Canada, 1922; Prof. of Public Health, University of Glasgow, 1923. *Publications:* Contributions to scientific journals; The Mustering of Medical Service in Scotland during the War, 1922; Text-Book of Hygiene, 1930; Manual of Public Health; Vol. I Laboratory Practice, 1936, Vol. II Hygiene, 1938; 2nd Edition (Currie and Mearns), 1945; 3rd Edition, 1947. *Recreations:* rowing, Oxford, fishing recently. *Address:* 40 Inverleith Place, Edinburgh 4. *T:* Edinburgh 84883. *Club:* Western (Glasgow).

Died 13 April 1949.

CURRIE, Patrick, CMG, 1919; DSO 1916; Col retd; Headmaster, New Farm State School, Brisbane; *b* 3 Aug. 1883; *s* of late D. Currie; *m* 1911, Kitty Gallwey. Served European War, 1914–19 (wounded twice, despatches twice, DSO, CMG, French Croix de Guerre). Served War of 1939–45, Asst O.-C. Troops, Queen Elizabeth and Aquitania, Middle East and Java; O.-C. Troops, Taroona and Awkui, New Guinea (twenty-six return voyages in all). *Address:* Marcinelle, Westacott Street, Toombul, Brisbane.

Died 7 Jan. 1949.

CURRIE, Sir Walter Louis Rackham, 4th Bt *cr* 1846; *b* 16 March 1856; *s* of 2nd Bt and Eliza Reeve, *d* of Matthew Rackham; *S* brother, 1930; *m* 1892, Bertha, *d* of late T. A. Mitford Freeman; one *s. Educ:* Haileybury; Keble College, Oxford. *Heir: s* Walter Mordaunt Cyril, *b* 3 June 1894. *Address:* Saxonholme, Newhaven, Sussex.

Died 5 Feb. 1941.

CURRIN, Richard William, DSO 1916; late Commanding 7th Batt. S African Coast Defence Corps; *b* 1872; *s* of late R. and Mrs E. J. Currin of East London, South Africa; *m* Ethel Cawood, 4th *d* of William and Johanna Glass of East London, and *g d* of late Sir Thomas Cawood; no *c. Educ:* Kleinemonde, Bathurst, SA. Farmed for many years in Bathurst district, SA, afterwards being connected with mining in Johannesburg as Compound Manager at New Rietfontein Estate Gold Mining Company; was in Johannesburg and took active part in Jamieson Raid under Reform Committee; served in Bechuanaland, 1897, with Kaffrarian Rifles, also through the Boer War, 1899–1902, and German South-West Africa as Capt. Commanding Company; reverted to 2nd Lieut and was sent over to England by Imperial Govt, 1915, and posted to 13th York and Lancs; went with them to Egypt, Dec. 1915, and to France, 1916 (DSO and bar, despatches); promoted to Captain before going to Egypt, and Major, 1916; Lt-Col 1917; commanded 8th Sherwood Foresters; commanded Kaffrarian Rifles, East London, South Africa, 1921–25; commanded 1st S African Infantry Brigade; 1925–31; on the outbreak of war, 1939, was appointed to command the Police Reserve, then the National Volunteer Brigade; Vice-Chairman British Empire Service League, 1937–38. *Recreations:* member of Algoa Rowing Club, and rowed many races on Zwantkops River, winning number of medals; capsized on one occasion and swam for 45 minutes with Coxswain (Nevay) on back and saved him. *Address:* 4 Albany Street, East London, South Africa. *Clubs:* Comrades, Kaffrarian Rifles Offices, East London.

Died 12 June 1942.

CURTEIS, Col Cyril Samuel Sackville, CMG 1919; DSO 1916; late RA; *b* 15 March 1874; *e s* of late Rev. Thomas Samuel Curteis, Rector of Sevenoaks; *m* Mabel de Stuteville, *d* of late William Easton of New York; three *s*. Served European War, Belgium and France, 1914–18, with 7th Division, Sept. 1914. Feb. 1915; subsequently commanding 25 SB, RGA, 1915–17; Commandant Fourth Army Artillery School, 1917; Commanding 83rd Brigade, RGA, 1917–18 (DSO, Bt Lt-Col, CMG, French Croix de Guerre, despatches six times, French citation); CRA, Malta, 1929–31; retired pay, 1931.

Died 8 Oct. 1943.

CURTIN, Rt Hon. John; PC 1942; Prime Minister of Australia since 1941; Minister of Defence since 1942; Minister of Defence Co-ordination, 1941–42; Chairman Advisory War Council since 1941; *b* 8 Jan. 1885; *s* of John Curtin and Katherine Bourke; *m* 1917, Elsie Needham, Hobart, Tasmania; one *s* one *d*. *Educ:* State Schools. Secretary, Timber Workers' Union, Victoria, 1911–15; Editor, Westralian Worker, Perth, 1917–28; Member House of Representatives, 1928–31 and since 1934; Australian Delegate to International Labour Conference, 1924; Member Commonwealth Royal Commission on Family Allowances, 1927–28; State Advocate for Gov. of Western Australia to Commonwealth Grants Commission, 1933–34–1935; Leader of Opposition, Commonwealth Parliament, 1935–41; Member, Western Australian War Industries Committee, 1941. Visited US, Canada, 1944; Prime Ministers' Conference, London, 1944. Freeman of London, 1944; Hon. LLD (Cambridge) 1944. *Publications:* Australia's Economic Crisis, 1931; The Heritage, 1925; various pamphlets for Labour Party. *Recreation:* walking. *Address:* Prime Minister's Lodge, Canberra, ACT; 24 Jarrad Street, Cottesloe, Western Australia. *TA:* Parliament House, Canberra.

Died 5 July 1945.

CURTIS, Sir (Edgar) Francis (Egerton), 5th Bt *cr* 1802; *b* 18 Dec. 1875; *s* of late J. E. Curtis, 3rd *s* of 3rd Bt, and Mary Ella, *d* of Marshall Wallace, Nova Scotia; *S* cousin, 1916; *m* 1st, 1903, Madeline (*d* 1941), 3rd *d* of late C. W. Alexander, ICS; 2nd, 1942, Ethel, *widow* of Arthur L. Warlow and *er d* of late E. C. Barlow. *Educ:* Shrewsbury. *Heir: cousin* Peter, *b* 9 April 1907. *Address:* 52 Pont Street, SW1. *Club:* Royal Thames Yacht.

Died 9 Aug. 1943.

CURTIS, Edmund, MA Oxon; LittD Dublin; Lecky Professor of Modern History, University of Dublin, since 1939; *b* 1881. Professor of Modern History, Univ. of Dublin, 1914–39. *Publications:* Roger of Sicily and the Normans in Lower Italy (1016–1154), 1912; Richard II in Ireland (1394–1395), 1927; A History of Ireland, 1936; A History of Mediæval Ireland, 1938; Calendar of Ormond Deeds, vols i–vi (1172–1603). *Address:* Trinity College, Dublin.

Died 25 March 1943.

CURTIS, Sir Francis; *see* Curtis, Sir E. F. E.

CURTIS, Very Rev. Canon George; Canon of Westminster, 1922–38, Hon. Canon since 1938; *b* 22 Jan. 1861; *s* of Richard Curtis and Mary Jane Wall. *Educ:* St Edmund's College, Ware; St Thomas' Seminary, Hammersmith. Ordained, 1885; Assistant Priest, Our Lady of the Rosary, Marylebone, 1885–99; Rector of SS. Peter and Paul, Clerkenwell, 1899–1917; Rector of St Paul's, Wood Green, 1917–36; Rural Dean, 1917–36; retired, 1936. *Address:* 4 Avenue Road, Herne Bay, Kent. *T:* Herne Bay 1211.

Died 22 April 1948.

CURTIS, Henry, FRCS (retired). Consulting Surgeon to the Metropolitan Hospital, E8. *Address:* c/o The National Provincial Bank, 250 Regent Street, W1.

Died 16 Feb. 1944.

CURTIS, Sir James, KBE 1919; DL Co. Warwick; JP, City of Birmingham and County of Warwick; Solicitor; *b* 5 July 1868; *m* Edith, *d* of George Rowe, of Enfield; one *s* one *d*. Fifty years in Local Government Service; Midland Divisional Food Officer, 1936–41 (unpaid); Advisory (unpaid) to Ministry of Food upon Divisional Organisation since 1941; Chairman Birmingham City Public Entertainments Committee, 1938–40; Vice-Pres. Royal Cripples' Hospital, Birmingham, and of Birmingham Citizens Society; Chairman Highbury Hospital Trust, 1915–36; Governor, Birmingham Blue Coat School; Vice-Chairman of Central Valuation Committee, Ministry of Health, 1928–38, and member of Railway Assessment Authority (England) and of Anglo-Scottish Railway Assessment Authorities; Food Commissioner of the Midland Division, 1917–21; Member of Departmental Committee on Unemployment Insurance; and of Local Government Reconstruction Committee. *Address:* Broadacre, Dorridge, near Birmingham. *Clubs:* Constitutional; Conservative, Birmingham.

Died 29 June 1942.

CURTIS-BENNETT, Sir (Francis) Noel, KCVO 1932 (CVO 1926); late Assistant Secretary HM Treasury; Welfare Adviser to Peter Merchant, Ltd; *b* 14 May 1882; *y s* of late Sir Henry Curtis-Bennett, JP, Chief Metropolitan Magistrate, of Boreham Lodge, nr Chelmsford, Essex, and Emily, *d* of late F. Hughes-Hallett, of Brooke Place, Ashford, Kent; *m* Dorothy, *widow* of Alfred C. Montagu of Essex Villas, Kensington, and The White House, Cowfold, Sussex. *Educ:* Tonbridge; privately. Entered Civil Service, 1905, as Inspector under Board of Agriculture and Fisheries; Private Secretary to Rt Hon. Lord Lucas, Parliamentary Secretary to the Board, 1911–12; transferred to National Health Insurance Commission (Eng.), 1912; Ministry of Health, 1920; Civil Commissioner's Department, 1925; Organising Secretary to Coalfields Distress Funds, 1928; HM Treasury, 1930; President, Secondary Public Schools Boxing Association; The Public Assistance Football League; Vice-President, English Rugby League, National Amateur Wrestling Association and numerous other sporting associations; Chairman, National Playing Fields Assoc., retired 1950; Vice-President, National Assoc. of Boys' Clubs; Vice-Chm. British Olympic Council; Chairman National Sporting Club Executive; Chairman National Council of Social Service Benevolent Fund; Directing Committee, National Institute for the Blind; Vice-Chairman Governing Body of Dockland Settlement; British Sports and Games Assoc.; Chairman Joint Committee of National Trust and Nat. Council of Social Service; represented Great Britain at the First International Congress on Recreation at Los Angeles, 1932; represented HM Government at World Congress on Recreation and Leisure Time, Hamburg, 1936, Rome, 1938, London, 1939; Vice-President British Empire Games, 1934; Member of the International Olympic Committee and International Playing Fields Committee; Member of National Advisory Committee for Physical Recreation; Lord Mayor's Red Cross Committee, 1940; Pres. Brighton and Hove ATC; Governor London Hospital and All Saints Hospital; Governor Hurstpierpoint College; Jubilee Medal, 1935; Coronation Medal, 1937. *Publication:* The Food of the People (preface by Lord Woolton), 1949. *Recreations:* cricket, motoring, swimming. *Address:* Oak Cottage, Telscombe Village, nr Lewes, Sussex. *T:* Rottingdean 8360; 118 Lexham Gdns, Kensington, W8. *T:* Western 8425. *Clubs:* Devonshire, Eccentric, Albany, British Sportsman, National Sporting.

Died 2 Dec. 1950.

CURWEN, Harold Spedding; Printer; Director of the Curwen Press Ltd, Plaistow E13; *b* Upton, Essex, 16 Nov. 1885; 3rd *s* of Joseph Spedding and Mary Jane Curwen; *g s* of Rev. John Curwen; *m* 1st, 1912, Rose Blanche Wenner; 2nd, 1923, Freda Margaret Simpson;

three d; 3rd, 1940, Marie Rasmussen. *Educ:* Abbotsholm School, Derbyshire. Worked at Hand Press at Abbotsholm School, 1902–03; trained in Printing Works of Curwen and Sons Ltd, Plaistow, 1904–05; one year in Leipzig in Printing Works, 1906; commenced work in Printing Works of Curwen and Sons Ltd, 1907; studied design in Printing at LCC Central School of Arts and Crafts; formed separate Company of Printing works as The Curwen Press Ltd, 1933. *Publications:* Processes of Graphic Reproduction; What is Printing. *Recreations:* carpentry and weaving. *Address:* Hope Cottage, Chetnole, near Sherborne, Dorset.

Died 6 May 1949.

CURWEN, Henry, CBE 1922; MB; medical practitioner; *b* 1879; *s* of Robert Ewing Curwen, The Elms, Frome, Somerset; *m* 1909, Marjorie Joan, *d* of late Rev. Xavier Peel Massy, The Rectory, Colinton, Midlothian; two *s* two *d*. *Educ:* Trinity College, Glenalmond; Edinburgh University, MB, ChB 1903; DPH Durham, 1905. Senior Medical Officer, Zanzibar, 1907; Principal Medical Officer, 1915; retired, 1922; 4th Class Order of El Aliyeh, 2nd Class Order of Brilliant Star of Zanzibar. *Address:* Kokstad, Griqualand East, Cape Colony.

Died 14 June 1946.

CURZON, Mrs Edith Basset Penn, CBE 1917; owner of Watermouth Castle, Berrynarbor, N Devon; *b* Umberleigh, N Devon, 1861; *d* of Chas. H. and Mrs Basset; *m* Major Ernest Penn Curzon (*d* 1938), late 18th Hussars, *e s* of Hon. E. G. Curzon; one *s* one *d*. *Educ:* home; Torquay. A good deal of travelling; had convalescent home for men, 1914–16; officers, 1916–19. *Address:* Watermouth, Berrynarbor SO; N Devon.

Died 30 April 1943.

CURZON, Hon. Francis Nathaniel, BA, FRGS; *b* 15 Dec. 1865; *e surv. s* of 4th Baron Scarsdale and Blanche, *d* of J. Pocklington Senhouse; *heir pres.* to 2nd Viscount Scarsdale; *m* 1922, Winifred Phyllis, *d* of Capt. Christian Combe, and of Lady Jane Seymour Combe; one *s* one *d*. *Educ:* Eton; Balliol College, Oxford. For 25 years a Member of the Stock Exchange, first with Chinnery Bros, and afterwards partner in Panmure Gordon & Co.; Director of Westminster Bank; Deputy Chairman, General and Commercial Trust Co., Chairman, National Mutual Life Assurance Society. *Recreations:* shooting, fishing. *Address:* 41 Eaton Place, SW. *T:* Sloane 1519; Hamilton House, Newmarket. *T:* Newmarket 200. *Clubs:* Carlton, Travellers', White's, Royal Automobile; County, Derby.

Died 8 June 1941.

CURZON-HOWE, Captain Leicester Charles Assheton St John, MVO 1935; RN; Naval Attaché British Embassy, Washington, since 1938; *b* 8 July 1894; *s* of late Admiral Hon. Sir A. G. Curzon-Howe, GCVO, KCB, CMG; *m* 1923, Rita Mackenzie; one *d*. *Educ:* RN Colleges, Osborne and Dartmouth. Entered RN 1907; Lieutenant, 1916; served in HMS Inflexible at Falkland Islands, Dardanelles, and Jutland (despatches, promoted, Italian Silver Medal); Lieutenant Commander, 1924; Fleet Signal Officer to C-in-C Mediterranean, 1926–28; Commander, 1928; Staff of Tactical School, 1928–30; RN Staff College, 1931; HMS Curacoa, 1932; HMS Boadicea, 1933; HM Yacht Victoria and Albert, 1934–36; Captain, 1935; commanded HMS Dundee, America and W Indies Station, 1937–38. *Recreations:* cricket, golf, shooting. *Address:* British Embassy, Washington, DC, USA; 16 Somers Crescent, W2. *T:* Paddington 2577. *Clubs:* United Service, MCC; RYS (Hon.).

Died Feb. 1941.

CURZON-SIGGERS, Ven. William, MA; Canon Emeritus, Dunedin; Archdeacon Emeritus, formerly Archdeacon of Southland, NZ; *b* 6 May 1860; *m* 1st, 1887, Annie Brook (*d* 1916); one *s*; 2nd, 1917, Edyth

Maude Hertslet. *Educ:* St Boniface College, Warminster; St Augustine's Coll., Canterbury (Senior Student); University College, Durham. First place in first class in Universities Preliminary Theology for Holy Orders. Ordained to position of Bishop's Vicar of St Alban's Cathedral, Pretoria; Vicar of Ravenswood and of Normanton, North Queensland; Vicar of St Stephen's, Ballarat, Victoria; Vicar of St Matthew's, Dunedin, 1896–1922; formerly Senior Chaplain NZ Forces, rank of Lieut-Col; founder and editor of New Zealand Guardian; President Society Protection of Women and Children and Prison Reform Association; FIGCM. *Publications:* God and Religion of Science and the Bible; Historical Review of the Immortality of the Soul; Scholar's Church Catechism; Teacher's Church Catechism; Lessons on Life of our Lord (3 vols); The Catholic Faith; Lessons for Sundays of the Year; Christianity and Man; Confirmation and its Preparation; Communicant's Manual with Music; Guide to Holy Communion; How to Teach the whole Counsel of God; Travels in Africa; Weekly Freewill Offering Schemes; Mothers' Unions; Reservation, its History and Development in the Anglican Communion; Archidiaconal Charges, 1926–1929. *Address:* 61 London Street, Dunedin, New Zealand. *T:* 10421.

Died 20 Sept. 1947.

CUTHBERTSON, Clive, OBE 1918; FRS 1914; BA; Fellow of University Coll., University of London; FInstP; *b* 29 Nov. 1863; *s* of William G. Cuthbertson and Jane Agnes Lister; *m* 1906, Mildred Maude Mary, *d* of Major Charles H. A. Gower. *Educ:* Trinity College, Glenalmond; University College, Oxford. Entered Indian Civil Service, 1884; Under-Secretary to the Government of Bengal, Financial and Municipal Department, 1888–90; retired, owing to ill-health, 1895; Assistant Private Sec. to late Marquess of Salisbury, 1900–02; Staff-Sergeant, Instructor of Musketry, 1914–15; Temporary Clerk, Foreign Office, 1915–19. *Publications:* A Sketch of the Currency Question, 1896; scientific papers. *Club:* East India and Sports.

Died 16 Nov. 1943.

CUTHBERTSON, Brig.-Gen. Edward Boustead, CMG 1915; MVO 1912; OBE 1942; JP; *b* 13 June 1880; *s* of Thomas Cuthbertson, 8 Devonshire Pl., W; *m* Cecily, *widow* of Captain Hon. G. F. Cumming-Bruce, and *d* of late T. H. Clifton of Lytham Hall, Lancashire, formerly Lady-in-waiting to Princess Christian of Schleswig-Holstein. *Educ:* Marlborough. Argyll and Sutherland Highlanders, 1899; served S African War, 1899–1902; Station Staff Officer (Queen's medal 4 clasps, King's medal 2 clasps); Major in the Isle of Wight Rifles, and Lt-Col commdg 2nd Monmouth Regt; Equerry to Princess Beatrice, 1908–14; served European War, 1914–18 (despatches, CMG); High Sheriff of Surrey, 1928; is a Knight of the Order of Military Merit (Spain), Knight of the Order of Philip the Magnanimous (Hesse), Commander of the Order of Isabel la Catolica (Spain); Awarded the Order of St Stanislaus (Russia) with crossed Swords. *Address:* Jermyns, Romsey, Hants. *T:* Braishfield 24. *Club:* Army and Navy.

Died 13 May 1942.

CUTLER, Elliott Carr, DSM (US); Hon. OBE; MD; Hon. FRCS 1943; Hon. FRCS Edin. 1945; Moseley Professor of Surgery, Harvard Medical School, since 1932; Surgeon-in-Chief, Peter Bent Brigham Hospital, since 1932; Consulting Surgeon, New England Peabody Home for Crippled Children and Children's Hospital, Boston; Civilian Consultant to the Secretary of War since 1946; *b* Bangor, Maine, 30 July 1888; *s* of George Chalmers Cutler and Mary Franklin Wilson; *m* 1919, Caroline Pollard Parker; four *s*. *Educ:* Pierce Grammar School and Volkmann School, Brookline, Mass; Harvard University, Cambridge, Mass (AB 1909); Harvard Medical School, Boston, Mass (MD 1913). Hon. Dr, Univ. of Strasbourg, 1938; Hon. DSc, Univ. of Vermont, 1941; Univ. of Rochester, 1946. Surgical

House Officer, Peter Bent Brigham Hospital, 1913–15; Resident Surgeon, Harvard Unit, American Ambulance Hospital, Paris, 1915; Resident Surgeon, Massachusetts General Hospital, 1915–16; Alumni Assistant in Surgery, Harvard, 1915–16; Voluntary Assistant, Rockefeller Institute, New York, 1916–17; Major, Medical Corps, US Army, 1917–19 (DSM); Instructor in Surgery, Harvard, 1921–24; Resident Surgeon, Peter Bent Brigham Hospital, 1919–21; Associate in Surgery, Peter Bent Brigham Hospital, 1921–24; Chairman, Dept of Surgery and Director of Laboratory of Surg. Research, Harvard, 1922–24; Professor of Surgery, Western Reserve University School of Medicine, 1924–32; Director of Surgical Service, Lakeside Hospital, Cleveland, 1924–32; Chief Surgical Consultant, European Theater of Operations, US Army, 1942–Feb. 1945; Chief of Professional Services Division, European Theater of Operations, US Army, Feb. 1945 to end of war (Legion of Merit, Croix de Guerre with palm, OBE (Hon.), Bronze Star, Oak Leaf Cluster to DSM 1947; Henry Jacob Bigelow Meda of Boston Surgical Soc. 1947). *Publications:* 262. *Recreations:* fishing, old medical books, stamps, golf, tennis. *Address:* 61 Heath Street, Brookline, Mass; (office) 721 Huntington Avenue, Boston 15, Mass. *T:* (office) Longwood 6226. *Clubs:* Harvard (New York); Harvard, Somerset (Boston); Country (Brookline); (Commodore) Vineyard Haven Yacht.

Died 16 Aug. 1947.

CUYLER, Sir George Hallifax, 5th Bt *cr* 1814; *b* 23 April 1876; *s* of 3rd Bt; *S* brother, 1919; *m* 1913, Amy, *d* of late Frederick Gordon, of the Briery, Sunderland, and *widow* of Gordon M'Kenzie. *Educ:* Repton. Late Temporary Captain in the Army. *Heir:* none. *Address:* c/o Westminster Bank, 65 Piccadilly, W1.

Died 30 April 1947 (ext).

D

D'ABERNON, 1st Viscount *cr* 1926, of Stoke D'Abernon; **Edgar Vincent,** PC, 1920; GCB 1926; GCMG 1917; KCMG 1887; FRS 1934; Bt *cr* 1620; 1st Baron *cr* 1914, of Esher; *b* Slinfold, Sussex, 19 Aug. 1857; *y s* of Sir Frederick Vincent, 11th Baronet; *m* 1890, Lady Helen Duncombe, *d* of 1st Earl of Feversham. *Educ:* Eton. Passed examination head of list for appointment of Student Dragoman at Constantinople, 1877, but did not take up appointment; joined Coldstream Guards, 1877; resigned, as Lieutenant, 1882; appointed Private Secry to Lord E. Fitzmaurice, Commissioner for Eastern Roumelia, 1880; Assistant to Her Majesty's Commissioner for Evacuation of Territory ceded to Greece by Turkey, 1881; appointed British, Belgian, and Dutch Representative on Council of Ottoman Public Debt, Constantinople, 1882; President of Council of Ottoman Public Debt, 1883; Financial Adviser to Egyptian Government, 1883–89; Governor of Imperial Ottoman Bank, Constantinople, 1889–97; MP (C) Exeter, 1899–1906; contested Colchester, 1910; Ambassador at Berlin, 1920–26; late Trustee of National Gallery; Trustee Tate Gallery; Chairman of Dominions Royal Trade Commission, 1912–17; Chairman Central Control Board (Liquor Traffic) 1915–20; Chairman Thorough-bred Horse-breeders' Association; Chairman Industrial Fatigue Research Board, 1926; Chairman Lawn Tennis Association; Member Racecourse Betting Control Board, 1928–32; Head of British Economic Mission to Argentine and Brazil, 1929; Chairman Medical Research Council 1929–33. *Publications:* A Grammar of Modern Greek, 1881; An Ambassador of Peace, vols i, ii and iii, 1929–1931; The Eighteenth Decisive Battle of the World, 1931; The Economic Crisis—Its Causes and the Cure, 1931; Portraits and Appreciations, 1931; (joint) Alcohol—its Action on the Human Organism. *Recreations:* racing, golf. *Heir:* none. *Address:* The Manor House, Stoke d'Abernon, Cobham, Surrey. *T:* Cobham 512. *Clubs:* Athenæum, Turf.

Died 1 Nov. 1941 (ext).

DABNEY, Hon. Charles William; retired; *b* Hampden Sydney, Virginia, 19 June 1855; *s* of Robert L. Dabney, Professor Union Seminary, and University Texas, Major Confed. Army, 1861–63, Stonewall Jackson's Chief of Staff and Biographer; *m* 1881, Mary Brent of Paris, Ky; two *d. Educ:* Hampden Sydney College, AB; University of Va.; University of Goettingen, PhD; LLD Yale and Johns Hopkins, University of Cincinnati, etc. Professor Chemistry and Min. Emory and Henry College Va, 1877–78; State Chemist and Director of the Agricultural Experiment Station of North Carolina, at Raleigh, 1881–87 inclusive; President of the University of Tennessee, 1887–1904; University of Cincinnati, 1904–20; Director Tennessee Station, 1887–90; Assist Sec. of Agriculture of the US Wash DC 1893–96; Chairman US Government Exhibits at Tennessee, 1897; Atlanta Expositions, 1895; Juror in Agronomie, Paris Exposition, 1900; Director of Bureau of Southern Education Board, 1902; President of Summer School of South, 1902–04; Member Washington Academy of Science; Officer Public Instruction, France; Chevalier Legion of Honour, France. *Publications:* Reports of N Carolina Agricultural Experiment Station, 1880–1887; on Phosphates, Pyrites, Black Tin in N Carolina, etc.; Reports of Tennessee Agricultural Experiment Station, 1887–1890; The Old College and the New, 1894; The National University, 1897; National Department of Science, 1897; History of Agricultural Education in America; Education and Agriculture, 1899; Condition of Public Schools in Southern States; Thomas Jefferson and Public Education; Educational Principles for the South; Man in the Democracy; The Meaning of the Solid South; Washington, Educationist; The Municipal University; A Star of Hope for Mexico, 1916; Fighting for a New World, 1919; Universal Education in the South, 2 vols, 1936. *Address:* 2917 Digby Avenue, Cincinnati, Ohio. *Clubs:* Authors'; Cosmos, Washington; University Literary, Cincinnati.

Died 15 June 1945.

DA COSTA, Brig.-Gen. Evan Campbell, CMG 1918; DSO 1918; late East Lancashire Regiment; *b* 1871; *y s* of late D. C. Da Costa, Barbados; *m* Jean, *e d* of late William Milne, Aberdeen. *Educ:* Harrow; RMC Sandhurst. Served Chitral Relief Expedition, 1895 (medal and clasp); served South African War, 1900–02 (Queen's medal and three clasps, King's medal and two clasps); European War, 1914–18 (CMG, DSO, despatches, Bt Lt-Col, and Bt Col, 3rd Class Order of the Nile); retired pay, 1924. *Club:* Naval and Military.

Died 24 Aug. 1949.

DA FANO, Mrs C.; *see* Landau, Dorothea.

DAFOE, Allan Roy, OBE 1935; MD; *b* 29 May 1883; *s* of William Allan Dafoe, MD, and Essa Van Deusen; *m* 1914, Bertha Morrison; one *s. Educ:* Madoc, Ont; University of Toronto. Practice of medicine as a general practitioner since 1907; in charge of Dionne quintuplets from their birth, 28 May 1934 until 1942; Hon. Life member of Academy of Medicine, Toronto; of Ontario Medical Association; and of Canadian Medical Association. *Publications:* Dr Dafoe's Guidebook for Mothers, 1936; How to raise your Baby; Through Baby's first years with Dr Dafoe. *Recreation:* student. *Address:* Callander, Ontario, Canada. *Clubs:* Canadian, New York.

Died 2 June 1943.

DAFOE, John Wesley, FRSC; Editor Free Press, Winnipeg, since 1901; Chancellor of University of Manitoba since 1934; *b* Canada, 8 March 1866; *m* 1890, Alice, *d* of late W. G. Parmelee, Ottawa; three *s* four *d.* Joined staff Montreal Star, 1883; first Editor Ottawa Journal, 1886; served on Staff of the Free Press, Winnipeg, 1886–92; Editor the Herald, Montreal, 1892–95; member of Editorial Staff Montreal Star, 1895, 1901; represented Canadian Dept of Public Information at Peace Conference, Paris, 1919; Member of Royal Commission on Dominion Provincial Relations, 1937–39. *Publications:* Over the Canadian Battlefields; Laurier; A Study in Canadian Politics; Clifford Sifton in Relation to His Times; Canada, An American Nation. *Address:* 1325 Wellington Crescent, Winnipeg, Canada. *Clubs:* Manitoba, Winnipeg.

Died 9 Jan. 1944.

DAGGAR, George. MP (Lab) Abertillery Division of Monmonthshire since 1929. *Publication:* Increased Production from the Workers' Point of View. *Address:* 25 High Street, Six Bells, Abertillery, Monmouthshire. *TA:* Miners' Office, Abertillery.

Died 14 Oct. 1950.

DAKERS, A. W., BA; Member of Whitley and Monkseaton UDC since 1935; Chairman, 1942; *b* 11 March 1868; *s* of Robert Dakers, Sedgefield, Co. Durham; *m* 1905, Janet G. Ker, schoolmistress, Newcastle-upon-Tyne. *Educ:* Bede College, Durham. Served as schoolmaster at Ryhope and at Newcastle-upon-Tyne; President of National Federation of Class Teachers, 1905–06; member of Northumberland Education Committee, 1909; BA (London), 1896; Vice-President, National Union of Teachers, 1912–13;

President, 1913–14. *Publication:* School Historical Reader, Hanoverian England. *Address:* Eastleigh, Collywell Bay, Seaton Sluice, Northumberland.

Died 16 Jan. 1947.

DAKIN, Prof. William John, DSc, FLS, FZS; Professor of Zoology, Sydney University, since 1929; *b* Liverpool, 1883; *s* of Wm Dakin, merchant; *m* 1913, C. M. G. Lewis, BSc. *Educ:* University of Liverpool; University of Kiel. Matriculated in Victoria University, England; Bsc, 1st class honours, in Zoology, Liverpool; Scholar in Zoology, University of Liverpool; MSc, 1907; awarded 1851 Exhibition Scholarship, 1907; studied in Germany and Italy, 1907–09. Assistant Lecturer in University of Belfast, 1909; Liverpool, 1910; DSc 1910; Senior Assistant in the Department of Zoology and Comparative Anatomy, University College, University of London, 1912; Professor of Biology in the University of Western Australia, 1913–20; Derby Professor of Zoology, University of Liverpool, 1920; Technical Director of Camouflage for the Commonwealth Government, 1941–45; President of Royal Society of Western Australia, 1913–15. *Publications:* Whalemen Adventurers (history of whaling), new edition, 1938; Text Books on Zoology; Osmotic Pressure and Blood of Fishes; various papers. *Recreations:* music, photography, yachting. *Address:* University, Sydney, NSW. *Club:* Australian (Sydney).

Died 2 April 1950.

DAKYNS, George Doherty, MA; *b* 6 Aug. 1856; *s* of Thomas Henry Dakyns of Rugby; *m* 1883, Augusta, *d* of Francis Field of Oxford; one *s*. *Educ:* Clifton College (Scholar); Magdalen College, Oxford, Demy, 1875–80; BA, 1879; MA, 1882; 2nd cl. Class. Mods; 2nd cl Lit. Hum.; 2nd cl. Modern History. Assistant Master and School House Tutor, High School, Newcastle, Staffs, 1881–89; Headmaster, South Shields High School, 1890–95; Headmaster of Morpeth Grammar School, 1896–1922. *Address:* The White House, Iffley, Oxford.

Died 22 April 1939.

DALAL, Sir Ardeshir Rustomji, KCIE 1946; Kt 1939; Director and Partner, Tata Sons, Limited, Bombay; Director in Charge, Tata Iron and Steel Co., Ltd, since 1931; Director: Andhra Valley Power Supply Co., Ltd; Associated Cement Companies, Ltd; Tata Oil Mills Co., Ltd; Taj Mahal Hotel, Bombay; Tata Chemicals, Ltd, till 1944; *b* 24 April 1884; *e s* of Rustomji Jehangir Dalal and Aimai Dorabji Bomanberam, Bombay; *m* 1912, Mane bai, *y d* of Jamsetji Ardeshir Wadia, Bombay; one *s* two *d*. *Educ:* Elphinstone College, Bombay; St John's College, Cambridge. Entered ICS, 1908; Asst Collector, and Collector, Bombay Pres.; Deputy Secretary, Government of Bombay; member Bombay Legislative Council, 1923; Acting Secretary, Government of Bombay; Acting Secretary, Government of India, Education, Health and Lands Departments; member Indian Legislative Assembly, 1927; Municipal Commissioner, Bombay, 1928–31; President, Rotary Club, Calcutta, 1937–38; Indian Chamber of Commerce, Calcutta, 1938–39, and Indian Science Congress Association, 1941; Member Governor-General's Executive Council, 1944–46. *Recreations:* swimming, shooting. *Address:* Gladhurst, Malabar Hill, Bombay. *TA:* c/o Ironco, Bombay. *T:* Bombay 42326 and 26041. *Clubs:* Royal Western India Turf, Willingdon Sports, Asian (Bombay); Calcutta, Royal Calcutta Turf (Calcutta).

Died 8 Oct. 1949.

DALAL, Sir Dadiba Merwanjee, Kt 1924; CIE 1923; *b* 12 Dec. 1870; *m* 1890; one *s* three *d*. *Educ:* Bombay. High Commissioner for India in the United Kingdom, 1923–24; gave evidence before Chamberlain Currency Commission, 1913; Member of the Committee on Indian Exchange and Currency (1919), and wrote Minority Report; Chairman of Government Securities Rehabilitation Committee Bombay, 1921; Member of

Council of Secretary of State for India, 1921; Delegate for India at the International Economic Conference, Genoa, and Representative for India at the Hague Conference, 1922; Member of Indian Retrenchment Committee, 1922; Delegate for India at the Imperial Economic Conference, 1923. *Recreation:* motoring. *Address:* c/o Imperial Bank of India, 25 Old Broad Street, EC2.

Died 4 March 1941.

DALCROZE, Emile J.; *see* Jaques-Dalcroze.

DALE, Benjamin James, FRAM, Hon. RCM, FRCO; Warden of the Royal Academy of Music, London; Member of Associated Board of the Royal Schools of Music, London; *b* London, 17 July 1885; *s* of Charles James Dale and Frances Ann Hallett, London; *m* Margit Kaspar, Munich. *Educ:* Stationers' Company's School, Hornsey; Oakfield School, Crouch End; Royal Academy of Music, London. Sir Michael Costa Scholar (Composition), RAM, 1902; Charles Mortimer Prize, 1902; Charles Lucas Medal, 1903; RAM Club Prize, 1905; Dove Prize, 1905. Before the war, held several positions as organist in London; interned in Ruhleben Camp, Germany, Nov. 1914–March 1918. *Publications:* Sonata in D minor, Pianoforte; Night Fancies, Pianoforte; Prunella, Pianoforte (also for Orchestra and for Violin and Pianoforte); A Holiday Tune, Pianoforte (also for Orchestra); Sonata in E, for Violin and Pianoforte; Ballade, for Violin and Pianoforte; English Dance, for Violin and Pianoforte (also for Orchestra); Suite in D for Viola and Pianoforte; Phantasy for Viola and Pianoforte; Introduction and Allegro, Six Violas; Romance and Finale, Viola and Orchestra; Before the Paling of the Stars, Chorus and Orchestra; Song of Praise, Chorus and Orchestra; Part-Songs for unaccompanied Choir; Two Shakespeare Songs, for voice and piano; Harmony (Musicianship for Students: Editor, Sir George Dyson). *Address:* 17c Abbey Road, NW8. *T:* Maida Vale 4353. *Club:* Authors'.

Died 30 July 1943.

DALE, Major Claude Henry, CMG 1938; OBE 1919; *b* 13 May 1882. *Educ:* King's College School, Wimbledon; Bedford School; Royal Military College, Sandhurst. Commission in Royal Welch Fusiliers, 1900; Retired' as Captain to Special Reserve Royal Warwickshire Regt; Mobilized for European War; Promoted Major; served on the Staff in France also UK (OBE); demobilized 1919 and finally resigned from Special Reserve in 1922; Deputy Commissioner, 1926, and Commissioner HM Eastern African Dependencies Office, London, 1933–40; Fellow Royal Soc. of Arts. *Address:* Norm, Seagrove Bay, Seaview, Isle of Wight. *Club:* Naval and Military.

Died 29 March 1946.

DALGLIESH, Theodore Irving; *b* Coventry. *Educ:* under Sir E. J. Poynter and A. Legros. One of the original members of the Royal Society of Painter-Etchers; first exhibited at the Academy, 1880. *Address:* Villa Beau-Site, Grasse, Alpes Maritimes, France.

Died 21 March 1941.

DALHOUSIE, 15th Earl of, *cr* 1633; **John Gilbert Ramsay;** Baron Ramsay, 1619; Lord Ramsay, 1663; Baron Ramsay (UK), 1875; late Lieut Scots Guards; *b* 24 July 1904; *e s* of 14th Earl and Lady Mary Adelaide Heathcote Drummond Willoughby, *d* of 1st Earl of Ancaster; *S* father, 1928. *Educ:* Eton. *Heir:* *b* Major Hon. Simon Ramsay, MC. *Address:* Brechin Castle, also Panmure House, Carnoustie, Angus; Dalhousie Castle, Bonnyrigg, Midlothian; 82 Eaton Square, SW1.

Died 3 May 1950.

DALLAS, Lt-Col Alexander Egerton, CMG 1917; OBE 1919; Indian Army, retired; *b* 1869; *m* 1894, Frederica Katherine, *d* of late Capt. William Montagu Leeds; one *d*. Served Burma, 1889–92 (medal with clasp); European War, 1914–17 (despatches, CMG).

Died 16 May 1949.

DALLIN, Dr Cyrus Edwin, AM, NA; Instructor in Sculpture, Massachusetts School of Art, Boston; *b* Springville, Utah, 22 Nov. 1861; English parentage; *s* of Thomas Dallin and Jane Hamer; *m* 1891, Victoria Colonna Murray, three *s*. *Educ:* common schools; École des Beaux Arts, Julian Academy, Paris. Numerous awards in USA and Paris. Member, National Academy of Designs, 1912; won first prize, and awarded contract for Soldiers' and Sailors' Monument, Syracuse, NY, 1907; Member of the Union International des Beaux Arts et des Lettres, Paris, 1913; member National Academy of Arts and Letters, 1916; Fellow National Academy of Arts and Science, 1933; Doctor of Fine Arts, Boston University, 1937; AM, Tuffs College, 1923. *Publication:* American Sculpture, its Present Aspects and Tendencies. *Recreations:* archery, golf, astronomy. *Address:* 69 Oakland Ave, Arlington Heights, Mass. *T:* Arlington 567. *Clubs:* St Botolph, Art, Boston; National Arts, New York.

Died 14 Nov. 1944.

DALLY, John Frederick Halls, MA, MD, BC Cantab; MRCP Lond.; FRSM (Pres. Sect. Hist. of Medicine); Consulting Physician to Mount Vernon Hospital; Senior Physician to St Marylebone and Western General Dispensary and Director of the Children's Supervisory Centre for Rheumatism and Rheumatic Heart Disease; Medical Supt Bromsgrove Emergency Hospital, Worcestershire; Consulting Physician to Sutton War Emergency Hospital, to Philanthropic Society's School, Redhill and to the Shriners Hospital, Montreal; Editor, West London Journal; Vice-President Chelsea Clinical Society; Member of St Marylebone War Committee; late Chairman, Special Neurological Board of Ministry of Pensions; *s* of late Frederick Dally; *m* 1909, Norah Willoughby, *γ d* of late Rev. Peregrine Edward Curtois, MA Cantab, Vicar of Hemingford Grey, Hunts; one *s*. *Educ:* Wolverhampton School; St John's College, Cambridge; St Bartholomew's Hospital; Florence. After graduating and before settling in practice held various resident Hospital appointments, including that of Medical Superintendent of the Royal National Hospital for Consumption, Ventnor. *Publications:* The Diaphragm in Man, 1908; The Comparative Value of Cardiac Remedies, a contribution to the discussion at the International Congress of Medicine, 1913; The Psychology of the Circulation; High Blood Pressure, its Variations and Control, 3rd ed., 1934; Low Blood Pressure, its Causes and Significance, 1928; Blood Pressure, 1931; Low Arterial Pressure, 1939; The Problem of Rheumatism in Relation to the National Health, 1939; Life and Times of Corvisart, 1941; numerous papers to scientific and medical journals. *Recreations:* travel, mountaineering, motoring. *Address:* 93 Harley Street, W1. *T:* Welbeck 7444. *Club:* Savage.

Died 4 Nov. 1944.

DALRYMPLE, Hon. Sir Hew Hamilton, KCVO 1932; HRSA, 1936; JP, DL; *b* 1857; *s* of 10th Earl of Stair, Late Major RS Fusiliers. *Educ:* Harrow. MP (U) Wigtownshire, 1915–18; was 32 years a member of Wigtownshire CC, and Convener, 1914–21; Captain in Royal Company of Archers, King's Bodyguard for Scotland; late Chairman Trustees of National Galleries, Scotland; Vice-Chairman of National Library of Scotland. *Address:* 24 Regent Terrace, Edinburgh 7. *Clubs:* Carlton; New, Edinburgh.

Died 11 July 1945.

DALRYMPLE, Joseph, CMG 1919; OBE 1918; LRCS&P Edinburgh; LRFP&S Glasgow; late Lieut-Colonel, RAMC; *b* 1869; *s* of George Dalrymple, Whitehaven, Cumberland; *m* Nora (*d* 1947), *e d* of late John Stevens, MHR, NZ; no *c*. *Educ:* Saint Bees School; Edinburgh Medical School. Served with Bechuanaland Field Force, Langeberg Rebellion, 1897 (medal and bar); South African War, 1900–01 (Queen's medal five bars); European War, 1914–19 (despatches thrice, CMG, OBE); late Surgeon-Captain South African

Constabulary. *Publications:* Restoration of Sick and Wounded to the Forward Area; Report on the treatment of malaria-infected troops in France. *Address:* c/o Standard Bank of South Africa Ltd 10 Clements Lane, EC4.

Died 17 July 1949.

DALRYMPLE, Col Sir William, KBE 1920; VD; LLD; Director, Anglo-French Exploration Co. Ltd; Chairman, Apex (Coal) Mines, Ltd; Rooiberg Minerals Development Co. Ltd, etc; Director: City Deep GM Co. Ltd, Van Ryn Deep Ltd, Modderfontein Deep Levels Ltd, Modderfontein East Ltd, etc; *b* 20 Sept. 1864; *s* of late William Dalrymple, Stirlingshire; *m* 1896, Isabel Rayner (*d* 1938), Tunbridge Wells; three *s*. *Educ:* Blair Lodge School, Stirlingshire; Dresden; London. Arrived Johannesburg, South Africa, 1888; Member Uitlander Council, 1897–99; Vice-President Chamber of Mines, 1899–1902, 1920, 1929, and 1931; Member Municipal Council, 1901–04; Member Legislative Council, 1907–10; Lieut-Col Commanding Scottish Horse, Transvaal Volunteers, 1902–07; President S African National Rifle Association; Hon. Col Transvaal Scottish 1st and 2nd Battalions (Infantry), Defence Force, SA, and SA Exped. Forces, SW Africa, 1914–15; Hon. Col 4th SAI (Scottish) SA Exped. Forces, France and Egypt, 1915–18; 9th SAI (Sportsmen), East Africa 1916–17; Chairman of Council, University of the Witwatersrand; Chairman, Council of Education, Witwatersrand; Medals: Boer War, Union of South Africa, and General Service (France and Flanders). *Address:* Glenshiel, Westcliffe, Johannesburg, SA. *TA:* Determined, Johannesburg. *Clubs:* Royal Societies, Caledonian; Caledonian United Service, Edinburgh; Rand, Johannesburg; Pretoria, Pretoria.

Died 20 June 1941.

D'ALTON, Rt Rev. Edward A., LLD, MRIA; Parish Priest of Ballinrobe since 1911; Vicar Forane of Ballinrobe deanery; Canon Theologian of the Chapter, Archdiocese of Tuam; Domestic Prelate to the Pope, 1921; Dean of Tuam and Vicar-General, 1930; *b* Lavallyroe, Co. Mayo, Nov. 1860. *Educ:* St Jarlath's College, Tuam; Maynooth College. Priest, 1887; served as curate in the parishes of Cong, Balla, and Athenry; Member of the Governing Body of University College, Galway, since 1908; LLD (Hon.) 1909; Senator of National University, 1914; Member of Galway Archæological Society; Fellow of the Royal Society of Antiquaries of Ireland; Member of the Royal Irish Academy since 1904. *Publications:* A History of Ireland from the earliest Times to the Present Day, 8 vols, 1910–1924; History of the Archdiocese of Tuam, 2 vols, 1928; many articles in reviews. *Recreations:* reading and foreign travel. *Address:* St Mary's, Ballinrobe. *TA:* Monsignor D'Alton, Ballinrobe.

Died Feb. 1941.

DALTON, Emilie Hilda, (Mrs J. E. Dalton), CBE 1919 (OBE 1918); *b* Charlbury, Oxon, 24 June 1886; *d* of F. T. and S. E. Horniblow; *m* 1941, John E. Dalton, OBE. *Educ:* Oxford High School; Univ. College, Reading. Chief Controller, Queen Mary's Army Auxiliary Corps; Headmistress of Fair Army Auxiliary Corps; Headmistress of Fair Street LCC Women's Evening Institute; HM Staff Inspector for Women's Subjects in Technical Institutions, 1935–42. *Address:* Allendale, Menston-in-Wharfedale, nr Leeds. *Club:* Ex-Service Women's.

Died 2 Jan. 1950.

DALTON, Comdr (E.) Lionel Sydney, DSO 1940; Royal Australian Navy; serving in HMAS Sydney since 1939; *b* 26 Oct. 1902; *s* of E. L. Dalton, Melbourne, Australia; *m* 1928, Margaret, *d* of A. S. Anderson, Inverurie, Scotland; one *s*. *Educ:* Royal Australian Naval College, Jervis Bay, NSW. On loan to Royal Navy, 1920–25; since served in Australian ships in Australian waters and abroad. *Recreations:* golf and tennis; ex-Rugby player. *Address:* Waitovu Street, Mosman, Sydney, NSW, Australia. *T:* XM6632. *Club:* Manly Golf.

Died 20 Nov. 1941.

DALTON, Sir Llewelyn Chisholm, Kt 1938; MA; *b* 21 April 1879; *o s* of late Rev. William Edward Dalton, Vicar of Glynde, Sussex; *m* 1st, 1906, Beatrice Templeton (*d* 1923), *d* of W. B. Cotton; one *s* three *d*; 2nd, 1931, Winifred, *o d* of late Edward Adams. *Educ:* Marlborough; Trinity College, Cambridge, BA (Hist. tripos) 1900; MA 1905. Barrister-at-law, Gray's Inn, 1901; Advocate ORC, 1903; entered Colonial Service, 1901; Legal Assistant Land Settlement Department Orange River Colony; Assistant Resident Magistrate, 1902–10; Registrar, British Guiana, 1910–19; puisne Judge since 1919; has acted on several occasions as Judge, Solicitor-General, Attorney-General, and Chief Justice; Puisne Judge, Gold Coast Colony, 1923–25; Ceylon, 1925–36; Chief Justice, Tanganyika, 1936–40; an official visitor, Internment Camps, Victoria, Australia, under Commonwealth War Dept. *Publications:* Law Reports, British Guiana (editor); Statutory Rules and Orders, British Guiana; The Civil Law of British Guiana; Digest of British Guiana Case Law; an assistant editor Burge's Colonial and Foreign Laws, Vol. IV. *Recreations:* golf, croquet. *Address:* c/o Barclays Bank Ltd, Lewes, Sussex.

Died 4 Jan. 1945.

DALTON, Ormonde Maddock, MA; FSA; Hon. FSA Scot.; FBA; Corr. Member of Société Nationale des Antiquaires de France; late Keeper of the Department of British and Mediæval Antiquities, British Museum; retired, 1927; *b* 1866. *Educ:* Harrow; New College, Oxford. *Publications:* Various Official, on Early Christian, Byzantine and Mediæval Antiquities, and The Treasure of the Oxus; also, Byzantine Art and Archæology; The Letters of Sidonius; East Christian Art; The History of the Franks of Gregory of Tours. *Address:* Holford, Somerset.

Died 2 Feb. 1945.

DALY, Major Denis St George; JP, DL; late joint MFH, Heythrop; *b* 1862; *m* 1896, Rose Zara, 2nd *d* of Albert Brassey, Heythrop Park, Co. Oxford; two *s* three *d*. *Recreations:* hunting and shooting. *Heir: e s* Bowes, Royal Horse Guards [*m* 1927, Diana, *y d* of late Major W. F. and Lady Sybil Lascelles]. *Address:* Over Norton Park, Chipping Norton, Oxon. *T:* Chipping Norton 42. *Clubs:* Naval and Military, Cavalry.

Died 16 April 1942.

DALY, Lt-Col Francis Augustus Bonner, CB 1900; MB, BCh Dip. State Med. Univ. Dublin, FRCSI; *b* 28 May 1855; *s* of Ulick James Daly. Entered Army, 1881; Lieut-Col 1901. Served Egypt, 1882 (medal, Khedive's Star); Soudan Frontier Field Force, 1885–86; Relief of Gordon (despatches); South Africa, 1899–1902 (despatches several times, King's and Queen's medals, 7 clasps, CB). *Address:* Portsea, Victoria, Australia. *Clubs:* University, Dublin; Australian, Melbourne.

Died 8 May 1946.

DALY, Francis Charles, CIE 1914; *b* 22 March 1868; *s* of Richard Mason Daly, Bengal Pilot Service; *m* 1906, Eily Kathleen, *d* of Henry Ramm, of Manchester; one *s* one *d*. *Educ:* Dedham Grammar School. Joined India Police Department, 1887; District Superintendent, 1897; Officiating Deputy Inspector-General, 1908; on Special Duty, 1909–11; Deputy Inspector-General of Police, CID, Bengal, 1913–18; retired 1920. Police Medal, 1911; served Lushai Hills, 1891–92 (medal); play, Who Knows, produced 1930 by Repertory Players. *Address:* c/o Grindlay and Co., 54 Parliament Street, SW1. *Club:* Royal Automobile.

Died 10 Jan. 1945.

DALY, Very Rev. Henry Edward; Privy Chamberlain to the Pope, 1916; retired through ill-health, 1942; *b* London. Assistant Sec. 1904–13; Diocesan Chancellor of Westminster, 1913–23. *Address:* 64 Barrowgate Road, Chiswick, W4.

Died 22 Nov. 1949.

D'AMADE, Albert; Général de Division; Membre du Conseil Supérieur de la Guerre; *b* Toulouse, Haute-Garonne, 24 Dec. 1856; *m* Marie de Ricaumont; one *s* two *d*. *Educ:* La Flèche. École Militaire de Saint-Cyr, 1874–76; Souslieutenant 3rd Tirailleurs; Lieutenant 143ᵉ Infanterie; Ecole Supérieure de Guerre, 1882–84; Campagne du Tonkin, 1885–87; attaché militaire en Chine, 1887–91; Chef de Bataillon, 1894; attaché militaire au quartier gᵃˡ des Forces Britanniques dans la Guerre Sud-Africaine, 1899–1900; attaché militaire à l'Ambassade de France à Londres, 1901–04; Colonel du 77ᵉ; Général de Brigade à La Rochelle; Commandant le Corps de débarquement du Maroc, 1907–09; Commandant la 9ᵉ; division à Orléans, 1910; Comᵗ le 13ᵉ Corps d'Armée, 1911; Commandant le 6ᵉ Corps d'Armée, 1912–14; Commandant l'Armée des Alpes, 1914; Commandant la groupe des divisions Territoriales du Nord, 1914; Commandant le Corps Français d'Orient, 1915; Mission militaire en Russie, 1915; Inspecteur Général du 5ᵉ Arrondissement à Lyon, 1916; Commandant la 10ᵉ Region à Rennes, 1917; Proprietaire Grand Cru Chateau Pontus-Fronsac, Bordeaux. *Address:* Château des Barayroux par Nègrepelisse, Tarn-et-Garonne; Château de Pontus par Fronsac, Gironde, France.

Died 11 Nov. 1941.

D'AMICO INGUANEZ, Baroness Mary Frances Carmen Maria Teresa Sceberras Trigona; 20th Baroness of Diar-il-Bniet *cr* 1350, and Bukana *cr* 1372, and 16th of Castel Cicciano; Premier Noble of Malta; *b* 1865; *d* of 15th Baron of Castel Cicciano, and *great-niece* of 19th Baroness of Diar-il-Bniet and Bukana; *m* 1890, Col A. C. M' Kean, CMG (*d* 1933). *Address:* Casa Inguanez, Notabile, Malta.

Died 26 Dec. 1947.

DAMPIER, Adm. Cecil Frederick, CMG 1919; *b* 1868; *s* of late Rev. A. Dampier; *m* 1913, Barbara Constance Anne, *d* of Walter Giffard, Chillington Hall, Staffs; two *s*. Entered Navy, 1881; retired list, 1922. *Address:* Highfield, Bishops Waltham, Hants. *T:* Bishops Waltham 19. *Club:* United Service.

Died 11 April 1950.

DAMROSCH, Walter; composer and musical director; *b* 30 Jan. 1862; 2nd *s* of Dr Leopold Damrosch, founder of the NY Oratorio Society, NY Symphony Society, etc. etc. Succeeded his father as Conductor of the above Societies and the Metropolitan Opera House, NY, 1885; founded a Wagner Opera Co. 1894, which produced the Nibelungen Trilogy in the United States; elected Conductor NY Philharmonic Society 1902; Conductor NY Symphony Society, 1885–1926; conductor of orchestral radio concerts and orchestral concerts, USA and Canada; Pres. of American Academy of Arts and Letters, 1941–48; member National Institute of Arts and Letters. *Publications:* The Scarlet Letter, Opera in three Acts; Cyrano, Opera in four Acts; Manila Te Deum; Violin Sonata; An Abraham Lincoln Song, for baritone solo, chorus and orchestra; The Man without a Country, opera; The Opera Cloak, opera in one act; Dunkirk, a ballad for baritone solo, chorus and stringed orchestra; My Musical Life, 1923; Songs, etc. *Address:* 168 East 71 Street, New York. *Club:* Century (New York).

Died 22 Dec. 1950.

DANBY, Vice-Adm. (Ret.) Sir Clinton Francis Samuel, KBE 1941; CB 1935; *b* 9 May 1882; *s* of late Rev. C. E. Danby and late S. E. Baddeley; *m* 1st, 1914, late Phyllis Antill-Pockley, Sydney, NSW; two *s* one *d*; 2nd, 1942, Alice Beatrice, widow of Capt. F. M.

Johnson, RN. *Educ:* Littlejohn's School, Greenwich; HMS Britannia. Served as Flag-Lieut to Admiral Sir Richard Porre, Bart, C-in-C The Nore 1912–14; during war in HMS Cleopatra and HM Ships Chatham and Courageous, Flagship of Adm. Sir Trevylyan Napier; Commander of RN Barracks, Chatham, 1919–21; Flag Captain to Adm. Sir Percy Addison, Commanding Australian Squadron 1922–25; Admiralty 1926–28; Commanded HMS Egmont, Malta, 1929–31, and Aircraft Carrier Furious, Home Fleet, 1931–33; Admiral Superintendent of HM Dockyard, Chatham, 1935–42; Commander 1915; Captain, 1921; Rear-Admiral, 1934; Vice-Admiral, 1937; retired list, 1937. *Recreation:* golf. *Address:* The Tower House, East Sutton, Kent. *Club:* United Service.

Died 30 June 1945.

DANCKWERTS, Rear-Adm. Victor Hilary, CMG 1936; RN; Deputy Commander-in-Chief, Eastern Fleet; Director of Plans, Admiralty, 1938–40; *s* of W. O. Danckwerts, KC; *m* 1915, Joyce Middleton; three *s* two *d*. *Educ:* Winchester; HMS Britannia. Served in Royal Navy from 1904; Present at Falkland Island action in HMS Kent, 1914; sinking of German cruiser Dresden, 1915; Captain, 1930; Rear-Admiral, 1940. *Address:* Merton Lodge, Emsworth, Hants. *T:* Emsworth 210. *Club:* United Service.

Died 1 March 1944.

DANDURAND, Rt Hon. Raoul, PC 1941; PC Canada, 1909; KC; LLD; Leader of the Government in the Senate, Canada, 1921–30 and since 1935; *b* Montreal, 4 Nov. 1861; *s* of Oedipe Dandurand, merchant, and Marie M. Roy; *m* Josephine (*d* 1925), 2nd *d* of late Hon. Félix G. Marchand, Prime Minister of Quebec Provincial Government; one *d*. *Educ:* Montreal College; Laval University. Received at the Bar, 1883; QC, 1897; called to Senate, 1898, for the De Lorimier Division; Speaker of the Senate, 1905–09; Minister without Portfolio, Canada, 1921–26 and 1926–30; Knight of Legion of Honour, 1891; Officer, 1907; Commander, 1912; Grand Officer, 1935; Commander of the Belgian Order Pour la Couronne; Grand Cordon de Saint Sava of the Kingdom of the Serbs, Slovenes, and Croats; Grand Cordon de la Pologne Ressuscitée; President, 6th Assembly of the League of Nations; a Liberal. Mrs Dandurand was Vice-President of the National Council of Women, and was made 'Officer d'Académie' by the French Government for her literary attainments. *Publications:* in conjunction with Ch. Lanctot, Treatise on Criminal Law, and a Manual for Justices of the Peace. *Address:* 462 St Catherine's Road, Outremont, Montreal. *Clubs:* Mount Royal, Montreal; Rideau, Ottawa.

Died 11 March 1942.

DANE, Sir Louis William, GCIE 1911; KCIE 1905; CSI 1904; Knight of Order of St John of Jerusalem; ICS, retired; *b* 21 March 1856; 5th *s* of late Richard Martin Dane, MD, CB; *m* 1882, Edith, Dame of Order of St John of Jerusalem, 3rd *d* of late Lieut-Gen. Sir F. B. Norman, KCB; one *s* three *d*. *Educ:* Kingstown School, Ireland. Entered ICS and posted to the Punjab, 1876; Private Secretary to the Lieutenant-Governor, 1879–82; revised the land revenue settlement of the Districts of Gurdaspur 1887–92, and Peshawur 1892–96; besides filling other offices, Chief Secretary to the Punjab Government, 1896–1900; served as Resident Magistrate at Tralee, County Kerry, 1900–01; recalled to India as Resident in Kashmir, 1901; was in charge of the British mission to Kabul, 1904–05; concluded the treaty with Amir Habibullah Khan, 1905; Sirdar-i-Afghanistan, 1905; Secretary to the Government of India in the Foreign Department, 1902–08; Lieut-Governor, Punjab, 1908–13; Chairman of the East India Association, 1925–32; President Thames Barrage Association; Chairman Attock Oil Co. *Address:* 24 Onslow Gardens, SW7. *T:* Kensington 1992.

Died 22 Feb. 1946.

DANGER, Frank Charles, CBE 1920; *b* 6 Aug. 1873; *s* of W. Danger, Liverpool; *m* 1905, Margaret Elizabeth Clarke; one *s*. *Educ:* King William's College, Isle of Man. Liverpool Shipping business, 1890–98; Hoare Miller and Co., East India Merchants, Calcutta, 1898–1922; retired, 1922. *Address:* Threeways, Churt, Farnham, Surrey.

Died 30 April 1943.

DANGIN, François T.; *see* Thureau-Dangin.

DANIEL, Sir Augustus Moore, KBE 1932; MA, MB, ChB; *b* 6 Dec. 1866; *o s* of Edward MacManus Daniel, MD; *m* 1904, Margery K, *d* of late William Welsh; one *s*. *Educ:* Repton School; Trinity College, Cambridge. Formerly JP Yorks, NR, and JP Scarborough; Assistant Director of the British School of Rome, 1906–07; Trustee of National Gallery, 1925–29; Director of the National Gallery, 1929–33; Hon. Associate, RIBA 1929; Hon. LittD Cambridge, 1931; Rede Lecture, 1940. *Address:* 2 Hampstead Hill Gardens, NW3. *T:* Hampstead 3817.

Died 7 Nov. 1950.

DANIEL, Lt-Col Charles James, CBE 1919; DSO 1900; late Loyal North Lancashire Regiment; *b* 3 Nov. 1861; *s* of late Rev. R. Daniel; *m* 1891, Agnes Margaret (*d* 1937), *d* of late Admiral Saumarez, CB; one *s* one *d*. Entered Army, 1882; Captain, 1892; Adjutant, 3rd Batt. The King's Own Royal Lancaster Regiment; served Zhob Valley Expedition, 1884; South Africa, 1900–02 (despatches, Queen's medal 2 clasps, King's medal 2 clasps, DSO); Assistant to Colonel in charge Records, Preston, 1905–16; Lt-Colonel in charge Infantry Record Office, Preston, 1917–19. *Club:* Army and Navy.

Died 3 July 1949.

DANIEL, Lt-Col Edward Yorke, CBE 1918; Secretary, Historical Section, Committee of Imperial Defence, 1914–39; *b* 2 July 1865; *s* of late Rev. R. Daniel; *m* 1899, Agnes (*d* 1934), *d* of Paymaster-in-Chief A. Turner, RN. *Educ:* York. Entered Royal Marine Light Infantry, 1884; Served in Naval Intelligence Department, 1901–10; retired, 1909. *Recreation:* golf. *Clubs:* United Service, Royal Automobile.

Died 26 Jan. 1941.

DANIELL, Mrs J. A. H.; *see* Young, E. H.

DANIELL, Maj.-Gen. Sir John Frederic, KCMG 1919; CMG 1916; late Royal Marine Light Infantry; *b* 20 Dec. 1859; *s* of late Rev. G. F. Daniell, Vicar of Aldingbourne, Sussex; *m* 1887, Constance, *d* of late G. Rosher, of The Knowle, Higham, Kent; one *s*. *Educ:* at home. Joined Royal Marine Light Infantry, 1878; at Staff College, 1885–86; Captain, 1886; served in Naval Intelligence Department, 1888–91; Staff Officer, Portsmouth Division, RM, 1891–96; Major, 1895; served on Instructional Staff, Royal Military Academy, Woolwich, 1898–1902, as Instructor and Professor of Military Topography; Lieut-Colonel, 1901; served in Naval Intelligence Department, 1903–09 (ADNI 1905); was one of British Delegates to International Conference on Wireless Telegraphy at Berlin, 1906; Colonel, 2nd Commandant, Portsmouth Division RM, 1909; Colonel Commandant, Chatham Division RM, 1910; Maj.-Gen. 1912; GOC Troops, West Africa, 1914; retired, 1920; Member of Royal United Service Institution, and Gold Medallist for Essay on Discipline, 1888. *Address:* The White House, Fernhurst, Sussex. *Club:* United Service.

Died 15 Sept. 1943.

DANIELL, Percy John, ScD (Camb.); Professor of Mathematics University of Sheffield since 1923; *b* Valparaiso, Chile, 9 Jan. 1889; *s* of W. J. Daniell; *m* 1914, Nancy Gertrude Hartshorne, Birmingham; two *s* two *d*. *Educ:* King Edward VI School, Birmingham; Trinity College, Cambridge. Senior Wrangler, 1909; Class 1 Nat. Sci. Tripos Part II, 1910; Asst Lecturer Liverpool University, 1911–12; Rayleigh Prizeman, 1912; Student Göttingen University, 1912–13; Asst Professor and then

Professor, Rice Institute, Houston, Texas, 1913–23. *Publications:* papers in scientific periodicals mainly on Stieltjes Integrals. *Recreation:* wireless.

Died 25 May 1946.

DANIELL-BAINBRIDGE, Rev. Howard Gurney; Hon. Priest in Ordinary to the King; *m* 1920, Ella Winifred, *γ d* of Dr Dodsworth, Queen's Gate. *Educ:* Winchester; Trinity College, Oxford; Cuddesden College. Ordained, 1880; MA, 1882; curate of Shepton-Beauchamp, 1880–83; St John Evangelist, Westminster, 1883–90; Priest in Ordinary, 1899; minor Canon and Sacrist of Westminster Abbey, 1890–1900; Precentor of Westminster Abbey, 1899–1909; Rector of Handsworth, Birmingham, 1909–28; Hon. Canon of Birmingham, 1910–28. *Address:* 27 The Close, Salisbury.

Died 26 Nov. 1950.

DANSEY, Lt-Col Sir Claude Edward Marjoribanks, KCMG 1943; CMG 1918; formerly Lancashire Fusiliers and Monmouth Regiment; *b* 1876; *s* of late Lt-Col E. M. Dansey; *m* 1945, Frances G. Rylander. *Educ:* Wellington College. Served Matabele Rebellion, 1896 (medal); Operations against Mohamed Salleh, in Borneo, 1899–1900 (medal); South African War, 1900–02 (despatches, two medals and five clasps); Somaliland (medal and clasp), 1909; European War, 1914–18; Major and Brevet Lt-Col Gen. Staff (despatches); Commander Légion d'Honneur (France); Chev. Ordre Léopold (Belgium). *Address:* Bathampton Manor, Bath. *Club:* Boodle's.

Died 11 June 1947.

DANSEY-BROWNING, Col George; *see* Browning.

DANSON, Rt Rev. Ernest Denny Logie; *b* 14 June 1880; *s* of Very Rev. J. M. Danson, DD, Dean of Aberdeen and Orkney, and Frances Ellen Rees; *m* 1918, Ada Irene Harvey, Murrurundi, NSW. *Educ:* Trinity College, Glenalmond; University of Aberdeen, MA, DD, 1921; Edinburgh Theological College. Ordained, 1906. Curate of Cathedral Church, Dundee, 1906–11; Singapore, 1911–12; Acting Chaplain in Java, 1913–14; Chaplain of Negri Sembilan, FMS, 1914–17; Bishop of Labuan and Sarawak, 1917–31; Assistant Bishop and Canon Residentiary of Carlisle, 1931–38; Assistant Bishop, and Provost of St Mary's Cathedral, Edinburgh, 1938–39; Bishop of Edinburgh, 1939–46; Primus of Episcopal Church in Scotland, 1943–46. *Address:* 4 Lansdowne Crescent, Edinburgh, 12. *Clubs:* Church Imperial; Caledonian United Service, Edinburgh.

Died 9 Dec. 1946.

DARBYSHIRE, Most Rev. John Russell, Hon. DD Glasgow University, 1932; LittD Sheffield; MA; Archbishop of Cape Town, 1938–48; *b* 1880; *s* of Edward Darbyshire, Claughton. *Educ:* Birkenhead School; Dulwich College; Emmanuel College, Cambridge (Classical Scholar), MA 1st Class Classical Tripos, 1902, 1st Class Theological Tripos, Pt I, 1904; Winchester Prize, 1903, Jeremie Sep Prize, 1904, Carus Greek Test Prize, 1905, Crosse Scholar, 1905. Deacon, 1904; Priest, 1905; Curate, St Andrew the Less, Cambridge, 1904–07; Vice-Principal of Ridley Hall, Cambridge, 1908–13; Vicar of St Luke, Liverpool, 1913–20; Canon Residentiary of Manchester Cathedral and Rector of St George, Hulme, Manchester, 1920–22; Vicar of Sheffield, 1922–31; Archdeacon of Sheffield, 1922–31; Rural Dean of Sheffield, 1927–31; Bishop of Glasgow and Galloway, 1931–38; Pilkington Lecturer, Liverpool, 1919; Examining Chaplain to Bishop of Bradford, 1920; Sub-prelate Order of St John of Jerusalem; Episc. Canon of Carmel St George's Coll. Ch Jerusalem. *Publications:* The Christian Faith, and some Alternatives, 1921; Our Treasury of Prayer and Praise, 1926; Jesus, the Messiah, in the Gospels, 1933. *Address:* Bishopscourt, Claremont, CP, South Africa. *T:* Cape Town 73689. *Club:* Civil Service (Cape Town).

Died 30 June 1948.

DARBYSHIRE, Ruth Eveline, CBE 1942; RRC 1st Class; Matron-in-Chief, British Red Cross Society and Order of St John of Jerusalem, 1940–43; *d* of late John Taylor Darbyshire. *Educ:* privately. Trained Wakefield Street Hospital, Adelaide, S Australia, and St Thomas's Hospital, London; Sister St Thomas's Hospital; Matron Royal Infirmary, Derby; Matron St Mary's Hospital, London; Principal Matron Territorial Army Nursing Service; Chief Lady Superintendent Lady Minto's Indian Nursing Association, India; Matron University College Hospital, London; Dame of Grace of St John of Jerusalem; Kaiser-i-Hind (1st Class). *Recreation:* extensive travel. *Address:* 92 Ember Lane, Esher, Surrey. *T:* Emberbrook 3864. *Club:* Cowdray.

Died 7 March 1946.

DARBYSHIRE, Taylor; author and journalist; London Manager of the Australian Press Association, 1919–35; *b* Lancashire, 5 July 1875; *s* of John Taylor Darbyshire; *m* Katharine Frances Broome Rickards; two *d. Educ:* Brisbane Grammar School; Sydney University. Went to Australia, 1885; read for the Bar, but abandoned a legal career in favour of journalism; joined staff of the Brisbane Newspaper Company, serving, there in all editorial capacities; joined The Age, Melbourne, becoming literary and dramatic critic as well as Editor of one of the paper's weekly periodicals; then transferred to the theatrical firm of J. C. Williamson, Ltd, of which he became General Manager and Associate Director; represented the Association at the Empire Press Union Conference in Canada, at the Washington Disarmament Conference, at several continental conferences, and throughout the world tour of the King and Queen when Duke and Duchess of York in 1927. *Publications:* King George VI, an authoritative biography, 1937; The Duke of York; The Royal Tour of the Duke and Duchess of York; Jamaica for Sport; In the Words of the King; A selection from the Speeches of King George VI, 1938. *Recreation:* carpentering. *Club:* Savage.

Died 5 July 1943.

D'ARCY, Dame Constance Elizabeth, DBE 1935; MB, ChM, FRACS. Lecturer in Clinical Obstetrics, Sydney University, since 1925; member of Senate of Sydney University, 1919–50; Deputy Chancellor, 1943. *Address:* 233 Macquarie Street, Sydney, NSW.

Died 25 April 1950.

D'ARCY, Rev. George James Audomar; Canon of Southwell; late Rural Dean of Workshop; Vicar of Worksop; *b* 1861; *s* of G. J. N. d'Arcy of Hyde Park, Killucan, Ireland, and Antoinette Jane, *d* of Anthony Dopping, DL, of Colmoyn, Co. Meath, Ireland; *m* 1911, Amy Louisa, *d* of J. Colley of Worksop and Sheffield; no *c. Educ:* The High School, Dublin; Oxford University. Curate of Freemantle, and All Saints, Southampton, Christ Church, Luton, St Margaret's, Anfield, Liverpool, St Michael's, Portsmouth; Vicar of St Patrick's, Birmingham. *Publications:* Drama of Life of St Patrick; Drama of Life of St Columba; Drama of Life of St Aidan. *Recreations:* pike fishing, dahlia growing. *Address:* The Vicarage, Worksop. *T:* Worksop 2180.

Died 10 Jan. 1941.

DAREWSKI, Herman; composer; *s* of late Edouard Darewski; *m* Madge Temple (*d* 1943). Musical Director, Spa Corporation, Bridlington, 1924–26; Musical Director, Winter Gardens, Blackpool, 1927–30; Winter Seasons, Royal Opera House, Covent Garden and Olympia; Hon. Organiser of National Collection of Music and Musical Instruments for YMCA Huts; Hon. Assistant Director of Paper Economy, The Paper Control; Hon. Organiser in Theatres, Music-Hall and Cinemas, War Loan Campaign for National War Savings Publicity Committee; Director of Music and Entertainment of entire British Medical Association Centenary Celebrations at BMA House, etc, and at the Royal Albert Hall, including production of Pageant Progress of Medicine, 1832–1918; Musical Director, Spa

Corporation, Bridlington, 1933–34–1935–36–1937; Inventor of Musical Strip Cartoons, Musical Midgets. *Publications:* Musical Memories, 1937; Music for revues and many popular songs, including: Sister Susie's sewing Shirts for Soldiers; Which Switch is the Switch, Miss, for Ipswich; When we've wound up the Watch on the Rhine: Where do Flies go in the Winter Time?; Patches; Mysterie; If you only knew; Whispering; My Mammy; Jubilee Valse; The Toast—King George. *Club:* City Livery.

Died 2 June 1947.

DARGAN, William J., MD; FRCPI; Physician to St Vincent's Hospital, Dublin; *s* of James Dargan, CE, and Teresa Johnson; *m* 1903, Tessie Ronayne; five *s* one *d*. *Educ:* St Vincent's College, Castleknock. House Surgeon and House Physician Mater Misericordia Hospital, Dublin; University Student, Royal University, Ireland. *Publication:* Secretory Diseases of the Stomach (Med. Press and Circ.). *Recreation:* golf. *Address:* 85 Eglinton Road, Dublin. *T:* Dublin 91187.

Died 3 Dec. 1944.

DARK, Sidney; *b* London, 1874; *e s* of late Harry Sidney Dark, of Lord's Cricket Ground; *m* 1895, Nellie Anders; one *s* one *d*. Began life as a professional singer, having been for a while a student at the Royal Academy of Music; afterwards for a year or two was on the stage; commenced journalism in 1899 by writing Green Room Gossip in the Daily Mail, and subsequently wrote in addition book notes, theatrical criticisms, and musical criticisms in this paper; joined the staff of the Daily Express in 1902 and was special correspondent of the paper during the Paris Peace Congress; Joint-Editor of John o' London's Weekly 1919–24; Editor of Church Times, 1924–41. *Publications:* Stage Silhouettes, 1901; Thackeray, 1912; The Man who would not be King, 1913; Thou art the Man, 1915; The Glory that is France; Afraid, 1916; Dickens, 1919; Books and the Man, 1921; The Child's Book of France, 1921; The Outline of Wells, 1922; Arthur Pearson of St Dunstan's, 1922; Child's Book of England, 1922; W. S. Gilbert; Life and Letters (with Rowland Grey), 1923; The Child's Book of Scotland, 1923; The Story of the Renaissance, 1923; How to Enjoy Life, 1924; London, 1924; The English Child's Book of the Church, 1925; Mainly About Other People, 1926; Elizabeth, 1926; Paris, 1926; The Prayer Book: What it Is and What it may Be, 1927; St Thomas of Canterbury, 1927; Twelve Bad Men, 1928; Five Deans, 1928; Archbishop Davidson and the English Church, 1929; Twelve Great Ladies, 1929; The Lambeth Conferences, 1930; How to Enjoy Leisure, 1930; London Town, 1930; Robert Louis Stevenson, 1931; Twelve More Ladies, 1932; (with late P. G. Konody) Sir William Orpen, 1932; The Jew Today, 1934; The World's Great Sermons, 1934; Lord Halifax, 1934; Newman, 1934; Manning, 1936; Mackay of All Saints, 1937; The War against God (with R. E. Essex), 1938; Inasmuch, 1939. Lift Up Your Hearts (with Enid Hobson), 1940; The Church Impotent or Triumphant? 1941; Not Such a Bad Life 1941; The Red Bible, 1942; If Christ Came to London, 1942; The People's Archbishop, 1942; I Sit and I Think and I Wonder, 1943; Best Short Stories, 1943; Seven Archbishops, 1944; The Laughing Cavalier of Christ, 1944; The Passing of the Puritan, 1946. *Club:* Savile.

Died 11 Oct. 1947.

DARLAN, Amiral de la Flotte Jean François, Médaille Militaire, Grand Croix Légion d'Honneur; GCVO 1938; Croix de Guerre; Chief of State in French Africa since 1942; *b* Nerac (Lot et Garonne), 7 Aug. 1881; *s* of Jean Baptiste Darlan and Marie Marguerite Espagnac; *m* 1910, Berthe Morgan; one *s*. *Educ:* Lycée St Louis, Paris. Entré à l'École Navale, 1899; Enseigne de vaisseau, 1902; Lieutenant de vaisseau, 1912; Capitaine de corvette, 1918; Capitaine de frégate, 1920; Capitaine de vaisseau, 1926; Contre Amiral, 1929; Vice Amiral, 1932; Trois citations pendant la grande guerre;

Campagnes de guerre en Chine et contre l'Allemagne et ses alliés; Commandements exercés; 4e Groupe de canonniers marins, Flottille du Rhin, avisos Altaïr, Chamois, Ancre, croiseur Jeanne d'Arc et Edgar Quinet, 1re division de croiseurs, Escadre de l'Atlantique; Commandant en Chef des Forces Maritimes Françaises; Minister of Navy and Mercantile Marine, France; Vice-President of the Council of Ministers, Secretary of State for Foreign Affairs and the Navy, Acting Secretary of State for War, and Minister for National Defence, Pétain Government, 1941–42; Commander-in-Chief of the land, sea, and air forces, Vichy, 1942. *Clubs:* Militaire, Interalliée, Automobile, Ile de France.

Died 24 Dec. 1942.

DARLING, Charles Robert, FIC, FInstP, ARCScI, WhEx; *b* 26 July 1870; *s* of Thomas Darling; *m* 1897, Florence, *d* of William Taylor, Rotherham, Yorks; two *s* one *d*. *Educ:* privately at Crewe; Royal College of Science, Dublin. Formerly Assist Professor of Science, Royal Military Academy, Woolwich; Lecturer in Applied Physics at Finsbury Technical Coll.; Past Vice-President and Member of Council of the Physical Society; Past Member of Council of the Faraday Society; during last war Chairman of the Admiralty Electric Welding Research Committee. *Publications:* Heat for Engineers; Pyrometry; Liquid Drops and Globules, Researches on Surface Tension, Thermo-Electricity, Electrochemistry, Fuels and Heat Insulation, in various scientific publications. *Recreations:* easy mountaineering, golf, and billiards. *Address:* Rosehill, Pant, Oswestry.

Died 12 Oct. 1942.

DARLING, Major John May, DSO 1916; MA, MB, ChB, FRCS; late SR, RAMC; Consulting Surgeon to Edinburgh Eye, Ear and Throat Infirmary; *b* 1878; *s* of late William Darling, Schoolmaster, Leith; *m* 1910, Jean (*d* 1934), *d* of late Neil Clark, JP, Argyllshire; two *s*. *Educ:* Royal High School, University, Edinburgh. *Address:* 1 Beaufort Road, Grange Road, Edinburgh. *T:* Edinburgh 52385.

Died 30 July 1942.

DARLING, Hon. Joseph, CBE 1938; Member of Legislative Council in Tasmania, since 1921; *b* 21 Nov. 1870; *s* of late John and Isabella Darling, Edinburgh; *m* 1893, Alice Minna Blanche Francis; eight *s* four *d*. *Educ:* Prince Alfred College, Adelaide. Pastoral pursuits; visited England with the Australian XI of Cricketers in 1896, 1899, 1902, and 1905; Captained the last three teams, also Captained Australia, in Australia, in Test Matches against England. In 1896, 1897, 1898 and 1899, obtained highest batting average for Australian XI teams. *Recreations:* Cricket, football, swimming. *Address:* Clare mount, Tasmania. *T:* Glenorch 25.

Died 2 Jan. 1946.

DARLINGTON, Rev. John, DD; Vicar of St Mark, Kennington, since 1897; President of St Mark's Traffic Workers' Brotherhood since 1904; Hon. Acting Chaplain, Belgrave Hospital for Children, since 1903; Surrogate; *b* London, 5 Dec. 1868; *o c* of John Darlington, Civil and Mining Engineer; *m* 1897, Lilian, *y d* of Dean Farrar, DD, FRS; one *s*. *Educ:* University College School; Lincoln College, Oxford; BA 1892; MA 1896; BD 1899; DD 1904. Trained for Holy Orders by Dean Vaughan, DD, at the Temple and Llandaff, 1892–93; Curate of Holy Trinity, Marylebone, 1893–94; St Margaret, Westminster, 1894–95; St George the Martyr, Southwark, 1895–97; holder of NUR and ASLE & F. Gold Medallions (presented, 1919). *Publication:* Effective Speaking and Writing, 2nd edition, 1925. *Recreations:* interchange of ideas with other workers, church architecture (especially Wren's); reading, music; interested in dachshunds. *Address:* St Mark's Vicarage, Kennington Oval, SE11; Stoneley, Curry Rivel, Somerset. *T:* Reliance 1801.

Died 15 March 1947.

DARRACOTT, Sir William, Kt 1932; JP Deal; President Deal, Walmer and District Conservative Association; *b* 1860; *s* of late Robert Gamon Darracott, Braunton, Devon; *m* 1885, Jane, *d* of late John Fogarty, Canterbury; one *s* one *d*. *Educ:* Chaloners, N Devon; Bideford Grammar School. Chairman Deal, Walmer and District War Memorial Hospital, 1922–33; Member House of Laity, National Assembly, Church of England, 1920–35; Chairman Conservative Party, Dover Division, 1923–36. *Address:* Laregan, Walmer, Kent. *Club:* Constitutional.

Died 2 March 1947.

DARWEN, 1st Baron *cr* 1946, of Heys-in-Bowland; **John Percival Davies;** a Lord-in-Waiting to the King since 1949; *b* 28 March 1885; *s* of Thos Pearce Davies and Lucy Dora Webb; *m* 1914, Mary Kathleen Brown; three *s* two *d*. *Educ:* Sidcot; Bootham; Manchester. Cotton Manufacturer; Adult School Work; contested (Lab) Blackburn 1922, 1923, Skipton 1929, 1931, 1933 Bye, 1935 and 1945. *Publications:* Politics of a Socialist Employer, 1929; Foundations of Peace (with Kathleen Davies), 1941; Glorious Banner, 1945. *Recreation:* gardening. *Heir:* *s* Hon. Cedric P. Davies [*b* 18 Feb. 1915; *m* 1934, Kathleen Dora, *d* of George Sharples Walker; two *s* one *d*. Sidcot; Manchester University]. *Address:* Wayside, The Ridgeway, Mill Hill, NW7. *T:* Finchley 4152.

Died 26 Dec. 1950.

DARWIN, Squadron Leader Charles John Wharton, DSO 1919; London Manager Bristol Aeroplane Co., Ltd; *b* 12 Dec. 1894; *s* of Charles Waring Darwin; *m* 1917, Sibyl Rose; one *s* two *d*. *Educ:* Winchester; Sandhurst. 2nd Bn Coldstream Guards, 1914; served European War, 1914–19 (despatches, DSO, wounded twice); joined Royal Flying Corps, 1916; RAF, 1927. *Address:* Elston Hall, Newark, Notts; 10 Montagu Mews, North, W1. *T:* Welbeck 1526; East Stoke 3, Nottingham. *Clubs:* Travellers', Royal Automobile, Royal Aero, Bath.

Died 26 Dec. 1941.

DARWIN, Major Leonard, late RE; *b* 15 Jan. 1850; 4th *s* of Charles Darwin, Down, Kent, and Emma Wedgwood, *d* of J. Wedgwood, Maer, Staffs; *m* 1st, Elizabeth (*d* Jan. 1898), *d* of late G. R. Fraser, 1882; 2nd, 1900, Charlotte Mildred (*d* 1940), *d* of late Edmund Langton. *Educ:* RMA, Woolwich. Entered RE 1871; Major, 1889; retired 1890; Instructor SME Chatham, 1877–82; Staff, Intelligence Dept WO, 1885–90; served on several scientific expeditions, including Transit of Venus of 1874 and 1882; MP (LU) for Lichfield Division, Staffs, 1892–95; contested that Division, 1895, 1896; President, Royal Geographical Society, 1908–11; President Eugenics Education Society, 1911–28; Chairman Bedford Coll. for Women, Univ. of London, 1913–20; Chairman Professional Classes War Relief Council throughout the War; Hon. ScD, Camb. *Publications:* Bimetallism, 1898; Municipal Trade, 1903; The Need for Eugenic Reform, 1926. *Address:* Cripps's Corner, Forest Row, Sussex. *Club:* Athenæum.

Died 26 March 1943.

DARYNGTON, 1st Baron *cr* 1923, of Witley; **Herbert Pike Pease,** PC 1917; DL, JP; an Ecclesiastical Commissioner since 1923; Ecclesiastical Estates Commissioner 1926–48; *b* 7 May 1867; *s* of late Arthur Pease, MP; *g s* of Joseph Pease, MP; *m* 1894, Alice (*d* 1948), 2nd *d* of the Very Reverend H. Mortimer Luckock, Dean of Lichfield; one *s* three *d*. *Educ:* Brighton College; Trinity Hall, Cambridge. MP (U) Darlington, 1898–1923; Unionist Whip, 1906–10 and 1910–15; Assist Postmaster-General, 1915–22; Pres. of the Church Army, 1917; for 25 years either Chm. or Vice-Chm. of House of Laity of Church Assembly. JP

North Riding of Yorks; JP Surrey. *Heir:* *s* Hon. Jocelyn Arthur Pike Pease, MA, *b* 1908. *Address:* 65 Onslow Gardens, SW7. *Club:* Athenæum.

Died 10 May 1949.

DASHWOOD, Col Edmund William, CBE 1919; late Northumberland Fusiliers; *b* 1858; *m* 1908, Geva Vereker (*d* 1942), MBE, *d* of late Comdr Henry James Stanley, RN. Served S Africa, 1899 (severely wounded, despatches, Bt Lt-Col); 4th Class Osmanieh. *Address:* The Avenue, Aspley Guise, Bletchley.

Died 5 Oct. 1946.

DASHWOOD, Elizabeth Monica; (*nom de plume* E. M. Delafield); JP Devon; *b* 9 June 1890; *er d* of late Count Henry de la Pasture of Llandogo, Monmouthshire; *m* 1919, Arthur Paul, 2nd *surv.* *s* of Sir George Dashwood, 6th Bt; one *d*. Served as a VAD in Exeter, 1914–17, and was then offered appointment under the Ministry of National Service in the South-Western Region at Bristol, remaining there until the end of the war; first novel published in 1917; Speaker for the Ministry of Information, 1940. *Publications:* Zella sees Herself; The War-Workers; The Pelicans: Consequences; Tension; The Heel of Achilles; Humbug; The Optimist; A Reversion to Type; Messalina of the Suburbs, 1924; Mrs Harter, 1924; The Chip and the Block, 1925; Jill, 1926; The Entertainment, 1927; The Way Things Are, 1928; What is Love? 1928; Women Are Like That, 1929; Turn Back the Leaves, 1930; Diary of a Provincial Lady, 1931; Challenge to Clarissa, 1931; Thank Heaven Fasting, 1932; The Provincial Lady Goes Further, 1932; General Impressions, 1933; Gay Life, 1933; The Provincial Lady in America, 1934; The Provincial Lady Omnibus, 1935; Faster! Faster! 1936; Straw Without Bricks, 1937; Nothing Is Safe, 1937; Ladies and Gentlemen in Victorian Fiction, 1937; As Others Hear Us, 1937; The Brontes, 1938; Three Marriages, 1939; Love Has No Resurrection, 1939; The Provincial Lady in War-time, 1940; No One Now Will Know, 1941; Late and Soon, 1943; three-act Comedy, To See Ourselves, Dec. 1930; three-act play, The Glass Wall, 1933; The Mulberry Bush (play), 1935. *Recreation:* reading. *Address:* Croyle, Cullompton, Devon.

Died 2 Dec. 1943.

DASHWOOD, Major Sir Robert Henry Seymour, 7th Bt *cr* 1684; DL; late 3rd Batt. Oxfordshire Light Infantry and 1st Batt. Royal Irish Rifles; *b* 19 July 1876; *s* of 6th Bt and Lady Mary Margaret Seymour, *d* of 5th Marquis of Hertford; *S* father, 1933; *m* 1903, Marjorie, *e d* of late Lt-Gen. G. Henry, CB; two *s* one *d*. *Educ:* Wellington. Served European War, 1915–16 (wounded, despatches twice). *Heir:* *s* Henry George Massy, *b* 11 May 1908. *Address:* Duns Tew Manor, Oxford.

Died 3 July 1947.

DATTA, Surendra Kumar; Principal Forman Christian College, Lahore; *b* 1878; *e s* of Nobo Gopal Datta and Shuruth Mohini Bose; *m* Alexandrena McArthur Carswell; one *s* one *d*. *Educ:* Forman Christian College, Lahore; Edinburgh University. BA (Punjab University); MB, ChB (Edinburgh). Lecturer in Biology, Forman College, Lahore; Member Senate, Punjab University, 1908–14 and since 1934; YMCA Welfare Officer in France with Indian Army, 1914–18 (despatches twice); National Secretary YMCA, India, Burma, and Ceylon, 1919–27; Member of the Lytton Committee on the Education of Indian Students in the United Kingdom, 1921–22; President All-India Conference of Indian Christians, 1923, 1933, and 1934; Member of the Indian Legislative Assembly, 1924–26; Staff of the World's Committee of YMCAs, Geneva, 1928–32; Member of the British Delegation at Institute of Pacific Relations, Kyoto, Japan, 1929; Member of the Indian Round Table Conference, 1931; Visiting Lecturer in USA under the International Institute of Education (Carnegie Foundation), 1935; Vice-President of the World's

Committee of YMCAs. *Publications:* Asiatic Asia; contributions to political and religious reviews. *Address:* Forman College, New Site PO Ichhra, Lahore, India.

Died June 1942.

DAUDET, Léon; Directeur de l'Action Française, et romancier; *b* Paris, 16 Nov. 1867; *s* of Alphonse Daudet et Julia Allard; *m* 1st, Jane Hugo; one *s*; 2nd, 1903, Marthe Allard, sa cousine; two *s* one *d*. *Educ:* Lycée Louis le Grand. A fait pendant dix ans ses études médicales, les a abandonnées pour la littérature en 1894; Depuis cette date n'a pas cessé d'écrire des romans et de nombreux articles; a collaboré au Figaro, au Gaulois, au Soleil, à la Libre Parole et finalement a fondé en 1908 avec Charles Maurras et un groupe d'amis patriotes un journal royaliste quotidien, organe du nationalisme intégral, l'Action Française dont la mission est de détruire la républiaque et de ramener en France le roi Jean III (Duc de Guise); membre de lé Acad. Goncourt. *Publications:* Hœrès; L'Astre noir; Les Morticoles; Les Kamtchatka; Les Idées en marche; Le Voyage de Shakspeare; Suzanne; La Flamme et l'Ombre; Alphonse Daudet; Sébastien Gouvès; Les Deux treintes; La Romance du temps présent; Le Pays des Parlementeurs; La France en alarmes; La Déchéance; Le Partage de l'enfant; Les Primaires; La Lutte; Le Bonheur d'être riche; La Mésentente; Ceux qui montent; Le Lit de Procuste; La Fausse Etoile; L'Avant guerre—publié le 4 mars 1913 et annonçant tout ce qui s'est passé depuis; Hors du joug allemand; L'Hérédo; Le Vermine du monde; Le Cœur et l'absence; Sylla et son destin; L'Amour est un Songe; Dans la lumière; Le Cœur brûlé; Le Napus; Un jour d'orage; Le sang de la nuit; Médée; Ariane; Phrynée; Le Panorama de la IIIème République; Le Bréviaire du Journalisme; Fièvres de Camargue; La Tragique Existence de Victor Hugo; La Vie Orageuse de Clemenceau; Les Lys Sanglants; Du Roman à l'Histoire; Mes Idées Esthétiques; Deux Idoles Sanglantes, la Révolution et son fils Bonaparte; *La série des souvenirs:* Fantômes et Vivants, Devant la douleur, Salons et journaux, L'Entre-deux-guerres, Au temps de Judas, Vers le Roi; la pluie de sang; Le stupide 19e; siècle; Alcofribas 2e Le drame des Jardies; l'Hérédo, Le Monde des images; Le Rêve éveillé; Moloch et Minerve; Charles Maurras et son temps; Au balcon de l'Europe; Notes d'un exilé; quatre volumes d'une série intitulée le *Courrier des Pays-Bas:* La ronde de nuit, Les Horreurs de la guerre, Mélancholia, Les Pèlerins d'Emmaüs; Flambeaux; Flammes; Paris-Vécu (en deux tomes); huit volumes de critique, *Écrivains et Artistes:* 29 mois d'exil; Clémenceau qui sauva la Patrie; Le Nain de Lorraine; Le Voyou de Passage; Le Garde des seaux; quatre volumes des Effondrements Sociaux, Les Rythmes de l'Homme, La Femme et l'Amour; Les Bacchantes, Goethe et la Synthèse. *Address:* 31 rue Saint Guillaume, Paris; Actiofran, 12–14 rue de Rome, Paris.

Died 1 July 1942.

DAUGLISH, Captain Edward Heath, CIE 1934; Royal Indian Navy, retired; *b* 1882; *s* of A. Dauglish, Oxted, Surrey; *m* 1927, Marguerita Lennox, *widow* of H. P. M. Rae and *d* of John Vincent de Coque, Sydney. *Educ:* St Edwards School, Oxford. Entered Royal Indian Navy 1904; served European War, 1914–19 (despatches twice); Chief of Staff and Capt. Superintendent Royal Indian Naval Dockyard, 1929–34; retired 1934. *Recreation:* field sports. *Address:* Highbury, Exeter Road, Exmouth. *T:* Exmouth 2744. *Club:* East India and Sports.

Died 19 Oct. 1950.

DAUKES, Lt-Col Sir Clendon Turberville, Kt 1935; CIE 1920; retd; *b* 1879; *s* of F. C. Daukes, CIE, Indian Civil Service, and Alice Bridget Daukes; *m* Dorothy Maynard Lavington Evans; three *s*. *Educ:* Haileybury College; Sandhurst. 1st Batt. York and Lancaster Regt at York, 1899; 2nd Batt. Agra, India, 1900; Indian Army, 1901; 39th Royal Garhwal Rifles, 1902; entered Political Dept, Gov. of India, 1903; acted Consul, Seistan, 1906;

Consul Turbat-i-Haidari, 1907; acted Political Agent Gilgit, 1911; returned military duty with 39th Garhwal Rifles, 1915; with General Malleson's Mission to NE Persia, 1918–19 (CIE); Political Agent. Loralai, Baluchistan, 1921–27; British Envoy, Nepal, 1929; HM Envoy Extraordinary and Minister Plenipotentiary at the Court of Nepal, 1934–35. *Address:* Packway, Bayley's Hill, near Sevenoaks. *Clubs:* Alpine Ski, MCC.

Died 17 Oct. 1947.

DAUKES, Sidney Herbert; (writes novels under pseudonym of Sidney Fairway), OBE, BA, MD (Cantab), DPH, DTM&H; late Director of Wellcome Museum of Medical Science and of Wellcome Historical Medical Museum; *b* April 1879; *s* of Rev. S. Whitfield Daukes, Vicar of Holy Trinity, Beckenham; *m* Emma (*d* 1944), *d* of William Kempsell, Reigate; one *s*; 1945, Ethel Maud, *widow* of E. J. T. Hoyle, late of The Anchorage, Doncaster. *Educ:* Lancing Coll.; Caius Coll., Cambridge (Honours, Science Tripos); London Hospital. Fellow of Royal Society of Tropical Medicine; and of R. Soc. of Medicine; Chairman of James Peek Trust. General practice for several years, then Public Health Work. Organized for British Government; Medical Section, Wembley, 1924; Ministry of Health Section, Wembley, 1925; Tropical Medical Exhibition, Antwerp, 1929; Medical Section, Paris Exhibition, 1931; RAMC 1915–19, Major; served France 1915–16 (despatches); organized for War Office the School of Military Hygiene, Leeds. *Publications:* The Medical Museum; Barrier Charts for Health Officers; The Pillar of Salt (Reminiscences), 1947; various articles and reviews; (Under Sidney Fairway) *Fiction:* The Yellow Viper; The Doctor's Defence; The Cuckoo in Harley Street; Reluctant Sinners; Dr Budleigh's Heritage; The Long Tunnel, 1935; We Live and Learn, 1936; Thanks to Doctor Molly, 1937; Quacks' Paradise, 1938; A Late Recovery, 1940; Dr Severin's Secret, 1943; It Came to Pass, 1944; He Loved Freedom, 1946. *Recreation:* golf. *Address:* Fairway, Brooklyn Avenue, West Worthing. *T:* Worthing, 1327. *Clubs:* Authors', Constitutional.

Died 3 Sept. 1947.

DAVENPORT, Charles Benedict; retired; Major Sanitary Corps, US Army, 1918–19; Reserve since 1922; Founder and Director (1943), Whaling Museum, Cold Spring Harbor; *b* Stamford, Conn, 1 June 1866; *s* of Amzi Benedict Davenport and Jane Joralemon Dimon of Brooklyn, NY; *m* 1894, Gertrude, of Burlington, Kansas, *d* of Wm Crotty, ranchman; two *d*. *Educ:* Brooklyn Polytechnic Inst.; Harvard Univ. On engineer corps, Survey Duluth, South Shore, and Atlantic Rly 1886; Assist in Zoology, Harvard Univ., 1888–93; Instructor Zoology, 1893–99; Director, Biological Laboratory of Brooklyn Institute, 1898–1922; Secretary since 1922; Assist Professor Zoology, University of Chicago, 1899–1901; Associate Professor, 1901–04; Director of the Department of Genetics, Carnegie Institution of Washington, 1904–34. *Publications:* Experimental Morphology, 1897, 1899; Statistical Methods, 1899 (4th ed. 1936); High School Zoology (with Gertrude C. Davenport), 1899, 2nd ed. 1911; Inheritance in Poultry and Canaries, Inheritance of Characteristics of Fowl, Carnegie Institution, 1906–1910; Eugenics, 1910; Heredity in Relation to Eugenics, 1911; Heredity in Negro-white Crosses, 1913; The Feebly Inhibited, 1915; Inheritance of Stature, 1917; Naval Officers; Their Heredity and Development, 1919; Physical Examination of First Million Draft Recruits, 1919; Defects found in Drafted Men, 1920; Army Anthropology, 1921 (last 3 with Lt-Col A. G. Love); Body Build and its Inheritance; Anthropometry and Anthroposcopy, 1927; Race Crossing in Jamaica (with Morris Steggerda), 1929; The Genetical Factor in Endemic Goitre; The Genetic Factor in Otosclerosis, 1933; How we came by our bodies, 1936. *Recreation:* walking. *Address:* Cold Spring Harbor, Long Island, USA.

Died 18 Feb. 1944.

DAVENPORT, Major Cyril James H., VD 1893; JP; FSA; late Superintendent of Bookbinding, British Museum; Major on retired list of Auxiliary Forces; Knight of Grace of the Order of St John of Jerusalem in England, commanded Unit of the National Reserve at the Coronation Procession, 23 July 1911; *b* Stirling, 5 June 1848; *e s* of Capt. Charles Davenport, DL, 1st Foot, late of Bramall Hall, Stockport, and *g s* of Admiral Sir S. P. Davenport, KCH, CB; *m* 1878, Constance (*d* 1932), *d* of Major Trevor Davenport, 1st Foot; one *d. Educ:* Charterhouse. Draughtsman in the Royal Engineer Dept of War Office, 1868; Lecturer at the Royal Institution, Eton Coll.; awarded silver medal Society of Arts, 1900; Brit. mem. of Internat. Jury, St Louis, USA, 1904 (Diploma and Gold Medal); Franco-British Exhibition, London, 1908; Imperial International Exhibition, London, 1909; Japan-British Exhibition, London, 1910; Coronation Exhibition, London, 1911; Esposizione Internazionale Torino, 1911; Member of Council, Society of Antiquaries, 1904–05; Bibliographical Society, 1904–09; Huguenot Soc. 1908–10; Royal Amateur Art Society, 1910–23; Burlington Fine Arts Club, 1900–13; Resident and Art Director, Toynbee Hall, 1910–12; MC to the Sette of Odd Volumes, 1909; editor Connoisseurs' Library, 1903 (London and New York); Little Books on Art, 1904. *Publications:* The English Regalia, 1897; Royal English Bookbindings, 1897; Cantor Lectures on Decorative Bookbindings, 1898; English Embroidered Bookbindings, 1899; Cameos, 1900; Life of T. Berthelet, 1900; Cantor Lectures on Personal Jewellery, 1902; Mezzotints, 1903; Bagford's Notes on Bookbindings, 1904; Jewellery, 1905; Leather for Libraries (joint), 1906; Life of Samuel Mearne, 1907; Miniatures, 1907; History of the Book, 1908 (London and New York); English Heraldic Book-Stamps, 1909; Jean Petitot, 1909; Cameo Book-Stamps, 1911; Cantor Lectures on Miniatures, 1913; Catalogue of Needlework Exhibition, Hastings, 1913; The Crown Jewels of England 1919 (with Sir G. Younghusband); British Heraldry, 1920; Architecture in England, 1924; The Art Student's Vade Mecum, 1925; Life of Roger Payne, 1927; Byways among English Books, 1927; Beautiful Books, 1929; contributor to The Anglo-Saxon Review, Bibliographica, The Connoisseur, Encyclopædia Britannica, etc. *Recreations:* painting, rug-making. *Address:* Bramall Lodge, St Leonards-on-Sea. *T:* Hastings 2107. *Clubs:* Sette of Odd Volumes, Whitefriars, Arts, University of London; East Sussex.
Died 15 Jan. 1941.

DAVENPORT, Sir Henry (Edward), Kt 1929; JP; Commendatore of Order of Crown of Italy, Commander Order of Astaur, etc; *b* 11 June 1866; 4th (*o surv.*) *s* of William Davenport; *m* 1st, 1889; 2nd, 1910, Annie Frances Smith. *Educ:* St Mark's, Tollington Park, N. Hackney Borough Council, 1906–28; Mayor of Hackney, 1912–13; Corporation of City of London, 1927; Sheriff of City of London, 1927–28; Prime Warden Basket Makers' Company, 1924; Master Horners' Company, 1939, 1940, 1941. *Address:* St Malo, Herne Bay.
Died 2 Aug. 1941.

DAVENPORT, Brig.-Gen. Sir William B.; *see* Bromley-Davenport.

DAVEY, Rev. Thomas Arthur Edwards; Canon Residentiary of Liverpool since 1931. *Educ:* University of Liverpool (Scholar); Ridley Hall, Cambridge. Deacon, 1916; Priest, 1917; Vicar of St Alban's, Bevington, 1929–31; Canon Treas. of Liverpool Cathedral, 1931. *Address:* 3 Parkfield Road, Sefton Park, Liverpool, 17. *T:* Lark Lane 964. *Clubs:* Athenæum, University, Liverpool.
Died 29 Oct. 1944.

DAVID, Rt Rev. Albert Augustus, DD; *b* Exeter, 19 May 1867; *s* of Rev. William David, Priest Vicar of Exeter Cathedral; *m* 1909, Eda Mary, *e d* of late T. W. Miles, PWD, India; three *s* one *d. Educ:* Exeter School; Queen's College, Oxford. Open Classical Scholarship, 1885; first in Classical Moderations, 1887; first in Lit. Hum. 1889. Lecturer at Queen's College, 1890; Assistant Master at Bradfield College, 1890–92; Rugby School, 1892–99; Fellow, Assist Tutor, Precentor, and Junior Bursar of Queen's College, 1899; Dean, 1904; Examining Chaplain to Bishop of Liverpool, 1901; Headmaster Clifton College, 1905–09; Headmaster of Rugby, 1909–21; Bishop of St Edmundsbury and Ipswich, 1921–23; Bishop of Liverpool, 1923–44; Select Preacher Oxford University, 1906–08, 1924; Hon. Canon and Chancellor of Coventry Cathedral, 1919; Hon. Fellow Queen's College, Oxford; Hon. DD Glasgow, 1937. *Publications:* Life and the Public Schools, 1932; Gems of Bible Poetry, 1939; Activity of God, 1941. *Recreations:* fishing, gardening. *Address:* Skippers Close, Trebetherick, Wadebridge, Cornwall. *T:* 188.
Died 24 Dec. 1950.

DAVID, W. T., MA (Cantab); ScD (Cantab); DSc (Wales); MInstCE, MIMechE; Professor of Engineering, Leeds University; *s* of late S. David, Laugharne, Carmarthenshire. *Educ:* University College, Cardiff; Trinity College, Cambridge. Research on Internal Combustion Engines under late Prof. B. Hopkinson of Cambridge; Assist Gas Engine Designer at works of Mather and Platt, Manchester; Inspector of Gun Ammunition Filling Factories (Military Appointment, Major, Inspection and Research Staff); Director of Dilution of Munitions Labour at Ministry of Munitions and later in charge of Dilution of Shipyard Labour at Admiralty; Assistant to Sir Robert Horne in War Cabinet (Demobilisation Section); HM Inspector of Technical Schools (Engineering); Professor of Engineering, University College, Cardiff; Dean of Faculty of Technology, Leeds University. *Publications:* Researches on Gaseous Explosions, published in Transactions and Proceedings of the Royal Society, and on Internal Combustion Engines, published in Proceedings Inst. Mechanical Engineers and Inst. Civil Engineers. *Recreations:* riding, motoring, and tennis. *Address:* The University, Leeds. *Club:* Leeds (Leeds).
Died 22 May 1948.

DAVIDS, Caroline A. F. Rhys, Hon. DLitt (Manchester), MA; *d* of John Foley, BD, Wadham College, and sometime Vicar of Wadhurst, Sussex, and Caroline E. Windham, of Felbrigg Hall, Cromer; *m* T. W. Rhys Davids (*d* 1922), FBA, LLD, DSc, etc.; two *d* (one *s* killed in war). *Educ:* at home; University College, London (John Stuart Mill and Joseph Hume Scholar). On staff of Economic Journal from its start till 1895; Lecturer on Indian Philosophy, Victoria University, Manchester, 1910–13; Lecturer on History of Buddhism, School of Oriental Studies, London, 1918–33; worked in various societies for child and working women's welfare, 1890–94, and for women's suffrage, 1896–1914; Hon. Secretary Pali Text Society (founded by husband 1881) since 1907; President of same since 1923. *Publications:* Buddhist Psychol: Ethics, 1900, 1923; various first editions of Buddhist canonical and other works; Buddhist Psychology, 1914, 1924; Buddhism (Home Univ.) 1912, 1934; Buddh. translations, 1910–1931; Old Creeds and New Needs, 1923; The Will to Peace, 1923; Will and Willer, 1925; Gotama the Man, 1928; The Milinda Questions, 1930; Sakya, 1931, etc.; A Manual of Buddhism, 1932; Indian Religion and Survival, 1934; Outlines of Buddhism, 1934; Birth of Indian Psychology, 1935; What is your Will?, 1937; To Become or not to Become?, 1937; What was the Original Gospel in Buddhism?, 1938; More about the Hereafter, 1940; Poems of Cloister and Jungle, 1941; Wayfarer's Words I-III, 1940–1942; (Editor) Lectures on

Psychology and Philosophy (Univ-Extn Series) by G. Croom Robertson, 1896. *Address:* Middleshaws, Chipstead, Surrey. *T:* Downland 485.

Died 26 June 1942.

DAVIDSON, Col Charles John Lloyd, DSO 1900; late Royal Inniskilling Fusiliers; *b* 6 Oct. 1858; *e s* of late James Brebner Davidson of Murlingden, Brechin, Forfarshire and Eglinton, Co. Derry; *m* 1st, 1890, Sophia Mary (*d* 1897), *d* of Major Burleigh Stuart of Dergmony, Omagh; 2nd, 1906, Mary Nathalie (*d* 1916), *d* of Col A. B. Cumberlege, Kingsfield, Southwick, Sussex; one *s* one *d*. *Educ:* privately; RMC, Sandhurst. Gazetted 27th Foot, 1879; Capt. Royal Inniskilling Fusiliers, 1888; Major, 1899; Lt-Col 1906; Bt-Col 1909; retired, 1910; served South Africa, 1899–1902 (severely wounded, despatches, Queen's medal five clasps, King's medal two clasps, DSO). *Address:* The Manor House, Eglinton, Co. Londonderry. *Club:* Naval and Military.

Died 13 March 1941.

DAVIDSON, Brig.-Gen. Charles Steer, CB 1915; S Staffs Regiment; retired; *b* 6 Sept. 1866. Entered Army, 1888; Captain, 1896; Major, 1906; Lt-Col 1911; Col 1915; commanded 123rd Infantry Brigade, 41st Division 1915–16; served South African War, 1900–02 (despatches twice, Bt Major, Queen's medal 3 clasps, King's medal 2 clasps); European War, 1914–15 (desp., CB). *Address:* White Lodge, Sheringham, Norfolk. *Club:* Naval and Military.

Died 29 Sept. 1942.

DAVIDSON, Lt-Col Colin Keppel, CIE 1935; OBE 1919; Officer of the Order of St John of Jerusalem, 1938; Officer of Order of Nichan-Iftikhar (N Africa), 1922; Clerk of the House of Lords since 1919, Taxing Master, 1933–39; Principal Clerk of Committees and Private Bills since 1939; *b* 1 Sept. 1895; *s* of late Col Leslie Davidson, CB, RHA, Gentleman Usher to King George V, and Lady Theodora, Dame of Grace of the Order of St John of Jerusalem (*e surv. d* of 7th Earl of Albemarle, PC, KCMG); *m* 1939, Lady Rachel Fitzalan-Howard, *e d* of 15th Duke of Norfolk; one *s* one *d*. Temp. commn and served in European war, 1914–18, as Captain, Royal Artillery, in France, Gallipoli, Mesopotamia (OBE, 1914–15 Star, 2 Medals, despatches twice); re-commissioned Oct. 1939, and is serving as temp. Lt-Col, Royal Artillery; is a Member of House Comm. of Westminster Hosp.; hon. Prison Visitor to HM Prison, Wormwood Scrubbs, 1938–39. *Address:* Angmering Park Farm, Littlehampton. *T:* Patching 66. *Clubs:* Turf, Marlborough, Beefsteak, Pratt's, MCC.

Died 2 March 1943.

DAVIDSON, Brig. Edmund, CMG 1919; late Royal Army Ordnance Corps; *b* 4 May 1875; *s* of late Major-Gen. Alexander Davidson, RE; *m* 1906, Edith, 6th *d* of late William Brodie, Milntown, Eastbourne; one *s* two *d*. *Educ:* Clifton College; RMA Woolwich. ADOS. War Office, 1928–31, and AAG 1929–31; Deputy Director of Ordnance Services, 1931–32; retired pay, 1932. *Address:* c/o Lloyds Bank, Ltd, 6 Pall Mall, SW1. *T:* Freshwater 264.

Died 30 May 1945.

DAVIDSON, James, DSc; Professor of Entomology, Waite Research Institute, University of Adelaide; *b* 27 July 1885; *s* of late James Davidson, Neston, Cheshire; *m* 1920, Johanne Therese, *y d* of late John Horneman, Copenhagen; three *s* one *d*. *Educ:* Birkenhead; University of Liverpool, BSc 1908; MSc 1910; Wolfe Barry Research Student in Entomology (Imperial College of Science and Technology) and Research Scholar in Zoology, Ministry of Agriculture; Research study in Berlin, Florence, and Paris; DSc (Liverpool), 1915. Served European War, Aug. 1914–June 1919; Lt Royal Irish Rifles; Capt. RAMC (1916); Sinai (despatches) and France; specialist officer (entomologist) attached War Office, 1918; investigations concerning

prevalence of mosquitoes in England; specialist Sanitation Officer with British Repatriation Commission for the evacuation of prisoners of war from Baltic Ports; Officer in charge of War Office Entomological Laboratory at Sandwich; assistant entomologist, Rothamsted Experimental Station, Harpenden, 1919–28. *Publications:* A list of British aphides and their food plants, and scientific papers dealing with the anatomy, biology, and experimental researches of insects and other arthropods in various scientific journals. *Address:* The University, Adelaide, Australia.

Died 3 Aug. 1945.

DAVIDSON, Sir Lionel, KCSL 1921; CSI 1913; *b* 19 Jan. 1868; *s* of William Davidson; *m* 1892, Emily Bryce, 2nd *d* of late Colonel Hugh Pearce Pearson, CB; one *s* one *d*. *Educ:* University College School, and University College, London; Balliol College, Oxford (MA). Entered ICS 1888; Under-Secretary to Government, 1896; Secretary to Land Revenue Comrs 1900; Comr and District Judge, Coorg, 1902; Collector and Magistrate, 1905; Secretary to Government, and Member of Legislative Council, Madras, 1910; Member Indian Legislative Council, 1916–17; Chief Secretary, Madras Government, 1918; member of the Executive Council of the Governor of Madras, 1918; Vice-President, 1920; resigned office, 1922; retired from ICS 1924; JP, Bucks County, 1927–38. *Address:* 20b Bradmore Road, Oxford. *T:* Oxford 47345.

Died 17 Sept. 1944.

DAVIDSON, Rev. Richard; Principal-Emeritus, Emmanuel College, Toronto; *b* 29 March 1876; *s* of Henry Davidson and Janet Craig Lillico; *m* 1906, Edith Mary, *d* of John McGregor Northwood and Harriet King, Chatham, Ont; two *s* two *d*. *Educ:* University of Toronto (BA 1899, MA 1900, PhD 1902); University of Berlin. Lecturer in Hebrew, Trinity College, Toronto, 1901–02; Fellow in Semitic Languages, University College, Toronto, 1904–05; Lecturer in Old Testament, Montreal Presbyterian College, 1905–06; Associate Professor, Semitic Languages, University College, Toronto, 1906–10; Professor of Old Testament, Knox College, Toronto, 1910–27; Professor of Old Testament, Union Theological College, Toronto, 1927–28; Professor of Old Testament, Emmanuel College, 1928–43, and Principal, 1932–43; DD Montreal Presbyterian College, 1914, Queen's Univ., 1941. *Publications:* The Book of Common Order of the United Church of Canada (joint author); A Faith to Live By, 1943; The Meaning of Baptism, 1943; articles in journals of Learned Societies. *Recreation:* travelling. *Address:* 120 Madison Avenue, Toronto, Canada.

Died 25 May 1944.

DAVIDSON, Col Stuart, CBE 1918; late RE; *b* 2 Oct. 1859. Entered Army, 1878; Col 1911; served European War, 1914–19 (CBE); retired pay, 1919. *Address:* c/o Lloyds Bank, Ltd, Cox & King's Branch, 6 Pall Mall, SW1.

Died 4 Oct. 1941.

DAVIDSON, William Tennent Gairdner, MB, ChB (Glas. Univ.); DPH (Camb.); MD 1918; *b* Shettleston, 26 April 1889; *e s* of late Dr Robert Davidson, Woodville, Shettleston; *m* 1917, Christian (decd), *o d* of late George Johnston, Edinburgh; one *s*; 1939, Elizabeth, *d* of late Martin Dowling, Greenock. *Educ:* Glasgow Academy; Glasgow Univ., Cambridge Univ. Graduated 1912, gaining Sir Wm Gairdner medal in Practice of Medicine. Acted as Casualty Surgeon Western Infirmary, Glasgow; also House-Surgeon, House-Physician and Senior resident at Royal Infirmary, Glasgow; travelled on the Continent; late Senior Assist-Physician City of Glasgow Fever Hospital, Ruchill. *Publications:* Some Observations on Advanced Pulmonary Tuberculosis; A Case of Cutaneous Anthrax in Man presenting Multiple Lesions; an investigation into the Phenomena of Serum Disease. Member of Clan Dhai Association. *Recreation:*

golf. *Address:* Woodville, Shettleston, Glasgow. *T:* Shettleston 1068. *Club:* Royal Scottish Automobile (Glasgow).

Died 7 May 1949.

DAVIE, Sir Henry Augustus Ferguson-, Kt 1930; CB 1924; late Principal Clerk, Public Bill Office, House of Commons; *b* 22 Aug. 1865; *brother* and *heir-pres.* of Sir William John Ferguson-Davie, 4th Bt; *m* 1897, Adeline, *d* of Thomas H. Newman, of Coryton Manor Lewdown, Devon; two *d. Address:* Bittiscombe Manor, Wiveliscombe, Somerset.

Died 31 Jan. 1946.

DAVIE, Maj. Sir William John F.; *see* Ferguson-Davie.

DAVIES, 1st Baron *cr* 1932, of Llandinam; **David Davies;** landed proprietor; JP Montgomeryshire; *b* Llandinam, 11 May 1880; *o s* of late Edward Davies of Plas Dinam, Llandinam, Mont, and Mary, *e d* of late Rev. Evan Jones of Brynhafren-Llandinam; *m* 1st, 1910, Amy (*d* 1918), 4th *d* of L. T. Penman, JP, of Broadwood Park, Lanchester; one *s*; 2nd, 1922, Henrietta Margaret (Rita), *y d* of late James Grant Fergusson of Baledmund; two *s* two *d. Educ:* Merchiston Castle School, Edinburgh; King's College, Cambridge. MA; 2nd Class Honours, Historical Tripos; FRGS; LLD (Hon.) Aberystwyth. President, National Library of Wales and University College of Wales, Aberystwyth; Member of Councils of University College of North Wales (Bangor), University College of South Wales (Cardiff), University College Swansea, and Normal College (Bangor); member of Court of University of Wales; Chairman of Ocean Coal and Wilson's; United National Collieries, Ltd; Burnyeat, Brown and Coy, Ltd; Cambrian and General Securities, Ltd; Director of Great Western Railway; Director of Midland Bank; President King Edward VII Welsh National Memorial Association and of the Welsh Housing and Development Association; President of Football Association of Wales; is closely associated with the work of the League of Nations Union and is Chairman, late President, of the Welsh Council of that Union; Founder and Chairman New Commonwealth Society; has visited Canada, Alaska, the Rockies, Japan, China and British East Africa; served European War; commanded 14th Batt. Royal Welch Fusiliers at home and in France, 1914–16, when he was appointed Parliamentary Private Secretary to Mr Lloyd George; MP (L) Montgomeryshire, 1906–29. *Publications:* The Problem of the Twentieth Century, 1930; Letters to John Bull, 1932; Suicide or Sanity, 1932; Force, 1934; Nearing the Abyss, 1936; Foundations of Victory, 1941; Facing the Future, 1942. *Recreations:* much interested in sport, including, hunting, and has foxhounds at Llandinam. *Heir: s* Hon. David Davies [*b* 16 Jan. 1915; *m* 1939, Ruth Eldrydd, 3rd *d* of Major W. M. Dugdale, DSO. Oundle; King's College, Cambridge, BA]. *Address:* Plas Dinam, Llandinam, Montgomeryshire. *Clubs:* Reform, Bath, National Liberal.

Died 16 June 1944.

DAVIES, 2nd Baron *cr* 1932, of Llandinam; **David Davies;** T/Major Royal Welch Fusiliers; *b* 16 Jan. 1915; *s* of 1st Baron and Amy (*d* 1918), 4th *d* of L. T. Penman, JP, of Broadwood Park, Lanchester, Co. Durham; *S* father, 1944; *m* 1939, Ruth Eldrydd, 3rd *d* of Major W. M. Dugdale, DSO, Llwyn, Llanfyllin, Mont; two *s. Educ:* Wellington House, Westgate-on-Sea; Oundle School; King's College, Cambridge, BA. Under articles to chartered accountants, 1936, till outbreak of war; with Army at home since 1st Sept. 1939. *Recreations:* fishing, shooting, hunting, music. *Heir: s* Hon. David Davies, *b* 2 Oct. 1940. *Address:* Llwynderw, Llandinam, Mont. *Clubs:* Bath, National Liberal.

Died 25 Sept. 1944.

DAVIES, Albert Emil; JP County of London; Chairman of several Investment Trusts; writer and lecturer on finance, economics, social problems, and railways; *b* London, 16 Nov. 1875; *m* 1898, Alice, *d* of J. Russell Berry, BA; two *s* three *d. Educ:* London elementary schools. Fellow of Royal Economic Soc. Alderman since 1919, and Chairman, 1940–41, Vice-Chairman, 1937–38, and Deputy Chairman (1926–27), London County Council; Trustee and Chairman Finance Cttee, Crystal Palace; Vice-Pres. Shaw Soc.; Mem. Executive Cttee Union Internationale des Villes; Member Board of Management Travel Assoc.; Chm. Claybury Hospital; Member Fabian Soc. Exec., 1911–47, Hon. Treas., 1936–47; Exec. Cttee Duke of Gloucester's Red Cross and St John Fund, 1939–45; Member Administrative Council Lord Mayor's National Air Raid Distress Fund, 1940–47; Chm. Joint Industrial Council for London Local Authorities (Manual Workers), 1936–37; Chm., 1930–36, of Nat. Cttee of Investigation under Coal Mines Act of 1930; First Chm., Finance Committee London and Home Counties Joint Electricity Authority, 1926–28; contested (Lab) Romford Division of Essex, 1922–24; Moss Side Division of Manchester, 1931; Chairman Labour Party Advisory Committee on Finance and Commerce, 1924–31; served on Government Committee, 1924, on Withheld Retired Pay of Naval and Marine Officers; at one time Hon. Lecturer in Business Economics at University of Leeds. City Editor, New Statesman, 1913–31. From Nov. 1941 to March 1942 did 15,000 mile speaking tour in USA and Canada to Civic authorities, etc., on behalf of Ministry of Information. *Publications:* The Foreign Correspondent, 1903; Tramway Trips and Rambles, 1905; Pitman's Guide to Business Customs and Practice on the Continent, 1908; The Nationalisation of Railways, 1909; State Purchase of Railways, 1910; The Money and the Stock and Share Markets, 1910; Off Beaten Tracks in Brittany, 1912; The Case for Railway Nationalisation, 1913; The State in Business, 1914; The Case for Nationalisation, 1920; (with Dorothy Evans) Land Nationalisation—The Key to Social Reform, 1921; The Treasure Book of Knowledge—a Guide to General Knowledge (Editor), 1923; British Railways, 1825–1924, 1924; The Story of the London County Council, 1925; What to Look For in a Prospectus, 1926; Foreign Investments, 1928; The Small Man and His Money, 1934; The London County Council, a Historical Sketch, 1889–1937; Our Ageing Population, 1938; I Wander, 1942; various articles in Encyclopædia Britannica, etc. *Recreation:* travel. *Address:* 54 Basildon Court, W1. *T:* Paddington 2021 and Welbeck 5216; 109 Handside Lane, Welwyn Garden City. *T:* Welwyn Garden 210. *Clubs:* National Liberal, Royal Empire Society Arts Theatre.

Died 18 July 1950.

DAVIES, Sir Alfred (Thomas), Kt 1931; CBE 1920; DL; JP; Hon. Colonel XIX London Territorial Regiment (St Pancras), 1934–36; *b* 17 July 1881; *m* Joanna Elizabeth, *d* of John and Mary Anne Lewis; one *s* one *d* (and one *s* killed during war of 1939–41). *Educ:* London Polytechnic. MP (U) Lincoln, 1918–24; Member LCC, 1931–37; Hon. Organiser Welsh Prisoners of War Fund; Member, Departmental Committee on Pensions, also of Agricultural, Housing Committees and League of Nations Union; undertook Government missions to Central European capitals and Balkan States; Arbitrator in Trade Disputes, 1921–23; selected National candidate for Rochester and Chatham Division, Nov. 1935; temporarily relinquished political activities, 1935–37, owing to serious illness; President, Holborn Conservative Assoc., 1939; Municipal Councillor St Pancras, 1913–19; Mayor, 1931–32; Member Kenwood Preservation Committee; Trustee St Pancras Church; Life Governor St Bartholomew's, Middlesex and London Fever Hospitals; Director Austin Motor Co., 1923; Glenbaudy Tin Plate Co., 1923; Pall Mall Gazette, 1922–23; Gerrard Trust and Allerdale Coal

Co.; on Council Royal Box Holders, Royal Albert Hall, London; Vice-President Trinity College of Music, London. *Address:* The Eagles, West Hill, Highgate, N6. *T:* Mountview 1696. *Clubs:* Carlton, Constitutional, Royal Automobile.

Died 16 Nov. 1941.

DAVIES, Sir Alfred Thomas, KBE 1918; CB 1917; DL and JP (retd), Denbighshire and Bucks; *b* 11 March 1861; *s* of late William Davies, silk mercer, Liverpool; *m* 1st, 1888, Margaret Esther (*d* 1892), *d* of late Thomas Christian Nicholas, Liverpool; 2nd, 1893, Mary (*d* 1947), *d* of late Charles Colton, Liverpool and Birkdale; three *s* one *d*. *Educ:* Waterloo High School, near Liverpool; University College of Wales, Aberystwyth. Admitted a solicitor, 1883; a notary, 1887; practised in Liverpool, 1883–1907; Cursitor of the County Palatine of Lancaster since 1895; Ex-Chairman of the County Licensing Committee and Compensation Authority for Buckinghamshire and Member of Appeals Committee of Bucks Quarter Sessions; Hon. Fellow of the University of Latvia; Organising Secretary of Technical Education for Waterloo-with-Seaforth (Lancs), 1891–96; Secretary of Lundie Memorial [Educational] Trust, Liverpool, 1895–1907; Permanent Secretary of the Welsh Department Board, of Education, 1907–25; also acting Chief Inspector of Education for Wales, 1920–25; Member of Imperial Education Conferences of 1907, 1911, and 1923; Founder and Hon. Director of the British Prisoners of War Book Scheme (Educational) in European War, 1914–18; Founder and Pres. of the Ceiriog Memorial Institute, N Wales; Past Pres. Temperance Collegiate Association (Incorporated); Past Governor of Mill Hill School. *Publications:* Handbook on the Licensing Acts and their Administration; Magisterial Responsibility and Duty in regard to the Licensing Acts; The Inspection of Licensed Houses; John Calvin and The Influence of Protestantism on National Life and Character; Sir Owen Edwards (Memoir); Robert Owen, Pioneer Social Reformer & Philanthropist; also numerous pamphlets on Licensing Administration; The Welsh Language and how to preserve it; The Cult of the Beautiful in the School; The Rural Lore Scheme. *Address:* 12 Lewes Crescent, Brighton, 7. *T:* Brighton 4545. *Club:* Royal Empire Society.

Died 21 April 1949.

DAVIES, Arthur Cecil, CIE 1937; Indian Civil Service, retd; *b* 28 May 1889. *Educ:* St Andrew's College, Dublin; Trinity College, Dublin. Entered Indian Civil Service, 1913; retired 1939. *Address:* c/o Lloyds Bank Ltd, 6 Pall Mall, SW1.

Died 2 Sept. 1947.

DAVIES, Arthur Vernon, OBE; MB, ChB; retired medical practitioner; *s* of E. E. and Catherine Davies, Bridgend, Glamorgan; *m* Annie Maude, *d* of J. Brooke Unwin, MD, of Dunchurch, Rugby; one *s* one *d*. *Educ:* privately, Cardiff; Owens College, Manchester. House Surgeon, Manchester Royal Infirmary and Northern Hospital; Medical Officer of Health Crompton UDC; MO Infant Welfare Centre, and Public Vaccinator (Oldham District); Certifying Factory Surgeon, Shaw, Lancs; MP (U) Royton Division, Lancashire, 1924–31; Knight of Grace of the Order of St John of Jerusalem. *Recreations:* music and ambulance work. *Address:* Compton House, Ashford, Kent.

Died 4 Aug. 1942.

DAVIES, Ben; tenor singer; Fellow RAM; Mus. Doc; *b* Pontardawe, Wales, 1858; *m* 1885, Clara Perry. *Educ:* Royal Academy of Music. With Carl Rosa Opera Company three years; sang title part in Ivanhoe and Italian Opera, Covent Garden; afterwards principal tenor of all festivals and concerts. *Address:* Oakhill, nr Bath.

Died 28 March 1943.

DAVIES, Rev. Canon Benjamin; Vicar of Wrexham; Cursal Canon of St Asaph since 1935; *b* 29 May 1880; *m* 1937, Antoinette Richards Parfitt; one *s*. *Educ:* St David's College, Lampeter; Worcester College, Oxford. Canon of St David's Cathedral, 1928–35. *Address:* The Vicarage, Wrexham.

Died 1 June 1941.

DAVIES, Lt-Col Charles Stewart, CMG 1919; DSO 1917; *b* 1880; *m* 1932, Margot Alexa, *d* of Dr A. T. Drake, London. Served South Africa, 1899–1901 (Queen's medal with three clasps, King's medal with two clasps); European War, 1914–19 (despatches, CMG, DSO, Croix de Guerre); commanded 1st Batt. Leicestershire Regt, 1927–31; half-pay, 1931; retired pay, 1932. Inspector of Training and Operations, Ministry of Public Security, Northern Ireland, 1940–42; ARP Officer, Gosport, 1942–45. *Address:* Palma, Lee-on-Solent, Hants. *T:* Lee-on-Solent 79206.

Died 10 Dec. 1946.

DAVIES, Clara Novello; specialist in voice-building and breath control; choral conductor; *b* Cardiff, 7 April 1861; *d* of Jacob Davies; *m* David Davies (*d* 1931); one *s* (Ivor Novello). Founder and Conductor of Royal Welsh Ladies' Choir which won highest honours at World's Fair, Chicago, 1893, and Paris Exposition, 1900; received Royal Command from late Queen Victoria, 1894, and choir taken under Royal patronage; also appeared before their Majesties King George and Queen Mary, April 26, 1928; Paris Exposition, 1937, the French Government bestowed on her the Médaille de Mérite, the gold medal of the Renaissance Française, and a bronze Palm of Honour; Founder of Services Musical Instrument Fund. *Publications:* Success in Singing; Songs: A Voice from the Spirit Land; Friend; Without Thee; The Vigil; Mother; Dear Memories; Comfort; No More War; Victory Song (in conjunction with John Morava); Memoirs; Voice-building; You Can Sing; The Life I Have Loved. *Address:* Brook House, 113 Park Lane, W1. *T:* Mayfair 2463.

Died 7 Feb. 1943.

DAVIES, Daniel James, CBE 1927; JP; BSc; FIC, etc.; Trade Commissioner for Newfoundland since 1934; Governor of the Imperial College of Science and Technology since 1936; Governor of Imperial Institute; *b* May 1880; *s* of late David and Mary Davies of Llangeler, Carmarthenshire; *m* 1912, Elizabeth Margaret, *d* of late D. J. Evans, Llandyssul, South Wales; three *d*. *Educ:* Pencader Grammar School; University College, Cardiff. Represented Newfoundland in Imperial Forestry Conference, 1920; Exhibition Commissioner for Newfoundland, BEE, Wembley, 1924–25; represented Newfoundland in International Committee for Fishery Research; one time Member Council Higher Education; on Newfoundland Delegation Imperial Conference, 1930; Acting High Commissioner in London for Newfoundland, 1930–33; Chairman Newfoundland Fishery Board, 1933–34; Officer d'Academie (France), 1928. *Publications:* various pamphlets and papers in connection with Newfoundland minerals. *Recreation:* fishing. *Address:* 58 Victoria Street, SW1. *Clubs:* Constitutional, East India and Sports.

Died 31 March 1946.

DAVIES, Rt Rev. David E.; *see* Edwardes-Davies.

DAVIES, David Percy, JP Herts; FJI; Deputy Chairman and Editor, News of the World Ltd; Hon. Treasurer, London Welsh Regimental Committee; Vice-President, Newspaper Press Fund and Society of Miniature Rifle Clubs; Member, Board of Management, Royal Free Hospital and Eastman Dental Clinic and Honourable Society of Cymnrodorion; *b* Cardiff, 25 Oct. 1891; *e s* of late David Davies, JP, Penallt, Sketty, Swansea; *m* 1916, Gladys Beatrice Woodman; two *s* one *d*. *Educ:* Llandovery College. Called to Bar, Gray's Inn, 1919; Welch Regiment (TA), 1910; served European War,

1914–18 in France and Italy, Major Commanding XIth Corps Cyclist Battalion (despatches twice); entered journalism 1910 on staff South Wales Daily Post and later George Newnes Ltd, London; Sub-editor News of the World, 1919; Deputy Editor, 1933; Director, 1935. High Sheriff of Glamorgan, 1943–44. *Publication:* Trades Unions and the Law, 1914. *Recreations:* shooting, motoring. *Address:* Charnwood, Radlett, Herts; 3 King's Bench Walk, EC4. *TA:* Worldly, Fleet, London. *T:* Radlett 6440, Central 3030. *Clubs:* Press, Royal Automobile.

Died 15 Oct. 1946.

DAVIES, Edward Harold, MusDoc, ARCO FRCM; Elder Professor of Music, University of Adelaide and Director of Music at the Elder Conservatorium since 1919; *b* Oswestry, 18 July 1867; 4th *s* of late John Whitridge Davies and Susan Gregory, of Wem, Salop; *m* 1893, Ina, *d* of Benjamin E. Deland of Gwaler, S Australia; two *s* two *d*. *Educ:* Oswestry Grammar School; University of Adelaide. Studied music under Dr Joseph Bridge, of Chester Cathedral; ARCO, 1890; went to Australia, 1887; MusBac, Adelaide Univ.; MusDoc, 1902, the first doctorate in music conferred by an Australian university. Founder and Conductor of the Adelaide Bach Society and the South Australian Orchestra. *Publications:* Anthems and Songs; Gramophone Records of Australian Aboriginal Melodies and Research Pamphlets on same. *Recreations:* swimming, golf. *Address:* University, Adelaide. *T:* Central 1691.

Died 1 July 1947.

DAVIES, Ernest, CBE 1918; *b* 1873; *m* 1903, Elizabeth Eleanor, *d* of late Rev. Isaac Taylor; two *s*. *Address:* Cheyne House, Rodborough, Stroud, Glos.

Died 31 March 1946.

DAVIES, Gen. Sir Francis John, KCB 1915; KCMG 1916; KCVO 1919; CB 1907; Vice-Lieutenant, JP Worcestershire; *b* 3 July 1864; *s* of late Lieut.-Gen. H. F. Davies, late Grenadier Guards, of Elmley Castle, Pershore; *m* 1896, Madalen, CBE 1920, *d* of late Major Hugh Scott of Gala; two *s* one *d*. *Educ:* Eton. Served in the Worcestershire Militia, 1881–84; joined Grenadier Guards, 1884; Adjutant, 2nd Batt., 1893–97; Capt. 1895; Maj. 1899; Lt-Col (brev.), 1900; Col (brev.), 1904; Col (subst.) 1907; Maj.-Gen. 1913; Lt-Gen. 1917; Gen. 1922; passed Staff College, 1891; served Suakin Expedition, 1885 (medal and clasp and Khedive's star); Jebu Expedition, 1892 (medal and clasp); South African War, 1899–1901 (despatches, Brev. Lieut-Col, medal with four clasps); European War, 1914–17 (despatches six times, KCB, KCMG, promoted Lt-Gen.); ADC Cork Dist, 1889; Special Service West Africa, 1892; DAAG Cape of Good Hope, 1897; S Dist, 1898; DAAG Intelligence Army Headquarters, South Africa, 1899; Act. Commissioner of Police, Johannesburg, 1900; Staff Captain, War Office, 1902; DAQMG, WO, 1902; Asst Director of Military Operations, 1904; one of British Delegates at International Conference on Wireless Telegraphy, Berlin, 1906; AQMG Western Command, 1907; General Staff Officer, 1st Division, Aldershot, 1908; GOC 1st (Guards) Brigade, Aldershot, 1909; Brig.-Gen. General Staff, Aldershot Command, 1910–13; Director of Staff Duties, War Office, 1913–14; served European War (France and Dardanelles and Egypt), 1914–17 (despatches, KCB, KCMG, prom. Lt-Gen.); Military Secretary War Office, 1916–19; GOC-in-C Scottish Command, 1919–23; Lieutenant of the Tower of London, 1923–26; ADC General to the King, 1922–26; retired pay, 1926. *Recreations:* fishing, shooting, and other field sports. *Address:* Elmley Castle, Pershore, Worcestershire. *Clubs:* Guards', Travellers', Beefsteak.

Died 18 March 1948.

DAVIES, Major Sir George Frederick, Kt 1936; CVO 1937; MA, JP; Alderman of Somerset County Council, 1938; *b* Honolulu, Hawaiian Islands, 19 April 1875; *s* of late Theophilus Harris Davies of Ravensdale, Tunbridge Wells, and late Mary Ellen, *d* of late George Cocking; *m* 1900, Mary Ellen, *e d* of late Col John Birney, RE; three *s* two *d*. *Educ:* Uppingham School; King's College, Cambridge. British Vice-Consul at Honolulu; European War (Glos Regt), 1914–19; MP (C) Yeovil Division of Somerset, 1923–45; Assistant Government Whip, Nov. 1931; a Lord Commissioner of the Treasury, 1932–35; Vice-Chamberlain of HM Household, 1935–37; Comptroller of HM Household, 1937–38. Landowner. *Recreations:* reading and gardening. *Address:* Courtfield, Norton-sub-Hamdon, Somerset. *T:* Chiselborough 246. *Club:* Carlton.

Died 21 June 1950.

DAVIES, George Maitland Lloyd; *b* 1880; *s* of John Davies, Liverpool; *m* 1916, Leslie, *d* of Michael Holroyd Smith; one *d*. *Educ:* Liverpool. Formerly an Officer in Volunteers; a bank manager, then Secretary of Welsh Housing Trust; gave up business career to become servant of the Fellowship of Reconciliation; imprisoned during War for preaching Christianity. MP (Christian Pacifist) University of Wales, 1923–24. *Publications:* numerous pamphlets, etc. on Peace. *Recreations:* gardening and walking.

Died 16 Dec. 1949.

DAVIES, Rev. Gilbert Austin, LLD, MA; *b* Shepherd's Bush, 15 Sept. 1868; *s* of Geo. Davies of Alderley Edge; *m* Beatrix Ida Whyte. *Educ:* Aldenham Grammar School; Owens College, Manchester; Trinity College, Cambridge (Major Scholar, 1887; Fellow, 1892–98). Gladstone Professor of Greek in University College, Liverpool, 1898–1906; Professor of Greek, Glasgow, 1906–34; Officer of the Order of St Sava. *Publications:* School Editions of Tacitus' Histories I and of Demosthenes' Philippics; Recension of Ovid's Fasti and (in collaboration) of Statius' Silvae (in Postgate's Corpus Poetarum Latinorum). *Address:* c/o Royal Bank of Scotland, St Andrews, Fife.

Died 26 July 1948.

DAVIES, Harold Whitridge, ED; Professor of Physiology, University of Sydney; *e s* of Professor E. Harold Davies; unmarried. *Educ:* Prince Alfred College, Adelaide; University of Adelaide. MB, BS Adelaide, 1917; FRACP, 1938. Captain Australian Army Medical Corps; War Service with 3rd Australian Division, France, 1917–18; Lt-Col AAMC; Reserve of Officers; Research Assistant with J. S. Haldane, CH, FRS, at New College, Oxford; Research Assistant and Lecturer in Department of Therapeutics, University of Edinburgh; Rockefeller Foundation Fellow and Assistant Physician, Hospital of the Rockefeller Institute, New York; Lecturer in Physiology and Pharmacology in the University of Leeds. *Publications:* (with J. C. Meakins), Respiratory Function in Disease, 1925; numerous contributions to Medical and Scientific Journals. *Recreations:* literature, art, music. *Address:* The University, Sydney. *Clubs:* British Empire; Imperial Service, University, Sydney.

Died 8 June 1946.

DAVIES, Maj.-Gen. Henry Rodolph, CB 1916; *b* 28 Sept. 1865; *s* of late Lt-Gen. H. F. Davies, Elmley Castle, Worcestershire; *m* Isabel Warwick, *d* of late Maj.-Gen. D. K. Evans. *Educ:* Eton. Served Burma, 1887–88 (medal, two clasps); NW Frontier, India, 1897–98 (medal with clasp); Tirah, 1897–98 (despatches, clasp); China, 1900 (medal); S Africa, 1901–02 (Queen's medal 4 clasps); European War (despatches eight times, Brevet Col, CB, Maj.-Gen.); commanded 52nd (2nd Oxf. and Bucks) Light Infantry, 1911–15; commanded 3rd Bde,

1915–16; 33rd Bde, 1917; 11th Div., 1917–19; 49th Div., 1919–23; retired pay, 1923. *Address:* 147 Coleherne Court, SW5.

Died 4 Jan. 1950.

DAVIES, Sir (Henry) Walford, KCVO 1937; Kt 1922; CVO 1932; OBE 1919; MusDoc (Camb.), 1898; FRCM (Lond.), 1926; Hon. LLD (Leeds), 1904; (Glasgow), 1926; FRCO (Lond.), 1904; Hon. FRAM 1923; Hon. MusDoc (Dublin), 1930; (Oxon), 1935; Master of the King's Music since 1934; Director of Music and Chairman of the National Council of Music, University of Wales, since 1919; Gresham Professor of Music since 1924; *b* Oswestry, Shropshire, 6 Sept. 1869; *y s* of late John Whitridge Davies and Susan, *d* of Thomas Gregory, Wem; *m* 1924, Margaret, *o c* of Rev. William Evans, Rector of Narberth. *Educ:* private tuition; St George's School, Windsor. Entered Choir of St George's, Windsor, 1882; assistant organist to Sir Walter Parratt, 1885–90; also organist of Windsor Park Chapel Royal; held a scholarship (for Composition) at the Royal College of Music, Kensington, 1890–94; organist and choirmaster at St Anne's, Soho, 1890–91; at Christ Church, Hampstead, 1891–98; Organist and Director of the Choir at the Temple Church, 1898–1923; Organising Director of Music, RAF, with rank of Major, 1918–19; teacher of Counterpoint at the RCM 1895; Prof. of Music at Univ. Coll. of Wales, Aberystwyth, 1919–26; Organist of St George's Chapel Windsor, 1927–32; Conductor of the Bach Choir, 1903–07; London Church Choir Association, 1901–13. *Publications: compositions:* an oratorio, 'The Temple' (Worcester Festival, 1902); a cantata, Everyman (Leeds Festival, 1904); Five Sayings of Jesus (Worcester Festival, 1911); Song of St Francis (Birmingham Festival, 1912); a Cantata, Hervé Riel; Cycle of Songs for children, a Merry Heart; Fantasy for tenor solo, chorus, and orchestra from Dante (Worcester Festival, 1920); Cantata, Heaven's Gate (People's Palace Festival, 1917); High Heaven's King (Worcester Festival), 1926; Parthenia Suite, Festival Overture and Holiday Tunes for Orchestra; a Children's Symphony; Christ in the Universe (Worcester Festival, 1929), and other works; *books:* Editor of the Fellowship Song Book; New Fellowship Song Book; A New Song Book (Llyfr Canu Newydd) Parts I and II, and other publications for Univ. of Wales Council of Music; A Students' Hymnal; Hymns of the Kingdom; (with Harvey Grace) Music and Worship, 1935; The Pursuit of Music, 1936, etc. *Address:* Cookham Dean. *Club:* Athenæum.

Died 11 March 1941.

DAVIES, John Bowen; KC 1926; Bencher of the Middle Temple, 1930; Autumn Reader Middle Temple, 1942; Stipendiary Magistrate at Merthyr Tydfil since 1935; *b* 1876; *s* of Henry Harries Davies, surgeon, Llandyssul, and Elizabeth Rosa, 2nd *d* of John Jones; *m* 1918, Mary, 2nd *surv. d* of Alderman D. L. Jones, JP, Derlwyn, Carm.; one *s. Educ:* Epsom; Downing College, Cambridge; MA, LLB (Honours). Called to Bar, Middle Temple, 1898; joined South Wales and Chester Circuit; Lieut Pembroke Yeomanry, Sept. 1914; Adjutant 2/1 Royal North Devon Hussars Yeomanry, 1916; served in France and Belgium with Royal West Surrey Regiment, 1917; invalided home, 1918; made Courts-Martial Officer and Deputy Judge Advocate, Northern Command, with substantive rank of Captain; Rector (lay) of St Peter's, Carmarthen; Magistrate for Cardiganshire, 1915; Chairman of Llandyssul Petty Sessional Division, 1924; Magistrate for Carmarthenshire, 1932; Recorder of Merthyr Tydfil, 1933–36; Vice-Chairman of Carmarthenshire Quarter Sessions, 1936; Magistrate for the Counties of Glamorgan, Monmouth and Brecon, 1936; Member of Carmarthenshire Agricultural Committee; Member of Glamorgan Standing Joint Committee, 1941; contested (C), Caernarvon Boroughs, 1929; Master of Vale of

Clettwr Fox Hunt, 1937. *Recreations:* hunting, fishing. *Address:* Derlwyn, nr Carmarthen; San Remo, Merthyr Tydfil; 3 Temple Gardens, EC4. *TA:* 87 Temple.

Died 12 Oct. 1943.

DAVIES, Col Percy George, CMG 1918; CBE 1927; late Royal Army Ordnance Corps; *y s* of late W. T. Davies of Old Charlton, Kent; *m* Annie, *y d* of Colonel Thomas Maxwell, JP, Natal; one *d. Educ:* privately. Joined Royal Garrison Artillery, and transferred to Army Ordnance Department; served in China, India, and South African War (despatches twice, Queen's and King's medals); European War (despatches three times, Bt Lt-Col, CMG), and in War of 1939–45; retired pay, 1927. *Recreation:* all forms of sport. *Address:* 4 Southampton Row, WC1.

Died 1 Dec. 1947.

DAVIES, Rachael Annie C.; *see* Cox-Davies.

DAVIES, Randall (Robert Henry), FSA; occasional writer; *b* 1866; *s* of late Rev. R. H. Davies, Incumbent of Chelsea Old Church; *m* 1910, Gladys Margaret, *y d* of late Sir Herbert Miles, GCB, GCMG; two *s. Educ:* Bradfield (Founder's Boy); Scoones's. For some time Art Critic to the Academy, Westminster Gazette, New Statesman, and Queen. Solicitor since 1898, and for some years Confidential Secretary to late Joseph Pulitzer, owner of the New York World. *Publications:* Chelsea Old Church, 1904; Portfolio Monograph, No. 48, 1907; Six Centuries of Painting, 1914; Stories of the English Artists (with Cecil Hunt), 1908; The Greatest House at Chelsey, 1914; A Lyttel Booke of Nonsense, 1912 and 1925; Monographs on Velasquez, Reynolds, and Romney; Black's Dictionary of Pictures, 1921; Chats on Old English Drawings, 1923; A Little More Nonsense, 1923; Thomas Girtin's Water Colours, 1923; The Railway Centenary, 1925; Notes upon some of Shakespeare's Sonnets, 1927; Less Eminent Victorians, 1927; Caricature, 1928; Out of the Ark, 1930; Advice to Young Ladies, 1933; Editor of the Old Water Colour Society's Club Annual Volume. *Recreation:* collecting. *Address:* 1 Cheyne Gardens, Chelsea, SW3. *T:* Flaxman 2549. *Club:* Burlington Fine Arts.

Died 24 Jan. 1946.

DAVIES, Col Thomas Arthur Harkness, CB 1909; DSO 1893; *b* Calcutta, 29 Nov. 1857; 3rd *s* of late Major-General Horatio Nelson Davies, Bengal Staff Corps, and Helena Adelaide, *d* of late John Anderson, HEIC, of Straquhan, Dumfries, Scotland. *Educ:* Wellington. Joined Devon Regt, 1876; Adjutant 2nd Batt., 1889–92; commanded 1st Batt. Devonshire Regt sixteen months in S African War, and in India, 1902–06; commanded 9th (Service) Batt. Devonshire Regt, Sept. 1914–Sept. 1915, July 1915–Sept. 1915 in France; SSO Madras command, 1892–94; DAAG Burma, 1894–97; Afghan War, 1880 (medal); Wuntho Expedition, Burma, 1892; commanded NE Column in Kachen Hills, Burma, 1892 (medal and clasps, DSO); commanded Sima Column in Kachen Hills, Burma, 1893; Tirah Expedition, 1897 (medal and 2 clasps); South Africa, 1899–1902, including operations Tugela Heights, Relief of Ladysmith, and Belfast (despatches, Brevet Lt-Col, medal and 3 clasps); European War, 1914–15.

Died 9 Nov. 1942.

DAVIES, Thomas Walton; Assistant Secretary, Colonial Office since 1945; *b* 14 Oct. 1907; *o s* of late David Davies, MB, Tunbridge Wells; *m* 1939, Joan, *o d* of late Lt-Col T. Eardley-Wilmot, DSO; one *s* two *d. Educ:* Tonbridge School; Balliol College, Oxford. Inner Temple, barrister-at-law. Asst Principal, Ministry of Transport, 1930; Colonial Office, 1931; seconded to Govt of Palestine, 1935; Assistant Private Secretary to Mr J. H. Thomas and Mr Ormsby-Gore, successive Secretaries of State for the Colonies, 1936; Secretary, Colonial Development Advisory Committee, 1937; Member of UK Trade Delegation to USA, 1938;

Colonial Office Observer, Eastern Group Conference, Delhi, 1940; Middle East Supply Centre, 1942; Colonial Secretary, Leeward Islands, 1943–45. *Address:* Dowches, Kelvedon, Essex. *Club:* United University.

Died 30 Jan. 1948.

DAVIES, Sir Walford; *see* Davies, Sir H. W.

DAVIES, Rev. Canon Watkin; Vicar of St Jude's, Swansea, since 1920; *b* 1869; *s* of David and Mary Davies; *m* 1893; one *d*. *Educ:* St David's College, Lampeter. Ordained, 1902; Curate, Pembrey, 1902; Llansamlet, 1906; St Mary, Swansea 1908; Hon. Chaplain of Swansea Workhouse 1912; Hon. Canon of Brecon Cathedral 1934; Hon. Secretary Evangelistic Temperance and Purity Committee of the Diocese; Past Provincial Grand Chaplain of South Wales, Eastern Division 1929. *Address:* St Jude's Vicarage, Swansea. *T:* 3191.

Died 17 Feb. 1943.

DAVIES, His Honour Judge William Frank de Rolante; Judge of County Court, Circuit 31, since 1926; Chairman of Carmarthenshire Quarter Sessions; Chairman of Quarter Sessions for the Town and County of Haverfordwest; *s* of late James Davies, JP; *m* 1926, Valerie Eileen, *d* of late Dr Hubert Thomas, JP, Swansea; one *s*. *Educ:* Llandovery School; Hertford College, Oxford. Called to Bar, Middle Temple, 1913; Capt., 4th Batt. The Welsh Regiment, 1915–19; served in Gallipoli, Egypt and Palestine (despatches). *Recreations:* golf, tennis. *Address:* Ucheldir, Carmarthen. *T:* 614. *Clubs:* United University; Carmarthen County.

Died 7 March 1942.

DAVIES, William John, CH 1917; Member of Brassworkers' and Metal Mechanics' Society; *b* 1848; *s* of Thomas Charles Davies; *m* 1869, *d* of Mark Cooke. Special war work in connection with recruiting and labour.

Died 12 Oct. 1934.

DAVIES, William Robert, CB 1909; *b* 1870; *m* 1898, Lucie Isabel, *d* of Henry Julian, Bolton. *Educ:* Manchester Grammar School; Balliol College, Oxford. Private Sec. to Pres. of Board of Education, 1903–05, and to Chief Sec. for Ireland, 1905–08; Prin. Assist Sec., Technological Branch, Board of Education, 1919–30. *Address:* c/o National Provincial Bank, 61 Victoria Street, SW1. *Club:* Athenæum.

Died 7 June 1949.

DAVIES, William Thomas Frederick, CMG 1920; DSO 1900; MD, BS (Lond.), MRCS (Eng.); Hon. LLD; late President S African Medical Council; Hon. Consulting Surgeon to Johannesburg Hospital; late Lt-Col Imperial Light Horse Volunteers; *b* 13 Aug. 1860; *s* of Ebenezer Davies; *m* 1886, Florence (*d* 1941), *d* of T. Dixon. Served South Africa as Surgeon-Major to Imperial Light Horse, 1899–1900 (despatches, DSO); commanded 2nd Imperial Light Horse in South-West Africa, 1914–15 (wounded); served in RAMC as Major, 1917–19; appointed Surgeon Specialist General Military Hospital, Colchester. *Address:* Glen Lynden, Mooi River, Natal. *Clubs:* Rand, Johannesburg.

Died 24 June 1947.

DAVIES-COOKE, Philip Tatton; *see* Cooke.

DAVIS, Alexander; *b* London, 1861; *m* 1st, Arabelle Selig (decd); 2nd, Mabel Hunt; five *s* one *d*. *Educ:* privately. Lived and travelled for many years in South Africa; a Swaziland pioneer under the late King Umbandine; founded the Bulawayo Sketch 1894, which he edited and illustrated as a pioneer organ until 1897; deputed to establish Rhodesian organ in London; edited Rhodesia, 1898, 1902; edited African Review, 1903–05; amateur artist and sculptor; first editor and later principal owner The Leader, Nairobi (later merged in the East African Standard). *Publications:* Umbandine, a Romance of Swaziland; The Native Problem in South Africa; A Layman's Philosophy, 1912; A Microcosm of Empire, 1917; Chronicles of Kenya, 1928; writer on Colonial subjects. *Address:* Nairobi, Kenya Colony.

Died 15 Oct. 1945.

DAVIS, Sir Charles, 1st Bt *cr* 1946; Kt 1944; DL, JP; one of HM's Lieutenants City of London; *b* 1878; 2nd *s* of George John and Harriet Davis; *m* 1900, Elsie Keeble, Westwood, Peterborough; two *s* one *d*. Member of Lloyd's; Freeman of London; Chm. Medway Conservancy, 1936–45; Member Port of London Authority, 1928–50; Commissioner of Taxes, City of London; High Sheriff of Kent, 1934–35; Sheriff, City of London, 1942–43; Lord Mayor of London, 1945–46. Formerly Hon. Colonel Kent (Fortress) Royal Engineers; 73rd Searchlight Regiment RA and 138th City of London Field Regiment RA; MInstCEI, MIMechE, MInstStructE, FRGS, FCS. *Publication:* One Hundred Years of Portland Cement, 1824–1924, etc. *Heir: s* Gilbert [*b* 2 Aug. 1901; *m* 1927; one *s* one *d*; *m* 1944]. *Address:* Barrington Hall, near Cambridge. *Clubs:* Constitutional, City Livery.

Died 27 Oct. 1950.

DAVIS, Dwight Filley; *b* St Louis, Missouri, 5 July 1879; *s* of John Tilden Davis and Maria Filley; *m* 1904, Helen Brooks, Boston; one *s* three *d*. *Educ:* Smith Academy, St Louis, Mo; Harvard University, AB 1900; Washington University (St Louis) Law School; LLB 1903. Member Public Baths Commission, St Louis, 1903–06; Public Library Board of Control, Museum of Fine Arts, 1904–07, 1911–12; Public Recreation Commission, 1906–07; St Louis House of Delegates, 1907–09; Board of Freeholders, 1909–11; City Plan Commission, 1911–14; Park Commissioner, 1911–14; Captain, Fifth Missouri Infantry, 1917; Major, 1917; Lieutenant-Colonel, 1918; Colonel, Officers' Reserve Corps, 1923; Member, Board of Overseers, Harvard University, 1915–21; Director, War Finance Corporation, Washington, DC, 1921–23; The Assistant Secretary of War, 1923–25; Secretary of War, 1925–29; Governor-General of the Philippine Islands, 1929–32; Director-General, Army Specialist Corps, 1942; Member, Board of Overseers, Harvard University, 1926–32; Hon. LLD Washington University, Univ. of Missouri and Penn. Military College. *Recreations:* tennis, golf, squash racquets. *Address:* Meridian Plantation, Tallahassee, Fla, USA. *Clubs:* Metropolitan, Burning Tree, Racquet, Washington; University, Harvard; New York; City, Racquet, Noonday, St Louis; Tennis and Racquet, Algonquin, Boston.

Died 28 Nov. 1945.

DAVIS, Eliza Jeffries, FSA; Fellow of University College, London; *b* 11 Feb. 1875; *e c* of John Jeffries Davis, farmer, Cross o' th' Hill, Stratford-on-Avon, and Catherine, *d* of Leacroft Freer; unmarried. *Educ:* private school; Cheltenham Ladies' College. BA London, Derby Prize for History, 1897; MA, 1913. Assistant Mistress, Bedford High School, 1898–1904, Stepney Pupil Teachers' School, 1904–08; Lecturer and Vice-Principal, Moorfields, LCC Training College, 1908–12; Research Assistant in the Dept of History, University College, London, 1914–19; Lecturer in the Sources of English History, 1919–21; Reader in the History and Records of London, University of London, 1921–40. Hon. Secretary to the Editorial Board of History from the beginning of the new series in 1916 to 1922; Editor, 1922–34; Hon. Librarian, Institute of Historical Research, 1921–23; Acting Secretary, 1939–40. *Publications:* articles in the Victoria County History of London, 1909; Tudor Studies presented to A. F. Pollard, 1924; historical journals, etc.; The Children's Rossetti (ed.), 1914. *Address:* Institute of Historical Research, University of London, WC1. *Club:* University of London.

Died 30 Oct. 1943.

DAVIS, Hon. Frank Roy, MD, CM, FACS; Minister of Public Health, Nova Scotia since 1933; *b* 25 Aug. 1888; *s* of Rev. J. H. and Eva Trueman Davis; *m* 1911, Elizabeth Balcon; two *s. Educ:* Halifax County Academy; University, Mt Allison and University, Dalhousie. Practised profession at Petite Riviere and Bridgewater; elected for Constituency of Lunenburg to the Nova Scotia Legislature, 1933; re-elected, 1937; Director, General Trust & Executor Corporation; Director Maritime Telegraph and Telephone Co. *Religion:* United Church of Canada. *Recreations:* golf, curling. *Address:* Bridgewater, Nova Scotia, Canada. *T:* 188. *Clubs:* Ashburn Golf and Country; Bridgewater Golf; Halifax, Halifax Curling.

Died 17 Sept. 1948.

DAVIS, Sir George Francis, Kt 1941; Chairman of Directors, Davis Gelatine Co. Pty Ltd, Cockatoo Docks and Eng. Co. Pty Ltd, Mount Frome Lime Co. Pty Ltd, Director Mercantile Mutual Insurance Co. Pty Ltd; *b* 22 Nov. 1883; *s* of late Charles George Davis, Hanley Hall, Worcester, England, later of New Zealand; *m* 1917, Elizabeth Eileen Schischka. *Educ:* King's College, Auckland. Joined Staff of New Zealand Glue Co., 1901, and has been actively engaged ever since, together with his brother, in directing the industry. *Recreations:* gardening, motoring, travel. *Address:* 54 Wentworth Road, Vaucluse, Sydney, NSW, Australia. *TA:* care Geodavis, Sydney. *T:* BU 5865 (Sydney). *Clubs:* Australian, Sydney.

Died 13 July 1947.

DAVIS, H. H.; *see* Haldin-Davis.

DAVIS, Lucien, RI; artist; *b* Liverpool, Jan. 1860; *s* of William Davis, artist, Liverpool. *Educ:* St Francis Xavier's College, Liverpool. Gained Studentship at Royal Academy, 1877; took several prizes. Commenced work as black-and-white artist in Cassell's publications, 1878; first important drawing published in Graphic, 1881; joined staff of Illustrated London News, 1885, since when many of the most important Christmas Number and 'great social events' drawings have been his; HM the Queen purchased a water-colour drawing, 1894; Badminton volumes on Cricket, Lawn Tennis, and Billiards are illustrated by him. *Recreations:* cricket, lawn-tennis, fishing. *Address:* Crayside, Tenterden, Kent.

Died 3 Jan. 1941.

DAVIS, Hon. Norman H.; United States Ambassador; Chairman, American Red Cross since 1938; *b* Bedford County, Tennessee; *s* of Maclin H. Davis and Christina Lee Shofner; *m* 1898, Mackie Paschall; four *s* four *d. Educ:* Vanderbilt University; Stanford University. DCL University of the South, 1921; LLD, Columbia University, 1933, Harvard University, 1935, Princeton University, 1937. Began business career in Cuba, 1902, became interested in banking, sugar and other enterprises; organized, 1905, The Trust Co. of Cuba and was president until 1917; adviser to Secretary of Treasury in connection with foreign loans, 1917; special US delegate to Spain and representative of Treasury in London and Paris, 1918; finance commissioner of US to Europe, 1919; American member Armistice Commission; member Supreme Economic Council (Chairman of finance section); financial adviser to Pres. Wilson and American Commission to Negotiate Peace; member of Reparations and Financial commissions; Assistant Secretary of United States Treasury, 1919–20; Under-Secretary of State, 1920–21; chairman, Commission of League of Nations to determine status of territory of Memel; Member of Board of Trustees of Vanderbilt University; trustee of Bank of New York; member of American Delegation to International Economic Conference, Geneva, 1927; formerly member League of Nations Financial Committee; member of the organizing committee for International Monetary and Economic Conference, 1932; delegate from US to Disarmament Conference, Geneva, Switzerland, 1932, and chairman of American delegation, 1933; head of American delegation to London Naval Conference, 1935; American delegate to Nine Power Treaty Conference, Brussels, Belgium, 1937; Chairman, Board of Governors, League of Red Cross Societies, 1938. *Recreation:* golf. *Address:* American Red Cross, National Headquarters, Washington, DC. *T:* Washington, DC Vic 8300. *Clubs:* Metropolitan, Burning Tree, Washington; Century, The Links, New York.

Died 2 July 1944.

DAVIS, Sir (Steuart) Spencer, Kt 1930; CMG 1919; Governor and Commander-in-Chief, St Helena, 1932–37; *b* 1875; *e s* of late Benjamin Shuttleworth Davis, MEC of St Kitts, West Indies; *m* 1915, Emma Agnes (*d* 1946), *o c* of late Nicholas Darnell Davis, CMG, of British Guiana; one *s. Educ:* Dean Close School, Cheltenham. Called to Bar, Gray's Inn, 1915; served in Customs and Treasury, St Kitts, West Indies, 1893–1901; Lieut St Kitts-Nevis Defence Force, 1898; Acting Adjutant, 1899; attached Exchequer and Audit Dept, London, July 1901; Assistant Treasurer, Gold Coast, Aug. 1901; Chief Assistant Treasurer, 1908; acted as PMG on three occasions, and as Treasurer, Member of Executive and Legislative Councils and Board of Education on many occasions between 1907 and 1916; Treasurer, April 1917, but did not take up appointment; Treasurer Tanganyika Territory, 1916; acting Chief Secretary, June–July 1919, and in Administrator's Deputy, April 1920; Treasurer, Palestine, 1922–32; Acting Chief Secretary, Palestine, June–Sept. 1923, Dec. 1924–Jan. 1925, April–May, and July–Aug. 1925; Chairman, Currency Committee, 1924; Delegate for Palestine at Constantinople in connection with Ottoman Public Debt, Oct.–Nov. 1924; Chairman, Commission on Finances of Orthodox Patriarchate of Jerusalem, Dec. 1925–June 1928; Chairman, Standing Committee for Commerce and Industry from 1928; Officer Administering Government of Palestine and Acting High Commissioner Trans.-Jordan, July–Sept., 1930. *Club:* East India and Sports.

Died 3 April 1950.

DAVIS, Rev. Canon Thomas Henry, MusDoc, BA, FRCO; Precentor, Canon Residentiary since 1920, and Organist, 1899–1933, of Wells Cathedral; *b* Birmingham, 1867; *m* 1900, Mabel (*d* 1936), 2nd *d* of Richard Child Heath, of Myton Grange, Warwick; one *s* one *d. Educ:* King Edward VIth School, Birmingham. Asst Mathematical Master, King Edward VIth School, Birmingham; Curate, St Mary's Church, Warwick, 1892–95; Priest-Vicar, Wells Cathedral, Assistant Master, Wells Cathedral Grammar School, 1895–1900; Prebendary of Combe VIIIth in Wells Cathedral, 1912. *Publications:* church music. *Address:* The Liberty, Wells, Somerset.

Died 9 Oct. 1947.

DAVISON, John Clarke; KC; Recorder of Londonderry since 1938; *b* 19 April 1875; *s* of late Samuel Davison, Armagh; *m* 1901, Alice M. (decd) *d* of late J. E. Peel, Armagh; two *s* one *d. Educ:* Coleraine Academical Institution (Scholar); Trinity College, Dublin (Exhibitioner, all three 1st prizes in Law School, BA, LLB); King's Inns, Dublin (Exhibitioner). Called to Irish Bar, 1898; called to Inner Bar, 1926; Senior Crown Prosecutor Co. Louth and Co. Antrim; Legal Adviser Government of Northern Ireland, 1922–25; MP (U) Co. Armagh, 1925–29, and for Mid-Armagh, 1929–38; Parliament of Northern Ireland; Chairman of Committees and Deputy Speaker, 1937; Parliamentary Secretary to Ministry of Home Affairs, 1937–38. *Recreations:* motoring, golf. *Address:* Kevock House, Knockbreda Road, Belfast. *T:* Belfast 41044. *Clubs:* Ulster, Belfast; Northern Counties, Londonderry.

Died 19 Feb. 1946.

DAVISON, Rt Hon. Sir Joseph, PC (N Ire.) 1940; Kt 1921; DL; Senator, N Ireland since 1935; *b* 1868. Contested (U) W Division, Belfast, 1923; formerly Alderman, retired 1924. *Address:* Thelma, Old Cavehill Road, Belfast.

Died 15 July 1948.

DAVRAY, Henry D., CBE; Officier de la Légion d'Honneur; Commander Nichan Iftikar and Ouissam Alaouite; RSL; Fellow and Silver Medal of the RSA; Editor Cross Channel; *b* 4 Aug. 1873. *Educ:* Paris University; Sorbonne; Ecole des Hautes Etudes. Translated Edmund Gosse's Modern English Literature, 1900, and Father and Son, 1912; W. G. Aston's Japanese Literature, 1901; Fitz Maurice Kelly's Spanish Literature, 1904; W. P. Trent's American Literature, and novels by G. Meredith, H. G. Wells, Arnold Bennett, Rudyard Kipling, Joseph Conrad, Maurice Hewlett, Mrs W. K. Clifford, Fiona Macleod and others; since 1898 has edited the Collection of Foreign Authors, published by the Mercure de France; contributes articles on English subjects to French, Swiss, Belgian, Italian dailies and periodicals; published La Littérature Anglo-Canadienne—Chez les Anglais pendant la Grande Guerre, English translation, Through French Eyes, Britain's Effort—L'Œuvre, et le Prestige de Lord Kitchener, English translation, Lord Kitchener: his Work and his Prestige; Oscar Wilde: La Tragédie Finale; Lecturer on English Literature, Ecole des Hautes Etudes Sociales, Paris, and Brussels Université Nouvelle; Literary Editor of Les Nouvelles, 1910–12; Editor of the Revue Sud-Américaine, 1913–14; special correspondent of Le Petit Parisien to the British front, 1915; special correspondent of Le Petit Journal in England, 1915–25; co-editor with J. L. May of The Anglo-French Review, 1918–21. *Address:* 14 Panton Street, Haymarket, SW1. *Club:* Savage.

Died 21 Jan. 1944.

DAVSON, Lt-Col Sir Ivan Buchanan, Kt 1942; OBE; TD; a Governor of the Imperial College of Tropical Agriculture; a Deputy Chairman of the West India Committee; *b* 1884; 3rd *s* of late Sir Henry Davson. *Educ:* Eton. City of London Yeomanry, 1904; RAF, 1916; Military Assistant to the Controller of Aircraft Production and Director of Foreign Services, 1918; served on West Indian Currency and Air Transport Committees; Deputy Chairman West India Com., 1928–36; Chairman, 1936–45. *Publications:* on West Indian Currency and British Colonial Sugar. *Address:* 29 St James's Street, SW1. *Clubs:* Carlton, Turf, White's, Beefsteak.

Died 27 Jan. 1947.

DAVY, Lila, CBE 1919; *b* 1873; *d* of late George Baynton Davy, JP of Owthorpe, Notts, and Spean Lodge, Spean Bridge, Scotland. *Educ:* at home. VAD, France, 1915–17; Queen Mary's Army Auxiliary Corps, with British Armies France and Flanders, 1917–20 (GHQ Sept. 1918–Jan. 1920) (despatches four times). *Club:* Service Women's (London and Edinburgh).

Died 6 Dec. 1949.

DAVY, Maurice John Bernard; Deputy Director and Keeper, Department of Air and Water Transport, Science Museum; *b* 12 Nov. 1892; *o s* of late Lieut-Col J. J. Davy; *m* 1924, Rosemary Mackintosh, *o d* of late Maj. H. A. Balbi; one *s* one *d*. *Educ:* Douai Abbey; privately. Served European War with 3rd Bn Connaught Rangers and as pilot officer Royal Flying Corps; entered Science Museum, 1920, specialising in the history of flight; Deputy Keeper, 1934; FRAeS; Officer, Order of St John of Jerusalem. *Publications:* Official Handbooks to the National Aeronautical Collections: Heavier-than-air Aircraft, 1929; Lighter-than-air Aircraft, 1934; Propulsion of Aircraft, 1936; Henson and Stringfellow, 1931; Interpretive History of Flight, 1937; Airpower and

Civilization, 1941; various papers on the history of aeronautics. *Address:* 51 Addison Avenue, W11. *T:* Park 6103. *Club:* Athenæum.

Died 1 June 1950.

DAW, Sir William Herbert, Kt 1923; one of the founders of the British Empire League (Vice-Chairman and Hon. Treasurer) and British Empire Club; *b* 1859; *s* of late Edmund Daw; *m* 1885, Amelia, *d* of late Henry Hobson. *Address:* Polruan, Chyngton Road, Seaford, Sussex.

Died 27 Feb. 1941.

DAWE, Sir Arthur James, KCMG 1942 (CMG 1938); OBE 1932; *b* 1891; *e s* of late A. H. Dawe, Tring; *m*; one *d*. *Educ:* Berkhamsted School; Brasenose Coll., Oxford. Editor of the Isis; Lt RNVR, War service, 1914–18; entered Colonial Office, 1918; Deputy Secretary to Imperial Economic Conference, 1923; Secretary to Commission of Enquiry into Affairs of Freetown Municipality, 1926; Secretary to Malta Royal Commission, 1931; Member of Commission of Enquiry into the Facilities for Oriental, Slavonic, East European and African Studies; Member Br Govt deleg. to Internat. Labour Conf., 1946; Asst Under-Sec. of State, Colonial Office, 1938–45; Deputy Under-Secretary of State, 1945–47; retired, 1947. *Club:* Authors'.

Died 14 July 1950.

DAWKINS, Lady Bertha Mabel; Woman of the Bedchamber to HM The Queen, 1907–35, Extra Woman of the Bedchamber since 1935; *b* 15 May 1866; 3rd *d* of Edward, 1st Earl of Lathom; *m* 1903, Major Arthur F. Dawkins, Fifth Fusiliers (*d* 1905); one *d*. *Educ:* home. *Address:* Wyck House, Wadhurst, Sussex.

Died 12 Nov. 1943.

DAWKINS, Charles William, CBE; *b* 1870; *m* 1901, Eleanor Selina, *d* of John Cranfield, Edmonton; one *s*. *Address:* Braeside, Uphill Road, NW7. *T:* Mill Hill 2373. *Club:* National Liberal.

Died 15 June 1948.

DAWKINS, Sir Horace Christian, KCB 1930; CB 1925; MBE 1918; Clerk of House of Commons, 1930–37; *b* 1867; *s* of late Clinton G. Dawkins, Foreign Office; *m* 1916, Marjorie, *d* of late Sir Vesey Holt, KBE, Mount Mascal, Bexley, Kent. *Educ:* Eton; Balliol College, Oxford. Entered House of Commons Office, 1891; second clerk assistant, 1918; Clerk Assistant, 1921–30. *Recreations:* shooting and golf. *Address:* Heale Cottage, Curry Rivel, Somerset.

Died 4 Feb. 1944.

DAWOOD, Khan Sahib Sir Adamjee Hajee, Kt 1938; merchant. *Address:* Stephen House, Dalhousie Sq., Calcutta.

Died 27 Jan. 1948.

DAWSON of Penn, of Penn, Bucks, 1st Viscount *cr* 1936; 1st Baron *cr* 1920; **Bertrand Edward Dawson,** PC 1929; GCVO 1918; KCB 1926; KCMG 1919; KCVO 1911; CB 1916; MD, BSc, FRCP; Physician-in-ordinary to HM the King and to Queen Mary; formerly Physician-in-Ordinary to King Edward VIII and King George V and also to King Edward VII; Consulting Physician to King Edward VII Sanatorium, Midhurst; Physician, London Hospital; Chairman Army Medical Advisory Board since 1936; President RCP, 1931–38; member of the Senate of the University of London; FRSM; *b* 9 March 1864; *s* of Henry Dawson, FRIBA; *m* 1900, Ethel, OBE, *y d* of Sir A. F. Yarrow, 1st Bt; three *d*. *Educ:* Univ. Coll.; London Hosp. Asst Physician London Hospital, 1896; Physician, 1906; Physician-in-ordinary to the Prince of Wales, 1923–36; member of Medical Research Council 1931–35; served European War, 1914–18 (CB); ScD Univ. of Pennsylvania, 1925; Hon. DCL Oxon, 1926; Hon. LLD Edin. 1927; Knight of Justice, Order of St John of Jerusalem, 1933. *Publications:* Influenza, Allchin's Manual of Medicine, vol. i; Diabetes Mellitus, Diabetes Insipidus, Rheumatoid Arthritis, *ibid.* vol. ii; Physical Examination of Stomach and Intestines, *ibid.* vol. v; contrib. Diseases of Lymphatic Vessels, Twentieth Century Practice of Medicine, 1895; Röntgen Rays as an Aid to the Diagnosis of Stricture of the Œsophagus, 1907; The Diagnosis and Operative Treatment of Diseases of the Stomach, 1908; Dyspepsia and the Conditions underlying it; and numerous articles to leading medical journals. *Heir:* none. *Address:* 149 Harley Street, W1. *T:* Welbeck 4444.

Died 7 March 1945.

DAWSON, Lady Aimée Evelyn, GBE 1918; *y d* of late Gordon Pirie, Château de Varennes, France; *m* 1st, Herbert Oakley; 2nd, 1903, Brig.-Gen. Sir Douglas Frederick Rawdon Dawson, GCVO, KCB, CMG (*d* 1933). *Address:* Remenham Place, Henley-on-Thames.

Died 24 Dec. 1946.

DAWSON, Sir Arthur James, Kt 1931; CBE 1924; OBE 1918; JP County of Durham, 1930; MA, DCL; late Director of Education, Durham; *b* 1859; *s* of late Richard Dawson, Eastham, Cheshire; *m* 1885, Elizabeth (*d* 1928), *d* of late William Moreton, Prees, Salop. *Address:* Hill Crest, Durham. *Clubs:* County, Durham.

Died 1 July 1943.

DAWSON, Geoffrey; Editor of The Times, 1912–19 and 1923–41; *b* 1874; *m* 1919, Cecilia, *y d* of 6th Baron Wenlock; one *s* two *d* [assumed name of Dawson by Royal Licence instead of Robinson, 1917]. *Educ:* Eton; Magdalen College, Oxford; Fellow of All Souls, 1898, and Estates Bursar, 1919–23. Colonial Office, 1898–1901; Private Secretary to Lord Milner in South Africa, 1901–05; Editor of Johannesburg Star, 1905–10; Secretary to the Rhodes Trust, 1921–22; one of the Rhodes Trustees, 1925; Fellow of Eton and Honorary Fellow of Magdalen, 1926; Hon. DCL Oxford 1934. *Address:* 24 Lowndes Street, SW1; Langcliffe Hall, Settle, Yorks. *Clubs:* Athenæum, Beefsteak.

Died 7 Nov. 1944.

DAWSON, Air Vice-Marshal Grahame George, CB 1942; CBE 1942; RAF. Chief Maintenance Staff Officer, Middle East, 1941 (despatches, CBE, CB). *Address:* The Warren, High Welwyn, Herts.

Died 14 Nov. 1944.

DAWSON, Lt-Col Henry King, DSO 1917; MD; late RAMC; *b* 1871; *s* of J. Dawson; *m* 1905, Mabel Mary, 3rd *d* of Rev. R. Pigott, JP, of Grendon Hall, Bucks; no *c. Educ:* Durham University. Served as Surgeon during S African War, and in European War, 1914–18 (despatches twice, DSO). *Address:* The Corner, Ashtead, Surrey.

Died 14 Nov. 1941.

DAWSON, John Miles; JP (WR); *b* 1871; *e s* of John Miles Dawson and Elizabeth Charlotte Russell, 3rd *d* of Lt-Col Wilford, HEICS; *m* 1899, Edith Marguerite, *d* of Sir Robert Gunter, 1st Bart, MP; two *s. Educ:* Eton; Trinity Hall, Camb. BA 1894. On Wetherby RDC 37 years, Chairman, 1934–37. Major 3rd Batt. W Yorkshire Regt; member of County Council for 33 years, County Alderman, Yorkshire (WR) for 18 years. *Address:* Heuthwaite Lodge, Wetherby, Yorkshire. *Clubs:* Union; Yorkshire (York).

Died 3 Dec. 1948.

DAWSON, Nelson, ARWS, RWA; Hon. ARCA Lond. *Address:* Staithe House, Chiswick Mall, W4.

Died 28 Oct. 1941.

DAWSON, Rear-Adm. Sir Oswald Henry, KBE 1944; *b* 9 March 1882; *s* of W. H. Dawson, MD, Malvern, Worcs; *m* 1922, Grace Swannell, *d* of J. T. Lefeaux, Cheltenham; one *s* two *d.* Entered RN 1898; Comdr 1916; Capt. 1923; Director of Navigation, Admiralty, 1927–30; Flag-Capt. and Chief Staff Officer, 2nd Battle Squadron, 1930–31; comd. Navigation

School, Portsmouth, 1932–41; retired as Rear-Adm., 1935; recalled as Commodore 2nd Class RNR in Sept. 1939, in charge of Mercantile Convoys; served till 1945. *Address:* Chalford Hill, Glos. *T:* Brimscombe 3128.

Died 11 May 1950.

DAWSON, Robert Arthur, ARCA London; FSAM, FRSA, DA (Manchester); practising artist; *m* Amelia J. Fox; two *s* one *d. Educ:* Royal College of Art; Bingley Grammar School. Formerly Headmaster, Municipal School of Art, Belfast, 1901–19; and Professor of Design, Queen's University (Technical Faculty); Government Art Examiner, Irish Schools; Assistant Master, Royal College of Art, 1899–1901; Art Master and Form Master, Bingley Grammar School; Principal, Municipal School of Art, Manchester, 1919–39; Exhibitor Royal Academy, Royal Hibernian Academy, New Gallery, Paris, etc. *Publications:* articles in various magazines and journals on art and art education. *Address:* The Studio, 12 York Street, Bingley, Yorks. *T:* Bingley 2138.

Died 16 Sept. 1948.

DAWSON, William Harbutt, Dr Phil, hon., Königsberg University 1936; *b* 27 July 1860; *y s* of John Dawson and Anne Hurd Harbutt of Skipton-in-Craven; *m* 1st, Anna Clara Auguste, *y d* of late A. W. Gruetz, of Charlottenburg; one *s*; 2nd, Else, *o d* of late Stadtrat Dr jur Emil Muensterberg (President of Berlin Poor Law Administration); (one *s* killed on active service, War of 1939–45) three *d. Educ:* Skipton (Ermysted) School; Private; Berlin University. Has been actively engaged in social and educational work; early books were written to interpret German life and institutions to the English. *Publications:* The German Empire, 1867–1914, 2 vols, 1919; Evolution of Modern Germany, 1908; German Socialism and Ferdinand Lassalle, 1888; Prince Bismarck and State Socialism, 1890; Germany and the Germans, 2 vols, 1894; Social Switzerland, 1897; German Life in Town and Country, 1901; Matthew Arnold and his Relation to the Thought of his Time, 1903; Protection in Germany (A History), 1904; The German Workman: A Study in National Efficiency, 1906; School Doctors in Germany 1906; The Vagrancy Problem, 1910; Social Insurance in Germany, 1883–1911, 1912; Industrial Germany, 1913; Municipal Life and Government in Germany, 1914; What is wrong with Germany (the causes of the War), 1915; Problems of the Peace, 1917; South Africa: People, Places, and Problems, 1925; Richard Cobden and Foreign Policy, 1926; A History of Germany, 1928; The Future of Empire, 1930; Germany under the Treaty, 1933; Cromwell's Understudy: the Life and Times of General John Lambert, 1938; History of Skipton, 1882; editor of After-War Problems, 1917; has contributed to Cambridge History of British Foreign Policy, 1922, Encyclopædia Britannica, the Palgrave-Higgs Dictionary of Political Economy, 1926, and the Columbia University Encyclopædia of Social Sciences; also to various journals. *Recreations:* gardening, walking, travelling. *Address:* 23 Latimer Road, Headington, Oxford.

Died 7 March 1948.

DAWSON, William Richard, OBE 1919; MD, FRCPI; Specialist Neurologist, Ministry of Pensions; Vice-President, Bath and Bristol Mental Health Society; *b* near Gilford, Co. Down, 11 Sept. 1864; *e s* of late Very Rev. A. Dawson, MA, Dean of Dromore; *m* 1898, Florence, *d* of late R. W. Shekleton, QC, Dublin. *Educ:* Royal School, Dungannon; Trinity College, Dublin; Berlin; Vienna. Specialised in Mental Disease; Assistant Physician, Royal Edinburgh Asylum, 1894; Resident Medical Superintendent, Farnham House, Dublin, 1899; Investigator under Royal Commission on Feebleminded, 1906; HM Inspector of Asylums in Ireland, 1911; President, Medico-Psychological Association of Great Britain and Ireland, 1911–12; Major, RAMC and Specialist in Nerve Disease to troops in Ireland, 1915 (promoted hon. Lt-Col, despatches); Pres., Special Medical Board, 1917; Co-Editor, Journal of Mental Science, 1920–21; Chief Medical Officer, Ministry of Home Affairs, Northern Ireland, 1922; retired, 1929. *Publications:* Elements of Pathological Histology; translated and edited from German of Weichselbaum; Insanities of Reproduction (Jellett's Manual of Midwifery); Report on Mentally Defective and Epileptic in Dublin, 1907, etc. *Recreations:* archæology, photography, literature. *Address:* 18 Brock Street, Bath. *T:* Bath 4162.

Died 17 June 1950.

DAY, Charles; Vice-Chairman Mirrlees Watson Co. Ltd, and of John Hall & Son (Oldham) Ltd; *b* 27 April 1868; *m* 1893, Harriet Jones Minshall; two *s* one *d. Educ:* Stockport Grammar School; Manchester Technical School; Manchester University. Whitworth Scholar; MSc (Tech.). Head of Engine Insurance and Consulting Departments of National Boiler Insurance Co. Ltd 1892; Manager, Cole Marchant and Morley Ltd, Bradford, Yorks, 1895; Manager and Director, Ferranti Ltd, 1898; Managing Director Mirrlees Watson Co. Ltd, Glasgow, 1902, and in 1910 also Managing Director Mirrlees Bickerton and Day Ltd; Past President of Institution of Mechanical Engineers, of Whitworth Society and of Manchester Association of Engineers. *Publications:* The Steam Engine Indicator and Engine Boiler Testing; many technical papers before Engineering Societies. *Recreations:* gardening and golf. *Address:* Highfield, 167 Buxton Road, Stockport. *T:* Stockport, Mile End 2795. *Clubs:* Constitutional; Royal Scottish Automobile (Glasgow); Engineers (Manchester).

Died 18 June 1949.

DAY, Rev. Edward Rouviere, CMG 1916; CBE 1919; MA; *b* 4 Jan. 1867; 4th *s* of late Robert Day, JP, FSA; *m* 1893, Constance Bremner; one *s* two *d. Educ:* Trinity College, Dublin. Ordained, 1891; Curate of Ballymacarrett, Co. Down, 1891–93; at the Curragh, 1893–96; Woolwich, 1896–99; S Africa, 1900–02 (despatches, Chaplain 3rd Class, Queen's medal 6 clasps, King's medal 2 clasps); St Helena, 1902; Pretoria, 1902–05; Dover, 1905–10; Lichfield, 1910–14; served European War, France and Belgium, 1914–18; in Egypt, 1918–21; ACG Third Army BEF, Principal Chaplain, EEF (despatches five times, CMG, CBE); Vicar of Steep, Hants, 1922–29; Rector of St Michael and all Angels, Boksburg, South Africa, 1929; St John's, Belgravia, 1932–34; All Saints, Bighton, 1935–37; late Chaplain to the Forces, 1st Class. *Address:* c/o Barclay's Bank (DC & O), West Street, Durban, Natal.

Died 26 Feb. 1948.

DAY, Rev. Ernest Hermitage, DD, FSA; Knight of the Order of St Sava of Serbia; Chap. St J; *b* 1866; 2nd *s* of Rev. Hermitage Charles Day, MA; *m* 1893, Doris Elinor, *y d* of late George Henry Philips, JP, DL; one *s* one *d. Educ:* Leamington College; Keble College, Oxford; Ely Theological College. Curate, Church of the Holy Redeemer, Clerkenwell, 1889; Vicar of Abbey Cwmhir, Radnorshire, 1891; Rector of Pickwell, Leicestershire, 1907–10; Editor of the Church Times, 1914–24. Examining Chaplain to the Bishop of Hereford, 1924. *Publications:* The Way of the Cross (translated from the French), 1893; Considerations for Advent, 1897; On the Evidence for the Resurrection, 1906; Gothic Architecture in England, 1909; Renaissance Architecture in England, 1910; Oberammergau and the Passion Play, 1910; Some London Churches, 1911; By Grace of the Christ Child, 1909; Memoir of Canon F. M. Williams, 1912; articles in Dictionary of the Prayer Book, 1912; In Our Lady's Praise, 1912; The Ministry of the Church, 1913; Monuments and Memorials, 1915; Saxon and Norman Churches in England, 1920; The First Christmas Crib, 1921; St Francis and the Greyfriars, 1926; The Sacristan's Handbook, 1931; The Subdiaconate, 1935; Editorial Secretary of Leicestershire Archæological Society,

1909–1916. *Recreations:* archæology, photography. *Address:* The Little Hermitage, Southway, Pinelands, Cape of Good Hope.

Died 18 Aug. 1946.

DAY, Samuel Henry; formerly a Master of the Supreme Court; *b* 14 May 1854; *e surv. s* of late Sir John Day; *m* Edith Higham; one *d. Educ:* Beaumont College. Called to Bar, Middle Temple, 1876; joined South Eastern Circuit and Sussex Sessions; had a large practice in election petitions. *Publication:* Day's Election Cases. *Address:* Le Chalet, Sea Lane, Rustington, Sussex.

Died 23 Dec. 1944.

DEACON, John Francis William; JP, DL; *b* 1859; *o s* of late John Deacon and Lucy Katharine, 2nd *d* of late Francis Pym, of Hasell Hall, Bedfordshire. *Educ:* Eton; Trinity College, Cambridge (MA). High Sheriff, Kent, 1904; Lord of the Manor of Southborough; Patron of three livings. *Address:* Mabledon, Tonbridge, Kent. *Clubs:* Carlton, National.

Died 9 Feb. 1941.

DEACON, Stuart; Stipendiary Magistrate of Liverpool, 1910–46; *b* 29 May 1868; *s* of late Henry Deacon, JP, of Appleton House, Widnes, Lancashire; *m* 1896, Winifred Mary Brunner; one *s* three *d. Educ:* Rugby; Trinity College, Cambridge. BA, LLB, 1890. Called to Bar, Inner Temple, 1892; JP Liverpool, 1903; JP Cheshire, and Wallasey Borough, 1910. *Recreation:* golf. *Address:* 1 Dudley Road, Wallasey. *T:* Wallasey 198.

Died 29 Nov. 1947.

DEAN, Frederic William Charles, CB 1932; CBE 1929; OBE 1925; late Superintendent Royal Gun and Carriage Factories, Woolwich; *b* 1867; *m* 1890. *Address:* Three Birches, Birchwood Road, Pett's Wood, Orpington.

Died 4 Feb. 1942.

DEAN, Herbert Samuel; *b* 8 March 1870; unmarried. Assistant Editor and later Acting Editor, Church Review, 1899; contributor to British, Dominion and American press, 1901–14; Assistant Editor, Dublin Review, 1915–16; Editor of The Universe, 1917–38; created Knight of the Order of St Gregory the Great by Pope Pius XI, 1931; Knight Commander, 1936. *Recreation:* music. *Address:* 23 Worple Road, Epsom.

Died 18 Aug. 1942.

DEAN-LESLIE, John; Sheriff-Substitute (retd); *b* 24 Sept. 1860; *s* of Alexander Davidson Dean, Engraver and Lithographer, Glasgow, and Jane Leslie. *Educ:* Glasgow Academy; Glasgow University (MA, LLB); University, Leipzig and University, Berlin. Advocate, 1886; Sheriff-Substitute of Stirling, Dumbarton, and Clackmannan at Alloa, 1901; at Stirling and at Alloa, 1915–40; served in 1st Lanarkshire RV and Queen's Brigade RV, Captain. *Recreations:* golf, shooting, curling. *Address:* 16 Victoria Place, Stirling. *T:* Stirling 257. *Clubs:* Stirling County; University, Edinburgh; Conservative, Glasgow.

Died 12 July 1946.

DEANE, Rev. Anthony Charles, DD (Lambeth) 1944; MA; FRSL; Canon of St George's, Windsor, since 1929 and Steward, since 1931; Chaplain to the King, since 1934; Proctor in Convocation, since 1932; Ecclesiastical Correspondent of The Times, since 1930; *b* 1870; *s* of H. C. Deane, barrister-at-law; *m* 1898, Maud, 2nd *d* of Colonel Versturme-Bunbury. *Educ:* Wellington College; Clare College, Cambridge (Seatonian Prizeman, 1905); Cuddesdon Theological College. Student of Lincoln's Inn, 1891. Ordained, 1893; editor of the Treasury Magazine, 1902–09; Vicar of Great Malvern, and Rural Dean of Powyke, 1909–13; Vicar of Hampstead, 1913–16; Vicar of All Saints, Ennismore Gardens, 1916–29; Chaplain Worcestershire Yeomanry, 1910–24; Hon. Canon of Worcester Cathedral, 1912–29; Chairman Inc. Society of Authors, 1918–21; Select Preacher, Oxford, 1936–38; Cambridge, 1937 and 1946.

Publications: Frivolous Verses, 1892; Holiday Rhymes, 1894; Leaves in the Wind, 1896; A Poet's Choice, 1898; New Rhymes for Old and Other Verses, 1901; A Little Book of Light Verse, 1902; Selected Poems of George Crabbe, 1903; At the Master's Side, 1905; St Columbia, 1905; St Paul and his Friends, 1906; The Reformation, 1907; The Society of Christ, 1908; New Testament Studies, 1909; Christmas Songs and other Verses, 1911; In My Study, 1913; Great Malvern Priory Church, 1914; A Library of Religion, 1918; Rabboni, 1921; Questioning Christ, 1922; How to Enjoy the Bible, 1925; Our Father, 1925; Various Verses, 1925; Life of Cranmer, 1926; Jesus Christ, 1927; How to Understand the Gospels, 1929; When Christ Came, 1931; The Valley and Beyond, 1935; Sixth-Form Religion, 1936; To an Unseen Audience, 1939; St Paul and his Letters, 1942; The World Christ Knew, 1944; Time Remembered, 1945. *Recreations:* fishing, chess, golf. *Address:* The Cloisters, Windsor Castle. *T:* Windsor 313; Church Cottage, Midhurst. *Club:* Athenæum.

Died 15 Sept. 1946.

DEANE, Major James, CMG 1903; DL, JP Beds; *b* 3 Oct. 1863; *s* of W. H. Deane of Fareham House, Fareham, Hants; *m* 1908, Phyllis Lucy, *d* of Mrs Hickman, Trunkwell House, Beach Hill, Berks, and *grand-daughter* of late Sir Alfred Hickman, Bart; two *d.* *Educ:* Eton; Sandhurst. Entered Black Watch, 1883; Captain, 1890; Major, 1899; served in Boer War as Adjutant of 4th Battalion Argyll and Sutherland Highlanders (Queen's medal 3 clasps, King's medal 2 clasps); Military Secretary to Sir Walter Hely-Hutchinson, Governor of Cape Colony, 1901; to HE the High Commissioner, South Africa, 1904–06. *Address:* Goldington Bury, Bedford. *T:* 3074. *Club:* Army and Navy.

Died 14 Nov. 1942.

DEANE, Percy Edgar, CMG 1920; *b* 10 Aug. 1890; *s* of J. H. Deane; *m* 1917, Ruth Marjorie, *d* of Herbert Manning, St Kilda, Victoria; one *d.* Served in AIF 1914–16; with Paris Peace Conference, 1919 (CMG); Secretary, Prime Minister's Department and External Affairs Dept, 1921–28; Secretary, Dept of Home Affairs, Commonwealth of Australia, 1929–32; acting Member of Commonwealth War Pensions Entitlement Appeal Tribunal, 1932–33; Member, 1933–36; Secretary to Australian Delegation at Imperial Conferences of 1918, 1921, and 1926. *Address:* 192 Punt Road, South Yarra, Melbourne, Victoria, Australia.

Died 17 Aug. 1946.

DEANS, Engr Rear-Adm. William Jordan, CB 1936; Royal Navy, retired. Served European War, 1914–19; Engineer Captain, 1927; ADC to the King, 1933; Manager Engineering Department, Portsmouth Dockyard, 1933–36; retired list, 1936. *Address:* Walnut Trees, Sissinghurst, Kent. *T:* Sissinghurst 236.

Died 20 Dec. 1947.

DEASE, Major Edmund J.; DL, JP, Queen's County; *b* 1861; *s* of Edmund Gerald Dease, MP, DL, JP (*d* 1904), of Rath House, Queen's County, and Mary (*d* 1918), 3rd *d* of late Henry Grattan, MP; *m* 1896, Mabel, *e d* of late Ambrose More O'Ferrall, of Balyna, Co. Kildare; (one *s* died on active service, 1940) one *d.* *Educ:* Oscott College, Birmingham. Major late 4th Bn Royal Irish Fusiliers; ex-Resident Magistrate Co. Kerry, Co. Tipperary, and City of Limerick. *Address:* Rath House, Ballybrittas, Queen's County. *TA:* Ballybrittas. *Clubs:* Kildare Street, Dublin.

Died 1 Oct. 1945.

DEASY, Major Henry Hugh Peter; *b* Dublin, 29 June 1866; 2nd and *o surv. s* of Rt Hon. Rickard Deasy, PC, Lord Justice of Appeal (Ireland); *m* 1901, Dolores, *y d* of late Col J. F. Hickie of Slevoyre, Co. Tipperary; one *s* one *d.* *Educ:* Bournemouth and Dublin. Gazetted to 16th Lancers, 1888; resigned commission, 1897; commenced

exploring in 1896 in Western Tibet; awarded Founders' Gold Medal by RGS for exploring and survey work in Central Asia during two expeditions lasting nearly three years; created a world's record in 1903 by driving his 14 hp motor car from Caux to Rochers de Naye in Switzerland. *Publications:* In Tibet and Chinese Turkestan, 1901; The Problem of Road Traffic: its Solution, 1914. *Address:* Cnoc Na Faire, Carrigahorig, via Birr, Eire. *TA:* Deasy, Lorrha.

Died 24 Jan. 1947.

DE BATHE, Sir Christopher Albert, 6th Bt *cr* 1801; Pilot Officer RAFVR; late 2nd Lieut Highland LI; *b* 17 Sept. 1905; *o s* of late Patrick Wynne De Bathe and Violet Lindsay, *d* of late Nicholas Wood, MP; *S* uncle 1940; *m* 1932, Edna Winifred, *o d* of late Arthur Terrell, Melbourne, Victoria; one *d.* *Educ:* Westminster; Rugby; RMC Sandhurst. Hon. Attaché in HM Diplomatic Service at Constantinople, 1930, and Brussels, 1931; Times Correspondent in Persia, 1932–33. *Club:* Naval and Military.

Died 3 June 1941 (ext).

DE BELABRE, Louis Fradin, Baron; Consul-General, retired; Knight of the Legion of Honour, Knight Commander of Medjidieh, Osmanieh, Abyssinia, Charles III (Spain); Officer of Public Instruction and seven other Orders; *b* 13 March 1862; *e s* of late Baron de Belabre, Col 20th Dragoons, French Army, and Ellen Martha Yorke; *m* 1st, 1889, Alexandra Janetta (*d* 1903), 4th *d* of Capt. George West, RN, and *g d* of Admiral Sir John West, GCB; one *d*; 2nd, 1905, Agnes Hepburn, *d* of Sir Robert McAlpine, Bt; one *d.* *Educ:* England; St Louis College, Paris. Entered the French Foreign Office, 1882; has held appointments in many parts of the world. *Publications:* Grand Canary and the Town of Las Palmas, 1900; Rhodes of the Knights, 1909; numerous articles in English and French press, also music and songs. *Recreations:* painting, music. *Address:* Dorset House, West Bay, Bridport, Dorset.

Died 18 May 1945.

DE BURGH, William George, FBA 1938; *b* 24 Oct. 1866; *s* of William de Burgh, Barr-at-law, of the War Office and Inner Temple, and Hannah Jane Monck Mason; *m* 1897, Edith Mary, *d* of W. F. Grace; one *s* and *d.* *Educ:* Winchester College; Merton College, Oxford; Classical Postmaster. 1st Class, Literæ Humaniores, 1889. University Extension Staff Lecturer; Resident at Toynbee Hall, Whitechapel, 1892; Lecturer in Classics, University College, Reading, 1896; Professor of Philosophy and Dean of the Faculty of Letters, University of Reading, 1907–34, and Deputy Vice-Chancellor till 1934; Professor Emeritus since 1935; Gifford Lecturer, St Andrews, 1937–38. *Publications:* The Legacy of Greece and Rome, 1912; The Legacy of the Ancient World, 1924; Towards a Religious Philosophy, 1937; From Morality to Religion (Gifford Lectures), 1938; Knowledge of the Individual (Riddell Memorial Lectures), 1939. *Address:* 5 Belle Avenue, Reading.

Died 27 Aug. 1943.

DECIES, 5th Baron *cr* 1812; **John Graham Hope de la Poer Beresford,** PC Ire. 1918; DSO 1904; 7th Hussars, 1887–1910; Representative Peer for Ireland; *b* 5 Dec. 1866; 2nd *s* of 3rd Baron Decies and Catherine Anne (*d* 1941), *d* of William Dent, RN, Shortflatt Tower, Northumberland; *S* brother, 1910; *m* 1st, 1911, Helen Vivien (*d* 1931), *d* of late George Jay Gould; one *s* two *d*; 2nd, 1936, *widow* of H. S. Lehr. *Educ:* Eton. Entered Army, 1887; was ADC to Lord Connemara, then Governor of Madras, and Adjutant of 7th Hussars; served under Colonel Plumer in operations against Matebele, 1896 (despatches); ADC to HRH Duke of Connaught, 1894–1900; commanded 37th Imperial Yeomanry, South Africa, 1902 (Lt-Col); Somaliland, 1903–04, commanded the Tribal Horse (Lieut-Colonel) (despatches, DSO); Military Order of Spain; Colonel Commanding South Irish Horse, 1911–16; AA and

QMG 1916; Chief Press Censor, Ireland, 1916–19; Member of the LCC 1922–25; Director Income Tax Payers' Society. *Recreations:* cricket, hunting, polo, racing. *Heir: s* Hon. Arthur George Marcus Douglas de la Poer Beresford, *b* 25 April 1915. *Address:* Leixlip Castle, Co. Kildare. *Clubs:* Kildare Street, Dublin.

Died 31 Jan. 1944.

DE CORDOVA, Rudolph; author, journalist, dramatist, motion picture scenario writer; *b* Kingston, Jamaica; *s* of late Altamont de Cordova and Katherine Lewis; *m* 1916, Alicia (*d* 1933), *o d* of late William and Isabel Royston and *widow* of Cecil Ramsey. *Educ:* University College School, College, and Hospital, London. Intended for Medicine; but in consequence of an admittedly mistaken diagnosis that he would go blind if he continued studying, had to give up all thought of practice; went on the stage and played leading parts in modern and classical drama in London, New York, etc.; recited plays from memory, The Merchant of Venice, Broken Hearts (by W. S. Gilbert), in London, New York, Boston, etc.; and all the male parts in The Antigone at the Bristol Musical Festival, 1902; writing in the intervals of acting, became chief descriptive writer on The Morning, 1897; has since written special articles for nearly every important daily London and provincial paper, and has contributed articles and short stories to magazines and many weekly papers both in England and the United States; for some years wrote special weekly features for The Sphere, The Graphic, and other papers; has written, among many others, the motion picture scenario of Romeo and Juliet, and assisted in its production on the screen. *Publications:* Royalties of the World; Parts I have Played; a series of biographies of leading actors; Contract (Bridge) in a Nutshell; *Plays:* Pandora's Box; Rapiers for two, Coffee for one; What will he do with it; The Green Spectacles; edited Dame Madge Kendal by Herself; with Alicia Ramsey (Mrs De Cordova) the following plays produced in London:—Monsieur de Paris, As a Man Sows, The Mandarin, Honor, The Password, Edmund Kean, The Price of a Hat, The Organ Grinder, The Mannequin, Doctor My Book, The Silver Candlestick, and seven sensational dramas for the London Hippodrome, The Bandits, The Redskins, The Golden Princess, The Earthquake, The Typhoon, The Volcano, The Sands o' Dee. *In the United States:* John Hudson's Wife, The Shadow behind the Throne, The Quicksands, The Password, The Price of a Hat; several of their plays have been broadcast, including Doctor My Book from 30 stations so far (translated into ten foreign languages), The Silver Candlestick, Edmund Kean, The Password, The Caretaker, The Royal Minstrel, etc. *Address:* 99 Oxford Gardens, North Kensington, W10. *T:* Ladbroke 1388. *Club:* Radio.

Died 11 Jan. 1941.

DEELEY, Sir Guy Meyrick Mallaby M.; *see* Mallaby-Deeley.

DEEPING, (George) Warwick; author; *b* Southend, Essex; *s* of George Davidson Deeping, JP, and Marianne Warwick; *m* Maude Phyllis, *d* of Captain Merrill, late of the Hussars. *Educ:* Merchant Taylors' School; Trinity College, Cambridge. BA, MA, and MB; studied at Middlesex Hospital. Practised as a doctor for a year; abandoned medicine for literature; joined RAMC, April 1915; on active service through Gallipoli Campaign, afterwards Egypt, then in France. *Publications:* Uther and Igraine; Love among the Ruins; The Seven Streams; Bess of the Woods; A Woman's War; Bertrand of Brittany; Mad Barbara; The Red Saint; The Rust of Rome; The Lame Englishman; Joan of the Tower; Fox Farm; Sincerity; The White Gate; The King behind the King; The Pride of Eve; The Slanderers; The Return of the Petticoat; The House of Spies; Marriage by Conquest; Unrest, 1916; Martin Valliant, 1917; Valour, 1918; Second Youth, 1919; The Prophetic Marriage, 1920; Lantern Lane; The House of Adventure, 1921; Orchards, 1922; The Secret Sanctuary, 1923; Apples of

Gold, 1923; Three Rooms, 1924; Suvla John, 1924; Sorrell and Son, 1925; Doomsday, 1927; Kitty, 1928; Old Pybus, 1928; Roper's Row, 1929; Exiles, 1930; The Road, 1931; Old Wine and New, 1932; Smith, 1932; Two Black Sheep, 1933; Seven Men Came Back 1934; The Man on the White Horse, 1934; Sackcloth into Silk, 1935; No Hero—This, 1936; Blind Man's Year, 1937; The Woman at the Door, 1937; The Malice of Men, 1938; Fantasia, 1939; Shabby Summer, 1939; The Man Who Went Back, 1940; The Dark House, 1941; Corn in Egypt, 1941; I Live Again, 1942; Slade, 1943; M. Gurney and Mr Slade, 1944; Reprieve, 1945; The Impudence of Youth, 1946; Laughing House, 1947. *Recreations:* tennis, golf, motoring, gardening, carpentering and all out-of-door work. *Address:* Eastlands, Weybridge, Surrey. *Club:* Lansdowne.

Died 20 April 1950.

DE FALLA, Manuel; composer; *b* Cadiz, Spain, 23 Nov. 1876. *Educ:* Madrid Conservatory; pupil of Felipe Pedrell (Composition) and José Tragó (Piano). *Works:* La Vida Breve; El Amor Brujo; The Three-Cornered Hat; El Retablo de Maese Pedro; Nights in the Gardens of Spain; Trois Mélodies; Siete Canciones Populares Españolas; Fantasia Baetica; Pièces Espagnoles; Homenaje a Debussy; Psyché; Concerto per Clavicembalo; Soneto de Gongora; Fanfare; Balada de Mallorca; Homenaje a Dukas, etc. *Address:* Alta Gracia, Cordoba, Argentina.

Died 14 Nov. 1946.

DE GEER, Baron Gerard; Professor Emeritus of Geology at the University Stockholms Högskola, now Director of its Geochronol. Institute; *b* 2 Oct. 1858; *s* of late Prime Minister, Louis De Geer, and Caroline Wachtmeister; *m* 1st, 1884, Mary Erskine; 2nd, 1908, Ebba Hult; two *s. Educ:* Gymnasium of Stockholm; University of Upsala. Assistant Geologist at the Geological Survey of Sweden, 1882; Geologist, 1885–97; Professor, University of Stockholm, 1897–1924; Member of the Swedish Parliament 1900–05; President of the 11th International Congress in Stockholm, 1910. *Publications:* about 400 papers and notes. *Recreations:* Scientific voyages to Spitzbergen (6 times), North America twice, the Alps twice, several Northern European countries. *Address:* Sveavägen 32, Stockholm, Sweden. *T:* 200254.

Died July 1943.

DE GREEF, Arthur; Commander Order of Leopold, Commander Legion of Honour, Grand Officer Order de la Couronne; member of the Royal Academy of Belgium; Principal Professor of Pianoforte at the Royal Conservatoire of Music in Brussels; President of the Jury Central of Belgium; *b* 10 Oct. 1862; *m* 1890, Emily Boichot Hulbert; one *d. Educ:* Brussels. Has toured as solo pianist throughout Europe and Russia; made his first appearance in London at the St James Hall with Dr Joachim and Piatti, 1888, and has since played at all the principal provincial cities in England, Scotland, and Ireland, and has been associated with the Albert Hall Orchestra, the Queen's Hall Orchestra, the London Symphony, Halle's several orchestra; was a personal friend of Edward Grieg. *Publications:* Ballad for String Orchestra; Suite for full Orchestra; Four Old Flemish Folk-Songs for Orchestra; two Pianoforte Concertos with Orchestra; Concertino pianoforte and orchestra; Pianoforte Fantasia with Orchestra; two Sonatas for piano and violin; Trio for violin, cello, and piano; Sonata for two pianos; several pianoforte pieces; several songs with orchestra or piano. *Address:* 110 rue Defacqz, Avenue Louise, Brussels. *Clubs:* artistique et littéraire, Brussels.

Died 29 Aug. 1940.

DE HOCHEPIED, 10th Baron; **Elbert Adrian William de Hochepied Larpent;** *b* 5 Dec. 1900; *s* of 9th B. de Hochepied and Bessie Cowill, *d* of J. Withycome of Pezweh, Postbridge, S Devon; *S* father,

1903. *Educ:* Bedford School. Served in Royal Air Force during latter part of European War. *Recreations:* tennis, rowing. *Heir: c* Lionel William Peppé Larpent [Captain late Connaught Rangers; *b* 10 Feb. 1877; *m* 1907, Marion Lucy, *d* of Lieut-Col G. F. A. Harris, MD].

Died 24 Jan. 1945.

DE JOUX, Lt-Col John Sedley Newton, CMG 1918; South Staffordshire Regt; retired; *b* 25 May 1876; *o s* of late Cephas Mark de Joux, late of HM's Civil Service, and Emma Mary, 3rd *d* of late Major John Somner Sedley, late Royal Staff Corps; *m* Mary Olivia, *y d* of late Lt-Col George MacCall, 8th Bengal Cavalry; two *d.* *Educ:* Clifton College; Royal Military Coll., Sandhurst. Joined 1st South Staffordshire Regt 1896; served South African War (Queen's medal 3 clasps, King's medal 2 clasps); European War (despatches twice, CMG). *Address:* Little Mead, Fleet, Hants.

Died 30 July 1949.

DE LABILLIERE, Rt Rev. Paul Fulcrand Delacour, DD, MA; FSA; Hon. MInstCE; Hon. CF; Order of St Sava (Class I); Dean of Westminster since 1938; Dean of the Most Hon. Order of the Bath since 1938; Member of Ecclesiastical Commission Board; Chairman of the Governors of Westminster School; Renter Warden and Member of Court of Glaziers Company; Hon. Fellow of Merton College, Oxford; *b* 1879; *s* of Francis Peter de Labilliere, Barrister-at-Law of Middle Temple, and Adelaide Ravenshaw; *m* 1909, Ester Elizabeth Morkel; one *s* one *d.* *Educ:* Harrow; Merton College, Oxford; Bishop's Hostel, Liverpool. Deacon, 1902; Priest, 1903; Domestic Chaplain to the Bishop of Durham, 1906–08; worked in S Africa, 1908–10; Clerical Superintendent of the Liverpool Scripture Readers, 1910–12; Chaplain of Wadham College, Oxford, 1914–20; TCF, 1916–19 (despatches); Vicar of St Andrews, Oxford, and Lecturer at Wycliffe Hall, 1919–27; Chaplain of Merton College, Oxford, 1920–27; Vicar of Christ Church, Harrogate, 1927–35; Bishop of Knaresborough, 1934–37; Archdeacon of Leeds, 1934–37; Rector of Methley, 1935–37; Examining Chaplain to the Bishop of Durham, 1914–27; Examining Chaplain to the Bishop of Ripon from 1931. *Recreation:* silence. *Address:* The Deanery, Westminster, SW1. *T:* Abbey 5228. *Club:* Athenæum.

Died 28 April 1946.

DELACOMBE, Lt-Col Addis, DSO 1916; retired list; *b* 1865; *s* of late Lt-Col Wm Addis Delacombe, RMLI, for many years Military Governor of the San Juan Islands, British Columbia, and later Chief Constable of Derby; *g s* of late General Henry Ivatt Delacombe, CB, RMLI, who lived to be 'the Father of the Army,' and of late Quarles Harris, of East Wickham Hall, Kent; *m* 1896, Emma Louise Mary, *o d* of late John Smallman Leland, MD of Kirkby Stephen, Westmorland; one *s* one *d.* *Educ:* Anglo-French College, Finchley. Enlisted in the Queen's Bays, 1887; obtained a commission in the Connaught Rangers, 1894; Captain in Royal Warwickshire Regt, 1900; Major in Royal Army Pay Corps, 1911; Lt-Col 1918; served with the Connaught Rangers in South African War, and with Intelligence Branch General Staff in the Dardanelles, Egypt, and Palestine, 1915–19, European War; placed on retired pay for age, 1922. *Address:* Shrewton Manor, near Salisbury, Wilts. *Club:* United Service.

Died 4 July 1941.

DELAFIELD, E. M.; *see* Dashwood, E. M.

de la FOSSE, Sir Claude Fraser, Kt 1922; CIE 1918; MA; DLitt 1922; *b* 10 Feb. 1868; *s* of late Maj.-Gen. de la Fosse, CB, DSO; *m* 1895, Minnie Caroline Briscoe (*d* 1943); one *d.* *Educ:* Bath College; Trinity College, Oxford. Principal, Victoria College, Kuch Behar, 1893–96; Professor, Queen's College, Benares, 1896–97; Inspector of Schools, 1897–1900; Assistant Director of Public Instruction, United Provinces, Allahabad,

1901–07; Director, 1908; Vice-Chancellor, Allahabad University, 1922; Member of the UP Legislative Council, 1909–19; on special duty with the Government of India, 1919; Member of Legislative Council of the Government of India, 1920; retired, 1923; Member Guildford Borough Council; Freeman Guildford Borough; Vice-Chairman RSPCA. *Publication:* A History of India for High Schools. *Address:* The Orchard, Merrow, Guildford, Surrey. *T:* Guildford 1070.

Died 17 Dec. 1950.

DELAHAYE, Col James Viner, DSO 1918; MC; psc; late RA; Southern (UK) Regional Representative for British Council, 1945; *b* 1890. *Educ:* Haileybury; Royal Military Academy, Woolwich. Served European War, 1914–18 (despatches twice, MC, DSO); North Russia; British Military Representative, Baltic States, 1920; General Staff, War Office, 1925–28; retired Dec. 1928; LNU, Hdqr. 1932 and 1933; Adv. Officer, Unemployment Nat. Council Social Service, 1933–34; commanded 122 Officer Cadet Training Unit, RA Larkhill, 1939–41; President, No. 1 War Office Selection Board (Experimental), 1942–43; Director Areas Division European Office of UNRRA, 1944. Contested Parly Div. of Exeter 1931, Dulwich, 1935, Buckingham 1937. *Publications:* Politics; contributor to various papers. *Address:* c/o Coutts and Co., 440 Strand, WC.

Died 7 Jan. 1948.

de la HEY, Rev. Richard Willis, MA; Rector of Hazelbury Bryan since 1938; *b* 3 June 1872; *s* of George de la Hey, Rector of Luddington cum Hemington, and Jessie, *d* of Richard Willis of the Hermitage, Woking; *m* 1905, Henrietta Green, *d* of George Harrison, Darlington; two *d.* *Educ:* Oundle School; University College, Oxford; Lichfield Theological College. Curate of St Paul's, Hull, 1899; Domestic Chaplain to Bishop (Jacob) of Newcastle, 1901; Vicar of St Jude's, South Shields, 1904–11; Silksworth, 1911–14; Vicar of Berwick-on-Tweed, 1914–38; Hon. Canon of Newcastle, 1927–38; Rural Dean of Norham, 1924–38; of Cerne, 1940–42. *Recreation:* walking. *Address:* Hazelbury Bryan Rectory, Sturminster Newton.

Died 21 Sept. 1942.

DELALLE, Rt Rev. Henry, OMI, PhD, DD; Titular Bishop of Thugga; Vicar Apostolic of Natal, South Africa, from 1903; Assistant to the Pontifical throne, 1947; retired, 1946; *b* Nancy (French Lorraine), 1 Dec. 1869. *Educ:* The Seminary of Pont-à-Mousson. A student at the Gregorian University in Rome; obtained the degrees of Doctor in Philosophy and Divinity; came over to Natal in 1896; Principal of St Charles' College, Pietermaritzburg; Private Secretary to Bishop Jolivet, Vicar Apostolic of Natal. *Address:* Sanatorium, Chelmsford Road, Durban, Natal.

Died 15 Feb. 1949.

DELAND, Margaret; *b* Pennsylvania, USA, 23 Feb. 1857; *d* of Sample Campbell; *g d* of Maj. William Wade; *m* Lorin Fuller Deland [author of Football, Imagination in Business, At the Sign of the Dollar], Boston, USA, 1880. *Educ:* Pelham Priory, a boarding-school kept by English ladies, near New York. *Publications:* The Old Garden, 1886; John Ward, Preacher, 1888; Florida Days, 1889; Sidney, 1890; The Story of a Child, 1892; Mr Tommy Dove, and other Stories, 1893; Philip and his Wife, 1894; The Wisdom of Fools, 1897; Old Chester Tales, 1898; Dr Lavendar's People, 1903; The Common Way, 1904; The Awakening of Helena Richie, 1906; R. J.'s Mother and some other People; An Encore, 1907; Where the Laborers are Few, 1909; The Way to Peace, 1910; The Iron Woman, 1911; The Voice, 1912; Partners, 1913; The Hands of Esau, 1914, Around Old Chester, 1915; The Rising Tide, 1916; The Vehement Flame, 1922; New Friends in Old Chester; The Kays,

1926; Captain Archer's Daughter, 1932; If This Be I, 1935; Old Chester Days, 1937; Golden Yesterdays, 1941. *Address:* Kennebunkport, Maine, USA. *T:* 74.

Died 13 Jan. 1945.

DELAP, Col George Goslett, CMG 1918; DSO 1900; LRCPI, LRCSI; *b* 13 April 1873; *s* of late Rev. Canon Delap; *m* 1912, Dorothy Mary, *y d* of late Major-Gen. W. J. Fawcett, CB; one *s* two *d.* Entered RAMC 1899; served South Africa, 1899–1902 (despatches twice, Queen's medal 4 clasps, King's medal 2 clasps, DSO); Salonica, Mesopotamia, Persia (despatches twice, 1915 medal, Allies War medal, Victory medal, CMG); Arab Rising, 1920 (medal); ADMS, Poona District, 1926–29; Hon. Surgeon on the personal Staff of the Viceroy, 1928; retired pay, 1929; Royal Humane Society bronze medal, 1916. *Address:* c/o Glyn Mills & Co., Kirkland House, Whitehall, SW1.

Died 26 June 1945.

de la PASTURE, Mrs Henry; *see* Clifford, Lady E. L. R.

DE LARGIE, Hon. Hugh; *b* Airdrie, Scotland, 1859; *s* of Archibald Hamilton de Largie; *m* Mary, *e d* of Charles M'Gregor, Townhead, Glasgow. *Educ:* St Margaret's School, Airdrie. Represented Western Australia in the Commonwealth Parliament, 1901–23; President first Labour Congress WA 1898; Joint Secretary Labour Party, 1906; Royal Commission on Navigation, 1904; Postal Affairs, 1908; and Pearling Industry, 1915; Member Parliamentary Delegation visiting Britain and France, 1916; Govt Whip in Senate, 1917–23; retired, 1923. *Publications:* Travel in Papua, 1911; some verse; articles on labour subjects. *Address:* 157 Brighton Road, St Kilda, Melbourne, S2, Australia.

Died 9 May 1947.

de la RUE, Sir Evelyn Andros, 2nd Bt *cr* 1898; *b* 5 Oct. 1879; *s* of 1st Bt and Emily Maria, *d* of late William Speed, QC; *S* father, 1911; *m* 1903, Mary Violet, *e d* of John Liell Francklin of Gonalston, Notts; two *s* three *d* (and one *s* decd; one *s* killed in action 1943). *Heir: s* Eric Vincent [*b* 5 Aug. 1906; *m* 1945, Cecilia, *d* of Lady Clementine Waring, CBE]. *Address:* Normans, Rusper, Sussex. *T:* Rusper 3; The Sol, Cookham, Berks. *T:* Bourne End 286.

Died 30 Nov. 1945.

DELEVINGNE, Sir Malcolm, KCB 1919 (CB 1911); KCVO 1932; late Deputy Permanent Under-Secretary of State, Home Office, retired 1932; *b* 11 Oct. 1868; 2nd *s* of Ernest Thomas Shaw Delevingne and Hannah Delevingne. *Educ:* City of London School; Trinity College, Oxford (Scholar); 1st Class Classical Moderations, 1889; 1st Class Lit. Hum. 1891; Proxime accessit Gaisford Greek Verse, 1888; BA 1891; MA 1925. Entered Home Office, 1892; Private Secretary to Secretary of State, 1896–98; British Delegate at the International Conferences on Labour Regulation at Berne, 1905, 1906, and 1913; a British Representative on the Labour Commission of the Peace Congress, 1919; a British Delegate at the International Labour Conferences at Washington, 1919, Geneva, 1923, 1928, and 1929; late Chairman Supervisory Body under the International Convention of 1931 for limitation of Manufacture of Dangerous Drugs; late Member of Permanent Central Board under Internat. Convention of 1925 relating to Dangerous Drugs; a British Delegate at the International Opium Conferences, Geneva, 1924–25 and 1931; Bangkok, 1931; and representative on the League of Nations Opium Committee, 1921–34; Member of Royal Commission on Safety in Coal Mines, 1936; Chm. of Departmental Committee on employment of women and young persons on the Two Shift System, 1934; Chairman of Inter-Departmental Committee on Rehabilitation of persons injured by accidents, 1936; Chm. of Central Emergency Committee for the Nursing Profession, 1939; Trustee of Czecho-Slovak Refugee Trust Fund; Chairman of Safety

in Mines Research Board, 1939–47; Member Council of Dr Barnardo's Homes. *Address:* 20 FitzGeorge Avenue, West Kensington, W14.

Died 30 Nov. 1950.

DE LISLE, Everard March Phillipps, JP, DL for Leicestershire; TD; Sheriff for Leicestershire, 1906–07; *e s* of late Ambrose C. March Phillipps de Lisle of Garendon Park and Gracedieu Manor, Leics., and 4th *d* of Sir Richard Sutton, 2nd Bt; *m* Mary (*d* 1945), 2nd *d* of late James Stebbings, of Stow Market, Suffolk; one *s* one *d. Educ:* Woburn Park (Lord Petre's School), Surrey. 24 years' service in LY; retired as Lieut-Col 1911; hunts with the LH, Quorn Hounds, and is owner of 25 fox covers in that country. *Recreations:* hunting, shooting, cricket, etc. *Clubs:* Cavalry; Leicester County, Leicester.

Died 6 Feb. 1947.

DE L'ISLE AND DUDLEY, 4th Baron *cr* 1835; **Algernon Sidney;** Bt 1818, late RA; *b* 11 June 1854; *s* of 2nd Baron and Mary, *d* of Sir William Foulis, Bt; *S* brother, 1922. *Educ:* Eton. Entered army, 1874; Lieut-Col 1900; Bt-Col 1904; retired pay, 1905; served South Africa on Staff, 1901–02 (Queen's medal 4 clasps). Owns about 10,000 acres. *Heir: b* Hon. William Sidney. *Address:* Penshurst Place, near Tonbridge, Kent; Ingleby Manor, Great Ayton, Yorkshire. *Clubs:* Naval and Military, Marlborough.

Died 18 April 1945.

DE L'ISLE AND DUDLEY, 5th Baron *cr* 1835; **William Sidney;** JP; *b* 19 Aug. 1859; 4th *s* of 2nd Baron and Mary, *d* of Sir William Foulis, Bt; *S* brother, 1945; *m* 1905, Winifred, *e d* of Roland Yorke Bevan and Hon. Agneta Kinnaird, 4th *d* of 10th Baron Kinnaird; one *s* one *d. Educ:* Eton; Trinity College, Cambridge. Called to Bar, Inner Temple, 1886; Mayor of Chelsea, 1906–08; Chairman of Chelsea Board of Guardians, 1919–22; Member of LCC for Chelsea, 1922–34; Chairman of the Mental Hospitals Committee, 1924–26; Chairman of the Parks Committee, 1932–34. *Heir: s* Capt. William Philip Sidney, VC. *Address:* 40 Lennox Gardens, SW1. *Club:* Carlton.

Died 18 June 1945.

DE LISSER, Herbert George, CMG 1920; late Editor, Jamaica Daily Gleaner; Gen. Secretary, and Member of Council, Jamaica Imperial Association; Chairman, West Indian section Empire Press Union, since 1923; *b* Falmouth, Jamaica, Dec. 1878; 2nd *s* of late Herbert George de Lisser, sometime editor of Jamaica Daily Gleaner, and Morisanna Isaacs; *m* Ellen, 3rd *d* of Thomas Gunter, late Assistant Director, Jamaica Government Railway; no *c. Educ:* Jamaica Collegiate School. *Publications:* Jamaica and Cuba, 1909; Twentieth Century Jamaica, 1913; Jane's Career, 1914; Susan Proudleigh, 1915; Triumphant Squalitone, 1917; Jamaica and the War, 1918; History and Geography of Jamaica, 1919; Revenge, 1920; White Witch of Rosehall, 1929; Under the Sun, 1937; founded Planters' Punch, an annual literary publication, 1920. *Recreation:* reading. *Address:* Kingston, Jamaica. *TA:* Empire, Jamaica. *Club:* Authors'.

Died 19 May 1944.

de MARGERIE, Pierre, Grand Croix Légion d'Honneur; KBE 1920; *b* Nancy, France, 6 Oct. 1861; 3rd *s* of Amédée de Margerie, Dean of the Catholic University, Lille, and Amélie, *d* of Count de Lespinats; *m* 1st, 1898, Jeanne (*d* 1922) *d* of Eugène Rostand, Member of the Académie des Sciences Morales, sister of Edmond Rostand, Member of the French Academy; one *s*; 2nd, 1924, Nicole Delorme (*d* 1928); one *d. Educ:* École des Sciences Politiques et Faculté de Droit, Paris. Entered the French Diplomatic Service, 1883; Secretary, Copenhagen, Constantinople; Counsellor of Embassy, Washington, 1901; Madrid, 1903; General Secretary of Algeciras Conference, 1906; French Delegate to European Danube Commission;

French Minister, Siam, 1907; China, 1909; Directeur adjoint des Affaires Politiques, 1912; President of the Financial Commission for Balkan Affairs, 1913; Directeur des Affaires Politiques; Conseiller d'Etat, Chef du Cabinet, 1914; French Ambassador, Brussels, 1919–22; Berlin, 1922–31; retired 1931. *Address:* 8 Boulevard de la Tour-Maubourg, Paris, VII.

Died 1 June 1942.

DE MAULEY, 4th Baron, UK, *cr* 1838; **Maurice John George Ponsonby;** *b* 7 Aug. 1846; 2nd *s* of 2nd Baron de Mauley and Lady Maria Jane Elizabeth, *d* of 4th Earl of Bessborough; *S* brother, 1918; *m* Hon. Madeleine Emily Augusta Hanbury Tracy (*d* 1938), 6th *d* of 2nd Baron Sudeley; one *s. Educ:* Eton; Christ Church, Oxford. 3rd in Law and Modern History. Curate, Leeds Parish Church; Vicar of Kirkstall, Leeds; St Paul's, Chichester; St Mark's, New Swindon; Wantage. *Heir: s* Hon. Hubert William Ponsonby [late Captain Gloucs. Hussars, Légion d'Honneur and Croix de Guerre; *b* 21 July 1878; *m* 1920, Elgiva, *d* of late Hon. Cospatrick Dundas and Lady Cordeaux; two *s* two *d*]. *Address:* Langford House, Lechlade. *T:* Lechlade 10.

Died 15 March 1945.

DE MERIC, Rear-Adm. Martin John Coucher, MVO 1921; RN; *b* 1887; *er s* of late Fleet-Surgeon E. V. de Meric, RN. *Educ:* HMS Britannia. Served European War, etc.; Commander, 1923; Capt. 1929; Rear-Admiral (retired), 1940; served in Royal Yacht, 1921–24. *Recreations:* usual games and sports. *Address:* Admiralty, SW1. *Club:* United Service.

Died 11 June 1943.

DEMERS, Marie Joseph; KC; one of the Judges of the Superior Court for the Province of Quebec since 1922; *b* Henryville, Co. Iberville, 31 May 1871; *s* of late Alexis Demers, MPP for Iberville, and Marie Goyette; *m* 1896, Berthe Gravel; four *s* one *d. Educ:* Henryville; St Hyacinth's College and St Mary's College, Montreal; Laval University. Admitted to the bar, 1895; advocate; member of the House of Commons, Canada, 1906. *Address:* St Jean, Province of Quebec. *T:* 23.

Died 28 July 1940.

DE MOLE, Lancelot Eldin, CBE 1920; AMIE Australia; *b* 13 March 1880; *s* of W. F. De Mole, CE, Adelaide, S Australia; *m* Josephine, *d* of G. F. Walter. *Educ:* Berwick Grammar School; Church of England Grammar School, Melbourne. *Address:* 25 Murdoch St, Cremorne, NSW. *T:* Sydney XY 1395.

Died 6 May 1950.

de MONTE, Frank Thomas, CIE 1934; Retired List; *b* 1 Dec. 1879; *s* of Francis William de Monte and Eva Eaton Flashman; *m* 1905, Louise Murrell; no *c. Educ:* Doveton College, Calcutta; Royal Indian Engineering College, Coopers Hill. Entered Indian Telegraphs Dept 1899; Deputy Director-General, Telegraphs, 1923; Postmaster-General of Burma 1924–25 and 1927; Postmaster-General of Bengal and Assam 1928; Chief Engineer Indian Posts and Telegraphs 1932–34. *Recreations:* big game shooting; travelling. *Address:* 21 Tanza Rd, Hampstead, NW3. *T:* Hampstead 4109. *Club:* International Adventurers (Los Angeles).

Died 17 April 1950.

DE MONTMORENCY, Major Hervey Guy Francis Edward, DSO 1917; *b* Gibraltar, 5 Nov. 1868; *o s* of Lt-Col Charles Anne Law de Montmorency and Elise Christine Motz; *heir pres.* to baronetcy held by 7th Viscount Mountmorres; *m* 1907, Evelyn, *d* of late Rev. E. Buchanan; no *c. Educ:* Royal Military Academy, Woolwich; France. Lieut Royal Artillery, 1886; resigned, 1890; served Boer War as volunteer; served European War as Captain then Major R. Field Artillery (despatches twice, DSO, Legion of Honour, Croix de Guerre, three citations). *Publications:* On the track of a Treasure; From Kant to Einstein; a monograph on the Montmorency family for private circulation; Sword and

Stirrup, 1936; occasional contributions to Saturday Review. *Recreations:* riding and swimming. *Address:* Bramblehurst, Hunsdon Road, Torquay.

Died 2 Sept. 1942.

DEMPSTER, Francis Erskine, CIE 1896; Indian Government Telegraphs, retired; *b* 9 July 1858; *e s* of Capt. H. L. Dempster, late Royal Madras Artillery; *m* 1883, Susan (*d* 1935), *d* of George Stuart, Edin.; one *d. Educ:* Edinburgh Academy, Institution, and University; Cooper's Hill College. Joined Indian Telegraph Department, 1878; Afghan War, 1879–80 (medal); Chin-Lushai Expedition, 1889 (medal and clasp); Chitral Expedition, 1895 (medal and clasp, despatches, CIE); Joint Delegate for India International Telegraph Conference, Lisbon, 1908, and Wireless International Conference, London, 1912; Director General Dec. 1911; retired July 1913. Decorated for services as Chief Telegraph Officer with the Chitral Relief Force, 1895. *Address:* c/o Thos Cook & Son, Berkeley Street, W1.

Died 14 June 1941.

DENE, Col Arthur Pollard, CMG 1919; DSO 1917; late Duke of Cornwall's Light Infantry; 2nd *s* of late Rev. John Dene, of Horwood House, Bideford, N Devon; *m* 1st, Elsie Beatrice Yvonne (*d* 1918), *y d* of late Major-Gen. F. W. B. Koe, CB, CMG; one *s* one *d*; 2nd, Dorothy, *er d* of late Capt. C. W. O'Brien, Tanderagee, Co. Armagh. *Educ:* Wellington College; St John's College, Oxford. Served European War, 1914–18 (CMG, DSO, Officer Legion of Honour); Commander 125th (Lancashire Fusiliers) Infantry Brigade TA, 1931–34; retired pay, 1934. *Address:* Odun House, Appledore, N Devon.

Died 26 March 1945.

DENHAM, 1st Baron *cr* 1937, of Weston Underwood; **George Edward Wentworth Bowyer;** 1st Bt *cr* 1933, of Weston Underwood, Kt 1929; MC; DL; *b* 16 Jan. 1886; *e s* of late Lieut-Colonel W. G. Bowyer, RE, of Weston Manor, Olney, Bucks; *heir-pres.* to Bowyer Baronetcy of Denham; *m* 1919, Hon. Daphne Mitford, 4th *d* of 1st Baron Redesdale; one *s* (elder son killed in action in the RAF) one *d. Educ:* Eton; New College, Oxford. Called to Bar, Inner Temple, 1909 (Midland Circuit); joined Bucks Batt. Oxford and Bucks LI (TF), 1910; served European War (wounded May 1915, despatches, MC); MP (C) Buckingham Division, Dec. 1918–37; Parliamentary Private Sec. to Sir Philip Cunliffe-Lister, 1921–24; Junior Lord of Treasury, 1926–29; Conservative Party Whip, 1925–35; Comptroller of HM Household, 1935; Parliamentary Sec. to Ministry of Agriculture, 1939–40; GSO (2 grade) Home Guard Directorate, War Office, 1940–45; Conservative Whip, House of Lords, 1945–47; Vice-Chairman, Conservative Party, 1930–35; President Urban District Councils Association; 1923–25, and since 1929. *Recreations:* hunting; tennis, cricket, shooting, golf. *Heir: s* Hon. Bertram Stanley Mitford Bowyer, Lieut, Oxford and Bucks, Light Infantry, *b* 3 Oct. 1927. *Address:* The Manor House, Weston Underwood, Olney, Bucks. *T:* Olney 281. *Clubs:* Carlton, International Sportsmen's, St Stephen's.

Died 30 Nov. 1948.

DENHAM, Hon. Digby Frank; *b* Langport, Somerset, 25 Jan. 1859; *m* 1884, Alice Maude Knight, Langport; one *s* two *d. Educ:* Grammar School, Langport. Went to Australia, 1881; a merchant; Governing Director Denhams Pty Ltd, Brisbane, etc., and Director other companies; Home Secretary and Secretary Agriculture; Secretary Public Works and Secretary Agriculture; Secretary Railways, subsequently Secretary Public Lands, 1903–11; Premier and Chief Secretary, Vice-President Executive Council in Queensland, 1911–15. *Address:* Ingleside, Annerley Road, S Brisbane. *Clubs:* Brisbane, Brisbane.

Died 9 May 1944.

DENHAM, Henry George, MA, DSc, PhD, FIC, FRSNZ; Professor of Chemistry, Canterbury University College, Christchurch, NZ, since 1923, Chairman of Professorial Board and Rector of the College since 1941; *b* Christchurch, 1880; *s* of James and Emma Denham, Langport, Somerset; *m* Helen Adrienne, *e d* of H. J. Horrell, Horrellville, NZ; one *s*. *Educ:* Canterbury College, Christchurch. After graduation at University of New Zealand, was awarded an 1851 Exhibition Science Scholarship; proceeded to University of Liverpool to study phy. chemistry; two years later went to Heidelberg for further study; joined staff of University of Queensland, 1912; during period of the war filled position of Acting-Professor of Chemistry there, subsequently becoming Assistant Professor at that institution; Professor of Inorganic Chemistry, Cape Town, 1921; Chairman of Council of Scientific Research (NZ); Member of the Academic Board and of the Senate of the University; Member of Council of Canterbury University College; Member of Committee of Dairy Research Institute and of the Wool Manufacturers' Research Association; Chairman of Wheat Research Institute of NZ; Fellow of Christ's College, Christchurch; Fellow of NZ and Australian Association for the Advancement of Science, Liversidge Lecturer for 1939; Fellow and ex-Pres. NZ Inst. of Chem.; Member and Past-President, Christchurch Rotary Club. *Publications:* numerous publications in British and German journals, mainly upon physical and chemical themes; Text-book of Inorganic Chemistry. *Recreation:* golf. *Address:* Canterbury University College, Christchurch, C1, NZ.

Died 15 Feb. 1943.

DENHAM-WHITE, Lt-Col Arthur; *see* White.

DENISON, Hon. Harold Albert; *b* 26 March 1856; 5th *s* of 1st Lord Londesborough; *m* 1899, Katherine, *d* of Sir T. V. Lister, KCMG; one *s*. Late Lieut RN. *Address:* Harpsden Close, Henley-on-Thames.

Died 2 Jan. 1948.

DENNING, Sir Howard, Kt 1932; CIE, ICS (retd); Secretary Iraq Currency Board; Director East Indian Railway Co; *b* Bristol, 20 May 1885; *s* of Henry Denning; *m* 1924, Margery Katherine Wemyss, *d* of Lt-Col E. W. Browne, IMS; one *s* one *d*. *Educ:* Clifton College; Caius College, Cambridge. 10th Wrangler, 1907. Entered ICS 1909, and posted as Assistant Collector Bombay Presidency; Under-Secretary to Government of India Finance Department, 1918; Joint-Secretary to Babington-Smith Currency Committee, 1919; Deputy Controller of the Currency, Bombay, 1920; Controller of the Currency, 1923; Additional Secretary to Government of India, Finance Department, 1929. *Recreation:* golf. *Address:* Cherry Close, Frithsden Copse, Berkhamsted, Herts. *T:* Berkhamsted 198.

Died 20 April 1943.

DENNIS, Sir Alfred Hull, KBE 1918; CB 1911; late Chief Assistant Solicitor to HM's Treasury, with allotted duty of legal adviser to War Office; retired, 1924; Chairman of the Northern Ireland Civil Service Committee, 1926–36; was Chief British Delegate to the International Committee of Experts on Private Aerial Law, 1926–33; *b* 31 July 1858; *s* of late John Dennis of Crowborough, Sussex; *m* 1905, Dorothy Caroline, *e d* of late Sir Henry Sutton; no *c*. *Educ:* Marlborough; Exeter College, Oxford. Called to Bar, Inner Temple, 1885. *Address:* Bepton Lodge, Midhurst. *T:* Midhurst 329.

Died 3 Feb. 1947.

DENNIS, John William; *b* near Boston, Lincs, 16 May 1865; *e s* of William Dennis, JP, of Kirton, Lincolnshire; *m* 1st, Evangeline Brewster (*d* 1919), *d* of late Dr Armstrong, Rochester, New York; no *c*; 2nd, 1922, Hilda Mary Clavering, *widow* of 8th Earl De la Warr. *Educ:* Kirton Grammar School; King's Coll. London. Entered Home Civil Service, 1883; resigned, 1891; founded London branch of W. Dennis and Sons, 1891; Member of Tariff Commission, 1904–20; Mayor of the City of Westminster, 1907–08; Land Tax Commissioner; Red Eagle 3rd Class; Officer of Legion of Honour; Potato Controller (unpaid) in the Ministry of Food, Feb.–Sept. 1917; MP (CU) Deritend Division of Birmingham, 1918–22. *Recreation:* golf. *Address:* 7 Grand Avenue, Hove, Sussex; Uffculme, Devon. *Clubs:* Carlton; Union, Brighton; Devon and Exeter.

Died 4 Aug. 1949.

DENNIS, Col Meade James Crosbie, CB 1918; Royal Artillery, retired pay; was Superintendent of the Royal Gun and Carriage Factories, Royal Arsenal, Woolwich, 1917–19; *b* 1865; *e surv. s* of late Meade Caulfield Dennis of Fortgranite, Baltinglass, Co. Wicklow; *m* 1892, Hon. Alice Handcock (*d* 1937), *y d* of 4th Baron Castlemaine of Moydrum Castle, Athlone; two *s* one *d*. *Educ:* Haileybury; RM Academy, Woolwich. Joined Royal Artillery, 1884; served in India to 1892; at home to 1899; South Africa, 1900 (despatches, Queen's medal and 5 clasps); European War (GS medal); in Royal Ordnance Factories as Asst Supt of Royal Laboratory, 1901–07; Assistant Supt Royal Gun Factory, 1907–17; Superintendent, 1917–19; Officer of the Legion of Honour; JP and DL Co. Wicklow. *Address:* Fortgranite, Baltinglass, Ireland. *T:* Baltinglass 8.

Died 27 Oct. 1945.

DENNIS, Trevor; Head Master, William Hulme's Grammar School, Manchester, 1921–47, retd; *b* 3 July 1882; *s* of William Robert Dennis and Jessie Anne Hodge; *m* 1911, Eveline Ada Walters; three *s*. *Educ:* Merchant Taylors' School; Clare College, Cambridge. Egyptian Irrigation service, 1905–07; assistant master, Rossall School, 1907–08; Sherborne School, 1908–13; Head Master, Lady Manners School, Bakewell, 1914–20. *Publications:* An Algebra for Preparatory Schools; An Arithmetic for Preparatory Schools. *Recreations:* cricket, Rugby football, music, drama. *Address:* 10 Waltham Road, Manchester 16. *T:* Moss Side 1589.

Died 17 Sept. 1950.

DENNISS, George Hamson, CBE 1920; Barrister-at-law; *b* 1854; *s* of Hamson George Denniss, Knight of the Imperial Order of the Rose of Brazil, and *g s* of Col George Hamson Denniss of the 43rd Light Infantry; *m* Jeanne Madeleine Dubouchet; one *s* two *d*. *Educ:* University College, London and School. Late Assistant Solicitor for the Customs and Excise; late Legal Expert, nominated under International Convention for the Simplification of Customs Formalities. *Publications:* (joint) An Article on Excise, in the Encyclopædia of English Law, 1906; reviser of 3rd editions of Highmore's Customs Laws and Excise Laws, 1923. *Address:* Kirkstyle, Westend, nr Southampton. *T:* Westend 67249.

Died 23 Nov. 1940.

DENNISTON, John Dewar, OBE; FBA; Fellow and Tutor of Hertford College, Oxford; *b* 4 March 1887; *s* of James Lawson Denniston, ICS; *m* 1919, Mary Grace, *y d* of late J. J. Morgan. *Educ:* Winchester; New College, Oxford. Served European War, 1914–18, 7th KOSB and General Staff War Office (Croix de Guerre, OBE; wounded twice). *Publications:* Greek Literary Criticism, 1924; edition of Cicero, Philippics i–ii, 1925; The Greek Particles, 1934; Euripides, Electra, 1939. *Address:* Hertford College, Oxford.

Died 2 May 1949.

DENNISTON, Sir Robert, Kt 1942; late Managing Director Best & Co., Ltd, Madras, East India merchants; *b* 3 Jan. 1890; *s* of Thomas Fairrie Denniston and Agnes Tayloe. *Educ:* Elstow School, Bedford. Joined Best & Co., Ltd, Madras, 1911; 2nd Lt RA 1915–18. *Recreations:* cricket, amateur theatricals. *Address:* The End Hose, Hythe, Kent. *Clubs:* Oriental, East India and Sports; Madras.

Died 19 Nov. 1946.

DENNY, Major Ernest Wriothesley, DSO 1918; JP and DL Norfolk; late 19th Royal Hussars; *b* 1872; *s* of T. Anthony Denny, 7 Connaught Place, W; *m* 1906, Lois Marjorie, *d* of late Lt-Col Hon. E. H. Legge, Coldstream Guards; four *s* two *d*. *Educ:* Wellington; New College, Oxford. Joined 13th Hussars, 1893; served South African War, 1899–1902 (despatches thrice, brevet of Major); Adjutant, 1901–04; exchanged into 19th Hussars, 1907; retired pay, 1910; rejoined 5 Aug. 1914, in command of South Cavalry Depot; Brigade Major Yeomanry, 1915–17; served with 25th Infantry Division, France, 1917–19, on Staff (despatches twice, DSO). *Recreation:* shooting. *Address:* Garboldisham Manor, Diss, Norfolk. *T:* Garboldisham 242. *Club:* Cavalry.

Died 20 Oct. 1949.

DENNY, Frederick Anthony; Chairman of E. M. Denny & Co. Ltd, Hibernia Chambers, SE1; *b* 12 Feb. 1860; *er s* of late E. M. Denny, 11 Bryanston Square, W1; *m* 1888, Maude Marian, *er d* of Sir Cuthbert Quilter, 1st Bt; one *s* three *d*. *Educ:* Eton. *Recreations:* hunting, shooting, fishing. *Address:* 22 Down Street, W1. *T:* Grosvenor 2983; Horwood House, Winslow, Bucks. *Club:* Orleans.

Died 18 Jan. 1941.

DENNY, Surg. Rear-Adm. Herbert Reginald Harry, CB 1933; RN retired; *b* 15 Dec. 1876; *s* of late Theophilus H. Denny; *m* 1906; two *s*. *Educ:* Eastman's; Guy's Hospital. Joined RN 1900; served European War in Grand Fleet, 1914–18; SMO of RN Hospital, Cape of Good Hope; Surg. Captain, 1926; Surgeon Rear-Admiral, 1931; Hon. Surgeon to the King, 1935; retired, 1935. *Recreations:* tennis, motoring. *Address:* Pendower, 42 Thorn Park, Mannamead, Plymouth. *T:* Plymouth 5766. *Club:* Overseas.

Died 20 April 1943.

DENNY, Hon. William Joseph, MC; *b* Adelaide; *s* of Thomas Denny; *m* W. Leahy; one *s* three *d*. *Educ:* Christian Brothers Coll.; Adelaide Univ. Formerly Member of Adelaide City Council; retired on election to Parliament, 1900; member for West Adelaide, 1900–02, 1902–05 and 1906–33; admitted to Bar; Attorney-General of South Australia, 1910–12; Attorney-General and Minister of Housing, South Australia, 1924–27; Minister of Irrigation and Repatriation, 1925–27; Attorney-General and Minister of Local Government and Railways, 1930–33; stroked winners of Torrens Fours; enlisted for active service with AIF, 18 Aug. 1916, as private (promoted to Captain, MC, wounded); appointed AIF representative, Military Mission to US, Sept. 1917. *Publications:* The Diggers; A Digger at Home and Abroad; The Australians' Effort. *Recreations:* walking, horse-racing, rowing. *Address:* Portrush Road, Toorak, South Australia. *Clubs:* Stock Exchange, Tattersall's, Commercial Travellers.

Died 2 May 1946.

DENT, Major John William; JP; *b* 18 Aug. 1857; *e s* of late John Dent Dent and Mary Hebden, *d* of John Woodall. *Educ:* Eton; Trinity College, Cambridge. Formerly Major 4th Dragoon Guards. *Address:* Ribston Hall, Wetherby, Yorks.

Died 8 Oct. 1943.

DENT-BROCKLEHURST, Maj. John Henry; *see* Brocklehurst.

DE PENCIER, Most Rev. Adam Urias, OBE, 1918; MA, DD, Chaplain to the Forces (T); 2nd Class, CEF, 1916–18; *b* 1866; *m* 1895, Nina Frederica (*d* 1936), *d* of Lieut Col Fred Wells; four *s* two *d*. *Educ:* Trinity University, Toronto. Ordained, 1890; Rector, St Matthew's, Brandon, 1904–08; St Paul's, Vancouver, 1908–10; Bishop of New Westminster, 1910–40; Metropolitan of British Columbia, 1925–40. *Address:* Vancouver, BC.

Died 31 May 1949.

de POURTALÈS, Count Guy; writer; *b* 4 Aug. 1881; *m* 1911, Helen Marcuard; one *s* two *d*. *Educ:* Geneva; University of Bonn; University of Berlin; University of Paris. 1st novel published 1913; correspondent to Revue de Paris and Revue des Deux Mondes; attached to BEF, 1914, as liaison-officer and interpreter (4th Division), gassed 1915 (French Croix de Guerre, Officer of the Legion of Honour, War medal, etc.). President to Revue Hebdomadaire, 1920–36. *Publications:* Solitudes (novel), 1913; Marins d'eau douce, 1919; Translation of Shakespeare's Measure for Measure, Hamlet and Tempest, 1922; Life of Liszt, 1925; Life of Chopin, 1926; Montclar (a novel), 1927; Nietzsche in Italy, 1929; R. Wagner (an artist's biography), 1932; Affinités instinctives (essays), 1934; La Pêche miraculeuse (a novel), 1937 (grand prix de l'Académie française, 1937 and Heinemann Prize 1938); Berlioz and romanticism, 1939, etc.; almost all of these have been translated into English, German, Czechoslovakian, Swedish, Hungarian, etc. *Address:* 14 rue François Ier, Paris, VIII. *T:* Élysées 73–40.

Died June 1941.

DE PREE, Maj.-Gen. Hugo Douglas, CB 1918; CMG 1916; DSO 1919; *b* Xmas Day, 1870; *s* of Col G. C. De Pree, Surveyor-General, India, and Mary, *d* of John Haig, Cameron Bridge, Fife; *m* 1st, Diones Margaret (*d* 1930), *d* of F. E. Thornhill, JP; two *s* one *d*; 2nd, 1937, Mary Putnam, *widow* of William F. Fisher, Tufton Place, Northiam, Sussex. *Educ:* Eton; RMA, Woolwich. Entered RA 1890; psc; served NW Frontier, India, 1897–98 (medal, 2 clasps); British East Africa, 1901 (medal with clasp); S Africa, 1901–02 (Queen's medal 5 clasps); European War, 1914–18 (despatches five times, CMG, Bt-Col, CB, DSO); commanded 13th Indian Infantry Brigade, 1920–23; General Officer Commanding 55th (West Lancashire) Division, TA, 1925–26; Commandant, Royal Military Academy, 1926–30; retired pay, 1931; Col Comdt RA, 1934–40. *Address:* Oak Hill House, Beckley, Sussex. *Club:* Army and Navy.

Died 30 March 1943.

DERAMORE, 4th Baron *cr* 1885; **George Nicholas de Yarburgh Bateson;** JP; Bt 1818; *b* 25 Nov. 1870; *s* of 2nd Baron and Mary, *d* of G. J. Yarburgh, Heslington, whose surname he assumed by Royal licence, 1876; *S* brother, 1936; *m* 1900, Muriel, *d* of late Arthur Duncombe, Sutton Hall, Easingwold; two *s* one *d*. *Educ:* Eton; Trinity College, Cambridge. JP East Riding, Yorkshire. *Heir:* *s* Hon. Stephen Nicholas de Yarburgh Bateson, Sqdn. Ldr RAFVR [partner in Cazenove, Akroyds and Greenwood & Co.; *b* 18 May 1903; *m* 1929, Nina Marion, *e d* of Alastair Macpherson-Grant, Broughton, Hants; one *d*]. *Address:* Deighton Grove, Crockey Hill, York. *Clubs:* Carlton; Yorkshire, York.

Died 4 Nov. 1943.

DERBY, 17th Earl of, *cr* 1485; **Edward George Villiers Stanley,** KG 1914; PC 1903; GCB 1920; GCVO 1908; KCVO 1905; CB (Mil.) 1900; JP; Bt 1627; Baron Stanley, 1832; Baron Stanley of Preston, 1886; Lord Lieutenant of Lancashire; Hon. Colonel 4th Batt. Manchester Regiment, 5th Bn King's Liverpool, 62nd Searchlight Regt and 5th Bn Loyal North Lancashire Regt, etc; *b* London, 4 April 1865; *e s* of 16th Earl and Lady Constance Villiers, *e d* of 4th Earl of Clarendon; *S* father, 1908; *m* 1889, Lady Alice Montagu, *d* of 7th Duke of Manchester, Lady of the Bedchamber to Queen Alexandra; two *s*. *Educ:* Wellington College. Lieut Grenadier Guards, 1885–95; ADC to Gov.-Gen. of Canada, 1889–91; served S Africa, first as Chief Press Censor, afterwards as Private Sec. to F.-M. Lord Roberts, 1899–1901 (despatches twice); one of the Lords of the Treasury, 1895–1900; Financial Secretary to the War Office, 1900–03; Postmaster-General, 1903–05; MP West Houghton Division of Lancashire, 1892–1906; Director-General of Recruiting, 1915–16; Under Secretary for War, 1916; Secretary of State for War,

1916–18, also 1922–24; Ambassador to France, 1918–20; Royal Victorian Chain, 1935. *Recreations:* racing, shooting; member of Jockey Club. *Heir: g s* Lord Stanley, MC. *Address:* Knowsley, Prescot, Lancashire; Coworth Park, Sunningdale. *Clubs:* Carlton, Guards', Turf, Travellers'.

Died 4 Feb. 1948.

DERHAM, Brig.-Gen. Frank Seymour, CB 1916; retired; East Lancs Regt; *b* 29 June 1858. Served Chitral, 1895 (medal with clasp); S Africa, 1902 (Queen's medal); European War, 1914–18 (despatches, CB). *Club:* United Service.

Died 27 Aug. 1941.

DERING, Comdr Claud Lacy Yea, DSO 1919; RN, retired; *b* 1885; *m* 1915, Winifred (*d* 1941), *d* of Edmund Gellibrand; one *d*. Served European War, 1914–18 (DSO).

Died 31 Oct. 1943.

d'ERLANGER, Baron Frederic A.; Chairman of Erlangers, Ltd, 4 Moorgate, EC2; *b* 1868. His activities are divided between business and music; his published compositions comprise several operas as well as symphonic choral works and ballets. *Address:* Park House, Rutland Gate, SW7. *T:* Kensington 0095.

Died 23 April 1943.

DERRICK, Col George Alexander, CBE, Civil, 1918, Military 1920, VD; *b* Southampton, 1860; *s* of George Derrick, Southampton; *m* 1905, Julia Anna, *d* of Jacob Hutkin, Poltava, Russia; no *c*. *Educ:* Southampton; privately. Public Accountant, Singapore, until 1915; commanded Singapore Volunteer Corps, 1912–19; retired with rank of Colonel, 1919; JP Singapore. *Address:* c/o Chartered Bank of India, Australia, and China, Bishopsgate, EC. *Clubs:* East India and Sports, Royal Automobile; Singapore.

Died 19 July 1945.

DE RUTZEN, Baron (John Frederick Foley); JP; Major in Welsh Guards; *b* 1909; *s* of late Lieut Alan Frederick James, Baron de Rutzen, Pembrokeshire Yeomanry (killed in action in European War), Slebech Park, Pembrokeshire, and Eleanor Etna Audley Thursby-Pelham of Abermarlais Park, Carmarthenshire, and Ridgeway, Pembrokeshire; *S* father, 1916; *m* 1932, Sheila Victoria Katrin, *o d* of Captain Sir Henry Philipps, 2nd Bt; one *d*. *Educ:* Eton; Trinity Hall, Cambridge. Pembrokeshire County Council, 1933–37 and since 1938; Welsh Guards, Supplementary Reserve, 1937. *Recreations:* fishing and shooting. *Address:* Slebech Park, Haverfordwest. *Clubs:* Guards', Pratt's, Farmers'.

Died 11 Oct. 1944.

DERWENT, 3rd Baron *cr* 1881; **George Harcourt Johnstone;** Bt 1795; President of the Yorkshire Liberal Federation; Co-Treasurer British Liberal International Council; Member of Council of the Georgian Group; Fellow of Royal Society of Arts; Fellow of Royal Asiatic Society; Member Royal Central Asian Society; *b* 22 Oct. 1899; 2nd *s* of late Hon. Edward Henry Vanden-Bempde-Johnstone, 2nd *s* of 1st Baron, and Hon. Evelyn Mary Agar-Ellis, *d* of 5th Viscount Clifden; *S* uncle, 1929; *m* 1929, Sabine (*d* 1941), *d* of General Iliesco, former Chief of the General Staff of the Roumanian Army, and Madame Iliesco, *née* Logadi. *Educ:* Charterhouse; Merton College, Oxford (BA 1920, Newdigate Prize). Hon. Attaché at Warsaw, 1923, at Brussels, 1927; Madrid, 1928; Berne, 1940. Served in RAF, 1942–44 (Defence Medal). *Publications:* Prosper Mérimée, 1926; Goya, 1930; Fifty Poems, 1931; Rossini, 1934; Return Ticket (under pseudonym George Vandon), 1940; Before Zero Hour (Poems), 1943. *Recreations:* fishing, golf, thinking the 20th century is just wonderful. *Heir: b* Hon. Patrick Robin Gilbert Johnstone, *b* 1901. *Address:* Hackness Hall, Scarborough, Yorks. *T:* Hackness 5. *Clubs:* St James', White's.

Died 12 Jan. 1949.

DE SALIS, Sir Cecil Fane, KCB 1935; CB 1931; MA; DL; *b* 1857; *m* 1889, Rachel E. F., *o c* of late Edmund Waller, Farmington Lodge, Glos; five *s* four *d*. *Educ:* Eton; Christ Church, Oxford, MA. Called to Bar, Inner Temple, 1881; Sheriff of Middlesex, 1905; County Alderman, County of Middlesex, 1910–37; Chairman, Middlesex County Council, 1920–25; Chairman, Territorial Army and Air Force Association, County of Middlesex, 1925–36. *Address:* Holly Cross House, Craizies Hill, Reading. *T:* Wargrave 241.

Died 9 March 1948.

DE SALIS, Rt Rev. Charles Fane, DD; Assistant Bishop of Bath and Wells since 1931; Prebendary of Shalford Wells Cathedral since 1938; *b* 19 March 1860; 3rd *s* of late Rev. H. J. A. Fane De Salis, of Portnall Park, and *d* of late Rt Hon. J. W. Henley, MP; *m* 1896, Lady Mary Alice Parker (*d* 1930), 3rd *d* of 6th Earl of Macclesfield; one *s* two *d*. *Educ:* Eton; Exeter College, Oxford. Ordained, 1883; Curate of St Michael, Coventry, 1883–88; Vicar of Milverton, 1888–96; East Brent, 1886–99; Prebendary of Coombe, 1900–11; Rector of Weston-super-Mare, 1900–11; Bishop Suffragan of Taunton, 1911; Residentiary Canon of Wells, 1915; retired as Suffragan and Residentiary Canon, 1930; Archdeacon of Taunton, 1911–38. *Address:* Bishop's Mead, Taunton. *T:* Taunton 2864. *Clubs:* Somerset County, Taunton.

Died 24 Jan. 1942.

DE SALIS, Lt-Col Edward Augustus Alfred, DSO 1900; late the Worcestershire Regt; *b* 2 June 1874; *s* of late Lt-Col Edward J. de Salis, Naval Ordnance Dept; *m* 1902, Emily Ethel, *e d* of late Col A. D. Geddes, 27th Regt Royal Inniskilling Fusiliers. Entered Militia, 1891; Army, 1899; Major, 1915; Lieut-Col 1919; served West Africa, 1897 (medal and clasp); South Africa, 1899–1901 (despatches twice, Queen's medal and 7 clasps); European War, 1914–18; retired pay, 1924. *Address:* 10 Magdalen Road, St Leonards-on-Sea. *Club:* Army and Navy.

Died 16 Dec. 1943.

DE SALIS, Lt-Col John Eugene, 8th Count de Salis; KJStJ; *b* 1891; *e s* of 7th Count de Salis, and Countess Helene de Riquet (*d* 1902), *d* of Prince de Caraman-Chimay; *S* father 1939; *m* 1947, Mary Camilla Presti; one *s*. *Educ:* Beaumont; Balliol College, Oxford, MA. Served European War in 1st Life Guards and Irish Guards, 1914–19 (twice wounded); attached British Embassy, Paris, as an assistant to military attaché, 1918–19; entered diplomatic service, 1920; appointed 3rd Secretary, Washington; transferred Tokyo, 1921; Aide-de-Camp to the Earl of Lytton when Governor of Bengal, 1925–27; Adjutant Indian Army Rifle Team, 1927–29; Commandant, 1930–34; served War of 1939–45; SCAO Asmara and Hamasien, Eritrea, 1943–44; Delegate of the Order of St John of Jerusalem for revision of Geneva Convention 1929; Chevalier Legion of Honour; Order of the Crown of Roumania; Bali Grand Cross, Order of Malta; Military Medal, Montenegro; FRGS. *Heir: s* John, *b* 16 Nov. 1947. *Address:* 10 Priory Walk, SW10. *T:* Freemantle 4176. *Clubs:* Pratt's, Bachelors', Royal Automobile, 1900.

Died 12 June 1949.

de SAUSMAREZ, Lady Annie Elizabeth, GBE 1920; *d* of Rev. F. W. Mann, Rector of St Mary de Castro, Guernsey; *m* 1896, Sir Havilland Walter de Sausmarez, 1st Bt (*d* 1941); no *c*. President of British Women's Work Association in China, 1914–19; médaille de la Reine Elizabeth. *Address:* Sausmarez Manor, Guernsey.

Died 15 March 1947.

DESBARATS, George Joseph, CMG 1915; BApSc; Hon. MEIC; Deputy Minister of National Defence, Canada, 1924–32; *b* 1861; *s* of George E. Desbarats and Lucianne Bosse; *m* Lilian, *d* of Sir Richard Scott; two *s* two *d*. *Educ:* Terrebonne College and Montreal

Polytechnic School; honour graduate, 1879. Various engineering positions on designing and construction of canals in Canada; railway construction in British Columbia; in charge hydrographic survey of river St Lawrence, 1899; Director of Government Shipyard at Sorel, 1901; Deputy Minister of Marine and Fisheries, 1909; Deputy Minister of the Naval Service of Canada, 1910; Plenipotentiary Delegate for Canada to the International Wireless Conference, London, 1912; Canadian Government representative Seamen's Conference, League of Nations, Genoa, 1920; President Engineering Institute of Canada, 1937; President Canadian Geographical Society, 1941. *Address:* 330 Wilbrod Street, Ottawa. *Clubs:* Rideau, Ottawa.

Died 28 April 1944.

DESBOROUGH, 1st Baron *cr* 1905, of Taplow; **William Henry Grenfell,** KG 1928; GCVO 1925; KCVO 1908; JP, DL, MA; late Chairman of Thames Conservancy Board; President and Chairman in the Bath Club, London, from its foundation of 1894 until 1942; Hon. Fellow Balliol College, Oxford, 1928; DCL Oxford, 1938; Ex-President, London Chamber of Commerce; Ex-President, British Imperial Council of Commerce; *b* 30 Oct. 1855; *s* of C. W. Grenfell, MP, and Georgiana, *d* of Lady Caroline and Rt Hon. W. Sebright Lascelles; *S* grandfather, C. P. Grenfell, MP; *m* 1887, Ethel, *co-heiress* to Barony of Butler, *d* of Hon. Julian and Lady Adine Fane; two *d* (two *s* killed in War, 1914–18). *Educ:* Harrow; Balliol College, Oxford. Played Harrow Eleven, 1873–74; represented Oxford in three mile race *versus* Cambridge, 1876; rowed *versus* Cambridge, 1877–78; President, OUAC and OUBC; climbed in the Alps and shot in the Rocky Mountains, India, etc.; swam twice across Niagara; stroked eight across the Channel; special correspondent second Suakim Campaign; MP Salisbury, 1880, 1885; MP Hereford, 1892 (resigned); Private Secretary to Sir W. Harcourt at Exchequer, 1892; Capt. of Yeomen of the Guard, 1925–29; High Sheriff, Bucks, 1890; Mayor of Maidenhead, 1895–97; MP (C) for Wycombe Div. of Bucks, 1900–05; member of Tariff Commission, 1904; Chairman of Pilgrims of Great Britain, 1919–29; President Central Association of Volunteer Regiments; Chairman of Fresh Water Fish Committee appointed by the Board of Agriculture, and Chairman of the Committee to enquire into the Police of England, Scotland and Wales appointed by the Home Office; won Epée prize Military Tournament, 1904–06; won Punting Championship three years. Owns about 12,000 acres. *Publications:* articles on Rocky Mountains, Rowing, House of Lords, Bimetallism. *Recreations:* hunting, rowing, punting, shooting, fishing. *Heir:* none. *Address:* Panshanger Park, Hertford, Herts. *Clubs:* Carlton, Bath.

Died 9 Jan. 1945.

DESBOROUGH, Arthur Peregrine Henry, CBE 1920; retired Civil Servant; *b* 10 Sept. 1868; 2nd *s* of late Major-General John Desborough, CB, RA; *m* 2nd *d* of late Major-General E. Bland, RE; no *c. Educ:* RM Academy, Woolwich. Entered Royal Artillery, 1887; Captain, 1897; Inspector of Explosives, Home Office, 1899; Superintendent, Royal Naval Cordite Factory, Holton Heath, 1915–28. *Recreation:* gardening. *Address:* Tulgey Wood, Broadstone, Dorset. *T:* Broadstone 51.

Died 19 July 1949.

DE SELINCOURT, Martin; *b* 26 Nov. 1864; *e s* of Charles Alexandre De Sélincourt and Theodora Bruce Bendall; *m* 1st, 1888, Mabel, 2nd *d* of William Speed, KC; four *s* one *d*; 2nd, 1933, Nancy, *e d* of Captain R. C. Brown, MC; one *s* one *d. Educ:* Mill Hill. Late Chairman of Swan and Edgar Ltd; late Chairman of the Geographical Magazine. *Recreations:* yachting, travelling. *Address:* Brooklands, Sarisbury Green, near Southampton. *T:* Locks Heath 2140. *Club:* Royal Cruising.

Died 8 Aug. 1950.

DESHUMBERT, Marius; formerly Professor of French at Staff College and Royal Military College; *b* Lyons, France, 1856. *Educ:* Lyons. Buddhist; Founder and Hon. Secretary of Comité International de Propagande pour la Pratique de la Morale fondée sur les Lois de la Nature; Founder and Hon. Secretary of the International League of Compassion. *Publications:* Dictionary of Difficulties met with in French; the Public Examination French Handbook; French-English List of Technical Military Terms; How to Teach and How to Learn Modern Languages; Grammaire Française Moderne (with M. Ceppi); Confucius, his Life and Doctrine; Ma Vie par Jésus de Nazareth; Morale de la Nature, translated into several languages; and several pamphlets on Ethics. *Address:* Dewhurst, Dunheved Road, Thornton Heath, Surrey.

Died 14 Feb. 1943.

DESIKACHARI, Diwan Bahadur Sir Tirumalai, Kt 1922; MRAS; Advocate; Chairman T. S. Electric Supply and E. T. Electric Corporations, etc., President The District Health Association; *b* 1868; *s* of Tirumalai Venkatachari and Komalammāl; *m* Pattammāl, *d* of late Diwan Bahadur T. M. Rangachariar, BA; one *s* three *d. Educ:* Presidency College, Madras. Chairman of the Municipality of Trichinopoly, 1909–11; first non-official Vice-President of the Trichinopoly District Board, 1914–17; first non-official President, 1917–25; non-official Member of the Madras Legislative Council under the Morley-Minto Scheme; was a Member of the newly reformed Legislative Council, Madras, and one of the panel of chairman till 1924; a Member of the Civil Justice Committee, India, 1924; Member, Malabar Tenancy Committee, 1927–28; awarded the title and badge of Diwan Bahadur for public work in 1911; the Kaisar-i-hind gold medal in 1920–21; certificate in 1921 for services during the War; Hon. Col 11th (Madras) Battalion, Indian Territorial Force, from 1938. *Publication:* South Indian Coins. *Recreations:* walking and driving; is a numismatist and coin collector. *Address:* Venkata Park, Cantonment, Trichinopoly, Madras Presidency, India; Enderley, Coonoor, RS Nilgris, S India. *Clubs:* Union, Trichinopoly; Cosmopolitan, Madras.

Died 9 July 1940.

DESPENCER-ROBERTSON, Lt-Col James Archibald St George Fitzwarenne, OBE; MP (U) Salisbury since 1931; *b* 7 Nov. 1893; *o surv. s* of late Sir Helenus Robertson. Assumed additional surname of Despencer in accordance with will of late Edmund Mortimer Despencer, who was killed in European War; unmarried. *Educ:* Eton; New College, Oxford. Royal Welch Fusiliers, 1914–19 (despatches thrice, OBE, Brevet Major); MP (U) West Islington, Nov. 1922–23; Parliamentary Private Secretary (unpaid) to Right Hon. C. C. Craig, Parliamentary Secretary to Ministry of Pensions, 1923; Major, Emergency Reserve, 1939. *Recreations:* shooting, walking, study of English historical antiquities. *Address:* Sydenham House, Lewdown, Devon. *T:* Chillaton 237. *Clubs:* Carlton, Leander.

Died 5 May 1942.

d'ESPEREY, Franchet; Maréchal de France since 1921; Voïvode de Yougoslavie; Membre du Conseil Supérieur de la Guerre; *b* 25 mai 1856; *s* of Louis d'Esperey et Louise de Dion; *m* 1892, Alice Dunsane de la Josserie; one *s* one *d. Educ:* École Spéciale Militaire de Saint-Cyr, 1874; École Supérieure de Guerre, 1882–84. S'lieutenant 1ers tirailleurs algériens, 1876; lieutenant, 1881; capitaine État Major du corps expéditionnaire du Tonkin, 1885; de l'Armée 1887; Adjutant major 4e tirailleurs algériens, 1893; Chef de Bataillon, 1893; L'Colonel, 1897; Colonel du 60e d'infanterie, 1903; Général de la 77e Brigade, 1907; 2e Division, 1911; 1er Corps d'Armée, 1913; Ve Armée, 1914; Groupe d'Armées de l'Est, 1915; du Nord, 1915; Commandant en chef des armées alliés en Orient, 1918; Inspecteur Général de l'Afrique du Nord, 1920; Grand Croix de St

Michel et St Georges; Grand Croix de l'Ordre de Victoria. *Address:* 34 rue de Lubeck, Paris. *Clubs:* Union, St Cloud Country.

Died July 1942.

DES VŒUX, Sir Edward Alfred, 8th Bt *cr* 1787; *b* 9 Nov. 1864; *s* of late Maj.-Gen. Alfred Anthony Des Vœux; *S* cousin, 1937. *Heir: cousin* Capt. William Richard de Bacquencourt Des Vœux, Grenadier Guards [*b* 1911; *m* 1939, Jean Margaret, *o d* of Lt-Col J. F. Elkington, DSO; one *d*].

Died 19 Dec. 1941.

DES VŒUX, Lt-Col Herbert, CSI 1919; *b* Portarlington, Queen's Co., Aug. 1864; *s* of late Major T. Des Vœux; *m* 1895, Minna, *d* of late Lieut-Col T. T. Haggard, RA; one *s* one *d*. *Educ:* Berkhamstead. Enlisted 1883; Commission, 1887; served with 1st Bengal Cavalry; joined Burma Military Police, Jan. 1890; Burma Commission, Dec. 1890; Inspector-General of Police, 1913; retired Indian Army, 1920. *Address:* c/o National Bank of India, 26 Bishopsgate, EC2. *Club:* Royal Automobile.

Died 26 March 1945.

DES VŒUX, Temp. Lt-Col Sir (William) Richard de Bacquencourt, 9th Bt *cr* 1787; Grenadier Guards; seconded Parachute Regt; *b* 27 Dec. 1911; *s* of Lt-Col Henry John des Vœux, OBE, and Dorothy Gladys Turner Farley; *S* cousin, 1942; *m* 1939, Jean Margaret Rew, *o d* of Lt-Col J. F. Elkington, DSO; three *d*. *Educ:* Eton; RMC, Sandhurst. Joined Grenadier Guards, 1931. *Heir:* none. *Address:* (wartime) Adbury Holt, Newbury, Berks. *T:* Newbury 187. *Club:* Guards'.

Died 20 Sept. 1944 (ext).

DEVALS, Rt Rev. Adrian; Bishop of Malacca since 1934; *b* Rodez, France, 19 Nov. 1882. Entered Foreign Missions Seminary Paris, 1900; priest, 1906; Came to Malaya, 1906; Parish priest Assumption Church, Penang, 1920. *Address:* 31 Victoria Street, Singapore, SS.

Died 17 Jan. 1945.

DEVAUX, J. Louis; KC; Chief Judge, Mauritius, since 1940; *b* 1884; 4th *s* of J. Devaux, St Lucia, BWI; *m* Eunice, *y d* of A. H. Bertrand, Winnipeg, Canada; three *d*. *Educ:* St Mary's College, St Lucia. Called to Bar, Lincoln's Inn, 1906 (Certificate of Honour); practised law, Winnipeg, Canada, 1906–15; St Lucia, 1915–19; acting Magistrate 1st District, St Lucia, 1917–18; Assistant Legal Adviser, Seychelles, 1919; Legal Adviser, 1920; acting Chief Justice, 1921–22 and 1923; Chief Justice of Seychelles, 1924–28; administered the Government, March–Sept. 1925, April–Aug. 1927, and Nov. 1927–March 1928; Resident Magistrate, Jamaica, 1928–31; Solicitor-General, Trinidad, 1931–35; Attorney-General, Trinidad, 1935–40. *Address:* Port Louis, Mauritius. *[Knighthood announced 1943 but died before receiving it.]*

Died Jan. 1943.

DEVERELL, Field Marshal Sir Cyril John, GCB 1935; KCB 1929; KBE 1926; CB 1918; Col The West Yorkshire Regiment (The Prince of Wales's Own) since 1934; *b* 9 Nov. 1874; *s* of late Major J. B. S. Deverell; *m* 1902, Hilda, *d* of late Col G. Grant-Dalton, The PWO West Yorkshire Regt; one *s* one *d*. *Educ:* Bedford School. 2nd Lieut The PWO West Yorkshire Regt, 1895; Adjutant 1st West Yorkshire Regt, 1904–06; passed Staff College, 1907; Brigade Major, India, 1908–12; General Staff, India, 1913–14; Brigade Major BEF, 1914–15; commanded 4th East Yorkshire Regt, 1915; 20th Infantry Brigade, 7th Division, 1915–16; 3rd Division, Aug. 1916–April 1919; Northern Div. British Army of the Rhine, 1919 (CB; Officer of the Legion of Honour; Croix de guerre with palm; Bt Major, 1915; Bt Lt-Col, 1916; Bt Col, 1917; Promoted Major-General for distinguished service in the field, 1919; despatches seven times); Welsh Division TA, 1919–21; Commanded United Provinces District, India, 1921–25;

Quartermaster-General in India 1927–30; Lieut-General, 1928; Chief of General Staff, India, 1930–31; GOC-in-C Western Command, 1931–33; General, 1933; GOC-in-C Eastern Command, 1933–36; ADC Gen. to the King, 1934–36; Field Marshal, 1936; Chief of Imperial General Staff, 1936–37; Hon. Director General Army and Royal Air Force Savings Associations; Member of National Savings Committee; DL Hampshire. *Address:* Court Lodge, Lymington, Hants. *T:* Lymington 304. *Club:* Army and Navy.

Died 12 May 1947.

DEVEREUX, Rev. Edward Robert Price, MA, LLB; Hon. Canon of Winchester Cathedral, 1917; Rector of Kegworth since 1922; Rural Dean of Akeley East Deanery since 1940; *s* of late Edward William Devereux, Camberwell; *m* 1897, Louisa Marian, *d* of late James Webb, Peckham Rye; one *s* one *d*. *Educ:* Mercers' School, London; Christ's College, Cambridge; 2nd Class Law Tripos and 2nd Class History Tripos, 1st Class Theol. Prelim. Ordained, 1895; Curate of All Saints, Southport, Lancs, and of Holy Trinity, Cambridge; Vicar of Christ Church, Woking, 1905–22; Member of the Archbishops' Mission of Help to Canada, 1912; Vice-Chairman Guildford Board of Guardians, 1913; Chairman Woking Education Committee, 1919–22; Proctor in Convocation and Member of Church Assembly, Diocese of Winchester, 1920–22; Diocese of Peterborough, 1923–25; Diocese, of Leicester, 1929–31, and from 1935. *Publications:* About the Feet of God; Two Courses of Confirmation Lectures; Things Worth Thinking Out. *Address:* The Rectory, Kegworth, nr Derby. *TA:* Canon Devereux, Kegworth. *T:* Kegworth 21. *Club:* National.

Died 23 Jan. 1941.

DE VILLIERS, Hon. Sir (Jean) Etienne (Reenen), Kt 1923; Judge of Appeal, Appellate Division, Supreme Court of South Africa since 1933; *b* 25 March 1875; *s* of late Rev. W. P. de Villiers of Carnarvon, Cape Province; *m* 1903, Minnie Edith, *d* of James Drummond of Somerset East, Cape of Good Hope; two *s*. *Educ:* South African College; Cape Town; St John's College, Cambridge, MA, LLD (formerly Fellow). Advocate of Supreme Court, Cape Town, 1900–13; Judge of Water Courts, 1913–19; KC 1919; Judge President OFS Provincial Division of Supreme Court of S Africa, 1920–33. *Publication:* The History of Legislation concerning Real and Personal Property. *Address:* Appeal Court, Bloemfontein. *Clubs:* Bloemfontein, Bloemfontein; Civil Service, Cape Town.

Died 4 Feb. 1947.

DEVITT, Sir Philip (Henry), 1st Bt *cr* 1931; JP; Sole Partner of Devitt and Moore; *b* 1876; *y s* of Sir Thomas Lane Devitt, 1st Bt; *m* 1919, Dorothy Maud, *d* of Rev. Frederic John Hall; five *d*. *Educ:* Loretto; Trinity Hall, Cambridge, MA. A founder of Nautical College, Pangbourne, and Chairman of the Board of Governors; a Governor of Loretto School; an Honorary Member and a Trustee of the Honourable Company of Master Mariners; Member of Committee of Royal Alfred Aged Merchant Seamen's Institution; a Vice-Pres. of Marine Society; a Member of the Board of the Sailors' Home, Dock Street; Chairman of the Annual National Service for Seafarers; Hon. Treasurer of the Institution of Naval Architects; Chairman London Local Marine Board. *Heir:* none. *Address:* Northaw Place, Northaw, Herts; Sandlea, Littlestone, Kent. *Clubs:* City of London, Royal Thames Yacht, Leander.

Died 5 June 1947 (ext).

DEVONSHIRE, 10th Duke of, *cr* 1694; **Edward William Spencer Cavendish,** KG 1941; Baron Cavendish, 1605; Earl of Devonshire, 1618; Marquess of Hartington, 1694; Earl of Burlington, 1831; Baron Cavendish (UK), 1831; High Steward of Cambridge University since 1938; Lord-Lieutenant of Derbyshire since 1938; Chancellor of Leeds University since 1938;

Chairman of Oversea Settlement Board, 1936; President Zoological Society of London, 1948; *b* 6 May 1895; *e s* of 9th Duke and Lady Evelyn Emily-Mary Fitzmaurice (GCVO 1937), *d* of 5th Marquis of Lansdowne; *S* father, 1938; *m* 1917, Lady Mary Cecil, CBE 1946, *d* of 4th Marquess of Salisbury, KG, GCVO; one *s* two *d* (*er s* killed in action, 1944). *Educ:* Eton; Trinity College, Cambridge. Hon. Colonel 40th (Sherwood) Foresters AA Battalion; Bt Lt-Col Derby Yeomanry; served Egypt, Dardanelles and France (despatches twice); attached Intelligence, 1916, and served War Office and British Mission, Paris; Member of British Peace Delegation, Paris, 1919; MBE; TD; LLD; Chevalier, Legion of Honour; contested NE Derbyshire, General Election, 1918, and West Derbyshire, 1922; MP (U) Western Division of Derbyshire, 1923–28; Parliamentary Under-Secretary of State for Dominion Affairs 1936–40; Parliamentary Under-Secretary of State for India and for Burma, 1940–42; Parliamentary Under-Sec. of State for the Colonies, 1943–45. Mayor of Buxton, 1919–21; JP Derbyshire. *Heir: s* Marquess of Hartington, MC. *Address:* Churchdale Hall, Bakewell, Derbyshire; Chatsworth House, Derbyshire; Compton Place, Eastbourne; Bolton Abbey, Yorkshire. *Clubs:* Brooks's, Turf, Flyfishers', 1900, Conservative, Athenæum.

Died 26 Nov. 1950.

DEVONSHIRE, Sir James Lyne, KBE 1920; MIEE; Vice-President of Tramways, Light Railways and Transport Association; *b* 4 Oct. 1863; 4th *s* of late Thomas Harris Devonshire, 1 Frederick's Place, Old Jewry, EC, and Mill Gap, Eastbourne; *m* 1889, Wilhelmina Walker, *d* of late Charles Sidey; two *d*. *Educ:* Eastbourne; Shrewsbury; London. Studied Electrical Engineering at City and Guilds (Engineering) College, South Kensington. Member Board of Trade Electrical Trades Committee; and subsequently of Electric Power Supply Committee; Member, Institution of Electrical Engineers (Vice-Pres. 1923–26); Council of Incorporated Association of Electric Power Companies; also Central Electricity Board, 1927–36. *Recreation:* golf. *Address:* 2 Wildcroft Manor, Putney Heath, SW15. *Club:* Royal Wimbledon Golf.

Died 13 April 1946.

DEW, Col Sir Armine Brereton, KCIE 1921; CSI 1915; CIE 1911; *b* 27 Sept. 1867; *s* of Major Frederick Napleton Dew, JP, DL, Herefordshire; *m* 1900, Esmé Mary, *d* of late Sir Adelbert Talbot, KCIE; one *s* one *d*. *Educ:* Wellington. Entered army, 1888; Captain Indian Army, 1899; Major, 1906; Lieut-Col, 1914; retired, 1922; served Hazara Expedition, 1891 (medal with clasp); attached to Gilgit Agency, 1894; joined Political Department, 1897; Political Assistant, 1898; Political Agent, 1905; Political Agent, Gilgit, 1908–12; Political Agent, Kalat, 1912–17; Revenue and Judicial Commissioner, Baluchistan, 1917; Agent to the Governor-General and Chief Commissioner, Baluchistan, 1919–22; retired; Victory medal, 1914–18; Afghan War medal, 1919; FRGS; Central Asian Society; British Institute International Affairs. *Clubs:* United Service, Alpine.

Died 7 June 1941.

DEW, Armine Roderick, MVO 1938; *b* 20 March 1906; *s* of late Lt-Col Sir Armine B. Dew, KCIE, CSI, and Esmé Mary, *d* of late Sir Adelbert Talbot, KCIE. *Educ:* Wellington; New College, Oxford. 3rd Secretary, 1928; Washington, 1928; transferred to Foreign Office, 1931; 2nd Secretary, 1933; transferred Paris, 1935; Moscow, 1938; 1st Secretary, 1939; Belgrade, 1940–41; Foreign Office, 1941. *Address:* Foreign Office, SW1.

Died 1 Feb. 1945.

DEWAR, Rev. Alexander, FRGS; Missionary Superintendent, Free Church of Scotland Mission, S Africa, since 1908; *b* Lochgilphead, Argyll, May 1864; *m*; two *s* one *d*. *Educ:* University of Glasgow; Free Church Divinity Hall. Appointed and ordained to the

Livingstonia Mission, Central Africa, 1893; pioneered the most northern mission station, Mwenzo, 1894; various translations into Chinamwanga and Kinkonde dialects; transferred to Karonga, north end of Nyasa, 1899; returned to Scotland, 1904, making the journey through Africa from the Zambesi to Cairo, being the first white man to accomplish this without an armed escort; Moderator of the General Assembly of the Free Church of Scotland, 1927. *Publications:* various school and religious books, including Catechisms, primers, Hymn books and gospels translated into native dialects, Chinamwanga and Kinkonde. *Recreations:* riding and gardening. *Address:* Free Church of Scotland, The Mound, Edinburgh; Hospital Hill, King William's Town, S Africa.

Died 10 Aug. 1943.

DEWAR, Michael Bruce Urquhart, OBE 1918; JP; MA; MIEE, AMInstCE; MSAE; a Vice-President, FBI; Chairman, British Timken, Ltd; *b* 5 Aug. 1886; *o s* of late William Dewar, Rugby; *m* 1910, Dorothy Gertrude (*d* 1943), *o c* of Sir Algernon F. Firth, 2nd Bart; two *s* (and *e s* killed, 1941, in action) three *d*; *m* 1945, Josephine Judith Mullins. *Educ:* Rugby; Trinity College, Cambridge. Mechanical Science Tripos (Hons), 1908. Served apprenticeship with Vickers Ltd, Sheffield; later joined T. F. Firth and Sons, Ltd, and became director; served European War, 1914–18, with RE; transferred to War Office for munition production, 1915; Ministry of Munitions 1916, and appointed director of National Projectile Factories and Assistant Controller of Shell Manufacture; deputy to Sir Glyn Hamilton West; Director General of Shell and Gun Manufacture, and served on several inter-Allied Committees, 1917; joined board, Leeds Forge Co. Ltd, 1919, and later became Managing Director; Managing Director of Metropolitan Carriage Wagon and Finance Co. Ltd, 1922–27; Mem. of Ministry of Labour Delegation which studied industrial conditions in Canada and USA in 1925; also of Committee of Enquiry into Employment Exchanges, 1920; Head of special mission on Tanks to USA, 1940; responsible in collaboration with US Ordnance for design and production of Sherman Tank; later Deputy Director General British Purchasing Commission and British Supply Mission till Dec. 1942; High Sheriff of Hertfordshire, 1944. *Recreations:* shooting, golf. *Address:* Little Horwood Manor, Bletchley, Bucks. *Clubs:* Carlton, Brooks's, Farmers'.

Died 21 Dec. 1950.

DEWAR, Vice-Adm. Robert Gordon Douglas, CBE 1922; retired; *s* of late Colonel Gordon Dewar of Harmony Hall and Mount Stewart, Jamaica, and late Emily Rodger of Parteen, Co. Limerick; *m* 1st, Sibyl Evelyn, *d* of late Vice-Admiral Orford Churchill; one *s*; 2nd, Eileen Violet, *d* of T. D. Atkinson, DL of Glenwilliam Castle, Ballingarry, Co. Limerick; one *s*; 3rd, Evelyn M. Barbara, *d* of late W. Russell of Hayes House, Keston, Kent. *Educ:* HMS Britannia, Dartmouth. Lieutenant, then Commander, and served as Commander of HMS Prince of Wales when that ship was Flagship of HSH Prince Louis of Battenberg, 2nd in command Mediterranean Fleet and as Flagship of Atlantic Fleet; Captain, 1913; served at Sea, 1914–19 in command of HM Ships, Venus, Euryalus, and Berwick; Captain in charge of Northern Area, Ireland, 1921–23; promoted to Flag rank, 1924. *Recreations:* fishing, shooting, cricket, skating, golf. *Address:* c/o Lloyds Bank, 6 Pall Mall, SW1.

Died 24 Aug. 1948.

DEWDNEY, Rt Rev. Alfred Daniel Alexander, BA; DD; *b* Toronto, Ont, Canada, 31 March 1863; *s* of Robert and Elizabeth Dewdney; great-grandfather, John Dewdney, came to Toronto from Devonshire, 1825; *m* 1st, Kathleen, *d* of Isaac Honsberger, Simcoe Co., Ont (decd); 2nd, Alice Ashwood Hanington, *d* of A. H. Hanington, KC, St John, NB; five *s* two *d*. *Educ:* Toronto Collegiate Institute; University of Toronto;

Wycliffe College; Queen's University. Deacon, 1886; Priest, 1887; Incumbent of Port Burwell, 1886–88; Rector of Durham 1888–90; Rector of Mitchell, 1890–94; Rector of St James' Church, St John, NB, 1894–1906; President of St John SS Teachers' Association for five years; Rector of St Alban's Cathedral, Prince Albert, Sask, 1906–11; Lecturer in Apologetics in Emmanuel College, 1907–21, and Acting Principal, 1912–13, 1918–19; Bishop of Keewatin, 1921–38; Rural Dean of Prince Albert, 1906–11; Archdeacon of Prince Albert, and Organiser of Missions, 1910–21; Examining Chaplain to the Bishop of Saskatchewan, 1907–21. *Address:* 315 Jedburgh Rd, Toronto, Ontario.

Died 21 April 1945.

DEWDNEY, Ven. Arthur John Bible; Archdeacon Emeritus, 1926; *m* Ina (*d* 1939), *d* of late Sir William Paulin; one *d*. *Educ:* Jesus College, Oxford, MA. Ordained, 1896; Curate of St Matthew's, Ponder's End, 1896–98; St Mark, Dalston, 1898–1900; Edmonton, 1901; Vicar of St Paul, Winchmore Hill, 1901–08; Hon. Chaplain to Bishop of Calgary, 1909; Hon. Canon of Calgary Pro-Cathedral, 1911; Archdeacon of Red Deer, 1912–16; Chief Missioner Diocese of Calgary, 1915–26; Archdeacon of Calgary, 1916–26. *Address:* 3430 Upper Terrace, Victoria, British Columbia, Canada. *T:* E 5495. *Clubs:* Union, Victoria.

Died 11 Jan. 1946.

DEWEY, Rev. Sir Stanley (Daws), 2nd Bt *cr* 1917; MA; FRMetS; Sub-Dean of Exeter Cathedral since 1930; *b* 12 Aug. 1867; *s* of 1st Bt and Clara, *d* of Thomas Daws of Pyrford Place, Surrey; *S* father, 1926; *m* 1st, 1891, Emily Rose (*d* 1940), *d* of late Rev. H. L. Pryce; four *s* two *d*; 2nd, 1940, Mary Violet (May) Jones, Bromley, Kent, *d* of late Rev. William Jones, Rector of Llansoy. *Educ:* Dulwich College; Pembroke College, Cambridge (Mathematical Scholar). Curate of St James, Norlands, 1891–94. Hambleden, 1894–96; Vicar of Geddington, 1896–1901; Rector of Moretonhampstead, 1901–27; Rural Dean of Moreton, 1920–27; Orgn Sec. and Lecturer Church Defence and Instruction, Diocese of Exeter, 1910–25; Clerical Hon. Sec. Exeter Diocesan Conf., 1930–43; Hon. Treas. Corporation of the Church House Westminster, 1934; Chairman Exeter Diocesan Dilapidations Board, 1934–43; Proctor in Convocation, Diocese of Exeter, 1932–36; Prebendary of Exeter Cathedral, 1935–43. High Sheriff of Devonshire, 1935. King's Silver Jubilee Medal, 1935. *Heir: g s* Anthony Hugh [*b* 31 July 1921; *s* of late Major Hugh Grahame Dewey, MC, and Marjorie Florence Isobell (who *m* 2nd, 1940, Sir Robert Bell, KCSI), *d* of Lt-Col Alexander Hugh Dobbs]. *Address:* Turnpike Field, Hartley Wintney, Hants. *T:* Hartley Wintney 58. *Club:* Athenæum.

Died 1 Jan. 1948.

DEWHURST, Wynford; Officier de l'Académie; Officier de l'Instruction Publique; Member, Society of Authors; Member, Bucks County Council, 1907–10; *b* Manchester; *m*; three *s* three *d*. *Educ:* private tutor; Mintholme College; intended for legal profession. Contributed pen-drawings and descriptive articles to Lancashire and Cheshire journals, the Pall Mall and St James's Budgets, etc., followed by five years' art study in Paris, at the École N. des Beaux Arts under Jérome, at Juliens and Colarossis Ateliers under Professors Bouguereau, Ferrier, Benjamin Constant; exhibitor at Salons, Champs de Mars, 1896; International Exhibitions of Munich, 1897, London, 1898 and 1899, Dresden, 1901, St Louis, 1904, New Zealand, 1906, Salon d'Automne, Paris, 1904, Brussels International Exhibition, 1905, Independent Art, Agnew Gallery, 1906; Venice, 1909, 1912, and 1914; Japan-British, 1910; Buenos Ayres, 1910; Rome, 1911; Exhibitor Royal Academy, 1914, 1915, 1916, 1920, 1924, and 1926; one-man show Walker Galleries, London, 1923; one-man show Fine Art Society, 1925; also a series of one-man shows throughout Germany, 1910, and in Paris at the Durand-Ruel Galleries, 1912; exhibitor of several frames of black-and-white sketches at the International Exhibition, South Kensington, 1903; is represented in the Luxemburg Gallery, Paris, the Manchester and Cardiff Municipal Art Galleries, and Whitworth Institute; gold medallist for landscape, London, 1908; Lecturer on Modern Painting; started a press campaign in France in 1922 which led Mr J. D. Rockefeller, jun., to offer £100,000 to save Versailles from destruction through neglect; it also led to the imposition of entrance fees for upkeep of the Palaces, hitherto free to the public; by means of lectures, pamphlets and Committees, urged the constitution of a Ministry of Art at Westminster; as a result of this the King has formed a Council of Royal Commissioners for Art; Life Member Royal Society of Arts. *Publications:* author illustrated articles on Picturesque France in the Artist, March 1900; Claude Monet, Impressionist, Pall Mall Magazine, June 1900; A Great French Landscapist, Artist, Oct. 1900; The Work of Didier-Pouget, Landscape Painter, Studio, January 1901; Impressionism, Genesis and Development, Studio, April and July 1903; Impressionist Painting, its Genesis and Development, 1904, etc. *Recreations:* sport in any form, music, literature. *Address:* 22 Queens Gardens, Hyde Park, W2. *T:* Regent 0927.

Died 9 July 1941.

de WINTON, Brig.-Gen. Charles, CMG 1916 (retired); *b* 23 Dec. 1860; sixth *s* of Ven. Henry de Winton, sometimes Archdeacon of Brecon; *m* 1898, Florence Rose (*d* 1922), *d* of Edmund Pepys, late Royal Dragoons; one *s* three *d*. *Educ:* Oxford Military College; RMC; Sandhurst. Joined the 37th Regt (afterwards 1st Hampshire), 1880; served in Ireland, Malta, India, Burma (medal with clasp); Aden Hinterland, 1903–04; Volunteer Adjt; Commanded 1st Hampshire Regt, 1907–11; Commanded East Midland Territorial Brig. (afterwards the 162nd), 1911; served European War, went with the Brigade to Gallipoli, and took part in the landing at Suvla Bay (severely wounded 15 Aug. 1915, CMG); Commanded 175th Infantry Brigade; retired 23 Dec. 1917. *Recreation:* ordinary. *Address:* Gate House, Midhurst, Sussex.

Died 19 March 1943.

de WINTON, Walter Bernard, CIE 1903; retired; *b* 30 Nov. 1850; *e s* of late Ven. Henry de Winton, Archdeacon of Brecon; *m* 1889, Emily Mabel, *e d* of late Maj.-Gen. J. A. Tillard, RA, CB; three *d*. *Educ:* Sherborne School; Royal Indian Engineering College, Coopers Hill. Entered Indian Public Works Department in Presidency of Madras, 1874; Chief Engineer and Secretary to Government of Madras in Public Works Dept 1897; retired, 1905. *Address:* Dunmovin, Upper Colwall, Nr Malvern, Worcs.

Died 13 March 1944.

DEWOLFE, Rev. Henry Todd, BA, DD, LLD; Professor NT Literature, Acadia University, 1912–37; Professor Emeritus, 1937; Principal Acadia Ladies' Seminary, Wolfville, NS, 1901–25; *b* 14 Sept. 1867; *m* 1893; one *s* (one *s* killed in action in France, 9 April 1917) two *d*. *Educ:* Acadia University; Newton Theological Seminary; Berlin. Instructor in NT Greek, Newton Theological Seminary, 1893–95; Pastor First Baptist Church, Foxboro, Mass, 1895–1901; removed to NS 1901; DD Acadia University, 1910; President Maritime Baptist Convention, 1915–16; President Maritime Religious Education Council, 1924–25; LLD Acadia University, 1925; Secretary of the United Baptist Board of Religious Education, 1916–36; First Vice-President NS Auxiliary of British and Foreign Society in Canada. *Publications:* occasional articles. *Recreations:* golf, tennis, walking. *Address:* Wolfville, Nova Scotia, Canada. *TA:* Wolfville, Nova Scotia, Canada. *T:* Wolfville 68.

Died 10 Sept. 1947.

DEWSNUP, Ernest Ritson, MA Manchester; Professor Emeritus, University of Liverpool, since 1940; Chaddock Professor of Commerce, University of Liverpool, 1919–39; *b* 1874; *s* of late Joseph Dewsnup and Annie Ritson; *m* 1897, Sarah Jane Gibbs; two *s* four *d. Educ:* Manchester and Owens College (Victoria University). Sikes Lecturer in Economics, and Head of Department of Higher Commercial Education, The Technical College, Huddersfield, 1899–1903; Special Lecturer in Railway Transport, and Stanley Jevons Student in Economic Research, University of Manchester, 1903–04; Professorial Lecturer in Railways, and Curator of Commercial Museum; Extension Professor in Railway Transport, Secretary of Advisory Board on Railway Education, University of Chicago, 1904–07; Professor of Railway Administration, and Head of Department of Transportation, University of Illinois, 1907–20; The Statistical and Finance Officer of the Department of Military Movements and Railways, War Office (London), 1918 and 1919. *Publications:* edited and contributed to Railway Organization and Working; The Housing Problem in England; Freight Classification; contributed to The State in relation to Railways; articles in various economic journals, society proceedings, and various periodicals. *Address:* Heybridge House, near Burton, Wirral, Cheshire. *TA:* Heybridge House, near Burton, Wirral, Cheshire. *T:* (Wirral), Burton 203.

Died 1 May 1950.

DEXTER, Walter; Editor (Hon.) of the Dickensian since 1925; *b* 1877; *m* 1911; two *s* three *d.* Took leading part in 1922 in securing for the benefit of the public No. 48 Doughty Street, London, the first house of Dickens's Married Life, opened in 1925 as a Library and Museum; Hon. Treasurer of The Dickens Fellowship, 1908–25; author of several Dickens plays, Principal organiser (Hon.) of The Pickwick Centenary Celebrations, 1936. *Publications:* The London of Dickens, The England of Dickens, Mr Pickwick's Pilgrimages, Dickens to his Oldest Friend, 1932, Days in Dickensland, 1933, Mr and Mrs Charles Dickens: his letters to her, 1935; The Love Romance of Dickens, 1936; (with J. W. T. Ley) The Origin of Pickwick, 1936; (Editor) The Letters of Dickens 3 vols, Nonesuch Edition, 1938; and other works of Dickensian interest and research, has contributed to the principal magazines and newspapers. *Recreations:* Dickens, the drama. *Address:* 77 Lakenheath, N14. *T:* Palmers Green 6244. *Club:* Savage.

Died 16 May 1944.

DEY, Rt Rev. Mgr James, DSO 1917; Bishop of Sebastopolis of Armenia since 1935, and Ordinary to HM Forces; late Principal Catholic Chaplain (Royal Air Force); Domestic Prelate to Pope, 1928; Protonotary Apostolic, 1931; *b* 1869; *s* of late James Dey, Walsall. *Educ:* Oscott. Priest, 1894; St Wilfrid's College, Oakamoor, 1894–1900 and 1902–03; St Edmund's Old Hall, 1900–02; served European War (despatches, DSO); Rector of Oscott College, Birmingham, 1929–35. *Address:* Cliffe, Great Austins, Farnham, Surrey.

Died 8 June 1946.

D'HERELLE, Dr Felix H.; *b* Montreal, Canada, 25 April 1873; *m* 1893, Mary Kerr, two *d. Educ:* Montreal; Paris. Bacteriologist, Government of Guatemala, 1901–06; Director Government Bacteriological Laboratory, Merida, Mexico, 1907–08; Assist. Pasteur Institute, Paris, 1908–14; Chief of Laboratory Pasteur Institute 1914–21; Chief of Lab., University of Leiden, 1921–23; Director of the Bacteriological Service, International Sanitary Council of Egypt, 1923–28; Professor of Bacteriology, Yale University, 1928–33; MD Hon. Leiden University, 1923; MA Hon. Yale, 1928; MD Hon. Montreal University, 1930; MD Hon. Laval University, 1930; Hon. Professor, University of Tiflis; Hon. Professor School of Medicine of Baku; Leeuwenhoek Medal, Amsterdam Academy of Science, 1925; Wood Gerhard Medal, 1928; Royal Asiatic Society Medal, 1930; Shaundin Medal, 1930; Member Royal Society of Canada, Harvey Society (New York), Société de Biologie (Paris), Société de Micobiologie (Leningrad), Deutsche Akademie der Naturforscher (Germany). *Publications:* Le Coccobacille des Sauterelles, Annales Institut Pasteur, 1914; Le Bactériophage, son rôle dans l'Immunité, 1921; The Bacteriophage, its rôle in Immunity, 1922; Immunity in Natural Infectious Disease, 1923; Le Bactèriophage et son Comportement, 1926; The Bacteriophage, 1927; The Bacteriophage and its therapeutical applications, 1930; Studies on Asiatic Cholera, 1930; Le Bactèriophage dans ses relations avec l'Immunité, 1934; Bacterial Mutations, 1934; Le phénomène de la Guérison, 1938; Étude d'une maladie, le Choléra, 1946. *Address:* 40 rue Olivier de Serres, Paris XV. *T:* Lec, 64.12.

Died 22 Feb. 1949.

DHONDUP, Rai Bahadur Norbhu, CBE 1941; British Trade Agent, Yatung, Tibet; *m* 1905; two *s* one *d. Educ:* Darjeeling High School. Entered Govt service, 1905. *Address:* Camp Lhasa, Tibet.

Died 22 Oct. 1943.

DHRANGADHRA, Major HH Maharana Shri Sir Ghanshyamsinhji, Maharaja Raj Saheb of, GCIE 1922; KCSI 1917; *b* 31 May 1889; *S* to the Gadi 1911. *Educ:* Rajkumar College, Rajkot; in England under the guardianship of Sir Charles Ollivant. Salute 13 guns. *Heir:* Maharaj Kumar Shri Mayurdhwajsinhji, *b* 1923. *Address:* Dhrangadhra, Kathiawar, India.

Died 4 Feb. 1942.

DIAMOND, Sir William Henry, KBE 1920; partner in Thomas Diamond & Co., ship repairers, engineers, and boilermakers, Cardiff; *b* 23 Sept. 1865; *s* of late Thomas Diamond; *m* 1889, Alice R. (decd), *d* of late T. M. Cottle, Cardiff; one *s* three *d. Address:* Deane House, Newport Road, Roath, Cardiff.

Died 3 Nov. 1941.

DIBDIN, Edward Rimbault; littérateur, artist, art expert; *b* Edinburgh, 25 Aug. 1853; 2nd *s* of late Henry Edward Dibdin; *m* 1833, Charlotte Elizabeth (*d* 1908), *d* of late Thomas Blott; two *s* two *d*; *m* 1912, Sara Beatrice, *d* of late William Guthrie, LLD, Advocate, Sheriff-Principal of Lanarkshire; one *s. Educ:* Edinburgh Institution. Trained for Scots law, 1870–77; Insurance Official, 1877–1904; Art Critic, Liverpool Courier, 1887–1904; Curator, Walker Art Gallery, Liverpool, 1904–18; organised and arranged the Baroda Art Gallery, 1919–21; Art-Director, North-East Coast Exhibition, 1929; Art-Director in Europe of Canadian National Exhibition of Toronto; Member of Council, Walpole Society and United Society of Artists; Hon. Member, Royal Society of Miniature Painters; President, Museums Association, 1914–18; President, Dickens Fellowship (Liverpool), 1924–27. *Publications:* Pictor Depictus, 1876; Editor of Vocal Melodies of Scotland, 1880; Notes on Pictures, 1896–1900; Bibliography of Charles Dibdin, 1901; The Magic Carpet, 1903; The Art of Frank Dicksee, RA, 1905; Liverpool Art and Artists in the 18th Century, 1918; The Art Gallery of Baroda, 1920; Thomas Gainsborough, 1923; G. F. Watts, 1923; Sir Henry Raeburn, 1925; numerous pamphlets, sheet-songs, etc. *Recreations:* music, gardening, study of theatrical history. *Address:* 64 Huskisson Street, Liverpool; 215 S Croxted Road SE21. *Club:* Artists (President 1896), Liverpool.

Died 28 Oct. 1941.

DICK, Col Sir Arthur Robert, KBE 1919; CB 1913; CVO 1919; *b* 1860; *s* of late Robert Ker Dick; *g s* of Mungo Dick, of Pitkerro, Forfarshire; *m* 1907, Susan, *d* of late Rt Rev. Charles Wordsworth, DD, DCL, Bishop of St Andrews, and *widow* of late John Stirling, of Muiravonside House, Stirlingshire. *Educ:* Sandhurst. Joined 26th Cameronians, 1881; 2nd Punjab Cavalry, 1884; Bt Lt-Col, 1903; Bt Col 1908; Col 1909. Served Waziristan, 1894–95 (medal with clasp); Malakand, action at Landakai (despatches), operations in Bajour and in Mohmand country (despatches, medal with clasp), 1897–98; China, 1900 (despatches, medal, Bt Lt-Col), operations in the Zakka Khel country, Base Commandant; operations in the Mohmand country, Base Commandant (despatches, Bt Col). Served with the Military Department of the Government of India, 1896–99; AQMG Northern Army, 1906; Military Secretary to GOC Northern Army, 1906–07; Inspecting Officer, Frontier Corps, NWFP India, 1908–14; served European War, 1914–19 (despatches); Officier Légion d'Honneur; Officier Ordre de Léopold. *Address:* 9 Wilbraham Place, SW1. *T:* Sloane 7773.

Died 30 June 1943.

DICK, Lt-Col Dighton Hay Abercromby, DSO 1915; late 3rd Batt. Royal Scots Fusiliers; *b* 26 Jan. 1869; *s* of Capt. Alfred Abercromby Dick, 11th Bengal Lancers (Probyn's Horse), and Fanny, *d* of Elliot Macnaghten, of Ovingdean, Sussex; *m* 1902, Lilian, *d* of Francis Ricardo, JP, DL, of The Friary, Old Windsor; one *s* one *d. Educ:* Wellington; Sandhurst. Entered Army, 1888; Major, 1910; retired, 1910; temp. Lt-Col 1915; Lt-Col 1917; resigned commission, 1924; served NW Frontier, India, 1897–98 (medal, two clasps); Tirah, 1897–98 (clasp); South Africa, 1899–1900 (severely wounded, despatches; Queen's medal, four clasps); European War, 1914–17 (despatches twice, DSO); Officier de l'Ordre de Léopold, Belgium, 1917; Croix de Guerre, Belgian, 1918. *Clubs:* Naval and Military; New, Edinburgh.

Died March 1941.

DICK, George Paris, CIE 1916; Barrister-at-law; *b* Clifton, 8 April 1866; *e s* of Lt-Col George Thomas and Parisina Lavinia Dick; *m* 1894, Effie Geraldine, *d* of Francis Newman; no *c. Educ:* Dulwich Coll. Called to Bar, Middle Temple, 1889; joined western circuit at Exeter; Advocate of the Calcutta High Court, 1893; of the Judicial Commissioner, Court Nagpur, 1891; Lecturer in Law to the Morris College, Nagpur, 1907–24; Standing Counsel 1911 and Government Advocate and *ex-officio* Standing Counsel to the Administration of the Central Provinces, 1912; Retired 1930; President of the Nagpur Civil Station Municipal Committee, 1918–24; Member of the Legislative Council for the Central Provinces, 1917–30; Delhi Durbar Medal, 1912; formerly President Anglo-Indian and Domiciled Community Association, Provincial Branch, Nagpur; Freemasonry PDGW Bombay, PDtJ Bombay. *Publication:* Fitch and his Fortunes, 1898. *Address:* c/o Grindlay & Co., 54 Parliament Street, SW1.

Died 27 Jan. 1941.

DICK, Henry Charles, CMG 1933; MBE 1920; JP Dorset; *b* 14 April 1872; *s* of Charles J. A. Dick; *m* 1906, Fanny, (*d* 1943), *d* of R. Neele; two *s. Educ:* privately. Entered Consular Service, 1904; served at Christiania, Bergen, Foreign Office, Lyons, Bratislava and Vienna; Consul-General, 1932; Assistant British Delegate on International Danube Commission, 1926–27, and 1932–34; retired 1934; engaged on relief work in Austria and employed on Saar Governing Commission. *Recreations:* sailing, shooting. *Address:* Brewery House, Wareham, Dorset.

Died 26 Oct. 1946.

DICK, Col James Adam, CMG 1919; VD; BA University of Sydney, 1886; MD, FRCS Edin.; AAMC; *b* 1866. Served S Africa, 1900 (despatches, Queen's medal with six clasps); European War, 1915–19 (despatches twice, CMG); Commander Order of St John, 1928. *Address:* Catfoss, 148 Belmore Road, Randwick, New South Wales, Australia. *Clubs:* Imperial Service, Sydney.

Died 23 Dec. 1942.

DICK, John Lawson, MD, MS, FRCS; *b* Edinburgh, 27 Nov. 1870; *m* 1911, Norah Winifred Duke; one *s* two *d. Educ:* Edinburgh University; St Bartholomew's Hospital, London. Buchanan Scholar and First Graduate of year 1892 in subjects of Diseases of Women and Children; Medallist in Physiology, Pathology, and Midwifery. Surgeon-Captain, South African War (Queen's medal); Surgeon, City of London Military Hospital, European War, 1914–18; late President of Medical Boards, Ministry of Pensions for the County of London. *Publications:* Defective Housing and the Growth of Children, 1919; Rickets, 1922; numerous articles scientific journals. *Recreations:* reading, travel. *Address:* 1 Chichester Road, Dorking, Surrey. *T:* 2548.

Died 13 June 1944.

DICK-CUNYNGHAM,   Sir   Colin   Keith; *see* Cunyngham.

DICKENS, Mary Angela; novelist; *b* London; *d* of *e s* of Charles Dickens. *Publications:* Cross Currents, 1891; A Mere Cypher, 1893; A Valiant Ignorance, 1894; Prisoners of Silence, 1895; Against the Tide, 1897; On the Edge of a Precipice, 1899; The Wastrel, 1901; Unveiled, 1907; The Debtor, 1912; Sanctuary.

Died 7 Feb. 1948.

DICKIE, Archibald Campbell, MA Manchester, ARIBA; Architect; Professor of Architecture, Manchester University, 1912–33, now Professor Emeritus; *b* Dundee, 1868; *s* of Charles Dickie, Dundee; *m* Mary Reich; one *d. Educ:* privately; Architectural Association School, London. Practised in London since 1898; Architect to Palestine Exploration Fund Expedition, 1894–97, and Member of Executive Committee since 1906; Secretary, 1910–12; Master in Design, Architectural Association School, London, 1906–11. *Publications:* Excavations in Jerusalem, 1894–1897 (Bliss and Dickie); numerous articles on Archæology and Architecture in PEF Quarterly Statements, Bible Encyclopædia, and elsewhere. *Recreation:* golf. *Address:* Long Crendon, Bucks.

Died 3 Sept. 1941.

DICKIE, Very Rev. John, MA; Hon. DD Aberdeen; Principal (since 1928) and Professor of Systematic Theology (since 1909), the Theological Hall, Knox College, Dunedin; Gunning Lecturer in Edinburgh University for term 1937–40; *b* Aberdeen, 20 May 1875; *s* of John Dickie; *m* 1906, Barbara Margaret, 2nd *d* of Thomas Trotter, Headmaster, Trinity Academy, Leith; three *s. Educ:* University of Aberdeen (MA Hons); University of Edinburgh; and University of Jena. University Assistant in Divinity, Edinburgh, 1905–06; ordained to the Parish of Tarland and Migvie, Aberdeenshire, 1906; Moderator of General Assembly, 1934–35. *Publications:* The Fundamental Principles of the Reformed Conception of the Church, 1924; joint-translator with Rev. Geo. Ferries, DD, of Haering's Dogmatik, 2 vols, 1913; The Organism of Christian Truth: a Modern Positive Dogmatic, 1931; (Japanese Translation) 1940; Fifty Years of British Theology, a Personal Retrospect (Gunning Lectures) Edinburgh, 1937; reviews of books; articles. *Recreation:* gardening. *Address:* Knox College, Dunedin, New Zealand.

Died 24 June 1942.

DICKINS, Col Vernon William Frank, DSO 1916; VD; late Commanding 1/9th Batt. London Regt (Queen Victoria's Rifles); *b* 15 Sept. 1867; 3rd *s* of late Lt-Col Henry Francis Dickins, VD; *m* 1901, Mary Sidney, *e d* of late Sidney Wilson; one *s.* Director of Dickins & Jones, Ltd, and other public companies; Member on Court of Assistants of Worshipful Company of Tylers and Bricklayers; joined Victoria Rifles, 1884; Capt. in Victoria and St George's Rifles, 1899; Major and 2nd in Command 1/9th Batt. London Regt Queen Victoria's Rifles, 1912; went out to France, Nov. 1914, with the 1/9th Batt. as Major 2nd in Command;

succeeded to Command of the 1st Batt., May, 1915, Lt-Col; served European War, 1914–18 (despatches four times, DSO); Col 1919. *Address:* Milford Bank, 39 Redington Road, Hampstead, NW3. *T:* Hampstead 1130.

Died 30 Nov. 1942.

DICKINSON, 1st Baron *cr* 1930, of Painswick; **Willoughby Hyett Dickinson,** PC 1914; KBE 1918; JP, DL; BA; *b* 9 April 1859; *s* of Sebastian Stewart Dickinson of Brown's Hill, Stroud, chairman of Quarter Sessions for county of Gloucester, and MP for Stroud; *m* 1891, Minnie Elizabeth, *d* of General Sir Richard Meade, KCSI, CIE; two *d. Educ:* Eton; Trinity College, Cambridge. Called to the Bar, 1884; LCC 1889–1907; deputy chairman, 1892–96; chairman, 1899; contested (L) Stepney, 1895; North St Pancras, 1900; MP (L) St Pancras, N, 1906–18; joined Labour Party, 1930; National Labour, 1931; served on Royal Commissions upon Superannuation of Civil Servants, 1901, Care of the Feeble-minded, 1904, on the Metropolitan Police, 1906, and London Cross-river Traffic, 1926; was a member of the Speaker's Conference on the Reform of the Franchise, 1916–17; one of the Originators of the League of Nations, 1915; Chairman of the London Liberal Federation, 1896–1918; Chairman of the League of Nations Society, 1915–18; Vice-President of the League of Nations Union, 1924; President of the International Union of League of Nations Societies, 1925; British Delegate (substitute) to the Assembly of the League of Nations, 1923; is Life President of the World Alliance for promoting International Friendship through the Churches, and is connected with various philanthropic enterprises; formerly a Commissioner (unpaid) of the Board of Control of the Mentally Defective; during the war was Chairman War Office Appeals Committee (Soldiers' Dependents). *Recreations:* fishing, bicycling, and golf. *Heir: g s* Richard Dickinson, *b* 1926. *Address:* Washwell House, Painswick, Glos. *T:* Painswick 3204. *Clubs:* Reform, National Liberal.

Died 31 May 1943.

DICKINSON, Sir Alwin Robinson, KCMG 1927; CMG 1922; *b* Cartmel, North Lancashire, 9 Feb. 1873; sixth *s* of late Thomas Dickinson; *m* Beatrice, *e d* of late John Burleigh; one *s* three *d. Educ:* Cartmel School; King's College, London. For many years Managing Director of the Pacific Phosphate Company; Commissioner, 1920–30, representing the interests of the British Government in the important phosphate undertaking acquired jointly by the British, Australian and New Zealand Governments; Director of public companies; is well known in business circles and has travelled widely; for many years Chairman Conservative and Unionist Association for Eastbourne Division of East Sussex. *Publications:* contributor to various periodicals on business and industrial subjects. *Recreation:* golf. *Address:* Temperley, Eastbourne. *T:* Eastbourne 1617. *Club:* Carlton.

Died 15 March 1944.

DICKINSON, Maj.-Gen. Douglas Povah, CB 1941; DSO 1917; OBE 1933; MC; Colonel of the Welch Regiment, since 1941; Secretary, National Rifle Association, since 1944; *b* 6 Nov. 1886; *e s* of late Col W. V. Dickinson, CMG; *m* 1924, Frances Mildred, *e d* of John Cracroft Wilson, of Cashmere, Christchurch, New Zealand; two *d. Educ:* Cheltenham College; RMC, Sandhurst. Joined Welch Regt 1906; Capt. 1914; Maj. 1926; Bt Lt-Col 1928; Bt Col 1932; Col 1936; Maj.-Gen. 1939; on Directing Staff of Staff College, Camberley, 1925–28; commanded 1st Bn The Welch Regt, 1934–36; Commandant Nigeria Regt, 1936–39; commanded East Africa Force, 1940; retired pay, 1944; psc, 1920; served in France Sept. 1914–July 1919 (despatches five times, Brevet of Majority, DSO, MC, 1914 Star, Victory and General Service Medals); served with Iraq Army in Kurdistan 1931 and 1932 (OBE, Mesopotamia General Service Medal, Order of Al

Rafidain 3rd Class and Iraq Active Service Medal); served War of 1939–45 despatches, 1939–45 Star, Africa Star, Defence Medal, War Medal, Bronze Star Medal of USA). *Address:* Bisley Camp, Brookwood, Woking, Surrey. *T:* Brookwood 3193. *Club:* Army and Navy.

Died 8 Jan. 1949.

DICKINSON, Robert Edmund; JP; *b* 1 Aug. 1862; *s* of E. H. Dickinson, Chapmanslade, Westbury, Wilts, and Emily Dulcibella, 3rd *d* of 3rd Baron Auckland, Bishop of Bath and Wells. *Educ:* Eton; Trin. Coll., Camb. BA History Tripos. MP (C) Wells Div. of Somerset, 1899–1906; contested (C) West St Pancras, 1910; Ex-Mayor of Bath; Major North Somerset Yeomanry. *Clubs:* Carlton, Beefsteak, Conservative.

Died 16 Nov. 1947.

DICKINSON, Thomas Vincent, Commander of the Crown of Italy; MD (Lond.), MRC) (Lond.); Consulting Physician to the Italian Hospital, London; Fellow, Royal Society of Medicine; Master, Society of Apothecaries, 1925–26; *b* 5 Jan. 1858; *m* 1892, Beatrice, *d* of late Captain Evens, Royal Fusiliers; one *s* one *d. Educ:* King's College, London; St George's Hospital; University of London. Founder of Anglo-Italian Literary Society; Royal Society of Arts' Medal for Italian. *Publications:* various medical works on diseases of women and children. *Address:* 2 Cadogan Mansions, SW1. *T:* Sloane 8809.

Died 21 Jan. 1941.

DICKS, Captain Henry Leage, CBE 1919; RN, retired; *b* 1870; *s* of late Henry Dicks; *m* 1896, Gwendoline (*d* 1940), *yr d* of Rev. Geldart Riadore. *Address:* Tranmere, 8 The Avenue, Bournemouth.

Died 12 Dec. 1942.

DICKSEE, Herbert; painter and etcher; Fellow of the Royal Society of Painter-Etchers; *b* 14 June 1862; *m* 1896, Ella M., *d* of late Sir William Crump; one *d. Educ:* City of London School; Slade School of Art. *Address:* Oak House, Kidderpore Avenue Hampstead, NW3. *T:* Hampstead 0871.

Died 20 Feb. 1942.

DICKSON, James; JP, DL Co. Tyrone; *b* 1859; *e s* of Right Hon. Thomas Alexander Dickson, PC, Dungannon; *m* 1884, Ella (*d* 1937), *y d* of William Tillie, HML, Londonderry; one *s* two *d. Educ:* Royal School, Dungannon, and in England. MP (L) Borough of Dungannon, 1880–85. *Recreations:* shooting, fishing, croquet. *Address:* Miltown House, Dungannon, County Tyrone. *Club:* Tyrone County.

Died 8 Aug. 1941.

DICKSON, Norman Bonnington, OBE; MICE; Chairman: The Merchants Trust Limited, The Traction and General Investment Trust Ltd, Monte Video Waterworks Company Ltd, Consolidated Water Works Co. of Rosario Ltd etc; *b* Glasgow, 19 Dec. 1868; *s* of Thomas Dickson, Edinburgh and Lebanon, Ceylon, and Mary Geddes, *d* of W. Borron, JP, Seafield Towers, Ardrossan; *m* 1902, Anne, *d* of Captain C. C. Higgins, JP, 13th Hussars, Boycott Manor, Buckingham; three *s* one *d.* Built railways in the Argentine, Siam, Brazil (Chief Engineer Leopoldina Railway 1898–1904) Cuba (General Manager Cuban Central Rlys 1904–08) Nyasaland; visited and reported in Spain for Ministry of Munitions, 1915; Vice-Chairman Priority Commission, Ministry of Munitions, 1915–18. *Recreations:* travel, shooting, golf. *Address:* Struan, Wimbledon Park, SW19. *TA:* Southfields. *T:* Putney 2309. *Clubs:* City of London; Royal Wimbledon.

Died 5 July 1944.

DICKSON, William Everard, MC; late Metropolitan Police Magistrate at Thames; *b* Geelong, Australia; *e s* of Thos Andrew Dickson; *m* 1933, Florence Hyde, *o d* of late Lieut-Col Jas Walker, CBE, DSO; one *d. Educ:* Geelong. Admitted Gray's Inn, 1912 (Holt Scholar,

Richards Essay Prize); called to Bar, 1914; Midland Circuit; served with Infantry and Machine Gun Corps throughout European War (Major, MC and bar, despatches); Military Legal Staff, Ireland, 1921; Secretary, Anglo-German Mixed Arbitral Tribunal under Part X. Treaty of Versailles, 1926; Hon. Legal Editor Medico-Legal Society, 1925–37. *Publications:* Assessment of Compensations; numerous articles. *Recreations:* golf, walking.

Died 10 Nov. 1945.

DICKSON, William Kirk, LLD; *b* Edinburgh, 24 Nov. 1860; *s* of William Dickson, Edinburgh; *m* 1897, Kathleen, *d* of Maj.-Gen. Sir Robert Murdoch Smith, KCMG; one surviving *s. Educ:* Merchiston Castle School, Edinburgh; Edinburgh Univ. (MA 1880). Advocate, 1887; Keeper of the Advocates' Library, Edinburgh, 1906; first Librarian of the National Library of Scotland, 1925–31; Sec. of the Society of Antiquaries of Scotland, 1905–08; Hon. LLD St Andrews, 1912; Rhind Lecturer in Archæology, 1914; Chairman of Edinburgh Centre of Franco-Scottish Society, 1930–36; Legion of Honour, 1939; Chairman of Council of the Scottish History Society, 1934–38. *Publications:* The Life of Major-Gen. Sir Robert Murdoch Smith, 1901; many articles, chiefly on history and bibliography. Editor of The Jacobite Attempt of 1719 (Scottish History Society, 1895); Historical Geography of the Clans of Scotland, 1899; The Surrender of Napoleon, 1904; The Register of the Great Seal of Scotland under the Commonwealth, 1904 (with J. H. Stevenson); War Record of the 2nd City of Edinburgh Battery RFA, 1923; Letters of Dr Alexander Monro (edited in Miscellany of Scottish History Society, 1933); Correspondence of Sir George Warrender, Lord Provost of Edinburgh, 1715 (Scottish History Society, 1935); Memories of Ayrshire, by Rev. John Mitchell, DD (edited in Miscellany of Scottish History Society, 1939), etc. *Address:* 8 Gloucester Place, Edinburgh. *Club:* University (Edinburgh).

Died 14 July 1949.

DIGBY, Hon. Gerald Fitzmaurice; *b* 20 Dec. 1858; 4th *s* of 9th Baron Digby; *m* 1906, Lady Lilian Mary Harriet Diana Liddell, *y d* of 2nd Earl of Ravensworth. Captain RN; retired. *Address:* Lewcombe Manor, Dorchester. *Club:* Travellers'.

Died 8 Dec. 1942.

DIGBY, Kenelm George; Hon. Mr Justice Digby; Puisne Judge High Court of Judicature at Nagpur, since 1943; *b* 23 March 1890; *s* of Col T. Digby, RE, and Alice Isabella Sherard; *m* 1926, Violet M. Kidd; one *s. Educ:* Haileybury College; Trinity College, Cambridge (Exhibitioner). 1st class 2nd Div. Classical Tripos, 1912. Passed for ICS 1913 and appointed 1914; military service in India, 1916–20; 2nd Lt IARO 95th Russell's Infantry, 1916; Lieut IARO 111th Mahars, 1917; attached Southern Command HQ Poona, 1918; Home Guard, London, 1940. *Recreation:* golf. *Address:* Nagpur, CP, India. *Club:* East India and Sports.

Died 25 Sept. 1944.

DIGBY, Rev. Stephen Harold Wingfield; Chaplain to the settlers in Kiambu District, Kenya Colony, East Africa, 1933; Canon of Nairobi Cathedral since 1934; Canon and Prebendary of Stratton in Salisbury Cathedral, 1919–32, Canon Emeritus since 1933; *b* 26 Sept. 1872; *y s* of late John Digby Wingfield Digby of Coleshill Park, Warwickshire, and Sherborne Castle, Dorset; *m* Eleanor Escreet Lewin, adopted *d* of Basil Richardson of Amwell, Bury, Herts; two *s* two *d. Educ:* Harrow School; Christ Church, Oxford. Curate to Canon Willink, Vicar of St Helens, Lancs; Chaplain in Missions to Seamen at Birkenhead and at San Francisco, California; Chaplain to the Forces at Royal Military Academy, Woolwich; Rector of Sheldon in Warwickshire; Vicar of Holy Trinity, Bordesley, Birmingham; Vicar and Rural Dean of Sherborne; served European War, chaplain to the 4th Cavalry Div.

1916–17; Surrogate; Proctor in Convocation and Member of National Church Assembly, 1922–24 and 1927–29; Exam. Chaplain to the Bishop of Mombasa, 1938. *Recreations:* rowing, cricket, shooting. *Address:* Kiambu, Kenya.

Died 4 Aug. 1942.

DIGGLE, F. Holt, OBE 1919; MB, ChB (Hons Manch.); FRCS (Eng.); FRCS (Edin.); Consulting Ear and Throat Surgeon, Ancoats Hospital, Manchester; Consulting Surgeon Manchester Ear Hospital; Laryngologist Holt Radium Institute, Manchester, Royal College of Music, Manchester, and Duchess of York Hospital, Manchester; *b* Heywood, May 1886; *s* of James Diggle, CE, FGS (consulting water-engineer) and Rachael Alice Diggle; *m* 1914, Mary Leah, *d* of Edward and Alice Horrox, Edinburgh; one *d. Educ:* Rossall College; Manchester University; St Bartholomew's and London Hospital, London. Medallist Anatomy and Gynæcology; Distinction Forensic Medicine, Honours MB, ChB; Bradley Surgical Scholarship; John Henry Agnew Scholarship Diseases of Children; Clinical Medicine Prize; Fellow of the Royal Society of Medicine (London), Member Otological and Laryngological Sections. Lecturer Practical Physiology (Otology) Manchester University; Captain (Temporary) RAMC; Surgical Specialist 33rd CCH and 77th CCS, EEF (despatches, OBE). *Publications:* Diseases of the Thyroid Gland in relation to Laryngology (Journal of Otology and Laryngology, Oct. 1923); Observations on Laryngofissure and its Technique (Practitioner, Nov. 1923); Laryngeal Malignant Disease and Radium (Journal of Otology and Laryngology, Vol. 46, 1931); Foreign bodies in the Oesophagus, Report on 67 cases (British Medical Journal, Feb. 1932); The Treatment of Intrinsic Laryngeal Cancer (Journal of Otology and Laryngology, Vol. 52, 1937). *Recreations:* golf, foreign travel. *Address:* Riverslea, West Didsbury, Manchester; 26 St John Street, Manchester (Private Clinic). *T:* Didsbury 1149, Blackfriars 0988. *Clubs:* Union, Manchester.

Died 30 Sept. 1942.

DILKE, Sir Fisher Wentworth, 4th Bt *cr* 1862; *b* 5 Jan. 1877; *e s* of late Ashton Dilke, MP, and Margaret Mary, *d* of T. Eustace Smith (she *m* 2nd, W. Russell Cooke); *S* cousin, 1918; *m* 1905, Ethel Clifford, *er d* of W. K.; three *s. Educ:* Trinity Hall, Cambridge, BA. *Publication:* Observer on 'Ranger,' 1938. *Heir: s* John Fisher Wentworth Dilke, [*b* 8 May 1906; *m* 1934, Sheila, *o d* of Sir William Seeds, KCMG; two *s*]. *Address:* Lepe Point, Exbury, Hampshire. *T:* Fawley 240. *Clubs:* Brooks's; Royal Yacht Squadron, Cowes.

Died 25 March 1944.

DILL, Field-Marshal Sir John Greer, GCB 1942; KCB 1937; CB 1928; CMG 1918; DSO 1915; American DSM (posthumous), 1944; Col Comdt Parachute Regt, Army Air Corps, since 1942; Col East Lancashire Regt since 1932; *b* Lurgan, N Ireland, 25 Dec. 1881; *s* of John Dill, Belfast, and Jane Greer, Lurgan; *m* 1st, Ada Maud (*d* 1940), *d* of Col W. Le Mottée; one *s*; 2nd, Nancy, *widow* of Brig. Dennis Furlong and *d* of late Henry Charrington. *Educ:* Cheltenham College; RMC, Sandhurst. Entered Army, 1901; Captain, 1911; Brig.-Maj. 1914; Col 1920; Maj.-Gen. 1930; Lt-Gen. 1936; Gen. 1939; Field-Marshal, 1941; served South Africa, 1901–02 (Queen's medal, 5 clasps); European War, 1914–18 (DSO, CMG, Bt Lt-Col, Bt Col); Officier Légion d'Honneur, Croix de Guerre, Croix de Couronne, Belgian Croix de Guerre; commanded 2nd Infantry Brigade, 1923–26; Army Instructor at the Imperial Defence College, 1926–28; Brigadier General Staff, India, 1929–30; Commandant Staff College, Camberley, 1931–34; Director of Military Operations and Intelligence, War Office, 1934–36; Commander British Forces in Palestine, 1936–37; GOC-in-C, Aldershot Command, 1937–39; Comdr of 1st Army Corps, in France, 1939–40; Vice-Chief of Imp. Gen.

Staff, 1940; ADC General to the King, 1940–41; Chief of Imperial General Staff, 1940–41; Governor-Designate of Bombay; Dec. 1941, British Chiefs of Staff visit to Washington with Prime Minister; remained in USA as Head of the British Joint Staff Mission. LLD (Univ. of Toronto, 1943; College of William and Mary, 1944; Princeton Univ. 1944). Howland Memorial Prize, Yale Univ. 1944. *Address:* Lloyds Bank, Cox's Branch, Waterloo Place, SW1; British Joint Staff Mission, Washington, DC.

Died 4 Nov. 1944.

DILLING, Walter James, MB, ChB (Hons) Aberdeen; Professor of Pharmacology and General Therapeutics, Liverpool University, since 1930; Major, RAMC (TF); *b* Aberdeen, 15 May 1886; *s* of Wm Dilling; *m* 1914, Vida J. B. Ducat; two *d*. *Educ:* Robert Gordon's College, Aberdeen; Aberdeen University. Second Assistant in Physiology, Aberdeen University, 1907; Carnegie Research Scholar in Physiology, 1907–09; Carnegie Research Fellow in Pharmacology, 1909–10; First Assistant Professor of Pharmacology and Physiological Chemistry, Rostock University, 1909–10; Lecturer in Pharmacology, Aberdeen University, 1910–14; Dr Robert Pollok Lecturer in Materia Medica and Pharmacology, Glasgow University, 1914–15, 1919–20; Lieut and Capt. RAMC (temp.) 1915–19, attached Royal Herbert Hospital, Woolwich; Lecturer in Pharmacology and General Therapeutics, Liverpool University, 1920–26; Examiner in Materia Medica, Pharmacology, etc., in the Universities of St Andrews, Oxford, Cambridge, Leeds, Belfast, Bristol, Sheffield, London, Cardiff, Birmingham; Dean of the Medical Faculty, Liverpool University, 1923–33, 1939–45, and Member of the University Council, 1923–29, 1940–41; Chairman, Liverpool Philharmonic Soc., 1937–40, 1945–48; formerly a Privy Council Representative on the Council of the Pharmaceutical Society; Member General Medical Council. *Publications:* Atlas of Crystals and Spectra of the Hæmochromogens, 1910; Charts of Blood Spectra, 1911; Pharmacology and Therapeutics of Materia Medica, 19th ed. 1950; Dental Materia Medica, Pharmacology and Therapeutics (with S. Hallam, LDS), 3rd ed. 1946; contributions to Scientific Journals on Pharmacological subjects. *Recreation:* music. *Address:* Kareol, Mines Avenue, Aigburth, Liverpool; Thwaite House, Coniston, Lancs. *TA:* 393 Garstonlancs. *T:* Garston 393. *Club:* University (Liverpool).

Died 19 Aug. 1950.

DILLINGHAM, Cyril Claud; DL Bedfordshire; JP County of Bedford and Borough of Luton; *b* 1 July 1886; *s* of Charles Dillingham and Ada Pestell; *m* 1910, Alice Maud, *d* of Wesley and Emily Blows, Luton; two *d*. *Educ:* Luton Higher Grade; Private School. Member of Bedfordshire County Council; Member of Standing Joint Committee for Bedfordshire; High Sheriff of Bedfordshire, 1940; Mayor of Luton, 1935–37; Deputy Mayor of Luton, 1937–42; Chairman of Electricity and Transport Committee of Luton, 1928–40; Chairman of Ministry of Food Slaughterhouse Tribunal for Bedfordshire and Huntingdonshire; Chairman of ARP Committee, Luton, 1938–40; Chief Air Raid Warden and Chief Fire Guard, Luton; Member of Navy League Sea Cadet Committee, Bedfordshire; and of Emergency Committee, Luton; Army Welfare Officer of Luton and Luton Rural; Member of Luton Town Council; Chairman of Luton Parliamentary Division Conservative Association; Chairman of Luton (Local) Conservative Association. *Address:* 25 Lansdowne Road, Luton, Beds. *T:* Luton 262. *Club:* City Livery.

Died 8 April 1943.

DILLON, 19th Viscount *cr* 1622; **Eric FitzGerald Dillon,** CMG 1919; DSO 1915; late Royal Munster Fusiliers; *b* 4 April 1881; *γ s* of late Hon. Conrad Dillon, *s* of 16th Viscount, and Ellen, *e d* of late Sir Henry Dashwood, 5th Bt, of Kirtlington; *S* brother 1934; *m* 1907, Norah Juanita Muriel (1915 Star and British War

and Victory medals), *d* of late Brig.-Gen. C. E. Beckett and Louisa Augusta, *d* of Gen. Rt Hon. Sir John Michel, PC, GCB, of Dewlish; one *s* one *d*. *Educ:* Rugby; Staff College, Camberley. Entered Army, 4th Batt. KO Lancaster Regt 1899; ASC 1900; Captain, 1905; Col, 1922; Royal Munster Fusiliers, 1908; Gen. Staff Officer, 3rd grade, War Office, 1912; served South African War, 1900–01 (Queen's medal 4 clasps); European War, 1914–18 (DSO, 1914 Star, CMG, despatches seven times, Bt Lt-Col, Chevalier and Officer of the Legion of Honour; Officier of the Order of Leopold; French and Belgian Croix de Guerre); GSO1, British Army of the Rhine; GSO1, I Division, Aldershot; Military Assistant to Chief of the Imperial General Staff, 1923–25; retired pay, 1925; recalled Sept. 1939; served in N Africa and England till 1941; one of HM Bodyguard of the Honourable Corps of Gentlemen at Arms, 1930; Member, Dorset Territorial Association. Patron of 2 livings. *Heir: s* Capt. Hon. Michael Eric Dillon [RHG, late 15th/19th Hussars and Transjordan Frontier Force; *b* 13 Aug. 1911; *m* 1939, Irene, *y d* of R. Merandon du Plessis, Whitehall, Mauritius; one *s* (*b* 18 Jan. 1945) one *d*. Eton; Sandhurst]. *Address:* 89 Eaton Square, SW1. *T:* Sloane 1819. *Club:* Turf.

Died 6 April 1946.

DILLON, Malcolm, MBE; DL, JP; *b* 1859; *s* of Anthony Dillon, JP, Wrexham; *m* 1884, Clara Elizabeth (*d* 1945), *d* of W. W. Palmer, of Southacre, Norfolk; three *s* one *d*. Chief Agent to the Marquis of Londonderry; Managing Director of the Londonderry Collieries, Limited, and Director of other Companies in the north of England; Mayor of Jarrow, 1903–06; Chairman, Seaham Bench of Magistrates, 1912–41; late Member Durham County Council; Member of Council of the Newcastle and Gateshead Chamber of Commerce; Hon. Associate of the Order of St John of Jerusalem; late Hon. County Secretary Soldiers and Sailors Families Association; Deputy Chairman, Durham County Sailors' Fund. *Publications:* The History of Irish Banking; a contributor to Banking and Economic Literature. *Address:* Dene House, Seaham. *Clubs:* Athenæum; Durham County, Durham.

Died 27 Sept. 1945.

DILNOT, Frank; author; *b* 1875; *s* of George Dilnot, Hayling, Hants; *m* Mary Margaret, *d* of Dr David Gregg, New York. *Educ:* privately. Descriptive writer Daily Mail, 1902–12; Editor, Daily Citizen, 1912–15; President Foreign Correspondents Association in America, 1916–19; Editor, Globe, 1919–20. Cross of Legion of Honour, 1919. *Publications:* Neame of Kent, 1928; The Squire of Ash, 1929; The Lady of Jean, 1930; The Storm-Riders, 1931; Mad Sir Peter, 1932; The Man from Argentina, 1940; Ghosts at Gossamer Street, 1945. *Recreations:* country life, cricket, and golf. *Address:* Splicing Oaks, Llanarth, Cardiganshire. *T:* Llanarth 238. *Club:* National Liberal.

Died 28 July 1946.

DINGLE, Aylward Edward; Mariner, retired; author (pen-name Sinbad); *s* of Robert Charles Dingle and Sarah Ann Cotterell; *m* 1st, 1904, Ethel Mean Tuckey; two *d*; 2nd, 1944, Nan Fassenden. *Educ:* Central School, Oxford. Followed the sea from age of 14 until 40, commanding in sail and steam; began writing for American Magazines then; returned to England in 1930, since when has published some 30 books, novels, biography, collections of short stories, autobiography; frequent broadcaster; sailed own schooner yacht in ocean races; at odd times built gasworks, managed a rope factory, was footman for J. Pierpont Morgan, and sold dictionaries to Negroes in New York; was also labourer in Thames Ironworks shipyard. *Publications:* Gold out of Celebes, 1920; Wide Waters, Fathomless, Flying Kestrel, 1927; The Silver Ship, Tares, 1930; Mary First Mate, Seaworthy, 1931; Not Wisely, 1932; A Modern Sinbad, 1934; Red Saunders, Spin a Yarn Sailor, 1934; Yellow Half-Moons, Sinister Eden, Sailors do Care, 1935; Pipe

All Hands, 1936; Mock Star, Old Glory, Nita of Martinique, 1938; Adrift, 1939; The Bomb Ship, 1942; Pirates May Fly, 1943; Calamity Jock, 1944, etc.; Desert Island Discord, Black Joker, 1945; The Age-old Kingdom, 1947; Reckless Tide, 1947; Moonshine and Moses, 1948; Out of The Blue, 1948. *Recreations:* deep sea yachting, Airedales, books. *Address:* The Shrubberies, Porthleven, Cornwall. *T:* Porthleven 244. *Clubs:* Seven Seas; Adventurers' (New York).

Died 30 Oct. 1947.

DIPPIE, Herbert, CIE 1936; DSO 1918; *b* 10 Dec. 1885; *s* of late Peter Dippie; *m* 1921, Mildred, *d* of late Richard Pigg, JP, Bellingham; two *d. Educ:* Cambridge University. BA 1908; MA, 1911. Entered Indian Educational Service, 1920; Director of Public Instruction, Orissa, 1936; retired 1940.

Died 26 July 1945.

DISBROWE-WISE,   Lt-Col   Henry   Edward Disbrowe; *see* Wise.

DITMARS, Raymond Lee, LittD; Curator of Mammals and Reptiles, New York Zoological Park, since 1899; *b* 20 June 1876; *s* of John V. H. Ditmars and Mary A. Knous; *m* 1903; two *d. Educ:* Barnard Military Academy. Assistant Curator of Entomology, American Museum of Natural History, 5 years; Court Reporter on New York Times, 1 year. *Publications:* The Reptile Book, 1907; Reptiles of the World, 1909; Snakes of the World, 1931; Strange Animals I have Known, 1931; Thrills of a Naturalist's Quest, 1932; The Forest of Adventure, 1933; Confessions of a Scientist, 1934; The Book of Zoography, 1934; The Book of Prehistoric Animals, 1935; The Book of Living Reptiles, 1936; The Reptiles of North America, 1936; The Book of Insect Oddities, 1937; The Making of a Scientist, 1937; The Fight to Live, 1938; Field Book of North American Snakes, 1939. *Address:* Scarsdale, New York.

Died 12 May 1942.

DITZEN,   Rudolf;   (pseudonym   Hans   Fallada); Schriftsteller und Landwirt; *b* Greifswald, Pommern, 21 July 1893; *m* 1st, 1929, Anna Issel; two *s* one *d*; 2nd, 1943, Ursula Boltzenthal. *Educ:* Verschiedene deutsche Gymnasien. Landwirtschaftliche Lehre, vielerlei Berufe, jetzt hauptsächlich Schriftsteller. *Publications:* Bauern, Bonzen und Bomben (Roman); Kleiner Mann—was nun? (Roman); Wer einmal aus dem Blechnapf frisst (Roman); Wir hatten mal ein Kind (Roman); Hoppelpoppel, wo bist du? (Kindergeschichten); Märchen vom Stadschreiber, der auf's Land flog; Altes Herz geht auf die Reise (Roman); Wolf unter Wölfen (Roman); Geschichten aus der Mürkelei—Der Eiserne Gustav (Roman); Kleiner Mann, Grosser Mann—alles vertauscht (Roman); Der Ungeliebte Mann (Roman); Damals bei uns daheim (Erinnerungen); Heute bei uns zu Haus (Erinnerungen); Der Alpdruck (Roman). English Editions: Little man—what now?; Who once eats out of the tin bowl, Once we had a child, Sparrow Farm, Old Heart goes on a journey, Wolf among Wolves,   Iron   Gustav.   *Address:*   Berlin-Niederschönhausen, Eisenmengerweg 19.

Died 6 Feb. 1947.

DIVER, (Katherine Helen) Maud; *d* of Col C. H. T. Marshall, Indian Army; *g d* of Lord Chief Baron Sir Frederick Pollock; *m* Lt-Col Diver (late) Royal Warwickshire Regiment (*d* 1941); one *s*. Born in India and spent most of her early life there and Ceylon; has been in England since 1896; has done a certain amount of journalistic work in the form of articles and short stories, which appeared in the Pall Mall, Longmans, Temple Bar, Cornhill, English Review, and other magazines. *Publications:* Capt. Desmond, VC, 1907; The Great Amulet, 1908; Candles in the Wind, 1909; Lilamani, 1911; The Hero of Herat, 1912; Judgment of the Sword, 1913; Desmond's Daughter, 1916; Unconquered, 1917; Strange Roads, 1918; The Strong

Hours, 1919; Far to Seek, 1921; Lonely Furrow, 1923; Siege Perilous, 1924; Coombe St Mary's, 1925; But Yesterday, 1927; A Wild Bird, 1929; Ships of Youth, 1931; The Singer Passes, 1934; Kabul to Kandahar, 1935; Honoria Lawrence: A Fragment of Indian History, 1936; The Dream Prevails, 1938; Sylvia Lyndon, 1940; In Royal India, 1942; The Unsung: A Record of British Services in India, 1944. *Recreations:* music, sketching, reading; riding and acting in her Indian days. *Address:* Tal an Vean, Parkstone, Dorset.

Died 14 Oct. 1945.

DIXEY, Charles Neville Douglas; JP Herts; *b* 7 Nov. 1881; *o s* of Charles Douglas Dixey; *m* 1913, Marguerite Isabel, *d* of Arthur W. Groser, barrister-at-law; three *s. Educ:* privately. Elected Member of Committee of Lloyd's, 1928; Deputy Chairman, 1930 and 1933; Chairman of Lloyds, 1931, 1934 and 1936; contested Acton (L), 1922, Southampton, 1923, Holderness Division of Yorkshire, 1924 and 1929. *Recreations:* tennis, golf, and fishing. *Address:* Culverwood House, near Hertford. *T:* Essendon 237. *Clubs:* Reform, Eighty, City.

Died 6 March 1947.

DIXIE, Sir (George) Douglas, 12th Bt *cr* 1660; *b* 18 Jan. 1876; *s* of 11th Bt and Lady Florence Caroline Douglas (*d* 1905), *y d* of 7th Marquess of Queensberry and Caroline, *d* of Gen. Sir William Robert Clayton, 5th Bt; *S* father, 1924; *m* 1902, Margaret Lindsay, *d* of Sir A. Jardine, 8th Bart of Applegirth; one *s* two *d. Educ:* Beaumont College; Stonyhurst College. Was a midshipman, RN, and late Lieut 3rd Batt. KOSB. *Heir:* *s* Alexander Archibald Douglas Wolstan [*b* 8 Jan. 1910; *m* 1940, Phyllis Pinnel, *d* of late Lt-Col Percy John Probyn, DSO]. *Address:* c/o Commercial Bank of Scotland, Annan, Dumfries-shire.

Died 25 Dec. 1948.

DIXON, Arthur Frederic William, CSI 1946; CIE 1942; ICS; Member, Board of Revenue, Madras, since 1944; *b* 11 May 1892; *s* of Rev. F. A. Dixon; *m* 1928, Gwendolen Mary Hamilton; one *s. Educ:* Monkton Combe School; Christ's College, Cambridge (MA). Served in 1/4th Border Regt in England and Burma, 1914–16, and in 1/4th Dorset Regt in Mesopotamia, 1916–19 (Capt., wounded, despatches). Rowed for Cambridge Univ. *versus* Oxford Univ. 1920, and for Cambridge Univ. representing Britain in the inter-allied games at Paris in 1919; joined ICS 1920; served as Assistant Collector, Sub-Collector, and Settlement Officer in Madras; Deputy Secretary Madras Govt, 1929; Collector and District Magistrate, 1933–36 and 1937–40; Secretary and Acting Chief Secretary and Revenue Commissioner, Orissa, 1936–37; Secretary Madras Govt, 1940–41; Dewan, Cochin State, 1941–43. *Recreations:* rowing, cricket, golf. *Address:* Cherwell, Adyar, Madras, India. *TA:* Prices Madras. *Club:* East India and Sports.

Died 29 April 1948.

DIXON, Augustus Edward, MD, Trinity College, Dublin; Emeritus Professor of Chemistry, University College, Cork; *b* Belfast, 1860; *e s* of Wakefield H. Dixon, JP; *m* 1890, Nina, *e d* of Wilfred Haughton, Dublin; one *s* one *d. Educ:* Royal Academical Institution, Belfast; Trinity College, Dublin; University of Berlin. Senior Moderatorship and Gold Medal in Experimental Science, TCD; Ekenhead Scholarship in Experimental Science, and Medical Scholarship in Chemistry and Physics, TCD. Late Assistant Lecturer in Chemistry, Trinity College, Dublin; subsequently Professor of Chemistry at Queen's College, Galway; Member of the Council, Chemical Society, 1900–05. *Publications:* numerous memoirs on chemical subjects published mostly in the Proceedings and Transactions of the Chemical Society of London. *Address:* 19 Hatherley Road, Sidcup, Kent.

Died 3 March 1946.

DIXON, Col Graham Patrick, CBE 1919; VD; MB, Chm, FRACS (Founder); Australian Army Medical Corps, retired; Surgeon, Repatriation Hospital, and Hon. Surgeon, Children's Hospital, Brisbane; *b* Brisbane, 16 May 1873; *s* of late Joseph B. Dixon; unmarried. *Educ:* Brisbane Grammar School; Sydney University. Served European War, ADMS Australian Mounted Div., 1914–19 (despatches twice, CBE). *Address:* 97 Wickham Terrace, Brisbane, Queensland; Clayton, Toowong, Brisbane. *Clubs:* Queensland, Brisbane; University, Sydney.

Died 7 Aug. 1947.

DIXON, Harry; *b* Watford, Herts, 1861; 2nd *s* of late Henry Dixon; *m* 1892; three *s*. *Educ:* London. First exhibited at Royal Academy, 1886; works shown include pictures in oil and water, animal, figure, and landscape subjects, and bronzes of animals; also exhibited for several years at New Gallery, occasionally at the Salon (Champs de Mars) and International Exhibitions, etc.; in 1891 large water-colour 'Lions', now in Tate Gallery, was purchased by Trustees of Chantrey Bequest. *Address:* Greenside, Village Road, Finchley, N3.

Died 31 Dec. 1941.

DIXON, John Edwin F.; *see* Fowler-Dixon.

DIXON, Rt Hon. Sir Thomas James, 2nd Bt *cr* 1903; PC for Northern Ireland, 1930; HML for the County of the City of Belfast since 1924; *b* 29 May 1868; *s* of 1st Bt and Lizzie, *d* of late Jas Agnew; *S* father, 1907; *m* 1906, Edith Stewart, DBE, 1921; *y d* of late Stewart Clark, of Dundas Castle, South Queensferry. DL Co. Antrim; High Sheriff Co. Antrim, 1912; Co. Down, 1913. *Recreations:* hunting, shooting. *Heir: half-brother* Baron Glentoran, PC (N Ire.). *Address:* Wilmont House, Dunmurry, Co. Antrim; Unicarval, Comber, Co. Down. *Clubs:* Carlton, Constitutional; Ulster, Union (Belfast); Kildare Street (Dublin).

Died 10 May 1950.

DIXON, William Macneile, MA, LLB, LittD; Hon. LLD (Aberdeen, Glasgow and Dublin); Hon. Fellow of Trinity College, Dublin; *b* India, 1866; *s* of Rev. William Dixon, MA; *m* 1891, Edith (*d* 1945), *d* of late G. F. Wales, MD, FRCSE; two *s* two *d*. *Educ:* Trinity College, Dublin. Twice Vice-Chancellor's prizeman in English Verse; Downes Prizeman; Elrington Prizeman; graduated First Class (1st Senior Moderatorship) in Modern Literature; Second Class (Junior Moderatorship) in Mental and Moral Science; President of the Library Association, 1902; re-elected, 1903; Professor of English Literature in the University of Birmingham, 1894–1904; Regius Professor of English Language and Literature in the University of Glasgow, 1904–35; on leave from the University of Glasgow for service in the Department of Information, 1916–18; Pres., Edinburgh Sir Walter Scott Club, 1931; Leslie Stephen Lecturer, University of Cambridge, 1915; Northcliffe Lecturer, University Coll., London; Warton Lecturer, British Academy; Ballard Mathews Lecturer, University College, Bangor; Donnellan Lecturer, Trinity College Dublin; Gifford Lecturer, University of Glasgow, 1935; Ker Memorial Lecturer, 1940. *Publications:* In the Republic of Letters; Trinity College, Dublin (College Histories Series); Thomas the Rhymer, a pageant play; English Epic and Heroic Poetry; The Edinburgh Book of Scottish Verse; Tragedy; Cinderella's Garden; The Fleets Behind the Fleet; Hellas Revisited; The Englishman; In Arcadia; The Human Situation, etc. *Recreations:* sailing, golf. *Address:* 16 Hythe Road, Worthing, W Sussex. *Club:* Athenæum.

Died 31 Jan. 1946.

DOBBIE, Sir Joseph, Kt 1920; *b* 1862; *s* of late James Dobbie. *Educ:* Ayr Academy; Edin. Univ. Head of Dalgleish, Dobbie & Co., SSC, Edinburgh. In favour of social reform; MP (L) Ayr Burghs, 1904–06; JP City of Edinburgh; Member Departmental Committee on

Housing, 1908; Chairman Royal Scots Recruiting Committee, 1914–16; Legal Member Edinburgh Military Tribunal; President Scottish Vernacular Association. *Address:* 42 Melville Street, Edinburgh. *TA:* Dalgleish, Edinburgh. *Clubs:* Scottish Liberal, Edinburgh.

Died 18 May 1943.

DOBBIE, William, CBE 1947; MP (Lab) Rotherham since 1933; *b* 28 Oct. 1878; *s* of a blacksmith; *m* 1902, Winifred, *d* of Charles Thomas, Shrewsbury; two *s* two *d*. *Educ:* Council School. Served RA, 1914–18. Pres. NUR, 1925–28 and 1930–33; Alderman, York City Council; past Lord Mayor and again, 1947. *Address:* House of Commons, SW1.

Died 19 Jan. 1950.

DOBBIE, William Herbert, CIE 1908; *b* 16 July 1851. *Educ:* Merchant Taylors' School. Joined Financial Department, Government of India, 1872; Assistant Accountant-General, Bengal, 1884; Punjab, 1885; Dep. Accountant-General, NW Prov. 1886; Controller, Assam, 1887; Dep. Accountant-General, NW Prov. and Oudh, 1890; Officiating Controller, Hyderabad, 1891; Deputy Controller-General, 1896; Accountant General, Madras, 1901–07; retired, 1907. *Address:* Mayfield, Littleham Cross, Exmouth. *T:* Exmouth 2877.

Died 17 Jan. 1941.

DOBBIN, Sir Alfred Graham, Kt 1900; *b* 10 Sept. 1853; *s* of late Leonard Dobbin of Rosemount, Cork; *m* 1st, 1876, Margaret Reid (*d* 1884), *d* of Peter Ogilvie; 2nd, 1887, Kate, *d* of William Wise of Clifton, Bristol; one *s* one *d*. High Sheriff, City of Cork, 1900; Chairman Imperial Hotel, Cork, Ltd; Trustee Cork Savings Bank; DL, Borough of Cork. *Address:* Imperial Hotel, Cork. *T:* Cork 1675.

Died 1 Feb. 1942.

DOBBIN, Brig.-Gen. Herbert Thomas, CBE 1925; DSO 1916; *b* 27 May 1878; *s* of Lieut-Col G. M. Dobbin; unmarried. *Educ:* Bedford; privately. Joined Duke of Cornwall's Light Infantry, 1899; Commandant Iraq Levies, 1922–26; commanded DCLI, 1926–30; Col, 1930; Officer in charge of Record and Pay Office, Exeter, 1931–35; retired pay, 1935.

Died 9 Sept. 1946.

DOBELL, Clifford, MA, ScD, FRS; Protistologist to the Medical Research Council, National Institute for Medical Research, Hampstead, NW3; *b* 22 Feb. 1886; *e s* of late Wm Blount Dobell and Agnes Thornely; *m* 1937, Monica, *d* of late Augustus Baker and Mrs Wm Bulloch. *Educ:* Sandringham School, Southport; Trinity College, Cambridge. Exhibitioner, 1905; Major Scholar 1906; BA 1906 (1st Class Nat. Sci. Tripos), MA 1910; pupil of Adam Sedgwick; Fellow of Trinity College, 1908–14; studied abroad at Zoological Institute, Munich (under R. Hertwig), 1907–08; Zoological Station, Naples, 1908; Ceylon, 1909; etc.; Walsingham Medallist, Cambridge, 1908; Rolleston Prizeman, Oxford and Cambridge, 1908; Belfour Student, Cambridge University, 1908–09. Lecturer and Assistant Professor of Protistology and Cytology at the Imperial College of Science, 1910–19. *Publications:* The Amœbae living in Man, 1919; The Intestinal Protozoa of Man (with F. W. O'Connor), 1921; Leeuwenhoek and his Little Animals, 1932; many papers dealing with researches on the Protozoa, Bacteria, and related organisms; several reports (dealing with amœbic dysentery, etc.) published by the Medical Research Council. *Address:* 161 West Heath Road, NW3.

Died 23 Dec. 1949.

DOBLE, Rev. Canon Gilbert Hunter, DD Oxon, 1943; Vicar of Wendron since 1925; *b* 26 Nov. 1880; *s* of John Medley and Fanny Doble; unmarried. *Educ:* Clifton College; Exeter College, Oxford (scholar); winner of Skeat Prize for English Literature, 2nd Class Honours, Final Hon. School of Modern History, 1903.

Ely Theological College, Deacon, 1904; Priest, 1907; Curate of Quron, S Mary Stoke (Ipswich), Berkeley, Madron, Tetbury, S Columb and Redruth; Examining Chaplain to the Bishop of Truro, 1924; Hon. Canon of Truro Cathedral, 1931. *Publications:* The Christian Child; The Cornish Saints series (49 numbers); The Welsh Saints series (5 numbers); Cornish Parish Histories series (8 numbers); A John Wesley of Armorican Cornwall; Two Cornish Parishes (Wendron and Sithney) in the 18th century; Breage in the 18th century; The Rector of Concoret, Les Saints du Cornwall; Fragments d'Hagiographie de la Cornouaille insulaire; Les relations durant les ages entre la Bretagne et le Cornwall; Les Saints Bretons; Some remarks on the Exeter Martyrology; The Pontificale Lanaletense; The Vita Pyrani; John Wesley and his work in Cornwall; Hagiography and Folk-lore; Dedications to Celtic Saints in Normandy, etc. *Address:* Wendron Vicarage, Helston, Cornwall.

Died 15 April 1945.

DOBSON, Bernard Henry, CIE 1938; CBE 1920; Indian Civil Service (retd); *b* 1 Jan. 1881; 4th *s* of late Austin Dobson; *m* 1916, Margaret Eleanor, *d* of late Col M. T. Sale, CMG, RE; no *c*. *Educ:* Clifton College; Emmanuel College Cambridge (Scholar). *Proxime accessit:* Porson Greek Verse Prize, 1902 and 1903; 1st class Cl. Tripos, 1902; passed ICS examn 1903. Settlement Officer, Chenab Colony, 1911–15; services lent to Home Govt, 1915–19; War Office, 1915–16; Asst Director (Russia and Roumania), Commission Internationale de Ravitaillement, 1916–19; 2nd Class, Order of St Anne, Russia; 2nd Class, Order of the Crown, Roumania; Gold Cross, Order of the Redeemer, Greece; Deputy Commissioner, Lyallpur, Punjab, 1919–23; Home Secretary to the Government of the Punjab and member of the Punjab Legislative Council, 1925–27; Commissioner, Rawalpindi, 1929 and 1933–34; Multan, 1930; Lahore, 1931 and 1936; Financial Commissioner Punjab, 1935–39. *Recreations:* travel, topography, fishing. *Address:* c/o Westminster Bank, St Martin's Place, Charing Cross, WC2. *Clubs:* Athenæum; United Service, Simla.

Died 7 June 1945.

DOBSON, Lt-Col Francis George, DSO 1919; MB, ChB; RAMC (TR); Medical Officer of Health, Beverley Rural District Council; Honorary Medical Officer, Beverley Cottage Hospital; President, Beverley Branch, British Legion; *b* 1879; *s* of Joseph Dobson, MD. *Educ:* Denstone College; University of Leeds. Formerly OC 1/2 West Riding Field Ambulance, 49th Division; served European War, 1914–19 (despatches twice, DSO, two medals, 1914–15 star). *Address:* Cross Street, Beverley, East Yorks. *T:* Beverley 111.

Died 28 July 1941.

DOBSON, John Frederic, MA; *b* 1875; *s* of William Cleaver Dobson, London, and Charlotte, 2nd *d* of F. A. Catty, MD; *m* 1911, Dina, *e d* of H. H. Portway, JP, of Bois Hall, Halstead, Essex; four *s* one *d*. *Educ:* St Paul's School; Trinity College, Cambridge (Scholar). First Class in Classical Tripos, Parts 1 and 2, 1896 and 1898. Assistant master at Clifton College, 1899; later, assistant lecturer in Classics at Manchester University; Professor of Greek, University of Bristol, 1910–40; Pro-Vice-Chancellor, 1931–40; Vice-President of Classical Association; Governor of Colston's School, Stapleton, and King's School, Bruton. *Publications:* various articles in Classical Quarterly, Classical Review, and other journals; Aristotle, de Spiritu (trans.), 1924; The Greek Orators, 1919; Ancient Education, 1932. *Recreations:* fly-fishing, cycling, etc. *Address:* Glaisters, Wrington, Somerset.

Died 31 Aug. 1947.

DOBSON, Col Sir William Warrington, Kt 1933; VD; TD; DL; Chairman of Parkers Burslem Brewery, Ltd; Hon. Colonel, 41st (North Stafford Regiment) AA Bn; Master North Stafford Foxhounds, 1903–04, 1906–07, and 1907–27; *b* Cheetham Hill, Manchester, 1861; *s* of Matthew Dobson and Louisa Warrington; *m* 1887, Alice (*d* 1936), 2nd *d* of William Meakin, of Westwood Manor, Wetley Rocks, Staffordshire; one *s* three *d*. *Educ:* Old Trafford School, near Manchester. Entered the office of Wallace and Co., Manchester, to learn office routine, 1879; entered father's business as a brewer and maltster, 1880; twice Mayor of Burslem; a County Councillor from the commencement of the Staffs County Council until the Potteries became a federated borough, when he became an Alderman of the new borough. Joined 1st Vol. Batt. North Staff Rgt. 1880; Captain, 1885; Major, 1890; Lt-Colonel, 1895; Colonel, 1900; commanded until 1908; Hon. Colonel, 1909; Chairman of Organisation Committee, Staffordshire Territorial Association. *Recreations:* hunting and shooting. *Address:* Seighford Hall, Stafford. *TA:* Seighford, Stafford. *T:* 107 Stafford. *Clubs:* Carlton, Junior Carlton.

Died 27 Nov. 1941.

DOCKER, Frank Dudley, CB 1911; Director, The Midland Bank, Ltd, the Electric and Railway Finance Corporation and the Birmingham Small Arms Co., Ltd; *b* 1862; *m* 1895, Lucy Constance, *d* of J. B. Hebbert, Edgbaston; one *s*. *Recreation:* golf. *Address:* Coleshill House, Amersham, Bucks. *Club:* Carlton.

Died 8 July 1944.

DOCKRILL, Col Walter Roy, CIE 1919; Transport Officer to Food Control Department, Hong Kong Government; Import, Export and Shipping Agent, and Manufacturer of Toys, Hong Kong; *b* Florence, Ontario, 1877; *s* of Joseph Dockrill of St Thomas, Ont, and Mary Kathleen O'Gorman of Kilrush; *m* 1st, 1902, Mabel Claire Palmer; two *d*; 2nd, 1936, Margaret Estelle Mayberry. *Educ:* New Westminster. Joined the Army, Dec. 1915; demobilised, Oct. 1919; went overseas with the 158th OSB; Transport Officer to the Canadian Forestry Corps until May 1917; transferred to Royal Engineers, and took charge of No. 4 Darse, Dunkirk; joined the Freeland Mission to Mesopotamia in Oct.; promoted to Major; Port Director for Basra, 1918, and promoted to Colonel; built and organised the Port of Basra; Pilotage Services and Conservancy Operations. *Recreations:* golf, fishing and hunting. *Address:* Hunghom, Kowloon, Hong Kong. *Clubs:* Vancouver, Shanghai, Shanghai Race, Zero, Shanghai.

Died 11 Aug. 1942.

DOD, Brig.-Gen. Owen Cadogan W.; *see* Wolley-Dod.

DODD, Francis, RA, 1935 (ARA 1927); RWS 1929 (ARWS 1923; *b* Holyhead, 29 Nov. 1874; 3rd *s* of Rev. Benjamin Dodd, Wesleyan Minister; *m* 1st, Mary Arabella (*d* 1948), *d* of J. Brouncker Ingle; 2nd, 1949, Ellen Margaret Tanner. *Educ:* Glasgow School of Art; Paris; Italy. Trustee of the Tate Gallery, Millbank, 1929–35. *Address:* 51 Blackheath Park, SE3. *T:* Lee Green 3647. *Club:* Athenæum.

Died 7 March 1949.

DODD, Frederick Henry, LRCP Lond., MRCS Eng., FGS; Psychological Physician; *b* 1890; *s* of late Thomas Henry Dodd, FIC, FCS; *m* 1925, Kathleen Elizabeth, *y d* of late Prof. Alfred Lodge; three *s* one *d*. *Educ:* St Dunstan's College; University of London (Guy's Hospital). Late House Physician, Evelina Hospital for Children; Assistant Physician, Queen's Hospital for Children; Chief Assistant, Children's Dept, Guy's Hospital; Medical Officer, Dr Barnardo's Homes, Blackheath; MO No. 1 Stores Depot, RAF; Outpatient Physician, South-Eastern Hospital for Children; Physician, Tavistock Psychotherapeutic Clinic;

Physician, Children's Psychological Dept and Dept Diseases of Children, Eastern Dispensary; Psychological Consultant, Woolwich ICAA; during European War, Captain RAMC, Heart Specialist and T. Med. Boards; during War of 1939–45 Psychiatrist to Hostels for evacuee children, N Dorset. *Publications:* Commonsense Psychology and the Home, 1934; papers on child psychology. *Recreations:* geology, mathematics, general science, tennis, cricket, and music. *Address:* 222 Woodstock Road, Oxford. *T:* Oxford 5623.

Died 17 Aug. 1950.

DODD, Sir Robert John Sherwood, Kt 1931; CSI 1928; *b* 26 July 1878; *s* of Rev. E. S. Dodd; *m* 1904, Gertrude E. M., *d* of late A. C. Evans, CE; one *s* one *d*. *Educ:* St Edmund's School, Canterbury. Joined Indian Police Service as Assistant District Superintendent, 1899; Superintendent, 1910; Secretary Police Committees, 1919–20; King's Police Medal, 1919; Principal Police Training School, 1921–23; Deputy Inspector-General, 1923; Inspector-General of Police, United Provinces, India, 1925–31. Member of Eastbourne Borough Council, 1941–50; Chairman of Education and Watch Cttees. Governor of several schools and colleges. Member of Hospitals Management Cttee and Eastbourne Executive Council, 1948–50. *Recreation:* golf. *Address:* Boostan, St Anne's Road, Eastbourne.

Died 3 Oct. 1950.

DODD, Stanley, MB, FRCP, FRCS; Consulting Surgeon, Chelsea Hospital; Consulting Gynæcologist to Bolingbroke Hospital for Women; Consulting Obstetric Surgeon to Westminster Hospital; 3rd *s* of late Arthur Dodd, 53 Elsworthy Road, NW; *m* 1912, Phyllis Embury; one *s*. *Educ:* Eastbourne College; Caius College, Cambridge. *Recreations:* shooting, fishing, golf. *Address:* Corner Farm, Chiddingfold, Surrey. *T:* Chiddingfold 105.

Died 21 April 1946.

DODD, Col Wilfrid T., DSO 1916; MC; TD; Commanding 4th Anti-Aircraft Divisional Signals, TA since 1938; *s* of W. H. Dodd, Liverpool; *m*; one *s* one *d*. *Educ:* St Francis Xavier's Coll. Liverpool. Served European War (despatches; DSO, MC, TD, Belgian Croix de Guerre); Deputy Chief Signal Officer, Western Command, 1921–29; commanded 55th (W Lancs) Divisional Signals, 1929–35; Colonel, 1925; DL County Lancaster, 1935; Hon. Col 55th (W Lancs) Divisional Signals, 1935. *Address:* 1 Shrewsbury Road, Oxton, Cheshire. *Club:* Junior Army and Navy.

Died 31 Aug. 1942.

DODDS, Stephen Roxby, MA, LLB; Solicitor and Commissioner for Oaths; Notary Public; JP; *b* Birkenhead, 29 Jan. 1881; *s* of T. L. Dodds, JP, Birkenhead, and Jane Widdifield Dodds; *m* Edith May, *d* of Johnston Bell of Heswall, Cheshire; no *c*. *Educ:* Rydal School, Colwyn Bay; Trinity Hall, Cambridge. Articled to late C. E. Stevens of Liverpool, 1903; admitted solicitor, 1906; became founder firm of Dodds, Ashcroft & Cook, 24 Fenwick Street, Liverpool, 1910; Liberal candidate for Wirral, 1922, 1924 and 1929; MP (L) Wirral Division of Chester Dec. 1923–Oct. 1924; President Liverpool Law Society, 1939–40; member of Council of Law Society (London); President of the Literary and Philosophical Society of Liverpool, 1925–26, and 1926–27; Chairman of Governors of Rydal School, Governor Wirral Grammar School and Wirral County School for Girls; Vice-Chairman Methodist Insurance Co. Ltd. *Publication:* The Writing of Modern History in Relation to Literature and Life (Presidential Address Birkenhead Literary and Scientific Society, 1914). *Recreation:* reading. *Address:* Heath Moor, Heswall, Cheshire. *Clubs:* National Liberal; Athenæum, Liverpool.

Died 10 Sept. 1943.

DODDS, Maj.-Gen. Thomas Henry, CMG 1918; CVO 1920; DSO 1902; Hon. Treasurer, Federal Executive of Returned Sailors' and Soldiers' Imperial League of Australia, since 1931; Councillor for City of Hawthorn, 1935–38; *b* 11 Dec. 1873; *s* of Thomas Dodds of Newcastle; *m* 1902, Elizabeth Jane, *d* of late George Hancock of Brisbane. Served South Africa with Queensland contingent, 1901–02 (despatches, Queen's medal 5 clasps, DSO); European War (CMG); Military Secretary Australian Commonwealth Forces, 1920–22; Australian Military Representative at War Office and Military Adviser to the High Commissioner for Australia in London, 1924–27; District Base Commandant and Commander 1st Division, NSW, 1927–29; Adjutant-General, Australian Military Forces, 1929–34. *Address:* 24 Currajong Avenue, Camberwell, Melbourne, E6. *Clubs:* Victorian Naval and Military, Melbourne; Imperial Service, Sydney.

Died 15 Oct. 1943.

DODGSON, Campbell, CBE 1918; MA; Hon. DLitt (Oxon); Hon. LittD (Camb.); Commander of Order of the Crown (Belgium); Officer of the Legion of Honour (France); Fellow of the British Academy; *b* Crayford, Kent, 13 Aug. 1867; *y s* of William Oliver Dodgson; *m* 1913, Frances Catharine, *e d* of late Rev. W. A. Spooner, DD. *Educ:* Winchester College (Scholar); New College, Oxford (Scholar). Keeper of Prints and Drawings, British Museum, 1912–32. *Publications:* Catalogue of German and Flemish Woodcuts in the British Museum, vol. i, 1903; vol. ii, 1911; introductory notes to publications of the Dürer Society, 1898–1911; Catalogue of Etchings by Muirhead Bone, 1909; Catalogue of Etchings by A. E. John, 1920; Old French Colour-Prints, 1924; Catalogue of Etchings by E. Blampied, 1926; Catalogue of Engravings by Dürer, 1926; Fifteenth Century Woodcuts in the Ashmolean Museum, Oxford, 1929; Catalogue of Etchings and Engravings by Robert Austin, 1931; Goya's Desastres de la Guerra (Roxburghe Club), 1933; Woodcuts of the Fifteenth Century in the British Museum, 1935; Catalogue of Etchings by Wilkie and Geddes, 1936; Dotted Prints and Metal-cuts (British Museum), 1937; Catalogue of Etchings by F. L. Griggs, 1941; Iconograpy of S. Gooden, 1944. *Address:* 22 Montagu Square, W1. *T:* Welbeck 5143. *Club:* Athenæum.

Died 11 July 1948.

DODGSON, Brig.-Gen. Colquhoun Scott, CB 1918; CMG 1915; ASC (retired); *b* 4 May 1867; *s* of J. C. Dodgson, BCS. *Educ:* Cheltenham College. Entered army, East Surrey Regt 1888; transferred to ASC 1892; served Zhob Field Force, 1890; South Africa, 1899–1902 (despatches twice, Queen's medal 4 clasps, King's medal 2 clasps); European War, 1914–18 (CMG, CB). *Club:* Army and Navy.

Died 4 Nov. 1947.

DODWELL, Henry Herbert; *b* 1879; *y s* of late Herbert Dodwell, of Long Crendon Manor, Bucks; *m* 1908, Lily May, *y d* of late Henry Mason, Deptford; two *s* two *d*. *Educ:* Thame Grammar School; St John's College, Oxford. Indian Educational Service; Curator of the Madras Record Office; Professor of the History of the British Dominions in Asia, Univ. of London, School of Oriental Studies; retired 1946. *Publications:* Dupleix and Clive, 1920; A Sketch of Indian History, 1858–1918, 1925; The Nabobs of Madras, 1926; Muhammad Ali the Founder of Modern Egypt, 1931; The Private Letter Books of Joseph Collet, 1933; India, 2 vols, 1936; Editor vols iv, etc., of The Diary of Ananda Ranga Pillai; Joint-Editor, Cambridge History of India; Editor of the Letters of Warren Hastings to John Macpherson; Editor and part author of Cambridge Shorter History of India, 1934. *Address:* Dover House, Chertsey, Surrey. *Club:* Athenæum.

Died 30 Oct. 1946.

d'OISLY, (Emile) Maurice; operatic and concert artist; Professor of Singing at Royal Academy of Music; Examiner for Associated Board of the Royal Schools of Music, London; *b* Tunbridge Wells, 2 Nov. 1882; French parentage; *m* 1919, Rosina Buckman (*d* 1948). *Educ:* Wellingborough School; Còllège de Blois. Studied Piano at RAM with Tobias Matthay and gained Potter Exhibition; Singing with Frederic King and gained Westmorland Scholarship. Drama with Rosina Filippi and Norman Forbes-Robertson; Light Opera engagement, Brussels, 1907; Grand Opera début, Royal Opera, Covent Garden, 1909, as David in Die Meistersinger; Covent Garden Grand Seasons, 1909–10–1911–12; Principal Tenor, Beecham Opera Company, 1910, 1915–20, Quinlan Opera Company, 1912–13; World Tour, 1922–23; tours have included Canada, USA, S Africa, Australia, NZ, Tasmania, Malta, India, S America and West Indies; Lead in Lilac Time (part of Schubert), Globe and Alhambra Theatres, 1932–33–1934; re-engaged, 1934–35–1936; Coliseum, 1936; Associate of the RAM, 1909; Fellow, 1919; Officier d'Académie. *Recreations:* swimming, shooting, fishing. *Address:* 39 Rokesly Avenue, Crouch End, N8.
Died 12 July 1949.

DOLAND, Lt-Col George Frederick, OBE 1919; DL, JP, Co. of London; Governing Director of companies; *b* 1872; *s* of Richard Doland; *m* 1895, Minnie Mary (OStJ), *d* of George Richardson, Balham. Served European War, 1914–19 as OC Co. of London RASC, Motor Transport Vols; MP (U) Balham and Tooting Division of Wandsworth, 1936–45; Alderman borough of Wandsworth (Mayor, 1928–29 and 1933–34); member LCC 1933. *Club:* Constitutional.
Died 26 Nov. 1946.

DONALD, Alexander Douglas, BL; Sheriff Substitute of Ross and Cromarty and Sutherland at Dingwall and Dornoch; *b* Kirriemuir, Angus; *m* Jessie Fairweather-Alexander; one *s*. *Educ:* Websters Seminary, Kirriemuir; University of Edinburgh. Vans Dunlop Law Scholar, Edinburgh University. Lecturer of Mercantile Law, Leith Technical College; Hon. Sheriff Substitute of the Lothians and Peebles and Lanark. *Publications:* contributions to various periodicals. *Recreations:* fishing, bowling, walking. *Address:* National Hotel, Dingwall; 16 Great King Street, Edinburgh 3.
Died 6 Oct. 1948.

DONALD, Sir John Stewart, KCIE 1915; CSI 1911; CIE 1894; *b* 8 Sept. 1861; *e surv. s* of late A. J. S. Donald, Punjab Provincial Civil Service; *m* 1905, Henrietta Mary, 2nd *d* of Col E. L. Ommanney, CSI; one *s* two *d*. *Educ:* privately; Bishop Cotton School, Simla. Appointed Extra Assistant Commissioner, 1882; Assistant Commissioner, 1890; was promoted for service in Gomal Pass and with Sherani Expedition (despatches); in charge of Gomal Pass, 1890–93; accompanied mission to Kabul under Sir H. Durand, 1893; on special duty NW Frontier, and British Commissioner for Domarcation of Kurram-Afghan boundary, 1894; Political Agent of the Tochi, and Deputy Commissioner of Bannu, 1899–1903; operations against Mahsud-Wazirs (medal with clasp); Chief Political Officer with force against Kabul Khel Wazirs and Gumati, 1902 (despatches); British Representative on Indo-Afghan Commission, 1903; Deputy Commissioner Dera Ismail Khan; Deputy Commissioner, Hazara, 1905; Resident in Waziristan, 1908; British Commissioner Anglo-Afghan Commission for Settlement of Border Disputes, 1910; chief Commissioner and Agent to the Governor-General in the NW Frontier Province, 1913–15; appointed an Additional Member of the Imperial Legislative Council of India, 1916; European War (Star of 1914–15, Victory Medal, and General Service Medal); retired from the service, 1920. *Recreations:* big-game shooting, golf. *Club:* East India and Sports.
Died 30 July 1948.

DONALDSON-HUDSON, Lt-Col Ralph Charles, DSO 1917; DL; JP; Landed Proprietor; *b* 20 Feb. 1874; *s* of Charles Donaldson-Hudson, MP for Newcastle, Staffs, 1880–85, and Sara Marie, *d* of Major S. R. Streatfield, 43rd Foot; *m* 1899, Muriel, *d* of R. D. Balfour, Sherrards, Welwyn, Herts; two *s* two *d*. *Educ:* Eton; RMC, Sandhurst. Lieut 12th Lancers, 1893–97; Lieut Shropshire Yeo., 1901–10; CC Shropshire, 1904–22 and 1931–40, Alderman since 1940; served with RFC and RAF European War (attained rank of Lt-Col, DSO, Chevalier Legion of Honour); High Sheriff, Shropshire, 1927. *Address:* Cheswardine, Market Drayton, Shropshire. *TA:* Hudson, Cheswardine. *T:* Hales 7. *Club:* Cavalry.
Died 25 April 1941.

DONE, Brig.-Gen. Herbert Richard, CMG 1919; DSO 1915; late the Norfolk Regiment; *b* 23 Sept. 1876; *y s* of Richard Done; *m* 1916, Elsie, *d* of late Samuel Kingan, DL, of Glenganagh, Co. Down; two *d*. *Educ:* Harrow. Entered army, 1896; Captain, 1904; Major, 1914; served S African War, 1900–02 (Queen's medal 3 clasps, King's medal 2 clasps); European War, 1914–18 (despatches nine times, DSO and bar, Bt Lt-Col and Col, CMG); retired pay, 1919. *Address:* Haygrass House, Taunton, Somerset. *Club:* Army and Navy.
Died 17 Jan. 1950.

DONERAILE, 6th Viscount *cr* 1785; **Edward St Leger,** MA; Baron Doneraile, 1776; *b* 6 Oct. 1866; *s* of Rev. Edward F. St Leger and Caroline, *d* of William R. Bishop; *S uncle* 1891. Anglican. Tory. *Educ:* Winchester; New College, Oxford. Barr. Inner Temple, 1891; Mayor of the City of Westminster, 1919–20. *Heir: b* Hon. Hugh St Leger, *b* 1869. *Address:* 91 Victoria Street, SW1. *T:* Victoria 3696. *Clubs:* Carlton, Bachelors', Oxford and Cambridge.
Died 7 Sept. 1941.

DONNAY, Maurice, Member of the French Academy; Commander, Legion of Honour; dramatic author; *b* Paris, 12 Oct. 1859; *m* Lucie Allard. *Educ:* Lycées de Vanves, Louis-le-Grand; Ecole Centrale des Arts et Manufactures. *Publications:* Phryné; Eux; La Vrille; Folle entreprise; Chères madames; Ailleurs; Lysistrata, 1892; Pension de famille, 1894; Amants, 1895; Douloureuse, 1897; L'Affranchie, 1898; Georgette Lemeunier, 1898; Le Torrent, 1898; Education de Prince, 1900; La Clairière, 1900 (with L. Descaves); La Bascule, 1901; L'Autre Danger, 1902; Le Retour de Jérusalem, 1903; Oiseaux de passage (with L. Descaves), 1904; L'Escalade, 1904; Paraître, 1906; La Patronne, 1908; Le Mariage de Télemaque (with J. Lemaître); Molière, 1911; Le Ménage de Molière, 1912; Les Eclaireuses, 1913; Le Cœur et la tête, 1913; Alfred de Musset, 1914; La Parisienne et la guerre, 1916; L'Impromptu du paquetage, 1916; Le Théâtre aux armées, 1916; Premières impressions, 1917; Lettres à la dame Blanche, 1917; Pendant qu'ils sont à Noyon, 1917; La chasse à l'homme, 1919. *Address:* 7 rue de Florence, Paris. *Clubs:* Union artistique, Cercle interallié, Escholiers, Cercle d'Anjon, Paris.
Died 29 March 1945.

DONNE, Col Henry Richard Beadon, CB 1908; CMG 1918; Grand Officer of the Portuguese Order of Christ, 1920; retired list; *b* 14 Nov. 1860; *y s* of late B. J. M. Donne, of Crewkerne, Somerset, and Exmouth, Devon; *m* 1891, Mary Amy (*d* 1947), *d* of late Sir C. A. Elliott, KCSI; one *d*. *Educ:* Sherborne. 2nd Lieut, 9th Foot, 1880; Lt Norfolk Regt, 1881; Captain, 1887; passed through Staff College, 1893; Major, 1897; Bt Lt-Col 1898; Col 1903; Station Staff Officer, 1st Class, India, 1894–97; DAAG, India, 1897–99; DAQMG, Malakand Field Force, 1897; DAAG Tirah Expeditionary Force, 1897–98; AAG, India, 1900–05; AAG Army Headquarters, 1907–11; served Burmese Expedition, 1887–89; served as Intelligence Officer in political expedition to Northern Shan States, 1888–89 and led attack and capture of insurgents stockades at Nawah; operations in the Chin Hills, 1889 (medal with clasp); North-West Frontier of India, 1897–98; on Staff with Malakand Field Force, operations in Bajaur, Mohmand (despatches, medal with clasp); Tirah, 1897–98; capture of Sampagha and Arhunga Passes, operations in the Bazar Valley (despatches, Bt Lt-Col, clasp), European War, 1914, special employment under the War Office (twice mentioned for valuable services). *Address:* c/o Glyn Mills & Co., Kirkland House, Whitehall, SW1; Hill Farm House, Seend, Wilts.

Died 14 March 1949.

DONNE, Thomas Edward, CMG 1923; Honorary Captain New Zealand Forces; *b* 4 Aug. 1859; 2nd *s* of William Donne, London; *m* 1883, *o d* of Henry Eldridge Lucas; three *s*. *Educ:* Public School, New Zealand. Entered NZ Civil Service, 1873; retired, 1923; General Manager New Zealand Government Tourist and Health Resorts; General Manager town of Rotorua Hot Lakes; Secretary Industries Commerce; Secretary to New Zealand Government, London, 1916–23; Royal Commissioner visit Duke and Duchess of York to New Zealand, 1901; Commissioner General for New Zealand to Louisiana Purchase Exposition, 1904–05; Vice-President and Executive Commissioner International Exhibition, Christchurch, New Zealand, 1907–08; Government Commissioner for Reception American Fleet, NZ, 1908; New Zealand Military Records Officer, London, 1914–16. *Publications:* Red Deer Stalking in New Zealand; The Game Animals of New Zealand, 1924; The Maori, Past and Present, 1927; Rod Fishing in New Zealand Waters, 1927; Moeurs et Coutumes des Maoris (Paris), 1938. *Recreations:* big-game shooting, angling, golf. *Address:* 50 King's Gardens, NW6. *T:* Maida Vale 1319.

Died 15 Feb. 1945.

DONNELLY, Patrick; MP (Nat.) South Armagh, 1918–22; solicitor. *Educ:* Queen's College, Belfast. *Address:* 4 Margaret Street, Newry, Co. Down.

Died 13 Aug. 1947.

DONOGHUE, Stephen, (Steve); *b* Warrington, Oct. 1884; *m* 1st, *d* of P. Behan; 2nd, 1929, Ethel Finn. Rode Derby winner six times. *Publication:* Donoghue Up! 1938.

Died 23 March 1945.

DONOHUE, Col William Edward, CBE 1918; MInstCE; *b* 1861; *s* of late Timothy Donohue, and *g s* of late John Donohue, Clonakilty, Co. Cork, and formerly of Co. Kerry; *m* 1890, Frances Martha, *d* of late John Everett and *g d* of late John Clayton of Wrockwerdine, Salop; one *d*. *Educ:* private schools and tutors; Royal College of Science, London (Whitworth Engineering Scholarship 1883); Université de Grenoble, France; School of Economics, London. Commission Royal Garrison Artillery, 1886, for duty as Inspector of Ordnance Machinery; transferred to RAOC, 1901, and to RASC for duty as Chief Inspector of Mechanical Transport, 1904; Member of Mechanical Transport Committee and Technical Adviser to Director of Transport, War Office, until outbreak of war, 1904–14; Inspector of Mechanical Transport Services, Eastern Theatres of operations (graded AQMG), 1916–19. *Publications:* on Mechanical Transport in undeveloped countries. *Recreation:* golf.

Died 23 Aug. 1945.

DONOUGHMORE, 6th Earl of, *cr* 1800; **Richard Walter John Hely-Hutchinson,** KP 1916; PC 1918; Baron Donoughmore, 1783; Viscount Suirdale, 1800; Viscount Hutchinson (UK), 1821; *b* 2 March 1875; *s* of 5th Earl and Frances, *d* of late Lieut-Gen. Stephens, HEICS; *m* 1901, Elena (*d* 1944), *d* of late M. P. Grace, New York; two *s*. *Educ:* Eton; New College, Oxford (Hon. Fellow 1931). Under-Secretary of State for War, 1903–05; Chairman of Committees, House of Lords,

1911–31; Chairman, National Radium Commission, since 1933; Hon. FFR 1945. *Heir: s* Visct. Suirdale, *b* 1902. *Address:* 7 Sloane Street (Flat I), SW1. *T:* Sloane 7857; Chelwood Beacon, Chelwood Gate, Sussex. *T:* Chelwood Gate 12; The Haven, Sandwich Bay, Kent. *T:* Sandwich 103. *Clubs:* Travellers', Beefsteak; Kildare Street (Dublin).

Died 19 Oct. 1948.

DONOVAN, Francis Desmond, CVO 1936; LDS, RCS Eng.; Surgeon Dentist to HM Household and to Queen Mary's Household; *b* 6 Dec. 1894; *s* of Captain Daniel Donovan, Cork. *Educ:* Kildare, Barry, South Wales; Middlesex Hospital and Royal Dental Hospital, London. Late Surgeon Dentist to HM Queen Alexandra, to King George V's Household and to King Edward VIII's Household. *Publications:* The Prevention of Pyorrhœa, 1927; Tooth Powders and Tooth Pastes, 1927. *Address:* 11 Mansfield Street, W1. *T:* Langham 1078.

Died 27 Dec. 1948.

DOORLY, Sir Charles William, Kt 1935; CBE 1930; *b* 20 Jan. 1875; *s* of J. G. and M. E. C. Doorly; *m* 1902, Marie C. Lofthouse; three *d*. *Educ:* Jamaica College. Clerk, Immigration Department, Jamaica, 1892; Protector of Immigrants Jamaica, 1909; Government Emigration Agent, Madras, 1913; Assistant Colonial Secretary, Jamaica, 1922; Administrator of St Lucia, 1928–35; Retired, 1935. *Address:* Halfway-Tree, PO Jamaica, BWI.

Died 5 Feb. 1942.

DOORLY, Most Rev. Edward; Bishop of Elphin, (RC), since 1920; *b* near Roscommon, 1870. *Educ:* Sligo, Maynooth Coll. Priest, 1895; Member of Elphin Chapter, 1912; Coadjutor Bishop of Elphin, 1923–26. *Address:* St Mary's, Sligo, Ireland.

Died 5 April 1950.

DORAN, Maj.-Gen. Beauchamp John Colclough, CB 1903; DL; late the Royal Irish Regiment; *b* 24 Sept. 1860; *e s* of late Gen. Sir J. Doran, KCB; *m* 1st, 1903, Mary (*d* 1932), *widow* of Wm M'Geough Bond; 2nd, 1933, Florence Fairchild, New York City. Entered army, 1880; Capt. and Bt Maj. 1887; Maj. 1899; Bt Lt-Col 1900; Bt-Col 1905; Brig.-Gen. 1912; Maj.-Gen. 1915; Lieut-Col Comdg 1st Batt. the Royal Irish Regiment, 1904–08; commanded 8th Infantry Brigade, 1912–15, 25th Division 1915–16; Southern District, Ireland, 1916–18; No. 5 Area, British Troops in France and Flanders, 1919; retired list, 1920; served Afghan War, 1880 (medal); Nile Expedition, 1884–85 (despatches, brevet Major, medal with clasp, Khedive's star); Hazara Expedition, 1888 (medal with clasp); Miranzai Expedition, 1891, as Brigade Major (clasp); NW F India, 1897 as Staff Officer (despatches); Tirah Expedition, 1897–98, as DAAG (despatches, medal, three clasps); South Africa, 1899–1902, on Staff, and subsequently commanding a mobile column of mounted troops, 1901–02 (severely wounded, horse killed, despatches twice, brevet Lieut-Col, Queen's medal 5 clasps, King's medal 2 clasps); European War, 1914–19, (despatches four times); High Sheriff of Co. Wexford, 1920–21. *Address:* Ely House, Wexford. *T:* 61. *Clubs:* Army and Navy, Royal Automobile.

Died 23 Nov. 1943.

DORAN, Edward; *b* Manchester, 1892. *Educ:* St Mary's, Failsworth, Manchester; Manchester Grammar School. Travelled extensively in Canada and USA; lecturer on the political, social, and industrial life of USA; authority on Western American History; was in turn Railway Worker and in British Film Production since the inception of that industry; responsible for Film Quota Act, 1927; contested (C) Silvertown, 1924; MP (U) Tottenham North, 1931–35; inventor of the Automatic Railway Level Crossing Control, Canada and USA, etc. *Publications:* The Abandoned Kingdom; Smiling Jim;

Fifty Million People *can* be wrong, etc. *Recreations:* cinematograph and landscape photography. *Address:* Wilgerwyn, Stocks Lane, East Wittering, Sussex. *Clubs:* Murrays, New Ambassadors, Unionist.

Died 15 Dec. 1945.

DORAN, Brig.-Gen. Walter Robert Butler, CB 1910; DSO 1902; retired pay; *b* 15 Dec. 1861; *s* of late General Sir John Doran, KCB, of Ely House, Wexford, Ireland; *m* 1911, Elsie, *e d* of late Emil Teichmann, of Sitka, Chislehurst; one *s*. Entered Army, the Royal Irish Regt, 1882; Captain, 1888; Major, 1901; served Egypt, 1882, including Kassassin and Tel-el-Kebir (medal with clasp, Khedive's star); Nile Expedition, 1884–85 (clasp); Hazara Expedition, 1888 (medal with clasp); Soudan, 1897–98, in charge of store depôt and hospital at Berber, and was present at the battle of Khartoum in command of an Egyptian battalion (despatches twice, Brevet Major, British and Khedive's medals with two clasps); also present in operations resulting in final defeat of the Khalifa; (in command of IXth Sudanese, despatches, Brevet Lieut-Col); served South Africa on the staff and in command of a column (Queen's medal with three clasps; King's medal with two clasps; despatches, DSO); commanded 2nd Bn Leinster Regt, 1904–08; GSO1 5th Div. 1909–12; European War, 1914–15 (despatches); Brigade Commander 17th Infantry Brigade 1912; Brig.-Gen. General Staff Aldershot Command, Sept. 1915–19. *Recreation:* golf. *Address:* Down House, Redlynch, Salisbury. *T:* Downton 47.

Died 6 Feb. 1945.

DORE, Ernest, MA, MD Camb.; FRCP London; Consulting Dermatologist, St Thomas's Hospital; Consulting Physician for Diseases of the Skin, Westminster Hospital; Consulting Physician St John's Hospital for Diseases of Skin; late Physician for Diseases of Skin, Hampstead General and North-West London Hospitals, and Consulting Physician for Skin Diseases to the Evelina Hospital for Sick Children; retd; *s* of late S. L. Dore of Pinner Hill, Middlesex. *Educ:* Mill Hill School; St John's Coll., Cambridge; St Mary's Hospital, London. *Publications:* Diseases of the Skin (with Dr Franklin), 1934; Light and X-Ray Treatment of Skin Diseases (jointly); Translator, Radium Therapy (Wickham and Degrais); articles on Skin Diseases in Practitioner's Encyclopædia of Medicine and Surgery, British Medical Journal, Lancet, and British Journal of Dermatology. *Recreation:* motoring. *Address:* 90 North End Road, NW11. *T:* Speedwell 0735. *Clubs:* Savage; Old Millhillians.

Died 27 June 1950.

DORMAN, Surg.-Gen. John Cotter, CMG 1900; MB, AMS; *b* 20 March 1852; *s* of E. B. Dorman of Kinsale; *m* 1883, Catherine Louisa, *d* of Rev. M. N. Thompson; one *s* two *d*. Entered army, 1875; Lt-Col 1898; Col 1903; Surg.-Gen. 1908; served Afghan War, 1878–80 (medal); Egypt, 1883 (medal, Khedive's star); South Africa, 1899–1902 (despatches, Queen's medal four clasps, King's medal two clasps); Hon. Physician to the King, 1910; retired, 1912. *Address:* Rampart House, Kinsale, Cork.

Died 30 Dec. 1944.

DORMER, Charles Walter C.; *see* Cottrell-Dormer.

DOTTRIDGE, Edwin Thomas, CBE 1920; *b* 1876; 2nd *s* of late Alfred James Dottridge; *m* Mabel Florence, *widow* of Clement Tulloch, *d* of Walter Hudson. Engaged in work in Italy on behalf of Foreign Office, 1916–19. Assisted Food Defence Plans Dept (Board of Trade) and Ministry of Food, 1939–41; Chevalier of the Crown of Italy, 1918. *Club:* Royal Automobile.

Died 20 Dec. 1947.

DOUGAL, Daniel, MC, TD; MD; FRCOG; Professor of Obstetrics and Gynæcology, University of Manchester; Hon. Surgeon to St Mary's Hospital, Manchester and Hon. Gynæcological Surgeon to Manchester Royal Infirmary; Examiner in Midwifery to University of Cambridge; sometime Examiner in Midwifery to Universities of Liverpool, Wales and the English Conjoint Board; *b* 4 Dec. 1884; *s* of James Dougal, MD, and Jessie Richards McLanachan; *m* 1916 Lilian Newton, *e d* of John Tweddell, Newcastle-upon-Tyne; no *c*. *Educ:* Glasgow High School; Manchester Grammar School; Manchester University, MD (Gold Medal) MB, ChB, University of Manchester. Prof. Tom Jones and Sydney Renshaw Exhibitioner; Foundation Fellow (Past Vice-Pres.) of Royal College of Obstetricians and Gynæcologists; Hon. Fellow of American Assoc. of Obstetricians, Gynæcologists and Abdominal Surgeons; Hon. Fellow of Edinburgh Obstetrical Society; Chairman of Directors, Journal of Obstetrics and Gynæcology of British Empire; Past Pres. Manchester Medical. Manchester Surgical, Manchester Pathological, and North of England Obstetrical and Gynæcological Societies; Col late RAMC (TA), Served European War in 52nd Field Ambulance and as DADMS 34th Division (MC, despatches twice, Croix de Guerre); and in War of 1939–45, as Officer Commanding Military Hospital, Davyhulme; President of the St Andrew's Society of Manchester; Member of the Society of Pewter Collectors. *Publications:* numerous papers in Obstetrical and Gynæcological subjects. *Recreations:* Collecting old pewter, fishing. *Address:* Southernhay, Fielden Park, West Didsbury. *T:* Didsbury 1434; 9 Lorne Street, Manchester 13. *T:* Ardwick 1055. *Club:* Fly Fishers'.

Died 4 June 1948.

DOUGAN, James Lockhart, CBE 1920; MA; *b* London, 1874; *s* of John Dougan, Belfast; and Margaret Lockhart, Lanark; *m* 1896, Margaret, *d* of John Morton, Glasgow; four *d*. *Educ:* Oxford University. Director of Missing and Wounded Department for Mediterranean Area British Red Cross, 1915–16; Assistant Commissioner Ministry of Food, 1917–18; member of Interallied mission of Relief to Southern Europe, Supreme Economic Council, 1919; Representative of Vienna Emergency Relief Fund, 1920–22; President, Anti-Tuberculosis Soc., Vienna; Institute for Research in Agricultural Engineering, University of Oxford, 1926; Medal of St Salvator, Vienna, 1921; Austrian Red Cross Decoration, 1921. *Publications:* Contributed to the *old* Economic Review quarterly article on the Economic position, etc.; occasional articles on economic subjects, to other publications; Editor, Abstracts of Current Literature, Agricultural Engineering; Joint Editor, Farm and Machine. *Address:* 324 Banbury Road, Oxford. *T:* Oxford 5717.

Died 27 Sept. 1941.

DOUGLAS, Lord Alfred (Bruce); *b* 22 Oct. 1870; *e surv. s* of 9th Marquess of Queensberry, and Sibyl, (*d* 1935), *y d* of Alfred Montgomery, *g d* of 1st Lord Leconfield; *m* 1902, Olive (*d* 1944; Opals, 1897; Rainbows, 1902; The Blue Bird, 1905; The Inn of Dreams, 1910), *d* of late Col F. H. Custance, CB, of Weston Hall, Norwich; one *s*. *Educ:* Winchester; Magdalen College, Oxford. Editor of the Academy, 1907–10; founder and editor of Plain English and Plain Speech; received into the Catholic Church, 1911. *Publications:* poetry: The City of the Soul, 1899; Sonnets, 1909; Collected Poems, 1919; In Excelsis, 1924; Complete Poems, 1928; New Edition in two vols, Sonnets and Lyrics, 1935; *light verse:* Tails with a Twist; The Duke of Berwick; The Placid Pug; The Pongo Papers; *biography:* Autobiography, 1929 (translated into French, German, and Spanish); Without Apology, 1938; *other:* Collected Satires, 1927; The True History of Shakespeare's Sonnets, 1933; Oscar Wilde, a Summing Up, 1940. *Address:* 1 St Ann's Court, Nizells Avenue, Hove Sussex.

Died 20 March 1945.

DOUGLAS, Archibald Campbell, FRGS; *b* 30 Dec. 1872; *e* and *o surv. s* of late Admiral Sir Archibald L. Douglas, GCB, GCVO, LLD McGill; unmarried. *Educ:* Radley; Oxford Military College. Member of the Honourable Society of Lincoln's Inn, 1889; called, 1912; served under the Foreign Office, 1894–1900, in what was then the Niger Coast Protectorate; Colonial Office in the Crown Colony of Nigeria, 1900–09; Member of the African Society, Royal Empire Society and The Japan Society; Juge britannique de la Zone Tanger, 1927; British Consul, Port Limon, 1928–29; Member of the North London Sessions; Central Criminal Court; Trinidad and Colonial Bar, WI. Served as a Transport Officer in the Benin Territories Expedition, 1898 (medal and clasp); a Political Officer to the Aro Field Force Expedition, 1901–02 (second medal and clasp); served 1902–03 (African General Service Medal); European War, served in City of London Police Reserve (medal, 1914–18); Freeman of the City of London. *Publications:* Niger Memories, by Nemo; Life of Admiral Sir Archibald L. Douglas, founder of the Japanese Navy; other contributions on African subjects in Journal West Africa and West Indies journals at Grenada and Jamaica. *Recreations:* all forms of sport, boat sailing. *Address:* 24 Old Buildings, Lincoln's Inn, WC; Castle House, N Warnborough, Basingstoke, Hants. *Clubs:* Authors', Cecil, The Knights of the Round Table.

Died 12 Dec. 1943.

DOUGLAS, Lt-Col Charles Edward, LLD (Ed.), MD, FRCSE, DPH (Camb.); retired; RAMC (T) (ret.); *b* 29 Dec. 1855; *s* of late Colonel Walter Douglas, Madras Staff Corps; *m* Elizabeth (*d* 1939), *d* of Dr J. R. Mackie; two *d. Educ:* Collegiate School and University of Edinburgh. For 47 years in medical practice, Cupar, Fife; MOH for 40 years there; volunteered for service in Boer War; attached MO 1st Batt. Worcestershire Regiment; retired active service Hon. Captain in Army; served as volunteer, territorial and regular officer for over 40 years (VD and TD); served European War 51st Div. Headquarters and commanding 51st Highland Casualty Clearing Station; Founder and for 45 years Secretary of Fife County Medical Association; has been Member of Council of British Medical Association 12 years and on many of its Committees. *Publications:* Two Medical Humorists (Harveian Oration); Observations on 70 years of Country Midwifery Practice; The Family Doctor as Specialist (Alexander Black Memorial Lecture); Lister and his contemporaries in Edinburgh, Ed. Med. Jl, Nov. 1939. *Recreations:* chess, literature. *Address:* 18 Queen's Gardens, St Andrews. *T:* St Andrews 371. *Clubs:* Royal and Ancient, St Andrews.

Died 28 Dec. 1943.

DOUGLAS, Claude, FRCS, LRCP; late Lieut-Col RAMC (T); Hon. Consulting Surgeon, Royal Infirmary, Leicester; *b* Bradford, 23 Aug. 1852; *s* of Dr Jas Douglas; *m* 1878, Louisa Bolitho, *d* of Dr Peregrine of Half Moon Street, W; one *s* one *d. Educ:* The Grange, Thorp Arch; St George's Hospital. Surgeon Leicester Provident Dispensary, 1879–86; Hon. Surgeon Royal Infirmary, Leicester, 1886–1911; late Medical Referee under Workmen's Compensation Act; ex-President, Midland Branch, BMA. *Publications:* Reports of Cases in Medical Journals. *Address:* 15 Marston Ferry Road, Oxford.

Died 9 June 1945.

DOUGLAS, Hon. Edward Archibald; Justice of the Supreme Court of Queensland since 1929; *b* Brisbane, 2 Nov. 1877; *e s* of late Hon. John Douglas, CMG, Premier of Queensland; *m* 1907, Annette Eileen, 2nd *d* of Hon. Virgil Power, formerly Justice of Supreme Court, Queensland; five *s* three *d. Educ:* St Benedict's College, Fort Augustus, Scotland. Associate to Sir Samuel Griffith, formerly Chief Justice of Queensland, 1897; to Mr Justice Power, Supreme Court, Queensland, 1900; admitted to Bar, Queensland, 1901;

commenced practice in Brisbane, 1904, and continued until 1929. *Recreations:* golf, tennis. *Address:* Ellan Vannin, Sutherland Avenue, Ascot, Brisbane, Australia. *Clubs:* Queensland, Brisbane.

Died 27 Aug. 1947.

DOUGLAS, (George) Keith; Chairman London Symphony Orchestra Concert Society; a Director of Ortus Films Ltd; Conductor of London Symphony and other orchestras; *b* 4 June 1903; *s* of late George Douglas, Chairman and Managing Director of Bradford Dyers Association, Ltd, and Elizabeth Scott; unmarried. *Educ:* Rugby; Exeter College, Oxford. Musician, now devoted to concert administration; Founder of: Bradford Philharmonic Concerts, Bradford Philharmonic Orchestra (conductor, 1925–31), Bradford Music Club; Hon. Sec. Royal Philharmonic Society, 1932–47; three years as conductor for Royal Carl Rosa Opera Company; Deputy Director of 1939 London Music Festival; Promoter of the Promenade Concerts, 1940 and 1941; owner and originator of the first Royal Albert Hall Stage set, which was made to improve the acoustics. *Publication:* Two arrangements for orchestra of extracts from Delius' opera, A Village Romeo and Juliet. *Recreation:* travelling. *Address:* North Lodge, Maze Hill, St Leonard's-on-Sea, Sussex. *Club:* Savage.

Died 4 Dec. 1949.

DOUGLAS, Lt-Col George Stuart, CIE 1919; Indian Army, retired; *b* 1879; 2nd *s* of late Arthur Douglas; *m* 1939, Mrs Lorna Osborne Mackellar, 2nd *d* of Judge Mocatta, Darling Point; two *s. Educ:* privately. Served SA War, 1899–1901; European War, 1914–19, France, E Africa and Persia (despatches, CIE, medal with clasp); Afghanistan NW Frontier, 1919; Mahsud Campaign, 1919–20; Waziristan, 1919–21 and 1921–24 (despatches, medal with 4 clasps); retired 1932. *Address:* Bowral, NSW, Australia. *Club:* United Service.

Died 28 April 1947.

DOUGLAS, Keith; *see* Douglas, George K.

DOUGLAS, O.; *see* Buchan, Anna.

DOUGLAS-HENRY, Major James, DSO 1918; OBE 1919; *b* 1881; *y s* of late Alfred Douglas-Henry, Herbert River, North Queensland; *m* 1927, Norma Margaret, 2nd *d* of late E. A. Mitchell Innes, CBE, KC. Served European War, 1915–18 (despatches, DSO, OBE).

Died Nov. 1943.

DOUGLAS-PENNANT, Hon. Violet Blanche. Commandant Women's Royal Air Force, 1918; National Health Insurance Commissioner, Wales, 1912–18; previously Member of the Education Committee, LCC; sister of 3rd Baron Penrhyn. *Publication:* Under the Searchlight, 1922. *Address:* 51 Onslow Square, SW7.

Died 12 Oct. 1945.

DOUGLASS, Walter John, LLM; late Puisne Judge of the Supreme Court of British Guiana; *b* 4 May 1863; 3rd *s* of Rev. Charles Edward Douglass, late of 14 Clifton Terrace, Brighton; unmarried. *Educ:* Brighton College; Trinity College, Cambridge. Articled to Trower, Freeling & Parkin of New Square, Lincoln's Inn, 1886; admitted Solicitor of the Supreme Court, 1889; partner in firm of Greenwood & Douglass, solicitors, Southampton, 1892–97; District Commissioner, Lagos, West Africa, 1897–1900; partner in firm of Macdonald & Douglass, St John's, Antigua, West Indies, 1901–07; called to Bar, Inner Temple, 1903; Stipendiary Magistrate, St Lucia, WI, and 1st Commissioner of Income Tax, 1907–12; Stipendiary Magistrate, British Guiana, 1912–20; Stipendiary Magistrate, Port of Spain, Trinidad, 1921–23. *Address:* Karatepi, Kennel Ride, Ascot. *Club:* Over Seas.

Died 1 Feb. 1945.

DOVE, Dame (Jane) Frances, DBE 1928; MA; JP; Governor of Girton College, Cambridge, and of Wycombe Abbey School, Bucks; *b* 27 June 1847; *d* of Rev. J. T. Dove, of Cowbitt Vicarage, Lincolnshire, 1862–1906. *Educ:* Queen's College, London; Girton College, Cambridge. Assistant Mistress Cheltenham Ladies' College and St Leonards School, St Andrews, Fife; Headmistress of St Leonards School, 1882–96; of Wycombe Abbey School, 1896–1910; Member of Bucks County Education Committee, 1910–28; received DBE in recognition of services to Education. *Publications:* part author of Work and Play, 1898; contributed to St Leonards School Gazette, 1877–1927, 1927. *Address:* 24 Priory Avenue, High Wycombe, Bucks. *T:* High Wycombe 331.

Died 21 June 1942.

DOVERDALE, 3rd Baron *cr* 1917; **Edward Alexander Partington;** *b* 25 Feb. 1904; *o s* of 2nd Baron and Hon. Clara Isabel Murray (*d* 1945), *d* of 1st Viscount Elibank; *S* father, 1935; *m* 1933, Audrey Ailsa, *d* of late Arthur Pointing, Sydney, Australia. *Educ:* Eton; Faraday House. Chairman and Managing Director Barrow Paper Mills Ltd; Chairman Brine Baths Park (Droitwich) Ltd; Borough Councillor of Droitwich, Worcs; Member Board of Governors of Hospitals for Diseases of the Chest; Cttee of Management, Brompton Hospital. *Recreations:* motoring, fishing, philatelist. *Heir:* none. *Address:* 14 Arlington House, Arlington Street, SW1. *T:* Regent 2330; Westwood Park, Droitwich Spa. *T:* Droitwich 2161. *Clubs:* Brooks's, Carlton.

Died 18 Jan. 1949 (ext).

DOW, Alexander Warren, BA; RBA 1916; artist; formerly Art Critic on the staff of Colour; writer of Palette and Chisel columns; *b* 1873; *s* of John Dow; *m* 1917, Emilie, *e d* of Rev. W. E. Smith; one *d*. *Educ:* Leys School, Cambridge; Clare College, Cambridge (prizeman). History Honours, 1895; engaged in business for 11 years; then studied Art under Norman Garstin; at the Polytechnic; under Frank Brangwyn, RA; and also in France; Vice-Pres. Old Dudley Art Society; exhibitor RA, ROI, International, RI, RHA, Liverpool, Paris Salon, RSA, NEAC, etc.; picture in the Manchester Whitworth Institute; Roman Catholic. *Publications:* articles on Art and other subjects; also many pictures for reproduction. *Recreations:* travel, opera. *Address:* 26 Temple Fortune Lane, NW11. *T:* Speedwell 4894. *Club:* Chelsea Arts.

Died 4 Oct. 1948.

DOWELL, Brig.-Gen. Arthur John William, CB 1919; CMG 1917; DL Devon; *b* 27 July 1861; *y s* of late Admiral Sir William M. Dowell, GCB of Ford, Bideford, Devon; *m* 1894, Amy Helen, *d* of late General T. C. Lyons, CB, 46 Lower Sloane Street. *Educ:* Wellington Coll.; RMC, Sandhurst. Received first commission in the Berkshire Regt, 1882; Capt. 1890; Maj. 1902; Lieut-Col, 1908; commanded 1st Batt. Royal Berkshire Regiment, to Aug. 1912; Commandant Royal Hibernian Military School, 1913–14; was ADC to Governor of Bermuda, 1894–96; Col, 1916; Brig.-General, 1916; commanded 6th Royal Berkshire Regiment, 1914–16; served Egyptian Expedition, 1882; surrender of Kafr Dowar (medal, bronze star); Soudan, Expedition, 1884–85, Nile, on transport duty (clasp); Soudan, 1885–86, Frontier Field Force, action of Giniss as ADC to Brig.-Gen. commanding 2nd Brigade; European War, 1914–16 (prom. Col, despatches twice, CMG); retired, 1918. *Address:* Tedstone, Lympstone, Devon. *Club:* Naval and Military.

Died 24 Jan. 1943.

DOWELL, Col George Cecil, CMG 1916; late Royal Artillery; *b* 28 July 1862; *s* of late Lieutenant-Colonel G. D. Dowell, VC, RM Artillery; *m* 1933, Katherine Ellen (*d* 1943), *widow* of Major W. A. Persse, RA, formerly of Roxborough, Co. Galway. *Educ:* Mannamead School,

Plymouth; Woolwich. Entered Army, 1882; was in India with British Mountain Artillery till 1914; Brigade-Major, 1898–1900; Capt. 1889; Major, 1900; Bt Lt-Col 1905; Col 1915 served Burma, 1885–86 (medal with clasp); Hazara Expedition, 1888 (clasp), and 1891 (clasp); Isazai Expedition, 1892; Chitral, 1895 (medal with clasp); Aden, 1903–04 (despatches, Bt Lt-Col); European War, 1914–18 (despatches 6 times, CMG, wounded, French Croix-de-Guerre). *Address:* Lloyds Bank, Ltd, 16 St James' St, SW1. *Club:* Naval and Military.

Died 4 Jan. 1949.

DOWLEY, Francis Michael, CIE 1941; MICE; late Regional Technical Adviser London Region Headquarters Office; *b* 29 Sept. 1885; *s* of E. Dowley, Tinvane House, Carrick-on-Suir, Ireland, and Mary Ursula Walshe; *m* 1922, Mary, *d* of Laurence and Frances Morrissey, Liverpool; two *s* three *d*. *Educ:* St Edmund's College, Ware; The Royal Indian Engineering College, Cooper's Hill. Joined Indian PWD 1907; served in Madras Presidency till 1915; served with Royal Engineers in Mesopotamia, 1915–20; in Madras PWD, 1922–40; Chief Engr Cauvey-Mettur Project, 1929–30; Chief Engr Madras, 1936–40. *Address:* Grinaun, Carrick-on-Suir, Co. Tipperary, Eire.

Died 31 May 1948.

DOWN, Captain Richard Thornton, CVO 1923; DSO 1919; RN (retired); *b* 1882; *e s* of late Capt. William Thornton Down, late of Spearpoint, Ashford, Kent. *Educ:* Tonbridge Castle School. Served South African War, 1899–1900 (medal with two clasps); China, 1900 (medal with clasp); European War, 1914–19 (despatches twice, DSO, Russian Orders of Vladimir and St Anne with swords, American Navy Cross, Italian Order of St Maurice and St Lazarus); Naval Attaché, Rome, 1922–26; retired list, 1928. *Club:* United Service.

Died 22 Aug. 1944.

DOWNES, Very Rev. Edmund Audley, MA; *b* Rawal Pindi, India, 17 Nov. 1877; *s* of late Edmund Downes, MD, Eastbourne; *m* 1906, Muriel Ashton, *e d* of late Cleland Lammimam, FRCS, Tunbridge Wells; one *s* (and 2 sons killed in the War) one *d*. *Educ:* Winchester College; University College, Oxford. 2nd Class Classical Hon. Moderations; 2nd Class Classical Hon. Finals; represented Oxford University in swimming and water polo, 1896–1900; played water polo for Sussex, 1899 and 1900; studied languages in Germany and France, 1900–02. Assistant Master at Wellington College, Berks, 1902–09; Deacon, 1905; Priest, 1906; Headmaster of St John's School, Leatherhead, 1909–32; Rector of Hadleigh, Suffolk, and Dean of Bocking, 1932–46; Rural Dean of Hadleigh, 1942–46; Member of Headmasters' Conference; Hon. Canon of Guildford, 1928. *Address:* No. 2 Cavendish Court, Blackwater Road, Eastbourne. *T:* Eastbourne 2091.

Died 19 Jan. 1950.

DOWNES, Maj.-Gen. Rupert Major, CMG 1918; VD; Knight of Grace of Order of St John of Jerusalem; AAMC; DMS to Australian Army; recently Chairman of Australian Red Cross Society; Commissioner St John Ambulance Brigade; *b* 10 Feb. 1885; *s* of late Maj.-Gen. M. F. Downes, RA, CMG; *m* 1913, Doris Mary, OBE, *d* of A. T. Robb, Toorak, Melbourne; one *s* two *d*. *Educ:* Haileybury; Ormond College, Melbourne University. MD, MS, FRACS; ADMS Anzac Mounted Division, 1916–17; DDMS Desert Mounted Corps and AIF in Egypt, 1918–19; DDMS Victoria, 1920–34. Director General of Medical Services, Australian Military and Air Forces, 1934–41; Inspector General Army Medical Services, 1941–42; Hon. Surgeon to Governor-General, 1927–31. *Address:* Iringa, Erskine Street, Malvern, Melbourne, SE3. *Clubs:* Melbourne, Naval and Military, Melbourne.

Died 5 March 1945.

DOWNIE, Major Fairbairn, CBE 1920; *b* 19 July 1880; 7th *s* of late Robert Downie of Dalmally and Newcastle-upon-Tyne; *m* Kathleen Mary, *e d* of late Rt Hon. C. A. O'Connor, last Master of the Rolls in Ireland; five *s* (and one killed on active service July 1946). *Educ:* School of Science and Art, Newcastle-upon-Tyne; privately; MIMarE. Lieut London Scottish; Capt., Oct. 1914; Staff Capt. War Office, 1916; Brevet Major, 1917; Major, 1917 (despatches, invalided from Belgium with shell concussion, Nov. 1914, 1914 Star, Allied and Victory medals); entered Ministry of Munitions, July 1915; Director and Superintendent Engineer of Ministry of Munitions, Ireland; acted as sole arbitrator in satisfactory settlement of twelve industrial strikes in Southern Ireland; visited and reported upon French and Belgian factories on behalf of War Office, 1918–19, received special mention for services in Ireland; late 14th Batt. London Regiment (London Scottish); Defence Medal. Travelled extensively in Europe, USA, Canada, Near and Far East. *Publications:* several articles on Germany and Japan. *Address:* 33 Stafford Court, Kensington, W8. *TA:* Einwod, Kens., London. *T:* Western 5357. *Club:* National Liberal.

Died 13 May 1949.

DOWNIE, John P., RSW; portrait, genre, and landscape painter; 4th *s* of late James Downie, merchant, Glasgow. *Educ:* High School, Glasgow; and Glasgow University; studied Art under Alphonse Legros at Slade School, Univ. Coll., London, 1889; also later under William Bougerau and George Ferrier in Paris. Represented in the Corporation collection of Glasgow by a portrait; and in the Permanent Collection, Paisley, by a picture. *Principal Works:* The Simple Life; A Scottish Pastoral; Nov. in Holland; is an exhibitor at the Royal Glasgow Institute, and at the various exhibitions throughout Great Britain, and—before the war—abroad. *Address:* 136 Wellington Street, Glasgow.

Died 4 April 1945.

DOWNING, George Henry, RBA 1920; Art Master Southern Boys' Secondary School, Portsmouth; *b* Portsmouth, 16 July 1878; *widower*, no *c*. *Educ:* Portsmouth. Painter in Water Colours and oils, both landscape and portraits; ARBA, 1917; Exhibitor RA, RBA, Salon, Paris; many provincial Corporation and other Art Galleries; been engaged in art teaching for over 40 years. *Publications:* Text book, The Drawing of Geometrical Models and their application to the drawing of common objects; Art applied to Window Display, 1929; contributor to Art Journals and lecturer on art subjects; many pictures reproduced in colour for publication. *Recreations:* bowls, fishing, billiards. *Address:* 102 Frensham Road, Southsea. *Club:* Southsea Waverley.

Died 10 Dec. 1940.

DOWNING, Henry Philip Burke, FSA, FRIBA (Vice-Pres. 1926–28); FSI; Member of Committee of Hon. Consulting Architects to the Incorporated Church Building Society and the London Diocesan Fund; Diocesan Surveyor for Chelmsford; Diocesan Architect for Chichester, 1918; *b* 1865; *e surv. s* of late Henry Downing and Emily, *y d* of late Captain Philip Burke; *m* 1st, 1894, Mary Florence (*d* 1932), *o d* of late Richard Latimer Southern; three *d*; 2nd, 1937, Katharine Mary, *yr d* of late D. J. Fitz-Patrick. *Educ:* S Olave's; Student of the Royal Academy. Formerly Member of Council and Vice-Chairman of the Art Standing Committee RIBA, and one of the Hon. Examiners in the History of Architecture and in Design. *Works:*—The Church of The Holy Spirit, Clapham; S Barnabas, Mitcham; S John, Walthamstow; All Saints, Hackbridge; S Augustine, Tooting, etc.; additions to Beddington, Gillingham, and Budleigh Salterton; and many works of preservation of ancient buildings, including Winchelsea Church, Sussex; Schools, among others for the Boroughs of Wimbledon; Bromley, Kent; and Bexhill; several Vicarages, houses at Kingswood, Surrey, etc. *Publications:* Architectural Relics

in Cornwall; Monograph on Church of St Bartholomew, Lostwithiel; Westminster Abbey and its Monuments; Monumental Brasses; Churches for the New Centres of Population; and Papers on Archæology of Architecture, especially Ecclesiastical. *Recreations:* walking, archæology, and sketching. *Address:* Avalon, Merton, Surrey; 12 Little College Street, Westminster Abbey, SW1. *Club:* Athenæum.

Died 26 March 1947.

DOWNS, James, OBE; JP; retired engineer; *b* Glasgow, 2 June 1856; *s* of James Downs, engineer, Hull, and Lilias Hall; *m* 1892, Ethel Ester, *o d* of William Wilson, merchant, Hull; one *s* one *d*. *Educ:* privately; Glasgow High School. During the last twenty-five years has given himself up to public (unpaid) work; during the War forged over a million shell and did extensive other work in munitions of war; commanded 5000 Special Constables under the Local Emergency Scheme for the defence of the East Coast; Vice-President of the University College of Hull. *Recreations:* cricket, golf, Rugby football, lawn tennis. *Address:* Dunedin, The Park, Hull. *Clubs:* Scottish Liberal, Edinburgh.

Died 28 Oct. 1941.

DOWSON, Sir Ernest MacLeod, KBE 1924; *b* India, 19 Nov. 1876; *o s* of late Ernest Dowson, Indian Telegraphs; *m* 1910, Hilda, *y d* of late Rev. S. Pascoe of Newquay, Cornwall; one *s*. *Educ:* Isle of Wight College; Central Technical College, London. Joined Egyptian Delta Light Railways as Asst Engineer, 1898; appointed to the Survey of Egypt, 1900; Director-General Survey of Egypt, 1909; Under-Secretary of State for Finance, Egypt, 1919; Financial Adviser to the Egyptian Govt, 1920–23; Advising the Palestine and Transjordan Governments on settlement and registration of rights to land and other land questions, 1923–28, and the Iraq and Zanzibar and Kenya Governments on the same problems, 1929–30 and 1935–40; Imperial Ottoman Order of the Osmania (4th Class) 1907; Imperial Ottoman Order of the Mejidia (3rd Class) 1912; despatches three times 1916–17; CBE 1918; Grand Cordon of the Order of the Nile, 1923; Brilliant Star of Zanzibar (2nd Class), 1937. *Address:* Downlands, Wrotham, Kent.

Died 26 June 1950.

DOWSON, Sir Hubert Arthur, Kt 1937; President of Law Society, 1936–37; Chairman Nottingham Trustee Savings Bank; *b* 26 Jan. 1866; *s* of Benjamin Dowson, Nottingham; *m* 1900, Lina Mary, *d* of Samuel Bourne, JP, Nottingham; one *s* two *d*. *Educ:* Newcastle, Staffs. Solicitor, 1888; President Nottingham Law Society, 1922 and 1936; Member Business of Courts Committee, 1934; County Court Rules Committee, 1935. *Recreations:* in former days, cricket, lawn tennis, Rugby football, hockey, lacrosse, later golf. *Address:* Lingwood Lodge, Norwich.

Died 20 July 1946.

DOXAT, Major Alexis Charles, VC; late 3rd Batt. Imperial Yeomanry; *b* 1867; 3rd *s* of late Edmund T. Doxat, Woodgreen Park, Herts; *m* 1903, Mrs Hugh Mair; no *c*. Joined Loyal Suffolk Hussars Yeomanry Cavalry in 1887, retired 1890, and then joined 7th Battalion Rifle Brigade (Prince Consorts' Own), 1892; Capt. 1894; retired 1896; served South African War (VC); European War, 1914–18; retired list with hon. rank of Major, 1918; JP, County of Southampton, 1918. *Address:* Crowthorne, Berkshire.

Died 29 Nov. 1942.

DOYLE, Col Sir Arthur Havelock James, 4th Bt *cr* 1828; retired; *b* 21 Feb. 1858; 3rd *s* of Sir Francis Hastings Doyle, 2nd Bt and Sidney, *d* of Rt Hon. C. W. Williams-Wynn, MP; *S* brother, 1933; *m* 1903, Joyce Etheldreda Mary, 2nd *d* of late Hon. Greville T. Howard; one *s* two *d*. *Educ:* RMC Sandhurst. Joined 85th King's Light Infantry, 1878; served Afghan War,

1879–80 (medal); Natal, 1881; formerly ADC to Prince Edward of Saxe Weimar; served West Coast of Africa, 1892, and with the King's Shropshire Light Infantry in South African War (Queen's medal four clasps, despatches); commanded 2nd Bt King's Shropshire Light Infantry, 1902–06; commanded 53rd District, 1914–18; JP Salop. *Publication:* 100 Years of Conflict, being a Record of 6 Generals of the Doyle Family, 1756–1856. *Recreations:* usual. *Heir:* s John, Captain Cameronians (Scottish Rifles) [b 3 Jan. 1912; m 1947, Diana, d of Col Steel. Served Palestine, 1937–38 (medal); in France, 1940 in Italy, 1943]. *Address:* Queen Manor, Boscombe, Salisbury. *Club:* Shropshire (Shrewsbury).

Died 19 Feb. 1948.

DOYLE, Sir Nicholas G.; *see* Grattan-Doyle.

D'OYLY, Sir (Hastings) Hadley, 11th Bt cr 1663; Indian Civil Service (retired) and Captain late Royal Defence Corps; b 26 Jan. 1864; s of 10th Bt and Henrietta Mary (d 1904), d of Sir Frederick Halliday, KCB; S father, 1921; m 1st, 1897, Beatrice Alice, d of F. B. Clerk, Mysore; two s one d; 2nd, 1910, Evelyn Maude, d of G. Taverner Miller; one s two d. *Educ:* Repton. Served ten years in the Behar Opium Agency and twenty years in the Andaman and Nicobar Islands Commission; Lieut in the Bihar Light Horse, 1884–94; in the Royal Defence Corps, 1914–19 (despatches). *Heir:* s Charles Hastings, b 1898.

Died 20 March 1948.

D'OYLY CARTE, Rupert; Chairman Savoy Hotel, Ltd, Berkeley Hotel Co., Ltd, and New Claridge's Hotel Co., Ltd; proprietor of the D'Oyly Carte Opera Co; b 3 Nov. 1876; y s of late Richard D'Oyly Carte; m 1907, Lady Dorothy Milner Gathorne-Hardy (against whom he obtained a decree nisi, 1941), y d of 2nd Earl of Cranbrook; one d. *Educ:* Winchester. *Club:* Garrick.

Died 12 Sept. 1948.

DOYNE, Dermot Henry; of Wells, Gorey, Co. Wexford; DL, MFH, Coollattin; b 1871; 2nd s of C. M. Doyne; m 1905, Alice Gertrude, d of Rt Hon. Frank Brooke, PC; two s two d. *Educ:* Magdalene College, Cambridge. High Sheriff, Co. Carlow, 1902. *Address:* Ardeen, Shillelagh, Co. Wicklow. *T:* Shillelagh 5. *Clubs:* Bachelors'; Kildare Street, Dublin.

Died 3 July 1942.

DRAKE, Bernard Harpur, CBE 1920; BA; Solicitor; Partner in Drake, Son and Parton, 108a Cannon Street, EC4; Member of the Council of the Law Society; b 8 June 1876; 2nd s of late Henry Drake, Winswood, Crediton, Devon; m 1900, Barbara, e d of late Daniel Meinertzhagen, Brockwood Park, Alresford, Hants; no c. *Educ:* Rugby; New College, Oxford. *Address:* 15 Sheffield Terrace, Kensington, W8. *T:* Park 6174. *Clubs:* United University, City University.

Died 14 Dec. 1941.

DRAKE, Hon. James George; b London, 26 April 1850; m 1897; one s three d. *Educ:* King's College School. Emigrated to Queensland, 1873; after few years' colonial experience entered journalism; worked for several papers, including Melbourne Argus; member of Queensland Hansard Staff; admitted to Queensland and Victorian Bars, 1882; entered Legislative Assembly, 1888; Federal Senator, 1901–06; Postmaster-General first Commonwealth Govt, 1901–03; Minister for Defence, 1903; Attorney-General of Commonwealth, 1903–04; Vice-President Federal Executive Council Australia, 1904–05; Major, late Commonwealth Defence Force. *Clubs:* Johnsonian, Brisbane.

Died 1 Aug. 1941.

DRAKE, Lt-Col Reginald John, DSO 1918; s of late Reginald Drake, ICS, and late Mrs George Shepherd, late of Becton House, Barton, Hants; m 1911, Lilian, d of T. Martin, Plympton, S Devon; two s. *Educ:* Haileybury; RMC, Sandhurst. Joined 2nd Prince of Wales (North

Staffordshire Regt), 1896; served S African War, 1900–02; European War, 1914–19 (despatches three times, DSO, American DSM, Officier Légion d'Honneur, Croix de Guerre, etc.); passed Staff College; served on Staff War Office and elsewhere in various capacities. *Address:* c/o Glyn Mills & Co., 67 Lombard St, EC3.

Died 15 Feb. 1948.

DRAKE-BROCKMAN, Maj.-Gen. Hon. Mr Justice Edmund Alfred, CB 1919; CMG 1915; DSO 1918; VD; Judge of the Commonwealth Court of Conciliation and Arbitration since 1927; Commonwealth Senator for Western Australia, 1920–26; Past President Employers' Federation of Australia; Government Whip in Senate, 1922–26; Chairman Central Coal Reference Board, 1942; b Busselton, W Australia, 21 Feb. 1884; e s of late Fredk. Slade Drake-Brockman, Surveyor-Gen. of Western Australia; m 1912, Constance, e d of W. Andrews of Hawthorn, Victoria; one s two d. *Educ:* Church of England Grammar School, Guildford. Barrister-at-law. Served European War (Dardanelles), 1914–15; France, 1916–18 (despatches, CMG); Order of Danilo, 4th Class; promoted Lieut-Col 11 May 1916; commanded 16th Batt. AIF 1916–18; commanded 4th Infantry Brigade AIF June 1918 to end of War (despatches six times, DSO); GOC 3rd Australian Division, 1939–42; an Australian representative at League of Nations Assembly, Geneva, 1925. *Recreation:* golf. *Clubs:* Melbourne, Victoria, Victoria Racing (Melbourne); Weld, Naval and Military (Perth, W Australia).

Died 1 June 1949.

DRAKOULES, Platon Soterios, LLD; University of Athens; writer, sociologist; founder of the Socialist Labour movement in Greece; Member of the Greek Parliament, 1910–11; b Ithaca, Ionian Islands, 1858; s of Eustathios Drakoules, Regent of Ithaca; m Alice Marie (d 1933), d of Henry Lambe, BA (Cantab), Truro, Cornwall. Founded in 1885 at Athens, Arden, the first journal in Greece to initiate ideals of social reform; represented Greece at the first International Socialist Congress at Paris, 1889; earliest advocate in Greece of Women's freedom and of food reform; lectured at Oxford University on Greek language and literature; founded 1901 at Oxford, Erevna, a Greek Review; translated into Greek works of Emerson, Ruskin, Krapotkin, Edward Carpenter, Henry George, George Bernard Shaw, H. S. Salt, Tolstoi; influenced public opinion towards Factory legislation and succeeded in having law against cruelty to animals passed; in European War supported the Entente; Missions: Constantinople, 1910, to promote Balkan Federation; Sofia, Belgrade, Bucarest, 1914, to promote inter-Balkan Labour entente; Lond., 1917, 1918, to represent Greece at the Labour Congress; America, 1919, to promote Labour and Hellenic Ideals; Amsterdam, 1924, New York, 1925, Vienna, 1926, Paris, 1928, Rome, 1929, and Berlin, 1931, as President of the Hellenic Garden Cities Association. *Publications:* The French Revolution, 1889; The Worker's Manual, 1891; Light from Within, 1893; Hygiene and Ethics, 1895; Crime and Humanity, 1908; The Housing Problem, 1926; Agrarian Commonwealth, 1927; Humane Education, 1932; and numerous articles on Near Eastern politics, especially in the Asiatic Review. *Recreations:* violin, chess. *Address:* Trentishoe Mansions, Charing Cross Road, WC2.

Died 27 May 1942.

DRAPER, Bernard Montagu, CB 1926; b 1875; er s of late H. M. Draper, Hemel Hempstead; m 1921, Sibyl, yr d of Rev. R. G. Carr. *Educ:* Rugby; University College, Oxford. Served in War Office from 1899; Director of Finance, War Office; retired, 1936. *Address:* The Red Cottage, Princes Risborough, Bucks.

Died 21 July 1950.

DRAPER, Hon. Thomas Percy, CBE 1918; b 29 Dec. 1864; s of Thomas Draper, of Lymm, Cheshire; m 1st, Mabel Constance (d 1930), d of late Hon. Sir Henry Parker, KCMG; four s two d; 2nd, widow of H. G. Barker. Educ: Tonbridge School; Clare College, Cambridge (Scholar), BA, Classical Tripos, 1886. Called to Bar, Inner Temple, 1891; West Australia Bar, 1892; Member of Legislative Assembly of Western Australia, 1908–12 and 1917–21; King's Counsel, 1910; Attorney-General of Western Australia, 1919–21; Judge of the Supreme Court of Western Australia, 1921–39. Address: 65 Mount St, Perth, W Australia. Clubs: Weld, Perth.

Died 11 July 1946.

DRAYTON, Miss Gertrude Drayton Grimké, CBE 1926; OBE 1918; Secretary of the Victoria League, since 1916; b 27 Dec. 1880; d of late Theodore Drayton Grimké Drayton, formerly of Clifford Manor, Newent, Glos; unmarried. Educ: private. Assistant Secretary of the Victoria League, 1911–16; Superintendent of King George and Queen Mary Victoria League Clubs for Men of the Overseas Forces in London, 1916–19 and of King George and Queen Elizabeth Victoria League Club, London, since 1939. Recreations: gardening and books. Address: Kinghams, Little Gaddesden, Herts. T: Little Gaddesden 37. Club: Ladies' Empire.

Died 18 April 1941.

DRAYTON, Sir Henry Lumley, Kt 1915; KC 1908; Chairman of the Liquor Control Board of Ontario since 1928; b Kingston, Ontario, 27 April 1869; s of Philip H. Drayton, KC, and Margaret, d of Charles W. Covernton, physician; m 1892, Edith Mary, (d 1938), d of late Joseph Cawthra, Toronto; three d; m 1943, Constance Louise Musgrave, d of late James M. Gavin, Edinburgh. Educ: England; Canada. Called to Ontario Bar, 1891; Counsel to the Railway Committee, Ontario Legislature, 1902; for the Corporation, City of Toronto, 1910; Commissioner for Ontario Government on Toronto Power Commission, 1911; Chief Commissioner, Board of Railway Commissioners, Canada, 1912–19; Member Canadian House of Commons, 1919–28; Minister of Finance, Canada, 1920–21; Minister of Immigration and Colonisation, Canada, July–Sept. 1926. Clubs: Toronto, Toronto Hunt (Toronto); Royal Ottawa Golf; Union (Victoria).

Died 29 Aug. 1950.

DREISER, Theodore; author; b Terrehaute, Ind, 27 Aug. 1871. Educ: public school, Warsaw, Indiana, and Indiana University. Began newspaper work, Chicago Globe, 1892; dramatic editor, St Louis Globe-Democrat, 1892–93; editor, Every Month, 1895–96; Smith's Magazine, 1905–06; Hampton's Magazine, 1906–07; Editor-in-Chief of the Butterick Publications, 1907–10; Merit Medal, American Academy of Arts and Letters, 1944. Publications: Sister Carrie, 1900; Jennie Gerhardt, 1911; The Financier, 1912; A Traveller at Forty, 1913; The Titan, 1914; The Genius, 1915; Plays of the Natural and the Supernatural, 1916; A Hoosier Holiday, 1916; Free and Other Stories, 1918; The Hand of the Potter, a Tragedy, 1918; Twelve Men, 1919; Hey, Rub-a-Dub-Dub; A Volume of Essays, 1920; Newspaper Days (A Book About Myself), 1922; The Color of a Great City, 1923; An American Tragedy, 1925; Moods; Cadenced and Declaimed, 1926; Chains, a second vol. of short stories, 1927; Dreiser Looks at Russia, 1928; A Gallery of Women, 1929; Dawn, 1931; Tragic America, 1932; Thoreau, 1939; America Is Worth Saving, 1941. Address: c/o G. P. Putnam's Sons, 2 W 45th St, NY City; 1015 N King's Rd, Hollywood, California.

Died 28 Dec. 1945.

DRESSEL, Otto; solo pianist; b London, 16 April 1880; y s of late Professor Richard Dressel. Educ: London; Weimar. Took up the piano as his profession, studying under his father; also a pupil of Arthur Friedheim; first appearance in London, 1902; has played in North and South America, Germany, and in France. Recreation: fond of studying ancient history. Address: 2 Sinclair Road, W14.

Died 30 Sept. 1941.

DREW, Brig.-Gen. Arthur Blanshard Hawley, CIE 1918; b 1865; s of Gen. H. R. Drew, Indian Army; m 1892, Violet, d of Maj. Walter Yeldham; four d. Educ: Wellington College. Served Hazara Expedition, 1888 (medal and clasp); Miranzai (1st and 2nd Expeditions), clasp; Chitral Relief Force, 1895 (medal and clasp); NW Frontier of India, 1897–98 (despatches, clasp) and 1901–02 (clasp); European War, 1914–16 (despatches, 1914–15 Star, British War Medal, Victory Medal, Bt-Col); Indian Frontier, 1917–18 (despatches, CIE). Address: Braemar, The Holt, Farnham, Surrey. T: Bentley 2151.

Died 24 Dec. 1947.

DREW, Hon. John Michael; Member of Legislative Council, W Australia for the Central Province, 1900–18 and since 1924; b 17 Oct. 1865; s of late Cornelius Drew; m 1895, late Mary Frances Commerford; one s. Educ: Northampton, and completed course of educational studies for journalistic career under private tuition at Fremantle, Western Australia. Commenced as a school teacher when eighteen years of age; at twenty became attached to the WA Record, eventually becoming sub-editor; manager of the Geraldton Express at twenty-five, and editor at twenty-seven; purchased the paper, 1895; Chief Secretary, W Australia and Leader of the Legislative Council, 1904–05, 1911–16, 1924–30, and 1933–36; Member Senate of WA University since 1930. Address: 18 Field Street, Mount Lawley, Western Australia. T: U 1757.

Died 17 July 1947.

DREWITT, Frederic George Dawtrey, MA, MD Oxon, FRCP, MRCS; Consulting Physician to the West London Hospital (retired); b 29 Feb. 1848; o s of Robert Dawtrey Drewitt and Frances, o d of Major C. Lane, 47th Regiment; m 1897, Hon. Caroline Mary (d 1940), y d of 3rd Baron Lilford. Educ: Winchester; Christ Church, Oxford, 2nd class Hon. Natural Science. Formerly House Physician St George's Hospital, and Gt Ormond Street Hospital for Sick Children; Physician and Asst Phys. to West London Hospital, 1882–1902; Physician to Victoria Hospital for Children, 1881–97; on Committee of British Ornithologist's Union, 1903; on Council of Zoological Society, 1904–08, 1910–16; Council of National Trust for places of Interest or Beauty since 1902; Council of Society for Promotion of Nature Reserves since 1912; on Board of Management, West London Hospital; Vice-Chairman of Committee of Management of Chelsea Physic Garden. Publications: Medical Papers and pamphlets; Bombay in Days of George IV (A Memoir of Chief Justice Sir Edward West), 2nd edn 1935; The Romance of the Apothecaries' Garden in Chelsea, 3rd ed. 1928; Latin names of Common Flowers, their Pronunciation and History, 1927; Life of Edward Jenner, Naturalist and Discoverer of Vaccination, 2nd edn 1933. Recreations: natural history, sketching and etching; Exhibited in Royal Academy, 1914–15. Address: 14 Palace Gardens Terrace, Kensington, W8. T: Bayswater 3538. Club: Savile.

Died 29 July 1942.

DREYFUS, Henry, DSc; Chairman and Managing Director of British Celanese Ltd; Director of Celanese Corporation of America; Director of Canadian Celanese, Ltd; b 7 Jan. 1882; s of late A. Dreyfus-Wahl; m 1938, Deborah Jenkinson. Educ: University of Bâle and University of Paris. Awarded Perkin Gold Medal, 1938. Address: Hyde Park Hotel, SW1. T: Sloane 9075. Clubs: British Empire, Royal Automobile, Queen's.

Died 30 Dec. 1944.

DRIESCH, Hans, PhD; Hon. LLD (Aberdeen) 1910; Hon. MD (Hamburg) 1922; Hon. ScD (Nanking, China), 1923; Professor Ordinarius Emeritus of Philosophy, University of Leipsic; *b* Kreuznach, Rhenish Prussia, 28 Oct. 1867; *s* of Paul Driesch, merchant in Hamburg; *m* 1899, Margarete Reifferscheidt; one *s* one *d*. *Educ:* Gymnasium of Hamburg; University of Freiburg; University of Munich; University of Jena (1886–89). On quitting Univ. made two expeditions (6 months each) to the Tropics (Ceylon, India, Burmah, Java); from 1891 until 1900 was spent almost entirely at Naples, at the Stazione Zoologica, founded by Dohrn, in work on the Physiology of Morphogenesis, and in private philosophical studies; in 1900 settled at Heidelberg; has made shorter or longer visits to Naples since that time; Gifford Lecturer, Aberdeen, 1907–08; Professor of Philosophy, Heidelberg, 1911; Foreign member of Linnean Society, 1912; member of Heidelberg Academy of Sciences, 1916; Professor of Philosophy, Cologne, 1920; Leipsic, 1921; visiting professor in China, Japan and USA, 1922–23; Carl Schurz Memorial Professor, Madison, Wis, 1926–27; President Society for Psychical Research, London, 1926–27; Hon. President Society for Psychical Research, Athens 1926; Member of Phi Kappa Phi (Wisconsin), 1927; Foreign Mem. Polish Acad. of Science (Krakow), 1930, of Society for Science and Art (Utrecht), 1930, of Hungarian Society of Philosophy (Budapest), 1931, of Psychological Society of Buenos Aires, 1931; Philosophical Society of England, 1934. *Publications:* Die mathematisch-mechanische Betrachtung morphologischer Probleme der Biologie, 1891; Die Biologie als Selbständige Grundwissenschaft, 1893, 2nd ed. 1911; Analytische Theorie der organischen Entwickelung, 1894; Die Localisation morphogenetischer Vorgänge: ein Beweis vitalistischen Geschehens, 1899; Die organischen Regulationen, 1901; Die Seele als elementarer Naturfactor, 1903; Naturbegriffe und Natururteile, 1904; Der Vitalismus als Geschichte und als Lehre, 1905; 2nd ed. 1923, English translation, 1914; The Science and Philosophy of the Organism, 1908, 2nd ed. 1929; German edition 1909, 4th ed. 1929, French edition, 1920; Zwei Vorträge zur Naturphilosophie, 1910; Ordnungslehre, 1912, 2nd ed. 1923; Die Logik als Aufgabe, 1913; The Problem of Individuality, 1914; Leib und Seele, 1916, 3rd ed. 1923, English translation, 1927; Wirklichkeitslehre, 1917, 3rd ed. 1930; Wissen und Denken, 1919, 2nd ed. 1922; Metaphysik, 1924; The Crisis in Psychology 1925, German 2nd ed., 1929; The Possibility of Metaphysics, 1926; Die sittliche Tat. 1927, English and Spanish translation, 1930; Der Mensch um die Welt, 1928, English translation, 1929, French and Spanish translation, 1930; Philosophische Forschungswege, 1930; Parapsychologie, 1932 (English translation); Philosophische Gegenwartsfragen, 1933; Psychical Research: the Science of the Super Normal, 1934; Die Ueberwindung des Materialismus, 1935; Die Maschine und der Organismus, 1935; Alltagsrätsel des Seelenlebens, 1938; about eighty articles in scientific and philosophical journals. *Address:* Leipsic, Zoellnerstrasse, 1. *T:* 10889.

Died 17 April 1941.

DRINKWATER, George Carr, MC, MA, RBA 1912; architect; portrait and figure painter; *b* Oxford, 10 July 1880; *s* of H. G. W. Drinkwater, FRIBA; *m* 1914, Carmen Hill, FRAM, singer; one *s*. *Educ:* Dragon School, Oxford; Rugby; Wadham College, Oxford. Pupil of Sir Thos G. Jackson, Bart, RA. Served South Africa, Trooper 59th Co. IY, 1900 (Queen's medal 3 clasps); Trooper 3rd Co. London Yeomanry, Aug. 1914; 2nd Lt East Anglian Brigade RFA, TF, 27 Jan. 1915; Brigade-Major RA, 54th Div., April 1917 to end of war; served throughout Palestine Campaign (MC, despatches twice); GSO2 Intelligence (on Egypt, HQRS) during Egyptian Rebellion, 1919; demobilised 31 May 1919; University Architecture, including New Buildings for Queens' College, Cambridge; Alterations to Brasenose College, Oxford; College Boat Houses at Oxford. *Publications:* Fifty Years of Sport, History of the University Boat Race; Centenary History of the Boat Race, 1929; The Boat Race, 1829–1938. *Recreations:* rowing (rowed in losing Oxford crews of 1902 and 1903); Leander crew, 1902. *Address:* 6 Radnor Place, W2. *T:* Paddington 5511. *Clubs:* Oxford and Cambridge, Leander.

Died May 1941.

DROWER, John Edmund, CBE 1919; *b* 1853; *s* of late George Marwood Drower; *m* Bessie Florence (*d* 1944), *d* of Edwin Chivers, Tavistock; two *s* one *d*. *Educ:* privately. In 1915 invited to enter the War Office and became Assistant Director of Army Contracts in Charge of Works until after the Armistice, when he organised the department of Building Materials Supply for the Ministry of Munitions, and became its first Director; a Fellow of the Royal Astronomical Society; Honorary corresponding member of the Fédération des Géomètres de Belgique, Officier d'Académie. *Address:* 48 Hurlingham Court, SW6.

Died 18 Jan. 1945.

DRUGHORN, Sir John Frederick, 1st Bt *cr* 1922; *b* 1862; *s* of John Drughorn; *m* 1883, Elisabeth, *d* of Lewis Berlips; four *d*. *Educ:* privately; Leiden University. Shipowner, established 1895; Director of The British and Continental Estates, Ltd. *Heir:* none. *Address:* Ifield Hall, Ifield, Sussex; The Wigwam, Gorleston-on-Sea. *T:* Crawley 73, Gorleston 140.

Died 23 Feb. 1943 (ext).

DRUMMOND, Cyril Augustus; *b* 1873; 3rd *surv. s* of Edgar Atheling Drummond (*d* 1893) and Hon. Louisa Theodosia Pennington (*d* 1886), *d* of 3rd Baron Muncaster; *m* 1st, 1898, Edith Belle (*d* 1919), *d* of Lancelot T. Wilkins; one *d*; 2nd, 1930, Mildred, *d* of Horace Humphreys; three *s* one *d*. *Educ:* Uppingham. Served South Africa 1899–1902; European War 1914–19 with Lanarkshire and 2nd Co. Lond. Yeo; Maj. 1917; DL JP Hants. *Address:* Cadland, Fawley, Southampton. *T:* Fawley 343. *Clubs:* Turf, White's; Royal Yacht Squadron, Cowes.

Died 7 Feb. 1945.

DRUMMOND, Lt-Comdr Geoffrey Heneage, VC; RNVR; Chevalier de Légion d'Honneur; with Imperial Chemical Industries, Victoria; since commencement of War has been with River Emergency Service; *b* 25 Jan. 1886; 3rd *s* of late Captain A. H. Drummond, Rifle Brigade, and Margaret Elizabeth, *d* of William Benson of Langtons, Alresford, Hants; *m* 1918, Maude Aylmer Tindal Bosanquet, of Claysmore, Middlesex; one *s* two *d*. *Educ:* Evelyn's; Eton; Christ Church, Oxford; SE Agricultural College. RNVR, Dec. 1915–Nov. 1919; served European War, 1915–18 (VC, Legion of Honour); Coronation Medal, 1937. *Address:* The Killick, Chalfont St Peter, Bucks. *T:* Victoria 4444.

Died 21 April 1941.

DRUMMOND, Isabella Martha, OBE 1934. *Educ:* Oxford Univ., MA. Headmistress Camden School for Girls, 1914–18; Headmistress North London Collegiate School for Girls, 1918–40. *Address:* c/o N London Collegiate School, Canons, Edgware.

Died 26 May 1949.

DRUMMOND, Maj.-Gen. Laurence (George), CB 1907; CBE 1919; MVO 1906; JP; DL Kent; *b* 13 March 1861; *s* of Adm. Hon. Sir James R. Drummond, GCB; *m* 1886, Katherine Mary, *d* of late Hugh Lindsay Antrobus; two *s* one *d*. *Educ:* Eton; RMC, Sandhurst. Page of Honour to Queen Victoria, 1874–77. Entered Army, Scots Guards, 1879; Captain, 1888; Major, 1897; Lt-Col 1904; Bt-Col 1904; Col 1908; Maj.-Gen. 1913; ADC to Maj.-Gen. Home District, 1892–97; Military Sec. to Governor-General of Canada, 1898–1900; Assistant Staff Officer to the Inspector-General of the

Forces, 1908; late Lt-Col commanding 3rd Batt. Scots Guards; served Bechuanaland Expedition in command of a troop of Methuen's Horse, 1884–85; commanded Guards Company in Special Service Corps; Ashantee Expedition, 1895–96 (star); Soudan Expedition, 1898 (despatches, Queen's and Egyptian medal and clasps); S Africa, on Staff 1st Division, and commanding Kimberley Mounted Infantry, 1899–1900 (despatches, Queen's medal two clasps); Commanding 7th Infantry Brigade, 1908–12; served European War, 1914–18 (despatches); retired pay, 1920. *Address:* Sissinghurst Place, Cranbrook, Kent. *Clubs:* Bath, Turf.

Died 20 May 1946.

DRUMMOND, Air Marshal Sir Peter R. M., KCB 1943; CB 1941; DSO 1918; OBE, MC; Air Member for Training on the Air Council since 1943; *b* Perth, Western Australia, 2 June 1894; *e s* of John Maxwell Drummond, Hawthornden, Western Australia; *m* 1929, Isabel Rachael Mary, *o d* of late P. F. Drake-Brockman, Inner Temple; one *s* two *d*. *Educ:* Scotch College, Perth. Served Australian Imperial Forces, Egypt and Gallipoli, 1914–15; Royal Flying Corps and RAF, Palestine, 1916–18; Sudan, 1919–20 (MC, despatches twice, DSO and bar 1918, medal with clasp, OBE); psa RAF Staff College, 1923; idc 1930; Deputy Air Officer, Commanding-in-Chief, Royal Air Force, Middle East, 1941–43. *Recreations:* winter sports, golf, tennis. *Club:* Royal Air Force.

Died 27 March 1945.

DRUMMOND, Rev. William Hamilton, DD, LLD; *b* Manchester, 1863; *e s* of late Dr James Drummond, Principal of Manchester College, Oxford; *m* 1890, Alice (*d* 1935), *d* of Walter Baily, MA; three *s* three *d*. *Educ:* University College School, University College, London (BA); studied theology at Manchester College and University of Jena. Entered ministry in Liverpool, 1887; subsequently Cross Street Chapel, Manchester, Warrington, and All Souls' Church, Belfast; Editor of the Inquirer, 1909–18; on active service with the YMCA, 1917–19; Secretary of the Hibbert Trust, 1919–38; Secretary of the International Congress of Free Christians and other Religious Liberals, 1920–29; Hon. President Manchester College, Oxford, 1938–42; Chevalier of the Order of Leopold for services to the Belgian wounded during the war; has travelled extensively since the War in Europe, America, and India in the interests of international brotherhood and peace. *Publications:* The Soul of the Nation, Essays on Religion, Patriotism and National Duty; The Book of the Hibbert Trust; numerous articles and reviews. *Address:* 15 Rawlinson Road, Oxford. *T:* 5278. *Club:* English-speaking Union.

Died 17 March 1945.

DRUMMOND-HAY, Francis Edward; *see* Hay, F. E. D.

DRURY, Alfred, RA 1913; ARCA; sculptor; *b* London, 11 Nov. 1856; *m* Phebe Maud (*d* 1928). *Educ:* New College School, Oxford. Studied in the Oxford School of Art; National Art Training School, South Kensington; Paris under Dalon. *Works include:* The Triumph of Silenus, 1885; Priestley and Lamp, 1899; Prophetess of Fate and Little Duchess, 1900; Gold Medal, Paris Exhibition, 1900; Sir John Cockburn, Alexander MacLeod, and Professor Schuster, 1902; King Edward VII, 1903; also colossal statues of Queen Victoria for Bradford and Portsmouth, 1903; Queen Victoria Memorial (Wellington), bronze statue of St George for Clifton College (Bristol), decoration for exterior of War Office (8 groups), 1905; War Memorial for Warrington, 1907; decoration for front of Victoria and Albert Museum, 1909; four bronze figures for Vauxhall Bridge, 1909; statue (bronze) of the late Duke of Devonshire for Eastbourne, 1910; marble statue of Elizabeth Fry for New Central Criminal Court, marble statue of King Edward VII for Birmingham University, 1912; King Edward VII Memorial, Aberdeen, 1913; King Edward

VII Memorial Statue for Sheffield, marble bust of Lieut-Gen. Sir Robert Baden-Powell, 1915; marble statue, Lilith (diploma work), 1916; Recumbent statue of Father Stanton for St Alban's Holborn, 1917; War Memorial for Hertford, Hart gazing; War Memorial for Pershore Abbey Church, Victory, 1921; London Troops Memorial, 1923; Kidderminster, 1922; Malvern College, 1924; Denstone College, 1925; Statue of Sir Joshua Reynolds, PRA, in quadrangle, Burlington House, 1931. *Recreations:* Rosearian, music. *Address:* Lancaster Lodge, Lancaster Road, SW19. *T:* Wimbledon 0704. *Clubs:* Arts, Royal Academy.

Died 24 Dec. 1944.

DRURY, Henry Cooke, MD, University of Dublin; FRCPI; Consulting Physician, Sir P. Dun's Hospital, Dublin; Consulting Physician, Rotunda Hospital; late Physician, Cork Street Fever Hospital; late FR Acad. Med. I, late FRSAI; *b* 28 Oct. 1860; 5th *s* of late Thomas Drury of Dartry, Rathmines, Dublin, JP, and Marion, *d* of John Girdwood of Corstorphine, Edinburgh; *m* 1891, Florence, *d* of late Edmund J. Figgis, JP, of Glenasmoil, Rathmines, Dublin; one *d*. *Educ:* Trinity Coll., Dublin. Late temp. Lieut-Col, RAMC, France. *Address:* 48 Fitzwilliam Square, W Dublin. *T:* 61379. *Clubs:* University, Dublin.

Died 11 Sept. 1944.

DRURY, Henry George, MVO 1904; *b* 1839; *m* 1871, Elizabeth Rose (*d* 1937), *d* of J. W. Seear. Was Superintendent of the Line, Great Eastern Railway; ex-Major Engineer and Railway Volunteer Staff Corps. *Address:* 32 Maxwell Road, Northwood, Middlesex. *T:* 192.

Died 28 Jan. 1941.

DRURY, Lt-Col William Price, CBE 1919; Royal Marines (retired); *b* 8 Nov. 1861; *s* of Naval, *g s* of Royal Marine officer; *m e d* of late Rev. and Mrs Pender-Cudlip (Annie Thomas). *Educ:* Brentwood School, Essex; Plymouth College. Served much at sea on China and Mediterranean Stations and elsewhere; was landed in command of the Marines of the Camperdown and Astræa for service in Crete on the occasion of the massacre of Christians and attack on the British camp by Bashi-Bazouks, Sept. 1898; Member of Naval Intelligence Department, 1900–01; rejoined the Royal Marines on out-break of war; served as Intelligence Officer on staff of Garrison Commander, Plymouth, and on staff of Naval C-in-C, Devonport; demobilised, March 1919; Mayor of Saltash, 1929–30; and 1930–31; Freeman of the Borough, 1935; Home Guard (Admin.) on formation. *Publications:* Bearers of the Burden, 1899; The Passing of the Flagship, 1902; The Shadow on the Quarter Deck, 1903; The Peradventures of Private Pagett, 1904; The Tadpole of an Archangel, 1904; Men at Arms, 1906; Long Bow and Broad Arrow, 1911; All the King's Men, 1919; The Incendiaries, 1922; Tales of Our Ancestors, 1925–1927; In Many Parts; the Memoirs of a Marine, 1926; A Book of St George, 1927; The Flag Lieutenant in China, 1929; Pagett Calling, 1930; Eight Bells, 1932; The Flag Lieutenant, 1934; King's Blood, 1935; A Regency Rascal, 1937; Fightingcocks, 1939. *Film:* The Further Adventures of the Flag Lieutenant. *Plays:* A Privy Council, 1905; The Flag Lieutenant, 1908; The Admiral Speaks, 1910; and several others. *Address:* Killigrew Cottage, Saltash, Cornwall. *T:* Saltash 2109.

Died 21 Jan. 1949.

DRURY-LOWE, Vice-Adm. Sidney Robert, CMG 1916, RN; *b* 19 Oct. 1871; 2nd *s* of Lt-Col R. H. Drury-Lowe, Grenadier Guards; *m* 1909, Clare Susan, *d* of Captain Hon. Fred. W. Charteris, RN, and Lady Louisa Charteris; one *d*. Joined HMS Britannia, 1885; HMS Calliope, 1889 (hurricane at Samoa); obtained five first-class certificates; Lieut 1892; Commander, 1902; served in Hyacinth in Somaliland Expedition, 1904; commanded Seamen Battalion of Naval Brigade at capture of Illig (despatches, medal, clasp); Captain, 1909; served European War, 1914–18, Mediterranean, German E Africa, Dardanelles, 1915–16 and Grand Fleet, 1916–19 (despatches, CMG); Rear-Adm. 1920; retired, 1921; Vice-Adm. retired, 1925. *Recreations:* tennis, golf. *Club:* United Service.

Died 24 Jan. 1945.

DRYLAND, Alfred, CBE 1930; MICE; Independent Chairman British Granite and Whinstone Fed; *b* 2 March 1865; *s* of William and Sarah Dryland; *m* 1885, Edith Rose Constance, *d* of H. R. Clarke, Magistrate and Collector, HM Indian Service; two *s* one *d. Educ:* Farnham Grammar School. Articled to A. W. Conquest, AMICE, 1880; Borough Surveyor of Deal, 1883; Assistant County Surveyor of Kent, 1890; County Surveyor of Hereford, 1898; Wilts, 1906; Surrey, 1908; County Engineer of Middlesex, 1920–32; Past President County Surveyors' Society and Institution of Municipal and County Engineers; Member Engineering Advisory Committee HM (late) Road Board; carried out the Great West, Great Cambridge, North Circular, Barnet and Watford Bypasses; Western Avenue and many other arterial roads and bridges in Middlesex; the Engineer to the joint Committee of Middlesex and Surrey for new bridges over the Thames at Chiswick and Richmond; Mayor of Royal Borough of Kingston on Thames, 1935–36–1937. *Publications:* many articles in the Technical press and papers to the Institutions on Engineering subjects, particularly roads and bridges. *Recreations:* golf, shooting. *Address:* 44 Crescent Road, Kingston Hill, Surrey. *T:* Kingston 2672.

Died 26 Nov. 1946.

DU BOULAY, Sir James Houssemayne, KCIE 1911; CIE 1906; CSI 1916; *b* 15 April 1868; *s* of late Rev. J. T. H. Du Boulay, Housemaster at Winchester; *m* 1901, Freda Elais, *d* of Alfred Howell; one *s* two *d. Educ:* Winchester; Balliol College, Oxford. Entered Indian Civil Service, 1889; Assistant Collector and Magistrate, Bombay Presidency; Deputy Municipal Commissioner on Plague Duty, Bombay, 1897–1900; acted as Private Secretary to Lord Northcote, Governor of Bombay, 1901; the Lord Lamington, Governor of Bombay, 1903–07; Secretary to Government, Bombay, 1909; Private Secretary to Viceroy (Lord Hardinge), 1910–196; Secretary to the Government of India, Home Department, 1916; Member Indian Jails Committee, 1919–20; Bursar Winchester College, 1927–35. *Address:* Oxenbourne, East Meon, Hants.

Died 26 Nov. 1945.

DUBUC, Arthur Edouard, DSO 1917; ADC; Chief Engineer Department of Railways and Canals, Ottawa, Ont, since 1924; *b* Montreal, 18 May 1880; *s* of late Arthur Dubuc and Angeline Racicot; unmarried. *Educ:* Mount St Louis Institute and Ecole Polytechnique, University of Montreal; BSc, MEIC, Corporations of Professional Engineers of Quebec and Ontario. Professional Institute of the Civil Service of Canada; Governor, Notre Dame Hospital, Montreal; with Dominion Government as Assistant Engineer Department of Public Works, 1901–12; District Engineer, Montreal, 1912–19; Superintending Canal Engineer, Quebec Canals, Department of Railways and Canals, Montreal, 1919–24; enlisted with 22nd French Canadian Battalion as Captain, Oct. 1914; Lt-Col 1917–18; was at Ypres, Vierstraat, Kemmel, Courcelette; commanded battalion at Regina trench, 1916; Vimy Ridge, 1917; Neuville-Vitasse, Mercatel, Amiens, Méharicourt and Arras to Chérisy, 1918 (wounded thrice, DSO and bar, Chevalier de la Légion d'Honneur, despatches twice); demobilised, 1919; Colonel in command of 11th Canadian Infantry Brigade, 1920; Reserve of Officers, 1924; Member of Royal Commission to investigate Soldiers' Pensions and Re-establishment, 1922–24; Hon. ADC to the Governor-General, 1923. *Address:* 63 Roxborough Apartments, Ottawa. *T:* Queen 6885. *Clubs:* Engineers', Canadian, University, Cercle Universitaire, United Services, Montreal; Hermitage Country, Magog, PQ; Rideau, Country, Ottawa; Laval sur le Lac, PQ.

Died 6 Sept. 1944.

DUCANE, Gen. Sir John (Philip), GCB 1928; KCB 1916; CB 1910; Deputy Chairman De Beers Consolidated Mines; Director other Diamond Mining Companies and African Explosives and Industries; *b* 5 May 1865; 2nd *s* of Sir Chas Du Cane; KCMG, of Braxted Park, Essex, and Hon. Georgina, *d* of Baron Lyndhurst; *m* 1914, Ethel, *widow* of Christopher Head, *d* of Hillyar Chapman of Kilhendre, Salop. Lieut RA 1884; Capt., 1893; Major, 1900; Lt-Col 1902; Col 1908; Maj.-Gen. 1915; Lt-Gen. 1919; General, 1926; DAAG Staff College, 1905–07; General Staff Officer, 1st Grade, Headquarters of Army, 1908–10; CRA 3rd Division, 1911–12; Staff Officer to Inspector-General of the Home Forces, 1913–14; served S Africa, 1899–1902 (despatches, Brevet Lt-Col, Queen's medal 5 clasps, King's medal 2 clasps); European War, Brig.-Gen., General Staff, III Corps, 1914; Maj.-Gen., RA, GHQ, 1915; Special Appointment, Ministry of Munitions, 1916; Commanded XV Corps, 1916–18; British Representative with Marshal Foch, 1918 (despatches 7 times); Master-Gen. of Ordnance, 1920–23; GOC in C, Western Command, 1923–24; General Officer Commanding-in-Chief British Army of the Rhine, 1924–27; ADC General to the King, 1926–30; Governor and Commander-in-Chief, Malta, 1927–31; retired pay, 1931. *Address:* 25 Berkeley Square, W1. *T:* Mayfair 4493. *Club:* Turf.

Died 5 April 1947.

DUCHEMIN, H(enry) P(ope); KC 1924; Editor Sydney Post-Record, Nova Scotia, since 1914; *b* Charlottestown, Prince Edward Island, Canada. *Educ:* Prince of Wales College, Charlottetown; Dalhousie University, Halifax, NS (University Medallist, high hons in Classics). English Master at Pictou Acad., 1896–1901; admitted to Bar of Nova Scotia, 1901; Pres. and Managing Director of Post Publishing Co., Ltd, Sydney, Nova Scotia; President of The Canadian Press, 1937–39, Hon. Pres., 1944–46; Governor of Dalhousie University since 1937. *Address:* 70 George Street, Sydney, Nova Scotia, Canada.

Died 21 May 1950.

DUCKWORTH, Sir Edward Dyce, 2nd Bt *cr* 1909; ICS; retired, 1927; *b* 10 July 1875; *e s* of Sir Dyce Duckworth, 1st Bt and 1st wife, Annie Alicia, *d* of A. Alexander Hopkins, Limavady, and *widow* of John Smith, of Mickleham Hall, near Dorking; *S* father 1928; *m* 1913, Cecil Gertrude, *y d* of Robert E. Leman; one *s* one *d. Educ:* Marlborough; Pembroke College, Oxford. Knight of Grace, Order of St John of Jerusalem. Formerly Judge High Court of Judicature at Rangoon, Burma; JP Suffolk; Member of Rating Appeal Committee and Chairman of County Licensing Committee of Quarter Sessions, East Suffolk; Member Standing Joint Committee County Council; represents Oxford University on Board of Governors of Ipswich School. *Recreations:* golf, shooting, fishing. *Heir: s* Richard Dyce, Capt. RA [*b* 30 Sept. 1918; *m* 1942, Violet Alison, *o d* of Lt-Col G. B. Wauhope, DSO; one *s*]. *Address:* Telport, Beccles, Suffolk. *Clubs:* East India and Sports; County, Ipswich.

Died 5 Aug. 1945.

DUCKWORTH, John; *b* 1 Nov. 1863; *s* of late George Duckworth; *m* 1890, Ruth, *d* of late William Sutcliffe, JP, Co. Lancaster. MP (L) Blackburn, 1923–29. *Address:* The Knolle, Wilpshire, nr Blackburn. *T:* 33; Greenbank, Grindleton, Yorks. *T:* 12. *Club:* National Liberal.

Died 22 Jan. 1946.

DUCLOS, Arnold Willard, BA, BCL, KC; Registrar of the Exchequer Court of Canada since 1919; Barrister; *b* 7 April 1874; *s* of Rev. R. P. Duclos and Sophie Jeanrenaud; *m* 1900; two *d*. *Educ:* Montreal High School; McGill University. Practised law, 1899–1919, first with Henry Aylen, KC, then EB Devlin, KC, MP, and since 1919 in present position; Asst Editor Quebec Law Reports for some years; Deputy Registrar and Law Reporter for few years; now Editor of the Exchequer Court Reports and Registrar; brought out 6th Ed. of Sir John Bourinot's work, How Canada is Governed. *Recreations:* golf, curling. *Address:* 195 James Street, Ottawa; c/o The Exchequer Court of Canada, Ottawa, Canada.

Died 30 Nov. 1947.

DU CROS, Alfred; *b* 10 Dec. 1868; *e s* of late W. H. Du Cros; *m* 1st, 1901, Mrs Louise Pemberton Hincks, New Orleans (*d* 1927); 2nd, 1933, Mrs Ethel Maude Hude. MP (C) Bow and Bromley, 1910. *Clubs:* Carlton, Devonshire.

Died 21 Dec. 1946.

DUDENEY, Mrs Henry; *m* Henry Ernest Dudeney (*d* 1930); one *d*. *Publications:* The Maternity of Harriott Wicken; The Orchard Thief; Maid's Money; Set to Partners; The Secret Son; Manhood End; Beanstalk; Quince Alley; Seed Pods; Brighton Beach; Traveller's Rest; The House in the High Street; Trundle Square; Portrait of Ellen; Put up the Shutters; Petty Cash; and other novels. *Address:* Castle Precincts House, Lewes, Sussex.

Died 21 Nov. 1945.

DUDGEON, Maj.-Gen. Frederick Annesley, CB 1915; South Lancs Regt; *b* 16 June 1866; *m* 1905, Florence Edith, *d* of late H. Black Stewart, Balnakeilly, Perth; one *s* one *d*. Entered Army, 1885; Captain, 1893; Adjutant, 1896–1900; Major, 1902; Lt-Col 1912; Colonel, 1916; Major-General, 1921; DAAG, India, 1900–05 and 1909–11; AAG, 1914; served European War, 1914–18; Battalion Commander, 1915; Brigade Commander, 1915–17; Divisional Commander, 1917–18 (despatches six times, CB); GOC 50th (Northumbrian) Division TA, 1923–27; retired pay, 1927; Officer Legion of Honour; Officer Order St Maurice and St Lazarus (Italy).

Died 28 May 1943.

DUDLEY, Col George de Someri; RAOC, retired; *b* Mount Aboo, Rajpootana, India, 29 Aug. 1874; *s* of Brig.-Surgeon Lt-Col W. E. Dudley, AMD, and A. M. Sealy; *m* 1900, Ruth Muriel, 2nd *d* of late Colonel J. R. Marett, ISC, Jersey; one *d*. *Educ:* Somerset and Bath Colleges; RMA, Woolwich. Entered Royal Artillery, 1894; transferred to Army Ordnance Dept 1907; served European War, France, and Belgium, 1915–18, Italy, 1918 (despatches five times, Bt Lt-Col, CMG); Disposal Board Commissioner, Italy, 1919–20; Commander, Crown of Italy; retired pay, 1931. *Address:* Highfield, Bonchurch, Isle of Wight.

Died 8 June 1941.

DUFF, Sir Arthur Cuninghame G.; *see* Grant-Duff.

DUFF, Col Charles de Vertus, CBE 1919; lawn tennis, golf and badminton coach and lecturer; *b* 4 Oct. 1870; *y s* of late Jekyl Chalmers Duff, JP, India; *m* 1st, 1895, Minnie (*d* 1932), *d* of Maj. G. C. Robinson, RA, India; no *c*; 2nd, 1935, Hilda Mary Dormer, *o d* of F. G. Gibson, Leamington Spa. *Educ:* Cranleigh. France and Germany for Consular Service. Magistrate, Brit. Central Africa, 1893–95; served South African War (OC French's Scouts) (despatches, Queen's medal five clasps, King's medal two clasps); received thanks of Colony of Natal, 1907; European War, 1915–19 (Colonel, South African Forces) (CBE, despatches); lecturer, with demonstrations and for BBC; maker of first Phonofilm picture demonstrating natural laws in lawn tennis; Inventor of Golf Doctor. *Publications:* Lawn Tennis; Spin and Swerve; You and Your Golf; Press contributor (Observer, Daily Mail, Evening Standard, etc.). *Recreation:* painting. *Address:* Corners, Florida Rd, Ferring, Worthing, Sussex. *T:* Goring 41022.

Died 6 Feb. 1950.

DUFF, Francis Bluett; *b* 6 Sept. 1875; *e s* of late Francis Bluett Duff, St Mary's Scilly, and Margretta Frances Sandys, Co. Waterford, Ireland; *m* Ione, *o d* of late Alfred Standring, JP, Leek, Staffs; two *d*. *Educ:* St Paul's School; King's College, Cambridge (Exhibitioner). Called to Bar, Inner Temple, 1901; Treasury Solicitors' Dept; Manager, Legal Dept, Northcliffe Press, 1907–16; Director Times Book Club, Ltd; commissioned Royal Flying Corps, 1916; service Ypres Salient; transferred War Office, Military Intelligence Staff; Court Martial Officer and Judge Advocate GHQ France, Captain; Legal Asst Board of Education, 1919; Legal Adviser Imperial War Graves Commission, France; British delegate International Law Congress, Buenos Aires, 1922. Senior Assistant Legal Branch, Ministry of Fuel and Power, 1943. *Publications:* numerous signed articles on special subjects in London and Provincial Press; contributor to Sir John Hammerton's Illustrated History of the Great War; author of radio plays for the BBC; The Trial of Eugene Aram; The Trial of Mary Blandy; The First Trunk Murder. *Recreation:* swimming. *Club:* Union Society (Cambridge).

Died 4 Dec. 1947.

DUFF, James Augustine; First Chairman Education Committee; Chairman Finance Committee; JP Co. Boro of Belfast; High Sheriff (County of Belfast), 1923; Past President, Belfast Scottish Association; *b* Glasgow, 27 Sept. 1872; *m* 1896, Jeanie McLean; one *s*. *Educ:* Board School, Glasgow; Glasgow and West of Scotland Technical College. Business in Belfast, 1892–1914; retired, 1914; given all time and energy since to public work in Belfast; President St Andrew's Society, 1925–26. *Publication:* Treatises on Non-Conducting Coverings and Robert Burns. *Recreations:* literature, golf, billiards. *Address:* Members' Club Room, City Hall, Belfast; Caroa, 186 Belmont Road, Belfast.

Died 4 March 1943.

DUFF, John Wight, FBA 1930; MA (Oxon and Aber.), Hon. DLitt (Durham), DLitt (Oxon), LLD (Aber.); Hon. Fellow of Pembroke College, Oxford; Professor of Classics, Armstrong College, Newcastle-on-Tyne, 1898–1933 now Emeritus Professor; Vice-Principal, 1918, 1921–24, 1926–33; Acting-Principal, 1918–19; Sather Classical Professor, Berkeley, California, 1935–36; a Co-editor of Oxford Classical Dictionary, in progress since 1937; *b* Dundee, 4 Sept. 1866; *s* of late William Duff, ironfounder, and Sarah Fergusson Wight; *nephew* of late Rev. Prof. Duff, DD, LLD, Edinburgh; *m* 1897, Lizzie Taylor Mackay, Bewdley, Worcestershire; one *s* one *d*. *Educ:* Aberdeen Grammar School (Latin dux); Aberdeen University (Simpson Greek Prizeman); Pembroke College, Oxford (scholar); 1st class Classical Modns; 1st class Lit. Hum.; Leipzig University. Assistant-Professor of Greek, Aberdeen, 1891–93; Professor of Classics and English, at Newcastle, 1893–98; and after the creation of separate chairs, Professor of Classics; Examiner in Classics for Universities of Aberdeen, Oxford, Manchester, Liverpool, Leeds, Sheffield, Bristol, and Birmingham. Vice-President of Classical Association of England and Wales; has visited many remains of classical antiquity in Provence, Italy, Greece, Crete, Asia Minor and Tunis; Pres., Society of Antiquaries, Newcastle, 1937–39; on governing bodies of several schools and on Tyneside Scottish Committee, 1914–19 and again 1939–44. *Publications:* reviews, papers on Greek travel, verse translations from German, French, and Latin, etc.; contributions to Journal of Roman Studies, Cambridge Ancient History, etc.; edition, with introduction, of Johnson's Lives of Milton and Addison, 1900; Byron; Selected Poetry, 1904; A Literary History of Rome (from Origins to Close of Golden Age), 1909

(2nd ed. 1910, 9th impression, 1931); Writers of Rome, 1923 (Spanish trans. 1928); A Literary History of Rome in the Silver Age, 1927; Minor Latin Poets (Loeb Library) (with A. M. Duff) 1934; Roman Satire: Its Outlook on Social Life, 1936. *Recreations:* book-buying, foreign travel. *Address:* 16 Victoria Square, Newcastle-upon-Tyne, 2.

Died 8 Dec. 1944.

DUFF, Stanley Lewis, CBE 1927; Secretary, Ancient Order of Foresters' Friendly Society since 1919; Secretary, National Conference of Friendly Societies since 1928; Chairman Insurance Unemployment Board; Chairman Advisory Committee to the Higher Education Sub-Committee of the LCC; Vice-President Insurance Institute of London; Member of Council Chartered Insurance Institute; *b* Fife, 1881; *s* of Peter Duff; *m* 1916, Rose, *d* of John Jackson, Biscot, Beds; four *d. Educ:* Addey and Stanhope School, London. Chairman of Consultative Council to Minister of Health upon National Health Insurance, 1924–29; Chairman Dental Benefit Joint Committee, 1926–29; President Faculty of Insurance, 1928–29. *Address:* 17 Russell Square, WC1; 35 Hills Lane, Shrewsbury. *T:* Shrewsbury 3506.

Died 28 April 1943.

DUFFERIN AND AVA, 4th Marquess of, *cr* 1888; **Basil Sheridan Hamilton-Temple-Blackwood;** Baron Dufferin and Claneboye, Ireland, 1800; Baron Clandeboye, UK, 1850; Earl of Dufferin, Viscount Clandeboye, 1871; Earl of Ava, 1888, and Bt; special mission abroad for Ministry of Information since 1942; *b* 6 April 1909; *o s* of 3rd Marquess and Brenda (who *m* 2nd, 1932, Henry C. S. A. Somerset, OBE), *e d* of Robert Woodhouse, Oxford House, Bishops Stortford; *S* father, 1930; *m* 1930, Maureen, 2nd *d* of Hon. (Arthur) Ernest Guinness, MA; one *s* two *d. Educ:* Eton; Balliol College, Oxford. Member, Indian Franchise Committee, 1932; Parliamentary Private Secretary to Marquess of Lothian, Under-Secretary of State for India, 1932; to Lord Irwin (now Viscount Halifax), President of the Board of Education, Nov. 1932–June 1935; to Viscount Halifax, Secretary of State for War, June–Nov. 1935; and to Viscount Halifax, Lord Privy Seal, 1935–36; Parliamentary Under-Secretary of State for the Colonies, 1937–40; 2nd Lieut Royal Horse Guards, 1940; Lord-in-Waiting, 1936–37; Director of Empire Division, Ministry of Information, 1941–42. *Heir: s* Earl of Ava, *b* 1938. *Address:* Clandeboye, Northern Ireland. *Clubs:* Carlton, White's, Buck's.

Died 25 March 1945.

DUGDALE, Col Arthur, CMG 1915; DSO 1919; late Commanding QO Oxfordshire Hussars; *b* 1869; *s* of late James Dugdale of Sezincote, Moreton-in-Marsh; *m* 1904, Ethel Innes, *e d* of late Col John Sherston, DSO, the Rifle Brigade; one *s. Educ:* Winchester; Christ Church, Oxford, MA. *Address:* Sezincote, Moreton-in-Marsh. *T:* Moreton-in-Marsh 22. *Club:* Cavalry.

Died 27 April 1941.

DUGDALE, Mrs Edgar T. S.; Blanche Elizabeth Campbell; *d* of late Lt-Col Eustace Balfour, *b* of 1st and 2nd Earls of Balfour, and of Lady Frances Balfour, *d* of 8th Duke of Argyll; *m* Edgar Trevelyan Stratford Dugdale, 2nd *s* of late W. S. Dugdale, Merevale Hall, Warwickshire; one *s* one *d. Educ:* privately. Employed from 1915 to 1919 in Naval Intelligence Dept 32; from 1920 to 1928 head of Intelligence Dept of League of Nations Union; Member of Executive Committee of League of Nations Union; Member of British Government's Delegation to League of Nations Assembly, 1932. *Publications:* Life of Arthur James Balfour, First Earl of Balfour, 2 vols 1936; Family Homespun, 1940. *Address:* 28 Albert Court, SW7. *Club:* Allies.

Died 16 May 1948.

DUGDALE, Rev. Sydney, MA; Prebendary Emeritus in Hereford Cathedral; 4th *s* of John Dugdale of Llwyn Llanfyllin, Montgomeryshire; *m* 1st, 1886, Edith, *d* of W. B. Marshall of Bellefield, New Brighton; 2nd, 1905, Phyllis (*d* 1935), *d* of Rev. R. E. Price, Rector of Moreton, Oswestry; two *s* four *d. Educ:* Rugby School; BNC Oxford, 2nd in Theology. Deacon, 1884; Priest, 1885; Curate St Anne, Limehouse, 1884–86; St Thomas, Salisbury, 1886–89; St Martin, Salisbury, 1889–91; Motcombe, 1891–92; Vicar of Motcombe, 1892–98; Westbury, Wilts, 1898–1904; Lower Beeding, Sussex, 1904–09; Whitchurch, Salop, 1909–19. *Address:* Aston Hall, Aston-on-Clun, Craven Arms, Shropshire. *T:* Little Brampton 2.

Died 10 Feb. 1942.

DUGGAN, Major Harold Joseph, DSO 1919; MC; Farmer; *b* 1896; *s* of Michael Joseph and Margaret Ballesty; *m* 1923, Mary Hope, Buenos Aires; three *s* two *d. Educ:* Clayesmore. Served European War, 1914–19 (despatches, DSO, MC and bar). *Recreations:* golf, tennis. *Address:* Bartolomé Mitre 441, Buenos Aires, Argentine. *Clubs:* Argentine; Strangers', Hurlingham, Buenos Aires.

Died 10 Jan. 1942.

DUGGAN, Hubert John; MP (C) Acton, Middlesex since 1931; *b* 24 July 1904; *s* of late Alfred Duggan and Marchioness Curzon of Kedleston, GBE. *Educ:* Eton. 2nd Lieut, Life Guards, 1924–28; contested (C) East Ham South, 1929; Parliamentary Private Secretary to Captain D. Euan Wallace, MC, MP, Civil Lord of the Admiralty, 1931–35; Lieut Life Guards, 1939, and Captain, 1940. *Clubs:* White's, Buck's.

Died 25 Oct. 1943.

DUIGAN, Maj.-Gen. Sir John Evelyn, KBE 1940; CB 1937; DSO 1917; *b* 30 March 1882; *m* Nora Hanley (*d* 1940), Tullamore. *Educ:* Wanganui College. Served S Africa, 1900–01 (Queen's medal and four clasps); European War, 1915–17 (despatches, DSO); OC Northern Command, New Zealand, 1931–37; CGS, NZ Military Forces, 1937–41.

Died 9 Jan. 1950.

DUKE, Lt-Col Augustus Cecil Hare, CMG 1919; DSO 1918; MA; Fellow of Balliol College, 1929; 2nd *s* of late Rev. Canon J. Hare Duke, DD; *m* 1908, Violet Elliott, Melbourne, Australia; no *c. Educ:* Bradfield College; Norwich Grammar School; St Catharine's College, Cambridge. 2nd Lieut Royal Artillery, 1900; retired, 1913; served S African War, 1901–02; served European War, DAQMG 57th Division, AA and QMG 50th Division (despatches, awarded CMG, DSO); Home Bursar, Balliol College, Oxford, 1920–39; Member of Committee on Physical Education (BMA), 1935–36; Oxford City Councillor, 1929–31; Governor the Radcliffe Infirmary, 1932–39; President Oxford Safety First Council, 1933–37; Senior Treasurer, President Oxford University Boxing Club, 1921–39; Member of Executive Committee Anti-Noise League, 1933–39; MA Oxon (by decree), 1924. *Recreations:* The Turf, gardening. *Address:* 39 Cromwell Road, Teddington. *T:* Kingston 0916.

Died 6 Feb. 1943.

DUKESTON, 1st Baron *cr* 1947, of Warrington; **Charles Dukes,** CBE 1942; Director of Bank of England since 1947; late General Secretary, National Union of General and Municipal Workers; Member of Consultative Comm. to Minister of Labour; *b* Stourbridge, 1881. MP (Lab) Warrington, 1923–24, and 1929–31; Member of the Trades Union Congress General Council, 1934–47. *Recreations:* photography and cinematography. *Heir:* none. *Address:* Woodfield, Copperkins Lane, Amersham, Bucks.

Died 14 May 1948 (ext).

DUMAS, Adm. Philip Wylie, CB 1914; CVO 1910; Royal Navy, retired; *b* 9 March 1868; 3rd *s* of late H. J. P. Dumas, JP; *m* 1911, Dorothy, *o d* of late Admiral Sir George Egerton, KCB, three *s* (and one missing, believed killed in action, Fleet Air Arm) one *d*. *Educ:* St Leonard's School; HMS Britannia. Entered Navy, 1881; Lieut, 1890; Commander, 1901; Capt. 1906; Ret. 1918; served Naval Attaché Germany, Denmark, and Holland, 1906–08; MVO, 1908; 2nd class Royal Danish Order Dannebrog; 2nd class Royal Prussian Order Red Eagle; 3rd class Japanese Order of Rising Sun; 4th class Russian Order St Vladimir; served as Secretary to Royal Commission on Oil Fuel and Engines, 1912–13; Assistant Director Torpedoes Admiralty, 1914; ADC to the King, 1918. *Address:* Moat House Farm, Brockham, Betchworth, Surrey. *T:* Betchworth 3383.

Died 12 Dec. 1948.

DUMMETT, Sir Robert Ernest, Kt 1940; Chief Metropolitan Magistrate since 1940; *b* 1872; *m* 1895, Emmie Welton; one *s* five *d*. *Educ:* Leys School and Clare College, Cambridge. Barrister Gray's Inn, 1896; Bencher since 1918; Treasurer, 1928; Recorder of South Molton, 1911–23; Recorder of Barnstaple and of Bideford, 1923–25; Metropolitan Magistrate, 1925–39; contested (L) Hornsey Div. of Middlesex, two elections of 1910. *Recreation:* golf. *Address:* 66 Witley Court, Woburn Place. *Club:* Garrick.

Died 17 Oct. 1941.

DUN, Robert Hay; *b* Latchford, Cheshire, 5 July 1870; *y c* of late John Dun, general manager of Parr's Bank, Ltd; unmarried. *Educ:* Loretto School, Musselburgh; Brasenose Coll., Oxford. (Classical scholar) 2nd class Mods and Greats, BA. Called to bar (Inner Temple), 1895; practised on Chancery side; was in cricket eleven and Rugby football fifteen at school and college, and in the University golf team; captain of Chislehurst Golf Club, 1902; served eight years as private and NCO in the 14th Middlesex (Inns of Court RV); has Order of the Nile 2nd and 3rd class; Advocate-General, Sudan, 1905–17; Chief Justice, 1917–26. *Recreation:* golf. *Address:* 13 Stanley Road, Hoylake, Cheshire. *Clubs:* United University; Royal Liverpool Golf, Hoylake.

Died 4 April 1947.

DUNALLEY, 5th Baron *cr* 1800; **Henry Cornelius O'Callaghan Prittie,** DSO 1916; late Rifle Brigade; *b* 19 July 1877; *s* of 4th Baron and Mary Frances, MBE, *o d* of Maj.-Gen. Onslow Farmer, RA, Aspley Guise, Bedfordshire; *S* father, 1927; *m* 1911, Beatrix Evelyn, *e d* of late James N. Graham, of Carfin, Lanarkshire; two *s*. *Educ:* Harrow; Trinity College, Cambridge. Served S African War, 1901–02; European War, S African War, 1901–02; European War, 1914–18 (despatches, DSO). *Publications:* Saddle and Steel, 1928; Khaki and Rifle Green, 1940. *Heir: s* Major Hon. Henry Desmond Graham Prittie. *Address:* Kilboy, Nenagh, Co. Tipperary. *Clubs:* Naval and Military; Kildare Street, Dublin.

Died 3 May 1948.

DUNBABIN, Robert Leslie, MA (Oxon); Emeritus Professor of Classics in the University of Tasmania; Head of Department of Classics in 1940; *b* 16 July 1869; unmarried. *Educ:* Hutchins School, Hobart; Corpus Christi College, Oxford (Exhibitioner). Tasmanian Scholar, 1888; 1st Class Classical Moderations, 1890; 1st Class Greats, 1892; Assistant Master at the Hutchins School and other schools; Acting-Professor of Classics in Adelaide, 1905; Lecturer, Assistant Professor, and Professor in the University of Tasmania from 1906–39; Vice-Chancellor, Feb.–April 1933. *Publications:* papers in the Classical Review, Classical Quarterly, and Mod. Lang. Rev. *Recreation:* reading. *Address:* 69 Federal St, Hobart, Tasmania.

Died 15 Oct. 1949.

DUNBAR, Sir George Alexander Drummond, 8th Bt *cr* 1697; *b* 10 May 1879; *s* of 7th Bt and Maria Louisa, *d* of late Hancorn Smith; *S* father, 1903; *m* 1916, Sophie Kathleen (*d* 1936), *d* of J. Benson Kennedy; one *s* one *d*. *Educ:* St Aidan's Coll., Granhamstown; Marist Brothers' School, Johannesburg. *Heir: s* Drummond Cospatrick Ninian, *b* 9 May 1917.

Died 25 June 1949.

DUNBAR, Sir Loraine Geddes, Kt 1915; formerly of Calcutta; *b* 1865; *s* of late Col W. M. Dunbar; *m* 1899, Liola Violet, *e d* of late Sir W. D. Cruickshank, CIE; four *s*. *Educ:* University, Paris and University, Edinburgh. *Address:* Whitehall Lodge, Harrogate. *Club:* Oriental.

Died 3 March 1943.

DUNBAR KILBURN, Bertram Edward, AICE, CIMechE, FCIPA, AIAE, MJIE, FRMetS; Chartered Patent Agent; JP Oxfordshire; *b* 1872; *o s* of Edward Dunbar Kilburn, London and Calcutta; *m* 1898, Emma Florence (*d* 1947), *d* of Col C. J. Mead, Bengal Artillery, ISC and PWD; one *s* two *d*. *Educ:* Eastbourne Coll.; Trinity Coll., Cambridge. Articled Clerk to late A. J. Boult, Ch. Patent Agent, 1893; then a Technical Assistant to him and partner, 1899–1905; started own business 1906 in which firm, now Kilburn and Strode, is still senior partner. Visiting Magistrate Oxford Prison since 1932 (except 1942–43); County Appeal Committee, 1935–46; Member of Area Probation Committee; Committee of Royal Humane Soc. since 1929; Council of Soc. for Nautical Research, 1933–37 and on previous occasions; Newcomen Society; Royal Society of Arts. Admiralty Secret Patent Dept, 1918–19. High Sheriff of Oxfordshire, 1942–43. Home Guard, June 1940–Dec. 1944. *Publications:* papers read before Junior Inst. of Engineers on Meteorology and Engineering and The Tides. *Recreations:* yachting and sailing; in Cambridge Univ. Hockey Team, 1891–92 and 1892–93. *Address:* Ledwell House, Sandford St Martin, Oxford. *TA:* and *T:* Great Tew 67. *Clubs:* United University, Royal Cruising, Royal Corinthian Yacht; Island Sailing, Oxfordshire (Oxford).

Died 18 July 1948.

DUNBOYNE, 26th Baron by Summons, 17th Baron by Patent; **Fitz-Walter George Probyn Butler,** Captain RN; retired; *b* 20 March 1874; *e s* of 16th Baron Dunboyne and Caroline Maude Blanche, *d* of Captain Probyn; *S* father, 1913; *m* 1915, Dora Isolde Butler, *e d* of late Comdr F. F. Tower, OBE; one *s* three *d*. Entered Navy, 1886; Lieut, 1895; Commander, 1906; served in Witu expedition, 1890 (medal and clasp); European War, 1914–18. *Heir: s* Hon. Patrick Theobald Tower Butler, Lieut late Irish Guards [*b* 27 Jan. 1917. Served War of 1939–45 (prisoner)]. *Address:* Vale House, Clewer, Windsor.

Died 9 May 1945.

DUNCAN, Alexander, CIE 1941. Agent and General Manager, Bengal-Nagpur Railway Co., Calcutta. *Address:* Bengal-Nagpur Railway Co., Calcutta, India.

Died 30 Jan. 1943.

DUNCAN, Claude Woodruff, CBE 1930; *s* of late Alexander Duncan, Crail, Fife; *m* Margaret, *o d* of late William Hislop, Goatfield, Haddington; no *c*. Joined Colonial Civil Service, British Guiana, 1899; British Guiana Police, 1901; Deputy Inspector-General of Police, Mauritius, 1912; Commissioner of Police, Malta, 1916; Inspector-General of Police, Nigeria, 1919–35; King's Police Medal, 1920; King's Jubilee Medal 1935. *Recreations:* golf, fishing, shooting. *Address:* Greenbank, Crail, Fife.

Died 15 July 1945.

DUNCAN, George, CBE 1941; LLD; Hon. FEIS; FSAScot; Advocate in Aberdeen; *s* of James Duncan, Architect, Turriff; *m* 1897, Eveline Louisa Crombie (decd); one *s* two *d*. *Educ:* Aberdeen University (MA). Was member of Aberdeen School Board; Chairman

Aberdeen Education Authority; President Scottish Association of Education Authorities; was Member of Aberdeen Town Council and is a JP; Member of Aberdeen University Court and of various other public bodies in Aberdeen; for many years Lecturer on Public and Private International Law in Aberdeen University. *Publications:* The Principles of Civil Jurisdiction according to the Law of Scotland (with Professor D. Oswald Dykes, KC), 1911; magazine articles. *Recreations:* public work; formerly mountaineering. *Address:* 60 Hamilton Pl., Aberdeen. *Club:* Scottish Mountaineering (Edinburgh).

Died 30 Sept. 1949.

DUNCAN, George B.; JP; editor of Weekly News since 1896 and Sunday Post since 1914; *b* Coupar-Angus, 12 Oct. 1869; *s* of John Duncan, journalist, and Elizabeth Brodie; *m* 1894, Christina, *e d* of Adam Simmers, Merle Grove, Downfield; one *s* two *d. Educ:* North Public School, Forfar; Forfar Academy. Reporter, Dundee Courier, 1887–90; sub-editor, Dundee Courier, 1890–96. *Publication:* On Sapphire Seas to Palestine—A Tour in the Holy Land of To-day. *Recreations:* travelling, bowling and curling. *Address:* Strathview, Broughty Ferry, Dundee. *T:* 7544 Broughty Ferry. *Clubs:* Eastern, Dundee.

Died 24 May 1941.

DUNCAN, Lt-Col James Fergus, DSO 1917; late RA; served European War, 1914–18 (despatches, DSO).

Died 26 Oct. 1941.

DUNCAN, John, RSA 1923; RSW 1930; *b* Dundee; two *d. Educ:* Dundee; London; Düsseldorf. Drew for magazines and book illustration in London; later executed decorative paintings in University Hall, Edinburgh; Associate Professor of the Teaching of Art in Chicago University, 1901–04; executed at St Peter's, Edinburgh, The Stations of the Cross; Church of the Good Shepherd, Altarpiece of the Ascension; Altarpieces at St Andrew's Episcopal Church, Aberdeen; at St Mary's, Broughty Ferry, at St Andrews, Darlington, at Rossal Hall, Fleetwood, Lancashire, at St Hilda's Priory, Whitby, and at Natal and Calcutta; mural paintings at St Cuthbert's Church, Edinburgh; pictures bought by the Modern Arts Association, for the Permanent Gallery of Dundee, by the Corporation of Glasgow and by the Royal Scottish Academy; stained glass windows at North Morningside Church, 1932; at Newbattle Parish Church, 1934; at Paisley Abbey, 1937; Carnoustie, 1937; Morar, 1939; ARSA 1910. *Address:* 29 St Bernard's Crescent, Edinburgh. *Clubs:* Scottish Arts, Edinburgh.

Died 24 Nov. 1945.

DUNCAN, Maj.-Gen. Sir John, KCB 1928 (CB 1918); CMG 1916; CVO 1923; DSO 1900; Bailiff Grand Cross, Order of St John of Jerusalem; late RS Fusiliers; *b* 24 Feb. 1872; *s* of Lieut-General J. Duncan; *m* 1st, 1896, Helen (*d* 1903), *d* of late William Boyd Buckle, BCS; one *d*; 2nd, 1906, Vivien, *d* of Emile R. Merton; two *d.* Entered Army, 1891; Capt. 1898; Maj. 1910; served North Frontier, India, 1897–98 (medal with clasp); S Africa (despatches, medal with five clasps, DSO); Great War, 1914–18; served as GSO 11th Division, Gallipoli; commanded 78th Infantry Brigade (1916–17), and later 22nd Div. (1917–19) in Macedonia; was Major-General, General Staff Army of Black Sea, April 1919–Dec. 1919 (despatches six times, CMG, CB, Bt Col, Maj.-Gen.); Grand Commander Order of Crown of Roumania, Grand Commander Order of Greek Redeemer, Grand Commander Crown of Italy, Commander Legion of Honour, Commander Servian White Eagle, French Croix de Guerre, Italian Croce di Guerra, Greek War Cross; passed Staff College; Brig. Major, Malta, 1902–03; General Staff Officer, Army Headquarters, 1903–08, Wessex Division, 1910; commanded Shanghai Defence Force, 1927–28; GOC 1st Division, Aldershot, 1928;

retired pay, 1928; Chief Commissioner St John Ambulance Brigade, 1931–43; Member of the Royal Company of Archers. *Address:* Marchfield, Binfield, Berks. *T:* Bracknell 338. *Clubs:* Brooks's, Turf.

Died 17 Sept. 1948.

DUNCAN, Comdr John Alexander, CB 1915; late RN; *b* 1878; *m* 1909, Beatrice Dorothy Percy, *d* of late Percy Weston, Greenfields, East Sheen; two *d.* Present at bombardment and capture of Sultan of Zanzibar's Palace, 1896; proof and experimental officer, Chemical Research Dept, 1910; qualified as interpreter in Swahili, 1896; Italian, 1900; Russian, 1903; German and Spanish, 1905; Turkish, 1907; Superintendent of Research, Woolwich, 1910–14; Chief Inspector of Naval Ordnance, 1914–19. *Address:* Parkhill, Arbroath, Angus. *Clubs:* New, Edinburgh.

Died 13 Aug. 1943.

DUNCAN, John Shiels, CBE 1938; *b* 19 Aug. 1886; *s* of late William Duncan, Newcastle, New South Wales; *m* 1911, Christina, *d* of J. Chalmers, Newcastle, New South Wales; one *d. Educ:* Hamilton, NSW; privately. Joined New South Wales Public Service, 1903; transferred to Commonwealth Public Service, 1923; called to Bar, NSW, 1925; Commonwealth Public Service Inspector for NSW, 1923–35; Deputy-Director Posts and Telegraphs, NSW, 1935–38; Official Secretary in Great Britain for the Commonwealth of Australia, 1938–42; Australian Govt Delegate, International Labour Conference, Geneva, 1939; Acting High Commissioner for Australia in London, Dec. 1938 to May 1939; Deputy High Commissioner for Australia, 1942–46; Australian Minister to Chile, 1946–48; Australian Minister Plenipotentiary to Chile, 1946–48. President Sydney Rotary Club, 1933–34; District Governor Rotary International, 1935. *Recreations:* golf, tennis, motoring. *Address:* 26 Onslow Gardens, Greenknowe Avenue, Pott's Point, Sydney, Australia.

Died 8 March 1949.

DUNCAN, Col Macbeth Moir, CMG 1916; DL; VD; TD; Advocate, Aberdeen; Hon. Sheriff-Substitute of Aberdeen, Kincardine and Banff; *b* 1866. *Educ:* Fettes College, Edinburgh; Clare College, Cambridge (Scholar, BA, Math. Tripos Hons). Served European War, 1914–19 (despatches, CMG); Col RFA (T); Hon. Cd. 75th (Highland) Field Brigade; RA, 1933–38; President, Society of Advocates, Aberdeen, 1928–30; Chairman County of the City of Aberdeen Territorial Army Association, 1922–25. *Recreations:* Cambridge University Rugby Union Football Team, 1885–88, all successful against Oxford (Captain, 1887–88); Scots RUF International, 1888; President Scottish Rugby Union, 1927–28. *Address:* Cults House, Cults, Aberdeenshire. *Clubs:* Royal Northern, Aberdeen; Conservative, Edinburgh.

Died 2 Oct. 1942.

DUNCAN, Rt Hon. Sir Patrick, PC 1937; GCMG 1937; CMG 1904; KC; LLD (Edinburgh and Cape Town); Hon. Fellow Balliol College, Oxford; Governor-General of Union of South Africa since 1937; *b* 21 Dec. 1870; *s* of John Duncan of Banffshire; *m* 1916, Alice Dold; three *s* one *d. Educ:* Balliol College, Oxford. Entered Service, 1894; Private Sec. to Sir A. Milner; Treas. of Transvaal, 1901; Colonial Secretary of the Transvaal, 1901; Colonial Secretary of the Transvaal, 1903–06; Acting Lt-Governor, 1906; Barrister of the Inner Temple and Advocate of the Supreme Court of South Africa; Minister of Interior, Public Health and Education, Union of South Africa, 1921–24; Minister of Mines, 1933–36. *Address:* Government House, Cape Town and Pretoria, S Africa. *Clubs:* Oxford and Cambridge, Athenæum; Rand, Johannesburg.

Died 17 July 1943.

DUNCOMBE, Col (Charles) William (Ernest), CBE 1918; DL, JP, TD; *b* 15 March 1862; *m* 1st, 1890, Lilian Bertha (*d* 1904), step *d* of Archibald Stuart-Wortley; 2nd, 1910, Adelaide (*d* 1934), *d* of Rev. H. M. Villiers and *widow* of A. F. Walrond. Served S Africa, 1900; Lt-Col Comdg and Hon. Col Yorks Hussars Yeomanry, 1908–12. *Publication:* (Editor) Ryedale, 1935. *Address:* Rievaulx, Helmsley, Yorks. *Clubs:* Cavalry; Yorkshire, York.

Died 8 May 1945.

DUNDAS, Lt-Col Frederick Charles, DSO 1917; late Argyll and Sutherland Highlanders; *b* 16 Jan. 1868; *s* of late Commander Frederick George Dundas, RN; *m* Elizabeth Drummond (*d* 1940), *e d* of late James Thomson, of Glenpark, Midlothian. *Educ:* Westminster; Sandhurst. Joined Argyll and Sutherland Highlanders, 1889; Captain, 1899; Major, 1911; Bt Lt-Col 1915 (for distinguished service in the field); Lt-Col 1917. *Clubs:* Army and Navy; New, Edinburgh.

Died 23 Jan. 1941.

DUNDAS, Robert Thomas, CIE 1916; late Indian Police; *m* 1st, Beryl Jessie, *d* of R. F. H. Pughe, Bengal Police; 2nd, 1917, Mary Tempest, *e d* of late E. N. Thompson, Parkstone. Assist Superintendent of Police, 1887; District Superintendent, 1895; Deputy Inspector-General, 1908; Inspector-General of Police, Bihar and Orissa, 1914; retired, 1923; Member of the Legislative Council, Bihar and Orissa; holds King's police medal. *Address:* c/o Grindlay & Co., 54 Parliament Street, SW1.

Died 24 April 1948.

DUNDAS-GRANT, Sir James; *see* Grant.

DUNEDIN, 1st Viscount *cr* 1926, of Stenton, Perthshire; **Andrew Graham Murray;** 1st Baron, 1905; PC 1896; GCVO 1923; KCVO 1908; QC 1891; Keeper of the Great Seal of the Principality of Scotland, since 1900; LLD Edinburgh, Glasgow, and Aberdeen; DCL Oxford; LLD Toronto, Chicago, Columbia; *b* Edinburgh, 21 Nov. 1849; *o c* of late Thomas Graham Murray, WS, Stenton, Perthshire, and Caroline, *d* of John Tod, WS, Kirkhill; *m* 1st, 1874, Mary Clementina (*d* 1922), *d* of Sir William Edmonstone, 4th Bt; two *d*; 2nd, 1923; Jean Elmslie, CBE, 1920 (Lady of Grace of St John of Jerusalem, Order of Queen Elizabeth, Belgium; Editor of Everyman, 1933–34; Director of Scottish Savings, 1916–23), *d* of late George Findlay, Aberdeen. *Educ:* Harrow; Trinity College, Camb. (Scholar) (MA). Scotch Bar, 1874; Advocate-Depute, 1888–90; Sheriff of Perthshire, 1890–91; Solicitor-General for Scotland, 1891–92, 1895–96; contested E Perthshire, 1885; Secretary for Scotland, 1903–05; Lord Advocate of Scotland, 1896–1903; MP (C) Bute, 1891–1905; Lord-Lieutenant of Bute, 1901–05; Lord Justice-General and Lord President, Court of Session, Scotland, 1905–13; a Lord of Appeal in Ordinary, 1913–32. *Recreation:* cine-photography. *Heir:* none. *Address:* 42 Lower Sloane Street, SW1. *Clubs:* Caledonian; New, Edinburgh.

Died 21 Aug. 1942 (ext).

DUNEDIN, Viscountess; Jean Elmslie, CBE 1920; Lady of Grace of St John of Jerusalem; Order of Queen Elizabeth, Belgium; *m* 1923, 1st Viscount Dunedin (*d* 1942); no *c*. Asst Editor, Everyman, 1914–16; First Director, Scottish War Savings, 1916–23; Editor, Everyman, 1933–34. *Publications:* translated The Barbarians in Belgium, 1915; and Three Aspects of the Russian Revolution, 1918. *Address:* 42 Lower Sloane Street, SW1. *Clubs:* Ladies Town and Country, Aberdeen (President).

Died 20 March 1944.

DUNHILL, Thomas Frederick, Mus. Doc. Dunelm (Hon.); FRCM; Hon. RAM; composer; Professor, Royal College of Music; Member, Associated Board of RAM and RCM; *b* Hampstead, 1 Feb. 1877; 3rd *s* of late Henry Dunhill; *m* 1st, 1914, Mary Penrose (*d* 1929), *d* of

Edward Arnold, of Pook Hill, nr Godalming, and *g g d* of Dr Arnold of Rugby; two *s* one *d*; 2nd, 1942, Isabella Simpson, *d* of late John Featonby, Scunthorpe, Lincs. *Educ:* a private school in Hampstead; Kent College, Canterbury; Royal College of Music, London (Open Scholarship for Composition, 1897). Studied with Franklin Taylor and Sir Charles Stanford. Pianoforte Professor at Eton College, 1900–08, and rejoined music staff in 1942; appointed on the staff of RCM 1905; visited Australasia as Examiner for Associated Board, 1906 and 1908; founded the Thomas Dunhill Concerts, 1907; lectures on musical subjects; adjudicates at musical festivals. *Publications:* Chamber Music, a Treatise, 1913; Mozart's String Quartets, 1927; Sullivan's Comic Operas, 1928; Sir Edward Elgar (Order of Merit Series), 1938; Principal compositions; Comrades (song for baritone and orchestra), 1905; Capricious Variations (cello and orchestra), 1911; The Wind among the Reeds (tenor song-cycle), 1912; Symphony in A minor (MS); Elegiac Variations (Gloucester Festival, 1922); opera The Enchanted Garden (Carnegie award, 1925); The Town of the Ford, Guildford Pageant Play, 1925; Tantivy Towers (comic opera, with libretto by Sir A. P. Herbert), 1931; Happy Families (comic opera, with libretto by Rose Fyleman), 1933; Gallimaufry (ballet) (Hamburg State Opera-house, 1937); Triptych (viola and orchestra), 1942; Overture, May-time, 1945; many chamber works and smaller pieces and songs. *Recreations:* travelling, swimming, acting. *Address:* 27 Platt's Lane, Hampstead, NW3. *T:* Hampstead, 4712. *Clubs:* Oxford and Cambridge Musical (President, 1938).

Died 13 March 1946.

DUNKIN, Major George William, MRCVS; DVH; Director, Agricultural Research Council Field Station, Compton, Berkshire, since 1937; *b* Canterbury, 26 July 1886; *s* of Charles Dunkin, Canterbury, and late Elizabeth Mary, *d* of late William Clark, Ospringe, Faversham; *m* 1915, Edith Beryl, *d* of late Peel C. H. Jay, Sutton, Surrey, and *g d* of late Capt. Charles Hawes Jay, RN. *Educ:* Simon Langton Schools; Royal Veterinary College, London; University of Liverpool. Practised veterinary surgery, Canterbury, specialising in canine work, 1910–14; Veterinary Officer in charge Troops, Canterbury, 1914–15; served European War in Egypt, 1915–19 (despatches); promoted Major, 1917, and commanded 20th Veterinary Hospital, EEF, 1917–19; Superintendent of Farm Laboratories of National Institute for Medical Research, Mill Hill, NW7, 1923–37, and engaged in research into certain animal diseases, *exempli gratia* Dog Distemper, Johne's Disease, Tuberculosis, etc.; Member of Council of Royal College of Veterinary Surgeons, 1929, National Veterinary Medical Association, 1920, and of Section of Comparative Medicine of Royal Society of Medicine, 1924; awarded Gold Victory Medal of Central Veterinary Society, 1929; President, Central Veterinary Society, 1925; President of South-Eastern Veterinary Association, 1923; Hon. Life Member, New York City Veterinary Medical Society; President Section of Comparative Medicine, Royal Society Medicine, 1936–37; Dalrymple-Champneys Award, 1936. *Publications:* various papers on prevention of Dog Distemper jointly with late Sir Patrick Playfair Laidlaw, and on the diagnosis of Johne's Disease, The Tuberculin Test in Cattle, and other papers of a scientific nature. *Recreations:* riding, golf, tennis, shooting. *Address:* Compton Manor, Compton, Berks. *TA:* Compton, Berks. *T:* Compton 57. *Club:* Savage.

Died 21 March 1942.

DUNLOP, Col Henry Donald B.; *see* Buchanan-Dunlop.

DUNLOP, James Crauford, MD, FRCP Edin.; FFA (Hon.); late Registrar-General for Scotland; *s* of Colin Hinton Dunlop, merchant in Glasgow, *s* of Henry Dunlop of Craigton, and Mina, *d* of James Crauford of Ardmillan, Lord Ardmillan; *m* Mary, *d* of John Morison

Duncan, Advocate; two s one d. *Educ:* Christ's Hospital; Edinburgh University. Assistant to Medical Adviser to Prison Commissioners, Scotland; Inspector, Inebriate (Scotland) Acts; Member, Royal Commission on Care and Control of Feebleminded; Director of Statistics in Department of Surveyor General of Supply, War Office; member of the King's Bodyguard for Scotland (Royal Company of Archers). *Publications:* various medical and statistical reports. *Address:* Drumbeg, Hamilton Road, North Berwick. *T:* North Berwick 239. *Clubs:* New, Edinburgh.

Died 10 April 1944.

DUNLOP, James Matthew; Chairman and Managing Director of Edwards Dunlop & Company Ltd, Sydney; Director of Edwards Dunlop & Company (London) Ltd; Chairman: Galwey & Co. Pty Ltd, Sydney; The Paget Mfg Co. Pty Ltd, Sydney; Simpson's Ink Pty Ltd, Sydney; *b* Edinburgh, 15 April 1867; *s* of John and Margaret Dunlop, Edinburgh, Scotland; unmarried. *Educ:* George Watson's College, Edinburgh, Scotland; Cooerwull Academy, Bowenfels NSW. Entered the business of Edwards, Dunlop & Company Limited as a boy and has been there ever since. Director Bank of NSW, 1927–30; President Sydney Chamber of Commerce, 1924–27, Associated Chambers of Commerce of Australia, 1926–27. *Recreations:* reading and stock breeding. *Address:* 123 Clarence St, Sydney, NSW, Australia. *T:* B0222; Munro Park, Sutton Forest, NSW. *T:* Moss Vale 108. *TA:* Care Dunloption, Sydney, NSW, Australia. *Club:* Australian (Sydney).

Died 21 Aug. 1949.

DUNLOP, Engr Rear-Adm. Samuel Harrison, CB 1940; MIMechE; *b* 2 July 1884; *s* of late Charles and Charlotte Dunlop; *m* 1916, Hilda, *d* of E. G. Jacobs; two *s*. *Educ:* Glasgow University. Entered Royal Navy by direct entry 1906; in various ships, 1906–09 and 1910–20; Russia to qualify as interpreter, 1909–10; Portsmouth Dockyard, 1920–24; Admiralty (Dockyard Dept), 1924–27; Queen Elizabeth, 1927–30; Admiralty (Engineer-in-Chief's Dept), 1930–34; Assistant Director of Dockyards, 1934–40; Deputy Director of Dockyards, Admiralty, 1940–46; retired list, 1947. ADC to the King, 1937–38. *Publication:* Oil from Coal, Institution of Engineers and Shipbuilders in Scotland, 1933. *Recreation:* cricket. *Address:* Glebe Lodge, Guildford. *T:* Guildford 62675. *Club:* Army and Navy.

Died 25 May 1950.

DUNLOP, William Louis Martial, CMG 1948; OBE 1920; MBE 1918; Head of King's Messengers and Communications Department, Foreign Office, 1940–47; *b* 3 Aug. 1882; *s* of late William Dunlop, Paisley; *m* 1911, Isabel Eveline, *γ d* of late Thomas Harrison; one *s* one *d*. Entered Foreign Office, 1903; Private Secretary to late Sir Mark Sykes, 1917–18; attached to British Delegation to Peace Conference at Paris, 1918 and 1919; Asst to Librarian and Keeper of the Papers, 1920–29; Senior Asst in Treaty Dept, 1929–40; attached to UK delegation to Peace Conference at Paris, 1946. *Address:* Ilsham, 32 Arundel Road, Cheam, Surrey. *T:* Vigilant 5766.

Died 23 April 1948.

DUNN, Edward; JP; MP (Lab) Rother Valley Division of Yorkshire since 1935; Parliamentary Private Secretary to Mr Arthur Henderson, Joint Parliamentary Under-Secretary at the War Office, since 1942; *b* 21 Dec. 1880; *s* of Harry and Jane Dunn; *m* 1914, Maggie Buckley; three *d*. *Educ:* Kiveton Park Council School. Secretary, Maltby Branch of Yorkshire Miners' Association, 1911–35; Member Miners' Federation Executive Committee, 1930–36; Member of WR County Council since 1918; Alderman since 1921; Chairman Maltby Parish Council, 1916–24; Chairman Maltby Urban Council since 1924; Member of Executive Committee

of County Council Association since 1934; Leader Labour Party in West Riding County Council, 1933–36. *Address:* 52 Blyth Road, Maltby, nr Rotherham.

Died 8 April 1945.

DUNN, John Shaw, MA, MD; Professor of Pathology, University of Glasgow, since 1936; *b* 22 March 1883; *s* of Hugh S. Dunn, Coalmaster, Kilmarnock; *m* 1914, Williamina, MD, DSc, *d* of Rev. R. H. Abel, Fettercairn; one *s* one *d*. *Educ:* Kilmarnock Academy; Glasgow High School; University of Glasgow. After graduation engaged mainly in study and teaching of Pathology in University of Glasgow as assistant to Professor; Lecturer on Clinical Pathology, 1914; RAMC 1915–19; Professor of Pathology, Birmingham, 1919–22; Manchester, 1922–31; Glasgow (Notman), 1931–36. *Publications:* on pathological subjects with special reference to renal disease. *Recreation:* angling. *Address:* 25 Bute Gardens, Hillhead, Glasgow. *T:* W London 2802.

Died 10 June 1944.

DUNN, Rev. Thomas Shelton, MA; Vicar of King's Norton, Birmingham, 1924–48, Canon Emeritus of Birmingham Cathedral; Surrogate for Diocese of Birmingham; *b* 4 Sept. 1875; *s* of late Nicholas John Dunn, JP, DL; *m* 1st, Constance Eaton Evans, Avallenau, Haverfordwest; 2nd, Noel Mary Medlicott Pryce, Montgomery; one *s* two *d*. *Educ:* Blundell's School; Keble College, Oxford; Leeds Clergy School. Curate Balsall Heath, Birmingham, 1899–1904; St Augustine's Edgbaston, 1904–09; Vicar of Church Stoke, Mont, 1909–14; Rector of Montgomery, 1914–19; Vicar of Lydbury North, Salop, 1919–24; Rural Dean of Church Stretton and Surrogate for Hereford Diocese, 1920–24; Rural Dean of King's Norton, 1926–33. *Address:* King's Norton Vicarage, Birmingham. *T:* King's Norton 1496.

Died 16 Jan. 1949.

DUNN, William, CBE 1934; JP; *b* 1876; *s* of John Dunn and Janet Carmichael; *m* 1905, Helen Erskine Dobbie (*d* 1941); two *s* four *d*. *Educ:* Alloa Academy; Dollar Academy. Timber Importer, Merchant and Sawmiller, first in Alloa, afterwards in Dundee; Member of Alloa Town Council 1909–16, Magistrate 1912–16; Member of Dundee Town Council 1928–33; Served two terms as Bailie of the City; Member of Harbour Board for three years and also several other Trusts; Chairman of Scottish Liberal National Assoc. and of East Fife Liberal Assoc. *Recreations:* golf, motoring and music. *Address:* Kinbrae, Newport, Fife. *TA:* Timber Dundee. *T:* Newport 3216, Dundee 81211–81212. *Club:* National Liberal (Edinburgh).

Died 6 March 1949.

DUNNE, Arthur Mountjoy; KC 1917; *b* 1859; *m* 1891, Alice Sidney (*d* 1945), *e d*, of late Sir John Lambert, KCIE; one *s*. Called to Bar, Middle Temple, 1881; BA, LLB Trinity College, Dublin; Bencher of the Middle Temple, 1925. *Address:* Enborne Lodge, Newbury, Berks. *Club:* Junior Carlton.

Died 18 June 1947.

DUNNE, Lt-Col Edward Marten; *b* 27 Aug. 1864; *s* of late T. Dunne, JP, DL, of Bircher Hall and Gatley Park, Herefordshire; *m* 1899, Hon. Grace Daphne Rendel, JP Herefordshire, 3rd *d* of 1st Lord Rendel; one *s* two *d*. *Educ:* Wellington College; RMC, Sandhurst. Entered army (Border Regt), 1884; graduated at the Staff College, 1891; left the army, 1896; Brigade-Major, Bedford Volunteer Brigade, 1898; Brigade-Major, Aldershot, during SA War; JP, DL and County Alderman Herefordshire; MP (L) Walsall, 1906–10; contested Melton Division, Leicesters, 1910; DAQMG Northumbrian Division, 1914–15; AAG (temp. Lt-Col) Headquarters Western Command, 18 Sept. 1915; High

Sheriff Herefordshire, 1922. *Recreations:* fishing, shooting. *Address:* Gatley Park, Kingsland, Herefordshire. *Club:* Brooks's.

Died 23 Feb. 1944.

DUNNE, John William; Fellow Royal Aeronautical Society; *e s* of late General Sir John Hart Dunne, KCB, of Cartron, Roscommon, and Julia Elizabeth Dunne; *m* 1928, Hon. Cecily Twisleton-Wykeham-Fiennes, *o d* of 18th Baron Saye and Sele; one *s* one *d. Educ:* private schools. Trooper, Imperial Yeomanry (Boer War), 1900. Sub-Lieutenant, Wiltshire Regiment (Boer War), 1901; attached HM Balloon Factory, 1906; member Royal Engineer Committee, 1907; Brigade Musketry-Instructor (temp. Captain), 63rd Brigade, 1914–15; Home Guard, 1940–41; began aeronautical experiments, 1900; invented (1904) the stable, tailless type of aerofoil which goes by his name; built and flew both monoplanes and biplanes of this type; designed and built (1906–07) the first British military aeroplane, tested secretly by HM War Office at Blair Atholl in 1907–08; is interested in philosophical problems, and is the discoverer of Serialism. *Publications:* Sunshine and the Dry-Fly, 1924; An Experiment with Time, 1927; The Serial Universe, 1934; The New Immortality, 1938; Nothing Dies, 1940. Children's books: The Jumping Lions of Borneo, 1937: An Experiment with St George, 1939. *Recreations:* fly-fishing, revolver shooting. *Clubs:* United Service, Flyfishers'.

Died 24 Aug. 1949.

DUNNING, Sir Leonard, 1st Bt *cr* 1930; Kt 1917; late Inspector of Constabulary, Home Office; *b* 17 June 1860; 2nd, *s* of late Simon Dunning, of Parliament Street, and Elizabeth Mary, *d* of late John Burder; *m* 1902, Edith Muriel, *e d* of William Tod, Drygrange, Allerton, Liverpool; one *s. Educ:* Eton; Exeter College, Oxon (BA 1881, honours in Jurisprudence). District Inspector Royal Irish Constabulary, 1882–95; Assist Head Constable of Liverpool, 1895–1902; Head Constable, 1902–12; one of HM Inspectors of Constabulary, 1912; retired 1930. *Heir: s* William Leonard [*b* 1903; *m* 1936, Kathleen Laurie, *o c* of J. Patrick Cuthbert, MC, Barclayhills, by Perth; one *s* one *d*]. *Address:* Beedinglee, Horsham, Sussex. *T:* Lower Beeding 8. *Club:* Conservative.

Died 8 Feb. 1941.

DUNSTAN, Hon. Sir Albert Arthur, KCMG 1948; *s* of Thomas Dunstan, Cope Cope, Vic.; *m* 1911, Jessie G., *d* of Alex. Chisholm, Swan Hill, Vic.; two *s* four *d.* Legislative Assembly, 1920–; MLA for Korong for many years; Member Country Party for 5 years after entering Parliament; formed, and was first leader of, Country Progressive Party, 1925; Minister for Lands and Forests, 1932–35; Premier of Victoria, 1935–45; Minister of Health, State of Victoria. Farmed in various places. *Address:* Parliament House, Melbourne, Victoria.

Died 14 April 1950.

DUNSTAN, Sir Wyndham Rowland, KCMG 1924 (CMG 1913); Hon. MA (Oxon), Hon. LLD (Aberdeen), FRS, Commander of Order of Leopold of Belgium; Director of the Imperial Institute, 1903–24; *b* Chester, 1861; *e s* of late John Dunstan, Constable and Governor of Chester Castle; *m* 1st, 1886, E. Fordyce, 2nd *d* of late G. F. Maclean; 2nd, 1900, Violet M. C., 3rd *d* of late Hon. F. Hanbury Tracy, MP Montgomery Boroughs, 5th *s* of 2nd Baron Sudeley. *Educ:* Bedford School; abroad. Demonstrator of Chemistry, University Laboratories, Oxford, 1884; University Lecturer in Chemistry in its Relations to Medicine, Oxford, 1885; Prof. of Chemistry, Pharmaceutical Soc., 1886; Professor of Chemistry, St Thomas's Hospital, 1892–1900; Director Scientific and Technical Dept Imperial Institute, 1896–1903; Examiner Hon. School Natural Science and for Medical Degrees, Oxford, Natural Science Tripos and for Medical Degrees Cambridge and in Univ. of London; Sec. Chemical Society, 1893–1903;

Vice-Pres. 1904–06; Pres. Chemical and Agricultural Section, British Association, 1906; Member of Council, Royal Society, 1905–07; Member of Council Royal Geographical Society, 1916; Governor London School of Economics, of Bedford College and of London School of Medicine for Women; Vice-Pres. Girls Public Day School Trust; Chairman Committee for National Memorial to Earl of Meath (Founder Empire Day); Hon. Sec. and Treas. Sudeley Cttee, from 1923; Hon. Member and one of the founders of the Aristotelian Society; Membre Correspondant de l'Institut d'Egypt; Hon. Member Agricultural Society of Trinidad; Pres. of the International Association for Tropical Agriculture, 1910; Pres. International Congress Tropical Agriculture, London, 1914; Member of Government Committee on Oil-Seeds, 1915–16; on Mineral Resources, 1917; on Empire Cotton Growing, 1917; visited Cyprus, 1904, Asia Minor, 1907, for Colonial Office; reports on agricultural and economic development presented to Parliament; visited Ceylon, 1910 and 1914, India, 1914, and Newfoundland, 1914, at request of Governments. *Publications:* British Cotton Cultivation, 1904 and 1908; The Agricultural Resources of Cyprus, 1906; Agriculture in Asia Minor, 1908; Cotton Cultivation of the World, 1910; Editor, Imperial Institute Handbooks to the Commercial Resources of the Tropics; Rubber, Ency. Brit.; Our Quest for Philosophy (the History of the Aristotelian Society), Hibbert Journal, 1942; numerous scientific papers in Transactions Royal Soc. and Chemical Soc. *Address:* East Burnham End, nr Slough. *T:* Farnham Common 13; 87 Chester Square, SW1.

Died 20 April 1949.

DUNSTERVILLE, Col Arthur Bruce, CMG 1916; CBE 1919; *b* 3 Nov. 1859. Served Soudan, 1885 (medal with clasp, bronze star); NW Frontier, India, 1897–98 (despatches thrice, medal two clasps); S Africa, 1899–1902 (Bt Lt-Col, Queen's medal five clasps); European War, 1914–18 (despatches six times, CMG, CBE, Chevalier Legion of Honour, 1914 Star, British War Medal, Victory Medal); Camp Commandant, 1914–16; Commander 1916–19.

Died 30 Oct. 1943.

DUNSTERVILLE, Maj.-Gen. Lionel Charles, CB 1916; CSI 1918; *b* 1865; *s* of Lt-Gen. Lionel D'Arcy Dunsterville; *m* 1897, Margaret, 2nd *d* of Col W. Keyworth, Bishopsteignton. Served Waziristan, 1894–95 (medal with clasp); NW Frontier, India, 1897–98 (medal with clasp); China, 1900 (despatches, medal); European War, 1914–19 (CB, CSI). *Publications:* The Adventures of Dunsterforce, 1920; And Obey, 1925; Stalky's Reminiscences, 1928; More Yarns, 1931; Stalky Settles Down, 1932. *Address:* Camelot, Barton, Torquay.

Died 18 March 1946.

DUNTZE, Sir George Puxley, 5th Bt *cr* 1774; *b* 6 Dec. 1873; *s* of 4th Bt and Harriet (*d* 1908), *e d* of Lloyd Thomas; *S* father, 1922; *m* 1908, Violet May, *d* of Henry M. Sanderson; one *s* two *d.* Heir: *s* George Edwin Douglas, *b* 1 June 1913. *Address:* PO Box 405, Pretoria, South Africa.

Died 20 May 1947.

DUNWOODIE, Lallah Bessie, CBE 1919; RRC (and bar); late Lady Superintendent Queen Alexandra's Imperial Military Nursing Service, India; *yr* of late John Dunwoodie, Director Inspector General, Royal Naval Medical Service. Served European War, 1914–19 (RRC, CBE). *Address:* Portchester, Hampshire.

Died 5 April 1950.

DU PARCQ, Baron *cr* 1946 (Life Peer), of Grouville; **Herbert du Parcq,** PC 1938; Kt 1932; a Lord of Appeal in Ordinary since 1946; *b* St Helier, Jersey, 5 Aug. 1880; *s* of Clement Pixley du Parcq and Sophia Thoreau; *m* 1911, Lucy, *d* of John Renouf, St Helier, Jersey; one *s* two *d. Educ:* Victoria College, Jersey; Exeter

College, Oxford (Scholar). MA; 1st class Classical Mods, 2nd Lit. Hum.; LLD (Hon.) Birmingham Univ., 1947. President of Oxford Union Society, 1902; King Charles I Senior Scholar, Jesus College, Oxford; BCL. Called to Bar, Middle Temple, and admitted to Jersey Bar, 1906; Member of General Council of the Bar, 1928–32; President, Hardwicke Society, 1910; Member of Western Circuit; KC 1926; Recorder of Portsmouth, 1928–29; of Bristol, 1929–32; Judge of the High Court of Justice (King's Bench Division) 1932–38; a Lord Justice of Appeal, 1938–46; Bencher of Middle Temple since 1931; Commissioner of Assize, Northern Circuit Spring Assize, 1931; Member, Home Office Committee on Persistent Offenders, 1931; appointed by Home Sec. to inquire into the recent disorders at Dartmoor convict prison, 1932; Hon. Fellow of Exeter and or Jesus Colleges, Oxford, 1935; Chairman of Royal Commission on Justices of the Peace, 1946; Chairman of Council of Legal Education since 1947. *Clubs:* Reform, Athenæum.

Died 27 April 1949.

DUPPUY, Rt Rev. Charles Ridley, DD; Assistant Bishop in Diocese of Worcester since 1936; Archdeacon of Worcester since 1938; Examining Chaplain to Bishop of Worcester, 1941; Canon of Worcester since 1932; Vice-Dean since 1940; *s* of late Rev. C. Duppuy; *m* 1925, May Kathleen, *d* of H. Baker-Munton. *Educ:* Keble College, Oxford (Second Class in Theology); Wycliffe Hall. Curate of Aston; Vicar of Christchurch, Bradford, 1909; joined Home Staff of the Church Missionary Society, 1911; Home Secretary, 1915–20; Chaplain to the Forces in France; Bishop of Victoria (Hong-Kong), 1920–32. *Address:* 10 College Green, Worcester.

Died 26 Sept. 1944.

DUPRÉ, Hon. Maurice; PC (Canada) 1930; KC (Quebec) 1922, (Dominion) 1930; member legal firm of Dupré, Gagnon, de Billy, Prévost & Home, 80 St Peter Street, Quebec; Vice-President and Director, Clinic Hardware Co.; Director: Caisse d'Economie Bank, Canadian Industrial Alcohol, Aldermac Copper Corporatio-Limited, Francoeur Gold Mines; *b* Levis, Quebec, 20 March 1888; *s* of H. Edmund Dupré, Officier de l'Instruction Publique (France), and Marie, *d* of late Hon. Dr J. G. Blanchet, former Speaker of the House of Commons, Ottawa, and Legislative Assembly, Quebec; *m* 1919, Anita Arden, *d* of James A. Dowd, New York; two *s* two *d*. *Educ:* Levis College; Laval University; Oxford. Called to Bar, 1911; started present legal firm, 1912; Conservative candidate, Kamouraska, 1925; MP Canadian House of Commons for West Quebec, 1930–35; Solicitor-General, Canada, 1930–35; Member of the Canadian delegation to the Imperial Conference in London, 1930; Chairman of the Arbitration and Disarmament Committee and Representative of Canada on the Lord Sankey Committee on constitutional matters; one of Canada's delegates to Assembly of the League of Nations and the Disarmament Conference at Geneva, 1932; elected Vice-President of the Naval Committee; joint Chairman of National Conservative Convention held in Ottawa, 1938; a Roman Catholic; a Conservative. *Recreations:* golf, tennis. *Address:* 144 Grande Allée, Quebec, Canada. *Clubs:* Garrison, Royal Quebec Golf, Canadian, Quebec; Murray Bay Golf, Montreal.

Died 4 Oct. 1941.

DU PRE, William Baring; JP, DL (Bucks); *b* 5 April 1875; *e s* of late James Du Pre, and *great-nephew* of late Caledon George Du Pre, DL, MP for Bucks; JP of Wilton Park, Beaconsfield; *m* 1st, 1903, Youri Wynyard (*d* 1942), *o d* of late Capt. H. Townley Wright, RN; three *d*; 2nd, 1945, Beryl, *widow* of Major Hon. Robert Dudley Ryder, 8th Hussars. *Educ:* Winchester College; Sandhurst. Late Lieut King's Royal Rifles and Lieut Imperial Yeomanry, S Africa (medal and 3 clasps); Lt-

Col Royal Horse Artillery (T); served European War, 1914–18; contested Loughborough Division, Leicestershire, 1906; MP (U) Wycombe Division, Bucks (S Bucks), 1914–23; High Sheriff, Bucks, 1911. *Recreations:* croquet, motoring. *Address:* Tetworth, Ascot, Berks. *T:* Ascot 1155. *Club:* Carlton.

Died 23 Aug. 1946.

DURBIN, Evan Frank Mottram; MP (Lab) Edmonton since 1945; Parliamentary Secretary to Ministry of Works since 1947; *b* 1 March 1906; *s* of Rev. F. and Mary Louisa Mellor Mottram Durbin; *m* 1932, Alice Marjorie Green; one *s* two *d*. *Educ:* Plympton and Exmouth Elementary Schools; Heles School, Exeter; Taunton School; New College, Oxford (Open Scholar). 1st Class Honours in the School of Philosophy, Politics and Economics. Lecturer at New College, Oxford; Junior and Senior Webb Medley Scholarships, University of Oxford; Ricardo Fellowship, University of London; Senior Lectureship in Economics at the London School of Economics; Temporarily on Economic Section of War Cabinet Secretariat, 1940; Temp. Appointment as Personal Assistant to Deputy Prime Minister, 1942. Parliamentary candidate (Lab) for E Grinstead, 1931, Gillingham, Kent, 1935. *Publications:* Purchasing Power and Trade Depression, 1933; The Problem of Credit Policy, 1935; Personal Aggressiveness and War (with Dr Bowlby), 1938; How To Pay for the War, 1939; The Politics of Democratic Socialism, 1940; What Have We to Defend?, 1942; Contributions to Economic Journal and other technical periodicals. *Recreations:* walking, tennis, squash, the cinema and detective stories. *Address:* c/o Midland Bank, 19 Marylebone High Street, W1.

Died 3 Sept. 1948.

DURELL, Col Arthur James Vavasor, CB 1917; CBE 1920; *b* 25 June 1871; 2nd *s* of late Rev. J. V. Durell, Rector of Fulbourn; *m* 1902, Alice Margaret, *e d* of Rev. Metcalfe Sunter; one *s* one *d*. *Educ:* Wellington College; RMC, Sandhurst (1st with honours). Entered army, Norfolk Regt 1890; Army Pay Department; Capt. 1898; Major, 1905; Lt-Col 1910; Col 1915; Chief Paymaster, 1915; Chief Paymaster, War Office, 1916; served S Africa, 1899–1902 (despatches, Queen's medal 5 clasps, King's medal 2 clasps); European War, 1914–19 (services mentioned twice); Bursar, Leys School, 1918–35. *Publication:* The Principles and Practice of the System of Control over Parliamentary Grants. *Address:* 2b Drosier Road, Cambridge.

Died 1 July 1945.

DURELL, Rev. John Carlyon Vavasour, CBE 1920; MA; BD; Residentiary Canon of Southwark Cathedral, 1936–40; now Canon Emeritus; Rector of Clapham since 1922; Surrogate for Diocese of Southwark; Warden of St Olave's School, 1923; *b* 1870; *s* of late Rev. J. V. Durell, Rector of Fulbourn; *m* Ellen Maud (*d* 1938), *d* of Henry Wood Payne, Bombay. *Educ:* Wellington College; Clare College, Cambridge (late Fellow). Bell University Scholar; Select Preacher, Cambridge. Formerly Rector of Patrington, E Yorks; Rector of Rotherhithe. 1907–22; Examining Chaplain to the Bishop of Southwark, 1910–36; Chaplain of Bermondsey Infirmary, 1914–22; Rural Dean of Clapham, 1922–36; Hon. Canon, Southwark Cathedral, 1920–36. *Publications:* The Historic Church; The Self-Revelation of our Lord; The Rotherhithe Church Pageant; Whizzbangs and Woodbines; Tales of Light and Shade on the Western Front, 1918; On the Road to Bethlehem, a Miracle Play of the Nativity; The Holy Places of Christendom; When Christ was Born; The Way of the Cross, a Miracle Play for Lent; Nowell, a Christmas Play; Arcady, a Midsummer Masque; The New Prayer Book in Relation to Life; The New Prayer Book in Relation to Life; The Old Testament Chronologically Arranged; Ecclesia Victrix, A Missionary Pageant; Faith and Freedom: A Wilberforce

Centenary Pageant. *Address:* The Rectory, Clapham, SW4. *TA:* Durell, Rectory, Clapham. *T:* Macaulay 1288.

Died 15 Aug. 1946.

DURHAM, Frances Hermia, CBE 1918; *b* 15 Aug. 1873; *y d* of late Arthur E. Durham, FRCS, Senior Surgeon, Guy's Hospital. *Educ:* Notting Hill High School; Girton College, Cambridge. Alexander Medallist, Royal Historical Society, 1899; Hon. Secretary, Registry and Apprenticeship Committee, Women's University Settlement, Southwark, 1900–07; Inspector and Organiser of Technical Classes for Women under the London County Council, 1907–15; Chief Woman Inspector, Employment Dept Board of Trade, 1915; transferred to the Ministry of Labour, 1917; Assistant Secretary in the Ministry of Labour, 1923–33; retired, 1933; co-opted member of the Devon County Education Committee, 1934. *Address:* Hawkern, Otterton, S Devon.

Died 18 Aug. 1948.

DURHAM, Lt-Col Frank Rogers, CBE 1922; MC; Chevalier Légion d'honneur; Chevalier de l'Ordre de la Couronne (Belgium); Secretary of the Royal Horticultural Society, 1926–46; *s* of Arthur Edward Durham, FRCS, late senior surgeon of Guy's Hospital; *m* Dorothy Ellis, *d* of Madame Ellis Browne, Calgary; one *d*. *Educ:* Rugby School; University College, London. MInstCE. Vice-President of Institution of Junior Engineers; for many years chief assistant to the late Sir William Lindley, MInstCE, practising civil engineering on the Continent under his service; Assistant Secretary to him on the Royal Commission of Waterways and Canals for foreign countries; reporter on Standardisation of Cast Iron Pipes on the Continent to the Engineering Standards Committee, etc.; in War joined up as private, 1914, 2nd Bn Royal Fusiliers; commissioned in Royal Engineers, 1916, and acted as Field Engineer to the CE 4th Army for water supply until 1919; Director of Works of Imperial War Graves Commission, 1919–26. *Address:* Gaybanks, Woolbrook, Sidmouth, South Devon. *T:* Sidmouth 468.

Died 30 March 1947.

DURHAM, Herbert Edward, ScD (Cantab), MB, BC (Cantab), FRCS (Eng.), ARPS; retired; lately engaged in the study of fermentation and allied problems; *b* 30 March 1866; *s* of late Arthur E. Durham, sometime Senior Surgeon to Guy's Hospital; *m* Maud Lowry, *d* of late Capt. Harmer, 81st Regt. *Educ:* University College School, London; King's College, Cambridge; Guy's Hospital, London; Hygiene Institute, Vienna. Working Member of Tsetse Fly Disease Committee of Royal Society; in charge of expeditions to investigate yellow fever in Brazil, organised by Liverpool School of Tropical Medicine, and beriberi, organised by London School of Tropical Medicine; Ex-President Herefordshire Association Fruit Growers and Horticulturists, and Woolhope Naturalists' Club; owing to considerable loss of vision had to give up active prosecution of research; introduced Derris as insecticide from Malaya; Medallist Royal Photographic Society, 1927. *Publications:* numerous papers on various medical, pathological, and hygienic subjects. *Recreations:* experiments in horticulture and fruit-growing and photography. *Address:* 14 Sedley Taylor Road, Cambridge. *Club:* United University.

Died 25 Oct. 1945.

DURHAM, Mary Edith; *b* 1863; *e c* of late A. E. Durham, FRCS. *Educ:* Bedford College; Royal Academy of Arts. Exhibited at Royal Academy, Royal Institute of Painters in Water-Colours, Institute of Painters in Oils, etc.; Illustrations to the Reptile volume of the Cambridge Natural History, and other books; lecturer; Fellow of the Royal Anthropological Institute and Member of Council; Member of Royal Institute of International Affairs. *Publications:* Through the Lands of the Serbs; The Burden of the Balkans, 1905; 2nd ed., 1912; High Albania, 1909; The Struggle for Scutari, 1914; Twenty Years of Balkan Tangle, 1920; The Serajevo Crime, 1925; Some Tribal Origins, Laws, and Customs of the Balkans, 1928; formerly correspondent of Times, Manchester Guardian, Nation, etc. *Address:* 36 Glenloch Road, Hampstead, NW3.

Died 15 Nov. 1944.

DURLEY, Richard John, MBE 1918; MaE, MInstCE; Secretary Emeritus, Engineering Institute of Canada, Montreal; *b* Bierton, Bucks, 11 Feb. 1868; *m* Elizabeth Schwill of New York; one *s* one *d*. *Educ:* Bedford Modern School; University College, Bristol; University College, London. With Earle's Shipbuilding and Engineering Co., Ltd, Hull, 1887–94; Whitworth Scholar, 1893; Professor of Mechanical Engineering, McGill University, Montreal, 1901–12; Officer i/c Gauges and Standards, Imperial Ministry of Munitions Department of Inspection, Canada, 1915–19; Secretary, Canadian Engineering Standards Association, 1919–25; Secretary, Engineering Institute of Canada, 1925–38. *Publications:* Kinematics of Machines, 1903; various technical papers in engineering journals and transactions. *Recreations:* sailing, fishing, shooting. *Address:* 3174 The Boulevard, Westmount, Quebec. *Club:* University (Montreal).

Died 13 Aug. 1948.

DU TOIT, Alexander Logie, FRS 1943; DSc, FGS; Consulting Geologist; formerly Consulting Geologist to De Beers Consolidated Mines; and Geologist to the Union Irrigation Department; Leader of the Government Expedition to Kalahari, 1925. *Educ:* Bishops College, Cape Town; Royal Technical College, Glasgow; Imperial College of Science, S Kensington. Received the Wollaston Fund for 1919 for research work in Cape Colony, etc.; at request of the Carnegie Institution made an extensive tour of South America on research work, 1923; South Africa Medal (Science Association), 1930; Murchison and Draper Medals, 1933. *Publications:* Physical Geography for South African Schools (1st ed. 1912, 2nd ed. 1926); Geology of South Africa (1st ed. 1926, 2nd ed. 1939); Our Wandering Continents, 1937; (joint) Geology of Cape Colony, 1909. *Address:* 2 Bye Way, Pinelands, Cape Town, South Africa.

Died 25 Feb. 1948.

DUTTON, Lt-Col Hugh Reginald, CIE 1930; FRCP (Lond.); DTM and H (Camb.); JP (Bombay), IMS (retd); late Member, Medical Board, India Office; *b* 21 Nov. 1875; *s* of late Rev. Alfred Dutton; *m* Harriet Agnes, *d* of late H. J. Brooker, Tonbridge, Kent. *Educ:* Ardingly College; Middlesex Hospital; London University. Served in Tibet Expedition, 1903–04 (medal and clasp); European War, 1914–18 (medal and Victory medal); Delhi Durbar, 1911 (medal); Jubilee Medal, 1935; Coronation Medal, 1937; Commissioned IMS 1902; retired, 1930; Principal and Professor of Medicine The Prince of Wales Medical College, Patna, Bihar and Orissa, India, 1925–30. *Publications:* Case Taking for Students; A Manual of Training for Nurses; Various contributions Indian Medical Gazette. *Recreations:* gardening, shooting. *Address:* c/o Grindlay's Bank Ltd, 54 Parliament St, SW1.

Died 5 July 1950.

DUVEEN, Edward Joseph, CBE 1929; *m* 1912, Vera, *d* of Percy Marsden; one *s* one *d*. *Publications:* Colour in the Home as applied to the Industrial Arts; An Imperial Parliament; Key Industries. *Address:* 54 Harley House, Regent's Park, NW1. *T:* Welbeck 3388.

Died 19 Dec. 1944.

DWYER, Hon. Sir Walter, Kt 1949; retired Judge; *b* 27 Aug. 1875; *s* of Walter and Mary Dwyer; *m* 1912, Maude Mary, *e d* of Charles Smith, Murchison, WA; two *d*. *Educ:* Christian Brothers' School; London

University. LLB (London Univ. (External)), 1906. Admitted to Bar (WA), 1907; Member of Legislative Assembly, WA, Perth Constituency, 1911–14; President, Court of Arbitration, 1926–45. *Recreations:* gardening, walking. *Address:* 28 Almondbury Road, Mount Lawley, Western Australia. *T:* U 2040. *Clubs:* Celtic (Perth, WA); WA Turf.

Died 23 March 1950.

DYALL, Clarence George; late Secretary Curator Royal Cambrian Academy of Art, Plas Mawr, Conway; retired, 1938; *b* Manchester, 23 Sept. 1858; *s* of Charles Dyall, first Curator of Walker Art Gallery, Liverpool; *m* Beatrice Helen Smiles; two *s. Educ:* Liverpool Institute. *Recreation:* work. *Address:* Plas Mawr, Conway. *T:* Conway 113. *Clubs:* Liverpool Artists, Liver Sketching (hon.) Liverpool.

Died 22 Sept. 1941.

DYALL, Franklin; actor and producer; *b* 3 Feb. 1870; *s* of Charles and Margaret Dyall; *m* 1st, Mary Phyllis Logan (marr. diss.); one *s*; 2nd, Mary Merrall. *Educ:* Liverpool Institute. First appearance, in The Masqueraders, St James's, 1894, and has since continued to appear on London stage. Played before Queen Victoria at Balmoral with George Alexander. Toured in Germany with Forbes-Robertson and Mrs Campbell, appearing before the Kaiser in Berlin; with E. S. Willard in America; with Miss Marie Tempest in America; toured in Daddy Longlegs, playing Jervis Pendleton; with Miss Mary Merrall ran Abbey Theatre, Dublin, for summer season; toured S Africa with Miss Merrall in Repertory. Other outstanding Parts: John Gabriel Borkman; Shylock; Cassius; Golaud, in Pelleas and Melisande (with Martin Harvey); Messenger from the Palace, in Reinhardt's prod. of Œdipus at Covent Gdn; Diaz, in Sacred and Profane Love; The Father, in Pirandello's Six Characters in search of an Author; The King, in Hamlet (with Martin Harvey and later with John Gielgud); Meister, in The Ringer; The Chinaman, in The Silent House; Weston, in White Cargo. In War of 1939–45, toured for 26 weeks in ENSA, 1941. Has produced many plays. Played in first straight 'talkie' made in England (Atlantic, 1929) and in many others afterwards. *Address:* 33 Carlton Hill, St John's Wood, NW8. *T:* Maida Vale 7500. *Clubs:* Garrick, Green Room, Chelsea Arts.

Died 8 May 1950.

DYDE, Samuel Walters; *b* 11 March 1862; *s* of Samuel Dyde, of Canada and Jane Christina Wardrope, Scotland; *m* 1888, Jane, *d* of late J. W. Farrell, Detroit; two *s* two *d. Educ:* Queen's University, Kingston; Germany. Professor of Mental and Moral Philosophy and Political Economy, University of New Brunswick, 1886–89; Professor of Mental Philosophy, Queen's University, Kingston, 1889–1911; Rector, Queen's University, 1911–14. Chaplain (Capt.) Canadian Militia, 1915; Principal Robertson College, Edmonton, Alberta, 1911–18; Principal Queen's Theological College, 1918–26; Professor Queen's Theological College, 1926–33. *Publications:* translated Hegel's Philosophy of Right, and Plato's Theaetetus. *Recreations:* camping, gardening. *Address:* Edmonton, Alberta, Canada.

Died 22 Jan. 1947.

DYER, Sir Alfred, Kt 1936; JP; Director, F. J. Parsons, Ltd, Hastings; Chairman of Directors, Hastings and East Sussex Building Society; Consulting Editor, Hastings and St Leonards Observer, Editor, 1902–42; *b* Dover, 9 Feb. 1865; *s* of Charles Dyer; *m* 1895, Edith Kate, (*d* 1946), *d* of George and Kate Havill, Devonshire; one *s* one *d. Educ:* St Leonards. Journalist on several Provincial papers; Editor Gravesend Standard for six years; Sports Editor Daily Mail two years. *Recreations:* bowls, golf. *Address:* The Wedge, Clinton Crescent, St Leonards. *T:* Hastings 4316. *Club:* Conservative (Hastings).

Died 15 Nov. 1947.

DYER, Bernard, DSc, FRIC, FCS, FLS; Official Agricultural Analyst for the Counties of Bedford, Cornwall, Dorset, Essex, Hants, Herts, Leicester, Rutland, Somerset, and West Suffolk; Consulting Chemist to the Essex and Leicester Agricultural Societies; Official Analyst to the London Corn Trade Association; Public Analyst (Food and Drugs Act, 1938) for the Counties of Essex, Herts, Leicester, Rutland, Dorset and Wilts, and the Boroughs of East Ham, Barking, Dagenham, Ilford, Leyton, Wanstead and Walthamstow; Past President of Society of Public Analysts; *b* London, 1856. *Educ:* City of London School; King's College; Royal Coll. of Science; Pharmaceutical Society; the private laboratory of the late Dr A. Voelcker. *Publications:* Fertilisers and Feeding Stuffs; Manuring of Market Garden Crops; Manuring of Hops; Analytical Determination of Available Mineral Plant Food in Soils (Journal of the Chemical Society, 1892); Kjehldahl's Method for Nitrogen (*ib.* 1895); Phosphoric Acid and Potash Contents of Wheat Soils of Broadbalk Field, Rothamsted (Philosophical Transactions of the Royal Society, 1901); Lawes Trust Lectures, 1901 (United States Department of Agriculture, Bulletin 106, 1902); various papers. *Address:* Peek House, 20 Eastcheap, EC3; 1 Lower Terrace, NW3. *T:* Hampstead 2713. *Clubs:* Savage, Chemical.

Died 12 Feb. 1948.

DYER, Edward Jerome, CBE 1920; interested in British overseas enterprises; *b* Australia; *s* of L. Dyer, Australian landowner and South Sea plantation owner; *m* Blanche, *o d* of Walter Lansby, Melbourne; one *s* one *d. Educ:* private tutors. Visited India and various far eastern countries as an Australian Trade Commissioner and on other occasions as newspaper correspondent; also visited various countries in N and S America; initiated and organised, and was Hon. Secretary for the Colonial Exhibition held in the Royal Exchange, 1902; in 1914, with Admiralty approval, organised and managed in honorary capacity the Vegetable Products Committee for Naval Supply throughout European War and for ten months after by request of the Admiralty for the benefit of the minesweepers in the North Sea. *Publications:* several magazine articles on Australia, Canada, and Far East. *Recreations:* travelling, riding and reading. *Address:* 19 Woodfield Road, Ealing, W5. *TA:* Mineurs, London. *T:* Perivale 2895.

Died 29 Dec. 1943.

DYER, Sir Leonard Whitworth Swinnerton, 14th Bt *cr* 1678; *b* 30 Oct. 1875; *o s* of Col Henry Clement Swinnerton Dyer, RFA (*d* 1898), of Westhope Manor and Amelia Susan (*d* 1903), *o d* of late John Ward of Otterington Hall, Yorkshire; *S* cousin 1940; *m* 1897, Lucy, *e d* of late Francis Schroeder, New York; one *s.* Served in RNVR Aug. 1914–Nov. 1916 (invalided). *Heir: s* Leonard Shroeder Swinnerton [*b* 30 March 1898; *m* 1925, Barbara, *d* of Hereward Irenius Brackenbury, CBE; one *s* one *d*]. *Address:* Westhope Manor, Craven Arms, Shropshire.

Died 19 Aug. 1947.

DYKES, David Oswald, KC 1926; MA, LLB; FRHistS; Professor of Constitutional Law and Constitutional History in the University of Edinburgh since 1925; *b* 1876; *s* of late Dr Oswald Dykes, DD, Principal of Westminster College, Cambridge; *m* Lucy *d* of late Samuel Waters, Ipswich; two *s. Educ:* University College School, London; University of Edinburgh; MA 1901; LLB 1903. Called to the Scots Bar, 1903. *Publications:* Edited Cooper on the Law of Defamation, 1906; joint author of Principles of the Law of Civil Jurisdiction, 1911; Source Book of Constitutional History from 1660, 1930. *Address:* 16 South Charlotte Street, Edinburgh.

Died 2 May 1942.

DYKES, Col Frescheville Hubert Ballantine-, CB
1945; DSO 1917; OBE 1923; DL, JP; retired list; late
Scots Guards; Lord Lieutenant of Cumberland since
1944; *b* 1881; *o s* of late Lamplugh F. Ballantine-Dykes
and Edith Georgina, *y d* of late Richard Howard Brooke,
Castle Howard, Co. Wicklow; *m* 1911, Winifred Mary,
e d of late W. Pitt Miller, Thistleton, Lancs; one *s* one *d*.
Late Lieut Scots Guards; Capt., 1915; Staff Capt., 1916;
DAAG, 1917–19; Brevet-Colonel, 1924; Col, 1926;
ADC Additional to King, 1926; served European War
(DSO, CB). *Address:* Kepplewray, Broughton-in-
Furness, Lancs.

Died 13 Jan. 1949.

DYKES, Brig. Vivian, CBE 1939; MBE 1928; Assistant
Secretary, War Cabinet; *b* 9 Dec. 1898; *s* of Alfred
Herbert and Annie Louise Dykes; *m* 1922, Ada
Winifred, *yr d* of Richard Smyth, Castle Widenham, Co.
Cork; one *s* one *d*. *Educ:* Dulwich College; RMA
Woolwich; Gonville and Caius College, Cambridge.
Commissioned in Royal Engineers, 1917; Captain 1928;
Bt Major 1936; Major 1937; Bt Lt-Col 1938; Col 1942;
served European War, France, 1918 (wounded); Wana
Column, Waziristan, 1920–21 (despatches); Shanghai
Defence Force, 1927 (MBE); Military Assistant
Secretary, Committee of Imperial Defence, 1936–38
(CBE); Instructor, Staff College, 1939. DSM from
President USA, 1943. *Address:* c/o Lloyds Bank (R.), 6
Pall Mall, SW1. *Club:* Army and Navy.

Died 29 Jan. 1943.

DYMOKE, Frank Scaman; DL, JP; The Hon. the
King's Champion, and Standard Bearer of England; *b* 24
July 1862; *m* 1st, 1893, Frances Anne (*d* 1906), 3rd *d* of
Charles Bell of Scamblesby, Lincoln; two *s*; 2nd, 1907,
Marion Royce (May), (*d* 1942), *y d* of late Charles
Josselyn of Colchester. *Address:* Scrivelsby Court,
Horncastle, Lincolnshire.

Died 28 Aug. 1946.

DYSON, Herbert Kempton; architect and consulting
civil engineer; specialist in structural engineering,
especially reinforced concrete and steel construction; *b*
24 Jan. 1880; *o s* of W. Franklyn Dyson, architect; *m*
1909, Nellie, *o d* of late George Cooper; one *s*.
MIStructE; Registered Architect; Past Member, British
Joint Committee on Reinforced Concrete; Hon.
Secretary of the Conference on the London Steel-Frame
Act; Sec. of the Concrete Inst., 1908–17; Hon. Sec.,
Institution of Structural Engineers, 1922–23; editor of
The Builders' Journal and Architectural Engineer, and of
Specification, 1904–08. *Works:* designer of numerous
structures of many kinds; Consulting Engineer for
Works of strengthening supports of Dome of St Paul's
Cathedral, 1914–18. *Publications:* The Everyday Uses of
Portland Cement; papers to technical societies. *Address:* 3
De Vere Gardens, Kensington, W8. *T:* Western 2393.

Died 15 Jan. 1944.

DYSON, William, OBE, TD; MD; Major RAMC (TA);
Consulting Dermatologist, Manchester Royal Infirmary;
Physician to the Manchester Hospital for Skin Diseases;
Consulting Dermatologist, Manchester Babies Hospital;
Past President, British Association of Dermatology;
Vice-President, Dermatological Section, Royal Society
of Medicine; *b* 19 May 1871; *s* of John Dyson,
Manchester; *m* Margaret Mabel, *d* of Dr Speirs, Cleator,
Cumberland; three *d*. *Educ:* Rossall School; Victoria
University of Manchester; Vienna. Late Hon. Physician,
Salford Royal Hospital; Assistant Physician, Manchester
Skin Hospital; House Surgeon, Manchester Royal
Infirmary, Manchester Northern Hospital, and Stockport
Infirmary; FRSM and various scientific societies;
graduated MB, ChB (Vict.) 1896; in 1910 presented
thesis for the degree of MD and was awarded the Gold
Medal; mobilised with the Territorial Force, 1914; went
overseas, Sept. 1914, with the 42nd Division; served in
Gallipoli, Egypt, and Palestine (OBE, despatches);
demobilised Feb. 1919. *Publications:* Cutaneous
Pigmentation in Normal and Pathological Conditions;
papers in medical journals. *Recreation:* fishing. *Address:*
Singleton House, Wilbraham Rd, Fallowfield,
Manchester. *T:* Rusholme 4780; *Consulting rooms:* 96
Mosley Street, Manchester. *T:* Central 4960. *Clubs:*
Clarendon, Manchester.

Died 5 Feb. 1947.

E

EACOTT, Canon Henry James Theodore, MA, Hon. CF; Rector of Kibworth since 1934; *b* 28 Dec. 1882; *s* of Rev. Caleb Eacott and Annie Siddons; *m* 1908, Elizabeth Osborn Liddell; one *d. Educ:* King's School, Peterborough; Oakham School; Hatfield Hall, Durham. Assistant Curate, St Chad's, Derby, 1906–09; Market Harborough, 1910–11; Vicar of Desborough, Northants, 1911–22; Market Harborough, 1922–29; Vicar of Hinckley, 1929–34; Chaplain to Forces, 1915–19; Hazebrouck, 1915; Salonica, 1915–18; Catterick, 1918–19; Rural Dean, Rothwell II, 1920–22; Gartree 1, 1922–29; Hon. Canon, Leicester Cathedral, 1932. *Recreations:* motoring and gardening. *Address:* Kibworth Rectory, Leicestershire.

Died 3 May 1943.

EADY, George Hathaway; JP; *s* of John Amos Eady; *m* Miss Mitchell; one *d. Educ:* Hartshead. Maker of dress goods; founder of G. H. Eady, Ltd, Managing Director; MP (U) Bradford Central 1931–35. *Recreations:* golf, angling, shooting, motoring. *Address:* Victoria Park, Shipley, Yorkshire. *T:* Shipley 528. *Club:* Constitutional.

Died 1 Sept. 1941.

EAGLESOME, Sir John, KCMG 1916 (CMG 1905); *b* 14 March 1868; *m* 1908, Evanna Constance (*d* 1945), *e d* of Kenrick Morton Lloyd, MRCS (Lond.). Entered PWD, India, 1890; was Assistant Engineer for construction of Khojak Tunnel, Afghanistan, 1892; and Godavari Bridge Madras, 1900 (thanked by Government); Director of Public Works, Northern Nigeria, 1900; in charge of Baro-Kano Railway, 1907; Director of Railways and Works, Nigeria, 1912–19; services lent to Ministry of Munitions, 1916; Officer of Legion of Honour, 1919; Member of First Council, Institute of Transport, 1919; Vice-President, Institute of Transport, 1923–24; Member of Colonial Economic Development Committee, 1919; Member of Committee on Inland Waterways; Member of West Riding County Council, 1922–24; Major, Engineer and Railway Staff Corps, RE (retd); President Leeds Chamber of Commerce 1933–34; Member of Colonial Development Advisory Committee, 1929–40. *Address:* c/o Lloyds Bank, Ltd (Cox's and King's Branch), 6 Pall Mall, SW1. *Club:* Union.

Died 3 April 1950.

EAGLESTON, Arthur John, CVO 1923; *b* 29 Oct. 1870; *o s* of late Joseph Eagleston, Oxford; *m* 1901, Fanny Congreve, *o d* of late Robert Edward Younger; one *s* one *d. Educ:* City of Oxford High School; Balliol College, Oxford (Scholar); 1st class Classical Mods. 1890; 1st class Final Classical School, 1892. Entered Civil Service and appointed to Home Office, 1894; Assistant Secretary, Home Office, 1913–32; retired, 1932; Acting Assistant Secretary, Home Office, 1940–41. *Address:* 6 Reynolds Close, NW11. *Clubs:* Reform, Hampstead Golf.

Died 23 Jan. 1944.

EARL, Frederick, OBE; KC 1912; Barrister; *b* Melbourne, 19 Dec. 1857; *m* 1891, Ethel Mildred, *d* of late Carl Schmitt, Professor of Music at Auckland University College; two *d. Educ:* Melbourne. Admitted to Bar, 1880; latterly specialised in cases relating to Maoris and their lands; was for several years President of the Auckland Club President Auckland District Law Society, and President Auckland Acclimatization Society; is President Auckland Cricket Association, and member of Committee of the Auckland Racing Club; during European War was Chairman Auckland Military Service Board. *Recreations:* angling, racing. *Address:* Remuera, Auckland, SE2, New Zealand. *T:* 24–255. *Clubs:* Northern, Auckland, Auckland.

Died 12 April 1945.

EARLE, Lt-Col Sir Algernon; *see* Earle, Lt-Col Sir T. A.

EARLE, Charles Westwood, CMG 1927; Managing Director of Wellington Publishing Co., Ltd; *b* Wellington, May 1871; *s* of Joseph Earle; *m* 1897, Katharine Hannah Wright; one *s* one *d. Educ:* Thorndon School; Wellington College. Editor of Referee, 1901; Associate Editor of Evening Post, 1906; Editor 1907–33, and Managing Director since 1912 of The Dominion; President of New Zealand Newspaper Proprietors' Association, 1921–48; Chairman United Press Association, 1939; on several occasions President of New Zealand Institute of Journalists. *Address:* Lower Hutt, NZ.

Died 28 March 1950.

EARLE, Gerald Frederick, CBE 1920; Agent Earle, Stoddart and Clayton Ltd, 2 Broadway, New York; *b* 1864; *s* of late Wm James Earle, Great Yeldham, Essex; *m* 1891, Louise, *d* of Horace Barnard, Utica, New York; one *s* one *d. Educ:* Uppingham. *Address:* 908 Watchung Avenue, Plainfield, New Jersey, USA.

Died 17 Sept. 1944.

EARLE, Herbert Gastineau, MA, MB (Cantab); LLD (Hon.) Hong Kong; Director of the Henry Lester Institute of Medical Research and Preventive Medicine, Shanghai, 1928; late Professor of Physiology, etc, University of Hong-Kong, 1915–27; Chairman, Research Council, Chinese Medical Association, 1926–34; Member Chinese Physiological Society; Member, the Physiological Society; FRSM; Fellow of the Royal Society of Tropical Medicine and Hygiene; Member of the British Medical Association; Member of the Universities China Committee; Member of the Royal Institute of International Affairs; *b* Acton, Middlesex, 10 Aug. 1882; *γ s* of Norwood Earle, Dover, and Jane Ann Livermore; *m* 1911, Audrey Mary, *e d* of C. G. Harrison; one *s* three *d. Educ:* City Freeman's School, City of London School; Downing College, Cambridge (Foundation Scholar); Westminster Hospital. 1st Class Natural Science Tripos, 1903; BA 1905; MA, MB 1913. Demonstrator of Physiology, Middlesex Hospital Medical School, 1904–15; Joint Lecturer on Biology, 1909–15; Temporary Honorary Assistant Physician, Royal Waterloo Hospital, 1914–15; Lecturer and Examiner Red Cross Society, 1914–15; Professor of Physiology 1915–27, Member of the Court and Senate, Dean of the Faculty of Medicine, and Member of Council, 1916–20, 1923, 1925, University of Hong-Kong; President Hong-Kong and China Branch, British Medical Association, 1919; Delegate Congress of British Universities, Oxford, 1921, Cambridge, 1926, and Edinburgh, 1931; General Adviser to the Lester Trust, Shanghai, 1928–34. Retired; interned, Shanghai; liberated at end of War. *Publications:* papers in medical journals. *Recreation:* tennis. *Address:* Henry Lester Institute, 1318 Avenue Road, Shanghai, China. *Clubs:* Hong-Kong; Shanghai.

Died 5 June 1946.

EARLE, Sir Lionel, GCVO 1933; KCB 1916; KCVO 1921; CB 1911; CMG 1901; JP; Order of the Crown of Belgium, 1920; *b* 1 Feb. 1866; *s* of late Capt. Charles William Earle, Rifle Brig., and late Maria Theresa Villiers; *m* 1926, Betty Strachey, (from whom he obtained a divorce, 1937), *d* of late W. E. Marriott and

Mrs Lindsay Jopling, *g d* of late Sir John Strachey, GCSI, KCIE. *Educ:* Marlborough; University of Göttingen and University of Paris; Merton College, Oxford. Assistant Secretary to Royal Commission Paris Exhibition, 1898–1900; an acting 2nd Secretary of Embassy, 1900; Private Secretary to the Lord Lieutenant of Ireland, 1902–03; to the Lord President of the Council (Earl of Crewe), 1907, to Secretary of State for the Colonies (Earl of Crewe), and Secretary of State for the Colonies, Rt Hon. L. Harcourt, MP, 1908–12; Permanent Secretary to HM Office of Works 1912–33; contested Brixton Division of Lambeth for the LCC, 1907; Member of the Royal Commission on Museums, 1927–30; Chairman of Ancient Monuments Board for England; Chairman of Government Hospitality; Member of the Sudeley Committee; late Trustee Wallace Collection and Chairman of Flowers and Shrubs Advisory Committee, 1934. *Publication:* Turn Over the Page, 1935. *Address:* 6 Wyndham House, Sloane Square, SW1. *T:* Sloane 2907. *Club:* St James's.

Died 10 March 1948.

EARLE, Rev. Canon Richard Cobden, BA; Rector of Stanford Rivers, Ongar, Essex, since 1934; Hon. Secretary of Diocesan Conference, 1924–34; Editor of Diocesan Chronicle, 1926–40; Hon. Canon of Chelmsford Cathedral since 1930; *b* 20 June 1867; *s* of late Edward Smith Earle, Brantwood, Burnt Ash Hill, SE, and Matilda, *d* of William Peploe, Tain; *m* 1898, Ethel Leader (*d* 1938), *e d* of Samuel Watson, Clapham Park; no *c.* Assistant Master at Whitgift Grammar School (temporary), Eliot Bank School and West Kent Grammar School, 1884–90; Army Coach at Dover, 1891–95; Deacon, 1895; Priest, 1896; Curate, All Saints, Clapham Park, 1895–98; Association Secretary of RTS, 1898–1905; Curate, All Saints, Clapham Park, 1905–08; Curate, Christ Church, Peckham, 1908–09; Rector of Quendon, 1909–34, and Vicar of Rickling, 1917–34 (by Archbishop's Licence); Diocesan Inspector, Chelmsford, 1916–33; Rural Dean of Newport and Stansted, 1927–34; also, concurrently, Assist Editor at RTS, 1905–17. *Recreations:* motoring and sailing. *Address:* Stanford Rivers Rectory, near Ongar, Essex. *T:* Ongar 139.

Died 26 Jan. 1942.

EARLE, Lt-Col Sir (Thomas) Algernon, 4th Bt *cr* 1869; TD, FSI; *b* 16 July 1860; 3rd *s* of Sir Thomas Earle, 2nd Bt, DL, JP, of Allerton Tower, co. Lancaster; *S* brother 1939; *m* 1901, Edith, *d* of General Disney Leith, CB, of Glenkindie, Aberdeenshire, and *sister* of 7th Lord Burgh; one *s* two *d. Educ:* Eton. Lt-Colonel commanding Lancashire Hussars Yeomanry, 1912–16; served in Egypt and on the Somme (British War Medal, Allied Medal and Territorial Medal); President Land Agents Society, 1918–19. *Publications:* papers, Historic Society of Lancashire and Cheshire, and Land agents Society Journal. *Recreations:* hunting, shooting, golf. *Heir:* *s* Hardman Alexander Mort [*b* 19 Aug. 1902; *m* 1931, Maie, *d* of John Drage, The Red House, Chapel Brampton; one *s* one *d*]. *Address:* Northcourt, Shorwell, Isle of Wight.

Died 5 Sept. 1945.

EASON, Sir Herbert Lightfoot, Kt 1943; CB 1919; CMG 1917; MD, MS (Lond.); FRCS; MD (Hon.) University of Dublin; late Superintendent and Senior Opthalmic Surgeon, Guy's Hospital and Dean of the Medical School and Warden of the College; *b* 15 July 1874; *m* 1st, 1908, Hon. Ierne Bingham (*d* 1917), *e d* of 5th Baron Clanmorris; one *d*; 2nd, 1920, Margaret, *e d* of R. G. Wallace, Quidenham, Attleborough, Norfolk; two *d. Educ:* University College, London; Guy's Hospital. Lt-Col late RAMC, Consulting Opthalmic Surgeon to Forces in the Mediterranean and Egypt, 1915–19; Member of Departmental Committee on the University of London (Board of Education), 1924–26; Member of Post Graduate Medical Education Committee (Ministry of Health), 1925–30; late Member

of the Governing Body of the British Post Graduate School; late Member (co-opted) of Hospitals and Medical Services Committee, LCC; a representative of the Faculty of Medicine on the Senate of the University of London 1911–37; representative of the Senate on the University Court, 1931–37; Vice-Chancellor, London Univ., 1935–36, and 1936–37; Principal of University of London, 1937–41; Ex-Officio Member of Central Health Services Council, 1948–49; Representative of the University of London on the General Medical Council (Pres., 1939–49); Member of General Council of King Edward's Hospital Fund for London; representative of the Ministry of Health on the General Nursing Council, 1933–37; Fellow of the Royal Society of Medicine; Member of the Opthalmological Society; Hon. Bencher, Inner Temple, 1938. *Address:* Newbridge Mill, Coleman's Hatch, Sussex. *Club:* Athenæum.

Died 2 Nov. 1949.

EASSIE, Brig.-Gen. Fitzpatrick, CB 1919; CMG 1916; DSO 1902; late Deputy Director of Vet. Services; *b* 15 Oct. 1864; 3rd *s* of late W. Eassie, CE; *m* (wife decd); one *s.* Entered Army, 1889; served Chin Hills, Burma, 1890; Manipur Expedition; Chin Hills, 1890–91, 1891–92, 1892–93, 1893–94 (despatches); Chitral, 1895 (medal with clasp); South Africa, 1899–1902, with Remount Department (despatches, DSO); European War; Director of Veterinary Services, British Salonika Force, 1914–18 (despatches, CMG, Bt Col, CB); Order of the Redeemer (Greece); Order of Military Merit (Greece); retired pay, 1921. *Club:* Naval and Military.

Died 10 Jan. 1943.

EAST, Col Charles Conran, CMG 1917; retired; *b* 1866; *s* of late General Sir Cecil James East, KCB; unmarried. *Educ:* Clifton College; Sandhurst. Royal Warwickshire Regiment, and Staff, India and Ireland; served Atbara and Khartoum (medal with clasps). *Address:* 15 Lansdown Place E, Bath. *Club:* Army and Navy.

Died 24 March 1942.

EASTERFIELD, Sir Thomas Hill, KBE 1938; MA (Cantab), PhD (Würzburg), FIC, FCS; FRS (NZ); *b* Doncaster, 4 March 1866; *s* of Edward Easterfield, Doncaster, and Susan Hill, Dymock, Gloucestershire; *m* 1894, Anna Maria Kunigunda Büchel; one *s* four *d. Educ:* Doncaster Grammar School; Yorkshire College, Leeds; Clare College, Cambridge (Foundation Scholar); Zürich Polytechnikum; University of Würzburg. Junior Demonstrator, Cambridge University Chemical Laboratory, 1888; University Extension Lecturer, 1891–93; Lecturer on Pharmaceutical Chemistry and Chemistry of Sanitary Science, Cambridge, 1894–98; Professor of Chemistry, Victoria University College, Wellington, NZ, 1899–1919; Director, Cawthron Institute, Nelson, NZ, 1919–33; President NZ Institute (now Royal Soc., NZ), 1920, 1921, Member of Council, 1902–41; President NZ Inst. of Chemistry, 1933. Hon. Life Governor British and Foreign Bible Soc. *Publications:* various papers on organic chemistry in the Journal of the Chemical Society; Trans. NZ Inst. & NZ Journal of Science and Technology. *Address:* Whernside, 48 Bronte Street, Nelson NZ. *T:* 529.

Died 1 March 1949.

EASTES, Arthur Ernest, CMG 1932; *b* 10 Nov. 1877; *s* of George Eastes, MB, FRCS, and Fanny Elizabeth Friend. *Educ:* Winchester College (Scholar); Magdalene College, Cambridge (Scholar). HBM Consular Service in China: Student Interpreter, 1901; 2nd Class Assistant, 1906; Vice-Consul (Acting), Hankow, 1908–10; 1st Class Assistant, 1910; Assistant Chinese Secretary, Peking, 1910–13; Consul (Acting), Harbin, 1913; Consul (Acting), Tengyueh, 1915–18; Vice-Consul, 1916; Consul, 1919; Consul-General (Acting), Chengtu, 1919–20; Consul, Amoy, 1922–23; Ichang, 1923–25; Chungking, 1926; Newchwang, 1927–29; Consul-

General, Harbin, 1929–30; Mukden, Manchuria, 1930–32; retired, 1933. *Address:* Fairholme, Marsham Way, Gerrard's Cross, Bucks. *Club:* Overseas.

Died 6 June 1948.

EASTMAN, Gen. William Inglefield; late RM Artil; *b* 3 Oct. 1856; 3rd *s* of Thomas Eastman, late Naval Instructor, RN; *m* 1891, Agnes Ida (*d* 1936), 2nd *surv. d* of Neil Lewis of Hobart; two *s. Educ:* privately. Lieutenant, 1873; Colonel Commandant, 1911; Maj.-Gen. 1912; Lieut-Gen. 1914; General, 1914; retired, 1921; Graduate of Staff College. *Address:* Hazeldean, Farncombe Road, Worthing.

Died 13 Oct. 1941.

EASTON, Brig.-Gen. Frederick Arthur, DSO 1918; late Royal Artillery; *b* 1871; *s* of late Captain F. Easton, 33rd (Duke of Wellington's) Regiment; *m* 1922, Francesca Catherine (*d* 1946), *d* of Col O. S. Smyth, DSO, Royal Artillery. *Educ:* Cheltenham College; RM Academy, Woolwich. *Address:* Fairholme, Bideford, N Devon.

Died 1 Jan. 1949.

EASTON, Col George, CBE 1920; TD; *b* 17 Oct. 1868; *e s* of John Huteson and Ellen Easton; *m* 1st, 1892, Alice Mary Hulbert; one *d*; 2nd, 1929, Norah Eve Kempe (*d* 1934); one *s. Educ:* Rossall School. 2nd Lieut Humber Volunteer Div. RE (Submarine Miners) 1888–91; Lieutenant 2nd East Riding of Yorkshire Artillery Volunteers, 1892–1908; Col 2nd Northumbrian Bde RFA, TA, 1908–12; rejoined 1914; Recruiting Officer Hull, 1914–15; Vice-Chairman and Secretary East Riding Territorial Army Association, 1915–19; County Adjutant East Yorkshire Volunteer Regiment, 1916–17; Hon. Lieut-Col East Yorkshrie RAMC (Vols.), 1917–19; County Director East Riding VAD, British Red Cross Society and Order of St John of Jerusalem, 1915–19; JP City of Kingston-upon-Hull, 1917–37; Member Hull City Council, 1906–16; Commander Order of St John of Jerusalem. *Recreations:* walking and horse exercise and foreign travel. *Address:* c/o B. C. Boulter, MA, Consitt House, Burford, Oxfordshire.

Died 27 March 1946.

EASTWOOD, Benjamin, CMG 1918; Chief Accountant, Uganda Railway, 1897; General Manager, 1914; now retired; Director of Railways, East Africa and Uganda, Head-quarters Staff, BEF1914; Colonel, Uganda Railway Military Unit, 1915 (despatches); Member of Legislative Council, British East Africa, 1914; of Executive Council, 1915; of Governor's War Council, 1915; *b* 1863. *Recreation:* big-game shooting. *Address:* Royal Empire Society, Northumberland Avenue, WC2. *Club:* Authors'.

Died 12 Oct. 1943.

EASTWOOD, Harold, CB 1939; a Principal Assistant Secretary, Admiralty, since 1936; *b* 3 April 1880; *yr s* of late John A. Eastwood, Chartered Acct; *m* 1912, Monica Coleridge, *d* of late Rev. W. Boyd, Vicar All Saints, Paddington, W; one *s. Educ:* Manchester Grammar School; Trinity College, Oxford (Scholar). BA 1903. Entered Admiralty as Clerk, Class I, 1904; Private Sec. to various members of the Board of Admiralty, 1907–14. *Recreation:* gardening. *Address:* Old Marks Holtye, Nr Cowden, Kent. *T:* Cowden 3117.

Died 14 April 1941.

EATON, Col Sir Richard William, Kt 1938; TD; DL; Alderman, City of London, since 1935; Sheriff, 1937–38; *b* London, 9 Aug. 1876; *e s* of Richard Henry Eaton; *m* 1st, 1905, Florence Ellen, *d* of Thomas Allwood; 2nd, 1937, Stella, *o d* of late Walter C. Michell; one *s* three *d. Educ:* privately. Member of Stock Exchange 1899; served with The Victoria and St George's Rifles, (now Queen Victoria Rifles), 1900–07; with the Sharpshooters, 3rd County of London Yeomanry, 1907–16; attached Egyptian Army, 1916–19; overseas, 1915–19 (despatches); Commanding XIX London Regiment, 1924–28, Hon. Colonel, 1928–33; Hon. Colonel 3rd County of London (Sharp-shooters) Yeomanry Regiment since 1939; Common Councilman for Ward of Coleman Street, 1930–35; Member of both the City and County of London, Territorial Army and Air Force Association; one of HM Lieutenants for City of London; DL County of London; a Treasurer of the Lieutenancy; life Fellow of Royal Empire Society; member of London Chamber of Commerce; Commandeur de l'Ordre de la Couronne, Belgian. *Recreations:* gardening; has shot big game and birds, and followed the Hounds, played polo, tennis, golf, cricket. *Address:* Oakfield, Langley Avenue, Surbiton; Warnford Court, EC2. *TA:* Eatonnay, Stock, London. *T:* Elmbridge 3289, London Wall 2452. *Clubs:* United Service, St James's.

Died 18 June 1942.

EBBLEWHITE, Ernest Arthur, Barrister-at-Law (Middle Temple); LLD (Hon.) Sheffield; JP (Middlesex); FSA, FRHS (Hon.); Member National Rose Society (Hon.); MBAA (Hon.); *b* 2 March 1867; *s* of late John Henry Ebblewhite and late Amy Louisa Price; *m* 1st, Blanche Amy (from whom he obtained a divorce 1927), *d* of late Frederic Charles George, Wells, Som.; two *d*; 2nd, 1927, Lizzie Blanche (Commander of the Order of St John of Jerusalem, Order of Mercy), *o d* of late Robert Hermann Ries, Clapham. *Educ:* privately, London and Brussels. Chairman of Highgate Petty Sessions, 1928–45; Assistant Chairman Middlesex Quarter Sessions since 1940; Member of Court of Governors Sheffield University; late Deputy Coroner, Middx; Past Master of Worshipful Companies of Ironmongers and (twice) Parish Clerks; an Ex-Mayor of Hornsey; Chairman of Criterion Restaurants Ltd; Director of London Insurance Brokers Ltd; Chairman and Treasurer of Order of St John Clinic; Late Treasurer Epson and Ewell Cottage Hospital; Vice-Pres. League of Mercy; Chairman of Governors of Epsom County School for Boys; Governor of Charing Cross Hospital; Trustee of Middlesex Victoria Fund; National Reservist; Special Police and Member of Returned Prisoners and Naturalization Revision Committees during European War, 1914–18; Clerk of Worshipful Companies of Gardeners 1902–37, Tin Plate Workers 1894–1937 and Framework Knitters 1931–37; Knight of Justice of St John of Jerusalem; Order of Mercy with Bar, Commander of the Order of the Crown of Belgium, Ordre Spéciale (1st class) of Belgium; Officer of Order of Mérite Agricole (France). *Publications:* Histories of Livery Companies and Masonic Lodges, Topographical books, Antiquarian tracts and Press contributions. *Recreations:* Archaeology, bowls. *Address:* The White Cottage, Epsom. *T:* Epsom 243.

Died 25 March 1947.

EBERTS, Edmond Melchior, MD (McGill, 1897), MRCS (Eng.), LRCP (London); Professor Emeritus, McGill University; Consulting Surgeon Montreal General Hospital; *b* Chatham, Ont, 27 May 1873; *s* of Hermann Joseph Eberts and Sarah Mary Gilbert Urquhart; *m* 1st, Beatrice Muriel Howard, Montreal, Que.; three *s* two *d*; 2nd, Grace Lindsay Codd, Waterloo, Que.; 3rd, Gertrude Arnoldi, Ottawa, Ont. *Educ:* High School, Winnipeg; St John's Coll., Winnipeg; McGill Univ., Montreal. Postgraduate work in London, 1898–99, in Vienna, Berne, and Bonn, 1906. Entered Montreal General Hospital as interne after graduation, 1897; Medical Superintendent (chief resident) Montreal General Hospital, 1899–1902; has since served continuously on the surgical staff of this hospital; Fellow Royal Canadian College of Physicians and Surgeons (charter member); Member of Association of Canadian Clinical Surgeons; Fellow of American Surgical Association; Member of Interurban Surgical Society; Clinical member American Association for Cancer Research; FACS (charter member). *Publications:* papers in the medical press. *Recreations:* gardening, trout fishing. *Address:* Lac Paquin, via Val David, County

Terrebonne, Que. T: Ste Agathe 13—W; Room 825, 1414 Drummond Street, Montreal, Canada. T: Marquette 7422. *Clubs:* Mount Royal, Montreal.

Died 24 May 1945.

EBRINGTON, Viscount; **Hugh Peter Fortescue;** Lieut Scots Greys; *b* 9 Dec. 1920; *o s* of 5th Earl Fortescue. *Educ:* Eton; RMC Sandhurst.

Died 17 July 1942.

ECCLES, William McAdam, MS Lond., FRCS Eng.; Consulting Surgeon to and Governor of St Bartholomew's Hospital; Fellow, Royal Society of Medicine; Past President, W London Medico-Chirurgical Society; Vice-President and late Member of Council, BMA (24 years); late Chairman, UK Council, International Hospital Association; Past President, University of London Medical Graduates Society; Past President, Paget Club; late Member of Council, Royal College of Surgeons of England; Bt Lt-Col RAMC, TF, attached to 1st London General Hospital; Examiner in Surgery to the University of Cambridge; Examiner in Surgery to University of Glasgow; Examiner in Surgery to Society of Apothecaries; Examiner in Anatomy for Fellowship of Royal College of Surgeons; Lecturer on Surgery, Clinical Applied Anatomy, and Anatomy, and Demonstrator of Operative Surgery, St Bartholomew's Hospital Medical College; Senior Assistant-Surgeon, West London Hospital and City of London Truss Society; *e s* of late W. Soltau Eccles, MRCS, of Norwood; *m* Coralie (*d* 1930), 2nd *d* of late E. B. Anstie, JP, Devizes; two *s. Educ:* Univ. College School; Univ. Coll.; St Bartholomew's Hospital. *Publications:* many works and papers on surgical subjects; late Joint Editor of St Bartholomew's Hospital Reports. *Address:* Glebelands, Bidborough, Tunbridge Wells, Kent. T: Southborough 765.

Died 30 May 1946.

ECKERSLEY, Eva Mary, CBE 1939; JP, FRGS; *b* 7 Feb. 1871; *d* of James Thorp, JP; Leigh, Lancashire; *m* 1902, William Eckersley (decd), of Tyldesley, Lancashire; one *s* one *d. Educ:* London and Berlin. *Address:* c/o Barclay's Bank, Leigh, Lancashire. *Clubs:* Town and Counties, Manchester.

Died 10 Feb. 1944.

ECKSTEIN, Captain Sir Bernard, 2nd Bt *cr* 1929; MA; late East Surrey Regt; Director Kassala Cotton Co. Ltd, Sudan Plantations Syndicate, Sudan Salt, Ltd; *b* 2 Nov. 1894; *s* of Sir Frederick Eckstein, 1st Bt and Catharine (*d* 1935), *d* of Henry Mitchell, Kimberley; *S* father, 1930. *Educ:* Eton; Trinity College, Oxford. Member of the Guild of Freemen. *Heir:* none. *Address:* Kya Lami, 25 South Street, W1. T: Mayfair 5588; Oldlands Hall, Uckfield, Sussex. T: Nutley 12. *Clubs:* Bath, City of London.

Died 10 May 1948 (ext).

EDDINGTON, Sir Arthur Stanley, OM, 1938; Kt 1930; FRS 1914; Plumian Professor of Astronomy, Cambridge University, since 1913; Director of the Observatory, Cambridge, since 1914; *b* Kendal, 28 Dec. 1882; unmarried. *Educ:* Owens Coll. (now Manchester Univ.) Trinity College, Cambridge. MA (Cantab), MSc (Manchester); BSc (Lond.); Hon. DSc (Manchester, Oxford, Dublin, Bristol, Leeds, Witwatersrand, Durham, Harvard, Allahabad, Benares and NUI); LLD (Edin. and Calcutta). Senior Wrangler, 1904; Class I. Div. I. Maths. Tripos Part II, 1905; Smith's Prizeman, 1907; Fellow of Trinity College, Cambridge, 1907; President of the International Astronomical Union; of the Physical Society, 1930–32; of the Royal Astronomical Society, 1921–23; Chief Assistant at the Royal Observatory, Greenwich, 1906–13; Romanes Lecturer, 1922; Gifford Lecturer, 1927; awarded Royal Medal of Royal Society, 1928; Hon. Freeman of Kendal, 1930. *Publications:* Stellar Movements and the Structure

of the Universe, 1914; Report on the Relativity Theory of Gravitation, 1918; Space, Time, and Gravitation, 1920; The Mathematical Theory of Relativity, 1923; The Internal Constitution of the Stars, 1926; Stars and Atoms, 1927; The Nature of the Physical World, 1928; Science and the Unseen World, 1929; The Expanding Universe, 1933; New Pathways in Science, 1935; Relativity Theory of Protons and Electrons, 1936; New Pathways in Science, 1935; Relativity Theory of Protons and Electrons, 1936; The Philosophy of Physical Science, 1939. *Address:* The Observatory, Cambridge. T: 4112. *Club:* Athenæum.

Died 22 Nov. 1944.

EDDISON, Eric Rucker, CB 1929; CMG 1924; author; *b* 24 Nov. 1882; *e s* of Octavius Eddison, of St Helen's, Adel, Yorkshire, and Helen Louisa, *d* of Daniel Henry Rücker, London; *m* 1909, Winifred Grace, *o d* of George Henderson, one *d. Educ:* Eton; Trinity College, Oxford; BA 1905 (2nd class Classical Moderations; 2nd class Lit. Hum.). Entered Board of Trade, 1906; Private Secretary to successive Presidents of the Board of Trade, 1915–19; Controller of the Profiteering Act Department, 1920–21; Secretary to the Imperial Economic Conference, 1923; Comptroller of the Companies Department, Board of Trade, 1924–28; Head of Empire Trades and Economic Division in Depart of Overseas Trade, 1928–30; Deputy Comptroller-General Dept of Overseas Trade, 1930–37; Member of Council for Art and Industry, 1934–37; retired from public service to devote whole time to literary work, 1938. *Publications:* Poems, Letters and Memories of Philip Sidney Nairn, 1916; The Worm Ouroboros, 1922; Styrbiorn the Strong, 1926; Egil's Saga (translation), 1930; Mistress of Mistresses, 1935; A Fish Dinner in Memison, 1941. *Recreations:* mountains and books. *Address:* Dark Lane, Marlborough, Wilts. *Club:* Athenæum.

Died 18 Aug. 1945.

EDDOWES, Alfred, MD (Edin.): MRCP (Lond.); LRCS (Edin.); retired; late Honorary Consulting Physician, Western Skin Hospital; late President, Dermatological section of British Medical Association, and New London Dermatological Society; Lecturer, Post-Graduates' College; *s* of W. Eddowes, surgeon, Pontesbury, Salop; *m*; one *s. Educ:* Shrewsbury; Edinburgh University; Medallist in Physiology; St Bartholomew's Hospital; Vienna; Hamburg and Paris. Resident Medical Officer (House-Surgeon) Royal Salop Hospital 4½ years; in general practice in Shropshire 11 years; late Physician for Diseases of the Skin, West End Hospital for Nervous Diseases; late Physician to skin department of St George's and St James's Dispensary; to St John's Hospital for diseases of the skin; late editor for skin department of Medical Press; corresponding member of Soc. Franç. de Dermatol., 1905, and of Soc. Italiana de Dermat. e Sifilo., 1925; Hon. Dermatologist, Stage Guild (Artists Section), 1925; Surgeon-Capt. (retired) 24th Middlesex (Post Office) Vol.; Hon. Capt. RAMC (V). *Publications:* Various contributions to special department of medicine; author of the Sundial and Shadow Almanac theory of Stonehenge. *Address:* 63 Palmerston Road, Buckhurst Hill, Essex.

Died 15 Jan. 1946.

EDDY, Sir (John) Montague, Kt 1944; CBE 1926; Director Bank of London & South America, Central Argentine Railway, Buenos Ayres Midland Railway, Australian Mercantile Land & Finance Co., Royal Insurance Co. (London Board), etc.; Member Executive Committee of British Council; *b* 1881; *s* of late Edward Miller Gard Eddy, 1st Chief Commissioner of Railways, New South Wales; *m* 1907, Dorothy Hilda, *d* of William Hall, MD, FRCS, Lancaster; two *s* one *d. Recreations:* yachting, golf. *Address:* Steyne Wood Battery, Bembridge, Isle of Wight. T: Bembridge 132. *Clubs:*

Athenæum, Royal Thames Yacht, Canning; Bembridge Sailing (Bembridge); Circulo de Armas, Jockey (Buenos Aires).

Died 22 Dec. 1949.

EDEN, Charles William Guy, CMG 1929; *b* 1874; *m* 1913, Hilda Marion, *d* of late R. J. Barton, Dalkey, Co. Dublin. Late Provincial Commissioner Uganda Protectorate. *Address:* Moorside, Hindhead, Surrey. *Club:* Windham.

Died 21 July 1947.

EDEN, Denis; *b* Liverpool, 20 July 1878; *s* of William Eden; *m* 1907, Helen Parry Eden, critic; one *s* two *d.* *Educ:* University College School. Began Art education under the late F. G. Stephens; studied at St John's Wood Art School at age of 16; from there entered Royal Academy Schools, 1897; first exhibited Royal Academy, 1899. *Principal Works*—The Sluggard, 1901; Robinson Crusoe, 1902; Exit, 1905; Eat to Live, 1904; Luxury of Vain Imagination, 1906; Peire de Valeria, 1907; Green Felicity, 1909; Princess of Kensington, 1910; Henry VII granting the charter to John Cabot and his three sons, historical panel in the Houses of Parliament, 1910; Griselda at the Wheatsheaf, bought for permanent collection, Liverpool, 1911; Ex-Voto, 1913; The Almspersons Parlour, 1914; The Old Apple Tree, 1915, Walker Gallery, Liverpool; The Boy in Brown Holland, 1916; Souvenir d'Hélène, Royal Academy, 1919; A Bowl of Lemons, Royal Academy, 1920; St Cosmas and St Damian; Good News from a Far Country, Royal Academy, 1921; The Province of the Woodpecker, Royal Academy, 1922; In the City of Palladio, Royal Academy, 1924; Sweet of the Year, 1928; illustrations to Whistles of Silver, 1933; to A Guide to Caper, 1943. *Address:* Corrán, Rathdrum, Co. Wicklow, Eire.

Died 30 Oct. 1949.

EDEN, Thomas Watts, MD, FRCS (Edin.), FRCP (Lond.); FRCOG; Past-President, Royal Society of Medicine; Consulting Obstetric Physician, Charing Cross Hospital; Consulting Surgeon to Queen Charlotte's Hospital and to Chelsea Hospital for Women; temp. Major RAMC; past Examiner in Midwifery, Universities of Oxford, Cambridge, Edinburgh, and Leeds, and Royal College of Physicians, London; past editor of The Journal of Obstetrics and Gynæcology of the British Empire; past President Obstetric Section of Royal Society of Medicine; *b* 8 May 1863; *o s* of late Alfred Thomas Eden of Evesham, Worcestershire; *m* 1900, May, *o d* of late John Dove Bain, late of Broughton Craggs, Cockermouth. *Educ:* privately; University of Edinburgh and University of Leipzig. Ettles Scholar, and James Scott Scholar (University of Edinburgh), 1888; Leckie-Mactier Fellow, 1889. Devotes himself entirely to the practice of midwifery and gynæcology. *Publications:* A Manual of Midwifery, 1915; Gynæcology (Eden and Lockyer), 1916; numerous articles in Green's Ency. Med., Quain's Dictionary of Medicine and medical papers; New System of Gynæcology, edited by Eden and Lockyer, 1917. *Recreations:* golf, riding. *Address:* Stoke Damerel, Thurlestone, Devon. *Club:* Savile.

Died 22 Sept. 1946.

EDGAR, Pelham, FRSC 1915; Professor Emeritus of English Literature Victoria College, University of Toronto; *b* Toronto, 17 March 1871; *s* of late Sir James Edgar, KCMG, etc., Speaker of the House of Commons, Canada; *m* 1st, 1893, Helen Madeline (*d* 1933), *d* of late G. D'Arcy Boulton, KC; 2nd, 1935, Dona Gertrude Cameron, *d* of late Rev. C. Cameron Waller; one *d.* *Educ:* Upper Canada College, University College in the University of Toronto (BA 1892); Johns Hopkins University (PhD 1897). On graduation was housemaster in Upper Canada College, 1892–95; went from there to Johns Hopkins University, Baltimore, US, where specialised in English studies; Fellow in the English Department, 1896–97; Lecturer in French,

Victoria College, Toronto, 1897; subsequently Professor of French, and later head of the English Department; President Canadian Authors' Association, 1936, 1937; President, Association of Canadian Bookmen, 1936, 1937; Chairman, Canadian Writers' Foundation Inc. *Publications:* Henry James, Man and Author, 1927; The Art of the Novel, 1934; Across My Path, a Literary Memoir, 1948; critical articles in various English and Canadian Reviews. *Recreations:* golf, billiards. *Address:* Port Hope, Ont, Canada. *Club:* University (Ottawa).

Died 7 Oct. 1948.

EDGE, Captain Sir William, 1st Bt *cr* 1937; Kt 1922; JP; *b* 21 Nov. 1880; *s* of late Sir Knowles Edge; *m* 1904, Ada, *d* of I. Ickringill, Keighley; one *s* one *d.* *Educ:* Bolton Grammar School. Middle Temple, London. MP (L) Bolton, 1916–23; Bosworth Division of Leicester, 1927–31, (LNat) 1931–45; Junior Lord of the Treasury, 1919–22; a National Liberal Whip, 1922–23; Charity Commissioner, 1932–35. *Heir:* *s* Knowles, *b* 31 Dec. 1905. *Address:* Riversleigh, Lytham, Lancs. *Club:* Reform.

Died 18 Dec. 1948.

EDGELL, Beatrice, PhD; DLitt; Emeritus Professor of Psychology, Bedford College, University of London; *b* 1871; *y d* of Edward Higginson Edgell, Tewkesbury. *Educ:* Notting Hill High School; University College of Wales, Aberystwyth; Würzburg, Bavaria. Member of Senate of University of London, 1906–10. *Publications:* Theories of Memory; Mental Life; Ethical Problems; papers in psychological journals; Proceedings of Aristotelian Society; Encyclopædia of Religion and Ethics. *Club:* University Women's.

Died 10 Aug. 1948.

EDGERLEY, Catherine Mabel, LRCP and S Edinburgh; Officer of the Order of St John of Jerusalem; Hon. Secretary of the Brontë Society; Fellow of Royal Society of Literature; *d* of late William Blackwood, Edinburgh; *m* 1907, Samuel Edgerley, MA, MD, late Medical Superintendent of Menston Mental Hospital, near Leeds. *Educ:* Edinburgh and Germany. Formerly Assistant Medical Officer at West Riding Mental Hospital, Sheffield; Surgeon Instructress to St John's Ambulance Brigade, Otley Division. *Publications:* papers on the Brontës; and medical articles. *Recreations:* literature, motoring. *Address:* Menston, near Leeds.

Died 21 Dec. 1946.

EDGEWORTH, Francis H., MD, MA (Cantab), DSc, Lond.; Emeritus Professor of Medicine, University of Bristol; Consulting Physician, Bristol Royal Infirmary; late Major RAMC(T); *b* Bristol, 20 April 1864; *s* of T. F. Edgeworth, MRCS; *m* 1896, Ethel (*d* 1931), *d* of T. Usher; one *s.* *Educ:* Clifton College; Gonville and Caius College, Cambridge. *Publications:* papers on clinical medicine, on vertebrate embryology and Cranial Muscles of Vertebrates, 1935. *Address:* Bristol University, Bristol.

Died 14 Jan. 1943.

EDINGTON, George Henry, MD, DSc, FRCS Eng., JP, DL; FRSE; Hon. Consulting Surgeon, late Visiting Surgeon, Western Infirmary, Glasgow, and Lecturer Clinical Surgery, University of Glasgow; Examiner in Surgery, University of Glasgow; Member of the King's Bodyguard for Scotland (The Royal Company of Archers); Member, Glasgow University Court since 1939; Member of Council of Scottish National Blood Transfusion Association, 1940; Member, Scottish Civil Nursing Reserve Advisory Council, 1940–43; President Royal Philosophical Society, Glasgow, 1940–43; President Glasgow Medico-Chirurgical Society, 1936–38; President Royal Faculty of Physicians and Surgeons, 1927–29 and Representative to General Medical Council, 1928–40; Medical Referee, Sheriffdom of Lanark; member of Council and of Executive British Red Cross Society, Scottish Branch, and was Chairman of Executive, 1930–42; Chairman, War Pensions Committee, Glasgow, since 1933; late Hon. Colonel RAMC Units Lowland Division; *b* Glasgow, 10 Jan. 1870; *e s* of late G. B. Edington, ironfounder, Glasgow, and Charlotte, *d* of late P. F. Watt, MD, Demerara; unmarried. *Educ:* Kelvinside Academy; Glasgow University; King's College, London. MB, CM, Glasgow (commended), 1891; and MD (commended), 1895; MRCS (Eng.) and LRCP (Lond.), 1896; FFPS, 1897; FSA (Scot.), 1909; DSc Glasgow, 1913; FRCS (Eng.), 1931; Fellow of Association of Surgeons of Great Britain and Ireland; Fellow Royal Society of Medicine. Hon. Physician to King George V, 1922–27; Professor of Surgery in Anderson's College; Lecturer in Anatomy, Western Medical School; afterwards Lecturer in Surgery; Assistant to Professor of Clinical Surgery, University of Glasgow; and Extra Hon. Surgeon, Royal Hospital for Sick Children, Glasgow; late Hon. Consulting Surgeon, Consumption Sanatoria and Orphan Homes of Scotland, Bridge of Weir; Editor, Glasgow Medical Journal; joined Vol. Medical Staff Corps, 1901; Capt. 1904; Major RAMCT, 1908; commanded detachment at Coronation, 1911 (medal); Lt-Col 1912; Commanded 1st Lowland Field Ambulance; Col AMS (TF), 1916; ADMS Lowland Division; Commanded 1/1st LFA, Gallipoli, Egypt, and 78th General Hospital, Egypt and Palestine (1914–15 Star, War Medal, and Victory Medal, and TD); Silver Jubilee Medal, 1935; Coronation Medal, 1937. *Publications:* papers in Anatomy and Surgery, in various Journals. *Recreations:* literature, fishing. *Address:* 20 Woodside Place, Glasgow. *Clubs:* Western, Royal Scottish Automobile, College, Glasgow.

Died 24 Sept. 1943.

EDLMANN, Col Francis Joseph Frederick, DSO 1916; OBE 1946; DL Kent; JP; *b* 22 Oct. 1885; *s* of late F. J. Edlmann, JP, Hawkwood, Chislehurst, Kent; unmarried. *Educ:* Bromsgrove School; Trinity College, Oxford, MA. Called to Bar, Inner Temple, 1911; served European War in the Northumberland Fusiliers, commanded 12th Service Batt. (twice wounded, despatches twice), ex-Hon. Col 5th Bn QO Roy. W Kent Regt; ex-Director (formerly Chm.) Merchant Banking House of Brown, Shipley & Co., Ltd; Governor and Trustee of Bromsgrove School; devotes much time to local work, particularly in connection with War Pensions and Military Welfare; Member of Kent County Council, 1937–44. High Sheriff of Kent, 1939–40. *Recreations:* shooting, cricket, lawn-tennis. *Address:* Hawkwood, Chislehurst, Kent. *T:* Imperial 94. *Clubs:* Carlton, United University, City of London.

Died 8 Dec. 1950.

EDMEADES, Lt-Col William Allaire, DSO 1918; late RA; *b* 1880; *s* of late Major-General H. Edmeades, Nurstead Court, Kent; *m* 1908, Winifred Elizabeth, *d* of W. E. A. James, of Barrock Park, Cumberland; one *s* one *d*. *Educ:* Wellington College. Served South African War, 1900–01 (despatches, Queen's medal and four clasps); European War in France and Belgium, 1915–18 (despatches, DSO); retired pay, 1929. *Address:* Wrotham Place, Wrotham, Kent. *TA:* Wrotham. *T:* Boro Green 145. *Club:* Army and Navy.

Died 27 March 1942.

EDMONDS, Garnham; JP; MP (L) North-East Bethnal Green, 1922–23; *b* 1866. A Member of LCC 1910–22; Mayor of Bethnal Green, 1908. *Address:* Carbis, King's Avenue, Woodford Green, Essex. *T:* Buckhurst 0508.

Died 9 April 1946.

EDMONDSTOUNE-CRANSTOUN, Charles Joseph; *see* Cranstoun, C. J. E.

EDMUNDS, Arthur, CB 1918; MB, MS, BSc, FRCS; Hunterian Professor, Royal College of Surgeons, 1926 and 1933; Fellow of King's College, University of London; late Consulting Surgeon, Royal Navy; late

temp. Surgeon Rear-Adm., RN; Consulting Surgeon, King's College Hospital, 1934; late Surgeon, Great Northern Central Hospital; Surgeon at Cuckfield and Hothfield EMS Hospital; *b* 17 April 1874; *s* of Joseph Edmunds and Anne Stroud Swift; *m* 1911, Maud Dampier, *d* of late Martin Stratford of Gloucester. *Educ:* King's Coll. and Hosp., London. Obtained the London University Exhibition in Zoology and Physiology, and Scholarship and Gold Medals in Physiology and Surgery. *Publications:* Glandular Enlargement; The Mechanism of Respiration in Pneumothorax; A New Method of Intestinal Anastomosis; Hypospadias; (part) Manual of Surgical Treatment; various papers on surgical and scientific subjects, etc. *Recreation:* sketching. *Address:* Bramley Cottage, Charing, Kent. *Club:* Savage.

Died 29 Nov. 1945.

EDMUNDS, Lewis Humfrey, KC; DSc; *b* 1860; *e s* of James Edmunds, MD; *m* 2nd, 1903, Elaine, *e d* of Capt. W. E. Burdett; two *s* two *d*. *Educ:* University College School; University College, London (of which a Fellow); St John's College, Camb. 1st class Final Natural Science Tripos, 1883; Mathematical Tripos, 1882; DSc London, 1881. Barr 1884; QC 1895; member and ultimately leader Oxford Circuit, 1885–1906; proprietor and editor Law Journal, 1893–1907, and has formerly owned and edited other newspapers, including the Saturday Review and the National Observer; contested NW Lanarks. (LU) 1900; Totnes Division of Devonshire (Liberal), 1906; Fellow of University College, London. *Publications:* Law and Practice of Letters-Patent for Inventions, 1890, 2nd ed. 1897; Copyright in Designs, 1895, 2nd ed. 1908; Patents, Designs, and Trade Marks Acts Consolidated; various articles on scientific and legal subjects. *Clubs:* Bath, Royal Automobile.

Died 27 April 1941.

EDVINA, Madame (Marie Louise); Prima Donna; French Canadian; *b* Quebec; *d* of F. X. Martin of Vancouver, BC; *m* 1st, James Buxton (decd), of Tamworth and Vancouver; 2nd, 1901, Hon. Cecil Edwardes, 3rd *s* of 4th Baron Kensington (Tank Corps; killed in action Dec. 1917); two *d*; 3rd, 1919 Nicholas Rothesay Stuart-Wortley (*d* 1926), MA, RAF, *s* of late Maj.-Gen. Hon. E. Stuart-Wortley. *Educ:* Convent of the Sacred Heart, Montreal; studied singing in Paris with Jean de Reszke, 1906–08. Debut, Royal Opera House, Covent Garden, as Marguerita in Faust, 1908; has since appeared at the Grand Opera and the Opera Comique in Paris, the Boston Opera House, the Chicago Opera, and the Metropolitan Opera House, New York.

Died 13 Nov. 1948.

EDWARDES, Lt-Col Alexander Coburn, CBE 1920; Indian Army, retired; *b* 1873; *s* of late Gen. Sir Stanley De Burgh Edwardes, KCB. Served Aden, 1903–04; European War, 1914–18 (despatches five times, Bt Lt-Col, 4th Class Order of White Eagle of Serbia with Swords); Afghanistan, 1919 (CBE); retired 1921. *Address:* 3 Glenside, Hr. Erith Rd, Wellswood, Torquay, Devon.

Died 27 Aug. 1948.

EDWARDES, Tickner; author and priest; Captain (retired), RAMC; *b* London, 21 Sept. 1865. Enlisted as private in the RAMC, Aug. 1915; went to Gallipoli and served there until the evacuation; promoted Staff Sergeant-Major, Jan. 1917, and attached to General Headquarters Staff, Egyptian Expeditionary Force; Lieut RAMC Jan. 1918; Captain, Jan. 1919; Medical Entomologist on Staff of Col Sir Ronald Ross, Malaria Consultant to War Office, April 1918–Feb. 1919; Rector of Folkington. 1925–27; Vicar of Burpham, Arundel, 1927–35; retired, 1935. *Publications:* Sidelights of Nature, 1898; An Idler in the Wilds, 1905; The Bee-Master of Warrilow, 1906; The Lore of the Honey Bee, 1908; Lift-Luck on Southern Roads, 1910; Neighbourhood—A Year's Life in and about an English Village, 1911; The Honey-Star, 1913; Tansy, 1914; Bees as Rent Payers, 1914; With the RAMC in Egypt, 1918; The Seventh Wave, 1922; Bee-keeping for All: a Manual of Honey-Craft, 1923, revised and enlarged 5th Ed., 1939; Bee-Keeping Do's and Dont's, 1925; Sunset Bride, 1927; Life's Silver Lining, 1927; A Country Calendar, 1928; Eve, the Enemy, 1931; A Downland Year, 1939. *Address:* The Cottage, Burpham, Arundel, Sussex.

Died 29 Dec. 1944.

EDWARDES-DAVIES, Rt. Rev. David, MA; *b* 30 May 1897; *m* 1931, May, *d* of Rev. David Lewis, Rector of Llanbedr, Ruthin. *Educ:* Hatfield Hall, Univ. of Durham (Scholar, Theological Exhibitioner), BA 1904, MA 1907; St Michael's College, Aberdare, 1905. Deacon, 1905; Priest, 1906; Curate of Oswestry, 1905–08; Wrexham, 1908–12; Vicar of Brymbo, 1912–19; Mold, 1919–28; Rhyl, 1928–34; Swansea (St Mary), 1934–44; RD of Swansea, 1937–44; Canon of St Asaph Cathedral and Chairman of Diocesan Education Committee, 1930; Canon of Brecon Cathedral, 1934–44; Chancellor, 1941–44; Bishop of Bangor, 1944–48; retired, 1948. Member of Governing Body and Representative Body of Church in Wales. *Club:* Rotary.

Died 15 May 1950.

EDWARDS, Agustin, Hon. LLD (Cantab); Knight Grand Cross of the British Empire; Grand Cross of Isabel la Catolica (Spain); Grand Cross of the Crown of Italy; Grand Cross of the Golden Harvest of China; Grand Cross of George I of Greece; Grand Cross of the Order of Polonia Restituta; Grand Cross of the Order of the Polar Star of Sweden; Knight Commander of the Legion of Honour of France; *b* Santiago de Chile, 16 June 1878; *m* Olga Budge of Santiago de Chile; one *s. Educ:* St Ignatius, Santiago de Chile. Member of the House of Representatives, 1899–1910; Vice-President of the House, 1902; Prime Minister, Minister for Foreign Affairs, Envoy Extraordinary and Minister Plenipotentiary in Spain, Italy, Switzerland, Sweden, and Great Britain; Envoy Extraordinary and Minister Plenipotentiary of Chile to the Court of St James, 1910–24, and Ambassador 1935–39; Special Envoy at the marriage of the King of Spain, 1906, and at the Coronation of King George V; Special Ambassador to Coronation of King George VI, President of Third Assembly of League of Nations, 1922; President of Council of League of Nations, 1936; President of the Chilean Delegation to the League of Nations; Representative of the Chilean Red Cross on the Board of Governors of the League of Red Cross Societies; President of Fifth Pan-American Conference held at Santiago de Chile, 1923; Ambassador Extraordinary and Plenipotentiary representing Chile in the Plebiscitary Commission, Tacna y Arica Arbitration, 1925–26; President of the Chilean Academy of History, and of the Chilean Historical and Geographical Society; Member of the Chilean Academy; correspondent of the Spanish Academy of the Tongue; Member of the Spanish Academy of Moral and Political Science; Member of the Historical Institute of Peru; Member of the Historical Academies of Colombia and of Venezuela; Member of Roxburghe Club, London. *Publications:* Spain (Voyages, 2 vols); Report of the Geneva International Conference (1 vol.); Notes on Sweden; My Native Land, 1928; Peoples of Old, 1929; Adventures of John Little Sparrowgrass, 1930; The Dawn, 1931; Four Presidents of Chile, 1932; The Life of Don Frederico Santa Maria, 1932; The Silver Problem, Historical Sketch of the Chilean Press; has founded 4 of the daily newspapers and 5 of the magazines published to-day in Chile. *Recreations:* golf, motoring. *Address:* Delicias, 1656, Santiago de Chile; Villa Serena, Viña del Mar, Chile. *Clubs:* Royal Automobile, Addington Golf.

Died 18 June 1941.

EDWARDS, Maj.-Gen. Sir Alfred Hamilton Mackenzie, KBE 1920; CB 1900; MVO 1904; *b* Naini Tal, India, 22 Sept. 1862; *y s* of the late William Edwards, late Bengal Civil Service, of Craigton, Ross-shire, NB; *m* 1st, 1892, Kate (*d* 1941), *d* of late John Henderson, Middlethird, Berwickshire; (*o s* killed in action 9th May 1915); 2nd, 1942, Maria, *widow* of Lt-Col M. C. Elderton, Indian Army. *Educ:* Craigmount, Edinburgh; Eton House, Tonbridge. Entered Army through Militia (3rd Bn Seaforth Highlanders), 1883; 1st Dragoon Guards, promoted Captain 1889; Major, 1896; transferred to 5th Dragoon Guards, 1897; Lieut-Colonel 1900; Colonel 1905. Served Hazara, 1888 (medal and clasp, despatches); S Africa 1899–1902; commanded Imperial Light Horse and 'A' Division South African Constabulary (despatches, Queen's medal 4 clasps, King's medal 2 clasps, Brevet Lieut-Col, and CB); commandant, Transvaal Volunteers, 1903–05; Military Secretary to Viceroy in India, 1905; AAG Northern India, 1905–06; Chief Constable Metropolitan Police, 1906–12; Commandant-General Rhodesian Forces, 1912–23; served World War (granted Hon. Rank of Major-General, KBE, despatches); retired, 1923. *Address:* 117 Barkston Gardens, SW5. *Club:* United Service.

Died 29 March 1944.

EDWARDS, Arthur James Howie, FSA Scot; Director of the National Museum of Antiquities of Scotland since 1938; *b* 15 Jan. 1884; *s* of late Capt. John Edwards, Dundee; *m* Margaret Jane, 3rd *d* of late William Cumming, Aberdeen; one *d. Educ:* Robert Gordon's College, Aberdeen. Assistant Keeper National Museum of Antiquities of Scotland, 1912; served European War, 1914–19, in Malta, Salonika, Egypt and Palestine. *Publications:* contributions to Archæological publications. *Recreations:* bowling, shooting. *Address:* 52 Strathearn Road, Edinburgh 9. *T:* 54443.

Died 26 July 1944.

EDWARDS, Arthur Tudor, MA, MD, MChir (Cantab), FRCS (Eng.); Surgeon-in-Charge, Department of Thoracic Surgery, London Hospital; Surgeon, Brompton Hospital for Diseases of the Chest; Consultant Adviser to Minister of Health for Chest Casualties; Civilian Consultant in Chest Surgery to Royal Air Force; Hon. Consulting Thoracic Surgeon to the Army; Consulting Surgeon, King Edward VII Sanatorium, Midhurst; Consulting Thoracic Surgeon, LCC and Mount Vernon Hospitals; Examiner in Surgery, University of Cambridge; Fellow of the Royal Society of Medicine and of the Association of Surgeons; President, Society of Thoracic Surgeons of Great Britain and Ireland; Hon. Fellow, American Association of Thoracic Surgeons; Corresponding Fellow, New York Academy of Medicine; Fellow (Foreign), Belgian Society of Surgery; Hon. MD Grenoble; *s* of late William Edwards, JP, Langland, Glam; *m* Evelyn Imelda Chichester, *d* of Dr Theo Hoskin, JP, London. *Educ:* Mill Hill School; St John's College, Cambridge; Middlesex Hospital (University Scholar). Senior Broderip Scholar in Medicine and Surgery. Hunterian Professor RCS; late Surgeon and Lecturer on Surgery, Westminster Hospital; served European War, 1915–19, surgical specialist No. 6 Casualty Clearing Station; Major RAMC. *Publications:* numerous papers in chest surgery in medical journals. *Address:* 139 Harley St, W1. *T:* Welbeck 7070. *Club:* United University.

Died 25 Aug. 1946.

EDWARDS, Ven. Bickerton Cross, MA; Hon. CF; Archdeacon of St David's, since 1942; Rector of Tenby with Gumfreston, since 1913; Canon of St David's Cathedral; Treasurer of St David's Cathedral, since 1941; *b* 1874; *s* of Rev. Bickerton A. Edwards, Vicar of Llanwonno; *m* 1902, Nora Elizabeth, *d* of Dr Philip Mules, Chester; one *s* one *d. Educ:* Llandovery; Oxford University. Ordained, 1897; Curate of Gresford, 1897–1900; Rhyl, 1900–02; British Chaplain, Madeira, 1902–09; Vicar of Sharnbrook, 1909–13; Commissary to

Bishop of Northern Africa, 1907; Judge of Provincial Court, of Church in Wales, 1934; Officiating Chaplain to the Forces, Sept. 1939. *Publication:* Short Sermons in War Time. *Recreations:* fishing, tennis, and motoring. *Address:* Rectory, Tenby. *T:* Tenby 68. *Club:* Tenby and County.

Died 13 May 1949.

EDWARDS, Brig. Brian Bingay, CBE 1944; MC; Chief Engineer Scottish Command; *b* 7 Oct. 1895; *s* of late Brig.-Gen. Richard Fielding Edwards, CMG, and Isabel Bingay; *m* 1928, Ena Russell Christopherson (Jun. Comdr ATS 1941–44); no *c. Educ:* Cheltenham; RMA, Woolwich. Commissioned RE 1914; France and Flanders, 1915–18 (MC, despatches); Malaya, 1923–26; Supt Air Defence Experimental Est., 1930–35; Hong-Kong, 1935–38; Campaign in France, 1939–40 (OBE, despatches); Deputy Chief Engineer Northern Command (Colonel), 1940–42, and Chief Engineer North Midland District, 1942–43; CEL of C to 1st Army and later in BNAF (CBE, despatches), 1942–44; Chief Engineer (temp. Brig.) No. 2 District CMF 1944; Director of Works AFHQ Central Mediterranean Force. *Recreation:* sailing. *Address:* 4 St Catherine's Gardens, Corstorphine, Edinburgh 12. *Club:* Little Ship.

Died 8 Nov. 1947.

EDWARDS, Lt-Gen. Frederick Charles; RM, retired; *b* 6 Oct. 1870; *e s* of Captain Frederick Edwards, RN, Ivybridge; *m* 1899, Nona Louisa, *d* of Robert White Stevens, Plymouth; two *s. Educ:* Plymouth College; Royal Naval School, New Cross. 2nd Lt RM 1890; Captain, 1898; Major, 1908; Lt-Col 1915; 2nd Commandant, 1921; Commandant Plymouth Division, 1924; ADC to the King, 1925; Major-Gen. 1926; Lieut-General, 1928; retired, 1929; Supt of Gymnasia, Gibraltar, 1900–03; Staff Officer Ports Div. RM 1908–10; OC Shetland Section RNR 1919–20; Grand Fleet, 1914–15; West Indies, 1915–16. *Recreations:* fishing, football. *Address:* 3 Nelson Gardens, Stoke, Devonport. *T:* Devonport 679. *Club:* Junior Naval and Military.

Died 9 Feb. 1947.

EDWARDS, George; JP County of London; HM Lieutenant City of London; FRIBA 1886; *b* Kensington, 2 Nov. 1854; *m* 1879, Florence, *d* of Joseph Hodgson; one *s* three *d.* Joined 1st Middlesex Volunteers, 1871; for 16 years Chairman of the St James's Bench. *Recreations:* rowing, golf, motoring. *Address:* Cheniston, Egham, Surrey. *T:* Egham 354.

Died 3 March 1946.

EDWARDS, Brig.-Gen. Graham Thomas George, CB 1915; late 20th Hussars; *b* 7 July 1864; *m* 1920, Mary, *d* of late Capt. Horatio Pettus-Batcheler. Entered Army, 1885; Captain, 1893; Major, 1900; Lt-Col 1911; Adjutant, Yeomanry Cavalry, 1899–1901; served S African War, 1899–1902 (despatches, Queen's medal 5 clasps); European War, 1914–15 (despatches, CB). *Address:* 22 Lincoln House, Basil Street, Knightsbridge, SW3. *Club:* Cavalry.

Died 30 April 1943.

EDWARDS, Col Herbert Ivor Powell, DSO 1919; TD, DL, JP; *b* 12 March 1884; *s* of late Howell Powell Edwards, JP, of Novington Manor, Lewes, and Katharine Elizabeth, *d* of Thomas Bonsall, DL, JP, Glanrheidol, Cardiganshire; *m* Nora Theodora Imogene, 2nd *d* of late Rev. A. J. Parsons; one *s* two *d. Educ:* Winchester; Oriel College, Oxford. Served in Sussex Yeomanry, 1906–29; European War, Staff Captain, 1st SE Mounted Brigade, 1914; Major 1/1 Sussex Yeomanry, 1914; Acting Lt-Col commanding 16th Sussex Yeomanry Batt., 1917–18; Gallipoli, Egypt, Palestine, France despatches, DSO); subsequently Brigade Commander 13th (Sussex Yeomanry) Army Brigade RA, and Battery and Brigade Commander 98th (Surrey and Sussex Yeomanry, Queen Mary's) Field

Brigade RA, 1921–29; Colonel, Territorial Army, 1929–41; CC, E Sussex, 1926; Chairman, E Sussex County Council, 1934–37; Member, Sussex T. Army Association. *Publication:* History of Sussex Yeomanry, 1914–1919. *Recreations:* hunting, shooting. *Address:* Novington Manor, and Odintune Place, Lewes, Sussex. *Club:* Bath.

Died 24 Sept. 1946.

EDWARDS, Sir John Henry Priestley Churchill, 3rd Bt *cr* 1866; late Lieut 23rd Batt. London Regiment; *b* 7 July 1889; *e s* of 2nd Bt and 2nd wife, late Laura Selina, 2nd *d* of late John Capes Clark; *S* father, 1896. *Heir: b* Henry Charles Serrell Priestley [*b* 1 March 1893; *m* 1916, Margarita Ethelyn, *d* of late J. B. King Kalvi. *Education* Rossall].

Died 13 Nov. 1942.

EDWARDS, John Hugh; JP Surrey; *e s* of late Councillor John Edwards, Aberystwyth; *m* Doris, *y d* of late Sir Samuel Faire, Glenfield-Frith Park, Leicester. *Educ:* University College of Wales. Late member of County Council, Cardiganshire; was a member of the Speaker's Commission on Devolution; Governor of the University Colleges at Aberystwyth and Cardiff; MP (L) Mid-Glamorgan, 1910–22; Accrington, 1923–29; Pres. Guildford and District Free Church Federal Council; Founder President of Surrey Federation of Ratepayers' Associations and of Confederation of Federated Ratepayers' Associations of England and Wales. *Publications:* From Village Green to Downing Street; The Life of D. Lloyd George, MP; The History of Wales. *Recreation:* golf. *Address:* Fairdene, Hindhead, Surrey. *Club:* Royal Automobile.

Died 14 June 1945.

EDWARDS, Rev. John Rosindale W.; *see* Wynne-Edwards.

EDWARDS, Brig.-Gen. Richard Fielding, CMG 1917; *b* 10 Jan. 1866; *s* of late General C. A. Edwards, CB, Colonel 18th (Royal Irish) Regiment; *m* Isabel, *d* of Jacob Bingay, Yarmouth, Nova Scotia. *Educ:* Cheltenham; RMA, Woolwich. Lieut RE 1885; Capt. 1894; Major, 1902; Lt-Col 1910; Col 1913; Secretary, RE Institute, Chatham, 1897–1902; Commanding Mersey Defences, 1914–18; Chief Engineer, Malta, 1919–22; Military Member of Executive Council of Malta, 1919–21; retired, 1923. *Address:* 10 Leigh Road, Southampton.

Died 19 Dec. 1942.

EDWARDS, Brig.-Gen. William Frederick Savery, CB 1919; CMG 1917; DSO 1901; DL; formerly Captain 3rd Batt. Devonshire Regiment; *b* 27 July 1872; *s* of late Rev. N. W. Edwards; *m* 1902, Evelyn Geraldine May, *o c* of late Major Denis Bingham, King's Royal Rifles; one *d. Educ:* Christ's Hospital. Employed with Sierra Leone Frontier Police, 1899–1901; served with Ashanti Field Force, 1900 (wounded twice, despatches twice, medal with two clasps, DSO); employed with South African Constabulary, 1901–06 (Queen's medal with 5 clasps); in command of Kioga Punitive Force, Uganda, 1907; Insp-Gen. of Police and Prisons in Uganda, 1906–08; Inspector-General of Police for the East Africa and Uganda Protectorates, 1908–22; awarded the King's Police Medal, 1911; served with East African Expeditionary Force, 1914–19, being Inspector-General of Communications, 1915–Feb. 1918, and a Brigade Commander, Feb. 1918–Feb. 1919, with rank of Brigadier-General in both appointments; took the surrender of the German Commander-in-Chief, General von Lettow Vorbeck, together with his forces at Abercorn on 18 Nov. 1918 (despatches 7 times CB, CMG, Brevet Major, 1915, 2nd class Russian Order of St Anne with Swords); commanded Turkana Punitive Force, East Africa, 1915 (despatches, African General Service medal with clasp, Bt Lt-Col); Grand Officer Portuguese Order of Aviz, 1920; County Director,

Devonshire Branch, British Red Cross Society, 1926, and Col-Comdt of Cadets for the County of Devon, 1931; FRGS, FRAI. *Recreations:* cricket, polo. *Address:* The Cottage, Whipton, Exeter, Devon. *Club:* Bath.

Died 9 June 1941.

EDWARDS, Rev. Canon William George, MA; *b* 1858; *s* of Rev. W. E. Edwards, Prebendary of Hereford and Vicar of Orleton, Herefordshire; *m* Charlotte Ann (*d* 1938), *e d* of Roland Hill; two *s* three *d*. *Educ:* Shrewsbury; Keble College, Oxford. Wells Theological College, Curate of Haslemere, 1882; Alverstoke, 1886; Vicar of St Augustine's, Southampton, 1889; Warden of St Thomas' Diocesan Home for the Friendless and Fallen, 1902–21; Rector of Wonston, Hants, 1921–31; Chaplain of Basingstoke Union, 1905; Hon. Canon of Winchester, 1916; Rural Dean of Winchester, 1921–28. *Address:* 8 Winsley Avenue, W Southbourne, Bournemouth. *T:* Southbourne 2042.

Died 16 July 1942.

EDWARDS, William Stuart, CMG 1935; KC 1927; *b* Thurso, PQ, 14 July 1880; *s* of Charles Fraser Edwards, Clarence, Ont, and Effie Kemp, Edinburgh; *m* 1914, Leslie Macintosh, *y d* of Dr Donald Marshall, Kenora, Ontario; two *s* two *d*. Called to Bar, Ontario, 1909; legal officer, Dept of Justice, Canada, 1910; Secretary Dept of Justice, 1913; Assistant Deputy Minister of Justice, 1914; Deputy Minister of Justice, 1924; retired, 1941. *Address:* c/o Dept of Justice, Ottawa, Canada.

Died 2 Sept. 1944.

EFFINGHAM, 5th Earl of, *cr* 1837; **Gordon Frederick Henry Charles Howard;** 15th Baron Howard of Effingham *cr* 1554; *b* 18 May 1873; *s* of late Capt. Hon. F. C. Howard, 2nd *s* of 2nd Earl; *S* cousin, 1927; *m* 1st, 1904, Rosamond Margaret (who obtained a divorce, 1914), *d* of late E. H. Hudson; two *s*; 2nd, 1924, Madeleine, *d* of William D. Foshay. *Heir: s* Lord Howard of Effingham.

Died 7 July 1946.

EGAN, William Henry; Secretary; JP; *b* Feb. 1869. MP (Lab) West Birkenhead, 1923–24, and 1929–31; Member of Birkenhead Town Council since 1911. *Address:* 49 Hamilton Square, Birkenhead.

Died Sept. 1943.

EGERTON, Lt-Col Arthur Frederick, DSO 1900; late Queen's Own Cameron Highlanders; *b* 15 Jan. 1866; *s* of late Lt-Col Hon. A. F. Egerton, and Helen, *d* of Martin Tucker Smith (she *m* 2nd, Sir W. J. Gascoigne, KCMG); *m* 1939, Helen, widow of Capt. Francis Dykes Walker. *Educ:* Radley. Entered Army, 1886; Captain, 1894; served Soudan, 1898, including Atbara and Khartoum (British medal, Khedive's medal with two clasps); South Africa, 1899–1900 (despatches, Queen's medal four clasps, King's medal two clasps, DSO); retired, 1902; DAAG Gallipoli, 1915. *Club:* Naval and Military.

Died 19 Feb. 1942.

EGERTON, Rev. Sir Brooke de Malpas Grey-, 13th Bt; 1617; MA; *b* 19 Aug. 1845; *s* of late Rev. William Henry Egerton, 4th *s* of 9th Bt, and Louisa, *d* of late Brooke Cunliffe; *S* cousin, 1937; *m* 1878, Alice Catherine (*d* 1913), *d* of late Rev. Edward Rose Breton. *Educ:* Brasenose College, Oxford. *Heir:* Philip Reginald de Belward Egerton, *b* 3 Sept. 1885. *Address:* Upper Berwick, Shrewsbury.

Died 5 Nov. 1945.

EGERTON, George, (Mrs Golding Bright), (Mary Chavelita); writer; *b* Melbourne, Australia, 14 Dec. 1859; *e d* of late Capt. John J. Dunne, Queen's Co., and Isabel George Bynon, Glamorganshire; *m* 1st, 1888, H. H. W. Melville (*d* 1889); 2nd, 1891, Egerton Clairmonte (*d* 1901); 3rd, 1901, Reginald Golding Bright (*d* 1941). *Educ:* privately. Went in sailing vessel to Valparaiso; then to Wales and Ireland; since worked in America and

London. *Publications:* Keynotes, 1893; Discords, 1894; Young Ofeg's Ditties, 1895; Symphonies, 1897; Fantasias, 1898; The Wheel of God, 1898; Rosa Amorosa, 1901; Flies in Amber, 1905; His Wife's Family (play), 1908; The Backsliders (play), 1910; The Rafale (adaptation), 1911; The Daughter of Heaven (adaptation from Pierre Loti and Judith Gautier's play), 1912; The Attack (adaptation), 1912; Wild Thyme, Flers et Caillavet (adaptation), 1914; Camilla States her Case (play), 1925. *Recreations:* languages, dialects, needlework; genealogy (Member Genealogical Society, Original Founder Member of the Irish Genealogical Research Society). *Address:* c/o Midland Bank, Cambridge Circus, Shaftesbury Ave, WC2.

Died 12 Aug. 1945.

EGERTON, Sir Walter, KCMG 1905; CMG 1901; Hon. LLD Edin.; *b* 1858; *m* 1905, Ada Maud, OBE (*d* 1934), *d* of Rev. George Lloyd Nash, and *widow* of C. W. Sneyd-Kynnersley, CMG. *Educ:* Tonbridge School. Cadet, Straits Settlements, 1880; Magistrate, Singapore, 1881; Collector, Penang, 1883; Acting Resident, Pahang, 1894; 1st Magistrate, Penang, 1897; British Resident Negri Sembilan, Malay Peninsula, 1902; High Commissioner, Southern Nigeria, 1903–04; Governor of Lagos, 1904–06; of Southern Nigeria, 1906–12; of British Guiana, 1912–17; represented the West African Colonies and Protectorates at Coronation, 1911; Member of Malta Royal Commission, 1931. *Address:* Fair Meadow, Mayfield, Sussex. *T:* Mayfield 32. *Clubs:* Junior Carlton, Royal Automobile.

Died 22 March 1947.

EGERTON, William Francis; *b* 1868; *e s* of late Adm. Hon. Francis Egerton and Lady Louisa Caroline, *d* of 7th Duke of Devonshire; *m* 1894, Lady Alice Susan, *e d* of 9th Duke of Leeds. Late Lieut 17th Lancers. *Address:* Gawithfield, Arrad Foot, Ulverston.

Died 21 March 1949.

EGERTON, Vice-Adm. Wion De Malpas, DSO 1917; JP Dorset; serving as Convoy Commodore RNR; *b* 1879; *o surv. s* of late F.-M. Sir Charles Egerton, GCB; *m* 1913, Anita Adolphine, *o d* of late A. R. David, Eastfield, Grimsby; one *s* two *d*. Served in Harwich Force, European War, 1911–17 (despatches twice, DSO); ADC to the King, 1928; Rear-Admiral, 1928; retired, 1930; Vice-Adm., retired, 1933. *Address:* Greenings, Chilfrome, Dorchester.

Died 1 Jan. 1943.

EGGAR, Sir Henry Cooper, Kt 1910; MVO, 1906; *b* Bramshaw, New Forest, 2 Jan. 1851; *s* of late Frederick Eggar, Aldershot; *m* 1st, 1874, Emilie (*d* 1920), *d* of late Thomas Hughes; two *s* one *d*; 2nd, 1923, Beatrice Clare, 2nd *d* of late Alfred Rixon, The Planes, East Sheen. *Educ:* privately; King's College, London. Admitted a Solicitor, 1876; formerly solicitor to the Government of India at Calcutta. *Address:* 6 Baring Crescent, Exeter.

Died 3 June 1941.

EGLINTON AND WINTON, 16th Earl of, *cr* 1507; **Archibald Seton Montgomerie;** DL; Lord Montgomerie, Baron Seton and Tranent, 1448; E. of Winton, 1600; Baron Kilwinning, 1615; Baron Ardrossan (UK), 1806; E. of Winton (UK), 1859; Hereditary Sheriff of Renfrewshire; Major, late Ayrshire Yeomanry; *b* 23 June 1880; *e s* of 15th Earl, and Janet Lucretia, DBE, LLD, (*d* 1923), *d* of B. A. Cunninghame; *S* father, 1919; *m* 1st, 1908, Lady Beatrice Dalrymple (who obtained a divorce, 1922), *e d* of 11th Earl of Stair; one *s* three *d*; 2nd, 1922, Marjorie, *widow* of Guy Vernon, and *d* of Thomas Walker McIntyre; one *s*. *Educ:* Eton. Late Lieut 2nd Life Guards; served European War, signalling officer, 1914–18 (despatches). *Heir: s* Lord Montgomerie. *Address:* Eglinton, Irvine; Skelmorlie Castle, Largs, Ayrshire. *Clubs:* Orleans, Boodle's.

Died 22 April 1945.

EISDELL, Hubert Mortimer; singer; *b* London, 21 Sept. 1882; *o s* of late John Arthur Eisdell, Hampstead; *m* 1910, Katharine, 3rd *d* of late Erskine Rainy Parker of Parknook, Lake River, Tasmania, and *g d* of late Hon. Joseph Leary, Minister for Justice, Australia; one *s. Educ:* Highgate; Caius Coll., Cambridge (Exhibitioner), MA. Canada, 1904–07; Chappell Ballad and Promenade Concerts, Queen's Hall, 1910; Liza Lehmann Tour, US and Canada, 1911; Royal Philharmonic Society's Concert, 1920; Royal Choral Society; Bach Choir; Three Choirs Festival; Norwich Festival; Boosey Ballad Concerts; Records for Columbia Company; Lieut RNVR (London Division), 1912; served throughout European War; at sea, 1915–17; Admiralty Staff, 1918; toured Australia, 1920–21; retired from RNVR 1921. *Recreations:* shooting, fishing, golf.

Died 30 May 1948.

ELDER, Sir James (Alexander MacKenzie), KBE 1925; JP; Director of National Bank of Australasia, Ltd; Director, Goldsbrough, Mort & Co., Ltd; *b* 10 Nov. 1869; *s* of James Elder, Elgin, Scotland; *m* 1898, Margaret Blyth Nicoll; one *s. Educ:* Elgin Academy. After finishing his articles in a law office in Elgin, went to Australia, 1891; associated in foundation of firm of John Cooke & Co., merchants, Melbourne, 1894; Commissioner for Australia in the United States of America, 1924–26; was first commercial member of the Australian Commonwealth Board of Trade; was Acting Chairman of the Australian Section of the Wembley Exhibition; has done voluntary national service for Australia in many directions. *Address:* Mayfair, South Yarra, Melbourne, SE1, Australia. *Clubs:* Melbourne, Australian, Melbourne.

Died 29 May 1946.

ELDERTON, Captain Ferdinand Halford, CMG 1918; DSO 1900; RN (Capt. Royal Indian Navy retired); *b* 25 Jan. 1865; *s* of late Capt. E. H. P. Elderton, 26th Cameronians; *m* 1901, Ada Alice, *e d* of A. M. Eckford, Chefoo, China; one *s* one *d. Educ:* Leamington College. Served Suakim, 1885 (medal with clasp, Khedive's star); as Lieutenant commanded the RIM river gunboat Pagan in Upper Burma Expedition, 1892–93 (medal and clasp for Chin Hills); China, 1900–01; was Senior Marine and Principal Transport Officer (despatches twice, DSO, medal, and clasp relief of Pekin); appointed to BEF in France, 1st Sept. 1914; Captain RN and Divisional Naval Transport Officer, Rouen, May 1916 (despatches twice); Senior Naval Officer, Rouen, April 1917; DNTO, Dover, 1918 (CMG and Legion of Honour, 1914 Star, General Service Medal, Victory Medal); Staff of Admiral Sup. Malta, as Naval Transport Officer for Chanak, 1922; Principal Sea Transport Officer with Shanghai Defence Force, 1927. *Recreations:* golf, yachting, motoring. *Address:* 3 King's Ride Gate, Richmond, Surrey.

Died 9 Dec. 1942.

ELDRIDGE, Captain George Bernard, CBE 1920; RN, retired. Served European War, 1914–19 (despatches, CBE, Officer Order of St Maurice and St Lazarus of Italy).

Died 25 Feb. 1944.

ELEY, Col Edward Henry, CMG 1916; CBE 1923; DSO 1918; TD; DL (London) 1929; *b* 1874; *s* of Henry Eley of Colnbrook, Bucks; *m* 1909, Beatrice Eleanor, *y d* of Colonel W. Narborough, of Woolwich; one *s* one *d.* Served European War, 1914–18 (despatches, CMG, DSO), ADC to the King, 1927–41. *Address:* 11 Court Rd, Eltham, SE9.

Died 2 Nov. 1949.

ELGEE, Frank, Hon. PhD; Consulting Curator, Dorman Memorial and Stewart Park Museums, Middlesbrough; *b* 8 Nov. 1880; *m* 1914, Harriet Wragg, BA. *Educ:* home. Hon. Member of Yorkshire Philosophical Society;

Member of Roman Antiquities Com. of Yorkshire Archæological Society. *Publications:* Moorlands of North-East Yorkshire, 1912; Romans in Cleveland, 1923; Early Man in North-East Yorkshire, 1930; Archæology of Yorkshire (with wife), 1933; Scarth Wood Moor (National Trust publication), 1936. *Address:* Weyhead, Basingstoke Road, Alton, Hants.

Died 7 Aug. 1944.

ELGOOD, Sir Frank Minshull, Kt 1943; CBE 1931; FRIBA; Chairman of Executive Board and Hon. Treasurer, Church Army; Chairman, Church Army Housing, Ltd; Chairman, Eagle Star Insurance Co. (W End Board); Chairman, Margaret Street Hospital for Diseases of the Chest; Commissioner for Income Tax; *b* 5 March 1865; 2nd *s* of George I and S. M. Elgood; *m* 1891, Isabel (*d* 1940), *d* of C. I. Allen; one *s* two *d. Educ:* King's College, London. Architect; Housing Commissioner (Ministry of Health), 1919–22. *Publications:* various articles on Housing and Town Planning. *Address:* 12 Silverdale Road, Eastbourne; 37 Welbeck Street, W1. *T:* Eastbourne 3404, Welbeck 2009.

Died 17 May 1948.

ELGOOD, George S., RI 1881; ROI 1883; painter and architect; *b* 26 Feb. 1851; *s* of Samuel Elgood, Cransford, and Jane, *d* of George Shirley, Tamworth; *m* Mary (*d* 1925) *d* of Edwin Clephan, JP. *Educ:* Bloxham; privately. Best known by his paintings of gardens and Architecture, both at home and abroad, exhibited principally at RI and Fine Art Society's Galleries. *Publications:* Some English Gardens, 1904; Italian Gardens, 1907. *Address:* Knockwood, Tenterden, Kent; Barnclose, Markfield, Leics.

Died 21 Oct. 1943.

ELGOOD, Lt-Col Percival George, CMG 1915; late Devonshire Regt; late Controller-General Food Supplies, Egyptian Government; *b* 30 July 1863; *s* of G. J. Elgood, JP; *m* Bonte, CBE, 1939, *d* of Professor Sheldon Amos, LLD. *Educ:* Marlborough. Entered army, 1883; Major, 1903; retired, 1903; Financial Secretary, Egyptian Army; has been in Ministries of Interior and of Finance, Egyptian Government; served European War, 1914–18 (despatches four times, CMG). Officier Légion d'Honneur, Corona d'Italia, White Eagle of Serbia, Saviour of Greece; 3rd class Mejideh, 3rd class Osmanieh, and 3rd class Nile. *Publications:* Egypt and the Army, 1924; The Transit of Egypt, 1928; Bonaparte's Adventure in Egypt, 1931; Egypt, 1935; The Ptolemies of Egypt, 1938; notices in DNB. *Address:* Villa Beata, Heliopolis, Egypt. *Club:* Army and Navy.

Died 20 Dec. 1941.

ELIASH, Dr Mordecai; Minister of Israel at the Court of St James since 1949; *b* 11 June 1892; *er s* of Akiba and Rachel Eliash; *m* 1926, Freda Locker (*d* 1938); one *s* one *d. Educ:* Oumagne; Yaroslavl; Berlin; Oxford. General Secretary, Zionist Commission to Palestine, 1919–21; Advocate, 1921–48; Lecturer and Examiner, Jerusalem Law School; City Magistrate, Jerusalem; Pres., Palestine Jewish Bar Assoc.; Member Israel Delegation to UN, 1948. *Publications:* contributions to Journal of the Palestine Oriental Society, on Oriental subjects. *Recreations:* chess, music. *Address:* 18 Manchester Square, W1. *T:* Welbeck 0164.

Died 12 March 1950.

ELIOT, Ven. Edward Francis Whately; Archdeacon in Italy and the French Riviera; Canon of Gibraltar; *b* 15 April 1864; *s* of William and Barbara Eliot; *m* 1896, Lady Kathleen Mary Cairns (*d* 1939). *Educ:* Haileybury Col; Trinity Col, Cambridge. Curate of St George's, Tufnell Park, N, 1887–91; Holy Trinity, Bournemouth, 1891–99; Vicar of St Matthew's, Southampton, 1899–1903; All Souls, Eastbourne, 1904–14; St

Richard's, Haywards Heath, 1916–21; Chaplain of St Michael's, Beaulieu, AM, France, 1921–34. *Address:* c/o Gibraltar Diocesan Office, 35 Great Peter St, SW1.

Died 29 June 1943.

ELIOT, Rt Rev. Philip Herbert; Hon. Canon of Christ Church, Oxford; *b* 1862; *e s* of late Very Rev. P. F. Eliot, Dean of Windsor; *m* 1900, Ethel Myra, *d* of late Rev. Stirling Marshall. Suffragan Bishop of Buckingham and Archdeacon of Buckingham, 1921–44. *Address:* Somerton, Slough. *T:* Slough 298.

Died 1 April 1946.

ELKINGTON, Frederick Pellatt; *b* 29 April 1874; *s* of A. J. Elkington, JP; *g s* of the inventor of Electro-Plate. *Educ:* Dover College; London University; France and Germany. Founded Naval and Military Magazine, 1900; Chairman Adelphi Play Society and Repertory Company, Little Theatre, producing Peer Gynt, The Father, The Poetasters of Ispashan and other plays never before produced in England; helped with Glasgow Repertory Company formation. *Recreations:* yachting and collecting military colours and flags.

Died 18 June 1940.

ELLENBOROUGH, 7th Baron *cr* 1802; **Henry Astell Law,** MC; DL Dorset; Major, late KOYLI; a Gentleman-at-Arms in HM's Body Guard since 1934; *b* 11 July 1889; *o s* of 6th Baron and Alice Caroline (*d* 1916), *d* of late John Harvey Astell, Woodbury Hall, Sandy, Bedfordshire; *S* father, 1931; *m* 1923, Helen Dorothy, *o d* of H. W. Lovatt; two *s. Educ:* Eton; Sandhurst. Served European War; retired pay, 1930. *Heir: s* Hon. Richard Edward Cecil Law, *b* 14 Jan. 1926. *Address:* Warmwell House, near Dorchester, Dorset. *T:* Warmwell 270. *Clubs:* Carlton, United Service.

Died 19 May 1945.

ELLERTON, Adm. Walter Maurice, CB 1917; RN; *b* 5 Aug. 1870; 5th *s* of late Canon Ellerton; *m* 1909, Gwendolen Mary, *e d* of late R. W. Kennard of North Leigh, Bradford-on-Avon; one *s* one *d.* Flag-Comdr to C-in-C, Devonport, 1908–10; Superintendent of Physical Training, 1912; Flag-Capt. Home Fleets, Devonport, 1913; Capt. of HMS Cornwall, 1914–17; HMS Erin, 1917–19; Director of Training and Staff Duties, Admiralty, 1919–21; Rear-Admiral in Charge and Admiral Superintendent, Gibraltar Dockyard, 1923–25; Comdr-in-Chief East Indies Station, 1925–27; ADC to the King, 1921; Rear-Admiral, 1921; Vice-Admiral, 1926; retired list, 1929; Admiral, retired, 1930. *Address:* Shipways Leaze, Kington Langley, Chippenham, Wilts. *T:* Kington Langley 74. *Club:* United Service.

Died 27 Nov. 1948.

ELLES, Gen. Sir Hugh Jamieson, KCB 1935; KCMG 1919; KCVO 1929; CB 1917; DSO 1916; Chairman International Sugar Council since 1938; Regional Commissioner SW England, 1939–45; Col Commandant Royal Tank Regt since 1934; Col Comdt RE since 1935; *b* 27 April 1880; *y s* of late Lt-Gen. Sir E. R. Elles, GCIE, KCB; *m* 1st, 1912, Geraldine (*d* 1922), *d* of late Lt-Gen. Sir Gerald Morton, KCIE, CB, CVO; two *d*; 2nd, 1923, May (*d* 1937), *widow* of Lt-Col George Franks, CMG, DSO, 19th Hussars; 3rd, 1939; Mrs A. H. Du Boulay. *Educ:* Clifton College; RMA, Woolwich. Gazetted to Royal Engineers, 1899; served SA War, 1901–02; Staff College, 1913–14, psc; France, Aug. 1914–19 (Officier de la Légion d'Honneur, 1917; Commandeur, 1920; Commandeur de la Couronne, 1917; French and Belgian Croix de Guerre, American Distinguished Service Medal; DSO CB, KCMG); Capt., 1908; Bt Major, 1915; Bt Lieut-Colonel 1916; Temp. Major-General, 1918–19; Bt Col 1918; Col, 1919; Maj.-Gen., 1928; Lt-Gen. 1934; General, 1938; Military Member of Garter Mission to Japan, 1929; Director of Military Training, War Office, 1930–33; Commander 42nd (East Lancs) Division, 1933–34; Master General of Ordnance, War Office, 1934–37; retired pay, 1938. *Address:* 15a Great Cumberland Place, W1. *Clubs:* United Service, Garrick.

Died 11 July 1945.

ELLESMERE, 4th Earl of, *cr* 1846; **John Francis Granville Scrope Egerton,** MVO; Viscount Brackley, 1846; *b* 14 Nov. 1872; *e s* of 3rd Earl of Ellesmere, and Lady Katharine Louisa Phipps, 2nd *d* of 2nd Marquess of Normandy; *S* father, 1914; *m* 1905, Violet, *e d* of 4th Earl of Durham; one *s* six *d. Educ:* Eton. Lieut-Col 3rd Batt. The Royal Scots; Bt Col 1918; served in South Africa with his regiment and ADC to Maj.-Gen. Sir W. G. Knox, KCB, 1900–02; Member of the Jockey Club; Member Racecourse Betting Control Board, 1928. Owns about 13,300 acres. *Recreations:* shooting, fishing, cricket. *Heir: s* Viscount Brackley. *Address:* Mertoun, St Boswells, Scotland; Bridgewater House, SW1. *T:* Whitehall 2093; Stetchworth Park, Newmarket.

Died 24 Aug. 1944.

ELLINGER, Barnard, CBE 1921; MA (Manchester, hon.); *b* Manchester; *s* of Alexander and Mathilda Ellinger; *m* Mabel Crouchley (*d* 1943); one *s. Educ:* privately. Lecturer and writer; formerly partner in Ellinger & Co., Shipping Merchants; ex-Pres. Manchester Statistical Society; Vice-President Royal Statistical Society, 1939–40 and 1943–45; Member of Disposal Board, 1919–20. *Publications:* This Money Business; Credit and International Trade; The City: The London Financial Markets; Your Money and Mine; Productivity of Labour after the War; Laissez Faire after the War; Our Trade with Germany; Lancashire's decline in Trade with China; Japanese Competition in the Cotton Trade; The Cotton Famine–History Supplement of the Economic Journal, contributions to the Times, Le Figaro, Manchester Guardian and other papers, etc. *Address:* 32a St John's Court, Finchley Road, NW3. *T:* Maida Vale 2572.

Died 12 Sept. 1947.

ELLIOT, Frederick Barnard, CBE 1920; Officer of the Orders of the Crown of Italy and Leopold II of Belgium, Chevalier of the Legion of Honour; late Director of the Hospital Saving Association; *b* 31 July 1877; *s* of late Lieut-Colonel G. A. Elliot, the Royal Irish Regiment, and Blanche, *d* of George Barnard of Cross Deep, Twickenham; *m* 1908, Ermyngarde, *d* of Edmond de la Poer of Gurteen le Poer Kilsheelan, Co. Waterford; one *s* two *d. Educ:* Eton; Trinity College, Oxford. Called to Bar, 1903; Capt. in 5th (Service) Battalion Royal Berkshire Regt, 1914; disabled from wounds received in France, Nov. 1915; Director of Shipping, Ministry of Food, 1917; Director of Freights, Ministry of Food, 1939–41. *Address:* Moulsford Grange, Berks. *Clubs:* Union, Leander.

Died 2 Jan. 1950.

ELLIOT, Maj.-Gen. Harry Macintire C.; *see* Cawthra-Elliot.

ELLIOT, Captain Mark F.; *see* Fogg Elliot.

ELLIOT, Lt-Col William Scott, DSO 1918; RASC retired; *b* 1873; *s* of late James Scott Elliot of Blackwood, Dumfriesshire; *m* 1902, Mary Theresa, *d* of Captain George Francis Lyon, of Kirkmichael, Dumfriesshire; one *s* one *d.* Served NW Frontier of India, 1897–98 (medal and clasp); European War, 1914–18 (despatches, DSO). *Address:* The Prelude, Coleman's Hatch, Sussex.

Died 11 Feb. 1943.

ELLIOTT, Charles Hugh Babington, MA, LLD; *b* 11 March 1852; *e s* of late Rev. Canon Elliott, Vicar of Winkfield, Windsor; *m* 1893, Annie Beatrice, *widow* of Commander Caesar H. Hawkins, RN, and *d* of late George Wills, Clifton; one *s* two *d. Educ:* Brighton College; Gonville and Caius College, Cambridge. 1st class Classical Tripos, 1875; 2nd class Theological Tripos,

1876. One of HM Inspectors of Schools, 1876; Divisional Inspector, 1904; retired, 1912. *Address:* Cliff Court, Frenchay, Bristol. *TA:* Hambrook.

Died 7 Sept. 1943.

ELLIOTT, Mrs John; *see* Elliott, Maud Howe.

ELLIOTT, Hon. John Campbell, PC Can. 1926; KC, BCL, DCL; *b* Ekfrid Tp., Middlesex Co., Ontario, Canada, 25 July 1872; *s* of Geo. Campbell Elliott and Jane Gunn. *Educ:* Ekfrid Public School, Strathroy, CI; Glencoe High School. Barrister-at-Law; Osgoode Hall, 1898; BCL, Trinity University, 1898; DCL, Toronto University, 1905; Ontario Legislature, 1908, 1911 and 1914; Crown Attorney and Clerk of the Peace for Middlesex County, 1922–24; elected to House of Commons, 1925; Minister of Labour, Health, etc., 1926; Minister of Public Works, Canada, 1926–30; Postmaster-General, Canada, 1935–39. *Address:* 286 Charlotte Street, Ottawa, Canada. *Clubs:* London, London Hunt and Country, London; Ontario, Toronto; Royal Ottawa, Country, Ottawa.

Died 20 Dec. 1941.

ELLIOTT, Maud Howe, (Mrs John Elliott); author, lecturer, campaign speaker; Secretary, Art Association of Newport; Hon. Vice-President, Society of the Four Arts, Palm Beach, Florida; *b* Boston, 9 Nov. 1854; *d* of Dr Samuel Gridley Howe and Julia Ward; *m* 1887, late John Elliott, painter. *Educ:* private Schools, Boston. Has lectured Chicago, Boston, Newport; President, Newport Co. Woman Suffrage League; member Executive Committee, NE Italian War Relief Fund; member RI Food Conservation Commission, 1917; member Miantonomi Memorial Park Commn; The Golden Cross of the Redeemer (Greek); Queen Mary's Needlework Guild (British). *Publications:* A Newport Aquarelle, The San Rosario Ranche, Atalanta in the South, Mammon, Phyllida, Laura Bridgman, 1903; Roma Beata, 1904; Two in Italy, 1905; Sun and Shadow in Spain, 1908; Sicily in Shadow and Sun, 1910; The Eleventh Hour in the Life of Julia Ward Howe, 1911; Life and Letters of Julia Ward Howe (with Laura E. Richards), 1915 (awarded Joseph Pulitzer prize, Columbia University, for best American biography teaching patriotism, 1917); Three Generations, 1923; Lord Byron's Helmet, 1927; John Elliott, the story of an artist, 1930; My Cousin, F. Marion Crawford, 1934; Uncle Sam Ward and His Circle, 1938; This was my Newport, 1944; What I Saw and Heard in Panama, ad 1930–1931, 1947. *Address:* Lilliput, Lovers Lane, Newport, RI, USA. *Clubs:* Cosmopolitan (New York); Chilton, Boston Authors (Boston).

Died 19 March 1948.

ELLIOTT, Robert Charles Dunlop, CMG 1942; Proprietor Chain Provincial Newspapers in Victoria; Director Spicers & Detmold Ltd and other companies; *b* 28 Oct. 1886; *s* of late Robert Cochrane Elliott; *m* 1912, Hilda, *d* of late Hon. Theodore Fink, Melbourne. Senator for Victoria, 1928–34; personal assistant to Lord Beaverbrook when Minister for Aircraft Production, 1940; accompanied Lord Beaverbrook on Missions to Moscow and Washington; Delegate to Imperial Press Conferences, London, 1930, S Africa, and Australia. Trustee National Library Museum and Gallery of Victoria. *Address:* c/o 395 Collins Street, Melbourne, Australia. *Clubs:* Devonshire; Athenæum, Naval and Military, Melbourne.

Died 6 March 1950.

ELLIOTT, Rowley; JP; DL Co. Tyrone; MP South Tyrone, Parliament of Northern Ireland, since 1929; Fermanagh and Tyrone, 1925–29; late Chairman Co. Tyrone County Council; *b* 23 April 1877; *m* 1906; one *s* two *d*. *Address:* Craigon House, Coagh, Co. Tyrone.

Died 17 Dec. 1944.

ELLIOTT, Col William, CB 1923; CBE 1919; DSO 1917; *b* Houghton, Sussex, 14 March 1879; 2nd *s* of William Elliott and Anne, *d* of Richard Cosens. Served S African War, 1900–02; commission to Army Service Corps from Paget's Horse (Imperial Yeomanry); served European War, 1914–18, Gallipoli and Senussi Campaigns, and later Deputy Director of Supplies and Transport, Egyptian Expeditionary Force; Deputy Food Controller, Upper Silesia; Plebiscite Commission, 1920; Irish administration, 1921–22; RAF Palestine, 1923; commanded Supply Reserve Depot, Deptford, 1925–29; Assistant Director of Supplies, War Office, 1929–30; Assist Director of Supplies and Transport, War Office, 1930–33; Assistant Director of Supplies and Transport, Southern Command, 1933–36; retired pay, 1936; re-employed, 1939–41; commanding 8th Wilts HG, 1942–45; White Eagle of Servia with Cross Swords (4th Class); Order of the Nile (3rd Class). *Address:* Lloyds Bank, R. Section, 6 Pall Mall, SW1.

Died 10 Dec. 1947.

ELLIOTT-COOPER, Sir Robert; *see* Cooper.

ELLIS; *see* Heaton-Ellis.

ELLIS, Anthony Louis; theatrical producer. Formerly dramatic critic of The Star and the Manchester Daily Dispatch; has also contributed critical articles on the drama to The World, The Academy, and various reviews and magazines; was a member of the Council of the Society of Dramatic critics, and twice President of the Dramatic Debaters; later entered into theatrical management in London and provinces; productions include—A Little Bit of Fluff, Our Mr Hepplewhite, The Daisy (Liliom), The Green Cord (part author), Marriage by Instalments; Jitta's Atonement; One Hour of Life; A House of Cards, Great Possessions; Iced Wings (part author), etc. *Publications:* Prisoner at the Bar; Story-Studies of the Criminal Mind; film version of The Burgomaster of Stilemonde; radio version of Trent's Last Case; The Tragical History of Admiral Byng; Brumaire; Edwin and Angelina; His Father's Sword, etc. *Recreations:* the theatre, walking.

Died 23 Sept. 1944.

ELLIS, Engr Rear-Adm. Ernest Frank, CB 1916; *b* 21 Dec. 1855; *e s* of Joseph Harrison Ellis, Chief Inspector Machinery, RN; *m* 1883, Caroline Ann (*d* 1925), *d* of Cornelius Rickard and Sarah Croad Baggs; one *s*. Served European War, 1914–17. *Address:* Calle de José Villalonga, El Terreno, Palma de Mallorca, España.

Died 31 Jan. 1944.

ELLIS, Sir (Samuel) Howard, Kt 1943; MBE 1919; *b* 2 June 1889; *s* of Howard J. S. Ellis; *m* 1918, Mary (decd), *d* of Sir Thomas Mackenzie; *m* 1926, Ellen, *d* of Alexander Brewster Joske; one *s* one *d*. *Educ:* Auckland Grammar School; NZ Univ. BA, LLB 1912. Called to NZ Bar, 1912; to Fiji Bar, 1912; served European War, Northumberland Fusiliers, RFC, RAF, 1915–19 (wounded); prisoner of war, 1916–17; Director of Man Power and National Service, Fiji, 1942–45. *Recreations:* cricket, tennis, squash racquets. *Address:* Tamavua, Suva, Fiji.

Died 19 Jan. 1949.

ELLIS, William, MusD Cantuar, 1929; MusB University of Durham; FRCO; Hon. Adviser on Music to diocese of Newcastle; *b* Tow Law, County Durham, 13 Oct. 1868. *Educ:* Old Elvet School, Durham; Durham Cathedral. Pupil of late Dr Philip Armes, first Professor of Music in the University of Durham, and organist of the Cathedral there, 1883–93; Sub-Organist (by Chapter appointment) of that Cathedral, 1903–18; Organist of Richmond Parish Church, Yorkshire, 1894–1903; Organist and Choirmaster of Newcastle Cathedral, 1918–38; Hon. Member of University College, Durham, 1916. *Address:* Gyseburn, Hexham, Northumberland.

Died Nov. 1947.

ELLIS, Sir William Henry, GBE 1918; Commander of the Crown of Italy; late Col Engineer and Railway Staff Corps RE; Master Cutler of Sheffield, 1914–18; *b* 20 Aug. 1860; *s* of J. D. Ellis, Thurnscoe Hall, Rotherham; *m* 1889, Lucy (*d* 1938), *d* of F. W. Tetley, Weetwood, Leeds; two *s* one *d*. Doctor of Engineering, Sheffield Univ.; JP Sheffield; Member of the University Council, Infirmary Board, Savings Bank, Town Trustees, Church Burgesses, all of Sheffield; in London, two years Deputy Chairman of the Disposals Board; Member Overseas Committee Board of Trade, 1920; President of the Institution of Civil Engineers, 1926; Past President of the Iron and Steel Institute, 1924–25; late Member of National Physical Laboratory and Cambridge University Appointments Board; Member of the Privy Council Committee of the Depart of Scientific and Industrial Research, 1925–26; late Member of the Governing Body of the Imperial College of Science and Technology and of Government Commission on Drainage, etc., in Doncaster Area. *Recreations:* climbing and organ music. *Address:* Weetwood, Ecclesall, Sheffield. *T:* Beauchief 70106. *Clubs:* Carlton, Alpine.

Died 4 July 1945.

ELLISON, Lt-Gen. Sir Gerald Francis, KCB 1922; KCMG 1919; CB 1904; CMG 1916; Colonel The Loyal Regiment, 1926–31; *b* 18 Aug. 1861; 2nd *s* of Canon Ellison; *m* 1894, Lilian Amy, *o c* of Col Robert Bruce, CB; one *s* one *d. Educ:* Marlborough. Joined army 1882; passed Staff College, 1889; attached Army Headquarters, 1890–92; Staff Captain Army Headquarters, 1894–97; DAAG Aldershot, 1897–99; Winner of Gold Medal of Royal United Service Institution, 1895; Staff service, S Africa, 1899–1900 (despatches, Brevet Lt-Col, Queen's medal 4 clasps); Special service, 1902–04; Secretary War Office Reconstitution Committee; AAG Army Headquarters, 1904–05; principal Private Secretary to Secretary of State for War, 1905–08; Director of Organisation, Army Headquarters, 1908–11; Staff Officer to Inspector-General, Oversea Forces, 1911–14; European War, 1914–16 (despatches, CMG); Major-General, General Staff, 1914–15; DQMG Gallipoli, 1915; MGA Aldershot, 1916–17; DQMG War Office, and Inspector-Gen. of Communications, 1917–23; has been a United Services Trustee; Lt-Gen., 1923; retired pay, 1925. *Publications:* Home Defence, 1896; The Perils of Amateur Strategy, 1926; The Sieges of Taunton, 1936. *Address:* Canons House, Taunton. *T:* Taunton 2926.

Died 27 Oct. 1947.

ELLISON, Rev. John Henry Joshua, CVO 1938; MVO 1913; Prebendary of St Paul's Cathedral since 1931; Chaplain in Ordinary to the King since 1910; Rector of St Michael, Cornhill, since 1913; *b* 18 March 1855; *s* of Rev. Canon Ellison, founder of the Church of England Temperance Society; *m* 1st, 1888, *d* of late Archbishop Tait (*d* 1888); one *s*; 2nd, 1901, Sara Dorothy Graham, *d* of late Walter Ewing Crum; three *s* two *d. Educ:* Eton College; Merton College, Oxford. Postmaster of Merton College; 1st class, Classical Moderations; 2nd class, Lit. Hum. Was domestic chaplain to Archbishop Tait; curate of Kensington; vicar of St Gabriel's, Pimlico, 1885–95; late Chaplain-in-Ordinary and Reader at Windsor Castle both to Queen Victoria and King Edward VII; Vice-Pres. SPG, 1905; was chaplain to Archbishop Davidson; Reader to the King at Windsor Castle, 1910–13; Select Preacher, Oxford University, 1905 and 1906; joint editor of Church and Empire, 1907; Vicar of Windsor, 1894–1913; Proctor in Convocation for Diocese of London, 1920; Hon. Treasurer of Sion College, 1926, and President, 1930; Hon. Chaplain to the London Stock Exchange, 1929; Chaplain to Lord Mayor of London, 1934–35, 1939–40, and 1941–42; Hon.

Chaplain to Hon. Company of Master Mariners, 1936. *Recreation:* golf. *Address:* Buscot, 14 Gills Hill, Radlett, Herts. *Club:* Athenæum.

Died 9 Jan. 1944.

ELLSON, George, CBE 1942 (OBE 1920); TD; MInstCE, MInstT; *b* 2 June 1875; *m* 1901, Frances Mabel, *d* of Septimus Ryott, Newbury, Berks; two *s* one *d. Educ:* Ripley College; Nottingham University College, etc. After engineering apprenticeship with the Butterley Co., Ltd, Derby, commenced service in Engineer's Office, SE Rly, 1898; Chief Assistant to Chief Engineer SE and C. Rly, 1913; and Engineer for Maintenance, 1920; Deputy Chief Engineer, Southern Railway, 1923; Chief Engineer, Southern Railway, 1927–44, Engineering Consultant, 1944–46; the principal works carried out under his supervision are the Civil Engineering works required for the extension of Electrified Working from London to Brighton, Worthing and Bognor Regis, and Portsmouth (via Horsham and via Guildford); the construction of the Train Ferry Dock, Dover, the construction of the Wimbledon and Sutton and the Motspur Park to Chessington Railways, and many new Stations and Goods and Locomotive Depots; has instituted much development in welding processes on railway track, and use of special rail steels, and has inaugurated system of technical training for railwaymen in engineering department; Telford Gold Medal and Premium 1921, and Telford Premiums 1927, 1938 and 1942; Fellow and Past President Permanent Way Institution; Lt-Col, Engineer and Railway Staff Corps, RE (TA). *Publications:* various papers published by Institution of Civil Engineers. *Address:* Chyngton Down House, Seaford, Sussex. *Clubs:* Transportation; Walton Heath Golf (Epsom).

Died 29 Sept. 1949.

ELLWOOD, Bt Col Arthur Addison, DSO 1917; OBE 1918; MC; TD; JP; *b* 20 March 1886; *s* Col Arthur Ellwood; *m* 1921, Winifred, *d* of J. N. Scorer; one *s* one *d. Educ:* Lincoln. Farming, Territorial Army and Volunteers; served European War, Lincolnshire Regiment and Machine Gun Corps (despatches, DSO, MC, OBE); Cologne until May 1919; India, Aug. 1919–21; commanded 4th Batt. Lincolnshire Regt 1929–33; County Council, Lindsey, since 1934. *Address:* Manor House, Mareham, Boston. *T:* Mareham 38.

Died 15 March 1943.

ELPHINSTONE, Sir (George) Keith (Buller), KBE 1920; Elect. Engineer; Chairman of Elliot Brothers (London) Ltd; *b* Edinburgh, 1865; *s* of Hon. Edward Buller Elphinstone, late Captain 92nd Highlanders; *m* 1st, 1899, Katharine Amy (*d* 1925), *d* of Colonel A. J. Wake (retired), RA; one *d*; 2nd, 1926, Isobel Penrose, *d* of late Sir Theodore Fry, Bt. *Educ:* Charterhouse. Served apprenticeship in electrical engineering works; worked on staff of well-known electrical engineers; took up manufacture of small electrical and mechanical apparatus in 1891, joining the firm of Elliot Brothers in 1893 as a partner. *Address:* 5 Kingston House South, Ennismore Gardens, SW7. *Club:* Windham.

Died 6 July 1941.

ELSDEN, John Pascoe; Barrister-at-Law; Recorder of Birkenhead since 1943; *b* 9 May 1887; *s* of Charles William and Amy Blanche Elsden; *m* 1911, Violet Mary Vernon-Harcourt; twin *s. Educ:* Abbey School, Beckenham. Called to bar, Inner Temple, 1909; 1914 RNAS (later Major RAF); Stipendiary Magistrate St Lucia, BWI, 1920; called to Bar, Trinidad and Tobago, 1921; joined Chester and North Wales Circuit; Chairman Chester and District Employment Committee; Chairman Assistance Board Appeals Tribunal. *Address:* 22 Hough Green, Chester. *T:* Chester, 1445. *Clubs:* Grosvenor, Chester City (Chester).

Died 14 April 1950.

ELSLEY, Rev. William James; Hon. Canon of Liverpool, 1925–34; Hon. Canon Emeritus since 1934; *b* 23 April 1870; *m* Alice Rowena, *d* of late Edward Coward, Bowdon, Cheshire; no *c. Educ:* Lincoln College, Oxford. Curate of St Bartholomew's, Armley, Leeds, 1901–08; Vicar of St Anne, Stanley, 1908–34; Hon. Secretary of St Edmund's, College, 1910–34. *Publications:* Difficulties in Personal Religion, 1932; Common Misunderstandings regarding the Church, 1929; Rome and England, some questions at issue, 1931; Established and Endowed, the meaning of the terms, 1928; Jesus Christ, God or Man? a vital question, 1934. *Recreation:* golf. *Address:* Cotmaton House, Sidmouth. *T:* Sidmouth 284. *Clubs:* Athenæum, Liverpool.

Died 12 Feb. 1942.

ELTISLEY, 1st Baron *cr* 1934, of Croxton; **George Douglas (Cochrane) Newton,** KBE 1919; JP; *b* 14 July 1879; *e s* of late George Onslow Newton of Croxton Park, Cambridgeshire, and late Lady Alice L. S., *d* of 11th Earl of Dundonald; *m* 1905, Muriel, *o c* of late Lieut-Col Jemmett Duke, late 17th Lancers; one *d. Educ:* Eton; Trinity College, Cambridge. Sheriff Cambridgeshire and Huntingdonshire, 1909; Vice-Chairman Cambridgeshire County Council, 1911–19; Chairman Cambridgeshire County Council, 1919 and 1920; Assistant Secretary (unpaid) to the Ministry of Reconstruction, 1917–19; MP (C) Cambridge Borough, 1922–34; Chairman Central Chamber of Agriculture, 1934; Chairman Council of Agriculture for England, 1922–23, and Water Companies Association, 1923–31; official Adviser for Agricultural Questions at the Imperial Economic Conference, Ottawa, 1932, and the World Monetary Economic Conference, London, 1933; Director Edmundson's Electricity Corporation, Ltd, Guardian Assurance Co., and other Companies. *Address:* Croxton Park Cambridgeshire. *T:* Croxton 205. *Club:* Carlton.

Died 2 Sept. 1942 (ext).

ELTON, Oliver, MA; Hon. DLitt Durham, Manchester, Oxford, Liverpool and Reading; Hon. LLD Edin.; FBA; Hon. Fellow of Corpus Christi College, Oxford, 1930; *b* 1861; *o s* of late Rev. C. A. Elton, BD; *m* 1888, Letitia, *d* of late Rev. Dugald MacColl, MA; two *s. Educ:* Marlborough; Corpus Christi Coll., Oxford (scholar; 1st class Lit. Hum. 1884). Lecturer on English Literature at Owens College, Manchester, 1890–1900; King Alfred Prof. of English Literature, Univ., Liverpool, 1900–25; Emeritus Professor, 1926; Special Lecturer, Panjab University, winter 1917–18; Special Lecturer, University College, London, winter 1922–23; Visiting Professor, Harvard University, 1926, and 1930–31; Lowell Lecturer, Boston, USA, 1926; Visiting Professor, Bedford College for Women, London, 1927–28; Lecturer in Rhetoric, Gresham College, 1929–30; President of English Association, 1932; Hon. member Mod. Lang. Assoc. of America, 1939. *Publications:* Mythical Books of Saxo Grammaticus' Historia Danica, translated, 1894; The Augustan Ages (Periods of European Literature), 1899; Michael Drayton, 1905; Life, Letters, and occasional Writings of Frederick York Powell, 1906; Modern Studies, 1907; Survey of English Literature from 1780 to 1830, 1912; from 1830 to 1880, 1920; and from 1730 to 1780, 1928; A Sheaf of Papers, 1922; Memoir of C. E. Montague, 1929; The English Muse, 1933; G. Saintsbury, 1933; Verse from Pushkin and Others, 1935; Pushkin's Evgney Onegin in English verse, 1938; Lascelles Abercrombie, 1939; Essays and Addresses 1939; Lyrics from Polish and Serbian (Slavonic Review, 1940–1944). *Recreation:* reading. *Address:* 293 Woodstock Road, Oxford. *T:* Oxford 5401. *Clubs:* University, Liverpool.

Died 4 June 1945.

ELTRINGHAM, Harry, FRS, MA (Cantab); MA, DSc (Oxon); FRES, FZS; entomologist; *b* South Shields, 1873; *e s* of late Jos. T. Eltringham, South Shields, and Eleanor, *d* of late Thomas Adshead, Macclesfield. *Educ:*

Durham; Trinity College, Cambridge. Honours Degree in Natural Science, 1894; rowed in First Trinity Eight and Four and in University Trials. Formerly partner in shipbuilding firm of Jos. T. Eltringham & Co.; is a Director of Manchester Dry Docks Co., Ltd; Trustee and late British Representative International Entomological Congresses; entered New College, Oxford, 1909; Secretary for Publications, Royal Entomological Society of London, 1922–25; Vice-President, 1914, 1918, 1926; President, 1931–32. *Publications:* African Mimetic Butterflies; Monographs of the Genera Acraea, Heliconius, Neptis, Larinopoda; Butterfly Lore; Histological and Illustrative Methods for Entomologists; Senses of Insects; The Mind of the Bees (translated from the French of Julien Françon); and numerous papers on Insect Vision, the Histology of Special Senses and Scent Organs in Insects, etc.; Joint Author of the Section Acraeinae in Catalogus Lepidopterorum and Genera Insectorum. *Recreations:* shooting, fishing, metal and cabinet work, music, photography. *Address:* Woodhouse, Stroud, Glos. *Clubs:* Leander, Royal Societies, Royal Automobile.

Died 26 Nov. 1941.

ELVEDEN, Viscount; Arthur Onslow Edward Guinness; *b* 8 May 1912; *o s* of 2nd Earl of Iveagh; *m* 1936, Lady Elizabeth Hare, *yr d* of 4th Earl of Listowel; one *s* (*b* 20 May 1937); two *d. Educ:* Eton; Trinity College, Cambridge. *Address:* The Old Rectory, Elveden, Suffolk, via Thetford.

Died 8 Feb. 1945.

ELVERSTON, Sir Harold, Kt 1911; FCII, JP; *b* 26 Dec. 1866; 3rd *s* of late James Booth Elverston, Manchester; *m* 1899, Josephine, *d* of J. J. Taylor of Rusholme, newspaper proprietor; three *s.* Contested Worcester, 1908; MP (L) Gateshead, 1910–18; Executive Committee of the National Liberal Federation, 1906–10 and 1921–25; member Manchester City Council; member Cheshire County Council, 1921; Hon. Secretary Lancashire and Cheshire Liberal Federation, 1906–25; Member Council Manchester Royal Coll. of Music; Member Advisory Committee, Royal London Mutual Assurance Society; Director Mutual Finance Ltd. *Address:* Plas Euryn, Colwyn Bay, N Wales; 231 Strand, WC2. *T:* Central 7120; 18 Booth Street, Manchester. *T:* Manchester 3874. *Clubs:* Reform, City Livery; Reform, Manchester.

Died 10 Aug. 1941.

ELVIN, Herbert Henry; General Secretary National Union of Clerks and Administrative Workers, 1910–41 (Hon. General Secretary, 1906–10); *b* 18 July 1874; *m* 1899, M. J., *d* of Rev. G. J. Hill; three *s. Educ:* Elementary School; Evening Classes at People's Palace, Birkbeck Institution, and City of London College. Before 17 years old summoned 7 times for open air preaching and last time sentenced to term of imprisonment; engaged for many years in Social and Religious activity in East End of London; Lay Preacher since 16th year and a foundation member of London Baptist Lay Preachers' Association; Member General Council TUC, 1925; Chairman, 1938, Vice-Chairman, 1939; Fraternal Delegate American Federation of Labour, 1939; attended many International Conferences of all kinds; 7 years British Labour Adviser International Labour Organisation, Geneva; Member League of Nations Union Executive for many years; International Association for Social Legislation; National Playing Fields Association; Central Council for Physical Recreation; Vice-President International Association of Workers' Leisure, National Peace Council; Vice-Pres. International Arbitration League; Vice-President, British Workers' Sports Association; Chairman, Workers' Temperance League; Vice-Chairman, China Campaign Committee; Member: Committee on Holidays With Pay and Royal Commission on Geographical Distribution of Industrial Population; Middlesex County Council; Vice-Chairman Employers' Side Middlesex Jt

Industrial Council; Chairman Middlesex Whitley Council for Local Govt Staffs, Member Nat. Whitley Council; Council of Working Men's Coll.; Chairman Drafting Cttee of Middlesex County Religious Syllabus; Prospective Parliamentary Labour Candidate, Bath, 1918, Watford, 1922, Spen Valley, 1929 and 1931; Governor, Ruskin College, Oxford; Member, British Association for Commercial and Industrial Education, WEA; on Hitler's list of wanted persons if Britain had been successfully invaded, etc. *Publications:* Socialism for Clerks, 1913; many articles for Press. *Recreations:* in early days all kinds of sport, now golf and chess. *Address:* 9 Bromefield, Stanmore, Middlesex. *T:* Edgware 3119.

Died 9 Nov. 1949.

EMANUEL, Frank Lewis; Acting President, Society of Graphic Art; late Instructor of Etching, Central School of Arts and Crafts; Member, Art-Workers' Guild, and Society of Marine Artists; President, British League for the Rescue of Art; *b* Bayswater, 1865; *s* of Lewis Emanuel, solicitor; *m* Florence Crawford Evans; one *s*. *Educ:* University College School; University College, London; Slade School of Art Académie Julian, Paris. 1st medal drawing from life and other awards, Slade School. First exhibited Salon, Paris, and RA in 1886; A Kensington Interior (oil), acquired 1912 by Chantrey Bequest for the nation; other official acquisitions by V and A Museum; Brit. Museum (etching); War Museum; Ashmolean Museum, Oxford; Liverpool (mezzotint); Durban; New Zealand, and Tel Aviv (oils); Ghent (drawing); Prague (etchings); Guildhall Library, London (lithographs), 1936; Nelson, New Zealand (presentation portrait of Lord Rutherford), 1936; Johannesburg Museum; 1937; work reproduced in Studio, Architectural Review, Graphic, Architect, Builder, Artist and many other publications; for many years special artist to the Manchester Guardian. *Publications:* Manchester Sketches; The Illustrators of Montmartre; William Roxby Beverley; Edward Duncan; William Callow; Etching and Etchings (1930); Art Gone Mad (from the French of Camille Mauclair); Original Engraving in Colours, from the French of R. Ligeron; Charles Keene, 1935; numerous articles and art critiques. *Recreations:* travel (has visited South Africa, Ceylon, France, Belgium, Holland, Spain); the collecting of prints and illustrated books; the exposing of those critics and art officials who are damaging Art and artists by aiding in Modernist-Art swindle. *Address:* 2 St John's Gardens, W11. *T:* Park 8427.

Died 7 May 1948.

EMBLETON, Dennis, MA, MB, MRCS, LRCP; Member of Central Medical War Committee; Pathologist Ashridge EMS Hospital; Lecturer in Bacteriology, University College Hospital Medical School, London; *b* Madeira, 1881; *s* of Dennis Cawood Embleton; MD; *m* 1907, Alys Faraday Boyd; one *s* one *d*. *Educ:* Tonbridge School; Christ's Coll., Cambridge. Assistant Pathologist Univ. Coll. Hospital, 1907; Bacteriologist, 1914; Major RAMC in charge Laboratory Royal Victoria Hospital, Netley, 1914; District Cerebrospinal Fever Officer; District Tetanus Inspector. *Publications:* papers in various Medical Publications. *Recreation:* sailing. *Address:* 47 Wimpole Street, W1. *T:* Welbeck 8861; Layton Manor, nr Richmond, Yorks.

Died 17 Sept. 1944.

EMBURY, Brig.-Gen. Hon. John Fletcher Leopold, CB 1919; CMG 1916; KC; Judge of the King's Bench, Saskatchewan, since 1918; *b* Canada, 10 Nov. 1875; *s* of Allan and Frances R. Embury; *m* 1904, Dora, A., *d* of E. E. Williams, Barrie, Ont; one *s* three *d*. *Educ:* Toronto University; Osgoode Hall. Practised Law at Regina, Canada; served European War, 28th Batt., 13th Infantry Brigade, 2nd Infantry Brigade, Canadian Contingent,

and British GHQ France (Canadian Section), 1914–19 (despatches, three times, CB, CMG). *Address:* Regina, Saskatchewan, Canada.

Died 15 Aug. 1943.

EMDIN, Engr Rear-Adm. Archie Russell, CMG 1918; retired; *b* 15 Aug. 1865; *y s* of William Henry Emdin, Bristol, and Mahalah Edwards, Hereford; *m* 1891, Kate Matilda, *e d* of late Chas. Malcolm Johnson, Chief Inspector of Machinery, Royal Navy; one *d*. *Educ:* City of London School; subsequently coached at King's College, London, for the Navy. Entered Royal Naval College, Keyham, as an engineer student, 1881; awarded Newman Memorial on passing into the Royal Navy, 1887; studied three sessions at Royal Naval College, Greenwich, and obtained Professional Certificate; Engineer Commander, 1903; held appointments in Engineer-in-Chief Department of the Admiralty, 1892–98 and 1900–05; was an Admiralty Member of Engineering Committee on Standardisation; Senior Assistant to the Manager of Devonport Dockyard, 1906–09; Lecturer in Marine Engineering and Design at Royal Naval Colleges at Greenwich and Keyham; specially commended by the Admirals Commanding for services in Pelorus and London; South African War (Queen's medal); Coronation medal, 1911; Resident Admiralty Engineer Overseer in the Midlands, 1912–14; Engineer Captain, 1914; Grand Fleet, 1915 and 1916; present at Jutland (despatches); Chief Engineer, HM Dockyard, Invergordon, 1916–17, and HM Dockyard, Malta, 1917–19; Engineer-Admiral on Technical and Administrative Staff of Commander-in-Chief, The Nore, 1919–22; retired list, 1923; Officer of the Légion d'Honneur, France; Order of St Anne, 2nd Class, with Crossed Swords. *Address:* Oak Lodge, Hailsham Road, Heathfield, Sussex. *T:* Heathfield 92.

Died 15 Feb. 1950.

EMERSON, Hon. Sir (Lewis) Edward, Kt 1944; KCSG, 1947; KC 1928; Chief Justice, Supreme Court of Newfoundland, since 1944; *b* 12 May 1890; 2nd *s* of late Hon. Mr Justice George H. Emerson and Katherine Maher; *m* 1920, Ruby Edith, *d* of late Fred. W. Ayre; one *d*. *Educ:* St Patrick's Hall and St Bonaventure's College, St Johns, Newfoundland; Ampleforth College, Yorks. Read law with Furlong and Conroy; admitted to practice, 1912; practised alone until 1918; partnership with late J. P. Blackwood, KC, 1918–32; Member of the Executive Council in the Hickman Government, 1924; contested St John's East in 1924; Member of the House of Assembly for Placentia East in 1928 and a Member of the House of Assembly for St John's East, 1932; Minister of Justice and Attorney General in the Alderdice Cabinet, 1932–34; attended Imperial and Economic Conference as Delegate for Newfoundland, 1932 and World Economic Conference, 1933; partnership with J. P. Blackwood, KC, and Eric Cook, 1934–37; Commissioner for Justice and Attorney-General for Newfoundland, 1937–44; Commissioner for Defence, 1940–44. *Recreations:* golf, salmon fishing, and motoring. *Address:* Virginia Waters, Logy Bay Road, St John's, Newfoundland. *T:* 3843. *Club:* Bally Haly Golf.

Died 19 May 1949.

EMERSON, Robert Jackson, RBS; *b* Rothley, Leicestershire; *m*; one *s* two *d*. *Educ:* Leicester. Studied at Leicester Art School under B. J. Fletcher and J. C. M'Clure; gold medalist; scholarships to Paris and London; designer to Collins & Co., Leicester. *Works include:* Portrait of a Boy (Leicester Art Gallery), Veritas, 1905; Morley Memorial (Leicester); Dawn (Sheffield), 1912; Flight (Kenilworth), 1913; Ceremonial Sword Hilt in Ivory, Gold, and Silver, 1917; Weaver Memorial (Wolverhampton), Silent Suffering (Lincoln), 1918; Public Memorial to John Henry Carless, VC (Walsall), Battlefield Memorial to 34th Division, La Boisselle, France, 1923; Battlefield Memorial to 34th Division, Mont Noir, Belgium, 1923; Major A. H. S. Waters, VC, DSO, MC, Portrait Bust (bronze), 1938; The Young

Aviator, Bronze Group (Wolverhampton Royal Hospital), 1940; Golden Youth, Bronze Lifesize (Wolverhampton Art Gallery), 1941. *Recreations:* boating, painting. *Address:* Wynn Road, Penn, near Wolverhampton; Studio, Castle Street, Wolverhampton. *Club:* Chelsea Arts.

Died 7 Dec. 1944.

EMERY, Brig.-Gen. William Basil, CB 1918; CMG 1915; late RA; *b* 14 Aug. 1871; *s* of late Ven. W. Emery, Archdeacon of Ely; *m* 1910, Joyce, *e d* of late A. C. Young, JP, OBE. Entered army, 1889; Captain, 1899; Major, 1905; Lt-Col, 1914; Col 1919; served South Africa, 1902 (Queen's medal 4 clasps); European War, including France, Salonica, and Palestine, 1914–18 (despatches, CMG, CB, Bt-Col); retired pay, 1923. *Address:* Roxwell, Buckingham. *Clubs:* United Service, Royal Automobile.

Died 5 Jan. 1945.

EMLEY, Herbert Barnes, CMG 1938; MILocoE; MInstT; Divisional Waterways Officer (NE Division) Docks and Inland Waterways Executive, since 1948; *b* 18 April 1891; *s* of Frank and Annie Emley, Johannesburg, SA; *m* 1st, 1916, Dorothy Margaret Horrocks (*d* 1941), Salkeld Hall, Cumberland; one *d*; 2nd, Mrs Frances Betty Cowper, *d* of W. L. Illingworth, Flower Bank, Thorner, Yorks. *Educ:* Charterhouse. Pupil Mech. Dept, NE Rly; Works Man, Gateshead, 1923–24; Chief Mech. Eng., Kenya Uganda Rly, 1924–30; Chief Mech. Eng., Sudan Rlys, 1930–32; General Manager Sudan Rlys., 1932–39; General Manager, Aire and Calder Navigation, Leeds, 1939–47. Served European War, France, 1914–18. *Recreations:* golf, shooting, fishing. *Address:* Bracken Lodge, Shadwell, nr Leeds. *Clubs:* Royal Automobile; Leeds (Leeds).

Died 1 Nov. 1948.

EMTAGE, William Thomas Allder, MA Oxford; *b* Barbados, WI, 1862; *s* of late Edmund Emtage, Barbados; *m* 1890, Mary Catherine, *d* of late N. L. Bynoe, Barbados; one *s* one *d*. *Educ:* Harrison College, Barbados; Pembroke College, Oxford (Scholar); 1st Class Math. Mods, 1881; 1st Class Math. Final Honours, 1883; 1st Class Natural Science Honours, 1885. Lecturer in Mathematics University College, Nottingham, 1885; Assistant Professor Mathematics and Physics, 1891; Professor Mathematics and Physics, 1893; Principal, Technical Institute, Wandsworth (LCC), 1895; Director of Public Instruction, Mauritius, 1900–20; Examiner, Oxford Locals, 1889, 1890; Examiner Final Honours School, Natural Science, Oxford, 1891, 1892; Fellow, Physical Society, London, 1893. *Publications:* Mathematical Theory of Electricity; Light; Mechanics of Solids; various short papers on Mathematics and Physics. *Recreations:* woodwork, bicycling. *Address:* Bankside, Deepdene Avenue, Dorking, Surrey.

Died 21 April 1942.

ENDICOTT, William; *b* Boston, Mass, 18 April 1865; *m* 1st, 1889, Helen Southworth Shaw (*d* 1910); 2nd, 1919, Ellice Mack; no *c*. *Educ:* Harvard; AB 1887. Entered office Kidder, Peabody & Co., Bankers, Boston and New York, on leaving College; admitted to partnership, 1897; retired, 1929; Member Board of Overseers, Harvard College, 1907–17; Pres. Boston and Albany Railroad Co.; Chairman of Directors New England Trust Co., Boston; Director Bigelow-Sanford Carpet Corporation; Member of Executive Committee Employers' Liability Assurance Corporation; Director American Employers' Liability Co.; Director American Employers' Fire Insurance Co.; American Red Cross Commissioner for Great Britain, 1917–19; Knight of Grace of Order of St John of Jerusalem. *Address:* 111 Devonshire Street, Boston, Massachusetts. *Clubs:* Somerset, Harvard, Boston; Harvard, New York.

Died 25 Aug. 1941.

ENGELBACH, Reginald; Technical Adviser to the Antiquities Department, Egyptian Government, since 1942; Commander of the Crown of Italy, 1934; Chevalier of the Order of the North Star (Sweden), 1935; Membre titulaire de l'Institut d'Egypte, 1935; Member of the German Archæological Institute, 1936; Chevalier of the Légion d'Honneur (France), 1937; *b* 1888; *s* of Frederick George Engelbach, MRCS, LRCP, and Marianne Wrench; *m* 1915, Nancy, *d* of James and Mary Lambert; one *s* one *d*. *Educ:* Tonbridge School; Central Technical College, London. After obtaining the diploma of Associate of the City and Guilds of London Institute in Civil and Mechanical Engineering in 1909, joined the British School of Archæology in Egypt as assistant to Sir Flinders Petrie; joined the Artists' Rifles, 6 Aug. 1914, and served in France until Feb. 1915; subsequently served at Suvla Bay, in Egypt, Palestine, and Syria in the Royal Engineers; in 1918 travelled extensively over Palestine and Syria as member of an Anglo-French military archæological mission to report on the antiquities; demobilised with the rank of Capt, 1919; retired from Territorial Force, 1939; became Chief Inspector of Antiquities for Upper Egypt, 1920, Assistant Keeper of the Cairo Museum in 1925, Acting Keeper in 1928, Keeper, 1928–41. *Publications:* Riqqeh and Memphis VI; Harageh; Gurob (in collaboration); The Aswan Obelisk, with some remarks on the ancient Engineering; A Supplement to the Topographical Catalogue of the private tombs of Thebes; The Problem of the Obelisks; A Suggestion for the transcription of Foreign Names into the Arabic Alphabet; Ancient Egyptian Masonry, the Building Craft (in collaboration); The Great Lake of Amenophis III at Medînet Habu (in collaboration); The Quarries of the Western Nubian Desert and the ancient route to Tushka; An Index of Egyptian and Sudanese sites from which the Cairo Museum contains antiquities; Mechanical and Technical Processes; Materials (in the Legacy of Egypt), 1940; Material for a revision of the history of the Heresy Period of the XVIIIth Dynasty, 1940; An Essay on the Advent of the Dynastic Race into Egypt, and its consequences, 1942; An Introduction to Egyptian Archæology (joint), 1945; and numerous articles on Egyptian and Coptic texts, history, and arts and crafts, in English and French archæological periodicals. *Address:* 14 Block C, Baehler Mansions, Zamâlik, Cairo. *T:* 42442. *Clubs:* Turf. Gezîra Sporting, Cairo.

Died 26 Feb. 1946.

ENGLAND, Col Abraham, CMG 1919; DSO 1917; TD 1921; DL; *b* Barrowford, 3 Jan. 1867; *m* 1895, Lucie, *d* of William Dunkerley. *Educ:* privately. Manchester merchant; served 42nd and 66th Division (TF), Egypt, Gallipoli, France, and Belgium (despatches thrice, DSO, CMG, TD); MP (NL) Heywood and Radcliffe Division 1922–31; President, Manchester Reform Club, 1934. *Recreations:* gardening, golf, sailing. *Address:* 15a Trafalgar Road, Birkdale, Lancs. *Clubs:* National Liberal; Reform (Manchester).

Died 4 Jan. 1949.

ENGLAND, Rev. Arthur Creyke, MA; Archdeacon of York and Canon Residentiary and Treasurer of York Minster, 1933–46; Examining Chaplain to the Archbishop of York; *b* Bolton Percy, 1872; *s* of Rev. George A. England; *m* 1901, Jessie, *d* of Francis Brangwyn; one *s* one *d*. *Educ:* St John's College, Cambridge. Curate of Grimsby; All Saints, Hull; Vicar of St Mary, Sculcoates, 1904–18; Vicar of Hessle, 1918–28; Rector of Kirby Misperton, Yorks, 1928–33; Rural Dean of Pickering, 1928–33; Canon of York, 1917–46; Canon Missioner, Diocese of York, 1929–33; Member Central Board of Finance; Chairman of Northern Organisation; Member C of E Pensions Board and York Diocesan Board of Finance; Chairman York and E

Riding Joint Industrial Council; Chairman Hessle Urban Council; JP East Riding; Rural Dean of Hull, 1924–28. *Address:* Levisham, Pickering, Yorks.

Died 30 Sept. 1946.

ENGLAND, Edwin Thirlwall, MA; *s* of late Edwin Bourdieu England, LittD; *m* Mary Elizabeth, *d* of Stephen Marshall of Skelwith Fold, Ambleside; two *s* four *d*. *Educ:* Manchester Grammar School; Trinity College, Cambridge (Major Scholar). First-Class, Second Division, Classical Tripos Part i; Second-class, Classical Tripos Part ii (Philosophy). Assistant Master Marlborough College, 1901–08; Head Master King Edward VI School, Bury St Edmunds, 1908–12; Exeter School, 1912–27; Owen's School, 1927–29; King Edward's School, Birmingham, 1929–41. *Recreations:* gardening, fishing. *Address:* Crossingfields, Exmouth, Devon. *T:* Exmouth 2373.

Died 2 May 1945.

ENGLAND, Henry Barren, FRHS; *b* 16 Aug. 1855. *Educ:* King's College School. Law and Literature. Editor of Fun, 1895–1900. *Recreation:* natural history. *Address:* 78 Lyndhurst Road, SE15.

Died 17 May 1942.

ENGLEDOW, Charles John; Peace Commissioner, Irish Free State, for Co. Cork; JP for Cos. Cork, Carlow, and Kildare (High Sheriff, Carlow, 1893); Member County Council; District Council; Board of Governors of the District Lunatic Asylum County Infirmary; Chairman of the Board of Guardians, Co. Carlow; *b* 30 Sept. 1860; *s* of Rev. W. H. Engledow, LLD, and Clara, *d* of John Boyd, JP; *m* 1883, Jeanie, *d* of William Hepburn, JP. *Educ:* Cambridge. Many years ADC to Governor of Grenada, and subsequently to Governor-in-Chief of the Windward Islands; MP N Kildare, 1895–1900. *Address:* Rostellan Castle, Co. Cork, Ireland. *TA:* Castle, Rostellan. *Clubs:* Reform; Royal Cork Yacht.

Died 1933.

ENGLEHEART, Lt-Col Evelyn Linzee, CBE 1919; retired; *b* 1862; 2nd *s* of late Sir John Gardner Engleheart, KCB; *m* 1924, Minnie Louise, widow of W. L. Davies; no *c*. *Educ:* Charterhouse; RMC Sandhurst. 2nd RW Fusiliers, 1882; Adjutant, 1893–96; Adjutant Queens Westminster Volunteers, 1896–1900; DAAG War Office, 1900–02; DAAG Malta, 1902–05; invalided out of Service as Major after Malta fever; attached War Office, 1914; Staff Captain, 1914; DAMS 1918; Bt Lt-Col 1918, (despatches twice, CBE). *Recreations:* shooting, fishing, painting and gardening. *Address:* c/o Lloyds Bank, Cox's and King's Branch, 6 Pall Mall, SW1. *Club:* MCC.

Died 4 Feb. 1943.

ENGLISH, Sir Crisp, KCMG 1918 (CMG 1917); MB, BS (Lond.) 1904; FRCS (Eng.) 1903; Consulting Surgeon St George's Hospital, Queen Alexandra Military Hospital, Millbank, Hospital of St John and St Elizabeth, King Edward VIIth's Hospital for Officers; Hon. Consulting Surgeon Royal National Orthopædic Hospital; *s* of Thomas Johnston English, MD; *m* 1905, Annie Gaunt (*d* 1946), *d* of Angus M'Leod, Edinburgh; one *d*. *Educ:* Westminster School; St George's Hospital (William Brown Scholar). MRCS, LRCP, 1900; Murchison Schol. RCP, 1900; Jacksonian Prize, RCS, 1902; MO in charge of Troops, Tower of London. Hunterian Professor of Surgery, Royal College of Surgeons, 1903–04; late Surgeon to Grosvenor Hospital for Women; served European War, 1914–18, operating surgeon in France, 1915; Consulting Surgeon to British Salonika Force, and to British Force in Italy (despatches four times); Member of War Office Medical Board, 1918–19; Col AMS, TFR (retd 1933); Prime Warden Worshipful Company of Goldsmiths, 1937–38; Hon. Member Inter State Post-Graduate Medical Assoc., North America; FRSM; Knight of Grace, St John of Jerusalem, Member of Chapter-General; Knight-Commander of Order of George I of Greece; Order of St Sava, Serbia. *Publications:* The Language of Facts (Hunterian Oration Medical Forum), 1933; Patients and Appendicitis, 1945; Diseases of the Breast, 1947, etc. *Address:* 82 Brook Street, W1. *T:* Mayfair 0123; Chilton Hall, Sudbury, Suffolk.

Died 25 Aug. 1949.

ENGLISH, Lt-Col Ernest Robert Maling, DSO 1917; *b* 2 Dec. 1874; 2nd *s* of late Major-General Frederick English, CB, 53rd Regt, and Ellen Sophia, *d* of late Commander R. S. Maling, RN; *m* 1905, Mabel Ianthe, *y d* of W. G. Lardner, late of 11 Fourth Avenue, Hove; one *d*. *Educ:* Wellington College; RMC, Sandhurst. Entered King's Shropshire, Lieut 1895; Capt. 1905; Major, 1915; retired, 29 Nov. 1919; served South African War, 1899–1902 (wounded, Queen's medal 4 clasps, King's medal 2 clasps); European War, 1914–18; APM 7th Div., Sept. 1915; APM 1st Corps, May 1916; APM (afterwards DPM) London District, May 1918 to Nov. 1919 (wounded, DSO, Croix de Guerre, despatches twice); on the Stage and has taken up film acting since 1920. *Recreations:* cricket, golf, tennis, etc. *Address:* 52 Melton Court, SW7. *T:* Kensington 2634. *Clubs:* Junior United Service, Garrick, MCC, Free Foresters.

Died 18 Aug. 1941.

ENGLISH, Col (Hon. Brig.-Gen.) Frederick Paul, CMG 1917; DSO 1905; Royal Dublin Fusiliers, retired; *b* 1859; *m* 1st, 1887, Elizabeth (*d* 1915), *d* of Hon. William Telfair of Bon Air, Mauritius; 2nd, 1917, Winifred, *d* of late John Crown, Roker, Sunderland. *Educ:* Cheltenham Coll.; RMC Sandhurst. Served SA 1899–1902 (wounded, despatches twice, brevet Lt-Col Queen's medal six clasps; King's medal two clasps); Aden Boundary Commission; in command of column, 1903–04 (DSO); ADC to Maj.-Gen. commanding troops in Egypt, 1885–87; Ceylon, 1887; European War, 1914–18 (despatches twice, CMG). *Address:* Lapswater, Yarcombe, Devon.

Died 2 May 1946.

ENGLISH, Lt-Col William John, VC 1900; Royal Ulster Rifles; Indian Army, retired; late RASC; *b* 6 Oct. 1882; *m* 1st, Linda (*d* 1918); 2nd, 1922, Mary Isabel, *d* of late William Pyper and Mrs Pyper, Knock, Belfast. Served in ranks; 2nd Lieut Army Service Corps, 1906; Lieut 1907; Captain, 1914; Major, 1924; transferred to Indian Army, 1928; retired, 1930; served with Scottish Horse, South Africa, 1901–02 (VC, Queen's medal 5 clasps). Decorated for bravery at Vlakfontein. *Address:* 10 King's Road, Knock, Belfast.

Died 4 July 1941.

ENNEVER, William Joseph; Founder of the Pelman Institute; *b* London, 1869; *e s* of late William Joseph Ennever and Teresa Ann, *d* of late John Sherrott; *m* 1895, Mary Margaret Oldacres (*d* 1904), *e d* of Basil Ranoldson Lawson; one *d*. *Educ:* private schools. Joined editorial staff of papers under Thomas Gibson Bowles; founded the first Pelman Institute in London in 1898, and subsequently visited and organised branches in India, Australia, S Africa, Canada, France and America; added the new word Pelmanism to the English language. *Publication:* Your Mind and How to Use It. *Recreations:* travel, golf. *Address:* 18 Caroline Terrace, SW1. *Club:* Devonshire.

Died 16 Aug. 1947.

ENSOR, Maj.-Gen. Howard, CB 1923; CMG 1918; CBE 1928; DSO 1900; BA 1895, MB, BCh 1897, University of Dublin; Col Comdt RAMC since 1937; *b* 20 March 1874; *s* of Edward Ensor, MA; *m* 1912, Gladys Marian, *y d* of Col Maurice Tweedie, late Indian Army; two *s* one *d*. Served with 1st Batt. West African Frontier Force, Nov. 1897 to March 1899; Senior Medical Officer Lapai Expedition, June 1898 (medal and two clasps); entered RAMC 1899; served in South Africa, 1899–1902 (despatches, Queen's medal 4 clasps, King's medal 2 clasps, DSO); present at following general actions—Magersfontein, Paardeberg, Poplar Grove, and Driefontein, and operations in Transvaal, 1900–02; seconded to Egyptian Army, May 1902; Fourth Class Osmanieh, 1910; Senior Medical Officer, Beir Expedition, 1911–12 (despatches, medal and clasp); 3rd Class Medjidieh, 1912; restored to establishment, 1912; served European War, 1914–19 (despatches seven times, Bt Lt-Col, CMG); Lt-Col March 1915; Bt Col June 1915; Col 1925; Maj.-Gen. 1929; Deputy Director of Medical Services, Eastern Command, 1929–33; Hon. Surgeon to the King, 1930–33; retired pay, 1933. *Address:* Osborne's, Hawkhurst, Kent.

Died 22 Nov. 1942.

ENTHOVEN, (Augusta) Gabrielle (Eden), OBE; Curator of the Gabrielle Enthoven Theatre Collection since 1925; *b* London, 12 Jan. 1868; *d* of late W. G. Romaine, CB, and Frances Phoebe Tennant; *m* 1893, Maj. C. H. Enthoven, RE (*d* 1910). Worked through the Great War from 1914; head of the records, War Refugee Committee, 1915; under Red Cross, head of whole of Records Department, Central Prisoners of War, to 1920; sent to New York for Red Cross, 1921; worked for Prisoners of War through the whole of War of 1939–45 on Records; gave Theatre Collection (of theatre material of London theatres) to Victoria and Albert Museum, South Kensington, 1924. *Plays Produced:* Montmartre, Alhambra, 1912; Ellen Young, Savoy, 1916; Honeysuckle, Lyceum, New York, 1921; The Confederates, Ambassadors, 1930. *Address:* 99 Cadogan Gardens, SW3. *T:* Sloane 7060.

Died 18 Aug. 1950.

ENTWISLE, John Bertie Norreys; JP, DL; *b* 1856; *S* 1868; *o s* of late John Smith Entwisle and Caroline, 2nd *d* of Robert J. J. Norreys of Davy Hulme Hall, Co. Lancaster; *m* 1st, 1881, Mynie Sophia Tuite (*d* 1916), *d* of G. T. Dalton and *niece* of late Baroness Lisgar of Bosworth Hall, Leicestershire; 2nd, 1919, Florence Augusta, *y d* of late Sir Alexander E. Ramsay, 4th Bart, of Balmain. High Sheriff, Leicestershire, 1888. *Recreations:* golf, hunting, shooting, fishing. *Address:* Foxholes, Rochdale; Kilworth House, Rugby. *TA:* North Kilworth.

Died 20 April 1945.

EPSTEIN, Mortimer, MA, PhD; FRGS. Editor of the Annual Register since 1921 and of the Statesman's Year Book since 1919. *Address:* 14 Brondesbury Park, NW6.

Died 23 June 1946.

ERRINGTON, Lt-Col Francis Henry Launcelot, CB 1916; VD; DCL; *b* 1857; *y s* of Gen. A. C. Errington; *m* 1st, 1884, Hon. Louisa Parnell (*d* 1933), *d* of 3rd Baron Congleton; one *s* one *d*; 2nd, Ruth Frances, widow of Charles Eaton, Montreal. *Educ:* abroad; Hertford College, Oxford. Called to Bar, 1882; Chancellor of Rochester, 1906; of Bath and Wells, 1910; of Newcastle, 1912; of London, 1922; Commissary of City and Diocese of Canterbury 1928; Commissary of St Paul's, 1930; Bencher of Lincoln's Inn, 1915; Commanded Inns of Court OTC 1913–16; served in France with XI Corps and with Independent Force, 1917–19. *Publications:* 5th, 6th, 7th, and 8th editions of Hanson's Death Duties; The Clergy Discipline Act 1892, with Notes. *Address:* The Red House, Berkhamsted; 15 Old Square, Lincoln's Inn, WC2. *T:* Holborn 4104. *Clubs:* Athenæum, Royal Air Force.

Died 8 July 1942.

ERROLL, 22nd Earl of, *cr* 1453; **Josslyn Victor Hay;** 25th Hereditary Lord High Constable of Scotland *cr* 1315; Baron Kilmarnock, with seat in House of Lords, 1831; *b* 11 May 1901; *er s* of 21st Earl and Mary Lucy Victoria, *o d* of Sir Allan Mackenzie, 2nd Bt, of Glen Muick, Aberdeenshire; *S* father, 1928; *m* 1st, 1923, Lady

Idina Gordon (who obtained a divorce 1930), *d* of 8th Earl De La Warr; one *d*; 2nd, 1930, Mrs Edith M. M. Ramsay-Hill (*d* 1939). Hon. Attaché, Berlin, 1920–22. *Heir:* (to Earldom) *d* of Lady Diana Denise Hay, *b* 5 Jan. 1926; (to Barony), *b* Hon. Gilbert A. R. Hay.

Died 24 Jan. 1941.

ERSKINE, Sir James Malcolm Monteith, Kt 1929; JP; *b* 18 July 1863; *g s* of Sir David Erskine, 1st Bt, of Cambo, Fife, and *heir-pres.* to Sir Thomas Erskine, 5th Bt; *m* 1898, Cicely, *d* of Rev. Charles Penrose Quicke; four *s* one *d*. *Educ:* Wellington College; abroad. MP (C) St George's Division of Westminster, 1921–29; was on a Sussex Rural District Council; member of Parish Council; Chairman of The Clan Erskine Society Committee. *Address:* 82 and 83 Eccleston Square, SW1. *Clubs:* Carlton, Junior Carlton.

Died 5 Nov. 1944.

ERSKINE, Adm. Seymour Elphinstone, CB 1918; *b* 23 June 1863; *s* of late Sir H. D. Erskine of Cardross, KCVO; *m* 1912, Florence Laetitia, 2nd *d* of late Rev. Sir Talbot Baker, 3rd Bt, of Ranston, Dorset. Entered Navy, 1875; Commander, 1897; Capt., 1902; Rear-Admiral, 1913; Vice-Admiral retired list, 1918; Admiral retired, 1921; ADC to HM, 1912–13; Commodore RN Barracks, Chatham, 1911–13; Rear and Vice-Admiral RN Barracks, 1915–18; served Benin Expedition, 1897; China, 1900; Armed Escort Service, 1918. *Address:* Holme Farm, Sway, Hants. *Club:* Army and Navy.

Died 23 Feb. 1945.

ERSKINE, Mrs Steuart; *d* of late H. Linwood Strong; *widow* of R. Steuart Erskine, FRGS. Fellow Royal Empire Society, Royal Central Asian Society and the Women Geographers, America. *Publications:* Lady Diana Beauclerk, her life and work; Beautiful Women in History and Art; Anna Jamieson; A Royal Cavalier; Twenty Years at Court; The Magic Plumes, The Wheel of Necessity (novels); The Vanished Cities of Arabia, 1925; Trans Jordan, 1925; The Bay of Naples, 1926; Vanished Cities of Northern Africa, 1927; In Search of Herself (novel), 1927; Twenty-Nine Years: The Reign of King Alfonso XIII of Spain, 1931; Palestine of the Arabs, 1935; wrote Memoirs of Edward, 8th Earl of Sandwich, those of Sir David Erskine, Sergeant-at-Arms to the House of Commons and of King Faisal of Iraq; a contributor to magazines and periodicals; has translated books and plays from the Spanish, and has written a book on Madrid, 1922; Portrait of Argentina, 1940 (Buenos Aires); My Latch Keys (Memoirs), 1948; translation from the Spanish, The Fall of a Throne, by Alvaro Alcalá-Galiano, 1933; original play, The Parasite, produced by Stage Guild, 1933; part author of The Flame, produced at Q Theatre, 1934. *Address:* c/o Royal Empire Society, Northumberland Avenue, WC2.

Died 10 Sept. 1948.

ERSKINE, Sir Thomas Wilfrid Hargreaves John, 4th Bt *cr* 1821; DSO 1916; Lt-Col late Cameron Highlanders; *b* 27 May 1880; *s* of 3rd Bt and Grace, *d* of Thomas Hargreaves; *S* father, 1912; *m* 1911, Magdalen Janet, *d* of Sir R. W. Anstruther, 6th Bt; one *s* six *d*. *Educ:* Eton. Joined Cameron Highlanders, 1900; Captain, 1910; Major, 1915. Served European War, 1914–18 (despatches, DSO). *Heir:* *s* Thomas David, *b* 31 July 1912. *Address:* Cambo, Kingsbarns, Fife.

Died 29 April 1944.

ERSKINE, Walter Hugh, CBE 1936; MBE 1920; Assistant Serjeant at Arms in the House of Commons, 1900–29 and Deputy-Serjeant at Arms, 1929–40; *b* 27 April 1870; *s* of late Sir H. David Erskine of Cardross, KCVO and Lady Horatia Seymour, *d* of 5th Marquis of Hertford; *m* 1929, Violet Emily, *d* of late Rev. R. S. Gregory, Rector of Much Hadham. *Educ:* Charterhouse. *Address:* Longmead, Mayfield, Tunbridge Wells. *T:* Mayfield 193.

Died 15 Feb. 1948.

ERSKINE-BOLST, Captain Clifford Charles Alan Lawrence, JP; FRGS; late 1st Batt. Black Watch; *b* Kelso, 1878; *s* of Charles Young Erskine-Bolst; *m* 1920, Blanche, *d* of Senator Maguire, of Mass, USA, and *widow* of Fletcher Ryer of California, USA. *Educ:* Blair Lodge, Polmont, Perthshire. MP (C) Hackney, South Division, Aug. 1922–Dec. 1923; MP (U) Blackpool 1931–35; deeply interested in the movement for promotion of closer relations between this country and the USA, Agricultural Adviser for the Principality of Wales, 1918; Freeman of the City of London. *Address:* Moon Field, Pluckley, Kent; Les Fal 'Eze, Eze-sur-Mer, Alpes Maritimes, France. *Clubs:* Carlton, St Stephen's, Pilgrims; Inter-Allié, Paris.

Died 11 Jan. 1946.

ERSKINE-HILL, Sir Alexander Galloway, 1st Bt *cr* 1945; KC 1935; DL; *b* 3 April 1894; *s* of Robert Alexander Hill and Marion Clark Galloway; *m* 1915, Christian Colville, *o d* of John Colville, MP, Cleland, Lanarkshire; two *s* two *d*. *Educ:* Rugby; Trinity College, Cambridge. Additional surname and arms of Erskine recognised by the Lord Lyon, 1943. Served European War with 6th Batt. Cameronians, subsequently with 3rd Cameron Highlanders; ADC to GOC-in-C Scottish Command, 1916–18; called to English Bar, 1919; Scottish Bar, 1920; Standing Junior Counsel to Department of Agriculture, Scotland, 1932; Advocate-Depute, 1932–35; MP (U) North Edinburgh, 1935–45; Private Parliamentary Secretary to the Lord Advocate, 1939; Hon. Colonel, 1940. Director of LNER. *Heir: s* Robert [*b* 6 Feb. 1917; *m* 1942, Christine Alison, *o d* of Capt. H. J. Johnstone, RN; two *d*]. *Address:* 39 Heriot Row, Edinburgh. *T:* Edinburgh 26886. *Clubs:* Carlton; New, Conservative, Edinburgh.

Died 6 June 1947.

ERSKINE-MURRAY, Lt-Col Arthur, CBE 1943; DSO 1916; late Royal Artillery; DL; County Army Welfare Officer, Warwickshire, since 1947; *b* 9 Oct. 1877; 4th *s* of Alexander Erskine Erskine-Murray, Advocate, of Aberdona, and *g s* of Hon. James Murray, who was a *y s* of 7th Lord Elibank; *m* 1906, Ena Nelson (*d* 1942), *d* of Dr Henry Trestrail, FRCS; one *s*. *Educ:* Kelvinside Academy, Glasgow; University, Glasgow and University, Edinburgh. Took the degrees of MA and LLB with the intention of being called to the Scottish Bar, but in 1900 was given a Commission in the Royal Artillery; served South Africa, 1901–02 (Queen's medal with 5 clasps); Adjutant Lowland (City of Edinburgh) Heavy Artillery, 1905–10; Adjutant RA, Weymouth, 1911–14; on outbreak of European War appointed General Staff Officer, Portland Fortress, and in Jan. 1915 appointed DAQMG Southern Command; proceeded to the Dardanelles as DAQMG, Sept. 1915 (despatches, DSO); Assistant Quarter-Master General, 2nd Australian and NZ Army Corps on the Staff of Lieut-General Sir Alex. Godley, GCB, Feb. 1916; served in this capacity in Egypt (Suez Canal Defences) and in France; Cavalier of the Order of the Crown of Italy for services on the Carso front, 1917; retired pay, 1923. Sec. Warwickshire TA and AF Assoc., 1924–43. *Recreations:* golf, tennis. *Address:* 28 Jurv Street, Warwick.

Died 1 Jan. 1948.

ESCOTT, Sir Ernest Bickham S.; *see* Sweet-Escott.

ESDAILE, Katharine Ada; author; *b* 23 April 1881; *d* of Andrew and Ada McDowall; *m* Arundell Esdaile; two *s* two *d*. *Educ:* Notting Hill High School; Lady Margaret Hall, Oxford (scholar). Hon. Mods, Oxford; took up classical archæology, then the history of English sculpture, 1540–1820; Medal of Society of Arts for studies in the subject, 1928, and subsequently awarded Leverhulme Fellowship, 1937. Edited first two vols of the Notebooks of George Vertue (for Walpole Soc.). *Publications:* English Monumental Sculpture since the Renaissance, 1927; Roubiliac's Work at Trinity College, Cambridge, 1925; Life and Times of L. F. Roubiliac, 1928; Temple Church Monuments (privately printed for the Benchers), 1933; English Monuments, 1935; History of St Martin's-in-the-Fields, 1942; English Church Monuments, 1510–1840, 1946. *Recreation:* visiting Churches. *Address:* Leams End, West Hoathly, East Grinstead, Sussex. *T:* Sharpthorne 31.

Died 31 Aug. 1950.

ESMONDE, Lt-Col Sir Laurence Grattan, 13th Bt *cr* 1629; *b* 3 Nov. 1863; 2nd *s* of 10th Bt, MP, and Louisa, *d* of Henry Grattan, MP; *S* nephew 1936; *m* 1st, 1906, Sarah May (*d* 1911), *d* of Alexander John Spittall; 2nd, 1928, Pauline (*d* 1941), *d* of late Joshua James Netterville, JP. *Educ:* Oscott. Called to Bar, King's Inns, Dublin, 1890; served S African War; Lt-Col (temp.) 27th Northumberland Fusiliers, 1914–15, and 10th and 11th Bn Royal Dublin Fusiliers, 1915–17. *Heir:* Capt. John L. Esmonde.

Died 1 Feb. 1943.

ESSENDON, 1st Baron *cr* 1932, of Essendon; **Frederick William Lewis;** 1st Bt *cr* 1918; JP; *b* 1870; *s* of late Edmund Lewis and Elizabeth, *d* of John and Hannah Muschamp Dent of Weardale; *m* Daisy Eleanor, *d* of R. H. Harrison of West Hartlepool; one *s* one *d*. Chairman of Furness, Withy & Co., Ltd and of 26 other Shipping and Insurance Companies associated with Furness, Withy & Co. Ltd; Chairman of Royal Mail Lines, Ltd, and Director of Cunard White Star, Ltd; Chairman of Houlder Bros & Co., Ltd; Director of Barclays Bank Ltd, and Sun Life and Sun Insurance Offices; Member of the Committee of Lloyd's Register of Shipping: President of Chamber of Shipping of the UK, 1922–23; Deputy Chairman of Ship Licensing Committee appointed by the President of the Board of Trade, Nov. 1915; Member of Shipping Control Committee appointed by Prime Minister in 1916 to consider the demands made upon British Merchant Shipping during the European War: Chairman of Departmental Committee on Co-operative Selling in Coal Mining Industry, 1926; Member of Channel Tunnel Cttee, 1929–30; Member Obsolete Tonnage Committee, 1930–31; Chairman of Development (Public Utility) Advisory Committee, 1930–32; Member of Advisory Shipping Council of Ministry of War Transport, 1939; Chairman of Committee for Sale of Empire Wool Abroad; Hon. Treas. King George's Fund for Sailors; Commander of the Legion of Honour; Commander of the Order of the Couronne; High Sheriff for Hertfordshire, 1926–27. *Recreation:* golf. *Heir: s* Hon. Brian Edmund Lewis [*b* 7 Dec. 1903; *m* 1938, Mary, *widow* of Albert Duffill and *d* of late G. W. Booker, Los Angeles]. *Address:* Essendon Place, Essendon, Herts. *T:* Essendon 259. *Club:* Reform.

Died 24 June 1944.

ESSEX, Sir (Richard) Walter, Kt 1913; JP Glos; *b* 13 Jan. 1857; *e s* of John Essex; *m* 1st, 1881, Marie (*d* 1883), *d* of late James Chinchen of Swanage, Dorset; 2nd, 1885, Lizzie (*d* 1934), 5th *d* of John Benson, Newcastle-on-Tyne; four *c*. *Educ:* privately. Entered upon a business career early in life; has been principally concerned in the wall-paper printing industry; active in municipal affairs in Wandsworth, etc., for many years; contested Kennington, 1900; MP (L) Cirencester Div. Gloucester, 1906–10; MP (L) Stafford, 1910–18; contested Burslem Division of Stoke-on-Trent, 1919; Hon. Freeman and final MP of Borough of Stafford, 1918. *Recreations:* travel, riding. *Address:* Dixcot, North Drive, Streatham, SW16; Bourton-on-the-Water, Glos. *Clubs:* Reform, National Liberal, English-Speaking Union.

Died 15 Sept. 1941.

ESTAUNIE, Édouard, DSO; Member of the French Academy, 1923; Commandeur de la Légion d'honneur et de l'ordre de Léopold; ingénieur; directeur du matériel et de la construction au sous-secrétariat des postes et télégraphes; homme de lettres; *b* Dijon, 4 Feb. 1862. *Publications:* romans: Un Simple, 1890; Bonne Dame, 1892; L'Empreinte, couronné par l'Académie française,

1896; Le Ferment, 1899; L'Epave, 1902; La Vie secrète, 1908, Prix de la vie heureuse; Les Choses Voient, 1913; Solitudes, 1917; L'Ascension de Mr Baslèvre, 1920; L'Appel de la Route, 1922; L'Infirme aux mains de lumière, 1923; Le Labyrinthe, 1924; Le silence dans la compagne, 1926; Tels qu'ils furent, 1927; Madame Clapain, 1932; Critique d'art: Impressions de Hollande; Petits-Maîtres, 1893; Science: Les Sources d'énergie électrique, 1895; Traité pratique de télécommunication, 1904. *Address:* 41 rue Raffet, Paris.

Died 3 April 1942.

ETCHES, Major Charles Edward, CB 1935; OBE 1919; late Royal Warwickshire Regt; *b* 1872; *m* 1st, 1902, Hon. Julia Caroline M. (marr. diss. 1917), 2nd *d* of 2nd Baron Norton; three *s* one *d*; 2nd, 1917, A. Jane Sylvester Hall (*d* 1938); one *s* (and one killed in action Dec. 1941) one *d*. *Educ:* Uppingham; RMC, Sandhurst. Served Nile Expedition, 1898; S Africa, 1899–1900; European War, 1914–19. *Club:* Naval and Military.

Died 30 May 1944.

ETESON, Col Harold Carleton Wetherall, CBE 1919; retired; Royal Garrison Artillery; *b* 24 Aug. 1863; *s* of late Major-General Francis Eteson and Isabella Adelaide Wetherall; *m* 1st, Emily Hall McMeekan; 2nd, Marian Elizabeth Jones; three *d. Educ:* Perceval House, Blackheath; RM Academy, Woolwich. After three years' service in the Royal Garrison Artillery obtained the position of Officer in Charge of Danger Buildings in the Royal Laboratory, Royal Arsenal; later, was an Assistant Inspector of Warlike Stores at Woolwich and Gibraltar; took over the duty of an Officer i/c Danger Buildings, 1896; and subsequently was promoted to Assistant Superintendent Royal Laboratory; went to Malta, 1902, and until 1915 was performing Regimental duty as Major and Lt-Colonel at home and Gibraltar; commanding the Thames Section of the Thames and Medway Garrison, 1915; retired list, 1919, with rank of Colonel. *Address:* Lloyds Bank, High Street, Portsmouth.

Died 4 April 1947.

ETHERTON, Sir George Hammond, Kt 1927; OBE 1919; DL Lancs; *b* 1876; *s* of late John Humphrey Etherton; *m* 1918, Mona Gertrude, *o c* of late Robert Roy, Inner Temple; two *s. Educ:* Horsham College; abroad. Solicitor, 1901; Deputy Town Clerk, Woolwich, 1902–03; Portsmouth, 1903–08; Town Clerk, Portsmouth, 1908–20; Liverpool, 1920–22; Clerk of the Peace for Lancashire, Clerk of the Lancashire County Council, County Solicitor, Clerk of the Lancashire Mental Hospitals Board, Clerk of the Lancashire Rivers Board, 1922–44. Member: Lord Newton's Departmental Committee on Rivers Thames and Lee, 1921; Royal Commission on Land Drainage, 1927; Viscount Chelmsford's Committee on Regional Development, 1931; Lord Finlay's Committee on Assize Towns, 1936; Railways Assessment Authority, 1930–47; Governing Body. Rossall School; Board of Trustees and Managers, Preston and District Savings Bank, 1923–44; Minister of Works and Planning Advisory Panel, 1942; War Damage Commission, 1944–48; Requisitioned Land and War Works Commission; Central Land Board, 1947–48; Local Government Boundary Commission, 1945–48. Board of Management Municipal Mutual Insurance Ltd; Director, Portsmouth and Brighton United Breweries, Ltd Visiting Fellow of Nuffield College, Oxford: Chairman, Society of Clerks of the Peace of Counties and Clerks of County Councils, 1935–44. Has Order of St Anne of Russia. *Address:* West End Farm, Bracknell, Berkshire. *Club:* Carlton.

Died 3 Dec. 1949.

EURICH, Prof. Frederick William, MD, CM; Hon. Consulting Physician Hythe (Hants) Cottage Hospital; late Professor of Forensic Medicine, University of Leeds, Emeritus Professor since 1932; Hon. Consulting Physician and Hon. Consulting Pathologist, Bradford Royal Infirmary; *b* 1867; *s* of late Richard Eurich; *m* Margaret Guendolen Carter-Squire; two *s* three *d. Educ:* Edinburgh, Heidelberg, Frankfort, Berlin; MD (Gold Medal). Member of the Home Office Departmental Committee on Anthrax, 1912–19; Medal of the Textile Institute, 1937; late Consulting Physician to Bradford Royal Eye and Ear Hospital, to the Ilkley Coronation Hospital, to Titus Salt Hospital, Saltaire, and to Bingley Cottage Hospital; late Specialist Medical Referee to the Home Office for Anthrax, Aniline, and Lead Poisoning; late Assistant Medical Officer and Pathologist Lancashire County Asylum, Whittingham; late Bacteriologist to the City of Bradford and to the Bradford Anthrax Investigation Board; Member of Howard League for Penal Reform. *Publications:* papers of neurological and bacteriological interest. *Recreations:* music, entomology. *Address:* Lanshawe Cottage, Dibden Purlieu, Southampton.

Died 16 Feb. 1945.

EUSTACE, Adm. John Bridges; *b* 20 Jan. 1861; *m* Helena, *d* of late Charles Robertson of Kindeace, Ross-shire. Entered Navy, 1874; Commander, 1896; Captain, 1903; Rear-Admiral, 1913; Vice-Admiral, 1918; Adm. 1922; served East Coast of Africa and Persian Gulf in suppression of slave trade, 1880–84; at the great fires at Valetta, 1891, and at Port St Louis, 1893; Commander of HMS Hood in Crete during 1899–1900; Principal Transport Officer to the China Expeditionary Force, 1900 (medal, despatches); in command of HMS Alert in the Fisheries in Newfoundland; took part in Venezuela Blockade, 1903; appointed to command of HMS Fox, 1904; and saw considerable service in Persian Gulf and Red Sea, and acted as Escort to Prince of Wales on his trip to India; appointed to HMS Cambridge School of Gunnery, 1907, from whence he commissioned HMS Vanguard in 1910; Commodore of RN Barracks, Portsmouth, 1912; Rear-Admiral, Dec. 1914–July 1916; employed under Ministry of Munitions, Aug. 1916–Jan. 1919; retired, Nov. 1918; JP, CC, Berks; Younger Brother of the Trinity House; Alderman, and Mayor of Wokingham, 1923–28. *Address:* Denton Lodge, Wokingham, Berks. *T:* Wokingham 158.

Died 9 Aug. 1947.

EUSTICE, John, BSc (Engineering) (Lond.); ARSM; AMICE; Professor Emeritus, formerly Professor of Engineering and Vice-Principal of University College, Southampton; *b* Camborne, 1864; *s* of late W. Eustice, Mining Engineer; *m* Evelyn Margaret, *d* of James Gay, Camborne; three *d. Educ:* School of Mines, Camborne; Royal College of Science, London. Trained as a mechanical and metallurgical engineer; Whitworth Scholar, 1887; National Science Scholar, 1888; Lecturer in engineering, Hampshire County Council, 1891–92; Head of engineering department of University College, Southampton, 1892–1931; directed the manufacture of shells and the testing of materials for the Ministry of Munitions in the College Laboratories, 1915–17; Technical Director of the Austin Motor Co., Birmingham; organised the Works School of the Company, 1917–18; lectured on engineering subjects for the YMCA in various centres in England and in France, 1918–19. *Publications:* Flow of Water in Curved Pipes, 1910, and Experiments in Stream Line Motion in Curved Pipes, 1911 (Proc. Roy. Soc.); Distribution of Heat-Energy in Internal Combustion Engines (Proc. Inst. Mech. Eng.), 1915; papers on engineering and engineering education in various publications. *Recreation:* golf. *Address:* Nyewoods, 330 Hill Lane, Southampton. *Club:* Southampton Golf.

Died 24 Feb. 1943.

EVAN-THOMAS, Llewelyn, CBE 1935; *b* 11 Sept. 1859; *s* of Charles Evan-Thomas, Gnoll, Neath, Glamorgan; *m* 1887, Mary Dulcie (*d* 1942), *d* of Thos William Booker; two *s. Educ:* Charterhouse; Balliol

College, Oxford. *Recreations:* shooting, fishing, horticulture. *Address:* Pencerrig, Builth, Breconshire. *T:* Builth-Wells 230.

Died 16 April 1947.

EVANS, Vice-Adm. Sir Alfred Englefield, KBE 1943; CB 1937; OBE 1919; Vice-Admiral, Head of Naval Technical Mission in Ottawa and Member of Supply Council (North America) since 1940; *b* South Africa, 30 Jan. 1884; 2nd *s* of Dr E. W. Evans, Tadley, Hants; *m* 1908, C. S., 2nd *d* of H. Macneil, Sydney, NSW; two *d*. *Educ:* Horris Hill School; HMS Britannia. Midshipman, 1900; Commander, 1917; Captain, 1924; Rear-Admiral, 1935; served European War, 1914–18; present at Jutland (despatches); Chief of Staff, Africa Station, 1927–29; Deputy Director of Naval Intelligence, 1929–30; Captain of the Fleet, Home Fleet, 1930–33; Commodore, South America, 1933–35; Rear-Admiral 2nd in Command 1st Cruiser Squadron, 1935–36; Rear-Admiral, Gibraltar, 1937–39; Vice-Admiral 1939; retired list, 1939; Commodore (RNR) of Convoys, 1939–40. *Recreations:* cricket (Hampshire and Royal Navy), golf. *Address:* Tregonwell Lodge, Cranborne, Dorset. *T:* Cranborne 9. *Clubs:* Naval and Military, Zingari, MCC.

Died 29 Dec. 1944.

EVANS, Sir Arthur, Kt 1911; DLitt Oxford; Hon. LLD Edin.; Hon. DLitt Dublin; MA; Hon. PhD Berlin, 1910; FRS, PSA, 1914–19; Fellow of Brasenose College, Oxford; Frazer Lecturer in Social Anthropology, Cambridge University, 1930–31; *b* Nash Mills, Herts, 8 July 1851; *e s* of late Sir John Evans, KCB; *m* 1878, Margaret (*d* 1893), *d* of late Prof. E. A. Freeman. *Educ:* Harrow; Brasenose Coll. Oxford; Göttingen; First class Modern History. Travelled in Finland and Russian Lapland, 1873, 1874; and in the Balkan countries, 1875 onwards; in 1882 imprisoned by Austrian Government on a charge of complicity in Crivoscian Insurrection in S Dalmatia; in 1884 made Keeper of the Ashmolean Museum in the University of Oxford, and superintended its reorganisation, at present Hon. Keeper; from 1893 onwards Archæological investigations in Crete resulting in discovery of præ-Phœnician Script; 1900–08 excavated the prehistoric Palace of Knossos; Keeper of Ashmolean Museum, 1884–1908; Hon. Keeper since 1890; Extraordinary Professor of Prehistoric Archæology; Royal Gold Medallist, RIBA, 1909; Petrie Medal, 1931; Copley Medal of Royal Society, 1936; Societies, Antiquaries (President, 1914–19), Hellenic, Numismatics, etc.; President of the British Association, 1916–19; foreign member of Royal Academy of Lincei, Rome, Bavarian Academy, Munich, R. Swedish Academy, R. Dutch Academy, Amsterdam, R. Society of Northern Antiquaries, Copenhagen, and of German Archæological Institute, of the Imp. Russian Archæological Society, Corr. of the Institute of France, and Officer de l'Instruction Publique. *Publications:* Through Bosnia, etc., 1895; Illyrian Letters (republication of letters to Manchester Guardian); Antiquarian Researches in Illyricum, 1883–1885; various Numismatic works (Horsemen of Tarentum, Syracusan Medallions, etc.); Cretan Pictographs and Præ-Phœnician Script, 1896; edited and supplemented Freeman's Sicily, vol. iv; The Horseman of Tarentum; The Mycenæan Tree and Pillar Cult, 1901; Reports on the Excavations of the Palace of Knossos; Tombs of Knossos, etc.; Scripta Minoa, 1909; Palace of Minos I, 1922, II (Parts I and II), 1928, III, 1930, IV, 1935; The Earlier Religion of Greece in the Light of Cretan Discoveries, 1931; Jarn Mound, 1933. *Recreations:* gardening, archæological exploration; private collection, Greek and Roman coins and gems, and prehistoric antiquities; Silver Wolf and Member Council Boy Scouts Association. *Address:* Youlbury, near Oxford. *T:* Boarshill 10. *Clubs:* Athenæum, Royal Societies.

Died 11 July 1941.

EVANS, Arthur Henry, OBE, MS, MD (Lond.), FRCS (Eng.); Surgeon, 1902–37, and Lecturer on Surgery Westminster Hospital; Hunterian Professor, Royal College of Surgeons of England, 1929; Senior Surgeon, Royal Masonic Hospital; late Surgeon the Royal Hospital for Diseases of the Chest; Consulting Surgeon to London Temperance Hospital, to Bethlem Royal Hospital, and to Cranleigh Village Hospital; Captain RAMC (T); Surgeon 4th London General Hospital; Surgeon to Hospital for Officers, Alford House, Park Lane; FRSM; 2nd *s* of Samuel Evans; *m* 1908, Dorothy, *y d* of Lawrence Briant; three *s* one *d*. Entered Westminster Hospital Medical School, 1890 (entrance scholarship); awarded Bird Gold Medal for diseases of women and children; MRCS (Eng.), LRCP (Lond.), 1895; held all the resident appointments at Westminster Hospital; graduated as MB, BS (Honours), in the London University, FRCS (Eng.), 1897; MD (Lond.) 1898; was surgeon in the Imperial Yeomanry Field Hospital in South Africa (despatches, medal, and three clasps); MS (Lond.) 1901. *Publications:* Nerve Injuries and their Treatment (with Sir James Purves Stewart) (2nd edition); papers in medical journals. *Address:* Littlebourne, Forest Green, Surrey. *T:* Forest Green 214.

Died 20 March 1950.

EVANS, Caradoc; novelist, playwright and journalist; *b* Pantycroy, Llandyssul, 1878; *s* of William Evans, sometime auctioneer at Carmarthen; *m* 1933, Countess Barcynska (Oliver Sandys), *d* of late Col Henry Pruce Jervis, IMS. *Educ:* Rhydlewis (Cardiganshire) Board School; Working Man's College, Crowndale Road, London. Apprenticed to a Carmarthen draper at age of thirteen, and employed for about twelve years at various London and provincial drapery shops; later joined editorial staffs of Everybody's Weekly, Harmsworth's History of the World, World's Great Books (Hulton's, Cassell's, etc.). *Publications:* My People, 1915; Capel Sion, 1916; My Neighbours, 1920; Taffy (a Play), 1924; Nothing to Pay (novel), 1930; Wasps (novel); This Way to Heaven, 1934; Pilgrims in a Foreign Land (stories), 1942; Morgan Bible (novel), 1943. *Recreations:* scene shifting and backstage odd jobs; sermon tasting.

Died 10 Jan. 1945.

EVANS, Maj.-Gen. Charles Harford B.; *see* Bowle-Evans.

EVANS, Charles Seddon; Chairman and Managing Director William Heinemann Ltd, Publishers, since 1932; *b* 1883; *s* of Charles Evans, lately one of HM Surveyors of Customs; *m* 1905, Rose Elizabeth, *d* of late William Callaghan; four *s* one *d*. *Educ:* East London College. Elementary School Master 1904–09; Educational Editor to Edward Arnold, Publishers 1909–13; General Manager William Heinemann 1914–21; Director 1921. *Publications:* Nash and Some Others 1913; many text books and literary criticism. *Address:* Bildens, Ewhurst, Surrey; 99 Great Russell Street, WC1. *Club:* Garrick.

Died 29 Nov. 1944.

EVANS, David, MusDoc (Oxon); Emeritus Professor; *b* 6 Feb. 1874; *s* of Morgan and Sarah Evans, Resolven; *m* 1899, Mary Thomas (*d* 1943), Plasycoed, Morriston; two *s*. *Educ:* privately; Univ. Coll., Cardiff. Mus. Bac. Oxon, 1895; Organist, Jewin Crescent, London, 1899; Lecturer in Music, and Head of Music Department, Univ. Coll., Cardiff, 1903; Professor of Music, University College of South Wales and Monmouthshire, 1908–39; Member of Academic Board, University of Wales; Examiner, University of Wales; Editor of Y Cerddor, 1916–21; Examiner for Central Welsh Board; Adjudicator at numerous National Eisteddfodau; Conductor of all the chief Cymanfaoedd in the Principality; Conductor of Eryri Music Festivals, etc. *Publications:* Orchestral Suite (prize, Merthyr National Eisteddfod, 1901); Rejoice in the Lord, Cantata for Chorus, Soli, and Full Orchestra; Orchestral Overture, 1906; The Coming of Arthur,

Dramatic Cantata, 1907; Deffro mae'n ddydd, Ode for Chorus and Orchestra; Confremant, Latin Ode for Chorus and Orchestra; Bro y Bugeiliaid (Operetta), 1917; Alcestis, for Choir and String Orchestra, 1929; Gloria, Cantata for Solo, Chorus and Orchestra; Editor of Moliant Cenedl; Editor of Moliant y Cysegr; Editor of Llyfr Emynau a Thonau; Music Editor of Church Hymnary Revised; Editor of University of Wales Students' Song Book; services, anthems, part-songs, songs, etc. *Address:* Plasycoed, Cefncoed Road, Cardiff.

Died 17 May 1948.

EVANS, David Owen, (Kt 1945, *but died before receiving the accolade*); MP (L) Cardiganshire since 1932; *b* 5 Feb. 1876; *s* of late William Evans and Elizabeth J. Owen; *m* 1899, Kate Morgan, *d* of late David Morgan. *Educ:* Llandovery School; Imperial College of Science. Civil Servant, Inland Revenue Dept, 1896; Barrister (Gray's Inn), 1909; practised in London until 1916; joined the Mond Nickel Co., Ltd, 1916; later Chief Administrative Director; a Vice-President, The International Nickel Co. of Canada, Ltd; Delegate Director, The Mond Nickel Co., Ltd; Director, Henry Gardner & Co., Ltd; Chairman, Council of Copper Development Association; Member of Council of the Honourable Society of Cymmrodorion, and of the Councils of the University Colleges of Aberystwyth and Swansea; Treasurer, University College, Aberystwyth, and National Museum of Wales, Cardiff; Member of the Court of Governors of the National Library of Wales (and of the Council). *Publications:* Law of Old Age Pensions; Finance Act, 1909–1910. *Recreations:* music and country rambles. *Address:* Flat 17, 32 Grosvenor Street, W1. *T:* Mayfair 6866; Cannon Hill, Bray Wick, Maidenhead, Berks. *T:* Maidenhead 2164; Rhydclomennod, Llangranog, Llandyssul, Cards. *T:* Llangranog 23. *Clubs:* Reform, National Liberal, Eighty, Farmers'.

Died 11 June 1945.

EVANS, Maj.-Gen. Sir Edward, KBE 1935; CB 1919; CMG 1918; DSO 1900; Col Wiltshire Regiment, 1929–42; *b* 28 June 1872; *s* of late Lt-Col E. W. Evans and Emily Sophia, *y d* of John Dudding, Lincoln; *m* 1907, Helen Beatrix, *d* of late E. Huth; one *s* one *d*. *Educ:* Sandhurst. Entered army, 1893; Captain, 1900; Major, 1910; Lt-Col, 1917; Col 1918; Maj.-Gen. 1928; Staff Captain, No. 10 District, 1905–08; DAA and QMG Home Counties Division TF 1908–09; DAA and QMG East Anglian Division TF, 1912; served South Africa, 1900–02 (severely wounded, despatches, Queen's medal with 3 clasps, King's medal 2 clasps, DSO); European War, 1914–18 (despatches five times, prom. Bt Lt-Col, ADC to His Majesty with Bt of Col, CB, CMG); AA and QMG 54th Div., 1915–17; AQMG, GHQ, EEF, 1917; DA and QMG XXth Army Corps, 1917–18; DQMG EEF, 1919–20; DQMG Ireland, 1920–22; Colonel on Staff i/c Administration Western Command, 1923–27; Director of Movements and Quartering, War Office, 1927–30; Major-Gen. in charge of Administration, Aldershot Command, 1930–34; retired pay, 1934. *Address:* Coastlands, Sidmouth, S Devon. *Club:* Army and Navy.

Died 16 Nov. 1949.

EVANS, Edwin, MBE; musical critic (Daily Mail since 1933, Liverpool Post, Time and Tide); Programme Annotator, Lecturer, etc.; President International Society for Contemporary Music, and Chairman its British Section, the London Contemporary Music Centre; *b* 1 Sept. 1874; *s* of Edwin Evans and Minnie Faultless; *m* 1st, 1899, Blanche Norman; one *s* one *d*; 2nd, 1940, Netta Lacey. *Educ:* Lille: Echternach, Luxembourg. Chairman, Camargo Society, 1930–34; Editor, The Music Lover, 1931–34; Ordre de la Couronne, Belgium; Palmes Académiques, France. *Publications:* Tchaikovsky, 1906, revised 1935; The Margin of Music; Stravinsky's Fire-Bird and Petrushka; translated Jean-Aubry's French Music of To-day; contributor to the Musical

Companion, Groves, etc. *Recreations:* music, detective novels, proto-history. *Address:* 1 Trinity Crescent, SW17. *T:* Battersea 1923. *Clubs:* Savage, Press.

Died 3 March 1945.

EVANS, Evan Jenkin, DSc (Lond.); BSc (Wales); ARCSc (Lond.); Professor of Physics, University College of Swansea since 1920; *b* 20 May 1882; *s* of late David Evans and late Mary Evans, Llanelly; *m* Elmira, *d* of late Captain Thomas Rees and Mrs Mary Rees, New Quay, Cardiganshire; two *s* three *d*. *Educ:* Llanelly County School; University College of Wales, Aberystwyth; Imperial College of Science and Technology, London. Demonstrator in Physics and Astro-Physics at the Imperial College of Science, 1906–08; Assistant Lecturer and Demonstrator in Physics at the University of Manchester, 1908, and in 1911 was appointed Senior Lecturer in Physics; Vice-Principal of University College of Swansea, 1935–37. *Publications:* numerous articles on Spectra, Magneto-Optics, and Electrical Conductivity of Alloys in the Philosophical Magazine and Astro-Physical Journal. *Address:* Firdene, Dillwyn Road, Sketty, Swansea; Wynnstay, Gilfachreda, near New Quay, Cards.

Died 2 July 1944.

EVANS, Evan Laming, CBE 1920; MA, MD (Cantab); FRCS (Eng.); Emeritus Surgeon, Royal National Orthopædic Hospital; Consulting Orthopædic Surgeon, British Post-Graduate Medical School, Hammersmith; Consulting Surgeon, West End Hospital for Nervous Diseases; *b* 3 Sept. 1871; *γ s* of late Worthington Evans and Susannah, *d* of late James Laming of Birchington Hall, Kent; *m* 1911, Vivien, *o d* of late Hugh Lloyd Roberts, CB. *Educ:* Eastbourne College; Trinity College, Cambridge (Honours in Natural Science Tripos). House Surgeon to St Bartholomew's and other hospitals, Physician South African War with the Welsh Hospital (medal and 3 clasps); Assistant Bacteriologist to the Royal Colleges of Physicians and Surgeons; obtained the University prize at Cambridge for MD thesis, 1902; Past President, Orthopædic Section, British Medical Association; Past President, Orthopædic Section Royal Society of Medicine and Harveian Society, London, etc. *Publications:* various articles on Orthopædic Surgery to the Medical Journals. *Recreations:* golf, climbing, ski-ing. *Address:* 33 Portland Place, W. *T:* Langham 2541. *Clubs:* Royal Mid-Surrey Golf; Tandridge Golf.

Died 5 April 1945.

EVANS, Frank Dudley, CBE 1938; MInstCE, MIStructE; T. Lt-Col RE, BTE; *b* 1883; *s* of Thomas Evans, Much Wenlock, Shropshire; *m* 1909, Rhoda Eliza Ashton; three *d*. *Educ:* Chelsea Polytechnic. Public Works Department, Federated Malay States, 1907–26; Nigeria, 1926–38, Director of Public Works; retired 1938. *Publications:* Engineering Operations for the Prevention of Malaria, InstCE 1914–1915; articles on roads to technical press. *Recreation:* rifle shooting. *Address:* c/o Barclay's Bank, Kasr el Nil, Cairo. *T:* Cairo 40277. *Club:* East India and Sports.

Died 1 Sept. 1941.

EVANS, Captain Frederic James, CBE 1919; RN; retired; *b* 1867; *s* of Captain Frederic John Evans; *m* 1900, Sarah Katharine, *d* of Robert Sherwood, New York; no *c*. *Clubs:* Junior Army and Navy; New York, New York.

Died 13 June 1945.

EVANS, Rev. Canon Frederic James, MA Dur.; *m* 1912, Mary (*d* 1946), 2nd *d* of late Harvey Scott-Smith, Handsworth. *Educ:* Hatfield Coll., Durham; St Stephen's House, Oxford. Curate of St Paul's, Jarrow, Co. Durham, 1893–96; Missionary (UMCA) at Masasi, E Africa, 1897–98; Principal, St Andrew's College, Kinugani, Zanzibar, 1898–99; Warden of St Mark's Theological Coll. Mazizini, Zanzibar, 1901; Examining Chaplain to Bishop of Zanzibar, 1902; Archdeacon of

Zanzibar, 1902–10; priest-in-charge of Cathedral, 1905; of Pemba, 1906; Subdean of Cathedral, 1908; Hon. Canon of Zanzibar, 1938. *Address:* 132 Ashburnham Road, Hastings, Sussex. *T:* Hastings 1959.

Died 21 Oct. 1946.

EVANS, Col George Henry, CIE 1911; CBE 1919; VD; FLS; FRES; *b* 28 Nov. 1863; *s* of late Major G. Evans, Devonshire Regt; *m* 1891, Rebecca Elizabeth (*d* 1940), *d* of late Captain J. Revill, Royal Artillery; no *c*. Entered Army Veterinary Dept 1884 Captain, 1894; Major, 1902; Lt-Col 1908; Colonel, 1913; retired, 1921; served Chin-Lushai Expedition, 1889–90 (despatches, medal with clasp); European War, 1914–18 (despatches, medal, CBE). *Address:* c/o National Bank of India, Ltd, 26 Bishopsgate, EC2. *Club:* Army and Navy.

Died 1 June 1948.

EVANS, Harold Muir, MD Lond., FRCS Eng. (by election); Major RAMC (T) (retired); Fellow of University College, London; Consulting Surgeon, Lowestoft and North Suffolk Hospital, Medical Referee, Workmen's Compensation Act; *b* 29 Sept. 1866; 3rd *s* of George Evans, Richmond, Surrey; *m* 1896, Violet, 2nd *d* of Nevile Reid, The Oaks, Hanworth, Middlesex; two *s* one *d*. *Educ:* Bute House; University College Hospital; Berlin University. Medical Officer for two years for the Cape Govt Railways on the Bloemfontein Vaal River Extension; Registrar, Central London Throat and Ear Hospital, 1892–93; in general practice at Lowestoft since 1894; served European War as Surgeon Specialist in Clearing Stations, 1915–17; JP Borough of Lowestoft. *Publications:* Brain and Body of Fish; A Short History of the Thames Estuary; Sting-fish and Seafarer, 1943; papers on physiology of fishes in Proc. Roy. Soc., etc., and numerous articles on Fish Venoms BMJ. *Recreations:* yachting, fishing and travel. *Address:* Greenbank, St Mary's Road, Beccles. *Clubs:* Royal Norfolk and Suffolk Yacht, Lowestoft.

Died 28 March 1947.

EVANS, Rev. J. T., MA, BD; Principal of the North Wales Baptist College, Bangor, and Special Lecturer in Semitics at the University College, Bangor, retired, 1943; Principal Emeritus, 1943; *b* Abercwmboi, Aberdare, 1 March 1878; *s* of William and Ann Evans; *m* 1907, Annie Humphreys; one *s* one *d*. *Educ:* Baptist and University Colleges, Bangor (Exhibitioner, Dean Edwards' Prizeman, Osborne Morgan Studentship); University of Leipzig; MA Wales; BD London. Formerly Examiner in Scripture for Central Welsh Board and University of Wales. *Publications:* articles in periodicals and magazines; Welsh Commentary on Amos (Welsh Baptist Sunday School Union); Old Testament Editor of the Welsh Bible Dictionary prepared by the Guild of Graduates, University of Wales; Welsh Handbook on the Religion of the Old Testament. *Recreation:* walking. *Address:* Llety'r Bugail, Clydach, Swansea, Glam.

Died 28 Feb. 1950.

EVANS, Col John, DSO 1919; TD, JP, DL Monmouthshire; *b* 1868; *m* 1898, Edith Mary, *d* of George Jones, JP, Abercarn. Served European War, 1914–19 (despatches, DSO); Brevet Colonel, 1920; Hon. Colonel 2nd Bn Monmouthshire Regt (TA), 1934–39; High Sheriff of Monmouthshire, 1931–32. *Address:* Grouville, Stow Park Circle, Newport, Monmouthshire.

Died 27 Sept. 1942.

EVANS, John Jameson, MD, FRCS; formerly Lecturer on Ophthalmology, University of Birmingham; Consulting Surgeon, Birmingham and Midland Eye Hospital, and Royal Institution for the Blind, Edgbaston, etc; *b* 1871; *s* of Benjamin Evans, Scythlyn, Pencader, Carmarthenshire; *m* Leta C., *d* of late Principal Edwards of Aberystwyth University College; two *s*. *Educ:* Lampeter College School; University of Edinburgh (Honours). Fellow and Member of the Royal College of

Surgeons, England, and Licentiate of the Royal College of Physicians, London, 1897. *Publications:* Bacterial Diseases of the Conjunctiva; Diseases of the Eye and the Workmen's Compensation Act, etc. *Recreations:* golf, tennis. *Address:* 51 Calthorpe Road, Birmingham 15; Farquhar Road, Edgbaston. *T:* Edgbaston 0090 and 1027; Froneithyn, Aberdovey. *T:* Aberdovey 100.

Died 13 Aug. 1941.

EVANS, John Owain, CBE 1918; Officer St John's Priory; retired Civil Servant; *b* 1875; *e s* of Owen Evans, Criccieth; *m* Margaret Ann, *d* of David Hughes, Finsbury; one *s* one *d*. Co-representative for Wales and Monmouthshire of War Cabinet Committee on Unemployment and Distress; Hon. Secretary of Lloyd George American Relief Fund, 1914–30; British Delegate on the Central Europe Interallied Reparations Commission (Trieste), 1919. *Address:* 205 Lauderdale Mansions, Maida Vale, W9.

Died 6 Nov. 1943.

EVANS, Hon. Sir John William, Kt 1926; CMG 1906; JP; Lieutenant-Governor of Tasmania since 1937; *b* Liverpool, 1 Dec. 1855; *s* of late George Matthew Evans, who settled in Hobart, 1859; *m* 1883, Emily M., *d* of late James Harcourt, Hobart; two *s* one *d*. *Educ:* Collegiate College, Hobart. Served several years in command of various steamers; appointed Manager Huddart Parker and Company's branch office, Hobart, 1894; a Director of the International Exhibition, 1894; elected House of Assembly for Kingborough, 1896, member for Franklin until 1937; Premier, Chief Secretary, Treasurer, and Minister for Education, Tasmania, 1904–09; Speaker, House of Assembly, Tasmania, 1913–14, 1916–25, and 1928–34; Master Warden and Warden Hobart Marine Board, 1891–1903 and 1909–39; President of Tasmanian Sanatorium for Consumptives since 1905; President of Boy Scouts Association; President of the Life Saving Association. *Address:* 31 Stoke Street, New Town, Hobart, Tasmania.

Died 2 Oct. 1943.

EVANS, Rev. John Young, MA (Oxford, London), BD (London); Senior Professor (Church History) of the United Theological College, Aberystwyth; *b* 16 Nov. 1865; *s* of late John Bennett Evans, Dowlais, Glamorgan; *m* Ellen (*d* 1940), *d* of late Alderman John Morgan, JP, Usk House, Brecon; one *s* two *d*. *Educ:* Merthyr Tydfil Grammar School; (after 4 years in business) University College of Wales, Aberystwyth (Senior Scholar, historical essay prize); Corpus Christi College, Oxford (Exhibitioner); First in Mods, Second in Greats; London: Prizeman (Scripture), Exhibitioner (Latin), University Scholar (Classics), Second place in MA (Classics, 1891). Professor of English and Classics, and later of Patristic Literature and New Testament at Trevecka Presbyterian College, 1892–1906; Assistant Examiner in Latin to the Central Welsh Board, 1901–08; Examiner to the Oxford Delegacy of Local Examinations in English 1908–35, and in Welsh, 1915–38; Examiner in Welsh to the College of Preceptors since 1931; Clerk of the Theological Senate of the University of Wales, 1907–21, and Dean of Divinity, 1922–26; Member of the Council and Court of the University College of Wales, Aberystwyth; Moderator of the North Cardiganshire Presbytery, 1924; Davies Lecturer to the General Assembly of the Presbyterian Church of Wales, 1928; Moderator of South Wales Association of Presbyterian Church of Wales, 1941–42; Hon. Treasurer of Aberystwyth Liberal Association since 1921. *Publications:* Pryderi Fab Pwyll and Dewrion Llys a Llan; Welsh Commentary on St Luke's Gospel, 2 vols, 1927–1928; numerous literary, theological, historical, biographical, and antiquarian pamphlets, essays and reviews, together with poems and short stories, in English and Welsh journals and magazines; articles, Erastianism in Hastings' Encyclopædia, NT Canon and Literature in the Welsh Bible Dictionary; Libretto of Cantata Gwen, 1890; Inter Salices (poems), 1891; Urddiad y Saint, 1907, and other

College plays not published; Editor of A Bookman in the Making (by James Evans), 1934. *Address:* Llwynhelyg, Caradog Road, Aberystwyth: Traethmeirion, Fairbourne, Merioneth. *T:* Aberystwyth 333.

Died 26 Dec. 1941.

EVANS, Rev. Lewis Herbert, MA (Oxon); Rector of Hitcham, Bucks, since 1930; Hon. Canon, Christ Church, Oxford; *b* 29 Oct. 1870; *s* of Rev. Canon Evans, DD, Master of Pembroke College, Oxford; *m* Geraldine Horatia, *d* of Rev. J. F. Kitson, Vicar of Antony, Cornwall; two *s. Educ:* Eton; Pembroke College, Oxford. Assistant Curate of Cirencester and St Augustine's, Edgbaston, Birmingham; Vicar of Eton, 1905–30; Rural Dean of Burnham, 1921–37. *Publication:* Stories from Fancy Land. *Recreation:* sketching. *Address:* Hitcham Rectory, Bucks.

Died 22 May 1942.

EVANS, Monsignor Canon Lionel Ella; *b* Tenby, Co. Pembroke, 1882; *s* of Thomas John Evans and Frances Sarah, formerly Griffith. *Educ:* St Joseph's Jesuit Col, Sarlat; Rome. Ordained Priest in Rome in 1907 for the Archdiocese of Westminster and since then at Archbishop's House, Westminster; Chaplain to the Forces during the War; Privy Chamberlain to the Pope, 1920; Domestic Prelate, 1934; Canon of Westminster Cathedral, 1928. Vicar-General of the Archdiocese of Westminster, 1937–39. *Address:* St Joseph's Nursing Home, Beaconsfield, Bucks.

Died 30 Aug. 1942.

EVANS, Rev. Sir Murland de Grasse, 2nd Bt *cr* 1902; FRGS; Major, late 5th London Brigade, RFA; Staff Lieut (1st class) 1915; Member of the International Commission for the purchase of supplies for the Allies, 1916–17; Member of the Royal Institution; Member of the Shipwright's Company; Rector of Tittleshall with Godwick and Wellingham since 1940; one of HM's Lieutenants for the City of London; Order of the Medjidieh, 2nd Class, of Takovo (Serbia), and of St Stanislas; sometime a member of the firm of Donald Currie and Co., Managers of the Union Castle Mail Steamship Company, Ltd; inaugurated the first All-British Steamship Service round Africa, 1910; *b* 8 Dec. 1874; *e s* of 1st Bt, KCMG, MP (*d* 1907), and Marie de Grasse, *d* of late Hon. Samuel Stevens, State Attorney, Albany, NY; *m* 1st, 1911, Evangeline Mary (*d* 1928), *d* of late Major Charles Newbourne, of Bombay; 2nd, 1934, Georgiana Constance, *d* of late Captain George Styles, DCLI. *Educ:* Elstree; Harrow; Germany. Deacon, 1934; priest, 1935. *Heir: b* Evelyn Ward [*b* 4 March 1883; *m* 1909, Primrose Mary, *d* of James Wyld Brown]. *Address:* Tittleshall Rectory, King's Lynn. *Club:* Reform.

Died 28 June 1946.

EVANS, Nevil Norton, MSc; LLD; Emeritus Professor of Chemistry, McGill University, Montreal, since 1936; *b* Montreal, 28 Sept. 1865; *s* of Walter Norton Evans and Nora Hunter, Wolverhampton; *m* 1902, B. V. O'Connor; two *s. Educ:* High School, Montreal; McGill University; Freiberg and Leipsic. After graduation from McGill was engaged in teaching in that institution for 50 years, except two years spent at the Royal Saxon School of Mines, Freiberg, and at the University of Leipsic; Fellow Canadian Institute of Chemistry. *Publications:* various analyses and descriptions of rocks, minerals, etc.; Elementary Chemistry for High Schools; Laboratory Manual of High School Chemistry; Handbook to Elementary Chemistry.

Died 9 Sept. 1948.

EVANS, Col Percy, CMG 1915; MB, late RAMC; late ADMS, London District; *b* 16 Nov. 1868; *m* 1909, Hilda Annie Drummond, *d* of late James Fergusson, MD. Capt. 1897; Major, 1906; Lt-Col 1915; Col 1917; served S Africa, 1900–02 (Queen's medal 3 clasps, King's medal 2 clasps); European War, 1914–18 (despatches four times, CMG, 1914 Star); Assistant Director of Medical Services,

BEF, Dec. 1915–March 1917; DDMS Lines of Communication, Mesopotamia, Sept. 1918–July 1919; retired pay, 1923. *Address:* Landfall, Fleet, Hants. *T:* Fleet 217.

Died 6 Nov. 1945.

EVANS, Peter MacIntyre, CBE 1933; MA Oxon, LLD (hon.) Leeds and London; FSA; JP (1926) Co. of London; *b* 3 Dec. 1859; *s* of John Evans; *m* 1893; three *d. Educ:* Winchester College; New College, Oxford. *Recreations:* shooting and fishing. *Address:* 190 Sussex Gardens, Hyde Park, W2. *T:* Paddington 6547. *Clubs:* Athenæum, Oxford and Cambridge, Bath, Hurlingham.

Died 21 Oct. 1944.

EVANS, (Richard) Stanley; Stipendiary Magistrate of Pontypridd, 1933; Chairman of Glamorgan Quarter Sessions, 1944, Vice-Chairman, 1934–44; DL, JP, Glamorgan; *b* 19 Aug. 1883; *s* of late David Richard Evans, JP Pontypridd, and Jane Davies, Ystradowen, Glam.; *m* 1927, Marjorie Scudamore, Pontypridd; one *d. Educ:* Llandovery School; Lincoln College, Oxford. BA (2nd Class Hist. Finals), 1907; MA, 1910. Called to Bar, Middle Temple, 1912; joined South Wales Circuit, 1912; served European War, Captain 5th Bn The Welch Regiment; Adjutant 5th (Res.) Bn The Welch Regt, 1915–16; Courts Martial Officer for South Wales, 1916–19; Chairman Courts of Referees (Unemployment Insurance), 1928–33. *Publication:* The Right of Recovery to Poor Law Relief. *Recreation:* golf. *Address:* Bronwydd, Pontypridd. *T:* Pontypridd 2178. *Clubs:* National Liberal; Cardiff and County (Cardiff).

Died 15 April 1949.

EVANS, Richard Thomas; *b* 1890; *m* 1918, Edith, *d* of Morgan Rhys Williams. *Educ:* University of Wales. Served European War, 1914–18; MP (L) Carmarthen Div. of Carmarthenshire 1931–35. *Publication:* Aspects of the Study of Society, 1923. *Address:* 20 Palace Road, Llandaff, Cardiff. *T:* Llandaff 21. *Club:* National Liberal.

Died 20 July 1946.

EVANS, Stanley; *see* Evans, R. S.

EVANS, Thomas, CBE 1920; JP; Director of Burnyeat, Brown and Co. Ltd, and United National Collieries, Ltd; Director, Ocean Coal Co. Ltd; Director Deep Navigation Collieries, Ltd, etc; *s* of late John Evans, Sychnant, Llanedie; *m* 1900, Lila, *y d* of Walter Evans, Hayston Hall, Johnston, Pembrokeshire. *Address:* Craig-y-Parc, Pentyrch, Glamorgan.

Died 24 Dec. 1943.

EVANS, Major Sir Thomas John Carey, Kt 1924; MC; FRCS (Eng.); late Medical Superintendent, Hammersmith Hospital; Consulting Surgeon, St Paul's Hospital for Genito-urinary Diseases; *b* 1884; *e s* of late Dr R. D. Evans, JP, Blaenau Festiniog; *m* 1917, Lady Olwen Lloyd-George, *e d* of 1st Earl Lloyd-George of Dwyfor, PC, OM; two *s* two *d. Educ:* University College, Cardiff; Glasgow; St Bartholomew's Hosp.; Vienna. Late House Surgeon Royal Southern Hospital, Liverpool; RMO Eastern Dispensary, London; Senior Clinical Assistant, Woodilee Asylum; entered Indian Med. Service, 1907; Surgical Specialist 8th Lucknow Division; Surgical Specialist Abor Expedition; Senior Med. Officer Mishmi Party, NE Frontier, India; during European War served Egypt, Anzac, and Mesopotamia (despatches thrice); Civil Medical Officer Baghdad; Resident Med. Officer, Mysore State; Surgeon to the Viceroy of India. *Publications:* surgical, in BMJ and Lancet. *Recreations:* fishing, etc. *Address:* Eisteddfa, Criccieth, N Wales. *T:* Criccieth 104. *Clubs:* Oriental, Royal Automobile.

Died 25 Aug. 1947.

EVANS, Timothy; *b* Sept. 1875; *s* of Thomas and Mary Evans; *m* 1900, Sarah, *d* of John Lewis Jones, Pencader, Carmarthenshire; one *s* one *d. Educ:* Llanelly Grammar School. One of the Founders of the London Welsh

Battalions 1914, and acted as Joint Hon. Secretary of the Committee; High Sheriff of Carmarthenshire 1935–36; Past Vice-President of the Welsh Rugby Union; Past President of the London Welsh Rugby Football Club; Past Chairman of the London Carmarthenshire Society; Patron of the Young Wales Association (London) Ltd; Member of the Worshipful Company of Horners; Freeman of the City of London; Past Grand Officer (Masonic) Grand Lodge of England. *Recreations:* golf and motoring. *Address:* 7 Park Road, Barry, Glamorganshire; 27 Bracknell Gardens, Hampstead, NW. *Club:* National Liberal.

Died 21 Feb. 1945.

EVANS, Brig.-Gen. Usher Williamson, CB 1915; CMG 1918; RE; *b* June 1864; 2nd *s* of Usher W. Evans, MD, Deputy Inspector-General Army Medical Department, Rockfield, Co. Westmeath; *m* 1st, 1907, Julia Gertrude (*d* 1918), 2nd *d* of Rev. W. S. Davis; 2nd, 1921, Flora E. (*d* 1925), *widow* of Lt-Col C. Sandes. Served Chin-Lushai Expedition, 1889–90 (medal with clasp); Tirah, 1897–98 (despatches, medal 2 clasps); European War, Mesopotamia, 1914–18 (despatches, CB, CMG, Croix de Guerre); siege and fall of Kut-el-Amara; GSO1. VIth Indian Division, and commanded 17th Brigade of same Division; Prisoner of War in Turkey, 2 years and 8 months; half-pay from 14 May 1919; retired, 1920; Organiser of Fire and Watch for 50 houses, 1940. *Address:* 27 Henleaze Gardens, Bristol. *T:* Bristol 67168.

Died 5 June 1946.

EVANS, Brig.-Gen. William, CMG 1918; DSO 1900; *b* 11 Feb. 1871; 3rd *s* of U. W. Evans, MD, Clifton; *m* 1908, Dora Rosamund, *d* of James Young, Bangalore; one *d. Educ:* Clifton College; RM Academy, Woolwich. Entered RA 1891; Captain, 1900; Major, 1909; Lieut-Col 1915; Temp. Brig.-Gen., CRA Guards Division, 1916–17; CRA 18th Division, 1917–18; Colonel, 1919; retired, 1920; Secretary Royal Artillery Institution, 1920–36; served S Africa, 1900–01 (despatches; Queen's medal 4 clasps, DSO); European War, 1914–18 (despatches six times, Bt Lt-Col, CMG; French Croix de Guerre); served in Home Guard, 1940–42. *Address:* 42 Exeter House, Roehampton, SW15.

Died 10 Sept. 1944.

EVANS, William James, CB 1922; CBE 1918; JP Co. London; Chairman Hampstead Bench, 1937–41; late Director of Establishments, Admiralty; *b* 1861; *m* 1884, Fanny Elizabeth, *d* of D. H. Jones. *Address:* Glencourt, Brondesbury Park, NW6.

Died 6 Nov. 1944.

EVANS-GWYNNE, Brig. Alfred Howel, CBE 1942; DSO 1918; late Royal Artillery; *b* 17 Nov. 1882; *s* of late Rev. G. F. J. G. Evans Gwynne; *m* 1914, Phyllis, *d* of late Lt-General Sir F. C. Shaw, PC, KCB; two *d. Educ:* Malvern College. Commission, RFA 1902; served in India and UK till 1915; Egypt, Macedonia, Serbia, France, and Belgium in European War, till wounded, Aug. 1918 (despatches, DSO); Staff College, 1919; psc; Commandant Senior Officers' School, Belgaum, 1935–37; retired pay, 1938; Deputy Military Secretary War Office, 1939–42. *Recreation:* hunting. *Address:* Manor Mead, Poulner Hill, Ringwood, Hants. *T:* Ringwood 653. *Clubs:* Army and Navy, Coaching.

Died 1 Dec. 1949.

EVATT, Brig.-Gen. John Thorold, DSO 1900; Indian Army, retd 1913; *b* 1 Aug. 1861; 4th *s* of late Henry Ashmore Evatt (90th LI and PWD Ceylon), and Mary Frances, *d* of Rev. John Hinde. *Educ:* Whitgift Grammar School. Entered army from the Militia, 1881; Capt. 1892; Maj. 1901; Brevet Lieut-Col 1901; Lieut-Col 1904; Brevet Col 1904; Brig.-Gen. 1907; served Burmah, 1892 (medal and two clasps); NW Frontier of India, 1897–98 (medal with two clasps); British East

Africa, 1898 (medal and clasp); Uganda, 1899 (in command, Capture of Kabarega and Mwanga, Kings of Unyoro and Uganda, despatches, DSO, clasp); Uganda, 1900 (in command) (despatches, Brevet of Lieut-Col, medal and clasp); raised and commanded first Indian Contingent for Uganda; commanded Uganda Military Force; raised and commanded 2nd Battalion, 39th Garhwal Rifles (now The Royal Garhwal Rifles); commanded Madras Brigade, 1907–10; re-employed Dec. 1914; Brigade Commander, 1914–15; Dep. Assist Censor, 1916–17; Area Comdt in France (British War Medal, Victory Medal). *Address:* c/o Lloyds Bank, Ltd, 23 Milsom Street, Bath.

Died 18 April 1949.

EVE, Arthur Stewart, CBE 1918; FRS 1917; MA, DSc; Hon. LLD (Queen's and McGill); Professor Emeritus of Physics, McGill University, Montreal, 1935; Dean Graduate Faculty, 1930–35; *b* Silsoe, Beds, 22 Nov. 1862; *s* of late J. R. Eve; *m* 1905, Elizabeth A. Brooks, Montreal; one *s* two *d. Educ:* Berkhamstead School (Exhibitioner); Pembroke College, Cambridge (Scholar); 14th Wrangler, BA, 1884; 1st Class, Part II; Science Tripos, 1885. Assistant Master, Marlborough College, 1886–1902; Bursar, 1897, 1902; Lecturer Mathematics, McGill University-Montreal, 1903; Assistant Professor, 1905, Associate Professor, 1909; Fellow of Royal Society of Canada, 1910; Captain, McGill COTC; Captain 3rd, 4th Overseas Universities Companies CEF reinforcing PPCLI; Major, 2nd in Command 148th Overseas Batt. CEF; 2nd in Command 20th Canadian Reserve Batt. RHC 1917; Director of Research, Admiralty Experimental Station, Harwich, 1917–18; Colonel (CEF), 1918; Lt-Col (reserve) 1920; Colonel (retired), 1928; Director of Physics, McGill University, 1919–35; President, Royal Society of Canada, 1929–30. *Publications:* (with Dr Keys) Applied Geophysics, 1929; Physics (Home University Library), 1934; (with Mendenhall and Keys) College Physics, 1936; Life of Lord Rutherford, 1939; (with C. H. Creasey) Life and Work of John Tyndall, 1945; various papers, mainly to Philosophical Magazine on radio-activity and ionization. *Address:* Overponds Cottage, Puttenham, nr Guildford, Surrey.

Died 24 March 1948.

EVERARD, Sir (William) Lindsay, Kt 1939; DL, JP Leicestershire; *s* of late T. W. Everard, DL, JP, of Bradgate Park, Leicester; *m* Ione, *e d* of late Capt. M. Beresford-Armstrong, DL, JP, of Moyaliffe Castle, Tipperary; one *s* one *d. Educ:* Harrow; Trinity College, Cambridge (MA). Served European War with Leicestershire Yeomanry and 1st Life Guards, 1914–19; MP (U) Melton Division, 1924–45; Hon. Air Commodore, 605th County of Warwick (Fighter) Squadron, Auxiliary Air Force; Director of Alliance Assurance Ltd (Leicester Office); Chairman of Directors of Everards Brewery, Ltd, Leicester; John Sarson & Son, Ltd. *Address:* Ratcliffe Hall, Leicestershire. *Clubs:* Carlton, Royal Aero.

Died 11 March 1949.

EVERETT, Rev. Bernard Charles Spencer, MVO 1931; MA; chief organizing secretary of SPCK since 1939; *b* Berry Pomeroy, Totnes, South Devon, 7 May 1874; 8th *s* of Rev. A. J. Everett; *m* Mary, *d* of Rev. C. R. Tollemache; no *c. Educ:* Newton College, South Devon; Gonville and Caius College, Cambridge. University Stewart of Rannock Scholar in Sacred Music and College Prizeman in Musical Composition. Deacon, 1899; Priest, 1900; Curate of Box, Wilts; Hon. Chaplain to the Forces, European War—Mediterranean and East African Expeditionary Forces (despatches); Minor Canon, St George's Chapel, Windsor Castle, 1901–32; Chaplain to British Legation, Copenhagen, 1932–36; Ridder of Dannebrog (Danish), 1925. *Publications:* songs, etc. *Recreations:* music and travel. *Address:* SPCK House,

Northumberland Avenue, WC2; Jacob's Ladder, Chinnor, Oxon. *T:* Kingston Blount 251. *Club:* Church Imperial.

Died 28 Aug. 1943.

EVERY, Rt Rev. Edward Francis, CBE 1936; DD; Rector of Egginton, Derbyshire, since 1937; Assistant Bishop and Hon. Canon of Derby since 1937; *b* 13 April 1862; 2nd *s* of Sir H. F. Every, 10th Bart, and Mary Isabella, *d* of Rev. E. Hollond. *Educ:* Harrow; Trinity College, Cambridge (2nd class Classical Tripos). Ordained, 1885; Curate of West Hartlepool, 1885–94; Vicar of New Seaham, 1894–99; St Cuthbert's, Gateshead, 1899–1902; Bishop of the Falkland Islands, 1902–10; Bishop of Argentine, etc., 1910–37. *Publications:* Twenty-Five Years in South America, 1929; South American Memories of Thirty Years, 1933. *Address:* The Rectory, Egginton, Derbyshire.

Died 16 Jan. 1941.

EVES, Reginald Grenville, RA 1939; ARA 1933; Hon. RI 1933; Member of the Royal Society of Portrait Painters and Royal Institute of Oil Painters; Official war artist to BEF, 1940; *b* 1876; *s* of W. H. Eves, JP, London; *m* 1903, Bertha Sybil, *y d* of late Philip Oxenden Papillon of Crowhurst Park, Battle, Sussex, and Lexden Manor, Colchester; one *s. Educ:* University College School. Won Trevellyan Goodall Scholarship at Slade School of Art under Professor Legros; entered the Slade School in 1891 and later gained the Slade Scholarship there under Professor Brown. Has exhibited at the RA and Salon; winner of Silver Medal, 1924; Gold Medal, 1926. *Works:* Queen of Spain; Princess Beatrice; Lord Leopold Mountbatten; Lord Cozens-Hardy, Master of the Rolls; Marquis and Marchioness of Winchester; Sir Cecil Clementi-Smith, for Mercer's Hall; Mr L. B. Sebastian, for Skinner's Hall; Viscountess Churchill; Hon. W. Cozens-Hardy, KC; Miss Julia Neilson; Mr Fred Terry; Viscount and Viscountess Falmouth; Marchioness of Bristol; Lord Knaresborough; Countess of Hardwicke; Lady Diana Manners; Marchioness of Granby; Lord Sherborne; Viscountess Curzon; Lord Alington; Lord and Lady Clifton; Rt Hon. Mr Justice Darling; Marquess and Marchioness of Carisbrooke; Sir Robert Connell; Lord Trevethin; Sir Eric Geddes; Lord Inverforth; Sir Benjamin Johnston; Lady Jane Grey; The Countess of Stamford; Lord Huntingfield; Rt Hon. Edward Shortt; Lady Constance Malleson; Duke of Norfolk; Rt Hon. Stanley Baldwin; Thomas Hardy, OM; The Very Rev. Lionel Ford; Gen. Sir Charles Townshend, KCB; Capt. Sir Acton Blake; Dr Cyril Norwood; Rt Hon. Sir Frederick Pollock, KC; Duke of Portland, Duchess of Portland, Earl Fitzwilliam, Marchioness Linlithgow, Earl of Hopetoun, The Bishop of Chester, Rt Hon. George Lambert, PC, Earl Jellicoe, Sir Stephen Killik, Lord Mayor; Lord Rea, Air Vice-marshal Sir Philip Game, The Bishop of Carlisle, Miss Elsie Fogerty, Max Beerbohm, Kellogg Fairbank, Viscount Runciman of Doxford, Admiral of the Fleet Lord Chatfield, Lord Russell of Killowen, Sir William Llewellyn, Leslie Howard, The Duchess of Leinster; Major-Gen. Lord Hutchison of Montrose, Lord Maugham, Lord Jessel, Viscount Vaughan, Lord Woodbridge, Sir Hugh Walpole; Marshal of the RAF Sir Cyril Newall, Gen. Sir A. F. Brooke, Gen. the Viscount Gort, Lieut-Gen. Sir Ronald Adam, Sir Vice-Marshal C. H. Blount. Represented in the Tate Gallery by portraits of Thomas Hardy, Max Beerbohm, Sir Frank Benson, and National Portrait Gallery by portraits of Thomas Hardy, Sir Ernest Shackleton, Earl Jellicoe; Luxembourg, Sir Frank Benson. *Address:* 149 Adelaide Road, NW3. *T:* Primrose 1316; Marsham Farm, Fairlight. *Club:* Arts.

Died 13 June 1941.

EWART, Lt-Col Ernest Andrew; *see* Cable, Boyd.

EWART, George Arthur, FRCS (Eng.); BA (Cantab); Surgeon St George's Hospital, London; Consulting Surgeon Hospital SS John and Elizabeth; Surgeon to Rupture Society; *b* 1 June 1886; *s* of J. Cossar-Ewart, FRS, Regius Professor of Natural History, Edinburgh Univ.; *m* 1914, Dorothy Hannah, *y d* of late Sir George Turner, KBE, CB, one *s* two *d. Educ:* Cargilfield; Clifton College; Edinburgh University (Vans Dunlop Scholar); Christ's College, Cambridge (Scholar, 1st Class Nat. Sci. Tripos, ran cross-country for Cambridge University, 1909); St George's Hospital (Brackenbury Prize in Surgery, Wm Brown Scholar, Herbert Allingham Surgical Scholar). Temp. Major RAMC (TF) during European War. *Publications:* articles on Abdominal Surgery in Medical Journals. *Recreations:* shooting, photography. *Address:* St George's Hospital, Hyde Park Corner, SW1. *Club:* United University.

Died 2 Oct. 1942.

EXHAM, Lt-Col Harold, DSO 1920; OBE 1919; late 7th Gurkha Rifles, Indian Army; *b* 13 Oct. 1884; *s* of late Colonel Richard Exham, CMG; *m* 1924, Estelle, *d* of late Livingston Crosby, New York; one *d. Educ:* Cheltenham College; RMC, Sandhurst. Joined York and Lancaster Regt in 1903 and transferred to Indian Army, 1907; retired, 1933. *Address:* Preston House, Iwerne Minster, Dorset. *T:* Child Okeford 273. *Clubs:* United Service, International Sportsmen's.

Died 27 Aug. 1950.

EXMOUTH, 7th Viscount *cr* 1816; **Charles Ernest Pellew;** Bt 1796; Baron, 1814; *b* 11 March 1863; *s* of 6th Viscount and Eliza, *d* of Hon. Judge William Jay, of New York; *S* father, 1923; *m* 1st, 1886, Margaret, *d* of Prof. C. F. Chandler, New York; 2nd, 1923, Mabel, *d* of Richard Gray, San Francisco. Demonstrator, Chemistry and Physics, Columbia University, 1892–97; Adjunct Professor of Chemistry, Columbia University, 1897–1911; Member Squadron A. National Guard, SNY, 1889–98, Captain US Vol. Signal Corps, 1898; 1st Lieut Depot Battalion, 12th Infantry, SNY, 1915–16; Chemist, Maxim Munitions Co., 1915–17; Alaska Products Co., 1917–19. *Publications:* Practical Medical and Physiological Chemistry, 1898; Dyes and Dyeing, 1912. *Heir: cousin* Edward Irving P. Pellew, OBE. *Address:* Highcombe Edge, Hindhead, Surrey. *T:* Hindhead 364. *Clubs:* Brooks's, Chemical Industry; Century, Chemists', New York.

Died 7 June 1945.

EYLES, Sir Alfred, KCB 1913; KBE 1919; *b* 8 Dec. 1856; *m* 1st, 1879, Emmeline (*d* 1914), *d* of William L. Kemp; 2nd, 1915, Catherine Crampton, *o d* of late J. R. S. Hayward, MD. Entered Admiralty, 1876; private secretary to Sir Gerald FitzGerald, KCMG 1885; Staff Officer for Estimates, 1891; Assistant Principal Clerk, 1897; Assistant Accountant-General, 1903; Deputy Accountant-General, 1904; Accountant-Gen. of the Navy, 1906–18; retired, 1918; CB 1908. *Address:* Wilton Lodge, Hillside Avenue, Worthing, Sussex. *T:* Worthing 3975.

Died 16 May 1945.

EYRE, John William Henry, FRS Edin., FZS, MD, MS (Dunelm); DPH (Camb.); Consulting Bacteriologist to Guy's Hospital; Emeritus Professor of Bacteriology, University of London, since 1935; Bacteriologist to the Worshipful Company of Fishmongers; President Royal Institute of Public Health and Hygiene, 1942; President, Hunterian Society, 1939; late Director of Bacteriological Depart, Guy's Hospital, and Lecturer on Bacteriology in the Medical School; *b* London, 18 July 1869; *o s* of John Eyre. *Educ:* private school; Whitgift Grammar School; Guy's Hospital; Univ. of Durham, graduated 1893; Berlin. Studied bacteriology of the eye whilst ophthalmic surgeon to St Mary's Children's Hospital and senior ophthalmic assistant to Guy's Hospital; went to Charing Cross Hospital as bacteriologist and lecturer, 1899; first Ernest Hart Memorial Research Scholar, 1900–02;

returned to Guy's as bacteriologist, 1902, and succeeded to the lectureship on bacteriology; co-opted by the Royal Society to Advisory Board of Commission on Mediterranean Fever, 1905–07; spent the summer of 1906 in Malta as chairman of the working party of the Commission; Erasmus Wilson Lecturer Royal College of Surgeons, and Milroy Lecturer Royal College of Physicians, 1908; Hunterian Professor Royal College of Surgeons, 1911–12; Bacteriologist to Royal Flying Corps Hospitals, American Red Cross Hospital for Officers, and HM Queen Mary's Royal Naval Hospital, etc.; Member War Office Trench Fever Committee, 1914–; Examiner, State Medicine London University, 1911–15; Bacteriology, 1923–28; Pathology and Bacteriology (Dental), 1926–33; Examiner Public Health, 1917–20, 1929–37 and 1940–42; also Tropical Bacteriology, 1911–20, RCS; a Manager MAB (Ministry of Health), 1928–30; Pres. of Royal Microscopical Society, 1920–21, Senior Secretary, 1911–20; Editor Society's journal, 1922–27. *Publications:* Bacteriological Technique (Third Edit.); Serums, Vaccines and Toxines (jointly); Editor English Edition Experimental Bacteriology by Kolle and Hetsch; Referee for volume Bacteriology throughout issue of International Catalogue Scientific Literature; Reports to the Mediterranean Fever Commission; papers on ophthalmological, pathological and bacteriological subjects. *Address:* 51 Portland Place, W1. *T:* Welbeck 5178. *Clubs:* Savage, Royal Automobile.

Died 17 Feb. 1944.

EYRE-BROOK, Canon Alfred; see Brook.

EYRES, Adm. Cresswell John, DSO 1918; OBE 1938; *b* 1862; 3rd *s* of Rev. Charles Eyres, Rector of Great Melton, Norfolk; *m* 1889, Rose (*d* 1940), *d* of J. Phipps Townsend of Walpole, Norfolk, and Downhills, Tottenham; three *d.* Entered Royal Navy as cadet, 1874; Commander, 1898; Captain, 1903; Naval Attaché with Russians during Russo-Japanese War, 1904–05; commanded HMS Jupiter, Spartiate, and Irresistible; Commodore-in-Charge, Hong-Kong, 1910–12; ADC to the King, 1912–13; commanded HMS Temeraire; Rear-Admiral, 1913; retired to take active service abroad, 1914 (DSO); Temp. Capt. RNR; Temp. Lieut-Colonel RGA; Admiral, retired, 1922; Commander Legion of Honour. *Address:* 6 Bede House, Manorfields, Putney, SW15. *Club:* East India and Sports.

Died 12 Oct. 1949.

EYRES, Sir Harry Charles Augustus, KCMG 1926; *b* 21 July 1856; *s* of Rev. C. Eyres, Rector of Great Melton, Norfolk, and Henrietta Maria Bullock of Faulkbourn Hall, Essex; *m* 1885, Penelope Louisa, *d* of Joseph Phipps Townsend, JP, of Walpole, Norfolk, and Downhills, Tottenham; two *s* two *d. Educ:* Marlborough College. Passed a competitive examination, 1877. Appointed Student Interpreter at Constantinople; Assistant at Constantinople, 1880; and at Scutari, Albania, 1881; Vice-Consul at Van, 1882; Acting Consul at Erzeroum, Nov. 1882–83; HM's Vice-Consul at Beyrout, 1885; Acting Consul-General there, 1886–87, 1890; Consul at Damascus, 1890; Acting Consul-General at Beyrout, 1894; HM's Consul-General at Constantinople, 1896–1914; retired, 1914; British Minister in Albania, 1922–26; retired, 1926. *Address:* Cut Heath, Farnham Royal, Slough, Bucks. *T:* Farnham Common 50. *Club:* Constitutional.

Died 19 July 1944.

EZECHIEL, Sir Percy (Hubert), KCMG 1935 (CMG 1923); Third Crown Agent for the Colonies, 1920–37; Member of East African Currency Board, 1919–37; Director of Colonial Scholars, 1921–37; Chairman of Palestine Currency Board, 1926–47; *b* 10 Aug. 1875; *s* of late Lt-Col James A. Ezechiel, OBE; *m* 1911, Ellen Mary (*d* 1931), *d* of Thomas Cowperthwaite, *widow* of J. Campbell Macmillan; two *s* one *d. Educ:* Bombay; Trinity College, Cambridge (BA 4th Wrangler, 1897). Entered Colonial Office, 1898; called to Bar, Middle Temple, 1903; Secretary to the Crown Agents for the Colonies, 1905–20; Member of Fair Wages Advisory Committee, 1909–20; Member of Currency Commission to Hong-Kong, 1931. *Address:* 17 Doran Drive, Redhill, Surrey. *T:* Redhill 4149.

Died 22 Oct. 1950.

EZRA, Sir David, Kt 1927; landed proprietor; *b* 1871; *s* of Elias David Ezra and Mozelle, *d* of Sir Albert Sassoon, Bart; *m* 1912, Rachel, *e d* of late Solomon D. Sassoon and late Mrs Flora Sassoon. *Educ:* Doveton College, Calcutta; privately. *Recreations:* aviculture and zoology. *Address:* 3 Kyd Street, Calcutta, India. *TA:* Enterprise, Calcutta. *Clubs:* Tollygunge, Jodhpur, Saturday, Calcutta, Calcutta.

Died 23 Aug. 1947.

F

FAGAN, Lt-Col Christopher George Forbes; (retired list) Indian Army; *b* 15 March 1856; *s* of late Major C. S. Fagan and Ellen, *d* of late Henry Denny of Tramore, Co. Waterford; *m* 1881, Florence Evelyn Jessie, *d* of late Surg.-Maj. J. W. R. Amesbury, IMS; two *s* one *d*. *Educ:* Harrow. Entered army, 1875; Lieut-Col 1901; served Afghan war, 1879–80 (medal); 63rd Foot, 1875; 10th Bengal Lancers, 1880; Assistant District Superintendent of Police, Punjab, 1885; Assistant Resident, Hyderabad, 1891; Assistant Political Agent and Consul, Basra, 1897; Political Agent and Consul, Muscat, 1898; Political Agent, Kotah, 1900; Alwar, 1901; Eastern States, Rajputana, 1904; retired 1907; Major RDC 1914–19 (despatches). *Address:* Old Job's, Chalfont St Peter, Bucks. *T:* Jordans 2177.

Died 9 July 1943.

FAGAN, Hon. Mark; MLC, Leader of the New Zealand Legislative Council and Minister without Portfolio, 1935–39, Speaker since 1939; *b* 17 Nov. 1873; *s* of Patrick Fagan and Maria Cribben; widower; no *c*. *Educ:* Waratah Tasmanian Public School. Miner; Miners' Representative as Workmen's Inspector of Mines; Miners Arbitration Court Advocate; elected Legislative Council 1930; attended as Legislative Councils Delegate the British Parliamentary Association Conference at London, 1935; Member of Wellington Harbour Board; Executive Member of NZ Labour Party. *Recreations:* cricket, football. *Address:* 119 Cuba St, Petone, NZ. *T:* 63330.

Died 31 Dec. 1947.

FAGAN, Sir Patrick James, KCIE 1922; CSI 1917; ICS; *b* 5 July 1865; *s* of late Maj.-Gen. W. T. Fagan, Bengal Staff Corps; *m* 1890, Emily Frances, 3rd *d* of late Walter A. Robinson, late Principal of Aitcheson College, Lahore; one *s* one *d*. *Educ:* Blundell's School, Tiverton; St John's College, Cambridge; BA Indian Languages Tripos, 1887. Entered ICS 1886; held executive posts, Deputy Commissioner, Settlement Officer, Commissioner; Financial Commissioner, Punjab, 1916; Member of the Imperial Legislative Council of India, 1918–19; retired, 1923; Fellow of the Royal Astronomical Society. *Address:* 45 Chiltern Court, Baker Street, W1. *T:* Welbeck 5544. *Club:* Athenæum.

Died 26 June 1942.

FAGAN, William Bateman, FRBS 1938; *m* 1899, Betty Maud Christian, ROI (*d* 1932), *d* of George Smith, JP; no *c*. *Educ:* Dulwich College. *Address:* 1 Wentworth Studios, Manresa Road, Chelsea, SW3. *T:* Flaxman 0570. *Club:* Chelsea Arts.

Died 9 April 1948.

FAHIE, Sen. Comdr Pauline Mary de Peauly, MBE 1942; FRMetSoc; Officer of the Order of St John of Jerusalem; *yr d* of Sir Robert (Vaughan) Gower, KCVO; *m* 1945, Wing-Comdr William Cusack Fahie, RAFVR; twin *s*. *Educ:* Convent of the Sacred Heart, Tunbridge Wells; Paris. Holder of following licences: 'A' and 'B' Pilot's (Air); 2nd Class Navigator's; Air Ministry Instructor's; GPO's Wireless Operator's Certificate. Commissioner of Girl Guides (Gillingham, Kent) since 1936; Commissioner (South Eastern Area), Civil Air Guard, 1938–39; Director of Women Personnel, Air Transport Auxiliary, 1939–45; Government Director British Overseas Airways Corporation, 1943–46; Member of Air Ministry's Departmental Committees on Civil Aviation (the Gorrel Committee), 1938–39; Member of Council of Women's Engineering Soc.; Hon. Lady Pres. Chatham and Gillingham Corps St John Ambulance Brigade since 1936; Hon. Freedom Company of Pattenmakers, 1943; Freedom of City of London, 1943; Member Committee 129th Squadron (Tunbridge Wells) ATC since 1939; for some years conducted with Miss Dorothy Spicer an Air Ferry Service; has piloted over 30,000 passengers; has frequently lectured on aviation. *Publications:* Piffling Poems for Pilots, 1934; Women with Wings, 1938; articles and stories in magazines and periodicals. *Recreations:* riding, ski-ing, and music. *Address:* 2 The Vale, Chelsea, SW3; Sandown Court, Tunbridge Wells. *T:* Flaxman 9056, Tunbridge Wells 593. *Clubs:* Ladies' Carlton, Forum.

Died 2 March 1947.

FAIR, Lt-Col James George, CMG 1916; DSO 1902; *b* 19 Nov. 1864; *s* of late James Fair of Hove; *m* 1901, Mary, *d* of late Lieutenant-General J. N. Sargent, CB. Joined 21st Hussars, 1885; retried, 1905; served as Staff Officer to General Gatacre during Atbara Campaign, 1898 (despatches, Khedive's medal and clasp); with 21st Lancers at Omdurman (Queen's medal clasp, 4th class Medjidieh); South African War, 1901–02 (despatches, DSO Queen's medal 5 clasps); Commanded Division SACE Transvaal, 1901–04; Division SAC Orange River Colony, 1904–08; Member of Inter-Colonial Council of Transvaal and Orange River Colony, 1906; Resident Commissioner and Commandant-General S Rhodesia, 1908–11; Deputy Assistant Director of Remounts, 1911–15; Deputy Director Remounts, Egypt, 1915–16; Deputy Assistant Director Remounts, Southern Command, 1916–29. *Address:* Sunnybourne, Cooden, Sussex. *T:* Cooden 126.

Died 7 Aug. 1946.

FAIRBAIRN, Sir George, Kt 1926; *b* 23 March 1855; *s* of George Fairbairn, of Victoria, Australia; *m* 1st, 1880, Jessie Kate Prell; 2nd, 1924, Lorna B. Robertson; one *s*. *Educ:* Geelong Grammar School, Australia; Jesus College, Cambridge. Member Parliament of Victoria, 1903–06; Australian House of Representatives, 1906–17; member of Senate, 1917–23; Agent-General for Victoria (Australia), 1924–27. *Address:* 3 Como Avenue, South Yarra, Melbourne SE1; Greenlaw, Mount Martha, Victoria, Australia. *Clubs:* Melbourne, Melbourne.

Died 23 Oct. 1943.

FAIRBAIRN, James; *b* Edinburgh; *s* of late James Fairbairn; *m* 1st, 1920, Winifred (*d* 1946), 2nd *d* of Adolphus Hallowes, MD, Maidstone; one *s*; 2nd, Helen Macfarlane Hamilton, 2nd *d* of late William Williamson Clelland, Glasgow. *Educ:* Royal High School, Edinburgh. Past Chairman of Council of Rubber Growers Assoc.; Vice-Chm. United Serdang Rubber Plantations Ltd; Director of British Rubber Development Board (Past Chm.); a Vice-Patron Great Ormond Street Hospital for Sick Children; a Vice-Pres. of the YMCA; Pres. Mansfield House University Settlement. *Recreations:* golf, riding. *Address:* St James' Court, Buckingham Gate, SW1. *T:* Victoria 2360. *Clubs:* MCC, Royal Automobile.

Died 7 June 1950.

FAIRBAIRN, John Shields, MA, BM, BCh Oxon, FRCP Lond., FRCS Eng.; MD (Hon.) University of Melbourne; MM (Hon.) Soc. Apoth.; Consulting Obstetric Physician and Gynæcologist, St Thomas's Hospital, and Consulting Physician to General Lying-in Hospital; Past President, RCOG; *b* Bathgate, West Lothian, 1868; *s* of Dr A. M. Fairbairn, 1st Principal of Mansfield College, Oxford; *m* 1913, Elma, 2nd *d* of late J. P. Stuart, Elgin, Morayshire. *Educ:* Bradford; Magdalen College, Oxford (Open Science Demyship, 1st Class in

Honour School of Natural Science, 1891); St Thomas's Hospital, London. Fellow of Royal Society of Medicine. Hon. Fellow Obstetrical Society, Edinburgh; formerly Examiner in Midwifery and Diseases of Women, Universities of Oxford, Cambridge, London, Glasgow, and Birmingham; Captain RAMC (T), 5th London General Hospital, 1914–18; Chairman of Central Midwives' Board, 1930–36; formerly editor, Journal of Obstetrics and Gynæcology of the British Empire. *Publications:* A Textbook for Midwives, 6th Edition, 1942; Gynæcology, with Obstetrics, etc.; papers on medical subjects in medical journals. *Address:* Blucairn, Lossiemouth, Morayshire. *T:* Lossiemouth 3004.

Died 22 Jan. 1944.

FAIRBAIRN, Richard Robert; JP; *b* 1867; *m*; six *s* three *d*. *Educ:* Toronto. Formerly Manager of Tramway and Omnibus undertakings in London, Birmingham, and Worcester; Midland Road Transport Officer during War; MP (L) City of Worcester Nov. 1922–23; contested Worcester 1910, 1918, 1922, 1923, 1924, 1929, 1931, and 1935. *Address:* Barbourne, Worcester. *T:* 2078.

Died Oct. 1941.

FAIRBROTHER, Ven. Rupert; Archdeacon Emeritus, 1936; *b* Carterton, Wellington, NZ; *m*; four *s* one *d*. *Educ:* Wellington College, NZ. Deacon, 1898; Priest, 1899; Curate of Grafton, 1898–99; Minister in charge, Bellinger and Nambucca, 1899–1901; Vicar of Inverell, 1901–15; Canon of St Peter's Cathedral, Armidale, 1914; Vicar of Tamworth, NSW 1915–34; Archdeacon of Tamworth, 1930–36. *Address:* Tamworth, New South Wales, Australia.

Died 21 Oct. 1947.

FAIRBURN, Charles Edward, MA; MICE, MIMechE, MIEE, MILocoE; Chief Mechanical and Electrical Engineer, LMS, since 1944; Lt-Col Engineer and Railway Staff Corps RE (TA); *b* 5 Sept. 1887; *o s* of Robert and Elizabeth Fairburn; *m* 1914, Eleanor, *d* of late Dr Cadman; one *s* one *d*. *Educ:* Brasenose College, Oxford. 1st Class Math. Mods. and Final Schools; 1st Class Engineering Final Schools; BA 1908; MA 1912; pupil to late Sir Henry Fowler of the then Midland Railway, Derby. Railway Dept of Siemens Dynamo Works, Ltd, 1912; War Service, RFC and RAF, finally with rank of Major; Head of Railway Dept of English Electric Co., 1919; General Manager, Dick Kerr Works, Preston, 1926; of Dick Kerr Works and Preston Car Works of English Electric Co., 1927; of Stafford and the two Preston Works of English Electric Co., 1928; Member of Executive Committee of English Electric Co., 1929; Chairman Contractors' Committee for the Electrification of the Polish State Railways, 1933; Electrical Engineer, LMS, 1934; also Deputy Chief Mechanical Engineer, 1937; Acting Chief Mechanical Engineer and Electrical Engineer, 1942. Member of London and Home Counties and North Wales and South Cheshire Joint Electricity Authorities. *Publications:* papers on Railway Electrification Work and Diesel Traction to Engineering Societies. *Recreations:* tennis and golf. *Address:* Claremont, Duffield Road, Derby. *T:* Derby 3596. *Club:* Transportation.

Died 12 Oct. 1945.

FAIRCHILD, Rev. John, MA; Principal North Wales Training College since 1884; Canon Bangor Cathedral, 1902. *Educ:* Queen's Coll., Oxford. Chaplain, Culham Coll., 1880–83; Vice-Principal York Training College, 1883–84. *Address:* N Wales Training College, Bangor.

Died 9 Dec. 1942.

FAIRCLOUGH, Col Brereton, CMG 1916; DSO 1918; TD; JP County of Cheshire and Borough of Warrington; *b* 1870; *e s* of late R. T. Fairclough; *m* 1907, Ethel C., *o d* of late H. Roberts; one *s* one *d*. *Educ:* Warrington Grammar School. Late S Lancashire Regt,

TF. Served S Africa, 1901–02 (Queen's medal 5 clasps); European War, 1914–18 (despatches five times, CMG, DSO). *Address:* Lane End, Hill Cliffe, Warrington.

Died 3 April 1945.

FAIRFAX, Col Bryan Charles, CMG 1918; *b* 12 Sept. 1873; 2nd *s* of late Colonel T. F. Fairfax, Grenadier Guards, and of Mrs Fairfax, *d* of Sir W. Milner of Nunappleton, Yorkshire; *m* 1915, Charlotte (*d* 1949), *d* of late Thomas Henry Ismay, Dawpool, Birkenhead. *Educ:* Winchester; Royal Military College, Sandhurst. Late Durham Light Infantry. *Address:* Whitwell Hall, York. *TA:* Whitwell-Welburn. *T:* Whitwell-on-the-Hill 33. *Clubs:* Army and Navy, Boodle's; Yorkshire (York).

Died 29 Jan. 1950.

FAIRFAX, Hon. Charles Edmund; *b* 29 April 1876; *brother* of 12th Baron Fairfax. *Address:* Northampton, Landover, Maryland, USA.

Died 6 April 1939.

FAIRFAX, Lt-Col William George Astell R.; *see* Ramsay-Fairfax.

FAIRFAX-LUCY, Sir Henry William Cameron-Ramsay-, 3rd Bt *cr* 1836; CB 1937; JP, DL Counties Roxburgh and Warwick; High Steward of the Royal Town of Sutton Coldfield, 1936; County Council Warwickshire and Roxburghshire; *b* 25 Sept. 1870; *e s* of 2nd Bt and Mary, *o d* of William J. Pawson of Shawdon, Northumberland; *S* father, 1902; *m* 1st, Ada Christina (*d* 1943), *d* and *heiress* of H. S. Lucy of Charlecote Park, 1892, and added the surname Lucy; three *s* two *d*; 2nd, 1944, Norah, *y d* of late Munro Mackenzie of Mornish. *Educ:* Eton. Lieut Royal Scots (Lothian Regt), 1890–91; Lieut 2nd Life Guards, 1891–92; Reserve of Officers, 1892–1921; Private Secretary to the Financial Secretary to the Treasury, Rt Hon. R. W. Hanbury, 1895–97; Private Sec. to the Solicitor-General for Ireland, Dunbar Barton, QC, MP, 1898–1900; Staff Lt served SA, 1900; Remount Department, War Office, 1901; called to the Bar, Middle Temple, 1902; passed special War Office course in Administration, 1907; Chairman Warwickshire Territorial Army Association, 1907–39, and Air Force Association; contested (U) South Leeds, 1906; (C) Holland-with-Boston Division of Lincolnshire, 1922; Inspector of Quartermaster-General's Services, Headquarters Scottish Command, 1915–18 with rank of Major; Major in the Army since 1918; President of Civilian Advisory Board to 4th Army, 1919; Chairman, Volunteer Service Committee, Coventry Area, Warwickshire; Hon. Col 48th SM Div. Train, RASC (T) since 1927. *Recreations:* hunting, shooting, polo. *Heir:* *s* Henry Montgomerie [MC, DL, Capt. Rifle Brigade and Argyll and Sutherland Highlanders, 1923; retired, 1925; *b* 20 Oct. 1896]. *Address:* Charlecote Park, Warwick; Maxton, St Boswells, Scotland. *Clubs:* Carlton, Hurlingham, Royal Automobile.

Died 20 Aug. 1944.

FAIRFIELD, 1st Baron *cr* 1939, of Caldy; **Frederick Arthur Greer,** PC 1927; Kt 1919; KC 1910; MA, LLD Aberdeen, 1926 and Liverpool, 1930; *b* 1863; *s* of late Arthur Greer, merchant, of Liverpool and Ballasalla House, Ballasalla, Isle of Man; *m* 1st, 1901, Katherine (*d* 1937), *d* of late E. van Noorden of Orangebury, South Carolina, USA; one *d*; 2nd, 1939, Mrs Mabel Neele. *Educ:* Ormskirk Grammar School; Grammar School, Old Aberdeen; Aberdeen University. First Class Honours in Philosophy, Fullerton Scholar; Bacon Scholar, and Arden Scholar at Gray's Inn. Called to Bar, 1886; joined Northern Circuit; practised locally till 1907, when removed to London; Justice of the High Court, 1919; Lord Justice of Appeal, 1927–38; Bencher of Gray's Inn, 1910; Treasurer, 1921. *Address:* Fairfield House, Caldy, Cheshire. *Club:* Athenæum.

Died 4 Feb. 1945.

FAIRHURST, James Ashton, TD, DL, JP, MA; *b* 1867; *o s* of Thomas Fairhurst (*d* 1912), Kilhey Court, Wigan, and Borness, Kirkcudbright; *m* 1894, Eva L. (*d* 1929), *e d* of William Ansell, JP, CC, Wylde Green, Warwickshire; one *s* two *d*. *Educ:* Rugby; Jesus Coll., Cambridge. MA 1892. Barrister, Inner Temple, 1892, Major and Hon. Lieut-Col, late of 5th Manchester Regiment; High Sheriff for Berkshire, 1923. *Recreations:* hunting, shooting, fishing, and all games. *Address:* Arlington Manor, Newbury; Fairhurst, Donnington, Berkshire. *T:* Chieveley 15. *Club:* Conservative.

Died 8 Jan. 1944.

FAIRTLOUGH, Maj.-Gen. Eric Victor Howard, DSO 1919; MC; *b* 6 Feb. 1887; *e s* of late Col F. Howard Fairtlough, CMG; *m* 1928, Agatha Zoë, 2nd *d* of G. C. Barker, Dulas Court, Pontrilas, Herefordshire; two *s* two *d*. Served European War, 1914–19 (despatches, MC, DSO, Orders of Redeemer of Greece and White Eagle of Serbia with swords); Temp. Maj.-Gen. 1941; retired pay, 1942. *Address:* The Manor House, Blandford St Mary, Dorset.

Died 30 Oct. 1944.

FAIRWAY, Sidney; *see* Daukes, S. H.

FALCON, Thomas Adolphus, RBA 1902, MA; landscape painter; *b* Pudsey, near Leeds, 24 July 1872; *s* of Thomas Falcon, MRCS, later of Bowdon, Cheshire; *m* 1901, Julie, *d* of E. Schwabe, Didsbury, Manchester; one *s* one *d*. *Educ:* Manchester Grammar School; Trinity College, Cambridge (Classical Tripos, 1893; Mediæval and Modern Language Tripos, 1894). *Publications:* Dartmoor Illustrated, 1900; Pictorial Dartmoor, 1902. *Address:* Hill Close, Braunton, North Devon.

Died 28 Jan. 1944.

FALCONER, John Downie, MA (Glas.), DSc (Edin.), FRSE, FGS, FRGS; geologist and geographer; *b* Midlothian, 1 Nov. 1876; *m* 1st, 1908, Edith (*d* 1934), *y d* of John Burman, Chelsea; one *s* two *d*; 2nd, 1941, Catherine Elizabeth, *d* of John and Mary Hughes, Saskatcon, Canada. *Educ:* University of Glasgow and University of Edinburgh. MA, 1898; BSc, 1901; DSc, 1906. Assistant to late Prof. James Geikie, 1901–04; Principal of the Mineral Survey of Northern Nigeria, 1904–09; Lecturer in Geography in Glasgow University, 1911–16; Temporary Assistant District Officer, Northern Nigeria, 1916–18; Director of Geological Survey, Nigeria, 1918–27; Geologist to the Republic of Uruguay, 1928–34. *Publications:* The Igneous Geology of the Bathgate and Linlithgow Hills (Trans. Roy. Soc., Ed. 1905–1906); The Geology of Ardrossan (*ibidem* 190); The Geology and Geography of Northern Nigeria, 1911; On Horseback through Nigeria, 1911; The Geology of the Plateau Tinfields (Nigeria), 1921; the Northern Tinfields of Banchi Province, Nigeria (with C. Raeburn), 1923; the Southern Plateau Tinfields, Nigeria, 1926; Geological Map of the Tinfields of Nigeria, 1927; the Gondwana Beds of the Department of Cerro Largo, Uruguay, 1930, and of the Department of Tacuarembó, Uruguay, 1931; the Gondwana System of NE Uruguay, 1937; Darwin in Uruguay, 1937. *Recreations:* travel, country life. *Address:* 43 Fordhook Avenue, Ealing Common, W5. *T:* Acorn 2195. *Club:* Royal Societies.

Died 16 April 1947.

FALCONER, Sir Robert Alexander, KCMG 1917; DCL (Oxon); DD, Edinburgh; LLD Glasgow, Dublin, Harvard, Princeton, Yale, Pennsylvania, Michigan, Western Reserve, Union, Rochester, USA, Toronto, McGill, and other Canadian Universities; DLitt, Manchester, Laval; CMG 1911; FRS Can; *b* Charlottetown, PEI, 10 Feb. 1867; *e s* of Rev. Alexander Falconer, DD, and Susan Douglas; *m* 1897, Sophie, *e d* of Rev. J. Gandier, Ontario; two *s*. *Educ:* Queen's Royal College School, Trinidad, BWI; University of Edinburgh; University of Leipzig; University of Berlin; and University of Marburg. As a boy spent eight years in Trinidad, BWI; W Indian Gilchrist scholarship, 1885; graduated BA London, 1888; MA 1889, BD 1892, DLitt 1902 (all from Edinburgh). Lecturer and Professor New Testament Greek in Pine Hill College, Halifax, NS, 1892–1907; during last three years Principal; Pres., University of Toronto, 1907–32; Pres. Emeritus, 1932; Pres., Royal Society of Canada, 1931–32; Pres., Royal Canadian Institute, 1933–35; Pres., Champlain Society, 1937–42; Hon. Pres. Canadian Association for Adult Education; Sir George Watson lecturer on American History in British Universities, 1925; Josiah Wood lecturer, Mt Allison University, 1928; Ingersoll Lecturer, Harvard University, 1930; Sharp Lecturer, 1933, Rockwell Lecturer, 1938, Rice Institute, Houston, Texas; Trustee Royal Ontario Museum; Former Trustee, Carnegie Foundation for the Advancement of Teaching; Jubilee Medal, 1935; Coronation Medal, 1937. *Publications:* articles in professional journals, encyclopædias, and dictionaries in Britain and America; articles on educational and public questions; The German Tragedy and its Meaning for Canada, 1915; Idealism in National Character, 1920; The United States as a Neighbour, 1925; Citizenship in an Enlarging World, 1928; Immortality and Western Civilisation, 1930; Two chapters in vol. vi Cambridge History of the British Empire, 1930; The Pastoral Epistles, 1937; Religion on My Life's Road, 1938. *Recreation:* travel. *Address:* 81 Glengowan Road, Toronto. *Clubs:* York, Toronto; Century, New York.

Died Nov. 1943.

FALKE, Prof. Otto von, Dr Phil; retired General Director of the Prussian State-Museums; *b* Vienna, 29 April 1862; *s* of Jakob v. Falke and Emma Stevenson, Dublin; *m* 1889, Luise Dreger (*d* 1935); two *d*. *Educ:* Vienna University. Directorial Assistant Museum Industrial Arts, Berlin, 1888; Director Museum Industrial Arts, Cologne, 1895; Director Museum Industrial Arts, Berlin, 1908; General Director of the Prussian State-Museums, 1920; retired 1927. *Publications:* Majolika, Handbook, 1896; Rhenish-Stoneware, 1908; Kunstgeschichte der Seidenweberei, 1913; Deutsche Porzellanfiguren, 1919; Möbel des Mittelalters u. d. Renaissance, 1924; Der Welfenschatz, 1930; Bronzegeräte des Mittelalters, 1935. *Address:* Berlin, Schlachtensee, am Schlachtensee 134.

Died 15 Aug. 1943.

FALLA, Norris Stephen, CMG 1918; DSO 1916; VD; Chairman and Managing Director Union Steam Ship Co. of NZ Ltd; Chairman Union Airways of NZ Ltd; Chairman Tasman Empire Airways; Director Peninsular and Oriental Steam Navigation Co.; British India Steam Navigation Co.; *b* Westport, NZ, 3 May 1883; *m* 1911, Audrey Stock, Dunedin, NZ; one *s*. *Educ:* Westport. FIA (NZ) degree (accountancy). Entered service Union Steam Ship Company of NZ, Ltd, 1898; NZ Manager, Federal S.N. Co., Ltd, 1931–34; enlisted B. Battery, NZFA, 1903; commissioned, 1909; Capt. 1911; left NZ, 1914; served Gallipoli, April–Dec. 1915 (DSO); commanded 4th (Howr.) Brigade, New Zealand Field Artillery, 1916; 3rd and 2nd Brigades, 1917–18 (CMG); Hon. Group Captain, NZ Territorial Air Force; Hon. ADC Governor General NZ, 1925–30; Brigadier Commandant Overseas Base, 2nd NZ Expeditionary Force, 1940–41. *Address:* Ministry of War Transport, W1; Wellington, NZ.

Died 6 Nov. 1945.

FALLADA, Hans; *see* Ditzen, Rudolf.

FANE, Lady Augusta; *e d* of 2nd Earl of Stradbroke; sister of 3rd Earl; *m* 1880, Cecil Francis William Fane (marr. diss. 1904; he *d* 1914); one *s* (and one *s* decd). *Publication:* Chit-chat, book of reminiscences, 1926. *Recreations:* hunting, golf, tennis, reading, travelling. *Address:* The Cottage, Swalcliffe, nr Banbury, Oxon.

Died 10 Feb. 1950.

FANSHAWE, Maj.-Gen. Sir Robert, KCB 1917; CB 1915; DSO 1900; Officer, Legion of Honour; *b* 5 Nov. 1863; *s* of Rev. H. L. Fanshawe; *m* 1903, Evelyne Katherine Isabel Knox (*d* 1943). *Educ:* Marlborough. Joined 2nd Bn Oxfordshire Light Infantry, 1883 and served with that regt till commencement of SA war; Adjt 1887, for 4½ years; service principally in India, including the war on NW Frontier, 1897–98 (Indian Frontier medal and two clasps); joined 6th Regt MI 8 Feb. 1900, as Adjutant; wounded at Paardeberg; commanded Mobile Column, South Africa, 1901, to end of war (despatches twice, Queen's medal 5 clasps, King's medal 2 clasps, DSO), and Bt Lt-Col DAAG 4th Division, 1903; European War, 1914–18 (despatches eight times, KCB); Commanded 52nd Oxfordshire Light Infantry, 1907–11; GSO1, 1st Division, 1911–14; commanding 6th Infantry Brigade, 1914–15; 48th South Midland Div. 1915–18; 69th Div. 1918–19; Chairman Oxfordshire County Territorial Assoc. and South Oxfordshire Hunt. JP, DL, Oxfordshire. *Recreations:* in India, polo and pig-sticking. *Address:* Lobbersdown, Milton Common, Oxon. *TA:* Lobbersdown, Tiddington. *T:* Ickford 247.

Died 24 Aug. 1946.

FARJEON, Herbert; author, dramatic critic and theatrical manager; *b* 5 March 1887; *s* of late Benjamin Leopold Farjeon, novelist, and Margaret, *d* of the American actor, Joseph Jefferson; *m* Joan, *d* of Sir Hamo Thornycroft; one *s* two *d*. *Educ:* Peterborough Lodge, South Hampstead; University College School. After acting one-night stands all over USA when 17 years old, became private secretary to Lady Wyndham; joined the Manchester staff of Daily Mail in 1907; then worked on Answers for three years; became dramatic critic to The World, 1910–13; Theatreland, 1912; Cartoon, 1915; Era, 1917–19; Sunday Pictorial, 1917–38; Daily Herald, 1919–23; Vogue, 1921–23 and 1927–35; Daily Express, 1923; Saturday Review, 1923; Weekly Westminster, 1923–26; Sphere, 1924–27; Graphic, 1927–32; Bystander (now incorporated with Tatler), 1936–42; John o' London's Weekly, 1943; dramatic critic to Time and Tide, and radio critic to The Listener, since 1943; dramatic critic to Sunday Graphic since 1944. Author of following plays and revues: Friends, Abbey Theatre, 1917; Advertising April (with Horace Horsnell), Criterion, 1922; Picnic, Arts Theatre, 1927; Many Happy Returns, Duke of York's, 1928; Pursuit of Adonis (with H. Horsnell), Festival Theatre, Cambridge, 1932; Why Not To-Night?, Palace, 1934; Spread It Abroad, Savile, 1936; The Two Bouquets (with Eleanor Farjeon), Ambassadors, 1936; Nine Sharp, Little, 1938; An Elephant in Arcady (with Eleanor Farjeon), Kingsway, 1938; Herbert Farjeon's Little Revue, Little, 1939; Diversion No. 1, Wyndham's, 1940; Diversion No. 2, Wyndham's, 1941; Big Top, His Majesty's, 1942; Light and Shade, Ambassadors, 1942; The Glass Slipper (with Eleanor Farjeon), St James, 1944. Entered into theatrical management at the Little Theatre in 1938, where he presented his own revues. Also presented An Elephant in Arcady at the Kingsway, The Country Wife at the Little (1940), and, with Bronson Albery, Diversion at Wyndham's all through the 'blitz' period. Member of Drama Panel of CEMA. *Publications:* Advertising April, 1921; Friends, 1922; Kings and Queens (with Eleanor Farjeon), 1932; Heroes and Heroines (with Eleanor Farjeon), 1933; Sketches from Spread It Abroad, 1936; The Two Bouquets, 1936; Sketches from Nine Sharp, 1938; Nine Sharp & Earlier (verses), 1939; Sketches from the Little Revue, 1939; The Herbert Farjeon Omnibus, 1942. Edited The Shakespeare Journal, 1922–1925, the Nonesuch Shakespeare, 1929, and the Limited Editions Club Shakespeare, 1939. *Recreation:* fishing. *Address:* 34 Loudoun Road, St John's Wood, NW8. *T:* Primrose 0467.

Died 3 May 1945.

FARMER, Sir John Bretland, Kt 1926; FRS; FRSE (Hon.); MA, DSc (Oxon), LLD (Edin.); Professor Emeritus of Botany and formerly Director of the Biological Laboratories, Imperial College of Science and Technology, London; formerly Member of Advisory Council to Committee of the Privy Council for Scientific and Industrial Research and of Agricultural Research Council; Member, Royal Commission for the 1851 Exhibition, etc.; has served as a Member of various Departmental and Inter-Departmental Committees; Hon. Member, Botanical Society Edin., Essex Field Club, and R. Microscopical Society, London; *b* 5 April 1865; *s* of J. H. Farmer, The Mythe, Atherstone; *m* 1892, Edith M., *d* of Rev. C. Pritchard, DD, Savilian Professor of Astronomy, Oxford; one *d*. *Educ:* Magdalen Coll., Oxford, 1883; 1st class Final Honour School Natural Science, 1887. Demonstrator of Botany, University of Oxford, 1887–92; Fellow of Magdalen College, Oxford, 1889–97; Assistant Prof. of Biology, Royal College of Science, London, 1892–95; awarded Royal Medal on recommendation of Royal Society, 1919. *Publications:* A Practical Introduction to the Study of Botany; Plant Life; also a number of memoirs, chiefly botanical and cytological; organised, and for some years edited, Science and Progress; one of the editors of The Annals of Botany; edited The Book of Nature Study, 6 vols; translated and edited (with A. D. Darbishire) De Vries, Die Mutations-theorie. *Recreations:* fishing, gardening. *Address:* Royal Beacon Hotel, Exmouth. *Clubs:* Athenæum; Bath and County, Bath.

Died 26 Jan. 1944.

FARMILOE, Ven. William Thomas, MA; Canon Emeritus of St Edmundsbury and Ipswich; *b* 15 Sept. 1863; *e s* of W. Farmiloe, London; *m* 1891, Edith Caroline (*d* 1921), *d* of Col Hon. Arthur Parnell. *Educ:* Queens' Coll., Cambridge; Ely Theological Coll. Curate of St Mary's, Barnes, 1887–90; Clerk in Holy Orders of St James', Piccadilly, 1890–94; Vicar of St Peter's, Great Windmill Street, Piccadilly, 1894–1905; St Augustine, Victoria Park, London, 1905–09; Nayland, Suffolk, 1909–14; Archdeacon of Sudbury, 1921–30; Canon Missioner of St Edmundsbury and Ipswich, 1914–30; Chaplain of All Saints, Rome, 1930–33; Hon. Secretary of the General Association of Church-School Managers and Teachers, 1895–1919. *Recreation:* travelling. *Club:* Athenæum.

Died 4 July 1946.

FARQUHAR, George Neil, CMG 1942; MC; Chief Secretary to Government of Uganda since 1945; Officer of the Colonial Administrative Service; *b* 26 Nov. 1896; *s* of J. N. Farquhar, MA (Oxon), DLitt (Oxon), DD, BD, writer, lecturer, and professor on Indian religions; *m* 1924, Helen Mary Erskine; one *s* one *d*. *Educ:* Mill Hill School; Hertford College, Oxford. Served European War with Royal Horse and Royal Field Artillery, 1915–19; France, on active service, 1916–19 (MC); Administrative Officer Ceylon Civil Service, 1920; transferred as Colonial Treasurer, Sierra Leone, 1934; Financial Secretary, Gold Coast, 1939; Financial Secretary, Nigeria, 1943. *Address:* Spurriers', Horsell Village, Woking, Surrey. *T:* Woking 919.

Died 10 April 1948.

FARQUHAR, Adm. Richard Bowles, CB 1917; retired 1918; *b* 12 Jan. 1859; 2nd *s* of late Admiral Sir Arthur Farquhar, KCB; *m* Mary (*d* 1944), *e d* of late R. Reade, HM Consul-General Ionian Isles; three *d*. *Educ:* Mr J. Graham's School, Greenock. Entered Navy, 1871; appointed to the Royal yacht Victoria and Albert, 1881, promoted Lieutenant; Comdr., 1893; Capt., 1899; Rear-Adm., 1909; Vice-Adm. 1914; Adm. 1917. Captain Naval Adviser to Inspector General of Fortifications, 1900–02; Captain and Rear-Admiral First Chief Inspector of Naval Ordnance; Commanding Devonport Sub-Division Home Fleet, 1911–12; Vice-Pres. of Ordnance Board, 1913–16; Admiralty representative and Naval Adviser on Commission Intern^lc de Ravitaillem^t, 1916–19. *Recreations:* golf, shooting, fishing. *Address:* Aboyne, Aberdeenshire.

Died 27 Nov. 1948.

FARQUHARSON, Bt Lt-Col Arthur Spenser Loat, CBE 1919; Vice-Master, Fellow, and Prel. in Logic, University College, Oxford; member of Delegacies for Military Instruction, University Police, and Local Examinations; Referee in Audit; 3rd *s* of Col M. H. Farquharson; *m* Agnes C. Raleigh; one *d. Educ:* Portsmouth Grammar School; Rochester King's School; University College, Oxford (Gunsley Exhibitioner). Secretary of JCR, 1892–93; Secretary of Cricket, 1892–93; First Class Hon. Mods, 1892; First Class Lit. Hum. 1894; passed 2nd into ICS 1894; Assistant Master, Trinity College, Glenalmond, 1896–97; Classical Lecturer, University College, Oxford, 1897; Fellow, 1899; Tutor, 1900; Dean, 1900–14; Lecturer in Philosophy, 1899–1914; Senior Proctor, 1913–14; attached GS War Office on mobilisation; GSO2, 1915; GSO1 and Chief Postal Censor, 1919–21; missions to France Belgium, and Italy; Territorial Army, 2nd Lieut 1902; Lieut 1904; Captain, 1905; Major, 1914; Bt Lt-Col 1918 (despatches twice, CBE); Officier Légion d'Honneur; Officier Ordre de Leopold; Officier d'Académie. *Publications:* Aristotle de motu et de incessu Animalium; articles in Classical Journals; editor of J. Cook Wilson's Statement and Inference. *Recreations:* golf and literature. *Address:* 3 Kybald Street, Oxford. *Clubs:* Leander; Oxford University Golf.

Died 5 Aug. 1942.

FARQUHARSON, Sir Arthur Wildman, Kt 1931; solicitor; banana and sugar planter; Chairman, Jamaica Banana Producers' Association and Imperial Association; *s* of Rev. J. S. Farquharson, Jamaica, and Anna Pengelly Coke; *m* 1890, Lilian M. Stone; two *d. Educ:* Marlborough College. Crown Solicitor of Jamaica, 1894–1911; Vice-President, British Empire Producers' Organisation; public work in and for Jamaica chiefly in connection with producers' co-operation, and the inauguration of a Jamaica-owned line of steamers to England. *Recreations:* gardening, motoring. *Address:* Fort George, Stoney Hill, Jamaica, BWI. *Club:* Royal Automobile.

Died 13 Nov. 1947.

FARQUHARSON, Lt-Gen. Henry Douglas, CMG 1919; RM (retired); *b* 3 July 1868; *m* 1900 (wife *d* 1944); one *s* one *d.* Served at defence of Antwerp; attached to Staff of General D'Amade, commanding the French Expeditionary Force, Dardanelles; Colonel Commandant of the Depot RM, 1920–22; Lieut-Gen. 1925; retired list, 1926; Croix de Guerre, 1916. Royal Humane Society's Medal, 1893. *Address:* Derryheen, Hook Heath, Woking. *T:* Woking 2576. *Club:* United Service.

Died 8 Dec. 1947.

FARR, Clinton Coleridge, FRS 1928; DSc; FInstP; Emeritus Professor of Physics at Canterbury College, Christ Church, NZ; *b* St Peter's Collegiate School, Adelaide, 22 May 1866; *s* of late Ven. Archdeacon Farr, MA, LLD Cantab, Headmaster of St Peter's Collegiate School, and Julia Warren, *d* of Sir Robert Ord, RA, of Greenstead Hall, Essex; *m* 1903, Maud Ellen Haydon of Christchurch, NZ; one *s. Educ:* St Peter's Collegiate School. Adelaide; University College, London; University of Adelaide; University of Sydney. Graduated in Science, 1888; Angus Engineering Scholar, 1889. Lecturer Mathematics and Physics, St Paul's College, University of Sydney, 1891–95; Lecturer Electrical Engineering, University of Adelaide, 1896; undertook magnetic survey of New Zealand, 1898; was engaged thereon till 1904; established magnetic observatory, Christchurch, NZ, for NZ Govt; Lecturer, Physics and Surveying, Canterbury College, University

of NZ, 1904–10; Professor of Physics, Canterbury University College, Christchurch, in the University of New Zealand, 1910–36. *Publications:* Some Expressions for the Radial and Axial Components of Magnetic Force a Solenoid, Roy. Soc. Proc.; Some Continuous Observations on the Rate of Dissipation of Electric Charges in the open air, Proc. Roy. Soc.; Interpretation of Milne Seismograms, Phil. Mag.; A magnetic survey of the Dominion of New Zealand and some of the outlying islands, etc.; The Porosity of Porcelain, with Special Reference to High Pressure Insulators for Electric Transmission Lines, NZ Journal of Science and Technology; The Viscosity of Sulphur, with D. B. MacLeod, Proc. Roy. Soc.; Tests and Investigation on High Tension Insulation, Jl American InstEE, etc.; Helium in NZ (with N. M. Rogers), NZ Journal of Science and Technology. *Recreation:* motor- and trout-fishing. *Address:* Canterbury. University College, Christchurch, C1, NZ.

Died 27 Jan. 1943.

FARRANT, His Honour Henry Gatchell; DL, Cambridgeshire, and Isle of Ely; *b* 1864; 2nd *s* of late Robert Farrant, Cullompton Court, Devon; *m* 1918, Marjorie Wyndham, *e d* of Arthur Lawrence, 30 Sussex Gardens, W; one *s* two *d. Educ:* Repton; New College, Oxford; MA 2nd Class Honour School of Jurisprudence; MA Corpus Christi College, Cambridge. Called to Bar, Inner Temple, 1890. Revising Barrister (Oxford Circuit), 1909; JP Worcestershire, 1904; Seven Commissioner, 1910; Bar Council, 1914; Remount Department, 1914; Military Service, Civil Liabilities Commissioner, 1916; Judge of County Courts on Circuit No. 35, 1918–37; Chairman Isle of Ely Quarter Sessions, 1921–41; a Governor of Repton School, 1925; Chairman, Cambridge Divisional Justices, 1927–41; President, Society of Chairmen of Quarter Sessions, England and Wales, 1930; Chairman Cambridgeshire Hunt Committee, 1928; Chairman Cambridgeshire Quarter Sessions, 1929–41. *Address:* Baytree Cottage, Thornham, King's Lynn, Norfolk.

Died 16 April 1946.

FARRAR, Rev. Canon Piercy Austin, LTh; Canon of St Michael's Cathedral, Barbados; *b* 1 Sept. 1873; *s* of Ven. Thomas Farrar, BD, Archdeacon of Demerara, B. Guiana, and Milicent Ann Farrar; *m* 1906, Mary, *d* of Very Rev. Dean P. L. Phillips, MA, Dean of St Michael's Cathedral, Barbados; one *s. Educ:* Queen's Coll., Demerara; Codrington Coll., Barbados. Deacon, 1896; Priest, 1898 (Guiana); Secretary to Bishop of Guiana and Diocesan Synod; Curate of Hawkchurch, Devonshire, 1900; Rector of St Andrew, Uddingston, Scotland, 1900; Curate of St Michael's Cathedral, Barbados, 1903; Vicar of St Paul's, Barbados, 1911; Rector of St James, Barbados, 1916; Rector of Christ Church, Barbados, 1917; Chaplain of House of Assembly, 1910; Rural Dean of St Michael's, 1929. *Address:* Allenby, Welches, Christ Church, Barbados, BWI.

Died 29 Oct. 1947.

FARRELL, James A.; *b* New Haven, Conn, 15 Feb. 1863; *m* 1889, Catherine M'Dermott. *Educ:* public schools, New Haven. Began work in steel-wire mill, New Haven, at 16; became general manager Oliver Iron and Steel Co.; President US Steel Products Export Co., 1903–11; President US Steel Corporation, 1911–32. *Address:* 944 5th Avenue, New York; South Norwalk, Conn, USA.

Died 28 March 1943.

FARRELL, Joseph Jessop, CBE 1924; late Deputy Chief Inspector of Taxes, Board of Inland Revenue; *b* 1866; *m* 1897, M. Emma Louise (*d* 1938), *d* of John Martyn; two *s* two *d. Educ:* Crossley School, Halifax; Bradford Grammar School. *Address:* 1 Eaton Road, Norwich. *T:* Eaton 606.

Died 27 April 1949.

FARRER, 3rd Baron cr 1893; **Cecil Claude Farrer;** Bt cr 1883, OBE 1917; Hon. Treasurer of the Commons Open Space and Footpaths Preservation Society; Member, Boxhill Committee and Leith Hill Committee, National Trust; b 8 May 1893; e s of 2nd Baron and Evelyn (d 1898), d of late Hon. Charles Spring-Rice; S father, 1940; m 1919, Evelyn Hilda Perry, e d of Edward T. Crook, Woodlands Hall, Bridgnorth. Educ: Eton; New College, Oxford, BA 1914. Formerly an Asst Secretary in Dept of Overseas Trade. Heir: half-brother Hon. Oliver Thomas Farrer, Sqdn. Leader RAFVR [b 1904; m 1931, Hon. Katharine Runciman, d of Viscount Runciman of Doxford, PC]. Address: High Hackhurst, Abinger Hammer, Dorking. Club: Brooks's.

Died 11 March 1948.

FARRER, Bryan; Bencher of Lincoln's Inn, 1920; JP Dorset; b 25 Nov. 1858; 3rd s of Oliver William Farrer, Binnegar Hall, Wareham, Dorset; m 1892, Mabel Gertrude, d of John Smith, Prince's Gate, SW; two s. Educ: Eton; Trinity College, Oxford. Called to Bar, Lincoln's Inn, 1894; practised at the Chancery Bar; retired from practice, 1925. Address: Binnegar Hall, Wareham, Dorset. T: Wareham 62.

Died 23 April 1944.

FARRER, Harold Marson; Senior Partner of Farrer & Co., Solicitors, Lincoln's Inn Fields, WC2; b 1882; s of Rev. William Farrer; m 1929, Helen Mary Cortlandt Benson; one d. Educ: Eton; Balliol College, Oxford. Eton VIII, 1900 and 1901; Oxford VIII, 1905. Called to Bar, 1907; solicitor, 1914; served in Gallipoli and France, 1915–18; Chairman Law Fire Insurance Society; Director of Equity and Law Life Assurance Society. Recreations: fishing, gardening, travel. Address: Hurley House, Hurley, Maidenhead. Clubs: Travellers', Oxford and Cambridge.

Died 19 July 1943.

FARRINGTON, Sir Henry (Anthony), 6th Bt cr 1818; late Woods and Forests Department, India; b 1 Oct. 1871; s of 5th Bt and Amy Florence, d of late Alexander Glendining; m 1906, Dorothy Marion, o d of Frank Farrington; one s one d. Educ: Haileybury and Coopers Hill College. Joined service, 1894; Deputy Conservator, 1901; charge of Andamans Forest Dept, 1908; Director of Forests School, 1911; Deputy Conservator, Bengal, 1912; Conservator, 1919; Chief Conservator, Central Provinces, 1923; retired, 1926. Heir: s Henry Francis Colden, b 25 April 1914. Address: Barrymores, Kintbury, Newbury, Berks.

Died 6 Sept. 1944.

FARTHING, Rt Rev. John Cragg; b 13 Dec. 1861; s of Richard Cragg Farthing; m Mary Elizabeth, d of John C. Kemp, Toronto; two s. Educ: Caius College, Cambridge. Deacon, 1885; Priest, 1886; Incumbent of Durham, Ont, 1885–88; Curate of Woodstock, Ont, 1888–89; Rec. of Woodstock, Ont, 1889–1906; Canon of St Paul's Cathedral, London, Ont, 1904; Prolocutor of the Lower House of the General Synod of Canada, 1905 and 1908; Dean of Ontario and Rector of St George's Cathedral, Kingston, Ont, 1906–08; Bishop of Montreal, 1909–39. Address: 310, 40th Avenue West, Calgary, Alberta, Canada.

Died 6 May 1947.

FARWELL, Sir Christopher John Wickens, Kt 1929; **Hon. Mr Justice Farwell;** Judge of Chancery Division of High Court of Justice since 1929; b 26 Dec. 1877; s of late Lord Justice Farwell; m Leslie, e d of late Dr T. C. Hope, Geelong, Australia. Educ: Winchester. Called to Bar, Lincoln's Inn, 1902; KC 1923; Bencher, 1928. Publication: Editor, Third Edition of Farwell on Powers. Address: 11 Kingston House South, Ennismore Gardens, SW7. T: Western 3090; Royal Courts of Justice, WC. Clubs: Athenæum, Windham, Flyfishers'.

Died 15 April 1943.

FASKEN, Brig.-Gen. William Henry, CB 1916; b 9 May 1863; s of late General Edward Thomas Fasken; m 1894, Lillian, d of late Col Sir Henry Thuillier, RE, KCIE. Educ: Marlborough; RM College, Sandhurst. Entered army (Lincolnshire Regt), 1882; 10th Bengal Lancers, 1885; Brigade Major to the IG of Cavalry in India, 1893–94; with Imperial Service Troops, 1894–1900; 10th Lancers (Hodson's Horse), 1901–09; in command 30th Lancers (Gordon's Horse), 1909–14; Colonel, 1912; commanded a brigade of Indian Cavalry in France, 1914–16 (despatches, CB); retired, 1920. Address: Hyde Grange, Chalford, Gloucestershire. T: Brimscombe 3246.

Died 24 April 1943.

FAUDEL-PHILLIPS, Sir Lionel Lawson Faudel, 3rd Bt cr 1897; Treasurer and Chairman of the Royal Hospital of Bethlem and Bridewell; Trustee of the Wallace Collection; Director of Faudels, Limited; b 1877; 2nd s of Sir George Faudel Faudel-Phillips, 1st Bt, GCIE and Helen (d 1916), d of late J. M. Levy, sister of 1st Lord Burnham; S brother, 1927; m 1908, Armyne Evelyn, o d of late Lord Granville Gordon; three d. Educ: Eton. One of His Majesty's Lieutenants of the City of London; Herts Territorial Reserve, 1914–17; Foreign Office, 1917–18; High Sheriff of Herts, 1933; Mayor of Hertford, 1928–29 and 1929–30; Master of Spectaclemakers; Member of Herts County Council; JP, DL Herts. Heir: none. Address: Balls Park, Hertford. T: Hertford 9. Clubs: Carlton, Brooks's.

Died 12 March 1941.

FAULKNER, Hon. James Albert, BA, MD, CM; Chairman Old Age Pensions Commission and Mothers' Allowances Commission for Province of Ontario; b 7 Oct. 1877; s of Dr George Washington Faulkner and Sarah Adelaide Young; m 1908, Helen A. Vermilyea; three s one d. Educ: Stirling Public and High School; University, McMaster and University, McGill. Physician and Surgeon; Minister of Health, Province of Ontario, 1934–37. Recreations: golf and fishing. Address: Parliament Buildings, Toronto, Canada. Clubs: Belleville, Bay of Quinte Golf and Country.

Died 27 April 1944.

FAUSSETT; see Godfrey-Faussett.

FAVIELL, Captain Douglas, RN (ret.); MVO 1915; OBE 1919; b 25 Nov. 1884; s of late Frederick H. Faviell of Highstanding, nr Barnstaple; m 1920, Dorothy Lennox, e d of late R. W. Wright of Pretoria and Marabastad, South Africa. Commanded HMS Oak, 1912–19, despatch vessel to C-in-C Home Fleets and Grand Fleet during that period; present at Battle of Jutland, and was commended for services in action; retired 1931; Order of the Sacred Treasure of Japan, 3rd class, 1918. Address: Amcotts, Bassett, Southampton.

Died 15 July 1947.

FAVIELL, Lt-Col William Frederick Oliver, DSO 1917; b 5 June 1882. Served S Africa, 1901–02 (Queen's medal with three clasps); Gallipoli, 1915–16; Mesopotamia, 1916–18 (despatches, DSO); commanded 1st Batt. Worcestershire Regt, 1927–31; retired pay 1932; Major of the Tower of London, 1933–45. Address: Mayhill, Bagshot, Surrey.

Died 14 Feb. 1950.

FAWCETT, Prof. Edward, FRS; MD, CM Edin.; Emeritus Professor of Anatomy, University of Bristol since 1934, Hon. Fellow, 1938; b 18 May 1867; s of Thomas Fawcett, BA Oxon; m Edith Dora, 2nd d of J. Wordsworth, Wakefield; one s one d. Educ: Blencow Grammar School; Edinburgh University; Edinburgh School of Medicine. MB, CM, Edinburgh, 1889; MD (Thesis Gold Medallist), 1906. Demonstrator of Anatomy, Edinburgh School of Medicine, 1887–89; Yorkshire College, Leeds, 1890–93; Professor of Anatomy in University College, Bristol, 1893–1909; Dean of the Faculty of Medicine, University College,

Bristol, 1905–09 and University of Bristol, 1909–34; University representative on General Medical Council, 1925–35; Examiner in Anatomy, University of Leeds, 1910–13; Honorary President Anatomical Section of the International Medical Congress at Buda-Pest, 1909; Long Fox Lecturer, 1909; Arris and Gale Lecturer, RCS, England, 1910; Vice-President, Anatomical Society of Great Britain and Ireland, 1913; Treasurer of Anatomical Society, Great Britain and Ireland, 1914–25; Examiner in Anatomy, Nat. Sci. Tripos, Univ. of Cambridge, 1914; late Examiner Queen's University, Belfast, in the National Univ. of Ireland, and in the Universities of Oxford, Manchester, Aberdeen, and London; National University, Ireland, Durham, Birmingham, and Liverpool; late Member of the Council and of the Court of the University of Bristol; FRS 1923; President Anatomical Society of Great Britain and Ireland, 1927–28 and 1928–29; President Bristol and Glos Arch. Society, 1936–37; Visitor in Biology of the General Medical Council. *Publications:* various contributions on anatomical and embryological subjects, more particularly concerning the development of the human skeleton and of the mammalian chondro-cranium, to the Journal of Anatomy and other journals; The Royal Arms in Glos Churches, Trans. Bristol and Glos Arch. Soc., 1934; Anthropophagous Figures on Glos, Som. and Wilts Churches and the Royal Arms in Bristol Churches, Trans. Bristol and Glos Arch. Soc., 1937; The Royal Achievements of Arms in Wiltshire Churches, 1938; Ditto Somerset Churches; Mayoral Sword Rests and an 18th Century Swordbearers Diary, Trans. Bristol and Glos Arch. Soc., 1940; numerous additional papers. *Recreations:* cycling, ecclesiastical architecture, photography. *Address:* 11 Leigh Road, Bristol 8.

Died 22 Sept. 1942.

FAWCETT, John, MD, BS (Lond.), FRCP (Lond.), FRCS Eng.; Consulting Physician to Guy's Hospital; Governor of Medical School, Guy's Hospital, and of Dulwich College; Member of Council, Medical School, St Thomas's Hospital; Member of Council of Epsom College; Invalid Children's Aid Association; Chairman Bermondsey Branch; Representative of Board of Education on General Nursing Council, 1928–32; Member of Senate of University of London, 1920–29; Senior Censor Royal College of Physicians of London, 1923–24; *b* 1866; *s* of John Bisdee Fawcett of Lloyd's; *m* 1899, May Fleming, *d* of late Herbert Fleming Baxter; one *s* one *d. Educ:* Dulwich College; Guy's Hospital. Formerly Member of Departmental Committee on Morphia and Heroin Addiction, and of Ministry of Pensions Disability Committee; Physician to and Dean of Medical and Dental Schools of Guy's Hospital, and Assistant Physician to the Royal Free Hospital; Bt Major, RAMC (T). *Publications:* contributions to medical Societies and journals. *Address:* 10 Chester Terrace, Regent's Park, NW1.

Died 18 Feb. 1944.

FAWCETT, Philippa Garrett; late Principal Assistant, Education Officers' Department, LCC; retired 1934; *o c* of late Professor Henry and late Dame Millicent Fawcett, GBE. Was Senior Wrangler. *Address:* 50 Lyttelton Court, N2.

Died 10 June 1948.

FAWCETT, William; author, journalist and sportsman; *o s* of late Sir William Fawcett, Stainton Grange, Yorks. *Educ:* Aysgarth; Uppingham. Served 4th Batt. Green Howards (The Yorkshire Regt) and Remounts; commenced Hunting career at 2½ with Cleveland and has since hunted with nearly every pack in England, Scotland and Ireland and written the histories of many of them in Booklet form; for some years bred hunters; trained and owned steeplechasers at Croft Spa, Yorks; hunted with the Zetland, Hurworth and Cleveland; always interested in Coursing; was one of the pioneers of Greyhound Racing in this country, and one of the first to broadcast a series of talks on the Greyhound; took up

literary career after writing a series of racing articles for the Newcastle Chronicle; succeeded the late Charles Richardson as Hunting and Racing Editor of The Field, 1928, being the youngest editor to be appointed to that position, leaving 1936, to devote himself to books and sporting research especially that dealing with horses, racing and hunting; Editor and Secretary United Services Association, 1938–39; Editor Hunts Assoc. *Publications:* Saddle Room Sayings; Turf, Chase and Paddock; Racing in the Olden Days; Thoroughbred and Hunter; Elements of Horsemanship; Horses and Ponies; The Devon and Somerset Staghounds; Hunting in Northumbria; Sporting Days in Tynedaleland; In St Wilfrid's City; Riding and Horsemanship; Foxhunting; A Romance of Transport; The Pytchley Hounds; The Young Horseman; Riding Schools; Punter's Pie; Star: the Story of a Foal; Sporting Spectacle; (with Sir W. Beach Thomas) Hunting England; contributor to the leading journals and papers on sport both here and in USA. *Recreations:* hunting, racing, coaching the Circus, sporting research, the collection of sporting trophies, sporting literature and anything to do with horses. *Address:* 20 Brampton Grove, Hendon, NW4. *T:* Hendon 8616. *Club:* United Hunts.

Died 18 May 1941.

FAWCETT, Maj.-Gen. William James, CB 1904; JP, DL; *b* 1848; *m* 1st, 1877, Mary (*d* 1881), *d* of Lt-Gen. W. T. Williams; 2nd, 1887, Alice (*d* 1943), *d* of Charles Lloyd. *Educ:* Dublin University, MB, MCh. Entered RAMC 1871; Colonel, 1899; Surg.-Gen. 1903; retired, 1908; Major-Gen. 1913; served Sudan Expedition, 1885 (medal and clasp, bronze star); Hazara Expedition, 1888 (despatches); Principal Medical Officer Irish Command, 1903–05; Deputy Director General of Army Medical Service, 1905. *Address:* St Andrews, Lustleigh, Devon.

Died 1 Dec. 1943.

FAWCUS, Lt-Gen. Sir Harold Ben, KCB 1931; CB 1928; CMG 1915; DSO 1917; DCL; late RAMC; *b* 20 May 1876; *s* of late John Fawcus, South Charlton, Northumberland; *m* Mary H. C. *d* of late Major J. J. Ross, PASLI; one *s* three *d. Educ:* Durham School and University. Lieutenant RAMC 1900; Captain, 1903; Major, 1911; Lieut-Col 1915; Col 1926; Maj.-Gen. 1926; Lt-General, 1929; Assist Prof., RA Medical Coll., 1912–14; Instructor, School of Army Sanitation, 1914; served South Africa, 1900–02 (Queen's medal 4 clasps, King's medal 2 clasps); European War, 1914–18 (despatches six times, CMG, DSO, Croix de Guerre); Deputy Director-General, 1926–29; Director-General Army Medical Services, War Office, 1929–34; retired pay, 1934; Col Commandant, Royal Army Medical Corps, 1938–41; Director-General, British Red Cross Society, 1934–38; a Commissioner of the Royal Hospital, Chelsea. *Recreations:* golf; a director of Roehampton Club. *Club:* Army and Navy.

Died 24 Oct. 1947.

FAWKES, Archibald Walter; late a Judge of the Supreme Court of South Africa (Free State Prov. Division); *b* 3 April 1855; *y s* of late Major Richard Fawkes; *m* Evelyn Fanny (*d* 1935), *y d* of late George J. Johnston of Castlesteads, Brampton, Cumberland. *Educ:* Repton; St John's College, Cambridge. Attorney-General of Gibraltar, 1892; Puisne Judge of the Orange River Colony, 1902. *Address:* Northroyd, Englefield Green, Surrey.

Died 19 Dec. 1941.

FEARFIELD, Joseph, CIE 1935; MICE; Manager, Bikaner State Railway; *b* 18 Dec. 1883; *m* 1910, Cicely Helen, *d* of late Rev. R. F. Follett; two *s* two *d. Educ:* Dean Close School, Cheltenham; Caius College, Cambridge, BA. MechSc Tripos, 1904. Assistant Engineer Jodhpur Bikaner Railway, 1904; Manager on Separation of Bikaner Railway, 1924. *Recreations:* Squash rackets, golf, lawn tennis, mismanaging railways. *Address:*

Webbington Paddock, Axbridge, Somerset; Bikaner, Rajputana, India. *T:* Winscombe 2287. *Clubs:* East India and Sports, Royal Automobile; Royal Bombay Yacht.

Died 17 June 1941.

FEARNLEY-WHITTINGSTALL, Francis Herbert, CIE 1929; *b* 8 June 1894; *e surv. s* of Rev. H. O. Fearnley-Whittingstall and Ailsie Mary, *e d* of Col O. P. Wethered, Great Marlow; *m* 1933, Leticia, *e d* of R. Chattock, MIEE. *Educ:* Cheltenham Coll.; RMC, Sandhurst. Joined Imperial Police in Burma, 1914; served in IARO, 1916–20; Private Sec. to the Governor of Burma, 1926–28; Dep. Comr of Police, 1929; Assistant Inspector-General of Police, Rangoon, 1931–36; King's Police Medal, 1921. *Recreation:* golf. *Club:* Junior Carlton.

Died 16 March 1945.

FEARON, Percy Hutton, (Poy); *b* Shanghai, China, 6 Sept. 1874; 4th *s* of late Robert Inglis Fearon. *Educ:* New York. Studied at the Art Student's League and Chase School of Art in New York, and subsequently under Prof. Hubert Herkomer at Bushey, Herts. First cartoons were published in London Judy; afterwards went to Manchester, 1905, as cartoonist for the Manchester Evening Chronicle, and later for the Sunday Chronicle and Daily Dispatch till 1913; Cartoonist, London Evening News, 1913–35; Cartoonist, Daily Mail, 1935–38. *Publications:* several collections of cartoons. *Recreation:* chess. *Address:* 15 Bellevue Road, Barnes, SW13. *T:* Prospect 7038. *Clubs:* Savage, Authors'.

Died 5 Nov. 1948.

FEETHAM, Rt Rev. John Oliver; Bishop of Queensland, North, since 1913; *b* 28 Jan. 1873; *s* of Rev. William Feetham, Vicar of Penrhôs, Raglan, Mon, Rural Dean and Proctor in Convocation, and Mary, *e d* of Ven. Archdeacon William Crawley. *Educ:* Marlborough; Trinity Hall, Cambridge (Scholar). Senior Optime in Math. Tripos, 1895; DD Camb. 1914. Resident at Oxford House, 1896–97; Wells Theological College, 1898; Deacon, 1899; Priest, 1900; Curate, St Simon Zelotes, Bethnal Green, 1899–1907; Principal of the Brotherhood of the Good Shepherd (in Bathurst Diocese), NSW, 1907–13. *Publications:* Editor, The Bush Brother, quarterly magazine, 1907–1913; Samarai to Ambasi, 1916; Editor North Queensland Jubilee Book, 1929; Imagination and Other Essays, 1940. *Recreations:* aeroplaning, riding. *Address:* Bishop's Lodge, Townsville, North Queensland. *Clubs:* Royal Societies; University, Sydney.

Died 14 Sept. 1947.

FEHR, Frank Emil, CBE 1920; Head of Frank Fehr & Co., colonial merchants; Underwriter at Lloyd's; *b* 1874; *s* of Henry Fehr, of Muswell Hill; *m* Jane, *d* of Thomas Poulter, JP; two *s* three *d. Educ:* privately. Pres. London Oil and Tallow Trade Assoc. 1919 and 1937; Asst Director Oilseeds Supply, Ministry of Food, 1917–19; contested Kent, Dartford Division (Ind U), March 1920; Pres. Kent County Football Assoc., 1920–30 and 1944–45; Chairman of the Incorporated Oil Seed Association, 1936–37; Chairman of The Baltic Mercantile and Shipping Exchange, 1937–39; President, London Cattle Food Trade Association, 1927–28 and 1940–41; Vice-Chairman London Copra Assoc.; Vice-Chairman Cocoa Assoc. of London. *Recreation:* Member W Kent Hunt. *Address:* Hatton House, Chislehurst; Upper Park, Lympne. *Clubs:* St Stephens', Constitutional.

Died 10 Jan. 1948.

FEILDEN, Major (Percy Henry) Guy; DL, JP Oxfordshire; late King's Royal Rifle Corps; *b* 1870; 4th *s* of late Lt-Gen. R. J. Feilden, CMG of Witton Park, Lancashire, and Jane Campbell, *d* of James Hozier of Mauldslie Castle, Lanark; *m* 1902, Hon. Dorothy Brand, 3rd *d* of 2nd Viscount Hampden; two *s* one *d.* Served

South African War; European War, Belgium and France; High Sheriff of Oxfordshire, 1938. *Address:* Cokethorpe, Witney, Oxon.

Died 24 March 1944.

FEILDEN, Col Wemyss (Gawne Cunningham), CMG 1917; retired; *b* 9 Aug. 1870; 3rd *s* of late Sir W. L. Feilden, Bart; *m* 1915, Winifred, *d* of late Rev. William Cosens, DD; two *s. Educ:* Marlborough College; Sandhurst. Entered Lancs Fusiliers 1890; Capt. 1898; Major, 1905; Lt-Col 1910; served S Africa, 1899–1902 (Queen's and King's medals 2 clasps); European War, 1914–17 (CMG); retired pay, 1921. *Address:* Rampyndene, Burwash, Sussex. *Club:* Junior United Service.

Died 21 June 1943.

FEILDEN, Sir William Henry, 4th Bt *cr* 1846; of Feniscowles, Lancashire, and Dilhorne, Staffordshire; JP; late Major, Derbyshire Yeomanry; *b* 8 March 1866; *s* of 3rd Bt and Catherine, *d* of late E. Pedder, Ashton Park, Lancs; *S* father, 1912; *m* 1891, Evelyn, *d* of Sir Morton Manningham-Buller, 2nd Bt, one *s* two *d.* Served South Africa, 1900 (medal with two clasps); European War, Major, Derbyshire Yeomanry, 1914–16, TFR, Acting Assistant Provost Marshal London District 1916, and APM Western Command, 1916–19. *Heir: s* William Morton Buller, MC [Captain, late Derbys. Yeomanry; *b* 1893; *m* 1st, 1922, Margery Hannah (*d* 1925), *o d* of Robert Knowles, Ednaston Lodge, near Derby; 2nd, 1927, Reva, widow of Major Guy Winterbottom; served European War, 1914–16 (despatches, MC)]. *Address:* East Lodge, Doveridge, Derbyshire. *T:* Uttoxeter 58. *Clubs:* Boodle's, Junior United Service, Royal Automobile; Yorkshire, York.

Died 23 Feb. 1946.

FEILDING, Lt-Col Rowland Charles, DSO 1917; late Coldstream Guards, Special Reserve; 3rd *s* of Rev. Hon. Charles William Alexander Feilding (4th *s* of 7th Earl of Denbigh) and Lucy, 4th *d* of John Grant of Kilgraston, Perthshire, and Lady Lucy Grant (*d* of 7th Earl of Elgin); *m* 1903, Edith Mary, *d* of Frederick Stapleton-Bretherton, of the Hall, Rainhill, Lancashire, and Isabella Mary (2nd *d* of 12th Lord Petre); four *d. Educ:* Haileybury College; Royal School of Mines (associate, 1893). Member of the Institution of Mining and Metallurgy; went to S Africa (Rhodesia and Transvaal), 1894; fought in Matabele Rebellion, 1896, in Gifford's Horse (wounded); has also practised as mining engineer in New Zealand, Ceylon, India, Burma, West Africa, Mexico, Argentine Republic, Republic of Colombia, Russia, Siberia, Canada, Newfoundland, Scandinavia, Spain, Italy, etc.; when war started was Captain in the City of London Yeo.; transferred, 1915, to Special Reserve Coldstream Guards, and went to France (despatches twice, DSO); commanded 6th Batt. The Connaught Rangers, 1916–18, and 1st Civil Service Rifles, 1918–19. *Publication:* War Letters to a Wife, 1929. *Club:* Guards'.

Died 5 Sept. 1945.

FELDMAN, Rev. Dayan Dr Asher, BA, PhD (London); Ecclesiastical Assessor to the Chief Rabbi; Senior Dayan of United Synagogue, 1902; now retired; *b* Russia, 1873; *m* Adeline Alice, *y d* of Rabbi Lubetski, Paris; one *s* one *d. Educ:* abroad; Jews' Coll.; Univ. College (Hollier Scholar), London. First Fellow of Jews' College, 1896; first English-trained student to receive Rabbinical Diploma, 1899, from the English Rabbinate. Minister, Stoke-Newington Synagogue, 1899–1902; acted jointly in office of Chief Rabbi during interregnum, 1911–13; formerly Hon. Secretary, Teachers' Training Committee and of Jews' College; Vice-Pres. Member of Council and Chairman Educn Committees of many communal institutions; Chairman of the Jewish Higher Educl Centre and Talmud Torah Trust since their foundation; Pres. for some years Jewish Aid Societies Metropolitan Hosp.; sometime Lecturer in

Homiletics at Jews' College, and for many years Lecturer to Jewish Teachers; Librarian of the United Synagogue Beth-Hamedrash and Jewish Institute. *Publications:* The Parables and Similes of the Rabbis (1924 and 1927); Jewish Teaching and Modern Life; The Teaching of Jewish Ideals; Papers on The Poetry of Jewish Observance; The Jewish Origin of Christian Ideals; Jewish Education in Rabbinic Simile (the Michael Friedlander Memorial Lecture); Jewish East London Organization (in Jewish Chronicle); Notes on the Early History of the Stoke Newington Synagogue and its precursor the New Dalston Synagogue and School (a link with the past). Sabbath Spice and Festival Fare (Talks to Children), 1927; contributor to the Jewish Quarterly Review, The Jews' College Jubilee Volume, and the Juridical Review (The London Beth-Din—The Jewish Court); occasional sermons and papers in the Jewish Press. *Address:* 5 Marlborough Mansions, Hampstead, NW6. *T:* Hampstead 4044.

Died 13 Dec. 1950.

FELKIN, Alfred Laurence, MA, FRSL, HM Inspector of Schools (Secondary Branch); retired, 1912; *b* Beeston, Notts, 29 Dec. 1856; *y s* of late Robert Felkin of Coombe Pyne, Branksome Park, Bournemouth, and Emily, *d* of Thomas Harrison of Ilkeston; *m* 1903, Hon. Ellen Thorneycroft Fowler (*d* 1929), *er d* of 1st Viscount Wolverhampton. *Educ:* Wolverhampton School; Magdalen College, Oxford. Demy, 1875; 1st class in Mods. (Math.), 1877, and 2nd class, Final Schools, 1879; BA 1879; MA 1882. *Publications:* On Heroes (a paper read before the Carlyle Society on the anniversary of Gen. Gordon's death, 1886); My Heart and Lute, 1901; Kate of Kate Hall (with his wife), 1904; Life of Sir Henry Hartley Fowler, Viscount Wolverhampton, in National Dictionary of Biography, 1912. *Recreations:* reading, music. *Address:* Mershire Lodge, Marlborough Road, Bournemouth. *Club:* Authors'.

Died 7 July 1942.

FELL, Aubrey Llewellyn Coventry, CBE 1920; MIEE; *b* Llangollen, N Wales, 8 July 1869; 5th *s* of late S. G. Fell, JP, Ickham Hall, Ickham, Canterbury; *m* 1st, 1895, Isabel Leckie Ewing (*d* 1925), *d* of late Thomas Mantel Fielding, Ingfield Manor, Billingshurst, Sussex; 2nd, 1926, Florence Ruby, *d* of Thomas Henry Wynn, late of Middlesborough, Yorks. *Educ:* Christ's College, Finchley; School of Electrical Engineering, Hanover Square. Electrical Engineer, Sheffield Corporation Tramways, 1897; General Manager, 1900; General Manager, London County Council Tramways, 1903–24. *Publications:* papers on Brakes for Tramcars, Tramway Corrugation, Mixed Systems of Traction, etc. *Recreations:* motoring, fishing, and bee-keeping. *Address:* Ripple Lodge, Ripple, nr Dover. *T:* Deal 806. *Clubs:* East India and Sports, Royal Empire Society.

Died 4 Oct. 1948.

FELL, Eleanor, ARE, 1908; 3rd *d* of Thomas Robinson Mitchell, MD, FRCS, and Sarah, *d* of Houghton Ainsworth of Darwin, Lancs; *m* Percy Herbert, *s* of J. J. Frampton Fell of S Norwood Park; one *d*. *Educ:* Preston; Tewkesbury. Studied at Westminster School of Art; gained figure prizes for the years 1902 and 1903, and the Gilbert-Garrat for animal and landscape. Exhibited at the Royal Academy Salon; International Society of Painters and Gravers; New English Art Club Institute; Brighton; Liverpool; Oldham; Leeds; Sweden; Barcelona. *Recreation:* stamp collecting. *Address:* The Chimes, Ambrose Place, Worthing.

Died 21 Jan. 1946.

FENTON, Brig.-Gen. Alexander Bulstrode, CB 1907; *b* 24 Jan. 1856. *Educ:* Marlborough. Entered Army, 66th (Berkshire) Regiment, 1873; transferred to Indian Staff Corps, Oct. 1876; Brigade Commander, Rangoon, 1906–09; retired 1911; served Burmese Expedition, 1886–89 (despatches, medal, two clasps, Brevet-Major); Chin Lushai, 1889–90 (clasp). *Address:* 12 Lansdown Place East, Bath. *T:* Bath 3635.

Died 10 Aug. 1942.

FENTON, Hon. James Edward, CMG 1938; *b* 4 Feb. 1864; *s* of John Philip Fenton and Catherine Taylor; *m*; one *s* one *d*. *Educ:* Public Schools, Victoria. Has occupied positions in municipal and public life for past forty years; printer and journalist by profession; a member of Federal Parliament for over twenty-two years; sat for several years on Parliamentary Committees; Minister for Trade and Customs in Scullin Government, 1929–31; Postmaster-General, Commonwealth of Australia, 1932–34; Australian delegate to London Naval Conference. *Publications:* several newspaper articles, etc. *Recreation:* earlier in life indulged in athletics and won several events. *Address:* Carinya, Box 1 Post Office, Merricks North, Victoria, Australia. *T:* Merricks 1.

Died 2 Dec. 1950.

FENTON, Sir Michael William, KCSI 1914; CSI 1911; *b* 5 July 1862; *m* 1888, Laura Harcourt, 4th *d* of late G. R. Elmsie, CSI; two *s* three *d*. *Educ:* Royal School, Armagh; Trinity College, Dublin (BA 1883). Appointed to the Indian Civil Service, 1883; held various posts under the Punjab Government, and represented the Province as Official Member on the Imperial Legislative Council, 1910; Financial Commissioner, 1912; retired, 1916. *Publication:* A Municipal Manual for the Punjab. *Address:* 63 Inverness Terrace, W2.

Died 27 Feb. 1941.

FENWICK, E. Hurry, CBE 1919; FRCS (Eng.); President, 1919–25, International Society of Urology; President, Second Congress of International Association of Urology; President, Section of Urology XVII International Medical Congress; Consulting Surgeon to Professor of Urology and late Lecturer on Clinical Surgery at the London Hospital; Consulting Surgeon to the West Herts Infirmary; *b* North Shields, 1856; *m* Annie (*d* 1937), *d* of Capt. John Fenwick, Elder Brother of the Trinity House; one *s* one *d*. *Educ:* privately; King's College and London Hospital; studied continental methods at Leipzig, Berlin, and other centres. Fellow of the Royal Society of Medicine and various foreign scientific societies. Late Examiner for the Conjoint Colleges; European War, 1914–19 (CBE, Brevet Major, Home Service mention); Lt-Col RAMC (TF); officer commanding Military Hospital, Bethnal Green, and Military Section London Hospital. *Publications:* several books and numerous papers. *Address:* 53 Bedford Gardens, W8. *T:* Park 8575.

Died 5 May 1944.

FENWICK, Ethel Gordon, (Mrs Bedford Fenwick); Editor of the British Journal of Nursing; *b* 26 Jan. 1857; *d* of late David Davidson Manson of Spynie House, Morayshire, Scotland; *m* 1887, Dr Bedford Fenwick (*d* 1939); one *s*. *Educ:* privately at Middlethorpe Hall, York. Registered Nurse, 1921; Children's Hospital, Nottingham, 1878; Royal Inf., Manchester, 1879; London Hosp. (Sister), 1879–81; St Bartholomew's Hosp. (Matron), 1881–87; Gordon House Home Hosp. (Managing Directress), 1889–96; Founder and First Member Brit. Nurses' Association; Member and Councillor Matrons' Council; Cross (Hon. Associate) of Order of St John of Jerusalem; President British Nursing Section, Chicago Exhibition (2 medals and diplomas 'for excellence of scientific exhibits'); commemorative medal of the Red Cross, Græco-Turkish War, 1899; Convener of Professional Section, International Congress of Women, London, 1899; Founder and Hon. Pres. International Council of Nurses, 1899; Hon. Pres. International Nurses' Congress, Buffalo, USA, 1901; Hon. Member Trained Nurses' Association of India; President National Council of Nurses Great Britain and Ireland, 1908; President International Congress of Nurses, London, and Hon. member American Nurses'

Association, 1909; President Society for State Registration of Trained Nurses; Hon. Sec. Central Registration Committee, President Society of Women Journalists, 1911; Hon. President International Congress of Nurses, Cologne, 1912; Hon. Treasurer French Flag Nursing Corps, 1915; and Hon. Superintendent, 1917; Hon. Member American National League for Nursing Education; Member General Nursing Council, Nurses Registration Act, 1920; Médaille Reconnaissance Française, 1921; Pres. British College of Nurses, Ltd, since 1926; Chevalier de l'Orde de Léopold, 1933; Hon. Pres. Florence Nightingale International Foundation, 1934. *Recreations:* armorial china collecting, travelling. *Address:* 19 Queen's Gate, SW7.

Died 13 March 1947.

FENWICKE, William Soltau, MD, BS (Lond.), MD (Strassburg); Income Tax Commissioner, West Sussex; Consulting Physician; Specialist in Diseases of the Stomach, etc; 3rd *s* of Samuel Fenwick, MD, of Harley Street, W; *m* 1896, Diana, *d* of late John Pearce of South Molton, Devon; two *s*. *Educ:* University College, London; Strassburg; Berlin. *Publications:* A series of monographs dealing with Diseases of the Digestive Organs; numerous articles on other subjects. *Recreations:* golf, sailing, fishing. *Address:* Bywell House, Worthing, Sussex.

Died 12 Feb. 1944.

FERARD, Arthur George, CBE, 1920; Officer of the Order of St John; MA (Oxon); *b* 6 May 1858; 2nd and *e surv. s* of late Charles Cotton Ferard, Ascot Place, Winkfield, Berks, and Emily, *d* of late Very Rev. Thomas Dale, Dean of Rochester; *m* 1895, Sarah Margaret (*d* 1923), *d* of late William Miller, 55 Lancaster Gate, W, and Halifax, Nova Scotia; one *d*. *Educ:* on the Continent; Brighton College; University College, Oxford. Entered Civil Service Grade I 1881; Assistant Secretary to Post Office Dept, general administration, special missions to Continent; during war organised the Post Office Relief Fund for dependents of PO servants called to the Colours, feeding of prisoners, PO hospital, etc.; retired 1919; joined Board of Queen Charlotte's Hospital, 1919; Marylebone Borough Council, 1919; Hon. Treasurer Marylebone Conservative and Constitutional Union; Chairman of Victoria Hospital for Children, Chelsea; Chairman of Handel Society; Chairman of House Committee of Queen Charlotte's Hosp.; Chairman Domestic Servants Benevolent Institution; member of Committees of Keats-Shelley Memorial Association, Royal Amateur Art Society, etc. *Publications:* miscellaneous articles, etc. *Recreations:* music, painting, travelling. *Address:* 101 Cadogan Gradens, SW3. *T:* Sloane 6767. *Clubs:* Oxford and Cambridge, Hurlingham.

Died 10 March 1943.

FERARD, John Edward, CBE 1918; *b* 1869; *s* of C. C. Ferard of Ascot Place, Winkfield; *m* 1912, Kathleen Marion, *d* of E. A. Dennys, late India Public Works Department; one *s*. *Educ:* Eton College (King's Scholar); Magdalen College, Oxford (Demy). Entered Local Government Board, 1892; Junior Clerk, India Office, 1893; Private Secretary to Mr G. W. E. Russell, the Lord Reay and the Earl of Onslow, Parliamentary Under Secretaries of State, and Sir A. Godley, Permanent Under-Secretary, 1894–1901; Senior Clerk, Public Works Dept 1901; Military Dept 1903; Judicial and Public Dept 1904; Assistant Secretary, Political and Secret Dept 1907; Judicial and Public Dept 1912; Secretary, Public and Judicial Dept, India Office, 1919–29; retired, 1929. *Address:* Pains Hill Corner, Limpsfield. *T:* Limpsfield Chart 3278. *Club:* Oxford and Cambridge.

Died 23 July 1944.

FERGUS, John F., MA, MD, FRFPSG, LRCP and S Ed.; Past President Royal Faculty of Physicians and Surgeons, Glasgow; Ex-Member Glasgow University Court; *b* Glasgow, 1865; *γ s* of Andrew Fergus, MD, MRCS, Glasgow, and Margaret, *d* of William Naismith of Auchincampbell, Hamilton; *m* 1890, Isabella Romanes, *e d* of late James A. Wenley, Treasurer, Bank of Scotland, Edinburgh; one *s* one *d*. *Educ:* Albany Academy and High School, Glasgow; University of Glasgow; University of Vienna; and University of Jena. Formerly Assistant Professor of Clinical Medicine, Glasgow University, and Assistant Professor of Medicine (Muirhead Chair), Glasgow University; Assistant Physician Glasgow Royal Infirmary; Visiting Physician Springburn-Woodside Red Cross Hospital; presently on Board of Managers Glasgow Royal Infirmary; Royal Technical College; Broomhill Home for Incurables; Glasgow and West of Scotland Convalescent Seaside Homes, Dunoon; Glasgow School of Art; VP Glasgow Ballad Club; Member Royal Philosophical Society, Glasgow; Member (formerly VP) Glasgow Royal Medico-Chirurgical Society. *Publications:* A Short Sketch of the History of Early Medicine; The Medical School of Salerno; Some Medicines of our Ancestors; and other papers on Medical History; and on medical subjects in medical journals; The Sodger and Other Verses (Scots Vernac.); Carmina Urbis et Ruris, etc.; Fancies of a Physician, Medical, and other Verses in Scots and English; Healing Waters; a three-act comedy produced in Athenæum Theatre, Glasgow, Nov. 1928. *Recreations:* verse writing, swimming, fishing. *Address:* 1 Parkgrove Terrace, Glasgow, C.3. *T:* Western (Glasgow) 5333. *Clubs:* Art, College, Glasgow.

Died 18 Feb. 1943.

FERGUSON, Brig.-Gen. Algernon Francis Holford; DL, JP; County Alderman; *b* 1867; *e surv. s* of Col John Stephenson Ferguson, 2nd Life Guards (*d* 1885), and Sophia, *y d* of late John Holford, of Rusholme Hall, Lancashire (she *m* 2nd, 1890, as 2nd wife, Sir Astley Paston Paston-Cooper, 3rd Bart); *m* 1897, Hon. Margaret Brand, *e d* of 2nd Viscount Hampden; one *s* one *d*. *Educ:* Eton. Has the Order of the Prussian Crown, 2nd Class, and Order of Swedish Sword, 2nd Class. *Address:* Polebrooke Hall, near Oundle.

Died 5 Nov. 1943.

FERGUSON, Hon. Sir David Gilbert, Kt 1934; *b* Muswellbrook, New South Wales, 7 Oct. 1861; *s* of John Ferguson and Elizabeth Johnston; *m* 1887, Alice, *d* of Robert Curtis; one *s* one *d*. *Educ:* University of Sydney, BA 1886; Levey Science Scholar. For some years occupied as a journalist in Sydney; Member of NSW and Queensland Hansard Staffs; Admitted to Bar, 1890; Puisne Judge, Supreme Court of New South Wales, 1912–32; Acting Chief Justice, 1929–30; retired, 1932; past Challis Lecturer in Law of Procedure, Evidence, and Pleading, in University of Sydney; Fellow of the University Senate, 1913–34; Vice-Chancellor of the University, 1919; Chairman of Royal Commission on Taxation; Chairman of Returned Soldiers and Sailors' Employment Board. *Address:* 16 Cranbrook Road, Rose Bay, Sydney, NSW. *T:* FM 3870. *Clubs:* Australian, University, Sydney.

Died 2 Nov. 1941.

FERGUSON, Fergus James, CBE 1920; Diplomatic Correspondent of Sunday Times; Reuter's Chief Diplomatic Correspondent in London (retired); *b* 27 Nov. 1878; *s* of late George Ferguson, Greenock; *m* 1920, Janet Smiles Nicholas, MA, BSc; one *d*. *Educ:* privately. Joined staff of Reuter's, Ltd, after short association with Daily Mail; has acted as Special Correspondent in Morocco, Persia, Egypt, and Near East generally; during War was attached as Accr. Correspondent on behalf of Reuter's and the Press Association to GHQ, Salonica, 1915–17; subsequently to GHQ, Palestine and Syria, during Lord Allenby's advance. President of Foreign Press Assoc., Switzerland,

1933–35. Publications: articles in magazines and press. *Recreations:* tennis, golf, motoring. *Address:* 410 Hood House, Dolphin Square, SW1.

Died 2 May 1948.

FERGUSON, Hon. (George) Howard, KC, BA, LLB, LLD; President, Crown Life Insurance Co.; Director: Toronto General Trusts Corporation; Brazilian Traction; Light, Heat and Power Corporation; Western Assurance Company; *b* Kemptville, Ontario, 18 June 1870; *s* of Dr Chas. F. Ferguson, MP (Scotch), and Elizabeth Wallace Bell (Irish); *m* 1896, Ella Cumming of Buckingham, Quebec; no *c. Educ:* Kemptville High School; University College, University of Toronto. Called to Bar, 1894; Councillor for three years and Reeve three years, Kemptville; Member Legislature of Ontario for the constituency of Grenville 1905–31; Minister of Lands, Forests and Mines, 1914–19; leader of the Conservative Party in the Legislature, 1920; Prime Minister and Minister of Education, 1923–31; High Commissioner for Canada in London, 1931–36. *Recreations:* history, fishing. *Clubs:* Marlborough, Athenæum; York, Hunt, Toronto; Albany, Rideau, Ottawa.

Died 21 Feb. 1946.

FERGUSON, Sir (Henry) Lindo, Kt 1924; CMG 1918; Commander of Order of St John of Jerusalem, 1937; MA, MD, Dublin; FRCSI; FRCSA; Hon. FACS; Hon. FRSM; Hon. MD Melbourne; Emeritus Professor of Ophthalmology, University of Otago; late Member of New Zealand Board of Health; Member of Council, Otago University, 1916–37; late Chairman of NZ Medical Council; President NZ Branch British Medical Association, 1919; a Fellow of NZ University, 1917–27; *b* 1858; *s* of William Ferguson, late of Ballybrack, Co. Dublin; *m* Mary Emmeline, *d* of John Leach Butterworth, Dunedin, NZ; one *s. Educ:* Kingstown School; Royal College of Science and Trinity College, Dublin (Senior Moderator in Natural Science). Dean of the Medical Faculty, University of Otago, 1914–37. *Address:* Wychwood, Dunedin, NZ.

Died 22 Jan. 1948.

FERGUSON, Hon. Howard; *see* Ferguson, Hon. G. H.

FERGUSON, James, CBE 1946; County Medical Officer, Surrey County Council, 1929–46; *b* 28 May 1879; *o surv. s* of late Thomas Ferguson, Muckamore, Co. Antrim; *m* 1915, Eleanor, *d* of late William MacCandless, JP, Londonderry; one *d. Educ:* Royal Academical Institution, Belfast; Queen's College, Belfast (Foundation Scholar in Classics, Foundation Scholar in Medicine); Univ. Exhibition in Classics and BA Honours Classics, 1902; MB, ChB, BAO, Royal Univ. of Ireland, 1908; DPH, Manchester Univ., 1914. Formerly Chief Assist County Medical Officer, Lancashire County Council; Examiner for MB and DPH, London and Manchester Universities; formerly Examiner for DPH, Conjoint Examining Board in England; formerly Member of Consultative Committee of Chief Medical Officer of Ministry of Health and Board of Education; Member of Prevention of Blindness Committee, of Tuberculosis Advisory Committee and of Nursing Advisory Committee of Ministry of Health; formerly Member of Advisory Committee of Director-General of the Emergency Medical Service, Ministry of Health; Member of Preventive Medicine Committee of Medical Research Council; Vice-Pres. (formerly Chairman of Council) of Royal Sanitary Institute; Fellow of Society of Medical Officers of Health, and of Royal Institute of Public Health; Member Medical Advisory Council, Nuffield Trust and Foundation; British Representative, European Conference on Rural Hygiene, Geneva, 1931; Member of Departmental Committees on Partially Sighted Children, 1932–34, and on Cost of Hospitals and other Public Buildings,

1933–38. KHP 1941–44. *Publications:* papers in medical journals; Reports to Surrey County Council, 1929–1945. *Address:* Cranleigh, Ashley Drive, Walton-on-Thames. *T:* Walton-on-Thames 1115.

Died 27 Aug. 1949.

FERGUSON, John Calvin, BA, PhD; LLD; Adviser to the Executive Yuan of the National Government of China; *b* 1 March 1866; *s* of Rev. John Ferguson; *m* 1887, Mary E. Wilson (*d* 1938); three *s* three *d. Educ:* Albert College, Belleville, Ont; Boston University. President, Nanking University, 1888–97; Nanyang College, 1897–1902; Secretary to the Chinese Ministry of Commerce, 1902; Member of Chinese Commission for Revision of Treaties with United States and Japan, 1902–03; Chief Secretary of the Chinese Imperial Railway Administration, 1903–05; sent on special missions to United States by Chinese Government; Member of Commission to Manchuria and Siberia, 1920; Delegate of Chinese Government to IX International Red Cross Convention, Washington, 1912; sent by Chinese Government to Washington Conference on Limitation of Armament and Far Eastern Questions, 1921; Councillor of the Viceroys at Nanking, 1898–1911, and at Wuchang, 1900–11; Foreign Secretary of the Board of Posts and Communications, 1911; Counsellor of the Department of State, China, 1915–17; Political Adviser to the Chinese Government, Peking, 1915–28; rejoined Chinese Government Service, 1936; Counsellor of the Red Cross Society of China 1912–22. Holds several decorations; editor Journal, North China Branch, RAS, 1903–11, President 1911; Hon. Member, 1919; Fellow in perpetuity of the Metropolitan Museum, New York, 1913; Hon. Fellow, 1923; Assoc. Editor of the China Journal of Science and Arts, 1923–31; Order of Merit of Red Cross Society of China, 1912; of Japan, 1913; received thanks of the Chinese Government for gift of his Art Collection to University of Nanking, 1935; Trustee of Boston Univ. since 1918; President of Phi Beta Kappa Association in North China since 1926; Pres. of Anglo-American Association, Peking, 1927–30. *Publications:* Outlines of Chinese Art; Chinese Mythology; Chinese Painting; Survey of Chinese Art; Noted Porcelains of Successive Dynasties; Catalogue of Recorded Paintings; Catalogue of Recorded Bronzes; numerous magazine articles. *Address:* Peking, China. *TA:* Ferguson Peking. *Clubs:* Century, India House, NY; Shanghai; Peking.

Died 3 Aug. 1945.

FERGUSON, Sir Lindo; *see* Ferguson, Sir H. L.

FERGUSON, Rev. Canon William Harold, MA; *b* 1 Jan. 1874; *s* of William Ferguson, Leeds; *m* 1933, Mabel Doreen, *yr d* of W. Stanley Earle; one *s* one *d. Educ:* Magdalen School; Keble College and Cuddesdon College, Oxford. Assist Master St Edward's School, Oxford, 1896–99; Bilton Grange, Rugby, 1899–1901; Lancing College, 1902–13; Warden St Edward's School, Oxford, 1913–25; Warden of Radley College, 1925–37; Canon and Precentor of Salisbury Cathedral, 1937–47; retired, 1947. *Address:* Farleigh, St Winefride's Rd, Littlehampton.

Died 18 Oct. 1950.

FERGUSON-DAVIE, Sir Henry Augustus; *see* Davie.

FERGUSON-DAVIE, Major Sir William John, 4th Bt *cr* 1641, and *re-created* 1849 for Gen. Henry Ferguson, husband of Juliana, *d* of Sir John Davie, 8th Bt of Creedy; *s* of 3rd Bt and Frances Harriet, 5th *d* of Sir William Miles, 1st Bt; *b* 17 June 1863; *S* father, 1915; *m* 1891, Phina (*d* 1939), *γ d* of late Thomas Nelson of Friars Carse, Dumfriesshire. Late Border Regiment. *Heir:* nephew Rev. Arthur Patrick Ferguson-Davie, *b* 1909. *Address:* Creedy Park, Crediton.

Died 12 July 1947.

FERGUSSON, Adm. Sir James Andrew, KCB 1925; KCMG 1920; CB 1918; *b* 16 April 1871; 2nd *s* of late Rt Hon. Sir James Fergusson, 6th Bt; *m* 1901, Enid Githa, *y d* of Thomas C. Williams, Wellington, NZ; four *d.* Served S African War (despatches, promoted Commander, Queen's medal, four clasps); European War, commanded 2nd Light Cruiser Squadron (despatches, Legion of Honour, CB); ADC to the King; commanded Devonport Reserve, 1919; A Lord Commissioner of the Admiralty, 1919–20; commanded the First Light Cruiser Squadron, 1920–22; Commander-in-Chief North America and West Indies Station, 1924–26; Admiral, 1926; retired list, 1928; St Anne, 2nd Class, Rising Sun, 2nd Class. *Clubs:* Marlborough, United Service.

Died 13 April 1942.

FERGUSSON, Surg. Rear-Adm. James Herbert, CBE 1928; MRCS, LRCP; RN, retired; *b* 1874; *s* of Robert Fergusson. *Educ:* St Paul's; privately; St George's Hospital. Fleet Medical Officer, Mediterranean Fleet; PMO RN Barracks, Chatham; Medical Officer in charge Royal Naval Hospital, Malta, 1930–32; retired list, 1932. *Recreations:* golf, tennis. *Clubs:* Junior Army and Navy, Roehampton.

Died 2 Aug. 1948.

FERGUSSON, Rev. John Moore, DD; Minister of the Presbyterian Church of England; Moderator of the Presbyterian Church of England, 1932–33; *b* Doune, Perthshire, 1863; *s* of Rev. Donald Ferguson; *m* Ethel Catherine Everett Evans; three *s. Educ:* University, St Andrews and University, Edinburgh; Princeton, USA; New College, Edinburgh. Served at Rockferry, Cheshire; St Andrew's, Woolwich; St George's, Southend-on-Sea; Christ Church, Wellington. *Address:* Dalnabreck, Highland Road, SE19. *Club:* Royal Empire Society.

Died 2 July 1944.

FERNYHOUGH, Col Hugh Clifford, CB 1924; CMG 1917; DSO 1900; late RAOC and Yorkshire Light Infantry; *b* 22 Sept. 1872; *m* 1903, Beatrice, *d* of late H. A. James, of Suffolk Hall, Cheltenham; two *s* one *d.* Gazetted Yorkshire Light Infantry, 1893; transferred to RAOC 1913; Captain, 1900; Major, 1913; Bt Lieut-Col 1916; Bt Col, 1919; Lt-Col, 1922; Col, 1927; served North-West Frontier, India, 1897–98 (medal with two clasps); S Africa, 1899–1902 (severely wounded, despatches thrice, Queen's medal 3 clasps, King's medal 2 clasps, DSO); European War, 1914–18 (despatches six times, 1914 Star with bar, CMG, Order of Leopold, Croix de Guerre, British war medal, Victory medal, Bt Lt-Col, Bt Col); retired pay, 1929. *Address:* Chalgrove, Ash Vale, Surrey.

Died 9 Oct. 1947.

FERRABY, H. C.; naval author and journalist; *b* London, 4 Aug. 1884. *Educ:* Warehousemen, Clerks, and Drapers Schools; Switzerland. Trained as a journalist under Commander C. N. Robinson, RN, on Navy and Army Illustrated and Army and Navy Gazette; served Daily Express, 1905–40; Official Naval War Correspondent, 1914–18; Naval Correspondent, Manchester Guardian, since 1934; Naval War Commentator to BBC, 1940–42. *Publications:* The Grand Fleet, 1918; The Imperial British Navy, 1919; The Immortal Story of Zeebrugge, 1920; Strange Intelligence (with HC Bywater), 1931; What We Imagine (a play), 1938. *Recreation:* going to sea as often as possible. *Club:* Press.

Died 31 Dec. 1942.

FERRAR, Lt-Col Henry Minchin, CBE 1919; *b* 25 March 1863; *s* of A. M. Ferrar, DL, Belfast; *m* Laura (*d* 1945), *d* of J. Hargreaves; one *d. Educ:* Royal Military Academy, Woolwich. Served European War, 1914–19 (despatches, CBE). *Club:* Army and Navy.

Died 5 Dec. 1949.

FERRARI, Ermanno W.; *see* Wolf-Ferrari.

FERRERO, Guglielmo; Man of Letters; Professor of Modern History, Geneva University since 1930; Professor of Military Institutions' History, Institut des Hautes Etudes Internationales, Geneva since 1930; *b* 1871; *m* Gina Lombroso; one *s* one *d. Educ:* Degrees in Literature and Laws. Has lectured in Paris (College de France) on Roman History, and in South and North America. Officer of Legion of Honour. *Publications:* Symbols; L'Europa Giovane; Militarism; The Greatness and Decline of Rome; Between the Old World and the New; La Guerre Européenne; The Tragedy of Peace; Democracy in Italy; The Women of the Caesars; The Ruins of the Ancient Civilisation; Words to the Deaf; Entre le passé et l'avenir; l'Unité du Monde (English Edition, 1931); Les Deux Vérités; La Révolte du fils; Sueur et Sang; Libération; The Third Rome, novel; La Fin des Aventures (English edition, 1933; War and Peace); Aventure, Bonaparte en Italie, 1796–1797, English edition, 1939; The Gamble; Reconstruction, Talleyrand à Vienne, 1814–1815, 1940; The Life of Cæsar; collaborated with Professor Lombroso in The Female Offender; with Leo Ferrero: La palingenesi di Roma; all the Italian books have been seized in 1935 by the Italian Government. *Address:* 8 Rue de l'Hôtel-de-Ville, Geneva. *T:* 47917; Villa Ulivello, Strada in Chianti, Florence, Italy. *TA:* Strada Chianti.

Died 3 Aug. 1942.

FESTING, Brig.-Gen. Francis Leycester, CB 1919; CMG 1916; (retired) Northumberland Fusiliers; RAF; *b* 25 July 1877; *e s* of late Maj.-Gen. Sir Francis W. Festing, KCMG, CB, and Selina Eleanor Mary, *d* of L. W. Carbonell, who *m* 2nd Col R. C. Drysdale, RA (*d* 1904); *m* 1901, Charlotte K. G. Festing; one *s. Educ:* Winchester College; Sandhurst. Joined Northumberland Fusiliers, 1896; served Soudan Campaign, 1898; Crete, 1899; S Africa, 1899–1900 (dangerously wounded, despatches); Hythe Staff, 1905–09; HQ Staff, Aldershot, 1912–14; RFC and RAF 1915–19 (CB, CMG, Bt Lt-Col, Bt Col). *Address:* Hyde House, Chalford, Glos. *Club:* Boodle's.

Died 17 Oct. 1948.

FETHERSTONHAUGH, Frederick Barnard; KC 1910; *b* 2 June 1864; *s* of Francis Fetherstonhaugh of Carrick House, County Westmeath, Ireland; *m* Marion Arabelle Rutledge, New York; one *s. Educ:* Toronto Collegiate Institute; privately; Law School of Upper Canada Law Society, affiliated with University of Toronto. Studied for mechanical engineer and afterwards law. Called to the Bar, 1889; founder and head of firm of Fetherstonhaugh & Co., patent barristers, engineers; Vice-President Royal Empire Society; Consul (Hon.) Argentine Republic, Toronto; Past President Empire Club of Canada. *Recreations:* yachting, motoring. *Address:* Lynne Lodge, Lake Shore Road, Toronto, Canada. *TA:* Invention, Toronto. *T:* Lakeside 0562 W. *Clubs:* Royal Canadian Yacht, Argonaut Rowing, National, Canadian Bar Association, Toronto Golf, Empire, Toronto.

Died July 1945.

FETHERSTONHAUGH, Lt-Col Timothy, DSO 1916; JP, DL, Cumberland; commanded 9th Batt. Seaforth Highlanders (Pioneers); *b* 1 Jan. 1869; *o* surv. *s* of late Timothy Fetherstonhaugh of the College, Kirkoswald, Cumberland, formerly 13th Hussars, and Hon. Maria Georgiana, 2nd *d* of 3rd Lord Dorchester; *m* 1st, 1899, Nancy (*d* 1917), *o d* of late J. M. Carr-Lloyd, Lancing Manor, Sussex; one *s* two *d*; 2nd, 1920, Bronwen Alicia Mary, *e d* of late St John Charlton; one *s.* Joined the Seaforth Highlanders, 1889; served Black Mountain Campaign, 1891, and Isazai Campaign; Chitral Campaign, 1895; South African War (severely wounded at Magersfontein); retired 1909–14; raised the 9th Battalion Seaforth Highlanders as a Pioneer Battalion and served with it in France (DSO, despatches thrice,

Brevet); served in the Westmorland and Cumberland Yeomanry, 1910–12; War Office Staff, 1917–19; High Sheriff, 1926; Chairman of Quarter Sessions, 1932. *Publications:* Our Cumberland Village; many magazine articles. *Address:* The College, Kirkoswald, Cumberland. *T:* Lazonby 7; Kinmel Manor, Abergele, N Wales. *Clubs:* Army and Navy, Carlton.

Died 1 Jan. 1945.

FETHERSTONHAUGH, Brig. William Albany, CB 1928; CBE 1920; DSO 1917; late Indian Army; *b* Melksham, 24 Oct. 1876; *e s* of late Lieut-Col W. A. Fetherstonhaugh; *m* 1915, Adela Mary, *e d* of late Claud Cayley; one *s* one *d. Educ:* Sandhurst. Entered service, 1896; Captain, 1905; Major, 1914; Lt-Col 1919; Col 1920; served Punjab Frontier, 1897–98 (medal and 2 clasps); European War (despatches 4 times, DSO, Légion d'Honneur, prom. Bt Lt-Col, 1914 Star and clasp, GS and Victory medals); Afghanistan and NW Frontier, 1919 (despatches, CBE, medal and clasp); commanded Lahore Brigade Area, 1926–29; retired, 1929. *Address:* Llanwenarth House, nr Abergavenny.

Died 25 Oct. 1947.

FEWTRELL, Maj.-Gen. Albert Cecil, CB 1938; DSO 1917; VD, OStJ; Chief Civil Engineer, Department of Railways, NSW; *b* 12 March 1885. Served European War, 1915–18 (despatches, DSO); Chief Engineer, Eastern Command, Australian Military Forces, 1939–40; GOC, 1st Aust. Div., 1940–42; GOC, L. of C. Area, New South Wales, 1942–43. *Address:* Railways Dept, Railway House, 19 York St, Sydney, NSW.

Died 16 Oct. 1950.

FFARINGTON, Henry Nowell, MA Oxon, FRMetSoc; succeeded to the Worden Estate, 1910, under the will of the late Susan Maria ffarington; *b* 21 March 1868; *s* of Richard Atherton ffarington and Everilda Mary Woodcock; unmarried. *Educ:* private tuition; St Edmund Hall, Oxford. Admitted a solicitor, 1901. *Recreation:* meteorological science. *Address:* Worden Hall, Leyland, Preston, Lancs. *Club:* Royal Societies.

Died 31 May 1947.

FFENNELL, Raymond William, Hon. Colonel South African Defence Force; FRCM; Director of the Central Mining and Investment Corporation, Ltd; *b* London, April 1871; *m* 1903, Hope Weigall. *Educ:* Harrow. In South Africa, 1894–1915; during that time Chairman of various companies including Rand Mines, Ltd, New Moderfontein, City Deep, etc.; took an active part in the formation of Defence Force after the South African War; became Lt-Col Commanding Witwatersrand Rifles, 1905; Founded the Empire Day Rifle Competition, 1908; a Vice-President National Rifle Association since 1910; Founded the Imperial Challenge Shield Competitions, 1910, to encourage rifle shooting among boys throughout the Empire; special trophies given by Earl Roberts, Earl Haig, Earl Jellicoe, the Viceroy of India, Lord Milner, the Governors-General of all the Dominions; with Mrs Ffennell founded the Hope Convalescent Home for Children in Johannesburg, 1915; since 1931 arranged for large numbers of elementary school children in the city of Oxford to receive a portion of their education on the Wytham Estate; in 1935 arrangements were made to receive London school children also; Sheriff of Berkshire, 1942. *Address:* Wytham Abbey, Oxford. *Club:* Carlton.

Died 5 June 1944.

FFOULKES, Charles John, CB 1934; OBE 1925; Hon. DLitt Oxon, 1936; BLitt; Lieut RNVR, 1914–18; Major Royal Marines, unattached, 1918–20; Trustee of Imperial War Museum, 1934–46; Member, War Office Committee on Military Museum; Hon. Freeman, Armourers' Company; Volunteer Warden, ARP, 1939; Sergeant of Pioneers, Home Guard, 20th Bn Middlesex Regt, 1940–45; Officer of the Order of St John of Jerusalem, 1929; *b* 26 June 1868; 2nd *s* of Rev. E. S. ffoulkes, BD, *g g s* of Sir Robt. Strange, the engraver; *m* 1942, Dorothy Agnes, MBE, *d* of Rev. C. F. Garratt, Little Tew, Oxon. *Educ:* Radley; Shrewsbury; St John's Coll., Oxford. Lecturer on Armour and mediæval subjects for the University of Oxford, etc.; Curator of the Tower Armouries, 1913–35; Master, 1935–38; First Curator and Secretary Imperial War Museum, 1917–33; Adviser to Admiralty on Heraldry and Design, 1918–36; Rhind Lecturer, Edinburgh, 1917; Royal Soc. of Arts, 1929, War and its Influence on the Arts; exhibitor at the RA Salon and RBA Exhibition, 1900, etc., Jubilee and Coronation and Defence Medals. *Publications:* Armour and Weapons, 1909; new edition, Gaya's Traité des Armes, 1911; Arms and Armour in the University of Oxford; The Armourer and his Craft, 1912; Ironwork, 1913; Survey and Inventory of the Tower of London, 1917; Catalogue of the Armourers' and Brasiers' Company; Notes on the Pierpont Morgan XIIIth Century Old Testament, 1927; The Gun-founders of England, 1936; Sword, Lance, and Bayonet, 1938; Arms and the Tower, 1939; Arms and Armament, 1945; many papers in Archæologia, Journal of Army Historical Research, etc. *Recreations:* all the above. *Address:* 60 Woodstock Road, Oxford.

Died 22 April 1947.

FFOULKES, Captain Edmund Andrew; *b* 1867; *e s* of late Rev. Edmund Salusbury Ffoulkes, BD, Vicar of St Mary the Virgin's, Oxford, and Anne, *d* of late Sir Thomas A. L. W. Strange, formerly Chief Justice of Madras. *Educ:* Shrewsbury School; Radley Coll. Was on the Roll for High Sheriff for Denbighshire; served as Captain, acted as Adjutant in European War, of the 2/ Volunteer Battalion The Oxford and Bucks Light Infantry. *Address:* Eriviat Hall, near Denbigh; 60 Woodstock Road, Oxford. *Clubs:* Junior Carlton, Royal Automobile.

Died 9 March 1949.

FFRENCH, Hon. John Martin Valentine; *b* 19 July 1872; *brother* and *heir-pres.* to 6th Baron ffrench; *m* 1915, Sophia, *y d* of Signor Brambilla, Villa Sucota, Como, Italy; two *s* three *d.* Formerly Lieut in 3rd Bn Connaught Rangers; served European War, 1915–19, as Capt. 7th (Service) Bn Leinster Regt; created Knight of Malta, 1932. *Heir:* *s* Peter Martin Joseph Charles John Mary, *b* 2 May 1926. *Address:* Castle ffrench, Ballinamore Bridge, Ballinasloe, Co. Galway. *Clubs:* St Stephen's Green, Dublin.

Died 7 May 1946.

FIDDES, Edward, Hon. LLD Manchester, 1931; Professor Emeritus, Manchester University; *b* Aberdeen, 31 July 1864; 2nd *s* of Edward Fiddes, Aberdeen. *Educ:* Aberdeen Grammar School; Aberdeen University (MA 1885); Peterhouse, Cambridge (MA 1892). Assistant Lecturer in Classics, Owens College, Manchester, 1890–95; Secretary to Council, Owens College, 1895–1903; Registrar of Manchester University, 1903–20; Senior Tutor for Men Students, 1912–20; Senior Pro-Vice-Chancellor, 1920–26; Ward Professor of History, 1926–31; Member of Cheshire Education Committee, 1923–31; FRHistS 1931; Chairman of Governors of Withington Girls' School since 1932; Member of Court of Governors of Manchester University, 1934. *Publications:* American Universities, 1926; Chapters in the History of the Owens College and Manchester University (1851–1914), 1937; various historical contributions. *Recreations:* walking, travel. *Address:* 173 Wilmslow Road, Withington, Manchester. *T:* Didsbury, 1819.

Died 9 March 1942.

FIEDLER, Hermann George, MVO 1914; MA, PhD; Hon. DLitt Oxford; Professor Emeritus, University of Oxford; Fellow of the Queen's College; Secretary of the Taylor Institution; *b* Zittau, Saxony, 28 April 1862; 2nd *s* of Musik-director August Fielder; *m* 1899, Ethel Mary (*d* 1933), *d* of Charles Harding; one *d*. *Educ:* Royal Johanneum, Zittau; University of Leipzig. Lecturer in German Language and Literature at Queen Margaret College and the Univ. of Glasgow, 1888–90; Professor of German Language and Literature in Mason College, Birmingham, 1890–1900; Professor of German Language and Literature in the University of Birmingham, 1900–07, also Dean of the Faculty of Arts, 1904–07; Taylor Professor of German Language and Literature in the University of Oxford, 1907–37; has acted as Examiner to the Universities of Oxford, Cambridge, Birmingham, Bristol, Leeds, Sheffield, Victoria University, Manchester, and University of New Zealand; Tutor to Prince of Wales, 1912–14; Vice-President of the English Goethe Society; Vice-Pres. and past President of the Society for the Study of Mediæval Languages and Literature; President of the Modern Humanities Research Association, 1936. *Publications:* A Third German Reader and Writer, 1896; A First German Course for Science Students, 1905; A Second German Course for Science Students, 1907; The Oxford Book of German Verse, 1911; enlarged edition, 1927; A Book of German Verse from Luther to Liliencron, 1916; German Short Stories, 1928; A Contemporary of Shakespeare on Phonetics and on the Pronunciation of English and Latin, 1936; Goethe's Faust, Part II, 1943; The Oxford Book of German Prose, 1943; A. W. Schlegel's Lectures on German Literature, 1944; has contributed articles to Brockhaus Konversations Lexikon, and to many philological reviews; Editor of Oxford Studies in Modern Languages and Literature since 1932 (15 vols); Editor of the German Mediæval Series, 1941–. *Recreations:* music, travelling. *Address:* The Lane House, Norham Road, Oxford. *T:* 3232. *Club:* Athenæum.

Died 10 April 1945.

FIELD, Adm. Sir (Arthur) Mostyn, KCB 1911; FRS, 1905; FRAS, FRGS; *b* 27 June 1855; γ *s* of late Captain John Bousquet Field, RN; *m* 1894, Laura Mary, *d* of late Captain George Herbert Hale, Bengal Army; one *d*. *Educ:* Royal Naval School. Naval Cadet, 1868; obtained three 1st class certificates and Beaufort testimonial; specially promoted Lieut 1875; Commander, 1889; Capt. 1895; Rear-Adm. 1906; Vice-Adm. 1910; Adm. 1913; served in HM Surveying Ships Fawn and Sylvia on East Coast Africa, Sea of Marmora, SE Coast of America, and Straits of Magellan, 1876–84; commanded HM Surveying Ships Dart, Egeria, Penguin, and Research on the Australian, China, and Home stations, 1885–1904; Hydrographer of Navy, 1904–09; Admiralty Representative on Port Authority of London, 1909–25; served as British Government Delegate for the Naval Section of the American International Scientific Congress held at Buenos Ayres, 1910; Acting Conservator of the River Mersey, 1910–30; Nautical Assessor to the House of Lords; Commissioner under the Pilotage Act, 1913. *Publications:* Sextant, Sounding and Nautical Surveying in Tenth Edition of Ency-Brit.; papers in Proc. Roy. Soc., etc.; Hydrographical Surveying (Wharton and Field). *Recreations:* motoring, carpentering. *Address:* Rest Harrow, Woodgreen, Salisbury. *T:* Breamore 214.

Died 3 July 1950.

FIELD, Frank Meade; KC (Can.) 1908; officer reserve Cobourg Heavy Battery; *b* Cobourg, Ont, 21 Jan. 1863; *s* of Corelli C. Field, merchant, Devonshire, and Mary Hossack; *m* 1895, Abbie, *d* of James M'Glennon, JP, Colborne, Ont; no *c*. *Educ:* Cobourg Collegiate Institute; Victoria College; Osgoode Hall, Toronto. BA 1884; 1st prize Natural Philosophy and Clarke prize. Called to Bar of Ontario, 1887; practised in Cobourg and Colborne; first President Northumberland County Conservative Association; contested West Northumberland for Ontario Legislature as a Liberal-Conservative, 1905; President Ontario Bar Association, 1914–15; Councillor

Canadian Bar Association; lectures on military, political and literary topics; travelled in America and Europe; Ontario representative to American Bar Association meetings at Chattanooga, 1910, Washington DC, 1914, and to New York State Bar Association, 1914; County Court Judge, Toronto, 1931–38; Judge in Admiralty for Ontario, 1932–38. *Publications:* writings in Canadian literary and legal publications. *Recreations:* hunting, travelling, curling. *Address:* Cobourg, Ontario, Canada. *Club:* Military Institute (Toronto).

Died 2 Aug. 1943.

FIELD, Adm. of the Fleet Sir Frederick Laurence, GCB 1933; KCB 1923; KCMG 1924; CB 1916; CMG 1919; *b* 19 April 1871; 2nd *s* of late Colonel Spencer Field, Royal Warwickshire Regiment; *m* 1902, Annie Norrington, 2nd *d* of late John Harris, Civil Service. Joined Royal Navy, 1884; Lieut 1893; landed from Barfleur in Boxer Rebellion, China, 1900 (wounded in taking Tientsin City, despatches, China medal, Relief of Pekin clasp); Commander, 1902; Captain, 1907; Rear-Admiral, 1919; Vice-Admiral, 1924; Admiral, 1928; Admiral of the Fleet, 1933; in command of HMS King George V at Battle of Jutland, 31 May 1916 (despatches, CB, CMG, 2nd Class of Russian Order of St Anne with Swords, Order of Crown of Roumania, Legion of Honour, American DSM); Chief of Staff to Admiral 2nd in Command, Grand Fleet, 1916–18; Director of Torpedoes and Mining, Admiralty, 1918–20; 3rd Sea Lord and Controller of the Navy, 1920–23; Rear-Admiral commanding Battle Cruiser Squadron, 1923; Vice-Admiral Commanding Special Service Squadron during World Cruise, 1923–24; Deputy Chief of the Naval Staff, 1925–28; Commander-in-Chief Mediterranean Fleet, 1928–30; First Sea Lord of the Admiralty and Chief of Naval Staff 1930–33. *Recreation:* golf. *Address:* Escrick Park, York. *Club:* United Service.

Died 24 Oct. 1945.

FIELD, His Honour Judge Henry St John; County Court Judge, Leicester Circuit, since 1945; *b* 22 Nov. 1883; *s* of Harry Field and Margaret Alexina Wentworth Bickmore; *m* 1914; one *d*. *Educ:* Rugby; Balliol, Oxon. Called to Bar, 1908; served European War, Lieutenant RA (temporary commission); KC 1936; Recorder of Warwick, 1937–45. *Recreations:* fishing, shooting. *Address:* 406 Collingwood House, Dolphin Square, SW1. *Club:* Garrick.

Died 9 Dec. 1949.

FIELD, Adm. Sir Mostyn; *see* Field, Adm. Sir A. M.

FIELD, Sid, (Sidney Arthur Field); comedian; *b* 1 April 1904; *s* of Albert Edward Field and Bertha Workman; *m* Constance Dawkins; one *s* two *d*. First London appearance, Holborn Empire, 1916; Melbourne, Australia, 1934. First West End success in Strike a New Note, Prince of Wales's, 1943–44; Strike It Again, Nov. 1944. Recent success in Harvey, Prince of Wales's. First appeared in films 1939. *Address:* c/o Archie Parnell & Co. Ltd, 3 Golden Sq., W1.

Died 3 Feb. 1950.

FIELDEN, Edward Brocklehurst; JP (Sheriff, 1911) Oxfordshire and Salop; Chairman, Lancs and Yorks Railway, 1919–23; Deputy Chairman London, Midland, and Scottish Railway since 1923; Chairman of Finance Committee Salop CC since 1920; *s* of late Joshua Fielden, MP, of Nutfield Priory, Surrey, and Ellen, *d* of Thomas Brocklehurst of The Fence, Cheshire; *m* 1st, 1884, Mary E. (*d* 1902), *d* of late Thomas Knowles, MP, of Darn Hall, Cheshire; 2nd, Mysie, MBE, 1918 (*d* 1942), *d* of William Theed. MP (C) Middleton Div. of Lancs, 1900–06, Exchange Division, Manchester, 1924–35. *Address:* Dobroyd Castle, Todmorden; Court of Hill, Ludlow, Salop. *Club:* Carlton.

Died 31 March 1942.

FIELDEN, Victor George Leopold, MD, QUB (Gold Medallist), MB, BCh, BAO, RUI; Senior Anæsthetist, Royal Victoria Hospital; Belfast Ophthalmic Hospital; Consulting Anæsthetist, Ulster Hospital for Women and Children; Medical Officer, Malone Training School; Chairman, NI branch St John Ambulance Association; late Captain (T.) RAMC, attached Belfast University OTC; *b* Plymouth, 1867; *e s* of late Immer Fielden, RN, late Board of Trade Surveyor; *m* Caroline Grant, *d* of late Chas. Henderson Ward, Solicitor, Belfast; one *s* five *d*. *Educ:* Queen's College, Belfast. Late Lecturer on Dental Materia Medica and on Practical Pharmacy, Queen's University, Belfast; Unionist; Church of Ireland. *Address:* 1 Cleaver Park, Malone Road, Belfast.

Died 5 June 1946.

FIELDING, Sir Charles William, KBE 1917; *b* 4 Oct. 1863; *s* of Thomas Mantell Fielding, and Eleanora Leckie-Ewing; *m* 1900, Florence, *d* of J. Willis Dixon, Hillsborough Hall, Sheffield; one *s* two *d*. *Educ:* Dover. Late Chm. of the Rio Tinto Company; Director General of Food Production, 1918–19; was on the Council of the Ministry of Reconstruction; Chairman of Committees of Ministry of Munitions; Member of Non-Ferrous Metals Committee of Board of Trade; was also a member of the Government Restriction of Imports Committee, Tonnage Priority Committee, Lord Milner's Committee on Production of Food, 1915, and the Committee which established the College of Science and Technology, 1906; owns 3000 acres of land in West Sussex; farms 1500 acres; is a writer on agricultural subjects, including production of the nation's food from British soil. *Publication:* Food, 1923. *Address:* Inglefield Manor, Billingshurst, Sussex.

Died 9 April 1941.

FIENNES, Hon. Sir Eustace (Edward), 1st Bt *cr* 1916; JP, Berks and Dorset; *b* 29 Feb. 1864; 2nd *s* of 14th Baron Saye and Sele; *m* 1894, Florence Agnes, OBE, *d* of John Rathfelde, of Constantia, Wynberg, Cape of Good Hope, and *widow* of A. W. Fletcher; one *s* (*e s* killed in war). *Educ:* Malvern College. Major, Oxfords Imperial Yeomanry, and Hon. Lieut in Army; served Riel Rebellion, 1885 (medal with clasp); Egypt, 1888 and 1889 (medal with clasp, bronze star); Pioneer Expedition to Mashonaland (medal); S Africa, 1900–02 (two medals with three clasps, despatches twice); European War, 1914–15; France with Oxfordshire Yeomanry, 1914; Antwerp with Royal Naval Division as Intelligence Officer; Dardanelles as GSO3 RN Div., 1915; DAAQMG Plymouth, 1916–18 (despatches, 2 medals, Mons Star); Hon. Lt-Col in Army; contested Banbury Div., Oxfordshire, four times; MP (L) 1906–10, and 1910–18; Governor of the Seychelle Islands, 1918–21; Governor and Commander-in-Chief of the Leeward Islands, 1921–29. *Heir: s* Ranulph Fiennes, *b* 12 Nov. 1902. *Address:* Wilbury House, Sunningdale Rise, Berks. *Club:* Orleans.

Died 9 Feb. 1943.

FIENNES, Lt-Col Sir Ranulph Twisleton-Wykeham-, 2nd Bt *cr* 1916; DSO 1944; commanding Royal Scots Greys since 1942; *b* 12 Nov. 1902; *o surv. s* of Lt-Col Hon. Sir Eustace Twisleton-Wykeham-Fiennes, 1st Bt; *S* father 1943; *m* 1931, Audrey Joan, *yr d* of Sir Percy Newson, 1st Bt; one *s* three *d*. *Educ:* RNC, Osborne; Eton College; RMC, Sandhurst. ADC, to Governor-General of Canada, 1928–30; Adjutant Royal Scots Greys, 1930. Served war of 1939–45, Middle East (wounded, despatches); British Member, Armistice Commission, Syria, 1941. *Recreations:* ski-ing and shooting. *Heir: s* Ranulph, *b* 7 March 1944. *Address:* Wilbury House, Sunningdale, Berks. *T:* Ascot 100. *Club:* Cavalry.

Died 24 Nov. 1943.

FIFE, Herbert Legard; JP, Co. Durham; 4th *s* of Wm Hy Fife of Lee Hall, Northumberland, and 2nd wife Caroline Jane, *d* of Sir Thos Legard of Ganton, Yorks; *m* 1st, 1897, Florence (*d* 1918) *d* of H. T. Toulmin, The Pre, Herts; two *d*; 2nd, 1931, Ada Dryden Trotter, *o d* of late Col Trotter, Langton Grange, Co. Durham; one *d*. *Educ:* Radley College. *Address:* Gainford House, Gainford, Darlington, Co. Durham.

Died 10 Aug. 1941.

FIFE, Lt-Col Ronald D'Arcy, CMG 1916; DSO 1917; DL, JP, North Riding, Yorkshire; *b* 19 March 1868; 4th *s* of W. H. Fife and Caroline Jane, *d* of Sir Thomas Digby Legard, 8th Bt of Ganton, Yorkshire; *m* 1st, 1898, Alice Louisa (*d* 1898), *d* of Arthur Duncombe of Sutton Hall, Yorkshire; 2nd, 1913, Margaret, *d* of Albert Rutson of 74 Eaton Square, SW. *Educ:* Radley and RMC Sandhurst. Entered army, 1887; served as Adjutant, Yorks Regt 1896–1900; ADC to Governor of Madras, 1901–05; Military Secretary to Governor of Cape Colony, 1906–08; served Kachin Expedition as Staff-Officer, 1893; Tirah Campaign, 1897, as Adjutant (medal, 2 clasps); European War, 1914–17, Commanding 7th Yorkshire Regt (despatches four times, CMG, DSO, severely wounded, Feb. 1917). *Recreations:* hunting, big game shooting, fishing. *Address:* Nunnington Hall, York. *Clubs:* Army and Navy; Yorkshire, York.

Died 17 Nov. 1946.

FIGG, Sir Clifford, Kt 1943; Business Adviser to Secretary of State for Colonies, 1939–45; *b* 16 Jan. 1890; *s* of William Henry Figg and Ethel Maud Hall; *m* 1920, Eileen Maud Crabb; one *s*. *Educ:* Charterhouse. Deputy Chairman, Ceylon Chamber of Commerce, 1928–30; Deputy Chairman, International Tea Committee, 1933–47, Chairman 1948; President, Ceylon Association in London, 1937; Member Imperial Economic Committee, 1937. *Recreation:* shooting. *Address:* Court Field House, Little Hampden, Great Missenden, Bucks. *T:* Hampden Row 38. *Clubs:* Oriental, City of London.

Died 24 Sept. 1947.

FIHELLY, Hon. John Arthur; *b* 7 Nov. 1883. *Educ:* Queensland State Schools and St Joseph's College, Brisbane. Entered Queensland Parliament, 1912; Minister of Justice, 1915–18; Minister for Railways, 1918–20; Acting Premier, 1919–20; Attorney General, Treasurer and Secretary for Public Works, 1920–22; Agent-General for Queensland, 1922–24; Senator Queensland Univ., 1916–22. *Address:* Brisbane.

Died 2 March 1945.

FILDES, Sir Henry, Kt 1932; JP; *b* 1870; *m*; one *s* one *d*. *Educ:* Partwood School and Harris Institute, Preston. MP (NL), Stockport, 1920–23; MP (LNat) Dumfries, 1935–45. *Address:* 2 Whitehall Court, SW1. *T:* Whitehall 3160; Endon House, Kerridge, Macclesfield. *TA:* Fildes, Kerridge, Macclesfield. *T:* Bollington, Macclesfield 3211. *Clubs:* White's, Reform.

Died 12 July 1948.

FINDLATER, Jane Helen; *b* Edinburgh; *d* of Rev. Eric Findlater, Lochearnhead, Scotland. *Educ:* home. *Publications:* Green Graves of Balgowrie; A Daughter of Strife; Rachel; The Story of a Mother; Stones from a Glass House; The Ladder to the Stars (with Kate Douglas Wiggin); The Affair at the Inn (with Mary Findlater); Tales that are Told; Crossriggs, 1908; Penny Monypenny, 1911; Seven Scots Stories, 1912; Content with Flies, 1916 (with Mary Findlater); Seen and Heard, 1916; A Green Grass Widow and other Stories, 1921; Beneath the Visiting Moon, 1923 (with Mary Findlater). *Address:* Viewfield, Comrie, Perthshire.

Died 20 May 1946.

FINDLAY, Col John, CB 1915; DSO 1917; VD; *b* 11 March 1869; *s* of late Charles Findlay, of Taieri, Otago. Late Canterbury Mounted Rifles Regiment, NZ Imperial Force; served S Africa, 1900–01 (despatches,

Queen's medal 5 clasps); European War (Dardanelles), 1914–17 (despatches, CB, DSO); ADC to the Governor-General, 1925–30; Colonel commanding Southern Mounted Rifle Bde, 1921–25. *Address:* Eiffelton, Ashburton, Canterbury, NZ.

Died 20 Sept. 1946.

FINDLAY, Leonard, MD, DSc, FRCP, FRFPSG; Consulting Physician, Queen Elizabeth Hospital for Children, London, and Radcliffe Infirmary, Oxford; *b* 1878; 3rd *s* of Dr William Findlay (George Umber), physician and essayist; *m* 1905, Gertrude, *e d* of James S. Binning, Blackheath; two *d*. Formerly Visiting Physician, Royal Hospital for Sick Children, Glasgow, and Professor of Pædiatrics, Glasgow Univ.; Hon. Member British Pædiatric Assoc.; American Pædiatric Soc.; Canadian Pædiatric Soc. Hon. Fellow Medical Society, Buda-Pest; Hon. Member Interstate Medical Association. North America; Hon. Member, Fellowship of Medicine; Corresponding Member Société de Pédiatrie de Paris; formerly Director Child Welfare Dept, League of Red Cross Societies, Geneva. *Publications:* Syphilis in Childhood; Rheumatic Infection in Childhood; (in collaboration): Poverty, Nutrition, and Growth; Finlayson's Clinical Manual; The Clinical Study and Treatment of Sick Children. *Address:* Amarah, Old Frensham Road, Farnham, Surrey. *T:* Frensham 274.

Died 14 June 1947.

FINDLAY, Lt-Col William Henri de la Tour d'Auvergne, DSO 1917; OBE 1919; Canadian ASC; *b* Nairn, Scotland, 3 Oct. 1864; *e surv. s* of Lt-Col Alex. Findlay, 3rd WI Regt and of Mill Bank, Nairn, and Alice Rachel de Ste Croix of St Heliers, Jersey; *m* 1st, Isobel, *y d* of Canon Hodgson, Horsham, Sussex; two *d*; 2nd, 1917, Josephine May, 2nd *d* of Thomas Vaughan Anthony, 14 Daleham Gardens, NW3. *Educ:* Dollar Academy; Edinburgh University. Served articles in Edinburgh as an architect and emigrated to S Africa, exploring and prospecting; went through the S African War with Royal Sussex Regt; settling in Sussex and emigrated to Canada; interested in improvement of stock and better cultivation of orchards; served European War, 1914–19 (despatches, DSO, OBE, Croix de Guerre); JP, Suffolk. *Address:* Ostlers, Curry Rivel, Somerset.

Died 18 March 1941.

FINDLAY-HAMILTON, George Douglas; of Westport, Linlithgowshire, and Carnell, Ayrshire; JP, DL, Ayrshire; member of Royal Archers King's Bodyguard for Scotland; *b* 11 March 1861; *y s* of Thomas Dunlop Findlay of Easterhill, Co. Lanark; *m* Georgina Julia (*d* 1923), *d* of Charles Vereker Hamilton Campbell of Netherplace, Ayrshire; one *d*. *Educ:* Fettes College, Edinburgh. *Recreations:* shooting, fishing. *Address:* Carnell, Hurlford, Ayrshire. *Clubs:* Conservative; New, Edinburgh; Western, Glasgow.

Died 12 March 1941.

FINDON, Benjamin William; (cousin of late Sir Arthur Sullivan); Lieut 1/11th Co. of London VR, 1917; *b* 6 Feb. 1859; *m* 1st, 1886, Elizabeth Sullivan (*d* 1896); two *s*; 2nd, 1920, Doris Fleetwood Chase; one *s*. *Educ:* private. Educated for musical profession. Organist of a country church at the age of eleven; became a journalist in 1889; musical critic of The Echo and Illustrated Sporting and Dramatic News; dramatic and musical critic of The Morning Advertiser, 1894–1909; Editor and Director Play Pictorial, 1906–33; president of the Playgoers Club, 1901. *Publications:* Life of Sir Arthur Sullivan, 1902. *Plays:* Troubles; Stella; Fancourt's Folly; The Primrose Path; Lady Wychling's Defence; The Marchioness, and other sketches; The Gates of Night, and other poems; History of the Playgoers' Club. *Recreation:* meandering Brighton cliffs and Downs. *Club:* Savage.

Died 20 July 1943.

FINK, Hon. Theodore; Australian lawyer, publicist, writer, and politician; Chairman of Directors of the Melbourne Herald and Weekly Times Newspapers Company, Ltd, and other companies; *b* Guernsey, Channel Islands, 3 July 1855; *s* of late Moses Fink, of Victoria; *m* Kate, *e d* of late George Isaacs, of South Yarra, Melbourne; three *s* two *d*. *Educ:* Geelong College and Melbourne Grammar School; University of Melbourne. Member of Legislative Assembly of Victoria for Jolimont and West Richmond for ten years until 1904, when he did not seek re-election; member without portfolio of the M'Lean Ministry, 1899; as member of the executive of the Australian Federal League helped the foundation of the Australian Commonwealth; President of the Royal Commission on Technical Education in Victoria, 1899–1901; and on the University of Melbourne, 1902–04; thanks of Parliament for his services to education, Aug. 1904; Member of the Melbourne University Council, 1906–23; Chairman of the Board of Inquiry into the Working Men's College, Melbourne, 1910; Vice-President of the Council of Public Education of Victoria; Delegate to the Imperial Press Conference, 1909; Delegate to the British University Conference, 1912; Vice-Chairman of the State War Council, Victoria; Chairman of the Commonwealth Repatriation Board for the State of Victoria, 1917–19; Delegate, Canadian Press Conference, 1920; Chairman of the Empire Press Union (Australian Section) since 1929. One of the original members in London of the Union, founded 1909; Attended all Conferences, London 1909 and 1930; Ottawa 1920, Melbourne 1925; Chairman, Apprenticeship Conferences, 1906–07 and 1911. *Address:* Weemala, Lansell Road, Toorak, SE2, Victoria, Australia. *T:* U1921. *Clubs:* Authors'; Yorick, Wallaby, Royal Melbourne Golf, Melbourne.

Died 23 April 1942.

FINLAISON, Maj.-Gen. John Bruce, CMG 1919; *b* 1870; *s* of late Alexander John Finlaison, CB; *m* 1901, Isabel, *d* of late Lieut-Gen. Sir John Hudson, KCB. Maj.-Gen., RM (retd), 1927; served European War, 1914–19. *Address:* Old Orchard, Dedham, Colchester.

Died 22 April 1950.

FINLAY, 2nd Viscount *cr* 1919, of Nairn; **William Finlay,** PC 1938; GBE 1945; KBE 1920; Baron *cr* 1916; **Rt Hon. Lord Justice Finlay;** Lord Justice of Appeal since 1938; Chairman of Wiltshire Quarter Sessions since 1937; Chairman Contraband Committee since 1939; *b* London, 1875; *o s* of 1st Viscount and Mary (*d* 1911), *y d* of late Cosmo Innes, Advocate, Inverleith House, Edinburgh; S father, 1929; *m* 1903, Beatrice (*d* 1942), *d* of late Edward Kirkpatrick Hall, Holly Bush, Staffordshire; one *d*. *Educ:* Eton; Trinity College, Cambridge. Barrister, 1901; Junior Counsel to Board of Inland Revenue, 1905–14; KC 1914; Commissioner of Assize, Northern Circuit, 1921; Midland and Oxford Circuits, 1922; Judge of the High Court of Justice (King's Bench Division), 1924–38. *Heir:* none. *Address:* Fairway, Great Bedwyn, Wilts. *Club:* United University.

Died 30 June 1945 (ext).

FINLAYSON, Surg. Captain Henry William, DSO 1916; RN, retired; *b* 1864. Served European War, 1916 (DSO, despatches, Russian Order of St Stanislas). *Address:* Belstone, Chiddingfold, Surrey.

Died 7 Dec. 1944.

FINNIS, Col Frank Alexander, CB 1930; OBE; Indian Army (retired); *b* 29 Nov. 1880; *e s* of late Col Henry Finnis, CSI, CBE, RE; *m* 1911, Hazel de Lona (*d* 1938), *yr d* of late Major-General L. W. Christopher, CB; no *c*. *Educ:* Wellington; RMA, Woolwich. Commissioned RGA 1900; Indian Ordnance Dept, 1906; Capt., 1912; Major, 1915; Bt Lieut-Col, 1919; Col, 1928; served S Africa, 1901–02; NW Frontier, India, 1908; European War, 1914–18 (Brevet Lieut-Col); 3rd Afghan War,

1919; Waziristan, 1919–20 (OBE); retired, 1935. *Address:* c/o Lloyds Bank, Ltd, 6 Pall Mall, SW1. *Club:* Junior United Service.

Died 29 Jan. 1941.

FINNIS, Gen. Sir Henry, KCB 1945; CB 1942; MC; *b* 21 April 1890; 3rd *s* of Col H. Finnis, CSI, CBE; *m* 1917, Cecile Violet D'Oyly, *o d* of Col A. D'Oyly O'Malley, CB; one *s. Educ:* Wellington College, Berks; RMC, Sandhurst. Joined Indian Army, 1909, Unit 3rd Royal Bn 12th Frontier Force Regt; served European War, Egypt, Aden, and Iraq (twice wounded, MC); command of 3rd Royal Bn 12th Frontier Force Regt, 1934; Colonel, 1935; Brigade Commander, 1938; Major-General, 1940; Lt-General, 1943; General, 1944; Military Secretary, General Headquarters, India; GOC-in-Chief, North-Western Army, India, 1943; Colonel 3rd Royal Bn 12th Frontier Force Regt since 1941. *Recreations:* riding, tennis, golf. *Club:* Naval and Military.

Died 31 May 1945.

FIRTH, Arthur Charles Douglas, MA, MD (Cantab), FRCP; Secretary to Committee appointed by University of Cambridge to organise post-graduate education in the Eastern Counties for medical officers returning from HM Forces; Fellow (supernumerary) Trinity Hall, Cambridge; Consulting Physician, King's College Hospital and Emeritus Lecturer in Medicine, King's College Hospital Medical School; Consulting Physician Victoria Hospital for Children, Edenbridge and District, Oxted and Limpsfield, West Herts and Norwood Cottage Hospitals, and the Warehousemen, Clerks and Drapers Schools; lately Principal MO to Alliance Insurance Co., North British and Mercantile Insurance Co., and National Provident Institution; Hon. Captain RAMC; *s* of Charles F. Firth, Leeds; *m* 1914, Violet Dorothea, *d* of Lieut-Col H. N. Reeves, Bombay Political Service; one *s* three *d. Educ:* Elstree; Harrow; Trinity College, Cambridge; St Thomas' Hospital. Lately Examiner in Medicine, Universities of London, Cambridge, and Glasgow and RCP; Assist Physician Royal Free Hospital, City of London Hospital for Diseases of the Chest and Royal National Orthopædic Hospitals. *Publications:* various papers in medical journals. *Recreations:* walking in the Lake District, Postal History. *Address:* 236 Hills Road, Cambridge. *T:* Cambridge 87765.

Died 9 Jan. 1948.

FIRTH, Sir Harriss, Kt 1933; FSI; late Chief Valuer to Board of Inland Revenue; *b* 1876; *s* of John William Firth, Leeds; *m* 1903, Nellie (*d* 1944), *d* of Charles Rawlinson, Huddersfield. *Address:* Old Oak Frant, Sussex.

Died 1 May 1950.

FIRTH, John B.; editorial staff of the Daily Telegraph; *b* 1868; *s* of late John B. Firth, of Bradford; *m* 1897, Helena Gertrude, *d* of late D'Ewes Lynam, Nottingham; one *s. Educ:* Queen's College, Oxford (Hastings Exhibitioner and Hon. Scholar). 1st Class. Mods. 1889; 1st Class. Lit. Hum. 1891. Joined the Daily Telegraph, 1897. *Publications:* Augustus Caesar; Constantine the Great; Middlesex Little Guide; Highways and Byways of Derbyshire; Highways and Byways of Nottinghamshire; The Minstrelsy of Isis; Highways and Byways of Leicestershire, 1926; compiler of The Daily Telegraph Miscellanies, Vols I–III; numerous articles in the Fortnightly Review and other magazines. *Club:* United University.

Died 23 May 1943.

FISCHER, Prof. Hans; Professor, Vorstand des Organisch-Chemischen Instituts der Technischen Hochschule München, since 1921; *b* Hoechst a. M., 27 July 1881; *m. Educ:* Lausanne, Marburg, München. DrPhil, Marburg, 1904; Dr Med. München, 1908. Privatdozent München Universität, 1912; ao Professor, München Universität, 1915; o. Professor Innsbruck Universität, 1916; o. Professor Wien Universität, 1918. *Publications:* Veröffentlichungen in Liebig's Annalen, Hoppe Seyler's Zeitschrift f. Physiol. Chemie; Berichte der Deutschen Chemischen Ges., und anderen Fachzeitschriften; (with H. Orth) Die Chemie des Pyrrols, Vol. II. *Address:* München, Lamontstrasse 1/Ir, Germany.

Died 31 March 1945.

FISH, Elizabeth, LLA, FEIS; President, Educational Institute of Scotland, 1913–14 (first lady president elected); Principal teacher of Modern Languages, Bellahouston Academy, Glasgow; retired, 1925; formerly Lecturer in Hygiene and Physiology at Royal Technical College, Glasgow, and at the Glasgow and West of Scotland College of Domestic Science; *b* Glasgow. *Educ:* Sharp's Institution, Perth; Practising School of the Church of Scotland Training College, Glasgow. Pupil-teacher, Henderson Street Public School; first for Scotland in Queen's Scholarship Examination for admission to Training College; student in Glasgow Church of Scotland Training College; teacher in Shields Road Public School, and in Pupil-Teachers' Institute, Glasgow; formerly conducted evening classes for the cure of stammering; member of many educational societies. *Publications:* papers on Educational Subjects in the Educational News. *Recreations:* reading, study of Italian, botany. *Address:* Morven, Milliken Park, Renfrewshire.

Died 21 March 1944.

FISH, Walter George, CBE, 1919; *b* Accrington, Lancs, 3 June 1874; *s* of late George Fish; *m* Margery, *d* of Ernest Townshend, Chalfont St Peter, Bucks. *Educ:* Westminster City School. Director Associated Newspapers, Ltd, 1919; Editor of Daily Mail until Jan. 1930; News Editor of Daily Mail, 1906–19; Hon. Director of Publicity, Coal Mines Department, Board of Trade, 1918; Hon. Press Adviser to Director-General of Press and Censorship Bureau, 1939–40; Member Advisory Committee, Ministry of Information, SW District, since 1940. *Address:* Old Manor, East Lambrook, S Petherton, Somerset. *T:* South Petherton 328; 90 Vicarage Court, Kensington, W8. *T:* Western 8221. *Club:* Devonshire.

Died 21 Dec. 1947.

FISHER, A. Hugh, ARE; artist and writer; *b* London, 1867; *s* of Alfred George Fisher and Isabella Fayle Smith; *m* 1909, Lilias Cecile (*d* 1930), *y d* of Edward Franck Wyman. *Educ:* City of London and University College Schools. After nine years in a city office relinquished business for art; studied at Lambeth, South Kensington, and Paris under Laurens and Constant; Exhibitor at RA, Paris Salon, New English Art Club, etc.; artist to the Visual Instruction Committee of the Colonial Office to travel for three years about the British Empire, 1907–10; has made three hundred etchings; has contributed articles, stories and poems to many periodicals. *Publications:* The Cathedral Church of Hereford, 1898; Yule's Book I., 1902; Through India and Burmah with Pen and Brush, 1911; Poems, 1913; The Marriage of Ilario, 1919; The Ruined Barn, and other Poems, 1921; Frolics with Uncle Yule, 1928; Quix, 1931; Callisto (a poem), 1934; Jemshid in Exile and other poems, 1935. *Address:* Westminster Bank, Ltd, 12 King Street, Hammersmith, W6. *Club:* The Art Workers' Guild.

Died 2 July 1945.

FISHER, Edwin; Chairman of Barclays Bank, Limited, since 1936; President of British Bankers' Association and Chairman of Committee of London Clearing Bankers, 1946–47; Director of Alliance Assurance Co. Ltd; Member of Council of Foreign Bondholders; *b* 1883; *y s* of late H. W. Fisher, Vice-Warden of the Stannaries; *m* 1920, Theodora Cecilia, *e d* of J. F. Hess; one *s* one *d. Educ:* Clifton College. Articled to Hills and Halsey, solicitors of Lincoln's Inn Fields; entered Barclays Bank; Assistant Secretary, 1908; Secretary, 1911; General

Manager, 1925; Vice-Chairman, 1932; Deputy Chairman, 1934; received commission 3rd KO Hussars, 1914; transferred to 1st Life Guards (SR), 1915; served in France with that Regiment, and as Captain with the 1st Life Guards Battalion Machine-Gun Guards, 1915–19; Life Governor of Birmingham University; Governor and Member of Council, Bedford College for Women; Vice-President of Institute of Bankers; Member of Sea-Fish Commission for United Kingdom, 1933–35; Member of Tithe Redemption Commission; High Sheriff of Sussex, 1943. *Address:* Kinnaird House, 1 Pall Mall East, SW1. *T:* Whitehall 6813; Barleys, Offham, near Lewes, Sussex. *T:* Lewes, 56. *Club:* Bath.

Died 27 Jan. 1947.

FISHER, Frank Lindsay, CBE 1923; *s* of Henry Edward Fisher, Blandford; *m* Ethel Owen Pugh; one *s. Educ:* Highgate. Disposals Board, 1921–23; President, Institute of Chartered Accountants, 1937–38. *Address:* Hayling Island. *T:* Hayling 77910.

Died 5 Jan. 1947.

FISHER, Adm. Sir Frederic William, KCVO 1909; CVO 1907; *b* Ceylon, 5 Oct. 1851; *s* of late Capt. W. Fisher of 78th Highlanders and 95th Foot, late of Ceylon. *Educ:* Lichfield Grammar School; North Grove House, Southsea; HMS 'Britannia,' at Dartmouth. Joined RN 1865; Senior Lieut of 'Teazer,' Persian Gulf and Red Sea, 1875–79; Senior Lieut of 'Amethyst,' SE Coast America, 1882–85; Senior Lieut of 'Rover,' Training Squadron, 1885–87; Commander 'Téméraire,' Mediterranean, 1887–91; commanded 'St Vincent,' 1891–93; 'Crescent,' China and Australia, 1894; 'Orlando,' Australia, 1895–98; 'Blenheim,' China, 1898; 'Grafton,' 1898–99; 'Collingwood,' 1899–1900; 'Alexandria,' 1900–01; 'Revenge,' 1901–03; Commodore, Jamaica, 1903; Captain of 'Canopus,' 1904; Admiral Superintendent of Malta Dockyard, 1907–10; President RN Coll., Greenwich, 1911–14; retired, 1914. *Publication:* Naval Reminiscences, 1938. *Recreations:* shooting, fishing, boat-sailing, etc. *Club:* United Service.

Died 23 Dec. 1943.

FISHER, Irving, AB, PhD, LLD; Professor Emeritus of Economics, Yale University; *b* Saugerties, NY, 27 Feb. 1867; *s* of Rev. George Whitefield Fisher and Ella Wescott; *m* 1893, Margaret (*d* 1940), *d* of Rowland Hazard, Providence, RI; one *s* one *d. Educ:* Yale University; Berlin; Paris. Tutor in Mathematics, 1890–93; Assistant Professor, 1893–95; Assistant Professor of Political Economy, 1895–98; Prof. of Political Economy at Yale Univ., 1898–1935; Prof. Emeritus, 1935; an Editor of Yale Review, 1896–1910; Hitchcock Lecturer, Univ. of California, 1917; lectured at Univ. of London School of Economics and Political Science, 1921; at Geneva School of International Studies, 1927; at Univ. of Southern California, 1941; Member Theodore Roosevelt's National Conservation Commission 1907; Chairman, Hygiene Reference Board, Life Extension Institute, since 1914; Chairman, Sub-Committee on Alcohol of Council of National Defence, 1917; Chairman of Board of Scientific Directors, Eugenics Record Office, 1917; President American Association for Labor Legislation, 1915–17; National Institute of Social Sciences, 1917; American Economic Association, 1918; Eugenics Research Association, 1920; American Eugenics Society, 1922–26 (and Founder); Econometric Society, 1931–34; American Statistical Association, 1932; FSS; member of many American and foreign learned societies; on Editorial Board, Econometrica; Advisory Editor Encyclopedia of Social Sciences; American Association for the Advancement of Science; National Association for Study and Prevention of Tuberculosis; Director of Remington Rand Incorporated and other companies. *Publications:* Mathematical Investigations in the Theory of Value and Prices, 1892, revised 1926; Elements of Geometry (with Prof. A. W. Phillips), 1896;

Bibliography of Mathematical Economics in Cournot's Mathematical Theory of Wealth, 1897; A Brief Introduction to the Infinitesimal Calculus, 1897; The Nature of Capital and Income, 1906; The Rate of Interest, 1907; National Vitality, 1909; The Purchasing Power of Money, 1911; Elementary Principles of Economics, 1910; How to Live (with Dr E. L. Fisk), 1915, 21st edition completely revised and rewritten (with Dr Haven Emerson), 1946; Stabilizing the Dollar, 1920; The Making of Index Numbers, 1922; League or War? 1923; America's Interest in World Peace, 1924; Prohibition at its Worst, 1926; The Money Illusion, 1928 (many foreign translations); Prohibition Still at its Worst, 1928; The Theory of Interest, 1930, translated into German; The Noble Experiment, 1930; The Stock Market Crash and After, 1930; Booms and Depressions, 1932; Inflation, 1933; Stamp Scrip, 1933; After Reflation, What? (British edition: Mastering the Crisis, with chapters on Stamp Scrip), 1934; Stable Money, a History of the Movement, 1934; 100% Money, 1935; Constructive Income Taxation, 1942; World Maps and Globes, 1944. *Recreations:* reading, walking. *Address:* Box 1825, New Haven 8, Connecticut, USA. *T:* 2–6186. *Clubs:* Faculty, New Haven; Yale, New York.

Died 29 April 1947.

FISHER, Brig.-Gen. John, CB 1912; *b* 9 March 1862; *s* of late Maj.-Gen. J. F. L. Fisher, Indian Army; *m* Mabel Edith (*d* 1912), *d* of late Maj.-Gen. C. T. Haig, RE. *Educ:* Marlborough; RMC Sandhurst. Lt Royal Irish Rifles, 1883; ISC, 1884; Captain, 1894; Major, 1901; Lt-Col, 1907; Colonel, 1911; served Manipur, 1891 (medal with clasp); Tirah, 1897–98 (medal with clasp); Waziristan, 1901–02 (clasp); Abor Expedition, 1912 (CB, medal and clasp); commanded 1st Batt. 2nd King Edward's Own Gurkha Rifles; commanded 79th Brigade, 1914–15; employed in France and Belgium, 1917–19; retired, 1919. *Address:* Sirmoor, Shortheath, Farnham, Surrey. *T:* Farnham 5136. *Club:* Naval and Military.

Died 7 Jan. 1942.

FISHER, John Campbell, CBE 1936; OBE 1918; Director of Colonial Audit since 1941; *b* 6 June 1880; *e s* of late Rev. Canon Robert Fisher, MA, Prebendary of York; *m* 1907, Agnes Beatrice, *d* of John Douglas Close, Nottingham; two *s* three *d. Educ:* Oakham School; Sidney Sussex College, Cambridge. Clerk, Colonial Audit Branch, Exchequer and Audit Department, 1902; Assistant Auditor various places in Nigeria, 1903; Local Auditor, Northern Nigeria, 1909; Examiner, Colonial Audit Branch, Exchequer and Audit Department, 1910; Second Class Clerk, Central Office, 1910; Auditor, Malta, 1913; Member of Control Board and Head of Food Control Office, Malta, 1917; Senior Clerk, Central Office, 1918; Assistant Director of Colonial Audit Central Office, 1928; Deputy Director, 1929–41. *Recreations:* golf, tennis (Cambridge Blue), fishing. *Address:* 20 Manor Road, Beckenham, Kent. *T:* Beckenham 1293. *Club:* Royal Empire Society.

Died 5 Feb. 1943.

FISHER, Brig. John Malcolm, CBE 1943; DSO 1919; OBE 1938; MC; TD; Col commanding 13th Light AA Regt RA (TA); *b* 7 June 1890; *e s* of Rev. William Fisher, Kingham, Oxfordshire; *m* 1919, Ailie, *y d* of late Sir W. J. and Lady Bell. *Educ:* Westminster School. Served European War, 1914–19 (despatches, DSO, MC). *Address:* Ladybower, Ashopton, Sheffield. *T:* Bamford 18.

Died 18 May 1943.

FISHER, Kenneth, MA, PhD; *b* 18 July 1882; *er surv. s* of late J. H. Fisher, Timperley, Cheshire; *m* 1911, Constance Isabel, 3rd *d* of late James Boyd, The Alton, Altrincham, Cheshire; three *s* one *d. Educ:* Manchester Grammar School; Magdalen College, Oxford (Demy, Senior Demy); Jena University; Manchester University. Member of Scientific Expedition to W Africa, 1906;

Assistant-Master, Clifton College, 1909–19; Head of Chemical Department, 1914; Head of Science Department, 1919; Manager of an explosive material factory for Brunner, Mond & Co., 1915–19; Senior Science Master, Eton College, 1920; Headmaster, Oundle School, 1922–45; JP Northants. *Publications:* chemical papers. *Recreations:* birds, member of British Ornithological Union. *Address:* Achurch Old Rectory, Oundle, Peterborough.

Died 2 Oct. 1945.

FISHER, Sir (Norman Fenwick) Warren, GCB 1923 (KCB 1919; CB 1916); GCVO 1928; Hon. DCL; Oxford; Hon. DSc, Reading; a Director of Royal and of Liverpool, London, and Globe Insurance Companies; a Director of Anglo-Iranian Oil Co.; a Director of Martin's Bank; Hon. Treasurer, Royal College of Mus; *b* 22 Sept. 1879; *o s* of late Henry Warren Fisher, 3 Ralston Street, Chelsea, SW; *m* 1906, Maysie, 2nd *d* of late Major E. C. Thomas; two *s. Educ:* Winchester; Hertford College, Oxford (Hon. Fellow). Entered Inland Revenue Department by open competition (Class I.) 1903; seconded for service with National Health Insurance Commission, 1912–13; Deputy Chairman, Board of Inland Revenue, 1914–18; Chairman, 1918–19; Permanent Secretary of HM Treasury and Official Head of HM Civil Service, 1919–39; Member of the Royal Commission on the Income Tax, 1919; Chairman, Industrial Transference Board, 1928; Chairman Colonial Services Committee, 1929–30; Member of Committee on Ministers' Powers, 1929–32; Regional Commissioner for Civil Defence, North-West Region, 1939–40; a Special Commissioner for London Region, 1940–42. *Address:* 7 Wythburn Court, Seymour Place, W1. *T:* Paddington 5984. *Clubs:* Brooks's, Athenæum.

Died 25 Sept. 1948.

FISHER, Sir Stanley, Kt 1922; *b* 1867; *s* of late George Henry Knapp-Fisher; *m* Susan Doveton, *d* of late Major-General William Maxwell, Royal Artillery. *Educ:* Westminster; Brasenose College, Oxford, MA. Called to Bar, 1890; President District Court, Kyrenia, Cyprus, 1902; Puisne Judge Supreme Court, Cyprus, 1911; Chief Justice Supreme Court, Cyprus, 1919–24; temporarily employed under the Foreign Office in Cairo, Egypt, 1924; Chief Justice of Trinidad and Tobago, and President of the West Indian Court of Appeal, 1924–26; Chief Justice of Ceylon, 1926–30. *Publication:* Ottoman Land Laws. *Address:* Lydney, East Terrace, Budleigh Salterton. *T:* Budleigh Salterton 222. *Club:* MCC.

Died 28 May 1949.

FISHER, Theodore, MD, FRCP Lond.; *b* 1863; *m* 1921, Edythe G., *d* of Henry Hope of Checkendon, Oxfordshire. *Educ:* privately; Guy's Hospital. Formerly Physician East London Hospital for Children, Shadwell; Physician to out-patients to the Bristol Royal Hospital for Sick Children and Women; Pathologist to the Bristol Royal Infirmary. *Publications:* The Heart and Sudden Death; papers in Medical Journals. *Recreation:* various forms of art. *Address:* Lynton, Cheltenham Road, Gloucester.

Died 13 July 1949.

FISHER, Sir Warren; *see* Fisher, Sir N. F. W.

FISKE, Rear-Adm. Bradley Allen; US Navy; *b* 13 June 1854; *s* of Rev. William Allen Fiske, LLD, and Susan Matthews Bradley; *m* 1882, Josephine Harper; one *d. Educ:* US Naval Academy. Commanded USS Minneapolis, Arkansas, and Tennessee; commanded 5th, then 3rd, then 1st Division US Fleet; invented Boat Detaching Apparatus; Electric Range Finder; Director System of Fire Control for Ships' Batteries; Naval Telescope Sight; Electric 4–arm Semaphore; Stadimeter; Turret Range Finder; System of steering Torpedoes by Hertzian Waves; Telescope Mount for Ships; Horizometer, Torpedoplane, the Fiskoscope and allied

apparatus of various kinds; Gun Director in 1890, and Telescope Sight, 1893; patented them in 1890 and 1893 in US, and about a year later in Great Britain; Elliott Cresson gold medal from Franklin Institute of Pennsylvania, 1893, for invention of Electric Range Finder; and the gold medal of the Aero Club of America for the invention of the torpedo plane in 1919; Aid for Operations of Navy, 1913–15; President US Naval Institute, 1911–23; Four years President Army and Navy Club of America; LLD University of Michigan, 1921. *Publications:* Electricity in Theory and Practice, 1883, 10 editions; War Time in Manila, 1913; The Navy as a Fighting Machine, 1916; second edition, 1918; From Midshipman to Rear-Admiral, 1919; The Art of Fighting, 1920; Invention, the Master-key to Progress, 1921; received gold medal from US Naval Institute, Jan. 1905, for prize essay on American Naval Policy. *Address:* The Waldorf Astoria, New York.

Died 6 April 1942.

FISKE, Rt Rev. Charles, DD, STD, LittD, LHD, LLD; retired Bishop of Central New York; prior to becoming Diocesan was Coadjutor, 1915; *b* New Brunswick, NJ, 16 March 1868; *m* 1902, Elizabeth Curlett Crampton; one *s. Educ:* St Stephen's College and General Theological Seminary. After several years in law and journalism, ordained Deacon, 1896; Priest, 1897; Rector of St Paul's, Westfield, NJ; St John's, Somerville, NJ; St John's, Norristown, Penna, and Church of St Michael and All Angels, Baltimore, Md; declined election as Bishop of Dallas, 1914. *Publications:* From Skepticism to Faith; The Confessions of a Puzzled Parson: and Other Pleas for Reality; The Christ We Know: a Study of the Life of Jesus for the New Generation; Cavalry To-day; The Real Jesus (with Rev. Prof. Burton S. Easton); The Perils of Respectability; The Faith by Which We Live; The Experiment of Faith; Sacrifice and Service; Back to Christ; The Religion of the Incarnation, etc.; was associate editor of The Churchman (New York), etc.; now Associate Editor of the Living Church; Lecturer at College of Preachers and Philadelphia Divinity School; contributor to symposia, Essays Towards Truth, magazines and reviews. *Recreation:* tennis. *Address:* 3405 Greenway, Baltimore, Md.

Died 8 Jan. 1942.

FISON, Captain Sir (Francis) Geoffrey, 2nd Bt *cr* 1905; MC; JP; late KRRC; *b* 12 March 1873; *er s* of 1st Bt and Isabella (*d* 1932), *d* of late Joseph Crossley, Broomfield, Halifax; *S* father, 1927. *Educ:* Harrow; Christ Church, Oxford (BA). Served European War, 1914–18 (wounded, MC). *Heir:* *b* William Guy, MC [*b* 25 Oct. 1890; *m* 1914, Gwladys Rees, *d* of John Robert Davies, Treborth, Bangor; two *s* one *d.* Eton; New College, Oxford, BA. Served European War, 1915–18 (despatches, MC)]. *Address:* Knoyle Place, East Knoyle, Salisbury.

Died 19 Jan. 1948.

FITCH, Charles Francis, CIE 1917; *b* Plymouth, 16 March 1860; *s* of late William James Fitch; *m* 1919, Emily Beatrice Gertrude Johnson. *Educ:* Park Grammar School, Plymouth. *Address:* Gutch Common, Semley, Wilts. *T:* Donhead 78. *Club:* Constitutional.

Died 30 May 1947.

FITZALAN OF DERWENT, 1st Viscount *cr* 1921, of Derwent, co. Derby; **Edmund Bernard Fitzalan-Howard,** KG 1925; PC 1918; GCVO 1919; MVO 1902; DSO 1900; JP; Lt-Col late 11th Hussars; DAAG S Africa (despatches); *b* 1 June 1855; *y s* of 14th and *uncle* and *heir-pres.* of 16th Duke of Norfolk; assumed name of Talbot in compliance with will of 17th Earl of Shrewsbury, 1876; reverted to Fitzalan-Howard, 1921; *m* 1879, Lady Mary Caroline (*d* 1938), *d* of 7th Earl of Abingdon; one *s* one *d. Educ:* Oratory School, Edgbaston. Contested Burnley, 1880; Brightside Div., Sheffield, 1883, 1886; a Lord of the Treasury, 1905; MP (Co. U.) Chichester, 1894–1921; Joint Parliamentary

Secretary to Treasury, 1915–21; Chief Unionist Whip, 1913–21; Viceroy of Ireland, 1921–22. *Heir: s* Capt. Hon. Henry Edmund Fitzalan-Howard. *Address:* Cumberland Lodge, Windsor. *T:* Egham 316. *Clubs:* Cavalry, Carlton, United Service.

Died 18 May 1947.

FITZGERALD, Denis P., MD, BA, NUI; Professor of Anatomy, 1909–42, now Emeritus Professor, University College, Cork; ex-Member of Board of Studies, NUI; *b* Cork, 29 April 1871; *m* 1908; four *s* four *d. Educ:* Univ. Coll., Cork (Scholar, Exhibitioner, and Prizeman); Presentation Brothers' College, Cork. Graduated in Arts in Royal University of Ireland, 1890, and in Medicine, 1896. For some years House Surgeon at Cork Eye, Ear, and Throat Hospital; Lecturer on Anatomy, University College, Cork, 1897–1908; ex-member of Senate, National University of Ireland; ex-member of Governing Body, University College Cork; ex-Lecturer on Artistic Anatomy, School of Art, Cork; ex-Dean of Medical Faculty, Univ. College, Cork. *Publications:* Some Abnormalities of the Ocular Muscles, 1898; A Persistent Left Superior Vena Cava, Notes on, 1908; The Pituitary Fossa and Certain Skull Measurements, 1909; Anomalies of the Vertebræ and their Significance, 1913; History of the Medical Profession in Ireland; History of Old Cork; The Churches and Abbeys of Old Cork, etc. *Address:* Dione, Well Road, Douglas Road, Cork. *T:* Douglas 29.

Died 9 April 1947.

FITZGERALD, Desmond; member of Senate of Eire since 1938. Participated in rising, 1916; MP (Sinn Fein), Pembroke Division, Dublin, Dec. 1918–22. Re-elected member of Dail Eireann, June 1922; Minister Foreign Affairs, Irish Provisional Government, Sept. 1922; Minister External Affairs, Irish Free State, 1922–27; Minister for Defence, 1927–32; was Editor of the Sinn Fein Bulletin. *Address:* Lonsdale, Temple Road, Dublin.

Died 9 April 1947.

FITZ-GERALD, Desmond Windham Otho; (28th Knight of Glin); *b* 20 Jan. 1901; *s* of Desmond Fitzjohn Lloyd Fitzgerald and Lady Rachel Wyndham-Quin, 2nd *d* of 4th Earl of Dunraven; *m* 1929, Veronica, 2nd *d* of late Ernest Villiers, and of Hon. Mrs Ernest Villiers, Homington House, Salisbury; one *s* two *d. Educ:* Lancing. *Address:* Glin Castle, Co. Limerick, IFS. *TA:* Knight Glin. *T:* Glin 3. *Clubs:* St James's; County (Limerick); Kildare Street (Dublin).

Died 2 May 1949.

FITZ-GERALD, Hon. Evelyn (Charles Joseph), CB 1919; Member of Panmure, Gordon & Co.; *γ s* of late Lord Fitz-Gerald, of Kilmarnock (Lord of Appeal); *m* 1923, Helen Gascoigne, *γ d* of late Lt-Gen. C. W. Drury, CB, of Halifax, Nova Scotia. *Educ:* Beaumont College, Old Windsor. Lieut RNR 1914; Private Secretary to General Sir John Cowans, Quartermaster-General to the Forces, War Office, SW, Dec. 1914–March 1919; Captain in the Army. *Address:* Thatched House, Swinley Forest, South Ascot, Berks. *T:* Ascot 517. *Clubs:* Turf, St James's.

Died 8 Oct. 1946.

FITZGERALD, Lt-Col Gerald James, CVO 1918; MVO 1910; late Royal Horse Guards; *b* 26 March 1869; *s* of R. A. Fitzgerald, Shalstone Manor, Buckingham; *m* 1st, Cecil Whitbread (*d* 1929); four *s*; 2nd, 1931, Joan (*d* 1943), *d* of late Edward Finch Dawson, Launde Abbey, Leicestershire. *Educ:* Wellington. Entered Royal Horse Guards, 1889; Adjutant, 1891–93; Captain, 1893; Major, 1906; served NW Frontier, India, 1897–98 (medal with clasp); commanded Royal Horse Guards Squadron, S Africa, 1900 (Queen's medal three clasps); Assistant Military Secretary, S Africa, 1909–11; commanded

Royal Horse Guards, 1915–19. *Recreations:* polo, big-game shooting, hunting. *Address:* Ridge House, Hindhead. *Club:* Turf.

Died 15 June 1944.

FITZGERALD, John Gerald; Professor of Hygiene and Preventive Medicine, and Director, Connaught Laboratories and School of Hygiene, University of Toronto, since 1913; *b* Drayton, Ontario, 9 Dec. 1882; *e s* of Wm Fitzgerald and Alice Woollatt; *m* 1910, Edna, *d* of Charles W. Leonard, London, Canada; one *s* one *d. Educ:* Harriston High School; University of Toronto, MB 1903, MD 1920, FRSC 1920, LLD 1925. Medical interne, Buffalo State Hospital, 1904–05; Clinical Assistant, Sheppard Hospital, Baltimore, 1905–06; Pathologist, Clinical Director, Toronto Hospital for Insane, Demonstrator, Psychiatry, Univ. Toronto, 1907–08; Research Student, Harvard University, 1908–09; Lecturer in Bacteriology, Univ. Toronto, 1909–11; Research Student, Pasteur Institute, Paris and Brussels, 1910; Research Student, University of Freiburg i/B, 1911; Associate Professor Bacteriology, Univ. California, 1911–13; Dean, Faculty of Medicine, University of Toronto, 1932–36; Major (Temp.), RAMC, BEF (France). *Publications:* Practice of Preventive Medicine; Numerous papers on Bacteriological subjects on Immunity, etc., in Pasteur Annales, Centralblatt für Bakteriologie, Journal of Infectious Diseases, etc. *Address:* University of Toronto, Toronto, Canada. *Clubs:* York, Toronto.

Died 20 June 1940.

FITZGERALD, Prof. Walter, MA (Liverpool and Manchester); Professor of Geography, Victoria University of Manchester, since 1944; *b* 16 July 1898; *s* of John Elliott and Johanna Brown Fitzgerald, Liverpool; *m* 1940, Sylvia Joan Wakeham, Sale, Ches.; one *s. Educ:* University of Liverpool. Served with Special Brigade, RE, in France and Belgium, 1917–18; 1st Cl. Hons (geography), Univ. of Liverpool, 1923; University Scholar, 1923–24; Lecturer in Geography, University of South Africa (Transvaal University College), 1924–25; Lecturer in Geography, Univ. of Manchester, 1928; External Examiner, at various dates, to Universities of London, Bristol, Training College Board, Civil Service Commission, etc. Travel in majority of European countries and African territories. *Publications:* Historical Geography of Early Ireland, 1926; Africa: a Social, Economic and Political Geography of its Major Regions, 1934, 7th edn 1950; The New Europe: An Introduction to its Political Geography, 1945, 3rd edn 1948; papers in scientific journals. *Address:* 21 Lynton Park Road, Cheadle Hulme, Cheshire. *T:* Cheadle Hulme 190.

Died 29 Nov. 1949.

FITZGIBBON, Hon. Mr Justice Gerald, LLD; Visitor Trinity College, Dublin, since 1931. *Educ:* Bassett's School; Clifton College; Trinity College, Dublin (Classical Scholar, Senior Moderator in Classics). King's Advocate, 1915–24; MP Southern Ireland, for Dublin University, 1921; re-elected TD for Dublin University, Dail Eireann, 1922–24; Judge of Supreme Court, Irish Free State, 1924–38. *Address:* 10 Merrion Square N, Dublin.

Died 6 Dec. 1942.

FITZGIBBON, Henry Macaulay, MA; Barrister-at-law; *b* Dublin, 30 June 1855; *o c* of Judge H. FitzGibbon, Recorder of Belfast; *m* Helen Rebecca (*d* 1924), *d* of J. K. Barton, Senior Surgeon, Adelaide Hospital, Dublin; two *d. Educ:* Bassett's School; Trinity College, Dublin. First Honourman in English and French Literature, and in Logics and Metaphysics; Senior Moderator and Gold Medallist in Modern Literature (TCD). Sometime Examiner in English to the Royal Univ. of Ireland, and to the Board of Intermediate Education in Ireland; formerly Captain 4th (old 5th) Connaught Rangers; Musketry Staff Officer, 1914–18. *Publications:* The Story of the Flute; The Early English and Scottish Poets and their Works; has edited Famous Elizabethan Plays and various other English Classics; also law books on Practice and on Local Government. *Recreations:* music, golf. *Address:* The Bungalow, Greystones, Co. Wicklow. *T:* Greystones 19.

Died 3 Feb. 1942.

FITZ HERBERT, Lt-Col Norman, CMG 1917; CBE 1919; *b* 1858; 4th *s* of late Lt-Col R. H. Fitz Herbert, JP, of Somersal Herbert, Derby; *m* 1908, Esther Beresford, 2nd *d* of late Henry Sproule of Ennis, Co. Clare. *Educ:* Wellington College. Went to New Zealand, 1876; took up land and engaged in sheep farming for 35 years; served with the third New Zealand Contingent in S African War, 1900–01 (Queen's medal and four clasps); with New Zealand Expeditionary Force, European War, 1914–19 (CMG, CBE, despatches twice); has travelled extensively in the British Dominions and the Far East. *Address:* 72 Kensington Court, W8. *T:* Western 1047. *Club:* Bath.

Died 21 Feb. 1943.

FITZMAURICE, Vice-Adm. Sir Raymond, KBE 1942; DSO 1916; *b* 7 Aug. 1878; *s* of late John Gerald Fitzmaurice, Barrister-at-law; *m* 1st, 1912, Evelyn Mary (*d* 1914), *d* of Charles Threlfall; 2nd, 1919, Beatrice Mary, *d* of late Adm. Sir Day H. Bosanquet, GCMG; one *d*. Entered Navy, 1893; Lieut 1901; Commander, 1913; 2nd in Command HMS Chatham, 1913–16; present at operations in East Africa and Dardanelles (DSO); Capt. 1918; in Command HMS Espiègle, 1916–18; Assistant Director of Naval Intelligence, 1918–19; Naval Adviser to Sir Reginald Tower, High Commissioner of Dantzig, 1919–20; commanded HMS Antrim, April 1921–April 1922, then HMS Yarmouth; Director of Signal Dept, Admiralty, 1923–25; Flag Captain and Chief Staff Officer HMS Resolution, 2nd Battle Squadron, and HMS Iron Duke, 3rd Battle Squadron, 1925–26; Vice-President Chemical Warfare Committee, 1927–29; a Naval ADC to the King, 1929; Rear-Adm. and retired list, 1929. *Club:* United Service.

Died 25 Oct. 1943.

FITZPATRICK, Rt Hon. Sir Charles, PC 1908; GCMG 1911; KCMG 1907; KC; *b* Quebec, 19 Dec. 1851; *s* of late John Fitzpatrick and Mary Conolly; *m* 1879, Corinne, *d* of late Hon. R. E. Caron, Ex-Lieut-Governor of Quebec, and sister of Sir Adolphe Caron. *Educ:* Quebec Seminary; Laval University (BA and LLB). Admitted to Bar, 1876; Member of Provincial Legislature for County of Quebec, 1890; re-elected, 1892; resigned as Prov. Member for Quebec County, 1896; and was elected to sit as Member for Quebec County in Dominion Parliament; Solicitor-General, 1896; Minister of Justice, Dominion of Canada, 1901–06; Chief Justice of Canada and Deputy Gov.-General, 1906–18; Lieutenant-Governor of the Province of Quebec, 1918–23. *Address:* 45 Ursula Street, Quebec. *Clubs:* Garrison, Quebec; St James's, Montreal; Rideau, Ottawa.

Died 17 June 1942.

FITZPATRICK, Brig.-Gen. Sir (Ernest) Richard, Kt 1946; CBE 1919; DSO 1917; DL Devon; Chevalier Légion d'Honneur; late Loyal Regt; *b* 12 Feb. 1878; *e s* of late Rev. Nicholas Richard Fitzpatrick, MA; *m* 1903, Georgina Ethel, *y d* of late Thomas Robison; one *s*. *Educ:* Marlborough, Trinity College, Cambridge. Entered Loyal North Lancashire Regt, 1899; served South African War (1899–1902), severely wounded (Queen's medal 4 clasps, King's medal 2 clasps); Brig.-Gen., 1916; served European War, 1914–19 (despatches 3 times, CBE, DSO, Bt Major, Bt Lt-Col, Legion d'Honneur); Deputy Adjutant-General, Forces in Great Britain, 1918; Deputy Director of Personal Services and Col on the Staff, War Office, 1919–21; retired pay, 1923; National Chairman, British Legion, 1943–47; Member Minister of Pensions Central Advisory Cttee; Member Board of Supervision Pensioners Savings

Scheme. *Recreations:* fishing, sailing. *Address:* 156 Sloane St, SW1. *T:* Sloane 4033. *Clubs:* Naval and Military; Bembridge Sailing (Bembridge).

Died 26 Aug. 1949.

FITZ PATRICK, Herbert Lindsay, CBE 1918; *b* 2 Dec. 1868. Controller-General of administration and finally Secretary-General, Egyptian Ministry of Finance (retired, 1924). Served European War under the Joint War Committee of the British Red Cross and Order of St John, 1914–19; as Director with the Dardanelles Expeditionary Force, Sept.–Dec. 1915; and as Commissioner with the Salonika Forces, 1916–19; Hon. Major, 1916; Lieut-Col 1917 (despatches four times, CBE, Knight of Grace of St John of Jerusalem). Holds several foreign orders and decorations including: Officer of the Legion of Honour and Croix de Guerre of France; Grand Officer Order of Nile, Egypt; Commander of Serbian Orders of White Eagle (with Swords) and St Sava; Commander of Redeemer and Croix de Guerre of Greece; Commander of Prince Danilo of Montenegro, etc. *Recreations:* languages and travel—world wide. *Address:* 16 St James's Square, SW1. *Clubs:* East India and Sports, Turf; Gezireh Sporting (Cairo).

Died 16 Jan. 1949.

FITZPATRICK, Brig.-Gen. Sir Richard; *see* Fitzpatrick, Sir E. R.

FITZROY, Captain Rt Hon. Edward Algernon, PC 1924; LLD Cambridge Univ.; DCL Oxford Univ.; JP, DL; Speaker of the House of Commons, since 1928; MP (C) S Northamptonshire, now Daventry Division, 1900–06, and since 1910; Deputy Chairman of Committees, House of Commons, 1922–24 and 1924–28; CC for Northamptonshire; *b* 24 July 1869; *s* of 3rd Baron Southampton; *m* 1891, Muriel, CBE, *d* of late Lieut-Col Douglas-Pennant; two *s* one *d*. *Educ:* Eton; Sandhurst. Formerly Page of Honour to Queen Victoria; late Capt. 1st Life Guards; Capt. Reserve Regt, 1st Life Guards; served European War, 1914–18 (wounded 1st Battle of Ypres, Klein Zillebecke). *Address:* Speaker's House, Westminster, SW1. *Club:* Carlton.

Died 3 March 1943.

FITZWILLIAM, 7th Earl *cr* 1716; William Charles de Meuron Wentworth-Fitzwilliam, KCVO 1912; CBE 1919; DSO 1900; JP; DL Co. Wicklow; Baron Fitz-William, 1620; Viscount Milton, 1716; Baron Milton (Great Britain), 1742; Earl Fitz-William, and Viscount Milton, 1746, KCVO 1912; CBE 1919; DSO 1900; JP Co. Wicklow and West Yorks; *b* Canada, 1872; *o s* of Viscount Milton, MP, and Laura, *d* of late Lord Charles Beauclerk; *S* grandfather, 1902; *m* 1896, Lady Maud Frederica Elizabeth Dundas, OBE, *d* of 1st Marquess of Zetland; one *s* four *d*. *Educ:* Eton; Trinity Coll., Cambridge. ADC to Marquis of Lansdowne in India, 1892–93; Major 3rd Batt. Oxford Light Infantry; Major West Riding Royal Horse Artillery, 1908; Brevet Lt-Col, 1913; served Army Headquarters Staff, South Africa, 1900 (despatches, DSO); European War, 1914–15 (despatches, CBE); travelled much in India and Europe; much interested in engineering, especially mining engineering. *Recreations:* hunting, riding, shooting, polo. *Heir: s* Viscount Milton. *Address:* 10 Chesterfield Street, W1. *T:* Mayfair 1692; Wentworth-Woodhouse, Rotherham, Yorkshire; Coollattin, Shillelagh, Co. Wicklow, Ireland. *Clubs:* Brooks's, York, Turf, Bachelors', Jockey; Royal Yacht Squadron, Cowes; Kildare Street, Dublin.

Died 15 Feb. 1943.

FITZWILLIAM, 8th Earl *cr* 1716; William Henry Lawrence Peter Wentworth-Fitzwilliam, DSC 1944; Baron Fitz-William, 1620; Viscount Milton, 1716; Baron Milton (Great Britain), 1742; Earl Fitz-William and Viscount Milton, 1746; Capt. Grenadier Guards; *b* 31 Dec. 1910; *o s* of 7th Earl and Lady Maud Frederica Elizabeth Dundas, OBE, *d* of 1st Marquess of Zetland; *S* father, 1943; *m* 1933, Olive Dorothea, *yr d* of late Hon. and Most Rev. Benjamin J. Plunket; one *d. Educ:* Eton. *Heir: cousin* Eric Spencer Wentworth-Fitzwilliam, *b* 1883. *Address:* 10 Grosvenor Street, W1. *T:* Mayfair 1774; Wentworth-Woodhouse, Rotherham, Yorkshire; Coollattin, Shillelagh, Co. Wicklow, Ireland. *Clubs:* Buck's, White's, Turf; Kildare Street, Dublin.

Died 13 May 1948.

FLANAGAN, William Henry; JP; Chairman and Managing Director of Imperial Patent Wadding Co., Ltd; Proprietor of Bates Bros, London; *b* 8 April 1871; *s* of late William Flanagan, JP; *m* Lillian M., *d* of late Edwin James Ashley, both of Manchester; two *d. Educ:* St Margaret's, Whalley Range; Manchester School of Technology. Member of the Buxton Borough Council, resigned 1922; contested Clayton Division, Feb. 1922; MP (C) Clayton Division of Manchester, Nov. 1922–23, and 1931–35. *Address:* Ribblehurst, Fairhaven, Lytham St Anne's. *T:* Lytham 6163.

Died 21 June 1944.

FLANNERY, Sir James F.; see Fortescue-Flannery.

FLAVIN, Michael Joseph; merchant; *b* 1861; *s* of James Flavin and Joan Mangan; *m* Mary Elizabeth Fitzgerald; three *s* two *d. Educ:* National schools and St Michael's College, Listowel. MP (N) North Kerry, 1896–1918; Member of Committee governing County Infirmary, Tralee, County Fever Hospital, Tralee, County Mental Hospital, Killarney. *Recreations:* fishing, gardening, handball, etc. *Address:* 119 Rock Street, Tralee, Co. Kerry. *TA:* Flavin, Tralee.

Died 3 May 1944.

FLECKER, Rev. William Herman, MA, DCL, JP; Vicar of S Peter's, Staines, since 1927; Surrogate; *b* Roade, Northants, 10 Dec. 1859; *s* of Rev. I. Flecker; *m* Sarah Ducat; one *s* one *d. Educ:* City of London (Cowper St) School. Vice-Master New College, Eastbourne; Head Master City of London College School; Headmaster Dean Close School, Cheltenham, 1886–1924; Examining Chaplain, late Bishop of Sodor and Man. *Publications:* Morning Prayer for Schools; Students' Prayer Book; British Church History to ad 1000. *Recreation:* reading. *T:* Staines 375.

Died 26 Aug. 1941.

FLEETWOOD-HESKETH, Charles Hesketh; *see* Hesketh.

FLEMING, Hon. Lord; David Pinkerton Fleming; Senator of the College of Justice in Scotland, since 1926; *b* 11 Feb. 1877; 4th *s* of late John Fleming, Writer, Glasgow; *m* Beatrice Joan, *y d* of James Swan, Edinburgh. *Educ:* Glasgow High School; University of Edinburgh and University of Glasgow. LLD Glasgow. Called to Scottish Bar, 1902; was on active service during European War (MC, Belgian Croix de Guerre); KC 1921; Solicitor-General for Scotland, 1922–23 and 1924–26; MP (C) for Dumbartonshire, 1924–26; Hon. Bencher of Middle Temple, 1940. *Address:* East Morningside House, Edinburgh. *Clubs:* Athenæum; University, Edinburgh; Western, Glasgow.

Died 20 Oct. 1944.

FLEMING, Sir Ambrose; *see* Fleming, Sir J. A.

FLEMING, Rev. Archibald, MA (Edin.); DD (Edin.); TD; HCF; Senior Minister of St Columba's (Church of Scotland), Pont Street, SW, since 1902; Member of RAF Chaplains' Advisory Board, Air Ministry, since 1918; Acting Chaplain, 9th VB The Royal Scots, 1901–03; Acting Chaplain, The London Scottish, 1903–22; *b* 27 Dec. 1863; *e s* of late Rev. Archibald Fleming of Inchyra, Minister of St Paul's Parish, Perth; *m* 1898, Agnes Jane, *d* of late R. C. Williamson; two *s* one *d. Educ:* Perth Academy (classical and mathematical medallist in the same year); Edinburgh University (First Prizeman in Divinity). Assistant Minister in St Cuthbert's,

Edinburgh, 1887; Minister of Newton Parish, Midlothian, 1888–97; of Tron Parish, Edinburgh, 1897–1902; Editor of Life and Work, the Church of Scotland Magazine, 1898–1902; was contributor, under W. E. Henley, to Scots Observer and National Observer; occasional preacher before Queen Victoria and King George V in Scotland; Past Grand Chaplain Grand Lodge of Freemasons (Scotland); Warrack Lecturer, Edinburgh and St Andrews Universities, 1933; Croall Lecturer (Edinburgh), 1935; received at Balmoral in 1897 Her Majesty's Diamond Jubilee Medal from Queen Victoria; Coronation Medal, 1937; Serbian Order of St Sava, 1919. *Publications:* frequent contributor to newspapers and magazines, usually anonymous. *Address:* 12 Beaufort Gardens, SW3. *T:* Kensington 5614; Inchyra, Perthshire. *Clubs:* Athenæum, Pilgrims (Hon. Chaplain), Caledonian (Hon.), Royal Air Force, Royal Societies (Hon.); University, Edinburgh.

Died 2 July 1941.

FLEMING, Col Archibald Nicol, DSO 1913; *b* Southend, Kintyre, Scotland, 9 Sept. 1870; *s* of J. N. Fleming; *m* 1903, *d* of Col A. H. Anthonisz, RAMC; three *s. Educ:* Fettes Coll., Edinburgh (Scholar); Edinburgh Univ. (Scholar). MBCM Ed., 1895; FRCS Ed., 1911. Entered Indian Medical Service, 1896; served Tirah Expedition, 1897 (medal and clasp); served for many years as MO, XX Deccan Horse, as well as in Civil employ, Madras, and under the Foreign Department; European War, commanded a Field Ambulance in France, 1914–18, and an Indian General Hospital in Egypt, 1918 (DSO, despatches twice, Mons Star, Allied and Victory medals); ADMS, Palestine, 1922–23; ADMS, Karachi Brigade Area, India, 1923–27; Hon. Surg. to the King, 1926–27; retired, 1927. *Recreation:* chess. *Address:* 5 Bright's Crescent, Edinburgh 9. *T:* 42344. *Clubs:* Junior Army and Navy; Caledonian United Service. (Edinburgh).

Died 27 June 1948.

FLEMING, Edward Lascelles; KC 1932; MP (U) Withington Div. of Manchester since 1931; *m* Rita; two *d.* Called to the Bar, Gray's Inn, 1921; Northern Circuit. *Publication:* Sheba's Ring, 1933. *Address:* House of Commons, SW1.

Died 17 Feb. 1950.

FLEMING, Edward Vandermere, CB 1925; *b* 31 March 1869; *s* of late James Fleming, formerly Surveyor-General of Customs; *m* Isabel Hector (*d* 1929), *d* of late Alexander Hector Taylor, JP, Aberdeen; one *s* two *d. Educ:* St Paul's School; Caius College, Cambridge; University Gold Medal for Latin Poem, 1891. Assistant Under-Secretary of State (Director of Establishments), War Office, 1924–29; Officier de la Légion d'Honneur, 1920; Member of General Committee, Research Defence Society, and or Council of the Poetry Society. *Publications:* The Science of Shaving (anon), 1931 (a translation published in Holland, 1932); Waters of Affliction (poems), 1934; St Martin's Aftermath (poems), 1947. *Address:* Wyldesmead, Morland Close, Hampstead Way, NW11. *T:* Speedwell 1097. *Club:* Athenæum.

Died 18 Oct. 1947.

FLEMING, Horace, MA; JP, Vice-President, Educational Settlements Association; *b* 1872; *e s* of Thomas Kingston Fleming, Liverpool; *m* 1899, Cecile A., 5th *d* of late W. J. Steele, Bratton, Wilts; one *s* one *d. Educ:* Wallasey Grammar School. Founder and first Hon. Warden, Beechcroft Settlement, Birkenhead; Assistant Director, Supplementary Rations Section Ministry of Food, 1918; Chief Executive Officer, Trade Organisation Section, Ministry of Reconstruction, 1918; Officer in charge Interim Industrial Reconstruction Committees, Ministry of Labour, 1919; Chairman, Educational Settlements Association, 1922–35; Chief Executive Officer, World Association for Adult Education, 1924–26; Member of Board of Education Adult Education Committee, 1925–34; Hon. MA,

Liverpool University, 1927; Hon. Warden, Mary Ward Settlement, 1929–34; Hon. Director Tavistock Little Theatre, 1932–34. *Publications:* The Lighted Mind; Beechcroft: An Experiment in Adult Education; Education through Settlements; articles on Adult Education in various journals. *Address:* Holme Lodge, Bratton, Westbury, Wilts.

Died 25 Jan. 1941.

FLEMING, Sir (John) Ambrose, Kt 1929; MA, DSc; Hon. DEng (Liverpool); FRS 1892; Consulting Electrical Engineer; Hon. Fellow of St John's College, Cambridge; Hon. Member of the Royal Philosophical Society of Glasgow; Fellow of University College, London; *b* Lancaster, 1849; *s* of Rev. James Fleming, DD; *m* 1933, Olive Franks. *Educ:* University College, London; Royal College of Chemistry; St John's College, Cambridge. Exhibitioner, Foundation Scholar, and Hon. Fellow at St John's College, Cambridge; Lecturer on Applied Mechanics in the University of Cambridge; has been intimately associated with the development of all the great applications of electrical science in the last twenty-five years, the Telephone, electric lighting, and wireless telegraphy; and is the inventor of the Thermionic valve; was departmental editor for Electricity in connection with the 10th ed. of the Encyclopædia Britannica, and wrote some 25 of the electrical articles for the 11th ed.; twice awarded the Institution Premium of the IEE; also Silver Medal of RS Arts for Scientific Investigations; Hon. MIEE, 1922; University Professor of Electrical Engineering in the University of London, 1910, and Professor in University College, 1885–1926; Hughes Gold Medallist of the Royal Society, 1910; awarded the Albert Medal RS Arts, 1921; Faraday Medal IEE, 1928; Duddell Medal of the Physical Society; 1930; Kelvin Medal, InstCE, 1935; Franklin Medal of the Franklin Institute, USA, 1935; gold medal of the Institute of Radio Engineers, USA. *Publications:* Short Lectures to Electrical Artisans, 1885; Treatise on the Alternate Current Transformer, 1889–1892; Electric Lamps and Electric Lighting, 1894; Electric Laboratory Notes and Forms, 1894; Magnets and Electric Currents, 1897; A Handbook for the Electrical Laboratory and Testing Room, 1901; Waves and Ripples in Water, Air, and Ether, 1902; The Principles of Electric Wave Telegraphy and Telephony, 1906; A Manual of Radiotelegraphy and Radiotelephony, 1908; a Pocket Book for Wireless Telegraphists; Propagation of Electric Currents in Telephone and Telegraph Conductors, 1911; The Wonders of Wireless Telegraphy, 1913; The Thermionic Valve in Radiotelegraphy, 1919; Fifty Years of Electricity, 1921; Electrons, Electric Waves and Wireless Telephony, 1923; The Interaction of Scientific Research and Electrical Engineering, 1927; Memories of a Scientific Life, 1934; besides some ninety scientific papers in last 42 years. *Recreations:* photography, travel, and experimental research. *Address:* University College, Gower Street, WC.

Died 18 April 1945.

FLEMING, Lt-Col John Kenneth Sprot, CBE 1929; *b* 1874; *s* of John Fleming, CSI; unmarried. *Educ:* Dulwich College; St Bartholomew's Hospital; MRCS (Eng.) 1898; LRCP (Lond.) 1898. Joined Indian Medical Service, 1901; Major, 1913; Lt-Col, 1920; served European War, 1914–21 (despatches twice, OBE); Deputy Director-General, IMS, 1925–29; retired 1929. *Address:* Dalreoch, Colmonell, Ayrshire. *Club:* Oriental.

Died 27 Dec. 1944.

FLEMING, Robert Alexander, MA (Edin.); MD (Edin.); Hon. LLD (Edin.); FRCPE; FRSE; Consulting Physician, Royal Infirmary, Edinburgh; Physician, Royal Incurable Hospital, Edinburgh; Examiner in Medicine, Royal College of Physicians, Edinburgh; Surgeon, King's Bodyguard for Scotland, RCA; *b* Dundee, 1862; *s* of Robert Fleming, merchant, Dundee; *m* 1897, Eleanor Mary, *d* of Canon W. L. Holland,

Rector, Cornhill-on-Tweed; three *s* one *d. Educ:* Larchfield Academy; Craigmount School; Edinburgh University; Vienna; Berlin. MD Thesis Gold Medal, MBCM 1st Class Hon., Edin. University. Formerly Pathologist Royal Infirmary, Edinburgh; Physician and Senior Lecturer on Clinical Medicine, Royal Infirmary, Edinburgh; Lecturer on Practice of Medicine, School of the Royal Colleges, Edinburgh; Examiner in Medicine and Clinical Medicine, Aberdeen and Edinburgh Universities; Consultant General Medicine and Neurology. Formerly Medical Adviser Prison and Borstal Dept for Scotland; retired, 1947; ex-Pres. Royal College of Physicians, Edinburgh. Major RAMC (T) retired; 1914–19, 2nd Scottish General Hospital and 42nd General Hospital, Salonika Expeditionary Force. *Publications:* Short Practice of Medicine; Diseases of Spinal Nerves, Allbut's System of Medicine; The Mental Element of Crime and Criminals; many papers on Neurological and other medical subjects. *Recreations:* shooting, fishing, archery. *Address:* 10 Chester Street, Edinburgh; Innerhadden, Perthshire. *T:* Edinburgh 20986. *Club:* New (Edinburgh).

Died 5 Dec. 1947.

FLEMING, Wilfrid Louis Remi, LRCP (London), MRCS (Eng.); JP, Surrey; medical practitioner; *b* 1 Oct. 1869; *s* of late Andrew Fleming of Kilmarnock; *m* Alice Mary, *d* of late Samuel Harley Kough of Church Stretton, Salop. *Educ:* privately; Edinburgh; Westminster Hospital and Rotunda Hospital, Dublin. Chairman of Managers, Pirbright Elementary Schools; late Assistant House Surgeon; House Surgeon and Resident Obstetric Assistant, Westminster Hospital; House Physician, Bethlem Royal Hospital; Medical Officer, Bisley Farm School and Shaftesbury Home; Medical Officer, Henley Park Auxiliary Military Hospital, 1915–19. *Recreations:* golf, lawn tennis, badminton. *Address:* Suffolk House, Pirbright, Surrey. *TA:* Pirbright. *T:* Brookwood 2119.

Died 13 Sept. 1944.

FLEMMING, Percy; Emeritus Professor of Ophthalmic Medicine and Surgery at University College, London; Consulting Ophthalmic Surgeon, University College Hospital; Consulting Surgeon, Royal London Ophthalmic Hospital (Moorfields). *Educ:* University College School and University College (Fellow). University Scholar in Medicine, 1887; BS University of London, 1887; MD 1888; Fellow of the Royal College of Surgeons of England, 1889. *Publications:* Harley St from Early Day; communications to medical papers, and to Transactions of Ophthalmological Society. *Address:* The Firs, Upper Basildon, Reading.

Died 19 Dec. 1941.

FLETCHER, Benton; *see* Fletcher, G. H. B.

FLETCHER, Charles Brunsdon; *b* Taunton, Somerset, 1859; *s* of Charles Fletcher; *m* 1889, Florence Mary, *e d* of late Hon. Sir Arthur Rutledge, KC; two *s* two *d. Educ:* Wesley College, Auckland, NZ; Newington College, Sydney, NSW. Went to New Zealand with parents, 1864; thence to Australia, 1872; entered Government Survey Department, New South Wales, 1879; Member of staff of Detail Survey of City of Sydney; Queensland Survey Department, 1883; joined Editorial staff, Brisbane Courier, 1893; Editor, 1898–1903, when took prominent part in the fight for federation; Queensland Correspondent, Melbourne Argus and Sydney Mail; Associate Editor, Sydney Morning Herald, 1903; Editor, Sydney Morning Herald, 1903; Editor, Sydney Morning Herald, 1918–38; Fellow Senate University of Sydney, 1925–40. *Publications:* The New Pacific, 1917; The Problem of the Pacific, 1919; and Stevenson's Germany, 1920; also section Literature in A Century in the Pacific; Standards of Empire, 1924; The Murray Valley, 1926; Coolah Valley, 1927; The Great Wheel, An Editor's Adventures, 1940. *Address:* Warinilla, Kirribilli, Sydney, NSW. *Clubs:* Australian, Sydney.

Died 17 Dec. 1946.

FLETCHER, Rev. Canon Denis, MA; Vicar of Swinton since 1926; Rural Dean of Eccles since 1933; b Atherton, Lancs, 6 Nov. 1881; 7th s of Ralph Fletcher, colliery proprietor. *Educ:* Rossall School; Queen's College, Oxford. Ordained, 1906; Curate of Saint Wilfrid's, Newton Heath, 1906–12; of Rochdale Parish Church, 1912–14; Chaplain to Forces, 1914–19 (despatches); served in Egypt, Gallipoli, Sinai Desert, France, and Belgium; Senior Chaplain, 42nd Division, 1916–19; Rector of S Wilfrid's, Newton Heath, 1919–26; Hon. Canon of Manchester Cathedral, 1930; Proctor in Convocation for Manchester Diocese since 1931. *Recreation:* golf. *Address:* The Vicarage, Swinton, Manchester. *T:* Swinton 1578. *Clubs:* Old Rectory, Manchester.

Died 27 April 1942.

FLETCHER, Frank Morley; artist; b Whiston, Lancashire, 1866; 3rd s of Alfred Evans Fletcher and Sarah, d of Richard Morley, Leeds; m 1895, Maud Evelyn, d of Jonah Brown of Walberswick. *Educ:* University College, Liverpool; Atelier Cormon, Paris. Exhibited paintings at Paris Salon, London RA, and International Society; Dresden, New York, etc., in USA; Medal World's Columbian Exhibition, British Section, 1893; Member of Council International Society of Sculptors, Painters, and Gravers, 1903–09; Head of Art Dept, University College, Reading, 1898–1906; HM Inspector of Schools of Art, 1906–08; Director of Edinburgh College of Art, 1908–23; Director of School of Art of Community Arts Association, Santa Barbara, California, 1923–30; Member Art Workers' Guild; Fellow of British Institute of Industrial Art; naturalised citizen of USA 1926. *Publications:* Wood-block Printing, 1916; Colour-Control, 1936; articles and pamphlets on Art Education. *Recreations:* outdoor work, travel, music. *Address:* Ojai, California, USA.

Died 2 Nov. 1949.

FLETCHER, (George Henry) Benton; Major (retired); artist, author, and traveller; b Merton, Surrey (with small prospects); y s of John Fletcher and Emily Bush Fletcher; unmarried. *Educ:* chiefly self-educated, but still ignorant on many subjects. Lived in slums of South London doing social work, 1889–99; became a licensed peddler; Adjutant, 1st Cadet Bn The Queen's, the first Cadet Bn raised in British Empire; now the Father of the Cadets as senior surviving officer of original Gazette; joined 5th Bn (Militia) The Sherwood Foresters, 1890; joined 1st Bn (Regular) South Staffordshire Regiment, 1900, and served as Staff-Officer in Boer War (medal with 3 clasps, invalided); joined Prof. Flinders Petrie's excavations, 1903; and worked in Egypt each season till 1914; discovered, single-handed, Temple of Seti I Abydos, now in Metropolitan Museum, New York; rejoined Army; Recruiting-Officer, London SW, 1914–15; RTO 1915–19; invited by King Hussein to visit Arabia, 1921; many other expeditions to Arabia, Libyan, Hedjaz, and Sahara Deserts; purchased Old Devonshire House, Bloomsbury (ad 1667), 1934, presented it to the National Trust (detroyed by enemy action in 1941 but replaced by 3 Cheyne Walk, Chelsea, purchased by Trust in 1943), together with unique collection of musical instruments, furniture, and pictures; endowed it as a centre for study of early keyboard and chamber music: harpsichords, virginals, and spinets are available for practice and concerts; included in LCC survey of London Museums. *Publications:* Artist Author, Royal Homes near London; History of Old Devonshire House; Story of Bourton House; Illustrator of colour books, Peeps in Arabia, Vanished Cities of Arabia, Vanished Cities of North Africa; Tunis, By the Waters of Egypt, Illustrator of books in line drawing, Jerusalem, Luxor, Bay of Naples, Pepys's Diary; various illustrations for Illustrated London News, Graphic, Sphere, Country Life, etc. *Recreations:* a nomad life, exploring. *Address:* 3 Cheyne Walk, SW3; The Cedar House, Cobham, Surrey.

Died 31 Dec. 1944.

FLETCHER, Herbert Morley, MA, MD (Cantab), LLD (Hon.); FRCP; Hon. Fellow Royal Australasian College of Physicians; late Senior Censor, Royal College of Physicians; Consulting Physician, St Bartholomew's Hospital; late Vice-President of Medical College of St Bartholomew's Hospital; Consulting Physician, Queen Alexandra's House, E London Hospital for Children, Queen Charlotte's Hospital, Royal Bucks Hospital; Hertford County Hospital and Infants Hospital; late Member of the Consulting Staff of Osborne Convalescent Home for Officers, and of the Medical Consultative Board of the Navy; Hon. Physician Metropolitan Convalescent Institution, Alexandra Hospital for Diseases of the Hip, and Florence Nightingale Hospital; Examiner in Medicine to Cambridge, Durham, Manchester, Sheffield, and Belfast Universities; to the National University of Ireland, to the Conjoint Board of the Royal College of Physicians and Surgeons, and to the Society of Apothecaries; Major, RAMC (T); 2nd s of Alfred Evans Fletcher and Sarah, d of Richard Morley of Leeds; m 1st, Ethel Frances (d 1918), d of late Joseph Crossley of Halifax; two s three d; 2nd, Mary Christina, d of late W. E. Willink, Liverpool; two d. *Educ:* Mill Hill School; Trinity College, Camb.; Freiburg and Vienna. *Publications:* contributions to various medical and scientific societies and journals. *Recreations:* fishing, shooting, and golf; Pres. of Cambridge University Athletic Club, 1888. *Address:* Burton Corner, Petworth. *T:* 3277. *Club:* Brooks's.

Died 9 Sept. 1950.

FLETCHER, Michael Scott, MA, BLitt; Professor of Philosophy, University of Queensland, Brisbane, since 1923; b Wesley College, Auckland, NZ, 28 May 1868; s of John Fletcher (principal) and Eliza Bale; m Winifred, RPAH, d of Robert Lumsden Davies; one s one d. *Educ:* Newington College; University, Sydney and University, Oxford. MA (Sydney), first class honours and University medal for Philosophy, 1902. Circuit work in the Methodist Church of NSW, 1892–1909; Tutor, NT Greek, Newington College, 1908; Research Student, Oxford, 1909–12; BLitt (Oxon) 1911; Master of King's College, University of Queensland, and Tutor in Greek and Philosophy, 1912–16; Master of Wesley College (University of Sydney) and Tutor in Philosophy, 1916–23; Examiner in NT Greek for final BD (Melbourne), 1917–22; Examiner for Sydney University in Department of Philosophy and Tutorial Lecturer to WEA Classes in Psychology, 1920–22; University Tutorial Lecturer to WEA Classes (Brisbane) in Philosophy, 1924–37. *Publications:* Psychology of New Testament, 1912; articles in Hastings' Dictionary of the Apostolic Church, 1915, 1918; Jewish Apocalypses, 1922; Hellenism and Judaism, 1926; articles in Australasian Journal of Psychology and Philosophy, 1924–1937. *Address:* The University, Brisbane, Australia. *Club:* United Service.

Died 6 Nov. 1947.

FLETCHER, Canon William Dudley Saul, BD; Member of General Synod, Church of Ireland; b 7 Nov. 1863; s of Rev. James Saul Fletcher, DD, and Annie Taylor; m 1899, Agnes Elizabeth Smythe; one s. *Educ:* Wesley College, Dublin; Trinity College, Dublin. Late Rector of grouped parishes of Leighlin, Wells, etc., Ireland; late Precentor of St Laserian's Cathedral, Diocese of Leighlin, and late Canon of St Canice's Cathedral, Diocese of Ossory; retired, 1947. *Address:* 1 Trimbleston Ave, Booterstown, Dublin.

Died 7 April 1948.

FLETT, Sir John Smith, KBE 1925; OBE 1918; FRS; MA, MB, CM, DSc, LLD; Director Geological Survey of Great Britain and Museum of Practical Geology, 1920–35; retired, 1935; *b* Kirkwall, Orkney, 1869; *m* Mary Jane, *d* of David Meason, Kirkwall; two *s* two *d*. *Educ:* Kirkwall Burgh School; George Watson's College, and University, Edinburgh. After leaving school studied Arts, Science, and Medicine at Edinburgh University, gaining many prizes and scholarships, including Falconer Fellowship, Baxter Science Scholarship, and Heriot Research Fellowship. Became Assistant to Professor James Geikie and Lecturer in Petrology in the University; joined HM Geological Survey, 1901; sent by Royal Society to West Indies along with Dr Tempest Anderson to report on the volcanic eruptions at the Soufrière, 1901; Petrographer to HM Geological Survey, 1903; Assistant to Director HM Geological Survey, in charge of Geological Survey of Scotland, 1911–20. *Publications:* Report on W Indian Eruptions (1902, Royal Society); Joint Author of many Memoirs of Geological Survey, including Land's End, Lizard, Bodmin and St Austell, Edinburgh, Ben Wyvis. *Address:* c/o Geological Museum, Exhibition Road, SW7. *Club:* Athenæum.

Died 26 Jan. 1947.

FLEXNER, Simon, MD; MA, Oxon, 1937; Fellow of Balliol College, Oxford; Director Emeritus Rockefeller Institute for Medical Research; Trustee, Johns Hopkins University, 1937–42; Carnegie Institution of Washington, 1910–14; Rockefeller Foundation, 1913–28; *b* Louisville, Ky, 25 March 1863; *s* of Morris Flexner and Esther Abraham; *m* 1903, Helen Whitall Thomas; two *s*. *Educ:* public schools, Louisville, Kentucky. MD, University of Louisville, 1889; DSc (Hon.) Harvard Univ., 1906; Yale University, 1910; Princeton Univ., 1913; University of Pennsylvania, 1929; National University of Ireland, 1936; University of Louisville, 1937; LLD (Hon.) University of Maryland, 1907; Washington University, Johns Hopkins University, Brown University, 1915; Cambridge University, 1920; Western Reserve University, 1929; Doctor, University Strasbourg, 1923; Doctor, Catholic University, Louvain, 1927; Doctor, Université Libre, Brussels, 1930; post-graduate student, Johns Hopkins University; Universities of Strasbourg, University of Prag, and University of Berlin. Member, American Medical Association, and many other societies; Chairman Research Fellowship Board (Physics, Chemistry, and Mathematics) National Research Council, 1919–37; foreign member many European and other medical and scientific societies; Member Medical Advisory Board, League of Red Cross Societies, Geneva; Commandeur, Legion of Honour, France; Order of the Sacred Treasure, Japan; Fellow and Associate in Pathology, Johns Hopkins University, Baltimore, 1891–95; Associate Professor of Pathology, 1895–98; Professor of Pathological Anatomy, 1898–99; Professor of Pathology, University of Pennsylvania, 1899–1903; Director, Ayer Clinical Laboratory, Pennsylvania Hospital, 1901–03; Pathologist, University Hospital and Philadelphia Hosp. Phila. 1900–03; Dir Rockefeller Inst. for Med. Res., New York, 1903–35; Col, Medical Reserve Corps, USA; Asst Surg.-Gen. US Public Health Service Reserve; Chairman, Public Health Council, New York State, since 1923; Eastman Visiting Professor, Balliol College, Oxford, 1937–38. *Publications:* (with James Thomas Flexner) William Henry Welch and the heroic age of American Medicine, 1941; many papers and monographs on pathological and bacteriological subjects. *Address:* 530 East 86th Street, New York. *Clubs:* Century Association, New York.

Died 2 May 1946.

FLICK, Brig.-Gen. Charles Leonard, CMG 1916; CBE 1918; VD; *b* Halesworth, Suffolk, 20 Dec. 1869; *s* of late Richard Flick, The Holt, Melton, Woodbridge, Suffolk; *m* 1904, Marie, *y d* of Joseph Milward, Skeleton Lake, Muskoka, Canada; one *s* two *d*. *Educ:* Yarmouth Grammar School; Felsted School. Served in Rhodesia, S Africa, 1899–1903 with South African Light Horse and Imperial Yeomanry (despatches, Queen's medal six clasps, King's medal two clasps); emigrated to British Columbia, 1903; raised, organized and commanded BC Horse, 1911; passed Militia Staff Course, 1913; mobilised BC Horse, 10 Aug. 1914, and proceeded to England with First Canadian Division; seconded to 12th Royal Fusiliers, 73rd Brigade, March 1915; commanded 7th Batt. Essex Regt in Gallipoli, 1915 (wounded, CMG); commanded 6th Batt. Devon Regt, Mesopotamia, 1916–19 (despatches, CBE); GOC Euphrates Defences, June 1918; raised, organized and commanded No. 2 Special Bn during Indian riots, 1919; subsequently employed on the NW Frontier, 1919 (medal and clasp); returned to Canada, May 1920; command of 5th Canadian Cavalry (BC Horse), 1920–24; retired 1929; Registrar of Enemy Aliens and Reporting Officer for Japanese resident on Gulf Islands, 1941. *Publications:* Twelve Months with Gen. Buller in Natal; Just what Happened—A Diary of the Canadian Mobilization, 1914; The Record of the Sixth Devons in the Great War of 1914–1919; A Canadian in Gallipoli; When I was a King; The Men of the Maple Leaf; History of British Columbia Horse; Canada War Ballads. *Address:* Mayne Island, BC. *Clubs:* Royal Victoria Yacht, Pacific (Victoria, BC).

Died 8 Feb. 1948.

FLINT, Robert Purves, RWS 1937; ARWS 1932; RSW; *b* Edinburgh, 1883; *s* of Francis Wighton Flint and Jane Purves. *Educ:* Daniel Stewart's College, Edinburgh. War service with Royal Scots in Flanders; Official Purchases, National Art-Collections Fund for the Queensland Art-Collections Fund; National Gallery, Melbourne; Scottish Modern Arts Association; represented at Birmingham, Sheffield, etc.; Exhibition of water-colours, Leicester Galleries, 1926. *Address:* Littlemead, Joy Lane, Whitstable, Kent. *T:* Whitstable 2475.

Died 1 March 1947.

FLOWER, Sir Archibald Dennis, Kt 1930; High Steward, Borough of Stratford-on-Avon; *s* of Edgar Flower, Stratford-upon-Avon, and Isabella Dennis, Ireland; *m* Florence (*d* 1946), *d* of Sir Richard Keane, 4th Bt Cappoquin, Co. Waterford; two *s* one *d*. *Educ:* Clifton and Bedford Modern School; Clare College, Cambridge; rowed for Cambridge University v. Oxford, 1886. Elected to Warwickshire CC, 1892; Mayor of Stratford, 1900–02, 1915–18, and 1931; Life Trustee of the Trustees of Shakespeare's Birth place in 1900. *Recreations:* travel, hunting, fishing, golf, and Shakespeare. *Address:* The Hill, Stratford-upon-Avon. *T:* Stratford-on-Avon 2396. *Club:* Garrick.

Died 22 Nov. 1950.

FLOWER, Robin Ernest William, CBE 1945; *b* Meanwood, Leeds, Yorkshire, 16 Oct. 1881; *s* of M. C. W. Flower, painter, and Jane Lynch; *m* 1911, Ida Mary Streeter, *d* of J. S. Streeter, Croydon; one *s* three *d*. *Educ:* Leeds Grammar School; Pembroke College, Oxford. BA Oxon; FBA; Hon. DLitt Celt., Nat. University, Ireland; Hon. DLitt Trin. Coll. Dublin; MRIA; FRHistSoc; Corresponding Fellow, Medieval Acad. of America. Assistant in the Department of MSS, British Museum, 1906; Deputy Keeper of MSS British Museum, 1929–44; Hon. Lecturer in Celtic, University College, London; Chairman of Council, Irish Texts Society; Hon. Acting Director, Early English Text Society; Member of Council, Irish Genealogical Society; Sir John Rhys Lecturer, Brit. Acad., 1927; Byron Foundation Lecturer, University of Nottingham, 1928; Lowell Lecturer, Boston, Mass, 1935; Woodward Lecturer, Yale University, 1935; Woodward Lecturer, Yale University, 1935; W. Vaughn Moody Lecturer, Chicago, 1935; Sir Israel Gollancz Lecturer, Brit. Acad., 1935; Giff Edmonds Lecturer, Roy. Soc. of Literature, 1939.

Publications: Catalogue of Irish MSS in British Museum, Vol. ii, 1928; Ireland and Medieval Europe, 1927; Introduction to T. F. O'Rahilly, Dánta Grádha, 1927; The Islandman (translation of T. O'Criomhthainn's An t-Oileánach), 1934; The Exeter Book of Old English Poetry (with R. W. Chambers and Max Förster), 1933; Laurence Nowell and the Discovery of England in Tudor Times, 1935; ire, 1910; Hymenæa, 1918; Love's Bitter-Sweet, 1925; Poems and Translations, 1931; Articles and reviews in Zeitschrift für Celtische Philologie, Ériu, The Times, Times Literary Supplement, etc. *Address:* 100 Ullswater Road, Southgate, N14. *T:* Palmers Green 4364. *Clubs:* Odd Volumes, Boston.

Died 16 Jan. 1946.

FLUX, Sir Alfred William, Kt 1934; CB 1920; MA (Cantab), Hon. LLD (Manchester); Assistant Secretary Statistics Department, Board of Trade, 1918–32; Guy (gold) Medallist (1930), and Hon. Vice-President (past President) of the Royal Statistical Society; Hon. Member of the International Institute of Statistics; of the American Statistical Association; of the Hungarian Statistical Society and of the Czechoslovak Statistical Society; Member of the League of Nations Committee of Statistical Experts; *b* Portsmouth, 8 April 1867; *m* Emilie, *d* of Direktör V. Hansen of Copenhagen. *Educ:* Portsmouth Grammar School; St John's College, Cambridge. Bracketed Senior Wrangler, 1887; Marshall Prize, 1889; Fellow of St John's College, Cambridge, 1889–95. Cobden Lecturer in Political Economy at Owens College, Manchester, 1893–1901; Stanley Jevons Professor of Political Economy at Owens College, 1898–1901; William Dow Professor of Political Economy in McGill University, Montreal, 1901–08. *Publications:* Economic Principles, 1904—new, revised, edition, 1923; New Edition of Jevons' Coal Question, 1906; The Swedish Banking System, 1910; The Foreign Exchanges, 1924; articles and papers on Statistical and Economic subjects in Economic Journal; Transactions of the Royal and Manchester Statistical Societies, etc. *Address:* Kronprinsensvej 12, Copenhagen.

Died 16 July 1942.

FLYNN, Alfred Axen Leonard, CIE 1936; VD; late Traffic Manager, Karachi Port Trust. *Address:* 52 Elmgrove, Thorpe Bay, Essex.

Died 18 Dec. 1943.

FOAKES-JACKSON, Rev. Frederick John, DD, DTh (Strasbourg); Hon. DLitt University of the South, USA; Hon. Correspondent Institut Historique et Héraldique de France (Medallist); FRHistS, FRLS; Fellow American Academy Arts and Sciences; Fellow of Jesus College, Cambridge, since 1886; Briggs Professor of Christian Institutions Union Theological Seminary, New York, 1916–34 now Emeritus; *b* Ipswich, 10 Aug. 1855; *s* of Rev. Stephen Jackson, Ipswich, and Catharine, *d* of Frederick Cobbold, 1st Dragoon Guards; *m* 1st, 1895, Anna M. Everett (*d* 1931); 2nd, Clara Fawcett, *widow of* Arthur Jackson Tomlinson, New York. *Educ:* Eton; Trinity College, Cambridge, BA 1879, MA 1882, BD 1903; DD 1905; Jeremie lxx Pri. 1877; Scholfield Prize (Bibl. Greek); 1st class Theol. Tripos, Crosse (Divinity) Scholar, 1879; Lightfoot (Eccl Hist.) Scholar, 1880. Ordained 1879–80 by Bishop of Winchester; Examining Chaplain to Bishop of Peterborough, 1897–1912; Hon. Canon, Peterborough, 1901–27; Hulsean Lecturer, 1902; GC Grand Lodge of Freemasons; Grand Superintendent Cambs (Royal Arch) till 1919; Junior Proctor, 1894; Senior, 1909; Lecturer, Jesus College, Cambridge, 1882–1916; Dean, 1895–1916; Lowell Lecturer, Boston, USA, 1916; Lecturer Jewish Institute of Religion, New York, 1924–27; Genera Theological Seminary (Church), 1925–26. *Publications:* History of Christian Church to ad 337, 1891; 7th ed. to ad 461, 1923; Christian Difficulties in the Second and Twentieth Centuries; A Biblical History of the Hebrews, 1903, 5th ed. 1924; article Christ in the Church, Cambridge

Theological Essays, 1905; chapter on Hooker, Cambridge History of Literature, vol. iii, 1908; chapter on Rise of Papal Power, Cambridge Mediæval Hist., vol. ii 1913; Biblical Hist. for Schools (OT 1912, 2nd ed. 1917, NT (with Rev. B. T. D. Smith) 1913); Society in England, 1750–1850; St Luke and a Modern Writer, 1916; Introduction to Church History (590–1314), 1921; Studies in the Life of the Early Church, 1924; Principles of Anglicanism, 1924; St Paul the Man and the Apostle, 1926, English edn, 1933; Gentile Christianity, 1927; Peter, Prince of Apostles, 1927; Josephus and the Jews, 1930; Commentary on the Acts of the Apostles (Moffatt series), 1931; The Christian Religion its Origin and Progress, part ii The Church in the Middle Ages, part iii The Church in England; Eusebius Pamphili, 1933; History of Church History, 1939; Editor of Parting of the Roads, essays by members of Jesus College, 1910, and of The Faith and the War, 1916; Origins of Christianity, vols i, ii and iii (with Kirsopp Lake); vol. ii of Outlines of Christianity, 1926; contributor to Records of Jesus College Boat Club, 1929; and to Christianity in the Light of Modern Knowledge, 1929; also to Cambridge Theological Essays, Cambridge History of Literature and Mediæval History. *Recreations:* formerly rowing, fishing, shooting, treasurer of the Cambridge University Boat Club, 1895–1910. *Address:* Englewood, NJ, USA. *Club:* United University.

Died 1 Dec. 1941.

FOGERTY, Elsie, CBE 1934; LRAM; Founder, Central School of Speech Training and Dramatic Art (Inc.); *d* of Joseph Fogerty, MICE, FRIBA and Hannah Cochrane. *Educ:* privately. Lecturer in English and Speech, Crystal Palace School of Art, 1889–1912; Lecturer on Speech and Dramatic Art, London County Council and University of London Extension Board; Tutor in Diction to Sir Frank Benson's London School of Acting; founded the Central School of Speech Training and Dramatic Art; Member of the Council of the British Drama League. *Publications:* Acting Editions of: As You Like it, Twelfth Night, Love's Labour Lost, The Princess, Alkestes, Antigone, Electra; Scenes from the Great Novelists; The Queen's Jest and other Plays; 1st Notes on Speech Training; trs Coquelin's Art of the Actor; Stammering; The Speaking of English Verse; Rhythm; Speechcraft; Speech Training in Schools, Practical Senior Teacher; Speech Training, The British Journal of Educational Psychology. *Recreations:* history and the theatre. *Address:* c/o 29 Queensberry Place, SW7.

Died 4 July 1945.

FOGG ELLIOT, Captain Mark, DSO 1940; RN (retd); *b* 30 Sept. 1898; *s* of C. T. Fogg Elliot, Staindrop, Co. Durham; *m* 1931, Barbara Mollie Stiles-Webb; one *d.* *Educ:* Sandroyd School; RNC, Osborne and Dartmouth. *Recreations:* hunting, shooting, fishing, and rowing. *Address:* Staindrop, Darlington, Co. Durham. *Club:* Leander (Henley-on-Thames).

Died 14 May 1950.

FOGGIE, David, RSA 1930; RSW; *b* Dundee, 1878; *m* 1902, Margaret Anne Jack, LLA; three *s* one *d.* *Educ:* High School, Dundee. Studied at Antwerp. Visited Belgium, Holland, Paris, Florence; represented in Public Galleries—Dundee, Paisley, Edinburgh, Stretford, Aberdeen, Glasgow. Secretary RSA, 1932. *Address:* 38 Danube Street, Edinburgh.

Died 2 June 1948.

FOGGITT, Mrs T. J.; *see* Bacon, Gertrude.

FOLEY, Blanchard, CSI 1927; VD 1928; *b* London, 15 June 1869; *s* of J. B. and R. A. Foley; *m* Amy Frances McNamara; no *c.* *Educ:* Highgate School; Merton College, Oxford, MA. Joined Indian Civil Service, 1893; Under-Secretary, Bengal, 1896–99; District Magistrate, Collector of Customs, Excise Com. etc., 1899–1916;

Commissioner Bihar and Orissa, 1916–24; Member of Board of Revenue, Bihar and Orissa, India, 1924–28; retired, 1928. *Publication:* Report on Labour in Bengal, 1906. *Address:* 20 Heene Way, Worthing, Sussex. *T:* Worthing 2843. *Clubs:* East India and Sports; Bengal United Service (Calcutta).

Died 2 May 1950.

FOLEY, Most Rev. Daniel; RC Bishop of Ballarat since 1916; *b* Co. Cork, 1865. *Educ:* Mt Melleray, Fermoy, and Maynooth. Ordained, 1889; went to Ballarat, 1890; served in a number of parishes; Rector of Terang, 1908–16. *Address:* Bishop's Palace, Ballarat, Australia.

Died 31 Oct. 1941.

FOLEY, Col Frank Wigram, CBE 1919; DSO 1900; late Royal Berkshire Regt; *b* 24 June 1865; 4th *s* of late Captain Edward Foley, RN; *m* 1903, The Baroness Berkeley; two *d*. *Educ:* Tonbridge School. Entered army, 1886; Capt. 1897; served with the Mounted Infantry, South African campaign, 1899–1901 (Queen's medal 4 clasps, DSO); European War, 1914–16 (severely wounded); retired pay, 1920; JP Surrey. *Address:* Fairlawn, Crawley Ridge, Camberley, Surrey. *Clubs:* United Service, Free Foresters, MCC.

Died 7 Oct. 1949.

FOLGER, Col Karl Creighton, CMG 1919, DSO 1917; late Canadian Ord. Corps; *m* 1905, Nancy, *d* of C. Moffitt, Newcastle; three *s*. *Educ:* RMC, Kingston, Canada. Served South African War, 1899–1902; European War, 1914–18 (despatches, DSO).

Died 22 Feb. 1941.

FOLLETT, Lt-Col Robert Spencer, DSO 1916; *b* 19 Oct. 1882; *s* of late W. W. S. Follett; *m* 1915, Dorothy, *d* of late W. J. Fanning; three *d*. *Educ:* Eton. Rifle Brigade, 1901–29; served S Africa, 1901–02 (medal with five clasps); European War (despatches four times, DSO, Bt Lt-Col). *Address:* Colchester's Farm, Ashleworth, near Gloucester. *Club:* Army and Navy.

Died 25 Sept. 1941.

FOORD, Francis Layton, CBE 1934; Government Secretary, Basutoland, 1930 and Deputy Resident Commissioner, 1931; retired 1934; Member of Home Guard; *b* 9 Oct. 1874; 4th *s* of Henry Robert Foord, Admiralty, and Gertrude Pagan Campbell, *d* of Dr Hutcheson; *m* 1906, Geraldine Christine Marie Trout; one *d*. *Educ:* The London International College; Private Coach. Cape Mounted Riflemen, 1893–1900; 1st South Staffordshire Regiment, 1900–02; Anglo-Boer War, 1899–1902 (Queen's Medal five clasps, King's Medal two clasps); Sub-Inspector Basutoland Mounted Police, 1902; Inspector of Police, 1913; Assistant Commissioner, 1915; accompanied a deputation of Basuto Chiefs to England in 1909 and 1919. *Recreations:* golf, tennis, badminton, fishing, shooting, bridge. *Address:* Henley, Exton, nr Exeter, S Devon.

Died 31 Dec. 1942.

FOOTT, Col (Hon. Brig.-Gen.) Cecil Henry, CB 1919; CMG 1916; *b* Bourke, Darling River, NSW, 16 Jan. 1876; *e s* of late T. Wade Foott of Springfort, County Cork, and of Dundoo Station, Queensland; *m* 1901, Isabel Agnes, *o d* of G. T. McDonald of Rocklea, Queensland; one *s* two *d*. *Educ:* Brisbane Boys' Grammar School. Mechanical engineer, 1890–96; Lieutenant, Queensland Permanent Artillery, 1896; posted to Royal Australian Engineers, 1901; Director of Engineers, Australia, 1909–11; MIVE Victoria, 1910; Staff College, Camberley, 1912–13, PSC; Royal Naval College, Portsmouth, 1914; DAQMG 2nd London Division (TF), Aug.–Oct. 1914; joined AIF in Egypt, 1915, served in Gallipoli, Egypt, and France (despatches seven times, Brevet Lt-Col, Brevet Col, CMG, CB); ADC to Gov.-General, 1921–24; ADC to the King, 1927–31; DEOS Australian Military Forces; Commanded 11th Mixed Brigade, Australian Military Forces, 1926–29; District Commandant, Victoria, 1929–31; Commander,

Home Guard, Victoria, 1940. *Publication:* Gold Medal Essay Commonwealth of Australia, 1913. *Address:* Upper Beaconsfield, Victoria, Australia. *Clubs:* Queensland United Service, Brisbane; R. Auto, Victoria.

Died 27 June 1942.

FORBES, Alexander, CBE 1919; Agent of Standard Oil Co. of New York and Rangoon; *b* 1860; *s* of Charles Forbes; *m* Elizabeth McGlashan, *d* of Captain Peter Low. *Address:* Craigatin House, Pitlochry, Perthshire.

Died 6 Jan. 1942.

FORBES, Arthur C., OBE 1920; FHAS, MRIA, FREFS; late Director of Forestry, Forestry Branch, Ireland; *b* 1866. *Publications:* English Estate Forestry; Development of British Forestry, etc. *Address:* Longleat, Killiney Road, Co. Dublin.

Died 7 Nov. 1950.

FORBES, Lt-Col Atholl Murray Hay, DSO 1917; late Royal Scots Fusiliers; *b* 1870; 4th *s* of late Major Frederick Murray Hay Forbes, BSC, and Honoria, *d* of Rev. W. K. Marshall, Prebendary of Hereford; *m* 1915, Alice Rose, *d* of late N. C. Tuely, widow of Major G. A. Keef, Royal Scots Fusiliers. Served NW Frontier of India, 1897–98; European War (despatches twice, wounded, DSO). *Address:* Morningside, Haslemere, Surrey.

Died 10 April 1942.

FORBES of Callendar, Charles William; JP, DL; *b* 27 Sept. 1871; *e s* of William Forbes and Edith Marian, 3rd *d* of late Rev. Lord Charles Amelius Hervey; *m* 1897, Jean, *o d* of late Admiral of the Fleet Sir Charles Frederick Hotham, GCB, GCVO; two *s* four *d*. *Educ:* Eton; Christ Church, Oxford. *Recreations:* shooting; Captain Stirling County Eleven, 1896–1909. *Address:* Callendar House, Falkirk, Stirlingshire. *T:* Falkirk 186 and 583; Earlstoun Lodge, Dalry, Kirkcudbrightshire. *T:* Dalry 213. *Clubs:* Carlton, Conservative, MCC; New (Edinburgh).

Died 31 July 1948.

FORBES, Rt Hon. George William; PC 1930; *b* Lyttelton, NZ, 12 March 1869; *m* 1895, Winnie, *d* of late Thomas Gee, Christchurch; one *s* two *d*. *Educ:* Boys High School, Christchurch, NZ. MP Hurunui, 1908–43; Minister of Lands and Agriculture, 1928–30; Minister of Finance, Customs, and Stamp Duties, 1930–31; Prime Minister, Minister of External Affairs, Minister in charge, Public Trust, Scientific and Industrial Research, and High Commissioner's Departments, New Zealand, 1930–35; also Minister for Railways, 1931–35; also Attorney-General, 1933–35; also Minister of Native Affairs, etc., 1934–35; Leader of Opposition, New Zealand, 1935–36; a Representative of New Zealand at Imperial Conference, 1930 and also at the World Economic Conference in 1932. *Address:* Crystal Brook, Cheviot, Canterbury, NZ.

Died 18 May 1947.

FORBES, James Graham, MA, MD, DPH (Camb.); FRCP; (retired); late Principal Assistant Medical Officer, LCC; *b* 24 March 1873; *s* of late Rev. Edward Forbes, MA, Clevedon, Somerset, and *g s* of Rev. Edward Forbes, DD, British Chaplain in Paris; *m* 1905, Muriel Watson, *d* of late Dr Watson Paul, Cowes; one *s* two *d*. *Educ:* Clifton College; Christ's College, Cambridge; St Bartholomew's Hospital. House Physician and Assistant Demonstrator Pathology, St Bartholomew's Hospital; Civil Surgeon attached Royal Horse Guards (Blue), and Medical Officer Anglo-French Boundary Commission, Gold Coast Colony, West Africa; Assistant Physician, Metropolitan Hospital and Royal Hospital for Diseases of Chest, City Road, EC; Pathologist and Bacteriologist, Hospital for Sick Children, Great Ormond Street; War service 1916–19; Capt. RAMC; Pathologist and Sanitary Officer, 36th General Hospital, British Salonika Force (despatches); Milroy Lecturer Royal College of Physicians, 1929; Member BMA. *Publications:*

Diphtheria—its Distribution and Prevention, 1932; Medical Report, Anglo-French Boundary Commission, West Africa, 1903 (and other contributions to St Bart's Hospital Reports); Fatal Lymphocythæmia in Early Life (jointly) (Proc. Roy. Soc. Med., 1908); Pollution of Swimming Baths (School Hygiene, 1912); Filarial Infection in Macedonia (RAMC Journal, 1919); Diphtheria Carriers in London Children (Public Health, 1923); Atmosphere of Underground Electric Railways of London in 1920 (Journal of Hygiene, 1924); Prevention of Diphtheria, Medical Research Council, Special Report Series No. 115, 1927; Progress of Diphtheria Control (Bull. of Hygiene, 1932); Survey of Diphtheria (Journal of State Medicine, 1923; Progress of Diphtheria Prevention (Brit. Med. Jl, Dec. 1937). Recreations: walking, travel, genealogy. Address: Tree Tops, Church Street, Wadhurst, Sussex.

Died 8 April 1941.

FORBES, James Wright, MA, LLB; b Edinburgh, 1866; s of late Alexander Forbes, Principal Keeper, HM Register of Deeds, Register House, Edinburgh; m 1903, Isabella Marion, d of James Cooper, dental surgeon, Edinburgh; two s. Educ: George Watson's College, Edinburgh; Edinburgh University. Won various prizes and scholarships. Called to Bar, 1891; Member of Edinburgh Parish Council and Board of Control, 1905–19; Sheriff-Substitute of Caithness, Orkney and Shetland at Lerwick, 1919; of Sutherland, Ross and Cromarty at Dornoch, 1922–35; of Dumfries and Galloway, 1935–42; JP, Sutherland, 1926; President, Watsonian Club, 1909. Publications: (with J. E. Graham, KC) Digest of LGB Arbitrations in Poor Law; contributor to Green's Legal Encyclopædia; Reporter of Cases for Scots Law Times, 1902–1915; Editor of Poor Law Magazine, 1909–1919. Recreations: fishing, gardening. Address: Bearlochan, Twynholm, Castle-Douglas, Kirkcudbrightshire. T: Twynholm 239. Clubs: Scottish Conservative, Edinburgh.

Died 18 March 1947.

FORBES, Lt-Comdr John Hay, DSO 1940; Royal Navy; HMS Spearfish; b 28 Aug. 1906; m 1930, Edith Sheilah Steel; one s one d. Educ: Ladycross, Seaford; RNC Dartmouth. Entered RNC Osborne, 1920; Lieut Cdr, 1937; Specialised in Submarines, 1928. Recreations: fishing, shooting, cricket, Scottish Rugby Trial, 1927–28. Address: West Coates, Village Road, Alverstoke. Club: Incogniti.

Died 2 Aug. 1940.

FORBES, Stanhope Alexander, RA 1910; Correspondent of the Institute of France; b Dublin, 18 Nov. 1857; s of William Forbes, then manager of Midland Great Western Railway of Ireland; m 1st, 1889, Elizabeth Adela, ARWS (d 1912), d of William Armstrong, Civil Service, Ottawa; 2nd, 1915, Maud Palmer, nephew of late Col Clubley, Indian Army. Educ: Dulwich; at Lambeth School of Art; Royal Academy Schools; Atelier of M. Bonnat in Paris; ARA, 1892. Among pictures exhibited in RA: The Fish Sale, The Village Philharmonic, The Health of the Bride, By Order of the Court, The Quarry Team, The Salvation Army, Forging the Anchor, The Lighthouse, The Smithy, Christmas Eve. Recreations: music, gardening. Address: Higher Faugan, Newlyn, Penzance.

Died 2 March 1947.

FORD, Ven. A. Lockett, MA, TCD; Archdeacon of Armagh since 1934; Rector and Vicar of Ardee; Hon. Chaplain the Lord Lieutenant, 1913; Chaplain of Ardee Mental Home; Chaplain of District Hospital, Ardee; b Newry, 3 April 1853; e s of late Rev. A. L. Ford, Vicar of Christ Church, Weston Point, Cheshire; m 1st, Annie, d of R. Richardson, Greenbank, Liverpool; 2nd, Hilda, d of Very Rev. H. Townsend Fleming, DD, Dean of Cloyne; three s one d. Educ: Royal Institution School, Liverpool; Trinity College, Dublin. Assistant Master, Royal Institution School, 1874–76; Curate of Dundalk,

1876–78; Rector of Camlough, 1878–93; Armagh Diocesan Representative Canon of St Patrick's (National Cathedral), Dublin, 1900–34; Rural Dean of Athirdee and Rural Dean of Drogheda to 1934; Member of Representative Church Body, 1934; Armagh Diocesan Secretary of Religious Education, 1901–07 and 1914; Lord-Lieutenant's Inspector of Endowed Schools, 1901–26; Member of General Synod; Hon. Secretary Diocesan Synod and Council, 1916; Governor of N Ireland's Inspector, 1922–26; Examining Chaplain to Lord Primate, 1934. Publications: Manual for Communicants; Advent Thoughts from the Lord's Prayer. Address: The Rectory, Ardee, Co. Louth. T: 20. TA: Ford, Ardee. Clubs: University, Dublin.

Died 16 April 1945.

FORD, Lt-Col Charles Hopewell, CMG 1915; late RA; b 14 Dec. 1864; m 1907, Ethel Mildred, d of late W. Knight Treves, FRCS. Entered army, 1884; Captain, 1893; Major, 1900; Lt-Col, 1913; served European War, 1914–18 (despatches, CMG); retired, 1919. Address: Claremont, Northdown Park Road, Margate. T: Margate 197.

Died 18 Dec. 1950.

FORD, Rev. Ernest Robert, MA; Prebendary Emeritus of St Paul's Cathedral, 1939; Prebendary, 1929–39; b 3 April 1863; y s of James Ford (law stationer) and Elizabeth Esther, d of William Kendra, Leeds; m 1897, Mary Susannah, d of John Hogben Cocksedge; one s two d. Educ: private schools; Fitzwilliam Hall, Cambridge. BA, 1887; MA, 1891. India Office, 1881–84; Curate of St Matthew's, Cambridge, 1887–91; Sub-Warden of SPCK Training College for Lay Workers, Stepney, and Curate of St Thomas', Stepney, 1891–93; Warden of above College, 1893–1904; Vicar and Rural Dean of Shoreditch, 1904–13; Rector of Christ Church, Brondesbury, NW6, 1913–29; Rural Dean of Willesden, 1924–29. Recreation: music. Address: The Knock, Rossall School, Fleetwood, Lancs. T: Fleetwood 8349.

Died 20 Nov. 1942.

FORD, Sir (Francis Charles) Rupert, 5th Bt cr 1793; b 5 April 1877; e s of 4th Bt and Frances Colville, e d of late William Ford, CSI (d 1905); S father 1890; m 1918, Katherine Olive, 2nd d of late J. C. Yorke of Langton, Dwrbach, Pemb.; two d. Educ: Sedbergh, Paris, and Bonn. Heir: cousin Capt. Aubrey St Clair-Ford. Address: Trecwn, Wilfred Road, Boscombe, Hants.

Died 28 Feb. 1948.

FORD, Col Frederick Samuel Lampson, CMG 1915; VD; MD; LMCC; RCAMC (retd); b 2 Feb. 1869; s of late James Morton and Ann Letitia Ford, Milton, Nova Scotia. Educ: Public School, Milton, NS; High School, Liverpool, NS; College of Physicians and Surgeons, University of Maryland; London Hospitals; MD (gold medallist) 1894. Served European War (France and Belgium) as OC 1st Canadian Casualty Clearing Station, Deputy Assistant Director Medical Services, Canadian Army Corps, and as Assistant Director Medical Services, 1st Canadian Division, BEF, 1914–18 (seriously wounded, despatches, CMG, 1914–15 Star, British War Medal, Victory Medal, Colonial Auxiliary Forces Officers' Decoration); Inspector Military Hospitals, Canada, 1918–19; District Medical Officer, Mil. District, No. 2, 1919–32. Address: 600 University Avenue, Toronto, Ont, Canada. Clubs: Military, Royal Canadian Yacht, Toronto.

Died 23 Nov. 1944.

FORD, Rev. George Paget, MA; Chaplain TA since 1921; Vicar of St Andrew's, Willesden Green, since 1935; Rural Dean of Willesden since 1940; Prebendary and Canon of Brownswood in St Paul's Cathedral, London, 1942; b 15 May 1883; s of an actor. Educ: St Andrew's College, Dublin; Mountjoy School, Dublin; Trinity College, Dublin (MA). Curate of Lismore Cathedral, Co. Waterford, 1906; of St Clement,

Barnsbury, London, 1909; Vicar of St Michael's Shoreditch, 1925. Chaplain to the Mothers' Union, 1944. *Publications:* What is Religion?, 1925; Why are you alive?, 1930; The Body Crucified, 1933; With Jesus to Calvary, 1935; Man's Desperate Need, 1938; Friendship with Jesus, 1941; How to Pray, 1945. Contributor Concise Oxford Dictionary, 1929. *Address:* St Andrew's Clergy House, Willesden Green, NW10. *TA:* and *T:* Willesden 2670.

Died 15 Oct. 1950.

FORD, Henry; Ford Motor Co.; *b* Dearborn Township, Michigan, 30 July 1863; *s* of William Ford and Mary Litogot; *m* 1888, Clara J. Bryant. *Educ:* district school. Organiser, 1903, and President, Ford Motor Company, to 1919 and since 1943; also General Manager, 1943–45; organised Peace Party to Europe, 1915; was Chief Engineer Edison Illuminating Co.; announced in 1914 a plan of profit sharing to employees; built the Henry Ford Hospital in 1919; Member of Society Automotive Engineers, and Detroit Board of Commerce. *Publications:* My Life and Work, 1922; (with Samuel Crowther) To-day and To-morrow, 1926; Moving Forward, 1930; Edison as I know Him, 1930. *Address:* Dearborn, Michigan, USA. *Clubs:* Detroit, Athletic, Country, Boat, Auto of America, Michigan Automobile, Detroit.

Died 7 April 1947.

FORD, Henry Justice; artist; *b* London, Oct. 1856; *s* of William Augustus Ford, solicitor; *m* 1921. *Educ:* Repton; Clare College, Cambridge (scholar); 1st class Classical Tripos, 1882. Studied art under Legros at the Slade School and under Herkomer at Bushey. Has exhibited at the Royal Academy, New Gallery, etc.; Illustrated the Andrew Lang Fairy Book Series; Lang's Tales of Troy and Greece; Fletcher and Kipling's School History of England; the Blue Door, a Fairy Tale by E. F. Benson; Pilot and other Tales by H. Plunkett Greene; The Pilgrim's Progress, English Church History, The Early History of the Christian Church, The Parables, St Peter and St Paul, by Rev. W. Lowther Clarke; Gripfast Series of History Books; Tales of Old France, by Mrs Creighton; painted the pictures for Longman's series of Historical Wall Pictures. *Works:* The Fisherman and the Mermaid; The Witch Maiden; La Belle Dame sans Merci; The Fairy Pool, etc.; also portraits and landscapes in oil, water-colour and pastel. *Recreations:* cricket, golf, billiards, and chess. *Address:* The Forge, Aldermaston, Berks.

Died 19 Nov. 1941.

FORD, Sir James, Kt 1930; JP; Clerk to Leeds Assessment Committee; *b* Leeds, 14 Nov. 1863; *s* of late James and Maria Ford, Leeds; *m* 1897, Ellen, *d* of late William H. Newill, Burton-on-Trent; one *d*. *Educ:* private schools in Leeds. Entered service of Leeds Board of Guardians, 1879; Clerk to Guardians, 1897–1930; Clerk to Assessment Committee, 1897–1942, and Clerk to former Leeds Rural DC, 1897–1913; Member Executive Council of Assoc. of Poor Law Unions, 1901–30; of (late) National Assoc. of Assessment Committees from formation until 1930. *Recreations:* formerly athletics of all descriptions (cyclist, football player, volunteer), gardening and literary pursuits. *Address:* 74 Headingley Lane, Leeds.

Died 10 Sept. 1943.

FORD, Maj.-Gen. John Randle Minshull-, CB 1933; DSO 1917; MC 1915; *b* 12 May 1881; *s* of late Capt. Minshull Ford, JP, 8th (The King's Regt, of Llewyngwyn, Montgomeryshire; *m* 1912, Dorothy, *y d* of Sir John Harmood Banner, 1st Bart, MP; one *s* one *d*. *Educ:* Twyford School, Winchester; Haileybury; Sandhurst. Joined 2nd Batt. Royal Welch Fusiliers, 1900; Capt., 1st Batt., 1911; Joined 1st Batt. Expeditionary Force, France, Oct. 1914; Commanded 1st, Nov. 1914–March 1915 (wounded at Neuve Chapelle); Staff, April 1915–Sept. 1915; Commanded 1st RWF, Sept. 15–Feb. 1916; Brig.-Gen. 3 Feb. 1916 (wounded thrice;

despatches, 6 times, DSO, MC, Brevets Major, Lt-Col and (Col); Bt Col commanded 1st Batt. South Stafford Regt, 1925–29; Commander 5th Infantry Brigade, Aldershot, 1930–32; ADC 1930–32; Major-General, 1932; Commander 44th Home Counties) Division and Area, TA, 1934–38; retired pay, 1938; Colonel Royal Welch Fusiliers, 1938–42; Lieut-Governor and GOC Guernsey and Alderney District, 1940. *Address:* The White Cottage, Windlesham, Surrey. *Club:* United Service.

Died 1 April 1948.

FORD, Sir Patrick Johnstone, 1st Bt *cr* 1929; Kt 1926; *b* Edinburgh, 5 March 1880; 2nd *s* of Jas Ford, Edinburgh, and Agnes Campbell, *d* of Alex. Cassels, WS; *m* 1905, Jessie Hamilton, *d* of H. Field, WS, Moreland, Kinross-shire, and Middlebluf, Manitoba; two *s* two *d*. *Educ:* Edinburgh Academy; New College, Oxford (MA); Edinburgh University (LLB). Advocate, 1907; contested Edinburgh East 1909 and Jan. 1910, and Inverness Burghs, Dec. 1910 (U); MP (U) Edinburgh North, April 1920–Dec. 1923, and 1924–35; Member Royal Company of Archers (King's Bodyguard for Scotland); Lieut 4th Batt. Cameron Highlanders, Nov. 1914; resigned on account of ill-health, April 1915; Hon. Lieut on Special Duties, 1917–19; Hon. Colonel Forth Heavy Brigade, Royal Artillery (T), 1926–35; resigned 1935; Hon. Member Royal Scottish Academy; FRSA 1939. *Publications:* Interior Paintings by Patrick W. Adam, RSA, 1920; Side Table, 1935; Christmas Thoughts and Other Poems, 1938. *Recreations:* various. *Heir:* *s* Henry Russell [*b* 30 April 1911; *m* 1936, Mary Elizabeth, *yr d* of Godfrey F. Wright, Whiddon, Bovey Tracey]. *Address:* 7 Moray Place, Edinburgh. *Clubs:* Carlton; Scottish Conservative, New, Edinburgh.

Died 28 Sept. 1945.

FORD, Gen. Sir Richard Vernon Tredinnick, KCB 1933 (CB 1928); CBE 1919; *b* 1878; *s* of late A. Vernon Ford, Sea View, Isle of Wight; *m* 1st, 1903, Diana (*d* 1911), *d* of late Rear-Admiral G. N. A. Pollard; 2nd, 1913, Mildred, *d* of late Capt. P. C. Underwood, RN; two *s* one *d*. Entered RM Artillery as 2nd Lieut 1896; ADC to the King 1929–30; Adjutant-General Royal Marines, 1930–33; retired list, 1933. *Address:* Eastney Lodge, Folkestone. *T:* Folkestone 2943.

Died 12 April 1949.

FORD, Sir Robert; *see* Ford, Sir F. C. R.

FORD, Worthington Chauncey, LLD, LittD; *b* Brooklyn, New York, 16 Feb. 1858; *s* of Gordon Lester and Emily Ellsworth Ford; *m* Bettina Fillmore Quin, of Washington, DC; two *d*. Historian and economist; Chief of Bureau of Statistics, US Dept of State, 1885–89; and of US Treasury Dept, 1893–98; Boston Public Library, 1898–1902; Chief Division of Manuscripts, Library of Congress, 1903–09; Lecturer in Harvard University and Univ. of Michigan; editor Massachusetts Historical Society; Director of the European Mission of the Library of Congress, 1929–35. *Publications:* Life of George Washington; American Citizens' Manual; edited Writings of George Washington; Letters of Henry Adams, 1858–1891, 1930; Writings of John Quincy Adams, Journals of the Continental Congress, and many historical works. *Recreations:* book and autograph collecting; golf and horseback riding. *Address:* c/o Morgan and Co., 14 Place Vendôme, Paris. *Clubs:* Royal Societies; Century, New York; Union, Odd Volumes, Boston; Union Interalliée, Paris.

Died 7 March 1941.

FORDHAM, Montague Edward, MA, FRHistS; FREconS; author; *b* 28 April 1864; *s* of Herbert and Constantia Elizabeth Fordham; *m* 1896, Sara Gertrude Worthington; two *s*. *Educ:* London International College; Trinity College, Cambridge. Lawyer 1886–1900; and concurrently lecturer on Social and Economic problems; Travelled 1892; Company director,

1896–1902; Director of an Arts and Craft Gallery in London, 1899–1908; Lecturer and writer on Social and Economic problems, 1907–14; Founder and subsequently Secretary to Land Club Union, 1907; served in British Red Cross and subsequently as a volunteer orderly in the hospital service of French Army, 1915–16; Government official, 1916–21; Reconstructor of Agriculture etc. in the devastated province of Drohicyzn, East Poland, 1922; Writer and Lecturer on Rural Problems since 1923; Council Sec. Rural Reconstruction Assoc., 1926–46. *Publications:* Mother Earth, 1907; A Short History of English Rural Life, 1916; The Rebuilding of Rural England, 1924; Britain's Trade and Agriculture, 1932; Monograph on The European Peasantry, 1600–1914, in Vol. V of European Civilisation, 1937; The Land and Life, 1942; The Restoration of Agriculture, 1945. *Recreations:* gardening and talking. *Address:* The Severals, Seer Green, Beaconsfield. *TA:* Fordham, Jordans. *Club:* Economic Reform.

Died 10 May 1948.

FORESTER, Francis William; b 1860; s of Henry William Forester of Somerby, Leicestershire; m 1894, Aline Laura, e d of Sir Powlett Milbank, 2nd Bart; one s three d. *Educ:* Eton. Served in 3rd Hussars; retired as Captain, 1891; was Lieut-Col West Somerset Yeomanry Cavalry, 1895–1900. *Address:* Hurdcott House, Salisbury. *T:* Wilton 36. *Clubs:* Naval and Military, Army and Navy, Royal Automobile.

Died 20 Sept. 1942.

FORMAN, Lt-Col Douglas Evans, CMG 1916; DSO, 1919; late RFA; b Edinburgh, 18 Sept. 1872; m 1918, Eunice Katharine Florence, d of late S. J. Fraser Macleod, KC. *Educ:* Edinburgh Academy; St Paul's School; RM Academy, Woolwich. 1st Commission in Royal Artillery, 1892; Captain, 1900; Major, 1909; Lt-Col 1915; served European War, 1914–18 (despatches, CMG); retired 1920; Army Remount Service, 1920–37. *Address:* Egerton Hotel, Buxton. *Club:* Naval and Military.

Died 13 March 1949.

FORMILLI, Cesare T. G.; Grande Ufficiale of the Crown of Italy; elected Professor of Arts by the Academy of Rome; artist, architect; b Rome; m Alice Eleanor, d of Morgan Morgans; two s one d. *Educ:* private tutors; Royal Academy of Arts, Rome. Appointed by the British Government as architect-contractor to the British section of the Turin Exhibition, 1911; appointed by the Italian Government as architect-contractor to the Italian Section of the Panama Exhibition, 1915; lectured on Art at the Stamford and Oakland Universities of California, also before the Royal Academy of British Architects in London; Royal Commissioner of the British section of the Fine Arts Exhibition, Rome, 1923; painted the ceiling of throne room at the Italian Embassy, London, representing Italy crowning the Arts; exhibitor at Royal Academy and Paris Salon; decorative artist of Brompton Oratory, London, also of the Middlesbrough and Leeds Cathedrals, etc. *Publication:* author and illustrator of The Stones of Italy and The Castles of Italy. *Recreation:* chess.

Died 8 Dec. 1942.

FORMOSA, Monsignor Canon John, BA, DD, JUD; late Senior Professor of Dogmatic Theology in the University of Malta; b 23 March 1869. *Educ:* University of Malta; University of Rome. First in order of merit both in Arts and Sciences and of Theology, thus winning the Government prizes of £20, and the £50 bequeathed by Marquis Bugeja for the first Theologian. Appointed in the Archiepiscopal Curia as Promotor Fidei; subsequently elected as Professor of Canon Laws at the Archiepiscopal Seminary; made a Lecturer of Canon Laws at the University; promoted a Canon of the Cathedral Chapter of Malta; examiner for Latin and Religious Doctrine in the Matric. Examination, examiner for Latin Literature in the Faculty of Literature

and for Dogmatic Theology in the Faculty of Theology in the University. *Publications:* A Latin Work, De Biblico Hexaemero; Publius in Latin verse, and other Latin poems; Italian works: I Fondamenti della Religione; Della Sacra Scrittura e della Divina Tradizione; Two Italian Pamphlets: L'Eucaristia e Malta, and L' Uomo e la Rivelazione. Essays: Il Sacrificio nella storia e nel dogma; Formazione del carattere della gioventù studiosa; La Madonna nel Soprannaturale e nell' Arte; Gesù Cristo nella Storia e nell' Arte; La Chiesa e xx Secoli di Storia; La Chiesa e la Civiltà; San Tommaso d' Aquino oracolo della Teologia; Un pellegrinaggio in Terra Santa; Un pellegrinaggio a Lourdes; Un pellegrinaggio per i Santuari di Spagna; La Svizzera e il Santuario di Einsiedeln; Orazione Panegirica: La Conversione prodigiosa di San Paolo Apostolo Patrono Principale di Malta; Orazione Panegirica: Il Provvidenziale Naufragio di San Paolo Apostolo in Malta, con l' aggiunta di annotazioni storiche su Malta. A Maltese work: a voyage from Munich to Oberammergau. *Recreations:* passes his summer holidays at Birzebbugia, sailing, rowing, fishing; spends one month in taking voyages in Europe. *Address:* 176 Strada Mercanti, Valletta, Malta.

Died 29 March 1941.

FORREST, George Topham; Superintending Architect of Metropolitan Buildings and Architect to the London County Council, 1919; retired 1935; o s of late George S. Forrest, Schoolmaster, Aberdeen; widower; one s. *Educ:* Aberdeen Grammar School and University. County Education Architect for the County of Northumberland, 1905–14; County Arch. for Essex, 1914–19; Past Fellow RIBA and Member of Council; Past Fellow Royal Society of Edinburgh; Hon. AIStructE; Member of Ministry of Health Committee for the Construction of Working Class Flats; Hon. Member of the British Engineering Standards Association; Member of the Steel Structures Research Committee of the Department of Scientific and Industrial Research. *Publications:* numerous papers dealing with the architectural work of County Councils, particularly Schools and Housing, and Lectures on various subjects, including the Early London Theatres with which Shakespeare was associated, The Rebuilding of Ypres, and The Architectural Development of American Cities.

Died 31 March 1945.

FORRESTAL, James; Secretary of Defence, Head of National Military Establishment, United States, 1947–49; b Beacon, New York, 15 Feb. 1892; s of James Forrestal and Mary A. Toohey; m 1926, Josephine Ogden; two s. *Educ:* Dartmouth College; Princeton Univ. With New Jersey Zinc Company, Tobacco Products Corp., 1915; William A. Read & Co., 1916; served US Navy, 1917–19; rejoined William A. Read & Co., 1919; Pres. Dillon, Read & Co., 1937–40; entered Govt service, 1940; Under Secretary of Navy, 1940–44; Secretary of Navy, 1944–47. *Address:* The Pentagon, Washington, DC. *T:* Republic 6700.

Died 22 May 1949.

FORRESTER, Peter; Director of Barclays Bank Ltd since 1920; Member of Manchester and Liverpool Local Boards of Barclays Bank Ltd; b 1864; s of Peter Forrester, Liverpool; m 1901, J. Meikle, d of Robert MacSymon, Knotty Ash, Lancashire; two s two d. *Educ:* privately. Commenced career in Bank of Liverpool, Liverpool; first Manager at Liverpool of Midland Bank Ltd; General Manager of The Union Bank of Manchester Ltd, 1902, Managing Director, 1916; Vice-Chairman, The Union Bank of Manchester Ltd, 1902, Managing Director, 1916; Vice-Chairman, The Union Bank of Manchester Ltd, 1937–39; Fellow of Institute of Bankers; Past President, Manchester Institute of Bankers; Vice-President, Cheshire Publicity and Industrial Development Council; Fellow of Royal Empire Society; Member of Council and Executive Committee, The Economic League (Lancashire and Cheshire Area).

Publications: Trade after the War; The Finance of the Cotton Trade, from Grower to Wearer; Banking in Cheshire; The Finance of General Merchandise; How the Banks help the Small Man in Business. *Recreations:* walking, motoring; interested in agriculture. *Address:* Kermincham Lodge, Holmes Chapel, Cheshire. *T:* Holmes Chapel 49; 39 Newton Road, W2. *Clubs:* Royal Automobile, Royal Empire Society.

Died 26 Nov. 1941.

FORSTER, Edward Seymour, MBE; MA (Oxon); FSA; Emeritus Professor of Greek, University of Sheffield; *b* 16 Dec. 1879; *s* of late Michael Seymour Forster, MA, BCL, of Woodhill, Crawthorne, Berks, and Elizabeth, *d* of George Humphrys of Ashcombe Park, Staffs; *m* 1907, Evelyn Beatrice, *d* of late John Taylor Davies; two *s* two *d*. *Educ:* Wellington College; Oriel College, Oxford (Scholar). 1st Class Classical Hon. Mods, 1900; 2nd Class Lit. Hum., 1902; Bishop Fraser Scholarship and Archæological Studentship, 1902; Student of the British School of Athens, 1902–04. Asst Lecturer in the University Coll. of N Wales, 1904–05; Lecturer in the Univ. of Sheffield, 1905–21; Prof. 1921–45; commissioned as temporary 2nd Lieut, 1915; on Active Service (attached General Staff Intelligence) with the British Salonica and Black Sea Forces 1915–19; Major, 1918 (despatches twice); Chevalier of the Serbian Order of St Sava. *Publications:* the Cyprian Orations of Isocrates (editor); The Speeches of Isaeus (Loeb Library); The Turkish Letters of Busbecq (translator and editor); A Short History of Modern Greece, 1941; contributions to the Oxford Translation of Aristotle, the Classical Review, the Classical Quarterly, the Journal of Hellenic Studies, etc. *Recreations:* field botany; walking. *Address:* Greatbatch Hall, Ashford, nr Bakewell. *T:* Bakewell 308; 28 Acol Road, NW6. *T:* Maida Vale 3786. *Club:* Authors'.

Died 18 July 1950.

FORSTER, Sir Martin (Onslow), Kt 1933; FRS 1905, DSc (London), PhD (Würzburg), FIC, FCGI; JP (Mysore); Research Chemist; *b* 8 Nov. 1872; *s* of late Martin Forster; *m* 1925, Elena (*d* 1941), *d* of late William Hall Haynes, of Cadiz, and *widow* of Horace P. Parodi, Barrister, Gibraltar. *Educ:* Dane Hill House, Margate; Finsbury Technical College; Würzburg University; Central Technical College. Salters' Company Research Fellow, 1894; Granville Scholar of the London University, 1899. Demonstrator, 1895–1902, and Assistant Professor of Chemistry, 1902–13, at the Royal College of Science, South Kensington; Hon. Secretary of the Chemical Society, 1904–10; Longstaff Medallist of the Chemical Society, 1915; Vice-President of the Institute of Chemistry, 1908–11, 1915–18; Convocation Member of Senate of London University, 1914–22; a director of British Dyes, Ltd, 1915–18; First Director of the Salter's Institute of Industrial Chemistry, 1918–22; Director, Indian Institute of Science, Bangalore, 1922–33; retired to Mysore; Treasurer, Chemical Society, 1915–22; Prime Warden, Worshipful Company of Dyers, 1919–20; President of Chemistry Section, British Association, Edinburgh, 1921; President of Indian Science Congress, 1925. *Publications:* contributions to the Journal of the Chemical Society. *Address:* Mysore City. *Clubs:* Athenæum, Savile, Savage.

Died 23 May 1945.

FORSTER-COOPER, Sir Clive, Kt 1946; MA, ScD (Cantab), FRS, FZS; Director of British Museum (Natural History), South Kensington, since 1938; Foreign Member of the New York Academy of Sciences; *b* 3 April 1880; *s* of John Forster Cooper and Mary Emily Miley; *m* 1912, Rosalie, *d* of R. Tunstall-Smith, Baltimore, Maryland, USA; two *s* one *d*. *Educ:* Rugby; Trinity College, Cambridge. Served on expeditions to Maldive and Laccadive Islands, 1900; Naturalist to North Seas Fisheries Commission Scientific Investigations, 1902–03; Expedition to the Seychelles, 1905, Fayum, 1907; took expeditions to Baluchistan, 1910 and 1911;

Director of University Museum of Zoology, Cambridge, 1914–37; Government war work on Malaria, 1915–18; late Reader in the Vertebrata; sometime Fellow of Trinity Hall. *Publications:* scientific papers in journals of Royal Society, Royal Society of Edinburgh, Indian Geological Survey, etc. *Address:* 8 The Vale, Chelsea, SW3. *T:* Flaxman 9843. *Club:* Arts.

Died 23 Aug. 1947.

FORSYTH, Andrew Russell, FRS, MA, ScD (Camb.), Hon. ScD (Dublin, Victoria, Oxford, Liverpool, Calcutta, Wales), Hon. LLD (Glasgow, Aberdeen), Hon. MathD (Christiania); Emeritus Professor, Imperial College of Science and Technology, SW; *b* Glasgow, 18 June 1858; *s* of late John Forsyth; *m* Marion Amelia (*d* 1920), *d* of late Henry Pollock. *Educ:* Liverpool College; Trinity College, Cambridge. Senior Wrangler, 1st Smith's Prizeman, 1881; Fellow of Trinity, 1881–1910. Professor of Mathematics, University College, Liverpool, 1882–83; Lecturer and Assistant Tutor, Trin. Coll. Camb., University Lecturer in Mathematics, 1884–95; Sadlerian Professor of Pure Mathematics, Cambridge, 1895–1910; Chief Professor of Mathematics, Imperial College of Science and Technology, South Kensington, 1913–23; FRS 1886; Royal Medallist, 1897; Member of Council Royal Society, 1893–95; Member of Council Senate of Camb. Univ., 1890–1910; Member of Treasury Committee on the Scottish Universities, 1909; President of Section A British Association (Toronto), 1897, (South Africa), 1905; President of the Mathematical Association, 1903–04, 1936; President of the London Mathematical Society, 1904–06; Hon. Fellow of the Royal Society of Edinburgh; Hon. Member of Manchester Lit. and Phil. Society, and of the Mathematical Society of Calcutta; Foreign Member of the Reale Instituto Lombardo, and of National Academy of Sciences, Washington; Corresponding Member of the Mathematical Society of Kharkow, and of the Reale Instituto Veneto. *Publications:* Treatise on Differential Equations (1st edit. 1885), and Solutions, 1918; Theory of Differential Equations, Part I 1890, Part II 1900, Part III 1902, Part IV 1906; Treatise on the Theory of Functions (1st edit 1893); Lectures on Differential Geometry (1st edit. 1912); Lectures on Functions of two or more Complex Variables (delivered in Calcutta), 1913; Calculus of Variations, 1927; Geometry of Four Dimensions, 1930; Intrinsic Geometry of Ideal Space, 1935; Editor of Quarterly Journal of Mathematics, 1884–1895; editor of Cayley's Collected Mathematical Papers, 1895–1898, and of Burnside's Theory of Probability, 1928; and mathematical papers in various transactions and journals. *Address:* Imperial College of Science and Technology, SW7; Bailey's Hotel, SW7. *T:* Frobisher 8131.

Died 2 June 1942.

FORSYTH, David, MD, DSc (Lond.), FRCP (Lond.), MRCS (Eng.); Consulting Physician to Charing Cross Hospital; Consulting Physician to Evelina Hospital for Children; late Senior Physician to the Psychological Clinic (Ministry of Pensions); Fellow, Royal Society of Medicine (Past President, Psychiatric Section); Member, British Psychological Society; International Psychoanalytical Association; Roger's Prizeman, University of London; *b* Greenwich, Kent, 24 Nov. 1877; *s* of late Alexander Forsyth, MD; *m* Kate (*d* 1940), *d* of late Frederick Neale; two *s*. *Educ:* Roan School; Guy's Hospital, London. *Publications:* Children in Health and Disease, 1909; History of Infant Feeding from Elizabethan Times, 1911; Psychoanalysis, 1913; Lectures on Medical Diseases, 1913; The Medical Inspection of Children (City of Westminster Health Society Annual Reports, 1912–1916); The Care of Children under School Age (Jl of State Medicine, 1916); The Rudiments of Character, 1921; Technique of Psycho-analysis, 1922; The Mental Health of the Child (Report of the Chief Medical Officer, Ministry of Health, 1925); Diagnosis of Neurotic Conditions in General Practice (Brit. Med. Jl

1933); Psychological Effects of Illness on Children (Lancet, 1934); Psychology and Religion, 1935, (2nd edit., 1936); The Consultant and Specialist in a State Medical Service (Medicine To-day and To-morrow, 1937); The Psychology of a Middle-aged Embezzler (British Journal of Medical Psychology, 1939); How Life Began, a Speculative Study in Modern Biology, 1939; Papers on Psychoanalysis in Proc. Roy. Soc. Med., Brit. Journal of Psychology, Psycho-analytical Review, etc. *Address:* 25 Weymouth Street, Portland Place, W1. *T:* Langham 3550.

Died 10 April 1941.

FORSYTH, Robert Sutherland, CMG 1933; Representative of Dominion of New Zealand on Empire Marketing Board and Imperial Economic Committee since 1925, and representative in United Kingdom of New Zealand Meat Producers' Board; Director of Imported Meat, Ministry of Food, Sept. 1939; *b* Dunedin, New Zealand, 1880; *s* of James Forsyth; *m* 1908, Margaret, *d* of Allan Hedley, Oamaru, New Zealand; one *s* two *d. Educ:* Dunedin. Chairman South Canterbury Chamber of Commerce, 1922–23; Adviser NZ Govt at Imperial Economic Conference, Ottawa, 1932; Pres. Brit. Assoc. of Refrigeration, 1934–35. *Address:* Morley House, 26 Holborn Viaduct, EC1; The Lyches, Hutton Mount, Essex.

Died 21 Aug. 1942.

FORTESCUE, Cecil Lewis, OBE, MA; MInstCE, MIEE; Emeritus Professor of Imperial College of Science and Technology and University of London; *b* 15 Jan. 1881; *e s* of late Lewis Fortescue of Barnack, Northants, and Bromsgrove, Worcestershire; *m* 1909, Mary Dorothea, 2nd *d* of R. T. Wright, Trumpington, Cambridge; one *s* one *d. Educ:* Oundle School; Christ's College, Cambridge (Natural Science Scholar); 1st Class Mechanical Sciences Tripos 1903. Two years' post graduate apprenticeship with Siemens Dynamo Works, Stafford; followed by one year on the staff at the same works; five years instructor in Electro-technics and Applied Mechanics at HM Torpedo and Gunnery Schools, Portsmouth; Professor of Physics, Royal Naval College, Greenwich, 1911–22; Professor of Electrical Engineering, Imperial College (City and Guilds College), London SW7. *Publications:* Wireless Telegraphy; several papers on wireless subjects before the Institution of Electrical Engineers and the Physical Society. *Address:* Gorseland, Keyhaven, Lymington, Hants. *Club:* Athenæum.

Died 22 Sept. 1949.

FORTESCUE, Brig.-Gen. Francis Alexander, CB 1911; CMG 1918; *b* 10 April 1858; 2nd *s* of late Captain Francis Fortescue, Scots Guards, and Katharine Frederica, 2nd *d* of Capt. A. Ellice, RN; *m* 1885, Mary Teresa (*d* 1935), *e d* of Henry T. J. Jenkinson, of Ower Fawley, Hants; one *d.* Entered Army, 1879; Capt. 1888; Major, 1895; Lt-Col 1902; Bt-Col 1905; Col 1907; ADC to GOC, Egypt, 1883–85; Military Secretary to GOC Egyptian Gendarmerie, 1886–87 (3rd Class Osmanieh); commanded 4th Battalion KRRC, 1902–06; General Staff Officer, 1st grade, South Africa 1908–09; commanded Devon and Cornwall Infantry Brigade, 1911–12; commanding Rifle Depot, 1912–14; General Staff Mediterranean Expeditionary Force, 1915; commanding Infantry Brigade, 1915–18; Adviser on Safety Services to Ministry of Munitions, 1918–22; served Afghan War, 1880 (medal, 2 clasps, bronze star); S Africa, 1881, 1896 (medal); 1899–1900 (despatches twice, Queen's medal four clasps); European War, 1914–18 (three medals, despatches twice); retired rank Brig.-Gen. 1918. *Club:* Brooks's.

Died 12 Oct. 1942.

FORTESCUE, Captain Hon. Sir Seymour (John), GCVO 1931; KCVO 1910; CMG 1900; CVO 1901; Extra-Equerry to HM since 1910; *b* 10 Feb. 1856; 2nd *s* of 3rd Earl Fortescue. Entered Navy, 1869; Commander,

1890; served bombardment Alexandria, 1882, and Egyptian War (Egyptian medal, Alexandria clasp, Khedive's bronze star); Eastern Soudan, 1885 (Suakim clasp); member of Naval Intelligence Department, 1891–93; Naval ADC to Commander-in-Chief in South Africa, 1899–1900 (despatches); Equerry-in-Waiting to King Edward VII 1893–1910; Serjeant-at-Arms House of Lords, 1910–36. *Publication:* Looking Back, 1920. *Address:* Friary Court, St James's Palace, SW1. *T:* Whitehall 6386. *Clubs:* Turf, St James', Orleans.

Died 20 March 1942.

FORTESCUE-BRICKDALE, Sir Charles, Kt 1911; JP Glos; barrister of Lincoln's Inn; a Verderer of the Forest of Dean; *b* 1 March 1857; *s* of late M. I. Fortescue-Brickdale of Lincoln's Inn, Conveyancing Counsel to the Court; *m* 1888, Mabel Beatrice (*d* 1944), *d* of G. L. M. Gibbs; two *s. Educ:* Westminster; Christ Church, Oxford; 2nd Class Lit. Hum. Called to Bar, 1883; Assist Barrister, Land Registry, 1888; Assistant Registrar, 1894; Registrar (title altered later to Chief Registrar), 1900; retired, 1923; served on (Sir John Dorington's) Departmental Committee on the Ordnance Survey, 1893, and (Lord Dunedin's) Royal Commission on Registration of Title in Scotland, 1907; Chairman Departmental Committee (1925) on Stewards' Fees under Law of Property Act 1922. *Publications:* Registration of Title to Land, 1886; The Practice of the Land Registry, 1891; Registration in Middlesex, 1892; Land Transfer in Various Countries, 1894; Parliamentary Report of 1896 on Registration of Title in Germany and Austria-Hungary; (jointly with William Robert Sheldon, barrister of Lincoln's Inn), The Land Transfer Acts, 1875 and 1897, 1899; Methods of Land Transfer, 1913; edited Sir Henry Hallam Parr's Recollections, 1917; (with Sir John Stewart Stewart-Wallace) The Land Registration Act 1925, 1927; article on Title to Land in Encyclopædia Britannica and on Ordnance Survey, Quarterly Review, Jan. 1895. *Address:* 10 Sheen Gate Gardens, SW14.

Died 20 Sept. 1944.

FORTESCUE-BRICKDALE, Eleanor, RWS; Member of the Royal Society of Painters in Water Colours; *y d* of late M. I. Fortescue-Brickdale, Barrister of Lincoln's Inn. *Educ:* Crystal Palace School of Art; Royal Academy Schools. Prize £40 for design for decoration of a Public Building, 1896; first picture exhibited at Royal Academy, 1897; pictures in permanent collections at Walker Art Gallery (Liverpool), Birmingham, Leeds, etc., stained glass windows in Bristol Cathedral, Brixham, etc. *Address:* 28 Palace Mansions, W14.

Died 10 March 1945.

FORTESCUE-FLANNERY, Sir James, 1st Bt *cr* 1904; Kt 1899; JP Surrey, Kent, Essex, and London; Lord of the Manor of Wethersfield and Patron of the Living; one of HM's Lieutenants for the City of London; MInstCE; Consulting Engineer; Director, Barclays Bank; *b* Liverpool, 16 Dec. 1851; *e s* of Captain John Flannery, Seacombe; *m* 1882, Edith Mary Emma (*d* 1936), *d* of Osborn Jenkyn; one *s* two *d. Educ:* Liverpool School of Science. Pupil at Britannica Engine Works, Birkenhead. Inspecting Engineer under Sir E. J. Reed; Ex-President Society of Consulting Marine Engineers; Ex-President Institution of Marine Engineers; ex-President Liverpool Shipbuilders' Guild; ex-President Junior Engineers' Institution; Associate of Lloyd's; Member of Technical Committee Lloyds Register; Brit. Comm. Brussels International Exhibition, 1897, and Milan Exhibition, 1906; MP (U) Shipley Division, Yorks, 1895–1906; Maldon Division, Essex, 1910–22. *Recreations:* cycling, riding, shooting, rowing. *Heir: s* Harold Fortescue-Flannery. *Address:* Wethersfield Manor, Essex. *T:* Shalford Green 219. *Clubs:* Carlton, Savage.

Died 5 Oct. 1943.

FORTEVIOT, 2nd Baron *cr* 1916; **John Dewar;** Bt *cr* 1907, OBE 1925; MC, TD; DL; Hon. Colonel 6/7 Black Watch; Director of John Dewar & Sons, Ltd; Chairman Distillers Co., Ltd; Extraordinary Director of Bank of Scotland; *b* 17 March 1885; *e s* of 1st Baron and Joan (*d* 1899), *d* of William Tod, Gospetry, Kinrosshire; *S* father 1929; *m* 1st, 1919, Marjory Heaton-Ellis, ARRC (*d* 1945), 2nd *d* of late Lt-Col Sir Charles Heaton-Ellis, CBE; 2nd, 1946, Muriel, *d* of late Lt-Col Sir Charles Heaton-Ellis, CBE; Wyddiall Hall, Herts, and widow of Major Alwyn Cavendish, The Rifle Brigade. *Educ:* Rugby; New College, Oxford (Oxford Eight, 1906). Served European War with Scottish Horse, 1914–18; Lord Provost of Perth, 1922–24; Brigadier, Royal Company of Archers, King's Bodyguard for Scotland. *Heir: half brother* Hon. Henry Evelyn Alexander Dewar. *Address:* Dupplin Castle, Perthshire. *Clubs:* Brooks's; Royal and Ancient, St Andrews.

Died 24 Oct. 1947.

FORTINGTON, Harold Augustus, OBE; *b* 19 Feb. 1890; *s* of William Henry Fortington, Ashridge, Ensbury, Dorset; *m* Edna Winifred (divorced 1940), *d* of Sir E. Jardine, Bt; one *d*; 2nd, 1943, Mary A. Crews, New York. *Educ:* King Edward's School, Birmingham. Ministry of Munitions, 1915–18 (OBE); Director-General Progress and Statistics, War Office, 1939–40. *Recreations:* fishing, flying. *Address:* Renfrew, Ontario, Canada. *Clubs:* Union; Racquet and Tennis, New York; Mount Royal, Montreal.

Died 29 Aug. 1944.

FORTUNE, Maj.-Gen. Sir Victor Morven, KBE 1945; CB 1936; DSO, 1916; *b* 21 Aug. 1883; *s* of late J. Fortune, Bengairn, Castle Douglas; *m* Eleanor, 2nd *d* of A. J. Steel Kirkwood, Lockerbie; one *s* two *d*. *Educ:* Winchester College; RMC, Sandhurst. Served European War, 1914–18 (despatches, DSO); War of 1939–40 (prisoner); commanded 1st Battalion Seaforth Highlanders, 1927–29; GSO 1st Grade 5th Division, 1930–32; Commander 5th Infantry Brigade, 1932–35; Major-General, 1935; Commander 52nd (Lowland) Division (Temp.), 1935–36; South-Western Area 1937; Commander 51st (Highland) Division TA, 1937; served War of 1939–45 (prisoner, 1940, liberated by American 1st Army, 1945); retired pay, 1945. *Clubs:* Army and Navy, Caledonian.

Died 2 Jan. 1949.

FOSBROOKE, Ven. Henry Leonard; Archdeacon of Lancaster since 1936; Prolocutor of Convocation of York, 1943; Chairman House of Clergy, National Assembly, Church of England, 1945; Church Commissioner, 1948; *m* 1905, Elizabeth Gardner, *d* of John and Mary Malcolm, Glasgow; two *s*. *Educ:* Clare College, Cambridge. Vice-President, Cambridge Union Society, 1905; BA, 1905; MA, 1912; Deacon, 1899; Priest, 1900; Rector of St Cyprian, Ordsall, 1906–13; Vicar of St Thomas, Pendleton, 1913–20; of North Somercotes, Lincoln, 1920–30; of St Michael-on-Wyre, 1930–38; of St Cuthbert's, Lytham, 1938–44; Rural Dean of Louthesk East, 1930; of Garstang, 1934–38; of the Fylde, 1939–44; Archdeacon of Blackburn, 1936. *Recreations:* shooting and fishing. *Address:* Warton Hall, West Lytham, Lancs. *Clubs:* United University; Union (Blackburn).

Died 10 March 1950.

FOSTER, Rev. Arthur Austin, MA; Rector of St Devenick's, Bieldside, Aberdeen, since 1910; Chaplain of Cluny Castle Chapel, Aberdeenshire, since 1908; Canon of The Diocese of Aberdeen and Orkney; Diocesan Librarian, Convener of Diocesan Overseas Missions Board; *b* Boston, Lincolnshire, 27 Dec. 1869; *m* 1896, Mary Ross Sutherland; one *s* one *d*. *Educ:* Moray House College, Edinburgh; University of Edinburgh. Schoolmaster Rochester and Edinburgh till 1901; Ordained, 1901; Curate at Workington and Maryport,

Cumberland, also Alnwick, Northumberland; Rector of Monymusk, Aberdeenshire, 1908. *Publication:* The Message of Robert Browning, 1912. *Recreation:* motoring. *Address:* The Rectory, Bieldside, Aberdeenshire. *T:* Cults 201.

Died 6 May 1942.

FOSTER, Sir Augustus Vere, 4th Bt *cr* 1831; *b* 31 March 1873; *s* of Maj. John Frederick Foster and Caroline, *d* of T. C. C. Marsh, Gaynes Park, Essex; *S* grandfather 1890; *m* 1894, Charlotte (*d* 1938), *d* of Rev. H. Ffolkes, Rector of Hillington, Norfolk, and *g d* of Sir W. Ffolkes, 2nd Bt; two *d*. *Educ:* Cheltenham College. Captain King's Own Norfolk Yeomanry during war. *Heir:* none. *Address:* Glyde Court, Ardee, Co. Louth.

Died 7 Nov. 1947 (ext).

FOSTER, Robert Frederick; Card Editor of the New York Tribune, New York Sun, Vanity Fair, Game and Gossip, etc; *b* Edinburgh, 1853; *m* Mary E. Johnson of New York. *Educ:* as an Architect and Civil Engineer, and practised until 1893, when he gave it up for literature. *Publications:* Foster's Whist Manual; Foster's Bridge Tactics; Foster on Bridge; Foster's Bridge Manual; Foster's Whist Tactics Foster's Duplicate Whist; Common Sense in Whist; Modern Whist; Whist at a Glance; American Leads; Common-Sense Leads; Whist and Its Masters; Foster's Encyclopædia of Indoor Games; Chess; Cinch; Poker; Hearts; Dice and Dominoes; Whist Inferences; Practical Poker; Call-Ace Euchre; Bidding No-Trumpers; Foster's Bidding Values; Foster's Bridge Maxims; The Bridge Player's Handbook; The Gist of Bridge; Foster's Skat Manual; Hoyle's Games, Autograph Edition; Five Hundred; Auction Bridge; Bridge Up to Date; Advanced Auction Bridge; Royal Auction Bridge; Nullos at Auction Bridge; Twenty-point Mah Jong; Foster on Mah Jong; The Laws of Mah Jong; Foster's Complete Pinochle, Foster's Complete Bridge; Foster on Auction; Auction Made Easy; Foster's Bridge Tactics; Foster's Russian Bank; Foster's Rotary Auction; Bridge for Beginners; also a philosophical work, The Coming Faith; and the novels, Cab No. 44; Not Guilty; numerous short stories in the magazines. He is also the Foster of the Pelman-Foster Memory System, and inventor of the Foster Fog-Signal. Inventor of the Foster Whist Markers and the Self-Playing Whist and Bridge Cards; the Pocket Card Player, etc.; originator of the eleven rule at Bridge and the no-trump bidding values. *Recreations:* golf, photography, and yachting. *Address:* 14th Floor, 135 William Street, New York.

Died 25 Dec. 1945.

FOSTER, Robert Spence, CMG 1946; OBE 1942; MA (Oxon); Brilliant Star of Zanzibar (3rd Class), 1943; Assistant Education Adviser to Secretary of State for the Colonies, Colonial Office, since 1946; *b* 11 June 1891; *s* of Myles Birket Foster, FRAM, FRCO, FTCL, and *g s* of Birket Foster, RWS; *m* 1929, Dulce Stella Amabel, *d* of late Mr Justice F. G. Gardiner, Judge President Cape Province, S Africa; two *s*. *Educ:* Magdalen College School, Oxford; St Edmund Hall, Oxford. Served European War 1914–18, Lt, King's Shropshire Light Infantry, Flanders and France (twice wounded); 1/3 King's African Rifles, 1917–19 (despatches); Supt of Education, Tanganyika Territory, 1922; Deputy Director of Education, Uganda, 1930; Director of Education, Zanzibar, 1939; Asst Education Adviser to S of S, 1943–44; Director of Education, Kenya, 1944–45. *Address:* Inglewood, Witley, nr Godalming, Surrey. *T:* Wormley 73.

Died 1 Sept. 1947.

FOSTER, William; JP; MP (Lab) Wigan Division since 1942; *b* 12 Jan. 1887; *m* 1911; two *s* one *d*. Parliamentary Secretary, Ministry of Fuel and Power, 1945–46. *Address:* 21 Newton Road, St Helens, Lancashire.

Died 2 Dec. 1947.

FOSTER, Sir William (Yorke), 3rd Bt *cr* 1838; CBE 1918; late Col RFA; *b* 1 April 1860; *e s* of 2nd Bt and Georgina, *d* of Richard Armit, of Dublin; *S* father, 1911; *m* 1885, Aileen Ethel, *d* of late Col Augustus Berkeley Portman; one *s* (*e s* died of wounds received in Great War, 1914) four *d. Educ:* Eton. Served South Africa, 1899–1900 (Queen's medal, four clasps). *Heir: s* Henry William Berkeley, MC [*b* 3 April 1892; *m* 1927, Janet Elizabeth, *d* of late Charles Bullen-Smith; one *s* one *d.* Late Major Northumberland Fusiliers]. *Address:* Priestwood House, Bracknell, Berks.

Died 14 June 1948.

FOTHERINGHAM, John Taylor, CMG 1916; Member of the Senate, Univ. of Toronto; Maj.-Gen. Canadian Militia; Maj.-Gen. CEF; ADMS 2nd Canadian Division, BEF; later, Director-General, Canadian Army Medical Service; Hon. Colonel, Canadian Army Med. Corps, 1924; *b* 5 Dec. 1860; *e s* of Rev. John Fotheringham, late of St Mary's, Ontario; *m* Jennie, *d* of George McGillivray of Whitby, Ontario; one *s* two *d. Educ:* University of Toronto—Arts, 1st class Honours in Classics; BA 1883. Trinity Medical College, Toronto; MD, CM silver medallist, 1891; MB Toronto, 1891; Hon. LLD Queen's University and University of Toronto, 1919; Fellow, American College of Physicians, 1923; Hon. Fellow American College of Surgeons, 1920; Fellow Royal College of Physicians, Canada, 1931. Assistant Classical Master, Upper Canada College, 1887–91; Physician on Consulting Staff of Toronto General Hospital and of the Hospital for Sick Children, Toronto; Professor Emeritus, History of Medicine, University of Toronto; Knight of Grace of the Order of St John of Jerusalem. *Address:* Airie House, 20 Wellesley Street, Toronto, Canada. *T:* Kingsdale 5390. *Clubs:* Canadian Military Institute, Toronto.

Died 19 May 1940.

FOUCHÉ, Leo, BA (Cape), DrPhil et Lett (Ghent); Minister of the Union of South Africa in the Netherlands and in Belgium, 1948; Chairman, S African Broadcasting Corporation, 1942; *b* 1880; *e s* of W. Fouché, Principal of Boys' High School, Robertson (Cape); *m* 1919, Ernestine, 2nd *d* of N. van den Berg, first Criminal Landdrost of Johannesburg; one *s* one *d. Educ:* Cape Univ.; University of Leiden; University of Ghent; University of Paris; and University of Berlin. Special service in Union Department of Defence, 1914–15; Professor of History, University of Pretoria, 1908; Professor of History, Witwatersrand Univ., 1934. *Publications:* Het Journal van Gijsbert Heeck; Die Evolutie van die Trekboer; The Diary of Adam Tas; Mapungubwe, etc. *Address:* Broadcast House, Commissioner Street, Johannesburg.

Died 19 March 1949.

FOUNTAINE, Vice-Adm. Charles Andrew, CB 1923; DL; *b* 1879; *s* of late Algernon Charles Fountaine of Narford Hall, Norfolk; *m* 1918, Louisa Constance Catherine, *d* of late Sir Douglas Maclean, of Maraekakaho, New Zealand. Naval ADC to the King, 1925–26; Rear-Adm. and retired list, 1926; Vice-Adm., retired, 1931; Lord of the Manor of Narford, Southacre and Newton. *Address:* Narford Hall, King's Lynn, Norfolk.

Died 24 March 1946.

FOWERAKER, A. Moulton, BA Cantab; landscape painter; *b* 1873; *o s* of Rev. E. T. Foweraker, Priest-Vicar of Exeter Cathedral. *Educ:* Exeter School; exhibitioner of Cavendish College, Cambridge, 1890; graduate of Christ's College, 1893, in Applied Science. RBA 1901–12. *Address:* c/o Lloyd's Bank, Swanage.

Died 14 Jan. 1942.

FOWKE, Sir Frederick (Ferrers Conant), 3rd Bt *cr* 1814; late Major Leics Imperial Yeomanry; *b* 13 May 1879; *s* of Frederick Gustavus Fowke, *e s* of 2nd Bt and Cecilia Eva, *d* of Edward Nathaniel Conaut, Lyndon

Hall, Oakham; *S* grandfather, 1897; *m* 1910, Edith Francis Daubeny, *d* of late Canon J. H. Rawdon; three *s* one *d.* Served with the Imperial Yeomanry in South Africa; Major Leicestershire Imperial Yeomanry, European War. *Heir: s* Captain Frederick Woollaston Rawdon Fowke, 2nd Derbyshire Yeomanry, *b* 14 Dec. 1910. *Address:* The White House, Kingswear, S Devon. *Club:* Cavalry.

Died 22 May 1948.

FOWLER, Sir Ralph Howard, Kt 1942; OBE; FRS 1925; MA; Fellow, since 1914, of Trinity College, Cambridge; Plummer Professor of Applied Mathematics in the University of Cambridge since 1932; Fellow of Winchester College; *b* 17 Jan. 1889; *e s* of Howard Fowler, of Glebelands, Burnham, Somerset; *m* 1921, Eileen Mary (*d* 1930), *d* of Baron Rutherford of Nelson, OM; two *s* two *d. Educ:* Winchester Coll.; Trinity Coll., Cambridge. Mathematical Tripos, Pt II, 1911; Rayleigh Prize, 1912; Adams Prize, 1925; Royal Medal of Royal Society, 1936. During War 1914–18, Capt. RM; Assistant Director, Anti-Aircraft Experimental Section, Munitions Inventions Dept; lately Stokes Lecturer in the University of Cambridge. *Publications:* Differential Geometry of Plane Curves; Statistical Mechanics; Statistical Thermodynamics (with Dr E. A. Guggenheim); papers on External Ballistics and Theoretical Physics. *Address:* Cromwell House, Trumpington, Cambs. *T:* Trumpington 222. *Club:* Athenæum.

Died 28 July 1944.

FOWLER-DIXON, John Edwin, FJI; Swedish Order of Merit; journalist, founder of the Athletic News Agency; *b* 3 Sept. 1850; *m* 1st, 1874, Rachel Sarah Elizabeth (*d* 1918), *d* of late William Fowler of Regent's Park, London, and Braybrooke, Market Harborough; three *s* one *d*; 2nd, 1927, Mary Helen Irene (*d* 1938), *er d* of Adam Kirk Ball, FSI. *Educ:* privately, in Suffolk. Present holder of forty miles' running record, 4 hours 46 mins 54 secs at Birmingham, 29 Dec. 1884. Ex-holder of fifty miles' amateur running record 6 hours 18 mins 26 secs, 1885; previously held record of 6 hours 20 mins 47 secs for same distance, 1884; fifty miles' amateur walking record, 8 hours 54 mins 40 secs, 1877; 100 miles' amateur walking record, 1877; President London Athletic Club, 1912; Vice-Pres. West London Lacrosse Club, etc.; member of Thames Hare and Hounds and other athletic institutions; Life Vice-President of Amateur Athletic Association, and assisted in its formation at Oxford, 1880; one of the British judges at Olympian Games, in Athens, 1906, Stockholm, 1912, Antwerp-1920, and Paris, 1924. *Publications:* Athletes and the War; verses, short stories, and articles on amateur sports and pastimes. *Recreations:* walking, cross-country running, golf, and lacrosse. *Address:* 5 Hillway, Highgate, N6. *Club:* Authors'.

Died 10 Oct. 1943.

FOX, Henry Benedict, CIE 1923; VD; *b* 1875; *m* 1925, Emily Anna, Auckland, NZ, 2nd *d* of late George Enderwicke Rose; one *d.* Chairman Surma Valley Branch, Indian Tea Association, and Member Assam Legislative Council, 1914–15 and 1919–22; served European War; Major, Acting Commandant, Surma Valley Light Horse, 1924; Member Legislative Assembly, India, 1931–33. *Address:* 55 Norfolk Road, Littlehampton, Sussex. *Club:* Bengal. Calcutta.

Died 11 Jan. 1944.

FOX, Sir John Charles, Kt 1921; JP Oxon; late Vice-Chairman of Quarter Sessions; Director, King's Lynn Dock Co.; *b* 29 May 1855; *e s* of John Fox, solicitor; *m* 1880, Mary Louisa, 2nd *d* of John Sutherland Valentine, CE; three *s* three *d. Educ:* Kensington Grammar School. Admitted a solicitor, 1876; member of the firm of Hare & Co., Agents to the Treasury Solicitor, 1881–91; Master, Chancery Division, 1891–1921; Senior Master, 1917–21; retired, 1921. *Publications:* Joint Editor of the

Yearly Practice of the Supreme Court, 1899–1908; General Williamson's Diary (for the Royal Historical Society); The Byron Mystery, 1924; The History of Contempt of Court, 1927; The Lady Ivie's Trial, 1929; Memoir of Percival Beevor Lambert, 1935; Handbook of English Law Reports, Part I; article, Contempt of Court, in The Laws of England; contributions to the Law Quarterly, English Historical and Modern Language Reviews. *Recreation:* walking. *Address:* Bridle Way, Goring, Reading. *T:* Goring 90. *Club:* Athenæum.

Died 21 March 1943.

FOX, Sir John Jacob, Kt 1944; CB 1938; OBE 1920; FRS 1943; DSc (Lond.); Fellow of Queen Mary College; Government Chemist; *b* 1874; *e s* of late Mark and Hannah Fox; *m* 1899, Amelia (Millie), *d* of Charles and Elizabeth Boas; one *s* one *d. Educ:* Royal College of Science; Queen Mary College. Appointed Chemist in Govt Laboratory, 1904; Past-Pres. Royal Institute of Chemistry; Past-Pres. Oil and Colour Chemists' Assoc. *Publications:* papers on physico-chemical subjects in technical and scientific journals. *Recreations:* swimming, golf. *Address:* Government Laboratory, Clement's Inn Passage, WC2. *Club:* Athenæum.

Died 28 Nov. 1944.

FOXCROFT, Miss H. C. *Publications:* Life and Works of Sir George Savile, Bart, First Marquis of Halifax; A Supplement to Burnet's History of my own Time; Life of Bishop Burnet (part author); A Character of the Trimmer (short life of first Marquis of Halifax), 1946; Verses appropriate to the War (privately printed); articles in the Historical, Quarterly, and Fortnightly Reviews, Scottish History Society Miscellany, Miscellany of the English Historical Society, Memorials of Old Wiltshire, Longman's Magazine, Rifleman, Quest, History; political pamphlets, articles, etc. *Address:* Innocks Lodge, Hinton Charterhouse, near Bath. *T:* Limpley Stoke 3125.

Died 6 July 1950.

FRAMES, Col Percival R.; *see* Ross-Frames.

FRAMPTON, Rev. Samuel, MA; Emeritus Minister of the Liverpool Old Hebrew Congregation; late Senior Jewish Minister of the Liverpool Community; retired 1932; *b* Portsea, Hants, 18 Aug. 1862; *m* 1894, Miriam Eva (*d* 1941), *e d* of late Rev. G. J. Emanuel, BA, Birmingham; one *s* one *d. Educ:* Aria College, Portsea. Minister of the Newcastle-on-Tyne Hebrew Congregation, 1886–91; sometime Lecturer in Hebrew to the Liverpool Board of Biblical Studies; Member of the Liverpool Education Committee; President of the Liverpool Hebrew Schools; Hon. Sec., Liverpool Jewish Board of Guardians since 1891; Vice-President of the Liverpool Port and Station Society; Founder of several Hebrew organisations of the city, etc. *Publications:* Joshua; An Annotated Hebrew Text, 1913; The Hebrew Scriptures and the Higher Criticism; contributor to the Commentary on the Prophetical Lessons in the Chief Rabbi's Edition of The Pentateuch and Haftorahs. *Address:* 15 Rosebery Avenue, Llandudno. *T:* Llandudno 7539. *Clubs:* Athenæum, Liverpool.

Died 4 July 1943.

FRANCE-HAYHURST, William Hosken; *see* Hayhurst.

FRANCIS, Francis, DSc, PhD; Professor Emeritus, University of Bristol, Foreign Correspondent of the Royal Academy of Medicine of Belgium; *s* of late Francis Francis; *m* 1910, Blanche, *d* of late Capt. Edward Montgomery Mason, 5th (Northumberland) Fusiliers. *Educ:* University of Liverpool and University of Erlangen. Assistant Lecturer in Chemistry, University College, Liverpool, 1895; Lecturer, University College, Bristol, 1896; Assistant Professor, 1903; Professor, 1906–36; Pro Vice-Chancellor, University of Bristol, 1919–31. *Publications:* Memoirs on chemical subjects, chiefly organic, published in the journals of the English

and German Chemical Societies; with J. M. Fortescue-Brickdale The Chemical Basis of Pharmacology, 1908; Notes on Inorganic Chemistry, 1921; Notes on Organic Chemistry, 1935. *Address:* Stuart House, The Royal Fort, Clifton, Bristol, 8. *Clubs:* Clifton, Bristol.

Died 14 April 1941.

FRANCIS, Grant Richardson, FSA; historian and novelist; *b* 17 Dec. 1868; *e s* of Attwell Francis, Swansea; and *g s* of Lt-Col George Grant Francis, FSA, Swansea; *m* Agnes Mary Baseley, Northampton; one *s* one *d. Educ:* privately. President British Numismatic Society, 1922–25 inclusive; Sanford Saltus triennial gold medallist of that body, 1926. *Publications:* The Silver Coins of the Tower Mint of Charles I; Jacobite Drinking Glasses; Old English Drinking Glasses, 1926; Scotland's Royal Line, 1928; Mary of Scotland (1561–1568), 1930; Romance of the White Rose, 1933; The Blood Feud, 1937, etc. *Recreations:* shooting, fishing. *Address:* Amberway, Guildford. *T:* 143.

Died 7 Dec. 1940.

FRANEY, John Sharman, BA; Barrister-at-law; Secretary of the Catholic Union of Great Britain, since 1919; *b* Burlingham, Norfolk, 1864; *o s* of late Rev. J. Franey, MA, The Grange, Ely and Emma, *d* of Robt Rushbrooke, of Hellesdon, Norfolk; *m* 1889, Mary Ethelind (*d* 1934), *d* of E. K. Harvey, JP, of Grey Friars, Norwich, and *g d* of Gen. Sir Robt Harvey, KCB, KTS; one *s. Educ:* Haileybury; Trinity Coll., Cambridge (BA). Studied in Paris and Berlin. Formerly assistant editor of the Fortnightly Review; Practises at the Chancery Bar; appointed in 1914 by Lord Bryce's Commission to take evidence of Belgian refugees, and subsequently to take the evidence of returned prisoners of war; awarded by HH Pius XI (1927) the Gold Medal of the Roman School of Christian Archæology; is Lord of the Manor of Lowestoft with Mutford and Lothingland in Suffolk. *Publications:* Hanson's Death Duties, 1915; and other legal works; contributions to Reviews, etc. *Address:* West Clandon, Surrey; 15 Old Square, Lincoln's Inn, WC2. *T:* Holborn 4104, Clandon 19. *Club:* Athenæum.

Died 12 June 1947.

FRANK, Dr Bruno; Schriftsteller; *b* Stuttgart, Württemberg, 13 Juni 1887; *s* of von Sigismund Frank und Lina Rothschild; *m* Elisabeth, *d* der berühmten Sängerin Fritzi Massary. *Educ:* Stuttgart Gymnasium; Haubinda (Thüringen); Universität in Tübingen, Universität in München, Universität in Strassburg und Universität in Leipzig. Unruhige Wanderjahre bis 1914; Kriegsdienst in Frankreich und Polen; dann zurückgezogene Jahre auf dem Lande in den bayerischen Bergen; nach seiner Verheiratung in München; seit dem Dritten Reich, ausserhalb Deutschlands; hat niemals ein Amt oder eine Stellung bekleidet; freier Schriftsteller von Anfangen. *Publications:* Erste Gedichte, 1905: Aus der Goldenen Schale. Erste Novellen, 1911: Flüchtlinge. Erster Roman, 1909: Die Nachtwache. Etwa dreissig Veröffentlichungen epischer, dramatischer und lyrischer Art: darunter die Romane: Trenck; Die Fürstin; Cervantes, 1934; Der Reisepass, 1937; Die Tochter, 1943; die Novellenbände: der Magier; Erzählungen; Tage des Königs; Politische Novelle; Aus vielen Fahren; der Gedichtband: die Kelter; die Theaterstücke: Zwölftausend, Perlen-Komödie, Das Weib auf dem Tiere, Die Schwestern und der Fremde, Sturm, im Wasserglas; Nina; Der General und das Gold. *Recreations:* Liebt tiefe Stille und ein gutes Gespräch zu zweien oder vieren, und die Lektüre von Flaubert, Turgenjew, Thomas Mann, Schopenhauer, Lytton Strachey. *Address:* 513 North Camden Drive, Beverly Hills, California.

Died 20 June 1945.

FRANK, Sir Howard Frederick, 2nd Bt *cr* 1920; Lt Grenadier Guards; *b* 5 April 1923; *er s* of Sir Howard Frank, 1st Bt, GBE, KCB, and Nancy Muriel (she *m* 2nd, 1932, Air-Marshal Sir Arthur Coningham, KCB), *e d* of John Brooks; *S* father, 1932. *Educ:* Harrow. Joined

R. Northumberland Fusiliers 1941; 2nd Lt Grenadier Guards, 1942. *Recreations:* shooting, sailing, fencing. *Heir: b* Robert John, *b* 16 March 1925. *Address:* c/o Mrs Robert Frank, Hepcote House, Findon, Sussex. *Club:* International Sportsmen's.

Died 10 Sept. 1944.

FRANKLAND, His Honour Judge Cecil J., LLB; Judge of County Circuit No. 13, 1933–36, No. 12 (Bradford, Halifax), since 1936; *b* 21 Oct. 1884; *s* of William and Mary Frankland; *m* 1916, Clare Hall. *Educ:* Leeds Church Middle Class School; Leeds University. Called to Bar, Middle Temple, 1915; served in Royal Artillery, Staff Captain Heavy Artillery, 17th Corps (despatches); joined North Eastern Circuit, 1919. *Address:* 38 Headingley Lane, Leeds, 6. *T:* 52728. *Clubs:* Athenæum; Union, Bradford; Halifax, Halifax.

Died 18 June 1942.

FRANKLAND, Grace Coleridge, (Mrs Percy Frankland); *b* Wimbledon, 4 Dec. 1858; *d* of late Joseph Toynbee, FRS; *m* 1882, Percy Faraday Frankland, CBE, FRS; one *s. Educ:* home; Germany; Bedford College, London. Authoress and journalist. Represented Bacteriology at Women's International Congress, London, 1899; elected member of Education Committee, 1903. *Publications:* various original researches on bacteria in scientific journals; Bacteria in Daily Life, 1903; joint-author of Micro-organisms in Water, 1894; Life of Pasteur, 1897. *Recreations:* music, gardening, travelling. *Address:* House of Letterawe, Loch Awe, Argyll.

Died 5 Oct. 1946.

FRANKLAND, Percy Faraday, CBE 1920; PhD, MSc, BSc, ARSM, FIC, LLD, St Andrews and Birmingham; ScD Dublin; DSc Sheffield; FRS; Fellow of Imperial College of Science and Technology; Professor of Chemistry 1900; Dean of Faculty of Science, 1913; Emeritus Professor, 1919; the University, Birmingham; *b* London, 3 Oct. 1858; 2nd *s* of late Sir Edward Frankland, KCB, JP, FRS; *m* 1882, Grace Coleridge Toynbee (*d* 1946); one *s. Educ:* Univ. Coll. School, London; Royal School of Mines; Würzburg University. Demonstrator and Lecturer on Chemistry, Royal School of Mines, 1880–88; Professor of Chemistry, Univ. Coll. Dundee, 1888–94; and in the Mason College, Birmingham, 1894–1900. Inaugurated monthly systematic bacteriological examinations of London Water-Supply for Local Government Board, 1885; formerly Examiner in Chemistry to London University, etc.; President of the Institute of Chemistry, 1906; President of the Chemical Society, 1911; Member of Admiralty Inventions Board, 1915; Member of Council of Royal Soc. 1903–05 and 1916–18; Vice-President, 1917–18; Davy Medal, 1919; Officer of the Order SS Maurice and Lazarus, 1919; 1915–18; Member of the Anti-Gas and Chemical Warfare Committees; Member of Royal Society Executive War Committee; Chairman Royal Society War Committee (Chemical Section); Chairman Royal Society Reserved Occupations Committee; Deputy Inspector of High Explosives (Birmingham Area). *Publications:* over eighty original Memoirs in scientific journals; Agricultural Chemical Analysis, 1883; Our Secret Friends and Foes, 1894; Micro-organisms in Water, 1894; Life of Pasteur, 1897; articles on Fermentation and Water in Thorpe's Dictionary of Technical Chemistry. *Address:* House of Letterawe, Loch Awe, Argyll.

Died 28 Oct. 1946.

FRANKLAND, Major Hon. Sir Thomas William Assheton, 11th Bt *cr* 1660; 15/19th Hussars; *b* 18 Aug. 1902; *e s* of The Baroness Zouche of Haryngworth, and of Sir Frederick Frankland, 10th Bt; *S* father, 1937; *m* 1st, 1931, Edna Maud (from whom he obtained a divorce, 1941), *y d* of Frederick Fox, JP, DL, Cheshire; no *c*; 2nd, 1942, Hon. Mrs Rous, *d* of late Capt. Hon. Edward Kay-Shuttleworth; one *s. Educ:* Royal Naval Colleges,

Osborne and Dartmouth. Joined Coldstream Guards, 1921; ADC to Lord Lloyd, High Commissioner of Egypt, 1925–26; transferred to 15/19th Hussars, 1926; Captain, 1936; Major, 1941; ADC to GOC-in-C, Southern Command, Salisbury, 1930–33. *Recreations:* hunting, shooting, cricket, golf. *Heir: s* James Assheton, *b* 23 Feb. 1943. *Address:* Monks Alley, Binfield, Berks. *Clubs:* Cavalry, White's.

Died 5 Aug. 1944.

FRANKLIN, Ernest Louis, JP, FSS; Fellow Royal Economic Society; partner in the firm of Samuel Montagu & Co., bankers and bullion merchants; *b* London, 16 Aug. 1859; 2nd *s* of late Ellis A. Franklin, partner in the same firm; *m* 1885, Hon. Henrietta Montagu, CBE 1950, *e d* of 1st Lord Swaythling, founder of firm of Samuel Montagu & Co.; three *s* two *d. Educ:* King's Coll. Sch., London. President for 50 years, now Vice-Pres. Home for aged Jews; Vice-Pres. Children's Country Holiday Fund (was Pres. of its Jewish Branch for 50 years); Vice-Pres. Jewish Home of Rest, etc. *Publications:* article on Foreign Exchange, 11th ed. Encyclopædia Britannica; article on Arbitrage, 14th ed.; articles chiefly on finance in British and American magazines and newspapers during a long period. *Recreations:* bridge and collecting works of art. *Address:* 50 Porchester Terrace, W2; Glenalla, Ray, Co. Donegal. *TA:* Elfranmont. *T:* Paddington 0212 and 2996. *Clubs:* Savile, Burlington Fine Arts.

Died 8 April 1950.

FRANKLIN, Brevet Col George Denne, CIE 1928; OBE 1919; Indian Medical Service, retired 1934; *b* 28 July 1877; *e s* of late George Cooper Franklin, MBE, FRCS, Leicester; *m* 1st, 1902, Dorothy Jessie Kemball-Cook; one *s* three *d*; 2nd, 1918, Ethel Janet Carver; one *s* (and a son, Sub-Lieut (A), RN, killed in 1940). *Educ:* Eastbourne College; King's College, Camb.; St Thomas's Hospital. KHS 1928–34; Mayor of Aldeburgh, 1934–35; JP, Suffolk, 1938. *Address:* Melbury, Aldeburgh, Suffolk.

Died 24 Dec. 1946.

FRANKLIN, Brig.-Gen. Harold Scott Erskine, CMG 1919; CBE 1942; DSO 1916; DL Kent; IA (ret.); *b* 25 Nov. 1878; *s* of late Surgeon-General Sir B. Franklin; *m* 1912, Kathleen Elizabeth, 2nd *d* of late Surgeon-Major W. Deane, IMS; two *s* (and two killed in action) one *d. Educ:* Marlborough; Sandhurst. First Commission, 1897; attached 1st Batt. Somerset LI 1897–98; joined 15th Sikhs IA 1898; served Tirah Expedition, 1897–98; China, 1900; European War, in France and Mesopotamia, 1914–18 (CMG, DSO, Bt Lt-Col); Afghanistan, 1919; Rebellion in Mesopotamia, 1920–21; retired, 1921; Zone Comdr Kent Home Guard, 1940–44. *Address:* 21 Waterloo Mansions, Dover, Kent.

Died 28 Feb. 1948.

FRANKLIN, Sir Leonard, Kt 1932; OBE; *b* London, 1862; 3rd *s* of Ellis A. Franklin, Banker, and Adelaide, *sister* of 1st Baron Swaythling; *m* Laura, *d* of W. Ladenburg, London; one *s* three *d. Educ:* King's College, London; Athenée Royale, Bruxelles. Called to Bar, 1894; senior partner in the firm of A. Keyser & Co., 31 Throgmorton Street, foreign bankers; keen social worker in the Jewish community; ardent Radical, and has fought North Paddington 1910 and 1918, SE St Pancras, 1922, Central Hackney, 1924, 1929, 1931; MP (L) Central Hackney, 1923–24; during the war was Local Government representative at Folkestone dealing with Belgian refugees (OBE, Officer of the Crown by the King of the Belgians); afterwards sent to France to report on the finances of the Hospitals; advocate and inventor of Percentage Proportional Representation. *Publication:* Percentage Proportional Representation, 1922. *Recreation:* social work. *Address:* The Grange, Goudhurst, Kent. *Clubs:* Reform, National Liberal, Eighty, Cobden.

Died 11 Dec. 1944.

FRANKLIN, Richard Penrose, MA; *b* Surbiton, Surrey, 28 Nov. 1884; *s* of S. Franklin, Solicitor; unmarried. *Educ:* St Paul's School, London (scholar); Pembroke College, Cambridge (scholar). 1st Class Hons Classics, Full Blue Athletics, 1907. Australia on business appointment, 1908; transferred to Schoolmaster, 1910; senior Classical Master, Sydney C. E. Grammar School, 1911–15; Headmaster Melbourne Grammar School, 1915–36; on leave with AIF (Lieutenant), 1917–19. *Recreations:* tennis, golf, fishing, motoring. *Clubs:* Melbourne, Melbourne; University, Sydney.

Died 12 Oct. 1942.

FRANKLIN, Col Will Hodgson, CMG 1933; CBE 1919; DSO 1916; Director of Companies; *b* 1871; *s* of William Franklin, Merchant, Liverpool; *m* Sarah (*d* 1941), *d* of Hon. George Knowling, St John's, Newfoundland; one *s* four *d*. *Educ:* Liverpool Institute. Settled in St John's, Newfoundland, 1891; engaged in export and import business; as Captain commanded and trained 1st Newfoundland Contingent, 1914; attached 1st Suffolk Regt Nov. 1914; served in France; Major, 1915; Lt-Col and commanded 6th Royal Warwickshire Regt 1916; Colonel 1919 (severely wounded; despatches twice, DSO, CBE); HM Trade Commissioner in East Africa, 1919–33; a Member of Imperial Reconstruction Committee, 1919, and of E African Inter-colonial Custom Conference, July 1921 (Chairman Nov. 1921, Dec. 1923, and March 1925 Conferences); Commissioner in London for HM Eastern African Dependencies', 1925–33; Colonial Reserve of Officers (Newfoundland). *Publication:* Mind and Method in Modern Minor Tactics, 1919 (with Brig. David Forster). *Address:* PO Box 1111, Nairobi, Kenya Colony; Satuini, Limuru, Kenya. *Clubs:* Muthaiga, Nairobi.

Died 22 Nov. 1941.

FRANKS, Col Kendal Fergusson, CIE 1943; DSO 1919; psc; Indian Army, retired; Assistant Director Recruiting, since 1940; ADR and Chief Civil Liaison Officer, since 1943; *b* 22 Sept. 1886; *s* of late Sir Kendal Franks, CB, and Jane Butt; *m* 1914, E. V. H. Catania; three *s* one *d*. *Educ:* Harrow; Sandhurst. R. Warwickshire Regt 1905–08; Zakka Khel Expedition (Medal); 117th Mahrattas (now the Royal Bn 5th Mahratta LI), 1908–34; served European War, 1914–18 (twice wounded, despatches, White Eagle of Servia. 3 medals); Royal Humane Society bronze medal, 1915; South Persia Expedition, 1918–19 (DSO, despatches); Staff College, Quetta, 1920–21; Brigade Major, Ferozepore Brigade, 1922–26; commanded Royal Bn 5th Mahratta LI, 1930–34; Gen. Staff Peshawar Dist, 1934–36; Recruiting Officer, Poona, 1936–40; Captain, 1914; Major, 1920; Bt Lt-Col 1929; Lieut-Col, 1930; Colonel, 1934; IRRO, 1940. *Address:* Poona, India.

Died 24 Dec. 1944.

FRASER, Agnes (Frances MacNab); author; *b* Halstead, Essex, 7 Dec. 1859; 4th *d* of late Rev. Canon Fraser, MA, and Mary Elizabeth, *d* of late Charles Parker, Springfield Place, Essex. *Educ:* at home. Studied Art at Heatherley's Studio, and at Slade School, London, 1882–84. Travelled to Algiers, 1889; Norway, 1891; travelled in South Africa, 1895; commissioned by British Columbian Government to write a book reporting on the resources of the province; travelled in British Columbia, 1897; in Morocco, 1901, and again 1902; visited Asia Minor in 1903. *Publications:* No Reply, 1888; Relics; Fragments of a Life, 1893; On Veldt and Farm in Bechuanaland, Cape Colony, the Transvaal, and Natal, 1897; British Columbia for Settlers, 1898; A Ride in Morocco among Believers and Traders, 1902. *Address:* Conyers, Churcham, Gloucester.

Died 14 Aug. 1944.

FRASER, Major Hon. Alastair (Thomas Joseph), DSO 1916; Deputy Lord Lieutenant, County of Inverness; Vice-Convener, County Council of Inverness; *b* 1 Aug. 1877; 4th *s* of 15th Baron Lovat; *m*

1915, Lady Sibyl Fraser, 5th *d* of 3rd Earl of Verulam; four *s* two *d*. *Educ:* Magdalen College, Oxford (BA). Served S Africa, 1901–02; European War, 1914–18 (wounded, despatches, DSO). *Address:* Moniack Castle, Kirkhill, Inverness-shire.

Died 14 Oct. 1949.

FRASER, Sir Colin, Kt 1935; mining geologist; Managing Director, Broken Hill Associated Smelters; Chairman, Electrolytic Zinc Co. of Australasia, Ltd; Chairman of Directors, Broken Hill South, Ltd; *b* New Zealand, 14 May 1875; *s* of John Cameron Fraser, Coromandel, Auckland, NZ; *m* 1913, Mary Helen, *d* of Patrick Butler Macnamara, Brockville, Ontario; two *d*. *Educ:* Auckland University College, New Zealand (MSc 1905). Was for some years in Dept of Geological Survey, NZ; went to London, 1911; to Australia, 1914. *Address:* 20 Albany Road, Toorak, Melbourne, SE2, Australia. *Clubs:* Australian, Melbourne.

Died 11 March 1944.

FRASER, Col Henry Francis, CMG 1917; DSO 1915; DL, Invernesshire; 21st Lancers; *b* 20 Nov. 1872; *s* of late John Fraser, Stratherrick, Inverness-shire, and Susan, *d* of General Webster, DL, JP, of Balgarvie, Co. Fife; *m* 1904, Anne (*d* 1947), *o d* of late Capt. Frederick Hardy, RN, JP, of Seafield, Co. Dublin; one *s*. *Educ:* Wellington College. 2nd Lieut 1895; Captain, 1901; Major, 1907; Lt-Col 1915; Col 1919; Temp. Maj.-Gen. 1920; ADC (extra) Viceroy of India, 1897; AMS to GOC Eastern Command, 1912–14; Assistant Adjutant-General, Egypt, 1920–24; served South Africa, 1899–1900 (despatches, Queen's medal 2 clasps); West Africa, Aro Expedition, 1901–02 (slightly wounded, despatches, medal with clasp); European War, 1914–18 (DSO, CMG, despatches, Legion of Honour); retired pay, 1924. *Address:* Wardlaw, Kirkhill, Inverness-shire. *T:* Drumchardine 18; 14 Ranelagh Avenue, SW13. *Club:* Cavalry.

Died 26 April 1949.

FRASER, Col Herbert Cecil, DSO 1918; OBE 1935; TD. Served European War, 1914–18 (wounded, despatches, DSO); commanded 4th Bn The King's Own Yorkshire Light Infantry, Hon. Col since 1939.

Died 11 Feb. 1943.

FRASER, Col Howard Alan Denholm, CB 1923; *b* 1867; *m* 1896, Edith Mary, *d* of W. D. Drake-Brockman; one *s* two *d*. *Educ:* Blundell's School. Royal Engineers; served Burma Expedition, 1891 (despatches, medal and clasp); European War, 1914–19 (despatches); Afghan War, 1919 (despatches); retired, 1924. *Address:* 32 Salisbury Road, Ringwood, Hants. *T:* Ringwood 404.

Died 14 Dec. 1948.

FRASER, Sir Hugh Stein, Kt 1911; formerly Partner in firm of Gordon Woodroffe, Madras; *b* 5 March 1863; 5th *s* of James Fraser of Mauritius and Newfield, Blackheath; *m* 1904, Fanny Louise, *d* of late John Bisdee Fawcett; two *d*. *Educ:* Blackheath Proprietary School; Rugby. A Member of Madras Port Trust for several years; additional Member of Council, Madras, 1910, 1911, 1914, 1915; Chairman Chamber of Commerce, Madras, 1910, 1911, 1914; Director of Bank of Madras; Sheriff of Madras, 1915. *Recreations:* shooting, fishing, golf, etc. *Address:* Selwood, Kemnal Road, Chislehurst, Kent. *T:* Chislehurst 17.

Died 29 Sept. 1944.

FRASER, Lt-Col James Wilson, CMG 1916; OBE 1919; DL and JP, Ross-shire; late 4th Batt. Seaforth Highlanders; late Maj. 1st Cheshire Regiment; *b* Farraline, Stratherrick, Inverness-shire, 31 May 1862; *s* of late Capt. John Fraser of Balnain and Farraline; *m* 1901, Edith, *d* of late Andrew Knowles of Swinton Old Hall, Lancs; four *s* two *d*. *Educ:* The College, Inverness; RM College, Sandhurst. Joined 1st Batt. Cheshire Regt 1882; retired as Major, 1903; joined 4th Seaforths, 1914, his two sons also joining Seaforth Battalions; served European War, 1914–19 (CMG); formerly owner of Balnain, Farraline, and Stronelairg, Inverness-shire; now of Leckmelm, Ross-shire. *Address:* Leckmelm, by Garve, Ross-shire.

Died 1 April 1943.

FRASER, Sir John, 1st Bt *cr* 1943; KCVO 1937; Order of Polonia Restituta, 1945; MC; MB, ChB, MD; ChM, FRCSE; FRSE; FRCP Ed (Hon.); Hon. LLD (Edin.); FACS (Hon.); FRAusCS (Hon.); Principal of Edinburgh University, since 1944; Member, His Majesty's Medical Household in Scotland; Member, Royal Company of Archers, King's Bodyguard in Scotland; Consulting Surgeon to Edinburgh Royal Hospital for Sick Children; Surgeon, Edinburgh Royal Infirmary; Consulting Surgeon, Royal Navy in Scotland; Member, Scientific Advisory Committee, Department of Health for Scotland, and International Society of Surgery; Hon. Consultant Adviser in Surgery, Department of Health for Scotland; Chairman, Medical Advisory Committee (Scotland); Hon. Fellow, American Surgical Association and Royal Medical Society, Edinburgh; Hon. Member, British Orthopædic Association; Member, Post-War Hospitals Committee (Scotland), 1942; Hugh Owen Thomas Lecturer Liverpool, 1934; Clubbe Memorial Lecturer, Sydney, Australia, 1935; *b* 1885; *s* of James Fraser, Tain, Ross-shire, and Margaret Mackay, Hilton, Tain; *m* Agnes Govane Herald, The Manse, Duns, Berwickshire; one *s* one *d*. *Educ:* Tain Academy; Edinburgh University; Graduated MB, ChB (with honours), Edinburgh, 1907; ChM 1910 (Lister Prizeman); FRCSE 1910; McCunn Scholar in Pathology, 1910; MD (gold medal) 1912; Freeland Barbour Fellow, 1914; Dawson Williams Memorial Prize, 1936. Captain RAMC, Special Reserve, 1914–18; Surgeon Edinburgh Royal Hospital for Sick Children, 1920–25; Assistant Surgeon, Royal Infirmary, 1919–25; Consultant for Surg. Tuberc. to Corporation of Edinburgh, 1922–25; Regius Prof. of Clinical Surg., Edin. Univ., 1925–44. *Publications:* Tuberculosis of Bones and Joints, 1914; Surgery at a Casualty Clearing Station, 1919; Surgery of Childhood, 1926; publications to surgical literature, especially on Tuberculosis, surgical shock, and surgical diseases of children. *Recreations:* golf and fishing. *Heir: s* James David, *b* 19 July 1924. *Address:* 20 Moray Place, Edinburgh; Forth Lodge, Gullane, East Lothian. *Clubs:* Athenæum; University (Edinburgh).

Died 1 Dec. 1947.

FRASER, John, BA (Cantab) MA Aber. and Oxon); Hon. LLD (Aber.); Fellow of Jesus College, Oxford, and Jesus Professor of Celtic; *b* Inverness, 19 Sept. 1882; *s* of John Fraser and Elizabeth Macdonald; *m* 1927, Frances Galloway Mordaunt; two *d*. *Educ:* University of Aberdeen; University of Cambridge; and University of Jena. Articles in English and foreign journals dealing with Classical and Celtic Scholarship and Comparative Philology. *Recreations:* golf, chess. *Address:* Jesus College, Oxford.

Died 18 May 1945.

FRASER, Sir John George, Kt 1924; CMG 1913; *b* 1864; *s* of late Alexander Fraser, Controller, Inland Revenue, Scotland; *m* 1888, Angela, *d* of late Edward Wallis, Berlin; one *d*. *Educ:* privately; Edinburgh Institution and University. Cadet Ceylon Civil Service, 1887; served therein, 1887–1923; retired from the post of Govt Agent, Western Province. *Address:* Villa Florenza, Denison Road, Launceston, Tasmania.

Died 21 July 1941.

FRASER, John Henry Pearson, DSO 1919; MC; MA, MB, LRCP; Hon. Consulting Physician, The Royal South Hants Hospital and Southampton Free Eye Hospital; *b* 1874; *s* of J. J. Fraser, MD; *m* 1908, Norah Sanders; one *s* one *d*. *Educ:* Jesus College, Cambridge (Exhibitioner); Addenbrooke's Hospital, Cambridge; St George's Hospital. Placed 1st in 1st part of final MB. Late

House Surgeon, House Physician, and Assistant Medical Registrar, St George's Hospital; House Physician, Victoria Hospital for Children, Chelsea; late Medical Referee Workman's Compensation Act for Home Office; Hon. Consulting Physician Royal South Hants and Southampton Hospital and Free Eye Hospital, Southampton; Member of Jersey Medical Society; served European War, attached 83rd Brigade RFA, 18th Division; 2nd in command 17th Field Ambulance, 6th Div.; Major, Jan. 1918; Lt-Col commanding 53rd Field Ambulance, 17th Division, May 1918 (DSO, MC and bar, despatches thrice, mentioned in the French order of the day, Croix de Guerre with Étoile); Hon. Surgeon, Hon. Life Member, and Associate, St John's Ambulance Association. *Address:* Les Augrès Manor Jersey.

Died 27 March 1949.

FRASER, Sir John Hugh Ronald, Kt 1932; CIE 1927; OBE 1919; *b* 15 March 1878; *m* 1906, Helen, *d* of General F. J. Davies, RE; two *d*. *Educ:* Haileybury; Pembroke College, Cambridge. Joined Indian Civil Service, 1902; Deputy Commissioner, Hazara, 1915; Judicial Commissioner, NWFP, India, 1923–33; retired, 1933. *Address:* Martlets, Fleet, Hants. *T:* Fleet 374.

Died 5 Dec. 1943.

FRASER, Sir (John) Malcolm, 1st Bt *cr* 1921; GBE 1923; Kt 1919; KStJ; Lord Lieutenant and Custos Rotulorum of Surrey since 1939; President, Surrey T & AFA; President, Surrey County Army Cadet Committee; *b* 24 Dec. 1878; *s* of W. J. Fraser, Hampstead; *m* 1907, Irene, *d* of C. E. Brightman of South Kensington; one *s* one *d*. *Educ:* Heidelberg Coll. Lieut attached Royal Naval Air Service, 1915; Lt-Comdr 1916; Comdr 1917; Captain, 1918, for special services, and requested by Admiralty to retain Naval Commission in connection with airships when other RNAS personnel was transferred to Royal Air Force; Deputy-Director of Airship Production at Admiralty, 1918–19, when over 100 airships were completed, including R34, the first airship to fly to America and back; formerly Assistant Editor The Standard; Editor of Evening Standard and St James' Gazette; Day Editor, Daily Express; Editor-in-Chief, Birmingham Gazette, Dispatch, etc.; Chairman of Embankment Trust Ltd; was Member Parliamentary Recruiting and War Savings Committees (1914); Adviser on Press Matters to Unionist Party, 1910; Reorganised Literature Department Unionist Party Headquarters, 1919; Honorary Principal Agent of Unionist Party, 1920–23; Vice-Chairman of Conservative Party, 1937–38; placed by the Government as its representative in charge of the production of the Government Daily Organ The British Gazette during the great strike of May 1926; High Sheriff of Surrey, 1937–38; V-L Surrey, 1938; DL 1936; County Alderman, Surrey CC, 1939–47; Hon. Colonel 67th Anti Tank Regt RA; Hon. Col 127th LAA Regt, RA (4th Queen's Royal Regt). *Heir: s* Basil Malcolm, Capt. RE [*b* 2 Jan. 1920. Eton; Cambridge. Serving MEF, CM Faud India since 1942]. *Address:* Brackenhill, Godalming. *Clubs:* Bath, Conservative, Constitutional, Royal Thames Yacht, Royal Motor Yacht; Royal Yacht Squadron (Cowes).

Died 4 May 1949.

FRASER, Kenneth; Vice Chairman and Managing Director of The Yorkshire Copper Works, Ltd, Leeds; *b* 22 Jan. 1874; *s* of Kenneth and Charlotte Fraser; *m* 1902, Alice Gertrude Woodall; three *s* two *d*. *Educ:* Quaker School, Stockton on Tees. Trained for a commercial career with Stockton Malleable Iron Co. Ltd (now part of South Durham Iron and Steel Co. Ltd); afterwards with Elliott's Metal Company Ltd, Selly Oak, Birmingham; Yorkshire Copper Works, Ltd, Leeds, since 1907; Vice President of Federation of British Industries (Chairman of Leeds and District branch); Fellow of Royal Society of Arts; Freeman of City of London. *Recreations:* curling, photography, philately, motoring, and the study of geography and peoples at first hand. *Address:* Tregullow, Oakwood, Leeds, 8. *T:* 66322. *Club:* British Empire.

Died 17 Feb. 1941.

FRASER, Leon, PhD, LLD; President, The First National Bank of the City of New York since 1937; *b* Boston, Mass, USA, 27 Nov. 1889; *s* of John Fraser and Mary Lovat; *m* 1922, Margaret M. Maury (decd). *Educ:* Trinity School and Columbia Univ., New York City. Instructor, Political Science, Columbia University, 1914–17; Major, US Army, 1917–19; Attorney-at-Law, 1919–24; General Counsel, Dawes Reparation Plan, 1924–27; practised law, New York, 1927–30; Director and Vice Pres., Bank for International Settlements, 1930–33; Pres. and Chm. of Board, Bank for International Settlements, 1933–35; Vice-Pres., The First National Bank of the City of New York, 1935–36; Director: General Electric Co., Internat. General Electric Co., United States Steel Corporation, New York Central Railroad Co., First National Bank, Federal Reserve Bank of New York, American Red Cross; Trustee: Mutual Life Insurance Co.; Acad. Polit. Sci.; Amer. Acad. in Rome; Amer. Hist. Assoc.; Carnegie Endowment for International Peace, Columbia University; New School for Social Research; Union College; Trinity School, NY; Pilgrims; British War Relief Society; Council on Foreign Relations. Grand Officer, Legion of Honour, France; Distinguished Service Medal, USA; Grand Officier Order of Leopold, Belgium; Off. Order of Saints Maurizio e Lazzaro, Italy; Officier d'Académie, France; Commander, Order of Saint Sava, Jugoslavia. *Publication:* English Opinion of the American Constitution, 1915. *Recreations:* riding, swimming. *Address:* 2 Wall Street, New York City. *TA:* Firstnat, New York. *T:* Rector 2–4000. *Clubs:* Century Association, Columbia University, The Creek, Knickerbocker, University, New York.

Died 8 April 1945.

FRASER, Malcolm, CVO 1935; OBE 1919; Chairman and Managing Director, Equitable Building and Investment Co. of Wellington, Ltd, since 1935; Member, Wellington City Council, 1938–47; Member, Board of Trustees, NZ Presbyterian Church, since 1921; *b* Inverness, 25 May 1873; *m* 1905; two *s. Educ:* Inverness. Joined NZ Govt Service, Land and Income Tax Dept, 1893; Accountant Public Service Superannuation Fund, 1908; New Zealand Govt Statistician, 1911–32; Commissioner for Unemployment, 1930–32; Under-Secretary, Department of Internal Affairs, 1932–35; devised and carried out system of ballot under Military Service Act, 1916–19 (OBE); Manager New Zealand tour of Duke of Gloucester, 1934–35 (CVO); Jubilee Medal, 1935. *Address:* 29 Rawhiti Terrace, Kelburn, Wellington, W1, NZ.

Died 29 Nov. 1949.

FRASER, Sir Malcolm; *see* Fraser, Sir J. M.

FRASER, Rt Hon. Peter, PC 1940; CH 1945; MHR for Wellington Central, 1918 (Electorate changed to Brooklyn, 1946); *b* Fearn, Ross-shire, Scotland, 1884; *m* (wife *d* 1945); no *c. Educ:* Board School. Local officer Liberal Party. Joined ILP in London, 1908; came to New Zealand, 1910; prominent positions in Labour Movement; Minister of Education, Health, Marine and Police, NZ, 1935–40; Minister i/c Police; Prime Minister of New Zealand, 1940–49; Minister of External Affairs and Minister of Island Territories, 1943–49; Minister of Maori Affairs, 1946–49. Attended Imperial War Council, London, and visited Western Front, Europe, as actg Prime Minister, 1939; attended meetings UK War Cabinet, 1941; visited USA, 1942; signed Canberra Pact, 1943; New Zealand delegate to Empire Parliamentary Association Conference, 1935; attended various Prime Ministers' Conferences; led NZ deleg. at San Francisco Conf., 1945, at first meeting of UN

Assembly, 1946, and at 3rd session, 1948; member of Wellington City Council, 1919–23 and 1933–36; of Wellington Harbour Board, 1933–38. Hon. LLD, Aberdeen Univ., 1941 and Univ. of Ireland, 1948. Holder of Special Grand Cordon of Order of Brilliant Star (China), 1947. Freedom of Cities of Aberdeen, Glasgow, Inverness, Edinburgh, London, Derby, Tain, Dingwall, Swansea. *Address:* 66 Harbour View Road, Northland, Wellington, NZ.

Died 12 Dec. 1950.

FRASER, William Donald; Headmaster, Grammar School, Burton-upon-Trent, since 1935; *b* 12 Oct. 1890; *s* of Donald Fraser and Christina Scott Thomson; *m* 1929, Ethel Mary McKay; one *d. Educ:* Emmanuel College, Cambridge; Glasgow University. Master, Grammar School, Batley, 1916–21; Perse School, Cambridge, 1922–28; Headmaster Grammar School, Barrow-in-Furness, 1928–35. *Recreations:* Scouting, camping. *Address:* Lynmoor, Stapenhill, Burton-upon-Trent. *T:* Burton 3172.

Died 10 Nov. 1941.

FRASER-SIMSON, Harold; composer; *b* 1878; *e s* of Arthur Theodore Simson and Catherine Fraser, of Reelig; *m* Cicely Devenish. *Educ:* Charterhouse; King's College; France. Formerly in the City; Chevalier of the Légion d'Honneur. *Publications:* has composed music of Bonita, 1911; The Maid of the Mountains, 1917; A Southern Maid, 1917; Our Peg, 1919; Missy Joe, 1921; Head over Heels, 1923; Our Nell, 1924; The Street Singer, 1924; Betty in Mayfair, 1925; Toad of Toad Hall, 1930; Ballets: A Venetian Wedding, 1926; The Nightingale and the Rose, 1927; 6 vols of When We were very Young songs, with A. A. Milne; a volume of songs from Alice in Wonderland, 1932; also a number of songs, part-songs, etc. *Recreations:* shooting, fishing, tennis, golf. *Address:* Dalcross Castle, Croy, Invernessshire. *TA:* Dalcross, Croy. *T:* Croy 8. *Clubs:* Garrick, Richmond Golf.

Died 19 Jan. 1944.

FRAZER, Hon. Sir Francis Vernon, Kt 1935; Chairman of New Zealand War Pensions Appeal Board since 1940; Deputy Chairman of Executive Commission of Agriculture, NZ, since 1940; Transport Appeal Authority and Industrial Appeal Authority since 1941; *b* 1880; *s* of John Dawson Frazer, Civil Servant, Dunedin, NZ; *m* 1905, Nina Jessie Black; two *s* one *d. Educ:* Nelson College; Otago and Canterbury University Colleges. LLB 1905; BA 1909; MA (honours in political science), 1910. Admitted barrister and solicitor, 1906; practised at Christchurch, NZ, 1907–11; Stipendiary Magistrate, 1911–20; Chairman Public Service Board of Appeal, 1918; Assistant Public Service Commissioner, 1920; Judge, Court of Arbitration, NZ, 1921–35; Temporary Judge Supreme Court, 1928–29; Chairman Transport Appeal Board, NZ, 1932–34; Chairman, Royal Commission for Dairying Industry, 1934; Chairman NZ School of Agriculture, 1940–43; Member of Senate of University of NZ, 1940–43. *Address:* 19 Portland Crescent, Wellington, N1, NZ. *Clubs:* Wellesley, Wellington, NZ.

Died 10 May 1948.

FRAZER, Sir James (George), Kt 1914; OM 1925; FRS 1920; Fellow of Trinity College, Cambridge; of the Middle Temple, Barrister-at-law and Hon. Bencher, 1931; Hon. Freeman of the city of Glasgow, 1932; Hon. DCL Oxford; Hon. LLD Glasgow and St Andrews; Hon. LittD Cambridge, Durham, and Manchester; PhD Athens; Doctor Honoris Causa of the Universities of Paris and Strasbourg; Fellow of the British Academy; Hon. Fellow of the Royal Society of Edinburgh; Associate Member of the Institut de France; Commandeur de la Légion d'Honneur; Commander of the Order of Leopold (Belgium); Corresponding Member of the Prussian Academy of Science; Extraordinary Member of the Royal Netherlands

Academy of Science; Zaharoff Lecture at Oxford on Condorcet, Feb. 1933; *b* Glasgow, 1 Jan. 1854; *m* 1896, Mrs Lilly Grove, author. *Educ:* Larchfield Academy, Helensburgh; Glasgow Univ.; Trinity College, Cambridge (Scholar). *Publications:* a revised edition of Long's Sallust, 1884; Totemism, 1887; The Golden Bough, 1890; 2nd ed. 1900; Passages of the Bible chosen for their Literary Beauty and Interest, 1895 (2nd ed. 1909; pocket edition 1927); Pausanias's Description of Greece, translated with a commentary, 1898; 2nd ed. 1913; Pausanias and other Greek Sketches, 1900; Lectures on the Early History of the Kingship, 1905; Adonis, Attis, Osiris, Studies in the History of Oriental Religion, 1906; 2nd ed. 1907; 3rd ed. 1914; Questions on the Customs, Beliefs, and Languages of Savages, 1907; The Scope of Social Anthropology, 1908; Psyche's task, a Discourse concerning the Influence of Superstition on the Growth of Institutions, 1909; 2nd ed. 1913; Totemism and Exogamy, 1910, re-issue, 1935; The Magic Art and the Evolution of Kings, 1911; Taboo and the Perils of the Soul, 1911; The Dying God, 1911; Letters of William Cowper, chosen and edited with a memoir and a few notes, 1912; Spirits of the Corn and of the Wild, 1912; The Belief in Immortality and the Worship of the Dead, vol. i 1913, vol. ii 1922, vol. iii 1924; The Scapegoat, 1913; Balder the Beautiful, 1913; Essays of Joseph Addison, chosen and edited with a preface and a few notes, 1915; The Golden Bough, vol. xii, Bibliography and General Index, 1915; Folk-lore in the Old Testament, 1918; Sir Roger de Coverley, and other literary pieces, 1920; Apollodorus, with an English translation, 1921; The Golden Bough, abridged edition, 1922; Folk-lore in the Old Testament, abridged edition, 1923; Sur Ernest Renan, 1923; The Worship of Nature, vol. i, 1926; The Gorgon's Head, and other literary pieces, 1927; Man, God, and Immortality, 1927; The Fasti of Ovid, 5 vols, 1929; Myths of the Origin of Fire, 1930; The Growth of Plato's Ideal Theory, 1930; Garnered Sheaves: Essays, Addresses, and Reviews, 1931; Lecture on Condorcet, 1933; The Fear of the Dead in Primitive Religion, 1933, Vol. ii, 1934, Vol. iii 1936; Creation and Evolution in Primitive Cosmogonies, 1935; Aftermath, a Supplement to the Golden Bough, 1936; Totemica, a Supplement to Totemism and Exogamy, 1937; Greece and Rome: a Selection from the Works of Sir James George Frazer, OM, 1937; Anthologia Anthropologica, a Selection of Passages for the Study of Social Anthropology, Vol. I Africa and Madagascar, 1938, Vol. II Australasia, 1939, Vol. III Asia and Europe, 1939, Vol. IV America, 1939. *Address:* Trinity College, Cambridge.

Died 7 May 1941.

FRAZER, John Ernest Sullivan, DSc, FRCS; Professor Emeritus in University of London, 1942; *b* London, 1870; *s* of late J. Frazer; *m* Violet Lowder, *d* of late Dr J. T. Jacques, Leicester; one *s*. *Educ:* Dulwich; St Bartholomew's Hospital. Holds several athletic cups and medals; after qualifying, spent seven or eight years in London and provincial hospitals; health injured by post-mortem wound; took up Anatomy as speciality, 1900; Demonstrator at St George's Hospital; transferred to King's College, 1905; Lecturer, St Mary's Hospital, from 1911 (retired); Prof. of Anatomy, University of London, 1914–41; Hunterian Professor, RCS, 1915–16; Harveian Lecturer, 1924; Ex-President and Member of Council, Anatomical Society; formerly Examiner Universities of London, Durham, Oxford, and Cambridge, and Primary FRCS; acting as OP Surgeon during war of 1914–18. *Publications:* Anatomy of Human Skeleton (4th ed. 1940); Manual of Embryology, 2nd ed. 1940; Practical Anatomy (with Dr R. Robbins); numerous papers, mainly Embryological in Journal of Anatomy and other Journals; editor of Buchanan's Anatomy. *Recreations:* reading and the less violent forms of exercise. *Address:* 8 Clydesdale Road, W11. *Club:* Royal Societies.

Died 15 April 1946.

FRAZER, Robert; American Minister to El Salvador since 1937; *b* Philadelphia, 8 Dec. 1878; *s* of Robert Frazer (Civil and Mining Engineer; president of railway) and Elizabeth Matilda McKibbin; *m* 1923, Mrs Edward William Howard (née Olivia Lansdale), San Mateo, California. *Educ:* Schools in Philadelphia and Germany; Massachusetts Institute of Technology, Boston. With banking firm in Porto Rico, 1899–1901; engaged in sugar-cane planting in Porto Rico, 1901–08; Consul at Valencia, Spain, 1909–12; at Malaga, Spain, 1912–14; at Bahia, Brazil, 1914–16; at Kobe, Japan, 1916–20; Consul-General at Large (Inspector), 1920–24; Consul-General at Zurich, Switzerland, 1924–25; Inspecting Consul-General in Far East, 1925–27; Consul-General at Calcutta, India, 1927–30; at Mexico City, 1930–32; at London, 1932–37. *Recreations:* golf, motoring. *Address:* American Legation, San Salvador, El Salvador; c/o Department of State, Washington, DC, USA. *TA:* American Minister, San Salvador. *T:* San Salvador 1077. *Clubs:* St James's; St Anthony, New York; Metropolitan, Washington.

Died 8 April 1947.

FREAKE, Sir Frederick Charles Maitland, 3rd Bt *cr* 1882; *b* 7 March 1876; *s* of 2nd Bt and Frederica (*d* 1932), *d* of Col F. T. Maitland, Holywich, Sussex; *S* father, 1920; *m* 1902, Alison, (*d* 1935), *d* of late Christopher Ussher of Eastwell, Co. Galway; one *s*. Sheriff of Warwickshire, 1939. *Heir:* *s* Charles Arland Maitland [*b* 13 Oct. 1904; *m* 1929, Claire M, *d* of H. T. S. Green, Hewlett, Long Island, USA; one *d*. Cantorist House, Childrey, Berks]. *Address:* Halford Manor, Shipston-on-Stour, Warwicks.

Died 22 Dec. 1950.

FREELAND, Maj.-Gen. Sir Henry Francis Edward, KCIE 1919; CB 1917; MVO 1911; DSO 1916; *b* 29 Dec. 1870; *m* 1897, Ethel Louise, *d* of Col T. Malcolm Walker, RA; one *s* three *d*. Entered RE 1891; Capt. 1902; Maj. 1911; Lt-Col 1915; Bt Col 1916; retired on Indian Pension, 1920; served Chitral, 1895 (medal with clasp); China Expeditionary Force, 1901–02; European War, 1914–17 (despatches eight times, DSO, CB); Honorary Associate The Priory of St John of Jerusalem; Officer Legion of Honour conferred by General Joffre personally. *Address:* The Malt House, Nayland, Suffolk. *T:* Nayland 254.

Died 29 March 1946.

FREELAND, Col John Cavendish, CB 1929; CBE 1925; *b* Charlottetown, Prince Edward Island, 22 Jan. 1877; 3rd *s* of Col R. G. Freeland; *m* 1909, Jeanie Wynyfryd, *d* of Jonathan Marshall, Traquair, Yelverton, S Devon; one *s*. *Educ:* Fauconberg Grammar School; Royal Military College, Sandhurst. 1st Commission, 1897; entered Indian Army (35th Sikhs), 1898; Lieutenant, 1899; Captain, 1906; Major, 1915; Brevet Lieutenant-Colonel, 1918; Substantive Lieutenant-Colonel, 1921; Colonel, 1922; served European War, 1914–18, France and Flanders and Mesopotamia (despatches four times, Bt Lt-Col); Afghanistan, NWF, 1919; AAG Army Headquarters, India, 1923–27; Staff-Officer, Military Department, India Office (GSO1), 1927–31; retired, 1931. *Address:* Playford, near Ipswich, Suffolk. *T:* Kesgrave 59.

Died 19 Sept. 1944.

FREELING, Sir Charles Edward Luard, 9th Bt *cr* 1828; *b* 1858; *s* of late Charles Rivers Freeling, 4th *s* of 1st Bt, and Amelia, *d* of Rev. Edward Luard; *S* cousin 1927; *m* 1913, Ethel Amy, *d* of late Iltid Nicholl. *Heir:* none. *Address:* Beenham Lodge, Reading.

Died 15 March 1941 (ext).

FREEMAN, Rev. Herbert Bentley, MA; Canon Residentiary in Bristol Cathedral, 1924–43, emeritus since 1943; *b* Uppingham, 1 Oct. 1855; *e s* of Frederick John Freeman, Vicar of Manton, Rutland (1st *cousin* of Prof. E. A. Freeman, Oxford, historian), and Mary

Cecilia Brown, descended from Dr Richard Bentley, Master of Trinity College, Cambridge; *m* 1896, Ida, *e d* of Prebendary J. H. Cardwell, Rector, St Anne's, Soho; one *s* (killed Menin Road, 1917), one *d*. *Educ*: Uppingham School; Trinity College, Oxford; 2nd Class, Classical Mods. Clerical work in Oxford (St Mary the Virgin); Christ Church, Bath; Algiers (Chaplain); St Anne's, Soho (Assistant-Curate); Vicar of Burton-on-Trent, 1899–1924; Rural Dean of Tutbury, 1903–24. *Recreations*: reading and being read to. *Address*: Bentley, 7 Clifton Hill, Bristol, 8. *T*: Bristol 34647.

Died 2 March 1950.

FREEMAN, Rt Rev. James Edward, DD, LLD, STD, DCL; Bishop of Washington since 1923; *b* 24 July 1866; *s* of Henry and Mary Morgan; *m* 1890; one *s* one *d*. *Educ*: Public School and by private tutors. Rector of St Andrew's Church, Yonkers, NY, 1894–1910; St Mark's Church, Minneapolis, 1910–21; Epiphany Church, Washington, 1921–23. *Publications*: Themes in Verse; If not the Saloon, What?; Every-day Religion; The Man and the Master; The Ambassador (Yale Lectures) Messages of Assurance; The Christ of the Byways. *Address*: Bishop's House, Washington, DC, USA. *T*: Woodley 0948. *Clubs*: Chevy Chase, Cosmos, Washington; Yale, New York.

Died 6 June 1943.

FREEMAN, Sir Ralph, Kt 1947; MInstCE, MAmSocCE, FCGI; Senior Partner Freeman Fox and Partners, Consulting Engineers; *b* 27 Nov. 1880; 3rd *s* of George James Freeman and Edith Henderson; *m* Mary, 2nd *d* of Joseph Lines and Jane Fitzhenry; three *s* one *d*. *Educ*: Aske's School, Hampstead; Central Technical Coll., Kensington (Siemen's Scholar, Siemen's Medal). Former Member: of Royal Fine Art Commission; of Council, Inst. Civil Engineers; Hon. Fellow of Imperial College of Science; Past Pres. Institute of Welding; Baker Medal, Telford Medal, Institution of Civil Engineers; Consulting Engineer, Sydney Harbour Bridge, Alfred Beit, Birchenough and Otto Beit Bridges, Rhodesia. *Publication*: Design or Sydney Harbour Bridge (InstCE Proceedings). *Address*: 68 Victoria Street, Westminster, SW1; Graden, Hendon Avenue, N3. *TA*: Traction, So-west, London. *T*: Victoria 9254. *Clubs*: Athenæum, Union.

Died 11 March 1950.

FREEMAN, Richard Austin; author; *b* 1862; *y s* of late Richard Freeman; *m* 1887, Annie Elizabeth, *d* of late Thomas Edwards; two *s*. *Educ*: various private schools; Middlesex Hospital Medical College. Entered Middlesex Hospital, 1880; Qualified, MRCS Eng. LSA Lond. 1886; House Physician, Middlesex Hospital, 1886; Assistant Colonial Surgeon, Gold Coast Colony, 1887; Medical Officer, Surveyor and Naturalist to the Expedition to Ashanti and Bontuku, 1889; Anglo-German Boundary Commissioner, 1890; invalided, 1891; Acting Surgeon in charge (temporary) of Throat and Ear Department, Middlesex Hospital, *circ*. 1892; Acting Deputy Medical Officer Holloway Prison, *circ*. 1901; Acting Assistant Medical Officer of Port of London, 1904; engaged in authorship until 1914; joined RAMC, TF; commanded 4th line 1st, 2nd and 3rd Home Counties Field Ambulances, 1916–17; brought to notice of S of S for War, 1918; placed on retired list, 1922; Freeman of the Society of Apothecaries of London, 1927; Elected to the Livery, 1929. *Publications*: Travels and Life in Ashanti and Jaman, 1898; The Golden Pool, 1905; The Red Thumb Mark, 1907; John Thorndyke's Cases, 1909; The Eye of Osiris, 1911; The Mystery of 31 New Inn, 1912; The Singing Bone, 1912; The Unwilling Adventurer, 1913; A Silent Witness, 1914; The Exploits of Danby Croker, 1916; The Great Portrait Mystery, 1918; A Savant's Vendetta, 1920; Social Decay and Regeneration, 1921; Helen Vardon's Confession, 1922; The Cat's Eye, 1923; Dr Thorndyke's Case Book, 1923; The Mystery of Angelina Frood, 1924; The Puzzle Lock, 1925; The Shadow of the Wolf,

1925; The D'Arblay Mystery, 1926; The Magic Casket, 1927; The Surprising Experiences of Mr Shuttlebury Cobb, 1927; A Certain Dr Thorndyke, 1927; Flighty Phyllis, 1928; As a Thief in the Night, 1928; Mr Pottermack's Oversight, 1930; Pontifex, Son and Thorndyke, 1931; When Rogues Fall Out, 1932; Dr Thorndyke Intervenes, 1933; For the Defence; Dr Thorndyke, 1934; The Penrose Mystery, 1936; Felo de Se?, 1937; The Stoneware Monkey, 1938; Mr Polton Explains, 1940; The Jacob Street Mystery, 1942. *Recreations*: painting, modelling in clay and wax, bookbinding and various handicrafts. *Address*: 94 Windmill Street, Gravesend.

Died 30 Sept. 1943.

FREEMAN-MITFORD, Maj. Hon. Thomas David; *see* Mitford.

FREESTON, Charles Lincoln, FJI, FRGS; author and journalist; *b* 14 April 1865; *s* of late Rev. Joseph Freeston; *m* 1891, Hilda (*d* 1933), *y d* of late Henry England; one *s* two *d*. *Educ*: Manchester Grammar School. Began journalism in the provinces, 1886; became connected with Pall Mall Gazette; secretary to Rt Hon. Sir Ughtred Kay-Shuttleworth, Bt, MP, during session of 1890; on editorial staff of Daily Graphic, 1890–98; chief sub-editor of Observer, 1891–95; and of Sunday Times, 1895–97; acting editor of The Car Illustrated, 1902–13; editor of The Motor-Owner, 1919–20; editor of The Anglo-Swiss Review, 1922–23; has acted as special correspondent to the Daily Telegraph in Italy and Austria, to the Daily Chronicle in France and Austria, and to the Daily Mail in France, Germany, and Spain. *Publications*: The Roads of Spain, a 5000 Miles Journey in the New Touring Paradise; The Passes of the Pyrenees; The High Roads of the Alps, A Motoring Guide to 100 Mountain Passes; Motoring on the Continent; The Alps for the Motorist; France for the Motorist; The Cream of Europe; Continental Touring, Hints for Travellers by Rail and Road; Cycling in the Alps; contributed five chapters to Badminton Motors; and numerous magazine articles. *Recreations*: foreign travel, motoring, golf and bowls. *Address*: Etwall, Baring Crescent, Beaconsfield. *T*: Beaconsfield 481. *Clubs*: Royal Automobile; Gerrards Cross Bowling.

Died 6 Jan. 1942.

FREETH, Maj.-Gen. George Henry Basil, CB 1919; CMG 1916; DSO 1900; *b* 31 Dec. 1872; *s* of Col W. Freeth; *m* 1903, Ruth Elaine, *d* of James W. Scott of Westlands, Queenstown; one *d*. *Educ*: Merchant Taylors' School, London; King William's Coll., Isle of Man; RMC, Sandhurst, 1891. Joined Lancashire Fusiliers 1892; Capt. 1899; Major, 1910; Bt Lt-Col 1912; Maj.-Gen. 1921; served in India; Nile Expedition, 1898 (medal and clasp, medal); occupation of Crete, and South Africa, 1899–1902 (Queen's medal 3 clasps, King's medal 2 clasps); European War, 1914–18 (despatches five times, CMG, CB, Brevet Col); psc; Major-General in charge of Administration, Southern Command, 1923–27; Deputy Adjutant General and Director of Personal Service in India, 1927–31; retired pay, 1931; Colonel The Lancashire Fusiliers, 1926–46. *Address*: The Close, Salisbury, Wilts.

Died 14 Dec. 1949.

FREMANTLE, Sir Francis Edward, Kt 1932; OBE; MA, MD, MCh, FRCS, FRCP, DPH, DL, JP; MP (U) St Albans, or Mid-Herts, since 1919; Chairman Parliamentary Medical Committee, of Unionist Health and Housing Committee, 1925–43; and of Select Committee on Publications and House of Commons Debates Reports; Lieut-Col RAMC, formerly Surgeon-Captain Herts Yeomanry (TA), retired; *b* 1872; *s* of late Dean of Ripon (Very Rev. the Hon. W. H. Fremantle); *m* 1905, Dorothy Marion Travers, *o d* of Henry Joseph Chinnery, JP, of Fringford Manor, Bicester; one *s*. *Educ*: Eton (King's Scholar); Balliol College, Oxford; Guy's Hospital. Plague Officer in India; served South African

War; War Correspondent Russo-Japanese War; County Medical Officer of Health for Hertfordshire, 1902–16; DADMS European War Gallipoli, Egypt, Mesopotamia (despatches twice); Member London County Council (Chairman of Housing Committee) 1919–22; President Incorporated Society of Medical Officers of Health, 1920–21; Member of the Industrial Health Research Board, 1930–34; Fellow and Vice-President, Royal Sanitary Institute, Member of Central Housing Advisory Committee, of the Inter-Departmental Committee on Nursing Services, of the Central Medical War Com., of the BMA Medical Planning Commission and of the Executive of several Health Organisations; a Trustee of Sutton Dwellings; Director of Rickmansworth and Uxbridge Valley and of St Albans Water Coys; Chairman Herts Pharmaceuticals Ltd; Member of St Albans Diocesan Conference and Church Assembly; Chairman of Enfield Chase Hunt Committee. *Publications:* A Doctor in Khaki; Health and Empire; The Housing of the Nation; The Health of the Nation. *Recreations:* hunting, lawn tennis. *Address:* Bedwell Park, Hatfield, Herts. *T:* Essendon 264. *Club:* Carlton.

Died 26 Aug. 1943.

FREMANTLE, Sir Selwyn Howe, Kt 1925; CSI 1920; CIE 1915; VD; ICS, retired; Member County Council, Buckinghamshire since 1934; *b* 11 Aug. 1869; 2nd *s* of late Adm. Hon. Sir E. R. Fremantle; *m* 1906, Vera Evelyn, *d* of late Henry Marsh, CIE; no *c. Educ:* Eton; Magdalen College, Oxford. Entered Indian Civil Service, 1890; Settlement Officer Rai Bareli, 1895; Bareilly, 1898; Magistrate and Collector, 1903; deputed to inquire into scarcity of labour in factories, 1905; Registrar Co-operative Societies, UP, 1907–12; Collector and Magistrate, Allahabad, 1913; Commissioner of Bareilly, 1918; appointed Controller of Passages, 1919; Commissioner of Meerut, 1919; Member of Council of Lt-Governor of United Provinces, 1920; Member Board of Revenue, UP 1921; retired 1925; served on Sanderson Committee on Emigration from India to Crown Colonies, 1909; deputed to inquire into financial results of military grass and dairy farms, 1910; specially appointed to Viceroy's Legislative Council for the purpose of the Factory Bill, 1911, and again for the purpose of the Co-operative Societies Bill, 1912. *Publications:* Rai Bareli Settlement Report, 1896; Bareilly Settlement Report, 1902; Report on Supply of Labour to Factories, 1905; A Policy of Rural Education, 1915. *Recreations:* tennis, golf. *Address:* Cheena House, Chalfont St Peter, Bucks. *Club:* East India and Sports.

Died 16 March 1942.

FRENCH, Captain Sir Frederick Edward, Kt 1942; RD; RNR; Captain P and OSN Company; *b* 4 Jan. 1882; 2nd *s* of late F. E. French, JP, Portsmouth; *m* Leila (*d* 1935), *y d* of late Benjamin Kent, Solicitor, Portsmouth; one *s.* Served European War, 1914–19, as Lieut RNR; Commander RNR, 1927; Captain RNR, 1932 Commodore of P and OSN Company since 1940. *Address:* 147 Macquarie Street, Sydney, Australia. *Club:* East India and Sports.

Died 6 July 1947.

FRENCH, Col George Arthur, CMG 1917; *b* Kingston, Canada, 21 Jan. 1865; 2nd *s* of late Major-General Sir George A. French; *m* 1899, Annie Elizabeth, *d* of late Thomas Jefferies of Newbay, Wexford; one *s. Educ:* St John's Coll. Winnipeg; Oxford Military College, Oxford. Lieut Royal Marines, 1882; Captain, Army Service Corps, 1890; Major, 1899; Lieut-Colonel, 1905; Col 1908; retired, 1912; Staff Employ—ADC to GOC Ceylon, 1893–94; DAAG Malta, 1898–99; DAAG Southern District, 1901–02; AQMG Western Command, 1909–12 and 1914–16; served on board HMS Achilles, Channel Squadron, 1884–85; HMS Ruby, S-E coast of America, 1885–89; Foreign Service in Army, Sierra Leone (twice), Malta, Crete, Ceylon,

South Africa, and Hong-Kong; Active Service: Cretan Insurrection, 1898; South African War, 1899–1900; European War, on Staff, Western Command, 1914–16, commanded Troops, Co. Wexford, during Irish Rebellion, 1916, and accepted surrender of Rebels at Enniscorthy on 1 May 1916, without any bloodshed; possesses also Royal Humane Society's Medal for saving life at sea. *Address:* Newbay, Wexford, Ireland. *Club:* United Service.

Died 15 Dec. 1950.

FRENCH, Lewis, CIE 1914; CBE 1919; *b* 26 Oct. 1873; *s* of David French of Eltham, Kent; *m* Margaret Ruth, *d* of late Sir C. L. Tupper, KCIE, CSI; one *s* one *d. Educ:* Merchant Taylors' School; St John's Coll. Oxford. 1st class Classical Moderations, Oxford; 2nd class Lit. Hum. ICS Exam., 1896. Assistant Commissioner, Punjab, 1897; Colonisation Officer, Chenab Colony, 1904–06; Director, Land Records, 1906; Director, Agriculture, 1907; Deputy Commissioner, Shahpur, 1908; Chief Minister, Kapurthala State, 1910–15; Special Commissioner, Defence of India Act, 1915; Director, Land Records, 1915; Additional Secretary, Punjab Govt 1916; Chief Secretary, 1918, 1920, and 1921; Financial Secretary, 1920; retired from ICS 1921; Director of Development in Palestine, 1931–32; Member, Board of Management Royal Hospital and Home for Incurables, Putney. *Publications:* Punjab Colony Manual; Annual Administration Reports of Kapurthala State; reports on Land Settlemeat and Agricultural Development, Palestine, 1932. *Address:* 20 Lytton Grove, Putney. *T:* Putney 1270.

Died 20 April 1945.

FRESHWATER, Douglas Hope, MA; MD Cambridge; MRCP Lond.; Consulting Physician to Skin Department and Lecturer on Skin Diseases, St George's Hospital; Consulting Dermatologist to LCC; Fellow Royal Society of Medicine, Member Senate, Cambridge University; *b* Colnbrook, Middlesex; *m* 1912, Ida Muriel Landale; one *s* one *d. Educ:* Westminster School; Trinity Coll., Cambridge; St George's Hospital; University, Berlin and University, Paris. Honours in Nat. Science Tripos, Cambridge, followed by entrance scholarship at St George's Hospital. After qualifying held various hospital appointments, then specialised in Diseases of the Skin after study in Paris, Berlin, and Aix-la-Chapelle Universities. *Publications:* numerous articles in the Lancet, Practitioner, British Medical Journal, Proceedings Royal Society of Medicine, etc., dealing with diseases of the skin and hair. *Recreations:* tennis, motoring, bridge. *Address:* 33 Wimpole Street, W1. *T:* Welbeck 1414. *Club:* Royal Thames Yacht.

Died 7 Feb. 1945.

FREUNDLICH, Herbert Max Finlay, Drphil; Drhc Utrecht; ForRS; Professor of Colloidal Chemistry, University of Minnesota, Minneapolis, Minn, since 1938; *b* Charlottenburg, Germany, 28 Jan. 1880; *s* of Philipp Friedrich Ernst Freundlich, Stolp, Prussia, and Ellen Elizabeth Finlayson, Cheltenham, England; *m* 1st, 1908, Maria Bertha Mann (*d* 1917); one *s* two *d*; 2nd, 1923, Maria Helene Gellert. *Educ:* University of München and University of Leipzig. DrPhil. Leipzig, 1903. Asst Physikalisch-Chemisches Institut, Univ. of Leipzig, 1903–11; Privatdozent, Univ. of Leipzig, 1906; Ausserordentlicher Prof. of Physical Chemistry, Technische Hochschule in Braunschweig, 1911; War work in gas protection at Kaiser Wilhelm Institut für physikal. Chemie und Elektrochemie, Berlin-Dahlem, 1916, Acting Director and Head of Dept of Colloidal Chemistry, 1919–33; Hon. Prof. Univ. of Berlin, 1923; Hon. Prof. Technische Hochschule, Berlin-Charlottenburg, 1930; Hon. Research Associate Univ. Coll., London, 1933–38. *Publication:* Kapillarchemie, Leipzig, 1909, 4th ed. in two vols 1930 and 1932, English trans Colloidal and Capillary Chemistry, London, 1926. *Recreations:* music, entomology, when young; in later years: history, archæology, psychology. *Address:* 521 Sixth Street, SE Minneapolis, Minn, USA. *T:* G1 1730.

Died 29 March 1941.

FREYER, Lt-Col Samuel Forster, CMG 1900; MD, RAMC; *b* 27 March 1858; *m* 1885, Charlotte Louisa, *d* of late William Burleigh, JP, Carrickfergus, Co. Antrim. Entered army, 1884; Major, 1896; served Soudan, James' Camel Corps, 1885 (medal with clasp, Khedive's star); Burma, 1886–87 (medal with clasp); Tirah Expedition, 1897–98; South African War, 1899–1902 (Relief of Ladysmith, despatches twice, Queen's medal, clasp, King's medal with two clasps, CMG).

Died 29 July 1947.

FRIEDMAN, Prof. Ignaz; Austrian Kammervirtuose; *b* Cracow, Poland, 14 Feb. 1882; *m* Maria de Schidlowsky; one *d*. *Educ:* Cracow; Vienna; Leipzig. Pupil of Riemann, Guido Adler, Leschetizky. Played on all Continents (over 2000 concerts); compositions for piano, chamber music, songs (Polish and German); Editions: Chopin, Liszt, Schumann (complete); Bach, Mendelssohn (partially). *Address:* c/o Steinway & Sons, 1 George Street, Conduit Street, W1.

Died 26 Jan. 1948.

FRIEND, Maj.-Gen. Rt Hon. Sir Lovick Bransby, PC Ireland, 1916; KBE 1919; CB 1908; *b* 25 April 1856; *s* of Frederick Friend of Woollet Hall, North Cray, Kent, and Fanny, *d* of G. Tyrrell and Frances Tyrrell; unmarried. *Educ:* Cheltenham College; RM Academy, Woolwich. Lieut Royal Engineers, 1873; Instructor RM College, Sandhurst, 1873; Instructor RM College, Sandhurst, 1883–84; Secretary RE Experimental Committee, 1885–89; Captain, 1885; Major, 1893; served Omdurman Campaign, 1898 (medal, clasps, despatches, 3rd class Osmanieh, 3rd class Medjidieh); Lt-Col 1900; Director of Works and Stores Egyptian Army, 1900–04; Egyptian Public Works, 1905; Assistant-Director Fortification Works, 1906–07; Pres. Claims Commission, British Armies in France, 1916–18 (despatches); General Officer commanding in Ireland, 1914–16; Maj.-Gen. in charge of Administration, Irish Command, 1912–14; commanding Scottish Coast Defences, 1908–12; President of the Claims Commission; retired pay, 1920; Commander Legion of Honour; Commander Belgian Couronne and Croix de Guerre. *Clubs:* United Service, MCC.

Died 19 Nov. 1944.

FRITH, Col Cyril Halsted, CBE 1919; *b* 1877; *m* 1925, Dorothy, *widow* of Capt. George Gardner, 21st Lancers, and *e d* of late Major H. G. Lyon-Campbell, 74th Highlanders, of Williamston, Perthshire. Served NW Frontier of India, 1897–98 (medal with two clasps); European War, 1914–18 (despatches, CBE). *Address:* Halsted House, Sunninghill, Berks.

Died 15 April 1946.

FRITH, Col (Hon. Brig.-Gen.) Herbert Cokayne, CB 1916; *b* Gainsborough, 12 July 1861; *s* of Rev. W. A. Frith; *m* 1895, Alice Isabel de Bilinski; one *s*. *Educ:* St Paul's College, Stony Stratford. Joined Somerset Light Infantry, 1882; commanded 1st Batt. 1909–13; employed with Egyptian Army, 1885–95; served with Egyptian Army, 1885–95; served with Egyptian Frontier Force in Sudan, action of Ginnis, 1885 (medal and Khedive's star); with Egyptian Frontier Force; action of Toski, 1889 (clasp, 4th Class Mejidieh); European War, served in Egypt, 1914–15; in Gallipoli Peninsula, 1915 (despatches twice, CB; 2nd Cl. St Stanislaus with swords); in Egypt, 1916–17; in France, 1917; Commander Oswestry Reserve Centre, 1917–18; Commander Mixed Brigade, 1918 (despatches); Colonel in Army, 1913; temp. Brig.-Gen., 1914; retired with

hon. rank Brig.-Gen., 1918; DL Somerset, 1930; JP Somerset, 1928; Member of VAD Council 1923–36. *Address:* Fons George, Taunton. *T:* 3207.

Died 5 March 1942.

FRITH, Walter; barrister, author, critic; *b* London; 3rd *s* of late W. P. Frith, CVO, RA; *m* 1898, Maud, widow of Rev. W. Law, and *d* of late J. S. Hill, JP, of Hawks Wick, Hertfordshire. *Educ:* Harrow; Trinity Hall, Cambridge. MA; LLB Cambridge. Barr, Inner Temple, 1880. *Dramatic Works:* Brittany Folk, 1889; The Barley Mow, 1889; The Verger, 1892; Midsummer Day, 1892; Molière, 1891; Flight, 1893; Her Advocate, 1895; Not Wisely, but Too Well, 1898; The Man of Forty, 1898; The Iron Duke, 1902; The Perils of Flirtation, 1904; Margaret Catchpole, 1910; The Bells of Lin-Lan-Lone, 1911; The Miniature, 1911. *Publications:* novels—The Sack of Monte Carlo; In Search of Quiet; The Tutor's Love Story. *Recreations:* golf, tennis, cricket, shooting. *Address:* 13 Harley Gardens, SW10. *Clubs:* Athenæum, MCC.

Died 25 July 1941.

FROHAWK, Frederick William, MBOU, FES; artist and zoologist; *b* Brisley Hall, Norfolk, 16 July 1861; *y s* of Francis William Frohawk; *m* 1st, 1895, Margaret Annie (decd), 7th *d* of Alexander Grant; two *d*; 2nd, 1911, Mabel Jane, 2nd *d* of A. Hart-Bowman; one *d*. *Educ:* private schools. FES 1891 (elected Special Life Fellow, 1926). Member of British Ornithologists' Union, 1895; zoological artist in oils, water-colours, lithography, wood drawing, and black and white; zoo. artist to The Field since 1881; illustrator of ornithology and reptiles for Encyclopædia Britannica, British Museum Catalogue of Fishes, Proceedings of Zoological Soc.; Trans. Ento. Soc. London; and other scientific journals; also various works on Entomology and Ornithology, including Birds of Sandwich Islands, Tegetmeier's Pheasants, Geese of Europe and Asia, and various subjects on Mammalia; entomologist to The Field since 1893; and assistant editor to The Entomologist, 1895; awarded the Civil List Pension of £200 in recognition for services to Natural History, and especially Entomology, 1932. *Publications:* various papers and illustrated articles on Zoology in the leading journals since 1882; Birds Beneficial to Agriculture (British Museum, Economic Series); Natural History of British Butterflies; The Complete Book of British Butterflies, 1935; Varieties of British Butterflies, 1938. *Recreations:* study of field natural history, collecting entomological specimens. *Address:* Essendene, Cavendish Road, Sutton, Surrey.

Died 10 Dec. 1946.

FROUDE, Ashley Anthony, CMG 1892, OBE 1919; BA; DL, JP Devon; Comdr, RNVR; *b* 28 June 1863; *s* of late James Anthony Froude; *m* 1897, Ethel Aubrey, *o d* of Captain A. P. Hallifax, Halwell House, Kingsbridge. *Educ:* Westminster; Oriel College, Oxford. Private Secretary to Sir R. Herbert, Colonial Office, 1886; Secretary to Behring Sea Commission, 1891; attached to Behring Sea Arbitration, 1892; Assistant Private Secretary, Colonial Office, 1896. Decorated for services in connection with Behring Sea Arbitration. *Recreation:* yachting. *Address:* Collapit Creek, Kingsbridge. *T:* Kingsbridge 2332.

Died 17 April 1949.

FRY, Rev. Canon Charles Edward Middleton, MBE 1939; Vicar of Littlewick, Berks, since 1947; Hon. Canon of Christ Church Cathedral, Oxford; a Proctor in Convocation and the Church Assembly; *b* 14 July 1882; *s* of late Very Rev. Thomas Charles Fry, DD, Dean of Lincoln and Julia Isabella, 3rd *d* of late Edward Greene, MP; unmarried. *Educ:* Berkhamsted; Christ Church, Oxford (Scholar). 2nd Class Honours History; 2nd Class Honours Theology; MA Oxford. Assist Curate Wantage, 1906–14; Vicar of St Luke, Maidenhead, 1914–47; Local Officiating Chaplain, 1915–18 and

1939–45. Rural Dean of Maidenhead; Chaplain Army Cadets; Member of Diocesan Conference; Member of Berkshire County Council; Joint Treasurer CETS; Chairman: Local Committee Slough Employment Exchange; Littlewick Youth Cttee etc. *Recreations:* fond of fishing, travel. *Address:* The Vicarage, Littlewick, Berks. *T:* Littlewick Green 132. *Clubs:* Church House; Union Society (Oxford).

Died 27 July 1950.

FRY, Sir Frederick Morris, KCVO 1919; CVO 1913; MVO 1911; *b* 9 July 1851; *s* of C. E. Fry of Compton House, Compton Bishop, Somerset; *m* 1910, Edith Headley, *d* of late Rev. H. H. Moore, vicar of St John's, Darwen; two *d*. *Educ:* King's College School, London. Called to Bar, Inner Temple, 1873; Member since 1898 of the Council (and 1898–1942 of the Distribution Committee) of King Edward's Hospital Fund for London (Hon. Secretary, 1907–11 and 1914–21); Past Master of the Merchant Taylors' Company; Member of the Court of the Sons of the Clergy Corporation, sometime Treasurer; Member of the Council of the City and Guilds of London Technical Institute. *Publications:* A Historical Catalogue of the Pictures, Herse-Cloths, and Tapestries at Merchant Taylors' Hall; An Illustrated Catalogue of the Silver Plate on the Merchant Taylors' Company; The Windows of Merchant Taylors' Hall; The Charters of the Merchant Taylors' Coy. *Address:* 150 Hamilton Terrace, NW8; Winbar, Bucklebury, Reading.

Died 3 Feb. 1943.

FRY, Matthew Wyatt Joseph, MA; Senior Fellow University of Dublin, 1924; Senior Lecturer, 1927, and Catechist, 1931; *s* of Rev. Henry Fry, MA, Corbally, Roscrea; *m* 1909, Margaret, *d* of late Col Sir Francis Barker; one *s* two *d*. *Educ:* Galway Grammar School; Trinity College, Dublin. Fellow of Trinity College, 1889. Tutor, 1891; Junior Dean, 1893–97; Assistant to Professor of Natural Philosophy, 1899; Editor of the University Calendar, 1900–24; Professor of Natural Philosophy in the University of Dublin, 1910–25; Representative of the Junior Fellows on the Board, 1911–17; Senior Proctor, 1918; Registrar, 1924. *Publications:* papers on Mathematics in the Proceedings of the Royal Irish Academy. *Recreation:* carpentry. *Address:* Willow Bank, Terenure, Dublin; 39 Trinity College, Dublin. *T:* 95323.

Died 2 Dec. 1943.

FRY, Theodore Wilfrid, OBE 1918; *b* 1868; 2nd *s* of Sir Theodore Fry, 1st Bt, and Sophia, *d* and *co-heiress* of John Pease, East Mount, Darlington, and Cleveland Lodge, Yorks. *Educ:* Clifton; New College, Oxford (exhibitioner; 1st class honours); FSA 1892. Bar, Inner Temple, 1893; North-Eastern Circuit; Stipendiary Magistrate, Middlesborough, 1908–20; Metropolitan Police Magistrate, Tower Bridge, 1920, Bow Street, 1926–41; contested Appleby Division, Westmorland, 1895; JP Yorks; Commissioner Military Service (Civil Liabilities) since 1916 (unpaid); Chairman Tees District Maritime Board 1918, and has acted as arbitrator in several industrial disputes. *Recreation:* sometime member Norwegian Club and Anglo-Norwegian Fishermen's Association Committees. *Address:* Park House, Hampton Court, Middlesex. *Clubs:* Reform, Brooks's.

Died 1 June 1947.

FRY, Windsor, RBA; *b* Torquay; *m* 1922, Gladys, *d* of F. Hardy-Syms, Rochester. *Educ:* Private Academy, Torquay; Royal Academy Schools (honours). Served European War, 1914–19 (wounded, Delville Wood); special lecturer on painting, LCC *Works:* Youth and Age, purchased by the Corporation of Liverpool, etc. *Address:* 5a Ranelagh Gardens, Hurlingham, SW6. *T:* Renown 2855.

Died 24 Jan. 1947.

FRYE, Frederick Robert, MusB (Cantab) FRCO; Hon. RCM; *b* Brook, Kent, 1851; 3rd *s* of Joseph and Eliza Frye; *m* 1891, Margaret E. S., *d* of John and Sarah Pattison, Colchester, Essex; one *s*. *Educ:* chiefly private. Organist and Choirmaster of the Cathedral, Chelmsford; retired, 1942, after 66 years as organist; Conductor, Chelmsford Musical Society 27 years; Choirmaster of the Chelmsford Association of Church Choirs; Hon. local representative of the RAM, RCM, TCML. *Publications:* songs, pianoforte and organ pieces. *Recreations:* reading and gardening. *Address:* St Mary's Lodge, Chelmsford.

Died 27 Aug. 1942.

FRYER, Edward Harpur; Secretary Automobile Association since 1942; *b* 24 June 1879; *er s* of late Edward Fryer, Architect, and Louisa Jane Harpur; *m* 1st, 1906, Minnie Jane Eugenie (*d* 1940), *e d* of late Frank Marshall, Derby; three *s* one *d*; 2nd, 1944, Winifred Blanche (Freda) Easton, Little Bilden, Banstead, *widow* of C. J. Easton, Tadworth. *Educ:* Diocesan School. Articled to late James Wright, FSI, and later in partnership with T. H. Thorpe, FRIBA, as Architect and Surveyor; commenced motoring in 1902; Hon. Secretary Derbyshire AC; temporary paid position with Motor Union, 1910; on its amalgamation with the AA first Midland Manager; transferred to London HQ as Chief of Staff, 1913; served European War, Staff Capt. RE, in Movements and Railways; demobilised, 1918; Road Manager AA, 1919; then Deputy Secretary; oft-times Chairman of varied and somewhat contentious Committees, in particular the Trunk Roads Joint Committee of the CPRE and RBA, whose Report was published in 1937; attended numerous Inquiries in England, Scotland, and Wales under the Motor Car Acts 1896 and 1903, the Roads Act 1920, the Road Traffic Acts 1930, 1933 and 1934, and the Trunk Roads Act 1936; gave evidence on many road matters before Parliamentary Committees; President Anglo-Franco-Hibernian Society. *Publication:* Bridge Across the Seas, 1942. *Recreations:* bridge, croquet, snooker, tennis, travel, and photography. *Address:* 8 Dorset Road, Cheam, Surrey. *T:* Vigilant 1238. *Clubs:* Devonshire, Arts, Royal Automobile; Royal Scottish Automobile (Glasgow); Royal Irish Automobile (Dublin).

Died 21 June 1948.

FRYER, Sir John Claud Fortescue, KBE 1946; FRS (1948); FRSE; LLD; MA; Secretary Agricultural Research Council; *b* 13 Aug. 1886; *s* of Herbert Fortescue Fryer and Mary Katherine Terry; *m* 1919, Constance Joan Denny-Cooke, MBE 1948; one *s* one *d*. *Educ:* Rugby; Gonville and Caius Coll. Cambridge. Fellow Gonville and Caius Coll. Scientific expeditions to Seychelles, Aldabra, Ceylon. Entomologist to Board of Agriculture; Director Plant Pathology Laboratory, Ministry of Agriculture; Secretary Agricultural Improvement Council (England and Wales). *Publications:* various on entomology and agriculture; also on geography, fauna and flora of the islands of South Indian Ocean. *Recreations:* entomology, fishing, shooting. *Address:* Chadsholme, Milton Road, Harpenden. *T:* Harpenden 504. *Clubs:* Athenæum, Farmers'.

Died 22 Nov. 1948.

FULLER, Adm. Sir Cyril Thomas Moulden, KCB 1928; CB 1919; CMG 1915; DSO 1916; Director Yorkshire Insurance, North-Eastern Airways and Martin Hearne, Ltd; *b* 1874; *s* of late Capt. Thomas Fuller, 18th Hussars; *m* 1902, Edith Margaret Connel. Entered RN 1887; Lieut 1894; Comdr 1903; Capt. 1910; Rear-Adm. 1921; Vice-Adm. 1926; Adm. 1930; served with Togoland and Cameroons Expeditionary Forces, 1914–16, as Senior Naval Officer (despatches); Commanded HMS Cumberland, Challenger, Astræa in succession, 1914–16, and HMS Repulse, 1916–17; Director of Plans Division, Naval War Staff, 1917–20; Head of British Naval Section, Peace Conference, Paris, 1919–20; Chief of Staff Atlantic Fleet, 1920–22; Assistant

Chief of Naval Staff, 1922–23; Third Sea Lord and Controller of the Navy, 1923–25; commanded Battle Cruiser Squadron, Atlantic Fleet, 1925–27; Commander-in-Chief America and West Indies Station, 1928–30; Second Sea Lord and Chief of Naval Personnel, 1930–32; retired list, 1935; Zone Commander, North Riding Home Guard, June–Oct. 1940; Member of Lord Willingdon's Mission to South America, Oct. 1940–Feb. 1941; Board of Trade Life-Saving Medal; Comdr Legion of Honour; Comdr Order of Crown of Italy; Order of Rising Sun; Croix de Guerre; United States Naval DSM. *Address:* Douthwaite Dale, Kirbymoorside, Yorkshire.

Died 1 Feb. 1942.

FULLER, Sir Francis Charles, KBE 1919; CMG 1906; *b* 22 Nov. 1866; *s* of late Captain Charles Fuller, 12th Royal Lancers, and Helen Bagge of Stradsett, Norfolk; *m* 1911, Elfrida Mary, *e d* of late W. H. Iremonger, Wherwell Priory, Hants. *Educ:* St Charles' College, London. Entered Colonial Civil Service as Cadet, 1884; remained in Fiji until 1892; was then named District Commissioner for Lagos; Resident of Ibadan, 1897; Assist Secretary to the Government of Malta, 1902; Chief Commissioner of Ashanti, 1905; retired, 1920. *Publication:* A Vanished Dynasty: Ashanti, 1921. *Club:* Royal Automobile.

Died 20 Sept. 1944.

FULLER, Rt Rev. John Latimer; *b* 1870; *s* of late Rev. John Fuller, BD, and Emmeline Jane, *e d* of late Rev. Richard Okes, DD, formerly Provost, King's Coll. Camb.; *m* 1914, Ethel Mary Cooper; two *s* one *d*. *Educ:* Emmanuel College, Cambridge. BA Cambridge, 1891; MA 1907. Ordained, 1893; Member of Community of Resurrection, Mirfield, 1902; in charge of Rand Native Mission, 1903; Archdeacon of the Northern Transvaal, 1909–13; Bishop of Lebombo, 1912–20; Rector of Pietersburg, N Transvaal, 1921–30; Chaplain to Khaiso School, Pietersburg, N Transvaal, 1930–44; retired, 1944. *Publications:* Romance of a South African Mission, 1907; South African Native Missions, 1908. *Address:* PO Gladdaklipkop, Pietersburg, N Transvaal, S Africa.

Died 25 May 1950.

FULLER, Walter Everard, CMG 1938; OBE 1924; *b* 10 Feb. 1879; *s* of Walter Fuller, Rye, Sussex; *m* 1908, Mabel Housden; one *d*. *Educ:* Rye Grammar School. Entered Foreign Office, 1898; Archivist, HM Embassy Constantinople, 1911–14; employed in Foreign Office, 1914–18; attached to British Delegation to Peace Conference, 1918–19; Archivist, HM Embassy, Rome, 1920–24; Superintending Archivist, HM Embassy, Paris, 1924–37; Foreign Office, 1937–38; retired, 1938. *Address:* Winchelsea, 46 Glenleigh Park Road, Bexhill-on-sea, Sussex.

Died 15 Feb. 1942.

FULLER, William Fleetwood, DSO 1918; DL Wilts; JP Wilts and Dorset; *b* 17 Sept. 1865; *e surv. s* of late George Pargiter Fuller, of Neston Park, Corsham; unmarried. *Educ:* Winchester College. Lt-Col in Royal Wiltshire Yeomanry, 1921–24; Member Wilts County Council, 1922–46; Member of Thames Conservancy Board, 1930–46; Master North Bucks Harriers, 1899–1905; Master (joint) Cattistock Fox Hounds, 1905–10; Master VWH (Cricklade) Fox Hounds, 1910–31; served European War (despatches, DSO). *Recreations:* hunting, shooting, fishing. *Address:* Neston Park, Corsham, Wiltshire. *Clubs:* Boodle's, Cavalry.

Died 19 Aug. 1947.

FURBER, Lt-Col Cecil Tidswell, DSO 1917; late Royal Tank Corps and King's Own Scottish Borderers; *b* 1883; *m* 1914, Evelyn Maisie, *d* of late Sir H. A. Crump, KCIE; one *s* two *d*. Served South African War, 1901–02 (Queen's medal and three clasps); European War, 1914–18 (despatches thrice, DSO and bar, Bt Major); retired pay, 1931; Acting Secretary National

Association for Employment of Sailors, Soldiers and Airmen, Essex Branch. *Address:* 62 Queensborough Terrace, W2.

Died 21 Dec. 1943.

FURKERT, Frederick William, CMG 1926; JP; *b* 1876; *s* of Geoffrey William Furkert of Ross, Westland, New Zealand; *m* 1902, Constance Mary (*d* 1928), *d* of Henry Plimmer; two *s* one *d*; 2nd, 1931, Catherine Annie Foley; one *s* one *d*. *Educ:* Ross State School; Hokitika High School; Wellington and Dunedin Technical Schools; Otago University. A Cadet, 1894–98; Assistant Engineer, 1898–1905; Resident Engineer-in-Charge, Province of Taranaki, 1905–06; Engineer-in-Charge of Construction North Island Main Trunk Railway, 1906–08; District Engineer Provinces of Otago and Southland, 1908–12; Inspecting Engineer, 1912–19; Assistant Engineer-in-Chief, 1919–20; Engineer-in-Chief and Under-Secretary of Public Works Department, New Zealand, 1924–32; Chairman Main Highways Board, 1924–32; now retired; Director of Military Works with rank of Hon. Col; during European War was in charge of construction of military semi-permanent camps and mobilisation bases. Also Commissioner of Defence Works with same rank in War of 1939–45 in Fiji, in charge of military works such as seaplane bases and aerodromes for Fiji, New Zealand, and USA armies, navies, and air forces, 1941–43. Wellington City Councillor and Member Wellington Hospital Board. Order of the Brilliant Star (China). *Publications:* papers for Institute of Civil Engineers, London, NZ Society of Civil Engineers, Royal Society of NZ. *Address:* 58 Matai Road, Hataitai, Wellington, E2, New Zealand.

Died 26 Sept. 1949.

FURNIVALL, Lt-Col Charles Hilton, CMG 1919; RAMC, retired; in medical charge Gloucestershire Regimental Depot, Horfield, Bristol; *b* 16 March 1873; *s* of Dr Charles Henry Furnivall and Lucy Francis Nodes Eager; *m* 1904, Daisy, *d* of D. MacBean, Quetta; two *s* two *d*. *Educ:* Epsom College; St Mary's Hospital. Entered Service beginning of South African War; served in India and at home; served European War (despatches thrice). *Recreations:* golf, billiards, motoring. *Address:* Yatton, Wellington Hill West, Bristol. *T:* Bristol 66860.

Died 19 March 1946.

FURST, Herbert Ernest Augustus; author and art critic; *b* 15 July 1874; *m* Ivy, *d* of Edward Hawkins; two *s* one *d*. *Educ:* privately, London; Berlin. Manager of Hanfstaengl, Fine Art Reproducers, London branch, 1897–1916; Member of the Court of the Fine Art Trade Guild from its foundation to 1914; one of the founders of the Arts League of Service; joint-founder and editor of The Apple, 1920–22; editor and publisher The Modern Woodcutters Series; editor of Arts and Crafts, 1927; editor of the Woodcut, an annual; regular contributor to Colour Magazine—pseudonym Tis—1916–26; editor of Apollo until out-break of war, 1939; contributor to Apollo; Connoisseur, The Field, etc. *Publications:* Songs of London; Songs of Town and Country; Chardin, 1908; Durer, 1909; Chardin and his Times, 1911; Individuality and Art, 1912; Frank Brangwyn, RA, 1918; Charles Shannon, RA, 1919; The Modern Woodcut, 1924; The Decorative Art of Frank Brangwyn, 1925; Anecdotes of Painters and Painting, 1926; Portrait Painting, 1927; Still Life Painting, 1927; Original Engraving and Etching: an Appreciation, 1931; Art Debunked, 1935; Essays in Russet, 1944; Leonard Campbell Taylor and this place in Art, 1945. *Recreation:* suspended. *Address:* Huggetts, Horney Common, Uckfield, Sussex. *Club:* PEN.

Died 16 Oct. 1945.

FYFE, David Theodore, MA (Cantab); FRIBA; Architect; Hon. Student of the British School at Athens; Convener, Panel of Architects for Air Raid Damage to Buildings of Historic Importance, Cambridgeshire, under Ministry of Works and Planning; *b* Yloilo,

Philippine Islands, 3 Nov. 1875; 2nd *s* of the late James Sloane Fyfe, Manila, and Jane Charlotte Abercrombie Fyfe; *g s* of Very Rev. Principal Brown, DD, Aberdeen; *m* 1911, Mary Nina, *o d* of late Robert Wright Brown and Anne E. Brown; two *s* two *d*. *Educ:* The Albany Academy, etc., Glasgow. Architectural Association Travelling Student, 1899; Architectural Student of the British School at Athens, 1900. Architect to the Cretan Exploration Fund and Sir Arthur Evans's excavations at Knossos, 1900–04; practised in London and assisted Sir John Burnet, 1905–15; Housing Architect for Ministry of Health, Queensferry and London, 1916–19; Architect to the Dean and Chapter of Chester Cathedral, 1919–38; Master and afterwards Director (1922–36) of the School of Architecture and Lecturer in Architecture (1926–41) in the University of Cambridge; Director of excavations at Glastonbury Abbey, 1926–27; RIBA Florence Bursar, 1932–33; Lt 4th Bn Cambridgeshire Home Guard, 1940–42. *Architectural Works:* Shaftesbury Inst., Lisson Grove, NW; Hall and Classrooms for Charlotte Mason College, Ambleside; works at Chester Cathedral; Memorial Chapels at Ashton Hayes, Chester, and St Clement's, Cambridge; Science Block at Chester Training College; Church Army Lodging Home, Cambridge; and various Memorials of the Great War, etc. *Publications:* Deeside Regional Planning Scheme (with Prof. Patrick Abercrombie); Hellenistic Architecture, 1936; Architecture in Cambridge, 1942; several articles. *Recreations:* sketching, fishing. *Address:* Longstowe Hall, Cambridgeshire. *T:* Caxton 203.

Died 1 Jan. 1945.

FYNES-CLINTON, Osbert Henry; late Professor of French and Romance Philology, University of Wales; *s* of late Rev. Osbert Fynes-Clinton, Rector of Barlow Moor, Didsbury; *m* 1907, Gwladys Mabel, *d* of Rev. William Hughes, Vicar of Llanuwchllyn; one *s*. *Educ:* MA, St John's College, Oxford; Taylorian Scholar in Spanish, 1892. French Master at King Edward School, Aston, Birmingham, 1896–1904; Examiner in Italian and Spanish, Birmingham University, 1905–07; Examiner in French, Aberdeen University, etc. *Publication:* The Welsh Vocabulary of the Bangor District, 1913. *Address:* Weirglodd Wen, Bangor.

Died 9 Aug. 1941.

G

GABAIN, Ethel Leontine, (Mrs John Copley), RBA 1932; ROI 1933; *b* Le Havre; *d* of late Charles Edward Gabain and Elizabeth Hutton Warden; *m* 1913, John Copley, RE; one *s. Educ:* Slade; Central School Arts and Crafts; Paris. Elected Associé of Salon des Artistes Français; Works purchased by Brit. Museum, Victoria and Albert Museum, Bibliothèque Nationale, Paris; Uffizi Gallery, Florence; Galleria Moderna, Rome; Royal Museum, Stuttgart; National Gallery, Ottawa; Public Library, New York; Public Library, Boston; City Art Gallery, Manchester; City Art Gallery, Bradford; Art Gallery, Melbourne; National Art Gallery, New Zealand, Oslo and Gottenburg City Art Galleries and others; awarded De Laszlo Silver Medal, 1933, for portrait of Miss Flora Robson, bought by City Art Gallery, Manchester; portrait of Miss Edith Evans in Restoration Comedy, bought by Municipal Art Gallery of Stoke on Trent and Hanley, 1935; portrait of Diana Wynyard, bought by Liverpool Art Gallery; portrait of Pamela Stanley in Two Bouquets, bought by Oldham Art Gallery; Official War Artist, 1940. *Publications:* Edition d'Art, Jane Eyre, illustrated with lithographs, 1923; Illustrations to The Warden (Trollope), 1925, etc. *Address:* 10 Hampstead Square, NW3. *T:* Hampstead 3001.

Died 30 Jan. 1950.

GABRIEL, Lt-Col Cecil Hamilton, CVO 1922; FRGS; late Foreign and Political Department, Government of India; *b* 16 Feb. 1879; *m* 1913, Harriet Mabel, *o surv. d* of late Colonel G. B. Renny; one *s.* Joined Army, 1900; transferred to Indian Army, 1902, and served with 37th Lancers (Baluch Horse); entered Indian Political Department, 1905; HBM's Consul, Bunder Abbas, 1906; Assistant Resident, Hyderabad, 1908; Assistant Political Agent, Chilas, 1909; British Joint Commissioner, Leh, 1912; Assistant Resident, Poonch, 1915; First Assistant to Resident in Kashmir, 1916; First Assistant to Resident in Persian Gulf, 1918; Deputy Secretary, Foreign and Political Department, Government of India, 1921; Secretary, Central India, 1924; Political Agent, Bhopal, 1925; Resident at Jaipur, and at Jodhpur, 1928; Gwalior, 1929; retired 1932. *Address:* Daneway, Cavendish Road, Bournemouth, Hants. *T:* 6634.

Died 25 Feb. 1947.

GABRIEL, Col Sir (Edmund) Vivian, Kt 1937; CSI 1911; CMG 1918; CVO 1906; CBE 1919; KJStJ 1910; VD 1921; TD 1948; MA, Camb.; DCL; FSA; FCS; Grand Comdr Order of Astor, Kt Comdr Holy Sepulchre. Commander of Orders of Orange Nassau and of St Agatha; Officer of the Orders of St Maurice and St Lazarus and of the Crown of Italy; Italian Croce di Guerra; Gentleman Usher to the King; Colonel ret. Royal Engineers (TA); Hon. Colonel 26 AA Regt (London Electrical Engineers); *b* 28 March 1875; *e s* of late Edmund Gabriel; *m* 1924, Mabel M. Preston (Commander of St John of Jerusalem, Med. d'Or de la Reconnaissance Française). Entered ICS 1897; served in Bengal, Rajputana, and Central India, 1898–1902; Asst Political ADC India Office, 1902; special service for Coronation and Coronation Durbar, 1902–03; Under-Secretary Foreign Department, India, 1903–07; Resident, Western Rajputana States, 1908; Chief Secretary North-West Frontier Province, 1909; Secretary Agent to Governor-General, Central India, 1910; Secretary, Coronation Durbar, 1911; Special Service, Nepal 1908, Libya 1912; Indian Political Dept, 1913; Bikaner 1914, Baroda 1920–21; War Office, Military Operations Branch, 1915; GSO1, British Military Mission with Italian Field Armies, 1915–17; Liaison Officer, British Aegean Squadron, 1917–18; Financial Adviser, Occupied Enemy Territory, 1918–19; British Air Commission, USA, 1940–46. *Clubs:* Marlborough-Windham, Athenæum; Royal Yacht Squadron; Racquet, Century (New York); Metropolitan (Washington, DC).

Died 14 Feb. 1950.

GADDUM, Arthur Graham, MBE; *b* 9 Jan. 1874; *s* of H. T. Gaddum, Bowdon, Cheshire; *m* 1929, Alice Muriel Behrens; one *d. Educ:* Rugby. High Sheriff of Pembroke, 1943. *Address:* Orielton, Pembroke, Pembrokeshire.

Died 7 Sept. 1948.

GADIE, Lt-Col Sir Anthony, Kt 1935; late RFA; Controller for City of Bradford; Chairman of Bradford Conservative and Unionist Association; Ex-Alderman of the city of Bradford; formerly Chairman of Waterworks Committee, Bradford, for over 40 years; Chairman of Yorkshire Branch of the Auctioneers and Estate Agents Institute, 1928; JP Bradford; auctioneer and valuer, Bradford; *m*; two *s* two *d*. Served in the Territorials pre-war; TD; served at home and in France during the War of 1914–18 (despatches); MP (U) Central Division of Bradford, 1924–29; Lord Mayor of the City of Bradford, 1920–21; Hon. Freeman, City of Bradford, 1944. *Address:* Oakwood, Toller Lane, Bradford.

Died 24 Aug. 1948.

GAGE, Andrew Thomas, CIE 1923; LLD (Aber.), MA, BSc, MB, FLS; Lt-Col, IMS, retired; formerly Director Botanical Survey of India; Superintendent Royal Botanic Gardens, Calcutta; *b* 14 Dec. 1871; *s* of Robert Gage; *m* 1900, Jean Stuart Bruce, Kildrummy. *Educ:* Grammar School, Old Aberdeen; University of Aberdeen. Assistant to Professor of Botany, University of Aberdeen, 1894–96; entered Indian Medical Service, 1897; retired, 1925; Curator of the Herbarium, Calcutta Botanic Gardens, 1898; Librarian and Assistant Secretary Linnean Society of London, 1924–29. *Publications:* A History of the Linnean Society of London, 1938; various technical papers on botanical subjects. *Recreation:* motoring. *Address:* Field End, Great Hallingbury, Essex.

Died 21 Jan. 1945.

GAGNON, Rt Rev. Mgr Cyrille, CMG 1944; LPh; DTh. Rector Laval University, Quebec. *Address:* Laval University, Quebec, Canada.

Died 1 Nov. 1945.

GAINFORD, 1st Baron *cr* 1917, of Headlam; **Joseph Albert Pease;** PC, 1908; JP, DL; Deputy Chairman of the Durham Coal Owners Association and Vice-Chairman of the Durham District Board (under Mines Act 1930); Director of Pease and Partners, Ltd; and other Colliery Companies; Chairman of Durham Coke Owners; Director of the County of London Electric Supply Company, Ltd; Chairman of South London Electric Supply Co.; late Chairman of the Tees Fishery Board; Chairman of the Trustees of the Bowes Museum; *b* Darlington, 17 Jan. 1860; 2nd *s* of Sir Joseph W. Pease, 1st Bart, MP, Hutton Hall Guisbro', and Mary, *d* of Alfred Fox, Falmouth; *m* 1886, Ethel (*d* 1941), *o d* of Sir Henry Havelock-Allan, 1st Bt; one *s* one *d. Educ:* Tottenham School; Trinity College, Cambridge (MA). Darlington Mayor, 1889; Private Secretary (unpaid) to Rt Hon. John Morley, Chief Secretary of Ireland, 1893–95; MP (L) Tyneside Division, Northumberland, 1892–1900; one of the Junior Whips to the Opposition, 1897–1905; a Junior Lord of the Treasury, 1905–08; Patronage Secretary to Treasury, 1908–10; MP (L) Saffron Walden Division, Essex, 1901–10; Chancellor

Duchy of Lancaster, 1910–11; President of Board of Education, 1911–15; Postmaster-General, 1916; MP (L) Rotherham Div., WR Yorks, 1910–16; on Claims Commission in France, 1915, 1917–20, and in Italy, 1918–19; Chairman of the British Broadcasting Co. Ltd, 1922–26, Vice-Chairman, 1926–32; President of Federation British Industries, 1927–28. *Publications:* sundry leaflets and pamphlets on Imperial Finance, Irish Affairs, Slavery in British Protectorates, the Coal Industry, etc. *Recreations:* golf, fishing, shooting, etc. *Heir:* s Hon. Joseph Pease, TD. *Address:* 18 Mansfield Street, Cavendish Square, W1. *T:* Langham 2816; Headlam Hall, Gainford, SO, Co. Durham. *T:* Gainford 207. *Clubs:* Brooks's, Turf, MCC.

Died 15 Feb. 1943.

GAIRDNER, Arthur Charles Dalrymple; *b* 16 June 1872; *e s* of late D. C. Gairdner; *m* Sylvia Jane Colquhoun, 2nd *d* of A. C. Balloch, Hook Heath. *Educ:* privately. General Manager and Director Union Bank of Scotland Ltd, 1910–19; Chairman British Overseas Bank Ltd, 1919–38; President Institute of Bankers (Scotland), 1917–19. Commander of Order of Polonia Restituta, Poland, 1935; Second Class of the Order of the Eagle Cross with Star, Estonia, 1936. *Recreation:* varied. *Address:* Hampton Lodge, Hurstpierpoint, Sussex. *Clubs:* Oriental; New (Edinburgh).

Died 21 March 1950.

GAIT, Sir Edward Albert, KCSI 1915 (CSI 1912); CIE 1907; PhD Patna, 1918; *b* 16 Aug. 1863; *m* 1897, Christian Maud (CBE, a Lady of Grace, St John of Jerusalem), *d* of late Col A. Stephen, JP; one *d.* *Educ:* Univ. College, London. Entered ICS 1882; Director of Land Records, Assam, 1893; Secretary to the Chief Commissioner of Assam, 1895; Magistrate and Collector, Bengal, 1897; Census Commissioner for India, 1903; Financial Secretary and Member of Legislative Council, Bengal, 1905; Commissioner of Chota Nagpur, 1905; Chief Secretary to Govt of Bengal, 1907; Census Commissioner for India, 1909; Member, Executive Council, Bihar and Orissa, 1912–15; Lieutenant Governor, Bihar and Orissa, 1915–20; Member of Council of India, 1922–27; Chairman of Council, Roy. Society of Arts, 1930 and 1931. *Publications:* A History of Assam; Report on the Census of Assam, 1891; Report on the Census of Bengal, 1901; Report (joint author) on the Census of India, 1901; Report on the Census of India, 1911, etc. Kt of Grace, St John of Jerusalem, 1917. *Address:* The Croft, Park Hill, Ealing, W5. *T:* Perivale 1219. *Club:* Athenæum.

Died 14 March 1950.

GALBRAITH, His Honour Judge James Francis Wallace; KC 1919; Judge of County Courts on Circuit No. 20 (Leicestershire, etc.) since 1935; JP; *b* 1872; 2nd *s* of Hugh James Galbraith; unmarried. *Educ:* Blackheath Proprietary School; Oriel College, Oxford (Scholar). President Oxford Union Society; President Hardwicke Society, 1909; called to Bar, Lincoln's Inn, 1893; Member of General Council of the Bar, of which Honorary Treasurer, 1921–35; Bencher of Lincoln's Inn, 1922; Contested Halifax, Jan. and Dec. 1910; MP (U) E Surrey, 1922–35. *Recreations:* lawn tennis and golf. *Address:* 3 New Square, Lincoln's Inn, WC. *T:* Holborn 1793; Monkswood, Kenley. *Club:* Constitutional.

Died 29 Jan. 1945.

GALBRAITH, Lt-Col James Ponsonby, OBE 1919; HM Lieutenant for County Tyrone, Northern Ireland, since 1945; *b* 27 March 1881; *yr s* of late Very Rev. George Galbraith, Dean of Derry, and Florence Acheson, *d* of late Acheson Lyle, HM Lieut for the City of Londonderry, The Oaks, Londonderry; *m* 1921, Henrietta Charlotte, *y d* of late Sir William Miller, MD, Londonderry; no *c.* *Educ:* Marlborough College; RMA Woolwich. 2nd Lt Royal Engineers 1899; Capt. 1908; Major 1916; Acting Lt-Col 1918–19; retired, 1924, with rank of Lt-Col. Served South Africa 1901–02 (Queen's

SA Medal and 4 clasps); European War, 1914–19, Gallipoli, Salonika, Batoum, Constantinople (1915 Star, War and Victory Medals, despatches twice, OBE); Major Home Guard, 1940–44 (Defence Medal). High Sheriff County Tyrone, 1926; DL 1928; Vice-Lieutenant, 1939. Member Representative Body of Church of Ireland, 1938; Hon. Sec.-Gen. Synod of Church of Ireland, 1940. *Address:* Clanabogan, Omagh, Co. Tyrone. *T:* Omagh 225. *Club:* Tyrone County (Omagh).

Died 1 Oct. 1950.

GALBRAITH, Col William Campbell, CMG 1916; TD; late RASC, TF; *b* Campbelltown, 11 Feb. 1870. Served European War, 1914–18 (despatches, CMG); served as officer in charge of Admiralty Housing and Labour for Great Britain; Col 1924; Hon. Sec. London Argyllshire Assoc. *Publications:* Commercial Side of Shipping (Harmsworth Encyclopædia); Airson tir agus Teanga, and other poems; Highland Heather, and other songs; soldier songs from Picardy.

Died 20 Feb. 1946.

GALE, Brig. Henry John Gordon, DSO 1918; *b* 3 July 1883; *s* of Col W. A. Gale, RE; *m*; one *d.* *Educ:* Malvern; RMA, Woolwich. Entered army 1902; Capt. 1914; Maj. 1917; Lt-Col 1932; Col 1936; Brigadier 1938; NWFP India, Mountain Artillery, 1912–16, 1920–36; Commander RA 43rd (Wessex) Division TA, 1936–39; retired, 1939; served European War, 1916–18 (wounded twice, despatches twice, DSO and Bar); North Russian Relief Forces, 1919; re-employed for active service, 1940–42; retired 1942. *Recreations:* fishing, tennis. *Address:* Onycha's, Netherhampton Road, Salisbury.

Died 12 Aug. 1944.

GALE, Norman; poet, story-teller, and reviewer; *m* 1st, Charlotte Mary (*d* 1922); 2nd, 1930, Edith Margaret. *Publications:* A Country Muse (2 vols), 1892; Orchard Songs, 1893; A June Romance, 1894; All Expenses Paid, 1895; Cricket Songs, 1894; Songs for Little People, 1896; Barty's Star, 1903; More Cricket Songs, 1905; A Book of Quatrains, 1909; Song in September, 1912; Solitude, 1913; Collected Poems, 1914; The Candid Cuckoo, 1918; A Merry-go-Round of Song, 1919; Verse in Bloom, 1925; A Flight of Fancies, 1926; Messrs Bat and Ball, 1930; Close of Play, 1936; Remembrances, 1937; Love-in-a-Mist, 1939. *Address:* Connemara, Headley Down, Bordon, Hampshire.

Died 7 Oct. 1942.

GALE, Walter Frederick, FRAS; *b* Sydney, 27 Nov. 1865; *s* of Henry Gale and Susannah Gordon Windeyer; *m* 1899, Violet Marion, *e d* of Joseph William Birkenhead, West Maitland, NSW; two *s* four *d.* *Educ:* Paddington House School. After five years' training in insurance and commercial offices, entered the service of the Savings Bank of New South Wales, afterwards amalgamated with the Government Savings Bank, and spent 38 years in various positions up to manager and chief inspector; interest in astronomy early developed by his father; at 19 he constructed a 7–inch reflecting telescope; several others up to 12 inches aperture were ground and polished in later years; observations of the planets, and particularly of Mars, commenced 1886; he discovered the small markings known as the oases of the planet, as well as hitherto uncharted canals, 1892; many later observations of clouds and markings interpreted as vegetation convinced him Mars is a world capable of bearing life; three new comets, some double stars and nebulæ, have also been discovered by him; advocates that the Argo Nebula is the centre of the galaxy and its two-armed spiral character; founder with R. T. A. Innes of the NSW Branch of the Brit. Astronomical Association; acted as first Secretary, and has been many times President. *Publications:* notes and observations in the Astronomische Nachrichten, the Monthly Notices of the Royal Astronomical Society, and in the Journal and Memoirs of the British Astronomical Association. *Recreations:* photography, boat-sailing, and fishing.

Address: Corunna, 142 Carrington Road, Waverley, NSW. *TA:* Observatory, Waverley. *T:* FW 1366. *Clubs:* Masonic, Sydney.

Died 1 June 1945.

GALES, Sir Robert Richard, Kt 1915; FCH, MInstCE, MAmSocCE; *b* 31 Oct. 1864; *s* of late Richard Smith Gales, of Littlehampton; unmarried. *Educ:* privately; Royal Indian Engineering College, Coopers Hill. Appointed to the Railway Branch of the Indian Public Works Department, 1886; received practical training on the Forth Bridge; on arrival in India in 1887 was employed on the Bannu Railway Survey, the Chenab Bridge at Sher Shah, the Mianwali Mari Railway extension, the Mari Attock Railway, and the reconstruction of the Ravi and Jhelum Bridges; appointed Assistant-Manager North Western Railway, 1895, and subsequently Assistant-Manager East Coast Railway, and Deputy-Manager Eastern Bengal Railway; Engineer-in-Chief Curzon Bridge over the Ganges at Allahabad, 1903; after conducting a reconnaissance of the Bombay Sind Railway Connection became Engineer-in-Chief Coonoor Ootacamund Railway, 1906; Engineer-in-Chief of the Hardinge Bridge over the Lower Ganges at Sara, 1908; Chief Engineer with the Railway Board, Govt of India Railway Department, 1915–17; Agent North-Western Railway of India, 1917–18; retired from Indian Railway Service, 1919; Partner, Rendel, Palmer & Tritton, Consulting Engineers, Westminster, 1919–37. *Publications:* various papers to InstCE. *Address:* St James's Court, Buckingham Gate, SW1.

Died 25 July 1948.

GALLICHAN, Walter M.; author and journalist; *b* St Helier, Jersey; *s* of John Gallichan and Elizabeth White, Reading; *m* 1st, Ada E., *d* of Dr H. White; 2nd, Norah Kathleen, *y d* of William Mutch, Aberdeen and London. *Educ:* Private School, Reading. Writer of social essays, novels, travel books; early contributions to National Reformer and assistant Editor of Free Review; Special Commissioner for Daily Mail in Spain and Scotland; Leader Writer, Publisher's Reader; a pioneer of sex education in England; Civil List Pension, 1934. *Publications:* Tales from the Western Moors, 1895; The Blight of Respectability, 1901; The New Morality, 1902; Seville, 1903; Conflict of Owen Prytherch, 1905; Modern Woman, 1909; Continental Towns, 1910; Fishing in Wales, and other angling books; The Great Unmarried, 1916; Religion of Kindness, 1916; Psychology of Marriage, 1917; Text-book of Sex Education, 1918; Letters to a Young Man, 1919; Critical Age of Woman, 1920; Our Hidden Selves, 1921; Pitfalls of Marriage, 1926; The Happy Fisherman, 1926; Sexual Apathy in Women, 1927; Youthful Old Age, 1929; The Poison of Prudery 1929; fifty-six volumes published. *Recreations:* trout fishing, gardening, cycling, travel. *Address:* 10 Meadway, Gidea Park, Essex. *T:* Romford 2666. *Club:* Savage.

Died 27 Nov. 1946.

GALLIE, Maj.-Gen. James Stuart, CB 1928; CMG 1918; DSO 1916; LRCP, LRCS, Edin., MScNU Ireland; late RAMC; *b* 20 March 1870; *s* of late John Gallie of Queenstown, Ireland; *m* 1903, Florence Ostle, *d* of late Col Charles Crighton of Hove, Sussex; two *s* two *d*. Served European War, 1914–18 (despatches, CMG, DSO, Bt-Col); Hon. Surgeon to the King, 1926–30; retired pay, 1930. *Address:* Marley House, Winfrith, Dorset. *Clubs:* Royal Dorset Yacht, Weymouth.

Died 1 May 1943.

GALLIER, William Henry, CBE 1920; late Principal Clerk, Exchequer and Audit Department; *b* 1855; *s* of late William Gallier, Storrington, Sussex. *Educ:* privately. *Address:* 29 West Street, Reigate, Surrey. *T:* Reigate 2031.

Died 6 Sept. 1946.

GALLOP, Rodney Alexander, CMG 1946; Foreign Office since 1940; *b* Folkestone, 26 May 1901; *yr s* of late Reginald G. Gallop, St Jean de Luz, France, and of Helen Marion Duffield; *m* 1925, Marjorie Dorothy Carmichael, *d* of Lieut-Col R. C. Bell, DSO, OBE; two *s*. *Educ:* Harrow; King's College, Cambridge. Diplomatic Service, 1923; 3rd Secretary Belgrade, 1923, Athens, 1926; 2nd Sec., 1928; Foreign Office, 1929; Lisbon, 1931; Foreign Office, 1933; 1st Sec., 1934; Mexico City, 1935; Copenhagen, 1938–40; Counsellor, 1944; Hon. Member of Danish Resistance Movement for his services during the occupation, 1945. *Publications:* A Book of the Basques, 1930; (with Miss Violet Alford) The Traditional Dance, 1935; Portugal: A Book of Folk Ways, 1936; Cantares do Povo Português, 1937; Mexican Mosaic, 1939; Music: Six Basque Folksongs, 1931; Eight Portuguese Folksongs, 1936. *Recreations:* travel, music, folklore research. *Address:* c/o Foreign Office, SW1. *Club:* United University.

Died 25 Sept. 1948.

GALLOWAY, Sir David, Kt 1924; MD, FRCPEd; JP; Physician Extraordinary to Sultan of Johore; Member of Executive and State Councils of State of Johore; *b* 8 May 1858; *e s* of late David Galloway, Edinburgh; *m* 1886, Rodney Mary, *e d* of late Joseph Murray, Edinburgh; one *s* one *d*. *Educ:* Daniel Stewart's College and University, Edinburgh. MB, CM 1884. Proceeded to Straits Settlements, 1885; accompanied late Sultan of Johore to Europe, 1895; decorated 2nd class Order of the Crown of Johore for service to late Sultan, 1896; promoted to 1st class, 1914; MRCPEd., 1899; MD (Gold Medal), 1900; FRCP, 1902; unofficial Member of Executive Council, Straits Settlements, 1903–14 and 1921; Vice-Chairman Straits Opium Commission, 1908; Ex-President Royal Asiatic Society, Straits Branch; Fellow of Royal Society of Medicine. *Publications:* On Splenic Abscess of Malarial Origin, BMJ, 1903; On the Etiology and Treatment of Sprue (2 papers), Journal Tropical Medicine, 1905; On the Otomycosis of the Malay Archipelago, Journal of Otology, 1903. *Recreations:* fishing, golf, motoring. *Address:* Johore Bahru, Malay Peninsula. *Clubs:* East India and Sports; University, Edinburgh; Johore, Singapore.

Died 5 March 1943.

GALLOWAY, Col Frank Lennox, CMG 1917; late RA; *b* 1869; *s* of late Major-General J. M. C. Galloway, Bournemouth; *m* 1899, Anna, 2nd *d* of late Albert Savory, Potters Park, Ottershaw; one *s* two *d*. *Educ:* United Services College, Westward Ho!; Royal Military Academy, Woolwich. Served with the Chitral Relief Force, 1895; Tirah Expeditionary Force, 1897; Brevet Lt-Colonel, 1916; Director Ministry of Munitions, 1916–19; Chief Inspector Armaments, Woolwich, 1919–21; Member Ordnance Committee, 1921–25. *Address:* Neatham, Sleepers Hill, Winchester. *T:* Winchester 4522.

Died 2 Nov. 1949.

GALPIN, Rev. Francis William, MA (Trinity College, Cantab); LittD; FLS; Hon. Canon of Chelmsford, 1917; Canon Emeritus, 1934; *b* 25 Dec. 1858; *m* 1889, Mary Maude Hawkins (*d* 1942); three *s* one *d*. *Educ:* King's School, Sherborne; Trinity College, Cambridge. Curate of Redenhall with Harleston, Norfolk, 1883–87; S Giles in the Fields, London, 1887–91; Vicar of Hatfield Regis, 1891–1915; Vicar of Witham, 1915–21; Rector of Faulkbourne, 1921–33; Hon. Freedom of Worshipful Company of Musicians, 1905; Surrogate and Rural Dean of Witham, 1915–33; Honorary Chaplain of the Forces; President, Essex Archæological Society, 1921–26; Vice-President, 1926; President, London Musical Association, 1938; writer on antiquarian subjects (monastic), and lecturer on ancient musical instruments. *Publications:* The Flowering Plants of Harleston in Norfolk, 1888; Descriptive Catalogue of the European Musical Instruments in the Metropolitan Museum of Art, New York, 1902; The Musical Instruments of the American

Indians of the NW Coast, 1903; Notes on a Roman Hydraulus, 1904; The Evolution of the Sackbut, 1907; Old English Instruments, 3rd edition, 1932; Household Expenses of Sir T. Barrington, 1911; Stainer's Music of the Bible (enlarged edition), 1913; co-author, The Church Plate of Essex, 1926; The Sumerian Harp of Ur, 1929; The Viola Pomposa, 1931; A Textbook of European Musical Instruments, 1937; The Music of the Sumerians, Babylonians and Assyrians, 1937; The Music of Electricity, 1938; The Romance of the Phagotum, 1941; In the Garden of the Lord, 1942; 'Neath the Trees of the Lord, 1945. *Address:* Stanmore, 164 Kew Road, Richmond, Surrey. *T:* Richmond 2063.

Died 30 Dec. 1945.

GALWAY, 8th Viscount *cr* 1727; **George Vere Arundell Monckton-Arundell,** PC 1937; GCMG 1935; DSO 1917; OBE 1919; Baron Killard, 1727; Baron Monckton (UK), 1887; late Lt-Col Life Guards; Hon. Col 42nd (Foresters) AA Bn since 1933; Col Comdt HAC, 1933–35 and since 1941; *b* 24 March 1882; *o s* of 7th Viscount and Vere (*d* 1921), *o d* of Ellis Gosling, Busbridge Hall, Godalming, Surrey; *S* father, 1931; *m* 1922, Hon. Lucia White, *yr d* of 3rd Baron Annaly; one *s* three *d. Educ:* Eton; Christ Church, Oxford. Sherwood Rangers Yeomanry, 1900–04; 1st Life Guards, 1904; Adjt, 1908–11; Capt. 1911; Staff Capt., 4th Cavalry Brigade, 1914–15; DAA and QMG, 2nd Cavalry Division, 1915–17; AA and QMG, 1917–19; Brevet Lt-Col, 1919; commanded Life Guards, 1925–29; retired pay, 1929; Gov.-Gen. of New Zealand, 1935–41; contested (C) Scarborough, 1910. *Heir: s* Hon. Simon George Robert Monckton-Arundell, *b* 11 Nov. 1929. *Address:* The Mantles, Blyth, Worksop, Notts. *T:* Ranskill 279; Serlby Hall, Bawtry, Yorkshire. *T:* Ranskill 1. *Clubs:* Guards', Carlton.

Died 27 March 1943.

GALWAY, Lt-Col Sir Henry Lionel, KCMG 1910 (CMG 1899); DSO 1896; *b* 25 Sept. 1859; *s* of late Lt-Gen. Sir T. L. Gallwey, KCMG, RE [assumed the present surname in place of Gallwey 1911]; *m* 1913, Marie Carola, CBE 1926, *d* of late Rt Hon. Sir Rowland Blennerhasset, 4th Bt, and *widow* of Baron Raphael D'Erlanger. *Educ:* Cheltenham; Sandhurst. Joined 30th Regiment, 1878; ADC and Private Secretary to Commander-in-Chief and Governor, Bermuda, 1882–89; Deputy Commissioner and Vice-Consul, Oil Rivers Protectorate, 1891; Acting Consul-General, 1896–98; Acting High Commissioner, S Nigeria, 1900; concluded treaty with King of Benin at Benin City, 1892; in command of Haussa force, under Sir Frederick Bedford, at attack on and capture of Nimbe, and during further operations against Brass chiefs, 1895 (despatches, DSO, medal with clasp); attached to Sir H. Rawson's intelligence staff, and also in command of a Haussa company during operations in Benin country, including capture of Benin City, 1897 (despatches, brevet of Major, clasp); chief political officer Aro expedition, 1901–02 (despatches, medal and clasp); present in several minor operations against natives in the Protectorate, 1891–1902; late Divisional Commissioner, Southern Nigeria; Governor of St Helena, 1902–11; of the Gambia. 1911–14; of South Australia, 1914–20. Hon. Col, 27th Australian Infantry, 1921–46. *Address:* 30 Lansdowne Road, Holland Park, W11. *Clubs:* Naval and Military, MCC, Pitt.

Died 17 June 1949.

GAMBLE, Sir David, 3rd Bt *cr* 1897; Mayor of St Helens, 1913–14, 1914–15 (1st and 2nd Barts were also Mayors of St Helens); *b* 1 May 1876; *e s* of 2nd Bt and Isabella (*d* 1937), *d* of George S. Sanderson of Claughton, Birkenhead; *S* father, 1908; *m* 1903, Eveline Frances Josephine, 2nd *d* of late Rev. Arthur R. Cole; four *s. Heir: s* David Arthur Josias [*b* 9 Dec. 1907; *m* 1932, Elinor Mary (Molly), *o d* of Henry E. Cole, Summers,

Long Sutton, Hants; one *s, b* 5 June 1933]. *Address:* White Lodge, Purton, Wiltshire. *TA:* Gamble, Purton. *T:* St Helens 16.

Died 17 July 1943.

GAMMELL, Sir Sydney James, of Countesswells, Kt 1928; JP, Co. Aberdeen and Co. Kincardine; *b* 1867; *e s* of late Rev. J. S. Gammell of Countesswells; *m* 1891, Alice Trench, *d* of Rev. H. Stobart; five *s* three *d. Educ:* Clifton; Pembroke College, Cambridge; BA, 1889. *Address:* 68 Gladstone Place, Aberdeen. *T:* 749.

Died 25 Feb. 1946.

GANDHI, Mohandas Karamchand; Editor of Young India; *b* 2 Oct. 1869. *Educ:* Rajkot; Bhavnagar; London. Called to Bar, 1889; practised as barrister and attorney in South Africa for 17 years; gave up a lucrative practice for service of the Indian settlers in South Africa in 1908; led Passive Resistance Campaign, and entered into a settlement with General Smuts in 1914; returned to India, 1915; Started Satyagraha movement 1918 and non-co-operation campaign 1920; inaugurated campaign for breach of Salt Laws, April 1930; interned 5 May 1930; released 26 Jan. 1931; held conversations with the Viceroy which resulted in the Delhi Pact, 1931; was a delegate to Second Round Table Conference, 1931; interned again 1932, went on a week's fast, while in jail, and got the premier's award altered in the interests of the untouchables; again went on a three weeks' fast for better treatment of untouchables and was released; started individual civil disobedience and was again imprisoned and released on declaring a fast for getting facilities to carry on the Anti-Untouchability campaign from prison, 1933; retired from active leadership of the Indian National Congress in 1934; advised the Congress to accept offices under the new Reforms, and continued to guide the policy and programme of the Congress Ministers under the new regime from Sevagram, the little village which he has made his headquarters in the interests of Rural Reconstruction work; led a Satyagraha Campaign for Freedom of speech and writing and action regarding War; suspended the campaign in 1942; wants now an orderly withdrawal of the British domination from India in the interest of both India and Britain. *Publications:* (Eng. trans.) The Story of My Experiments with Truth, 1949 (posthumous); etc. *Address:* Sevagram, Wardha (CP), India.

Died 30 Jan. 1948.

GANGE, Edwin Stanley; JP, a Bristol merchant; *b* 1871; *s* of a Baptist minister; *m* 1895, Alice, *d* of Henry Denning, MP (Co. L) North Bristol, 1918–22. Sheriff of Bristol, 1931–32.

Died 29 Feb. 1944.

GARCKE, Sidney, CBE 1941; MIMechE; A pioneer of the Motor movement; Chairman, Eastwoods, Ltd; Dennis Bros Ltd, Electrical Press Ltd; Director of British Electric Traction Co. Ltd; *b* London, 1885; *s* of late Emile Garcke, MIEE; *m* 1908, Clare, *d* of late J. G. Lorrain, MInstCE, MIMechE, MIEE; one *s* one *d. Educ:* University of London. Past President of Institute of Transport; Upper Warden, Worshipful Company of Pattenmakers. *Address:* Felhurst, Grand Avenue, Hove; 26 Harcourt House, Cavendish Square, W1. *Clubs:* Garrick, Royal Automobile; Brighton Union (Brighton); Royal Motor Yacht (Poole).

Died 3 Oct. 1948.

GARDINER, Alfred G.; JP, Bucks; *b* Chelmsford, 1865; *s* of Henry James Gardiner; *m* Ada, *d* of Peter Claydon, of Witham; two *s* four *d.* Editor of The Daily News, 1902–19; President Institute of Journalists, 1915–16. *Publications:* Prophets, Priests, and Kings; Pillars of Society; The War Lords; Certain People of Importance; The Anglo-American Future; The Life of Sir William Harcourt, 1923; The Life of George Cadbury, 1923; John Benn and the Progressive Movement, 1925; and works under pen name of Alpha of the Plough. *Recreation:* golf. *Address:* Whiteleaf, Princes Risboro'. *T:* Princes Risboro' 23. *Club:* Reform.

Died 3 March 1946.

GARDINER, Col (Hon. Maj.-Gen., retired) Henry Lawrence, CB 1917; *b* 16 April 1860; *s* of Rev. T. Gardiner, Old Aberdeen; *m* Isobel Violet (*d* 1941), *e d* of J. Dunlop, of Brockloch, Ayrshire; one *s* two *d*. *Educ:* Chanonry School, Old Aberdeen; Aberdeen University; RM Academy, Woolwich. Received Commission in the RA, 1879, gaining the Toombs' Memorial Scholarship; Captain, 1887; Major, 1897; Lt-Col 1905; Col 1912; Instructor, School of Gunnery, 1898–1903; Chief Instructor, 1908–12; Col in Charge, RGA Records, 1912–13; Commandant, School of Gunnery, 1913–14; commanded Scottish Coast Defences and Forth Garrison, 1914–17 (temporary Maj.-Gen., despatches, CB); served Afghan War, 1878–80 (despatches, medal with clasp); Zhob Valley Expedition, 1884. *Address:* c/o Mrs R. L. Barton, The Little House, Sheringham, Norfolk.

Died 24 Feb. 1946.

GARDINER, John Stanley, FRS, 1908; MA (Cantab), FLS, FRGS; Emeritus Professor of Zoology in Cambridge University, 1909–37; Trustee of British Museum since 1931; Standing Commission on Museums and Galleries since 1942; *b* Belfast, 24 Jan. 1872; *s* of late Rev. Jephson Gardiner, Black Torrington, Devon; *m* 1st, 1900, Rachel Florence (*d* 1901), *d* of late Richard Dening, Ottery St Mary; 2nd, 1909, Edith Gertrude, *d* of R. A. Willcock, Goldthorn, Wolverhampton, formerly Fellow of Newnham Coll., Camb. (DSc Dub.), and author of numerous papers in bio-chemistry; two *d*. *Educ:* Marlborough College; Gonville and Caius College, Cambridge. Coral Reef Boring Expedition to Funafuti, 1896; Fellow of Gonville and Caius College, 1898; Dean of Gonville and Caius College, 1903–09; Balfour Student, 1899–1901; Maldive and Laccadive Expedition, 1899–1901; Murchison Award, RGS, 1902; Indian Ocean Expedition in HMS Sealark, 1905; Demonstrator of Animal Morphology, 1902–08; Senior Proctor of University, 1907–08; Member of (Treasury) Committee on Fishery Investigations, 1907–08; Seychelles Expedition, 1908; University Lecturer in Zoology, 1909; Member Government Advisory Committee on Fisheries, 1913; Director of Scientific Investigations, Ministry of Fisheries; 1920; Agassiz Medal of National Academy of Sciences (USA); Linnean Medal of Linnean Society; Darwin Medal of Royal Society, 1944. *Publications:* Coral Reefs and Atolls, 1931; editor of The Fauna and Geography of the Maldive and Laccadive Archipelagoes, 1902–1906; numerous papers; Natural History of Wicken Fen. *Recreations:* travel, fishing, gardening, yachting. *Address:* Bredon House, Cambridge. *Club:* Cambridge Cruising.

Died 28 Feb. 1946.

GARDINER, Linda; Secretary Royal Society for the Protection of Birds, 1900–35; *b* Gorleston, Suffolk; *yr d* of late W. S. Gardiner, Managing Editor of Darlington and Stockton Times and of Hampshire Observer; *g d* of late Robert Harrison, Hull. *Educ:* home. Some journalistic experience. *Publications:* Several novels, numerous contributions to magazines and newspapers; Editor of Bird Notes and News, and organiser of Bird and Tree Nature Study scheme. *Recreation:* bird-watching. *Address:* 82 Victoria Street, SW1.

Died 1 March 1941.

GARDINER, Robert Strachan, CBE 1946; FRICS; FLAS; MRASE; lately Secretary to Central Landowners' Association; *b* 1874; *s* of Robert Gardiner, late Agent for the Earl of Lisburne; *m* 1st, Kate Louise (*d* 1926), *d* of Henry Crossley; one *d*; 2nd, 1929, Hilda Grace, *d* of Thomas Lucas. *Educ:* Aberystwith Grammar School; University College of Wales; Aspatria Agricultural Coll.

Late Agent for agricultural estates, including Hawarden Castle Estate, Flintshire, and Burton Manor Estate, Cheshire. *Address:* 8 Bicton Place, Exmouth. *T:* Exmouth 3576. *Club:* Farmers'.

Died 17 Oct. 1950.

GARDINER, Rev. Thory Gage, MA; *b* 1857; *s* of late Stephen Gage Gardiner and Susan, *d* of Thory Chapman; *m* Dorothy, *e d* of late Sir John A. Kempe, KCB. *Educ:* Cheltenham College; Brasenose College, Oxford (BA 1880). Ordained, 1881; Curate, St Jude's, Whitechapel, 1881; Sub-Warden, Toynbee Hall, 1885–89; Rector of All Saints, Colchester, 1890–92; St George-the-Martyr, Southwark, 1892–97; Somerleyton with Ashby, 1897; Farnham, 1897–1904; St Michael Paternoster Royal London, 1907–10; Lambeth, 1910–17; Chaplain to Archbishop of Canterbury, 1903–28; Hon. Canon of Southwark, 1915; Residentiary Canon of Canterbury, 1917–37; Chairman, Southern Section Co-operative Union, 1891–96; Secretary to Education Committee of Co-operative Union, 1891–95; served on the Colchester, the Southwark, and the Farnham Board of Guardians; on the Colchester and on the Farnham School Board; Chairman (elected) St-George-the-Martyr, Southwark, Vestry, 1894–97; served on the Poor Law Commission, 1909. *Address:* 53 St Peter's Street, Canterbury. *T:* Canterbury 2587.

Died 29 Oct. 1941.

GARDINER, Walter, FRS 1890; MA, ScD; Honorary Fellow and sometime Fellow and Bursar of Clare College, Cambridge; *b* 1 Sept. 1859; *o surv. s* of late Stephen T. Gardiner; *m* 1893, Isabella Whitehead, *d* of late James Campbell, Glasgow; one *s* one *d*. *Educ:* Bedford; Clare College, Cambridge (Scholar); Würzburg University. Scholar of Royal Agricultural Society of England, 1874–76; First Class Natural Science Tripos, 1881. Science Lecturer at Girton College, 1883; University Demonstrator in Botany, 1884; University Lecturer in Botany, 1889; with Prof. M. C. Potter, ScD, reinstituted University Botanical Museum founded by Prof. Henslow; Rolleston Prize, Oxford, 1888; Royal Medal of the Royal Society, 1898; has given courses of lectures at the Royal and London institutions; lectures at the Royal and London Institutions; lecturer to British Association (Newcastle), 1889; one of the Vice-Presidents of the Botany Section at the Cambridge meeting of the Brit. Assoc. 1904. *Publications:* author of various papers, dealing mainly with Histological and Physiological Botany, in the Royal, Linnean, and other Societies. *Recreations:* fishing, gardening, natural history.

Died 31 Aug. 1941.

GARDNER, Hon. Mrs Alan; President, Herefordshire Women's Liberal Association; Vice-President, Women's Liberal Federation for England; Vice-President, Ladies' Committee of Congress on Tuberculosis; President, Lydney Women Federation; Vice-President, Essex Needlework Guild; a President of The Children's Happy Evening Association, of the Soldiers and Sailors Family Association for the Dean Forest, of the Liberal Social League, of the Surrey Ladies Garden Club; *e d* of Lord Blyth of Blythwood; *m* 1885, Col Alan Gardner, MP, DL, JP, 11th Hussars of Clearwell Castle, Glos (*d* 1907); two *s* one *d*. Has seen much of wild life in unexplored countries, and big-game shooting; in company with her husband, has made many shooting expeditions to Africa, Northern India, Nepaul, Assam, North America, and Australasia; has explored interior of Somaliland and the Abyssinian frontier; done much work among unemployed ex-soldiers, running cooking and training classes for them for domestic service. *Publications:* Rifle and Spear with the Rajpoots; Life in Somaliland, etc. *Recreations:* gardening, embroidery, cooking, hunting, biggame shooting, sketching. *Address:* The Old Malt House, Worplesdon, Guildford. *T:* Worplesdon 8.

Died Jan. 1944.

GARDNER, Benjamin Walter; *b* 1865; *s* of W. B. Gardner, Halstead, Essex; *m* 1890. MP (Lab) Upton Division, 1923–24, 1929–31 and 1934–45. *Address:* 205 Shakespeare Cres., E12.

Died 13 Jan. 1948.

GARDNER, Henry Willoughby, MBE; *b* 1861; *m* 1909, Mary Louisa, *d* of late Rev. E. F. Rambaut. *Educ:* Charterhouse; St Bartholomew's Hosp. MD Lond.; FRCP Lond. Consulting Physician Salop Infirmary; Consulting Physician Shropshire Orthopædic Hospital; late President of the Midland Medical Society. *Publications:* The Treatment of Phthisis for the County of Shropshire; contributions to medical journals. *Address:* Coombehurst, Church Stretton.

Died 27 Feb. 1948.

GARDNER, John Addyman, MA, FRIC; consulting chemist; *b* 1867; *e s* of late Thomas Gardner of Bradford; *m* 1903, Mrs Henrietta White (*d* 1926), *d* of late Lieut and Adjt Arthur Henry Lews, 65th Regt. *Educ:* Bradford Grammar School; Magdalen College, Oxford (Demyship); Heidelberg. 1st Class (Chemistry) Hon. School of Natural Science, 1889. Demonstrator in Chemistry, Oxford, 1891; Lectureship in Chemistry, Medical School, St George's Hospital, 1894; Lecturer in Organic Chemistry, London School of Medicine for Women until 1935; Reader in Physiological Chemistry, London Univ.; Lecturer in Chemistry and Biochemist, St George's Hospital; retired, 1942; sometime Examiner in Chemistry in Final Hon. School, Oxford Univ., London University, Royal Colleges of Physicians and Surgeons, Soc. of Apothecaries, etc.; Hon. Treas. of the Biochemical Soc., 1912–44; Member of Council of Chemical Society, 1919–22; for many years has taken an active interest in the teaching of science in schools. *Publications:* article on Blood (with Dr Buckmaster), and on Cholesterol in Allen's Commercial Analysis; numerous papers on chemical, biochemical, and physiological subjects in the Proceedings of the Royal Society, the Transactions of the Chemical Society, the Journal of the Physiological Society, and in the Biochemical Journal. *Recreation:* fishing. *Address:* 11 St Paul's Road, Manningham, Bradford. *T:* Bradford 655. *Clubs:* Savile, Knights of the Round Table.

Died 13 May 1946.

GARLAND, Lester V. L.; *see* Lester-Garland.

GARMOYLE, Viscount; Hugh Wilfrid John Cairns, DSO 1941; Brigadier late Rifle Brigade; *b* 9 June 1907; *er s* and *heir* of 4th Earl Cairns; *m* 1936, Barbara Elisabeth, *yr d* of Capt. Arden Franklyn, New Place, Shedfield, Hants, and 33 Bryanston Square, W. ADC to GOC-in-C, Southern Command, 1937–38; served War of 1939–45 (DSO and Bar). *Address:* Farleigh-Hungerford, Bath.

Died July 1942.

GARNEAU, Sir (John) George, Kt 1908; LLD, DCL; Chairman of the National Battlefields Commission, 1908–39; *b* Quebec, 19 Nov. 1864; 2nd *s* of late Hon. Pierre Garneau, Member of the Legislative Council of the Province of Quebec, and Charlotte Cecile Burroughs; *m* 1892, Marie Alma (*d* 1936), *d* of Major A. Benoit of Ottawa; three *s* three *d. Educ:* Quebec Seminary; Montreal Polytechnic School of Engineering; BAppSc (High Honours), Laval University. Professor Emeritus (Laval); LLD (hon.) Toronto University, 1917; McGill University, 1921; DCL (hon.) Bishop's University, 1931. Abandoned practice of engineering to go into business, and is President of Garneau, Ltd, wholesale woollens and staples; Mayor of Quebec, 1906–10; Chairman of Executive Committee which organised Quebec Tercentenary celebration; Acting Chairman of the Quebec Public Service Commission, 1910–21; Member of the National Research Council (Canada), 1918–32; President of La Caisse d'Economie de Quebec, Vice-President of La Banque Canadienne

Nationale, Director Bell Telephone Company of Canada, General Trust of Canada, Continental Life Insurance Co. and Donacona Paper Company Ltd; a Knight of the Legion of Honour of France, 1908; Knight Commander of the Order of St Gregory the Great, 1919. *Recreations:* golf, hunting, fishing, photography. *Address:* 136 Grande Allée, Quebec. *Clubs:* University Montreal; Garrison, Quebec.

Died 6 Feb. 1944.

GARNETT, Martha; *b* 3 Dec. 1869; 3rd *c* of Richard Roscoe, solicitor, of Shaen, Roscoe, Massey & Co., 8 Bedford Row; *m* 1896, Robert Singleton Garnett (*d* 1932); two *s* three *d. Educ:* Queen's College, Harley Street; Miss Norton's, Holly Hill, Hampstead (private school); Newnham College, Cambridge. *Publications:* The Infamous John Friend, novel, 1909; Amor Vincit, novel, 1912; Samuel Butler and his family relations, 1926; Unrecorded, novel, 1931. *Recreations:* gardening, country life. *Address:* Hardown, Morcombelake, Bridport, Dorset.

Died 8 Aug. 1946.

GARNETT, Lt-Col William Brooksbank, DSO 1917; DL, JP Co. Tyrone; late Royal Welch Fusiliers; High Sheriff for County Tyrone, 1941, and Officer of Ulster Home Guard; Member Representative Body of Church of Ireland; *b* 31 July 1875; 3rd *s* of late Frederick Brooksbank Garnett, CB, FSS, and of late Mary C., *d* of Lt-Col John Laurie, RA, of Maxwelton; *m* 1915, Eleanor Constance, *e d* of late John Benjamin Story, KHS; *one son* killed in action, Belgium, 23rd May 1940; one *d. Educ:* Charterhouse. Entered Civil Service (Inland Revenue Dept); served as 2nd Lieut 24th Middlesex (Post Office) Rifles, 1895; Lieut CIV, 1900; received Hon. Freedom of City of London; served S Africa, 1900 (Queen's medal and four clasps); joined Royal Welch Fusiliers, 1900; served 2nd RWF, China and India, 1901–07; 1st RWF, Ireland, 1908–12; Adjutant 7th RWF, 1913–14; served European War with 1st RWF, 1914; commanded 20th (Public Schools) Bn Royal Fusiliers, 1916 and 2nd Bn RW Fusiliers, 1917–18; Brig.-General Commanding 121st Inf. Brig., May–Sept. 1918; Commanded 2nd Bn The Welch Regt, Oct. 1918–May 1919 (despatches four times, DSO, Bt Lt-Col); retired pay, 1927; Secretary, Flint and Denbigh Territorial Army Association, 1927–36. *Address:* Corick, Clogher, Co. Tyrone, Northern Ireland. *T:* Clogher 216. *Club:* Naval and Military.

Died 17 Aug. 1946.

GARRATT, Geoffrey Theodore, MBE 1942; JP; Capt. Pioneer Corps; *b* 1888; of Rev. C. F. Garratt; *m* 1920, Anne Beryl Benthall. *Educ:* Rugby School, Hertford College, Oxford. ICS 1913–23; served with Indian Cavalry during European War, MEF, 1916–19; Berlin Correspondent Westminster Gazette; Political Secretary Indian Round Table Conference; Organised welfare work Bengal; Correspondent Manchester Guardian in Ethiopia, 1936, in Finland, 1940; Hon. Administrator, NJC for Spanish Relief, 1937–38; Contested (Lab) Cambridgeshire, 1925, 1929, 1931, Wrekin, 1935. *Publications:* Hundred Acre Farm; An Indian Commentary; Rise and Fulfilment of British Rule in India; Life of Lord Brougham; The Two Mr Gladstones; Musolini's Roman Empire; The Shadow of the Swastika; Gibraltar and the Mediterranean; What has Happened to Europe (USA only); Europe's Dance of Death; Edited: The Legacy of India. *Recreation:* travel. *Address:* Bishopsteignton House, near Teignmouth, S Devon. *TA:* Bishopsteignton 30. *Club:* Authors'.

Died 28 April 1942.

GARRETT, Col Arthur Newson Bruff, CBE, 1919, TD, JP; *b* 1868; *s* of late Major N. D. Garrett, RA, Aldeburgh, Suffolk; *m* 1st, 1895, Elise Grant (*d* 1921), *d* of late Kenneth Mackenzie of Borlum-Beg, Inverness-shire; 2nd, 1926, Helen Guy, *widow* of Rev. Dr A. G. Pentreath, DD, late Rector of Stockton, and *d* of late C.

Guy Carleton, Beech Mount, Co. Cork. *Educ:* Portsmouth Grammar School. Colonel 4th Batt. King's Shropshire LI, 1914–18; GSO Strait Settlements, 1916–17; Command of 2/1 Royal North Devon Hussars, 1918; Command of 2nd Cyclist Brigade, Athlone, 1919. *Recreations:* shooting, fishing, gardening. *Address:* The Barton, St Feock, Truro, Cornwall. *T:* Feock 281.

Died 24 April 1942.

GARRETT, Sir Douglas Thornbury, Kt 1947; BA; Solicitor; Senior partner of Parker, Garrett and Co., St Michael's Rectory, Cornhill, EC3; *b* 23 July 1883; *s* of late Samuel Garrett, Solicitor, JP; *m* 1907, Gwendoline Frieda Isabella, *d* of late ACF Calaminus; one *s* one *d*. *Educ:* Rugby School; Emmanuel College, Cambridge (Scholar). Admitted as Solicitor, 1909 (honours); Lieut RNVR, 1917–19; Pres. of Law Society, 1946–47; Member of Council since 1926; Member of Disciplinary Committee since 1933; Member of Supreme Court Rule Committee since 1938; President of Law Association; Secretary of London General Ship-owners Society since 1920; Director of Legal and General Assurance Society Ltd, Williams Deacon's Bank Ltd, and Solicitors' Law Stationery Society Ltd; Member of Council of Bedford College for Women since 1926; Member Governing Body of Rugby School since 1941; Member, Chancellor of the Exchequer's Committee on Banking and Insurance, 1942; Pres. of Fisheries Organization Society, Ltd, 1948–. *Recreations:* reading, music, pictures, architecture, sailing, walking. *Address:* Brewsters, Lamarsh, Bures, Suffolk. *T:* Bures 255; 8 Briardale Gardens, NW3. *T:* Hampstead 2741. *Clubs:* City of London, Savile, MCC; Aldeburgh Yacht (Aldeburgh).

Died 22 Oct. 1949.

GARRETT, Herbert Leonard Offley, CIE, 1937; ED; MA; Esquire Bedell of the University of Cambridge since 1936; Supervisor ICS Probationers and Secretary Board of ICS Studies, Cambridge, since 1937; *b* 16 June 1881; *s* of late Dr G. M. Garrett, Organist of St John's College, Cambridge and of the University, composer of church music; *m* 1922, Sibyl, *d* of late H. H. Young, Normanton; two *d*. *Educ:* Charterhouse; St John's College, Cambridge. BA 1902. Colonial (Educational) Service, Hong Kong, 1904–12; Indian Educational Service, 1912; professor Government College, Lahore, 1912; military duty, 1917–18; secretary publicity department, 1919; Lt-Col commanding 4th (Lahore) University Training Corps, 1924–36 (ED 1933); Keeper of records of government of Punjab, 1924–36; Principal Government College, Lahore, 1927; retired from IES, 1936. *Publications:* Cunningham's History of the Sikhs (new edition); Moghul Rule in India; The Mohammedan Period of Indian History; General Editor Punjab Government Record Office Publications and numerous articles etc. on Indian History. *Recreations:* golf, lawn tennis. *Address:* Waynekirke, 18 Fendon Road, and St John's College, Cambridge. *Clubs:* Punjab, Lahore; Union, Cambridge.

Died 6 Dec. 1941.

GARRETT, Captain Peter Bruff, CBE 1919; RN, retired; *b* 14 July 1866; *s* of Major N. D. Garrett, RA; *m* 1891, Alice Maude Mary (*d* 1930), *e d* of late John Stone; (one *s* killed on Service in 1942) one *d*. *Educ:* St Mark's School (now Imperial Service College); Stubbington, Fareham. Joined Navy, Naval Cadet, 1879; went to sea in HMS Nelson, 1881; Sub-Lieut 1886; Lieut 1890; retd Commander, 1911; served European War as DNTO at Newhaven, and at Portsmouth (OBE, CBE, promoted Captain RN, General African medal (Vitu Clasp), Victory medal, 1919). *Address:* 62 Kensington Road, Westonsuper-Mare, Somerset.

Died 11 Feb. 1950.

GARSIDE, Oswald, RI 1916; painter in water colours; *b* Southport, Lancashire, 3 Aug. 1869; *s* of Thomas Garside, FCS, scientific chemist and analyist, Southport, and Elizabeth, *d* of Samuel Smith, master cotton-spinner, of Bury and Heywood, Lancs. *Educ:* Took up the study of art at the age of twenty-three; obtained Lancashire County Council Scholarship, and studied three years at Julian's, Paris; obtained extension of one year which was spent in Italy. Regular Exhibitor at Royal Academy, Paris Salons, and other exhibitions, since 1902; Pictures in Public Galleries at Birkenhead, Blackpool, Derby, Southport, Liverpool, Oldham, Warrington, Eastbourne, Bury, Lancashire, Kettering, Worcester, Kidderminster, Dudley, Conway, Reading, Doncaster, Newcastle, Northampton, and Bolton; Member Royal Cambrian Academy, Royal British Colonial Society, Manchester Academy of Fine Arts, and Liverpool Academy of Arts, Ulster Academy of Arts, and Royal West of England Academy; President Midland Sketching Club and Warrington Art Society; Director, Artists General Benevolent Institute and Orphan Fund. *Publication:* Landscape Painting in Water Colours. *Address:* The Studio, 1 White Hart Lane, Barnes, SW13; 20 Kensington Gore, SW7. *Clubs:* Arts; Liverpool Artists.

Died 10 Dec. 1942.

GARSTANG, Walter, MA, DSc, FLS, FZS; Professor of Zoology in the University of Leeds, 1907–33, Emeritus Professor since 1933; Pro-Vice-Chancellor, 1929–31; Vice-President, Marine Biological Association, 1940; *b* Blackburn, 9 Feb. 1868; *e s* of late Walter Garstang, MD, MRCP; *m* 1895, Lucy Ackroyd (*d* 1942); one *s* five *d*. *Educ:* Blackburn Grammar School; Jesus College, Oxford. Berkeley Fellow of the Owens College, Manchester, 1891–92. Fellow and Lecturer of Lincoln College, Oxford, 1893–97; Chief Naturalist to the Marine Biological Association, 1897–1907; Médaille de la Société d'Aquiculture et de Pêche, Paris, 1900; Delegate of HM Government to International Conference on Exploration of the Sea, Christiania, 1901; Scientific Adviser to British Delegates on the International Council, 1902–08; Convener of the International Committee on Trawling Investigations, 1902–08; Member of Advisory Committee of Development Commission on Fishery Research, 1919–45; 1st Buckland Professor of Fish Culture, 1929. *Publications:* 70 memoirs on Marine Biology and Sea Fisheries; The Return to Oxford: a Memorial Lay, 1919; Songs of the Birds, 1922 (3rd Ed., 1935); The Students' Opera 1922; The Theory of Recapitulation, 1922; Wordsworth's Interpretation of Nature, 1926; Frank Buckland's Life and Work, 1929; Doliolids and Copelata of the Terra Nova, 1933–1935; Spolia Bermudiana, 1939; The Siphonophora 1945. *Recreations:* gardening, birds and the Muses. *Address:* 18 Apsley Road, Oxford. *T:* Oxford 59788.

Died 23 Feb. 1949.

GARVIE, Rev. Alfred Ernest, Hon. DD Glasgow, London and Berlin; Principal of New College, 1907, of Hackney College, 1922, and of Hackney and New College, 1924–33; Principal Emeritus since 1933; *b* Zyrardow, Russian Poland, 29 Aug. 1861; *s* of Peter Garvie, linen manufacturer, and Jane Kedslie Garvie; *m* 1893, Agnes (*d* 1914), 4th *d* of late William Gordon, Glasgow; two *d*. *Educ:* private school in Poland; home tuition; George Watson's College, Edinburgh. MA with 1st Class Honours in Philosophy, Glasgow, 1889; BA with 1st Class Honours in Theology, Oxford, 1892; BD Glasgow, 1894; MA Oxford, 1898; hon. DD Glasgow, 1903, Berlin, 1931, London, 1934. Edinburgh Univ. 1878–79; business in Glasgow, 1880–84; Glasgow Univ. 1885–89 (1st Prizeman in Greek, Latin, Logic, Literature, Moral Philosophy, Logan Gold Medal); Oxford University, 1889–93. Minister of Macduff Congregational Church, 1893–95; President Congregational Union of Scotland, 1902; Minister of

Montrose Congregational Church, 1895–1903; Professor of Philosophy of Theism, Comparative Religion, and Christian Ethics in Hackney and New Colleges, London, 1903–07; Chairman of the Congregational Union of England and Wales, 1920; President of the National Free Church Council, 1923; Deputy Chairman of the Lausanne Conference on Faith and Order, 1927; Moderator of the Federal Council of the Free Churches, 1928. *Publications:* The Ethics of Temperance, 1895; The Ritschlian Theology, 1899; Commentary on Romans, 1901; The Gospel for To-day, 1904; The Christian Personality, 1904; My Brother's Keeper, 1905; Religious Education; A Guide to Preachers, 1906; Studies in the Inner Life of Jesus, 1908; Commentary on Luke; The Christian Certainty, 1910; Studies of Paul and his Gospel, 1911; Handbook of Christian Apologetics, 1913; The Joy of Finding; The Missionary Obligation, 1914; The Evangelical Type of Christianity, 1915; The Master's Comfort and Hope, and the Minister and the Young Life of the Church, 1917; The Purpose of God in Christ, 1919; The Christian Preacher, 1920; Tutors unto Christ, 1920; The Holy Catholic Church; Congregational View; The Old Testament in the Sunday School, 1921; The Beloved Disciple, 1922; The Way and the Witness, The God Man Craves; The Christian Doctrine of the Godhead, 1925; The Preachers of the Church, 1926; The Christian Ideal for Human Society, 1930; The Christian Belief in God, 1933; Can Christ Save Society? 1934; Revelation through History and Experience, 1934; The Fatherly Rule of God, 1935; The Christian Faith, 1936; Memories and Meanings of My Life, 1937; Christian Moral Conduct, 1938; Editor of the Westminster New Testament. *Address:* 34 Sevington Road, Hendon, NW4. *T:* Hendon 6834.

Died 7 March 1945.

GARVIN, James Louis, CH 1941; Hon. LLD, Edinburgh; Hon. LittD Durham; *b* 12 April 1868. Writer on world-issues for The Daily Telegraph; Editor-in-Chief of the Encyclopædia Britannica, fourteenth edition, 1926–29; Editor, Pall Mall Gazette, 1912–15, and of the Outlook, 1905–06; Editor of The Observer, 1908–42. *Publications:* The Economic Foundations of Peace; The Life of Joseph Chamberlain, Vol. I, 1836–1885, 1932; Vol. II 1885–1895, 1933; Vol. III 1895–1900, 1934; contributions to the Encyclopædia Britannica, Fortnightly Review, National Review, Quarterly Review, etc. *Address:* Gregories, Beaconsfield. *Clubs:* Athenæum, Garrick.

Died 23 Jan. 1947.

GARWOOD, Edmund Johnston, FRS 1914, MA, ScD, Hon. DSc Sheffield, 1933, Hon. DSc Leeds, 1938; *b* 1864; *s* of Rev. William Garwood. *Educ:* Trinity College, Cambridge. Director Jarrow Chemical Co., 1887–92; Lecturer, Cambridge University Extension Syndicate, 1891–98; Hon. Secretary Geological Society of London, 1905–12, President, 1930–32; Lyell Medalist, 1915; Gill Memorial Royal Geographical Society, 1898; Yates-Goldsmid Prof. of Geology and Mineralogy in the University of London, 1901–31; Emeritus Professor since 1931; President Geographical Association, 1913; President Section C British Association, 1913; President Yorks Geological Society 1925–26, and 1938. Explorations in Spitsbergen (with Sir Martin Conway), 1896–97; and in Sikhim Himalayas (with Mr Douglas Freshfield), 1899. *Publications:* The Geological Structure and Physical Features of Sikhim with maps, in Douglas Freshfield's Round Kangchenjunga, 1903; The Geology of Northumberland and Durham, Jubilee Vol. of Geologist's Association, 1910; Geological Chapters in A History of Northumberland, Vols I-XV, 1893–1939; numerous papers, including descriptions of Fossil Calcareous Algæ,

in the Quart. Jl of Geol. Soc. and in other scientific journals. *Address:* 90 Adelaide Road, NW3. *Clubs:* United University, Alpine.

Died 12 June 1949.

GARWOOD, Engr Rear-Adm. Hugh Sydney, CB 1928; OBE 1919; *b* 6 June 1872; *y s* of late Inspector of Machinery, Henry Daniel Garwood, RN; *m* Edna Mary, *y d* of late Rev. Henry J. Coachafer, Rector of North Huish, Devon; (one remaining *s* killed by enemy action, Sept. 1942) two *d. Educ:* privately; RNE College, Keyham. Submarine Service, 1904–10; served S African War, 1901–03; European War, 1914–19; Admiralty, 1910–14; retired list, 1931. *Address:* Barton-on-Sea, Hants. *T:* New Milton 316. *Club:* Royal Naval (Portsmouth).

Died 15 March 1948.

GARWOOD, Lt-Col John Reginald, DSO 1918; *b* 1873; *m* 1912, Helen Winifred, *o c* of late Frank Lloyd; two *d. Educ:* Marlborough; RMA Woolwich. Served European War, 1914–18 (despatches, DSO); retired. *Address:* Coombe Farm, Croydon. *T:* Addiscombe 2310.

Died 20 Nov. 1948.

GASCOIGNE, Brig.-Gen. Sir (Ernest) Frederick (Orby), KCVO 1927; CMG 1918; DSO 1898; JP, DL, Surrey; Standard Bearer HM's Body Guard, Hon. Corps Gentlemen-at-Arms; Chairman Army and Navy Stores; Director British Empire Trust Co., East Surrey Water Co., and Frederick Hotels Co.; President Union Jack Club and Union Jack Hostel; *b* 19 April 1873; *s* of late Lieut-Col Gascoigne, formerly Grenadier Guards; *m* 1902, Cicely, 3rd *d* of late Gen. Edward Clive, formerly Grenadier Guards; four *s* one *d. Educ:* Eton; RMC, Sandhurst. Entered Grenadier Guards, 1892; Adjt 1st Batt. 1898; Captain, 1899; Brigade Major of 16th (Guards) Brigade, 1900–02; DAAG (Musketry), 1903; retired, 1907; DAQMG, MEF, 1915; AQMG, MEF, 1915–16; DA and QMG Eastern Force, EEF, 1916–17; Assistant to DQMG, EEF, 1917; served Soudan, 1898, including Khartoum (despatches, DSO, British medal, Khedive's medal with clasp); South Africa, 1900–02 (despatches, Queen's medal three clasps, King's medal two clasps, Brevet Major); European War (Dardanelles), 1915 (despatches, Brevet Lt-Col; St Anne, 2nd class, with swords (Egypt), 1916 (despatches); (Palestine) 1917 (despatches, CMG, Col hon. rank Brig.-Gen. 1918). *Address:* Ashtead Lodge, Ashtead, Surrey. *T:* Ashtead 26.

Died 16 Jan. 1944.

GASCOIGNE, Laura Gwendolen, CBE 1918; Lady of Justice of the Order of St John of Jerusalem; Commandant of Lotherton Auxiliary Military Hospital; *d* of late Sir Douglas Galton, KCB; *m* 1892, Colonel F. R. T. Gascoigne, DSO (*d* 1937); one *s* one *d. Publications:* La Fenton; A Step Aside; Among Pagodas and Fair Ladies. *Address:* Lotherton Hall, Aberford, Yorkshire. *TA:* Lotherton, Aberford. *T:* Aberford 213.

Died 10 July 1949.

GASELEE, Sir Stephen, KCMG 1935; CBE 1918; MA, Hon. DLitt (Liverpool); Hon. Fellow of King's College, Cambridge; FSA; FBA; Corr. Member of the Roumanian Academy, and of Utrecht Provincial Society of Arts and Sciences; Hon. Librarian of the Athenæum; Librarian and Keeper of the Papers at the Foreign Office since 1920; *b* 9 Nov. 1882; *s* of late H. Gaselee, Barrister-at-law; *m* 1917, May Evelyn, *d* of E. Wyndham Hulme, late Librarian of the Patent Office; three *d. Educ:* Eton (Scholar); King's College, Cambridge (1st class Classical Tripos, 1904). Fellow of Magdalene College, Cambridge, since 1908, and Librarian, 1908–19; temporary Clerk in Foreign Office, 1916–19; President, Bibliographical Society, 1932–33, and Classical Association, 1939–40; Sandars Reader in Bibliography, Cambridge, 1935; Commander Order of St John of Jerusalem; Grand Cross, Military Order of Christ of Portugal. *Publications:* The Codex Traguriensis of

Petronius, 1915; Apuleius (Loeb Classics), 1916; Achilles Tatius (Loeb Classics), 1917; Stories from the Christian East, 1918; Anthology of Medieval Latin, 1925; Oxford Book of Medieval Latin Verse, 1928; The Foreign Office, 1933; The Costerian Doctrinale of Alexander de Villa Dei (Roxburghe Club), 1938; The Language of Diplomacy, 1939; articles on classical and oriental studies. *Recreations:* shooting, tennis. *Address:* 24 Ashburn Place, SW7. *T:* Frobisher 4218. *Clubs:* Athenæum, Carlton, Beefsteak.

Died 15 June 1943.

GASK, Rear-Adm. (S) Walter, CB 1916; *b* 1870; *s* of late Henry Gask of Bromley, Kent; *m* Edith Ethel, *d* of late James Winter of Dhurringile, Australia; one *d. Educ:* Dulwich College. Entered Navy, 1887; Secretary to Admiral, Dover Patrol, 1914–17; Deputy Paymaster Director-General, Admiralty, 1923–25; retired list, 1925. *Address:* Bruncketts, Waltham St Lawrence, Berks. *Club:* Junior United Service.

Died 27 July 1949.

GASKELL, Ven. Albert Fisher; Vicar of Littleborough, Lancs, since 1911; Archdeacon of Rochdale since 1935; *b* 10 Feb. 1874; *s* of James and Eliza Gaskell; *m* 1910, Mary Ann Mabel Fairhurst; two *s. Educ:* Bath College; Hertford College, Oxford (scholar). 1st Class Mods, 1896; Aubrey Moore Theological Stud. and 1st Class Lit. Hum. 1898; Ellerton Prize 1899; MA 1901. Vicar of S Jude, Preston, 1909; Rural Dean of Rochdale, 1917; Hon. Canon of Manchester, 1928. *Address:* The Vicarage, Littleborough, Lancs. *T:* Littleborough 8334.

Died 20 Dec. 1950.

GASTRELL, William Shaw Harriss; *b* 4 Dec. 1862; *e s* of late J. P. H. Gastrell, Minister in HM's Diplomatic Service; *m* 1890, *d* of Lieut-Col Wade, formerly Scottish Rifles (90th LI); two *d.* Entered HM Consular service, 1890; HBM Consul Tenerife, 1895; Commercial Attaché to HM's Embassy at Berlin, and to Legations at The Hague, Stockholm, Christiania, and Copenhagen, 1896–1907; Foreign Office, 1907–12; HBM's Consul-General at Paris, 1912–14; retired, Nov. 1914. *Publications:* Our Trade in the World in Relation to Foreign Competition, 1885–1895; The German Empire of To-day, 1902. *Clubs:* Devon and Exeter, Exeter.

Died 23 Sept. 1948.

GATES, Caleb Frank, BA, BD, DD, LLD; *b* Chicago, Ill, 18 Oct. 1857; *s* of Caleb Foote Gates and Mary Eliza Hutchins; *m* 1883, Mary Ellen Moore (*d* 1937); three *s. Educ:* Beloit Coll.; Chicago Theological Seminary. Missionary ABCFM, 1881–94; at Mardin, Turkey in Asia, 1881–94; President of Euphrates College, Harpoot, 1894–1903; Pres. Robert Coll., Constantinople, 1903–32; acquired three Oriental languages, Arabic, Turkish, and Armenian; Administrator of famine relief after the Armenian massacres of 1895–96; Chairman near East Relief Committee Constantinople, 1917–19; accompanied American High Commissioner to Lausanne as Adviser on the Peace Treaty; LLD Edin. Univ. and Beloit College; Order of Alexander III and II, Bulgaria; Order of George I., Greece. *Publications:* A Christian Business Man: the Life of Caleb Foote Gates; Not To Me Only (record of half a century in Turkey); Chapter on The Caliphate, in the Modern Moslem World; magazine articles. *Recreations:* golf, tennis, riding. *Address:* 1640 E 3rd Avenue, Denver, Colorado, USA.

Died 10 April 1946.

GATES, Sir Frank Campbell, KCIE 1913; CSI 1906; late Financial Commissioner of Burma; *b* Croydon, 9 Nov. 1862; *s* of late George Gates of Croydon; *m* 1899, Alice Grisell, *d* of late Archibald Tod of Woolton, Liverpool; one *d. Educ:* Cheltenham Coll.; Balliol Coll., Oxford. Barrister-at-Law, Lincoln's Inn, 1891. Entered Indian Civil Service by open competition, 1880; posted to Lower Bengal, 1882; transferred to Burma, 1884; served as Assistant Commissioner, Deputy

Commissioner, Secretary and Revenue Secretary to Govt of Burma; Commissioner of Division; Chief Secretary to Govt of Burma; Financial Commissioner; Member of Burma Legislative Council, 1897–98 and 1903–12; Additional Member of Governor-General's Legislative Council, 1910–12; retired 1914. *Recreations:* gardening and reading. *Address:* Fairlight Lodge, Fairseat, Nr Sevenoaks, Kent. *T:* Fairseat 7.

Died 12 Jan. 1947.

GATHORNE-HARDY, Gen. Hon. Sir (John) Francis, GCB 1935 (KCB 1929; CB 1918); GCVO 1935; CMG 1919; DSO 1915; *b* 14 Jan. 1874; 2nd *s* of 2nd Earl of Cranbrook; *m* 1898, Lady Isobel Stanley (Lady Isobel Gathorne-Hardy, DCVO), *d* of 16th Earl of Derby; one *d. Educ:* Eton; Sandhurst (Sword of Honour). Joined Grenadier Guards, 1894; Captain, 1900; Bt Major, 1902; Brevet Lt-Col 1913; Bt Col 1916; Major-Gen. 1919; Lt-Gen. 1928; General 1933; served South African War, 1900–02 (despatches twice, Queen's medal, King's medal, Bt Maj.); European War, 1914–18 (despatches eleven times, Promoted Major-General, Bt Col, CB, CMG, DSO); Legion of Honour, Croix de Guerre (French), Order of Savoy, Croix de Guerre (French), Order of Savoy, Croix de Guerre (Italian), Montenegrin Medal for Merit; Staff College, 1905–06; Brigade Major, 1st Guards Brigade, Aldershot, 1908–11; General Staff Officer, 2nd Grade, War Office, 1913–14; General Staff Officer, 2nd Grade, 2nd Corps, 1914–15; 2nd Army, 1915; 1st Grade, 7th Division, 1915–16; Brig.-General, General Staff, XIV Corps, 1916–18; Major-General, General Staff, British Forces in Italy and Tenth Italian Army, 1918–19; Commanding Field Troops, Egypt, 1921–22. Director of Military Training, 1922–25; commanded Deccan District, 1926–28; GOC-in-C Northern Command, 1931–33; GOC-in-C Aldershot Command, 1933–37; ADC General to the King, 1934–37; retired pay, 1937. DL Wiltshire. *Address:* Lockeridge House, Marlborough. *Club:* Turf.

Died 21 Aug. 1949.

GATTY, Nicholas Comyn; musical composer; *b* 13 Sept. 1874; 2nd *s* of late Rev. Reginald A. Gatty, Rector of Hooton Roberts, Yorkshire; *m* Margreths Helen, *d* of late Adolph Borgen of Copenhagen. *Educ:* privately; Downing College, Cambridge. BA 1896; MusB 1898; MusD 1927; studied at Royal College of Music (principally composition, with Sir Charles Stanford). Published works include the operas Duke or Devil, Prince Ferelon, King Alfred and the Cakes, and The Tempest; odes for chorus and orchestra, suite for strings, violin sonata. In MS the operas, Greysteel, Macbeth, First Come, First Served, and Gammer Gurton's Needle; variations and overture for orchestra, variations for string quartet, pianoforte trio, etc.

Died 10 Nov. 1946.

GAUDET, Col Frederick Mondelet, CMG 1918; *b* 1867; *m* 1898, Margaret Grant (*d* 1941). *d* of Andrew Thomson, Quebec; no *c. Educ:* RMC, Kingston. Commissioned R. Canadian Art 1887; Superintendent Dominion Arsenal, 1895–1913; Canadian Overseas Forces, 1914–19 (despatches, CMG, Officer Legion of Honour); Director of Public Safety, City of Montreal, 1919–21; Director of Advisory Council for Scientific and Industrial Research, 1921–22; on Board of Canadian Industrial Alcohol Co. 1922–29; Consultant Canadian Car Munitions, Ltd; retired, 1945. *Club:* University (Montreal).

Died 3 Nov. 1947.

GAUDIN, Engr Rear-Adm. Edouard, CB 1918. Entered navy as Assistant Engineer, 1886; Engineer-Comdr, 1901; Naval Intelligence Dept, 1905–08; Engineer Comdr of Dreadnought, 1908–11; Eng.-Capt., 1911; served at Admiralty, 1911–14; served European War (CB); Deputy Engineer-in-Chief of the Navy and Superintendent of Naval Engineering, 1918–20; retired.

Died 8 March 1945.

GAUMONT, Léon Ernest; Ancien Industriel; Officier de la Légion d'Honneur; *b* 10 May 1864; *s* of Ferdinand Gaumont and Marguerite Dupanloup; *m* 1888, Camille Maillard (décédée); three *s* two *d*. *Educ*: Collège Sainte Barbe, Paris. Président d'Honneur de la Chambre Syndicale française de la Cinematographie; Ancien Président du Conseil d'Administration de la Société Francaise de Photographie et de Cinematographie; Fondateur et ancient Président du Conseil d'Administration de la Société des Etablissements Gaumont à Paris; Fondateur et ancien Président de Conseil d'Administration of the Gaumont Co. Ltd in London devenue la Gaumont British Distrib. Co.; Promoteur et realisateur des premiers filmsparlants synchrones présentés à l'Academie des Sciences de Paris 1910, et à la Royal Institution of Great Britain 1912; Promoteur et realisateur du film cinematographique en couleurs naturelles (par le méthode trichrome). Le Défile de la Victoire le 14 juillet 1919 aux Champs Elysées à Paris présenté à l'Academie des Sciences de Paris, 1919. *Address*: Sainte Maxime-sur-Mer, Var, France. *T*: 2.49. *Club*: Yacht de France.

Died 11 Aug. 1946.

GAUNT, Mary; author; *b* Chiltern, Victoria; *d* of late Judge Gaunt, Melbourne, Victoria; *m* 1894, Hubert Lindsay Miller, MD, of Warrnambool, Victoria (*d* 1900); no *c*. *Educ*: Grenville College, Ballarat; Melbourne University. Wrote as a girl because she always wanted 'to do something' and felt that every woman should be economically independent; contributed to Argus and Age in Melbourne; at her husband's death, finding herself with very small means, she came to England to make her livelihood by her pen; after many vicissitudes she at last succeeded in making enough money to travel to West Africa; went to China, Siberia, and Saghalien, 1913–14; Jamaica, 1919; returned to France, 1921; to Italy, 1922. *Publications*: Dave's Sweetheart; The Moving Finger; Kirkham's Find; Deadmans; 3 books with J. R. Essex, The Arm of the Leopard, Fools Rush In, and The Silent Ones; The Mummy Moves; The Uncounted Cost; Alone in West Africa; Every Man's Desire; A Woman in China; The Ends of the Earth; A Broken Journey; A Wind from the Wilderness; The Surrender; Where the Twain Meet; As The Whirlwind Passeth; The Forbidden Town; Saul's Daughter; A Lawless Frontier; Joan of the Pilchard; Reflection in Jamaica; Harmony; Worlds Away. *Recreations*: bridge playing, travelling, more especially in little-known lands. *Address*: Villa Camilla, Bordighera, Italy. *TA*: Gaunt, Bordighera.

Died 19 Jan. 1942.

GAUVAIN, Sir Henry, Kt 1920; Medical Superintendent and Founder of Morland Clinics, Alton, now largely occupied by Belgian evacuated crippled children, and Med. Supt of Lord Mayor Treloar Cripples' Hospital and College, Alton and Hayling Island, since its foundation, 1908; Founder and Director of Overbury Court Residential School for evacuated Belgian cripple children; CStJ; Hon. Consulting Surgeon to the King Edward VII Welsh National Memorial Association for the Treatment of Tuberculosis, to Papworth Village Settlement, and to King George's Sanatorium for Sailors, Bramshott; late Consulting Surgeon (Tuberculosis) to the London and Essex County Councils; hon. Consulting Surgeon to Hampshire County Council; late Examiner in Tuberculosis, University of Wales; *b* 1878; *o surv. s* of late William Gauvain, of Alderney, CI; *m* 1913, Louise Laura, *d* of late William Butler, JMS; one *d*. *Educ*: St John's College, Cambridge (Scholar); St Bartholomew's Hospital, London (Senior Science Scholar). BA 1st Class hons. Nat. Sci. Tripos; MA, MD, MCh (Cantab); FRCS (Eng.); Hon. MD (Melbourne); JP Hants; FRSM (late President of the Electrotherapeutic and Diseases of Children sections), etc. Late Chairman of the Joint Tuberculosis Council; Vice-President of the National Association for Prevention of Consumption and of the International Light Committee, etc.; Pres. Alderney Evacuee Relief Committee; Recipient of the Golden Key of American Physical Therapy Association. *Publications*: contributions to medical journals. *Recreations*: travel, sailing, and fishing. *Address*: Alton Park, Alton, Hants; Morland Hall, Alton, Hants. *TA*: Gauvain, Alton. *T*: Alton 2198 and 3333. *Clubs*: Oxford and Cambridge; Cambridge University Cruising.

Died 19 Jan. 1945.

GAVIN, William Aloysius; retired; *b* Pontefract, Yorkshire; *s* of George Fitzpatrick Gavin, Surgeon. *Educ*: Hull Grammar School. Official publisher to Lloyds Register, 1896–99; Proprietor and Managing Director of Vanity Fair, 1899–1908; President Gavin-Armour Steel Corporation of America, 1915–22; Chairman International Housing Trust, Sport: Chairman of Board of Directors and Timekeeper of National Sporting Club, 1896–1904. In 1919 drafted the Bill which legalised boxing—then prohibited—in the State of New York, and in face of great opposition organised the support necessary for its passage through the Senate at Albany. So successful was the administration of this Bill that it was adopted by 44 other States of the Union. In 1919 drafted the rules governing boxing in the USA and founded the National Boxing Association of America (NBA), of which body he was made first President. Founded the International Sporting Club, New York. Was one of the two judges in the Willard-Dempsey contest at Toledo for the Heavyweight Championship of the world. In 1897 crossed Norway in a balloon with the explorer Nansen. *Recreations*: golf, yachting, racing. *Address*: 69 Trinity Court, Gray's Inn Rd, WC1.

Died 4 Jan. 1948.

GAY, Maj.-Gen. Sir Arthur William, KCMG 1919; CB 1916; CMG 1917; DSO 1900; *b* 22 March 1863; *s* of late John Gay, FRCS; *m* 1893, Maud, *e d* of Col R. C. Evanson; one *s* one *d*. Entered RA 1882; Capt. 1891; Major, 1900; Lt-Col 1909; Col 1912; passed Staff College, 1899; Staff Captain Hd. Qr. of Army, 1899; Brig.-Major, RA, Curragh, 1900; Brig.-Major, RA, Head Qr. Staff, Ireland, 1902; Gen. Staff Officer Wessex Division, 1908; CRA W Lancs Dn., 1914; served Burmah, 1885–87 (medal with clasp); South Africa, 1900 (despatches, medal with four clasps, DSO); European War, 1914–17 (despatches, CB).

Died 16 Dec. 1944.

GAY, Edwin Francis; Research Staff of Huntington Library, San Marino, California, since 1936; *b* Detroit, Mich, 27 Oct. 1867; *s* of Aaron F. Gay and Mary L. Loud; *m* 1892, Louise Fitz Randolph; one *s* one *d*. *Educ*: AB University of Michigan, 1890; PhD University of Berlin, 1902; Honorary LLD Harvard University, 1918, University of Michigan, 1920, North-Western University, 1927, Tulane Univ., 1935, Occidental Univ., 1940; Hon. LittD, Manchester Univ. (England), 1933. Instructor at Harvard Univ., 1902–03; Assistant Professor, 1903–06; Professor Economics, 1906; Professor Economic History at Harvard University 1924–36; Dean Graduate School of Business Administration, Harvard University, 1908–19; Director of Research, National Bureau of Economic Research (New York City), 1924–33; President New York Evening Post, Inc. Nov. 1919–Jan. 1924; Member American Academy Arts and Sciences, American Philosophical Society, American Economic Assoc., American Historical Assoc., American Statistical Association; Member Commercial Economy Board of Council National Defence, 1917–18; War Trade Board, Feb. 1918–19. *Address*: Huntington Library, San Marino 15, California, USA. *Clubs*: Century, New York.

Died 8 Feb. 1946.

GAY, Maisie; Actress; *b* 7 Jan. 1883; *d* of Peter Munro-Noble. *Educ*: Germany; North London Collegiate School. First appeared on the stage in the chorus of The Cherry Girl at Blackpool, 1903; toured in several George

Dance and George Edwardes' musical comedy productions before making first appearance in London as Fifi in The Waltz Dream; subsequently in Girls of Gottenberg, and for two years in Our Miss Gibbs; visited America in Oct. 1911 to play in The Quaker Girl in New York; afterwards played in 160 towns in USA in 266 days; later played in Phyllis, High Jinks, and Pins and Needles in America; in Dec. 1919 made début in revue in The Whirligig; other revues include: A to Z, Snap, London Calling, and the Charlot Revues, This Year of Grace, and the Cochran 1930 Revue; played in principal Australian cities in 1929; first talkie as Mrs 'Arris in To Oblige a Lady; later played Mrs 'Arris in Edgar Wallace's The Old Man, subsequently in the film version of play by the same author; series of talks for invalids for BBC, 1941. *Publication:* Laughing Through Life, 1932. *Recreations:* reading and listening to wireless. *Address:* c/o Brown, Shipley & Co., 123 Pall Mall, SW1.

Died 13 Sept. 1945.

GAYDA, Virginio; Editor of Giornale d'Italia 1926–43; *b* Rome, 12 Aug. 1885. *Educ:* University of Turin. Took part in the political direction of the Italian press, which followed the annexion of Bosnia-Herzegovina; sent to the Balkan Peninsula and Turkey, where he made various journeys, and finally in Austria, where he stayed for over five years; after the beginning of war was actively occupied in Rome to direct—together with the principal Italian politicians exiled from Austria—the Italian policy towards the intervention on the side of the Entente Powers; went to Russia special envoy of Corriere della Sera (Milan), after of Messaggero (Rome); remained there, 1915–18, witnessing the fall of Imperial Russia; went to Stockholm and to London as envoy of Messaggero and to Paris and Berlin; editor of Messaggero, 1921–26. *Publications:* La Crisi di un Impero, 1913, translated into English under title of Modern Austria, 1915; L'Italia d'oltre confine. The Italy of beyond the confine, 1914; Il crollo russo, The Fall of Russia (translated into Spanish), 1919; La Germania contro la Francia, Germany against France (translated into French), 1922; La Jugoslavia contro d'Italia, 1933; Italia, Inghilterra, Etiopia, 1936; Construzione dell' Impero, 1936; Problemi siciliani, 1937, I quattro anni del Terzo Reich, 1938. *Address:* Palazzo Sciarra, Rome.

Died 14 March 1944.

GAYER-ANDERSON, Major Robert Grenville; *b* 29 July 1881; *s* of late Henry Gayer-Anderson, The Lodge, Old Marston, Oxon. *Educ:* Tonbridge School; Guy's Hospital; MRCS and LRCP London, 1903. Joined RAMC 1904; seconded Egyptian Army, 1907–17; served Tagoi Punitive Expedition, 1910 (Soudan medal and clasp, despatches, Order of the Mejedie); Soudan Sleeping Sickness Commission, Leprosy Mission, and Anthropological Research, 1910–13; AAG for Recruiting, Egyptian Army, 1914; served European War, 1914–18, Egypt, Gallipoli, Arabia, Arab Bureau, Political Officer Red Sea Patrol (wounded, despatches, Orders of the Nile and the Nahada); Egyptian Revolution, 1919; retired from Army, 1920; Senior Inspector Ministry of the Interior, Egyptian Government; Oriental Secretary the Residency, Cairo, 1922; retired, 1924, but resided in Cairo till 1942, when he handed over to Egyptian nation the Bayt-el-Kredlea (a 16th-century Arab house in Cairo) as The Gayer-Anderson Pasha Museum of Oriental Arts and Crafts; Sub-Commissioner (Middle East) British Red Cross Society and Order of St John of Jerusalem (War Organisation), 1941–42; Leva (Maj.-Gen.) with title of Pasha, 1943. *Address:* The Little Hall, Lavenham, Suffolk. *Clubs:* Turf, Cairo.

Died 16 June 1945.

GAYFORD, Air Cdre Oswald Robert, CBE 1941; DFC; AFC; FRGS; late RAF; *b* 18 May 1893; *s* of Ernest Robert Gayford, Hadleigh, Suffolk; *m* 1941, Irene Helen Davies, *d* of Reginald William Andrews. *Educ:* Bishop's Stortford School. Served as Seaman RNVR in RN Armoured Trains, France and Belgium, 1914–15, and in North Sea in 7th Destroyer Flotilla and 10th Sloop Flotilla, 1915–16; commissioned in RNVR as Observer RNAS Sept. 1916; served C Squadron, No. 2 Wing, 1917–18 (DFC) and in No. 221 Squadron, RAF, and Caspian Sea, Russia, 1918–19 (Bar to DFC); RAF Operations in British Somaliland, 1919–20 (despatches); permanent commission in RAF, 1920; RAF Headquarters, Constantinople, 1922–23; No. 1 Fighter Squadron in Iraq, 1924–26 (Despatches); No. 47 Bomber Squadron, Sudan, 1926–29 (commanded third of RAF Flights from Cairo to Cape and back, 1928); psa, 1930; in charge of RAF long range experiments, 1931–33; first non-stop flight, England to Egypt, 1931; world's long-distance record, Cranwell to Walfis Bay, 5,339 miles in 57 hrs 25 mins, 1933 (AFC and Royal Aeronautical Society's Silver Medal for British Aviation); idc, 1934; No. 58 Bomber Squadron, 1935; Air Ministry, 1936–37; in command RAF Long Range Development Unit (World's Long Distance Record by three Vickers Wellesley Bombers Ismailia to Port Darwin, 7,162 miles in 52 hours), 1938–39; commanded RAF Wattisham Station, 1939–41 (CBE), commanded No. 231 Wing, Middle East, 1942, and 208 Group, Middle East, 1943; No. 33 Base in Bomber Command, 1943–44; retired list, 1944. *Recreations:* shooting, golf, gardening. *Address:* Naughton Hall, Nedging Tye, Suffolk. *TA:* Naughton Hall, Suffolk. *T:* Bildeston 278. *Club:* Royal Air Force.

Died 10 Aug. 1945.

GEACH, William Foster; Member of Stock Exchange of Melbourne, since 1907; Senior Partner of J. B. Were and Son, Share, Finance and Exchange Brokers; *b* St Kilda, Melbourne, 31 July 1859; *s* of late William Geach and Geraldine Nicholson, Melbourne; *m* 1912, Ada, *o d* of Gustav Thureau, Castlemaine, Victoria; two *s* three *d*. *Educ:* Wesley College, Melbourne. With Hobson's Bay Railway Co., 1877; legal profession, 1877–89; joined J. B. Were and Son to take charge of the International Exchange Department of the firm's business, 1889; Partner, 1906; Senior Partner, 1926. *Recreations:* artist, photography, literature, motoring. *Address:* 39 Point Nepean Road, Elsternwick, Victoria, Australia. *Clubs:* CTA, Savage, Stock Exchange, Royal Automobile, Melbourne.

Died 26 Oct. 1940.

GEARY, Sir William Nevill Montgomerie, 5th Bt *cr* 1782; MA, DL; *b* 7 April 1859; *S* father 1895; *m* 1906, Florence Mary, 2nd *d* of late G. E. Burke of Danesfield, Galway. *Educ:* Eton; Christ Church, Oxford. Barrister, Inner Temple, 1884; Attorney-General Accra, Gold Coast, 1895–97; Legal Practitioner, Nigeria; contested Durham City (L), 1900; Gravesend, 1906; Temporary Captain, Manchester and R. Warwick Regiments; attached Staff Simla and Mesopotamia. Owns about 2400 acres. *Publications:* Chitty on Contract, 12th ed. 1890, with J. M. Lely; The Law of Marriage and Family Relations, 1892; A Lawyer's Wife, 1896; Nigeria under British Rule, 1927. *Recreations:* hunting, planting. *Heir:* none. *Address:* Oxon Hoath, Tonbridge. *TA:* Hadlow. *T:* Hadlow 232; 6 Pump Court, Temple, EC4. *Club:* Travellers'.

Died 26 Dec. 1944 (ext).

GEDDES, Rt Rev. William Archibald, BA, DD; Bishop of Yukon since 1933; *b* Magdalen Islands, Que., 18 Feb. 1894; *s* of David and Annie L. Geddes; *m* 1929, Beatrice Rose, *d* of Thomas C. and Amelia Terry, Toronto. *Educ:* Dalhousie University, Halifax; Wycliffe College, Toronto. Served European War in France as a gunner in 8th Canadian Siege Battery; ordained as missionary to the Eskimo at Herschel Island, Diocese of Yukon, 1920; Archdeacon of Yukon, 1927; Bishop of Mackenzie River, 1928–33; DD (hon.) St John's College, Winnipeg, and Wycliffe College, Toronto. *Address:* Dawson, Yukon Territory, NW Canada.

Died 16 April 1947.

GEDYE, Nicholas George, OBE, 1919; MInstCE; Consulting Civil Engineer in Westminster since 1921; *b* Bristol, 1874; *o s* of late Joseph Gedye. *Educ:* Bristol Grammar School; Birmingham University (BSc). Engineer-in-chief, Tyne Improvement Commission, 1910–15; served European War, France and Belgium, 1917–18, Lieut-Colonel, RE (OBE, Officer of Belgian Order of the Crown); Chief Engineer for Docks, Harbours and Waterways, Ministry of Transport, 1919–21; British Government representative on Permanent International Commission of Navigation Congresses since 1935; Chairman of Association of Consulting Engineers, 1930; Vernon Harcourt lecturer, Inst. of Civil Engr, 1931; British Govt delegate, World Power Conference, Washington, 1936; Regional Works Adviser to Regional Commissioner for SW England, 1940–46. *Publications:* Articles on Docks Harbours, etc. in Encyclopædia Britannica; other technical papers. *Address:* Alliance House, Caxton Street, SW1. *T:* Whitehall 8700. *Club:* Athenæum.

Died 19 May 1947.

GEIJER, Eric Neville, MC, FSA; Rouge Dragon Pursuivant of Arms, since 1926; *s* of C. E. de Geijer and Lila, *d* of late Sir W. A. White, PC, GCB, GCMG, and *widow* of 5th Lord Abinger; *m* 1933, Ethel Mary, *d* of Wm Trueman. *Educ:* Wellington College; Trinity College, Cambridge (BA). Formerly Lieut (SR) Grenadier Guards; ADC to Governor of Bombay (Lord Willingdon), 1915–16; served European War (MC). *Address:* Little Bowstridge, Chalfont St Giles, Bucks; College of Arms, Queen Victoria Street, EC4. *T:* City 6229. *Clubs:* Guards', Pratt's.

Died 14 Jan. 1941.

GEIKIE-COBB, Rev. William Frederick, DD, Rector of St Ethelburga's, Bishopsgate, in the City of London; *b* Danbury, Essex, 1857; *m* 1st, 1885, Harriette Emily White (*d* 1936); two *s* one *d*; 2nd, 1939, Elizabeth Smart, *d* of late Dugald Colquhoun, Meigle, Perthshire. *Educ:* Chelmsford Grammar School; Trinity College, Dublin. Assistant Curate of Send, Surrey; Addlestone; Holy Trinity, Winchester; St Luke's, Kentish Town; Assistant Secretary, English Church Union, 1891–98; Indian Church Aid Association, 1898–1905; Chairman, Marriage Law Reform League since 1928. *Publications:* Origines Judaicae; Theology Old and New; Mysticism and the Creed; The Path of the Soul; The Humanist's Hornbook, etc. *Recreations:* gardening, walking, brass-rubbing. *Address:* 15 West Hill Court, Highgate, N6.

Died 14 Dec. 1941.

GELDER, Sir (William) Alfred, Kt 1903; JP; *b* 12 May 1855; *s* of William Gelder of North Cave, Brough, Yorks; *m* 1877, Elizabeth (*d* 1934), *d* of Thomas Parker of Hull; two *s* one *d*. Mayor of Hull, for 5 years, 1899–1903; carried out large schemes of City Improvement during 43 years of active service as Alderman of the City; received the Honorary Freedom of the City, 1930; MP (L) Brigg Division, Lincolnshire, 1910–18. *Address:* West Parade House, Hull. *Club:* Reform.

Died 26 Aug. 1941.

GELL, Hon. Mrs Edith Mary; *b* 1860; *d* of William, 8th Viscount Midleton, and Augusta, *d* of 1st Baron Cottesloe; *m* 1889, Philip Lyttelton Gell (*d* 1926). Lady of the Manors of Hopton-Carsington and Middleton. *Publications:* The Cloud of Witness, 1891; Squandered Girlhood, 1892; The More Excellent Way, 1898; The Vision of Righteousness, 1899; The Forces of the Spirit, 1908; The Menace of Secularism, 1912; The Happy Warrior, 1914; Problems for Speakers, 1915; The Empire's Honour; Influence of Women of the Early Church in Britain; Conquering and to Conquer; The Blessèd Company, 1916; Wedded Life, 1917; The Church-woman's Vote, 1917; The Empire's Destiny, 1918; The New Girl, 1919; Womanhood and Fellowship, 1919; The Resurrection of a Nation, 1919;

The Liberation of Spiritual Force, 1919; Womanhood at the Crossroads, 1919; The New Crusaders, 1920; Our Mother Earth, 1921; The Spirit of the Home, 1922; Look Before You Leap, 1924; Under Three Reigns, 1927; Heaven in Daily Life, 1929; John Franklin's Bride, 1930; Ways and Signposts, 1930; The Ideal of Stillness, 1931; Live Gloriously, 1932; Build, 1933; Hopton Hymns, 1934; Jubilee Musical Masque, 1935. *Address:* Hopton Hall, Wirksworth. *Clubs:* Ladies' County, Derby.

Died 17 April 1944.

GELLIBRAND, Maj.-Gen. Sir John, KCB 1919; CB 1917; DSO 1916; late Manchester Regt; *b* 5 Dec. 1872; *s* of Thomas Lloyd Gellibrand; *m* Elizabeth Helena du Breul; one *s* two *d*. *Educ:* King's School, Canterbury; Royal Military College, Sandhurst. Commissioner of Police, Victoria, 1920–22; Member for Denison in the Federal Parliament, 1925–28; served South African War, 1900 (medal, two clasps); European War, 1914–18 (DSO and Bar, CB); Officer Legion of Honour, Croix de Guerre avec Palme, American Distinguished Service Medal. *Address:* Risdon, Tasmania. *TA:* Lindisfarne, Tasmania.

Died 3 June 1945.

GEMMELL, George Harrison, FIC; Lecturer on Chemistry at the School of Medicine, Edinburgh, and Examiner in Chemistry for the Royal Colleges, Edinburgh; Professor of Chemistry, Royal (Dick) Veterinary College, Edinburgh, and Public Analyst for Counties of Midlothian, East Lothian, West Lothian and Peebles, Clackmannan and many Burghs; Official Analyst NB Association of Gas Managers; *b* Birkenhead, 20 Aug. 1860; *s* of Alexander Gemmell, Shipbuilder and Marine Architect; *m* 1885, Mary A. Drust. *Educ:* Hull Grammar School; Royal School of Mines, London. Pupil Teacher and Assistant Master, Hull School Board, 1874–82; Student at Royal School of Mines, 1882–83; Assistant in Chemical Laboratory of Prof. J. Campbell Brown, City Analyst, Liverpool, 1883–87; Research Chemist, 1887–1900; researches on manufacture of phosphorus and cyanogen from the air. *Publications:* Gemmell's Chemical Notes and Equations, and many communications to Society of Chemical Industry and Royal Scottish Society of Arts, including Detection of Arsenic in Foodstuffs; The Economic Utilisation of Peat; Chemical and Mechanical Testing of Portland Cement; Smoke Abatement and Atmospheric Pollution; Moisture in Wood Pulp. *Address:* Chemical Laboratory, 4 Lindsay Place, Edinburgh. *T:* Edinburgh 22921.

Died 1 Feb. 1941.

GENT, Sir (Gerard) Edward (James), KCMG 1946; CMG 1941; DSO 1919; OBE 1935; MC; High Commissioner for the Federation of Malaya since 1948; *b* 1895; 4th *s* of late Judge Gent; *m* 1923, Guendolen Mary Wyeth; two *s* two *d*. *Educ:* King's School, Canterbury; Trinity College, Oxford. Served in Flanders and Italy with Duke of Cornwall's LI, 1914–18; Assistant Principal Colonial Office, 1920; Private Secretary to the Parliamentary Under-Secretary of State (Rt Hon. W. Ormsby Gore, MP), 1924; Principal, 1926; Asst Secretary, 1939; Assistant Under-Secretary of State, 1942–46; Governor and C-in-C Malayan Union, 1946–48. *Address:* King's House, Kuala Lumpur.

Died 4 July 1948.

GENTLE, Sir William Benjamin, Kt 1916; JP; *b* Ashwell, Herts, 8 Sept. 1864; *o s* of late Wm Gentle; *m* 1891, Elizabeth (*d* 1941), *d* of Frederick Steward, West Dereham, Norfolk; two *s*. *Educ:* Merchant Taylors' School. Entered Ordnance Survey, 1882; went to So. Africa, 1883; served in Cape Mounted Rifles, 1883–86; joined Metropolitan Police, 1887; Reading Police, 1897; Chief Constable of county borough of Brighton, 1901–20; High Sheriff of Norfolk, 1938; Mayor of Thetford, 1932–35, 1936–37, 1940 and 1941. Hon. Freeman Borough of Thetford; Colonel of Sussex

Yeomanry Cadets which corps he raised; Knight of Grace of the Order of St John of Jerusalem in England member of many charitable institutions; has Queen Victoria, King George V, and King George VI medals; President local corps, St John Ambulance Brigade; Staff Assistant Commissioner, St John's Ambulance Brigade; JP County of Norfolk and member of Norfolk County Council; Commissioner of Income Tax; High Steward of Norwich Cathedral. *Publication:* Police Instruction Book and Police Officers' Guide to the Children Act, 1908. *Address:* Ford Place, Thetford, Norfolk. *Clubs:* Carlton, Royal Automobile; Norfolk, Norwich; Royal Norfolk and Suffolk Yacht, Lowestoft.

Died 2 Sept. 1948.

GENTLES, Thomas A., KC 1921; MA, LLB; Chairman of Regional Coal Valuation Board for Scotland; *b* 1867; *s* of Rev. Thomas Gentles, MA, DD, of Paisley Abbey; *m* Katherine, *d* of late Duncan MacLaren of Bracklinn, Callander, and sometime of Ledard, Aberfoyle; one *d.* *Educ:* George Watson's College, Edinburgh; Glasgow Academy; Glasgow University. Enrolled Law Agent, 1889; Assistant Solicitor to Caledonian Railway Company, 1895–1908; called to Scottish Bar, 1910. *Recreations:* curling, golf. *Address:* 56 Manor Place, Edinburgh. *T:* 203271. *Clubs:* Scottish Conservative, Edinburgh Royal Burgess, Edinburgh; Luffness New Golf.

Died 27 June 1943.

GEOFFRION, Aimé; Barrister; Professor of Civil Law, McGill University, 1905–20, now Emeritus Professor; *b* 13 Nov. 1872; *s* of late Hon. C. A. Geoffrion and Eulalie, *d* of late Sir A. A. Dorion, Kt; *m* 1896, Marguerite, *e d* of late Hon. J. R. Thibaudeau; two *s* two *d.* *Educ:* St Mary's College; McGill University. Advocate, 1894; KC 1903; Bâtonnier (President) Montreal Bar, 1917–18; BCL McGill University; DCL (Hon.) Bishop's University and University of Montreal; Liberal; Roman Catholic. *Address:* 815 Upper Belmont, Westmount, PQ, Canada. *Clubs:* St James's, Mount Royal, Reform, Montreal; Rideau, Ottawa.

Died 15 Oct. 1946.

GEOGHEGAN, Col Francis Edward, CIE 1918; *b* 14 Aug. 1869; *s* of late Capt. T. P. Geoghegan, Roy. Warwick. Regt; *m* 1899, Laura Louise (*d* 1945), 3rd *d* of late David Muir Munn, FRS, Duddingston, Midlothian; one *d.* *Educ:* St Charles College (Roman Catholic); RMC, Sandhurst. 2nd Lieut Gloucestershire Regt 1889; transferred to Indian Army, 1891; served NW Frontier, 1897–98 (medal with clasp); China, 1900 (despatches, medal with clasp, Relief of Pekin); European war, 1914–18; with Indian Contingent, France (1914 star); as ADST Embarkation, Karachi and Bombay, 1915–18 (name brought to notice of the Govt of India, CIE); retired, 1922. *Recreations:* all outdoor games and sport. *Address:* Valleyfield, Ringford, Kirkcudbrightshire.

Died 11 Feb. 1945.

GEOGHEGAN, Joseph, MD Edin., FRCS Edin.; Physician to Out Patients, Royal Hospital, Richmond; *b* 9 June 1888; *s* of Alexander Geoghegan and Mary Davidson Clark; *m* 1912, Muriel Kerr-Brown; one *s* one *d.* *Educ:* George Watson's College and University, Edinburgh. *Publications:* numerous professional articles. *Recreation:* squash. *Address:* 22 Wimpole Street, W1. *T:* Langham 1216; 5 Akenside Road, NW3. *T:* Hampstead 7022. *Club:* RAF.

Died 4 Feb. 1948.

GEORGE, Sir Anthony Hastings, KCMG 1943; CMG 1938; Consul-General at Shanghai, 1940–41, and at Boston, Mass, USA since 1943; *b* 3 Nov. 1886; *s* of late William Edwards George, JP, of Downside, Stoke Bishop, Bristol. Entered Consular Service in China, 1908. *Address:* British Consulate-General, Boston, Mass, USA.

Died 9 Jan. 1944.

GEORGE, Sir Edward James, Kt 1939. Chairman Orconera Iron Ore Co. Ltd; and member of Council Federation of British Industries. *Address:* The County Hotel, Rothbury, via Morpeth, Northumberland.

Died 25 Oct. 1950.

GEORGE, Rev. Canon George Frank, FRSA, FRIBA, FRGS; Commissary for Bishop of Nyasaland; Vicar of St Francis', Gladstone Park, NW10, since 1939; Chaplain General Guild of St Barnabas for Nurses; *b* 14 Sept. 1873; *s* of George Francis George and Alice Filmer; unmarried. *Educ:* Royal Academy Schools; Bishops' College, Cheshunt. Honours Building Construction, South Kensington, British Institution Scholarship in Architecture; Member of the Society of Architects; Diocesan Architect Universities Mission to Central Africa; Captain, Nyasaland Field Force (temp.); Architect of Likoma Cathedral and numerous churches; Deacon, 1916; Priest, 1917; Archdeacon of Nyasa, 1928–35, and Canon Emeritus of Likoma Cathedral; Vicar of St Peter's, Devizes, Wilts, 1935–39. *Recreations:* climbing, swimming, walking. *Address:* St Francis' Vicarage, Gladstone Park, NW10. *T:* Gladstone 1287.

Died 15 Nov. 1942.

GEORGE, Rt Rev. Monsignor Thomas, DD, PhD; Canon Theologian, 1928; *b* Sutton, St Helens, Lancs; 12 Sept. 1872. *Educ:* St Edward's College, Liverpool; St Joseph's College, Upholland; Gregorian University, Rome. Priest, 1897; Professor of Divinity, St Joseph's College, 1902–09; Rector of St Joseph's Church, Liverpool, 1910; Domestic Prelate to His Holiness Pope Pius X, 1911; Superior of the Collegio Beda, Rome, 1911–18. *Address:* St Joseph's, Birkdale, Southport. *T:* Birkdale 6313.

Died 23 Nov. 1943.

GERALD; see Fitz-Gerald.

GEROTHWOHL, Prof. Maurice Alfred, PhD, LittD (Dublin); publicist; writes on international affairs; London Diplomatic Correspondent to the Star and to Universal Service, USA; is a Grand Officer of the Order of the Crown of Roumania; a Commander of the Star of Roumania and the Holy Redeemer of Greece; an Officer of the Crown of Belgium and the White Rose of Finland; a Knight of the Crown of Italy; *b* London, 1877; *s* of late B. S. Gerothwohl, city merchant, and late Stéphanie, *d* of Lieut-Col Vuillien, of French army. *Educ:* Paris; Brussels; Heidelberg. Literary and Dramatic Critic in Paris, 1898–1900; has acted as an Examiner or Inspector in Modern Languages to Civil Service Commission, Admiralty, Scotch Education Department, Irish Intermediate Board, Oxford and Cambridge Joint Board, Cambridge Syndicate, LCC, Central Welsh Board, etc.; Professor of the Romance Languages, Trinity College, Dublin, 1905–09; Head of French and Romance Department, University of Bristol, 1909–12; Fellow, Vice-President, and first Professor of Comparative Literature, Royal Society of Literature, 1911–20; led the press campaign for the administrative reform of Bristol University, 1912; Diplomatic Correspondent of the Daily Telegraph and leader writer on foreign affairs, 1919–35; has attended in a journalistic capacity most of the Peace Conferences since the 1918 armistice; contested (L) West Leicester, 1924; Faversham, 1929. *Publications:* numerous articles on foreign politics in the daily, weekly, and monthly press, etc.; on Education and on French Literature; Nero in Modern Literature, 1905; Chatterton, a play in four acts, 1909; Co-Editor of Lord D'Abernon's Diary; numerous school and University French texts.

Died 11 Nov. 1941.

GERVIS, Henry, MA, MB, BCh; Surgeon (retired); JP for Brighton; Captain RAMC, T (retired); *b* 1863; *s* of late Henry Gervis, MD, London, and Louisa Pollard; *m* Matilda Martha (*d* 1938), *d* of late William Death, Burnt Mill, Essex; two *s* one *d.* *Educ:* Mill Hill School; Trinity

College, Cambridge; St Thomas's Hospital. Practised at Bishop's Stortford, Herts, and at Brighton; Mayor of Brighton, 1906; served European War from outbreak to singing of Peace, on Staff of 2nd Eastern General Hospital at Brighton, and 20 General Hospital in France; formerly Provincial Grand Master of Mark Master Masons in Sussex. *Publication: Arms* and the Doctor. *Recreation:* wood-carving. *Address:* 14 Stanford Avenue, Brighton. *T:* Preston 2472.

Died 13 Oct. 1941.

GETHIN, Col Sir Richard Walter St Lawrence, 9th Bt *cr* 1665; CMG 1919; DSO 1917; Légion d'Honneur, Croix de Chévalier, 1918; RA, retd; *b* 16 Feb. 1878; *s* of Sir Richard Gethin, 8th Bt, and Catharine, *d* of F. E. B. Scott, Ingham Lodge, Cheshire; *S* father, 1921; *m* 1906, Helen, *d* of W. B. Thornhill, Castlebellingham, Ireland; two *s* one *d*. *Educ:* Radley Coll.; R. Military Academy, Woolwich. 2nd Lt Royal Field Artillery, 1897; Lieut 1900; Capt. 1902; Major, 1914; Bt Lt-Col 1916; Lt-Col 1917; Col 1920; served S African War, 1899–1901 (wounded at Battle of Colenso, 15 Dec. 1899, Queen's medal 5 clasps); Staff College, 1913–14; European War in France, 1914–18 (CMG, DSO, and Legion of Honour); Staff Capt. 1914; DAA and QMG 1915; AQMG 1915; Inter-Allied Military Commission of Control, Austria, 1920–21; Hungary, 1921–22; AQMG Scottish Command, 1924–28; Officer in Charge RA Record and Pay Office, 1929–33; retired pay, 1933; District Commissioner Eltham Branch Boy Scouts, 1937–39; Kenya Defence Force, 1940–42. *Heir: s* Richard Patrick St Lawrence, Lieut-Col REME, *b* 15 May 1911. *Address:* Sotik, Kenya Colony.

Died 27 Aug. 1946.

GIANNINI, Amadeo Peter; *b* San José, California, 6 May 1870; *s* of Luigi Giannini and Virginia Demartini; *m* 1892, Clorinda Agnes, *d* of Joseph Cuneo, San Francisco; three *c*. *Educ:* Public School and Business College. Began at twelve years of age with L. Scatena and Co., Wholesale Commission Merchants, San Francisco, and at nineteen was admitted to firm; became manager, Estate of Joseph Cuneo and director, Columbus Savings and Loan Society; founder, Bank of Italy (now Bank of America NT and SA), 1904; Chairman of Board of Directors, Bank of America NT and SA and Transamerica Corporation, successor to Bancitaly Corporation of which he was also founder in 1919; Director, National City Bank, New York; City Bank Farmers Trust Co., New York. *Address:* 485 California Street, San Francisco, California, USA; Seven Oaks, San Mateo, California. *TA:* Ameritrans, San Francisco, California. *T:* San Mateo 465, Douglas 6112. *Clubs:* Olympic, Bohemian, Commonwealth, Commercial, Union League, Golf, San Francisco; Los Angeles Country, Athletic, California, Los Angeles; Broad Street, Athletic, New York; Congressional Country, Washington; Union Interalliée, Paris.

Died 3 June 1949.

GIBB, Maj.-Gen. Sir Evan, KBE 1936; CB 1927; CMG 1915; CBE 1919; DSO 1902; late RASC; *b* 12 March 1877; *e s* of late William Gibb of Rubislaw, Aberdeen; *m* 1st, 1902, Beatrice Ramsay (*d* 1928), *o c* of late Major-General H. Jardine Hallowes; 2nd, 1940, Irene Marguerite, *d* of late F. G. Johns, Enfield. *Educ:* Rossall; RMC Sandhurst. Entered West India Regiment, 1898; transferred to ASC, 1899; served Sierra Leone, 1898 (medal with clasp); South Africa, 1899–1902 (despatches, Queen's medal 5 clasps, King's medal 2 clasps, DSO); European War, 1914–18 (despatches six times, CMG, Bt Lieut-Colonel and Brevet Colonel); Adjutant, Army Service Corps, Aldershot, 1905; Staff Captain, War Office, 1907; Deputy Assistant Director, War Office, 1910; Assistant Instructor, Army Service Corps Training Establishment, 1911; DAQMG France, 1914; Assistant Director of Transport, France, Nov. 1914; AQMG, GHQ France, 1915; Brig.-Gen. QMG's branch, GHQ France, 1919; DA and QMG, GHQ, British Troops in France and Flanders, Nov. 1919; GOC British Troops in France and Flanders, 1 Jan. 1920; Temp. Brig.-Gen. and Director of Labour in France, 1916; Controller of Salvage in France, 1918; Lt-Col 1920; Col 1923; Colonel Commandant, 1924; Maj.-Gen., 1927; ADS and T. Aldershot Command, 1923–27; Director of Supplies and Transport, War Office, 1929–33; Hon. Col 47th Divisional RASC, 1929–34; Hon. Col FANY, 1933–47; retired pay, 1933; Col Comdt RASC, 1933–47; Member Herring Industry Board, 1938–47; Director, 1939–40; Pres. London Chamber of Commerce, 1943, 1944 and 1945; Vice-Pres. 1946; Vice-Pres. Assoc. of British Chambers of Commerce, 1945. Comdr of the Crown (Belgium); Croix de Guerre (France); Cruz de Boyaca (Colombia). *Address:* Braeside, Hove Park Road, Hove, Sussex. *Clubs:* United Service, Royal Automobile, MCC.

Died 13 July 1947.

GIBB, James Rattray; Sheriff-Substitute of Perth and Angus at Dundee, 1941–46; *b* 14 March 1884; *s* of D. M. Gibb, SSC, of Edinburgh; *m* Isobel, *y d* of Andrew Cockburn, Edinburgh; one *s*. *Educ:* Perth Academy; Royal High School, Edinburgh, and Edinburgh University. Advocate, Scotland, 1915; Sheriff-Substitute of the County of Sutherland, 1935–41; and of the County of Ross and Cromarty, 1937–41; formerly of Zetland; sometime Captain RAF; Lecturer on Veterinary Jurisprudence at Royal (Dick) Veterinary College, Edinburgh; Editor of the Scots Law Times (Sheriff Court) Reports. *Recreations:* philately, golf, shooting. *Address:* Viewbank, 6 Hill Street, Broughty Ferry, Angus. *T:* Broughty Ferry 79251.

Died 4 Dec. 1946.

GIBB, Maurice Sylvester, CBE 1920; MIMechE; Commander of the Belgian Order of the Crown; Managing Director, Special Areas Reconstruction Association, Ltd since 1936 and now Joint Liquidator; Director of William Gray & Co., Ltd, West Hartlepool; Deputy Chairman of Hartlepool Gas and Water Co.; Member of Council of the British Employers' Confederation; President, 1937–38; *b* 28 March 1878; *s* of James Foote Gibb; *m* 1913, Honor, *d* of late Dr J. W. Browne; two *s* two *d*. *Educ:* London; Retford. Engineering training at Central Marine Engine Works, West Hartlepool; Marine Engineer, Thompsons Aberdeen White Star Line, 1899–1903; Board of Trade Chief Engineer's Certificate; Outside Machinery Superintendent to North Eastern Railway, 1903–07; General Manager and Managing Director at Central Marine Engine Works, West Hartlepool, 1907–36; member of Management Board and Council of the Engineering and Allied Employers' National Federation, 1917–37; Past President of the North-East Coast Engineering Employers' Association; Past President of the North-East Coast Institution of Engineers and Shipbuilders; Past President Hartlepools Incorp. Chamber of Commerce; Director of Munitions Supply at the Ministry of Munitions 1916, and afterwards Representative of the Ministry in charge of the National Projectile Factory at Birtley, 1917–18; Member of Technical Committee of Lloyd's Register of Shipping, 1917–37; Chairman of the BOT Committee on examinations of Engineers in the Mercantile Marine, 1937. *Address:* Longdown Cottage, Guildford.

Died 6 May 1950.

GIBB, Robertson Fyffe; Hon. Captain, Royal Naval Reserve; Director of the Union Castle Mail Steamship Co., Ltd; *b* 15 June 1868; *m* Marjorie Moon Peddie; three *s*. Joined Union Steamship Co., 1883; Joint Manager of Union Castle Co., 1912; Director, 1929; Chairman, 1932–39; Director of Bullard, King & Co., Ltd, African Lands and Hotels, Ltd, and Elders Insurance Co., Ltd, etc.; Chairman of Manica Trading Co., Ltd; Pres. of Chamber of Shipping of the UK, 1939–40; Member of General Purposes Committee of Shipping Federation, of General Committee of Lloyds' Register of

Shipping; Chairman of Royal Alfred Aged Merchant Seamen's Institution; Fellow of Royal Empire Society; has made frequent visits to South and East Africa. *Recreations:* golf, travelling and reading. *Address:* Longfeld, Hersham, Surrey. *T:* Walton-on-Thames 1787.

Died 26 Sept. 1944.

GIBB, Lt-Col Ronald Charles, CBE 1919; late RASC; *b* 24 July 1873; *s* of George Gibb; *m* Marion Winifred, *d* of late Lt-Col C. W. Thiele, RA, MC; one *d. Educ:* Harrow; RMC Sandhurst. Entered Army, 1894; served Tirah, 1887–88 (medal and two clasps); S Africa, 1901–02 (Queen's medal with clasp); retired pay, 1911; served European War, 1914–19 (despatches, CBE). *Address:* The Green Corner, Wade Court, Havant, Hants.

Died 1 Oct. 1946.

GIBBON, Sir (Ioan) Gwilym, Kt 1936; CB 1931; CBE 1918; BA, DSc (Lond.); late Director of Local Government Div., Ministry of Health; *b* Treherbert, Glamorgan, 1874; *s* of David Gibbon, mining engineer. *Educ:* High School, Oswestry; London School of Economics and Political Science. Was in the Savings Bank Department and the Secretary's Office, General Post Office, and in the Local Government Board; retired, 1936. *Publications:* Unemployment Insurance; Medical Benefit in Germany and Denmark; Infant Welfare Centres; The Expenditure and Revenue of Local Authorities; The Public Social Services; Problems of Town and Country Planning; History of the London County Council (with Reginald W. Bell), 1939; Reconstruction and Town and Country Planning; articles on public administration. *Recreation:* golf. *Club:* Reform.

Died 4 Feb. 1948.

GIBBON, Brig.-Gen. James Aubrey, CMG 1919; *b* 1864; 4th *s* of Rev. Canon William Wynter Gibbon, Ripon; *m* Madeline, *d* of late E. M. Denny of 11 Bryanston Square, W; three *s* one *d. Educ:* Haileybury; Royal Military Academy, Woolwich. Commission, Royal Engineers, 1884; served Tirah Campaign, 1897–98 (medal and 2 clasps); Chief Engineer, Aldershot, 1914–15; Chief Engineer VIII Corps, Gallipoli and Egypt, 1915–16; Chief Engineer, Southern Command, 1916–20; Lay Reader in 4 Dioceses. *Address:* Ditcheat Manor House, Bath, Somerset. *T:* Ditcheat 216.

Died 4 Jan. 1947.

GIBBS, Charles, FRCS Eng.; Senior Surgeon to Lock Hospitals and Consulting Surgeon to Charing Cross Hospital; *m* Kate (*d* 1940), *d* of H. T. Northcroft, Lancing; one *s* one *d.* Entered as student Charing Cross Hospital, 1885; held all the minor appointments; Assistant Surgeon, 1896; Capt. RAMCT in European War; Surgeon-in-Chief to the Langman Field Hospital, South African War, 1900. *Publications:* Diseases of the Penis, Gonorrhœa, Impotence and Sterility (Quain Dictionary); Results of treatment in syphilis by English and French Salvarsan Products; various articles on surgery in medical journals and medical societies. *Address:* 3 Upper Wimpole Street, Cavendish Square, W1.

Died 5 Oct. 1943.

GIBBS, Hon. Michael Patrick, KC 1911; BL, MLC; President Legislative Council, 1930–33; *b* St John's, Newfoundland, 25 March 1870; *s* of John and Margaret Gibbs; widower. *Educ:* Christian Brothers' School of St John's. Called to Bar, 1896; Secretary of the Tenants' League, 1892; Editor Terra Nova Advocate, 1893; Member for District St George, 1897; one of the counsel for Newfoundland Government on Royal Commission on French treaty rights, 1898; Governor of the Newfoundland Savings Bank, 1898; Mayor of St John's, 1906–10; Legislative Council with rank of Cabinet Minister, 1909; Leader of Government Legislative Council Sessions, 1911–13; took evidence and reported to Government upon the land tenure system of Newfoundland; Cabinet Minister without portfolio in National Government formed prosecute war, 1917; on Reconstruction declined seat in Cabinet, 1918; Leader of Opposition in Legislative Council, 1918; President of Newfoundland Fisherman's Star of the Sea Association, 1936–40; Member of the American Branch of the International Law Association; Catholic. *Recreation:* fishing. *Address:* 57 Le Marchant Road, St John's, Newfoundland. *TA:* Gibbs St John's.

Died Nov. 1943.

GIBSON, Alexander George, DM, FRCP; Consulting Physician, Radcliffe Infirmary and County Hospital, Oxford; *b* Hull, 21 Sept. 1875; *s* of William and Elizabeth Gibson; *m* Constance Muriel (*d* 1942), *d* of late J. T. Jones, JP of Tenby; two *s* one *d. Educ:* University College, Aberystwyth; Christ Church, Oxford; St Thomas's Hospital, London. *Publications:* The Radcliffe Infirmary, 1926; The Heart, 1926; Clinical Methods, 1927; The Mycoses of the Spleen, 1930; The Physician's Art, 1933. *Address:* 27 Banbury Road, Oxford. *T:* 3228.

Died 11 Jan. 1950.

GIBSON, Charles Dana; artist; *b* Mass, USA, 14 Sept. 1867; *s* of Charles De Wolf and Josephine Elizabeth Gibson; *m* 1895, Irene Langhorne, of Richmond, Va. *Educ:* Flushing High School; Art Student League, NY First drew for Life, 1886. *Publications:* Drawings by C. D. Gibson; Pictures of People; Sketches and Cartoons; The Education of Mr Pipp; Americans; A Widow and her Friends; The Social Ladder. *Address:* 127 East 73rd Street, New York. *Clubs:* Century Association, NY City.

Died 23 Dec. 1944.

GIBSON, Sir Charles Granville, Kt 1937; *b* 8 Nov. 1880; *m*; one *d. Educ:* Leeds Central High School; Leeds University. Lord Mayor of Leeds, 1924–25; Member of Leeds City Council for 12 years; MP (C) Pudsey and Otley Division of West Riding, 1929–45; Managing Director S. Gibson & Sons, Ltd, and Director of various Companies; Chairman of the Yorkshire Automobile Club, 1929; Chairman, Leather Producers Association, 1921–24; President, Light Leather Tanners and Curriers Federation, 1923–24; Life Member of Court, Leeds University; Chairman, Leather Insdustries Department, Leeds University; President Assoc. of British Chambers of Commerce, 1939–40; Chairman of Executive Council, Federation of Chambers of Commerce of the British Empire, 1938–40; Member British National Committee of International Chambers of Commerce; President Leeds Chamber of Commerce, 1940–41; Member Advisory Cttee on Debts Clearing Office and Import Restrictions Act, 1934; Chairman British Glacé Kid Tanners Assoc., 1944–45. Member of British Mission to South America, 1940–41, with Marquess of Willingdon. *Recreations:* golf, motoring, and travel. *Address:* Oakwood Hall, Roundhay, Leeds, 8. *TA:* Gibson, Bramley, Leeds. *T:* Leeds 58335. *Club:* Constitutional.

Died 17 July 1948.

GIBSON, Charles Stanley, OBE 1919; FRS 1931; Emeritus Professor of Chemistry, London University, Guy's Hospital Medical School, SE1, since 1949 (Professor, 1921–49); *b* 8 Feb. 1884; 7th *s* of late Joshua Gibson, Manchester; unmarried. *Educ:* Manchester Grammar School; Corpus Christi Coll., Oxford (Natural Science Scholar). Honours in Chemistry, 1905; MA (Oxford and Cambridge), ScD (Cambridge), BSc (Oxford), MSc (Tech.) (Manchester); FRIC. Membre d'honneur de la Société de Chimie Industrielle; Mem. of Sidney Sussex Coll., Cambridge; Senior Research Student of the Goldsmiths' Company, Oxford University, 1909–12; Assistant Lecturer and Demonstrator in the University Chemical Laboratory,

Cambridge; Professor of Chemistry, The Maharaja's College, Trivandrum, S India, 1912–19; Honorary Advisor to the Chemical Warfare Committee of the Ministry of Munitions, 1916–19; Professor of Chemistry, The Egyptian Government School of Medicine, Cairo, 1919–20; Hon. Secretary of the Chemical Society, 1924–33; President, Chemistry Section of British Association, 1938; Senior Gas Adviser in SE England, 1939–45. *Publications:* author of Essential Principles of Organic Chemistry, and numerous papers dealing with Stereo-Chemistry, The Chemistry of Natural Products; The Organic Chemistry of Arsenic, Sulphur, Selenium and Gold, production of films of Gold, chemotherapy, etc. *Recreations:* gardening, music, golf. *Address:* Greenaway, Warren Drive, Kingswood, Surrey. *T:* Mogador 2414. *Club:* Athenæum.

Died 24 March 1950.

GIBSON, Wing-Comdr Guy Penrose, VC 1943; DSO 1942, and bar, 1943; DFC 1940, and bar, 1941; RAF; commanding 617 Sqdn; *b* 12 Aug. 1918; *s* of Alexander James Gibson and Nora Mary Strike; *m* 1940, Evelyn Mary Moore. *Educ:* St Edward's School, Oxford. Left school, 1936. Joined RAF, 1936, as Pilot Officer; Flight Lt 1940; Squadron Leader, 1941; Wing Cmdr 1942. *Publication:* Enemy Coast Ahead, 1946. *Recreations:* squash, swimming, sailing. *Address:* RAF, c/o Air Ministry, Kingsway, WC2. *Clubs:* RAF, Adastral.

Died 19 Sept. 1944.

GIBSON, Harvey Dow, LLD; President, 1931, Manufacturers Trust Company, New York, NY; Director of many other companies; *b* North Conway, NH, 12 March 1882; *s* of James L. Gibson and Addie Dow; *m* 1st, 1903, Carrie Hastings Curtis, Newtonville, Mass; 2nd, 1926, Helen Whitney Bourne, New York; no *c. Educ:* Bowdoin College. AB 1902; LLD 1919. Trustee and Chairman Finance Cttee; Hon. degrees; Univ. of New Hampshire, LLD 1933; Northeastern Univ., LLD 1945. American Express Company, Boston; Asst Mgr financial department, New York; Raymond and Whitcomb Co., Vice-Pres. and Member of controlling group; Liberty National Bank, New York, Asst to Pres. 1912, Vice-Pres. 1913, Pres. 1917; New York Trust Company, Pres. 1921; American Red Cross: Chairman, New York Chapter, 1917, General Manager, 1917, Commissioner for France, 1918, for Europe, 1919; for Great Britain, 1942–45; and for Western Europe, 1944–45; Member of the Pres. War Council and War Finance Com. 1917–19; Chairman, New York City Emergency Unemployment Relief Committee, 1931–33; National Chm., Amer. Red Cross campaign, 1946 and 1947; Bd of Governors of Amer. Nat. Red Cross. Officer of the Legion of Honour (France); Commander, Order of the Crown (Belgium); Knight, Order of Vasa (Sweden); Commander, Order of the Crown (Rumania); United States of America Medal for Merit; Assoc. Commander, Order of St John of Jerusalem (Great Britain). *Recreations:* fox hunting (Ex-MFH Meadow Brook Hounds), riding, ski-ing, etc. *Address:* 52 East 69th Street, New York; Locust Valley, New York; 55 Broad Street, New York. *Clubs:* Buck's; Advertising, Bankers' Club of America (Governor), Bond, Creek (Pres. and Governor), The Links, Links Golf, Madison Square Garden (Pres. and Governor), Meadow Brook, National Golf Links of America, Newcomen Society of England (American Branch), New York Yacht, Coffee House, Piping Rock, Racquet and Tennis, River, Turf and Field, Recess, Union League, University, Wall Street (New York); Union Interalliée, Travellers' (Paris).

Died 11 Sept. 1950.

GIBSON, Sir Henry James, KCB 1912 (CB 1902); *b* 7 Oct. 1860; *s* of late Rev. H. A. Gibson, Vicar of Linslade, Bucks; *m* 1901, Ethel Margaret (*d* 1917), *o d* of late Thomas Allen Green; two *s* three *d. Educ:* Rossall; St John's Coll. Oxford. Casberd Scholar, 1st Class Classical Moderations. Appointed War Office Clerk, 1885;

Senior, 1896; Principal, 1897; Assistant Accountant-General, 1900; Resident Clerk, 1893–1900; Private Secretary to Mr Woodall, Financial Secretary, 1894–95; and to Hon. St John Brodrick, MP, Under-Secretary of State for War, 1895–96; Deputy-Accountant-General, War Office, 1903; Assistant Director of Army Finance, 1904; Assistant Comptroller and Auditor, 1905–11; Comptroller and Auditor-General, 1911–21; Chairman of Policy and Parliamentary Committee National Union of Manufacturers, 6 Holburn Viaduct, EC, 1921–25. *Recreations:* lawn tennis, golf and bowls. *Address:* The Rectory, Emsworth, Hants.

Died 22 Nov. 1950.

GIBSON, Rear-Adm. Isham Worsley, OBE 1919; MVO 1901; *b* 1882; 3rd *s* of late Dr J. E. Gibson of Cowes; *m* 1914, Phyllis, *d* of late Captain Morrish, RN; one *s* one *d.* Entered Navy, 1896; Mid-Shipman of Windsor, RN Guard of Honour, Queen Victoria's Funeral (MVO); Lieut 1902; Lieut-Comdr, 1910; Comdr, 1914; Capt., 1920; Rear-Adm., 1932; served European War, 1914–18; Dardanelles, 1915 (despatches, OBE); Naval War College, 1922–24; commanded HMS Dragon, Mediterranean Fleet, 1924–26; Naval Staff, Admiralty, 1927–30; HMS Dorsetshire, Atlantic Fleet, 1930–31; HMS Exeter 1931–32; retired list, 1932. *Address:* Greenmoor Cottage, East Boldre, Hants.

Died 30 Nov. 1950.

GIBSON, Prof. James, MA, DLitt; Emeritus Professor of Logic and Philosophy, University College of North Wales; sometime Fellow of St John's College, Cambridge; *b* 31 Dec. 1864; *s* of Samuel and Jane Gibson; *m* 1895, Margaret Beatrice Harris (*d* 1943). *Educ:* Trinity Coll., Dublin; St John's Coll., Cambridge. *Publications:* Locke's Theory of Knowledge and its Historical Relations, 1917; articles and reviews in philosophical journals. *Address:* Bron Hwfa, Bangor.

Died 1 Aug. 1943.

GIBSON, John Ashley; author and journalist; Originated and Edits Outward Bound Library; *b* 10 Jan. 1885; *e s* of late J. K. Gibson, of the General Post Office; *m* 1918, Doris, *e d* of late Ireson Freer; two *s* one *d. Educ:* Mercers' School. Assist Editor, Literay World; TP's Weekly; The World; The Tramp; and on staff of Daily News and Leader; visited West Africa 1910, looking for copy and a gold mine, finding one but not the other; toured Malayan Archipelago and the Moluccas as Special Correspondent, 1924; Leader Writer and Assistant Editor, Times of Ceylon, 1912–15 and 1919–21; Editor, the Malay Mail, 1923–26; Press Sec., Coalfields Distress Funds, 1928–29; War Service, 1915–18 in France and East Africa with Royal Fusiliers (Company Comdr) and 1st KAR; RAFVR (Flight Lieut and Adjt, Fighter Command), 1940–44; Asst Curator and Secretary, Imperial War Museum, 1918–19; Ministry of Information, 1945–46. *Publications:* The Twilight Drummers, 1914; Children of the Lion, 1920; Cinnamon and Frangipanni, 1923; The Malay Peninsula and Archipelago, 1928; Ceylon, 1929; Postscript to Adventure, 1930; The Death of the Lion (with Justin Pieris), 1935; discovered and edited, MS Journal of Sieur Jean de Lacombe of Quercy, with the relation of his East Indian Voyages, 1668–1676, 1937; contributor to Fortnightly Review, English Review, Blackwood's, The Nation and Athenæum, Bookman, Outlook, Spectator, etc. *Address:* 585 Finchley Road, NW3. *T:* Hampstead 4986.

Died 6 April 1948.

GIBSON, Sir John Watson, Kt 1945; OBE; Director Pauling & Co. Ltd; Chairman Acton Bolt Ltd; *b* Middlesborough, 9 Aug. 1885; *s* of Robert Elwin Gibson and Ruth Eleanor Hugill; *m* 1911, Lilian Gindle Armstrong; two *s* three *d. Educ:* Middlesbrough High School. Pupil in civil engineering on Middlesbrough Dock with Sir John Scott, 1900–08; 1910–25. Engaged on civil engineering projects in various parts of world with Lord Cowdray (S. Pearson & Son, Ltd), including construction King George Dock, Hull, Queen Mary Reservoir, Staines, Sennar Dam and Irrigation Works, Blue Nile, Sudan. During European War: Director Shell & Gun Production in USA; Special Mission to India; Controller Aircraft Requirements and Review. 1933–37, built Gebel Aulia Dam, White Nile, Sudan. During War of 1939–45: Controller Building Construction, Ministry of Supply, 1940–41, responsible for construction of Royal Ordnance Factories. Technical Adviser to President Board of Trade, 1942, initiated opencast coal working; Deputy Director-General Civil Engineering (Special), Ministry of Supply, 1943–44, responsible for construction of breakwater for Mulberry Harbour. *Recreations:* cricket, golf, farming. *Address:* Stanwell Place, Stanwell, nr Staines. *T:* Ashford (Middlesex) 2025. *Clubs:* Royal Thames Yacht, Royal Automobile.

Died 19 March 1947.

GIBSON, Walcot, FRS (L. and E.), FGS (L. and E.); DSc; Director for Scotland HM Geological Survey of Great Britain; retired, 1925; *b* 24 Aug. 1864; *m* 1895, Annie Olive Landon; no *c*. *Educ:* Bromsgrove School; Mason Science College; Royal College of Science. Geological Work, South Africa, 1889–91; East Africa, 1891–93; HM Geological Survey, 1893–1925. *Publications:* Geology of Coal and Coal Mining; Coal in Great Britain; several papers to scientific societies, author and part author of numerous Geological Survey Memoirs. *Address:* Pathways, Fairlight Road, Hythe, Kent.

Died 28 Nov. 1941.

GIBSON, William John, CBE 1926; *b* 1865; *s* of Josias Gibson; *m* 1895, Mary Simpson, *d* of Alexander Laird; one *d*. *Educ:* Glasgow University, MA 1888; Glasgow Technical College Course Certificate in Agricultural Science, 1894. Headmaster of Nicolson Institute, Stornoway, 1894–1925; retired, 1925. *Publications:* Science in the School, 1904; Education in Scotland, 1912; In the Near East, 1926. *Recreations:* geology and archæology. *Address:* 15 Plewlands Avenue, Edinburgh.

Died 24 Nov. 1944.

GIBSON, William Sumner, CMG 1934; Partner, Gibson and Pelloe, 31 Lemon Street, Truro; *b* 21 June 1876; *s* of Right Rev. E. C. S. Gibson, late Bishop of Gloucester and Mary Grace Philpott; *m* 1925, Dorothea Rose, *d* of late Adrian Rapley; one *s*. *Educ:* Marlborough; Keble College, Oxford (scholar); 1st class Modern History 1899. Eastern Cadetship, Colonial Civil Service, 1899; held various appointments; Legal Adviser, Federated Malay States, and Member of Federal Council, 1922–33; retired, 1935; Barrister-at-Law, Lincoln's Inn, 1913–36; admitted Solicitor, 1938. *Address:* Bella Vista, Penryn, Cornwall.

Died 7 Aug. 1946.

GICK, Sir William John, Kt 1941; CB 1936; CBE 1920; OBE 1918; *b* 1877. Naval Store Officer, Grand Fleet, during European War; Deputy Director of Stores, 1933–34; Director of Naval Stores, 1934–40. *Address:* 21 Melcombe Court, Dorset Square, NW1. *T:* Paddington 7271.

Died 31 Aug. 1948.

GIDDINGS, William John Peter, FJI, FRSA; journalist, attached staff The Advertiser, Adelaide; *b* North Adelaide, 29 June 1861; *o s* of late William Giddings, and *nephew* of Major J. L. Giddings, one of the Lucknow garrison; *m* 1897, Aurora, *y d* of late Captain Killicoat; one *d*. *Educ:* St Peter's College, Adelaide. Joined staff of Adelaide Advertiser, 1880, and acted as Special Commissioner for that paper at Colinderies, London, 1886; editor and proprietor of the Silver Age, 1890; editor Tamworth News, 1894; on Golden Age, 1895; went to England, 1896; joined staff of British Australasian; acted as Special Commissioner for

Newcastle Morning Herald at Diamond Jubilee Celebrations in London, 1897; returned to Australia and acted as Special Commissioner for British Australasian on visit of Prince and Princess of Wales, 1901; editor Faulding's Journal, 1899–1913, and of The Standard, Adelaide, 1913–18; a Member of South Australian Royal Commission on Inebriety, 1906; Commissioner to report on experiments by Dr Danysz, of the Pasteur Institute, Paris, for destroying rabbits in Australia by means of disease; Chairman of the South Australian Corps of Veterans, and Founder of Veteran Movement in Australia; Life Member, Council SA District Trained Nursing Society and Royal British Nurses Association; suggested and arranged Lucknow Relief Jubilee Celebrations in Australia, 1907; induced Commonwealth Govt to grant annual dinner to active-service veterans and right of military funerals to all Crimean and Mutiny veterans dying in Australia; represented South Australia at Jubilee of District Trained Nursing at Liverpool, 1909, and International Congress on Alcohol and International Nursing Congress, London, the same year; one of the founders of Royal SA Aero Club; has travelled extensively in Europe, Mauritius, Ceylon, and Australia. *Recreation:* motoring. *Address:* Talunga, Glenelg, South Australia. *T:* Glenelg X 1276. *Clubs:* Authors', Press; Commercial, Returned Soldiers, Adelaide.

Died 2 Aug. 1938.

GIDNEY, Lt-Col Sir Henry Albert John, Kt 1931; FRCSE; FRS (Edin.); DPH (Cantab); DO (Oxon); IMS, retd; MLA, India, since 1921; *b* 9 June 1873. *Educ:* Calcutta; Edinburgh; University College Hospital, London; Cambridge. Entered Indian Medical Service, 1898; served China Expedition, 1900–01; North-East Frontier, 1913; North-West Frontier, 1914–15 (wounded); President, Anglo-Indian and Domiciled European Association All India and Burma; Leader of Anglo-Indian Deputation to London, 1925; Member, Indian Sandhurst Committee, 1931; Anglo-Indian Delegate to the Indian Round Table Conference, 1930–32; British Indian delegate to Joint Parliamentary Committee, 1933; Chairman, Legislative Assembly pending election of Speaker, 1935; Member, Central Advisory Board of Health, 1937. *Address:* 87a Park Street, Calcutta, India.

Died 5 May 1942.

GIE, S. F. N.; Dr Phil; Minister Plenipotentiary and Envoy Extraordinary of Union of South Africa to USA since 1944; *b* Worcester, Cape Province, 13 July 1884; *s* of C. J. C. Gie and M. Naudé; *m* 1911, Johanna Jordaan, Cradock CP; two *s*. *Educ:* Boys' High School, Worcester; Victoria College, Stellenbosch; University of Amsterdam; University of Berlin. Professor of History, University of Stellenbosch, 1918–26; Secretary for Education, Union of South Africa, 1926–34. Minister Plenipotentiary and Envoy Extraordinary of the Union of South Africa to Germany 1934–39; to Sweden, 1934–44. *Address:* South African Legation, 3101 Massachusetts Avenue, Washington, DC, USA.

Died 9 April 1945.

GIFFARD, Very Rev. Agnew Walter Giles, MA (Oxon); Rector of St Peter Port, Guernsey, since 1931; Dean of Guernsey and its Depdendencies since 1931; officiating Chaplain to troops (stationed in Guernsey), 1935; *b* Guernsey, 28 April 1869; 3rd *s* of Agnew Giffard, CE and Henrietta Delicia Godfray; *m* 1896, Ethel Denbow (*d* 1942), *e d* of Joseph William Gullick, CMG; two *s*. *Educ:* Elizabeth College, Guernsey; Queen's College, Oxford. Deacon, 1894; Priest, 1895; Curate of Aylesford, Kent, 1894; Rector of Manton, 1896; Vicar of Messingham with E. Butterwick, 1900; Vicar of Sparsholt with Kingston Lisle, 1918; Diocesan Organising Secretary, ACS Lincoln Diocese, 1914; Oxford Diocese, 1918–29; Commissioner of Sewers, County and City of Lincoln, 1907–18; Chairman of the British Hospitals Association Regional Committee,

Oxon, Berks and Bucks, 1931. *Publication:* editor, Liber Vitae Reginensium, 1914–1919. *Recreations:* rowing, sea-fishing. *Address:* The Deanery, Guernsey. *TA:* Dean of Guernsey. *T:* Guernsey 36.

Died April 1947.

GILBERT, James Daniel; DL, JP; Member of Thames Conservancy, 1901–38, Chairman, 1937–38; MP (L) West Newington, London, Jan. 1916–Dec. 1918; Central Southwark, 1918–24; Member London County Council for West Newington (now Central Southwark), 1898–1928; *b* West Newington, 1864; *m* 1st (wife *d* 1921); 2nd, 1926, Jessie, *y d* of W. Bromley, JP. *Educ:* privately. Hon. Secretary Liberal Association, 1885–98; Chairman of LCC Committees Corporate Property, 1899–1900; Fire Brigade, 1900–02; Rivers, 1903–06; General Purposes, 1906–07; Chief Progressive Whip, 1901–07; proposed resolution for Circular Overbridge and Embankment Trams; secured Steamboats Bill and organised first services; suggested site for New County Hall at Westminster Bridge; Land Tax Commissioner, 1907; Member Port of London Authority, 1913–39; Chairman Stores Committee, 1919–34, River Committee, 1934–39; Member County of London Territorial Association, 1918; has travelled considerably, visited India, Burmah, Australia, New Zealand, Canada, United States, Egypt, Morocco, Russia, French and Belgian Battle Fronts (1918), etc.; Presented with vote of thanks (on vellum) by British Red Cross Society and Order of St John of Jerusalem, 1918, for organising River Trips for Wounded Soldiers, 1915–18; Member Select Committee on Transport, 1918; Chairman London Liberal MP's Group, 1919, 1922 and 1924; Member Select Committee on London Traffic, 1919; Chairman Kennington Park Extension Committee, 1921; a Chairman of Standing Committees, House of Commons; 1923 and 1924; Trustee, Crystal Palace, 1924, River Wandle Advisory Committee, 1928–35; LCC nominee on Morley College Council; SE1; Trustee and Manager Lambeth Savings Bank, 1935. *Publications:* Two-and-a-Half Years' Record of the Moderate Party, 1909; The Record of the Second Moderate Council, 1912. *Recreation:* travelling. *Club:* National Liberal.

Died 26 Sept. 1941.

GILBERT, Jean. *Publications:* The Girl in the Taxi; The Cinema Star; The Joy-Ride Lady; Mam'selle Tralala; Puppchen; Tango Princess; Modern Eve; Lady of the Rose; Katja the Dancer; One Must be Young; The Prettiest of All; Dorine; The Way to Fortune; The Lady in Purple; The Bride of Lucullus; Uschi; The Game of Love. *Address:* c/o International Copyright Bureau, Ltd, Dewar House, Haymarket, SW.

Died 20 Dec. 1942.

GILBERT, Lt-Col Leonard Erskine, CIE 1919; Indian Medical Service, retired; *b* 1874; *s* of Edward G. Gilbert, Harleston, Norfolk; *m* 1900, Louisa M. Carruthers, Inverness; one *s* two *d*. *Educ:* St Thomas's Hospital; London University; MD, 1910. Entered IMS, 1900; ADMS, BEF Mesopotamia; Inspector General of Civil Hospitals, Burma; retired, 1929. *Address:* 63 St George's Square, SW1.

Died 12 Sept. 1946.

GILBERT, Walter; sculptor, metal worker and designer; art adviser to several firms whose manufactures embrace industrial art; *b* 12 Aug. 1871; *s* of Henry Edward Gilbert and Jane Isabella Gilbert; *m* Ina MacGeoch; one *s* one *d*. *Educ:* Studied Art Birmingham Municipal Art School; South Kensington; France, Belgium and Germany. Formerly taught art in Rugby School and in Harrow School; travelled in USA and in India; principal works designed and in conjunction with the late Louis Weingartner executed the Great Gates to Buckingham Palace and the Victoria Memorial under Sir Aston Webb, architect, the sculpture in the Great Reredos and other work in Liverpool Cathedral under Sir Giles

Gilbert Scott, RA, architect; Great Doors to the Grand Temple Masonic Peace Memorial under H. V. Ashley and Winton Newman, FFRIBA, architects; all bronze doors in Main Restaurant and private dining rooms on the Queen Mary, also moulded glass panels in Main Restaurant; war memorials, Eccleston Park, Liverpool; Liverpool Exchange; Masonic Hall, Liverpool; Crewe; Troon; Burnley; and Morley, Yorks, etc.; sculpture and metal work Commercial Union Assurance, Cornhill; and Kingston Guildhall (Sir Aston Webb and Son, architects); carved doors, Cornhill Insurance Co.; great bronze doors, New Scottish Government Offices, Edinburgh; The Shrine, Masonic Peace Memorial; all sculpture and bronze doors, etc., in the great building, 44 Main Street, Johannesburg, South Africa (F. Lorne, FRIBA, of Sir John Burnet Tait and Lorne, Architects), etc. *Publications:* writer on industrial art (sculpture and metal work). *Address:* (temp: c/o Rev. Canon Cragg, Tandridge Vicarage, nr Oxted, Surrey); 35a Addison Road, Kensington, W14. *Club:* Constitutional.

Died 23 Jan. 1946.

GILBEY, Sir (H.) Walter, 2nd Bt *cr* 1893; Chairman of W. & A. Gilbey, Ltd, and of Royal Agricultural Hall Co., Ltd; *b* 1 Oct. 1859; *e s* of 1st Bart and Ellen (*d* 1896), *d* of late John Parish, Bishop Stortford, Herts; *S* father, 1914; *m* 1st, 1884, Ella (who obtained a divorce, 1926), *d* of late John Coutts Fowlie, Coombe Warren, Kingston Hill; (second *s* killed in action, March 1915); 2nd, 1934, Mrs Marion Broadhead; one *s*. *Educ:* Harrow. *Recreations:* racing, shooting, golf. *Heir: g s* Walter Derek, 2nd Lt Black Watch [*b* 11 March 1913; *s* of late Walter Ewart Gilbey and Alice Dora Coysgarne, *o d* of A. Coysgarne Sim]. *Address:* Orchard Court, Portman Square, W1. *T:* Welbeck 8330. *Clubs:* Orleans, Garrick.

Died 11 April 1945.

GILBEY, Tresham; JP, Director of John Barker & Co., Ltd; *b* 6 Aug. 1862; 3rd *s* of Sir Walter Gilbey, 1st Bt; *m* 1886, Annie (*d* 1941), *o c* of late Sir John Barker, 1st Bt. *Educ:* Harrow. Studied for law; took up journalism; joint-author of The History of the Essex Foxhounds; Founder and late proprietor of Baily's Fox-Hunting Directory; Past President and Member of Council Polo Pony Society; Past President and on Council of the County Polo Association. *Recreations:* hunting, polo, shooting. *Address:* Whitehall, Bishop's Stortford, Herts. *T:* Bishop's-Stortford 58. *Clubs:* Hurlingham, Orleans.

Died 16 Feb. 1947.

GILBEY, Sir Walter; *see* Gilbey, Sir H. W.

GILCHRIST, Lt-Col Walter Fellowes Cowan, CIE 1918; MVO, 1921; late 4th Sikhs 12th Frontier Force Regt; Indian Army, retired; *b* 1879; *s* of W. G. Gilchrist, MICE, PWD, India; *m* 1910, Myra, *d* of late Major-Gen. R. A. Carew Hunt; one *s* two *d*. *Educ:* Cheltenham College; Sandhurst; Staff College, Camberley. Served Somaliland, 1903–04 (medal and two clasps); European War (Mesopotamia), 1914–19 (despatches, CIE); Operations in Waziristan, 1919–20 (despatches). *Address:* Sid Abbey, Sidmouth. *T:* Sidmouth 104.

Died 28 Dec. 1943.

GILDER, Joseph B.; journalist; *b* St Thomas's Hall, Flushing, NY, 29 June 1858; *s* of late Rev. Wm H. Gilder; *m* 1892; one *s* one *d*. Entered US Naval Academy, 1872; resigned, 1874. Resigned assistant city-editorship New York Herald, Dec. 1880, and with sister, Jeannette L. Gilder, started The Critic, Jan. 1881, holding co-editorship for twenty-one years; literary adviser, Century Co., 1895–1902; United States Government Despatch Agent at London, 1902–04; Editor Putnam's Magazine, 1906–10; Editor New York Times Review of Books, 1910–11; banking and brokerage business, 1911–14; Secretary, Industrial Finance Corporation, 1914–28; Secretary, The Morris Plan Insurance Society, 1917–28; Treas. Am. Copyright League, 1886; an organiser and Secretary of Univ.

Settlement Society of New York; contributor of prose and verse to periodicals; travelled in Europe, 1928–35. *Publications:* The American Idea, 1902; Andrew Carnegie's Gospel of Wealth; James Russell Lowell's Impressions of Spain; Addresses of John Hay, etc.; also (with J. L. Gilder) Essays from The Critic, and Authors at Home. *Address:* 7 West 43rd Street, New York, USA. *TA:* (cable): Gilderjo. *Clubs:* Athenæum, Authors, Whitefriars; Century, New York.

Died 9 Dec. 1936.

GILES, Major Godfrey Douglas, OBE; artist, military and sporting subjects; *b* Kurrachee, India, 9 Nov. 1857; *s* of Capt. Edward Giles, late Indian Navy; *m* Evelyn, *d* of George Barclay, Edinburgh; one *d*. *Educ:* Cheltenham. Entered Army, 1875; went direct from Sandhurst to India; joined Bombay Staff Corps; served in Afghan War, 1879–81 (medal), seconded for service in Egyptian Gendarmerie, 1883; commanded Turkish Cavalry at battle of El Teb; attached to 10th Royal Hussars, and present at second battle of El Teb (medal and clasp, Khedive's Star, and Osmanieh 4th Class); left the army, 1884; studied painting in Carolus Duran's studio, 1885; war correspondent for Graphic in South African war, 1900; with Cavalry Division at relief of Kimberley and capture of Cronje; Capt. in Loyal Suffolk Hussars (Imperial Yeomanry). *Publications: pictures published:* Saving the Guns at Maiwand; The Canal Turn, Grand National Steeplechase; Life of a Racehorse; Quorn Hunt; The Derby; and various military and sporting pictures. *Address:* 9 Forres Street, Edinburgh.

Died 1 Feb. 1941.

GILES, Margaret M.; *see* Jenkin, Mrs Bernard.

GILES, Sir Robert (Sidney), Kt 1922; *b* 2 Dec. 1865; *s* of late Richard William Giles; *m* 1914, Mary Louisa (MBE 1924), *widow* of Hugh Seaborne May, RE, and *d* of late Captain Charles H. Marillier, Rifle Brigade; no *c*. *Educ:* Clifton College; Magdalen College, Oxford, MA. Called to Bar, Middle Temple, 1890; practised in Rangoon; Assistant-Government Advocate, Burma, 1900–05; Government Advocate, Burma, 1905–07; member of Burma Legislative Council, 1905–07 and 1922–24; President, 1924–27; Vice-Chancellor, University of Rangoon, 1921–27; Hon. LLD, University of Rangoon, 1927. *Recreations:* shooting, fishing. *Address:* Rossall Hall, Bicton Heath, Shrewsbury. *TA:* and *T:* Montford-Bridge 28. *Club:* Oxford and Cambridge.

Died 25 Aug. 1944.

GILFORD, Hastings, FRCS England; Fellow, Royal Society of Medicine; *b* Melton Mowbray, 1861; *m* 1887, Lilian Adele Hope; two *s* two *d*. *Educ:* private school. Formerly Hunterian Professor, Royal College of Surgeons of England; formerly Surgeon in charge of Sutherland War Hospital and Hospital for Pensioners; author of Progeria (Med-Chir. Trans. 1897) and Ateleiosis (Med-Chir. Trans. 1902). *Publications:* Disorders of Post-natal Growth and Development, 1911; Tumors and Cancers: A Biological Study, 1925; Cancer, Civilization, Degeneration, 1932; The Cancer Problem and its Solution, 1934; The Hysterozoa, 1936; various articles. *Recreation:* tennis. *Address:* 47 Cressingham Road, Reading. *TA:* Hastings Gilford, Reading; The Clinic, 49 Cressingham Road, Reading.

Died 6 Sept. 1941.

GILL, Rt Rev. Charles Hope, MA, DD; *b* 11 Feb. 1861; *s* of late Rev. Wm Gill, Rector of Hertingfordbury, Hertford, and Anna Maria, *d* of late Rear-Admiral Charles Hope, RN; *m* 1893, Margaret Mary, *d* of late Rev. Gervase Thorp; two *s* two *d*. *Educ:* St Edmund's School, Canterbury; King William's College, Isle of Man; Queens' College and Ridley Hall, Cambridge. Curate of St Peter's, Tynemouth, 1884–86; missionary, CMS at Shikarpur, Bengal, 1887–90; Jubbulpore, 1890–97; Secretary, CMS and Hon. Chaplain to

Cathedral, Allahabad, 1898–1905; Bishop of Travancore and Cochin, 1905–24; Vicar of Gerrard's Cross, 1926–30; British Chaplain, Hyères, 1930–38. *Address:* Grosvenor Court, Croft Road, Torquay.

Died 29 June 1946.

GILL, Col Douglas Howard, CMG 1918; DSO 1917; late RA; Establishment Officer, University of London, University College; *b* 21 Feb. 1877; *s* of late Rev. T. Howard Gill, MA, formerly Chaplain to British Embassy, Paris; *m* 1st, 1912, Sallie (whom he divorced 1930), *widow* of Woodbury Kane, USA; no *c*; 2nd Gwendolyn, *yr d* of late Lupton Adamthwaite, Cirencester. *Educ:* Tonbridge School; RMA, Woolwich. 2nd Lieut Royal Artillery, 1897; served South African War in RHA and RFA batteries (2 medals 7 clasps, including Siege of Ladysmith, severely wounded); subsequently served as Captain in India and at home; went out to France as Major commanding a Field Artillery Battery in 4th Division of original Expeditionary Force, Aug. 1914; subsequently commanded Field Artillery Brigade in France, and then Anti-Aircraft of 1st Army (despatches, DSO, CMG, Bt Lt-Col, Chevalier Légion d'Honneur); Commandant of 26th (London) Air Defence Brigade, Territorial Army, 1922–26; retired pay, 1926. *Recreations:* fishing, shooting, golf. *Club:* Army and Navy.

Died 18 Sept. 1949.

GILL, Sir Frank, KCMG 1941; OBE 1919; Director and Vice-President, International Standard Electric Corporation; Chairman, Standard Telephones and Cables, Ltd, Creed & Co. Ltd, International Marine Radio Co. Ltd, Standard Telecommunication Laboratories, Ltd; *b* 4 Oct. 1866; *y s* of Henry Corlett Gill, Advocate, Castletown, Isle of Man, and G. H. Claxton, Liverpool; *m* 1895, C. Maude, 3rd *d* of C. W. Beckwith, Advocate, Douglas, Isle of Man; one *s* one *d*. *Educ:* private schools; Engineering, evenings at Finsbury; Royal College of Science, Dublin; Liverpool University; University College, London. With National Telephone Co., Ltd (District Manager, SW Lancashire, Dublin and S Ireland, Provincial Superintendent for Ireland, Engineer-in-Chief), 1902–13; Consulting Engineer (Gill and Cook); Assistant then Controller, Central Stores Dept, Ministry of Munitions, 1917–19; European Chief Engineer, International Western Electric Co., International Standard Electric Corporation; Vice-Pres. in charge of operations National Telephone Co. of Spain; Vice-President in charge of Shanghai Telephone Co.; MICE; Past Pres. and Hon. MIEE; Hon. Member Consultative Cttee Internat. Telephony; Knight Commander Spanish Royal Order of Isabella la Católica, 1926. Chinese Order of Brilliant Star, special Rosette, 1949. *Publications:* (with W. W. Cook) Principles involved in computing the Depreciation of Plant, 1917; Presidential address to the IEE, 1922; Address to IEE Students on Engineering Economics, 1923; Joint Meeting of IEE, ICE, IME, Engineering Economics, 1943; Inst. Struct. Engrs, Engineering Economics, 1947. *Address:* 63 Aldwych, WC2. *TA:* Instanelco London. *T:* Holborn 8765. *Club:* Athenæum.

Died 25 Oct. 1950.

GILL, MacDonald, FRIBA, FRGS; architect, mural painter and cartographer; *b* Brighton, 1884; *s* of Rev. A. T. and Cicely Rose Gill; *m* 1915, Muriel Bennett; one *s* two *d*; 1946, Priscilla, *d* of Edward Johnston. *Educ:* Royal Naval Academy, Bognor; Central School of Arts and Crafts, London. Articled to L. Pilkington, 1901–03; Assistant to Sir Charles Nicholson and H. C. Corlette, 1903–08; Lecturer in Architecture and Calligraphy; Designer to Imperial War Graves Commission; Cartographer to Empire Marketing Board, Underground Railway Company, the GPO and Ministry of Information; Member of Art Workers' Guild, Guild of Memorial Craftsmen, RS Arts, Society for the Protection of Ancient Buildings. Principal works in architecture: in St Paul's and Chichester Cathedrals; in

Sussex churches; Parkstone and Bude; St Paul's School, London; Bladen Estate, Dorset; Oxford Colleges; Netherfield and West Wittering, Sussex. In mural painting: in Lincoln Cathedral; Rocker Church; Lindisfarne and Howth Castles; Scott Polar Inst. and Guildhall, Cambridge; Houses of Parliament; University of London; RMS Queen Mary and RMS Queen Elizabeth. *Publications:* decorative maps, etc. *Address:* 1 Hare Court, Temple, EC4. *T:* Central 3947. *Club:* Savage.

Died 14 Jan. 1947.

GILL, Air Cdre Napier John, CB 1936; CBE 1919; MC; General Manager, Marine Mountings Ltd, Swindon; *b* 5 April 1890; *s* of late Robert T. Gill. *Educ:* Rugby School; RMA, Woolwich. 2nd Lieut RA 1910; learnt to fly on Dopudassin Monoplane at Brooklands, 1911–12; Royal Aero Club Certificate No. 174, 1912; seconded to RFC 1913; transferred to RAF on its formation with rank of Wing-Commander; Commanding Officer Martlesham Heath experimental establishment, 1922–24; Deputy Director of Technical Development, Air Ministry, 1927–31; Air Commodore, 1932; SASO, Coastal Command, 1932–36; AOA, Fighter Command, 1936–37; retired, 1937. With Boulton Paul Aircraft Ltd, 1937–42. *Address:* Marine Mountings Ltd, North Wroughton, Swindon.

Died 20 Oct. 1948.

GILLAM, Brig.-Gen. Reynold Alexander, CMG 1918; DSO 1918; late RE; *b* 1872; 2nd *s* of late F. A. Gillam; *m* 1906, Gwladys, *d* of late T. Lindsay Watson of Briery Yards, Roxburghshire, and Leaburn, Hawick; two *s* one *d*. *Educ:* privately; RMA, Woolwich. Served operations in Chin Hills, Burma, 1893–96; NW Frontier of India, Tirah, 1897–98 (medal and two clasps); S African War, 1900–02 (Queen's medal and two clasps; King's medal and two clasps); Anglo-Belgian (Rhodesia-Congo) Boundary Commission, as Chief British Commissioner, 1911–12; European War, 1914–18; temp. Brig.-Gen. 1917–18 (wounded, despatches three times, CMG, DSO, Bt Col, French Croix de Guerre, 1914–15 Star, General Service and Victory medals); retired pay, 1927. *Address:* Weekhayes, Milverton, Somerset.

Died 26 Jan. 1942.

GILLAN, Sir Robert Woodburn, KCSI 1916; CSI 1911; late Controller, Appointments Department, Ministry of Labour; *b* 2 Aug. 1867; *e s* of late Rev. George Gillan, Carmunnock; *m* 1889, Mary (*d* 1936), *o d* of late Wm van Baerle; one *s* one *d*. *Educ:* Ayr; Christ's College, Cambridge. Joined Indian Civil Service, 1888; attached to United Provinces, filling executive and chiefly revenue posts; Settlement Officer, Meerut, 1895; Secretary to the Board of Revenue, 1902; Financial Secretary to Government, 1907; Comptroller and Auditor-General, 1910; Finance Secretary to the Govt of India, 1912; Member of the Royal Commission on Indian Finance and Currency, 1913; Member Railway Board, 1914; President, 1915–18; retired, 1920. *Recreations:* tennis, photography. *Address:* Camlarg, Warwick's Bench, Guildford.

Died 2 July 1943.

GILLANDERS, Hon. John Gordon; Justice of Court of Appeal for Ontario (and *ex officio* Judge of the High Court); *b* 26 Aug. 1895; *s* of Angus Gillanders and Helen Learmonth; *m* 1927, Kathleen M. White, London, Ont; one *s* one *d*. *Educ:* Osgoode Hall, Toronto. Served European war with RFC and RAF, Captain (DFC, despatches); practised law, London, Ontario; Chairman Commission for the Investigation of Cancer Remedies; Chairman Mobilization Board Division B since 1940. *Recreations:* fishing, golf. *Address:* Osgoode Hall, Toronto, Ontario. *Clubs:* London Hunt and Country, London, London, Ontario.

Died 15 May 1946.

GILLESPIE, Brig.-Gen. Ernest Carden Freeth, CB 1915; CMG 1917; late RASC; *b* 20 May 1871; *m* 1928, Una, *widow* of Major W. P. R. Wheatley, DSO. *Educ:* Sandhurst. Entered army (Leinster Regt), 1890; Capt. ASC 1897; Maj. 1903; Lt-Col 1912; Col 1916; Brig.-Gen., 1917–20; Officier de la Légion d'Honneur, 1920; ADST Cavalry Corps, France, 1915–16; DDST 5th and 4th Armies, France, 1916–19; DST Egypt. Ex Force, 1919–20; ADST Scottish Command, 1920–21; retired 1921; served European War, 1914–18 (CB, CMG, despatches). *Clubs:* Somerset County, Taunton.

Died 19 Jan. 1942.

GILLESPIE, Ven. Henry Richard Butler, LLB, MA, BD, Vicar of Morrinsville since 1930; Archdeacon of Waikato; *b* 23 Dec. 1880; *s* of late Very Rev. H. J. Gillespie, DD, Dean of Killaloe, and Mary Eleanor, *d* of late Frank Sheppard; *m* 1912; Edith Mary, *d* of late Adam Burr; two *s* one *d*. *Educ:* Portora Royal School; Trinity College, Dublin. Curate assistant Cahir Union 1905–07; Fiddown Union 1908–12; Incumbent Aghancon, 1912–23; Vicar Helensville, NZ, 1923–25; Okato 1925–29; Examining Chaplain to Bishop of Waikato since 1928; Examiner to Board of Theological Studies NZ since 1928; Member of the Board, 1937; Member of General Synod and of Standing Committee of General Synod since 1932; Tribunal of General Synod, 1934; Vicar General, 1941. *Recreation:* gardening. *Address:* The Vicarage, Morrinsville, New Zealand. *T:* 60.

Died 24 Aug. 1943.

GILLESPIE, Robert Dick, MB, MD (Hons Gold medal), FRCP, DPM; Physician for Psychological Medicine, Guy's Hospital, and Lecturer in Psychological Medicine, Guy's Hospital Medical School; Air Commodore, late RAFVR; Corr. Member of American Psychiatric Association; Member of the Association of Physicians; Examiner in Psychological Medicine to the Royal College, and University of London; McNeill Lecturer to the University of Aberdeen, 1935; Consulting Physician to the Cassel Hospital; Salmon Lecturer, New York, 1941; *b* 15 Dec. 1897; *s* of Campbell Gillespie, Glasgow; *m* 1930, Audrey Margaret Mary, *er d* of late C. R. Howard, OBE, MD; one *d*. *Educ:* Hutcheson's Grammar School and University, Glasgow. House Surgeon and House Physician, Western Infirmary, Glasgow, 1920–21; McCunn Research Scholar in Physiology, 1922–24; Assistant Resident Psychiatrist, Johns Hopkins Hospital, 1923–25; Henderson Research Scholar in Mental Diseases, 1925; Pinsent-Darwin Research Student in Mental Pathology, University of Cambridge, 1926–29. *Publications:* Books and Papers on functional, nervous, and mental diseases and physiological subjects; etc. *Address:* Nuffield House, Guy's Hospital, SE1. *T:* Hop 1864; Brown's Copse, Heyshott, Sussex. *T:* Midhurst 218. *Club:* Athenæum.

Died 30 Oct. 1945.

GILLESPIE, Sir Robert Winton, Kt 1941. Chairman, Gillespie Bros, Pty, Ltd; President Bank of New South Wales; Chairman Knox Grammar School; one of the founders of the Fairbridge Farm Schools in Commonwealth of Australia. *Address:* Redhall, Stuart Street, Wahroonga, NSW, Australia.

Died 2 Aug. 1945.

GILLIBRAND, Brig. Albert, DSO 1917; TD; Active List, Territorial Army; Deputy Director Supplies and Transport HQ, BTE, Cairo; *b* 5 Feb. 1884; *s* of John Gillibrand and Jane Bailey; *m*; one *s* three *d*. *Educ:* Monton. Served European war, 1914–20, Gallipoli (wounded), Egypt (attack on Suez Canal and Senussi operations), Sinai, Palestine, Syria; Officer i/c Transport, Cairo; Officer i/c Rail Transport, The Force in Egypt; acting DAQMG, 42nd Division; Senior Supply Officer, 42nd Division; Officer i/c Supply and Transport, Western Frontier Force EEF; OC Advanced Horse Transport Depot, Egyptian Expeditionary Force; Deputy Assistant-Director of Supplies and Transport, GHQ,

EEF; Assistant-Director of Supplies and Transport, 21st Corps; ADS and T., North Force (Palestine, Syria, and Cilicia); ADS and T, Palestine. During the General Strike appointed Officer i/c Supplies and Transport, War Office (Civil Constabulary Reserve); commanded the 42nd Divisional Train, RASC, 1922–30 (DSO, despatches thrice, Brevet Lt-Col, Brevet Colonel). *Recreations:* riding, golf. *Address:* Courtlands, Hayes Road, Bromley, Kent. *T:* Ravensbourne 5084. *Clubs:* Junior Army and Navy, Eccentric; Constitutional, Manchester.

Died 27 Sept. 1942.

GILLIE, Rev. Robert Calder, MA; DCL; Minister Emeritus of Presbyterian Church of England; Ex-President National Council of the Evangelical Free Churches; ex-Moderator of the Presbyterian Church of England; *b* 1865; *s* of John Gillie, Examiner in Navigation and Seamanship for Tyne and Wear ports, and May Calder; *m* Emily Genn Dalrymple, *d* of John Japp, Liverpool; three *s* one *d*. *Educ:* Durham College of Science, and University; Presbyterian Theological College (now Westminster College, Cambridge); Tübingen; Berlin. Assistant minister to the late Rev. John Watson, DD (Ian Maclaren), Sefton Park Church, Liverpool, 1891–93; Minister of Willesden Presbyterian Church, London, NW, 1893–99; Minister of St Andrew's Presbyterian Church, Eastbourne, 1899–1910; Minister of Marylebone Presbyterian Church, London, 1910–28; Minister of Trinity Presbyterian Church, Bath, 1928–38. *Publications:* The Story of Stories, a Life of Christ for Children, 1902; The Kinsfolk and Friends of Jesus, 1904; God's Lantern-bearers, the Story of the Hebrew Prophets, 1908, 1924; Little Sermons to the Children, 1909; Talks on Temperance, 1910; Evangeliealism: Has it a Future?, 1912; What I said to the Children, 1912; The Minister in the Modern World, 1923; For Listening Children, 1923; The Bible for Youth (with Rev. James Reid), 1924; The Gospel for the Modern Mind, 1928; The Later Story of the Hebrews, 1930. *Address:* 1 Barton Close, Cambridge. *T:* Cambridge 55346. *Club:* English-Speaking Union.

Died 29 Nov. 1941.

GILLILAN, Major Edward Gibson, DSO 1918; DL, JP; High Sheriff of Leicestershire, 1932; *b* 25 Feb. 1880; *s* of late William Gillilan; *m* Mary Morris (*d* 1946); one *s* two *d*. *Educ:* Eton. Joined Coldstream Guards, 1899; served South African War; European War (despatches twice, DSO). *Recreations:* hunting, shooting. *Address:* The Upper House, Great Bowden, Market Harborough. *T:* Market Harborough 9. *Clubs:* Guards', Boodle's.

Died 9 Jan. 1947.

GILLMAN, Clement, CBE 1937; *b* 26 Nov. 1882; *e s* of Frederic Gillman, London; *m* 1908, Eva Kerber; two *s*. *Educ:* Freiburg; Technical High School, Zürich. Joined Contractors for Survey and Construction of Central Rly in E Africa, 1905; civilian prisoner of war, 1914–16; served European War, EA Expeditionary Force, 1916–19 (despatches); Captain Rly Corps; in the Rly Dept of Tanganyika Territory, 1919–37; Water Consultant to the Tanganyika Territory Government, 1938–41. *Publications:* many papers on technical, geographical and geological subjects. *Recreations:* mountaineering, walking. *Address:* PO Box 389, Dar-es-salaam.

Died 5 Oct. 1946.

GILMOUR, David, CBE 1918; MInstCE; Past President S African InstE; retired; War Supplies Department, Union of South Africa, since 1939; *m* 1895, Agnes Roy (*d* 1943); one *s* one *d*. *Educ:* Schools and professional training, Glasgow. Consulting Engineer various Mining Groups, Johannesburg, New York, South America, New Zealand, etc.; Director Explos. Supply Factories, Ministry of Munitions, 1914–19; President Standard Chemical Co., Toronto, 1919–24; Construction

Director Santander Mediterranean Govt Railway, Spain, 1924–26; private consulting practice since 1926. *Clubs:* Civil Service, Cape Town; Rand, Johannesburg.

Died 30 Jan. 1946.

GILMOUR, James Pinkerton; Pharmacist; retired; *b* 31 Aug. 1860; *s* of Alexander Gray Gilmour and Jessie Hutchison; *m* 1888, Annie S. F. Forrester; one *d*. *Educ:* Brisbane Andersonian College, Glasgow School of Pharmacy. Qualified as chemist and druggist, 1899; in practice as hospital dispenser, and pharmacist in business; Chairman Executive North British Branch Pharmaceutical Society, 1908–15; member and office-bearer in all representative pharmaceutical professional and trade organisations; member of several Departmental Committees under the Insurance Acts; Hon. Member, Philadelphia College of Pharmacy and Science; Chairman, Board of Directors Rationalist Press Assoc. since 1926; Hon. Treasurer, Divorce Law Reform Union. *Publications:* Chapters on Dyestuffs and Photographic Chemicals, in Raw Materials of Commerce, and of numerous papers on a wide range of subjects in pharmaceutical and Rationalist journals; Editor, Chemist and Druggist's Year Book for Scotland, 1911–1915; Biographical sketch of the author in The History of Freethought, by the Rt Hon. J. M. Robertson; The Discovery of the Anæsthetic Properties of Chloroform; Editor, Pharmaceutical Journal, 1916–1933; General Editor Champion of Liberty (Bradlaugh Centenary Volume, 1933). *Recreations:* walking, boating, foreign travel. *Address:* 96 Hillway, Highgate, N6. *T:* Mountview 2346.

Died 10 March 1941.

GILMOUR, Major John, CMG, 1934; MC; Hon. MA Univ. of Michigan; *b* 25 Sept. 1884; *e s* of late John Gilmour, Edinburgh; *m* 1919, Marjorie J., *o d* of Leonard Turner, Ipswich; two *s*. *Educ:* George Watson's College and University, Edinburgh. MB, ChB, 1906; FRCS (Edin.), 1909. Entered Royal Army Medical Corps, 1910; seconded to the Public Health Dept, Egyptian Civil Service, 1911; Capt., 1913; served European War 1914–18, Dardanelles, East Africa, France, Palestine; Member War Mission to United States, 1917 (1914–15 Star, Allied and Victory Medals, MC); retired from army, 1919; League of Nations Mission to Persia, 1924; President, Quarantine Board, Egypt, 1929–39; Grand Officer Order of Ismail; Grand Officer Order of the Nile; Commander, Order of George I., Greece; Chevalier, Legion of Honour. *Publications:* Report on Investigations into Sanitary Conditions in Persia, League of Nations, 1924; Rapport annuel sur le Pilgrimage au Hedjaz, International Health Office, Paris. *Recreations:* golf, fishing. *Address:* Home Office, 24 Heriot Row, Edinburgh 3; Waveney Cottage, Gt Bealings, nr Woodbridge, Suffolk. *Clubs:* Savile, Pilgrims; Union, Alexandria; Turf, Cairo.

Died 22 Nov. 1943.

GILMOUR, William Henry, Emeritus Professor since 1935; LLD Penn; MDS Liverpool; LDS Eng.; Vice-President Fédération Dentaire Internationale, 1936; *b* Liverpool, 31 Dec. 1869; *m* 1897, Amy Carr, Liverpool; one *s* one *d*. *Educ:* Liverpool Institute; Liverpool Dental Hospital (Fletcher Scholarship, operating), 1894; Royal Dental Hospital, London; University College (Victoria University), Liverpool. House Surgeon, Liverpool Dental Hospital, 1892–93; private practice in Bordeaux, France, 1893–94; Hon. Dental Surgeon, 1897; Warden, 1898, which became merged in title of Director of Dental Education, 1912; Lecturer in Dental Surgery, 1906–07; Professor of Dental Surgery and Director of Dental Education, University of Liverpool, 1920–35; Secretary, Board of Dental Studies, 1905–35; Hon. Director, Liverpool Dental Hospital; Master in Dental Surgery *ex officio* Hon. Degree, 1908; Doctor of Laws, University, Pennsylvania, Honoris Causa, 1926; took a leading part in the establishment of dental degrees and diplomas, Liverpool University, and to building of new

Dental Hospital, 1910, and University Dental School, 1922; President British Dental Association, 1927; Hon. Consulting Dental Surgeon, Western General Hospital, 1914–19; Member Dental Board of the United Kingdom, 1921–24 and since 1939; additional member General Medical Council, 1921–24 and since 1939; External Examiner (Dental), University of Birmingham, 1922–25, University of Leeds, and for Dental Degrees, University of New Zealand, 1922–25; Member Dental Benefit Council, Ministry of Health, 1929; Fellow of the International College of Dentists, 1929. *Publications:* numerous publications in British and foreign dental scientific journals. *Recreations:* gardening, shooting, motoring. *Address:* 47 Rodney Street, Liverpool. *T:* Royal 2456.

Died 6 April 1942.

GILPIN, Brig.-Gen. Frederic Charles Almon, CB 1911; CBE 1919; retired pay; *b* 31 Oct. 1860; *s* of late Col Bradney T. Gilpin, the Wiltshire Regt; *m* 1889, Georgiana (*d* 1945), *d* of late Rev. Canon Stephenson; one *d*. *Educ:* Wellington College; RMC, Sandhurst. Entered Army, 1881; Capt. 1888; Major, 1897; Lt-Col 1904; Col 1908; DAAG Belfast District, 1894–97; S Africa, 1900; Gibraltar, 1901–03; AQMG Western Command, 1908–09; served S Africa, 1899–1900 (despatches, Queen's medal 5 clasps, brevet Lt-Col); European War, 1914–18 (despatches). *Address:* Leaves, Horsham Rd, Cranleigh, Surrey.

Died 17 Dec. 1950.

GILPIN, Sir Harry (Edmund Henry), Kt 1949; Commander, Order of the Crown of Italy, 1920; Director, Baker Perkins Ltd, since 1912; *b* 4 Feb. 1876; *s* of Edmund and Margaret Ann Gilpin; *m* 1901, Olive Elizabeth Capper; two *s*. *Educ:* Friends' School, Ackworth. Contested Finsbury (L.), 1922; Chairman Liberal Party National Executive, 1943–46. Chairman Industrial Co-partnership Assoc., 1946–; Member Board of Trade Advisory Council on Export Credits, 1931–. *Recreations:* reading, snooker. *Address:* Kentmere House, Castor, Peterborough. *T:* Castor 269. *Clubs:* Reform, National Liberal, Omar Khayyam.

Died 24 July 1950.

GILSON, Major Charles J. L.; author; *b* Dedham, Essex, 1878; *e s* of Charles Rawlinson Gilson, of Halstead, Essex; *m* Barbara Marion, *e d* of Guy Hamilton Ashwin, of Coverleigh. Wath-upon-Dearne; one *s*. *Educ:* Dulwich College. Entered the Sherwood Foresters, 1899; served in Malta, Hong-Kong, Tientsin, and Singapore; took part in the S African War, 1899–1901; five times wounded (despatches twice, medal and five clasps); placed on retired pay for wounds. R. Naval Division, 1914. Antwerp; Commandant First Class Detention Barracks (despatches); travelled Japan, the American continent, Australia, the South Sea Islands, East Indies, and East Africa. *Publications:* Wild Metal, Barry Royle, The Cat and the Curate, Chances and Mischances, and over fifty books for boys; contributor to Adventure and other American magazines, to Blackwood's, Chambers's, etc.

Died 18 May 1943.

GILSON, Paul; *b* Brussels, 15 June 1865. *Educ:* Brussels Athenæum. First Prix de Rome, 1889; Teacher Brussels Royal Conservatorium, 1900–10; Antwerp Royal Conservatorium, 1904–10. Musical critic, Le Soir, 1910–14; Midi, 1923; General Inspector of the Belgian Musical Schools, 1912–30; Director of the Revue Musicale Belge, 1925–32. *Publications:* three operas; three ballets; about fifty orchestral works; about forty vocal works; manuals of harmony, orchestra, etc. *Address:* 33 Voltaire Avenue, Brussels III.

Died 3 April 1942.

GIMLETTE, Surg. Rear-Adm. Sir Thomas Desmond, KCB 1911; CB 1907; RN; *b* 27 Nov. 1857; *s* of late Fleet-Surgeon Hart Gimlette; *m* 1st, 1888, Mary Ann (*d* 1923), *d* of George and Elizabeth Nichols; two *s*; 2nd, 1934, Mabel, *widow* of Rev. R. Gardner-Smith, Scarborough, and *er d* of late Joseph and Mary Nicholson, Castleford. *Educ:* St Thomas's Hospital. Instructor to Surgeons on entry into Haslar Hospital, 1896–1901; in charge of Royal Naval Hospital, Hong-Kong, 1904–07; Inspector-General in charge of Royal Naval Hospital, Haslar, 1908–11. Served Egypt, 1882 (medal, bronze star); Soudan, 1884 (despatches, promoted, two clasps); accompanied Admiral Sir W. Hewett as Medical Officer on Mission to King John of Abyssinia, 1884; Deputy Inspector-General Hospitals and Fleets, 1901; in charge of Admiralty Recruiting Headquarters, 1914–17; awarded Sir Gilbert Blane's Gold Medal, 1887. *Address:* 15 St Martin's Avenue, Epsom.

Died 4 Oct. 1943.

GINNETT, Louis, ROI; painter of mural decoration and portraits; designer in stained glass; *s* of John Frederick Ginnett, Brighton; *m* 1901, Lillian Emma Carden; one *s* one *d*. *Educ:* Brighton Grammar School. Studied, London and Paris. Works at Victoria and Albert Museum, Brighton Corporation Gallery, Harrogate Corporation Gallery, National Gallery (modern) of Japan. *Address:* Rookeryfield, Ditchling, Sussex. *T:* Hassocks 115.

Died 12 Aug. 1946.

GIORDANO, Sua Eccellenza Umberto; composer; accademico d'Italia; *b* Foggia, 27 Aug. 1867. *Educ:* Naples Conservatoire. *Works:* Marina, Mala Vita, Regina Diaz, André Chenier, Fedora, Siberia, Marcella, Mese Mariano, Madame Sans-Gêne, Cena delle Beffe, Il Re, etc. *Address:* Reale Accademia d'Italia, Rome.

Died 12 Nov. 1948.

GIRAUD, Gen. Henri Honoré; Médaille Militaire, 1949; *b* Paris, 1879. *Educ:* St Cyr. Served European War, 1914–18, Captain of Zouaves (prisoner; escaped); Major; Chief of Staff Moroccan Division (Croix de Guerre with 4 bars). Served Riff Campaign, Morocco; commanded Sixth Region; Military Governor of Metz. War of 1939–45, Commander Seventh and Ninth Armies successively (prisoner; escaped); reached unoccupied France, 1942; escaped from France in a British submarine; commanded French Forces in N Africa, later High Commissioner as well; met General de Gaulle at Inter-Allied Conference, N Africa, Jan. 1943, later reaching agreement; until Nov. they were joint chairmen of the French committee for National Liberation; Giraud then retired from the Presidency but remained C-in-C until spring 1944, when post abolished. Declined to be Inspector-General of the French Armies. Right-Wing Deputy, Second Provisional Assembly, France, 1946.

Died 11 March 1949.

GIRDLESTONE, Gathorne Robert, MA, DM Oxon; FRCS Eng.; Cons. Orthopædic Surgeon; Hon. Surgeon, Wingfield-Morris Orthopædic Hospital, Headington; Hon. Consulting Orthopædic Surgeon to the Army; Hon. Consulting Orthopædic Surgeon-Radcliffe Infirmary, Oxford, etc.; FRSM; sometime Nuffield Professor of Orthopædic Surgery, University of Oxford, and Fellow of New College; Past President British Orthopædic Association; Corresponding Member of the American Orthopædic Association and American Academy of Orthopædic Surgeons; *s* of Rev. R. B. Girdlestone, Hon. Canon, Christ Church, Oxford; *m* Ina M., *d* of George Chatterton, JP, Wimbledon. *Educ:* Charterhouse; New College, Oxford; St Thomas's Hospital (University Scholar). Captain RAMCT 1915–19. *Publications:* Tuberculosis of Bone and Joint; Oxford Medical Publications; The Place of Operations for Spinal Fixation, British Journal of Surgery; The Cure of Crippled Children (with Sir Robert Jones) British Medical Journal; The Union and Consolidation of a Fracture, American Journal of Surgery; Arthrodesis and other Operations for Tuberculosis of the Hip, Robert Jones Birthday Volume; The Operative Treatment of Potts Paraplegia, British Journal of Surgery; Dislocations, Fractures, Fracture-dislocations, British Encyclopædia of Medical Practice. *Address:* Fir Corner, Frilford Heath, nr Abingdon, Berks. *T:* Frilford Heath 301.

Died 30 Dec. 1950.

GIRLING, John Henry, CVO 1930; *e s* of late Rev. George Girling, Vicar of Westhall, Suffolk; *m*; one *s* one *d. Educ:* King's College, London. *Address:* c/o Coutts & Co., 440 Strand, WC2.

Died 4 Dec. 1948.

GIROUARD, Hon. Dr Jean; late Member of Legislative Council, Province of Quebec, Canada; *b* St Benoit, 7 March 1856; *s* of Jean Joseph Girouard, notary, and Marie Emelie Berthelot; *m* 1883, Lydia, *d* of Hon. J. G. Laviolette; two *s* two *d. Educ:* Sulpician College, Montreal. Practising medicine, 2 years at St Philippe d'Argenteuil, Province of Quebec; 2 years at St Marthe C. of Vaudreuil, and since at Longueuil; School Commissioner for years; Member of Municipal Councils for 4 years; President of Longueuil Tramway Company; Vice-President of Montarville Land Company, Limited; Maitre de Chapelle de l'Eglise St Antoine de Longueuil; and promoter of plain chant reform according to motu proprio of Pope Pius X. *Address:* 68 St Charles Street, Longueuil, Quebec. *T:* 4. *Clubs:* Bourbonnais Fish and Game, Le Moyne.

Died 12 Nov. 1940.

GLADSTONE OF HAWARDEN, Lady; Maud Ernestine Gladstone, CBE; Dame of Grace of St John of Jerusalem, Queen Elizabeth Medal (Belgium); 2nd *d* of Stuart, Baron Rendel; *m* 1890, Henry Neville, Baron Gladstone of Hawarden (*d* 1935). President of the Flintshire County Nursing Association; President of the Flintshire Orthopædic Voluntary Organisation; Lady President Priory Order in Wales (County of Flint) of the Order of St John of Jerusalem; Founder and organiser and Chairman of Committee of the Wirral and Eddisbury Musical Competition and Festival since 1911; now President of the Festival which is known as the Chester Musical Festival; Founded during the war The Chester Chamber Concerts; Member of Catherine Gladstone Maternity Home Joint Committee Flintshire CC; co-opted member of Public Health and Tuberculosis Committee Flintshire CC; lent Sealand, Littlestone Kent, as a Hospital for Post Officer Soldiers, 1914–19; Organised and controlled Parkgate Auxiliary Military Hospital, 1914–19; controlled and managed Hoole Bank, and Hoole House Hospitals, Chester, 1916–19. *Address:* 78 Eaton Sq., SW1; Plas Warren, Broughton by Chester; Villa Thorenciel, Cannes, AM, France.

Died 23 July 1941.

GLADSTONE, Sir Hugh Steuart, Kt 1941; JP, LL; FZS, FRSE, FSA Scot.; Lord Lieutenant of Dumfriesshire since 1946; *b* 30 April 1877; *o s* of late S. S. Gladstone, Capenoch; *m* 1907, Cecil Emily, *e d* of late Gustavus Talbot, MP; three *s* one *d. Educ:* Eton; Trinity Hall, Cambridge (MA). Late Lieut, 3rd KOS Borderers; served S Africa, 1900–02 (two medals, five clasps); County Councillor (Dumfriesshire), 1904–46; Chairman of Finance Committee, 1911–30; Vice-Convener of County, 1920–30; Convener, 1930–46; Vice-Pres. Association of County Councils in Scotland, 1932, Pres. 1933–35; Capt. 2/5th KOS Borderers, 1914–19 (attached to General Staff at War Office, 1914–19, despatches); Member of Council of Zoological Society of London, 1916–22, 1922–28, 1929–33, 1934–37, and 1938–41; VPZS, 1925–26 and 1932–33; Chairman Wild Birds Protection Advisory (Scotland) Com. since 1921;

Member of the Departmental Committee on Rating of Machinery in England and Scotland, 1923–25; Chairman International Committee for Protection of Birds (British Section), 1923–29; Member of the Departmental Committee on Revision of Poor Law (Scotland), 1935; Member of Wild Birds Protection Advisory (England) Com. since 1937. *Publications:* The Birds of Dumfriesshire, 1910; Catalogue of the Vertebrate Fauna of Dumfriesshire, 1912; Maria Riddell, the Friend of Burns, 1915; Birds and the War, 1919; Record Bags, 1922, 2nd edn, 1930; Shooting with Surtees, 1927; Thomas Watling, Limner of Dumfries, 1938; etc.; articles on birds in The Scottish Naturalist, British Birds (Magazine), etc. *Recreations:* shooting and fishing. *Address:* Capenoch, Penpoint, Dumfriesshire. *T:* Thornhill 261. *TA:* Gladstone, Penpont. *Clubs:* Bath; New (Edinburgh).

Died 5 April 1949.

GLADSTONE, Sir John Evelyn, 4th Bt *cr* 1846; MA, JP, DL; *b* 23 Nov. 1855; *s* of Capt. J. N. Gladstone, RN, MP, 3rd *s* of 1st Bt; *S* cousin, 1926; *m* 1888, Gertrude Theresa (*d* 1937), *d* of Sir Charles Hayes Miller, 7th Bt; three *d. Educ:* Eton; Christ Church, Oxford. High Sheriff of Wilts., 1897; contested (C.) Spen Valley Division of WR of Yorkshire, 1885; was Assistant Private Secretary to Postmaster-General. *Heir: cousin* Albert Charles Gladstone. *Address:* Bowden Park, Chippenham. *Club:* Junior Carlton.

Died 12 Feb. 1945.

GLADSTONE, Reginald John, MD, FRCS, FRSE; retired; late Reader in Anatomy and Lecturer in Embryology, University of London, King's College; *b* 9 June 1865; *s* of Thomas H. Gladstone, DPh, and Matilda, *d* of Joshua Field, FRS; *m* 1912, Ida Millicent Field; one *s* one *d. Educ:* Clapham Grammar School; Gymnasium, Aberdeen; Marischal College, University of Aberdeen; Middlesex Hospital Medical School. Formerly Lecturer on Embryology at Middlesex Hospital Medical School. *Publications:* The Pineal Organ (with CPG Wakeley), 1939; contributions to the Journal of Anatomy and Physiology; Annals of Surgery; Encyclopædia Britannica; Lancet; British Medical Journal; Journal of the Anthropological Institute, and British Journal of Surgery. *Address:* Greenhayes, Sway Road, Brockenhurst, Hants. *T:* Brockenhurst 2206.

Died 12 Feb. 1947.

GLANELY, 1st Baron *cr* 1918; **William James Tatem;** Bt *cr* 1916, LLD, University College of South Wales and Monmouthshire; DL, Co. Glamorgan; JP, Cos. Glamorgan and Wilts.; High Sheriff Glamorgan, 1911–12; *b* 1868; *s* of late Thomas Tatem, of Appledore; *m* 1897, Ada Mary, CBE 1920 (*d* 1930), *d* of late Thomas Williams, Cardiff. Governor of the Cardiff Royal Infirmary; presented with the Freedom of the City of Cardiff, 1928; Chairman of W. J. Tatem, Ltd, The Tatem Steam Navigation Co., Ltd, The Atlantic Shipping and Trading Co., Ltd, The Dulverton Steam Ship Co., Ltd, Mount Stuart Dry Docks, Ltd; a Director of The Great Western Railway Co.; Lobitos Oilfields, Ltd, Anglo-Ecuadorian Oilfields, Ltd; British Corporation Register of Shipping and Aircraft, West of England Protection and Indemnity Association, Shipping Federation, Ltd, Cardiff Exchange, Ltd, Coal and Shipping Exchange (Cardiff), Ltd, British Steamship Owners' Association, and Chepstow Race Course Co.; Ex-Chairman of the Cardiff Shipowners' Association; President University College, S Wales and Monmouth, and Bristol Channel District Association of Chartered Shipbrokers; President Royal Hamadryad Seamen's Hospital and Royal Porthcawl Golf Club. *Heir:* none. *Address:* 12 Hill Street, Mayfair, W1; Exning House, Exning, nr Newmarket. *Clubs:* Bath, White's, Carlton; Jockey, Newmarket.

Died 28 June 1942 (ext).

GLANUSK, 3rd Baron *cr* 1899; **Wilfred Russell Bailey; Bt** *cr* 1852, DSO 1916; Lord Lieutenant Brecknock; late Grenadier Guards; *b* 27 June 1891; *o s* of 2nd Baron and Editha Elma, CBE 1920 (*d* 1938), *o d* of late Warden Sergison of Cuckfield Park, Sussex; *S* father, 1928; *m* 1942, Margaret Eldrydd, *d* of late Maj.-Gen. T. H. Shoubridge, CB; one *d. Educ:* Eton; RMC, Sandhurst. Served European War, 1914–18 (DSO and bar); retired from army, 1924; rejoined, 1939; commanded Training Bn Welsh Guards; Colonel GHQ, 1942. *Heir: cousin* David Russell Bailey, Lieut RN, *b* 1917. *Address:* Glanusk Park, Crickhowell, S Wales.

Died 12 Jan. 1948.

GLASFURD, Col Alexander Inglis Robertson, CMG, 1917; DSO 1916; Indian Army, retired; *b* Betul, CP India, 4 Dec. 1870; *s* of Maj.-Gen. C. L. R. Glasfurd; *m* 1894, Mabel, *d* of Rev. E. Hignett; two *s. Educ:* Fettes College; RMC, Sandhurst. First Commission in Loyal North Lancashire Regt, 1890, transferred to Indian Army, 1892 and joined 4th Infantry, Hyderabad Contingent; Adjutant for 4 years. Passed Staff College, 1907; Brigade-Major Jhelum and Rawalpindi Infantry Brigades, 1907–11; Brigade-Major, 3rd Brigade, Mohmand FF, 1908 (medal and clasp); transferred to 46th Punjabis, 1912; Gen. Staff Officer Derajat and Bannu Frontier Brigades, 1912–13; served European War (France) as Brigade-Major 27th Infantry Brigade (9th Scottish Division) first formation, Aug. 1914–Sept. 1915 (despatches, DSO); GSO 2nd grade, 3rd Div. Sept. 1915–Aug. 1916; GSO 1st grade, 48th Div. (despatches, CMG) Aug. 1916–17; E African Campaign, 1917–18; Commanded 40th Pathans, 1917–21; served in operations in Afghanistan, 1919; Brig.-Gen. commanding 72nd Indian Brigade, 1920 (Mesopotamia); retired, 1921. *Publications:* Leaves from an Indian Jungle, 1904; Rifle and Romance in the Indian Jungle, 1905; Sketches of Manchurian Battlefields, 1908; Musings of an old Shikari, 1928. *Recreations:* big-game hunting, shooting, fishing. *Address:* The Old Court, Cranleigh, Surrey. *Club:* Shikar.

Died 29 March 1942.

GLASGOW, Brig.-Gen. Alfred Edgar, CB 1923; CMG 1918; DSO 1916; *b* 1870; *s* of late W. J. Glasgow of Old Court, Co. Cork; *m* 1913, Amy Gertrude, *d* of late Colonel W. Moore-Lane (late Postmaster General, Punjab, India) and *widow* of Major J. H. Burbury, Royal Sussex Regiment. *Educ:* Nelson and Wellington Colleges, New Zealand. Joined Royal Sussex Regt 1891; Adjutant, 1895–99; Commanded 2nd Bn 1919–23. Served Relief of Chitral, 1895; NW Frontier of India, 1897–98; Tirah, 1897; France and Belgium, Sept. 1914–Nov. 1918; Commanded 58th Brigade, Jan. 1917 till end of war (wounded twice, Brevets of Lt-Col and Col, despatches seven times, DSO, CMG, CB Croix de Guerre); retired pay, 1927. *Address:* Rannoch, Summersdale, Chichester.

Died 1 Feb. 1950.

GLASGOW, Ellen; author; *b* 22 April 1874; *d* of Francis Thomas and Anne Gholson Glasgow. *Educ:* home. Doctor of Literature, University of North Carolina, 1930; Doctor of Laws, University of Richmond, 1938; Duke University, 1938, College of William and Mary, 1939; Member of American Academy of Arts and Letters; National Institute of Arts and Letters; Society of Authors, Playwrights and Composers; Phi Beta Kappa Society; Colonial Dames of America; Modern Language Association; American Humane Association; and PEN Club; Pres. of Richmond Society for the Prevention of Cruelty to Animals; awarded, in 1940, by American Academy of Arts and Letters, Quinquennial Howells Medal 1941, The Saturday Review of Literature's Special Award; Southern Authors Award; Pulitzer Prize, 1941. *Publications:* The Descendant, 1897; Phases of an Inferior Planet, 1898; The Voice of the People, 1900; The Battleground, 1902; The Freeman and other Poems, 1902; The Deliverance, 1904; The Ancient Law, 1908;

The Romance of a Plain Man, 1909; The Miller of Old Church, 1911; Virginia, 1913; Life and Gabriella, 1916; The Builders, 1919; One Man in His Time, 1922; Dare's Gift, 1924; Barren Ground, 1925; The Romantic Comedians, 1927; They Stooped to Folly, 1929; The Sheltered Life, 1932; Vein of Iron, 1935; In This Our Life, 1941; A Certain Measure: An Interpretation of Prose Fiction, 1943. *Address:* One West Main Street, Richmond, Virginia, USA. *Clubs:* English Speaking Union; Cosmopolitan, New York.

Died 20 Nov. 1945.

GLASGOW, Brig.-Gen. William James Theodore, CMG 1917; Queen's Royal Regt; *b* 18 April 1862; *s* of late W. J. Glasgow of Old Court, Co. Cork; *m* 1903, Sibyl, *d* of late John A'Deane, 17 Radnor Place, W2. *Educ:* Sherborne; RMC Sandhurst. Entered Army, 1885; Major, 1903; retired, 1912; served Burma, 1885–87 and 1887–89 (medal, 2 clasps); NW Frontier, 1897–98 (medal, 2 clasps); European War, 1914–18 (despatches thrice, Brevet Lt-Col, CMG). *Address:* Shedfield Grange, Botley, Hants. *T:* Wickham 3157. *Club:* Army and Navy.

Died 9 Feb. 1944.

GLASPELL, Susan; *b* Davenport, Iowa, 1 July 1882; *d* of Elmer S. Glaspell and Alice Keating; *m* 1st, 1913, George Cram Cook (*d* 1923); 2nd, 1925. *Educ:* Drake Univ., Iowa; Univ. of Chicago. Newspaper reporter in Des Moines, Iowa; short story writer; identified with the Little Theatre movement through the Provincetown Players. *Publications:* The Glory of the Conquered, 1909; The Visioning, 1911; Lifted Masks, 1912; Fidelity, 1915; Trifles, 1917; (with George Cram Cook) Suppressed Desires, 1917; Plays (including Bernice and other plays), 1920; Inheritors, 1921; Verge, 1922; The Road to the Temple, 1926; The Comic Artist (with Norman Matson), 1927; Brook Evans, 1928; Fugitive's Return, 1929; Alison's House, play produced, 1930; Ambrose Holt and Family, 1931; The Morning Is Near Us, 1940; Norma Ashe, 1942; Prodigal Giver, 1946. *Address:* Provincetown, Mass, USA.

Died 27 July 1948.

GLEADOWE, Reginald Morier Yorke, CVO 1943; MA, NRD, Head of Honours and Awards Branch, Admiralty; Admiralty representative, War Artists Committee; Member of Court of Goldsmiths' Company and Freeman of City of London; *b* London, 6 May 1888; *o s* of G. E. Y. Gleadowe, CMG, of HM Treasury, Assistant Auditor and Controller-General; *m* 1921, Cecil Mary, *d* of John Rotton, Solicitor to Westminster City Council; one *s* one *d. Educ:* Winchester College (Prefect of Hall and Goddard Scholar); New College, Oxford (Scholar). First in Greats; Slade School, 1912. Entered Civil Service by open competition; Inns of Court Squadron; Private Secretary to Secretary of the Admiralty; Principal, Admiralty; Secretary, First Inter-Allied Naval Conference; King's Messenger, Eastern Mediterranean (Hon. Captain RM); Orders of Rising Sun and S Anne of Russia; Asst to Director, National Gallery, 1919–23; Master, Winchester College; Lecturer, National Gallery; Examiner and Lecturer, London University; Winchester City Councillor (Chairman Housing and Town-planning Committee, 1938); Slade Professor of Fine Art, Oxford University, 1928–33; Hermione Lecturer, Dublin, 1931; Lecturer in Fine Arts, University of Belfast, 1928; Exhibitor, World's Fair, New York, 1939 and 1940, Paris International (Diploma), 1937, New English, Royal Academy, Grosvenor Galleries, BIIA, etc.; gold and silver plate etc. for Royal Victorian Order in King's Chapel, Savoy (HM The Queen), Goldsmiths Company, City of London Corporation, Cathedrals, Churches, Colleges, etc.; Portrait Drawings at Trinity College, Cambridge, New College, Oxford, etc. Designer Stalingrad Sword. *Publications:* Oxford University and the Fine Arts (1928); Amrbose McEvoy, etc. *Recreations:* sailing and silence. *Address:* Admiralty, Whitehall, SW1; The College,

Winchester. *T:* Winchester 739; Calamansac, Porth Navas, Cornwall. *Clubs:* Athenæum, Royal Cruising, Architectural Association; OUYC (Commodore, 1933–35).

Died 9 Oct. 1944.

GLEDHILL, Gilbert; Company Director; *b* 1889; *y s* of late George H. and Mary A. Gledhill; *m* 1920, Philippa Amy, *y d* of late Ralph Seddon and Marjory S. McC. Holmes, Berwick-on-Tweed; one *s* two *d. Educ:* Perse School, Cambridge; Bradford and Bridlington Grammar Schools. Served European War, 1914–19 with 5th Cheshire Regiment, BEF (wounded), 1915–17; with Ministry of Munitions, 1917; with Aircraft Production Dept, London, 1918–19; MP (C) Halifax, 1931–45. *Address:* Heatherlea, 13 Elmfield Terrace, Halifax. *T:* Halifax 3107. *Clubs:* Constitutional; Halifax, Halifax.

Died 2 Sept. 1946.

GLEED, Sir John Wilson, Kt 1939; MA; DL Lincolnshire; JP Holland, Lincs; *b* 15 March 1865; *s* of late Richard Gleed; *m* 1890, Mary Bengough, *d* of late Rev. Joseph Clark, Rector of Kegworth, sometime Fellow of Christ's College, Cambridge; one *d. Educ:* Uppingham; Jesus College, Cambridge. Chairman of Holland County Council since 1915. *Address:* West Elloe, Spalding, Lincs. *TA:* Westelloe, Spalding. *T:* Spalding 2012.

Died 30 July 1946.

GLEICHEN, Lady Helena, OBE; FRSA; artist; Imperial Arts League; *d* of late Admiral Prince Victor of Hohenlohe-Langenburg and Lady Laura Seymour, *d* of Admiral Sir George Seymour, and sister of Francis, Marquis of Hertford. *Educ:* Calderon's, Rollshoven and Brangwyn's schools, and Arthur Lemon; exhibitor Royal Academy, etc. Served European War ten months in France, and two years Joint Commandant (with Mrs. Hollings) British X-ray Section, Italian Front; holds medal for military valour (Italy); Lady of Grace St John of Jerusalem. *Publication:* Contacts and Contrasts, 1940. *Address:* St James's Palace, SW1. *T:* Whitehall 7187; Ashmead House, Cam, Glos. *T:* Dursley 2491.

Died 28 Jan. 1947.

GLENARTHUR, 2nd Baron *cr* 1918; **James Cecil Arthur;** of Carlung, Ayrshire; Bt *cr* 1903; *b* 2 June 1883; *o s* of 1st Baron and Janet Stevenson Bennett, OBE, JP Co. Ayr, Hon. President Ayrshire Branch British Red Cross Society, *y d* of late Alexander Bennet M' Grigor, LLD, of Cairnoch, Stirlingshire; *S* father, 1928; *m* 1907, Evelyn, *e d* of late Henry March-Phillips, Fairby, Tiverton, N Devon; one *s* one *d. Educ:* Eton; Christ Church, Oxford. Late Capt. Ayrshire Yeomanry, and Lieut 4th Bn Argyll and Sutherland Highlanders. *Heir: s* Hon. Matthew Arthur, Acting Major Scots Greys [*b* 12 May 1909; *m* 1st, 1931, Audrey, *o d* of George Lees-Milne, Wickhamford Manor, Evesham; one *d*; 2nd, 1939, Margaret, *d* of late H. J. J. Howie, of Stairaird, Mauchline, Ayrshire]. *Clubs:* Western, Glasgow.

Died 11 Dec. 1942.

GLENDINNING, John Clements; late Senator, Northern Ireland; DL County Borough of Londonderry; *b* Londonderry, 1866; 2nd *surv. s* of late William Glendinning, Proprietor of the Derry Standard; *m* 1897, four *s. Educ:* Foyle College, Londonderry. Provincially associated with Unionist and Loyalist work; Vice-President, under the then Marquis of Hamilton's Presidency, and President for several years of the City of Derry Unionist Association. *Recreations:* formerly rowing; later, golf and travel. *Address:* Glendearg, Dhu Varren, Portrush, Co. Antrim, N Ireland.

Died 18 Dec. 1949.

GLENTORAN, 1st Baron *cr* 1939, of Ballyalloly; **Capt. Herbert Dixon;** Bt *cr* 1903, PC N Ire. 1923; OBE 1919; DL; High Sheriff, Co. Kildare, 1916; 6th Inniskilling Dragoons; *b* 23 Jan. 1880; 4th *s* of late Rt

Hon. Sir D. Dixon, Bart, MP, DL; *S* to baronetcy of half-*brother*, 1950; *m* 1905, Hon. Emily Ina Florence Bingham, *d* of 5th Baron Clanmorris; one *s* three *d. Educ:* Rugby; RMC, Sandhurst. Served S African War, 1901–02 (Queen's medal 5 clasps); in Remounts during European War (despatches, OBE); MP for East Belfast, Ulster Parliament, 1921–29, Bloomfield Division since 1929; MP (U) Pottinger Division of Belfast, Dec. 1918, East Belfast, 1922–39; Chief Whip Unionist Party, 1921–42; Minister of Agriculture, N Ireland, 1941–43. *Recreations:* hunting and racing, Steward of the Irish National Hunt Committee. *Heir: s* Major Hon. Daniel Stewart Thomas Bingham Dixon, Grenadier Guards [*b* 19 Jan. 1912; *m* 1933, Lady Diana Mary Wellesley, *d* of 3rd Earl Cowley; two *s* one *d*]. *Address:* Draycot Cerne, Chippenham, Wilts; Ballyalloly, Comber, Co. Down, Northern Ireland. *Clubs:* Carlton; Kildare Street (Dublin); Ulster (Belfast).

Died 20 July 1950.

GLOVER, Halcott; playwright and novelist; *s* of late J. H. L. Glover and Mary Emma Cooper, Manchester; *m* Henrietta Louise (*d* 1947), *d* of late F. R. Gilder, London. *Educ:* Manchester. Early days in the Lancashire Cotton Business; Captain, RAF, European War, 1914–18. *Publications:* Wat Tyler; The King's Jewry; Hail Caesar; The Second Round; God's Amateur; Wills and Ways; Bellairs; Drama and Mankind; On the Quota; Exodus (with H. F. Rubinstein). Novels: Morning Pride; Dead Man's House; Both Sides of the Blanket; Louise and Mr Tudor; Louise in London. *Address:* c/o Curtis Brown Ltd, 6 Henrietta St, WC2.

Died 5 May 1949.

GLOVER, Terrot Reaveley, Hon. LLD Queen's Univ. 1910, McMaster Univ., Canada, 1917, Glasgow Univ., 1930; Hon. DD St Andrews Univ., 1921; Hon. LittD Trinity College, Dublin, 1936; *b* Bristol, 23 July 1869; *s* of late Dr Richard Glover; *m* 1897, 2nd *d* of late H. G. Few, Cambridge; two *s* four *d. Educ:* Bristol Grammar School; St John's College, Cambridge (Fellow, 1892–98, 1901). Professor of Latin, Queen's Univ., Kingston, Canada, 1896–1901; Classical Lecturer, St John's College, Cambridge, 1901–39; Public Orator in the University, 1920–39, Orator Emeritus, 1939; Wilde Lecturer in Natural and Comparative Religion, Oxford, 1917–21; Lowell Lectures, Boston, 1922; Sather Professor of Classics, University of California, 1923; President of Baptist Union of Great Britain and Ireland, 1924; Donnellan Lecturer, Trinity College, Dublin 1932. *Publications:* Life and Letters in the Fourth Century, 1901; Studies in Virgil, 1904; second edition entitled Virgil, 1912; The Conflict of Religions in the Early Roman Empire, 1909; The Jesus of History, 1917; From Pericles to Philip, 1917; Jesus in the Experience of Men, 1921; The Pilgrim, 1921; Progress in Religion, 1922; Latin Translation of R. L. Stevenson's A Child's Garden of Verses, 1922; Herodotus, 1924; Paul of Tarsus, 1925; Saturday Papers, 1927; Democracy in the Ancient World, 1927; The Influence of Christ in the Ancient World, 1929; The World of the New Testament, 1931; Greek Byways, 1932; Horace, 1932; The Ancient World, a Beginning, 1935; A Corner of Empire (with D. D. Calvin), 1937; The Disciple, 1941; The Challenge of the Greek and other Essays, 1942; Cambridge Retrospect, 1943. *Address:* 67 Glisson Road, Cambridge. *T:* 4125.

Died 26 May 1943.

GLOVER, Thomas, CBE 1920; *b* 1862; *s* of Thomas Glover; *m* 1st, 1893; 2nd, 1929, Lydia Elizabeth, *y d* of Edward Bolton JP, Charlbury, Oxon. Was Technical Adviser to Controller of Coal Mines during European War. *Address:* 224 Unthank Road, Norwich.

Died 18 Feb. 1942.

GLYN, Sir Arthur Robert, 7th Bt *cr* 1759; *b* 5 Aug. 1870; *s* of 4th Bt and Henrietta Amelia (*d* 1903), *d* of Richard Carr Glyn; *S* brother, 1921. *Educ:* Pembroke College, Cambridge. Alderman of Surrey County Council; JP Surrey. *Heir:* Sir Richard Fitzgerald Glyn, Bt, DSO. *Address:* The Well House, Ewell, Surrey.
Died 4 Jan. 1942.

GLYN, Mrs Clayton, (Elinor); *y d* of late Douglas Sutherland of Toronto, Ontario; *m* 1892, Clayton Glyn, JP (*d* 1915), of Durrington House and Sheering, Harlow, Essex. *Publications:* The Visits of Elizabeth, 1900; The Reflections of Ambrosine, 1902; The Damsel and the Sage, 1903; The Vicissitudes of Evangeline, 1905; Beyond the Rocks, 1906; Three Weeks, 1907; The Sayings of Grandmamma, 1908; Elizabeth Visits America, 1909; His Hour, 1910; The Reason Why, 1911; Halcyone, 1912; The Contrast, and Other Stories, 1913; The Sequence, 1913; Letters to Caroline, 1914; Three Things, 1915; The Career of Katherine Bush, 1917; Destruction, 1919; Points of View, 1920; The Philosophy of Love, 1921; Man and Maid, 1922; The Great Moment, 1923; Six Days, 1924; Letters from Spain, 1925; This Passion called Love, 1926; Love's Blindness, 1926; It, 1927; The Flirt and the Flapper, 1930; Love's Hour, 1932; Sooner or Later, 1933; Did She?, 1934; Romantic Adventure, 1936; Has produced following films: The Great Moment, Beyond the Rocks, 1922; Three Weeks, 1923; His Hour, 1924; Man and Maid, 1925; The Only Thing, 1926; It, Ritzy, 1927; Knowing Men, 1929; The Price of Things, 1930. *Address:* 105 Carrington House, Hertford Street, W1. *T:* Grosvenor 2729. *Club:* Bath.
Died 23 Sept. 1943.

GLYNN, Lt-Col Thomas George Powell, CMG 1900; OBE 1918; late The King's Regiment; *b* 13 July 1863; *s* of late Lt-Col T. G. H. Glynn; *m* 1st, 1893, Mary, *e d* of late Wm Ford; one *d*; 2nd, 1911, Beatrice Emily, *d* of late Ernest Ford. Joined 3rd Batt. Royal Munster Fusiliers; transferred to 1st Batt. King's Regt May 1885; Adjutant of King's Regt 1887–92; Adjutant of the London Rifle Brigade, 1892–96; sent to Natal early in the South African War on special service; later, Staff Officer Volksrust Sub-District, Transvaal, during 1900–02 (despatches, Queen's medal three clasps, King's medal two clasps, CMG); retired, 1912; served European War, 1914–19 (despatches, OBE). *Address:* Newtown House, Branksome Park, Bournemouth. *T:* Bournemouth 5346.
Died 3 May 1949.

GLYNTON, Col Gerard Maxwell, DSO 1919; *s* of late Charles Maxwell Glynton, Bath; *m* 1st, Irene Mary (*d* 1924) *yr d* of B. J. Hall, Eastcote, Middlesex; 2nd, 1929, Audrey, *o d* of G. A. Linck, Nab Wood, Shipley, Yorks. *Educ:* Bath College; RMC, Sandhurst. Gazetted to Indian Army, 1899; appointed to 3rd QAO Gurkha Rifles, 1901; graduated at Staff College, 1910; served European War in Mesopotamia, Egypt, and Palestine (despatches, DSO); Commandant 1/6th Gurkha Rifles, 1922–26; General Staff Baluchistan District, 1927–31; retired 1932. *Address:* The Priory, Follifoot, Yorkshire. *T:* Harrogate 81537.
Died 26 Jan. 1942.

GOBLE, Air Vice-Marshal Stanley James, CBE 1924; DSO 1917; OBE 1918; Australian liaison Officer for Empire Air-training Scheme in Canada since 1940; *b* Croydon, Victoria, Australia, 21 Aug. 1891; *s* of George and Anne Goble; *m* 1922, Kathleen, *d* of Col F. W. Wodehouse, CIE. three *s. Educ:* Graduated RAF Staff College, 1925–26. Imperial Defence Coll., 1927. Royal Naval Air Service and Royal Air Force; transferred Royal Australian Air Force, 1921; served European War (Croix de guerre, DSC, DSO, despatches twice, promoted, OBE); ADC to Governor-General of Australia, 1922–26; Air Member for Personnel, Air Board, Australia, 1928–32; Chief of Air Staff, 1933–34; Deputy Director of Operations, Air Ministry, 1935–36; Air Officer Commanding No. 2 (Bomber) Group, 1936–38; Acting Chief of Staff of Royal Australian Air Force, 1939–40; MIAeE, 1924. *Recreations:* golf, tennis. *Clubs:* Athenæum, Melbourne.
Died 24 July 1948.

GOBLE, Warwick; *b* London; *s* of Burkitt and Mary Ann Goble. *Educ:* City of London School; Westminster School of Art. Earlier years occupied in chromo-lithography; afterwards contributed to illustrated papers, magazines, etc.; on staff of Pall Mall Gazette and Westminster Gazette; illustrated fairy tales and books on travel in colour and black and white; exhibited water-colours at Royal Academy, Walker Art Gallery, Liverpool, etc.; worked in drawing office, Woolwich Arsenal, during European War; and after, gave voluntary service in British Red Cross Society in France. *Publications:* contributed illustrations to Constantinople, The Greater Abbeys of England. Water Babies, Japanese Fairy Tales, Bengal Folk Tales, Pentamerone, The Fairy Book, The People's Chaucer, The Book of Fairy Poetry, etc. *Recreations:* travel, sculling, and cycling. *Address:* The Glade, Beech Road, Shepherd's Hill, Merstham.
Died 22 Jan. 1943.

GODDARD, Lt-Col Gerald Hamilton, DSO 1917; *b* 18 Jan. 1873; *s* of Lt-Col Thomas Goddard of Clyffe Pypard, Wilts, Indian Army, and Harriette Coleman; *m* 1st, 1903, Ida Rose Laura (*d* 1934), *d* of Edmund Howard Reynolds, Chiswick; two *s*; 2nd, 1936, Mildred Jeanie, *yr d* of late Rev. G. E. Gilbanks; one *s. Educ:* Univ. Coll. School; University College and University College Hospital, London. MRCS England, LRCP London, 1895. Surgeon, Brit. India SN Coy, 1896–97; House Surgeon, Sheffield Royal Infirmary, 1898–99; entered RAMC, 1899; served S African War, 1899–1902 (Queen's medal 3 clasps, King's medal 2 clasps; severely wounded, Paandeberg); received thanks of Commander-in-Chief for services; passed exam. for Major, RAMC, with six months' acceleration, 1906, obtaining special certificate; MO Alderney CI Troops, 1907–10; OC Helena Hospital, Shorncliffe, 1910–13; promoted Lt-Col, RAMC, 1915; European War, OC 38th Field Ambulance, BEF, and later OC 23rd Casualty Clearing Station, and OC Military Hospital and Acting DDMS Gibraltar (despatches 4 times, DSO); Knight of Grace Order of St John of Jerusalem, 1919; invalided on pension, 1923; re-employed on retired pay at Worcester, 1923–38 and Sept. 1939 and since 1940; Chairman Brit. Med. Assoc., Worcester and Bromsgrove Division, 1936–37; Chairman National Service Medical Board, Worcester; Vice-Chairman Worcestershire County Joint Committee, BRCS and Order of St John, 1940–47; Emergency Officer BMA Freemasonry, PGD England. *Address:* Beuna Vista, Barneshall Avenue, Worcester. *TA:* Barneshall, Worcester. *T:* Worcester 2866.
Died 20 April 1948.

GODFREY, Brig. Arthur Harry Langham, DSO 1941; MC 1916; ED; Brigade Commander 24 Aust. Inf. Bde AIF (ME) since 1941; *b* 26 Jan. 1896; *s* of C. E. R. Godfrey, born Newton Abbot, Devon; *m* 1918, Mabel Sophia Barrett-Lennard; three *s* one *d. Educ:* Central College, Geelong, Victoria. Wool and Stock Auctioneer, Strachan & Co., Ltd, Geelong, Victoria; European War, 1914–18, enlisted 1914; embarked from Australia, 1915; Commissioned, 1916, 58 Bn AIF and Staff Capt. 14 Aust. Inf. Bde 1917 (MC); War of 1939–45; commanded 2/6 Aust. Inf. Bn 1939–41 (DSO and bar). *Recreations:* cricket, football, tennis. *Address:* 6 William Street, Newtown, Geelong, Victoria, Australia. *Clubs:* Naval and Military, Melbourne; Corio, Geelong, Victoria.
Died 5 Nov. 1942.

GODFREY, Sir George Cochrane, Kt 1919; VD, BA, Assoc. MInstCE; MIE (Ind.); Chairman Bengal-Nagpur Rly Co. and Foster Yates & Thom Ltd; *b* 27 Sept. 1871; *s* of George B. and Hester Ann Godfrey; *m* 1900, Ethel Beatrix Kingsford; one *d. Educ:* Harrow; Trinity College, Cambridge. Civil Engineer appointed to Bengal Nagpur Railway, India, 1895; served till 1917, when lent to Govt of India as a Member of the Railway Board; Coal Controller for India, 1917–19; Indian Railway Committee, 1921; Howrah Bridge Committee, 1922; member Legislative Council, Bengal, 1923–25; General Manager Bengal-Nagpur Railway, India, 1911–25; Council of State, India, 1928–30; Partner Bird & Co., Calcutta, 1925–31. *Address:* 4 Upper Cheyne Row, Chelsea, SW3. *Clubs:* Oriental; Bengal, Calcutta.
Died 18 March 1945.

GODFREY, Vice-Adm. Harry Rowlandson, CB 1919; DSO 1916; *b* 11 Oct. 1875; fifth *s* of late Lt-Col C. J. Godfrey, Madras Staff Corps; *m* 1911, Mary Caroline Pearl, 2nd *d* of W. Barrett Lennard of Vancouver; one *s* one *d. Educ:* Stubbington House, Fareham. Entered Britannia, 1890; Lieut 1898; served in HMS Daphne in China during Boxer Rising (China medal, 1900); Royal Humane Society Testimonial, 1902, for saving a man from drowning at Invergordon whilst in HMS Anson; served in HMS Porpoise during operations against Mullah, 1903–04 (Somaliland medal and clasp); Commander, 1910; served in HMS Beagle, destroyer, during Dardanelles operations, 1914–15 (despatches twice, DSO for his services as Senior Commander afloat of destroyer flotilla in those waters); Captain, 1915; Captain commanding a Destroyer Flotilla of Grand Fleet March 1917 (despatches, CB); Commanded HMS Valiant, 1st Battle Squadron, Mediterranean Fleet (retired list, 1926); Vice-Adm., retired, 1931; awarded United States Naval DSM 1919; Naval ADC to the King, 1926. *Recreation:* golf. *Address:* Aviemore, Heathfield, Sussex.
Died 17 Feb. 1947.

GODFREY, Hon. John M.; *b* Hastings, Ont, 23 July 1871; *s* of Rev. Robert and Mary Jane Godfrey; *m* 1900, Lily Connon; two *s* two *d. Educ:* Toronto University; Osgoode Hall. BA Toronto Univ., 1891, LLB 1893. Called to Bar, 1894; practised in Toronto, Ont; Chairman Public School Board, Toronto, 1903; defeated as Liberal Candidate in Peel, 1908; KC 1921; Justice of the Supreme Court of Ontario, 1938–42; LLD from Ottawa University and made Officer L'Instruction Publique, France, 1928; Ontario Securities Commissioner, 1934. *Recreations:* golf and fishing. *Address:* Port Credit, Ontario. *Clubs:* Mississaga Golf, National, Toronto.
Died 29 Aug. 1943.

GODFREY, Percy; *b* Derbyshire, 1859; *m* 1908, Lily (*d* 1935), *widow* of Leonard Sidgwick Howell, and *d* of late George Clowes. Musical training private. Gained Lesley-Alexander Prize for Piano Quintette, 1900; and Musician's Comp. Prize for Coronation, 1902; Choral Ballade Prize, Dover Festival 1904; orchestral works: Canterbury Festival, 1929, Folkestone Festival, 1932; Torland, overture, and other orchestral works broadcast; Member of Musicians' Company. *Address:* 32 Bouverie Square, Folkestone, Kent.
Died 30 Jan. 1945.

GODFREY, Lt-Col Stuart Hill, CIE 1908; FRGS; *b* 2 June 1861; *s* of late John R. R. Godfrey; *m* 1896, Guendolen, *d* of late Lt-Col Sir Adelbert Talbot, KCIE; two *s* two *d. Educ:* Westminster School (Queen's Scholar). 2nd Queen's RWS Regt, and Indian Army, Indian Political Department and Persia, North-West Frontier, and Central India States. Entered Army, 1881; Captain, 1892; Major, 1901; Waziristan, 1901–02 (medal); served Mohmand expedition, 1908 (CIE); retired from Indian Army, 1916; appointed to General

Staff, War Office, 1916. *Publications:* Trans. of Pushkin's Kapetauskaya Dochka; Report on Gilgit, Chitral, Hunza, and Nagar.
Died 29 Nov. 1941.

GODFREY-FAUSSETT, Captain Sir Bryan Godfrey, GCVO 1932; KCVO 1919; CMG 1908; CVO 1911; MVO 1906; RN, retired; has the Orders of the Dannebrog, Leopold of Belgium, Rising Sun of Japan, Crown of Italy, and White Eagle of Serbia; Equerry to King George V, 1901–36, Extra Equerry to King Edward VIII, 1936, and to King George VI since 1937; *b* 1863; *e s* of late Godfrey Trevelyan Godfrey-Faussett, of Heppington, Kent; *m* 1907, Eugénie F. E., 3rd *d* of late William Humble Dudley Ward, and Eugénie, *o d* of 1st Viscount Esher; one *s.* Entered Navy, 1877; Lieut 1887; Commander, 1899; retired as Capt. 1906. *Address:* The Ranger's Lodge, Hyde Park, W2. *Club:* Turf.
Died 20 Sept. 1945.

GODFREY-FAUSSETT, Brig.-Gen. Edmund Godfrey, CB 1919; CMG 1915; late RE; FSA; *b* 25 Aug. 1868; *s* of late Thomas Godfrey-Faussett, Barrister-at-law, Auditor to the Dean and Chapter of Canterbury Cathedral, FSA; *m* 1897, Mabel Gertrude, 2nd *d* and *co-heir* of late Sir Augustus W. Lawson Hemming, GCMG; one *s* one *d. Educ:* Winchester; RMA Woolwich. Entered army, 1888; Capt. 1898; Major, 1906; Lt-Col, 1914; Staff Capt. War Office, 1908–10; served South African War, 1899–1902 (despatches twice, Queen's medal 4 clasps, King's medal 2 clasps); European War, 1914–18 (despatches six times, CMG, CB, Bt Col); retired pay, 1922; Chairman, and Vice-President Sussex Archæological Society. *Address:* Hadlow Down, near Uckfield, Sussex. *T:* Hadlow Down 202.
Died 29 May 1942.

GODLEY, Brig.-Gen. Francis Clements, MVO 1904; *b* 8 March 1858; 2nd *s* of late Rev. James Godley, Rector of Carrigallen, Co. Leitrim; *m* 1886, Maud Adeline (*d* 1941), *d* of Surgeon-Major R. Whittall, IMS; one *s* two *d. Educ:* Marlborough. Entered army, 1876; Colonel, 1903; retired, 1907; served Sikkim Expedition, 1888; South Africa, 1899–1901 (Queen's medal 3 clasps); late commanded 2nd Batt. The Sherwood Foresters, 12th Sherwood Foresters, and 91st Infantry Brigade. *Recreations:* shooting, fishing. *Address:* Chalmore, Wallingford, Berks.
Died 13 Nov. 1941.

GODLEY, John Cornwallis, CSI 1914; Director of Public Instruction, Punjab, 1907–17; *b* 9 Feb. 1861; 3rd *s* of late Rev. James Godley, Carrigallen, Co. Leitrim; *m* 1st, 1895, Mary Blanche (*d* 1941), *d* of William MacNaught; one *s* one *d;* 2nd, 1940, Sybil Pinder, *widow* of F. Stuartson Collard, FRCS Eng. *Educ:* Marlborough; Corpus Christi College, Oxford. *Address:* c/o Lloyd's Bank, 6 Pall Mall, SW1.
Died 19 Aug. 1946.

GODMAN, Dame Alice Mary, DBE 1918; *b* 1868; *d* of late Major Percy Chaplin; *m* 1891, Frederic Du Cane Godman, DCL, FRS, FLS (*d* 1919). Late Deputy President, British Red Cross Society; County Commissioner for Girl Guides; President, Women's Branch, Horsham and Worthing Division Conservative Association; Hon. Treasurer SE Area; Chairman of Approved and also Village Schools. *Address:* 45 Pont Street, SW1. *T:* Kensington 2711; South Lodge, Horsham, Sussex. *T:* Lower Beeding 3.
Died 3 Oct. 1944.

GODMAN, Col Charles Bulkeley; *b* 1849; *m* 1st, 1893, Adelaide, *d* of Adm. Hon. F. A. C. Foley, of Packham, Fordingbridge, Hants; 2nd, 1903, Maud, *d* of Rev. D. Robertson, Henfield, Sussex. Served S Africa, 1901–02 (Queen's medal five clasps); late Master of the

Chiddingfold and of the Crawley and Horsham Fox-hounds; DL, JP, Sussex. *Address:* Woldringfold, Horsham, Sussex.

Died 18 Jan. 1941.

GOFF, Thomas Clarence Edward; JP, DL; *b* 28 May 1867; *e s* of late Capt. Thomas William Goff, MP, and Dorothea, *d* of late Rev. Lord Augustus FitzClarence; *m* 1896, Lady Cecilie Heathcote-Drummond-Willoughby (author of A Woman of the Tudor Age, 1930), 4th *d* of 1st Earl of Ancaster; one *s* one *d. Educ:* Eton; Christ Church, Oxford. Major 3rd Battalion Royal Scots Regt. Served S African War, 1900–02 (Queen's Medal, 4 clasps); served European War, 1914–18 (3 medals); contested Buckrose Div. E Yorks (C), 1905; Member LCC 15 years; Vice Chairman of Council, 1930–31. *Address:* The Court, Holt, Wilts. *T:* N Trowbridge 40.

Died 12 March 1949.

GOLDFINCH, Sir Arthur Horne, KBE 1918; Chairman of London Board of British-Australian Wool Realisation Association, 1921–26; *b* Valparaiso, Chile, 10 May 1866; unmarried. *Educ:* privately. Entered the service of Duncan, Fox & Co., General Merchants, Valparaiso, 1881; became a partner of that firm (Liverpool, London, Chile, and Peru), 1903; retired from business, 1913; Liberal candidate for Colchester, 1914–18; Director of Raw Materials, War Office, 1917–21. *Address:* 53 Dunstan Road, NW11. *T:* Speedwell 8040. *Club:* Devonshire.

Died 9 Nov. 1945.

GOLDFINCH, Sir Philip Henry Macarthur, KBE 1934; General Manager and a Director of Colonial Sugar Refining Company, Ltd, in Australia, New Zealand and Fiji; Chairman of British Settlers' Welfare Committee, Sydney; *b* Gosport, 1884; *s* of late Lt Comdr H. E. Goldfinch, RN, New Zealand; *m* 1911, Mary M., *d* of William Robert Cowper, NSW; one *s* two *d. Educ:* Sydney Grammar School. MLA for Gordon, NSW, 1935–37. *Recreations:* golf and tennis. *Address:* Buckhurst New South Head Road, Double Bay, NSW. *TA:* care Sugar, Sydney. *Clubs:* Union, Australian Pioneers, Royal Golf, Sydney.

Died 7 April 1943.

GOLDIE, Barré Algernon Highmore, CBE 1930; TD; *b* 9 May 1870; *e s* of late Rev. Alexander Robert Goldie, Elvaston, Derbyshire, and Margaret Elizabeth Holme; *m* 1892, Bertha Hollis (*d* 1938); two *s* two *d. Educ:* Shrewsbury. Private Secretary to Thomas Charles Baring, MP for City of London, 1889–92, later Trustee and Executor. Herts Yeomanry, 1901–06, 1914–20 (Col 1926–31); Hon. Col 86th Field (Herts Yeomanry) Brigade Royal Artillery, 1931–45. *Recreations:* hunting, golf, fishing. *Address:* The Old Rectory, Brampton, Huntingdon. *T:* Huntingdon 160. *Club:* White's.

Died 2 Dec. 1949.

GOLDING, Captain John, DSO 1917; Chevalier du Mérite Agricole, FIC; Lecturer on Agricultural Chemistry, University of Reading; *b* Plaxtol, nr Sevenoaks, Kent, 21 April 1871; *e s* of late Thomas Golding, The Tree House, Plaxtol, and late Sally, *d* of Thos Barton, Royton Chapel, Lenham; *m* Florence, *d* of John Mundella, Nottingham. *Educ:* Queen Elizabeth's Grammar School, Sevenoaks; Pharmaceutical and other Laboratories, London. Assistant to Dr J. A. Voelcker, RASE Laboratories, Hanover Square; Lecturer Agricultural Chemistry and Bacteriology, University College, Nottingham, 1894–1900; Head of Chemical and Bacteriological Departments, Midland Agricultural and Dairy College, 1900–12; Research Chemist National Institute for Research in Dairying (University of Reading), Shinfield, nr Reading, 1912–37; Recorder of Section M (Agriculture) British Association Australian visit, 1914; served in France, 1915–19, with 18th Division as Sanitary Officer; XVIII Corps, XIII Corps,

and V Army as Agricultural Officer (despatches twice, DSO, French decoration for harvesting crops in evacuated area). *Publications:* over 100 scientific papers and articles; Research work on Agricultural Chemistry, Dairy Chemistry, and Bacteriology, including, Nitrogen Assimilation by Leguminous Plants, Causes of Faults in Milk and Cheese, Disposal of By-products and Vitamins of Milk. *Recreation:* motoring. *Address:* Shirley, Plaxtol, near Sevenoaks, Kent; 5 Wellington Avenue, Reading. *T:* Reading 81434.

Died 22 Sept. 1943.

GOLDSCHMIDT, Lt-Col Sidney George, TD; Managing Director, Goldschmidt, Hahlo & Co., Ltd, Manchester; *b* 5 April 1869; *s* of Alderman Philip Goldschmidt, JP, Mayor of Manchester, 1883–84, 1885–86; *m* 1896, Jane Maud Grieve, *d* of late Sir Walter Thorburn, JP, MP; two *s* two *d. Educ:* privately; Manchester College of Technology. Trained as an engineer; Manager Director in above firm of yarn and machinery exporters, 1895; joined 7th Lancs Volunteer FA, 1889; retired, 1910, with rank of Lt-Colonel; joined 20th Battalion Manchester Regiment, 1914; transferred to the Royal Field Artillery, 1915; invalided from the army, June 1919; Vice-Pres., Duchess of York Hospital for Babies; Council National Pony Society (35 years). *Publications:* Bridle Wise; Stable Wise; Fellowship of the Horse; An Eye for a Horse; Skilled Horsemanship; Random Jottings of a Horseman; numerous articles both in England and America; numerous broadcasts on sport and old furniture. *Recreations:* collecting Old English furniture and Chinese porcelain (exhibited in Manchester Art Gallery, 1925–26). *Address:* Ollerton House, nr Knutsford, Cheshire. *T:* Knutsford 371. *Clubs:* Devonshire; Clarendon (Manchester).

Died 27 Feb. 1949.

GOLDSMITH, Herbert Symonds, CMG 1912; Lt-Governor Northern Provinces Nigeria, 1918–21; *b* 18 Aug. 1873; *s* of late F. W. Goldsmith, Hampstead and Eastbourne; *m* 1913, Beatrice Maude, *d* of late Arthur M. Case, Faringdon and Eastbourne; two *d. Educ:* Cranbrook; Eastbourne College. Entered Nigeria Civil Service, 1899; retired 1921; Chairman West Africa Exhibition Committee, 1924–25; Hon. Secretary, Macgregorlaird Centenary, 1932; Officer of the Legion d'Honneur. *Address:* Barncroft, Eastergate, Chichester, Sussex. *TA:* Fontwell. *T:* Eastergate 42. *Club:* Royal Automobile.

Died 7 March 1945.

GOLIGHER, William Alexander, LittD; Regius Professor of Greek, University of Dublin (Trinity College), 1934–40; Senior Fellow since 1935; Fellow and Tutor of Trinity College, 1902–35; Senior Tutor, 1927–35; Registrar of Trinity College, 1930–37, Vice-Provost, 1937; Irish Barr, 1905; *b* Londonderry, 30 Dec. 1870; 3rd *s* of John Goligher, JP, of Londonderry, and Matilda, *d* of late James Hunter, Gorticross, Co. Londonderry; *m* Sara, *y d* of late Jonathan Bolton Stott of Manchester, 1897; one *d. Educ:* Academical Institution (now Foyle College), Londonderry; Trin. Coll., Dublin (Classical Scholar); Stewart Scholar in Modern Literature, 1891. Vice-Chancellor's Prizeman in English Verse, 1892; Student in Classics with large gold medal in Modern Literature, 1892; Professor of Ancient History in Dublin Univ., 1904–09 and of Ancient History and Classical Archæology 1909–34; Honor Lecturer in Classical Composition, 1903–07. *Publications:* contributions to Kottabos, Hermathena, Classical Review, English Historical Review, etc.; compiled (with Dr Mahaffy) the Greek volumes in H. Spencer's Sociological Data series. *Recreations:* walking, novels, music. *Address:* 25 Trinity College, Dublin; The Chalet, Sutton, Co. Dublin. *T:* Sutton 78. *Clubs:* Fellows', Trinity College, Dublin.

Died 15 Aug. 1941.

GOLLAN, Sir Henry Cowper, Kt 1921; KBE 1918; KC; LLD (Hong Kong University); *b* Coquimbo, Chile, 8 Jan. 1868; *s* of late Sir Alexander Gollan, KCMG; *m* 1908, *d* of James Nelson Norris, of St Louis, USA; no *c*. *Educ:* Charterhouse; Edinburgh University. Called to Bar, 1891, Northern circuit; practised in London till 1899, when he became Private Secretary to Brig.-Gen. Lugard, CB (now Lord Lugard), High Commissioner of Northern Nigeria; went to Northern Nigeria with him and became Attorney-General; Chief Justice of Northern Nigeria, 1901; transferred to Bermuda as Chief Justice and President of the Legislative Council, 1904; Attorney-General of Trinidad, 1911–18; Attorney-General of Ceylon, 1918–24; Chief Justice of Hongkong, 1924–30; retired 1930. *Address:* 1 Brick Court, Temple, EC4. *Club:* Savile.

Died 5 Aug. 1949.

GOLLIN, Alfred, CBE 1920; *b* Liverpool, 29 May 1861; unmarried. Joined the Metropolitan Special Constabulary, Aug. 1914, appointed Commander of Y Division, Oct. 1914, and resigned the Command, 1919; MBE 1918; OBE 1919; Member of The Worshipful Company of Gardeners; Freeman of the City of London; Fellow of The Royal Institution. *Recreations:* yachting, golf, and travel. *Address:* 41 Parkside, Knightsbridge, SW1. *T:* Sloane 2753. *Clubs:* Royal Thames Yacht, Royal Automobile.

Died 29 Dec. 1946.

GONDAL, His Highness Maharaja of, Sir Bhagvat Sinhjee, GCSI 1937; GCIE 1897; KCIE 1887; *b* 24 Oct. 1865; *s* of late Thakore Saheb Sagramji of Gondal; *m* 1881, Nandkuverba, CI, *d* of H. H. Maharana of Dharampore; three *s* three *d*. *Educ:* Rajkumar College, Rajkot; Edin. University Hon. LLD (Edin.) 1887; MB and CM (Edin.) 1892; MRCP (Edin.) 1892; DCL (Oxon) 1892; MD (Edin.) 1895; FRCP (Edin.) 1895; FCP and SB 1913; Fellow of the University of Bombay, 1885; FRSE 1909; MRAS, MRI (Great Britain and Ireland); HPAC. *Publications:* Journal of a Visit to England, 1883; A Short History of Aryan Medical Science, 1895. *Address:* Gondal, Kathiawar, India. *TA:* Gondal, India.

Died 10 March 1944.

GONTHIER, George, Hon. DCS (Montreal), 1934; Hon. LLD (Ottawa), 1935; formerly Auditor-General of Canada; Gonthier & Midgley, chartered accountants, and St Cyr, Gonthier & Frigon, bankers and brokers, Montreal; *b* Montreal, 21 Nov. 1869; *s* of Louis Gonthier and Adeline Charbonneau; *m* 1892, Lumina (*d* 1918), *d* of Antoine Da Sylva, Quebec; two *s* three *d*; 2nd, 1927, Kathleen, *d* of late Rt Hon. C. J. Doherty; one *s*. *Educ:* Commercial Schools, Montreal; private tuition. Accountant, 1893–1924; ex-Treasurer and Member of Council Chamber of Commerce since 1902; one of the Organisers and Member of the first Executive of the Investment Bankers' Association of Canada; Founder and first President of the Institute of Accountants and Auditors of the Province of Quebec; Council of the Ecole des Hautes Etudes Commerciales of the University of Montreal; Commissioner Censor Crédit Foncier Franco-Canadien, Chairman Board of Audit of Canada, 1924–25; has lectured and written on financial and accounting subjects; has promoted measures of commercial and public utility. *Address:* Montreal, Canada. *Clubs:* Montreal, Canadian, Montreal.

Died 29 Jan. 1943.

GOOCH, Sir Thomas (Vere Sherlock), 10th Bt *cr* 1746; *b* 10 June 1881; *s* of 9th Bt and Alice Elizabeth, *d* of E. Williams of Honeycombe House, Calstock, Cornwall; *S* father, 1899; *m* 1902, Florence Meta (*d* 1932), *y d* of late James Draper of St Heliers; three *s* two *d*. Owns about 7200 acres. *Heir:* *s* Lt-Col Robert Eric Sherlock Gooch, DSO. *Address:* Benacre Hall, Wrentham, Suffolk. *Clubs:* Carlton, Royal Automobile.

Died 7 July 1946.

GOOD, Christopher Frank, CB 1948; MRCS Eng., LRCP Lond.; Principal Medical Officer Insurance Medical Service, Ministry of Health. Fellow of Society of Medical Officers of Health; late Medical Assessor, Ministry of Pensions; Clinical Assistant Med. Out-patients, Resident Anæsthetist, Emergency Officer and House Physician, London Hospital. *Address:* Medical Staff, Ministry of Health, Whitehall, SW1.

Died 16 Jan. 1949.

GOOD, Percy, CBE 1941; FCGI. Hon. Fellow Imperial College of Science and Technology; Director, British Standards Institution. *Address:* 1 Vincent Square, Westminster, SW1. *T:* Victoria 7357. *Club:* Athenæum.

Died 2 Dec. 1950.

GOODALL, Alexander, MD, FRCP; Major, late RAMC (TC); Past President, Royal College of Physicians of Edinburgh; Physician, Royal Infirmary and Ministry of Pensions' Hospital, Edenhall; Lecturer on Clinical Medicine, University, and on Physiology, Surgeons' Hall, Edinburgh; *b* 1876; *s* of Rev. Charles Goodall, BD, minister of Barr, Ayrshire; *m* 1904, Ada Durell Martin; two *s* three *d*. *Educ:* George Watson's Coll.; Edinburgh Univ. *Publications:* The Blood: a Guide to its Examination and to the Diagnosis and Treatment of its Diseases (with Dr Gulland), 1912; Aids to Histology, 1912; numerous articles, chiefly on blood diseases and testing of drugs. *Recreations:* shooting, golf. *Address:* 14 Walker Street, Edinburgh. *T:* 23596.

Died 6 Oct. 1941.

GOODALL, Lt-Col Edwin, CBE 1919; MD; FRCP; Hon. Consulting Physician, late Medical Superintendent, Cardiff Mental Hospital; *b* 1863; *s* of E. B. Goodall, Solicitor, Calcutta; *m* 1898, Anna Filippa Jönsson, Halmstad, Sweden. *Educ:* Guy's Hospital; University of Tübingen. Served European War, 1914–19 (despatches, CBE). *Publications:* Pathology of Mental Disorders (Croonian Lectures), Lancet, 1915; Pathology of Insanity (8th Maudsley Lecture), Journal of Mental Science, 1927, etc. *Address:* Fairlawn, Kingsway, Hove, Sussex.

Died 29 Nov. 1944.

GOODE, Sir William (Athelstane Meredith), KBE 1918; Director of Communications, Ministry of Food, Assistant Secretary, 1941; Head of Cable Branch, 1939; Chairman Council of British Societies for Relief Abroad; Chairman Newfoundland War Contingent Association; Director Provincial Insurance Co.; *b* Newfoundland; *s* of the Rev. T. A. Goode; *m* 1899, Cecilia (*d* 1938), *d* of Dr C. A. Sippi, London, Ontario; one *d*. *Educ:* Doncaster Grammar School; Foyle College, Ireland. Unofficial Financial Adviser to Hungarian Government, 1923–41; Pres. of and British Representative on Austrian Section of Reparation Commission, Vienna, 1920–21; British Director of Relief in Europe, Feb. 1919–June 1920; Liaison Officer of Ministry of Food with United States and Canadian Food Administrations and Director Ministry of Food Cable Department, 1917–19; Member of Newfoundland and West Indian Military Contingent Committees, 1916; Hon. Sec. and Organiser of National Committee for Relief in Belgium, 1915; Hon. Sec. British Committee Panama Pacific Exposition, 1913–14; Joint News Editor Daily Mail, 1911; News and Managing Editor Morning and Evening Standard, 1904–10; with Associated Press of America, 1896–1904, representing them on Admiral Sampson's flagship throughout Spanish-American War, and in England for six years, as Special Correspondent. Commander Order of Crown of Belgium; Commander Order of Queen Isabella the Catholic. *Publications:* Economic Conditions in Central Europe; With Sampson through the War, a History of the Naval Operations in the West Indies during the Spanish-American War; short stories in magazines. *Recreations:* fishing, cabling and advising. *Address:* 49 Westbourne Gardens, W2. *T:* Bayswater 1026; 3 Whitehall Court, SW1. *T:* Whitehall 3160.

Clubs: Reform, West Indian, Pilgrims'; Royal Cornwall Yacht, Falmouth; British Schools and Universities, New York.

Died 14 Dec. 1944.

GOODENOUGH, Ethel Mary, CBE 1943; Supt Women's Royal Naval Service, on staff of Adm. Sir Bruce Fraser, C-in-C Eastern Fleet, since 1944; *d* of late Lt-Col H. L. Goodenough, Indian Army. *Educ:* privately. Joined Admiralty Staff, 1918; Chief Woman Officer, 1937; Deputy Director, 1939. *Address:* Flat 4, 46a Kings Road, Chelsea, SW3.

Died 10 Feb. 1946.

GOODENOUGH, Adm. Sir William Edmund, GCB 1930; KCB 1919; CB 1916; MVO 1912; *b* 2 June 1867; 2nd *s* of Commodore J. G. Goodenough, CB; *m* 1901, Hon. Margaret Stanley, OBE, *e d* of 4th Lord Sheffield; two *d.* Went to sea, 1882; Captain 1905; commanded RN College, Dartmouth, 1905–07, and subsequently HMS Albemarle and HMS Duncan; HMS Cochrane; HMS Colossus; present at relief-operations after earthquake at Messina; went with escort to His Majesty to India; commanded HMS Southampton; Commodore 2nd Light Cruiser Squadron; in command of 2nd LCS at action with Germans at Heligoland Bight, 1914; and at action of Dogger Bank, 24 Jan. 1915 (St Vladimir of Russia, 3rd cl.); battle of Jutland, 1916 (despatches); Superintendent, Chatham Dockyard, 1918–20; Vice-Admiral, 1920; Commander-in-Chief on the Africa Station, 1920–22; Vice-Admiral commanding Reserve Fleet, 1923–24; Commander-in-Chief, the Nore, 1924–27; Admiral, 1925; First and Principal Naval ADC to the King, 1929–30; retired list, 1930; President, Royal Geographical Society, 1930–33; Commander of St Maurice and St Lazarus (Messina); Croix de Guerre. *Address:* Parson's Pightle, Coulsdon, Surrey. *T:* Downland 566. *Club:* Travellers'.

Died 30 Jan. 1945.

GOODHART, Gordon Wilkinson, MA, MD, FRCP; Pathologist LCC in charge of St Mary Abbots Group Laboratories; *b* 24 July 1882; *y s* of late Sir James Goodhart, Bt, and Emma Sandford, *d* of W. Bennett, JP, Ashford, Herefordshire; *brother and heir-pres.* to Sir Ernest Goodhart, Bt; *m* 1914, Alice Stransham, *d* of Lieut-Gen. W. P. LaTouche, IA; one *s* two *d. Educ:* Westminster; Trinity College, Cambridge; Guy's Hospital; Freiburg. House Physician, Gull Research Student, Demonstrator of Pathology, Senior Assistant Bacteriologist, Guy's Hospital; Clinical Pathologist, University Coll. Hosp.; Capt. RAMC; Pathologist, 2nd London General Hospital; Pres., Section of Pathology, Royal Society of Medicine; Ex-Pres. Medical Society of London and Association of Clinical Pathologists, Fellow Pathological Society of Great Britain and Ireland. *Publications:* contributions to Medical Journals. *Address:* 40 West Cromwell Road, SW5. *Club:* United University.

Died 16 July 1948.

GOODMAN, Paul, FRHistS; Secretary of the Spanish and Portuguese Jews' Congregation, London; *b* 10 April 1875; *m* 1907, Romana Manczyk; two *s* one *d.* Member of Council of Jewish Agency for Palestine; Hon. Treasurer and Chairman of Political Committee, Zionist Federation of Great Britain and Ireland; Chairman Sir Moses Montefiore Commemoration Committee for Chair of English at the Hebrew University in Jerusalem; Hon. Treasurer of the International Confederation of General Zionists; Hon. Secretary of the international Portuguese Marranos Committee, formed in 1926; Member of the Council of the Jewish Historical Society of England and of the Jewish Memorial Council; Hon. Secretary of the first Zionist Political Committee formed in London in 1916; Vice-Pres. of the English Zionist Federation, 1919–27. *Publications:* The Synagogue and the Church, 1908; A History of the Jews, 1911, 7th revised edition, 1939; Die Liebestätigkeit im Judentum, 1913; Zionism and the Jewish Diaspora, 1921; Moses

Montefiore, 1925; Theodor Herzl, 1927; Zionism in England, 1930; Joint Author, Think and Thank, Montefiore Endowment, Ramsgate, 1933; B'nai B'rith, 1936; Joint Editor, Zionism: Problems and Views, 1916; Editor, The Jewish National Home (1917–1942), 1943; Editor of the Department of Anglo-Judaica of the Universal Jewish Encyclopedia (New York); Editor of the Zionist Review since 1920; since 1897 has contributed to the Jewish and general Press on Zionist, theological and historical subjects. *Recreations:* reading, walking. *Address:* Hatikvah, 10 The Ridgeway, Golders Green, NW11.

Died 13 Aug. 1949.

GOODRICH, Edwin Stephen, FRS 1905; MA, DSc, LLD; Fellow of Merton College, Oxford; Linacre Professor of Zoology and Comparative Anatomy, University Museum, Oxford; *b* 1868; *m* 1913, Helen L. M. Pixell, MA, DSc. *Educ:* Awarded Gold Medal of Linnean Society, 1932, and Royal Medal of Royal Society, 1936. *Publications:* Vertebrata Craniata, 1909; Living Organisms, 1924; Structure and Development of Vertebrates, 1930; and other works in zoology. *Address:* 12 Park Town, Oxford. *T:* Oxford 2982.

Died 6 Jan. 1946.

GOODWIN, Col Frank, CIE 1911; VD; Locomotive Superintendent Rajputana-Malwar Railway, India, 1898; retired, 1912; Commandant 2nd Batt. Bombay, Baroda, and Central India Railway Volunteer Rifles, 1908–11; granted rank of Colonel in the Indian Volunteer Force on appointment as ADC to HM the King Emperor, 1911; *b* 26 March 1857; *s* of William John Goodwin, London; *m* 1882, Isabella Ann, *d* of Rev. James Cumine, Rector of Preban, Co. Wicklow. *Address:* Mevagissey, Cornwall.

Died 23 May 1943.

GOODWIN, Major George Alfred, CMG 1900; Cape Railway Pioneer Regiment; *b* 10 June 1857; *m* 1897, Martha Alice, *d* of Robert Wagstaffe; one *d. Address:* Birken, Prestatyn, Flintshire. *T:* 17.

Died 31 Dec. 1945.

GOODWIN, Engr Vice-Adm. Sir George Goodwin, KCB 1918; CB 1913; *b* 1862; *s* of late Charles Frederick Goodwin; *m* 1885, Mary (*d* 1926), *d* of late Thomas Sagar, Fleet Engineer, RN; one *s* one *d.* Chief Engineer, Chatham Dockyard, 1904; Deputy Engineer-in-Chief, Admiralty, 1907; Engineer-in-Chief of the Fleet, 1917–22; retired list, 1922; Hon. LLD Birmingham University; Past President Institute of Metals; Past President Institute of Marine Engineers; Hon. Vice-President Institution of Naval Architects; Hon. Life Member Institution of Mechanical Engineers; holds the Russian Order of St Stanislas 1st Class, the Distinguished Service Medal of the United States of America. *Address:* Pen Dre, South Leigh Road, Havant, Hants.

Died 2 April 1945.

GOODWIN, William Lawton, BSc (Lond.); DSc (Edin.); LLD (Mount Allison); FRSC; *b* Baie Verte, New Brunswick, 30 April 1856; *s* of Edward Chappell Goodwin (descended from a Massachusetts family of that name, members of which came to New Brunswick with Monckton's army, 1754) and Margaret Carey, *g d* of John Carey, and officer in a Highland regiment; *m* 1885, Christina Murray, *d* of Rev. Wm Murray, of Earltown, Nova Scotia, and of Kingston, Jamaica; one *s* three *d. Educ:* Mount Allison Academy and University, Sackville, New Brunswick; Edinburgh University; Heidelberg; London. Canadian Gilchrist Scholar, 1877–80. Demonstrator of Chemistry in University of Edinburgh, 1879–80; Demonstrator of Chemistry with Prof. Wm Ramsay, University College, Bristol, 1881–82; Prof. of Chemistry, etc., Mount Allison, 1882–83; Professor of Chemistry, Queen's University, 1883–1921; Dean of the School of Mining, Queen's University, Kingston, Canada, 1893–1913; Dean of the Faculty of Applied

Science, Queen's University, Kingston, Canada, 1913–21; retired, 1921. *Publications:* A Text-book of Chemistry, 1886; Handbook for Prospectors, 1924, 1929, 1932; Manuel de Prospecteur, 1930; Geology and Minerals of New Brunswick, 1928; Geology and Minerals of Ontario, 1929; Geology and Minerals of Quebec, 1929; Geology and Minerals of Manitoba, 1930; Everyday Science, 1931; papers in Transactions of Royal Society, Edinburgh; Berichte der deut. chem. Gesellsch.; Chemical News; Nature; Canadian Mining Review, etc. *Recreations:* rowing, fishing, music, study of birds and their songs. *Address:* Ste Anne de Bellevue, PQ, Canada.

Died Jan. 1941.

GOODWIN, Sir William V. S. Gradwell, Kt 1919; JP, CC, Co. Stafford; Chairman of Newcastle, North-West Staffordshire Employment Committee, Ministry of Labour, of the Newcastle Endowed Schools and Staffordshire Compensation Authority; *b* Bocking, Essex, 1 Feb. 1865; *s* of J. G. Goodwin, of Bocking Manor, Essex, and Newark House, Notts. *Educ:* Magnus School, Notts. Lord of the Manor of Cheddleton; Hon. Freeman of Newcastle. *Address:* Westwood Manor, Wetley Rocks, Staffs. *TA:* Westwood, Stoke-on-Trent. *T:* Wetley Rocks 202. *Club:* Royal Automobile.

Died 26 Jan. 1942.

GOODYEAR, Robert Arthur Hanson; writer of Yorkshire rural plays and books for boys; *b* Barnsley, 1877; *m* 1906. *Educ:* Archbishop Holgate's Grammar School. *Publications:* Forge of Foxenby, 1920; Songs of a Seaside Village, 1920; Boys of Castle Cliff School, 1921; The White House Boys, 1921; Topsy-Turvy Academy, 1922; The Greenway Heathens, 1922; The Four Schools, 1922; The Captain and the Kings, 1923; Jack o' Langsett, 1923; Tom at Tollbar School, 1923; The Life of the School, 1923; Yorkshire Recitations, 1923; Dramatic Monologues, 1923; Humorous Monologues, 1923; The Fifth Form at Beck House, 1924; Young Rockwood at School, 1924; The Sporting Fifth at Ripley's, 1924; Battle Royal School, 1924; Three Joskins at St Jude's, 1925; The Boys of Ringing Rock, 1925; The School's Best Man, 1925; Boys of the Valley School, 1925; Blake of the Modern Fifth, 1926; The New Boy at Baxtergate, 1926; Boys of the Mystery School, 1926; The Hope of his House, 1926; Fellows of Ten Trees School, 1927; Up Against the School, 1927; His Brother at St Concords, 1927; Romance of Scarborough Spa, 1927; With Wat at Wintergleam, 1928; Rival Schools at Schooner Bay 1928; Luck of the Lower Fifth, 1929; Clare of Glen House, 1929; Hardy Brockdale Boys, 1929; Too Big for the Fifth, 1929; Our Bessie (play), 1929; All Out for the School, 1930; Tringle of Harlech, 1930; Lady Hard-to-Please (play), 1930; At Sunflower Cottage (play), 1930; Grammar School Hotspurs, 1930; School Before All, 1931; Plain English (play), 1931; Something like a Chum, 1932; Tales They Tell (play), 1932; Mullion's Millions (play), 1932; Jolly for Jennifer (play), 1933; Once in a Blue Moon (play), 1933; Rivals at St John's, 1933; The School's Airmen, 1934; The Old Golds, 1934; Who Is This Woman? (play), 1934; Isle of Sheer Delight, 1935; The Captain of Glendale, 1935; Tudorvale Colours, 1936; The School's Airmen, 1936; Broom and Heather Boys, 1937; Pulling Templestone Together, 1937; The Vanishing Lady (play), 1938; Parry Wins Through, 1938; Fenshaven Finds its Feet, 1939; House Prefect, 1940; Peace at Nobody's Price (play), 1940; Red shall the Heather Bloom (play), 1944. *Recreation:* village play production. *Address:* Wheatcroft, near Scarborough. *T:* 2211.

Died 24 Nov. 1948.

GOOLDEN, Rear-Adm. Francis Hugh Walter, CB 1942; (retd); *b* 22 Aug. 1885; *s* of E. R. Goolden, Cookham Grove, Berks, and Eva Sophia, *d* of William Massey, Cahervillahow, Tipperary; *m* 1911, Dorothy

Melian, *d* of Savage French, Cuskinny, Queenstown, Ireland; one *s* two *d*. *Educ:* Bradfield College; HMS Britannia. Royal Navy; Commander, 1918; Captain, 1926; Rear-Admiral, 1937; retired. *Address:* The Brookside, Bedhampton, Hants. *TA:* and *T:* Havant 281. *Club:* Army and Navy.

Died 13 June 1950.

GOPATHI NARAYANASWAMI CHETTY, Diwan Bahadur Sir, Kt 1945; CIE 1929; JP Province of Madras; Landlord and Merchant; *b* 28 Sept. 1881; *s* of Gopathi Mahadeva Chetti; *m*; one *s*. *Educ:* Madras. Member, Council of State, 1930–36; Pres. Madras Corp., 1927 and 1928: Councillor, 1907–36; now Alderman; Pres. Madras Railway Passengers' Assoc.; ex-Pres. District Secondary Education Board; Hon. Inspector of Certified Schools; Pres. Depressed Classes Mission Soc.; Vice-Pres. Prevention of Cruelty to Animals, Soc. for the Protection of Children and Madras Children's Soc.; ex-member Board of Industries; member of Senate, Univ. of Madras; ex-Pres. South Indian Liberal Federation (Madras Branch); Member Madras Labour Advisory Board; Sec., Madras Presidency Discharged Prisoners' Aid Soc., Provincial Jail visitor; special First-class Magistrate, Bangalore Civil and Military Stations, 1940–44; Pres. Madras Assoc. for the Blind; Member and Pres. Exec. Cttee of the Countess of Dufferin's Fund; ex-Chairman War Propaganda Cttee, Saidapet; Special 1st Class Magistrate, Saidapet; Pres. Tirumalai Tirupathi Devasthanam Cttee; Chairman, Provincial Welfare Fund; Ex-Pres. and Trustee of Pachaiyappa's Trust Board; Member of the Council of the Victoria Technical Institute, Madras; Member Advisory Board, M & SM Railway; Chairman, V. P. Hall Trust; Title of Rao Bahadur conferred, 1909; Diwan Bahadur, 1922; Certificate of Merit awarded, 1911; Kaisar-i-Hind Medal, 1926. *Address:* Gopathi Villa, San Thome, Madras, India. *T:* 2451. *Club:* Cosmopolitan (Madras).

Died 10 Oct. 1945.

GORDON, Alban Godwin, BSc, FCS; Barrister-at-law; *b* 1890; *s* of John Gordon, MD, Aberdeen; *m* 1st, Lilian Clotilde (*d* 1930), *d* of William Bradburn, Wolverhampton; two *s* one *d*; 1937, Patricia Betty Astrid, *d* of late Louis Meyer. *Educ:* King Edward's School, Birmingham; Birmingham University. Lecturer to National Insurance Commission, 1912; Founder of the Association of Approved Societies, 1913; Member of London Insurance Committee, 1913–20; of Executive of Fabian Society; of Brighton Town Council; of Gray's Inn (Lee Prizeman, 1926); Labour candidate for Brighton, 1923, 1924, 1935; for the Lewes Division of Sussex, 1929, 1936 (by-election); served in Army, 1915–19 (despatches twice); Capt. and Adjt 1917. *Publications:* Social Insurance; The Commonsense of Socialism, 1924; Russian Year, 1935; Russian Civil War, 1936; pamphlets and articles on National Insurance; articles in New Statesman, etc.; various songs. *Plays:* The Pedigree Shop, 1921; Peace; Eve Triumphant, 1922. *Recreation:* tennis. *Address:* Beech Corner, Chipstead, Surrey. *T:* Downland 441; 3 Hare Court, Temple, EC. *T:* Central 7742.

Died 4 April 1947.

GORDON, Hon. Sir Alexander, Kt 1930; KC 1904; *b* Sydney, 22 May 1858; *s* of Alexander Gordon, QC; *m* 1906, Margaret Thomas, of New Quay, South Wales; one *s* one *d*. *Educ:* Repton. Became associate to the late Mr Justice Hargrave, one of the Judges of the Supreme Court of NSW; called to the Bar of NSW, 1882; Judge of the Supreme Court of New South Wales, Australia, 1910–28; retired 1929. *Recreations:* greatly interested in every kind of sport, especially football, cricket, and tennis; fond of music and the theatre. *Clubs:* Australian, Union, Sydney.

Died 7 Jan. 1942.

GORDON, Major Archibald Alexander, CBE 1917; MVO 1908; Member King's Bodyguard for Scotland (Royal Company of Archers); late Major 9th (Highlanders) Royal Scots: CA (resigned 1943) and JP of Edinburgh; was from 1906 until he resigned 14 years later, Private Secretary to the Duke of Wellington, KG, GCVO; *b* 1867; 2nd *s* of late Dr William Eagleson Gordon, Bridge-of-Allan, Stirlingshire; *m* Maude (*d* 1929), twin *d* of late Major-General E. Davidson Smith. *Educ:* Edinburgh Collegiate and University. Has acted as Hon. Secretary of several home and foreign movements for which he holds various acknowledgments. In European War as Major, Special List; served with Staff of RN Division during siege of Antwerp, after which as Attaché à la Maison Militaire de SM le Roi des Belges and Belgian King's Messenger (1914–19). Cited in Belgian and French Army Orders of the day. (Holds among foreign war awards the 1st Class of the Belgian Croix Civique with swords and bar, 1914–15, and the Belgian and French Croix de Guerre, both with palms.). *Publications:* Transactions of the Franco-Scottish Society, 1897–1905 (with late Professor John Kirkpatrick, LLB, LLD); The Church of the Multiplying of the Loaves and Fishes at Tabgha on the Lake of Gennesaret, and its mosaics, edited the English Edition, 1937; Culled from a Diary, 1941. *Recreations:* archæology, gardening. *Address:* Jessamine, Bridge of Allan, Stirlingshire.

Died 9 Aug. 1949.

GORDON, Cora Josephine, RBA, artist, author, lecturer, traveller, and musician; Member of Royal Society of British Artists, Society of Women Artists, Woman's International Art Club, and American Society of Women Geographers; a Vice-President of the Alpha Club; *d* of Fredric Turner, MRCS, and Sarah, *d* of C. Partington; *m* Jan Gordon, RBA (*d* 1944). *Educ:* London, Brussels; Slade School of Art. *Exhibitions:* London, Ghent, Paris, Munich, New York, Los Angeles, and San Francisco; Ex-member of the Société des Artistes Decorateurs; served as nurse and interpreter, Serbia, 1915. Represented British Museum, Albanian Chieftain's Head (drawing); Oldham Municipal Gallery, Flatford Pool (Oil). *Publications:* numerous articles; (and with Jan Gordon) The Luck of Thirteen, reprinted as Two Vagabonds in Serbia and Montenegro (Penguin), 1939; Poor Folk in Spain, Misadventures with a Donkey in Spain; Two Vagabonds in the Balkans; Two Vagabonds in Languedoc; Two Vagabonds in Sweden and Lapland; Two Vagabonds in Albania; On Wandering Wheels; Star Dust in Hollywood; Three Lands on Three Wheels; A London Roundabout, 1933; Portuguese Somersault, 1934. *Recreation:* the Spanish lute. *Address:* 48d Clanricarde Gardens, W2. *Club:* Forum.

Died 1 July 1950.

GORDON, Hon. Sir David John, Kt 1925; Member of the Legislative Council of South Australia, 1913–44, President, 1932–44; *b* Riverton, South Australia, 4 May 1865; *m* 1888, Anna Louisa (*d* 1933), *d* of late Henry Peel, Semaphore, S Australia; two *s* two *d*. *Educ:* Stanley Grammar School, Watervale, S Australia. After commercial experience joined Staff of S Australian Register and for some years Commercial Editor, subsequently member of Editorial Staff and Chief of Parliamentary Staff; was Member of Federal Parliament, 1911–13; Ex-President, Associated Chambers of Commerce of Australia; ex-President Adelaide Chamber of Commerce; ex-Director, Broken Hill South, Ltd; North Broken Hill Co. Ltd; Adelaide Electric Supply Co., Ltd; Goldsbrough Mort and Coy., Ltd; Chm. of Australian Delegation at International Economic Conference, Geneva, 1927; Employers Representative at International Economic Conference, Geneva, 1927; Employers Representative at International Labour Conference, Geneva, 1927. *Publications:* The Central State; History of South Australia; Handbook of South Australia; Official Year-Book of South Australia; The Nile of Australia; Conquering the Desert—Conservation, Reclamation, Irrigation; The War and its Aftermath. *Recreations:* tennis, golf. *Address:* 17 Victoria Avenue, Unley Park, Adelaide, South Australia. *TA:* David Gordon, Adelaide. *T:* Unley 1309. *Clubs:* Adelaide, Stock Exchange, Commercial Travellers', Adelaide.

Died 12 Feb. 1946.

GORDON, George Stuart, MA; Hon. DCL (Oxon) 1941; LLD (Glasgow); DLitt (Leeds); FRSL; President of Magdalen College, Oxford, since 1928; Hon. Fellow of Merton College; Hon. Fellow of Oriel College; Fellow of Eton College; *b* 1881; *e s* of William Gordon, Falkirk; *m* 1909, Mary *e d* of J. W. Biggar, Polmont; three *s* one *d*. *Educ:* Glasgow University; Oriel College, Oxford; Paris. First Class Classical Moderations, 1904; Stanhope Prize, 1905; First Class Literæ Humaniores, 1906; Fellow of Magdalen College, 1907–15. University Lecturer in English, 1907–13; Professor of English Language and Literature, University of Leeds, 1913–22, and Dean of the Faculty of Arts, 1920–22; Merton Professor of English Literature, University of Oxford, 1922–28; Professor of Poetry, 1933–38; Vice-Chancellor, University of Oxford, 1938–41; Warton Lecturer, 1922, 1930; Andrew Lang Lecturer, 1928; Sir George Watson Lecturer, 1931; Rede Lecturer, University of Cambridge, 1931; Taylorian Lecturer, 1932; Clark Lecturer, Trinity Coll., Cambridge, 1933; Gresham Prof. of Rhetoric, 1930–33; President of the Classical Association of Scotland, 1934; President of the English Association, 1941–42; Leslie Stephen Lecturer, University of Cambridge, 1941; Member of General Advisory Council and Chairman of the Spoken English Committee of the BBC; 2nd Lieutenant, 6th Battalion West Yorkshire Regiment, Aug. 1914; Captain, Nov. 1914; served European War (wounded; mentioned for services); on the Staff of the Official Military History, 1919–22; Major TF Reserve. *Publications:* The Fronde (Stanhope Essay), 1905; Peacham's Complete Gentleman, 1906; Plays of Shakespeare, 1909–1911, etc.; English Literature and the Classics, 1912 (a collection of Oxford lectures); Mons and the Retreat, 1918; Charles Lamb, 1921; Shelley and the Oppressors of Mankind (Warton Lecture), 1923; The Discipline of Letters, 1923; The Trojans in Britain, 1924; Medium Ævum and The Middle Age, 1925; Companionable Books, 1927; Three Oxford Ironies, 1927; Shakespeare's English, 1928; Andrew Lang (Lang Lecture), 1928; Warton Lecture on Virgil, 1931; Poetry and the Moderns, 1935; articles in The Times Literary Supplement. *Address:* The President's Lodgings, Magdalen College, Oxford. *Club:* Athenæum.

Died 12 March 1942.

GORDON, James Scott, CBE 1923; OBE 1918; *b* 10 Dec. 1867; *s* of late Robert Gordon, Stragullen, Strabane, Co. Tyrone; *m* 1913, Martha Jane, *d* of late Alexander Moore, Milecross, Newtownwards, Co. Down; three *s* one *d*. *Educ:* Edinburgh University (DSc); Victoria University, Manchester. Principal, Agricultural and Horticultural College, Holmes Chapel, Cheshire, 1895–1900; Chief Inspector Dept of Agriculture, Dublin, 1900–11; Deputy Assistant Secretary, 1911–20; Permanent Secretary to Ministry of Agriculture, Northern Ireland, 1921–33; Chairman to Pig Marketing Board, Northern Ireland, 1933–38; President of Agricultural Section British Association, 1928. *Address:* Stragullen, Strabane, Co. Tyrone.

Died 4 Sept. 1946.

GORDON, Jan, RBA; artist, author, lecturer, traveller, and folk musician; Art Critic to the Studio, Liverpool Daily Post and Christian Science Monitor; Member Royal Society of British Artists; *b* 11 March 1882; *s* of Rev. A. Gordon and Blanche, *d* of Rev. J. Graham; *m* Cora Josephine Gordon, RBA; no *c*. *Educ:* Marlborough Coll.; Truro School of Mines. Lieutenant RNVR, 1917–18. *Exhibitions:* London, Ghent, Paris, Munich,

New York, Los Angeles, and San Francisco; Official Artist, War Museum, Naval Medical Section. Represented British Museum, The Waterless Mountains, Albania (water colour); Oldham Municipal Gallery, Regent Street (tempera); Imperial War Museum, Transport of wounded on the Turkish front during the Spring, etc.; Wellcome War Museum, Operation on Wounded in Battleship, etc. *Publications:* A Balkan Freebooter; Bernard Meninsky; Modern French Painters; Buddock against London; Catalogue of the Preston Harrison Collection; A Girl in the Art Class; On a Paris Roundabout; Piping George; Some Craftie Arts; Beans Spilt in Spain; A Stepladder to Painting; Elementary Introduction to the Ostwald Colour System, 1938; (and with Cora J. Gordon), The Luck of Thirteen, reprinted as Two Vagabonds in Serbia and Montenegro (Penguin), 1939; Poor Folk in Spain; Two Vagabonds in the Balkans; Two Vagabonds in Languedoc; Two Vagabonds in Sweden and Lapland; Two Vagabonds in Albania; On Wandering Wheels; Star Dust in Hollywood; Three Lands on Three Wheels; A London Roundabout, 1933; Portuguese Somersault, 1934; Art Aint All Paint (with H. M. Bateman), 1943. *Recreations:* Spanish guitar, music, and folk-poetry. *Address:* 48d, Clanricarde Gardens, W2. *Club:* Savage.

Died 2 Feb. 1944.

GORDON, Brig.-Gen. Laurence George Frank, CB 1915; DSO 1900; late RFA; *b* 21 May 1864; *s* of late Col G. G. Gordon, CVO, CB; *m* 1st, 1895, Florence Juliette (*d* 1924), *d* of C. A. Walters, and *widow* of Alexander M'Hinch, CIE; one *d*; 2nd, 1926, Violet, *d* of C. T. Murdoch, MP, *widow* of A. Y. Lethbridge. Served South Africa, 1899–1900 (despatches, Queen's medal five clasps, King's medal two clasps, DSO); European War, 1914–15 (despatches, CB). *Address:* The Manor, Homington, near Salisbury. *T:* Combe Bissett 323.

Died 15 Jan. 1943.

GORDON, Lt-Col Ramsay Frederick Clayton, CIE 1911; Indian Army, retired; late Commandant of Military Police; *b* 17 Nov. 1864. Lieut 18th Hussars, 1884; Captain, ISC, 1895; Major Indian Army, 1902; Lieut-Col 1910; retired, 1920.

Died 14 April 1943.

GORDON, Ronald Grey, MD, DSc, FRCPE; Physician, Royal United Hospital, Bath; Physician, Bath and Wessex Orthopoedic Hospital Bath; late Member of Medical Advisory Board, Institute of Medical Psychology, Malet Place, WC; Neurologist Stoke Park Colony for Mental Defectives, Bristol; late Medical Director Child Guidance Council; Member of Council, British Medical Association; *b* 25 March 1889; *s* of Alexander Gordon, JP, DL, and Amy Grey Irvine; *m* 1913, Agnes Theodora Henderson; two *s. Educ:* Charterhouse; Edinburgh University. BSc, MB, ChB, MD, DSc. Started in practice as physician at Bath, 1913; served RAMC, 1915–19, MEF and BEF; Neurologist Ministry of Pensions SW Area, 1919–24; Physician Royal Mineral Water Hospital Bath, 1920–29; Morison Lecturer, Royal College of Physicians, Edinburgh, 1937; Lieut-Colonel RAMC, TA, 1938; Temp. Col AMS, 1939; Hon. Col RAMC, 1945. *Publications:* Personality; The Neurotic Personality; Autolycus; The Neurotic and his Friends; Abnormal Behaviour; The Philosophy of a Scientist: (Jointly) Chronic Rheumatic Diseases; Paralysis in Children; Introduction to Medical Psychology; The Mental Defective; The Physiological Principles of Hydrology; The Uses and Limitations of Psychotherapy. *Recreation:* gardening. *Address:* 23 Queen Square, Bath; Woodex, Limpley Stoke, nr Bath. *T:* Bath 2390, Limpley Stoke 3296. *Club:* Caledonian.

Died 26 April 1950.

GORDON, Sir Thomas Stewart, Kt 1938; retired; *b* 26 April 1882; *m* 1909, Victoria, *d* of C. B. Fisher; three *d. Educ:* Broughton, Victoria; Commercial Coll., Adelaide. Late Chm. and Managing Director of Birt and Co. (Pty)

Ltd, Sydney and Brisbane; Australian Director Federal Steam Navigation Co., Ltd, London; Director Bellambi Coal Co., Ltd, Australian General Insurance Co., Ltd, Cockatoo Docks and Engineering Co. Pty Ltd, Darling Island Stevedoring and Lighterage Co. Ltd, Newstead Wharves and Stevedoring Co. Ltd, Ready Mixed Concrete Co. Ltd etc.; Director of Shipping in Australia, 1942–45; Australian representative, British Ministry of Transport, 1939–46; President King George's Fund for Sailors (NSW), 1940–46; ex-Pres.: Australian Merchant Seamen's Relief Fund, Corps of Commissionaires (NSW) and Adult Deaf and Dumb Society (NSW). *Address:* 25 Wunulla Road, Edgecliffe, Sydney, NSW.

Died 5 July 1949.

GORDON, Webster Boyle, CIE 1904; *b* 3 June 1859; *m* 1894, Rose Ethel, *d* of Col D. G. Pitcher, ISC. *Educ:* RIEC, Cooper's Hill. Appointed PWD, India, 1879; Sanitary Engineer, Government of UP, 1899–1901; Secretary to Indian Irrigation Commission, 1901–03; Director of Irrigation Works, Cape Colony, 1903–07; Chief Engineer and Secretary to Govt Punjab, 1908–11; Secretary to Govt of India, PWD, and Member of Imperial Legislative Council, 1911–13; retired, 1913. *Recreations:* fishing, golf. *Address:* Sheerwater, Monkstown, Co. Cork.

Died 12 Oct. 1943.

GORDON, Hon. Wesley Ashton; PC Canada, 1930; KC 1926; Barrister-at-law; Bencher Law Society of Upper Canada since 1931; *b* Owen Sound, Canada, 11 Feb. 1884; *s* of Charles Gordon and Josephine Gimby; *m* 1909, Jean, *d* of John Harkness, New York City; two *s* three *d. Educ:* Owen Sound Collegiate; Osgoode Hall, Toronto. Called to Bar, 1908; Minister of Labour 1932–35, and Mines, Immigration and Colonization 1930–35; Member of Parliament, 1930–35. *Address:* Haileybury, Canada.

Died 9 Feb. 1943.

GORDON, Col William Eagleson, VC; CBE 1920; ADC to the King, 1913; *b* 4 May 1866; *e s* of late William Eagleson Gordon, MD, Homehill, Bridge of Allan, Stirlingshire; *m* 1910, Margaret Katherine, *o c* of late James Blair, of Cluny, Victoria, and *g d* of W. A. Lauder of Bonnyhee House, County Leitrim; one *d.* Appointed The Gordon Highlanders, 1888; served Chitral campaign, 1895 (wounded); Malakand Pass (medal with clasp); Tirah campaign, 1897–98 (clasp); South African War, 1899–1902 (dangerously wounded, Magersfontein; wounded, Paardeberg; despatches, VC; promoted Bt Lt-Col, Queen's medal five clasps, King's medal two clasps); Adjutant 1st Batt. Gordon Highlanders, 1899–1903; Staff-Capt. No. 1 District, Scottish Command; DAQMG Highland Div. (TF); European War (wounded, CBE, 1914 Star, General Service and Victory medals, despatches); Br. Col 1913; commanded No. 1 District, Scottish Command, 1917–20. *Clubs:* Naval and Military, MCC.

Died 10 March 1941.

GORDON, William Thomas, MA, DSc (Edin.), MA (Cantab), FRSE; FGS; FLS; Professor Emeritus of Geology, University of London, 1949; *b* Glasgow, 27 Jan. 1884; *e s* of late William Gordon, engineer, Edinburgh, and Mary Paterson, Edinburgh; unmarried. *Educ:* George Heriot's School, Edinburgh; Edinburgh Univ. Graduated, 1906, MA, BSc; DSc 1911; Carnegie Research Scholar in Geology, 1906; Falconer Fellow in Geology and Palæontology, 1908; Emmanuel College, Cambridge, BA (Cantab) in research, 1910; Sudbury-Hardyman Prize, 1912; Makdougall Brisbane Medal, Royal Society of Edinburgh, 1922. Lecturer in Palæontology and Assistant in Geology, Edinburgh University, 1910–13; Lecturer in Geology, University of London, King's College, 1914; Reader in Geology, 1919; Univ. Professor of Geology, 1920–49; Fellow, 1929. *Publications:* scientific papers in Transactions Royal Society of Edinburgh, Trans Geological Society of

Edinburgh, Trans Botanical Society of Edinburgh, Annals of Botany Trans Philosophical Society of Cambridge. *Recreations:* walking, antiquarian study. *Address:* 50 Addison Gardens, West Kensington, W14. *Club:* Athenæum.

Died 12 Dec. 1950.

GORDON-CLARK, Lt-Col Craufurd Alexander, CMG 1918; DSO 1917; *b* 2 March 1864; 2nd *s* of late Gordon Wyatt Clark of Mickleham Hall, Surrey; *m* Lilias (*d* 1939), *d* of late Horace Cockerell, CIE; two *s. Educ:* Winchester; Sandhurst. King's Royal Rifles, 1884–1905; Queen's Westminster Rifles, 1905–10 and 1914–18; served NE Frontier India (medal and clasp); South African War, 1899–1902 (Queen's medal and four clasps); European War, France, Salonika, and capture of Jerusalem (despatches, DSO, CMG). *Address:* Appletons, Cobham, Surrey.

Died 8 March 1950.

GORDON-HALL, Col Frederick William George, CB 1916; MB, AMS; RP; *b* Benares, 28 Aug. 1861; *e s* of late Dr F. W. Hall, Indian Army, and Matilda Gordon; *m* 1897, Clare Frances, *d* of F. Taylor; one *s* one *d. Educ:* privately; Edinburgh University. MB, CM 1883. Entered AMS through Netley Hospital, 1886; served European War, 1914–18 (CB). *Publications:* articles in RAMC Journal. *Recreations:* tennis and swimming; collects Oriental porcelain. *Address:* Fairfield Lodge, Stoke Poges, Bucks. *T:* Fulmer 1942.

Died 12 May 1942.

GORDON LENNOX, Lady Algernon, (Blanche), DBE; Lady of Grace, St John of Jerusalem; *d* of late Col Hon. Charles Henry Maynard; *m* 1886, Col Lord Algernon Gordon Lennox (*d* 1921); one *d. Address:* 5 Radnor Place, W2.

Died 17 Aug. 1945.

GORDON-LENNOX, Lord Esme Charles, KCVO 1939 (MVO 1907); CMG 1919; DSO 1918; DL, JP; Brig.-General, late Scots Guards; Yeoman Usher of the Black Rod, and Secretary to the Lord Great Chamberlain, 1929–46; *b* 1875; 2nd *s* of 7th Duke of Richmond; *m* 1st, 1909, Hon. Hermione Frances Caroline Fellowes (who obtained a divorce for desertion, 1923, *m* 2nd, 1923, Baron Rolf Cederström), *d* of 2nd Baron de Ramsay; one *s*; 2nd, 1923, Rosamond Lorys, *d* of late Admiral N. C. Palmer, CVO; one *d.* Served South Africa, 1900–02, on Staff (Queen's medal 3 clasps, King's medal 2 clasps); West Africa, 1903 (medal with clasp); European War, 1914–18 (wounded Ypres, 1914; 2nd time, 1918; Bt Lt-Col 1917, DSO, CMG; Italian order of St Maurice and St Lazarus, 1918); Brig.-Gen. 1916. *Address:* c/o Lloyds Bank Ltd (Cox's and King's Branch), 6 Pall Mall, SW1. *Club:* Turf.

Died 4 May 1949.

GORDON-WATSON, Maj.-Gen. Sir Charles Gordon, KBE 1919; CMG 1915; FRCS Eng.; Hon. FACS; KStJ 1917; AMS; Governor and Consulting Surgeon, St Bartholomew's Hospital, Metropolitan Hospital, St Mark's Hospital, St Andrew's Hospital, Jockey Club, and National Hunt Committee; late Vice-President, Royal College of Surgeons; *b* April 1874; *s* of late Rev. H. G. Watson, MA Oxon; *m* Geraldine (*d* 1935), *d* of late Charles James Teevan; one *s. Educ:* St Mark's, Windsor; St Bartholomew's Hospital. Served S Africa, 1899–1901 (medal and 3 clasps); European War, 1914–20 (KBE, CMG); Consulting Surgeon to Forces in France, 1914–18; Cons. Surgeon to the Army at Home 1939–42. *Clubs:* White's, Garrick; Yorkshire, Golf (York).

Died 19 Dec. 1949.

GORE, Charles Henry, MA; *b* Liverpool, 1862; *s* of late Rev. Canon Gore, DD, Vicar of Bowdon, Cheshire; *m* 1st, Mary Lynn, *d* of late Bulkeley Allen, JP, West Lynn, Altrincham, Cheshire; 2nd, Eva Lois, *d* of late William Wood, Pickering, Yorks, and Mrs Wood, The Valley,

Scarborough. *Educ:* Owens College, Manchester; King's College, Cambridge (Exhibitioner, 1882); twenty-second wrangler and honours in science, Cambridge, 1884–85; MA 1888. Master at Durham School, 1886; Senior Mathematical Master and Vice-Principal, Liverpool College, 1887–93; Headmaster of Hymers College, Hull, 1893–1927; President of the Hull Literary and Philosophical Society, 1899–1901. *Address:* Westbourne Grove, Scarborough.

Died 6 June 1945.

GORE, Hon. Seymour Fitzroy O.; *see* Ormsby-Gore.

GORE, Col Sir St John Corbet, Kt 1930; CB 1901; CVO 1925; CBE 1918; late commanding 5th Dragoon Guards (retired); *b* 10 Dec. 1859; *m* 1892, Isabella Charlotte (*d* 1937), *d* of late P. G. Van der Byl. *Educ:* Elizabeth Coll., Guernsey; Winchester. Gazetted to 5th Dragoon Guards, 22 Jan. 1879; served with Heavy Camel Regt in Soudan in 1884 (medal and star), to India in 1893 with 5th Dragoon Guards; served as Military Secretary to both Sir Baker Russell and Sir George Luck in Bengal, 1897–99; commanded cavalry at battle of Elands Laagte, 21 Oct. 1899; siege of Ladysmith (despatches thrice, Queen's medal 4 clasps, King's medal 2 clasps, CB); Brigade Comm., 2nd South Midland Mounted Brigade, 1908–11; served in European War as Military Secretary to Sir Archibald Hunter and to Sir Archibald Murray, 1914–19; Honourable Corps of Gentlemen-at-Arms, 1909; Clerk of the Cheque and Adjutant, 1920; Standard Bearer, 1922; The Lieut, His Majesty's Body Guard of Hon. Corps of Gentlemen-at-Arms, 1926–38. *Address:* Hemingford Grey House, Huntingdon. *Club:* Cavalry.

Died 5 Nov. 1949.

GORE-BOOTH, Sir Josslyn (Augustus Richard); *see* Booth.

GORGES, Brig.-Gen. Edmund Howard, CB 1915; CBE 1919; DSO 1902; FRGS; *b* 23 Nov. 1868; 2nd *s* of late Capt. Gorges, RMA; *m* 1921, Irene Maud, *widow* of Capt. C. H. Dinnen, the King's Regt. *Educ:* St Helen's Coll., Southsea; RM Coll., Sandhurst. Entered army, 1887; served with 2nd Batt. Manchester Regt in E Indies, 1887–96; with 1st Batt. Aldershot and Mediterranean, 1897–98, and in E Indies, 1908–12; Captain, 1896; Major, 1902; Bt Lieut-Colonel, 1906; Bt Col 1910; Substantive Lt-Col 1912; Substantive Colonel, 1917; served with King's African Rifles, 1898–1908; served Maluka Expedition, BE Africa, 1898; Uganda Mutiny, 1898–99 (medal with 2 clasps); South Africa, 1900 (medal and 3 clasps; Uganda, 1900 (medal with 2 clasps); commanded force against Suk and Turkana tribes, BE Africa, 1901 (despatches, DSO); commanded camel corps and mounted infantry in Somaliland, 1904; commanded 1st Batt. King's African Rifles, 1905; Nandi Field Force, 1905 (despatches, brevet Lt-Col, clasp); East Africa, 1906 (despatches); Commandant West African Regt 1912–16; Brig.-Gen. 1916; European War (Cameroons), 1914–16 (despatches twice, and twice mentioned for valuable services, CB, CBE, Officier Légion d'honneur); commanded 1st Eastern Brigade, Army of the Rhine; ret. 1919; granted a special pension for distinguished military services. *Publication:* The Great War in West Africa, 1930. *Address:* 14 Woodbury Avenue, Petersfield, Hants.

Died 26 Oct. 1949.

GÖRING, Field-Marshal Hermann; Commander-in-chief of the German Air Force, 1933–45; Prime Minister of Prussia, 1933; Reichsjägermeister, 1934; Commissioner for the Four Year Plan, 1936; member Ministerial Council for Reich Defence, 1939; President General Council for War Economy, 1940; *b* 12 Jan. 1893; *s* of Judge Göring, member of Foreign Office and Commissioner in German South-West Africa; *m* 1st, Karin Freiin von Fock (*d* 1931), Stockholm; 2nd, 1935, Frau Emmy Henny (née Sonnemann); two *d.*

Volunteered as Lieutenant in Infantry Regiment, 1914; transferred to Air Force, commanded Richthofen Squadron, 1918; air adviser in Denmark, director of Svenska Lufttrafik; one of earliest National Socialist collaborators of the Führer; severely wounded in the Rising of 9 Nov. 1923; National Socialist member of the Reichstag, 1928; President of the Reichstag, 1932; Prussian Minister of the Interior, 1933; Reich Minister for Air, 1933, responsible for the creation of German Air Force; given rank of General by President von Hindenburg, 1933; Air Chief Marshal, 1935; Field-Marshal, 1938. *Address:* Leipziger Strasse 3, Berlin W8.

Died 15 Oct. 1946.

GORMANSTON, 16th Viscount *cr* 1478; **Jenico William Richard Preston;** Baron Loundres, 1478; Baron Gormanston (UK), 1868; Premier Viscount of Ireland; 2nd Lieut KOYLI; *b* 7 Oct. 1914; *s* of 15th Viscount and Eileen (who *m* 2nd, 1934, John Black Atkins, MA), *y d* of late Lt-Gen. Sir W. Butler; *S* father, 1925; *m* 1939, Pamela, *o d* of Capt. Dudley Hanly, and Lady Marjorie Heath (by her 1st marriage); one *s. Educ:* Downside. Served War of 1939–45. *Heir: s* Hon. Jenico Nicholas Dudley Preston, *b* 19 Nov. 1939. *Address:* Gormanston Castle, Co. Meath; 4 Coulson Street, SW3. *Club:* St James'.

Died 9 June 1940.

GORRINGE, Lt-Gen. Sir George F., KCB 1915; KCMG 1918; CB 1912; CMG 1900; DSO 1896; *b* Southwick, Sussex, 10 Feb. 1868; 2nd *s* of late Hugh Gorringe, JP, Kingston-by-Sea, Sussex. *Educ:* Lee's School, Brighton; Wellington College. Joined RE at Chatham, 1888; Egyptian Army, 1893; DAAG Headqr. Staff, EA, Dec. 1895; Dongola Expeditionary Force, 1896 (medal, DSO, clasps Firket and Hafir); on staff of GO commanding at actions of Abu Hamed and Atbara (Brevet clasps, 1897, Abu Hamed and Atbara); DAAG, Headquarters Staff, Khartoum Expeditionary Force, 1898 (clasp Khartoum, 4th class Medjidieh, British medal); Gedaref relief column, 1898 (clasp Gedaref); commanded irregulars at actions of Abu Adel and Om Debrikat, death of Khalif (2 clasps, Brevet Lieut-Colonel); specially employed in charge of reconstruction of Khartoum, 1899; ADC to Lord Kitchener, 1900; DAAG Headquarters Staff, S Africa, 1900 (despatches); commanded flying column, Cape Colony, 1901 (despatches, Queen's medal, three clasps, CMG); commanding operations, Southern Sennar, 1904 (clasp, Jerok); Brevet-Colonel, 1904; 3rd Class Osmanieh, 1904; Director, Movements and Quartering, War Office, 1906–09, Substantive Colonel and temporary Brigadier-General; Brig.-Gen. commanding 18th Infantry Brigade, 1909–11; Major-Gen. 1911; Commanding Bombay Brigade, India, 1912–15; Commanding 12th Indian Division; Commanding operations Southern Arabistan and Euphrates Valley, terminating with capture of Nasiriyeh, Mesopotamia, March 1915–Jan. 1916 (KCB, despatches); Chief of Staff Tigris Force, Jan. 1916–March 1916 (severely wounded); Commanding 3rd Indian Army Corps (Kut relief force), March 1916–July 1916; Commanding 47th Division (London) in France, 1916–19 (KCMG, despatches); Commanding 10th Div., Egypt, 1919–21; Lt-Gen., 1921; retired pay, 1924; Col Comdt RE 1927–38. *Recreations:* hunting, polo, shooting. *Address:* (temp. Kingston Lane, Southwick, Sussex); Kingston House, Kingston-by-Sea, Sussex. *Club:* United Service.

Died 24 Oct. 1945.

GORST, Rev. Ernest Freeland, MA; Hon. Canon of Chester Cathedral since 1926; *b* 27 Nov. 1871; *s* of Peter Freeland Gorst, MA, JP, Leicestershire; *m* Ethel Margaret, (*d* 1940), *d* of Canon Cartmell, MA; one *d. Educ:* St John's College, Cambridge. Curate of Asfordby and Kirby Bellars, 1895–98; Vicar of Kirby Bellars, 1898–99; Vicar of Bickley, 1899–1935; Rural Dean of Malpas, 1917–35; Private Chaplain to the Marquess of

Cholmondeley, 1899–1935; Rector of Waverton, 1935–36. *Recreations:* lawn tennis, shooting. *Address:* Coney Grove, Christleton. *T:* Christleton 246.

Died 25 Jan. 1942.

GORST, Harold E.; author; *b* 1868; *s* of late Rt Hon. Sir John Gorst, and *brother* of late Sir Eldon Gorst, KCB; *m* Dorothy, *d* of late Edmund Russell Bevan; two *d*; also two *s* and one *d* by former marriage. *Educ:* Eton; Halle a Saale, Germany; studied music at the Leipzig Conservatoire. For several years Parliamentary correspondent in the Press Gallery of the House of Commons; lectured in the United States and Canada during 1909; Parliamentary candidate, 1911–17; served European War (wounded). *Publications:* Without Bloodshed, 1897; Sketches of the Future, 1898; China, 1899; The Earl of Beaconsfield (Victorian Era Series), and Farthest South, 1900; The Curse of Education, 1901; Compromised (written in collaboration with Miss Gertrude Warden), 1902; The Fourth Party, 1906; The Philosophy of Making Love, 1908; The Proofs of Christ's Deity, 1927; Much of Life is Laughter, 1936. *Address:* Walberton, Arundel, Sussex.

Died 13 Aug. 1950.

GORT, 6th Viscount (Ireland *cr* 1816; UK *cr* 1945); **John Standish Surtees Prendergast Vereker,** VC 1918; GCB 1940; KCB 1938; CB 1937; CBE 1928; DSO 1917; MVO 1910; MC 1915; Baron Kiltarton, 1810; Field-Marshal; late Grenadier Guards; High Commissioner and Commander-in-Chief for Palestine and High Commissioner for Transjordan, 1944–45; Col Comdt HAC since 1943; *b* July 1886; *s* of 5th Viscount and Eleanor (*d* 1933), *d* and *co-heiress* of R. S. Surtees of Hamsterley Hall, Co. Durham [she *m* 2nd, 1908, Col S. M. Benson]; *S* father, 1902; *m* 1911, Corinne (whom he divorced 1925), *d* of George Medlicott Vereker; one *d. Educ:* Harrow; Sandhurst. Entered army, 1905; Capt. 1914; Brevet Major, 1916; Bt Lt-Col 1921; Col 1926; Maj.-Gen. 1935; Gen. 1937; Field-Marshal, 1943; Chief of Imperial General Staff, 1937–39; C-in-C of British Field Force, 1939–40; Inspector-General to the Forces for Training, 1940–41; and Inspector-General Home Guard; ADC Gen. to the King, 1940–44; Governor and Commander-in-Chief of Gibraltar, 1941–42; Governor and Commander-in-Chief of Malta, 1942–44; served European War, 1914–18 (despatches 9 times, MC, DSO 2 bars, VC). *Heir: b* Hon. Standish Robert Gage Prendergast Vereker, MA. *Address:* 23 Down Street, W1. *Clubs:* Guards', Turf, Army and Navy, White's; Royal Yacht Squadron, Cowes.

Died 31 March 1946.

GORTON, Brig.-Gen. Reginald St George, CB 1922; CMG 1919; DL, Rutland; *b* Madras, 1866; *s* of late Venerable Archdeacon John Gorton, Kirkby Lathorpe, Lincs; *m* 1906, Dorothea, *d* of T. H. Burroughes, Ketton Cottage, Stamford; no *c. Educ:* Felsted. Entered Royal Artillery, 1886; served Miranzai Expedition, 1890; Hunza Nagar Expedition, 1891; Relief of Chitral, 1895; South African War 1899–1902; European War, 1915–18; Chief of British Military Mission to Hungary, 1919–22; retired pay, 1922. *Address:* Ketton Priory, Stamford.

Died 30 March 1944.

GOS, Charles; Écrivain; Lauréat de l' Académie Française; *b* Genève, Suisse, 7 Oct. 1885; fils d'Albert Gos, célèbre peintre de montagne, et de Jeanne Monnerat; *m* 1918, Edmée de Coulon (*d* 1930); 1947, Laetitia Lovey. *Educ:* Genève et Paris. Écrivain et journaliste; directeur littéraire de la Collection Montagne qu'il a fondée en 1933 aux Éditions Victor Attinger, Neuchâtel et Paris; a fait de 1925 à 1937 de nombreuses tournées de conférences littéraires tant en Europe qu'aux États-Unis sous les auspices notamment de l' Alliance Française. *Publications:* La Croix du Cervin, 1918; La Nuit des Drus, 1920; Généraux Suisses, 1925; Voyageurs Illustres en Suisse, 1937; Tragédies Alpestres (Eng. Ed.

Alpine Tragedy), 1940; Solitude Montagnarde, 1942; L'Épopée Alpestre, 1944; Notre-Dame des Neiges (Eng. Ed. Our Lady of the Snows), 1947; Le Cervin (2 vols), 1948, etc.; plusieurs de ses livres sont traduits en anglais, en allemand, en italien, et en espagnol. *Address:* La Fouly, val Ferret (Valais), Suisse. *Club:* (Hon.) Alpine.

Died 14 April 1949.

GOSCHEN, Sir Harry (William Henry Neville), 1st Bt *cr* 1927; KBE 1920; Director, Agricultural Mortgage Coop. Ltd; Director Atlas Assurance Co; *b* 1865; *s* of Henry Goschen of Heathfield, Addington, Surrey; *m* Christian, *d* of late Col J. A. Grant, CB, CSI. *Educ:* Eton. Late Partner of Goschens & Cunliffe; late Chairman of National Provincial Bank, Limited; Director-Chartered Bank of India, Australia and China; Prime Warden of Goldsmiths Co., 1919–20; Hon. Major 24th Middlesex, RV (Post Office); DL Essex; JP; OBE 1918. *Address:* Durrington House, Harlow, Essex.

Died 7 July 1945 (ext).

GOSCHEN, Hon. Sir William Henry, KBE 1917; partner in Goschens and Cunliffe; Chairman of Sun Insurance Office, of Sun Life Assurance, and of Union Discount Co. of London; *b* 7 June 1870; *y s* of 1st and *brother* and *heir-pres* of 2nd Viscount Goschen; *m* 1896, Geraldine Elizabeth (*d* 1918), *y d* of Rt Hon. J. W. Mellor, KC, of Culmhead, Taunton; two *s* two *d*. *Educ:* Rugby; New College, Oxford. Knight of Grace of the Order of John of Jerusalem; Commissioner of Public Works Loan Board; Warden of the King's Chapel of the Savoy; Chairman of London Hospital since 1931. *Recreation:* golf. *Address:* 47 Cadogan Gardens, SW3. *T:* Kensington 2451. *Clubs:* Garrick, Beefsteak, Royal Automobile, I Zingari.

Died 16 June 1943.

GOSLING, Cecil; *b* 13 Feb. 1870; *e s* of late Sir Audley Gosling, KCMG, and Ida, *grand-nephew* of Count Axel Fersen and *d* of Count August Gyldenstolpe, Chamberlain to King of Sweden; *m* 1st, 1896, Hélène (marr. diss.), *y d* of André Bauër, Paris; 2nd, 1921, Baroness Christine de Linden, *o c* of late Baron de Linden. Honorary Attaché to the Legation at Guatemala, 1890. Served with Mounted Police in Matabeleland, 1893–94 (medal); Vice-Consul at Havana, 1896; and transferred to Hamburg, 1897; HM Consul for Republic of Paraguay, 1899–1904; Chargé d'Affaires, Asuncion, 1904; Santiago, 1909; Envoy Extraordinary and Minister Plenipotentiary to Bolivia, 1910; British Consul-General at Gothenburg, 8 Jan. 1916, for duration of the War; Consul-General at Frankfort-on-the Main, 1919–24; Chargé d'Affaires on special mission to the Czecho-Slovak Republic, 1918; Coronation Medal, 1911; Grand Cross Order of the Mehdania, Spain, 1939. *Publication:* Travel and Adventure in Many Lands, 1927. *Recreations:* riding, shooting, and fishing. *Address:* Santa Christina, El Charf, Tangier, Morocco.

Died 23 Nov. 1944.

GOSSAGE, Alfred Milne, CBE 1920; FRCP; 2nd *s* of William Herbert Gossage; *m* Bertha Pillans, 3rd *d* of Pillans Scarth Stevenson, Montreal, Canada; one *s* one *d*. *Educ:* Clifton; Oxford. *Address:* Apple Tree Shott, Chalfont St Giles, Bucks. *T:* Chalfont St Giles 79.

Died 8 June 1948.

GOSSAGE, Air Marshal Sir Leslie, KCB 1941 (CB 1937); CVO 1937; DSO 1919, MC; RAF (retired); late Royal Artillery; *b* 3 Feb. 1891; *er s* of late Lt-Col E. F. Gossage of Winwood, Budleigh Salterton, Devon; *m* 1917, Eileen Gladys, *d* of late Brig.-Gen. E. O'Brien, CB, CBE; one *s* (and one *s* killed on active service). *Educ:* Rugby School; Trinity College, Cambridge. 1st Commission, Royal Field Artillery, 1912; seconded for service with RFC, 12 May 1915; Flight Commander and temp. Capt., 5 Sept. 1915; Squadron Commander and temp. Major, 1 June 1916; Wing Commander and temp. Lieut-Colonel, 5 Dec. 1917; Service in France during

war 3 years 7 months, at home 8 months (MC, DSO, despatches four times); granted permanent commission in RAF as Squadron Leader, 1 Aug. 1919; Wing Commander in RAF 1921; Group Capt., 1928; Air Commodore, 1932; Air Vice-Marshal, 1936; Air Marshal, 1940; Directing Staff, Staff College, Camberley, 1925–27; Deputy Director of Staff Duties, Air Ministry, 1928–30; Air Attaché, British Embassy, Berlin, 1930–31; Senior Air Staff Officer, Air Defence of Great Britain, 1931–34, and in Iraq 1934–35; AOC British Forces, Aden, 1935–36; Air Officer Commanding No. 11 Group, 1936–40; Member of Air Council for Personnel, 1940; Air Officer Commanding, Balloon Command, 1941–44; Chief Comdt and Director-General of Air Training Corps, 1944–46. *Address:* Abbotswood, Buxted, Sussex. *Clubs:* United Service, Royal Air Force.

Died 8 July 1949.

GOSSELIN, Rt Rev. Mgr Amédée; Archivist of Laval University; *b* St Charles de Bellechasse, PQ, 1863. Priest, 1890; was Professor, Prefect of Studies, Superior of the Quebec Seminary, and Rector of Laval University. *Address:* Laval University, Quebec.

Died 21 Dec. 1941.

GOSSET, Lt-Col Allen Butler, CMG 1919; *b* 1868; *s* of late Col William Butler Gosset, RE; *m* 1923, Olive Elizabeth Wilson; one *s*. Served S Africa, 1899–1902 (Bt Major, Queen's medal four clasps, King's medal two clasps, despatches four times); European War, 1914–19; AAG War Office, and AQMG France (Bt Lt-Colonel, despatches 3 times, CMG); Lt-Col 2nd Batt. The Cheshire Regt, 1917–21. *Club:* Junior United Service.

Died 28 July 1948.

GOSSLING, Archibald George; Manager East Anglian Trustee Savings Bank, Wymondham, Norwich; *b* London, 1878; *s* of Harry Russell Turner Gossling; *m* 1903, Anne Elizabeth Tweed. *Educ:* Westbourne Park Schools, Paddington. Joiner; MP (Lab) Yardley Division of Birmingham, 1929–31; Member, General Council AS Woodworkers, 1917–20; Member, Executive Council AS Woodworkers, 1920–29; Member, Executive National Federation Building Trades Operatives; Member, Executive National Joint Council Building Industry; Member of Govt Commission on Prices of Timber; Member, National Conciliation Board Building Trades, 1917–20; Member, Executive WEA; Member, Executive National Housing and Town Planning Council, etc. War-work: Auxiliary Coast Guard; Site Officer at Essential Works. *Address:* Gibbs Flat, Market St, Wymondham, Norfolk. *Club:* Parliamentary Labour.

Died 19 May 1950.

GOTCH, John Alfred, MA (Hon.) Oxon; FSA, FRIBA; JP; Past President, Royal Institute of British Architects; Past Member of Royal Fine Art Commission; Hon. Corresponding Member, American Institute of Architects; Past Vice-President, Society of Antiquaries of London; Chairman of Quarter Sessions, Northamptonshire (retd); *b* 1852; 3rd *s* of Thomas Henry Gotch, Kettering; *m* Annie, *e d* of J. M. Perry, Nottingham; one *d*. *Educ:* private school; Kettering Grammar School; University of Zürich. Articled to R. W. Johnson of Melton Mowbray; travelled in Switzerland, Belgium, France, Italy; served on Committee of Architectural Association, 1883–87; President of Architectural Association, 1886–87; Member of Council, RIBA, 1886–1904, 1905–23, 1930; Vice-Pres., 1914–19, Pres., 1923–25; Pres., Northants Assoc. of Architects, 1911–22; principal works—houses, schools, banks, war memorials. *Publications:* The Buildings of Sir Thomas Tresham, 1883; Architecture of the Renaissance in England, 1894; Early Renaissance Architecture in England, 1901; The Growth of the English House, 1909; The English Home from Charles I to George IV, 1918; The Original Drawings for the Palace at Whitehall, attributed to Inigo Jones, 1912; Old English Houses, 1925; Inigo Jones, 1928; (Editor) The

Growth and Work of the Royal Institute of British Architects, 1823–1934, 1934; The Old Halls and Manor Houses of Northamptonshire, 1936; Squires' Homes and other Old Buildings of Northamptonshire, 1938. *Recreations:* formerly walking, climbing. *Address:* Weekley Rise, nr Kettering. *TA:* Weekley, Kettering. *T:* Kettering 3086. *Clubs:* Arts'; Northampton.

Died 17 Jan. 1942.

GOTT, Acting Lt-Gen. William Henry Ewart, CB 1942; CBE 1941; DSO 1941; MC; Corpus Commander; *b* 13 Aug. 1897; *e s* of late Lt-Col W. H. Gott, Armley House, Leeds; *m* 1934, Pamela Frances Mary, *yr d* of late Brig.-Gen. Walpole Kays, CMG; two *d. Educ:* Harrow. 2nd Lt King's Royal Rifle Corps, 1915; Lt-Col commanding, 1938; Brigadier, 1940; Maj.-Gen., 1941; Lt-Gen., 1942; served European War, 1914–18 (wounded, MC); Adjutant 13th London Regt, TA, 1925–28; psc, 1930–31; served war of 1939–45 (DSO and bar, CBE, CB). *Recreation:* travel. *Address:* Waverley Avenue Lodge, Fleet, Hants; Cowesby Hall, Thirsk, Yorkshire. *T:* Fleet 842. *Club:* Naval and Military.

Died 7 Aug. 1942.

GOUDIE, Hon. Sir George Louis, Kt 1939; JP; *b* 30 March 1866; *s* of George Goudie, formerly of Braefield, Dunrossness, Shetland; *m* 1890, Alice Maud, *d* of Joseph Watson; five *s. Educ:* State Schools; private. Farming and Grazing, later Merchant; elected Leg. Council of Victoria, 1919; Minister for Public Works and Mines, 1923–27; Minister Water Supply and Labour and Electricity, 1932–35; Commissioner Public Works, Victoria, 1935–43; Minister for Immigration, 1935–43; Chairman State Employment Council, 1932–43; Chairman State Air Raid Shelters' Committee, 1941–45. *Recreations:* natural history, angling, bowls, photography. *Address:* 49 Elizabeth Street, Elsternwick, Victoria, Australia. *T:* L 5545. *Club:* Elsternwick Social.

Died 1 May 1949.

GOUDIE, William John, DSc, LLD, MIMechE, MIES, MASME, AMInstCE; *b* 6 Nov. 1868; *s* of William Goudie and Agnes Rhind. *Educ:* Girvan Parish School; Kilmarnock Academy; University of Glasgow. Trained as mechanical engineer in works of Glasgow and South-Western Railway, Kilmarnock, then experience in marine consulting engineer's service, 1884–1906; Assistant Professor, then University Reader, Univ. Col, London, 1907–19; Emeritus James Watt Professor of Theory and Practice of Heat Engines, University of Glasgow. *Publications:* Steam Turbines, 2nd edition, 1922; Ripper's Steam Engine Theory and Practice, 8th edition, 1932; various papers in Engineering Societies Transactions and technical press. *Recreations:* music, gardening. *Address:* Bellevue, 1 Kay Park Terrace, Kilmarnock, Ayrshire. *T:* Kilmarnock, 501.

Died 4 Oct. 1945.

GOUGH, Lt-Col Hugh Augustus Keppel, CIE 1918; Indian Army, retired; *b* 1871; *s* of late Gen. Sir Hugh Henry Gough, VC, GCB; *m* 1901, Helen Isabel (*d* 1942), *d* of Augustus Gore. *Educ:* Wellington College. Served Chitral Relief Force, 1895 (despatches, medal and clasp); Consul at Shiraz, Persia, 1916; Political Agent, Malwa, 1920. *Address:* The Red House, Goring, Oxon. *Club:* Public Schools.

Died 8 Oct. 1950.

GOUGH, William, FRCS; Emeritus Professor of Gynaecology, University of Leeds; *b* 1876; *m* 1905, Agnes Innes Crane Fraser; one *s* four *d. Educ:* Leeds. Obstetrician and Gynaecologist; Vice-President RCOG 1942. *Recreations:* gardening and golf. *Address:* Dunearn, Wood Lane, Leeds, 6. *T:* 51203.

Died 29 June 1947.

GOULBURN, Brig.-Gen. Cuthbert Edward, DSO 1900; *b* 6 Feb. 1860; *s* of Col Goulburn, Betchworth House, Betchworth, Surrey; *m* 1902, Grace Ethel, *e d* of W. H. Foster, Apley Park, Bridgnorth; two *s. Educ:*

Cheltenham College; RMA, Woolwich. Served in India and Africa; commanded the 42nd Battery RFA from the commencement till 1 May 1901, South African War; present at Elandslaagte, Reitfontein, Farquhar's Farm, throughout the siege of Ladysmith on Cæsar's Camp; with Gen. Buller's operations north of Natal, Belfast and Lydenburg (despatches, DSO); commanding RA (Terrl), North Midland Division, 1909–14; Master of the Albrighton Hounds, 1905–10; retired RA 1905; Brig.-Gen. 1918. *Address:* Betchworth House, Betchworth, Surrey. *Clubs:* Travellers', Bachelors'.

Died 18 Dec. 1944.

GOULD, Alec Carruthers, RBA, RWA; marine and landscape painter, and illustrator; *b* Woodford, Essex, 17 March 1870; *e s* of late Sir Francis Carruthers Gould. *Educ:* private schools and Prisca Coborn's. Exhibitor at RA, RBA, NEAC, and International, and provinces; work represented, National Collection, South Kensington, Porlock Vale. *Recreations:* outdoor sketching, fly-fishing, and society of children. *Address:* Upway, Porlock, Somerset.

Died 5 Sept. 1948.

GOULD, Barbara Ayrton, JP; *d* of late Professor W. E. Ayrton, FRS, and late Mrs Hertha Ayrton, MIEE; *m* Gerald Gould (*d* 1936); one *s. Educ:* Notting Hill High School; University College, London. Publicity Manager, Daily Herald, 1919–21; Organising Secretary National Society of Lunacy Reform till 1923; Parliamentary candidate for Northwich, Cheshire, 1924, 1929, and 1931, for Hulme Div. of Manchester Gen. Election, 1935; Member of the Royal Commission on the Civil Service, 1929–31; Member Labour Party Distressed Areas Commission, 1936–37; Executive Member of the Labour Party, 1929–50; Vice-Chairman Labour Party, 1938, Chairman, 1939–40; MP (Lab) Hendon North, 1945–50; Member of Standing Joint Committee of Working Women's Organisation, Chairman, 1932–33; Member Arts Council, 1950; Vice-Chairman of British Council. *Address:* 74a Philbeach Gardens, SW5.

Died 15 Oct. 1950.

GOULD, James Childs; *b* 1882; *s* of Richard Gould; *m* 1905, May Blanche Flagg, New Brunswick; two *d.* Member of Lloyds. Gave his residence at Radyr as a hostel for wounded soldiers; Governor of King Edward VII Hospital; Member Executive, Prince of Wales Hospital; City Councillor, City of Cardiff, 1917; MP (U), Central Cardiff, 1918–24. *Recreations:* cricket, tennis, riding, golf, and shooting. *Address:* 18 Chaldon Way, South Coulsdon, Surrey.

Died 2 July 1944.

GOULD, Col Philip, DSO 1915; late R. Irish Fusiliers; *b* 22 Aug. 1870; *m* 1914, Maria Augusta, *d* of late Major Alexander Frederick Stewart, Worcestershire Regt; three *s* one *d.* Entered army, 1891; Captain, 1900; Adjutant, 1900–04; Major, 1910; served South Africa, 1899–1902 (despatches, Bt-Major; Queen's medal 5 clasps; King's medal, 2 clasps); European War, 1914–19 (DSO); Temp. Lt-Col 1916; retired with rank of Lt-Col, 1920. *Address:* Wolverdene, Andover, Hants. *Club:* Junior United Service.

Died 1 July 1942.

GOULD, Lt-Comdr Rupert Thomas, RN (ret.); author and broadcaster; *b* Portsmouth, 16 Nov. 1890; *s* of W. Monk Gould, composer, and Agnes H. Skinner; *m* 1917, Muriel Hilda Estall; one *s* one *d. Educ:* Eastman's, Southsea; RN College, Dartmouth. Joined RN 1906; served in Mediterranean, on Yangtse, and in Home Fleet; Invalided, 1915; Naval Assistant in Hydrographic Department, Admiralty, 1916–27; broadcast since 1934 as Star Gazer of London Regional Children's Hour, and since Oct. 1942 in BBC Brains Trust. In 1920 offered to clean and reconstruct the four marine time-keepers, belonging to the nation, with which John Harrison, in 1764, won the Parliamentary reward of £20,000 for finding longitude at sea; completed this work, 1933; the machines are normally on exhibition, going, in the National Maritime Museum, Greenwich; founded (1927 onwards) a private collection of early typewriters, now on loan to Chiswick Polytechnic. *Publications:* The Marine Chronometer: its History and Development, 1923; Oddities: a Book of Unexplained Facts, 1928; Enigmas: another Book of Unexplained Facts, 1929; The Case for the Sea-Serpent, 1930; The Loch Ness Monster, and others, 1934; Captain Cook, 1935; A Book of Marvels, 1937; The Stargazer Talks, 1943; Communications, Old and New, 1945; various monographs on points of horological and geographical research. *Recreations:* billiards, table tennis, kite-flying; repairing all forms of mechanism; collecting ancient typewriters. *Address:* at The Grange, Harbledown, Canterbury. *T:* Canterbury 3136. *Club:* Sette of Odd Volumes.

Died 5 Oct. 1948.

GOULDER, George Frederick; Editor; *b* Jan. 1863; *m* 1892, Annie Secunda Poole, Southampton; one *s. Educ:* City of London School. Editor and Proprietor of the News and Book Trade Review, a journal devoted to the newspaper, book, and publishing trade generally, for 55 years. *Recreation:* work. *Address:* 37 Strand, WC2. *T:* Temple Bar 5761.

Died 20 July 1942.

GOUMENT, Charles Ernest Vear, CSI 1911; *b* 26 Oct. 1857; *m* 1891, Annie, *d* of late William Hodgson Oliver, FRCS, of Stockton-on-Tees, Co. Durham; two *s* one *d.* Entered Public Works Department, India, as Assistant Engineer, 1880; Executive Engineer, 1893; Under-Secretary to Government of Punjab, Public Works Department, 1899; Superintending Engineer and Sanitary Engineer to Government of Punjab, 1902; Chief Engineer and Secretary to Government of the United Provinces, Public Works Department since 1908; Member of the Legislative Council, United Provinces, 1908; retired 1912. *Address:* c/o Thos Cook & Son, Berkeley Street, W1.

Died 9 Nov. 1941.

GOUR, Sir Hari Singh, Kt 1925; MA, DSc, DLitt, DCL, LLD; Barrister-at-law; Founder (1946) and Vice-Chancellor, University of Saugor. Elected Member Indian Constituent Assembly; *b* Saugor, Central Provinces, India, 26 Nov. 1866; *s* of Thakur Takhat Singh Gour; *m* (wife *d* 1941); four *d. Educ:* Government High School, Saugor; Hislop College, Nagpur; Downing College, Cambridge; Inner Temple, Lond. BA 1892; MA 1895; LLD 1905; is also LLD of Trinity College, Dublin; Hon. DLitt and First Vice-Chancellor, Delhi University. Vice-Chancellor Nagpur University, 1936; Leader of the Opposition, Legislative Assembly, 1921–34; President High Court Bar Association, Nagpur; President Hindu Association; Indian Delegate to Joint Parliamentary Committee on Government of India Bill, 1935; Chairman Quinquennial Conference Universities of the Empire, 1936; is a social reformer, speaker, and jurist. *Publications:* Law of Transfer in India and Pakistan, 2 vols (7th ed. 1948); Penal Law of India, 2 vols (5th ed. 1936); Hindu Code (4th ed. 1938, 2nd reprint revised 1940, now being codified by the Legislature); Future India, 1934; Random Rhymes; Stepping Westward; The Spirit of Buddhism, 14th reprint, 1929, 21st reprint 1940; His Only Love, 1930; Passing Clouds, 1930; Lost Souls, The Story of Indian Revolution, 1935–1936; The Truth about India, 1943; Facts and Fancies, 1948; contributor to English magazines. *Address:* Model House, Saugor (CP), India. *T:* 3, 3A.

Died 25 Dec. 1949.

GOURAUD, Gen. Henri, Hon. GCMG 1915; *b* Paris, 17 Nov. 1867. *Educ:* College Stanislas, Paris; St Cyr, 1888–90. Second-Lieutenant, 21st Battalion Chasseurs à pied, 1890; In the Soudan, 1894–99 (wounded twice);

Capture of Samory, 29 Sept. 1898; Chef de bataillon, 1899; served Zinder, Tchad, Mauritanie, and Adrar, 1900–10; Morocco Campaign, 1911–14; General de Brigade, 1912; served European War, 1914–19; General 10th Div. of Infantry, wounded 7 Jan. 1915; Gen. commanding 1st Corps Colonial Army, Jan. 1915–May 1915; Expeditionary Corps, Dardanelles, May 1915–June 1915; wounded, 30 June 1915; Gen. commanding 4th Army, Dec. 1915–Dec. 1916; Resident General in Morocco, Dec. 1916–May 1917; commanding 4th Army, May 1917–Sept. 1919; Governor of Strasbourg, Sept. 1919; High Commissioner for France in Syro-Cilicia, and Commander-in-Chief of the Army of the Levant, Nov. 1919; Membre du Conseil Supérieur de la Guerre, 1922; Military Governor of Paris, 1923–37; Chevalier de la Légion d'Honneur, Oct. 1897; Médaille Militaire, July 1915; Grand Croix de la Légion d'Honneur, Dec. 1918. *Address:* 90 bis, Rue de Varenne, Paris VIIe.

Died 16 Sept. 1946.

GOVER, Brig. Charles Rhodes, DSO 1917; late RA; *b* 6 March 1881; *s* of late Alfred Greatbatche Gover. Served NW Frontier of India, 1908 (medal with clasp); European War, 1914–18 (despatches, DSO); Commander, Royal Artillery, 55th (West Lancashire) Division, TA, 1934–38; retired pay, 1938; re-employed in the RA 1939–41; retired pay, 1942. *Club:* Army and Navy.

Died 29 Dec. 1942.

GOVER, John Mahan, KC 1919; LLD; *s* of late John Richard Gover, Bromley, Kent; *m* 1893, Rachel Cleland Brudenell Ernest, *d* of late Mr Justice Downing Bruce, of HM High Court in Jamaica; one *s* one *d. Educ:* University of London; Law Exhibitioner, 1887. Called to Bar, Middle Temple, 1889; sometime holder of Inns of Court Studentship in Roman Law and International Law; joined Northern Circuit, 1891; a Bencher of the Middle Temple, 1925; sometime Member of the Senate of the University of London. *Recreations:* fishing, golf. *Address:* 5 New Square, Lincoln's Inn, WC2; 23 Wetherby Mansions, Earl's Court Square, SW5. *T:* Holborn 6171, Flaxman 0579.

Died 18 April 1947.

GOW, Lt-Col Peter Fleming, DSO 1916; late Indian Medical Service; FRCOG 1934; *b* 28 June 1885; *s* of James C. Gow, Oakbank, Maryfield, Dundee; unmarried. *Educ:* Morgan Academy; University College, Dundee; St Andrews University (MA 1905; MB, ChB 1909; DPH 1910); FRCSE 1924. Entered IMS as Lieut 1912; served with 16th and 17th Cavalry; proceeded with Indian Exped. Force A to France, Sept. 1914 (Captain, despatches, 1915); joined Indian Expeditionary Force D in Mesopotamia, Jan. 1916 (DSO); Special Infectious Diseases Officer on Staff of 1st Army Corps, May to July 1916; Staff-Surgeon, Headquarters, 1st Indian Army Corps, Mesopotamia, July 1916; DADMS 6th Indian Division; Resident Surgeon Eden Hospital for Women, Calcutta, 1921–33; Professor of Clinical Obstetrics, Medical College, Calcutta, and 2nd Surgeon Eden Hospital, Calcutta, 1926; Professor of Midwifery and Gynecology Medical College, Calcutta, and 1st Surgeon Eden Hospital, Calcutta, 1933–40. *Address:* Oakbank, Maryfield, Dundee. *T:* Dundee 82191. *Clubs:* East India and Sports, Oriental.

Died 3 April 1949.

GOWANS, Hon. Lt-Col James, DSO 1902; Durham Artillery Militia; *b* 23 April 1872; *m* 1902, Erin Laura Muriel, *d* of William Wheelwright of Durban, Natal; one *s* two *d. Educ:* Harrow; Clare College, Cambridge. Served South Africa, 1900–01 (despatches, Queen's medal 3 clasps, King's medal 2 clasps, DSO). *Recreations:* in Harrow cricket and football XIs; Camb. Rugby XV 1892 and 1893; Scotland Rugby XV 1893, 1894, 1895, and 1896.

Died 27 April 1936.

GOWER, Granville Chas. Gresham L.; *see* Leveson-Gower.

GOWLLAND, Lt-Col Edward Lake, DSO 1917; MB (Lond.); TD 1918; late RAMC; *b* 14 Dec. 1876; *s* of late Richard Sankey Gowlland, Chief Secretary HM Office of Works; *m* Mary Florence Alexander; twin *s*. *Educ:* Christ's Hospital; St Mary's Hospital. In general practice at Faversham, Kent, 1901–14; Major RGA (TF), commanding the Kent Heavy Battery and Ammunition Column, 1909–15; Member Territorial Association for Kent; temp. Com. RAMC 1915 (despatches twice); Lt-Col RAMC(TA) commanding County of London Field Ambulance; Supt, Ministry of Pensions Hospital, Orpington, 1921–23; President Harveian Society of London, 1933; Commandant, Star and Garter Home, Richmond, Surrey, 1924–41. *Publication:* Surgery in its Modern Aspect, Harmsworth Ency., 1922, etc. *Recreation:* sailing. *Address:* Star and Garter Home, Richmond, Surrey. *Club:* Royal Burnham Yacht.
Died 1 Nov. 1942.

GRACE, Harvey, MusDoc (Cantuar); FRCO; Editor of the Musical Times since 1918; Organist East Grinstead Parish Church since 1941; *b* Romsey, 25 Jan. 1874. Organist and Director of the Choir, Chichester Cathedral, 1931–38. *Publications:* The Organ Works of Bach; The Complete Organist; French Organ Music, Past and Present; The Organ Works of Rheinberger; Ludwig van Beethoven; A Musician at Large; A Handbook for Choralists; Choral Society Training and Conducting; A little life of Bach; (with Sir Walford Davies) Music and Worship, 1935; Organ Music, Songs, and Choral Music. *Address:* 21 Cantelupe Road, East Grinstead, Sussex. *T:* East Grinstead 381.
Died 15 Feb. 1944.

GRACE, Sir Valentine Raymond, 5th Bt *cr* 1795; DL Queen's County; High Sheriff, 1907; JP Co. Dublin; formerly Capt. 4th Bn Leinster Regt; *b* 21 Jan. 1877; *s* of 4th Bt and Margaret, *d* of V O'Brien O'Connor, Dublin; *S* father, 1903; *m* 1900, Mildred (*d* 1935), *d* of late Major Eustace Jameson; one *s* four *d*. *Educ:* Downside; Trinity Hall, Cambridge. *Recreations:* motoring, acting, and cricket. *Heir: s* Raymond Eustace, *b* 6 Jan. 1903. *Address:* Boley, Monkstown, Co. Dublin. *Clubs:* Royal St George's Yacht, Kingstown.
Died 3 May 1945.

GRAHAM, Alexander; Recorder of Bridgnorth since 1905; *b* 1861; *s* of John Graham, Dundalk; *m* 1904, Mary Adeline, *d* of J. Cock. Called to Bar, 1887. *Address:* Whitehouse, Kingsland, Shrewsbury.
Died 26 July 1941.

GRAHAM, Allan James, CBE 1920; BA; Solicitor; *s* of John Graham and Mary Gilkison Allan; *m* 1913, Norah Russell Delafield; three *s*. *Educ:* Marlborough College; Trinity College, Oxford. *Recreations:* golf, racquets, cricket. *Address:* Brentwood, Hoylake, Cheshire.
Died 27 June 1941.

GRAHAM, Sir Aubrey Gregor, Kt 1927; *b* 17 Dec. 1867; *m* 1904, Mabel Hammond. Chief Construction Engineer, Govt Railways, Nigeria, 1919–28. *Address:* Saiwa, Kitale, Kenya.
Died 13 Sept. 1947.

GRAHAM, Sir Cecil William Noble, Kt 1911; *b* 19 Sept. 1872; 2nd *s* of Sir John Graham, 1st Bt; unmarried. *Educ:* Eton College; Trinity College, Oxford. President of the Calcutta Chamber of Commerce, 1909–10, 1911–12; Trustee of the Victoria Memorial, 1909–12; Member Bengal Legislative Council, 1909, and Imperial Legislative Council, 1909–12. *Recreations:* rowing, Eton VIII, 1891; 9th man for Oxford, 1894–95; Leander, 1895, 1896, 1897; winning crews Henley Regatta Grand Challenge Cup, 1896; Steward's Cup, 1897; Polo,

Indian Championship, played in winning Calcutta team 1908–09 and 1909–10. *Address:* Ayr County Club, Sandgate, Ayr. *Clubs:* Leander; Royal Turf, Calcutta.
Died 25 Feb. 1945.

GRAHAM, Rear-Adm. Cosmo Moray, CB 1942. Served European War, 1914–18; Captain, 1930; Rear-Adm., 1941; retired list, 1941; Flag Officer Commanding Humber Area. *Address:* Monks Park, Wadhurst, Sussex.
Died 5 Nov. 1946.

GRAHAM, Sir Crosland; *see* Graham, Sir J. C.

GRAHAM, Duncan MacGregor; MP (Lab) Hamilton Division, Lanarkshire, since Dec. 1918; *b* Rawyards, Airdrie, 1867; *s* of Malcolm Graham and Mary MacGregor; *m* 1st, Isabella Miller, *d* of Thos Gillies, Holytown; 2nd, Isabella, *d* of Wm Moore, Newarthill; five *s* (*e s* killed in the War) two *d*. *Educ:* Whiterigg and Longrigg Board Elementary Schools. Started work as a miner at the age of eleven, 1878; check-weigher at Thankerton Colliery, Holytown, and Eddlewood Colliery, Hamilton, for a period of sixteen years; political organiser to the Scottish miners, 1908–18; General Secretary, Lanarkshire Miners' County Union, 1918–23; Member of National Executive, Scottish Miners, 1918–30. *Recreations:* reading and walking. *Address:* 37 Cardigan Street, Lambeth, SE11; 37 Bothwell Road, Hamilton.
Died 19 Oct. 1942.

GRAHAM, George, RBA 1948; ROI 1918; RI 1922; RSW 1927; *b* Leeds, 1 June 1881; *s* of late Michael Graham, Leeds; *m* 1915, Catherine, *d* of late Rev. C. Pauli, Vicar of Redmire, Yorkshire; no *c*. *Educ:* Rounday, Leeds. From the age of 18 to 20 studied architecture under Thomas Dyer of Leeds; went to Leeds Sch. of Art for drawing; later studied drawing and painting in London under Sir Frank Brangwyn, RA, J. M. Swan, RA and Sir William Nicholson; pictures in the following public collections: Bradford, Leeds, Worthing, Sheffield, Eastbourne, Swansea, Blackpool, Newcastle-upon-Tyne, Oldham, Southport, Paisley, Brighton, Birmingham, Hastings, Liverpool, Darlington, Hove. *Recreation:* music. *Address:* Salt Dykes, Winchelsea, Sussex.
Died 1 Jan. 1949.

GRAHAM, Rt Hon. George Perry, PC 1925; PC Canada, 1907; LLD; Senator, 1927; Hon. Colonel, Brockville Rifles; Vice-President Canada Foundries and Forgings, Ltd; President Recorder Printing Co., Ltd; Director Brockville Trusts and Savings Co., Ltd; *b* Eganville, Ontario, 31 March 1859; Irish descent; *m* Carrie L., *d* of Nelson Southworth of Morrisburg. *Educ:* High Schools in Morrisburg and Iroquois, Ontario. Managed the Morrisburg Herald for eleven years, and was Associate Editor of the Ottawa Free Press for a short time; Grand Master of the AOUW of Ontario for two years; former National President, Victorian Order of Nurses; elected to Legislature for Brockville, 1898, 1902, and 1905; Provincial Secretary, 1904; Leader of Opposition in Ontario Legislature, 1907; MP Brockville, 1907 and 1908; MP South Renfrew, 1912; South Essex, Ontario, 1921–25; Minister of Railways and Canals, Canada, 1907–11; Minister of National Defence, 1922; Minister of Railways and Canals, Canada, 1923–26. *Address:* 350 King Street West, Brockville, Ont; The Kenniston Apartments, Ottawa. *Clubs:* Brockville Rowing and Country, Brockville; Brockville; Ontario, Toronto; Reform, Press, Mt Stephen, Montreal; Country, Rideau, Chaudiere, Royal Golf, Ottawa.
Died 2 Jan. 1943.

GRAHAM, H. E.; *see* Hamilton, Col E. G.

GRAHAM, Lady Helen Violet, DCVO 1937; Extra Woman of the Bedchamber to the Queen since 1939; National President YWCA of Great Britain since 1942; *b* 1879; *d* of 5th Duke of Montrose. Lady-in-Waiting to Duchess of York, 1926; Woman of the Bedchamber to the Queen, 1937–39. *Address:* 114 Cranmer Court, Sloane Avenue, SW3. *T:* Kensington 0462.
Died 27 Aug. 1945.

GRAHAM, Very Rev. John Anderson, CIE 1911; VD, FRGS; Kaiser-I-Hind Gold Medallist (Delhi-Durbar, 1903, Bar, 1935); Silver Jubilee Medal; MA (Edin.), DD (Edin. and Aberdeen); Moderator of Church of Scotland, 1931–32; Missionary of the Church of Scotland, at Kalimpong, Bengal, since 1898; Hon. Superintendent of the St Andrew's Colonial Homes for poorer Anglo-Indian children; *b* 8 Sept. 1861; *s* of David Graham, formerly of HM Customs, London, latterly of Cardross, NB; *m* 1889, Kate M'Conachie (*d* 1919), Edinburgh (Kaiser-I-Hind Gold Medallist, 1916); two *s* four *d*. *Educ:* Cardross Parish School; Glasgow High School; Edinburgh University. Was in the Home Civil Service in Edinburgh, 1877–82; graduated, 1885; ordained, 1889. *Publications:* On the Threshold of Three Closed Lands; Missionary Expansion of the Reformed Churches; Education of the Anglo-Indian Child; Possibility of a Universal Religion. *Address:* Kalimpong, Bengal.
Died 15 May 1942.

GRAHAM, John Fuller; *b* 4 Nov. 1872; *s* of late Robert Fuller Graham; *m* 1897; one *s* one *d*. *Educ:* King's School, Bruton; University College, London. Entered ICS, 1896; Assistant Commissioner in Assam; District and Sessions Judge, 1909; Officiating Superintendent and Remembrancer of Legal Affairs, Assam, 1917–18; Secretary to Government of Bengal, Legislative Department, 1919–20; Puisne Judge of the High Court of Judicature at Calcutta, 1927–32. *Address:* c/o Grindlay & Co., Ltd, 54 Parliament Street, SW1.
Died 24 Jan. 1946.

GRAHAM, Captain John Irvine, CBE 1920; RN retd; *b* 1862; *s* of Col J. H. Graham, 22nd (Ches.) Regt; *m* 1st, 1893, Florence Sarah (*d* 1918), *d* of Walter Hills; 2nd, 1919, Hazel Dorothy, *d* of late Maj.-Gen. Sir Thos Graham, KCB; no *c*. *Educ:* Elizabeth College, Guernsey. Naval Cadet, 1875; Lieut 1885; Commander, 1897; lent to Customs, 1907; retired from Navy with rank of Captain on permanently joining Customs as Inspector of Waterguard, London, 1909; Inspector-General of Waterguard under Board of Customs and Excise, 1912–22; retired from Customs, 1922. *Address:* Digby Croft, Chilbolton, Hants. *Club:* Army and Navy.
Died 10 Dec. 1947.

GRAHAM, Sir (Joseph) Crosland, Kt 1929; JP Denbighshire; *b* Huddersfield, 1866; *s* of late Joseph and Annie Graham, Broadgreen, nr Liverpool; *m* 1st, 1895, Marah Bond Robinson (*d* 1927); one *s*; 2nd, 1929, Violet Kathleen, 2nd *d* of late Major C. M. E. Brinkley; two *d*. *Educ:* privately. Director, Union Marine Insurance Co.; Chairman, Duff Development Co., and Birkenhead Brewery Co. *Recreations:* shooting, tennis, golf. *Address:* Clwyd Hall, Ruthin, Denbighshire. *T:* Ruthin 48. *Club:* Arts.
Died 30 April 1946.

GRAHAM, Col Malcolm David, CB 1915; CMG 1918; CVO 1919; *b* 14 July 1865; *s* of late Hon. R. Graham of Fintry; *m* 1896 (wife *d* 1903); one *s* [*m* 1921, Constance Mary, *o c* of Lt-Col T. E. Carew Hunt, DSO]. *Educ:* Haileybury College; Sandhurst. Entered army (Northants Regt), 1885; Captain, 1893; Major, Duke of Cornwall's Light Infantry, 1906; Lt-Col Royal Berks Regt 1912; served Mashonaland Expedition 1890 (Medal and Clasp); served European War, 1914–18 (CB, CMG, 1914 Star; Russian order of St Anne, 3rd class,

with swords; Serbian order of the White Eagle, 3rd class, with swords; 3rd Class Crown, Belgium; 3rd Class Officier Legion of Honour, France; 2nd Class Order of Wen-Hu, China; Croix de Guerre, Belgium; severely wounded, despatches thrice); Deputy Military Secretary War Office, 1916–20; O. i/c London Infantry Record Office, 1921; ADC to King, 1918–22; retired pay, 1922. *Address:* Lloyds Bank, Ltd, Cox's Branch, 6 Pall Mall, SW1. *Club:* Army and Navy.
Died 16 Nov. 1941.

GRAHAM, Norval Bantock; JP; Chairman, Midland News Association, Ltd; Chairman, Royal Hospital, Wolverhampton; late Consultative Board of Press Association Ltd; late Director of Reuters Ltd; Past President, Newspaper Society; *b* Wolverhampton, 1 Aug. 1870; *s* of late Thomas Graham, JP; *m* Ethel Esther Gertrude Bratt; one *d*. *Educ:* Tettenhall College, Staffs. Studied engineering, and for several years with Carnegie Steel Co., Pittsburg, Pa; later joining his father, on the death of whom succeeded him as Chairman. *Address:* Endhall, Compton, near Wolverhampton. *T:* Tettenhall 51077. *Clubs:* Reform, Royal Thames Yacht.
Died 11 Feb. 1944.

GRAHAM, Sir Robert, Kt 1935; retired East India Merchant; *b* 14 March 1876; *s* of Robert Graham and Mary Breck; *m* 1908, Caroline Barkly Hay; one *s* one *d*. *Educ:* Daniel Stewart's College, Edinburgh. Vice-Chairman, Indian Tea Association, Calcutta, 1913–14 and 1917–19, Chm., 1914–16; Chm. Indian Tea Cess Committee, Calcutta, 1913–15 and part 1921; Chairman, South Indian Association in London, 1922–24; Vice-Chairman, Indian Tea Association, London, 1930–31, Chairman, 1931–34; Chairman, International Tea Committee, 1933–47. *Recreation:* golf. *Address:* 28 Sheldon Avenue, Highgate, N6. *T:* Mountview 4988. *Club:* City of London.
Died 15 Oct. 1947.

GRAHAM, Col Robert Blackall, CBE 1919; Indian Army, retired; *b* 1874; *s* of Col R. B. Graham. *Educ:* Wellington College; RMC, Sandhurst. Served NW Frontier of India, 1897–98 (medal and clasp); South Africa, 1899–1900 (wounded, Queen's medal and clasp); European War, 1914–19 (despatches, CBE); retired 1924.
Died 12 April 1944.

GRAHAM, Rt Hon. Sir Ronald (William), PC 1921; GCB 1932 (CB 1910); GCMG 1926 (KCMG 1915); GCVO 1923; Trustee of British Museum since 1937, and on its Standing Committee; *b* 24 July 1870; *e s* of late Sir H. J. L. Graham, KCB, and Edith, *d* of 1st Earl of Cranbrook; *m* 1912, Lady Sybil Brodrick (*d* 1934), 2nd *d* of 1st Earl of Midleton. *Educ:* Eton. Attaché, Diplomatic Service, 1892; appointed to Embassy in Paris, 1893; 3rd Secretary, 1894; transferred to Teheran, 1897; 2nd Secretary, 1897; transferred to Petrograd, 1899; 1st Secretary, 1904; employed in Foreign Office, 1903–07; British Agent before Muscat Arbitration Tribunal at The Hague, 1905; on Special Service, Crete, 1906; Councillor of Embassy, Egypt, 1907; acted as Agent and Consul-General, 1907–08–1909; Adviser to Ministry of Interior, Egyptian Government, 1910–16 (despatches); Minister Plenipotentiary, 1916; Assist Under-Sec. Foreign Office, 1916–19; Acting Permanent Under-Secretary Jan.–Sept. 1919; HBM Minister to Holland, 1919–21; HBM Ambassador to Italy, 1921–33; British Government Director of Suez Canal Co., 1939–45; Chairman, Lincolnshire & Central Electricity Supply Co., 1939–48; holds Grand Cordon of the Order of the Nile, and of the Order of St Maurice and St Lazarus. *Recreations:* shooting, fishing, golf. *Address:* 4 Down Street, Piccadilly, W1. *T:* Mayfair 5759. *Clubs:* Turf, MCC, Beefsteak.
Died 26 Jan. 1949.

GRAHAM, Walter Armstrong, FRGS; *b* 2 May 1868; *e s* of John Graham, JP, Grasmere, Westmorland; *m* 1898, Maude, *d* of late Henry Carver of Wilmslow, Cheshire; one *s* one *d*. *Educ*: Stratford-on-Avon; Ghent; Tübingen; Edinburgh University. Entered Burma Civil Service, 1889; Assistant Political Officer, Northern Shan States, 1893; commenced by Govt of India for services, 1895; services lent by Indian Government to Siam, 1897; Director, Bangkok Revenue Department, 1898; Director, Land Records Department, Siam, 1901; resigned Burma Civil Service, 1903; Commander, Order of the White Elephant, 1903; HSM's Resident Commissioner, Kelantan, 1903; Adviser to His Siamese Majesty's Minister of Lands and Agriculture, 1909; retired, 1926; Kt Commander Order of Crown of Siam, 1912; Kt Grand Cross Crown of Siam, 1913; Knight Grand Cross White Elephant, 1925; President of the Siam Society, 1920–26. *Publications*: The French Roman Catholic Mission in Siam, 1901; Kelantan, a Handbook, 1908; various articles under *nom-de-plume* Pinya; Siam, 2 vols, 1st edition, 1912, 3rd edition, 1924; contributions to Ency. Brit. *Address*: Buckland House, Buckland Newton, Dorset. *Club*: Dorset County (Dorchester).

Died 7 May 1949.

GRAHAM, William; Solicitor (Nicholson Graham and Jones, 19/21 Moorgate, EC2); *b* 7 July 1862; *s* of Walter and Susan Scovell Graham; *m* 1898, Mary Beatrice, Dame of Grace of Order of St John of Jerusalem, *d* of late John Francis Cockburn Lee; one *d*. *Educ*: King's College School, London; matriculated London University, 1880. Articled to Geo. E. Philbrick, Solicitor; admitted solicitor, 1884; Master, Merchant Taylors' Co., 1930–31. Director of Associated Newspapers Ltd; Law Debenture Corporation Ltd; London General Investment Co. Ltd; River Plate Electricity Co. Ltd; Wm Whiteley & Co. Ltd and Charrington and Co. Ltd. Member of Council of Royal Albert Hall and of Executive Committee of British Council for Relations with Foreign Countries. Governor of St Bartholomew's Hospital. CStJ 1931. *Recreations*: reading, travelling. *Address*: 8 Park Crescent, W1; Telegraph Cottage, Coombe Warren, Kingston-on-Thames. *Clubs*: Carlton, Junior Carlton, Gresham.

Died 17 Nov. 1943.

GRAHAM, Winifred, (Mrs Theodore Cory); author; 2nd *d* of late Robert George and Alice Graham, of St Albans, Hampton-on-Thames; *m* 1906, Theodore J. Cory, MA (Cantab), *e surv. s* of late Richard Cory, JP, Cardiff. *Educ*: home. Appointed to be a British Delegate at the third World's Christian Citizen Conference at Pittsburg, Nov. 1919, and elected Chairman of a World Commission on Mormonism during that period; Divisional Vice-President of the British Red Cross Society, Middlesex County Branch. *Publications*: On the Down Grade; A Strange Solution; The Star Child; Meresia; Beautiful Mamma; The Zionists; A Child at the Helm; The Great House of Castleton; Mayfair; Angels and Devils and Man; A Social Pretender; The Beautiful Mrs Leech; When the Birds Begin to Sing; Wickedness in High Places; The Vision at the Savoy; Emma Hamilton's Miniature; A Miracle of the Turf; World without End; Ezra, the Mormon; Christian Murderers, 1908; Mary, 1909; The Enemy of Woman, 1910; The Love Story of a Mormon, 1911; The Sin of Utah; Her Husband's Secret; The Spectre of the Past; Sons of State; The Mormons (a Popular History), 1913; The Gods of the Dead, 1913; The Pit of Corruption, 1914; The Imperial Malefactor, 1915; Judas of Salt Lake, 1916; Falling Waters, 1919; The Daughter Terrible, 1921; Breakers on the Sand, 1921; Sealed Women, 1922; John Edgar's Angels, 1922; And it was So. 1923; Eve and the Elders, 1924; Ninety and Nine Just Persons, 1924; In Fear of a Woman, 1925; The Diamond Heels, 1926; A Sinner in a Surplice, 1926; My Letters from Heaven, More Letters from Heaven (psychic books), 1926; Unholy Matrimony, 1927; Fame and Shame, 1927; Till

Divorce us do Part, 1928; After Hell, 1928; Consummated, 1929; Tumbling Out of Windows, 1929; A Wolf of the Evenings, 1930; The Last Laugh, 1930; Wolf-net, 1931; The Power behind the Throne (in collaboration), 1931; Vacant Possession, 1932; The Life of a Nobody, 1932; Identity, 1933; Experimental Child, 1933; Tongues in Trees, 1934; Hallowmas Abbey, 1935; The Man Behind the Chair, 1935; What Thinkest Thou, Simon? 1936; Ghostly Strength, 1936; The Wise Man hath Said, 1937; Dr Julian, 1937; The Frozen Death, 1938; Glenvirgin's Ghost, 1938; All Fires go out, 1939; Sacrifice & Co., 1940; The River of Thought, 1941; Christopher Carol, 1942; A Spider never falls, 1944; What Next?, 1945; That Reminds Me, 1945; Observations, 1946; I Introduce (autobiography), 1948. *Recreation*: swimming. *Address*: St Albans, Hampton-on-Thames. *T*: Molesey 216. *Club*: English-Speaking Union.

Died 5 Feb. 1950.

GRAHAM BROWN, Rt Rev. George Francis, OBE 1931; DD (Lambeth); Hon. DD (Edin.); Bishop in Jerusalem since 1932; Hon. Fellow St Catharine's College, Cambridge, since 1937; *b* 27 Jan. 1891; 2nd *s* of G. Graham Brown, China Inland Mission, Edinburgh; *m* 1929, Jane Pasley Hay,*o d* of late J. J. Graham Brown, MD, FRCPE, Edinburgh; one *s*. *Educ*: Glasgow Academy; Monkton Combe School; St Catharine's College, Cambridge (Exhibitioner). BA 1913; MA 1919; MA Oxon by incorporation, 1922. 2nd Lieut KOSB Aug. 1914; Belgium, 1916; Captain and Adjutant, KOSB (SR); invalided out of service, 1918; History Master, Monkton Combe School, 1918–21; Wycliffe Hall, 1921; ordained 1922; Chaplain of Wycliffe Hall, Oxford, 1922–23; Vice-Principal, 1923–25; Principal, 1925–32; Lecturer, Wadham College, Oxford, 1923–25; Examining Chaplain, Bishop of Ripon, 1925–32; Proctor in Convocation, 1931; Sub-Prelate (*ex-officio*) of Order of St John of Jerusalem. *Recreations*: rowing, golfing, tennis. *Address*: St George's Close, Jerusalem; 12 Warwick Square, SW1. *TA*: Biblandic, London. *T*: Victoria 3232. *Clubs*: National, Athenæum.

Died 23 Nov. 1942.

GRAHAM-CAMPBELL, Sir Rollo Frederick, Kt 1933; *b* 2 Jan. 1868; *s* of late John Graham-Campbell of Shirvan, Argyllshire, NB, and Jessie, *d* of late Charles Saunders of Fulwood Park, Liverpool; *m* 1899, Catharine Ellen, *d* of late Sir Walter Sherburne Prideaux; three *s* three *d*. *Educ*: Eton; Trinity College, Cambridge; 2nd class Law Tripos; LLB 1891; LLM 1894. President of the Cambridge Union, 1891; called to Bar, Inner Temple, 1892; Counsel for the Attorney-General in Legitimacy Cases, 1901–08; one of the Junior Counsel for the Director of Public Prosecutions at the CCC, 1908–13; Metropolitan Police Magistrate, 1913–33; Chief Magistrate of the Police Courts of the Metropolis, 1933–40. *Address*: Oaksend, Oxshott, Surrey. *T*: Oxshott 21. *Clubs*: Oxford and Cambridge, Garrick.

Died 3 June 1946.

GRAHAM-HARRISON, Sir William Montagu, KCB 1926; KC 1930; DCL Oxon 1932; Chancellor of Diocese of Gloucester since 1937; Member of National Mark Committee, 1934; Chairman since 1937; Chairman, National Committee of Investigation under Coal Mines Act, 1930, since 1936, and N Ireland Civil Service Committee since 1937; *b* 4 Feb. 1871; *s* of Capt. T. A. J. Harrison, RA; *m* 1900, Violet Evelyn Cecilia, *er d* of late Sir Cyril Clerke Graham, Bart, CMG; two *s* one *d*. *Educ*: Wellington College; Magdalen College, Oxford. Fellow of All Souls College, Oxford, 1895. Hon. Fellow of Magdalen Coll., Oxford, 1938; Barrister, 1897; Solicitor for HM Customs and Excise, 1913–17; Second Parliamentary Counsel to Treasury, 1917–28; First, 1928–33; retired, 1933; Chancellor of Diocese of Durham, 1934–40; of Diocese of Truro, 1935–40; and of

Diocese of Portsmouth, 1938–40; Member of London School Board, 1900–03. *Clubs:* Athenæum, United University.

Died 29 Oct. 1949.

GRAHAM-LITTLE, Sir Ernest Gordon; *see* Little.

GRAHAM-SMITH, George Stuart, FRS 1919; MD, MA; Reader Emeritus in Preventive Medicine, University of Cambridge. *Educ:* Pembroke College, Cambridge; Guy's Hospital; MD 1905. *Address:* Pathological Laboratory, Cambridge; c/o Pembroke College, Cambridge.

Died 30 Aug. 1950.

GRAHAM-STEWART, Alexander, MB, ChB (Hons Aber.); Medical Officer in charge of Details, Regent's Park Barracks, since 1939; late Physician to Lawn House, Convent of the Daughters of the Cross; Orphan Working School, Margate; Medical Officer to Wellington House, Westgate-on-Sea; late Medical Officer in Charge, British Red Cross, Wanstead Auxiliary Military Hospital, Margate, etc.; Captain, Royal Army Medical Corps; Medical Referee to Royal Insurance Company; Scottish Provident Institution; and Sun Life Assurance Company of Canada, etc.; late Lecturer in Cardio-pathology, Military Hospital, Maghull; *b* 1879; *s* of late Rev. Dr Stewart; *m* Letta, *e d* of J. D. Walker, Dumbreck, Glasgow; two *s. Educ:* Gordon's College; Aberdeen University. Late House Physician and House Surgeon, Royal Infirmary, Aberdeen; Hunterian Medallist, 1912; late Examiner British Red Cross Society. *Publications:* medical articles on cardiac and pulmonary and intestinal diseases and on disorders of the blood-pressure. *Recreations:* fishing, shooting, golf. *Address:* 26 Ulster Place, Upper Harley Street, NW1. *T:* Welbeck 1204.

Died 27 Feb. 1944.

GRAIN, His Honour Judge Sir Peter, Kt 1928; *b* 25 Sept. 1864. Called to Bar, Middle Temple, 1897; Member of Bar Council, 1902–06; Resident Magistrate at Zanzibar, 1906; Judge of the Court of Appeal for E Africa, 1906; Assist Judge of HBM Court for Zanzibar, 1906; Legal Member of Council and Attorney-General to the Govt of Zanzibar, 1907; Acting First Minister of the Government of Zanzibar, Aug. 1907 to April 1908; Assistant Judge to HM Supreme Court for the Dominions of the Sublime Porte at Constantinople, 1910; Acting Judge, 1911 and 1912; Judge of Special Court for trial of German and Austrian subjects in Egypt, 1914; Judge HBM Prize Court, Egypt, 1914; Judge of Special Court for trial of civil cases of German and Austrian subjects in Egypt, 1915; Assistant Judge, Supreme Court, Egypt, 1915–19; Acting Judge, 1917–18; Judge, 1919–21; Assistant Judge, HBM Supreme Court for China, 1921–27; and Judge of High Court of Wei-hai-Wei, 1926; holds Order of the Alijah, 1st Class, Zanzibar. Past Grand Deacon, England. *Address:* Farnham Common, Bucks. *Club:* East Indian and Sports.

Died 6 May 1947.

GRANARD, 8th Earl of, *cr* 1684; **Bernard Arthur William Patrick Hastings Forbes,** KP 1909; PC Great Britain, 1907 (PC Ireland, 1918); GCVO 1915; Bt 1628; Viscount Granard and Baron Clanehugh, 1675; Baron Granard (UK), 1806; HM Lieutenant, Co. Longford; a Deputy Speaker of the House of Lords; Director of the Bank of Ireland; Vice-Admiral of Connaught; Grand Cross of the Order of St Maurice and Lazarus of Italy; Grand Cross of the Order of the Star of Roumania; Grand Cross of Order of Charles III of Spain, and Companion of Spanish Order of Military Merit; Grand Cross of the Order of Isabel the Catholic of Spain; Grand Cross of the Order of Christ of Portugal, and of the North Star of Sweden; Grand Cross Order of Dannebrog; Grand Cross of the Order of Ethiopia;

Commander of the Order of the Redeemer of Greece; Lieut-Colonel in the Reserve of Officers, Scots Guards; Member of the Council of State of Ireland; *b* 17 Sept. 1874; *s* of 7th Earl and Hon. Frances Mary Petre, *e d* of 12th Baron Petre; *S* father, 1889; *m* 1909, Beatrice, OBE, *d* of Ogden Mills of Staatsburg, Dutchess County, USA; two *s* two *d. Educ:* Oratory School. Formerly Lieut 3rd Batt. Gordon Highlanders; ADC to Lord-Lieut of Ireland (Earl Cadogan); Lieut, Scots Guards, 1899; Capt. 1905; resigned, 1911; served S African War, 1900–02 (Queen's medal 3 clasps, King's medal 2 clasps), Special Ambassador to announce Accession of King George V at Court of Lisbon, Madrid, The Hague, Brussels, Copenhagen, Stockholm and Christiania, 1910; commanded 5th Batt. R. Irish Regt in European War, 1914; Lord-in-Waiting to King Edward VII, 1905–07; Master of the Horse, 1907–15 and 1924–36; HM Comptroller at Ascot, 1936–45; Assistant Postmaster-General, 1906–09; a member of the Irish Senate, 1921–34; late Lt-Col comdg 8th City of London Regt (Post-Office Rifles); Chairman Food Control Committee for Ireland; a Member of the Irish Convention; Assistant Military Secretary to Commander-in-Chief British Salonika Force (Grand Officier of the Legion of Honour; White Eagle of Serbia (4th Class); despatches four times). *Heir:* *s* Viscount Forbes, AFC. *Address:* Castle Forbes, Newtown Forbes, Co. Longford; 73 Rue de Varenne Paris. *Clubs:* Turf; Jockey (Paris).

Died 10 Sept. 1948.

GRAND, Sarah; novelist; Mayoress of Bath, 1923, 1925, 1926, 1927, 1928, 1929; *b* Ireland, of English parents; *d* of Edward John Bellenden Clarke, Lieut RN, and Margaret Bell, *d* of late George Henry Sherwood, lord of the manor of Rysome Garth, Yorkshire; *m* at 16, Brigade-Surgeon Lieut-Col M'Fall (*d* 1898); one *s*. Travelled for five years in the East, China, and Japan; wrote Ideala at 26, and has since interested herself in the Woman's Movement. *Publications:* Singularly Deluded; A Domestic Experiment; Ideala; The Heavenly Twins, 1893; Our Manifold Nature, 1894; The Beth Book, 1897; The Modern Man and Maid, 1898; Babs the Impossible, 1900; Emotional Moments, 1908; Adnam's Orchard, 1912; The Winged Victory, 1916; Variety, 1922. *Recreations:* sociology, music, and a country life. *Address:* 7 Sion Hill Place, Bath.

Died 12 May 1943.

GRANDE, Julian; author, lecturer, and formerly English newspaper correspondent in Switzerland; accredited to the League of Nations; *b* 9 Nov. 1874; *m* 1st, 1911, Constance Alice (*d* 1922), *d* of Hon. J. W. Barnicoat, Nelson, NZ; 2nd, 1938, Irene, widow of Lt-Col E. A. Wallinger, DSO, and *d* of late Harrison Benn, Bradford and Dawlish. *Educ:* on the Continent and in Ireland. Has been an Alpine climber since the age of 14; has travelled throughout the world; toured India for 4th time as guest of various Indian Princes, 1935–36; lectures on his travels and on mountaineering all over the UK and in most leading public schools. Acted as foreign correspondent abroad for the London Times, 1910–16, Birmingham Post Sheffield Telegraph, 1910–23; War correspondent for the New York Times, 1914–23; during World War (1914–18) was voluntarily engaged in counter-acting enemy propaganda in Switzerland; edited and published on behalf of British Govt nearly 100 publications in German, French and Italian, 1914–18; staff correspondent of the Daily Telegraph, 1922–33; Has represented the Press at 78 meetings of the Council of the League of Nations, 16 Assemblies, Economic Conferences, Locarno Treaty Conference, Reparation Conferences, and all Disarmament Conferences, including the Three-Power Naval Conference. *Publications:* edited and revised The Land and the Book, 1910; The Bernese Oberland in Summer and Winter, 1911; A Citizen's Army: the Swiss System, 1916; L'Empire britannique et la Guerre; edited England in

War Time, 1918; (with Mrs Grande) translated into English Dr Nicolai's Biology of War, 1918; Geneva, its Place in the World, 1920; Constance Grande, 1925; Japan's Place in the World, 1934. *Recreation:* mountaineering. *Address:* Knowle, Cuckfield, Sussex. *TA:* Grande, Cuckfield. *T:* Cuckfield 51. *Club:* Authors'.

Died 6 Jan. 1946.

GRANET, Sir (William) Guy, GBE 1923; Kt 1911; *b* 13 Oct. 1867; *s* of late William Augustus Granet; *m* 1892, Florence Julia, 2nd *d* of 1st Viscount Selby; one *d.* *Educ:* Rugby; Balliol College, Oxford. Called to Bar, Lincoln's Inn, 1893; Secretary, Railway Companies' Association, 1900; General Manager, Midland Railway Co., 1906; Member of the Royal Commission on the Civil Service, 1911–14; Controller of Import Restrictions, 1915; Director-General of Movements and Railways, and Member of Army Council, 1917; Chairman, British and Allied Provisions Commission, and Representative of the Ministry of Food in USA and Canada, 1918; Member of the National Economy (Geddes) Committee, 1921–22; Chairman of the London, Midland, and Scottish Railway, 1924–27; Chairman of South Africa Railway Commission, 1933. *Address:* Burleigh Court, Stroud, Glos. *T:* Brimscombe 119. *Clubs:* Brooks's, Athenæum; Royal Yacht Squadron, Cowes.

Died 11 Oct. 1943.

GRANGER, Col Thomas Arthur, CMG 1918; MB; Indian Medical Service (retired). *Educ:* Edinburgh University. First commission, 1894; Captain, 1897; Major, 1906; Brevet Lt-Col, 1914; Lt-Col, 1914; Col 1922; served Mekran Expedition, 1898; NW Frontier of India, 1898–99; ADMS Army Headquarters, India, 1911–14; Hon. Surgeon to the Viceroy of India, 1914–19; European War, 1914–18; ADMS Headquarters Egyptian EF and Mediterranean EF, 1915–16; ADMS 4th Cavalry Division, BEF, France, 1916–18 (despatches twice, CMG); retired, 1922. *Address:* 16–19 Piccadilly, SW1.

Died 4 Aug. 1942.

GRANNUM, Reginald Clifton, CMG 1925; *b* 17 April 1872; 3rd *s* of late E. T. Grannum, CMG; *m* 1902, Ada, *d* of James Austin, Glastonbury, Somerset; two *s* two *d.* Treasurer and Member of Executive and Legislative Councils of British Guiana, 1908–22; Treasurer and Member of Executive and Legislative Councils of Kenya Colony, 1922–30; retired 1930. *Address:* St Helier, Jersey, CI.

Died 7 Jan. 1946.

GRANT, Alexander; KC 1908; *b* Bolton, Lancashire, 5 Sept. 1866; *m* 1st, Lilian R. A. *d* of late W. Farr, of Petersborough; 2nd, Isabel, *d* of late J. Sharples, of Prestwich, Manchester; two *d.* Attended Bank Street British Schools, Bolton, 1870–78, for the last two years as a half-timer; obtained a Thomasson Exhibition providing three years' education at Manchester Grammar School and an allowance for maintenance; obtained Foundation Scholarship and Langworthy Scholarship, 1881; Head of the school and Lawson Gold Medallist, 1884; elected to a Postmastership at Merton College, Oxford, 1884; 1st Class Classical Moderations, 1885; 1st Class Literæ Humaniores, 1888; 1st Class Final School of Law, 1889; 2nd Class BCL, 1890; Fellow of All Souls College, 1890–97; Eldon Law Scholar; Lecturer in Roman Law and Jurisprudence, Victoria University, Manchester, 1892; called to Bar, Inner Temple, 1894; Bencher of the Inner Temple, 1918, Treasurer, 1940. *Address:* 1 New Square, Lincoln's Inn, WC2. *T:* Holborn 5011.

Died 21 March 1941.

GRANT, Arthur James, MA; Emeritus Professor, Leeds University; ex-President of Historical Association; *b* Farlesthorpe, Lincolnshire, 21 June 1862; *s* of Samuel and Hannah Grant; *m* 1901, Edith Radford (*d* 1929). *Educ:* Boston Grammar School; King's Coll., Cambridge. Professor of History in the University of Leeds, 1897–1927; Professor of Modern History in the University of Egypt, Cairo, 1930–32. *Publications:* Greece in the Age of Pericles; The French Monarchy; English Historians; Scott; A History of Europe; History of Europe in Nineteenth Century (with H. V. Temperley), 1926; Europe in the Sixteenth Century, 1931; The Huguenots, 1935. *Address:* 4 Oak Bank, Leeds 6.

Died 24 May 1948.

GRANT, Major Sir Arthur Lindsay, 11th Bt *cr* 1705; Grenadier Guards; *b* 8 Sept. 1911; *er s* of 10th Bt and Evelyn, *y d* of late Collingwood L. Wood, of Freeland, Perthshire; *S* father, 1931; *m* 1934, Priscilla Jean Fortescue, *yr d* of Brig. Alan F. Thomson, DSO; two *d.* Entered Grenadier Guards, 1931; resigned commission, 1936; rejoined Grenadier Guards, 1939. *Heir: b* Francis Cullen, *b* 5 Oct. 1914. *Address:* House of Monymusk, Aberdeenshire.

Died 18 July 1944.

GRANT, Rev. Cecil, MA; retired; *b* 1870; *s* of John Grant, Linton, Kent; *m* Lucy (*d* 1937), *d* of W. Thompson, Ipswich; no *c. Educ:* Sutton Valence School, Kent; Wadham Coll., Oxford (Classical Scholar). Assist Master, Allhallows School, Honiton, and Queen Mary's School, Walsall; Headmaster of Keswick School (on its re-establishment as a Co-educational School in 1898) till 1907; Founder and Headmaster of St George's School, Harpenden, 1907–36; Member of Head Masters' Conference, 1921–36. *Publications:* Articles on Co-education, in Special Reports of the Board of Education, vol. xi and elsewhere; A School's Life, 1903; The Case for Co-education (with Norman Hodgson), 1913; English Education and Dr Montessori, 1913; edited with Francis House abridgment of A. Clutton Brock's, What is the Kingdom of Heaven?, 1929. *Recreation:* golf. *Address:* Maldon Lodge, Harpenden.

Died 3 April 1946.

GRANT, Gen. Sir Charles John Cecil, KCB 1937 (CB 1930); KCVO 1934; DSO 1915; DL, JP; of Pitchford and Cotes; *b* 16 Aug. 1877; *s* of late Lt-Gen. Sir Robert Grant, GCB; *m* 1903, Lady Sybil Myra Caroline Primrose, *e d* of 5th Earl of Rosebery; one *s.* Entered Coldstream Guards, 1897; Adjutant, 1902–05; Capt. 1903; Major, 1913; Lt-Col (Brevet), 1916; Col (Brevet), 1919; subst. 1922; Major-General, 1930; Lieut-Gen. 1934; General, 1937; served South Africa, 1899–1902 (wounded, Queen's medal three clasps, King's medal two clasps); European War, 1914–18 (wounded, DSO, Bt Lt-Col, Bt Col, despatches seven times); psc; Brigade-Major Brigade of Guards, 1909–12; Gen. Staff Officer, 3rd Grade, War Office, 1912–13; Brigade Major, France, 1914; GSO2, 1914–15; GSO1, 1915–17; Brig.-Gen. and commanded 1st Infantry Brigade, 1917–18; Brig.-Gen. General Staff, 1918–19; commanded 3rd Batt. Coldstream Guards, 1919–21; Colonel on the Staff, Egypt, 1921–25; commanded 137th (Staffordshire) Brigade, 1925–27; commanded 8th Infantry Brigade, 1927–30; Commander 53rd (Welsh) Division, TA, 1930–32; General Officer Commanding London District 1932–34; General Officer Commanding-in-Chief Scottish Command, 1937–40; Governor of Edinburgh Castle, 1937–40; retired, 1940; Colonel of the King's Shropshire Light Infantry, 1931–46; Commander Legion of Honour; Commander of the Crown; Belgian and Italian War Crosses; 1914 Star and clasp; British War Medal; Victory Medal; Coronation Medal, 1911; Silver Jubilee Medal, 1935; Coronation Medal, 1937. *Recreations:* hunting, fishing, golf, shooting. *Address:* The

Durdans, Epsom; Pitchford Hall, Shrewsbury; Bearnoch, Glen Urquhart. *Clubs:* Turf; Shropshire (Shrewsbury); New (Edinburgh).

Died 9 Nov. 1950.

GRANT, Lt-Gen. Harold George; b 1884; m 1913, Norah Lindsey Bucknall, d of Lindsey Barker; two s. Col Commandant Plymouth Division Royal Marines, 1936–39; Maj.-Gen., 1939; Lt-Gen., 1940; retired, 1940; served as Major RM, 1941; to Retired List, 1944. *Address:* Ryburn, Tilford, Farnham, Sy.

Died 31 Oct. 1950.

GRANT, Adm. Henry William, CB 1917; Director Cable and Wireless (Holding) Ltd, and telegraph companies associated therewith; Director Globe Telegraph and Trust Co. Ltd; b 24 Jan. 1870; e s of late Admiral H. D. Grant, CB; m Mabel Blanche Edith, d of late Captain A. R. Wonham, RN; no c. Capt. of Dryad and in command of Navigation School, Portsmouth, 1910–12; Commanded HMS Hampshire, China and Grand Fleet 1914, 1915; Assist Director and Deputy Director Operations Divisions Naval Staff, 1915–18; Rear-Adm. retired, 1919; Vice-Adm. retired, 1925; Adm. retired, 1929; Chairman and Managing Director Marconi's Wireless Telegraph Co. Ltd and Marconi's International Marine Communication Company Ltd and their subsidiary companies, 1941–46. *Address:* Beech Trees, Lynchmere, Haslemere, Surrey. *T:* Liphook 3227. *Clubs:* United Service; (hon.) Royal Yacht Squadron, (Cowes).

Died 15 April 1949.

GRANT, Sir James Dundas-, KBE 1920; MA, MD, FRCS (Eng. and Ed.); retired; Hon. Consultant in Aural Diseases to Ministry of Pensions; Consulting Surgeon (Throat and Ear), to Brompton Hospital for Consumption, Central London Nose, Throat, and Ear Hospital, The Cancer Hospital, West End Hospital for Diseases of the Nervous System, The Royal Freemasons Hospital, and The Sussex (Brighton) Throat and Ear Hospital; late Teacher of Laryngology and Otology, University of London; Vice-President, Royal Institution; Hon. Surgeon Royal Academy of Music; Hon. Admiral Surgeon to Royal Society of Musicians, Scottish Hospital and Caledonian Asylum; Surg.-Maj. (retired) 24th Middlesex (Post Office) Rifle Volunteers; Principal Medical Officer 6th Brigade, London Division National Reserve; Hon. member of American and Foreign Special Societies; late Aurist and Laryngologist, King George Military Hospital, Lord Knutsford's Hospitals for Officers, New Zealand Military Hospital, Walton-on-Thames, Endsleigh Palace, and Russian Hospitals for Officers, etc., during European War, 1914–18; b Edinburgh, 13 June 1854; s of James Dundas Grant, Advocate; m 1890, Helen (d 1944), d of Edward Frith; two s. *Educ:* Edinburgh Academy; Dunkirk College (France); University of Edinburgh; University of Würzburg (Bavaria); London, St Bartholomew's Hospitals, and other medical schools. General practitioner of medicine till 1886; then aurist and laryngologist. *Publications:* various contributions to his special departments of medicine and surgery. *Recreations:* walking, orchestral conducting. *Address:* Flat 4, 29 Sheffield Terrace, W8.

Died 13 Nov. 1944.

GRANT, Maj.-Gen. Sir Philip Gordon, KCB 1931; CB 1918; CMG 1916; b 10 Dec. 1869; y s of late Col J. M. Grant, RE; m 1907, Annette, 4th d of John Coventry, of Burgate Manor, Fording-bridge, Hants; two s three d. *Educ:* privately; RM Academy, Woolwich. Joined RE 1888; Capt. 1899; Major, 1906; Lieut-Col, 1915; was for five years with Egyptian Army as Director of Military Works; served Chitral, 1895 (medal with clasp); S Africa, 1899–1902 (despatches, Queen's medal 3 clasps, King's medal 2 clasps), Aden, 1903; East Africa, 1904; Somaliland (despatches, medal with clasp); European War, 1914–18 (despatches, CMG, CB,

Major-General); Director of Public Works in Palestine, 1921–23; Commandant, School of Military Engineering, Chatham, and GOC, Chatham Area, 1923–27; also Inspector of RE 1926–27; Director of Works, War Office, 1927–31; retired pay, 1931. *Address:* The Long House, Hurstbourne Priors, Hants.

Died 14 July 1943.

GRANT, His Honour Judge Robert; b 24 Jan. 1852; s of Patrick and Charlotte Bordman Grant; m Amy Gordon, e d of Sir Alex. T. Galt, GCMG, Montreal, 1883; three s. *Educ:* private school in Boston; Public Latin School, Boston; Harvard (AB 1873; PhD 1876; LLB 1879); LittD Columbia, 1921; LittD Harvard, 1922. Practised Law from 1879; was one of the Water Commissioners of City of Boston, 1888–93, and Chairman of the Board, 1889–93; Judge Probate Court and Court of Insolvency, Boston, Mass, 1893–1923; now retired; Member American Academy of Arts and Letters; Fellow American Academy of Arts and Sciences; Member Massachussetts Historical Society; Overseer of Harvard College, 1895–1921; Member of Sacco-Vanzetti Advisory Commission, 1927. *Publications:* The Little Tin Gods on Wheels (verse), 1879; The Confessions of a Frivolous Girl, 1880; The Lambs (verse), 1882; An Average Man, 1883; Face to Face, 1886; Jack Hall, or The Schooldays of an American Boy, 1887; Jack in the Bush, or a Summer on a Salmon River, 1888; The Reflections of a Married Man, 1892; The Opinions of a Philosopher, 1893; The Bachelor's Christmas, 1895; The Art of Living, 1895; Search-Light Letters, 1899; Unleavened Bread, 1900; The Undercurrent, 1904; The Orchid, 1905; The Law-Breakers, 1906; The Chippendales, 1909; The Convictions of a Grandfather, 1912; The High Priestess, 1915; Their Spirit, 1916; Law and the Family, 1919; The Bishop's Granddaughter, 1925; Occasional Verses (1873–1923), privately printed, 1926; The Dark Horse, 1931; Fourscore: An Autobiography, 1934. *Recreations:* fishing, golf. *Address:* 211 Bay State Road, Boston, Mass, USA. *TA:* 211 Bay State Road, Boston. *T:* Kenmore 2026. *Clubs:* Somerset, Harvard, Tavern, Boston.

Died 19 May 1940.

GRANT, Sir Robert McVitie, 2nd Bt cr 1924; JP; Hon. LLD Edinburgh University; Chairman of McVitie & Price, Ltd; b Edinburgh, 7 Dec. 1894; o s of Sir Alexander Grant, 1st Bt; S father 1937. *Educ:* George Watson's College, Edinburgh. *Recreations:* golf, fishing, shooting. *Heir:* none. *Address:* Glenmoriston, Edinburgh 10; Aldenham Cottage, Letchmore Heath, Herts; Logie House, Dunphail, Morayshire. *Clubs:* Marlborough, Royal Automobile; New, Edinburgh.

Died 26 Jan. 1947 (ext).

GRANT, Rt Hon. William; JP; MP (U) North Belfast, Parliament of Northern Ireland, 1921–29, Duncairn Division since 1929; first Minister of Health and Local Government in Northern Ireland since 1944; Belfast; 4th s of Martin and Mary A. Grant; m 1906; two s two d. *Educ:* National School. Shipwright; Chairman of the Belfast District Shipwrights Association; Parliamentary Secretary to Ministry of Labour, N Ireland, 1938–41; Minister of Public Security, N Ireland, 1941–43; and Minister of Labour, N Ireland, 1943–44. *Address:* 75 Dunlambert Drive, Belfast.

Died 15 Aug. 1949.

GRANT, William, MA (Aberdeen), BA (London), LLD (Aberdeen); Editor of The Scottish National Dictionary, and Secretary of the Scottish National Dictionary Association Limited; b Elgin, 19 Sept. 1863; e s of late Robert Grant, Surveyor, Kirkcudbright; m 1899, Janet Cameron Robertson, 2nd d of James Holm, The Grange, Carlton Curlieu, Leicester; no c. *Educ:* Elgin Academy; Fordyce School; Aberdeen University. Teaching English and Classics in the Academy, Elgin, 1884–86; in Albany Academy, Glasgow, 1886–91; studying in France, Belgium, Germany, 1891–93;

teaching English and Classics in Garnethill Girl's High School Glasgow, 1893–95; Modern Language Master, High School, Arbroath, and Headmaster, Ladyloan School, 1895–1903; Lecturer in English and Modern Languages, FC Normal College, Aberdeen, 1903–08; Lecturer in Phonetics, Teachers' Training Centre, Aberdeen, 1908–28; Lecturer on the History of the English Language, University of Aberdeen, 1916–20; Convener of the Scottish Dialects Committee, 1907–29. *Publications:* Pamphlet, What still remains to be done for the Scottish Dialects; Introduction to Chambers' Scots Dialect Dictionary; Phonetic Tests for the Scottish Dialects; Scottish Dialects of Avoch and Cromarty; Pronunciation of English in Scotland; Manual of Modern Scots (joint author); Transactions of the Scottish Dialects Committee I-IV (1914–1921); Speech Training for Scottish Students (joint author). *Recreations:* walking and word-hunting. *Address:* Ashfield, Cults, Aberdeen. *T:* Cults, Aberdeen 133.

Died Dec. 1946.

GRANT-DUFF, Sir Arthur Cuninghame, KCMG 1924; *b* 23 May 1861; *e s* of late Rt Hon. Sir M. E. Grant Duff, GCSI; *m* 1906, Kathleen, *y d* of late General Powell Clayton, formerly US Ambassador in Mexico. *Educ:* Balliol College, Oxford. Nominated Attaché, 1885; 3rd Secretary, 1887; 2nd Secretary, 1892; employed at Madrid, 1885; Vienna, 1888; Stockholm, 1891; Pekin, 1892; Caracas, 1900; Berne, 1901; sent to Caracas on special service, 1902; Secretary to HM's Legation, Mexico, 1902; sent to Stockholm, 1905, to be HM's Chargé d'Affaires during absence of HM's Minister; has been also HM's Chargé d'Affaires at Caracas, Berne, and Mexico; Secretary to HM's Legation, Brussels, 1905; Chargé d'Affaires, Darmstadt, 1906; Councillor of Embassy in HM Diplomatic Service; Minister Resident and Consul-General at Havana, 1906–09; Minister Resident at Dresden and Coburg, and Chargé d'Affaires at Waldeck-Pyrmont, 1909–14; employed in Intelligence Department, Admiralty, 1916–19; Envoy Extraordinary and Minister Plenipotentiary to Republics of Peru and Ecuador, 1920–23; Republic of Chile, 1923–24; Envoy Extraordinary and Minister Plenipotentiary at Stockholm, 1924–27; Grand Cross, Star of the North (Sweden). *Address:* 3 Adelaide Court, Adelaide Crescent, Hove, Sussex. *Club:* English-Speaking Union.

Died 11 April 1948.

GRANT-STURGIS, Sir Mark Beresford Russell, KCB 1923; late Presiding Special Commissioner of Income Tax; *b* 1884; *s* of late Julian Sturgis; took by deed poll additional surname of Grant, 1935; *m* 1914, Lady Rachel Montagu-Stuart-Wortley, *d* of 2nd Earl of Wharncliffe; one *s* (and one killed on Active Service, 1944) one *d*. Assist Private Sec. to Rt Hon. H. H. Asquith, 1906–08, when Chancellor of the Exchequer, and one of his Private Secretaries when Prime Minister, 1908–10; Special Commissioner of Income Tax, 1910; Chairman, Treasury Selection Board, 1919–20; joint Assistant Under-Secretary for Ireland, 1920–22; Asst Under-Sec. of State for Irish Services, 1922–24. *Address:* Hillersdon House, Cullompton, Devonshire; 1 Manson Place, Queen's Gate, SW7. *Clubs:* Brooks's, Beefsteak.

Died 29 April 1949.

GRANTHAM, William Wilson, KC 1923; LCC since 1913, Deputy Chairman, 1935; VD; DL; Recorder of Deal since 1905; one of HM Lieutenants for the City of London; *b* S Norwood, 7 Jan. 1866; *e s* of late Hon. Mr Justice Grantham; *m* 1897, Sybil, *o d* of late Sir Andros de la Rue, 1st Bt; five *s* three *d*. *Educ:* Harrow School; Trinity College, Cambridge (BA 1889, MA 1895). President Cambridge Union and the ADC, 1888; Capt. CURV; represented Cambridge Undergraduates at the Octo-Centenary Bologna Univ. Called to the Bar, Inner Temple, 1890; travelled in North and South America, Mexico, Africa, Greenland, Iceland, China, Japan, Siberia, Newfoundland, Labrador, Palestine, etc.; Major,

Inns of Court, OTC, and subsequently Major 6th (Cyclist) Bn Royal Sussex Regt; Depôt Adjutant City Imperial Volunteers, 1900; Chairman of Governors of Hackney Downs School, 1926–36; Master Grocers' Co. 1906; Licensed Lay Reader, Diocese of Chichester, 1911. *Publications:* Stool-ball Illustrated and how to play it; List of the Wardens of the Grocers' Company from 1345–1907, with MS notes; (part) Will Adams, the Pilot-Major and first Englishman to Japan. *Recreations:* stool-ball, etc. *Address:* Balneath Manor, near Lewes. *Clubs:* Carlton, Royal Automobile, MCC.

Died 18 Feb. 1942.

GRANTLEY, 5th Baron *cr* 1782; **John Richard Brinsley Norton,** DL, JP, FSA; Baron of Markenfield, 1782; *b* Florence, 1 Oct. 1855; *s* of 4th Baron and Maria, *d* of Signor Federigo, Capri; *S* father, 1877; *m* 1st, 1879, Katharine (*d* 1897), *d* of W. H. McVickar, New York; one *s* three *d*; 2nd, 1899, Alice, (*d* 1942), 2nd *d* of late Viscount Ranelagh. *Educ:* Harrow; Dresden. Owns about 520 acres. *Recreations:* shooting, fishing, collects ancient and modern coins and other antiquities. *Heir:* s Hon. R. H. Brinsley Norton. *Address:* Weeke Manor, Winchester. *T:* Winchester 192; Markenfield Hall, Ripon. *Club:* White's.

Died 5 Aug. 1943.

GRANVILLE-BARKER, Harley Granville, Hon. DLitt (Oxon); LLD (Edin.); LittD (Reading); FRSL and member of its Academic Committee; Director, British Institute, University of Paris, 1937–39; Visiting Professor, Yale, 1940; Harvard, 1941–43, 1944, lecturer 1945; *b* London, 1877; *s* of Albert James Barker and Mary Elisabeth Bozzi-Granville; *m* Helen, *d* of I. E. and Ellen Huntington Gates, of New York. *Publications:* Prunella (with Laurence Housman), 1906; A National Theatre (with William Archer), 1907; Three Plays, 1909 (The Marrying of Ann Leete, 1901; The Voysey Inheritance, 1905; Waste, 1907); The Madras House, 1910; Anatol (a paraphrase from the German of Arthur Schnitzler); Souls on Fifth, 1916; The Red Cross in France, 1916; an English version of Sacha Guitry's Deburau; Three Short Plays (Rococo, Vote by Ballot, Farewell to the Theatre), 1917; The Harlequinade (with Dion Clayton Calthrop), 1918; The Exemplary Theatre, 1922; The Secret Life, 1923; Doctor Knock (from the French of Jules Romains); Prefaces to Shakespeare, Series one, 1927, two, 1929, three, 1936, and four, 1945; Henry V to Hamlet (British Academy Lecture, 1925); His Majesty, 1928; On Dramatic Method, 1931 (the Clark Lectures for 1930); The Study of Drama (Cambridge Inaugural lecture), 1934; on Poetry in Drama (Romanes Lecture), 1937; The Perennial Shakespeare (Broadcast National Lecture), 1937; Quality (Presidential Address to the English Association, 1938); The Use of the Drama (Spencer Trask lectures, Princeton, 1944); editor (with G. B. Harrison) of The Companion to Shakespeare Studies; and author (with Helen Granville-Barker) of the following English versions of Spanish plays: by G. Martinez Sierra, The Romantic Young Lady, Wife to a Famous Man, The Kingdom of God, The Two Shepherds, 1923; Take Two from One, 1931; by Joaquin and Serafin Alvarez Quintero: The Women have their Way, A Hundred Years Old, Fortunato, The Lady from Alfaqueque, 1927, Love Passes By, Don Abel wrote a Tragedy, Peace and Quiet, Doña Clarines, 1932. *Address:* 18 Place des États-Unis, Paris, XVIme. *Clubs:* Athenæum, Garrick; Cercle de l'Union, Travellers', Paris; Century, New York.

Died 31 Aug. 1946.

GRANVILLE-BARKER, Helen; author; *d* of I. E. Gates and E. M. Huntington-Gates; *m* 1918, Harley Granville-Barker (*d* 1946). *Publications:* Novels: Ada, 1923; Wives and Celebrities, 1926; Living Mirrors, 1928; Come, Julia, 1931; Moon in Scorpio, 1932; Traitor Angel, 1935; The Locked Book, an anthology, 1936. Poems: Folk Songs from the Spanish; Songs in Cities and Gardens; Cities Remembered, 1939;

Nineteen Poems, 1944. Plays: translated from the Spanish (with Harley Granville-Barker), The Romantic Young Lady; The Kingdom of God, etc., by Gregorius Martinez-Sierra; The Women have their Way; A Hundred Years Old; Fortunato; The Lady from Alfaqueque; Love Passes By; Don Abel Wrote a Tragedy; Peace and Quiet; Doña Clarines, by S. and J. Alvarez-Quintero. *Address:* 18 Place des États-Unis, Paris, France. *Clubs:* English-Speaking Union; Colony (New York); St Cloud Country, Union Interalliée (Paris).

Died 16 Feb. 1950.

GRATTAN-BELLEW, Lt-Col Sir Charles Christopher, 4th Bt *cr* 1838; MC; late King's Royal Rifle Corps Reserve; *b* 23 Aug. 1887; *s* of Sir Henry Grattan-Bellew and Lady Sophia Maria Elizabeth Forbes (*d* 1942), *d* of 7th Earl of Granard; *S* father 1942; *m* 1923, Maureen Peyton, *niece* and *adopted d* of late Sir Thomas Segrave, Shenfield, Essex; one *s* one *d*. *Educ:* Oratory School; RMC, Sandhurst. Served European War, 1914–18 (MC, Brevet-Major). Served OC Troopship, 1941–46. *Recreations:* hunting, fishing. *Heir:* *s* Henry Charles, *b* 12 May 1933. *Address:* The Bungalow, Malahide, Co. Dublin. *T:* Malahide 19. *Club:* Kildare Street (Dublin).

Died 6 Nov. 1948.

GRATTAN-BELLEW, Sir Henry Christopher, 3rd Bt *cr* 1838; JP, DL; late Capt. 5th Connaught Rangers; late Lieut 5th Dragoon Guards; *b* 1 June 1860; *s* of Thomas Arthur Grattan-Bellew and Pauline, *d* and *co-heiress* of Henry Grattan, MP; *S* uncle, 1867; *m* 1885, Lady Sophia Maria Elizabeth Forbes, *d* of 7th Earl of Granard; three *s* three *d*. *Educ:* Beaumont; Downside. *Heir:* *s* Charles Christopher, MC, Lt-Col late King's Royal Rifle Corps [*b* 23 Aug. 1887; *m* 1923, Maureen Peyton; one *s* (*b* 12 May 1933) one *d*]. *Address:* Tennehinch, Enniskerry, Co. Limerick. *Club:* St James's.

Died 20 Jan. 1942.

GRATTAN-DOYLE, Sir Nicholas, Kt 1924; DL, JP Co. Durham; JP Hertfordshire and Middlesex; *b* 18 Aug. 1862; 3rd *s* of John Doyle, Ballyroe House, Co. Wexford; *m* 1st, 1899, Kathryn Deering Nevins (*d* 1902), Holly Hall, East Orange, New Jersey; 2nd, 1907, Gwendoline F. Mackusick, Lyttel Hall, Surrey; two *s* two *d*. *Educ:* privately; St Aidan's Academy, Enniscorthy. One of the founders of the Northern Tariff Reform Federation and hon. Secretary since its formation, 1905; Joint Chairman Tynside Irish Brigade Committee until Brigade taken over by War Office; Joint Chairman Newcastle War Savings Committee; Freeman of the City of London; Member of the Guild of Feltmakers; Deputy Director Education and Propaganda, Ministry of Food, 1918; contested Gateshead as Unionist, Jan. 1910; MP (U) Newcastle-on-Tyne (North), 1918–40; Director Northern Newspapers Co. Ltd. *Recreations:* hunting, golf, and all sports. *Address:* Highfield, Hadley Wood, Barnet. *T:* Barnet 3113. *Clubs:* Carlton, Royal Automobile.

Died 14 July 1941.

GRAVES, Charles L.; *b* 15 Dec. 1856; 4th *s* of late Right Rev. Charles Graves, DD, Hon. DCL (Oxford), FRS, Bishop of Limerick and Selina, *e d* of John Cheyne, MD, Physician Gen. to the Forces in Ireland; *m* 1889, Alice (*d* 1936), *e d* of late Lieut-Col G. H. Grey. *Educ:* Marlborough College; Christ Church, Oxford. Assistant editor of the Spectator, 1899–1917; member of Punch Staff, 1902–36, Assistant Editor, 1928–36; retired, 1936. *Publications:* The Hawarden Horace, 1894; More Hawarden Horace, 1896; Life and Letters of Sir George Grove, 1903; Humours of the Fray, 1907; Life and Letters of Alexander Macmillan, 1910; Party Portraits, 1910; The Brain of the Nation, 1912; War's Surprises, 1917; Lauds and Libels, 1918; Mr Punch's History of the Great War, 1919; Horace Odes, Book V, English versions, with Rudyard Kipling, 1920; New Times and Old Rhymes, 1921; Punch's History of Modern England (4 vols), 1921, 1922; More Lauds and Libels, 1925; Life of Sir Hubert Parry (2 vols), 1926; Eulogies and Elegies, 1927; and (in collaboration with E. V. Lucas) Wisdom while you Wait, Signs of the Times, Hustled History, etc. *Club:* Athenæum.

Died 17 April 1944.

GRAVES, Rt Rev. Frederick Rogers; *b* Auburn, NY, 24 Oct. 1858; *s* of Samuel S. and Elizabeth Anna Graves; *m* 1883, J. H. Roberts; one *s* three *d*. *Educ:* Hobart College; General Theological Seminary of New York. Missionary in China since 1881; Deacon, 1881; Priest, 1882; Missionary Bishop, Shanghai, 1893–1937; translator of Theological and Biblical works into Chinese; Professor in Divinity School; DD Hobart College, General Theol. Seminary 1893, Oxford, 1908. *Publications:* Eight Books Gingham's Antiquities; Commentary on Isaiah; Commentary on the Psalms; numerous smaller works, all in Chinese. *Address:* c/o St John's University, Shanghai, China.

Died 17 May 1940.

GRAVES, George; *b* London, 1 Jan. 1876. First appearance on stage at Portsmouth; London stage, 1898. *Publication:* Gaieties and Gravities, 1931. *Club:* Savage.

Died 2 April 1949.

GRAVES, John George, Hon. LLD Sheffield; Alderman and JP for City of Sheffield, and Chairman of J. G. Graves, Ltd; *b* Horncastle, Lincolnshire, 22 Aug. 1865; *e s* of Thomas Graves; *m* 1891, Lucy, *e d* of James Dawson, Roxby, Lincolnshire; one *d*. *Educ:* Grammar School, Batley, Yorks. Founder of Mail Order firm of J. G. Graves, Ltd; Lord Mayor of Sheffield, 1926; Hon. Freedom of City of Sheffield, 1929, in recognition of public services and many valuable benefactions to the city. *Recreations:* books, works of art, travel, country walks. *Address:* Riverdale, Ranmoor, Sheffield 10. *T:* Sheffield 31713. *Clubs:* National Liberal; The Club, Sheffield.

Died 18 July 1945.

GRAY, Baroness, 22nd in line *cr* 1445; **Ethel Eveleen Gray-Campbell;** *b* 16 Jan. 1866; *d* of Eveleen Smith, Baroness Gray (*d* 1918); *S* brother, 1919; *m* 1888, Henry Tufnell Gray-Campbell (*d* 1945), *s* of J. T. Campbell and Lady Anne Campbell; one *s*. *Heir:* *g s* Master of Gray, *b* 3 July 1931. *Address:* 73 Pont Street, SW1.

Died 2 Oct. 1946.

GRAY, Master of; Lindsay Stuart Campbell-Gray, MC; Major, late RA; *b* 4 May 1894; *er s* of Baroness Gray; *m* 1930, Doreen McClymont, *er d* of late Cyril Tubbs; two *s* two *d*. *Educ:* Eton; Magdalen College, Oxford. Served European War, 1914–19 (despatches, MC); ADC to Governor of Nigeria, 1924–25; ADO Nigerian Administrative Service 1925–27. *Recreations:* hunting, steeplechasing, and polo. *Clubs:* Naval and Military, Leander.

Died 7 Sept. 1945.

GRAY, Arthur Wellesley; Minister of Lands, British Columbia, since 1933; Minister of Municipal Affairs since 1934; *b* 6 Oct. 1876; *s* of Thomas W. Gray and Hyslop Baird; *m* 1913, Margaret H. A. Davidson (decd), Kirkcaldy, Scotland; two *d*. *Educ:* New Westminster Public and High Schools. Alderman, New Westminster, BC, 1907–12; Mayor, 1913–19, 1927–33; Government Commission South Vancouver, 1921–23; BC Legislature since 1927. *Recreations:* lacrosse, football, cricket. *Address:* Parliament Buildings, Victoria, BC, Canada. *Clubs:* Westminster, BPOE No. 4, New Westminster.

Died 7 May 1944.

GRAY, Lt-Col Clive Osric Vere, CMG 1919; DSO 1916; one of HM's Body Guard of Hon. Corps of Gentlemen at Arms since 1932; *b* 7 July 1882; *s* of Evelyn Gray, Indian Civil Service, and Violet, *d* of General Wilkins, RE; *m* 1908, Vere, *d* of late Sir Elwin Palmer,

KCB, KCMG, Governor of National Bank of Egypt; one *s* one *d*. *Educ:* Cheltenham College; Sandhurst. Seaforth Highlanders, 1901; served Frontier Expedition against Mohmands, 1908, ADC to Sir James Willcocks (dangerously wounded, medal with clasp); European War, 1914–18 (despatches eight times, Bt Lt-Col, CMG, DSO, Chevalier Legion of Honour).

Died 3 Dec. 1945.

GRAY, Donald, MA; Headmaster Bootham School, York, since 1927; *b* 5 May 1893; *s* of late Albert A. Gray, MD, Glasgow, and Mabel Henderson; *m* 1st, Esther S. Henderson (*d* 1922); 2nd, J. Kathleen Wright; three *s*. *Educ:* Glasgow Academy; Bootham School, York; Glasgow University; Merton College, Oxford. *Address:* Bootham School, York.

Died 2 Aug. 1943.

GRAY, Lt-Col George Douglas, CBE 1925; MD; late Medical Attaché, HM Foreign Office, and RAMC; *s* of late Robert Collie Gray, JP, Edinburgh; *m* 1900, Lucy Agnes, RRC, *d* of late Charles Harrison; one *s* one *d*. *Educ:* Edinburgh University, MB CM, 1894, MD Hons, 1897. Served British Central Africa, 1894–98 (medal with clasp) and British East Africa, 1899 (medal with clasp); Ashanti, 1900 (medal with clasp); European War, 1914–19 (despatches thrice); Principal Medical Officer, British Central Africa Administration, 1897–1902; Physician to British Legation, Peking, 1902–26; received a letter of thanks and an Imperial gift from the Chinese Throne for services rendered during the Plague Epidemic, 1910–11; appointed British Delegate to the International Pneumonic Plague Conference, Manchuria, 1911; British Delegate to the International Finance Commission for Administration of Maritime Customs Surtax for Famine Relief, 1922; during European War raised and commanded the Chinese General Hospital (despatches twice); received the Medaille d'Honneur en Argent, and Chinese Order of Wen Hu for war services, also Order (with sash) of Chia Ho; Hon. Member Royal Central Asian Society. *Publication:* All about the Soya Bean: In Agriculture, Commerce and Industry, 1936. *Address:* Dunallan, Dalkeith, Midlothian. *Clubs:* New, Edinburgh.

Died 12 Sept. 1946.

GRAY, George Kruger, CBE 1938; ARCA, FSA 1921; *b* Kensington, 25 Dec. 1880; *s* of late Edwin Charles Kruger of St Heliers and Frances Hester Harris; *m* 1918, Audrey Gordon, *d* of Ven. J. H. Gray, DD, Archdeacon of Hong-Kong; one *s*. *Educ:* Merchant Taylors' School, Gt Crosby; Royal College of Art (Royal Exhibition Scholar). Landscape and portrait painter (water-colour); designer and painter of stained glass and of ecclesiastical work, including altar-pieces, war memorials, and seals and other heraldic work of all kinds; exhibitor at Royal Academy, New Gallery, Paris, Ghent, etc.; designer of the collar of the Order of the British Empire, the Processional Cross of the Archbishop of Wales, the two maces of the Ulster Parliament, the Heraldic Panels for gates of King George's Playing Fields, and designer and sculptor of the coinage of Union South Africa, the badge of the Knights Bachelor, Reverse of Great Seal of Ulster, the new Great Seal, George VI, of the four new Baronet's Badges, Imperial Silver Coinages of Georve V and George VI, New Coins for Commonwealth of Australia and Dominion of Canada; several Colonial Flag Badges, and of the official seals of the Union of South Africa, The Province of Nova Scotia and Northern Rhodesia, New Silver Coinages of S Rhodesia, 1933, New Zealand, 1934, and Mauritius, 1934, Exchequer Seal, 1938, Great Seal for Canada, 1939, etc.; Historical Costumes and Heraldry, Aldershot Tattoo, 1935, 1936, 1937, 1938 and 1939; Designer of Her Majesty's Personal Message to Householders, 1940, Admiralty Badge for M/S and A/S, 1940; Fiery-Cross War Savings Poster and Stamp, 1941; served in the 2nd Artists Rifles

and RE Camouflage School; Member of the Arts and Crafts Society and Art Workers' Guild; Liveryman, Worshipful Company of Glaziers, 1936; Freeman of the City of London, 1937; Officer of the Order of St John; Jubilee Medal, 1935; Coronation Medal, 1937. *Publications:* Vanity Fair cartoons, posters, book illustrations. *Address:* The Studio, 11 Addison Crescent, W14; Three Chimneys, Fittleworth, Pulborough, Sussex. *T:* Western 1544 and 3553.

Died 2 May 1943.

GRAY, Howard Alexander, MA; *b* Aberdeen, 28 Jan. 1870; *e s* of Henry Gray, merchant, Aberdeen; *m* Harriet Emily, *y d* of late Henry Jones, Birmingham, 1898; two *s*. *Educ:* Aberdeen Grammar School; University of Aberdeen and University of Edinburgh. MA (Aberdeen) 1888, with Honours in Mental Philosophy; Seafield Gold Medallist in English Literature. A working journalist since 1890; engaged successively on the editorial staffs of Scottish Leader (Edinburgh) Northern Daily News and Northern Evening News (Aberdeen), and Birmingham Daily Mail; assistant-editor of Birmingham Daily Post, 1894–99; editor of the Birmingham Daily Argus and Birmingham Evening Despatch, 1899–1902; leader-writer, Pall Mall Gazette, 1902–23; assistant-editor and leader-writer of Observer, 1920–41. *Recreations:* walking, fishing. *Address:* 208 Bath Road, Hounslow. *T:* Hounslow 1624. *Club:* Devonshire.

Died 3 Oct. 1942.

GRAY, James Hugo; Professor of Anatomy in University of London and Head of Department of Anatomy at St Mary's Hospital Medical School, London, since 1941; *b* Adelaide, South Australia, 14 March 1909; *s* of James Tinsley and Mary Hannah Gray of South Australia; *m* 1934, Leonore Elizabeth, *d* of Rev. Wiebusch of South Australia; three *d*. *Educ:* St Peter's Collegiate School, Adelaide; St Mark's University Residential College, University of Adelaide. MB, BS, 1932, Adelaide. Demonstrator of Anatomy, University of Adelaide, 1934; Cancer Research Fellow and Hon. Demonstrator of Anatomy, St Bartholomew's Hospital, London, 1935–36; Demonstrator and Senior Demonstrator of Anatomy, University College, London, 1936–41; MD, Adelaide, 1939. *Publications:* Research papers on physical anthropology of Australian Aborigines, 1930–1936; Research papers in British Empire Cancer Campaign Reports, in British Journal of Surgery, and in Journal of Anatomy on lymphatic spread of cancer and on growth and regeneration of lymphatic vessels, 1935–1940. *Recreation:* field natural history. *Address:* 24 Christchurch Mount, Epsom, Surrey. *T:* Epsom 9625.

Died 20 Dec. 1941.

GRAY, Lt-Col John Anselm Samuel, CMG 1918; DSO 1916; *b* 22 July 1874; *m e d* of Alexander Gray, Cape Town; one *s* one *d*. *Educ:* privately. Served South African War, Dragoon Guards, Colonial Division and Imperial Yeomanry, 1899–1902 (Queen's and King's medals 5 clasps); West Africa, Southern Nigeria, 1907–13; with Army in France, Sept. 1914–March 1919 (despatches six times); Chevalier of the Legion of Honour; Assistant Director, Ministry of Transport, 1919–21. *Recreation:* fishing. *Address:* 25 Grosvenor Place, SW1. *Club:* Junior Carlton.

Died 26 Sept. 1950.

GRAY, Milner, CBE 1937; *b* Luton, 1871; *s* of Rev. Arch. Campbell Gray; *m* 1902, Elizabeth Eleanor, *d* of Mark Samuel Luck, Lewisham; no *c*. *Educ:* Greenwich. MP (L) Mid Beds Parliamentary Division 1929–31; Parliamentary Secretary, Ministry of Labour, 1931. *Address:* Beacon Lodge, Kinsbourne Green, Harpenden. *T:* Harpenden 951. *Club:* National Liberal.

Died 10 April 1943.

GRAY, Lt-Col Sir Vivian Beaconsfield, KBE 1945; CBE 1939; MC; Chairman of Middle East Board of Directors of UKCC and General Manager, Associated British Manufacturers (Egypt) Ltd; *b* 25 May 1885; 4th *s* of James Cooke Gray; *m* 1911, Lucy, *d* of James Broadfoot, Jordanhill, Glasgow; one *s* one *d*. *Educ:* Blairlodge School, Stirlingshire. Served European War, commanded at end of war 2nd Bn The Cameronians (The Scottish Rifles) (twice wounded); in Egypt since 1920; Past President, British Chamber of Commerce in Egypt; Grand Officer Order of the Nile. *Recreations:* golf, fishing, shooting. *Address:* Zamalek, Gezireh, Cairo. *Clubs:* Turf, Cairo.

Died 16 March 1948.

GRAY, Major William Bain, CBE 1935; Regional Officer for Health Services, Ministry of Health, No. 1 Region; *b* 1886; *s* of George Gray and Jessie Hossack; *m* 1916, Ursula Elizabeth Campbell Johnstone; no *c*. *Educ:* George Watson's College; University of Edinburgh; New College, Oxford. MA (Edin.), First Class in History and Gladstone Prize; BLitt (Oxon); Carnegie Research Fellow; PhD (Edin.). Held educational appointments in Scotland and England; 2nd Lieut 6th Bn The Royal Scots, and served in Territorial and Regular Army till 1923; General Staff, Aldershot Command, 1918–23; Major, Army Educational Corps, 1920; R of O 1923; Colonial Service, 1924; Director of Education, British Guiana; member of Court of Policy (*i.e.* legislature) and British Guiana Constitution Commission, 1927; Member of first executive and legislative councils under new constitution, 1928; Chairman of many Government Commissions and Committees appointed to report on Gold and Diamond Industries; Electoral Districts; Unemployment; Reorganisation of Medical Services, etc.; acted as Colonial Secretary and Governor's Deputy on many occasions, 1928–38; Administrator St Vincent, 1938–41; acted as Governor of the Windward Islands, May to July 1939; Governor and Commander-in-Chief of St Helena, 1941–46. *Publications:* historical and other articles. *Address:* c/o Cox's and King's Branch, Lloyds Bank, 6 Pall Mall, SW1.

Died 3 Feb. 1949.

GRAY, William Forbes, FRSEdin, FSAScot; author, journalist; Vice-President of Old Edinburgh Club, 1947, and Editor of its Publications, 1923–36; *b* Edinburgh, 14 April 1874; *m*; one *d*. On literary staff of Edinburgh Evening News, 1894–98; News Editor, British Weekly, 1898–1905; Sub-editor, British Monthly, 1903–05; Acting Editor, Scottish Review, 1906–09; Editor, Sir Walter Scott Quarterly, 1927–28; Editor of Transactions of East Lothian Antiquarian and Field Naturalists' Society, 1937–45; contributor to leading journals and magazines; formerly Vice-President of Edinburgh Bibliographical Society; prepared Bibliographies on various subjects. *Publications:* Introduction to Alexander Smith's A Summer in Skye, 1912; Edited Books that Count: a Dictionary of Useful Books, 2nd ed., 1923; The Poets Laureate of England: Their History and their Odes, 1914; Some Old Scots Judges, 1914; History of Scottish Union and National Insurance Company, 1924; An Edinburgh Miscellany; Chapters mainly in the Social and Literary History of the City, 1925; A Printing House of Old and New Edinburgh, 1925; Catalogue of Gray Library, Haddington: Introduction and Descriptive Notes, 1929; Scott in Sunshine and Shadow: The Tribute of his Friends, 1931; Five Score: A Group of Famous Centenarians, 1931; Scott Centenary Handbook, 1932; Index Vol. to Publications of Old Edinburgh Club, 1936; partly compiled, and wrote Introduction to Bibliography of East Lothian, 1936; Historic Churches of Edinburgh, 1940; Edited and wrote introduction to Comments and Characters, by John Buchan, 1940; East Lothian Biographies, 1941; A Short History of Haddington, 1944; abridged and edited with notes, Henry (Lord) Cockburn's Memorials of His Time, 1945; Short History of Edinburgh Castle, 1948;

(conjointly with Miss Margaret Tait) George Square: Annals of an Edinburgh Locality, 1948; numerous memoirs in Dictionary of National Biography, Nelson's Encyclopædia, etc. *Recreations:* antiquities and book-collecting. *Address:* 8 Mansionhouse Road, Edinburgh. *T:* 41657.

Died 12 May 1950.

GRAYBURN, Sir Vandeleur Molyneux, Kt 1937; Chief Manager, Hong-Kong and Shanghai Banking Corporation, Hong Kong; *b* 28 July 1881; *s* of late William Echlin Grayburn and Margaret Ellen Markham; *m* 1st, Ruth Danvers Higgs; 2nd, Minnie Doris Robson (who obtained a decree nisi, 1939); one *s* one *d*; 3rd, Muriel Mary, *e d* of C. B. Mellor, Chester. *Educ:* Denstone College. 41 years in Hong-Kong and Shanghai Banking Corporation. *Recreations:* golf and tennis. *Address:* Hong-Kong.

Died 21 Aug. 1943.

GREAVES, John Ernest, CBE 1918; JP, TD, DL Co. Merioneth; High Sheriff, 1884; High Sheriff of Carnarvonshire, 1885; Lord-Lt Carnarvon 1886–1933; late Hon. Col 6th Batt. Royal Welsh Fusiliers; President, Carnarvonshire Territorial Association; Chairman, Quarter Sessions, 1890–1929; *b* 1847; *s* of John Whitehead Greaves, Plas Weunydd, and Edith, *d* of G. Steadman, Pakenham Manor; *m* 1875, Marianne (*d* 1934), *d* of late E. Rigby, MD; one *d*. *Address:* Broneifion, Criccieth, N Wales. *Club:* Royal Automobile.

Died 27 Feb. 1945.

GREAVES-LORD, Sir Walter, Kt 1927; KC 1919; Member of Gray's Inn and Middle Temple; Bencher of Gray's Inn, 1920; Treasurer, 1933; Vice-Treasurer, 1934; Member Council of Legal Education, 1924; Chancellor of the Primrose League, 1926–27; a Freeman of the City of London; Member of the Court of the Feltmakers Company; Master, 1933–34; *b* Sept. 1878; *s* of Simeon Lord, of Ince, Lancashire, and Southport; *m* 1903, Caroline Ethel, *o d* of late Sir Albert Stephenson; one *s* one *d*. *Educ:* Wigan Grammar School; Victoria University, Manchester. Tyrer Prizeman in Common Law and winner of Thompson Yates Cup for English Oration, University College, Liverpool; LLB Victoria, 1899; Arden Scholar, Gray's Inn, 1900. Called to Bar, Gray's Inn, 1900; joined Northern Circuit; Recorder of Manchester, 1925–35; Judge of High Court of Justice, King's Bench Division, 1935–40; retired, 1940; contested (U) Ince, Lancashire, Jan. and Dec. 1910; MP (C) Norwood Division of Lambeth, 1922–35. *Recreations:* golf, motoring. *Address:* Sanderstead, Surrey.

Died 18 June 1942.

GREEN, Albert; JP; *b* 3 Nov. 1874; *m* 1900, *d* of Godfrey Turner, Derby; two *s*. *Educ:* Local Schools. Manufacturer at Derby; Member Derby Council, 1911; Mayor, 1915–16; Alderman, 1917; MP (Ind U) Derby Boro', 1918–22. *Club:* Eccentric.

Died 25 Sept. 1941.

GREEN, Arthur George, FRS; MSc, FIC, FCS; formerly Director of Research, British Dyestuff Corporation; late Professor of Applied Chemistry (Dyestuffs), University of Leeds; *b* 1864; *s* of late William John Green, FRIBA, architect; *m* Constance Fanny (*d* 1941), *d* of late Henry Charles Heath, miniature painter to Queen Victoria; two *d*. *Educ:* Lancing College, Sussex; University College, London. On leaving college, entered works of Brooke, Simpson, and Spiller, aniline colour manufacturers, of London, as research and manufacturing chemist; chief chemist and manager of the colour works of the Clayton Aniline Co. of Manchester, 1894–1901. Inventor of a number of new coal-tar colouring-matters; Perkin Gold Medallist and Research Medallist of the Dyers Company of London; has held advisory appointments to Dye-stuff manufacturing Firms in England, United States, France, Germany, and Italy;

Member of Dyestuffs Development Committee of Board of Trade, Industrial Solvents Committee of Medical Research Council. *Publications:* A Systematic Survey of the Organic Colouring-Matters, 1905; The Analysis of Dyestuffs and their Identification in Dyed and Coloured Materials, 1915; Article upon Synthetic Dyes in the Encyclopædia Britannica. Also a large number of researches on the chemistry of colouring-matters published in the scientific journals. *Address:* Conarth, Ashley Drive, Walton-on-Thames, Surrey. *T:* Walton-on-Thames 523. *Club:* English Speaking Union.

Died 12 Sept. 1941.

GREEN, Rt Rev. Arthur Vincent, MA, LLD; *b* Albury, Surrey, 1857; *s* of Rev. Samuel Dutton Green, Colac, Victoria; *m* 1880, Matilda, *d* of Ven. J. K. Tucker, Archdeacon of Beechworth and Sale; one *s*. *Educ:* Trinity Coll.; Univ. of Melbourne; Univ. of Sydney. Ordained, 1880; Curate of St Andrews, Brighton, and St Peter's, Melbourne, 1880–85; Incumbent of Holy Trinity, Maldon, 1885–88; St Paul's, Geelong, 1889–90; Archdeacon of Ballarat, and Vicar of Christ Church Pro-Cathedral, 1890–94; Examining Chaplain to Bishop of Ballarat, 1891–94; Bishop of Grafton and Armidale, 1894–1900; of Ballarat, 1900–15; Canon of St Paul's Cathedral, Melbourne, 1916–23; Theological Lecturer, Trinity College, Melbourne University, 1920–43. *Publications:* The Ephesian Canonical Writings (Moorhouse Lectures for 1910), 1910; Australian Sermons, 1914; Australian Sermons (2nd series), 1930. *Address:* Lis Escop, Heidelberg, Victoria, Australia.

Died 24 Sept. 1944.

GREEN, Rt Rev. Charles Alfred Howell, DD; DCL; Bishop of Bangor since 1928; Archbishop of Wales, 1934–44; *b* 19 Aug. 1864; *e s* of late Rev. A. J. M. Green, MA; *m* 1899, Katharine Mary, *e d* of Rt Hon. 1st Baron Merthyr of Senghenydd, GCVO; no *c*. *Educ:* Charterhouse School; Keble College, Oxford (Classical Scholar). Librarian and President of the Oxford Union Society; Degree with honours in Literæ Humaniores, 1887; Curate of Aberdare, 1888–93; Vicar, 1893–1914; Rural Dean, 1902–14; Archdeacon of Monmouth, and Canon Residentiary of Llandaff Cathedral, 1914–21; Bishop of Monmouth, 1921–28; Member of the School Board, 1898–1903; elected Proctor for the Clergy in Convocation, 1913; appointed a General Commissioner of Income Tax for the Division of Miskin, 1913; Member of the Court of Governors of the University College of South Wales, 1914; Member of the Theological Board of the University of Wales, 1915; Member of Council and of Court of Governors, of University College of North Wales, 1933; Hon. Fellow of Keble College, Oxford, from 1935; Member of the Council and Court of Governors of the National Library of Wales, 1936; BD 1907. DD 1911, BCL 1938, DCL 1938, Oxford; Select Preacher, University of Cambridge, 1923; Select Preacher, University of Oxford, 1927 and 1928. *Publications:* Notes on Churches in the Diocese of Llandaff; The Church's Title to its Endowments; The Relation of the Church of England to the Church of Rome in Pre-Reformation Times; The Setting of the Constitution of the Church in Wales, 1937, etc.; contributor to Episcopacy, Ancient and Modern; several Welsh articles in Y Geninen and Yr Haul. *Recreation:* travelling. *Address:* Bishopscourt, Bangor, North Wales. *Club:* Oxford and Cambridge.

Died 7 May 1944.

GREEN, Engr Rear Adm. Sir (Donald) Percy, KCMG 1919; CB 1916; RN, retd; *b* 12 March 1866; 4th *s* of S. R. Green, Sandal; *m* 1928, Mildred Isobel, *d* of David Thomas, Councillor of Cowbridge, Glamorgan. *Educ:* private school, Folkestone. Joined HMS Marlborough Training School for Engineer Officers, RN, 1881; has had a great deal to do with training naval cadets as follows: HMS Brittania, 1894–99; RN College,

Dartmouth, 1907; HMS Cornwall, 1908–10; also engineer cadets, RN College, Keyham, 1901–04; HMS Lion, 1910–15; in charge of machinery; Engineer Captain on Staff of Vice-Admiral Commanding Battle Cruiser Fleet; served European War, 1914–19; in the Lion during the actions, 28 Aug. 1914, and 24 Jan. 1915 (specially promoted); in the Tiger during Battle of Jutland Bank; on staff of Commander-in-Chief, Grand Fleet (Sir David Beatty in Queen Elizabeth), 1916–19; retired list, 1922. *Recreations:* Rugby football, cricket, racquets, polo, golf. *Address:* Glenleigh, Northfield Road, Minehead.

Died 7 March 1950.

GREEN, Col Sir Edward Arthur Lycett, 3rd Bt *cr* 1886; TD; *b* 1 April 1886; *e s* of Sir Lycett Green, 2nd Bt, and Ethel Mary, OBE (*d* 1934), 2nd *d* of A. Wilson, of Tranby Croft, Hull; *S* father 1940; *m* 1909, Elizabeth (from whom he obtained a divorce, 1922), *d* of David Williams; two *s*. *Educ:* Eton. *Heir:* *s* Edward Stephen Lycett [*b* 1910; *m* 1935, Constance Mary, *d* of Ven. H. S. Radcliffe; one *d*]. *Address:* Ken Hill, Snettisham, King's Lynn. *T:* Snettisham 202. *Clubs:* White's, Cavalry.

Died 4 March 1941.

GREEN, George Alfred Lawrence; Editor or Editor-in-Chief, Cape Argus, Cape Town, 1910–37; retired, 1937; *b* Portsmouth; *s* of late G. L. Green; *m* 1899, Katherine Muriel Bell, *d* of Rev. G. E. Bell, Vicar Henley-in-Arden; one *s* two *d*. *Educ:* Portsea Diocesan Grammar School. Settled in S Africa, 1894, joining staff of Cape Times; Editor Diamond Fields Advertiser, Kimberley, 1898–1910; MP for Kimberley, 1908–10; awarded King's Medal for service in connection with Union in S Africa; Delegate to Empire Press Union Conferences, Australia, 1925, United Kingdom, 1930, South Africa, 1935. *Publications:* The Siege of Kimberley; An Editor Looks Back: South African and other Memories; Juta & Co., C Town. *Address:* Cape Argus Office, Cape Town. *Club:* City (Cape Town).

Died 9 Aug. 1949.

GREEN, Lt-Col Harold Philip; DL Beds; JP Berks; Chairman J. W. Green Ltd, Luton Brewery; *b* 2 Dec. 1877; *s* of late John William Green, Luton; *m* 1930, Joyce, 2nd *d* of late His Honour Sir Thomas Colpitts Granger and *widow* of Commander C. G. Naylor, RN. *Educ:* Bedford. Joined 3rd Bn Bedfordshire Regt, 1898; served European War, 1914–18, with 1st Bn Bedfordshire Regt and X Corps HQ; Lt-Col 1918; High Sheriff, Berkshire, 1943. *Recreations:* shooting, tennis. *Address:* Queens Hill, Ascot, Berks. *T:* Ascot 160. *Clubs:* Carlton, Bath; Travellers', Paris.

Died 25 March 1944.

GREEN, Rev. James, CMG 1918; VD; Ex-President NSW Conference, and Senior Methodist Chaplain, Australian Defence Forces; *b* 1868; *s* of Wm and Isabella Green, Newcastle-on-Tyne; *m*; two *s*. *Educ:* Rutherford College, Newcastle-on-Tyne. Minister in the Methodist Church of Australia, various parishes in Newcastle, NSW, and Sydney districts; served as Chaplain during the South African War in 1st Bushmen's Contingent and the 1st Australian Commonwealth Horse Queen's medal 5 bars, king's medal 2 bars); served as senior Chaplain with the Australian Imperial Force in Egypt, Gallipoli, and France (Gallipoli Star, CMG); served four years as Senior Chaplain with the AIF; on service within Australia during the War until 31 May 1942. *Publications:* An Australian History of the South African War (5 chapters), 1901; The Story of the Bushmen, 1901; the Selector, a novel, 1907; the Lost Echo, a novel, 1910; News from No Man's Land, a narrative of Australian campaigning in France, 1917; Through My Hospital Window, 1935. *Address:* 131 Cook Road, Centennial Park, Sydney, NSW.

Died 6 Nov. 1948.

GREEN, Adm. Sir John Frederick Ernest, KCMG 1919; CB 1916; *b* 1866; *s* of late Henry Green, Blackwall; *m* 1901, Maud Kathleen (*d* 1935), *yr d* of late Col C. McInroy, CB, Edzell. Rear-Admiral 1917; Vice-Admiral 1922; served European War, 1914–17, including Jutland Bank (CB); Senior Naval Officer, White Sea, 1918; Admiral Superintendent, Rosyth, 1920–23; and Commanding Officer, Coast of Scotland, 1922–23; retired list, 1925; Adm. retd, 1927. *Address:* The Hill House, Dunfermline, Fife. *Club:* Naval and Military.

Died 30 Oct. 1948.

GREEN, Kathleen (Mary) Haydn; *d* of Sir Frank Green, 1st Bt; *m* 1905, Henry Newton Veitch (*d* 1925), author of Sheffield Plate, its History, Manufacture, and Art, 1908. Lady Mayoress of London, 1900–01. *Publications:* The Poet's Crown, and Other Verses, privately printed in 1895; Poems, 1899; Twelve Allegories, 1901; also lyrics to songs, etc. *Address:* Ivy Cottage, Otford, Kent.

Died 25 Jan. 1944.

GREEN, Eng. Rear Adm. Sir Percy; *see* Green, Eng. Rear Adm. Sir D. P.

GREEN, Hon. Robert Francis; Senator since 1921; *b* Peterboro, Ontario, 14 Nov. 1861; *s* of Benjamin Green and Rebecca Lipsett; *m* 1889, Celia Elizabeth McDannell; one *s. Educ:* Peterboro, Ontario. Came to Winnipeg, 1882, and followed the construction of the CPR to Revelstoke; engaged in general merchandise business in the Kootenays till 1904; opened a real estate and insurance business in Victoria, under the firm name of Green and Burdick Bros, 1908; retired from firm, 1917; first Mayor of Kaslo, BC, 1893; re-elected, 1896 and 1897; representative of the Kaslo and Slocan Riding in the Local Legislature, 1898–1906; MP Kootenay, 1912–21; a Minister of the Crown, 1903–06 (Minister of Mines, Provincial Sec., Minister of Lands and Works, resigned, 1906). *Address:* Victoria, BC. *TA:* Victoria, BC. *T:* Empire 6746. *Clubs:* Union, Victoria.

Died 5 Oct. 1946.

GREEN, Walford Davis, MA; Barrister, Inner Temple; *b* 24 Aug. 1869; *e s* of late Rev. Walford Green, ex-Pres. Wesleyan Conference; *m* Annie (*d* 1940), *d* of late C. E. Carpenter; two *d. Educ:* Leys School; King's College, Cambridge. MP (C) Wednesbury, 1895–1906. *Publications:* Political Career of George Canning; William Pitt, Earl of Chatham, 1901. *Recreations:* cricket, golf. *Address:* Courtenwell, Langton, Tunbridge Wells. *Clubs:* Carlton, Constitutional.

Died 17 Nov. 1941.

GREEN, Maj.-Gen. William, CB 1937; DSO 1916; *b* 1 Aug. 1882; *s* of late Col Sir William Green, KCB; *m* 1914, Lesley Kathleen Hannaford; one *d. Educ:* Fettes College; RMC, Sandhurst. Gazetted Black Watch, 1900; Capt., 1906; Major, 1915; Bt Lt-Col, 1919; Lt-Col, 1928; Col 1931, Maj.-Gen. 1935; served S Africa, 1901–02 (Queen's medal 4 clasps); Commanded 9th Royal Scots (Temp. Lieut-Col), 1916–18; 153 Infantry Brigade (51st Highland Division), Temp. Brig.-Gen., 1918–19 (DSO and two bars, Officer Légion d'Honneur, Croix de Guerre Belge, despatches five times); passed Staff College, 1920; commanded 2nd Batt. Loyal Regt, 1928–31; General Staff Officer, 1st grade, Scottish Command, 1931–33; Commander 9th Infantry Brigade, 1933–35; Commander South-Western Area 1938–40; retired pay, 1940. *Recreations:* golf, won Army Championship, 1911 and 1921. *Address:* c/o Lloyds Bank, Cox and King's Branch, 6 Pall Mall, SW1.

Died 4 Dec. 1947.

GREEN, William Kirby, CMG 1929; retired; Member of the International Legislative Assembly for the Tangier Zone; *b* London, 5 May 1876; *s* of Sir William Kirby Green, KCMG, Diplomatic Corps, and Mary, *d* of Sir Thomas Reade, KCMG; *m* Ada Gresham Bois; three *s.*

Educ: Eton; English College, Bruges. Served in 37th Imperial Yeomanry in Boer War; went to Nyasaland in the Administrative Service under the Foreign Office, 1901; remained in the same service until he retired. *Recreations:* natural history, cricket, etc. *Address:* Tangier, Morocco.

Died 31 Jan. 1945.

GREEN-WILKINSON, Brig.-Gen. Lewis Frederic, CMG 1919; DSO 1917; Hon. Brigadier-General; *b* 1865; *e s* of late Lt-Gen. F. Green Wilkinson, CB, and Annie, *e d* of William Cuthbert, Beaufront Castle, Hexham; *m* 1904, Hon. Sarah May Trench (*d* 1934), *sister* of 3rd Baron Ashtown; two *d. Educ:* Wellington College; Sandhurst; Staff College. Served with Rifle Brigade, 1886–88 and 1888–89; Burmese expeditions; Dongola expedition, 1896 (4th class Medjidieh); Nile expedition, 1897 (4th class Osmanieh); S African War, 1899–1902 (Brevet Major); Private Secretary to Duke of Connaught (Inspector General of the Forces), 1906–07; Major Rifle Brigade, 1903–08; served European War, 1914–19 (Brevet Lt-Col, Brevet Col, DSO, CMG, Chevalier Legion of Honour); commanding a Brigade, 1916–19. *Recreations:* shooting, fishing, farming. *Address:* 10 Westminster Mansions, SW1. *T:* Abbey 6564. *Club:* Royal Empire Society.

Died 11 April 1950.

GREENE, Charles Henry, MA, FRHistS; *b* 12 Jan. 1865; 2nd *s* of late William Greene, of East Lodge, Bedford; *m* 1895, Marion Raymond, *d* of Rev. Carleton Greene, Vicar of Great Barford; four *s* two *d. Educ:* Bedford Grammar School; Wadham College, Oxford (exhibitioner). Assistant Master, Berkhamsted School, 1889; Second Master, 1896; Headmaster, 1910–27; President of the Incorporated Association of Assistant Masters, 1906. *Address:* Incents, Crowborough, Sussex. *T:* Crowborough 146.

Died 4 Nov. 1942.

GREENE, Col Hon. Edward Mackenzie, CMG 1909; VD; KC 1902; JP; Hon. Col in British Army; late Commissioner of Railways and Harbours, S Africa; *b* Pietermaritzburg, 18 Nov. 1857; *s* of James Green, DD, Dean of Maritzburg, Natal, and Charlotte Mary Moodie; *m* Jane Maud, *d* of Capt. Joseph Nourse, RN; four *s* one *d. Educ:* Lancing Coll. Served Zulu War with Natal Carbineers, 1879–80 (medal, clasp); Member of Legislative Assembly of Natal for Lion's River Division, 1897–1910; served Boer War in command of Natal Carbineers, 1899–1900 (Queen's medal 3 clasps, King's medal 1 clasp, siege of Ladysmith); Minister of Railways and Harbours, Natal, 1908–10; Member of South African National Convention for Natal; Delegate from Natal to Imperial Defence Conference, 1909 (CMG). *Recreations:* farming, speciality breeding South Devon cattle. *Address:* Dawn Cliff, Westville Road, Durban, Natal. *Clubs:* Victoria, Pietermaritzburg; Rand, Johannesburg.

Died 22 Aug. 1944.

GREENE, George Ball, CBE 1924; *b* 1872; *s* of Hugh McNiele Greene; *m* 1909; one *s* one *d.* Principal Clerk and Clerk of Executive and Legislative Councils, British Guiana, 1911; Assistant Colonial Secretary, 1917 (retired). *Address:* Littlewood, West Byfleet, Surrey. *T:* Byfleet 367. *Clubs:* Royal Automobile, British Empire, West Indian.

Died 28 Jan. 1945.

GREENE, Sir Graham; *see* Greene, Sir W. G.

GREENE, John Arthur; Technical Adviser to industrial concerns; *b* Southport, Lancs, 18 Feb. 1879; *e surv. s* of late Rev. Henry Greene, MA. Trained as journalist, ultimately specialising in the investigation of British Industries; has devoted much time to the better utilisation of coal for the production of pulverised fuel, oil, smokeless fuel, and the generation of power; has investigated natural resources in many countries;

Technical Assistant to Senior Geologist HM Petroleum Research Department (Admiralty), 1917–18; Technical Adviser on Minerals and Supplies (and Hon. Sec.) to Special Committee appointed by Institution of Petroleum Technologists, 1918–19; founded a National Fuel Research and Coal Treatment Station, and by private subscription raised £100,000 for its establishment, 1920; conducted researches into oxygen and carbon dioxide therapy, 1934–37, and introduced Open-Top Oxygen Hood (now known as St George's Hospital Oxygen Tent), 1938. *Publications:* Treatise on British Mineral Oil in collaboration; Patent, Smokeless and Semi-Smokeless Fuels; numerous papers and articles on the better utilisation of coal and the production of oil. *Recreation:* welfare work. *Address:* Royal Empire Society, Northumberland Avenue, WC2.

Died June 1945.

GREENE, Sir (Walter) Raymond, 2nd Bt *cr* 1900; DSO 1916; JP; *b* 1869; *s* of 1st Bt and Anne, *d* of Rev. Preb. C. Royds; *S* father, 1920. *Educ:* Eton; Oriel College, Oxford (MA). Lt-Col-commanding DYO Loyal Suffolk Hussars, 1906–11; served South Africa, 1899–1900 (Queen's medal 3 clasps); European War, 1914–15 (DSO) served with 9th Lancers in France; Lt-Col commanding 2/3 County of London Yeomanry, 1915–16; GSO 1918; MP (C) Chesterton Division, Cambridgeshire, 1895–1906; MP (C) North Hackney, 1910–23; Member of London County Council, North Hackney, 1907–10; Chairman Housing Committee, 1910. *Heir: b* Edward Allan, *b* 12 Sept. 1882. *Address:* Burrough-on-the-Hill, Melton Mowbray. *Clubs:* Carlton, Turf.

Died 24 Aug. 1947.

GREENE, Sir (William) Graham, KCB 1911 (CB 1899); *b* 16 Jan. 1857; *s* of William Greene (*d* 1881), East Lodge, Bedford. *Educ:* Cheltenham College. Entered Admiralty, 1881; private secretary to First Lord of the Admiralty, 1887–1902; Principal Clerk, Admiralty, 1902–07; Assistant Secretary, 1907–11; Permanent Secretary of the Admiralty, 1911–17; Secretary Ministry of Munitions, 1917–20; JP County of London and Cambridge; Alderman (retired) Cambridge CC. *Address:* Harston House, Harston, Cambs. *T:* Harston 262. *Club:* Travellers'.

Died 10 Sept. 1950.

GREENER, Lt-Col Herbert, DSO 1900; South African Union Defence Force (retired); *b* 10 Nov. 1862; *s* of Thomas Greener, Tulse Hill, London; *m* 1898, Helen Olive, *d* of C. Bennett, late Isle of Wight; one *s. Educ:* private school; Rev. J. C. C. Pipon, Chester. Civil Service, Cape Colony, 1884; on Staff, Administrator British Bechuanaland, 1888; Receiver of Revenue and Acting Postmaster-General, British Bechuanaland, 1889; Staff High Commissioner, Cape Town, 1890; Captain and Paymaster BB Police, 1891, and Chief Customs Officer for Bechuanaland Protectorate to 1900; Matabeleland Campaign, 1893; Boer War, 1899–1902 (despatches); Financial Adviser Military Governor, Bloemfontein, 1901; Chief Paymaster and Accountant-General South African Constabulary, 1901; Registrar, Rhodes Univ. Coll., Grahamstown, 1912–25; University of South Africa. Decorated for war services, 1899–1900, in connection with Siege of Mafeking. *Recreations:* shooting, motoring, and outdoor exercise. *Address:* Village de Putron, Guernsey, CI. *Clubs:* Grange, Guernsey; Salisbury, Rhodesia.

Died 27 Feb. 1943.

GREENLEY, William Alfred, CMG 1919; DSO 1917; Member of London Stock Exchange; *b* 1 Jan. 1884; *m* 1st, 1919, Kathleen Mary, *o d* of late George Henry Grimshaw, of Gorton, Manchester; two *s* one *d*; 2nd, 1938, Mrs Sadie Levy. *Educ:* privately. Joined the Army, Oct. 1914; served in France and Belgium until 23 Jan. 1919 (despatches three times, CMG, DSO); rejoined

Army, Temp. Major, 1939; Lt-Col 1941; relinquished commission, 1943. *Address:* 104 Eaton Place, SW1. *Clubs:* Conservative, City Livery, Royal Automobile.

Died 28 March 1949.

GREENLY, Lt-Col Sir John Henry Maitland, KCMG 1941; CBE 1919; MA; MIMechE; MIEI; FInstF; FIM; FInstMet; Chairman, since 1937 and Director, since 1929, Babcock & Wilcox, Ltd; Director: Power Securities Corp., Ltd, Cape Asbestos Co., Ltd, Phoenix Assurance Co. Ltd; Chairman, British Non-Ferrous Metals Research Association, 1937–49; Member of Advisory Council to Committee of Privy Council for Scientific and Industrial Research, 1937–43; Member, Industrial Advisory Panel to Air Ministry, 1938–39; Chairman, Prime Minister's Advisory Panel of Industrialists on Rearmament, 1938–39; Controller-General, British Supply Board in Canada and USA, 1939–40; Deputy Chairman and Administrator, Fire Prevention Executive, 1941–45; Member, National Advisory Council for Fire Prevention, 1941–45; Vice-Chairman, Fire Prevention (Operational) Committee, 1941–45; Member, Fuel Research Board, 1942–47; President, Institute of Metals, 1942–44. Past President (1938–41) and Fellow, Institute of Fuel; Chairman, Coal-Burning Appliances Joint Consultative Board, 1936; Member of Council, British Coal Utilisation Research Association, 1938–46; Member, Provisional General Purposes Committee, Coal Utilisation Joint Council, 1939–46; Member, Fuel and Power Advisory Council, 1944–46; Member of Council, British Welding Research Association, 1946–50; *b* 25 July 1885; 2nd *s* of late Edward Howorth Greenly, JP, DL, and Sarah, 2nd *d* of late Lt-Gen. Bowes Forster; *m* 1910, Joan Isabel, 2nd *d* of late Owen R. Dunell; two *s. Educ:* Charterhouse; Trinity College, Oxford, MA. Trained as Civil Engineer; commissioned Herefordshire Regt (TF), 1906; Captain, 1912; Major, 1916; Staff Captain and Brigade Major, 1916; served European War, 1914–18 (despatches twice); Lieut.-Colonel, 1917; Assistant Controller of Inspection of Munitions of War at Ministry of Munitions, 1916–19; in 1920 became Joint Managing Director of William Foster, Pascoe, Grenfell and Co., copper manufacturers and smelters, London and Swansea, and subsequently Joint Managing Director of British Copper Manufacturers Ltd. *Recreations:* fishing, shooting, motoring, and golf. *Address:* 34 Farringdon Street, EC4. *T:* Central 3282; Calcot Hill, Calcot, nr Reading. *T:* Reading 67433. *Clubs:* Athenæum, Flyfishers'; Berkshire County (Reading).

Died 31 Dec. 1950.

GREENSHIELDS, R. A. E., LLD, DCL; Chief Justice Superior Court, PQ since 1929; Chancellor of Bishop's College; *b* Danville, PQ; *s* of John Greenshields and Margaret Naismith Greenshields; *m* Maude A. Gooderham; one *d. Educ:* St Francis College; McGill University. Barrister; Judge of the Superior Court, 1910; Judge of Court of King's Bench, 1919. *Recreation:* golf. *Address:* 3465 Simpson Street, Montreal, PQ, Canada. *Clubs:* Mount Royal, Montreal.

Died 28 Sept. 1942.

GREENWELL, Allan; Hon. (corresponding) member Canadian Institute of Mining and Metallurgy; hon. member Mining and Geological Institute of India; *b* Radstock, Somersetshire, 27 Dec. 1860; *y s* of late George Clementson Greenwell, FGS, MInstCE; *m* Elizabeth Frances (*d* 1940), *y d* of late James Leader; one *d. Educ:* Malvern College. Editor Colliery Guardian, 1900–13; joined staff of The Times, 1913; Private Secretary to Lord Milner, Supervisor of the Supply and Distribution of Coal, 1916–17; in charge of Statistics, Coal Mines Department, 1917–20; Imperial Mineral Resources Bureau, 1920–22; Safety in Mines Research Board, 1922–29. *Recreation:* travelling.

Died 19 March 1944.

GREENWOOD, 1st Viscount *cr* 1937, of Holbourne; **Hamar Greenwood;** PC 1920; PC (Ireland) 1920; 1st Baron *cr* 1929; Bt *cr* 1915; KC 1919; Chairman, Anglo-Egyptian Chamber of Commerce; President, The Pilgrims Society; *b* Whitby, Ontario, 7 Feb. 1870; *s* of John Hamar Greenwood, Barrister-at-law, and *g s* of William Greenwood, of Llanbister, Radnorshire; *m* 1911, Margery (DBE 1922, CBE 1920, OStJ), *d* of late Walter Spencer, Fownhope Court, Herefordshire; two *s* two *d. Educ:* Public School, Whitby, Canada; BA Toronto University, Hon. LLD 1938. Eight years Lieut in Canadian Militia; sometime in Department of Agriculture of Ontario; Captain King Edward's Horse, and General Reserve of Officers; Lieut-Col commanding 10th Service Batt. South Wales Borderers (1st Gwent); served European War, 1914–16; BEF 1915; made DAAG on Lord Derby's Staff, War Office, 1916; Hon. Colonel Winnipeg Grenadiers; Under-Secretary of State for Home Affairs, 1919; Secretary of Overseas Trade Dept, 1919–20; Chief Secretary for Ireland, 1920–22; Barrister-at-law of Gray's Inn; a Bencher of Gray's Inn, 1917; Treasurer, 1930; Barrister-at-law of New South Wales, South Australia, and New Brunswick; Senior MP (L) York, 1906–10; Sunderland, 1910–22; MP (C) East Walthamstow, 1924–29; Treasurer of Conservative Party, 1933–38; President of British Iron and Steel Federation, 1938–39; Grand Cordon of the Order of Ismail, Egypt. *Recreations:* golf, shooting, and fishing. *Heir: s* Hon. David Henry Hamar Greenwood, *b* 30 Oct. 1914. *Address:* 47 Kingston House, Princes Gate, SW7. *Clubs:* Carlton, 1900, British Empire, Beefsteak.

Died 10 Sept. 1948.

GREENWOOD, Col Charles Francis Hill, CB 1935; DSO 1918; OBE 1923, TD; DL County of London; Hon. Colonel 6th Bn the Queen's Royal Regt since 1937; *b* 4 Dec. 1871; *s* of late Charles F. T. Greenwood, 32 Russell Square, WC. Member of the Stock Exchange; joined Artists' Rifle Volunteers, 1894; served in South African War with the City of London Imperial Volunteers; European War with the Artists' Rifles, 23rd London Regt and 22nd London Regt; commanded 1st/22nd London Regt, Jan. 1917–March 1918, and Sept. 1918 to end of War (DSO). *Address:* 30 Langley Avenue, Surbiton, Surrey. *Club:* Bath.

Died 20 April 1944.

GREENWOOD, Col Harry, VC; DSO 1918; OBE 1944; MC; *b* Windsor, 1881; *e s* of Charles Greenwood, Notts, and Margaret Abernethy, Co. Tipperary; *m* 1909, Helena, *d* of Daniel G. Anderson, Newcastle-upon-Tyne; two *d. Educ:* privately. Served S African War, 1899–1901; with Territorial Force until 1914; rejoined Forces from Reserve of Officers and appointed to KOY Light Infantry, 1915–19, when retired with rank of Lt-Col (wounded thrice, despatches thrice, VC, DSO with bar, MC); civil life since 1901 with Sir Robert Williams & Co. and associated companies; Director of Zambesia Exploring Co., Ltd, Benguela Railway Co., Ltd, Benguela Estates, Ltd, Angola Estates, Ltd, etc. *Recreations:* golf and shooting. *Address:* 77 Home Park Road, Wimbledon Park, SW19. *T:* Wimbledon 2360.

Died 6 May 1948.

GREENWOOD, Major, FRS 1928; FRCP, 1924; DSc Lond. 1928; Professor Emeritus of Epidemiology and Vital Statistics, London School of Hygiene and Tropical Medicine (University of London), since 1945; President of Royal Statistical Society, 1934–36; *b* 9 Aug. 1880; *s* of late Major Greenwood, MD, and late Annie, *d* of late P. L. Burchell, MB; *m* 1908, Rosa, (*d* 1945), *d* of late Andreas Baur; two *s. Educ:* Merchant Taylors' School; London Hospital; University College, London. Demonstrator of Physiology, London Hospital Medical College, 1905–10; Statistician to Lister Institute, 1910–19; Captain RAMC (TF); in charge of Medical Research Subsection of Ministry of Munitions, 1917–19; Medical Officer, Ministry of Health, 1919–27; Hon.

Secretary of Royal Statistical Society, 1919–34, and Member of the International Statistical Institute; Hon. Member of the American Statistical Association and of the Indian Nat. Acad. of Sciences; Consultant in Medical Statistics to Essex CC. *Publications:* Epidemics and Crowd-Diseases, 1935; The Medical Dictator, 1936; Some British Pioneers of Social Medicine, 1948; Medical Statistics from Graunt to Farr, 1948; Treatises on the Physiology of the Special Senses, 1910; and on the Health of the Industrial Worker (with Prof. Collis), 1921; numerous papers on physiological, epidemiological and statistical subjects. *Address:* Hill Crest, Church Hill, Loughton, Essex.

Died 5 Oct. 1949.

GREENWOOD, Robert Morrell, CBE 1918; MA, LLM; JP; a Treasurer of St Mary's Hospital, Paddington; *yr s* of John Broadley Greenwood of Morton, Bingley, Yorkshire; *m* Margaret Emma, 2nd *d* of Rev. C. E. Leir, Rector of Ditcheat; no *c. Educ:* Trinity College, Cambridge. Director of the Law Courts Branch, Treasury Solicitor's Department, 1921–28; a Taxing Master of the Supreme Court, 1928–43. *Address:* 13 Gloucester Square, W2. *T:* Paddington 2030. *Club:* Oxford and Cambridge.

Died 28 Feb. 1947.

GREER, Sir Harry, Kt 1922; DL; *b* 18 Sept. 1876; 3rd *s* of late William Greer, Dundalk, Co. Louth; *m* 1906, Marguerite Charlotte, 2nd *d* of Louis Roche, Emperor's Gate, SW; three *d.* MP (C) Clapham, 1918; Wells Division of Somerset, 1919–22; Chairman Board of Trade Committee Merchandise Marks Acts. *Recreations:* travelling, golf. *Address:* 45 Lowndes Square, SW1. *Clubs:* Carlton, Royal Thames Yacht, Junior Carlton.

Died 20 March 1947.

GREER, Richard Townsend, CSI 1904; *b* 14 Oct. 1854; *s* of Rev. Geo. S. Greer, The Rectory, Kirkcubbin, Co. Down; *m* 1901, Alice Mary Pugh, *e d* of Sir Griffith Pugh Evans, DL, KCIE, Lovesgrove, Aberystwyth, Wales; two *s* two *d.* Entered ICS 1877; Assistant Secretary to the Chief Commissioner of Assam, 1883; Commissioner of Chittagong, 1893; Inspector-General of Police, Bengal, 1899; Chairman of Calcutta Corporation, 1901; Member of Legislative Council, Bengal, 1901; Commissioner of Orissa, 1906; Commissioner of Patna, 1907; Member of Board of Revenue, Bengal, 1908; Member of Executive Council, Bengal, 1911; JP, Cardiganshire, 1917. *Address:* Dolau, Llanbadarn, Aberystwyth.

Died 31 Jan. 1942.

GREG, John Ronald, CBE 1918; *b* 1866; *e s* of late Albert Greg of Escowbeck, Caton, Lancaster; *m* 1897, Esther, 6th *d* of late John Fell, DL, of Flan How, Ulverston; one *s* one *d. Educ:* Rugby; privately. Member Warwickshire Territorial Force Association; O/C South Midland (Warwick) RGA 1908–15; European War, 1915; took active part in Tank production; Conservative candidate for Nuneaton Div., Warwickshire, 1912–13. *Recreations:* shooting and fishing. *Address:* Corriehead, by Kirriemuir, Angus. *T:* Cortachy 50. *Club:* Overseas League.

Died 29 April 1950.

GREG, Lionel Hyde, CIE 1934; Kaisar-I-Hind medal, 1920; *b* 19 Jan. 1879; *s* of Eustace Greg; *m* Marjory Elaine Watson; no *c. Educ:* St Paul's School; Royal Engineering College, Cooper's Hill. Indian Service of Engineers; Assistant Engineer, 1900; Chief Engineer, 1929; retired 1934. *Recreation:* gardening. *Address:* Downside, Houndean Rise, Lewes, Sussex. *T:* Lewes 316. *Club:* Overseas.

Died 15 Feb. 1945.

GREGGE-HOPWOOD, Edward Robert; *b* 1846; *o s* of late Edward John Gregge-Hopwood and Susan Fanny, *d* of John Baskervyle-Glegg of Withington Hall and Gayton Hall, Cheshire; *m* 1875, Mary Brenda

Madeline, *y d* of George Beauchamp Cole of Heatham House, Twickenham, and *g d* of 12th Earl of Derby. Hon. Colonel Lancashire Hussars Imperial Yeomanry; Lord of the Manor of Hopwood. *Club:* Turf.

Died 6 July 1942.

GREGORY, Rev. Benjamin, DLitt; *b* 18 Jan. 1875; *s* of Rev. J. Robinson Gregory (theological writer) and Caroline Plommer of Blean, Boughton, Kent; *g s* of Dr Benjamin Gregory, fifth generation of Wesleyan Methodist Ministers; *m* 1922; Edith Mary, *widow* of Erskine A. Crossley, Capt. 5th Sherwood Foresters, Quarndon Hill, Derby, and *o d* of Sir Norval Helme; one *s. Educ:* Douglas Grammar School; Kingswood School, Bath; Didsbury College. Member of Public Bodies in Manchester and Salford; Superintendent, Huddersfield Mission, 1912–17; on Military Service Tribunal; Superintendent of East End Mission; associated with Lady Askwith in initiating Communal Kitchens in London; Governor British Film Institute, 1936; Hon. Sec. Religious Film Society; Editor, The Methodist Times, 1918–37; Methodist Recorder, 1937–50; Director Religious Films Ltd and GHW Productions. *Recreation:* golf. *Address:* Gatesgarth, Selsey, Sussex. *T:* Selsey 57. *Club:* National Liberal.

Died 20 July 1950.

GREGORY, Maj.-Gen. Charles Levinge, CB 1918; CMG 1919; Indian Army, retired; *b* 22 Aug. 1870; *e surv. s* of H. C. Gregory, West Court, Callan, Ireland; *m* 1900, Irma (*d* 1940), *o d* of late Major E. Harran, 4th Dragoon Guards. 2nd Lieut Royal Irish Fusiliers, 1889; joined Indian Army, 1892. Served NW Frontier of India (Zakkha Khel Country), 1908 (despatches, medal with clasp); European War, 1914–18 (CB, CMG, despatches six times); retired 1923. *Address:* Adcote, Fleet, Hants.

Died 24 July 1944.

GREGORY, Sir Holman, Kt 1935; KC 1910; *b* 30 June 1864; *m* 1st, 1891, Ada (*d* 1930), *d* of Mark Whitwill, JP; 2nd, 1935, Nannette Evelyn, *d* of C. Evelyn O'Leary. Admitted a Solicitor of the Supreme Court, 1886; called to Bar, Middle Temple, 1897; Bencher, 1920; Master Treasurer, 1933; Recorder of Bath, 1916–24; Bristol, 1924–29; Judge of Mayor's and City of London Court, 1929–32; Common Serjeant of the City of London, 1932–34; Recorder of City of London, 1934–37; MP (L) S Derbyshire, 1918–22; Chairman of Departmental Committee dealing with Workmen's Compensation Acts, 1918–20; Chairman of Royal Commission on Unemployment Insurance, 1930–32. *Address:* 7 Cottesmore Court, W8. *T:* Western 9146.

Died 9 May 1947.

GREGORY, Jackson; author; *b* 12 March 1882; *s* of Judge D. S. Gregory and Amelia Hartnell Gregory; *m* 1910, Lotus McGlashan, Truckee; two *s. Educ:* University of California. Reader in English at the University. Principal of high schools; reporter and correspondent for various periodicals in US and Canada; author of short stories and serials, American and British magazines; author of numerous photoplays; novelist. *Publications:* Under Handicap; The Splendid Outlaw; The Short Cut; Wolf Breed; Six Feet Four; The Joyous Trouble Maker; Man to Man; Desert Valley; Daughter of the Sun; Judith of Blue Lake Ranch; The Bells of San Juan; Ladyfingers; The Everlasting Whisper; The Wilderness Trail; Bab of the Backwoods; The Desert Thoroughbred; Captain Cavalier; Emerald Trails; Redwood and Gold; Sentinel of the Desert; Rapidan; The Trail to Paradise; The Island of Allure; The Silver Star; Riders Across the Border; Red Rivals; The First Case of Mr Paul Savoy; The Second Case of Mr Paul Savoy; Ru, The Conqueror; The Third Case of Mr Paul Savoy; White Water Valley; Mountain Men; Into the Sunset; Lords of the Coast; Sudden Bill Dorn; Dark Valley; Powder Smoke; Mysterious Rancho; Marshal of Sundown; Secret Valley; Ace in the Hole; The Far Call; Girl at the Crossroads; I Must Ride Alone; Guardians of

the Trail. *Recreations:* travel; excursions into desert and mountainous regions of the west and south-west; motoring. *Address:* 597 Fifth Avenue, New York. *Club:* Authors'.

Died 12 June 1943.

GREGSON, Edward Gelson, CMG 1917; CIE 1911; *b* 10 June 1877; *s* of Rev. J. Gelson Gregson; *m* 1903, Ella Corisande Hilleary, *d* of Dr Frederic Edward Hilleary, LLD, Stratford, Essex; one *d. Educ:* Portsmouth Grammar School. Assistant Blockade Officer, Waziristan, India, 1900; Political Officer, Mohmand Border (medal with clasp), 1908; Commandant Border Military Police, Peshawar, 1902–07; Personal Assistant to the Inspector-General of Police, NW Frontier (India General Service medal two clasps); on special duty Persian Gulf, for the suppression of the arms traffic, 1909–14 (Naval General Service Medal, Indian General Service Clasp, Persia); holds Durbar Coronation medal, 1911; European War, 1914–15 (General Service, Victory medal, King's Police Medal, Valour); Commissioner of Police, Mesopotamia Expeditionary Force; Deputy Inspector General of Police, Punjab, 1926; retired 1931; late Lieut-Colonel Indian Army Reserve of Officers. *Recreations:* riding, shooting. *Address:* Buncrana, Liss, Hants.

Died 23 Feb. 1942.

GREGSON, Col Henry Guy Fulljames Savage, CMG 1917; late RAOC; *b* 28 Oct. 1872. Entered East Kent Regt 1892; Capt. 1899; Major, 1910; Lt-Col 1914; Col 1923; served S Africa, 1899–1900 and 1902 (severely wounded, Queen's medal and clasp); European War, 1914–17 (CMG); Commandant RAOC School of Instruction, 1924–29; retired pay, 1929. *Address:* Whitelackington, Ilminster, Somerset.

Died 28 April 1949.

GREIG, Sir Alexander, Kt 1947; Director of Retail Co-ordination and Retail Trade Adviser to Min. of Food; *b* 1878; *m* 1904, Jeanie Duncan McNab (*d* 1949); one *s* one *d*. Over 50 years connected with Food Trades; until retirement, Dec. 1946, a Managing Director of Allied Suppliers group of companies; Member of London Provision Exchange; Fellow of Inst. of Certificated Grocers. *Address:* Torcroft, Torfield Road, Eastbourne. *T:* Eastbourne 4033.

Died 5 May 1950.

GREIG, Alexander Rodger, BASc; *b* 18 Dec. 1872; *s* of William Greig and Elizabeth Rodger; *m* 1897, Jessie Shaw; one *d. Educ:* McGill Univ., Montreal. Chief Draughtsman, Mechanical Dept, Canada Atlantic Railway, Ottawa, 1895–1902; Chief Draughtsman and Mechanical Engineer, Canadian Northern Railway, 1902–06; Prof. Agricultural Engineering, Manitoba Agricultural College, Winnipeg, 1906–09; Prof. of Mechanical and Agricultural Engineering, Univ. of Saskatchewan, 1909–37; member of various engineering societies; retired, 1937; Acting Professor of Mechanical Engineering, University of Alberta, Edmonton, Alta, 1939–41 and 1942–43. *Publications:* bulletins on Farm Buildings and Wall Insulation. *Address:* University, Saskatoon. *TA:* Saskatoon. *T:* 4565, 10130.

Died 21 July 1947.

GREIG, Lt-Col Edward David Wilson, CIE 1914; MD, DSc, FRSE; FRCPE; Indian Medical Service (retd); late Director, Pasteur Institute, Shillong; *b* Edinburgh, 20 March 1874; *y s* of late David Greig, FRCSE, JP; unmarried. *Educ:* Edinburgh Academy; University of Edinburgh. Graduated MB CM, 1895; BSc, 1898. Assistant to Professor of Pathology, University College, London, 1898; entered Indian Medical Service, 1899; Military duty till 1902; Plague Research, Bombay, 1902–03; Member (sometime Director) of Sleeping Sickness Commission of Royal Society in Uganda, 1903–05; Member (sometime Director) of Enteric Fever Research Committee of

Government of India, 1906–08; investigated for Government of India the etiology of Dysentery, 1908–09; Epidemic Dropsy, 1909–11; Cholera, 1912–16; Membre correspondant de la Société de Pathologie exotique; Delegate Interallied Sanitary Commission, Paris, 1919; active service in Mesopotamia during 1914–18 War; Director of Medical Research, India, 1921–23; Joint Editor, Indian Journal of Medical Research, 1921–23; Physician-Consultant on Diseases of Tropical Climates, Royal Infirmary, Edinburgh, 1929–39; Lecturer on Diseases of Tropical Climates, Edinburgh University, 1924–39. *Publications:* Reports to the Royal Society of Sleeping Sickness; to the Government of India on Enteric Fever, Dysentery, etc.; various contributions to Scientific Journals. *Recreations:* walking, golf. *Address:* 38 Coates Gardens, Edinburgh, 12. *T:* Edinburgh 61241. *Club:* Caledonian United Service (Edinburgh).

Died 13 April 1950.

GREIG, James, RBA, artist; *b* Arbroath, 1861; *s* of Alexander Greig. Came to London, 1890; went to Paris, 1895; returned to London, 1896; for many years Art critic of the Morning Post. *Publications:* Life of Gainsborough; Life of Raeburn; Farington's Diary; Diaries of a Duchess; Drawings for Punch, etc. *Club:* Savage.

Died 13 Oct. 1941.

GREIG, Sir Robert Blyth, Kt 1919; MC; LLD, DSc, MSc, FRSE; Director London Midland & Scottish Railway since 1937; Director Scottish Motor Traction Co. and David Macbrayne Ltd; Member of Carnegie Trust for Universities of Scotland; *b* Balcurvie, Fife, 23 March 1874; *s* of George Greig of Balcurvie and Helen, *d* of late John Martin, Greenock; *m* 1903, Maud, 2nd *d* of late Sir George B. Hunter, KBE; three *s* one *d*. *Educ:* Edinburgh Univ. Lecturer in Cheshire Agricultural Coll., 1897–99; Durham College of Science, Newcastle-on-Tyne, 1899–1903; Fordyce Lecturer in Agriculture, Aberdeen University, 1903–10; Staff Inspector in Agriculture, Board of Education, Whitehall, 1911; Commissioner, Board of Agriculture for Scotland, 1911; Chairman, 1921–28; Permanent Secretary, Department of Agriculture for Scotland, 1928–34; retired 1934; joined the army (Royal Scots), 1914; served in France, 1916–17. *Publications:* numerous papers and articles. *Address:* Shaws, Barnton, Midlothian. *Clubs:* Reform; University (Edinburgh).

Died 29 Nov. 1947.

GRESLEY, Sir Herbert Nigel, Kt 1936; CBE 1920; DSc; MInstCE; MIMechE, MIEE, MInstT; Chief Mechanical Engineer, L & NE Railway; *b* 19 June 1876; 4th *s* of late Rev. Nigel Gresley; *m* 1901, Ethel Frances (*d* 1929), *d* of late W. P. Fullagar, of St Anne's, Lancashire; two *s* two *d*. *Educ:* Marlborough. Engineering pupil of Sir John A. F. Aspinall, L and Y Railway, Horwich; Locomotive Engineer, Great Northern Railway, Doncaster, 1911–22; Lt-Col Engineer and Railway Staff Corps, RE (TF); Governor, Queen Mary College; Chairman of Board of Trade Committee on Steering Gear of Ships; Member of Committees appointed by Ministry of Transport on Automatic Train Control, and Committee on Railway Electrification. *Publications:* papers before the Institution of Civil Engineers, Institution of Mechanical Engineers, Institute of Transport. *Recreations:* shooting, golf. *Address:* Watton House, Hertford. *T:* Watton at Stone 252. *Clubs:* Junior Carlton, Brooks's.

Died 5 April 1941.

GRETTON, 1st Baron *cr* 1944, of Stapleford; **John Gretton,** PC 1926; CBE 1919; ex-Chairman Bass, Ratcliff and Gretton, Ltd; Colonel Territorial Army, retired; *b* 1867; *e s* of John Gretton, Bladon House, Burton-on-Trent; *m* 1900, Hon. Maud Helen de Moleyns (*d* 1934), *γ d* of 4th Baron Ventry; one *s* two *d*.

Educ: Harrow. MP (C) Derbyshire, S, 1895–1906; Rutland, 1907–18; Burton Division of Staffordshire, 1918–43. *Recreations:* yachting, literature, architecture, travelling. *Heir: s* Hon. John Frederic Gretton. *Address:* Stapleford Park, Melton Mowbray; Burton-on-Trent. *Clubs:* Carlton; Royal Yacht Squadron, Cowes.

Died 2 June 1947.

GREVILLE, Hon. Louis George; *b* 1 Jan. 1856; 3rd *s* of 4th Earl of Warwick; *m* 1887, Lily (*d* 1898), *d* of J. H. Gordon; one *s*, killed in France, 1918. Second Secretary Diplomatic Service, 1882–87; High Sheriff of Wilts, 1920–21. *Address:* Heale House, Woodford, Salisbury. *TA:* Middle-Woodford. *Club:* Fly Fishers.

Died 6 March 1941.

GREVILLE, Dame Margaret Helen Anderson, (Hon. Mrs Ronald Greville), DBE 1922; *d* of late Rt Hon. William McEwan, MP Central Edinburgh; *widow* of Capt. Hon. R. Greville (*d* 1908), *e s* of 2nd Baron Greville. *Address:* 16 Charles Street, Berkeley Square, W1. *T:* Grosvenor 2357; Polesden Lacey, Dorking. *T:* Leatherhead 2103.

Died 15 Sept. 1942.

GREW, Edwin Sharpe, MA (Cantab); *b* 4 Nov. 1866. *Educ:* Cowper St; Christ's Coll. Camb. BA Mathematical Tripos, 1888. Joined staff, Educational Times, 1889; Daily Graphic, 1890; editor, Illustrated Scientific News, 1901; editor, Knowledge, 1903. *Publications:* War with the Boers, 1901–1902; The Struggle in the Far East, 1905–1906; Romance of Modern Geology, 1908; The Court of William III; The English Court in Exile; James II at St Germains (last two with Marion E. Grew, FRHistS); The Growth of a Planet; articles and stories in reviews and magazines. *Recreation:* golf. *Address:* 47 Oakley St, SW3. *Club:* Devonshire.

Died 31 Dec. 1950.

GREY, Clifford; author; *b* 5 Jan. 1887; *s* of George Davis, Birmingham; *m* Dorothy Gould (*d* 1940), two *d*. *Educ:* King Edward VI's School, Birmingham. Commenced as an actor at the age of 19, and toured in various small companies in England and the Colonies till the age of 25; gave up the stage and took to writing entirely, and in 1916 obtained a footing in the West End by supplying the lyrics to The Bing Boys are Here; since then has been connected with a number of musical plays and films in London and America, including: Heart's Desire; Queen of Hearts; The Bing Boys are Here; The Bing Girls; Theodore and Co.; Pell Mell; Arlette; Yes, Uncle; Hullo America; The Kiss Call; Baby Bunting; Kissing Time; The Bing Boys on Broadway; Who's Hooper; Johnny Jones; A Night Out; Sally; Little Miss Raffles; Phi Phi; Lady Butterfly; Mr Cinders; Hit the Deck; Love Parade; Rogue Song; Smiling Lieutenant; Out of the Bottle; A Kiss in a Taxi; Rome Express; Facing the Music; Jack o' Diamonds; Accidentally Yours; Love Laughs; At the Silver Swan; Land without Music; Mr Whittington; Lilac Domino; Man Inside; Southern Roses; Pearls Bring Tears; Oh, Letty; Yes, Madam; Hold My Hand; Luck of the Navy; Lambeth Walk. *Recreations:* reading, motoring, and golf. *Address:* 38 Sandringham Court, W9.

Died Sept. 1941.

GREY, Egerton Spenser, CB 1922; Officier de la légion d'Honneur, 1924; Barrister-at-law (Inner Temple); late Controller of Clearing Office (Germany); Administrator of German, Austrian, Hungarian, and Bulgarian Property under the various Treaties of Peace; Director of Russian Claims Department, 1920–26; *b* 1863; *γ s* of Col F. D. Grey; *m* 1890, Ethel Harriett, (*d* 1949), *γr d* of Sir Frederick Wigan, 1st Bt; five *s* one *d*. *Educ:* Radley College. Served in Bechuanaland Expedition (Methuen's Horse), 1884–85; Bankruptcy Department, Board of Trade, 1885–1919; supervised liquidation of enemy businesses under Trading with the Enemy Acts,

1916–19. *Recreations:* dry-fly fishing, golf. *Address:* The White House, Cobham, Surrey. *T:* Cobham 248. *Club:* Travellers'.

Died 11 May 1950.

GREY, Francis Temple; Deputy Coroner, East Middlesex; Serving Brother of Order of St John of Jerusalem; *b* London, 10 Feb. 1886; *e s* of late Col Arthur Grey, CIE; *m* 1928, Eglantine, *y d* of late Major Edward Charles Ellice, DSO, of Invergarry; six *s* two *d. Educ:* privately; Wadham College, Oxford. Barrister-at-law, Lincoln's Inn; Surgeon, Royal Navy, retired; Inspector, Metropolitan Special Constabulary. *Publications:* contributed the following articles to the Ency. Brit.; Capital Punishment, Coroners, Extradition, Legal Aspects of Insanity, Medical Jurisprudence and the article The Coroner and his Inquest, to the Ency. of Medicine; edited 5th ed. Pitt Cobbett's Cases in International Law (Part I). *Recreations:* travel, yachting, swimming. *Address:* Lowood, Upper Norwood. *Clubs:* Royal Automobile; Malta Union.

Died 23 Jan. 1941.

GREY, Captain George Charles; MP (L) Berwick-on-Tweed since 1941; serving Supplementary Reserve of Officers Grenadier Guards since 1938; *b* 2 Dec. 1918; *e s* of Maj.-Gen. W. H. Grey, CB. *Educ:* Winchester; Hertford College, Oxford. *Address:* 1 Cheltenham Terrace, SW3. *Clubs:* Guards', Boodle's, Reform, National Liberal.

Died 30 July 1944.

GREY, Samuel John; partner, S. J. Grey and Willcox, Solicitors, Birmingham; *b* 1878; *s* of Samuel Grey and S. A. John; *m* 1904, Jessie Bridgman, Stoney Stratford; one *s* two *d. Educ:* Chepstow Grammar School. Admitted a Solicitor, 1903; Elected to Birmingham City Council, 1919; Alderman, 1930; Warden for Birmingham King George's Jubilee Trust; Lord Mayor of Birmingham, 1934–36; JP; Chairman of Finance Committee Birmingham City Council; Hon. Treas. and Chm. of Finance Committee, Birmingham Univ.; Director of Joseph Lucas, Ltd, Wesleyan and General Assce Society, Halford Cycle Co. Ltd; Member of Council of Birmingham Chamber of Commerce. *Recreations:* golf and motoring. *Address:* Broadmeadow, Solihull, Warwickshire. *T:* Solihull 0082, (Office) Central 7906. *Clubs:* Union, Midland, Birmingham.

Died 31 Dec. 1942.

GREY-EGERTON, Rev Sir Brooke de Malpas; *see* Egerton.

GRIBBLE, Francis Henry; man of letters; *b* Barnstaple, 15 July 1862; *e s* of Henry Gribble, Old Bank, Barnstaple; *m* 1st, Maria Evertje Aleida (*d* 1928), *d* of Christian Hermann Schanze, Inspector-General of the Netherlands State Railways; 2nd, 1937, Minnie Maud Battell. *Educ:* privately; Exeter College, Oxford (BA; 1st class Lit. Hum., 1884). Classical master, Warwick Grammar School; came to London, 1887, to write for newspapers; original editor of Phil May's Annual; contributor to Fortnightly Review, etc. *Publications:* The Red Spell, 1895; The Things that Matter, 1896; The Lower Life, 1896; Only an Angel, 1897; Sunlight and Limelight, 1898; The Early Mountaineers, 1899; Lake Geneva and its Literary Landmarks, 1901; a Romance of the Tuileries, 1902; Stromboli, 1904; The Story of Alpine Climbing, 1904; The Dream of Peace, 1904; The Pillar of Cloud, 1906; Madame de Stael and her Lovers, 1907; George Sand and her Lovers, 1907; Rousseau and the Women he Loved, 1908; Chateaubriand and his Court of Women, 1909; The Passions of the French Romantics, 1910; The Romance of the Oxford Colleges, 1910; The Love Affairs of Lord Byron, 1910; Double Lives, 1911; Rachel: her Stage Life and her Real Life, 1911; The Romantic Life of Shelley, 1911; The Comedy of Catherine the Great, 1912; The Romance of the Men of Devon, 1912; Romances of the French

Theatre, 1912; The Tragedy of Isabella II, 1913; The Court of Christina of Sweden, 1913; The Life of the Emperor Francis Joseph, 1914; The Royal House of Portugal, 1915; In Luxembourg in War Time, 1916; Women and War, 1916; The History of Ruhleben (with Joseph Powell), 1919; Seen in Passing, 1929; Balzac: The Man and The Lover, 1930; Dumas, Father and Son, 1930; Emperor and Mystic, 1931; The Fight for Divorce, 1932; What America Owes Europe, 1932. *Recreation:* Continental travel. *Address:* 76 West Bay Road, Bridport. *Clubs:* Authors'; Bridport and West Dorset, Bridport.

Died 10 Oct. 1946.

GRIBBON, Brig. Walter Harold, CMG 1918; CBE 1919; psc; *b* 1881; *yr s* of late Walter Galt Gribbon, MA Oxon; *m* 1st, Edith Margaret (*d* 1934), *d* of Dr J. B. Stuart, JP; two *s* one *d*; 2nd, 1935, Doris May, *d* of A. A. Davies. *Educ:* Rugby School; Leicestershire Militia; Quetta Staff College, Imperial Defence College. General Staff, Mesopotamia, War Office and Constantinople, 1914–21; served European War, 1914–18 (despatches, CMG, CBE); Brevet Lt-Col 1917; Brevet Col 1921; Lt-Col 1928; Col 1921; commanded 2nd Bn The King's Own Royal Regiment (Lancaster), 1928–31; Commander Canal Brigade, Egypt, 1931–32; Officer-in-Charge of Infantry Record and Pay Office, Lichfield, 1932–36; retired pay, 1936; Comdg 8th (Cinque Ports) Bn Kent Home Guard since 1942. *Address:* Galt, Seabrook Rd, Hythe, Kent. *Club:* Junior United Service.

Died 18 Dec. 1944.

GRIER, Brig.-Gen. Harry Dixon, CB 1916; DSO 1918; late RA; *b* 31 May 1863; *s* of Captain Alexander Dixon Grier, late 89th Regiment; *m* 1901, Jane Bertram, *d* of late W. Sanderson, JP; one *s* two *d*. Served Burma, 1889–91 (medal with clasp); Isazai Expedition, 1892; Chitral, 1895 (honourably mentioned, medal with clasp); NW Frontier, India, 1897–98 (despatches, clasp); Tirah, 1897–98 (despatches, Bt-Major, clasp); European War, 1914–18; one of the garrison of Kut Al Amara (despatches five times, CB, DSO, twice wounded); retired pay, 1919. *Address:* Wymering Lodge, Farnborough, Hants.

Died 22 Oct. 1942.

GRIER, John Arthur Bolton, CIE 1935; *b* 17 Feb. 1882; *s* of John William MacGregor Grier and Emily Louisa Flavell; *m* 1915, Elsie Mary Streeten; one *s* one *d. Educ:* Christ's Hospital; St John's College, Hurstpierpoint. Worked with W. J. and H. Thompsons, Tea Brokers, Mincing Lane, 1902–06; Tea planting on Lankapura Estate, Dooars, 1906–08; joined Bombay Company Ltd 1908 and worked in their Cotton Mills at Sholapur; retired from India, 1937. *Recreations:* shooting, fishing, tennis, golf. *Clubs:* Western India, Poona; Royal Bombay Yacht, Bombay.

Died 8 Dec. 1946.

GRIER, Sir Selwyn Macgregor, KCMG 1936; Kt 1934; CMG 1929; MA; *b* April 1878; *s* of late Rev. R. M. Grier, Vicar of Hednesford and Prebendary of Lichfield; *m* 1922, Florence, *o d* of late Dr C. G. Heard, Hunmanby, Yorks. *Educ:* Marlborough College; Pembroke Coll., Cambridge (Classical Scholar); 2nd Class Classical Tripos, 1900. Ass. Master, Berkhamsted School, 1901–02; Cheam School, 1902–05; Assistant Resident, Northern Nigeria, 1906; 3rd Class Resident, 1908; 2nd Class Resident, Nigeria, 1917; Secretary for Native Affairs, Nigeria, 1921; seconded as Director of Education, Southern Provinces, Nigeria, 1925; Colonial Secretary, Trinidad, 1929–35; acting Governor, Trinidad, Aug. 1929–March 1930, July–Nov. 1932 and May–Sept. 1934; Governor and Commander-in-Chief, Windward Islands, 1935–37; retired, 1937; called to the Bar, 1910. *Address:* Grangeside, Bramley, nr Guildford, Surrey.

Died 8 Nov. 1946.

GRIERSON, Charles MacIver, RI; *b* Queenstown, Ireland, 8 Dec. 1864; *s* of late Charles Grierson, manager of the Cunard Company; *m* Ethel, *d* of late Cochran Davys, Clerk of the Crown and Peace, Sligo, Ireland; one *s* two *d*. *Educ:* Plymouth. Studied Art under F. Brown at Westminster, late Slade Professor, and in the Royal Institute Schools; Member Royal Institute, 1892; Pastel Society, 1904; Exhibitor Royal Academy; Royal Institute, Liverpool; Birmingham, etc. *Recreations:* breeding of Cairn Terriers, and collecting English silver coins. *Address:* 61 Pavilion Way, Eastcote, Ruislip, Middlesex.

Died 25 Sept. 1939.

GRIERSON, Sir George Abraham, OM 1928; KCIE 1912; CIE 1894; ICS (retired); *b* Glenageary, Co. Dublin, 7 Jan. 1851; *e s* of late George Abraham Grierson, LLD; *m* Lucy Elizabeth Jean, *d* of late M. H. Collis, MD, 1880. *Educ:* St Bees and Shrewsbury; Trinity College, Dublin; Mathematical Honours, and Hindustani and Sanskrit Exhibitioner; BA, Dublin University; PhD (Hon. Causa), Halle University, 1894; LittD (Hon. Causa), Dublin University, 1902; LLD (Hon.) Cambridge University, 1920; DLitt (Hon.) Oxford University, 1929; Vagisha (Bihar and Orissa), 1921; late Fellow of Calcutta University. Appointed member of Indian Civil Service, 1873; landed in India, 1873; Assist Mag. and Collector; Inspector of Schools, Bihar Circle, 1880; Officiating Magistrate and Collector of Gaya, 1887; Magistrate of Howrah, 1892; additional Commissioner of Patna, 1896; opium agent of Bihar, 1896; on special duty with Government of India, in charge of Linguistic Survey of India, 1898–1902 (retired, 1903); Superintendent of the Linguistic Survey of India; holds certificates of high proficiency in Bengali and Sanskrit; Fellow of the British Academy; Hon. Fellow of Royal Asiatic Society of Bengal, of the Bombay Branch of the Royal Asiatic Society, and of the Royal Danish Academy of Sciences; Hon. Member of American Oriental Society, Benares Nāgarī Prachāriṇī Sabhā, Société Finno-Ougrienne, International Phonetic Association, Bihar and Orissa Research Society, Modern Language Association, Linguistic Society of India, Deutsche Morgenländische Gesellschaft, Bangiya Sahitya Parishad; Correspondant Etranger de l'Institut de France (Académie des Inscriptions et Belles Lettres); Hon. Foreign Associate Member of the Société Asiatique de Paris; Corresponding member of the Königliche Gesellschaft der Wissenschaften zu Göttingen; late President Gypsy Lore Society; Hon. Vice-President Royal Asiatic Society; Prix Volney (Académie Française), 1905; Gold Medallist, Royal Asiatic Society, 1909; Campbell Memorial Medal (RAS Bombay), 1923; Gold Medal, British Academy, 1928; Sir William Jones Gold Medal (Royal Asiatic Society of Bengal), 1929; Church of Ireland. *Publications:* Handbook of the Kaithi Character; Grammar and Chrestomathy of the Maithili Language; Seven Grammars of the Bihar Dialects; Bihar Peasant Life; The Modern Vernacular Literature of Hindustan; The Satsaiya of Bihari; Essays on Kashmiri Grammar; The Languages of India; Linguistic Survey of India; Pisaca Languages of North-Western India; Manual of the Kashmiri Language; Lallā Vākyāni (with L. Barnett); Ishkāshmī, Zebaki, and Yāzghulāmi; Editor and Translator of Hātim's Tales; the Torwali Language; Editor and translator of the Kashmiri Srī Krishnāvatāra Līlā; Editor of Kashmiri Siva Parinaya and Srī Rāmāvatāra Carita; Editor of Waterfield's Lay of Alha; Dictionary of the Kashmiri Language; translator of Vidyapati's Purusha Parīkshā, under the title of The Test of a Man; and many papers in the journals of Oriental Societies. *Recreations:* the study of philology and the various Indian vernaculars; music. *Address:* Rathfarnham, Camberley. *T:* Camberley 43. *Club:* Royal Societies.

Died 7 March 1941.

GRIESBACH, Maj.-Gen. Hon. William Antrobus, CB 1919; CMG 1918; DSO 1916; KC 1919; *b* Fort Qu'Appelle, NW Territories, 3 Jan. 1878; *s* of late Lt-Col Arthur Henry Griesbach, Royal North-West Mounted Police, and Emma Hodgins; *m* 1906, Janet Scott McDonald Lauder; no *c*. *Educ:* St John's College, Winnipeg. Served South African War, 1900; Lieut 19th Alberta Dragoons, 1906; Mayor of Edmonton, Alberta, 1907; President Union of Alberta Municipalities, 1908; Conservative candidate, House of Commons, 1911; seconded from the 19th Alberta Dragoons with rank of Major for Divisional Cavalry, 1st Canadian Contingent, 1914; Commanded 49th Canadian Batt. (Edmonton Regiment), which he raised, 1915–17; Brig.-Gen., 1917; Maj.-Gen., 1921; nominated Conservative candidate, House of Commons, 1915; MP West Edmonton, 1917; Senator since 1921; Commanded 1st Canadian Infantry Brigade, BEF, France (despatches six times); Inspector-General of Canadian Active Service Force in the four Western Provinces, 1940–43. *Publications:* Hints to Western Canadian Cavalrymen, 1914; Memoranda and Extracts from Operation Orders, 1916. *Recreations:* hunting, shooting, and canoeing. *Address:* Edmonton, Alberta, Canada. *TA:* Griesbach, Edmonton, Canada. *Club:* Edmonton.

Died 21 Jan. 1945.

GRIFFITH, Hon. Arthur; Patent Attorney; *b* Gortmore, Co. Westmeath, Ireland; *m* 1st; one *s*; 2nd; one *s* one *d*. *Educ:* Scots College, Melbourne; Sydney University. Six years Master, Sydney Grammar School; Minister for Public Works, NSW, 1910–14; Education and Local Government, 1915–16; granted title Honourable for life, 1917; holds National Shipwreck Society's Medal for saving life at sea; thirty years practising as Patent Attorney; two years Pres. Institute of Patent Attorneys of Australia; ten years Trustee of the Savings Bank of New South Wales; at present a member of Australian Air Force Recruiting Committee. *Address:* Asbestos House, York St, Sydney, NSW.

Died 1 Sept. 1946.

GRIFFITH, Arthur Donald, MB, BS (Lond.), FRCS (Eng.); Senior Ophthalmic Surgeon and Lecturer on Ophthalmology, Westminster Hospital; Senior Surgeon, Royal Eye Hospital (late Dean of its Medical School); Consulting Ophthalmic Surgeon, St David's Home for Disabled Soldiers, Ealing; Fellow of the Royal Society of Medicine; Member of the Ophthalmological Society of the United Kingdom; Brevet Major (retired), RAMC (TF); Cavaliere, Corona d'Italia; *b* 1882; *s* of Arthur Griffith, solicitor, London; *m* Aurora, *d* of late Conte Mocenigo Soranzo, of Venice. *Educ:* King's College, London (Scholar and Exhibitioner). King's College Hospital (formerly House Surgeon, House Physician and Surgical Registrar); also House Surgeon and Registrar, Royal Eye Hospital; Senior Resident Medical Officer, Royal Free Hospital; late Ophthalmic Surgeon, Italian Hospital, London; served World War in Malta, Salonika and Italy, 1914–19 (despatches); Senior Ophthalmic Specialist, Malta Command, and Officer i/c Military Hospital, Hamrun; Surgical Specialist, British Salonika Force; Senior Medical Officer, Faenza Area, Italy. *Publications:* articles on ophthalmic subjects in medical journals and publications. *Address:* 7 Queen Street, Mayfair, W1. *TA:* Oculist, Phone, London. *T:* Grosvenor 1488. *Club:* Savile.

Died 5 March 1944.

GRIFFITH, Arthur Stanley, CBE 1939; retired; *b* 20 March 1875; *s* of Joseph Griffith, farmer, Eccleston, Lancs; *m* 1927, Anna Nellie Beech (widow), *d* of late Robert Henry Scott; one *s*. *Educ:* Royal Institution, Medical School and Royal Infirmary, Liverpool. MB and ChB 1897, MD 1901 (Vict.); DPH, RCPS London, 1902; PhD Camb., 1926; Derby Exhibition in Medicine, 1897, Liverpool School of Medicine. Resident House Physician, Royal Infirmary, and Medical Officer, Lock Hospital, Liverpool, 1898; Alexander Fellow in Pathology, Liverpool, 1899–1902; Resident Scientific Investigator, Royal Commission on Tuberculosis,

1903–10; Grocers' Research Scholar, 1911–14; Weber-Parkes Prize and Medal (Tuberculosis work) RCP London, 1927; Member Scientific Staff, Medical Research Council, 1914–40; Member of Cattle Diseases Committee, Economic Advisory Council, 1932–34. *Publications:* articles on Human and Animal Tuberculosis, Meningococcus, Spirochaeta icterohaemorrhagiae, etc., in various journals. *Address:* Paradise House, Newnham, Cambridge. *T:* 55881.

Died 9 April 1941.

GRIFFITH, Brig.-Gen. Charles Richard Jebb, CB 1918; CMG 1915; DSO 1900; *b* 4 Oct. 1867; *s* of Col R. Griffith. *Educ:* Clifton; Oundle; RMC, Sandhurst. Entered army, Bedfordshire Regt, 1887; Captain, 1895; Adjutant, 1895; served South Africa, 1899–1902 (despatches, Queen's and King's medals with 4 clasps, DSO); European War, 1914–18; commanded Battalion in France and Flanders, 1914–15; commanded Brigade in France and Flanders, 1915–18 (despatches 8 times, CB, CMG, Bt-Colonel; Officer Legion of Honour). *Address:* c/o Holt & Co., Kirkland House, Whitehall, SW1.

Died 4 Aug. 1948.

GRIFFITH, Sir Francis Charles, Kt 1931; CSI 1923, OBE 1919; Chief Constable New Scotland Yard since 1933; *b* 9 Nov. 1878; *s* of late F. R. Griffith, of Corsley, Wiltshire, and of the PWD, India; *m* 1906, Ivy Morna, *d* of George Jacob, ICS; one *s* one *d*. *Educ:* Blundell's School, Tiverton. Joined the Indian Police, 1898; served for 9 years as a District Officer; held Staff appointments at Headquarters, 1908–12; Deputy Commissioner of Police in charge of the CID, Bombay City, 1913–18; Commissioner of Police, Bombay City, 1919–21; Inspector-General of Police, Bombay Presidency, 1921–32; King's Police Medal, 1916. *Recreations:* shooting, golf, lawn tennis. *Address:* 2 Girton House, Manor Fields, Putney Hill, SW15. *T:* Putney 5042. *Club:* East India and Sports.

Died 16 Nov. 1942.

GRIFFITH, George Herbert, CBE 1927; *b* 1877; *s* of late Rev. J. W. Griffith, Pentraeth, Anglesey; *m* 1907, Mary St Lo (*d* 1934), *d* of late Captain William St Lo Malet, 8th Hussars; no *c*. *Educ:* Oswestry School. Was in the London and North-Western Railway, 1895–1902; joined Egyptian State Railways, 1902; Deputy General Manager, 1924; retired, 1928; General Manager Pullman Car Co., Ltd, 1928, retired, 1945; served European War, 1914–19, Hon. Major RE Rail Transport Dept (despatches OBE, CBE, 3rd class orders of the Nile and Ismail, 4th class order of the Medjidie). *Address:* 1 First Avenue, Hove. *Club:* Constitutional.

Died 11 April 1947.

GRIFFITH, Rev. Henry Allday, MA; Residentiary Canon of St Albans, since 1939; *b* 2 Sept. 1875; *s* of late Y. H. Griffith of Plasgwynfwyn, Llanbedr, Merioneth; *m* 1901, Margaret, *d* of Rev. H. J. Cheales, late Vicar and Rural Dean of Friskney, Lincs. *Educ:* Trinity College, Oxford, MA; Queen's Coll., Birmingham, 1903. Called to the Bar at the Middle Temple, 1900; Deacon, 1904; priest, 1906; Vicar of Warton, 1908–12; Arcadia, Transvaal, 1912–16; CF 1917–19; served in France; Priest-in-charge, Watermoor. Cirencester, 1919–20; Vicar of All Saints, Gloucester, 1921; Archdeacon of Pretoria, 1921–24; Hon. CF 1920; Examining Chaplain to the Bishop of Pretoria; Vicar of Wolverton St Mary, 1924–26; Rector of Ashwell, 1926–33; Rural Dean of Baldock, 1929; Rector of Dunstable, 1933–39; Rural Dean of Dunstable, 1933–36; Hon. Canon of St Albans, 1934–39; Diocesan Missioner of St Albans, 1939–41. *Address:* Abbey Lodge, St Alban's.

Died 22 Jan. 1942.

GRIFFITH, Thomas Wardrop, CMG 1918; LLD Aber. 1922; Hon. DSc Leeds, 1929; MD Aber.; FRCP Lond.; retired; Emeritus Professor, University of Leeds; Hon. Consulting Physician, General Infirmary at Leeds

and Leeds Public Dispensary; 8th *s* of late Charles Fox Griffith, JP, Aberdeen; *m* Louisa, (*d* 1937), *γ d* of Grosvenor Talbot, Leeds; two *s*. *Educ:* Grammar School and University of Aberdeen. Professor of Medicine, 1910–25, Professor of Anatomy, 1887–1910, University of Leeds; Hon. Physician General Infirmary at Leeds, 1892–1925; Hon. Consultant for Yorkshire in Cardiac Affections to the Ministry of Pensions; Member of the General Medical Council, 1918–27; Lieut-Col late RAMC(T). *Address:* 7 Stainbeck Lane, Chapel Allerton, Leeds. *T:* Chapeltown 41170.

Died 21 Oct. 1946.

GRIFFITH, W. St Bodfan; *b* Henfaes, Aber, 31 Oct. 1876; *o s* of late John and Mary Griffith; *m* 1907, Doli, *d* of late John Roberts, MD of Plas Eryr, Llanddeiniolen; one *s* two *d*. *Educ:* Christ's Hospital (Scholar); University Colleges of Bangor and Aberystwyth (open Exhibitioner); Trinity College, Cambridge (foundation Sizar) MA Cantab; BSc Wales; 1st Class Parts 1 and 2 Natural Sciences Tripos, Cambridge. Formerly Assistant Master at King Edward VII School, Sheffield, and at Uppingham; Headmaster of Friars School, Bangor, 1919–34; Church of England. *Publications:* (with Mr T. Petrie) work on Practical Physics. *Recreations:* natural history, mountaineering, shooting. *Address:* Aber, Caernarvonshire.

Died 24 Sept. 1941.

GRIFFITH, Walter Spencer Anderson, CBE 1920; MD, FRCP, FRCS; retired; *b* 1854; *s* of Rev. John Griffith, LLD, sometime Headmaster, Brighton Coll; *m* 1st, 1885, Mary Anne, *γ d* of T. Kinder, JP, Sandridge Bury, St Albans; one *s*; 2nd, 1918, Ella F., *d* of late W. Jackson Kennedy, MD, Lisaghmore, Kirkcaldy, Fife. *Educ:* Brighton College; Downing College, Cambridge. Consulting Physician, Queen Charlotte's Lying-in Hospital; Consulting Obstetric Physician, St Bartholomew's Hospital. *Address:* 19 Cheyne Walk, SW3. *T:* Flaxman 8712; The Brae Cottage, Grayswood, Haslemere, Surrey. *T:* Haslemere 565.

Died 26 Feb. 1946.

GRIFFITH-BOSCAWEN, Rt Hon. Sir Arthur Sackville Trevor, PC 1920; Kt 1911; JP, MA; Member of the Inland Transport War Council; *b* Trevalyn Hall, near Wrexham, 18 Oct. 1865; 2nd *s* of late Capt. Griffith-Boscawen and late Helen Sophia, *e d* of late Admiral Norwich Duff; *m* 1st, 1892, Edith Sarah (*d* 1919), *e d* of late S. Williams, Boons Park, Edenbridge, Kent; 2nd, 1921, Phyllis Maud, *e d* of late William Dereham, Rawdon Hall, Holyport, Berks; one *d*. *Educ:* Rugby; Queen's College, Oxford. 1st Class Classics, 2nd Class History. President Oxford Union Society, 1888; Lt-Col late commanding 3rd Batt. RW Kent Regiment, with which he served at Malta during the embodiment, 1899–1900; Private Secretary to Chancellor of Exchequer, 1895–1900; JP Kent and Berkshire; MP (C) Tonbridge Division, Kent, 1892–1906; (Co. U) Dudley, 1910–21; (Co. U) Taunton, 1921–22; Parliamentary Charity Commissioner, 1900–06; Member of London County Council, 1910–13, and was Chairman of the Housing of the Working Classes Committee; during European War commanded 3rd Batt. RW Kent Regt (Special Reserve) at Chatham, and later served in France in command of a battalion of the Hampshire Regt (despatches and also in Sec. of State's list); Parliamentary Secretary to Ministry of Pensions, 1916–19; Parliamentary Secretary of Board of Agriculture and Fisheries, 1919–21; Minister of Agriculture and Fisheries, 1921–22; Minister of Health, 1922–23; Chairman of Commissioners under Welsh Church Act, 1923–45; Chairman, Royal Commission on Transport, 1928–31; Chairman of Transport Advisory Council, 1936–45; is Hon. Treasurer of the Church Army and one of the Trustees of the Whiteley Homes; a Member of the Church Assembly, late Chairman of the Church of England Pensions Board. *Publications:* Fourteen Years in Parliament, 1907; Memories 1925. *Recreations:* travelling;

has visited America, Japan, China, Egypt, South Africa, etc.; shooting, fishing, motoring, etc. *Address:* Pangbourne Lodge, Berkshire. *Club:* Carlton.

Died 1 June 1946.

GRIFFITH-JONES, Ebenezer, BA (Honours), London, 1882; DD Edin., 1912; Principal Emeritus of United Independent College Bradford; *b* Merthyr Tydvil, 5 Feb. 1860; *s* of Rev. E. Ayron Jones, Congregational Min., and Mary Ann, *d* of late Rev. D. Griffith, Missionary to Madagascar; *m* Carita (*d* 1936), *d* of T. F. Stoner, Frithknowl, Elstree, Herts; one *s* one *d.* *Educ:* Emlyn Grammar School, Newcastle-Emlyn; Presbyterian College, Carmarthen; New and University Colleges, London. Congregational Minister at St John's Wood, 1885–87; Llanelly, 1887–90; Mount View, Stroud Green, 1890–98; Balham, 1898–1907; Principal and Professor of Dogmatics, Apologetics, Homiletics, and Practical Theology at Yorkshire United Independent College, Bradford, 1907–32; Minister-in-Charge English Congregational Church, Llandilo, 1932–36; Chairman of the Congregational Union of England and Wales, 1918–19; Chairman of Yorkshire Congregational Union, 1924–25; President, National Free Church Council, 1931–32. *Publications:* The Ascent through Christ, 1899; Types of Christian Life, 1901; The Master and His Method, 1903; Economics of Jesus, 1904; Faith and Verification, 1907; The Challenge of Christianity to a World at War, 1915; Faith and Immortality, 1916; The Unspeakable Gift, 1918; Providence Divine and Human, vol. i; Some Problems of Divine Providence, 1925; vol. ii, The Dominion of Man, 1926. *Recreations:* photography, golf, motoring, chess. *Address:* Bryn, Manordillo, Llandilo, S Wales.

Died 22 March 1942.

GRIFFITHS, George Arthur; MP (Lab) Hemsworth Division of Yorkshire since 1934; a checkweighman at the Monkton Colliery; secretary and organizer to the Labour Party in the Hemsworth Division; Member of Royston UDC since 1910, Chairman 7 times; Member of WRCC since 1925; *b* 1880; *m* 1902; three *d.* *Educ:* Buckley C of E School. Member of Coalowners and Workmen Joint Board for 14 years; Member of South Yorkshire Miners' Welfare Committee 10 years; Miner's Delegate for Monckton YMA for 21 years. *Address:* 14 Park View, Royston, Yorks.

Died 15 Dec. 1945.

GRIFFITHS, Lt-Col George Cruickshank, CMG 1919; CBE 1937; Director of Produce; Maize, Potato, and Rice Controller; *b* 1884; *m* 1926, Catherine Marion, *o d* of Ernest Alexander Walker, MD, CM, New Plymouth, New Zealand. Served European War, 1915–19 (despatches, CMG). *Address:* Box 921, Nairobi, Kenya Colony.

Died 1 Sept. 1949.

GRIFFITHS, John, MA (Lond.); BA (Wales); BD (London and Wales); Professor of New Testament Greek at the Baptist College, Cardiff; *s* of Ioan and Jane Griffiths; *m* 1908, Edith Davies, Rhos, Wrexham; one *s* one *d.* *Educ:* Old College School, Carmarthen; Bangor Baptist College; University College, Bangor. Started life as a miner; after seven years training at Bangor, settled as Pastor of Ebenezer Baptist Church, Ammanford, 1908; edited Seren Gomer Welsh Baptist Bimonthly, 1917–20 and Heuwr Welsh Baptist Sunday School Magazine, 1922–23; conducted University tutorial classes, 1919–28. *Publications:* over 200 articles to various Welsh magazines and periodicals, including The Contributions of Glamorganshire Baptists to Religious Doctrine and several articles in the Welsh Bible Dictionary. *Recreations:* golf and walking.

Died 13 Feb. 1947.

GRIFFITHS, Col Joseph, CMG 1918; MD, FRCS (Eng.); late Col OC 1st Eastern General Hospital. *Educ:* Edinburgh University. Surgeon Addenbrooke's Hospital; Consulting Surgeon, St Leonard's Hospital, Sudbury, and County Hospital, Huntingdon; Hunterian Professor R. College of Surgeons, 1894–95; Reader in Surgery, Cambridge University, 1897–1902. *Address:* 6 Union Road, Cambridge. *TA:* and *T:* Cambridge 56638.

Died 4 Jan. 1945.

GRIFFITHS, Brig.-Gen. Thomas, CMG 1917; CBE 1919; DSO 1916; *b* Presteigne, Radnorshire, 29 Sept. 1865; *m* Delia, *d* of Wm Macnamara of Kew, Victoria; two *d.* *Educ:* Old Vicarage, Wrexham. Joined Permanent Military Forces, Victoria, 1886; served continuously in that Force and Defence Dept of Australia; World War, 1914–18 (CMG, CBE, DSO); served on General Birdwood's Staff, Military Administrator, German New Guinea, 1920–21; Administrator of the Island of Nauru, Central Pacific, 1921–27; retired 1927; Member Commonwealth War Pension Entitlement Appeal Board, 1929–32; Acting Administrator of New Guinea, 1932–33; Administrator, 1933–34. *Address:* 15 Lempriere Avenue, East St Kilda, Melbourne, Australia.

Died 10 Nov. 1947.

GRIGGS, Clare H., FCIS; General Secretary, Ideal Benefit Society; Ideal Insurance Company Ltd, Ideal Bank Ltd; Vice-Chairman, Birmingham Executive Council; *d* of Francis Wm Daniels, JP and Charlotte Smith; *m* 1st, 1913, H. Ireton Hands (Architect and Surveyor); 2nd, 1930, Wilfrid H. Griggs (Company Director). *Educ:* King Edward's Grammar School, Birmingham. Director of Maypole Developments Ltd; originally Assistant Secretary to the Ideal Benefit Society. *Recreation:* golf. *Address:* Aspley House, Tanworth-in-Arden, Warwickshire. *T:* Tanworth-in-Arden 222.

Died 2 Jan. 1950.

GRIGSON, Air Cdre John William Boldero, DSO 1920; DFC; Royal Air Force; *b* 26 Jan. 1893; *e s* of late Canon W. S. Grigson; *m* 1933, Mary Isabel, *o d* of R. T. D. Sayle, JP, Langtons, Ottershaw, Surrey; two *s.* *Educ:* Leatherhead. Served European War, 1914–20 (DSO, DFC and bar, despatches); Egypt and Iraq, 1920–22 (bar to DFC); Iraq, 1925–29; Staff College, Andover, 1925; Imperial Defence College, 1930. *Recreation:* fishing. *Club:* Royal Air Force.

Died 3 July 1943.

GRIGSON, Sir Wilfrid Vernon, Kt 1947; CSI 1945; ICS, retd; *b* 11 Oct. 1896; 3rd *s* of late Rev. Canon W. S. Grigson, Vicar of Pelynt, Cornwall, and late Mary Beatrice Boldero; *m* 1920, Phyllis May Holt (Kaisar-i-Hind Silver Medal, 1945), *d* of late Edgar Percy Bainbridge; one *s* one *d.* *Educ:* Leatherhead; Christ Church, Oxford (Classical Scholar, 2nd Class Hon. Mods 1916, BA 1919, MA 1945). 5th Officer Cadet Bn, Cambridge, 1916; served with Machine-Gun Corps (Lt), 1916–19 (France and Mesopotamia 1917, Palestine, France and Belgium 1918). Entered ICS 1919. Asst Commissioner, Central Provinces, 1920, served as Deputy Commissioner of Seoni (1925), Hoshangabad (1926–27 and again 1935–36), Nagpur (1931–34), Jubbulpore (1936–38); Administrator, Bastar State, 1927–31; Member, Indian Legislative Assembly, Delhi Session, 1936; acted as Commissioner, Jubbulpore, 1937, and Addtl Commissioner, Nagpur, 1940. Director-General Revenue Hyderabad State, and Special Duty there, 1938–40; Joint Secretary in Ch. Sec.'s Depts, Nagpur, 1940–41; Governor's Secretary CP and Berar, 1941–42; Aboriginal Tribes Enquiry Officer in addition, 1940–42; Member Executive Council of the Nizam of Hyderabad and Berar (Revenue, Police, Supply, Local Government and Rural Reconstruction portfolios), 1942–46; Revenue Minister in charge Revenue, Customs, Excise, Rural Reconstruction, Backward Classes, Town and Country Planning, 1946–47; Leader of the House, Hyderabad Legislative Assembly, 1947; released from service, 1947; Secretary, Ministry of Refugees, Government of Pakistan, 1947. *Publications:* The Maria Gonds of Bastar, 1938; The Aboriginal Problem in the Central Provinces and Berar (Nagpur, 1944); The Aboriginal in the Future India (Royal Anthropological Institute), 1945; The Challenge of Backwardness (Hyderabad), 1947; various other reports and articles on the aboriginals of the CP and Hyderabad. *Recreations:* Fellow, Royal Anthropological Institute, Royal Society of Arts, Indian Anthropological Institute, (Pres.) Deccan History Assoc.; golf and shooting. *Address:* 239 Staff Lines, Bonus Road, Karachi; c/o Lloyds Bank, 6 Pall Mall, SW1.

Died 26 Nov. 1948.

GRILLO, Dr Ernesto N. G.; First Stevenson Professor of Italian Language and Literature, University of Glasgow, 1925–40; Director of Italian Studies, University of Glasgow, 1910–40; Head of Italian Department, Athenæum Commercial College, Glasgow, 1911–40; Interim Italian Lecturer, University of Edinburgh, 1918–20; Professor of English and German, University of Urbino, 1903–05; Director, Anglo-American Institute, Florence, 1905–09; Italian Examiner to Civil Service Commission, 1912–40; Italian Examiner to Royal Society of Arts, since 1919; Italian Examiner to University of Edinburgh, 1919–25; Interim Italian Consul-General for Scotland, 1921; Professor of Comparative Literature, University of Perugia Summer Sessions, 1927–30; Knight Officer of the Crown of Italy; *b* Italy, Dec. 1877; *s* of late Don Vincenzo Grillo, of S. Angelo Lombardi and S. Gennaro; *m*; one *s* one *d. Educ:* Italy, Switzerland, England, Germany. MA Urbino; DLit (Royal University of Florence); LLD (University of Perugia); MA (Hon.) Glasgow University. *Publications:* Lezioni d'Inglese, 1903; Lezioni di tedesco, 1904; Chaucer and Boccaccio, 1903; De Luci Acci Vita et Scriptis, 1907; De Joanne Cassiano, 1910; Italy and the War, 1914; The Italian Poets, 1917; The Italian Prose-Writers, 1917; A New Italian Grammar, 1918; La Dolce Favella, 1918; The Teaching of English, 1918; Fiume; The Only Possible Solution, 1919; Pre-Dante Poetical Schools, 1919; The Dawn of Italian Prose, 1920; a new Italian Dictionary, 1921; Dante the Prophet, 1921; The Univ. of Padua, 1922; Tasso's Aminta, 1923; The Univ. of Naples, 1924; The Univ. of Pavia, 1925; Girolamo Savonarola, 1925; Shakespeare in Italy, 1925; Ugo Foscolo, I Sepolcri, 1928; Machiavelli, 1928; Gemme e Fiori, 1929; Italian Studies, 1929; Studies in Modern Italian Literature; Studies in Modern Italian Literature, Second Series; Italy Under Fascism; Studies in Italian Romanticism; Relazioni Culturali tra l'Italia e la Gran Bretagna, 1940; odd papers, articles, short poems on various subjects. *Recreations:* interest in agriculture, walking. *Address:* Asker, Cardross, Scotland; Casa Grillo, S Angelo Lombardi, South Italy.

Died 6 July 1946.

GRIMMER, Hon. W. C. Hazen, MA, KC; LLD; Judge, Court of Appeal and Chancery Court, New Brunswick, 1914; Court of Divorce and Matrimonial Causes, 1932; *b* 31 Oct. 1858; *s* of Geo. S. and Mary A. Grimmer; *m* 1884, Bessie Emily Gove, Saint Andrews, New Brunswick; one *s* one *d. Educ:* University of New Brunswick, Fredericton. Studied law at Saint Andrews. Admitted to Bar, 1880; Barrister, 1881; KC, 1902; moved to Saint Stephen's, 1881; Mayor, 1889; elected to Legislative Assembly, 1903; re-elected, 1908–12; Surveyor-General in Hazen Government, 1908; Attorney-General, New Brunswick, 1911–14. *Address:* Saint John, New Brunswick. *T:* 4571. *Clubs:* Cliff, St John.

Died 3 Oct. 1945.

GRIMSDALE, Harold Barr, MB, BC (Cantab), FRCS (Eng.); Consulting Ophthalmic Surgeon, St George's Hospital; Consulting Surgeon, Royal Westminster Ophthalmic Hospital; Consulting Ophthalmic Surgeon,

Bushey Cottage Hospital; Hon. Ophthalmic Surgeon to Royal Normal College for Blind, to Governesses' Benevolent Institution, to Artists' Annuity Fund; *b* Liverpool, 1866; *s* of Dr T. F. Grimsdale; *m* Mabel, *d* of S. E. Todd. *Educ:* Winchester (Entrance Exhibition); Caius College, Cambridge (Exhibition); St George's Hospital (Entrance Scholarship). Hon. Consulting Ophthalmic Surgeon to Military Hospitals in London; Member of Departmental Committee on Welfare of the Blind. *Publications:* Lectures on Nursing of Diseases of the Eye; Elementary Lectures on Errors of Refraction; Chief Operations of Ophthalmic Surgery; (with Elmore Brewerton, FRCS) A Text-Book of Ophthalmic Operations, 1907; third edition, 1937.

Died 5 May 1942.

GRIMSTON, Col Lionel Augustus, CIE 1921; OBE 1919; VD 1908; Chairman and Director, Upper Assam Tea Co., Ltd, Eastern Assam (Tea) Co., Ltd and New Columbia Rubber Co., Ltd; *b* 18 April 1868; *s* of Colonel Oswald Grimston and Frances Campbell; unmarried. *Educ:* All Saints School, Bloxham. United Services College, Westward Ho! Assistant at Chowkidinghi, Dibrugarh Combination (Tea) Co., Assam, 1886–91; Manager, Rajghur Division, Eastern Assam (Tea) Co., Ltd, Assam, 1891–97; Superintendent, Eastern Assam (Tea) Co., Ltd, 1897–1921; Lakhimpur Mounted Rifles (Volunteers), Assam, 1888–91; Assam Valley Mounted Rifles (Volunteers), 1891–96; Assam Valley Light Horse (Volunteers), 1896–1917; 6th Assam Valley Light Horse (Indian Defence Force), 1917–20; Assam Valley Light Horse (Auxiliary Force India), 1920–21; in command, 1916–21, with rank of Lt-Col; retired with honorary rank of Colonel, 1921; Hon. ADC to Viceroy of India, 1918–21. *Address:* Sedgemoor, 2 Mill Road, Eastbourne, Sussex. *T:* Eastbourne 1429. *Club:* Golfers'.

Died 12 Nov. 1943.

GRIMWADE, Maj.-Gen. Harold William, CB 1918; CMG 1917; VD; *b* 18 May 1869; *s* of late Hon. F. S. Grimwade, MLC; *m* 1896, Winifred (*d* 1939), *d* of John Thornton; two *s* one *d.* Served European War (despatches four times, CB, CMG, Croix de Guerre); commanded 4th Division Australian Commonwealth Forces, 1926–30; retired 1931; Hon. Colonel Univ. Rifles Regt, Melbourne. Member Felton Bequest Cttee. *Address:* Marathon, Frankston, Victoria, Australia. *Clubs:* Melbourne, Australian (Melbourne).

Died 3 Jan. 1949.

GRINDELL-MATTHEWS, Harry; Occupied in Research Work, particularly Air Defence; *b* 17 March 1880; *s* of Daniel Matthews and Jane Rymer Grindell. *Educ:* privately; Merchant Venturers' College, Bristol. On outbreak of Boer War 1899, volunteered for service with Cape Mounted forces and served throughout campaign (twice wounded); wireless Telephone and Broadcasting; in 1911 on Ely Racecourse, Cardiff, established wireless telephonic conversation with aeroplane in flight and sent first Press message by Radio Telephone from Westgate Hotel, Newport, Mon, to Western Mail, Cardiff; list of inventions; Automatic pilot for flying machine; in 1912 gave Command demonstration of wireless Telephone between motor cars at Buckingham Palace; in 1914 controlled boats by means of searchlight (this invention was acquired by the British Government for the Admiralty); Submarine Detecting Devices, 1915–17; Talking Films, photographing Sound Records simultaneously with pictures on same film, the late Sir Ernest Shackleton's farewell being so recorded, 1918–24; Sky projector 1925, first demonstration given in Germany and later in New York; Luminaphone—an organ played by light, 1926; consulting expert on Sound Film Production to Warner Bros, USA, 1926–27; engaged upon methods of

Defence from Air Attack and Underwater Craft since 1930. *Recreation:* flying. *Address:* Tor Cloud, Clydach, Glam.

Died 11 Sept. 1941.

GRISWOLD, Rev. H. D., DD, PhD; *b* 24 May 1860; *s* of Benjamin Griswold and Laura Hurd; *m* 1890, Fannie Sheldon; one *s* two *d. Educ:* Union College, Schenectady, NY, Union Theological Seminary, NY City, Oxford, Berlin and Cornell Universities. Missionary in India, 1890–1927, appointed by the Board of Foreign Missions of the Presbyterian Church, USA; Missionary, Jhansi, India, 1890–94; Professor of Philosophy, Forman Christian College, Lahore, Punjab, 1894–1913; Secretary of the Council of the three India Missions of the Presbyterian Church in the USA, 1914–18 and 1922–25; Visiting Lecturer in Columbia University, New York, on Modern Hinduism, 1928–29. *Publications:* Brahman, a Study in the History of Indian Philosophy, 1900; The God Varuna in the Rig Veda, 1910; The Religion of the Rig Veda, 1923; Ancestors and Descendants of Edward Griswold of Dryden, NY, 1930; Insights into Modern Hinduism, 1934; articles in Encyclopædia of Religion and Ethics on the Arya Samaj and Indian Pessimism; and in Encyclopædia of Social Sciences on Brahmanism and Hinduism; Monographs on the Chet Rami and Radha Swami Sects, and on the Qadiani Movement. *Recreations:* reading, genealogical research. *Address:* c/o Dr Arthur Griswold, 4611 Main Street, Stratford, Conn, USA. *Clubs:* Phi Delta Theta, Phi Beta Kappa.

Died 11 May 1945.

GRITTEN, William George Howard, MA, FRGS; barrister and writer; MP (C) The Hartlepools, 1918–22, and since 1929; *o s* of William and Annie Howard Gritten, father, architect; *m* 1918, Helena Blanche Paget, widow of Commander Webb, RN; one *s. Educ:* Brasenose College, Oxford (Classical Scholar and Exhibitioner, Hons Class. Mods, Bridgman Essay Prize, Hons Lit. Hum.). Called to Bar, Inner Temple, 1899; Northern Circuit and CCC; contested (C) the Hartlepools, Jan., June (by-election), and Dec. 1910–22, and 1923; has the record of having fought nine contested elections in the same constituency; Freeman City of London, and Liveryman Painters' Company. Has travelled in Asia, Africa, America, and round the world. *Publications:* many articles on political and other subjects in monthly magazines and weekly and daily press. *Recreations:* sculling, cycling. *Clubs:* Carlton, Pratts', 1900 (Deputy Chairman).

Died 5 April 1943.

GROGAN, Brig.-Gen. Edward George, CB 1902; CBE 1919; JP Co. Fife; *b* 21 June 1851; *o s* of George Grogan, JP, of Seafield, Co. Dublin, Carabineers and 7th Royal Fusiliers; *m* 1st, 1874, Meta (*d* 1881), *d* of Admiral Sir W. King Hall, KCB; 2nd, 1883, Ida (*d* 1943), *d* of J. R. Forman of Craig Park, Midlothian; five *s* two *d. Educ:* Cheltenham Coll. Served in 42nd Royal Highlanders (the Black Watch) in expedition to Coomassie, 1873–74 (wounded at battle of Amoaful, medal with clasp); South African campaign in command of 1st Batt. the Black Watch (despatches, medal with 4 clasps, CB); Colonel Commanding Black Watch Brigade Territorial Force; retired, 1907; appointed to Command a Brigade with temporary rank of Brigadier-General 16 Nov. 1914; retired. *Address:* Torrevagh, St Andrews. *Clubs:* Royal and Ancient, St Andrews.

Died 24 April 1944.

GROGAN, Lt-Col George Meredyth, DSO 1916; on retired pay; *s* of late Rev. John Grogan, MA, of Ballardin, Co. Meath, and Clyde Road, Dublin; *m* 1927, Eva Augusta Elizabeth, *d* of Ernest F. L. Ellis, of St Austins, Co. Wexford; one *s.* Gazetted to the Royal Irish Regt, 1890; served S African War (Queen's medal 3 clasps, King's medal 2 clasps); European War continuously at the Front for three years; took part in

Gallipoli operations, including Suvla Bay landing, also in Salonika Front, including operations at Dorian and Struma Valley; Palestine campaign, including Gaza line, and fall of Jerusalem, also in France (Vimy Ridge) (despatches twice, DSO, 1915 Star, Brit. War medal, Victory medal, Officer, Order of the Crown of Italy). *Recreations:* shooting and lawn tennis. *Address:* Plattenstown, Arklow, Co. Wicklow. *T:* Arklow 28. *Clubs:* Kildare Street, Dublin.

Died 4 July 1942.

GRONOW, Albert George, CBE 1920; Chairman and Managing Director Burrup, Mathieson and Company, Limited; *b* 30 April 1878; *s* of Sylvanus and Rhoda Gronow; *m* 1909, Alice Mabel, 3rd *d* of Lieut-Commander G. R. Stone, RN; one *s. Educ:* Maindee School, Newport, Mon. Served apprenticeship to printing from 1890 with R. H. Johns, Ltd, Newport, Mon; Director and General Manager of Waterlow Bros and Layton, Ltd, 1910–19; whilst with this Company was responsible for production of emergency Paper Money on the outbreak of war in 1914, the development of New Paper Money by photogravure process 1916, produced the whole of the Food Rationing printing for this country, 1918, was technical adviser on Government Printing Works to Controller of HM Stationery Office, 1919–21; Director and Joint General Manager of Waterlow & Sons Ltd, 1919–21. *Recreations:* golf, tennis. *Address:* Charnwood, Harrow Weald. *Clubs:* Royal Automobile; Moor Park.

Died 21 April 1950.

GROSE, Frank Samuel, CBE 1938; retired; *b* 15 Oct. 1881; *s* of late Dr S. Grose, FRCS. *Educ:* Brighton College. Northern India Salt Revenue Dept and Burma Frontier Service, 1904–37. *Recreations:* golf, walking. *Address:* Eversley, Highweek, Newton Abbot. *T:* Newton Abbot 294. *Club:* East India and Sports.

Died 25 Dec. 1941.

GROSE, Sir James Trevilly, Kt 1934; President, Boy Scouts Association New Zealand; Chairman, Imperial Chemical Industries (New Zealand) Ltd; Chairman, New Zealand Board, National Mutual Life Association of Australasia Ltd; Director, Imperial Chemical Industries (Australia) & New Zealand Ltd, Bryant & May, Bell & Co., Ltd, British Australian Lead Manufacturers (New Zealand) Ltd; Local Director in Wellington, New Zealand Insurance Co. Ltd Trustee Department; General Manager, National Bank of New Zealand Ltd, 1928–37, Advisory Director in New Zealand, since 1937; *b* 13 April 1872; *s* of Edward Giddy Grose and Mary Eliza Ball; *m* 1st, 1907, Annie Jane Hartley; one *s* one *d*; 2nd, 1927, Fannie Jane Sendall. *Educ:* Brisbane Grammar School. Entered service of Bank of New South Wales, 1889; loaned to Commonwealth Government, 1918; Finance Secretary to Defence Dept, 1918–19; returned to service of Bank of New South Wales; Chairman of Associated Banks, NZ, 1929 and 1932–33. *Recreations:* golf, fishing, gardening. *Address:* 27 Orchard Street, Wadestown, Wellington, NZ. *Clubs:* Wellington, Wellington.

Died 5 Dec. 1944.

GROSVENOR, Lady Henry, (Rosamund Angharad), CBE 1918; *o c* of late Edward Lloyd of Castella, Glamorgan; *m* 1st, Edward Seymour Greaves of Glen Etive, Argyll, Watchbury, Warwickshire and Quenby Hall, Leicestershire; 2nd, 1911, Lord Henry Grosvenor, 3rd *s* of 1st Duke of Westminster (*d* 1914).

Died 16 April 1941.

GROVE, Henry Montgomery, CBE 1929; *b* 27 Feb. 1867; *e s* of Maj.-General Henry Leslie Grove, Madras Staff Corps; *m* 1906, Lilian Mabel, *d* of Rev. Canon A. Hall Hall; four *s. Educ:* Clifton College; RMC, Sandhurst. 2nd Lieut Devonshire Regiment, 1887; Lieut 1st Bengal Cavalry, 1890; left Indian Army consequent on illness, 1897; acting Consul at Moscow, 1900; HBM

Consul, Moscow, 1901–13; Consul at Warsaw, 1913–15; left when Germans took Poland; in charge of Consulate of Helsingfors, Finland, 1915–18 (Russian Revolution, Finnish Red and White fighting, advent of Germans in Finland, etc.); Consul-General at Gothenburg, Sweden, 1919–20; Special Employment Department of Overseas Trade, 1920–21; HBM Consul-General and Senior Assistant Agent with the British Mission at Moscow, 1921–23; HBM Consul-General, Reval, Estonia, 1923–28; retired 1928; employed in the Foreign Office, 1930–37. *Publication:* Moscow. *Address:* Wayside Cottage, Brasted Chart, Kent. *T:* Brasted 3.

Died 1 April 1942.

GROVE, Col Reginald Parker, CMG 1917; *b* 23 Aug. 1859; *s* of late Philip Grove, Eastcote, Pattishall, Northamptonshire, and Laura, *d* of late Thomas Lynes; *m* 1891, Mary Donaldson (*d* 1940), *d* of William Young Craig; one *s* two *d*. *Educ:* private school; Royal Military College, Sandhurst. 2nd Lieut 22nd Cheshire Regiment, 1879; Brevet-Colonel, 1909; Colonel, 1910; Commanded Territorial Brigade, 1911; retired, 1912; served Burmese Expedition, 1888–89 (medal with clasp); South African War, 1900–02 (despatches twice, Queen's medal with three clasps, King's medal with two clasps); served on Staff in France in European War (despatches twice, 1914 Star, CMG). *Address:* Lloyds Bank, Ltd, 6 Pall Mall, SW1.

Died 20 April 1942.

GROVER, Gen. Sir Malcolm Henry Stanley, KCB 1914; KCIE 1911; CB 1906; *b* 19 July 1858; 6th *s* of late Charles Ehret Grover of Hemel Hempstead, Herts; *m* 1891, Helen Grace (*d* 1912), *y d* of late Alexander John Lawrence, CIE, Indian Civil Service; one *s* one *d*. *Educ:* Charterhouse; Roy. Mil. College, Sandhurst. Entered Army, 1876; Captain, 1887; Major, 1896; Brevet Lt-Col, 1898; Subst. Lt-Col, 1902; Subst. Col, 1902; Maj.-General, 1907; Lt-Gen., 1912; Gen. 1917; on staff of the Cesarevitch of Russia during his visit to India, 1890–91; DAAG Punjab Frontier Force, 1894–95; DAQMG Punjab Command Headquarters, 1895–98; AAG Punjab Frontier Force, 1898–1900; AQMG Eastern Command Headquarters, 1902–05; DAG Eastern Command Headquarters (officiating), 1905; Afghan Campaign, 1879–80 (medal); Sudan Campaign, 1885, action of Tamai, affair at Thakool (medal with clasp, bronze star); NW Frontier India; Waziristan, 1894–95, as DAAG, Headquarters Staff (medal with clasp, despatches); Tochi, 1897–98, as DAQMG 2nd Brigade (medal with clasp, despatches); South African War, 1901–02, special service (medal with three clasps); commanded Cavalry Brigade, Punjab, 1906–08; Inspector-General of Cavalry in India, 1908–11; Secretary to Government of India, Army Department, 1911–12; commanded 4th (Quetta) Division, India, 1912–16; War Medal, 1914–18; retired, 1919. *Address:* 42 Lingfield Road, Wimbledon Common, Surrey. *Club:* United Service.

Died 17 Nov. 1945.

GROVER, Montague Macgregor; *b* Melbourne, 1870; *s* of Harry Grover, Hemel Hempstead; *m* Regina, *y d* of Reginald Varley. *Educ:* State School; Church of England Grammar School; Queen's College. Articled to Melbourne firm of architects, 1888–92, joined the Melbourne Age, 1894; on the literary staff of the Melbourne Argus, 1896–1907; visited England as Secretary to the late J. C. Williamson, theatrical manager, 1902–03; sub-editor Sydney Morning Herald, 1907–10; started as editor Daily Sun, 1910–16; Sunday Sun, Sydney, 1917; London Representative, 1920–21; edited Sydney Sun, 1921–22; started as editor Melbourne Sun Pictorial, first pictorial daily in Australia, Sept. 1922; started as editor Melbourne Evening Sun, May 1923; six months in USA writing for Melbourne Herald, 1926; Editor of the World, Sydney, 1931–32; Melbourne representative Sydney Bulletin. *Publications:* The Minus Quantity and other short plays, 1914; The Time is Ripe (Economic); numerous short stories and verses, and for many years a regular contributor to the Sydney Bulletin; Socialist. *Recreation:* surf bathing. *Address:* 9 Copelen Street, South Yarra, Melbourne, SE1, Australia.

Died 7 March 1943.

GROVES, Charles Nixon, CBE 1920; OStJ; MA, MD, BCh Oxford; general practitioner; *b* 1871; *m* Frances (decd), *d* of Dr F. M. Miller, JP; one *s* one *d*. *Educ:* Bradfield College School; Oxford University; London Hospital. Fellow and late Member of the Council of Medical Society of London and of Harveian Society; medical officer in charge of Darell Hospital for officers during the War, 1915–19; twice mentioned in lists of Sec. of State for War. *Recreation:* golf. *Address:* 16 Pembridge Crescent, W11. *T:* Bayswater 0380. *Clubs:* Athenæum; Royal West Norfolk Golf.

Died 8 Nov. 1950.

GROVES, Ernest William Hey, MS and MD, London, DSc, (Hon. Brist), FRCS, England; FRACS; LLD (Hon. Belfast); Emeritus Professor of Surgery in the University of Bristol; Consulting Surgeon to Bristol General Hospital; Cons. Editor British Journal of Surgery; *b* 20 June 1872; *s* of Edward Kennaway Groves, Civil Engineer in India, Kingston Cottage, Coonoor; *m* 1896, Frederica Margaret Louise, *d* of Rev. E. Anderson, Vicar of Berwick Bassett, Swindon; no *c*. *Educ:* Redland Hill House, Bristol; London University; gained Scholarship to St Bartholomew's Hospital, EC. House Surgeon to Sir Francis Champneys there; Surgeon to the Bristol General Hospital 1913; President of the British Orthopedic Association, 1928–29; Vice-President of the Royal College of Surgeons, England, 1928–29; President of the Association of Surgeons of Great Britain and Ireland, 1929–30; Hunterian orator, 1930. *Publications:* Synopsis of Surgery; Textbook for Nurses; Surgical Operations for Nurses and Students; Modern Methods of treating Fractures; and other articles. *Recreations:* golf, swimming. *Address:* 25 Victoria Square, Clifton, Bristol.

Died 22 Oct. 1944.

GROVES, Herbert Austen, CBE 1919; LLB (Lond.); Solicitor and Parliamentary Agent, retired; *b* 1880; *s* of late Rev. W. H. Groves. Home Office (Prisoners of War Branch), 1915–17; Member of Committee on Proposals for Employment of Prisoners of War, 1916–17; Admiralty, 1917–19, and Assistant Secretary (Board), 1919; Parliamentary Agent to HM Government, 1932–34. *Recreations:* gardening, travel. *Address:* 33 Circus Road, NW8. *T:* Primrose 1268. *Club:* Royal Automobile.

Died 25 Feb. 1943.

GROVES, Col John Edward Grimble, CMG 1916; TD; JP; late 5th Batt. Cheshire Regt (TF); *b* 1863; *y s* of late William Peer Grimble Groves, Salford, Lancashire; *m* 1st, 1888, Ethel Lloyd (*d* 1934), *e d* of late C. J. Allen, 20 Bedford Row, WC; three *s* four *d*; 2nd, 1936, Florence, 5th *d* of George Kitchener and widow of R. J. Tickle. Served European War 1914–18 (despatches, CMG). *Address:* Lydstep Haven, Pembrokeshire. *T:* Manorbier 29. *Club:* Junior United Service.

Died 29 July 1948.

GRUBER, Rudolph, MD, MRCS; Consulting Ophthalmic Surgeon to the German Hospital, London; *b* 1868; *s* of late Professor Dr Joseph Gruber of the University of Vienna; *m* Dorothy H. Tabor, *d* of S. Brock; no *c*. *Educ:* University of Vienna. Senior Assistant Surgeon to the first Ophthalmic Clinic of the University of Vienna and lecturer on the Diseases of the Eye; Consulting Ophthalmic Surgeon to the German Hospital, London. *Publications:* several papers on ophthalmological subjects, mostly Graefe's Archiv für Ophthalmologie. *Recreations:* gardening and chess. *Address:* 81 Harley Street, W1. *T:* Welbeck 6486; Joyden Crest, Bexley, Kent.

Died 15 April 1945.

GRUNDY, Cecil Reginald; late Editor of The Connoisseur; *b* 31 May 1870; *s* of Edwin Landseer Grundy, art critic of Liverpool; *m* Clara Beatrice (*d* 1914), *d* of Henry Rawlings Smith of New Zealand; one *d. Educ:* High School, Liverpool Institute; Liverpool School of Art. Initiated the scheme for local war museums adopted throughout the Kingdom and in several British Colonies; Hon. Sec. Local War Museums Association; visited USA on behalf of the Museums Association and lectured at some of the principal Universities and Art Museums there, 1926. *Publications:* Life of James Ward, 1909; Local War Museums, a Suggestion, 1916; Frederick William Hayes, 1922; The Lady Lever Art Gallery, 1923 (2nd ed., with S. L. Davison, 1929); Lessons from America in Museum Organisation and Upkeep, 1927; English Art in the 18th Century, 1928; Libretto of Gainsborough, opera by Albert Coates, 1938; The Sacristy of Westminster Abbey, 1930; Catalogue of Pictures and Drawings in the F. J. Nettlefold Collection, 1933–; joint-author, History of the Innholders' Company, 1922; reviews and magazine articles on art. *Recreation:* chess. *Address:* 4 Earls Terrace, Kensington, W8. *T:* Western 5994.

Died 10 Dec. 1944.

GRUNDY, Sir Cuthbert Cartwright, Kt 1919; JP, RCA, RI, RWA, FLS; a Vice-President Royal West of England Academy, Royal British Colonial Society of Artists; Manchester Academy of Fine Arts; South Wales Art Society; Fylde Art Society; initiator of Lake District Artists Society; Hon. Member Royal Art Society of New South Wales, W Australian Society of Arts, New Zealand Academy of Fine Arts, Royal Society of Miniature Painters, etc.; originator of the Wayside Pulpit; Hon. Freeman of County Borough of Blackpool; *b* 1846; *y s* of late Thomas Grundy, and Eliza Relph-Greenhow. *Educ:* Stand Grammar School; Owens College (Victoria Univ.). President for 21 years of Royal Cambrian Academy. Interested in institutions and public work for the welfare of the people; donor of Bury children's Holiday Home, Manchester Special School for Phthisic children, Children's Convalescent Home, Blackpool, Bury Schools' Holiday Camp, Unsworth Children's Playing Field, Unitarian Church Hall, Blackpool; Land at Ambleside to National Trust, etc.; joint-donor with brother, J. R. G. Grundy, of the Grundy Art Gallery, Blackpool, Public Recreation Ground and Reading Room, Blackpool, the Public Institute, Pleasure Grounds Children's Recreation Ground and Grundy Park, Cheshunt, Herts; silver medal Royal Humane Society. *Publications:* An Introduction to the Study of Chemistry; Notes on the Food of Plants; How does a Plant grow?; pamphlets on the Fine Arts. *Recreations:* music, reading. *Address:* Homefield, Blackpool.

Died 1 Feb. 1946.

GRUNDY, George Beardoe, MA, DLitt Oxon; Hon. Fellow of Corpus Christi College, Oxford, since 1931; *s* of Rev. G. F. Grundy, Aspull, Lancs; *m* Mabel, *d* of Dr G. R. Ord, Streatham; one *s* one *d. Educ:* Brasenose Coll., Oxford; 2nd class Classical Moderations, 1890; 2nd class Lit. Hum. 1891; Geographical Student of the University of Oxford, 1892. Hon. mention for Conington Prize, 1897; Proxime Accessit, Arnold Historical Essay, 1899; Conington Prize, 1900. Lecturer for Professor of Ancient History, Oxford, 1897–1903; Fellow and Tutor of Corpus Christi College, Oxford, 1903–31; at one time University Lecturer in Classical Geography and Lecturer at Brasenose College. *Publications:* The Great Persian War, 1902; The Battle of Platæa, 1893; Thucydides and the History of his Age, 1911; Ancient Gems in Modern Settings, 1913; A History of the Greek and Roman World, 1926; Fifty-five years at Oxford, 1945; The Saxon Land Charters of Berkshire, Hampshire, Wiltshire, Somerset, Worcestershire, Gloucestershire and Dorsetshire; The Ancient Highways of Somerset, Dorset, Wilts, Hants, Berks, Oxon, Worcs, Gloucs in The Archaeological Journal; articles on Ancient History in Journal of Philology and Hellenic Journal. *Recreations:* golf, croquet. *Address:* 17 Parks Road, Oxford.

Died 6 Dec. 1948.

GRUNDY, Thomas Walter; *b* 1864; *m* 1885, Eliza Metcalfe. Mayor of Rotherham, 1915–16; MP (Lab) Rother Valley Division of Yorks, Dec. 1918–35; was an official of the Miners' Association. *Address:* 15 Godstone Road, Rotherham.

Died 28 Jan. 1942.

GRYLLS, Charles John Tench Bedford, CB 1927; CBE 1920; *b* 1874; *o s* of late Rev. Henry Borlase Grylls, MA, Vicar of Marystowe, Devon; *m* 1901, Florence Thompson; one *s* two *d. Educ:* Kelly College, Tavistock; Trinity College, Cambridge, BA, 1896. Entered Civil Service, 1897 (Public Record Office of Ireland); transferred to Inland Revenue Dept 1901; thence to Customs and Excise Dept 1909; Assistant Secretary to Board of Customs and Excise, 1919–25; Commissioner and Joint Secretary, Board of Customs and Excise, 1926–35. *Address:* 49 Fairacres, Roehampton Lane, SW15. *T:* Prospect 3271.

Died 16 Sept. 1946.

GUBBAY, Moses Mordecai Simeon, CSI 1918; CIE 1916; Indian Civil Service (retired); *b* Shanghai, 1876; *s* of M. S. Gubbay; *m* Ella Halford (*d* 1915); no *c. Educ:* Clifton; Caius College, Cambridge. Under-Secretary to the Govt of India Commerce Department, 1906–10; Collector of Customs, Bombay, 1910–15; Wheat Commissioner for India, 1915; Controller of Currency, India, 1916; Financial Secretary to the Government of India, 1920. *Address:* 117 Leadenhall Street, EC3. *Clubs:* East India and Sports; Bengal, Calcutta.

Died 14 May 1947.

GUEDALLA, Philip, MA, JP; *b* 12 March 1889; *o s* of late David Guedalla and late Louise Soman; *m* 1919, Nellie Maude Reitlinger. *Educ:* Rugby School; Balliol College, Oxford (Exhibitioner, 1st Class Honour Moderations, 1910; 1st Class Modern History 1912). President Oxford Union Society, 1911; Barrister, Inner Temple, 1913; retired from practice, 1923; served as legal adviser Contracts Department, War Office, and Ministry of Munitions; organised and acted as secretary to Flax Control Board, 1917–20; contested (L) North Hackney, 1922; North-East Derbyshire, 1923 and 1924; Rusholme, 1929; Withington, 1931; Squadron Leader, RAF, 1943; Hon. Director, Ibero-American Institute of Great Britain; Chairman, Ibero-American and Films Committees, British Council; Member of the Cinematograph Films Council, Board of Trade. *Publications:* Ignes Fatui, a Book of Parodies, 1911; Metri Gratia, Verse and Prose, 1911; The Partition of Europe, 1715–1815, 1914; Supers and Supermen, 1920; The Industrial Future, 1921; The Second Empire, 1922; Masters and Men, 1923; A Gallery, 1924; A Council of Industry, 1925; Napoleon and Palestine (Davis Lecture), 1925; Independence Day, 1926; Palmerston, 1926; Conquistador, 1927; Gladstone and Palmerston, 1928; Bonnet and Shawl, 1928; The Missing Muse, 1929; The Duke, 1931: Argentine Tango, 1932; The Queen and Mr Gladstone, 1933; The Hundred Days, 1934; The Hundred Years, 1936; The Hundredth Year, 1940; Mr Churchill: A Portrait, 1941; The Liberators, 1942; The Two Marshals, 1943; Middle East, a Study in Air Power, 1944. *Address:* The Laundry, Easton Park, Dunmow, Essex. *Clubs:* Athenæum, Garrick, Beefsteak.

Died 16 Dec. 1944.

GUIBAULT, Joseph Alexandre; KC; Judge Puisne of the Superior Court for the Province of Quebec, since 1934; *b* 23 Oct. 1870; *s* of Joseph Guibault and Olive St Germain; *m* 1897, Dinorah Desrosiers; one *s* one *d. Educ:* Seminary of Joliette. Admitted to practice, 1895;

Conservative candidate for the County of Joliette in the 1908 Federal Election; a member of the local City Council for three years; Mayor of the City of Joliette, 1909–20; was appointed to the Council of the Montreal Bar, 1919; President of both the Joliette Liberal Conservative Association and of L'Idée Conservatrice, since the foundation of these two associations, and attending delegate to the National Convention of Winnipeg, 1927; a director and legal adviser of the Union St Joseph of Canada, 1911–34; President of Joliette Fish and Game Club; Knight of Columbus (Joliette Council 1468), of which he was Grand Knight. *Publications:* was editor of the weekly newspaper L'Etoile du Nord, of Joliette, and was a contributor to local newspapers. *Recreations:* hunting, fishing, and travelling. *Address:* Court House, Montreal; 5 de Lanaudière Street, Joliette, PQ, Canada. *T:* Joliette 121. *Clubs:* Canadien, Société des Oliviers, Montreal; Joliette Fish and Game.

Died 25 Aug. 1940.

GUIDER, James Adolphus, CIE 1911; JP; *b* 6 June 1862; *s* of Michael Guider, of Knock, Roscrea, Ireland; *m* Marie Louise (*d* 1939), *d* of F. Morris; no *c. Educ:* St Paul's School, Belgaum. Indian Police, retired; Deputy Inspector-General of Police, Criminal Investigation Department, Bombay Presidency, 1910–20; Superintendent, Watch and Ward Dept, BB and CI Rly, India, 1921–32. *Address:* 4 Prince of Wales Road, Poona, India. *Clubs:* Western India, Poona.

Died 22 Sept. 1943.

GUILBERT, Yvette; lyric artist; Chevalier of the Legion of Honour; *b* Paris, 1865; *m* Dr M. Schiller. *Educ:* Paris; St Mandé. Served two years in the Magasin du Printemps; trained for the stage by Landrol; made *début* at Les Bouffes de Nord; has appeared at Cluny Theatre, Eldorado, Eden Concert, etc.; has visited England and United States. *Publications:* Struggles and Victories; 2 novels: La Vedette, Les Demi-Vieilles; How to Sing a Song, 1919; L'Art de chanter une chanson, 1927; La Chanson de Ma Vie (Memoires), 1927; English Version: The Song of My Life, 1929; La Passante Emerveillée (Mes voyages), 1929; Mes Lettres d'Amour, 1932; Collections of Songs edited by Schott, Augener, Enoch Hengel, Rouart, Ditson, etc. *Address:* 120 Rue de Courcelles, Paris. *T:* Carnot 28–79.

Died 3 Feb. 1944.

GUILFORD, 8th Earl of, *cr* 1752; **Frederick George North;** DL; JP Kent; Baron Guilford, 1683; late Lt-Col Royal East Kent Yeomanry; *b* 19 Nov. 1876; *s* of 7th Earl and Georgiana, 2nd *d* of Sir George Chetwynd, 3rd Bt; *m* 1901, Violet (*d* 1947), *e d* of W. Hargrave Pawson of Shawdon, Northumberland, and Hon. Mrs Howard of Sibton Park, Kent; two *s. Heir: g s* Lord North. *Address:* Home Farm House, Waldershare Park, Dover.

Died 9 Nov. 1949.

GUILLAMORE, 8th Viscount *cr* 1831; **Richard O'Grady;** Baron O'Grady of Rockbarton *cr* 1831; *b* 9 Aug. 1867; *s* of late James Waller O'Grady and Ada, sister of Sir W. C. Bruce, 9th Bt; *S* cousin, 1930. *Heir: b* Standish Bruce O'Grady, *b* 17 March 1869. *Address:* Rathfredagh, Newcastle West, Co. Limerick.

Died 28 Nov. 1943.

GUINNESS, Hon. (Arthur) Ernest; *b* 2 Nov. 1876; 2nd *s* of 1st Earl of Iveagh; *m* 1903, Marie Clotilde, *d* of Sir George Russell, 4th Bt; three *d. Educ:* Eton; Cambridge University, MA. Late Lieut London Rifle Brigade. *Address:* 17 Grosvenor Place, SW1. *T:* Sloane 7447; Holmbury House, Holmbury St Mary, Surrey; Glenmaroon, Chapelizod, Co. Dublin. *Clubs:* Carlton, Bachelors'; Kildare Street (Dublin).

Died 22 March 1949.

GUINNESS, Benjamin Seymour; Chairman of British and Foreign Trust Ltd; *b* Dublin, 18 Nov. 1868; *s* of Richard Seymour Guinness JP; *m* 1st, 1902, Bridget Henrietta Frances (*d* 1931), *d* of Sir Richard Lewis

Mostyn Williams-Bulkeley, 11th Bart, Baron Hill, Beaumaris, Anglesey; one *s* two *d*; 2nd, 1936, Donna Maria Nunziante, Principessa di Mignano, *d* of the Duca di Mignano (through this marriage Mr Guinness became Prince di Mignano, since confirmed by Royal Decree). *Educ:* Royal Navy. Royal Navy 1882–91, when retired with rank of Lieutenant; went to USA, where became prominent in various phases of business life; was Director of New York Trust Company; Lackawanna Steel Co.; Kansas City Southern Rly; Seaboard Air Line; Duquesne Light Company, Pittsburgh; United Railroads of San Francisco; retired in 1929. *Recreations:* shooting, fishing, yachting; race horse breeder. *Address:* 69 rue de Lille, Paris; 11 Carlton House Terrace, SW1. *Clubs:* Army and Navy, St James's.

Died 15 Dec. 1947.

GUINNESS, Hon. Ernest; *see* Guinness, Hon. A. E.

GUINNESS, Henry Seymour; *b* 24 Nov. 1858; *e s* of Henry Guinness of Burton Hall, Stillorgan, Co. Dublin; *m* 1900, Mary Middleton, *d* of Robert S. Bainbridge, of Keverstone, Co. Durham; four *d. Educ:* Winchester College. Royal Indian Engineering College, Coopers Hill; Argyll Scholar, 1879. Public Works Department, India, 1880–95; Lieutenant, Burma State Railway Volunteer Rifles, 1884; Burma Medal and three clasps, 1885–92; Associate Member Institution Civil Engineers, 1894–1934; High Sheriff, Co. Dublin, 1899; Council, Alexandra College, Dublin, 1899–1940 (Vice-Warden, 1913–40); Director, Great Northern Railway, Ireland, 1902–24; Director, Bank of Ireland, 1910–24 (Governor, 1922–24); Assistant Managing Director, Arthur Guinness, Son & Co. Ltd, 1924–30; Member, Royal Irish Academy, 1911; Representative Church Body, Ireland, 1916–31; Senator, Parliament of the Irish Free State, 1921–34. *Address:* Broadwater House, Tunbridge Wells. *T:* Tunbridge Wells 1375.

Died 4 April 1945.

GUISE-MOORES, Maj.-Gen. Sir Guise, KCB 1925; KCVO 1931; CB 1915; CMG 1918; MRCS Eng., LRCP Lond., DPH Lond; *b* 24 Dec. 1863; *s* of Col S. Guise-Moores, late Devon Regiment; *m* Kate Louise, *d* of Captain Wood, RE; one *s. Educ:* Cheltenham College; St Thomas's Hospital. Captain RAMC 1890; Major, 1900; Surgeon-Major Scots Guards, 1901; Lt-Col RAMC 1912; Colonel AMS 1915; Maj.-Gen. 1920; DADMS, 7th Division, Sept. 1914; ADMS 1st Div. 1914; 14th Div. 1915; 29th Div. 1916; Guards Div., 1916–17; DDMS II Corps, 1917; DMS second Army, 1917; Army of the Rhine, 1917–18; Commandant RAM College, SW, 1919–20; on Council Officers' Assoc., British Legion; House Governor and Medical Superintendent, Osborne Convalescent Home for Officers of the Navy and Army, Air Force, and Indian Army, 1924–31; Principal Medical Officer National Rifle Association, 1908–14; DMS British Empire Exhibition, Wembley; Hon. Surgeon to the King, 1923; DDMS Aldershot Command, 1920; served Chitral, 1895 (medal with clasp); South Africa, 1899–1902 (despatches twice, promoted Major; Queen's medal 6 clasps, King's medal 2 clasps); European War, 1914–18; with 7th Division for relief of Antwerp, Oct. 1914; First Battle of Ypres, 1914; Battle of Neuve Chapelle, March 1915; with 50th Division, First gas attack on Ypres, April 1915; with 29th Division Battles of Somme, July 1916; with II Corps, third battle of Ypres, 1917; with II Corps, battles leading up to Passchendaele, Oct. 1917; fourth Battle of Ypres with II Army, 1918 (despatches five times, CB, CMG, promoted Major-General); retired pay, 1923; Colonel Commandant RAMC 1927–33; Knight of Grace of Order of St John of Jerusalem, 1925; Officer, Order of Leopold; Croix de Guerre, Belgium; Croix de Guerre avec palme, France; Life member of Council of Cheltenham College. *Publications:* Manual of Hygiene and Sanitation (British Red Cross Society); Veld Sore, British Medical Journal, 1901; Medical Science Progress during 1904, Scientific Year Book, 1905; South Africa as a Health Resort, Knowledge and Scientific News, 1905; The Medical Appreciation of Campaigns (Journal of the Royal Army Medical Corps). *Address:* Wilton Lodge, Cheltenham.

Died 3 Oct. 1942.

GULLAND, George Lovell, CMG 1917; LLD Edin.; MA, BSc, MD, FRCPE; Emeritus (retired, 1928) Professor of Medicine, Edinburgh University, 1915–28; Consulting Physician to the Royal Infirmary, 1911–27, retired, 1928; Physician to the Victoria Hospital for Consumption and Diseases of the Chest since 1896; Consulting Physician to Chalmers Hospital; Principal Medical Officer to the Scottish Widows' Fund, 1911–28; past President Royal College of Physicians at Edinburgh; Major late RAMC (T); sometime Colonel, AMS; *b* Edinburgh, 1862; *s* of John Gulland, for some time one of the magistrates of that city; *m* 1888, Helen, 2nd *d* of late Professor Masson; one *s* one *d*. *Educ:* Royal High School, Edinburgh; University of Edinburgh and University of Halle. Graduated as MB and CM 1886. Resident Physician in the Royal Infirmary and Royal Hospital for Sick Children, Edinburgh; Private Assistant to late Sir Thomas Grainger Stewart; in practice since 1888; Examiner in Medicine, University of Glasgow, 1888; Examiner in Biology and later in Materia Medica, Royal College of Physicians, Edinburgh; Freeland-Barbour Research Fellow, RCPE. *Publications:* numerous papers in medical and scientific journals, many of which deal with diseases of the blood and of the chest. *Recreations:* golf, fishing, and sketching. *Address:* 11 Chester Street, Edinburgh. *T:* 22328.

Died 4 May 1941.

GULLAND, John Masson, FRS 1945; MA (Oxon); PhD (St Andrews); DSc (Edin.); FRSE; FRIC; Sir Jesse Boot Professor of Chemistry, University College, Nottingham, since 1936; *b* Edinburgh, 1898; *o s* of late Prof. G. L. Gulland, CMG, Professor of Medicine, Edinburgh University; *m* 1924, Ruth Madeline Ida Russell, MA, LLB (Edin.), *d* of late Sir Jas A. Russell, LLD; two *d*. *Educ:* Edinburgh Academy; Edinburgh University. Served European War as 2nd Lieut RE 1917–19, with a Divisional Signal Co. in France; BSc (Edin.), 1921; carried out research in Organic Chemistry at the Universities of St Andrews and Manchester; Carnegie Research Scholar, 1922 and 1923; University Demonstrator in Chemistry, Oxford University, 1924–31; Lecturer in Chemistry, Balliol Coll., 1926–31; in charge of teaching of Organic Chemistry in its special relationship to Physiology and Medicine, 1930–31, and Examiner in this subject, 1927–31; Senior Assistant in Biochemistry, The Lister Institute of Preventive Medicine and Reader in Biochemistry in the University of London, 1931–36; Hon. Secretary of the Chemical Society, 1933–36; Hon. Secretary, 1932–34, and Recorder, 1935–37, of Section B (Chemistry) of British Assoc. for the Advancement of Science; External Examiner in Chemistry, Universities of Cambridge, Aberdeen and Edinburgh; Senior Gas Adviser, Ministry of Home Security, North Midland Region, 1939–43; Assistant Director, Chemical Research and Development, Ministry of Supply, 1943–44. *Publications:* chemical and biochemical papers in scientific journals. *Recreations:* fishing, golf, walking, sketching.

Died 26 Oct. 1947.

GUMLEY, Sir Louis Stewart, Kt 1937; DL; LLD (Edin.); JP; *b* Dublin, 1872; *s* of Thomas Frank Sadleir Gumley, Dublin, and Wilhelmina Moffat Tait, Edinburgh; *m* 1901, Catherine Horne Lindsay, Edinburgh; three *s* one *d*. *Educ:* Edinburgh. Entered Leith Parish Council, 1904; Chairman of Leith Parish Council, 1913; Magistrate of Leith, 1919; Magistrate of Edinburgh, 1920–23; Treasurer of Edinburgh, 1931–34; Lord Provost of Edinburgh, 1935–38; Senior Partner of Gumley and Davidson, Valuators, Surveyors and

Property Agents. *Address:* 52 Inverleith Row, Edinburgh. *T:* 83702. *Clubs:* Scottish Conservative, Edinburgh.

Died 30 Sept. 1941.

GUN, William Townsend Jackson, FRHistS, FSG; *b* 30 May 1876; *o s* of Capt. Henry Allen Gun, RE, and *g s* of Wilson Gun, DL, of Rattoo, Lixnaw, Co. Kerry; *m* 1908, Ethel Winifrid (author of Somerset stories and poems), *y d* of Rev. Charles Young, MA, Vicar of Chewton-Mendip, Somerset. *Educ:* Harrow; Trinity College, Cambridge; BA 1898. Barrister, 1901; High Sheriff Co. Kerry, 1902; Hon. Treasurer Co. Kerry Society, 1922–34; Joint Editor of the Genealogists' Magazine, 1928–42; engaged in genealogical research with special reference to the descent of ability and characteristics in families. *Publications:* Studies in Hereditary Ability, 1928; Harrow School Register (1571–1800), 1934; articles in various magazines on genealogical and cognate subjects. *Address:* 55 Wetherby Mansions, SW5. *Club:* Bath.

Died 16 Feb. 1946.

GUNN, Major Alistair Dudley, DSO 1919; Indian Army, retired; *b* 17 April 1884; *s* of Colonel William Donald Gunn and Louisa Massey; *m* 1924, Marjory May Adamson; two *s*. *Educ:* Oundle; Sandhurst. 1st Devons, 1904–05; Indian Army, 110th Mahratta Light Infantry, 1905–28; IEF. 'D,' 1915–16; Siege of Kut, 1915–16 (despatches, Prisoner of War, Turkey, 1916–19, DSO, 1914–15 Star, General Service, Victory); NW Frontier India, 1921–22 (despatches, medal and clasp). *Recreations:* motoring, shooting. *Address:* c/o Lloyds Bank, 112 High Street, Kensington, W8.

Died March 1943.

GUNN, Battiscombe George, FBA 1943; MA; Professor of Egyptology, University of Oxford, since 1934; *b* London, 30 June 1883; *e s* of late George Gunn, London Stock Exchange, and Julia Alice, *d* of John Moore Philp; *m* 1st, Lillian Florence Hughes; one *s*; 2nd, 1948, Constance Anna Rogers. *Educ:* Westminster, Bedales, and other schools. Took part in excavations at El-Harageh (by British School of Archæology in Egypt), 1913–14; El-Amarna (by Egypt Exploration Soc.), 1921–22; Sakkara (by Antiquities Dept of Egyptian Govt), 1924–27; Assist Keeper, The Egyptian Museum, Cairo, 1928–31; Curator of Eygptian Section, University Museum, Philadelphia, 1931–34. Fellow of The Queen's College, Oxford, since 1934. *Publications:* The Instruction of Ptah-hotep, 1906; (with R. Engelbach) Harageh, 1923; (with T. Eric Peet and C. Leonard Woolley) The City of Akhenaten, I, 1923; Studies in Egyptian Syntax, 1924; (with Cecil M. Firth) Excavations at Sakkara: Teti Pyramid Cemeteries, 1926; translations of Egyptian stories in Land of Enchanters (ed. Bernard Lewis), 1948; various articles in archæological periodicals; editor Journal of Egyptian Archæology, 1934–1940. *Address:* 24 Wellington Square, Oxford. *T:* Oxford 3356.

Died 27 Feb. 1950.

GUNN, John William Cormack, MA, MB, ChB; FRSSAf; Professor of Pharmacology in the University of Cape Town since 1919; Curator, Wernher & Beit Medical Laboratories, Head of Medical Students' Residence, and Dean of the Faculty of Medicine, University of Cape Town; *b* Kirkwall, Scotland, 1889; *s* of late John R. Gunn; *m* Marian, *e d* of late Joseph Lambe; two *s*. *Educ:* Kirkwall Burgh School; Edinburgh Univ. Marquis of Zetland Bursar, 1905; Neil Arnott Prizeman in Experimental Physics, 1908; Assistant in Materia Medica, University of Edinburgh, 1912; Assistant in the Department of Pharmacology, University College, London, 1913; served in RAMC 1914–19; Major, RAMC, in charge of Medical Division 19th General Hospital, Dec. 1917–June 1919 (despatches); Lecturer in Pharmacology, Queen's University, Belfast, June 1919. *Publications:* several on Pharmacological subjects in the Journal of Pharmacology; Transactions of the Royal Society of South Africa, etc. *Recreations:* golf (Captain of Mowbray Golf Club, Cape Town, 1936–37). *Address:* University, Cape Town, South Africa.

Died 4 May 1941.

GUNNING, Brig.-Gen. Sir Charles Vere, 7th Bt *cr* 1778; CB 1918; CMG 1917; *b* 31 Oct. 1859; *s* of 5th Bt and Isabella, *d* of Col Chester Master, Knole Pk, Bristol, and The Abbey, Cirencester; *S* brother, 1906; *m* 1888, Ethel Beatrice, *d* of late Rev. W. R. Finch-Hatton; one *d. Educ:* Radley College. Formerly Capt. Durham Light Infantry; served South Africa, 1899–1902, in Remount Department (despatches, Queen's medal three clasps, King's medal two clasps, prom. Major); European War, in Remount Dept since Aug. 1914; promoted Temp. Brig.-Gen. to command of British Remount Commission, Canada, Aug. 1916 (despatches, CMG, CB); Hon. Brig.-Gen., 1927; JP County of Northants. *Heir: cousin* Robert Charles Gunning. *Address:* 31 Kensington Court, W8. *T:* Western 6739. *Club:* Junior United Service.

Died 29 Jan. 1950.

GUPPY, Henry, CBE 1937; MA (Vict.); DPhil et Litt (Louvain); LittD (Manchester); Médaille du Roi Albert; Librarian of the John Rylands Library, Manchester, since 1899; President (1926–27) and Hon. Fellow of the Library Association; Member of the Roxburghe Club; inaugurated the reconstruction of the Library of the University of Louvain, Dec. 1914; *b* London, 31 Dec. 1861; *e s* of Henry Guppy; *m* 1886, Matilda, 2nd *d* of John Bumby, RN; one *d. Educ:* City of Lond. MC School, and privately. Sub-Librarian of Sion Coll., London; Joint-Librarian of the John Rylands Library, Manchester. *Publications:* editor of the Library Association Record, 1899–1903, and of the Bulletin of the John Rylands Library 1903–1947; Hand List of Proclamations, George I to Victoria; The John Rylands Facsimiles; The Public Library: its History and its Functions, 1906; The Books of the Middle Ages and their Makers, 1908; Life and Times of Shakespeare, 1916; Brief Record of Twenty-one Years Work in the JRL, 1921; Dante Alighiere, 1321–1921: an appreciation, 1921; Brief Summary of the History of the First-Folio of Shakespeare, 1923; The John Rylands Library, 1899–1924: a Record of its History, 1924; William Tindale and the Earlier Translators of the Bible into English, 1925; Suggestions for the cataloguing of Incunabula, 1924; The Reconstruction of the Library of the University of Louvain, Great Britain's contribution, 1926; A Brief Sketch of the History of the Transmission of the Bible down to the Revised English Version of 1881–1895, 1926; Stepping-stones to the Art of Typography, 1928; Seventy-five Years, 1850–1925, of Public Library Development, 1926; John Bunyan, 1628–1928: His Life, Times, and Writings, 1928; The Art of Reading, 1929; The Beginnings of Printed Book Illustration to 1500, 1933; The French Journals of Mrs Thrale and Dr Johnson (with M. Tyson), 1932; Miles Coverdale and the English Bible, 1935; The John Rylands Library, 1899–1935: a brief record of its history, 1935; Erasmus, 1936; Manchester University: a retrospect and an appeal, 1937; The Royal Injunctions of 1536 and 1538, and the Great Bible, 1539–1541, 1938; Medieval Manuscripts and Jewelled Book Covers, 1939; Twice Raped Louvain, 1940; The Evolution of the Art of Printing in Commemoration of 500th Anniversary of the Invention of Typography, 1940; The Dawn of the Revival of Learning, 1942; Human Records ... from the beginning, 1943. *Address:* The John Rylands Library, Manchester; Sunwick, Lansdowne Road, Buxton.

Died 4 Aug. 1948.

GURDON, Lt-Col Bertrand Evelyn Mellish, CIE 1900; DSO 1895; Indian Army, retired, 1918; *b* 2 Sept. 1867; 3rd *s* of Maj.-Gen. Evelyn Pulteney Gurdon, late Indian Staff Corps, and Mary, *d* of late General

Sandeman; *m* 1907, Evelyn Agnes, *d* of late Frederick Clarke, and *widow* of Capt. Frank Duncan, Indian Army; two *d. Educ:* Haileybury; Royal Military College, Sandhurst. Took part in defence of Chitral Fort, March and April 1895 (despatches, medal with clasp, DSO); FRGS. *Address:* Heatherfield, Warren Rd, Crowborough, Sussex. *T:* 266. *Club:* Alpine.

Died 6 Oct. 1949.

GURDON, Lt-Col Philip Richard Thornhagh, CSI 1911; late Commissioner Assam Valley Districts; and sometime acting Chief Commissioner of Assam; *b* 2 Feb. 1863; *e surv. s* of late Maj.-Gen. E. P. Gurdon; *m* 1889, Ada Elizabeth, OBE, *d* of late James M'Naught, Belfast; one *d. Educ:* Charterhouse; Royal Military College, Sandhurst. Entered Army, 1882; Assam Commission, 1886; Capt. ISC 1893; retired, 1919; Member Royal Asiatic Soc.; School of Oriental Studies. *Publications:* The Khasis, 1914; and other works.

Died 28 Dec. 1942.

GURNER, Vice-Adm. Victor Gallafent; retd; *b* 5 Oct. 1869; *γ s* of late Henry Field Gurner, sometime Crown Solicitor of the Colony of Victoria, Australia; *m* 1900; Edith Mary, *d* of late Henry Collins, Reading; one *d. Educ:* Geelong; HMS Britannia. 1st Lieut of Royalist during operations in Samoa, 1898; in command of Philomel during operations in the Persian Gulf, 1909–10; in command of Armed Merchant Cruiser Laurentic and Armoured Cruiser Antrim during European War; Commodore in charge, Hong Kong, 1918–20; Rear-Adm. retd, 1921; Vice-Adm. 1926. *Recreations:* cricket, football, shooting. *Address:* Burrswood, Groombridge, Kent.

Died 18 Oct. 1950.

GURNEY, Maj.-Gen. Russell, CB 1944; ADC to the King since 1944; *b* 8 Oct. 1890; *s* of Rev. T. A. Gurney; *m* 1928, Margaret Emily Thorp; two *s. Educ:* Clifton College. Director of Personal Services, War Office, 1943–47; retired, 1947. Late Northamptonshire and Suffolk Regts; European War, 1914–19, France, Belgium, Italy (despatches twice, Legion of Honour, Order of Crown of Belgium, French and Belgian Croix de Guerre). *Publication:* History of the Northamptonshire Regiment, 1935. *Recreations:* fishing, golf. *Address:* Hayne House, Seaton, Devon. *T:* Seaton 51. *Club:* United Service.

Died 29 June 1947.

GUTHRIE, Captain Sir Connop, 1st Bt *cr* 1936; KBE 1918; Grenadier Guards (SR); Hon. Air Commodore Balloon Barrage; Special Representative of British Ministry of Shipping in USA, 1916–19; and Member of the United States Government's Shipping Control Com., 1918; *b* 6 July 1882; *m* 1913, Eila, *d* of late Sir Malcolm McEacharn of Galloway House, Wigtownshire; one *s* one *d.* Served 1914–15 (wounded); Chevalier Légion d'Honneur; Commendatore, Crown of Italy; Distinguished Service Medal (USA). *Recreations:* shooting, golf. *Heir: s* Lt-Comdr Giles Connop McEacharn Guthrie, DSC, Fleet Air Arm [*b* 21 March 1916; *m* 1939, Rhona, *d* of Frederick Stileman; two *s* Eton; Magdalene College, Cambridge]. *Address:* Brent Eleigh Hall, Lavenham, Suffolk. *T:* Lavenham 202. *Club:* Guards'.

Died 28 Sept. 1945.

GUTHRIE, Mrs Murray, (Olive Louisa Blanche); JP; Director of the Chelsea Book Club; *d* of Sir John Leslie, 1st Bt and Lady Constance Leslie; *m* 1894, (Walter) Murray Guthrie, late MP for Bow and Bromley (*d* 1911). Chairman of Chalmers, Guthrie & Co., merchant bankers; Chairman Torosay Parish Council; Chairman Committee of Education for Mull; Member of Committee of Management of West Highland Rest (poorhouse). *Recreations:* deerstalking, golf and collecting books and autographs. *Address:* Torosay Castle, Isle of Mull. *TA:* Craignure. *Clubs:* Ladies' Automobile; Queen's, Edinburgh.

Died 3 July 1945.

GUTHRIE, Ramsay; *see* Bowran, Rev. J. G.

GUTHRIE, Thomas Maule; Solicitor; partner in David Guthrie and Sons, and other industrial concerns; *s* of late James Guthrie of Pitforthie, Brechin; *m* 1927, Ella Kate, 2nd *d* of late W. G. Leete, Merchant, Liverpool. *Educ:* Edinburgh University. Provost of Brechin, 1902–09; Town-Clerk, 1909–20; MP (Nat. Liberal) Moray and Nairn, 1922–23; served throughout European War, and later on Upper Nile. *Recreations:* shooting, fishing, golf, tennis, music. *Address:* Rosehill, Brechin. *TA:* Guthrie, Brechin. *T:* Brechin 66. *Clubs:* Bath; University, Edinburgh.

Died 30 March 1943.

GUTIERREZ-PONCE, Don Ignacio; Envoy Extraordinary and Minister Plenipotentiary from the Republic of Colombia to the Court of St James's, 1901–09, and 1915–23; Corresponding Member of the Royal Spanish Academy of History, the Colombian Academy and other scientific and literary societies; *b* Bogotá (Colombia); *s* of Don Ignacio Gutiérrez Vergara, Statesman, and Doña Maria Ignacia Ponce de León; *m* Doña Rosa Maria Ribon del Corral (*d* 1928); two *d.* *Educ:* Bogotá, where he was Professor of Mathematics at the Seminary; New York University, MD and Gold Medal; Paris, MD; London (Univ. Coll.), MRCS England. Surgeon to the Ophthalmic Clinic of Trocadéro, Paris; Great-officer of the Colombian Order of Boyaca; Officer of the Legion of Honour and Officer of Public Instruction; Hon. Member of the Colombian National Academies of History, Medicine, and Natural Sciences; Member of the International Diplomatic Academy and the Society of Americanists, Paris; founded the Polytechnic Society of Colombia. Entered the Diplomatic service as Secretary to the Colombian Legation at Paris, 1883, and acted as Chargé d'Affaires, 1884; Secretary of Legation to London and Berlin, 1884; proceeded in the same capacity of Madrid, 1886; returned to the Legation at Paris, 1888; Chargé d'Affaires, 1889; Envoy Extraordinary and Minister Plenipotentiary to the German Court, 1901–10; Special Envoy from the Colombian Govt to the Coronation of King Edward and Queen Alexandra, 1902 (Coronation medal); Envoy Extraordinary and Minister Plenipotentiary on special mission to the Vatican, 1903; Envoy Extraordinary and Minister Plenipotentiary to the Court of Vienna, 1908–14; Envoy Extraordinary and Minister Plenipotentiary to the Court of the Netherlands, 1908–15; Member of the Permanent International Court of Arbitration at the Hague; exchanged with Sir Edward Grey the ratifications of an Extradition Treaty with Great Britain, 1909; negotiated and signed a Treaty of Commerce and Navigation with Austria-Hungary, 1912; Delegate from Colombian Government to several International Conferences; Paris, 1883, 1890, and 1900; Copenhagen, 1884; London and Berlin, 1907; London, 1912 and 1914; has held Special Commissions from Governments of Salvador and Bolivia, and from Free Academy of Medicine of Lima (Peru); Head of Special Diplomatic Mission to Paris in connection with the Peace Conference, 1919; signed on behalf of his Government the Declaration of Accession of the Republic of Colombia to the Covenant of the League of Nations. *Publications:* Vida de Don Ignacio Gutiérrez Vergara y episodios históricos de su tiempo; Apuntaciones al Diccionario por la Real Academia Española; Apuntes para la Historia de Santa Fe de Bogotá; Les Races, la végétation, les animaux et les productions minérales de Colombie; Reminiscencias de Vida diplomática. *Address:* 2 Avenue Pierre I de Serbie, Place d'Iéna, Paris. *T:* Kléber 82–30. *Clubs:* Union Interalliée, Paris.

Died July 1942.

GUY, William, FRCS, LRCP, LDS, Hon. HDD, FDS, FRSE; LLD (Penn); Consulting Dental Surgeon, Royal Infirmary and Edinburgh Dental Hospital; late Member of Dental Board of United Kingdom; Lecturer, Dental Anatomy; Assessor to Examiners Royal College Surgeons, Edinburgh; Chairman Dental Tribunal for Scotland (Dangerous Drugs Act); Vice-President BDA, President, 1914; Vice-President Sixth International Dental Congress; President Section of Anæsthesia; *b* 1859; *s* of Wm Guy, MD; *m* 1895, Helen Beatrice (*d* 1944), *d* of John Smith, MD, LLD; no *c. Educ:* Norwich Grammar School; Edinburgh Univ. and Med. School. Dean Edinburgh Dental Hospital and School, 1899–1933; Member of General Medical Council, 1921–29; Vice-President Federation Dentaire Internationale; Major 2nd Scottish General Hospital, RAMC (TF), retired; has devoted much attention to dental education, dental legislation, and the technique of anæsthetics. *Publications:* autobiography: Mostly Memories—Some Digressions, 1949; numerous contributions to Medical and Dental Journals. *Recreations:* shooting, photography, occasional verse. *Address:* 11 Wemyss Place, Edinburgh. *T:* Central 20568. *Club:* Scottish Conservative (Edinburgh).

Died 28 May 1950.

GWATKIN, Rev. Walter Henry Trelawny Ashton-, MA; *b* 1861; 5th *s* of late Frederick Gwatkin of Grove House, Twickenham; *m* 1888, Frances Lilian, *o c* of Frank Ashton, JP, Middlesex and Lancashire; one *s. Educ:* Shrewsbury; King's College, Cambridge. Curate, Farnborough, Hants, 1886–87; Curate-in-Charge, Wye, Kent, 1890–95; Vicar of Margate, Kent, 1895–1902; Rector of Wrotham, Kent, 1902–13; Rural Dean of Shoreham, 1909–13; Chaplain to Bishop of Rochester, 1905–13; Canon Residentiary, 1915–19, Treasurer, 1919–20, of Truro Cathedral; Rector of Bishopsbourne, 1923–32. *Address:* Davington Priory, Faversham, Kent.

Died 6 May 1945.

GWATKIN-WILLIAMS, Captain Rupert Stanley, CMG 1918; Captain, Royal Navy (retired); *s* of Joseph Baylis Williams, ICS, and Sutton Ann Trimnell; *m* 1st, 1903, Evelyn Gwatkin; two *s* one *d*; 2nd, 1920, Florence Margaret Cross Scott, (*d* 1948), Dundee; one *d. Educ:* Portsmouth Grammar School; HMS Britannia, Dartmouth. Midshipman in HMS Imperieuse on the China Station, 1891; served as Lieutenant at the taking of the Taku Forts, and throughout the Boxer War, 1900; retired from the active list of the Royal Navy with the rank of Captain, 1912; rejoined on the outbreak of the War; in Nov. 1915 his ship, HMS Tara, was torpedoed and sunk in the Gulf of Sollum; crew were made prisoners by the submarine whose Commander handed them over to the Senussi Arabs, amongst whom they endured five months of captivity; spent nearly two years in command of HMS Intrepid on the Murman Coast of Russia (CMG); in command of HMS Edinburgh Castle, the Commodore and Ocean Escort of the American Convoys bringing troops across the Atlantic, 1918. *Publications:* Prisoners of the Red Desert; Under the Black Ensign, 1922; numerous magazine and press articles. *Recreation:* natural history and outdoor life generally. *Address:* 43 Lebanon Park, Twickenham, Middlesex. *T:* Popesgrove 1184.

Died 2 Aug. 1949.

GWYN-THOMAS, Brig.-Gen. Gwyn, CMG 1918; DSO 1916; Colonel and Hon. Brig.-Gen. (retd) Indian Army; *b* 1871; *s* of late Colonel Edgar Hastings Thomas; *m* 1st, Alice Laura (*d* 1920), *widow* of A. W. Bird; 2nd, 1924, Helen Margaret, *d* of late Col Alexander Baird, and *widow* of Lt-Colonel Archibald John Saltren-Willett, Royal Artillery, of Petticombe, North Devon. psc, 1907. Served European War, 1914–18; 3rd Afghan War and Indian Frontier, 1920–21 (wounded, despatches seven times, DSO immediate award, CMG, Bt Col); retired,

1923; has assumed the additional surname of Gwyn. *Address:* Petticombe, Monkleigh, Bideford, N Devon. *Club:* East India and Sports.

Died 20 April 1946.

GWYNN, Edward John, LittD (Dublin, Oxford, Durham, and Wales), LLD (Glasgow), DLitt Celt. (NUI); Provost of Trinity College, Dublin, 1927–37; Fellow 1893–1927; Honorary Fellow, 1937; *b* 1 April 1868; *s* of Rev. John Gwynn, DD, Regius Professor of Divinity in the University of Dublin; *m* 1906, Olive Mary, *d* of Colonel J. G. Ponsonby; three *s* two *d*. *Educ:* St Columba's College; Trinity College, Dublin (Scholar, 1888; Univ. Student and Senior Moderator, 1889). Todd Lecturer in Celtic Languages in the Royal Irish Academy, 1899–1904; Commissioner of National Education (Ireland), 1905–15; Lecturer in Celtic Languages in the University of Dublin, 1907–28. *Publications:* The Metrical Dindshenchas, Parts i, ii, iii, iv and v (Todd Lecture Series); Catalogue of Irish MSS in Trinity College, Dublin (with late T. K. Abbott); The Rule of Tallaght; articles on Irish literature and philology. *Address:* Trinity College, Dublin.

Died 10 Feb. 1941.

GWYNN, Stephen (Lucius); *b* 13 Feb. 1864; *s* of Rev. John Gwynn, DD; *m* 1889, Mary L., *d* of Rev. Jas Gwynn; two *s* one *d*. *Educ:* St Columba's Coll. Rathfarnham; Brasenose Coll. Oxford (Scholar), 1882; 1st Mods and Lit.Hum. 1884–86. Teacher of Classics, etc., in various places, 1887–96; did a little writing also from 1890 on; came to London, 1896, and commenced author, definitely, as journalist, magazine writer, etc.; drifted rather into book-writing of later years; left London to live in Ireland, 1904; MP (N) Galway City, 1906–18, when the constituency was merged; joined 7th Leinster Regt as private, Jan. 1915; Lieut 6th Connaught Rangers, April 1915; Capt. July 1915; served in France with 16th Irish Div. 1915–17 (Chevalier, Legion of Honour, 1917); Officier de l'Instruction Publique, 1929; Member of Irish Convention, 1917–18; DLitt National Univ. of Ireland 1940, Dublin Univ. 1945. *Publications:* translation, De Musset's Comedies; edition of Odes of Horace; An XVIIIth Century Portrait Painter (Northcote), 1898; The Repentance of a Private Secretary, 1898; Tennyson, 1899; Highways and Byeways in Donegal and Antrim, 1899; The Decay of Sensibility, 1900; The Old Knowledge, 1901; The Queen's Chronicler (verses), 1901; To-day and To-morrow in Ireland, 1902; A Lay of Ossian and Patrick (verse), 1903; John Maxwell's Marriage, 1903; Fishing Holidays, 1903; The Masters of English Literature, 1904; Thomas Moore, 1904; The Fair Hills of Ireland, 1906; The Glade in the Forest, 1907; A Holiday in Connemara, 1909; Robert Emmet: A Historical Romance, 1909; The Famous Cities of Ireland, 1916; For Second Reading (essays), 1918; John Redmond's Last Years; Irish Books and Irish People, 1919; The Irish Situation; Garden Wisdom, 1921; Collected Poems, 1923; The History of Ireland, 1923; Ireland, A Survey of Historical Forces (Modern World Series), 1924; Duffer's Luck (fishing sketches), 1924; Experiences of a Literary Man, 1926; In Praise of France, 1927; Ireland (Kitbag Travel books), 1927; Saints and Scholars, biographical essays, 1929; Robert Falcon Scott: a Study, 1929; The Letters and Friendships of Sir Cecil Spring Rice, 1929; The Life of Sir Walter Scott, 1930; Burgundy, 1930; The Life of Horace Walpole, 1932; Mary Kingsley, 1932; Life and Friendships of Dean Swift, 1933; Claude Monet and his Garden, 1934; Mungo Park, 1934; Memoirs of Sir Lowry Cole (with Maud Lowry Cole), 1934; Ireland in Ten Days; Life of Oliver Goldsmith, 1935; Irish Literature and Drama, 1936; The Happy Fisherman, 1936; From River to River, 1937; Fond Opinions (essays), 1938; Dublin Old and New, 1938; Two in a Valley (with Roy Beddington), 1938; Henry Grattan and His Times, 1939; Robert Louis Stevenson, 1939; Salute to Valour (wartime verses), 1941; edited Memoirs of Sir

Charles Dilke (with Miss G. Tuckwell), 1917; The Anvil of War, letters between F. S. Oliver and his Brother, 1914–1918, 1936; Memories of Enjoyment (essays), 1946; Aftermath (verses), 1946. *Address:* 23 Palmerston Road, Dublin. *Club:* Stephen's Green (Dublin).

Died 11 June 1950.

GWYNNE, Comdr Alban Lewis, CB 1918; RN (retired); *b* 1880; *s* of Alban Gwynne, Monachty, Cardiganshire; *m* 1912, Ruby, *d* of Col Hodson Bond; one *s* one *d*. Lent for duty under Turkish Government 1909–11; served European War (CB). *Club:* United Service.

Died 5 July 1942.

GWYNNE, Brig. Alfred Howel E.; *see* Evans-Gwynne.

GWYNNE, H. A., CH 1938; *b* Kilvey, 1865; *s* of R. Gwynne of Kilvey; *m* 1907, Edith Douglas, *o surv. d* of late Thomas Ash Lane. *Educ:* Swansea Grammar School; abroad. Acted as correspondent for the Times in the Balkans; became Reuter's correspondent in Roumania, 1893; went to Ashanti for Reuter's Agency, 1895; accompanied Lord Kitchener's Expedition to Dongola in 1896 as Reuter's chief war correspondent, in which capacity he followed the operations of the Turkish-Greek war in 1897, the expedition to Berber in the same year; went to Peking in Jan. 1898, remaining there till May 1899, whence he sailed directly to South Africa, organised Reuter's war service for the Boer war, followed Lord Methuen's operations, present at Magersfontein; he joined Lord Roberts on his arrival, followed his operations to the capture of Pretoria, and then took part in many of the minor operations till the end of the war; returned England Nov. 1902; sailed again for South Africa same month to accompany Mr Chamberlain on his visit to South Africa; went to Belgrade on occasion of murder of King and Queen; visited Macedonia during disturbances; Foreign Director of Reuter's Agency, 1904; appointed editor of the Standard 1904, resigned 1911; editor of the Morning Post, 1911–37. *Publications:* The Army on Itself; The Will and the Bill. *Recreations:* all outdoor games and exercises. *Address:* Mawbyns, Little Easton, Dunmow, Essex. *Club:* Carlton.

Died 26 June 1950.

GWYNNE, Paul; *see* Slater, Ernest.

GWYNNE, Brig.-Gen. Reginald John, CMG, 1918; *b* 16 Sept. 1863; *s* of late J. E. A. Gwynne, JP, and Mrs Gwynne, Folkington Manor, Polegate, Sussex; *m* 1894, Mary Mayall, *d* of late S. Taylor, JP, of Oldham; one *d*. *Educ:* Eton; Pembroke College, Oxford. Commanded 16th Horse, 1906–11; commanded a Cavalry Brigade, 1911–13; Director-Gen. of Mobilisation in Canada, 1914; Adjutant-General, 1917 (despatches thrice): retired, 1921. *Address:* Ardmore Grange, Sidney PO, Vancouver Island, BC.

Died 20 March 1942.

GWYNNE-JONES, Howell, CVO 1935; MRCS; LRCP; Medical Practitioner; Major late RAMC Militia; *b* 4 Dec. 1890; *s* of late William Howell and Gwladys Gwynne-Jones; *m* 1922, Harriett Marshman, *d* of late Dr George Petrie Hay, Forres; one *d*. *Educ:* Taunton School; London Hospital. Senior Hon. Medical Officer Gerrards Cross and Chalfont St Peter Hospital; sometime Medical Attendant to the late Princess Victoria; late Demonstrator of Anatomy, Senior Resident Accoucheur, House Surgeon, House Physician, Emergency Officer, Receiving Room Officer and Resident Anaesthetist, London Hospital; served European War with RAMC (SR), 1914–19 (1914 Mons Star). Freeman and Liveryman Glass Sellers Company. *Recreations:* fishing, golf. *Address:* The White House, Packhorse Road, Gerrards Cross. *T:* Gerrard's Cross 2992.

Died 15 Nov. 1946.

H

HAAG, Norman C.; *b* London, 8 Dec. 1871; 3rd and *y s* of late Carl Haag, RWS; *m* 1920, Doris Maud de Winton, *e d* of Sir Ernest Salter Wills, Bt of Meggernie Castle, Glenlyon, Perthshire, and Littlecote, Hungerford, Wilts; one *s* two *d*. *Educ:* Blairlodge School, Scotland; Lausanne University; Paris. Employed in the Consulate at Marseilles, 1893–95; Vice-Consul at Cherbourg, 1895; transferred to Marseilles, 1899; placed in charge of the Vice-Consulate at Toulon as Acting Vice-Consul, 1900; Vice-Consul for the Department of Var, with the exception of the town of Hyères, to reside at Toulon, 1903; given a Royal Commission, 1906; Vice-Consul at Bremerhaven and Geestemunde, 1906; employed War Office, 1914; Consul at Flushing, 1914; employed at Admiralty, 1915; Acting Consul-General Barcelona, 1915–16; Acting Consul at Madrid, 1918–19; HM's Consul at Basle, 1920–32; given the personal rank of Consul-General, 1929; retired 1932, and was granted a pension; holds hon. certificate, on vellum, of the Royal Humane Society, for saving two lives at personal risk. *Recreations:* fishing and motoring. *Address:* Penwood, Branksome Park, Bournemouth, W. *T:* Westbourne 63610.

Died 8 Dec. 1950.

HÄBERLIN, Dr Henry; *b* 6 Sept. 1868; *s* of Henry Häberlin, Member of National Council, and Anne Gmünder; *m* 1897, Paula Freyenmuth; two *s*. *Educ:* Weinfelden and Frauenfeld; University of Zürich; University of Leipzig; University of Berlin. Member of Great Council of Thurgovia, 1905; Member of National Council, 1904, President, 1919; Federal Councillor, 1920–34; President of the Swiss Confederation, 1926 and 1931; Colonel of Infantry. *Recreations:* mountaineering, letters. *Address:* Blumenrain, Frauenfeld, Switzerland. *T:* Frauenfeld 7–25–50.

Died Feb. 1947.

HACKENLEY, Most Rev. John, DD; Bishop Coadjutor of Nova Scotia, 1925–34, Bishop, 1934–39; Archbishop of Nova Scotia since 1939; *b* Colne, Lancs, 4 Aug. 1877. *Educ:* University of King's College, Windsor, NS. Curate of Digby Neck, 1904–05; Rector of Granville, 1905–08; of Indian Harbour, 1908–16; of La Have, 1916–21; of North Sydney, 1921–24; Chancellor of University of King's College, 1937. *Address:* Church of England Institute, Barrington St, Halifax, NS.

Died 15 Nov. 1943.

HACKET-THOMPSON, Brig.-Gen. Frederick; *see* Thompson.

HACKETT, Walter; *b* Oakland, California, 11 Nov. 1876; *m* Marion Lorne. Has written the following among many other plays: The Prince of Dreams, 1904; The Regeneration, 1908; The Invaders, 1908; The White Sister (with F. Marion Crawford), 1909; Get Busy with Emily, 1910; In the Mountains, 1911; Fine Feathers (with Eugene Walter), 1912; Our World, 1911; Honest Jim Blunt, 1913; Don't Weaken, 1914; It Pays to Advertise (with Roi Cooper Megrue), 1914; He Didn't Want to Do It (with George Broadhurst), 1915; Mr and Mrs Ponsonby, 1915; The Barton Mystery, 1916; £150, 1917; The Invisible Foe, 1917; The Freedom of the Seas, 1918; Mr Tod's Experiment, 1920; Ambrose Applejohn's Adventure, 1921; Pansy's Arabian Night, 1924; The Wicked Earl, 1927; Other Men's Wives, 1928; 77 Park Lane, 1928; Sorry you've been troubled, 1929; opened Whitehall Theatre with The Way to Treat a Woman, 1930; Good Losers (with Michael Arlen), 1931; Take a Chance, 1931; The Gay Adventure, 1931;

Road House, 1932; Afterwards, 1933; Hyde Park Corner, 1934; Espionage, 1935; The Fugitives, 1936; London After Dark, 1937; Toss of a Coin, 1938.

Died 22 Jan. 1944.

HACKING, 1st Baron *cr* 1945, of Chorley; **Douglas Hewitt Hacking;** PC 1929; 1st Bt *cr* 1938, OBE; JP; DL for County of Surrey; *b* Clayton-Le-Moors, 4 Aug. 1884; *s* of late J. Hacking, JP, Clayton-le-Moors; *m* 1909, Margery Allen, *e d* of late H. H. Bolton, JP, Newchurch-in-Rossendale; two *s* one *d*. *Educ:* Giggleswick School; Manchester University. Commission in East Lancashire Regt, Aug. 1914; served two years in France (despatches, OBE); MP (U), Chorley Div. of Lancs, Dec. 1918–June 1945; Parliamentary Private Sec. to late Sir James Craig, Bart, MP (Lord Craigavon), at Ministry of Pensions, 1920, and Admiralty, 1920–21; Parliamentary Private Sec. to late Sir L. Worthington-Evans, Bart, MP, Secretary of State for War, 1921–22; Vice-Chamberlain of the Royal Household, 1922–24, and Nov. 1924–Dec. 1925; Conservative Whip, 1922–25; Parliamentary Under-Secretary of State for Home Dept, and Representative of the Office of Works in the House of Commons, 1925–27; Secretary, Department of Overseas Trade, Parliamentary Secretary Board of Trade, and Parliamentary Under-Secretary of State for Foreign Affairs, 1927–29; Parliamentary Under-Secretary Home Office, 1933–34; Financial Secretary to War Office, 1934–35; Parliamentary Under-Secretary of State for Dominion Affairs, 1935–36; Member of Empire Parliamentary Delegation to South Africa, 1924; Chairman of Home Office Committee on Compensation for Silicosis, 1926; Chairman of Home Office Committee on Taxicabs (Conditions of Licensing, etc.), 1927; Chairman of Committee on redistribution of Royal Ordnance Factories, 1934; Founder, Travel Association of Great Britain and Ireland, 1928; Chancellor of the Primrose League, 1931; Vice-Chairman, National Union of Conservative and Unionist Associations, 1930–32; Govt Delegate to League of Nations, Geneva, 1933; Chairman Conservative Party Organisation, 1936–42; Member General Medical Council, 1932–47; 5th Bn Surrey Home Guard, 1940–44. A Governor of Cranleigh School; JP County of Surrey. *Recreations:* tennis, golf. *Heir: s* Hon. Douglas Eric Hacking [*b* 7 Dec. 1910; *m* 1936, Daphne, *d* of Leslie Finnis, Kensington, W; two *s* one *d*]. *Address:* 25 Westminster Gardens, SW1. *T:* Victoria 6118; Mannings Hill Cottage, Cranleigh, Surrey. *T:* Cranleigh 482. *Club:* Carlton.

Died 29 July 1950.

HADDOCK, Captain Herbert James, CB 1902; late ADC to HM; Capt. Royal Naval Reserve, 1914; *b* 27 Jan. 1861; *s* of late James Haddock; *m* 1893, Mabel (*d* 1935), *d* of Francis Baines Bouchette, Quebec. *Address:* 18 Furzedown Road, Highfield, Southampton.

Died 4 Oct. 1946.

HADDON, Archibald; theatrical journalist; Ironbridge, Shropshire; *m* 1st, Mary Jones (*d* 1913); 2nd, Johanna Simonsen; one *s* three *d*. *Educ:* Birkenhead School; The Old Hall, Wellington, Shropshire. Journalist since 1889; dramatic critic of Liverpool Review, 1890–1902; Daily Express, 1902–23; St James's Gazette, 1904; Standard and Evening Standard, 1909–14; Sporting Times, 1917; Empire News, 1917–23; Sunday Express, 1918–23; The Democrat, 1921; World's Pictorial News, 1923; Vaudeville critic of the Theatre World, 1933 and the Sunday Referee, 1933–34; Editor and Proprietor, Liverpool Review, 1900–02; News Editor and Librarian,

Daily Express, for late Sir Arthur Pearson; Dramatic critic to the British Broadcasting Company, 1923–24, reappointed to British Broadcasting Corporation, 1933; general publicity officer for Fellowship of Freedom and Reform, 1923–24; Entertainments Protection Association, 1924; Stoll Theatres Circuit, 1924–33; Stage and Allied Arts League, 1933–39; Gilbert Miller Productions, 1934–35; Bertram Mills' Circus, 1936–38; Butcher's Film Service, Ltd, since 1936; The Pageant of Surrey, 1937; and various stage and film producers and numerous world-famous stars. *Publications:* Green Room Gossip, 1922, a volume of dramatic criticism and comment; Hullo, Playgoers! 1924, a volume of theatre talks broadcast to the British Isles from 2 LO; The Story of the Music Hall, 1935, and a brochure on Pictorial Press Publicity. *Recreation:* home life. *Address:* Denland, The Chart, Oxted, Surrey. *T:* Limpsfield Chart 2118.

Died 15 Oct. 1942.

HADDON, Trevor, RBA. Paints principally portraits and Spanish and Venetian subjects. *Educ:* Studied at the Slade School, obtained 3 years' scholarship of £50 a year in 1883, age 19; medal (1885) for painting from life, and landscape prize. Travelled in Spain, 1886–87; studying in Madrid; worked with Sir Hubert Herkomer, 1888–90; stayed in Rome, 1896–97; worked in Venezuela, 1921; Life Membership of Royal Society of British Artists conferred, 1922; painted portraits and held exhibitions in Victoria, BC, San Francisco, Honolulu, etc., 1926–30; one-man shows in London, Leicester Galleries, 1902, Chenil Galleries, 1906, Doré Galleries, 1908; 'Brother Savages,' 1910; 100 Pastel Sketch Portraits at the Kodak Gallery. *Publications:* The Old Venetian Palaces; Southern Spain, etc. *Address:* 67a St Andrew's Street, Cambridge. *Club:* Savage.

Died 13 Dec. 1941.

HADDOW, Sir (Robert) Renwick, Kt 1943; Senior Resident Partner, Mackinnon Mackenzie & Co., Calcutta; *b* 14 Nov. 1891; *s* of John Haddow, JP, and Elizabeth Campbell; *m* 1st, 1921, May Anderson (*d* 1927); one *s* one *d*; 2nd, 1931, Isabel Robb. *Educ:* Bellahouston Academy, Glasgow. Apprenticed to Bell Brothers & Co., shipowners, Glasgow, 1909; came to India, 1913, to Mackinnon Mackenzie & Co.; President, Bombay Chamber of Commerce, 1930–31; Member, Bombay Legislative Council, 1929–31; President, Bengal Chamber of Commerce and Associated Chambers of Commerce, 1942–43 and 1945–46; Member, Bengal Legislative Assembly, 1940–41, and Council of State, 1941–43. *Recreation:* golf. *Address:* 16 Strand Road, Calcutta; Gleniffer, West Kilbride. *TA:* Xavga, Calcutta. *Clubs:* Oriental, Bengal, Byculla, Bombay; Royal Calcutta Turf.

Died 18 Feb. 1946.

HADDY, Engr Rear-Adm. Frederick George, MVO 1911; RN, retired; Director Peter Brotherhood, Ltd, Peterborough; *b* 1875; *s* of Eng.-Rear-Adm. George A. Haddy, late RN, of St Germans; *m* 1st, 1905, Ellen Maud Annie, *d* of Lewis G. Davies, RCNC; 2nd, 1935, Janette, 2nd *d* of Henry Allman-Newcastle. *Educ:* private school; RN Engineering College, Keyham. Royal Yacht Victoria and Albert, 1905–11; Medina, 1911, 1912; London Overseer for the Admiralty, 1929; retired list, 1930. *Address:* White Gates, Farnham Royal, Bucks.

Died 30 Dec. 1950.

HADFIELD, Sir Ernest, Kt 1938; OBE 1920; JP Lancs; solicitor; *b* 1873; *m* Annie Mary, *yr d* of late James Butterfield; one *s. Educ:* Queen Elizabeth Grammar School, Blackburn. Mayor of Southport, 1925–26. *Address:* 86 Park Road, Southport, Lancs.

Died 17 July 1947.

HADFIELD, Walton John, CBE 1931; MInstCE; *s* of James Hadfield, Norton, Sheffield, and Elizabeth Ruth Walton, Heslington, York; *m* Caroline Anne Wilkinson, Sheffield; three *d. Educ:* Royal Grammar School,

Sheffield. Articled to previous City Engineer, Sheffield; Dep. City Engineer; City Engineer, Sheffield, 1915–36; Pioneer of modern methods of road construction; responsible for important drainage schemes; in recent years has been responsible for construction of great arterial roads and Town Planning developments, as well as other Municipal Works; President of the Institution of Municipal and County Engineers, 1934–35; a member of the Ministry of Transport Technical Advisory Committee on Experimental Work; and a member of the British Standards Institution; Chairman, British Road Tar Association and National Road Tar Committee. *Publications:* numerous papers and articles on professional subjects; a volume entitled Highways and their Maintenance. *Address:* 304 Western Bank, Sheffield. *T:* Broomhill 61566.

Died 25 Jan. 1944.

HADLEY, Wilfred James, MD, FRCS Eng., FRCP Lond., DPH Camb.; Consulting Physician to London Hospital and Victoria Park Chest Hospital; *b* Gloucester, 28 March 1862; *m* Mrs Ernest Charrington, MBE, *d* of H. T. Wells, RA; one *d. Educ:* University, Durham (first in honours, MB, and gold medal, MD) and University, Göttingen; London Hospital. Late Pathologist to Victoria Park Chest Hospital; Curator of Museum, Lecturer on Bacteriology, Hygiene, Pathology and Medicine, London Hospital; Physician Chest Hospital, Victoria Park. *Publications:* Fibroid Diseases of the Lung, including Fibroid Phthisis (with Sir Andrew Clark and Dr Chaplain; Diseases of Respiration, Medical Annual; Nursing, General Medical and Surgical, 1901; various papers in medical and scientific journals. *Recreation:* outdoor sports. *Address:* Parkside, Reigate, Surrey. *T:* Reigate 2045.

Died 6 July 1944.

HAIG, Lt-Col Patrick Balfour, CB 1917; MB, CM Edin., MRCS, LRCP London; late IMS; *b* 1866; *s* of late W. J. Haig of Dollarfield, Clackmannanshire, and Margaret, *d* of Rev. P. Balfour; *m* 1909, Evelyn Georgiana (*d* 1941), *d* of late J. T. Brooke of Haughton Hall, Shifnal, and of Lady Wilhelmina Brooke; two *s* one *d. Educ:* Loretto School; University, Edinburgh and University, Paris. Entered IMS, 1892; Kaiser-i-Hind Medal, 1st class, 1913; served Waziristan, 1894–95 (medal and clasp); NW Frontier, India, 1897–98, Malakand and Utman Khel, Buner, action of Tangi Pass (medal and clasp); Uganda, 1899 operations against rebels and Sudanese Mutineers in Unyaro, final defeat and capture of Kings Kabarega and Mwanga (despatches, medal and clasp); Uganda, 1900 operations against Nandi Tribes (despatches, medal and clasp); European War, 1914–18 (despatches, CB); retired, 1921. *Address:* Lethington, Nairn. *Club:* Caledonian United Service (Edinburgh).

Died 18 Oct. 1949.

HAIGH, Bernard Parker, MBE 1917; DSc; MInstCE; Professor of Applied Mechanics, Royal Naval College, Greenwich, since 1921; *b* 8 July 1884; *s* of William Rylance Haigh, Engineer, Edinburgh; *m* 1915, Mildred Cole; one *s. Educ:* Allan Glen's School, Glasgow; University of Glasgow. After nine years of practice as Engineer, at home and overseas, entered Admiralty Service; RN College, Greenwich, and at Portsmouth during War; Consulting Engineer in Civil Practice; Inventor of weapons and processes, scientific instruments and machines for testing materials. *Publications:* scientific papers on Engineering subjects, on Fatigue in Metals, Welding Practice, etc. *Address:* RN College, Greenwich, SE10. *T:* Lee Green 5325.

Died 18 Jan. 1941.

HAIGH, Ernest Varley-, CBE 1918; MIMechE; FTI; FIIA; *m* 1927, Hedvig Gabriella de Poor, Budapest, Hungary. *Educ:* Huddersfield College. As Manager for J and P Coats, Ltd, resided for various periods abroad, Italy, Russia, Spain, and Mexico; Deputy (later acting)

Director General and Controller, Trench Warfare Supply Dept, Controller, Department of Engineering, Ministry of Munitions, 1916–18. *Recreations:* sailing, climbing, golf. *Address:* 60 Knightsbridge, SW1. *Club:* Royal Thames Yacht.

Died 24 May 1948.

HAILSHAM, 1st Viscount *cr* 1929, of Hailsham; **Douglas McGarel Hogg;** Baron *cr* 1928, PC 1922; Kt 1922; KC 1917; DCL Oxford; LLD Birmingham; Hon. LLD Cambridge; Hon. DLitt Reading; Hon. LLD Belfast; JP Sussex, 1923; *b* 1872; *e s* of late Quintin Hogg, *g s* of Sir James Weir Hogg, Bart, PC, and William Graham, MP; *m* 1st, 1905, Elizabeth (*d* 1925), *d* of Judge Trimble Brown, Nashville, Tennessee, USA, and *widow* of Hon. A. J. Marjoribanks; two *s*; 2nd, 1929, Mildred, *d* of Rev. Edward Parker Dew and *widow* of Hon. Clive Lawrence. *Educ:* Eton (Captain of Oppidans). Studied sugar-growing in West Indies and British Guiana, and was for eight years with the firm of Hogg, Curtis, Campbell & Co., West India merchants; served in S African War with 19th (Lothian and Berwick) Yeomanry (medal and 4 clasps); called to Bar, 1902; Vice-President and Vice-Chairman since 1902 of the Polytechnic (founded by his father); President West India Committee since 1943. Capt. and Group Adjutant, West Group, County of London Volunteer Regiment, 1914–19; Director Legal and General Insurance Co., 1920–22, 1929–31 and since 1939; Bencher, Lincoln's Inn 1920; Attorney-General, to Prince of Wales, 1920–22; Attorney-General, 1922–24, and Nov. 1924–28; Lord Chancellor, 1928–29; Secretary of State for War, 1931–35 and Leader of the House of Lords; Lord Chancellor, 1935–38; Leader of the Opposition in the House of Lords 1930–31; Chairman, British Delegation to the Institute of Pacific Relations Meeting at Kyoto, 1929; Member of Council of State, 1928–29; Acting Prime Minister Aug.–Sept. 1928; President Old Etonian Association, 1928; President Sussex County Cricket Club, 1931; President MCC, 1933; a British delegate to the Ottawa Conference, 1932; A British delegate to the World Economic Conference, 1933; Hon. Col Inns of Court Regiment, 1935–48. Pres. Professional Classes Aid Council since 1936; Chairman of British Empire Cancer Campaign since 1936. *Publication:* Editor of the Hailsham edition of Halsbury's Laws of England. *Recreation:* travel. *Heir: s* Capt. Hon. Quintin McGarel Hogg, MP. *Address:* Carter's Corner Place, Hailsham, Sussex. *T:* Hurstmonceux 3119. *Clubs:* Athenæum, Carlton, MCC.

Died 16 Aug. 1950.

HAINES, Henry Haselfoot, CIE 1919; FCH, FLS, FASB; *s* of Frederick Raines, FSA; unmarried. *Educ:* University Coll School; Coopers Hill Coll. Indian Forest Service, 1888; made a Fellow of Coopers Hill, 1889; Imperial Forest Botanist, 1906; Principal, Imperial Forest College, 1907; Conservator of Forests, 1909; retired, 1919; served for 30 years as a volunteer and in Indian Defence Force, receiving a commission, 1907. *Publications:* Forest Flora of Chota Nagpur and Santal Pargannahs; Forest Flora of Southern Circle, Central Provinces, India; Botany of Bihar and Orissa. *Recreations:* gardening, botany, and natural history, formerly also riding and polo. *Address:* Glyn Cogan, Berriew, Montgomery. *T:* Tregynon 38.

Died 6 Oct. 1945.

HAKING, Gen. Sir Richard Cyril Byrne, GBE 1921; KCB 1916; KCMG 1918; CB 1910; Colonel of Hants Regiment, 1924–45; JP, DL for Wilts; *b* 24 Jan. 1862; *m* 1891, Rachel Violette, (*d* 1939), *d* of late Sir Henry Burford-Hancock, CMG, Chief Justice of Gibraltar. Entered army, 1881; Captain Hants Regiment, 1889; Major, 1899; Lieutenant-Colonel, 1903; Colonel, 1905; Brigadier-General, 1908; Major-General, 1914; Lieut-General, 1915; General, 1925; DAAG, Cork District, 1898–99; South Africa, 1899–1901; Professor, Staff College, 1901–04; DAAG Staff College, 1904–06;

General Staff Officer, 1st Grade, 3rd Division, 1906–08; Brig.-Gen. General Staff, Southern Command, 1908–11; commanding 5th Infantry Brigade, 1911–14; commanding 5th Brig. 1914; 1st Division, 1915; XIth Corps, 1915–18; Chief of the British Section Armistice Commission, 1918–19; commanding British Military Missions, Russia and Baltic Provinces, 1919; commanding Allied Troops Plebiscite Area, East Prussia and Danzig, 1920; High Commissioner League of Nations Danzig, 1921–23; served Burmah, 1885–87 (despatches, medal with clasp); South Africa, 1899–1900 (despatches, Queen's medal 3 clasps); European War, 1914–18 (promoted Major-General for distinguished conduct in the field, despatches eight times, GBE, KCB, prom. (temp.) Lt-Gen., KCMG); General Officer commanding the British Troops in Egypt, 1923–27; retired pay, 1927. *Address:* Mill Cottage, Bulford, Wilts. *T:* Bulford 2121. *Club:* Army and Navy.

Died 9 June 1945.

HALDANE, Gen. Sir J. Aylmer L., GCMG 1922; KCB 1918 (CB 1906); DSO 1898; *b* 17 Nov. 1862; *o s* of late D. Rutherford Haldane, MD, LLD. *Educ:* Edinburgh Acad.; Wimbledon School; RMC Sandhurst. Joined Gordon Highlanders, 1882; Adjutant 3½ years; ADC to Gen. Sir W. Lockhart, 1896–99; served Waziristan, 1894–99 (medal and clasp); chitral, 1895 (medal and clasp); Tirah, 1897–98; DAAG Headquarters Staff; actions of Chagru Kotal, Dargai, Saran Sir, Dwatoi; capture of Sampagha and Arhanga Passes; operations against Chamkanis and in Bara and Bazar Valleys (despatches, DSO and 2 clasps); South Africa, 1899–1900, with 2nd Gordon Highlanders; battle of Elandslaagte (severely wounded); in command of Chieveley armoured train, 15 Nov.; captured and escaped from Pretoria; battles of Lang's Nek and Belfast (despatches, brevet Lieut-Colonel, medal and 4 clasps); Military Attaché with Japanese Army, Russo-Japanese War, 1904–05; present at battles of Liao-yang, Sha Ho, and Mukden (medal and clasp); European War, 1914–19 (despatches nine times, promoted Major-General and Lieut-General, KCB, 1914 Star, General Service and Victory medals); General Officer C-in-C Mesopotamia 1920–22 during extensive Arab insurrection, which was suppressed (GCMG, medal and 2 clasps); Defence Medal, 1939–45 (medal); General, 1925; retired pay, 1925; Knight of Grace of St John of Jerusalem, 1912. *Foreign decorations:* Grand Officier de l'ordre de la Couronne (Belgian), Commander Legion of Honour, 1918; 3rd Class, Sacred Treasure; Croix de Guerre (French and Belgian). *Publications:* How we Escaped from Pretoria, 1900; A Brigade of the Old Army, 1920; The Insurrection in Mesopotamia, 1922; The Haldanes of Gleneagles, 1929; A Soldier's Saga. *Recreations:* shooting, travelling, golf. *Address:* 107 Westbourne Terrace, W2. *T:* Paddington 0522. *Club:* Naval and Military.

Died 19 April 1950.

HALDANE, James Brodrick C.; *see* Chinnery-Haldane.

HALDAR, Hiralal, MA, PhD; *b* 30 April 1865; *s* of Kamal Chand Haldar; *m* 1891, Subala Datta; three *s*. *Educ:* General Assembly's Institution, Calcutta. Teacher, City Collegiate School, Sova Bazar, 1888–90; Professor of Philosophy and English, Raj Chunder College, Barisal, 1890–92; Professor of Philosophy and English Literature, Berhampur College, 1892–1911; Professor of Philosophy, City College, Calcutta, and Lecturer in Philosophy, Calcutta University, 1911–14; Lecturer in Philosophy, Calcutta University, 1914–21; Professor of Philosophy in the University of Calcutta, 1921–31; George V Professor of Philosophy, Calcutta University, 1931–33; President, Council of Post-graduate Teaching in Arts, 1933–34; Fellow of the Calcutta Univ., 1913–23, 1926–38. *Publications:* Neo-Hegelianism; Two Essays on General Philosophy and Ethics, Psychical Research and Man's Survival of Bodily Death; various articles on philosophical subjects in the Philosophical Review, Monist, Madras Christian College Magazine, Modern Review, etc. *Recreation:* light reading. *Address:* P49 Manicktolla Spur, Calcutta, India.

Died 15 Sept. 1942.

HALDIN-DAVIS, H., FRCS, MD, FRCP; Consulting Dermatologist to the Royal Free Hospital and Dermatologist, Willesden Borough Council; Physician Hospital for Diseases of the Skin, Blackfriars; Medical Referee to Home Office; Dermatologist to Ministry of Pensions; *m* 1924, Lily V. Samuel, of Castlemount, Eastbourne, *widow* of Frank Samuel. *Educ:* Charterhouse; Balliol College, Oxon; St Bartholomew's Hospital. *Publications:* Skin Diseases in General Practice (3rd ed.); Modern Skin Therapy. *Address:* Green's End, Forest Row. *T:* Forest Row 239. *Club:* Reform.

Died 2 Feb. 1949.

HALDON, 5th Baron *cr* 1880; Bt 1782; **Edward Arthur Palk;** *b* 1854; 4th *s* of 1st Baron; *S* great-nephew, 1938; *m* 1883, Charlotte Frances (*d* 1931), *d* of late Rev. Sir Frederick Shelley, 8th Bt. Served South Africa, 1901–02.

Died 1939 (ext).

HALE-WHITE, Sir William, KBE 1919; MD London and Dublin; FRCP; Hon. LLD, Edinburgh, 1927; Hon. FRCP, Edinburgh, 1931; late President of the Royal Society of Medicine; Physician to Guy's Hospital since 1890 (now Consulting Physician); late Vice-Chairman Queen's Institute of District Nursing; late Councillor, British Red Cross Society; late Chairman, now Fellow, Bedford College; late Treasurer, Epsom College; *b* London, 7 Nov. 1857; *e s* of late William Hale White (Mark Rutherford); *m* E. J. S. (*d* 1945), *d* of A. D. Fripp, RWS; one *s.* Entered Guy's Hospital, 1875; Assistant Physician, 1885; Lecturer on Medicine, 1899; Croonian Lecturer to the Royal College of Physicians, 1897; Harveian Orator, 1927; Col RAMC (T); Chairman, Queen Mary's Hospital. *Publications:* Text-Book of General Therapeutics, 1889; Materia Medica, 26th ed. 1945; Text-Book of Pharmacology and Therapeutics, 1901; Common Affections of the Liver, 1908; Bacon, Gilbert and Harvey, 1927; Laennec, 1923; Great Doctors of the Nineteenth Century, 1935; Keats as Doctor and Patient, 1938. *Address:* 24 Warnborough Road, Oxford. *T:* Oxford 4232. *Club:* Athenæum.

Died 26 Feb. 1949.

HALES, Harold Keates; Sole Proprietor, Hales Brothers, Shippers, Export and Import Merchants, Audrey House, Ely Place, EC1; *b* Manchester, 22 April 1868; *s* of Lewis George Hales, Manchester; *m* 1915, Ethel, *d* of J. King, Clapham; one *s. Educ:* Chorlton High School, Manchester; Endowed School, Burslem, Staffs. Apprenticed 1885 to Gildea & Walker, Earthenware Manufacturers, Burslem, going through all processes of earthenware manufacture; later employed as cashier at Hammersley & Co., China Manufacturers, Longton, Staffs; afterwards Country Representative for Gibson & Sons for 4 years, and Wade & Co., Burslem, for 9 years; in March 1897 entered motor-car business in Burslem; elected a Councillor of the Federated Area of Stoke-on-Trent, 1910; on outbreak of war joined up Oct. 1914 with the Royal Naval Armoured Car Division and took part in the Landing at Gallipoli, 25 April 1915 (3 medals); returned to England and was demobilised, 1916; travelled India and the Far East representing British Manufacturers, 1916–28, visiting India, Burma, Ceylon, Malaya, Dutch East Indies, Siam, China, Japan, Korea, Manchuria and Philippine Islands; opened a London Shipping office under title of Hales Brothers, 1929; MP (C) Hanley, 1931–35; is a pioneer of motor industry since 1897, and has taken considerable interest in aviation; presented the Trophy for the Blue Riband of the Atlantic, 1935, for the fastest crossing between Europe and America, held formerly by the Italian Steamship Rex, and later by the French Steamship

Normandie. *Publications:* Harold's Adventures, 1926; Chariots of the Air, 1935; Autobiography of 'The Card,' 1936; The Road to Westminster, 1936; acts as journalist, contributing to 26 newspapers in England and India and the Far East. *Recreations:* violin, motoring, chess, and cello, and in earlier life football, tennis and cricket. *Address:* Selahdale, 6 West Heath Avenue, Golders Green, NW11. *TA:* Selahbros, London. *T:* Speedwell 1456.

Died 7 Nov. 1942.

HALFORD, Rt Rev. George Dowglas, DD, MA Oxon; Queensland order of witness since 1921; *b* 1865; *s* of Edward Halford, MD, of Hammersmith, W, and Frances Trist Douglas; unmarried. *Educ:* Felsted; Keble Coll., Oxford; Leeds Clergy School. Assistant Curate St Peter's, Jarrow, 1890–94; of St Andrew with St Anne, Bishop-Auckland, 1894–95; Vicar of St Peter, Jarrow, 1895; was one of the men who placed themselves without reserve in the hands of Bishop Westcott of Durham; head of St Andrew's Bush Brotherhood, 1897–1902, and Rector of Mitchell, diocese of Rockhampton, Q, 1897–1902; Archdeacon of Mitchell, 1898–1902; Rector of Rockhampton, 1902–09; Archdeacon of Rockhampton, 1902–07; Bishop of Rockhampton, 1909–20. *Recreations:* at school played cricket and football, in Football Eleven three years; at Oxford rowed all four years, and was captain of College Eight. *Address:* The Priory, Grange, Brisbane, Queensland.

Died 27 Aug. 1948.

HALFORD, Jeannette, OBE 1928. *Educ:* Notting Hill High School; Germany. Secretary, 1900–08, to the International Co-op. Alliance in connection with which the organisation of four International Congresses was carried out, Hon. Secretary, National Association for the Prevention of Infant Mortality and of the Association of Maternity and Child Welfare Centres, 1909–37; founder and Hon. Secretary, Cookham Child Welfare and Nursery Centres, 1939–46. *Publications:* The Bachelor Girl's Cookery Book; editing of reports in English, French and German of International Congresses on Co-operation, and in English only of reports of National Conferences on Infant Mortality, 1913–1933. *Recreation:* gardening. *Address:* Cottesloe, Cookham. *T:* Bourne End 739.

Died 27 Feb. 1950.

HALL, Rev. Abraham Richard, MA; Hon. Canon of Carlisle Cathedral; *b* Doncaster, 1851; *m* 1898, M. A. Bowers (*d* 1928), of Bollington Cross, near Macclesfield. *Educ:* Doncaster Grammar School; St Catharine's College, Cambridge. Ordained, 1876; Curate of Bollington, Macclesfield, 1876–80; Christ Church, Bootle, 1880–84; St George's, Barrow-in-Furness, 1884–86; St Mary's, Carlisle, 1886–93; Vicar of Wreay, 1893–1940; Rural Dean of Carlisle, South, 1904–25; Proctor in Convocation for Diocese of Carlisle, 1902–22; has taken much interest in the educational work of diocese of Carlisle; at one time Chairman of the Diocesan Board of Examiners and afterwards Secretary of the Education Society. *Address:* at St Edmund's Rectory, Salisbury.

Died 7 Dec. 1942.

HALL, Sir (Alfred) Daniel, KCB 1918; FRS; MA; Hon. DSc Oxon; Hon. LLD Aberdeen and Cambridge; VMH; Hon. Fellow of Balliol College; late Director John Innes Horticultural Institution; late Chief Scientific Adviser Ministry of Agriculture; *b* 22 June 1864; *s* of Edwin Hall of Rochdale; *m* 1st, Mary Louisa (*d* 1921), *d* of John Brooks of Edgbaston, Birmingham; one *s*; 2nd, 1922, Ida S. A., *d* of Alfred Beaver. *Educ:* Manchester Grammar School; Balliol College, Oxford. First Principal, South-Eastern Agricultural College, Wye, 1894–1902; Director of the Rothamsted Experimental Station (Lawes Agricultural Trust), 1902–12; Foreign

Member, Royal Academy of Agriculture, Sweden; Commissioner under the Development Act, 1909–17; British Government Delegate International Labour Conference, Geneva, 1921; Chm. of Commission on Agriculture, Kenya Colony, 1929; Rede Lecturer (Univ. of Camb.), 1935; Heath Clark Lecturer, University of London, 1935; Earl Grey Lecturer, King's College, Newcastle-upon-Tyne, 1939; Member of Economic Advisory Council; Vice-President, Royal Horticultural Society. *Publications:* The Soil, 4th edition, 1931; The Book of the Rothamsted Experiments, 1919; Fertilisers and Manures, 3rd edition, 1928; The Feeding of Crops and Stock, new edition, 1936; The Agriculture and Soils of Kent, Surrey and Sussex (with E. J. Russell) 1911; A Pilgrimage of Brit. Farming, 1913; Agriculture after the War, 1916; The Book of the Tulip, 1929; Digressions of a Man of Science, 1932; The Apple (with W. B. Crane), 1933; The Frustration of Science (with others), 1935; The Pace of Progress, 1935; The Improvement of Native Agriculture, 1936; Our Daily Bread, 1938; The Genus Tulipa, 1940; Reconstruction and the Land, 1941; various papers in Proceedings Royal Society, Transactions Chemical Soc., Journal Agricultural Science, etc. *Recreations:* fishing, gardening, Oriental art. *Address:* (temp.): Long Sutton House, nr Basingstoke. *Club:* Athenæum.

Died 5 July 1942.

HALL, Arthur Henry, CB 1937; CBE 1918; MICE; FRAeS; *b* 17 Aug. 1876; *e s* of late H. S. Hall, mathematical author; *m* 1910, Maud Henrietta Webster; two *s. Educ:* Clifton; Trinity Hall, Cambridge (1st class Mechanical Science Tripos). Apprenticed to Wm Denny and Bros, Dumbarton; Assistant Mechanical Engineer, Woolwich Arsenal, 1905–14; Assistant Superintendent, Mechanical Engineering Dept, Woolwich Arsenal, 1914–17; Director of Mine and Torpedo Production; in charge of production of the above and other Anti-Submarine Devices at the Admiralty, 1917–19; Controller, Miscellaneous Stores, Disposal, Ministry of Munitions, 1919; Controller, Aircraft, Factory Consumable Stores and Miscellaneous Stores Disposal, Ministry of Munitions, 1920; Controller, Ferrous and Non-Ferrous Metals and Chemical Disposals, Disposal and Liquidation Commission, 1921; Supt of Production Royal Airship Works, Cardington, 1926–28; Chief Superintendent, Royal Aircraft Establishment, Farnborough, 1928–41. *Publications:* articles on Fly-fishing and Photography. *Recreations:* dry-fly fishing, ornithology, and photography. *Club:* Authors'.

Died 10 Sept. 1949.

HALL, Sir Daniel; *see* Hall, Sir A. D.

HALL, Hon. David Robert, late MLA; Solicitor; Company Director; *b* Bright, Victoria, 5 March 1874; *s* of Thomas and Marion Hall of Dumfries, Scotland; *m* Cassie Jackes (*d* 1928), Armidale, NSW; two *s; m* 1944, Myra Perkins. *Educ:* Forest Lodge Public School and University Law School. Entered State Parliament of New South Wales, 1901; called to NSW Bar, 1903; later represented Werriwa in Federal Parliament for five years; resigned to become Solicitor-General of New South Wales with life seat in Legislative Council; resigned to contest seat in Legislative Assembly; succeeded and accepted office as Attorney-General, 1914–19; Minister for Housing, 1919–20; introduced and administered Acts seizing whole wheat crop of the State and necessary commodities Control (Price-fixing) Act. *Recreations:* walking and swimming. *Address:* 82 Portland Place, W1; 77 King Street, Sydney, Australia. *Clubs:* City Livery; Masonic, Sydney.

Died 6 Sept. 1945.

HALL, Col Edward, DSO 1917; TD, JP, Derbyshire; *b* 1872; *s* of Col Edward Hall, JP, of Horwich House, Whaley Bridge; *m* Margaret Ethel, *d* of C. A. Johnstone of Glen Albyn, Whaley Bridge; no *c.* Served European War, 1914–18 (despatches, DSO). *Address:* Shall-cross Manor, Whaley Bridge. *T:* Whaley Bridge 88.

Died 20 March 1941.

HALL, Edward Laret, CMG 1939; *b* 24 Oct. 1864; *s* of Charles Wallace Hall and Eliza Scott; *m* 1st, 1891, Kate Edith Lovett; one *s;* 2nd, 1908, Catherine Mary Walch (*d* 1941); one *d;* 3rd, 1944, Jessie Stewart Williams. *Educ:* various schools in Tasmania and New Zealand. Admitted as a barrister, Attorney, Solicitor and Proctor of Supreme Court of Tasmania, 1887; practised as such till 1892; Commissioner of Courts of Requests, Stipendiary Magistrate, and Coroner, 1892–1938, also Warden of Mines, 1893–1938; at various times, 1928–38, acting puisne Judge of Supreme Court; retired, 1938. *Recreations:* golf and motoring. *Address:* 38 Lyttleton Street, Launceston, Tasmania. *T:* Launceston, Tas. 175.

Died 29 Nov. 1947.

HALL, Col Ernest Frederic, CMG 1916; late RA; *b* 25 Nov. 1865; *s* of late Arthur Hall, Madras Civil Service; *m* 1st, 1901, Daisy Gordon (decd), *d* of late H. M. Chase, Bengal Civil Service; no *c;* 2nd, 1920, Lilian Dora (*d* 1942), *widow* of Edward D. Ritchie, MD, and *d* of Rev. F. M. Middleton, Rector, Old Alresford. *Educ:* Bradfield College; RM Academy, Woolwich. Entered Army, 1884; Capt. 1895; Major, 1900; Lieut-Col 1911; Commanded 36th Brigade, RFA, France and Flanders, Aug. 1914–July 1915 (despatches, CMG); ADA War Office, 1916–20 (Legion of Honour, Croix d'Officier); Colonel, 1919; retired, 1920; JP, Hampshire since 1927; Member of House of Laity of the National Assembly of the Church of England since 1930; Chairman, Eastleigh County Bench. *Address:* Woodley Cottage, Romsey, Hants. *T:* Romsey 35.

Died 21 June 1942.

HALL, Frederick; *b* Stillington, nr York, 1860; 2nd *s* of Frederick Hall, MRCS, of Stillington, Yorkshire; *m* Beryl, *d* of Capt. Dodd, Moulmein, Burma; one *d. Educ:* Lincoln School of Art; The Academy, Antwerp, under Verlat. Exhibits at the Royal Academy, London, since 1886; awarded a medal by Société des Artistes Français; worked for fifteen years at Newlyn in Cornwall; figure and landscape painter. *Address:* Speen, Newbury, Berks.

Died 21 Aug. 1948.

HALL, Sir Frederick Henry, 2nd Bt *cr* 1923; Underwriter at Lloyds; *b* 11 April 1899; *er s* of Sir Frederick Hall, 1st Bt, KBE, DSO, MP, and Annie Ellen (*d* 1929), *d* of Henry Hall, MD; *S* father 1932; *m* 1924, Olwen Irene, *yr d* of late Alderman Frank Collis, Stokeville, Stoke-on-Trent, and Deganwy, Llandudno; two *s* one *d;* 1947, Constance Phyllis Duff. *Educ:* Marlborough; RMC, Sandhurst; Cambridge University. *Recreations:* golf, motoring. *Heir: s* Frederick John Frank, *b* 14 Aug. 1931. *Address:* Little Simons, Gt Horkesley, Essex. *Club:* Carlton.

Died 22 June 1949.

HALL, Col Frederick William George G.; *see* Gordon-Hall.

HALL, George A., Architect; FRIBA; *s* of late George Hall, Architect; *m* Marion (*d* 1937), *y d* of Charles Preston, solicitor; one *s.* Articled to his brother, the late Edwin T. Hall; a general practitioner; has executed many works in town and country in all branches of his profession; Councillor for the City of Westminster, 1913–37; Governor of various charities; PM in Masonry; contributed scientific articles and dramatic and musical criticisms. *Recreations:* music, sketching, and out-of-door sports. *Address:* 1 Victoria Street, SW1. *T:* Abbey 6580.

Died 19 Jan. 1945.

HALL, George Thompson, CMG 1918; CBE 1919; VD; retired; *b* Malton Yorkshire, 1865; *s* of Edwin Hall; *m* Eliza Camilla Townshend; one *s* one *d. Educ:* Rawlings Academy, Malton; Nunthorpe Hall College, York. Emigrated to NZ 1884; took up business; deeply interested in local government; Treasurer, Woodville Jockey Club, five years; Captain, Woodville Rifles, 1897; Adjutant, 1902; Ruahine Battalion, 1902–04; Captain, main body, NZEF, to 1915; Camp Commandant, Egypt, to April 1916, rank Lieut-Colonel; Chief of Staff, HQ, Egypt, to May 1916; AQMG and Chief of Staff, NZ, HQ, London, to July 1920, rank Colonel (despatches twice). *Recreations:* volunteering, football, cricket, golf. *Address:* 136 The Terrace, Wellington, NZ. *T:* 43785.

Died 2 Dec. 1948.

HALL, Henry Noble, CBE 1939; American Correspondent News of the World since 1941; *b* 11 Dec. 1872; *s* of Henry Nissen Hall and Lillian Porter; *m* 1st, 1893, Suzanne Arot (*d* 1919); 2nd, 1920, Jean Oertel; no *c. Educ:* King's School, Canterbury; Victoria College, Jersey; Sorbonne, Paris. Journalist; Paris Correspondent The Cyclist, The Irish Cyclist, 1890; joined staff The Standard, 1892, with Pierre Lafitte founded La Bicyclette, worked on French papers; visited West Indies, 1901, owner-editor The Pioneer and Trinidad Magazine; Philadelphia North American, 1905; assistant editor New Orleans Item, 1907; staff correspondent New York World, 1908, won Panama libel suit; War Correspondent, 1914–15, interviewed King Albert; in 1912 and 1916 seconded by New York World to Democratic National Committee for Woodrow Wilson's campaigns; Asst Sec. of Commission to Honour and Welcome British French War Missions in 1917; actg corr. The Times in Washington, 1917, War Correspondent with American Expeditionary Forces, covered Peace Conference and meetings Supreme Council; Editor Revue Hebdomadaire Presse Anglaise, Paris, 1921; Public Relations Officer, International Chamber of Commerce, 1925; Paris Manager TIDA, 1930, and since its creation representative British Council in charge British propaganda in France; First Secretary, temporary, HM Embassy, Paris, 1939; associated with Lord Bessborough in French Welfare Work, 1940; Officer Legion of Honour; Order of Leopold (Belgium). *Address:* 150 East 49th Street, New York. *Clubs:* National Press, Washington; Dutch Treat, Silurians, Adventurers, Overseas Press, Lotos, New York.

Died 26 March 1949.

HALL, Hubert, formerly of HM Public Record Office; LittD; FSA; *b* Hesley Hall, Yorks, 1857; *s* of late Richard Foljambe Hall. *Educ:* Shrewsbury School; Wren's. Appointed to the Public Record Office, 1879; Assistant Keeper of the Public Records, 1912; Resident Officer, 1892; an Inspecting Officer of Records, 1905; retired, 1921; Secretary to the Royal Commission on Public Records, 1910–18; Hon. LittD Camb. 1920; Literary Director of the Royal Historical Society, 1891–1938, and Hon. Vice-President, 1939; Vice-President of the Historical Association, 1925–29; Member of the Board of Celtic Studies (Legal and Historical Committee); Foreign Member of the American Antiquarian Society and Corresponding Member of other Societies; Vice-Chairman of the American Historical Association Head quarters in London, 1912–20; Hon. Auditor, 1894–1938, of the Selden Society, member of Council, 1927, and Vice-President, 1939–42; Hon. Auditor of the New Palæographical Society (1894–1927); Reader in Palæography and Economic History in the University of London (London School of Economics and King's College, 1896–1925), Special Lecturer, London School of Economics, 1926–30; Special Examiner University of London and member of the Palæography Sub-Committee, Institute of Historical Research, 1930–38; Author or Editor of numerous historical works, and

contributions to the London Reviews and Historical or Antiquarian Journals, 1880–1941. *Recreations:* natural history, fishing, and gardening. *Address:* Cartref, Walderslade, near Chatham.

Died July 1944.

HALL, James Henry; MP (Lab) Whitechapel Division of Stepney, 1930–31 and since 1935; Alderman, Stepney Borough Council; *b* 24 March 1877; *s* of James Hall; *m* Theresa Ellen, *d* of George Coleman, Leyton; one *s* three *d. Address:* Cooden, 101 Fyfield Road, Walthamstow, E17. *T:* Larkswood 4230.

Died 6 June 1942.

HALL, Surg. Rear-Adm. John Falconer, CMG 1919; MB, RN, retired; Commissioner, Board of Control, 1931–38; *b* 1872; *s* of late William Hall; *m*; one *s* one *d.* Served China, 1900 (despatches, medal, specially promoted); second-in-charge at Haslar Hospital, 1920–23; Deputy-Director of the Medical Department at the Admiralty, 1919–20; in charge of Royal Naval Hospital at Malta, 1923–26; Hon. Surgeon to the King, 1925; Retired List, 1927; European War, 1914–19 (despatches, CMG); Gilbert Blane Gold Medallist, 1902. *Address:* The Dial, Chudleigh, S Devon. *T:* Chudleigh 3136. *Club:* Caledonian.

Died 15 Jan. 1946.

HALL, (Miss) Radclyffe; writer; *b* Bournemouth, Hants, 12 Aug. 1880; *née* Marguerite Antonia Radclyffe-Hall; *d* of Radclyffe Radclyffe-Hall. *Educ:* King's College, London; Germany. Began by writing verses: many were set to music, notably, The Blind Ploughman, set by Coningsby Clarke, several by Coleridge Taylor, Liza Lehmann, Woodeforde Finden, Mrs George Batten, and others; has for many years taken a great interest in Psychical Research, having been for some time a Member of the Council of the Society for Psychical Research; Fellow of the Zoological Soc. *Publications:* Short stories for periodicals, etc.; Poems of the Past and Present (poems); Songs of Three Counties and other Poems (poems); The Forgotten Island (poems); The Forge (novel, 1924); The Unlit Lamp (novel, 1924); A Saturday Life (novel, 1925); Adam's Breed (novel, 1926), awarded the Femina-Vie-Heureuse prize and James Tait Black Memorial Book Prize for that year; also gold medal of Eichelbergher Humane Award, 1930; The Well of Loneliness (novel, 1928); The Master of the House (novel, 1932); Miss Ogilvy Finds Herself (short Stories, 1934); The Sixth Beatitude (novel), 1936. *Recreations:* dog-breeding, riding, travelling, first nights, collecting antique oak. *Address:* The Wayside, Lynton, N Devon.

Died 7 Oct. 1943.

HALL, Adm. Sir Reginald; *see* Hall, Adm. Sir W. R.

HALL, Robert, FLS, CMZS; Hon. Fellow, American Ornithologists' Union; late Curator of Tasmanian Museum; *b* Lal Lal, nr Ballarat, 1867; *s* of Capt. I. J. Hall, Victoria; *m* Edith, *d* of late Hon. W. R. Giblin, Puisne Judge of Supreme Court, Tasmania, sometime Premier and Attorney-General for that State. *Educ:* Scotch College and University, Melbourne; University of Tasmania. Secretary of Royal Society, Tasmania; resigned, 1913; accompanied the Consul for Norway to Kerguelen Land as Naturalist to the Expedition, 1897; travelled 2500 miles up Lena River (Siberia) to the mouth—probably first English naturalist to do so—collecting birds, etc., for scientific purposes, which were in Tring Museum, 1903 and later sold to Smithsonian Inst., Washington, DC, Hon. Foundation Mem. Austr. Geog. Soc., est. 1946. *Publications:* Key to Birds of Australia, 1899; Insectivorous Birds of Victoria, 1900; Nature Studies in Australia (with W. Gillies), 1903; Useful Birds of South Australia, 1907; Australian Bird Maps, 1922. *Address:* Littlegrange, 395 Sandy Bay Road, Hobart, Tasmania.

Died 17 Sept. 1949.

HALL, Adm. Sir (William) Reginald, KCMG 1918; CB 1915; DCL; RN; *b* 28 June 1870; *m* 1894, Ethel (*d* 1932), *d* of late Sir William de Wiveleslie Abney, KCB; one *s* one *d*. Inspecting Captain of Mechanical Training Establishments, 1906–07; Naval Assist to Comptroller of Navy, 1911–13; commanded HM ships Cornwall, Natal, and Queen Mary; Director of Intelligence Division Admiralty War Staff, 1914–18; MP (U) West Derby Division of Liverpool, 1919–23; Eastbourne, 1925–29; Principal Agent of the Unionist Party, 1923–24; Officer Legion of Honour; Rear-Admiral, 1917; retired, 1919; Vice-Admiral retired, 1922; Admiral, 1926. *Address:* Dockhead, Beaulieu, Hants. *T:* 281; 36 Curzon Street, Mayfair. *Club:* Beefsteak.

Died 22 Oct. 1943.

HALL-THOMPSON, Adm. Percival Henry, CB 1924; CMG 1917; *b* 1874; *s* of late Henry Hall Thompson, Eling, Hants; *m*; two *s* two *d*. Entered Service, 1887; Capt. RN 1913; Rear-Adm. 1923; Vice-Adm. 1928; Adm. 1932; served European War, 1914–19 (despatches, thanks of Indian Government, CMG); ADC to the King, 1922; Naval Adviser to the New Zealand Government, 1919–21; First Naval Member of Royal Australian Naval Board, 1923–26; Vice-Admiral commanding Third Battle Squadron, Atlantic Fleet, 1927–28; Vice-Admiral commanding Reserve Fleet, 1929–30; retd list, 1932. *Address:* Hotel Imperial, Hythe, Kent. *T:* Hythe 6433. *Clubs:* United Service; (hon.) Royal Yacht Squadron (Cowes); Royal Naval (Portsmouth); Cinque Ports (Hythe).

Died 6 July 1950.

HALLETT, Rev. Canon Cyril, MA; Chaplain to the Sisters of Bethany, Lloyd Square, since 1941; Canon of Zanzibar Cathedral since 1911; *b* 1 May 1864; *s* of James Alfred Hallett. *Educ:* Westminster; Abingdon; Oriel College, Oxford. Priest, 1888; Assistant Curate, Odd Rode, Cheshire 1887–90, St Mary's, Slough, 1890–96; All Saints, Notting Hill, 1896–1902; Vicar of St Barnabas, Oxford, 1902–11; Archdeacon of Rovuma, UMCA 1911–21; Chaplain, E African Forces, 1917–19; Archdeacon of Zanzibar, UMCA, 1921–30; Warden of the House of Mercy, Highgate, 1931–40; Chaplain St Helena's Home, Ealing, 1940. *Address:* 10 Lloyd Street, WC1.

Died 30 Oct. 1942.

HALLETT, Rt Rev. Mgr Philip Edward, BA (Lond.); Protonotary Apostolic ad instar, 1935; *b* 3 May 1884. *Educ:* St Mary's, Woolhampton; Wonersh; University of Innsbruck. Priest, 1907; various curacies until 1915; Rector of English Martyrs, Walworth, 1915–24; Rector of St John's Seminary, Wonersh, 1924–47. *Publications:* A Son a Priest, 1946; Translator of Stapleton's Life of Sir Thomas More, 1928; St John Fisher's Defence of the Priesthood, 1935, and Blessed Robert Southwell's Spiritual Exercises, 1931; Editor of St Thomas More's Utopia, 1937, Dialogue of Comfort, 1937; and History of the Passion, 1941; pamphlets, articles, etc. *Address:* The Grange, Ashtead, Surrey. *T:* Ashtead 78.

Died 27 July 1948.

HALLIFAX, Charles Joseph, CSI 1921; CBE 1918; Indian Civil Service, retired. *Educ:* Blundell's School, Tiverton; Balliol College, Oxford. Entered ICS, 1888; Commissioner, 1912; Financial Commissioner, Punjab, 1921; retired, 1923.

Died 22 Aug. 1946.

HALLIFAX, Edwin Richard, CMG 1925; CBE 1922 (OBE 1918); *b* Darjeeling, 17 Feb. 1874; *s* of Benjamin Wilson Hallifax, Dhajea Tea Estate, Darjeeling, and Wellington, Som; *m* 1906, Eveline (*d* 1948), *d* of John Wilson, of Wilson, Guthrie & Co., Glasgow; one *s* one *d*. *Educ:* Blundell's School, Tiverton (Scholar); Balliol College, Oxford; BA 1896. Cadet, Hong Kong, 1897; passed cadet, 1900; acting police magistrate, New Territory, 1899; police magistrate, Hong Kong, 1899;

JP, 1900; asst supt of police, and police magistrate, New Territory, 1900; acting registrar-general, 1902; seconded as Transvaal emigration agent at Chinwangtao, 1905; dist officer, New Territory 1907; acting 1st police magistrate, 1909 to 1911; acting deputy supt of police and asst supt of fire brigade, 1911; acting registrar-general and MLC, 1911; MEC, 1912; registrar-general 1912; title altered to Secretary for Chinese Affairs, 1913; private secretary to Governor, in addition, 1914 to 1915; comsnr, Hong Kong section British Empire Exhibition, 1924–25; acting Colonial Secretary on various occasions, 1926–32; retired, 1933. *Address:* Mountview, Tiverton, Devon.

Died 4 May 1950.

HALLIFAX, Rear-Adm. Guy Waterhouse, CMG 1938; RN Retd; Director of Seaward Defence Union Defence Force; *b* 21 June 1884; *s* of late Rear-Admiral John Salway Hallifax and of Charlotte Annie, *d* of Maj.-Gen. de Courcy Hamilton, VC; *m* 1930, Madeleine Summer Theed, *d* of George Simms, Sunningdale; no *c*. *Educ:* privately; HMS Britannia. Joined Britannia, 1899; Lieut 1905; Lt-Comdr 1913; Comdr 1917; Captain, 1924; Rear-Admiral, 1935; Retd 1935; Commanded HMS Carlisle, China Squadron, 1926–28; Naval Attaché, Paris, 1928–31; HMS Malaya, Home Fleet, 1932–34; Director Signal Division Admiralty, 1934–35; Secretary to Governor-General of Union of S Africa, 1936–37. *Address:* Fair View, Highwick Drive, Kenilworth, Cape Town. *Clubs:* Army and Navy, Civil Service, Cape Town.

Died 28 March 1941.

HALLIFAX, Vice-Adm. Ronald Hamilton Curzon, CB 1940; CBE 1943; Flag Officer Red Sea and Canal Area; *b* 24 July 1885; 2nd *s* of late Rear-Admiral John S. Hallifax, Old Alresford, Hants; *m* 1923, Joanne Mary, 3rd *d* of R. H. Hughes, Yelverton, Devon; one *s* two *d*. *Educ:* Stubbington House; HMS Britannia. Captain, 1927; Commanded 5th Destroyer Flotilla, 1929–31; Imperial Defence College, 1932; Naval Attaché, South America, 1933–36; Commanded HMS Rodney, 1936–38; ADC to the King, 1938; Rear-Admiral, 1938; Rear-Admiral Commanding Home Fleet Destroyers, 1938–41; Vice-Admiral, 1942. *Address:* Red House, Shedfield, Hants. *T:* Wickham 3145. *Club:* United Service.

Died 6 Nov. 1943.

HALLOWES, Col Francis William, CB 1920; CIE 1918; late Supply and Transport Corps; *b* 1866; *s* of late Lt-Col W. Hallowes, 2nd Batt. KSLI; *m* 1891, Martha Musgrave, 2nd *d* of late Maj.-Gen. E. M. Beadon, 2nd Batt. KSLI; two *s* one *d*. Served Hazara Expedition, 1888 (medal and clasp); Chitral Relief Force, 1895 (medal and clasp); Somaliland, 1904 (medal and clasp); European War, 1914–18 (two medals); retired, 1920. *Address:* Otterhead, Ruiru, Kenya.

Died 11 May 1942.

HALLWARD, Reginald; artist; *b* 18 Oct. 1858; *s* of Charles Berners Hallward; *m* 1887, Adelaide Bloxam, artist and author; two *s* three *d*. *Educ:* private tuition; student at Slade and RCA Schools. Painter, decorator, illustrator, stained glass designer; Principal work: Decoration of Oldham Parish Church, Lustleigh Church, Devon; Gt Warley, Essex; Little Lever Church; Holy Trinity Church, Bury; Altar pieces Werneth Church, St Margaret's Church, Leicester, etc.; Memorial stained glass windows at Ingestre Church; S Transept window St Andrew's Parish Church; series of nave windows, St Etheldreda's Church, Fulham; other principal windows at: Cobham, Kent, Ealing, Gt Warley, Tilbury; American Memorial Chapel, Brookwood; Series of windows American Memorial Chapel, Suresnes, Paris; also at Ingestre, Coventry, and Ingatestone; Altarpiece in St Margaret's Church, Leicester, etc.; series of windows for Abberley Hall School Chapel; executed War Memorials in England, France and Belgium; Principal Exhibitions at the

Dowdeswell Galleries, 1913; collected exhibition at Galleries of the Royal Institute of British Architects, Oct. 1925, when 231 pictures, etc., were included; other minor exhibitions. *Publications:* Children's books; Rule Britannia; Quick March; Flowers of Paradise; Poems: Wild Oats; Apotheosis; The Religion of Art; The Next Step; writes on Art for the Press, etc. *Recreations:* music, walking. *Address:* 2 Mawddach Crescent, Arthog, Merioneth.

Died 30 March 1948.

HALSBURY, 2nd Earl of, *cr* 1898; **Hardinge Goulburn Giffard;** Baron Halsbury, 1885; Viscount Tiverton, 1898; KC, 1923; late Major in RAF; *b* 20 June 1880; *e s* of 1st Earl and Wilhelmina, *d* of late Henry Woodfall; *S* father, 1921; *m* 1907, Esmé, *d* of late James Stewart Wallace; one *s* one *d*. *Educ:* Eton; New College, Oxford. Contested (C) Carmarthen Boroughs, 1910; Barrister (Inner Temple); Recorder of Carmarthen, 1923–35. *Publication:* 1944 (a novel), 1926. *Heir: s* Viscount Tiverton.

Died 15 Sept. 1943.

HALSEY, Sir Laurence Edward, KBE 1919; JP Surrey; late hon. Accountant Prince of Wales National Relief Fund; Auditor of the Duchy of Cornwall; *b* 1871. *Educ:* Haileybury. Member of the Royal Commission on Wheat Supplies, 1918–20; Sheriff of Surrey, 1935. *Address:* Worplesdon, Surrey. *Clubs:* Union, City of London.

Died 13 Sept. 1945.

HALSEY, Adm. Sir Lionel, GCMG 1925 (KCMG 1918; CMG 1913); GCVO 1920 (KCVO 1919); KCIE 1922; CB 1916; DL, JP; Extra Equerry to the King since 1936; Member of Council of Duchy of Cornwall; Hon. Commodore Sea Cadet Corps in England and Wales, 1942; *b* 26 Feb. 1872; 4th *s* of late Rt Hon. Sir Frederick Halsey of Gaddesden, Herts, 1st Bt; *m* 1905, Morwenna, *y d* of late Major Bevil Granville of Wellesbourne, Warwick; two *d*. *Educ:* Stubbington House, Fareham. Joined HMS Britannia, 1885; Lieutenant from Royal Yacht, 1893; served in defence of Ladysmith, 1899–1900 (despatches, South African medal and clasp, defence of Ladysmith); specially promoted for these services to Commander, 1901; Captain, 1905; Rear-Admiral, 1917; Vice-Admiral, 1921; Admiral (retired), 1926; commanded HMS New Zealand during Empire Cruise of that ship, 1913 (CMG), and during action in Heligoland Bight, 1914, and at Dogger Bank, 1915 (despatches); served in HMS Iron Duke at Jutland as Commodore 1st Class and Captain of the Fleet; ADC 1914–17; Good Service Pension, 1915; Third Sea Lord, 1917–18; commanded Royal Australian Navy, 1918–20; Chief of Staff to Prince of Wales during Canadian Tour 1919, Australian and New Zealand Tour, 1920, and India and Japan, 1921–22; Comptroller and Treasurer to the Prince of Wales, 1920–36; retired list, 1922. Pres. Eastern Area British Legion since 1934; Chm. Navy League, 1941–45, Pres., 1945–47; County Director BRCS (Beds), 1939–45, County Pres., 1945–. *Recreations:* shooting, fishing, golf. *Address:* Mount Pleasant, Old Warden, Biggleswade Beds. *Club:* Bath.

Died 26 Oct. 1949.

HALSEY, Lt-Col Sir Walter Johnston, 2nd Bt *cr* 1920; OBE 1920; *b* 1868; *e s* of Rt Hon. Sir Frederick Halsey, 1st Bt, and Mary Julia (*d* 1922), *d* of late F. O. Wells; *S* father, 1927; *m* 1896, Agnes Marion, *d* of William Macalpine Leny; two *s* one *d*. *Educ:* Eton; Magdalen College, Oxford, BA. *Heir: s* Capt. Thomas Edgar Halsey, DSO, RN (retd). *Address:* Gaddesden Place, Hemel Hempstead; 32 St James's Place, SW. *Club:* United University.

Died 2 Sept. 1950.

HALSEY-BIRCHAM, Sir Bernard Edward, GCVO 1936; KCVO 1925; Solicitor and Parliamentary Agent; senior partner in Bircham & Co., 46 Parliament Street and 50 Old Broad Street; *b* 1 Jan. 1869; 2nd *s* of Edward Joseph Halsey of Henley Park, Surrey; JP; Chairman of Surrey County Council; assumed additional surname of Bircham in 1895; *m* 1897, Ivy Clelia, *e d* of Arthur Powys Vaughan, late 60th Rifles and Home Office; one *s*. *Educ:* Eton. Admitted a Solicitor, 1891; JP Surrey; private solicitor to the King, 1922. *Recreations:* gardening, cricket, golf. *Address:* Chilmark, Wilts. *Clubs:* Union, Travellers'.

Died 11 July 1945.

HAM, Wilbur Lincoln; KC, Victorian Bar, Australia; *b* 14 Nov. 1883; 3rd *s* of Hon. C. J. Ham; *m* 1918, Aileen Marjorie Wren; two *s* one *d*. *Educ:* Melbourne Grammar School; Toorak Grammar School; Ormond College, Melbourne University. Admitted to the Bar, 1906; served European War, 1915–18; Major 13th Australian Light Horse Regiment; KC 1927. *Recreation:* lawn tennis. *Address:* Eildon, Williams Road, Toorak, Australia. *Clubs:* Melbourne, Melbourne.

Died 30 Jan. 1948.

HAMBLEDEN, 3rd Viscount *cr* 1891; **William Henry Smith,** MA Oxon; Governing Director W. H. Smith & Son Ltd; Chairman of Council of Royal College of Art; Chairman, King's College Hospital; President Sadler's Wells Foundation; *b* 25 July 1903; *e s* of 2nd Viscount and Lady Esther (Caroline Georgiana) Gore, 3rd *d* of 5th Earl of Arran; *S* father, 1928; *m* 1928, Lady Patricia Herbert, *o d* of 15th Earl of Pembroke; three *s* two *d*. *Educ:* Eton; Oxford. *Heir: s* Hon. William Herbert Smith, *b* 2 April 1930. *Address:* Strand House, Portugal Street, WC2. *T:* Holborn 4343; The Manor House, Hambleden, Henley-on-Thames. *T:* Hambleden 35.

Died 31 March 1948.

HAMBRO, Sir Eric, KBE 1919; Chairman of Council of Royal National Pension Fund for Nurses; formerly partner in C. J. Hambro & Son; *b* 30 Sept. 1872; *s* of late Sir Everard A. Hambro, KCVO; *m* 1st, 1894, Sybil Emily (who obtained a divorce 1929; she *d* 1942), 3rd *d* of Martin R. Smith, of Warren House, Hayes; two *s* two *d*; 2nd, 1929, Mrs Estelle Elger, *y d* of Cecil Beresford Whyte, of Newtown Manor, Sligo, and Hartley Manor, Carrick on Shannon, Ireland. *Educ:* Eton; Trinity Coll., Cambridge. MP (C) Wimbledon Div., Surrey, 1900–07.

Died 28 Dec. 1947.

HAMER, Rev. Charles John; Canon Emeritus of Bradford since 1935; Licensed Public Preacher, Diocese of St Alban's since 1935; Hon. Life Governor of the Church Missionary Society; *b* 8 Sept. 1856; *e surv. s* of John Edward Bridges Hamer, Eccleston Square, London; *m* 1886, Margaret, *y surv. d* of George Winn, Normanby, Lincolnshire; one *s* four *d*. *Educ:* private school; London College of Divinity; Pembroke College, Oxford. Ordained, 1880; Curate of Christ Church, Harrogate, 1880–83; of St Luke, Manningham, Bradford, 1883–86; Vicar of St John's, Bowling, Bradford, 1886–98; Hon. Chaplain to the Bishop of Newcastle, 1907–15; Vicar of St Paul's, Newcastle, 1898–1920; Hon. Canon of Newcastle, 1906–20; Vicar of Ilkley, 1920–35; Hon. Canon of Bradford, 1922–35; Surrogate for Diocese of Bradford, 1922; Proctor in Convocation, 1924–35; Hon. Secretary of Bradford Diocesan Conference, 1922–35; Editor Bradford Diocesan Year Book, 1921. *Publications:* Old Testament History; New Testament History; Notes on St Matthew; Notes on St Mark; Notes on St Luke. *Address:* 90 Clarence Road, St Albans. *T:* St Albans 856.

Died 5 Aug. 1943.

HAMER, Sam Hield, CBE 1935; *s* of late John Hamer, JP. *Educ:* City of London School. On the editorial staff of Cassell & Co., 1886–1907; editor of Little Folks, 1895–1907; Secretary of the National Trust for Places of

Historic Interest or Natural Beauty, 1911–34. *Publications:* The Story of the Ring; Whys and other Whys; A Way-farer in the Dolomites; The Jungle School; The Magic Wand, and many other children's books. *Address:* Ladywell, 69 Dartmouth Park Hill, NW5. *T:* Gulliver 3777.

Died 6 Feb. 1941.

HAMILTON; *see* Rowan-Hamilton.

HAMILTON, Cosmo; dramatist and novelist; 2nd *s* of late Henry James Gibbs, Board of Education, and Helen Hamilton; assumed mother's name by deed poll. Worked with Lord Roberts on the NSL; Captain Legion of Frontiersmen; edited the World; gazetted Sub-Lieut RNAS Sept. 1914; served with US Government Liberty Loan Campaign, 1917–18; Head Warden ARP, recruiting officer, 1938–39; Censorship, Sept. 1939. *Publications:* Novels—Adam's Clay; Brummell; The Blindness of Virtue; Duke's Son; The Infinite Capacity; The Outpost of Eternity, 1912; The Door that has No Key, 1913; A Plea for the Younger Generation; The Miracle of Love, 1915; His Friend and His Wife, 1920; The Rustle of Silk, 1922; The Laughing Mask; Unwritten History, 1924; Caste, 1925; The Three Passions, 1928; The Little Gold Ring, 1929; The Pleasure House, 1930; Happiness, 1931; People worth talking about; The Splendour of Torches, 1934; Pillion, 1935; Adam and Evelyn, 1936; The Armour of Light, 1937; Discord and Harmony, 1938; Everyman to His Wife, 1938; Drama Within Drama, 1939; Thy Lamp, O Memory, 1939; The Brief Flower, 1942. Plays—The Wisdom of Folly; A Sense of Humour; The Mountain Climber; Scandal, Parasites, The Silver Fox; The Belle of May-fair; The Catch of the Season; The Beauty of Bath; Florabella; Castles in Spain; Bridge (produced in Paris in French); Arsène Lupin; Mrs Skeffington; The Blindness of Virtue; Mr Pickwick; The Aunt of England, with Anthony Gibbs, 1935. *Club:* Savile.

Died 14 Oct. 1942.

HAMILTON, Captain David Monteith, CMG 1917; RN, retired; *b* 12 Oct. 1874; *s* of Colonel J. G. Hamilton; *m* 1935, Letitia L., widow of Adam Mackay, Hamilton, Ontario. Retired Captain, 1912; Officer of Legion of Honour, 1917. *Address:* Hamara, La Négresse, Biarritz, France. *Clubs:* Army and Navy; Travellers', Paris.

Died 18 May 1942.

HAMILTON, Maj.-Gen. Sir Edward Owen Fisher, KCB 1911; CB 1902; *b* 17 Feb. 1854; *s* of late William James Hamilton of Fiddown, County Kilkenny, Ireland; *m* 1886, Isabel (*d* 1944), *d* of late Gen. Philip H. F. Harris, CB; one *s* two *d*. Gazetted as Lieutenant to 1st Battalion The Queen's, 1873; served Afghan War, 1878–80 as Major-Gen. Primrose (despatches, medal and clasps); Captain, 1883; served with 2nd Batt. Burmah War, 1886–87, and April to Aug. 1887 as Brigade Major to Sir Wm Lockhart commanding a brigade (medal with 2 clasps); was Brigade Major at Cawnpore, 1887–88, and Inspector of Signalling, Punjab and Bengal, 1888–93; served in Hazara Expedition, 1891, as Superintendent of Signalling (despatches, clasp); served with Sir Wm Lockhart in Tochi Valley, 1895 (clasp); served with the Malakand Field Force, 1897, as DAAG 2nd Brigade, under Brig.-Gen. Jeffreys (despatches); served with 2nd Batt. The Queen's as 2nd in command in Tirah Expeditionary Force, 1897–98 (medal 2 clasps, Bt of Lt-Col); served in command 2nd Batt. The Queen's in S Africa, 1899, and from April 1900 to end of the war as Brigadier-General commanding a Brigade (despatches several times, medal with 5 clasps, brevet of Colonel, CB); commanded a Brigade in India, 1902–07; Maj.-Gen. 1906; GOC Troops, West Africa, 1908–11; Lt-Governor and GOC

Troops, Guernsey and Alderney District, 1911–14; retired from the service, 1914. *Address:* Broom Cottage, Wokingham, Berks. *T:* Wokingham 243.

Died 30 March 1944.

HAMILTON, Edwin J.; architect (retired); *b* London, 8 June 1852; *y s* of Rev. Robert Hamilton, a Congregational minister. *Educ:* private school in Brighton. Articled to late Thomas Simpson (architect to the Brighton Education Committee); subsequently worked as assistant in Surrey and the west of England; commenced practice in Brighton in 1878; elected a member of the Society of Architects in 1887, and served as Pres. 1894–95, 1895–96, and 1908; Chairman of the Sussex Congregational Union, 1907; Hon. Secretary of same, 1913–25. *Works:* mostly private country houses, schools, and some church work in the home counties. *Address:* Highbury House, 13 Wellington Road, Brighton 7. *T:* Brighton 4446.

Died 29 Dec. 1946.

HAMILTON, Col Ernest Graham, CMG 1919; DSO 1916; MC; late The Connaught Rangers and Cheshire Regt; *s* of Charles George Hamilton; *m* 1907, Ethel Marie, (*d* 1945), *d* of James Moore Frith of Lawnakilla, Enniskillen; two *s*. *Educ:* Wellington College; Sandhurst. Joined Connaught Rangers, 1902; served in India, 1902–06; West Africa, 1906–07; returned to India, 1908; Capt., 1911; Lt-Col, 1924; Col 1928; in France with Expeditionary Force, Aug. 1914–Feb. 1915; Staff Captain, Feb. 1915; Brigade-Major, Sept. 1915; went to Mesopotamia with Indian Corps, Dec. 1915, having served continuously since outbreak of war (despatches five times, DSO, CMG, MC, promoted); commanded 148th (3rd West Riding) Infantry Brigade, TA, 1929–33; retired pay, 1933; recalled to Army, June 1940, Gen. Staff, Aldershot Command. Manager Administration in Royal Ordnance Factory, 1942; commanded 12th E Lancs Bn HG, and finally No. 24 Sector, NW District. *Publications:* under nom de plume H. E. Graham; The Defence of Bowler Bridge; The Battle of Dora. *Address:* Basingbourne, Fleet, Hants.

Died 10 April 1950.

HAMILTON, Gavin Macaulay, CMG 1921; MVO 1920; *b* 1880; *s* of late Sir Robert G. C. Hamilton, KCB, LLD; unmarried. *Educ:* Wellington House, Westgate-on-Sea; Bradfield College, Berks. Entered the service of the Bank of England, 1899; resigned 1907 to join the Staff of the Lord Lieutenant of Ireland (Earl of Aberdeen); held successively the positions of Assistant Chamberlain, additional Private Secretary and Vice-Chamberlain on Vice-regal Staff; Secretary to the Governor-General of New Zealand (Earl of Liverpool), 1912; retired on conclusion of HE's term of office, 1920. *Recreations:* shooting and fishing. *Address:* 16 Combe Park, Bath. *Club:* Caledonian.

Died 13 June 1941.

HAMILTON, Sir George Clements, 1st Bt *cr* 1937; Kt 1922; electrical engineer; *b* 1 Nov. 1877; *y s* of late Ven. George Hans Hamilton, DD, Archdeacon of Northumberland and Canon of Durham, and Lady Louisa Hamilton; *m* 1906, Eleanor *d* of late Henry Simon and late Mrs Simon of Lawnhurst, Didsbury; one *s* one *d*. *Educ:* Aysgarth; Charterhouse. Apprenticed to Scott and Mountain for 5 years, and represented that firm in India, Bulgaria, Greece, Russia, and Egypt; Major Queen's Westminster Rifles, Jan. 1915; MP (C) Altrincham Division of Cheshire, 1913–23, and for Borough of Ilford, 1928–37; resigned 1937; Director of Enrolment National Service, 1917; Controller of Contract Claims, Ministry of Munitions, 1918; Parliamentary Private Secretary (unpaid) to the Minister of Pensions, 1919–20; Chairman of Officers' Pensions Warrant Committee, 1920; Chairman of War Office Committee for Combination of Pay Office and Records Office, 1921; Member of East Suffolk CC; Chairman of Expanded Metal Co.; Chairman The National Group of Fixed

Trusts, etc. *Recreations:* shooting, tennis. *Heir: s* Patrick George [*b* 1908; *m* 1941, Winifred Mary, *o d* of Hammond B. Jenkins, Maddings, Hadstock]. *Address:* Cransford Hall, Saxmundham. *T:* Rendham 26. *Club:* Carlton.

Died 12 Jan. 1947.

HAMILTON, George Douglas F.; *see* Findlay-Hamilton.

HAMILTON, Col Gilbert Claud, CMG 1919; DSO 1915; late Grenadier Guards; *b* 21 April 1879; *o s* of late Rt Hon. Lord Claud Hamilton; *m* 1st, 1911, Enid Awa (*d* 1916), *d* of Charles Elgar, NZ; 2nd, 1916, Mary, *d* of J. A. Blair of New York. Entered army, 1898; Capt., 1905; Adjutant, 1906; Major, 1914; Col, 1923; employed with SA Constabulary, 1900–01; with Macedonian Gendarmerie, 1904–06; Military Secretary to Governor of NZ, 1910–11; employed with NZ Military Forces, 1911–13; served S Africa, 1899–1902 (despatches, Queen's medal 6 clasps, King's medal 2 clasps); European War, 1914–19 (despatches thrice, CMG, DSO); retired pay, 1925.

Died 30 March 1943.

HAMILTON, Gen. Sir Ian ((Standish Monteith), GCB 1910; GCMG 1919; KCB 1900; CB 1896; DSO 1891; ADC; late Col Queen's Own Cameron Highlanders and Gordon Highlanders; Col 3rd Battalion Manchester Regiment; *b* Corfu, 16 Jan. 1853; *e s* of Col Christian Monteith Hamilton and Corinna, *d* of 3rd Viscount Gort; *m* 1887, Jean (*d* 1941), *e d* of Sir John Muir, 1st Bt. *Educ:* Cheam; Wellington. Entered Army, 1873; served Afghan War, 1878–80 (despatches twice, medal with 2 clasps); served Boer War, 1881 (despatches); Nile Expedition, 1884–85 (despatches, brevet of Major, medal with 2 clasps; and Khedive's star); Burmese Expedition 1886–87 (despatches, brevet of Lieut-Col, medal with clasp); Colonel, 1891; Chitral relief force, 1895 (despatches, CB, and medal with clasp); commanded 3rd Brigade Tirah Campaign, 1897, 1898 (despatches, medal with clasp); commandant, Hythe, to 1899; served South Africa, 1899–1901, Elandslaagte, defence of Ladysmith (including Waggon Hill), Diamond Hill, etc., etc. (despatches several times, promoted Maj.-Gen.); Mil. Sec. Headquarters, 1901–03; Chief-of-Staff to Lord Kitchener, 1901–02; from that time to end of war commanded mobile columns in western Transvaal, including actions at Roodival, etc. (despatches, promoted Lt-Gen.); QMG to Forces, 1903–04; served as Military Representative of India with the Japanese Field Army in Manchuria 1904–05; GOC-in-Chief Southern Command, 1905–09; Adjt-Gen. to Forces (2nd military member of Army Council), 1909–10; GOC-in-Chief Mediterranean and Inspector-General Oversea Forces, 1910–15; commanded Mediterranean Expeditionary Force, 1915; General, 1914; 1st class Order of the Crown of Prussia, 1902; Grand Cordon of Order of Sacred Treasure, Japan, 1905; Grand Cordon Military Order of Merit, Spain, 1905; 1st class Order Red Eagle, Prussia; Grand Officer, Legion of Honour; Lieut of the Tower of London, 1918–20; Pres. British Legion (Scotland); Lord Rector of Edin. University, 1932–35; Freedom of Royal and Ancient Burgh of Inverness, 14 June 1947. *Publications:* Icarus; A Jaunt in a Junk; Fighting of the Future; A Ballad of Hadji; A Staff Officer's Scrap-Book, 1906; The Millennium? 1913; Gallipoli Diary, 1920; Friends of England; Soul and Body of an Army; (with Victor Sampson) Anti-Commando, 1931; When I Was a Boy, 1939; Jean—a Memoir, 1942; Listening for the Drums, 1944. *Address:* 1 Hyde Park Gardens, W2. *T:* Paddington 5104.

Died 12 Oct. 1947.

HAMILTON, Air Vice-Marshal John Beresford C.; *see* Cole-Hamilton.

HAMILTON, Brig.-Gen. John George Harry, DSO 1900; DL, JP; late the Black Watch; *b* 6 Aug. 1869; *o s* of late George Hamilton, JP, DL, Skene, Aberdeenshire; *m* 1912, Sybil Irene, OBE 1943, *d* of late E. Montefiore Micholls; (one *s* killed in action in Crete, 1941) one *d.* *Educ:* Cheltenham College. Entered Army, 1890; Captain, 1899; served South Africa, 1899–1902 (despatches twice, Queen's medal 5 clasps, King's medal 2 clasps, DSO); European War, 1914–18 (despatches six times, Bt Lt-Col); Major, 1909; Lt-Col 1916; Brig.-Gen. 1916; retired pay, 1921; Durbar medal, 1912. *Address:* Skene House, Aberdeenshire. *T:* Lyne of Skene 25. *Clubs:* New, Edinburgh.

Died 24 Sept. 1945.

HAMILTON, His Honour Sir Orme R.; *see* Rowan-Hamilton.

HAMILTON, Brig. Robert Sydney, CB 1922; CMG 1915; DSO 1918; RAOC; *b* 5 March 1871; *s* of late Ven. F. C. Hamilton, Archdeacon of Limerick; *m* 1902, Mary Eleanor, *d* of late Sir Alexander Shaw. Entered RA 1891; Captain, 1899; Major, 1905; Lt-Col 1911; Col 1918; Ordnance Officer, 4th Class, 1898–1905; 3rd Class, 1905–11; 2nd Class, 1911; served South Africa, 1899–1902 (Queen's medal 5 clasps, King's medal 2 clasps); European War, 1914–18 (despatches, CMG, DSO); Directing Ordnance Officer, RAOC 1926–28; retired pay, 1928.

Died 1 July 1945.

HAMILTON, Sir Robert William, Kt 1918; MA, FRGS, FSA (Scot.); *b* 26 Aug. 1867; 2nd *s* of late Sir R. G. C. Hamilton, KCB; *m* 1925, Gertrude, *d* of late John Williamson, Kirkwall, Orkney. *Educ:* St Paul's School; Trinity Hall, Cambridge; Inner Temple. Secretary Commission of Enquiry Dominica, 1893; District Commissioner, Lagos, 1895; Registrar East Africa Protectorate, 1897; Secretary of Famine Relief Committee, 1899; Assistant Judge and Administrator-General, 1900; Judge of the High Court, 1902; Secretary Land Commission, 1904; Chief Justice British East Africa, and President HM Court of Appeal for Eastern Africa, 1905; Chairman Civil Service Commission, 1918; retired, 1920; MP (L) Orkney and Shetland, 1922–35; Parliamentary delegate to South Africa, 1924, Canada, 1928, Iceland, 1930; Indian Round Table Conference, 1930; Joint Select Committee, East Africa, 1931; Parliamentary Under Secretary, Colonial Office, 1931–32; Scottish Liberal Whip, 1934. *Publications:* East Africa Law Reports. *Recreations:* fishing and yachting. *Address:* The Grange, Hadlow Down, Sussex. *T:* Hadlow Down 231. *Clubs:* Reform; Mombasa; Nairobi.

Died 15 July 1944.

HAMILTON, Sir William Stirling-, 11th Bt *cr* 1673; *b* 4 Dec. 1868; *s* of 10th Bt and Eliza, *d* of late Major-Gen. Barr; *S* father, 1913; *m* 1902, Mabel Mary, *d* of late Maj.-Gen. Henry Tyndall, CB; one *s.* *Heir: s* Robert William [Capt. RN; *b* 5 April 1903; *m* 1930, Eileen, *o d* of late Rt Rev. H. K. Southwell, CMG; one *s* two *d*]. *Address:* Rascals, Southwater, Horsham, Sussex.

Died 7 Oct. 1946.

HAMILTON-RUSSELL, Hon. Claud Eustace; JP, DL; *b* 4 March 1871; 3rd *s* of 8th Viscount Boyne; *m* 1899, May, *d* of Sir Lindsay Wood, 1st Bt; one *s* one *d.* Master of the Wheatland Foxhounds, 1902–19. *Address:* Bayards, Steyning, Sussex. *Club:* Boodle's.

Died 7 May 1948.

HAMILTON-RUSSELL, Hon. Frederick Gustavus; JP, DL; *b* 12 June 1867; 2nd *surv. s* of 8th Viscount Boyne; *m* 1897, Lady Margaret Rachel Scott (*d* 1938), *y d* of 3rd Earl of Eldon. *Address:* 3 Cambridge Gate, Regent's Park, NW1. *T:* Welbeck 3966.

Died 3 Oct. 1941.

HAMLEY, Herbert Russell; Professor of Education, Institute of Education, University of London, since 1932; Acting Director, 1937–38; *b* Ballarat, Victoria, Australia, 6 Sept. 1883; *s* of David John and Eliza Mary Hamley; *m* 1920, Edna Florence Robinson; one *s* one *d*. *Educ*: Wesley College, Melbourne; Queen's College, University of Melbourne (Scholar). MA, MSc, DipEd, Melbourne; MA (Hon.), Sydney; PhD Columbia University; Government of Victoria Scholar; Dixson Final Honour Scholar in Natural Philosophy, University, Melbourne; Twice Research Scholar in Natural Philosophy. Lecturer in Mathematics and Natural Philosophy, Queen's College, University of Melbourne; Principal, University High School, Melbourne; Principal, Secondary Training College, Bombay, 1924–29; Professor of Physics, Wilson College, Bombay, 1915–24; Lecturer in Mathematics, Teachers College, Columbia University, New York, 1929–30–1931; Reader in Education, University of London, 1931–32; Visiting Professor of Education, University, Cairo, 1942–43; Educational Adviser to Government of Iraq, 1943–44. *Publications*: Relational and Functional Thinking in School Mathematics (National Council of Teachers of Mathematics, USA); Intelligence and Intelligence Testing; The C Child (Year-book of Education); The Magnetic Properties of Stalloy; School Discipline; The Teaching of Arithmetic; The Fundamental Formulæ of Physics; Joint Ed., The Year Book of Education; Editor of Teaching, an educational Journal published in Bombay; articles in educational journals. *Recreations*: swimming, walking. *Address*: University of London Institute of Education, WC1. *T*: Museum 5525.

Died 5 June 1949.

HAMMAN, Lt-Col Jacob L., DSO 1916; MP South-West Africa since 1926; farmer; *b* 28 Sept. 1876; *s* of Eduard Christian Hamman, late member Volksraad, Transvaal Republic, and MGS Munhingh; *m* Anna Elizabeth Retief; one *s* three *d*. *Educ*: South African schools. Joined telegraph service Transvaal Republic; served on President Kruger's Staff during Anglo-Boer War; was taken prisoner of war; served during European War in command of Middelburg A Commando in SWA under General Botha (despatches, DSO); MP Middelburg, Transvaal, 1915–20; Member of Legislative Assembly since 1928. *Address*: PO Box 18, Kalkfeld, South-West Africa.

Died 31 Aug. 1948.

HAMMERTON, Sir John (Alexander), Kt 1932; author and editor; founded World Digest, 1939; *b* Alexandria, Scotland, 27 Feb. 1871; *s* of late James Hammerton of Oldham; *m* 1st, 1895, Rhoda Lawrence (*d* 1948); 2nd, 1949, Mrs Kate Janet Maitland. *Educ*: Glasgow. Assistant Editor Scottish Reformer, 1888–93; Glasgow Daily Echo, 1893–94; editor Blackpool Herald, 1894–95; Nottingham Daily Express, 1895–97; Birmingham Weekly Post, 1897–1900; General Editor, S. W. Partridge and Co., 1900–05; editor London Magazine, 1905–07; Punch Library of Humour (25 vols), 1907; Harmsworth History of the World, 1907–09; World's Great Books, 1909–10; Charles Dickens Library (18 vols), 1910; The Fine Art Scott (28 vols), 1911; editor, The War Illustrated, The Great War, 1914–19; The Masterpiece Library of Short Stories (20 vols), 1920, new edition, 1934; Harmsworth's New Atlas, 1920; Harmsworth's Universal Encyclopaedia, 1920–22; People of All Nations, 1922–24, new ed. 1934–35; Universal History of the World, 8 vols, 1927–29; Manners and Customs of Mankind, 1931–32; New Book of Knowledge, 1937–38, postwar edn (8 vols), 1949; editor New Universal Encyclopedia, 1947–49; and many similar publications; wrote, spoke and enacted commentary to the War Film, Forgotten Men, 1935; editor, The War Illustrated, 1939–47; The Second Great War, 1939–46; FRSA; Pres., Robert Louis Stevenson Club (London), since 1945. *Publications*: The

Actor's Art, 1897; J. M. Barrie and his Books, 1900; Tony's Highland Tour, 1901; Stevensoniana, 1903; The Call of the Town: A Tale of Literary Life, 1904; Humorists of the Pencil, 1905; English Humorists of To-day; In the Track of R. L. Stevenson; George Meredith: His Life and Art, 1909; The Argentine through English Eyes, 1916; Wrack of War, 1918; An Outline of English Literature, 1925; Memories of Books and Places, 1928; Barrieland, 1929; Barrie: The Story of a Genius, 1929; With Northcliffe in Fleet Street, 1932; As the Days Go By, 1941; Other Things than War, 1943; Books and Myself: Memoirs of an Editor, 1944; Child of Wonder: A Biography of Arthur Mee, 1946; The Rubáiyat of a Golfer, 1946; many serial works anonymously and several books under a *nom de plume*. *Recreations*: reading for pleasure, motoring, foreign travel. *Address*: John Carpenter House, Whitefriars, EC4; De Walden Lodge, Eastbourne, Sussex. *T*: Central 8080, Eastbourne 3416. *Clubs*: Reform, Savage.

Died 12 May 1949.

HAMMICK, Brig. Robert Townsend, DSO 1917; DL Wilts; Chairman Wilts TA Association; *b* 1882; *o s* of late W. M. Hammick. *Educ*: Marlborough; Royal Military Academy, Woolwich. Served European War, 1914–19 (despatches five times, DSO, Bt Lt-Col, 3rd class Order of Nile); commanded 19th Field Brigade, Royal Artillery, Bordon, 1931–34; Col 1935; CRA 46th (North Midland) Division, 1935–36; Comm 30th (Northumbrian) AA Group, 1936–38; retired pay, 1938. *Address*: Red Poulden, Tisbury, Wilts. *T*: Tisbury 287. *Club*: Army and Navy.

Died 26 Nov. 1947.

HAMMOND, Brig.-Gen. Dayrell Talbot, CB 1909; CBE 1919; late Hon. Col 4th Batt. Connaught Rangers; *b* 24 Dec. 1856; *e s* of J. H. Hammond, JP, of Preston, Lancashire; *m* Emma Adelaide, *d* of late W. Ince Anderton, DL, Euxton Hall, Chorley, Lancs. Major, retired pay, Connaught Rangers; JP for Co. Meath and for Co. Roscommon. *Address*: Corballis, Dunsany, Co. Meath. *Clubs*: East India and Sports; Stephen's Green, Dublin.

Died 9 Jan. 1942.

HAMMOND, John Lawrence Le Breton, on editorial staff of Manchester Guardian since Sept. 1939; Hon. Fellow St John's College, Oxford; Hon. DLitt Oxford and Manchester; FBA; Officer of the Legion of Honour; *b* 1872; 2nd *s* of late Rev. V. F. Hammond, Vicar of Drighlington, Yorkshire; *m* 1901, Lucy Barbara Hammond. *Educ*: Bradford Grammar School; St John's Coll., Oxford (Classical Scholar). Editor of the Speaker, 1899–1906; leader-writer on Tribune, 1906–07, Daily News, 1907; Sec. Civil Service Commission, 1907–13; 2nd Lieut Lowland Division RFA Sept. 1915–Aug. 1916; employed by Ministry of Reconstruction until Armistice; Special Correspondent for Manchester Guardian at Peace Conference, 1919. *Publications*: Charles James Fox, 1903; Life of C. P. Scott, 1934; Gladstone and the Irish Nation, 1938; joint-author with his wife of The Village Labourer, 1760–1832, 1911; The Town Labourer, 1760–1832, 1917; The Skilled Labourer, 1760–1832, 1919; Lord Shaftesbury, 1923; The Rise of Modern Industry, 1925; The Age of the Chartists, 1930; James Stansfield, 1932; The Bleak Age, 1934. *Address*: Oatfield, Piccotts End, Hemel Hempstead. *Club*: Reform.

Died 7 April 1949.

HAMMOND, Captain Leslie Jennings Lucas, CBE 1935; RN, retired; *b* 15 Oct. 1877; *s* of Joseph Hammond and Susan Georgina Lucas; *m* 1903, Edythe Adelaide White, Quebec, Canada; one *s* two *d*. *Educ*: Newton College; HMS Britannia. In HMS Orlando, Flagship Australian Squadron, 1894–97; at college at Greenwich and Portsmouth, 1897–98; on North American Station in HMS. Crescent, Flagship of Admiral Sir Frederick Bedford; after 2 years at college was Gunnery Lieut of HMS Duke of Edinburgh; joined Naval Ordnance Inspection Dept, 1907; Assistant Inspector at Elswick Ordnance Works, 1908–11; Admiralty, Whitehall, 1911–27; Deputy Chief Superintendent, Research Dept, Woolwich, 1927–28; Superintendent of Royal Naval Cordite Factory, Holton Heath, 1928–35. *Recreations:* cricket, tennis, Rugby (played for Devon County and the Harlequins), shooting. *Address:* Middle Copse, Wareham. *T:* Wareham 101.

Died 18 Dec. 1943.

HAMMOND, Thomas Edwin; Surgeon, Cardiff Royal Infirmary; Consulting Surgeon, Welsh National Memorial Association; President, Section of Urology, Royal Society of Medicine; Ex-President, Cardiff Medical Society; *b* 5 Aug. 1888; *s* of Edwin Hammond and Jane Jenkins. *Educ:* Cheltenham College; St Bartholomew's Hospital Medical School. Open Scholarship Anatomy and Physiology Inter-MB London; FRCS 1913. *Publications:* The Constitution and its Reaction in Health; Principles in the Treatment of Inflammation, 1934; Infections of the Urinary Tract; Vitality and Energy in Relation to the Constitution; Surgical Subjects various scientific journals. *Recreation:* fishing. *Address:* 34 Newport Road, Cardiff. *T:* Cardiff 4262.

Died 25 March 1943.

HAMPDEN, Ernest Miles H.; *see* Hobart-Hampden.

HAMPSHIRE, Dugan Homfray, CMG 1942 for public services in Federated Malay States; *yr s* of late Dr F. K. Hampshire.

Died April 1942.

HAMPSHIRE, Frederick William; Chairman and Managing Director of F. W. Hampshire and Co. Ltd, Sunnydale, Derby, and Globe Works, Riddings, Derbyshire; *b* 13 April 1863; *s* of Matthew William Hampshire, railway contractor and Esther Moody; *m* 1st, 1903, Elizabeth Katie Walters; 2nd, 1927, Jessie Deakin; one *s* two *d*. *Educ:* Board School. Founded and built up the firm of F. W. Hampshire and Co. Ltd, manufacturing chemists; during the war, founded and edited Le Courier Belge which was the means of providing news to the Belgian refugees and of re-uniting thousands of families scattered throughout this country; Founder and President of Union of Commonweal; Fellow of Chemical Society; Vice-President and Life Governor, University College Hospital and Cromer Hospital; Vice-President Derby YMCA; Trustee and Member of Management Committee of Derbyshire Hospital for Women; Trustee and Member of Committee of Woodhouse Hostel, Derby; Trustee Derbyshire Children's Seaside Home. *Recreations:* travelling, photography. *Address:* Overstrand Lodge, Overstrand, Norfolk.

Died 20 July 1941.

HANBURY, Daniel; *b* 3 June 1876; 2nd *s* of late Sir Thomas Hanbury, KCVO of La Mortola, Italy; *m* 1st, 1901, Sylvia Dorothea (*d* 1931), *y d* of late G. Dymond; two *d*; 2nd, 1932, Ruth, *yr d* of late Rev. Sheffield Hardinge. *Educ:* privately; Trinity College, Cambridge. *Address:* Castle Malwood, Lyndhurst, Hants; Villa della Pergola, Alassio, Italy. *Clubs:* Royal Cruising, All England Lawn Tennis; Royal Yacht Squadron (Cowes).

Died 21 July 1948.

HANBURY-WILLIAMS, Maj.-Gen. Sir John, GCVO 1926; KCB 1917; KCVO 1908; CMG 1899; CVO 1902; Colonel Oxford and Bucks Light Infantry; Extra Equerry to the King since 1934; *b* 19 Oct. 1859; *y s* of late Ferdinand Hanbury-Williams of Coldbrook Park, Monmouthshire; *m* 1888, Annie Emily (*d* 1933), Lady of Grace Order of St John of Jerusalem, *e d* of Emil Reiss; one *s* three *d*. *Educ:* Wellington Coll. Joined 43rd Light Infantry, 1878; ADC to Lt-Gen. Sir E. Hamley, in Egypt, 1882; battle of Tel-el-Kebir, horse shot

(despatches, medal with clasp, bronze star, 5th class Medjidie); extra ADC to Sir M. E. Grant Duff, Governor of Madras, 1884 and 1885; extra ADC to Lt-Gen. Sir H. Macpherson, Burma, 1886; adjutant 3rd Oxford Light Infantry, 1892–97; Military Sec. to His Exc. Sir A. Milner, 1897–1900; Secretary to Secretary of State for War, 1900–03; served South Africa, 1899, 1900 (despatches, medal and 3 clasps, promoted Lt-Col, half-pay); Governor-General's Secretary, and Military Secretary, Canada, 1904–09; Brigadier-General in charge of administration, Scotland, 1909–14; Employed Gen. Staff, 1914; Chief of British Military Mission with Headquarters Russian Army in the Field, 1914–17; (despatches, war medals); in charge of British Prisoners of War Department at the Hague Aug. 1917–March 1918, and at Berne April 1918–Dec. 1918; Marshal of the Diplomatic Corps, 1920–34; Knight of the Legion of Honour; Commander of the Order of San Bento d'Aviz (Portugal); Commander First Class Order of Danebrog (Denmark); Order of St Vladimir, 3rd Class; Order of Saint Anne. *Publication:* The Emperor Nicholas II as I knew Him, 1922. *Recreations:* hunting, shooting. *Address:* Henry III Tower, Windsor Castle. *Clubs:* Marlborough, Boodle's.

Died 19 Oct. 1946.

HANCOCK, His Honour Ernest, MC 1918; Judge of the County Courts, Circuit No. 45 (Wandsworth and Kingston-upon-Thames), 1941–50; *b* 30 Nov. 1887; 3rd *s* of Robert Hancock; *m* 1914, Louisa Maud Mary, *d* of John George Woolland Reddaway; two *s*. *Educ:* Exeter School; Lincoln College, Oxford. Called to Bar, Inner Temple, 1913; Judge of County Courts, 1937; Member of Standing Committee for framing County Court Rules; served European War as Lieutenant with RGA, and in France with South African Heavy Artillery, 1917–18 (MC). *Recreations:* motoring and golf. *Address:* Kepier Cottage, Kingston Hill, Surrey. *T:* Kingston 3528. *Club:* Oxford and Cambridge.

Died 26 Dec. 1950.

HAND, Rt Rev. George Sumner; Rector of St George's, Basseterre, St Kitts, since 1944. *Educ:* St John's College, Oxford; Ely Theological College. Dean of St John's Cathedral, Antigua, 1930–37; Bishop of Antigua, 1937–43; Priest-in-charge of St Mary's, Antigua, Jan.–May 1944. *Address:* S George's Rectory, S Kitts, BWI.

Died 26 July 1945.

HANDLEY, Tommy; *b* 12 Jan. 1896; *m* 1929, Jean Allistone. Articled to Corn Trade, Liverpool; first professional engagement, Maid of the Mountains, 1917; toured in revues; ran sketch The Dis-orderly Room. First Broadcast 1924; Command Performances: Coliseum, Disorderly Room, 1924; Victoria Palace, as commentator to the Broadcast of Variety Command Performance, 1927; Windsor Castle (on occasion of Princess Elizabeth's 16th birthday), ITMA (It's That Man Again), 1942. *Recreations:* golf, cycling, reading. *Address:* 34 Craven Rd, W2. *Club:* Savage.

Died 9 Jan. 1949.

HANDMAN, Frederick William Adolph, CBE 1935; MInstCE 1928; retired Chartered Civil Engineer; *b* 13 Dec. 1876; *s* of late Adolph Marion and Elizabeth Handman; *m* 1900, Beatrice Annie Dunell; one *s* three *d*. *Educ:* private. Railway construction in Brazil, 1909–21; Chief Engineer on Irrigation works and Port works for Brazilian Government, 1921–24; Agent and Chief Engineer on Hydro-Electric Works for New Zealand Government, 1924–28; Resident Engineer on construction of Lower Zambezi Bridge, Portuguese East Africa, 1929–36; Member New Zealand Society of Civil Engineers, 1928; American Society of Civil Engineers, 1930; Telford Premium, Institution of Civil Engineers, 1929 and 1937; Silver Jubilee Medal, 1935. *Publications:* Reconstruction of a Viaduct, The Arapuni Hydro-Electric Development, and The Lower Zambezi Bridge in Proceedings, Institution of Civil Engineers. *Recreations:* big game hunting, golf. *Address:* Sunnyside Blantyre, Nyasaland. *TA:* Handman Blantyre.

Died 31 July 1948.

HANDOVER, Alderman Lt-Col Sir Harry George, Kt 1921; OBE, DL, JP; *b* 1868; *s* of William H. Handover; *m* 1895, Emmeline Kate, *d* of Dr Stamford Felce; two *s.* Mayor of Paddington, 1912–20, 1931–35; Member of Metropolitan Water Board and Thames Conservancy Board. *Address:* Upton, Chevening Rd, NW6.

Died 12 Nov. 1948.

HANDS, Sir Harry, KBE 1919; *b* 18 Sept. 1860; *s* of Josiah Hands, The Gables King's Norton, Birmingham; *m* 1886, Aletta Catherine, OBE (*d* 1935), *d* of Philip A. Myburgh, MLA Mayor of Cape Town, 1912–13. Greater Cape Town, 1915–18; Commander Order of Leopold II of Belgium. *Address:* Talana, Claremont, Cape Town, South Africa. *Clubs:* City, Royal Automobile (Cape Town).

Died 17 March 1948.

HANDS, William Joseph, CBE 1920; HM Divisional Inspector of Schools (East Central Division), Board of Education (retired). Assistant Director, Dilution of Labour Branch, Ministry of Munitions, 1916; Deputy Director-General of National Labour Supply, Ministry of National Service, 1917; Controller of Ministry of National Service, 1918; Member of War Cabinet Committee on the staffs of Government Departments, 1919; Secretary of Ministry of National Service, 1919; Controller of Profiteering Act Department, Board of Trade, 1919. Educational Adviser, Columbia Graphophone Co., and His Master's Voice, 1929–39; Assistant-Controller of Labour and Member of Secretariat, Ministry of Munitions, Commonwealth of Australia, 1940–46. *Address:* c/o Lloyds Bank, Derby.

Died 24 Feb. 1947.

HANFORTH, Thomas William, MusB (Dunelm); Hon. RCM; Fellow Royal College of Organists; *b* Hunslet, nr Leeds, 6 March 1867; *s* of late William Hanforth, wheelwright and carriage builder; *m* 1893, Alice, *d* of late Frank Arrowsmith, York, *niece* of John and Henry Sotheran, booksellers and publishers; two *s.* *Educ:* York Commercial College; York Minster Choir School. Chorister, Leeds Parish Church, under late R. S. Burton; Chorister, York Minster, under late Dr E. G. Monk; Assistant Organist, York Minster, under late Dr John Naylor; Organist and Master of the Choir, Sheffield Cathedral, 1892–1937; Professor of Music, Yorks School for the Blind; Conductor, York Madrigal Society, Countess of Harewood's Ladies' Choral Society; Philharmonic Orchestra and Cathedral Oratorio Choir; Grand Organist of England (Freemasons), 1923–24 and 1937–38; Organist to the Corporation of the City of Sheffield, 1932–37. *Publications:* church services, anthems, etc.; music for the Three Craft Degrees in Freemasonry; pieces for the organ, pianoforte, etc.; songs. *Recreation:* photography. *Address:* Clarendon Road, Fulwood Park, Sheffield. *T:* Broomhill 31761.

Died 5 June 1948.

HANKEY, Basil Howard Alers, CBE 1919; 2nd *s* of late E. A. Hankey of Notton House, Lacock, Wilts; *m* Maud Wyndham, *o d* of late Col J. R. P. Goodden, JP, of Compton House, Sherborne; one *d.* *Educ:* Sherborne. County Director of Red Cross in Wilts during European War, 1914–18; formerly in the Wilts Yeomanry. *Address:* Stanton Manor, Chippenham Wilts. *TA:* Hankey, Stanton, Chippenham. *T:* Kington Langley 40.

Died 10 June 1948.

HANKEY, Lt-Col Cyril, CBE 1919; MVO 1918; *m* 1940, Mrs George McClintock. Entered Royal Artillery, 1891; Captain, 1900; retired, 1906; Equerry to Prince Christian, 1908–14; served European War, 1914–18, as King's Messenger, 1914–15; Lt-Colonel, 1915; GSO 1 London Air Defences, 1916–18 (CBE). *Address:* 125 Mount Street, W1. *T:* Grosvenor 2880. *Club:* Turf.

Died 1 Nov. 1945.

HANKEY, Mabel; RMS; *b* Bath; *d* of Henry Eddington Hobson, artist. *Educ:* Bath. *Works:* Summer Days, 1907, purchased by Canterbury Society of Arts, New Zealand, 1907; New Gallery—The Empty Chair. *Publication:* Black and White portraits.

Died 5 Jan. 1943.

HANKINS, George Alexander, DSc (Eng.), ARCS, MICE, MIMechE; Director of Mechanical Engineering Research, Department of Scientific and Industrial Research, since 1947; *b* 25 April 1895; *y s* of late Henry Hankins; *m* 1920, Gladys, *yr d* of late A. J. Schooley; one *d.* *Educ:* Royal Dockyard School, Portsmouth; Imperial College of Science and Technology, University of London. Royal Scholar; Whitworth Exhibitioner; Engineer apprentice, HM Dockyard, Portsmouth. Served European War, 1914–18, in Army, 1914–15; engineering inspector, Admiralty, 1916; junior scientific officer, Nat. Physical Lab., 1917; Superintendent, Engineering Div., 1944. Crompton Medal, Institution of Automobile Engineers, 1935; Andrew Laing Memorial lecturer, NEC Inst., 1943; Centenary lecturer on Fluid Mechanics, Institution of Mechanical Engineers, 1947. Member of numerous Govt and other cttees on research in engineering and applied science. *Publications:* 30 or more papers in proceedings of scientific and professional societies. *Recreation:* golf. *Address:* 19 Pine Walk, Surbiton, Surrey. *T:* Elmbridge 4431.

Died 2 Nov. 1950.

HANNA, Hon. Henry; KC; Judge of the High Court, Eire, 1925–43; *b* 4 Jan. 1871; *m.* *Educ:* Belfast Royal Academy; Queen's Univ., Belfast; London Univ. Called to Irish Bar, 1896; KC Ireland, 1911; called to English Bar, Middle Temple, 1913; Bencher of King's Inns, Ireland, 1915; Serjeant-at-Law, 1919; Hon. Member American Bar Association; Hon. Member Canadian Bar Association; Member, Executive Committee, International Academy of Comparative Law, The Hague; Ex-Pres. Photographic Society of Ireland; Ex-President Irish Kennel Club. *Publications:* several legal treatises; The Pals at Suvla Bay, being an historical record of the 7th Royal Dublin Fusiliers during the campaign at Suvla Bay in 1915. *Address:* 83 Pembroke Road, Dublin. *Club:* London University.

Died 21 March 1946.

HANNA, Very Rev. Robert K., MA, DD; Moderator of the General Assembly of the Presbyterian Church in Ireland, 1926–27; Minister of Adelaide Road Church, Dublin, since 1914; *b* Kildrum, Ballymena, Co. Antrim, 8 Oct. 1872; *m* 1898, Nora, *o d* of Henry Pringle, Clones; three *d.* *Educ:* Royal Academical Institution, Belfast; Queen's College, Galway; Trinity College, Dublin; Theological Course at Belfast, Princeton (New Jersey) and Edinburgh; Hon. DD Glasgow University, 1927. Ordained 1898; Minister of Whiteabbey, a suburb of Belfast, till 1914; during the War worked with the YMCA, first at Gillingham and afterwards at Abbeville; on return from France, made Convener of the Committee in charge of Work among Sailors and Soldiers; visited the American and Canadian Church Assemblies as Irish Delegate, 1925; a Catechist in Trinity College, Dublin, and a Member of the Board of Managers in St Andrew's College, Dublin. *Publications:* occasional pamphlets and papers. *Recreations:* golf and fishing. *Address:* 63 Upper Leeson Street, Dublin. *T:* Ballsbridge, Dublin 202. *Clubs:* Dublin Rotary; Royal Dublin, Royal County Down Golf.

Died 29 April 1947.

HANNAH, Ian Campbell, MA, FSA, JP Peeblesshire; MP (U) Bilston division of Wolverhampton since 1935; *b* 16 Dec. 1874; *s* of John Julius Hannah, Dean of Chichester; *m* 1904, Edith Browning Brand; three *s*. *Educ:* Winchester; Trinity College, Cambridge. Master of English School, Tientsin, China, 1897–99. Assistant at Michaelhouse, Natal, 1901; President of King's College, Nova Scotia, 1904–06; Professor of Church History, Oberlin College, Ohio, 1915–25; Extra-mural lecturer, Cambridge University (with breaks) since 1900. *Publications:* Eastern Asia, a History; The Sussex Coast; Berwick and Lothian Coast; Capitals of the Northlands; Heart of East Anglia; Arms and the Map; Christian Monasticism; Voadica; Story of Scotland in Stone; History of British Foreign Policy; History of Trinity College, Cambridge; History of Sedgley, etc. *Recreations:* cycling, archaeology. *Address:* Whim, West Linton, Peeblesshire. *TA:* Hannah, Lamancha; Sandyfields House, Sedgley, Staffordshire. *TA:* Hannah, Sedgley. *T:* Sedgley 2221.

Died 7 July 1944.

HANNAH, Flight-Sgt John, VC 1940; RAF; *b* 27 Nov. 1921; *m* 1941. *Educ:* Victoria Drive Secondary School, Glasgow. *Address:* 51 Sycamore Rd, Birstall, Leics.

Died 7 June 1947.

HANNAH, William George; *b* 20 Sept. 1868; *s* of William Hannah and Sarah Ann George; *m* 1907, Edith Mary, *d* of late William Thomas Crank, Clifton. *Educ:* United Westminster Schools and privately. Called to Bar, Middle Temple, 1899; Official Asst Solicitor to Queen Anne's Bounty, 1905–21; Official Solicitor, 1921–25; Asst Sec., 1925–35; Secretary, 1935–42; Acting Sec. of Legal Board of Church Assembly. *Publications:* pamphlets and papers on Church law and ecclesiastical subjects. *Recreations:* travel and music. *Address:* Pilgrims Cottage, Merstham, Surrey. *T:* Merstham 194; 15 Old Square, Lincoln's Inn, WC2. *T:* Holborn 4104.

Died 27 Nov. 1945.

HANNAY, Brig.-Gen. Frederick R.; see Rainsford-Hannay.

HANNAY, Rev. James Owen, MA; DLit Dublin (Honoris Causa), 1946; Hon. Fellow, Imperial College of Science, London University; Vicar of Holy Trinity, Kensington Gore, since 1934; *b* 16 July 1865; *s* of Rev. Robert Hannay, DD, Vicar of Belfast; *m* Ada (*d* 1933), *e d* of Rt Rev. F. R. Wynne, DD, Bishop of Killaloe; two *s* two *d*. *Educ:* Temple Grove, East Sheen; Haileybury; Trinity College, Dublin. BA, 1887. Deacon, 1888; Priest, 1889; Curate of Delgany, Co. Wicklow; Rector of Westport, Co. Mayo, 1892–1913; MA, 1895; Donellan Lecturer, Dublin University, 1901–02; Member of General Synod of Church of Ireland, 1905–15; Canon of St Patrick's Cathedral, 1912–21; Temporary Chaplain to Forces, 1916; Chaplain to British Legation, Budapest, 1922–24; Rector of Mells, 1924–34; University Preacher, Durham, 1926; Oxford, 1927. *Publications:* The Spirit and Origin of Christian Monasticism; The Wisdom of the Desert; A Wayfarer in Hungary, 1925; Murder Most Foul, 1929; Pleasant Places, 1934; Isaiah, 1937; God's Iron: A Life of the Prophet Jeremiah, 1939; Novels (as George A. Birmingham)—The Seething Pot; Spanish Gold; Lalage's Lovers; The Adventures of Dr Whitty, 1913; The Search Party, 1913; The Lost Tribes, 1914; From Connaught to Chicago, 1914; Minnie's Bishop and Other Stories, 1915; Gossamer, 1915; The Island of Mystery, 1918; Up the Rebels, 1919; Good Conduct, 1920; Inisheeny, 1920; Lady Bountiful, 1921; The Lost Lawyer, 1921; A Public Scandal, 1922; Found Money, 1923; King Tommy, 1923; The Grand Duchess, 1924; Bindon Parva, 1925; Goodly Pearls, 1926; Fidgets, 1927; The Runaways, 1928; The Major's Candlesticks, 1929;

Wild Justice, 1930; Fed Up, 1931; The Silver-Gilt Standard, 1932; Angel's Adventure, 1933; Two Fools, 1934; Millicent's Corner, 1935; Mrs Miller's Aunt, 1936; Magilligan Strand, 1938; Appeasement 1939; Over the Border, 1942; Poor Sir Edward, 1943; Good Intentions, 1945; Laura's Bishop, 1949; Editor of Irish Short Stories, 1932. Plays—Eleanor's Enterprise, 1911; General John Regan, 1913; Send for Dr O'Grady, 1923; (with Sydney H. Nicholson) romantic light opera, The Mermaid, 1927. *Recreation:* yachting. *Address:* 187 Queen's Gate, SW7. *Clubs:* Garrick, Athenæum, Allies.

Died 2 Feb. 1950.

HANNAY, Maj.-Gen. Robert Strickland, CB 1926; CMG 1917; DSO 1900; LRCP, LRCS Ed., LFP&S (Glasgow); *b* 27 Aug. 1871; *s* of E. A. Fuhr and Dora Hannay; *m* 1st, 1896, Maud Lilian (*d* 1939), *d* of H. H. Bottomley; one *s* (*d* on active service); 2nd, 1944, K. D., *d* of late Comdr Hannay, RN. *Educ:* Queen's University; Edinburgh. Entered army, 1898; served South Africa, 1899–1901 (despatches, Queen's medal with six clasps, DSO); European War, 1914–19 (despatches five times, CMG, Bt Col 1 Jan. 1919); Major-General, 1926; KHS 1926; Col Comdt RAMC 1939–41. Changed name by deed poll to Robert Strickland Hannay, 1919; retired pay, 1930. *Address:* 56 Wynnstay Gardens, W8.

Died 5 Oct. 1948.

HANNEN, Lancelot, CBE 1919; BA; late senior partner of Christie, Manson & Woods, art auctioneers; *b* 10 Dec. 1866; 3rd *s* of late Benjamin Hannen; *m* 1897, Delia Mary, *d* of late Thomas Ramsey Dennis; one *s* one *d*. *Educ:* Radley; Trinity Hall, Cambridge. *Recreations:* rowing, shooting, and fishing; rowed in the following winning crews: Cambridge University Crew, 1888–89; Trinity Hall Head of the River, 1886–87–1888; Cambridge University Fours, 1886–87–1888; Henley Regatta Grand Challenge, 1886–87; Visitors Fours, 1887; Stewards Fours, 1888. *Address:* 2 Mansfield Street, W1. *T:* Langham 2169.

Died 24 Aug. 1942.

HANNON, Rt Rev. Daniel Joseph, DD; RC Bishop of Menevia since 1941; *b* 12 June 1884; *s* of Patrick Hannon and Elizabeth McGlynn. *Educ:* Cardiff; Valladolid; Oscott; Rome. After ordination was Bishop's Agent in Rome; Curate St David's Cathedral, Cardiff; eventually became Administrator; was Parish Priest, subsequently in Aberavon and Penarth. *Address:* Bishop's House, Wrexham. *T:* Wrexham 2054.

Died April 1946.

HANOTAUX, Gabriel; late Foreign Minister, France; Membre de l'Académie française; Délégué de la République française à l'Assemblée et au Conseil de la Société des Nations; Membre pour la France de la Haute Cour Internationale d'arbitrage; Doyen et Président du cinq centième anniversaire de l'Académie française en 1935; *b* Beaurevoir, Aisne, France, 19 Nov. 1853; *m* 1913, Marie de la Crompe de la Boissière. *Educ:* Saint-Quentin; Paris. *Publications:* Études historiques sur le XVIᵉ et XVIIᵉ siècles en France; L'Affaire de Madagascar; Histoire du Cardinal de Richelieu; L'Énergie française; Le Choix d'une carrière; La Paix latine; Histoire de la France contemporaine; Fachoda; La Démocratie et le travail; Jeanne d'Arc; La France en Amérique du Nord; Histoire de la guerre de 1914, 18 vol.; L'Histoire et les historiens; le Traité de Versailles; Histoire de la nation française, 15 vol.; La Jeunesse de Balzac; Sur les chemins de l'histoire; Histoire des colonies françaises, 6 vols; Histoire de la nation égyptienne, 7 vols; Histoire de la nation égyptienne, 7 vols; Pour l'empire colonial français; Mon Temps, souvenirs de ma vie. *Address:* 4 avenue Hoche, Paris. *T:* Carnot 40–73; Villula, à Roquebrune-Cap-Martin, Alpes Maritimes; Le Prieuré d'Orchaise (Loir-et-Cher).

Died 11 April 1944.

HANSELL, Rev. Arthur Lloyd; *b* 21 June 1865; *s* of Peter E. and Emily Hansell; *m* 1906, Mary Ellen Julius; two *d. Educ:* Charterhouse; Magdalen College, Oxford; Cuddesdon Theological College. Curate Wantage, 1891–98; Vicar Karori, NZ, 1899–1914; Vicar Lower Hutt, NZ 1914–33; Archdeacon of Wairarapa, 1922–34; Archdeacon of Wellington, NZ 1934–40. *Address:* Homewood Crescent, Karori, Wellington, NZ.

Died 16 Feb. 1948.

HANSEN, Hans; artist; 2nd *s* of H. P. Hansen, Consul for Montevideo, Leith. *Educ:* Royal High School, Edinburgh. Started painting at the age of 13; studied art under Mr Hodder at the School of Art, Princes Street, Edinburgh; water-colour painting under R. B. Nisbet, RSA, and late Joe Ross, ARSA; first exhibited at Royal Academy at the age of 20; favourite sketching ground Morocco and Spain; painted for the Queen's Dolls House by Royal Command; Silver Medal International Exhibition, Salzburg. *Recreations:* yachting (Gold Medal, Firth of Forth), cycling. *Address:* 9 Ponds Cottages, Church Road, Barling, Southend-on-Sea.

Died 4 Dec. 1947.

HANSON, Sir Gerald Stanhope, 2nd Bt *cr* 1887; *b* 23 April 1867; *s* of 1st Bt and Constance Hallett, *d* of late C. B. Bingley, Stanhope Park, Greenford; *S* father, 1905; *m* 1st, 1899, Sylvia (*d* 1909), *d* of late E. Dutton Cook; one *s*; 2nd, 1912, Dorothy (*d* 1918) (whom he divorced 1917), *d* of late Alfred Peel, Lincoln; 3rd, 1922, Flora, *er d* of late Lt-Col W. A. R. Blennerhassett, Clifton, Bristol; one *s. Educ:* Magdalene College, Cambridge. *Heir: s* Richard Leslie Reginald, *b* 21 Nov. 1905. *Address:* Grovelands, Wineham, Henfield, Sussex. *Club:* Public Schools.

Died 18 Jan. 1946.

HANSON, Hon. Richard Burpee, KC, BA, LLB, LLD; *b* Bocabec, NB, 20 March 1879; *s* of Richard B. Hanson, English-Canadian, and Hannah P. Mann, Scotch; *m* 1906, Jean Balfour, *d* of James S. Neill, Fredericton, NB; one *d. Educ:* Public Schools, Bocabec, NB; High School, St Andrews, NB; Mt Allison University, Sackville, NB; Dalhousie University, Halifax, NS, BA, LLB. A Barrister-at-Law; Director Fraser Companies Ltd, Restigouche Co. Ltd, New Brunswick Telephone Co. Ltd, Ganong Bros Ltd, and other corporations; General Counsel and Chief Solicitor for Fraser Cies. Ltd, and associated and Subsidiary Companies; Mayor of Fredericton, 1918–19 and 1919–20; MP York-Sunbury, 1921–35 and 1940–45; Chairman Standing Committee of H of C on Railways, Shipping, Session 1932; Chm. Banking and Commerce Committee H of C, Session 1934; Sworn of the Privy Council, 1934; Minister of Trade and Commerce and Chm. of the Committee of Privy Council on Scientific and Industrial Research 1934–35; Leader of Opposition in House of Commons, 1940–43 and Leader of Conservative Party in Canada, 1940–43; retired from public life, 1945. Conservative. *Recreations:* golf, motoring, fishing. *Address:* 270 Church St, Fredericton, NB. *T:* 60. *Clubs:* City, Golf, Fredericton; Rideau, Ottawa.

Died 14 July 1948.

HANSON, Rev. Robert Edward Vernon, OBE, 1915; MA; *b* 29 March 1866; *s* of late Joseph and Catherine Hanson; *m* 1896, Margaret (*d* 1938), *d* of late Thomas Fox Simpson, solicitor, Tunbridge Wells; two *s. Educ:* King's College, London; Emmanuel College, Cambridge. Assistant Curate, St John's, Richmond, Surrey, 1894–1900; Chaplain to the Forces, 1900–18; served South African War, Aldershot, Egypt, Dublin, Deepcut, Malta, European War (despatches, OBE); Dep. Chaplain-in-Chief, RAF, 1918; Chaplain-in-Chief, Royal Air Force, 1926–30; retired list, 1930. *Address:* 2 Holmesdale Road, Sevenoaks. *Club:* Royal Air Force.

Died 7 Feb. 1947.

HARAN, James Augustine, CMG 1909; MA, MD, University of Dublin; College Historical Society's Gold Medal in History; sometime Resident Medical Officer, Barrington's Hospital, Limerick; Chairman, Mombasa Town Planning Committee, 1909; Nursing Service Unification, 1914; Medical Officer, Troops on Duty (5th Aug. 1914); Sociological Records, 1917; late Deputy Principal Medical Officer, East Africa Protectorate; late of the EAMS Corps, etc. *Publications:* occasional papers, etc. *Address:* 10 Upper Oldfield Park, Bath.

Died 17 April 1940.

HARARI, Sir Victor (Pasha), Kt 1928; CMG 1905; late Director-General of Accounts, Egyptian Ministry of Finance; Chairman, Mortgage Company of Egypt, Ltd; Director Agricultural Bank of Egypt and National Bank of Egypt; *b* 1857; *m* 1887, Emma Aghion, Alexandria. *Educ:* Paris; London. Holds Cross of Legion of Honour. *Address:* Harari Villa, Cairo.

Died 21 Feb. 1945.

HARBEN, Guy Philip, OBE 1917; Ex-Chairman, St Mary's Hospital, W2; *b* 28 Oct. 1881; *s* of Henry Andrade Harben and Mary Frances James; *m* 1905, Marie Hamilton (*d* 1939); one *s. Educ:* Rugby; Royal Agricultural Coll.; Slade School of Art. Artist in Italy; Board of Trade Commissioner for Italy, 1915; special attaché at Rome Embassy for blockade purposes; joined the Prudential Assurance Co. on cessation of war, Deputy Chairman, 1936–48. *Recreations:* fishing (dry fly), orchid growing. *Address:* Colbury House, Hillstreet, Totton, Hants. *T:* Ower 10.

Died 3 Dec. 1949.

HARBERTON, 7th Viscount *cr* 1791; **Ernest Arthur George Pomeroy;** Baron Haberton, 1783; *b* 1 Dec. 1867; *e s* of 6th Viscount Harberton and Florence, *o d* of William Wallace Legge, Malone House, Co. Antrim; *S* father, 1912; *m* 1932, Fairlie Harmer. *Educ:* Charterhouse; Trinity College, Cambridge. Formerly Lieutenant 20th Hussars, and Captain 3rd Battalion Royal Dublin Fusiliers; served South Africa, 1900 (medal). *Publications:* Worse than Scripture, or the Truth about Science, 1924; How to Lengthen our Ears, 1917. *Heir: b* Hon. Ralph Legge Pomeroy. *Address:* 101 Cheyne Walk, SW10.

Died 22 April 1944.

HARBORD, Alderman Sir Arthur, Kt 1939; CBE 1935; JP; Alderman of the Borough of Great Yarmouth; MP (Liberal) Great Yarmouth, 1922–24 and 1929–31 (Liberal Nationalist) since 1931; *b* 1865; *s* of Robert Harbord; *m* Charlotte Nellie, *d* of J. M. Belward, Croydon; two *d. Educ:* British School and Winchester House School, Great Yarmouth. Elected on the Board of Guardians, 1894 (chairman for four years); elected to Town Council, 1898; Alderman, 1916; Mayor, 1917–18, 1918–19 and 1934–45; Ex-Pres. local British Legion, and Chairman Licensing Justices; Chairman of Corporation Town Planning Committee; during the War served on War Emergency Committee, Norfolk Red Cross Executive Committee, Recruiting Officers' Advisory Committee, Food Control, Coal Control, and many other committees; Hon. Secretary, 1903–05, and now President Great Yarmouth and Lowestoft War Pension Committee; Chairman Great Yarmouth Charity Trustees; Member of the Great Yarmouth Port and Haven Commission. *Address:* 60 St Peter's Road, Great Yarmouth. *TA:* Alderman Harbord, Great Yarmouth. *Clubs:* National Liberal; Great Yarmouth Central Liberal.

Died 24 Feb. 1941.

HARBORD, Frank William, CBE 1918; Officier, Légion d'honneur; FIC; Associate Royal School of Mines; Consulting Metallurgist; Senior Partner Riley Harbord and Law; Civil Member of Ordnance Committee; Past President, Iron and Steel Institute; Past

President of Institution of Mining and Metallurgy; Fellow of the Institute of Chemistry; Fellow of the Chemical Society; *b* Norwich; *s* of J. M. Harbord and Emily, *d* of Wm Riches of Oxwick; *m* 1887, Marian (*d* 1942), *d* of Vernon Smith; two *s* four *d*. *Educ*: privately; Royal School of Mines. For ten years engaged in iron and steel manufacture in the Midlands, and afterwards Consulting Metallurgist to Indian Government; at Royal Indian Engineering College, Cooper's Hill, 1892–1905; in private practice as Consulting Metallurgist since 1905; acted as Metallurgist to the Canadian Commission sent over to investigate Electric Smelting in Europe, 1903; investigated and reported on the manufacture of iron and steel in Transvaal for the Government of the Colony, 1909; during the 1914–18 war Hon. Adviser in Metallurgy to the Ministry of Munitions. *Publications*: Metallurgy of Iron and Steel, 5th edition; Edited and Revised second edition of Sir W. R. Austen's Introduction to the Study of Metallurgy. *Address*: Parliament Mansions, Abbey Orchard Street, Victoria Street, SW1. *TA*: Harbordlab, Phone, London. *T*: Abbey 3104; Englewick, Englefield Green, Surrey. *Club*: St Stephen's.

Died 27 Dec. 1942.

HARCOURT, Lady; *see* Suart, Evelyn.

HARCOURT, George, RA 1926; Hon. Corresponding Member Société des Artistes Français; President of the Royal Society of Portrait Painters; Chairman and Hon. Art Director Royal Drawing Society; *b* Dumbartonshire, 11 Oct. 1868; *m* 1897, Mary Lascelles Lee Smith. ARA 1919. *Works*: The Leper's Wife, at Winchester College; Forgiven, bought by South Australian Government for National Gallery, Adelaide; The Wanderer, bought by New Zealand Academy of Fine Arts for Wellington; The Birthday, Gold Medal, Amsterdam International Exhibition, 1912; Dawn, hon. mention, International Exhibition, Paris, 1900; Thought-reading, Medal, Paris Salon, 1896; The Birthday, Gold Medal, Paris Salon, 1923; three fresco paintings in Royal Exchange; The Founding of the Bank of England, 1694; Abel Smith, MP, Founder of Smith's Bank; and Pascoe Grenfell, MP, Governor of Royal Exchange Assurance; Spring 1915, bought by Australia for National Gallery, Sydney; Portrait of Miss Anne Harcourt (Diploma Gallery, RA). *Address*: High Sparrows Herne, Bushey, Herts.

Died 30 Sept. 1947.

HARCOURT-SMITH, Sir Cecil; *see* Smith.

HARDCASTLE, Ven. Edward Hoare; Archdeacon Emeritus of Canterbury since 1939; *b* 6 March 1862; *s* of Edward and Priscilla Buxton Hardcastle of New Lodge, Hawkhurst, Kent; *m* Hon. Alice Goschen (*d* 1941), 2nd *d* of 1st Visc. Goschen; one *s* four *d*. *Educ*: Winchester College; Trinity College, Cambridge. Ordained 1887; Priest, 1889; Curate at St George's, Ramsgate, 1887–91; Vicar of Weston, Bath, 1891–1901; Rector of St Martin's and St Paul's, Canterbury, 1901–04; Vicar of Maidstone, 1904–24; Archdeacon of Canterbury and Canon Residentiary of the Cathedral, 1924–39. *Address*: 1 Selbourne House, Chatham Place, Brighton.

Died 20 May 1945.

HARDIE, Sir David, Kt 1913; MD Aberdeen; FRACS; LLD; *b* Elgin, Scotland, 4 June 1856; *s* of late John Hardie, Pluscarden, Elgin, and Margaret Masson; *m* 1883, Marianne, *d* of Alexander Jeans, Nairn; one *s* two *d*. *Educ*: Aberdeen Grammar School and University. Consulting Physician Sick Children's Hospital, Lady Bowen Hospital; temp. Lieut-Col RAMC 1915–16. *Publications*: several in medical journals. *Recreations*: golf, gardening. *Address*: Blythsdale, 11 Arran Avenue, Hamilton, NE2, Brisbane, Queensland. *T*: M 3961. *Club*: Queensland.

Died 11 Nov. 1945.

HARDIE, Robert Purves, MA, Edin. and Oxon; *b* Edinburgh, 1864. *Educ*: Edinburgh University; Merton College, Oxford. 1st Class Math. Mods, 1885, 2nd Class Lit. Hum., 1888. Assistant, Edinburgh University, 1889; Lecturer in Philosophy, 1892; Reader in Ancient Philosophy, 1921–32. *Publications*: R. Adamson's Development of Greek Philosophy (edited with Professor W. R. Sorley), 1908; A. H. Douglas's Pietro Pomponazzi (edited with Charles Douglas), 1910; The Tobermory Argosy, A Problem of the Spanish Armada, 1912; Aristotle's Physica, I-IV (Oxford trans.), 1930; Ferox and Char in the Lochs of Scotland: An Inquiry, Part I, 1940; Roads of Mediæval Lauderdale, 1941. *Recreations*: fishing, golf, naval history. *Address*: 13 Palmerston Road, Edinburgh.

Died 9 March 1942.

HARDIE, Most Rev. William George, CBE 1950; MA (Camb.), DD; *b* Sydney, NSW, 20 Aug. 1878; *s* of George Hardie, Sydney; *m* 1905, Alice Annie Somerville; two *s*. *Educ*: Giggleswick Sch.; Emmanuel Coll. and Ridley Hall, Cambridge. Ordained, 1902; Curate Holy Trinity, Cambridge, 1902–04; Christ Church, Greenwich, 1904–06; Assistant Secretary CMS, 1906–07; Curate Sherborne Abbey, 1908–11; Vicar Holy Trinity, Swansea, 1911–15; S John's, Lowestoft, 1915–22; S Luke's, Finchley, 1922–28; Assist Bishop of Jamaica, 1928–31; Bishop of Jamaica, 1931–49; Archbishop of West Indies, 1945–49. *Recreations*: Rugby football, cricket, golf, fishing. *Clubs*: Royal Empire Society, West India Committee, National.

Died 21 Feb. 1950.

HARDIMAN, Alfred Frank, RA 1944; ARA 1936; RS, FRBS, sculptor; *b* 1891; *e s* of Alfred William and Ada Hardiman. Entered the Royal College of Art 1912, studying under the late Prof. Lantéri, gaining his diploma, 1916; continued study at the Royal Academy Schools; Rome Scholar, 1920. Works include Stone Groups for the County Hall Extension, Westminster; Memorial Statue of late Field Marshal Earl Haig, Whitehall; Stone and Bronze Sculpture for new Norwich City Offices, Norwich; medal of Royal Society of British Sculptors, 1939; Gold Medal of Royal Society of British Sculptors, 1946, for bronze fountain for the New Council House, Bristol. *Recreation*: fishing. *Address*: Farthing Green, Church Lane, Stoke Poges, Bucks. *T*: Farnham Common 536. *Club*: Arts.

Died 17 April 1949.

HARDING, Harold Ivan; *b* Toronto, 29 Jan. 1883; *s* of Edwin John Harding and Grace Elizabeth Lesslie; *m* 1911; no *c*. *Educ*: Switzerland; Elizabeth College, Guernsey; Germany. Entered British Consular Service in China, 1902; stationed at Peking, Shanghai, Canton, Wuchow, Changsha, Shanghai, Hoihow, Pakhoi, Ichang, and Foochow, in various capacities, until 1913; thence until 1922 Chinese Second Secretary at Peking, save for three months in 1917, when he was in charge of Consulate at Harbin; Vice-Consul at Kashgar, in Chinese Central Asia, 1922–23; Consul at Tengyueh on Sino-Burman Frontier, 1923–27; subsequently Consul at Changsha and Foochow and Consul General, Tsinan and Yunnanfu; retired, 1937; FRGS and Fellow of Royal Central Asian Society. *Publications*: has written for New Age, New East (Tokyo), Golden Hind, etc. *Recreations*: walking, climbing, riding, swimming, rowing, canoeing, travelling. *Address*: Te Puhapa, Mamáo, Tahiti.

Died 29 Dec. 1943.

HARDING, Most Rev. Malcolm Taylor McAdam. Curate of Mattawa, Ontario, 1887; Brockville, Ontario, 1888; Assistant Minister of St George's Cathedral, Kingston, Ont, 1889; Rector, and Rural Dean of Brandon, Man, 1893; Archdeacon of Assiniboia, 1903; Coadjutor Bishop of Qu'Appelle, 1909–11; Bishop of

Qu'Appelle, 1911–35; Chancellor of St John's College, Winnipeg, 1935; Archbishop of Rupert's Land, 1935–42; retired. *Clubs:* Union (Victoria, BC).

Died 22 April 1949.

HARDING, Walter Ambrose Heath, MA, FLS, FZS; Hon. Capt. retired; Cambs Vol. Regt; *b* April 1870; *o s* of late Col T. Walter Harding, DL, JP, of Madingley Hall, Cambs; *m* 1895, Ethel Adela (author of The Dominant Chord, A Daughter of Debate; she died 1942), *e d* of late James Audus Hirst of Adel Towers, Adel, W Yorks; one *s* one *d. Educ:* Cheltenham; Peterhouse, Cambridge. *Publications:* Papers on zoological subjects in various scientific journals; part author of volume on Hirudinea in Fauna of British India series. *Recreations:* travel, book-collecting, sketching. *Address:* Madingley Hall, Cambridge. *TA:* Madingley. *T:* Madingley 252. *Club:* Carlton.

Died 16 Oct. 1942.

HARDING, Lt-Col William, CBE 1919; MD. *Educ:* Edinburgh University (MB, CM). MRCP London; late Medical Superintendent County Asylum, Berry Wood, Northampton; served European War, 1914–19 (despatches, CBE). *Address:* 3 Silverton Terrace, Rothbury, Northumberland.

Died 23 Jan. 1945.

HARDINGE OF PENSHURST, 1st Baron *cr* 1910; **Charles Hardinge,** KG 1916; PC; GCB 1910; GCSI 1910; GCMG 1905; GCIE 1910; GCVO 1905; KCMG 1904; KCVO 1904; CB 1895; CVO 1903; ISO 1906; Chain of Victorian Order, 1912; DL; LLD (hon.) Cambridge; *b* 20 June 1858; *brother* of 3rd Viscount Hardinge; *m* 1890, Hon. Winifred Sturt (*d* 1914), *d* of 1st Baron Alington; one *s. Educ:* Harrow; Trinity College, Cambridge. Entered Diplomatic Service, 1880; 3rd Sec., 1882; 2nd Sec., 1885; Sec. of Legation, Teheran, 1896; Sec. of Embassy, Petrograd, 1898–1903; Assistant Under-Secretary for Foreign Affairs, 1903–04; Permanent Under-Secretary of State for Foreign Affairs, 1906–10, and 1916–20; British Ambassador at Petrograd, 1904–06; Viceroy of India, 1910–16; British Ambassador in Paris, 1920–23; Grand Officer, Legion of Honour, 1903; Grand Cross of the Crown of Italy, 1903; Grand Cross of Our Lady of Portugal, 1903; Grand Cross of Greek Order of St Saviour, 1906; Grand Cross of Spanish Order of Charles III, 1907; Grand Cross of Danish Order Dannebrog, 1908; Grand Cross of Swedish Order Vasa, 1908; Grand Cross of Norwegian Order St Olaf, 1908; Grand Cross of the Austrian Order of Leopold, 1908; Grand Cross of Russian Order Alexander Nevski, 1908; Grand Cross of the German Order of the White Eagle, 1908; Grand Cross of the Legion of Honour, 1922. *Publication:* On Hill and Plain, 1933. *Heir:* s Major Right Hon. Sir A. H. L. Hardinge, PC, GCB. *Address:* 3 Down Street, Piccadilly, W1; Oakfield, Penshurst.

Died 2 Aug. 1944.

HARDY, Edgar Wrigley C.; *see* Cozens-Hardy.

HARDY, Col Edwin Greenwood, CMG 1919; DL, JP Somerset; *b* 1867; *s* of late Lt-Gen. W. Hardy, CB; *m* 1893, *d* of late J. Brooking and late Lady M'Mahon; two *d. Educ:* Winchester. The Royal Dragoons, 1887–94; served in S Africa with Imperial Yeomanry; European War, in Gallipoli, 1915; Salonika, 1915–16; France, 1916–19; DD Remounts, Cavalry Corps, 1916–19; Chairman Somerset Territorial Army Association, 1935–39. *Address:* Lattiford House, Wincanton, Somerset. *T:* Wincanton 2213. *Club:* Cavalry.

Died 31 March 1944.

HARDY, Godfrey Harold, FRS, FRAS; MA Oxford and Cambridge; Hon. DSc Athens, Harvard, Manchester, Sofia; LLD Birmingham, Edinburgh; DPhil Marburg, Oslo; Fellow of Trinity College, Cambridge; Hon. Fellow of New College, Oxford; Fellow, Cambridge Philosophical Society; Royal Medal, 1920,

Sylvester Medal, 1940, and Copley Medal, 1947, Royal Society; De Morgan Medal, London Mathematical Society, 1929; Chauvenet Prize, American Mathematical Association, 1933; President of Section A, British Association, 1922; President, National Union of Scientific-Workers, 1924–26; President, Mathematical Association, 1924–26; President, London Mathematical Society, 1926–28, 1939–41; Visiting Professor at Princeton University and California Institute of Technology, 1928–29; Hon. or Corr. Member various Academies of Sciences and mathematical Societies, etc; *b* 7 Feb. 1877. *Educ:* Winchester; Trinity College, Cambridge; Fellow, 1900–19. Lecturer, 1906–19; Cayley Lecturer in the University of Cambridge, 1914–19; Fellow of New College and Savilian Prof. of Geometry in the University of Oxford, 1919–31; Sadleirian Professor of Pure Mathematics in the University of Cambridge, 1931–42. *Publications:* A Course of Pure Mathematics, 1908 (9th ed., 1944); Inequalities (with J. E. Littlewood and G. Pólya, 1934); Introduction to the Theory of Numbers (with E. Maitland Wright, 2nd ed., 1945); Ramanujan, 1940; A Mathematician's Apology, 1940; Cambridge Math. Tracts, Nos 2, 12, 18, 38; papers in various mathematical periodicals. *Address:* Trinity College, Cambridge.

Died 1 Dec. 1947.

HARDY, Gen. Hon. Sir (John) Francis G.; *see* Gathorne-Hardy.

HARDY, Air Cdre Stephen Haistwell, CBE 1944; RAF; Commandant Officers Advanced Training School, Royal Air Force College, Cranwell, Lincs, since 1944; *b* 29 Jan. 1905; *er s* of Charles C. Hardy, late Major RE, and of late Georgina Hardy; *m* 1934, Margaret, *d* of late J. D. Nimmo, Sparrows Herne Hall, Bushey Heath, Herts; no *children. Educ:* Malvern College; RAF College, Cranwell. Commissioned RAF 1924; Sqn Ldr 1937; Wing Comdr 1940; Group Capt. 1942; Air Commodore, 1944. Aeronautical Engineering Specialist Course, RAF, Henlow, Beds, 1929–30; RAF Staff College, 1936; War of 1939–45 (despatches, CBE). *Recreations:* golf, tennis, squash, etc. *Address:* c/o Mrs Nimmo, Sparrows Herne Hall, Bushey Heath, Herts. *Club:* RAF.

Died 8 April 1945.

HARE, Alfred Thomas, MA; *b* 13 Sept. 1855; 2nd *s* of Evan Hare, solicitor; *m* 1886, Florence Edith, 3rd *d* of late Jabez Church, FGS, MICE; three *s. Educ:* Merchant Taylors' School; Wadham Coll., Oxford (Scholar 1874; 1st Class Honours, Math. 1877; Phys 1878). Member of the firm of Hare & Co., Solicitors, 1881–96; Principal of the Law Courts Branch of the Treasury Solicitor, 1897–1920; late Vice-Chairman, Brentford Board of Guardians. *Publication:* Construction of Large Induction Coils, 1900. *Address:* The Orangery, St Margaret's, Twickenham. *T:* Popesgrove 1860.

Died 9 June 1945.

HARE, Brevet Lt-Col Charles Tristram Melville, CBE 1919; late The Leicestershire Regt; *b* Grantham, Lincolnshire, 9 Feb. 1879; *e s* of Charles Edward Hare; *m* 1911, Maria Geertruida, *e d* of late Ary Volker Van Waverveen of Klarenbeek, Doornspyk, Holland; (son killed in Burma 29 April 1945) one *d. Educ:* Stamford School; RMC, Sandhurst. Joined The Leicestershire Regiment, 1898; served Boer War, 1900–02; passed Staff College, 1914; served European War as Regimental and Staff Officer, 1914–18 (despatches thrice, Bt Lt-Col, CBE). *Address:* Highway House, Beaconsfield, Bucks. *Club:* United Service.

Died 30 June 1950.

HARE, Brig. George Ambrose, CIE 1934; Indian Army, retired; *b* 5 Feb. 1880; *s* of Charles Edward and Agnes Marian Isabel Hare; *m* 1st, 1912, Mabel Rose Spring (*née* O'Brien) (*d* 1921); one *d*; 2nd, 1930, Edith Margaret Constance (*d* 1939), *d* of late Lt-Col Arthur

Williamson Alsager Pollock, 13th Somerset LI. *Educ:* Stamford School; RMA, Woolwich. 1st Commission RFA, 1899; S African War (Queen's medal three clasps); Indian Ordnance, 1909; European War (Victory medal, 1914–18); Director, Indian Ordnance and Clothing Factories, 1930–35; retired 1935. *Address:* Moola House, Nutbourne, nr Chichester. *T:* Bosham 3134.

Died 30 Jan. 1948.

HARE, Brig.-Gen. Robert Hugh, CB 1919; CMG 1916; DSO 1902; MVO 1907; late RA; *b* 4 Dec. 1867; *s* of Edward Hare, CSI, Deputy Inspector-General of Hospitals, HEICS; *m* 1908, Lillian Louisa, *e d* of James Mellor; one *s* one *d. Educ:* Hermitage School, Bath; RMA, Woolwich; Staff College, 1899. Served Chitral, 1895 (medal with clasp); South African Campaign, 1899–1902 (despatches, DSO, Queen's medal 3 clasps, King's medal 2 clasps); European War, 1914–18 (despatches, CB, CMG); Brig.-Gen., Nov. 1916; Colonel, 1917; Col-Commandant area, India, 1920; retired pay, 1924. *Address:* Markway Lodge, Burley, Ringwood, Hants.

Died 2 Oct. 1950.

HARE, Sir Thomas Leigh, 1st Bt *cr* 1905; MVO, JP, DL; *b* 4 April 1859; *s* of late Sir Thomas Hare, 2nd Bt; *m* 1886, Ida (*d* 1929), *d* of 3rd Earl Cathcart; one *d. Educ:* Eton. Served in Scots Guards and 24th Regt; Major and Hon. Lieut-Col, Norfolk Artillery Militia; MP (C) Norfolk, SW, 1892–1906; contested same Division, 1910. *Heir:* none. *Address:* Stow Hall, Downham, Norfolk. *Clubs:* Carlton, Arthur's.

Died 22 Feb. 1941 (ext).

HARE, William Loftus; author, lecturer and editor; *b* 30 April 1868; 2nd *s* of Thomas Matthews Hare, Ipswich and London, and Ada Mary Hare, Ballina; *m* 1915, May, *o c* of Henry and Elizabeth Forshaw, Derby. On the death of his father, entered the business of engraving and printing with his three brothers, known as Hare and Co., until 1899; worked with Bemrose and Sons, Ltd, of Derby and London as manager of photo-engraving and chromo-collotype printing department till 1912; and other firms till the war period, when his business career closed; became lecturer in comparative religion to the Theosophical Society for five years, and in 1924 helped with the organisation of a Conference of Living Religions within the Empire which led to the foundation in 1930 of the Society for Promoting the Study of Religions; Editor of the Society's Journal Religion, 1930–35; editorial work for the Garden Cities and Town Planning Association, 1921–37; took a leading part in the defence of the Foundling Hospital Site against building of flats there, and has written its history; member of the Society of Friends. *Publications:* Works on Comparative Religion; Religions of the World, 1908; Mysticism of East and West, 1923; Systems of Meditation in Religion, 1936; joint author of Who wrote the Mahatma Letters?, 1936; and other works on religions, philosophy and economics. *Address:* 27 Westholm NW11.

Died 25 Feb. 1943.

HAREWOOD, 6th Earl of, *cr* 1812; **Henry George Charles Lascelles,** KG 1922; GCVO 1934; DSO 1918; TD; Baron Harewood, 1796; Viscount Lascelles, 1812; Personal ADC to the King since 1936; Lord Lieutenant and Custos Rotulorum West Riding Yorks since 1927; Royal Trustee British Museum since 1930; Grand Master of United Grand Lodge of England since 1943; Chancellor of Sheffield University since 1944; *b* 9 Sept. 1882; *e s* of 5th Earl and Lady Florence Katherine Bridgeman (*d* 1943), *d* of 3rd Earl of Bradford; *S* father 1929; *m* 1922, HRH Princess Mary (Princess Royal); two *s. Educ:* Eton; Sandhurst. Late Captain Grenadier Guards; late Major, Yorkshire Hussars; Hon. Attaché, Rome, 1905–07; ADC to Governor-General of Canada, 1907–11; contested (U) Keighley Division of Yorkshire,

1913; served European War, 1914–18 (wounded three times, DSO and Bar, French Croix de Guerre); Hon. Col 1st City of London Battalion Royal Fusiliers and 5th Battalion West Yorkshire Regt; Member of the Jockey Club. Owns about 29,700 acres. *Heir: s* Viscount Lascelles, *b* 7 Feb. 1923. *Address:* Harewood House, Leeds. *Clubs:* Turf, St James's, Carlton; Yorkshire, York.

Died 24 May 1947.

HARGEST, Brig. James, CBE 1943; DSO 1918; MC; VD; MP Invercargill, 1931–35, Awarua since 1925; sheep farmer; *b* 4 Sept. 1891; *s* of James Hargest and Mary Prosser; *m* 1917, Sister M. H. Wilkie, ARRC; two *s* one *d. Educ:* Mandeville and Gore, New Zealand. Served European War, 1914–18; 2nd Lieutenant with main body New Zealand Expeditionary Force (wounded Gallipoli); France, 1916 to end of war; Lieut-Colonel, 1918; appointed to command 2nd Otago Regiment (DSO, MC, Legion of Honour, Cross Chevalier, despatches); Commd 3rd NZ Infantry Brigade, 1927–31; left NZ, 1940, with NZEF as Brigadier 5th Infantry Brigade; commanded 5th Infantry Brigade, 1940–41 (prisoner but escaped, two bars to DSO, CBE); served on various local bodies. *Address:* Rakahauka, Southland, NZ. *Clubs:* Gentlemen's, Invercargill, New Zealand.

Died 12 Aug. 1944.

HARI KISHAN KAUL, Raja Pandit, CSI 1922; CIE 1912; MA; Rai Bahadur, 1905; Raja, 1926; *b* 22 Aug. 1869; Revenue and Development Minister, Patiala; *s* of Raja Pandit Suraj Kaul, CIE; *m d* of Pandit Kashi-Nath; two *s* one *d. Educ:* Government College, Lahore. Many gold medals; Fuller Exhibition, Aitchison Ram Rattan Scholarships; BA 1888; MA 1890. Assistant Commissioner, 1890; Junior Secretary to Financial Commissioner, 1893–97; Settlement Officer, Muzaffargarh, 1898–1903; Mianwali, 1903–08; Deputy Commissioner, 1906; Deputy Commissioner and Superintendent Census Operations, Punjab, 1910–12; acted as manager Badshahi mela (people's fête), Coronation Durbar, Delhi, 1911; Deputy Commissioner, Montgomery, 1913; Deputy Commissioner in charge of Criminal Tribes, Punjab, 1916; Deputy Commissioner, Jhelum, 1919; Commissioner, Rawalpindi, 1919; Commissioner, Jullundur, 1920; member Royal Commission Superior Civil Services in India, Nov. 1923; Commissioner Rawalpindi, April 1924; retired from service, Aug. 1924; Member Indian Economic Enquiry Committee, 1925; Member Indian Tariff Board (Cotton Textile Enquiry), 1926–27; Diwan Bharatpur State, 1927; Prime Minister Jammu and Kashmir State, 1931–32; Prime Minister, Patiala, 1936; Revenue and Development Minister, Patiala, 1937–38. *Publications:* Assessment and Settlement Reports and Customary Law of the Muzaffargarh and Mianwali Districts; Gazetteer of the Muzaffargarh District; Punjab Census Report, 1911; Revised Glossary of Multani. *Address:* 29 Lawrence Road, Lahore, Punjab.

Died 26 Jan. 1942.

HARINGTON, Brig.-Gen. John, CB 1927; CMG 1919; DSO 1915; JP, Salop; *b* 10 April 1873; 5th *s* of late Sir Richard Harington, 11th Bart; *m* 1908, Lady (Frances) Aline Gore-Langton, 4th *d* of late 4th Earl Temple of Stowe; one *s* one *d.* Joined Rifle Brigade, 1895; Capt., 1901; Major, 1914; Commanded 2nd and 3rd Battalions, 1919–23; with King's African Rifles, 1903–07; Adjutant TF, 1909–12; served Nile Expedition, 1898 (Queen's medal, Khedive's medal with clasp); South Africa, 1899–1902 (Queen's medal 3 clasps, King's medal 2 clasps); Somaliland, East Africa, 1903–04 (medal 2 clasps); Nandi, 1905–06 (clasp); European War, 1914–18 (CMG, DSO, Bt Lt-Col, despatches 4 times, wounded three times, Légion d'Honneur (Chevalier); BGC 139 Infantry Brigade, 1918–19; Inspector Gen. of the King's African Rifles, 1923–27; commanded 139th Territorial Infantry Brigade, 1928–30; retired pay, 1930;

Reward for Distinguished Military Services, 1933. *Address:* Chelmarsh Hall, Bridgnorth, Salop. *T:* Quatt 2. *Club:* Army and Navy.

Died 11 April 1943.

HARKER, Rowand; KC 1926; Chairman Road and Rail Traffic Act Appeal Tribunal; *b* 18 Jan. 1879; *s* of late Thomas Parkinson Harker, Brighton; *m* Lucy Millicent, *d* of William Hudson Scott, Carlisle; two *d. Educ:* Brighton. Admitted Solicitor, 1900; called to Bar, Middle Temple, 1905; served European War, RAOC and DAAG to Judge Advocate-General; South-Eastern Circuit. *Recreations:* golf, fishing. *Address:* 1 Brick Court, Temple, EC. *TA:* 97 Temple. *T:* Central 1687; 89 Barkston Gardens, SW5. *T:* Frobisher 2430. *Clubs:* Royal Ashdown Forest; Royal Mid-Surrey Golf.

Died 1 June 1946.

HARLAND, Henry Peirson; MP for East Belfast, 1939–45; Director of Harland and Wolff, Ltd, Shipbuilders and Engineers; Chairman of Heaton Tabb and Co. Ltd; Director of Short and Harland, Ltd, and of Ocean Transport Co. Ltd; *b* 1 Sept. 1876; *s* of Rev. A. A. Harland, Uxbridge, Middlesex; *m* 1917, 2nd *d* of J. D. Barbour; one *s* four *d. Educ:* Rugby. Apprenticed to Harland and Wolff, Ltd, 1893; on staff of Chinese Engineering Co. in Tientsin, Northern China; returned to Harland and Wolff, Belfast, in 1910; transferred to Govan Works in 1914; on Lord Pirrie's staff when he was Controller of Merchant Shipbuilding during War of 1914–18; Chairman Committee of technical advisers superintending completion ex-German liner Bismarck (renamed Majestic); MInstCE, MINA, and MIME; Member of Court of Company of Shipwrights and a member of General Committee of Lloyd's Register: also served on Consultative Committee of Shipbuilders and Engineers appointed to confer with Marine Department of Board of Trade; Vice-Chairman Watford Conservative Association. *Recreations:* riding, shooting, and golf. *Address:* Oakwood, The Warren, Radlett, Herts. *T:* Radlett 5968. *Club:* Union.

Died 11 Aug. 1945.

HARLEY, Rev. Alfred W. M., MA; DCL; *b* Bridgewater, Nova Scotia, 1862; *s* of late John Harley; *m* 1891, Margaret S., *d* of late John D. McClearn, Liverpool, Nova Scotia; two *s. Educ:* King's College, Windsor. BA 1884; MA 1887; DCL (hon.) King's College, Windsor, 1923. Deacon, 1886; Priest, 1887; Curate of Trinity Church Liverpool, NS, 1886; Rector, 1891–1906; Rural Dean of Shelburne, NS, 1891–1906; Professor of English Literature, King's College, Windsor, Nova Scotia, 1906–18; Priest in charge of Conquer-all, Nova Scotia, 1918–32. *Address:* Bridgewater, Nova Scotia.

Died Nov. 1941.

HARLEY, John Hunter, MA; FRHistS, FRGS; Officers' Cross of the Polish Order of the Polonia Restituta; Chevalier Legion of Honour; *b* 1865; *s* of James Harley and Janet Hunter; *m* 1897, Flora Dent. *Educ:* University of Glasgow and University of Oxford. Graduated with 1st Class Honours in Mental and Moral Philosophy. Entered journalism on the Literary Staff of the London Echo; Parliamentary representative of the Echo in the Press Gallery and Lobby, 1904; Special Commissioner of Echo to Ireland, 1905; Press Representative of Labour Party in Press Gallery of the House of Commons, 1908; President of the National Union of Journalists in 1911 and again in 1912; Alderman of the St Pancras Borough Council, 1912; Chairman of Women's Work Committee of the Central (Unemployed) Body for London, 1914; Member of St Pancras Tribunal under the Military Service Act and of the St Pancras Food Control Committee, 1915; Editor Polish Review, 1915; Editor New Poland, 1917; Member of the LCC 1919; General Editor of the Polish Press Bureau and of the Polish Economic Bulletin, 1920.

Publications: The New Social Democracy, 1911; Syndicalism (People's Books Series), 1913; Poland—Past and Present, 1915; Colonel Beck, 1939; Towards a Free Europe, 1945; many articles in reviews and newspapers; philosophical papers, printed by the Aristotelian Society. *Address:* 59 Parliament Hill, Hampstead, NW3; Stoke Albany Lodge, Bromham Road, Bedford. *T:* Hampstead 1147, Bedford 5282. *Clubs:* National Trade Union, Royal Societies, PEN.

Died 11 Jan. 1947.

HARLEY, Lt-Col Thomas William, CIE 1926; Indian Medical Service, retired; *b* 10 Dec. 1876. *Educ:* Dublin University, MB, Bch. Joined Indian Medical Service; 1902; retired, 1931.

Died 13 Nov. 1950.

HARMAN, N. Bishop, MA, MB, FRCS; Hon. LLD; Consulting Ophthalmic Surgeon, West London Hospital; Lecturer in Ophthalmology and late Dean of the West London Post Graduate College; Ophthalmic Surgeon to the Belgrave Hospital for Children; Consultant, National Institute for the Blind; late Ophthalmic Consultant LCC Education Department; member, Government Committee on Causes and Prevention of Blindness, 1920–22, and 1938; President, Section of Ophthalmology, Winnipeg; Chairman of National Ophthalmic Treatment Board; Vice-President, BMA; late Direct Representative General Medical Council; Member and Treasurer of Dental Board of the UK; President, Manchester College, Oxford; CMO South African War; *b* 1869; *s* of late Walter John Harman of Highgate; *m* Katherine, *d* of Arthur Chamberlain, JP, Moor Green Hall, Birmingham; two *s* two *d. Educ:* City of London School; St John's College, Cambridge (Scholar and Research Student); Middlesex Hospital. *Publications:* Congenital Cataract; Preventable Blindness; Analysis of 4288 Cases of Blindness; The Eyes of our Children; Aids to Ophthalmology, edn 9; Science and Religion; etc. *Address:* Crockham Hill, Kent.

Died 13 June 1945.

HARMAR, Fairlie; Member of New English Art Club; *m* 1932, 7th Viscount Harberton (*d* 1944). *Principal Works:* The Bridge, Monxton (Walker Gallery, Liverpool); After a Game of Lawn Tennis (presented to Birmingham Art Gallery by Contemporary Art Society); Sarson Farm (Manchester Art Gallery); Chelsea China, Pietermaritzburg Public Art Gallery; L'Aveyron bought by Contemporary Art Society for Belfast Art Gallery; Cheyne Walk Gardens, bought by Earl of Derby; Bowl of Flowers in Cottage Window, bought by Contemporary Art Society, 1936; Boats on the Thames, bought by Wolverhampton Public Gallery, 1936; 42 Cheyne Walk, bought by Harrogate Art Gallery, 1938; Cheyne Walk, bought by Bradford Art Gallery, 1938; Oxen in Brittany, bought by Hamilton Bequest for Corp. of Glasgow, 1938; Cheyne Walk, April 1939, bought by Newport Art Gallery, 1943. *Address:* 101 Cheyne Walk, SW10.

Died 13 Jan. 1945.

HARMER, Rt Rev. John Reginald, DD; *b* 11 Aug. 1857; *s* of Rev. George Harmer, Vicar of Maisemore; *m* 1895, Mary Dorothy, *d* of Arthur H. Somers-Cocks, CB, Bengal CS; one *d. Educ:* Eton (Captain of the School and Newcastle Scholar, 1877; King's College, Cambridge (Scholar). Bell's Scholar; Carus prizeman; BA, 5th Classic, 1881; 1st Class in Theology, 1883; Fellow of King's Coll. and Corpus Coll., Camb. Honorary Fellow of Corpus College, Camb.; Vice-Principal, Clergy Training School, Cambridge, 1891–93; Dean of Corpus, 1892–95; Librarian, 1890–95; Bishop of Adelaide, 1895–1905; Bishop of Rochester, 1905–30; formerly chaplain to Bishop Lightfoot of Durham, and editor of his posthumous works; Lady Margaret Preacher, Cambridge, 1914. Commander of the Order of Leopold II, 1919, for services rendered as a member of the Executive of the National Committee for Relief of Belgians in Belgium. *Address:* 3 Eversfield Road, Kew Gardens, Richmond, Surrey. *Club:* Church Imperial.

Died 9 March 1944.

HARMER, Sir Sidney Frederic, KBE 1920; FRS; ScD (Camb.), BSc (Lond.), Hon. Fellow and previously Fellow of King's College, Cambridge; Fellow of University College, London; Former President of the Linnean Society of London; *b* Norwich, 9 March 1862; 2nd *s* of late Frederic William Harmer, JP, MA, FGS; *m* 1891, Laura, *d* of A. P. Howell, BCS; one *s* one *d*. *Educ:* University College, London; King's College, Camb. Natural Sciences Tripos, Part II, Class I; distinguished in Zoology and Comparative Anatomy, Camb. 1883. Lecturer in Natural Science, King's Coll., Camb. 1886; Asst Tutor, 1890–1908; Director of the Natural History Departments of the British Museum, 1919–27; formerly Superintendent of University Museum of Zoology, Cambridge; Vice-Chairman of Discovery Committee; Foreign Member of K. Norske Vid. Akad., and of Roy. Swedish Acad. Sci.; Hon. Member of Boston Society Nat. Hist. and of Soc. Zoologique de France; Gold Medal of Linnean Society, 1934. Served for many years on SS Discovery Cttee. *Publications:* Report on Polyzoa collected by (Dutch) 'Sibolga' Expedn, 4 vols (Text and plates); Reports on Stranded Whales; papers on Zoological subjects; joint editor of Cambridge Natural History. *Recreation:* gardening. *Address:* 5 Grange Road, Cambridge. *T:* Cambridge 4702.

Died 22 Oct. 1950.

HARMOOD-BANNER, Major Sir Harmood, 2nd Bt *cr* 1924; (retired; late 3rd S Wales Borderers); *b* Liverpool, 28 Oct. 1876; *e s* of Sir John Sutherland Harmood-Banner, 1st Bart, and Elizabeth, *d* of late Thomas Knowles of Darnhall, Cheshire, MP for Wigan; *S* father, 1927; *m* 1907, Frances Cordelia, *d* of late George Duberly, JP, of Plansworth, Co. Durham; one *s* two *d*. *Educ:* Wellington College, New College, Oxford; MA, Honours in Law. Joined 4th S Wales Borderers; while reading for the Bar was called up for service during the S African War, first at Aldershot and then in S Africa (medal with 5 clasps, granted Hon. Captaincy in Army); Musketry Instructor, 4th S Wales Borderers, 1902–08; served with 3rd S Wales Borderers (Special Reserve), 1908–13, when retired on account of ill-health, and granted Major's rank and right to wear uniform; served with 7th R. Welsh Fusiliers at the depôt, Newtown, 1914–17; JP Montgomeryshire, 1917; High Sheriff, 1920; Member Montgomeryshire TA Association, 1919–34; Member Governing Body Welsh Church, and the Conservancy Board of the Severn; a Director, Moss Hall Coal Co., and Pearson and Knowles Coal and Iron Co., and representative on the Mining Association of Great Britain, and Lancashire and Cheshire Coal-owners' Association, 1906–20; Member Montgomeryshire County Council, 1927–33; Mayor of Montgomery, 1928–29, 1929–30, 1930–31, and 1931–32. *Recreations:* shooting, fishing. *Heir: s* George Knowles Harmood-Banner, *b* 1918. *Address:* Boughrood Castle, Radnorshire. *T:* Llyswen, 6. *Clubs:* Union, Royal Automobile.

Died 5 July 1950.

HARMSWORTH, 1st Baron *cr* 1939, of Egham; **Cecil Bisshopp Harmsworth;** *b* London, 28 Sept. 1869; 3rd *s* of late Alfred Harmsworth, Barrister-at-law; a yr brother of late Lord Northcliffe and of late Lord Rothermere; *m* Emilie Alberta (*d* 1942), *d* of William Hamilton Maffett, Barrister-at-law, St Helena, Finglas, Co. Dublin; two *s* one *d*. *Educ:* Trinity College, Dublin. BA, 1891; MA 1911; LLD (Hon.) 1938; Senior Moderator in Modern Literature; Stewart Scholar in Literature. Visitor of the College and University, 1943; Contested Droitwich, 1900; NE Lanarkshire, 1901; MP (L) Droitwich, 1906–10; South Bedfords. (Luton), 1911–22; Under-Secretary of State for the Home Office,

1915; member of the Prime Minister's Secretariat, 1917–19; Under-Secretary of State for Foreign Affairs, 1919–22, and Acting Minister of Blockade, 1919; a member of the Superior Council of the Blockade (Paris, 1919), and Supreme Economic Council; British Member of the Council of the League of Nations, Jan. 1922; Pres., Commons Footpaths and Open Spaces Preservation Soc.; Pres., Town and Country Planning Assoc.; Treasurer, Empire Press Union. *Publications:* Pleasure and Problem in South Africa, 1908; Immortals at First Hand, 1933; A Little Fishing Book, 1942. *Recreation:* fly-fishing. *Heir: s* Hon. Cecil Desmond Bernard Harmsworth, MA Oxon [*b* 1903; *m* 1926, Dorothy Alexander, *d* of Hon. J. C. Heinlein, Bridgeport, Ohio, USA; one *d*]. *Address:* 13 Hyde Park Gardens, W2. *T:* Paddington 6860. *Clubs:* Reform; University (Dublin).

Died 13 Aug. 1948.

HAROON, Seth Haji Sir Abdoola, Kt 1937; general merchant; proprietor, Motipur Sugar Factory and Motipur Estate; Director, Indian Trans-Continental Airways; Director, Daily Gazette; President, all India Muslim Conference; Member, Executive Committee Muslim League; Member, Central Legislative Assembly, India, since 1926; President, All India Postal and Telegraph Union; Chairman, Hajiani Hanifabai Girls High School, and Jamia Islamia Orphanage; Member, Executive Committee, St John Ambulance Association Indian Council, and of Mobilization Plan; *b* 1872; *m* 1914, Begum Nusrat; three *s* five *d*. *Recreation:* bridge. *Address:* Seafield, Victoria Road, Karachi, Sind. *TA:* Shadman. *T:* 5128 and 2738. *Club:* Karachi.

Died 27 April 1942.

HARPER, Charles G.; artist, author, and journalist; *b* 1863. Well-known magazine and book illustrator; an enthusiastic pedestrian, cyclist, and lover of the countryside. *Publications:* English Pen Artists of To-day; The Marches of Wales; A Practical Handbook of Drawing for Reproduction; Some English Sketching Grounds; From Paddington to Penzance; Revolted Woman; The Brighton Road; The Portsmouth Road; The Dover Road; The Bath Road; The Exeter Road; The Great North Road; The Norwich Road; The Holyhead Road; Cycle Rides round London; The Cambridge, Ely, and King's Lynn Road; Stage Coach and Mail in Days of Yore; The Ingoldsby Country; The Hardy Country; The Newmarket, Bury, Thetford, and Cromer Road; The Oxford, Gloucester, and Milford Haven Road; The Hastings Road; The Manchester and Glasgow Road; The Dorset Coast; The South Devon Coast; The North Devon Coast; The Somerset Coast; The Cornish Coast (North); The Cornish Coast (South); The Kentish Coast; The Sussex Coast; The Old Inns of Old England; Love in the Harbour; a Novel; Rural Nooks round London; Haunted Houses; Half-Hours with the Highwaymen; The Autocar Road Book; The Tower of London; The Smugglers; Thames Valley Villages; Summer Days in Shakespeare Land; Motor Runs round London; The RAC Guides; Overheard at the Front; Talks with T. Atkins, Esquire; Motor Coach Route Books I–II; On the Road in Holland; The Downs and the Sea, 1923 (with J. C. Kershaw); Queer Things about London; The Smugglers (with Lord Teignmouth); More Queer Things about London; The City of London Guide; Round and about London by Tram, the London County Council Guide; London, Yesterday, To-day and To-morrow; A Literary Man's London; A Londoner's Own London; Mr Pickwick's Second Time; The Bunyan Country, Landmarks of the Pilgrim's Progress; Abbeys of Old Romance, 1930; Mansions of Old Romance, 1930; Southwark, Past and Present. *Address:* Rookwood, Hazel Lane, Petersham, by Richmond, Surrey.

Died 8 Dec. 1943.

HARPER, Sir Charles Henry, KBE 1930 (OBE 1919); CMG 1921; *b* 24 Feb. 1876; 7th *c* of Dr J. Harper, Barnstaple, Devon, and Augusta, *d* of Captain John De Lancey Robinson, RN; *m* 1910, Marjorie, *d* of Rev. Gerard Ford, MA, Ideford Rectory, Devon; one *s* one *d*. *Educ*: Blundell's School, Tiverton; Exeter College, Oxford, MA. Entered the Colonial Service as a Cadet in the Gold Coast Civil Service, 1900; attached to the Ashanti Field Force, 1900; called to Bar, Inner Temple, 1909; Togoland Field Force; Senior Political Officer, occupation by the British, till Dec. 1914; Chief Commissioner of Ashanti, 1920–23; Governor and Commander-in-Chief, St Helena, 1925–32; Ministry of Food, 1939–41. *Recreation*: formerly Rugby football (Oxford and England). *Address*: Broomhill, Christow, nr Exeter. *T*: Christow 323.

Died 13 May 1950.

HARPER, George McLean, AM, PhD (Prin.), Woodrow Wilson Professor of Literature, Princeton University 1926; Professor Emeritus 1932; Special Lecturer in English Literature, 1932–34; *b* Shippensburg, Pennsylvania, 31 Dec. 1863; *s* of William Wylie Harper and Nancy J. McLean; *m* 1895, Belle Dunton Westcott of Princeton; one *s* one *d*. *Educ*: University of Princeton; University of Göttingen and University of Berlin. AB Princeton, 1884. Reporter on New York Tribune, 1884; studied abroad, 1885–87; employed on Scribner's Magazine, 1887–89; Instructor, 1889–91; Assistant Professor, 1891–94; Professor of Romance Languages, 1894–1900, Professor of English, 1900–26, in Princeton; Member of the National Institute of Arts and Letters; Delegate of the Commission for Relief in Belgium, 1915; hospital orderly in France, 1917; advocate of Anglo-American Union; Officer of the Order of the Crown of Belgium. *Publications*: The Legend of the Holy Grail, 1893; Masters of French Literature, 1901; A Life of Charles Augustin Sainte, Beuve, 1909; William Wordsworth, his Life, Works, and Influence, 1916; John Morley and other Essays, 1920; Wordsworth's French Daughter, 1921; Dreams and Memories, 1922; Spirit of Delight, 1928; Literary Appreciations, 1937; one-volume edition of the Life of Wordsworth, 1929; joint-translator, from the German, of Rein's Japan, volume ii; editor of several French texts, and of President Wilson's Addresses, 1918; Selections from Wordsworth, 1923; Introduction to the Standard text of Wordsworth, 1934; Chapter in the Coleridge Memorial Volume, 1934; numerous articles in Quarterly Review, Atlantic Monthly, Scribner's Magazine, Yale Review, and other periodicals in England and America. *Address*: Princeton, New Jersey, USA.

Died 14 July 1947.

HARPER, George Milne, CIE 1941; MA; Chairman Public Service Commission, United Provinces, since 1942; *b* 27 Aug. 1882; *s* of Rev. W. Harper; *m* 1912, Madeline C. C. Irvine; one *s* one *d*. *Educ*: Dollar Academy; Royal High School, Edinburgh; Edinburgh University; Oriel College, Oxford. Entered Indian Civil Service, 1906; Secretary to Government, Revenue and Public Works Dept, United Provinces, 1931; Commissioner, 1934; Senior Member, Board of Revenue, United Provinces. *Recreations*: tennis, golf. *Address*: Public Service Commission, Allahabad, UP. *Club*: East India and Sports.

Died 1 Dec. 1943.

HARPER, Vice-Adm. John Ernest Troyte, CB 1926; MVO 1913; *b* 29 May 1874; 5th *s* of late Leonard Harper of Bruton, Somerset, late of Christchurch, New Zealand; *m* 1904, Dorothy, *o d* of late Captain Alexander Meldrum, RN; one *s*. *Educ*: Christ's College, New Zealand. Entered Navy, 1888; Lt 1896; Comdr 1906; Capt. 1913; Rear-Adm. 1924; Vice-Adm. retired, 1929; served S African War, 1899–1900 (medal, Natal clasp); Ogaden Somali Expedition, 1900–01 (medal, Jubaland clasp); Commander (N) of HM Yacht Victoria and Albert, 1911–14; compiled Official Record of battle of Jutland; Master-of-the-Fleet for the Naval Review on 20th July 1914; commanded ships afloat during European War; Director of Navigation Admiralty, 1919–21; Member Anglo-American Arbitration Board 1921–22; Naval ADC to the King, 1923–24; retired list, 1927; Nautical Assessor to House of Lords, 1934–46; Home Guard, 1940–42; has orders of Dannebrog of Denmark and Redeemer of Greece. *Publications*: The Truth about Jutland, 1927; (with Langhorne Gibson) The Riddle of Jutland, 1934; The Royal Navy at War, 1941. *Address*: Ilam, Hawkhurst, Kent. *T*: Hawkhurst, 110. *Club*: United Service.

Died 27 May 1949.

HARPER, Lt-Col John Robinson, CBE 1919; TD 1914; RAMC, TF; JP Barnstaple; Fellow of the Royal Society of Medicine; *b* 7 Nov. 1867; *e s* of late Dr Joseph Harper and Augusta, *d* of Captain John Delancey Robinson, RN; *m* Evelina, *d* of late Joseph Hucks Gibbs; one *s* one *d*. *Educ*: Blundell's School, Tiverton; St Thomas's Hospital. Served British Exped. Force, France, 1914–19 (despatches, CBE); o/c 14 Stationary Hospital; Consulting Surgeon, North Devon Infirmary; formerly House Surgeon and Resident Accoucheur, St Thomas's Hospital; Mayor of Barnstaple, 1912–13; Commander of the Military Order of Aviz (Portugal), 1919. *Publications*: Clinical Aspects of Enteric Group Infections as modified by Protective Inoculation, Lancet, 1920; Congenital Hypertrophic Stenosis of Pylorus, Lancet, 1905; Influence of Rainy Winds on Phthisis (with W. Gordon), British Medical Journal, 1907; other medical papers. *Address*: Pilton Cottage, Pilton, Barnstaple. *T*: 2112.

Died 30 April 1947.

HARRAGIN, Alfred Ernest Albert, DSO 1918; *b* 4 May 1877; *s* of Alfred Ernest Albert Harragin and Clementina Collins; *m* 1908, Rosina, *d* of H. A. Green, engineer, Trinidad; one *s* two *d*. *Educ*: Queen's Royal College, Trinidad. Passed Trinidad Civil Service Examination, and held acting appointment at HM Customs, Trinidad; joined the staff as local clerk of Colonial Bank; joined staff of New Colonial Co., Trinidad, as accountant; joined Royal Mail Steam Packet Co.; Inspector of Trinidad Constabulary, 1905; toured England with West Indian Cricket Team, 1906; left Trinidad with first contingent BWI as Captain, 1915; Lieut in 1st BWI, 1915; Captain, 1916; arrived in Egypt, 1916; Major, 1917; served with 1st BWI in Egypt and Palestine until April 1919 (DSO); returned to Trinidad, 1919; Inspector of Constabulary, Trinidad Constabulary, BWI, 1912–34; Senior Insp. 1934–36; Deputy Inspector-General, 1936–37; retired, 1937; awarded King's Police Medal for gallantry, 1936. *Recreations*: cricket, tennis. *Address*: Trinidad Constabulary, BWI. *T*: 1530. *Clubs*: Union, Trinidad.

Died 21 May 1941.

HARRINGTON, Charles; painter. *Educ*: Brighton. Exhibited at RA and provincial exhibitions; represented in Victoria and Albert Museum, Ashmolean Museum, Oxford; Whitworth Institute, Manchester; Fitzwilliam Museum, Cambridge; Rochdale Art Gallery; Sargent Gallery, Wanganui, NZ, etc.

Died 12 Feb. 1943.

HARRINGTON, Ernest John, CBE 1924; *b* London, 1864; *s* of late George Harrington; *m* 1898, Augusta Elkington, *d* of late Tate Mansford; no *c*. Entered General Post Office, 1882; Deputy Comptroller and Accountant-General, 1921; retired, 1924. *Address*: Greensand, Heath Road, Petersfield.

Died 31 Dec. 1944.

HARRINGTON, Col Hon. Gordon Sidney, KC 1915; LLD 1938; *b* Halifax, NS, 7 Aug. 1883; *s* of Charles Sidney Harrington, KC, and Mary S. R. De Wolf; *m* Katherine Agnes MacDonald, Glace Bay, CB. *Educ*: Dalhousie University, Halifax, LLB. Mayor of

Glace Bay, 1913-15; served in CEF 1915-20; Colonel, 1918; Deputy Minister, Overseas Military Forces of Canada, 1918-20; Premier of Nova Scotia, 1930-33; Minister of Public Works and Mines, Nova Scotia, 1925-33; Chairman of Canadian Commission to Administer Unemployment and Social Insurance Act, 1935-36; Nova Scotia Parliament, 1925-37. *Address:* 238 Jubilee Road, Halifax, NS. *Clubs:* Thatched House; Rideau, Ottawa; Halifax, Halifax, NS.

Died July 1943.

HARRINGTON, Rt Hon. Sir Stanley, PC Ireland, 1919; Kt 1907; BA, JP; *b* 15 May 1856; *s* of late William Harrington, JP, of Lee View, Cork; *g s* of late William Stanley (formerly Comptroller Inland Revenue Department, Ireland), of Dublin; *m* 1882, Catherine (*d* 1911), *d* of late Thomas Lyons, JP of Waterview, Co. Cork; two *s* two *d. Educ:* Beaumont College, Windsor; Royal University. President Cork Incorporated Chamber of Commerce and Shipping, 1892-93; Director Munster and Leinster Bank, Ltd; has taken a prominent part in the Irish Industrial Revival. *Address:* Araglin, Queenstown. *Clubs:* Cork, Royal Cork Yacht.

Died 31 July 1949.

HARRIOTT, George Moss, CSI 1911; CIE 1900; late Chief Engineer Indian Public Works Department, and Secretary Public Works Department to the Chief Commissioner Central Provinces, retired 1913; Consulting Engineer for Irrigation to the Government of Mauritius, 1913-15; *b* 11 July 1858; *s* of late John Thompson Harriott of Ormskirk, Lancashire; *m* 1891, Charlotte Mary, *e d* of Col J. W. MacDougall, ISC; one *s.* Joined the Indian Public Works Department, 1878; and served in the Central Provinces of India. Decorated for services in connection with the famine of 1896-97, and the public works of the feudatory states of Chattisgarh in the Central Provinces of India during the years 1893-99. Also for introducing and establishing irrigation, as well as for the direction and administration of all public works, in the Central Provinces 1901-13. Major Indian Volunteers; Volunteer Officers' Decoration, 1907. *Recreations:* shooting, golf, tennis. *Address:* Micklehithe, Stevenage, Herts. *T:* 153.

Died 4 Dec. 1943.

HARRIS, Albert Henry; Managing Director, Harris Publications, Ltd; *b* Croydon, 13 Sept. 1885; *s* of Albert E. Harris, late of Cassell & Co., Ltd; *m* Thora Amy, *d* of Geo. Henry Legge, Southampton; one *s. Educ:* International College, Hampstead; Institution Fauvel, Neuilly-sur-Seine. Entered T. B. Browne's Advertising Agency, 1902; Secretary, Globe Press, 1905; joined Benn Brothers as Manager Goldsmith's Review, 1907; Managing Editor, World's Hotel Blue Book, and Who's Who in the Hotel World, 1909; founded Philatelic Magazine, 1911, and Who's Who in Philately, 1914; Trench Warfare Transport Section, 1915-18; Disposals Board, 1919-22. *Publications:* Editor, Philatelic Magazine, Philatelic Trader, Who's Who in Philately, Philatelic Magazine Handbooks; Stamp Collectors Annual; Standard Index to Philatelic Literature; Meter Postage Stamp Catalogue. *Address:* 112 Strand, WC2. *Club:* Constitutional.

Died 29 Nov. 1945.

HARRIS, Sir Alexander; *see* Harris, Sir C. A.

HARRIS, Sir Charles, GBE 1920; KCB 1913; CB 1911; late Permanent Head of the Finance Department, War Office; *b* 2 March 1864; 2nd *s* of late John Harris of Ivybridge, Devon; *m* 1891, Lisbeth, *d* of late Ferdinand Schiller, Calcutta; two *s* one *d. Educ:* Bradford Grammar School; Balliol College, Oxford (Scholar). BA First in competition for the Civil Service, 1886; Clerk, War Office, 1887; Principal Clerk, 1900; Assistant Financial Secretary, 1908; Joint Secretary of the War Office, 1920;

retired, 1924; Commander, Legion of Honour, 1921. *Recreations:* rowing, climbing, fishing. *Address:* Hillcote, Cookham, Berks. *T:* Bourne End 45.

Died 10 June 1943.

HARRIS, Sir (Charles) Alexander, KCMG 1917; CB 1904; CMG 1900; CVO 1917; MVO 1911; BA; *b* Wrexham, 28 June 1855; *e s* of Rev. G. Poulett Harris, formerly Vicar of Hawes, Yorkshire, and Martha, *d* of Alexander McCarroll of Brighton; *m* 1879, Constance Maria (*d* 1941), *y d* of John Shute, Glenavon House, Clifton; two *s* one *d. Educ:* Richmond School, Yorkshire; Christ's College, Cambridge; also of Lincoln's Inn. Scholar of Christ's College; Porteus medallist; special notice for Bell University Scholarship; 12th Classic, 1878; Tancred student in Common Law, Lincoln's Inn. Entered Colonial Office, as result of open competition, 1879; secretary to West India Royal Commission, 1882; in the West Indies till 1883; assistant secretary to International Conference on Sugar Bounties, 1887-88; private secretary to Mr Sydney Buxton, as Under-Sec. of State for the Colonies, 1894; also to Lord Selborne, 1895; resigned on promotion, 1896; specially detailed for the preparation of the case of HM Government in the Venezuela boundary matter, and attached to the Attorney-General's staff in Paris, 1899; member of Advisory Committee on Commercial Intelligence (Board of Trade), 1900-17; charged with the conduct of British case in Brazilian boundary question, 1901-04; Principal Clerk, Colonial Office, 1898-1909; Chief Clerk, 1909-17; Governor of Newfoundland, 1917-22; on Managing Committee of Imperial Institute, 1909-16; Chairman of Tropical Diseases Secretion, Ghent Exhibition, 1913; Governor of New England Co., 1930-38. *Publications:* articles on finance and economics to Dictionary of Political Economy; various lives to Dictionary National Biography; Edited for Hakluyt Society, Storm Van's Gravesande (with J. de Villiers); Harcourt's Voyage to Guiana. *Recreations:* athletics, sport and natural history. *Club:* National.

Died 26 March 1947.

HARRIS, Col Sir David, KCMG 1911; CMG 1900; VD, Cape Colonial Forces; *b* City of London, 12 July 1852; *s* of Woolf and Phœbe Harris; *m* 1873, Rosa Gabriel of Prussia. *Educ:* Coxford's College, City of London. Went to Diamond Fields, 1871; Lieutenant Diamond Fields Horse, 1876; Captain, 1878; served in Gaika Galecka campaign, 1877-78 (despatches, medal and clasp); served in Griqua campaign, 1878; Major, Kimberley Regiment, 1890; Lieut-Colonel commanding Griqualand West Brigade, 1896; commanded column that quelled large native rising in Bechuanaland, 1896-97 (thanks of Government); commanded Town Guard defence of Kimberley, 1899-1900 (despatches, thanked by High Commissioner, CMG). *Publication:* Pioneer, Soldier, and Politician, 1931. *Recreations:* hunting, shooting. *Address:* Kimberley, Cape Colony. *Clubs:* Kimberley, Kimberley; Civil Service, Cape Town.

Died 23 Sept. 1942.

HARRIS, Henry; Member Advisory Council of Victoria and Albert Museum; *s* of late Henry Harris, Steventon Manor, Hants, and Janet, *d* of Rt Hon. Lord Young, PC; unmarried. *Educ:* Eton; Christ Church, Oxford. Hon. Secretary to the Legation to the Vatican, 1917-21; a Trustee of the National Gallery, 1934-41; Chairman of Decorative Committee of Westminster Cathedral. *Address:* 23 Cheyne Walk, SW3. *T:* Flaxman 9706. *Clubs:* St James', Garrick.

Died 20 May 1950.

HARRIS, Sir Henry Percy, KBE 1917; *b* 8 Sept. 1856; *s* of late Sir George David Harris, JP, LCC; *m* 1st, 1908, Ethel Alice (*d* 1933), *d* of late E. Chivers Bower, Broxholme, Scarborough; 2nd, 1934, Eva Margaret, *er d* of late Arthur E. Stearns. *Educ:* Eton; Christ Church,

Oxford (BA). Barrister, Lincoln's Inn, 1881; MP (U) S Paddington 1910–22; LCC Paddington, 1892–1910; leader of Moderate Party, 1904–06; Deputy-Chairman of the London County Council, 1898; Chairman, 1907–08; late Chairman London War Pensions Committee; sometime Chairman London Municipal Society; Chairman Select Committee on War Pensions, 1920; JP, DL London. *Address:* 98 Gloucester Terrace, W2. *T:* Paddington 6629. *Club:* Carlton.

Died 23 Aug. 1941.

HARRIS, James Rendel, MA; Hon. LittD Dublin; Hon. LLD Haverford; Hon. Dr Theol. Leyden; Hon. LLD Birmingham; Hon. DD Glasgow; Hon. Fellow of Clare College, Cambridge; FBA 1927; *b* Plymouth, 1852; *m* 1880, Helen Balkwill. *Educ:* Plymouth Grammar School; Clare College, Cambridge (3rd Wrangler, ex-Fellow). Moderator and Examiner Mathematical Tripos; Professor at Johns Hopkins University (1882–85); Professor at Haverford College (1886–92); University Lecturer in Palæography, Cambridge University (1893–1903); Professor of Theology, University of Leyden, 1903–04; Director of Studies at the Friends' Settlement for Social and Religious Study, Woodbrooke, near Birmingham, 1903–18; Curator of MSS at the John Rylands Library, Manchester, 1918–25; Pres. Free Church Council, 1907–08; Haskell Lecturer at Oberlin College, 1910. Travelled extensively in the East in search of MSS. *Publications:* The Teaching of the Apostles and the Sibylline Books, 1885; Fragments of Philo, 1886; The Origin of the Leicester Codex, 1887; The Teaching of the Apostles, 1887; The Rest of the Words of Baruch, 1889; Biblical Fragments from Mount Sinai, 1890; The Diatessaron, 1890; The Acts of Perpetua, 1890; A Study of Codex Bezae, 1890; The Apology of Aristides, 1891; Codex Sangallensis, 1891; Some Syrian and Palestinian Inscriptions, 1891; Memoranda Sacra, 1892; Popular Account of the newly recovered Gospel of St Peter, 1892; Origin of the Ferrar Group, 1893; Stichometry, 1893; The Four Gospels from the Syriac Palimpsest (co-editor), 1894; Lectures on the Western Text of New Testament, 1894; Fragments of Ephrem Syrus, 1895; Union with God, 1895; Hermas in Arcadia, 1896; Letters from Armenia, 1897; the Homeric Centones, 1898; the Legend of Ahikar, 1898 (co-editor); Life of Francis William Crossley (editor), 1899; Double Text of Tobit, 1899; The Gospel of the Twelve Apostles, 1900; Verse Division of New Testament, 1900; Tract on Triune Nature of God, 1900; Further Researches into the History of the Ferrar Group, 1901; Annotators of the Codex Bezae, 1901; The Dioscuri in Christian Legend, 1903; The Guiding Hand of God, 1905; The Cult of the Heavenly Twins, 1906; Aaron's Breastplate, 1908; Side-lights on New Testament Research, 1909; Some Woodbrooke Liturgies, 1909; The Odes and Psalms of Solomon, 1910; An Early Christian Psalter, 1910; Boanerges, 1913; The Sufferings and the Glory, 1914; Origin of the Cult of Dionysos, 1915; Origin of the Cult of Apollo, 1915; Origin of the Cult of Artemis, 1916; Origin of the Cult of Aphrodite, 1916; Odes and Psalms of Solomon (Rylands' Lib. Ed. Co-editor), Vol. I 1916; Vol. II 1920; Ascent of Olympus, 1917; Testimonies (with Vacher Burch), Part I 1917; Part II 1920; Picus who is also Zeus, 1917; Origin of the Prologue to St John's Gospel, 1917; Origin of Apple-Cults, 1919; Return of the Mayflower, 1919; Origin of Doctrine of the Trinity, 1919; The Mayflower Song-Book, 1919; The Last of the Mayflower, 1920; The Finding of the Mayflower, 1920; An Apple Masque, 1920; Metrical Fragments in iii Maccabees, 1920; The Pilgrims Press (Co-editor), 1922; A New Christian Apology, 1923; Tatian, Perfection according to the Saviour, 1923; The Quest for Quadratus, 1924; As Pants the Hart, 1924; Scylla and Charybdis, 1925; The Sources of Barlaam and Joasaph, 1925; Apollo and his Birds, 1925; Apollo at the Back of the North Wind, 1926; The Stature of our Lord, 1926; Early Colonists of the Mediterranean, 1926; Bar Salibi

against the Melchites (Co-editor), 1927; Traces of Egypt in the Mediterranean, 1927; What was the Afikoman, 1927; Jesus and Osiris, 1927; Further Traces of Hittite Migration, 1927; St Paul and Greek Literature, 1927; a Primitive Dye-stuff, 1927; Egypt in Britain, 1927; Glass Chalices of the First Century, 1927; The Twelve Apostles, 1927; Eucharistic Origins, 1927; St Winefred, 1928; Egypt and the Atlantic Seaboard, 1928; St Bees, 1928; Watling Street, 1928; The Voyage of Hanno, 1928; Watendleth, 1928; Go West, 1928; Origin of the Cult of Hermes, 1929; Go East, 1929; St Mildred's Hair, 1929; Early Map of Britain, 1929; North and South, 1929; A New Stonehenge, 1929; Barley, 1929; Minster, 1929; Rutupiae, 1929; Waymarks, 1930; Peg O'Nell, 1930; Tenedos, 1930; Horus, 1930; Augmentation, 1930; Fomors and Firbolgs, 1930; Runnymede, 1931; Egypt and the Volga, 1931; St Kilda, 1931; Maeldune, 1931; Semo Sancus, 1931; Bast, 1931; Josephus and His Testimony, 1931; The Magi, 1932; Nicodemus, 1932; The Masts of the Mayflower, 1932; Denderah, 1933; Justin Martyr and Menander, 1933; The Builders of Stonehenge, 1933; Who Discovered North America?, 1934; A Temple in Tennessee; Wordsworth's Lucy; Hundreds and Hides, 1935; Emendations to the Greek of the New Testament, 1935; The Migration of Culture, 1936; Isis and Nephthys in Wiltshire, 1938; An Egyptian Cat Goddess in Britain, 1938. *Recreation:* travel. *Address:* 210 Bristol Road, Birmingham. *T:* Selly Oak 0562.

Died 1 March 1941.

HARRIS, Hon. Sir John Richards, KBE 1937; MD; Member Legislative Council, Victoria, for North-eastern Province since 1920; *b* 24 Jan. 1868; *s* of late Thomas H. Harris, Rutherglen; *m* 1897, Jessie Lily (*d* 1937), *d* of James Prentice; three *s*. *Educ:* Grenville College, Ballarat; Melbourne University. MB 1890, Melbourne University, ChB 1891, MD 1902. RMO Melbourne Hospital, 1891–92; in practice at Rutherglen, 1892–1917; served in European War, 1917–18; MO No. 1 Squadron Aust. Flying Corps, Palestine; Hon. Minister in Allan Ministry, 1925–27; Unofficial Leader of Legislative Council, 1928–35; Minister of Public Instruction and Public Health, Victoria, 1935–41. *Recreations:* bowls, golf. *Address:* Trahna, Norong, Via Rutherglen, Victoria, Australia.

Died 16 Sept. 1946.

HARRIS, Percy Graham; Resident Cameroons Province, Nigeria; *b* 4 March 1894; *s* of W. J. Harris, Liverpool; *m* 1923, Enid King; one *s*. *Educ:* St Bees School, Cumberland. Studied law until outbreak of war, 1914. Served throughout that war with King's (Liverpool) and Nigeria Regts; joined Nigerian Administrative Service, 1919; Senior Resident, 1938; awarded Anthropological Diploma, London University, 1933; HM Consul-General at Duala, Cameroons, under French Mandate, 1940–43. Fellow RAI; Member Royal African Society; Fellow Navy League. *Publications:* several monographs in Journal RAI, Royal African Society, and Man; contributions to West Africa and West African Review; compiled Gazeteer of Sokoto Province, Nigeria, 1937. *Recreations:* tennis, golf, music, sketching, writing. *Address:* The Residency, Buea. *Club:* East India and Sports.

Died 25 Feb. 1945.

HARRIS, Rev. Samuel Collard; Vicar of St John the Evangelist, Leeds, 1936; *b* 9 April 1869; unmarried. *Educ:* New College, Oxford, Third Class Hon. Mods., Third Class Lit. Hum.; Salisbury Theological College. Curate of Leeds, 1893–97; Precentor of Brisbane Cathedral, 1897–1901; Mission Chaplain in the Diocese of Brisbane, 1901–05; Curate of St Luke, Heywood, Manchester, 1905; Vicar of Kirkstall, 1907–36; Hon. Canon of Ripon, 1922. *Address:* Kenmure, 29 Cumberland Road, Headingley, Leeds 6. *T:* Headingley, Leeds 51424.

Died July 1940.

HARRISON, Albert John, CIE 1912; *b* 31 Dec. 1862; *s* of William Henry and Frances Sarah Harrison, Oxendon House, Northants; unmarried. *Educ:* Rugby, Harrow. Trained as Mechanical Engineer, Airedale Foundry, Leeds, and Hyde Park Loco Works, Springburn, Glasgow; left England for Assam, 1890, to join Jokai Tea Co. as Engineer; managed Tippuk Tea Garden, 1895–1902; Manager, Meckla Nuddee Sawmills, Dibrugarh, Assam, 1902; medals; Durbar and Abor. *Recreations:* polo, riding, shooting.

Died 7 Dec. 1941.

HARRISON, Archibald Walter, MCBA, BSc, DD (London Univ.); President of Methodist Conference; Secretary, Methodist Education Committee; *b* 20 Aug. 1882; *s* of Rev. J. T. Harrison, Wesleyan Minister; *m* 1910, G. Elsie, *d* of Dr J. S. Simon, Principal of Didsbury College; one *s* two *d*. *Educ:* Loughborough Grammar School; Nottingham University College. Ordained Wesleyan Methodist Ministry, 1909; Minister in Burnley, Bristol and Highgate; 2nd Lieut in 2nd Devons; later Chaplain to the Forces in France and Italy; Vice-Principal Westminster Training College, 1921–30; Principal, 1930–40; Chairman of the Sunday School Lessons Council; Governor of the Leys School and of several other secondary boarding schools. *Publications:* Arminianism (Duckworth Library of Theology); Liberal Puritanism; The Evangelical Revival and Christian Reunion. *Address:* 89 Elers Rd, W13. *T:* Ealing 1021.

Died 8 Jan. 1946.

HARRISON, Brig.-Gen. Arthur Howarth Pryce, CSI 1919; Indian Army; reitred; *b* 1871; *s* of Robert Devereux Harrison, Fron Llwyd, Welshpool; *m* 1907, Coela Elizabeth le Strange, *d* of Captain le Strange Herring; one *s* one *d*. Served Waziristan Expedition, 1894–95 (medal and clasp); NW Frontier of India, 1897–98 (medal and clasp) European War, 1914–19 (Bt Lt-Col CSI); Afghan War, 1919 (despatches, medal with clasp). *Address:* Braiswick, Colchester. *T:* Colchester 2679.

Died 22 May 1949.

HARRISON, Charles; humorous black and white artist for various periodicals; *m* Harriet Shephard; two *s* two *d*. *Educ:* St Thomas's College, Hackney. Family connected with the stage; started as a youth to draw for the Red Lion House publications; on the staff of Cassell & Co. as humorous artist for a number of years; was cartoonist for the old Pall Mall Gazette when under the editorship of the late W. T. Stead; has drawn cartoons (non-political) for the Daily Mail, The Evening News, The Daily Express, etc.; started to draw for Punch, 1895; contributor to nearly every humorous periodical; has drawn for the principal advertisers, invented several advertisement characters. *Publications:* as illustrator, Master Charlie, by S. H. Hamer; Accidents Will Happen, in collaboration with W. K. Hasleden; The Swoop, by P. G. Wodehouse; History Retold, London Japanned, verses and pictures; Six Plays for Children. *Recreations:* walking, lingering in old book and curio shops. *Address:* 7 Wormholt Road, Uxbridge Road, W12. *T:* Shepherd's Bush 4706. *Club:* London Sketch.

Died Dec. 1943.

HARRISON, Col Charles Edward, CVO 1909; CMG 1916; MB Lond., FRCS; *b* 19 Oct. 1852; *s* of late Surg.-Maj. John Harrison, Grenadier Guards. *Educ:* Wellington College; St Bart's Hospital and London Univ. (MB Honours, 1876). Entered Army, 1874; appointed Medical Officer, Grenadier Guards; Brevet Col 1907; retired, 1909; served with the regt in Egyptian Expedition, 1882; present at action at Mahuta and at battle of Tel-el-Kebir (medal with clasp, bronze star); Brig.-Surg. Lieut-Col Brigade of Guards, 1891–1909, and Medical Officer in charge of the Queen Alexandra Mil. Hospital, 1905–09; Hon. Surgeon to King Edward VII; Officer commanding 1st Lond. (City of Lond.)

General Hospital, 1909; Assistant Director of Medical Services, 2nd London Division, Territorial Force, 1912; served European War in France as Officer commanding No. 23 General Hospital, American (Chicago) Medical Unit (despatches, CMG, 1914–15 bronze star, war medal, and victory medal); Officer Commanding Prince of Wales' Hospital for Convalescent Officers, Great Central Hotel, NW, 1916; Deputy Commissioner of Medical Services, Ministry of National Service, 1918; represented the War Office at the Surgical Congress in Paris in 1892; served in the Territorial Force Reserve, 1918–23. *Address:* Woolborough Farm, Outwood, near Redhill, Surrey.

Died 25 Jan. 1944.

HARRISON, Lt-Col Edgar Garston, CB 1907; DSO 1899; *b* 11 May 1863; *s* of Daniel Harrison of the Abbey, Staveby, Kendal. *Educ:* Haileybury. Joined Dorset Militia, 1881; gazetted to Duke of Wellington's West Riding Regt, 33rd, 1885; served in Ireland, India and England, 1885–95; commanded HH the Sultan of Zanzibar's forces during Mazarui-Arab Rebellion, 1895–96 (Sultan of Zanzibar's medal, Brilliant Star of Zanzibar); East African Rifles during Uganda Mutiny, 1897–98 (Brevet Major, DSO, medal with 2 clasps); Nandi Field Force, 1905–06 (medal with clasp, CB); commanded 3rd Batt. King's African Rifles, 1903–09; 2nd Battalion Duke of Wellington's Regiment in France, Oct. to Dec. 1914; 12th Service Battalion Manchester Regiment, in France, 1914–17 (despatches, twice wounded, Bt Lt-Col). *Address:* Hundhow, Kendal. *TA:* Burneside. *T:* Staveley 48. *Club:* Army and Navy.

Died 22 June 1947.

HARRISON, Ven. Edward Stanley; Rector of Montego Bay Parish Church, Jamaica, and Hon. Canon of the Cathedral since 1932; Rural Dean of St James and Archdeacon of Cornwall, Jamaica, since 1933; *b* April 1889; *s* of Edward Harrison and Matilda Harford. *Educ:* King's College, London; St Peter's College, Jamaica. Deacon, 1916; Priest, 1917; Curate Parish Church, Sav-la-Mar and George's Plain, Jamaica, 1916–17; Rector, All Saints' Church, Kingston, Jamaica, 1917–25; in charge St Peter's, Port Royal, Jamaica, 1917–25; Chaplain to Troops, Port Royal, Jamaica, 1917–25; Rector of Lucea, Jamaica, 1925–28; Rural Dean of Hanover, Jamaica, 1925–28; Rector and Senior Canon of the Cathedral Church of St Jago de la Vega, Spanish Town, Jamaica, 1928–32; Rural Dean of St Catherine, 1928–32. *Recreations:* golf and sea bathing. *Address:* The Rectory, Montego Bay, Jamaica, BWI. *Club:* Royal Empire.

Died 27 Dec. 1948.

HARRISON, Ernest, MA (Cambridge); Hon. LLD (Glasgow); Fellow of Trinity College, Cambridge, since 1900; Registrary of the University since 1925; Editor of the Classical Review since 1923; *b* 4 June 1877. *Educ:* St Paul's School; Cambridge. Craven Scholar, 1898; Chancellor's First Classical Medal, 1900. Lecturer of Trinity College, 1904–25; Tutor, 1914–25; Senior Tutor, 1920–25; Lieut RNVR, 1917–19. *Address:* Trinity College, Cambridge. *T:* Cambridge 3441.

Died 28 March 1943.

HARRISON, Sir Fowler; *see* Harrison, Sir J. F.

HARRISON, Sir John, KBE 1923; *b* 1866; *s* of late John Christopher Harrison, Hartlepool, Durham; *m* 1899, Edith Avice, *d* of late Thomas Moran, Malvern, Victoria; one *s* one *d*. *Educ:* Church of England School, Shildon; James Reed's School, Bishop Auckland. Went to Australia, 1885, with his father where they founded the firm of J. C. Harrison & Son, master builders; retired; Chairman of Disposals Board, War Service Homes, NSW, 1922–24; Chairman of the Board of Control, Matraville Garden Village for Disabled Soldiers, Sydney, 1917–30; a member of Federal Capital Commission,

Canberra, 1924–29. *Recreation:* bowls. *Address:* Lealhome, Chandos Street, Ashfield, NSW. *Clubs:* Tattersalls (Life), New South Wales, Millions, Sydney.

Died 22 June 1944.

HARRISON, Sir (John) Fowler, 2nd Bt *cr* 1922; *b* 8 Feb. 1899; *o s* of Sir John Harrison, 1st Bt, and Clara Elizabeth, *d* of late Jonathan Fowler; *S* father 1936; *m* 1930, Kathleen, *yr d* of late Robert Livingston, The Gables, Eaglescliffe, Co. Durham; two *s* one *d. Educ:* New College, Harrogate. Served in Royal Flying Corps and Royal Air Force, 1918–19. *Heir: s* John Wyndham, *b* 1933. *Address:* The Red Cottage, Nunthorpe, Middlesbrough, Yorks. *T:* Marton 56225.

Died 24 May 1947.

HARRISON, Lt-Col Norman, CMG 1918; DSO 1917; MIEE; Hon. Col SA Corps of Signals; *m* 1907, Marguerite Ethel Dorey, Jersey; two *s.* Engineer-in-Chief Postal Telegraphs, Union of South Africa, 1910–14; Director of Army Signals, German South-West Africa Campaign, 1914–15; Assistant Director, Army Signals, BEF, France, 1915–19, and Commanding Officer, SA Signal Units; Under-Secretary, Department of Postal Telegraphs, Union of S Africa, 1922–23; Resident Director, Standard Telephones and Cables, Ltd, 1924–39. *Address:* Widmore Cottage, Hermanus, Cape Province, S Africa. *Club:* Civil Service (Capetown).

Died 21 April 1949.

HARRISON, Brig.-Gen. Robert Arthur Gwynne, CMG 1900; RA; retired; *b* 11 Jan. 1855; 2nd *s* of late Rev. C. R. Harrison, BCL, Vicar of North Curry, Somerset; *m* 1885, Alice, *e d* of late J. W. Yardley, Chesterfield Lodge, Lichfield. *Educ:* Clifton College; RMA, Woolwich. Entered army, 1875; Lt-Col 1900; served South Africa, 1899–1902 (despatches thrice, Queen's medal 5 clasps, King's medal 2 clasps, CMG); Commanded 68th (Welsh) Divisional Artillery, Jan. 1915–Jan. 1916, European War. *Address:* The Old Rectory, King's Worthy, Winchester, Hants.

Died 10 Nov. 1943.

HARRISON, Robert Tullis, CSI 1929; Chief Engineer for Irrigation and Secretary to Government of Bombay in Public Works Department, 1920–31; *b* 18 Sept. 1876; 2nd *surv. s* of late Hon. James Harrison of Hoodley Estate in the Parish of St Thomas, Jamaica, and Susan McDermott; unmarried. *Educ:* privately; Royal Indian Engineering College, Coopers Hill (ACH). An Assistant Engineer in the Indian Public Works Dept (now the Indian Service of Engineers), 1899; posted to the Province of Bombay; Under-Secretary to Govt in the PWD, 1911; Superintending Engineer, 1915. *Recreations:* shooting, tennis, motoring. *Clubs:* East India United Service; Byculla, Royal Bombay Yacht (Bombay); Club of Western India (Poona).

Died 27 March 1950.

HARRISON, Rosamond Mary, OBE; Hon. Organising Secretary for Staffordshire Red Cross and St John Joint War Organisation Prisoners of War Department; Member, Staffordshire Agricultural Committee and War Agricultural Committee; Master, North Stafford Fox-Hounds since 1930; Chairman, Staffs County Women's Land Army; 3rd *d* of late Frederic James Harrison of Maer Hall, nr Newcastle, Staffordshire. *Educ:* privately. Organising Hon. Secretary North Staffs Regt Prisoners of War Association, 1914–18 (OBE); Chairman, Staffordshire Federation of Women's Institutes; Chairman West Midland Area Women's Advisory Committee, 1933–36 and 1945–47, President, 1936–44; Branch Secretary, RSPCA, North Staffordshire, 1935–47. *Recreations:* hunting, light horse breeding, farming, women's institutes. *Address:* Maer Hall, Newcastle, Staffs. *T:* Whitmore 207.

Died 8 Sept. 1948.

HARRISON, William John, MB, BS Durh., MRCS Eng., LRCP London; Hon. Surgeon, Ear, Nose, and Throat Hospital, Newcastle-on-Tyne; Hon. Consulting Surgeon, Ear, Nose and Throat Department, Ingham Infirmary; Hon. Surgeon in charge of the Ear, Nose, and Throat Department, Fleming Memorial Hospital for Sick Children; Aural Surgeon, Ministry of Pensions Hospital; *o s* of late W. Harrison, Newcastle-on-Tyne; unmarried. *Educ:* privately; Durham Univ. College of Medicine; St Thomas's Hospital, London. FRSM; Ex-President Otological Section; Ex-Vice-President Newcastle-on-Tyne and Northern Counties Medical Society; Major TD (retired), RAMC, TA (despatches, wounded, 1915). *Publications:* numerous articles in various medical journals. *Recreations:* golf, fishing, hunting. *Address:* Clewer Lodge, Akenside Terrace, Newcastle-upon-Tyne 2. *T:* Jesmond 823. *Club:* Naval and Military.

Died 29 Sept. 1943.

HARRISON, Sir William Montagu G.; *see* Graham-Harrison.

HART, Albert Bushnell; Eaton Professor of Science of Government, Harvard, 1910–26, now Emeritus; *b* Clarksville, Pennsylvania, 1 July 1854; *s* of Albert Gailord Hart; *m* Mary Hurd Putman; two *s. Educ:* Cleveland Schools; Harvard University; Berlin University; University of Freiburg; École des Sciences Politiques, Paris. AB Harvard, 1880; PhD Freiburg i/B, 1883; LLD Richmond, Tufts, Western Reserve; doc.-ès-lettres, University of Geneva. Instructor in History, Harvard, 1883–87; Assistant Professor, 1887–96; Professor of History, 1896–1910; Member and Historian US Geo. Washington Bicentennial Commission. *Publications:* American History told by Contemporaries (5 vols); Commonwealth History of Massachusetts (5 vols); Salmon P. Chase; Formation of the Union; Essentials of American History; New American History; Guide to American History (joint); Actual Government; Slavery and Abolition; National Ideals Historically Traced; American Citizen Series (ed); American Nation—a History, 28 vols (ed); The Southern South; The Obvious Orient; George Washington Pamphlets, 1930–1932; Cyclopædia of American Government, 3 vols (joint ed); The War in Europe; Monroe Doctrine; American History Maps; American Patriots and Statesmen (5 vols); School History of the US; We and our History; America at War; Handbook of the War (joint), etc. *Address:* Harvard University, USA. *Clubs:* Harvard, Boston; Century, New York; Faculty, Cambridge; Cosmos, Washington.

Died 16 June 1943.

HART, Arthur W.; *see* Woolley-Hart.

HART, Lt-Col Eric George, DSO 1918; MA (Dublin); *b* Mangalore, 6 Feb. 1878; *s* of late Henry Hart, MBE, of Southern India and 44 Lennox Road, Southsea; *m* 1909, Audrey Doreen Davis (whom he divorced 1921); one *d*; 1942, Lilian Mary Webb. *Educ:* Victoria College, Jersey; Wellington Coll.; RMA, Woolwich. 2nd Lt RA, 1897; Captain, 1902; transferred to Indian Army (S and T Corps), 1906; Major, 1915; Bt Lt-Col, 1919; Lt-Col 1923; retired, 1924; served China, 1900–01; Mekran, 1901–02 (despatches); Aden Hinterland, 1904; Persia, 1911–13; European War, Mesopotamia (despatches four times, DSO, Bt Lt-Col); Afghanistan, 1919; NW Frontier, 1919; Prof. of Arabic, Persian, and Hindustani, and Reader in Indian History, Dublin Univ., 1926–38; Cipher Officer attached RAF, July 1939–Sept. 1940. *Publications:* A Manual of Office Work, 1908; Examinations: How to Pass them, 1911; Gandhi and the Indian Problem, 1931; The Art and Science of Organization, 1933. *Recreations:* yachting, making masks, painting portraits. *Address:* Polwheveral, Constantine,

Falmouth. *T:* Constantine 282. *Clubs:* Naval and Military, Overseas; Royal Cornwall Yacht, Falmouth; Royal Bombay Yacht.

Died 8 Oct. 1946.

HART, Heber Leonidas, KC 1913; LLD; *y s* of late Percy M. Hart of Putney; *m* 1941, Mabel Neal. *Educ:* private schools, Univ. of London. Recorder of Ipswich, 1915–36; Bencher of the Middle Temple, Treasurer, 1937; British Member of the Anglo-German, Anglo-Austrian, Anglo-Bulgarian, and Anglo-Hungarian Mixed Arbitral Tribunals established under the Treaties of Peace, until the completion of their work in 1931; Liberal candidate for Windsor, Jan. 1910; President of the Johnson Club, 1943; past Chairman of the Eighty and 1920 Clubs; Hon. Capt. *Publications:* The Law of Banking, 1904, 4th ed. 1931; The Bulwarks of Peace, 1918, 2nd ed. 1933; Reminiscences and Reflections, 1939; The Way to Justice, 1941. *Address:* 9 Putney Hill, SW15. *T:* Putney 1638. *Club:* Reform.

Died 4 Feb. 1948.

HART, Lt-Col Henry Travers, CBE 1919; *e s* of late Col E. C. Hart, RE and Maria Eliza, *e d* of late Col J. B. Travers; *m* 1908, Phyllis Hope (*d* 1941), 4th *d* of Col H. M. Matthews; one *d*. *Educ:* Sedbergh; RM Academy, Woolwich. Entered Royal Artillery, 1893; Captain, 1900; Brevet Major, 1912; Major, 1914; Lt-Col, 1917; retired, 1922; Head Quarters Army, 1902–06, 1908–12; served European War, 1914–18 (three medals, CBE). *Publications:* Harts of Donegal; Slide Rule made easy. *Recreations:* shooting and fishing. *Address:* c/o National Provincial Bank Ltd, Honiton, Devon.

Died 25 Feb. 1948.

HART, Sir William Edward, Kt 1926; OBE; LLD; *b* 14 Feb. 1866; *m* 1893, Jane Elizabeth Ogden, Leeds; one *s*. *Educ:* Leeds Grammar School. Assistant Solicitor, Leeds Corporation, 1897–1900; Deputy Town Clerk, Sheffield, 1900–07; Solicitor to National Telephone Co. Ltd, 1907–13; Town Clerk of Sheffield, 1913–31; Deputy Licensing Authority, North-Western Area, 1934–39. *Address:* Orchard House, Dunham Massey, Cheshire.

Died 5 March 1942.

HART-SYNNOT, Brig.-Gen. Arthur Henry Seton, CMG 1919; DSO 1900; FRGS; late East Surrey Regiment; *b* 19 July 1870; *e s* of late Major-General FitzRoy Hart-Synnot, CB, CMG; *m* Violette, *d* of J. E. Drower, CBE. *Educ:* Clifton College; King William's College; RMC, Sandhurst; Staff College, psc. Served Relief of Chitral, 1895, in command of Maxim gun section (medal with clasp); Tirah campaign, 1897–98, as ADC to the GOC 1st Brigade (2 clasps); Boer War, 1899–1902, first with the Mounted Infantry and afterwards as Brigade Major of the Irish Brigade, and subsequently as DAAG (twice wounded, despatches, DSO, medal with 7 clasps, King's medal with 2 clasps); European War, 1914–18 (Bt Lt-Col, bar to DSO, French Croix de Guerre, Chevalier Légion d'Honneur, very severely wounded); Chasseur-Alpin première classe (honoraire), 1938; British Military Attaché with the Japanese Army, Manchuria, 1905; received from the Mikado the 4th class of the Order of the Sacred Treasure and Japanese War Medal. *Club:* Army and Navy.

Died 22 Nov. 1942.

HARTFORD, Captain George Bibby, DSO 1918; RN, retd; *b* 11 April 1883; *s* of late Henry W. Hartford and late Mrs Hartford, both Christchurch, Hants; *m* 1st, Alice Wells (*d* 1920), *o d* of late James Walter, Yokohama; one *s* one *d*; 2nd, 1922, Eveline Isabel, *widow* of late Charles H. Ross. *Educ:* Northwood Park, Winchester; HMS Britannia. Served European War, 1914–18 (despatches, DSO); retd 1922; recalled to active service, 1939 (despatches, Bar to DSO); Member of

Royal Toxophilite Society. *Publication:* Commander RN, 1927. *Address:* Snakemoor, Botley, Hants. *T:* Durley 7. *Club:* United Service.

Died 14 Aug. 1941.

HARTINGTON, Marquess of; William John Robert Cavendish; Lt late Coldstream Guards; *b* 10 Dec. 1917; *er s* of 10th Duke of Devonshire, KG; *m* 1944, Kathleen, 2nd *d* of Joseph P. Kennedy.

Died 9 Sept. 1944.

HARTLAND, George Albert; MP (U) Norwich, 1931–35; *b* 1884; *s* of late J. F. Hartland, MD. *Educ:* St Francis Xavier's College, Liverpool. *Address:* Tavistock Residential Club, Tavistock Square, WC1. *T:* Euston 4855. *Clubs:* Constitutional, 1900.

Died 18 July 1944.

HARTLAND-SWANN, Louis Herbert, CBE 1922; *b* 1878; *s* of Joseph William Swann, Ipswich; *m* 1907, Edith Mildred, *e d* of late John Cumming Nimmo, *g d* of Joseph Whitaker, founder of Whitaker's Almanack; two *s* one *d*. *Educ:* Ipswich. Director Lever Bros and Unilever, Ltd, 1923–38; late Joint Head Official Agencies Section, National War Savings Committee; Director of Advertising, Coal Mines Department, Board of Trade; Director of Advertising, Victory Loan Campaign, etc.; formerly Deputy President British Association of Advertising; Vice-Chairman, Sales Managers' Association, etc.; (formerly Louis Herbert Swann, assumed by Deed Poll 1921 the additional surname of Hartland). *Address:* c/o Lloyds Bank Ltd, Holborn Circus, EC1. *Clubs:* East India and Sports, Royal Automobile.

Died 18 July 1947.

HARTLEY, Christiana, CBE 1943; JP; Hon. MA Liverpool, 1943; Director of W. P. Hartley Ltd, Aintree and London; *d* of late Sir William Hartley. *Educ:* governess; private schools. Poor Law Guardian for 18 years; Member of Southport Town Council, 12 years; Mayor of Southport, 1921–22; gave Christiana Hartley Maternity Hospital, Colne, 1935; Southport Maternity Hospital, 1932, and Nurses Home, Southport, 1940; Freedom of Colne (Lancs), 1927, of Southport, 1940. *Address:* 4 Lord St, West, Southport. *T:* Southport 2841.

Died 14 Dec. 1948.

HARTLEY, Harold T.; *b* London, 28 Oct. 1851; *e s* of T. H. P. Hartley, Brondesbury; *m* 1st, 1878, Katie, *e d* of Francis Brewer, Kensington; 2nd, *e d* of R. M. Ordish, CE; one *s*. *Educ:* City of London College. Partner in firm of Emmott, Hartley and Co., Fleet Street, publishers; founders of The Textile Manufacturer, Chambers of Commerce Chronicle and Warehousemen and Drapers' Trade Journal; one of the founders of the Burlington Magazine; afterwards Director of Venice in London, the Indian, Victorian Era, Greater Britain, and Military Exhibitions, etc.; Life Governor of Charing Cross Hospital; Knt. of the Order of St Sava; Commander of the Order of Danilo of Montenegro. *Publication:* Eighty-Eight Not Out, 1939. *Recreations:* gardening and fishing. *Address:* Brook House, North Stoke, Oxford. *Clubs:* Junior Constitutional, Authors'.

Died 29 Sept. 1943.

HARTOG, Sir Philip Joseph, KBE 1930; Kt 1926; CIE 1917; MA, BSc; L-ès-Sc., Paris; Hon. LLD, Dacca; Director of the International Institute Examinations Enquiry, 1932; *b* London, 2 March 1864; 3rd *s* of late Alphonse Hartog and Marion, *d* of Joseph Moss; *m* 1915, Mabel Hélène (author of Living India, 1935, and India in Outline, 1944, 2nd ed. 1945), *d* of H. J. Kisch; three *s*. *Educ:* University College School; Owens College, Manchester; University of Paris and University of Heidelberg; Collège de France. Assistant Lecturer in Chemistry in Owens College, 1891–1903; Lecturer in the Victoria University, Manchester, 1898–1903; Secretary to Victoria Univ. Extension Scheme, 1895–1903; member of Court of the Victoria University,

1901–03; Academic Registrar of the University of London, 1903–20; late Berkeley Fellow of the Owens College, Manchester; Secretary to the Mosely Commission of Educational Enquiry, 1902–03; Secretary to the Treasury Committee on the Organisation of Oriental Studies in London, 1907–09, and to the India Office Committee on the same subject, 1910–17: Crown Member of the Governing Body of the School of Oriental Studies since 1916; Member of Viceroy's Commission on University of Calcutta, 1917–19; first Vice-Chancellor of the University of Dacca, Bengal, 1920–25; Member of Indian Public Service Commission, 1926–30; Member of Committee of Enquiry on Aligarh University, 1927; Chairman of the Auxiliary Committee on Education of the Indian Statutory Commission, 1928–29; Chairman of Linguists Committee of Appointments Register, Ministry of Labour and National Service, since 1939. *Publications:* papers on chemical and physical subjects in various journals; many biographies of chemists and physicists in the Dictionary of National Biography; articles in the Special Reports on Educational Subjects of the Board of Education; The Owens College, a history and description of, 1900; The Writing of English, 1907; new ed. 1908; Examinations in their bearing on National Efficiency, 1911; Examinations and their Relation to Culture and Efficiency, 1918; The Relation of Poetry to Verse, 1926; Pascal, 1927; Priestley, 1931; An Examination of Examinations (with E. C. Rhodes), 1935, 2nd edition, 1936; The Marks of Examiners (with E. C. Rhodes and Cyril Burt), 1936; Secondary School Examinations, etc., with suggestions for Reform (an address to the NUT), 1937; A Conspectus of Examinations (with Gladys Roberts), 1938; The Purposes of Examinations, A Symposium (edited), 1938; Some Aspects of Indian Education, 1939; The Marking of English Essays (in collaboration), 1941; Words in Action, 1945. *Address:* 5 Inverness Gardens, W8. *T:* Bayswater 4294. *Club:* Athenæum.

Died 27 June 1947.

HARTOPP, Sir George Francis Fleetwood Cradock-, 8th Bt *cr* 1796; *b* 20 July 1870; 4th *s* of Sir John William Cradock Hartopp, 4th Bt and Charlotte Frances, *e d* of E. G. Howard; *S* brother, 1937; *m* 1909, Ethel, *widow* of Captain B. Gunston; no *c*. *Educ:* Wellington College. Member London Stock Exchange, now retired from active business. *Heir: cousin* John Edmund Cradock- [*b* 1912; *s* of late F. G. Cradock-Hartopp and Elizabeth Ada Mary, *o d* of late John Windsor Stuart, Foley House, Rothesay]. *Clubs:* Turf, White's.

Died 5 Sept. 1949.

HARTRICK, Archibald Standish, OBE 1948; RWS 1910; painter; black and white artist; *b* Bangalore, Madras, 7 Aug. 1864; *e s* of late Capt. William Hartrick, 7th Royal Fusiliers, and Josephine, *d* of Dr Archibald Smith, Edinburgh; *m* Lily Blatherwick, RSW (*d* 1934). *Educ:* Fettes Coll. Edinburgh; Edinburgh University. Studied painting under A. Legros, Slade School, London, 1884–85; Paris, under Boulanger and Cormon, 1886–87; exhibited Salon, 1887. Staff of Daily Graphic, 1890; staff of Pall Mall Budget, 1893; member New English Art Club, 1893; Official War Artist (Land Work), 1940; International Society of Sculptors, Painters, and Gravers, 1906; Vice-President and one of founders of Senefelder Club; silver medal Milan International Exhibition, 1906–07; medal Chilean Centenary Exhibition, 1910; Set of drawings of Cotswold types acquired for British Museum through National Arts Collection Fund and some friends; The Penitent's Bench, water-colour bought by Chantrey Bequest, 1933; water-colours Whitworth Art Gallery, Manchester, 1944; Drawings in Melbourne National Gallery, Sydney, NSW, and Aberdeen Gallery; Lithographs in Victoria and Albert Museum, Liverpool and Manchester Galleries; Los Angeles Museum; Royal Library, Stuttgart; bronze

medal of California Print Makers, Los Angeles, 1929; Drawings of lesser examples of English Mediæval Stained Glass, Victoria and Albert Museum; Lithographs: British Museum and Gallery of South Australia, Adelaide. *Publications:* Drawing, 2nd Edition, 1928; Lithography as a fine art, 1932; A Painter's Pilgrimage through Fifty Years, 1939. *Address:* 75 Clancarty Road, Fulham, SW.

Died 1 Feb. 1950.

HARTWELL, Sir Brodrick Cecil Denham Arkwright, of Dale Hall, Essex; 4th Bt *cr* 1805; late Lieut-Col, 1st Garrison Batt. Oxfordshire and Buckinghamshire Light Infantry; Major, late 2nd Garrison Batt. Northumberland Fusiliers; late Lieutenant and Captain Leicester Regiment; *b* 10 July 1876; *s* of Captain Edward Hughes Brodrick Hartwell, RN, Inspector-General Constabulary, Jamaica, and HBM Consul for Naples and South Italy, *s* of 2nd Bt, and Augusta, *d* of Stewart Henry Paget; *S uncle* 1900; *m* 1st, 1902, Georgette Madeleine (marr. diss. 1907), *d* of M. Pilon Fleury of Djenan Saka, El Biar, Algiers; one *d*; 2nd, 1908, Joan Amy, *o d* of Robert Milne Jeffrey, Esquimault, Vancouver; one *s* one *d*. Served South Africa (medal with two clasps); European War, in Gallipoli, 1915. *Heir: s* Brodrick William Charles Elwin, Lieut Leicestershire Regiment [*b* 7 Aug. 1909; *m* 1937, Marie Josephine, *d* of S. P. Mullins; one *s* (Francis Antony Charles Peter, *b* 1 June 1940)]. *Address:* 220 Rodney House, Dolphin Square, SW1.

Died 24 Nov. 1948.

HARTY, Sir (Herbert) Hamilton, Kt 1925; MusDoc, TCD, 1925, Victoria University Manchester, 1926 and De Paul University, Belfast, 1936; LLD Queen's University, Belfast, 1933; Hon. FRCM; Gold Medal, Royal Philharmonic Society, 1934; composer-conductor; regularly conducts all leading English orchestras in addition to touring USA as Guest Conductor, and in 1934 undertook extensive tour in Australia; *b* 4 Dec. 1880. Permanent Conductor Hallé Orchestra, Manchester, 1920–33. *Works:* An Irish Symphony; A Violin Concerto in D Minor; A Pianoforte Concerto in B Minor; Comedy Overture, 1907; With the Wild Geese (orchestra); The Children of Lir (orchestra); The Mystic Trumpeter (chorus and orchestra); songs, piano, violin, and 'cello solos, etc. *Address:* 1 Norfolk Road, St John's Wood, NW8.

Died 19 Feb. 1941.

HARTY, Most Rev. J. M., DD; Archbishop of Cashel since 1914; *b* Murroe, Co. Limerick, Ireland, 1867. *Educ:* St Patrick's College, Thurles; St Patrick's College, Maynooth; Gregorian University, Rome. Priest, 1894; Professor of Dogmatic Theology, St Patrick's College, Maynooth, 1895; Professor of Moral Theology, 1904; Professor of Canon Law, 1909; one of the Editors of The Irish Theological Quarterly, 1906–14; Theological Correspondent of Irish Ecclesiastical Record, 1903–14; Hon. Secretary, Maynooth Union, 1904–14; President of The Catholic Truth Society of Ireland, 1914. *Publications:* various articles on Theological subjects in Irish Theological Quarterly, Irish Ecclesiastical Record, and Catholic Encyclopedia. *Address:* The Palace, Thurles, Co. Tipperary, Ireland.

Died 11 Sept. 1946.

HARVEY, Maj.-Gen. Alexander William Montgomery, CB 1937; MB; IMS; retired; *b* 4 April 1881. Lieut, IMS, 1903; Capt. 1906; Major, 1915; Bt Lt-Col, 1917; Lt-Col, 1923; Bt Col, 1926; Col 1932; Maj.-Gen., 1935; retired, 1937.

Died 2 Dec. 1942.

HARVEY, Conway, CBE 1938; JP; Farmer, Koru, Kenya Colony; *b* 5 Feb. 1880; *s* of E. J. Harvey, Bockingfold Manor, Goudhurst, Kent; unmarried. *Educ:* Bethany House, Goudhurst. Served throughout Boer War; served European War with East African Mounted Rifles; Chairman, Passion Fruit Board; Vice-Chairman,

Coffee Board of Kenya; Member, Transport Licensing Board; member of Kenya Legislative Council for Nyanza, 1921–38; Member Legion of Frontiersmen and British Legion; Jubilee and Coronation Medals. *Recreations:* riding, fishing, golf, bridge. *Address:* Koru, Kenya Colony. *Clubs:* Muthaiga Country, Nairobi, Nairobi; Rift Valley Sports, Nakuru; Karen Country, Ngong.

Died 21 June 1943.

HARVEY, Col Francis George, CBE 1918; DSO 1918; *b* 1872. Served Matabeleland, 1893 and 1896; S African War, 1899–1902; European War, 1914–18 (despatches, DSO, CBE, Officer of Legion of Honour).

Died 3 Aug. 1944.

HARVEY, Harold, ARCA; *e s* of Francis M'Farland Harvey of Penzance, Cornwall; *m* Gertrude Bodinnar. *Educ:* privately. Studied with Norman Garstin and later at Juliens, Paris, under Benjamin Constant and Jean Paul Laurens. First exhibited at Royal Academy 1898, since then regularly; also at principal London and Provincial Exhibitions, such as The International, Goupils, The Grosvenor, Liverpool, Glasgow, Oldham, etc., also at Carnegie Institute, Pittsburgh, and most of the great American cities, also Venice; represented in municipal galleries, Cardiff, Swansea, S Shields, Birmingham, Oldham, Vancouver, Trafford Park, Stretford, Truro, Brighton, Northampton, Leamington Spa; one-man shows, Leicester Galleries, 1918, 1920, and 1926; Barbizon House, 1932. *Recreation:* fishing. *Address:* Maën Cottage, Newlyn, Penzance.

Died 19 May 1941.

HARVEY, Sir (Henry) Paul, KCMG 1911; CB 1901; *b* 1869; *m* 1896, Ethel Frances, *d* of Colonel Edward Persse; one *d*. *Educ:* Rugby; New College, Oxford. 1st Cl. Honours, Lit. Hum. Assistant Private Secretary and Private Secretary to Marquess of Lansdowne while Secretary of State for War, 1895–1900; British Delegate to international Commission on Greek Finance, 1903; British Representative on International Commission for Control of Macedonian Finance, 1905; Financial Adviser to Egyptian Government, 1907–12 and 1919–20; Director of Prisoners of War Information Bureau, 1914–16; Secretary to the Air Board, 1916–18, and Chief Auditor of National Health Insurance, 1912. *Publications:* compiled and edited The Oxford Companion to English Literature, 1932, and Oxford Companion to Classical Literature, 1937. *Club:* Oxford and Cambridge.

Died 30 Dec. 1948.

HARVEY, Hon. Horace, LLD; Chief Justice of Alberta since 1910; *b* Malahide, Elgin Co., Ontario, 1 Oct. 1863; *s* of William Harvey, MP, and Sophronia Mack; *m* 1893, Louise Palmer (*d* 1948), Toronto; one *s*. *Educ:* University of Toronto. Called to the Bar of Ontario, 1889; Practised profession in Toronto till 1893, when moved to Calgary, and called to bar of NWT; Registrar of Land Titles at Calgary, 1896; Deputy Attorney-General, of NWT 1900; Puisne Judge of Supreme Court of NWT, 1904; of Supreme Court of Alberta, 1907, upon its establishment; Chief Justice of Trial Division, 1921, on establishment of that Division; Chief Justice of Appellate Division, 1924; Chairman of Board of Governors of University of Alberta, 1917–40. *Address:* Edmonton, Alberta, Canada.

Died 9 Sept. 1949.

HARVEY, Rev. James, DD; Senior Minister of Lady Glenorchy's North Church; *b* Aberdeen, 10 March 1859; *s* of George Thompson Harvey merchant there, and Harriet Smith; *m* 1897, Alexandra Georgeina (*d* 1924), *d* of Alexander Peddie-Waddell, WS, of Balquhatstone, Stirlingshire; one *s* two *d*. *Educ:* Grammar School and Univ., Aberdeen, MA, DD; Free Church Coll. at Aberdeen; University, Göttingen; University, Strasbourg. Minister of Duntocher Free Church, Dumbartonshire, 1885–90; Clerk of Edinburgh

Presbytery of Free Church (afterwards United Free Church) for twelve years; Principal Clerk of General Assembly of United Free Church, May 1919, and later Church of Scotland, resigned 1939; Moderator of General Assembly of UF Church of Scotland, 1925. *Publications:* How can I help Scotland? a pamphlet on House of Lords' judgment on Church case, Aug. 1904, and various sermons. *Recreation:* water-colour sketching. *Address:* 7 Western Terrace, Edinburgh. *T:* Edinburgh, 62889.

Died 15 Feb. 1950.

HARVEY, Sir John Martin-, Kt 1921; Hon. LLD; FRSL; Hon. Lieut Legion of Frontiersmen; Hon. NCO Royal Highlanders of Canada; *b* Wyvenhoe, Essex, 22 June 1863; *s* of John Harvey, member of Institute of Naval Architects, and Margaret Diana Mary, *d* of late Rev. D. G. Goyder; *m* 1889, Angelita Helena de Silva, *o d* of late Don Ramon de Silva Ferro; one *s* one *d*. *Educ:* King's College School, London. Intended for father's profession of naval architecture, but developed early predilection for stage; studied elocution under late John Ryder; made first appearance at Old Court Theatre under John Clayton; then joined one of Sir C. Wyndham's companies for 'Betsy'; subsequently joined Sir Henry Irving, and remained with him for many years, accompanying him on his various tours through America; has managed Lyceum, Prince of Wales, Covent Garden Opera House, and other theatres; made Hon. Lieut of the Legion of Frontiersmen for services in recruiting; made a Chief of Sarcee Tribe of NW America with title of Ta-Decasze (Red Feather), 1924. *Productions:* The Only Way; Don Juan's Last Wager; Ib and Little Christina; A Cigarette Maker's Romance; Eugene Aram; The Exile; Pelléas and Mélisande; The Breed of the Treshams; Hamlet; The Corsican Brothers; Great Possessions; The World and His Wife; The Last Heir; A Tragedy of Truth; The Conspiracy; Richard III; Œdipus; The Taming of the Shrew; The Faun; Armageddon; Henry V; The Burgomaster of Stilemonde, Via Crucis; The Death of Tintagiles; The Showing up of Blanco Posnet; Scaramouche; The Lyons' Mail; The Lowland Wolf; The King's Messenger; The Bells, etc. *Publication:* Autobiography, 1933. *Recreations:* drawing and painting (studied under Slade Prof. Brown, and at Heatherley's Studio), objets d'art, member of the Meyrick Society. *Address:* Primrose Cottage, Fife Road, East Sheen, Surrey; Bonchurch, IOW. *T:* Prospect, 4502. *TA:* Unfurl, London. *Clubs:* Green Room, Royal Automobile, Eccentric (Hon.), Stadium (Hon.).

Died 14 May 1944.

HARVEY, Sir Paul; *see* Harvey, Sir H. P.

HARVEY, Sir Percy Norman, KBE 1946; CB 1944; Government Actuary since 1944; *b* 1 Nov. 1887; *s* of late George Alfred Harvey, Hornchurch, Essex; *m* 1912, Ethel Elizabeth Maud, *d* of late W. S. J. Smith, Hornchurch, Essex; two *s* one *d*. *Educ:* Grocers' Company School. FIA 1913; entered Civil Service 1913; Actuary in Govt Actuary's Dept 1920; Principal Actuary, 1928; Deputy Govt Actuary, 1936–44; seconded to Ministry of War Transport as Statistical Adviser in 1939 and as Joint Statistical Adviser and Director of Statistics and Intelligence Division, 1942–44. Member of Council of Institute of Actuaries, 1930–38, 1939–42, and 1944–, Vice-Pres. 1935–38; Member of Council of Royal Statistical Soc. 1942–; Member of Statistical Committee of Medical Research Council, 1930–; Chairman Civil Service Nursing Aid Assoc. 1944–. *Recreation:* walking. *Address:* Wetherby, Red Down Road, Coulsdon, Surrey. *T:* Downland 509. *Club:* Reform.

Died 30 Aug. 1946.

HARVEY, Ven. Richard Charles Musgrave; *b* 8 Sept. 1864; *e s* of late Prebendary C. M. Harvey, Hillingdon Vicarage, Uxbridge; *m* Laura (*d* 1931), *y d* of late Henry Willmer, JP, Eastleigh, Hants; no *c*. *Educ:* Marlborough;

Keble College, Oxford. Ordained, 1888; Curate of Portsea, 1888–94; Vicar of Eastleigh, 1894–1901; Vicar of Dewsbury, 1901–13; Archdeacon of Huddersfield, 1914–27; Hon. Canon of Wakefield Cathedral, 1909–35, Emeritus since 1935; Archdeacon of Halifax, 1927–35; Prolocutor of York Convocation, 1929–35; Vice-Chairman of the House of Clergy, 1929–32. *Address:* The White House, Milford, Godalming. *T:* Godalming 961.

Died 20 Oct. 1944.

HARVEY, Alderman William Alfred, OBE 1933; MM; *b* 2 Dec. 1883; *s* of William Fowler and Mary Ann Harvey; *m* 1912, Bertha Jessie Turner; one *d*. *Educ:* Bethany School, Goudhurst, Kent. Served in British Expeditionary Force in France, 1916–19 (MM); Mayor of Guildford, 1931–32, and 1932–33; initiated a Work for Wages Scheme at Guildford which was widely adopted by other municipalities and public bodies throughout the country, 1932; created an Hon. Freeman of the Borough of Guildford for public services in addition to those of the mayoralty, 1933. *Recreation:* rose growing. *Address:* Abbots Copse, Guildford. *T:* Guildford 42.

Died 27 Nov. 1946.

HARVEY, Lt-Col William Frederick, CIE 1921; MA, MB, FRCPE, DPH; FRSE; Indian Medical Service (retired); Director histopathology research and lately Superintendent Royal College of Physicians' Laboratory, Edinburgh; Sectional editor Tropical Diseases Bulletin; *b* 1873; *s* of R. Harvey, MA, LLD; *m* 1910, Jean, *d* of Donald Sutherland, chartered accountant, Edinburgh; one *s* one *d*. *Educ:* Dollar Academy; Edinburgh University; Univ. College, London. Graduated Medicine, first class Honours, Edinburgh University. Deputy Sanitary Commissioner, Punjab, 1902–05; Director Pasteur Institute, Kasauli, 1905–11; Director Central Research Institute, Kasauli, India, 1911–25; Assistant Director Medical Services, Sanitary; Mesopotamian Expeditionary Force, 1916 (despatches). *Publications:* Theory and Practice of Antirabic Immunisation, Sc. Mem. Govt of India; Vaccine Lymph, Indian Medical Gazette; Notes on Immunity, Scott. Med. and Surg. Jl; Opsonic Index, Biometrika; various other papers in the Indian Journal of Medical Research and Edinburgh Medical Journal; co-author articles Rabies and Cholera in Brit. Syst. Bacteriology and of Debateable Tumours. *Address:* 56 Garscube Terrace, Edinburgh.

Died 11 Sept. 1948.

HARWOOD, Basil, MA; DMus Oxon; *b* 11 April 1859; *s* of Edward Harwood, JP, of Woodhouse, Olveston, Gloucestershire; *m* 1899, Mabel Ada, *d* of George Jennings of Ferndale, Clapham, and Castle Eve, Parkstone, Dorset; two *s*. *Educ:* Charterhouse; Trinity College, Oxford. Organist of St Barnabas', Pimlico, 1883–87; Ely Cathedral, 1887–92; Christ Church Cathedral, Oxford, 1892–1909; Precentor of Keble College, Oxford, 1892–1903; Choragus of the Univ. of Oxford 1900–09; Examiner for Musical Degrees, Univ. of Oxford, 1900–01, 1904–05, 1908–09, and 1914–15. *Publications:* Church Services, Anthems and Hymn Tunes; 2 Organ Sonatas and other Organ Pieces; Songs; Cantatas; 'Inclina Domine' (Gloucester Festival, 1898); As by the Streams of Babylon (Oxford Bach Choir, 1907); Jesus, Thy Boundless Love (Festival of Sons of the Clergy, St Paul's Cathedral, 1909); Concerto for Organ and Orchestra in D (Gloucester Festival, 1910); Song on May Morning (Leeds Festival, 1913); Love Incarnate (Gloucester Festival, 1925); Motet, Ye Choirs of New Jerusalem (Gloucester Festival, 1928); Church Cantata, Sacrifice triumphant, 1939; Musical Editor of the Oxford Hymn Book, 1908. *Address:* 50 Courtfield Gardens, SW5; Woodhouse, Almondsbury, Gloucestershire. *T:* Frobisher 3987. *Club:* Authors'.

Died 3 April 1949.

HARWOOD, Adm. Sir Henry Harwood, KCB 1939; OBE 1919; *b* 19 Jan. 1888; *s* of late Surtees Harwood Harwood, Ashmans Hall, Suffolk; *m* 1924, Joan, *d* of late Selway Chard, Magnolia House, West Tarring, Sussex; two *s*. *Educ:* HMS Britannia. Midshipman, 1904; Lieut 1908; Commander, 1921; Capt. 1928; commanded HMS Warwick and 9th Destroyer Division, 1929; Imperial Defence College, 1931–32; HMS London, 1932–34; Staff of RN War College, 1934–36; Commodore Commanding South America Division and HMS Exeter, 1936–39; Rear-Admiral Commanding South America Division, 1940; commanded HM Forces in action against Graf Spee, Dec. 1939 (promoted to Rear-Admiral, KCB); a Lord Commissioner of the Admiralty and an Assistant Chief of Naval Staff, 1940–42; Commander-in-Chief, Mediterranean (acting Admiral), 1942; Commander-in-Chief, Levant, 1943; Vice-Admiral, 1943; Flag Officer commanding Orkney and Shetlands, 1944–45; Admiral, 1945; retired medically unfit, 1945. *Recreations:* shooting, fishing, golf. *Address:* White Cottage, Goring, Berkshire. *T:* Goring (Oxon) 212. *Club:* United Service.

Died 9 June 1950.

HASKETT-SMITH, W. P.; *see* Smith.

HASLAM, Henry Cobden; retired; *b* 1870; *s* of Henry Haslam of Lloyds and 1 Portland Place, W1; *m* Julie Henriette, *d* of Edward Dupont, part Founder and 41 years Director of Brussels Natural History Museum; one *s* one *d*. *Educ:* Gonville and Caius College, Cambridge; ScD, MB, BCh Cantab. Engaged for many years in scientific research at Medical Schools, Cambridge University; MP (U) Horncastle Division, 1924–45. *Publications:* papers in journals of Physiology, Biochemistry, Pathology and others. *Recreations:* boating, sailing, and lawn tennis. *Address:* 15 Cranmer Rd, Cambridge. *T:* Cambridge 4094. *Club:* Constitutional.

Died 7 Feb. 1948.

HASLEHUST, Ernest William, RI; RBA; RWA; artist; Member of The Ridley Art Club; Royal Society of Arts; Imperial Arts League; *e s* of late William Henry Haslehust, and Rosine Haslehust, of Lee, Kent. *Educ:* Manor House, Hastings; Felsted. Studied art at the Slade School University College under Professor Legros. Has exhibited at the principal galleries in London—also in the provinces, and abroad; works in the collections of the Queen, Duke of Portland, Earl of Romney, Lord Savile, etc.; picture purchased for the permanent Art Collections of Wellington, Auckland, New Zealand, Port Elizabeth, Oldham, Huddersfield, Swansea, Bristol, Bootle, Vancouver City, Sheffield, Lincoln, Newport (Mon), Mansfield, Colombo, Nottingham; Master of the Worshipful Company of Cordwainers, 1943–44. *Publications:* Illustrator of Beautiful England series of books; Silvery Thames; Water-colour painting; I wish I could paint (with Percy V. Bradshaw). Series of illustrated articles in the Artist; part illustrator of many other publications and magazine articles; Illustrations and Posters for the LNER, etc. *Recreations:* mechanics and gardening. *Address:* 3 The Orchard, Blackheath, SE3. *T:* Lee Green 2029. *Clubs:* Arts, Langham Sketch.

Died 3 July 1949.

HASLETT, Very Rev. Thomas, MA, DD; Senior Minister, First Ballymena Presbyterian Church, N Ireland. Moderator of the Presbyterian Church in Ireland, 1925. *Address:* c-o Mrs George Smith, 84 Maryville Park, Belfast.

Died 1 Aug. 1947.

HASSALL, John, RI, RWA; *b* 1868; *s* of late Christopher Clark Hassall, RN; *m* 1st, 1893, Isobel Dingwall; one *s* two *d*; 2nd, 1903, Constance Maud, *d* of Rev. A. Brooke-Webb; one *s* one *d*. *Educ:* Newton Abbot College, Devon; Neuenheim College, Heidelberg. Started as farmer in Manitoba; studied in Antwerp and Paris, 1891–94. *Publications:* posters, illustrations, book-covers, and children's books. *Recreation:* archæology. *Address:* 88 Kensington Park Road, W11. *T:* Park 5826. *Clubs:* London Sketch, Odd Volumes, Savage, Knights of ye Round Table, Masonic Pen and Brush Lodge.

Died 8 March 1948.

HASSANEIN, Sir Ahmed Mohamed Pasha, KCVO 1927; Governor of the Egyptian Royal Household since 1936; *b* Cairo, 31 Oct. 1889; *s* of late El Sheikh Mohamed Hassanein El Boulaki; *m* 1926, Loutfia, *d* of Yousry Pacha and Princess Chivekiar of Egypt; two *s* one *d. Educ:* Royal School of Law, Cairo; Balliol College, Oxford. Attached to the Staff of General Sir John Maxwell, Commander-in-Chief in Egypt, 1914–16; Ministry of Interior, 1916; on the Official Mission to the Senussi, 1916–17; Order of the Nile and MBE; Inspector, Ministry of Interior, 1918; Champion Fencer of Egypt, and represented Egypt in Olympic Games, Antwerp, 1920; President Egyptian Fencing Federation; made journey across Libyan Desert to the Oases of Kufra, 1920–21 (Egyptian Medal of Merit); Secretary to the Egyptian Official Delegation to London, 1921; crossed the Libyan Desert from Sollum to Darfur, and discovered the Oases of Arkenu and Owenat, 1922–23 (Commander of the Order of the Nile); First Secretary to the Egyptian Legation, Washington 1923; First Chamberlain to King Fouad I of Egypt 1925; Comptroller to Prince of Saïd, 1935–36; Founder's Medal of the Royal Geographical Society, London, and Elisha Kent Kane Medal of Geographical Society of Philadelphia, 1924; Gold Medal of the French Geographical Society, 1928; First Secretary to the Egyptian Legation, London, 1924; Vice-Pres. of the International Geographical Union, 1925; Grand Cross of the Orders of The Crown of Italy, Leopold II of Belgium and Ashtur of Afghanistan; Grand Officer of the Orders of the Nile, Maurice and St Lazare of Italy, Crown of Belgium, Rising Sun, Japan; White Lion, Czechoslovakia; St Sauveur, Greece; Pius IX; St Trinité of Abyssinia; Commander of the Order of Polonia Restituta; Commander of the Légion d'Honneur, Officier of the French Palmes Académiques. *Publications:* The Lost Oases; articles on travel and exploration in geographical magazines. *Recreations:* fencing; represented Oxford University against Cambridge, 1911–13, riding, shooting, and aviation; Vice-President, Aero Club of Egypt. *Address:* Abdin Palace, Cairo. *Clubs:* Royal Societies; Mohamed Aly, Cairo; Royal Yacht, Alexandria.

Died 19 Feb. 1946.

HASTED, Lt-Col John Ord Cobbold, DSO 1917; *b* 20 Aug. 1890; *s* of late J. E. H. Hasted, Madras Police; *m* 1st, 1918, Phyllis Mary (*d* 1921), *d* of late Field-Marshal Sir Arthur Barrett, GCB, GCSI, KCVO; one *s*; 2nd, 1922, Barbara, *widow* of Edmund Hartley, Lancs Fusiliers. *Educ:* Cheltenham College; Sandhurst. ADC to the Viceroy, India, Nov. 1914–March 1916; Adjutant, 1st Durham LI, 1917–19; Adjutant, 3rd Reserve Bn Durham LI, 1921–22; Adjutant, 1st Batt. Durham Light Infantry, 1922–25; commanded 2nd Bn Durham Light Infantry, 1936–38; retired pay, 1938; Comdg ITC The Durham Light Infantry since Sept. 1939. Served European War (despatches, DSO); 3rd Afghan War, 1919; Producer, Northern Command Tattoo, 1934. *Address:* c/o Glyn, Mills & Co., Kirkland House, Whitehall, SW1.

Died 3 Jan. 1942.

HASTIE, Edward, FRIBA; *b* 1876; *m* 1904, Nellie Bond Newton; one *d. Educ:* Burgess School; private tutor. Pupil of Ernest Newton, ARA, FRIBA, 1896. Joined Sir Frank M. Elgood, 1904; became partner 1919; firm now Hastie, Winch and Kelly; work almost entirely domestic architecture. Principal works; Bisley Pavilion for the National Rifle Association; The Lord Roberts Memorial Workshops at Brompton Road, Fulham, and Liverpool; Gordon House, Welbeck Street; Eastgate House, Eastcastle Street, Nos 72–74a and Nos 79–80, Margaret Street; designed Power Stations at Peterborough,

Blackburn, Preston and Hams Hall, Birmingham. *Recreations:* water colour sketching, yacht racing, ski-ing and skating. *Address:* 1 Bentinck Street, Welbeck Street, W1. *T:* Welbeck 8863; Boyle Lodge, Thames Ditton. *T:* Emberbrook 2239.

Died 23 March 1947.

HASTINGS, Frank, CBE 1919; *b* 1869. Chairman of Serbian Red Cross in Great Britain; Order of White Eagle of Serbia. *Address:* 40 Hillfield Road, W Hampstead, NW6.

Died 22 Oct. 1940.

HASTINGS, Col Sir George, Kt 1910; MD, VD; Knight of Grace of the Order of St John; *b* 1853; *s* of George Hastings of Terrington, Norfolk; *m* 1878, Alice (*d* 1931), *d* of late W. P. Frith, RA, CVO; two *d. Educ:* London University; St Bartholomew's Hospital. For many years physician to Banks; late consulting physician to the Gas Light and Coke Co.; late Surgeon Colonel Middlesex Hussars; Chairman of Ranelagh Club for 40 years; President of Coaching Club. *Publications:* various medical works. *Recreation:* sport of all kinds. *Address:* 1 The Albany, Piccadilly, W1. *T:* Regent 1997.

Died 13 Aug. 1943.

HASWELL, Col John Francis, CIE 1920; VD; TD; MD; late Commanding 2/4th Border Regiment; *b* 1864; *s* of late Francis Robert Newton Haswell, Monkseaton; *m* 1895, Frances Mary, *d* of William Little, JP, Hutton Hall, Penrith. *Educ:* Leys School, Cambridge; Edinburgh University, MB, CM 1886, MD 1898. Served S Africa, 1900–01 (Queen's medal with three clasps); European War, 1914–19; Afghan War, 1919 (CIE). *Address:* The Friarage, Penrith.

Died 3 Feb. 1949.

HATFIELD, William Herbert, FRS 1935; Director of Research, Director of Thos Firth and John Brown, Ltd, Sheffield; Director of Firth Vickers Stainless Steels, Ltd, Sheffield; *b* 10 April 1882; *s* of Francis Albert Hatfield and Martha Sheppard; *m* 1907, Edith Marian Seagrave; no *c. Educ:* Sheffield University College; Sheffield University. DMet (Sheffield), FCS, FInstP, MInst MechE; Fellow Institution Chemical Engineering. Vice-President Iron and Steel Institute; Chairman Heterogeneity Committee and Corrosion Committee, Iron and Steel Inst.; Member Iron and Steel Research Council; Mappin Medallist (Sheffield), 1902; Bessemer Gold Medal Iron and Steel Inst., 1933; Compton Medal Institution of Automobile Engineers, 1929; Campbell Memorial Lecturer, Philadelphia, USA, 1928; Commenced industrial experience in the works of Sir Henry Bessemer and Co. Ltd, Sheffield. *Publications:* Cast Iron in the Light of Recent Research, 1912; The Application of Science in the Steel Industry, 1928; many scientific and technical papers to various Institutions, including Royal Society, Royal Institution, Iron and Steel Institute, Institute of Mechanical Engineers, Royal Aero Society, Institute of Automobile Engineers, etc. *Recreations:* golf and literature. *Address:* Brincliffe House, Osborne Road, Sheffield. *Club:* Athenæum.

Died 17 Oct. 1943.

HATHAWAY, Frank John, MD; Surgeon, King Edward VII Hospital Windsor; *s* of late John Hathaway, Allahabad; *m* 1902, Rose Mabel Bunyard; two *s* one *d. Educ:* Aldenham; Edinburgh University. House Surgeon several hospitals; Civil Surgeon, South African War; practice in Windsor as a surgeon since 1903; Surgical Specialist in France during European War for two years. *Publications:* contributions to various medical periodicals. *Recreation:* golf. *Address:* Langholm, Osborne Road, Windsor. *T:* Windsor 51.

Died 28 Jan. 1942.

HATHAWAY, Maj.-Gen. Harold George, CB 1914; late Army Medical Service; *b* 30 June 1860; *s* of late T. Hathaway; *m* 1899, Cécile Marie, *d* of late W. B. Scomes, of 82 Queen's Gate, South Kensington; one *s.*

Educ: King's School, Rochester; St Bartholomew's Hospital, London. Joined Army 1885; Active Service in Burma, including Ruby Mine Expedition, 1885–89 (medal and two clasps); Chitral Relief Expedition, 1895 (medal and clasp); Punjab Frontier and Tirah Expedition (two clasps); South Africa as Medical Officer, Cavalry Divisional Staff, took part in all engagements with Cavalry Division throughout war; dangerously wounded at Diamond Hill (promoted for distinguished conduct in the field, medal with five clasps); European War, 1914–16 (despatches); Kut-al-Amara. *Recreation:* for four years master of Peshawar Vale Hounds. *Address:* Tan y Castell, Deganwy, North Wales.

Died 3 Sept. 1942.

HATHERTON, 4th Baron *cr* 1835; **Edward Charles Rowley Littleton;** DL, JP; *b* 6 Aug. 1868; *e s* of 3rd Baron and Charlotte (*d* 1923), 7th *d* of Sir Charles R. Rowley, 4th Bt; *S* father, 1930; *m* 1897, Hester Edith, *d* of late T. T. Hoskins, MD, of Tasmania; *three s* five *d. Educ:* Eton. Late Lieut 3rd Bn North Staffs Regt; in service of Rajah Sarawak, 1890–96. *Heir: s* of Hon. Edward Thomas Walhouse Littleton, RN (retired), [*b* 13 Aug. 1900; *m* 1925, Ida Guendolen, *d* of Robin Legge; two *d.* Davan Hollow House, Denham, Bucks]. *Address:* Hatherton Hall, Cannock, Staffs; Teddesley Park, Penkridge, Staffs.

Died 10 Nov. 1944.

HATTEN, Rev. Prebendary John Charles Le Pelley, MA, Hon. CF; Prebendary of Colworth in Chichester Cathedral since 1931; *b* 17 Aug. 1875; *s* of late Rev. Charles William Hatten, Rector of Bodle Street Green, and Rozalie Jane Palmer De Verinne; *m* 1909, Lilian Frances Susan Kingsford (decd); no *c. Educ:* Grantham Grammar School; Selwyn College, Cambridge, MA; Scholae Cancellanii, Lincoln. Curate of S Wilfrid's, Haywards Heath, Sussex, 1899–1904; Dallington, Sussex, 1904–06; S Michael's, Headingley, Yorkshire, 1906–08; Ewhurst, Sussex, 1908–11; T. C. F. 1917–18; Rector, 1911–34 and Rural Dean, 1924–34, of Dallington; Rector of Uckfield, 1935–38; Prov. Grand Chaplain of Sussex (Freemasons), 1933. *Address:* 78 West Hill, St Leonards-on-Sea.

Died 30 Jan. 1943.

HAULTAIN, Hon. Sir Frederick William Gordon, Kt 1916; *b* Charlton, Kent, 25 Nov. 1857; *s* of late Lieut-Col F. W. Haultain, RA; *m* 1938, *widow* of W. B. Gilmour, Montreal. *Educ:* Toronto Univ. Member of North-West Council, 1887–88; Member of North-West Legislative Assembly, 1888–1905; Premier, Attorney-General and Commissioner of Education, North-West Territories, Canada, 1891–1905; Member of Legislative Assembly, Province of Saskatchewan, and Leader of Opposition, 1905–12; Chief Justice of Supreme Court, Saskatchewan, 1912–38. *Address:* Regina, Saskatchewan, Canada. *Clubs:* Assiniboia, Regina.

Died 30 Jan. 1942.

HAUPTMANN, Gerhart Johann Robert; Hon. Dr, Oxford 1905, Leipzig 1909, Prague, 1921, Columbia University 1932; Senator of the German Academy Munich 1925; Ehrenmitglied der Universität Wien; Mitglied der Preusz. Academy, Abtlg.f.Dichtkunst; Corr. Mitglied der Acad. der Columbia University; Correspond. Mitglied der Academy Athen.; Hon. President, German Society, Oxford; German dramatist, novelist and poet; *b* Ober-Salzbrunn, Silesia, 15 Nov. 1862; *s* of Robert Hauptmann, and Marie Strähler; *m* 1st, 1885, Marie Thienemann; *three s*; 2nd, 1904, Margarete Marschalk; one *s. Educ:* Acad. of Arts, Breslau; University of Jena. Received; Grillparzer-Preis of the kaiserl. Akad. der Wissenschft. Wien 1896, 1898, 1900; Nobel-Prize for Literature 1912; Goethe-Preis, 1932; Ordre Royal du Sauveur Athen 1909; Maximilian-Orden f.Wiss.u.Kunst 1911; Roter-Adler-Orden mit der Krone IV Kl. 1915; Rote-Kreuz-Medaille Adlerschild d. Deutschen Reiches 1922; Pour le mérite (Friedensklasse), Burgtheater-Ring Wien 1929; Preusz. Staats-medaille für Verdienste um den Staat, Berlin 1932; Groszes Ehrenzeichen mit dem Stern Austria 1932; Ehrenbürger: Hirschberg 1912; Breslau 1922. *Publications: Dramas:* Vor Sonnenaufgang, 1889; Das Friedensfest, 1890; Einsame Menschen, 1891; Die Weber, 1892; College Crampton, 1892; Der Biberpelz, 1893; Hanneles Himmelfahrt, 1894; Florian Geyer, 1896; Die versunkene Glocke, 1897; Fuhrmann Henschel, 1899; Helios, 1899; Schluck und Jau, 1900; Michael Kramer, 1900; Der rote Hahn, 1901; Der arme Heinrich, 1902; Rose Bernd, 1903; Elga, 1905; Und Pippa tanzt, 1906; Das Hirtenlied, 1906; Die Jungfern vom Bischofsberg, 1907; Kaiser Karls Geisel, 1908; Griselda, 1909; Die Ratten, 1911; Gabriel Schillings flucht, 1912; Festspiel in deutschen Reimen, 1913; Der Bogen des Odysseus, 1913; Die Winterballade, 1917; Der weisze Heiland, Indipohdi, 1920; Peter Brauer, 1921; Veland, 1924; Dorothea Angermann, 1925; Spuk, 1929; Vor Sonnenuntergang, 1932; Die goldene Harfe, 1933; Hamlet in Wittenberg, 1935. *Epik works:* Promethidenlos, 1885; Der Apostel, Bahnwärter Thiel, 1892; Griechischer Frühling, 1908; Der Narr in Christo Emanuel Quint, 1910; Atlantis, 1912; Lohengrin, Parcival (for children) 1913; Der Ketzer von Soana, 1918; Anna, 1921; Fasching, Phantom, 1922; Ausblicke, 1922; Die Insel der Groszen Mutter, 1923; Die blaue Blume, Till Eulenspiegel, 1927; Wanda, 1928; Buch der Leidenschaft, 1929; Spitzhacke, Drei Reden 1930; Hochzeit auf Buchenhorst, 1931; Um Volk und Geist, 1932; Das Meerwunder, 1934; Im Wirbel der Berufung, 1935; Das Abenteuer meiner Jugend, 1937. *Lyrik:* Bas bunte Buch, 1888; Sonette, 1920; Gesammelte Werke: deutsch: Ges. W. in 12 Bdn 1922; engl.: The Dramatic Works 9 vol. New York, 1913–1929; Ulrich von Lichtenstein, Komödie, 1939. *Address:* Der Wiesentein, Agnetendorf im Riesengebirge, Germany. *T:* Hermsdorf-Kynast 325.

Died 8 June 1946.

HAVILAND, Ven. Francis Ernest. Curate of St Peter's Cathedral, Armidale, 1883; Incumbent of Woodburn, 1883–87; St Matthew's, South Grafton, 1887–92; St Luke, Gulgong, 1892–1904; Rector of Bourke, 1904–07; Cobar, 1907–18; Coonamble, 1918–23; O'Connell, 1923–25; Portland 1925–32; Rural Dean, Rylstone, 1902–04; Archdeacon of Bourke, 1904–23; Archdeacon of Mudgee 1923–32; retired as Archdeacon Emeritus. *Address:* Austinmer, NSW.

Died 14 Aug. 1945.

HAWES, Col Benjamin Reddie, CB 1902; *b* 17 March 1854; *s* of late Captain Hawes, 2nd Bengal Fusiliers; married. *Educ:* Stonyhurst Coll. Entered 2nd Royal Munster Fusiliers (then 104th Bengal Fusiliers) from the Militia, 1875; served Burmese campaign, 1886–88, and South African War, 1900–02 (despatches, Queen's medal 2 clasps, King's medal 2 clasps, CB); promoted Lieut-Colonel, 1900; commanding 2nd Batt. Royal Irish Rifles, 1900–04, 26th Batt. Manchester Regt, 1915–16. *Address:* Clifton House, Monkstown, Co. Dublin. *Clubs:* Royal St George Yacht, Kingstown.

Died 22 Dec. 1941.

HAWK, William, CBE 1918; late Chairman of the Cornwall County Council, and Chairman Cornwall War Agricultural Executive Committee; *b* 1851; *m* 1890, Florence, *d* of John Clemence, Howton, Cornwall. *Address:* Kernock, St Mellion, Cornwall.

Died 6 Jan. 1944.

HAWKE, Sir (John) Anthony, Kt 1928; KC 1913; **The Hon. Mr Justice Hawke;** Judge of the King's Bench Division since 1928; a Bencher of the Middle Temple; *b* 1869; *s* of Edward H. Hawke; *m* 1894, Winifred, *d* of late N. H. Stevens; one *s* one *d. Educ:* Merchant Taylors' School; St John's College, Oxford (scholar, MA, 1st Cl. Law, Hon. Fellow of the College). Called to bar, Middle Temple, 1892; joined Western Circuit, 1893; late

Attorney-General to the Prince of Wales; late Recorder of Plymouth; MP (U) St Ives Division of Cornwall, 1922–23, and 1924–28; Member of Bar Council since 1908; Vice-Chairman, 1926. *Recreation:* golf. *Address:* 1 Essex Court, Temple, EC4; 76 Carlisle Mansions, SW1. *Clubs:* Carlton, Garrick; Devon and Exeter, Exeter; Royal Western Yacht, Plymouth.

Died 30 Oct. 1941.

HAWKEN, Roger William Hercules, BA, ME (Sydney), MInstCE; MIEA; Professor of Engineering, University of Queensland, since 1919; *b* 12 May 1878; *s* of late Hon. Nicholas Hawken, MLC; *m* Adelaide, *d* of late Charles Mott, Armidale, NSW; five *d*. *Educ:* Public Schools Darlington, Newtown; Newington College, Sydney, Univ. of Sydney, BE, 1900; BA, 1902; ME, 1919. With Public Works Dept, Sydney, 1902–03; Acting Professor of Engineering, Sch. of Mines, Ballarat, 1904; Federated Malay States, 1905–09; Shire Engineer, NSW, 1910–11; Locum Tenens Prof. of Engineering, Sydney, 1912; Lecturer and Acting Professor Univ. of Queensland, 1912–18; President Institution of Engineers, Australia, 1923; President Roy. Soc. of Queensland, 1925; Chairman Cross-River Commission, Brisbane City Council, 1925–26; Representative of State of Queensland to Council Standards Association of Australia. *Publications:* papers on Influence Lines, Deflections using Two Origins, Columns, Earth Pressure, Flood Discharge, Bridge Location, Traditions, Economy of Purchase, Imperfect Supports, University and the Professions. *Recreation:* bowls. *Address:* Kidston Street, Albion Heights, Brisbane, Queensland. *T:* M 1914. *Clubs:* University (Sydney); Johnsonian (Brisbane).

Died 18 Oct. 1947.

HAWKES, Maj.-Gen. Sir Henry Montague Pakington, KCB 1911; CB 1904; CSI 1909; Indian Army; *b* 28 Aug. 1855; *s* of late Col R. Hawkes, 80th Regt; *m* 1889, Mary Isabel Jessie, *d* of Charles Woodgate, late of Under River, Kent. *Educ:* Wellington College. Entered army, 1872; Captain, 1884; Major, 1892; Lieut-Col 1898; Col 1901; Maj.-Gen. 1905; served Afghan War, 1879–80, present at march from Kabul to Kandahar and battle of Kandahar (despatches, medal with clasp, bronze star); Isazai Expedition, 1892; Tirah, 1897–98 (medal with two clasps). *Club:* United Service.

Died 3 April 1946.

HAWKESWORTH, Sir (Edward) Gerald, KCMG 1948 (CMG 1943); MC 1918; *s* of Rev. John and Frances Hawkesworth; unmarried. *Educ:* St Bees School; Queen's College, Oxford. Grenadier Guards, 1916–19; Nigerian Administrative Service, 1921–41; Chief Commissioner of Ashanti, Gold Coast, 1941–46; Governor and C-in-C, British Honduras, 1947–48; retired 1948. *Recreation:* golf. *Club:* Guards'.

Died 14 Aug. 1949.

HAWKESWORTH, Lt-Gen. Sir John Ledlie Inglis, KBE 1945; CB 1943; CBE 1940; DSO 1943 (and Bar, 1945); *b* 19 Feb. 1893; *m* 1919, Helen Jane, *d* of D. N. McNaughton; one *s*. *Educ:* St Bees School; Queen's College, Oxford. Served European War, 1914–16 (wounded thrice, OBE); Director of Military Training, War Office, 1940; Comdr of 4th Division BNAF, 1942–43; commanding 46th Div., 1943–44; comd. 10 Corps, 1944–45; commander Legion of Merit, 1945. *Address:* Littlecote, Firwood Drive, Camberley, Surrey. *T:* Camberley 1526. *Club:* Army and Navy.

Died 3 June 1945.

HAWKINS, Percy, CIE 1926; MInstCE; *b* 10 Sept. 1870; *s* of late Frederic Charles Hawkins; *m* 1898, Edith Maud (*d* 1908), *d* of late William Pendlebury; one *s* one *d*. *Educ:* King's College; The Royal Indian Engineering College, Cooper's Hill. Joined the Indian PWD, 1894; Under Secretary for Public Works, Government of Madras, 1908; Under Secretary for Public Works,

Government of India, 1911; Deputy Secretary for Public Works, Government of India, 1913; Secretary for Public Works and Chief Engineer for Irrigation, 1923; Member of the Legislative Council, 1924. *Address:* 37 Ellesmere Road, Chiswick, W4. *T:* Chiswick, 3937.

Died 15 May 1949.

HAWKINS, Col Thomas Henry, CMG 1917; late RMLI; *b* 3 May 1873; *s* of T. H. Hawkins, FRCS; *m* Margaret, *d* of James Whishaw, Petrograd; four *s* four *d*. *Educ:* Clifton College, 1884–90. 2nd Lieut RM 1891; Captain, 1899; Major, 1910; Lt-Col, 1917; Col retired, 1919. *Address:* Locksley, Formby, Lancs. *T:* Formby 19.

Died 28 Dec. 1944.

HAWLEY, Willis Chatman, AM; *b* Monroe, Oregon, 5 May 1864; *e s* of Sewel R. Hawley and Emma A. Noble; *m* 1885, Anna M. of Albany, Oregon, *e d* of John Geisendorfer; two *s* one *d*. *Educ:* Willamette University, Salem, Oregon; AB, AM, LLB; hon. LLD 1909. Principal, Umpqua Academy, Wilbur, Oregon, 1884–86; President Oregon State Normal, Drain, Oregon, 1888–91; Professor Mathematics Willamette University, 1891–93; President of Willamette Univ., 1893–1902; Vice-Pres. and Dean, 1902–07; Professor of American History and Economics, 1893–1907; Member of Congress First District of Oregon, 1907–33; Head Manager Woodmen of the World, 1896–1936; was regularly admitted to the Bar in Oregon and to district and circuit courts of the United States and of the United States Supreme Court; Member of Committee on Ways and Means; Member of National Forest Reservation Commission; appointed as Member of Joint Committee of the Senate and House of Representatives on Federal Farm Loans, created by Act of 1915, and of the Select Committee on the Budget, and a member of Joint Commission of the Senate and House on the Celebration of the Two Hundredth Anniversary of the Birth of George Washington; Member of the Federal Tax Commission; Chairman of Caucus of the Republicans of the House of Representatives for the Sixty-ninth, Seventieth, Seventy-first and Seventy-second Congresses; taxation and tariff expert. *Recreation:* flower gardening. *Address:* 989 Oak Street, Salem, Oregon, USA. *Club:* The Elks (Salem).

Died 24 July 1941.

HAWORTH, Sir Arthur Adlington, 1st Bt *cr* 1911; JP Co. Chester and Shropshire; *b* 22 Aug. 1865; *e s* of late Abraham Haworth, JP, Altrincham; *m* Lily, *y d* of late John Rigby, Altrincham; one *s* two *d*. *Educ:* Rugby School. Business in Manchester; Chairman Manchester Grammar School; Chairman Manchester League of Nations Union; Treasurer, Mansfield College, Oxford; MP (L) South Manchester, 1906–12; Junior Lord of the Treasury, Feb.–April 1912; Chm. Manchester Royal Exchange; Major 1st Vol. Bn Cheshire Regt. *Recreations:* hunting, shooting, fishing. *Heir:* *s* Arthur Geoffrey [*b* 5 April 1896; *m* 1926, Emily Dorothea, *er d* of H. E. Gaddum, The Priory, Bowdon]. *Address:* Normanby, Altrincham. *Clubs:* Reform, National Liberal; Reform, Union, Manchester.

Died 31 Aug. 1944.

HAWORTH, Rev. James, MA; Hon. Canon of Durham Cathedral, 1903; *b* Bank Hey, Blackburn, 17 Dec. 1853; *m*. *Educ:* Foundation Scholar of Durham University; BA 1878, MA 1881. Vice-Principal of the Diocesan Training College, Winchester, 1879–84; Deacon, 1879; Priest, 1880; Curate of Wyke, 1879–81; Vice-Principal St Hild's College, Durham, 1885–89; Curate in charge of St Mary-le-Bow, Durham, 1888–1910; Principal of St Hild's College, Durham, 1889–1910; Vicar of Haswell, Sunderland, 1910–13; Vicar of South Hetton, 1913–38; Hon. Sec. Durham Diocesan Board of Education, 1892–1906. *Recreation:* walking. *Address:* Gordon Mount, The Peth, Durham. *TA:* Gordon Mount, Durham. *T:* Durham 323.

Died 6 April 1942.

HAWORTH, Sir (Walter) Norman, Kt 1947; FRS 1928; DSc, PhD; Hon. DSc Belfast, Zürich and Oslo; Hon. ScD (Cantab); Hon. LLD Manchester); *b* 19 March 1883; 2nd *s* of Thomas Haworth, White Coppice, Chorley, Lancashire; *m* 1922, Violet Chilton, 2nd *d* of late Sir James Dobbie, LLD, FRS; two *s*. *Educ*: Schools in Chorley and Preston, and privately; University of Manchester and University of Göttingen. Senior Demonstrator in Chemistry, Imperial College, S Kensington, London, until 1912; Reader in Chemistry, University of St Andrews, until 1920; Professor and Director of the Chemistry Department of Kings College, Newcastle, University of Durham, 1920–25; Professor of Chemistry and Director of Department of Chemistry in University of Birmingham, 1925–48; Vice-Principal, University of Birmingham, 1947–48; President, Chemical Society, 1944–46, Longstaff Medallist, 1933; Davy Medallist, Royal Society, 1934, Royal Medallist, 1942; Bakerian Lecturer, Roy. Society, 1944; Vice-Pres., Roy. Society, 1947–48; Nobel Prize for Chemistry, 1937; Mem. Atomic Scientists' Assoc.; Chm. Chemistry Research Board, 1947. Hon. Mem. Acad. Sciences, Haarlem, Brussels, Munich, Vienna, Finland, India, Dublin and Swiss Chemical Soc. *Publications*: scientific papers, published mainly in the Journal of the Chemical Society, on Vitamin C, and on the Constitution of the Terpenes and Carbohydrates. *Address*: Thurcroft, Burnt Green, nr Birmingham. *Club*: Athenæum.

Died 19 March 1950.

HAWTHORN, Brig.-Gen. George Montague Philip, CBE 1923; DSO 1916; *b* 16 Dec. 1873; *s* of late James Kenyon Hawthorn, Sandown, Isle of Wight. *Educ*: Harrow. Entered army, 1894; Bt Col, 1919; Col, 1920; served Ashanti, 1900 (medal); Somaliland, 1902–04 (medal with two clasps); East Africa and Nyasaland, 1914–19 (despatches, DSO, Bt Lt-Col, Bt Col, Croix de Guerre); Inspector-General, King's African Rifles, 1919–23; retired pay, 1923. *Address*: Little Barraer, Newton-Stewart, Wigtownshire.

Died 5 March 1945.

HAY, Maj.-Gen. Arthur Kenneth, DSO 1917; OBE 1919; late RA; *y s* of late Major-General E. O. Hay, CB; *m* 1938, Joan Barbara, *y d* of late N. J. Hughes-Hallett, OBE, DL; one *s*. *Educ*: United Services Coll., Westward Ho!; Royal Military Academy, Woolwich. Entered RH and RFA, 1902; served European War, 1914–18 (despatches four times, DSO, OBE); Staff Coll., Camberley, 1919; Lt-Col 1929; Col 1931; Asst Adjt-General, War Office, 1931–33; Brigadier, General Staff, 1934–35; Commander 8th Infantry Brigade, India, 1935–38; retired pay, 1938; Recalled on outbreak of war as Brigadier, General Staff; Acting Major-General, 1941; reverted to retired pay, 1942. *Address*: The Malt House, Warmington, nr Peterborough.

Died 19 April 1949.

HAY, Clifford Henderson, CMG 1921; CBE 1928; MVO 1920; President of Superannuation Board of NSW since 1940; *b* 22 April 1878; *s* of Thomas Davidson Hay, of Woodville, South Australia; *m* 1907, Lucille, *d* of George Herbert Westcott, Sydney; three *s*. *Educ*: Sydney Grammar School. Chief Clerk and Accountant of the Premier's Department, 1914; Under-Secretary and Permanent Head of the Premier's Department of New South Wales, and General Secretary of Conferences of Premiers of the Australian States, 1916–38; Agent-General for New South Wales, 1938–40; organised the visit of the French Mission, 1918, the Prince of Wales, 1920, the British Special Service Squadron, 1924, the United States Battleship Fleet, 1925, the Duke and Duchess of York, 1927, the Duke of Gloucester, 1934; King's Silver Jubilee Medal, 1935; Coronation Medal, 1937; Officer of the Order of Nichan Iftikhar (French), 1924; FRGS (Australia) 1919;

FRCI (London), 1921, FIIS 1933; JP 1916. *Recreations*: fishing and bowls. *Address*: 43 Milson Road, Cremorne, NSW. *Clubs*: Royal Automobile; Millions (Sydney).

Died 16 Dec. 1949.

HAY, Douglas, MC, BSc Hons Lond. MInstCE; Chief Mining Engineer to National Coal Board since 1946; Hon. Professor of Mining, Sheffield University; *s* of W. Hay, mining engineer, Sheffield, and Emily, *d* of late R. Rhodes of Canterbury. *Educ*: King Edward VI Grammar School, E Retford; Nottingham University College. 1st Class Colliery Manager's Certificate, 1910; James Forrest Medallist and Miller Prizeman of Institution of Civil Engineers, 1912; Manby Premium, 1927. HM Inspector of Mines in Durham, 1912–14; active service in France, RFA and latterly Royal Engineers, Field Survey, 1914–19; HM Inspector of Mines, Durham and N Staffs, 1920–22; Professor of Mining, Sheffield University, 1922–25; Member Departmental Committee on Training and Qualification of Mine Officials, 1929–30; Consulting Engineer on Ventilation of the Mersey Tunnel, 1929–37; Past Pres., Institution of Mining Engineers. *Publications*: various contributions to Proceedings of Institution of Mining Engineers, and Institution of Civil Engineers. *Address*: Wimborne, Guildford Road, Woking.

Died 24 Feb. 1949.

HAY, Ven. Edgar; Archdeacon of Barnstaple, 1935–45, Archdeacon Emeritus since 1945; *b* 14 Dec. 1863; *s* of Richard H. Hay, Mutford Hall, Suffolk, and Augusta, *d* of Joseph Edgar; *m* 1895, Emily (*d* 1949), *d* of Captain Francis James Hugonin, Nursted House, Hants. *Educ*: S Paul's School; Corpus Christi College, Cambridge. BA, 1885; MA, 1889. Deacon, 1886; Priest, 1887; Rector Carlton Colville, Lowestoft, 1894–97; Plymtree, Devon, 1897–1929; Rector of S Lawrence with All Hallows (Goldsmith Street), S Martin, S Paul and S Stephen, Exeter, 1929–45; Prebendary of Exeter Cathedral, 1920–45. Rural Dean of Ottery, 1908–20; Proctor in Convocation since 1918; Mem. in charge of Church Assembly measures, Ecclesiastical Dilapidations, 1923, Widows' Pensions, 1936, etc.; Mem. Central Board of Finance, 1916–48, Central Board of Pensions 1929–47, Vice-Chairman, 1939, and Chairman Widows Pensions Committee, 1936; Honorary Sec. Diocesan Board of Finance, 1905–08 and 1922–27 and of Diocesan Clergy Maintenance Committee, 1905–45; Honiton RDC and Guardians, 1917–22. *Publication*: Plymtree in Devon, its Parish Church, etc. *Recreations*: formerly: rowing (TRC), swimming, golf, chess. *Address*: Wedderlie, 30 Mount Ararat Road, Richmond, Surrey. *Club*: United University.

Died 19 Dec. 1949.

HAY, Lord Edward (Douglas John); late Major 2nd Bn Grenadier Guards; *brother* and *heir-pres.* of 11th Marquess of Tweeddale; *b* 2 Nov. 1888; *m* 1st, 1917, Bridget (*d* 1926), *o d* of Major Cameron Barclay, 10th Royal Hussars; one *s* one *d*; 2nd, 1928, Audrey Birkin, *yr d* of Sir Thomas Latham, 1st Bt; one *d*. *Educ*: Eton; Magdalen College, Oxford. Lieut Grenadier Guards, 1913; Acting Capt. 1918; Capt. 1920. Served European War, France, Gallipoli, Egypt, 1918; Major, 1928; retired pay, 1930; served on Peace Conference, Paris, 1918–19; Special Missions to Austria, Hungary, and Bulgaria; Staff Captain to Gen. Sir Edmund Ironside on special mission to Hungary and Roumania, 1921; Military Secretary to Rt Hon. Sir Herbert Samuel, High Commissioner in Palestine, 1921–23. *Address*: Hill Hall, Theydon Mount, Essex. *Clubs*: Turf, Guards'.

Died 18 June 1944.

HAY, Maj.-Gen. Edward Owen, CB 1903; RA; retired 1908; *b* 24 Oct. 1846; *e s* of late Admiral J. B. L. Hay; *m* 1870, Helena (*d* 1915), *d* of late Admiral Sir J. Crawford Caffin, KCB; three *s*. *Educ*: Rugby; Clifton College; RMA, Woolwich. Entered army, 1867; Captain, 1879; Major, 1884; Lt-Colonel, 1894; Colonel, 1898; served

Egypt, 1882, including Tel-el-Kebir (despatches, bt Major, medal with clasp, 4th class Medjidie, Khedive's Star); commanded troops at Ladysmith, Natal, 1897–99; AAG, RA, War Office, 1899–1903; Major-General on Staff commanding RA of 2nd Army Corps, 1903–05; Administrative General Southern Command, 1905–07; Colonel Commandant Royal Artillery, 1917. *Address:* Brent Tor, Tunbridge Wells. *Club:* National.

Died 3 May 1946.

HAY, Francis Edward Drummond, MVO 1908; *b* 17 Aug. 1868; *s* of late Sir Francis R. Drummond-Hay; *m* 1895, Eveline Anstey-Bennett, MBE; two *s. Educ:* Marlborough. Was employed in the Consulate-General at Tripoli, and the Consulate at Cadiz, 1887–91; was employed as clerk to the Legation at Tangier, 1891; passed an examination, and was appointed Vice-Consul at Algiers, 1895; Acting Consul-General, 1895, 1896, 1898, 1899, 1900, 1902, 1903, 1904, 1905; Vice-Consul, Taranto, Italy, 1897; Vice-Consul, Bremerhaven, 1905; Consul in the Faröe Islands, 1906; Consul for Southern Morocco, 1906; Consul for Norway, 1906–10; Loanda, 1910–13; Dantzig, 1913–14; Bahia, 1915; Acting Consul-General, Rio de Janeiro, 1915–19; Consul-General, Lyons, 1919–24; Consul at Nantes, 1924–28, and Consul-General, 1928–29; retired, 1929; Member Royal Company of Archers (King's Body Guard for Scotland); Jubilee Medal, 1935; Coronation Medal, 1937. *Address:* Tigh Grianach, Dunkeld, Perthshire. *T:* Dunkeld 260.

Died 31 Jan. 1943.

Hay, Col George Lennox, CBE 1919; DSO 1917; late Royal Army Ordnance Corps; *b* 1873; *s* of the late Col Sir George Jackson Hay, KCB, CMG; *m* 1904, Edith Almena, *d* of the Hon. Clarence Peniston, Bermuda. Served European War, 1914–18 (despatches five times, DSO, CBE); retired pay, 1922.

Died 3 Nov. 1946.

HAY, Captain John Primrose, MA, BSc; *b* 1878. *Educ:* University, Glasgow and University, London. Lecturer in Mathematics, Manchuria Christian College, 1906–15; MP (Lab) Cathcart Division of Glasgow, 1922–23. *Address:* 10 Stamperland Crescent, Clarkston, Glasgow.

Died 5 Dec. 1949.

HAY, Rt Rev. Robert Snowdon; Bishop of Tasmania since 1919; *b* Bishop Auckland, Durham, 1867; *γ s* of late James Hay of Bishop Auckland; *m* 1897, Maud Caroline, 2nd *d* of late William Joseph Glenny, of King's College, London; three *s* four *d. Educ:* Bishop Barrington's School; King James I Grammar School, Bishop Auckland; Hatfield Hall, Durham University (Open Theological Scholar and Exhibitioner); LTh (3rd class), BA, DD (Hon.) Fellow of Australian College of Theology. Master at Durston House School, Ealing; Deacon, 1891; Priest, 1894; held curacies at Leadgate and South Hylton, Sunderland; Rector of Laidley, 1897 (Brisbane, Queensland); then of Bundaberg and Warwick; Member of Australian General Synod, and Queensland Provincial Synod; Member of Diocesan Council; Hon. Canon of Brisbane, 1909–16; Rector, St Andrew's, South Brisbane, 1911–16; Dean of St David's Cathedral, Hobart, 1916–19; Chaplain 1st Class, Australian Military Forces; (Military decoration); Member of Royal Society, Tasmania; President British and Foreign Bible Society, Tasmania; President United Social Service of Tasmania. *Recreations:* represented University, also Durham County, in Assoc. football; cricket, hockey, etc. *Address:* Bishopscourt, Hobart, Tasmania. *T:* Central 1728. *Clubs:* Rotarian, Hobart.

Died 3 Feb. 1943.

HAY, Stephen Moffatt, MD, CM, LSA, MCPSO; *b* Wellington Co., Canada, 1857; *s* of Robert Hay, JP, and Mary Moffatt Hay; *m* 1887, Carrie, *d* of Dr W. W. Ogden; two *d. Educ:* Guelph; St Catherine's, Toronto; London, England. Born on farm; worked there until 21

years old; studied medicine in Toronto, Canada, London, and Edinburgh; for some years examiner on Diseases of Women for College of Physicians and Surgeons of Ontario; Chief of Surgical Service, Toronto Western Hospital; Associate Professor of Clinical Surgery, Toronto University; Consulting Surgeon, Toronto Orthopedic Hospital; retired. *Publications:* General Septic Peritonitis; Diagnosis and Treatment of Acute Perforations of Stomach and Duodenum; The Language of the Abdomen, etc. *Recreations:* motoring, golf, launching. *Address:* 224 Dunvegan Road, Toronto, Canada. *T:* Mohawk 6840.

Died 11 June 1943.

HAY, Col Westwood Norman, CIE 1917, DSO 1918; *b* 1871; *m* 1899, Violet Maud, *d* of A. W. Cowdell; two *s* three *d. Educ:* Haileybury; Royal Military Academy, Woolwich. Served China, 1900 (medal); East Africa, 1917–18 (DSO, wounded); Afghanistan, 1919; NWF India, 1919–20; Waziristan, 1920–21; retired, 1923. *Address:* Hayfield, Lerwick, Shetland.

Died 3 Sept. 1946.

HAY, Will; actor (film, stage and radio); *b* 6 Dec. 1888; *s* of late W. R. Hay, Aberdeen, and late Elizabeth Ebden, Spennymoor; *m* 1907; one *s* two *d. Educ:* London; Manchester. Apprenticed to Engineering trade; went on Stage, 1909; into Films, 1934; toured the world, 1923–24; USA 1927; S Africa, 1928–29; Sub-Lieut RNVR Special Branch, 1942, as Instructor to Sea Cadet Corps; Lieut 1945. *Publication:* Through my Telescope, 1935. *Recreations:* flying, civilian pilot 1925 onwards; astronomy (FRAS, Member British Astronomical Association). *Clubs:* Savage, Eccentric, Royal Automobile.

Died 18 April 1949.

HAY, William Gosse, BA; novelist; *b* Linden, Burnside, South Australia, 17 Nov. 1875; *surv. s* of late Hon. Alexander Hay, MLC, Member first elected Parliament of S Australia, and Agnes Grant, *d* of W. Gosse, MD, FRCS, Colonial Surgeon, South Australia; *m* 1901, Mary Violet, 3rd *d* of late Rev. Francis Williams, MA, Headmaster of St Peter's College, Adelaide; three *s. Educ:* Church of England Grammar School, Melbourne; Trinity College, Cambridge. *Publications:* Stifled Laughter, 1901; Herridge of Reality Swamp, 1907; Captain Quadring, 1912; The Escape of Sir William Heans, 1918; An Australian Rip van Winkle, 1921; Strabane of the Mulberry Hills, 1929; The Mystery of Alfred Doubt, 1937. *Recreations:* has enjoyed deep-sea fishing, fencing, tennis, and real tennis; now walking, reading, woodcarving, golf. *Address:* Nangawooka, Victor Harbour, South Australia; Cragend, Marino Rocks, Adelaide, SA. *T:* Victor Harbour, 61. *Club:* Authors'.

Died 21 March 1945.

HAYDEN, Arthur; Knight of the Order of Dannebrog, 1912; *b* 1868; *m* 1905, Katherine Isabella Poole. Entered Civil Service, Exchequer and Audit Department, 1888; Senior Auditor (Air Ministry), 1921–28. *Publications:* Wedgwood Exhibition Catalogue, 1909; Royal Copenhagen Porcelain, 1911; Bye-Paths in Collecting, 1919; Spode and his Successors, 1925; Old English Porcelain, The Lady Ludlow Collection, 1932; and the following vols in Chats Series for Collectors: English China, 1904; Old Furniture, 1905; Old Prints, 1906; English Earthenware, 1909; Cottage and Farmhouse Furniture, 1912; Old Silver, 1915; Old Clocks, 1917; Royal Copenhagen Porcelain, 1918; Old Sheffield Plate, 1920. *Recreation:* angling. *Address:* 8 Dartmouth Park Road, NW5. *T:* Gulliver 1518.

Died 9 Aug. 1946.

HAYDEN, Mary Teresa, MA; *b* Dublin; *d* of Dr Thomas Hayden, a Dublin physician. *Educ:* various convent schools; Alexandra College, Dublin. Graduated in Royal University of Ireland, taking scholarship in

Modern Languages; BA, 1885; MA, 1887; Junior Fellowship in English and History, 1895; DLitt (Hon.), 1935. Acted as Advising Examiner in History for Intermediate Education Board of Ireland, 1907 and 1912; Professor of Modern Irish History to University College, Dublin, 1911–38; on foundation of National University of Ireland, 1909, was appointed a member of the Senate (the only woman member), and remained a member till 1924; was for many years a member of the Executive of the Gaelic League. *Publications:* (with G. Moonan) A Short History of the Irish People, 1921; various articles on literary and historical subjects. *Address:* 26 Cambridge Road, Dublin.

Died 12 July 1942.

HAYES, Cdre Sir Bertram Fox, KCMG 1920; CMG 1917, DSO 1918; DL; Commodore on retired list, RNR; Master of Hon. Co. of Master Mariners, 1940; *b* 25 April 1864. Served European War, 1914–18 (CMG, DSO). Retired as Commodore of the White Star Line Fleet, Dec. 1924; Director Marconi International Marine Communication Co. Ltd; DL County Palatine of Lancaster, 1931. *Publication:* Hull Down, reminiscences of Windjammers, Troops, and Travellers, 1925. *Address:* Formby Lodge, Blundellsands, Liverpool. *Clubs:* Golfers; Liverpool Constitutional.

Died 15 May 1941.

HAYES, Lt-Col Edwin Charles, CBE 1919; RAMC retired; *b* 1868; *s* of Edwin T. C. Hayes, Solicitor, Dublin; *m* 1909, Minnie Albina (*d* 1920), *d* of late Major Lennard Barrett, RA; one *s* one *d*. *Educ:* High School, Dublin; RC Surgeons, Dublin. LRCP and S Ed. 1894; DPH London, 1905. Entered RAMC, 1896; retired as Lt-Col 1919; served Boxer Expedition, China, 1900–02 (medal); European War, 1914–19 (despatches, CBE); OC 21st Field Ambulance, 7th Division, 1914–15; OC No. 9 General Hospital; OC No. 47 General Hospital. *Recreations:* cricket, golf, tennis, and ski-ing. *Address:* 17 Sion Hill, Bath.

Died 10 Feb. 1942.

HAYES, John Henry; Secretary of British Optical Association; Registrar of Joint Council of Qualified Opticians; Member, Editorial Board of Police Review; *b* 14 Oct. 1889; *s* of Inspector J. W. Hayes, Wolverhampton Police; *m* Ethel, 2nd *d* of St Thomas A. Stroudley, schoolmaster, Albrighton, nr Wolverhampton; one *d*. *Educ:* Formerly Member of Metropolitan Police; contested Edge Hill, Liverpool, 1922; MP (Lab) Edge Hill, Liverpool, 1923–31; Parly Private Secretary, Ministry of Pensions, 1924; a Labour Whip, 1925–31; Vice-Chamberlain of HM Household, 1929–31. *Address:* 65 Brook Street, W1. *T:* Mayfair 3382; 44 Holders Hill Road, Hendon, NW4. *T:* Finchley 2230.

Died 25 April 1941.

HAYES, Lt-Col Joseph, DSO 1918; MD, CAMC; practising specialist, Electro- and Physiotherapy, Halifax, Nova Scotia, Canada; *b* Wingate, County Durham, 23 March 1864; *s* of James Hayes and Mary Jane Patterson; *m* 1888; four *s* two *d*. *Educ:* Public Schools, United States, England, and Nova Scotia; Special Student, University Mount Allison, Sackville, NB, 1884 and 1885; Doctor of Medicine, University Pennsylvania, 1888. Active practice of Medicine, County of Cumberland, Nova Scotia, 1888–1915; Secretary and Organiser, Nova Scotia Liberal-Conservative Association, 1908–15; Unit Medical Director Dept Soldiers Civil Re-establishment, Maritime Provinces, 1919–21; Commissioner, Supreme Court of Nova Scotia; contested Victoria County in the Provincial General Elections of 1915; Surgeon-Major, Canadian Militia, 1893; Lieut-Col 1911; joined CEF Aug. 1915; ADMS Camp, Aldershot, 1915–16; Medical Officer of the 85th Battalion, 8 Feb. 1917; saw continuous service along the Western front from Arras to Passchendaele until 12 April 1918; transferred to No. 12 British General

Hospital, Rouen; Senior Medical Officer Central Group Canadian Forestry Corps, for organisation and administration of the sanitary and medical services; Commanding Officer No. 2 Canadian Stationary Hospital, Outro-sur-la-Boulogne; demobilized Halifax, 19 May 1919 (despatches twice, DSO). *Publications:* The 85th in France and Flanders, 1920; Report of the Tuberculosis Commissioner on a survey of Public Health Centres with reference to Tuberculosis Control, 1927; numerous Public Health and general articles in pamphlets and in press; Nova Scotia Medical Services in the Great War, 1920, as chapter xxvi in Nova Scotia's Part in the Great War. *Address:* 82 Oxford Street, Halifax, Nova Scotia, Canada. *T:* B-5834.

Died 1 March 1944.

HAYES, Lt-Col Robert Hall, CMG 1915; *b* 11 April 1867; *m* 1913, Catherine, *d* of Rev. Hussey Burgh Macartney; one *d*. Entered army, 1885; Captain, 1893; Major, 1902; Lieut-Col, 1912; Commandant Mounted Infantry School, India, 1905–09; served Hazara Expedition, 1891 (medal with clasp); European War, 1914–16 (despatches twice, CMG); Commanded 2nd Batt. Middlesex Regt; retired list, 1917. *Address:* Radipole Manor, nr Weymouth.

Died 23 Aug. 1946.

HAYES, Rt Rev. Romuald; RC Bishop of Rockhampton since 1932; *b* Malvern, Victoria, 1892. *Educ:* St F. Xavier's College, Melbourne; Propaganda College, Rome. Priest, 1917. *Address:* Rockhampton, Queensland, Australia.

Died 25 Oct. 1945.

HAYHURST, William Hosken France-, JP; CC; *b* 1873; *o surv. s* of late Charles Hosken France-Hayhurst and 1st wife, Mary Halsted, *d* of William H. Poole, of Terrick Hall, Salop; *m* 1918, Renée Elizabeth (*d* 1919), *y d* of Gordon Cloëte, Rosebank, Cape Town; one *d*. *Educ:* Eton. Late Capt. Cheshire Yeomanry; High Sheriff of Cheshire, 1929; DL Cheshire, 1930. *Address:* Bostock Hall, Middlewich. *T:* Middlewich 7; Davenham Hall and Whatcroft Hall, Northwich. *Club:* Junior Carlton.

Died 4 March 1947.

HAYLER, Guy; *b* Battle, Sussex, 5 Nov. 1850; *y s* of late George Hayler, Battle, and Mary, *e d* of late John Brignall, Wittersham, Kent; *m* 1874, Ann Elizabeth (*d* 1941), *o d* of late Henry Hartley Harriss, of Maidstone, and *nephew* of late Henry Chambers, JP, of London; four *s* four *d*. *Educ:* Battle and London. World's Electoral Superintendent and Past Grand Counsellor of the International Order of Good Templars; Vice-President of the United Kingdom Alliance; General Secretary North of England Temperance League, 1889–1907; Hon. Sec. Nat. Prohibition, Convention, 1897; Hon. Secretary National Temperance Federation, 1895–1919; President World Prohibition Federation, 1909–39; has travelled extensively. Special Press Commissioner, American Liquor Enquiry, 1901; founded Temperance Institute, Newcastle, 1899. *Publications:* many books and pamphlets on temperance and prohibition. Editor of the Internat. Record; Temperance Witness, 1890–1907; Northern Temperance Year Book, etc. *Recreations:* chess and reading (has one of the most complete private libraries of books on the liquor question in England). *Address:* Courtfield, South Norwood Park, SE25; 32 Buckingham Palace Road, SW1. *T:* Livingstone 2833.

Died 23 Sept. 1943.

HAYMAN, Rev. Canon Henry Telford, MA, TD; Hon. Canon of Wakefield Cathedral, 1933–40; Canon Emeritus, 1940; *b* 20 Nov. 1853; *s* of Charles Christopher Hayman, MD, and Elizabeth Hughes Norton; *m* 1879, Ellen Maria Elizabeth Cobham (*d* 1939), *d* of Dr Cobham Brewer, lexicographer; two *s* one *d*. *Educ:* Bradfield College; Corpus Christi College, Cambridge. Assistant Master of Framlingham College, Suffolk, 1876; ordained 1877; Curate of St Andrew's,

Nottingham, 1877–79; Vicar of Ruddington, Notts, 1879; Vicar of Edwinstowe with Carburton and Perlethorpe, 1884; Rector of Thornhill, 1907–40; 30 years a clergyman in Nottinghamshire and 32 in Yorkshire; 27 years Prov. Grand Superintendent of Royal Arch Masons, Notts; Chaplain of the Robin Hoods, 7th Batt. Sherwood Foresters, for 25 years; 30 years Deputy Provincial Grand Master of Notts; installed Prov. Grand Master of Nottinghamshire, 1933; PG Chaplain of England. *Recreations:* cricket (played in 1874 for Kent), tennis. *Address:* Springfield House, Charlton Kings, Gloucestershire.

Died 8 Feb. 1941.

HAYMES, Lt-Col Robert Leycester, DSO 1915; late RA; *b* 31 Dec. 1870; *o* surv. *s* of Rev. Robert Evered Haymes, formerly of Great Glen, Leicestershire; *m* 1897, Minnie Kathleen, *d* of late Major Wilmot Ellis, RA; three *s* two *d*. *Educ:* Bedford Modern School; Oxford Military College; RMA Woolwich. Entered Army, 1891; Captain, 1899; Instructor in Gunnery, 1905–09; Adjutant, 1909–11; Lt-Col 1917; 2nd in command Malay States Guides, 1911–14; served in Native Mountain Artillery, NW Frontier, India, 1897–1903; European War, 1914–18 (despatches twice, DSO); retired on account of wounds, 1919. *Address:* Pine Cone, New Haw, Weybridge. *T:* Byfleet 450.

Died 16 May 1942.

HAYNES, Edmund Sidney Pollock; *b* London, 26 Sept. 1877; *s* of Edmund Child Haynes, solicitor, and Grace Mary Nicolas, *d* of Sir Richard Pollock, KCSI; *m* 1905, Oriana Huxley Waller; three *d*. *Educ:* Eton College (Scholar); Balliol College, Oxford (Brackenbury Scholar). Articled to Hunter and Haynes of Lincoln's Inn, solicitors, 1900; Knight Commander of the Holy Sepulchre, 1926. *Publications:* Standards of Taste in Art, 1904; Religious Persecution, a Study in Political Psychology, 1904 (popular edition, 1906); Early Victorian and Other Papers, 1908; Divorce Problems of To-Day, 1912; The Belief in Personal Immortality, 1913 and 1925; A Study in Bereavement, a Comedy in One Act, 1914; Divorce as it might be, 1915; The Decline of Liberty in England, 1916; Personalia, 1918 and 1927; The Case for Liberty, 1919; Concerning Solicitors, 1920; The Enemies of Liberty, 1923; Fritto Misto, 1924; Lycurgus or The Future of Law, 1925; Much Ado about Women, 1927; A Lawyer's Notebook, 1932; More from a Lawyer's Notebook, 1933; The Lawyer's Last Notebook, 1934; (with Derek Walker-Smith) Divorce and its Problems, 1935; Life, Law, and Letters, 1936; and articles in various periodicals on anomalies of the marriage laws. *Recreations:* swimming, sculling, music, divorce law reform, and occasional journalism. *Address:* 5 Marlborough Hill, NW8; 9 New Square, Lincoln's Inn, WC. *T:* Primrose 1253, Holborn 3907. *Clubs:* Athenæum, Garrick, Johnson.

Died 5 Jan. 1949.

HAYNES, Brig.-Gen. Kenneth Edward, CMG 1917; CBE 1919; RA; *b* 2 Aug. 1871; *m* 1901; one *s*. *Educ:* Malvern Coll.; R. M. Academy, Woolwich. Entered RA 1890; Captain, 1899; Major, 1911; Brevet Lieut-Col, 1915; Col, 1919; Assistant Superintendent of Experiments, 1901–05; Assistant Superintendent R. Carriage Factory, 1907–12; Superintendent of Experiments, 1913–18; Member of Ordnance Committee, 1918; Vice-President, 1920–23; Superintendent of Design, 1924–25; President Royal Artillery Committee, 1925; Vice-President of the Ordnance Committee, 1927–28; Member, 1925–27; retired pay, 1928; served S Africa, 1900 (Queen's medal 3 clasps); China, 1900 (medal); European War, 1914–17 (CMG). *Address:* High Barn, Charing, Kent. *T:* Charing 77. *Club:* Army and Navy.

Died 28 June 1944.

HAYS, Very Rev. Father Francis; *b* Liverpool, 21 May 1870; *e s* of Francis Hays, London, and Rosanna, *d* of J. Nugent, Co. Westmeath, Ireland. *Educ:* private tutor; London Univ. Schools; Roman Seminary. Primarily intended for the legal profession, he was induced by his friend, Cardinal Manning, to enter the RC priesthood; ordained priest, 1894; ministered at St Barnabas Cathedral, St Patrick's, Nottingham, and founded the Missions at Bridgford and West Leicester; his life-work has been his Christian Social Crusade; he founded the World's Catholic Temperance Crusade, of which he is still the first President, 1896; Vice-Pres. of the United Kingdom Alliance; travelled extensively preaching 'Crusades.' Pope Leo XIII conferred upon him the title of 'The Apostle of Temperance,' 1900; whilst Pope Pius X bestowed upon him his highest commendation and apostolic benediction, and the two succeeding Pontiffs have blessed his work. *Address:* St Peter's Rectory, Beeston, Nottingham.

Died 19 May 1943.

HAYS, Sir Marshall, Kt 1928; JP County of London; Chairman and Managing Director London United Laundries, Ltd; President, North Hammersmith Conservative Association; admitted an Hon. Freeman of the Borough of Hammersmith, 29 Oct. 1934; *b* Ealing, 1872; *s* of Richard Baker Hays; *m* 1906, Edith, *e d* of Wm Douglas Lamb, N Shields; no *c*. *Educ:* Harrow View School, Ealing. Five times Mayor of Hammersmith, 1920–25; County Councillor, 1925–31; Chairman of the Chiswick Hospital; Member of Council of the London Municipal Society; Chairman and Hon. Treasurer, West London Hospital; Chairman of the Home Counties Approved Soc.; Chairman of the Hammersmith District Nursing Assoc.; Chairman of the Latymer Road Mission; Chairman West London Philanthropic Society; Vice-Chairman, Goldhawk Mutual Benefit Building Society, Chiswick; Chairman, Whitton Park Club House, Ltd; Chairman of the Hammersmith Branch of the British Legion; Chairman of Governors of the Upper Latymer Foundation School and of the Godolphin and Latymer Girls' School; Vice-Chairman St Clement Danes Holborn Estate Grammar School. Chairman, Fowey and Lanteglos Memorial to Sir Arthur Quiller-Couch; President, League of Mercy, District of Hammersmith. *Address:* 22 St Peter's Square, W6. *TA:* Milkwhite Hammer London. *T:* Riverside 2306; 1 Harbour Terrace, Fowey, Cornwall. *T:* Fowey 139. *Club:* Royal Fowey Yacht (Fowey).

Died 24 Jan. 1948.

HAYTER, 1st Baron *cr* 1927, of Chislehurst, Kent; **George Hayter Chubb;** 1st Bt *cr* 1900, Kt 1885; JP Kent; Chairman of Chubb and Sons' Lock and Safe Co., Ltd, from its formation as a company in 1882 until 1940, a managing director since 1940; Director to six other Companies; *b* London, 29 Aug. 1848; 2nd *s* of late John Chubb, Brixton; *m* 1870, Sarah Vanner (*d* 1940), *o d* of Charles Early, JP, Witney, Oxon; two *s* two *d*. Appointed Commissioner of Royal Patriotic Fund, 1890; member of Council of Royal United Service Institution, 1893; Member of Governing Body, Leys School, Cambridge, since 1896; Member of Executive Council, Royal Naval Fund; connected with several philanthropic institutions. *Heir: s* Hon. Charles Archibald Chubb [*b* 11 Nov. 1871; *m* 1898, Mary, *d* of late J. F. Haworth of Withens, Sutton Coldfield, Warwickshire; two *s*]. *Address:* Newlands, Chislehurst. *Clubs:* Carlton, Constitutional.

Died 7 Nov. 1946.

HAYWARD, Arthur Canler, CBE 1933; late Director of Audit, Exchequer and Audit Department; *b* 1870; *e s* of late Edward and Agnes Hayward, Leeds; *m* 1911, Annie Ball, *o d* of late Henry Wainwright, Leeds; one *s* two *d*. *Address:* The Nook, Sandsend, Whitby, Yorks. *T:* Sandsend 27.

Died 15 Sept. 1945.

HAYWARD, Alderman Sir Fred, Kt 1931; JP; General Manager and Secretary, Burslem and District Co-operative Society since 1902; Alderman, Stoke-upon-Trent, (Mayor 1926); *b* 1876. *Address:* The Hollies, High Lane, Burslem. *T:* Potteries, Central 7230.
Died 19 Dec. 1944.

HAYWOOD, Horace Mason, CIE 1922; formerly Secretary Bengal Chamber of Commerce, Calcutta. *Address:* 73 Culverden Park, Tunbridge Wells.
Died 11 March 1942.

HAZEL, Alfred Ernest William, CBE 1918; KC 1930; MA, BCL, LLD; Principal of Jesus College, Oxford, since 1925; Recorder of Burton-on-Trent, 1912–38; Hon. Fellow of Queen's College, Oxford; Assessor of the Chancellor's Court, Oxford; *s* of John Hazel, West Bromwich; *m* 1919, Ethel, *e d* of Rev. W. G. Percival; one *s. Educ:* West Bromwich Wesleyan School; King Edward's School, Birmingham; Jesus College, Oxford. Scholar, First Class Honours, Classics and Law, Eldon Law Scholar; Inns of Court, Prizeman. Barrister-at-law, Lincoln's Inn, 1898; KC 1930; Senior Proctor, Oxford University, 1910–11; Reader in Constitutional Law at the Inns of Court, 1910–26; All Souls Reader in English Law, Oxford, 1922–33; Examiner in Law at the Universities of Oxford, Cambridge, Glasgow, London, and Wales; MP (L) West Bromwich, 1906–10; University Lecturer on Criminal Law and Law of Evidence, Oxford, 1915–22; Deputy Controller Priority Department, Ministry of Munitions, 1915–19. *Address:* Jesus College, Oxford; Oxenford House, West Bromwich.
Died 20 Aug. 1944.

HAZLERIGG, 1st Baron *cr* 1945, of Noseley; **Arthur Grey Hazlerigg;** 13th Bt *cr* 1622; *b* 17 Nov. 1878; *o c* of Major Arthur Grey Hazlerigg and Janet Edith (*m* 2nd, 1888, Major Henry Pelham Burn), *e d* of Sir Archibald Orr-Ewing, 1st Bt; *S* grandfather, 1890; *m* 1903, Dorothy Rachel, *e d* of John Henry Buxton of Hunsdonbury Ware; three *s* three *d. Educ:* Eton; Trinity College, Cambridge (BA 1902). Contested (C) Melton Mowbray Division of Leicestershire; High Sheriff, 1909. Lieutenant, RNVR 1915; Captain, General List, 1916–19: Lord Lieutenant, Leicestershire; member of Leicestershire County Council since 1906; Chairman, 1923–24; Chairman Quarter Sessions; Hon. Col 115th Regt RA (TA); Coroner's Commission, 1934–35; Home Office Advisory Committee under Regulation 18b, 1939–41. President Royal Agricultural Society, 1931; Chairman Council of Agriculture, 1932. KStJ. *Recreations:* cricket, shooting, fishing. *Heir: s* Major Hon. Arthur Grey Hazlerigg, MC, DL [*b* 24 Feb. 1910; *m* 1945, Patricia, *e d* of late John Pullar, High Seat, Fields Hill, Kloof, Natal; one *d*]. *Address:* Noseley Hall, Leicester. *TA:* Billesdon. *Clubs:* Travellers', National; Leicester County (Leicester).
Died 25 May 1949.

HAZLETON, Richard; General Secretary, The Institution of Production Engineers since 1929; *b* Dollymount, Co. Dublin, 5 Dec. 1880; *s* of late Thomas Hazleton, Dublin and Dungannon; unmarried. *Educ:* Blackrock College, Co. Dublin. Entered politics as Nationalist; contested South Dublin, 1906; MP (N) North Galway, 1906–18; North Louth, 1911; travelled extensively on lecture tours in USA, New Zealand, Australia, and South America; served on Prime Minister's Reconstruction Committee, 1917; Balfour of Burleigh Committee on Commercial and Industrial Policy, 1916–18; Hon. Secretary, Irish Parliamentary Party, 1907–18, and Chairman of its Industrial Committee, 1917–18; Secretary, Society of Technical Engineers, 1921–29. *Address:* 36 Portman Square, W1.
Died 26 Jan. 1943.

HEAD, Most Rev. Frederick Waldegrave, MC; Archbishop of Melbourne since 1929; *b* 18 April 1874; *s* of late George Frederick Head, Vicar of Clifton and Hon. Canon of Bristol, and late Mary Henrietta Head; *m* 1904, Edith Mary Colman; one *s. Educ:* Alton School, Plymouth; Windlesham House, Brighton; Repton School; Emmanuel College, Cambridge. 1st Class Historical Tripos, 1896; Lightfoot Scholar and Whewell Scholar, 1897; Prince Consort and Seeley Medals, 1900; MA 1900. Fellow and Lecturer in History, Emmanuel College, Cambridge, 1900; Ordained 1902; Dean and Tutor, 1903; Senior Tutor and Chaplain, 1907; Life Fellow, 1927; Vicar of Christ Church, Greenwich, 1922–26; Canon and Sub-dean of Liverpool Cathedral, 1926–29; Temporary Chaplain to the Forces, 1916–19; Senior Chaplain to the Guards' Division, 1917–19 (MC and Bar); Hon. CF 1920; Chaplain to HM the King, 1922–29; Examining Chaplain to the Bishop of Leicester; Lecturer in Pastoral Theology, Cambridge, 1928. *Publications:* The Fallen Stuarts, 1901; (Part) The Heart of the Empire; Six Great Anglicans. *Recreations:* bicycling and walking. *Address:* Bishopscourt, Clarendon Street, East Melbourne, C2, Australia.
Died 18 Dec. 1941.

HEADFORT, 4th Marquess of, *cr* 1800; **Geoffrey Thomas Taylour;** Bt 1704; Baron Headfort, 1760; Viscount Headfort, 1762; Earl of Bective, 1766; Baron Kenlis, (UK) 1881; Senator Irish Free State 1922–28; President RHS of Ireland since 1920; Fellow of the Linnean Society, 1930; Victoria Medal of Honour, 1940; served World War, 1915–19, Gallipoli, Salonika, France; retired as Captain (despatches); late Lieut 1st Life Guards; JP, DL Co. Meath; *b* 12 June 1878; *s* of 3rd Marquis and 2nd wife Emily, *d* of Rev. Lord John Thynne and *widow* of Captain Wilson Patten; *S* father, 1894; *m* 1901, Rose, *d* of late Charles Boote; two *s* one *d. Heir: s* Earl of Bective. *Address:* Headford, Kells, Co. Meath.
Died 29 Jan. 1943.

HEADLAM, Rt Rev. Arthur Cayley, CH 1921; MA, DD, Hon. DD (Aberdeen, Trinity College, Dublin, Durham, London, Oslo); Order of St Sava (Serbia) 4th Class; Order of the Crown of Serbia, 2nd Class; Knight Commander Order of the White Rose of Finland, 1st Class; *b* Whorlton, Durham, 2 Aug. 1862; *e s* of late Rev. A. W. Headlam; *m* 1900, Evelyn Persis (*d* 1924), *d* of Rev. George Wingfield, Rector of Glatton, Hunts. *Educ:* Winchester College (scholar); New College, Oxford (scholar), 2nd class, Class Moderations; 1st class, Final Classical School. Fellow of All Souls' Coll., Oxford, 1885–97 and since 1924; Theological Lecturer Oriel, Queen's, and Trinity; Birkbeck Lecturer Trinity Coll., Cambridge, 1897–98; Examining Chaplain to the Bishop of Southwell, 1891–1904; Select Preacher to the University of Oxford, 1899–1901, 1915–17; of Cambridge, 1918–19; Rector of Welwyn, Herts, 1896–1903; Member of the Senate of London University, 1903–13; Bampton Lecturer 1920; Fellow of King's Coll. London, 1905; editor of the Church Quarterly Review, 1901–21; Principal of King's College, London, 1903–12; Professor of Dogmatic Theology, King's College, London, 1903–16; Regius Professor of Divinity, Oxford University, and Canon of Christ Church, Oxford, 1918–23; Bishop of Gloucester, 1923–45; FRHortS. *Publications:* Ecclesiastical Sites in Isauria, 1893; joint author with Professor Sanday of a Critical and Exegetical Commentary on the Epistle to the Romans, 1895; Teaching of the Russian Church, 1897; contributor to Authority and Archæology, 1899; to New Testament Criticism, 1902; to London Theological Studies, 1911; and to Hastings' Bible Dictionary; Sources and Authority of Dogmatic Theology, 1903; History, Authority, and Theology, 1909; St Paul and Christianity, 1913; The Miracles of the New Testament, 1914; The Revenues of the Church of England, 1917; The Study of Theology, Inaugural Lecture, 1918; The Doctrine of the Church and

Christian Reunion (Bampton Lectures), 1920; The Life and Teaching of Jesus the Christ, 1923; The Church of England, 1924; Jesus Christ in Faith and History, 1925; Economics and Christianity, 1926; The New Prayer Book, 1927; The Building of the Church of Christ (Sermons), 1928; Christian Unity, 1930; What it Means to be a Christian, 1933; Christian Theology; The Doctrine of God, 1934; The Task of the Christian Church (an address), 1942; Why I am Satisfied: An Open Letter to Professor C. E. M. Joad, 1944; The Holy Catholic Church, 1945. *Recreation:* gardening. *Address:* Whorlton Hall, Barnard Castle. *T:* Whorlton 25. *Club:* Athenæum.

Died 17 Jan. 1947.

HEADLAM, Captain Sir Edward James, Kt 1928; CSI 1924; CMG 1919; DSO 1916; RIN (retired); *b* 1 May 1873; 4th *s* of late Morley Headlam of Gilmonby Hall, Yorkshire, and Whorlton Grange, Durham; *m* 1918, Nancey Benyon (*d* 1932), widow of Stanley Hobson, Nigeria. *Educ:* Durham School; HMS Conway. Sub-Lt RIM, 1894; Lt 1900; Comdr 1913; Marine Survey of India, 1897–1914; Naval Transport Officer E African Forces, 1914–17; Principal Naval Transport Officer, South and East Africa, 1917–19; Director Royal Indian Marine, 1922–28; retired 1929. Assistant Marine Transport Officer, British Expeditionary Force, N China, 1900–01 (medal, despatches); Royal Humane Societies Medal; Hon. Member American Military Order of Dragon; FRGS; gun running operations, Persian Gulf, 1912 (Naval General Service medal and clasp); served European War (despatches four times, CMG, DSO, special promotion to Captain, 1914–15 Bronze Star, British War and Victory Medals). *Publications:* History of Sea Service under the Government in India; occasional articles in Royal Geographical Society's Journal, and United Service Journal. *Recreations:* various. *Address:* c/o Lloyds Bank, 6 Pall Mall, SW1.

Died 14 July 1943.

HEADLAM, Maj.-Gen. Sir John Emerson Wharton, KBE 1919; CB 1913; DSO 1900; *b* 16 April 1864; *e s* of late Morley Headlam of Gilmonby Hall, Yorkshire, and Whorlton Grange, Durham; *m* 1890, Mary, *e d* of late Percival Wilkinson of Mount Oswald, Durham; two *d*. Entered army, 1883; Captain, 1892; Major, 1900; Lt-Col, 1902; Col, 1905; Maj.-Gen., 1915; Instructor, School of Gunnery, 1892–97; Headquarters, 1903–06; Headquarters, India, 1908–13; Headquarters Staff, South Africa, 1900–02 (despatches twice, brevet Lt-Col, Queen's medal four clasps, King's medal two clasps, DSO); European War, 1914–18, (wounded, despatches four times, promoted Major-General for distinguished service in the field; Order of St Anne of Russia, 1st class with swords; Commander of the Legion of Honour; American Distinguished Service Medal); retired pay, 1921; Col-Comdt RA, 1928–34; JP, DL, Shropshire; DL Co. Durham. *Publication:* History of the RA from the Indian Mutiny to the Great War, Vol. I, 1931, (with Sir Charles Callwell), Vol. II, 1937, Vol. III, 1940. *Clubs:* Shropshire County, Shrewsbury.

Died 14 Oct. 1946.

HEADLAND, Isaac Taylor, DD, AM, STB, PhD, LittD; Professor of Philosophy in Mt Union College; *b* Pennsylvania, USA, 16 Aug. 1859; 3rd *s* of Jacob Headland of Lincolnshire; *m* 1894, Mariam, MD, *d* of William Sinclair, AM, of Sarnia, Canada; one *s* one *d*. *Educ:* Mt Union College, AB, AM, PhD; Boston University, STB 1890. Professor of Science and Psychology in Peking University, 1890–1907. Has made a careful study of Chinese porcelain, bronze, jade, cloisonné, and painting, and is preparing a work on The Pictorial Art of China; has a collection of more than 500 paintings of the Sung, Yüan, Ming, and present dynasties; has given courses of lectures in cities, colleges, universities, at Chautauquas, Bible Schools, summer conferences, and College Commencements; Hazlett

Lecturer and Stinson Prof. of Missions in Wesley College of North Dakota Univ., 1919–20; charge of Department of Chinese Art, Methodist Centenary, Exposition, Columbus, 1919. Member (Φ BK) Phi, Beta, Kappa. *Publications:* Chinese Mother Goose Rhymes, 1900; Chinese Boy and Girl, 1901; Chinese Heroes, 1902; Our Little Chinese Cousin, 1903; A Tourist's Guide to Peking, 1907; Court Life in China, 1909; Some By-Products of Missions, China's New Day, The Young China Hunters, 1912; Home Life in China, 1914; Chinese Rhymes for Children, 1933; articles for Munroe's Encyclopedia of Education; article on Sex Life in China for Encyclopedia Sexualis; many contributions to magazines. *Recreation:* the study of things Chinese. *Address:* 1696 Arch Avenue, Alliance, Ohio, USA. *T:* 3509. *Club:* Authors'.

Died 2 Aug. 1942.

HEALY, Rev. George White, MA, BD, TCD. Canon of Cork, retired. *Address:* Ahakista, Birchington, Kent.

Died 14 Oct. 1943.

HEALY, Ven. John, LLD; Treasurer since 1935 and Canon of St Patrick's Cathedral, Dublin, since 1897; *b* 1850; *s* of Abraham Healy, JP, Dublin; *m* 1st, Eunice, *d* of M. le Pasteur Lelièvre; 2nd, Mary, *d* of late Dr Thornton of Ballinasloe; three *s* three *d*. *Educ:* Trinity College, Dublin. Took Holy Orders, 1873. Successively Curate of Cootehill; Rector of Killersherdiny, Ballyboy, Ratoath and Kells; Archdeacon of Meath, 1914–28; devoted to historical and antiquarian studies, especially those relating to Ireland; Secretary for N Meath of the Royal Society of Irish Antiquaries. *Publications:* The Ancient Irish Church; Art Teaching of the Ancient Irish Church; The Vikings in Ireland; St Patrick; History of the Diocese of Meath; antiquarian and historical articles in various magazines. *Address:* Drakestown Rectory, Navan, Co. Meath.

Died 8 March 1942.

HEALY, Maurice; KC 1931; Recorder of Coventry since 1941; Bencher, Inner Temple, 1938; *b* 16 Nov. 1887; *er s* of late Maurice Healy and Annie, *d* of late A. M. Sullivan. *Educ:* Christian Brothers College, Cork; Clongowes Wood College; University College, Dublin. Called Irish Bar, Dublin, 1910; called to English Bar, Gray's Inn, 1914; served with Royal Dublin Fusiliers (4th and 1st Bns.), 1915–19, also at 29th Division Headquarters, Captain (MC); contested West Waterford as a Parliamentary Candidate (Ind Nat.), Dec. 1910. *Publications:* Claret and the White Wines of Bordeaux, 1934; The Old Munster Circuit, 1939; Stay me with Flagons, 1940. *Recreations:* talking and listening to music.

Died 9 May 1943.

HEARD, Maj.-Gen. Richard, CIE 1924; Indian Medical Service, retired; *b* 1870. *Educ:* Trinity College, Dublin, BA, MB, BCh. Entered IMS, 1893; Professor of Midwifery, Lahore Medical College, 1909; Inspector-General of Prisons, Assam, 1922; Punjab, 1922; Surgeon-General with Govt of Bengal, 1924; retired, 1927.

Died 16 Aug. 1950.

HEARNSHAW, Fossey John Cobb, MA, LLD, LittD; Emeritus Professor of History in the University of London; *b* Birmingham, 31 July 1869; *s* of Rev. John Hearnshaw, Wesleyan Minister; *m* 1904, D. M. Spencer, MA; one *s* one *d*. *Educ:* Walsall and Manchester Grammar Schools; London University (MA); Peterhouse, Cambridge University (Historical Scholar, MA, LLM); Dublin University (LLD); LittD (Camb.). External Examiner in History in London University, 1909–13; Durham University, 1912–13; Manchester University, 1914–17; Bristol University, 1921; University of Wales, 1930; Professor of History at University College, Southampton, 1900–10; Professor of Modern History in the Armstrong College of the University of Durham, 1910–12; Professor of Mediaeval

History in the University of London, 1913–34; Hon. Secretary Royal Historical Society, 1931–34 and President of the Historical Association, 1936–38; Fellow of King's College, 1926. *Publications:* Southampton Court Leet Records, 1905–1907; Leet Jurisdiction in England, 1908; Life of Sir Henry Vane, 1910; History of Southampton, 1910; Legal Literature (in Cambridge History of English Literature), 1912; England in the Making, 1913; Editor of King's College Lectures on Colonial Problems, 1913; First Book of English History, 1914; Freedom in Service, 1916; Main Currents of European History, 1917; Democracy at the Crossways, 1918; Europe in the Nineteenth Century, 1919; Democracy and British Empire, 1921; Historical Atlas of Modern Europe, 1921; Editor of King's College Lectures on Mediæval Civilisation, 1921; The European Revolution, 1848 (in Cambridge History), 1922; History of Newcastle, 1924; Democracy and Labour, 1924; World History, 1924; Development of Political Ideas, 1927; A Survey of Socialism, 1928; British Prime Ministers, 1928; Editor of Cassell's Dictionary of English History, 1928; The Centenary History of King's College, London, 1929; The 'Ifs' of History, 1929; The Social and Political Ideas of some Great French Thinkers of the Age of Reason, 1930; of the Revolutionary Era, 1931; of the Age of Reaction and Reconstruction, 1932; and of the Victorian Age, 1933; Conservatism in England, 1933; Edwardian England, 1933; The Place of Surrey in the History of England, 1936; The Prelude to 1937, 1937; Outlines of the History of the British Isles, 1938; Germany the Aggressor, 1940; Sea Power and Empire, 1940. *Address:* Hammerwood, Oxted, Surrey. *T:* Oxted 327.

Died 10 March 1946.

HEARST, Hon. Sir William Howard, KCMG 1917; KC 1908; *b* Tp Arran, Co. Bruce, Ont, 15 Feb. 1864; *s* of Wm Hearst and Margaret M' Fadden; *m* 1891, Isabella Jane Dunkin; two *s* two *d*. *Educ:* Tara Public School; Collingwood Collegiate Institute; Osgoode Hall, Toronto. Admitted to Bar, 1888; commenced practice of law, Sault Ste Marie, 1888; head of firm of Hearst and Hearst, Toronto; Bencher of the Law Society, 1913; Member of Ontario Legislature for Electoral District of Sault Ste Marie, 1908–19; Minister of Lands, Forests, and Mines, Province of Ontario, 1911–14; Premier, 1914–19; LLD Toronto University, 1915; member International Joint Commission for settlement of disputes between the United States and Canada, 1920. *Address:* 80 Glen Road and 25 King Street, West Toronto. *T:* Randolph 3188, Elgin 2471.

Died 29 Sept. 1941.

HEASLETT, Rt Rev. Samuel, MA, DD (Hon.) Durham University; Assistant Bishop of Sheffield since 1943; Bishop of South Tokio, 1922–40; Presiding Bishop of the Church in Japan, 1933–40; *b* Belfast, 1875; *m* Hilda (*d* 1936); one *s*. Deacon, 1900; Priest, 1903; Tutor Divinity School, Osaka, 1900–03; Missionary Tokushima, 1904–10; CMS Missionary Tokyo, 1910–21; Professor in the Central Theological College, Tokyo, 1913–21; Lieut (2nd) Labour Corps, Dec. 1917; France with Chinese Labour Corps, 1918–19; Acting-Captain, Dec. 1918–June 1919; demobilised, June 1919; Gen. Secretary, CMS work in Japan, 1920–21; retired Oct. 1940; on outbreak of war Dec. 1941, arrested; four months in Japanese prison; repatriated Oct. 1942. *Publication:* From a Japanese Prison. *Address:* Wyaston House, Grenoside, Sheffield. *T:* Ecclesfield 38588. *Club:* National.

Died 16 Oct. 1947.

HEATH, Arthur Raymond; JP; *e s* of late Admiral Sir L. G. Heath of Anstie Grange and Kitlands, Holmwood, Surrey; *m* 1881, Flora, Jean, *y d* of late Edward Baxter of Kincaldrum, Forfar, and Gilston, Fife; one *s*. *Educ:* Marlborough; Trinity Coll., Cambridge; LLB 1877. Called to Bar, Inner Temple, 1879; MP (C)

Lincolnshire, Louth Division, 1886–92. *Address:* Kitlands, Coldharbour, Surrey. *TA:* Kitlands, Coldharbour.

Died 8 June 1943.

HEATH, Col Edward Charles, CVO 1935; DSO 1917; Chevalier de la Légion d'Honneur, 1939; *b* 1873; *s* of late William Fitzhenry Heath, PWD, India; *m* Mary Beatrice, *d* of late William Halliday. 2nd Lieut 3rd Sherwood Foresters, 1893; Director of Army Classes, Folkestone, 1899–1914; Lt-Colonel commanding 3rd Sherwood Foresters, 1912–16, and 8th King's (Liverpool Irish), 1916–19; served European War, 1914–19, in France and Flanders (despatches, DSO, promoted Colonel); Commandant, Army General and Commercial College, Cologne, 1919–20; Officer in Charge of Education, Rhine Army, 1920–21; First General Secretary, British Legion, 1921–40; joined LDV (River Patrol), 1940; Organised and Commanded 'Heath's Machine Gun Battalion' and 34th County of London—London River (South)—Bn Home Guard, 1940–43; Supervising Military Liaison Officer R Sector HG, 1943–44. Organised and directed British Legion Festival of Empire and Remembrance, 11 Nov. 1929–38; New Year Festival and Grand Pageant of the Empire and Her Allies, 1942 and 1943, and Festival of Empire, May 1945. *Address:* 143 Rivermead Court, Hurlingham, SW6. *T:* Renown 1066.

Died 7 Sept. 1946.

HEATH, Sir (Henry) Frank, GBE 1927; KCB 1917; CB 1911; Fellow of University College, London, 1896; Hon. ARIBA, 1926; Officier de l'Instruction Publique, 1904; Member of Council, Royal Albert Hall, 1929–45; Crown Governor of the Imperial College of Science and Technology and Member Finance and Executive and other Committees, 1931–45; appointed Governor by City and Guilds of London Institute, 1945; thereafter re-appointed member of the above Committee, 1945; Hon. Secretary, British National Committee for Intellectual Co-operation under the League of Nations, 1929–45; Member, Royal Commission for the 1851 Exhibition, since 1924; Member of Council, Queen Alexandra House, 1931–45; Member of Universities China Committee in London, since 1932; Chairman, General Council, 1938–39, Vice-Chairman, 1939–44, and Chairman Mark Committee, since 1935, of British Standards Institution; *b* London, 11 Dec. 1863; *e s* of late Henry Charles Heath, miniature painter to Queen Victoria; *m* 1st, 1892, Antonia Johanna Sophie Theresa (*d* 1893), *y d* of F. G. Eckenstein, Canonbury; 2nd, 1898, Frances Elaine, (*d* 1939), 5th *d* of late J. H. Sayer, High Barnet and Hastings; two *s*. *Educ:* Westminster School; Univ. College, London, 1884–88; Strassburg Univ., 1888–90. Professor of English, Bedford College, London, 1890–95; Lecturer in English Language and Literature at King's College, London, 1891–95; Assistant-Registrar and Librarian, University of London, 1895–1901; Academic Registrar and Acting-Treasurer, University of London, 1901–03; Member of the Advisory Committee to the Treasury on Grants to University Colleges, 1909–11; Joint Secretary to the Royal Commission on University Education in London, 1909–13; Director of Special Inquiries and Reports under the Board of Education, 1903–16; Principal Assistant Secretary of the Universities Branch of the Board, 1910–16; Education Correspondent to the Government of India, 1904–16; Secretary to the Department of Scientific and Industrial Research, 1916–27; Secretary to the Advisory Council for Scientific and Industrial Research, 1915–27; Governor of the Imperial Institute, 1925–27; President, British Electrical and Allied Industries, Research Association, 1931–32; Secretary, Universities Bureau of the British Empire, 1929–30; Hon. Director 1930–34; member of Colonial Office Research Committee, 1924–33; Member of the Commission on Educational and Cultural Films, 1929–33; Member of Executive

Committee of the International Commission on Intellectual Co-operation, League of Nations, and of the Comité de Direction of the International Institute for Intellectual Co-operation, Paris, 1930–39. *Publications:* chapters on English Language and Literature to the time of Elizabeth, in 'Social England'; co-editor with A. W. Pollard and others of the Globe Chaucer; editor of the Modern Language Quarterly, 1897–1903; editor of the Yearbook of Universities of the Empire, 1930–1934. *Address:* 2 Morpeth Mansions, SW1. *Club:* Athenæum.

Died 5 Oct. 1946.

HEATH, Sir James, 1st Bt *cr* 1904; JP; ironmaster and colliery proprietor; Colonel of Staffordshire Yeomanry Cavalry; *b* 26 Jan. 1852; *s* of late Robert Heath (MP Stoke-on-Trent, 1874–80) of Biddulph Grange, Congleton, and Anne, *d* of James Beech of Tunstall, Stafford; *m* 1st, 1881, Euphemia Céléna (*d* 1921), *d* of P. G. Vanderbyl, Cape Town, and High Beeches, Farnborough; (one *s* killed in action Sept. 1914); one *d*; 2nd, 1924, Joy Nitch Smith (marriage annulled, 1927 on his petition); 3rd, 1927, Sophie Mary Eliott-Lynn (from whom he obtained a divorce, 1932; she died 1939); 4th, 1935, Dorothy Mary Hodgson, BSc, *er d* of C. M. Hodgson, Indian Forest Service, retired, and Mrs Hodgson, Beech, Alton, Hampshire. *Educ:* Clifton College. MP (C) Staffordshire, NW, 1892–1906. *Heir:* none. *Address:* 48 Lowndes Square, SW1. *T:* Sloane 5654. *Clubs:* Carlton, Junior Carlton.

Died 24 Dec. 1942 (ext).

HEATH, Brig.-Gen. Ronald Macclesfield, CMG 1919; DSO 1902; Col of Middlesex Regt since 1932; *b* 5 March 1876; *s* of Lieut-Col J. M. Heath, CMG; *m* 1938, Marian Ross, *d* of late Ross Porter, Marchwood Park, Hampshire. *Educ:* Marlborough. Served S Africa, 1899–1902 (despatches twice, Queen's medal 6 clasps; King's medal 2 clasps, DSO); Operations in Southern Kordofan, 1908; commanded Camel Corps of Egyptian Army in Soudan, 1908–12; Egyptian Medal and Clasp and Osmanieh (4th Class); Operations in Southern Kordofan, 1910; Sudan 1910 Medal and Clasp; Mejidieh (3rd Class), and Osmanieh (3rd Class); European War, 1914–18 (despatches six times, Croix de Guerre); commanded 10th Batt. Royal Warwickshire Regt 1916–18; Brig.-General commanding 56th Infantry Brigade, 1918–19; commanded 1st Bn Middlesex Regt, 1920–24; commanded Tientsin Area, 1926–30; retired pay, 1930. *Recreations:* shooting, music. *Address:* Danesford Grange, near Bridgnorth, Salop. *Club:* Army and Navy.

Died 21 April 1942.

HEATH-CALDWELL, Maj.-Gen. Frederick Crofton, CB 1910; *b* 21 Feb. 1858; 2nd *s* of late Admiral Sir Leopold George Heath, KCB; *m* 1889, Constance Mary, *d* of Col H. Helsham-Jones; one *s*. Entered RE, 1877; Captain, 1888; Brev. Major, 1888; Major, 1895; Lt-Col 1903; Col 1906; AAG, S Africa, 1900–02; AAG, RE, Headquarters of Army, 1906–08; Inspector of RE, 1908–13; Commanding Scottish Coast Defence, 1913–14; Director Military Training, War Office, 1914–15; GOC Portsmouth Garrison, 1916–18; GOCSE Area Royal Air Force since 1918; served Egypt, 1882 (medal with clasp, bronze star); Soudan, 1885 (despatches, clasp brevet Major); S Africa, 1899–1902 (despatches, brevet Lt-Col, Queen's medal two clasps, King's medal two clasps); took the additional name of Caldwell on succeeding his great-uncle James Stamford Caldwell; JP County Palatine of Chester. *Address:* Linley Wood, Talke, Staffordshire. *Club:* Army and Navy.

Died 18 Sept. 1945.

HEATH-JONES, Edgar, CBE 1919; was Financial Secretary, Central Prisoners of War Committee; Financial Adviser to the Disposal Board in Paris, 1919–21; *m* 1911, Elsie Grace Plummer. *Educ:* Merchant

Taylors' School; Brasenose College, Oxford. *Address:* Efford Cottage, Bude, North Cornwall. *T:* Bude 474. *Clubs:* Reform; Stoke Poges Golf (Slough).

Died 6 Aug. 1949.

HEATHCOTE, Brig.-Gen. Charles Edensor, CB 1919; CMG 1918; DSO 1915; formerly the King's Own (Yorkshire Light Inf.); *b* 8 April 1875; *er s* of Lt-Col C. L. Heathcote, 2nd Durham Light Infantry; *m* 1909, May, 2nd *d* of late Edmund Severne of Wallop in Shropshire, and Thenford, Northants; one *s*. Entered army, 1st KOYLI, 1894; Capt., 1900; Major, 1913; Lt-Col, 1922; Col, 1924; Supt Gymnasia, Malta, 1900–02; with West African Frontier Force, 1904–09; Superintendent Gymnasia, Eastern Command, 1911–14; served S Nigeria, 1904–05, 1905–06, 1906, 1908 (despatches thrice, medal 2 clasps); European War, 1914–18 (DSO, CB, CMG, despatches 6 times, Bt Lieut-Colonel Order of the Nile 3rd Class); in Command successively of 2nd KOYLI, 1st KOYLI, 4th Lincoln Regt, 7th Infantry Brigade, 9th KOYLI, 7th Leicester Regt and 231st Infantry Brigade, 2/4 and 2/5 KOYLI; succeeded to command of 2 KOYLI, 1922; Inspector of Physical Training, 1924–27; Brigadier 1st Rhine Brigade, British Army of the Rhine, 1928–29; Brigadier 15th Infantry Brigade, York, 1929–32; retired pay, 1932. *Address:* Ryst End, Forest Row, Sussex. *Club:* United Service.

Died 6 Sept. 1947.

HEATHCOTE, John Norman; JP; *b* 21 June 1863; *e s* of J. M. Heathcote of Conington Castle, and Louisa Cecilia MacLeod of MacLeod. *Educ:* Eton; Trinity College, Cambridge. BA Classical Tripos, 1885; Gold Medal, Royal Agricultural College, Cirencester, 1889; JP Huntingdonshire, 1906. County Councillor, 1913; High Sheriff for Cambs and Hunts, 1917. *Publication:* St Kilda, 1900. *Recreations:* sketching, photography, shooting, yachting. *Address:* Conington Castle, Peterborough. *T:* Sawtry 32. *TA:* Sawtry. *Clubs:* Oxford and Cambridge, MCC.

Died 16 July 1946.

HEATHCOTE-DRUMMOND-WILLOUGHBY, Brig. Gen. Hon. Charles Strathavon; *see* Willoughby.

HEATHER, Henry James Shedlock, BA, MInstCE, MInstEE; Professor of Electrotechnics at the University of Witwatersrand, Johannesburg, 1914–24; resigned under superannuation, Dec. 1924; *b* 9 May 1863; *s* of late Jas Heather, Solicitor, London; *m* 1904, Ethel Kate (decd), *widow* of late H. C. Wood and *d* of Wilberforce Wilson, formerly Surveyor-General of Hong-Kong; no *c*. *Educ:* St Paul's School; Balliol College, Oxford. Has carried out much electrical engineering work in S Africa, and in particular equipped the mines of the Rand Mines and Central Administration Groups (now the Central Mining and Investment Corporation, Ltd) for the use of purchased electrical power. *Publications:* Electrical Engineering for Mechanical and Mining Engineers; various papers for the Institutions of Civil Engineers, Electrical Engineers, Mining and Metallurgy, etc. *Recreations:* formerly rowing (College Eight), now shooting. *Club:* Rand (Johannesburg).

Died 3 Jan. 1939.

HEATHERSHAW, James Thomas, CBE 1927; *b* Beaufort, Victoria, 7 May 1871; *s* of late Rev. H. Heathershaw; *m* 1901, Rosa Ethel Rodway; one *s* one *d*. *Educ:* Flinders Sch., Geelong. Joined Victorian Treasury, 1889; transferred Commonwealth Treasury, 1902; Accountant to the Treasury, 1916–26; Secretary to the Commonwealth Treasury, 1926–32; Commissioner of Invalid and Old Age Pensions, 1932; retired 1936. *Recreation:* golf. *Address:* Melbourne, Australia.

Died 28 July 1943.

HEATLEY, David Playfair, MA; Reader Emeritus in Political Science and in History, University of Edinburgh; retired 1935; *b* Northumberland, 1867; 2nd *s* of John Heatley and Helen, *d* of David Playfair. *Educ:* Royal High School and (1884–90) University of Edinburgh. Vans Dunlop Scholar in History, 1889. Engaged in historical research, 1889–92; Assistant in History, University of Edinburgh, 1892; University Lecturer in History and Political Science, 1900; Official Adviser (of Studies) in the Faculty of Arts, 1907–15; for several years represented the Civil Service Commissioners on committees for appointments. *Publications:* Studies in British History and Politics, 1913; Diplomacy and the Study of International Relations, 1919; Viscount Grey of Fallodon by Politicus, 1934; articles in several quarterlies. *Recreations:* fishing, golf. *Address:* 28 Minto Street, Edinburgh. *Clubs:* Scottish Arts, Edinburgh.

Died 20 Sept. 1944.

HEATLY-SPENCER, Col John, CBE 1937; MD, FRCP, DTM and H Cantab; *b* Windsor, 1880; *m* 1915, Margaret McInnes; two *d*. *Educ:* New Zealand; University of London. Commissioned 1906; Service United Kingdom, Gibraltar, India, France, Macedonia, Turkey; Professor of Medicine RAM College, 1929–34; Professor of Tropical Medicine, Royal Army Medical College and Consulting Physician to the British Army, 1934–37; Hon. Physician to the King, 1935–37; retired pay, 1937. *Publications:* various Medical Monographs. *Address:* c/o Glyn Mills & Co., Ltd, Kirkland House, Whitehall, SW1.

Died 31 Dec. 1946.

HEATON, Sir (John) Frederick, Kt 1942; Chairman and Managing Director, Thomas Tilling, Ltd, and Chairman of many other Companies mainly associated with road passenger transport; *b* 18 Oct. 1880; *m* 1st, 1908; 2nd, 1927; three *s* two *d*. *Educ:* Bradford Technical College. Took an active part in the inauguration and development of provincial motor omnibus operations. Founded, 1918, on behalf of Thomas Tilling, Ltd, Road Transport and General Insurance Co., Ltd, and, 1922, Motor Credit Services, Ltd Appointed, 1943, on behalf of the Government, Chairman of group of aircraft manufacturing companies associated with Short Brothers Ltd Member of Inland Transport War Council, 1941–44; Member Finch Committee set up by Army Council, 1941; Chairman, Watford and District Peace Memorial Hospital. *Recreation:* agriculture. *Address:* The Firs, Croxley Green, Herts; Can Court, Cirencester. *Clubs:* St James's, Royal Thames Yacht.

Died 27 April 1949.

HEATON, William Haslam, MA, MIEE; late Principal, University College, Nottingham; *s* of late R. Heaton, Bolton, Lancashire; *m* A. S., *d* of late Walton Turner, Ipswich; one *s* two *d*. *Educ:* Manchester Grammar School; Brasenose College, Oxford (1st Classes Math. Mods 1876; Math. Final School, 1878; Natural Science School, 1880). Demonstrator in Physics, Clarendon Laboratory, Oxford, 1881–84. *Recreation:* mountaineering. *Address:* 19 Lenton Road, Nottingham. *T:* Nottingham, 41644. *Club:* Alpine.

Died Oct. 1941.

HEATON-ELLIS, Lt-Col Sir Charles Henry Brabazon, Kt 1926; CBE 1919; DL, JP; *b* 11 May 1864; *e s* of Edward H. F. Heaton-Ellis, of Wyddiall Hall, and Louisa Harriott, *d* of Colonel Kingscote, of Kingscote, Glos; *m* 1st, 1898, Marion (*d* 1935), *e d* of Herbert T. S. M'Carthy, of Somerton, New South Wales; four *d*; 2nd, 1936, Margaret, *d* of R. C. MacCulloch, Ballyarton, Londonderry. *Educ:* Harrow; Trinity College, Cambridge. Commission in 4th Batt. Bedfordshire Regt since 1885; served S Africa (Queen's medal and clasp); under Admiralty, 1914–19 (CBE, 1914–15 Star (Royal Navy), British War Medal and Victory Medal); Chairman North Herts (Hitchin Division) Conservative

Association, 1906–32; Member of Herts County Council, 1903–19; Secretary to the Puckeridge Hunt, 1894–95; travelled extensively in Africa, Australasia, and South Sea Islands. *Recreations:* hunting, shooting, fishing. *Address:* Wyddiall Hall, Buntingford, Herts. *T:* Buntingford 28. *Club:* United Service.

Died 24 June 1945.

HEATON-ELLIS, Vice-Adm. Sir Edward Henry Fitzhardinge, KBE 1920; CB 1916; CBE 1919; MVO 1907; *b* 19 Nov. 1868; *s* of Edward Heaton-Ellis, Wyddiall Hall, Herts; *m* 1896, Gertrude, OBE, *d* of Arthur Holme-Sumner; two *s* (both died in the war). Entered Navy, 1882; Sub-Lieutenant, 1889; Lieutenant, 1892; Commander, 1903; Captain, 1908; Rear-Adm., 1919; Vice-Admiral (retired), 1925; commanded HMS Sentinel as a Commander; Naval Attaché, France, Spain, Portugal, and Belgium, 1907–11; Assistant Director of Intelligence Division, Admiralty, War Staff 1914–15; Naval Liaison Officer, Paris, 1917–19; Commanded as Captain HM Ships Good Hope, Prince of Wales, King Edward VII, and Inflexible, 1915–16, present at Battle of Jutland; Chief of Staff in Battle Cruiser Fleet, 1916–17; retired, 1920; in 1937 was elected President of the Navigators and Engineer Officers Union, and on outbreak of war, 1939, took over duty of Superintendent of Watts Naval Training School in Norfolk for two years; Comm. of Order of Legion of Honour; Commander of Order of Rising Sun; Commander of Order of Crown of Italy. *Address:* Falcon House, Twyford, Guist, Norfolk. *Clubs:* St James's; Travellers', Paris.

Died 23 Feb. 1943.

HEAWOOD, Edward, MA; Librarian to the Royal Geographical Society, 1901–34, Librarian Emeritus since 1934; *b* Newport, Salop, 26 Aug. 1863; 2nd *s* of Rev. J. R. Heawood; *m* 1895, Lucy, *d* of Rev. James Cookson; two *s*. *Educ:* Queen Elizabeth's School, Ipswich; Gonville and Caius College, Cambridge. 1st div. 3rd class Classical Tripos, 1886. Assisted in settlement of Santal Colony in Bengal Duars, 1890–92; Assistant at Royal Geographical Society, 1894–1900; Recorder, Sect. E, British Association, 1903–04 and 1906–07; Research Medal, Royal Scottish Geographical Society, 1933; Victoria Medal, Royal Geographical Society, 1934. *Publications:* Geography of Africa, 1896; Geographical Discovery in the 17th and 18th Centuries, 1912; papers in Geographical Journal, The Library, etc. *Recreations:* gardening, rugmaking, study of old papermarks. *Address:* Briarfield, Merstham, near Redhill, Surrey.

Died 30 April 1949.

HEBB, Sir John Harry, Kt 1941; CB 1937; CBE 1928; OBE 1918; BA, MB, BCh Oxon; Hon. Physician to the King, 1937–41; *b* 21 June 1878; *s* of late Rev. H. A. Hebb; *m* 1907, Ethel Kathleen Wolfgang; no *c*. *Educ:* Kelly Coll.; St John's Coll., Oxford; Westminster Hosp. MB, BCh Oxon, 1905; BA, 1900; University Scholar, Westminster Hospital. Senior House Surgeon, Westminster Hospital, 1905; House Physician, Bethlem Royal Hospital, 1906; Assistant Medical Officer, Stretton House Asylum, 1907; Private Practice, 1907–19; late temp. Major, RAMC (April 1915–Nov. 1918; service with MEF, and subsequently 107 Field Ambulance in France). *Recreations:* golf and carpentry. *Address:* Trewint, West Byfleet, Surrey. *T:* Byfleet 229. *Clubs:* Union, Oxford.

Died 15 Feb. 1942.

HECKSTALL-SMITH, Major Brooke, TD; Secretary to the International Yacht Racing Union and Yacht Racing Association, and Yachting Correspondent of the Daily Telegraph and Yachting World; *b* 30 Nov. 1869; 2nd *s* of late Brig.-Surg. Lieut-Col Heckstall Smith; *m* 1896, Teresa (*d* 1943), *d* of E. H. Stanfield; one *s*. Succeeded the late Dixon Kemp as Secretary YRA (in 1898) and Yachting Editor of the Field newspaper

(1900–28); in 1904 proposed to the Yacht Club de France the unification of all Rules of Yacht measurement, a proposal which resulted in the formation of the International Yacht Racing Union in Paris in 1907, to which twenty-nine nations became affiliated; was secretary to International Conferences held in 1906, 1907, 1919, 1924, 1928, and 1933; at the 1928 Conference the Delegates of America attended and adopted the same Rules as all the European nations; the series of Conferences resulted in complete harmony of all nations, and upwards of 2000 racing yachts have been built to the Rules; served European War, RASC, Aug. 1914–May 1919. *Publications:* The Manual of Yacht and Boat Sailing and Architecture, 11th edition; The Helmsman's Handbook; Yacht Racing, A Text-Book on the Sport; All Hands on the Main Sheet; Yachts and Yachting in Contemporary Art; The Britannia and her Contemporaries; The Complete Yachtsman, 6 editions; The Etiquette of Flags. *Recreations:* yachting, trout fishing. *Address:* Rowlands, St Mary Cray, Kent. *T:* Orpington 176. *Clubs:* Royal Victoria Yacht; Mudhook Yacht.

Died 6 March 1944.

HEDGES, Killingworth, MInstCE; MIEE retired; *s* of late W. Killingworth-Hedges of Streatham and Wooton, Oxfordshire; *m* 1918, Ivy Frances, 2nd *d* of late John Hewetson; one *s*. *Educ:* privately. Articled to late James Easton, CE; five years with Easton and Anderson. Made a bicycle in 1865 and model engine, both exhibited S Kensington Science Museum; Assist Engineer, North Holland Sea Canal, and on Denver and Rio Grande Railway; obtained two Miller prizes at Inst. CE for description of these works; designed the Aerated Bread Co.'s plant (Daugleish system); suggested the pioneer tea shops, opened 1878; Director of the Lambeth Waterworks until taken over by the Metropolitan Water Board; first to introduce electric lighting for dock work, installing Gramme dynamos at Liverpool Docks, 1878; established the Lightning Research Committee of the RIBA and Surveyors' Institution, 1901, acted as Hon. Sec.; started the collection of electric lighting exhibits, now at South Kensington; Livery, The Draper's Co.; Freeman, City of London; Founder of the 25 Club, 1906. *Publications:* Useful Information on Practical Electric Lighting, 1879, 2nd edition, 1881; The Supply of Electricity by Local Authorities; Precautions on Introducing the Electric Light; Modern Lightning Conductors; Central Station Lighting, 1887 (Telford Premium); edited (with Sir Oliver Lodge, FRS) the Lightning Research Committee's Report, 1905; article on Lightning Conductors to the Encyclopedia Britannica, 11th and 14th editions. *Address:* 10 Cranley Place, SW7. *T:* Kensington 6703. *Club:* Royal Automobile (founder member).

Died 20 Jan. 1945.

HEDWORTH, Rev. Thomas, MA TCD; late Vicar of Wellesbourne; formerly Headmaster, Ellesmere College, Shropshire; 3rd *s* of Hardy C. Hedworth and Louisa Phipp, late of Oasby Manor, Grantham; unmarried. *Educ:* Denstone College, Staffs; Trinity College, Dublin. *Address:* Wellesbourne Hastings, Warwickshire.

Died 16 Jan. 1950.

HEENAN, Hon. Peter; Minister of Lands and Forests, Ontario, since 1934; *b* Tullaree, Co. Down, 19 Feb. 1875; *s* of Peter Heenan and Margaret Rogers, both of Ireland; *m* 1907, Annie, *d* of D. T. Fawcett, Beausejour, Manitoba; three *s* two *d*. *Educ:* Public School, Workington, Cumberland. Came to Canada, 1902; was a locomotive engineer; represented Ontario Independent Labour Party at British Commonwealth Conference, London, July 1925; Alderman of Kenora for five years, and Chairman of the Brotherhood of Locomotive Engineers for eight years; first elected to Ontario Legislature at general election, 1919; re-elected, 1923; resigned seat to accept nomination for House of Commons; elected at general election, 1925, as a Liberal-

Labour, and 1926; Minister of Labour, Canada, 1926–30; represented Canada at International Labour Conference, Geneva, 1928; Roman Catholic. *Address:* 420 Rosemary Road, Toronto, Ontario, Canada. *Clubs:* Elks, Ontario, Canadian (Ottawa).

Died 11 May 1948.

HEGEDUS, Ferencz; violinist; *b* Funfkirchen, nr Budapest, 26 Feb. 1881; father Hungarian, mother Spanish; *m* Kate Buckley, violinist; three *d*. *Educ:* Funfkirchen Academy; Budapest Conservatoire; Royal Hungarian Academy of Music. Conductor at Opera Comique, Budapest School for the Blind; appeared in London, 1900; has visited Berlin, Leipzig, Hanover, and many other German towns; has done tours in United Kingdom, Germany, Austria, Hungary, Italy, etc.

Died 12 Dec. 1944.

HEILBUTH, George Henry; Director, H. Stodart & Co., Ltd, Wine Merchants and Shippers, 20 and 21 Suffolk Street, SW1, Director Hotel York, Ltd, Sacratinta Ltd; Partner, G. Heilbuth & Co., 15 Walbrook, EC4; *s* of Samuel Heilbuth; *m* Florence, *d* of late John Sankey. One of HM's Lieutenants City of London; elected a member of Corporation of London, 1899; Past Chairman, Accounts, Street, Guildhall School of Music, Sanitary, City of London Schools, Overseers, Gresham Committee (City Side), etc.; Chairman West Ham Park Committee, 1926; Chairman City of London Police Committee, 1929; A Trustee of Prison Charities; Deputy Alderman (Ward of Walbrook), 1909–29; Past Overseer, St Stephen's, Walbrook and Past Overseer and Churchwarden St John the Baptist, Walbrook; Guardian City of London, 1904–30, and City of Westminster Guardians, 1905–14; Liveryman Company of Spectacle-makers and member Court of Loriners Company, Master 1940 and 1941; late member Metropolitan Asylum Board; Gov. of Bridewell and Bethlem and Middlesex Hospitals; Member City Dispensary Comm. and the Honourable Society of Gray's Inn; past President United Wards Club, City of London; Chairman and Hon. Treasurer Brixton Prison Discharged Prisoners' Aid Society; Vice-President Royal London Discharged Prisoners' Aid Society; Member Westminster City Council since 1906; Mayor of the City of Westminster, 1925–26; Deputy Mayor, 1926–27; Pres. Westminster Philanthropic Society, Westminster Health Society, and Westminster National Savings Committee, 1925; Chm. Westminster King's Roll Committee, 1925; Vice-Pres. Royal Sanitary Institute Congress, 1926, and Member Jubilee Committee; Chairman Metropolitan Mayors Association, 1925; a Commissioner of Taxes, City of London; Appointed by the City of London Corporation as its representative on the Governing body of the City of London College, 1932; also Metropolitan Boroughs' Standing Joint Committee, 1941; Member, Grand Council Travel and Industrial Development Association of Great Britain; Original Founder Guildhall Lodge No. 3116 and its First Secretary, 1905–33. Member Board Management Freemasons Hospital; a Founder and Past Master United Wards Lodge; Hon. Member Sir Edward Clarke, Honor Deo, Londinium, and Portsoken Lodges. *Address:* 20 and 21 Suffolk Street, Pall Mall, SW1. *TA:* Liveryman-Cannon-London. *T:* Whitehall 8881. *Club:* Junior Carlton.

Died 3 Oct. 1942.

HEILGERS, Actg Lt-Col Frank Frederick Alexander; JP; MP (C) Bury St Edmunds since 1931; *b* 25 June 1892; *s* of Alexander Frederick Heilgers, Wannock, Polegate, Sussex; unmarried. *Educ:* Harrow; Magdalen College, Oxford; MA. Served in European War in Gallipoli, Egypt, and Palestine, 1914–19 (despatches); War of 1939–45, DAQMG 11 Corps, 1940; DAQMG War Office, 1942; Parliamentary Private Sec. to Rt Hon. Walter Elliot when Min. of Agriculture, 1935–36; to Rt Hon. Herwald Ramsbotham, when Minister of Pensions, 1937–39, and First Comr of Works, 1939–40; Alderman West Suffolk

County Council; JP, Suffolk, 1923; Area Vice-Pres. Eastern Area, British Legion; Silver Medal RSPCA for promoting the passage into law of the Riding Establishments Act, 1939. Farms over 1000 acres in West Suffolk; Breeder of British Friesian cattle and Large Black pigs. *Address:* Wyken Hall, Bardwell, Bury St Edmunds, Suffolk. *TA:* Stanton, Suffolk. *T:* Stanton 4. *Clubs:* Carlton, Boodle's, Travellers'.

Died 16 Jan. 1944.

HEINZ, Howard; President and Chairman of the Board of H. J. Heinz Co., Pittsburgh, USA, and H. J. Heinz, Co. Ltd, London, since 1919; *b* Sharpsburg, Pa, USA, 27 Aug. 1877; *s* of late Henry John and Sarah Sloan Heinz; *m* 1906, Elizabeth Granger Rust, Saginaw, Michigan; two *s*. *Educ:* Shady Side Academy, Pittsburgh; Yale University; Hon. Degree of Doctor of Law, Juniata College, 1926. Entered the business established by his father, 1900; Advertising Manager, 1905; Sales Manager, 1907; Chairman of the Board of Directors, 1919; during War, gave his time and services to his country; served as United States Food Administrator for Pennsylvania; Chairman, Food Supply Committee, National Council of Defence, Pennsylvania; Zone Chairman, United States Food Administration for Pennsylvania, Ohio, Virginia, West Virginia, Maryland, and the district of Columbia; Member of the War Industries Board at Philadelphia; after signing of Armistice, became head of the American Relief Administration of South-eastern Europe and Asia Minor, and representative of the United States Grain Corporation, with headquarters at Constantinople, his post requiring his presence in Europe; President of, and, with other members of his family, maintains the Sarah Heinz House (Pittsburgh), a business training school for working boys and girls; Member of the Board of Trustees of the West Penn Hospital, the University of Pittsburgh, the Carnegie Institute, Shady Side Academy, and the Western Pennsylvania School for the Blind (Pittsburgh). He is a Director of the Pennsylvania Railroad Company; the Mellon National Bank, Pittsburgh; Boys' Clubs of America (Director); President of Pittsburgh Regional Planning Assoc.; Member, Executive Committee, of National Industrial Conference Board, Inc., and of the American Relief Association Children's Fund; Trustee of the Carnegie Endowment for International Peace, and of the CRB Educational Fund; Member of the Japan Society; and a Governor of the Yale Publishing Association. *Recreations:* golf and fishing. *Address:* Morewood Heights, Pittsburgh, Pa., USA. *Clubs:* American; Duquesne, Allegheny Country, Rolling Rock, Fox Chapel, Pittsburgh Golf, Harvard Yale-Princeton, Pittsburgh; University, Yale, Recess, New York; Chicago, Chicago; Ristigouche Salmon, Quebec.

Died 10 Feb. 1941.

HELE-SHAW, Henry Selby, Hon. DEng Liverpool, 1931; DSc, LLD, FRS; Past President and Hon. Life MIMechE; Hon. MIChemE; Hon. Fellow Society of Engineers; Hon. Member Bristol Naturalists' Society; MInstCE; FRMetSoc; Emeritus Professor of Liverpool University; *b* Billericay, Essex, 29 July 1854; *m* Ella Marion, *d* of late S. G. Rathbone, JP, Liverpool; one *d*. Engineer apprentice; Senior Whitworth Scholar, 1876; Miller Scholarship, Watt Gold Medal and Telford premium of Institution of Civil Engineers; Gold Medallist InstNA, 1899; Silver Medallist Society of Arts, 1908; Scholar and afterwards 1st Professor of Engineering at Bristol, University College, 1881–85; 1st Professor of Engineering, Harrison Chair, University College, Liverpool, 1885–1904; President of the Liverpool Engineering Society, 1894–95; Chairman of the Liverpool Automobile Club, and Self-Propelled Traffic Association; Hon. Consulting Engineer to Royal Lancashire Agricultural Society, 1896–1904; Chairman of Management Committee, Liverpool School of Technology, 1900–03; 1st Professor of Civil,

Mechanical, and Electrical Engineering at Transvaal Technical Institute, 1903–04; Principal of Transvaal Technical Institute, 1904–05; Organiser of Technical Education in Transvaal, 1905; Member of Council of Royal Society of South Africa, 1905; President of Mechanical Section British Association; Founder Member and Member of Committee of Royal Automobile Club; Past President, Institution of Automobile Engineers; Past President, Association of Engineers in Charge; Past President, Society of Model and Experimental Engineers; inventor of clutches, pumps, and other machines; Gold medal International Inventions Ex. 1885; Vice-President Auto-Cycle Club; Chairman Aircraft Sub-Committee in the War. *Publications:* 100 papers on mathematical, physical, and engineering subjects, contributed to various scientific societies. *Recreations:* reading, walking, and sketching. *Address:* 3 Cherrington Villas, Ross-on-Wye. *Club:* St Stephen's.

Died 30 Jan. 1941.

HELLINGS, Robert Bailey, CMG 1922; *b* 1863; *s* of Robert Carnal Hellings, Cheltenham; *m* 1895, Marie Rosa, *d* of Otto von Vietinghoff, Glogau, Germany. Entered Ceylon Civil Service, 1885; Govt Agent, Sabaragamuwa, 1906; Govt Agent, S Province, and a MLC, 1912; MEC 1914; retired, 1921. *Address:* 27 Somerset Street, Grahamstown, S Africa.

Died 29 Aug. 1947.

HELLINS, Rev. Edgar William James, MA, LLB, DD; Rector of Marnhull, Dorset, since 1908; *b* 7 March 1872; 2nd *s* of Rev. Chas. T. Hellins, late Vicar of Thriplow, Cambs; *m* 1903, Eva Gwenelin (*d* 1942), 2nd *d* of Adam Eyton, JP, of Plas Llanerch-y-Mor, Flints. *Educ:* King's School, Ely; St Catharine's College, Cambridge (Scholar); Theol. Tripos Class II; Law Tripos Class II 1898. Deacon, 1901; Priest, 1902; Curate of Oxton, Birkenhead, 1901–02; Sub-Dean, Librarian and Director of Law Studies, St Catharine's Coll., Cambridge, 1902–08; Prebendary of Grimston and Yatton in Sarum Diocese, 1918; Proctor in Convocation for the Diocese of Sarum, 1918; Captain Cambridge Univ. RV, 1897–99; Chaplain, 1905–08; Camb. Univ. OTC, 1908–13; Director of Ecclesiastical Insurance Office. *Recreation:* motoring. *Address:* Marnhull Rectory, Dorset. *TA:* Rector, Marnhull. *T:* Marnhull 47.

Died 26 Dec. 1946.

HELLIWELL, Maj.-Gen. John Percival, CBE 1919; MRCS Eng.; LRCP Lond.; LDS Eng.; Consulting Dental Surgeon to the London County Council, 1936; Member of the Army Advisory Committee on Maxillo-facial injuries; *b* 24 May 1884; *s* of late James Helliwell, Manchester; *m* Ida Violet Zurcher, *d* of late Ernest Honner Hunter; one *s* one *d*. *Educ:* Owens College, Manchester; St Mary's Hospital. House Dental Surgeon, Manchester Dental Hospital, 1908–09; Demonstrator in Orthodontics, 1910; Dental Surgeon, British Troops in India, 1910–14; Inspecting Dental Officer, London District, Eastern Command and War Office, 1915–20; Inspector of Dental Services, War Office, 1921–27; Assistant Director-General, Army Medical Services (for the Dental Service) War Office, 1927–35; Director, Army Dental Service, 1935–36; retired pay, 1936. Colonel Commandant The Army Dental Corps, 1932–46. *Address:* Doonholm, Beaconsfield, Bucks. *T:* Beaconsfield 493. *Club:* Army and Navy.

Died 7 Nov. 1948.

HELY-HUTCHINSON, Victor; Director of Music, BBC, since 1944; *b* Cape Town, 26 Dec. 1901; *y s* of late Rt Hon. Sir Walter Hely-Hutchinson; *m* 1925, Marjorie Hugo; two *s*. *Educ:* Eton; Balliol College, Oxford. DMus Oxon 1941. Lecturer in Music, University of Cape Town, 1922–25; on music staff of BBC, 1926–34; Peyton-Barber Professor of Music, University of

Birmingham, 1934–44; pianist, composer, conductor and lecturer. *Publications:* various musical works. *Recreation:* golf. *Address:* 26 Queen's Grove, NW8.
Died 11 March 1947.

HELYAR, Lt-Comdr Kenneth Cary, DSO 1918; RN; retired; *b* 1887; *s* of late Colonel Charles William Hawker Helyar, 3rd Hussars; *m* 1924, Cynthia, *d* of J. S. Phillimore, 5 The College, Glasgow; two *s* one *d.* Served European War, 1914–18 (despatches, DSO). *Address:* Poundsford Lodge, Pitminster, Taunton.
Died 18 June 1941.

HEMINGFORD, 1st Baron *cr* 1943, of Watford; **Dennis Henry Herbert**, PC 1933; KBE 1929; DL; JP; *b* 25 Feb. 1869; *e s* of late Rev. Henry Herbert of Hemingford Abbots, Hunts, and Mary, *d* of Rev. Edward Grevile Ruddock; *m* 1903, Mary Græme, *d* of late Valentine Græme Bell, CMG; three *s. Educ:* The King's School, Ely; Wadham College, Oxford (Hon. Fellow, 1933). Admitted solicitor, 1895; member of firm of Beaumont & Son, and Clarke, Rawlins & Co., Gresham House, London, EC; Chairman, Equity and Law Life Assurance Society, 1931–40; MP (U) Watford Division of Herts, 1918–43; Deputy Chairman of Ways and Means, House of Commons 1928–29; Chairman of Ways and Means and Deputy Speaker, 1931–43; Chairman of Select Committee on Offices of Profit under the Crown, 1941, and Chairman or Member of other Select or Departmental Committees; member of Herts County Council since 1912; Alderman, 1933; member of Council of the Law Society, Vice-President, 1940–41, President, 1941–42. *Publications:* The Law as to Solicitors, 1932; Back Bencher and Chairman, 1946; What Parliament is and does. *Recreations:* shooting, fishing, and boating. *Heir: s* Hon. Dennis George Ruddock Herbert, MA. *Address:* Clarendon Lodge, Watford. *Clubs:* Carlton, City of London, United.
Died 10 Dec. 1947.

HEMINGWAY, Charles Robert, CBE 1920; JP; *b* Cardiff, 26 Sept. 1860; *s* of James Hemingway; one *s* (and one killed at battle of Festubert, 1915) six *d. Educ:* Macclesfield Grammar School. Retired. *Recreations:* golf, shooting, fishing. *Address:* Ards Place, Aberlady, East Lothian. *T:* 49.
Died 13 Jan. 1947.

HEMMERDE, Edward George; KC; Recorder of Liverpool since 1909; *b* 1871; *s* of late Manager of Imperial Ottoman Bank; *m* 1903, Lucy Elinor (whom he divorced 1922), *y d* of late C. C. Colley; one *d. Educ:* Winchester; University College, Oxford (1st class Mods.). Called to Bar, Inner Temple, 1897; joined Northern Circuit; contested Winchester, 1900; Shrewsbury, 1906; and Portsmouth, 1910; MP (L) East Denbigh, 1906–10; NW Norfolk, 1912–18; (Lab) Crewe Division of Cheshire, 1922–24. *Publications:* A Maid of Honour (Play), under pseudonym, Edward Denby; (with Francis Neilson), A Butterfly on the Wheel (Play); (with Francis Neilson) The Crucible (Play); Proud Maisie (Play); A Cardinal's Romance (Play); (with Cicely Fraser) The Dead Hand (Play). *Recreations:* golf and river (winner of Diamond Sculls, 1900), and cricket (Winchester XI 1890). *Address:* 1 Hare Court, Temple, EC4. *T:* Central 4640.
Died 24 May 1948.

HEMMING, Gen. Edward Hughes, CMG 1915; late RE; retired; *b* 13 May 1860; *e surv. s* of G. W. Hemming, KC; *m* 1889, Blanche Alice (*d* 1942), *e d* of Col A. W. Macnaghten, Bombay Cavalry; one *s* one *d. Educ:* Clifton College; RM Academy, Woolwich. Entered Army, 1880; served Zhob Valley Expedition, 1884; European War, 1914–18 (despatches, CMG); Major-Gen., 1919; Deputy Commissioner Housing, Lancs and Cheshire, Ministry of Health, 1919–21. *Address:* Castle House, Newbury. *T:* Newbury 2.
Died 20 April 1943.

HEMMING, Col Norman Mackenzie, CB 1916; Superintendent of Building Works, Royal Arsenal, 1911–21; retired pay, 1921; *b* 28 Oct. 1868; *s* of George Wirgman Hemming, KC; *m* 1897, Evelyne Marian, *e d* of Lt-Col Charles Mountstuart Erskine; two *d. Educ:* Wellington College. 2nd Lt, Royal Engineers, 1888; Capt. 1899; Major, 1907; Lt-Col 1916; Col 1921; served in India, 1894–1902; QO Sappers and Miners, 1894–99; PWD, Rajputana, 1899–1902; Assistant Superintendent Building Work Dept, Royal Gun Powder Factory, Waltham Abbey, 1905; served Tirah Campaign, 1897–98; special duty in Indian famine, 1897. *Address:* St Winnins, Bourne End, Bucks.
Died 1 Jan. 1950.

HENDERSON OF ARDWICK, 1st Baron *cr* 1950, of Morton Park, Carlisle; **Joseph Henderson**; JP; Lord of the Treasury since 1945; *m;* one *d.* First Labour Mayor of Carlisle, 1927–28; an employee of the LNER, and has held official positions in the National Union of Railwaymen. President, 1933–36; MP (Lab) Ardwick Division of Manchester, June–Oct. 1931 and 1935. *Heir:* none. *Address:* Rowanby, Eskdale Avenue, Morton Park, Carlisle. *T:* Carlisle 73.
Died 26 Feb. 1950 (ext).

HENDERSON, Rev. Alexander Roy, MA, DD (Edin.); Principal of Paton Congregational College, Nottingham, 1921–37; Principal Emeritus since 1937; *b* 11 June 1862; *s* of George and Isabella Henderson, King Edward, Aberdeenshire; *m* 1891, Jean Boyd Galbraith, Greenock; two *s* two *d. Educ:* King Edward School; Edinburgh University; Edinburgh Theological Hall. Assistant at George Square Congregational Church, Greenock, 1887–89; Minister of Montrose Congregational Church, 1889–95; Minister of Augustine Congregational Church, Edinburgh, 1895–1902; Minister of Castle Gate Congregational Church, Nottingham, 1902–19; Minister of Queen Street Congregational Church, Wolverhampton, 1919–21; Chairman of Congregational Union of England and Wales, 1923–24. *Publications:* Character in Common Life; History of Castle Gate Congregational Church, Nottingham; The Life of J. M. Jarvie of Greenock; God and Man in the Light of To-Day. *Recreation:* golf. *Address:* 6 Villa Road, Nottingham. *T:* 64458.
Died 21 Feb. 1950.

HENDERSON, Very Rev. Edward Lowry; *b* 1873; *s* of Peter Lindsay Henderson of Woodfield House, Kingsbury; *m* 1907, Sibyl Marjory, *y d* of late Preb. Bernard Reynolds; three *s* one *d. Educ:* Radley; Oriel College, Oxford (BA 1896; 3rd Class Modern History; MA 1899). Trained at Oxford House, Bethnal Green, and Wells Theological College; Curate of Limehouse Parish Church, 1899–1906; Vicar of St James, Derby, 1906–10; Rector of Lowestoft, 1910–17; Residentiary Canon of Gloucester and Canon Missioner, 1917; Provost of St Mary's Cathedral, Edinburgh, 1919–25; Dean of St Albans 1925–35; Dean of Salisbury, 1936–43; Dean Emeritus from 1943. *Address:* Fritham Lodge, nr Lyndhurst, Hants.
Died 26 Sept. 1947.

HENDERSON, Sir Frederick Ness, KBE 1918; Chairman, Iron Trades Employers Insurance Association Ltd; Chairman, North West Rivet Bolt & Nut Factory, Airdrie; Director, A. & J. Inglis, Ltd, and J. & A. Stewart, Ltd; *b* 23 Dec. 1862; *s* of William Henderson, Shipbuilder, Glasgow; *m* 1888, Jessie Miller (*d* 1943), *d* of Alexander Strathern, Sheriff-Substitute of Lanarkshire; four *s* one *d. Educ:* Albany Academy; Glasgow University. *Address:* Crosbie House, Monkton, Ayrshire. *T:* Troon 153. *TA:* Monkton, Ayrshire.
Died 11 April 1944.

HENDERSON, George Cockburn, MA; Emeritus Professor of History in the University of Adelaide; Research Professor of History, University of Sydney; *b* Hamilton, NS Wales, 1 May 1870; *s* of Richard and Anne Henderson of Newcastle, England. *Educ:* Sydney University; Balliol College, Oxford. Gold Medallist in Philosophy; Fraser Scholar in History; and James King of Irrawang Travelling Scholar in Sydney University; went to Balliol College in 1894 and won Brackenbury Scholarship. Lecturer under Oxford University Extension Delegacy; Acting-Professor of History and Philosophy in Sydney University, 1899–1900; Professor of History, Adelaide University, 1902–24; Member of Board of Governors of Public Library, Museum and Art Gallery of South Australia, 1903–23; Chairman, Public Library Committee, 1907–23; Founded South Australian Archives. *Publications:* Life of Sir George Grey, 1907; Reflections on the War, 1916; The British Navy at War, 1917; Fiji and the Fijians, 1931; The Discoverers of the Fiji Islands, 1933; Fijian Documents, 1938; (Editor) The Journal of Thomas Williams, 2 vols, 1931. *Recreations:* golf, travel. *Address:* Dora Creek, Lake Macquarie, NS Wales, Australia. *Clubs:* Authors'; Adelaide, Adelaide.
                                                    Died 9 April 1944.

HENDERSON, George Gerald, FRS 1916; MA, DSc (Glasgow), Hon. LLD (St Andrews and Glasgow), Hon. DSc Belfast, FIC, FCS; Emeritus Professor; *b* Glasgow, 30 Jan. 1862; *e s* of George Henderson, Glasgow, and Alexandrina Kerr; *m* 1895, Agnes Mackenzie, *d* of late John Crawfurd Kerr. *Educ:* private school; University of Glasgow (Clark Fellowship), and University of Leipzig. Lecturer and demonstrator in Chemistry, University of Glasgow, 1884–92; Lecturer in Chemistry, Queen Margaret College, Glasgow, 1889–92; Professor of Chemistry, The Royal Technical College, Glasgow, 1892–1919; Regius Professor of Chemistry, Glasgow University, 1919–37; for eight years Hon. Secretary, and then Chairman of the Scottish section of the Society of Chemical Industry; Secretary, 1901–04, 1905 Recorder, and 1916 President of section B, British Association; Past President of Society of Chemical Industry; Past President Chemical Society; Past President Institute of Chemistry; Hon. Member Society of Public Analysts. *Publications:* numerous papers in organic and inorganic chemistry in Transactions of Chemical Society Proceedings of Royal Society, Journal of Society of Chemical Industry, Transactions of Royal Society of Edinburgh, and Analyst; An Introduction to Analytical Chemistry (with Prof. M. A. Parker); Catalysis in Industrial Chemistry; Report on Chemical Industries of West of Scotland; etc. *Recreations:* fishing, golf. *Address:* Horsaclett, Tarbert, Isle of Harris.
                                                    Died 28 Sept. 1942.

HENDERSON, George Hugh, OBE; FRS 1942; FRSC, PhD; Professor of Physics, Dalhousie University, Halifax, since 1924; Chief Superintendent, Naval Research Establishment, Halifax, since 1948 (Joint Supt, 1939–48); *b* 8 Dec. 1892; *s* of John A. Henderson; *m* 1929, Ruth, *o d* of late Senator W. B. Ross; two *d*. *Educ:* Pictou Academy; Dalhousie University; Gonville and Caius College, Cambridge. Lieut CE, 1916–18; Fellow National Research Council of Canada, 1918–19; 1851 Exhibitioner, 1919–22; Asst Prof. Univ. of Saskatchewan, 1922–24. Member of Nat. Research Council of Canada; Governor of Nova Scotia Research Foundation. *Publications:* various papers on radio-activity and allied subjects. *Recreations:* fishing, shooting. *Address:* 74 Morris Street, Halifax, NS, Canada. *Clubs:* Halifax (Halifax, NS).
                                                    Died 19 June 1949.

HENDERSON, Col Harry Dalton, CB 1925; DSO 1918; VD 1902; TD 1919; DL Perthshire, 1925; Member of Education Committee, Perthshire County Council; Chairman Perthshire Local Employment Committee (Ministry of Labour); *b* Lydney, Gloucestershire, 1858; *s* of late William Henderson,

Mining Engineer, Oakengates, Salop, and Paulina, *d* of John Dean; *m* 1884, Mary, *d* of Robert Moffat, Collector of Inland Revenue, Gloucester; two *s* two *d*. *Educ:* Rev. M. S. Ridley's, Lydney; Newland Grammar School; Shuthonger House, Tewkesbury. Civil Service (Inland Revenue Department), 1880–1921; has served continuously in Volunteer and Territorial Forces since 1875; 2nd VB Gloster Regiment, 1875–87; 6th Batt. (The Black Watch) RH, 1888–1908; RASC since 1908; European War, 1914–19; commanded 51st (Highland) Divisional Train in France and Flanders, 1915–18; commanded East Yorks RASC District, 1918, and Highlands RASC District, 1918–19 (despatches thrice, VD, DSO, TD, CB); Chairman, Perthshire Territorial Army Association 1923–36. *Publications:* The Episcopal Church in Scotland, 1903; Boy Scout Stories in The Empire Annual for Boys, 1910–1913; miscellaneous reviews and general journalistic work for The Record and other newspapers. *Recreations:* golf and gardening. *Address:* The Orchard, Perth, Scotland. *T:* Perth 617.
                                                    Died 13 May 1945.

HENDERSON, Lt-Col Henry Cockcroft P.; *see* Page-Henderson.

HENDERSON, Herbert Stephen, VC 1896; Mining and Mechanical Engineer; Manager, the Ulster Finance and Investment Co. Ltd, Johannesburg and Bulawayo; ranching on Doddieburn Ranch, S Rhodesia; *b* Hillhead, Glasgow, 30 March 1870; 4th *s* of William Henderson, Bishop Street Engineering Works, Glasgow; *m* 1924, Ann Davison, BA, Pretoria; two *s*. *Educ:* Kelvinside Academy, Hillhead, Glasgow. Five years apprenticeship with J. and J. Thomson, engineers, Glasgow; afterwards connected with Workman, Clark, and Co., Belfast, and Harland and Wolff; left Belfast 1892, for the Rand; connected professionally with Langlaagte, Primrose, Crœsus, and George and May Gold Mines; left Rand, 1894, for Rhodesia, as engineer to Queen's Mine, etc.; when rebellion broke out, joined Rhodesia Horse as Scout under Capt. M'Farlane; on 28 March (Sunday) left Bulawayo, and when about 35 miles from town, Colliers and himself, who formed the advance guard, were fired at and cut off by rebels; Colliers' horse, shot five places, ran 200 yards, then dropped; Colliers shot through knee; put him on his pony; only reached Bulawayo Wednesday, dodging Matabele; had nothing to eat from Sunday morning till Wednesday morning, and never wishes to spend another birthday like it. Decorated by Lord Milner at opening of Bulawayo railway. *Recreations:* yachting, riding, and shooting, gymnastics. *Address:* PB Farvie Mine, Bulawayo. *Club:* Bulawayo.
                                                    Died Aug. 1942.

HENDERSON, James; JP; Director, The United Steel Cos Ltd; Deputy Chairman, Appleby-Frodingham Steel Co. Ltd; *b* 12 May 1868; *m* 1905; two *s* one *d*. *Educ:* West of Scotland Technical College, Glasgow. Past-President, British Iron and Steel Federation; Honorary Treasurer, Iron and Steel Institute. *Address:* Holmer Ridings, Holmer Green, Bucks. *Club:* Union.
                                                    Died 20 Nov. 1945.

HENDERSON, Sir James Blacklock, Kt 1920; LLD, DSc; MIEEn; FInstP; Associate Institution of Naval Architects; *b* 5 March 1871; *e s* of late James Henderson, MA, Headmaster of Whitehill High School, Glasgow; *m* 1898, Annie M. (*d* 1949), *d* of Joseph Henderson, Esp Hill, Haydon Bridge, Northumberland. *Educ:* by father; Allan Glen's School, Glasgow; University of Glasgow; and University of Berlin. Lecturer in Physics in Yorkshire College, Leeds, 1894–98; Head of Scientific Department, Barr and Stroud, Glasgow, 1898–1901; Lecturer on Electrical Engineering and University Assistant in Engineering, Glasgow University, 1901–05; Professor of Applied Mechanics, Royal Naval College, Greenwich, 1905–20; Adviser upon Gyroscopic Equipment to Admiralty 1920–25; Inventor of many improvements in gunnery used by the British Navy; Past President of the Engineering Section of the British Association for the Advancement of Science, and Member of its Council, Member of the Parliamentary and Scientific Committee and of its executive committee. *Publications:* scientific papers published in Proceedings of the Royal Society, Institution of Electrical Engineers, Institution of Naval Architects, Physical Society, Philosophical Magazine, Wiedemann's Annalen, Electrician, etc. *Recreations:* motoring, golf, lawn tennis. *Address:* Vine Cottage, Park Gate, SE3. *T:* Lee Green 2748. *Clubs:* Royal Automobile; Royal Blackheath Golf; Royal Institution.

Died 7 April 1950.

HENDERSON, John, MD, ChB, FRFPS (Glas.); Consulting Physician; *b* 5 Oct. 1876; *s* of John Henderson, late of Fordell, Burnside; *m* Jenny, *d* of D. D. Martin, Edinburgh; one *s* one *d.* *Educ:* Allan Glen's School, High School, and Univ., Glasgow. Registered in 1898; Hon. Consulting Physician to Glasgow Royal Infirmary; Professor of Medicine in St Mungo's Coll., Glasgow, 1913–47; formerly Lecturer in Clinical Medicine in Glasgow University; Assistant to Muirhead Chair of Medicine in Glasgow University, 1911–13; retired Major, RAMC, TF; war service overseas in Salonica and France, 1916–18; Formerly President of Royal Faculty of Physicians and Surgeons of Glasgow; Member Association of Physicians. *Publications:* Wheeler and Jack's Handbook of Medicine, 9th edn, 1932; 10th edn 1937; Bence-Jones' Proteinuria, 1912; Medicine for Nurses, 1921; Catechism Series in Medicine; High Blood-pressure and its Treatment, 1923; Oral Sepsis—a Cause and Result of Disease, 1924; The Position of Extramural Teaching in Glasgow in 1828 and its Progress during the Century, 1928. *Recreations:* golf, motoring. *Address:* 6 Newton Place, Glasgow, C3. *T:* Douglas 5035. *Club:* Royal Scottish Automobile (Glasgow).

Died 1 June 1949.

HENDERSON, John Cochrane, MB, BCh; JP Westmorland; *b* 1881; *s* of late William Thomson Henderson, Glasgow; *m* 1927, Ethel Briggs-Bury, Easedale, Windermere. *Educ:* Glasgow Academy; Glasgow Univ. Served as MO attached Armoured Cars. Western Desert, Egypt, 1916–17. High Sheriff for Westmorland, 1944. *Address:* St Andrews, Bowness-on-Windermere. *T:* Windermere 19.

Died 5 Feb. 1946.

HENDERSON, Kingsley Anketell, CMG 1937; FRIBA; FRAIA; A. & K. Henderson and Associates; Chairman of Directors Argus and Australasian, Ltd; Official Referee under City of Melbourne Building Act; Member Town Planning Association of Victoria; *b* Melbourne, 15 Dec. 1883; *s* of late Anketell Matthew and Mary Louisa Henderson, Melbourne; *m* 1909, Ruve Cutts, *d* of late Frederick William Poolman. *Educ:* Cumloden, East St Kilda; Melbourne University. Past President Federal Council Australian Institute of Architects and Royal Victorian Institute of Architects; Member of Malvern City Council for six years. *Recreations:* motoring, politics. *Address:* Charter House, 4 Bank Place, Melbourne, Victoria. *TA:* Henalmar. Melbourne. *T:* M. 1181, 1182, 1183. *Clubs:* Royal Societies; Melbourne, Savage, Athenæum, Melbourne.

Died 6 April 1942.

HENDERSON, Rt Hon. Sir Nevile Meyrick, PC 1937; GCMG 1939; KCMG 1932; CMG 1923; 2nd *s* of late Robert Henderson, Sedgwick Park, Horsham, and Emma Caroline (*d* 1931), *d* of John Hargreaves of Cuffnells, Lyndhurst. *Educ:* Eton. Attaché in HM Diplomatic Service, 1905; 3rd Secretary, St Petersburg, 1905–08; Tokio, 1909–11; St Pettersburg, 1912–14; Rome, 1914; Nish, 1915; Foreign Office, 1915; 1st Secretary, Paris, 1916; Counsellor in Constantinople, 1921; acting British High Commissioner in Constantinople, Nov. 1922 to Feb. 1924, and from June

to Sept. 1924; appointed to the Residency, Cairo, with the rank of Minister Plenipotentiary in HM Diplomatic Service, 1924; HM Minister Plenipotentiary at the British Embassy, Paris, 1928–29; Envoy Extraordinary and Minister Plenipotentiary at Belgrade, 1929–35; British Ambassador to Argentine Republic and Minister to Paraguay 1935–37; British Ambassador in Berlin, 1937–39; since 1941 Group Commander (Colonel) in Home Guard. *Publications:* Failure of a Mission, 1940; Hippy, 1943. *Recreations:* shooting, fishing, golf. *Club:* St James's.

Died 30 Dec. 1942.

HENDERSON, Richard; Shipowner; *b* South America, 23 April 1854; 3rd *s* of late John Henderson, Glasgow; *m* 1887, Hildegard, *d* of late Henry Oelrichs, New York; one *s* two *d.* *Educ:* Glasgow and St Andrews. Chairman Anchor Line SS Co., 1899–1912; Trustee Rangoon Tramway Co., 1903–23; Member Mersey Docks and Harbour Board, 1900–07; Deputy Chairman Liverpool, London and Globe Insurance Company, 1907. *Recreations:* music, golf, motoring. *Address:* 348 Foul Bay Road, Victoria, BC. *TA:* Anchor, Victoria, BC. *Clubs:* Constitutional; Western, Glasgow.

Died 24 Feb. 1945.

HENDERSON, Thomas, CBE 1933; JP; FRSE; Actuary of the Savings Bank of Glasgow, 1924–35; *b* 23 Jan. 1870; *s* of David Henderson and Sarah Brodie; *m* 1909, Margaret Gertrude, *o d* of late William Mort Thompson, London; one *s* one *d.* *Educ:* Penrith; Glasgow. Joined the staff of the Savings Bank of Glasgow, 1883; passed through every grade in the service; Assistant Actuary, 1917; Hon. Secretary of the Trustee Savings Banks Association, 1929–35; Vice-President of the Trustee Savings Banks Association; Vice-Chairman of the Executive of the International Thrift Institute, Milan, 1925–35; former member Scottish Savings Committee. *Publications:* Trustee Savings Banks: their Origin and Purpose; Among Savings Bank Friends in America; Trustee Savings Banks: the Case for Disinterested Service; The Savings Bank of Glasgow; One Hundred Years of Thrift; numerous brochures; also contributions on Thrift Subjects to the Press. *Recreations:* reading, motoring, public service, charitable, philanthropic, and religious organisations. *Address:* 5 Belmont Crescent, Glasgow, W2. *T:* Western 660. *Clubs:* Scottish Automobile, Glasgow; Scottish Conservative, Edinburgh.

Died 23 March 1945.

HENDERSON, Velyien Ewart, MA, MB; FRSC; Professor of Pharmacology and Toxicology, University of Toronto, since 1909; Major, 198th Battalion CEF, 1916; Captain, CAMC 1918; *b* Cobourg, 1877; *s* of Joseph Henderson; *m* 1911, Edith E. van der Smissen; two *s.* *Educ:* Upper Canada College; University of Toronto. BA, 1899; MB, 1902; MA, 1903. Demonstrator of Physiology, University of Pennsylvania, 1902–03; student in the Universities of Prague and Marburg, 1903–04; Demonstrator of Physiology, University of Toronto, 1904–06; Lecturer in Pharmacy and Pharmacology, 1906–09. *Publications:* various scientific papers in Physiology and Pharmacology. *Address:* 111 Admiral Road, Toronto. *T:* Randolf 4668. *Clubs:* York, Toronto.

Died 6 Aug. 1945.

HENDERSON, Brig. William Alexander, CMG 1919; DSO 1918; VD; FRIBA; Assistant Chief Architect, State Savings Bank, Melbourne (granted leave during war), retired 1947; *b* Richmond, Melbourne, 28 Nov. 1882; *s* of James Alexander Henderson, Sackville Street, Kew, Melbourne; *m* 1912, Ella Rose Mary, *d* of Charles F. Oberfuchshuber, Ulmarra, Clarence River, New South Wales; one *s* one *d.* *Educ:* Ulmarra Public School. Articled architectural pupil to Mr John Little, 1899–1903; Verdon Prize, Melbourne Technical College, also Bronze and Silver Medals of the Royal

Victorian Institute of Architects. Assistant Instructor Architectural Classes, Melbourne Technical College, 1902; Instructor Building Construction Melbourne Technical College, 1912–33; ARVIA 1906; ARIBA 1922; FRVIA 1924; FRIBA 1926, resigned membership, 1947; in partnership with late R. J. Haddon, 1910–29; enlisted as Sapper in Australian Military Forces, 1906; served European War in Egypt and France with 2nd Division, Engineers, AIF, as Major, 1915; Lt-Colonel commanding 1st Pioneer Batt., 1917; transferred to Divisional Staff and commanding 1st Divisional Engineers, 1918 (CMG, DSO, despatches four times); commanding 4th Divisional Engineers, Australian Military Forces, 1922; Colonel and commanding 4th Infantry Brigade, 3rd Division, Australian Military Forces, 1926–30; Chief Engineer, Southern Command, 1940–42; Chief Engineer, 2nd Aust. Army, 1942; Retired List, 1944. *Recreations:* gardening, politics; Nationalist; Creed, Methodist. *Address:* Harwood, 112 Yarrbat Avenue, Balwyn, Melbourne, E8, Victoria, Australia.

Died 20 Sept. 1949.

HENDRICK, James, BSc, LLD, FRIC; Emeritus Professor of Agriculture, University of Aberdeen; formerly Director of Studies and Research, North of Scotland College of Agriculture; *b* Belfast, 1867; parents Scottish; *m* 1897, Fräulein Borsche (*d* 1941); one *s* one *d*; 1942, C. Diack. *Educ:* Belfast; King's College, London; Univ. of Leipzig. Chief Asst to Professor of Chemistry, R. Agricultural Coll., Cirencester, 1890–93; Lecturer in Agricultural Chemistry, Technical College, Glasgow, 1893–96; Lecturer in Agricultural Chemistry, University of Aberdeen, 1896–1912; Lecturer in Agricultural Chemistry, North of Scotland College of Agriculture; formerly Chemist to Highland and Agricultural Society of Scotland; Strathcona-Fordyce Professor of Agriculture, University of Aberdeen, 1912–42. *Publications:* The Farmer's Raw Materials; many papers on Chemical, Agricultural, and Educational subjects; Journal of the Society of Chemical Industry; Analyst; Journal of Agricultural Science; Transactions of the Highland and Agricultural Society of Scotland, etc., many articles in the Standard Cyclopedia of Modern Agriculture; rewrote and revised many sections of last edition, 5th, of Stephen's Book of the Farm. *Recreations:* fishing, walking, motoring. *Address:* 72 Queen's Road, Aberdeen. *T:* Aberdeen 2122. *Club:* University (Aberdeen).

Died 25 Feb. 1949.

HENDRIE, Herbert, ARCA; artist in stained glass and landscape painter; *b* Manchester, 1887; *s* of William Laidlaw Hendrie; *m* 1924, Constance Gough, London; one *d*. *Educ:* The Royal College of Art; Slade School. Went up to London from Manchester, 1910; studied under Prof. Lethaby at the Roy. Coll. of Art; held a commission in the Army, 1915–18 (4th Batt. Manchester Regt); served in France, 1916–17 (Chevalier Mérite Agricole); studied under Professor Tonks, the Slade School, 1919; exhibited at the Royal Academy, New English Art Club, etc.; designed and executed stained-glass windows for St Peter, Mancroft, Norwich; St Winifred's Church, Welbeck Abbey; St John's Church, Perth; Buckfast Abbey; Ampleforth Abbey, Liverpool Cathedral, Lincoln's Inn Hall, London; St Mary's Cathedral, Johannesburg, Glasgow Cathedral, etc. *Recreations:* tennis, gardening, and travel. *Address:* Chelsey, Smiley Knowes, North Berwick. *T:* 414. *Club:* Chelsea Arts.

Died 23 May 1946.

HENDRY, James, MBE, JP, MA, BSc MB; FRFPSG; FRCOG; Regius Professor of Midwifery, University of Glasgow, since 1943; Medical Director, Royal Maternity and Women's Hospital, Glasgow; Gynæcological Surgeon, Royal Infirmary, Glasgow; *b* 25 Sept. 1885; *e s* of John Hendry, Beith, Ayrshire; *m* 1914, Harriet Elizabeth, *o d* of Joseph Williamson, São Paulo, Brazil,

and Glasgow; three *s*. *Educ:* University of Glasgow (MB, ChB 1910); University of Freiburgim Breisgau; University of Baden. Asst to Prof. of Physiology, Univ. of Glasgow, 1910–12; Volunteer Assistant Univ. Frauenklinik, Univ. of Freiburg, 1912–13; served throughout European War, 1914–18, first as Adjutant OTC Univ. of Glasgow and, 1916–19, with RAMC in France; demobilised as Major; Assistant in Univ. Departments of Obstetrics and Gynæcology, 1919; Muirhead Prof. of Obstetrics and Gynæcology, Univ. of Glasgow, 1927; Examiner Queen's Univ., Belfast, Universities of Aberdeen, Durham, and Edinburgh; Pres. Obstetrical Socs of Edinburgh and Glasgow; Deputy Chairman Central Midwives Board for Scotland; Member Interdepartmental Committee on Medical Schools, 1942–44; Medical and Scientific Advisory Committees to the Secretary of State for Scotland; Chairman Medical Committee of Scottish Advisory Committee of the Nuffield Provincial Hospitals Trust. *Publications:* Combined Textbook of Obstetrics and Gynæcology (joint), 1923, 4th ed. 1944; many papers in medical and scientific journals since 1913. *Address:* 7 Clairmont Gardens, Glasgow, C3. *T:* Douglas 5260.

Died 9 Sept. 1945.

HENEAGE, Lt-Col Hon. Henry Granville, DSO 1902; late 12th Lancers; *b* 17 March 1868; 2nd *s* of 1st and *brother* and *heir-pres.* to 2nd Baron Heneage, OBE; *m* 1904, Gladys Mary, 3rd *d* of late Sidney Cuthbert of Beaufront Castle, Hexham. *Educ:* Eton. Entered 3rd Lincoln Regiment 1885; 12th Lancers, 1888; Major, 1900; served as ADC to Governor of Bombay, 1895–98; served South Africa, 1899–1902 (DSO, medal with six clasps, despatches, King's medal two clasps); retired from army, 1905; Hon. Sec. Duhallow Hunt Club, 1909–11; served European War as R. of O., Aug. 1914–April 1919; commanded 2/1 Lincolnshire Yeo., 1915–16; Staff appointment in France, 1917–19 (1914 Star, General and Victory medals). *Address:* 7 Montpelier Square, SW7. *T:* Kensington 2015.

Died 15 June 1947.

HENLEY, Col Frank Le Leu, DSO 1917; OBE 1919; VD; Deputy Director Supply and Transport, Southern Command HQ, Melbourne; *b* 7 Dec. 1888; *s* of James Robert Henle; *m* Elizabeth Elder Wisdom. Served European War, 1914–18 (despatches, DSO, OBE). *Address:* 5 Vincent Street, Surrey Hills, Victoria. *Clubs:* Naval and Military, Melbourne.

Died 25 Dec. 1941.

HENNESSY; *see* Pope-Hennessy.

HENNIKER, Col Alan Major, CBE 1919; late RE; *b* 1870; *m* 1902, Blanche Marie, *d* of late James Gadsden of Lannion, Brittany; one *s* one *d*. *Educ:* RMA. Served South African War, 1899–1902; European War, Aug. 1914–Feb. 1919; retired pay, 1926. *Address:* Carlinwark, Middleton Road, Camberley, Surrey.

Died 11 April 1949.

HENRIQUES, Sir Philip Gutterez, KBE 1918; DL; *b* 2 Nov. 1867; *s* of late Alfred G. Henriques, JP, DL, of Hove, Sussex; *m* 1892, Beatrice, *e d* of Sir George Faudel-Phillips, GCIE, 1st Bt, of Balls Park, Hertford. *Educ:* Wellington College; Trinity College, Cambridge, Historical Honours. Called to Bar, Inner Temple, 1892; practised Common Law and Parliamentary Bar; DL, JP Surrey; one of HM Lieutenants for the City of London; Alderman and Vice-Chairman, 1934–37, Chairman, 1937–40, of the Surrey County Council. Assistant Financial Secretary, Ministry of Munitions, until 1920; Alderman of the London County Council, 1921–25; Chairman, Works and Navigation Committee of Thames Conservancy, 1934–47; Officer of the Legion of Honour; Officer of the Crown of Italy. *Address:* 37 Eaton Square, SW1. *T:* Sloane 7432; Normandy Park, nr Guildford. *Club:* Athenæum.

Died 26 April 1950.

HENRY, George, RA 1920; RSA; *b* Ayrshire, 1858. *Educ:* Glasgow School of Art; Paris. Travelled China, Japan, Egypt, India, 1893–94; Painter, pastel, water-colour and oil. *Works:* Sundown; A Galloway Landscape; Springtime; Harmony; Goldfish; Symphony; The Samisen Player; The Mousumé; Salutations; Japanese Baby; Geisha; East and West; Pearl Necklet; The Black Hat; Afternoon Tea; The Mirror; At the Window; The Black Dress; The Blue Gown; The Blue Veil; Poinsetta, etc.; many portraits. *Address:* 26 Glebe Place, Chelsea, SW3. *T:* Flaxman 4675. *Clubs:* Thatched House, Chelsea Arts; Glasgow Arts.

Died 23 Dec. 1943.

HENRY, Maj. James D.; *see* Douglas-Henry.

HENRY, Prof. Robert Mitchell; Hon. Professor of Classical Literature, University of Dublin; Hon. LittD (Dublin); Hon. LLD (Belfast and St Andrews); Member of Royal Irish Academy; President, Classical Association of Ireland, 1920; President, Classical Association of England and Wales, 1936; *b* 11 Feb. 1873; *e s* of late Rev. Robert Mitchell Henry, Belfast, and Kate, *e d* of late Rev. Thomas Berry, Athlone; *m* 1st, Margaret Jane, *γ d* of late John MacFarland, Omagh, Co. Tyrone; 2nd, Kathleen Elizabeth Raleigh, *e d* of Herbert Watson, BE, AMICE, Belfast. *Educ:* Methodist College, and Queen's College, Belfast; graduated with First Class Honours in Classics, Royal University of Ireland, 1893; with First Class Honours in Classics, London University, 1895; MA, and Studentship in Classics, RUI, 1898; Junior Fellowship in Classics, RUI, 1900. Professor of Latin, 1907–38, and late Secretary to the Academic Council, University, Belfast; Pro-Vice-Chancellor, Belfast University, 1938–39; Professor of Humanity, St Andrews University, 1939–47; Pres. of the Classical Association of Northern Ireland, 1929–38; late Lord Lieutenant's Inspector of Endowed Schools, Ireland; late Chairman of Trade Boards, Irish Free State. *Publications:* Livy, Book xxvi, edited, with Introduction, Notes, and Appendices, 1905; Selections from Livy with Introduction, 1906; (with Rev. F. W. O'Connell) An Irish Corpus Astronomiae, edited with Introduction, Translation, Notes and Glossary, 1914; The Evolution of Sinn Fein, 1920; (with T. W. Dougan) Cicero Tusculan Disput. iii–v edit. with Introd., apparatus criticus and commentary, 1934; Virgil and the Roman Epic, 1938; articles in Classical Review, etc. *Address:* Trinity College, Dublin. *Club:* Royal Societies.

Died 21 Dec. 1950.

HENSON, Rt Rev. Herbert Hensley; *b* London, 8 Nov. 1863; 4th *s* of late Thomas Henson, Broadstairs, Kent, and Martha Fear; *m* 1902, Isabella Caroline, *o d* of J. W. Dennistoun of Dennistoun, Scotland. *Educ:* privately and at Oxford. First class Modern History; Fellow of All Souls College, Oxford, 1884–91; re-elected, 1896; BD 1898; Hon. DD Glasgow, 1906; Durham, 1913; Oxon. 1918; LLD St Andrews, 1932. Head of the Oxford House, Bethnal Green, 1887–88; Vicar of Barking, Essex, 1888–95; select preacher at Oxford, 1895–96, 1913–14; Cambridge, 1901; Incumbent of St Mary's Hospital, Ilford, 1895–1900; Chaplain to Lord Bishop of St Alban's, 1897–1900; Canon of Westminster Abbey and Rector of St Margaret's, 1900–12; Sub-Dean of Westminster, 1911–12; Dean of Durham, 1912–18; Bishop of Hereford, 1918–20; Bishop of Durham, 1920–39; Canon of Westminster Abbey, 1940–41; late Hon. Professor of Modern History in Durham Univ.; Proctor in Convocation, 1903–18; Gifford Lecturer, 1935. *Publications:* Light and Leaven, 1897; Apostolic Christianity, 1898; Cui Bono: an Open Letter to Lord Halifax, 1899; Ad Rem, Thoughts on the Crisis in the Church, 1900; ed. Church Problems, a View of Modern Anglicanism, by various authors, 1900; Dissent in England, two lectures, 1901; Godly Union and Concord, 1902; Cross Bench Views of Current Church Questions, 1902; The Education Act and After, 1903; Preaching to the Times, 1903; Sincerity and Subscription, 1903; English Religion in the 17th century, 1903; The Value of the Bible, and other sermons, with a letter to the Bishop of London, 1904; Moral Discipline in the Christian Church, 1905; Religion in the Schools, 1906; Christian Marriage, 1907; The National Church; Christ and the Nation, 1908; The Liberty of Prophesying (Lyman Beecher Lectures), 1909; Westminster Sermons, 1910; Puritanism in England, 1912; The Creed in the Pulpit, 1912; War-Time Sermons, 1915; Robertson of Brighton, 1816–1853, 1916; Christian Liberty, 1918; edited The Naked Truth by Bishop Croft, 1919; edited Sir William Anson: a Memoir, 1920; Anglicanism, 1921; Byron: the Rede Lecture, 1924; In Defence of the English Church, 1923; Quo Tendimus, 1924; Notes on Spiritual Healing, 1925; Church and Parson in England, 1927; The Book and the Vote, 1928; Disestablishment, 1929; Sibbes and Simeon, 1932; The Oxford Groups, 1933; Christian Morality, 1936; Ad Clerum, 1937; The Church of England, 1939; Last Words in Westminster Abbey, 1941; Retrospect of an Unimportant Life, Vol. 1, 1942, Vol. 2, 1943; Bishoprick Papers, 1946. *Recreations:* motoring, walking. *Address:* Hyntle Place, Hintlesham, Ipswich, Suffolk. *Club:* Athenæum.

Died 28 Sept. 1947.

HENSON, John James, CBE 1920; *b* 1868; *m* 1896. *Address:* The Chalet, Rhiwbina, near Cardiff.

Died 20 Dec. 1948.

HENVEY, Col Ralph, CMG 1919, DSO 1917; late RA; *b* 1876. Served South African War, 1899–1900 (despatches, Queen's medal and five clasps); Northern Nigeria, 1901–03 (despatches twice, two medals and two clasps, Brevet-Major); European War, 1914–17 (despatches, DSO); retired pay, 1923. *Address:* White Cottage, Upper Shirley Road, Shirley, Croydon, Surrey.

Died 5 Dec. 1945.

HEPBURN, Malcolm Langton, MD; BS (London); FRCS (England); LRCP (London); Ophthalmic Surgeon; Consulting Surgeon to the Royal London Ophthalmic Hospital since 1910; late Dean of the Medical School (Royal London Ophthalmic Hospital); Consulting Ophthalmic Surgeon, Royal Free Hospital, since 1913; Ex-President of the Ophthalmological Section of the Royal Society of Medicine; Hon. Secretary, Council of British Ophthalmologists; late Lecturer on Ophthalmology to London School for Medicine for Women; late Examiner in Ophthalmology Conjoint Board of Royal College of Surgeons and Physicians; *b* 20 Oct. 1866; *s* of Augustus Paull Hepburn of Bermondsey; *m* 1896, Ruby, *d* of James Worthington, JP, Lowestoft; one *s* three *d. Educ:* Uppingham School; St Bartholomew's Hospital, London. House Surgeon at St Bartholomew's Hospital, London, 1893–94; started in general practice in Lowestoft, 1895; held the post of Assistant Surgeon, and later (1900) Surgeon to the Lowestoft Hospital; returned to London, 1904; after studying Ophthalmology became first Assistant Surgeon to the Central London Ophthalmic Hospital, 1909; late Assistant Opthalmic Surgeon, Hampstead Hospital; FRGS. *Publications:* The Ophthalmology of General Practice, 1922; several contributions to Ophthalmic literature; and some on the subject of Mountain Sickness in the Alpine Journal, etc. *Recreations:* cricket, fives, lawn tennis, mountaineering. *Address:* 111 Harley Street, W1. *T:* Welbeck 9450. *Club:* Alpine.

Died 16 May 1942.

HEPBURNE-SCOTT, James Cospatrick; *see* Scott.

HEPWORTH, Joseph; JP; MP (U) Bradford East since 1931; *e s* of Elijah and Charlotte Hepworth; one *s* one *d*. Director of several companies; Vice-Pres. of the Institute of British Foundrymen; Chairman of Bradford Northern Rugby League Football Club. *Address:* Woodhall Grange, Calverley, near Leeds. *T:* Pudsey 2381.

Died 11 May 1945.

HERBERT, Brig.-Gen. Edmund Arthur, CMG 1919; MVO 1904; DL, JP; *b* 5 Aug. 1866; *s* of Edmund Herbert, Llansantffraed, Abergavenny, and Elinora, *d* of Col Gwynne Holford; *m* 1898, Ethel, *o d* of late Sir John Rodger, KCMG; two *d*. Entered army, 1886; Capt., 1897; Major, 1902; Lieut-Colonel, 1904; Col, 1907; commanded Inniskilling Dragoons, 1904–08; Welsh Border Mounted Brigade, TF, 1912; served Zululand, 1888; S Africa, 1899–1902 (Queen's medal 2 clasps, King's medal with clasp); served European War, 1914–18 (CMG, Order of White Eagle (Serbia). *Address:* Moynes Court, Chepstow. *T:* Chepstow 368. *Club:* Army and Navy.

Died 29 May 1946.

HERBERT, Col Hon. Sir George Sidney, 1st Bt *cr* 1937; TD, JP; ADC to the King (Additional) since 1936; Groom in waiting to the King, since 1937; Gentleman Usher to the King; DL and Vice-Lieutenant, Wilts; *b* 8 Oct. 1886; 2nd *s* of 14th Earl of Pembroke. *Educ:* Eton College; Magdalen College, Oxford. Served European War, 1914–19; a Volun. or Territ. since 1905; Director of Wilton Royal Carpet Factory; Director of Wessex Assoc. News Ltd, and of Western Gazette Co. Ltd; local Director, Liverpool, London & Globe Insurance Co. Ltd 1932, etc. *Recreation:* shooting. *Address:* Knoyle House, Salisbury, Wilts. *TA:* East Knoyle. *T:* East Knoyle 28. *Club:* Carlton.

Died 30 Jan. 1942 (ext).

HERBERT, Lt-Col Herbert, FRCS; Indian Medical Service, retired; Consulting Surgeon, Nottingham and Midland Eye Infirmary; and Consulting Ophthalmic Surgeon, Worthing Hospital; Consulting Pathologist, Sussex Eye Hospital; ex-Vice-President, Ophthalmological Society of the United Kingdom; *b* 1865. Late Professor of Ophthalmology, Grant Medical College, Bombay; Fellow and Syndic, Bombay University; War service with Indian troops on Hospital Ship, at Brockenhurst and at Karachi, India. *Publications:* The Practical Details of Cataract Extraction, 1903; Cataract Extraction, 1908; The Operative Treatment of Glaucoma, 1923; numerous papers, particularly on Glaucoma and Tropical Ophthalmology. *Address:* 6 Southview Drive, Worthing.

Died 19 March 1942.

HERBERT, John Alexander, BA, FSA; *b* Gateshead, 26 Aug. 1862; *e s* of Rev. S. A. Herbert, Rector of St James's, Gateshead; *m* 1896, Alice (*d* 1941), *d* of Lt-Col R. Aufrère Baker, RA, and *widow* of Walter H. Low, MA; one *d*. *Educ:* Royal Grammar School, Newcastle-upon-Tyne; St John's College, Cambridge (BA 1883). Assistant Keeper of MSS, 1912; Deputy Keeper, 1921–27. *Publications:* Titus and Vespasian, 1905; vol. iii of the Catalogue of Romances in the Department of MSS, 1910; Illuminated MSS, 1911; Guide to the Exhibited MSS, part iii, 1912, 1923; Schools of Illumination, parts i-vi, 1914–1930; Sherborne Missal, 1920; French Text of Ancrene Riwle, 1944; various articles in Romania, Walpole Society, etc. *Address:* c/o Westminster Bank, 214 High Holborn, WC1.

Died 7 Dec. 1948.

HERBERT, Lt-Col Sir John Arthur, GCIE 1939; DL, JP, Governor of Bengal, 1939–43; *b* 1895; *s* of late Sir Arthur Herbert, GCVO, and Helen Louise Gammell, Providence, RI, of Coldbrook, Abergavenny, Mon; *m* 1924, Lady Mary Theresa Fox-Strangways, *d* of 6th Earl of Ilchester, OBE; one *s*. *Educ:* Wellington; Harvard, USA. MFH Monmouthshire, 1921–25; Lieut, Royal Horse Guards, 1916; Major, 1930; retired 1934; MP (C) Monmouth, 1934–39; Assistant Whip (unpaid), 1937–39; ADC to Viceroy, 1926–28. *Address:* Llanover, Abergavenny, Mon. *Clubs:* Buck's, Turf, Carlton.

Died 11 Dec. 1943.

HERBERT, Lt-Col Norman F.; *see* Fitz Herbert.

HERBERT, Maj.-Gen. William Norman, CB 1936; CMG 1919; DSO 1917; DCL 1946; *b* 1880; *s* of John Herbert, Kenilworth; *m* 1925, Frieda (*d* 1933), *o d* of late A. T. Venn, MD; one *d*. Served S African War, 1901–02 (Queen's medal with five clasps); N Nigeria, 1906 (medal with clasp); European War, 1914–19 (despatches, DSO with bar, Brevet Lt-Col, CMG); Iraq rebellion, 1920 (Medal and clasp); General Staff Officer, 1st Grade, Northern Command, 1930–32; Commander 10th Infantry Brigade, 1932–34; Comdr 50th (Northumbrian) Division TA, 1935–39; Col Royal Northumberland Fusiliers, 1935–46; retired pay, 1939; Commander 23rd (Northumbrian) Division, 1939–40, Operations France and Belgium, 1940 (despatches); retired pay, 1940. *Address:* Manor Farm House, Stanton, Glos, nr Broadway, Worcs. *Club:* Naval and Military.

Died 26 April 1949.

HERBERT-SMITH, His Honour Charles, LLD (Lond.); Freeman of City of York; late County Court Judge, Circuit No. 32; retired 1934; *b* York, 1862; *s* of Thomas Smith; *m* Ella, *d* of Rev. J. Mostyn; one *s* three *d*. *Educ:* Elmfield College, York; London University. Barrister-at-Law; joined Gray's Inn, 1885; winner of a First Class Studentship and the Arden Scholarship; Doctor of Laws of London University; Bencher of Gray's Inn. *Recreation:* gardening. *Address:* 10 Albemarle Road, Norwich.

Died 7 Jan. 1944.

HERCY, Sir Francis Hugh George, Kt 1921; CBE 1918; *b* 14 May 1868; *s* of late Thomas Joseph Hercy, DL, JP, of Churchfield and Winkfield, Berks. Formerly Captain 3rd Batt. (Militia) The Queen's RW Surrey Regt; Temp. Capt. in Army, 8 Aug. 1914; on Recruiting Staff; thanked for his services by Earl Kitchener, 1915, and by Earl of Derby, 1915; mentioned for valuable services in connection with the war, 1917; DAAG War Office during transfer of recruiting to civil control; then in Ministry of National Service; DL County of London. *Address:* 80 South Audley Street, W1.

Died 13 Feb. 1947.

HERDMAN, Major Sir Emerson Crawford, KBE 1921; Senator, Northern Ireland; HML, Co. Donegal; *b* 2 Jan. 1869; *m* 1895, Olive May, *d* of late Emerson Tennent Herdman of Sion House, Co. Tyrone. *Educ:* Uppingham; Christ Church, Oxford. Served World War, 1914–16. *Recreations:* hunting and golf. *Address:* Carricklee, Strabane, Co. Tyrone.

Died 10 Feb. 1949.

HERNAMAN-JOHNSON, Francis, MD; FFR; Physician to the Charterhouse Rheumatism Clinic; Chairman Council British Rheumatic Association; Consulting Radiologist to the French Hospital, London (Chevalier de l'Ordre de la Santé Publique, République Française), and to Croydon General Hospital; Consulting Radiologist, Aldershot Command, 1915–18 (despatches); *b* Crosby, Lancashire, April 1879; *s* of late J. Hernaman-Johnson, BA (Cantab), barrister-at-law of the Inner Temple; *m* Janet Eleanor, *d* of Thos Francis Townend; one *s* one *d*. *Educ:* Merchant Taylors' (Lancs); University of Aberdeen; St Bartholomew's Hospital. MD (Aberdeen), 1910; MB, ChB (Honours), 1904; Liddell (First Medical) Bursar, 1899–1902; Duthie Scholar, 1903–05. Past President, Section of Radiology, Royal Society of Medicine; Past Warden and Examiner in Medicine, Faculty of Radiologists; Fellow American Electro-therapeutic Association; DMRE (Camb.) 1921; served in RN, 1904–07; Surgeon, RN Hospital,

Plymouth, 1904–05. *Publications:* Behold, the Axe! (novel) 1948; Radiotherapy in relation to General Medicine, 1926; and numerous contributions to the British Medical Journal, Lancet, and Practitioner; contributor to the London Evening Standard under the pen-name of Francis Wimbrook. *Recreation:* writing plays and novels. *Address:* Charterhouse Clinic, 56 Weymouth St, W1. *T:* Welbeck 1264. *Club:* Arts Theatre.

Died 3 Sept. 1949.

HERON, Hon. Col Alexander Robert, CMG 1919; DSO 1917; VD; Pharmaceutical Chemist; *b* 25 Dec. 1888; *m*; one *s* (elder son killed in action) two *d*. Served European War, 1915–19 (despatches, DSO, CMG). Served in 1939–45 war, 1940–46. *Address:* Hilton St, East Brisbane, Australia.

Died 18 Oct. 1949.

HERON, Lt-Col Davis, CIE 1918, MB, FRCSE, IMS, retired; *b* 1878; *m* 1921, Nesta, *d* of late Capt. Pennell Hill, Indian Army; one *d*. Vice-Consul Seistan and Kain; Residency Surgeon, Udaipur, Mewar, India, 1927; retired 1930. *Address:* The Cottage, Ley Hill, nr Chesham, Bucks.

Died 24 June 1941.

HERON, Edward Thomas; JP; *b* 1867; *s* of Thomas Heron; two *s*. *Educ:* Haberdashers' School. Apprenticed to Hutchings & Crowsley, Ltd; manager Chevens & Son, and later started The Advertiser, W London; started as printer in Tottenham Street, 1893, and absorbed the business of Coxill & Co., Ltd, J. H. Kennett & Co., Ltd, A. Page & Co., Ltd, Pitcher & Co., Ltd, R. F. Hunger & Co.; started the first two papers in the world for the Gramophone and Moving Pictures—the Talking Machines News and the Kinematograph Weekly; among many other periodicals founded the Millinery Trades Journal, Ballooning and Aeronautics, Bowling and Curling, the Concert Artists' Journal; Chairman E. T. Heron & Co., Ltd, Maxclif Publishing Co., Ltd, Olympic Publications Ltd, Melina Estates Ltd, and other private Companies; Alderman and Mayor of St Pancras, 1908–09. *Publications:* many handbooks, including Scott's Machinery Index, The Kinematograph Handbook, The Showman's Guide. *Address:* Silver End, St Leonards-on-Sea. *T:* Hastings 2574, Museum 4777.

Died 10 April 1949.

HERON-ALLEN, Edward, FRS 1919; FLS, FGS, FZS, FRMS, MRIrish Academy, etc; Hon. Member, Accad. St Cecilia, Rome; President, Royal Microscopical Society, 1916–18; Hon. Member, Manchester Micr. Society; Marine Biologist and Zoologist; Lieut 6th Vol. Bn Royal Sussex Regt, 1917 (France, 1918); *b* London, 17 Dec. 1861; *s* of George Allen and Catherine Heron; *m* 1st, 1891, Marianna, *d* of Rudolf Lehmann, painter; 2nd, 1903, Edith, *d* of William Brown Pepler, MD; one *d*. *Educ:* Harrow. Admitted Solicitor of Supreme Court, 1884; Special Commissioner of Music Section of Colonial Exhibition to Italy, 1885; lecturing and writing in United States, 1886–89; since then Student of, and Lecturer upon, Protozoology; attached to Staff Intelligence Dept War Office (MI 7 B1 and 4), 1918; District Commissioner SW Sussex for National Service, 1916–17; District Commissioner of Boy Scouts for SW Sussex, 1910–19; President of the Sette of Odd Volumes, 1927–28; President of the National Auricula Society, 1928. *Publications:* Violin-making, 1882; Bibliography of the Violin, 1890–1896, and De Fidiculus Opuscula, i-viii, 1882–1895; ix, The Nefer Sign, 1941; Rubáiyat of Omar Khayyám, Literal Translation of Bodleian MS, 1898; Fitzgerald's Omar Khayyám with the original Persian, 1899; A Commentary upon Omar Khayyám, 1905; Quatrains of Omar Khayyám; Nicolas and Corvo, edited 1924; The Lament of Bábá Táhir, 1902, and others; A Manual of Cheirosophy, 1885; The Science of the Hand, 1886, and others; Selsey Bill, Historic and Prehistoric, 1911; Selsey Map and Guide, 1912; The

Parish Church of St Peter, Selsey, 1935, and others; A Study of Chalk Foraminifera, 1893; The Foraminifera of Selsey Bill, 1908–1911; of Kerimba Archipelago, 1915; of West Scotland, 1916; of Cornwall, 1916; of the North Sea, 1911–1914, and many others; Bionomics of the Foraminifera, Phil. Trans. Roy. Soc., London, 1915; Alcide d'Orbigny, his Life and Work; Presidential Address, R Micr. Soc., 1917; Purpose and Intelligence in the Foraminifera, R Inst. Great Britain, 1915; R Micr. Soc. 1915–1916, and Brit. Assoc. Rep. 1915; Foraminifera of the Eocene of Biarritz (Halkyard), 1919; of the Terra Nova Expedition, 1922; of Lord Howe Id., 1924; of Moorabool Quarry, 1924; of Plymouth, 1930; of the Falkland Islands (Discovery Expedition Report), 1932; Barnacles in Nature and Myth, 1928; Madame de Sévigné, 1928; The Gods of the Fourth World, 1931; fiction and verse (chiefly under various pseudonyms). *Recreations:* Persian literature; Marine Zoology; Meteorology; Heraldry; Bibliography; Occasional Essays and Scientific Romances; Auricula and Asparagus Culture. *Address:* Large Acres, Selsey Bill, Sussex. *T:* Selsey 1. *Club:* Garrick.

Died 28 March 1943.

HERRIES, Lady, (12th in line, *cr* 1490); **Gwendolen Mary Fitzalan Howard, (Duchess of Norfolk);** *b* 11 Jan. 1877; *d* of 11th Baron and Hon. Angela Mary Charlotte Fitzalan-Howard, 2nd *d* of 1st Lord Howard of Glossop; *S* father, 1908; *m* 1904, 15th Duke of Norfolk (*d* 1917). Owns about 18,900 acres. *Heir: to Barony:* s Duke of Norfolk, KG. *Address:* Everingham Park, York; Kinharvie, New Abbey, Dumfries.

Died 28 Aug. 1945.

HERSCHEL, Rev. Sir John Charles William, 3rd Bt *cr* 1838; FRAS; *b* 22 May 1869; *s* of 2nd Bt and Anne Emma Haldane, *d* of Alfred Hardcastle, Hatcham House, Surrey; *S* father, 1917; *m* 1908, Catharine Margaret, *y d* of late Col E. T. Browell, late RA; no *c. Educ:* Winchester; Christ Church, Oxford (MA); Wells Theological College. Ordained, 1906; Curate of Bracknell, 1906–08; Wooburn, 1908–10; Crowthorne, 1910–14; Perpetual Curate of Braywood, 1914–19; Rector of West Clandon, 1919–34; Vicar of Perranzabuloe, 1934–39; Vicar of Westbury, Bucks, 1939–45. *Heir: none. Address:* Observatory House, Slough.

Died 15 June 1950.

HERTZ, Alfred; Hon. Citizen of San Francisco; *b* Frankfurt am Main, 15 July 1872; *s* of Leo Hertz and Sarah Koenigswerther; *m* Lilly Dorn; no *c. Educ:* Frankfurt Raff Conservatory. Conductor: Altenburg, Elberfeld, and Breslau; Conductor of German Opera at the Metropolitan Opera House, New York, 1902–15; Conductor of San Francisco Symphony Orchestra, 1915–30; Regional Director Federal Music Project, 1937–40. *Recreations:* motoring, bridge. *Address:* 770 Camino del Mar, San Francisco, California, USA. *T:* Bayview 7707. *Clubs:* Argonaut, Family, Musicians, San Francisco.

Died 17 April 1942.

HERTZ, Very Rev. Joseph Herman, CH 1943; Chief Rabbi of the United Hebrew Congregations of the British Empire since 1913; Commander of the Order of Leopold II and Columbia University medal for outstanding service; *b* Rebrin, Slovakia, 25 Sept. 1872; and emigrated as a child to New York; *s* of Simon Hertz, Hebraist; *m* Rose Freed (*d* 1930), New York; two *s* three *d. Educ:* New York City College (BA); Columbia University (PhD); Jewish Theological Seminary of America (Rabbi, Doctor of Hebrew Literature, honoris causa); hon. LLD (University of London); Rabbi at Syracuse (NY) till 1898; of the Witwatersrand Old Hebrew Congregation, Johannesburg, 1898–1911. Expelled by President Kruger for pro-British sympathies and for advocating removal religious disabilities of Jews and Catholics in South African Republic, 1899; Member of the High Commissioner's Consultative Committee, 1900; Professor of Philosophy, Transvaal Univ. Coll., 1906–08; Pres., Jews College, London since 1913, Acting Principal, 1939–45; Pres. of the Jewish Historical Society of England, 1922–23; of Conference of Anglo-Jewish Preachers; on Board of Governors of Univ. of Jerusalem and Chairman of the Governing Body of its Institute of Jewish Studies; Vice-Pres. Anglo-Jewish Association, London Hosp., The League of Nations Union, National Council of Public Morals, King George's Fund for Sailors, etc. *Publications:* A Book of Jewish Thoughts, twenty-five eds; Affirmations of Judaism, The Pentateuch and Haftorahs with Commentary; Commentary on the Jewish Prayer Book; Sermons, Addresses and Studies, 4 volumes; contributor to the Jewish Encyclopædia, Encyclopædia Britannica, and member of original Board of Translators, 1896–1903, of the American Jewish Bible Version. *Address:* Chief Rabbi's Office, 4 Creechurch Place, Aldgate, EC3; 103 Hamilton Terrace, NW8. *Club:* Athenæum.

Died 14 Jan. 1946.

HERTZ, William Axel, CSI 1911; *b* Moulmein, 1 Oct. 1859; *s* of late A. W. T. Hertz and Anne Fairweather; *g s* of Bishop Hertz of Ribe, Denmark. *Educ:* St Xavier's College, Calcutta. Entered Government Service, 1886; saw active service as Political Officer Burma War, 1886–89 (medal and two clasps); on special duty against dacoits, 1889–90; promoted to Burma Commission; Deputy Commissioner, 1903; Commissioner, 1919; studied Chinese in Peking, 1897–98, and passed prescribed examination; Settlement Officer, Magwé, 1900–03; in charge of Hpimaw Expedition, 1910–11 (thanked by Government of India, CSI); Kachin Hills Operations, 1914–15; additional member of the Viceroy of India's Council, 1919; retired from the Service, 1921. *Publications:* articles in the Graphic, Field, Asia, Pioneer, etc. *Address:* 10 Lennox Garden Mews, Knightsbridge, SW1.

Died 15 March 1950.

HERTZBERG, Maj.-Gen. Charles Sumner Lund, CB 1943; MC 1916; VD 1924; Chief Engineer, 1st Canadian Army, 1942–43; *b* Toronto, 12 June 1886; 2nd *s* of Anton Lund Hertzberg and Helen McMaster; *m* 1910, Jessie Todd Alexander; two *s. Educ:* St Andrew's College, Toronto; University of Toronto. Civil engineering; served European War, 1914–18 (wounded, MC, Czechoslovak War Cross), and War of 1939 in Royal Canadian Engineers. *Address:* 9 Barton Avenue, Toronto, Canada. *Club:* Toronto Cricket.

Died 9 Jan. 1944.

HERTZOG, Gen. Hon. James Barry Munnik, BA, LLD; *b* 3 April 1866; *s* of Johannes Albertus Munnik Hertzog; *m* 1894, *d* (*d* 1942) of C. Neethling, Stellenbosch; three *s. Educ:* Victoria College, Stellenbosch; Amsterdam University. Advocate at Bloemfontein; Judge, Orange Free State, 1895; commanded Boer Forces of South-Western Division, South African War, 1899–1902; Minister of Justice, first Union Cabinet, 1910–12; Minister of Native Affairs, 1924–29; Prime Minister, 1924–39, and Minister of External Affairs, 1929–38; formerly leader of Nationalist Party, and leader of United South African National Party from inception, 1933–39. *Address:* 21 Bryntirion, Pretoria, SA.

Died 21 Nov. 1942.

HERVEY, Lord Walter John; *b* 29 Jan. 1865; 3rd *s* of late Lord Augustus Hervey, and Mariana, *d* of W. P. Hodnett; *brother* and *heir-pres.* to 4th Marquess of Bristol, MVO; *m* 1903, Hon. Hilda Calthorpe, *d* of 6th Baron Calthorpe. Late Lt Suffolk Imp. Yeomanry; JP Notts and Wilts; Major Army Remount Service, 1915–19. *Address:* Rumsey House, Calne, Wilts. *Club:* Bachelors'.

Died 13 July 1948.

HERZFELD, Ernst Emil; DrPhil; Professor Emeritus at Institute for Advanced Study, Princeton, NJ; Professor Ordinarius, Berlin University, 1920–35; *b* Celle, Hanover, 23 July 1879. *Educ:* Dom-Gymnasium Verden Hannover; Joachimsthalsches Gymnasium, Berlin; Technische Hochschulen; University of Charlottenburg; University of München; University of Berlin. Explorations and travels in Kurdistan and Luristan, 1905–06; Constantinople-India, 1908; Syria, 1908, 10, 14; Paikuli, Kurdistan, 1910, 13, 23; Turkey, Persia, 1916–17; Afghanistan, 1924; Persia, 1923–31; Commander of the Order of Wasa (Swedish); Commander, Order of the House of Hohenzollern (German); Fellow of the Royal Asiatic Society, British Academy, Kern Institute (Leyden), Académie Arabe de Damas, Medieval Academy of America, Archaeological Survey of India. *Excavations:* Assur, 1903–05; Cilicia, 1907; Samarra, Iraq, 1910–13; also 1931; Pasargadae, Persia, 1928; Kûh i Khwâja, Sistan, 1929; Persepolis, 1931–35. *Publications:* Reise durch Luristan, etc, 1907; Parsargadae, Klio, 1908; Iranische Felsreliefs (with Prof. F. Sarre), 1910; Genesis der Islamischen Kunst. Der Islam, 1910; Archaeolog. Reise im Euphrat-u. Tigris-Gebiet (with Prof. Sarre), 1911 and 1920; Am Thor von Asien, 1920; Die Ausgrabungen v Samarra I–V, 1923, 25, 26, etc.; Paikuli, Mon. and Inscr. of the Sassanian Empire, 1924; Iranische Denkmaeler since 1932; Iran in the Ancient East, 1941; Zoroaster and His World, 1946; Monuments et inscriptions d'Alep, 1947–1948, etc. *Address:* Institute for Advanced Study, Princeton, NJ, USA.

Died 21 Jan. 1948.

HESELTINE, Lt-Col Christopher, OBE; DL; JP; *b* 26 Nov. 1869; *s* of J. P. Heseltine, 91 Eaton Square, SW1; *m* 1923, *widow* of Percy Howes; one *s. Educ:* Eton; Trinity Hall, Cambridge. Played Association Football, Cambridge, 1891–92; cricket with Lord Hawke's Teams in India, South Africa and West Indies; Master of New Forest Foxhounds, 1899; served South African War, 1899–1902, with Hampshire IY; ADC to Lord-Lieutenant of Ireland, 1902–06; served European War, 1914–19, with Royal Fusiliers, and at War Office as King's Messenger (despatches twice, OBE, Chevalier Legion of Honour); DL, JP Hants, 1925; President of Hampshire County Cricket Club, 1925–26, and 1936, and Committee of MCC, 1925–29, 1930–34, 1935–38, 1941–43. *Recreations:* cricket, football, hunting, shooting. *Address:* Brambridge Park, Eastleigh, Hants. *TA:* Brambridge, Otterbourne. *T:* 2211 Twyford, Hants; Walhampton Cottage, Lymington Hants. *T:* Lymington 68. *Clubs:* Carlton, White's.

Died 13 June 1944.

HESKETH, 1st Baron *cr* 1935, of Hesketh; **Thomas Fermor-Hesketh;** 8th Bt *cr* 1761; Director County Fire Office Ltd; Chairman and Director of 8 Private Companies; *b* 17 Nov. 1881; *e s* of Sir Thos George Fermor-Hesketh, 7th Bt, and Florence, *d* of W. Sharon, San Francisco; *S* father, 1924; *m* 1909, Florence Louise, *d* of late J. W. Breckinridge, and *g d* of General J. C. Breckinridge, etc., former Vice-President USA; two *s* two *d. Educ:* Eton; Sandhurst; Cambridge, BA. 2nd Lt Royal Horse Guards, 1900–03; Capt. Lancs Hussars Yeomanry, 1910–17; Hon. Major TF; Advisory Engineer, Lancashire War Agricultural Committee, 1917–19; MP (U) Enfield Division of Middlesex, Nov. 1922–Nov. 1923; High Sheriff, Northants, 1932; JP for counties of Lancaster and Northampton; owns about 15,000 acres; contested Ormskirk Division Lancs as Co. U, 1918. *Heir: s* Capt. Hon. Frederick Fermor-Hesketh, Scots Guards, *b* 8 April 1916. *Address:* Easton Neston, Towcester; 7 Rutland Gate, SW7. *Clubs:* Marlborough, Carlton.

Died 20 July 1944.

HESKETH, Charles Hesketh Fleetwood-; JP, DL, Co. Lancaster; *b* 13 Oct. 1871; *o surv. s* of late John Bibby of Hart Hill, Allerton, Liverpool, and second wife, Anna Maria Emily Fleetwood, *e d* of late Rev. Charles Hesketh, MA, Rector and Lord of the Manor of North Meols, and Anna Maria Alice, *d* of Richard Saunders of Wennington Hall, Lancaster; *m* 1st, 1900, Anne Dorothea, *e d* of late Sir Thomas Brocklebank, Bt; three *s* three *d* (separation deed, 1923, marr. diss., 1934); 2nd, 1935, Gladys Victoria, *y d* of late Capt. Charles Alfred Howard McPherson, 2nd West India Regt. *Educ:* Eton; Trinity College, Cambridge. BA, 1893; MA, 1897. Called to Bar, Inner Temple, 1895; High Sheriff of Lancashire, 1901; served in South African War, 1900; European War, 1914–17; invalided out with rank of Major in the Army; Lord of the Manor of North Meols and of Holcombe Court; Patron of four Livings; took surname and arms of Hesketh by Royal Licence, 1899; and by a subsequent Royal Licence, 1907, surname and arms of Fleetwood-Hesketh. *Address:* Holcombe Court, Holcombe Rogus, nr Taunton; Meols Hall, Southport, Lancashire. *Clubs:* Cavalry; Royal Yacht Squadron, Cowes.

Died 13 April 1947.

HETT, Geoffrey Seccombe, MB Lond., FRCS Eng.; FRGS; MBOU; FZS; Consulting Surgeon, Royal Ear Hospital, and Ear, Nose, and Throat Department, University College Hospital, London; Consulting Surgeon, Ear, Nose, and Throat Hospital, Eastbourne; Consulting Surgeon to the Cassell Hospital for Nervous Diseases; Consulting Surgeon to the National Institute for the Blind; Plastic Surgeon to the Queen's Hospital, Sidcup, Surgeon to British Red Cross, Surgeon to French Red Cross; Major RAMC retd; *b* 14 Aug. 1878; *s* of late Geoffrey Hett, MD; *m* 1st, Aeddan Blanche Muriel (*d* 1942), *g d* of Hon. Robert Arundell; one *s* one *d*; 2nd, 1943, Cynthia Crowdy. *Educ:* St Paul's School; University College, London. After completing his medical education and holding various Hospital appointments, devoted himself to the study of diseases of the ear, nose, and throat; studied in London, Vienna, Freiburg, etc., and was subsequently appointed Assistant Surgeon to the London Throat Hospital and the Throat Hospital, Golden Square; has held the post of Curator of the Anatomical Museum and Assistant in the Department of Anatomy, University College, London, and carried out researches on the Comparative Anatomy of the Tonsils; has lectured before the Zoological Society, etc. OC, Lord Methuen's Convalescent Hosp. for Officers, Corsham Court, Wilts; OC Middleton Park Red Cross Hospital for Officers and other ranks (Head Injuries). *Publications:* papers on subjects relating to his speciality in medical journals, etc. *Recreations:* big game hunting, shooting, fishing, zoology. *Address:* 8 South Parks Road, Oxford. *Clubs:* Bath, Shikar.

Died 3 May 1949.

HETT, Walter Stanley; British Council Representative, Cyprus; *b* 8 April 1882; *s* of Geoffrey Hett, MD (Ed.), and Mary Hett; *m* 1911, Dorothy Bourdillon; two *s* two *d*. *Educ:* St Paul's School (scholar); Wadham College, Oxford (scholar). Asst Master, King's School, Grantham, 1906–07; Asst Master, Brighton College, 1907–33; Second Master, Brighton College, 1933–38; Headmaster, Brighton College, 1939–44. *Publications:* Short History of Greece, 1908; Alexander the Great, 1934; Greek Reader, 1933; Loeb Translator—Aristotle Minor Works, 1935, 1936, 1937. *Club:* Public Schools (Hon. Vice-Pres.).

Died 24 Jan. 1948.

HEWARD, Leslie Hays, ARCO, Hon. ARCM; *b* 8 Dec. 1897; *s* of Herbert Heward, Bradford; *m* 1925, Lenore, *d* of Arthur Shepherd, artist, London; one *d*. *Educ:* Manchester Cathedral Choir School, Manchester Grammar School; Royal College of Music. Assistant Organist, Manchester Cathedral, 1914; Organist, St Andrews Church, Ancoats, Manchester, 1914; Organist,

Garrison Church, Windsor, 1917; Music Master, Eton College, 1917; Musical Director, Westminster School, 1920; Conductor, British National Opera Co. 1922–28; Musical Director, Capetown Municipal Orchestra and Cape Peninsula Broadcasting Association, 1924; Musical Director, City of Birmingham Orchestra, 1930–43. *Publications:* many musical compositions. *Recreation:* walking. *Address:* 44 Harborne Road, Edgbaston, Birmingham. *Clubs:* Savage, MM; Birmingham Garrick.

Died 3 May 1943.

HEWART, 1st Viscount *cr* 1940, of Bury, in County of Lancaster; **Gordon Hewart,** PC 1918; Kt 1916; Lord Chief Justice of England, 1922–40; *b* Bury, 7 Jan. 1870; *e s* of late Giles Hewart, Bury; *m* 1st, 1892, Sara Wood (*d* Nov. 1933), *e d* of J. Hacking Riley, Bury; one *s* one *d* (eldest son killed and second son invalided in European War); 2nd, Dec. 1934, Jean, *d* of James Reid Stewart, Wanganui, New Zealand. *Educ:* Manchester Grammar School; University College, Oxford (Scholar 1887; BA 1891; MA 1893; Honorary Fellow, 1922); Hon. LLD Manchester University, 1922; Toronto, 1927; Sheffield, 1927; Birmingham, 1928; Johannesburg, 1936. Hon. DCL Oxford, 1926; Pres. of Classical Assoc., 1926; of English Assoc., 1929; a Vice-Pres. of Oxford Society. Called to Bar, Inner Temple, 1902; joined Northern Circuit; KC 1912; contested NW Manchester at by-election, 1912; Bencher of the Inner Temple, 1917; Treas., 1938; MP (CL) E Leicester, 1913–22; Solicitor-Gen. 1916–19; Attorney-Gen. 1919–22; attended Peace Conference in Paris, 1919, as HM Attorney-Gen.; Pres. of Commission on War Criminals; Cabinet Min. 1921–22; one of the British signatories of the Irish Peace Treaty, 1921; received Freedom of Borough of Bury, 1922, and of Hastings, 1930; Pres. of the War Compensation Court, 1922–29; a Trustee of the British Museum, The Times, Reform Club, Chequers, and National Police Fund; Hon. Member of the Canadian and American Bar Associations; Hon. Member of the Average Adjusters' Association; Master of the Curriers' Company, 1926–27; member of many Masonic Lodges; PGW of England; JP Herts; President of Hertfordshire Golf Union. *Publications:* The New Despotism; Essays and Observations, 1930; Not without Prejudice, 1937. *Heir: s* Hon. Hugh Vaughan Hewart, *b* 11 Nov. 1896. *Address:* Garden Hill, Totteridge, South Herts; 2 Harcourt Buildings, Temple, EC4. *T:* Hillside 2517, Temple 67, and Central 679. *Clubs:* Reform, Savage, United Service; Hadley, Moor Park, and Woking Golf.

Died 5 May 1943.

HEWBY, William Petch, CMG 1902; *b* Notting Hill, 1 March 1866; *e s* of late John Petch Hewby, BA Oxon, MRCS; *m* 1910, Jeannette Claudine, *e d* of Arthur Stowell, London. *Educ:* private tuition. Entered service of the Royal Niger Co. (then National African Co.), 1883; (Royal Niger Company's Medal, etc.); Resident (1st Class) Northern Nigeria, 1900; retired, 1914. *Address:* Prestbury Cottage, Bovey Tracey, S Devon.

Died 12 Feb. 1946.

HEWETT, Sir Harald George, 4th Bt *cr* 1813; *b* 24 Oct. 1858; *s* of 3rd Bt and Clara, *d* of Gen. W. von Pochhammer of the Prussian Army; *S* father, 1876; *m* 1st, 1887, Emma (*d* 1889), *d* of T. Pope; 2nd, 1892, Eleanor (*d* 1946), *d* of Captain Studdy, RN, and Mrs W. T. Summers; two *s* one *d. Heir: s* John George [*b* 23 Oct. 1895; *m* 1926, Yuilleen, *o c* of Samuel F. Smithson, Kipkoris, Kitale; two *s.* Major KAR; MC; served British East Africa, 1914–19. Ol'Morogi, Naivasha, Kenya Colony]. *Address:* Newbury, Berks. *T:* Newbury 48.

Died 5 March 1949.

HEWETT, Sir John (Prescott), GCSI 1911; KCSI 1907; CSI 1899; KBE 1917; CIE 1891; Bailiff of Egle in the Venerable Order of St John of Jerusalem; MP (U) Luton, 1922–23; *b* Barham, Kent, 25 Aug. 1854; *e s* of Rev. John Hewett and Anna Louisa Lyster, *d* of Captain Hammon; *m* 1879, Ethel Charlotte, 2nd *d* of Henry

Binny Webster, BCS; one *s* two *d*. *Educ*: Winchester; Balliol Coll., Oxford. Joined Bengal Civil Service, 1877; served in North-Western Provinces and Oudh, 1877–86; Under-Secretary to Government of India in the Home Department, 1886; acted Private Secretary to Viceroy and Governor-General of India, 1888, 1890; Deputy-Secretary to Government of India in Home Department, 1886; acted Private Secretary to Viceroy and Governor-General of India, 1888, 1890; Deputy-Secretary to Government of India in Home Department, Dec. 1890; Magistrate and Collector in North-Western Provinces, 1893; Secretary to Royal Commission on Opium, 1893; member of the Indian Plague Commission, Nov. 1898; Secretary to Government of India, Home Department, 1894–1902; Chief Commissioner of the Central Provinces, 1902; Ordinary Member of Governor-General's Council, India, in charge of Department of Commerce and Industry, 1904; Lieut-Gov. United Provinces of Agra and Oudh, 1907–12; Pres. Coronation Durbar Committee, 1911. *Publication*: Jungle Trails in Northern India, 1938. *Address*: The Court House, Chipping Warden, Banbury. *T*: Chipping Warden 12. *Clubs*: Carlton, Oriental.

Died 27 Sept. 1941.

HEWITT, Surg. Rear-Adm. Alfred James, CB 1931; CBE 1927; LRCP, LRCS, Edin.; *m* Lilian Mary Beatrice (*d* 1934). Served European War, 1914–19; retired list, 1932.

Died 11 Jan. 1947.

HEWITT, Brig. Charles Caulfield, DSO 1918; MC; *b* 20 March 1883. *Educ*: Sandroyd House; Charterhouse; Sandhurst. Joined Roy. Inniskilling Fusiliers, 1902; Instructor, School of Musketry, Hythe, 1913; served European War, 2nd Royal Inniskilling Fusiliers, 1914–15; Machine Gun Training Centre, 1915–16; 11th Machine Gun Company, BEF, 1916–17; Corps Machine Gun Officer, VI Corps, 1917; commanded 46th Batt. Machine Gun Corps, 1917–18; Army Machine Gun Officer, 3rd Army, with rank of Colonel, 1918 (wounded twice, despatches twice, DSO, MC); Chief Instructor Machine Gun School, 1923–24; transferred to the Royal Welsh Fusiliers, 1929; Bt Lt-Col 1927; Lt-Col 1931; commanded 2nd Battalion The Royal Welch Fusiliers, 1931–34; Col 1935; Assistant Director (Small Arms) War Office, 1935–38; retired pay, 1938; called up from RARO, 1940, to command an Infantry Brigade; placed on retired list, 1941. Commandant, National Fire Service College, 1941–45. *Club*: United Service.

Died 17 June 1949.

HEWLETT, Sir (William) Meyrick, KCMG 1931; CMG 1915; *s* of late William Oxenham Hewlett; *m* 1906, Eveleen Macdonald Nash; two *s* one *d*. *Educ*: Harrow. Student Interpreter in China, 1898; served Defence of the Legations at Peking, 1900 (China Medal and clasp); Acting Consul at Chiangsha, 1908, 1909, 1910; Ichang, 1911, 1912, 1913, 1914, 1915, 1916; Acting Consul-General at Tientsin, 1913; at Chengtu, 1916–22; Local rank Consul-General; Acting Consul at Newchwang, 1913, 1914; Shanghai, 1914; Consul at Amoy, 1923–27; Consul-General, Nanking, 1927–31; Consul-General, Hankow, 1931–35; retired 1935. *Publication*: Forty Years in China, 1943. *Address*: Two Gates, Gerrards Cross. *T*: Gerrards Cross 2338.

Died 16 March 1944.

HEYGATE, Rev. Ambrose, MA; Canon Emeritus of Chester; *b* 2 Oct. 1852; *s* of Rev. William Edward and Maria Elizabeth Heygate; *m* Jennie MacNab. *Educ*: Winchester; Keble College, Oxford. Vice-Principal of St John's, Newfoundland Theological College, 1876–82; Senior Curate of St John's Cathedral, 1882–91; Chaplain to P. Egerton Warburton, Arley Hall, 1892–96; Vicar of

Ashton Hayes, 1896–1904; Vicar of St James, Congleton, 1904–18; Rector of Willersey, 1918–24; Rural Dean of Congleton, 1907–18.

Died 6 Feb. 1941.

HEYGATE, Rev. William Augustine; late Prebendary of Fordington and Writhlington, in the Cathedral of Salisbury; Examining Chaplain to the Bishop of Salisbury, 1902–24; *b* 29 May 1847; *e s* of Canon W. E. Heygate, Rector of Brighstone, Isle of Wight; *m* Frances Sophia, *d* of Thomas Ffooks, JP; no *c*. *Educ*: Winchester College; New College, Oxford (scholar). 2nd Class Mods, 1867; 2nd Class Lit. Hum. 1869; BA, MA. Assistant Master Lancing College, 1874–81; Deacon, 1881; Priest, 1882; Curate of S Edmund's, Salisbury, 1881–84; Domestic Chaplain to Bishop Moberly, 1883–84; Vicar of Leigh, Dorset, 1884–90; Burbage, Wilts, 1890–99; Gillingham, Dorset, and Rural Dean of Shaftesbury, 1899–1905. *Address*: Totnell, Broadstone, Dorset.

Died 21 Jan. 1941.

HEYTESBURY, 4th Baron *cr* 1828; **Leonard Holmes A'Court;** Bt *cr* 1795; Colonel, late Wilts Regt; *b* 11 June 1863; *s* of Hon. William Leonard and Isabella, *d* of Rev. Richard A'Court Beadon, of Cheddar; *S* brother, 1903; *m* 1896, Sybil Mary (*d* 1937), *d* of late Capt. F. B. Morris; one *s* two *d*. *Heir*: *s* Hon. William Leonard Frank Holmes A'Court. *Address*: Green House, Crockerton, Warminster, Wilts. *T*: Warminster 129.

Died 2 Feb. 1949.

HEYWARD, DuBose; writer; *b* Charleston, S Carolina, USA, 1885; *m* 1923, Dorothy H. Kuhns, playwright; one *d*. *Educ*: public schools. Member firm Heyward and O'Neill, Charleston, General Insurance Under-writers, until 1924; from 1924 devoted entire time to writing; Hon. LittD University of North Carolina, 1928; Hon. Phi Beta Kappa Fraternity, 1931; member, Authors' League of America, American Society of Composers, Authors and Publishers; American Institute of Arts and Letters. *Publications*: Carolina Chansons—Poetry, 1922; Skylines and Horizons—Poetry, 1924; Porgy—Novel, 1925; Angel—Novel, 1926; Porgy—Play (dramatised), 1927; Mamba's Daughters—Novel, 1929; Brass Ankle—Play, 1931; Jasbo Brown—Poems, 1931; Peter Ashley—Novel, 1932; Porgy and Bess—opera (music by George Gershwin) 1935; Lost Morning—novel, 1936; Mamba's Daughters—Play (dramatised), 1939; Star Spangled Virgin—Novel, 1939. *Address*: 24 South Battery, Charleston, S Carolina, USA. *Club*: St John's Hunting.

Died 16 June 1940.

HEYWOOD, Charles Christopher, MA, MB, MRCP; Consulting Physician, Royal Manchester Children's Hospital; Consulting Physician, Salford Royal Hospital; Consulting Physician to Manchester Warehousemen and Clerks' School; late Consulting Physician to Chetham's Hospital, Consulting Physician, Alderley Edge Cottage Hospital; *b* 3 May 1865; *s* of Henry R. Heywood (Hon. Canon of Manchester and Vicar of Swinton) and *g s* of Sir Benjamin Heywood, 1st Bt; *m* 1893, Mildred Ella, *e d* of late Capt. P. R. Lempriere, RA; four *s* two *d*. *Educ*: Harrow; Trinity College, Cambridge. Was for nine years an officer of the 2nd VB Manchester Regt and the 6th Batt. Manchester Regt (Territorial); late Lt-Col (temp.) Commanding 2/9th Batt. Manchester Regt; Major, RAMC. *Publications*: sundry papers read before scientific societies. *Address*: Earnscliffe, Alderley Edge. *T*: Alderley Edge 2119. *Club*: Old Rectory (Manchester).

Died 10 March 1948.

HEYWOOD, Sir (Graham) Percival, 4th Bt *cr* 1838; CB 1946; DSO 1918; TD, JP, DL; Lieutenant-Colonel Commanding 1/1 Staffordshire Yeomanry, 1916–18 and 1920; Barrister-at-Law; *b* 14 July 1878; *s* of 3rd Bt and Margaret Effie, *e d* of Rt Rev. G. H. Sumner (Bp. of Guildford); *S* father, 1916. *Educ*: Sherborne; Trinity College, Cambridge, MA. Served European War

(DSO). *Heir: nephew* Oliver Kerr Heywood, *b* 1920. *Address:* Doveleys, Rocester, Uttoxeter, Staffordshire. *TA and T:* Rocester 214. *Club:* Naval and Military.
Died 29 June 1946.

HEYWOOD, Maj.-Gen. Thomas George Gordon, CB 1940; OBE 1919; *b* Caen, France, 27 Dec. 1886; *m* 1st, Louise Orr Sutherland; two *d*; 2nd, Joan Morgan, *d* of H. R. Bromley Davenport. 2nd Lieut RA, 1905; Capt. 1914; Bt Major, 1917; Major, 1925; Bt Lt-Col, 1923; Col, 1932; Maj.-Gen., 1939; Military Attaché, Paris, 1932–36; Brig. RA, Aldershot Command, 1936–39; Commander 7th Anti-Aircraft Division, 1939; Army Representative on British Military Mission to Russia, Aug. 1939; in command of Military Mission to Holland, 1940 and to Greece, 1940–41; Commander Presidency and Assam District, India, 1941–42; Commander 26 Indian Division, 1942–43; retired from Army, 1943; took up post under Supply Dept, New Delhi; served European War, 1914–18 (despatches twice, Bt Major, OBE, Legion of Honour, Order of the Redeemer, Order of the White Eagle); War of 1939–45 (CB), Grand Officer Order of King George the First of Greece and Greek Military Cross, 1941. *Club:* Army and Navy.
Died 27 Aug. 1943.

HEYWOOD-LONSDALE,   John   Pemberton Heywood, DSO 1918; OBE 1926; Lt-Col commanding Shropshire Yeomanry, 1922–28, Hon. Colonel, 1938–40; now Hon. Colonel RA, TA; Master of the Bicester Foxhounds, 1899–1922 and 1931–33; *b* 1869; 2nd *s* of late A. P. Heywood-Lonsdale; *m* 1905, Hon. Helen Annesley, 3rd *d* of 11th Viscount Valentia; one *s* one *d*. *Educ:* Eton; New College, Oxford, BA. Sheriff, Co. Louth, 1902; Lt-Col Shropshire Yeomanry; served European War (DSO, despatches); JP; County Councillor Buckinghamshire, 1925; granted rank of Brevet-Colonel, 1926; Member of the University Eight, 1889–90–1891–92. *Address:* Poundon, Marsh Gibbon, Bicester. *T:* Stratton Audley 12. *Clubs:* Orleans, Oxford and Cambridge.
Died 12 Aug. 1944.

HICHENS, Robert Smythe, FRSL, 1926; journalist, novelist; *b* Speldhurst, Kent, 14 Nov. 1864; *e s* of late Canon F. H. Hichens. *Educ:* Tunbridge Wells; Clifton; RCM; studied at Bristol and in London for some years to be a musician. Meanwhile wrote and published many lyrics for music, some recitations and short stories; finally resolved to abandon music for literature; studied for a year at the London School of Journalism; since then has written much for various newspapers. *Publications:* The Coastguard's Secret (written at age of 17); The Green Carnation, 1894; An Imaginative Man, 1895; The Folly of Eustace, 1896; Flames, 1897; The Londoners, 1897; Byeways, 1897; The Slave, a Romance; Tongues of Conscience, 1900; The Prophet of Berkeley Square, 1901; Felix, 1902; The Woman with the Fan, 1904; The Garden of Allah, 1905; The Black Spaniel, 1905; The Call of the Blood, 1906; A Spirit in Prison; Egypt and its Monuments, 1908; Barbary Sheep, 1909; Bella Donna, 1909; The Holy Land, 1910; The Dweller on the Threshold, 1911; The Fruitful Vine, 1911; The Way of Ambition, 1913; The Near East, 1913; In the Wilderness, 1917; Snake-Bite, 1919; Mrs Marden, 1919; The Spirit of the Time, 1921; The Last Time, 1922; December Love, 1923; After the Verdict, 1924; The God within Him, 1926; The Bacchante and the Nun, 1927; The Streets, 1928; Doctor Artz, 1929; On the Screen, 1929; The Gates of Paradise, 1930; The Bracelet, 1930; My Desert Friend, 1931; The First Lady Brendon, 1931; Mortimer Brice, 1932; The Paradine Case, 1933; The Gardenia, 1934; The Power to Kill, 1934; The Afterglow, 1935; Susie's Career, 1935; The Sixth of October, 1936; Daniel Airlie, 1937; Secret Information, 1938; The Journey Up, 1938; That Which is Hidden, 1939; The Million, 1940; Married or Unmarried, 1941;

A New Way of Life, 1942; Veils, 1943; Harps in the Wind, 1945; Yesterday (memoirs), 1947; Too Much Love of Living, 1947; Incognito, 1947; also The Daughters of Babylon, with Wilson Barrett. Collaborated in The Medicine Man, Lyceum Theatre; Becky Sharp, Prince of Wales's Theatre; The Garden of Allah, New Century Theatre, New York, and Drury Lane, 1920. Wrote also The Real Woman, produced at the Criterion Theatre; and adapted from the French Les Affaires sont les affaires, produced in New York under the title Business is Business; Press the Button, 1916; The Voice from the Minaret, 1919. *Recreations:* lawn tennis, golf, riding, travelling. *Address:* Muralto, Nüscheler Strasse, Zürich, Switzerland. *Clubs:* Athenæum, Royal Automobile.
Died 20 July 1950.

HICKIE, Maj.-Gen. Sir William Bernard, KCB 1918 (CB 1914); *b* 21 May 1865; *e s* of late Col J. F. Hickie, late Royal Fusiliers, of Slevoyre, Borrisokane. *Educ:* Oscott College; Sandhurst (graduate of the Staff College). Joined Royal Fusiliers, 1885; served throughout Boer War, 1900–02, on the Staff, in command of a Mounted Infantry Corps and of a Mobile Column (Bt Lt-Col); DAQMG 8th Division, 1903–06; commanded 1st Batt. Royal Fusiliers; AQMG Irish Command, and promoted substantive Colonel, 1912; Brig.-Gen. 1914; served European War, in command of a Brigade and of 16th (Irish) Division, 1914–18 (despatches, promoted Maj.-Gen., KCB, Croix de Guerre); retired pay, 1921; Senator, Irish Free State, 1925–36; President British Legion South Ireland Area since 1920. *Clubs:* Army and Navy; Kildare Street (Dublin).
Died 3 Nov. 1950.

HICKING, Sir William Norton, 1st Bt *cr* 1917; DL, JP Notts; *b* 12 Dec. 1865; *s* of late George Hicking, Nottingham; *m* 1890; Mabel, *d* of W. G. Eking, Beeston, Notts; two *d*. High Sheriff, Notts, 1913–14. *Heir:* male issue of 2nd daughter (Jonathan Frederick North). *Address:* Brackenhurst Hall, Southwell, Notts. *TA:* Southwell. *T:* 2224. *Clubs:* Boodle's, Carlton.
Died 18 April 1947.

HICKLEY, Adm. Cecil Spencer, CB 1920; MVO 1909; RN; *b* 22 Jan. 1865; *s* of late Admiral Victor Grant Hickley; *m* 1919, Diana, *widow* of Richard R. Ramsden. Entered Navy, 1878; Commander, 1899; Captain, 1904; Rear-Adm., 1916; Vice-Admiral, 1920; retired, 1920; Admiral (retired), 1925. *Address:* 39 Hyde Park Gate, SW7. *T:* Western 6478. *Clubs:* United Service, MCC.
Died 1 May 1941.

HICKLING, Lt-Col Horace Cyril Benjamin, CBE 1937; DSO 1917; MC, late RE; late Member Legislative Council, Trinidad and Tobago; Director, Apex (Trinidad) Oilfields, Ltd, Trinidad; British-Borneo Petroleum Syndicate; Ste Madeleine Sugar Co; *b* 1879; *e s* of late Horace Hickling, Little Firs, Woking; *m* 1917, Katharine, 3rd *d* of Fred. W. Portal, The Lodge, Eliot Bank, Forest Hill; four *d*. *Educ:* Haileybury. Served European War, 1914–18 (despatches, DSO, MC); Mining Engineer. MIMM, MIPT, MJIE. *Address:* Cowleaze, Binley, near Andover, Hants. *T:* St Mary Bourne 326. *Club:* Public Schools.
Died 13 Sept. 1948.

HICKMAN, Hon. Albert Edgar; *b* Grand Bank, Newfoundland, 2 Aug. 1875; *s* of Henry Hickman; *m* 1906, Marie Louise, *d* of Robert Laurie, Scotland; one *s* three *d*. *Educ:* Mount Allison College, Sackville, New Brunswick. Premier of Newfoundland, 1924; Consul-General for Greece in Newfoundland. *Recreations:* boating, fishing. *Address:* Bartra, Circular Road, St John's, Newfoundland. *Clubs:* British Empire Society; City, St John's; Bankers, New York.
Died 9 Feb. 1943.

HICKMAN, Major Sir Alfred (Edward), 2nd Bt *cr* 1903; late 4th (RI) Dragoon Guards; retired pay, 1921; Shropshire Yeomanry, 1922–37, retired as Major; *b* 8 May 1885; *s* of Alfred, *e s* of 1st Bt, and Mary Whitby, *d* of late William Hickin, of Audmore House, Stafford; *S* grandfather, 1910; *m* 1st, 1919, Lilian Brenda, *o d* of late B. Howard Mander and Mrs Mander, of Trysull Manor, Wolverhampton; two *s*; 2nd, 1940, Nancie Beryl, *e d* of Capt. T. G. Morse-Evans, The Parc, Bridgend, Glam. *Educ:* Marlborough Coll.; Sandhurst. Served European War. *Recreations:* polo, hunting, shooting. *Heir: s* Alfred Howard Whitby, *b* 29 Jan. 1920. *Address:* Charringworth Court, Winchcombe, Glos. *TA:* Hickman, Winchcombe. *T:* Winchcombe 173. *Club:* Cavalry.

Died 11 March 1947.

HICKMAN, Captain Charlie Steward, DSO 1916; Royal Indian Navy; *b* 12 July 1868; *s* of Major Robert John Hickman, late 60th Rifles; *m* 1900, Jessie Beatrice, *d* of late A. A. Duke, MD, Worthing; one *s* one *d*. *Educ:* Rossall; HMS Worcester. Joined Royal Indian Marine, 1889; Marine Survey Dept, 1895–1915, last 5 years in charge; served European War: sailed to India, 11 Aug. 1914, in HT Dongola; Mesopotamia, 1915 (despatches twice, DSO); Port Officer, Bombay, 1915–20; retired, 1921. *Recreations:* secretarial work, tennis, croquet. *Address:* Pemberley, Pemberley Lane, Bedford. *Clubs:* Town and County, Croquet, Bedford.

Died 31 May 1941.

HICKMAN, Brig.-Gen. Harry Otho Devereux, CB 1919; *b* 1860; *o s* of late Henry Thomas Hickman, of Chorlton House, Leamington, and Katharine, *d* of late John Barker, of Albrighton Hall, Shropshire; *m* 1890, Louisa, 4th *d* of T. R. Cochrane, Calder Glen, Lanarkshire; two *d*. Late Colonel Royal Inniskilling Fusiliers; Second in Command of the Royal Military College, Sandhurst, 1910–12; Assistant Director of the Territorial Forces, 1912–13; DL Warwickshire. *Address:* 12 Kenilworth Road, Leamington. *T:* Leamington 219.

Died 5 April 1946.

HICKMAN, Robert St John, CIE 1922; VD; *b* 11 Feb. 1867; *s* of Major Robert John Hickman, late 60th Rifles, and Anne, *d* of late Charles St John; *m* 1902, Agnes Beatrice, *d* of D. Turner of Hammersmith House, Dublin; three *d*. *Educ:* Rossall; Burgoyne House, Southsea. Went to India as a tea planter, 1884; joined the newly formed Volunteer Corps Surma Valley Light Horse, 1885; was ADC to the Viceroy of India; Col Commanding Surma Valley Light Horse, Indian Auxiliary Force; member of Assam Legislative Council, 1917–20; attended War Conference held at Delhi as representative of Assam, 1918. *Recreations:* polo, shooting, tennis, golf. *Address:* Minstead, Haslemere, Surrey. *Club:* Junior Army and Navy.

Died 22 Jan. 1947.

HICKS, Sir (Edward) Seymour, Kt 1935; actor-manager and author; Controller, Entertainments National Service Association, since 1939; Chevalier, Legion of Honour, 1931; Chevalier, Order of the Crown of Stuart; *b* St Helier, Jersey, 1871; *e s* of Major Hicks, 42nd Highlanders, and Grace Seymour; *m* Ellaline Terriss (Lewin) (author of By Herself and with Others 1928), *d* of late William Terriss; one *d*. *Educ:* Prior Park College, Bath; Victoria College, Jersey. Originally intended for the Army, but entered the dramatic profession 11 Nov. 1887; principal light comedian, Gaiety Company; concerned in building the Globe, Queen's, and Aldwych Theatres; originated concert parties in European War, taking out first company to the front in 1914; toured with own company, Africa, Australia, Canada. *Publications:* written and produced sixty-four plays, including Under the Clock, One of the Best, Catch of the Season, Earl and the Girl, Sporting Life, With Flying Colours, Sleeping Partners, The Man in Dress Clothes, Good Luck, Bluebell in Fairyland, The Gay Gordons, The Beauty of Bath, Vintage Wine, The Miracle Man, etc. *Books:* Twenty-four Years of an Actor's Life, 1910; If I were Your Father, 1919; Difficulties, 1922; Chestnuts Re-Roasted, 1924; Hullo, Australians! 1925; Between Ourselves, 1930; Acting: A Book for Amateurs, 1931; Laugh with Me, 1936; Night Lights, 1938; Me and My Missus, 1939; Not Guilty, M'Lord, 1939; Vintage Years, 1943. *Recreations:* fishing, shooting. *Clubs:* Beefsteak, Garrick, Buck's.

Died 6 April 1949.

HICKS, Rt Rev. (Frederick Cyril) Nugent, DD; Bishop of Lincoln since 1933; Chaplain and Sub-Prelate of the Order of the Hospital of St John of Jerusalem, 1928; Order of St Sava (1st Class) of Yugoslavia, 1932; Cross of the Order of the Redeemer (Greece), 1933; Grand Cross of the Order of the Star of Roumania, 1935; Governor of Harrow School, 1927; Visitor Eton College and King's College, Cambridge, Brasenose and Lincoln Colleges, Oxford; Hon. Fellow of Keble College, Oxford, 1933; Member of Council of Keble College, 1934; Select Preacher, Oxford University, 1934; *b* Dunstable, 28 June 1872; *o c* of Charles Cyril Hicks, MD, and Agnes Nugent, *o d* of Frederick Ayrton; *m* 1909, Ethel Kathleen, *d* of late Canon Francis Forbes Savage, late Vicar of Flushing, Falmouth. *Educ:* Harrow; Balliol College, Oxford; Cuddesdon Theological College. Scholar of Balliol College, 1891; 2nd Class Classical Moderations, 1893; 1st Class Literæ Humaniores, 1895; Liddon Theological Studentship, 1895. Lecturer of Keble College, 1896; Tutor, 1897–1909; Dean, 1901–09; ordained 1897; Principal of Bishops' College, Cheshunt, 1909–20; Rector of Toddington, Beds, 1921–24; General Secretary Central Advisory Council of Training for the Ministry, 1913–24; Vicar of Brighton and Rector of West Blatchington, 1924–27; Rural Dean of Brighton, 1924–27; Bishop of Gibraltar, 1927–33; Examining Chaplain to Bishop (Stubbs) of Oxford, 1899–1901; to Bishop (Paget) of Oxford, 1901–09; to Bishop (Jacob) of St Albans, 1913–19; to Bishop (Furse) of St Albans, 1920–24; to Bishop of Chichester, 1924–27; Hon. Canon of St Albans, 1914–24; Prebendary of Waltham in Chichester Cathedral, 1924–28; Proctor in Convocation for Diocese of St Albans, 1921–24; for Diocese of Chichester, 1924–27, and Member of National Assembly of Church of England; Commissary to Bishop of Bombay, 1908–27; to Bishop of Nyasaland, 1915–27; in command of Oxford University Officers' Training Corps, 1908–09; Lt-Col (unattached list) Territorial Force, 1909; retired, 1912. *Publications:* Consecration Prayers: a Sermon preached at Consecration of Bishops of British Honduras, Zanzibar, and Khartum, 1908; The Fullness of Sacrifice, an Essay in Reconciliation, 1930. *Address:* The Old Palace, Lincoln. *T:* Lincoln 1430. *Club:* Athenæum.

Died 10 Feb. 1942.

HICKS, George Dawes, MA, PhD, LittD; FBA 1927; Professor of Philosophy, University College, London, 1904–28; Emeritus Professor since 1928; *b* Shrewsbury, 14 Sept. 1862; *e s* of Christopher Hicks, Solicitor; *m* 1st, 1902, Lucy Katharine (*d* 1908), *d* of late William Henry Garrett, Highbury, London; 2nd, 1923, Frances Jane (*d* 1935), *widow* of Edward Corrado Aguggia, DLitt, and *d* of Mrs Campbell-Strickland, of Broadwater. *Educ:* Royal Grammar School, Guildford; Owens College, Manchester (BA Vict. 1st Class Honours in Philosophy, 1888; MA, 1891; LittD, 1904), Manchester College, Oxford; University of Leipzig (PhD, 1896). Hibbert Scholar, 1891–96; BA Cambridge, by research, 1909; MA 1912. Minister of Unity Church, Islington, 1897–1903; Lecturer for London School of Ethics and Sociology, 1897–98; Vice-President of Aristotelian Society, 1901; President, 1913; Sec. 1915; Assistant Editor of Hibbert Journal, 1902; Examiner in Logic and Moral Philosophy in University of Glasgow, 1903; Examiner in Philosophy in the University of London, 1905; Examiner in Logic in the University of Bristol,

1910; Examiner in Moral Science Tripos, Cambridge, 1913, 1914, 1920, 1921, 1928, and 1929. Examiner in Mental Philosophy in the University of Aberdeen, 1915; Examiner in Philosophy in University of London, 1930; Hibbert Lecturer, 1931; Upton Lecturer in Philosophy, 1933; Essex Hall Lecturer, 1934; Hobhouse Memorial Lecturer, 1936. *Publications:* Die Begriffe Phänomenon und Noumenon in ihrem Verhältnis zu einander bei Kant, 1897; English Philosophy in Nineteenth Century in Ueberweg—Heinze's Geschichte der Philosophie, 1897, 12th ed. 1928; Memoir of James Drummond in J. D.'s Pauline Meditations, 1919; Ways towards the Spiritual Life, 1928; Art. on Theory of Knowledge, Ency. Brit. 14th ed. 1929; Berkeley (Leaders of Philosophy Series), 1932; Human Personality and Future Life, 1934; Thought and Real Existence, 1936; The Philosophical Bases of Theism, 1937; Critical Realism: Studies in the Philosophy of Mind and Nature, 1938; various articles and reviews in Mind, Proceedings of Aristotelian Society, Hibbert Journal, Journal of Psychology, and other periodicals. *Recreations:* gardening, climbing. *Address:* 9 Cranmer Road, Cambridge. *Club:* Savile.

Died 16 Feb. 1941.

HICKS, Sir Seymour; *see* Hicks, Sir E. S.

HICKSON, Oswald Squire; Practising Solicitor; *b* 2 April 1877; *s* of William and Catherine Sarah Hickson; *m* 1926, Dorothy Eleanor, *widow* of Capt. John Henderson Begg; three *d. Educ:* University College School, Gower Street, London. Articled 1895 to James Jackson, Solicitor, Northampton; Qualified, 1900; Admitted Solicitor, 1902; commenced practice in London, 1907; Senior partner, firm Oswald Hickson, Collier and Co.; served on Lord Chancellor's committee to report on Law of Defamation, 1939. *Recreations:* golf; played cricket for Northamptonshire, 1897, 1898. *Address:* 11 South Lodge, St John's Wood, NW. *T:* Cunningham 4238.

Died 9 Jan. 1944.

HIDAYAT HOSAIN, M., Shamsul Ulama, 1919; Khan Bahadur, 1922; PhD; Prin. of the Calcutta Madrasah; Registrar, Central Madrasah Examination Board, Bengal; retired from Government Service, 1935; *b* 1887; *e s* of late Shamsul Ulama Vilayat Hosain, Head Moulvi, Calcutta Madrasah; *m* 1905, Kamrun Nisa Begum, *d* of Khan Bahadur Fazlur Rahman. *Educ:* Calcutta Madrasah. Lecturer in Arabic and Persian, Presidency College, Calcutta, 1908; Senior Professor of Arabic and Persian, 1914–28; Lecturer in Arabic Post-Graduate Depart, Calcutta University; Fellow of Calcutta University; Fellow and Philological Sec. of the Royal Asiatic Society of Bengal since 1925; Member of the Arabic and Persian Board, Dacca University and Andhra Univ.; Member of the Governing Bodies, Presidency College, and Islamia College; Member of the Committee for Film Censorship in Bengal; Member of the Bengal Publicity Board; Pres. Moslem Institute; President, Arabic and Persian Board, Calcutta University, 1929; Vice-President of Muhammadan Orphanage, Refuge, and Anjuman Mufidul Islam; Member of the Executive Committee of various charitable societies. *Publications:* Catalogue Raisonné of Arabic Manuscripts in the Buhar Library, Calcutta; Maathir-i-Rahimi, a History of India; Kashful Hujub, a Bibliography of Shia Literature in Arabic; Biographies of Calligraphers in Persian; Tarikh Mubarak Shahi, a History of India in Persian; Tarikh Shahi, a History of Afghan rulers of India in Persian; Chemistry in Iraq and Persia in the 10th Century AD, Memoirs of the Asiatic Society of Bengal, Vol. XI No. 5; Three Arabic Treatises on Alchemy, Memoirs of the Asiatic Society of Bengal, Vol. XII, No. I; Tabaqat Akbari, Vol. III, a History of India in Persian; Tadhkira-i-Shushtar, a local history of Shushtar in Persian; A Grammar of Modern Persian; besides contributions to the

Encyclopædia of Islam, Journal of the Royal Asiatic Society of Bengal, the Islamic Culture, the Concordance et Indices de la tradition Musulmane. *Address:* 96/3 Collin Street, Calcutta, India.

Died 27 Nov. 1941.

HIDAYATALLAH, Hon. Khan Bahadur Shaikh (Sir) Ghulam Husain, KCSI 1933; Kt 1926; BA, LLB. Governor of Sind since 1947; President Advisory Council to Governor of Sind, 1936; late Minister for Local Self-Government, Bombay; Member of Executive Council, Bombay, 1928–34; Premier of Sind, 1937–38 and 1942–47. *Address:* Karachi, India.

Died 4 Oct. 1948.

HIGGINBOTTOM, Frederick James, FJI; *b* Accrington, 21 Oct. 1859; *s* of Matthew Fielding Higginbottom, mathematical tutor; *m* 1884, Anne Elizabeth (*d* 1922), *d* of Edwin H. Neville. *Educ:* privately. Entered journalism 1875, Southport Daily News; editor Southport Critic, 1879–81; sub-editor and special correspondent, Press Association, 1881–91; London correspondent, Dublin daily National Press, 1891–92; Parliamentary correspondent, Pall Mall Gazette, 1892–99; founded London Press Exchange, Ltd, 1892; managing editor Pall Mall Gazette and manager Pall Mall Magazine, 1900–09; editor Pall Mall Gazette, 1909–12; director of Press Intelligence, Ministry of National Service, 1917; assistant (honorary) to secretariat, Ministry of Food, 1918; Parliamentary Correspondent, The Daily Chronicle, 1919–30; member of deputation of British Editors to Sweden, 1906, and of that to Germany, 1907; delegate on Empire Press Union World tour, 1925; Trustee and Chairman, Institute of Journalists Provident Fund; Mem. Church Assembly, House of Laity. Royal Naval Artillery Vols, 1876–82. *Publications:* The Vivid Life: A Journalist's Career, 1934; Islington Year Book, 1898; many Parliamentary handbooks. *Recreations:* country pursuits, rowing. *Address:* The Lawn, Briston, Melton Constable. *Clubs:* Press, Church House.

Died 12 May 1943.

HIGGINS, Edward John, CBE 1920; *b* Highbridge, Som, 1864; *m* 1888, Catherine Price, Penarth; four *s* three *d. Educ:* Dr Morgan's School, Bridgwater. Entered Salvation Army as an Officer, 1882; held various positions in Evangelical and Staff work in United Kingdom, including appointment on Staff of International Training College; Chief Secretary, United States, America, 1896–1905; Assistant Foreign Secretary at London Headquarters; Commissioner for Field Work, Great Britain and Ireland, 1911–19; Chief of the Staff, 1919–29; General of The Salvation Army 1929–34; elected by its High Council to succeed W Bramwell Booth, 1929. Retired from Generalship of the Salvation Army, 1934. *Address:* Sebring, Florida, USA.

Died 14 Dec. 1947.

HIGGINS, Frederick Robert; Poet; *b* Foxford, Co., 24 April 1896; *s* of late Joseph Thomas and Annie Higgins; *m* 1921, Beatrice May, *d* of late James Moore, Dublin. *Educ:* various country schools in Mayo. At fourteen years of age went to work for a building provider's office in Dublin, and after some years at clerical work became an official in the Irish Labour Movement, where contact with mechanical industry intensified a passion for primitive nature; from secretarial work turned in 1920 to the editing of various Irish periodicals, economic and literary; frequent contributor of poetry and critical studies to English, American, and Irish literary journals, joint editor with W. B. Yeats of Broadsides, 1935; Foundation Member of the Irish Academy of Letters; Managing Director of the Abbey Theatre, Dublin; A Deuce of Jacks, play produced 1935. *Publications:* Salt Air, Poems, 1924; Island Blood, Poems, 1925; The Dark Breed, Poems, 1927; Arable Holdings, Poems, 1933;

The Gap of Brightness, Poems. *Recreation:* gallivanting in the country. *Address:* Durlas, Lower Dodder Road, Rathfarnham, Dublin.

Died 8 Jan. 1941.

HIGGINS, Sir George; *see* Higgins, Sir S. G.

HIGGINS, Air Marshal Sir John Frederick Andrews, KCB 1928; KBE 1925; CB 1918; DSO 1900; AFC; RAF; Officer Legion of Honour; *b* 1 Sept. 1875; *s* of William Higgins of The Chestnuts, Farnham; *m d* of late Edward Singleton, Quinville, Co. Clare. Entered RA 1895; Captain, 1901; Major, 1911; served South Africa, 1899–1902 (wounded, despatches, Queen's medal 4 clasps, King's medal 2 clasps, DSO); European War, 1914–18 (wounded, despatches, Bt Lt-Col and Col); Air Officer commanding Forces in Iraq, 1924–26; Air Member for Supply and Research of Air Council, 1926–30; retired list, 1930; Air Officer Commanding-in-Chief, India, 1939–40. *Address:* c/o Air Ministry, Adastral House, Kingsway, WC2. *Clubs:* Army and Navy, Bath.

Died 1 June 1948.

HIGGINS, Sir (Sydney) George, Kt 1919; CBE 1918; a Shipowner; Director Wm France Fenwick & Co., Ltd; Committee London General Shipowners Society; Lloyd's Register of Shipping; Director Denaby and Cadeby Main Collieries, Ltd, retd 1946; Vice-President King George's Fund for Sailors; *b* 26 Jan. 1867; *s* of late Warner Charles Higgins of Portlane, Sunbury-on-Thames; *m* 1890, Ida Blanche (*d* 1946), *d* of late James Hollway, JP, DL, of Stanhoe Hall, Norfolk; one *s* two *d.* Assistant Accountant-General (unpaid) Ministry of Shipping, 1917–19; formerly on Council of the Chamber of Shipping, on Pilotage Committee of the Trinity House, on Shipowners Parliamentary Committee, and Advisory Committee on new Lighthouse Works; Member of the Board of Referees in the Royal Mail Group Scheme, 1932; Chairman of Police Pay (New Entrants) Committee set up by Home Office and Scottish Office, 1932; President of the Institute of Marine Engineers, 1933. *Address:* Brooklands, Sunbury-on-Thames. *T:* Sunbury 2509.

Died 30 Aug. 1947.

HIGGINSON, Captain Archibald Bertram Watson, CB 1919; DSO 1917; RN (retired). Served European War, 1915–19 (despatches, DSO, Croix de Guerre, CB, Officer of Legion of Honour). *Address:* The Bungalow, Naas, County Kildare.

Died 25 July 1950.

HIGHAM, Lt-Col Bernard, CIE 1935; IMS (retd); MB, BS (Lond.), MRCS, LRCP; Secretary Willingdon Sports Club, Bombay; *b* 14 Dec. 1880; *s* of late Charles Higham, Bookseller, London and Alice Mary Brown; *m* 1906, Florence (*d* 1941), *e d* of late Richard Parsons, Ootacamund, S India; three *s. Educ:* Wilson's Grammar School, London. St Thomas's Hospital, 1898–1905; Clinical Assistant Skin Department, 1904; House Physician, 1904–05; Casualty Officer, 1905; Indian Medical Service, 1906–35; served NW Frontier, 1908 (Medal and clasp); European War (1915 Star, Victory and General Service Medals); Chemical Analyser to Government of Bombay, 1920–35; Retired 1935. *Recreation:* golf. *Address:* Willingdon Sports Club, Bombay, India. *T:* Bombay 42001. *Clubs:* Byculla, Royal Bombay Yacht, Willingdon Sports, Bombay.

Died 8 Nov. 1944.

HIGHAM, Sir Thomas, Kt 1934; High Sheriff, Co. of Lancaster, 1934; DL, JP, County Alderman Lancs County Council; head of firm of Highams, Ltd, Cotton Manufacturers, Woodnook Mills, Accrington; *b* 3 Oct. 1866; *s* of Eli and Selina Higham; *m* 1893, Lizzie, *d* of late A. Ashworth, JP; two *s. Educ:* Silcoates; privately. Entered Accrington Town Council 1901; Mayor of

Accrington 1906–07 and 1927–28; First Freeman of Borough of Accrington; Chairman of Mid-Lancashire Electricity Board; Chairman of Ribble Board of Conservators; President of Accrington and District Blind Society; President of Amateur Opera Society; was at one time organist to Accrington Choral Society and also organist at Oak Street Congregational Church. *Recreations:* fishing, shooting, golf, music. *Address:* Bank House, Accrington. *TA:* Higham 2458, Accrington. *T:* 2458.

Died 22 Jan. 1947.

HIGHFIELD, John Somerville; Senior Partner in Highfield and Roger Smith, Consulting Engineers; *b* Nov. 1871; *s* of late Samuel and Sarah Highfield; *m* 1st, 1900, Martha A. Ritchie (*d* 1902); 2nd, 1908, Marina Julia Stretch; two *d. Educ:* Rydal School; King's College, London. A Director of Central London Electricity, The London Power Company, and Chairman of The Fuller's Earth Union; Past President of Institution of Electrical Engineers, of Institution of Junior Engineers, and of Association of Supervising Electrical Engineers; Vice-Pres. of Royal Institution of Great Britain and of Royal Society of Arts, London. *Publications:* numerous Presidential Addresses, scientific papers in the technical and general press. *Recreations:* yachting, shooting, and fishing, agriculture. *Address:* Sterlings, Cookham Dean, Berkshire. *Clubs:* Athenæum, Royal Thames Yacht (Vice-Commodore); Brixham Yacht (Vice-Commodore), and other Yacht Clubs.

Died 15 Aug. 1945.

HIGNELL, Harold, CMG 1936; retired; *b* 16 May 1879; *s* of Thomas Evans Hignell, The Shrubbery, Downend, Glos; *m* 1st, 1911, Ann Mary McMillan; 2nd, 1927, Catherine Elizabeth Hill; three *s* one *d. Educ:* Denstone; Jesus College, Cambridge. Farming in S Africa and Kenya, 1905–13; served European War in East Africa, 1914–16 (despatches); Political Officer German East Africa and Administrative Officer Tanganyika, 1916–36; retired as Senior Provincial Commissioner, 1936. *Recreations:* golf and gardening. *Address:* The Chalet, Alveston, nr Bristol. *TA:* Alveston nr Bristol.

Died 30 June 1943.

HIGNETT, Mrs Dorothy Eleanor Augusta, CBE 1920; OBE 1918; JP Southampton County; *d* of Thomas Lawes Rogers, Rainhill, Lancashire; *m* 1897, Arthur Holland Hignett. Deputy Directress, Central Irish War Hospital Supply Depôt, Irish Branch British Red Cross Society, during European War; a Lady of Grace of Order of St John of Jerusalem; Bronze Life Saving medal, 1916. *Address:* Odiham, Hants.

Died 20 May 1946.

HILEY, Sir (Ernest) Haviland, KBE 1928; CBE 1919; Chairman of the Traffic Commissioners (Eastern Area), since 1931. Joined North-Eastern Railway, 1891; occupied positions of District Traffic Superintendent at York, Divisional Goods, Mineral and Docks' Manager at Hull and Newcastle-on-Tyne; Passenger Manager Great Northern Railway (London), 1905–08; left North-Eastern Railway, 1913, to reorganise and take up General Managership of New Zealand Government Railways, 1913–19; Colonel New Zealand Forces HQ Staff, 1914–19; Member of Indian Government Commission on administration of Indian Railways, 1920; member of Royal Commission on Local Government of Greater London, 1921–23; appointed to investigate conditions in Mexico, 1923; appointed to report upon transport conditions in Rhodesia and prepare scheme of future development, 1925; Rhodesian Government Adviser on Railway Questions, 1926; Chairman of the Rhodesian Railway Commission, 1927–28. *Address:* Sussex House, Cambridge. *Club:* Travellers'.

Died 30 March 1943.

HILEY, Sir Ernest Varvill, KBE 1918; Chairman, Glover & Main, Ltd and associated Cos; *b* 11 Oct. 1868; *s* of Charles Hiley, Yeadon, Wharfedale, Yorks; *m* 1908, Edith Caroline, *d* of late James H. Beckingham, Priestfield, Lintz Green, Co. Durham, and *widow* of Walter Whetstone, Knighton; no *c*. Solicitor, 1891; Town Clerk of Leicester, 1902–08; Town Clerk of Birmingham, 1908–16; Deputy Director-General of National Service 1917; MP (U) Duddeston Division of Birmingham, 1922–23; Member Royal Commission on Lunacy and Mental Disorder, 1924–26; Member Royal Commission on Transport, 1928. *Address:* 6 Berkeley House, Hay Hill, W1. *T:* Mayfair 3276. *Club:* Carlton.

Died 19 July 1949.

HILL, Sir Albert, 2nd Bt *cr* 1917; Director of Sir James Hill & Sons Ltd; *b* 4 Nov. 1877; *s* of Sir James Hill, 1st Bt; *S* father, 1936; *m* 1900, Ellen, *d* of Thomas Sowden; one *s*. *Heir: s* James [*b* 1905; *m* 1930, Marjory, *d* Frank Croft, Apperley Grange, Rawdon, near Leeds; one *s* four *d*]. *Address:* Throstle Nest, Bradford.

Died 13 May 1946.

HILL, Sir Alexander Galloway E.; *see* Erskine-Hill.

HILL, Alfred; Welwyn, Herts. *Educ:* Welwyn Vicarage School. MP (Lab) West Leicester, 1922–23. *Address:* 119 Willow Brook Road, Leicester. *T:* 21120.

Died 14 July 1945.

HILL, Lady Arthur; 3rd *d* of late J. Fortescue-Harrison, MP, of Crawley Down Park, Sussex; *m* 1877, Rt Hon. Lord Arthur William Hill (*d* 1931). Composer of the song: In the Gloaming. *Address:* East-hampstead Park, Wokingham, Berks.

Died 12 Feb. 1944.

HILL, Sir Arthur Norman, 1st Bt *cr* 1919; Kt 1911; solicitor and notary; Member of Hill, Dickinson & Co., Liverpool; *b* 8 Aug. 1863; *s* of G. Birkbeck Hill, DCL Oxon; *m* 1889, Elen Mary Stratford, *d* of J. T. Danson, FSA, Grasmere, Westmorland; one *s* three *d*. *Educ:* Bruce Castle. Secretary and Treasurer of Liverpool Steamship Owners Association, 1893–1923; Manager and Secretary, Liverpool and London Steamship Protection Association, Ltd, 1914–23; Manager and Secretary, Liverpool and London War Risks Insurance Association, Ltd, 1913–23; Chairman of Board of Trade Advisory Committee on Merchant Shipping, 1907–37; British Delegate International Conference Safety of Life at Sea, 1913–14 and 1929; and on Load Line, 1930; Chairman Port and Transit Executive Committee, 1915–19; Vice-President Chamber of Shipping, 1924; Chairman Seamen's National Insurance Society since 1911; Chairman Governing Body of Seamen's Pension Fund since 1919; Member of the Committee on Industry and Trade; British Delegate at Economic Conference, Geneva, May 1927. *Heir: s* Norman Gray, *b* 1894. *Address:* Green Place, Stockbridge, Hants.

Died 7 Jan. 1944.

HILL, Sir Arthur William, KCMG 1931; CMG 1926; FRS; MA; ScD; DSc (Adelaide); VMH; FLS; Hon. Member Royal Society, NZ; Hon. Member of New York Academy of Sciences; Director of Royal Botanic Gardens, Kew, since 1922; Assistant Director, 1907–22; *b* 11 Oct. 1875; *s* of late D. Hill, Herga, Watford. *Educ:* Marlborough; King's College, Cambridge. 1st class Natural Sciences Tripos, Pt I 1897, Pt II 1898. Senior Demonstrator, 1899; University Lecturer in Botany, 1905–07; Fellow of King's College, Cambridge, 1901; Dean, 1907; Hon. Fellow, 1932; travelled in Iceland, 1900; the Andes of Bolivia and Peru, 1903; West Indies, 1911 and 1924; West Africa, 1921; Australia, New Zealand, Java, Malaya, and Ceylon, 1927–28; South and East Africa, 1930–31; India, 1937; Captain, DGR & E; Veitch Gold Medal of Royal Horticultural Society,

1937. *Publications:* botanical papers in scientific journals; Memoir of Canon HN Ellacombe. *Address:* The Royal Gardens, Kew. *Club:* Athenæum.

Died 3 Nov. 1941.

HILL, Brig.-Gen. Cecil, CB 1917; *b* 25 Oct. 1861; *s* of Capt. T. Hill, Romanby, Northallerton; *m* 1893, Edith P. M. Lambert; one *s*. *Educ:* Richmond, Yorks; RM Academy, Woolwich (passed out 1st of his term, 1881, gaining Pollock Medal and Riding Prize). Commission in Royal Engineers, 1881; served in Nile Expedition, 1884–85 (medal and Khedive's Star); Ceylon, 1886–90 and 1897, 1900; Gibraltar, 1904–08; Field Master of Calpe Hunt, 1904–08; Chief Engineer, Plymouth, 1912–14; commanded South Irish Coast Defences as Brigadier-General, 1914–15; served European War, 1915–18 (CB). *Recreations:* hunting, polo, fishing. *Address:* The Old House, Sutton Courtenay, Berks.

Died 20 Dec. 1942.

HILL, Charles Alexander; Past Chairman, and Managing Director of The British Drug Houses, Ltd, 1909–43; *b* 18 Aug. 1874; *s* of Arthur Bowdler Hill and Fanny Pember; *m* 1898, Ruth (*d* 1945), *d* of Walter Fletcher; three *s* one *d*. *Educ:* Winchester. BSc London; FIC. Vice-President, and Member of Council of Association of British Chemical Manufacturers (Chairman, 1926–28, President, 1930–31–1932–33); Chemical Soc.; Institute of Chemistry; Soc. of Public Analysts (and Vice-Pres.); three times President of the British Pharmaceutical Conference; has taken leading interest in developing the fine chemical industry in this country. *Publications:* various publications on chemical and technical subjects. *Recreations:* tennis, golf. *Address:* 13 Buckingham Palace Road, SW1. *Clubs:* Carlton, Conservative, Portland.

Died 23 Oct. 1948.

HILL, Sir Enoch, Kt 1928; JP; FCIS; late President and Managing Director, Halifax Building Society, Commercial Street, Halifax; *b* Leek, Staffs, 10 Sept. 1865; *m* 1st, 1887; 2nd, 1906; one *s*. *Educ:* privately. Engaged for some years in journalism, and from 1885, partly with the Leek United Building Society, and partly with the Halifax Building Society; Chairman Yorkshire Board, Union Bank of Manchester, Limited; Chairman, Yorkshire and Derbyshire Board, Alliance Assurance Company, Limited; Member of Barclays Bank, Leeds Board; Advisory Director, Head Office, Barclay's Bank; Chairman, National Association of Building Societies, 1921–33. *Publications:* A History of the Ancient Parish of Alstonefield, Staffs; a number of pamphlets upon phases of Building Society work in the United Kingdom and in the United States of America. *Recreations:* football, cricket, motoring, photography, golf, gardening. *Address:* Willow Hall, Halifax, Yorks. *TA:* Enoch Hill, Halifax. *T:* Sowerby Bridge 81308. *Clubs:* Constitutional, City Livery, 1900; Halifax.

Died 13 May 1942.

HILL, Col Eustace, DSO 1918; TD; DL; Sheriff, 1926; *b* 30 April 1869; 3rd *s* of James Duke Hill, Terlings Park, Harlow, Essex; *m* 1913, Barbara le Grand, *d* of George J. Gribble, 34 Eaton Square, SW, and of Kingston Russell House, Dorset; one *s* two *d*. *Educ:* Harrow. Essex Yeomanry, 1901; served European War, 1914–18 (DSO, despatches); commanding Essex Yeomanry, 1920–27; MFH East Essex Hunt, 1922–30. *Recreations:* hunting, shooting. *Address:* Elbrook House, Ashwell, Baldock, Herts. *Club:* Cavalry.

Died 21 Oct. 1946.

HILL, Lt-Col Frank William Rowland, CMG 1917; DSO 1900; OBE 1919; Royal Army Ordnance Corps; *b* 19 Feb. 1875; *m* 1904, Susan, *d* of Colonel J. Moutray Read. Joined Dorsetshire Regt 1895; served North-West Frontier, India, 1897–98 (medal with two clasps); S Africa, 1899–1901 (despatches twice, Queen's medal five clasps, DSO); European War, 1914–17 (despatches, Bt Lt-Col, CMG); retired 1926. *Address:* Amberley, Gloucestershire.

Died 21 Aug. 1942.

HILL, Sir George (Francis), KCB 1933 (CB 1929); MA; DCL (Oxon). LittD (Cambridge and Manchester); LLD (Edin.); Fellow of the British Academy; FSA, Hon. FSA Scot.; Member of Royal Commission on Historical Monuments (England); *b* Berhampur, India, 22 Dec. 1867; *γ s* of Rev. Samuel John Hill; *m* 1897, Mary (*d* 1924), *e d* of John Dennis Paul, FGS, Leicester. *Educ:* University College School and University College, London; Merton College, Oxford (Exhibitioner, Hon. Fellow, 1931). First-class Classical Moderations, 1889; first-class Literæ Humaniores, 1891. Assistant in the British Museum, 1893; Keeper of the Department of Coins and Medals, 1912–30; Director and Principal Librarian of British Museum, 1931–36; Fellow of Univ. Coll., London; Medallist (1915) of Royal Numismatic Society, (1923) of American Numismatic Society and (1934) of Société Française de Numismatique; Serena Medallist of British Academy, 1948; Hon. Member several European numismatic societies; Vice-President Hellenic and Roman Societies; editor of the Journal of Hellenic Studies, 1898–1912, and of the Numismatic Chronicle 1912–30; Rhind Lecturer, 1915. *Publications:* Six volumes of the British Museum Catalogue of Greek Coins, 1897–1922; Handbook of Greek and Roman Coins, 1899; Coins of Ancient Sicily, 1903; Pisanello, 1905; Historical Greek Coins, 1906; Historical Roman Coins, 1909; Portrait Medals of Italian Artists, 1912; Development of Arabic Numerals in Europe, 1915; Medals of the Renaissance, 1920; Medallic Portraits of Christ, 1920; Becker the Counterfeiter, 1924–1925; Select Greek Coins, 1927; A Corpus of Italian Medals of the Renaissance before Cellini, 1930; Treasure Trove, 1936; History of Cyprus, Vols I-III, 1940–1948; other works on Numismatics. *Address:* 23 Whitehall Court, SW1. *Clubs:* Athenæum, Authors'.

Died 18 Oct. 1948.

HILL, Gerard Robert, CB 1935; MA; *b* 19 Feb. 1872; *s* of Henry Hill, JP, The High Hall, Thornton-le-Dale and F. D., *d* of Rev. H. Pixell; *m* 1903, S. Dorothea, *d* of E. G. Place of Skelton Grange, York, and Loch Dochart House, Perthshire; one *s. Educ:* Eton; Balliol College, Oxford. Barrister, Inner Temple, 1899; Ministry of Health (legal branch), 1921–29; Assistant Solicitor, 1926–29; a Parliamentary Counsel to the Treasury, 1929–37; JP and CC Yorkshire NR; Chairman of the Statutory Committee of the Pharmaceutical Society of Great Britain; member (1942–45) of Central Valuation Committee and of Railway Assessment Authority. *Publications:* edited various works on Local Government and Public Health Law. *Address:* The High Hall, Thornton-le-Dale, Pickering, Yorks. *T:* Thornton-le-Dale 222. *Club:* National.

Died 28 Aug. 1946.

HILL, Grace Livingston, (Mrs Thomas Franklin Hill); author and public speaker; *b* 16 April 1865; *d* of Rev. Charles Montgomery Livingston, and Marcia Macdonald; *m* 1892, Rev. Thomas F. Hill; two *d. Publications:* Marcia Schuyler; Phoebe Deane; Miranda; Dawn of the Morning; The City of Fire; The Tryst; Cloudy Jewel; Exit Betty; The Search; The Red Signal; The War Romance of the Salvation Army; The Enchanted Barn; The Girl from Montana; Lo, Michael!; The Mystery of Mary; The Best Man; The Obsession of Victoria Gracen; The Finding of Jasper Holt; Ariel Custer; Not Under the Law; A New Name; Coming Through the Rye; Job's Niece; The White Flower; The Witness; The Voice in the Wilderness; The Man of the Desert; Crimson Roses; Blue Ruin; Duskin; The Prodigal Girl; Ladybird; The Gold Shoe; Silver Wings; The Chance of a Lifetime; Kerry; The Challengers; Happiness Hill; The Patch of Blue; The Ransom; Matched Pearls; The Beloved Stranger; Rainbow Cottage; Amorelle; Christmas Bride; Beauty for Ashes, 1935; White Orchids, 1935; The Strange Proposal, 1935; April Gold, 1936; Mystery Flowers, 1936; The Substitute Guest, 1936; Sunrise, 1937; Daphne Deane, 1937; Brentwood, 1937; Marigold, 1938; Homing, 1938; Maris, 1938; The Seventh Hour, 1939; Patricia, 1939; Stranger Within the Gates, 1939; Head of the House, 1940; Rose Galbraith, 1940; Partners, 1940; By Way of the Silverthorns, 1941; In Tune with Wedding Bells, 1941; Astra, 1941; Girl of the Woods, 1942; Crimson Mountain, 1942; The Street of the City, 1942; Spice Box, 1943; The Sound of the Trumpet, 1943; Through These Fires, 1943; More than Conqueror, 1944; Time of the Singing of Birds, 1944; All through the Night, 1945; A Girl to come Home to, 1945; Bright Arrows, 1946; Where Two Ways Met, 1946. *Address:* 215 Cornell Avenue, Swarthmore, Pa, USA. *T:* Swarthmore 464.

Died 23 Feb. 1947.

HILL, H. Lancelot H., MA, FCA, Senior Partner in the firm Hill, Vellacott and Co., Chartered Accountants, London, and elsewhere; Director of Electric and Musical Industries Ltd, The Gramophone Co., Ltd, Columbia Graphophone Co. Ltd, Tubbs, Lewis & Co. Ltd, United Elastics, Ltd; The Progressive Finance and Investment Co. Ltd; *b* 23 May 1883; *s* of Arthur J. Hill, St Keverne, Harrow-on-the-Hill, and Downderry, Cornwall; *m* 1915, E. S. Penelope Packe, The Vicarage, Feering, Essex; one *s* one *d. Educ:* Harrow; Pembroke College, Cambridge. President of the Institute of Chartered Accountants, 1931–32 and 1933–34; Supervising Accountant for Eastern Counties appointed by Ministry of Food; Sundry appointments by Board of Trade under Trading with the Enemy Act, 1914–18; Member of Committee to enquire into position of Co-operative Societies in relation to Income Tax, 1932; An Assessor under Midland (Amalgamated) District (Coal Mines) Scheme, 1932; Chairman Executive Committee of 4th International Congress on Accounting, London, 1935; An Accountant to Joint Committee set up by British and Argentine Governments to enquire into the condition of Anglo-Argentine Meat Trade, 1935; Member of London Passenger Transport Arbitration Tribunal, 1935; Member of Voluntary Hospitals Commission, 1935; Member of Sugar Commission, 1936; Member of Committee of Inquiry into Coal Distribution Costs, 1938; Ministry of Food, 1939. *Club:* City of London.

Died 20 Aug. 1944.

HILL, His Honour Henry Staveley S.; *see* Staveley-Hill.

HILL, J. Smith, BA, BSc; JP Cumberland; *b* 12 May 1866; *s* of P. L. Hill, Trowbridge, Wilts; *m* 1896, Annie, *d* of late John Todd, Mereside, Bromfield, and *widow* of Dr H. J. Webb, BSc; one *s* three *d. Educ:* Corsham School, Wilts; Cowley College, New Barnet; London University. Matriculated at London Univ. 1882; BA Degree, 1885; graduated BSc 1889, with honours in Botany. Member Cumberland County Council, 1907–10; co-opted as External Member of County Education Committee, 1913–34; Income Tax Commissioner, 1913; life member, by examination (Second Prizeman), Royal Agricultural Society of England; awarded Vellum of Royal Humane Society, 1891; and Council Gold Medal of Surveyors' Institution, 1905; Principal of Aspatria Agricultural College, near Carlisle, 1894–1916; Resident Agent for Greystoke Castle Estate, Cumberland, 1916–26. Hon. Treasurer Cumberland Nursing Association since 1933. *Recreations:* fell walking, gardening. *Address:* Spring Bank, Braithwaite, Keswick. *T:* Braithwaite 216.

Died 5 Dec. 1944.

HILL, Rt Rev. John Charles, DD; *b* 22 May 1862; *e s* of late John Sheriff Hill; *m* 1893, Rosomond, *d* of Weston Parry; one *d. Educ:* Harrow; Trinity College, Cambridge. Ordained, 1887; Curate of the Harrow

School Mission, Latimer Road, Kensington, 1887–90; Rotherham, 1890–93; Rector of Halesowen, 1893–1909; Rural Dean of Dudley, 1903–09; Hon. Canon of Worcester, 1907–09; Rector of Bury, 1909–30; Rural Dean of Bury, 1912–24; Bishop Suffragan of Hulme, 1924–30; Chairman of the Council of Rossall School, 1919–32; Hon. Canon of Coventry, 1920–22; Hon. Canon of Manchester, 1922–24; Proctor in Convocation, 1922–24. *Address:* Harrow Cottage, Long Ditton, Surrey. *T:* Emberbrook 1890.

Died 29 March 1943.

HILL, Joseph, FRIBA, FIArb, MIStructE; Practising Architect; *b* 7 Jan. 1888; British parents; *m* 1917, Enid Yetts; two *s* one *d. Educ:* Newcastle Grammar School; Armstrong College (Durham University); Royal Academy School of Architecture. Spent 7 years in office of City Architect of Newcastle-upon-Tyne; Glover Travelling Studentship, Testimonies of Study Prize and Sketches Prize, Northern Architectural Assoc., 1910; Distinction in Thesis, RIBA Final Examination, 1913; came to London, 1909; worked in offices of Henry W. White, Henry Tanner, Mountford and Dare Clapham, J. S. Gibson and Gordon; partner, Yetts, Sturdy and Usher, 1913, afterwards going into individual practice; responsible for variety of structures, including commercial buildings, theatres, flats, library and fire-station, factories, inns; also domestic and restoration work; has specialised in Licensing work and has wide experience as expert technical witness in Court applications, appeals, etc.; joined Architectural Assoc., London, 1910 (Member Council many years, Pres. 1940); Member of Practice Committee RIBA and of Discipline Committee Architects' Registration Council of UK; has belonged to HAC since 1914 and holds rank of Capt.; served throughout European war 1914–18, and a portion of war of 1939–45. *Recreations:* Territorial Army work; archæology and sketching; also natural history. *Address:* 124 Sloane Street, SW1; Babergh Hall, Great Waldingfield, Sudbury, Suffolk. *T:* Sloane 5126, Long Melford 259. *Club:* Cavalry.

Died 13 Jan. 1947.

HILL, Leonard R.; *see* Raven-Hill.

HILL, Lt-Col Sir Norman Gray, 2nd Bt *cr* 1919; MC; MB, BS; RAMC; *b* 24 Aug. 1894; *o s* of Sir Norman Hill, 1st Bt, and Elen Mary Stratford, *d* of J. T. Danson, FSA, Grasmere; *S* father 1944. Served European War, 1914–18 as Lieut Duke of Lancaster's Yeomanry (MC with Bar). *Heir:* none.

Died Feb. 1944.

HILL, Philip Ernest; Chairman and Managing Director Philip Hill & Partners, Ltd, Philip Hill Investment Trust Ltd, Second Covent Garden Property Co. Ltd; Chairman Beecham Maclean Holdings, Ltd, J. C. Eno Limited, Prichard & Constance (Manufacturing) Limited, Strong & Co. of Romsey Limited, Eno Proprietaries, Ltd, Macleans, Ltd, Covent Garden Properties, Ltd, Olympia, Ltd, Timothy White's and Taylor's, Ltd, and subsidiary Companies, Beecham's Pills, Ltd, Veno Drug Co., Ltd, Scribbans & Co., Ltd, R. Hovenden & Sons, Ltd; Director Armstrong Siddeley Development Co., Ltd, Hawker Siddeley Aircraft Co., Eagle Star Insurance Co., Ltd, Quadrant Trust Ltd, etc; *m* 1934, Phyllis Lytton Hill. *Recreation:* golf. *Address:* Windlesham Moor, Windlesham, Surrey. *T:* Bagshot 368. *TA:* Hilbermarl, Piccy, London. *Club:* Royal Thames Yacht.

Died 15 Aug. 1944.

HILL, Maj.-Gen. Walter Pitts Hendy, CB 1934; CMG 1919; DSO 1916; Col of Royal Fusiliers (City of London Regiment) since 1933; *b* 10 June 1877; *s* of J. Ledger Hill, JP, late of Bulford Manor, Wilts; *m* 1910, Phyllis Gertrude Sandars of Scampton, Lincolnshire; one *s* one *d. Educ:* Marlborough College. Served S African War, 1899–1902 (Queen's medal three clasps, King's

medal two clasps); European War, 1914–18 (despatches, Bt Lt-Col, DSO, CMG); to command 2nd Loyal Regiment, 1924; Major-Gen. 1933; retired pay, 1938; Maj.-Gen. i/c Administration, 1939–40. *Address:* West Amesbury House, Amesbury, Wilts.

Died 26 July 1942.

HILL, William Kirkpatrick, BA Lond.; *b* Edmonton, 1862; 3rd *s* of Rev. S. J. Hill of Berhampore; *m* 1895, Eleanor Margaret, *d* of J. L. Childs, JP, Portsmouth; one *d. Educ:* School for Sons of Missionaries, Blackheath; University College School; University College, London. Prizeman, University of London. Assistant Master, University College, School, and Second Master of its Hampstead Preparatory Branch; Head Master, Kentish Town High School, BPDS Co.; Editor of Educational Review; Examiner and Inspector of Schools, Superintendent of Examinations; House Secretary, and Secretary to Finance Committee, University of London; retired, 1922. *Publications:* William Henry Widgery, Schoolmaster (biography); Modern Ideals of Education (Contemporary Review); Responsibility of Parents for Failure in Modern Education; Essential Equality of Man and Woman (Westminster Review); Educational Movements in England (School Review, Chicago); various articles in Educational Review of America, Journal of Education and Educational Times; Under Three Kings (historical romance, 1907); Edwin Trafford, Altruist (economic romance, 1908); The Valley Farm (poem, Cornhill, January 1934). *Recreations:* music and painting. *Address:* 14 Downshire Hill, Hampstead, NW3.

Died 26 Jan. 1944.

HILL-WALKER, Major Alan Richard, VC; late Northampton Regt; *b* 12 July 1859; *e s* of late Capt. Hill, Chief Constable North Riding of Yorkshire, and Frances Miriam, *d* of T. Walker, Maunby Hall, Thirsk; *m* 1902, Muriel Lilias Oliphant, *d* of late T. S. Walker of Maunby Hall, Thirsk [assumed the additional name of Walker, 1902]; one *s.* Joined North York Rifles, 1877; 58th Regt, 1879; served Zulu War, 1879 (medal); Boer War, 1881; Battles of Laing's Nek (despatches, VC), Ingogo, Majuba Hill (severely wounded); AAG, Mandalay, Burma, 1897; Tirah Campaign, 1897. *Recreations:* hunting, shooting—sport of all kinds. *Address:* Maunby Hall, Thirsk, Yorkshire. *T:* Kirkby Wiske 203. *Clubs:* Army and Navy, United Service; Yorkshire, York.

Died 21 April 1944.

HILL-WOOD, Major Sir Samuel (Hill), 1st Bt *cr* 1921; JP, DL; *b* 1872; *e s* of late Samuel Wood, Moorfield, Derbyshire; *m* 1899, Hon. Decima Bateman Hanbury, 6th *d* of 2nd Lord Bateman; four *s.* Contested High Peak Division, Jan. 1910; MP (C) High Peak Division, Derbyshire, 1910–29; assumed surname of Hill-Wood in lieu of Wood, 1910. *Heir: s* Basil Samuel Hill, 2nd Lieut Grenadier Guards [*b* 5 Feb. 1900; *m* 1925, Hon. Joan Brand, *e d* of 3rd Viscount Hampden; one *s* one *d.* Eton; Trinity Coll., Cambridge. 58 Montagu Sq., W]. *Address:* 52 Eaton Pl., SW; Moorfield, Glossop Derbys. *Clubs:* Carlton, Bachelors'.

Died 4 Jan. 1949.

HILLHOUSE, Prof. Percy Archibald, DSc; MINA; MIES; Professor of Naval Architecture, Glasgow University since 1921; *b* Derby, 4 March 1869; *s* of late Archibald Hillhouse, General Goods Manager, Caledonian Railway, and Annie Adamson; bachelor. *Educ:* Partick Academy; Albany Academy; Glasgow University. Draughtsman, A. and J. Inglis, Shipbuilders and Engineers, Pointhouse Shipyard, Glasgow, 1889–93; Draughtsman, Clydebank Shipyard, 1893–98; Professor of Naval Architecture Tokio Imperial University, Japan, 1898–1902; Naval Architect to Fairfield Shipbuilding and Engineering Company Ltd, 1902–37; Vice-President, Institution of Naval Architects since 1928; President Institution of Engineers and Shipbuilders in Scotland, 1935–37. *Publications:* Ship Stability and Trim; Various papers to Technical Societies and in Technical

Journals. *Address:* Whitworth, Busby, Glasgow. *TA:* Hillhouse, Busby. *Clubs:* Royal Scottish Automobile, College, Glasgow.

Died 28 Sept. 1942.

HILLIAM, Maj.-Gen. Edward, CB 1919; CMG 1917; DSO 1916; *b* Willesby Hall, Spalding, Dec. 1863; *s* of Capt. T. Hilliam, Royal South Lincoln Militia; *m* Letitia, *d* of Arthur Wallace of London, Ont; no *c. Educ:* Spalding Grammar School. Soldier in 17th Lancers, 1883–93; RNWM Police, Canada, 1893–1900; served South African War, 1900–02; SA Constabulary, 1902–05; retired and took to fruit ranching in British Columbia; immediately on outbreak of war, 1914, rejoined and went to France as Adjutant 5th Canadian Batt.; served European War, 1914–18 (despatches 11 times, DSO and bar, CMG, CB, Officer Legion of Honour, Croix de Guerre with three Palm leaves); Maj.-Gen., Imperial Army, 1917; with Imperial Forces until 1919. *Address:* 3614 Blenheim Street, Vancouver, BC, Canada.

Died 21 May 1949.

HILLIAR, Harry William, CBE 1920. Superintending Examiner in Patents, Designs, and Trade Marks Office, 1932–37. *Address:* 18 Balcaskie Road, Eltham, SE9.

Died 15 July 1941.

HILLIER, George Lacy; Member London Stock Exchange; *b* Sydenham, 6 June 1856; *e s* of Frederick and Maria Ann Hillier. *Educ:* privately, through ill-health. Amateur Champion at all distances, bicycle and tricycle, 1881; one of the founders of the National Cyclists' Union and Cyclists' Touring Club. *Publications:* The Cycling Volume, Badminton Library; The Art of Ease in Cycling; Training, published in Germany; The Potterers Club, novel; The Weston Diamond, novel, etc. *Recreations:* cycling, walking, running, swimming. *Address:* 4 Queen Victoria Street, EC4. *TA:* Gervase, Stock, London. *T:* City 5456. *Clubs:* CTC, NCU, Stanley, Brixton Ramblers' Cycle, Fellowship of Old Time Cyclists.

Died 11 Feb. 1941.

HILLS, Adam; MP (Lab) Pontefract since 1935; *b* 10 Aug. 1880; *s* of Adam and Ellen Hills; *m* 1906, Isabella Lillie Buck; one *s. Educ:* Elementary School. Employed L and NE Rly Coy until election to Parliament. *Address:* 102 Weldon Crescent, Newcastle-on-Tyne.

Died June 1941.

HILLYARD, Comdr George Whiteside, RN retired; late Secretary of All England Lawn Tennis Club; *b* Hanwell, Middlesex, 6 Feb. 1864; *m* Blanche, *d* of Charles Bentley Bingley. *Publication:* Forty Years of First-class Lawn Tennis. *Address:* Pulborough, Sussex.

Died 24 March 1943.

HILTON, Harold Horsfall; Editor of Golf Illustrated, 1913; Amateur Golf Champion, 1900, 1901, 1911, and 1913; runner-up, 1891, 1892, and 1896; Open Golf Champion, 1892 and 1897; Irish Open Champion, 1897, 1900, 1901, 1902; Amateur Champion, USA, 1911; *b* W Kirby, Cheshire, 12 Jan. 1869. *Educ:* Norfolk County School. *Publications:* Modern Golf (America); My Golfing Reminiscences, 1907. *Clubs:* Golfers'; Royal Liverpool Golf, Hoylake; Formby; Ashford Manor; Royal North Devon.

Died 5 May 1942.

HILTON, John, MA; Professor of Industrial Relations in the University of Cambridge since 1931; *b* Bolton, 28 Dec. 1880; *m* 1902; one *s* two *d. Educ:* elementary schools, scholarship to Bolton Grammar School. Apprenticed mill mechanic, 1896; evening classes at Bolton Technical School; foreman and manager of engineering works at Bury and Heywood, 1902–07; studies in Russia, 1907–08; lecturer and technical journalist, 1908–12; acting secretary Garton Foundation, 1912–18; Assistant Secretary and Director of Statistics,

Ministry of Labour, 1919–31; Member of Council, Royal Statistical Society; Member of International Institute of Statistics; Secretary Committee on Trusts, 1919; President of third and fourth Conferences of Labour Statisticians and of Textile Wages and Hours Commission, ILO, Geneva; Chairman, Committee on Consumers' Co-operation in Great Britain, 1935–38; Weekly Broadcasts, This and That, 1934–36; This Way Out, 1936–37, John Hilton Talking, 1940–43, Director of Home Publicity, Ministry of Information, Sept. 1939–June 1940. *Publications:* Why I go in for the Pools, 1936, This and That, 1938; Rich Man, Poor Man, 1944 (posthumous); articles in reviews and official reports; joint Editor, Are Trade Unions Obstructive? 1935; weekly articles and daily questions and answers in News Chronicle, 1936–1939; Director, News of The World Industrial Advice Bureau, 1942. *Recreations:* manual work, drama, broadcasting. *Address:* 24 De Freville Avenue, Cambridge. *T:* Cambridge 2273.

Died 28 Aug. 1943.

HILTON, Sir Robert Stuart, Kt 1942; OBE 1919; Deputy Chairman and Managing Director The United Steel Companies Limited, Sheffield, since 1928; *b* 28 Dec. 1870; *s* of Thomas Hilton, Wigan, Lancs; *m* 1899, Julia McBryde; one *s* one *d. Educ:* Sedbergh School. Managing Director and Deputy Chairman of Metropolitan-Vickers Electrical Co. Ltd, Trafford Park, Manchester, 1919–28. *Address:* Little Wolford Manor, Shipston-on-Stour, Warwickshire. *Clubs:* Junior Carlton, Burlington Fine Arts.

Died 10 Oct. 1943.

HIME, Maj.-Gen. Henry Charles Rupert, CB 1934; DSO 1917; MB, ChB (Vict. Univ.), DPH, Leeds; late RAMC; *b* 8 Nov. 1877; *s* of late T. W. Hime, MD; *m* 1934, Hilda Margaret, *yr d* of late E. Moore. Served S African War, 1899–1902; European War, 1914–18 (DSO); retired pay, 1934. *Address:* c/o Holt & Co., Kirkland House, Whitehall, SW1.

Died 24 April 1945.

HINCHLIFFE, Richard George, PRCA 1939; RCA 1930; portrait and genre painter; President Royal Cambrian Academy; President Liverpool Academy of Arts since 1931; *b* Manchester; *s* of George and Louisa Hinchliffe, Manchester; *m* Florence, *d* of George and Alice Williams, Liverpool; one *d. Educ:* privately. Studied painting and drawing at the Liverpool School of Art, Slade School, London, Atelier Julien, Paris, Munich; gained scholarship at Royal Academy, Munich; won the King's Medal at Royal Academy School, Munich, 1910. Frequent Exhibitioner at Royal Academy of Arts, London, and provincial galleries; late President of the Liver Sketching Club, Liverpool; President of the Artists' Club, Liverpool, 1929. *Recreations:* yachting, motoring. *Address:* 11 Grove Park, Liverpool, 8. *Clubs:* Artists, Liverpool.

Died 7 Jan. 1942.

HIND, Sir Jesse (William), Kt 1934; DL County of and City and County of Nottingham; MA (Oxon); head of firm of Wells and Hind, solicitors, Nottingham; Director of Sherwood Colliery Co., Ltd, Mansfield, and other companies; Hon. Secretary to Nottinghamshire and Derbyshire Local Committee, Department of Scientific and Industrial Research, Fuel Research (Coal Survey), 1937–45; *b* 1866; *e s* of Jesse Hind, JP, Nottingham and Edwalton, Notts; *m* 1892, Lilian Frances, *er d* of Henry Doughty Browne, JP, 10 Hyde Park Terrace, W, and Tilgate Forest Lodge, Sussex (one *s* killed in action, 1916). *Educ:* Clifton College; Trinity College, Oxford. Admitted a Solicitor, 1891; during the European War rendered valuable service in hospital work; Chairman of West Bridgford VAD Hospital and founder of Monty Hind Orthopaedic Ward (pioneer ward of its kind); awarded certificate of Secretary of State for War for Red Cross services; after the War rendered further public service by assisting and training some 200 ex-service men, etc. and training, and starting in life, some 40 destitute War Orphans at Vimy Ridge Farm, Kinoulton. *Publications:* (with Harry Knox, BA Oxon) Law of Copyright in Designs, 1899; Articles, Letters, and Book Reviews in the Press. *Address:* The Elms, Newcastle Circus, The Park, Nottingham; Vimy Ridge Farm, Kinoulton, Nottingham. *Clubs:* Carlton, Royal Automobile; Notts, Nottingham Borough Notts; United Service, Nottingham.

Died 4 May 1946.

HINDE, Brig.-Gen. Alan, CMG 1919; *b* 1876; *m* 1910, Sara Maud Gladys, *d* of John Leland, Drogheda. Served S Africa, 1899–1902 (despatches, Queen's medal with three clasps, King's medal with two clasps); European War, 1914–19 (despatches, CMG). *Address:* Prospect House, Great Cornard, Suffolk.

Died 24 Aug. 1950.

HINDLEY, Sir Clement D. M., KCIE 1929; Kt 1925; MA; MInstCE, MInstT, MIE (Ind.); Chairman, Racecourse Betting Control Board since 1928; Chairman, Codes of Practice Com. for Civil Engineering and Building under the Minister of Works and Planning since 1942; Member of Central Council for Works and Buildings; Member of Inland Water Survey Committee; Member of Fuel Efficiency Com., Ministry of Fuel and Power; Hon. Col RE; Member of Council of Institute of Welding; *b* 19 Dec. 1874; *s* of late Charles Hugh Hindley; *m* 1899, Anne *d* of late Henry Rait; three *s. Educ:* Dulwich College; Trinity Coll., Cambridge. Engineer East Indian Railway, 1897–1914; Secretary, 1914–18; Deputy Agent, 1918–20; Agent E India Ry (General Manager), 1920–21; Chairman of the Commissioners for the Port of Calcutta, 1921–22; Chief Commissioner of Railways, Railway Board, India, 1922–28; Member of the Channel Tunnel Committee, 1929–30; Chairman Steel Structures Research Com., 1929–36; Member Forest Products Research Board, 1929–33; Member of Cambridge Univ. Appointments Board, 1930–34; Member of the Development (Public Utility) Committee, 1929–30; Member of Building Research Board, 1929–39; Member of Advisory Council for Scientific and Industrial Research, 1932–37; Member of General Board of National Physical Laboratory, 1935–36 and 1939–40; Pres., InstCE, 1939–40; Regional Works Adviser, London Civil Defence Region, Min. of Home Security, 1939–42; Chairman of Committee on the more efficient use of Fuel under the Mines Department, 1940; Pres. of the Alleyn Club, 1931; Colonel Auxiliary Force, India; VD 1913; Volunteer Long Service Medal; Commander Ordre de Leopold, 1926. *Address:* High Elms, The Green, Hampton Court. *T:* Molesey 1977. *Clubs:* Oriental, Athenæum.

Died 3 May 1944.

HINE, Harry, RI; landscape painter, especially of English and foreign cathedrals; *b* London, 27 Feb. 1845; *s* of H. G. Hine, VPRI; *m* 1874, Victoria (*d* 1926), *d* of S. D. Colkett, Norwich. *Educ:* North London Collegiate School. Went to sea at 13; began to paint at 25; settled down ashore. *Publication:* My five voyages in 'sail' from January 1859 to 1869, in The Seagoer, September 1936 onwards. *Recreations:* music; outdoor sports in moderation. *Address:* Pulborough House, Botesdale, Suffolk.

Died 20 Oct. 1941.

HINE, Reginald Leslie, FSA, FRHistS; historian and solicitor; *b* 25 Sept. 1883; *s* of Neville Joseph and Eliza Hine, Newnham Hall, Herts; *m* 1912, Florence Lee Pyman; one *d. Educ:* privately and The Leys School, Cambridge. *Publications:* Anima Celtica, 1910; Dreams and the Way of Dreams, 1913; The Cream of Curiosity, 1920; The History of Hitchin (2 vols), 1927–1929; Hitchin Worthies, 1932; Natural History of the Hitchin Region, 1934; Confessions of an Un-Common Attorney (4th edn), 1948. *Recreation:* exploring every

nook and cranny of Hertfordshire. *Address:* Willian Bury, Willian, Hertfordshire. *TA:* Hine, Hitchin. *T:* Letchworth 532. *Club:* The Tomorrow.

Died 14 April 1949.

HINGE, Maj.-Gen. Harry Alexander, CB 1919; CMG 1916; DSO 1918; late KHS; retired; *b* 18 Oct. 1868; *s* of Lt-Col D. I. Hinge; unmarried. Served NW Frontier, India, 1897–98 (medal with clasp); S Africa, 1902 (Queen's medal three clasps); European War, 1914–18 (despatches five times, CB, CMG, DSO); retired pay, 1926. *Club:* Junior United Service.

Died 15 Sept. 1948.

HINGSTON, Surg. Captain William Percival, CB 1924; late RN; *b* Edinburgh, 1879; *s* of Col C. W. J. Hingston, Indian Army; *m* Myfwany Dora, *d* of Geo. W. Marsden; one *s. Educ:* private; Middlesex Hospital. Served World War; in charge of the RN Establishments, Yokohama, during the earthquake, Sept. 1923; retired list, 1929. *Recreations:* hunting and yachting. *Address:* The Cottage, Montagu Road, Datchet, Bucks.

Died 16 Jan. 1950.

HINKS, Arthur Robert, CBE 1920; FRS 1913; MA, Chevalier de l'Ordre de la Couronne, 1920; Secretary, Royal Geographical Society since 1915; *b* London, 26 May 1873; *e s* of Robert and Mary Hinks; *m* 1899, Lily Mary (*d* 1928), *e d* of Jonathan Packman, MICE; two *s. Educ:* Whitgift Grammar School, Croydon; Trinity College, Cambridge. Second Assistant, Cambridge Observatory, 1895; Chief Assistant, 1903–13; Demonstrator in Practical Astronomy, 1895–1913; Royal Geographical Society Lecturer in Surveying and Cartography, 1908–13; Secretary of the Royal Astronomical Society, 1909–13; Vice-President, 1913; Gresham Lecturer in Astronomy, 1913–41; Assistant Secretary, RGS, 1913–15; Prix Leconte de l'Académie des Sciences, 1910; Gold Medal of the Royal Astronomical Society, 1912; Victoria Medal of the Royal Geographical Society, 1938; Cullum Medal, American Geog. Soc., 1943. *Publications:* Astronomy; Map Projections; Maps and Survey; many papers on the Determination of the Solar Parallax and other astronomical subjects (Monthly Notices RAS, etc.); Catalogue photographique des Etoiles observées avec la planète Eros ... (Académie des Sciences, 1913); papers and reviews on Boundary Treaties, Geodetic and Stereographic Survey, Antarctic exploration, and Map Projections, etc. in Geographical Journal. *Address:* Royal Geographical Society, Kensington Gore, SW7; The White Cottage, Royston, Herts. *T:* Kensington 5466, Royston 3140. *Club:* Travellers'.

Died 18 April 1945.

HINSLEY, His Eminence Cardinal Arthur; Archbishop of Westminster since 1935; *b* 1865. *Educ:* Ushaw; English College, Rome. Professor at Ushaw, 1893–97; Assistant Priest Keighley, 1898; Headmaster of St Bede's Grammar School, Bradford, 1899–1904; Pastor of Sutton Park, 1904–11; Pastor of Sydenham, 1911–17; Rector of the English College, Rome, 1917–28; Visitor Apostolic to the Catholic Missions in Africa, 1927; Titular Archbishop of Sardis, 1930; Apostolic Delegate in Africa, 1930–34; Canon of the Patriarchal Basilica of St Peter's Rome, 1934–35; Cardinal, 1937. *Address:* Archbishop's House, Westminster, SW1. *Club:* Athenæum.

Died 17 March 1943.

HINTON, Arthur; Fellow and Professor of Harmony and Composition at the Royal Academy of Music; *b* Beckenham, 1869; *m* Katharine Goodson. *Educ:* Shrewsbury; Royal Academy of Music, under M. Prosper Sainton, M. Sauret, F. W. Davenport; Munich, under Prof. Rheinberger; Vienna; Rome. Visited Australia thrice, also Tasmania, New Zealand, Ceylon, Jamaica, and Canada, as Examiner for Associated Board of RAM and RCM. *Compositions:* Two Symphonies;

Porphyria's Lover; Dramatic Scenes, Seraph of Heaven, Semele for Voice and Orchestra; Pfte Concerto; Pfte Quintet and Trio; Song Cycles, Butterflies, and White Roses, and numerous other pieces for voice, pfte solo, etc. *Address:* Greenlands, Rottingdean, Sussex.

Died 11 Aug. 1941.

HINTON, Wilfred John, MA; LLD (Hon.); Director of Studies, Institute of Bankers, since 1929; *b* 7 Nov. 1887; *s* of late William James Hinton of Cardiff and Esther Virgo of Walton-in-Gordano; *m* 1914, Helen Louise, *d* of Rev. David S. Murray; one *s*. *Educ:* Howard Gardens School, Cardiff; University of Wales; Jesus College, Oxford; Treasury Fellow, University of Wales, 1910. Professor of Political Economy, Dean, Member of Court and Council University of Hong-Kong, 1913–29; British Commercial Commissioner in Siberia, March–Aug. 1919; Conferences at Honolulu (IPR), Mont Tremblant (IPR), Hot Springs, Bretton Woods; lectures in various English and American Universities, 1929–39; Member of Council Royal Institute of International Affairs, 1929–32; Member of Executive Council Universities Bureau of the British Empire, 1932–34; Ministry of Information, 1940–45; one of the Directors of British Information Services, New York, 1942–45. *Address:* Institute of Bankers, 11 Birchin Lane, EC3. *Clubs:* English-Speaking Union; Century Association (New York).

Died 20 June 1949.

HIPWOOD, Sir Charles, KBE 1926; CB 1917; *b* July 1869; *e s* of late Lacey Hipwood, Hampstead; *m* 1904, Margaret Helen, 2nd *d* of late Daniel McLeish, Fort William; one *s* one *d*. *Educ:* Christ's Hospital; Wadham College, Oxford. Entered Board of Trade, 1893; Head of Mercantile Marine Dept, 1916–29; Second Secretary, 1929–32; retired, 1932; Director National Union of Manufacturers, 1932–45. Officer, Legion of Honour; Officer, Crown of Belgium; Commander, Crown of Italy. *Address:* Heatherbank, Chislehurst, Kent.

Died 11 March 1946.

HIRD, Norman Leslie; JP; General Manager since 1920 and Director of the Union Bank of Scotland, Ltd, Glasgow; Chairman Central Committee of Scottish Chambers of Commerce, 1944–; *b* 22 April 1886; *s* of late Captain William Hird of the Mercantile Marine; *m* 1911; Mabel Mary, *d* of late Samuel Fuller, Woodford, Essex; two *d*. *Educ:* London University. Vice-Pres. British Bankers' Assoc. (various periods); Pres. Institute of Bankers in Scotland, 1926–28; Representative of Board of Trade on Regional Board for Scotland of the Cabinet Production Executive, 1940–42; Deputy Chairman, Administrative Committee of Empire Exhibition, Scotland, 1938; President Glasgow Chamber of Commerce, 1943–44; Director of Scottish Amicable Life Assurance Society. *Publications:* various articles on Banking and economic subjects. *Recreations:* ski-ing, tennis, mountaineering. *Address:* Beechwood House, Stirling. *T:* 738. *Clubs:* Conservative; Western, Glasgow; University, Edinburgh.

Died 2 March 1946.

HIRSCH, Lt-Col Leonard, CIE 1919; IMS, retd; *b* 1879. *Educ:* MRCS England and LRCP London; FRCS Edinburgh. Served European War, 1914–19 (CIE).

Died 23 April 1942.

HIRST, 1st Baron *cr* 1934 of Witton; **Hugo Hirst;** 1st Bt *cr* 1925; Chairman of The General Electric Co., Ltd; President of the Radio Manufacturers Association; Honorary Member Institution of Electrical Engineers; Hon. Treasurer Empire Industries Association; *b* 26 Nov. 1863; *m* 1892, Leontine (*d* 1938), *d* of Herman Hirsch; two *d*. Member of the Prime Minister's Trade and Employment Panel; Economic Adviser to the Cabinet Research Committee; the Board of Trade Advisory Council, 1922–25, 1929–32, 1936–39; the Committee on Unemployment Insurance, 1925–26; Committee on

Co-operative Selling in the Coal Industry, 1926; of British Economic Mission to Australia, 1928–29; the Melchett-Turner Conference, the Committee on Industrial Research; Representative of HM Government on League of Nations, Sub-Committee of Experts for Scientific Property; Master of the Worshipful Company of Glaziers, 1929 and 1930; Past President of Federation of British Industries, Past President of the Association of Technical Institutions; the Institute of Fuel, the British Export Society, the British Electrical Development Association, the Incorporated Society of British Advertisers, and the Decimal Association. *Heir:* none (his grandson, H. H. Hirst, died on operational duties with the RAF May 1941). *Address:* Claridge's Hotel, Brook Street, W1; Fox Hill, Earley, nr Reading. *T:* Reading 61400. *Clubs:* Carlton, St James's, Portland.

Died 22 Jan. 1943 (ext).

HIRST, William; JP; *b* 1873. President of City of Bradford Co-operative Society, Ltd. Contested South Bradford three times; MP (Lab) South Bradford 1924–31. *Address:* 13 Nurser Place, Little Norton, Bradford.

Died 5 May 1946.

HIRST, William Alfred; author and traveller; *b* Huddersfield, 1870; *e s* of late Alfred Hirst, of Dalton Lodge, Huddersfield; *m* 1898, Catherine, *d* of late George Thompson, Harrogate; one *s*. *Educ:* Clifton Coll.; Worcester Coll., Oxford. Arrived in India, 1894; officiated as Professor of History at the Govt College, Lahore, 1895–96; First Professor Meerut College, 1896–1902; Principal of Gujerat College, Ahmedabad, 1902–07; served in various Yeomanry Regiments since Aug. 1914, and in Middlesex Regiment (wounded on Somme in 1916); received temp. Commission, 1917. *Publications:* Survey of Ethics, 1902; Argentina, 1910; A Guide to S America, 1915; Rambles in the Home Counties, 1927; Real Self-Government for India, 1933. *Recreations:* reading and study; riding, cricket; used to play Rugby football and run long distance races. *Address:* 19 Upper Park Road, Hampstead, NW. *Club:* United University.

Died 4 Sept. 1948.

HITLER, Adolf; Head of the German State since 1934, and Chancellor of the German Reich since 1933; Commander-in-Chief of the German Fighting Forces since 1938; Personal Commander of Army since 1941; Supreme War Lord; Supreme Law Lord since 1942; *b* Braunau on the Inn, Upper Danube, 20 April 1889, of an old Upper Austrian peasant and artisan family; *m* 1945, Eva Braun. religion, Catholic. *Educ:* secondary schools in Linz and Graz; studied painting and architecture in Vienna; settled at Munich in 1912 to study painting, supporting himself as artisan in building trade. Volunteer in German Army, 1914; wounded, 1916; gassed and temporarily blinded, 1918; Iron Cross, 1st Cl. and 2nd Cl., Western Front; after Revolution of 1918–19 devoted himself to politics, becoming President and Leader of the National Socialist German Workers' Party; took part in rising of 9 Nov. 1923 and was sentenced to fortress detention until Dec. 1924; re-founded National Socialist Movement, 27 Feb. 1925; appointed Chancellor of the German Reich by President von Hindenburg, 30 Jan. 1933; member of the Reichstag from 5 March 1933; became Head of the German State by law of 1 Aug. 1934, confirmed by Referendum of 19 Aug. 1934. *Publication:* Mein Kampf, vol. I, 1925, vol. II, 1927. *Address:* Wilhelmstr, 77, Berlin, W8. *T:* 11 6191; Ober-Salzberg Berchtesgaden, Bavaria.

Died 30 April 1945.

HJORT, Johan, FRS, PhD, ScD, Professor at the University of Oslo, Norway; *b* Kristiania, 18 Feb. 1869; father was Professor of Medicine at the University there. *Educ:* Kristiania; Munich; Naples. Lecturer in Zoology at the University of Kristiania until 1900; Director of Norwegian Fisheries, 1900–16; work was divided between practical administration for the development of the fishing industry and the part participation in oceanographical expeditions and research in North European, Atlantic, and Canadian waters; since 1916, engaged in studies of more general biological character. *Publications:* several papers on embryology and life history of marine animals; for later years in the publications of the International Council for the Study of the Sea; (with Sir John Murray) The Depths of the Ocean, 1912; The Unity of Science, 1921; The Emperor's New Clothes, 1931. *Recreation:* has spent all time free from bureau work on marine expeditions. *Address:* University, Oslo, Norway.

Died 7 Oct. 1948.

HOADLEY, Charles Archibald, CBE 1936; MSc; BME; Principal Footscray Technical School since 1916; *b* 1 March 1887; *s* of Abel Hoadley and Susannah Anne Barrett; *m* 1931, Rita Cadle McComb; two *s*. *Educ:* Wesley College; Queens College, Melbourne University. Graduated BME 1910; BSc, 1911; MSc, 1914. Geologist to Australasian Antarctic Expedition, Queen Mary Land, 1911–13; Senior Technical Instructor in Engineering, Ballarat School of Mines, 1914–15; Joined Scout Association, 1920; Appointed Camp Chief of Victoria, 1924; Chief Commissioner, 1928. *Recreations:* scouting, tennis. *Address:* 10 Geelong Road, Footscray, Melbourne, W12, Australia. *Club:* Rotary.

Died 27 Feb. 1947.

HOADLEY, Jane, CBE 1919; RRC; *d* of George Hoadley. Formerly Matron, Principal Matron (Hon.) 1915–19, Queen Alexandra's Imperial Military Nursing Service; served S Africa, 1899–1902 (Queen's and King's medals, RRC); European War, 1914–19 (medal, bar to RRC, CBE). *Address:* Mount Hawke, Truro.

Died 11 Feb. 1946.

HOARE, Douglas; *b* 28 June 1875; *s* of late Canon Gurney Hoare and Alice Woodfall. *Educ:* Repton; Trinity College, Cambridge. Joint-editor of the By the Way Column in the Globe; Wrote Musical Criticism in the Times, the Globe, the Daily Telegraph, etc.; *Plays:* Think of a Number; with Sydney Blow: Where Children Rule, Little Miss Llewellyn; Oh, I Say; Lord Richard in the Pantry; The Officers Mess; Kiki; The Live Wire; Old Jig; with J. E. Hoare: The Wolves, Dancing Shadows. *Publications:* Politics for the Pocket (with H. W. Goldberg); Arctic Exploration; Murder to Music (with Percy Colsen). *Recreations:* walking, golf, swimming. *Address:* 25 St Cross Hospital, Winchester.

Died 1 March 1947.

HOARE, Sir Henry (Hugh Arthur), of Stourhead, Wilts, 6th Bt *cr* 1786; JP; *b* 19 Nov. 1865; *o s* of H. A. Hoare of Wavendon House, Bucks, and Julia Lucy, *e d* of T. V. Lane, and *g d* of 2nd Viscount Exmouth; *S* cousin, 1894; *m* 1887, *cousin* Alda, *d* of William Henry Purcell Weston. *Educ:* Harrow. Owns 6000 acres. *Heir: cousin* Peter William Hoare, *b* 1898. *Address:* Stourhead, Warminster, Wilts. *TA:* Stourton, Wilts. *Club:* Boodle's.

Died 25 March 1947.

HOARE, Brig.-Gen. Reginald, CMG 1919; DSO 1918; late 4th Hussars; *b* 18 Sept. 1865; 7th *s* of late Thos Rolls Hoare; *m* 1918, Violet Eliza Reid, *d* of late John Reid Walker, Ruckley Grange, Shifnal; three *s* one *d*. *Educ:* Eton Coll. Served South African War, 1901–02 (Queen's medal five clasps); European War, 1914–18 (wounded, despatches, DSO, CMG). *Address:* Badger Heath, near Wolverhampton. *Club:* Cavalry.

Died 14 Oct. 1947.

HOBART, Lt-Col Sir (Claud) Vere Cavendish, 2nd Bt *cr* 1914; DSO 1898; OBE 1919; DL Isle of Wight since 1913 and for Co. Southampton since 1932; *b* 12 March 1870; *o s* of late Sir Robert Henry Hobart, 1st Bart, KCVO, CB, *g s* of George, 3rd Earl of Buckinghamshire, and Hon. Julia Trollope, *e d* of 1st

Baron Kesteven; *S* father, 1928; *m* 1st, 1900, Violet Verve, MBE, (*d* 1935) 2nd *d* of late John Wylie; one *s*; 2nd, 1936, Lois Anne (*d* 1947), *e d* of late Rev. Albert Popham. *Educ:* Eton; Sandhurst. Entered Army (Grenadier Guards), 1890; Captain, 1899; served Uganda, 1897–99 (despatches, DSO, medal with clasp); served South Africa as DAAG, 1899–1900 (medal with clasp); Major, 1906; retired, 1906; Lieut-Col Commanding Princess Beatrice's IW Rifles, 1908–13; on Staff, British Forces in France and Flanders, 1914–19 (despatches 3 times, OBE, 1914 Star, British and Victory medals); contested (L) Westminster, 1906 and 1910; JP Co. Southampton. *Heir: s* Lieut-Comdr Robert Hampden Hobart, RN [*b* 7 May 1915; *m* 1942, Sylvia, *d* of H. Argo, Durban, Natal; two *s*]. *Address:* Gatcombe Park, Isle of Wight. *Clubs:* Household Brigade Yacht; Bembridge Sailing.

Died 29 Nov. 1949.

HOBART, Henry Metcalf, MInstCE, MIEE, MIMechE of Great Britain; Fellow AmIEE, MAmSocME; at present engaged in a private consulting engineering practice; *b* Boston, Mass, 1868; *m*. *Educ:* Massachusetts Institute of Technology. Carried on a consulting practice in London, 1903–11; Chief Designer of Continuous Current Machinery for the Union Electricitäts Gesellschaft, Berlin, 1900–03; Technical Expert, The British Thomson-Houston Co., London, during their carrying out of Central London Railway Contract, Middlesbrough Tramways, Dublin Tramways, etc., 1895–1900; the General Electric Co. of America, and the Thomson-Houston Co., 1889–95; BSc Massachusetts Institute of Technology, 1889; Lecturer on Dynamo Design at University College and at Northampton Institute, and in special Electrical Engineering subjects at Faraday House, 1908–11; Consulting Engineer to the General Electric Company of Schenectady, New York, 1911–40. *Publications:* Electric Railway Engineering; Continuous Current Dynamo Design; Armature Construction; Electric Machine Design; Steam Turbine Engineering; High-Speed Dynamo Electric Machinery; Heavy Electrical Engineering; Electricity; Electric Trains; Electric Motors (3rd edition); The Electric Propulsion of Ships; Design of Static Transformers; Design of Polyphase Generators and Motors; editor of A Dictionary of Electrical Engineering. *Address:* 10 Balltown Road, Schenectady, New York.

Died 11 Oct. 1946.

HOBART, Lt-Col Sir Vere C.; *see* Hobart, Lt-Col Sir C. V. C.

HOBART-HAMPDEN, Ernest Miles, CMG 1914; *b* 11 Nov. 1864; *s* of late Hon. G. A. Hobart-Hampden; *m* 1901, Hélène (*d* 1938), *d* of late Rev. Louis Langel; one *s*. *Educ:* Clifton; Brasenose College, Oxford. Entered Consular Service China, 1888; transferred to Japan, 1889; Vice-Consul, Yokohama, 1904; second Secretary (local rank) and Japanese Secretary to British Embassy, Tokio, 1909; first Secretary (local rank), 1916; retired, 1919. *Publication:* English-Japanese Dictionary of the Spoken Language (in collaboration with H. G. Parlett). *Address:* 25 Coleherne Court, SW5. *T:* Frobisher 6218.

Died 1 May 1949.

HOBDAY, Alfred; *b* Faversham, Kent, 1870; *m* 1895, Ethel Sharpe, pianist. *Educ:* Royal College of Music (Open Scholarship for violin), and studied under Holmes for violin and viola, Dr Bridge for harmony and counterpoint, Dr Gladstone for organ, and Mr Herbert Sharpe for piano. Made a speciality of the viola as a solo instrument, and gave many concerts with his wife, at the St James's Hall, Aeolian Hall, and in the provinces; at the Monday and Saturday Popular Concerts he frequently appeared with the Joachim Quartet and also with Lady Hallé, Ries, and Piatti; principal viola in Queen Victoria's private band, 1895, and holds the Diamond Jubilee silver medal and the Coronation medals of King

Edward and King George; was principal viola in the London Symphony Orchestra from its formation in 1905 to 1930, and has played with most of the great conductors; engaged as solo viola and viol d'amore at the Royal Opera, Covent Garden, 1900–14; principal viola in the Royal Philharmonic Society; Three-Choir Festivals of Gloucester, Hereford, and Worcester, etc.; was engaged as principal viola at the Leeds Festival twice with Sullivan, and since with Stanford, Nikisch and Albert Coates; is on the staff of Examiners for the Associated Board of the RAM and RCM, and has three times visited South Africa as Music Examiner to the University. *Address:* 26 St Anne's Road, Tankerton-on-Sea, Kent.

Died 23 Feb. 1942.

HOBHOUSE, Rt Hon. Sir Charles (Edward Henry), 4th Bt *cr* 1812; PC 1909; JP; TD; *b* Sussex, 30 June 1862; *e s* of Sir C. P. Hobhouse, 3rd Bt, and Edith Lucy, *d* of Sir Thos Turton, Bt; *S* father, 1916; *m* 1st, 1890, Georgina Fleetwood (*d* 1927), *o d* of late G. P. Fuller of Neston Park; 2nd, 1931, Aimee Gladys, *widow* of B. A. Brendon, ICS. *Educ:* Eton; Christ Church, Oxford. Lieut 60th Rifles, 1884–90; MP (L) East Wilts, 1892–95; East Bristol, 1900–18; Private Secretary at Colonial Office, 1892–95; County Alderman, Wilts, 1893–1924; a Church Estates Commissioner, 1906–07; Parliamentary Under-Secretary for India, 1907–08; Financial Secretary to Treasury, 1908–11; Chancellor of the Duchy of Lancaster, 1911–14; Postmaster-General, 1914–15; an Hon. Col Royal Tank Regiment. *Recreations:* hunting, shooting. *Heir:* half-brother, Reginald Arthur Hobhouse. *Address:* Monkton Farleigh, Wilts. *Club:* Brooks's.

Died 26 June 1941.

HOBHOUSE, Sir Reginald Arthur, 5th Bt *cr* 1812; *b* 4 May 1878; 2nd *s* of Sir C. P. Hobhouse, 3rd Bt; *S* half-brother 1941; *m* 1905, Marjorie Chisholm, *e d* of F. Spencer, Pondsmead, Oakhill, Somerset; four *s* two *d.* *Educ:* Marlborough. JP and County Alderman, Somerset; High Sheriff, Somerset, 1932. *Heir: s* Charles Chisholm, Major N Somerset Yeo. (TA), *b* 1906. *Address:* Pondsmead, Oakhill, near Bath. *T:* Oakhill 3. *Club:* Brooks's.

Died 9 July 1947.

HOBKIRK, Brig.-Gen. Clarence John, CMG 1918; DSO 1916; *b* 16 July 1869; *s* of late John Hobkirk, Drummond Place, Edinburgh, and late Baroness Farina Firrao; *m* Nora Louisa, *d* of late Arthur Bosanquet, ICS, of Cleddon Hall, Trelleck, Monmouth; one *s* one *d.* *Educ:* Cheltenham College, Sandhurst. Joined 1st Batt. Essex Regt 1890; served S African War, 1900–02 (Queen's medal 5 clasps, King's medal 2 clasps, despatches twice); Military Attaché, Rome and Berne, 1914; at War Office, 1914; served European War, 1915–16, as temp. Lt-Col commanding 11th Essex Regt; 1916–18 as temp. Brig.-Gen. commanding 14th Australian Infantry Brigade and 120th (Highland) Infantry Brigade (despatches six times, Brevet Lt-Col, CMG, DSO); Subst. Lt-Col commanding 2nd Batt. Essex Regt 1919; retired 1920 with rank Brig.-Gen.; HG Service, 1940. *Address:* Cleddon Hall, Trelleck, Monmouth. *Club:* Army and Navy.

Died 9 Sept. 1949.

HOBLEY, Charles William, CMG 1904; *b* 1867; *s* of William Hobley, Chilvers Coton, Warwickshire; *m* 1905, Alice Mary (*d* 1940), *d* of late Thomas Turner, Sutton Coldfield; one *s* one *d.* *Educ:* Mason College, Birmingham University. Geologist, Imperial British East Africa Co., 1890; Sub-Commissioner, East Africa Protectorate, 1894; Assistant Deputy Commissioner, 1902; Acting Commissioner, 1904; Acting Deputy Commissioner, 1903–04, and 1906–07; Acting Senior Commissioner, 1907; Provincial Commissioner, Seyidieh Province, 1912; Official Member, Legislative Council, East Africa Protectorate, 1912–20;

Commissioner of Mines; Chief Political Officer to Expeditionary Force, British-German East Africa, 1914–15 (despatches); retired from Colonial Service, 1921; Fellow Royal Anthropological Institute and Corr. Fellow Zoological Society; awarded Back Grant of Royal Geographical Society, 1915; Member of Advisory Board of Geological Survey, 1930; Council, Royal Geographical Society, 1931; Council, Royal Anthropological Institute, 1931; Council, Geological Society, 1930; Secretary Society for Preservation of the Fauna of the Empire, 1923–36; Vice-President Geologists Association, 1935–39; AMInstCE; FGS; FRGS. *Publications:* Ethnology of A-Kamba, 1910; Bantu Beliefs and Magic, 1922, 2nd Edition, 1938; Kenya from Chartered Company to Crown Colony, 1929. *Address:* Woodfield, Quarry Road, Oxted, Surrey. *T:* Oxted 710. *Club:* East India and Sports.

Died 31 March 1947.

HOBSON, Geoffrey Dudley, MVO; Director of Sotheby & Co., 34–35 New Bond Street, W1; *b* 17 March 1882; 4th *s* of Richard and Mary Eleanor Hobson, The Marfords, Bromborough, Cheshire; *m* 1920, Gertrude Adelaide (*d* 1938), *d* of Rev. T. Vaughan, Rhuddlan Rectory, Flintshire; one *s.* *Educ:* Harrow; University College, Oxford. Joined Sotheby & Co. (then Sotheby Wilkinson & Hodge), 1909. *Publications:* Maioli, Canevari, and others, 1926; Thirty Bindings, 1927; Bindings in Cambridge Libraries, 1929; English Binding before 1500, 1929; Les reliures à la fanfare, Le Problème de l'S fermé, 1936; Art After The War, 1946. *Address:* 11 Chelsea Park Gardens, SW3. *T:* Flaxman 7594. *Clubs:* Athenæum, Windham, Oxford and Cambridge.

Died 5 Jan. 1949.

HOBSON, Robert Lockhart, CB 1931; BA; *b* 26 July 1872; *s* of Canon W. T. Hobson; *m* Hon. Daisy Denison, *d* of Adm. Hon. A. D. S. Denison; four *s* one *d.* *Educ:* St John's, Leatherhead; Jesus College, Cambridge (Scholar). First-Class Classical Tripos, 1893. Assistant in British Museum, 1897; Deputy Keeper of Department of British and Mediæval Antiquities, 1921; Keeper of Dept of Oriental Antiquities and of Ethnography; retired 1938. *Publications:* Catalogue of English Pottery, 1903; Guide to English Pottery and Porcelain, 1904; Catalogue of English Porcelain (1905) in British Museum; Worcester Porcelain, 1910; Chinese Pottery and Porcelain, 1915; The Wares of the Ming Dynasty, 1923; The Art of the Chinese Potter, 1923; Guide to the Pottery and Porcelain of the Far East, British Museum, 1924; the Later Ceramic Wares of China, 1925; Catalogue of the Eumorforpoulos Collection, 1925–1928, etc. *Recreations:* lawn tennis and gold. *Address:* Correen, Pondtail Road, Horsham.

Died 5 June 1941.

HOCKLEY, Ven. Guy Wittenoom, MA Oxon; Archdeacon of Cornwall and Warden of Community of the Epiphany since 1925; Prebendary of Trehaverock in Prebendal Church of St Endellion since 1946; Hon. Canon of Truro since 1946; *b* 16 Feb. 1869; *s* of Major Julius Joseph Hockley and Emma Annie Mary, *d* of Rev. J. T. Darby. *Educ:* Blundell's School, Tiverton; Balliol College, Oxford; Cuddesdon Theological College. Deacon, 1892; Priest, 1893; Curate of Hawarden, 1892–97; of St Matthew, Westminster, 1897–1903; Diocesan Chaplain to Bishop of Worcester, 1903–05; to Bishop of Birmingham, 1905–06; Vicar of St Saviour, Hoxton, 1906–08; Vicar of St Matthew, Westminster, 1908–14; Rector of Heathfield, 1914–16; Rector of Liverpool, 1916–25; Rural Dean of Liverpool North; Proctor in Convocation; Hon. Canon of Liverpool; of Truro Cathedral, 1925–30; Canon Residentiary of Truro Cathedral, 1930, 1946. *Address:* Trevrea, Truro. *T:* Truro 2021.

Died 16 Sept. 1946.

HOCKLIFFE, Ernest, MA, JP; *b* 1863; *s* of Frederick Hockliffe, Bedford; *m* 1890, Marian Isabella Napier, *y d* of Sir J. C. Robinson, CB, of Newton Manor, Swanage; no *c*. *Educ:* Bedford School; Lincoln College, Oxon (Scholar). 1st Class Classical Moderations, 1883; 2nd Class Literæ Humaniores, 1886. Master at Uppingham School, 1889–1922; Prof. of English Literature, Queen's College, London, 1922–26; Member of Rutland County Council and JP, 1908–22. *Publications:* Diary of Ralph Josselin, Royal Historical Society, 1908; (part author) A Rhymer's Ring, 1922; Editor and part author of a History of Bedford School. *Address:* Barrow Court Farm, Tickenham, Clevedon, Somerset.

Died 19 May 1944.

HODGE, Francis Edwin, RI, ROI, RP, RWA; painter, portraits and decorations; *b* S Devon, 1883; *e s* of late E. Hodge; *m* Hazel Bruce, *d* of Captain A. R. Dunlop. *Educ:* privately; Westminster School of Art. Assistant to Prof. G. Moira (Royal College of Art) for three years; Brangwyn, John and Orpen, and Slade Schools; Paris. Exhibitor at the RA International Society, NEAC, RBA (as member); RPS, ROI, Carnegie Institute, Pittsburg, Canadian Imperial Exhibition, etc.; Salon, Paris, Hon. Mention 1927, Silver Medal, 1938. Represented in following public galleries: Imperial War Museum, Victoria and Albert Museum, Derby, Plymouth, Doncaster, Kidderminster, Auckland, New Zealand, and National War Collection. War service in France (Captain RA). *Publications:* Illustrated History of the Fourth Army; History of the 9th Scottish Division; Figure Painting, The Artist, Illustrations for the Graphic, Cassells, and other magazines. *Recreations:* riding, fishing. *Address:* Studio: 2a Sydney Close, SW3. *Clubs:* Arts, Authors'.

Died 6 Feb. 1949.

HODGE, Harry; Managing Director of William Hodge & Co., Ltd, Printers and Publishers, Glasgow, and of Hodge & Chilver, Ltd, London; *b* Edinburgh, 5 Aug. 1872; *m* Agnes Hunter, *d* of John Moffatt, CA; one *s* two *d*. *Educ:* Glasgow Academy; University, Leipzig and University, Glasgow. Founded the Notable British Trials Series, 1905, and has acted as general editor ever since; Editor Scottish Law Review; President Edinburgh Music Club; although a business man, finds time to write music; a number of his compositions for pianoforte have been published in Germany and Scotland. *Publications:* Toccatina in G major, A Tune with Changes, A Coffee Trifle, Variations in G minor, Gavotte in A minor, Waltz in A flat, Allegro in G minor, Suite in A flat major, Prelude in E flat, Waltz Sketches (3 sets), Choral Preludes for strings; The Black Maria; Famous Trials (Penguin), etc. *Recreations:* music, criminology, and travel. *Address:* 58 Murrayfield Avenue, Edinburgh; 86 Hatton Garden, EC1. *Clubs:* Savage, Constitutional, Royal Automobile, Scottish Conservative, Musicians (Edinburgh); Royal Scottish Automobile (Glasgow).

Died 10 Dec. 1947.

HODGE, Lt-Col James Philip; MP (L) Preston, 1922–24; *b* 1879; 2nd *s* of late Archibald Hodge of Hoole Park, Chester, formerly a Fifeshire miner; *m* 1917, Anna Fortunée (*d* 1944), 2nd *d* of late Michel Venture, shipowner of Marseilles; one *d*. *Educ:* Chester Cathedral Choir School. Practised as a Chartered Accountant in Chester at the age of 21; relinquished this profession for that of the Bar, to which he was called by the Inner Temple in 1917, and is on the Northern Circuit; served prior to the War as private in Inns of Court OTC; obtained commission in APD and went to France in 1914; served also in Salonika and in Egypt, being subsequently appointed Inspector of Pay Offices with rank of Lt-Col. *Recreations:* sculling, golf, studies in Theology.

Died 12 July 1946.

HODGE, Sir Rowland Frederic William, 1st Bt *cr* 1921; Director of Canning Town Glass Works, Ltd, etc; *b* 15 Sept. 1859; *s* of John Rowland Hodge of Newcastle-on-Tyne; *m* 1st, 1898; Mabel (*d* 1923), *d* of William Edward Thorpe; two *s* two *d*; 2nd, 1930, Vera, Countess Cathcart. *Educ:* Houghton-le-Spring. Was a prominent shipbuilder on Tyneside; Founder and Managing Director for over twenty years of Northumberland Shipbuilding Co. Ltd. *Heir:* *s* John Rowland, MBE [*b* 1 May 1913; *m* 1939, Joan, *o d* of late S. F. Wilson; three *d*]. *Address:* Chipstead, Churt, Surrey. *T:* Headley Down, 2276. *Clubs:* Junior Carlton, Constitutional, Royal Automobile.

Died 21 Sept. 1950.

HODGES, Arthur Harris, CMG 1938; Colonial Treasurer, Jamaica, BWI, since 1934; Privy Councillor, Jamaica, 1940; *b* 16 Dec. 1884; *m* 1916, Florence Marguerite Mann Ogden; one *s*. Treasury service in South Africa, 1901; Australia, 1908; West Africa, 1901. *Address:* Treasury, Kingston, Jamaica. *Club:* British Empire.

Died 26 Oct. 1941.

HODGES, Lt-Col Aubrey Dallas Percival, CMG 1910; MD Lond.; MRCS, LRCP Lond; *b* 1861; *s* of Herbert Busy Hodges; *m* 1st, 1909, Helena Riddick (*d* 1925); one *d*; 2nd, 1927, Hilda Margaret, *y d* of late Rev. F. S. Legg, MA. *Educ:* Epsom Coll.; London Hospital. Late Assistant Resident Medical Officer, South-East Fever Hospital, New Cross; House Physician, House Surgeon and Resident Accoucheur, London Hospital; Medical Officer in charge Sleeping Sickness extended Investigation; Fellow Royal Institute of Public Health; Fellow Royal Society of Tropical Medicine and Hygiene; PMO Uganda Protectorate, 1908–18; Lieut-Colonel Commanding Uganda Medical Service and ADMS for Uganda, 1914–18 (despatches); holds Sudanese Mutiny medal, 1898. *Address:* Alfold, Neville Road, Bognor.

Died 17 May 1946.

HODGES, Barbara K.; (pseudonym, Elizabeth Cambridge); *b* Rickmansworth, 7 Oct. 1893; *d* of H. W. Webber, MD, MS; *m* 1914, G. M. Hodges, MB, BS; two *s* one *d*. *Educ:* Moorfields, Plymouth; The Eyrie, Westgate on Sea; Les Marroniers, Paris. Writer of short stories, 1910–14; short service with VAD during war; began writing again 1930. *Publications:* Hostages to Fortune; Sycamore Tree; Susan and Joanna; The Two Doctors; Spring Always Comes; Portrait of Angela (all novels). *Recreations:* gardening, reading. *Address:* The Blocks, Deddington, Oxon. *TA:* Hodges, Deddington, Oxon. *T:* Deddington 257.

Died 3 March 1949.

HODGES, Frank; JP; Member of Central Electricity Board; *b* Woolaston, Gloucestershire, 30 April 1887; *s* of Thomas and Louisa Hodges; *m* Henrietta, *d* of John and Jemima Carter, Abertillery; one *d*. *Educ:* Queen Street Elementary School, Abertillery; Ruskin and Labour College, Oxford. Oxford Labour Colleges, 1909–10. Miners' Agent, Garw, Glam., 1912; Civil Lord of the Admiralty, 1924; MP (Lab) Lichfield Division of Staffs, 1923–24; Member of Royal Commission on Coal Mines, 1919; Secretary International Miners' Federation, 1925–27; General Secretary Miners' Federation of Great Britain, 1918–24; Fellow of Royal Economic Society. *Recreations:* golf, tennis, walking. *Address:* 62 Dorset House, Gloucester Place, NW1. *T:* Welbeck 3269. *Clubs:* Bath, Royal Automobile; New, Glasgow.

Died 3 June 1947.

HODGES, Rev. William Herbert; *b* 13 Oct. 1873; *e s* of late W. A. Hodges, JP; *m* 1915, Annie Helen, 2nd *d* of Richard Lett, Buenos Aires; one *s* one *d*. *Educ:* Bainster Court School, Southampton; Wadham College, Oxford, MA (open Classical Exhibition); Marburg University; Paris. Classical Master Walsall Grammar School,

1898–1901; Modern Languages Master Loretto, 1902–04; ordained, 1904; Curate of St Anne, Highgate Rise, 1904–07; Assistant Master Merchant Taylors' School, 1904–07; Chaplain and Assist Master St Lawrence College, Ramsgate, 1907–09; Curate Dewsbury Moor, 1909–11; Huddersfield; 1911; Archdeacon in Argentina and Rector of St John's Pro-Cathedral in Buenos Aires, 1912–32; Rector of Betteshanger-with-Ham, Kent, 1932–35; Rector of St Alphege with St Margaret, Canterbury and Master of Eastbridge Hospital, 1935–45. *Recreations:* formerly football and a little mountaineering. *Address:* Silverhaze, Broadstone, Dorset. *T:* 461.

Died 27 Jan. 1948.

HODGKIN, Lt-Col Harry Sidney, DSO 1915; late 4th (Royal Irish) Dragoon Guards; *b* 13 June 1879; *m* 1912, Elsie, *d* of late R. J. McMordie, MA, MP, and late Mrs McMordie, CBE, LLD; two *d.* Served one year in ranks of Imperial Yeomanry; 2nd Lt Cheshire Regt, 1901; West African Regt, 1903–06; Captain, 1908; 4th Dragoon Guards, 1914; Adjutant Territorial Force, 1914; served South Africa, 1900–02 (Queen's medal 3 clasps, King's medal 2 clasps); European War, 1914–18 (wounded, despatches 3 times, DSO, Bt Major); taken prisoner 1918; commanded column Irish Rebellion, 1916; retired pay, 1922. *Address:* King's Cliffe, Northants.

Died 26 May 1943.

HODGSON, Lt-Col Greenwood, CBE 1918; *b* 18 Jan. 1875; *s* of late James Hodgson; *m* 1st, 1897, Elizabeth Alice Mills; 2nd, 1928, Doris Agnes Hinds. Served South Africa, 1899–1902; European War, 1914–19 (CBE). *Club:* Civil Service (Cape Town).

Died 12 March 1950.

HODGSON, (John) Stuart; *b* Rochdale, 1877; *s* of W. J. Hodgson, MD; *m* Emily, *d* of Robert Storr Best of Goole; one *d.* *Educ:* Richmond, Yorks; Christ's College, Brecon; Queen's College, Oxford; BA 1900. Editor Daily News, 1921–31. *Publications:* A Summary of the Liberal Industrial Report, 1928; Portraits and Reflections, 1929; The Man who made the Peace, 1939; Lord Halifax, A Study, 1941. *Address:* 98 Croydon Road, Beckenham. *T:* Beckenham 0677.

Died 10 May 1950.

HODGSON, Alderman Sir William, Kt 1935; JP. Chairman Lancashire County Council; Chairman Public Assistance Committee. *Address:* The Sycamores, Poulton-le-Fylde.

Died 26 Feb. 1945.

HODGSON, Mrs Willoughby, FRSA; author and journalist; 3rd *d* of late John Gibson, of Delcombe Manor, Dorset; *m* 1st, late Edmund Copleston Gay-Roberts, Turlake, Devon; 2nd, late Joseph Willoughby Hodgson; one *s* one *d.* *Educ:* St Hilda's College, St John's Wood. Sometime political worker in connection with the Woman's Liberal Unionist Association in Westminster, The City of London in Wilts, Somerset, and at Huddersfield; Hon. Sec. Society of Women Journalists, 1909–12; lecturer on antiques. *Publications:* How to Identify Old China, 80th edition, 1903; How to Identify Old Chinese Porcelain, 4th edition, 1905; The Book of Old China, 1912; Old English China, 1913; The Quest of the Antique, 1924; contributor to The Times, Evening Standard, The Connoisseur, The Queen, The Ladies' Field, Apollo, etc. *Recreations:* archery, croquet, the study of antiques. *Address:* c/o Lloyd's Bank Ltd, Exmouth.

Died 8 Jan. 1949.

HODSON, Sir Arnold Wienholt, KCMG 1932; CMG 1922; Knight of Justice Order of St John of Jerusalem; Vice-President NRA; *b* 1881; *e s* of late Algernon Hodson, and Sarah Wienholt, formerly of Llanwern Park, Monmouthshire; *m* 1928, Elizabeth, *e d* of Major Malcolm V. Hay; two *d.* *Educ:* Italy; Mulgrave Castle;

Felsted. Central Queensland, 1900–02; joined Queensland contingent for South African War, 1902; Transvaal, 1902–04; Bechuanaland Protectorate, 1904–12; specially employed in connection with Damara War (medal and clasp); Somaliland, 1912–14; HBM Consul, Southern Abyssinia, 1914–23; served European War (two medals); attached to Abyssinian Army in expedition against Tigre (medal); African General Service Medal; 3rd class star of Ethiopia; HBM Consul, South-Western Abyssinia, 1923–26; Governor of Falkland Islands, 1926–30; Sierra Leone 1930–34; Governor and Commander-in-Chief of Gold Coast, 1934–41; has explored in various parts of Africa. *Publications:* Trekking the Great Thirst; Seven Years in Southern Abyssinia, 1927; Where Lion Reign, 1929; A Practical Galla Grammar; (Play) The Downfall of Zachariah Fee; etc. *Recreations:* big game shooting, big game fishing, yachting, golf, rifle shooting, etc. *Clubs:* Travellers', St James's, Shikar; Royal Yacht Squadron, Cowes.

Died 26 May 1944.

HOERNLÉ, Prof. R. F. Alfred, MA, BSc (Oxon); Professor of Philosophy at the University of the Witwatersrand, Johannesburg, South Africa; President, South African Institute of Race Relations; Lt-Col Active Citizen Force, as Chief Organizer of SA Army Educational Scheme, for duration of the Second World War; *s* of late A. F. Rudolf Hoernlé; *m* 1914, Agnes Winifred, *d* of W. K. Tucker, CMG; one *s.* *Educ:* Gymnasium Ernestinum, Gotha; Pforte nr Naumburg, a.S.; Balliol College, Oxford (Jenkyns Exhibitioner); 1st class Lit. Hum., 1903; John Locke Scholar, 1903; Senior Demy of Magdalen College, 1904. Assistant to the Professor of Moral Philosophy in the University of St Andrews, NB, and Lecturer, 1905–07; Professor of Philosophy at the South African College, Cape Town, Cape Province, Union of South Africa, 1908–11; Professor of Philosophy at Armstrong College (Newcastle-on-Tyne), in the University of Durham, 1912–14 and 1920–23; Assistant Professor of Philosophy at Harvard Univ., Cambridge, Mass, USA, 1914–20; S African Delegate to the second British Commonwealth Relations Conference near Sydney, NSW, 1938. *Publications:* Studies in Contemporary Metaphysics, 1920; Matter, Mind, Life and God, 1923; Idealism as a Philosophical Doctrine, 1925; Idealism as a Philosophy, 1927; South African Native Policy and the Liberial Spirit, 1939; articles and reviews in Mind and other philosophical periodicals. *Address:* 38 St Patrick Road, Houghton Estate, Johannesburg, South Africa.

Died 21 July 1943.

HOFMEYR, Hon. Gysbert Reitz, CMG 1914; *b* 12 Feb. 1871; *s* of late Jan Hendrik Hofmeyr, Riversdale, Cape Province; *m* 1895, Ydie, *d* of P. A. P. J. Nel, Bruintjes Hoogte, Somerset East; four *s* two *d.* *Educ:* Riversdale and Victoria College, Stellenbosch. Entered Civil Service of Cape Colony in 1890; Clerk Assistant of Cape House of Assembly, 1897; Registrar to the Special Tribunals Court, 1900–02; co-proprietor and editor of Het Zuid-Afrikaanse Jaarboek, 1905–07; Clerk of Transvaal House of Assembly upon formation of Parliament in that Colony under Responsible Government in 1907; Transvaal Secretary to the SA National Convention, 1908–09 (Union medal); Secretary to Delimitation Commission, 1909–10; Clerk of House of Assembly, Union of South Africa, 1910–20; Administrator of the Territory of South-West Africa, 1920–26; is a Commissioner of Oaths for the Union; in 1912 accompanied General Beyers on mission to attend military manœuvres and inspect military institutions in England, Switzerland, France, and Germany; attended the meetings of the Permanent Mandates Commission at Geneva as the Union Government's representative in respect of the Mandated Territory of South-West Africa, and later the Fifth Assembly of the League of Nations as a member of the South African Delegation, 1924;

Member of Angola-South-West Africa Boundary Commission, 1926. *Publications:* The First Sketch of Practical Plan for Union of SA, 1907; edited for publication the Minutes of the SA National Convention, 1911; wrote criticism on manuscript record of the Inner History of the National Convention by Sir Edgar Walton, KCMG, 1912; An Undivided White South Africa, 1916. *Recreation:* golf. *Address:* Welgemeend, 9 Camp Street, Gardens, Capetown.

Died March 1942.

HOFMEYR, Rt Hon. Jan Hendrik; PC 1945; Member Union House of Assembly for Johannesburg (North) since 1929; *b* 20 March 1894; *s* of late Andries Brink Hofmeyr, Capetown; unmarried. *Educ:* South African College School, and South African College, Capetown; Balliol College, Oxford. Hon. Fellow of Balliol Coll., 1946; Rhodes Scholar, First Classical Moderations, Oxford, First Greats. Professor of Classics, University of the Wit-watersrand, 1917–24; Principal, 1919–24; Administrator of the Transvaal Province, Union of South Africa, 1924–29; Minister of Interior, Public Health, and Education, South Africa, 1933–36; Minister of Mines, Labour, Education, and Social Welfare, 1936–38; Minister of Finance and of Education, 1939–48; Deputy Prime Minister and Minister of Mines and Education, 1948; Vice-Chancellor of the University of the Wit-watersrand 1926–30, Chancellor since 1938; President of the Classical Association of South Africa, 1927–29 and 1934; Vice-President, Classical Association (Great Britain), 1934; President of the South African Association for the Advancement of Science, 1928–29; Pres. of National Council of YMCA of South Africa since 1939. *Publications:* The Life of Jan Hendrik Hofmeyr (Onze Jan), 1914; National Debts, 1917; Studies in Ancient Imperialism (with Prof. T. Haarhoff) 1921; The Open Horizon, 1929; South Africa (Modern World Series), 1931; various papers. *Recreations:* tennis, motoring. *Address:* 191 William Street, Pretoria, South Africa. *T:* Pretoria 2–7862. *Clubs:* Rand (Johannesburg); Pretoria (Pretoria).

Died 3 Dec. 1948.

HOG, Steuart Bayley, BA; JP; DL; proprietor of Newliston, Linlithgowshire, and Kellie, Fife; Vice-Lieutenant for County of West Lothian since 1935; Lt-Col West Lothian Volunteers, retired; *b* 11 Sept. 1864; *s* of late Thomas Alexander Hog and Harriet, 2nd *d* of late Steuart Bayley Hare of Calder Hall; *m* 1892, Jemima Christian, 2nd *d* of Ralph Dundas; two *s*. *Educ:* Trinity College, Cambridge. Scottish Bar. *Heir: e s* Major Roger Thomas Alexander Hog, MC, RA [*b* 1893. Winchester; RMA, Woolwich]. *Address:* Newliston, Kirkliston, West Lothian. *Clubs:* New, Edinburgh.

Died 28 Nov. 1944.

HOGAN, James H., RDI 1936; FSGT; Chairman and Art Director Whitefriars Glass Works; *b* 20 Dec. 1883; *s* of Edmond Hogan; *m* 1909, Maud, *d* of George Russell; one *s* one *d*. *Educ:* Ashburnham School; Westminster School of Art; LCC Central School of Arts and Crafts; Camberwell School of Arts and Crafts. Honours award for design, 1909. Served European War, 1915–18. Silver Medal, Royal Society of Arts; Master of the Faculty of Royal Designers in Industry, 1941–43; Master Art Workers Guild, 1945; Fellow Society of Master Glasspainters; FRSA; Fellow Soc. of Glass Technology; Fellow Soc. of Industrial Artists; Member Arts and Crafts Society. Exhibited RA Arts and Crafts Exhibition Society, Ghent, Milan, Brussels, Paris International Exhibitions. Principal works: Stained glass windows in the Great Central Space, Liverpool Cathedral; Windows in Hereford, Exeter, Rochester, Carlisle, Winchester, Perth, Australia, and Dunedin, New Zealand Cathedrals; St Thomas' Church Fifth Avenue, the Church of The Heavenly Rest, New York City, and St Luke's Cathedral, Evanston, USA; many designs for Decorative and Table glassware including Commemorative Bowls presented to King George V at his Jubilee by Glass Sellers

Company. *Publications:* Royal Society of Arts Journal; Papers on History and Design of Glass, Stained Glass; Journal of Society of Glass Technology; Papers on design and History of Glass. *Address:* 17 Bute Gardens, Brook Green, Hammersmith, W6. *T:* Riverside 2539. *Club:* Savage.

Died 12 Jan. 1948.

HOGARTH, Alfred Moore, FCIS; FRES; Entomologist and Bacteriologist; Professor, Institute of Micro-Biology (Inc.); Founder and Governor of College of Pestology; Founded, with Earl of Denbigh, Imperial Cash on Delivery Association; *b* Darlington, 29 June 1876; *m* Agnes Palmer, *e d* of Austin Palmer, Bristol; five *s* one *d*. Assumed name of Hogarth by deed poll, 1925. *Educ:* Pitman's Coll.; Northampton Institute. With Sir Charles Higham and Douglas Charrington founded in early part of 1915 the National Volunteer Reserve; subsequently joined Army overseas, Salonica, 1914–15 Star; resigned Commission (Lieut TA), 6 Aug. 1924; lectured on Pests, at the request of the War Office and the Admiralty, at Aldershot and Deptford, 1921, on the Rat Problem, as a guest of the Government, in the Isle of Man, 1922; and on the Rat, an International Menace, at the Royal Institute of Public Health Congress at Portsmouth, 1930; author of the first Rats' Bill, 1908; one of the first Fellows of the Society of Tropical Medicine and Hygiene (London), 1909. *Publications:* The Rat a World Menace, 1929; The Rat and its Repression; British Mosquitoes and How to Eliminate them; Disinfectants and Disinfection. *Recreations:* bio-chemistry, music. *Address:* 143 Golders Green Road, NW11. *T:* Speedwell 1061. *Club:* Junior Army and Navy.

Died 11 March 1947.

HOGG, Col Conrad Charles Henry, CMG 1916; RE; *b* 4 Aug. 1875; *s* of late Col Arthur Melvile Hogg, Indian Staff Corps. Served South Africa, 1890–1902; European War, 1914–18 (despatches twice, CMG); 3rd Afghan War, 1919; retired, 1925. *Club:* Army and Navy.

Died 20 May 1950.

HOGG, Sir Gilbert Pitcairn, KCIE 1939 (CIE 1932); CSI 1936; Chief Secretary to Government, Bengal, from 1933; *b* 2 Feb. 1884; *s* of late John Hogg, General Manager and Director, Merry & Cunningham, Coal Masters, Glasgow, and Janet Pitcairn; *m* 1912, Isobel, *d* of late James M. Davidson, The Mains, Giffnock, Renfrewshire; one *s* one *d*. *Educ:* High School and University, Glasgow. Entered ICS 1907; retired 1938. Chief Sec., Govt of Bengal, 1933–37; Home Member, Bengal, 1937; Act. Governor, Assam, 1938. Asst Controller, Ministry of Labour, Edinburgh, 1941–43; Chairman, Co-ordinating Cttee Sales, Scottish Coalmasters, 1943–46; Coal Supplies Officer, Scottish Division, Ministry of Fuel and Power, 1943–46; Deputy Director Sales, Nat. Coal Board, Scottish Division, 1946–47; Retired 1947. *Address:* Towerwood, Newton Mearns, Renfrewshire. *T:* Newton Mearns 2191. *Clubs:* Overseas; Conservative (Glasgow).

Died 15 April 1950.

HOGG, Guy Weir; *b* 24 Oct. 1861; *e s* of late Charles Swinton Hogg and Harriet Anne, *d* of Sir Walter George Stirling, Bt; *m* 1892, Constance Piercy (*d* 1920), *d* of late Henry Joseph Marsden; one *s* one *d*. *Educ:* Eton; Christ Church, Oxford. Was Consul at St Helena for Portugal, Sweden and Norway, and the Netherlands; Vice-Consul for Russia; Acting Consul for Germany, Austria, and Denmark; British Vice-Consul at Monaco, 1925–28; managing partner of the firm of Solomon, Hogg & Co.; a JP and Sheriff of St Helena; Managing Director of SA Advertising Contractors (Ltd) of Cape Town, and Secretary of Civil Service Club, Cape Town: General Manager Uganda Company, Ltd; twice President Uganda Chamber of Commerce: founder and first Editor of Uganda Herald; Editor East African Leader.

Died 5 April 1943.

HOGG, Wing-Comdr Henry Robert William, CIE 1936; OBE 1929; with RAFVR in India; Adviser in Physical Education to Punjab Government (Education Department); Deputy Chief Commissioner, All India Boy Scouts Association; Provincial Secretary, Punjab Boy Scouts' Association; *b* 25 Jan. 1886; *s* of late Henry Robert Hogg, Merchant, Glasgow; *m* 1912, Katherine Eliza Reid, *d* of C. M. Henry, Tea Planter, Alton, Ceylon, and Inverurie, Scotland; one *s* one *d*. *Educ:* St George's Academy, Glasgow. Served in France with 8th/10th Bn Gordon Highlanders; YMCA International Secretary, 1914 with the Fleet, Invergordon; Member of Lahore Board of Film Censors, 1933–39; Punjab Rural Community Board, 1931–39; Hon. Secretary Lahore SPCA; Leader of All-India Contingent of Boy Scouts to World Jamborees, Arrowe Park, Birkenhead, 1929; Frankston, Victoria, Australia, 1934; World Rover Moot, Scotland, 1939; organised Relief Work in the Quetta Earthquake Disaster and undertook with Rover Scouts the removal of the dead from its ruins. Awarded Boy Scout Medal of Merit in 1920 (Scotland); Kaiser-i-Hind Medal, 1926; Kaiser-i-Hind Gold Medal, 1941; Order of the Silver Wolf, Punjab; Officer Brother, Order of St John of Jerusalem. *Publications:* Scoutmasters Hand-Book; New Urdu Physical Training Courses I–II; New Urdu Book of Games. *Address:* Montmorency Park, Walton PO, Lahore; Yandoit, 189 Craigcrook Road, Edinburgh, 4. *Clubs:* Punjab, Lahore Gymkhana, Rotary (President, 1936–37), Lahore.

Died 20 June 1942.

HOGG, Sir Malcolm (Nicholson), Kt 1920; Director, Forbes Campbell & Co. Ltd, Westminster Bank, Ltd, and Union Bank of Australia, Ltd; Beaumont Property Trust Ltd (Chairman); *b* 17 Jan. 1883; *s* of late Quintin Hogg, 5 Cavendish Square, W, and late Alice Anna, *d* of William Graham, formerly MP for Glasgow; *m* 1910, Lorna, *yr d* of late Sir Frank Beaman; one *s* one *d*. *Educ:* Eton; Balliol College, Oxford. Joined Forbes, Forbes Campbell & Co. Ltd, 1904; went to their Bombay office, 1905; Deputy Chm. Bombay Chamber of Commerce and Member Legislative Council of Governor of Bombay, 1915–17; Chairman Bombay Chamber of Commerce and Member Legislative Council of Viceroy of India, 1917–19; Member of Southborough Indian Franchise Committee, 1918; Member of India Council, 1920–25. *Address:* 41 Lothbury, EC2. *T:* Royal 2011; 20 Melton Court, SW7. *T:* Kensington 4068. *Clubs:* Travellers', Beefsteak.

Died 14 Feb. 1948.

HOGG, Robert Henry, CMG 1937; OBE 1919; MB, ChM; MRCS Eng.; MRCP; FRACS. *Educ:* Otago Boys' High School, Dunedin; Otago University, Dunedin. Served European War, 1915–19 with New Zealand Medical Corps (despatches twice, promoted Major, OBE); President New Zealand Branch British Medical Association, 1936. *Address:* Queen Street, Blenheim, NZ.

Died 24 Aug. 1949.

HOHLER, Sir Thomas Beaumont, KCMG 1924; CB 1916, CMG 1914; JP; *b* 15 March 1871; *s* of H. B. Hohler, Fawkham Manor, Kent; *m* 1922, Cynthia, *d* of late William Astell, Woodbury Hall, Sandy, and Lady de L'Isle and Dudley, Penshurst Place, Kent; one *s* one *d*. *Educ:* Eton; Trin. Coll., Cambridge. Attaché, 1894; 3rd Secretary, 1897; 2nd Secretary, 1901; 1st Secretary, 1908; Constantinople, 1895; Cairo, 1896; Constantinople, 1896; Petrograd, 1897; Cairo, 1899; Tokyo, 1901; Cairo, 1906; Adis Ababa (Charge d'Affaires), 1907; Constantinople, 1908; in charge of Legation, Mexico, 1911; Washington, 1917; Counsellor of Embassy, 1914–18; Political Agent in High Commission in Constantinople with rank of Envoy Extraordinary and Minister Plenipotentiary; at Buda Pesth as High Commissioner, 1920; Minister 1921–24; appointed to go on Special Mission to Mexico, 1924; British Minister at Santiago, 1924–27; British Minister to

Denmark, 1928–33; Special emissary to Colombia, 1938. High Sheriff of Kent, 1944; has received the Chilian Order of Merit and the Grand Cross of the Danebrog. *Publications:* Oasis of Siva, 1900; Diplomatic Petrel, 1942. *Recreations:* yachting, shooting, fishing, polo, rowing. *Address:* Fawkham Manor, Kent. *Club:* Carlton.

Died 23 April 1946.

HOLBERTON, Sir Edgar Joseph, Kt 1921; CBE 1919; *b* 10 May 1874; *s* of John Lidstone Holberton of Greenbank, Wordesley, Staffordshire; *m* 1911, Mary Renée, *d* of Judge Romney Kane of Glandree, Co. Clare; one *s* two *d*. *Educ:* Sherborne School (Scholar); Magdalene College, Cambridge (Scholar). Joined Bombay-Burma Trading Corporation, Rangoon, 1899; Manager, 1908–21; Chairman Burma Chamber of Commerce, 1918–20; Member Burma Legislative Council, 1918–20; Member of Council of State of India, 1920–23. *Recreations:* riding, tennis, golf, fishing. *Address:* 14 Avenue Court, Draycott Avenue, SW3. *T:* Kensington 2624.

Died 22 May 1949.

HOLBROOK, Col Sir Arthur (Richard), KBE 1918; VD 1892; JP, DL; *b* Bath, 28 April 1850; *s* of late Richard Holbrook, Southsea; *m* 1878, Amelia Mary (*d* 1944), *d* of late Alexander Parks, Southsea and Constantinople; six *s* four *d*. *Educ:* Portsmouth. Newspaper proprietor; founder of Southern Daily Mail; Fellow of the Institute of Journalists; President Newspaper Society, 1913–14; Chairman Portsmouth Conservative Association, 1885–98; President Portsmouth Chamber of Commerce, 1907–12; Commanded Royal Army Service Corps, Salisbury Plain District, 1914–19; late Hon. Colonel 44th (Home Counties) Divisional RASC; formerly Lieut-Colonel Commandant and Hon. Col 3rd (Duke of Connaught's Own) Volunteer Battalion the Hampshire Regt; Military Member of Hampshire Territorial Association since 1906; MP (U) Basingstoke Division of Hampshire, 1920–23 and 1924–29; is Member of Council National Rifle Association; Representative of Hampshire on Grand Council of Primrose League; President, London Hampshire Society, 1930–35; Provincial Grand Master of Mark Freemasons, Hampshire and the Isle of Wight since 1921. *Address:* Kingston Hill, Surrey. *Clubs:* Carlton, Constitutional, Savage.

Died 24 Dec. 1946.

HOLDEN, Hon. Sir Edward Wheewall, Kt 1946; BSc, MIEA; MLC, S Australia, since 1935; Chairman of Directors of General Motors—Holden's Ltd since 1934; Chairman Australian Cotton Textile Industries Ltd; Deputy Chairman Bank of Adelaide; *b* 14 Aug. 1885; *s* of Henry James Holden, Adelaide; *m* 1908, Hilda Mary, *d* of Robert John Lavis, Adelaide; one *s* two *d*. *Educ:* Prince Alfred College, Adelaide; University of Adelaide. Managing Director of General Motors—Holden's Ltd, 1929–34. President SA Chamber of Commerce, 1929–30; President SA Chamber of Manufactures, 1936–39; President Associated Chambers of Manuf. of Aust., 1938–39; Member of Council Univ. of Adelaide; Alderman City Council of Adelaide; Controller-General of Australian Army Canteens Service (Hon.) for duration of war; President SA Committee, Council for Scientific and Industrial Research. *Recreations:* tennis, golf. *Address:* 52 Brougham Place, North Adelaide, S Australia. *Clubs:* Australian, Melbourne; Stock Exchange, Naval and Military, Adelaide.

Died 18 June 1947.

HOLDEN, Rt Rev. John, MA, DD; Assistant Bishop in Diocese of Truro since 1938; Archdeacon of Cornwall since 1947; Proctor in Convocation since 1944; *b* 1882; *m* 1911, Elsie Maud, *y d* of Canon E. L. Roxby, no *c*. *Educ:* St John's Coll., Durham, MA. Archdeacon of Kwangsi, 1919–23; Bishop of Kwangsi-Hunan, 1923–33; Bishop of Szechwan, 1933–37; Bishop of Western Szechwan, 1937–38; Vicar of St Budock,

1938–44; Residentiary Canon, Truro Cathedral, 1944–47; Treasurer, 1944–46; Canon Missioner, 1946–47. *Address:* Gwaylin, Truro.

Died 14 Aug. 1949.

HOLDEN, Norman Edward, LLB, BA, OBE 1918; senior partner in Haes & Sons; *b* Manchester, 30 Nov. 1879; 2nd *s* of late Sir Edward Holden, Bart; *m* Marion (*d* 1946), *d* of late G. S. Munro, Wellington, NZ, formerly Secretary for Industry and Commerce. *Educ:* Lyceé Condorcet, Paris; Berlin; Trinity Hall, Cambridge. Served in South African War (Queen's medal three clasps); European War—France and Dardanelles. *Address:* Norton Priory, nr Chichester. *T:* Selsey 22. *Clubs:* Bath, Buck's, Reform.

Died 29 Sept. 1946.

HOLDER, Sir Henry (Charles), 2nd Bt *cr* 1898; *b* Edgbaston, 1 May 1874; *s* of 1st Bt and Geraldine Augusta, *d* of John Williams Knipe, of Worcester; *S* father, 1923; *m* Evelyn, *d* of Sir Robert Ropner, 1st Bt; two *s* three *d*. *Educ:* Repton; Brasenose Coll., Oxford (MA). *Heir: s* John Eric Duncan [*b* 1899; *m* 1927, Evelyn Josephine, *er d* of late William Blain and Mrs Blain, the Old Manor House, Combe Florey; one *s* (*b* 12 March 1928), two *d*]. *Address:* Penwood Farm, Burghclere, Newbury. *T:* Highclere 121.

Died 3 Aug. 1945.

HOLDGATE, Rev. William Wyatt, MA; *b* 1872; *s* of R. Holdgate of Stoke-on-Trent; *m* 1899, Rowena Margaret (*d* 1938), *d* of J. H. Tucker of Bank of England; one *s* three *d*. *Educ:* High School, Newcastle, Staffs; Trinity College Cambridge (Exhibitioner); 1st Class Nat. Sci. Tripos, 1894. Assist Master Trent Coll. 1895, Head, Magdalen College School, Brackley, 1900; Headmaster, Sutton Valence School, Kent, 1910–31; Rector of Otham, 1931–34; Vicar of Sutton-on-the-Hill, Derby, 1934–38; Vicar of Tong, Salop, 1939–44. *Recreation:* astronomy. *Address:* Arnold School, Blackpool.

Died 24 Feb. 1949.

HOLDSWORTH, Benjamin George, CIE 1941; Secretary to Indian Food Department, since 1942; *b* 31 July 1892; *s* of Rev. J. Forster Holdsworth; *m* 1920, Ellen May, *d* of late James Hill, Poltimore, S Devon; one *s* one *d*. *Educ:* Bristol Grammar School; Brasenose College, Oxford. Entered Indian Civil Service, 1916; served in Mesopotamia and Palestine with 1/155 Pioneers during European War; Settlement Officer Tanjore, Kistna, and Godavari Districts, 1920–27; Secretary, Board of Revenue, Madras, 1927–30; Joint Secretary, First Indian Round Table Conference, 1930–31; Administrator Pudukkottai State, 1931–34; Collector Salem and Coimbatore Districts, 1934–37; Revenue Secretary to Govt of Madras, 1937–41; Establishment Officer, Govt of India, 1941. *Recreations:* golf and tennis. *Address:* c/o Finance Dept, Govt of India Secretariat, New Delhi/ Simla. *Clubs:* Madras, Madras.

Died 19 April 1943.

HOLDSWORTH, Brig.-Gen. George Lewis, CB 1917; CMG 1919; JP; *b* 1862; *s* of late George Holdsworth, Dartmouth, S Devon; *m* Alice (*d* 1940), widow of G. W. Duff-Assheton-Smith, DL, JP, of Vaynol, Carnarvonshire. *Educ:* Eton; Trinity College, Cambridge; Sandhurst. Joined 21st Hussars, 1884; transferred to 7th Hussars, 1885; served S African War, 1899–1902 (Bt Lt-Col 1902, despatches); Bt Col 1906; Lt-Col commanding 7th Hussars, 1907–11; during European War served on British Remount Commission in Canada and America, 1914–15; Assistant Director of Remounts, Egypt, 1916; Director of Remounts, Mesopotamia, 1916–18; Temp. Brig.-Gen. 1916 (despatches, CB); Servian Order of White Eagle with swords, 1916; France, 1918–19 (despatches, CMG); retired, 1919, with rank of Brig.-General. *Recreations:* racing, hunting, and shooting; has done a good deal of big-game shooting in India. *Address:* 14 Great Stanhope Street, W1. *T:* Grosvenor 1439; Glynde Place, Glynde, Sussex. *Clubs:* Marlborough, Naval and Military, Boodle's.

Died 21 Aug. 1942.

HOLDSWORTH, Sir Herbert, Kt 1944; JP Bradford; Director; Holdsworth Bros (Waste Material Dealers), Ltd, Provincial Building Society, Jackson's Stores Ltd, West Riding Realty Co. Ltd; *b* Liversedge, Yorkshire, 1890; *s* of late Sam Holdsworth and Annie Holdsworth; *m* 1914, Beatrice, *d* of late William Lee and Harriet Lee, Bradford; one *d*. *Educ:* Batley Grammar School. MP (L) Bradford South, 1931–45, (Nat. L) 1938–45; Chief Whip Liberal Nationals, 1940–42; Asst Govt Whip (unpaid), 1940–42. Contested Rothwell Division, Yorks, 1929. *Address:* Moorfields, 108 Leeds Road, Eccleshill, Bradford. *T:* Bradford 411. *Clubs:* National Liberal; Bradford Liberal (Bradford).

Died 8 July 1949.

HOLDSWORTH, Sir William Searle, Kt 1929; OM 1943; KC 1920; Bencher of Lincoln's Inn; Vinerian Professor in English Law, University of Oxford, since 1922; Fellow, All Souls College; Hon. Fellow, St John's College; Reader in Constitutional Law (English and Colonial) and Legal History at the Inns of Court, since 1937; *b* Elmers End, Beckenham, 7 May 1871; *s* of Charles Joseph Holdsworth, solicitor; *m* 1903, Jessie A. A. G., *d* of Gilbert Wood (one *s* killed on active service, 1942). *Educ:* Dulwich College; New College, Oxford (History Exhibition, 1890); 1st Class History School, 1893; 1st Class Law School, 1894; Barstow Scholar Inns of Court, 1895; Studentship Inns of Court, 1895. Lecturer, New College, 1895; Vice-President of St John's Coll., 1902–03; Professor of Constitutional Law, University Coll., London, 1903–08; Fellow St John's College, 1897–1922; All Souls Reader in English Law, 1910–22; BA 1893; MA and BCL, 1897; DCL, 1904; FBA, 1922; Hon. LLD Cambridge, 1926; Northwestern Univ. of Chicago, 1927; University of South California, 1927; Birmingham, 1928; Edinburgh, 1931; Upsala, 1933; DLitt, Leeds; Hon. DL Calcutta, 1938; Ames medal, Harvard University, 1927; Swiney Prize, RS Art, 1934; Member of Indian States Committee, 1928; Tagore Professor, Calcutta, 1938. *Publications:* Law of Succession, Testamentary and Intestate, 1899; History of English Law, vol. i 1903, vols ii and iii 1909; new and revised edition in 9 vols—vols i–iii 1922; vols iv, v, vi 1924; Vols vii and viii 1925; vol ix 1926; vols x–xii 1938; Charles Viner and the Abridgments of English Law, 1923; Creighton Lecturer, 1924, The Influence of the Legal Profession on the Growth of the English Constitution, 1924; Sources and Literature of English Law, 1925; Historical Introduction to the Land Law, 1927; The Historians of Anglo-American Law, 1927; Charles Dickens as Legal Historian, 1928; Some Lessons from our Legal History, 1928; Some Makers of English Law, 1938; articles in various English and American Law Reviews and papers. *Address:* All Souls College, Oxford; Grandpont House, Folly Bridge, Oxford. *T:* 2043. *Club:* Athenæum.

Died 2 Jan. 1944.

HOLE, Lt-Col Hugh Marshall, CMG 1924; late Secretary of British South Africa Co; *b* 16 May 1865; *o s* of late Charles Marshall Hole, Tiverton, Devon; *m* 1st, 1890, Ethel (*d* 1924), *d* of late T. Rickman of Longfleet, Dorset; 2nd, 1927, Olive Mary Torin, of Lumley Mill, Emsworth. *Educ:* Blundell's School; Balliol College, Oxford, BA. Entered service of BSA Co., 1890; joined Civil Service of Rhodesia in 1891 as Secretary to Administrator (Dr Jameson), and from then to 1914 filled many public offices in that territory, including Civil Commissioner of Bulawayo, and Acting Administrator NW Rhodesia; served Matabele Rebellion, 1896, Boer War, 1899, 1900, and European War, 1915–19; at close of War rejoined BSA Co. in London; represents Rhodesia on Headquarters Council of British Empire Service League. *Publications:* (Joint) Reports on Native

Disturbances in Rhodesia, 1896–1897; The Making of Rhodesia, 1926; Old Rhodesian Days, 1928; Lobengula, 1929; The Jameson Raid, 1930; The Passing of the Black Kings, 1932; numerous articles and pamphlets on subjects connected with Rhodesia. *Recreation:* travel. *Clubs:* Authors', British Empire; Salisbury, Rhodesia.

Died 18 May 1941.

HOLE, S. Hugh F.; *b* 16 Oct. 1862; *o s* of late Very Rev. S. R. Hole, Dean of Rochester, and of Caunton Manor, Notts; *m* 1889, Geraldine, *e d* of C. Markham of Tapton House, Chesterfield; one *s* one *d*. *Educ:* Eton; abroad. Late Major Royal Sherwood Foresters (Notts Militia); Barrister Inner Temple; FRGS; Lord of the Manor of Caunton; served S Africa as a Lieut CIV, 1900; present at all engagements with his regiment up to the fall of Pretoria, afterwards in the Military Government of the ORC; is a Life Member of the Royal Hunting Club of Sweden; Senior Vice-President of the London Notts Society; ex-member of the Federal and Legislative Councils of the Leeward Islands; served in Flanders, 1914 (despatches, Officer Crown of Belgium, Knight of Legion of Honour, Croix de Guerre). *Publication:* Looking Life Over. *Recreations:* tree culture and travel. *Address:* Caunton Manor, Newark.

Died 14 May 1948.

HOLFORD, Mrs Gwynne, CBE 1918; Mary Eleanor; Lady of Grace of St John of Jerusalem; *d* of late P. R. Gordon Canning of Hartpury; *m* J. P. Gwynne Holford (*d* 1916), of Buckland, Breconshire; one *d*. Originator of scheme for supplying artificial limbs to sailors and soldiers in European War, 1914–18, at Queen Mary's Hospital, Roehampton. *Address:* Hartpury House, Gloucester.

Died 18 Dec. 1947.

HOLLAMS, Frederick William, MA Oxofrd; JP Kent; Barrister, Inner Temple; High Sheriff of Kent, 1917–18; *b* 1 June 1848; 2nd *s* of late Sir John Hollams; *m* 1873, Mary Owen (*d* 1929), *d* of Sir Charles Lanyon of the Abbey, Co. Antrim; one *d*. *Educ:* Blackheath School; Trinity College, Oxford. Called to Bar, Inner Temple, 1872; lecturer on Common Law to the Incorporated Law Society in 1880 and 1881; Counsel to the Law Society, 1877–1910; retired from practice, 1910. *Address:* Dene Park, Tonbridge, Kent. *TA:* Shipbourne. *T:* Tonbridge 192.

Died 21 Nov. 1941.

HOLLAND, Vice-Adm. Cedric Swinton, CB 1945; Commander of the Legion of Merit, 1946; *b* 13 Oct. 1889; *s* of late Admiral Swinton Holland and Eva Williams; *m* 1925, Barbara, *o d* of Sir Charles Venables-Llewelyn, CB; one *s* one *d*. *Educ:* HMS Britannia. Served European War, 1914–18 (despatches); Naval Attaché, Paris, 1938–40; commanded HMS Ark Royal, 1940–41 (despatches); Director, Signal Dept, Admiralty, 1942–43; retired, 1946. *Recreations:* shooting, fishing, sailing, travelling. *Address:* 1 Albert Place, W8. *T:* Western 5261. *Clubs:* White's United Service; Royal Naval (Portsmouth); Royal Yacht Squadron (Cowes).

Died 11 May 1950.

HOLLAND, Charles Thurstan, LLD (L'pool), DL, TD, ChM, FRCS; Hon. Fellow, American College of Radiology; Lecturer on Radiology, Liverpool University, 1920–31; Hon. Member of the American Roentgen Ray Society; of the Nordisk Förening for Medicinsk Radiologie; of the Societas Radiologiae Medicae Italica; of the British Association of Radiologists; of the Deutsche Roentgen-Gesellschaft; Hon. Member Die Österreichische Gesellschaft für Röntgenkunde und Strahlenforschung; Hon. Member The Swiss Radiological Society; Hon. Consulting Radiologist, King Edward VII Welsh National Memorial Association, The Liverpool Royal Infirmary, and the Shropshire Orthopædic Hospital; *s* of late Alderman William Thomas Holland, Bridgwater; *m* Lilian (*d* 1924), *d* of late James Fergusson, Liverpool; one

s. Educ: privately; University College Hospital, London. Major (retired) RAMC (T); Member of War Office Committee on Radiology, 1918; Expert attached to the Western Command, 1918; Radiologist to First Western General Hospital, 1914–19; Hon. Radiologist to the Royal Southern Hospital, Liverpool, 1896–1904; Hon. Radiologist to the Royal Infirmary, Liverpool, 1904–23; Hon. Radiologist to the Royal Liverpool Children's Infirmary, 1907–32; President of the First International Congress of Radiology, London, 1925; President (Section of Radiology) Congress of Radiology and Physio-therapy, London, 1922; President of the Roentgen Society of London, 1904 and 1916; President (Electro-therapeutic section) British Medical Association, Liverpool, 1912, and Royal Society of Medicine, 1913; President Liverpool Medical and Literary Society, 1895; President Lancashire and Cheshire Photographic Union, 1906–07; President Liverpool Amateur Photographic Association, 1905 and 1916; President Liverpool Wayfarers' Club, 1910–12; Vice-President (section of Radiology) International Congress of Medicine, London, 1913, President of British Institute of Radiology 1929–30; Hon. Member Liverpool Medical Institution; Hon. Fellow American Electro-therapeutic Association; Member of the British Orthopædic Association; Fellow (three medals) of the Royal Photographic Society. *Publications:* Article on Radiology in the Medical Annual, 1914 to 1930 inclusive; many papers on radiology in various books and journals since 1898. *Recreations:* mountaineering, photography. *Address:* 43 Rodney Street, Liverpool. *T:* Royal 7441. *Clubs:* Royal Automobile, Alpine.

Died 16 Jan. 1941.

HOLLAND, Henry, CBE 1919; JP; Chairman Advisory Committee for the Blind; Trustee Citizens Benevolent Association; *b* Nafferton, Yorkshire, Dec. 1859; *s* of Robert and Anne Holland; *m* 1885, Jane Eastwood, OBE, JP; three *s* three *d*. *Educ:* private; State schools. MP (Reform) Christchurch North, 1925–35; Justice of Peace; Member of Christchurch City Council, 1911; Mayor of Christchurch, 1912–19; 15 years a Member of Christchurch Drainage Board; 15 years Member of Christchurch Fire Board and for 2 years its Chairman; 19 years Member Lyttelton Harbour Board and one year its Chairman; Chairman Canterbury Patriotic Fund, 1914–40; Chairman Disabled Soldiers League, 1920–41; Trustee of Fund for disabled soldiers since 1911; Government Representative Waimakariri River Trust, and Red Cross Executive; Chairman Christchurch Fire Board Sinking Fund Commissioners. Retired from active business, 1944. *Address:* PO Box 807, Christchurch, C1, New Zealand. *T:* 34,104.

Died 26 Dec. 1944.

HOLLAND, Col Lancelot, DSO 1915; late Seaforth Highlanders; *b* 17 July 1876; *m* 1925, Enid Anstruther (from whom he obtained a decree of divorce for desertion, 1931), *d* of late Lord George Campbell. *Educ:* Merchiston Castle School, Edinburgh. Entered Army, 1896; Captain, 1901; Colonel, 1923; Adjutant Volunteers, 1904–07; Brigade-Major 5th Brigade, Aldershot, 1912–13; General Staff Officer 3rd Grade Northern Command, 1913–14; served Nile Expedition, 1898; S Africa, 1901–02 (despatches, Queen's medal 5 clasps); European War, 1914–18 (despatches, DSO, Bt Lt-Col); Brigade Commander 152nd (Seaforth and Cameron) Infantry Brigade, 1924–27; GSO1 Rawalpindi District, India, 1929; retired pay, 1930. *Club:* Army and Navy.

Died 29 July 1943.

HOLLAND, Vice-Adm. Lancelot Ernest, CB 1939; *b* 1887; *s* of late Tom Wilkinson Holland; *m* 1913, Phyllis Margaret Wales, *d* of late Dr Arthur John Smith; no *c*. *Educ:* HMS Britannia. Head of Naval Mission to Greece (Commander of the Order of the Redeemer), 1930–31; Assistant Chief of Naval Staff, 1937–38; Rear-Admiral,

Second Battle Squadron, 1939. *Recreations:* polo, ski-ing. *Address:* 37 Grosvenor Square, W1. *T:* Mayfair 8322. *Clubs:* United Service, Lansdowne, Royal Automobile.

Died 24 May 1941.

HOLLAND, Sir (Reginald) Sothern, 1st Bt *cr* 1917; Kt 1912; JP; Chevalier de l'ordre de Leopold, 1917; a Rhodes Trustee since 1932; *b* Alexandria, Cape Province, 15 March 1876; *y s* of late Ben Herbert Holland, late Registrar of Deeds for Cape Colony, and late Agnes Hope, 3rd *d* of late Charles Hugh Huntly, CMG; *m* 1910, Stretta Aimée, *d* of E. G. Price, Broadwater, Godalming, Surrey; two *s. Educ:* St Andrew's College, Grahamstown. Entered Cape Civil Service, 1894; Colonial Office, 1896; Native Affairs Department, 1899; Prime Minister's Department, 1902; Private Secretary to Rt Hon. Sir J. Gordon Sprigg, Prime Minister, 1904, to Rt Hon. Sir Starr Jameson, Bt, Prime Minister, 1904; Permanent Head, Prime Minister's Department, 1905; resigned, 1908; Secretary to South African Shipping Freights Conference, 1905–06; accompanied Prime Minister to London at Coronation, 1902 (medal); on special Railway Mission, 1906; and to Imperial Conference, 1907; HM Trade Commissioner in S Africa, 1908–13; at outbreak of war organised campaign on German trade, and exchange meetings between British manufacturers and traders; in Nov. 1914 organised High Explosives Dept as a branch of War Office; late Deputy Director General Explosives Supplies under Ministry Munitions; Director-General of Munitions Inspection, 1915; at Admiralty, Board of Inventions, 1917; Member of Royal Commission on Paper Supplies and of Council to advise on disposal of War Property and Stores; Controller Cultivation Department of Food Production Department, April 1918; retired from Chairmanship of the Central Mining and Investment Corporation, Ltd, 1931, reappointed, 1943–45; Sheriff of Oxfordshire, 1943. *Recreations:* hunting, shooting, farming. *Heir: s* Jim Sothern [*b* 1911; *m* 1937, Elisabeth Hilda Margaret, *o d* of T. F. Vaughan Prickard, CVO]. *Address:* Westwell Manor, Burford, Oxford.

Died 14 Sept. 1948.

HOLLAND, Richard, CBE 1934; Secretary of National Society, 1918–36; *m* 1924, Hetty Lee-Holland. *Address:* Park Corner, Heathfield, Sussex.

Died 17 June 1942.

HOLLAND, Sir Sothern; *see* Holland, Sir R. S.

HOLLAND, Theodore, OBE; FRAM; Hon. Doctor of Music, Cincinnati Conservatory of Music, USA; Composer; Professor of Harmony and Composition, RAM, London; Member, Associated Board of Royal Schools of Music, of Incorporated Society of Musicians, of Royal Philharmonic Society and of Composers' Guild; Hon. Treasurer, Royal Musical Association; Member, Mendelssohn Scholarship Committee; *b* 25 April 1878; 5th *s* of late Sir Arthur Holland, JP, DL; *m* Isména Schwann. *Educ:* Westminster School; RAM; Hochschule für Musik, Berlin. Studied with Joachim, Corder, Robert Kahn, and Stillman-Kelley. Served War, 1914–18 (despatches twice, OBE); Pres. RAM Club, 1936–37. *Publications:* Santa Claus, musical play (Scala Theatre, London, 1912); King Goldemar, children's operetta, 1902; additional numbers Leo Fall's The Merry Peasant (Strand Theatre, London, 1909); incidental music Two Gentlemen of Verona, 1911; A Pastoral Medley, cantata, 1907; Evening on a Lake, for small Orchestra, 1908; Songs of Nyasaland, for Bass-Baritone and Orchestra, 1924; Ellingham Marshes, for Viola and Orchestra, 1940; String Quartet No. 1 in C minor, 1933; String Quartet No. 2 in E minor, 1938; Trio for Piano, Violin and 'Cello, 1935; Suite in D for Viola and Piano, 1935; Cortège, for Orchestra of 'Cellos, 1939; Four Fancies, for Violin and Piano, 1923; Variations on an Original Theme, for Violin and Piano, 1927; Variations on Swedish Air, for Piano, 1906; Variations in F sharp

minor, for Piano, 1941; Sonatina for Piano, 1938; Toccata for Piano, 1938; 2 Shelley Songs, 1908; 3 Flecker Songs, 1938; Spring, Sinfonietta for Orchestra, 1943; Trio for Piano, Violin, and 'Cello No. 2 in C minor, 1943; Preludes for Piano, 1944; Threnody, for 'Cello and Orchestra, 1945; Autumn Voices, for Violin and Piano, 1947. *Recreations:* sketching and reading. *Address:* 10 Eldon Rd, W8. *Clubs:* Authors', Garrick, Savage.

Died 29 Oct. 1947.

HOLLAND, Sir Thomas Henry, KCSI 1918; KCIE 1908; FRS 1904; DL County of Edinburgh; Knight Commander, Polonia Restituta; Hon. DSc Calcutta and Melbourne; Hon. LLD Manchester, Glasgow, St Andrews, Edinburgh, Aberdeen, Queen's (Ont); Hon. DSc (Eng.) Witwatersrand; FGS, FRSA; Principal and Vice-Chancellor, University of Edinburgh, 1929–44; Member of Governor-General's Council, India, 1920–21; President, IME, 1915–16; Indian Industrial Commission, 1916; Board of Munitions, India, 1917; InstMM 1925–27; Institution of Petroleum Technologists, 1925–27; Chairman of Council, RS Arts, 1925–27; President, British Association 1929; Geological Society, 1933–34; Chairman of Empire Council Mining and Metallurgical Institutions, 1927–30; of Departmental Committee on Qualifications of Colliery Officials, 1930; Vice-President, Royal Society, 1924–45; President, Mineralogical Society of London, 1933–36; Geographical Association, 1938; Albert Medal, RS Arts, 1939; *b* Helston, Cornwall, 22 Nov. 1868; *s* of late John Holland, Springfield, Canada; *m* 1896, Frances Maud (*d* 1942), *d* of late Chas. Chapman, Deputy Commissioner in Oudh; one *s* one *d. Educ:* National Scholar, 1885; Murchison Medallist and Prizeman, 1887; Assoc. Roy. Coll. Sci., 1888; Berkeley Fellow of Owens Coll., 1889. Joined Indian service, 1890; Pres. Royal Asiatic Society of Bengal, 1909; President, Mining and Geological Institute of India, 1906, 1907; Director of Geological Survey, India, 1903–09; President, Burma Oil Reserves Committee, 1908; Fellow and Reader of the Calcutta University; Dean of Faculty of Science, 1909; Prof. of Geology and Mineralogy Manchester University, 1909–18; President, Indian Mining and Geological Club, and of Roy. Coll. of Sci. Old Students' Association, 1910; Member of the Royal Commission on Oil Fuel and Engines, 1911–13; Major and Commandant Manchester Univ. OTC, 1913–16; Rector, Imperial College of Science and Technology, 1922–29; Member of Advisory Committee, Imperial Institute, 1910–16; Bigsby Medallist, Geological Society of Lond., 1913; Gold Medal, InstMM, 1930; Pres., Geological Section, British Assoc., 1914 and of the Education Section, 1926; Trueman Wood Lecturer, RS Arts, 1929; Ludwig Mond Lecturer, Manchester University, 1930; Huxley Memorial Lecturer, Imperial Coll. of Science, 1937; Fison Memorial Lecturer, Guy's Hospital, 1938; Bruce-Preller Lecturer, RSE, 1941; Hon. Pres. Royal Scottish Society of Arts and Mining Inst. of Scotland. *Publications:* The Mineral Sanction, an aid to International Security and various memoirs on mineral questions, Petrology, Geology, and Anthropology. *Club:* Athenæum.

Died 15 May 1947.

HOLLINS, Alfred, MusD; FRCO; Organist and Choirmaster, St George's West, Church of Scotland, Edinburgh, since 1897; *b* Hull, 11 Sept. 1865; *s* of late John Hollins of York and Hull, and Mary Evans; *m* Helen, *d* of late G. Lawson. *Educ:* Yorkshire School for the Blind; Royal Normal College for the Blind, London. Studied the Organ under the late Dr E. J. Hopkins; Piano under Prof. Fritz Hartvigson, Hans von Bülow (Berlin and Frankfort), and Prof. Max Schwartz. Organist, St John's, Redhill, 1884–88; St Andrew's, Upper Norwood, 1888–97; First Organist, People's Palace, E London, 1888–89; Professor at the Royal Normal College, 1886–94; began public career as solo pianist, appearing at the Crystal Palace Concerts, Royal

Philharmonic, and with Joachim and Piatti at the London Saturday Pops; in 1885 played three Concertos at one Concert (Beethoven Emperor, Schumann A minor, and Liszt E flat) with the Berlin Philharmonic Orchestra under Klindworth; visited America in 1886 and 1888, playing with the New York Philharmonic and Boston Symphony Orchestras; gave a series of Organ Recitals in the Town Hall, Sydney, NSW, 1904, afterwards visiting New Zealand for further Recitals; Fellowship Diploma, Honoris Causa, of the Royal College of Organists, 1904, and in 1907 was invited by the RCO to give an example of the Art of Improvisation on the organ, at the distribution of Diplomas; toured South Africa (Organ Recitals), 1907, 1909, 1916; has given numerous Organ Recitals practically all over the United Kingdom; has devoted much time to the study of Organ Construction and Specification; Mus. D (Hon.) Edinburgh University, 1922; Extensive Organ Recital Tour, Canada and USA 1925–26. *Publications:* A Blind Musician Looks Back, 1936; church and concert organ music, anthems, songs, piano pieces, etc. *Recreations:* concerts, reading, walking, machinery. *Address:* 3 Grosvenor St, Edinburgh. *T:* Edinburgh 23524.

Died 17 May 1942.

HOLLIS, Rt Rev. George Arthur, MA; Bishop Suffragan of Taunton since 1931; Residentiary Canon of Wells since 1918; Prebendary of Wanstrow, 1940; *b* 17 April 1868; *e s* of late Henry William Hollis, JP, Managing Director of the Weardale Coal and Iron Co; *m* 1898, Mary Margaret (*d* 1941), 4th *d* of Charles Marcus Church, Canon of Wells Cathedral; four *s*. *Educ:* Keble College, Oxford. Ordained, 1894; Curate of St James, Wednesbury, 1894–95; Chaplain Wells College, 1895–98; Lecturer, 1898–1903; Vice-Principal, 1903–09; Priest Vicar of Wells Cathedral, 1904–09; Perpetual Curate of Armley, 1909–13; of Headingley, 1913–18; Principal of Wells Theological College, 1919–30; Prebendary of Coombe 13th, and Chancellor of Wells Cathedral, 1918–35; Archdeacon of Wells, Prebendary of Huish and Brent, 1935–40. *Recreations:* tennis, etc. *Address:* East Liberty, Wells, Somerset. *T:* Wells 246.

Died 20 March 1944.

HOLLOND, Maj.-Gen. Spencer Edmund, CB 1920; CMG 1919; DSO 1916; *b* 19 March 1874; *o surv. s* of late John Robert Hollond of Wonham, Devon; *m* 1st, 1905, Lula (*d* 1911), *d* of Charles Pfizer, New York; 2nd, Mrs Hubert Crichton, *widow* of late Major Hubert Crichton, Irish Guards; one *s*. *Educ:* Harrow; Cambridge. Entered Rifle Brigade, 1895; ADC to Duke of Connaught, 1901–04; Major, 1913; served S African War, 1899–1900 (despatches, Queen's medal four clasps); European War, 1914–18 (despatches, CB, CMG, DSO, Legion of Honour); Bt Lt-Col 1 Jan. 1917; Bt Col 1918; Commanded 8th Infantry Brigade, 1921–25; Colonel-Commandant Seniors Officers' School, Sheerness, 1925–27; Maj.-Gen. 1927; retired pay, 1928. *Address:* 59 Whitelands House, SW3. *T:* Sloane 6848. *Club:* Army and Navy.

Died 15 Feb. 1950.

HOLLOWAY, Basil Edward, CB, 1921; *s* of late Rev. Edward John Holloway of Clehonger, Hereford; *m*; one *s*. *Educ:* Marlborough; Trinity College, Cambridge. Joined War Office, 1900; Director and Assistant Controller of Munitions Finance, Ministry of Munitions, 1917; Principal Clerk Air Ministry, 1918; Principal Assistant Secretary 1920; Director of Contracts, Air Ministry, 1932–37; retired, 1937. *Address:* Long Meadow, Pinner, Middlesex. *T:* Pinner 308.

Died 25 March 1947.

HOLLOWAY, Rev. John Ernest, FRS 1937; FRSNZ; DSc (NZ); Lecturer in charge of Botany Department, University of Otago, Dunedin, NZ, since 1924; *b* Christchurch, NZ, 12 Feb. 1881; *s* of John and Anna Holloway; *m* 1908, Margaret Brenda North; two *s* three *d*. *Educ:* Nelson College, NZ; Auckland University College, NZ; St John's Theological College, Auckland, NZ. Deacon, 1907; priest, 1908; assistant curate, Hawera, NZ, 1907–08; Wanganui, NZ, 1909; Barnsley, Yorks, 1909–11; Vicar Oxford, NZ, 1912–15; Hokitika, NZ, 1916–21; Leeston, NZ, 1922–23; licensed to officiate in Diocese of Dunedin since 1924. *Publications:* various research papers on New Zealand botanical science from 1909 in Trans. Roy. Soc. NZ, and in Annals of Botany (English). *Address:* University of Otago, Dunedin, NZ.

Died 6 Sept. 1945.

HOLM, Alexander, CMG, 1934; CBE, 1926; *b* 1878; *s* of late Alexander Holm, Buckland, Betchworth, Surrey; *m* 1905, Jessie Neilson, *d* of late Daniel Crawford, Potterells, Hatfield; three *d*. *Educ:* University School, Reigate; Wye College, Kent. Gold Medallist, Royal Agricultural Society of England; Fellow Highland and Agricultural Society of Scotland. Principal and General Manager, Agricultural College and Experimental Farm, Potchefstroom, Transvaal, 1903–12; Under-Secretary for Agriculture, Union of South Africa, 1912–19; Director of Agriculture, Kenya, 1919–33; Chairman Wheat Commission, SA, 1917; Member of Executive, Legislative and Inter-Colonial Railway Councils; Economic and Finance Committee: and Central Advisory Committee European Education; President Royal Agricultural and Horticultural Society of Kenya, 1919–33; Exhibition Commissioner (Kenya), British Empire Exhibition, 1924; Chm. Labour Commission, 1927; Chairman Food Control Board, 1929; Member Central Agricultural Advances Board; Chairman Coffee and Sisal Industries Committee, 1931; Chairman Board of Agriculture; Member Butter Levy Board, 1932; Vice-Chairman Joint East African Board; Chairman East African Group (Overseas League), 1939; Chairman Weybridge Branch RSPCA. *Publications:* articles on Agriculture and Agricultural Education. *Address:* Kenlawn, Weybridge, Surrey.

Died 24 Jan. 1943.

HOLMAN, Lt-Gen. Sir Herbert Campbell, KCB 1920 (CB 1918); CMG 1915; DSO 1901; psc; late Devonshire Regt and 16th Cavalry; *b* 3 May 1869; *s* of the late William Laban Holman; *m* 1902, Annie Ethel Talbot (*d* 1948), 2nd *d* of late Maj.-Gen. W. Howey; one *s* one *d*. *Educ:* Dulwich; Sandhurst. Entered army, 1889; Captain, 1900; Major, 1907; Bt Lt-Col 1914; Lt-Col 1915; Bt Col 1916; Maj.-Gen. 1919; Lt-Gen. 1926; served with Wuntho Expedition, 1891 (wounded); operations of Irrawady column as staff officer (despatches, medal with clasp); China, 1900, as 1st class officer interpreter and Special Service officer, graded as DAAG (despatches, DSO, medal); Attaché with Russian Forces in Manchuria, 1905 (Order of St Stanislaus, 2nd class, with swords, and Russian war medal); served European War, 1914–18 (despatches 9 times, CB, CMG, promoted Bt Col and Major-Gen.; Legion of Honour); Chief of British Military Mission to South Russia, 1919–20 (KCB, Order of St Anne, 1st class, with swords; Order of St Stanislaus, 1st class, with swords, Order of St Vladimir, 4th class, with swords); Assist Secretary, Military Department, Government of India, 1901; staff captain, Intelligence Department, War Office, 1902; DAQMG General Staff, 1904; awarded Royal Humane Society's medal, 1907; General Staff Officer, Army Headquarters, India, 1910; Deputy Quartermaster General in India, 1921–22; GOC Sind-Rajputana District, 1922–24; GOC Mhow District and 4th Indian Division, 1924–27; retired, 1928; Private in Home Guard, 1940–44. Hon. Treasurer to The Bible Speaks to Britain, Bible monthly. *Address:* 18 Tongdeau Ave, Hove, Sx.

Died 25 July 1949.

HOLMAN-HUNT, Hilary Lushington Holman, CIE 1917; MICE; MIME; CMZS; *b* 6 May 1879; *s* of late W. Holman-Hunt, OM, DCL, and Marion Edith (*d* 1931), *g d* of Alexander Waugh, DD; *m* 1905, Gwendolyn Norah, *d* of late G. M. Freeman, KC; one *d*; 1941, Winifred Clare Waterworth (*d* 1946). *Educ:* Wellington; Heidelberg; RIEC, Coopers Hill. Joined Public Works Dept, Burma, 1901; served European War, 1914, in India and France, Capt. IARO (despatches); Chief Engineer and Secretary to Government, 1923; retired, 1933; awarded Royal Humane Society's Medal, 1907. *Publications:* engineering articles and pamphlets. *Recreations:* sculling, shooting, polo and racing. *Address:* Rockland-All-Saints, Attleborough, Norfolk. *T:* Caston 244. *Clubs:* East India and Sports, Royal Automobile.

           Died 10 Sept. 1949.

HOLMDEN, Sir Osborn George, KBE 1918; DL City of London; JP; Director, H. Clarkson Co., Ltd, and Furness Withy Co., Ltd; during the war of 1914–18 was Director of the Inter-Allied Chartering Executive, and served on several Committees; British Delegate at Peace Conference; Member of Committee of Enquiry into Coastguard Organisation, 1931; Commander of the Crown (Belgium); Commander Crown of Italy; Officer, Légion d'Honneur; Commander of St Olaf, Norway; *b* 24 Nov. 1869; *m* 1897, Mary Mildred, *d* of J. A. Swanston; one *s* one *d*. Past Grand Steward and Past Grand Deacon in Freemasonry; Master Spectacle Makers, 1929. *Recreation:* golf. *Address:* Fraser Heath, Tadworth. *T:* Betchworth 16. *Clubs:* Conservative, Bath, Royal Thames Yacht.

           Died 16 April 1945.

HOLME-SUMNER, Captain Berkeley, CBE 1919; OBE 1919; RN (retired); *b* 1872; *m* 1895, Margaret Joan, *d* of late James Harvey; one *s* three *d*. Served European War, 1914–19 (OBE, CBE, Legion of Honour). *Address:* Old Graingers, Plaxtol, Kent.

           Died 10 Dec. 1943.

HOLMES, George Augustus; Director of Examinations of the London College of Music from 1887 and founder of its scheme of Local Examinations in Music; Organist, St George's, Camberwell, 1880–1903; *b* Peckham, 10 May 1861. *Educ:* privately. Took part in Music (Organ Recitals) at Fisheries Exhibition, 1883, and Inventions Exhibition, 1885; Composer of a large number of Pianoforte works, including Tarentelle Brilliant, Tarentelle Chromatique, six Melodious Studies, Miniature Recreations, six Characteristic Duets, etc.; also author of the Academic Manual of the Rudiments of Music (1045th Thousand) and Three Hundred and Fifty Questions and Exercises on the same; Joint-Author (with Dr F. J. Karn) of the Academic Manual of Musical History, 1899, and other editions up to 1943; Historical Chronology of Music with 800 Questions, 1900, and editions to 1939; Musical Art Forms, 1901, and ten following editions, revised and enlarged; Standard Studies for Pianoforte, 15 Books, annotated; Technical Studies for Pianoforte, 15 Books, annotated; Classified Studies for Pianoforte, 12 Books, annotated; Standard Studies for Violin, annotated; Standard Studies for American Organ; Technical Training for the Pianoforte, Book I (71st Edition), Book II (15th Edition); Academic Manual of Musical Information; Analyses of Pianoforte Compositions, 5 Books; an analysed edition of Classics for the Pianoforte (Academic Classics); a 2nd selection (Students' Classics); a 3rd selection (Pianoforte Classics); four series of compositions from the modern composers entitled (1) Contemporary Pianoforte Music, (2) Pianoforte Recreations, (3) Selected Pianoforte Pieces, and (4) The Modern Series, with critical remarks upon the form and construction; The Academic Series of Violin Music, analysed and annotated; Preparatory Manuals for the Pianoforte, Books I to IV; Primary

Pianoforte Manuals, Books I and II; Academic Pianoforte Primers, Books I and II; Preparatory Manuals for the Violin, Books I and II; Rudimentary Musical Knowledge; The Academic Manual of Harmony, and (2) Key to same; The Student's Rudiments of Music and (2) 460 Questions and Exercises on the same; also Primary Exercises in Singing, and other miscellaneous works for students. *Recreations:* horticulture, the study of the old masters of music, and the collecting of their works. *Address:* Kelso House, Worcester Road, Sutton, Surrey; Breeze Holm, Broadstairs, Kent; Lond. Coll. of Music, Great Marlborough St, W1.

           Died 26 Nov. 1943.

HOLMES, Harold Kennard, CBE 1928; *b* 9 Nov. 1875; *s* of Henry James Holmes and Jeannie Foster Kennard; 1st marr. diss; *m* 1938, Ellen Florence Jordan; one *s*. *Educ:* Bloxham. Solicitor Supreme Court, Hong-Kong, 1900; served with KRRC, Somme, 1916; wounded, Guillemont; with 20th London Regt Salonika, Palestine, France, and Rhine; 2nd Lieut 1918; Hong-Kong Civil Service, 1919; Assistant Land Officer; Crown Solicitor, Hong-Kong, 1922–35. *Address:* Hoblets, Pebmarsh, Essex.

           Died 13 Jan. 1942.

HOLMES, Paymaster Rear-Adm. John Dickonson, CBE, 1919; *b* 1875. Assistant Clerk, 1892; served European War, 1914–19 (despatches, CBE); retired, 1930. *Address:* Saville House, Billingshurst, Sussex. *T:* Billinghurst 109.

           Died 6 Jan. 1947.

HOLMPATRICK, 2nd Baron *cr* 1897; **Hans Wellesley Hamilton,** DSO 1919; MC; *b* 8 Aug. 1886; *s* of 1st Baron and Lady Victoria Alexandrina (*d* 1933), *d* of Gen. Lord Charles Wellesley and *sister* of 3rd and 4th Dukes of Wellington; *S* father, 1898; *m* 1925, Lady Edina Ainsworth, 4th *d* of 4th Marquess Conyngham; one *s* one *d*. Served European War, 1914–18 (wounded, despatches). *Heir: s* Hon. James Hans Hamilton, *b* 29 Nov. 1928. *Address:* Abbotstown, Castleknock, Co. Dublin. *TA:* Castleknock. *Clubs:* Cavalry; Kildare Street, Dublin.

           Died 5 Sept. 1942.

HOLMS, John Mitchell, CSI 1906; Indian Civil Service (retired); Barrister (Inner Temple); *b* 25 June 1863; *e s* of late James Holms; *m* Gwendolyn, *y d* of late M. L. Ferrar, Indian Civil Service; one *d*. *Educ:* Blairlodge School; Balliol College, Oxford. Served in the UP since 1883, as district officer; Joint Secretary to the Board of Revenue, Commissioner of Excise, Financial Secretary and Chief Secretary to Government, and as Commissioner, Meerut and Fyzabad Divisions; member of the Excise Committee appointed by the Government of India, 1905–06; member of the Governor-General's Legislative Council, 1908–11; member Board of Revenue, and Vice-President Legislative Council, UP; Officiating Lieut-Governor, UP, 1917; retired, 1918. *Address:* Farringford, London Road, Cheltenham.

           Died 18 July 1948.

HOLMS, William Frederick, CIE 1918; *b* 1866; 3rd *s* of James Holms; *m* 1st, 1920, Muriel Beatrice (*d* 1944), *o d* of late Major R. E. Firminger; 2nd, 1944, Dorothy Topham, *d* of late Canon S. N. Perry. *Educ:* Blairlodge School; Coopers Hill College. Indian Public Works Department, 1888; Superintending Engineer in Punjab Irrigation Department, 1910; Chief Engineer and Secretary to Punjab Government Irrigation Branch, 1916–19. *Recreations:* fishing; formerly golf, cricket and football; Scottish Rugby International in 1886, 1887, and 1889. *Address:* 8 Park Close, Eastbourne. *Clubs:* Royal Eastbourne Golf, Devonshire (Eastbourne).

           Died 30 Sept. 1950.

HOLNESS, Col Harold James, DSO 1918; late RAVC; *b* 22 Sept. 1882. Served European War, 1914–18 (despatches twice, DSO); Commandant RAV School and School of Farriery, 1930–32; Deputy Director of Veterinary Services, Southern Command, India, 1933–34; retired pay, 1938.

Died 30 April 1941.

HOLT, Sir Follett, KBE 1934; MInstCE, FCGI; Chairman of the Entre Rios Railways and Chairman and Director of other railways and undertakings; *b* 4 Dec. 1865; *s* of late Robert Hallett Holt, barrister-at-law, head of the Land Registry Department, and Clara Rush; *m* 1896, Eliza Robertson Leitch; one *s*. *Educ:* Merchant Taylors' School; City and Guilds Technical College under Professors Ayrton and Perry. Articled to W. Adams of the L. and SW Railway; then an Assistant to Sir Alexander Rendel, Consulting Engineer; in 1889 joined the Buenos Aires and Rosario Railway and became subsequently General Manager and Chief Engineer of the Great Western of Brazil and the Entre Rios Railways; built the lines joining the latter with the North and with Buenos Aires, and the train-ferry system; in 1894 and 1897 played in the winning team of the River Plate Polo Championship; in the war a Financial Adviser to the Coal Mines Department, and member of HM Special Diplomatic and Commercial Mission to the ten South American Republics. Member of the Advisory Council to the Board of Trade, 1931–34; London Chairman of the British Exhibition in Buenos Aires, 1931; Chairman of the Frozen Pesos Committee under the United Kingdom and Argentine Convention, 1933. *Publication:* Report on the British Diplomatic and Commercial Mission to South America, 1918. *Address:* Riffhams, Danbury, near Chelmsford. *Clubs:* Athenæum, Argentine.

Died 20 March 1944.

HOLT, Captain Sir Henry Gisborne, Kt 1923; JP, late 4th Suffolks; *b* 1864; *e s* of late Captain William Frederic Holt, 3rd Somersets, and Elizabeth Sykes Boyd; *m* 1st, 1888, Alethea R. A. (*d* 1920), *d* of late General W. H. Scott, Scots Guards, of Thorpe, *g d* of 1st Baron Stanley of Alderley, and *widow* of Sir Edward Blackett, 6th Baronet; 2nd, 1925, Patience Alice (*d* 1929), 2nd *d* of late W. C. Scott, Thorpe House, Chertsey. *Educ:* Rev. Stephen Hawtrey's, Windsor. Comptroller of the Household to the Lord-Lieut of Ireland, 1921–22; served European War, 1914–19.

Died 26 Jan. 1944.

HOLT, Sir Herbert S., Kt 1915; LLD (McGill), DCL (Bishop's); Chairman of the Board, Royal Bank of Canada, Montreal; Montreal Light, Heat and Power Co.; President, Montreal Trust Company; Vice-President, Dominion Textile Co., Ltd, and Montreal Cottons Ltd, and Director of numerous companies; *b* County Kildare, Ireland, 12 Feb. 1856; *s* of late William Robert Grattan Holt; *m* 1890, Jessie (*d* 1939), *e d* of late Andrew Paton, of Sherbrooke, Quebec, Canada; three *s*. *Educ:* Dublin. A member of American and Canadian Societies of Civil Engineers; engaged for several years on engineering and construction of the Canadian Pacific Railway, Calgary and Edmonton Railway, Regina and Long Lake Railway, and several other railways in Canada and the United States. *Recreations:* motoring, and fishing. *Address:* 3459 Stanley Street, Montreal; Ballycrystal House, Nassau, Bahamas. *TA:* Herbholt, Montreal and Nassau. *T:* Plateau 3042, Montreal: 275 Nassau. *Clubs:* Mount Royal, Montreal; Mount Bruno Country; Manitoba, Winnipeg; Rideau, Ottawa; Toronto, Toronto.

Died 28 Sept. 1941.

HOLT, Sir Richard Durning, 1st Bt *cr* 1935; Hon. LLD, University of Liverpool, 1933; partner, Alfred Holt & Co., shipowners; Member, 1896, Chairman, 1927, Mersey Docks and Harbour Board; Chairman Elder Dempster Lines, Ltd since 1932; JP; *b* 1868; *s* of late Robert D. Holt of Sefton Park, Liverpool, and High Borrans, Westmorland; *m* 1897, Eliza Lawrence, *e d* of late John Wells, New Brunswick, New Jersey; three *d*. *Educ:* Winchester; New College, Oxford. MP (L) Hexham Division, Northumberland, 1907–18. *Address:* 54 Ullet Road, Liverpool.

Died 22 March 1941.

HOLT-WILSON, Brig. Sir Eric Edward Boketon, Kt 1933; CMG 1919; DSO 1900; Commandant, War Department Constabulary since 1942; *b* 26 Aug. 1875; *e s* of late Rev. Thomas Holt-Wilson, Rural Dean, JP, Redgrave, Suffolk, and Helen Emily, *sister* of late Sir E. Walter Greene, Bt, MP, of Nether Hall, Suffolk; *m* 1st, 1903, Susannah Mary Shaw (*d* 1927); one *s* one *d*; 2nd, 1931, Audrey, *o d* of late H. R. Stirling; two *d*. *Educ:* Harrow; RMA, Woolwich (cricket XI, football XI, champion revolver shot). Entered RE 1895; Instructor, School of Military Engineering, 1903–06; Cadet Company Commander and Instructor in Military Engineering, Royal Military Academy, Woolwich, 1909–12; Imperial Security Intelligence Service, 1912–40 (Chief Staff Officer, 1917–40); inception and organisation, through Home Office, of official registration by the Police of alien residents in UK; General Staff Officer, Imperial General Staff, 1914–24 and 1939–40; Lt-Col 1917; Hon. Brig. 1939; Secretary, Lord Chancellor's Sub-Committee on War Emergency Legislation, Cttee of Imperial Defence, 1924–38; formulated all military Defence Regulations for war; served South Africa, 1899–1902 (despatches twice, Queen's medal, 5 clasps, King's medal, 2 clasps, DSO); European War, 1914–19; inception and organisation of Field Security Intelligence Police duties, France, 1914, Egypt, Greece, Germany; Member of Inter-Allied Intelligence Bureau, Paris, 1915; Chief of Police Commission, British Occupied Rhineland, 1919 (despatches, Bt Major, Bt Lieut-Col, CMG, Legion of Honour, Crown of Belgium); Deputy Commandant War Dept Constabulary, 1927–42; British Delegate for Navy, Army, and Air Force, International Convention on Treatment of Prisoners of War, Geneva, 1929; special intelligence service in India, Dominions, and Colonies, 1929, 1930, and 1938; Visiting Lecturer, Staff College, Camberley, 1921–39; Jubilee Medal, 1935; Coronation Medal, 1937; Defence and War Medals, 1939–45. *Publications:* Field Entrenchments, 1914; revision of the Army Manual of Field Engineering, and author of all pre-war official papers and manuals on Security Intelligence Police Duties in Peace and War. *Recreations:* shooting and ski-running (President Ski Club of Great Britain, 1934–35). *Address:* Spye Arch House, Lacock, Wilts. *Club:* Army and Navy.

Died 26 March 1950.

HOLTHOUSE, Edwin Hermus, MA, MB (Camb.), FRCS (Eng.); Consulting Surgeon to the Western Ophthalmic Hospital; *b* Smyrna, 18 Nov. 1855; 2nd *s* of late Carsten Holthouse, FRCS, sometime Surgeon to the Westminster Hosp.; *m* Harriet Emily (*d* 1940), *e d* of late Robert Hesketh, FRIBA, of Earlswood Mount, Redhill, Surrey; two *s*. *Educ:* Westminster School; Trinity College, Cambridge (Exhibitioner), Natural Sciences Tripos (2nd class), 1878. Late Surgeon St Pancras and Northern Dispensary. *Publications:* Convergent Strabismus: an Essay, 1897; papers on ophthalmic subjects; contribution to Cambridge Medieval History (Vol. iii); articles on historical subjects. *Address:* 6 Gilbert Road, Ramsgate, Kent.

Died 2 Jan. 1949.

HOLTZ, Alfred Christian Carlsen, FCIS (Eng.); *b* Melbourne, 1 March 1874; *m* 1899, S. A. Thompson, Brighton, Victoria, Australia; one *s* two *d*. *Educ:* The Grammar School, Brighton; St Kilda Grammar School, Melbourne. Over five years on staff of P. and O. SN Co., Melbourne; entered service of Wilson and Mackinnon, proprietors of The Argus and the Australasian newspapers, Melbourne, 1894; was secretary a number of years; General Manager, The Argus, and the Australasian, 1920–36; Secretary to Newspaper Proprietors-Association of Melbourne from its establishment in 1917 until 1919, when he became representative of The Argus on that body; President of the Rotary Club of Melbourne, 1925–26, and of the 1st Australian Official Rotary Conference, 1926; District Governor for Rotary International for the Common, wealth of Australia, 1929–30, and Chairman of the 3rd Pacific Rotary Conference-Sydney, 1930; Chairman of the Audit Bureau of Circulations, from its establishment in 1931 till 1939, State Chm. for Toc. H. (Victoria), 1931–32; Represented the Australian Press at the Conference of Press Experts held at Geneva in 1927; Chm., Board of Governors, Normal College for Sunday School Teachers, since 1929; Chairman Congregational Union of Victoria 1938–39; Chm. of the Australian Newspapers Conference from its foundation, 1924–36; Executive Chairman, 1936–39; Manager Australian Press Association, 1920–36; Foundation Director, Australian Associated Press (which includes the former), 1939. Chairman Board of Management Freemasons' Hospital, Melbourne, 1938–41; Deputy Director for Victoria, Commonwealth Department of Information, 1939–41; Deputy Chairman, Nursery Kindergarten Extension Board, 1940–42; District Air Raid Warden, City of Kew, since 1939; Editor, The Southern Congregationalist, 1944–; King's Jubilee Medal. *Recreations:* Literature, philately, photography, horticulture, motoring. *Address:* 25 Grange Road, Kew, Melbourne, E4, Australia. *TA:* Holtz, Kew, Melbourne. *T:* Haw 6446. *Clubs:* Royal Automobile of Victoria, Rotary, Overseas League, Melbourne Cricket, English-Speaking Union (Melbourne).

Died 18 March 1948.

HOMBERSLEY, Ven. Arthur; *b* 1855; *s* of Rev. W. Hombersley, MA; *m* 1898, Anne Georgina (*d* 1929), St George; one *s* one *d.* Ordained, 1880; Curate of Deddington, 1880–82; Normacot, 1882–89; Rector of St Andrew, Grenada, 1890–94; Rector of All Saints, Port of Spain, 1894–1930; Canon of Trinidad Cathedral, 1892–1914; Archdeacon of Trinidad, 1914–29. *Address:* Trinidad. *Clubs:* Savannah, Trinidad.

Died 29 Aug. 1941.

HOME, Col James Murray, CBE 1919; DL, JP Berwickshire; retired Indian Army; *b* Feb. 1866; *e s* of late Colonel Robert Home, CB, RE; *m* 1893, *o d* of late James Fergusson; one *s* one *d. Educ:* Winchester; Staff College, Camberley. Entered RA 1886; transferred Indian Army, 1889; served Chin-Lushai, 1889–90; NE Frontier, 1891; Waziristan, 1901–02; Russo-Japanese War, 1904–05; European War, 1914–19 (despatches, CBE, Brevet Colonel); Staff Capt. and DAQMG HQ Army in India, 1902–05; Military Attaché Russo-Japanese War; DAAG Aldershot Command, 1905–09; GSO1, 65th Division; AA and QMG 71st Division; SO1, Royal Air Force; Chairman TA Assoc. of Roxburgh, Berwick and Selkirk since 1928; St Anne of Russia, 2nd class with swords. *Address:* Bassendean, Gordon, Berwickshire. *Clubs:* United Service; New, Edinburgh.

Died 19 Feb. 1946.

HOME, Col Robert Elton, CBE 1919; DSO 1902; retired; late RGA; *b* 29 May 1869; *e s* of late Col Robert Home, CIE; *m* 1904, Delphine (*d* 1942), *y d* of late W. J. Etheridge; two *d. Educ:* Cheltenham. Entered Army, 1888; Captain, 1898; Major, 1908; Lt-Col 1916; Col 1917; retired pay, 1921; served Waziristan Expedition, 1894–95 (medal with clasp); Punjab Frontier, 1897–98 (medal with 2 clasps); S Africa, 1890–1902 (despatches thrice, medal with 5 clasps, King's medal 2 clasps, DSO); services in connection with the War, 1914–18 (Bt Col, CBE). *Address:* 3 Hadley Grove, Barnet.

Died 17 April 1943.

HOMER, Louise; Opera and Concert Singer, Contralto; *b* Pittsburg; *d* of William Beatty, clergyman; *m* Sidney, *s* of G. Homer; one *s* five *d. Educ:* Philadelphia; Boston; Paris. Début as leading Contralto at Vichy; leading Contralto at La Monnaie, Covent Garden, Chicago Opera; nineteen seasons of Metropolitan Opera in New York; MA Tufts College, 1931, Smith College, 1932; Doctor of Letters, Miami Univ., Oxford, Ohio, 1933; Doctor of Music, Middlebury College, 1934. *Address:* Bolton-on-Lake George, New York, USA.

Died 6 May 1947.

HOMFRAY, Lt-Col John Robert Henry, CBE 1919; *b* 23 Oct. 1868; *s* of Lieut-Col J. R. M. Homfray, IA; *m* 1st, 1897, Margaret Emily (*d* 1928), *d* of Captain Bonham Ward Bax, RN; two *d;* 2nd, 1935, Mary Amelia, *widow* of Lieut Francis Maunsell. *Educ:* RN Academy, Gosport. PGS Lieut RMA 1886; Capt. 1897–1908; Major and Bt Lieut-Col (retired), 1919; War service, Grand Fleet, 2nd BS 1914–16; second in command, Cromarty, RM Garrison, 1916–17; OCRM defences West Indies, 1917–19 (despatches, CBE, Lieut-Col). *Address:* Burnside, 2 Cole Park Road, Twickenham, Middlesex.

Died 26 Feb. 1944.

HONEY, Sir de Symons Montagu George, Kt 1932; CMG 1919; *b* Alexandria, Cape Province, 1 Nov. 1872; *s* of J. W. Honey, sen., retired Civil Commissioner and Resident Magistrate, Cape Service; *m* 1904, Violet Marguerite, *d* of Charles Jones, Stellenbosch; two *s. Educ:* Public School, Carnarvon. Served with BSA Coy.'s Police, Mashonaland; British Central Africa Administration; Beira Mashonaland Railway Construction, and in Boer War; joined Transvaal Civil Service, 1901; Secretary to the Governor of the Transvaal for Swaziland affairs, 1904; Government Secretary of Swaziland, 1907; and, in addition, Deputy Resident Commissioner, 1910; Resident Commissioner of Swaziland, 1917–28; Governor and Commander-in-Chief, Seychelles, 1928–33.

Died Jan. 1945.

HONYWOOD, Sir Courtenay John, 9th Bt *cr* 1660; *b* 29 May 1880; *s* of 8th Bt and Zaidee, *d* of J. B. Sparrow, Gwyndu, Anglesey; *S* father, 1907; *m* Constance Mary, *d* of late Rev. C. H. Vincent Pixell, Vicar of St Faith, Stoke Newington. Owns about 5700 acres. *Heir:* *b* Lt-Col William Wynne Honywood. *Address:* Puerto Saavedra, Chile.

Died 4 July 1944.

HOOD, Paymaster-Captain Basil Frederick, CBE 1937; DSO 1916; RN; *b* 20 Sept. 1886; 2nd *s* of Mrs C. du plat Hood, *née* Richardson Griffiths, and late Rev. J. F. Hood, BA. *Educ:* St John's School, Leatherhead. Entered Royal Navy, 1904; Assistant Paymaster, 1907; Paymaster, 1911; Secretary to Admiral of Patrols, 1912–14; Secretary to Vice-Admiral commanding Eastern Mediterranean during Gallipoli campaign, 1915–16 (despatches twice, DSO); specially promoted to Paymaster Lieut-Commander, 1917; Paymaster-Commander, 1923; Paym.-Capt. 1934. *Club:* Junior United Service.

Died 10 Jan. 1941.

HOOD, Lt-Col Hon. Neville Albert, CMG 1918; DSO, 1917; late RA; *b* 4 Oct. 1872; 4th *s* of 4th Viscount Hood; *m* 1908, Eveline Mary, *o d* of Herman Ustioke Pender of Tresillian, Falmouth; one *s* three *d. Educ:* Clifton College; Royal Military Academy, Woolwich. Served South African War, 1900–02 (despatches twice, 2 medals 6 clasps); European War 1914–18 (despatches three times, CMG, DSO); DL Cornwall. *Address:* Grove Hill House, Falmouth, Cornwall. *T:* Falmouth 893.

Died 24 Jan. 1948.

HOOD, Thomas, CMG 1917; LRCP Lond.; MRCS Eng.; *b* 1870. Senior Medical Officer, Gambia, 1913; Director of Med. and Sanitary Service, Nigeria, 1913–20; retired, 1920. *Address:* Miramar, Pelham Gardens, Folkestone.

Died 1 July 1949.

HOOPER, Col Arthur Winsmore, CMG 1916; DSO 1900; late RAMC; *b* 22 Feb. 1869; *m* 1910, Amy Harriet, *d* of late Sir B. T. Brandreth Gibbs. Served S Africa, 1899–1902 (despatches, Queen's medal six clasps, King's medal two clasps, DSO); European War, 1914–18 (despatches, Bt Lt-Col, CMG); retired pay, 1921. *Address:* 15 Grove Park Road, Weston-super-Mare.

Died 23 Dec. 1945.

HOOPER, David, LLD; FRIC, FCS; late Wellcome Historical Medical Museum, Euston Road; late Research Chemist, Bio-Chemical Laboratory, University of Bristol; late Chemist in Ministry of Munitions, Westminster; *b* Redhill, Surrey, 1 May 1858; *m* 1887, Hannah, *d* of Rev. Thomas Evans; two *s* three *d*. *Educ:* Chelmsford; London; The Hague. Quinologist to the Government of Madras, India, 1884–97; Curator of Industrial Section Indian Musuem, Calcutta, 1897–1912; Economic Botanist to the Government of India, 1912–14; late Treasurer and Vice-Pres. of Asiatic Society of Bengal; Fellow of the Calcutta Univ.; Hanbury Gold Medallist, 1907; Pres. British Pharmaceutical Conference, 1916. *Publications:* (joint) Pharmacographia Indica; editor of Materia Medica of Madras; joint-editor Materia Medica for India; Chinese Drugs of the Malay Peninsula; Some Persian Drugs. *Address:* The Vicarage, Winscombe, Som.

Died 31 Jan. 1947.

HOOPER, Reginald Stewart; Editor of The Tatler since 1940, and of The Bystander since 1932; *b* 4 Dec. 1889; *s* of late Henry Stewart Hooper and Beatrice Everitt; *m* 1st, 1917, Marjorie Rose (*d* 1934); one *s* two *d*; 2nd, 1935, Marguerite Mary Duff Joy. *Educ:* Uppingham; Brasenose College, Oxford (First Hulme Exhibitioner in Law). Sub-Editor of the Tatler, 1913–14; Herefordshire Regt and Staff, 1914–18; edited The Illustrated Sporting and Dramatic News, 1937–40. *Publications:* And the Next; One at a Time. *Recreation:* farming. *Address:* 152 Marsham Court, Westminster, SW1. *T:* Victoria 8181; Polefields, Markbeech, Edenbridge. *T:* Cowden 2131. *Club:* United University.

Died 2 Sept. 1945.

HOOPER, William Henry; Taxing Master Supreme Court since 1935; *b* 1876; *s* of William and Emma Hooper, Brighton; *m* 1902, Emma Florence, *d* of Edward and Caroline Mitchell, Brighton; two *d*. *Educ:* privately. Solicitor; Member of Law Society; Assistant Official Solicitor to the Supreme Court, 1920; Assistant Master (Management and Administration Dept), 1933; Served European War, 1916–19, Capt. and Adjutant 38th Welsh Divisional Train (despatches). *Recreations:* riding, golf. *Address:* 44 Northampton Road, Addiscombe; Room 252, Royal Courts of Justice, WC2. *T:* Addiscombe 1957.

Died 29 July 1946.

HOOPS, Albert Launcelot, CBE, 1931; LMS Hon. Singapore, 1931; MD, DPH, BA, Univ. Dublin; Senior Medical Officer, Malacca Agricultural Medical Board, Malacca; *b* 1876; *s* of Dr S. Mostyn Hoops; *m* 1901, *d* of late T. Stringer; two *s* three *d*. *Educ:* King William College, Isle of Man; Trinity College, University of Dublin; London School of Tropical Medicine. Served South African War, 1901–02 (Queen's medal four clasps, despatches); Malayan Medical Service, 1904–31; organised Medical, Prison and Labour Depts, Malay State of Kedah, 1906–20; acted twice as Adviser to the Government of Kedah; Principal Civil Medical Officer, Straits Settlements, 1921–31, and President Council College of Medicine, Singapore; President, 5th Congress Far Eastern Association of Tropical Medicine, Singapore, 1923 (joint editor of Congress Transactions); Vice-President of 6th Congress, Tokyo, 1925, 7th Congress, Calcutta, 1927, 8th Congress, Bangkok, 1930, 9th Congress, Nanking, 1934; represented British Colonies and Protectorates on League of Nations Eastern Bureau Advisory Council, 1928–31; Member, Legislative Council, Straits Settlements, 1923–31; Chairman of Tuberculosis Committee, 1923; Member of the Federated Malay States Medical Enquiry Committee, 1925; Chairman of Malayan Standing Medical Advisory Committee, 1924–31; President of Malayan Branch, British Medical Association, 1926–27 and 1930–31; Fellow Royal Society Tropical Medicine and Hygiene; Arnott Gold Medal, 1913. *Publications:* Some Aspects of Health Work and Medical School Organisation in the United States, 1925; Present Day Public Health in India, 1928; Lectures on the History of Medicine, 1930; The History of Malaria, 1934. *Recreation:* yachting. *Address:* Malacca, Straits Settlements. *Clubs:* Sports; Royal Singapore Yacht.

Died 16 Nov. 1940.

HOPE, Collingwood, CBE 1918; KC 1901; JP; DL; FRGS; High Steward, Borough of Southwold, Suffolk, 1905–45; Recorder of Bolton, 1903–25; late Chairman Agricultural Wage Board; *b* 10 Nov. 1858; 5th *s* of late Thomas Arthur Hope of Cheshire; *m* 1887, Alice Therese (*d* 1925), *e d* of late R. N. Dale, Bromborough, Cheshire; two *d*. *Educ:* Rugby; Germany; Pembroke College, Oxford. Called to Bar (Inner Temple), 1882; a Revising Barrister for Lancashire, 1892–97; a county councillor for Cheshire, 1898–1901; Chairman Essex Quarter Sessions, 1921–35. *Address:* Crix, Hatfield Peverel, Essex.

Died 5 May 1949.

HOPE, Edward William, OBE; MD, DSc, LRCP; Emeritus Professor of Public Health, University of Liverpool; late Medical Officer of Health, City and Port of Liverpool; late Examiner in Public Health, Royal College of Physicians of London, Royal College of Surgeons of England, and in the Universities of Cambridge, Edinburgh, London, Manchester, and Belfast; President of the Society of Medical Officers of Health and of the Liverpool Medical Institution; *b* 1854; *s* of late Robert Wallis Hope, formerly of War Office; *m* 1899, C. Rennie, *d* of late John Bowring of Liverpool and Newfoundland; one *s* two *d*. *Educ:* Royal School of Mines; Edinburgh University. *Publications:* Health at the Gateway; Industrial Hygiene and Medicine; Manual of School Hygiene; Manual of Public Health; Report on Physical Welfare of Mothers and Children, Carnegie UK Trust; various Reports on the Health of Liverpool. *Address:* Coppice, Caldy, West Kirby, Cheshire; University of Liverpool.

Died 27 April 1950.

HOPE, John Deans; JP Haddingtonshire; *b* 8 May 1860; *s* of late James Hope, Eastbarns, Dunbar, the eminent agriculturist; *m* 1899, *y d* of late R. K. Holmes-Kerr, Glasgow, and of Underbank, Ayrshire; one *d*. *Educ:* Fettes College; Edinburgh University. Contested West Perthshire 1895; MP (L) West Fife, 1900–10; Haddingtonshire, 1911–18; Berwick and Haddington, 1918–22; served on ten Parliamentary Commissions. *Recreation:* shooting. *Address:* Haddington, Scotland. *Club:* Northern (Edinburgh).

Died 13 Dec. 1949.

HOPE, Lt-Col John William, DSO 1915; late RA; *b* 29 Jan. 1876; *s* of late James Hope, ICS; *m* 1st, 1906, Ethel Obre Wallis, *widow*, *d* of late Col A. Wintle, RA; one *s* one *d*; 2nd, 1928, Irma Marguerite Burton, *widow*, *d* of H. Seedorff. Entered army, 1896; Capt. 1902; Adjutant, 1905–08; Major, 1912; Lt-Col, 1916; Brigade-Major, India, 1911–14; served European War, 1914–18 (wounded, despatches, DSO, Belgian Croix de Guerre); retired pay, 1922. *Address:* Southview, Aveley Lane, Farnham, Surrey.

Died 5 Oct. 1942.

HOPKINS, Sir Frederick Gowland, OM 1935; Kt 1925; MA Cantab; MB, DSc, Lond.; Hon. DSc Cantab, London, Oxford, Manchester, Dublin, Sheffield, Glasgow, Leeds, Reading, Harvard; LLD Birmingham, Aberdeen and St Andrews; DCL Durham; Hon. MD Louvain, Brussels, Budapest, Lausanne; Doctor hc Paris, 1945; FRCP, FRS 1905; Professor of Bio-chemistry, University of Cambridge, 1914, Sir William Dunn Professor, 1921–43; Fellow and late Prælector in Biochemistry, Trinity College; Hon. Fellow of Emmanuel College; an original Member of the MRC, retired 1930; Member of Agricultural Research Council; Chairman Animal Diseases Committee Economic Advisory Council; Member of several European Academies and learned societies; Vice-President, Chemical Society, 1921; Baly Medal, RCP, 1915; Croonian Lecturer, Royal Society, 1915; Dunham Lecturer, Harvard; Royal Medal, 1918; Copley Medal, 1926; Albert Medal, 1934; Harben Medal, 1937; Nobel Prize for Medicine, 1929; Huxley Memorial Lecturer, 1920; Herter Lecturer New York and Baltimore, 1921; Cameron Prizeman University Edinburgh, 1922; late one of the Official Analysts to the Home Office; President, Royal Society, 1930–35; President, British Association, 1933; President, Cambridge Phil. Society, 1936–39; *b* 1861; *s* of late Frederick Hopkins; *m* 1898, Jessie Anne Stevens; one *s* two *d*. Author of many contributions to Biochemistry; a pioneer in vitamin research. *Address:* Saxmeadham, Grange Road, Cambridge. *T:* Cambridge 4031. *Club:* Athenæum.

Died 16 May 1947.

HOPKINS, Harry L., DSM 1945; *b* Sioux City, Iowa, 1890; *m* 1942, Mrs Louise Gill Macy. *Educ:* Grinnell College (LLD 1935). Began as Supervisor of Association for Improving Conditions of Poor; Executive Secretary, Board of Child Welfare, 1915–17; Directing Manager, New Orleans, for American Red Cross, 1917–22; then Assistant Director of Association for Improving Condition of the Poor; then Director, New York Tuberculosis and Health Association Executive Director of New York State Temporary Emergency Relief Administration, 1931, Chairman, 1932; Federal Administrator of Emergency Relief, 1933; Works Progress Administrator, 1935–38; Secretary of Commerce, 1938–40; until 1945, Special Adviser and Assistant to President of United States; Member of US War Production Board; Chairman of Munitions Assignments Board; Member Central Committee American Nat. Red Cross. *Address:* 3340 N Street, NW, Washington, DC, USA.

Died 29 Jan. 1946.

HOPKINS, Sir John Wells Wainwright, 1st Bt *cr* 1929; *b* 1863; *s* of John B. Hopkins; *m* 1894, Ethelind, 3rd *d* of Charles Mackern, Buenos Aires; (*er s* killed in action in European War, 1916, and *yr s* killed in action, 1942) one *d*. MP (U) South-East St Pancras, 1918–23 and 1924–29. *Heir:* none. *Address:* New Place, Lingfield, Surrey. *T:* Lingfield 27.

Died 16 Feb. 1946 (ext).

HOPKINS, Lt-Col Lewis Egerton, DSO 1917; OBE 1919; RE (retired); *b* 21 Jan. 1873; *s* of Thomas Hopkins, Limber Grange, Lincolnshire; *m* 1906, Carrie Estoteville (*d* 1938), *e d* of Sir Peyton Skipwith, Bart; two *s*. *Educ:* Repton; RMA, Woolwich. Employed on railways under the Government of India, 1894–1926; retired as Chief Engineer to the Railway Board. Travelled in Turkey and Persia in 1903, and again 1911–13 in connection with Trans-Persian Railway; Commanded 83rd Field Company, 20th Division, and RE 39th Division, France, 1914–17; and later East Persia,

1917–20 (despatches 3 times DSO, OBE); retired, 1927. *Publications:* Universal Railway Statistics, 1910; The Truth about Gold, 1933; Elementary Politics and Reform, 1935; Political Finance. *Recreation:* fishing. *Address:* Upton House, Upton, Huntingdonshire. *Club:* Junior United Service.

Died 7 Jan. 1945.

HOPKINSON, Sir Frederick Thomas, KBE 1925; MInstCE; *b* 1863; *s* of James Hopkinson, of Bury, Lancashire; *m* 1st, 1891, Lilian (*d* 1932), *d* of late James Thomas, JP, Rock House, Haverfordwest; one *s*; 2nd, 1936, Nora Mary, *yr d* of late J. P. Middleton, Woking, and *widow* of Lionel Hethorn Booth, LRCP, MRCS. Partner with late Lord Cowdray in the firm of S. Pearson and Son, Limited, Contractors for Public Works; at Ministry of Munitions and Air Board during the War; Member of the Gattie Committee (1919) for Ministry of Transport; rendered special services to Sudan Government in connection with Sennar Dam, Sudan, afterwards constructing same and Gezira Irrigation Scheme; Member of the Mears Committee (1926) to report and advise the Indian Government on the Bombay Back Bay Reclamation. *Clubs:* Reform; Walton Heath and Royal Wimbledon Golf.

Died 19 Sept. 1947.

HOPKINSON, Col Henry Charles Barwick Pasha, CMG 1913; CBE 1919; rank of Major-General in Egyptian Service; *b* 1867; *s* of G. H. Hopkinson and B. I. Somerset; *m* 1898, Hon. Mabel Parnell, *d* of 3rd Lord Congleton; one *s*. *Educ:* Winchester. Served Seaforth Highlanders; Egyptian Army and Police; Sudan Campaign, 1896–98 (despatches twice; twice wounded; 2nd Medjidie, 3rd Osmanie, 2nd class Order of the Nile, Sudan medal 4 clasps); retired, 1906. Called up from Reserve of Officers and granted local and temporary rank of Colonel, 1915; acted as Provost-Marshal and Military Control Officer, Alexandria (despatches four times); Col 1920. *Address:* Trelough, Wormbridge, Herefordshire. *Club:* Army and Navy.

Died 19 April 1946.

HOPTON, Ven. Charles Ernest, MA; Archdeacon of Birmingham, 1915–44; Canon of Birmingham, 1910; Surrogate for Marriages; Warden of the SIES Saltley, 1929; *b* 13 Feb. 1861; *s* of late Captain C. E. Hopton, 23rd Royal Welsh Fusiliers, and late Mrs Hopton of Kemerton Court, Tewkesbury; *m* 1890, Lucy Ann Barlow, *d* of late F. B. Osborn, FRIBA, VD, Edgbaston; no *c*. *Educ:* Clifton College; Hereford Cathedral School; St John's College, Cambridge (Somerset Exhibitioner). Curate of St Mary, Selly Oak, 1884–87; St George's, Redditch, 1889–91; Vicar of Stretton Grandison with Ashperton, Herefordshire, 1891–98; St Stephen's, Worcester, 1898–1907; Rural Dean of East Worcester, 1906–07; Rural Dean of King's Norton, 1909–15; Vicar of Moseley 1907–27. *Address:* 66 Hagley Road, Edgbaston, Birmingham, 16.

Died 20 Dec. 1946.

HOPWOOD, Edward Robert G.; *see* Gregge-Hopwood.

HOPWOOD, Vice-Adm. Geoffrey, CBE 1919; RN, retd; *b* 6 May 1877; *s* of late Rev. Canon Frank Edward Hopwood; *m* 1902; Mabel Kennedy; one *s* one *d*. Assistant Director of Mobilisation, Admiralty, 1916–17; served European War, 1914–19 (despatches, CBE); Deputy Director of Naval Intelligence, 1920–22; commanded HMS Diomede on China Station, 1922; in command of the Royal Naval Barracks at Chatham, 1925–27; commanded aircraft-carrier Hermes, 1927–28; Naval ADC to the King, 1928; Rear-Adm., 1929; retired list, 1930; Vice-Adm., retired, 1934. *Address:* 15 Romney Court, West Worthing, Sussex.

Died 14 Aug. 1947.

HOPWOOD, Adm. Ronald Arthur, CB 1919; retired; *b* 7 Dec. 1868; 3rd *s* of late John Turner Hopwood of Ketton Hall, Stamford; *m* 1915, Gladys, *e d* of Rev. H. B. Wolryche Whitmore of Thedden Grange, Alton; two *d. Educ:* Cheam School. Specialised in Gunnery; Vice-President of Ordnance Committee, 1917–18; General Secretary Navy League, 1919–22. *Publications:* The Old Way; The Secret of the Ships; The New Navy. *Address:* 7 Sloane Gardens, SW1. *Club:* United Service.

Died 28 Nov. 1949.

HORAN, Gerald; KC 1915; Master of the High Court, Eire, 1926–49; *b* 3 May 1879; *s* of M. L. Horan, solicitor, Dublin; *m* Kathleen, *d* of William Scallan, solicitor Dublin; one *s* one *d. Educ:* Catholic University School; Trinity College, Dublin. President, University Philosophical Society; Irish Bar, 1901; Revising Barrister, Dublin, 1912; Crown Prosecutor for Counties Meath and Louth, 1913–15; Clerk of Crown and Hanaper and Permanent Sec. to the Lord Chancellors of Ireland, 1915–21. *Publications:* Courts of Justice Act, 1924 (Ireland); Circuit Court Practice, 1932. *Recreation:* gardening. *Address:* Saint Peter's, Ailesbury Road, Dublin.

Died 9 May 1949.

HORDERN, Sir Archibald Frederick, Kt 1946; CBE 1942; AFC; Chief Constable of Lancashire since 1935; *b* 15 June 1889; *s* of late Peter Hordern, Bury House, Alverstoke, Hants; unmarried. *Educ:* Cheltenham; RMC, Sandhurst. Served European War, 1914–19, with South Staffordshire Regiment and RFC; Chief Constable of ER Yorks, 1926–34, of Cheshire, 1934–35. OStJ; King's Police Medal, 1933; Liveryman Worshipful Company of Coachmakers and Coach Harness Makers. *Address:* County Chief Constable's Office, Preston; Holme Mead, Lindle Lane, New Longton, near Preston, Lancs. *TA:* Ecilop, Preston. *T:* Preston 4811. *Clubs:* United Service, City Livery, Royal Automobile.

Died 17 April 1950.

HORDERN, Rev. Arthur Venables Calveley, CMG 1916; CBE 1919; *b* 12 April 1866; *s* of Rev. J. C. Hordern, RN; *m* 1898, Hilda Leigh Slater; four *s* (and one killed in action, 1942) two *d. Educ:* Grammar School; private tutor. Deacon, 1890; Priest, 1891; Chaplain to the Forces, 1894–1920; served South African War (Queen's and King's medals seven clasps, despatches, specially promoted); at Aldershot, Plymouth, Preston, South Africa (Senior Chaplain), Colchester; European War, Principal Chaplain MEF and EEF March 1915–June 1918; (despatches six times, CMG, CBE, Serbian Order, Karageorge, 3rd Class, 1916); Assistant Chaplain-General Northern Command, 1918–20 (mentioned for valuable services); awarded £50 a year for Distinguished Military Service, 1932; Rural Dean of Hodnet, 1920–30. *Address:* Merrington, Lavender Rd, Maybury, Woking.

Died 30 Oct. 1946.

HORDERN, Captain Edward Joseph Calveley, CIE 1920; Royal Indian Navy, retired; *b* 24 July 1867; 3rd *s* of late Rev. J. C. Hordern, RN; *m* Margaret Emily (*d* 1933), *o d* of Edward Francis Murray, MICE; three *s. Educ:* Bury Grammar School; HMS Conway. Apprentice to sea, 1883–88; 3rd grade Officer Indian Marine, 1889; Commander, 1907; Special promotion, Captain, 1912; held post as Assistant Director RIM 1913; Deputy Director, 1914; Principal Port Officer, Burma, 1918; held temp. rank Royal Navy as Lieut 1897–98, serving in HMS Magdala, Plassey, Eclipse and Racoon; Captain RN 1918–19; DNTO Burma, 1917–18; HMS Excellent and Vernon, 1892; served in China during Boxer Rising; Somali Expedition, European War, Kuki Operations (despatches, CIE). *Address:* c/o National Provincial Bank, Berkhamsted.

Died 29 Aug. 1944.

HORDERN, Brig.-Gen. Gwyn Venables, CB 1918; CMG 1916; late KRRC; *b* 27 June 1870; *m* 1916, Lady Violet E. H. Milles, *d* of 1st Earl Sondes. Served Nile Expedition, 1899 (medal and clasp); South Africa, 1899–1902 (despatches twice, Bt Major, Queen's medal five clasps, King's medal two clasps); European War, 1914–18 (despatches seven times, Bt Lt-Col and Col, CMG, CB); retired pay, 1923. *Address:* Baughurst House, Basingstoke.

Died 15 July 1945.

HORDERN, Rt Rev. Hugh Maudslay, MA; *b* 28 Sept. 1868; *s* of Herbert L. C. Hordern of Throwley House, near Faversham, Kent, and Emily Maria, *d* of Thomas Henry Maudslay of Banstead Park, Surrey; *m* 1895, Edith Augusta, *d* of John Glas Sandeman of 73 Sussex Gardens, Hyde Park; two *s* one *d. Educ:* Winchester; Christ Church, Oxford. Assistant Curate, Warnham, Sussex, 1892–94; Rector of Singleton, 1894–1910; Vicar of S Nicholas, Brighton, 1910–24; Diocesan Inspector of Schools, 1904–09; TCF 1913–18. Prebendary of Heathfield in Chichester Cathedral, 1922; Surrogate for Diocese of Chichester, 1922; Proctor in Convocation, 1924–30; Archdeacon of Lewes, 1923–30; Bishop of Lewes, 1929–46. Treasurer of Chichester Cathedral, 1929. *Address:* Brook Cottage, Slaugham, Sussex. *T:* Handcross 225.

Died 25 March 1949.

HORE, Sir (Charles Fraser) Adair, KBE 1925; CB 1919; *b* 8 Nov. 1874; *s* of Lieut-Col Fraser Salter Hore, Bombay, and Isabella, *d* of Rev. Charles Dawes, Mount Ephraim, Kent; *m* 1st, 1912, Elizabeth (*d* 1936), *widow of* late J. I. Belisha; 2nd, Jeanette (Polonia Restituta, 4 class, Poland), *d* of Johann Schärer von Rufs, Basle. *Educ:* Merchant Taylors' School; St John's College, Oxford (BA honours, Lit. Hum. 1897, Modern History, 1898). Entered Local Government Board, 1898; special investigator on Poor Law Administration abroad to Poor Law Commission, 1909; National Health Insurance Commission, 1912; Principal Assistant Secretary Ministry of Pensions, 1919–35; Permanent Secretary, Ministry of Pensions, 1935–41; Ministry of Petroleum, 1941–42. Polonia Restituta, 4 Class, Poland. *Publications:* Public Health and Social Conditions, 1909; Foreign and Colonial Systems of Poor Relief, 1911. *Recreations:* golf, travel. *Address:* Apple Tree Cottage, South-Godstone, Surrey. *T:* South-Godstone 2105. *Clubs:* Oxford and Cambridge, Roehampton.

Died 23 Jan. 1950.

HORMASJI BHIWANDIWALLA, Khan Bahadur Sir Dosabhai, Kt 1934. Landlord. *Address:* Bombay, India.

Died April 1940.

HORN, Sir Arthur Edwin, Kt 1937; CMG 1922; MD (London), BSc (London), MRCP; Consulting Physician to Colonial Office; Medical Secretary, Colonial Advisory Medical and Sanitary Committee, Colonial Office, 1923–24; *s* of William Horn, Forest Hill; unmarried. *Educ:* City of Westminster School; St Mary's Hospital; London University. Medical Officer, West African Medical Staff, in Gold Coast, Gambia, and Nigeria; Principal Medical Officer, Tanganyika Territory; Director of Medical and Sanitary Services, Malaya; Medical Secretary to Advisory Medical and Sanitary Committee for Tropical Africa (Colonial Office), 1910–12. *Publications:* An Investigation of Cerebro-spinal Meningitis in the Northern Territories of the Gold Coast (Society of Tropical Medicine and Hygiene, 1908); Health of Europeans in West Africa (Lancet, 1912); Health of Europeans in East Africa (Lancet, 1912). *Recreations:* shooting, sailing, golf. *Address:* 14 Wimpole Street, W1. *T:* Langham 3938; Cecil Lodge, Limpsfield, Surrey. *T:* Oxted 61. *Club:* East India and Sports.

Died 19 Dec. 1943.

HORN, Dr Gunnar; Norwegian Geologist and Explorer; Knight of the Royal Order of the North Star (Swedish); Geologist to the Norway Svalbard and Polar Sea Research Institution since 1924; *b* 25 June 1894; *e s* of late Fin Horn, Architect. *Educ:* Technical University, Trondheim. Royal School of Mines; Berlin Doctor's Degree. Mining Engineer, Spitsbergen, 1917–19; Oil Geologist, Trinidad and Venezuela, 1920–23; expeditions to Bear Island, 1924 and 1925; to Transcaspia (USSR), 1925; Spitsbergen, 1926; Leader expeditions to Franz Josef Land, 1929 and 1930, the latter year with the sealer Bratvaag, during which expedition Andrée's camp on White Island was discovered; Greenland, 1932; Lecture tour USA, 1931–32. *Address:* 13 Anton Schjoethsgate, Oslo, Norway.

Died 15 July 1946.

HORNBY, C. H. St John, BA, FSA; Director of W. H. Smith & Son, Ltd; Trustee of British Museum since 1936; Trustee of the Wallace Collection since 1933; *b* 25 June 1867; *e s* of Rev. C. E. Hornby of Ashendene, Herts; *m* 1898, Cicely, *e d* of Charles Barclay of Bayford, Herts; three *s* two *d*. *Educ:* Harrow; New College, Oxford. Rowed in Oxford University VIII, 1890. Called to the Bar, 1892. *Address:* Chantmarle, Dorset. *T:* Evershot 27. *Clubs:* Oxford and Cambridge, Athenæum, Royal Automobile, Beefsteak, MCC, Hurlingham.

Died 26 April 1946.

HORNBY, Brig.-Gen. Edmund John Phipps, VC 1900; CB 1911; CMG 1916; *b* 31 Dec. 1857; 2nd *s* of Admiral of the Fleet Sir G. Phipps Hornby, GCB; *m* 1895, Miss Jay of Blendon Hall, Bexley; two *d*. Was ADC to Earl Roberts, 1901–03; entered Royal Artillery, 1877; Captain, 1886; Major, 1896; Lt-Col 1903; Colonel, 1908; served Bechuanaland Expedition, 1884–85; South Africa, 1900 (VC, despatches, brevet Lieut-Col); European War, 1914–15 (despatches thrice, CMG); Brig.-Gen. commanding 4th Divisional Artillery, 1909–13; DL, JP Berkshire. *Address:* Thatched Cottage, Sonning, Berks. *T:* Sonning 3251.

Died 13 Dec. 1947.

HORNBY, Brig.-Gen. Montague Leyland, CB 1922; CMG 1917; DSO 1895; FRGS; late East Lancs Regt; late Comm. Lancashire Fusiliers Brig. (TF) with rank of Col; *b* 23 July 1870; *m* 1902, Harriet Millicent, *d* of Major Corbett Winder of Vaynor Park; four *d*. *Educ:* Shrewsbury; Royal Military College, Sandhurst. Entered army, 1889; Capt. 1900; Bt Maj. 1904; Bt Lt-Col 1916; Bt Col 1918; Col 1920; formerly employed with the Punjab Frontier Force and with the King's African Rifles, and as Staff Officer to HM Commissioner and Commander-in-Chief, Somaliland Protectorate (local Lieut-Colonel, 1904–07); Brigade Major 70th Brigade, 1914–15; commanded 8th (Service) Batt. Yorks and Lancs Regt (temp. Lt-Col), 1915–16; Brig. Commander, 1916–19; served with Waziristan Delimitation Escort, 1894 (severely wounded, despatches, DSO, medal with clasp); North-West Frontier, India, 1897–98 (medal with two clasps); Jubaland, East Africa, 1898 (medal with clasp); operations in Unyoro, Uganda, 1899 (clasp); Nandi Expedition, East Africa, 1900 (despatches, medal with clasp); Somaliland, 1902–04 (despatches, Bt Major, clasp); European War, 1914–18 (severely wounded, despatches 6 times, Bt Lt-Col and Col, CMG); retired pay, 1927; JP Salop. *Publications:* How to March, 1914; The Platoon Roll-Book, 1915; How to Buy Land in Canada, 1913; A Plan for British Community Settlements in Canada, 1931; The Empire Builders, 1935; The Migration Impasse, 1935; Canada and British Immigration, 1936; The Case for Organised Empire Migration, 1937; Canada and Post-War Immigration, 1946. *Address:* Lethbridge, Alberta, Canada. *Club:* Army and Navy.

Died 21 Nov. 1948.

HORNE, Sir Allan; *see* Horne, Sir J. A.

HORNE, Sir Edgar; *see* Horne, Sir W. E.

HORNE, Edward Butler, CMG 1934; OBE 1928; Colonial Civil Service, retired, 1934, as Senior Commissioner, Kenya Colony; *b* 1881; *s* of H. J. D. Horne and Margaret, *d* of Rev. Hon. G. Hastings; *g s* of Sir William Horne; *m* M. R. Wade; one *s*. *Educ:* Bedford Grammar School. Major Home Guard, 1940–45. *Address:* St Helens, Galway, Eire. *Club:* East India and Sports.

Died 16 Jan. 1947.

HORNE, Col Edward William, CB 1936; CMG 1919; CBE 1918; Vice-Lieutenant for County of Caithness; *b* 1857; *e surv. s* of Major James Horne, of Stirkoke, Caithness; *m* 1882, Marjorie, *d* of late George Miller Cunningham of Leithen, Peeblesshire; one *d*. *Educ:* King's College School; Sandhurst. Joined 71st Highland Light Infantry, 1877; retired, 1882; joined 3rd Batt. Seaforth Highlanders, 1883; retired, 1911; rejoined 1914 and served till termination of the War; Chairman Territorial Force Association of Caithness and of County Council, 1929–38. *Address:* Thuster, Wick, Caithness. *T:* Wick 140.

Died 16 April 1941.

HORNE, Frederick Newman; Chairman and Managing Director of Horne Brothers, Ltd; *b* 4 March 1863; *s* of George Francis Horne, Bedfont, Middlesex; *m* 1893, Anna Florence Mary Wright, Weston-super-Mare; four *s* one *d*. *Educ:* Bramham House, Surbiton. Devoted to the building up of Horne Brothers, of which business, until it was turned into a Limited Liability Company in 1923 with a capital of £1,000,000, he was the sole proprietor. *Recreations:* shooting, motoring, farming. *Address:* North Frith, Tonbridge, Kent. *TA:* and *T:* Tonbridge 372. *Club:* Royal Automobile.

Died 3 Oct. 1946.

HORNE, Sir (James) Allan, Kt 1919; *b* 1876; *e s* of late Arthur Horne; *m* 1924, Auriol (*d* 1930), *o c* of late Hon. Alistair George Hay and *widow* of Capt. Noel Barran, 2nd Life Guards; one *s*. *Educ:* privately. Formerly senior resident partner of Jardine, Skinner & Co., East India merchants, of Calcutta; was Controller of Munitions, Bombay, during the latter part of European War of 1914–18. *Address:* 74 Park Street, W1. *T:* Mayfair 2269. *Club:* Oriental.

Died 3 Feb. 1944.

HORNE, Maynard, MA, MBBC (Cantab), LRCP, MRCS; Consulting Anaesthetist to St George's Hospital, SW, and Hospital for Women, Soho Square; *b* 30 March 1870; *s* of late Rev. William Horne, MA (Cantab), and Florence Walpole Maynard; *m* 1894, Lillie, *y d* of late Thomas Pearson; one *s* two *d*. *Educ:* Haileybury; Trinity College, Cambridge; St George's Hospital. Held house appointments at St George's Hospital for two years; formerly senior anæsthetist to Seamen's Hospital, Greenwich; National Orthopædic Hospital, and other hospitals in London; Capt. RAMC (T), 2nd London General Territorial Hospital, attached to 26th British General Hospital, BEF, for 18 months; served with 53rd General Hospital, BEF. *Recreations:* shooting, fishing, lawn tennis. *Address:* 55 Ennismore Gardens, SW7. *T:* Kensington 8775.

Died 7 Feb. 1944.

HORNE, Sir (William) Edgar, 1st Bt *cr* 1929; Chairman Prudential Assurance Co.; JP, London; DL, Sunderland; *b* 21 Jan. 1856; *s* of Edgar Horne; *m* Margery (*d* 1939), *d* of George Anderson May, of Elford, Staffordshire; two *s* one *d*. *Educ:* Westminster. Past President of the Surveyors' Institution; Alderman of the Westminster City Council; Mayor, 1923–24; contested N Devon (LU), 1906; MP (U) Guildford Division of Surrey, 1910–22. *Recreations:* travel, golf, shooting. *Heir: s* Alan Edgar [*b* 19 Sept. 1889; *m* 1st, 1915, Henriette Kelly (*d*

1919); one *d*; 2nd 1923, Roslyn, *d* of John Brian Robinson; one *s*]. *Address:* 46 Orchard Court, Portman Square, W1. *T:* Welbeck 8690; The Cottage, Shackleford, Surrey; The Lodge, Lairg, Sutherland. *Clubs:* Carlton, City of London, Arts.

Died 26 Sept. 1941.

HORNE, William Ogilvie, CSI 1912; *y s* of Major James Horne, of Stirkoke, Caithness; *m* 1900, Hope Helena, *d* of late Henry Irwin, CIE; two *s* two *d. Educ:* Clifton College; Trinity College, Oxford. Entered Indian Civil Service, 1882; served in Madras; Collector, District Magistrate and Agent to the Governor in Vizagapatam, 1896–1901; Inspector-General of Police, 1902–08; Commissioner of Separate Revenue, 1908; Commissioner of Land Revenue and Forests, Madras, 1910; retired, 1914. *Publication:* Work and Sport in the Old ICS, 1928. *Address:* Oakbank, Birnam, Perthshire.

Died 10 Jan. 1943.

HORNELL, Vice-Adm. Sir Robert Arthur, KBE 1941; DSO 1918; Croix de Guerre with palm; RN, retired; Naval Officer in charge of a British Base Port; *b* 1877; *e s* of late Robert Hornell, Barrister-at-law; *m* May Augusta Emmerson Sheean; one *d. Educ:* Cheam School; HMS Britannia. Entered Navy, 1894; served continuously at sea, 1894–1928; ADC to the King, 1929; promoted and retired as Rear-Admiral, 1929; Vice-Admiral, retired, 1934; rejoined at the outbreak of the War; Commodore of Convoys for 2½ years. Vice-Chairman NB Apostleship of the sea. *Address:* Lodge Hill Way, Lower Bourne, Farnham, Surrey. *Clubs:* Junior United Service; Royal Naval (Portsmouth).

Died 4 May 1949.

HORNELL, Sir William (Woodward), Kt 1931; CIE 1918; LLD (Hong Kong); *b* 18 Sept. 1878; 2nd *s* of Robert Hornell, Barrister-at-law, Inner Temple, and Elizabeth Brooking Cornish; *m* 1946, Kathleen Veronica, *widow* of Arthur Brown. *Educ:* Radley; Trinity College, Oxford. Appointed to Indian Educational Service, 1901; Professor of English, Presidency College, Calcutta, 1902; Inspector of European Schools, Bengal, 1903; Assistant Director of Public Instruction, Bengal, 1906; resigned Indian Educational Service and joined Board of Education, Whitehall, 1908; Assistant Director of Special Inquiries and Reports, Board of Education, 1910; Secretary Imperial Education Conference, 1911; Director of Public Instruction, Bengal, 1913–24; Vice-Chancellor, University of Hong Kong, 1924–37; Member of the Calcutta University Commission, 1917–19. Hon. Resident Adviser, College of the Sea, Selwyn House, Endsleigh Street, WC1, 1942–46. *Address:* c/o National Bank of India, Ltd, 26 Bishopsgate, EC2. *Club:* United University.

Died 22 Sept. 1950.

HORNIBLOW, Col Frederick, CB 1917; *b* 27 Oct. 1862; *s* of George Horniblow, MD, late 72nd Highlanders; *m* 1889, Ellen Augusta, *d* of late Patrick Scott, HEICS. *Educ:* Malvern. Entered army, 1883; Col 1908; DAAG, Ceylon, 1895–99; Officer in charge of ASC Records, 1914–18; served South Africa, 1900–02 (Queen's medal and clasp). *Address:* Glendon Cottage, Tekel's Avenue, Camberley, Surrey. *T:* Camberley 268. *Club:* United Service.

Died 10 April 1945.

HORNIMAN, Benjamin Guy; journalist and author; President, Indian Journalists' Association; *b* Dovercourt, Essex, 1873; *s* of William Horniman, Paymaster-in-Chief, RN; unmarried. *Educ:* Portsmouth Grammar School and Queen's Service House. Editor Southern Daily Mail, 1897–1900; subsequently on leading English journals; Assistant Editor Calcutta Statesman, 1906–12; Special Correspondent Eastern Bengal, 1907–08; met Dalai Lama on his flight from Lhassa in 1910; Delhi Durbar, 1911; founded, with Sir Pherozeshah Mehta,

Bombay Chronicle, 1913; a leader of Home Rule for India movement; deported to England, 1919; after continued exclusion for over six years, landed Colombo and India Jan. 1926; Founder and Editor Indian National Herald, 1926–29; later associated with conduct of Bombay Chronicle and associated journals; Editor-in-Chief, Bombay Sentinel, 1933–45. *Publications:* Amritsar and our Duty to India; The Agony of Amritsar (with Helena Normanton); various pamphlets and lectures. *Recreations:* housework and loafing. *Address:* Bombay, India. *Cables:* Horniman Bombay.

Died 16 Oct. 1948.

HORNSBY, Sir Bertram, Kt 1926; CBE 1919; Grand Cordon Order of the Nile (Egypt). *Address:* The Old Rectory, Ifield, near Crawley, Sussex. *Club:* Oriental.

Died 30 June 1943.

HORNSBY-WRIGHT, Lt-Col Guy Jefferys, DSO 1919; MA; *b* 1872; *e s* of late Deputy-Surgeon-General J. C. Hornsby-Wright; unmarried. *Educ:* Eastbourne College; University College, London; Emmanuel College, Cambridge. Assistant Master at Felsted School (House-Master and Senior Master of Army Side), 1897–1926; Fellow and Secretary of Emmanuel College, Cambridge and Secretary of Board of Military Studies, Cambridge University, 1926–38; served European War, 1914–19, commanded 2/5 Bn Essex Regt and (in France) 15th Bn Essex Regt (despatches twice, DSO). *Publication:* Alumni Felstedienses (1852–1903). *Address:* 9 Broadwater Down, Tunbridge Wells. *Club:* Athenæum.

Died 4 Oct. 1941.

HORROCKS, Walter James Hodgson, MC; *b* 1897; *s* of late R. H. Horrocks, JP, Salkeld Hall; *m* 1929, Mary, 3rd *d* of late J. Park, Benton, Northumberland. *Educ:* Harrow. Straight from Harrow to commission in Gordon Highlanders; later transferred to RFC and served two years in France, MC 1917; High Sheriff of Cumberland, 1939. *Recreations:* golf, lawn tennis, cricket, shooting, fishing. *Address:* Salkeld Hall, Penrith. *T:* Langwathby 224. *Clubs:* County, Carlisle.

Died 5 Jan. 1946.

HORROCKS, Col Sir William Heaton, KCMG 1918; CB 1917; MB, BSc; Editor of RAMC Journal; *b* 25 Aug. 1859; *m* 1894, Minna (*d* 1921), *d* of Rev. J. C. Moore, Connor, Co. Antrim; one *s* one *d.* Captain RAMC 1887; Major, 1899; Lieut-Col 1911; Col 1915; Brig.-Gen. (temp.) 1919; Hon. Surgeon to HM 1914; Chadwick Gold Medal, 1914; Stewart Prize of British Medical Association, 1916; Member Mediterranean Fever Commission, Royal Society, 1904–05; Chairman Anti-Gas Committee; Director of Hygiene, War Office, 1919, and Chairman of the Army Hygiene Committee; Fellow of the Royal Sanitary Institute; Hon. Fellow of Society of Medical Officers of Health. *Publications:* Bacteriological Examination of Water; joint-Editor 2nd edition of Notter and Firth's Theory and Practice of Hygiene; medical papers and reports. *Address:* Birch Mead, Hersham.

Died 26 Jan. 1941.

HORSBURGH, Benjamin, CMG 1921; VD 1920; *b* 10 April 1868; unmarried. *Educ:* Heriot's School and University, Edinburgh; MA. Entered Ceylon Civil Service, 1889; served as Chairman, Municipal Council, and Mayor of Colombo; Government agent, North Central, North-Western, and Northern Provinces; Excise Commissioner, Food Controller, 1919–20, and Controller of Revenue; acted for several periods as Colonial Secretary and once as Governor; retired, 1923; Major (retired) Ceylon Garrison Artillery. *Publications:* papers on Place Names for the Ceylon Antiquary. *Recreations:* fishing, shooting, sailing, golf. *Address:* 25 Nile Grove, Edinburgh.

Died 10 April 1935.

HORSLEY, Terence Beresford; Editor Sunday Empire News; *b* 2 April 1904; *e s* of late Albert Beresford Horsley, W Hartlepool; *m* 1932, Judith Rhoda Cartmell Ridley; two *s* one *d. Educ:* Dragon's, Oxford; Rugby. From 1930 to present day spent in many branches of journalism with a break between 1940 and 1946 when served as pilot in Fleet Air Arm with rank of Lt-Comdr (A) RNVR Took up soaring, 1935; Holder of Silver 'C'. *Publications:* Odyssey of An Out of Work, 1930; Round England in an £8 Car, 1932; Fishing for Trout and Salmon, 1944; Soaring Flight, 1945; Sporting Pageant, 1947; The Long Flight, 1947; Flying and Fishing, 1948; Find, Fix and Strike, 1944; Gliding and Power Flying (under name of String-Bag), 1946. *Recreations:* soaring, wild-fowling, fishing, tennis (*not* Lawn), and curiosity. *Address:* Southwold, Southdowns Rd, Hale, Cheshire. *T:* Altrincham 2010. *Clubs:* Royal Aero; Clarendon, Tennis and Racquets (Manchester).

Died 24 April 1949.

HORSNELL, Horace; author; Dramatic Critic to Observer since 1920; Tatler since 1942; *b* 12 June 1882. Served with Royal Engineers, BEF, 1914–19 (despatches twice); Dramatic Critic to Outlook, 1927–28; Punch, 1930–31. *Publications:* Novels: The Bankrupt, 1913; The Talking Woman, 1922; Man Alone, 1940; Castle Cottage, 1940; Miss Fanny, 1941; The Cool of the Evening, 1942. Memoirs: The Album, 1945. Plays: Advertising April, 1923, and Pursuit of Adonis, 1933 (with Herbert Farjeon); The Queen's Pleasure, 1937. Verse: The Tyro's Vade Mecum, 1934; The Horoscope, 1934; The Olympic Game, 1939; The Phoenix' Nest, 1947. *Address:* 7 Stone Buildings, Lincoln's Inn, WC2.

Died 10 Feb. 1949.

HORTON, Sir Henry, Kt 1935; Chairman and Managing Director, Wilson and Horton, Ltd, Publishers of New Zealand Herald and Weekly News; *b* Timaru, NZ, 14 May 1870; *e s* of late Alfred George and Jessie Haliburton Horton; *m* 1897, Jessie Buchanan, *d* of James Thomson, Auckland; two *s. Educ:* Christ's College, Christchurch, NZ; Auckland University College; BA, NZ University. Director of NZ Insurance Co.; local Director, Colonial Sugar Co.; Member Auckland Patriotic Society; Commander Brother of Order of St John of Jerusalem. *Recreations:* golf and angling. *Address:* 240 Remuera Road, Auckland, SE2, NZ. *TA:* Herald, Auckland, NZ. *T:* 24,596. *Clubs:* Northern, Auckland.

Died 19 July 1943.

HORTON, William; JP Staffordshire and Denbighshire; *b* 1854; *m* 1885, Edith M. (*d* 1943), *d* of W. H. Sabin, Moseley. *Educ:* Birmingham Grammar School; London. High Sheriff of Denbighshire, 1935. *Address:* Bryndinarth, Colwyn Bay, Denbighshire.

Died 25 Jan. 1944.

HORTON-STARKIE, Rev. Prebendary Le Gendre George, MA; Vicar of Wellow, near Bath, since 1886; Prebendary of Combe 10th in Wells Cathedral since 1916; *b* 12 July 1859; *o s* of late George William Horton, MA, Vicar of Wellow, Somerset, and Anne Elizabeth, *d* of late Le Gendre Nicholas Starkie of Huntroyd and Ashton Hall, Lancashire; *m* 1891; Mabel Augusta Hawksworth (*d* 1933), *e d* of Rev. Frederick Fawkes, Farnley Hall, Yorks; two *s. Educ:* Eton; Trinity College, Cambridge; Wells Theological College. Second-Lieutenant 1st Somerset Militia, 1877; Curate of Bilton, Warwickshire, 1883–86; assumed by Royal licence additional name of Starkie, 1918. *Recreations:* rowing, shooting, hunting. *Address:* Wellow Vicarage, near Bath, Somerset. *TA:* Wellow, Bath. *T:* Combe Down 3049. *Clubs:* Carlton, MCC.

Died 9 May 1943.

HORWOOD, Hon. Sir William Henry, KCMG 1944; Kt 1904; Chief Justice, Newfoundland, 1902–44; Representative on Peace Commission established under treaty between Great Britain and USA, May 1916; *b* 5 Nov. 1862; *m* 1908, Julia, OBE 1941, *d* of Rev. Geo. Hutchinson. Barrister, 1885; Bencher, Law Society, 1891; QC 1895; elected to House of Assembly, 1894, 1897, and 1900; Colonial Secretary, 1894–95; member of Executive Council, 1894–97, and 1900–02; Acting Attorney-General, 1897; Minister of Justice and Attorney-General for Newfoundland, 1900–02; delegate from Government of Newfoundland to Ottawa Conference to discuss with members of Canadian Cabinet terms of proposed union of the Colony with Canada, 1895; acted as Leader of Government in 1901; Chief Justice of Newfoundland, 1902; Administrator of the Government, Sept. 1902 to Feb. 1903, and May to Sept. 1904, also 1909–12–1913–14 and on subsequent occasions and also in 1935 and 1938 during absence of the Governor served as Administrator and Chairman of the Commission of Government; Knight of Grace of the Order of St John, 1920. *Address:* 15 Church Hill, St John's, Newfoundland.

Died 7 April 1945.

HORWOOD, Brig.-Gen. Sir William Thomas Francis, GBE 1928; KCB 1921; CB 1919; DSO 1917; retired; late 5th Lancers; *b* Nov. 1868; *y s* of late C. Horwood, of the Manor House, Broadwater, Sussex; *m* Violet (*d* 1941), *e d* of late Lieut-General J. G. Fife, of Goring on Thames; one *d.* Recruiting Officer and Adjutant 49th Regimental District, 1900–02; 2nd Provisional Battalion, 1902; Brig.-Maj. 24th Field Army Brigade, 1902–04; War Office, 1902–10; Chief of Police, London and North-Eastern Railway, 1911–14; DAAG War Office, 1914–15; late Provost-Marshal, General Headquarters, BEF (Officer Legion of Honour, Order of Leopold, Order of Crown and Croix de Guerre of Belgium; Commander Order of Dannebrog, 2nd Class Rising Sun (Japan), Grand Cordon Crown of Roumania, Crown of Italy, and Star of Ethiopia, despatches seven times); Asst Commissioner, Metropolitan Police, 1918–20; Commissioner, Metropolitan Police, 1920–28. *Recreations:* shooting, yachting. *Club:* Naval and Military.

Died 16 Nov. 1943.

HOSE, Edward Shaw, CMG 1924; *b* 25 Nov. 1871; *s* of late George Frederick Hose, DD, Bishop of Singapore, Labuan and Sarawak; unmarried. *Educ:* Blundell's School, Tiverton. Junior Officer in the Civil Service of the State of Perak, 1891; held various appointments in the Malayan Civil Service; British Resident, Negri Sembilan, Federated Malay States, 1922; Acting Chief Secretary to Government, Federated Malay States, 10 May 1923 to 25 Oct. 1923; Colonial Secretary, Straits Settlements, 18 July 1924–24 Dec. 1925; Officer Administering the Government of the Straits Settlements and High Commissioner for the Malay States, 8 May 1925 to 6 Nov. 1925. *Address:* The Manor House, Normandy, Guildford, Surrey.

Died 12 Sept. 1946.

HOSKEN, Clifford; see Keverne, R.

HOSKIN, Alan Simson; Assistant Secretary, Board of Trade; *b* 16 Sept. 1886; *e s* of late William Hoskin; *m* 1919, Estelle Painter; one *d. Educ:* Mill Hill School; Trinity College, Cambridge. *Address:* 36 Meadway, NW11. *T:* Speedwell 8323. *Club:* Reform.

Died 24 Oct. 1945.

HOSKINS, Maj.-Gen. Sir (Arthur) Reginald, KCB 1919; CMG 1916; DSO 1902; *b* 30 May 1871; *s* of Thomas Hoskins of Belgrave Road, SW; *m* 1914, Myfanwy, *d* of Thomas Williams, N Wales; one *d. Educ:* Westminster; Sandhurst; Staff College, Camberley. Entered army, 1891; Capt. 1900; served Dongola Expedition, 1896 (despatches), Nile Expedition, 1897–99 (despatches thrice, 4th class Medjidie, Khedive's medal 9 clasps, Bt Major, British medal); South Africa, 1899–1902 (despatches, Queen's medal 3 clasps, King's medal 2 clasps, DSO); East Africa, 1902–03 (despatches, medal and clasp); European War, 1914–18 (despatches twice, KCB, CMG, prom. Lt-Gen.); Commander-in-Chief, East Africa, 1917; Inspector-General, King's African Rifles, 1913–15; Commanding N Midlands TF, 1919–23; retired pay, 1923; Colonel N Stafford Regiment, 1921–36; Principal, Philip Stott College, Overstone, 1928; Principal, Bonar Law College, 1929–38. *Address:* Quenington Court, Fairford, Glos. *Club:* Carlton.

Died 7 Feb. 1942.

HOSKYN, Col John Cunningham Moore, CBE 1918; DSO 1918; Order of the Crown of Italy; Indian Army; retired; *b* 20 Dec. 1875; *s* of John T. Hoskyn, Lieut RN, and Mary Moore; *m* Dorothy Mary ffolliott Powell (*d* 1920). Served European War, 1914–18 in Mesopotamia Persia and Caucasus (CBE, DSO, Bt Lieut-Col, despatches four times); Military Attaché, HBM Legation, Teheran, 1918–20; Commandant 10/4th Bombay Grenadiers, 1921–24; retired, 1925. *Club:* United Service.

Died 19 Oct. 1941.

HOSKYNS, Sir Chandos Wren, 14th Bt *cr* 1676; Flying Officer in RAF; *b* 14 Dec. 1923; *e s* of Rev. Canon Sir Edwyn Hoskyns, 13th Baronet, and Mary Trym Budden; *S* father, 1937. *Educ:* Winchester Coll. *Heir: b* John Chevallier, *b* 1926. *Address:* 11 Millington Road, Cambridge. *T:* Cambridge 4822.

Died 3 April 1945.

HOSTE, Dixon Edward; *b* Aldershot, 23 July 1861; *s* of Major-General Hoste, CB; *m* 1894, Amelia Gertrude Broomhall, *d* of the General Secretary of the China Inland Mission; three *s. Educ:* Clifton College; RMA Woolwich. Commission in Royal Artillery, 1880; resigned commission, 1884, having served four years in England; went out to China as a missionary in connection with the China Inland Mission, 1885; accompanied six young Cambridge men, being thus one of The Cambridge Band, who made some stir at the time; worked eleven years in Shansi (North China), at that time a month's journey from Shanghai, wearing Chinese dress, eating Chinese food and living in a Chinese house; Superintendent of the Mission in Shansi, 1894; on returning from furlough in 1898, was appointed Superintendent of the Mission in the province of Honan (North Central) and in 1901 became acting General Director of the China Inland Mission; General Director of the China Inland Mission, 1902–35. Was interned in Shanghai, War of 1939–45. *Publications:* numerous articles on topics connected with Missionary work in China; also devotional articles. *Recreations:* reading, used to play lawn tennis when younger. *Address:* c/o China Inland Mission, Newington Green, N16.

Died 11 May 1946.

HOTSON, Sir (John) Ernest (Buttery), KCSI 1930; CSI 1926; OBE 1918; MA; *b* 17 March 1877; *s* of late Hamilton Andrew Hotson, Manager, British Linen Bank; *m* 1924, Mildred Alice, *d* of late A. B. Steward, ICS. *Educ:* Edinburgh Academy; Magdalen College, Oxford. Entered Indian Civil Service (Bombay), 1900; Assistant Collector; Political Service in Kathiawar; Under and Deputy Secretary, Bombay; Private Secretary to the Governor of Bombay; Collector; military duty 1914–18, attaining rank of Lieut-Col; Commandant Mekran Levy Corps; Consul at Shiraz; Secretary and Chief Secretary, Bombay; Member of Council of Governor of Bombay, 1926–31; acting Governor of Bombay, 1931. *Publication:* Editor, Philatelic Journal of India, 1923–1928. *Recreations:* golf, natural history, stamp collecting. *Address:* c/o Grindlay & Co., Ltd, 54 Parliament Street, SW1. *Clubs:* East India and Sports; University, Edinburgh; Byculla, Bombay.

Died 13 May 1944.

HOUGHTON, Alanson Bigelow; *b* Cambridge Mass, USA, 10 Oct. 1863; *s* of Amory Houghton, jr, and Ellen Ann Bigelow; *m* 1890, Adelaide Wellington of Corning, New York; one *s* three *d. Educ:* BA Harvard, 1886; Post-Graduate work, Göttingen, Berlin, Paris. Entered manufacture of glass at Corning, New York, 1889; 2nd Vice-President, 1903–10; President, 1910–18; since Chairman Board Corning Glass Works; Director Metropolitan Life Insurance Co., Carnegie Endowment for International Peace, Brookings Institution, Washington, DC; Institute for Advanced Study, Princeton, NJ etc.; Ex-Pres. Board of Education, Corning; twice Representative Presidential Elector, Member 66th and 67th Congresses (1919–23) 37th NY District; resigned to become Ambassador Extraordinary and Minister Plenipotentiary to Germany, Feb. 1922–Feb. 1925; American Ambassador at the Court of St James's, 1925–29. *Recreation:* golf. *Address:* The Knoll, Corning, New York; 3003 Massachusetts Avenue, Washington, DC, USA. *Clubs:* Century, Union, Harvard, Metropolitan, University, New York; Metropolitan, Chevy Chase, Burning Tree, Washington; Somerset, Boston.

Died 16 Sept. 1941.

HOULDSWORTH, Sir Henry Hamilton, 2nd Bt *cr* 1887; landed proprietor; member of various Councils and Committees; Major (retired), Princess Louise's 4th Batt. Argyll and Sutherland Highlanders; Capt. Special Reserve; *b* 17 Sept. 1867; *s* of 1st Bt and Elisabeth, *d* of Walter Crum, Thornliebank, Renfrewshire; *S* father, 1917. *Educ:* Eton College; Christ Church, Oxford (MA). Patron of one living. Served S African War, 1900–01 (Queen's medal and three clasps). *Heir: b* William Thomas Reginald, CBE. *Address:* Coodham, Kilmarnock. *Clubs:* Conservative; County, Ayr; Prestwick Golf; Troon Golf.

Died 18 Dec. 1947.

HOULDSWORTH, J. Hamilton; DL; JP; *b* 11 Aug. 1867; *o surv. s* of James Houldsworth of Coltness and Katharine J., *d* of Canon H. McGrath; *m* 1891, Albinia Mary, *d* of Rev. Filmer Sulivan; two *s* one *d. Educ:* Eton; Trinity College, Cambridge. Joined the Royal Scots Greys, 1889; retired 1895; served European War on the Staff; Chairman and Director of Coltness Iron Co., and other companies. *Recreations:* shooting, fishing, golf, etc. *Address:* Castlebank, Lanark. *Clubs:* Army and Navy; New, Edinburgh.

Died 5 Dec. 1941.

HOUSE, George; MP (Lab) St Pancras, North, since 1945; Vice-Chairman Parliamentary Committee of the LCC; *b* 7 March 1892; *m* 1921; two *d. Educ:* Queen Elizabeth Hospital, Bristol. Printer, then Constructional Steelwork Erector, then trade union organiser. *Address:* Wrythe Green, Carshalton, Surrey. *T:* Wallington 4082.

Died 8 Feb. 1949.

HOUSSEMAYNE DU BOULAY, Brig.-Gen. Noel Wilmot, CMG 1916; *b* 25 Dec. 1861; 2nd *s* of late Rev. J. T. H. Du Boulay and Alice Mead, *y d* of Rev. G. J. Cornish. Served Sudan, 1884–85 (medal 2 clasps, bronze star); Japan and China War, 1894–95 (Japanese War medal); attached to Japanese Army Headquarters; China, 1900 (medal with clasp); European War, 1914–18 (despatches twice, CMG). *Address:* c/o Lloyds Bank, Cox's and King's Branch, 6 Pall Mall, SW1.

Died 25 Nov. 1949.

HOUSTON, George, RSA; landscape painter and etcher; *b* Dairy, Ayrshire. Has exhibited in Canada, Australia, New Zealand, America, and on the Continent. Representative works acquired by Glasgow, Walker Art Gallery, Liverpool, Preston, Oldham, Scottish Modern Art Association, Canterbury Art Society, and

Wellington, NZ. *Recreations:* fishing, shooting. *Address:* Dalry, Ayrshire. *T:* Dalry, Ayrshire 2129. *Club:* Glasgow Art (Glasgow).

Died 5 Oct. 1947.

HOUSTON, Sir Thomas, Kt 1927; OBE 1919; BA, MD; Major; Ex-President of Ulster Medical Society; late Lecturer in Medical Jurisprudence, now Pro-Chancellor, Queen's University, Belfast; Consulting Clinical Pathologist, Royal Victoria Hospital, Belfast. *Educ:* Queen's College, Belfast. *Publications:* on Hæmatology, Pathology, and Bacteriology. *Recreations:* golf and tennis. *Address:* 75 University Road, Belfast. *T:* 22556. *Club:* Union (Belfast).

Died 21 June 1949.

HOWARD DE WALDEN, 8th Baron *cr* 1597; **Thomas Evelyn Scott-Ellis;** Baron Seaford, 1826; late Lieut 10th Hussars; *b* 9 May 1880; *s* of 7th Baron and Blanche, *e d* of William Holden, Palace House, Lancashire [she married, 2nd, 2nd Baron Ludlow (*d* 1922), and died 1911]; *S* father, 1899; *m* 1912, Margherita, CBE 1920, *d* of late Charles van Raalte of Brownsea Island, Dorset; one *s* five *d*. *Educ:* Eton; Sandhurst. Served South Africa, 1899–1901; European War, 1914–19. *Operas:* (with J. Holbrooke) The Children of Don; Dylan; Bronwen and (plays) Lanval; Heraclius. *Heir:* *s* Major Hon. John Osmael Scott-Ellis [*b* 27 Nov. 1912; *m* 1934, Countess Irene Harrach, *y d* of Count Hans Albrecht Harrach; three *d*].

Died 5 Nov. 1946.

HOWARD, Sir Albert, Kt 1934; CIE 1914; MA; ARCS, FHS; Hon. Fellow of the Imperial College; *b* 8 Dec. 1873; *s* of Richard Howard; *m* 1st, 1905, Gabrielle L. C. Matthaei (*d* 1930), Fellow of Newnham College, Cambridge; no *c*; 2nd, 1931, Louise Ernestine Matthaei, Chief of Agricultural Section, International Labour Office, formerly Fellow and Director of Studies, Newnham College, Cambridge. *Educ:* Royal College of Science, London; St John's College, Camb. (Foundation Scholar). First Class Hons Nat. Science Tripos, 1898; BA 1899; MA 1902. Mycologist and Agricultural Lecturer, Imperial Department of Agriculture for the West Indies, 1899–1902; Botanist to the South-Eastern Agricultural College, Wye, 1903–05; Imperial Economic Botanist to the Government of India, 1905–24; Director of the Institute of Plant Industry, Indore, and Agricultural Adviser to States in Central India and Rajputana, 1924–31; Editor of Soil and Health. *Publications:* Crop Production in India, 1924; The Development of Indian Agriculture, 1928; The Application of Science to Crop Production, 1929; The Waste Products of Agriculture, 1931; An Agricultural Testament, 1940; Farming and Gardening for Disease or Health, 1945; numerous papers on botanical and agricultural subjects in Journal of Agricultural Science, Agricultural Journal of India, Memoirs of Dept of Agriculture of India. *Recreation:* travel. *Address:* 14 Liskeard Gardens, Blackheath, SE3. *T:* Greenwich 2879. *Club:* Farmers'.

Died 20 Oct. 1947.

HOWARD, Col Francis James Leigh, CBE 1918; DSO 1917; retired; *b* Delhi, 19 May 1870; *s* of Lieut-Colonel T. Howard, RE, and H. C. Plummer; *m* 1905, Mrs M. E. Campbell; no *c*. *Educ:* Dulwich College; Sandhurst. 8th The King's (Liverpool) Regt, 1890–93; RASC, 1893–1923; Egyptian Army, 1895–1905; Expedition to Dongola, 1896; Nile Expeditions, 1897, 1898 and 1899 (despatches thrice, 4th class of the Medijie, Brevet of Major); Governor of Red Sea Litoral, 1904–05, 4th class of the Osmanieh; served European War. *Recreations:* fishing, shooting and golf. *Club:* United Service.

Died 27 April 1942.

HOWARD, Col Henry Cecil Lloyd, CB 1946; CMG 1919; DSO 1917; one of HM Body Guard of Hon. Corps of Gentlemen-at-Arms since 1935; Colonel 16th/5th Lancers, 1943; *b* 30 Aug. 1882; *o s* of late Col H. R. L. Howard, CB, 16th Lancers, and Violet Mary Barnard, *d* of late Capt. H. B. Hankey; *m* 1912, Irene F. N., *d* of late Col Hon. George Gough, CB. *Educ:* Eton; Royal Military College, Sandhurst. 2nd Lt 16th Lancers, 1901; served South African War (Queen's medal with four clasps); passed Staff College, 1911; served European War, 1914–18 (wounded, despatches nine times, DSO and bar, CMG, Brevets of Major and Lt-Col, Order of Crown of Italy and Croce di Guerra, French Croix de Guerre); Lt-Col commanding 16th Lancers and 16/5th Lancers, 1921–25; Col, 1922; Assistant Commandant Royal Military College, Sandhurst, 1925–29; commanded 6th (Midland) Cavalry Brigade, 1929–31; AQMG, Eastern Command, 1931–34 and 1939–41 (re-employed); retd 1934; ADC to the King, 1933–34; High Sheriff of Flintshire, 1937. DL Denbighshire, JP Flintshire. *Address:* Wigfair, St Asaph, N Wales. *T:* Trefnant 314. *Club:* Cavalry.

Died 24 Jan. 1950.

HOWARD, Sir Henry Fraser, KCIE 1923; CSI 1919; CIE 1913; Fellow of St John's College, Cambridge, and Senior Bursar since 1923; *b* 1874; *m* 1913; Mabel Rosa (*d* 1923), *d* of R. J. Roney-Dougal; two *s* three *d*. *Educ:* Aldenham School; Trinity Hall, Cambridge. Classical Tripos, 1895, Class 1, Division 1. Indian Civil Service, 1896; Superintendent, Revision of Imperial Gazetteer for Bengal, 1904; Under-Secretary to Government of India, Finance Department, 1905; Collector of Customs, Calcutta, 1909–13; Controller of Currency, India, 1914–16; Officiating Secretary to Government of India, Commerce and Industry Department, 1916; Sec. Govt of India, Finance Dept 1917–20; Temporary Finance Member of the Viceroy's Executive Council, 1919; Controller of Finance, India Office, 1920; Sec. Indian Retrenchment (Inchcape) Committee, 1922–23. *Publications:* India and the Gold Standard; Finances of St John's College, Cambridge, 1511–1926. *Address:* Traverston, 9 West Road, Cambridge. *Clubs:* East India and Sports, Leander; Bengal, Calcutta.

Died 19 Oct. 1943.

HOWARD, Leslie; actor; *b* London, 3 April 1893; *m* Ruth Evelyn Martin; one *s* one *d*. *Educ:* Dulwich. Bank Clerk; served in Army, discharged, 1917; first appearance on stage as Jerry in Peg o' My Heart, 1917; toured as Charley in Charley's Aunt, 1917; first London appearance, New Theatre, 1918; played in Our Mr Hepplewhite, Mr Pim Passes By, The Young Person in Pink, etc.; first New York appearance, Henry Miller Theatre, in Just Suppose, 1920; on New York stage, 1920–25; at The Queens, London, in The Way You Look at It, 1926; New York, 1927–28; in London produced and played in Her Cardboard Lover, 1928, and Berkeley Square, 1929; New York, 1929–33; William Shakespeare in This side Idolatry, Lyric, London, 1933; Alan Squier in The Petrified Forest, which he produced with Gilbert Miller, New York, 1935; his own play, Murray Hill, was produced in New York, 1927, and in London, 1928, as Tell Me the Truth; entered films, 1930; films include Outward Bound, Service for Ladies, Smilin' Through, Berkeley Square, Of Human Bondage, British Agent, The Scarlet Pimpernel, The Petrified Forest, Pygmalion, Gone With the Wind, Intermezzo, 49th Parallel, Pimpernel Smith, The First of the Few. *Address:* Stowe Maries, Westcott, near Dorking, Surrey. *Clubs:* Lotos, Coffee House, New York.

Died 1 June 1943.

HOWARD, Lady Mabel, CBE 1920; JP; *b* 1878; 2nd *d* of 5th Earl of Antrim; *m* 1878, Henry Charles Howard (*d* 1914). *Address:* Greystoke Castle, Penrith.

Died 31 Dec. 1942.

HOWARD, Russell John, CBE 1919; late Surgeon London Hospital; Surgeon Poplar Hospital; *b* 26 Jan. 1875; unmarried. *Educ:* King's College School. Master in Surgery, London University; Fellow of the Royal College of Surgeons of England. *Publications:* Practice of Surgery; House Surgeon's Vade Mecum; Surgical Nursing; Surgical Emergencies, 1924. *Recreation:* farming. *Address:* Manor House, Oving, Nr Aylesbury, Bucks.

Died 2 Dec. 1942.

HOWE, Captain Leicester Charles Assheton St John C.; *see* Curzon-Howe.

HOWEL-JONES, Lt-Col Walter, CMG 1919; DSO 1917; retired from Royal Artillery; *b* 16 April 1868; *s* of Major-General Howel-Jones, Royal (late Bengal) Artillery; *m* Léonie, *d* of Admiral Forbes, RN; one *d.* *Educ:* Cheltenham College. Entered Royal Artillery 1887; served Miranzai Expedition, 1891; Isazai Expedition, 1892 (India medal and clasp); Chitral Relief Force, was present at the taking of the Malakand Pass, 1895, and with the Mohmand Expedition, 1897 (India medal, 1895, and two clasps); European War in Belgium and France, 1915–18, in command of an Artillery Brigade and as Brig.-Gen. 2nd Anzac Heavy Artillery; in Germany with the Army of Occupation until the end of 1919 (despatches four times, CMG, DSO, 1915 Star, Victory and Allies' medals); retired, 1919. *Address:* c/o Lloyd's Bank (Cox's Branch), 6 Pall Mall, SW1. *Club:* Junior United Service.

Died 27 July 1948.

HOWELL, Lt-Col Geoffrey Llewellyn Hinds, CMG, 1919; *b* 7 March 1875; *e s* of late Conrad Goodridge Howell; *m* 1946, Maria Eugenie Morel. *Educ:* Marlborough; RMA, Woolwich. 2nd Lt RA, 1895; Lt, 1898; Capt., 1901; served S African War, 1899–1902 (Queen's medal 5 clasps, King's medal 2 clasps); resigned commission, 1906; received temporary commission in Mechanical Transport, RASC, 1914–19; served in France, Flanders, 1915–19 (despatches six times, Brevet Lieut-Col, CMG); Associate of Institution of Mechanical Engineers; Member of West India Committee. *Recreations:* shooting, fishing, cricket, photography, wireless experimenting. *Address:* Arden, Tobago, BWI. *Clubs:* Army and Navy, MCC.

Died 19 Nov. 1948.

HOWELL, John, CBE 1920; MB; FRCS; Consulting Surgeon Dean Close School, Evesham Hospital and Bourton Cottage Hospital, Cheltenham General Hospital; late Surgeon, Cheltenham College and Cheltenham Ladies' College; Mayor of Cheltenham, 1938–39–1940–41; Deputy Mayor, 1941–42; Member of Cheltenham Town Council; Chairman Medical Advisory Committee of Gloucestershire County Council; *b* 1871; *s* of late W. G. Howell; *m* 1902, Margaret Ida Rees (*d* 1932), Newport, Pembrokeshire; three *s* one *d.* *Educ:* Guy's Hospital. Chairman Cheltenham Chamber of Commerce, 1931–32; President Cheltenham Rotary Club, 1926; Hon. Freedom of Cheltenham, 1943; WM Foundation Lodge (82) 1911, PPSGD. *Address:* 7 Imperial Square, Cheltenham. *T:* Cheltenham 3739; Parcygors, Llechryd, Cardiganshire. *Clubs:* New, Cheltenham.

Died 4 March 1945.

HOWELL, William H., PhD, MD, ScD, LLD; Emeritus Director, School of Hygiene and Public Health, Johns Hopkins University; retired, 1931; Chairman, National Research Council, 1932–33; Dean of Medical Faculty, 1899–1911; Professor of Physiology, 1893–1931; *b* Baltimore, Md, USA, 20 Feb. 1860; *s* of G. H. Howell and Virginia Magruder Howell; *m* 1887, Anne Janet Tucker of Baltimore; one *s* two *d.* *Educ:* The Johns Hopkins Univ. Graduated, 1881. Held successively the positions of Fellow, Assistant Associate, and Associate Professor in the department of Biology; accepted the Chair of Physiology and Histology in the University of Michigan; subsequently became Associate Professor in Harvard University for one year; Pres. 13th International Physiological Congress. *Publications:* Text-Book of Physiology; numerous researches in physiology in Phil. Trans. Roy. Soc., etc.; editor of An American Text-Book of Physiology, and a Text-Book of Physiology for Medical Students. *Recreations:* golf, tennis, boating. *Address:* 112 St Dunstan Road, Baltimore, USA. *Clubs:* Johns Hopkins, Baltimore; Yacht, Portland.

Died 6 Feb. 1945.

HOWELL-JONES, Col John Hyndman, CIE 1919; DSO 1915; *b* 1877; *s* of late Hon. B. Howell-Jones, CMG, British Guiana; *m* 1905, Florence, *d* of late Edmund Severne, of Wallop, Salop, and Thenford, Northants. Entered RMA 1896; Capt. Army, 1902; transferred to Army Ordnance Department, 1915; Brevet Major, 1916; Brevet Lt-Col, 1918; Lt-Col, 1927; Brevet Colonel, 1929; Col, 1931; served European War, 1915–17 (despatches six times, DSO, Brevets Major and Lieut-Colonel, CIE); Assistant Director of Ordnance Services, War Office, 1932–34; retired pay, 1934; re-employed ADOS 1939. *Club:* United Service.

Died April 1941.

HOWIE, Hon. Sir Archibald, Kt 1938; MLC New South Wales; Chairman of Directors, Port Jackson and Manly Steamship Co. Ltd; North Shore Gas Co. Ltd; Howie, Moffat & Co. Pty Ltd; Governing Director, Navua Pty Ltd; Director of a number of other Companies; Chairman of Advisory Panel on Defence Works, Defence Co-ordination Department, Commonwealth of Australia, since 1940; President of Federal Council and of New South Wales Branch Australian Jersey Herd Society; President, Royal Agricultural Society of NSW; *b* Glasgow, 1879; one *s.* Lord Mayor of Sydney, 1936 and 1937. President, Sydney Chamber of Commerce, 1938–40. *Address:* Box 2116–L, GPO, Sydney, NSW. *Clubs:* Australian, New South Wales, Royal Sydney Yacht Squadron, Sydney.

Died 26 Oct. 1943.

HOWKINS, Col Cyril Henry, CBE 1919; DSO 1917, TD; DL (Warwick); *b* 1876; *m* 1905, Ann, *d* of late Henry Shaw, Birmingham; two *s* one *d.* *Educ:* Mason College and Birmingham Univ. MRCS, LRCP 1901; LDS (Eng.), 1900. Served S African War, 1901–02 (Queen's medal 4 clasps); commanded 1st S Med. Field Ambulance (TF), 1910–17; Assistant Director of Medical Services, BEF, 1917–19 (despatches four times, DSO); Civil Consulting Dental Surgeon to RN; Member examining Board for Dental Nurses and Assistants; late Examiner in Dental Surgery the Royal College of Surgeons (England); and to the Universities of Sheffield, London and Birmingham; Consulting Dental Surgeon to Children's Hospital; Vice-Chm. and Hon. Dental Surgeon to Birmingham Dental Hospital; Vice-Chm. to Dental Hospitals Assoc.; Past-President Odontological Section, Royal Society of Medicine; Member of British Medical and Dental Associations; Past-President of the CC Branch BDA. *Address:* 83a Edmund Street, Birmingham; Hagley Court, Hagley Road, Birmingham.

Died 31 Oct. 1947.

HOWLAND, Hewitt Hanson; *b* Indianapolis, 8 Oct. 1863; *s* of John D. Howland and Desdemona Harrison; *m* Manie Cobb, Paducah, Ky. *Educ:* Indianapolis Classical School. In literary work since 1898; late editor and literary adviser of The Bobbs-Merrill Co., publishers; editor of the Century Magazine, 1925–31. *Address:* 117 E 77th Street, New York City. *Clubs:* Players, National Arts, Town Hall, PEN (New York); University (Indianapolis).

Died 10 May 1944.

HOWLETT, Rt Rev. Monsignor Martin, DD, PhD, LLD; Domestic Prelate to the Pope; Canon of Westminster Cathedral, 1908; Canon Theologian, 1927; Protonotary Apostolic ad Instar, 1931; *b* Inistioge, Co. Kilkenny, 3 May 1863; *e surv. s* of John Howlett, JP, of Russellstown House, Co. Kilkenny. *Educ:* Downside, Bath; Pontifical Roman University and Academia of Noble Ecclesiastics, Rome. Ordained priest by Cardinal Parocchi, 1886; appointed secretary by Leo XIII to Cardinal Satolli for the opening of the Washington University and the Centenary of the American Hierarchy; made Cameriere Segreto to HH Pope Leo, 1890; Rector of Our Lady and St Joseph, Kingsland, 1892–1905; Westminster Cathedral, 1905–47. *Publication:* Ed. Westminster Cathedral Chronicle, 1907–1918. *Address:* Cathedral Clergy House, Francis Street, Westminster, SW1.

Died 17 Feb. 1949.

HOWLETT, Brig. Reginald, CBE 1939; DSO 1917; MC; *b* 1882; *s* of late W. R. C. Howlett, Old Catton, Norfolk; *m* 1924, Helen, *d* of late Walter A. Clark, of Crutherland, Lanarkshire. Served S African War, 1901–02 (Queen's medal with five clasps); European War, 1914–18 (despatches, MC, DSO and bar); Lt-Col 1928; commanded 2nd Batt. Royal Fusiliers, 1928–32; Col 1932; Commander 162nd (East Midland) Infantry Brigade TA, 1932–35; Inspector-General of West Indian Local Forces and Officer Commanding the Troops, Jamaica, 1936–39; retired pay, 1939. *Address:* Horseleas, Bradfield, Berks. *Club:* Army and Navy.

Died 20 Oct. 1942.

HOWLEY, John F. W., MA; *b* 1866; *e s* of late Richard Irwin Howley; unmarried. *Educ:* Summerhill College, Sligo; St Stanislaus' College, Tullabeg; University College, Dublin, BA 1888; MA 1889; DLitt 1925. Professor of Education at St Patrick's Training College, Drumcondra, 1908; Professor of Philosophy at University College, Galway, 1914–36; Examiner in English to Intermediate Board, 1912; Substitute Professor and Intern. Examiner in English, Univ. College, Galway, 1917; Librarian, 1917; Member of Governing Body, 1928; represented University College, Galway, at the Catholic Emancipation celebrations, 1929; President of the Library Association of Ireland, 1941; Member of Hospitals Library Council, 1937–41. *Publications:* Psychology and Mystical Experience, 1920; Mysticism in Everyday Life, 1923; Humanism and Mystical Experience, 1925–1926; Faith and Reason in Relation to Truth, 1926; various broadcasts, Radio Eirann, 1937–1940. *Address:* Cepeda, Goatstown Road, Dundrum, Co. Dublin.

Died Sept. 1941.

HOWLEY, William John Joseph, CSI 1920; MInstCE; MIE (Ind.); *b* 1865; *e s* of late Lieut-Col John Howley, DL, of Rich Hill, Lisnagry, Co. Limerick; *m* 1898, Evelina Rivers, *e d* of late John Edward Kilburn, MRCS; no *c. Educ:* Oscott College; RIEC Coopers Hill. Assistant Engineer, Indian Public Works Department, 1889; Executive Engineer, 1900; Superintending Engineer, 1914; Chief Engineer and Joint Secretary to Government, 1917; Secretary to Government, 1919; retired, 1921; Member of the Madras Legislative Council, 1917–20; Member, Committee of Arbitration, Madras-Mysore Cauvery dispute, 1929; DL County of the City of LImerick, 1888. *Address:* Rich Hill, Lisnagry, Co. Limerick. *Clubs:* East India and Sports; County (Limerick).

Died 15 July 1948.

HOWLEY, William Richard, CMG 1938; KC 1911; Registrar of Supreme Court, Newfoundland; *b* 1875; *m* 1905, Mary Patricia, *d* of Edward Ryan, St John's. Was Commissioner for Justice, Newfoundland. *Address:* Killowen, Circular Road, St John's, Newfoundland.

Died 18 April 1941.

HOWORTH, Col Henry Godfrey, CMG 1918; late RA; *b* 6 June 1870; *s* of late Sir Henry Hoyle Howorth, KCIE, FRS; *m* 1898, Alice Caroline Mary, *d* of Capt. William Gibson, JP, DL, and *widow* of Egerton Griffin Carrol; two *s* one *d. Educ:* Haileybury. Entered Army, 1889; served European War, 1914–19 (despatches, Bt Lt-Col, CMG); Col 1919; retired pay, 1923. *Address:* Forest Hill, Bideford, Devon. *T:* Bideford 172.

Died 5 Jan. 1947.

HOWSON, Ven. George John, MA Camb.; *b* 1 May 1854; Archdeacon and Canon Emeritus of Liverpool since 1934; *e s* of Very Rev. J. S. Howson, Dean of Chester; *m* Ethel (*d* 1937), *d* of Ven. Archdeacon Dealtry, Vicar of Maidstone; two *s* one *d. Educ:* Liverpool College; Haileybury College; Trinity College, Cambridge. 1st Class Theological Tripos, with Evans Prize. Curate of Maidstone; Rector of Overton, Flints; Vicar of Crewe; Rector of Christ Church, Salford; Rector of St Mary, Crumpsall; Vicar of St Andrew, Southport; Rector of Woolton, near Liverpool; Archdeacon of Warrington, 1916–33; Residentiary Canon of Liverpool, 1933–34; Archdeacon of Liverpool, 1933–34; examining chaplain to Bishop of Liverpool, 1904–34; chaplain to High Sheriff of Lancashire, 1911–12 and 1923–24; Chaplain of the Order of St John of Jerusalem. *Publication:* Overton in Days Gone By. *Address:* Llys Cyngar, Morfa Bychan, Portmadoc.

Died 20 May 1943.

HOWSON, Captain John, CBE 1919; RD, RNR (retired); *b* Whitehaven, Cumberland, 22 Nov. 1871; *e s* of late Commander John Howson, CB, RNR; *m* 1926, Emily, *d* of Joseph Howson, Whitehaven. *Educ:* private schools; Nautical Academy. Entered Mercantile Marine, 1887, doing service in sailing vessels until 1895; obtained Extra Master's Certificate in that year and joined the Pacific Steam Navigation Co.; obtained commission in the Royal Naval Reserve, 1896; served in a chartered Naval Transport during S African War, 1900–02 (medal and clasp); served Royal Navy, 1902–03; transferred to Royal Mail Steam Packet Co., 1906; commanding several of their vessels, 1910–14; served in Royal Navy, 1914–18 (CBE); commanded Hospital Ship attached to Black Sea Naval Squadron, 1919, and Royal Mail Steam Packet Company's vessels until 1921, when retired from sea service; placed on the retired list with the rank of Captain RNR, 1923. *Address:* Farleton Rise, Burton, Westmorland. *T:* Burton 48.

Died 9 May 1948.

HOYSTED, Col Desmond Murree Fitzgerald, CBE 1930; DSO 1916; *b* 7 Aug. 1874; *s* of late Surg.-Gen. T. N. Hoysted; *m* 1904, Sybil (*d* 1942), 2nd *d* of Colonel Hoysted of Greta, Sidcup; two *s* two *d. Educ:* Rugby. Lieutenant 26th Field Com. RE 1894; served SA War, 1899–1902 (Queen's medal 3 clasps, King's medal 2 clasps); returned home in command of 26th Field Co. RE 1904; Division Officer RE and acting CRE Dublin District, and then in the Alexandria Garrison of British Army of Occupation; in Egypt till Feb. 1914; Staff Officer RE London District, Feb. 1914 till outbreak of war; served European War, France, 8 Aug. 1914, with 4th Infantry Division in command of 9th Field Co. RE till Sept. 1915; CRE 22nd Infantry Division, Serbian Expeditionary Force, 1915–17; Chief Instructor Fortification RE Training Centre, Deganwy, till 1918; CRE II Army Defence Lines, BEF, France, 1918; Instructor, Senior Officers' School, woking, 1919; CRE West Lancashire and Cheshire, 1920; CRE Lancashire Area (Cheshire to Scottish Border), 1922; Chief Technical Examiner of RE Works, War Office, 1926–30; retired pay, 1930; Secretary of Royal Asiatic Society, 1930–40; Research and Experiments Branch, Ministry of Home Security, 1940–42. *Address:* c/o Cox's Branch, Lloyd's Bank, 6 Pall Mall, SW1.

Died 3 Oct. 1945.

HRDLIČKA, Aleš, MD, ScD; in charge Division of Physical Anthropology, US National Museum, Smithsonian Institution, 1903; Curator, 1910–42; retired, 1942, since then Associate in Anthropology, Smithsonian Institution; Founder and Editor, American Journal of Physical Anthropology since 1918; Founder and first President of the American Association of Physical Anthropologists, 1929; *b* Humpolec, Bohemia, 29 March 1869; Czech parentage; immigration to USA, New York City, 1882; *m* 1896; no *c. Educ:* Old Country; New York; Paris. MD 1892, '94 (Ecl., Homoeop., Allop.). Interne (research), State Hosp. for Insane, Middlet., NY, 1894–96; Assoc. in Anthrop., State Pathol. Inst., NY, 1896–99; in charge Phys. Anthrop., Hyde Expeditions, Amer. Mus. Nat. Hist., NY, 1899–1903; Sec. Gen. XIX Intern. Congr. Americanists, 1915; Sec. Sect. Anthropol. Pan-American Sc. Cong., 1916; Sec. Com. Anthrop. Nat. Res. Counc., 1917–18; Assoc. Edit. Amer. Naturalist, 1901–08; ScD (hon.), Karlova Universita, Prague, Bohemia, 1920; Dr Sc. nat. (hon.) University of Brno, 1929; Member National Academy of Sciences, USA, and of the Czech Academy of Sciences and Arts; Hon. Member Royal Anthropological Institute, etc.; Huxley Medal, 1927; extensive scientific travels, North and South America, Europe, Asia, Australia, Egypt, South Africa, Alaska. *Publications:* Ancient Man in North America; Ancient Man in South America; Medical and Physiological Studies among Indians; Anthropology of Florida; Anthropometry; Anthropology (USA) The Old Americans; Skeletal Remains of Early Man; Animal-like Manifestations in the Human Child; Practical Anthropometry; Memoirs and papers on Man's Evolution, Skeletal Remains of Man; Egyptians (Kharga); Tuberculosis among Indians, Origin of the American Indian; Evolution and Variation of Teeth; Skeletal Variation, etc. *Recreations:* formerly all outdoor sports; lately, mainly gardening. *Address:* US National Museum, Washington, DC.

Died 5 Sept. 1943.

HUBBACK, Brig.-Gen. Arthur Benison, CMG 1916; DSO 1918; *b* Liverpool, 13 April 1871; *e s* of late Joseph Hubback, JP, Liverpool; *m* 1901, Margaret Rose Frances, 2nd *d* of late Sir Gordon Blennerhassett Voules, Kt; one *s* one *d. Educ:* Fettes College, Edinburgh. Articled to T. Shelmerdine, City Architect of Liverpool; Public Works Department, Federated Malay States, 1895; Government Architect; Designed many of principal Public Buildings in the FMS; ARIBA 1905; FRIBA 1910; Malay States Volunteer Rifles, 1902; Captain, 1902; Major, 1910; Lt-Col 1913; in command of contingent representing Federated Malay States at Coronation of King George V; Major 19th Batt. London Regiment TF Sept. 1914; Lt-Col commanding 20th Batt. London Regt TF, 47th Division, BEF, Feb. 1915; Brig.-Gen. 2nd Infantry Brigade, 1st Division BEF, 1916; Brig.-Gen. 118th Infantry Brigade, 39th Division, BEF, 1918; Brig.-Gen. 63rd Infantry Brigade, 37th Division, BEF, 1918; Colonel, TF, 1919 (despatches six times, CMG, DSO, wounded); Colonel commanding 5th London Infantry Brigade, TA, 1920–24; retired, 1924, with rank of Brig.-Gen. *Address:* 4 The Hollies, High Road, Broxbourne, Herts. *T:* Hoddesdon 2813. *Clubs:* East India and Sports; Royal Wimbledon Golf (Wimbledon).

Died 8 May 1948.

HUBBACK, Mrs Eva M., MA; Principal, Morley College, Westminster Bridge Road; Member, LCC Education Committee and Chairman of LCC Schools Sub-Committee; Hon. Secretary, Association for Training in Citizenship; Chairman, Family Endowment Society; Joint Editor, Universities quarterly; *b* 1886; *d* of late Sir Meyer A. Spielman; *m* 1911, F. W. Hubback (killed in France, 1917); one *s* two *d. Educ:* St Felix School, Southwold; Newnham College, Cambridge; Economics Tripos, Part II, 1908, Class I. *Publications:*

(with Lord Simon of Wythenshawe) Education in Citizenship; The Population of Britain; articles in daily, weekly, and monthly press. *Address:* 19 Wellgarth Road, Golders Green, NW11. *T:* Speedwell 1294.

Died 15 July 1949.

HUBERMAN, Bronislaw; violinist; *b* Czestochowa, Poland, 19 Dec. 1882; *m;* one *s. Educ:* Warsaw; Berlin under Joseph Joachim. Appeared 1892 in the Vienna International Musical Exhibition and in a court-concert before Emperor Francis Joseph, the farewell concert of Adelina Patti in Vienna; his first interpretation of the Brahms Violin-Concerto in Vienna in 1896, with Brahms himself present; played in public as the only living violinist on the violin of Paganini in Genova, 1908, and was presented with a gold medal by the Lord Mayor, specially coined for that occasion; Director of Violin Master School at State Music Academy in Vienna, 1934. *Publications:* Vaterland Europa; Mein Weg zu Paneuropa; Aus der Werkstadt des Virtuosen; many newspaper articles and public speeches on art and politics.

Died 15 June 1947.

HUCKIN, Victor Henry St John; 21 July 1880; *b* 21 July 1880; *s* of late Dr Henry Robert Huckin, Headmaster of Repton School; unmarried. *Educ:* Eton; Balliol Coll., Oxford. Has held Consular appointments in Norway, Sweden, French West Africa, Colombia, Peru, Argentina, Chile, Bolivia, USA, and Italy; HM Consul-Gen. Buenos Aires, 1930–37. *Address:* Wensleydale, Worcester Park, Surrey.

Died 11 Oct. 1943.

HUDD, Hon. Sir Herbert Sydney, BE, 1937; MC; *b* 25 Feb. 1881; *s* of late William Hudd; *m* 1919; Mabel Law, 4th *d* of late Richard Smith, Woodlands, Glenelg, South Australia; no *c. Educ:* Grote Street School, Adelaide, South Australia. Member of S Australian House of Assembly, 1912–15, 1920–38, and since 1941; Commissioner of Public Works, Minister of Railways, and Minister of Marine, South Australia, 1933–38; Sec., Parliamentary Liberal Party, 1912–15; 1921–27; Government Whip, 1927–30; President, SA Literary Societies Union, 1913–15; Member Adelaide Hospital Board, 1912–15; Adelaide University Council, 1921–24; served European War with 43rd Batt. AIF as NCO, Lieutenant and Captain (MC). *Recreations:* tennis, golf. *Address:* 27 Pier Street, Glenelg, South Australia. *Clubs:* Adelaide, Adelaide.

Died 30 April 1948.

HUDDLESTON, Sir Arthur James Croft, Kt 1933; CMG 1927; OBE 1919; LLD (Glas.); *b* 6 July 1880; *e s* of late Tristram Frederick Croft Huddleston and Bessie, *d* of late Rev. J. Chataway; *m* 1910, Mary Ellen (*d* 1947), *e d* of late Edmond Symonds of Kronstaad, S Africa, and Thaxted, Essex; three *d. Educ:* Eton (King's Scholar); King's Coll., Cambridge. Joined Sudan Political Service, 1904; Gov. Khartoum Province, 1920–22; Gov. Blue Nile Province, Sudan, 1922–27; Financial Sec. Sudan Government, 1928–31; Economic Adviser, 1931–32; retired, 1932; Director Royal Technical Coll., Glasgow, 1933–45; 4th Class Osmanieh, 1914; 2nd Class Order of the Nile, 1930. *Recreations:* rowing, lawn tennis. *Address:* 8 Bute Gardens, Glasgow, W2. *T:* Glasgow (Western) 2101. *Clubs:* Leander; Western (Glasgow).

Died 18 Feb. 1948.

HUDDLESTON, George, CIE 1903; Director of Assam-Bengal Railway, 56 Victoria Street, SW1; formerly General Traffic Manager, East Indian Railway; *b* 14 Feb. 1862; 3rd *s* of late Major G. E. Huddleston, East Surrey Regiment; *m* 1883, Agnes (*d* 1934), *d* of William O'Reilly; one *s. Educ:* Bedford School. Was Lieut-Colonel (VD) East Indian Railway Volunteer Corps; retired, 1911; employed as Railway Transport Officer, holding a temporary commission in the army, 1914–17. *Publications:* History of the East Indian Railway

Part I, 1906, Part II, 1939; Tales for the Train; The White Fakir; Kissed by the Sun; Daughter of India. *Address:* 21 Princes Court, SW3. *Club:* Oriental.
Died 12 May 1944.

HUDDLESTON, Maj.-Gen. Sir Hubert Jervoise, GCMG 1947 (KCMG 1940; CMG 1918); GBE 1946; CB 1925; DSO 1917; MC; *b* 1880; *s* of late Thomas Jervoise Huddleston, Norton, Suffolk; *m* 1928, Constance Eila, *o d* of late F. H. M. Corbet; one *d. Educ:* Bedford; Felsted. Served South African War, 1899–1902 (despatches, Queen's medal and four clasps, King's medal and two clasps); Sudan, 1910 (medal and clasp); European War, 1914–18 (despatches, MC, DSO and bar, Bt Lt-Col, CMG); GOC Sudan, 1924–30; Commander 14th Infantry Brigade 1930–33; Maj.-Gen., 1933; Commander Presidency and Assam District, Eastern Command, India, 1934–35; Commander Baluchistan District, Western Command, India, 1935–38; retired pay, 1938; Lieut-Governor and Secretary Royal Hospital Chelsea, 1938–40; GOC N Ireland District, 1940; Governor-General of Anglo-Egyptian Sudan, 1940–47; Col of Dorsetshire Regt, 1933–46. *Address:* 7 Cleveland Row, SW1. *T:* Whitehall 5920. *Club:* Army and Navy.
Died 2 Oct. 1950.

HUDLESTON, Ven. Cuthbert, MA; Archdeacon of Perth, West Australia, 1910–40; *m*; two *s* one *d. Educ:* New College, Oxford. Ordained 1887; Curate of St Dunstan, Stepney, 1887–92; Walworth Mission, 1892–98; Priest in charge Norseman, 1898–1900; Coolgardie, 1900–03; Rector of Kalgoorlie, 1903–05; Rector of St John, Perth, 1905–07; Rector of St Alban, Perth, 1907–19. *Address:* Church Office, Perth, West Australia.
Died 1 Dec. 1944.

HUDSON, Albert Blellock; Judge of Supreme Court of Canada since 1936; *b* Pembroke, Ont, 21 Aug. 1875; *s* of Albert and Elizabeth Hudson; *m* 1st, 1908, Mary B. Russell; 2nd, 1936, Marjorie G. Runciman. *Educ:* Portage la Prairie; Winnipeg; Manitoba University, LLB 1898. Barrister, 1899; KC 1914; Bencher Law Society, 1912; MPP Winnipeg South, 1914; Attorney-General, Manitoba, 1915; resigned 1917; MP for South Winnipeg, 1921–25. *Clubs:* Manitoba, Winnipeg; Rideau, Ottawa.
Died 6 Jan. 1947.

HUDSON, Arthur, KC; MA; *b* 1861; *s* of late Henry Hudson, Walsoken, Norfolk; *m* 1899, Mary Rose (*d* 1944), *d* of Captain Donald Hay M'Barnet, Cameron Highlanders and Norfolk Regt; one *s. Educ:* Balliol Coll., Oxford, MA. Barr. Inner Temple, 1892. District Commissioner Sierra Leone, 1896; Solicitor-General, 1897; Attorney-General, 1901; Puisne Judge, 1903; Attorney-General Gold Coast, 1908; KC Gold Coast, 1910; retired, 1912; a Legal Adviser in the Ministry of Food, 1917–18; Municipal Reform candidate LCC (S Islington) 1922; (N Battersea) 1925; Kensington Board of Guardians, 1922; Member of Kensington Borough Council 1928; A Director of various Companies; has travelled extensively in Colonies, in India, in Central and S America. *Publications:* The Call of the Nation, etc.; an occasional contributor of articles to the principal London newspapers. *Recreation:* foreign travel. *Address:* 2 Vicarage Gardens, W8. *Clubs:* St James's, United, Pegasus.
Died 10 Sept. 1948.

HUDSON, Lt-Col Charles Tilson, CMG 1918; MRCS, LRCP Lond.; DPH, DTM; *b* 1865; *s* of late Charles Thomas Hudson, Clifton; *m* 1901, Christina Mabel, *d* of late Capt. Frank Corbett. Served NW Frontier of India, 1897–98 (medal with two clasps); European War, 1914–18 (despatches). *Address:* The Church House, Lyonshall, Herefordshire.
Died 8 Feb. 1948.

HUDSON, Engr Rear-Adm. George William, CB 1919; *b* 8 Feb. 1861; *m* 1884, Victoria Harriet Fisher (*d* 1940), *d* of late Henry Fisher Jackson, Southsea; one *d. Educ:* privately. Served European War, 1914–19; retired list, 1919. *Address:* 9 Whitwell Road, Southsea.
Died 30 Jan. 1941.

HUDSON, Gen. Sir Havelock, GCB 1928; KCB 1918; KCIE 1919; CB 1914; CIE 1903; 19th Bengal Lancers; *b* 26 June 1862; *s* of late Lieut-Gen. Sir John Hudson, KCB; *m* 1901, Kate, *d* of Maj. J. Hawkins. Entered Army, 1881; Capt. 1892; Major, 1901; Lt-Col 1907; Col 1911; Maj. Gen., 1915; General, 1921; served Second Miranzai Expedition, 1901 (medal with clasp); NW Frontier, 1897 (medal and clasp); China, 1900 (despatches, medal, brevet of Major); European War, 1914–18 (despatches, prom. Major-General, KCB); late Assistant QMG and Member of Executive Committee, Coronation Durbar, Delhi, 1903; Commandant Cavalry School, Sangor, 1912; Brig.-Gen. General Staff, Northern Army, 1912–14; Adjutant-General, India, 1917–20; General Officer Commanding-in-Chief, Eastern Army in India, 1920–24; ADC General to the King, 1922–24; retired, 1924; Member of Council of India, 1924–29; Colonel, Northamptonshire Regiment, 1925–31; Colonel, 19th Lancers IA, 1931–32. *Address:* 5 The Close, Winchester. *T:* Winchester 1158. *Club:* United Service.
Died 25 Dec. 1944.

HUDSON, James Frank, MA, BSc; Principal, Technical College, Huddersfield, 1904–37; *b* Camberwell, 19 Sept. 1872; *o s* of late J. Hudson, VMH, of Acton, W; *m* 1905, Lilian, *d* of late J. Snook, Cotham, Bristol; two *s* one *d. Educ:* Acton Collegiate School; St Paul's School; Jesus College, Oxford (Open Exhibitioner, Scholar, and Prizeman; 1st class, Math. Mods; 1st class, Math. Finals; Honours in Physics; BA 1895; MA 1898). Assistant Lecturer at Jesus College, and Demonstrator of Physics in the Clarendon Laboratory, 1896–1900; Lecturer in Mathematics, Univ. College, Bristol, 1900; Professor of Mathematics, Hartley Univ. Coll., Southampton, 1900–04; Hon. Secretary, Southampton and District Teachers Guild, 1901–04; Hon. Secretary, Conference on Science Teaching and Nature-Study, June 1902; Member of Council, Teachers' Guild of Great Britain and Ireland, 1903–04; Member of Court of Governors, Hartley University College, 1903–04; Hon. Secretary, National Dahlia Society, 1897–1903. *Recreations:* boating, cycling, tennis, gardening. *Address:* Springlands, Wendover Road, Stoke Mandeville, Bucks. *T:* Stoke Mandeville 127.
Died 29 Nov. 1949.

HUDSON, Sir Leslie S., Kt 1925; *b* 25 Nov. 1872; *s* of late Thomas Moore Hudson of Castleacre, Norfolk. *Educ:* Christ's Hospital. Joined the service of P & OSN Co., 1889; proceeded to India, 1894, and thence to Japan, China, and Australia, returning to India, 1915; joined the firm of Mackinnon, Mackenzie & Co., 1916; Vice-Chairman Bombay Chamber of Commerce, 1923–24; President, 1924–25, 1927–28; Member Legislative Council Bombay Presidency, 1924–26, 1929–30; Member Legislative Assembly, India, 1932–37; a representative of Indian Central Legislature at Coronation, 1937. *Recreations:* shooting, golf. *Address:* 86 St James's Street, SW1. *Clubs:* Thatched House, Oriental; Byculla, Royal Bombay Yacht, Bombay.
Died 25 March 1946.

HUDSON, Lt-Col Ralph Charles D.; *see* Donaldson-Hudson.

HUDSON, Stephen; novelist. *Publications:* Richard Kurt, 1919; Elinor Colhouse, 1921; Prince Hempseed, 1922; Tony, 1924; Myrtle, 1925; Richard, Myrtle and I, 1926; A True Story, 1930; Céleste and Other Sketches, 1930;

Time Regained, translation of Marcel Proust's Le Temps Retrouvé, 1931; The Other Side, 1937. *Address:* Abinger Manor, near Dorking.

Died 29 Oct. 1944.

HUDSON-KINAHAN, Sir Robert Henry; *see* Kinahan.

HUGGINS, Sir George Frederick, Kt 1937; OBE. Director of Ste Madeleine Sugar Co., Ltd. *Address:* Port of Spain, Trinidad.

Died 7 June 1941.

HUGHES, Alfred James, CIE; Postmaster-General, Bengal and Assam, retired; *s* of late Dr James Hughes, Civil Surgeon, Nowgong, Assam; *m* Edith Vera, *d* of Major F. Goldney, IA; one *s*. Joined Indian Postal Service, 1895; services lent to Government of Bombay for famine duty for two years; served as Chief Superintendent, Field Post Offices, in the Somaliland Campaign, 1902; on deputation as Deputy Director in charge of Indian Field Post Offices, Egypt, 1914–16; gazetted Temporary Major, RE, and Director, Field Post Offices, Mesopotamia, 1917 (despatches thrice, CIE). *Address:* 23 Wimborne Gardens, Ealing, W13.

Died 24 Oct. 1947.

HUGHES, Col Arbuthnott James, CMG 1919; late RFA; *b* 1856; *m* 1st, 1886, Caroline Mabel (*d* 1924), *d* of T. R. Leadam, MD, York Place, W; 2nd, 1927, Ethel J., *widow* of Capt. Robert H. Stewart, RN. Served European War, 1914–19 (despatches, CMG). *Address:* Presteign, Warwick Park, Tunbridge Wells.

Died 20 April 1945.

HUGHES, Charles Evans; *b* Glens Falls, New York, 11 April 1862; *s* of David Charles Hughes and Mary Catherine Connelly; *m* 1888, Antoinette Carter; one *s* two *d. Educ:* Colgate University; Brown University, AB, AM; LLB Columbia Law School, 1884; LLD Brown University, 1906; Columbia, Knox, and Lafayette, 1907; Union, Colgate, 1908; George Washington, 1909; Williams College, Harvard, and University of Pennsylvania, 1910; Yale University, 1915; University of Michigan, 1922; Dartmouth College, 1923; Amherst College, Princeton University and University of the State of New York, 1924; Pennsylvania Military College, 1928; Doctor of Civil Law, New York University, 1928; Dr (Hon.) Brussels and Louvain, 1924. Admitted to NY Bar, 1884; prize fellowship, Columbia Law School, 1884–87; practised law, New York, 1884–91, 1893–1906; Professor of Law, 1891–93; Special Lecturer, 1893–95, Cornell; Special Lecturer, New York Law School, 1893–1900; Counsel Stevens Gas Committee, 1905, and Armstrong Insurance Committee, 1905–06 (New York Legislature); Special Assistant to US Atty-Gen., Coal Investigation, 1906; Governor of NY two terms, 1907–08, 1909–10; resigned, 1910; Associate Justice, Supreme Court of US, 1910–16; nominated for President of the United States in Republican National Convention, Chicago, June 10, 1916; Secretary of State, United States, 1921–25; Chairman, International Conference on the Limitation of Armament at Washington, 1921; Member, Permanent Court of Arbitration at the Hague, 1926–30; Judge of Permanent Court of International Justice, The Hague, 1928–30; Chief Justice of the United States, 1930–41; Member, Law firm, Hughes, Rounds, Schurman & Dwight, NY City, 1917–21 and 1925–30; Chairman, US Delegation to Sixth Pan-American Conference at Havana, 1928; Master of the Bench, Middle Temple, London; Fellow, Brown University; Trustee, University of Chicago; Chairman, Draft Appeals Board, New York City, 1917–18; Pres. NY State Bar Association, 1917–18; Legal Aid Society, New York, 1917–19, New York County Lawyers' Association, 1919–20; President, American Bar Association, 1924–25; President, Association of the Bar of the City of New York,

1927–29; President, American Society of International Law, 1925–29. *Publications:* Conditions of Progress in Democratic Government, Yale Lectures, 1909; The Pathway of Peace, and other Addresses, 1925; The Supreme Court of the United States, Columbia University Lectures, 1927; Our Relation to the Nations of the Western Hemisphere (Princeton University Lectures), 1928; Pan American Peace Plans (Yale University Lectures), 1929. *Address:* 2223 R Street, Northwest, Washington, DC, USA. *Clubs:* University, Union League (President, 1917–19), Century, Lawyers', Brown, Delta Upsilon, Nassau County, New York.

Died 28 Aug. 1948.

HUGHES, Col Edmund Locock, DSO 1916; OBE 1919; Librarian Royal United Service Institution since 1927; *b* Feb. 1880; 3rd *s* of Robert H. Hughes, MB, and Laetitia Hughes of Down House, Whitchurch, Tavistock; *m* 1906, Mary, *e d* of W. Tatham Hughes, ISO; one *s. Educ:* Kelly College, Tavistock; Marlborough College; Clare College, Cambridge. Entered Army, 1st Northamptons, in India as a 'varsity candidate, 1900; Capt. 1908; Major, 1915; Adjutant to the 5th Batt. Durham Light Infantry, 1910–13; served European War, 1914–18 (wounded at battle of the Marne); retired pay, 1926. *Recreation:* golf. *Address:* Royal United Service Institution, Whitehall, SW1.

Died 3 April 1945.

HUGHES, Rev. Ernest Selwyn; *b* Cobram, Victoria, 12 May 1860; *s* of Charles William Hughes and Ellen Man; *m* 1904, Isabel Janet Thomson (*d* 1933); no *c. Educ:* Melbourne Grammar School; Trinity College, University of Melbourne. On leaving school received appointment from Lords of the Treasury in Royal Mint; resigned in 1883 to enter Trinity College; BA 1887; Holy Orders, 1887; Curate, Fitzroy, 1887–90; Mission of Holy Redeemer, 1890–93; St Peter's, Melbourne, 1893–1900; Vicar, 1900–26; Canon of St Paul's Cathedral, Melbourne, 1911–39; great interest in social questions. *Recreation:* President of the Victorian Cricket Association. *Address:* 410 Albert St, Melbourne, C2. *Club:* Athenæum.

Died 16 June 1942.

HUGHES, Maj.-Gen. Frederick Godfrey, CB 1916; VD (Victoria); late Australian Forces; *b* 26 Jan. 1857; *s* of late Charles W. Hughes; *m* 1885, Agnes Eva Snodgrass (*d* 1940); two *s* two *d. Educ:* Church of England Grammar School, Melbourne. Served European War, 1914–16 (despatches, CB); commanded 3rd Light Horse Brigade AIF; was in command of dismounted 8th, 9th, and 10th Light Horse, Gallipoli. *Address:* 43 Alma Road, St Kilda, Victoria, Australia.

Died 23 Aug. 1944.

HUGHES, Rev. Harold; *b* 1884; *s* of late H. H. Hughes, Abingdon, Berks; *m* 1926, Beatrice Serena, *d* of late Dr W. J. Bowden. *Educ:* Pembroke College, Oxford (Classical Scholar); BA 1907; MA 1919. Headmaster of King's College, Taunton, 1919–29; Vicar of Godney, 1930–34; Vicar of Pilton, Somerset, 1934–45; Vicar of Benson, Oxford, 1945–48. Member of English Association, Historical Association. *Publication:* A Chaplet of Prayers for War-Time, Gathered from the Eikon Basilike, 1917. *Recreations:* music, walking, boating. *Address:* 31 Gravel Hill, Ludlow, Shropshire.

Died 15 Feb. 1950.

HUGHES, Brig.-Gen. Henry Thoresby, CMG 1916; DSO 1919; Royal Canadian Engineers (R of O); *b* 1873; *m* 1900, Sarah H. Porter, of Montreal. Served European War, 1914–19 (despatches four times, CMG, DSO). *Clubs:* Union, Victoria, BC.

Died 4 June 1947.

HUGHES, (Mary) Katherine H. P.; *see* Price Hughes.

HUGHES, Sir Reginald Johnasson, 11th Bt *cr* 1773; *b* 22 June 1882; *s* of 10th Bt and Elsie (*d* 1932), *d* of John Johnasson, 55 Queen's Gate, London SW7; *S* father, 1932. *Educ:* Trinity College, Cambridge. *Heir: uncle* Robert Heywood.

Died 6 May 1945.

HUGHES, Talbot, ROI; Member of Royal Society of Oil Painters and the Pastel Society; *b* 1869; *s* of William Hughes, painter of still life; *m* 1912; two *s*. *Works:* A Stolen Meeting; Played Out; The End of the Game; When Thieves Fall Out; Mrs Siddons as Lady Macbeth; A Masque at Ranelagh. *Address:* Lanecote, Osmington, near Weymouth.

Died 6 Feb. 1942.

HUGHES, Sir Thomas, Kt 1916; JP Glamorgan; *b* 29 June 1863; *m* 1891, Phyllis May, OBE, 2nd *d* of J. F. Edisbury; two *s*. *Educ:* Mill Hill School. Clement's Inn Law Prizeman, 1885; Chairman of Governors, Bridgend Glamorgan County School, 1898–1911; Vice-Chairman, Glamorgan County Council, 1902–11; Clerk and Solicitor to Bridgend Urban District Council, 1887–1908; Chairman, Welsh National Education Campaign Committee, 1900–04; Member Departmental Committee Imperial and Local Taxation, 1910–12; Member Departmental Committee Liquor Trade Finance (England and Wales), 1917; Member Council and Sustentation Executive Baptist Union, 1916–39; Hon. Sec. South Glamorgan Liberal Association, 1886–1911; Chairman South Wales Joint Sustentation Board since 1916; President Penarth Boys' Club since 1929; JP Glamorgan; Chevalier d'ordre de Couronne (Belgian); Chairman National Health Insurance Commission (Wales), 1912–19; Joint Treasurer Cardiff Belgians' Relief Committee, 1917–19; Chairman Welsh Board of Health (HM Ministry of Health), 1919–28; Chairman Court of Referees, HM Ministry of Labour, 1928–38; Member of Executive Committee, Prince of Wales' Hospital, Cardiff, 1920–40; has been Chairman Penarth Panel of Justices for Juvenile Courts; Chairman Glamorganshire County Personal Service League, 1928–40; Member Welsh YMCA Council; Vice-President of South Wales Federation of Boys' Clubs. *Recreation:* bowls. *Address:* Cartref, Clinton Road, Penarth. *T:* Penarth 681.

Died 9 April 1942.

HUGHES, Thomas Cann, MA, FSA; Freeman of London, Chester and Lancaster; retired Town Clerk; *b* Chester, 14 Aug. 1860; *o s* of Thomas Hughes, FSA, Sheriff of Chester, 1872–73; *m* 1911, Ada Heywood; one *d*. *Educ:* King's School, Chester (Platt Exhibitioner); Pembroke College, Cambridge. BA 1882; MA 1890. Admitted Solicitor, 1885; Assistant Solicitor, Manchester, 1887–96; Town Clerk of Lancaster, 1896–1922; Jubilee Master Rowley Lodge, Lancaster, 1914; MWS Philips Rouge-Croix Chapter, 1916; Centenary Provincial Grand Registrar, West Lancashire, 1927; Member of Law Committee Association of Municipal Corporations, for 14 years; President Lancashire and Cheshire Antiquarian Society, 1917; Vice-President British Archæological Assoc., 1906, etc.; Governor Lancaster Royal Grammar School, 1911–46; Pres. Lancaster Astronomical Soc., 1915–19; Vice-Chm., Ancient Monuments Committee for Lancashire; VP Brontë Soc. *Publications:* J. K. S. Lapsus Calami, 1891; Corporate Insignia of Lancaster, 1897; Registers of Chester Cathedral, 1904; The Literary Associations of the County Town of Lancaster and its Surrounding Districts, 1929; Stanley John Weyman, 1933; Lancaster Freemen, Part I, 1935, Part II, 1938; Westmorland Clockmakers, Part I, 1935, Part II, 1937, Part III, 1939; etc. *Recreations:* reading; collecting Devonshire Literature and old china. *Address:* Oakrigg, Scotforth, Lancaster. *TA:* Oakrigg, Lancaster. *T:* Lancaster 50. *Clubs:* Authors'; Union (Cambridge); Manchester Literary (Manchester).

Died 21 May 1948.

HUGHES-BULLER, Ralph Buller, CIE 1908; CBE 1920; King's Police medal, 1914; ICS (retired); *b* 1871; *s* of Gen. Sir W. T. Hughes, KCB, and Katharine, *d* of Capt. Buller; *m* Elizabeth, *γ d* of late Very Rev. Dr Norman Macleod, DD, Dean of the Thistle and Dean of the Chapel Royal; one *d*. *Educ:* Marlborough; Balliol College, Oxford. Assumed name of Buller as heir of late James Buller of Dunley, Bovey Tracey. Entered ICS, 1892; retired, 1917; Political employ, 1898; Assist to Gov.-Gen.'s Agent in Baluchistan, 1899; special duty in connection with Census and Gazetteer, 1901–06; Magistrate and Collector, Secretary to Government, and Inspector-General of Police, Eastern Bengal and Assam, 1907–12; Inspector-General of Police, Bengal, 1912–16; Offg Director of Criminal Intelligence in India, 1913; special duty New Scotland Yard, 1916–17; Director National Service, South-Western Region, 1917–18; Chairman, Exeter and District Local Employment Committee, 1920; Vice-President, National Institute for the Blind, etc. *Publications:* Census Report, Baluchistan; Provincial Gazetteer of Baluchistan; articles and pamphlets. *Address:* Southdown Lodge, Brighton Rd, Lewes, Sussex. *T:* Lewes 400.

Died 13 Dec. 1949.

HUGHES-MORGAN, Maj. Sir David; *see* Morgan.

HUGHES-ROBERTS, John Gwyndeg, MVO 1928; Government Cinematograph Adviser since 1934; *b* London, 1894; *s* of late William Hughes-Roberts; *m* 1935, Isobel Violet, *d* of William Bryce. Served European War, 1917–19 (wounded, France, 1918); Private Secretary to Controller HM Stationery Office, 1921–34; Custodian of Imperial War Museum Films; Chairman Services Training Films Committee; Member National Film Library Committee; British Standards Institution, Cinematograph Industry Standards Cttee, and Ministry of Education Cttee for Production of Visual Aids. *Recreations:* the film, chess, swimming. *Address:* 85 Taymount Grange, Taymount Rise, Forest Hill, SE23. *T:* Forest Hill 6583; HM Stationery Office, 65 Whitehall, SW1. *T:* Whitehall 8855.

Died 28 Feb. 1949.

HUGO, Lt-Col James Henry, DSO 1897; MRCS (England); LRCP (London); MB, BS (London); DPH; Legion of Honour, Croix de Chevalier (1918); IMS, retired; *b* 16 July 1870; *m* 1902, Minnie Alice Muriel (*d* 1940), *d* of Col C. Dempster, Indian Army. *Educ:* Foyle College, Londonderry. St Bartholomew's Hospital. interim House Physician; Clinical Assistant Orthopædic Department; House Surgeon General Hospital, Nottingham; Assist Medical Superintendent Dulwich Infirmary; entered Netley in IMS 1896; attached to 31st Punjab Infantry, 1897; siege of Malakand; Expedition into Upper Swat; Expedition against Mahmuds (DSO, medal two clasps); Residency Surgeon, Kashmir, 1914; retired, 1925; Director of Medical Services, Jammu and Kashmir State Government, 1925–32. *Address:* Byways, The Ridgeway, Guildford, Surrey.

Died 28 Feb. 1943.

HULIN de Loo, Georges Charles Nicolas Marie, Hon. CBE, Art historian; *b* 10 Dec. 1862; *s* of Jules François de Paule Hulin de Loo and Léonie-Marie Hulin; unmarried. *Educ:* Ghent (Athénée); Ghent University (Docteur en Philosophie et Lettres, Docteur en Droit); Berlin, Strasbourg, Paris. Doctor (Hon.) University of Utrecht. Professor at the University of Ghent, 1889–1932; Member (and for 1935 President) of the Académie Royale des Sciences, des Lettres et des Beaux Arts de Belgique; Correspondant de l'Institut de France; Chairman of the Committee of the Museum of Fine Arts of Ghent; Chairman of the Committee of Modern painting of the Royal Museum of Fine Arts of Belgium; Chairman of the Society: Les Amis du Musée, Ghent, etc. *Publications:* Jan Provost, 1902; Catalogue Critique de l'Exposition de Bruges, 1902; Primitifs Français, 1904; P. Bruegel l'Ancien (with René van

Bastelaer), 1907; Heures de Milan, 1911; Comment j'ai retrouvé Hozenbaut, 1939; Le sujet du rétable des frères Van Eyck à Gand: la Glorification du Sauveur, 1941; Pedro Berruguete et les portraits d'Urbin, 1942; Traces de Hubrecht van Eyck: empreintes contemporaines en Suisse et en Allemagne, 1943; numerous articles in Burlington Magazine, Bulletin de l'Académie Royale de Belgique, Bull. de la Soc. d'Histoire et d'Archéologie de Gand, Pantheon, Jahrbuch der Koen. preuss. Kunstsammlungen, Revue Archéologique, Paris, Art in America, etc. *Recreations:* pictures, travelling. *Address:* 3 Place de l'Evêché, Ghent, Belgium; Loo-ten-Hulle (Fl. Or.) Belgium. *Clubs:* Burlington Fine Arts (Hon.); Société littéraire Le Club, Ghent.

Died Feb. 1946.

HULL, Henry Mitchell, CMG 1902; *b* 19 March 1861; *γ s* of late Rev. John Winstanley Hull; *m* 1891, Adela Rachel (*d* 1942), *d* of Rev. H. Fiennes-Clinton, Rector of Cromwell, Notts. *Educ:* Charterhouse. Private Secretary to Governor Gold Coast, 1888–91; Travelling Commissioner, Gold Coast, 1891–99; one of the British Commissioners for delimitation of boundary between Gold Coast Colony and German Protectorate of Togo, 1892; has acted on two occasions as Director of Telegraphs and Comptroller of Customs; Assist Colonial Secretary, 1899; raised and armed 3500 native levies during Ashanti Rising, 1900 (medal); Secretary for Native Affairs, Gold Coast Colony, 1902–07. *Address:* Belvedere, Castle Road, Walmer, Kent.

Died 3 Oct. 1946.

HULME, Rev. Thomas Ferrier, MA; LLD; DD; *b* Torquay, 1856; *s* of late Rev. Thomas Hulme; *m* Lucy Moore, *d* of George Alcock, Mansfield, Notts; two *d*. *Educ:* Kingswood School, Bath; Headingley College, Leeds. Graduated at Trinity College, Dublin. Entered Wesleyan Ministry, 1878; Governor of Kingswood School, Bath, 1901–03; Chairman of Wesleyan Synod in Bristol and Bath District, 1907–32; President of Wesleyan Conference, 1923–24; visited the Wesleyan Churches in Italy and Sicily, Dec. 1923–Jan. 1924; Representative to S African Conference, 1925, and extended tour of six months to visit the Wesleyan Mission Centres in the different countries of S Africa; Representative to General Conference of the Methodist Episcopal Church of America, 1928; Representative to Sesquicentennial celebration of Methodist Episcopal Church in America, 1784–1934, 1934; Representative to Australian Conference to commemorate the centenary of Methodism in Victoria, and extended tour of eight months to visit the Churches in New Zealand, South India, Ceylon and Canada, 1936; Hon. LLD Bristol, 1925; Hon. DD North-Western Univ., USA. *Publications:* John Wesley and his Horse; Voices of the New Room, 1933. *Address:* 16 Blenheim Road, Bristol 6. *T:* 34731.

Died 30 Oct. 1942.

HULTON, Col Frederick Courtenay Longuet, CB 1918; *b* 1864. Served South Africa, 1901–02 (Queen's medal with five clasps); European War, 1914–18 (despatches, CB, Order of Wen Hu of China).

Died 25 Dec. 1940.

HULTON, Lt-Col Henry Horne, DSO 1918; late RA; Government Secretary, Jersey; *b* 3 Nov. 1882; *e s* of late Rev. William Hulton of Watlington, Oxon, and 45 Lancaster Gate; *m* 1908, Isobel Hope Millicent, *γ d* of late J. Jackson, JP, DL, of the Homemead, Heacham, Norfolk; one *d*. *Educ:* Eton. Commissioned in the RH and RFA from the PWO, Norfolk Artillery, 1900; seconded to IY in SA 1902; seconded to S Nigeria Regt, WAFF 1905–07; RHA, S Africa and India, 1909–12; Inter-Allied Military Commission of Control, Germany, 1920–24; retired pay, 1927; Queen's SA medal; Delhi Durbar Coronation medal; went to France 14 Aug. with 2nd Division; Brig.-Major, RA, 6th Division, Dec. 1916; Brig.-Major, RA, 5th Australian Division, June

1917; Act. Lieut-Col 161st Yorks Brigade RFA, Aug. 1918 (twice wounded; despatches four times; DSO; 1914 Star). Actions—Mons, Basse Maroilles, Villers Cotteret, Marne, Aisne, first Ypres, Givenchy, Festubert, Somme, 1916; Vimy Ridge, Hill 70, third Ypres, Amiens, Villers Bretonneux, Hamel, Amiens, crossing River Somme, St Quentin, Hindenburg line, Fonsomme line, crossing of River Sambre, Avesnes. *Address:* Waldegrave Beaumont, Jersey, CI. *Club:* Cavalry.

Died 8 Dec. 1941.

HULTON, Col John Meredith, CBE 1919, DSO 1918; *b* 1882; *m*; two *s* one *d*. Served S Africa, 1901–02 (Queen's medal with three clasps); European War, 1914–19 (CBE, DSO, Order of the Nile, Crown of Italy, Rising Sun of Japan); Lt-Col 1927; Col 1931; Chief Instructor, Royal Tank Corps Central Schools, 1931–35; retired pay, 1935. *Address:* c/o Lloyds Bank, Ltd, Cox & Co.'s branch, Pall Mall, SW1.

Died 13 July 1942.

HULTON, Sir William (Rothwell), 2nd Bt *cr* 1905; *b* 16 Feb. 1868; *e s* of 1st Bt and Sarah Matilda, *o d* of Ralph Rothwell, Ribbleton House, Co. Lancaster; *S* father, 1907; *m* 1890, Ethel Marguerite, 3rd *d* of E. Braddyll; one *s* one *d*. *Educ:* Harrow; Clare College, Cambridge (BA 1890). *Heir: s* Roger Braddyll [*b* 30 March 1891; *m* 1918, Hon. Marjorie Evelyn Louise de Montmorency, *o c* of 6th Viscount Mountmorres; one *s* one *d*]. *Address:* Hulton Park, near Bolton.

Died 27 June 1943.

HUMBLE-BURKITT, Col Bernard Maynard, CMG 1919; DSO 1917; JP; retired; landowner; *b* Bath, 21 April 1864; 4th *s* of late Rev. Michael Maughan Humble, MA, Emmanuel College, Cambridge, Rector of Sutton Scarsdale; *g g s* of John Anderson of Swinnithwaite Hall, Yorks; *m* Vera, *d* of late Joseph Mason, Victoria, British Columbia; no *c*. *Educ:* Derby; abroad. Served North-West Rebellion, Saskatchewan, 1885 (medal); World War with British Columbia Regt, 1914–18 (DSO, CMG, despatches twice); assumed by Royal licence the surname of Burkitt, 1921. *Recreations:* shooting, fishing. *Address:* Cowden Hall, Horam, Sussex. *Clubs:* Arthur's, Bath.

Died 12 Feb. 1945.

HUMBY, Lt-Col James Frederick, CMG 1916; DSO 1902; late commanding 12th Batt. Sherwood Foresters; *b* 21 July 1860; *e s* of late Fred. Peter Humby, Southbroom, Devizes, Wilts; *m* 1883, Bertha Elizabeth, *γ d* of late Canon Rich-Jones, The Vicarage, Bradford-on-Avon. *Educ:* Paris. Joined 3rd Batt. Royal Irish Rifles as 2nd Lieut 1891; Captain, 1896; Major, 1901; commanded 54th (Ulster) Imperial Yeomanry Feb. 1900; 74th (Dublin) Imperial Yeomanry June 1901; 8th Batt. Imperial Yeomanry May 1902, South Africa; taken prisoner at Lindley with 13th Batt. May 31; escaped 30 Aug. 1900 (despatches twice; Queen's medal four clasps, King's two clasps; DSO); European War, 1914–16 (CMG). *Address:* Theomore, Swakeleys Road, Ickenham, Middlesex.

Died 23 May 1943.

HUME, Sir George Hopwood, Kt 1924; MIEE; JP; Barrister-at-Law, Middle Temple; *b* 1866; *s* of George Hume, sometime British Vice-Consul in South Russia; *m* 1st, 1901, Jeanne Alice (*d* 1922), *d* of Professor A. Ladrierre, Lausanne; 2nd, 1932, Dorothy Hunt, *yr d* of Mrs S. J. Blundell, Liverpool. *Educ:* Russia, England, France, Switzerland, Germany. MP (U) Greenwich, 1922–23, 1924–29 and 1931–45; Leader of Municipal Reform Party, London County Council, 1917–25; Member LCC since 1910; Chairman of London CC 1926–27; Alderman since 1922; Member of Thames Conservancy Board since 1916; Chairman London Electricity Committee, 1913–26; Chairman of Highways Committee, 1913–19; Member Ministry of

Transport, London and Home Counties Traffic Advisory Committee, 1924–25, and of London Home Counties Joint Electricity Authority, 1925–26. Chairman of Mildmay Mission Hospital. *Address:* 83 Lee Road, SE3. *T:* Lee Green, 2547. *Club:* Junior Carlton.

Died 13 Sept. 1946.

HUME, James Gibson, AM (Harvard), PhD (Germany); Professor Emeritus of History of Philosophy in the University of Toronto, Canada; *b* near Toronto, 1860; *s* of James Hume and Marion Brown; *m* 1892, Margaret Alice, *y d* of Thomas Bunting and Sarah Ward, St Catharines; four *s* one *d. Educ:* University of Toronto; Johns Hopkins; Harvard; Freiburg in Baden. BA, University of Toronto, 1887 with double Honours in Classics and in Philosophy; Governor-General's Gold Medal; in Johns Hopkins, Fellow elect., 1888; at Harvard, Thayer's Fellow and AM, 1889; Roger's Fellow, 1890. Prof. of History of Philosophy in Univ. of Toronto, 1889, and of Ethics in Univ. Coll., PhD Summa cum laude, Germany, 1891; visited Oxford, and the Scottish Universities, 1891; returning to University of Toronto, 1891–92. *Publications:* chiefly Articles and Reviews in American and Canadian journals; Value of a Study of Ethics; Political Economy and Ethics; Introduction to Works of Schopenhauer; Introduction to Psychology for Teachers (International Series), GP Young's Ethics of Freedom; Socialism; Evolution and Personality in Memorial Volume to Professor John Watson, Queen's University, Kingston. *Address:* 58 Spadina Road, Toronto, Canada. *Clubs:* Toronto; Harvard; Exchange (Pontiac, Mich).

Died 28 Jan. 1949.

HUME, William Fraser, DSc, FRSE, ARSM, ARCS, FGS (Lyell Medallist, 1919); FRGS; Associé Étranger of Geological Society of France; President, RGS of Egypt, 1926–40; President, Institute of Egypt, 1928–29; Technical Counsellor, Geological Survey of Egypt, till retirement on pension in 1940; *b* 1867; *y s* of George Hume of London; *m* Ethel Gladys, *y d* of James Williams of Bryn Glas, Newport; one *s* one *d. Educ:* Collège Galliard, Lausanne; Royal College of Science and Royal School of Mines, London. On teaching staff of the Royal College of Science, 1890, passing through all stages to Senior Demonstrator; Examiner in Geology, Royal Indian Engineering College, Coopers' Hill; Geological Survey of Egypt, 1897, becoming in turn Superintendent and Director; studied various economic problems; advising on Water Supply to British Army in Egypt, 1915–17. *Publications:* Notes on Russian Geology (Cretaceous Rocks, Black Earth, and Loess), 1892; Chemical and Micro-Mineralogical Researches in the Cretaceous Rocks of the South of England, 1893; Genesis of the Chalk, 1894; Cretaceous Strata of County Antrim, 1897; (with Mr Barron) Topography and Geology of Eastern Desert of Egypt, 1903; Topography and Geology of South-Eastern Sinai, 1906; Notes on Petrography of Egypt, 1908; Distribution of Iron Ores in Egypt, 1909; Study of Soils in Egypt, 1910; Building Stones of Cairo, 1910; Petroleum; its Occurrence and Origin, 1910; Nitrate Shales of Egypt, 1915; Report on Oilfield Region of Egypt, 1916; Geology of Egypt, vol. i, Surface Features of Egypt and their Determining Causes; vol. ii, The Fundamental Pre-Cambrian Rocks of Egypt and the Sudan, 1934; Terrestrial Theories (Egyptian Government), 1947; numerous other papers. *Recreations:* reading and family life. *Address:* The Laurels, Rustington, Sussex. *T:* Rustington 233.

Died 23 Feb. 1949.

HUME-COOK, Hon. James, CMG 1941; Secretary Australian Industries Protection League since 1922; *b* New Zealand, 23 Sept. 1866; *m* 1902, Nellie, *d* of Thomas Maine; two *s* one *d.* Member Legislative Assembly, Victoria, Australia, 1894–1900; House of Representatives, Commonwealth of Australia, 1900–10; Hon. Minister, 1908–10. *Address:* Girrahween, 13 Manor Street, Brighton, Melbourne, S5, Australia.

Died 7 Aug. 1942.

HUME-WILLIAMS, Rt Hon. Sir Ellis, PC 1929; 1st Bt *cr* 1922; KBE 1918; KC 1899; a Knight of Grace of the Order of St John of Jerusalem; *b* 19 Aug. 1863; *s* of J. W. Hume-Williams, Barrister-at-law, and Agnes, *d* of James Malet Charter, JP, DL, of Lynchfield Hall, Bishop's Lideard, Somerset; *m* 1886, Lucy Arnette, *d* of late J. J. Satow, Riga. *Educ:* Trin. Hall, Camb., BA, LLB, Cressingham prize, 1879. Called to the Bar, 1881; contested North Monmouthshire (Unionist), 1895; Frome Division of Somerset, 1900; North Kensington, 1906; MP (U) Bassetlaw Division, Notts, 1910–29; Recorder of Bury St Edmunds, 1901–05; of Norwich, 1905–44; served in Flanders, 1914–15, with Munro Ambulance Corps at Nieuport; Red Cross Commissioner in Russia, 1916, 1917; Executive of Central Prisoners of War Committee; Visiting Officier to exchanged prisoners in Switzerland; Liaison Officer between War Trade Department and Commission internationale de Ravitaillement. *Publications:* The Taking of Evidence on Commission; The Irish Parliament from 1782 to 1800; 10th edition of Taylor on Evidence; The World, The House and The Bar, 1930. *Heir:* s Roy Ellis, *b* 1887. *Address:* 2 Ryder Street, SW1. *Club:* Carlton.

Died 4 Feb. 1947.

HUMPHERY, John Edward, Hon. LLD (Leeds); A Managing Director of the Proprietors of Hay's Wharf, Limited; Royal Exchange Assurance and other Companies; Treasurer of Guy's Hospital since 1944; High Sheriff of Surrey, 1940–41; *b* 9 Nov. 1873; *s* of R. P. Humphery, Godstone, and M. Clayworth; *m* 1899, St George Frances, *d* of C. Innes Taylor; two *d. Educ:* Rugby. *Recreations:* yachting, hunting, shooting. *Address:* Santon, Reigate. *T:* Reigate 3260. *Clubs:* Travellers', Royal Thames Yacht.

Died 24 April 1946.

HUMPHREY, Douglas, BA, BSc; *b* London, 1880; *m* Dorothy, 2nd *d* of late Rev. E. Albany Clarke, Dikoya, Ceylon. *Educ:* Merchant Taylors' School; Sidney Sussex College, Cambridge—1st Class Natural Science Tripos, 2nd Class Honours Mathematics; BSc London. Assistant Master, Trinity College, Stratford-on-Avon, and Clayesmore School; Senior Science Master, Macclesfield Grammar School, 1907–14; war service with the Cheshire Regiment, 1914–19; Head of Department of Mathematics and Physics, The Polytechnic, 1919–32; Director of Education, The Polytechnic, W1, 1932–44. *Publications:* Advanced Mathematics for Students of Physics and Engineering, 1928; Intermediate Mechanics, 1930; Elementary Mechanics, 1939; Revision Mathematics for School Certificate, 1940. *Address:* 1 Brangwyn Drive, Patcham, Brighton, 6. *T:* Preston 3914.

Died 19 Dec. 1945.

HUMPHREYS, Arthur L., FSA, FRGS; *b* Wellington, Som, 1865. Editor and founder of Books of To-day and Tomorrow, which he conducted 1894–1924 and contributed largely to under the nom de plume of Arthur Pendenys; Vice-President of the British Record Society; late senior partner in the firm of Hatchards; retired, 1924; contributor to the Daily and Weekly Press. *Publications:* Materials for the History of Wellington (Somerset), 1889; Piccadilly Bookmen; Memorials of the House of Hatchard, 1893; Love's Garland, 1894; The Somerset Roll, 1897; The Private Library, 1897; Somersetshire Parishes, 1905; Estimates of Thomas Spencer Baynes and F. T. Elworthy, an Address to Taunton Field Club, 1905; Salt and Sincerity, 1908; Handbook to County Bibliography, 1917; East Hendred: A Berkshire Parish Historically Treated, 1923; The Art of Life, an Address to the Reading Rotary Club, 1925; Elias Ashmole and his Work for Berkshire, 1925; The History of Caversham Bridge, 1231–1926; Eccentric Characters of Berkshire, 1926; The Streets and Street Lore of Reading, 1926; Old Decorative Maps and Charts, 1926; How to write the History of a Village, 1930; Bucklebury, a Berkshire Parish, the Home of Bolingbroke, 1932; When I was a Boy, 1933; Berkshire in Song, Rhyme and Steeple Chime, 1935; History of Crockfords Club, 1828–1844, 1940. *Club:* Devonshire.

Died 21 March 1946.

HUMPHREYS, Cecil Lee Howard, OBE, TD; Director of Works, Ministry of Works and Buildings; *b* 7 Sept. 1893; *s* of late Henry Howard and Alice Page Humphreys; *m* 1918, Ailsa, *d* of late Sir James Yoxall, MP; one *d. Educ:* Westminster School. Pupil under his father, 1911–14. Joined 1st Bn HAC Aug. 5, 1914 and served in France, 1914, 1916, Salonica, 1916–17, Palestine, 1917–18, France, 1918–19; commissioned in London Regt, 1915; served continuously in Territorial Army and in the second German war, was in command of 2 Corps Signals from Sept. 1939 to July 1940 when he became Chief Signal Officer 3 Corps; evacuated from Dunkirk, May 1940; released from military service Dec. 1940 to take up post of Director of Works; until end of 1940 senior partner in firm of Howard Humphreys and Sons, Consulting Engineers, 17 Victoria Street, Westminster; has travelled a great deal in British Crown Colonies as Consulting Engineer to Crown Agents for the Colonies, especially in Africa and near East; Member of Council of Institution of Civil Engineers; MIMechE, MAmSocCE; Member of Council (British Section) of Société des Ingénieurs Civils de France; MInstWE; Member of Territorial Association of the County of London; Member of Westminster City Council; awarded Telford Premium of Institution of Civil Engineers. *Publications:* (with his brother G. Howard Humphreys) The Training of a Civil Engineer, 1932; a number of engineering papers. *Recreations:* The Territorial Army and bad golf. *Address:* The Union Club, London. *T:* Whitehall 9841. *Clubs:* Bath, Union.

Died 18 July 1941.

HUMPHREYS, Brig.-Gen. Gardiner, CB 1915; CMG 1918; DSO 1900; *b* 2 March 1865; *m* 1906, Lady Emily Nugent (*d* 1935), *d* of 10th Earl of Westmeath; two *s.* Entered RA 1884; Captain, 1893; Major, 1900; Colonel, 1914; Brig.-General, 1915; served South Africa, 1899–1902 (wounded twice, despatches, Queen's medal 6 clasps); European War, 1914–18 (despatches, CB, CMG, Légion d'honneur (croix d'officier), Croix de Guerre). *Club:* Naval and Military.

Died 6 Feb. 1942.

HUMPHREYS, George Alfred, FRIBA, LLD; FSA, RCA; JP Carnarvonshire. Member of the Town Planning Institute; Fellow of the Land Agents Soc.; Chief Agent to Rt Hon. Lord Mostyn, Exors. Col Hon. H. Lloyd Mostyn, decd., and others; Governor Univ. of Wales; Life Governor Univ. College of N Wales and Chairman of Council; Trustee Royal Cambrian Academy; Member Council of Agriculture for Wales; Past Chairman Caernarvonshire Standing Joint (Police) Committee; and present Chairman of Finance and General Purposes Committee; Vice-Chairman Caernarvonshire County Licensing Committee. *Address:* Mostyn Estate Office, Llandudno. *TA:* Humphreys, Architect, Llandudno. *T:* (Office) 6977, (Private) 6078.

Died 8 May 1948.

HUMPHREYS, Sir George William, KBE 1927; CBE 1920; TD; Chevalier Légion d'Honneur; MInstCE; Consulting Engineer; *b* 1863; *s* of late Thos Wm Humphreys; *m* Helen McGilliwie (*d* 1942), *y d* of late Robt Sinclair; one *d. Educ:* Mill Hill School. Trained on railway work for GWR and with the late Mr Woodman Hill; engaged on dock and harbour work in England and France prior to obtaining (1902) in open competition the position of Manager of Works to the LCC; Chief

Engineer of the LCC, 1912–30; during the War was Vice-Chairman and Chairman of the Munitions Works Board of the Ministry of Munitions; a member of the last Committee of experts and of the Representative Committee entrusted with the preservation of St Paul's Cathedral; Chairman of the Building Research Board of the Department of Industrial and Scientific Research, 1928–33; Past President Institution of Civil Engineers; Colonel, late Engineer and Railway Staff Corps RE (TA). *Publications:* communications to Institution of Civil Engineers. *Address:* 59 Drayton Gardens, SW10. *Club:* Reform.

Died 9 March 1945.

HUMPHRIES, Sir Sidney Richard White, Kt 1921; JP, late Alderman late City Councillor, Member of Dock Board, and other Committees for 30 years, retired, 1938; JP County and City of Bristol, since 1905; *b* 7 Sept. 1857; *s* of late George Humphries of Bath, and late Sarah, *d* of late Richard White, of Stratton, St Margaret's, Wilts; *m* 1890, Kate, *d* of late Charles Gibbs; one *s. Educ:* Allesley Park College, Warwickshire. Formerly connected with Flour Milling Industry; established the Castle Flour Mills, Bristol, 1895; President Bristol Incorporated Chamber of Commerce and Shipping, 1905–08; President National Association of British and Irish Millers, 1912; President Bristol Channel and West of England Corn Trade Association, 1914; Chairman Agricultural Development Movement (Bristol Centre), 1909–14; First President Gloucestershire Old Spots Pig Society; Bristol Representative at Chamber of Commerce Conferences, Montreal, 1904; Buda Pesth and Milan, 1907; Liège, 1908, Cape Town, 1927. *Recreations:* hunting, motoring. *Address:* Eastfield Lodge, Westbury-on-Trym, Bristol. *T:* Westbury-on-Trym, 66942. *Clubs:* Constitutional, Bristol.

Died 3 March 1941.

HUMPHRIES, Sydney S.; *see* Sidney-Humphries.

HUMPHRIS, Francis Howard, MD (Brux., Honours), FRCP (Edin.), DMRE (Camb.), MRCS (Eng.), LRCP (Lond.), LM; Major RAMC, TF, retired; Commander St John of Jerusalem; Chevalier of the Order of Leopold I; Freedom of the City of London; Livery Apothecaries Company; Prime Warden Blacksmiths Company, 1941–43; Third London General Hospital, Officer in Charge X-Ray Department and Department of Electro-Therapeutics Land Tax Commissioner for division of City of Westminster; Governor of Christ's Hospital; Member of Lloyd's; *b* Croydon, May 1866; *s* of F. H. Humphris, JP; *m* Ethel Marion, *d* of Col Hesketh, ISC. *Educ:* Highgate School; privately; Edinburgh University; RCS; UCH. Tutor at Univ. of Brussels, 1895–98; 10 years in Honolulu; Supt Insane Asylum; Senior Staff Physician, Queen's Hospital, Honolulu; Exam. for Licence to Practice; Pres. of the Hawaiian Territorial Medical Society, etc.; came to London, 1908; for 6 months was Clinical Assistant X-Ray and Electro-Therapeutic Department, W London Hospital; Served European War (Mons Star, 1914 War Medal, Victory Medal, despatches); sent to Egypt by War Office with rank of Major, RAMC, to reorganise X-Ray Depts of Military Hospitals Golden Key for distinguished services to Physical Therapy; FRSM; Past Pres. Hunterian Society; Past Chairman of Council and President Irish Medical Graduates' Association; Consulting X-Ray Physician to East and West Molesey and Hampton Court Cottage Hosp., and Guildhall School of Music; Hon. Consulting X-Ray Physician and Electrotherapist to Christ's Hospital; late Hon. Consultant Shell Shock Hospital (Lord Knutsford's Com.); Special Correspondent of Physical Therapeutics, USA; Consulting Physician Specialising in X-Rays and Electro-Therapeutics; Hon. Consulting X-Ray Physician and member Honorary Advisory Medical Board St John's Clinic and Institute of Physical Medicine. *Publications:* Electro-Therapeutics for

Practitioners, 2nd edition, 1921; Artificial Sunlight and its Therapeutic Uses, 5th edition, 1929; Physiotherapy, Its Principles and Practice, 1930; Emanotherapy, 1937. *Recreation:* golf. *Address:* Aloha, 12 Arnison Road, East Molesey, Surrey. (For letters and appointments: c/o Dr Stuart Webb 86 Brook St, W1). *Clubs:* Savage, Marlborough-Windham, Lansdowne, Pilgrims; Bath and County, Bath.

Died 17 June 1947.

HUMPHRYS, Brig.-Gen. Charles Vesey, CBE 1919; retired pay; *b* 1 Oct. 1862; *s* of late John Winter Humphrys, of Ballyhaise House, Cavan and Priscilla Cecilia, *d* of Rev. J. P. Garrett, of Kilgarron, Co. Carlow; *m* 1st, 1892, Florence, *d* of James Humphrys, and *g d* of Christopher Humphrys, of Clareview, Co. Fermanagh; one *s*; 2nd, Marion, *d* of Edwin Owen, Editor and journalist. *Educ:* Cheltenham College; Sandhurst. Lieut Duke of Wellington's Regt, 1882; Adjutant, 1891–95; commanded, 1908–12; served in S African War, 1901–02 (Queen's medal 3 clasps, despatches); appointed Commandant Central School of Musketry, India, 1912; commanded Bangalore and Southern Brigades, 1915–16; commanded various brigades in England and France, 1916–19. *Recreations:* hunting, shooting, fishing, golf. *Address:* The Old Manor House, Chilworth, Surrey.

Died 21 April 1944.

HUNKIN, Rt Rev. Joseph Wellington, OBE 1919; MC; DD; Bishop of Truro since 1935; *b* 25 Sept. 1887; *s* of late Joseph Weston and Elizabeth Hockin Hunkin; *m* 1914, Ruth Christobel Beer; two *s* two *d*. *Educ:* Truro School; Leys School and Gonville and Caius College, Cambridge. Mathematical Tripos, 1908 (bracketed 12th Wrangler); Part I Theological Tripos, 1910 (1st Class Honours); Carus Greek Testament Prize, 1910; Crosse Scholarship, 1910; Jeremie Septuagint Prize, 1912. Assistant Curate, St Andrew's, Plymouth, 1913–14; Fellow of Gonville and Caius College, 1913; Vice-Principal, Wycliffe Hall, Oxford, 1914; TCF, 1915–19 (MC and bar, OBE); Dean, Gonville and Caius College, 1919; Examining Chaplain to Bishop of Exeter and Bishop of Chelmsford, 1919; Tutor, Gonville and Caius College, 1920; Secretary to the General Board of Studies, 1924–26; Senior Proctor, 1925–26; Archdeacon of Coventry and Rector of St Andrew's with Holy Trinity, Rugby, 1927–35; Chaplain to the King, 1926–35; Hulsean Preacher, 1931. *Publications:* Essay in Palestine in General History (Schweich Lectures), I and II Maccabees in SPCK Commentary, The Earliest Christian Church, Episcopal Ordination and Confirmation; The Spirit of Man and the Spirit of God; The New Testament, a Conspectus; papers in Theological Journals, etc. *Recreation:* gardening. *Address:* Lis Escop, Truro. *T:* Truro 2183.

Died 28 Oct. 1950.

HUNLOKE, Major Sir Philip, GCVO 1936; KCVO 1928; CVO 1921; MVO 1916; JP; Extra Groom-in-Waiting to the King since 1936; *b* 1868; *e s* of Capt. Philip Perceval, late RHG (*d* 1897), and 2nd wife Hon. Ernestine Wellington Sidney, 2nd *d* of 1st Lord de L'Isle and Dudley; *m* Sylvia, OBE 1918, *d* of J. P. Heseltine, of Walhampton, Lymington, Hants; two *d* one *s*. Served in South African War, 1899–1901; European War, 1914–18; hon. Capt. in the Army, 1901; late Major in Bucks IY; assumed by royal licence name of Hunloke, 1905; Groom-in-Waiting to the King, 1911; younger brother of Trinity House, 1931; Légion d'Honneur (Officier); Order of St Stanislaus (2nd Class); Redeemer of Greece; Crown of Belgium (2nd Class). *Recreations:* yachting, hunting, shooting, etc. *Address:* Hides Close, Beaulieu, Hants. *Clubs:* Turf; Royal Yacht Squadron (Commodore), Island Sailing (Commodore), Cowes.

Died 1 April 1947.

HUNN, Major Sydney Arthur, MVO 1919; OBE 1918; MC; Major, 10th Australian Light Horse Regiment; Reserve of Officers; *b* 1889; *m* 1921, Dorothy, *e d* of late Lt-General Sir J. Talbot Hobbs, KCB, KCMG; one *s* one *d*. Served European War, 1915–19 (despatches twice, MC, OBE, MVO, 1914–15 Star (2 medals) French Croix de Guerre); acted as ADC to Prince of Wales during his stay with Australian Corps in France and Belgium. *Address:* 169 Walsh Street, South Yarra, Victoria, Australia. *Clubs:* Weld, Naval and Military, Turf, Perth; Naval and Military, Melbourne.

Died 25 Feb. 1942.

HUNT, Dame Agnes Gwendoline, DBE 1926; RRC 1918; Founder Shropshire Orthopædic Hospital, now known as Robert Jones and Agnes Hunt Orthopædic Hospital, Oswestry, 1900 and Founder Derwen Cripples Training College, 1927; *b* 31 Dec. 1866; 7th *c* of Rowland Hunt, Boreatton Park, Shropshire. *Educ:* at home. Entered Royal Alexandra Hospital, Rhyl, as lady pupil, 1887; completed nursing training at Salop Infirmary, 1890; joined Queen's Jubilee Nurses, 1891; acted as Commandant of Auxiliary Orthopædic Hospital, Baschurch, Aug. 1914–July 1919; inaugurated scheme of Orthopædic after care clinics; made Hon. Member of the British Orthopædic Association, 1925. *Publications:* Reminiscences, 1935; This is my Life, 1938; The Story of Baschurch; various articles published in the Cripples Journal. *Address:* Boreatton, Baschurch, Shropshire. *T:* Baschurch 207.

Died 24 July 1948.

HUNT, Adm. Sir (Allen) Thomas, KCB 1924; CB 1918; CSI 1911; *b* 14 Feb. 1866; 3rd *s* of late Rt Hon. G. Ward Hunt; *m* 1924, Dorothy, 2nd *d* of late Rev. Horace Waller. *Educ:* Marlborough College. Entered Navy, 1879; Commander, 1900; Captain 1906; Vice-Adm. 1922; served Egyptian War, 1882 (medal, bronze star); Witu, 1890 (despatches, general Africa medal, clasp); Dongola Expedition, 1896 (Khedive's medal); Crete, 1897 (despatches); South Africa, 1899–1900 (medal and clasp); Somaliland, 1908–09 (medal and clasp); Persian Gulf, 1909–11 (CSI, medal and clasp); 1914–15 (Star, War Medal, Victory Medal); Coronation, 1911 (medal); 3rd class Order of Rising Sun, Japan, 1912; Rear-Adm. 1917; European War, 1914–18 (CB); C-in-C, S America, 1919–21; retired list, 1924; Admiral, 1926. *Recreations:* shooting, fishing, billiards, golf, lawn tennis. *Address:* Byne House, Warminster. *Clubs:* United Service, Shikar.

Died 24 Feb. 1943.

HUNT, Major Edwin Watkin, DSO 1916; MC, JP; Farmer; Director of the Land and Agricultural Bank of South Africa; Life President, Transvaal Agricultural Union; Member, South African Shipping Board; Deputy Chairman, South African Live Stock and Meat Industries Control Board; *b* 10 Jan. 1869; *s* of George Henry Hunt and Elizabeth Davies; *m* 1903, Hetty Sheasby. *Educ:* Public School, Sydney. Represented a Johannesburg constituency in the First Provincial Council of the Transvaal; Member of the Johannesburg Municipal Council for several years; Member of Parliament for Turffontein, for several years; Life Member of the Executive Committee of the TAU; President South African Agricultural Union on seven occasions, member, Education Committee; President Johannesburg Poultry Club; Member of the Advisory Board of Agriculture, SA; Chairman of Producers Advisory Committee under the Marketing Act, 1937; served throughout Anglo-Boer War; raised and commanded Hunt's Scouts, German West African Campaign (despatches, DSO); Second in Command 9th South African Horse, East African Campaign (despatches, MC); for some time Commandant Kilwa Kisawani and other posts, East African Campaign; affiliated Life Member Empire Parliamentary Association; Life Fellow of the Royal Empire Society. *Recreations:* gardening, bowls. *Address:*

M'tamba Ranch, PO Huntleigh, N Transvaal, SA. *Clubs:* Pretoria, Pretoria; Union, Wanderers, Johannesburg.

Died 28 Nov. 1945.

HUNT, Brig. Frederick Welsley, CB 1923; CMG 1915; CBE 1919; RAVC; *b* 28 Nov. 1871; *m* 1910, Kathleen, *d* of late Col R. F. Williamson, CB; one *d.* Captain Army Veterinary Corps, 1902; Major, 1910; Lieut-Col 1915; Colonel, 1921; served NW Frontier, India, 1897–98 (medal with clasp); S Africa, 1899–1902 (Queen's medal and clasps; King's medal 2 clasps); European War, 1914–17 (despatches twice, CMG, Bt Col); Director Veterinary Services in India, QMG Branch, 1925–28; retired pay, 1928. *Address:* Rockmount, Co. Waterford.

Died 23 Dec. 1944.

HUNT, Gerard L.; *see* Leigh-Hunt.

HUNT, Henry Ambrose; *b* London, 7 Feb. 1866; *s* of E. J. Hunt; *m* 1889, W. E. Linden; two *d. Educ:* Dartford Grammar School. Joined the Sydney Observatory Staff, 1884; won the Prize Essay on Southerly Bursters given by the late Hon. Ralph Abercromby, 1892; inventor of the Cube Pressure Anemometer, 1902; Acting Meteorologist for State of New South Wales, 1904; Meteorologist for the Commonwealth of Australia, 1906–31; retired, 1931; organizer of the existing service. *Publications:* Types of Australian Weather, 1893; numerous papers on Australian Climate. *Recreations:* chess, mechanics, motoring. *Address:* 34 Martin Street, Elsternwick, Melbourne, Australia. *T:* Brighton 1331. *Club:* Australian (Melbourne).

Died 7 Feb. 1946.

HUNT, Hilary Lushington Holman H.; *see* Holman-Hunt.

HUNT, Hubert Walter, MusD; FRCO; Hon. RCM; LRAM; Organist and Master of the Choristers of Bristol Cathedral since 1901; *b* Windsor, 1865; *s* of Thomas Hunt, Lay-Clerk of St George's Chapel, Windsor Castle; *m* Clara Harriett, *d* of James Clements; one *s* one *d. Educ:* St George's School, Windsor Castle, and privately. Chorister at St George's, 1874–80; principal solo boy for two years; articled to Sir Geo. Elvey, 1880; articles transferred to Mr (Sir) Walter Parratt, 1882; Organist and Choirmaster Clewer Parish Church, 1883; Christ Church, Clapham, 1886; St Jude's, South Kensington, 1887; studied the violin under J. S. Liddle and J. T. Carrodus; public performances chiefly in Chamber Music; Director (Conductor) of the Bristol Madrigal Society, 1915. *Publications:* Male Voice Chant Book; A Short Account of Bristol Cathedral Organ. *Address:* 14 Belgrave Road, Bristol 8. *Club:* Bristol Music.

Died 7 Oct. 1945.

HUNT, Sir John, Kt 1923; OBE 1918; Town Clerk of the City of Westminster, 1900–28; Honorary Clerk of the Metropolitan Boroughs Standing Joint Committee, 1913–28; *b* Derby, 19 Oct. 1859; *e s* of late Henry Hunt; *m* 1899, Annie Jane Creed (*d* 1943), *d* of John Arthur; two *s. Educ:* Gloucester and Southampton Grammar Schools. Barrister-at-law of the Middle Temple; an Assistant-Commissioner under the London Government Act 1899. *Publications:* London Local Government, 2 vols; The London Government Act, 1899; Metropolitan Borough Council Elections. *Address:* Ruskin House, Orpington, Kent. *Club:* Constitutional.

Died 31 Jan. 1945.

HUNT, Lt-Col Reginald Seager, DSO 1918; *b* 24 Feb. 1874; *s* of Walter Freeman Hunt and Alice Mortimore. *Educ:* Haileybury College. Served South African War, 1899–1902 (Queen's medal with three clasps); European War, 1914–18, France, Egypt, Syria, Mesopotamia (DSO, despatches twice); Iraq, 1920 (medal); 3rd KO

Hussars, and 1st King's Dragoon Guards. *Address:* The Old Manor House, Walcott, Norwich. *TA:* Walcott, Bacton. *T:* Walcott 237.

Died 1 April 1942.

HUNT, Rowland; MP (U) Ludlow Div. Shropshire, 1903–18; JP, DL; *b* 13 March 1858; *e s* of late Rowland Hunt of Boreatton, and Florence Marian, *d* of R. Humfrey of Stoke Albany; *m* 1st, 1890, G. Veronica (*d* 1924), 4th *d* of late Duncan Davidson of Tulloch; two *s* one *d*; 2nd, 1932, H. Evelyn, 3rd *d* of late Rev. T. H. Hunt, Ruyton Park, Shropshire. *Educ:* Eton; Magdalene College, Cambridge. Hunted Eton College beagles for two years, and also Trinity College beagles for two years; hunted Wheatland hounds for ten years, Shropshire hounds for two years and Wheatland hounds for three years; served with Lovat's Scouts in South Africa; Major in City of London Rough Riders. *Publication:* pamphlet on Import Duties and Imperial Preference called Free-trade or Freedom: Which? *Address:* Linley Green, Broseley, Shropshire. *T:* Iron Bridge 153.

Died 30 Nov. 1943.

HUNT, Adm. Sir Thomas; *see* Hunt, Adm. Sir A. T.

HUNT, Lt-Col Thomas Edward C.; *see* Carew-Hunt.

HUNT, Rev. Thomas Henry, DD; Alexandra Professor of Divinity, King's College, Halifax, Nova Scotia, since 1907; Fellow since 1938; *b* St Eleanors, PEI, 1865; *e s* of William T. de V. Hunt. *Educ:* St Peter's School; Charlottetown, PEI; King's College, Windsor, NS. Deacon, 1888; Priest, 1889; Headmaster of St Peter's Boys' School, 1888–1904; Assistant Priest, St Peter's Cathedral, 1889–1904; Lecturer in Hebrew and Divinity, Trinity College, Toronto, 1904–07. *Address:* King's College, Halifax, Nova Scotia.

Died Aug. 1941.

HUNT, Violet; *b* Durham, *d* of the late Alfred William Hunt, RWS, and Margaret, *d* of James Raine, DCL; *m* 1911. *Publications:* The Maiden's Progress, a novel in Dialogue, 1894; A Hard Woman, 1895; Unkist, Unkind! 1897; The Human Interest, 1899; Affairs of the Heart, 1900; The Celebrity at Home, 1904; Sooner or Later, 1904; The Cat (Animal Autobiographies), 1905; White Rose of Weary Leaf, 1908; The Wife of Altamont, 1910; Tales of the Uneasy, 1910; The Doll, 1911; The Desirable Alien, 1913; The House of Many Mirrors, 1915; Their Lives, 1916; The Last Ditch, 1918; Their Hearts, 1921; The Tiger Skin, 1924; More Tales of the Uneasy, 1925; The Flurried Years, 1926; The Wife of Rossetti, 1932. *Address:* 80 Campden Hill Road, W8. *T:* Western 4460.

Died 16 Jan. 1942.

HUNTER, Maj.-Gen. Sir Alan John, KCVO 1937; CB 1934; CMG 1919; DSO 1918; MC; Director, Prisoners of War, War Office, 1940–41; *b* 5 Oct. 1881; *s* of John Turner Hunter; *m* 1913, Joan, 4th *d* of Hon. Arden Adderley; three *s* two *d. Educ:* Wellington College. 2nd Lieut Huntingdon Militia (5th Bn KRRC), 1900; 2nd Lieut KRRC, 1901; Captain, 1913; Major, 1916; Lieut-Col (Brev.), 1917; Colonel, 1921; Maj.-Gen. 1933; ADC to Lieutenant-General and General for Ireland, 1908–10; served South African War, 1901–02 (Queen's medal 2 clasps); Brigade-Major, France, 1915–16; DAQMG April–Oct. 1916; GSO2 Oct.–Nov. 1916; Commandant School of Instruction (temp. Col), Nov. 1916–April 1917; Brigade Commander (temp. Brig.-Gen.), April 1917–May 1919 (despatches seven times, Brevet Lieut-Col, MC, DSO, CMG, Belgian Croix de Guerre, 1914–15 Star, two medals); GSO2 War Office, 1919–21; GSO1 War Office, 1921–23; Commandant Small Arms School (temp. Col Cdt.), 1923–26; Brigade Commander, Northern Command, 1926–28; AA and QMG 3rd Division, 1928–31; Brigadier, General Staff, Eastern Command, 1931–33; Director of Personal Services, War

Office, 1934–38; retired pay, 1938; Secretary, National Rifle Association, 1938. *Address:* Cowshot Farm, Bisley Camp, Brookwood, Surrey. *Club:* United Sports.

Died 5 March 1942.

HUNTER, Henry Hamilton, CBE 1931; LLD (Dub.); Advocate; *b* Dublin, 1875; *s* of late William Adams Hunter, Glenvar, Clontarf, Dublin; *m* 1914, Izabel Langford Guilbride; one *s*. *Educ:* Trinity College, Dublin, 1st Senior Moderator and gold medallist in History and Political Science. Advocate of the Supreme Court of the Cape of Good Hope, Court of the Eastern Districts of the Cape of Good Hope, and the High Court of Uganda; served with the Rhodesia Regiment in the South African War (Queen's medal and three clasps); served European War (East Africa); temporary Captain; Senior Unofficial Member of the Legislative Council of Uganda, 1921–33; Unofficial Member of the Kenya and Uganda Inter-Colonial Railway Council until 1934 and of the Kenya and Uganda Harbour Board, 1932–34; represented Uganda at Coronation, 1937; Silver Jubilee Medal; Coronation Medal. *Publication:* Planting in Uganda (with E. Brown, FLS). *Recreations:* golf and sailing. *Address:* PO Box 26, Kampala, Uganda.

Died 20 Jan. 1944.

HUNTER, Hon. John McEwan; retired; Chairman of Board of Investment and Finance of Australian Presbyterian Church Incorporated, Queensland, since 1927; Member of Judicial Committee of Australian Presbyterian Church Incp., since 1930; Governing Director, Hunters Pty Ltd, since 1890; President of Queensland Chamber of Agricultural Associations, 1929; *b* 14 Feb. 1863; *m* 1890, Helen Guthrie, *d* of Archibald Moffat, Toowoomba; one *d*. Agent-General for Queensland, 1919–22. *Address:* Brisbane, Queensland, Australia.

Died 18 April 1940.

HUNTER, Matthew, CIE 1916; Indian Educational Service (retired); *s* of late William Hunter, Cowside, Settle, Yorkshire; unmarried. *Educ:* Giggleswick School; Queen's College, Oxford; University, Strasburg; University, Heidelberg; Honours, Final School of Natural Science, Oxford; Burdett-Coutts University Scholarship in Geology; MA 1890. Lecturer in Chemistry and Physics, Rangoon College, 1890–1909; Chemical Examiner to the Government of Burma, 1890–1905; Acting Principal, Rangoon College, 1905 and 1909–11; Principal, Rangoon College (now University College, Rangoon), 1911–23; Hon. DSc Rangoon, 1922. *Address:* 28 Westbourne Park Villas, W2. *Club:* East India and Sports.

Died 18 May 1941.

HUNTER, Robert Lewin, MA; *b* 1852; *s* of late Richard Hunter, Wimbledon, SW; *m* 1st, 1877, *d* of Thos Devas, of Mount Ararat, Wimbledon; two *s* two *d* (two *s* killed in war); 2nd, Margaret Montgomery Pirrie (*d* 1926), *yr d* of Rt Hon. A. M. Carlisle; 3rd, 1933, Hon. Elaine Augusta Villiers, *widow* of Ernest Villiers and *d* of 1st Baron Wimborne. *Educ:* Winchester; BNC, Oxford. Admitted a Solicitor, 1877; late Warden of Bradfield College; Law Debenture Corporation, Meux's Brewery Co. (Deputy Chairman), and British Medical Bureau. *Clubs:* United University, Prince's.

Died 16 May 1942.

HUNTER, Samuel Robert, JP, Antrim; BA, MD, BCh, BAO; General Practitioner of Medicine in Dunmurry, Co. Antrim; Divisional Surgeon St John's Ambulance Brigade, 1940; *b* 3 March 1877; *s* of William and Margaret Hunter; *m* 1911, Kathleen Sophia, *d* of late Rev. Andrew Macafee, Omagh, Co. Tyrone; two *s* one *d*. *Educ:* Upper Sullivan School, Holywood, Co. Down; Royal Academical Institution, Belfast; Queen's University, Belfast. Civil Surgeon to Royal Artillery at Fort Dunree, Co. Donegal, 1902; House Surgeon and

Extern Surgeon Royal Victoria Hospital, Belfast, 1903; Temp. Captain RAMC (Salonica and Mesopotamia), 1916–18; Medical Officer to Post Office, Dunmurry, since 1927; Chairman Belfast Division of British Medical Association, 1932–33; Treasurer Belfast Division of British Medical Association since 1933; President of Ulster Medical Society, 1934–35. *Recreations:* golf, archæology. *Address:* Baroni, The Green, Dunmurry, Co. Antrim. *T:* Dunmurry 2239.

Died 9 July 1948.

HUNTER, Walter King, MD, DSc, FRFPSG; LLD, Emeritus Professor University of Glasgow; Consulting Physician, Glasgow Royal Infirmary; late Consulting Physician Glasgow Royal Mental Hospital; Major, RAMC (TF) (retired); late Physician Glasgow Royal Infirmary; late President, Royal Medico Chirurgical Society of Glasgow; *b* Glasgow, 1867; *s* of late William Hunter, merchant, Glasgow; unmarried. *Educ:* Glasgow Academy; Glasgow University; King's College, London; Paris. Has held following appointments—Foulis Memorial Scholarship; Resident Medical Officer, Royal Hospital for Sick Children; Resident Physician, Glasgow Royal Infirmary; Assistant Physician, Glasgow Royal Infirmary; Extra Physician, Royal Hospital for Sick Children; Lecturer in Practice of Medicine, Queen Margaret College, Glasgow University; Muirhead Professor of Medicine, University of Glasgow, 1911–34; Member of the Association of Physicians. *Publications:* Recent Advances in Hæmatology, 1911; Acute Degenerative Changes in the Nervous System, as illustrated by Snake-venom Poisoning, in Proceedings of the Royal Society of Medicine, 1910; Certain Chronic Glandular Enlargements, Lancet, 1912; and many other papers. *Recreations:* golf, fishing, yachting. *Address:* Thirladene, Bridge of Allan, Stirlingshire. *T:* Bridge of Allan 2262. *Clubs:* Art, Western (Glasgow).

Died 7 Nov. 1947.

HUNTER-BLAIR, Captain Sir Edward, 6th Bt *cr* 1786; RN; JP; *b* Edinburgh, 14 March 1858; 4th *s* of late Sir Edward Hunter-Blair, 4th Bt, and Elizabeth, *d* of late George Wauchope; *S* brother, 1939; *m* 1886, Cecilia Dora, 3rd *d* of late Sir W. J. Farrer; one *s*. *Educ:* HMS Britannia. Joined Britannia, 1870; Lieut 1882; Comdr 1895; succeeded to the property of Blairquhan, 1896; retired, 1899; Chairman of the Carrick District Committee of the Ayrshire County Council, 1909–30; Vice-Lieut for Ayrshire, 1925–42; served as Captain, 1915–19. *Heir: s* James Hunter-Blair. *Address:* Milton, Maybole, Ayrshire.

Died 11 April 1945.

HUNTINGTON, Emily Mabel, CBE 1929; 2nd *d* of late William Balle Huntington, DL, 143 Piccadily, W, and Blackmore Park, Hanley Swan, Worcester. *Educ:* Coed-Bel, Chislehurst, Kent; Dresden. *Recreations:* hunting, tennis, golf. *Address:* Bricklehampton Hall, Pershore, Worcs. *TA:* Pershore. *T:* Elmley Castle 213. *Clubs:* Ladies' Automobile, Ladies' Carlton.

Died 20 Jan. 1948.

HUNTON, Sidney W., MA; Professor of Mathematics, Mount Allison University, Sackville; Professor Emeritus since 1935; *b* Ottawa, Ontario; *s* of Thomas Hunton, merchant, and Amelia Hunton; *m* Annie, *d* of Dr J. R. Inch, Chief Superintendent of Education for New Brunswick; three *s* two *d*. *Educ:* McGill University (scholar); University College, London. Won the Canadian Gilchrist Scholarship; graduated in Arts in the University of London; Prizeman in Mathematics and won Rothschild Scholarship in Mathematics, University College. Assistant to Professor Rowe in University College; Delegate to Congress of the Universities of the Empire in London, 1912. *Address:* Sackville, New Brunswick, Canada.

Died 28 Nov. 1941.

HURD, Sir Percy Angier, Kt 1932; 3rd *s* of late William Hurd, solicitor; *m* Hannah (*d* 1949), *d* of late Rev. Dr Cox, Dundee; two *s.* Was chiefly concerned in the establishment of The Outlook, 1898; editor and managing director until change of proprietors, 1904; London editor Montreal Star and associated Canadian journals; editor Canadian Gazette and later Canada's Weekly; Sec. Tariff Commission; Delegate to Devastated Regions of France on Allied Relief Committee of Royal Agricultural Society, 1915–18; Alderman of Hornsey until 1945; MP (U) Frome, Dec. 1918–23; MP (C) Devizes, 1924–45; Vice-Chairman Departmental Committee on Agricultural Produce (Linlithgow Committee); Member, Departmental Committee on Municipal Service; Pres. Rural District Councils Association, 1925–45. *Publications:* The Empire, A Family Affair; The New Empire Partnership: Defence, Commerce, Politics (joint with Sir Archibald Hurd); Next Steps in Empire Partnership; The War and the Future; Canada, Past, Present and Future; The Fighting Territorials (2 vols). *Address:* Hillside, Jackson's Lane, Highgate, N6. *T:* Mountview 1920. *Club:* Constitutional.

Died 5 June 1950.

HURDON, Elizabeth, CBE 1938; MD, FACS; *d* of John and Anne Coom Hurdon, Cornwall. *Educ:* privately; The Ladies' College (defunct), Hamilton, Canada; Toronto University. Past Director of Medical Services and Research, Marie Curie Hospital; formerly Associate in Gynæcology in the Johns Hopkins University, Baltimore, USA; Medical Officer, attached RAMC Malta and Salonica, 1916, 1917, 1918; Member, British Empire Cancer Campaign; Member, Advisory Council of the Marie Curie Hospital; Hon. Member, Medical Women's Federation (British); Fellow Royal Soc. of Medicine. *Publications:* The Vermiform Appendix and its Disease (with H. A. Kelly), 1905; Pathology of the Reproductive Organ, Operations for disease of the Appendix, in Gynæcology and Abdominal Surgery, 1908; Contributions to medical journals in Great Britain and America. *Recreation:* gardening. *Address:* Rockleigh, Exeter. *T:* Exeter 3660. *Club:* Forum.

Died 29 Jan. 1941.

HURLE, John A. Cooke-; JP, Devon; *b* 1863; 2nd *s* of late J. Cooke-Hurle, Brislington; *m* 1902, Alice Mary, 2nd *d* of late Thomas Davey, Leigh Woods, Bristol; one *s* three *d. Educ:* Uppingham. Served with the 7th Battalion Imperial Yeomanry in South Africa, retiring with the rank of Captain; Major North Somerset Yeomanry, 1914; served European War, 1914–17; Master of the Lamerton Foxhounds, 1906–11; New Forest Foxhounds, 1911–13; South Devon Foxhounds, 1913–15. *Recreation:* hunting. *Address:* Holne Cott, Ashburton, S Devon.

Died 30 May 1941.

HURST, Sir Arthur Frederick, Kt 1937; MA, DM Oxon, FRCP, London; University Lecturer in Medicine, Oxford; Consulting Physician and Governor of Guy's Hospital and Medical School; Physician (temp.) to Radcliffe Infirmary, Oxford; Lt-Col, late RAMC; late Member of Medical Advisory Committee (MEF), Cons. Physician at Salonica and Neurologist to Netley Hospital and Officer in Charge of the Seale Hayne Military Hospital for functional nervous disorders; late President, Medical Section, Royal Society of Medicine; President, International Society of Gastro-Enterology; Vice-President, Anglo-Soviet Medical Society; Hon. Fellow, Ulster and Manchester Medical Societies, and Hon. Member, Association of British Physicians, American Medical Association, Swedish Medical Society, American and Mexican Gastro-Enterological Associations, and the Sociétés de Gastro-Entérologie of Paris and Belgium; *b* Bradford, Yorkshire, 23 July 1879; *m* Cushla, *y d* of late Frederick Riddiford, Hawera, New Zealand; one *s* two *d. Educ:* Bradford and Manchester Grammar Schools; Magdalen College, Oxford (Demy); Guy's Hospital (University Scholar). 1st class final honour School of Physiology, Oxford, 1901; gold medals in medicine and surgery, Guy's Hospital (University Scholar). 1st class final honour School of Physiology, Oxford, 1901; gold medals in medicine and surgery, Guy's Hospital, 1904; Radcliffe Travelling Fellow 1905–08, Radcliffe Prize, 1909 and Osler Memorial Medal, 1935, Oxford University. Formerly Demonstrator in Physiology and Neurologist, Guy's Hospital; Goulstonian Lecturer Royal College of Physicians, 1911; Croonian Lecturer, RCP, 1920; Harveian Orator, RCP, 1937; Moxon Medallist, RCP, 1939. *Publications:* books and papers on Medical Subjects. *Address:* Red Gables, Headington, Oxford. *T:* Oxford 6916. *Club:* Athenæum.

Died 17 Aug. 1944.

HURST, Bertram Lawrance, MInstCE; MIMechE; MLStructE; Chartered Consulting Civil Engineer in private practice since 1907; *b* 21 March 1875; *er s* of Arthur Allen and Julia Sarah Charlotte Hurst, Willingdon, Sussex; *m* 1920, Constance Warren; two *s. Educ:* St Saviours School, Eastbourne; City of London College. Pupil of J. Westwood, CE, Contractors, Millwall, E 1890–95; draughtsman, Chief Engineer's Office, Great Western Railway, 1895–96; designing engineer, J. Westwood and Co. 1896–97; Civil Engineering Assistant, Chief Engineer's Office, Great Western Railway, 1897–99; Engineering Assistant, Admiralty, 1889–1903; Assistant Civil Engineer, HM Dockyard, Portsmouth, 1903–07. *Recreations:* walking, sailing. *Address:* White Lodge, Sunningfields Road, Hendon, NW4; Gloucester House, 19 Charing Cross Road, WC2. *Club:* Constitutional.

Died 19 May 1943.

HURST, Dr Charles Chamberlain, ScD (Cantab), PhD; TD; DL, JP, Leics; Biologist and Pioneer in Genetics; *b* 1870; *s* of late Benjamin Hurst, JP, CA, Burbage, Leics; *m* Rona, *y d* of late William Hurst, JP, CA, Earl Shilton, Leics; one *s. Educ:* Wesley College, Sheffield; Research Student and Fellow Commoner, Trinity College, Cambridge. Late Member of the Regent House and the Faculty of Biology, University of Cambridge; Examiner in Genetics, Univ. of Madras; Corr. Member Carnegie Inst., Washington, DC; Scientific Member of the Horse-breeding Committee of the Board of Agriculture, 1910; Governor of the Midland Agricultural College, 1920; Scientific Member of the Wool-breeding Council of the Ministry of Agriculture and the Dept of Agriculture for Scotland, 1926–31; Member of Scientific and Orchid Committees of RHortS of London. Member of Council of International Bureau of Human Heredity. Awarded Royal Pension 1941 in recognition of valuable discoveries in science of Genetics. Served in Leicestershire Regt (V & T), 1893–1909; rtd Captain and Hon. Major; served European War, 2nd Officer i/c Records, Lichfield, 1914; OC Signals RE 59th and 71st Divs, 1915–18; Inspector Army Food Production, Eastern Command, 1918–19; retired Major RE Signals 46th Div. 1921. Served in Royal Observer Corps, Sussex, 1939–41; AAO Civil Defence Control, Horsham, 1942–45. *Publications:* The Orchid Stud Book, Kew, 1909 (with late R. A. Rolfe); Experiments in Genetics, 1925; The Mechanism of Creative Evolution, 1932; A Genetical Formula for the Inheritance of Intelligence in Man, 1932; The Genetics of Intellect, 1934; Heredity and the Ascent of Man, 1935; numerous papers to the Royal Society, London, and other societies on the Continent and in America. *Recreations:* music, gardening, biographies and philosophy. *Address:* Broomhurst, Worthing Road, Horsham, Sussex. *T:* Horsham 941.

Died 17 Dec. 1947.

HURST, William M.; *see* Martin-Hurst.

HUSKINSON, Edward; Director Illustrated Newspapers, Ltd; Director Illustrated London News and Sketch, Ltd; *b* 1877; 9th *s* of late William L. Huskinson, of Epperstone Manor, Notts. *Educ:* Oakham. Editor of The Tatler, 1908–40. *Recreations:* tennis, golf, sailing. *Clubs:* Bath; Bembridge Sailing.

Died 14 Nov. 1941.

HUSKINSON, Richard King; *see* King, Richard.

HUSKISSON, Hon. Maj.-Gen. (retired) William, CMG 1916; *b* Greenwich, 9 Feb. 1859; *e s* of late Francis Huskisson, Royal Naval College, Greenwich; *m* 1890, Caroline, *d* of late Col David Ward, Royal (Bengal) Engineers; three *d*. *Educ:* Compton House, Brighton; RM Academy, Woolwich. Entered RE 1878; Capt. 1888; Major, 1896; Lt-Colonel, 1904; Colonel, 1907; temp. Maj.-Gen. 1915; Professor of Fortification, RM College Kingston, Canada, 1890–95, and at RM College, Sandhurst, 1898–1903; served European War, 1914–17 (despatches, CMG); Officer of Order of St John of Jerusalem, 1938. *Address:* 13 St Mark's Road, Alverstoke, Hants. *T:* Gosport 8112.

Died 24 July 1946.

HUSKISSON, Lt-Col William Gordon, CBE 1919; DSO 1917; late RASC; *b* 23 Dec. 1877; *s* of late Col Samuel George Huskisson, CB. Entered Army, 1900; served S Africa, 1900–02 (Queen's medal with three clasps, King's medal with two clasps); Somaliland, 1903–04 (medal with clasp); European War, 1914–17 (despatches, CBE, DSO, Order of the Nile). *Address:* Woodcroft, Waterloo, Portsmouth.

Died 9 Feb. 1949.

HUSSAIN, Wajahat, CIE 1943; Deputy Governor, Reserve Bank of India, since 1943; *b* 23 Aug. 1894; *s* of Chaudhri Karamat Hussain; *m* 1924, Saida Mohamad Said; two *s* two *d*. *Educ:* Zillah School, Arrah; St Xavier's College, Calcutta; Presidency College, Calcutta; Gonville and Caius College, Cambridge. Called to Bar, Lincoln's Inn, 1923; joined ICS 1919 and was posted to UP; usual work as a revenue officer and magistrate in several districts; Settlement Officer, 1927; Sec. of Rural Indebtedness Enquiry Committee, 1932; lent to Kashmir, 1932, Home Minister there till 1937; Sec. to Govt of UP in PWD 1937–42; Commissioner, Gorakhpur, 1942–43. *Publications:* Rent Rate Reports of Salone, Rae Bareli & Musafirkhana, Sultanpur. *Recreations:* tennis and riding. *Address:* Reserve Bank of India, Bombay. *TA:* Reservbank, Bombay. *T:* 30981. *Clubs:* Dilkusha, Lucknow.

Died 4 Dec. 1945.

HUSSEY, Sir George Alfred Ernest, Kt 1901; *b* 14 Dec. 1864; *s* of George Hussey, Southampton; *m* 1st, 1885, Annie (*d* 1906), *d* of William Read, Acocks Green, Worcestershire; 2nd, 1912, Melville (*d* 1942), *d* of Thomas Laurie, Kirkcudbright; 3rd, 1944, Christine, *d* of Robert Leathes, Gateshead, Durham. *Educ:* Cranleigh School. Mayor of Southampton, 1898–1901; Freeman of the Boro'; a past master of Worshipful Company of Distillers. Lieut-Col commanding 5th Batt. Hampshire Regt 1907–12. *Recreations:* yachting, shooting. *Address:* Tarakai, The Crescent, Surbiton; Georgeville, Penfold Rd, Clacton-on-Sea. *Clubs:* Constitutional; Royal Southampton Yacht (Commodore); Yacht Racing Association.

Died 20 Aug. 1950.

HUTCHEN, Frank, FRGS; FJI; Managing Editor of Northamptonshire Evening Telegraph since 1903; *b* Kettering, 1 March 1870; *γ s* of Joseph Hutchen; *m* 1894, Carrie (*d* 1939); *γ d* of Frederick Smith, Kettering; two *s* one *d*. *Educ:* Wellingborough Grammar School. Trained as a journalist on the Kettering Leader; founded the Northamptonshire Citizen, and the Football Telegraph. *Publications:* Under the Southern Cross; Travel Articles. *Recreation:* travel. *Address:* Dryden House, Kettering. *T:* Kettering 2347. *Club:* Royal Automobile.

Died 14 Feb. 1942.

HUTCHEN, Lt-Col James William, CMG 1917; CBE 1919; in charge of War Graves Division, Department of Internal Affairs, New Zealand, since 1929; *b* 1880. *Educ:* Wellington College, New Zealand. Secretary to Administration W Samoa, 1920–29. *Address:* Marama Terrace, Eastbourne, Wellington, NZ.

Died 12 May 1943.

HUTCHINGS, Charles Henry, CMG 1931; OBE, KC, JP; *b* 1 Oct. 1869; *s* of Charles and Euphemia Hutchings; *m* 1893, Annie Maud White; one *s* six *d*. *Educ:* Methodist College, St John's; Mount Allison University, Sackville, NB. Enrolled Solicitor, 1891; admitted to Bar, 1892; Master in Chancery to Legislative Council, 1897; Deputy Minister of Justice, 1900–04, and 1908–17; Member of Legislature for district Bav-de-Verde, 1904–08; acting Judge, Central District Court, 1916–17; Inspector-General, Newfoundland Constabulary, 1917–34; during War had charge of internment of enemy subjects; Member of Home Defence Committee in conjunction with Admiralty on coast patrol; in charge of Forces for protection of St John's during threatened enemy raid; Member of Military Service Board and chairman of various committees in connection with War matters previous to organisation of Department of Militia; brought to notice of Secretary of State for valuable services rendered, 1919; Member of Commission appointed to investigate high cost of living, 1919; Member of Economic Commission appointed to enquire into the matter of unemployment, its causes and remedies, 1929; appointed member of Public Utilities Commission, 1930; retired from commanding Constabulary Force, 1934, and resumed legal practice; Director of Civil Defence, 1940–41. *Recreations:* shooting and fishing. *Address:* Longstop, Winter Avenue, St John's, Newfoundland. *T:* 171–921. *Clubs:* Masonic, St John's.

Died 17 June 1946.

HUTCHINGS, Harold Varlo, CBE 1942; MBE, 1936; *b* 5 March 1885; *s* of George A. Hutchings, St John's, Nfld; *m* 1914, Julia May, *d* of William H. Crowdy, St John's, Nfld; one *s* two *d*. *Educ:* Bishop Field College. Civil servant, 1907; Chm. Board of Customs, Chm., Board of Liquor Control, Chief Commissioner of Immigration, until end of 1944; Imperial Trade Correspondent, Dept Overseas Trade (Board of Trade) until 30 June 1945. *Recreations:* fishing and shooting. *Address:* 111 Fresh-water Road, St John's, Newfoundland. *TA:* St John's. *T:* 5.

Died 4 Feb. 1948.

HUTCHINS, George D'Oyly, CBE, 1920; Director of Woodall-Duckham (1920), Ltd; *b* 15 Oct. 1866; *s* of late George Albert Hutchins; *m* Maude (*d* 1938), *d* of A. Newman; one *s*. *Educ:* Bedford Grammar School. *Address:* Clive House, Knott Park, Oxshott, Surrey.

Died 22 April 1949.

HUTCHINSON, Brig. Alan George Caldwell, CB 1931; OBE; *b* 25 July 1879; *s* of late Col J. B. Hutchinson, CSI, CIE; *m* 1909, Suzanne Bayford Conyers, *d* of late Major W. Lindsay; two *s*. *Educ:* Haileybury College. Appointed Inniskilling Fusiliers, 1898; joined Indian Army, 1900; Adjutant Indian Volunteers, 1909–14; BM, 1915–16; DAAG, EEF, 1916; specially employed War Office, 1916–17; GSO2, Home Forces, 1917; DAQMG, 1921; AQMG, 1927–31; Brigade Commander 1931–35; served NW Frontier of India, Waziristan, 1901–02; East Africa, 1903–04; NW Frontier of India, 1908; European War, 1914–21 (despatches); Afghanistan, NWF, 1919 (despatches); Waziristan, 1919–20, 1921–23 (despatches,

OBE); retired, 1935. *Recreations:* shooting, tennis, golf. *Address:* Middleton, Stonegate, Sussex. *Club:* Junior United Service.

Died 21 May 1947.

HUTCHINSON, Claude Mackenzie, CIE 1920; *b* 29 April 1869; *e s* of late Rev. Edward Hutchinson; *m* 1914, Alice Muriel, *e d* of late Major J. W. Leather. *Educ:* Trinity Coll., Glenalmond; St John's College, Cambridge. Lecturer Agricultural Chemistry, Colonial College, 1898–1904; Scientific Officer Indian Tea Association, 1904–09; Imperial Agricultural Bacteriologist to Government of India, 1909–26; Chief Scientific Adviser for India, Imperial Chemical Industries, 1926–31; retired, 1931. *Publications:* Numerous Memoirs and Papers on Bacteriology of Soil; Plant Pathology, Bacteriology of Indigo Manufacture, Pebrine in India, Saltpetre, Green Manuring and Fertilizers, Electrolysis of Brine; Kala Azar. *Recreations:* golf, Cambridge blue 1889, cricket, tennis, hockey, painting. *Address:* Alde End, Aldeburgh, Suffolk. *Clubs:* Bengal, Tollygunge, Calcutta.

Died 2 Aug. 1941.

HUTCHINSON, Rev. Francis Ernest, DLitt; FBA 1944; *b* 17 Sept. 1871; 3rd *s* of Rev. Charles Pierrepont Hutchinson, Rector of Wonston, and Louisa, *d* of Rev. Alleyne H. Barker, JP; *m* 1904, Julia Margaret, *d* of Col G. A. Crawford, RA; one *s* one *d*. *Educ:* Lancing; Trinity College, Oxford (BA 1894, MA 1897, DLitt 1942); King's Coll. Cambridge (MA (incorp.), 1904). Assistant Master at Radley College, 1895–1900; Chaplain and Tutor Cooper's Hill College, 1900–03; Chaplain of King's College, Cambridge, 1903–12; Lecturer of Magdalene College, Cambridge, 1907–09; Select Preacher, Cambridge, 1906 and 1917, and Oxford, 1938–40; Vicar of Leyland, 1912–20; Secretary to the Delegacy for Extra-Mural Studies, Oxford University, and Staff Lecturer, 1920–34; Chaplain of All Souls College, 1928–35, Fellow, 1934–35; Canon of Worcester, 1934–43; Hulsean Lecturer, Cambridge, 1918–19; President, Preston Branch of Workers' Educational Association, 1916–20, Worcester Branch, 1936–43. *Publications:* The Sacred Poets (Herbert, Crashaw, and Vaughan), The Growth of Liberal Theology, and other chapters in The Cambridge History of English Literature; Christian Freedom (Hulsean Lectures), 1920; contributor to Seventeenth Century Studies, 1938, to Cambridge Bibliography of English Literature, 1940: Works of George Herbert, 1941; Milton and the English Mind, 1947; Henry Vaughan, 1947. Editor of the Cambridge Review, 1906–1907. *Address:* 3 Church Walk, Oxford. *T:* Oxford 3930.

Died 21 Dec. 1947.

HUTCHINSON, Col Francis Patrick, CB 1912; Indian Army retired; *b* 15 April 1858; *s* of Gen. C. W. Hutchinson, RE; *m* 1891; Mabel Ada Hay (*d* 1938), *d* of late J. Ferguson, Advocate, Aberdeen; one *s*. Entered Army, 1878; Capt. ISC 1889; Maj. Indian Army, 1898; Lt-Col 1904; Col 1908; served Afghan War, 1879–80 (medal); Chin-Lushai Expedition, 1889–90 (medal with clasp); Lushai, 1890–91 (clasp); NW Frontier, India, 1897–98 (medal with clasp); Tirah, 1897–98 (clasp); Waziristan, 1901–02 (despatches, clasp); Commanded 13th Bn Royal Fusiliers, 1914–15. *Address:* Sirmoor, Lymington, Hants.

Died 25 Dec. 1944.

HUTCHINSON, George Thomas, MC; *b* 30 July 1880; *s* of late Herbert Hutchinson; *m* 1st, Isabella Rose (*d* 1920), *d* of late Rev. H. B. Wolryche Whitmore, Royal Hill, Tewkesbury; one *d*; 2nd, Leland Mary (*d* 1927), *d* of late J. Hone, Donnybrook, Co. Dublin; 3rd, Mary Evelyn, *d* of late W. Lloyd Thomas, Tredilion Park, Abergavenny. *Educ:* Marlborough College; Magdalen College, Oxford (History Demy); 1st Class Hon. School Modern History 1903. Barrister-at-law, Inner Temple, 1906; Assistant Secretary, Duchy of

Cornwall, 1908; Treasurer of Christ Church, Oxford, 1910–45; served in France with Queen's Own Oxfordshire Hussars (Yeomanry), 1914–18; a Rhodes Trustee; Member of the General Claims Tribunal; Chairman of Curators of Oxford Botanic Garden. *Publications:* From the Cape to the Zambesi; The Heythrop Hunt. Contributions to Times and Quarterly Review on agricultural subjects. *Recreations:* sport and travel. *Address:* Sarsden Glebe, Churchill, Oxon. *Club:* Travellers'.

Died 17 Jan. 1948.

HUTCHINSON, St John; KC 1935; Barrister-at-law; Recorder of Hastings since 1930, of Hythe, 1928–30; *b* 8 April 1884; *o s* of late Sir Charles Hutchinson, MP, of Mayfield, Sussex; *m* 1910, Mary, *o d* of late Sir Hugh Barnes, KCSI, KCVO; one *s* one *d*. *Educ:* Elstree School; Winchester; Magdalen College, Oxford. BA History Honours. Barrister-at-law, Middle Temple, 1909; contested (L) Rye Division (Sussex) in both 1910 elections; Isle of Wight in 1929; London County Council, Member for Poplar (Progressive), 1912–16; Assistant Legal Adviser to Ministry of Re-construction, 1917; Executive Committee of Contemporary Art Society; Prosecuting Counsel to the Post Office at the Central Criminal Court, 1931–35. *Recreation:* shooting. *Address:* 3 Prince Albert Road, NW1. *T:* Gulliver 4648; 1 Plowden Buildings, Temple, EC4. *T:* Central 2516. *Clubs:* Garrick, Buck's, Beefsteak.

Died 24 Oct. 1942.

HUTCHINSON, Victor H.; *see* Hely-Hutchinson.

HUTCHINSON, Walter Victor, MA, FRGS, FRAI, FRSA, FRES, FZS; barrister-at-law; Order of the Crown of Belgium (Palms in Gold); publisher, printer, bloodstock breeder and farmer, etc; *b* 16 May 1887; *s* of Sir George Thompson Hutchinson, Kt, and Frances Octavia Cornwall; *m* 1st, 1932, Violet May Hewart; one *d*; 2nd, 1939, Marjorie Denson, *o d* of late John Edge and Mrs Edge, of Ulverston and Chester; one *d*. *Educ:* Highgate College; Haileybury College; St John's College, Oxford. Honours in Jurisprudence; Honours at Bar (Inner Temple). Hon. Private Secretary to the Secretary of the War Office, 1915–19; Secretary of the War Office Memorial Plaque and Scroll Committees: Chairman and Managing Director of Hutchinson & Co. (Publishers), Ltd, Hutchinson Printing Trust, Ltd and some 78 allied publishing, printing, and other businesses. Founded and edited the Coalition Party's paper Popular View; President, Printers' Pension Corporation, 1943; Vice-President Newspaper Press Fund; President, Book-binders' Pensions Fund, 1944; Founder of National Gallery of British Sports and Pastimes. *Publications:* Editor of Wonders of the World, Hutchinson's Story of the Nations, Britain Beautiful, Birds of our Country, 1001 Wonderful Things, Hutchinson's Pictorial Encyclopædia, Hutchinson's Pictorial History of the War, etc. *Recreations:* fishing, riding, racing, yachting, motoring, tennis. *Address:* 70 Ennismore Gardens, SW7. *T:* Kensington 6226 and 9211; Stanbridge Earls, nr Romsey, Hants. *T:* Romsey 403; Woodcote Stud, Hants; Carvers, Haslemere, Surrey. *T:* Haslemere 864. *Clubs:* Junior Carlton, Pilgrims, Bath; Royal Southern Yacht; Royal Motor Yacht; Bibury; Sandown; Kempton; Newbury; Hurst Park; Windsor, etc.

Died 30 April 1950.

HUTCHISON OF MONTROSE, 1st Baron *cr* 1932, of Kirkcaldy, co. Fife; **Maj.-Gen. Robert Hutchinson,** PC 1937; KCMG 1919; CB 1918; DSO 1915; Hon. Treasurer Liberal National Organization; *b* 5 Sept. 1873; *m* 1st, 1905, Agnes Begbie (*d* 1941), *o d* of late William Drysdale of Kilrie, Fife; 2nd, 1942, Mrs Drysdale of Kilrie, Fife, *widow* of J. C. Drysdale of Kilrie. Entered 7th Dragoon Guards, 1900; Captain 11th Hussars, 1905; Major 4th Dragoon Guards, 1912; General Staff Officer, 3rd Grade, 1912–14; 2nd Grade, 1914; served South Africa, 1900–02 (Queen's medal 3 clasps, King's medal 2 clasps); European War, 1914–19 (despatches six times, KCMG, DSO, CB, Bt Lt-Col, Bt Col, Croix de Guerre, Order of Crown of Italy); Legion D'Honneur, American Distinguished Service medal; GSO 1st Grade, 1915–17; temp. Maj.-Gen. and Director of Organisation at the War Office, May 1917–19; DAG 1919; retired pay, 1923; MP (NL) Kirkcaldy, 1922–23; (L) Montrose, 1924–31, (LNat), 1931–32; Scottish Whip (NL), 1923; Liberal Whip (L), 1924–26; Chief Liberal Whip, 1926–30; Paymaster-General, 1935–38; Director: National Bank of Australasia, Phœnix Assurance Co., Fife Coal Company, R. Hutchison & Co. Ltd. *Address:* Kilrie, By Kircaldy, Fife. *Clubs:* United Service, Reform, White's; New (Edinburgh).

Died 13 June 1950 (ext).

HUTCHISON, Acting Brig. Colin Ross Marshall, DSO 1918, MC; Major Reserve of Officers; *b* 16 Jan. 1893; *s* of James David Hutchison and Emma Mary Marshall; *m* 1927, Jovine Helen Trevor, *d* of E. Trevor Williams, JP, Dromenagh, Iver Heath, Bucks; one *s* two *d. Educ:* Merchiston Castle, Edinburgh; RMA, Woolwich. RFA 1912; Expeditionary Force, Aug. 1914; Capt., 1916; Acting Major, 1916–19 (DSO and bar, MC and bar, wounded three times, despatches four times); Captain Royal Horse Artillery, 1919–30; Retired 1930. *Address:* The Larches, Iver Heath, Bucks. *T:* Iver 21. *Club:* Junior United Service.

Died 29 April 1943.

HUTCHISON, George William, CMG 1934; Public Accountant; *b* 3 April 1882; *s* of Joshua Hutchison and Maria Beirne; *m* 1910, Amy Angus; one *s* one *d. Educ:* Auckland Grammar School. JP; Fellow and Past-Pres. of NZ Society of Accountants; Fellow and Past-President of Australasian Institute of Secretaries; Fellow and Past Pres. of NZ Branch, the Chartered Institute of Secretaries, London; Mayor of Auckland, 1931–35; Chevalier of the Legion of Honour. *Address:* 45 Portland Road, Remuera, Auckland, SE2, New Zealand. *TA:* Auditus.

Died 14 Feb. 1947.

HUTCHISON, Lt-Col Graham Seton, DSO 1918; MC; FRGS; FRHistS; *b* 20 Jan. 1890; *s* of late James Alexander Hutchison, Inverness, and late Beatrice Jameson, *d* of A. J. W. Waterlow; *m* 1919, Emilie Beatrice, *d* of late C. H. Durham; two *s* one *d. Educ:* Bradfield College; RMA, Woolwich. Entered King's Own Scottish Borderers, 1909; served Egypt, Sudan, and India; Staff Officer to Durbar Committee, 1911 (medal); Lieut 3rd A. & S. H. 1913; Trooper, BSAP; Personal Assistant to Commandant-General, Rhodesia Defence Force; Intelligence Officer, Organiser Cadet System; European War, 1914–19—93rd Highlanders, 33rd Batt. MGC; Capt. 1915; Major, 1917; Lieut-Col 1918 (MC, DSO, despatches four times, 1914 Star and clasp, wounded thrice); political work, 1919–20; first Chairman Old Contemptibles Association, 1919; Member British Legion from foundation; Chairman, MGCOCA, since 1934; ADC and Secretary to British Commissioner, Upper Silesian Commission, 1920–21; arranged Armistice between Korfanty's Polish Insurgents and German Defence Corps, May 1921; Genoa Conference, 1922; contested Uxbridge Division (L), 1923; Lord Mayor and Sheriff's Committee of London, 1929–30; Founded Paladin League, 1930; First Principal, Shri Shivaji Military School, Poona, 1932; founded National Workers Movement, 1933; Ehrenmitglied Leib-Regts Kameradschaft, München; Air Ministry, 1939; Executive Council National Playing Fields Association; Executive Committee, Gordon Boys' School. Landscape Painter; Exhibitor ROI, etc. *Publications:* (under own name), Footslogger: an autobiography; Warrior; Meteor; Arya; Challenge; God's Image; Pilgrimage; History of the 33rd Division; Machine Gun Corps; Silesia Revisited; Machine Guns: their History and Tactical Employment; Challenge to Youth; Kitchener—The Man; Cecil Rhodes—The

Man; Gordon and the Gordon Boys; These were Men; The British Army; The 51st Division can save Scotland; (under name of Graham Seton) The W Plan (and for the Talking Film version); The Governor of Kattowitz; Colonel Grant's Tomorrow; Life without End; Eye for an Eye; The Viper of Luxor; Blood Money; Minos Magnificent; Pelican Row; Scar 77; The K Code Plan; The Secret Circle; According to Plan; Tiger's Cub; The V Plan; The Red Colonel; Biography of a Batman; and other tales; Military Correspondent and regular press contributions. *Recreations:* mountaineering, collecting sculpture and paintings of the human figure, travel. *Address:* Booker Hill Farm, High Wycombe, Bucks. *T:* High Wycombe 503. *Club:* United Service.

Died 3 April 1946.

HUTCHISON, Sir James, Kt 1936; Editor of the Otago Daily Times, Dunedin, since 1909; *b* 1867; *s* of William Hutchison, a New Zealand journalist and politician; *m* 1893, Anna Pearson, *d* of late James Copland, MD, PhD; three *s. Educ:* private tuition; Wellington College, NZ; University of Otago. Entered journalism as member of staff of Evening Herald, Dunedin, 1885; transferred to Otago Daily Times staff, 1889; delegate from NZ to Imperial Press Conference, Canada, 1920; delegate from NZ to Imperial Press Conference, London, 1930. *Club:* Dunedin.

Died 12 June 1946.

HUTIN, Marcel; formerly day by day contributor to the Echo de Paris; *b* Wissembourg, Bas Rhin, 22 June 1869; *m* Jeanne Combé; two *s* (one killed in War). *Educ:* Lycée de Vesoul; Paris University. Barrister-at-law; contributor to the Figaro, Gaulois, and (for twenty years) Echo de Paris; among French journalists was the first to give to the interview, which he practised in nearly every European capital, a great development in the field of political and military matters; followed from Petrograd the Russo-Japanese War, and wrote daily on the War, 1914–18; Grand Officer of the Legion of Honour and possessor of many Foreign Orders. *Recreations:* music, travel. *Address:* 10 Rue Lesueur, Paris. *T:* Passy 31–32.

Died 20 Oct. 1950.

HUTSON, Sir John, Kt 1943; OBE 1936; VD; BA Dun. 1879; MB, CM Edin. 1883; DPH Camb. 1905; *b* 13 July 1859; *s* of Ven. Eyre Hutson, British Consular Chaplain, St Thomas, Danish WI; *m* 1st, 1884, Mary Ellen Webb; one *s;* 2nd, 1932, Constance Mary Starling. *Educ:* Codrington College, Barbados; Edin. Univ. Resident Surgeon and Senior Resident Surgeon Barbados General Hospital, 1885–88; Poor Law Inspector, Barbados, 1901–25; Public Health Inspector, Barbados, 1912–25; MLC Barbados, 1920–43; President Legislative Council, Barbados, 1941–43; member and President General Board of Health, 1895–1943; MEC 1936–42. *Recreations:* golf, bridge. *Address:* Rhodesia, Pine Hill, Barbados, BWI.

Died 29 March 1950.

HUTTON, Alfred Eddison; *b* 1865; *s* of J. Hutton, Eccleshill. *Educ:* Mill Hill School; Trin. Coll. Camb. MP (L) Morley Div. Yorkshire, 1892–1910. *Club:* Brooks's.

Died 30 May 1947.

HUTTON, Rev. John Alexander, MA, DD; Editor of the British Weekly, 1925–46; *b* Coatbridge, Lanarkshire, 21 April 1868; *m* Margaret Johnstone (*d* 1946), *d* of Rev. Robert Cameron, Glasgow; one *s. Educ:* Dundyvan Acad.; High School of Glasgow; Glasgow Univ. Ordained to the ministry in Alyth, Perthshire, 1892; called to Bristo Church, Edinburgh, 1898; to Jesmond, Newcastle-on-Tyne, 1900; to Belhaven, Glasgow, 1906; Minister of Westminster Chapel, Buckingham Gate, SW, 1923. *Publications:* Guidance from Robert Browning in Matters of Faith; Pilgrims in the Region of Faith; The Authority and Person of our Lord; The Fear of Things; At Close Quarters; The Winds of God; The Weapons of Our Warfare; If God be for Us; Ancestral

Voices; Loyalty, The Approach to Faith; Our Only Safeguard; On Accepting Ourselves; The Proposal of Jesus; Discerning the Times; The Persistent Word of God; That the Ministry be not Blamed; The Victory over Victory; Our Ambiguous Life; There they Crucified Him: As at the First; The Dark Mile; Guidance from Francis Thompson in Matters of Faith; Guidance on Russia from her Literature; Finally; with Paul to the End. *Address:* Ash, Seven-oaks, Kent. *T:* West Ash 310. *Club:* Reform.

Died 13 Jan. 1947.

HUTTON, Stamford, OBE 1928; MBE 1918; JP and Chairman of Quarter-Sessions, Co. Gloucester; *b* 1866; *s* of late Crompton Hutton of Harescombe Grange, Gloucs., Judge of County Courts, 1872–88, and late Harriet S. Hutton, *e d* of late Edward Holland of Dumbleton Hall, Gloucestershire; *m* 1895, Helen Frederica, 2nd *d* of late J. Fenwick-Fenwick of The Verzons, Ledbury, and *g d* of late Sir Thomas Gabriel, Bart; one *s*. *Educ:* Winchester; Trinity College Cambridge, BA 1888; MA 1893. Called to the Bar, Inner Temple, 1891; joined Oxford Circuit; Recorder of Lichfield, 1905–38. *Address:* Harescombe Grange, Gloucester. *T:* Painswick 3260.

Died 6 Nov. 1941.

HUXHAM, Hon. John; *b* Devon; widower. *Educ:* Devon. Entered Queensland Parliament as senior Member for South Brisbane, 1908; was a Minister of the Crown for over nine years, holding the offices of Home Secretary and Minister for Public Instruction; was a Member of the Senate of the Queensland University for several years, up to the time of appointment as Agent-General; Agent-General for Queensland, 1924–29; JP for the States of Queensland and New South Wales; interested in social work, especially education and reformatory, and the welfare of women and children. *Address:* Parliament House, George Street, Brisbane.

Died 4 Aug. 1949.

HUXLEY, Mrs Lindsey Kathleen, CBE 1941; *b* 6 July 1894; *d* of late Brig.-Gen. R. M. Foot, CB, CMG, DSO, and late Frances Sophy Daniell; *m* 1919, Gervas Huxley (marr. diss. 1930); no *c*. *Educ:* Wycombe Abbey School, Bucks. Hon. Treasurer National Federation of Women's Institutes, 1927–38; Member Reorganisation Commissions for Eggs and Poultry for England and Wales and for Great Britain, 1933–36; Member Poultry Technical Committee for Great Britain, 1937–38; Chief Regional Administrator, WVS for Civil Defence, 1938–45. *Address:* Stocks, Blewbury, Berks. *Club:* Forum.

Died 15 Nov. 1945.

HYAMSON, Moses, BA, LLD (both of London University); Rabbi of the Orach Chaim Congregation, New York, since 1913; Professor of the Codes at the Jewish Theological Seminary of America, 1915–40; Emeritus Professor since 1940; *b* Russia, 1862; *s* of a Rabbi; *m* 1892, Sara, *e d* of Rev. A. E. Gordon, Precentor of the Great Synagogue, Duke's Place, Aldgate, EC; no *c*. *Educ:* Jews' College and University College, London. 5 years Minister at Swansea; 3 years at Bristol; 10 years at Dalston Synagogue, Poets' Road, Canonbury; Ecclesiastical Assessor to the late Chief Rabbi, 1901–11; Acting in the Chief Rabbinate, 1911–13; former co-editor of the Jewish Forum, New York; Founder and President of the League for safeguarding the Fixity of the Sabbath. *Publications:* The Oral Law and other Sermons, 1910; First and only English Edition of the Collatio Mosaicarum et Romanarum Legum, 1913; The Jewish Concept of Wine and its Use, 1920; The Jewish Method of Slaughtering Animals from the Point of View of Humanity, 1923; edition of Hebrew Text and English Translation of Bachya's Duties of the Heart, Introduction and Part I, 1924; Parts II and III in 1941; Parts IV and V in 1943; Parts VI, VII and VIII in 1945;

Parts IX and X; also, in poetic form, List of Contents, Rebuke and Exhortation, 1947; Proposed Reform of the Calendar, 1929; Reply to Marvin and Cotsworth's Moses the greatest of Calendar Reformers, 1930; The Blank Day Device in Proposed Reforms of the Calendar, memorandum to the League of Nations, 1931; Sabbath and Festival Addresses, 1936; edition of Book I of The Mishneh Torah, 1938; essays in Jewish Quarterly Review, the Menorah Journal, and the Jewish Forum. *Recreation:* travel. *Address:* 65 East 96th Street, New York.

Died 9 June 1949.

HYAT-KHAN, Hon. Lt-Col Sirdar Sir Sikander, KBE 1933; MBE 1920; Premier, Punjab, since 1937; Deputy Governor, Reserve Bank of India, since 1935; Representative of the Reserve Bank of India in London; *b* 5 June 1892; *s* of late Nawab Muhammad Hyat-Khan, CSI, KIH, Khan Bahadur, of Wah (Attock District); *m* 1912; five *s* five *d*. *Educ:* MAO College, Aligarh; University College, London. Recruiting Officer European War, 1914–18; commission in 2–67th Punjabis (now 1/2nd Punjabis); served NWF and in Third Afghan War, 1919; appointed to Brigade Headquarters Staff; first Indian to command a Company on active service; Vice-Chairman, Attock District Board; First Class Honorary Magistrate, 1919–30; Member of the Punjab Legislative Council since 1921; non-official member of the Police Enquiry Committee, 1926; Personal Assist to Mela Officer during Prince of Wales' visit; elected by Punjab Council to Provincial Simon Committee which elected him as its chairman; was connected with Boards of 11 Companies including Messrs Owen Roberts, the Punjab Portland Cement Co., Wah Stone and Lime Company, North India Constructional Engineers and the Frontier Mining Syndicate; temporary Revenue Member for three months, 1929, Revenue Member, Punjab Government, 1930–35 and 1936–37; Acting Governor of the Punjab, 1932 and 1934. *Recreations:* shooting, riding, and gardening. *Address:* Wah PO, Attock District, India; 98 Upper Mall, Lahore; The Boundary, Simla E, India.

Died 26 Dec. 1942.

HYDARI, Rt Hon. Sir Akbar Nawab Hydar Nawaz Jung Bahadur, PC 1936; Kt 1928; DCL (Oxford); LLD (Osmania and Madras); Member for Information, Governor-General's Executive Council, India, since 1941; President Hyderabad State Executive Council 1937–41; *b* 8 Nov. 1869; *s* of Nazerally Hydari of Cambay, India; *m* 1893, Amena (*d* 1940) (Kaiser-i-Hind Gold medal), *d* of Najmuddin Tyabji, Bombay; four *s* two *d*. *Educ:* St Xavier's College, Bombay. Joined Indian Finance Dept 1888; Assistant Accountant-General, UP, 1890; Deputy Accountant-General, Bombay, 1897; Madras, 1900; Examiner, Govt Press Accounts, 1901; Comptroller, India Treasuries, 1903; CP, 1900; lent as Accountant-General, Hyderabad, State, 1905; Financial Secretary, 1907; Secretary to Govt Home Dept (Judicial Police, Education, etc), 1911; Ag. Director-General of Commerce and Industries, 1919; Accountant-General, Bombay, 1920; Finance and Railway Member Hyderabad State Executive Council, 1921–37; also Member for Co-operative Credit and Mines Departments, 1927; Official Director, Singareni Collieries Co. Ltd 1922 and Mining Boards, 1925; Chairman, Inter-University Board, 1925; Vice-Chancellor, Osmania University, Hyderabad, 1935; First President, Hyderabad Educational Conference, 1915; President, All-India Mahomedan Educational Conference, Calcutta, 1917; President, Nizam's State Railways; Head of Hyderabad Delegation to the Indian Round Table Conferences, London, 1930–31, 1931 and 1932, and to the Parliamentary Joint Select Committee on Indian Constitutional Reform, 1933; Chairman, Committee of Indian States Ministers, 1934–41; President, External Relations Committee, Constitutional Reforms Secretariat, Hyderabad, 1936;

delivered Punjab University Convocation Address, 1925; Fellow of the Bombay, Dacca, Aligarh Muslim and Hyderabad Osmania Universities; conceived and organised Osmania University, Hyderabad; helped in the production of Urdu Nastaliq type; organised State Archæological Department; negotiated the State purchase of railways; especially interested in Ajanta frescoes and Indian paintings. *Publications:* Hyderabad State Budgets and Educational Addresses. *Address:* Delhi, Simla, India. *Clubs:* United Service, Secunderabad.

Died 8 Jan. 1942.

HYDARI, Sir Muhammad Saleh Akbar, KCIE 1944 (CIE 1935); CSI 1941; late ICS; Governor of Assam, 1947; *b* 12 Oct. 1894; *s* of late Rt Hon. Nawab Sir Akbar Hydari; *m* 1918, Sigrid, *d* of W. Westling, Pitea, Sweden; one *s* two *d. Educ:* Bombay University; Balliol College, Oxford. Served as District Officer in the Madras Presidency, 1920–23; Under Secretary to the Government of Madras, Development Department, 1923; Under Sec. to the Government of India, Education, Health and Lands Department, 1924; Agent of the Government of India in Ceylon, 1927–29; Secretary to the Imperial Council of Agricultural Research, New Delhi, 1929–31; Joint Secretary to the Indian States Delegation to the Indian Round Table Conference, London, Second Session, 1931; Adviser to Delegation from Hyderabad (Deccan) to the Indian Round Table Conference, London, and Joint Parliamentary Committee on Indian Constitutional Reforms, Third Session, 1932–34; Joint Secretary to the Government of India, Department of Education, Health and Lands, 1934–38; Secretary to the Government of India, Dept of Labour, 1938–41; Representative of India on the Eastern Group Supply Council, 1941, and Chairman, 1942–43; Sec. to Govt of India, Dept of Industries and Civil Supplies, April 1943–Oct. 1945; member of the Viceroy's Executive Council, Nov. 1945–Aug. 1946. *Recreations:* tennis, golf, and shooting. *Address:* Government House, Shillong, Assam. *Clubs:* Imperial, Delhi Gymkhana (New Delhi); United Service (Simla).

Died 28 Dec. 1948.

HYDE, Sir Charles, 1st Bt *cr* 1922; OBE; LLD; Knight of Justice of the Order of St John of Jerusalem; Order of St Sava (2nd class); Proprietor Birmingham Post and other newspapers; *b* 23 Oct. 1876; *y s* of late George Edwin Hyde, Surgeon, and late Mary, *d* of late John Frederick Feeney; unmarried. *Educ:* Clifton College; Exeter College, Oxford. Six years Chairman, Queen's Hospital, Birmingham; Ex-Chairman, Birmingham Pensions Hospitals; Past President, Children's Hospital, Birmingham; Birmingham Dispensary; Ex-Warden, Guild of Undergraduates, Birmingham University, 1923–25; Ex-President United Hospital, Birmingham; President, Birmingham Blue Coat School, Warwickshire County Cricket Club; High Sheriff of Warwickshire, 1933–34. *Address:* The Moat, Berkswell, nr Coventry; The Manor House, Whitsbury, Wilts. *Clubs:* Royal Automobile, Bath; Union, Birmingham.

Died 26 Nov. 1942 (ext).

HYDE, Douglas; (known in Ireland as 'An Craoibhin Aoibhinn'); historian, poet, and folklorist; President of Ireland, 1938–45; *b* 17 Jan. 1860; *y s* of late Rev. Arthur Hyde, Frenchpark, Co. Roscommon. *Educ:* Trin. Coll., Dublin, BA (with first Senior Moderatorship and large Gold Medal), 1884; LLD 1887; DLitt (Hon.) RUI 1906; DLitt University of Wales (Hon.), 1927; DLitt Trinity College, Dublin (Hon.), 1933; Interim Prof. Mod. Lang. State University of New Brunswick, 1891. President of Irish National Literary Society, 1894–95; President of Gaelic League since its foundation, 1893, till 1915, when he resigned; President Irish Texts Society; Examiner in Celtic to Royal University of Ireland; assist editor, New Irish Library, 1897; received honorary freedom of cities of Dublin, Cork, and Kilkenny, 1906, on returning from USA with £11,000 for the Gaelic League, 1906;

Member of Royal Commission on Irish University Education, 1906; Freedom of Limerick, 1909; Member of the Senate, 1909–19, and Professor of Modern Irish in the National University of Ireland, 1909–32; and Dean of the Celtic Faculty; Senator in the Irish Parliament, 1925 and 1938; Chairman of the Folklore Institute of Ireland, 1930–34; Gregory Medal, 1937; Freedom of Galway, 1939. *Publications:* Leabhar Sgeuluigheachta, 1889; Beside the Fire, 1890; Cois na teineadh, 1891; Love Songs of Connacht, 1894; Three Sorrows of Story-telling, 1895; Story of Early Irish Literature, 1897; An Sgeu luidhe Gaodhalach, cuid I 1898, cuid II 1899, cuid III 1901, republished in Irish type 1933 (French translation, 1901); A Literary History of Ireland, 1899; Mediæval Tales from the Irish, being Vol. I of Irish Texts Society, 1899; Ubhla den Chraoibh (a volume of poems in Irish), 1900; Casadh an tsugàin, a play in Irish, produced in the Gaiety Theatre, Dublin, Oct. 1901; Tri Sgéalta, edited for Oireachtas Committee, 1902; Filidheacht Ghaedhalach, 1903; Raftery's Poems, 1904; enlarged edition 1933; The Bursting of the Bubble, An Pósadh, An Cleamhnas, King James, The Tinker and the Fairy, all Irish plays, 1905; The Religious Songs of Connacht, 1906; Sgéaluidhe Fíor na Seachtmhaine, 1909; Maistin an Bheurla, a play, 1913; Legends of Saints and Sinners from the Irish, 1915; The History of Charlemagne, edited and translated from the Book of Lismore and other vellum MSS, being Vol. XIX of Irish Texts Society, 1919; An Leath-rann, 1922; editor of Lia Fail, 1925; Ocht Sgéalta ó Choillte Maghach, 1936; Imeasg na n Gaedheal ins an Oileán úr, 1937; Mise Agus an Connradh, 1938; Sgéalta Thomáis Uí Chathasaigh, 1939. *Address:* Ratra, Phoenix Park, Dublin.

Died 12 July 1949.

HYDE, Rev. Canon Henry Edward; Home Secretary of the Missionary Council of the Church Assembly since 1930; Canon of St George's Cathedral, Perth, W Australia, 1930; Commissary for Archbishop of Perth, 1930; for Bishop of Bunbury, 1933; for Bishop of Rockhampton, 1936; for Bishop of Kalgoorlie, 1937; *b* Raywood, Victoria, Australia, 30 Aug. 1884; *e s* of Charles Edward Hyde, JP; *m* 1st, 1911, Florence Adela (decd), *e d* of late William and Margaret Gardner, Edinburgh; one *s* two *d*; 2nd, 1934, Hettie Hayden, *d* of Andrew and Hettie Pannell, Claygate; one *d. Educ:* Moore College, Sydney; Durham University. Deacon, 1909; Priest, 1910; Curate, St John's Darlinghurst, Sydney, 1910–11; Marley Hill, Co. Durham, 1911–12; All Saints, Mile End, London, 1912–14; Rector of Cobargo cum Tilba Tilba, NSW, 1914–17; LT St John's, Fremantle, WA, 1917–19; organising secretary of Church Extension Fund and the Diocesan Board of Finance, Diocese of Perth, W Australia, 1919–30; came to England as Commissary for the Province of W Australia, 1925; founded the Australian New Settlement Fund at S. P. G., Tufton Street, SW1, and raised £40,000 and sent to WA, 50 Priests for spiritual work amongst British Ex-Servicemen in W Australia; Naval Chaplain, Fremantle, 1917–19; a member of the Perth Diocesan Council Board of General Purposes and Church of England Emigration Committee. *Publications:* The Church's Chance in the Australian Bush; The Brittains go to Australia; Out back in the bush. *Recreations:* football, boxing, tennis, played inter-State football. *Address:* Missionary Council, Church House, Deans Yard, Westminster, SW1. *T:* Abbey 4355. *Club:* Church Imperial.

Died 13 Feb. 1941.

HYDE, William, CBE 1938; DL; JP; MA (Hon. Oxford); Alderman, Oxford County Council; Registrar, Oxford University Provident Association; Trustee, Nuffield Provincial Hospitals Trust; Manager, Nuffield Provident Guarantee Fund; *b* 1889; *s* of Thomas W. Hyde; *m* 1913, Gladys, *d* of Chas F. White, MP; no *c. Educ:* Toddington, Dunstable, Beds. County Councillor, Oxfordshire, 1919–31; County Alderman, Oxfordshire, from 1931; Chairman, Oxfordshire Public Assistance and Regional Planning Committees; and Public Health Committee; Chairman, Oxford Employment Committee; Chairman, Reading and Oxford Area Committee, Unemployment Assistance Board; Chairman, Minister of Health's Consultative Council on National Health Insurance, 1935–36; served European War with RNAF. *Publications:* various articles on Social Insurance, Agricultural Co. operation and Hospital Organisation. *Recreations:* walking, brass-rubbing. *Address:* The Cottage, Shirburn, Oxford. *TA:* Shirburn, Watlington, Oxon. *T:* Watlington (Oxon) 6. *Clubs:* National Liberal: Oxfordshire, Oxford.

Died 21 April 1945.

HYETT, Sir Francis Adams, Kt 1919; *b* 18 Nov. 1844; *s* of William Henry Hyett, FRS, and Anne Jane, *d* of Joseph Biscoe; *m* 1870, Ellen Maria (*d* 1928), *d* of Charles Carpenter, formerly of Moditanham, Cornwall; three *d.* *Educ:* Eton; Trinity Hall, Cambridge. Barrister-at-law, Inner Temple, 1872; Deputy Chairman, 1886–1904, and Chairman Glos Quarter Sessions, 1904–29; Vice-Chairman Glos County Council, 1904–18; Chairman, 1918; Chairman Glos Education Committee, 1908–19; Chairman Govs Barnwood House Hospital for the Insane, 1895–1937; Chairman Appeal Tribunal for Glos; Chairman of Council, Bristol and Glos Archæological Association, 1917–20. *Publications:* Florence: Her History and Art; Gloucester in National History; (Joint) A Manual of Gloucestershire Bibliography; Glimpses of the History of Painswick. *Recreations:* hunting, till incapacitated by an accident in 1884, since, literature and bibliography. *Address:* Painswick House, Painswick, Stroud.

Died 19 May 1941.

HYLTON, 3rd Baron *cr* 1866; **Hylton George Hylton Jolliffe;** Bt 1821; Capt. of HM's Body Guard of the Yeomen of the Guard until 1924; *b* 10 Nov. 1862; *e s* of 2nd Lord Hylton and Agnes, *d* of 2nd Earl of Strafford; *S* father, 1899; *m* 1896, Lady Alice Adeliza Hervey, *d* of 3rd Marquess of Bristol; one *s* one *d.* *Educ:* Eton; Oriel Coll., Oxford. (BA Honours, 1885; MA 1891). Formerly in Diplomatic Service; MP (C) Somerset, Wells, 1895–99; Lord-in-Waiting to the King, 1915–18. Owns about 6,000 acres. *Publication:* (edited) The Paget Brothers (1790–1840), 1918. *Heir: s* Hon. W. G. H. Jolliffe. *Address:* Ammerdown, Radstock. *Clubs:* Carlton, Brooks's.

Died 26 May 1945.

HYMANS, Paul, GCMG 1927; Minister of State; *b* Brussels, 1865; *s* of late Louis Hymans, former Member House of Representatives and Member of the Belgian Royal Academy, and Louise de l'Escaille; *m* 1898, Thérèse Goldschmidt. *Educ:* Brussels University. Barrister at the Court of Appeals in Brussels, 1885; Member of the House of Representatives for Brussels since 1900; Member of the Belgian Royal Academy since 1921; Hon. Professor at the Brussels University and Pres. of this University's Board; Belgian Envoy Extraordinary and Minister Plenipotentiary to the Court of St James, 1915–17; Minister of Foreign Affairs, 1918–20, 1924–25, 1927–34 and 1934–35; Minister of Justice, 1926–27; Member of the Council of Ministers, 1935–36; First Belgian Plenipotentiary to the Peace Conference of Paris, 1919; late Member of the Council of the League of Nations; President of first assembly of the League of Nations, Geneva, 1920; President of the Extraordinary Assembly of the League for China and Japan, 1932; Belgian Delegate to the Disarmament Conference, 1932; President of the Commission of Conciliation and Arbitration between Finland and Norway, and between Switzerland and Rumania. *Publications:* Histoire parlementaire de la Belgique; Bruxelles moderne; Frère Orban—Biographie; Portraits, Essais et Discours; Pages Libérales; Fragments d'histoire, impressions et souvenirs. *Address:* 15 rue Ducale, Brussels.

Died 8 March 1941.

HYNE, Charles John Cutcliffe Wright; novelist and traveller; was interested in mining in Mexico; *b* Bibury, Gloucestershire, 11 May 1865; *e s* of late Rev. Charles Wright Noble Hyne and late Frances, *o d* of late Robert Wootton; *m* 1897, Elsie (*d* 1938), *d* of late John Haggas of Ingrow, one *d.* *Educ:* Bradford Grammar School, Clare College, Cambridge (MA). Rowed in winning University Trial Eight, 1887. Wrote for magazines; travelled in Balearic Islands, Europe, Canary Islands, Congo Free State, Gold Coast, Arctic Sea, Russian Lapland, North America, San Thomé, Mexican Gulf Keys, Algeria, Tunisia, Southern Morocco, Western Mexico, Cameroons, North Brazil, Senegal, Spanish Main, West Indies, etc.; also much at sea; is now engaged on a Research into the causes of Congenital Deafness. *Publications:* The New Eden, 1892; The Recipe for Diamonds, 1894; Honour of Thieves, 1895 (republished as The Little Red Captain, 1902); The Stronger Hand, 1896; The Paradise Coal-Boat, 1897; Adventures of Captain Kettle, 1898; Through Arctic Lapland, 1898; Further Adventures of Captain Kettle, 1899; The Lost Continent; The Filibusters, 1900; Prince Rupert the Buccaneer, 1901; Mr Horrocks, Purser, 1902; Thompson's Progress, 1902, Captain Kettle, KCB, 1903; McTodd, 1903; Atoms of Empire, 1904; Trials of Commander M'Turk, 1906; Kate Meredith, 1907; Empire of the World, 1910; The Escape Agents, 1911; The Marriage of Kettle, 1912; Firemen Hot, 1913; Captain Kettle on the Warpath, 1916; Red Herrings, 1918; Captain Kettle's Bit, 1918; Admiral Teach, 1920; The Reverend Captain Kettle, 1925; Ben Watson, 1926; President Kettle, 1928; Abbs, 1928; People and Places, 1930; Mr Kettle, 3rd Mate, 1931; But Britons are Slaves, 1932; West Highland Spirits, 1932; Captain Kettle, Ambassador, 1932; Man's Understanding, 1933; Absent Friends, 1938; My Joyful Life, 1935; Don't You Agree? 1936; Ivory Valley: an adventure of Captain Kettle, 1938; Wishing Smith, 1939; Steamboatmen, 1942, etc. *Recreations:* big-game shooting abroad, and all other shooting available in the British Islands; an enthusiastic cave-hunter. *Address:* Heaton Lodge, Bradford. *TA:* Hyne 2274, Bradford; Kettlewell, by Skipton-in-Craven. *TA:* Hyne, Kettlewell. *T:* Bradford 2274, Kettlewell 226. *Club:* Authors'.

Died 10 March 1944.

HYSLOP, Lt-Col Francis, CBE 1920; late The King's Regt; *m* Katherine Nicola, *d* of late Bagot Blood, Rockforest and Gleninagh, Co. Clare. Lieut-Col 1918; served S Africa, 1899–1902 (Queen's medal with three clasps, King's medal with two clasps); European War, 1914–18 (1914–15 Star); Afghan War, 1919 (despatches, medal with clasp, CBE). *Address:* c/o Lloyds Bank, 6 Pall Mall, SW1.

Died 26 Dec. 1944.

I

IGGLESDEN, Sir Charles, Kt 1928; DL, Kent; JP, FSA, FJI; OStJ; author and journalist; *b* Ashford, 1861; *s* of Henry Igglesden; *m* 1885, Nellie (*d* 1939), *d* of George Swatman, CE; four *s. Educ:* privately; Paris. Editor Kentish Express since 1881; President Institute of Journalists, 1927; Past Chairman British Section International Association of Journalists; Chairman Kent National Health Insurance Committee; Past Vice-Chm. Kent Higher Educ. Committee; Alderman, Kent County Council; member Kent Territorial Association; Honorary Recruiting Officer for East Kent, 1914–18; Past Grand Assistant Director of Ceremonies in Freemasonry; played for leading cricket clubs, and regularly took elevens to France previous to War; at one time prominent lawn tennis player; played chess for his county. *Publications:* A Saunter through Kent with Pen and Pencil, and other topographical books; Out There, a Visit to the Trenches, 1915; A Mere Englishman in America; The Demon Eleven, and other Cricket Stories; Those Superstitions, 1932; Novels—Crimson Glow, A Flutter with Fate, Clouds, Law the Wrecker, and Downs Valley Farm. *Recreation:* fishing. *Address:* Heathfield, Ashford, Kent. *T:* 23. *Clubs:* Authors', Press, Band of Brothers.

Died 26 June 1949.

ILIFF, Rt Rev. Geoffrey Durnford, DD; Prebendary Emeritus of Hereford Cathedral since 1942; *b* 7 Oct. 1867; 5th *s* of Rev. George Iliff, Headmaster of Hall School, Sunderland; *m* 1898, Florence Sophia (decd), *e d* of T. Stephens of Deal; four *s. Educ:* St Edmund's School, Canterbury; St Augustine's College, Canterbury. 1st Class Univ. Prelim. for candidates for Holy Orders, 1889. Deacon, 1891; Priest, 1892; Missionary at Tai An Fu, 1890–94; Peking, 1894–95; Ping Yin, 1895–97; Tientsin, 1898–1903; acting chaplain to the Forces, Tientsin, 1900–03 (China medal); 1st Bishop of Province of Shantung (exclusive of Territory ceded to Germany in 1898), 1903–20; Hon. Fellow St Augustine's College, Canterbury, 1904; Surrogate, Rural Dean of Snaith, 1921–28; Vicar of Goole, 1920–28; Rector of Pencombe, 1928–32; Archdeacon of Hereford, 1929–41; Rector of Eaton Bishop, Hereford, 1932–41. *Address:* Cold Norton Priory, Chipping Norton, Oxon.

Died 10 June 1946.

ILLINGWORTH, 1st Baron *cr* 1921, of Denton; **Albert Holden Illingworth;** PC 1916; JP; *b* 25 May 1865; *s* of late Henry Illingworth and Mary, *d* of late Sir Isaac Holden, Bart, of Lady Royde Hall, Bradford; *m* 1st, 1895, Annie Elizabeth (whom he divorced 1926; she died 1930), *d* of late Isaac H. Crothers, Chevalier of the Légion d'Honneur, of Le Château, Croix, Nord, France; 2nd, 1931, Margaret Mary Clare, *o d* of late W. B. Wilberforce, Markington Hall, Yorkshire. *Educ:* The London International College, and in French Switzerland. President Bradford Chamber of Commerce, 1910; Postmaster-General, 1916–21; MP (Co. L) Heywood Division of South-East Lancashire, 1915–18; Heywood (Radcliffe Division), Dec. 1918–May 1921; joined Conservative Party 1930; was a Member of Departmental Committee on Anthrax; Advisory Committee to Ministry of Munitions for dealing with Labour Problems; Excess Profits Board; Textile Committee for Trade after War; War Office Contracts Committee; Lord Balfour of Burleigh's Committee on Commercial and Industrial Policy; Chairman of Cabinet Committee on the Acceleration of Turn-round of Ships during European War; Upper Warden of the Weavers Company; Director National

Provincial Bank, Ltd; Lloyds and National Provincial Foreign Bank Ltd, Ford Motor Co., Ltd; Chairman, United States Metallic Packing Co., Ltd. *Heir:* none. *Address:* Markington Hall, Yorkshire. *T:* Bishop Monkton 11; 44 Grosvenor Square, W1. *T:* Grosvenor 2660. *Clubs:* Boodle's, Hurlingham; Travellers, Paris.

Died 23 Jan. 1942 (ext).

IMBERT-TERRY, Lt-Col Claude Henry Maxwell, DSO 1916; retired; *b* 1880; *e s* of Claude Alexander Imbert-Terry; *m* 1921, Ethel Mary, *e d* of late W. H. Monckton. *Educ:* Charterhouse. Entered Devonshire Regt, 1901; served South African War (Queen's medal with three clasps); European War, 1914–18 (despatches, DSO); Lieut-Col Commanding a Bn King's Own Yorkshire Light Infantry, 1916. *Address:* Rosemount, St Heliers, Jersey, CI. *Clubs:* United Service, Naval and Military.

Died 20 March 1942.

IMMS, Augustus Daniel; Hon. Fellow of Downing College and Reader in Entomology, Cambridge University, 1931–45; *b* 24 Aug. 1880; *s* of late Walter Imms of Moseley; *m* 1913, Georgiana Mary, *γ d* of late T. W. French, Resident Magistrate, County Tyrone; two *d. Educ:* University of Birmingham; Christ's College, Cambridge. BSc (Lond.), 1903; BA (Cantab), 1907; MA 1913; DSc 1907; FRS. President Royal Entomological Society, 1937–38; 1851 Exhibition Science Research Scholar, 1905–07; Assistant Demonstrator in Zoology, University of Birmingham, 1903; Professor of Biology, University of Allahabad, 1907–11; Forest Zoologist to the Government of India, 1911–13; late Fellow of the University of Allahabad; Reader in Agricultural Entomology, Manchester University, 1913–18; Chief Entomologist, Rothamsted Experimental Station, Harpenden, 1918–31; late President, Association of Economic Biologists; Corresponding Member Académie d'Agriculture de France; Foreign Member Amer. Acad. Arts and Sci., and of Entomological Society, Finland; Hon. Member Netherland Entomological Society and Entomological Society of India. *Publications:* A General Text-book of Entomology and other books; Articles in Encyclopædia Britannica and Chambers's Encyclopædia; various scientific papers, principally on the Structure and Biology of Insects and other Arthropods. *Address:* Faldonside, Tipton St John, near Sidmouth. *T:* Ottery St Mary 58.

Died 3 April 1949.

IMPERIALI, Marquis Guglielmo, dei Principi di Francavilla; Senator of the Realm; *b* 19 Aug. 1858; *s* of Marquis Francesco; *m* Maria Giovanna dei Principi Colonna, *d* of Eduardo Colonna, Prince of Summonte. *Educ:* Naples; Doctor juris, Univ. of Naples. Foreign Office, Rome; Secretary, Berlin, Paris; 1st Secretary Washington, Bruxelles; Councillor of Embassy, Berlin; Minister Plenipotentiary, Sofia; Ambassador, Constantinople; Italian Ambassador to the Court of St James, 1910–20; Italian Representative to the Council of the League of Nations at Geneva, 1921–23. DC (Hon.) University of Sheffield. *Address:* Palazio Colonna, Rome. *Clubs:* Turf, St James'.

Died 20 Jan. 1944.

IMPEY, Lt-Col Lawrence, CSI 1917; CIE 1911; CBE 1920; *b* 17 June 1862; *s* of Col E. C. Impey, CIE. *Educ:* Marlborough; Sandhurst. Lieutenant in Derbyshire Regt 1883; Indian Army, 1885; employed under Government of India in the Political Department, 1887; has held appointments of Political Agent in Alwar, Bhopal, Eastern States, Rajputana, Bundelkhand, and Resident at Baroda; retired, 1917. *Recreations:* riding, golf, bridge.

Died 6 June 1944.

IMRIE, Lt-Col Hew Francis Blair, CMG 1915; OBE 1919; JP Angus; late 5th Royal Highlanders (TF); *b* 10 July 1873; *m* Selina Gladys, *d* of late Brig.-Gen. Eyre Crabbe, CB; two *s* two *d. Educ:* Wellington College; Cambridge University, PASI. Served S Africa, 1900–03, with 1st Batt. Fifth Fusiliers (2 medals); European War, 1914–17, in command of 5th Royal Highlanders (CMG, despatches). *Address:* Lunan House, Montrose. *Club:* United Service.

Died 1 Feb. 1942.

INCE, Edward Lindsay, MA (Camb.), DSc (Edin.); FRAS, FRSE; Lecturer in Technical Mathematics, University of Edinburgh; *b* Amblecote, Staffs, 30 Nov. 1891; *s* of Edward Ince, late of HM Customs and Excise; *m* 1924, Phyllis, *d* of late John Fry, of Benhall, Suffolk; two *d. Educ:* Perth Academy; Edinburgh University; Trinity College, Cambridge; Paris. Senior President of the Students' Representative Council, Edinburgh, and Convener of the International Academic Committee, 1913–15; Smith's Prizeman, Cambridge, 1917; Lecturer in the University of Liverpool, 1920–26; Professor of Pure Mathematics in the Egyptian University, 1926–31; Examiner in the Universities of London, Edinburgh, and St Andrews. *Publications:* A Handbook on Foreign Study, 1914; Descriptive Geometry and Photogrammetry (No. 1 of the Edinburgh Mathematical Tracts, 1915); Ordinary Differential Equations, 1927; Principles of Descriptive Geometry, 1933; Cycles of Reduced Ideals in Quadratic Fields, 1934; Integration of Ordinary Differential Equations, 1939; original papers, mainly on the theory and applications of Differential Equations. *Recreations:* book-collecting, microscopy. *Address:* 5 Greenhill Place, Edinburgh, 10. *T:* 52921. *Club:* Authors'.

Died 16 March 1941.

INCE, Evelyn Grace, ARWS 1937; *y d* of late Rev. J. C. Ince, Gurnard, IW. *Educ:* privately. Art Training at Byam Shaw School of Art (Scholarship, 1913). Land worker, 1917–18; First exhibited at RA 1917; Exhibitor also at Royal Society of Painters in Water Colours, New English Art Club, Royal Society of British Artists, British Artists Exhibitions, Carnegie Institute, Pittsburg, International Watercolour Exhibitions, Chicago. Flower Piece (Tempera) purchased under terms of Chantrey Bequest, 1934, etc. *Address:* White Lodge, Meadow Way, Letchworth.

Died 7 May 1941.

INCLEDON-WEBBER, Brig.-Gen. Adrian Beare, CMG 1919; DSO 1916; DL Somerset; Colonel Royal Irish Fusiliers, 1937–46; *b* 23 June 1876; *y s* of late Edward Chichester Incledon-Webber of Buckland House and St Brannock's, Devonshire; *m* 1923, Gladys Emily, *d* of Rev. Worthington Jukes of Shobrooke, and *widow* of Lieut J. R. Wissman, RFA; one *d.* Served S African War, 1900–02 (Queen's medal 3 clasps, King's medal 2 clasps); European War, 1914–19 (despatches five times, DSO, CMG); Major, Royal Irish Fusiliers, 1915; Temp. Brig.-General, 1917; brevet Lieut-Colonel, 1918; commanded 1st Batt. Essex Regiment, 1923–27; 130th (Devon and Cornwall) Infantry Brigade, 1928–31; retired, 1931, with rank of Brig.-Gen. *Address:* Clifford Lodge, Cannington, Somerset. *Club:* Army and Navy.

Died 25 Oct. 1946.

INGHAM, Major Samuel, VC 1915; late RAOC and West Yorkshire Regt; Sales Representative John Player & Sons; *b* 16 Sept. 1893; *m* 1916, Bertha Elizabeth Charlotte, *y d* of G. F. Duval, Bradford; two *s* one *d.* Name changed by Deed Poll, 1941, to Ingham. Retired

from Corps of Military-Accountants, 1926. *Recreations:* golf, tennis, swimming. *Address:* Penrhiw Villas, Oakdale, Mon.

Died 8 Dec. 1950.

INGILBY, Sir William Henry, 4th Bt *cr* 1866; Bt Lieut-Col late Scots Guards; *b* 28 Dec. 1874; *e s* of 3rd Bart and Eleanor Isabella, *d* of late Henry Macdowall of Garthland, Co. Renfrew; S father, 1918; *m* 1906, Hon. Alberta Diana, 3rd *d* of 1st Baron Swansea; one *s.* Served South African War, 1899–1902 (Queen's medal six clasps, King's medal two clasps); Commanded Guards Depot, 1914–19. *Heir: s* Joslan William Vivian [Major Scots Guards; *b* 1 Sept. 1907; *m* 1948, Diane, *o d* of Sir George Colvin, CB. Eton]. *Address:* Ripley Castle, Harrogate. *T:* Ripley 253.

Died 20 Sept. 1950.

INGLEFIELD, Rear-Adm. Sir Edward Fitzmaurice, KBE 1919; CBE 1918; Royal Navy (retired); Secretary of Lloyd's, 1906–21; Hon. Member, 1922; *b* 10 April 1861; *y s* of late Admiral Sir Edward Inglefield, KCB, DCL, FRS; *m* 1887, Julia Katharine Margaret (*d* 1944), Belgian Médaille de la Reine Elizabeth 1918, OBE 1920, Order of Mercy, 1928, Dame of Grace of St John of Jerusalem, 1931, *e d* of late J. Christopher Wilson, Ambleside, Westmorland; one *s. Educ:* privately. Entered RN, 1874; served as Lieut with Nile Expedition, 1884–85 (medal, clasp, and bronze star); commanded a first-class torpedo boat during combined international blockade of coast of Greece under Duke of Edinburgh, 1886 (4th class of Medjidie); First Lieutenant of HMS Victoria when she foundered off the coast of Syria, 1893, but was then in Malta Hospital owing to an accident; afterwards First Lieutenant of HMS Ramillies and Commander of HM ships Trafalgar and Royal Sovereign in the Mediterranean; Assistant Director of Naval Intelligence, 1901–05; Commanded HMS Antrim, 1905–06; a Younger Brother of Trinity House; Member of Council Royal Geographical Society, 1922–25; Member of Advisory Committee to Board of Trade on Lighthouses, etc., since 1907; Committee of the Marine Society since 1908. *Address:* 49 Lennox Gardens, SW1. *T:* Kensington 5972; Burke House, Beaconsfield, Bucks. *Clubs:* United Service; Royal Yacht Squadron, Cowes (hon. mem.); Royal Yacht of Belgium (hon. mem.).

Died 19 July 1945.

INGLIS, Sir Hugh Arbuthnot, Kt 1942; *b* 28 June 1890; *m* 1922, Sylvia Stewart, *d* of Gilbert Blane, Folijon, Windsor; no *c. Educ:* Fettes College, Edinburgh. Entered Indian Police, 1910; Principal, Police Training School, Moradabad, 1931; Inspector-General of Police, United Provinces India, 1940; retired, 1945. *Recreations:* polo and zoology. *Address:* Alltan Donn, Nairn, Scotland. *Club:* East India and Sports.

Died 19 July 1948.

INGLIS, Rev. James W., MA, DD; Principal Emeritus, Theological College; *b* 12 Sept. 1861; *s* of Rev. James Inglis and Frances Wordley; *m* 1900. *Educ:* Glasgow Academy and University. Missionary in Manchuria, 1891–1938. *Publications:* Christ not Mythical; Articles on Buddhism in Journal of Royal Asiatic Society (China); (in Chinese) Commentaries on NT; Christ the Supreme Revelation; Handbook of Comparative Religion; Translations of: St Augustine (Selections); De Imitatione Christi; Pensées de Pascal. *Recreation:* music. *Address:* 20 Little Road, Edinburgh 9.

Died 15 Jan. 1943.

INGLIS, John Alexander; KC 1926; King's and Lord Treasurer's Remembrancer in Scotland; *b* 3 Feb. 1873; *e s* of late Dr Alexander Inglis of Auchindinny and Redhall, Midlothian; *m* 1903, Margaret Isabella (*d* 1932), *d* of William Stuart Fraser, WS; one *s* two *d. Educ:* Cheltenham College; Christ Church, Oxford (Scholar), MA; Edinburgh University (Lord Rector's Prizeman, 1898), LLB. Passed Advocate of the Scottish Bar, 1898.

Ensign in the Royal Company of Archers (King's Bodyguard for Scotland); JP Midlothian; Chairman of Colinton School Board, 1914–19; Assistant Commissioner for Food Control, 1918–20; a Trustee of the National Library of Scotland since 1925; Vice-President of the Royal Society of Edinburgh; Chairman of Scottish History Society. *Publications:* edited for the Faculty of Advocates the Faculty Digest of Case Law, 1868–1922. *Address:* Auchindinny House, Milton Bridge, Midlothian. *Clubs:* Oxford and Cambridge; New, Edinburgh.

Died 13 Aug. 1941.

INGRAM, Rt Rev. and Rt Hon. Arthur Foley Winnington, PC 1901; KCVO 1915; DD, LLD; *b* Worcestershire, 26 Jan. 1858; 4th *s* of Rev. E. Winnington Ingram, Stanford Rectory and Ribbesford House, and Louisa, *d* of Rt Rev. Bishop Pepys, Worcester; unmarried. *Educ:* Marlborough Coll. and Keble Coll., Oxford. 1st class Mods., 2nd class Greats, Oxford. Private Tutor, 1881–84; Curate at St Mary's, Shrewsbury, 1884–85; Private Chaplain to Bishop of Lichfield, 1885–89; Head of Oxford House, Bethnal Green, Chaplain to Archbishop of York and to Bishop of St Albans, 1889; Rector of Bethnal Green, 1895; Rural Dean of Spitalfields, 1896; Canon of St Paul's Cathedral, 1897–1901; Bishop of Stepney (Suffragan to Bishop of London), 1897–1901; Bishop of London, 1901–39; Dean of the Chapels Royal, 1901–39; Chaplain London Rifle Brigade, 1901; Prelate of Order of British Empire, 1918–39; Chaplain NAVR; Grand Cross of the Royal Order of the Redeemer of Greece, 1919; St Sava, 1st Class of Serbia, 1919. *Publications:* Work in Great Cities; Old Testament Difficulties; New Testament Difficulties; Church Difficulties; Messengers, Watchmen, Stewards; The Men who Crucify Christ, 1896; Christ and His Friends, 1897; Banners of the Christian Faith, 1899; The Church in Time of War, 1915; The Potter and the Clay, 1917; Rays of Dawn, 1918; Victory and After, 1919; The Spirit of Peace, 1921; Re-Building the Walls, 1922; The Spirit of Jesus, 1925; The Sword of Goliath, 1926; Some World Problems, 1927; Holiday Recollections of a World Tour, 1928; Good News from God; Has God Spoken to Man?; Every man's doubts and difficulties, 1937; What a Layman Should Believe, 1938; The Secrets of Happiness, 1939; Fifty Years' Work in London, 1940; Secrets of Fortitude, 1940. *Recreations:* squash rackets, golf tennis. *Address:* The Boynes, Upton on Severn, Worcestershire. *Clubs:* Athenæum, Royal Societies, Bath (Hon.), Devonshire (Hon.).

Died 26 May 1946.

INGRAM, Edward Maurice Berkeley, CMG 1934; OBE 1918; Diplomatic Adviser to Ministry of Economic Warfare; *b* 14 Dec. 1890; *s* of late Major E. R. B. Ingram, Welch Regiment. *Educ:* Eton; King's College, Cambridge. General Staff, War Office, 1914–18; entered Foreign Office and Diplomatic Service, 1919; Private Secretary to Additional Parliamentary Under-Secretaries of State for Foreign Affairs, Sir Arthur Steel Maitland and Sir Hamar Greenwood; Assistant Secretary to Lord Milner's Special Mission to Egypt and Private Secretary to Chairman; 2nd Secretary, 1920; transferred to Christiania (now Oslo), 1924; First Secretary, 1924; acted as Chargé d'Affairs in 1924 and 1925; transferred to Berlin, 1926; acted as Chargé d'Affaires in 1926 and 1927; transferred to the Foreign Office, 1927; Acting Counsellor and transferred to Peking, 1929; acted as Chargé d'Affaires in 1931, 1933 and 1934; Counsellor 1932; transferred to Rome, 1935; acted as Chargé d'Affaires in 1935, 1936 and 1937; transferred to the Foreign Office, 1937; and to Ministry of Economic Warfare, 1939. *Address:* c/o The Foreign Office, Downing Street, SW1. *Clubs:* Athenæum, Travellers', MCC.

Died 21 May 1941.

INGRAM, William; KC 1929; *b* Morayshire, 1865; *s* of late Rev. Gordon Ingram, Minister of Urquhart, near Elgin; *m* 1901, Jessie, *d* of late Hugh McLardy, Howrah, Calcutta; one *d*. *Educ:* Fettes College; University of Edinburgh. MA, LLB, DSc; Rhind and also Vans Dunlop Scholar in Philosophy, 1891. Called to Bar, 1893; has specialised in Indian Law Appeals to the Judicial Committee of the Privy Council; is a Knight Templar according to the Scottish Rite; Conservative; Fellow of the Scottish Antiquarian Society; Editor, Manse Fellowship Magazine. *Recreations:* travelling and antiquarian research. *Address:* Normanhurst, North Berwick. *T:* North Berwick 232; 44 Great King Street, Edinburgh. *T:* 23888. *Club:* Overseas (Edinburgh).

Died 13 July 1943.

INKSON, Col Edgar Thomas, VC, DSO 1917; late RAMC; *b* 1872; *m*; one *s* one *d*. Served South Africa, 1899–1904 (despatches twice, promoted Captain, Queen's medal 5 clasps, King's medal 2 clasps, VC); European War, 1914–18 (DSO, despatches thrice); retired pay, 1926. *Address:* Briarwood, Summersdale, Chichester.

Died 19 Feb. 1947.

INNES; *see* Mitchell-Innes.

INNES, Lt-Col James Archibald, DSO 1900; *b* 30 July 1875; *s* of late James Innes of Roffey Park, Horsham; *m* 1st, 1909, Marjorie (*d* 1912), 3rd *d* of Abraham John Roberts; 2nd, 1914, Lady Barbara Lowther (whom he divorced 1921), *e d* of 6th Earl of Lonsdale; one *s* one *d*; 3rd, 1927, Evelyn, *e d* of Nigel W. Dawnay; three *s* one *d*. Served S Africa, 1899–1902 (despatches, Queen's medal with 5 clasps, King's medal with 2 clasps, DSO); Captain Rifle Brigade, 1901–09; High Sheriff of Suffolk, 1943. *Address:* Horringer Manor, Bury St Edmunds; Inchgarry, North Berwick.

Died 16 Aug. 1948.

INNES, Sir James Bourchier, 14th Bt *cr* 1628; *b* 1883; *s* of late Thomas Innes, of Valparaiso (5th *s* of 11th Bt), and Virginia, *d* of late Col Hugh Plunkett Bourchier; *S* uncle, 1919. Heir: *cousin* Walter James, *b* 8 Aug. 1903. *Address:* Edingight House, Keith, Banffshire.

Died 20 Dec. 1950.

INNES, Rt Hon. Sir James R.; *see* Rose-Innes.

INNES, John Robert, CMG 1920; Barrister-at-law, Lincoln's Inn; *b* 4 Sept. 1863; *s* of James Innes of Wroxton, Banbury; *m* Edith (*d* 1938), *e d* of T. W. Offin of Hockley, Essex. *Educ:* abroad; Edinburgh University. Entered Civil Service of the Straits Settlements by public competition, 1886; held various administrative and legal posts; acted as Attorney-General and Public Prosecutor, Straits Settlements, 1906; Judicial Commissioner Federated Malay States, and Judge of the Court of Appeal, Straits Settlements, 1907; retired on pension, 1919. *Publication:* Registration of Title in the Federated Malay States. *Recreations:* lawn tennis and cycling. *Address:* Montrose, Branksome Wood Road, Bournemouth.

Died 1 Oct. 1948.

INNES, Hon. Reginald Heath L.; *see* Long-Innes.

INNESS, William James Deacon, CMG 1929; MRCS Eng.; LRCP Lond.; DPH; Director of Medical and Health Services, West African Medical Staff, retired, 1932; *b* 1877; *s* of William Francis Inness; *m* 1910, Elsie, *d* of Dr Walter K. Loveless, Stockbridge, Hants; one *s*. *Educ:* Exeter School; St Mary's Hospital. Entered West African Medical Staff in Northern Nigeria, 1905; served in Nigeria, Sierra Leone, and Gold Coast. *Address:* The Parsonage Farm, Horwood, Bideford, Devon.

Died 30 May 1948.

INSKIP, J. Henry, RBA; a landscape artist and painter of interiors; *m* Kate, 2nd *d* of George Brough of Pickering, Yorks. A constant exhibitor at the Royal Academy, RBA, and most of the principal art exhibitions of the country; an hon. member of the Old Cheltenham Fine Art Society, and an occasional writer of art criticism for the press; a member of Fylingdales Group of Artists; Hon. Vice-Pres. Scarborough Sketching Club. *Works:* Walmer, Whitstable, both purchased by Rochdale Corporation for permanent collection; The Mill at Canterbury, purchased by Corporation of Whitby, for permanent collection at Pannett Gallery; In the Heat of the Day, RA 1908; Sussex Cottages, RA 1910; Lower Street, Pulborough, and The Bridge at Brandon, RA 1911; Nov. Feeding, Combe Lands, Sussex, RA 1912. *Address:* 19 The Esplanade, Scarborough.

Died 3 Jan. 1947.

INSKIP, Rt Rev. James Theodore, DD; *b* Clifton, Bristol, 6 April 1868; *e s* of late James Inskip, Clifton, Bristol; *m* 1894, Lilian Hamilton (*d* 1940), 3rd *d* of late Charles Buchanan Ker, Clifton, Bristol; one *s* two *d*. *Educ:* Clifton College; Corpus Christi College, Cambridge (Classical Tripos, 1889; BA 1889, MA 1893, DD 1919); Ridley Hall, Cambridge. Ordained 1891; Curate of St James', Hatcham, SE 1891–94; Manager on two groups under London School Board; Vicar of St Paul's, Penzance, 1894–1900; Member of Penzance Board of Guardians; Vicar of Leyton, E, 1900–07; Special Lecturer in Pastoral Theology, King's College, London, 1904–05; Vicar of Jesmond, Newcastle-upon-Tyne, 1907–16; Chaplain to High Sheriff of Northumberland, 1913–14; Hon. Secretary of Newcastle High School, 1907–16; Hon. Canon of Newcastle, 1914–16; Examining Chaplain to Bishop of Chelmsford, 1914–19; Vicar of Christ Church, Southport, 1916–19; Hon. Canon of Liverpool, 1917–19; Proctor for Archdeaconry of Liverpool in Convocation of York, 1919; Bishop of Suffragan of Barking, 1919–48; Archdeacon of Essex (renamed West Ham, 1922), 1920–48; Chairman of West Ham and District Educational Conference, 1920–29; Member of Essex County Education Committee, 1923; Golden Lecturer, 1932–33; Vice-Chairman, LCC Church of England Advisory Board, 1936–48. *Publications:* The Pastoral Idea, 1905; The Harvest of the River, 1930; Evangelical Influence in English Life, 1933; The One Foundation, 1933; Our Faith, 1942; (Joint) Memoir of Charles Vickery Hawkins, of King's College, Cambridge, 1896; (Joint) Confirmation and After, 1934; After Confirmation, 1946; A Man's Job, 1948. *Club:* Athenæum.

Died 4 Aug. 1949.

IONIDES, Basil, FRIBA; Architect; *b* 17 Upper Phillimore Gardens, June 1884; 4th *s* of late L. A. Ionides; *m* 1930, Hon. Nellie Levy, *d* of 1st Viscount Bearsted; no *c*. *Educ:* Tonbridge. Apprenticed to Alexander Paterson of Glasgow and afterwards worked in London; Interiors Savoy Theatre, Claridges restaurant and numerous other places in London; also sundry gardens and country houses. High Sheriff of Sussex, 1944. *Publications:* two books on interior decoration; numerous articles. *Recreations:* farming, collecting porcelain, and gardening. *Address:* Buxted Park, Sussex; Riverside House, Twickenham. *Club:* Burlington Fine Arts.

Died 23 Sept. 1950.

IRVINE, Dr Alexander; *b* Antrim, Ireland, 19 Jan. 1863. Minister and writer. Joined the Marines; served Gordon Relief Expedition; went to the United States, 1888, lectured to troops of the Expeditionary Force in France. *Publications:* From the Bottom Up; My Lady of the Chimney Corner; God and Tommy Atkins; The Souls of Poor Folk, 1921; The Carpenter and his Kingdom,

1922; A Fighting Parson, 1930; My Cathedral, 1937; Anna's Wishing Chair, 1938. *Address:* 333 S Gramercy Place, Los Angeles, California. *T:* 2858.

Died 15 March 1941.

IRVINE, Lt-Col Gerard Beatty, CB 1916; late Indian Medical Service; *b* 18 Aug. 1863. Capt. IMS 1887; Major, 1899; Lt-Col 1907; served Waziristan Expedition, 1894–95 (medal with clasp); NW Frontier, India, 1897–98 (medal with clasp); East Africa, 1903–04 (medal with clasp); European War, Mesopotamia, 1914–18 (despatches, CB). *Club:* Naval and Military.

Died 13 Feb. 1947.

IRVINE, James Mercer, KC Scot., LLD; Sheriff of Renfrew and Bute since 1918. Advocate, 1889; Lecturer in Civil Law, Glasgow University, 1895–1907; Additional Advocate-Depute, 1905–06; Professor of Law, Aberdeen University, 1907–19. *Publication:* (joint) Law of Rights in Security. *Address:* 3 Royal Circus, Edinburgh.

Died 1 June 1945.

IRVINE, Lt-Col Richard Abercrombie, CMG 1912; DSO 1917; late 3rd Batt. (Res.) Lancs Fusiliers; late Provincial Comr, Northern Territories, Gold Coast; retired. Served European War, 1915–18 (DSO, Bt Lt-Col).

Died 10 Oct. 1946.

IRVINE, Hon. Sir William (Hill), GCMG 1936; KCMG 1914; KC, LLD; *b* Newry, Ireland, 6 July 1858; *s* of Hill Irvine, JP, and *nephew* of John Mitchel; *m* 1891, Agnes Somerville, *e d* of Hon. T. D. Wanliss, MLC; one *s* two *d*. *Educ:* Royal School, Armagh; Trin. College, Dublin. BA Dublin; MA; LLM, Melbourne. Left Ireland for Australia, 1879; called to Bar, Melbourne, 1884; entered Parliament, 1894; Attorney-General of Victoria, 1899–1900; Premier and Attorney-General Victoria, 1902–03; entered Federal Parliament, 1906; Attorney-General of the Commonwealth, 1913; Chief Justice of Victoria, 1918–35, Lieut-Governor, 1918–35. *Publication:* Irvine's Justices of the Peace, 1887. *Address:* 25 Wallace Avenue, Toorak, Melbourne, SE2, Victoria, Australia. *Clubs:* Melbourne, Melbourne.

Died 20 Aug. 1943.

IRVING, Ven. Edward Arthur; *b* Southsea, Hants, 20 Dec. 1850; *s* of late Edward George Irving, MD, FRGS, RN, and Lucy E. H. Morrell; *m* 1st, 1876, Margaret Hamilton; no *c*; 2nd, 1917, Alexandra M'Kechnie. *Educ:* Christ's Hospital. Came to Canada, 1872; Deacon, 1881; Priest, 1882; Licensed Lay Reader and Curate, Orangeville (Dio. Niagara), 1880–82; Curate, St George's, Guelph, 1882–86; Curate in charge, Dundas, 1886; (1st) Rector, St James, Dundas, 1895–1916; Rural Dean, Co. of Wentworth, 1897, 1899, and 1908; Hon. Canon, Christ Church Cathedral, Hamilton, 1911; Archdeacon of Wentworth and Haldimand, 1912; retired, 1916. *Address:* Apartment, 12, 210 Aberdeen Avenue, Hamilton, Ontario, Canada.

Died 10 Feb. 1943.

IRWIN, Robert; Lieutenant-Governor Nova Scotia, 1937–40; *m* 1894, Mary P. McGill; two *s*. *Educ:* Shelburne Academy. Business Career. *Address:* Shelburne, Nova Scotia. *T:* 50.

Died 16 May 1941.

ISAAC, Charles Leonard, TD, DL, Co. Glam; BA, MB, BC, (Cantab); FRCSE, MRCS, LRCP; Consulting Surgeon; Consulting Surgeon, Brecon County Hospital; Colonel, AMST, Bt-Col, 1924; ADMS, 53rd Welsh Division (ret.); Hon. Col 53rd Welsh Divisional RAMC; *s* of David Isaac, Solicitor, Swansea; *m* Dorothy Margaret, *d* of Fred. Williams, Neath; one *s* one *d*. *Educ:* Swansea Grammar School; Christ's College, Blackheath; St John's College, Cambridge. Senior Surgeon, Swansea Hospital; Consulting Surgeon, Clydach War Hospital and Gorseinon Hospital; Medical Referee, County

Court Circuit, No. 30; Member, British Medical Association, and Fellow London Medical Society; Member of the Surgical Union of Great Britain; Examiner of General Nursing Council of England and Wales; Past President, College of Nursing, South Wales and Monmouth; late Chairman, Swansea Branch, BMA; mobilised 14 Aug. 1914, BEF; Surgical Specialist Casualty Clearing Station; Hon. Surgeon to the King, 1930–34; Vice-President British Legion, Swansea Branch; Patron RNVR and RND Association Western Division. *Publications:* Value of Surface Signs in Diagnosis of Deepseated Disease, BMJ, 1909; Five Cases of Ileocæcal Resection, Ib. 1928; Successful Re-section of Intussusception in Child of two years, Lancet, 1913; A Case of Bennett's Fracture, BMJ, 1912; Case of Keratodermia Blennorrhagia in a Woman, Brit. Jl Dermat., 1920; Clinical Aspects on Acute Pancreatitis, Clinical Journal, 1929. *Address:* Machen Lodge, Gower Road, Swansea. *Clubs:* Junior Army and Navy; Bristol Channel Yacht.

Died 6 Nov. 1944.

ISAACS, Rt Hon. Sir Isaac Alfred, PC 1921; GCB 1937; GCMG 1932; KCMG 1928; Member of Judicial Committee of PC, 1924; *b* Melbourne, 6 Aug. 1855; *s* of late Alfred and Rebecca Isaacs of Auburn, Victoria; *m* 1888, Daisy Jacobs; two *d. Educ:* Beechworth Grammar School; Melbourne University. LLB, LLM; graduated as Scholar in Law with 1st Class honours at University. Admitted to Victorian Bar, 1880; QC 1899; member of Victorian Legislative Assembly as representative of Bogong, 1892–1901; retired, having become member of Federal Parliament. Solicitor-General of Victoria, 1893; Attorney-General, 1894 and 1900; retired, 1901, on ceasing to be a member of State Parliament; member of Australian Federal Convention, 1897, which framed the Commonwealth Constitution; of Royal Commission on Parliamentary Procedure, 1894; member of House of Representatives of Australian Commonwealth Parliament, 1901–06; Attorney-General of Australia, 1905–06; Justice of High Court of Australia, 1906–30; Acting Chief Justice, 1927 and 1929; Chief Justice of Australia, 1930–31; Gov.-Gen. of Australia, 1931–36; Knight of Grace of the Order of St John of Jerusalem, 1931; Hon. Bencher Inner Temple, 1932. *Address:* Maranie, Mount Macedon, Victoria, Australia.

Died 11 Feb. 1948.

ISAACS, Susan Sutherland, CBE 1948; MA, DSc (Vict.), Hon. DSc (Adelaide); Psychologist to the London Clinic of Psycho-Analysis since 1931; *b* 24 May 1885; *d* of William Fairhurst, Bolton, Lancs, and Miriam Sutherland; *m* 1st, 1914, W. B. Brierley; 2nd, 1922, Nathan Isaacs. *Educ:* Bolton Secondary School; University of Manchester and University of Cambridge. Graduate Scholar, University of Manchester, 1912; Research student, Cambridge Psychological Laboratory, 1912–13. Lecturer in Psychology, Darlington Training College, 1913–14; Lecturer in Logic, Univ. of Manchester, 1914–15; Tutor of Tutorial Classes in Psychology, Univ. of London, 1916–33; Principal, Malting House School, Cambridge, 1924–27; Head of Dept of Child Development, Univ. of London Institute of Education, 1933–43; Member of Training Committee, Institute of Psycho-Analysis, 1944–46, and Member of its Board, 1945–47; Hon. Joint Secretary, 1919, 1921, and Chairman, 1928–31, Education Section, British Psychological Society; FRAI 1923–39; Assistant Editor, British Journal of Psychology, since 1921; Editorial Board, British Journal of Educational Psychology, since 1931, and British Journal of Medical Psychology since 1936; Fellow, British Psychological Soc.; Editor, Contributions to Modern Education. *Publications:* An Introduction to Psychology, 1921; The Nursery Years, 1929; American edition awarded Parents' Magazine Medal, 1937; Intellectual Growth in Young Children, 1930; Health and Education in the Nursery (with Dr Victoria Bennett), 1931; The Children We Teach, 1932; Social Development in Young Children, 1933; The Psychological Aspects of Child Development, 1935; Chapters in Handbook of Child Psychology, 1931, On the Bringing Up of Children, 1936, Educational Guidance of School Child, 1937, in Children in War-Time, 1940, in Cambridge Evacuation Survey, 1941, in The Family in a World at War, 1942, and in Fatherless Children, 1945; Childhood and After: Essays and Clinical Studies, 1948; Troubles of Children and Parents, 1948; articles and reviews in scientific and educational journals. *Recreations:* gardening, walking, and ornithology. *Address:* 30a Primrose Hill Road, NW3. *T:* Primrose 2861.

Died 12 Oct. 1948.

ISACKE, Maj.-Gen. Hubert, CB 1922; CSI 1919; CMG 1915; The Queen's Own (Royal West Kent Regiment); *b* 28 Oct. 1872; *s* of late Col H. W. Isacke, Royal Artillery; *m* Mildred, *d* of late Sir Charles P. Layard, Chief Justice of Ceylon; two *s.* Entered Army, 1892; Captain, 1902; Bt Major, 1902; Major, 1912; Bt Lt-Col 1913; Col 1917; Maj.-Gen. 1923; General Staff Officer, 2nd Grade, War Office, 1910–12; Staff College, Quetta, 1913–14; General Staff Officer, 1st Grade, 1915–16; Br.-Gen. General Staff, AHQ, India 1916–20; Brigade Commander, India, 1920–23; District Commander, India, 1925–27; Commander 56th (1st London) Division TA, 1927–31; retired pay, 1931; served with Malakand Field Force 1897–98 (severely wounded, medal with clasp); S African War, 1899–1902 (despatches twice, Bt Major Queen's medal 3 clasps, King's medal 2 clasps); European War, 1914–18 (CMG, despatches four times, Bt Col). *Address:* Polhampton, Overton, Hants. *Club:* Army and Navy.

Died 12 Feb. 1943.

ISBISTER, William James, MBE, KC; *b* Adelaide, South Australia, 1866; *er s* of late William Isbister. *Educ:* St Peter's School, Adelaide; University of Adelaide; graduated there in Law, 1887. Afterwards became a student at the Inner Temple (Common Law Scholarship, 1891, First Common Law Prize, Council of Legal Education, 1892), and was called to the Bar, 1893; KC South Australia, 1916; Australian Red Cross Representative in Egypt; a member of the Council of the University of Adelaide. *Recreation:* golf. *Address:* 21 Strangways Terrace, North Adelaide, South Australia. *Club:* Adelaide.

Died 16 Dec. 1950.

ISHAM, Sir Vere, 11th Bt *cr* 1627; *b* 10 May 1862; *s* of late John Vere Isham; *S* cousin, 1903; *m* 1895, Millicent, *d* of Henry Halford Vaughan, Regius Professor of Modern History, Oxford; one *s* one *d. Educ:* Eton; Sandhurst. Formerly Captain in 2nd Battalion Suffolk Regiment. *Heir: s* Gyles. *Address:* Lauriston, St Leonards-on-Sea.

Died 11 Feb. 1941.

ISHERWOOD, Sir William, 2nd Bt *cr* 1921; Managing Director Sir Joseph W. Isherwood and Co. Ltd, 4 Lloyd's Avenue, EC3; *b* 28 Jan. 1898; *s* of Sir Joseph W. Isherwood, 1st Bt, and Annie Mary Fleetham; *S* father 1937; *m* 1932, Nenette, *d* of C. Pittolo; two *d. Educ:* Gresham School; Cambridge University; Armstrong College. Naval Architect from 1921; Director of Sir Joseph W. Isherwood & Co. Ltd, 1927; Chairman and Managing Director of same Company, 1937; Member of Worshipful Company of Shipwrights, of Institution of Naval Architects, of North-East Coast Institution of Engineers and Shipbuilders. *Recreations:* golf, riding, motoring. *Heir:* none. *Address:* Boiling Common Cottage, The Midway, Felpham, Sussex. *TA:* Ishercon, London. *T:* Bognor Regis 166, Royal 2777.

Died 29 May 1946 (ext).

IVES, George (Cecil), Author and Criminologist; MA, FZS; *b* 1867; adopted and brought up from babyhood by late Hon. Emma Ives, *d* of 3rd Viscount Maynard and *widow* of late J. R. Ives of Bentworth Hall, Alton; unmarried. *Educ:* home; Magdalene College, Cambridge; London. *Publications:* Book of Chains, 1897; Eros' Throne, 1900; History of Penal Methods, 1914; Extra-Organic Habits of Animals, 1918; The Continued Extension of the Criminal Law, 1922; The Græco-Roman View of Youth, 1926; Obstacles to Human Progress, 1939. *Recreations:* chess, swimming, cricket, anything to get hot and work hard at. *Club:* Royal Societies. MCC.

Died 4 June 1950.

IVES, Harry William Maclean, CIE 1921; MICE; *b* 14 Aug. 1867; *s* of William Barnett Edward Ives, Chertsey; *m* 1st, Frances Mary (*d* 1934), *d* of Thomas Adams Palmer, Barrister-at-law; no *c*; 2nd, 1935, Muriel, widow of T. G. F. Palmer and *er d* of late Lt-Col J. F. C. Thatcher, Bombay Staff Corps. *Educ:* Bishop Cotton's School, Simla; Thomason Civil Engineering College, Roorkee. Obtained the Thomason Gold Medal for the best project of his year; and after obtaining one of the four guaranteed Government posts in his year was appointed an Assistant Engineer to the PWD, Punjab Irrigation, 1889; Executive Engineer, 1900; Superintending Engineer, 1909; Chief Engineer and Secretary to Government, Punjab, 1918; retired, 1922; was on the construction of the Head Works of the Upper Chenab Canal (K-I-H Gold Medal, CIE). *Recreations:* cricket, tennis and rowing. *Clubs:* East India United Service; Punjab, Lahore.

Died 21 June 1941.

IVIMEY, Mrs Fairfax; *see* Matthews, Julia B.

J

JACK, Adolphus Alfred, MA, LLM; Hon. LLD; b 8 Oct. 1868; s of late Professor Wm Jack of Glasgow University; m 1902, Lucy, d of late John Nichol, Professor of English Language and Literature, Glasgow University, 1862–89. *Educ:* Fettes College, Edinburgh; Glasgow University; Peterhouse, Cambridge. Barrister-at-Law, Lincoln's Inn, 1895; Fellow of Peterhouse, 1898–1905; Lecturer on English Language and Literature, Queen Margaret College (Women's Department), University of Glasgow, 1895–1902; Clark Lecturer in English Literature, Trin. Coll., Cambridge, 1914–15; Chalmers Professor of English Literature, University of Aberdeen, 1915–37. *Publications:* Thackeray, a Study; Essays on the Novel; The Prince, a Play; Shelley, an Essay; Mathilde, a Play; Poetry and Prose, being Essays on Modern English Poetry; A Commentary on the Poetry of Chaucer and Spenser; The Angry Heart, a Domestic Drama; Four Plays in One Volume. *Address:* 22 Queen's Road, Aberdeen; Bohally, Pitlochry, Perthshire. *T:* Tummel Bridge 25.

Died 21 Feb. 1946.

JACKMAN, Mgr Canon Arthur, DD; in charge of Church of the Holy Rood, Watford; Canon of Westminster Cathedral since 1920; b Shoreham, Sussex, 1878; s of William Jackman, Devonport. *Educ:* Wonersh and Rome. Ordained Priest, 1902; in same year appointed assistant secretary to Cardinal, then Bishop, Bourne of Southwark; followed his Eminence to Westminster as his private secretary, 1903–26, and Archivist of the same Archdiocese; editor of the Catholic Directory, 1909–27; Rural Dean of St Alban's Conference; Editor of Holy Roodlets; named Cameriere Segreto to Pius X, 1910, to Benedict XV, 1914, and to Pius XI, 1922; Domestic Prelate, 1933. *Address:* Holy Rood, Watford. *TA:* Holyrood, Watford. *T:* Watford 4085.

Died 22 May 1945.

JACKSON, Rev. Canon Brice Lee, MA; Rector of Kilcommon Erris; b 21 March 1864; s of Colonel James Jackson, HM Indian Army, and Ellen Weldon; m Louisa Mary, d of John Blakeney King and Hadley Horne; two s. *Educ:* Heath Mount School, Hampstead; Sandhurst (Queen's India Cadet); Trinity College, Dublin. Took Holy Orders, 1888; entire service in Church of Ireland, except one year in Australia. *Publication:* Sermons in Church of England Pulpit. *Address:* The Rectory, Belmullet, County Mayo. *TA:* Belmullet.

Died 8 Feb. 1941.

JACKSON, Sir Ernest; *see* Jackson, Sir J. E.

JACKSON, Lt-Col Ernest Somerville, CMG 1918; DSO 1917; late Welch Regt; b 1872; s of late T. H. Jackson, The Manor House, Birkenhead. *Educ:* Harrow. Egyptian Army, 1898–1914; European War, 1914–18 (despatches, DSO, CMG, Bt Maj.); has Osmania 4th Class and Medijia 3rd Class. *Club:* Army and Navy.

Died 10 March 1943.

JACKSON, F. Ernest, ARA 1944. *Address:* 96 Holywell Street, Oxford.

Died 11 March 1945.

JACKSON, Rt Hon. Sir (Francis) Stanley, PC 1926; GCSI 1932; GCIE 1927; b 21 Nov. 1870; y s of 1st Lord Allerton; m 1902, Julia Henrietta (Kaisar-i-Hind Medal 1st class, 1932), e d of late H. B. Harrison-Broadley, MP, Welton House, Brough; one s. [m 1927, Diana, o d of late Dr A. P. Beddard]. *Educ:* Harrow; Trinity College, Cambridge, BA Hon. DLitt Calcutta Univ. 1932 and Dacca Univ.; Hon. LLD Sheffield Univ. Knight of Grace

St John of Jerusalem; MP (U) Howdenshire Division of Yorkshire, 1915–26; Financial Secretary to the War Office 1922–23; Chairman of the Unionist Party, 1923–26; Governor of Bengal, 1927–32; Harrow Eleven, Cambridge Eleven (Capt. 1892–93), Yorkshire Eleven; has repeatedly played for Gentlemen *versus* Players, and All England teams; served in South Africa, 1900–02; Captain 3rd Royal Lancaster Regt; raised and commanded 2/7th West Yorks Regt, 1914–17; DL West Riding, Yorks. Chairman of Governors of Harrow School since 1942. *Recreations:* cricket, golf, shooting. *Club:* Carlton.

Died 9 March 1947.

JACKSON, Rev. Frederick John F.; *see* Foakes Jackson.

JACKSON, Brig.-Gen. Geoffrey Meinertzhagen; DL, JP; Managing Director Clay Cross Company; b 9 April 1869; 3rd s of Thomas Hughes Jackson, JP of the Manor House, Birkenhead; m 1893, Jessie Cowper Coles (d 1945), d of late Henry Hyndman Laird, Birkenhead; two s three d. *Educ:* Harrow. JP Derbyshire, 1900; DL Derbyshire, 1916; High Sheriff of Derbyshire, 1924; Hon. Brig.-General; sometime Lieut-Col Commanding 6th Bn The Sherwood Foresters; Col Commandant 2/1st Lincoln and Leicester Brigade, 1915–16. *Recreations:* golf, hunting. *Address:* Clay Cross Hall, Chesterfield. *Clubs:* Bath; Royal St Davids Golf.

Died 9 Sept. 1946.

JACKSON, Rev. George; b Grimsby, 15 Oct. 1864; 2nd s of William and Eliza Jackson; m 1892, Annie, d of J. Hyslop Bell, JP, Darlington; two s one d. *Educ:* Collegiate School, Grimsby; Wesleyan Methodist College, Richmond, BA, London University; DD Aberdeen University. Entered Wesleyan Methodist ministry, 1887; one year in the Clitheroe Circuit; Superintendent of the Wesleyan Methodist Mission, Edinburgh, 1888; Pastor of Sherbourne Street Methodist Church, Toronto, 1906; Professor of English Bible, Victoria College, Toronto, 1909–13; Resident Tutor, Didsbury College, Toronto, 1909–13; Resident Tutor, Didsbury College, Manchester, 1913–16; Brixton Hill, London, 1916–19; Professor of English Language, Literature and Bible, Didsbury College, Manchester, 1919–28; Governor John Rylands Library. *Publications:* First Things First, 1894; The Table Talk of Jesus, 1896; Judgment, Human and Divine, 1897; The Ten Commandments, and A Young Man's Book Shelf, 1898; A Young Man's Religion, 1900; Memoranda Paulina, 1901; The Old Methodism and the New, 1903; The Teaching of Jesus, 1903; The Fact of Conversion, 1908; Studies in the Old Testament, 1909; The Preacher and the Modern Mind (Fernley Lecture), 1912; In a Preacher's Study, 1914; Leaves of Healing, 1916; Reasonable Religion, 1922; Collier of Manchester, 1923; The Guests of God, 1925; A Parson's Log, 1927; Half-Hours in a Library, 1933. *Recreations:* reading and walking. *Address:* Rowanbrae, Teignmouth. *T:* Teignmouth 113.

Died 16 April 1945.

JACKSON, Lt-Col George Scott, CBE 1919; DSO 1916; TD, MD; 2nd s of Daniel Jackson, MD, Hexham; m 1st, Maud, e d of late C. Harrison Stanton, Newcastle; one s two d; 2nd, M. A. Dodds. *Educ:* Durham School; Glasgow University. Medical Practitioner in Alnwick for twenty-five years; served European War, including 2nd battle of Ypres (despatches six times, Bt Maj., DSO and bar, Bt Lt-Col); transferred to RAMC Jan. 1918, and commanded 39th General Hospital till June 1919;

commanded 1/7 Batt. Northumberland Fusiliers, TF, 1915–21. Retired from practice, 1944. *Publications:* several contributions to the Lancet. *Recreations:* played for Northumberland County at cricket and tennis, and for University at Rugby football, held West of Scotland Championship and Lanarkshire Championship for tennis for three years. *Address:* 42 Thalassa Road, Worthing.

Died 21 Oct. 1946.

JACKSON, Captain Harold Gordon, CBE 1929; RN retired; *y s* of late Admiral Sir T. S. Jackson, KCVO; *m* Louie, *d* of late Inspector-General Thomas Browne, RN; one *s* two *d. Educ:* HMS Britannia. Served at sea till 1907, when joined Naval Ordnance Inspection Department; Inspector of Steel, 1912–19; Superintendent of Design, Naval Ordnance, 1919; Superintendent of Design, 1925; Member of Ordnance Committee, 1929; Assistant Inspector, under CIA, 1940–45. *Address:* 274 Dorchester Road, Weymouth.

Died 13 Feb. 1950.

JACKSON, Harold Gordon, DSc; Master of Birkbeck College since 1943; Professor Emeritus of Zoology, 1948; Deputy Vice-Chancellor, 1949–50; Chairman of Collegiate Council, University of London 1947–50; *b* Shoreham, Sussex, 1888; *s* of Rev. Joseph Jackson, Liverpool; *m* 1919, Marion Poole; one *d. Educ:* Merchant Taylors' School, Crosby; University of Liverpool (Isaac Roberts Scholar). Research Assistant, University of Liverpool, 1911; Lecturer, University of Birmingham, 1913. Served in Royal Warwickshire Regt, 1915–19; Reader, University of London and Head of Zoology Dept, Birkbeck College, 1921; Professor of Zoology, Univ. of London, 1928–48. *Publications:* Papers chiefly on Crustacea, in the publications of the British Museum; Smithsonian Institution; Musée Royal de Belgique; Proc. Zool. Soc.; Quart. Jl Micros Sci.; and other scientific journals. *Recreations:* various literary and antiquarian pursuits, but mainly music. *Address:* Northlands, Hadley Green, Barnet, Herts. *T:* Barnet 2066. *Club:* Athenæum.

Died 5 Aug. 1950.

JACKSON, Sir Henry Mather-, 3rd Bt *cr* 1869; CBE 1918; JP, DL; *b* 19 Oct. 1855; *S* father, 1881; *m* 1886, Ada, CBE 1939, JP, *d* of late Gen. Somerset, CB, Troy House, Monmouthshire; one *s* three *d. Educ:* Harrow; Trinity College, Cambridge (MA). Barrister Lincoln's Inn, 1881; Lord Lieutenant and formerly Chairman Quarter Sessions for Monmouthshire; contested (L) S Division of Monmouthshire, 1885, and Flint Boroughs (LU), 1886. *Heir: s* Edward Arthur [*b* 1899; *m* 1932, Cecilia, *er d* of late Capt. Christopher Balfour, DSO, and of late Mrs Lowry-Corry. Eton. Late Lieut Scots Guards. Served European War, 1917–18. Pratt's]. *Address:* St Mary's Hill, Abergavenny. *T:* Nantyderry 74. *Club:* Brooks's.

Died 23 March 1942.

JACKSON, Holbrook; author; Editorial Director of National Trade Press, Ltd; and Heywood & Co., Ltd, 1917–45; *b* Liverpool, 31 Dec. 1874; *m* 1900; one *d. Educ:* various schools. Joint-editor of New Age, 1907; editor The Beau, 1910; acting editor of T. P.'s Magazine, 1911–12, and T. P.'s Weekly, 1911–14; editor T. P.'s Weekly, 1914–16; Editor of To-day, 1917–23; contributor to various journals, and lecturer; Chairman, British Colour Council, 1933–34. *Publications:* Edward FitzGerald and Omar Khayyám, an Essay and a Bibliography, 1899; The Eternal Now, a book of verses, 1900; Everychild, an anthology of verses for children, 1906; Bernard Shaw: a study, 1907; William Morris: a biography, 1908; revised edition, 1926; Great English Novelists, 1908; Platitudes in the Making, 1911; Romance and Reality, 1911; All Manner of Folk, 1912; Town: an Essay, 1913; The Eighteen Nineties, 1913; Southward Ho! and Other Essays (Wayfarer's Library) 1914; Occasions, 1922; Joint-author, A Brief Survey of

Printing, 1923; Essays of To-day and Yesterday, 1928; The Anatomy of Bibliomania, 1930, vol. ii, 1931; The Fear of Books, 1932; William Caxton, 1933; Maxims of Books and Reading, 1934; The Printing of Books, 1938; Bookman's Holiday, 1945; The Reading of Books, 1946; The Complete Nonsense of Edward Lear, 1947; Dreamers of Dreams, 1948. *Recreations:* reading and talking. *Address:* 1 Winterstoke Gardens, Mill Hill, NW7. *T:* Mill Hill 1177. *Club:* Athenæum.

Died 15 June 1948.

JACKSON, Sir (John) Ernest, Kt 1924; CIE 1918; *b* 26 Nov. 1876; *m d* of late Maj.-Gen. G. F. A. Harris, CSI; one *s* two *d. Educ:* Marlborough College. *Address:* Fairways, Farnham Royal, Bucks.

Died 18 Oct. 1941.

JACKSON, Sir John Peter Todd, Kt 1933; JP, DL; *b* 1868; *m* 1902, Florence, *d* of William Christopher Wood; one *s* one *d. Address:* Wheelton, Chorley, Lancs.

Died 14 Sept. 1945.

JACKSON, Maj.-Gen. Sir Louis (Charles), KBE 1918; CB 1917; CMG 1906; RE; Commander of the Legion of Honour, 1917; Knight of St Stanislas (1st class), 1918; *b* 7 March 1856; *s* of late Sir Louis Steuart Jackson, CIE, BCS; *m* 1885, Bessie (*d* 1938), *d* of late W. Vivian; one *s* one *d. Educ:* Somersetshire Coll., Bath; RMA, Woolwich. Served Afghanistan, 1879 (medal); ADC to Governor of Leeward Islands, 1883; Instructor in Fortification and Military Engineering, SME, Chatham, 1895–1902; Commissioner for Anglo-German Boundary of Northern Nigeria, Central Africa, 1902–04; CRE Dublin, 1904–06; Assistant Director of Fortifications and Works, War Office, 1907–10; Chief Engineer, London District, 1910–13; retired 1913; reappointed Assistant Director, War Office, Aug. 1914; a Director-General in Ministry of Munitions, 1915; Controller Trench Warfare Research, 1916–17; visited Russian Front on duty, 1916; employed by WO on special duty in Canada, 1918; retired as Hon. Maj.-General, Nov. 1918. *Publications:* History of the United Service Club, 1937; Fortification and Siegecraft, in Encyclopædia Britannica, 11th ed. articles Poison Gas and Military Mining in Supplement. *Club:* United Service.

Died 8 Oct. 1946.

JACKSON, Sir Percy Richard, Kt 1925; JP; Hon. LLD Leeds and Sheffield; *b* 1869; *s* of William Michael Jackson, Sheepridge, Huddersfield; *m* 1st, 1892, Mary Elizabeth (*d* 1938), *d* of Thomas Blacker, Skelmanthorpe; two *s* four *d*; 2nd, 1939, Jessie Ewen, *d* of Robert Robertson, Logie Easter. *Educ:* Huddersfield Collegiate. Member of West Riding Council, 1904–37; Chm. of West Riding Education Committee 1917–37; Chm., County Councils Association, 1929–35; Pres. of Association of Education Committees, 1924; Trustee and Vice-Chm. of United Kingdom Carnegie Trust since 1924; Chairman Land Settlement Association, 1934–39; Member of Council and Court of Leeds University since 1918; of Consultative Committee of Board of Education, 1922–38; Member of Royal Commission on the Civil Service, 1930–31. *Address:* Woodland's, Scissett, nr Huddersfield. *TA:* Jackson, Woodlands, Scissett. *T:* Skelmanthorpe 2217.

Died 24 Dec. 1941.

JACKSON, Sir Ralph, Kt 1929; MRCVS, late Chief Veterinary Officer, Ministry of Agriculture; *b* 1872; *o s* of late James Richard Jackson, RN; *m* Evelyn, 3rd *d* of Thomas Horsfall, Roefield, Clitheroe, Lancs; three *d. Educ:* Probus School, Cornwall; Royal (Dick) Veterinary College, Edinburgh; Royal Veterinary College, London. Joined Ministry of Agriculture, 1897; retired, 1932. *Recreation:* golf. *Address:* Roefield, Meadfoot Road, Torquay.

Died 2 Aug. 1943.

JACKSON, Sir Richard Hoyle, Kt 1932; Chairman Lancashire Indian Cotton Committee; Chairman, Empire Cotton-Growing Corporation; Member of Executive British Cotton Growing Association; JP Co. Lancaster; *b* 1869; *e s* of William Jackson; *m* 1897, Alice Prockter, *d* of William Scott; one *s* two *d*. *Educ:* Oldham High School. *Address:* 105 Windsor Road, Oldham. *T:* 1952 Main Oldham. *Clubs:* Albion, Oldham.
Died 24 Jan. 1944.

JACKSON, Lt-Col Richard Rolt Brash, DSO 1918; Retired Pay; *b* 15 Dec. 1874; *s* of Francis William Jackson, MA, Cork, and Sara Susanna Fitton; *m* 1903, Angelina Lefebure, *o d* of Capt. Willie Keene, Co. Cork; one *s*. *Educ:* Queen's College, Cork; Royal Military College, Sandhurst. Gazetted R. Munster Fusiliers, 1895; served SA war 1899–1902 (despatches, Queen's medal with three clasps, King's medal and two clasps); transferred RASC; served European War, 1914–18 (despatches twice, DSO, 1914 Star, General Service Medal, Victory Medal). *Recreations:* fishing and shooting. *Address:* c/o Lloyds Bank, 6 Pall Mall, SW1.
Died 21 Dec. 1943.

JACKSON, Maj.-Gen. Robert Edward, CMG 1919; DSO 1918; *b* 1886; *s* of Samuel Jackson, Mount Lawley, Perth, W Australia; *m* 1914, Edith Marguerite, *d* of late H. D. Vautin, Sydney, NSW; two *s* one *d*. *Educ:* Brisbane Grammar School. Served European War, 1915–19 (despatches thrice, DSO, Chevalier of Legion of Honour, CMG); General Officer Commanding, 1st Division, NSW, 1939–40; GOC Northern Command, Australia, 1940–41; GOC Western Command, 1941–42; retired, 1946. *Address:* 68 Elizabeth Bay Road, Sydney, NSW, Australia.
Died 24 Nov. 1948.

JACKSON, Rt Hon. Sir Stanley; *see* Jackson, Rt Hon. Sir F. S.

JACKSON, Adm. Sir Thomas, KBE 1923; CB 1906; MVO 1906; *b* 20 Feb. 1868; *s* of Admiral Sir T. Jackson, KCVO; *m* Mona Anna (*d* 1945), *d* of Col Henry Murray; two *s* two *d*. Entered Navy, 1881; Commander, 1899; Captain, 1905; Vice-Admiral, 1920; Admiral, 1925; was Naval Attaché, Tokio, 1906 (2nd class Order Sacred Treasure, Japan); Director of Intelligence Division of the War Staff, Jan. 1912 to Oct. 1913; Director of Operations Division, Jan. 1915–June 1917; Commanded Egypt and Red Sea Division of Mediterranean Squadron July 1917–Jan. 1919; retired list, 1923. *Address:* Waterside, Uplyme.
Died 7 July 1945.

JACKSON, Lt-Col Vivian Archer, DSO 1917; late York and Lancaster Regt; *b* 1882; *s* of J. A. Jackson; *m* Dorothea Gartside-Spaight; one *s*. *Educ:* Wellington College. Served European War, 1914–17 (despatches, DSO, Bt Lt-Col, Croix de Guerre); psc. *Address:* Newton House, Blisland, Bodmin, Cornwall.
Died 2 April 1943.

JACOB, Maj.-Gen. Arthur Le Grand, CB 1923; CMG 1918; CIE 1907; CBE 1924; DSO 1898; Indian Army, retired; Colonel 10th Baluch. Regt; *b* Bhuj, India, 19 Feb. 1867; *s* of Major-General W. Jacob, IA; *m* Mary Hilston, *d* of late Fleet Paymaster J. T. Sueter, RN. *Educ:* Sherborne School; RMC, Sandhurst. Lt 1st North Lancashire Regt, 1886; transferred Indian Staff Corps, 1887; served in Zhob Field Force, 1890; Mekran Expedition, 1898; action at Gok Parosh (despatches, DSO); NW Frontier of India, Waziristan, 1901–02 (medal with clasp); European War, 1914–18 (despatches, CMG, Brevet-Colonel and ADC to the King, 3 medals); Iraq Rebellion, 1920 (despatches, medal with clasp); Waziristan, 1922–23; commanded Razmak Field Force (despatches, CBE, medal with clasp); commanded Kohat

District, 1922–24; Waziristan District, 1924–26; retired, 1926. *Address:* c/o Lloyds Bank, King's Branch, 6 Pall Mall, SW1. *Club:* United Service.
Died 10 Aug. 1942.

JACOB, Lt-Col Arthur Leslie, CSI 1920; CIE 1914; OBE 1918; Indian Army, retired; *b* 1870; *m* 1896, Jenny Coke Mickleburgh. British Army, 1891; Indian Army, 1892–95; Indian Foreign and Political Dept, 1895–1923; served European War, 1914–18; Afghan War, 1919 (CSI). *Address:* 58 Napier Court, Hurlingham, SW6.
Died 21 June 1944.

JACOB, Mrs Arthur, (Violet), Hon. LLD Edinburgh, 1936; *b* Scotland; *d* of William Henry Kennedy-Erskine, of Dun; *m* Major Arthur Otway Jacob, late 20th Hussars. *Publications:* The Sheepstealers; The Interloper; Verses— The History of Aythan Waring; The Fortune Hunters, 1910; Flemington, 1911; Songs of Angus, 1915; More Songs of Angus, 1918; Bonnie Joann, 1922; Tales of My Own Country, 1922; The Northern Lights, 1927; The Good Child's Year Book, 1927; The Lairds of Dun, 1931; Scottish Poems, 1944. *Address:* Marywell House, Kirriemuir, Angus, Scotland. *Club:* Ladies' Empire.
Died 9 Sept. 1946.

JACOB, Field-Marshal Sir Claud (William), GCB 1926; GCSI 1930; KCB 1917; KCSI 1924; KCMG 1919; CB 1915; late IA; Colonel of the Worcestershire Regiment, 1927–38; Colonel of 2/10th Baluch. Regiment, 1928; *b* 21 Nov. 1863; *s* of late Major-General W. Jacob, IA; *m* 1894, Clara Pauline, *d* of late Rev. J. L. Wyatt; one *s*. *Educ:* Sherborne School; RMC, Sandhurst. Entered Army, 1882; Captain, ISC, 1893; Major, Indian Army, 1901; Lt-Col 1904; Col 1908; General Staff Officer, 1st Grade, India, 1912; Brig.-Gen. Commanding Dehra Dun Brigade, 1915; Commanding Meerut Division, 6 Sept. 1915; 21st Division, 18 Nov. 1915; 2nd Army Corps, 1916–19; Chief of General Staff, India, 1920–24; General Officer Commanding-in-Chief, Northern Command, India, 1924–25; Commander-in-Chief in India, 1925; Secretary of Military Department, India Office, 1926–30; Constable of Tower of London, 1938–43; served Zhob Valley, 1890; North-Western Frontier, India, 1901–02 (medal with clasp); European War, 1914–18 (CB, wounded, despatches ten times, promoted Major-Gen., Lieutenant-General, 3 June 1917); General, 1920; ADC General to the King, 1920–24; Field-Marshal, 1926; Order of St Vladimir 4th class with, swords (Russia); Grand Officier de l'ordre de la Couronne (Belgium) with Croix de Guerre; Grand Officier Légion d'Honneur, Croix de Guerre, France, Grand Officier de l'ordre de Leopold, Distinguished Service Medal (American). *Address:* 7 Ovington Court, SW3. *T:* Kensington 4684. *Clubs:* Army and Navy, Naval and Military.
Died 2 June 1948.

JACOBS, William Wymark; *b* London, 8 Sept. 1863; *s* of William Gage Jacobs; *m* 1900, Agnes Eleanor Williams; two *s* three *d*. *Educ:* private schools. Entered Civil Service, Savings Bank Dept, 1883–99. *Publications:* Many Cargoes, 1896; The Skipper's Wooing, 1897; Sea Urchins, 1898; A Master of Craft, 1900; Light Freights, 1901; At Sunwich Port, 1902; The Lady of the Barge, 1902; Odd Craft, 1903; Dialstone Lane, 1904; Captains All, 1905; Short Cruises, 1907; Salthaven, 1908; Sailors' Knots, 1909; Ship's Company, 1911; Night Watches, 1914; The Castaways, 1916; Deep Waters, 1919; Sea Whispers, 1926; one-act plays; Establishing Relations, The Warming Pan, A Distant Relative, Dixon's Return, etc.; (joint) Beauty and the Barge, The Monkey's Paw, etc. *Address:* 203 Elm Tree Road Mansions, St John's Wood, NW8. *T:* Cunningham 5212. *Club:* Garrick.
Died 1 Sept. 1943.

JACOBS-BOND, Carrie; *see* Bond, C. J.

JACOBSEN, Thomas Owen; JP County of London; LCC North Lambeth, 1919–22; MP (L) Hyde Division of Cheshire, 1916–18; *b* Liverpool, 1864; *s* of R. B. Jacobsen, Merchant, Liverpool, and Elizabeth Victoria Owen; *m* 1890, Annie Amelie Pauline (*d* 1941), *d* of Marius Veillard, Banker, London; no *c. Educ:* Liverpool Institute. Travelled extensively throughout Colonies, United States, India, etc.; President Federation of Envelope Makers and Manufacturing Stationers, 1925–27; Vice-President Labour Co-partnership Association; President Stationers' Association of Great Britain and Ireland, 1929–31; contested (L) City of London, 1929. *Recreations:* politics and travelling. *Address:* Westminster Bank, Ltd, 173 Victoria Street, SW1. *Club:* National Liberal.

Died 15 June 1941.

JACOBSON, Ernest (Nathaniel Joseph), CBE 1917; formerly Comdt and Chairman Discipline Board, Metropolitan Special Constabulary; *b* London, 1877; *s* of S. N. Jacobson, London; *m* 1907, Gladys, *d* of Walter Ellis, 94 Portland Pl., W; (one *s* killed in the Middle East, 7 April 1941) two *d. Educ:* City of London School. Admitted a Solicitor, 1901; a partner in the firm of Jacobson Ridley and Co., Solicitors; joined Metropolitan Special Constabulary, Aug. 1914; on Staff of Sir Edward Ward (Chief Staff Officer), Sept. 1914; Chairman Discipline Board, Metropolitan Special Constabulary, 1914–46. *Recreations:* golf, tennis. *Address:* 68 Pall Mall, SW1; 121 Gloucester Place, Portman Square, W1. *T:* Welbeck 6768. *Clubs:* Reform, Garrick.

Died 30 Dec. 1947.

JAFFRAY, Rev. William Stevenson, CMG 1915; CBE 1919; DD Edin.; *b* 30 March 1867; *s* of late William Stevenson Jaffray of Greystones, Aberdeenshire; *m* 1901, Ethel Annie Duncan, *d* of late Major James Law, RE. *Educ:* privately; Edinburgh Univ. Entered Army, 1891; served South Africa, 1899–1901 (despatches, Queen's medal 6 clasps, prom. Chaplain, 3rd Class); European War, 1914–18; Assistant Principal Chaplain V. Army; Principal Chaplain British Salonika and Black Sea Forces (ranking as Brigadier-General) (despatches four times, CMG, CBE, Order of St Sava, 2nd Class, Serbia, 1920 star, War medal and Victory medal); Deputy Chaplain-General, 1920–25; Hon. Chaplain to the King 1921; retired, 1925, as Principal Chaplain (Brigadier-General); Chaplain Commandant of Royal Army Chaplains' Dept, 1932–37; awarded Distinguished Service Pension, 1935; King's Silver Jubilee Medal, 1935; Coronation Medal, 1937. *Publications:* contributions to magazines. *Address:* c/o Glyn, Mills and Co. (Holt's Branch), Kirkland House, Whitehall, SW1. *Club:* Richmond Golf.

Died 7 Nov. 1941.

JAGGARD, Captain William; *e s* of William Jesse and Elizabeth Ada Jaggard; *m* 1898, Emma Frances Cooke; three *s* one *d. Educ:* Leamington; Cambridge. Passed twenty-two years preparing his main life-work—the Shakespeare Bibliography; has lectured in England and America; on active service, 4 Aug. 1914–May 1920; a Governor, Shakespeare Memorial at Stratford-on-Avon, also of Stationers' School, Hornsey; member of the Livery of the Worshipful Company of Stationers, and Freeman of the City of London; founded at Stratford-on-Avon the Avon Literary Club; Shakespeare Glee Club; Amateur Dramatic Society; discovered in 1935 Shakespeare's original annotated set of Holinshed's Chronicles, 1585–1587, 3 vols. *Publications:* Kyriologio, or Vegetarian's Alpha and Omega, 1905; Liverpool Literature, 1905; Folk-lore, Superstition and Witchcraft in Shakespeare, 1906; Shakespeare's First Play, 1907; Shakespeare's Publishers, 1907; Birth and Growth of Printing, 1908; Dunbar Pedigree, 1910; Shakespeare Bibliography, 1911; Shakespearean Frauds, 1911; Stratford-on-Avon from a Student's Standpoint, 1914; Roll of Honour of Fifty Thousand Repatriated Overseas Officers and Soldiers, 1919; Army Records—Human

and Humorous, 1920; Jaggard Jottings from Olden Days, 1921; Shakespeare's Private Faith, 1921; Shakespeare's honour, 1921; Shakespeare's enemies, 1922; Bookmen and Book-borrowers, 1922; With Queen Elizabeth to Westminster, 1922; National Theatres 1922; Shakespeare's Radiance, 1923; Shakespeare to the Ordinary Man, 1923; Shakespeare Treasure, Known and Unknown, 1923; Shakespeare Survey, 1924; Book-edge Adornment, 1924; Memoir of Richard Savage, 1924; Shakespeare's Almanack, 1925; Dyes and Dyeing, 1926; Co-compiler of Pollard and Redgrave's Catalogue of English Books from 1475 to 1640 (Civil War), 1926; Shakespeare Memorial at Stratford-on-Avon: Fifty Years' Illustrated Retrospect, 1926; Rollright Stones, Prehistoric Temple, 1928; Haunted Hillborough, 1928; Shakespeare Societies, Old and New, 1929; Literary Secrets: Authorship of Duty of Man, 1931; Shakespeare and the Tudor Jaggards, 1934; Shakespeare once a Printer and Bookman, 1934; Shakespeare in private and public life, 1935; sundry big bibliographical indexes, and other works; editor of Book Queries, 1894–1912. *Recreations:* Old books, drama, music, travel, and gardening. *Address:* Rose Bank, Tiddington Road, Stratford-on-Avon. *TA:* Jaggard, Stratford-on-Avon. *Club:* Authors'.

Died 27 April 1947.

JAGGER, John; MP (Lab) Clayton division of Manchester since 1935; Parliamentary Private Secretary to Mr Herbert Morrison since 1940; General President of National Union of Distributive and Allied Workers since 1920; *b* 1 Oct. 1872; *s* of James and Mary Jagger; *m* 1898, Martha Southern; two *s. Educ:* Elementary School, Oldham. Visited Burma, 1892–97; Departmental Manager Co-operative Society, York, to 1915; Yorkshire Divisional Officer to the Amalgamated Union of Co-operative Employees, 1915–20. *Address:* 4 Endsleigh Gardens, WC1. *T:* Euston 3191. *Clubs:* Labour, Trades Union.

Died 9 July 1942.

JAMES, Alderman Alfred Henry, CBE 1918, JP; Traffic Commissioner for West Midland Area appointed by Minister of Transport, 1931; Chairman Birmingham Safety First Council since 1924; Lord Mayor of Birmingham, 1926–28; Deputy Lord Mayor, 1929; *b* Birmingham, 1868; *s* of Henry and Ann James; *m* 1894, Jessie, *d* of Josiah Swingler; one *s. Educ:* Higher Grade School, Aston. A teacher 1883; a jeweller and general outfitter since 1895; member Aston Board of Guardians, 1898; chairman, 1908–12; member Aston Town Council, 1902–11; chairman Education Committee, 1904–11; member Birmingham City Council, since 1911; Alderman, 1911; member of Watch, Tramways and Assessment Committees; chairman Technical Education Sub-Committee, 1912–20; Continuation Schools Sub-Committee, 1918–20; Fire Brigade Sub-Committee, 1916–18; Judicial Sub-Committee, 1918–20; Watch Committee, 1920–23, chairman of Gen. Purposes Committee, 1928; member of Tame and Rea District Drainage Board, 1923; trustee of Mason's Orphanage, 1912, and Almshouses, 1914; Governor of Birmingham Blue Coat School, 1914; hon. Divisional Director of Training (Ministry of Labour) for West Midland Area, 1918; chairman of Training Committee (Ministry of Pensions) for West Midlands, 1916–18; chairman Aston Manor Conservative Club, 1913; member of National Police Council, 1921; hon. secretary and joint hon. treasurer Police Aided Association for Clothing Destitute Children since 1923; chairman Tramways Committee since 1930; chairman Police Committee of the Association of Municipal Corporations, 1926–29; President Birmingham General Hospital and Birmingham General Dispensary, 1929–30; chairman, Birmingham Hospital Saturday Fund; governor Birmingham University; chairman Assessment Committee since 1927; Trustee Evans's Cottage Homes since 1927; Chairman of Birmingham Airport Committee since 1934. *Recreations:* various. *Address:* 94 Clifford Street, Lozells, Birmingham. *T:* Northern 0199.

Died 16 Jan. 1941.

JAMES, Brig.-Gen. Alfred Henry Cotes, DSO 1915; MVO 1916; *b* 30 Aug. 1873; *m* 1910, Edith Mary Bray; one *s. Educ:* Sherborne; Merton College, Oxford, BA. 2nd Lt 1st South Staffordshire Regt, 1897; Captain, 1902; Major, 1915; Col 1919; served South African War, 1899–1902 (despatches twice, Queen's medal 3 clasps, King's medal 2 clasps); European War, 1914–18; APM 3rd Corps; Provost Marshal, 3rd Army, 1915; Provost Marshal, Forces in Great Britain, Aug. 1918 (despatches four times, DSO, MVO, Bt Lt-Col, Officier de la Légion d'honneur); commanded 2nd Batt. The South Staffordshire Regt; retired, Jan. 1921; JP Surrey, 1937. *Address:* Water House, Bletchingley, Surrey. *Club:* Army and Navy.

Died 21 April 1947.

JAMES, Arthur L.; *see* Lloyd James.

JAMES, Col Cecil Polglase, DSO 1917; late Argyll and Sutherland Highlanders; *b* 5 March 1879; *s* of late Col W. James; *m* 1923, Helen, *d* of John Henry Springman; one *s* one *d.* Entered Army from Militia A. & S. Highlanders, 1900; Bt Lieut-Col 1918; Lieut-Col 1924; Col 1928; served European War, 1914–18 (despatches 3 times, temp. Lt-Col 1916–19; Bt Lt-Col, DSO with bar, twice wounded; prisoner Nov. 1917; retired pay, 1932. *Address:* Meadowfield, Cranleigh, Surrey.

Died 30 Oct. 1943.

JAMES, Lt-Col Charles Henry, CIE 1912; late IMS; Assistant Commissioner East Surrey Area St John Ambulance Brigade; *b* 4 Aug. 1863; *s* of late Lieut-Col L. H. S. James, RA; unmarried. *Educ:* Cranleigh; St Thomas's Hospital, London. MRCS and LRCP 1887. Assistant House Surgeon, House Surgeon and Resident Accoucheur St Thomas's Hospital, 1888–89; House Physician Gen. Lying-in Hospital, 1889–90; entered Indian Medical Service, 1891; Deputy Sanitary Commissioner Punjab, 1894–1900; Kaisar-i-Hind, First Class, for plague work, 1901; Medical Adviser Patiala State, 1903–12; FRCS England, 1908; Major, 1903; Lieut-Colonel, 1911; Civil Surgeon, Simla, 1912–16; Civil Surgeon and Chief Medical Officer, Delhi Province, 1917–21; retired Oct. 1921. *Publications:* Manual for Vaccinators in the Punjab, 1895; Report of Plague in Bombay, 1897; Report of the Outbreak of Plague in the Punjab, 1897; articles on Medical and Surgical subjects. *Address:* St Rowans, The Chase, Reigate, Surrey. *T:* Redhill 1155. *Club:* East India and Sports.

Died 27 Oct. 1944.

JAMES, Engr Rear-Adm. Charles John, CB 1919; *b* 1862. Served Suakim, 1884–85; China, 1900–03; European War, 1914–19 (despatches, CB, Order of Sacred Treasure of Japan).

Died 16 April 1943.

JAMES, Brig.-Gen. Cyril Henry Leigh, CB 1916; CMG 1918; *s* of late Rev. R. Lee James, LLB, BCL, Vicar of Watford, Herts, 1855–1915. *Educ:* RMC, Sandhurst. Joined 5th Fusiliers; commanded 1st Batt.; served Nile Expedition, 1898 (medal with clasp, Khedive's Soudan medal); occupation of Crete, 1898; South African War, 1899–1902 (Queen's medal 3 clasps, King's medal); European War, in command of a Brigade, 1914–19 (despatches four times, CB, CMG, Commandeur of the Order of The Star of Roumania, 1914–15 Star, Victory medal, Allies medal); also (R) reward in recognition of distinguished service. *Clubs:* United Service; Royal Yacht Squadron, Cowes.

Died 8 Nov. 1946.

JAMES, Sir Edward Albert, 5th Bt *cr* 1823; *b* 5 Sept. 1862; *s* of late Francis Edward James and Helen Donald Fullarton; *S* brother 1937. *Heir: b* Captain Fullarton James, CBE. *Club:* Constitutional.

Died 6 Dec. 1942.

JAMES, Sir Francis; *see* James, Sir J. F. W.

JAMES, Very Rev. Henry Lewis; *b* 18 March 1864; *s* of Peter and Mary James; *m* 1901, Ada Isabella Williams (*d* 1917); two *s* two *d. Educ:* Ystrad Meurig School; Christ College, Brecon; Jesus Coll. Oxford (Scholar). 2nd class Mods, 2nd class Lit. Hum., BA 1886; MA 1891; BD 1924; DD 1924. Deacon 1887, Priest 1888; Curate of Llandudno 1887–90; Llanddeiniolen 1890–93; Llanfair-is-gaer 1893–95; Warden of Bangor Church Hostel 1895–1901; Surrogate 1901; Rector of Llangefni w Tregaian 1901–07; Tredington, Worc. 1907–10; Aberffraw 1910–26; Rural dean of Malltreath 1918–26; Examining Chaplain to Bishop of Bangor 1918–34; Rector, Dolgelley 1926–30; Llanwrin 1930–34; Hon. Canon of Bangor 1928–30; Prebendary of Penmynydd 1930–33; Chancellor of Cathedral 1933–34; Dean of Bangor 1934–40. *Publications:* Ymholiad a Diolch, 1895; Nodiadau ar y Llyfr Gweddi Gyffedin, 1900; Arweinydd yr Athro i'r Catecism, 1925; Pregethau Plaen, 1928; Esboniad ar Epistol Cyntaf St Ioan, 1929; contributor to Geiriadur Beiblaidd, Haul. *Address:* Bodfair, Glanrafon Hill, Bangor, N Wales. *TA:* Bodfair, Bangor. *T:* Bangor 518.

Died 17 Jan. 1949.

JAMES, Col Herbert, CB 1911; *b* 12 Nov. 1859; *s* of late Thomas James; *m* 1883, Margaret Isabella (Meta) (*d* 1938), *d* of late Capt. C. B. S. Neill, Madras Staff Corps, and *g d* of late Brig.-Gen. J. G. S. Neill, CB, and Lady Neill. *Educ:* Clifton College. Entered Army, 1878; Capt. ISC 1889; Major, Indian Army, 1898; Lt-Col 1904; Col 1908; served S Africa, 1879 (medal with clasp); Afghan War, 1879–80 (medal); Hazara Expedition, 1888 (despatches, medal with clasp); NW Frontier of India, 1897–98 (despatches, medal with clasp); Waziristan, 1901–02 (clasp); retired, 1911. *Address:* 5 Godwyn Road, Folkestone.

Died 1 March 1943.

JAMES, Lt-Col Herbert Lionel, CB 1915; late 2nd Batt. Manchester Regt; *b* 11 March 1863; *m* 1st, 1895, Lilla Cornelia, *d* of Rev. H. Huleatt; one *s*; 2nd, 1903, Mary Katharine, *d* of John Heelis, Pendleton; one *d.* Entered army, 1885; Captain, 1892; Major, 1901; Lt-Col, 1908; served South African War, 1900–01 (despatches, Queen's medal 4 clasps); European War, 1914–19 (despatches, CB); retired, 1919. *Address:* 28 Linden Road, Bedford.

Died 20 March 1946.

JAMES, Sir (John) Francis (William), Kt 1938; MA (Christ Church, Oxford); JP Cornwall; Barrister (MT); *b* 3 June 1879; *e s* of late William James; *m* Flora Louise, *d* of late Charles Francis Hicks of Silverdale; one *s* one *d.* Entered Indian Civil Service, 1903; District and Sessions Judge, 1918; additional Judge, Patna High Court, 1928; Judge, Patna High Court, 1931–39. *Address:* Tamar Bank, Saltash, Cornwall.

Died 11 Dec. 1950.

JAMES, Lewis Cairns; retired Professor Royal Academy of Music; Royal College; Guildhall School of Music, and City of London School; *b* Edinburgh, 23 Sept. 1865; *s* of Rev. Alexander T. James; *m* 1st, Jessie (*d* 1910), *d* of Edward Moore of Brighton; 2nd, Catherine Mary, *d* of John Maitland Marshall of The Grove, Dulwich; one *s* one *d. Educ:* Watson's College, Edinburgh; Kingswood School Bath. Started life as Assistant Master in Preparatory School went on the stage in 1886 at the Savoy Theatre; thence to America and for four years after with the Savoy Operas; played leading parts at the Opera Comique, Globe, Strand, Vaudeville, Lyric, Prince of Wales's, Gaiety, etc., under the management of R.

D'Oyly Carte, William Greet, Horace Sedger, A. and S. Gatti, Charles Frohman, Willie Edouin, H. J. Leslie, and George Edwardes; also played in South Africa, Canada and America; Professor of Elocution; stage manager and producer of operas and plays. *Publications:* part author of several one-act comedies; editor of the Golden Reciters and Lectures on Elocution and Voice Production. *Recreations:* music, the drama, and golf. *Address:* St Winifred's, 34 Denmark Road, Gloucester.

Died 7 Oct. 1946.

JAMES, Lionel, MA; *b* 1868; *s* of late George Coulson James of Penzance; *m* 1912, Ethel, *d* of late Arthur Clabburn, Gordon Highlanders; three *s* two *d. Educ:* Westminster (Queen's Scholar, 1882–87; Captain, 1886–87); Christ Church, Oxford. 1st Class Classical Moderations, 1889; 2nd Class Literæ Humaniores, 1891. Assistant Master at St Peter's College, Radley, 1892–1906; Headmaster Monmouth Grammar School, 1906–27. *Publications:* Acting Editions of the Aulularia, Captivi, and Rudens of Plautus; the Andria of Terence (with trans.); the Frogs of Aristophanes (with trans.), and the Wasps; Jubilate Deo, a Sequence of Daily Prayers for Schools, 1921, 3rd Edition with Warren Hastings prayers, 1940; Hints on Running; Hints on Latin Prose; Songs of Zion; Founder's Faith—a Calendar of Thoughts of William Sewell (Founder of St Columba's and of Radley), 1938; A Forgotten Genius (William Sewell), 1945. *Address:* Trevabyn, Barcombe Heights, Paignton, S Devon. *T:* 82300.

Died 28 April 1948.

JAMES, Lt-Col Sydney Price, CMG 1935; FRS 1931; MDLond. 1906; DPH 1907; League of Nations Prix Darling Laureate, 1934; Indian Medical Service (retired); Member of the permanent Committee and President of the Yellow Fever Commission of the Office International d'Hygiène Publique; Member of the Malaria Commission of the League of Nations, Geneva; Member of the Chemotherapy Committee of the Medical Research Council and the Tropical Diseases Committee of the Royal Society; Member of the combined War Office and MRC Malaria Committee; Past President, Royal Society of Tropical Medicine and Hygiene. Joined Indian Medical Service, 1896; served in military campaigns on the NW Frontier of India (Tochi Valley), 1897–98, and in China (Boxer Campaign), 1900–01; appointed to the Government of India's Bacteriological Department and was a member of the Royal Society's Malaria Commission in India, 1902–03; Statistical Officer with the Government of India in the Sanitary and Medical Departments, 1904, and engaged in research work, particularly on malaria, kala-azar, and yellow fever in various countries until 1914; served in the European War, 1914–18 (ADMS Indian Expeditionary Force in Mesopotamia; despatches); retired from IMS, 1918, and joined the Local Government Board (now the Ministry of Health) as Medical Inspector and Adviser on Tropical Diseases; represented the British Government on the League of Nations Epidemic Commission to Poland, 1922; Expert Member of League of Nations Malaria Commission in 1923, and took part, 1923–27, in inquiries on malaria in Russia and other countries of Europe, the near East, and the United States; deputed to India in 1927 as a member of the Fletcher Committee on the organisation of medical research; deputed to East Africa in 1929 on behalf of the Colonial Office; retired from Ministry of Health, 1936; joined Molteno Research Institute, Cambridge. *Publications:* Malaria at Home and Abroad; various publications on Filariasis, Malaria, Kala-Azar, and Medical Zoology, etc. *Recreation:* yachting. *Address:* Sea View, Old Bosham, nr Chichester. *T:* 2154. *Club:* East India and Sports.

Died 17 April 1946.

JAMES, Hon. Sir Walter Hartwell, KCMG 1931; Kt 1907; KC 1902; *b* Perth, W Australia, 28 March 1863; *m* 1892, Gwenyfred, OBE, JP (*d* 1938), *d* of Dr Hearder of Carmarthen. *Educ:* Perth State and High School. Called to Bar, 1888; MLA East Perth, 1894–1904; one of the Delegates of the State to and Member of Judiciary Committee at Federal Convention, 1897–98, when Commonwealth Constitution framed; Minister without Portfolio, 1901–02; Premier of W Australia, 1902–04; Agent-General for Western Australia, 1904–06; Pro-Chancellor of University of Western Australia, 1929; Chancellor, 1930–36; Hon. LLD 1936. *Address:* 69 Mount Street, Perth, Western Australia.

Died 3 Jan. 1943.

JAMES, Winifred Lewellin, (Mrs Henry de Jan); novelist, travel writer, lecturer, journalist; *b* Windsor, Victoria, Australia; 12th *c* of Rev. Thomas James, Liskeard, Cornwall, and Gertrude, *d* of Frederick Peterson, Hull, England, and Melbourne, Victoria; *m* 1913, Henry de Jan of Louisiana, US, and Almirante, Panama. *Educ:* privately at St Kilda, Victoria. Began to write, 1904; came to London, 1905; interested in home-making for young workers; exhibited at National Economies Exhibition in 1916 a Three Pound Room; in 1922 established for one year a free demonstration of a Home in the Room at 114 Fulham Road, SW; has taken this work up permanently; Journalism, special articles to Yorkshire Post, London Daily Chronicle, Evening Standard, etc. *Publications:* Bachelor Betty, 1907; Patricia Baring, 1908; Saturday's Children, 1909; Letters to my Son, 1910; More Letters to my Son, 1911; Letters of a Spinster, 1911; A Sweeping, 1911; The Mulberry Tree, 1913; A Woman in the Wilderness, 1915; Out of the Shadows, 1924; Three Births in the Hemingway Family, 1929; London is My Lute; A Man for England, 1930; Gangways and Corridors, 1936.

Died April 1941.

JAMESON, Rt Hon. Andrew; PC Ireland, 1921; DL, JP; Chairman John Jameson & Son, Ltd; Director Bank of Ireland; Chairman of Irish Lights Commissioners; *b* 17 Aug. 1855; 2nd *s* of Andrew Jameson of Walk House, Alloa, and Margaret, *d* of James Cochrane, Glen Lodge, Sligo; *m* 1st, 1877, Grace E. A. M. (*d* 1922), *d* of Will Burke, MD, Registrar-General of Dublin; two *d*; 2nd, 1924, Ruth, *y d* of late George Vaughan Hart, KC. *Educ:* London International College; Trinity College, Cambridge (BA); MA Trinity College, Dublin. High Sheriff, Co. Dublin, 1902; Governor of Bank of Ireland, 1896–98; a Senator Irish Free State, 1922–36. *Address:* Sutton House, Sutton, Co. Dublin. *TA:* Sutton House, Baily, Dublin. *T:* Howth 52. *Clubs:* Windham; Kildare Street, Dublin.

Died 15 Feb. 1941.

JAMIAT RAI, Diwan, Rai Bahadur, Diwan Bahadur, CIE 1911; *b* 1861; *s* of Mehta Santokh Rai, of Bhown in the Jhelum District, Punjab, India; *m* 1890, Shrimati Chanodevi (*d* 1922), *e d* of Rai Gobind Lall, Bahadur, Assistant Engineer, Military Works Service; one *s. Educ:* Bhown, Kohat and Gujrat. Entered Government service, 1880; served in the Political office with the Kuram Field Force, 1880; accompanied Major McIvor to Helmund in connection with the Afghan Boundary Commission, 1885–86; special duty, boundary settlement of Laghari Barkhan, 1897; Assistant to the Superintendent of Gazetteers of Baluchistan, 1902–07; assisted Major Jacob in the inquiry into the working of offices in Baluchistan, 1910; and services specially commended by the Local Government, and acknowledged by the Government of India; Assistant to the Superintendent of Census operations, Baluchistan, 1910–11; Extra Assistant Commissioner, 1902; Settlement Officer, Baluchistan, 1912–15 and 1916–19; Census Superintendent, Baluchistan, 1920–22; retired from service, 1922; received the title of Rai Sahib, 1898; Rai Bahadur, 1908; and Diwan Bahadur, 1925; Kaisar-i-Hind Gold Medal, 1930, Bar, 1935; one of the founders and vice-patron of Sandeman Library, and Browne Gymkhana, Quetta; Vice-President of MacMahon Museum; Patron Hindu Panchayat and Sanatan Dhramsabha, Quetta; Member Quetta Municipal Council. *Publications:* Municipal Manual of Quetta (1926); Memo on the Land Revenue System, Levies and Police of Quetta; Conversation Manual in Pushtu; Helps to the Study of the Brahui Language; translated into English, Mr Dame's Textbook of Balochi; notes on the domiciled Hindus of Baluchistan, 1924; Hindus of Ghazni and Kandahar, and Menial Indian Castes, 1918; Barech Afghans, 1922; Freemasonry in Quetta, 1908; Reports on the Settlements of Duki, 1913, and Barkhan, 1915; a paper on the Frontier Crimes Regulations 1917; Report on the revenue rates and economic condition of certain villages in Baluchistan, 1920; Notes on Natts—a wandering tribe, 1921; Notes on the Achakzai Afghans, 1921; Afghan Pawindahs, 1922; The Administration of Justice in Rural Areas of Baluchistan, 1927; Manual of Customary Law for Baluchistan, 1932; written several pamphlets on temperance and kindred subjects. *Address:* Quetta, India.

Died 14 June 1941.

JAMIESON, Sir James (William), KCMG 1923; CMG 1910; Hon. LLD Hong-Kong University, 1918; FRGS; *b* 11 Sept. 1867; unmarried. Joined the Consular Service in China, 1886; served as Chinese adviser to the Burma-China Frontier Delimitation Commission during the season 1898–99; Commercial Attaché to HM's Legation in China, 1899–1909; seconded for service under Colonial Office as Supt of Chinese labour in the Transvaal, 1905–08; Consul-General, Canton, 1909–26, when transferred to Tientsin; Coronation Medal, 1911; retired 1930. *Club:* Thatched House.

Died 8 Jan. 1946.

JAMIESON, John Kay, MA, ChM (Dublin); Hon. LLD (Leeds); MRIA; Professor of Anatomy and Chirurgery, University of Dublin, 1936–47; retd 1947; *b* 20 July 1873; 4th *s* of late Robert and Barbara Jamieson, Sandness, Shetland; *m* Elisabeth (*d* 1936), *y d* of R. P. Goodworth, MRCS Winterton, Lincs; one *s* one *d*. *Educ:* Sandness Madras School; Edinburgh University. MB, CM 1894. Formerly demonstrator of anatomy, Surgeon's Hall, Edinburgh, and School of Medicine, Leeds; Professor of Anatomy, Univ. of Leeds, 1910–36; Pro. Vice-Chancellor, 1923–25. Acting Vice-Chancellor, 1923–24; Dean of Faculty of Medicine, 1915–36; Member of General Medical Council, 1928–36; Examiner in Universities of Edinburgh, Aberdeen, Liverpool, Manchester, Sheffield, Birmingham, Bristol, Wales, Dublin, Belfast, National and Irish Conjoint. *Publications:* various papers on anatomy of Lymphatic System. *Recreations:* golf, sea-fishing. *Address:* Trinity College, Dublin.

Died 20 Aug. 1948.

JAMIESON, R. Kirkland, RBA and NS; landscape painter; *b* Lanark, 1881; *m* 1920, Dorothea Selous, RBA. *Educ:* Lanark, Glasgow, Paris. Headmaster Westminster School of Art, 1934–39; Acting Principal St Martin's School of Art, 1945–47. *Recreations:* reading, walking. *Club:* Chelsea Arts.

Died 3 Sept. 1950.

JAN, Mrs Henry de; *see* James, Winifred L.

JANET, Pierre, MD; Membre de l'Institut (Académie des sciences morales et politiques); Professor honoraire de Psychology in the Collège de France; Director of the Journal de Psychologie Normale et Pathologique; *b* 1859. *Publications:* L'automatisme psychologique, 1889; L'état mental des hystériques, 2 vol. 1893; Névroses et idées fixes, 2 vol. 1898; Obsessions et la psychasthénie, 2 vol. 1903; Les Névroses, 1908; The Major Symptoms of Hysteria, 1908; Les Médications psychologiques, 3 vol. 1919, Traduction anglaise, psychological healing, 2 vols; La médecine psychologique, 1923, Traduction anglaise,

Principles of psychotherapy; De l'angoisse à l'extase 1er vol., un délire religieux, la croyance, 1926; 2me vol., les sentiments fondamentaux, 1928, Cours sur l'évolution de la mémoire et de la notion de temps, 1929; Cours sur l'évolution de la personnalité, 1930; Cours sur la force et la faiblesse psychologiques, 1932; Cours sur l'amour et la haine, 1933; Les Débuts de l'intelligence, 1933; L'intelligence avant le langage, 1936; La psychologie de la croyance et le Mysticisme, 1937; Les troubles de la personnalité sociale, 1937; L'examen de conscience et les interprétations des hallucinations de l'ouïe voix, 1938. *Address:* Rue de Varenne, 45, Paris vii. *T:* Littré 99–55.

Died 24 Feb. 1947.

JAORA STATE, Lt-Col HH Fakhr-ud-Daulah Nawab Sir Mohammad Iftikhar Ali Khan Bahadur Saulat Jang, GBE 1937; KCIE 1911; Hon. Lt-Col in the Indian Army; *b* 1883. The State covers an area of about 601 square miles, and has a population of 116,953. H.H. served in the European War, 1914–18, by paying a large contribution towards war expenditure and by placing the entire resources of the State at the disposal of the British Government; he did the same in the War of 1939–45; the administration is controlled by a Council of State, of which His Highness the Nawab is President, and is assisted by his Chief Minister and four other Members. *Address:* Jaora State.

Died 18 Dec. 1947.

JAQUES-DALCROZE, Emile; Mus. Doc; Principal of the Institut Jaques-Dalcroze, Geneva; and visiting Principal of the London School of Dalcroze Eurhythmics since 1913; *b* 6 July 1865; *s* of Jules Jaques of Ste Croix (Vaud); *m* Nina Faliero (*d* 1946); one *s*. *Educ:* Pupil of R. Fuchs, Anton Bruckner and Leo Delibes. Professor of Harmony at the Conservatoire, Geneva, 1892–1910; Principal of the Jaques-Dalcroze College at Hellerau-Dresden, 1910–14. *Publications: Principal Works:* For soli, chorus, and orchestra, La Veillée, 1893; Poème Alpestre, 1896; Festival Vaudois, 1903, and Fête de Juin, 1914; Lyric Comedies, Janie 1893, Sancho Panza, 1897; also fragments of an opera, Le Violon maudit, 1893; operas-comiques, Le Bonhomme Jadis, 1907, and Les Jumeaux de Bergame, 1908; Evocation, Les Premiers Souvenirs, 1918; Écho et Narcisse, 1920; La Fête de la Jeunesse et de la Joie, 1923; Les Belles Vacances; Notre petite vie à nous; Le Petit Roi qui Pleure, 1932; Le Joli Jeu des Saisons, 1934; Rythmes de chant et de danse (vocalises), 1935; La Jolie musique, 1935; co-ordination des mouvements; Au jardin fleuri; Entrons dans la ronde; Chansons de gosses, 1936; Elle et lui; duos; Les trois âges; Pour leurs petits doigts; Genève chante, 1937; suites, concertos songs, etc. *Address:* Institut Jaques-Dalcroze, 44 Terrassière, Geneva, Switzerland.

Died 1 July 1950.

JARDINE, Sir Alexander, 10th Bt of Applegirth, 1672; *b* 1 Aug. 1868; 2nd *s* of 8th Bt and Henrietta, 3rd *d* of William Younger of Craigielands, Dumfriesshire; *S* brother, 1915; *m* 1914, Winifred Mary Hamilton, *d* of late Major Young, Lincluden House, Dumfries; one *s* one *d*. *Educ:* Repton. Has spent most of his time in Virginia, N Alaska, and British Columbia. *Heir: s* William Edward, *b* 15 April 1917. *Address:* Craig Gowan, Lockerbie, Dumfriesshire.

Died 27 March 1942.

JARDINE, Sir Douglas (James), KCMG 1938; CMG 1932; OBE 1918; *b* 13 Oct. 1888; *e s* of late James Jardine, MD, Richmond, Surrey; *m* 1923, Jessie Mary (*d* 1943), 2nd *d* of late Lachlan Andrew Macpherson of Corriemony, Glen Urquhart, Inverness-shire, and Little Wyrley Hall, Staffordshire; two *d*. *Educ:* Westminster School; Trinity College, Cambridge, BA Classical Honours, 1910; MA 1914. Assistant Secretary to Government of Cyprus, 1910–16; Secretary to Administration, Somaliland, 1916–21; accompanied British Mission to Coronation of Empress Zauditu of Abyssinia (3rd Class Star of Ethiopia), 1917; Officer in

Charge HQ Services, Somaliland Expeditionary Force, 1920 (African General Service medal and clasp, despatches); Senior Assistant Secretary, Nigerian Secretariat, 1921–27; Deputy Chief Secretary, Tanganyika, 1927–28; Chief Secretary to Government, Tanganyika, 1928–34; accredited representative of HM Government to Permanent Mandates Commission, Geneva, 1929, 1930 and 1931; acting Governor, Tanganyika, in 1929, 1931, 1933, and 1934; Governor and Commander-in-Chief, North Borneo, 1934–37; Sierra Leone, 1937–41; Leeward Islands, 1941–44. *Publications:* The Mad Mullah of Somaliland, 1923; (joint) The Handbook of Cyprus, 1913 and 1919. *Address:* Quarries, Bashurst Hill, Itchingfield, Sussex. *T:* Slinfold 247. *Clubs:* United University; Surrey County Cricket.

Died 11 Dec. 1946.

JARDINE, Sir Ernest, 1st Bt *cr* 1919; JP; Chevalier de la Légion d'Honneur; *b* Nottingham, 23 Sept. 1859; *s* of John Jardine, lace-machine builder; *m* Ada Jane (*d* 1926), *d* of James Fletcher, Nottingham; one *s* two *d*. *Educ:* Lycée Imperial, Saint Omer, France; Tudor House School, Nottingham. MP (LU) East Somerset, 1910–18; High Sheriff of Notts, 1928–29. President of Nottinghamshire Football Assoc. *Recreation:* bowls. *Heir:* *s* John, *b* 1884. *Address:* Gwedon, The Park, Nottingham. *TA:* Jardine, Nottingham. *T:* Nottingham 41483. *Club:* Carlton.

Died 26 April 1947.

JARDINE, His Honour Judge James Willoughby; KC 1927; Judge of Bow County Courts since 1940; *b* 29 Oct. 1879; *o s* of late James Jardine, KC; *m* 1910, Lettice Joyce, *y d* of Sir Henry Sutton; three *s* one *d*. *Educ:* Eton; King's College, Cambridge. Classical and Law Tripos (1st Class); called to Bar, Inner Temple, 1904; North Eastern Circuit; served Great War, 1914–18, Dardanelles and France, Major RAF; Recorder of Halifax, 1923–31; of Newcastle-upon-Tyne, 1931–32; of Leeds, 1932–40; Solicitor-General of County Palatine of Durham, 1932–39; Attorney-General of County Palatine of Durham, 1939–40; Bencher of the Inner Temple, 1935. *Address:* 41 Sloane Gardens, SW1. *Clubs:* United University, Alpine.

Died 15 Oct. 1945.

JARDINE, Malcolm Robert; *b* 1869; 2nd *s* of late William Jardine, Barrister and Acting Judge, Allahabad High Court; *m* 1898, Alison (*d* 1936), 2nd *d* of Robert Moir, MD; one *s*. *Educ:* Fettes College, Edinburgh; Balliol College, Oxford. BA Oxford, 1893. Barrister, Middle Temple, 1893; practised at Bombay Bar, 1894–1916; Perry Professor of Jurisprudence and Roman Law, 1898–1902; Principal, Government Law School, 1902–03; Clerk of the Crown, 1903–14; Advocate-General Bombay, 1915–16. *Address:* 63 Cornwall Gardens, SW7. *Club:* United University.

Died 16 Jan. 1947.

JARDINE, William Ellis, CIE 1909; FRGS, FRAS, MRCAS; *b* 1867; *s* of William Jardine, Judge High Court, Allahabad, and Elinor Georgina Ellis; unmarried. *Educ:* Fettes College, Edinburgh; Wren's; Trinity College, Cambridge. ICS 1886–1924. Served in Madras, Hyderabad, Central India; Resident at Baroda and Gwalior, 1912–24; Knight of Grace of Order of St John of Jerusalem; Order of Mercy. *Club:* East India and Sports.

Died 14 Nov. 1944.

JARMAN, Charles, CBE 1946; Acting General Secretary, National Union of Seamen, since 1946; *b* 19 Jan. 1893; *s* of late Charles and Annie Jarman; *m* 1915, Flora Pocock (decd); one *s* one *d*. *Educ:* St Nicholas, Bristol. Merchant Navy, as boy; joined Navy; invalided 1911; rejoined Merchant Navy; elected Delegate Nat. Union of Seamen, 1915; served all British districts as Sec.

and Organiser; American Internat. Organiser. *Address:* 42 Nelson Road, New Malden, Surrey. *TA:* Searoving Clapcom London. *T:* Malden 1751.

Died 30 May 1947.

JARMAY, Sir John Gustav, KBE 1918; FCS, FIC; *b* 31 Dec. 1856; *s* of late Gustav de Jármay; *m* 1882, Charlotte E. (*d* 1938), *d* of late George Wyman, MD; one *s*. *Educ:* private; technical schools; University of Zurich. Inventor of processes which are in use in several industries in England and abroad; special study the Ammonia Soda Process, with which industry he has been connected since its infancy; Director of Brunner, Mond & Co., Limited, and Director of other chemical works in England. *Recreations:* shooting, hunting, mountaineering. *Clubs:* Royal Societies, Royal Automobile.

Died 22 Aug. 1944.

JARRETT, James Henry; KC; Chief Justice, Windward and Leeward Islands since 1940, also Member of West Indian Court of Appeal; *b* 31 March 1895; *s* of Henry and Caroline Mary Jarrett; *m* 1924, Ida Alexandra Dutfield; one *s* one *d*. *Educ:* Lancing College. Called to Bar, Gray's Inn; HAC, 1914; served European War, 1914–19; Asst District Commissioner Uganda, 1919; Seconded Judicial Dept as Magistrate, 1922; Magistrate, 1924; Asst Attorney-General, 1926; Crown Counsel, 1927; Attorney-General, Grenada, 1929; Acting Administrator and Acting Chief Justice St Vincent, 1930 and 1931; Attorney-General Bahamas, 1933; Acting Chief Justice, 1934; Colonial Secretary, 1935–40; Deputy Governor, 1935; Acting Governor on several occasions, 1936–39. *Publication:* Law Finder—A Guide to Legislation in force in the Bahama Islands on the 1st November 1934, 2nd Ed. 1936. *Recreations:* tennis, squash and bridge. *Address:* Supreme Court, Windward Islands and Leeward Islands, Grenada, BWI.

Died 7 April 1943.

JARVIS, Edward Blackwell, CMG 1920; *b* 9 April 1873; *s* of late Thomas Jarvis of Mount Jarvis, Antigua, BWI, and *g s* of late Col Sir Stephen John Hill, KCMG, CB; *m* 1st, Alice, *d* of General Wm Hill; one *s* one *d*; 2nd, Edith Ruby, *d* of Major W. H. Ledeatt. Entered Colonial Civil Service as second clerk, Colonial Secretary's Office, Leeward Islands, 1890; Clerk, Governor's office, 1891; Chief Clerk, 1901; Assistant Colonial Secretary, 1903; Assistant Chief Secretary, Uganda, 1912; Chief Secretary, 1918; Acting Governor, 1921, 1922, 1923, 1925, 1926, 1927; Croix Commander Order of Leopold II for services rendered during war, despatches; Commander of Leopold, 1928; retired, 1927. *Recreations:* shooting, fishing, tennis, golf. *Address:* Waynflete, Merrivale, Ross-on-Wye, Herefordshire. *T:* Ross-on-Wye 426.

Died 17 Nov. 1950.

JARVIS, Sir John, 1st Bt *cr* 1922; MP (U) Guildford Division of Surrey since 1935; Hon. Col RAMC; Hon. DCL (Durham); DL County of Surrey, 1936; Chairman, J. & A. Churchill, Ltd, publishers, Sir W. G. Armstrong Whitworth (Ironfounders) Ltd, and other companies; initiator of the Surrey Scheme to help the Distressed Area of Jarrow, subsequently starting five new industries on Tyneside, employing over 5000 men, of which companies he is Hon. Chairman; Freeman of the Borough of Jarrow; *b* 25 March 1876; *e s* of late Joseph Charles Jarvis, of The Bourne, Harpenden; *m* 1901, Bessie, 3rd *d* of late Edwin Woodfield, Enfield; one *s* two *d*. High Sheriff of Surrey, 1934–35; an organiser and a keen sportsman with many interests and wide sympathies; holder of Jackson Cup (Curling), 1937 and 1938. *Recreations:* gardening, curling. *Heir:* *s* Arnold Adrian Jarvis, *b* 25 Oct. 1904. *Address:* Hascombe Court, nr Godalming, Surrey. *TA:* Jarvis, Hascombe. *T:* Hascombe 54. *Club:* Carlton.

Died 3 Oct. 1950.

JARVIS, William Rose, MVO (5th Class) 1937; Private Trainer to HM the King and Lord Harewood's race-horses since 1925; *b* 21 June 1885; *s* of William Arthur Jarvis; *m* 1913, Isabel Grace, *d* of Joseph Butters, Kremlin, Newmarket; one *s* one *d*. *Educ:* Cranleigh. Served European War in France, Lieut in South Notts Hussars and attached to 23rd Middlesex Regt; started training racehorses, 1911; previously assistant trainer to late J. H. Houldsworth; with his uncle James Ryan at Green Lodge, Newmarket, 1902–10. *Recreation:* golf. *Address:* Egerton, Newmarket. *T:* 1. *Club:* MCC.

Died 27 Jan. 1943.

JAST, L. Stanley, MA; late Chief Librarian, Manchester Public Libraries; *b* Halifax 1868; *m* Millicent Murby. *Educ:* Halifax; London. Library appointments at Halifax, Peterborough, and Croydon; Hon. Secretary Library Association, 1905–15; Past President of the Library Association; Past President, Unnamed Society, Manchester; represented British Librarians at Conferences in USA in 1904 and 1913, and member of Manchester Corporation delegation in 1929; author of various plays, produced by the Unnamed Society; Festival Theatre, Cambridge, etc. *Publications:* The Lover and the Dead Woman, and five other plays in verse, 1923; The Child as Reader, 1927; The Planning of a Great Library, 1927; The Provision of Books for Children in Elementary Schools, 1928; Libraries and Living, 1932; Shah Jahan: a play, 1934; The Library and the Community, 1939; What It All Means, 1941; (American edition, 1944, under title: Reincarnation and Karma); Editor, Live Books Resurrected Series; various pamphlets and papers on library and literary subjects. *Recreations:* thinking and reading. *Address:* Penrhyn House, 3 Riverdale Road, Twickenham Park, Middlesex. *T:* Popesgrove 5596.

Died 25 Dec. 1944.

JAWAHIR SINGH, Sardar Bahadur Sir Sardar, Kt 1934; CIE 1925; MLA Punjab. *Address:* Mustafabad, Ambala, Punjab.

Died 3 May 1947.

JAY, Major Charles Douglas, DSO 1917; Royal Sussex Regt, late Machine Gun Corps; *s* of Rev. W. P. Jay, former Vicar of St Anne's, Eastbourne; *m* 1st, 1917, Kathleen Horatia (*d* 1930), *γ d* of late David Lionel Beddington, Longstock Park, Stockbridge; two *s* one *d*; 2nd, 1930, Ada (Peggy), *o c* of Dr W. W. Nuttall, JP, Latch Gate, Sandgate, Kent; two *d*. *Educ:* Haileybury; MA Cantab. Served European War (DSO, despatches); relinquished commission, owing to ill health, 1921. *Address:* Bycliffe, Sandgate, Kent.

Died 7 May 1941.

JAYATILAKA, Sir Don Baron, KBE 1943; Kt 1932; Representative of Ceylon Government in India; Vice-Chairman of Board of Ministers and Leader of State Council and Minister for Home Affairs Ceylon; *b* 13 Feb. 1868; *s* of D. D. Jayatilaka; *m* Mallika (*d* 1929), *d* of Sri Devaraksita Batuntudawe, Pandit; no *c*. *Educ:* Vidyalankara Oriental College, Kelaniya; Wesley College, Colombo; Jesus College, Oxford (BA Cal. 1898; BA Oxon 1913, MA 1916). Barrister-at-law (Lincoln's Inn), 1913; Advocate of the Supreme Court of Ceylon, 1913; Principal of Dharmaraja College, Kandy, 1890–98; Principal of Ananda College, Colombo, 1900–10; President Young Men's Buddhist Association, Colombo, since 1898; Member of the Legislative Council of Ceylon, 1924–31; Member of State Council since 1931; has revised and edited number of old Sinhalese works; is Hon. Chief Editor of the Sinhalese Etymological Dictionary. *Address:* Ceylon Govt Office, New Delhi.

Died 31 May 1944.

JAYS, Tom, MRCS, LRCP; *b* 29 Dec. 1868; *s* of John Robert Jays; *m* Sarah (*d* 1939), *d* of Thomas Coles. *Educ:* Islington College; St Thomas's Hospital. Missionary of CMS in West Africa, 1892–1905; Travelling Secretary of Student Volunteer Movement, Britain, 1900–01; Student Missionary Union, North America, 1902–03 and 1910–11; Service in RAMC, 1915–19 (Egypt, Gallipoli, Salonika, East Africa, India); Vice-Principal, Livingstone College, 1919–21; Principal, 1921–46. *Recreation:* golf. *Address:* 34 Chigwell Road, Woodford, E18.

Died 2 Feb. 1947.

JEANS, Sir James Hopwood, OM 1939; Kt 1928; MA, DSc (Hon.) Oxon, Manchester, Benares; LLD (Hon.) Aberdeen, Johns Hopkins, St Andrews; ScD (Hon.) Dublin; DL (Hon.) Calcutta; Hon. Fellow Inst. Physics; Hon. Fellow of Trinity College, Cambridge; FRS; Professor of Astronomy in the Royal Institution; Member Advisory Council of the Department of Scientific and Industrial Research, 1924–29 and 1934–39; Member of Royal Commission for the 1851 Exhibition, and Chairman of Science Committee; *b* 11 Sept. 1877; *s* of W. T. Jeans, London; *m* 1st, 1907, Charlotte Tiffany (*d* 1934), *d* of Alfred Mitchell, New London, Conn; one *d*; 2nd, 1935, Susi, *e d* of Oskar Hock, Vienna; two *s* one *d*. *Educ:* Merchant Taylors' School; Trinity Coll., Cambridge (Fellow, 1901, Hon. Fellow, 1942). Univ. Lecturer in Mathematics, 1904; Prof. of Applied Mathematics in Princeton Univ. 1905–09; Stokes Lecturer in Applied Mathematics in the University of Cambridge, 1910–12; Secretary of the Royal Society, 1919–29; Research Associate, Mt Wilson Observatory, 1923–44; President of the Royal Astronomical Society, 1925–27; President of the British Association for the Advancement of Science, 1934; President of the Indian Science Congress Association (Jubilee Meeting) 1938; awarded Royal Medal of the Royal Society, 1919; Gold Medal of the Royal Astronomical Society, 1922; Franklin Medal of the Franklin Institute, 1931; Mukerjee Medal of the Indian Association for the Cultivation of Science, 1937; Calcutta Medal of the Royal Asiatic Society of Bengal, 1938. *Publications:* The Dynamical Theory of Gases, 1904; Theoretical Mechanics, 1906; The Mathematical Theory of Electricity and Magnetism, 1908; Radiation and the Quantum-Theory, 1914; Problems of Cosmogony and Stellar Dynamics, 1919; Atomicity and Quanta, 1926; Astronomy and Cosmogony, 1928; Eos, or the Wider Aspects of Cosmogony, 1928; The Universe Around Us, 1929; The Mysterious Universe, 1930; The Stars in their Courses, 1931; The New Background of Science, 1933; Through Space and Time, 1934; Science and Music, 1937; Introduction to the Kinetic Theory of Gases, 1940; Physics and Philosophy, 1942, etc. *Address:* Cleveland Lodge, Dorking. *T:* Dorking 2117. *Club:* Athenæum.

Died 16 Sept. 1946.

JEBB, Brig.-Gen. Gladwyn Dundas, CB 1930; CMG 1916; CBE; DSO 1902; *b* 27 March 1877; *γ s* of late J. G. Jebb of Barnby Moor House, Notts, and Alice Caroline Dundas, *sister* of 5th Viscount Melville; *m* 1912, Norah, *o c* of Maj.-General Lomax; one *s*. Entered army, 1896; Captain, 1902; Major, 1913; Lt-Col, 1920; Col, 1923; served South Africa, 1899–1902 (despatches twice, Queen's medal 3 clasps, King's medal 2 clasps, DSO); European War, 1914–18 (despatches five times, Bt Lt-Col, CMG); Brig.-General in charge of Administration, 1918; Deputy Director of Recruiting and Organisation, War Office, 1925–27; commanded 126th East Lancashire Infantry Brigade, 1928–30; retired pay, 1930. *Address:* The Birks Bellingham, Northumberland.

Died 19 Aug. 1947.

JEEJEEBHOY, Sir Byramjee, Kt 1928; JP; owner of 9000 acres in Salsette; large landed proprietor; *b* 28 Feb. 1881; *s* of Rustomjee Byramjee Jeejeebhoy, JP, and Avabai, *d* of Sir Jamsetjee Jeejeebhoy, 2nd Bt; *m* 1908;

two s. Educ: St Xavier's College. Hon. Presidency Magistrate, 1908–15; Delegate of the Parsi Chief Matrimonial Court, 1909–25; Member of the Bombay Municipal Corporation; Chairman of the Standing Committee, 1924; President Parsi Pioneer Boy Scouts, 32nd Bombay; Chairman Byramjee Jeejeebhoy Charitable Institution; Member of the Jail Committee for Conditional Release of Prisoners; Member Bombay Board of Film Censors, 1924–37; Vice-President Released Prisoners' Aid Society, Member Bombay Vigilance Society, and Bombay Presidency Nursing Association; Trustee Prince of Wales' Museum, 1921–23; Vice-President Society for Protection of Children in Western India; Founder Byramjee Jeejeebhoy Hospital for Children, the first Children's Hospital in India; Sheriff of Bombay, 1927; Director several Joint-Stock Companies; President, Imperial Bank of India; Provincial Commissioner, Boy Scouts, Association, Bombay Presidency; President, Bombay Boy Scouts' Local Association, 1932–38. Address: The Cliff, Malabar Hill, Bombay, India. TA: Jeruby, Bombay. T: 41814 Residence, 20035 Office. Clubs: Willingdon Sports, Orient, Asian. Bombay; Ladies', Poona.

Died 31 March 1946.

JEFFREY, Sir John, KCB 1934; CB 1929; CBE 1927; FRSE; b 1871; s of John Jeffrey of Chirnside, Berwickshire; m 1898, Jean Stewart (d 1942), d of James Sneddon, Mus. Bac. (Cantab), Edinburgh; three s. Secretary, Departmental Committee on Medical Relief (Scotland), 1903; Assistant Secretary, Royal Commission on Poor Laws, 1905–09; General Superintendent of Poor, Northern Highland District, 1909–12; Secretary, Scottish National Health Insurance Commission, 1912–19; Secretary, Scottish Board of Health, 1919–28; Department of Health for Scotland, 1929–33; Under-Secretary of State for Scotland, 1933–37; Chairman, General Board of Control for Scotland, 1939–45; Chairman, Scottish Civil Nursing Reserve Advisory Council, 1939–45; Chairman, Local Government and Public Health Consolidation (Scotland) Committee, 1937–39. Address: 9 Cluny Gardens, Edinburgh. T: 52145. Clubs: Northern, Edinburgh.

Died 19 June 1947.

JEFFREY, William; author and journalist; b 1896; m Margaret W. J. Graham; one s one d. Educ: Glasgow University. Publications: Verse: Prometheus Returns; The Wise Men come to Town, 1923; The Nymph, 1924; The Doom of Atlas, 1926; The Lamb of Lomond, 1926; Mountain Songs, 1928; The Golden Stag, 1932; Eagle of Coruisk, 1933; Fantasia written in an Industrial Town (poem), 1933; Sea Glimmer: Poems in Scots and English, 1945. Joint Author, Pageant of Empire, Empire Exhibition, 1938. Address: 733 Shields Road, Pollokshields, Glasgow, S1.

Died 11 Feb. 1946.

JEFFREY-WADDELL, John, ARSA, FSA Scot; Architect; b 4 May 1876; s of R. G. Waddell and J. L. Jeffrey; m 1903, J. L. Swan; two d. Educ: home; School of Art and Technical College, Glasgow. Architect, especially of Ecclesiastical Buildings; has been employed in the restoration of Iona Cathedral; Dornoch Cathedral; The Town Church, St Andrews; Fowlis Wester Church; Dunino Church; and the building of many modern churches such as the Scots Church, Brussels, Belgium; Banff; Lockhart Memorial, Edinburgh; Denny; Plean; Stewarton; Monkton; Gigha; Kilmonivaig; St Bride's, Sanquhar; St Bride's, Bothwell; St Andrews, Castle-Douglas; Kilsyth, etc.; in addition he has built many church halls; restored Provand's Lordship, and done a considerable amount of domestic work and general practice, including the reparation of Gilbertfield Castle. Publications: By Bothwell Banks; Rambles through Lanarkshire; The Reparation of Provand's Lordship; Alexander (Greek) Thomson; Architecture of Glasgow; Bothwell Castle; Glasgow Cathedral. Recreations:

archæology, sketching and etching, study of mediæval architecture, pictures and antique furniture. Address: 95 Bath Street, Glasgow. T: Douglas 654; Caldergrove House, Hallside, Lanarkshire. T: Blantyre 80. Clubs: Royal Automobile, Overseas; Athenæum, Glasgow.

Died 4 Dec. 1941.

JEFFREYS, Maj.-Gen. Henry Byron, CB 1904; CMG 1917; b 9 Feb. 1854; s of late Gen. E. R. Jeffreys, CB, and Mary, d of Col Patrick Vans Agnew of Barnbarroch, Wigtownshire; m 1888, Marian, o c of late Capt. W. F. Burlton-Bennet, 6th Warwickshire Regt and g d of Sir John Hawkshaw; two s one d. Educ: Marlborough. Entered Royal Artillery, 1873; Staff College, 1887–88; AAG Madras Army, 1890–94; Brigade Major, RA, Aldershot, 1896–98; served South Africa, 1899–1901 (medal with six clasps, despatches twice, Brevet Colonel); commanded RHA Aldershot, 1901–03; Chief Staff Officer, S Africa, 1904–06; retired, 1910; Commissioner of Boy Scouts, Sussex and London; called up for service at the outbreak of European war; Colonel Commandant RA, 1923. Address: 30 Adelaide Crescent, Hove. T: Hove 4429. Club: Union (Brighton).

Died 4 Dec. 1949.

JEHU, Thomas John, MD (Edin.), MA (Camb.), FGS; FRSE; Regius Professor of Geology and Mineralogy, Edinburgh University, 1914–42; b Llanfair-Caereinion, Montgomeryshire, 1871; s of late John Jehu, JP, Llanfair; m 1904, Annie, 2nd d of late Very Rev. Principal Stewart, DD, St Mary's College, St Andrews; two s. Educ: The High School, Oswestry; Univ. of Edin.; St John's College, Cambridge (Exhibitioner, Foundation Scholar, and Prizeman in Natural Science). Studied Medicine and Science at the University of Edinburgh; took Degrees of MB, CM, 1893, BSc 1894, and was medallist in the Class of Geology. At the University of Cambridge took 1st Class Natural Science Tripos, Parts I and II, 1897–98; 2nd Class Moral Science Tripos, 1899; Newcombe Prize for Natural Science and Philosophy of St John's College, 1898; Arnold-Gernsternberg Studentship, 1900. Heriot Fellow of the University of Edinburgh, 1901. Member Royal Commission on Coast Erosion, 1906; Lecturer in Geology, St Andrews Univ., 1903–14. Publications: several papers on the Geology of Wales and of Scotland (Trans. Roy. Soc. Edin.). Recreations: travelling, walking. Address: University, Edinburgh.

Died 18 July 1943.

JELF, Sir Arthur Selborne, Kt 1932; CMG 1927; b 10 Oct. 1876; s of Rev. Dr Jelf, Master of the Charterhouse; m 1st, Blanche (d 1917), d of John Connell; 2nd, Evelyn Mary, d of A. E. Hardcastle; two s one d. Educ: Marlborough; Exeter College, Oxford. Malayan Civil Service, 1899–1925; Seconded for Military Service (Intelligence), 1917–19; Colonial Secretary, Jamaica, 1925–35; retired, 1935; Acted as Governor of Jamaica on several occasions for varying periods of time. Hythe Borough Council, 1936–40; Mayor of Hythe, 1938–39. Address: The Priory, The Bayle, Folkestone. Club: Royal Empire Society.

Died 26 Feb. 1947.

JELF, Sir Ernest Arthur, Kt 1939; b 3 Oct. 1868; s of late Hon. Mr Justice Jelf, and Jane, y d of late Rev. William Clark King, Vicar of Norham; m Rose Frances (d 1923), 2nd d of late R. W. C. Reeves, DL, of Besborough, Co. Clare; one s one d. Educ: Haileybury; New College, Oxford. Called to Bar, Inner Temple, 1893; South Eastern Circuit; sometime a Commissioner for Trial of Municipal Election Petitions and a Revising Barrister; King's Remembrancer, 1937–43; and Senior Master of the Supreme Court, retired, 1943. Publications: Editor of third ed. of Encyclopædia of Laws of England; The Wonderful Pagoda and other children's ballets; Jill's Magic Island and other children's ballets; The Little Old Woman, children's ballet; The Shadow of the Inn and other Nativity Plays for dancing children; Eileen's

Journey, history in fairyland; Stories sworn to be true; Pope Pacificus; Corrupt and Illegal Practices, with notes; Where to find your Law; London Institutions of Public Importance; Evidence in Criminal Cases; The Law of Innkeepers; Fifteen Decisive Battles of the Law; The Education Act with notes; After the Journey's End, in National Review; and Time and Place in Practical Politics in the Hibbert Journal. *Recreation:* writing ballet-plays for children and arranging for their production. *Address:* St Mary's Cottage, Waxwell Lane, Pinner, Middlesex. *T:* Pinner 431; Goldsmith's Building, Temple, EC4. *T:* Central 2980. *Club:* Athenæum.

Died 1 Sept. 1949.

JELF, Herbert William; Master of the Supreme Court of Judicature, Chancery Division, since 1925; *b* 5 Aug. 1882; *s* of late Sir Arthur Richard Jelf, a Judge of the High Court; unmarried. *Educ:* Eton; Christ Church, Oxford; MA. Rowed in the Oxford University Eight, 1904; held Commission in RNVR (and served afloat) during European War. *Recreations:* rowing, travelling abroad. *Address:* 177 St James Court, SW1. *T:* Victoria 2360. *Clubs:* Royal Thames Yacht, Leander.

Died 24 March 1943.

JELLETT, Henry, MD, FRCPI; Consulting Gynæcologist, Rotunda Hospital, Dublin; *b* 1872; *γ s* of Very Rev. Henry Jellett, DD, Dean and Ordinary of St Patrick's Cathedral, Dublin; *m* 1903, Mary Gwendoline, *e d* of Francis H. M. Leader, JP, of Classas, Coachford, Co. Cork; one *s* one *d*. *Educ:* Dublin University. External Assistant and Assistant Master, Rotunda Hospital, Dublin, 1895–98; Extern Examiner, Dublin Univ., 1900–01 and 1918–19; Extern Examiner, RUI, 1902–05; Censor, RCP, 1906–08; Gynæcologist to Dr Steevens' Hospital, Dublin, 1903–09; Master Rotunda Hospital, Dublin, 1910–19; Kings' Professor of Midwifery, Dublin University, 1909–11; Gynæcologist to Sir Patrick Dun's Hospital, 1909–11; late Gynæcological Surgeon, North Canterbury Hospital, Christchurch; late External Examiner in Midwifery and Gynæcology, Manchester University and University of New Zealand; late Consulting Obstetrician to Health Department of NZ; President Obstetrical Section, Royal Academy of Medicine in Ireland, 1910–11; Commandant of Munro Ambulance Corps, Northern Flanders, 1914–17 (despatches, Chevalier de l'Ordre de la Couronne de Belgique, Croix de Guerre Française with two stars, 1914–15 Star; Victory and War medals). *Publications:* A Manual of Midwifery (4th ed. with D. G. Madill), 1929; A Short Practice of Midwifery (10th ed.), 1930; A Short Practice of Midwifery for Nurses (13th ed.), 1945; A Short Practice of Gynæcology for Students (6th ed. with R. E. Tottenham), 1930; A Practice of Gynæcology (5th ed.), 1925; The Causes and Prevention of Maternal Mortality, 1929; (novel) The Nursing Home Murder (with Ngaio Marsh), 1936; (play) Wisha, God Help Us! 1941; (novel) Much To-Do, 1946; numerous papers relating to Obstetrics and Gynæcology. *Recreations:* fishing and motoring. *Address:* Rosnalee, Fendalton Road, Christchurch, NW1, NZ. *TA:* Jellett, Fendalton. *Club:* University (Dublin).

Died 8 June 1948.

JENCKEN, Maj.-Gen. Francis John, CB 1918; Knight of Grace of the Order of St John of Jerusalem, BA, MB, BCh, DPH, University of Dublin; *b* 4 April 1858; *s* of F. E. Jencken, MD; *m* 1st, Frances Susan, *d* of Dawson Westropp, JP of Mellon, Co. Limerick; 2nd, Gertrude May, *d* of William Goodenough Bayly; no *c*. *Educ:* Portarlington; Foyle College; Trinity College, Dublin (Medical Scholar). Entered army, 1882, Major RAMC 1894; Lt-Col 1902; Col 1911; (Surg.-Gen.) Maj.-Gen. 1915; Administrative Medical Officer, EC; Assistant Director of Medical Services, 1911–14; 3rd Army Home Forces, 1914–15; Deputy Director of Medical Services, Eastern Command, 1915; served Sudan, 1884, Battles of

El Teb and Tamaai, The Nile, 1885; European War (despatches twice); retired, 1918. *Recreations:* botany, walking. *Address:* Fedamore, Searle Road, Farnham, Surrey. *Club:* Junior United Service.

Died 14 Dec. 1943.

JENKIN, Mrs Bernard, (Margaret M. Giles); retired; *b* 1868; 2nd *d* of Richard W. and Frances E. Giles; *m* 1898, Bernard M. Jenkin; one *d*. *Educ:* Kensington High School; Brussels; Heidelberg. Studied eight years at National Art Training School (now Royal College of Art, South Kensington) chiefly under Professor E. Lantéri; visited galleries at Paris, Milan, Florence, Venice, Rome, Athens, Lahore, and Calcutta; designed and executed marble and stone memorials for Clifton, Stockport, etc.; modelled frieze and spandrils for terracotta and designed finials for stone, and other architectural decoration; exhibited groups and portraits and reliefs at Royal Academy; The Old Salon, Paris, Edinburgh, Glasgow, and Bristol; modelled portrait busts and medallions; a member of the Royal West of England Academy, and of the Society of Mural Decorators and Painters in Tempera; designed and modelled medals for the Royal Horticultural Society and the Royal Horticultural Society and the Society of Chemical Industry, and a seal for the Institution of Electrical Engineers and the University of Rangoon. *Address:* 25b Durdham Park, Bristol 6.

Died 31 March 1949.

JENKINGS, Adm. Albert Baldwin; *b* 2 March 1846; *m* 1898, Augusta Isabel Kitty, 2nd *d* of Henry Langley, 31 Queen's Gate Terrace, SW. Entered navy, 1859; Captain, 1882; Rear-Adm., 1897; Vice-President Ordnance Committee, 1897–1900; commander of Inflexible at bombardment of Alexandria, 1882, during Egyptian war (medal, clasp, Khedive's star); second in command of the Channel Squadron, 1900–01; Admiral 1907; retired, 1907. *Address:* 11 Belgrave Road, SW1. *Club:* United Service.

Died 5 Oct. 1942.

JENKINS, Arthur; MP (Lab) Pontypool division of Monmouth since 1935; Parliamentary Secretary, Ministry of Education, Aug.–Oct. 1945; Alderman, Monmouth County Council; Miners' Agent (Eastern Valley District), South Wales Miners' Federation, since 1918; Chairman of a local appeal board at a Royal Ordnance Factory; *m*; one *s*. *Educ:* Varteg Council School; Ruskin College, Oxford; private school in France. Worked as miner in South Wales coalfield until 20 years of age; Member of Monmouth County Council since 1919; late Vice-President South Wales Miners' Federation; Member County Councils' Association; Member EC South Wales Miners' Federation; Member Royal Commission on Licensing; Parliamentary Private Secretary to Rt Hon. C. R. Attlee, 1940–45; Parliamentary Secretary, Ministry of Town and Country Planning, 1945. *Publications:* press articles mainly on local government and coal mining subjects. *Address:* Greenlands, Pontypool, Mon. *T:* Pontypool 331.

Died 25 April 1946.

JENKINS, Charles Elliott Edward; KC 1897; *b* 1859; *s* of late Charles Jenkins, ICS; *m* 1938, Violet Evelyn St Hill, *e d* of late Rev. W. St Hill Bourne. *Educ:* Lancing College; Lincoln College, Oxford. Called to Bar, Lincoln's Inn, 1885; Treasurer, 1927; retired from Bar, 1935. *Address:* Turville Heath House, Henley-on-Thames. *T:* Turville Heath 2. *Club:* Oxford and Cambridge.

Died 23 Sept. 1946.

JENKINS, Major Edward Vaughan, DSO 1900; late Duke of Wellington's Regt; *b* 14 Oct. 1879; *s* of late Lt-Col Vaughan Jenkins. *Educ:* Clifton. Entered Army, 1899; served S Africa, 1900–02 (despatches, Queen's medal, 4 clasps, King's medal 2 clasps, DSO); served E Africa and Uganda, 1902–12 (despatches, AFGS medal, with 2 clasps); European War, 1914–16. *Club:* MCC.

Died 20 Feb. 1941.

JENKINS, Herbert Riches, MA; *b* 23 Dec. 1880; *s* of William Jenkins and Kate Elizabeth Riches; *m* 1911, Margaret Florence Jones; one *d. Educ:* Clifton College; St John's College, Cambridge. Mining Engineer; High Sheriff of Herefordshire, 1935; Member of Herefordshire County Council, 1937; Vice-President Herefordshire General Hospital; Governor of Royal Agricultural Society of England; Director of Universal Grinding Wheel Co. Ltd, Stafford; JP County of Hereford. *Recreations:* shooting, golf, tennis. *Address:* Westhide, Hereford. *T:* Bartestree 60. *Club:* United University.

Died 8 Feb. 1944.

JENKINS, Joseph Barclay; JP; ex-Moderator of South Wales Presbyterian Church; Chairman Cardiganshire County Council; Ex-Mayor Borough of Aberystwyth; *b* 5 June 1870; *γ c* of William and Elizabeth Jenkins; *m* 1914, Florence A. Taylor Malin; no *c. Educ:* Cwmystwyth School. Bookseller and Stationer; Newspaper Correspondent; Pres. Aberystwyth YMCA; Member Courts of Welsh Univ., University College of Wales, Welsh National Library and Central Welsh Board. High Sheriff of County of Cardigan, 1943. *Publications:* articles in Welsh magazines and periodicals. *Recreation:* travelling. *Address:* Henley, North Road, Aberstwyth.

Died 1 April 1950.

JENKINS, Alderman Sir William, Kt 1931; JP; MP (Lab) Neath Division of Glamorgan since 1922; Chief Agent, Afan Valley Miners' Federation; *b* Cymmer, Glamorgan, 1871; father, miner; *m*; two *s* two *d. Educ:* Glyncorrwg National School. Commenced working at 11½ on the railway; underground as miner at 12 years of age; checkweigher, 1898; elected Glyncorrwg School Board, 1900; Glyncorrwg Urban Council, 1904; Chairman, 1908–16, 1927; Glamorgan County Council, 1906; Chairman, CC, 1919–21; Chairman, Education Committee since 1918; Secretary, Western Miners' Association, 1906; Sub-Agent, 1908; Agent for Afan Valley Miners, 1912; Member of Council, University of Wales; Congregationalist; Deacon and Precentor of Welsh Church; Chairman, Federation of Education Authorities for Wales, May 1926; Chairman Glamorgan School for Blind; Chairman Glamorgan Standing Joint Committee; Vice-Pres. County Council Association England and Wales. *Recreations:* golf, bowls. *Address:* Cymmer, Port Talbot.

Died 8 Dec. 1944.

JENKINSON, John Edward; JP; *b* Dunedin, NZ, 17 Oct. 1858; *s* of J. Hartley Jenkinson, Halifax, Yorkshire, and Jane Matthews, Aberdeen; *m* 1st, 1891, Annie (decd), *d* of James Eaton, Christchurch; two *s*; 2nd, 1919, Nellie, *d* of Col M. McCredie. *Educ:* State schools, Otago. Entered the employ of Dunedin Ironworks as an apprentice to boilermaking and iron shipbuilding, 1875; made a member of the Boilermakers' Society in Dunedin, and in a few months was elected President; returned to New Zealand from a visit to Australia, 1884; entering the Government Railway service, was instrumental in forming a union (Boilermakers') in Christchurch, and soon afterwards the Canterbury Trades Council, which was the forerunner of similar councils now firmly established and federated throughout New Zealand; was Pres. of Trades Council, Eight-Hour Day Committee, political committees, etc.; inaugurated scientific trade lectures under management of Union, which has done much to popularise Unionism; assisted as a delegate to form and draft rules of Amalgamated Society of Railway Servants of New Zealand, now some thousands strong; Member (Labour) Legislative Council, 1892–1914; started business in

Wellington as a bicycle manufacturer and motor importer, 1896. *Address:* Sandon Road, Feilding, New Zealand.

Died 29 Jan. 1937.

JENKS, Sir Maurice, 1st Bt *cr* 1932; Kt 1931; Kt Commander of the Order of Dannebrog; *b* 25 Nov. 1872; *s* of late Robert Isaac Jenks; *m* 1st, 1903, Martha Louise Christabel (*d* 1938), *d* of late George Calley Smith; three *c*; 2nd, 1939, Constance Edith, *d* of W. R. Currie, Beckenham, Kent. Court of Common Council Ward of Cheap, 1910; Alderman Ward of Cheap, 1923; Senior Sheriff City of London, 1930–31; Lord Mayor of London, 1931–32; one of HM's Lieutenants for the City of London; Hon. LLD University of London; Member of Governing Body and Hon. Treasurer of the School of Oriental and African Studies; Chairman and Trustees of Modern College; prominently connected with the principal Masonic bodies and Livery Guilds; Member of the Court of the University of London; Member of the Post Office Advisory Council; Member of the Railway Rates Tribunal (specially added unpaid); formerly Head of the firm of Maurice Jenks, Percival & Co., Chartered Accountants (retired, 1939). *Recreations:* golf, yachting, fishing. *Heir: s* Richard Atherley [*b* 26 July 1906; *m* 1932, Marjorie Suzanne Arlette du Cros; two *s*]. *Address:* 26 Parkside, Knightsbridge, SW1. *T:* Sloane 7766. *Clubs:* Carlton, Gresham, Royal Thames Yacht.

Died 19 May 1946.

JENNER, Sir Walter (Kentish William), 2nd Bt *cr* 1868; DSO 1918; Lt-Col (Retired Pay), formerly Major 9th Lancers and Bt Lieut-Col; JP Co. Somerset; *b* 12 Oct. 1860; *e s* of Sir William Jenner, 1st Bt, GCB, MD, FRS, and Adela, *d* of Stephen Adey; *m* 1893, Flora (*d* 1921), *d* of Field-Marshal Sir Donald Stewart, 1st Bt. *Educ:* Charterhouse; Sandhurst; Staff College, Camberley. Rejoined Army, Aug. 1914 (despatches three times, DSO, Bt Lt-Col); Lt-Col (RP), 1918; Brevet Lt-Col, 1919. *Recreation:* music. *Heir: b* Lt-Col A. V. Jenner, CMG. *Address:* Lytes Cary, Kingsdon, Somerset. *Clubs:* Naval and Military, Cavalry.

Died 12 Oct. 1948.

JENNEY, Col Archibald Offley, CBE 1919; *b* 1864; *s* of late Arthur Henry Jenney, Ditchingham Lodge, Norfolk; *m* 1907, Doreen Mary, *d* of Col Gerald Paul Townshend; two *d.* Served European War, 1914–19 (despatches twice, CBE). *Address:* Guildown, Goodrich, Ross, Herefordshire.

Died 7 Dec. 1946.

JENNINGS, Herbert Spencer; Walter Professor of Zoology and Director of the Zoological Laboratory, Johns Hopkins University, Baltimore, Md, USA 1906–38, Professor Emeritus since 1938; *b* 8 April 1868; *s* of George Nelson Jennings and Olive Taft Jenks; *m* 1st, 1898, Louise Burridge; one *s*; 2nd, 1939, Lulu Plant Jennings. *Educ:* University of Michigan; Harvard University; University of Jena. Professor of Botany and Bacteriology, Montana State College, 1897–98; Instructor in Zoology, Dartmouth College, 1898–99, and University of Michigan, 1899–1903; Assistant Professor of Zoology, University of Pennsylvania, 1904–06; Visiting Professor at Keio University, Tokyo, Japan, 1931–32; Eastman Visiting Professor at Oxford University, 1935–36; Visiting Professor, University of California, Los Angeles, 1939, and Research Associate since 1939; PhD (Harvard); AM (Oxford); Hon. LLD (Clark University, Pennsylvania, University of California); Hon. DSc (Michigan, Pennsylvania, Oberlin, Chicago). *Publications:* Anatomy of the Cat (with J. Reighard); Behaviour of the Lower Organisms; Life and Death, Heredity and Evolution in Unicellular Organisms; Prometheus, or Biology and the Advancement of Man; Genetics of the Protozoa; The Biological Basis of Human Nature; The Universe and Life; Genetics; Genetic Variations in Relation to

Evolution. *Recreations:* motoring, travel. *Address:* 10531 Wellworth Avenue, Los Angeles, 24, California, USA. *T:* AR 32834.

Died April 1947.

JENNINGS, James George, CIE 1919; MA; Indian Educational Service (retired); *b* 14 June 1866; *s* of James Jennings; *m* 1894, Maud Walrond, *d* of Gateward Coleridge Davis, Bar-at-law; two *d. Educ:* Lincoln College, Oxford. Indian Educational Service, 1892; Director of Public Instruction, Bihar and Orissa 1913–17 and 1920–21; Vice-Chancellor, Patna University, 1917–20; Member of the Legislative Council, Bihar and Orissa, 1913–16 and 1917–20; Additional member (temporary) of the Viceroy's Legislative Council, 1917. *Publications:* Sakuntala; Marcus Aurelius; Duty to the State; Metaphor in Poetry. *Address:* 38 Morrab Road Penzance, Cornwall.

Died 3 April 1941.

JENSEN, Ernest T., MB London; MRCS England; LRCP London; Fellow of Royal Society of Medicine; Member of British Medical Association; Member of Harveian Society of London; *b* London, 1873; *s* of Peter and Sara Jensen, of Copenhagen and London. *Educ:* Guy's Hospital. A founder (with Dr G. W. Pailthorpe), Chairman of Council, Member of Scientific Committee, and a Vice-President of Institute for Scientific Treatment of Delinquency; Vice-Pres. Medical Soc. for Study of Radiesthesia; was Hon. Treasurer of Brunswick Trust (for Cancer Research); Civil Surgeon to Herbert Hospital, Woolwich; served with Field Force in S African War; travelled in British East Africa and Uganda with shooting expedition; Registrar to Harold Fink Officers' Hospital and Londonderry House; Fellow of Society of Tropical Medicine and Hygiene; a founder and Hon. Secretary the Tropical Disease Prevention Association. *Publications:* Treatment of the Urethra for Locomotor Ataxy, British Medical Journal, 11 March 1911; Fear and Disease, Lancet, 30 Jan. 1915; Treatment through the Sympathetic System, Radiesthesia, 1942. *Recreations:* philosophy and furnishing. *Address:* 25 Berkeley Square, W1. *T:* Mayfair 1120.

Died 30 July 1950.

JEROME, Col Henry Joseph Walker, CB 1900, CMG 1915; late commanding RE, South Aldershot; retired 1907; *b* 7 Jan. 1854; *s* of late Maj.-Gen. John Jerome; *m* 1892, Harriet Elizabeth (*d* 1935), *d* of late George Yule. Entered army, 1873; Capt. 1885; Maj. 1893. Served Afghan war, 1878–80 (medal with clasp); served S Africa, 1899–1902 (despatches, Queen's medal with 4 clasps, CB); European War, 1914–15 (despatches, CMG).

Died 8 Nov. 1943.

JEROME, Lucien Joseph; *b* Chacrata, India, 20 March 1870; *o s* of late Maj.-Gen. Henry Edward Jerome, VC; *m* 1st, Ethel Frances Blakeney (decd); 2nd, Vivienne Fane Savile (*d* 1912); one *s*; 3rd, Maria de las Mercedes Arredonda; one *d. Educ:* Lycée de Tours, France; Tutors. Unpaid British Vice-Consul at Nice, 1891; in charge of the Vice-Consulate, Monaco, 1897; Vice-Consul, Havana, 1897; Acting Consul-Gen., Havana, 1898–99; in charge of United States Interests in Cuba during the Spanish-American War, 1898; Consul for the United States of Mexico, 1899; Acting Consul-General, Port-au-Prince, 1905–06; re-appointed to Mexico, 1906; Acting British Chargé d'Affaires, Lima, 1908, 1909, and 1911; at La Paz, 1910; Consul-General, Callao, 1907–13; Ecuador, 1913–18, First Secretary, Legation at Quito and Chargé d'Affaires during absence of HM Minister; FRGS; Acting Consul at Vigo, 1918; Consul-General at Seville, 1918–19; retired, 30 Oct. 1919; Hon. Fellow of the Society of Geography and Statistics of Mexico; Corresponding Fellow Geographical Society of Lima; received the Coronation Medal, 1911. *Address:* Grabador, Esteve 36, Valencia, Spain.

Died 23 April 1943.

JERSEY, Dowager Countess of; (Margaret Elizabeth), DBE 1927; CBE 1920; JP 1920; *b* 29 Oct. 1849; *d* of 2nd Lord Leigh; *m* 1872, 7th Earl of Jersey (*d* 1915); one *s* two *d.* Life Dame Pres. Grand Council of Primrose League; travelled in France, Italy, Egypt, Holy Land, Greece, Turkey, Samoa, New Caledonia, China, Japan, Canada, etc.; followed her husband when he went as Governor to New South Wales, 1891. *Publications:* Sleeping Beauty, a play for children; Maurice, or the Red Jar, 1894; Eric, Prince of Lorlonia, 1895; St George of England-drama for children, 1899; Augustus: The Adventures of a Little Boy, 1909; Poems and Hymns for Young Children, 1910; John Alexander and the Little Man, 1915; Fifty-one Years of Victorian Life, 1922; several poems; articles descriptive of travels in India, New Caledonia, Samoa, and Japan, in Nineteenth Century, etc.; (with Hon. Emily Ward) Hannibal's Tribunal, A drama of the Eastern Pyreness. *Club:* Ladies' Empire.

Died 22 May 1945.

JERVIS, Sir Henry (Felix) Jervis-White-, 5th Bt *cr* 1797; *b* 1859; *s* of Col Henry Jervis-White-Jervis, 3rd *s* of 2nd Bt; *S* brother 1943; *m* 1885, Sarah Ann Danbrook; three *d. Address:* Callander, Ontario, Canada.

Died 18 Sept. 1947.

JERVIS, Col Sir John Henry Jervis-White-, 4th Bt *cr* 1797; RA; *b* 4 July 1857; *S* uncle 1887; *m* 1887, Margaret, *d* of Capt. G. Campbell, RHA, Madras. Entered Army, 1877; Capt. 1885; Major, 1895; Lt-Col 1902; Colonel, 1918; served Zulu war, 1879 (medal with clasp); South Africa, 1899–1902 (despatches thrice, Bt Lt-Col, medal 6 clasps, King's medal 2 clasps); retired, 1903. *Heir: b* Henry Felix [*b* 1859; *m* 1885, Sarah Ann Danbrook; three *d*]. *Address:* Blake Dene, Parkstone, Dorset.

Died 18 Jan. 1943.

JERVIS, Col Nicholas Gordon Mainwaring, DSO 1919; *b* 1881; *s* of Col Walter Neil Jervis, RA, of Chatcull, Eccleshall, Staffordshire; *m* 1909, Louisa Amy Stella, *d* of late Roland Cotton, of Etwall Hall, Derby; one *s. Educ:* Cheltenham; RMA, Woolwich. Served European War, 1914–19 (despatches, DSO); Commander Royal Artillery, 53rd Welsh Division, Territorial Army, 1928–32; retired pay, 1932; Hon. Secretary, E Essex Hunt, 1933. *Address:* Pitchards, Halstead, Essex. *T:* Halstead 97.

Died 6 March 1943.

JERVOISE, Rear-Adm. Edmund Purefoy Ellis, CBE 1918; *b* 1861; *y s* of F. J. E. Jervoise of Herriard Park, Hants; *m* 1904, Alice Flora Mary, *d* of George Christian, Bighton Wood, Hants. JP Hampshire, 1924. *Address:* Farringdon Hurst, Alton, Hants. *T:* Tisted 210. *Club:* Junior United Service.

Died 4 Jan. 1950.

JESPERSEN, Otto, PhD, LittD, LLD; late Professor of English in the University of Copenhagen; *b* 16 July 1860; *s* of Judge Jespersen; *m* 1897, Ane Marie Djörup (*d* 1937); one *s. Educ:* Frederiksborg; Copenhagen. PhD, 1891. Professor, 1893; Volney Prize of the Institut de France, 1906; Visiting Professor Columbia University, NY, 1909–10; honorary LittD *ibid.* 1910 and Paris, 1927; LLD St Andrews, 1925; member of the Academies of Copenhagen, Oslo, Helsingfors, Ghent, Prague, Amsterdam, and Lund; Fellow of British Academy; hon. mem. of Philological Society, of Modern Language Association, etc.; President of Modern Humanities Research Association, 1921; Rector of University of Copenhagen, 1920–21. *Publications:* Progress in Language; Fonetik; How to teach a Foreign Language; Growth and Structure of the English Language; Lehrbuch der Phonetik; A Modern English Grammar on Historical Principles; Language, its Nature, Development, and Origin; Philosophy of Grammar; Mankind, Nation and Individual; International

Language; Novial Lexike; Essentials of English Grammar; Linguistica, selected papers; Analytic Syntax; Autobiography in Danish. *Address:* Lundehave, Elsinore, Denmark.

Died 30 April 1943.

JESS, Lt-Gen. Sir Carl Herman, Kt 1935; CB 1939; CMG 1919; CBE 1920; DSO 1917; Chairman of Australian Man-Power Committee since 1940; *b* 1884; *m* 1914, Marjory, *d* of D. McGibbon, Melbourne; one *s* (and one killed on active service, 1941) one *d*. *Educ:* Bendigo. Served European War, 1914–17 (despatches thrice, DSO, Serbian Order of the White Eagle); Col 1926; Commanding Field Troops and District Base Commandant, 5th Military District (Western Australia), 1927–31; Commandant 3rd Military District, Victoria, 1932–34; Adjutant-General, Australian Military Forces, 1934–39; Lt-Gen. 1940; on leave 1933–34, as Organiser Melbourne Centenary Celebrations. *Clubs:* Naval and Military, Melbourne.

Died 16 June 1948.

JESSE, Col John Leonard, CMG 1919; CBE 1929; DSO 1916; *b* 4 April 1876; *s* of William and Florence Jesse; *m* 1903, Mary Henrietta, *o d* of F. Mandy, JP. *Educ:* Lancing; Pembroke Coll., Oxford. Royal Marine Light Infantry, 1897; Lieut ASC 1900; Captain, 1902; Adjutant, 1910; Major, 1914; Lt-Col 1920 Col 1925; served S African War, 1901–02 (despatches, Queen's medal 2 clasps, King's medal 2 clasps); Somaliland, 1908–10 (despatches, medal with clasp); European War, France and Italy, 1914–18 (despatches thrice, DSO, CMG); retired pay, 1930. *Address:* c/o Lloyds Bank, Cox and King, Pall Mall, SW1. *Club:* Flyfishers'.

Died 23 May 1944.

JESSE, William, MA; *b* 7 Sept. 1870; *e s* of William and Florence Jesse, Ingatestone, Essex; *m* 1894, Grace Grant, *e d* of Alan C. G. Cameron; one *s*. *Educ:* Crewkerne; Hereford Cathedral School; Selwyn College, Cambridge. Assistant Master, Bedford Modern School, 1891–94; La Martinière College, Lucknow, 1894–1903; Principal, Meerut College, 1903–23; Headmaster, Kenton College, Kenya, 1924–29; Fellow and Syndic, Allahabad University; Member, UP Light Horse, formerly Captain, Lucknow Vol. Rifles. *Publications:* various pamphlets and papers on Indian ornithology and on Indian education. *Recreations:* shooting, fishing, tennis, and natural history. *Address:* 4a Collingham Place, SW5. *T:* Frobisher 6188. *Club:* Athenæum.

Died 6 Dec. 1945.

JESSEL, 1st Baron *cr* 1924, of Westminster; **Herbert Merton Jessel;** 1st Bt *cr* 1917, CB 1919; CMG 1918; TD; MP (U) St Pancras (South), 1896–1906, and 1910–18; contested St George's Westminster bye-election, June 1921; late Capt. 17th Lancers and Major Royal Berks Yeomanry; Hon. Col 1st Royal Fusiliers (City of London Regt), 1905–23; *b* Brighton, 27 Oct. 1866; *y s* of late Rt Hon. Sir George Jessel, Master of the Rolls; *m* 1894, Maud, 5th *d* of late Rt Hon. Sir Julian Goldsmid, Bt, MP; one *s* two *d*. *Educ:* Rugby; New Coll., Oxford. Joined 17th Lancers, 1886; served in India, 1887–90; retired shortly after being elected for St Pancras (South), 1896; carried through the House of Commons, Old Age Pensions Act, 1911, Municipal Elections Act, 1911, and Affiliations Order Act, 1914; carried through the House of Lords, Road Traffic (Driving Licences) Act, 1936; Member of the Public Accounts Committee of the House of Commons, 1910–18; appointed to Government Committee on Prevention and Relief of Distress, Aug. 1914; a Chairman Military Services Committee Panel (Ministry of National Service), June 1918; appointed to Crown Lands Advisory Committee, April 1933; an Alderman for the City of Westminster; Mayor, 1902–03; Hon. Freedom of Westminster, 1948; Emergency Committee, Oct. 1939; DL, JP County of London; Chairman, Hanover Square Division Bench, Westminster,

1930–35; President (Chairman, 1903–15) London Municipal Society; President Metropolitan Mayors' Association; Chairman Budget Protest League, 1909; Hon. Arbitrator Hearts of Oak Benefit Society, 1901–27; rejoined the Army, Oct. 1914, as Remount Conducting Officer; promoted Assistant Commandant, Dec., and Commandant Army Remount Service, with the rank of Lieut-Col, Jan. 1915 (despatches twice, CB, CMG); Deputy Director of Remounts, War Office, Nov. 1918; retired June 1919 with the rank of Colonel in the Army; Controller Horses and Animals Disposals Board, unpaid, 1919–20, Ministry of Supply; London Whip, Unionist Central Office, 1920–27; Officer of Legion of Honour of France; Officer of Order of Leopold, Belgium. *Recreation:* shooting. *Heir: s* Hon. Edward Herbert Jessel. *Address:* 40 Parkside, Knightsbridge, SW1. *Clubs:* Army and Navy, Garrick, Carlton, Beefsteak.

Died 1 Nov. 1950.

JEUDWINE, Lt-Gen. Sir Hugh Sandham, KCB 1918; KBE 1922; CB 1915; TD; RA; Colonel Commandant, RA, since 1923; Hon. Colonel 59th (4th West Lancs) Medium Regiment RA since 1920; DL Surrey; *b* 9 June 1862; *m* 1891, Mary Grace, *d* of late David Meynell; one *d*. *Educ:* Eton; RMA, Woolwich. Entered Army, 1882; Capt. 1891; Major, 1900; Lt-Col 1908; Col 1912; Maj.-Gen. 1916; Lt-Gen. 1923; Instructor School of Gunnery, 1894–99; DAQMG, Cape Colony, 1902; Assist Supt of Experiments, School of Gunnery, 1904; General Staff Officer, War Office, 1904; Dep. Assist Adjt-General, Aldershot Command, 1909; General Staff Officer, 2nd Grade, Staff College, 1912; 1st Grade, Staff College, 1913; served S African War, 1899–1902; District Commandant, and in command of Mobile Column; (Queen's medal 2 clasps; King's medal 2 clasps); European War, 1914–18; General Staff Officer, 1st Grade, First Corps, 1914; 1st Grade, 1st Div., 1914; Brigadier-General, General Staff, Fifth Corps, 1915; Commanded 41st Infantry Brigade, 1915; 55th (West Lancs) Division, 1916–19, Lancashire Division, British Army of the Rhine, 1919 (despatches nine times, promoted Maj.-Gen., CB, KCB, Commander of the Legion of Honour, Commander of the Order of Leopold, Belgian Croix de Guerre); Chief of the General Staff, British Army of the Rhine, 1919; commanded 5th Division on active service in Ireland, 1919–22; (KBE); Director-General of the Territorial Army, 1923–27; retired pay, 1927; gold medallist of the Royal Artillery Institution, 1897, 1907, and 1908; gold medallist of United Service Institution of India, 1908; Fellow of the Huguenot Society of London. *Club:* United Service.

Died 2 Dec. 1942.

JEUDWINE, Lt-Col Wilfrid Wynne, CMG 1916; MD; FRCS (Edin.); late IMS; *b* 19 May 1877. Served NW Frontier, India, 1908 (medal with clasp); European War, 1914–18 (despatches, CMG); Civil Surgeon and Chief Medical Officer, Delhi Province, 1922–23; Prof. Ophthalmic Surgery, King Edward's Medical College, Lahore, 1920–21; Civil Surgeon, Jullundur, 1922; Civil Surgeon, Simla W, 1923–25; retired, 1928. *Address:* Lochaber, Field End, Eastcote, Mx.

Died 22 Jan. 1943.

JHALAWAR, Lt HH Maharaj Rana Sir Shri Rajendra Singh Ji Dev Bahadur of, KCSI 1938; MRAS, ARPS, FRGS, FZS, FRHortS, FRAgS; *b* 15 July 1900; *S* father, Maharaj Rana Sir Bhawani Singh Bahadur, 1929; *m*; one *s*. *Educ:* Mayo College, Ajmer; School of Rural Economy, University of Oxford. Late Lieut in the ITF 11th/19th Hyderabad Regimen (Russel's), now Lt 1/19th Hyderabad Regiment; is a keen Shikari, and has shot many tigers and a few bisons in South India; record shot three tigers in five minutes. Interested in mass education; has a taste for music, agriculture, poetry (Urdu and Hindi, writes under nom de guerre, Makhmoor, and Sudhakar) and fine arts; Member of the Royal Institution of Great Britain, British

Society of Dowsers (is himself a keen Dowser), Royal Agri.-Horticultural Society of India, Calcutta, etc. Is a Knight of the Round Table (England); member of the Standing Committee of the Chamber of Princes, 1932–37; President of All India Khsatriya Mahasabha, 1934–36. Receives a salute of 13 guns. *Recreations:* big-game hunting, shooting, clay-pigeon shooting, photography, fishing, tennis (also interested in cricket, badminton, croquet, squash rackets), and motoring. *Heir:* s Yuvraj Shri Harischandra, *b* Oxford, 27 Sept. 1921. *Address:* Brijnagar, Rajputana, India. *TA:* Jhalendra. *Clubs:* Eccentric; Pinewood Gun, Bisley Gun, London Gun, Stratford-on-Avon Gun, Shri Bhawani, Brijnagar.

Died 2 Sept. 1943.

JIND, Brig. HH Farzand-i-Dilband Rasikh-ul-Itikad Daulat-i-Inglishia, Raja-i-Rajgan Maharaja Sir Ranbir Singh Rajendra Bahadur, GCSI 1937; GCIE 1916; KCSI 1909; *b* 1879; *S* 1887; *m*; two *s*. Belongs to Phulkian family of Sidhu Jats, descended from Phul. State is 1282 square miles in extent, and has a population of 361,812. Enjoys a salute of 15 guns; contributes an infantry batt. to Imperial Defence Contingent, which took part in frontier expeditions of 1897, and served in East Africa, 1914–18, and Afghan frontier in 1919. Offered all resources of State for service of the Crown during European War, 1914–18; placed all resources at HM's disposal at commencement of War of 1939–45. Jind Infantry unit left for intensive training, 19 July 1940, in British India and therefrom proceeded overseas. Raised 2 companies for garrison duty in India—one as an Indian Army Unit and one as Indian States' Forces Unit. Celebrated Diamond Jubilee, March 1947. *Heir: er s* Yuvraj Rajbir Singh, *b* 1918. *Address:* Sangrur, Jind State, Punjab.

Died 31 March 1948.

JINKIN, Paymaster Rear-Adm. Robert Alfred, CB 1930; OBE 1925; RN (retired); *b* 17 Nov. 1876; *e s* of late A. J. Jinkin, Plymouth; *m* 1913, Florence Ruby, *d* of Thornton Fell KC, Victoria, BC; two *d. Educ:* Plymouth Grammar School. Entered RN 1894; served European War (HMS Centurion and King George V), 1914–19 (1914–15 Star, General Service Medal, Victory Medal); Naval Assistant to Accountant General of Navy, 1919–22; Fleet Accountant Officer, Atlantic Fleet, 1922–24; Deputy Paymaster Director General, 1925–29; Port Accountant Officer, Portsmouth, 1930–31; retired list, 1931. *Recreations:* golf, garden. *Address:* The Little Field, Tavistock, Devon.

Died 25 Aug. 1944.

JINNAH, Mahomed Ali; Quaid-i-Azam; Governor-General of Pakistan since 1947; President of Pakistan Constituent Assembly since 1947; *b* 25 Dec. 1876. *Educ:* In India; Lincoln's Inn, England. Called to Bar, 1896; enrolled Advocate, Bombay High Court, 1897. Member Imperial Legislative Council from 1910. President All India Muslim League, 1916, 1920 and since 1934; attended Round Table Conference, 1929–30; Member, Indian Central Legislative Assembly and Leader of Muslim League Party until Aug. 1947. *Publication:* Pakistan.

Died 11 Sept. 1948.

JOB, William Carson; late Member Legislative Council, Newfoundland; *b* St John's, Newfoundland, 4 June 1864; *m* 1892, Edith Warren, St John's, NF; one *s* three *d. Educ:* Uppingham. Newfoundland Shipowner and Merchant; partner in Job Bros, Liverpool, England; Job Bros and Co., St John's, Newfoundland; Member Imperial Economic Committee, London. *Recreations:* fishing, shooting, golf. *Address:* c/o Trade Commissioner for Newfoundland, 58 Victoria Street, SW1. *Club:* Junior Carlton.

Died 25 June 1943.

JODHPUR, Air Vice-Marshal HH Raj Rajeshwar Sarmad-I-Rajhai Hindustan Maharaja Dhiraj Sri Sir Umaid Singhji Sahib Bahadur of, GCSI 1936; GCIE 1930; KCSI 1925; KCVO 1922; Hon. ADC to the King, 1936–46; LLD (Hon.), 1939; Air Vice-Marshal in RAF, 1945; Sovereign of the Marwar State; Head of the Rathor Rajput clan, and one of the leading ruling Princes of India; is Honorary Lt-Gen. in the Army; the younger offshoots of this family are the ruling Princes of Bikaner, Kishengarh, Idar, Rutlam, Sailana, Sitamau, and Jhabua; *b* 8 July 1903; *s* of HH the late Maharaja Dhiraj Sri Sir Sardar Singhji Sahib Bahadur, GCSI; *m* 1921, HH Maharaniji Sri Badan Kanwarji Sahiba, *d* of Rao Bahadur Thakur Jai Singhji of Umednagar; five *s* one *d. Educ:* Mayo College, Ajmere. Ascended the Gaddi, 1918; invested with full ruling powers, 1923; reorganised the Judicial Department and the State Military Forces; introduced a scheme for the extension of primary education; revised land revenue settlement; introduced Provident Fund for the benefit of Raj servants. *Recreations:* polo, fishing, pig-sticking, rackets, and flying. *Heir:* Maharaj Kumar Sri Hanwant Singhji Sahib, *b* 16 June 1923. *Address:* Jodhpur, Rajputana, India.

Died 9 June 1947.

JODRELL, Lt-Col Henry Ramsden, CMG 1917; retired; RH and F. Artillery; 4th *s* of Capt. J. C. F. Ramsden, Willinghurst, Guildford; assumed name of Jodrell by Royal Licence, 1920; *m* 1902, Dorothy Lynch, CBE, *e d* of late Col Sir Edward Thomas Davenant Cotton-Jodrell, KCB; three *d. Educ:* Eton; RM Academy, Woolwich. Joined R. Artillery, 1891; retired, 1907; rejoined RFA European War, 2nd Division Expeditionary Force; invalided Ministry of Munitions, 1916–19 (CMG, Mons medal with clasp, two GS medals, 2nd class Order of St Anne of Russia). *Recreations:* estate management, shooting, fishing, etc. *Address:* Donhead Lodge, Shaftesbury. *T:* Donhead 264.

Died 3 Sept. 1950.

JOEL, Dudley Jack Barnato, MA; MP (C) Borough of Dudley since 1931; *b* 1904; *y s* of late Lt-Col S. B. Joel, JP; *m* 1936, Mrs Esme Ritchie (*d* 1939), *o d* of late J. M. Oldham, Ormidale, Ascot. *Educ:* Repton School; King's College, Cambridge. Travelled extensively in S Africa. *Recreations:* racing, shooting. *Address:* Moulton Paddocks, Newmarket, Suffolk. *T:* Newmarket 218; 74 Brook Street, W1. *T:* Mayfair 4693. *Club:* Royal London Yacht.

Died 28 May 1941.

JOGENDRA SINGH, Sir Sardar, KCSI 1946; Kt 1929; *b* 25 May 1877. Was Minister of Agriculture in the Punjab for 11 years. Minister of Education, Health and Lands, Governor-General's Executive Council, India, 1942. Taluqdar Aira. *Address:* Delhi/Simla, India; Aira Holme, Simla E.

Died 3 Dec. 1946.

JOHNS, Lt-Col Whitfield Glanville, DSO 1918; a General Manager, Lloyds Bank; Chairman of West London Hospital since 1933, and Chairman of the Bankers' Health Insurance Society; *b* 1877; *m* 1st, Margaret (*d* 1932), 3rd *d* of Josiah Wilkinson; two *s*; 2nd, 1933, Dr Nora Leesmith. Served European War, 1914–18 (despatches, DSO). *Address:* 71 Lombard Street, EC3; Old Parsonage, Fernhurst, Haslemere. *Clubs:* Devonshire, Alpine.

Died 8 March 1941.

JOHNSON, Amy, CBE 1930; BA, ARAeSI; FRGS; FSE; MWES; aviator; *e d* of John William Johnson and Amy Johnson, Hull; *m* 1932, J. A. Mollison (from whom she obtained a divorce, 1938). *Educ:* Sheffield University (Degree in Economics). Commenced flying, Sept. 1928; took Pilot's A Licence at London Aeroplane Club; Engineer's Licence A (for rigging), C (for engines) also obtained; made an Associate of the Royal Aeronautical Society, April 1930, and a member of the Women's

Engineering Society, May 1930; obtained Pilot's Commercial Licence in Australia, June 1930; first woman to fly alone from London to Australia, 1930, setting up a new record for a solo flight to India (Karachi in six days); flew to Japan and back, setting up records both ways, 1931; flew solo to Cape Town and back, making new records both ways, 1932; England to America non-stop via North Atlantic, with J. A. Mollison, in 39 hours, July 1933; President's gold medal from Society of Engineers, 1931; Egyptian gold medal for valour, 1930; International League of Aviators' Women's Trophy for 1930; Segrave Trophy for 1932; Holder (with J. A. Mollison) of present England-India record of 22 hours; regained London-Cape records in solo flight to Capetown via West Coast, and return via East Coast, 1936; Winner of Royal Aero Club's Gold Medal, 1936; President Women's Engineering Society, 1935–36–1937; Member of Guild of Air Pilots and Navigators of the British Empire. *Publication:* Sky Roads of the World, 1939. *Recreations:* flying, riding, swimming. *Clubs:* Royal Aero, Forum (Pres. Technical Section).

Died 5 Jan. 1941.

JOHNSON, (Arthur) Basil (Noel), MusD, Lambeth, 1928; BA (Oxon); Hon. FRCO; *b* Oxford, 1861; *γ s* of late Very Rev. G. H. S. Johnson, Dean of Wells, and Lucy, *d* of late Admiral Robert O'Brien; *m* 1891, Elizabeth Ann, *d* of Right Rev. Bishop Percival, late Bishop of Hereford; no *c. Educ:* Malvern College (Classical Exhibitioner, Organist to the School, 1876–79); Magdalen College, Oxford (Academical Clerkship). Second Class Classical Moderations; BA 1882; Royal College of Music, 1883–84. Organist, St James', Norlands, and St Gabriel's, Pimlico, 1885; Organist and Music Master, Rugby School, 1886–1914; Conductor, Rugby Philharmonic Society 27 years, Rugby Orchestral Society 8 years, Rugby School Subscription Concerts 17 years; Precentor and Organist, Eton College, 1914–26; Examiner Associated Board, RAM and RCM. *Publication:* Part-Songs. *Recreations:* used to be painting in water-colours, tennis, cycling, motoring. *Address:* Judge's Lodgings, Wells, Somerset. *T:* Wells 2249.

Died 10 Dec. 1950.

JOHNSON, Col Arthur Morrell, CBE 1939; MC, TD, MD; *b* 22 Nov. 1887; *s* of late Dr Daniel McIntosh Johnson, Tatamagouche, Nova Scotia, Canada; *m* 1919, Hilda Mabel Moscrop, *d* of Hugh Moscrop Robinson; one *s* one *d. Educ:* Dalhousie University, Halifax, Nova Scotia. Served European war, 1914–18; saw active service in Egypt, Gallipoli, Sinai, France, Belgium (MC); served in War of 1939–45, France, Belgium, MEF; joined Territorial Army, 1914; in practice in Bury, Lancs, as physician and surgeon since 1911; Hon. Consulting Surgeon, Bury Infirmary. *Address:* Hazeldene, Bury, Lancs. *T:* Bury 384. *Clubs:* Palatine, Bury.

Died 18 March 1946.

JOHNSON, Sir Arthur Palmer, Kt 1932; MA; *b* 1865; *s* of late Sir Samuel George Johnson, Nottingham; *m* 1894, Annie, *d* of Richard Challands, Nottingham; two *d. Educ:* Emmanuel College, Cambridge. Admitted Solicitor, 1891; Town Clerk of Hampstead, 1893–1931; President of National Association of Local Government Officers, 1924–31, and Chairman of the National Executive, 1911–32; First Hon. Freeman, Borough of Hampstead, 1931. *Recreation:* golf. *Address:* The Wong, 70 Maresfield Gardens, NW3. *T:* Hampstead 3084. *Club:* Oxford and Cambridge.

Died 21 June 1944.

JOHNSON, Basil; *see* Johnson, A. B. N.

Johnson, Borough; *see* Johnson, E. B.

JOHNSON, Dennis R.; *see* Ross-Johnson.

JOHNSON, Eric Townsend, BA, LLB; Colonial Civil Servant (retired); *b* 13 Nov. 1875; *s* of late Peter Johnson; *m* Ruby Violet, *d* of late Leopold Yates; two *s* one *d. Educ:* Sedbergh; Trinity Hall, Cambridge. Barrister-at-law, 1902; joined Northern Circuit; Resident Magistrate, Kenya, 1915–29; Acting Judge, Kenya, 1924–25 and 1928–29; Puisne Judge, HBM Court for Zanzibar, 1929–34; Member of Court of Appeal for Eastern Africa; Judge of High Court, Nyasaland, 1934–37; retired 1937. *Recreations:* sailing, fishing. *Address:* Ragleth House, Little Stretton, Church Stretton, Shropshire. *T:* Church Stretton, 138. *Clubs:* Oxford and Cambridge Musical; Mombasa Yacht; English, Zanzibar.

Died 17 June 1942.

JOHNSON, (Ernest) Borough, RP; Master Draughtsman with the lead pencil; Ex-Member Royal Society of British Artists, PS, RI, ROI, RBC, Original Member Society of Graphic Art, Art Workers' Guild, etc; *b* Shifnal, Salop; *γ s* of late Dr C. H. Johnson, JP; *m* Esther, *e d* of Rev. James George, of Norfolk. *Educ:* Slade under Legros, and Herkomer's School. Formerly Art Prof. Univ. of London (Bedford College), and Headmaster of Art Dept at the South-Western Institute, Chelsea, and other London Art Schools; Exhibitor for many years and Silver Medallist for portraits at Paris Salons, New Gallery, Roy. Acad., Internat. Soc. and Royal Society of Portrait Painters, London, and various International Exhibitions; Painter of figure subjects of a realistic and dramatic type; works bought for the Melbourne Nat. Gall., Adelaide Nat. Galls., also French Government for Municipal Gallery at St Quentin, Aberdeen Municipal Gallery, Nottingham Art Gallery, Wolverhampton Municipal Art Gallery, 1948, and other public Galleries, etc.; represented by drawings and lithographs in the British and South Kensington Museums; National Portrait Gallery with a portrait of Prof. Herkomer, RA, and in Moscow Municipal Gallery by The Spirit of Russia; sixty water-colour drawings and many pencil drawings of Blitzed London acquired by the Corporation of the City for the Guildhall Museum, 1945. *Publications:* Drawings of Michael Angelo; The Woodcuts of Frederick Sandys; The Technique of the Lead Pencil, 1927; Figure and Portraiture in Pencil, Chalk and Charcoal; A Portfolio of Rapid Studies from the Nude; The Art of the Pencil; and articles in The Studio Magazine, etc. *Recreations:* travelling abroad, painting and sketching, with his artist wife, collecting antiques and curios, old English furniture and Chinese porcelain. *Address:* 22 Westbourne Park Road, W2. *T:* Bayswater 7029.

Died 30 July 1949.

JOHNSON, Francis H.; *see* Hernaman-Johnson.

JOHNSON, Maj.-Gen. Frank Ernest, CSI 1919; CMG 1915; DSO 1900; RA; *b* 29 Jan. 1861; *m* 1903, Alexa, *e d* of late Sir W. Macpherson, Judge of the High Court, Calcutta; two *s.* Entered Army, 1880; Capt. 1889; Major, 1898; Lt-Col 1905; Colonel, 1910; AQMG, 2nd Division, 1911; Brig.-Gen.; commanding RA Lahore Division, Dec. 1911; Major-Gen. RA 3rd Army, BEF, France, Oct. 1915; Inspector RH and RFA in India, Oct. 1916; served NW Frontier, India, 1897–98 (medal with two clasps); China, 1900 (despatches, medal with clasp, DSO); European War, 1914–18 (despatches, CMG); retired, hon. rank of Maj.-Gen., 1918. *Address:* Holt Bank, Alverstoke, Hants.

Died 12 July 1945.

JOHNSON, Lt-Col Sir Frank William Frederick, KBE 1941; DSO 1918; *b* 1866; *s* of F. W. Johnson, MRCS; *m* Jane, *d* of Capt. J. H. Day, Cowes. Commanded Pioneer Corps for occupation of Rhodesia, 1890; Chief Staff Officer Langberg Rebellion, 1896 (despatches, thanked by Cape Govt); European War, 1914–18, as Lieut-Col Royal Sussex Regt (despatches, DSO); commanded troops and administered martial law,

Lahore, 1919 (thanked by Punjab Govt); Member Legislative Assembly, Southern Rhodesia, 1927–28. *Publication:* Great Days, 1940. *Clubs:* East India and Sports, Royal Automobile; Norfolk, Royal N and S Yacht.

Died 6 Sept. 1943.

JOHNSON, Sir George, Kt 1936; MIEE; JP; Chairman of Johnson and Fletcher Ltd, Engineers, Bulawayo, S Rhodesia; *b* 30 Sept. 1867; *s* of William Johnson, JP, and Mildred Matilda Dawson; *m* 1906, Florence Payne; two *s* one *d. Educ:* King's Lynn; Bury St Edmunds. Has been in business at Bulawayo, S Rhodesia, since 1897; Founder of Assoc. Chambers of Commerce of Rhodesia, 5 times President; also 19 times President of Bulawayo Chamber of Commerce; Chairman of Defence Commission, Southern Rhodesia, 1916, and of Customs and Tariff Commission, 1935. *Address:* Box 224, Bulawayo, S Rhodesia. *TA:* Motor, Bulawayo. *Clubs:* East India and Sports; Bulawayo, Bulawayo.

Died 10 July 1947.

JOHNSON, George Lindsay, MA, MD, BS, FRCS Eng.; late Capt. SAMC; Ophthalmic Surgeon to HM Forces in Natal; *b* 10 July 1853; *y s* of late William H. Johnson of Manchester; *m;* one *s. Educ:* Owens College, Manchester; Caius Coll., Cambridge. FRS, Italy. Corresponding Member Fred Wilhelm Academy of Scientific Research, Berlin; late Examiner in Theoretical and Applied Optics to the SM Co., London; late Surg. to New Coll.; Consulting Ophthalmic Surg. Western General Dispensary; Hon. Fellow American Academy of Ophthalmology; late Member of Council, Royal Photographic Society. *Publications:* Treatise on Glaucoma; contributions to Knapp's Archives of Ophthalmology; Photographic Optics and Colour Photography, 5th ed.; Pocket Atlas and Textbook of the Fundus Oculi, 2nd ed.; The Weird Adventures of Prof. Delapine; The Land of the Little Moons; various articles in Proceedings of the Royal Zoological Society, London; author of Observations on European Leprosy; and Ophthalmology of the Mammalia, Phil. Trans. Royal Society, 1901; Ophthalmology of the Reptilia and Amphibia, Transactions Royal Society, 1924; The Great Problem and the Evidence for its Solution, 2nd ed., 1935, American ed., 1936; Photography in Natural Colours (4th ed.); also inventor of the macula sensitometer and various other optical instruments of precision. *Recreations:* chiefly scientific experimental work and research; also motoring, photography and exploring. *Address:* 28 Onslow Gardens, SW7.

Died Aug. 1943.

JOHNSON, H. C. Brooke; Director of Rubber and Coconut Companies; Governor of St Edward's School; *b* 30 May 1873; *s* of Capt. W. F. Johnson, RN; *m* 1918, Phyllis Loveday, *d* of Col F. J. H. Wynch, Indian Army; two *s. Educ:* St Edward's School, Oxford; Nancy, France; Cannstadt, Germany. Chartered Mercantile Bank of India, London, and China, 1891–93; Assistant Treasury Department, Sarawak Civil Service, 1894; Acting Postmaster-General and Magistrate Court of Requests, 1897; Acting Treasurer, 1898; Clerk to the Supreme Court Judge, 1900; member of committee administering the Government of Sarawak during the absences of HH the Rajah, 1898–99, and 1901–02; retired from Sarawak Civil Service, 1902; European Adviser to the Pangeran of Lawas (Borneo), 1904, retiring from position and receiving compensation through Foreign Office when Lawas was taken over by the Rajah of Sarawak, 1905; Assistant Commander Special Constabulary, R Division, Metropolitan Police Area, Aug. to Oct. 1914; Ordinary Seaman, Royal Naval Division, Oct. 1914 to Jan. 1915; Lieut Army Service Corps, Jan. 1915; Captain, Aug. 1915; Assistant Secretary Ministry of Information, 1918; demobilised,

May 1919. Secretary and Manager, The Hurlingham Club, 1925–34. *Address:* 9 Glenmore House, Richmond Hill, Surrey. *Club:* Hurlingham.

Died 30 Nov. 1949.

JOHNSON, Brig.-Gen. Sir Henry (Allen William), 4th Bt *cr* 1818; CB 1917; Col and Hon. Brig.-Gen. in the Army; retired pay; late Col of General Staff 8th Division Irish Command, 1902–06; late Lt-Col commanding 1st Batt. Yorks Light Infantry; AAG Central Force, HD, 5 Aug. 1914–19 May 1915; DAG Central Force, HD 29 May 1915 to 11 March 1916; and DAG Eastern Command, 12 March 1916 to 31 March 1918; *b* 9 Oct. 1855; *S* father, 1883; *m* 1st, Ella, *d* of T. Dyson, Bank of Bengal, 1886 (drowned in wreck of SS Roumania off coast of Portugal, 1892); one *s;* 2nd, Georgina, *d* of late Hon. A. C. Orde-Powlett of Thorney Hall, Leyburn, Yorkshire, 1897; one *d. Educ:* Cheltenham. Served in Jowaki campaign, 1877; Afghanistan, 1878–80; Burmah, 1886–87. *Heir: s* Henry Allen Beaumont [*b* 3 Jan. 1887; Lt-Col late Commanding 8th KGO Light Cavalry, Indian Army; retired; *m* 1917, Dorothy Nora, *y d* of late M. C. Gurney, CMG, MVO; two *d*]. *Address:* 12a Barkston Gardens, SW5. *T:* Frobisher 3253.

Died 10 April 1944.

JOHNSON, Henry Harrold; author; *b* Leicester, 14 Dec. 1869; *s* of Joseph Johnson and Frances Harrold; Freeman of Leicester; *m* 1903, Gertrude Helen Watson; three *s* two *d. Educ:* Wyggeston Boys' School, Leicester; BA (London), 1889, the Prizeman, 1st Class Hons, English Language and Literature; Trinity College, Cambridge; La Sorbonne, Paris (University of France); Leipzig University; Manchester College, Oxford. French and German Master, Merchant Taylors' School, Crosby; Minister of Waverley Road Church, Small Heath, Birmingham, 1897–1900; travelled and lectured in USA, 1900–01; conducted the negotiations with Board of Education, which resulted in the introduction of Moral Instruction and Training in Schools, and wrote Report on Moral Instruction and Training in French State Schools; Secretary of the Moral Education League, 1902–13; Hon. Secretary International Moral Education Congress Executive Council, 1912–13; Minister of Oat Street Chapel, Evesham, 1914–19; started the first model Interdenominational Social Service Union, Evesham, 1916; Minister of Cross Street Chapel, Manchester, 1919–28; originated the Wayside Pulpit Thought for the Week, 1920; Minister of Hartington Road Church, Buxton, 1929–39. *Publications:* The Road-Makers and other poems, 1902; The Bridge-Builders and other poems, 1907; The House of Life (Interpretations of the Symbolical paintings of G. F. Watts), 1911; Moral Instruction in Elementary Schools in England and Wales, 1908; A Short Life of Jesus, 1933; Collected Poems in eight volumes, The Voice of One (1) English Lyrics, 1933; (2) Love Lyrics, 1934; (3) Labour Lyrics, 1934; (4) Devotional Lyrics, 1935; (5) Nature Lyrics, 1936; (6) Empire Lyrics, 1937; (7) World Lyrics, 1937; (8) Human Lyrics, 1938; In French—Le Problème d'un Enseignement moral efficace (Lecture at Sorbonne, Paris); sundry articles in Contemporary Review, Hibbert Journal, International Journal of Ethics, etc. *Recreations:* music and walks. *Address:* Iona, Wye Grove, Buxton.

Died 9 Aug. 1940.

JOHNSON, Henry Langhorne, MA, CBE 1918; Chairman and Managing Director of Midland Coal and Cannel Company, 10 Arthur Street, EC4; Chairman HR Howes & Co., Ltd; Chairman of Managing Director Fakenham Gas Co; *b* Whitkirk, 30 Jan. 1874; *s* of J. E. Johnson; *m* 1906, Muriel, *d* of Worthington Church, of Warlingham; two *d. Educ:* Leeds Grammar School; Keble College, Oxford (Scholar). Assistant-Master Hurstpierpoint College; Second Master, 1902–05; Head of all Church Army Work on the Western Front, 1916–18. *Publications:* Hurst Register; Love the Logician; various Essays and Poems. *Recreations:* music and gardening. *Address:* (temp.): Coombe Lea Hotel, Bickley. *TA:* Warleigh, London. *T:* Mansion House 5139.

Died 12 Nov. 1945.

JOHNSON, Herbert; JP; *b* 1856; 2nd *s* of Rev. H. I. Johnson; *m* 1912, Violet Charlotte, MBE (*d* 1921), *e d* of late John Fletcher of Saltoun, and *widow* of Capt. Bertram Meeking, 10th Hussars. High Sheriff of Hampshire, 1920. *Address:* Meadowlands, Weeke, Winchester.

Died 2 April 1949.

JOHNSON, Hiram Warren; Senator of United States since 1917; *b* Sacramento, California, 2 Sept. 1866; *s* of Grove Laurence Johnson and Annie de Montfredy; *m* 1886, Minnie L. McNeal, of Sacramento. *Educ:* University of California. Began as shorthand reporter; studied law in father's office; admitted to Californian Bar, 1888; practised in Sacramento and San Francisco; Governor of California, 1911–15; re-elected for term 1915–19, but resigned in 1917; a founder of Progressive Party, 1912. *Address:* 857 Green Street, San Francisco, California.

Died 6 Aug. 1945.

JOHNSON, John Charles S.; *see* Sperrin-Johnson.

JOHNSON, Raymond, OBE 1919; MB, BS (Lond.), FRCS (Eng.). Consulting Surgeon to University College Hospital. *Publications:* various publications on surgical subjects. *Address:* Burdenshot Gate, Worplesdon, Guildford. *T:* Worplesdon, 144.

Died 26 Oct. 1944.

JOHNSON, Hon. William Dartnell; Director, Central Co-operative Organisation of the State (WA); Organiser of Co-operative Federation of Australia, Canberra, Dec. 1943; *b* Wanganui, New Zealand, 9 Oct. 1872; *s* of George G. Johnson; *m* Jessie, *y d* of Duncan McCallum, Woy Woy, New S Wales; one *s* three *d*. *Educ:* State School, Turakina, NZ. Carpenter by trade; migrated to Western Australia; followed his trade and gold-mining for number of years on Eastern gold-fields. Became active wheat and wool farmer and was first Member for Kalgoorlie in Legislative Assembly; Minister for Works, 1904–06 and 1911–14; Minister for Lands and Agriculture, 1914–17; re-entered Parliament as Member for Guildford, 1924; Speaker of Legislative Assembly, Western Australia, 1938–39; Chm. Western Australian Parliamentary Labour Party since 1924. *Recreations:* riding, bowling. *Address:* 58 Ord Street, West Perth, Western Australia.

Died 26 Jan. 1948.

JOHNSTON, Edward, CBE 1939; *b* Uruguay, 11 Feb. 1872; 2nd *s* of Fowell Buxton Johnston, Captain 3rd DG; *m* 1903, Greta Kathleen Greig; three *d*. *Educ:* privately. Studied Medicine, Edinburgh University, 1896–97 (gave up on account of health); studied pen shapes of letters in early MSS. Brit. Museum, 1898–99. Teacher of the first classes in Formal Penmanship and Lettering, LCC Central School, 1899–1912; Teacher at RCA since 1901; Designed block letters based on classical Roman Capital proportions (for London Electric Railways) 1916; Pres. Arts and Crafts Exhibition Society, 1933–36. *Publications:* Writing and Illuminating, and Lettering, 1906; Manuscript and Inscription Letters, 1909. *Address:* Cleves, Ditchling, Sussex.

Died 26 Nov. 1944.

JOHNSTON, Edward Hamilton, DLitt; Boden Professor of Sanskrit, Oxford, since 1937; *b* 26 March 1885; 2nd *s* of late R. E. Johnston, Governor of the Bank of England, 1909–11; *m* 1924, Iris Olivia Helena, 3rd *d* of late Sir Henry May, GCMG, Clare Priory, Suffolk; three *s* three *d*. *Educ:* Eton; New College, Oxford. Indian Civil Service (Bihar and Orissa), 1909–24.

Publications: Editions and translations of Sanskrit poems of Asvaghosha, 1928–1936; Early Samkhya, 1937. *Address:* Balliol College, Oxford. *T:* Oxford 47244.

Died 24 Oct. 1942.

JOHNSTON, Lt-Col Francis Gawen Dillon, CMG 1919; DSO 1916; TD; RA; *b* 1875; *s* of W. H. Johnston, Ealing; *m* 1908, Jessie Muriel (*d* 1929), *er d* of late David S. Carson, St Oswald's, Kilmacolm; two *s* three *d*. *Educ:* Clifton College. Engineer, Sir W. G. Armstrong Whitworth & Co., Elswick, 1894–1927; served South African War, 1900–01 (Queen's medal 3 clasps); European War, 1915–19 (CMG, DSO). A Baron of the Holy Roman Empire in right of his great-grandmother, Elizabeth Dillon, *d* of Sir John Dillon, 1st Bt of Lismullen, Co. Meath. *Address:* c/o Lloyds Bank, Newcastle-on-Tyne.

Died 8 Dec. 1945.

JOHNSTON, Sir Frederick William, KCIE 1927; CSI 1913; CIE 1911; *b* 2 Nov. 1872; *s* of late Reverend A. Orrock Johnston, DD; *m* 1905, Gertrude Helen, *d* of Lt-Col J. Young; one *s*. *Educ:* Kelvinside Academy, Glasgow; Trinity Hall, Cambridge (BA 1894). Agent to the Governor-General and Chief Commissioner in Baluchistan, 1922–27; Resident in the Persian Gulf, Bushire, 1928–29. *Recreations:* golf, lawn tennis. *Address:* Southern Lodge, St Andrews, Fife. *T:* St Andrews 676. *Clubs:* Royal and Ancient Golf, St Andrews.

Died 1 May 1947.

JOHNSTON, George Francis, MD Edin.; MRCP London; *b* St John, New Brunswick, 1860; *s* of Hugh Johnston; *m* Mary Alice, *d* of late James Merryweather; one *s*. *Educ:* King William's College, Isle of Man; Edinburgh University; Paris. Hon. Consulting Physician to the National Sanatorium Association; Consulting Physician to the Hospital for Diseases of the Nervous System, Maida Vale, W; Consulting Physician, Mount Vernon Hospital for Consumption. *Publications:* various articles in Lancet, Practitioner, etc., on Diseases of the Nervous System. *Address:* Tilmore Croft, Petersfield.

Died 1 Nov. 1943.

JOHNSTON, Maj.-Gen. George Jameson, CB 1915; CMG 1917; CBE 1920; VD; *b* 24 Oct. 1868; *m* 1894, Margaret, *d* of Charles Hobson, Melbourne; two *s* one *d*. Served S African War, 1899–1900 and 1902 (Queen's medal 3 clasps); European War, Dardanelles and France, 1915–17 (despatches, CB), also 1916–18 (CMG); Military Administrator, German New Guinea, 1917–20; GOC 3rd Australian Div. 1922–27; Major-General, 1923. *Address:* 7 Balaclava Road, East St Kilda, Melbourne, Australia. *Club:* Athenæum (Melbourne).

Died 23 May 1949.

JOHNSTON, Brig.-Gen. George Napier, CB 1924; CMG 1918; DSO 1916; late Royal Artillery; *b* Quebec, Canada, Aug. 1867; *s* of late Peter Johnston, JP, Quebec; *m* Hilda Stairs (*d* 1940), Halifax, Nova Scotia; one *s* one *d*. *Educ:* Royal Military Coll., Kingston. Commissioned, 1888; since then Adjutant, five years; Gunnery Instructor, Punjab, India, three years; Artillery Staff Officer, New Zealand, 1904–07; served in West Indies, Canada, United Kingdom, India, Egypt, New Zealand; Director of Artillery, New Zealand, 1911; when European War broke out organised New Zealand Divisional Artillery, and commanded the Artillery of the New Zealand and Australian Division throughout Gallipoli campaign, and New Zealand Artillery in France and Flanders till end of War; commanded New Zealand Division, Cologne, Germany, till demobilisation; commanded RA 52nd Lowland Division, 1920–24; retired, 1924 (DSO, CB, CMG, Bt Col, despatches eight times, Legion of Honour, Croix d'Officier). *Recreations:* fishing, golf, sailing. *Clubs:* Dar-es-Salaam, Tanganyika.

Died 3 April 1947.

JOHNSTON, Major Robert, VC; late Capt. Imperial Light Horse; *b* 13 Aug. 1872; *s* of Robert Johnston, QC, of Laputa, Co. Donegal. *Educ:* King William's College, Isle of Man. 5th Batt. Royal Inniskilling Fusiliers, 1890–94; served S Africa, 1899–1901 (dangerously wounded siege of Ladysmith); VC at Elandslaagte (King's and Queen's medals); Commandant Concentration Camp, Middelburg, 1902; District Land Commissioner, Eastern Transvaal, 1903; Irish Prison Service, 1911; Commandant Prisoners of War, Oldcastle, and Major, General List, 1914–15; Governor HM Convict Prison, Maryborough, 1915; Resid. Magistrate, Co. Roscommon, 1918; Co. Clare, 1920; retired on change of Government; Farming 1922; Thoroughbred cattle breeding 1926. *Recreations:* Irish Rugby 1893; English Rugby XV in South Africa, 1896, Transvaal, 1897; fly-fishing, golf, etc. *Address:* Ballygallon, Innistiogue, Co. Kilkenny.

Died 24 March 1950.

JOHNSTON, Sir Thomas Alexander, 11th Bt *cr* 1626, of Caskieben; *b* 15 Dec. 1857; *S* cousin, 1921; *m*; five *s* two *d*. Mobile Bar Pilot; retired 1933. *Recreation:* fishing. *Heir: s* Thomas Alexander, *b* 3 May 1888. *Address:* 406 Eslava Street, Mobile, Alabama, USA.

Died 20 Dec. 1950.

JOHNSTON, Maj.-Gen. Walter Edward Wilson-, CB 1927; CIE 1919; CBE 1923; DSO 1916; Indian Army, retired; Colonel of 4/11th Sikh Regiment, 1932–46; *b* 27 Oct. 1878; *s* of late Lt-Col J. Wilson-Johnston, IMS, Oxton, Cheshire; *m* 1919, Edith Maud, *d* of late Capt. Francis Gilbert Jones, RN; one *s* two *d*. *Educ:* Rugby; RMC, Sandhurst. Served China, 1900 (medal); European War (Mesopotamia), 1915–18 (despatches five times, CIE, DSO, Bt Lt-Col, Order of White Eagle of Serbia with swords); Waziristan, 1919–21, 1921–23 (medal, two clasps, despatches, CBE); Dep. Dir of Staff Duties, AHQ, India, 1923–24; GSO 1, India Office, 1924–27; Comdr Razmak Bde, India, 1927–29; Commander Ambala Brigade Area, 1929–31; Maj.-Gen. 1931; retired, 1933. Defence Medal, 1940–45. *Address:* c/o Grindlay & Co., 54 Parliament St, SW1.

Died 30 July 1948.

JOHNSTON, Hon. Mr Justice (William John), KC 1911; MA, LLB; *b* 1869; *s* of late James Johnston, JP, Dunarnon, Belfast; *m* 1894, Kathleen, 2nd *d* of late William King, Belfast; one *s*. *Educ:* National School, Magherafelt; Methodist College, Belfast; Queen's College, Belfast. BA (Royal University) 1888; MA 1889; LLB 1891. Called to Bar, 1892; joined North-East Circuit; Editor of the New Irish Jurist, 1900; Irish Law Times, 1906; Counsel to the Irish Commissioners of Public Works and the Treasury in Ireland, 1907; contested (Lib.) South Derry, Dec. 1910; entered the Pembroke (Dublin) Urban Council as a Reform Candidate, Jan. 1911; CC Judge of Monaghan and Fermanagh, 1911, and of Monaghan and Louth, 1921–24; Judge of High Court, Irish Free State, 1924–39; Judge of Supreme Court, Eire, 1939–40; retired from judiciary, 1940; Member of the Irish Judiciary Committee, 1923; Chairman of the Compensation (Personal Injuries) Committee, 1923; Commissioner of Charitable Donations and Bequests, 1940. *Publications:* Law of Local Government in Ireland, 1899; Handbook of Land Purchase, 1903; The Labourers (Ireland) Acts, 1906. *Recreation:* walking. *Address:* 61 Lansdowne Road, Dublin. *T:* Dublin 63056.

Died 29 Nov. 1940.

JOHNSTONE, Lt-Col Bede, DSO 1918; *b* 15 Aug. 1877; *e surv. s* of late J. J. S. Johnstone, MA, MD; *m* 1912, Gladys, *y d* of late John Fort Jowitt, Ceylon; no *c*. *Educ:* Prior Park, Bath; Ampleforth, Yorks. Enlisted Gloucestershire Regt, 1895; gazetted R. W Kent Regt, 1901; West African Frontier Force, 1905–09; served S African War (King's and Queen's medals, despatches);

European War, 1914–19 (wounded, despatches thrice, 1914–15 medal, British and Allied War medals, DSO); retired pay, 1931. *Address:* c/o Lloyds Bank, 6 Pall Mall, SW1.

Died 21 Dec. 1942.

JOHNSTONE, Brig.-Gen. Francis Buchanan, DSO 1900; *b* 2 Feb. 1863; *s* of late David Johnstone of Croy, Row, Dumbartonshire; *m* 1887, Edith Arethusa, *d* of late Frederick Padwick of West Thorney, Sussex; one *d*. Entered Army, RA, 1882; Capt. 1890; Major, 1899; Lt-Col 1908; served South Africa, 1899–1900 (despatches, DSO); European War, 1914–15; Balkan Expedition (wounded); retired pay. *Club:* Naval and Military.

Died 14 Nov. 1947.

JOHNSTONE, Rt Hon. Harcourt; PC 1943; MP Middlesbrough West since 1940; Secretary, Department of Overseas Trade, since 1940; *b* 19 May 1895; *o s* of late Hon. Sir Alan Johnstone, GCVO. *Educ:* Eton; Balliol College, Oxford, MA. Served European War; MP (L) East Willesden, 1923–24, South Shields, 1931–35. *Address:* 23 Gayfere Street, SW1. *T:* Abbey 4703.

Died 1 March 1945.

JOHNSTONE, J. Alfred; Hon. Fellow TCL; *b* Ireland, 1861; *s* of late Rev. J. W. Johnstone, MA, Rector of Michelstown; *m d* of late Ven. P. Teulon Beamish. *Educ:* Dublin University. *Publications:* Dreams that were not all Dreams; Touch, Phrasing and Interpretation; Modern Tendencies and Old Standards in Musical Art; The Art of Teaching Pianoforte-playing; Elementary Phrasing, with Examples; How to Use the Pedal; Essentials in Pianoplaying; Individuality in Piano Touch; Rubato; Notes on Beethoven's Sonatas; The Beauty of Life (Poems), 1936; Everybody's Guide to Optimism; and many other works. *Recreations:* motoring, travelling. *Address:* Killinear, Sidmouth.

Died 21 March 1941.

JOHNSTONE, Robert, CMG 1917; ISO 1912; *b* 1861; *s* of J. M. Johnstone, MD, and Susannah Pierce; *m* 1886, Helena Victoria Orrett (*d* 1924); one *s* one *d*. *Educ:* Bath; Edinburgh. Joined Civil Service, Jamaica, 1878; Assist Colonial Secretary, 1906; Collector General of Excise, Internal Revenue and Customs, Stamp Commissioner and Comptroller Widows' and Orphans' Pensions, Jamaica, 1919; retired, 1923; acted Colonial Sec. numerous occasions, including period of Great War; held dormant Commission (29 Aug. 1916) to administer Government of Jamaica in absence of Governor and Colonial Secretary; acted as Governor of Jamaica three and a half months in 1917, one month 1918, and two months 1919; was a nominated Member of the Privy Council, and *ex officio* Member of the Legislative Council, and President of the Marine Board, and member of other official Boards; JP Kingston; represented the West Indies at Imperial Statistical Conference in London, 1920; one of three Members of Legislative Council, Jamaica, appointed to attend Canada-West Indies Trade Conference at Ottawa, 1920; at one time Rear-Commodore Royal Jamaica Yacht Club. *Publications:* Nelson and the West Indies; papers in local journals. *Clubs:* West Indian; Royal Jamaica Yacht.

Died 21 Aug. 1944.

JOICEY-CECIL, Lord John (Pakenham); *see* Cecil.

JOLL, Cecil Augustus, MS, MB, BSc (Lond.), MCh, MD, BSc (Bristol); FRCS (Eng.); Senior Surgeon to the Royal Free Hospital and Lecturer on Surgery; Senior Surgeon to the Miller Hospital; Senior Surgeon to Royal Cancer Hospital; Consulting Surgeon to the Royal Bucks Hospital, St Luke's Hospital, Melton Mowbray Hospital, Welwyn Garden City Hospital, Thames Ditton Cottage Hospital, The Manor House Hospital, Golders Green, and to the Horton Hospital, Epsom; Hunterian Professor, Royal College of Surgeons, 1923 and 1939, and Member of Council, 1939; 2nd *s* of W. F. Joll, Bristol; *m* 1st, 1924, Laura Merriall (*d* 1931), *d* of late

Louis Winsole, JP, Liverpool, and Frodsham, Cheshire; one *s*; 2nd, 1936, Antonia, *yr d* of F. H. Ramsden, Lanchester Court, W2; one *s*. *Educ*: privately; University College, Bristol; University College Hospital, London; London Hospital; Paris. Marshall, Tibbits Martyn and Clark Prizeman, Committee's gold medal, University gold medal at MB, BS, with honours in Medicine, Surgery, Pathology, and Forensic Medicine and Hygiene. Senior House Surgeon, Royal Infirmary, Leicester; House Physician, General Hospital, Birmingham; Senior Resident Medical Officer, Royal Free Hospital; Surgeon-in-Chief, Majestic Hospital, Paris, 1914–15; Senior Surgeon to the Richmond Military Hospital, and Surgeon to the End sleigh Place Hospital for Officers; Surgeon to the Michie Hospital and to the Maxillo-Facial Hospital; Consulting Surgeon to the Richmond Military Hospital; Operating and Consulting Surgeon to the Brook War Hospital; Temporary Captain RAMC (Surgical Specialist); FRSM. *Publications*: The Diseases of the Thyroid Gland, 1932; Recent Advances in the Aetiology, Diagnosis, and Treatment of Cancer, Fox Memorial Lecture, 1933; The Diagnosis and Treatment of Carcinoma of the Stomach; The Technique of Operation for Carcinoma Coli; A Plea for an Eclectic Attitude; Tinel's Nerve Wounds (Editor); co-author Aids to Surgery; co-author Thyroid Grafting and Treatment of Exophthalmic Goitre; co-author Article, Thyroid Surgery, Encyclopædia of Surgery; Gunshot Wounds of Skull; various articles in Medical Annual, etc. *Recreation:* ornithology. *Address:* 64 Harley Street, W1. *T:* Langham 4242 and 2514. *TA:* Thyroid, Wesdo, London.

Died 25 Jan. 1945.

JOLLIFFE, Arthur Ernest, MA Oxon; *b* Oxford, 23 Jan. 1871; 6th *s* of Henry Jolliffe, Oxford; *m* Eliza, 2nd *d* of James Ostler, Oxford; one *s* two *d*. *Educ:* City of Oxford Sch.; Balliol Coll., Oxford, Scholar. Fellow of Corpus Christi College, Oxford, 1891–1920. Hon. Fellow, 1931; Assistant-Tutor, Jesus College, Oxford, 1903–20; Hon. Fellow, 1934; Fellow of King's College, London, 1934; Professor of Mathematics, in University of London, Royal Holloway College, 1920–24, King's College, 1924–36; Emeritus Professor since 1936. *Publications:* papers in Mathematical Journals and Encyclopædia Britannica. *Address:* 64 Park Town, Oxford.

Died 17 March 1944.

JOLLIFFE, Lt-Col Thomas William, CMG 1917; Finance Member, Military Board, Australian Military Forces, 1923–37; *b* 16 March 1873;

Died 12 June 1944.

JOLLY, John Catterall; KC 1939; Chairman, Preston, Liverpool and Manchester County Quarter Sessions since 1938; Chairman, Lancaster County Quarter Sessions since 1944; Recorder of Preston since 1938; Member Home Secretary's Advisory Council on Treatment of Offenders since 1945; Chairman, Agricultural Land Tribunal, Lancashire; *b* 1887; *s* of Thomas Jolly, JP, of Preston, Lancs; *m* 1914, Jennie, *d* of Arthur Birtwistle of Blackburn; two *d*. *Educ:* Aldenham; King's College, Cambridge. BA 1909. Called to Bar, Inner Temple, 1911; Bencher, 1946. *Address:* 1 Essex Court, Temple, EC4. *T:* Central 6717; 23 West Cliff, Preston, Lancs. *T:* Preston 4770. *Clubs:* Oxford and Cambridge; Winckley (Preston); County (Lancaster).

Died 22 Jan. 1950.

JOLY, John Swift, BA, MB, BCh, BAO, MD (Dublin University), FRCS Eng.; Consulting Surgeon; Senior Surgeon St Peter's Hospital for Stone; Consulting Urologist (Civilian) to HM Navy; *γ s* of late Rev. John Swift Joly, Rector of Athlone; *m* Mary, *e d* of S. A. O. FitzPatrick, Dublin; one *s*. *Educ:* Trinity College, Dublin; 1st Senior Moderator (large gold medallist) in Experimental Science, Medical Scholar, Surgical Travelling Prizeman, etc.; Berne and Vienna. Fellow of the Royal Society of Medicine (Ex-President of the Section of Urology). Delegate for Great Britain to the Société Internationale d'Urologie; Corresponding member of the American, French and Italian Urological Societies; Major, RAMC; served in Egypt and Palestine, European War (despatches). *Publications:* Stone and Calculous Disease of the Urinary Organs, 1929; various articles on Urology in Medical Papers. *Recreations:* golf, fishing, mountaineering, photography. *Address:* 80 Harley Street, W1. *T:* Langham 1080. *Club:* Savage.

Died 14 Dec. 1943.

JOLY DE LOTBINIÈRE, Maj.-Gen. Alain Chartier, CB 1917; CSI 1911; CIE 1906; RE, Kaisar-i-Hind gold medal; Officier Légion d'Honneur, 1917; retired; late Chief Engineer and Secretary to Government Bengal, and Member Legislative Council of Bengal; *b* Quebec, Canada, 31 Oct. 1862; *s* of late Sir Henry Joly de Lotbinière, KCMG; *m* 1887, Marion Helen Campbell; one *s*. *Educ:* RM College, Kingston, Canada. Entered RE 1886; Captain, 1895; Major, 1903; Lt-Col 1911; Maj.-Gen. 1918; retired, 1919; proposed and carried out the first large Hydro-Electric Transmission Power Scheme in the East, *i.e.* the Cauvery Falls Transmission of Power to the Kolar Goldfields in Mysore, SI; for a short time this was the longest power transmission line in the world; designed and carried out the Jhelum Power Installation in Kashmir, and built a fleet of electrically operated dredges which were employed in grading the Jhelum River, in order to free the valley from floods; Chief Engineer of the Anzacs, 1914; served with this corps in Gallipoli and France; was Engineer-in-Chief of the Army of the Peninsula throughout the evacuation (despatches five times). *Recreations:* fishing, shooting and golf. *Address:* Greystoke, Crowthorne, Berks. *T:* Crowthorne 57.

Died 14 April 1944.

JONES, Abel John, CBE 1920; MA (Cantab), BSc (Wales), PhD (Jena), LCP; HM Inspector of Schools, retired; *b* Rhymney, Mon; *s* of David Rees Jones and Hannah Evans; *m* 1910, Rhoda May Williams, BSc, Cardiff; three *s*. *Educ:* University College, Aberystwyth; University of Jena; Clare College, Cambridge. First Class Moral Sciences Tripos, 1908. During war 1914–18 Hon. County Organiser for Glamorgan under the National War Savings Committee. Adjudicator (literary) at several National Eisteddfodau. *Publications:* Character in the Making; Rudolf Eucken: A Philosophy of Life (People's Books); John Morgan, MA (a biography); Abbrevia (a system of phonetic shortwriting); Deffrod Mae'n Ddydd (30 letters to the people of Wales); Dysgu'r Gymraeg; Y Llyfrau Elfennol; Heriaf fy Hen Syniadau, 1942; I was Privileged (Reminiscences), 1943; From an Inspector's Bag (More Reminiscences), 1944; In Search of Truth, 1945 (Nelson's Discussion Books); For a Human Advance; articles in English and Welsh. *Recreation:* literature. *Address:* Hedd-Annedd, New Road, Porthcawl, Glam. *T:* 259.

Died 8 May 1949.

JONES, Captain Benjamin Henry, CBE 1919; Royal Indian Navy, retired; *m* 1905, Gladys Herbert Orpen; one *d*. *Address:* 22 Limes Road, Folkestone. *T:* Cheriton 85387.

Died 7 July 1949.

JONES, Cecil Charles, MA, PhD, LLD, DCL; Hon. Lieut-Col; *b* 11 Feb. 1872; *s* of Abel and Catherine Jones, Moncton, NB; *m* 1899, Margaret Baird, Chipman, NB; five *d*. *Educ:* University of New Brunswick; Harvard University; University of Chicago. Instructor Mathematics and Physics, Acadia University, Nova Scotia, 1898; Associate Professor Mathematics and Physics, 1900; Professor of Mathematics, 1904; Professor of Mathematics, Univ. of New Brunswick, 1906; Chancellor, Univ. of New Brunswick, 1906–31; Member Board of Education for New Brunswick, 1906–40; President, 1931–40; retired; Chairman

Committee on Fisheries, Game, and Fur-Bearing Animals, Commission of Conservation, Canada, 1910–21; Member University Site Commission. Province of British Columbia, 1910. *Publications:* articles and pamphlets, education and mathematics. *Address:* Fredericton, NB, Canada. *T:* 425. *Club:* Royal Empire Society.

Died 19 Aug. 1943.

JONES, Charles Hugh LePailleur, CMG 1946; OBE 1917; VD; MEIC; CStJ; President and Managing Director of Price Brothers & Co. Ltd, Mersey Paper Co. Ltd, and subsidiaries of both companies; *b* Montreal; *s* of Charles Goode Jones and Marie Barker; *m* Elisabeth, *d* of John Kennedy, Montreal; four *s* one *d*. *Educ:* Public Schools, Montreal; McGill University. Formerly with CPR Shops, Mech. Dept, Trainmaster, Asst Supt; AC Rly various positions and Asst Gen. Manager; various positions and General Manager, Lake Superior Corporation and subsidiary companies, Sault Ste Marie, Ont; General Manager, Sault Ste Marie Pulp and Paper Co.; Vice-President and General Manager of: Spanish River Pulp and Paper Co. Ltd, and subsidiary companies, Fort William Paper Co., Kaministiquia Power Co., Manitoba Paper Co. Served European War, 1914–18, Canada, England, France; raised and commanded 227th Bn CEF, OC Central Group, CEF France (despatches twice, OBE); West Nova Scotia Regt; R of O Canada; Life Member and Director, Canadian Legion; Director, Canadian Legion War Services, Inc. King's Jubilee, Coronation, Long Service medals. *Recreations:* golf, fishing (fresh-water and sea), riding, yachting, historical investigation, collector. *Address:* La Ferme de la Bonne Entente, 3400 Ste Foy Road, Ste Foy, PQ. *T:* 2–8251. *Clubs:* British Empire; St James's (Montreal); Cruising Club of America (New York); Canadian Military Institute (Toronto); Royal Quebec Golf (Quebec); Halifax, Halifax Aero, Halifax Curling, Halifax Golf and Country, Royal Nova Scotia Yacht Squadron (Halifax, NS); Liverpool Golf and Country, (Commodore), Liverpool Yacht (Liverpool, NS).

Died 22 May 1949.

JONES, Sir (Charles) Sydney, Kt 1937; Hon. LLD (Liverpool); JP; *b* 7 Feb. 1872; *e s* of late Charles William Jones, Liverpool, and Georgina, *d* of late Sidney Potter, Manchester; unmarried. *Educ:* Charterhouse; Magdalen College, Oxford. Shipowner; member of firm of Alfred Holt and Co., Liverpool; member of Liverpool City Council and Education Committee; formerly Treasurer, President, and Pro-Chancellor, Liverpool University; MP (L) West Derby Div. of Liverpool, Dec. 1923–Oct. 1924; has been Chairman of Liverpool Steamship Owners' Association; High Sheriff of Lancashire, 1929–30; Lord Mayor of Liverpool, 1938–42. *Address:* Eastbourne, Prince's Park, Liverpool. *T:* Lark Lane 2168. *Clubs:* Reform, Eighty; Exchange, University, Liverpool.

Died 16 Feb. 1947.

JONES, Clifford T.; KC 1913; barrister; *b* Liverpool, NS, 19 April 1873; *s* of Rev. Joseph E. and Elizabeth Jones; *m* 1901, Elizabeth J. White, Banff; one *s* three *d*. *Educ:* Acadia College, Wolfville, NS. Came to Alberta, 1893; taught school, Banff, 1894–95; called to Alberta Bar, 1899; Secretary, Calgary Law Association, 1902–11, President, 1912, now Hon. Vice-Pres.; Alderman, Calgary, five years; School Trustee, four years; President, Archæological Society, 1913; Hon. President, Apollo Choir, 1914; Chairman, Legislative Committee City Planning Commission; Secretary, Liberal Association, 1908; Liberal Candidate South Calgary Constituency, 1912; Chm. Finance Committee Public School Board, 1922–23; Vice-Chm. 1923; Member Power Committee Alberta Development Board, 1927; Executive Committee United Empire Loyalists, 1928–43; Vice-President, 1929; Archivist, 1931–43; Member of the Classical Association of Great Britain; Life Member

Archæological Institute of America. *Recreation:* horticulture. *Address:* 1302 Prospect Avenue, Calgary, Alberta.

Died 24 Feb. 1948.

JONES, Col Conwyn M.; *see* Mansel-Jones.

JONES, Rev. Canon David A.; *see* Akrill-Jones.

JONES, Very Rev. David John; Dean Emeritus of Llandaff; *b* 31 Dec. 1870; *s* of William and Ann Jones; *m* 1908, Constance Rose Sutherland; one *s* one *d*. *Educ:* Jesus College, Oxford. Curate of Llanelly, 1894–96; Chaplain of S Michael's College, Aberdare, 1897–1901; Vicar of Port Talbot, 1901–20; Vicar of Roath, 1920–31; Dean of Llandaff, 1931–48. *Address:* Deanery, Llandaff. *T:* Llandaff 331.

Died 14 March 1949.

JONES, Ven. David Morgan, BA; Rector of Llanddowror, Carmarthen, since 1945; Archdeacon of Carmarthen and Canon of Llanrhian, 1938–49, Archdeacon Emeritus, 1950; *b* 28 Dec. 1874; *s* of James Jones, Master Mariner and Catherine Jones of Llanrhystyd, Cardiganshire; *m* 1904, Margaret Jane, 2nd *d* of George Clark, steel and tin works proprietor, Morriston, Glamorganshire, and Alice Clark; one *s* three *d*. *Educ:* Llanrhystyd National School; Aberayron Grammar School; Llandovery College; St David's College, Lampeter and St Michael's College. Deacon, 1899; Priest, 1900; Curate of Llangyfelach, 1899–1905; Curate of St John's, Swansea, 1905–08; Rector of Aberporth, 1910–17; Vicar of Cardigan, 1917–31; Vicar of Llanelly, 1931–45; Rural Dean of Sub-Aeron, 1920–31; Surrogate, 1920; Canon of Mathry, 1930–38; Secretary of St David's Diocesan Board of Finance, 1931, also of Dilapidations; of Diocesan Conference and Diocesan Board of Patronage; Member of Governing Body, also of Representative Body of The Church-in-Wales. *Recreation:* fishing. *Address:* Llanddowror Rectory, St Clears, Carmarthen.

Died 19 Sept. 1950.

JONES, E. Alfred; *b* Llanfyllin, N Wales, 1872. Member of the Honourable Society of Cymmrodorion; Hon. Bard of the National Gorsedd of Wales, with the title of Kelvyth Maldwyn; Fellow Commoner of Clare College, Cambridge; Hon. MA Oxford, Cambridge, Univ. of Wales; Rutgers Univ. USA; FSA; 2nd Lieut Royal Welch Fusiliers; sometime hon. Curator of Silver, Yale Univ. Art Museum; and Assist Prof. of Fine Art at Yale; Liveryman of the Goldsmiths Company and Freeman of the City of London; Hon. Friend of St George's Chapel, Windsor. *Publications:* The Church Plate of the Diocese of Bangor; the Old Church Plate of the Isle of Man; Old English Gold Plate; the Old Silver Sacramental Vessels of Foreign Protestant Churches in England; the Old Plate in the Jewel House at the Tower of London; the Old Plate of the Cambridge Colleges; the Old English Plate of the Emperor of Russia; the Gold and Silver of Windsor Castle; Editor of Memorials of Old North Wales; The Emperor of Russia's Collection of Old English Watches; Old English Furniture Makers, from Charles II to Queen Anne; The Old Silver of American Churches; The Journal of Alexander Chesney; American Members of the Inns of Court; The Loyalists of New Jersey; The Loyalists of Massachusetts; Old Silver, European and American; Newcome's Academy and its Plays, 1933; joint author of the Plate of Eton College; the Plate wrought by the Courtauld family of Goldsmiths; many illustrated catalogues of plate (mainly privately printed); contributor to the Encyclopædia Britannica, etc. *Club:* Oxford and Cambridge.

Died 23 Aug. 1943.

JONES, Ebenezer G.; *see* Griffith-Jones.

JONES, Edgar H.; *see* Heath Jones.

JONES, Edward William M.; *see* Milner-Jones.

JONES, Ernest L.; see Lancaster-Jones.

JONES, Captain Sir Evan, Kt 1935; JP, DL, MIME; Fellow Institute of Quarry Managers. Sheriff of Merioneth, 1924; Deputy Chairman Merionethshire Quarter Session, 1948; served European War, 1914–19 (despatches, twice). *Address:* Brynmeirion, Festiniog.
Died 5 June 1949.

JONES, Sir Evan Davies, 1st Bt *cr* 1917; MICE; LLD; Lord Lieutenant of Pembrokeshire, 1932–44; *b* 18 April 1859; *s* of Thomas Jones, Pentower, Fishguard; *m* 1st, 1884, Cecilia Ann (*d* 1913), *d* of Jacob Evans; one *s* (and two *s* killed in European War, 1918) two *d*; 2nd, 1914, Lily (*d* 1945), *d* of James Railton. Chairman County Council, 1926; Chairman Standing Joint Committee, 1928–36; Vice-President National Library of Wales, 1928–39; (retired) Major in the Engineer and Railway Staff Corps, RE (TF); one of the Committee of three appointed to deal with the organisation of Civilian Labour for defence purposes in the London area during the War; Governing Director of Topham, Jones & Railton, Ltd, Civil Engineering Contractors; High Sheriff, Pembrokeshire, 1911–12; Petrol Controller, 1917–18; MP (Co. L) Pembrokeshire, Dec. 1918–22; Chairman of the Road Transport Board, 1918–19; Commissioner for Dyes (Board of Trade), 1917–19; Controller of Coal Mines, 1919; President of the Federation of Civil Engineering Contractors, 1935 and 1936. *Heir: s* Tom Barry Jones [*b* 1888; *m* 1922, Jean Costain, *widow* of Lieut Herbert Costain, RAF. Trinity College, Cambridge, MA. Served European War, Lieut Roy. Fusiliers; was prisoner of war in Germany, May 1917–Dec. 1918]. *Address:* Pentower, Fishguard, Pembrokeshire; 171 Victoria Street, SW1.
Died 20 April 1949.

JONES, Sir Francis (Adolphus), KBE 1925; CB 1917; *b* 29 May 1861; 3rd *s* of Charles Edward Jones, 20 Cornwall Gardens, SW, and Maria, *d* of John Adolphus Young of Hare Hatch, Berks; *m* 1899, Ada Charlotte (*d* 1944), *e surv. d* of Thomas Vaughan Roberts; one *s* one *d*. *Educ:* Winchester; Univ. Coll. Oxford. Lincoln's Inn, 1886; Assistant Legal Adviser, Board of Agriculture 1893; Legal Adviser, Ministry of Agriculture and Fisheries, 1915–25, and Solicitor to HM Commissioners of Woods, etc., 1916–25. *Address:* c/o Young Jones & Co., 2 Suffolk Lane, Cannon Street, EC4.
Died 21 Sept. 1947.

JONES, Rt Rev. Frank Melville, CBE 1938; DD; *b* 1866; *s* of Rev. Francis Innes Jones, Incumbent of All Saints, Nelson, NZ; *m* 1895, F. Higgins, Lady Principal of CMS Girls' Seminary, Lagos; no *c*. *Educ:* Nelson College, University of New Zealand (BA); Ridley Hall, Cambridge. Ordained, 1890; Curate of Holy Trinity, Cheltenham, 1890–92; CMS Missionary, Onitsha, 1893; transferred to Yoruba Mission as Principal of Lagos Training College, 1894; removed college to the Hinterland at Oyo, 1896; Principal CMS Training College, Oyo, 1895–1919; Secretary Yoruba Mission, 1902–19; Archdeacon of Yoruba country, 1906–19; Bishop of Lagos (Nigeria), 1919–40; Examining Chaplain to Bishop Tugwell, 1900. *Publications:* papers for the Pan-Anglican Congress.
Died 8 Jan. 1941.

JONES, Frank Newling, FJI, JP; *s* of Rev. J. C. Jones, MA, Spalding, Lincs; *m* 1895, Bertha Newling, *d* of late W. A. Newling, JP, Outwell; two *s*. *Educ:* Spalding Grammar School. Served apprenticeship on Lincolnshire Free Press; junior reporter on Surrey Comet, 1890–94; Western Morning News, 1894–1900; South Wales News and Echo, 1900–20; Director and Editor Surrey Comet, 1920–40. *Recreation:* golf. *Address:* Melbourne, Outwell, Wisbech.
Died March 1942.

JONES, Frederick Archibald L.; see Leslie-Jones.

JONES, Frederick James, MVO 1927; ISO 1927; MInstCE; retired; *b* 24 May 1874; *s* of Frederick Jones; *m* 1906, Margaret Jane Davidson; three *s* four *d*. *Educ:* Otago Boys' High School; Canterbury College. In New Zealand Railways, 1889–1928; District Engineer, 1901–20; Supervising Engineer, 1920–21; Assistant Chief Engineer, 1922–23; Chief Engineer, 1924; Chairman, Board of Management, 1925–28; President, New Zealand Society of Civil Engineers, 1925. *Publications:* Papers for Society of Civil Engineers; The Strength of New Zealand Timbers; Calculation and Strength of New Zealand Railway Bridges; The Economics of Railway Transportation as applied to New Construction. *Recreation:* golf. *Address:* Raumati Beach, NZ. *Clubs:* Wellington, Wellington, NZ.
Died 25 March 1943.

JONES, Frederick L.; see Llewellyn-Jones.

JONES, Col Frederick William C.; see Caton-Jones.

JONES, George Basil Harris, MC, MA, Headmaster, Southern Grammar School, Portsmouth; *b* 3 April 1896; *s* of Thomas Jones, Treorchy, S Wales and Elizabeth Harris Jones; *m* 1939, Freda Parris; one *d*. *Educ:* Christ Coll., Brecon; Sidney Sussex College, Cambridge (MA). 2nd Cl. (Div. 1) Historical Tripos, 1921. Called to Bar, Gray's Inn, 1928; served European War, Lieutenant 1st Welsh Horse, 1916–19 (MC); TARO Royal Artillery, 1932, Assistant Master, Preston Grammar School, 1921–23; High Storrs Grammar School, Sheffield, 1923–31; Emanuel School, SW11, 1931–34; member of Cambrian Archæological Association. *Recreation:* archæology. *Address:* Southern Grammar School, Portsmouth.
Died 22 Nov. 1946.

JONES, Vice-Adm. George Clarence, CB 1943; RCN; Chief of Naval Staff, Naval Service HQ, Ottawa, since 1944; *b* Halifax, NS, 24 Oct. 1895; *e s* of J. C. and H. R. Jones; *m* 1932, Helen Fordham Johnson; two *s* one *d*. *Educ:* RN College of Canada. Cadet HMS Berwick, 1913; Vanquisher, 1918; RN College of Canada, 1920; Lieut in Command HMCS Patrician and Patriot, 1921–24; RN Staff College, 1925; HMS Resolution, 1926; Lieut Comdr Naval Service HQ, 1927–29; HMS Iron Duke, 1929; Comdr Imperial Defence College, 1930; Comdr in charge, Halifax, 1931–32, later, Esquimalt; Capt. 1938; COAC, Halifax, 1941–42; Rear-Admiral, 1941; Vice-Adm. 1944. *Recreations:* golf, tennis. *Address:* 301 Metcalfe St, Ottawa, Canada.
Died 8 Feb. 1946.

JONES, George William; *b* Upton-on-Severn, Worcestershire, 18 May 1860; *s* of George Jones; *m* Eliza Sophia Ann, *d* of Charles Walker Durham, New Whittingham, Derbyshire. Written largely and lectured throughout Great Britain and the United States of America and in Canada on The History and Craft of Printing; Member of the Roxburghe Book Club of San Francisco and the Zamorano Book Club of Los Angeles; Member of the Winnipeg Branch of the Craftsman's Union of the United States of America and Canada; Printer by appointment to the King and Queen of the Belgians; Member of the Worshipful Company of Stationers; the Representative of the Federation of Master Printers of Great Britain and Ireland on the Committee appointed by the Lords of the Treasury to advise HM Stationery Office on the Faces of Types and Modes of Display of Government Printing; Designer of Linotype Granjon, Linotype Estienne, Linotype Georgian, and other type faces; Member of The Royal Society of Arts Committee on Book Production; a Representative of the Federation of Master Printers of Great Britain and Ireland on the Industrial Art Committee of the Federation of British Industries; has been appointed by the Board of Education to inspect and report on Composing and Letterpress Machine work at many of the principal technical schools in England. *Publications:* for many years editor and proprietor of The Printing World. *Recreations:* golf, the collecting of early printed books. *Clubs:* City Livery, Whitefriars.

Died 14 May 1942.

JONES, Maj.-Gen. Guy Carleton, CMG 1916; *b* Halifax, Nova Scotia, 1864; *s* of Hon. A. G. Jones; *m* 1st, Susan (*d* 1926), *d* of late Robert Morrow; 2nd, 1928, Contessina Ginevra Mannini (*d* 1943), *d* of late Conte Mannini, of Florence. *Educ:* Merchiston Castle School, Edinburgh; Galt Collegiate Institute; King's College, London. MD, CM, MRCS Col RCAMC; Hon. Fellow American College of Surgeons. Served S African War (Queen's medal 2 clasps); European War, 1914–18 (CMG); Director-General, Canadian Medical Service, 1906–17; retired, 1920; Knight of Grace, Order of St John of Jerusalem; Officier Légion d'honneur, 1916. *Address:* 34 Plewlands Gardens, Edinburgh 10. *Clubs:* Royal Societies, Reform.

Died 23 Oct. 1950.

JONES, Henry Albert, CMG 1943; MC; Director of Public Relations, Air Ministry, since 1944. Served European War, 1914–18; in Army and RAF; in Historical Section of Committee of Imperial Defence, 1918; Director of air branch there, 1920; Official Air Historian, 1922; was in Air Staff Secretariat, 1939; Senior Administrative Officer, United Kingdom Air Liaison Mission, Ottawa, and with RAF delegation, Washington. *Address:* Public Relations Dept, Air Ministry.

Died 27 March 1945.

JONES, Lt-Gen. Henry Albert H.; late Royal Marines, retired list, 1933. *Address:* The Manor House, Compton, nr Winchester. *T:* Twyford 3156.

Died 6 Oct. 1944.

JONES, Sir Henry Haydn, Kt 1937; Alderman, Merioneth CC; *b* 1863; 2nd *s* of Joseph David Jones of Ruthin; *m* 1903, Gwendolen, *o d* of Lewis D. Jones of Chicago; one *d*. *Educ:* Board School and Academy, Towyn. MP (L) Merioneth, 1910–45. *Address:* Pantyneuadd, Towyn, Merioneth.

Died 2 July 1950.

JONES, Ven. Henry James Church, MA; Archdeacon of Brecon since 1923; Vicar of Builth Wells since 1919, and Curate-in-Charge of Alltmawr since 1921; *b* Aberporth, Cardiganshire, 30 Aug. 1870; *s* of late Rev. John Jones, Vicar of Penbryn, Cardiganshire; unmarried. *Educ:* Christ's College, Brecon; St John's College, Oxford. Curate of St John's and St Mary's, Brecon, 1893–1919; Vicar of Battle, Breconshire, 1904–19; Rural Dean of Brecon, Part I, 1916–19; Curate-in-Charge of Llanddewir Cwm, 1919–21; Canon of Brecon Cathedral since 1923; Vice-Chairman Breconshire Education Committee since 1934; Chairman, Governors of Christ's College, Brecon, since 1934. *Recreation:* book collecting. *Address:* The Vicarage, Builth-Wells, Breconshire. *T:* Builth-Wells 219. *TA:* Archdeacon, Builth-Wells.

Died 18 Jan. 1941.

JONES, Howell G.; *see* Gwynne-Jones.

JONES, Idris Deane, MA, Fellow and Senior Tutor of Merton College, Oxford; member of Hebdomadal Council, Oxford University, since 1941; *b* 20 Aug. 1899; *s* of Rev. I. Jones, Bristol; *m* Muriel, *d* of W. H. Cooper, W Bromwich; two *d*. *Educ:* Bristol Grammar School. Probationary Flight Officer, RAF, 1917–18; Classical Scholar of New Coll., Oxford, 1918–21, 1st Class Mod. Hist. Final School, 1921; Prize Fellowship at Merton, 1921; Tutor, 1923; Senior Tutor since 1932; Univ. Lecturer in Modern History, 1929–34; Proctor, 1933–34; Examiner, Modern History Final Honour

School, 1936–38; Laura Spelman Rockefeller Fellowship, Harvard University, 1924–25. Acting Flight Lieut, RAFVR (T), 1939–46, commanding No. 150 Squadron, ATC. *Publications:* The English Revolution; an Introduction to Stuart history (1931). *Recreations:* various. *Address:* Postmasters' Hall, Merton Street, Oxford. *T:* Oxford 4015.

Died 27 March 1947.

JONES, Principal J. Morgan, MA, Congregational minister; Professor of Church History and Religious Education, 1914–26, Principal since 1926, Independent College, Bangor; *b* 23 Oct. 1873; *m* 1902, Lucy Evans, of Bridgnorth, Salop; two *s* one *d*. *Educ:* Cardiff, Brecon, Oxford, and Berlin. Congregational Minister at Aberdare, 1900–13; Chairman of North Wales District of WEA; Warden of Guild of Graduates of Univ. of Wales, 1930–33; Chairman of N Wales Congregational Union, 1933–34, and of Union of Welsh Independents, 1939–40; Dean of Divinity of Univ. of Wales, 1940–43; Vice-President Univ. College of North Wales. *Publications:* The New Testament in Modern Education, 1922; Welsh books: The Pilgrim Fathers, 1920; The Teaching of Jesus Christ, 1921; The Reformation Treatises, 1926; The New Testament: its History and Meaning, 1929; The Fourth Gospel, 1930; Walter Cradoc and his Contemporaries, 1939; Editor of Y Cofiadur (Historical Society of Welsh Independents). *Recreation:* golf. *Address:* Bala-Bangor Independent College, Bangor, North Wales. *T:* Bangor 402.

Died 7 March 1946.

JONES, Rev. John Daniel, CH 1927; MA (Vic.), DD (St Andrews, Wales, Manchester); *b* 13 April 1865; *s* of J. D. Jones of Ruthin, schoolmaster-musician; *m* 1st, Emily (*d* 1917), *d* of Joseph Cunliffe of Rookwood, Chorley; one *d*; 2nd, 1933, Edith Margery, *d* of W. W. Thompson. *Educ:* Towyn Academy; Chorley Grammar School; Owens College; Lancashire Independent Coll. Settled as Congregational Minister in Lincoln, 1889; Minister at Lincoln 9¼ years; Minister of Richmond Hill Congregational Church, Bournemouth, 1898–1937; Chairman of Lincolnshire Congregational Union, 1898; Chairman of Hants Congregational Union, 1903; Chairman Congregational Union of England and Wales, 1909–10 and 1925–26; Hon. Secretary Congregational Union of England and Wales, 1919; Moderator of Federal Council of Free Churches, 1921–23; Moderator of International Congregational Council, 1930; President of National Free Church Council, 1938–39. *Publications:* Birthday of Hope; The Model Prayer; The Way into the Kingdom; The Glorious Company of the Apostles; The Elims of Life; Christ's Pathway to the Cross; The Gospel of Grace; Things Most Surely Believed; The Hope of the Gospel; The Gospel of the Sovereignty; If a Man Die; The Lord of Life and Death; Devotional Commentary on St Mark (4 vols); The King of Love; Watching the Cross; The Inevitable Christ; Richmond Hill Sermons; Morning and Evening; Keep Festival; Three Score Years and Ten. *Recreation:* golf. *Address:* Brynbanon, Bala. *T:* Bala 65. *Club:* National Liberal.

Died 19 April 1942.

JONES, Paymaster Rear-Adm. John Edward, CBE 1922; retired; *b* 4 Sept. 1866; *m* 1903, Margaret Jessie (*d* 1943), *d* of John Jones, Lota, Chile; two *s* three *d*. *Educ:* Dedham School; Hope House Academy, Southsea. Entered Royal Navy as Asst Clerk, 1883; Paymaster Captain, 1921; Paymaster Rear-Admiral, 1923, retired; took part in International Blockade of Greece, 1886; China Boxer rising, 1900; European War, 1914–18, North Sea Grand Fleet. *Address:* New Croft, Record Road, Emsworth, Hants.

Died 21 Jan. 1948.

JONES, Col John Hyndman H.; *see* Howell-Jones.

JONES, John Joseph; MP (Lab) Silvertown Division of West Ham, 1918–40; late General Organiser National Union of General and Municipal Workers; Member of West Ham Town Council since 1904; *b* Nenagh, Tipperary, 8 Dec. 1873; *s* of John and Margaret Jones; *m* 1902, Kate, *d* of J. H. Holden; two *s* three *d*. *Educ*: Christian Brothers Schools, Nenagh. Active in Socialist and Trades Unionist Movement for the last 45 years; helped in the organisation of unskilled labour in London District; Secretary of London Transport Workers Federation District Committee, 1911–13; attended as delegate various National and International Trades Union and Socialist Congresses. *Publications*: My Lively Life; Bidden to the Feast, 1938. *Recreations*: interested in football, cricket, etc. *Address*: 9 Wanlip Road, Plaistow, E13.

Died 21 Nov. 1941.

JONES, Dr (John) Share, MBE 1948; Professor of Veterinary Anatomy, Surgical and Applied Anatomy, and Operative Veterinary Surgery, 1919–38; in charge of Department of Human Anatomy, 1919–24; now Professor Emeritus, University of Liverpool; late Director of Veterinary Studies; MD (V; hc, Berne); DVSc; MSc; MRCVS (1900); FRCVS (1907); *s* of Thomas Jones; *m* Mary S., BA, LLB, MB, ChB, MD (Public Health), *d* of W. Howell Jones, Wrexham. *Educ*: Univ. of Liverpool; King's College (proxime accessit Logic Prize), Univ. College, Royal Veterinary College, London (Centenary Prizeman, etc.).; Paris. Tutor in Surgery and Demonstrator of Anatomy, RVC, 1900–04; awarded Steel Memorial Medal by RCVS, 1928; Bronze Medal, Berne; Victory Medal Central Vet. Soc. London; formerly Member of Council (for 38 years) and Vice-Pres. RCVS (Pres., 1928–29); Hon. Vice-Pres. Nat. Federation of Meat Traders' Assoc., Great Britain; First President Welsh Branch National VM Assoc. of Great Britain and Ireland; Hon. Fellow Central VM Assoc., London, and North Wales VM Assoc., Governor University College of North Wales; Member of Court of Governors Royal Veterinary College, London; formerly Examiner to Universities of Aberdeen, Edinburgh, and London; Member of Colonial Office Committee on Colonial Veterinary Services, and of the Departmental Committee of the Ministry of Agriculture on the Reconstruction of the Royal Veterinary College, London; Chairman Land Settlement and Training Association for Rural Development; Chairman of the North Wales Live Stock Joint Committee; Hon. Local Fuel Overseer, etc.; was for some years a manufacturer of Welsh Woollen Goods and Director of the Mills Glyn Ceiriog; gave evidence before the Royal Commission on University Education in Wales; contested (L) Shropshire (Oswestry Division), 1929. *Publications*: four vols on Surgical Anatomy, 1904–1914; Superficial Anatomy of the Limbs, 1906; Comparative Anatomy of Supernumerary Digits in Ungulates as Evidence of the Interrelationship existing between the various Species; Points in the Anatomy of the Llama as compared with Capra and Equus; Higher Agricultural Education in Wales, 1914; The Education of the Veterinary Student, Brussels, 1919; Local Health Authorities and Animal Diseases, Bordeaux, 1924; Veterinary Science, 1910–1925; The Encyclopædia Britannica; Animal Husbandry and Public Health, with a plea for a National System of Live Stock Insurance, Ghent, 1927; The Relationship of the Veterinary Surgeon to Animal Husbandry, International Veterinary Congress, 1930; The Domestic Animals in relation to our Food and Industries, 1935; Settlement on the Land—Der Ausweg, Paris; Wales and the Animal Industry; formerly Editor Veterinary Student and Editor-in-chief Veterinary News; numerous contributions to Scientific Journals. *Address*: Bryn Offa, Wrexham. *T*: Wrexham 2149. *Clubs*: University (Liverpool); Exchange (Wrexham).

Died 2 Dec. 1950.

JONES, Joseph, CBE 1932; JP; Member of Coal Commission since 1938; Adviser on Social Insurance to National Coal Board since 1947; *b* St Helens, Lancs; *s* of Benjamin and Joanna Jones; *m* 1912, Edith Hannah, *d* of John and Emma Morritt; one *s* six *d*. *Educ*: Parr (St Helens) National School; Sir D. Gamble Technical College, St Helens; Sheffield University. Local Miners' Official, 1914; Treasurer, YMA, 1922; General Secretary, Yorkshire Miners' Association, 1923–38; HM Coal Mines Reorganisation Commissioner, 1930–38; Executive Committee MFGB, 1923; gave evidence for MFGB to Samuel Coal Commission, 1925; Executive Committee National Labour Party, 1926–31; Member Committee of Inquiry into Cotton Industry, 1929; served on West Riding County Council and Barnsley Town Council between 1919 and 1933; Vice-President Miners' Federation of Great Britain, 1932, President, 1934–38; First Chairman Workers' Temperance League. *Publications*: The Coal Scuttle; Organise for Victory (pamphlet); Why I am in the Labour Party (pamphlet). *Recreations*: golf, bowls, swimming, and walking. *Address*: Hillcrest, 15 Huddersfield Road, Barnsley, Yorks. *T*: Barnsley 926. *Club*: National Labour.

Died 1 April 1948.

JONES, Lawrence, MS, FRCS; late Assistant Surgeon and Joint Lecturer on Operative Surgery, St George's Hospital, and Assistant Surgeon Seamen's Hospital, Greenwich; *s* of Rev. W. Morgan Jones, Marks Tey, Essex. *Educ*: St Paul's School; St George's Hospital. MRCS Lond., LRCP England, 1900; MB Lond. 1901; FRCS Eng. 1902; BS Lond. (1st class honours) 1902; MS Lond. 1904. *Publications*: contributions to the medical journals, and to the Transactions of the Royal Medico-Chirurgical and Medical Societies. *Recreations*: natural history, fishing, gardening. *Address*: Little Seeleys, Beaconsfield. *T*: Beaconsfield 34.

Died 11 July 1949.

JONES, Col Llewellyn Murray, CMG 1919; DSO 1900; late King's Regt (Liverpool); *b* 23 Nov. 1871; *s* of late Maj.-Gen. R. Godfrey Jones, Madras Cavalry; *m* 1902, Ida St George, 4th *d* of late John W. Nicholson of St John, New Brunswick; one *s*. Entered Army, 1891; Capt. 1900; Major, 1909; Col 1924; Adjt 1898; served South Africa, 1899–1902 (despatches four times, Queen's medal three clasps, King's medal two clasps, DSO); European War (Bt Lt-Col, CMG); retired pay, 1926. *Address*: Little Paddock, Chobham, Surrey. *Club*: Junior United Service.

Died 7 Feb. 1946.

JONES, Llewellyn Rodwell, MC, BSc, PhD; *b* Bristol, 28 Aug. 1881; *s* of late Rev. W. Rodwell Jones and Sarah, *e d* of late Thos Cuthbertson; unmarried. *Educ*: Kingswood School, Bath; London University. Schoolmaster, 1904–12; Leeds University, Geography Department, 1913–14; served in France, West Yorkshire Regt, 1914–19 (Major); London School of Economics, 1919; Visiting Lecturer to the Geography Dept of Chicago University, 1925; Professor in Geography in the University of London, 1925–45; Head of Geography Department in the London School of Economics; retired, 1945. *Publications*: North England, 1921; North America, 1925, 7th edition, 1946 (with P. W. Bryan, PhD); The Geography of London River, 1931; numerous articles to the British and American Geographical Journals. *Address*: c/o London School of Economics, Houghton Street, Aldwych, WC2.

Died 15 Aug. 1947.

JONES, Brig.-Gen. Morey Q.; *see* Quayle-Jones.

JONES, Captain Owen, CBE 1919; RD, RNR; retired; a Director of the London Assurance; *b* 20 June 1866; 2nd *s* of Lieut-Col A. S. Jones, VC, of Finchampstead, Berks; *m* 1902, Lillian, *d* of Wm Stevenson, of The Lea, Bridge of Allan; two *d*. *Educ*: privately; HMS Conway. 28 years in P & O Co.'s service, 9 years in command; Elder

Brother, Trinity House, EC; served during the South African War, 1900–01, in the Elswick Battery of Field Artillery as Driver, Bombardier, Corporal, and Sergeant (despatches twice, Queen's medal and 4 clasps). *Address:* Worplesdon Chase, Guildford.

Died 2 Feb. 1941.

JONES, Sir Pendrill Charles V.; *see* Varrier-Jones.

JONES, Penrhyn Grant, CBE 1928; Assistant Judge HBM Supreme Court for China since 1931; *b* 28 May 1878; *s* of F. Topham Jones; *m* 1926, Silvia Norman. *Educ:* Malvern; Vienna. Student Interpreter in China, 1902; called to Bar, Inner Temple, 1912; Consul at Harbin, 1927–29; Amoy 1930–31. *Address:* HBM Supreme Court, Shanghai, China. *Club:* Thatched House.

Died 15 July 1945.

JONES, Rev. Percy Herbert, CBE 1919; Chaplain and Instructor Commander RN, retired; *b* 1864; 2nd *s* of Staff Commander James Owen Jones, RN; unmarried. *Educ:* Christ's Hospital; Christ Church, Oxford. Chaplain and Instructor in HM Navy, 1896–1920; served European War, 1914–19 (despatches, CBE). *Address:* 4 Wexford Road, Wandsworth Common, SW12. *T:* Battersea 6269. *TA:* 4 Wexford Road, Wandsworth Common.

Died 27 Feb. 1941.

JONES, Raymond R.; *see* Ray-Jones.

JONES, Rev. Richard Charles Stuart. Hon. Canon of Gloucester; Vicar of Fairford, 1918–36. *Address:* The Little Cloister, Gloucester.

Died 28 Jan. 1941.

JONES, Sir Robert Armstrong-, Kt 1917; CBE 1919; MD Lond., BS, DSc Hon. (Wales); FRCS England, FRCP London; FSA; DL County of London and Carnarvonshire; JP Essex, Co. Carnarvon and County of London; High Sheriff of Carnarvonshire, 1929; *b* 2 Dec. 1857; *e s* of Rev. Thomas Jones, Eisteddfa, Criccieth, N Wales, and Jane Elizabeth, *o d* of Robert Jones, Eisteddfa; *m* 1893, Margaret Elizabeth, Dame of Order of St John of Jerusalem, *e d* of Sir Owen Roberts, MA, DCL, LLD; one *s* two *d*. Was one of the Lord Chancellor's Visitors in Lunacy, 1921–31; expert in mental diseases; was temporary Lt-Col, RAMC European War and was Consulting Physician in mental diseases to Military Forces in London and Aldershot Commands, and to American Red Cross Hospital for Officers, Lancaster Gate; visited asylums in France, Germany, Italy, Switzerland, Austria, Poland, Russia, and Norway, and published experience; late Secretary and President of Royal Medico-Psychological Association; Hon. Associate and Knight of Grace, Order of St John of Jerusalem; late member of Advanced Board of Medical Studies, University of London, and late member of the Board of Philosophical Studies; lectured upon Mental Diseases at the Post-Graduate Medical College and Polyclinic, London, and at the Westminster Hospital; late Examiner in Mental Diseases and Psychology to London University; late Gresham Professor of Physic and also Lecturer on Mental Diseases, St Bartholomew's Hospital, 1921–31; President of Section Psychological Medicine, British Medical Association, 1903; President Psychiatry Section Royal Society of Medicine, 1929; late Resident Physician to London County Council Asylum, Claybury, Woodford, 1892–1916; formerly Resident Physician to Royal Earlswood Institution, Surrey; formerly Secretary of Psychology Section, Congress of Hygiene and Demography in London; has served on the Archbishop of Canterbury's Special Committee on Spiritual Healing, 1920–23, and has contributed papers to XIXth Century and Contemporary Review also to Eugenics Society, Society for Study of Childhood, Medico-Legal, and numerous others, and also articles upon the treatment of mental diseases to English and American journals and reviews of Psychological and Philosophical works; has published investigations into the question of Mental and Physical Deterioration and given evidence before the Departmental Committee of the Privy Council, 1903, and of the Home Office *re* Juvenile Delinquency, 1925, also the Royal Commission on Divorce and Matrimonial Causes; Vice-Pres. of Hon. Society of Cymmrodorion; and of several other learned societies; Life Governor of the Royal Hospitals of Bethlem and Bridewell, Westminster, Poplar, etc. *Recreation:* gardening. *Address:* 27 Phillimore Gardens, W8. *T:* Western 8888; Plâs Dinas, Carnarvon, N Wales. *T:* Llanwnde 14. *Club:* Athenæum.

Died 30 Jan. 1943.

JONES, Robert Noble, CBE 1928; *b* Belfast, 1 Aug. 1864; *m* 1890; one *s* three *d*. *Educ:* Public Schools, New Zealand. Admitted Solicitor of Supreme Court, New Zealand, 1890; enrolled as Barrister, 1899; Judge of Native Appellate, Native Land Validation, and Native Land Courts, 1903; Under-Secretary for Native Affairs, New Zealand, 1921–33; Chief Judge of Native Land Court, 1918–39. *Address:* Box 86, Gisborne, New Zealand.

Died 29 June 1942.

JONES, Rufus M., BA, MA, DLitt DD; LLD; DTheol; STD; LHD Heb. LittD; Professor of Philosophy in Haverford College, 1904–34; *b* South China, Maine, USA, 25 Jan. 1863; *s* of Edwin Jones and Mary Hoxie; *m* 1st, 1888, Sarah H. Coutant; 2nd, 1902, Elizabeth Bartram Cadbury; one *s* one *d*. *Educ:* Haverford College; University, Harvard; University, Heidelberg; University, Oxford; University, Marburg. Principal of Oak Grove Seminary, 1889–93; Editor The American Friend, 1893–1912; Editor Present Day Papers, 1913–15; Trustee of Bryn Mawr College since 1898; President of the Board, 1917–37; Trustee of Brown University since 1927; Chairman of American Friends Service Com. for European Reconstruction, 1917–28, 1933–44; Trustee Yenching University in China since 1934; Minister of Society of Friends; Member of Phi Beta Kappa Society; Chairman of the Fellowship of Christian Co-operation, 1930–34; University Preacher, Harvard University; joint recipient of Philadelphia Award for Public Service, 1939; Theodore Roosevelt Medal for public service, 1942. *Publications:* A Dynamic Faith, 1901; Social Law in the Spiritual World, 1904; Studies in Mystical Religion, 1909; The Quakers in the American Colonies, 1911; Spiritual Reformers in the 16th and 17th centuries, 1914; The Inner Life, 1917; The World Within, 1918; A Service of Love in War Time, 1920; The Later Periods of Quakerism, 1921; Spiritual Energies in Daily Life, 1922; Religious Foundations, 1923; The Fundamental Ends of Life, 1924; The Church's Debt to Heretics, 1925; Finding the Trail of Life, 1926; The Faith and Practice of the Quakers, 1927; New Studies in Mystical Religion, 1927; The New Quest, 1928; The Trail of Life in College, 1929; Some Exponents of Mystical Religion, 1929; George Fox: Seeker and Friend, 1930; Pathways to the Reality of God, 1931; A Preface to Christian Faith in a New Age, 1932; Mysticism and Democracy in the English Commonwealth, 1932; joint author of Rethinking Missions, 1932; Haverford College: a History and an Interpretation, 1933; The Trail of Life in the Middle Years, 1934; Rethinking Religious Liberalism, 1935; The Testimony of the Soul, 1936; Some Problems of Life, 1937; The Eternal Gospel, 1938; The Flowering of Mysticism in the Fourteenth Century, 1939; A Small Town Boy, 1941; Spirit in Man, 1941; New Eyes for Invisibles; The Radiant Life, 1944; The Luminous Trail, 1947. *Recreation:* golf. *Address:* Haverford, Pennsylvania, USA.

Died 16 June 1948.

JONES, Rev. S. M.; *see* Martin-Jones.

JONES, Dr Share; *see* Jones, Dr J. S.

JONES, Rev. Spencer John; *b* The Waldrons, Croydon, 2 Feb. 1857; *s* of Jenkin and Sarah Jones; *m* 1885, Elizabeth Barbara (*d* 1934), *d* of Edward Coxwell, solicitor, Southampton; one *s* one *d. Educ:* Chatham House, Ramsgate; Worcester College, Oxon; Wells Theological College. BA 1880. Ordained, 1880; Curate of Pitminster, Taunton, 1880–83; Woking, Surrey, 1883–84; Millbrook, Southampton, 1884–85; Battersea, 1885–87; Rector of Batsford with Moreton-in-Marsh, 1887–1932; Hon. Diocesan Missioner, 1893–1900; Proctor in Convocation, 1898–1900. *Publications:* The Clergy and the Catechism, 7th edition; England and the Holy See, 2nd edition; Now and Then, vol. of sermons; Our Lord and His Lessons; Method; The Counter-Reformation in the Church of England; Introduction to Christian Monism by Erich Wasmann; Benito Mussolini, an Introduction to the Study of Fascism, 1927; Catholic Reunion, 1930. *Club:* Authors'.

Died 28 Jan. 1943.

JONES, Sir Sydney; *see* Jones, Sir C. S.

JONES, Sir Thomas, Kt 1944; MRCS Eng., LRCP Lond. 1896; JP Anglesey; Chairman Anglesey Education Committee; Deputy Chairman Anglesey Quarter Sessions; *b* 1870; *m* 1900, Elizabeth Jane Williams; two *s* one *d. Educ:* Liverpool Institute; Owens College, Manchester. *Address:* Gwyndy, Amlwch, Anglesey. *T:* Amlwch 240. *Club:* National Liberal.

Died 30 July 1945.

JONES, Captain Thomas Alban, DSO 1918; RD; RNR (retired); JP; *b* Llanon, Cardiganshire, 1869; *m* Anne Elizabeth, *d* of late Alderman John Roberts, JP, Rhayader; two *d. Educ:* Llanon Grammar School. Served European War as a Naval Transport Officer on the Admiralty Pier, Dover, 1914–17; Commodore of Convoys plying between Liverpool and Port Said and vice versa, 1917 to Armistice; Nautical Adviser the Union Castle Mail Steamship Co., Ltd, London, retired, 1922; High Sheriff of Radnorshire, 1927–28; Freeman City of London. *Publication:* Courses and Distances in European Waters. *Address:* 68 Bishopsgate, EC2.

Died 3 May 1945.

JONES, His Honour Sir Thomas Artemus, Kt 1931; KC 1919; LLD (Hon.), 1938; Bencher of the Middle Temple, 1926, Lent Reader, 1937; late County Court Judge for the District of North Wales (retired 1942); late Chairman of Caernarvonshire Quarter Sessions; Vice-President University College of North Wales; Ex-Chairman of Conscientious Objectors Tribunal for North Wales; *b* Denbigh; *y s* of late Thomas Jones, stone-mason; *m* 1927, Mildred Mary [called to Bar, Middle Temple (J. J. Powell Prize), 1932. Bedford College, graduated with honours at London University], *e d* of T. W. David, JP, Llandaff. Called to Bar, Middle Temple, 1901; joined the Welsh Circuit (N Wales Division), 1902; Freeman of the City of London and Member of the Gardeners Company; formerly on the parliamentary staff of the Daily Telegraph and the Daily News; contested (L) Macclesfield, 1922; East Swansea, 1923; and Keighley, 1924; served on the Anglo-Mexican Claims Commission, on which he represented Great Britain in 1928 and 1929. *Publication:* Without my Wig, 1944. *Recreations:* golf and fishing. *Address:* Bryn Gwyn, Bangor, N Wales. *T:* Bangor 18.

Died 15 Oct. 1943.

JONES, Sir Thomas George, KBE 1921; Newspaper Proprietor; Chief Divisional Food Officer, Wales, Midland and North-Western Divisions, Ministry of Food, until June 1945; *b* Pontnewydd, Monmouthshire, 5 Jan. 1881; *o s* of late George and Jane Jones, Blænavon, Mon; *m* 1901, May, 2nd *d* of late Alfred Matthews, Porthcawl, Glam.; three *d.* Director and Chairman of several public companies; Unionist candidate Pontypool Division, 1922; National Conservative candidate Ogmore Division, 1931; Director of Ships' Stores,

Ministry of Food, 1917–20; Director National Kitchens, 1918–21; served, 1914–21, upon several Government Department Committees, including National Salvage Council, Disposals Board, etc. Divisional Food Commissioner, South Wales Division, 1921–41. *Publication:* The Unbroken Front, 1944, etc. *Address:* Beachside, Porthcawl, Glamorgan. *T:* Porthcawl 25, S Wales area. *Clubs:* Constitutional, 1900.

Died 30 Nov. 1948.

JONES, Thomas Gwynn, CBE 1937; MA (Wales); DLitt (Wales); DLitt (Eire); Emeritus Professor, University College of Wales, Aberystwyth; *b* 1871; *e s* of late Isaac Jones, Gyffylliog, Denbighshire, and Jane Roberts, Betws-yn-Rhos, Denbighshire; *m* 1899, Margaret Jane, *d* of Thomas Davies, Denbigh; two *s* one *d. Educ:* schools; privately. Literary work and journalism (Wales, England, and Egypt); cataloguer, National Library of Wales; reader and lecturer, afterwards Professor of Welsh Literature, University College of Wales, Aberystwyth; retired, 1937; Member of Board of Celtic Studies (University of Wales), the Folk-lore Society, the Folk-lore of Ireland Society, Vice-President and Medallist of the Honourable Society of Cymmrodorion, etc. *Publications:* Dante and Beatrice (a play, with Daniel Rees), 1903; Ymadawiad Arthur a Chaniadau Eraill (poems), 1910; Emrys ap Iwan (biog.), 1912; Thomas Gee (biog.), 1913; Rhieingerddi'r Gogynfeirdd (study of traditional poetry), 1915; Tir na n-Og (lyrical ode for music), 1916; Tudor Welshmen's English, 1919; Dychweledigion (trans. of Ibsen's Gjengängere), 1920; Cultural Bases (study of Tudor period in Wales), 1921; Faust, Tragoedia gan Goethe (a metrical trans.), 1922; Awen y Gwyddyl (trans. from Irish Gaelic verse), 1922; Gwaith Tudur Aled (works of 16th cent. bard), 1926; Blodau o Hen Ardd (Greek and Latin Epigrams, with Prof. H. J. Rose), 1927; The Culture and Tradition of Wales, 1928; Y Gelfyddyd Gwta (Welsh Epigrams, ed. with intro.), 1929; Welsh Folk-lore and Folk Custom, 1930; Pobun (trans. of Von Hofmannsthal's Jedermann), 1933; Llwyfan y Byd, The Theatre of the World (Welsh and English versions of Von Hofmannsthal's Das Grosse Welttheater), 1936; Y Dwymyn (Poems), 1944; Brithgofion (Early Reminiscences); also fiction, plays, juveniles; collected works: Manion, 1931; Cymeriadau, 1933; Caniadau, 1934; Beirniadaeth a Myfyrdod, 1935; Astudiaethau, 1936; Dyddgwaith, 1937; Visions of the Sleeping Bard (trans. fr. the Welsh of Ellis Wynne, 1940); Macbeth, A Welsh translation, 1942. *Address:* Willow Lawn, Caradog Road, Aberystwyth, Cardiganshire.

Died 7 March 1949.

JONES, Sir Thomas M.; *see* Miller-Jones.

JONES, Lt-Col Walter H.; *see* Howel-Jones.

JONES, Hon. Wendell Phillips; KC 1905; Mayor of Woodstock, 1913, 1914; President St John and Quebec Railway Co. 1917; President New Brunswick Barristers Society, 1923; *b* 25 Nov. 1866; *s* of Randolph K. and Gertrude H. Jones; *m* 1888, Grace J. Jordan; two *s* five *d. Educ:* Woodstock Grammar School; Dalhousie College, Halifax, NS; Boston University Law School. Admitted as Attorney-at-law, 1896; sworn in as Barrister-at-law, 1897; Member Legislative Assembly of NB 1903–08; Solicitor-General of the Province of New Brunswick, 1905–08; Director of Old Age Pensions for New Brunswick, 1935–40; Chairman of New Brunswick Board of Public Utilities, 1940; Chairman of New Brunswick Motor Carrier Board, 1940; Chairman of New Brunswick Securities Board, 1940. *Recreation:* golf. *Address:* Woodstock, NB, Canada. *T:* 74.

Died 29 Sept. 1944.

JONES, William Henry, CBE 1921; Financial Director; British Ministry of War Transport Representative in USA; *b* 1873; *s* of Henry Jones, Cardiff; *m* Bessie, *d* of John Baker, Brooklyn, New York; one *d. Educ:* Lewis

School, Pengam; Cardiff College. Was Director-General, British Ministry of Shipping, New York. *Address:* 115 Bay View Avenue, Atlantic Highlands, New Jersey, USA. *T:* 235.

Died 9 Oct. 1944.

JONES, Rev. William Hudson M.; *see* Macnaughton-Jones.

JONES, William Llewellyn; Chairman and Managing Director of Lloyd's Packing Warehouses Ltd; a Past President and for many years an Executive Director of Manchester Chamber of Commerce; Director: London & Lancashire Insurance Co. Ltd; Manchester Ship Canal Co. and other Companies connected with transport, timber, paper and cloth working; *b* 16 Oct. 1881; *o s* of William Jones, Bramhall, Cheshire, and Margaret Tennant; *m* 1907, Mary H. Stocker, Liverpool; one *s* one *d.* High Sheriff for County of Denbigh, 1944–45. JP Denbighshire. *Recreations:* yachting, motoring, golf, and gardening. *Address:* Bryn Eisteddfod, Glan Conway, Denbigh County. *T:* Llandudno Junction 81175. *Clubs:* National Liberal; Reform, Clarendon (Manchester).

Died 19 July 1950.

JONES, Mrs William Neilson; *see* Rayner, M. M. C.

JONES, William Tudor, MA, DPhil; *b* Strata Florida, Cardiganshire, 8 Sept. 1865; *m* 1892, Helen Clarke, Northampton. *Educ:* University of Wales and University of Jena. Graduated as Doctor of Philosophy in Jena under Rudolf Eucken; MA University of Bristol. Minister of the Unitarian Churches in Swansea, Wellington, NZ, Islington and Bristol; travelled, lectured, and preached in Australia and New Zealand, 1906–10; Lecturer to the Board of Education, the War Office, and the Ministry of Labour, 1916–19. *Publications:* Eucken's Truth of Religion, Knowledge, and Life, The Nature of Religion, The Permanent and the Transient in Christianity, The Ethics of the Spiritual Life (edited); The History of Free Religious Thought in Swansea; The Place of Thought and Feeling in Religion (Welsh); The Parables of Jesus; The Idea of Personality in the English Thinkers of the Present (Jena dissertation in German); An Interpretation of Rudolf Eucken's Philosophy; Rudolf Eucken's Philosophy of Religion; The Philosophy of Rudolf Eucken in the series Philosophies Ancient and Modern; The Spiritual Ascent of Man; The Reality of God; The Training of Mind and Will; The Making of Personality; What Philosophy is; Metaphysics of Life and Death; Nature, Thought, and Personal Experience; The Reality of the Idea of God; Contemporary Thought of Germany, vols i and ii; Editor of the Library of Philosophy and Religion; Editor of the Library of Contemporary Thought; The Status and Destiny of Man in the Cosmos. *Address:* Riviera House, Lower Erith Road, Torquay.

Died 12 June 1946.

JONES, Rt Rev. William Wynn, MA; ThL (Hons); Bishop in Central Tanganyika since 1947; *b* 10 Nov. 1900; *s* of Matthew Tertius Jones, Swansea, and Margaret Veale Ford; *m* 1933, Ruth Lemprière Taylor; two *s* two *d. Educ:* Queen's College, Taunton; Sydney University (MA 1925); Australian College of Theology (ThL Hons 1925). Housemaster Trinity Grammar School, 1922; Ordained, 1925; Curate Dulwich Hill; Principal Training College for Teachers at Kongwa, 1928; Headmaster the Arusha School for Europeans, Tanganyika, 1933; Chancellor, Diocese of Central Tanganyika, 1941; Assistant Bishop in Central Tanganyika, 1943–47; Hon. CF 1941. *Publication:* Barua za Msafiri, Part I 1939, Part II 1944. *Recreations:* tennis, golf. *Address:* 6 Salisbury Square, EC4; Dodoma, Tanganyika, E Africa. *TA:* Kikuyu Dodoma. *Club:* Royal Empire Society.

Died 29 May 1950.

JONES MITTON, Col George, CBE 1920; *b* 25 March 1860; *o s* of George Jones of Mitton Manor, Penkridge, Staffs; *m* 1885, Alice (*d* 1942), *d* of Lt-Col G. Wilbraham Northey, JP, DL, of Ashley Manor, Box, Wilts; one *s* two *d. Educ:* Clifton College. Served South African War (medal 3 clasps); Bt Col and Colonel commanding 3rd South Staffs Regt, 1911–19; European War, 1914–19 (despatches, CBE); assumed name of Mitton, 1881. *Recreations:* fishing, travelling, golf. *Address:* c/o Lloyds Bank, Wolverhampton.

Died 17 Feb. 1949.

JORDAN, Elizabeth, LittD; author and playwright; *b* Milwaukee; *d* of William Francis and Margaretta Garver Jordan; unmarried. *Educ:* Convent of Notre Dame, Milwaukee, Wisconsin; graduate. Given Hon. Degree of Doctor of Letters by Mount Mary College and University, Milwaukee, 1932; winner of St Mary's Cross of Honour. Vice-Pres. Notre Dame Alumnæ Association. Ten years on editorial staff of New York World; three years Assistant Editor of the New York Sunday World; Editor of Harper's Bazaar, 1900–13; literary adviser to Harper and Brothers, 1913–18. *Publications:* Tales of the City Room; Tales of the Cloister; Tales of Destiny; May Iverson—Her Book; Many Kingdoms; May Iverson Tackles Life; May Iverson's Career; Lovers' Knots; The Wings of Youth; The Girl in the Mirror; The Blue Circle; The Lady of Pentlands; Red Riding Hood; Miss Blake's Husband; Black Butterflies; Miss Nobody from Nowhere; The Devil and the Deep Sea; The Night-Club Mystery; The Four-flusher; The Playboy; Young Mr X; Page Mr Pomeroy; Daddy and I; The Life of The Party, 1935; The Trap, 1936; Three Rousing Cheers (autobiography), 1938; First Port of Call, 1939; Faraway Island, 1941; Young John Takes Over, 1942; Herself, 1943; Miss Warren's Son, 1944; and many magazine stories; The Whole Family (with others); The Story of a Pioneer (with Anna Howard Shaw); author of play: The Lady from Oklahoma, produced 1912; Dramatic critic of Weekly, America; author of two editorials a week, syndicated in leading American newspapers. *Recreations:* reading, music, and the theatre; outdoor and athletic habits; golf, horseback riding, motoring, mountain climbing, walking, and rowing. *Address:* 36 Gramercy Park, New York City, USA; (summer home) Spread-wings, Florence, Mass, USA. *T:* Gramercy, New York 5–2389. *Cable Address:* Jordgram New York. *Clubs:* Colony, Cosmopolitan, New York; Northampton Country, Northampton, Mass.

Died 24 Feb. 1947.

JORDAN, Hon. Sir Frederick Richard, KCMG 1936; Chief Justice of New South Wales, since 1938; Lieutenant Governor of New South Wales, 1938–46; *b* 13 Oct. 1881; *s* of Frederick Jordan and Sarah Noble; *m* 1928, Bertha Maud Clay; no *c. Educ:* Sydney High School; University of Sydney. BA Sydney, 1904; Wigram Allen Scholar, 1905; Harris Scholar, 1906; LLB Sydney, 1907. Called to Bar, 1907; Lecturer in Equity, etc. at Sydney University, 1910–21; KC, 1928. *Publications:* Chapters on Equity in New South Wales; General Principles of the Administration of Justice; Admiralty Jurisdiction in New South Wales. *Recreations:* fencing, swimming, reading, travel. *Address:* Supreme Court, Sydney, NSW.

Died 4 Nov. 1949.

JORDAN, Herbert William; Director Jordan & Sons, Ltd, 1895–1942; member Court of Stationers' and Newspaper Makers' Company (Master, 1946–47); *b* 17 March 1874; *s* of William and Elizabeth Ann Jordan; *m* 1906, Alice Mary Wakeman; one *s* one *d. Educ:* Stationers' School. *Publications:* Company Law and Practice, 1908, edns 1–17; Companies Diary, 1908, edns 26–59; Debentures, 1913, edns 1–13; How to Form a Company, 1913, edns 1–21; Private Companies, 1914, edns 1–17; Duties of Secretaries, 1915, edns 1–11; Reminders for Secretaries, 1917, edns 1–17;

Registration of: (a) Business Names, 1917, edns 1–8, (b) Directors' Names, 1917, edns 1–7; Converting into a Private Company, 1922, edns 1–12; National Profit Sharing, 1933; Sixty Years of Company Registration, 1924, edns 1 and 2; New Company Law: (a) in England, 1929, (b) in Northern Ireland, 1932; joint publications: Companies Act, 1907, Annotated, 1907, edns 1–8; Law of Stamp Duties, 1914, edns 13–21; Handbook on Companies, 1925, edns 36–38; Guide to Companies Act 1928, 1928; Voluntary Liquidation, 1931. *Recreations:* usual. *Address:* 28 Norfolk Street, Strand, WC2; 23 Arlington Road, Eastbourne. *T:* Eastbourne 2511. *Clubs:* Royal Empire Society, City Livery, Rotary.

Died 22 Sept. 1947.

JORDAN LLOYD, Dorothy, MA, DSc; FRIC; Director of the British Leather Manufacturers' Research Association since 1927; b 1889; d of late Professor Jordan Lloyd, MD, FRCS, JP, Birmingham, and late Mrs Jordan Lloyd, Highfield, Selly Hill. *Educ:* King Edward's High School, Birmingham; Newnham College, Cambridge (Fellow, 1914–20). Biochemical research under the Medical Research Council at the Biochemical Laboratory, Cambridge, 1915–20; Member of the Staff of the British Leather Manufacturers' Research Association, 1920–27. *Publications:* The Chemistry of the Proteins; numerous original papers on biochemical subjects in the Biochemical Journal, the Proceedings of the Royal Society, etc. *Recreations:* climbing, riding. *Address:* 11 Pelham Place, SW7. *T:* Kensington 8909. *Clubs:* International Sportsmen's, Ladies' Alpine.

Died 21 Nov. 1946.

JOSCELYNE, Rt Rev. Albert Ernest, DD; Archdeacon of Sherborne, 1919–41; b 1866. *Educ:* Merchant Taylors' School; Jesus College, Oxford (Scholar). Curate St George's in the East, 1890–95; Vicar of St George's, Millom 1895–1903; Vicar of St Peter's, Islington 1903–05; Bishop Coadjutor of Jamaica, 1905–13; Vicar of St Mark's, Salisbury, 1913–19; Vicar of Chardstock, 1919–30; Prebendary of Yatesbury in Salisbury Cathedral, 1919–41; Vicar of Preston, near Weymouth, 1930–37. *Publications:* Words to Workers, 1910; The Voices of God, 1911; Words to Worshippers, 1912. *Address:* Rheola, 16 Icen Road, Weymouth.

Died 3 May 1945.

JOSEPH, Horace William Brindley, MA, FBA, 1930; Fellow of New College, Oxford; b 28 Sept. 1867; s of Rev. Alex. Joseph and Janet Eleanor Acworth; m 1919, Margaret (d 1926), 2nd d of Robert and Monica Bridges. *Educ:* Wimborne Grammar School; All Hallows School, Honiton; Winchester College; New College, Oxford (Scholar). Fellow and Lecturer of New College, 1891; Tutor, 1892; Fellow of Winchester College, 1942; Senior Proctor, 1906–07; Public Examiner, Lit. Hum., 1910–12, 1921–22; University Lecturer in Philosophy, 1927–32. *Publications:* An Introduction to Logic; The Labour Theory of Value in Karl Marx; The Concept of Evolution; A Comparison of Kant's Idealism with that of Berkeley; Some Problems in Ethics; Essays in Ancient and Modern Philosophy; various articles in Mind, etc. *Address:* 33 Northmoor Road, Oxford.

Died 13 Nov. 1943.

JOSEPH, Sir Samuel George, 1st Bt cr 1943; Kt 1934; a Lieutenant and Alderman of the City of London; b 15 Aug. 1888; yr s of A. Joseph and S. Gluckstein; m 1916, Edna Cicely, yr d of late P. A. S. Phillips, Portland Place, W1; one s. *Educ:* City of London School. Served European War, 1914–19, Salonika, Egypt, France; Captain Royal Irish Regiment, acted Staff Captain (despatches); Chairman and Managing Director Bovis, Ltd; Extraordinary Director Scottish Equitable Life Assurance Society; Underwriting Member of Lloyds; elected to St Marylebone Borough Council, 1922; Mayor, 1928–30; Alderman Ward of Portsoken, 1933; Sheriff of the City of London, 1933–34; Lord Mayor, 1942–43; formerly Hon. Col 56th (1st London)

Divisional RE; Governor of St Bartholomew's Hosp., Christ's Hospital, St Thomas's Hospital, Bridewell and Bethlem Hospital; Liveryman of the Worshipful Company of Cutlers. *Heir:* s Keith Sinjohn Joseph, Capt. RA, b 17 Jan. 1918. *Address:* Claridge's Hotel, W1; 1 Stanhope Gate, W1. *T:* Mayfair 8860, Grosvenor 4030. *Clubs:* Carlton, MCC, etc.

Died 4 Oct. 1944.

JOSSELYN, Col John, CMG 1919; DSO 1917; OBE 1918; TD; b 28 Oct. 1872; s of Frederic Josselyn and Mary Elizabeth, d of Rev. Henry Lloyd Oswell; m 1900, Lilian Bella, d of Ven. William Weston Elwes, Archdeacon of Madras; one s one d. Chairman Dinding's Rubber Co., and East India Distilleries and Sugar Factories, Ltd; Lond. Chairman State Assurance Co. Ltd, and other Directorships; Practised as a Solicitor in Madras, and Ipswich; served in Suffolk Yeomanry, Madras Guards, Madras Artillery Volunteers, and the Suffolk Regt, TF; mobilized, 1914; Brigade Major, 1915; Lt-Col 1916; Col 1918; Commanded 2/5th West Yorks in England and France; went to N Russia June 1918; served Murmansk Railway; Commanded North Dvina River Force, Archangel; President Allied Claims Commission, N Russia (TD, DSO, OBE, CMG, Croix de Guerre and Russian Order St Vladimir, 3rd class with swords, St Anne, 2nd class with swords, despatches four times); Deputy Director Russian Claims Dept, Board of Trade, 1920–22; Lt-Col (Home Guard). *Address:* St James' Court, SW1. *Club:* Carlton.

Died 11 Oct. 1943.

JOWETT, Rt Hon. Frederick William; PC 1924; JP; b Bradford, 1864; s of Nathan Jowett, Bradford. For fifteen years City Councillor and eight years Chairman of Public Health Committee; twice President of ILP; Chairman of Labour Party Conference, Edinburgh, 1921; Chairman of Public Accounts Committee, 1932; MP (Lab) West Bradford, 1906–18; East Bradford, 1922–24, and 1929–31; First Commissioner of Works, 1924. *Publication:* The Socialist and the City. *Address:* 10 Grantham Terrace, Bradford.

Died 1 Feb. 1944.

JOYCE, Rt Rev. Gilbert Cunningham, DD; b 1866; s of Rev. F. Hayward Joyce, Vicar of Harrow; unmarried. *Educ:* Harrow School; Brasenose College, Oxford. Ordained to be Subwarden of S Michael's Theological College, Aberdare, 1892; appointed by late Right Hon. W. E. Gladstone to be warden of his foundation, S Deiniol's Library, Hawarden, 1896; Principal of S David's College, Lampeter, 1916–22; Chancellor of S Asaph Cathedral, 1924–27; Archdeacon of S David's, 1927–28; Bishop of Monmouth, 1928–40; Hon. Fellow of Brasenose College, Oxford, 1937; Pro-Chancellor of the University of Wales, 1934; Hon. LLD University of Wales, 1937. *Publications:* The Inspiration of Prophecy; contributor to Hastings' Encyclopædia of Religion and Ethics, etc. *Address:* 31 Victoria Street, Tenby, Pem.

Died 22 July 1942.

JOYCE, James; writer; b Dublin, 2 Feb. 1882; s of John Joyce and Mary Murray; m 1904, Nora, d of Thomas Barnacle and Ann Healy, Galway; one s one d. *Educ:* Clongowes Wood College and Belvedere College, Ireland; Royal University, Dublin, BA. Has lived in Paris, Rome, Trieste and Zürich. *Publications:* Chamber Music (verses); Dubliners (fiction); A Portrait of the Artist as a Young Man (fiction); Exiles (play); Ulysses (fiction); Pomes Penyeach (verses); Finnegans Wake (fiction). *Recreation:* singing. *Address:* 34 rue des Vignes, Paris XVIᵉ.

Died 13 Jan. 1941.

JOYCE, Rt Rev. Monsignor T. J.; PPVG; parish priest and domestic prelate. *Educ:* Christian Brothers' School, Nenagh; Mungret Lay College; St Patrick's College, Carlow. Ordained, 1896; Curate in Portumna; Curate in Ballinasloe, 1897; Administrator, 1901; was appointed parish priest of Ballymacward; returned to Ballinasloe as Vicar Forane, 1912; parish priest of Portumna, 1919; Domestic Prelate to Pius XI, 1928. *Address:* St Brigid's, Portumna, County Galway.

Died 20 Feb. 1947.

JOYCE, Thomas Athol, MA; OBE 1918; *b* 1878; *e s* of late T. Heath Joyce. *Educ:* Dulwich; Hertford College, Oxford. Entered British Museum, 1902; Deputy Keeper, Department of Ethnography, 1921, Sub-Keeper, 1932; retired, 1938; Hon. Secretary, Royal Anthropological Institute, 1903–13; Vice-President, 1913–17 and 1923–25; President, 1931–33; Hon. Lieutenant, attached General Staff, 1916; Captain, 1917; Hon. Secretary Hakluyt Society, 1923; led archæological expeditions to British Honduras, 1926, 1927, 1929, 1931; President Section H. British Association, 1934. *Publications:* Les Bushongo, 1910; Handbook to the Ethnographical Collections in the British Museum, 1910; South American Archæology, 1912; Mexican Archæology, 1914; Central American Archæology, 1916; Maya and Mexican Art, 1927; various papers on Anthropology and Archæology in Scientific Journals. *Recreations:* fishing, yachting. *Address:* c/o British Museum, WC; Escampobar, Magagnose, AM, France. *T:* Magagnose 28.

Died 3 Jan. 1942.

JUDD, Thomas Langley, CBE 1920; OBE 1918; partner in J. Earle Hodges, Wright, Judd & Co., Incorporated Accountants, Ridgway House, 41–42 King William Street, EC; *b* 1880; *m* Hilda (*d* 1943); three *s* one *d. Educ:* privately. Served in the Ministry of Munitions during the War; Assistant Director of Accounts, 1917; Deputy Director of Accounts, 1917; Assistant Controller of Accounts, 1918; Deputy Controller of Accounts, 1918; Assistant to Member of Council, 1918; Elected to Court of Common Council of City of London, 1935. *Address:* Aldeburie, St Martha's, Guildford, Surrey.

Died 31 March 1945.

JULIUS, Sir George Alfred, Kt 1929; Hon. DSc University of NZ; BSc, BE, MIMechE; MIEAust; Consulting Engineer, Sydney, NSW, since 1907; Chairman of Commonwealth Council for Scientific and Industrial Research; Chairman, Australian Council for Aeronautics; *b* Norwich, 29 April 1873; *e s* of late Churchill Julius, late Archbishop and Primate of New Zealand; *m* 1898, Eva, 3rd *d* of late C. Y. O'Connor, CMG, Engineer-in-Chief for West Australia; two *s. Educ:* Church of England Grammar School, Melbourne; University of New Zealand. Engineer in Locomotive Department, Western Australian Government, 1896–1907; inventor various calculating devices, including Automatic Totalisators, in use in many countries; Hon. Lecturer in Engineering, University of Sydney; Past President of Institution of Engineers, Australia, 1925; Past President, Engineering Association of NSW, 1911, 1912, 1913; Past President of Electrical Association, NSW, 1918; Chairman, Standards Association of Australia, 1926–40. *Publications:* Physical Characteristics of Australian Hardwoods, 1906, and various scientific papers on engineering and economic problems in Australia. *Recreation:* tennis. *Address:* Culwalla Chambers, 67 Castlereagh Street, Sydney. *TA:* Jupag, Sydney. *Clubs:* Australian, University, Rotary, Sydney.

Died 28 June 1946.

JURY, Sir William Frederick, Kt 1918; *b* 5 Dec. 1870; *m* 1891, Ellen, *d* of William C. Marshe; no *c. Educ:* British and foreign schools. Organised supply of cinema films for the War on the Western Front, Italy, Salonica, Mesopotamia, Egypt, and Palestine, 1915–18; did work on War Loan and organising War Charities; Director of Cinema Propaganda, Ministry of Information; President of the Cinematograph Trade Benevolent Fund, and Glebelands Home. *Address:* Sherwood House, Reading. *T:* Reading 4278.

Died 2 Aug. 1944.

K

KADOORIE, Sir Elly, KBE 1926; Comdr de la Légion d'Honneur, Grand Médaille d'Or de l'Académie Francaise, Médaille de la reconnaissance de France; Médaille d'Honneur du Mérite Syrien de Première Classe-Or, 1933; Chinese Decorations: Order of the Brilliant Jade; First Class gold medal of the Chinese National Government, etc; *b* 1867; *s* of Silas Kadoorie, Bagdad; *m* 1897, Laura, *d* of A. Mocatta, London; two *s*. Left Bagdad, 1880; proceeding to India and China, founded firm of E. S. Kadoorie & Co. in Hong-Kong and Shanghai, and later Sir Elly Kadoorie & Sons; general finance and directorships of public companies; greatly interested in causes of charity and education, having, in conjunction with his brother, the late Sir Ellis Kadoorie, Kt, founded schools and hospitals in all parts of the world, more especially in the Near and Far East. *Address:* Marble Hall, Shanghai, China; 6 Princes Gate, SW7; St George's Buildings, Hong Kong. *TA:* Kadoorie Shanghai; Kadoorie Hong-Kong. *T:* Kensington 6019. *Clubs:* Royal Automobile; Hong-Kong, Hong-Kong Race, Hong-Kong; Shanghai, Shanghai Race, Cercle Sportif Française, Shanghai.

Died 8 Feb. 1944.

KALININ, Mikhail Ivanovich; Chairman of the Presidium of the Supreme Soviet of the USSR since 1938; member of Supreme Soviet of the USSR; member of Political Bureau of CPSU; *b* in Tver district, 20 Nov. 1875; peasant family. *Educ:* Village school. Started as metal worker, Petrograd, 1889; joined League of Struggle and Emancipation of Working Class, 1895; joined Russian Social Democratic Labour Party, 1898; first arrested for political activity, 1899; organised workers' circles in Tiflis and Revel, 1899–1903; exiled to Olonets district, 1904; participated in first Revolution, Petrograd, 1905; delegate of Russian Social Democratic Labour Party at 4th Stockholm Congress, 1905; trade union and underground Party press organisation, Moscow and Petrograd, 1906–17; elected candidate member of Central Committee of Bolshevik Party, Prague Conference, 1912; activities in connection with the Oct. Revolution, 1917; Chairman of All-Russia Central Executive Committee of the Soviets, subsequently the Central Executive Committee of the USSR; with agitational train, Civil War, 1919–20 (two Orders of the Red Banner); headed commission for famine relief, 1919–22; awarded Order of Lenin for services to first Socialist State. *Address:* Palace of the Soviets, Moscow, USSR.

Died 3 June 1946.

KALLAS, Dr Oskar Philipp; retired, 1934; *b* 25 Oct. 1868; *s* of late Mihkel Kallas, Saaremaa, Estonia; *m* 1900, Aino Julia Maria Krohn, two *s* two *d*. *Educ:* Candidatus Philologiæ of the Tartu (Dorpat) Univ.; Dr Philosophiæ of the Helsinki Univ. Lecturer in higher schools at Narva, Petrograd, Tartu; Lecturer in Finno-Ougric languages and ethnography at the University of Petrograd; one of the founders and Chairman (1908–18) of the Estonian National Museum at Tartu; one of the founders and Director of the first Estonian higher School for Girls; Sub-Editor of the Estonian daily newspaper, Postimees, 1903–18; Corresponding Member of the Imperial Geographical Society in Petrograd, the Magyar Neprajzi Tarsasag in Budapest, the Finno-Ougric Society and the Society for Finnish Literature in Helsinki; Hon. member of the Learned Estonian Society and other scientific Societies in Tartu; Dr Philos. (Hon.), of the Tartu University, etc.; since the independence of Estonia in the Diplomatic Service; Estonian Minister in Finland, 1918–22; Estonian Envoy Extraordinary and Minister Plenipotentiary to the Court of St James,

1922–34, and The Hague, 1923–34. *Publications:* works and articles on Ethnography and Folklore, published mostly in Estonian, also in German, Finnish, and English. *Address:* Parnu Maantee 23, Tallinn, Estonia.

Died 26 Jan. 1946.

KAMAT, B. S.; *b* 1871; *m* Yamunabii Gawaskar. *Educ:* Deccan College, Poona. Entered mining and building trade; did civic work on municipal and local bodies for ten years; Member of the Bombay Legislative Council, 1913–16 and 1917–20; Member Legislative Assembly, 1921–23; Member Royal Commission on Indian Agriculture, 1926–28; served on the Bombay Textile Labour Committee, 1928–29; Member Bombay Provincial Banking Enquiry Committee of the Government of India, 1929–30; visited England as a member of a delegation of the Indian Liberal Party in connection with the Montagu-Chelmsford Reforms, 1919, and on a political mission, 1923; ex-Member Legislative Council, Bombay, India; served on the Governing Boards of various educational bodies; did social work, also for agricultural reform. *Recreation:* gardening. *Address:* Ganeshkhind Road, Poona, India. *Clubs:* National Liberal; Deccan Liberal, Poona.

Died 11 July 1945.

KANE, Albert Edmond, CBE 1935; JP; *b* 17 Aug. 1867; *s* of Hugh Smiley Kane, MD, Antrim, and Ellen Malone, Antrim; *m* 1891, Kathleen A. Peel; three *d* two *s*. *Educ:* Cliftonville Academy, Belfast. Served apprenticeship in Mercantile Marine with Thos Dixon and Sons, Belfast; settled in Australia, 1888; Melbourne City Council, 1922–35; retired 1935; served with Red Cross Society during European war; Hon. Treasurer of Victorian Division of Australian Red Cross. *Club:* Commercial Travellers' (Melbourne).

Died 24 May 1949.

KANIKA, Raja of, Raja Bahadur Sir Rajendra Narayan Bhanja Deo, Kt 1933; OBE 1918; MRAS, FRSA; Member Legislative Assembly of Orissa; Member Advisory Council of Orissa, 1936; Member of Executive Council, Bihar and Orissa, 1929–34, Vice-President, 1931–34; *b* Aul, Orissa, 24 March 1881; 2nd *s* of the Raja of Aul, adopted to Kanika family in 1896; *m d* of the Raja and Feudatory Chief of Nayagarh in Orissa, 1899; one *s* one *d*. *Educ:* Ravenshaw Collegiate School and College, Cuttack. Received the management of Killah Kanika from Court of Wards, 1902; President of Utkal Union Conference, 1906; member of the Bengal Legislative Council, 1909–12; Member of the Bihar and Orissa Legislative Council, 1912–16; Member Imperial Legislative Council, 1916–20; Co-opted member of the Committee on the division of functions between Central and Provisional Governments; member Reformed Legislative Council of Bihar and Orissa, 1921; member Reformed Legislative Assembly of India, 1922; member of the Bihar and Orissa Legislative Council, 1923–28; Fellow, Patna University, 1917–19; Elected Member, Patna University Senate, 1919–22; Nominated Member, 1927–29 and since 1932; Ex-officio Member, 1929–32; Member of Committee to co-operate with Simon Commission, 1928; member of the Bengal Fishery Board; Governing Body, Ravenshaw College, Cuttack; Title of Raja conferred (as personal distinction), 1910, and (as hereditary distinction), 1919; Title of Raja Bahadur conferred as personal distinction, 1934; received Coronation Medal, 1911. *Recreations:* billiards, tennis, shikar. *Heir: s* Tikayet Sailendra Narayan Bhanja Deo. *Address:* Cuttack, Orissa, India.

Died 14 Dec. 1948.

KAPADIA, Dr Shaporji Aspaniarji, MD, LRCP, LRCS; Barrister-at-law (Inner Temple), called 1893; late Lecturer and Examiner on Gujarati language at University College, London; *b* Bombay, 12 June 1857; *o s* of Parsi merchant. Arrived in London from Bombay, 1881. *Educ:* Elphinstone High School and Grant Medical College, Bombay; Life Member St Thomas's Hospital, London. Late Senior Clinical Assistant at Royal Westminster Ophthalmic Hospital and Lecturer on Materia Medica and Pharmacology, Zenana Medical College, London; Oriental editor and founder of the Orient Library and Wisdom of the East Series. *Publications:* The Teachings of Zoroaster and the Philosophy of the Parsi Religion; Editor (Oriental) of 60 volumes of the Wisdom of the East Series and the Orient Library. *Recreations:* studying science and psychology. *Address:* 22 Redcliffe Gardens, S Kensington, SW10. *T:* Flaxman 7242.

Died 10 March 1941.

KAPURTHALA, HH Jagatjit Singh Bahadur, Maharajah, *cr* 1911; **Raja-i-Rajgan of,** GCSI 1911; GCIE 1921; GBE 1927; Hon. Brig. in Army; Hon. Colonel of 3/11th Sikhs; *b* Sept. 1872; *S* father, 1877; *m*; three *s*. Grand Cross of the Legion of Honneur; Grand Cross of the Order of St Maurice and St Lazare of Italy; Grand Cross of Charles III of Spain; Grand Cross of the Star of Roumania; Grand Cordon of the Order of the Nile; Grand Cordon of the Crown of Persia; Grand Cross of the Star of Ethiopia; Grand Cordon of the Order of Morocco; Grand Cordon of the Order of Tunis, Grand Cross of the Order of Cambodia; Grand Cross of the Sun of Peru; Grand Cross of the Order of the Merit of Cuba; Grand Cross of the Order of Chili. The State has an area of 652 square miles and a population of about 378,380; besides the State of Kapurthala he possesses landed property in the Province of Oudh, having a population and area of nearly fifty per cent more than those of the State in the Punjab; entitled to a salute (personal) of 15 guns and salute (local permanent) of 15; attended Queen Victoria's Diamond Jubilee, 1897; Silver Jubilee of King George V, 1935; and Coronation of King George VI and Queen Elizabeth, 1937. Heir: *s* Tika Raja Paramjit Singh, *b* 18 May 1892. *Address:* Kapurthala, Punjab.

Died 19 June 1949.

KARAULI, Maharaja of, HH Maharaja Sir Bhom Pal Deo Bahadur Yadukul Chandra Bhal, KCSI 1935; *b* 18 June 1866; *s* of Thakur Sugan Palji of Pardampura; *m* 1st, *d* and 2nd, *sister* of late Raja Bahadur Bhagwan Singh; 3rd, *d* of Thakur Chiman Singh; one *s* one *d.* Accession to the Gadi, 1927. *Recreation:* big game shooting. Heir: Maharaj Kumar Shri Ganesh Pal. *Address:* Karauli, Rajputana, India. *TA:* Maharaja Karauli.

Died 6 April 1947.

KARSLAKE, Lt-Gen. Sir Henry, KCB 1937; KCSI 1935; CB 1929; CMG 1916; DSO 1902; Colonel Commandant, RA, since 1937; *b* 10 Feb. 1879; *o s* of late Lewis Karslake; *m* 1905, Florence Clare, *d* of Vice-Adm. E. Rooke; two *s. Educ:* Harrow; Royal Military Academy, Woolwich. Joined 10th Co. WD RGA, 1898; joined 83rd Field Battery, 1899; posted to T Battery RHA, 1901; posted on promotion to 100th Battery RFA, 1906; officer of a company of Gentlemen Cadets, Sandhurst, 1907; posted to 116th Battery RFA, 1911; Staff College Student, 1912–13; posted 129th Howitzer Battery, 1914; Brig.-Major, Dec. 1914; General Staff Officer, 2nd grade, Aug. 1915; GSO 1st Grade, June 1916; Brig.-Gen. Tank Corps, Oct. 1918; GSO1, British Army on Rhine, April 1919; Colonel, June 1919; GSO 1st Grade, HQ, Peshawar, 1920–23; GSO1 War Office, 1923–25; Colonel on the Staff, General Staff, Southern Command, 1925–28; served S Africa, 1900–02 (despatches twice, Queen's medal 4 clasps, King's medal 2 clasps, DSO); European War 1914–18 (despatches, CMG, Légion d'Honneur, Bt Lt-Col Jan. 1917; Bt Col June 1919); Brigadier RA, Western Command, India,

1928–31; ADC to the King, 1930–31; Maj.-Gen. 1931; Maj.-Gen. RA, Army Headquarters, India, 1931–33; Comm., Baluchistan District, India, 1933–35; Lt-Gen. 1936; retd pay, 1938; GOC France, May–June 1940. *Address:* c/o Lloyds Bank, 6 Pall Mall, SW1.

Died 19 Oct. 1942.

KARSLAKE, Lt-Col John Burgess Preston, TD, MA, FSA; JP; DL; *b* 1868; *o s* of late Preston Karslake of White Knights, near Reading, Berks; *m* 1898, Mary Leonore, *er d* of Edward Darell; two *s* three *d. Educ:* Eton; Trinity College, Oxford. Called to Bar, Middle Temple, 1892; joined Western Circuit; Member of LCC for South Paddington, 1910–31; Vice-Chairman, 1925; Member of Metropolitan Water Board since 1903; Chairman, 1920–22; Mayor of Paddington, 1937–38 and 1940; JP and DL, County of London; joined Berks Yeomanry, 1895; Lieutenant-Colonel, 1914; served in France in European War. *Publications:* papers in Proceedings of Society of Antiquaries. *Recreations:* yachting, shooting, and motoring. *Address:* 22 Westbourne Terrace, W2. *T:* Paddington 6468; Silchester, near Reading. *Club:* Junior Carlton.

Died 3 Sept. 1942.

KATRAK, Khan Bahadur Sir Kavasji Hormusji, Kt 1942; OBE 1935; merchant and landlord, Karachi, Sind. *Address:* 245 Staff Lines, Karachi, India.

Died 24 June 1946.

KAUNTZE, William Henry, CMG 1937; MBE 1918; KStJ; FRCP (Lond.); BA, MD, ChB (Victoria University); MB, BS (Lond.); MRCS (Eng.); Medical Adviser to Secretary of State for the Colonies since 1944; *b* 1887; *s* of W. G. Kauntze; *m* 1919, Edith Davidson, *d* of J. Johnston, Capetown; one *d. Educ:* Victoria University, Manchester; London University. House Surgeon, Manchester Royal Infirmary, 1911–12; Resident Medical Officer, Salford Union Infirmary, 1912–13; Medical Officer, West African Medical Staff, 1914–16; served with West and East African Forces, 1914–19 (Major, East African Medical Staff); Senior Bacteriologist and Deputy Director of Laboratory Services, Kenya Colony, 1919–32; Director of Medical Services, Uganda, 1932–41; Asst Medical Adviser, Colonial Office, 1941–44; Deputy Medical Adviser, Colonial Office, 1944. *Publication:* (with N. Jewell) Handbook of Tropical Fevers, 1931. *Clubs:* Royal Empire, Authors'.

Died 4 Nov. 1947.

KAVANAGH, Lt-Gen. Sir Charles Toler McMurrough, KCB 1917; (CB 1909); KCMG 1919; CVO 1909 (MVO 1906); DSO 1902; Governor of Military Knights of Windsor since 1932; *b* 25 March 1864; 3rd *s* of late Rt Hon. A. McMurrough Kavanagh of Borris, Co. Carlow; *m* 1895, May, 2nd *d* of S. Perry, Woodrooff, County Tipperary; two *d.* Entered Army, 1884; Capt. 1890; Maj. 1900; Lt-Col 1904; Col 1908; Maj.-Gen. 1915; Lt-Gen. 1915; served S Africa, 1901 (despatches twice, Bt Lieut-Col, Queen's medal 5 clasps, King's medal 2 clasps, DSO); European War, 1914–18 (wounded, despatches, prom. Maj.-Gen.); command, 10th Hussars, 1904; Commanding 1st Cavalry Brigade, 1909–13; late 10th Hussars; commanded 7th Cavalry Brigade, 2nd Cavalry Division, 5th Div., 1st Army Corps, Cavalry Corps; retired pay, 1920. *Address:* Governor's Tower, Windsor Castle. *T:* Windsor 537. *Club:* Cavalry.

Died 11 Oct. 1950.

KAY, James, RSA 1938; ARSA 1933; RSW; *b* Lamlash, Isle of Arran, 22 Oct. 1858; *m* Ada B. E. Laval; one *d. Educ:* School of Arts, Glasgow. First exhibited at RA, 1889; Paris Salon, 1894, and Art Exhibitions of Great Britain, Ireland, Europe and America; silver medal and diploma by The Société des Amis des Arts de Rouen, 1903; gold medal and diploma of the Société des Artistes Français, 1903; gold medal and diploma by the Jury of the 37th Exposition-Municipale des Beaux-Arts de Rouen, 1906. *Chief works:* Une Rivière du Nord, purchased by French Government for National Gallery of Luxembourg; Winter; Launch of the Lusitania; Launched—River Clyde; Un Canal—Ecosse; A Dutch Canal; In Search of Grist; Between the Bridges, River Clyde; Phosilipo, Naples; Nocturne, Oban Bay; Rambla de las Flores Barcelona, Spain; The Thames, London; Nocturne, River Clyde; Rouen Cathedral, Gibraltar, Hills of Morvern from Oban, all purchased for various collections and public galleries. *Recreations:* music and reading. *Address:* Crimea, Whistlefield, Dumbartonshire. *T:* Garelochead 276.

Died 26 Sept. 1942.

KAY, Sir Robert Newbald, Kt 1920; *b* York, 6 Aug. 1869; *s* of William Kay and Ann Newbald; *m* 1899, Alice May, *d* of Rev. Thomas Thornton Lambert, Wesleyan Minister; five *s* one *d*. *Educ:* Priory St Higher Grade School, York. Articled to Fredk. A. Camidge, Solicitor, York; admitted a Solicitor, 1893; commenced practising on his own account at York, 1893; large professional practice, principally amongst agriculturists; MP (L) Elland Division of Yorks, 1923–24; Sheriff of York, 1913–14; Chairman of the York Recruiting and Advisory Committee, 1914–18; Lord Mayor of York, 1924–25. *Address:* 2 Newlands Drive, Boroughbridge Road, York. *T:* York 78542.

Died 24 Feb. 1947.

KAYE, Cecil William, MA; *b* 25 June 1865; *s* of late James Kaye, Barrister-at-law, of Lincoln's Inn; *m* Dora Millicent, *d* of late Judge William Barber, QC; one *s* one *d*. *Educ:* Marlborough; University College, Oxford; University of Würzburg. Assistant Master Uppingham School; Headmaster Loughborough Grammar School, 1893–1900; Headmaster Bedford Modern School, 1901–16; Principal of Bedford Evening Institution, 1901–16; Headmaster, St Bees School, 1916–26; formerly on Council of IAHM; Hon. Treasurer of National Froebel Union; Representative of IAHM on Public School Emigration League; Diocesan Lay Reader; late Representative of Carlisle Diocese on Central Board of Lay Readers. *Recreations:* bees, gardening. *Address:* Millbeck Towers, Underskiddaw, Keswick.

Died 15 May 1941.

KAYE, George William Clarkson, OBE; FRS; MA (Cantab), DSc (Lond.), FInstP; Superintendent Physics Department, The National Physical Laboratory, Teddington, since 1922; *b* 8 April 1880; *s* of late George Kaye, architect; *m* Ethel Gertrude, *d* of late Prof. A. R. Willis, MA, DSc, of the Imperial College of Science; one *s* two *d*. *Educ:* Royal College of Science; Trinity College, Cambridge. Captain RE (T), 1910; Major, RAF, 1917; Territorial Decoration, 1919; British War medal; despatches twice; Chief Inspector of Materials, Air Ministry, 1917–20; President of the Röntgen Society, 1917–18; Hon. Editor of the British Journal of Radiology, 1919–32; Hon. Editor Radiography, since 1935; Cantor Lecturer, 1921 and 1926, Aldred Lecturer, 1936, Royal Society of Arts; British delegate, International Congress of Radiology, 1925, 1928, 1931 (Chairman), 1934, 1937; Tyndall Lecturer Royal Institution, 1926; Visitor and Manager of Royal Institution, 1929–35, 1939–41; Sec. of International X-Ray and Radium Protection Committee since 1928; Mackenzie Davidson Lecturer and Medallist, Royal Society of Medicine, 1921; Silvanus Thompson Lecturer and Medallist, 1935, President, British Inst. of Radiology, 1928–29, Hon. Member, 1929; Hon. Fellow, Society of Radiographers, 1937, Pres., 1937–41, Stanley Melville Memorial Lecturer and Medallist, 1940; Corresp. Editor for British Empire of the International Critical Tables, 1923; Caldwell Lecturer (1927) and Hon. Member (1928) American Roentgen Ray Society; Hon. Member Nordisk Förening för Medicinsk Radiologi, 1933; Member National Radium

Commission, 1929–33, Secretary, 1935–39; Member Inter-Services X-Ray advisory Committee since 1926; Member Grand Council British Empire Cancer Campaign; Chairman, Noise Investigation Committee, Ministry of Transport; Chairman Acoustics and Noise Committee, British Standards Institution; Chairman League of Nations International Commission on Noise and Housing, Geneva; Pres. Section A, British Association, 1937, and International Conference on Concert Pitch, 1939. *Publications:* X-Rays; High Vacua; Physical and Chemical Constants (jointly); The Acoustics of Buildings (jointly); numerous papers on physics, Royal Society, Philosophical Magazine, Encyclopædia Britannica, etc. *Recreation:* gardening. *Address:* 13 Waldegrave Park, Strawberry Hill, Middlesex. *T:* Popesgrove 2281. *Club:* Athenæum.

Died 16 April 1941.

KAYE, Levett Mackenzie, CIE; *b* 9 Feb. 1869; *s* of late James Kaye, Barrister-at-law; *m*; one *d*. *Educ:* Marlborough College. Joined UP Police as an Assistant Superintendent, 1889; Superintendent of Police, 1892; Personal Assistant to the Inspector-General, 1903; Deputy Inspector-General, 1912; Inspector-General of Police, United Provinces, India, 1919–24; retired, 1924; awarded the King's Police medal, 1921. *Recreations:* fishing and shooting.

Died 24 July 1941.

KAYS, Brig.-Gen. Horace Francis, CB 1918; *b* 1861; *m* Emily, *d* of late Sir Auckland Colvin. *Educ:* Harrow. Commanded 2nd Batt. Highland Light Infantry, 1908–12. Served Hazara Expedition, 1891 (medal, clasp); Miranzai Expedition, 1891 (despatches, clasp); S African War, 1899–1902 (Queen's medal 3 clasps, King's medal 2 clasps); European War (despatches, CB). *Clubs:* New, Edinburgh.

Died 17 Jan. 1945.

KAYS, Brig.-Gen. Walpole Swinton, CMG 1917; retired; *b* 1858; *m* Margaret, *d* of late H. Harris, Steventon Manor, Hants; two *d*. *Educ:* Harrow. Commanded 2nd Battalion, KRRC, 1903–07; served Ashanti, 1895 (Star); South Africa, 1899–1902 (wounded Spion Kop, despatches twice, brevet Lieut-Col, Queen's medal five clasps, King's two clasps); Brigadier-General, 1914. *Address:* Firgrove House, Farnham, Surrey. *T:* Farnham 225. *Club:* Naval and Military.

Died 14 Dec. 1941.

KAYSER, Charles William; JP Notts; *b* 1870; *s* of Charles William Kayser, Endcliffe Grange, Sheffield; *m* 1912, Kathleen Langley, *d* of Frank Lee Price, Sheffield; two *d*. *Educ:* privately; abroad. Chairman and Managing Director of Kayser, Ellison & Co., Ltd, Carlisle Steel Works, Sheffield. *Recreations:* hunting and shooting. *Address:* Eaton, nr Retford, Notts. *Clubs:* Royal Automobile; Sheffield, Sheffield.

Died 23 Nov. 1947.

KEAN, Captain Abraham, OBE 1934; Master of HMS Prospero; Spring Time Master SS Stephano; *b* Flowers Island, Bonavista, Newfoundland, 1855; *m d* of William and Emma Yetman, formerly of Cape Freels; six *s* two *d*. MP Bonavista Bay, 1885–89; Bay-de-Verde District, 1897; Minister of Marine and Fisheries, 1897. *Address:* 25 Prescott Street, St John's, Newfoundland.

Died 18 May 1945.

KEANE, Most Rev. David, DD; RC Bishop of Limerick since 1924; *b* Ballygran, Limerick, 27 Feb. 1871. *Educ:* St Colman's College, Fermoy; St Munchin's College, Limerick; St Patrick's College, Maynooth. Ordained, 1895; Professor Diocesan College, 1896–1909; President of College, 1909–20; Chancellor of Cathedral Chapter, 1918; parish priest of Glin, 1920–24. *Address:* The Palace, Corbally, Limerick.

Died 14 March 1945.

KEANE, Major Gerald Joseph, CMG 1930; DSO 1917; MD; DPH; DTM; RAMC; retired; late Director Medical and Sanitary Services, Uganda; *b* 18 Dec. 1880; 2nd *s* of J. H. Keane; *m* 1923, Auriol Frances Kyrle, *y d* of late H. D. Chapman, Kilhendre, Ellesmere, Salop; one *s. Educ:* Mount St Mary's College, Chesterfield; Liverpool University. Entered Army, 1908; Capt. 1911; served European War (despatches, DSO). *Address:* Mardon, Moretonhampstead, Devon.
Died 18 June 1943.

KEAY, Lt-Col John, CBE 1919; MD; FRCPE; JP. *Educ:* Glasgow University (MB, CM, MD); FRCP Edin. Served European War, 1914–19 (despatches, CBE). *Address:* Champions, Beaminster, Dorset.
Died 21 Jan. 1943.

KEDDIE, Col Herbert William Graham, CBE 1919; DSO 1917; late RA and RAOC; *b* 24 July 1873; *e s* of J. Keddie, Executive Engineer, Public Works Dept, India; *m* 1903, Ella Cameron; one *s. Educ:* Oswestry; RM Academy, Woolwich. Joined Royal Artillery, 1894; transferred to Army Ordnance Dept, 1906; served Boer war, 1899–1902; Somaliland, 1902; European War, 1914–18 (despatches twice, CBE, DSO); retired pay, 1927. *Address:* c/o Glyn, Mills and Co. (Holt & Co.), Kirkland House, Whitehall, SW1.
Died 27 Nov. 1943.

KEELING, Rev. William Theodore; *b* 22 March 1871; *e s* of Rev. W. H. Keeling; *m* Julia, *e d* of late B. Moss; two *s* one *d. Educ:* Bradford Grammar School; Jesus College, Cambridge. 2nd class Honours in Classics, 1893; and in Theology, 1895. Assist Master at Liverpool College, 1895–97; Epsom College, 1897–1901; Weymouth, 1901–02; Head Master, Warwick School, 1902–06; Headmaster, Grantham School, 1906–10; Cordwalles School, 1910–12; Professor of Old Testament, Anglican Theological College of British Columbia, 1912–32; Rector of St John's Vancouver, 1928–41; Chaplain, Classical and Modern Language Master, St George's School, Vancouver, BC, 1941–45. Deacon, 1897; Priest, 1898. *Recreations:* croquet, cricket, tennis. *Address:* 11 Spencer Road, East Molesey, Surrey.
Died 29 Nov. 1946.

KEEN, Col Frederick Stewart, CB 1926; DSO 1915; Indian Army, retired; *b* 22 June 1874; 3rd *s* of late Colonel Sir Frederick John Keen, KCB; *m* 1904, Mabel Mary, *d* of late Frederick Crowder; one *s* one *d. Educ:* Haileybury; Sandhurst. Attached to 1st Bn Royal Welch Fusiliers, 1894; joined the 45th Rattray's Sikhs, 1895; served NW Frontier of India, 1897–98; East Africa and Uganda, 1898–1901; NW Frontier 1902, and European War, 1914–18 (East Africa, India and Mesopotamia); NW Frontier of India, 1921–22 (CB, DSO, Brevet of Lt-Colonel, despatches several times); graduated at the Staff College, Quetta, 1909 and 1910; retired, 1926. *Address:* Swallowcliffe, Seaton, Devon. *T:* 150.
Died 7 Aug. 1949.

KEEN, Col John Fred, CMG 1918; TD; retired; *b* 1881; *s* of late John Reynolds Keen, JP, Chewton Mendip, Bath; *m* Nellie Nicholson, Cambridge, Ohio, USA; two *s* one *d. Educ:* Summerleaze Collegiate School, Bristol. *Recreations:* big game, rifle shooting (international), and philately. *Address:* 6446 Churchill Street, Vancouver, Canada. *T:* Kerrisdale 0398. *Club:* Terminal City (Vancouver).
Died 18 May 1949.

KEEN, Col Sidney, DSO 1917; TD; RE (TF); was Chief Engineer, 4th Area British Troops in France and Flanders; late CRE 27th Division and Lines of Communication in France; *b* Chewton Mendip, Somerset, 1868; *e s* of late J. R. Keen, JP of Chewton Mendip; *m* 1895, Rosalie Augusta Ada, *y d* of Henry Flower of Ston Easton and Litton, Somerset; two *d.* Joined the 1st Gloucester Engineer Volunteer Cadet Corps, 1881; all ranks to Sergeant; commissioned in the 1st Gloucester Engineer Volunteers, 1888 (name changed to 1st Devon and Somerset Engineer Volunteers, 1889); Lieut 1889; Captain, 1892; Major, 1903; Adjutant of the Corps, 1904–06; Lieut-Col 1908; became CRE Wessex Division on the formation of the Territorial Force, 1908; volunteered for active service on outbreak of war, and took the 1st line RE of the Wessex Division to France, Dec. 1914, having been appointed CRE the 27th Division (despatches thrice); has done much hard work in connection with the Volunteer and Territorial movements; was a member of the Territorial Force Association for the County of Somerset; Chairman of Directors of the Clevedon Water Company, Clevedon Gas Company, and Clevedon Constitutional Club Company; Director of other companies; Proprietor of the Clevedon Potteries, Brick and Tile Works, etc.; President the Clevedon Branch of the British Legion. *Address:* Glen View, Walton St Mary, Clevedon, Somerset. *T:* 411. *Clubs:* Junior Army and Navy; Bristol Constitutional; Clevedon (President).
Died 17 Oct. 1941.

KEETON, George Haydn, MA; *b* 13 Oct. 1878; *s* of Haydn Keeton, Mus. Doc., and Eliza Southam; *m* 1911; one *d. Educ:* Oakham School; Emmanuel College, Cambridge. 1st Class Classical Tripos. Assistant Master at Reading School, 1901–03; VIth Form Master at Fettes College, Edinburgh, 1903–10; Headmaster of Pocklington School, E Yorks, 1910–14; Headmaster of Reading School, 1914–39; Acting VIth Form Master, Fettes College, Edinburgh, Jan.–July 1940; Acting Asst Master, Trinity College, Glenalmond, 1942–43; Former Member of Headmasters' Conference; Cambridge University Rugby XV, 1899 and 1900; English International Rugby XV, 1904. *Recreations:* fishing and gardening. *Address:* Beacon Cottage, Victoria Hill, Fleet, Hants.
Died 7 Jan. 1949.

KEIGHLY-PEACH, Adm. Charles William, DSO 1919; *b* 1865; *m* 1901, Kathleen, *d* of Fleet Paymaster J. R. Dennis; one *s* five *d.* Capt., RN, 1907; Rear-Adm., 1918; retired list, 1918; Vice-Adm., retired, 1924; Admiral, retired, 1928. *Address:* Imber Cottage, Station Approach, West Byfleet.
Died 27 Nov. 1943.

KEIGHTLEY, Sir Samuel Robert, Kt 1912; MA, LLD; barrister and novelist; *b* Belfast, 13 Jan. 1859; *e s* of late Samuel Keightley, JP, Bangor, Co. Down; *m* 1st, 1892, Gertrude Emily (*d* 1929), *y d* of late Henry Smith, Northampton; one *s* two *d;* 2nd, 1930, Anne, *widow* of Col Vowell. *Educ:* private school; Queen's College, Belfast. Scholar in Classics and Law. Irish Bar, 1883; contested South Antrim as Independent Unionist, 1903; was presented with service of plate in recognition of services; contested (L) South Derry, 1910; Member of the First Senate of Queen's University of Belfast. *Publications:* Poems, A King's Daughter, 1881; The Crimson Sign, 1895; The Cavaliers, 1896; The Last Recruit of Clare's, 1897; The Silver Cross, 1898; Heronford, 1899; The Pikemen, 1904. *Recreations:* golf, gardening. *Address:* Parkside Hotel, Dublin.
Died 14 Aug. 1949.

KEIR, Surg. Rear-Adm. William Wallace, CMG 1918; MB; RN, retired; *b* 1876. *Educ:* Glasgow University. Served European War in charge of hospital ships Rewa and China; Hon. Surgeon to the King, 1934–35; in charge of the RN Hospital at Haslar, 1932–35; retired list, 1935; Chevalier Legion of Honour.
Died 12 June 1949.

KEIRSTEAD, Wilfred Currier, MA, PhD, DCL (Acadia Univ.) 1931; LLD (Univ. of NB) 1942; Professor of Philosophy and Economics, University of New Brunswick, NB, Canada, 1908–31; Philosophy and Education, 1931–44; *b* 12 June 1871; 2nd *s* of James W.

Keirstead and Malvina Dunfield; *m* 1904, Gertrude Lydia Seely; one *s*. *Educ:* Provincial Normal School; Univ. of New Brunswick (BA 1898, MA 1900); Univ. of Chicago (PhD 1903). Taught in the common schools about two years; studied in St Martin's Seminary for one year and matriculated into Univ. of New Brunswick, 1894, and was graduated First Division, 1898; took one year at Bates Coll. and Divinity School; entered Univ. of Chicago, 1899, taking combined Divinity and graduate courses, took PhD 'magna cum laude,' 1903; was Pastor First Baptist Church, Rockford, over two years, then came to Woodstock, NB, as Pastor of United Baptist Church until 1908; FREconS; at one time Examiner in Economics for Civil Service of Canada; Chairman Provincial Commission on Mothers' Allowances and Minimum Wage Legislation; Representative and Provincial Administrator of Canada Food Board during European War, 1914–18; member of various Welfare Organisations; President, Children's Aid Society (Fredericton) for many years. *Publications:* Report of the Proceedings of the Canadian Political Science Association for 1934; Magazine articles. *Recreation:* the usual sports but no special recreations. *Address:* Fredericton, NB, Canada. *T:* 1252–1241.

Died 5 Nov. 1944.

KEITH, Arthur Berriedale, DCL, DLitt; Hon. LLD (Leeds); Barrister-at-law and Advocate; Regius Professor of Sanskrit and Comparative Philology, Edinburgh University, since 1914; Lecturer on Constitution of the British Empire since 1927; Crown Member of Governing Body of School of Oriental Studies, London, 1916–35; *b* 5 April 1879; *s* of late Davidson Keith and Mrs Keith of St Margaret's, Dunbar; *m* 1912, Margaret Balfour (*d* 1934), *d* of late Charles Allan, Town Clerk of Bathgate. *Educ:* Royal High School and University, Edinburgh; Balliol College, Oxford. MA Edin. (1st class honours in Classics), Guthrie Fellowship in Classics; Ferguson Scholarship in Classics (Glasgow); BA Oxon (1st class honours in Classical Moderations, Literæ Humaniores, Sanskrit and Pāli); Boden Scholarship, 1898; DCL 1911; DLitt Edin. 1914. Called to Bar, Inner Temple (Certificate of Honour), 1904; admitted to Faculty of Advocates, 1921; Lecturer in Ancient History at Edinburgh, 1907; Deputy Boden Professor of Sanskrit at Oxford, 1907–08; took first place Civil Service competition, 1901; appointed to Colonial Office; was Secretary to Crown Agents for the Colonies, 1903–05; reappointed to Colonial Office, 1905; was a representative of His Majesty's Government at Colonial Navigation Conference, 1907; Joint-Secretary to Imperial Copyright Conference, 1910; Clerk Imperial Conference, 1907; Junior Assistant Secretary to Imperial Conference, 1911 (Coronation medal); Private Sec. to Permanent Under-Sec. of State, 1912; represented Colonial Office on Committee of Visual Instruction; Member of Committee on Home Administration of Indian Affairs, 1919; Examiner in British Constitution and Public Administration and Finance, University of London, 1923–32. *Publications:* Responsible Government in the Dominions (first in 1909 and completely rewritten and enlarged to 3 vols in 1912); revised to 1927 and rewritten, 2 vols, 1928; State Succession in International Law, 1907; 3rd edition of Sir C. Lucas's Historical Geography of West Africa, and South Africa (vol. iii), 1913; Catalogues of the Sanskrit and Prakrit MSS in the Bodleian and Indian Institute Libraries at Oxford, 4 vols, 1904–1911; editions of the Aranyakas of the Rigveda, 1908 and 1909; Vedic Index of Names and Subjects (with Prof. Macdonell, 2 vols, 1912); Taittirīya Samhitā, translated, with introduction and notes, 2 vols, 1915; Imperial Unity and the Dominions, 1916; Indian Mythology, 1917 (vol. vi of Mythology of All Races); The Sāmkhya System, 1918, 2nd ed., 1924; Home Administration of Indian Affairs (Cmd. 207, 1919); The Belgian Congo and the Berlin Act (based on a Monograph written for the Historical Section of the Foreign Office during the War), 1919;

Selected Speeches and Documents on British Colonial Policy, 1763–1917, 2 vols 1918; Rig-Veda Brahmanas translated, 1921; Dominion Home Rule in Practice, 1921; War Government of the British Dominions, 1921; The Karma Mīmāmsā, 1921; Indian Logic and Atomism, 1921; Treatise on the Conflict of Laws (with Prof. A. V. Dicey, 3rd ed.), 1922; 5th ed., 1932; Speeches and Documents on Indian Policy, 2 vols, 1922; Buddhist Philosophy, 1923; Classical Sanskrit Literature, 1923, 2nd edition, 1927; Sanskrit Drama, 1924; Constitution, Administration, and Laws of the Empire, 1924; The Religion and Philosophy of the Veda and Upanishads, 2 vols, 1925; Notes on Imperial Constitutional Law, Journal of Comparative Legislation, vols i–xxiv; History of Sanskrit Literature, 1928; 6th edition of Wheaton's International Law, largely rewritten, 2 vols, 1929; 7th edition of vol. 2, 1944; The Sovereignty of the British Dominions, 1929; Dominion Autonomy in Practice, 1929; Constitutional History of the First British Empire, 1930 (awarded Royal Empire Society's Gold Medal, 1931); Law of Contracts, 1931; British Constitutional Law, 1931; Speeches and Documents on the Dominions, 1918–1932; Constitutional Law of the British Dominions, 1933; art on Dominions, &c, in Halsbury's Laws of England, vol. xi 1933; 5th ed., largely rewritten, of Ridges' Constitutional Law of England, 1934, 7th ed., 1939; 4th ed. of Anson's Law and Custom of the Constitution: The Crown, 1935; Letters on Imperial Relations, Indian Reform, Constitutional and International Law, 1916–1935, 1935; The Governments of the British Empire, 1935; Catalogue of the Sanskrit and Prakrit MSS of the India Office, vol. ii, 1935; The Privileges and Rights of the Crown, 1936; A Constitutional History of India, 1600–1935, 1936, 2nd ed., 1939; The King and the Imperial Crown, 1936; Letters and Essays on current Imperial and International Problems, 1936; Speeches and Documents on International Affairs, 1918–1937; The Dominions as Sovereign States: their Constitutions and Governments, 1938; The King, The Constitution, the Empire and Foreign Affairs: Letters and Essays, 1936–1937; The British Cabinet System, 1938; Constitutional Law, 1939; Constitution of England from Queen Victoria to George VI, 2 vols, 1940; The Causes of the War, 1940; The British Commonwealth, 1941; Federation: its Nature and Conditions, 1942; The Constitution under Strain, 1942. *Address:* 4 Crawfurd Rd, Craigmillar Park, Edinburgh.

Died 6 Oct. 1944.

KEITH, Sir Henry Shanks, GBE 1942; Kt 1920; DL County of Lanark; LLD St Andrews; JP; Hon. Sheriff-Substitute of Lanarkshire; *b* Holytown, 25 Dec. 1852; *s* of James Keith and Helen Hamilton; *m* 1885, Elizabeth (*d* 1934), *d* of John Hamilton; two *s* two *d*. *Educ:* St John's and Gilbertfield, Hamilton. Commenced business with father, 1868; Chairman; James Keith, Ltd, Merchants, Hamilton; entered Town Council of Hamilton, 1892; succeeded father as Provost in 1902–08; re-elected, 1919 and 1922; member of Lanarkshire Education Authority; Chairman, 1919–23–1930; President of Scottish Education Authorities' Association, 1920–25; Member County Council, Lanarkshire; Chairman Education Committee, 1930–43; Chairman, National Committee for Training of Teachers, 1927–43; was member of numerous Committees and Advisory Councils during European War; Chairman of National Insurance Committee of Hamilton since 1911; Unionist candidate for Falkirk Burghs, 1906 and 1910; for Mid-Lanark, Dec. 1910; Coalition candidate for Hamilton Division in 1918; Coalition candidate, 1922; Conservative candidate for Camlachie, 1923; been a member of the Convention of Royal Burghs of Scotland, as representative of Hamilton Town Council, since 1895. *Publications:* numerous reports and memoranda on municipal and social subjects, Rating and Taxation. *Recreation:* reading. *Address:* Avonholm,

Hamilton. *TA:* Keith, Avonholm, Hamilton. *T:* Hamilton 471. *Clubs:* Constitutional, 1900; Glasgow Conservative; Edinburgh Conservative.

Died 9 July 1944.

KELL, Maj.-Gen. Sir Vernon (George Waldegrave), KBE 1919; CB 1917; late South Staffordshire Regiment; *b* 21 Nov. 1873; *s* of late Major Waldegrave C. F. Kell; *m* Constance Rawdon, *d* of late James Scott, Westlands, Queenstown; two *s* one *d. Educ:* home; Sandhurst. Entered army, 1894; Captain, 1901; Major, R of O, 1913; served China, Boxer Campaign, 1900 (medal with clasp, despatches); Language Officer in China, 1902–03; Staff Captain, War Office, 1904–07; Imperial Defence Committee, 1907–09; retired, 1909; re-employed, War Office, 1909–14; served European War, GSO first grade, Directorate of Military Intelligence, War Office, 1914–24 (despatches, CB, Bt Lt-Col, KBE); Re-employed, War Office, 1924–40; Commandant War Department Constabulary; Knight, 1st Class, Order of St Olaf (Norway); American Order of the Chinese Dragon; Officer Legion of Honour; Officer Order of Leopold; Officer Order of St Maurice and St Lazarus; Jubilee Medal, 1935; late Chairman, Japan Society. *Recreation:* fishing. *Address:* 67 Evelyn Gardens, SW7. *T:* Kensington 1726. *Club:* Naval and Military.

Died 27 March 1942.

KELLETT, Adelaide Maud, CBE 1919; R.R.C. Served European War 1915–19 (despatches, CBE, RRC); Principal Matron Australian Army Nursing Staff, 2nd District Base; Matron Sydney Hospital, 1921; retired 1944. Jubilee Medal, 1935; Coronation Medal, 1937; Florence Nightingale Medal. *Address:* Sydney Hospital, Macquarie Street, Sydney, NSW.

Died 12 April 1945.

KELLETT, Lt-Col Edward Orlando, DSO 1943; MP (U) Aston Division of Birmingham since 1939; serving with his Regiment during War of 1939–45; *b* 19 May 1902; *o surv. s* of late Major-General R. O. Kellett, CB, CMG, Clonacody, Fethard, Co. Tipperary; *m* 1926, Myrtle, *d* of late Arthur Atherley, of Languard Manor, Isle of Wight; one *d. Educ:* Cheltenham; RMC Sandhurst. Entered Irish Guards, 1922; Nottingham (Sherwood Rangers) Yeomanry, 1930; Major, 1936; Lt-Col 1940; travelled extensively throughout the world; motored in 1934 from London to Cape Town and in 1935 from London to Calcutta via Afghanistan, etc.; FRGS; Fellow Royal Empire Society. *Recreations:* hunting, big game shooting, travelling. *Clubs:* Guards', White's, MCC.

Died March 1943.

KELLETT, Ernest Edward, MA (Oxon); *b* 1864; 3rd *s* of late Rev. Featherstone Kellett; *m* 1907, Josephine, *y d* of late Dr Joseph Laidler, Stockton-on-Tees; one *d. Educ:* Kingswood; Wadham College, Oxford. Senior English Master at Leys, Cambridge, until 1924; literary critic and author; editor of Book of Cambridge Verse, 1911. *Publications:* (joint) translation of Bie's History of the Pianoforte; The Passing of Scyld, and other poems; The Religion of our Ancestors; Suggestions; Reconsiderations; Short History of the Jews; The Whirligig of Taste; The Story of Myths, 1928; The Conflict (a saga of the seventh century), 1930; Fashion in Literature, 1931; The Northern Saga; Literary Quotation and Allusion, 1933; Short History of Religions; As I Remember; A Pageant of History, 1936; Story of Dictatorship, 1937; Aspects of History, 1938; Ex Libris, 1940; articles in Encyclopædia Britannica and Dictionary of Religion and Ethics. *Recreation:* chess. *Address:* Lantern House, Meadvale, Redhill.

Died 23 Oct. 1950.

KELLY, Annie Elizabeth, CBE 1938; artist; portrait painter; *b* 12 April; *d* of late Thomas G. Abbott and Maude Laura, *d* of William Mason, barrister (both from England); *m* 1908, Cecil Fletcher Kelly. *Educ:* privately;

Canterbury University College School of Art. Exhibited at Paris Salon, awarded Silver Medal, 1934; exhibited at RA, RSA, Royal Soc. of Portrait Painters, Royal West of England Acad., Royal Cambrian Acad., Royal Inst. of Oil Painters, London Portrait Soc. and also at other galleries; represented by work in portrait and landscape in National Gallery of New Zealand and Robert McDougall Art Gallery, Christchurch and Canterbury Society of Arts Gallery, Dunedin Public Art Gallery and Scottish National Portrait Gallery (portrait of Emeritus Prof. James Park, FGS). Member of Council of Canterbury Society of Arts. *Address:* 245 Montreal Street, Christchurch, C1, New Zealand. *T:* 35654 Christchurch, C1, New Zealand.

Died 4 Oct. 1946.

KELLY, Col Courtenay Russell, CMG 1919; DSO 1917; Colonel, Retired List, late RA; *b* 1872; 2nd *s* of late Henry Russell Kelly, Dungannon, Co. Tyrone, and late Mary Howard, *d* of Courtenay Newton, JP; *m* 1938, Violet Ruth Wallace. *Educ:* Charterhouse. Entered army, 1892; Col 1920; served Somaliland, 1903–04 (medal and clasp); European War, 1914–17 (despatches, DSO, and Legion of Honour); retired pay, 1929. *Address:* 83 Barkston Gardens, Earls Court, SW5. *T:* Frobisher 0611. *Club:* Army and Navy.

Died 16 June 1945.

KELLY, Francis Michael; author and consulting expert; *b* Liverpool, 9 April 1879; *s* of Joseph William Kelly, master-mariner and Mary Anne Crolly, both of Drogheda, Co. Louth, Ireland; *m* 1928, Laura, *d* of George E. Baldwin, Barholm, Lincs; no *c. Educ:* France (Toulouse, Bourges); Germany (Bonn, Düsseldorf); Stonyhurst; Balliol College, Oxford (Exhibitioner, Honours in Classical Moderations); Slade School of Art. Asst to late C. Wilhelm as designer at Empire Theatre and in various West End productions for four years; worked independently as designer, actor and author till 1914; incapacitated for active service through motor accident; National Service during war, joined Rifle Brigade, 1918, also as sergeant interpreter; since then free-lance journalist and author; also expert adviser on artistic and historical problems; Imperial Censorship, 1939–40. *Publications:* Historic Costume (with Prof. R. Schwabe), 1925, 2nd Ed. (revised) 1929; A Short History of Costume and Armour (with Prof. R. Schwabe), 1931; Shakespearian Costume for Stage and Film, 1938; Seasons of the Year; part author of Robes of Thespis; Mediaeval Costume and Life, etc.; various articles in Burlington Magazine, Connoisseur, Apollo, Times (Lit. Sup.), Observer, etc. *Recreations:* antiquities, history, the theatre, research work, reading and talking, travelling and visiting Continental museums and galleries. *Address:* 37 Hollywood Road, SW10. *T:* Flaxman 0893. *Club:* Mermaid.

Died 6 Feb. 1945.

KELLY, Rev. Herbert Hamilton, SSM; Member, Society of Sacred Mission; Tutor, Kelham Theological College, Newark-on-Trent, 1919 (emeritus); *b* 18 July 1860; *s* of Rev. J. Davenport Kelly (afterwards Canon of Manchester) and Margaret Alice Eccles, of Blackburn. *Educ:* Manchester Grammar School; RMA, Woolwich; Queen's College, Oxford, 3rd Class Math. Mods; 4th Hon. Hist. MA. Ordained Deacon, 1883; Priest, 1884; Curacies, Leeds, 1884–85; S Barnabas, Southfields, 1886–90; Warden of Theological College of Sacred Mission, 1891–1910 (at Brixton till 1897, transferred to Mildenhall, Suffolk, 1897–1903, now at Kelham, Newark-on-Trent); Director of Society of the Sacred Mission, 1893–1910; Prof. Theological College, Ikebukuro Tokyo, 1913–19. *Publications:* History of the Church of Christ, 2 vols, 1901, 1902; England and the Church, 1904; The Church and Religious Unity, 1913; The Gospel of God, 1928; Catholicity, 1932; various magazine articles, etc. *Address:* House of the Sacred Mission, Kelham, Newark-on-Trent, Notts.

Died 31 Oct. 1950.

KELLY, Howard Atwood; Surgeon; *b* Camden, NJ, 20 Feb. 1858; *s* of Henry Kuhl Kelly and Louisa Warner Hard; *m* 1889, Laetitia Bredow; five *s* four *d*. *Educ:* University of Pa. BA 1877; MD 1882. Founder of the Kensington Hospital for Women, Phila., 1883; Associate Professor of Obstetrics, 1888–89, University of Pa; Professor of Gynecology and Obstetrics, 1889–90, Gynecology, 1899–1919, Emeritus Professor since 1919, Johns Hopkins University; Gynecol. Surgeon, 1899–1919, Consulting Gynecologist since 1919, Johns Hopkins Hospital; founder of the Howard A. Kelly Hospital, Baltimore, 1892, incorporated 1913; LLD Aberdeen, 1906, Washington and Lee, Va, 1906, University of Pa, 1907, Washington College, 1933, and Johns Hopkins, 1939; Fellow and Ex-President (1907) Southern Surgical and Gynecological Association; Hon. Fellow of the Obstetrical Society of London; Fellow American College of Surgeons; Hon. Fellow Royal College of Surgeons (Edin.); Hon. Member Royal Medical Society of Edinburgh; the Italian Society of Obstetrics and Gynecology, Rome; Society of Gynecology and Obstetrics, Paris; Société Française de Gynécologie; Society of Obstetrics and Gynecology, Berlin; Society of Obstetrics, Leipzig; KK Gesellschaft der Aerzte in Wien; Hon. Fellow of the Edinburgh Obstetrical Society; Royal Academy of Medicine, Ireland; Glasgow Obstetrical and Gynecological Society; Chicago Gynecological Society; Associate Foreign Member, Society of Obstetrics, Gynecology, and Pediatrics, Paris; Member French Association of Urology, Paris; Fellow British Gynecological Soc.; Hon. Fellow and ex-President (1912) American Gynecologica Society, Hon. Fellow Roentgenological Society; Fellow American Radium Society; Member International Society of the History of Medicine; Hon. Member Peruvian Surgical Society, 1920; Corresponding Member étranger de la Société de Chirurgie de Paris; Academy of Rumania, 1921; Hon. Member of the Obstetric and Gynecological Society of Moscow, 1923; Honorary Fellow American Urological Association; Hon. Fellow Gynecological and Obstetrical Society, Kiev, 1924; Hon. Fellow, Seabord Med. Association of Virginia and North Carolina; Fellow American Assoc. for the Advancement of Science; Associate, The Victoria Inst. or Philosophical Soc. of Great Britain, 1925; Member of the British Mycological Soc.; Academy of Natural Science of Philadelphia; New York Zoological Society; New York Botanical Gardens; American Museum of Natural History; American Society Ichthyologists and Herpetologists; Life Member, National Association of Audubon Societies; Deutsche Gesellschaft für Pilzkunde; Comdr of the Order of Leopold, Belgium, 1920; Order of the Cross of Mercy, Serbia, 1922; Cross of Charity of the Kingdom of the Serbs, Croats, and Slovenes, 1926; Lecturer Hunterian Society, London, Jan. 1928. *Publications:* Operative Gynecology, 2nd edit. 1906; The Vermiform Appendix and its Diseases (with E. Hurdon), 1905; Walter Reed and Yellow Fever, 3rd edit., 1923; Gynecology and Abdominal Surgery (ed. with C. P. Noble), vol. i 1907; vol. ii 1908; The Surgical Stereo Clinic, representing work of eminent surgeons in Great Britain and the US, 84 Sections, 1908 *et seq.*; Appendicitis and other Diseases of the Vermiform Appendix, 1909; Medical Gynæcology, 2nd edit., 1912; Cyclopedia of American Medical Biography, 2nd edit. 1920 (with W. L. Burrage); Myomata of the Uterus (with T. S. Cullen), 1909; Some American Medical Botanists, 1914; Diseases of Kidneys, Ureters, and Bladder, 2 vols, 2nd edit. 1922 (with C. F. Burnam); A Scientific Man and the Bible, 1925; Gynecology, 1928; Dictionary of American Medical Biography (with W. L. Burrage), 1928; Electrosurgery (with Grant E. Ward), 1932; Snakes of Maryland, 1936; some 500 scientific articles. *Recreations:* mycology, lichenology, herpetology, canoeing. *Address:* 1406 Eutaw Place, Baltimore, Md, USA.

Died 12 Jan. 1943.

KELLY, Hon. Hugh Thomas; KC 1907; KCSG 1937; a Justice of the Supreme Court of Ontario, High Court Division, 1911–37; *b* Simcoe County, Province of Ontario, 1 March 1858; *s* of John Kelly and Anne M'Laughlin; *m* 1890, Mary, *d* of late M. Hynes; one *s* two *d*. *Educ:* public schools; St Michael's College, Toronto (whence graduated with Gold Medal for General Proficiency); University of Toronto. Called to Bar, 1886; President of the County of York Law Association and the Toronto Bar Association, 1910 and 1911; Member of Board of Trustees of Toronto Public Library since 1893; Member of Board of Governors, University of Toronto since 1906, and for some years chairman of its Finance Committee; Charter member of Board of Governors of Catholic Church Extension Society of Canada; Member of the Commission to revise the statutes of the Province of Ontario, 1924; Chairman of Conciliation Board to settle question of wages between Canadian Pacific Railway Co. and Canadian National Railway and their employees, 1926; Member continuously since 1896 of the Board of the Toronto Savings Bank Charitable Trusts; Hon. LLD, University of Toronto, 1926. *Address:* 33 Maple Avenue, Toronto, Canada. *Clubs:* Royal Canadian Yacht, Toronto.

Died 8 Dec. 1945.

KELLY, Mr Justice James Gerald; Judge of the High Court of Justice for the Province of Ontario since 1938; *b* 28 May 1897; *s* of James Kelly and Cecilia MacIsaac; *m* 1922, Margaret Ellen Simpson; four *s* two *d*. *Educ:* Prince of Wales College, Charlottetown, PEI; University of Toronto; Osgoode Hall, Toronto. Served European War, Canadian Expeditionary Force, 1915–19, with 26th New Brunswick Infantry (wounded, MC); BA University of Toronto, 1923; LLB 1928; called to Bar with honours, 1926; KC 1937. *Publications:* Contributed to Canadian Encyclopaedic Digest; Editor Holmested's Judicature Act. *Recreation:* reading. *Address:* Osgoode Hall, Toronto. *T:* Hudson 2542.

Died 31 July 1942.

KELLY, Major John Upton, DSO 1916; *b* 1882; *s* of Richard Kelly, Summerhill, Enniskerry; *m* Eileen Miriam, *d* of late Henry Adams, Cannon Hill, Bray, Berks. *Educ:* Uppingham. Royal Fusiliers; Wiltshire Regt; RFC; served S Africa, 1900–01; ADC General Munro and General T. Capper, 1907–12; Adjutant Malta Militia, 1912–14; European War, France, 1915–16 (despatches, DSO); placed on retired pay owing to wounds, 1919; General Inspector, Local Govt Board of Ireland (retired). *Recreations:* steeplechasing, hunting, fishing, yachting. *Address:* Bucklands, Lymington, Hants. *Clubs:* United Service; Royal Lymington Yacht; Union, Malta.

Died 23 July 1943.

KELLY, Brig.-Gen. Philip James Vandeleur, CMG 1917; DSO 1917; late 3rd Hussars; *s* of Brigade Surgeon Lt-Col William Pierce Kelly, FRCSI, JP, Inspector General HM Prisons Burmah and the Andaman Isles, of Erinagh House, Castle Connell, Co. Limerick, and Elinor Charlotte Beatty of Borodale, Co. Wexford; unmarried. Served S Africa, 1901–02 (Queen's medal 4 clasps); Sudan, 1908 and 1910 (two medals two clasps); European War, 1914–18 (despatches, CMG, DSO); commanded Darfur Campaign, 1916 (despatches twice); Appointed First Military Governor of Darfur; joined the Australian Mounted Division in Palestine, 1917; GSO (I) and subsequently commanded the 5th and 13th Cavalry Brigades, 1917–18; 5th Cavalry Brigade, Territorial Army, 1925–29; retired pay, 1929. *Clubs:* Cavalry; Yorkshire, York.

Died 31 Dec. 1948.

KELLY, Robert Alsop, CMG 1935; *b* 3 Aug. 1881; *s* of late Patrick Kelly and late Mary Helen Alsop; *m* 1915, Olivia Christabel McLean Wait; one *s* one *d*. *Educ:* George Heriot's School, Edinburgh. Associate of the Society of Auditors and Accountants (England); Deputy

Treasurer, Northern Rhodesian Government, 1911–29; Treasurer and Currency Officer, Gold Coast Colony, 1929–36; retired, 1936; re-appointed to Colonial Service, as Treasurer, etc., Grenada, 1940; Acting Colonial Secretary, Grenada, May 1940 and Jan.–May 1941; Treasurer, etc., Bermuda; Member Executive Council, Bermuda, 1943–46; retired, 1946. Secretary, Gold Coast Chamber of Mines and Mining Member of Legislative Council, Gold Coast, 1936–37; served South Africa (Queen's Medal, 5 clasps); Lieutenant NR Rifles, 1916–21; Acting Adjutant NR Rifles, 1917–18; Jubilee Medal, 1935; Coronation Medal, 1937. *Recreation:* golf. *Clubs:* Royal Empire Society; Royal Scots (Edinburgh).

Died 11 July 1950.

KELLY, Sir Robert (Ernest), Kt 1939; CB 1919; MD, BSc, FRCS; Consulting Surgeon, Liverpool Royal Infirmary; Emeritus Professor of Surgery, University of Liverpool; Council of the Royal College of Surgeons (ex-Vice-President) till 1944; Ex-President, Liverpool Medical Institution; Member, General Medical Council; Member, Army Council Medical Advisory Board, till 1944; *b* 7 April 1879; *s* of Robert Kelly, Liverpool; *m* Averill Edith Irma, *d* of Dr J. Edlington M'Dougall, Limpsfield; one *d. Educ:* Liverpool Institute and University of Liverpool; Junior and Senior Lyon-Jones Scholar, Kanthack Medal in Pathology; Medals in Surgery and Forensic Medicine; Derby Exhibitioner. Col Army Medical Service; Consulting Surgeon to the British Forces in Greece, 1917–18; Médaille d'honneur des Epidémies, 1919. *Publications:* Intra-tracheal Anæsthesia, British Journal of Surgery, 1913; Surgery in Salonika, British Medical Journal, 1918; and other surgical publications. *Address:* 80 Rodney Street, Liverpool. *T:* Royal Liverpool 7590. *Club:* Wallasey Golf.

Died 16 Nov. 1944.

KELLY, His Honour Judge Sir Stanley Anthony Hill, Kt 1936; *b* 1869; *s* of late S. W. Kelly, JP, The Elms, nr Cardiff. Called to Bar, 1893; joined S Wales and Chester Circuit, 1893; Legal Adviser, Gov. of Seychelles, 1903; Judge of County Courts Circuit No. 24, 1910–26; Additional Judge of Metropolitan County Courts and Judge of Uxbridge County Court, 1926; Judge of Bloomsbury County Court, 1926–39. *Address:* 18 Norfolk Crescent, W2. *T:* Paddington 3367. *Club:* Reform.

Died 21 Oct. 1949.

KELLY, Sir Thomas, Kt 1931; Lord Provost of Glasgow, and Lord Lieutenant of the County of the City of Glasgow, 1929–32; *b* Carluke, Lanarkshire, 1862; *s* of William Kelly; *m* 1890, Anne (*d* 1929), *d* of John Cameron, Findon, Ross-shire; one *s* two *d. Educ:* Braidwood, Carluke. A Chartered Accountant by profession; a member of the Town Council of Glasgow, 1912–32; held office successively as a Magistrate, City Treasurer, Chairman of the Tramways and Finance Committees; during European War served on the Military Tribunal, and on the Committee entrusted with the reception and maintenance of the Belgian refugees; DL for County of City of Glasgow; LLD Glasgow University; President Institute of Accountants and Actuaries, Glasgow, 1932–34. *Recreations:* golf, bowling. *Address:* 17 Cleveden Road, Glasgow, W2. *T:* Western 2144.

Died 29 Nov. 1947.

KELLY, Thomas Dwyer, CMG 1937; Member of Public Service Board, New South Wales since 1938; *b* Molonglo, NSW, 31 May 1880; *s* of late John Joseph and late Mary Kelly, Molonglo and Sydney; *m* 1914, Irene Mabel Welch; no *c. Educ:* St Joseph's College, Hunters Hill, Sydney. Entered New South Wales Public Service, as clerk, Treasury Department, 1900; Expenditure Accountant and Chief Accountant, Treasury; Under Secretary and Comptroller of Accounts to the Treasury, New South Wales, 1935–38; Vice-

President, Metropolitan Water Sewerate and Drainage Board since 1935 and the Hunter District Water Board, since 1938; Fellow, Commonwealth Institute of Accountants; Fellow, Institute of Public Administration (New South Wales Division). *Recreations:* golf, motoring, gardening, cricket, football.

Died 1 Nov. 1949.

KELLY, William, Hon. ARSA (retd), Hon. LLD Aberdeen. Architect; Past-President of the Institute of Scottish Architects; a Vice-President of the Scottish Ecclesiological Society. *Address:* 62 Rubislawden North, Aberdeen.

Died 10 March 1944.

KELLY, Captain William Henry, CBE 1918, DSO 1917, RD, Royal Naval Reserve (retd); Marine Superintendent, the Pacific Steam Navigation Company, Liverpool, 1921–33; *b* Chester, 22 Aug. 1873; *e s* of late W. H. Kelly, Chester; unmarried. *Educ:* King's School, Chester. After 10 years' experience in various grades in sailing ships, joined the Pacific Steam Navigation Co., 1898; Freeman of City of Chester and member of Joiners and Turners' Company; Freeman of the City of London and of the Livery of the Hon. Company of Master Mariners; Younger Brother of Trinity House; served European War, 1914–18. *Address:* 9 University Road, Bootle, Lancs. *T:* Bootle 3799.

Died 8 June 1941.

KELLY, William Thomas; JP; MP (Lab) Rochdale, 1924–31 and 1935–40; Alderman LCC since 1934; *b* 21 June 1874; *m* 1896, Mary (*d* 1930), *d* of C. Gillett. *Educ:* Manchester. Engineer; Trade Union Officer; Industrial Officer; Vice-Chairman Trinity House Whitley Council; Vice-Chairman War Department Industrial Whitley Council; Member Burnham Committee for Teachers' Salaries; Deputy-Chairman London Advisory Council for Juveniles; Member of Trade Boards. *Address:* 101 Dewhirst Road, Rochdale. *Club:* National Labour.

Died 13 March 1944.

KELYNACK, Theo. N., MD, ChB, MRCP; Consulting Physician and Hon. Governor, Mount Vernon Hospital; late Visiting Physician, Harpenden Sanatorium for Children; Medical Adviser, National Children's Home and Orphanage; Medical Adviser, Shaftesbury Society; late Hon. Secretary, Society Study of Inebriety; *b* Wells, Somerset, 26 June 1866; *s* of late Rev. N. Kelynack; *m* 1904, Violet McLaren, MB, ChB (Edin.) (*d* 1940); one *d. Educ:* Univ. Coll. School, London; Owens College, Manchester. Fellow Royal Society of Medicine. Editor of British Journal of Tuberculosis, 1907–34; British Journal of Inebriety since 1903; The Child, 1910–27; Member of Council of Royal Institute of Public Health and Hygiene. *Publications:* Pathology of Vermiform Appendix, 1893; Renal Growths; their Pathology, Diagnosis, and Treatment, 1898; Pathologist's Handbook, 1899; The Sanatorium Treatment of Consumption, 1904; The Alcohol Problem, 1906; Editor of The Drink Problem in its Medico-Sociological Aspects, 1907; Editor of Tuberculosis in Infancy and Childhood, 1908; National Health Manuals, 1910–1914; Medical Examination of Schools and Scholars, 1910; The Tuberculosis Year Book and Sanatoria Annual, 1913; The Year Book of Open Air Schools and Children's Sanatoria, 1914; Human Derelicts, 1914; Defective Children, 1915; The Drink Problem of To-Day, 1916; Child Welfare Annual, 1916; Pro Patria, 1916. *Address:* Homecot, 9 Arden Grove, Harpenden, Herts. *T:* Harpenden 66. *Club:* Royal Empire Society.

Died 23 Dec. 1944.

KEMBALL, Lt-Col Charles Arnold, CIE 1903; Indian Army (retired); late Political Department Government of India; *b* 27 June 1860; 2nd *s* of late Charles Gordon Kemball, JP, of Mettingham, Suffolk; *m* 1895, May, 2nd *d* of late Joseph Askew Turner; one *s. Educ:* Charterhouse; Sandhurst. 2nd Lieut 15th Regt (East

Yorkshire Regt), 1881; Bombay Staff Corps, 1882; Consul-General, Bushire, 1900–04; Resident, Gwalior, 1910–12; JP Norfolk, 1927. *Address:* Denton Lodge, Harleston, Norfolk. *TA:* and *T:* Homersfield 206.

Died 25 Jan. 1943.

KEMBALL, Maj.-Gen. Sir George Vero, KCMG 1916; CB 1903; DSO 1902; Royal Artillery (retired); Col Comdt RA 1927–29; *b* 22 Oct. 1859; *s* of late Major-General John Shaw Kemball, Fairseat, Wrotham; *m* 1889, Hattie, OBE, *d* of Gilbert Elliot, ICS; one *s.* *Educ:* Harrow. Joined RA 1878; Col 1904; Inspector-General, W African Frontier Force, 1901–05; Assistant Director and Director at War Office, 1909–13; Maj.-Gen. 1914; Brigade Commander, India, 1914; Divisional Commander, India, 1917–19; served Afghanistan, 1879–80 (medal); Chitral Relief Force, 1895 (despatches, brevet of Maj., medal with clasp); North-West Frontier India, 1897–98 (despatches, clasp); West Africa, 1901 (medal and clasp); commanded expedition against Kontagora and Bida, 1900 (despatches, DSO, medal, clasp); and Kano Sokoto expedition, 1903 (CB, despatches, clasp); European War, 1915–16, Mesopotamia (wounded, KCMG, despatches five times). *Address:* 24 Milnthorpe Road, Eastbourne.

Died 8 Jan. 1941.

KEMBALL-COOK, Sir Basil Alfred; *see* Cook.

KEMMIS BETTY, Lt-Col Paget, CMG 1919; DSO 1915; late RE; *b* 12 May 1876; *s* of late Col Joshua F. K. Betty; *m* 1910, Frances Enid Gwenllian, *d* of late Judge John Bishop, Dolygarreg; one *d.* Entered army, 1895; Capt. 1904; Major, 1914; Lt-Col 1921; served South Africa, 1900–02 (Queen's medal 4 clasps, King's medal 2 clasps); European War 1914–18 (DSO, Bt Lt-Col, CMG); retired pay, 1923. *Address:* Puddletown, Dorset.

Died 11 May 1948.

KEMP, Rev. Frederick James; *b* 11 Feb. 1885; *s* of J. T. Kemp; *m* Thyrza Maud, *o d* of Edward Noyes; no *c.* *Educ:* Christ's Hospital; Jesus College, Oxford. Penarth School; Warwick School; King Edward VII School, Lytham, and Clifton College. Headmaster, Haberdashers' Aske's Hampstead School, NW2, 1920–40. *Recreations:* outdoor, mainly golf, walking. *Address:* BM/FJK, London, WC1.

Died 27 Sept. 1943.

KEMP, Henry Thomas, KC 1904; LLM, MA, JP; *b* Hull, 7 Dec. 1852; *s* of late Rev. Henry William Kemp, MA, Hon. Canon of York and Master of the Charterhouse, Hull; *m* 1887, Jessie, *d* of late James Melrose, JP, Clifton Croft, York. *Educ:* Shrewsbury School; St John's College, Cambridge. 1st Class, Law Tripos, 1877. Called to Bar, Inner Temple, 1879; admitted *ad eundem* Middle Temple, 1892; Bencher, Middle Temple, 1912; Recorder of York, 1911–17; of Kingston-upon-Hull, 1917–28. *Address:* 59 Inverness Terrace, W2.

Died 12 Jan. 1943.

KEMP, Sir Joseph Horsford, Kt 1927; CBE 1918; *b* Drogheda, 23 Dec. 1874; *s* of P. Kemp; *m* Mary Stuart; one *s.* *Educ:* High School, Dublin; Cape University (BA). Barrister, Lincoln's Inn; Cadet, Hong Kong, 1898; Chief Justice of Supreme Court, Hong Kong 1930–33. *Address:* Camborne, Langley Park Road, Sutton, Surrey. *T:* Vigilant 0412.

Died 13 Sept. 1950.

KEMP, Sir Kenneth McIntyre, Kt 1937; Barrister-at-law; *b* 13 Dec. 1883; *s* of David Skinner Kemp; *m* 1915, Margaret, *e d* of Lieut-Col Ashton Street, IMS; one *s* one *d. Educ:* George Watson's College, Edinburgh; Dulwich College; Corpus Christi College, Cambridge. Called to Bar, Inner Temple, 1908; practised in Bombay from 1909 onwards; acted Chief Presidency Magistrate, 1912; Lecturer, Government Law College, 1913–14; served

with Indian Army in Aden, Mesopotamia and Salonika, 1915–19 (despatches); Editor, Indian Law Reports, Bombay, 1919; acted Judge High Court for periods during 1927, 1928 and 1929; Advocate-General, Bombay, 1935–37; resigned, 1937; Legal Adviser to Secretary of State for India and Burma and thereafter to Secretary of State for Commonwealth Relations, 1938–48. *Recreations:* tennis and golf. *Address:* Carfax, 21 Parkside, Wimbledon, SW19. *T:* Wimbledon 1413. *Clubs:* East India and Sports; Royal Bombay Yacht (Bombay).

Died 9 May 1949.

KEMP, Stanley Wells, FRS 1931; ScD (Dublin); Secretary to Marine Biological Association of the United Kingdom and Director of the Plymouth Laboratory since 1936; *b* 14 June 1882; *s* of Stephen Kemp, FRAM; *m* 1913, Agnes, *d* of W. Spotswood Green, CB; one *d. Educ:* St Paul's School; Trinity College, Dublin. Assistant Naturalist, Department of Agriculture and Technical Instruction for Ireland, Fisheries Branch, 1903–09; Superintendent of Zoological Section of Indian Museum, Calcutta (afterwards the Zoological Survey of India), 1910–24; attached as Zoologist to Abor Punitive Expedition, 1911–12; Director of Research to the Discovery Committee, Colonial Office, 1924–36. *Publications:* papers on zoological subjects, mainly on Crustacea, in various scientific journals. *Address:* The Laboratory, Citadel Hill, Plymouth. *Club:* East India and Sports.

Died 16 May 1945.

KEMPLING, William Bailey, FRSL; Institute of Journalists; *b* Hull; *m* Elizabeth Watts, Windermere. Over 25 years on the Daily Chronicle (14 years as Assistant Literary Editor). *Publications:* The Poets Royal of England and Scotland; The Shakespeare Memorials of London; Shakespeare; The Unending Quest; ed. 4 vols of anthology; numerous contributions to The Fortnightly Review, The Graphic, The Book Monthly. *Recreation:* Shakespeare in work and play. *Address:* 7 Exhall Close, Stratford-on-Avon.

Died 31 Jan. 1941.

KEMPSON, Eric William Edward; 2nd *s* of Frederick Robertson Kempson, formerly of Birchyfield, Bromyard, Herefordshire; *m* Beatrice Hamilton, 3rd *d* of L. T. Ashwell of Warlingham, Surrey; one *s* one *d. Educ:* Shrewsbury; Trinity College, Cambridge. Naval Instructor, RN, 1904–07; a Master RN College, Dartmouth, 1907–11; a Master Rugby School, 1911–19; HM Inspector of Schools, 1919–27; Headmaster of RN College, Dartmouth, 1927–42; served in Royal Engineers in Palestine (MC, despatches twice). *Address:* 29 Bywater St, SW3. *T:* Kensington 8706. *Club:* Garrick.

Died 23 July 1948.

KEMPSTER, Christopher Richard, consulting physician; MRCS; LRCP; Freeman of City of London; Liveryman Society of Apothecaries; FRSM; *b* London, Nov. 1869; *s* of late William Henry Kempster, MD; *m* Hilda, *d* of late William E. Oakes; no *c. Educ:* Cavendish College, Cambridge; Westminster Hospital; King's College Hospital; London Hospital. Medical Officer i/c X-ray and Electro-therapeutic Dept, Hampstead General and North-West London Hospital; Medical Officer i/c X-ray and Physio-therapeutic Dept, Manor House Orthopædic Hospital; Physician i/c X-ray and Electro-therapeutic Dept, and Lecturer to St John's Hospital for Skin, London; Hon. Senior Assist, X-ray and Radium Dept, Royal Cancer Hospital, London; MO i/c X-ray and Electro-therapeutic Dept, City of London Military Hospital; Medical Officer i/c X-ray Dept, Cambridge Heath Military Hospital; Medical Officer i/c Hendon Cottage Hospital; Civil Surgeon to War Office; Staff Captain, City of London National Guard. *Publications:* papers in medical journals. *Recreation:* foreign travel.

Address: 46 Portland Court, W1. *T:* Museum 9660. *Clubs:* City Livery, United Wards, Cambridge Graduates.

Died 7 Sept. 1948.

KEMPSTER, Lt-Col Herbert William, CMG 1917; late RASC; Director of London and Northern Estates Co. Ltd, Reunion Properties Co. Ltd, David Stuart Ltd (Edinburgh); *s* of late Lieut-General F. J. Kempster of Tiptree Hall, Essex; *m* 1902, Elizabeth Ellen, *d* of late E. A. Mammatt, Prior Park, Ashby-de-la-Zouche; one *s*. Served South Africa, 1899–1902 (Queen's medal with six clasps, King's medal with two clasps); European War, 1914–18 (despatches, CMG, Brevet Major, Order of SS Maurice and Lazarus of Italy, 1914 star with bar, two medals). *Address:* c/o Barclays Bank (Dominion, Colonial and Overseas), Wall, EC2. *Club:* Junior Naval and Military.

Died 26 Nov. 1944.

KEMPSTER, John Westbeech, DL, MIEE; *b* Birmingham, 1864; *s* of late John Kempster, JP; *m* 1897, Eleanor Mabel, *d* of late John Meredith Jones, JP; two *d*. *Educ:* Dulwich College; Neuwied-on-the-Rhine; City and Guilds of London Institute. A Principal of Harland & Wolff, Ltd, Belfast, 1906; Chairman of Managing Directors, 1911; has been President of Clyde Shipbuilders' Association, President of Greenock Chamber of Commerce, Chairman of Greenock Provident Bank. *Publications:* Britain's Financial Plight, 1928; Banking, Credit, and the Crisis, 1932; Our Rivers, 1946; various addresses and articles on Industrial and Economic subjects. *Recreation:* fishing. *Address:* Chalk Hill, Guildford, Surrey. *T:* Guildford 4664.

Died 24 Jan. 1947.

KEMPTHORNE, Rt Rev. John Augustine, DD; *b* 26 May 1864; *s* of John Kempthorne, MA, Fellow of Trinity, Head Master of Blackheath School, and Vicar of Trumpington, and Eliza Gertrude, *d* of Theophilus Thompson, MD; *m* 1890, Hester Mary, *d* of late John Peile; no *c*. *Educ:* Haileybury; Trinity College, Cambridge (Scholar); Abbott University Scholar; Hon. Mention Chancellor's Medal for Classics; 1st Class in Classical Tripos; Part I 1884, Part II 1886. Curate of St Aidan's, Gateshead, 1890; Vicar of St Mary's, Rochdale, 1895; Vicar of St Thomas's, Sunderland, and Examining Chaplain to Bishop Westcott, 1900; Rector of Gateshead, 1901; Rector of Liverpool and Hon. Canon, 1904; Examining Chaplain to Bishop of Liverpool, 1904; Member of Liverpool Education Committee and of Council of Liverpool University; Vicar of Hessle, 1910–13; Bishop of Hull, 1910–13; Bishop of Lichfield, 1913–37. *Publication:* Pastoral Life and Work To-day, 1919. *Address:* Maris House, Trumpington, Cambridge.

Died 24 Feb. 1946.

KENDALL, Captain Charles James Cope, CIE, 1919; DSO 1904; late Royal Indian Marine; *b* 1864; *s* of late Surg.-Gen. H. Kendall; *m* 1901, Lilian Mary (*d* 1909), *y d* of late Rev. W. Maule; one *s*. *Educ:* Epsom. Entered RIM 1885; served Burma, 1885–89 (medal with two clasps); Marine Survey, India, 1889–97; China, 1900 (medal); Somaliland, 1904 (medal, DSO); served as Marine Transport Officer in Egypt during European War, Aug. 1914–March 1919 (CIE and Order of Nile, 3rd Class). *Address:* Lickeen House, Glencar, Co. Kerry, IFS.

Died 11 Dec. 1943.

KENEALY, Most Rev. Anselm E. J.; Archbishop of the titular Metropolitan See of Ratiaria since 1936; *b* 1864. Entered the Franciscan Order, 1879; Priest, 1887; appointed to the Chair of Logic and Metaphysics, English Franciscan (Capuchin) Province, 1888; sometime editor of the Franciscan Annals; Guardian of the Franciscans, Crawley, Sussex, 1899; President of the Roger Bacon Society; Minister Provincial for England, 1902; first Rector of the Franciscan College, Cowley,

Oxford, 1906; elected a life member of the Oxford Union, 1907; called to Rome, 1908, as member of a Commission on the Affairs of his Order, and there, the same year, elected Definitor-General to represent the English-speaking provinces; Visitator-General, Irish Province, 1910; Archbishop of Simla, 1910–36. *Address:* Franciscan Friary, Crawley, Sussex.

Died 18 Dec. 1943.

KENMARE, 5th Earl of, *cr* 1800; **Valentine Charles Browne,** CVO 1904; Bt 1622; Viscount Kenmare, Baron Castlerosse, 1689; Viscount Castlerosse, 1880; Baron Kenmare of Killarney, (United Kingdom), 1856; *b* 1 Dec. 1860; *e s* of 4th Earl, and Gertrude Harriet, *o d* of Rev. Lord Charles Thynne; *S* father, 1905; *m* 1887, Hon. Elizabeth Baring, *d* of 1st Baron Revelstoke; two *s* (and one *s* killed in action, 1915) two *d*. *Educ:* Oratory School. Lieut Co. Kerry. Owns 140,000 acres. *Heir:* Viscount Castlerosse. *Address:* Kenmare House, Killarney, County Kerry; 117 Eaton Square, SW1; The Coast House, Walmer, Kent. *T:* Sloane 5050, Deal 31. *Clubs:* Turf, Brooks's, MCC; Kildare Street, Dublin.

Died 14 Nov. 1941.

KENMARE, 6th Earl of, *cr* 1800; **Valentine Edward Charles Browne;** Bt 1622, Viscount Kenmare, Baron Castlerosse, 1689; Viscount Castlerosse, 1800; Baron Kenmare of Killarney, (United Kingdom), 1856; late Captain Irish Guards; Director of Evening Standard, Daily Express, and Sunday Express; *b* 29 May 1891; *e s* of 5th Earl of Kenmare and Hon. Elizabeth Baring, *d* of 1st Baron Revelstoke; *S* father, 1941; *m* 1st, 1928, Doris (from whom he obtained a divorce, 1938; she died 1942), *d* of Edward Charles Delavigne; 2nd, 1943, Viscountess Furness. *Educ:* Royal Naval College, Osborne; Downside; Trinity College, Cambridge, BA. Served European War, 1914 (wounded). *Publication:* Valentine's Days, 1934. *Heir:* *b* Hon. Gerald Ralph Desmond Browne, OBE 1923, Major (retired), 1st Roy. Dragoons [*b* 20 Dec. 1896. Oratory School]. *Address:* Kenmare House, Killarney, County Kerry. *Clubs:* Carlton, Guards', White's, St James', Orleans, Beefsteak, Press.

Died 20 Sept. 1943.

KENNARD, Sir Coleridge (Arthur Fitzroy), 1st Bt *cr* 1891; in Diplomatic Service; *b* London, 12 May 1885; *o s* of Hugh Coleridge Kennard, Grenadier Guards, and Helen, *d* of James Wyllie, Hove, and Eilenroc, Antibes, France; granted the baronetcy conferred on his grandfather, Coleridge Kennard, who died before receiving the patent; *m* 1st, 1911, Dorothy Katharine (who obtained a divorce 1918), *y s* of late Sir George Head Barclay, KCSI, KCMG; two *s*; 2nd, 1924, Mary Graham (*d* 1931), *d* of late Sir Frederick Orr-Lewis, 1st Bt, Montreal. *Educ:* Eton. Entered Foreign Office, 1908; appointed Rome, 1909; transferred to Teheran, 1909; 3rd Secretary, 1910; transferred to Foreign Office, 1914; appointed to Stockholm, 1916; 2nd Secretary, 1918; 1st Secretary, 1919; Chargé d'Affaires, Helsingfors, Aug. 1919. *Publications:* Level Crossings, 1924; Suhaïl, 1927; Public Gardens, 1929; Olympia, 1934; Farewell to Eilenroc, 1935. *Heir:* *s* Lawrence Ury Charles, *b* 6 Feb. 1912. *Address:* 9 avenue de Suffren, Paris. *Club:* St James'.

Died 7 Oct. 1948.

KENNARD, Col Henry Gerard, CBE 1919; on London staff of The Christian Science Monitor; 2nd *s* of Adam S. Kennard, Crawley Court, Winchester; *m* Annie, *e d* of Col R. Poyser, DSO; two *d*. *Educ:* Eton; Sandhurst. Gazetted to 5th Dragoon Guards, 1890; commanded, 1907–11; retired, 1911; commanded Dublin Garrison, 1915–18. *Address:* 54b Warrington Crescent, W9. *T:* Cunningham 4696. *Club:* United Service.

Died 1 March 1946.

KENNEDY, His Honour Judge Alfred Ravenscroft, KC 1919, BA; Judge of County Courts on Circuit No. 49 (Kent) 1929–30, Circuit No. 53 (Gloucestershire, etc.) since 1930; *b* 15 Feb. 1879; *e surv. s* of late Rt Hon. Lord Justice Kennedy and *d* of George Richmond, RA; *m* 1908, Daisy *d* of Alfred Chapman, MICE. *Educ:* Eton; King's College, Cambridge, BA. Called to Bar, Lincoln's Inn, 1903; Legal Adviser at the Foreign Office during War; Recorder of Burnley, 1924–29; MP (U) Preston, 1924–29; Bencher of Lincoln's Inn, 1922; Commissioner of Assize, 1933 and 1934; Deputy Chairman Gloucestershire Quarter Sessions, 1936; Chairman, County Probation Committee; President, Corporation of Certified Secretaries, 1927–37; Life Governor, Cheltenham College, 1939; Arbitrator under Coal Mines Act; Aliens Tribunal, 1939; Chairman, Gloucestershire Quarter Sessions, Appeals, Rating and Licensing Committees; Vice-Chairman, Home Office School, Ashton Keynes, 1941. *Publications:* Contracts of Sale CIF; editor of Kennedy's Law of Civil Salvage; editor of Benjamin on Sale; contributor to Halsbury's Laws of England. *Address:* Ablington House, Bibury, Glos. *T:* Bibury 17.

Died 10 Feb. 1943.

KENNEDY, Lt-Col Andrew Campbell, DSO 1917; late RA; *b* 1872; *s* of late Admiral A. J. Kennedy, RN; *m* 1927, Peggie (*d* 1940), 2nd *d* of John McNeill of Shalaney, Cork, and *widow* of Dr A. H. Vassie. Served European War, France, 1914–16 (despatches); Mesopotamia, 1916–17 (despatches, DSO). *Address:* Grange Lodge, Furness Road, Eastbourne.

Died 5 Jan. 1941.

KENNEDY, Charles Rann, Hon. LLD, Saint Mary's College, California; dramatist, actor, producer; formerly with wife, trustee and head of Drama Department, the Bennett Junior College, Millbrook, NY; *b* Derby, 14 Feb. 1871; *s* of Annie Leng Fawcett and Edmund Hall Kennedy; *m* Edith Wynne Matthison. *Educ:* College School, Saltley, Birmingham. Formerly engaged in mercantile life; first appearance on stage, 28 April 1897; first appearance in New York, 1903; leading parts in Shakespeare, Greek Drama, Shaw, etc., and in own plays. *Plays:* What Men Dare; The Servant in the House; The Winter Feast; The Terrible Meek; The Flower of the Palace of Han; The Necessary Evil; The Idol Breaker; The Rib of the Man; The Army with Banners; The Fool from the Hills; The Chastening; The Admiral; The Salutation; Old Nobody; Crumbs; Flaming Ministers; Face of God; Beggar's Gift; Isles of the Blest; The Seventh Trumpet. *Poems:* Sonnets for Armageddon. *Address:* 10678 Rochester Avenue, Los Angeles 24, California.

Died 16 Feb. 1950.

KENNEDY, Major Francis Malcolm Evory, CB 1917; DL, JP Somerset; Alderman of the Somerset County Council; *b* 12 Nov. 1869; *y s* of late Tristram Kennedy, MP, for Co. Louth; *m* 1925, Lucy Caroline, *e d* of late Rev. T. H. Gregory of Whalley, Lancashire. Joined the Somerset Light Infantry, 1891; Captain, Worcestershire Regt, 1900; retired, 1908; joined W Somerset Yeomanry, 1908; retired 1921; served NW Frontier of India, 1897–98; Mohmand (medal with clasp); S African War, 1900–02; served as Adjutant, 16th Batt. MI, 10 Feb. 1901 to 31 May 1902; operations in Orange River Colony, 30 Nov. 1900 to 31 May 1902 (Brevet of Major, Queen's medal with 4 clasps); CB 1917, in recognition of services during the war. *Address:* Crossways, Kingston, Taunton. *T:* Kingston 230. *Clubs:* Somerset County, Taunton.

Died 28 Jan. 1945.

KENNEDY, Col James Crawford, CBE 1924; MD, late RAMC; Medical Inspector, P & O and allied Steamship Cos; *b* 1879; *s* of late Rev. D. W. Kennedy, Perth; *m* 1912, Eileen, *d* of Daniel Woodruffe, Market Harborough; one *s* two *d*. *Educ:* Edinburgh Univ. MB,

ChB (Edin.), 1900; MD (Edin.), Gold Medal, 1908; DTM and H (Camb.), 1909; MRCP (Edin.), 1925. Lieut RAMC, 1900; Captain, 1903; Major, 1912; Lieut Colonel, 1918; temp. Colonel, 1922; Brevet Colonel, 1923; Col 1928; was Member Mediterranean Fever Commission; Late Assistant Professor of Pathology and Professor of Tropical Medicine, RAM College; Consulting Physician to the British Army, 1922–29; ADMS Poona, 1930–32; retired pay, 1932; served European War, India (despatches) and Mesopotamia; Consulting Physician to British Forces in Turkey, 1922–23; Hon. Physician to HM, 1923–32. *Publications:* contributions to medical literature on general and tropical medicine and bacteriology. *Recreations:* golf, tennis, yachting. *Address:* Ravenscroft, Ash, Surrey.

Died 4 April 1944.

KENNEDY, Maj.-Gen. Sir John, GBE 1946; KBE 1937; CB 1932; CMG 1918; DSO 1916; Lieutenant of the Tower of London, 1945–48; Vice-Chairman Executive Committee British Red Cross Society; *b* 1878; *s* of late Lt-Colonel John Kennedy, 5th Dragoon Guards, Tyrnon, Dumfriesshire; *m* 1919, Mrs C. R. Pawson, *d* of Captain Upton Gaskell, JP, Ingersley Hall, Cheshire. *Educ:* Haileybury. Entered Argyll and Sutherland Highlanders, 1898; Major-General, 1931; retired ill-health, 1936; Egyptian Army, 1909–14; served European War, France and Belgium, 1914–18 (twice wounded, despatches six times, DSO and bar); Brevets Lt-Col and Col, CMG; 1914 star and two medals; Commanded 7th Seaforth Highlanders, 1916, 26th (Highland) Brigade, 1917–18; Inspector of Infantry, 1918; Instructor Senior Officers School, 1919; Commanded 2nd Buffs, 1923, 19th Indian Infantry Brigade, 1926, 44th Home Counties Division TA, 1932, 1st Division, 1934–36; Colonel of the Buffs, 1937–43; Vice-Chairman Exec. Committee of Red Cross and St John War Organisation, 1939–47; Kt Grand Cross of Dannebrog; Kt Comdr of the Royal Order of St Olaf; Order of the Nile; the Prince Carl Gold Medal; Grand Officer of Royal Order of George I; Grand Officer of Order of Orange Nassau. *Address:* 32 Hereford House, Park Lane, W1. *T:* Mayfair 1963. *Club:* Army and Navy.

Died 5 Sept. 1948.

KENNEDY, Lt-Col John Ross, DSO 1940; OBE 1942; AMICE, AMIEE; RE (TA); CRE 50 (Northumbrian) Division, 1940–42; *b* 14 Jan. 1905; *s* of R. S. Kennedy, Chalkmead, Ferring, Sussex; *m* 1930, Lucretia Thrale Martin; two *s*. *Educ:* Oundle; Durham University. Student Apprentice, North Eastern Marine Engineering Co. Ltd, 1922–25; College Apprentice Metropolitan-Vickers Electrical Co. Ltd, 1926–29; Junior Engineer, Merz and McLellan, 1929–33; Senior Engineer, Merz and McLellan, 1933–38; Head of Electrical Power Station Section, Merz and McLellan, 1938–39; CRE 50 (N) Div., 1939–40. *Publications:* technical papers only. *Recreations:* ski-ing, mountain climbing. *Address:* HQ 50 (N) Div. RE, c/o Army Post Office.

Died 14 June 1942.

KENNEDY, Rt Rev. Kenneth William Stewart, DD, MB; in charge Rathmichael Parish, Dio. Dublin since 1936; *s* of Very Rev. T. Le Ban Kennedy, DD, Dean of Clogher; *m* 1904, Mary Elizabeth, *d* of Rev. H. R. Poole, DD, Senior Fellow, Trinity College, Dublin; no *c*. *Educ:* Royal School, Armagh; Trinity College, Dublin (Classical Scholar). Divinity Test, 1890; BA, 1888, Biblical Greek Prize, 1888; Downes Div. Prem. Extemp. Sp. and Written Composition 1889, MB, BCh and BAO, 1891, BD and DD (jure dig.) 1926, Kaisar-i-Hind Medal (1st Cl.), 1933. Ordained, 1890; Curate of St Ann's Dublin, 1890–91; Missionary Dublin University Mission to Chota Nagpur, 1892–1904; SPG Missionary in Chota Nagpur, 1904–26; Examining Chaplain to Bishop of Nagpur, 1904–10; to Bishop of Chota Nagpur, 1904–26; Commissary Chota Nagpur, 1906 and 1913–14; Secretary Medical Missions SPG, 1913–14; Bishop of Chota Nagpur, 1926–36; Member of Legislative Council, Bihar and Orissa, 1922–25. *Address:* Rathmichael Rectory, Shankill, Co. Dublin. *T:* Shankill 72.

Died 9 Dec. 1943.

KENNEDY, Patrick James; first Chairman of Meath County Council; *b* 19 Dec. 1864; *s* of Brian Kennedy; *m* 1888, Cornelia, 3rd *d* of late P. A. Duncan, Professor in University of Vienna. *Educ:* Castleknock College, Dublin. MP North Kildare, 1892–95; JP Co. Meath; MP (N) for North Westmeath, 1900–06; High Sheriff of Meath, 1910. *Address:* Rathcore House, Enfield, Meath.

Died 10 March 1947.

KENNEDY, Vincent; Solicitor; *b* 15 Feb. 1876; *s* of late Hugh Peter Kennedy, Crown Solicitor, Cavan, and Catharine R., *d* of Dr P. Maginnis, London; *m* 1st, 1912, Cecilia Beatrice Mary (*d* 1919), *d* of Adolphe Boursot, 12 Vicarage Gate, Kensington; five *s* four *d*; 2nd, 1921, Grace, *d* of Dr Jeffries, late of Brighton. *Educ:* Clongowes Wood College. Qualified as Solicitor, 1900; MP (N) West Cavan, 1904–18; practises in all Courts in Dublin and surrounding counties. *Recreations:* golfing, tennis, and motoring. *Address:* 45 Seapoint Avenue, Monkstown, Co. Dublin. *T:* Dun Laoghaire 82876. *Clubs:* National Liberal; Leinster, Dublin; National Yacht, Dun Laoghaire.

Died 18 Nov. 1943.

KENNEDY-PURVIS, Adm. Sir Charles Edward, GBE 1946; KCB 1939; CB 1935; a Lord Commissioner of the Admiralty and Deputy First Sea Lord, 1942–46. Commanded First Cruiser Squadron, Mediterranean Fleet, 1936–38; Pres., Royal Naval College, Greenwich, and Vice-Admiral Commanding RN War College, 1938–40; Commander-in-Chief America and West Indies, 1940–42. *Address:* Admiralty, SW1.

Died 26 May 1946.

KENNET, Lady; (Kathleen Kennet), (Lady Scott), ARBS 1928; sculptor [given rank as widow of KCB in recognition of her husband's work]; Vice-President, Artists Benevolent Association; *d* of Canon Lloyd Bruce; *m* 1st, 1908, Captain Robert Falcon Scott, CVO, RN, explorer (*d* 1912); one *s*; 2nd, 1922, Edward Hilton Young (1st Baron Kennet, PC, GBE, DSO, DSC); one *s*. *Educ:* convent. Five years student in Paris; travelled in Greece, Turkey, Egypt, Algeria, Mexico, Arizona, Norway, New Zealand, Australia, S Africa, Ceylon, Society Islands, Ecuador and West Indies, etc.; Private Secretary to Permanent Secretary of Ministry of Pensions, 1916; Medallist, Paris Salon; made following public monuments, War Memorials in Market Place, Huntingdon, and at Oundle School; Hon. C. S. Rolls at Dover; Captain Smith of the Titanic at Litchfield; Dr Wilson at Cheltenham; Captain Scott in Waterloo Place and at Portsmouth; Hon. Edwin Montagu, Calcutta; Lord Northcliffe in Fleet Street; Bishop Browne, Bristol Cathedral; Lord Milner, Rhodes House, Howson at Holt School, Adam Lindsay Gordon in Westminster Abbey, HM King George V (Hearts of Oak), etc.; also busts of King George VI, Mr Asquith (Tate Gallery), Mr Lloyd George (War Museum), Mr Stanley Baldwin, The Earl of Reading, Bernard Shaw, John Galsworthy, Lord Knutsford, Colonel House, Mr Ambassador Davis, Mr Stanley Bruce, Sir John Simon, Colonel Lawrence, James Maxton, Sir John Reith, Nansen, Chelmsford, Hailsham, Neville Chamberlain, Montagu Norman, Dr David (Bishop of Liverpool), Peter Scott, Lord Woolton, etc.; Ideal figures at Welwyn Garden City, Cambridge, etc. *Publication:* Homage: A Book of Sculptures, 1938. *Address:* Leinster Corner, Lancaster Gate, W2. *T:* Paddington 3886; Fritton Hithe, Great Yarmouth. *T:* Fritton 247.

Died 25 July 1947.

KENNION, Lt-Col Roger Lloyd, CIE 1918; *b* 1866; *s* of late Lt-Col T. E. Kennion, Bengal Artillery; *m* 1900, Alice Marion, *d* of Maj.-Gen. F. M. Kenyon-Stow; one *s* one *d*. *Educ:* Repton; Sandhurst. King's Own Scottish Borderers, 1887; Central India Horse, 1890; joined Indian Foreign and Political Dept, 1893; served in Central India, Kashmir, Gilgit, Leh; sent on Mission into Tibet, 1900; served in Rajputana and Chitral; Consul-General, Meshed, Persia, 1906; Consul, Seistan and Kain, 1906–09; Political Agent, Dir, Swat, and Chitral, 1911–14; served Kurram Field Force, 1889; Tirah Expedition (Press Correspondent), 1897; Indian Expeditionary Force, France, 1914–15; Mohammerah, Persian Gulf, 1915–16; mission with the Russian Troops, North-West Persia, 1916–17 (Order of St Vladimir with swords and St Anne with swords); Consul and Political Officer, Kermanshah, 1917–18; Political Officer, North Persian Force, 1918; British Envoy, Nepal, 1919; retired, 1921. *Publications:* Sport and Life in the Further Himalaya; By Mountain, Lake, and Plain, being sketches of Sport in Persia; Diversions of an Indian Political, 1932. *Address:* Durford Wood, Rogate, Sussex. *TA:* Kennion, Rogate.

Died 26 March 1942.

KENNY, Augustus Leo, CBE 1938; Private Chamberlain to The Pope (Popes Pius X, Benedict XV, Pius XI, Pius XII). Knight Grand Cross of the Order of St Gregory the Great, with Plaque; MB, ChB (Melb.); FRACS; Specialist Diseases Eye, Ear, Nose, Throat, Member of Medical Board of Victoria; Senior Official Visitor in University for Government of Victoria; *b* Salford, Lancashire, England, 29 July 1863; *s* of John Kenny, Fort Brown, Galway, Ireland, and Mary Naughton, Nenagh, Tipperary, Ireland; *m* 1912, Olga Constance Zichy-Woinarski, *d* of Gustavus George Zichy, ADC Prince Worionetski, Captain of Kossuth's Cavalry, 1848, and Henrietta Woijnarska; two *s* two *d*. *Educ:* Christian Brothers, Salford and Melbourne; Jesuit Fathers, Melbourne; University of Melbourne. Member of Suite of Papal Legate for International Eucharistic Congress at Sydney, 1928; Hon. Surgeon for Diseases of Eye, Ear, Nose and Throat at St Vincents Hospital, Melbourne; Senior Vice-Pres. of Lord Mayor's Fund for Hospitals and Metropolitan Charities, Melbourne; FRS of M, England; Member of Deutsche Ophthalmologischen Gesellschaft. *Publications:* contributions to Medical Journals and Catholic Magazines. *Recreations:* music, riding. *Address:* 18 Collins St, Melbourne, Australia. *Club:* Melbourne.

Died 27 Sept. 1946.

KENNY, Matthew J.; KC 1914; *b* 1 Feb. 1861; *s* of Michael Kenny, solicitor, and Bridget, *d* of W. H. Frost, Ballymorris, Co. Clare; *m* 1887, Elizabeth, *d* of Walter Robertson Stewart, of Lairshill, Aberdeenshire; two *s* two *d*. *Educ:* Ennis College; Queen's University, Ireland. MP for borough of Ennis, 1882, as a supporter of Mr Parnell, being then the youngest member; Mid-Tyrone, 1885–95; called to English Bar, Gray's Inn, 1886; Irish Bar, 1889; Senior Crown Prosecutor for Co. Kerry, 1916; Circuit Court Judge for Cork City and County, 1925–33. *Recreations:* breeder of pedigree horses, cattle, and sheep. *Address:* Freagh Castle, Miltown Malbay, Co. Clare.

Died 8 Dec. 1942.

KENT, Col Herbert Vaughan, CB 1917; late RE; *b* Hersham, 14 July 1863; *s* of late George Barton Kent, of Ruislip Park, Middlesex; *m* 1891, Helen Chauncey Tiffany (*d* 1942), Washington, DC, USA; one *s* two *d*. *Educ:* Clifton College; RM Academy, Woolwich. On Intelligence Staff at War Office, 1899–1900; Assistant-Inspector of Submarine Defences, 1903–05; CRE Straits Settlements, 1906–09; commanding NE Coast Defences, 1910–12; Assistant-Director of Fortifications and Works at War Office, 1914–18; 2nd Class Order of St Stanislas. *Publications:* Dancing on Skates; Combined Figures and Ice Valsing; My Racing Log. *Recreations:* yachting, skating. *Address:* Lake View House, Coburg, Ontario, Canada. *Clubs:* Junior United Service; Bembridge Sailing.

Died June 1944.

KENWOOD, Lt-Col Henry Richard, CMG 1918; MB, FRSE, DPH, FCS; Emeritus Professor of Hygiene and Public Health in the University of London; Honorary Lieut-Colonel, RAMC; Late Member of Army Hygiene Consultative Committee; late Civilian Member of the Army Medical Advisory Board; Ex-Medical Officer of Health to the County Council of Bedfordshire; *b* Bexhill, Sussex, 22 Dec. 1862; γ *s* of late John Kenwood of The Olives, Wadhurst, Kent; *m d* of J. Jocelyne, Taunton. *Educ:* Collegiate School, Tunbridge Wells. Studied Medicine, Public Health, and Chemistry at the London Hospital Medical College, Edinburgh University, Paris Institutions, and Univ. Coll., London. Demonstrator, under the late Prof. Corfield, 1890; Assistant Professor, 1896; appointed Medical Officer of Health for the Finchley District, London, 1893; resigned, 1904. *Publications:* articles in medical journals; communications to Scientific Societies; Public Health Laboratory Work; Hygiene and Public Health (with Prof. H. Kerr). *Recreations:* golf and horseriding. *Address:* Wadhurst, 126 Queen's Drive, N4.

Died 7 June 1945.

KEOGH, Col James Blair, CIE 1919; DSO 1917; Indian Army (ret.); *b* 1871; *s* of Major A. R. Keogh, formerly 14th Regt. Served European War, 1914–19 (wounded, despatches, DSO); Mesopotamia 1920–21. *Address:* La Retraite, Millbrook, Jersey, Channel Islands; c/o Lloyd's Bank, 6 Pall Mall, SW1.

Died 11 July 1944.

KEOGH, Joseph Wiseman, CMG 1936; OBE 1920; JP; *e s* of George Keogh, JP DL of Geevagh and of Glencourt, Co. Wicklow (*d* 1909) and Teresa, *e d* of late William Osborne Carroll; *m* 1885, Ella Douglas (*d* 1941), *o d* of late Admiral Douglas Curry, of Shottery Hall, Warwickshire; two *d. Educ:* Oscott College; Trinity College, Dublin (BA and Honourman). Formerly Capt. Instructor of Gunnery, 6th Brig., S Irish Div. RA; British Vice-Consul Monaco, 1896–1910; HM's Consul for the Alpes Maritimes, France, and for the Principality of Monaco, 1910–36.

Died 9 May 1947.

KEPPEL, Adm. Sir Colin (Richard), GCVO 1930; KCIE 1911; KCVO 1908; CB 1898; DSO 1898; CVO 1906; Extra Equerry to HM; late Equerry-in-Ordinary; retired, 1913; *b* 3 Dec. 1862; *s* of late Hon. Sir H. Keppel; *m* 1889, Henrietta Mary, *d* of late Major-General R. Blundell; two *d. Educ:* HMS Britannia. Joined HMS Britannia, 1875; midshipman of Inconstant during Egyptian war, 1882 (medal, Khedive's bronze star); Sublieutenant of Invincible; served with Naval Brigade landed for service in Soudan with Nile Expedition, 1884–85; Lieutenant, 1885; Equerry and Flag Lieutenant to the Duke of Edinburgh during HRH's command in the Mediterranean, 1886–89; and afterwards at Devonport, 1890–93; Commander, 1895; lent to Egyptian Government for service on the Nile, 1897–98; commanded gunboat flotilla (despatches, after occupation of Berber, DSO; despatches after the fall of Khartoum, CB, 1898); Captain, 1899; received thanks of both Houses of Parliament for Soudan, June 8, 1899 Rear-Admiral in Atlantic Fleet, 1909–10; Sergeant-at-Arms, House of Commons, 1915–35; Admiral, retired, 1917. *Address:* Grove Lodge, Bracknell, Berks. *T:* Winkfield Row 23. *Clubs:* Brooks's, Turf.

Died 6 July 1947.

KEPPEL, Hon. Sir Derek, GCVO 1916; KCB 1932; KCVO 1911; CMG 1901; CIE 1906; CVO 1910; MVO 1901; *b* London, 7 April 1863; 2nd *s* of 7th Earl of Albemarle; *m* 1898, Hon. Bridget Harbord, γ *d* of 5th

Baron Suffield; two *d. Educ:* Charterhouse. Late Lieut-Col Prince of Wales' Own Civil Service Rifles; VD 1900; JP, retired 1938; Equerry-in-Ordinary to George Duke of York and Prince of Wales, 1893–1910, and to King George V, 1910–12; Master of HM's Household and Extra Equerry to King George V, 1912–36, and to King Edward VIII, 1936; retired, 1936; Extra Equerry to King George VI since 1936. *Recreations:* shooting, yachting, golf. *Address:* Kensington Palace, W8. *T:* Western 1927; Bramshott Lodge, Liphook, Hants. *T:* Liphook 3166. *Clubs:* Turf, Carlton; Royal Yacht Squadron (Hon.), Cowes.

Died 26 April 1944.

KEPPEL, Frederick Paul, LittD, LLD; President Carnegie Corporation of New York, 522 Fifth Avenue, New York City, 1923–41, Educational Adviser since 1941; *b* 2 July 1875; *s* of Frederick and Frances M. Keppel; *m* 1906, Helen Tracy Brown; five *s. Educ:* Columbia. Columbia University, Secretary, 1902–10, Dean College, 1910–18; 3rd Assistant Secretary of War, 1918–19; Vice-Chairman American Red Cross, 1919–20; International Chamber Commerce, 1920–22; Secretary Plan of New York, 1922–23. *Publications:* Columbia University, 1913; Undergraduate and his College, 1917; Four volumes of miscellaneous papers. *Recreations:* fishing, tree culture. *Address:* Montrose, Westchester County, New York. *TA:* Carncor, New York. *T:* Peekskill 1839, (Office) Vanderbilt 6–5525. *Clubs:* Athenæum; Century, University, New York.

Died 8 Sept. 1943.

KEPPEL, Lt-Col Hon. George, MVO 1908; *b* 1865; 3rd *s* of 7th Earl of Albemarle; *m* 1891, Alice Frederica (*d* 1947), *d* of Admiral Sir W. Edmonstone, 4th Bt; two *d. Educ:* Sandhurst. in Gordon Highlanders, 1886–92; late PWO Norfolk Artillery; served European War, 1915–16; late 10th (Service) Batt. Royal Fusiliers, 1914–16; Lt-Col commanding 2/4 East Lancashire Regt, 1916–17; late Lt-Col commanding 2/5 Highland Light Infantry; Lt-Col Reserve of Officers. *Recreations:* shooting, yachting, golf. *Address:* Villa dell' Ombrelliso, Bellosguardo, Florence, Italy. *Clubs:* Boodle's, Turf, St James's.

Died 22 Nov. 1947.

KEPPIE, John, RSA 1937; ARSA 1920; FRIBA (Retired); JP; Architect; *b* Glasgow, 1862; *s* of James Keppie, tobacco importer, and Helen Cuthbertson Hopkins; unmarried. *Educ:* Ayr Academy; Glasgow University; Atelier-Pascal, Paris. Late Senior Member of the firm of John Keppie & Henderson, Architects, Glasgow; Past Vice-President, RIBA; Past President of Royal Incorporation of Architects in Scotland; Past Chairman of Governors, Glasgow School of Art. *Address:* Haddington Park, W Prestwick, Ayrshire. *T:* Prestwick 78086. *Clubs:* Art, Glasgow.

Died 25 April 1945.

KER, Richard William Blackwood; JP, DL; *b* 1850; *e surv. s* of late David Stewart Ker and Hon. Anne Dorothea Blackwood, *d* of 3rd Lord Dufferin and Clandeboye; *S* brother, 1877; *m* 1876, Edith Louisa, γ *d* of William George Rose of Wolston Grange, Dunchurch, Co. Warwick; one *s. Educ:* Sandhurst. Formerly Capt. 1st R. Dragoons; High Sheriff, Co. Down, 1880; MP Co. Down, 1884–85; E Down, 1885–90. *Address:* Prospect House, Donaghadee, Co. Down. *Club:* Carlton.

Died 19 June 1942.

KER, William Pollock, CMG 1913; *b* 12 Dec. 1864; *s* of late Rev. W. T. Ker, Deskford, Banffs; *m* 1897, *e d* of late Dr Charles Murray, Sussex, New Brunswick; two *s. Educ:* Aberdeen Univ. (MA). Student Interpreter, China, 1888; Consul at Wuhu, 1902; Nanking, 1905; called to Bar, Middle Temple, 1903; Commercial Attaché, China,

1909–17; Consul-Gen., Tientsin, 1917–26; retired 1927. *Address:* The Malt House, East Horsley, Surrey. *T:* East Horsley 30.

Died 6 Aug. 1945.

KERN, Jerome; composer; *b* NY City, 27 Jan. 1885; *s* of Henry Kern and Fanny Kakeles; *m* 1910, Eva, *d* of George Draper Leale, Walton-on-Thames, Surrey. *Educ:* graduated Newark (NJ) High School, 1902; studied music, New York College of Music, piano under Alexander Lambert, Paolo Galico; harmony under Dr Austin Pierce, and under private tutors in Germany, 1904–05. Began as composer in England, 1905; member American Society Composers and Authors; Dramatists' Guild; Authors' League of America Inc.; Society Authors, Playwrights, Composers; specialises in application of modern school of harmony to lighter forms of opera. *Compositions:* Nobody Home, 1914; Very Good, Eddie, 1915; Theodore & Co., 1916; Oh, Boy, 1917; Oh Lady, Lady, 1918; Head over Heels, 1919; Sally, 1920; Good Morning, Dearie, 1921; Cabaret Girl, 1922; The Bunch and Judy, 1922; Beauty Prize, 1923; Stepping Stones, 1923; Sitting Pretty, 1924; Sunny, 1925; Criss Cross, 1926; The Cat and the Fiddle, 1932; Music in the Air, 1933; Three Sisters, 1934; and many others. *Address:* Cedar Knolls, Bronxville, NY; 62 W 45th Street, New York.

Died 11 Nov. 1945.

KERNAHAN, Coulson; writer and ex-Territorial Officer; was for many years literary adviser to Ward, Lock and Co; *b* Ilfracombe, 1 Aug. 1858; *e s* of Dr James Kernahan, MA, FGS; *m d* (*d* 1941) of late S. G. Gwynne and *widow* of Prof. G. T. Bettany, MA, BSc; one *d. Educ:* St Albans School; privately by his father. Collaborated with late Frederick Locker-Lampson in *Lyra Elegantinarum;* contributed to Nineteenth Century, Fortnightly Review, National Review, Punch, Spectator, Army Quarterly. *Publications:* A Dead Man's Diary; A Book of Strange Sins; God and the Ant; The Child, the Wise Man, and the Devil; Captain Shannon; A World Without a Child; Visions; An Author in the Territorials (with Foreword by Lord Roberts); In Good Company; Black Objects; Plain Facts and Painful Speaking about Spiritualism; Six Famous Living Poets; Celebrities; Little Stories about Famous Folk; The Garden of God (Nature Studies and Fancies), 1928; Five More Famous Living Poets, 1928; Begging the Moon's Pardon, 1930; The Sunlight in the Room, 1932; A Dog and his Master, 1932; A World without the Christ, 1934; Chatter about Dogs (Foreword by Warwick Deeping), 1936. His books have been translated into eighteen languages, into Esperanto, and Braille type for the blind. *Recreations:* his pipe and his tyke. *Address:* Frognal, Fairlight, near Hastings. *T:* Pett Hastings 2127. *Clubs:* Savage, Whitefriars, Omar Khayyam.

Died 17 Feb. 1943.

KERNAHAN, Mrs Coulson; novelist; *o d* of late S. G. Gwynne, mathematical master at Taunton College; *widow* of the late Prof. G. T. Bettany, MA, BSc; one *s* three *d. Educ:* by her father; University College, London. *Publications:* House of Rimmon; Trewinnot of Guy's; Frank Redland, Recruit; The Avenging of Ruthanna; No Vindication; An Unwise Virgin; Devastation; A Beautiful Savage; The Fate of Felix; The Whisperer; A Village Mystery; The Sinnings of Seraphine; An Artist's Model; The Mystery of Magdalen; The Disappearance of the Duke; A Case for the Courts; The Sin of Gabrielle; The Graven Image; The Fraud; Ashes of Passion; The Gate of Sinners; Quixote of Magdalen; Under Seal of the Confessional; The Thirteenth Man; The House of Blight; The Vagrant Bride; The Hired Girl; The Go-Between; Bedtime Stories (with Coulson Kernahan); The Mystery of Mere Hall; A Fair Sinner; The Blue Diamond; The Chance Child; The Stolen Man; The Woman Who Understood; The Trap; Peg of the Prairie; The Temptation of Gideon Holt; Talks to Women; The

Secret of Home Happiness; Tales of Our Village; The Whip of the Will; More Tales of Our Village; The Wireless Call; Five Minutes to Spare. *Recreation:* riding. *Address:* Frognal, Fairlight, Sussex. *T:* Pett 127.

Died 17 Jan. 1941.

KERR, Rev. Prof. F. W., DD; LLD; called to St Andrew's Church, Westmount, Montreal, 1932; *b* Oxford County, Ontario, 19 Feb. 1881; *s* of Donald and Elizabeth Kerr; *m* Elizabeth, BA, *d* of Dr Grady, Miami, Mo, USA; two *s* one *d. Educ:* St Mary's Collegiate; University of Manitoba; Knox College, Toronto (graduated with travelling scholarship, 1908); Postgraduate in Glasgow UF College; University of Marburg; University of Chicago. Pastor at Prince Rupert and New Westminster, BC; delegate to Universities' League of Nations Society at Geneva, 1925; Professor Religious Education and Pastoral Theology, Manitoba College, Winnipeg, 1920–32; President, Winnipeg Canadian Club, 1931. *Recreations:* tennis, golf. *Address:* St Andrew's Church, Westmount, Montreal, Canada. *Club:* Rotary.

Died 7 June 1945.

KERR, James, MA, MD, DPH Cambridge; late Consulting Medical Officer, Medical Research Officer, Medical Officer (Education), LCC and School Medical Officer for London; Major, RAMC; Glasgow. *Educ:* Grammar School, Manchester; Science Scholar of St John's Coll., Cambridge and St Bartholomew's Hosp. Formerly Member of Hon. Medical Staff, Bradford Royal Infirmary and Bradford Eye and Ear Hospital; Medical Superintendent, Bradford School Board; Medical Officer, LSB. Howard Medallist, Royal Statistical Soc. and Ingleby Lecturer, University of Birmingham. Secretary, Second Internat. Congress on School Hygiene; Member of Examination Board and Examiner in Hygiene for English Board of Education. Officier de l'Instruction publique de France. *Publications:* various medical papers and Reports of the Medical Officer to the Education Authorities, London, 1902–11; School Vision; The Fundamentals of School Health, 1926; The Air we Breathe, etc. *Address:* 9 Regent Terrace, Edinburgh.

Died 5 Oct. 1941.

KERR, James Rutherford, CBE 1920; ChM, MB (Glasgow); Hon. Consulting Surgeon, Southport Infirmary; Surgeon, EMS Hospital, Southport; Medical Referee, Workmen's Compensation Acts; *b* 14 June 1878; *s* of John G. Kerr, MA, LLD, Glasgow. *Educ:* Allan Glen's School; University of Glasgow. House Surgeon, Sir William Macewen's Wards, Western Infirmary, Glasgow; House Surgeon, House Physician, Senior Resident Medical Officer, House Surgeon to Out-Patient Department, Royal Hospital for Sick Children, Glasgow; Chirurgien-Chef, Hôpital de l'Alliance, Yvetot, France (Médaille d'Honneur en Vermeil); Surgeon-in-Charge, Orthopædic and Limbfitting Centre (Ministry of Pensions), St Helens, Lancs, with supervision of affiliated out-patient clinics in north-western area; Joint Secretary, section Industrial Diseases BMA Conference, Glasgow, 1922; Joint Hon. Secretary, Industrial Hygiene Section, Royal Institute of Public Health Congress, 1923; President the St Helens Medical Society; Chairman, Southport Division British Medical Association. *Publications:* Modern Surgery in its Association with Engineering, Engineering, 1909; Med. Exam. and Workmen's Compensation, ibid., 1910; Labour Exchanges and Workmen's Compensation, ibid.; Orthopædics in Relation to Man-Power, ibid., 1919; Thoracoplasty for Chronic Empyema, with Notes of Two Cases, Prac. 1912; The Suturing of Tendons, ibid., 1912; The Treatment of Industrial Accidents, BMJ, 1922; The American Industrial Doctor, Journal of State Medicine, 1923; The Physiotherapy Treatment of Industrial Accident Cases, Journal of State Medicine,

1923; Chronic Joint Disease as a Cause of Industrial Invalidity, Lancet, 1924. *Address:* 70 Scarisbrick New Road, Southport. *T:* Southport 3821.

Died 21 Sept. 1942.

KERR, Lt-Col Mark Ancrum, CB 1904; *b* 2 May 1859. *Educ:* Cheltenham College. Entered army, 1879; Captain, 1890; Major, 1899; Lieut-Colonel, 1904; served Thibet, 1903–04 (despatches, CB). *Address:* 115 The Promenade, Cheltenham.

Died 19 Nov. 1941.

KERR, Adm. Mark (Edward Frederic), CB 1913; MVO 1903; RN; Chairman of Allenby Club and Member of Council of United Services Corps; Committee, Veterans Association; *b* 26 Sept. 1864; *s* of Admiral Lord Frederic Kerr; *m* 1906, Rose, OBE 1938, *d* of late Wilfred Gough, Royal Dragoons; two *d*. Entered RN 1877; served Egyptian War in Naval Brigade, 1882, and Soudan, 1891; Naval Attaché in Italy, Austria, Turkey, and Greece, 1903 and 1904 (Egyptian medal, Khedive's Star, and clasp, 1891); C-in-C, Greek Navy, 1913–15; C-in-C Adriatic Squadron, 1916–17 (wounded and gassed, 24 May 1917); wrote 10 Oct. 1917, memo that persuaded Cabinet to form RAF; Deputy-Chief Air Staff and Major-General in RAF, and commanded SWRAF Area, 1918; retired from Navy and RAF, 1918; flew from Phalerum to Porus Island and back, longest sea flight up to that time, 1914; attempted Atlantic Flight, made 2nd and 3rd longest flights made across country and sea, 1919; President RN Old Comrades Association; Royal Humane Society's medal for saving life at sea; Knight Commander Russian Order of S Stefan and Stanislas; Grand Officer Italian Order of Maurice and Lazarus, 1917; Commander of the Crown of Italy; Grand Cross of George I of Greece, 1936; Knight Commander of the Order of the Redeemer (Greek); Spanish Naval Order of Merit, 3rd Class; Iron Cross of Lombardy, 2nd Class; Military Cross of Savoia, 1917; Coronation medal; took pilot's flying certificate, Royal Aero Club, on a Sopwith seaplane, July 1914. *Publications:* Land, Sea, and Air, 1927; The Sailor's Nelson, 1932; The Navy in my Time, 1933; Prince Louis of Battenberg, Admiral of the Fleet, 1934. Poems: The Destroyer and a Cargo of Notions; Nelson; Prayer of Empire; Flying; The Rubaiyat of Kram Rerk, 1927. Essays: The Spirit of Nelson, How Helson's Memorandum was carried out at Trafalgar (Nineteenth Century, 1911). *Recreations:* flying, polo, race-riding, hunting, shooting, fishing. *Address:* 19 Draycott Avenue, SW3. *T:* Kensington 7396. *Clubs:* Allenby Services; Royal Yacht Squadron, Cowes.

Died 20 Jan. 1944.

KERR, Philip Walter, MVO, 1937; Pilot Officer, RAFVR, serving War of 1939–45; Rouge Croix Pursuivant of Arms since 1928; *s* of late Admiral of the Fleet Lord Walter Kerr, GCB, and Lady Amabel Cowper; *m* 1936, Dorothy, *o d* of Charles J. P. Cave, MA. *Educ:* Oratory School, Edgbaston, Birmingham; Pembroke College, Cambridge; BA 1908. Served European War, Imperial Light Horse, German South-West Africa Campaign; Captain RFA, 25th Brigade, 1st Division, France; Egyptian Civil Service, 1919–24; FSA; Knight of Honour and Devotion of the Sovereign and Military Order of Malta. *Recreations:* rowing, gardening. *Address:* Martlets, Knebworth. *T:* Knebworth 19. *Clubs:* Travellers, Royal Automobile.

Died Feb. 1941.

KERR, Brig.-Gen. Robert S.; *see* Scott-Kerr.

KERR, William Richard; ISO 1914; late Principal Clerk in Office of Works; *b* 1853; *s* of late William Kerr, Dublin, and Mary, *d* of Francis Caulfield Moore; *m* 1880, Sarah Emily (*d* 1930), *o c* of James Newling Thompson. Office of Works, 1871; Principal Clerk, 1909; resigned, 1914. *Address:* Avoca, St Leonard's Road, Deal.

Died 26 March 1943.

KERR, William Warren, CMG 1924; CBE 1918; JP Victoria; Managing Director of Richardson Kerr Proprietary Ltd, Insurance Brokers, 465 Collins Street, Melbourne, Victoria; Chairman Commissioners State Savings Bank of Victoria; Chairman Directors, Mutual Store; *b* Victoria, 15 Dec. 1864; *y s* of late John Wilson Kerr; *m* 1887, Janie Buchanan (*d* 1945), 3rd *d* of late Rev. Alexander Gosman, DD; one *s* (and one killed in action at Gallipoli, May 2, 1915) one *d*. *Educ:* Church of England Grammar School, Melbourne. President Associated Chambers of Commerce of Australia, 1918–20; Pres. Melbourne Chamber of Commerce, 1916–18; Chm. Congregational Union of Victoria, 1905–06; Mayor of Kew, 1907–08; Chm. of Commonwealth Royal Commission on Taxation; a Representative of Australia at Geneva Economic Conference, 1927; President Charity Organisation Society of Melbourne for 23 years; Past Grand Master of Freemasons of Victoria (Grand Master, 1932–33; 1933–34; 1934–35); King's Silver Jubilee Medal, 1935; Coronation Medal, 1937. *Publications:* sundry lectures and addresses. *Recreations:* photography, bowls. *Address:* 32 Belmont Avenue, Kew, Melbourne, E4, Australia. *TA:* Insbrok, Melbourne. *Clubs:* Constitutional, Rotary (Melbourne).

Died 2 July 1949.

KERR-SMILEY, Peter Kerr; *b* 22 Feb. 1879; *s* of late Sir Hugh Smiley, 1st Bart of Drumalis, Larne, Co. Antrim; *m* 1905, Maud Gaines, *o d* of Ernest L. Simpson, of New York; one *s* one *d*. *Educ:* Eton; Trinity Hall, Cambridge. Gazetted 21st Lancers, 1900; served South African war, 1901–02, with French's Scouts and later 5th Lancers and Staff (medal four clasps); European War, 1914–18, in France with 14th Bn Royal Irish Rifles; contested (U) South Down, 1906; MP (LU) North Antrim, 1910–22; assumed additional name of Kerr, 1905; Officier Légion d'Honneur; Order of Merit, Chili (2nd Class). *Publication:* The Home Rule Peril. *Recreations:* yachting, fishing, shooting. *Address:* Mill House, Astwick, Arlesey, Beds. *Clubs:* Marlborough, Carlton.

Died 23 June 1943.

KERRISON, Lt-Col Edmund Roger Allday, CMG 1902; OBE; late commanding 4th Batt. Norfolk Regt (Militia); JP Norfolk; *b* 25 Dec. 1855; *s* of Roger Allday Kerrison, Banker, of Norwich; *m* 1885, Jessie Matilda (*d* 1944), *d* of Admiral Greville; two *s*. *Educ:* Harrow; Repton; RMA Woolwich. Entered RA, 1875; passed Staff Coll., 1890; Brigade-Major, Royal Artillery, 1890; Major, 1892; retired, 1897; contested (C) South Norfolk, 1910; High Sheriff of Norfolk, 1927. *Address:* Bird's Place, Buxton, Norwich. *Club:* Army and Navy.

Died 12 July 1944.

KERSEY, Major Henry Maitland, DSO 1902; TD; *b* 1859; *s* of late S. Overbury Kersey of Overbury Hall, Kersey, Suffolk. *Educ:* Repton and abroad. Served in South Africa, 1900–02; first on staff of Gen. St George Henry, CB, afterwards with the 15th Batt. Imperial Yeomanry, finally comm. battalion (despatches, DSO); served World War; Major Herts Yeomanry and Hon. Major Herts Yeomanry and Hon. Major in the Army; retired. *Address:* Nelholme, Felixstowe; 7 Carlton Gardens, SW1. *Clubs:* White's, Carlton, MCC, Cavalry.

Died 18 Dec. 1941.

KERSHAW, Sir Leonard William, Kt 1921; *b* 18 Nov. 1864; *o surv. s* of late Rev. J. C. Kershaw, Vicar of Walton-le-Dale, Lancashire, and of Hartburn, Northumberland; *m* 1904, Ruth Agnes, 2nd *d* of late J. P. Grain, barrister-at-law; no *c*. *Educ:* Rossall; Queen's College, Oxford. BA 1885. Called to bar, 1886; practised at the Central Criminal Court, London Sessions, and on the Northern Circuit; one of the Examiners of the Court, 1904–08; Lecturer at the Imperial Inst., 1908–09; Assist Registrar of the Court of Criminal Appeal, 1908; King's Coroner and Attorney;

Master of the Crown Office, King's Bench Division, and Registrar of Court of Criminal Appeal, 1912–33. *Publications:* joint-editor of 7th edition of Russell on Crimes; 4th ed. of Wise on Riots; 7th and 8th eds of Wigram's Justice's Note Book. *Address:* Walton, Oval Way, Gerrard's Cross. *T:* Gerrard's Cross 3481.

Died 9 Feb. 1949.

KERSHAW, Sir Louis (James), KCSI 1921; CSI 1918; CIE 1911; *b* 1869; *m* 1892 (wife *d* 1942). *Educ:* Belfast Methodist Coll.; Trinity Coll., Dublin. Entered ICS 1890; served in various capacities in Bengal and Assam till 1905; Sec. to Govt, Eastern Bengal and Assam, 1905; Sec. to Government, Bihar and Orissa, 1912; Commissioner, Tirhut, 1913; Sec. India Revenue and Agricultural Dept, 1914; Sec. Revenue Statistics Dept India Office, 1915; on special duty Peace Conference, 1919; Delegate at International Labour Conferences, 1919, 1920, 1922, 1923, 1924, 1925; Delegate at International Conference on Communications and Transit, Barcelona, 1920; Representative of India on the Governing Body of the International Labour Organisation, 1923–26; Sec. Industries and Overseas Dept India Office, 1921; Assistant Under-Secretary of State, India Office, 1924–33; Deputy Under-Secretary of State, 1933–34; Member Federal Finance Committee, 1932; Member Committee on Indian Reserve Bank. 1933; Member Committee on Indian Statutory Railway Authority, 1933; retired 1934; on special duty with Government of Burma, 1934–35. *Address:* 23 Queen's Gate Gardens, SW7. *Club:* Oriental.

Died 15 Feb. 1947.

KESSELL, Ernest, CBE 1929; Hon. Organiser of Pearson's Fresh Air Fund, 1892–1946; Treasurer of St Dunstan's (for Blinded Soldiers, Sailors and Airmen), 1915–32; *b* 22 Feb. 1868; 2nd *s* of late Thomas Kessell, Penzance; *m* 1st, 1891, Agnes Mary, *d* of James Richardson Crowe; 2nd, 1906, Emma Jane, *d* of late Peter Keary; two *s* two *d*. *Educ:* Penzance. Staff of Cornish Telegraph, 1883–84; Tit-Bits, 1885–90; Secretary of C. Arthur Pearson, Ltd, 1890–99; Secretary of Daily Express Limited, 1900–15; resigned to help in care of blinded soldiers and sailors who were then coming back from European War; Treasurer and General Superintendent until 1932; Hon. Secretary of Pearson's Fresh Air Fund from its inception in 1892; Councillor of Royal Borough of Kingston-upon-Thames, 1935–46; member of Wireless for the Blind Cttee since inception in 1929; Chm. Kingston and District Branch NSPCC Hon. Treasurer Parliamentary Borough of Kingston-upon-Thames Conservative and Unionist Assoc., 1939–44. *Recreations:* golf, and sports generally, gardening. *Address:* 20 Geneva Road, Kingston-on-Thames. *T:* Kingston 1614.

Died 30 June 1948.

KETTLEWELL, Arthur Bradley, CIE 1916; CBE 1920; late ICS; *b* 1871. *Educ:* Cheltenham; New College, Oxford. Entered ICS 1890; Political Officer, Wano, 1898–99; Deputy Commissioner, 1903; Secretary to Govt, Punjab, 1903–07; Additional Secretary to Govt, Punjab, 1915–16; retired, 1917. *Address:* Graffham, Sussex.

Died 20 Oct. 1945.

KETTLEWELL, Rev. Percy W. H., MA; *b* 1868; *e s* of W. J. Kettlewell; *m* Nina Mary, *d* of D. L. Clarke, Hatfield, Highlands, Cape; one *s* two *d*. *Educ:* Chigwell School (Head of School, Football XI); Keble College, Oxford (Capt. of Boats). BA Classical honours, 1892; MA 1897. Assistant Master Clifton Coll., 1894–1908; Deacon, 1894; Priest, 1895; Headmaster of St Andrew's College, Grahamstown, S Africa, 1909–33; Canon of Grahamstown Cathedral; Member of the Education Commission appointed by the Government of the Cape Colony, 1910; Vice-Chairman of Council of Rhodes University College, SA till 1933; Member of Joint Matriculation Board of the SA Universities, 1911–22;

Captain, Union Cadet Force; Inspector of Schools in Oxford diocese, 1934; Vicar of Buckland, Aylesbury, 1934–44; Canon Emeritus of Grahamstown Cathedral, 1945. *Publications:* Rivington's Books of the Bible—Ruth, 1 Samuel, Ezra, and Nehemiah. *Address:* Argyll, West Hill, Grahamstown, CP, S Africa.

Died 25 April 1950.

KEVENHOERSTER, Most Rev. John Bernard, OSB, DD; Titular Bishop of Camuliana since 1933; Prefect Apostolic in the Bahamas since 1932; Vicar Apostolic since 1941; *b* 1 Nov. 1869; *s* of Bernard Kevenhoerster and Agnes Plantenberg. *Educ:* Germany; Parochial and Public Schools, Minneapolis; St John's College, Collegeville, Minn (BA); St John's Seminary, Collegeville, (PhB); Post Graduate Courses in the University of the State of Minnesota. Ordained 1896; Professor St John's College; Chaplain, St John's College; Rector, St John's Seminary; Pastor, St Anselm's Church, New York City, 1907–29; Vicar Forane, Bahama Islands, 1929–32. *Address:* PO Box 187, Nassau, Bahamas; 673 Tinton Avenue, Bronx, NY. *TA:* Bernard Nassau. *T:* Nassau 46.

Died 9 Dec. 1949.

KEVERNE, Richard; (pen name of Clifford Hosken); author and journalist; *b* 29 Aug. 1882; *yr s* of late James J. Hosken; *m* 1911, Emma Harris, *yr d* of late E. K. Foster, Florida, USA; no *c*. *Educ:* privately. For many years on Editorial staff of Daily Mirror; served during European War in RFC and RAF (Captain SO3); began writing novels in 1925. *Publications:* Eighteen novels and four volumes of short stories including: William Cook, Antique Dealer, 1928; The Sanfield Scandal, 1929; The Man in the Red Hat, 1930; Crook Stuff, 1935; White Gas, 1937; Open Verdict, 1940; The Black Cripple, 1941; Crooks and Vagabonds, 1941; The Lady in No. 4, 1943; also Tales of Old Inns, 1939; numerous short stories and articles in principal newspapers and magazines. *Recreations:* shooting, fishing, and the study of old inns. *Club:* Savage.

Died 9 June 1950.

KEWLEY, Ven. John, MA; Archdeacon Emeritus of Man, 1938; *b* 1 May 1860; *s* of R. Kewley of Castletown. *Educ:* King William's College; Sidney Sussex College, Cambridge (Scholar); Wrangler, 1883. Ordained 1883; Curate of St Paul, Ramsey, 1883–91; Vicar of Kirk Arbory, 1891–1912; Rural Dean of Castletown, 1897–1912; Canon of Man, 1899–1912; Archdeacon of Man, 1912–38; Rector of Kirk-Andreas, 1912–38; Examining Chaplain to Bishop of Sodor and Man, 1912–24; Member of the Manx Legislative Council, 1912–19, and Executive Council, 1912–38; Chairman of the Council of Education of the Isle of Man, 1918–19; JP Isle of Man, 1913; President of the Isle of Man Licensing Appeal Court, 1926–38; Chairman of JP's of Ramsey District, 1933–38, of Castletown District, 1939. *Address:* 74 Malew Street, Castletown, Isle of Man. *TA:* Archdeacon Kewley, Castletown-Man. *T:* Castletown 3159.

Died 6 Nov. 1941.

KEY, Carl Axel Helmer, DPh University of Upsala; *b* Sweden, 26 April 1864; *m*; three *d*. Lecturer at Upsala 1894–96; Editor and Chairman of Svenska Dagbladet Publishing Co., Stockholm, 1897–1907, 1908–34; Member of the Board of Royal Opera, Stockholm, 1909–14, and of Chamber of Commerce, Stockholm, 1902–16; President of Swedish Press Club, 1917–20, and Swedish Newspaper Proprietors Association, 1903–05; Member of the Swedish Overseas Institute since 1927. *Publications:* Alessandro Manzoni, 1894; China and its Commercial Relations in the Last Centuries, 1900; La Vie Economique de la Suède, 1913; Life of A. O. Wallenberg, 1916; Travels in USA, 1922, German edn 1923; European Bankruptcy and Emigration, Swedish edn 1923, English and German edns 1924; A New Colonial Policy, 1926, Swedish and English edns 1927,

German edn, with preface of President of German Reichsbank, Dr Luther; Coffee, Sugar, and Bananas, Swedish edn 1928, 4th enlarged edn 1930, 5th revised edn, 1934, German edn 1929; The Pacific—the World's New Focus, 1932; Japan and the White Race: A World Problem, 1934. *Recreations:* riding and golf. *Address:* 7 Ostermalmsgatan, Stockholm. *Club:* Stora sällskapet.

Died 23 April 1938.

KEYES, 1st Baron *cr* 1943, of Zeebrugge and of Dover; **Roger John Brownlow Keyes;** Bt *cr* 1919, GCB 1930; KCB 1918; KCVO 1918; CB 1911; CMG 1916; CVO 1918; MVO 1906; DSO 1916; ADC 1914; DCL Oxford; LLD Cambridge, Aberdeen, St Andrews, and Bristol; *b* 1872; *s* of late Gen. Sir Charles Keyes, GCB; *m* 1906, Eva Mary Salvin Bowlby, Red Cross Order of Queen Elizabeth of Belgium, *d* of late Edward Salvin Bowlby, DL, of Gilston Park, Herts, and Knoydart, Inverness-shire; one *s* (*e s* Lt-Col Geoffrey C. T. Keyes, VC, MC, killed 1941, leading commando raid) three *d*. Entered Navy 1885; Commander, 1900; Captain, 1905; Rear-Admiral, 1917; Vice-Admiral, 1921; Admiral, 1926; Admiral of the Fleet, 1930; served Witu, 1890 (medal, clasp); China, 1900 (despatches, promoted to Commander, medal, two clasps); was Naval Attaché, Rome, Vienna, Athens, and Constantinople, 1905–07; Captain and Commodore in charge of the Submarine Service, 1910–14; Chief of the Staff Eastern Mediterranean Squadron, 1915 (despatches, CMG, DSO, and Commander Legion of Honour); Grand Fleet Captain and Rear-Admiral, 1916–17; Director of Plans, Admiralty, 1917; Acting Vice-Admiral in command of Dover Patrol, 1918; in command of operations against Zeebrugge and Ostend, 23 April 1918 (KCB, KCVO, Grand Cross Order of Leopold, Grand Officer Legion of Honour, Croix de Guerre, French and Belgian, American DSM); commanding Battle Cruiser Squadron, Atlantic Fleet, 1919–21; Deputy Chief of Naval Staff and a Lord Commissioner of the Admiralty, 1921–25; C-in-C Mediterranean Station, 1925–28; C-in-C Portsmouth Station, 1929–31; retired list, 1935; MP (Nat. C.) Portsmouth (North) division, 1934–43; replaced on Active List, 1940; Special Liaison Officer to King of Belgium, 1940; Special Liaison Officer to King of Belgium, 1940; Director of Combined Operations, 1940–41; Hon. Colonel Commandant of Portsmouth Division Royal Marines, 1932–43. *Publications:* Naval Memoirs: vol. i The Narrow Seas to the Dardanelles, 1934, vol. ii Scapa Flow to the Dover Straits, 1935; Adventures Ashore and Afloat, 1939; The Fight for Gallipoli, 1941; Amphibious Warfare and Combined Operations, 1943. *Heir: s* Hon. Roger George Bowlby, Lieut RN, *b* 1919. *Address:* Tingewick House, Buckingham. *Clubs:* Naval and Military, United Service.

Died 26 Dec. 1945.

KEYNES, 1st Baron *cr* 1942, of Tilton; **John Maynard Keynes,** CB 1917; MA, FBA; leader of British Delegation which negotiated the American Loan in Washington, Sept.–Dec. 1945, and Feb. 1946 was appointed a Governor of the International Bank for Reconstruction and Development; Fellow and Bursar of King's College, Cambridge; Fellow of Eton College; a Director of the Bank of England; a Trustee of the National Gallery; Chairman of Council for the Encouragement of Music and the Arts; High Steward Borough of Cambridge since 1943; President, Royal Economic Society; Member of Chancellor of the Exchequer's Consultative Council; Chairman, Arts Theatre of Cambridge; Officier de l'Ordre de Léopold; *b* Cambridge, 5 June 1883; *e s* of John Neville Keynes, and Florence Ada, *d* of late Rev. John Brown, DD; *m* 1925, Lydia Lopokova. *Educ:* Eton; King's College, Cambridge. Twelfth Wrangler, 1905. President of Cambridge Union Society, 1905; India Office, 1906–08; Treasury, 1915–19; Member of Royal Commission on Indian Finance and Currency, 1913–14; principal Representative of the Treasury at the Paris Peace Conference and Deputy for the Chancellor of the Exchequer on the Supreme Economic Council, Jan.–June 1919; Member of Committee on Finance and Industry, 1929–31; Editor of Economic Journal, 1911–44. *Publications:* Indian Currency and Finance, 1913; The Economic Consequences of the Peace, 1919; A Treatise on Probability, 1921; A Revision of the Treaty, 1922; A Tract on Monetary Reform, 1923; A Short View of Russia, 1925; The End of Laissez-Faire, 1926; A Treatise on Money, 2 vols, 1930; Essays in Persuasion, 1931; Essays in Biography 1933; The General Theory of Employment, Interest and Money, 1936; How to Pay for the War, 1940. *Address:* King's College, Cambridge; 46 Gordon Square, WC1. *T:* Euston 3875; Tilton, Firle, Sussex. *Clubs:* Athenæum, United University.

Died 21 April 1946 (ext).

KEYNES, John Neville, MA, ScD; Registrary Emeritus of the University of Cambridge; Hon. Fellow of Pembroke College; *b* Salisbury, 31 Aug. 1852; *o s* of late John Keynes and Anna Maynard Neville; *m* 1882, Florence Ada, *d* of Rev. John Brown DD; one *s* one *d*. *Educ:* Amersham Hall School; University College, London; Pembroke College, Cambridge; Senior Moralist (Cambridge), 1875; Gold Medallist (London), 1876. Fellow of University College, London, 1875; Fellow of Pembroke College, Cambridge, 1876. University Lecturer in Moral Science, Cambridge, 1884–1911; Secretary of the Local Examinations and Lectures Syndicate, 1892–1910; Registrary Univ. of Cambridge, 1910–25; Member of Council of Senate of Univ. of Cambridge, 1892–1924, and Secretary of Council, 1893–1925; Chairman of Special Board for Moral Science, 1906–12; Chairman of Special Board for Economics and Politics, 1908–20. *Publications:* Studies and Exercises in Formal Logic, 1884 (4th ed. 1906, reprinted 1928); Scope and Method of Political Economy, 1891 (4th ed. 1917, reprinted 1930); articles in the Encyclopædia Britannica, and in Palgrave's Dictionary of Political Economy. *Address:* 6 Harvey Road, Cambridge. *T:* Cambridge 4578.

Died 15 Nov. 1949.

KEYSER, Agnes, (Sister Agnes), RRC; *d* of Charles Keyser. Founded King Edward VII's Hospital for Officers; St John of Jerusalem, Coronation medals, King Edward VII, King George V, and King George VI; King's Jubilee Medal, 1935. *Address:* 17 Grosvenor Crescent, SW1. *T:* Sloane 9101.

Died 11 May 1941.

KEYSERLING, Count Hermann, PhD, Dr hc; writer and lecturer; President-founder of the School of Wisdom, Darmstadt; *b* Koenno, Estonia, 21 July 1880; *s* of Count Leo Keyserling and Baroness Jane Pilar von Pilchau; *m* 1919, Countess Goedela von Bismarck-Schoenhausen; two *s*. *Educ:* Pernau, Dorpat, Geneva, Heidelberg and Vienna. Studied after finishing the Russian Gymnasium at Pernau, Zoology, Chemistry, and Geology, PhD at Vienna in 1902; years of independent study in Paris and London and Berlin. inherited the estates of Koenno, Kerkau and Raykull in Russia in 1908, lived there until 1918 when was dispossessed by Russian Revolution; foundation of the school of Wisdom at Darmstadt, 1920; lecture tours during many years to many countries; now retired. *Publications:* The Travel Diary of a Philosopher, 1918; Creative Understanding, 1922; The Recovery of Truth, 1927; The World in the Making, 1925; The Book of Marriage, 1925; Europe, 1928; America Set Free, 1929; South-American Meditations, 1932; Problems of Personal Life, 1933; Das Gefuege der Welt, 1906; Politik, Wirtschaft, Weisheit, 1922; Philosophie als Kunst, 1920; Menschen als Sinnbilder, 1925; La Révolution mondiale et la responsabilité de l'Esprit, 1934; The Art of Life, 1937; Das Buch vom persönlichen Leben, 1936; Immortality, 1907; From Suffering to

Fulfilment, 1938. *Recreations:* country life and sea voyages. *Address:* 4 Prinz Christiansweg, Darmstadt. *TA:* Graf Keyserling, Darmstadt. *T:* Darmstadt 2042.

Died 26 April 1946.

KHAN, Major Sir Khan Hashmatullah, Kt 1933. Major in Gwalior State Forces, and Member Council of Regency, Gwalior State. *Address:* Gwalior, Central India.

Died 23 Dec. 1936.

KHAN, Sir Shafa'at Ahmad, Kt 1935; Member for Health, Education and Arts Indian National Government, Sept.–Oct. 1946; *b* Moradabad, UP, India, 1893; *s* of Sajjad Amad Khan, Zemindar, Moradabad; *m* 1924, Fahmida, *yr d* of late Justice Shah Din, of Lahore; two *d. Educ:* Government High School, Moradabad; Trinity College, Dublin; Sidney Sussex College, Cambridge; University of London. First Class Honours in History, 1914; Gold Medallist of Dublin University, 1914; LittD 1918. Assistant Professor of Indian Economics, University of Madras, 1919–20; organised the publication of Allahabad University Studies in History; a member of the United Provinces Legislative Council, from Moradabad, UP, since 1924; President several Muhammadan Educational Conferences; President, Conference of Muslim members on Local bodies and Legislative Council, 1928; Representative of UP Muslim Members of the Legislature in England, 1927; President, Bengal Muslim Conference, 1930; Delegate to the three Round Table Conferences in London, 1930–32; Delegate to Parliamentary Joint Committee on India, May–Nov. 1933; Hon. Secretary to the Muslim Delegation to the Round Table Conferences, 1930–31; President of the Muslim Youth League, Calcutta, May 1931; Chairman All-India Muslim Conference, 1933–34; presided over All-India Modern History Congress, Poona, June 1935; Officiating Member, Federal Public Service Commission, Govt of India, May–July 1940; Member GIP Railway Committee, appointed by Govt of India, Aug.–Dec. 1940; High Commissioner for India in South Africa, 1941–44. *Publications:* The East India Trade in the XVIIth Century in its Political and Economic Aspects, 1923; Anglo-Portuguese Negotiations relating to Bombay, 1660–1667; Sources for the History of British India in the XVIIth Century, 1926; John Marshall in India, 1668–1672; The Indian Federation, 1937; Federal Finance, 1939; Founder and Editor, Journal of Indian History, and the weekly, later on, daily, Star (English), Allahabad; contributions to periodicals. *Recreations:* walking and motoring. *Address:* New Delhi, India.

Died July 1947.

KHAN, Hon. Lt-Col Sirdar Sir Sikander H.; *see* Hyat-Khan.

KHUNDKAR, Sir Nurul Azeem, Kt 1946; **Hon. Mr Justice Khundkar;** BA, LLB (Cantab); Judge, High Court, Calcutta, since 1937; *b* 17 March 1890; of Eusuf Ali Khundkar, of the Middle Temple, Barrister-at-Law, Advocate of the High Court at Calcutta, and of Dora Maxwell, *o d* of Rev. Henry Erskine, of County Cavan, Ireland; *m* 1932, Rose Marcar, grandniece of Dr N. S. P. Aganoor, OBE, British Consul at Ispahan; no *c. Educ:* St Xavier's College, Calcutta; Peterhouse, Cambridge. Called to Bar, 1918, Lincoln's Inn; acted as Sub-Editor on Editorial Staff of The English and Empire Digest, 1918; acted as lecturer in LCC Senior Commercial Institutes, 1919; Assistant Editor of Looker-on, East and West, and Indian Business, 1920–21; Lecturer in Mercantile Law, Calcutta University, also Presidency Magistrate and acted as Judge, Court of Small Causes, Calcutta, 1921–24; Deputy Superintendent and Remembrancer of Legal Affairs, Bengal, 1924; Vice-President All India Society for Prevention of Cruelty to Animals, 1939; President Calcutta Society for Prevention of Cruelty to Animals, 1942; Member: Governing Body, Presidency College, Calcutta; Advisory Committee

Bengal War Purposes Fund, etc. *Publications:* various articles on subjects of economic and topical interest. *Recreations:* golf, gardening. *Address:* 1 Victoria Terrace, Calcutta. *Club:* Calcutta.

Died 10 May 1947.

KIDD, Rev. Beresford James, DD; Hon. Canon of Christ Church, 1915; *b* Birmingham, 1 Jan. 1864; *s* of Rev. James and Mary Kidd; *m* 1894, Agnes, *d* of W. T. Walker; no *c. Educ:* Christ's Hospital; Keble College, Oxford. 2nd Class, Hon. Mods; BA 2nd Class, Lit. Hum.; 1st Class, Honour Theology. Ordained, 1887; Assistant Curate of SS Philip and James, Oxford, 1887–1900; Chaplain of Pembroke College, Oxford, 1894–96; Lecturer in Theology at Pembroke Coll., 1902–11; Examiner in Hon. School of Theology, 1902–04 and 1917–19; Examining Chaplain to Bishop of Oxford, 1912, and to Bishop of London, 1927; Proctor in Convocation, 1917; Vicar of St Paul's, Oxford, 1904–20; Warden of Keble College, 1920–39, Hon. Fellow, 1940; Tutor of Non-Collegiate Students, 1889–1920; Order of St Sava (5th Class), 1919; Prolocutor of the Convocation of Canterbury, 1932–36. *Publications:* The Later Mediæval Doctrine of the Eucharistic Sacrifice, 1898; The Thirty-nine Articles, 1899; The Continental Reformation, 1902; Letters of Dr W. Bright, 1903; Documents Illustrative of the Continental Reformation, 1911; Documents Illustrative of the History of the Church, vol. i to ad 313, 1921; vol. ii to ad 461, 1923; vol. iii ad 500–1500; A History of the Church to ad 461, 3 vols, 1922; The Churches of Eastern Christendom from ad 451, 1927; The Counter-Reformation, 1933; The Primacy of the Roman See, 1936. *Address:* 35 Belsyre Court, Oxford. *T:* 3922.

Died 15 May 1948.

KIDD, Lt-Col Bertram Graham Balfour, DSO 1919; Indian Army, retired; *b* 6 Dec. 1875; *s* of Surg.-Gen. Leonard Kidd, Keady, Armagh; *m* 1908, Violet Mary Alice, *d* of John H. Bott, Cheltenham; one *s* one *d. Educ:* Wellington College; RMC, Sandhurst. Commissioned 1895; joined 23rd Bombay Rifles, Indian Army, 1896; Adjutant 123rd Outram's Rifles, 1901–05; Commandant 3/153rd Rifles, 123rd Rifles, and Training Battalion, Rajputana Rifles, 1918–24; served NW Frontier of India, Waziristan, 1901–02; Aden Boundary Commission, 1903–04; European War, 1914–21, EE Force, 1917–18, commanded Allied Guards (British, French, Italian, and Indian) at Jerusalem (despatches, DSO); Iraq, 1920 (despatches); Waziristan, 1923–24 (despatches); retired, 1924. *Address:* Strathmore, Camberley, Surrey. *T:* Camberley 422.

Died 1 Aug. 1943.

KIDD, Percy M., MD Oxford; Fellow of Royal College of Physicians of London; Consulting Physician to the London Hospital; Consulting Physician to Hospital for Consumption and Diseases of the Chest, Brompton; *b* 1851; *s* of late Joseph Kidd, MD; *m* 1881, Gertrude (*d* 1940), *d* of late Maj.-Gen. T. B. Harrison, West Hay, Wrington, Somersetshire; three *s. Educ:* Uppingham; Balliol Coll. Oxford. First Class Final School of Natural Science, Oxford, 1873; Radcliffe Travelling Fellow, Oxford University, 1878. *Publications:* on various medical subjects in Quain's and Allbutt's Dictionaries of Medicine, and medical Journals and Transactions of medical societies. *Recreations:* golf, fishing, music. *Address:* 22 Montagu Street, Portman Square, W1. *T:* Paddington 2940.

Died 21 Jan. 1942.

KIDDLE, Captain Kerrison, CBE 1919; *b* 27 Dec. 1876; *m* 1909, Hjordis, *d* of Consul-General O. Holter, Oslo; one *s* two *d. Educ:* Eastmans, Stubbington; HMS Britannia. Sub-Lt of HMS Ardent, 1897–98; took part in operations in Crete; specialised as Torpedo Lieut; Comdr 1911; Captain, 1918; commanded HMS Contest, Destroyer, Grand Fleet, 1914–16; served in Dover Patrol and in command of HMS Active, 1916–17;

command of HMS Greenwich, Depôt Ship, Grand Fleet Flotillas, 1917–19; command of 5th Destroyer Flotilla, 1 March 1919 (despatches, CBE); retired list, 1922; served War of 1939–45; dept of Chief Inspector of Naval Ordinance, 1942–45. *Address:* 35 Grimston Avenue, Folkestone, Kent.

Died 26 Dec. 1949.

KIDDY, Arthur William; Contributor to Encyclopaedia Britannica, Palgrave's Dictionary of Political Economy and various financial periodicals; *b* Belper, Derbyshire, 1868; *s* of late John Kiddy; *m* 1903, Ann (*d* 1941), *d* of late Richard Clapham of Maryport. *Educ:* York House, Southampton; Collegiate School, Belper. With accountants and business firms, 1883–89; commenced journalism on financial editorial staff of the Daily News, 1890; assistant City Editor of Daily News, 1891–99; City Editor, Standard, 1899–1914; City Editor of the Morning Post, 1915–37; City Editor of the Spectator, 1917–37; London Financial Correspondent of the New York Evening Post, 1895–1933; Editor of the Bankers' Magazine, 1895–1945; Associate City Post, 1937–46. 4th Order of Rising Sun, 1908. *Recreations:* photography, billiards. *Address:* Green Acre, Hadley Highstone, Barnet, Herts. *T:* Barnet 5412.

Died 18 Feb. 1950.

KILBRACKEN, 2nd Baron *cr* 1909; of Killegar; **Hugh John Godley,** CB 1931; KC 1924; MA; *b* 12 June 1877; *o surv. s* of 1st Baron and Hon. Sarah James (*d* 1921), *d* of 1st Lord Northbourne; *S* father, 1932; *m* 1st, 1919, Helen Monteith (marr. diss. 1936), *d* of Vereker Monteith Hamilton and *widow* of N. F. Usborne; two *s* one *d*; 2nd, Leonora (*d* 1948), *d* of P. C. Taylor, Brighton. *Educ:* Eton; Balliol College, Oxford. Barrister, Lincoln's Inn, 1902. Member Central Control Board (Liquor Traffic), 1917–21; Counsel to the Chm. of Committees (House of Lords), 1923–44; formerly Asst Parliamentary Counsel to the Treasury. *Heir: s* Hon. John Raymond Godley, Lt-Comdr (A) RNVR, DSC [*b* 17 Oct. 1920; *m* 1943, Penelope Anne, *y d* of Rear-Adm. Sir C. N. Reyne, KBE; one *s*]. *Address:* Killegar, Killeshandra, Co. Cavan. *T:* Killeshandra 9. *Clubs:* Athenæum; Kildare Street (Dublin).

Died 13 Oct. 1950.

KILBURN, Bertram Edward D.; *see* Dunbar Kilburn.

KILBY, Reginald George, CIE 1916. *Educ:* Winchester; Pembroke College, Oxford. Entered ICS 1895; Magistrate and Collector, 1910; Magistrate and Collector, Balasore, Bihar, and Orissa, 1912; retired, 1925. *Address:* Broadview, Brimley, Bovey Tracey, Devon.

Died 21 Sept. 1949.

KILGOUR, Rev. Robert, MA (Glas.); BD (Glas.); DD (Glas.) 1909; Chaplain to the Scots Guards and other Church of Scotland and Presbyterian Troops in London District since 1933; *b* 29 April 1867; *e s* of Robert Kilgour; *m* 1891, Agnes Elizabeth, *e d* of Ebenezer Horn; two *s*. *Educ:* Miller's Academy, and Broomloan Road Public School, Govan; City Public School, Glasgow; Glasgow University, Black Bursar in Divinity. Student Missionary at Cardonald, Govan Parish, and at Carrick Castle, Lochgoilhead. Licensed, Presbytery of Dunoon, 1889; Missionary of the Church of Scotland, Darjeeling, 1889–1909; Superintendent of the Translating and Editorial Department of the British and Foreign Bible Society, 1909–32; Acting Chaplain, Church of Scotland, Darjeeling; Municipal Commissioner and Secretary and Treasurer of many charitable schemes in Darjeeling; Examiner in Nepali for the Universities of Calcutta and Allahabad; one of the two translators of the Old Testament into Nepali. *Publications:* Four Ancient Manuscripts; The Gospel in Many Tongues; The Gospel in Many Years; The Bible throughout the World; (with Dr A. S. Geden), Introduction to Ginsburg's Hebrew OT; (with others), Nepali Dictionary. *Recreation:* golf. *Address:* 3 Stanway Gardens, Acton, W3. *T:* Acorn 1224. *Club:* Overseas.

Died 28 Jan. 1942.

KILLIN, Robert, CBE 1918; JP; General Superintendent, Northern Division, London, Midland and Scottish Railway (retired); *b* 14 Oct. 1870; *s* of James and Mary Killin; *m* 1895, Jane Emily Kerry; two *s* four *d*. *Educ:* Scots School, Rutherglen. Joined Caledonian Railway and worked through the different grades; Assistant District Superintendent for Western District, 1908; District Superintendent, 1910; Assistant Superintendent of the Line, 1912; Superintendent of the Line, 1916; General Superintendent (Midland Division), London, Midland and Scottish Railway, 1923; General Superintendent (Northern Division), London, Midland and Scottish Railway, 1924; Chairman Stelar Oil Co., Glasgow, 1936; Chairman Ailsa Shipbuilding Co., 1940. *Address:* Avondale Lodge, West Kilbride, Ayrshire. *T:* West Kilbride 2154. *Clubs:* Conservative, Royal Scottish Automobile, Glasgow.

Died 26 Dec. 1943.

KILMAINE, 5th Baron *cr* 1789; **John Edward Deane Browne;** Bt 1636; Representative Peer for Ireland since 1911; *b* 18 March 1878; *s* of 4th Baron and Alice Emily, *d* of Col Deane-Shute; *S* father, 1907; *m* 1901, Lady Aline Kennedy, *d* of 3rd Marquess of Ailsa; one *s* one *d*. *Educ:* abroad; Magdalen College, Oxford. *Heir: s* Hon. J. F. A. Browne, MA. *Address:* Corner House, 73 Dorset Road, Bexhill, Sussex. *Clubs:* National; Royal St George Yacht, Kingstown; East Sussex, Hastings.

Died 27 Aug. 1946.

KIMBALL, Katharine, retired ARE, artist; former Sociétaire salon d'automne, section de gravure; *b* New England, 1866. *Educ:* Jersey Ladies' College, St Helier; National Academy of Design, New York; Elliott Medal Antique Class, 1897. Bronze Medal Panama—Pacific International Exposition, San Francisco, 1915. Exhibitor Royal Academy, Royal Society of Painter-Etchers, Salon des Artistes Français, Salon d'automne Walker Art Gallery, Liverpool; Art Institute of Chicago; Coronation Exhibition (George V); Royal Swedish Academy, Stockholm, etc. Represented in the permanent collections: Congressional Library, Washington, New York Public Library, Boston Art Museum, Philadelphia, Museum of Art, Melbourne Gallery and Museum, Oakland Public Museum, British Museum, Victoria and Albert Museum, Bristol Museum and Art Gallery, Victoria Art Gallery and Municipal Libraries, Bath, Newark Public Library, Bibliothèque d'Art et d'Archéologie, Jacques Doucet, Paris. *Publications: illustrated:* Okey's Paris, 1904; Gilliat Smith's Brussels, 1906; Sterling Taylor's Canterbury, 1912; Rochester (Artists Sketch-Book Series), 1912; illustrations in Century, Studio, Artist, Gazette des Beaux Arts; Queen. *Recreation:* reading. *Address:* c/o Brown, Shipley & Co., 123 Pall Mall, SW1.

Died 19 March 1949.

KIMBER, Sir Henry Dixon, 2nd Bt *cr* 1904; MA Oxon; *b* 8 Nov. 1862; *e s* of Sir Henry Kimber, 1st Bt, and Mary Adelaide (*d* 1901), *d* of late Gen. Chas Dixon, RE; *S* father, 1923; *m* 1st, 1890, Florence Sarah (*d* 1907), *o d* of late Charles B. N. Snewin; two *d* (son killed European War); 2nd, 1910, Lucy Ellen, *y d* of late G. W. Crookes; one *s* one *d*. *Educ:* Epsom College; Lincoln College, Oxford. Solicitor; senior partner in Kimbers, Williams, Sweetland, Stinson & Co., 34 Nicholas Lane, EC; a DL of the City of London; Commander of the Order of the Crown of Italy; a Governor of St Thomas' Hospital; a member of the Court of Common Council. *Heir: s* Charles Dixon, [*b* 7 Jan. 1912; *m* 1933, Ursula, *er d* of late Ernest Roy Bird, MP]. *Address:* 51 Cadogan Pl., SW1. *T:* Sloane 9466. *Clubs:* Junior Carlton, Royal Automobile.

Died 4 Sept. 1950.

KIMBER, Sir Sidney (Guy), Kt 1935; JP; *b* 5 Nov. 1873; *s* of late Richard Kimber; *m* 1898, Helen Sarah Walker; two *d*. *Educ:* King Edward VI School, Southampton. Entered Borough Council as Councillor, 1910; Alderman, 1916; Sheriff, 1917–18; Mayor, 1918–20; Given Freedom of the Borough, 1932; President Southampton Camera Club, The Southampton Golf Club, etc. *Recreation:* bowls. *Address:* 2 Welbeck Ave, Southampton. *T:* Southampton 75316.
Died 8 Oct. 1949.

KIMBERLEY, 3rd Earl of, *cr* 1866; **John Wodehouse,** CBE 1925; MC; JP; Bt 1611; Baron Wodehouse, 1797; *b* 11 Nov. 1883; *e s* of 2nd Earl and Isabel Geraldine (*d* 1927), *d* of Sir Henry Stracey, 5th Bt; *S* father 1932; *m* 1922, Margaret Montagu, *d* of late Colonel Leonard Howard Irby; one *s*. *Educ:* Eton; Trinity Hall, Cambridge. Captain 16th (The Queen's) Lancers; served European War, France, Aug. 1914–17; Italy, 1918–19 (MC, Croce de Guerra, despatches twice, wounded once); MP (L) Mid Norfolk, 1906–10. Owns about 11,200 acres. *Heir: s* Lord Wodehouse. *Address:* Kimberley House, Wymondham, Norfolk. *Clubs:* Turf, Bath.
Died 16 April 1941.

KIMENS, Richard Edward, CMG 1923; *b* 22 Oct. 1872; *s* of Richard and Louise Whitmore-Perks; unmarried. *Educ:* Russia; Germany. Before the European War, 1914–18, was British Vice-Consul at Warsaw; Commissioner for Russia of the British Red Cross Soc., 1916–18; Asst Commissioner to British Mission in Poland, 1918–19; Commercial Secretary at HM Embassy at Warsaw, 1919–33; retired, 1933; employed in Ministry of Economic Warfare, Sept. 1939–Dec. 1940. Officer of the Order Polonia Restituta (Poland). *Club:* Travellers'.
Died 5 April 1950.

KIMMINS, Charles William, MA (Cantab), DSc (Lond.); 2nd *s* of late James Kimmins; *m* Grace Thyrza, CBE, *d* of James Hannam; two *s*. *Educ:* Owens College, Manchester; University College, Bristol; Downing College, Cambridge. Chief Science Master Leys School, Cambridge; Staff Lecturer Cambridge University Extension Scheme; Inspector of Schools for Mr Llewellyn Smith's report on Technical Education to the London County Council, 1892; Inspector of Science Teaching to the Technical Education Board of the London County Council, 1894; Director of University Extension in London 1895; Chief Inspector of Technical Education Board of LCC 1900; Chief Inspector of Education Department LCC 1904–23; Chairman of the University Extension Board, 1923; Member of the Senate of the University of London since its reconstitution in 1900; Deputy Vice-Chancellor, 1933–34; President of the Education Section of the British Association, 1929; Member of the Governing Body of St Paul's Schools; Member of the Roedean School Council. *Publications:* original papers on the Periodates published in the Transactions of the Chemical Society; The Chemistry of Life and Health; Children's Dreams, 1920; The Child's Attitude to Life, 1926; The Child in the Changing Home, 1926; The Mental and Physical Welfare of the Child, 1927; The Springs of Laughter, 1928; The Triumph of the Dalton Plan, 1931; The Wonderland of Dreams, 1937. *Recreations:* reading and writing books and articles. *Address:* The Old Heritage, Chailey, Sussex. *Clubs:* Athenæum, National Liberal.
Died 12 Jan. 1948.

KINAHAN, Sir Robert Henry Hudson-, 3rd Bt *cr* 1887; *b* 13 Sept. 1872; 2nd *s* of 1st Bt; *S* brother 1938. *Educ:* Trinity College, Dublin. *Heir:* none. *Address:* The Manor, Glenville, Fermoy, Co. Cork.
Died 26 Dec. 1949 (ext).

KINCAID, Col William Francis Henry Style, CB 1906; *b* 3 Jan. 1861; *s* of John Henry Kincaid, Dublin; *m* 1904, Rosamund Humphreys. *Educ:* Harrow; France. Entered RE 1880; Captain, 1889; Major, 1899; Colonel, 1903; employed with Egyptian army, 1893–99; AAG, S Africa, 1900–02; served Soudan, 1884–85 (medal with two clasps, bronze star); Expedition to Dongola, 1896 (despatches, Brevet-Major, medal two clasps); Nile Expedition, 1897 (despatches, two clasps); Nile Expedition, 1898 (despatches, Brevet Lieut-Col, 4th class Osmanieh, two clasps and medal); S Africa, 1899–1902 (despatches, Brevet-Colonel, Queen's medal five clasps, King's medal two clasps); retired, 1911; re-employed, 1915–19. *Address:* 1 Ilchester Place, Holland Park, W14. *Club:* United Service.
Died 19 Dec. 1945.

KINCAID-SMITH, Brig.-Gen. Kenneth John, CB 1919; CMG 1916; DSO 1900; late RA; *b* 7 Aug. 1871; *s* of Major J. Kincaid-Smith of Polmont, Falkirk. Entered RA 1891; Captain, 1900; served South Africa, 1899–1902 (despatches twice, Queen's medal 5 clasps, King's medal 2 clasps, DSO); European War, 1914–18 (despatches, CMG, CB, Bt Col, Chevalier Legion of Honour); late Hon. Col Essex Heavy Brigade RGA, TA; JP, DL, Essex; High Sheriff, Essex, 1929. *Address:* St Osyth's Priory, Colchester.
Died 15 July 1949.

KING, Sir Alexander Freeman, KCB 1911; CB 1908; *b* 1851; *s* of Rev. W. King, Fordham, Essex; *m* 1927, Sarah Ansell (*d* 1937), *d* of late John Cook, Hadleigh, Suffolk. Assist Sec. PO 1903–05; Joint 2nd Sec. 1905–07; 2nd Sec. 1907–11; Secretary to PO 1911–14. *Address:* 50 Wood Vale, SE23.
Died 8 May 1942.

KING, Lt-Col Alexander James, CMG 1918; DSO 1900; late The King's Own Royal Regiment and Fife and Forfar Yeomanry; *b* 15 July 1863; *o s* of late Rev. Edward King, BA, FRHS, FSA Scot. *Educ:* Radley College. Joined the King's Own Regiment, 1884; Capt. 1892; Major, 1902; served with Egyptian Army in Camel Corps in Dongola Expedition, 1896; Nile Expedition, 1897; Khartoum Expedition, 1898 (despatches three times, order of 4th class Medjidie, Brevet-Major); South African Campaign 1899–1900, was present during the siege of Ladysmith, and commanded the Kimberley Mounted Corps in the relief of Mafeking (despatches three times, Queen's medal 5 clasps, DSO); European War (CMG, despatches three times); DL, JP Aberdeenshire. *Address:* Tertowie House, Kinellar, Aberdeenshire. *Clubs:* Naval and Military, Boodle's; New, Edinburgh.
Died 9 July 1943.

KING, Brig.-Gen. Algernon D'Aguilar, CB 1916; CMG 1918; DSO 1900; RHA; retired; *b* 28 May 1862; *s* of late Maj.-Gen. A. H. King, CB, RA; *m* 1894, Lilian, *d* of late Thos Hargreaves of Arborfield Hall, Berks; one *d*. *Educ:* Cheltenham Coll.; RMA, Woolwich. Entered army, 1882; Major, 1900; served South Africa, 1900–02 (despatches, Queen's medal 4 clasps, King's medal 2 clasps, DSO); European War, Egypt, 1914–15 (despatches); Dardanelles, 1915–16 (despatches, CB); Palestine, 1916–18 (despatches 4 times, CMG). *Address:* 33 Buckingham Palace Mansions, SW1. *T:* Sloane 5079. *Club:* United Service.
Died 2 Feb. 1945.

KING, Cecil, TD, 1922; RI 1924; ROI 1932; RBA 1910–14; RBA 1910–14; Vice-President, Society of Marine Artists; Member, Société Nationale des Beaux Arts de la Mer, Paris; marine and landscape painter and writer; *b* 6 Aug. 1881; *s* of G. Frederic King and Alice Elizabeth, *d* of Henry Francis Bowker. *Educ:* Haileybury. Studied engineering; subsequently at Goldsmith's Institute, Westminster Art School and in Paris under Laurens and Steinlen. Pictures in Imperial War Museum (naval events in Baltic, 1918–19); Musée de Marine, Paris, etc.; Marine Painter to Royal Thames Yacht Club since 1932; formerly a regular contributor to Illustrated London News; Member (and former Councillor) of Society for Nautical Research, and originator and designer of the SNR Van de Velde Memorial; designer of the Zeebrugge, Armada, and other historical ship models used in Admiralty Theatre, etc., Wembley, 1924; Capt. TF (retd); served European War, 1914–19. *Publications:* Rule Britannia, 1941; HMS and their Forbears, 1940; The History of British Flags, 1914; magazine and newspaper articles, chiefly on art, travel and flags; light verse. *Recreations:* sailing and travel. *Clubs:* Chelsea Arts, Royal Thames Yacht (Hon.).

Died 9 Dec. 1942.

KING, Brig.-Gen. Sir Charles Wallis, KCVO 1932; Kt 1914; CB 1915; CMG 1918; CVO 1922; MVO 1904; *b* 10 Feb. 1861; *s* of Charles Ley King, Burlington, Plymouth; *m* 1st, 1884, Sarah Ann Lincoln; one *s* one *d*; 2nd, 1914, Phoebe Beatrice Redman. Lt Worcestershire Regt, 1886; Capt. ASC 1891; Major, 1899; Lieut-Col 1906; DAAG Home District, 1894–97, and 1901–03; Woolwich, 1897–1900; Assist-Director Supplies and Transport 4th Army Corps, 1903; AQMG London District, 1911; Assistant Director Military Transport, 1912–14; Director of Supplies, British Expeditionary Force, 1914 (despatches, CB); DAA & QMG 3rd Army Home Defence, 1916; DAA & QMG Northern Army Defence, 1917; Chairman GPS Committee of Royal Tournament. *Address:* 66 Victoria St, SW1. *Club:* United Service.

Died 20 April 1943.

KING, David Wylie; Acting Assistant-Editor, 1941, and Mining Editor The Financial Times since 1920; *b* Kilwinning; *e s* of John King; *m* 1918, Gertrude, *d* of J. Parkinson, Liverpool; two *s* one *d*. *Educ:* privately. Sub-Editor The Financial Times, 1899–1902; Asst Mining Editor, 1902–20; toured principal South African mining fields, 1925; travelled Canada, visiting all important mining districts, 1927. *Address:* 79 Marlborough Mansions, Cannon Hill, NW6. *T:* Hampstead 5940. *Club:* Mining and Metallurgical.

Died 8 April 1945.

KING, Rt Rev. George Lanchester; *b* 1860; *s* of late William Norman King; *m* 1921, Louisa Beatrice, *y d* of late William Henry Bewley, Rockville, Co. Dublin. *Educ:* Clare College, Cambridge (DD). Curate of Tudhoe Grange, Durham, 1884–89; Holy Trinity, Gateshead, 1889–90; St Mary, South Shields, 1890–94; Vicar, 1894–99; Bishop of Madagascar, 1899–1919; Secretary of the Society for Propagation of the Gospel, 1919–24; Canon Residentiary of Rochester Cathedral, and Canon Missioner, 1923–40; Assistant Bishop in the Diocese of Rochester, 1928–39. *Publications:* God and Ourselves; What is the Church; A self-made Bishop. *Address:* 33 Walden's Park Road, Horsell, Surrey.

Died 26 Jan. 1941.

KING, Humphrey Hastings, MA, LLB, Barrister-at-Law (Chancery and conveyancing); Chancellor of Dioceses of Sheffield, Chester, and Carlisle; Chairman of Legal Board of Church Assembly; one of Conveyancing Counsel of High Court; *b* 9 Jan. 1880; *s* of Henry Sampson King and Ada Charlotte Mapping; *m* 1908, Marjorie Mary, *er d* of Edward Alfred Webb, FSA; two *s* three *d*. *Educ:* Charterhouse (Sen. Scholar and leaving Exhibitioner); Pembroke College, Cambridge (Scholar). Class. Tripos 1901, Law Tripos (Pt 2) 1902; University Trial Eights, 1900 and 1901. Served 1914–19, RNVR (Anti-Aircraft) and RGA (demobilised rank Major); called to Bar 1904. *Publications:* original and editorial works of a legal character. *Recreations:* various. *Address:* 5 New Square, Lincoln's Inn, WC2; Orchard House, Holywell Hill, St Albans, Herts. *T:* Holborn 6430; St Albans 166. *Clubs:* Athenæum, Leander.

Died 3 Aug. 1950.

KING, James Foster, CBE 1920; LLD; Chief Surveyor, British Corporation Register of Shipping and Aircraft, 1904–40; Hon. Vice-President, INA; Hon. Fellow, NEC Institute; Hon. Member, Institution of Engineers and Shipbuilders in Scotland, and Society of Naval Architects and Marine Engineers in America; *b* Erskine, 1862; *s* of James Foster King. *Educ:* Glasgow High School. Apprenticeship with Russell & Co. and John Reid & Co., Port Glasgow; experience with Earles and Harland & Wolff; principal surveyor to Brit. Corporation Register, 1890. *Publications:* numerous papers dealing with technical subjects relative to shipbuilding. *Address:* 27 Kingsborough Gardens, Glasgow. *T:* West 1025. *Clubs:* Royal Scottish Automobile, Glasgow.

Died 11 Aug. 1947.

KING, John Hampden, CBE 1922; *b* 1865; *s* of John Hampden King, High Court Judge, British Guiana; *m* 1901, Ella Lindon, *d* of Captain Claude Kerr, Royal Dublin Fusiliers. Assistant Colonial Secretary, British Guiana, 1900; Immigration Agent-General, 1911. *Address:* Georgetown, British Guiana.

Died 25 Feb. 1945.

KING, Joseph; *b* 31 March 1860; *e s* of Joseph King, MRCS, of Liverpool; *m* 1st, 1887, Maude Egerton (*d* 1927), *y d* of Henry G. Hine, artist, VPRI; one *d*; 2nd, 1928, Helena G. Martins. *Educ:* Uppingham School; Trinity College, Oxford; Airedale College, Bradford; University, Giessen and University, Berlin. MP (L) N Somerset, 1910–18. *Publications:* Various pamphlets and books from 1892 to 1941, on political and foreign affairs, on education and artistic subjects; The German Revolution, 1933, etc.; Invasion Today, 1941. *Address:* Brownholm, Tilford, Farnham, Surrey. *TA:* Joseph King, Elstead, Surrey. *T:* Elstead 2250. *Clubs:* Reform, National Trade Union.

Died 25 Aug. 1943.

KING, Sir Kelso, Kt 1929; Managing Director, Mercantile Mutual Insurance Company, since 1907; Managing Director, Australian General Insurance Co. Ltd; Chairman, Morts Dock and Engineering Co.; Director, Illawarra, and South Coast SN Co., Australian Fertilizer Proprietary Co. Ltd, Colonial Mutual Life Assurance Society; Chairman, Walter and Eliza Hall Trust and Boy Scouts Association, NSW Branch; President of the New South Wales Branch, The St John Ambulance Association, since 1919; Trustee, Royal Naval House; *b* Sydney, NSW, 30 Dec. 1853; *s* of Rev. George King, LLD; *m* Alice Kirk; one *s* three *d*. *Educ:* Calder House, Sydney. Served on Pastoral Station in Queensland as a Jackaroo, 1870; entered service Bank New South Wales, 1871; transferred to Commercial Banking Company of Sydney, 1872; Secretary, Mercantile Mutual Insurance Co., 1877; Manager, 1899; Member of the Council of the Canberra Grammar School, the King's School and Trinity Grammar School. *Recreation:* all spare time spent in the Boy Scouts and other welfare movements. *Address:* Kilbronae, Point Piper, Sydney, NSW. *TA:* Kelso, Sydney. *Clubs:* Australian Pioneers (President), Australian, Union, Sydney.

Died 7 Feb. 1943.

KING, Lt-Col Lancelot Noel Friedrick Irving, CBE 1928; OBE 1919; late RE; *b* 25 Dec. 1878; *s* of late Aelian Armstrong King, Ceylon Civil Service; *m* 1923, Ester, *d* of Joseph Stäck, Gothenburg, Sweden. Entered Army, 1899; Lt-Col, 1924, served Aro Expedition, 1901–02 (medal and clasp); European War, 1914–19 (despatches thrice, OBE); was Senior British Commissioner Jubaland Boundary Commission; retired pay, 1929. *Address:* Storskärsgatan 4, Stockholm, Sweden.

Died 29 May 1947.

KING, Preston, MD, Alderman and JP, Bath; *b* 1862; *s* of late Wm Norman King of Gt Barton, Suffolk, JP; *m* 1898, Margaretta Baring, *d* of late Rev. Frederick Bond. *Educ:* Bury St Edmunds Grammar School; Cambridge; St Thomas's Hospital. Mayor of Bath, 1913–14 and 1917–18; Practising Medicine, specialising in Electro-therapeutics and X-rays; Consulting Physician and Governor to the Royal Mineral Water Hospital; late Hon. Electrician Royal United Hospital and Bath Ear and Throat Hospital. *Publications:* various professional and other articles. *Recreations:* workshop, carpentry, turning, etc. *Address:* 19 The Circus, Bath. *T:* Bath 2555.

Died 29 Jan. 1943.

KING, Richard, (Richard King Huskinson); *b* 1879; 10th *s* of late William Lamb Huskinson, of Epperstone, Notts. *Publications:* With Silent Friends; Passion and Pot Pourri; Second Book of Silent Friends; Over the Fireside; Below the Surface; Some Confessions of an Average Man, 1922; Folded Hands, 1923; The Return Journey, 1924; New Silent Friends, 1925; One Quiet Evening, 1927; At the Close of the Day, 1929; Soul's Dark Cottage, 1930. *Address:* c/o Hodder & Stoughton, St Paul's House, Warwick Square, EC4.

Died 3 April 1947.

KING, Sir Wilfred Creyke, Kt 1935; Chairman and Managing Director of The Exchange Telegraph Co. Ltd, 64 Cannon Street, EC4; *s* of Henry Stavely King, MD Lond. *Address:* The Chalet, Roehampton, SW15. *Club:* Union.

Died 22 Feb. 1943.

KING, Maj.-Gen. William Birchall Macaulay, CMG 1918; DSO 1915; VD; late Canadian Field Artillery; Hon. Colonel 8th Field Regt, RCA; *b* 1878; *s* of Colonel Frank King, MD, St Catherine's, Ontario, Canada; *m* 1909, Nora Beatrice, *d* of Lieutenant-Colonel R. Z. Rogers; one *s* one *d.* Served South African War, 1900–02, present at relief of Mafeking (Queen's medal and 4 clasps, King's medal and 2 clasps); European War, 1914–18 (despatches 6 times, DSO, CMG, Belgian Order of the Crown, Belgian Croix de Guerre); DOC Military District No. 1, 1923–26; District No. 4, 1926–31; retired 1931; resident JP at Ventersdorp, South Africa, 1902–06. *Address:* 72 Heath St W, Toronto 12. *Clubs:* United Service; Albany (Toronto); United Service (Montreal).

Died 23 June 1950.

KING, Rt Hon. W(illiam) L(yon) Mackenzie; PC (UK), 1922; PC (Can.), 1909; OM 1947; CMG 1906; *b* Berlin (now Kitchener), Ontario, 17 Dec. 1874; *e s* of John King, KC, and Isabel Grace, *γ d* of William Lyon Mackenzie; unmarried. *Educ:* Undergraduate course, Arts and Law, University of Toronto (BA, 1895; LLB, 1896; MA, 1897); postgraduate course, Fellow in Political Economy, University of Chicago, 1896–97; Fellow in Political Science, Harvard Univ., 1897–1900, including travelling fellowship abroad (AM, Harvard, 1898; PhD, Harvard, 1909). Deputy Minister of Labour, Canada, and editor of the Labour Gazette, 1900–08; MP (L) North Waterloo, Ontario, 1908–11; Prince, PEI, 1919–21; North York, Ontario, 1921–25; Prince Albert, Saskatchewan, 1926–45; Glengarry, Ontario, 1945–49; Minister of Labour of Canada in Laurier Administration, 1909–11; President, The General Reform Association of Ontario, 1912–14; engaged upon investigation of industrial relations under auspices of the Rockefeller Foundation, 1914–17; Member, National Executive, Canadian Patriotic Fund, 1914–20; selected as the late Sir Wilfrid Laurier's successor as Leader of the Liberal Party of Canada at National Liberal Convention, Ottawa, Aug. 1919; Leader of the Opposition, 1919–21 and 1930–35; Prime Minister, President of the Privy Council, Canada, 1921–30 (except from 28 June–25 Sept. 1926) and 1935–48; Secretary of State for External Affairs, 1935–46; retd as Leader of Liberal Party, 7 Aug. 1948; retd as Prime Minister and Pres. of Privy Council,

15 Nov. 1948. Rep. Canada at Imperial Conferences, London, 1923, 1926 and 1937, at meeting of Prime Ministers, London, 1944, 1946 and 1948; at signing Multilateral Treaty for Renunciation of War, at Paris, 1928; Member Council Assembly, League of Nations, Geneva, 1928 (Vice-Pres. 1928 and 1936); Chm. Canadian Deleg. to the UN Conf., San Francisco, 1945, to Conf. of Paris, 1946, and to Gen. Assembly of UN, Paris, 1948; signed Washington Declaration on Atomic Energy, with President Truman and Prime Minister Attlee, at the White House, Washington, 15 Nov. 1945; UN Charter at San Francisco, 26 June 1945. Attended Coronation of King George VI and Queen Elizabeth, 1937; Minister in Attendance on the King on Their Majesties' visit to Canada and USA, 1939; concluded with President Roosevelt the Ogdensburg Agreement (17 Aug. 1940) and the Hyde Park Declaration (20 April 1941). Hon. LLD: Queen's, Toronto, and McGill Univs (Can.); Harvard, Yale, Princeton and Columbia Univs and Coll. of William and Mary (USA); Edinburgh, Cambridge and London Univs (UK); Univs of Brussels and Louvain (Belgium); Univ. of Amsterdam (Netherlands); Hon. DCL, Oxford. Fellow, Royal Soc. of Can., 1910; Hon. Life Member, Can. Legion, 1934; Fellow, Can. Geog. Soc., 1943. Hon. FRIBA, 1944; Hon. Life Member, Parly Press Gallery, Ottawa, 1944; Hon. Bencher of Gray's Inn, 1946; Hon. Bencher, Law Soc. of Upper Can., 1947; Mem. Bar of Ontario, 1947; Mem. Académie des Sciences Morales et Politiques of Institut de France, 1948. Freedom of City of London, 1923, Sheffield, 1923, Manchester and Edinburgh, 1926, Aberdeen, 1937, Derby, 1944; Citoyen d'Honneur de la Ville de Dieppe, 1946. A Presbyterian. *Publications:* The Secret of Heroism, 1906; Industry and Humanity—a Study in the Principles underlying Industrial Reconstruction, 1918, abridged ed., 1935; re-issued, 1947; The Message of the Carillon and Other Addresses, 1927; Canada at Britain's Side, 1941; Canada and the Fight for Freedom, 1944. *Address:* Laurier House, Ottawa.

Died 22 July 1950.

KINGAN, William Sinclair; Member of Senate of Northern Ireland; DL, JP, Co. Down; *b* 6 Dec. 1876; *er s* of late Samuel Kingan, DL, JP, Glenganagh, Bangor, Co. Down; *m* 1921, Catherine Elizabeth Margaret, *er d* of Alfred E. Brett, Richmond Lodge, Strandtown, Co. Down; two *s* one *d.* *Educ:* Rugby. Formerly in Business. *Recreations:* hunting, golf. *Address:* Glenganagh, Bangor, Co. Down. *T:* Bangor 43. *Clubs:* Junior Carlton; Ulster, Belfast.

Died 8 Dec. 1946.

KINGCOME, Engr Vice-Adm. Sir John, KCB 1946 (CB 1943); RN retd; *b* 20 April 1890; *s* of G. H. E. Kingcome, Calcutta; *m* 1915, Elsie Furse, *d* of B. Parken, Plymouth; one *s* one *d.* *Educ:* Plymouth; RNE College, Keyham. Joined RNE College, 1905, and RN College, Greenwich, 1909; served European War, 1914–18; Engineer Captain, 1935; Fleet Engineer Officer, Home Fleet, 1939–40 (despatches); Engineer Rear-Admiral, 1941; Eng. Vice-Adm. 1945; Engineer-in-Chief of the Fleet, 1945–47; retired, 1947. *Recreations:* golf, tennis, etc. *Address:* 10 Sydney Place, Bath. *T:* Bath 2778. *Club:* Army and Navy.

Died 15 July 1950.

KINGHORN, Col Harry Jackson, CB, 1935; *b* 14 April 1867; *s* of James Kinghorn JP, and Margaret Eaton; *m* 1894, Elizabeth) *d* 1940), *d* of George Watson, Aberdeen. *Educ:* West End Academy and Grammar School, Aberdeen. Enlisted 4th Gordon Highlanders, 1885; commissioned 1st Aberdeenshire RE (V), 1894; Commanded 2nd Highland Field Company RE (Major), 1910; took Company to France 1914—7th Division; severely wounded 10 March 1915, Neuve Chapelle; Lt-Colonel, 1916; CRE 64th Highland Division March, 1916 till Armistice; CRE the 51st Highland Division, 1921; Colonel, 1923; retired, 1924; Hon. Colonel 51st

Highland Division RE, 1926–30; Chairman City of Aberdeen Territorial Army Association, 1927–31; JP and DL for County and City of Aberdeen. *Recreations:* golf, shooting, fishing. *Address:* Auchenhove, Lumphanan, Aberdeenshire; 5 Bon Accord Crescent, Aberdeen. *Club:* Thatched House.

Died 24 March 1947.

KINGSFORD, A. Beresford, MD, retired; *s* of late Montague Kingford; *m* Esther Gilfillan, ARCM; no *c*. *Educ:* King's School, Canterbury; University College, London. MRCS Eng. 1889, DPH Cantab 1890, MD Durham, 1906; Anæsthetist University College Hospital (now Consulting). *Publications:* Comparative Psychology of Murder by Poisoning, in The Police Journal, October 1929; on 1st Aid, ibid. October 1933. *Address:* 60 The Drive, NW11. *T:* Speedwell 4105.

Died 23 Jan. 1944.

KINGSFORD, Adm. Henry Coare; Admiral (retired); *b* 1858; *s* of Montague Kingsford of Littlebourne, Kent; *m* 1901, Isabel Evelyn (*d* 1911), *d* of Thomas Sworder of Hertford; one *d. Educ:* R. Hammond, Dover. Entered Navy, 1870; Lieut, 1880; served in Orontes in Egyptian War (medal and Khedive's star); Commander, 1894; Captain, 1899; received order Knight Commander St Maurice and St Lazarus of Italy, 1905; Rear-Admiral, 1908; retired, 1912; Admiral retired 1917. *Recreation:* motoring. *Address:* Stanford Lodge, South Canterbury. *T:* Canterbury 3525.

Died 1 March 1941.

KINGSMILL, Hugh, (Hugh Kingsmill Lunn); author; *b* 21 Nov. 1889; 2nd *s* of late Sir Henry Lunn; *m* 1st, Eileen FitzGerald Turpin; one *d*; 2nd, Dorothy Vernon; two *s* two *d. Educ:* Harrow; New College, Oxford; Trinity College, Dublin, MA. *Publications:* The Will to Love, 1919; The Dawn's Delay, 1924; Blondel, 1927; Matthew Arnold, 1928; After Puritanism; The Return of William Shakespeare, 1929; Behind Both Lines, 1930; Frank Harris, 1932; The Table of Truth; Samuel Johnson, 1933; The Sentimental Journey, 1934; D. H. Lawrence, 1938; The Fall, 1940; The Poisoned Crown, 1944; (with William Gerhardi) The Casanova Fable, 1933; (with Hesketh Pearson) Skye High, 1937; This Blessed Plot, 1942; Talking of Dick Whittington, 1947; (with Malcolm Muggeridge) Brave Old World, 1936; Next Year's News, 1937; Anthologies; Invective and Abuse, The Worst of Love, Johnson without Boswell, etc. *Address:* c/o Eyre and Spottiswoode, 15 Bedford Street, WC2.

Died 15 May 1949.

KINGSNORTH, Engr Rear-Adm. Sir Arthur (Frederick), KCB 1922; CB 1916; *b* 1864; *y s* of late John and Eleanor Kingsnorth of Woolwich, Kent; *m* 1911, Helen, *e surv. d* of late Charles Smith, Hartlepool. Engineer Rear-Admiral, 1918; was Engineer Captain on the Staff of the late Rear-Admiral Sir Robert Arbuthnot, Bart, KCB, MVO, first cruiser squadron, in the Battle of Jutland, 31 May 1916 (despatches, CB); retired list, 1922. *Address:* c/o Lloyds Bank, Devonport.

Died 23 April 1947.

KINGSTON, 9th Earl of, *cr* 1768; **Henry Edwyn King-Tenison;** Bt 1682; Baron Kingston, 1764; Viscount Kingsborough, 1766; Baron Erris, 1800; Viscount Lorton, 1806; Representative Peer for Ireland since 1917; late Lt Irish Guards; late Capt. 5th Batt. Connaught Rangers; *b* 19 Sept. 1874; *s* of 8th Earl, and Florence, *d* of Colonel Edward Tenison, Kilronan Castle; *S* father, 1896; *m* 1897, Ethel Lisette, *y d* of Sir Andrew Barclay Walker, 1st Bt; one *s* two *d*. Owns about 33,000 acres. *Heir:* s Viscount Kingsborough. *Address:* Kilronan Castle, Carrick-on-Shannon. *Clubs:* Carlton; Kildare Street, Dublin.

Died 11 Jan. 1946.

KINGSTON, 10th Earl of, *cr* 1768; **Robert Henry Ethelbert King-Tenison;** Bt 1682; Baron Kingston, 1764; Viscount Kingsborough, 1766; Baron Erris, 1800; Viscount Lorton, 1806; Representative Peer for Ireland since 1917; late Lieut Royal Scots Greys; *b* 27 Nov. 1897; *s* of 9th Earl of Kingston and Ethel Lisette, *y d* of Sir Andrew Barclay Walker, 1st Bt; *S* father 1946; *m* 1st, Gwyneth (from whom he obtained a divorce, 1947), *d* of W. H. Evans, Tenby; one *s* one *d*; 2nd, 1947, Jean Sinclair Alexander. *Educ:* Eton; RMC, Sandhurst. Served European War, 1915–18; retired, 1927. Owns about 33,000 acres. *Heir:* s Viscount Kingsborough. *Address:* Kilronan Castle, Carrick-on-Shannon.

Died 17 July 1948.

KINGSTON, Most Rev. George Frederick, DD, MA, PhD, DCL, LLD; Archbishop of Nova Scotia and Primate of All Canada since 1947; *b* Prescott, Ont, 1889; *s* of Richard and Elizabeth Newman Kingston; *m* 1919, Florence Brown, NS; one *s* two *d. Educ:* Trinity Coll., Univ. of Toronto, BA 1913, MA 1914; PhD 1923; Harvard; Oxford BD King's College, NS, 1917. Professor of Philosophy, King's College, Nova Scotia, 1920–22; Professor of Moral Philosophy, Trinity College, Toronto, 1922–40; Dean of Men Students, Trinity College, Toronto, 1926–40; Canon of St James Cathedral, Toronto, 1937–40; Bishop of Algoma, 1940–44; Bishop of Nova Scotia, 1944. DD Trinity College, Toronto, 1940; King's College, Halifax, NS, 1940; DCL Bishop's College, Lennoxville, 1945; LLD, Univs of Western Ontario and Toronto, 1948; DD, Wycliffe Coll., Toronto, 1948. *Publication:* The Foundations of Faith, 1925. *Recreation:* golf. *Address:* Bishop's Lodge, 402 Tower Road, Halifax, NS, Canada.

Died 20 Nov. 1950.

KINLOCH, Brig.-Gen. Sir David (Alexander), 11th Bt *cr* 1686, of Gilmerton; CB 1900; MVO; late Grenadier Guards; *b* 20 Feb. 1856; *s* of 10th Bart and Lucy (*d* 1903), *d* of Sir Ralph Anstruther, 4th Bt of Balcaskie; *m* 1897, Elinor Lucy (*d* 1943), *d* of Colonel Bromley Davenport of Capesthorne, Cheshire; one *s* two *d. Educ:* Eton; University College, Oxford (BA 1877). Entered army, 1878; Capt., 1889; Maj., 1894; Adjutant 1st Batt. Grenadier Guards, 1885–90; Lieut-Colonel commanding 1st Batt. Grenadier Guards, 1900; Brevet-Col 1904; served South Africa, 1899–1900 (despatches, Queen's medal, 3 clasps, CB); commanded 6th Brigade 2nd London Division Territorial Forces, 1908–12; offered his services at commencement of the war and was appointed temporary Brig.-Gen. 1914, commanding 70th Infantry Brigade of the new army; served France, 1915 (despatches, Hon. Brig.-Gen., March 1917); Member of the King's Body Guard of Scotland (Royal Archers); is a Director of Leslie and Godwin, Insurance Brokers. *Heir:* s Alexander Davenport [Major Special Reserve Grenadier Guards; *b* 17 Sept. 1902; *m* 1929, Alexandra, *d* of Frederick Y. Dalziel, New York; two *d*]. *Address:* Gilmerton House, Drem, East Lothian; 20 Eaton Place, SW1. *Clubs:* Turf; New, Edinburgh.

Died 27 Oct. 1944.

KINLOCH, Sir George, 3rd Bt *cr* 1873, of Kinloch; OBE 1918; *b* 1 March 1880; *e s* of 2nd Bt and Jessie Montgomerie Lumsden; *S* father 1910; *m* 1906, Ethel May, *y d* of late Major J. Hawkins; one *s* one *d. Educ:* Charterhouse; Trinity College, Cambridge (BA). *Heir:* s John [*b* 1 Nov. 1907; *m* 1934, Doris Ellaline, *er d* of C. J. Head, Shanghai; one *s*]. *Address:* Garrymore, Blairgowrie, Perthshire. *T:* Blairgowrie 205. *Clubs:* Royal City and County, Perth.

Died 16 March 1948.

KINLOCH-COOKE, Sir Clement, 1st Bt *cr* 1926; KBE 1919; Kt 1905; BA, LLM; Hon. ARIBA; *o s* of Robert Whall Cooke; *m* Florence (*d* 1944), *y d* of late Rev. Lancelot Errington. Assumed additional surname of Kinloch. *Educ:* Brighton College; St John's College,

Cambridge Mathematical Tripos; Law Tripos. Barr Oxford Circuit; Treasury Prosecuting Counsel for Berkshire; legal adviser to House of Lords Sweating Commission; Private Secretary to Earl of Dunraven (Under-Sec. of State for the Colonies); Examiner under CS Commission for HM's Factory Inspectorships; edited English Illustrated Magazine, The Observer, Pall Mall Gazette, New Review; many years leader writer on Morning Post; founder, and editor, 1901–41, of the Empire Review; Member of Council and Executive Committee of Festival of Empire; MP (U) Devonport, 1910–23; East Cardiff, 1924–29; Member of LCC, 1907–10; of Educational Authority for County of London; of London (Central) Unemployed Body; Governor of Imperial College of Science and Technology; Chairman Central Emigration Board; and of SW Advisory Committee London Secondary School for Girls; Member of Council Royal Empire Society; served on numerous committees in House of Commons; Chairman of the Naval and Dockyard Committee, 1910–24; twice Chairman of the Expiring Laws Continuance Act Committee; Chairman of Queen Mary's Holiday Home for Governesses, and Princess Mary's Memorial Home; has travelled extensively in the Dominions; Director (London Board) of Colonial Mutual Life Assurance Society, Ltd (of Australia); Director of Associated British Picture Corporation, Ltd, and Associated British Cinemas. *Publications:* Australian Defences and New Guinea; Authorised Memoir of Princess Mary Adelaide, Duchess of Teck; Life of HM Queen Mary; numerous political essays on imperial and colonial subjects. *Recreations:* yachting, hunting, cricket, football, athletics, lawn tennis. *Address:* 32 Grosvenor Street, W1. *T:* Mayfair 1820. *Clubs:* Athenæum, Carlton, MCC.

Died 4 Sept. 1944 (ext).

KINLOSS, 8th Baroness *cr* 1602; **Mary Morgan-Grenville,** CI; *b* 30 Sept. 1852; *S* father, 3rd and last Duke of Buckingham and Chandos, 1889; *m* 1884, Maj. Luis Ferdinand Harry Courthope Morgan (*d* 1896), *e s* of George Manners Morgan, Biddleston Park, Bucks; assumed additional name of Grenville, 1890; three *s* one *d*. Heir: *g d* Beatrice Mary Grenville Morgan-Grenville, *b* 1922. *Address:* Moreton Lodge, near Buckingham.

Died 17 Oct. 1944.

KINLOSS, Master of; Rev. Hon. Luis Chandos Francis Temple Morgan-Grenville; *b* 10 Oct. 1889; *e surv. s* and *heir* of 8th Baroness Kinloss, CI; *m* 1921, Catharine, *d* of John Jackman, The Kennels, Stowe; three *d*. *Educ:* Exeter Coll., Oxford; Lichfield Theological College. Deacon, 1914; Priest, 1930; Curate of St Sepulchre, Northants, 1914–19. *Address:* Sunnyside, Elmswell, Bury St Edmunds.

Died 2 Aug. 1944.

KINNAIRD, Hon. Emily, CBE 1920; OBE 1918; *d* of 10th Baron Kinnaird. *Educ:* at home under old-fashioned system. Member of National Overseas YWCA and of YWCA Training College; and of the Committee for Indian Students and Visitors of the International YWCA Service Dept; Vice-Pres. of Scottish Branch Zenana Bible and Medical Mission and of Scottish Division of the British YWCA; has frequently worked in India to take part in establishing friendly Christian relations with its men and women and help them to attain their national aspirations, and has taken part in the work of Missionary Schools and of Indian YWCA work through the country. *Publications:* Reminiscences Emily Kinnaird, being Recollections of Victorian Ideals in contrast with To-day; My Adopted Country, meaning India; Youth's Opportunity, being especially addressed to Indian Youth in 1948; contributor to Every Member (India), and The Zenana. *Address:* 62 Berkeley Court, Marylebone Road, NW1. *TA:* Emily Emmisarius, London. *T:* Welbeck 8147.

Died 9 Sept. 1947.

KINNAIRD, Hon. Patrick, MC; Director Barclays Bank; *b* 4 Dec. 1898; *γ s* of 11th Baron Kinnaird; *m* 1925, Violet, *d* of late Captain Frances Sandford. *Educ:* Eton; RMC, Sandhurst. Joined Scots Guards, 1917 (wounded); ADC to Governor General of Canada, 1920–21; Regimental Adjutant Scots Guards, 1939–43; Governor of Charterhouse; Treasurer and Member of Council of Bedford College for Women; Chairman of St Peter's Hospital, Covent Garden; Treasurer of National Rifle Association; Treasurer of St Thomas' Hospital. *Recreations:* shooting, golf, etc. *Address:* 1 Pall Mall East, SW1. *TA:* Ember Lesquare, London. *T:* Whitehall 5664. *Club:* Guards'.

Died 31 March 1948.

KINSLEY, Albert, RI 1896; *b* Hull, Yorks, 26 June 1852; *s* of Elisha and Elizabeth Kinsley; *m* 1883, Eliza Randles of Leeds. *Educ:* Baker Street Grammar School, Hull; Darley Street School, Leeds. Served apprenticeship with Messrs Lawson and Son, engineers and machine makers, Leeds; came to London, 1876; exhibited first picture RA 1882, and constantly since; also all important exhibitions, including Antwerp and Paris, 1900; elected member of Dudley, 1882; RBA 1889; RCA 1913. *Recreations:* cricket, swimming, billiards. *Address:* 22 Campdale Road, Tufnell Park, N. *Club:* London Sketch.

Died 1 May 1945.

KINSMAN, Frederick Joseph; *b* 27 Sept. 1868; *s* of Frederick Kinsman and Mary Louisa Marvin. *Educ:* St Paul's School, Concord, New Hampshire; Keble College, Oxford. DD Oxon; DD Berkeley; LLD Washington and Seton Hall. For twenty-five years, clergyman in the Episcopal Church; Bishop of Delaware, 1908–19; resigned to become a Roman Catholic. *Publications:* Salve Mater, 1920; Trent, 1921; Americanism and Catholicism, 1924; Reveries of a Hermit, 1936. *Address:* Hospice, Marcotte, Lewiston, Maine, USA.

Died 19 June 1944.

KIPPING, Frederic Stanley, FRS 1897; Emeritus Professor of Chemistry, University College, Nottingham; *b* Manchester, 1863; *e s* of James Stanley Kipping and Julia, *d* of C. A. Duval, artist; *m* Lily, 2nd *d* of W. T. Holland, JP, Bridgwater; two *s* two *d*. *Educ:* Manchester Grammar School; Lycée de Caen; Owens Coll.; Univ. of Munich. PhD (Munich); DSc (London). Chemist in Manchester Corporation Gas Works, 1882–85; studied in Germany; Assistant under Professor Perkin, FRS, for three years, Heriot-Watt College, Edinburgh; six years Lecturer in Chemical Department of Central Technical College; Longstaff Medal of the Chemical Society, 1909; Member of Council of the Royal Society, 1911; Davy Medal of the Royal Society, 1911; Davy Medal of the Royal Society, 1918. Hon. DSc (Leeds). *Publications:* many papers published in Transactions of the Chemical Society; joint-author with late Prof. Perkin, FRS, of Inorganic and Organic Chemistry. *Recreations:* lawntennis; formerly played for Lancashire and for Manchester; golf, billiards. *Address:* 11 Marine Terrace, Criccieth, N Wales.

Died 30 April 1949.

KIRBY, Brig.-Gen. Arthur Durham, CB 1919; CMG 1917; *b* 21 Oct. 1867; *m* 1921, Mary Muriel, 2nd *d* of late William Wilson, 52 Princes Gate, SW, and Las Delicias, Uruguay. *Educ:* Haileybury; RMA, Woolwich. 2nd Lieut RA 1887; Lieut 1890; Capt. 1898; Major, 1903; Lt-Col 1914; Brig.-Gen. 1915; Bt Col 1918; served South African War, 1899–1900 and 1902 (despatches, Queen's medal 7 clasps, Bt Maj.); European War (CMG, CB, Bt Col, despatches 6 times); Col-Comdt Royal Artillery, Eastern Command, India, 1921–24, also Western Command, 1923–24; retired pay, 1924. *Recreations:* big-game shooting, polo, and cricket. *Address:* Whitehills, Newton Stewart, Scotland. *Clubs:* Army and Navy, Royal Automobile, MCC.

Died 30 Oct. 1948.

KIRK, Harry B., MA, Professor of Biology, Victoria University College, Wellington, 1903–45, Professor Emeritus since 1945; *b* Coventry; *m* 1885. *Educ:* Auckland Grammar School and College. Honours in zoology and botany. Entered Education Department, 1879; Assistant Inspector of Native Schools, 1885. *Address:* Victoria University College, Wellington, NZ.
Died 15 July 1948.

KIRKE, Gen. Sir Walter Mervyn St George, GCB 1939 (KCB 1934; CB 1919); CMG 1918; DSO 1916; DL, JP, Surrey; Colonel Comdt, Royal Artillery, 1934–46; Hon. Colonel 70th A-A Regt (now 470th HAA Regt TA) 1934–39; and 2/5th The Queen's Royal Regiment, 1939; President, Witley and District Branch of British Legion and RA Association, Surrey; Vice-President, RUSI and Old Contemptibles, Godalming; *b* 19 Jan. 1877; *s* of late Col St G. M. Kirke, RE; *m* Lilian Ethel (*d* 1945), *o d* of J. Macliesh; two *s* four *d*. *Educ:* Haileybury; RM Academy, Woolwich. Entered Royal Artillery, 1896; Capt. 1901; Bt Major, 1914; Major, 1914; Bt Lt-Col 1915; Bt Col 1917; Maj.-Gen. 1924; Lt-Gen. 1931; Gen. 1936; served in Waziristan Campaign, 1901–02 (medal and clasp); Commandant Bhamo Bn Burma Military Police; commanded Wellaung, Punitive Expedition in S Chin Hills, 1905–06; psc; GSO, 3rd Grade, at War Office, 1912; 2nd Grade on mobilisation, 1914; served European War, 1914–18 (despatches six times, Bt Lt-Col, Bt Col, CB, DSO, CMG, Order of the Crown of Belgium, Officer Legion of Honour, French and Belgian Croix de Guerre, White Eagle of Serbia, Comdr, George I of Greece); Deputy Director Military Operations, 1918–22; Colonel on the Staff, GS Aldershot, 1922–24; head of British Naval, Military, and Air Force Mission to Finland, 1924–25 (Commander White Rose of Finland, Grand Cross 1939 and Finnish Meritorious Service Medal 1939); President Inter-Allied Commission of Investigation for Hungary; Deputy Chief of the General Staff in India, 1926–29; Commander 5th Division and Catterick Area, 1929–31; General Officer Commanding-in-Chief Western Command, 1933–36; Director-General of Territorial Army, 1936–39; Inspector-General of Home Defences, 1939; Commander-in-Chief of Home Forces, 1939–40; ADC General to the King, 1937–40; retired pay, 1940. *Address:* Oaks Cottage, Enton Green, Godalming. *Club:* Army and Navy.
Died 2 Sept. 1949.

KIRKHOPE, Lt-Col Kenneth Macleay, CIE 1919; VD; MICE, MIE (Ind.); late Flt Lt RAFVR/T; late Chief Controller of Stores and Director of Inspection, Indian Stores Department; *b* 9 April 1877; *s* of late W. G. Kirkhope, Glasgow; *m* 1st, 1905, Bertha Norah Freeman (*d* 1934); one *d*; 2nd, 1944, Annie May Hough. *Educ:* Public School; Royal Technical College. *Address:* Galway Lodge, Farnborough, Kent.
Died 20 Aug. 1950.

KIRKMAN, Frederick Bernulf Beever, BA Oxon; author, naturalist, school examiner; *b* Natal, 16 Feb. 1869; *s* of late John Kirkman; *g s* of Rev. T. P. Kirkman, FRS, and of J. F. Beever; *m* 1910, Kathleen Helena Willis; two *s*. *Educ:* Beaumaris Grammar School; Lincoln College, Oxford; Paris University. Formerly Assistant Master at Bromsgrove, Radley College, Merchant Taylors, EC; took an active part in introducing into English schools reformed methods of modern foreign language teaching; has written and edited a number of books for schools based on those methods; in 1898 gave up teaching owing to medical advice; has since been engaged chiefly in authorship, linguistic and ornithological, and in original investigation into the life-history of certain species of birds; Examiner (temp.) Board of Education, 1917–22; School Examiner for Oxford, Cambridge, London Universities; Hon. Treas. Inst. for the Study of Animal Behaviour; Civil List pension, 1943; FBPsS 1943. *Publications:* Linguistic: The Teaching of Foreign Modern Languages, 1909; La Première Année de Français, 1905; 13th edition; and other school-books. Ornithological: editor and part author of the British Bird Book, 4 vols 1911–1913; British Birds, 1930 (with F. C. R. Jourdain), 2nd edition, 1938: Bird Behaviour, 1937; The Highway History, 4 vols, 1936–1938. *Recreations:* walking, reading. *Address:* 94 Princes Avenue, Watford.
Died 1 May 1945.

KIRKNESS, Lewis Hawker, CIE 1936; DSO 1918; OBE 1919; MA, MInstT; (Lt-Col); late Member Permanent Commission, International Railway Congress; *b* 1881; *s* of late William Kirkness; *m* 1917, Idonea Frances, 2nd *d* of late James Armstrong. *Educ:* King's College School; St John's College, Cambridge (exhibitioner and scholar). Entered service Madras Railway, 1904; Assistant Traffic Superintendent, 1905; District Traffic Superintendent, 1909; Secretary to Agent, Madras & Southern Mahratta Railway, 1911; Served European War, 1914–19 (DSO, OBE, despatches, Order White Eagle, Serbia, Order of Military Merit, Greece); Deputy Transportation Superintendent, Madras & Southern Mahratta Railway, 1924; Principal, Railway Staff College, Dehra Dun, 1929; Secretary, Railway Board, India, 1933–36; Joint Secretary, Wedgwood Committee on Indian Railway Finance, 1936–37; served War of 1939–45, Movement Control, War Office. *Publications:* Principles of Absolute Block System, 1929; (with Sir Kenneth G. Mitchell) Report on Road and Rail Competition in India. *Address:* Little Kenwyn, Liphook, Hants. *T:* Liphook 3200. *Clubs:* Junior Carlton, Overseas.
Died 24 Jan. 1950.

KIRKPATRICK, Lt-Col Alexander Ronald Yvone, CMG 1918; DSO 1916; late RA; *b* 1868. Entered RA 1888; Lieut-Col 1916; served European War, 1914–18 (despatches, DSO, CMG).
Died 3 Feb. 1950.

KIRKPATRICK, Gen. Sir George (Macaulay), KCB 1918 (CB 1911); KCSI 1917; *b* 23 Aug. 1866; *s* of late Sir George Airey Kirkpatrick, KCMG, ex-Lieut Governor of Ontario; *m* 1896, Mary Lydia (*d* 1945), 3rd *d* of J. F. Dennistoun; three *d*. *Educ:* Trinity College School, Port Hope, Canada; Haileybury; Royal Military College, Kingston, Canada. Entered RE 1885; Capt. 1894; Major, 1903; Col 1906; Lt-Gen. 1921; General, 1927; ADC to GOC Thames District, 1892–95; DAAG S Africa, 1899–1902; DAQMG Canada, 1902–04; Headquarters, 1904–06; General Staff Officer, 1st Grade, India, 1906–10; served S Africa, 1899–1902 (despatches twice, brevet of Major and Lt-Col; Queen's medal 5 clasps, King's medal 2 clasps); European War, 1914–15 (prom. Maj.-Gen.); passed Staff College; Inspector-General Military Forces of Australia, 1910–14; Director Military Operations, India, 1914–16; Chief of General Staff, India, 1916–20; General Officer Commanding HM Forces in China, 1920–21; General Officer Commanding-in-Chief, Western Command, India, 1923–27; Colonel Commandant Corps of Royal Engineers, 1927–39; retired pay, 1930. *Address:* 10 Rodway Road, SW15.
Died 6 Feb. 1950.

KIRKPATRICK, Major William, DSO 1902; Indian Army, retired; *b* 2 Feb. 1863; *s* of late Dy-Surg.-Gen. James Kirkpatrick; *m* 1906, Lillias Elizabeth, *d* of Captain Robert Steuart, DL, of Westwood, Linlithgowshire. Entered army, 1883; Capt. 1894; Major, 1901; served Burmese Expedition, 1885–87 (despatches, medal and clasp); 1st Miranzai Expedition, 1891; NW Frontier, India, 1897–98 (medal with clasp); Mahsud Waziri operations, 1901–02 (despatches twice, DSO, clasp). *Address:* St Lawrence House, Haddington, East Lothian.
Died 24 June 1941.

KIRKPATRICK, William, CIE 1941; BE, BA, MICE; late Chief Engineer, Sind; *b* 15 Sept. 1886. Joined Indian Service of Engineers, 1910. Served in both Wars (1916–20 and 1941–43). *Address:* c/o Lloyds Bank Ltd, 6 Pall Mall, SW1.

Died 15 May 1947.

KIRWAN, Hon. Sir John Waters, KCMG 1947; Kt 1930; JP; *b* 2 Dec. 1866; 2nd *s* of late Nicholas John Kirwan of Sandymount House, Co. Galway; *m* 1912, Gertrude, *d* of late Hon. T. F. Quinlan, CMG; two *s.* Travelled extensively; did literary work for Dublin and London press; went to West Australian gold-fields in 1895; part proprietor Editor-in-Chief, 1895–1926, of Kalgoorlie Miner (daily) and Western Argus (weekly); advocate of Australian federation; at first federal elections was returned member for Kalgoorlie in House of Representatives, of which he was Deputy Chairman of Committees and Member of Elections and Qualifications Committee, 1901–03; Member of Royal Commission on Iron Bonuses, 1902–03; Honourable for life since 1904; Member East Coolgardie Licensing Bench, 1906–23; Member Legislative Council of WA for South Province, 1908–46, when he retired; Chairman of Committees, 1923–26; President of Legislative Council of Western Australia, 1926–46. Delegate from WA to first Imperial Press Conference, and during that Conference hon. sec. to over-sea delegates, 1909; delegate to second Imperial Press Conference at Ottawa, 1920; delegate to third Imperial Press Conference at Melbourne, 1925; represented Australia at Seventeenth Conference Parlementaire Internationale du Commerce at Prague, 1931; and at Eighteenth Conference at Rome, 1933; member of Senate of University of Western Australia, 1912–34; Director of Hocking & Co., Ltd. *Publications:* An Empty Land, Pioneers and Pioneering in Australia, 1934; My Life's Adventure, 1936; articles in Nineteenth Century, The Times, etc., dealing chiefly with Imperial and Australian questions; several papers for WA Historical Society. *Recreations:* golf, travelling. *Address:* Savoy Hotel, Perth, West Australia. *Clubs:* Hannans (Kalgoorlie); Weld (Perth); Kildare Street (Dublin).

Died 9 Sept. 1949.

KISCH, Temp. Brig. Frederick Hermann, CB 1942; CBE 1919; DSO 1916; Chairman Palestine-British Trade Association; RE; *b* Aug. 1888; *s* of H. M. Kisch, CSI; *m* 1927, Ruth Laura, *d* of Sir Leonard Franklin, OBE; two *s. Educ:* Clifton College; RMA, Woolwich. Entered R. Eng., 1909; served European War, France, 1914–15; Mesopotamia, 1916–17 (despatches thrice, wounded thrice, DSO, Croix de Guerre, Bt Maj., Bt Lt-Col); Officier de la Légion d'Honneur, 1918; British Deleg. Versailles Peace Conference, 1919; retired pay, 1922; rejoined Lt-Col RE, 1939; Chairman, Palestine Zionist Executive, 1922–31. *Publication:* Palestine Diary, 1938. *Club:* Bath.

Died 7 April 1943.

KISCH, Hermann Michael, CSI 1905; Barrister-at-law; *b* 1 Dec. 1850; *s* of late Joseph Kisch, surgeon; *m* Alice Charlotte (*d* 1917), *d* of late J. L. Elkin; two *s* one *d. Educ:* City of London School; Trinity College, Cambridge. ICS, Bengal, 1873; sometime Under-Secretary to Government of Bengal, and Under-Secretary and Deputy Secretary to Government of India; employed in Famine Relief, Bengal, 1874; Madras, 1877; Postmaster-General of Bengal from 1884, and in that capacity organised posts for Sikkim Campaign, 1888 (medal and clasp); officiated for four years as Director-General of Post Office of India; Member of Council of Lt-Governor of Bengal, and Acting Financial Secretary to Government of Bengal, 1901–02; Commissioner of a Division from April 1902; retired, 1904; represented India at International Postal Congresses, Vienna, 1891; Washington, 1897; Berne, 1900; Rome, 1906; and at Imperial Penny Postage Conference, London, 1898; author of Statistical Accounts of Chittagong and other

districts and State of Hill Tippera. *Address:* 51 Campden Hill Road, Kensington, W8. *T:* Western 1384. *Club:* East India and Sports.

Died 7 Nov. 1942.

KITCHIN, Shepherd Braithwaite; KC; Advocate of Supreme Court of South Africa; *b* Dalton-in-Furness, Lancs; *m* 1914, Jean, *d* of late Allan Forsyth Stark, Edinburgh. *Educ:* Univ. of the Cape of Good Hope (BA, LLB); Trinity Hall, Cambridge (Scholar, LLB). Prizeman in Law and Lit. (Latham Essay). Acting Crown Prosecutor for Griqualand West, 1910; Member of Cape Provincial Council for Kimberley, 1912–13; Editor of South African Law Journal, 1913–18; was Chairman, Kimberley Public Library, Member of Board of Trustees, SA Public Library, Member of School Board. *Publications:* A History of Divorce, 1912; Reports of the Supreme Court (Griqualand West Local Division) from 1905. *Address:* 6 Market Street, Kimberley, South Africa.

Died 6 May 1944.

KITSON, Charles Herbert, MA, DMus Oxon, FRCO (Hon.); FRCM; *b* Leyburn, Yorkshire, 13 Nov. 1874; *s* of late James Kitson; *m* 1908, Lucy, 2nd *d* of late W. P. Viccars, JP, of Anstey Pastures, Leicester. *Educ:* Ripon School; Selwyn College, Cambridge (Organ Scholar). Organist and Choirmaster, Christ Church, Cathedral, Dublin, 1913–20; Professor of Music, Univ. College, Dublin, 1915–20; Senior Theory Professor, Royal Irish Academy of Music, 1918–20; Professor of Music in the Univ. of Dublin, 1920–35; Hon. Member Conference of Cathedral Organists; sometime Examiner for degrees in music in the Universities of Oxford, Durham, Wales, New Zealand, Manchester and London; late Dean of the Faculty of Music, London University. *Publications:* The Art of Counterpoint; Applied Strict Counterpoint; Studies in Fugue; The Evolution of Harmony; Elementary Harmony; Additional Exercises to Harmony; Rudiments of Music; Counterpoint for Beginners; Invertible Counterpoint; Rudiments for Juniors; Six Lectures on Accompanied Vocal Writing Elementary Contrapuntal Harmony; Elements of Composition; various compositions for Organ, Church Music, Part-songs, etc. *Address:* c/o Royal College of Music, SW7.

Died 13 May 1944.

KITSON, Maj.-Gen. Sir Gerald Charles, KCVO 1912 (CVO 1905); CB 1910; CMG 1901; *b* 6 Oct. 1856; *s* of Rev. J. B. Kitson and Harriet Buller, Morval, Cornwall; *m* 1894, Gwendolen (*d* 1934), *d* of Horace D'Oyly Moule, CSI; one *d. Educ:* Winchester. Entered Army, 1875; Lieut-Col 1896; DAAG Meerut, 1890–92: AAG Umballa, 1892–94; served Manipur, 1891 (medal, despatches); Staff College, 1885–86; late Commandant of Royal Military College, Kingston, Canada; Military Attaché, British Embassy, Washington; Commandant of Royal Military Coll., Sandhurst, 1902–07; commanding Brigade, Jubbulpore, 1907; Jullundur, 1908; Quartermaster-General in India, 1909–12; Commanded 2nd Division, India, 1912; retired, 1918. *Address:* Old East Haxted, Edenbridge, Kent. *T:* Edenbridge 2276. *Club:* Naval and Military.

Died 3 March 1950.

KITSON, Hon. James Clifford; *b* 6 Dec. 1864; 2nd *s* of 1st Baron Airedale; *brother* and *heir-pres.* to 2nd Baron. *Address:* 3 Cadogan Square, SW1.

Died 25 Sept. 1942.

KLEINWORT, Herman Greverus; *b* 3 July 1856; *e s* of late A. F. H. Kleinwort of The Glebe, Denmark Hill, and Sophie Charlotte, *d* of H. D. Greverus; *m* Marguerite M. J., *d* of late O. Günther, Antwerp. *Educ:* privately in London; Realgymnasium, Karlsruhe; Institut Supérieur de Commerce, Antwerp. *Address:* 45 Belgrave Square, SW1. *T:* Sloane 7905; Wierton Place, Maidstone.

Died 18 June 1942.

KLUGH, Ven. Leonard; b 24 Dec. 1859; s of C. W. Klugh, Secretary Governesses' Benevolent Institution, and Sarah Kingdom Klugh; m Ada Lindsay Robson (d 1940), d of Commander Plummer, Indian Marine Navy; no c. Educ: Philological School and King's College, London. Deacon 1895; Priest 1896; Curate at Egloshayle, Margate Parish Church, and Saltwood successively; Chaplain on Bengal Ecclesiastical Establishment, 1889–1912; Archdeacon of Lucknow, 1911–13; Rector of Kenchester with Bridge Sollers, 1913–16; Chaplain to Malakand and Buner Field Forces, 1897–98 (medal and clasp); Indian Long Service Volunteer Medal; Chaplain, Cavalry Division Delhi Durbar (medal); editor, Lucknow Diocesan Chronicle, 1907–09; Secretary, Board of Missions, 1893–96; Diocesan Inspector of Schools, Hereford; Chaplain to the Forces, 4th Class (temp.), 1915; Hon. CF, 1919; Chaplain St Maxime, Var, 1927–28; Chaplain of the Estorils, Portugal, 1929 and 1930; Vicar of Ewshott, Hants, 1918–30; Public Preacher, Rochester Diocese, 1930; Chaplain, Sliema, Malta, 1931; Chaplain, Marseilles, winter season, 1933. Address: Lloyd's Bank, High Street, Rochester, Kent.

Died 13 Jan. 1943.

KNAGGS, Col Henry Thomas, CB 1919; CMG 1917; late RAMC; b 26 July 1863; m 1893, Violet Geraldine (d 1934) d of late Robert Keating Clay, JP, Killiney, Co. Dublin. Capt. 1886; Maj. 1898; Lt-Col 1906; Col 1915; S Africa, 1899–1902 (Queen's medal 3 clasps, King's medal 2 clasps); served European War, 1914–18; retired pay, 1919. Address: Eversleigh, Parabola Road, Cheltenham.

Died 14 March 1946.

KNAGGS, Col Morton Herbert, CMG 1918; late Army Ordnance Department; b 1871; s of Col H. Knaggs, RAMC. Served South African War, 1900–02 (despatches, Queen's medal and three clasps, King's medal and two clasps); Assistant Director at War Office, 1916–19; Dist Officer Bureau de Liquidation de Matériel de Guerre, Germany, 1920–22. Club: United Service.

Died 4 March 1948.

KNAGGS, Robert Lawford, MA, MD; m 1st, 1926, Adrienne Ernestïne Blanche, née Blouet-Dargonne (d 1931), widow of Morton William Smith, Recorder of Rochester; 2nd, 1933, Anne, d of John Simpson, Hunmanby. Hunterian Professor, Royal College of Surgeons of England; Professor of Surgery, the University, Leeds 1910–19; Consulting Surgeon, Leeds General Infirmary; and House Physician, Guy's Hospital. Address: Glenburnie, 20 Forde Park, Newton Abbot.

Died 16 April 1945.

KNAPP, Brig.-Gen. Kempster Kenmure, CB 1919; CMG 1916; late RA; b 16 Jan. 1866; s of Rev. John Knapp, RN; m 1906, Lilian W. Cowan; (one s killed in action, 1945) one d. Served Manipur, 1891; Burma, 1891–92 (medal with clasp); Lushai, 1892 (clasp); Waziristan, 1894–95 (clasp); NW Frontier, India, 1897–98 (medal 2 clasps); European War, 1914–18 (despatches six times, CB, CMG, Bt Col); temp. Brig.-Gen. 1916; retired pay, 1923. DL Northants, 1946–47. Address: Brooke Lodge, Weadon, Northants.

Died 12 April 1948.

KNATCHBULL, Brig.-Gen. George Wyndham Chichester, CMG 1916; Indian Army; b Morah, Gwalior, India, 3 March 1862; e s of Lt-Gen. Reginald Edward Knatchbull, RA, and Sarah Emma, d of Capt. Owen Lomer, IA; m 1900, Constance (d 1913), d of Alexander Marsden, MD, FRCSE; one s. Educ: Private School, Jersey; Sandhurst. Lieut the Welsh Regt 1883; joined the Indian Army, 1885; Capt. 1894; Major, 1901; Lt-Col 1909; served Burma Campaign, 1886–87 (despatches); China Expeditionary Force, 1900–02; European War, 1914–16; first in command of 6th Batt.

The King's Own Royal Lancaster Regt, and then in command of 38th Brigade, 13th Division (promoted temp. Brig.-Gen., wounded, despatches, CMG); retired Oct. 1918 with hon. rank of Brigadier-General.

Died 2 June 1943.

KNEBWORTH, Viscount; Alexander Edward John Lytton, MBE 1940; Major, The Queen's Bays; son and heir of 2nd Earl of Lytton, KG; b 10 March 1910. Educ: Royal Naval College, Dartmouth; Trinity College, Cambridge. Owns about 3500 acres. Address: Royal Armoured Corps Depot, Catterick Camp, Yorkshire. Club: Cavalry.

Died 4 July 1942.

KNIGHT, Charles, CB 1920; b 1863; s of late David Knight, Roche, Cornwall. Assistant Secretary, Local Government Board and Ministry of Health, 1918–22. Address: Higher Town, Tremodrett, Roche, Cornwall.

Died 25 March 1941.

KNIGHT, Charles Andrew R. B.; see Rouse-Boughton-Knight.

KNIGHT, Charles Joseph, CBE 1935; Traffic Commissioner in South-Eastern Area; Alderman of County Borough of Eastbourne; Director of Eastbourne Waterworks Co; b 10 July 1863; s of Joseph Hobbs Knight and Ann Upham; m 1889, Estelle Ianthe Hyland; one s. Educ: privately. Mayor of Eastbourne, 1925–26. Recreations: cricket and golf. Address: Rosalyn, Pevensey Bay, Sussex.

Died 6 Feb. 1950.

KNIGHT, Clara Millicent, DLit; writer; late Reader in Classics in University of London (King's College); e d of late Cornelius J. Knight. Educ: privately; University College and King's Coll., London. Lectureships in Classics in the Univ. of London; Member of Council of the Hellenic Society; formerly Member of the Council of the Classical Association; Member of Cambridge Philological Society. Publications: Various articles on Comparative Philology and Classical Literature in English and American periodicals; edition of Plautus Menaechmi; Joint-Editor of the Animal Year-Book, Vols I–III. Recreation: music. Address: 40 Silverston Way, Stanmore, Middlesex. T: Grimsdyke 1794.

Died 31 July 1950.

KNIGHT, Eric; Major, Army United States; b Menston, Yorkshire, 10 April 1897; s of Frederic Harrison Knight and Marion Hilda Creasser; m 1st, 1917, Dorothy Noyes Hall; three d; 2nd, 1932, Jere Knight. Educ: Beverly School, Yorks; Boston Museum of Fine Arts, USA; New York Academy of Design. Served European War, Princess Patricia's Canadian Light Infantry. Publications: Song on Your Bugles, 1936; The Flying Yorkshireman, 1938; You Play the Black and the Red Comes Up, 1940; Now Pray We for Our Country, 1940; This Above All, 1941; Lassie, Come Home, 1942; Sam Small Flies Again, 1942. Recreation: farming. Address: c/o Curtis Brown, Ltd, 6 Henrietta Street, WC2.

Died 15 Jan. 1943.

KNIGHT, Eric Ayshford; JP, DL; b 1863; 2nd s of Capt. E. Lewis Knight and Henrietta Mary, d of E. A. Sanford, of Nynehead Court, Wellington, Som; m 1897, Constance Ida (d 1932), d of J. W. H. Wilson, Winnipeg; one s one d. Educ: Cheltenham. Ranched in Canada till 1896; served (Yeomanry) South Africa (medal); contested Droitwich Division, 1906; MP (C) Kidderminster, 1910–18; Kidderminster Division of Worcestershire, 1918–22; Major in Worcester Imperial Yeomanry. Recreations: fishing, hunting, shooting, chess. Address: Wolverley House, Kidderminster. TA: Wolverley. T: Wolverley 234. Clubs: Carlton; County, Worcester.

Died 10 Aug. 1944.

KNIGHT, Brig.-Gen. Henry Lewkenor, CMG 1918; DSO 1917; late Royal Irish Fusiliers; *b* 1874; *s* of late Rev. Charles Edward Knight, Chawton, Hampshire; *m* 1901, Sybil Madeleine Howard; one *d*. *Educ:* Haileybury. Served South African War, 1899–1900 (despatches, Queen's medal and five clasps); European War, 1914–18 (despatches, DSO, CMG); Colonel-Commandant 12th Indian Infantry Brigade, Rawalpindi, 1923–27; retired pay, 1929. *Address:* Le Court, Greatham, Liss, Hants.

Died 28 March 1945.

KNIGHT, Prof. Nicholas, AB, AM, PhD, FFSc; Emeritus Professor of Chemistry, Cornell College; *b* Mexico, New York, 2 April 1861; *s* of George and Mary McDonald Knight; *m* 1887, Anna May Audas; two *s*. *Educ:* Mexico, New York, Academy; University, Syracuse; University, Harvard; University, Cornell; University, Johns Hopkins; and University, Strassburg. Professor of Natural Science, Cazenovia Seminary, New York, 1882–92; Professor of Chemistry, Randolf-Macon College, Virginia, 1895–98; Cornell College, 1899; Member Editorial Board of the Chemical News; Fellow and Chairman for USA of the Faculty of Sciences. *Publications:* Quantitative Chemical Analysis; Blow-Pipe Analysis; Chemical Arithmetic; Chemistry of Colloids; about 350 scientific and other articles in scientific journals and magazines. *Address:* Cornell College, Mount Vernon, Iowa, USA. *Clubs:* American Chemical Society, German Chemical Society, Iowa Academy of Science (President, 1920–21), Phi Beta Kappa, Phi Lambda Upsilon, Delta Upsilon.

Died 29 July 1942.

KNIGHT, William George, MA, CIE 1911; late Indian Educational Service; *b* 18 June 1858; *m* E. M., *d* of Robert Knight, proprietor of Statesman, Calcutta; two *s* two *d*. *Educ:* Edinburgh University, MA 1st Class Hons Maths; Ferguson Scholar for Scottish Universities; BA Cambridge University, Wrangler and 1st Class Finals, 1885. Professor, Presidency College, Calcutta, 1885; also Patna College and Sibpur Engineering College; Inspector of Schools, Bengal, 1906; Director of Public Instruction, Bengal, 1908; retired, 1913; assumed by deed poll surname of Knight in lieu of Kuchler, 1919. *Address:* Woodland Rise, Reigate, Surrey. *T:* Reigate 998.

Died 4 Nov. 1943.

KNIGHT, William Stanley Macbean, BLitt (Oxon); Barrister-at-law; *b* 1869; *s* of William Richard Irwin Knight; *m* Winifred Ida, *d* of late Major P. J. O'Sullivan, MD, RAMC; one *s* four *d*. Solicitor, 1893; called to Bar, Inner Temple, 1899; Tutor, New College, Oxford, 1920; member of London County Council and Vice-Chairman, Local Government Committee, 1907–10; Alderman and Chairman of Parliamentary Committee of St Pancras Borough Council, 1906–17; prospective Parliamentary Conservative candidate for Poplar until 1909; in 1910 left the Conservative and Municipal Reform parties, becoming Chairman Liberal Association, East St Pancras, resigning 1916; member of Central Unemployed Body for London, 1908–10; formerly a Vice-President of Council of Tariff Reform League; Corresponding Member, Netherlands Vereniging voor de uitgave van Grotius; de Jong van Beek Prize of the Royal Netherlands Academy, 1931. *Publications:* The Business Encyclopædia, 1902 (last ed. 6 vols, 1936); A History of Britain during the Great War, 1916; The History of the Great European War, 10 vols, 1914–1920; translated and edited Selections from Grotius' De Jure Belli ac Pacis, 1922; Life and Works of Hugo Grotius, 1925; contributor to Encyclopædia of Social Sciences, 1934. *Address:* 3 Clifton Road, Brighton, Sussex.

Died 21 March 1950.

KNIGHT, Maj.-Gen. Sir Wyndham (Charles), KCIE 1919; CB 1916; CSI 1917; DSO; *b* 30 Nov. 1863; *s* of Capt. W. B. Knight, late Queens' Bays; *g s* of Edward Knight of Chawton, Hants; *m* 1st, 1896, Harriet Monica (*d* 1927), *d* of Francis John Johnston; two *s*; 2nd, 1928, Alice Hariot Margaret (*d* 1938), *d* of Major-Gen. H. C. Johnstone, CB, and *widow* of Sir Alfred Kensington; 3rd, 1938, Georgina Helen, *d* of late Maj.-Gen. H. Pipon, CB and *widow* of Lt-Col H. G. Stainforth, CMG. *Educ:* Cheltenham. Served NW Frontier of India, 1897; Mohmand expedition, as Road Commandant (medal and clasp, despatches); Tirah, 1897–98 (clasp, despatches); S African War, 1900–02 (medal and 5 clasps, King's medal and 2 clasps, despatches twice, brevet majority, DSO); chief staff officer Imperial Yeomanry in South Africa, 1900–02; DAAG, 8th Division in India, 1904–08; ADC to King George V, 1912–17; GSO1, Army Headquarters, India, 1912–15; Brigade Commander and Embarkation Commandant, Bombay, 1915–17; and in command of Bombay District, 1917–19; Major-General i/c Administration, Southern Command, India, 1919–22; retired, 1922; JP Hants. *Address:* Pamber Place, Basingstoke.

Died 10 June 1942.

KNIGHTLEY, Captain Percy Frank, DSO 1918; *b* Aldershot, 1874; *s* of late Major Edward Knightley, RW Fusiliers; *m* 1896, Sophie, *d* of John Fletcher, Birkenhead; one *d*. *Educ:* King's College, London. Is an Associate of Chartered Institute of Secretaries; a trustee of the HAC Compassionate Fund; Vice-Pres. Kenton Branch, British Legion; Member of the Company of Pikemen, HAC; Hon. Secretary of HAC Westmeath Committee and Poor Children's Fund; Hon. Sec. of R. W. Fusiliers Officers' Association; served European War 1914–18 with HAC and Royal Welch Fusiliers (despatches, DSO). *Publications:* The Practical Company Secretary, 1931; Notes on Company Work, 1935; Company Correspondence, 1936; Articles on Joint Stock Company procedure. *Recreations:* hard work, motoring, and an unbounded interest in all military matters. *Address:* 98 Northwick Avenue, Kenton, nr Harrow.

Died 10 April 1942.

KNOBLOCK, Edward; playwright; *b* New York City, 7 April 1874. *Educ:* Harvard University, BA, 1896. *Plays:* The Faun, 1911; Kismet, 1911; Milestones, with Arnold Bennett, 1912; The Headmaster, with Wilfred T. Coleby, 1913; My Lady's Dress, 1914; Marie-Odile, 1915; Paganini, 1916; Home on Leave, 1916; Tiger, Tiger, 1918; Mumsee, 1920; One, 1920; Cherry, 1920; The Lullaby, 1923; London Life (with Arnold Bennett), 1924; Mr Prohack (with Arnold Bennett from his novel), 1927; The Mulberry Bush, 1930; (with J. B. Priestley) The Good Companions, 1931; Grand Hotel, from Vicky Baum's novel, 1931; (with Beverley Nichols) Evensong, 1932; Hatter's Castle, from A. J. Cronin's novel, 1932; The Edwardians, from the novel by V. Sackville West, 1934; Rolling Stone, 1936; The Henry Irving Centenary Matinee, 1938; Bird of Passage, 1943. *Films:* Three Musketeers for Douglas Fairbanks, 1921, and The Thief of Bagdad, 1923; Red Waggon (from Eleanor Smith's novel), 1933; Chu Chin Chow, 1934; Evensong (from Beverley Nichols' novel), 1934. *Publications:* Kismet, Milestones, My Lady's Dress, London Life, The Lullaby, Tiger, Tiger, Marie-Odile, in play form; Cot 5, a book of verses, 1918; The Ant Heap (novel), 1929; The Man with Two Mirrors (novel), 1931; The Love Lady (novel), 1933; Round the Room, an autobiography, 1939; Inexperience (novel), 1941. *Address:* 21 Ashley Place, Westminster, SW1. *Clubs:* Beefsteak, Pratt's.

Died 19 July 1945.

KNOOP, Douglas, MA, Hon. ARIBA; Professor of Economics, University of Sheffield, 1920–48; *b* Manchester, 16 Sept. 1883; 2nd *s* of late H. L. Knoop, Manchester. *Educ:* Hulme Gram. School and Owens College, Manchester. Travelled in Canada and USA,

1906–07; Acting Investigator, Labour Depart, Board of Trade, 1907–08; Assistant Lecturer in Economics, University of Manchester, 1909–10; Lecturer in charge of Economics Depart, University of Sheffield, 1910–20; Dean of the Faculty of Arts, Univ. of Sheffield, 1922–25; AK Travelling Fellow, 1913–14. *Publications:* Industrial Conciliation and Arbitration; American Business Enterprise; Municipal Trading; Outlines of Railway Economics; Colour Impressions; The Riddle of Unemployment; (with G. P. Jones) The Mediæval Mason, The London Mason in the Seventeeth Century, The Scottish Mason and The Mason Word, A Short History of Freemasonry to 1730, A Handlist of Masonic Documents, The Genesis of Freemasonry, and An Introduction to Freemasonry; various contributions to economic, masonic, and architectural journals; (with G. P. Jones and Douglas Hamer) The Two Earliest Masonic MSS, The Early Masonic Catechisms, Early Masonic Pamphlets, and The Wilkinson Manuscript. *Address:* 25 The Grove, Totley, Sheffield. *T:* Sheffield 72515.

Died 21 Oct. 1948.

KNOTT, Sir Thomas Garbutt, 2nd Bt *cr* 1917; *b* 14 July 1879; *s* of Sir James Knott, 1st Bt, and Margaret Annie (*d* 1929), *d* of late Rev. Thomas Garbutt; *S* father, 1934. Served S Africa, 1899–1902; European War, 1914–18. *Heir:* none. *Clubs:* Manor, Exmouth.

Died 10 April 1949 (ext).

KNOWLES, Frances I.; *see* Knowles, M. H. F. I.

KNOWLES, Sir George Shaw, Kt 1939; CBE 1928; OBE 1919; High Commissioner for Australia in the Union of South Africa, since 1946; *b* Brisbane, 14 March 1882; *s* of late G. H. Knowles, Ipswich, Queensland; *m* 1908, Eleanor, 2nd *d* of John S. Bennett, Registrar Land Court, Brisbane; three *s* one *d*. *Educ:* Toowoomba Grammar School; Trinity College, Melbourne, MA, LLM. Barrister and Solicitor, Australia, 1916; Entered Queensland Public Service 1898; transferred to Commonwealth Public Service 1902 and joined Law Department in 1907; acted as Solicitor-General of the Commonwealth for two and a half years during 1918–19, 1923–24, and 1930–31; Solicitor-General, Permanent Head of the Law Dept and Parly Draftsman, 1932–46; Legal Adviser to Australian Delegation to First Assembly of League of Nations 1920, and to Fifth Assembly 1924; Secretary for Australia in British Empire Delegation to Washington Disarmament Conference, 1921–22; Legal Adviser to Australian Delegation to Imperial Conference, 1937; member of Australian Patent Attorney's Examination Board, 1915–46; member of Council of Canberra University Coll., 1930–46 (Acting Pres., 1933); member of Australian National Debt Commission, 1932–46. *Publications:* Annotated Edition of Commonwealth Acts 1901–1911; the Australian Constitution (with notes), 1936. *Recreations:* golf, motoring. *Address:* Australian High Commissioner's Office, Pretoria, S Africa.

Died 22 Nov. 1947.

KNOWLES, Ven. Kenneth Davenport, MA Oxon; DD Oxon, 1924; HCF; Archdeacon of Huntingdon, 1921–43; Archdeacon Emeritus, 1943; Vicar of Diddington since 1938; Surrogate; *b* 9 March 1874; *s* of Thomas Knowles of Poynton, Cheshire, and Mary Frances Knowles; *m* 1906, Dorothy Laing, *d* of Robert Falkner, Manchester; two *d*. *Educ:* King's School, Canterbury; Bedford School; Worcester College, Oxford; Ely Theological College. Solicitor, admitted 1900; deacon, 1905; priest, 1906; first curacy Ramsey, Hunts; Rector Woodwalton, 1907–12; Rector of Brampton, 1912–22; Rector of Upton with Copmanford, 1924–38; Chaplain to Hunts Cyclist Batt. Territorials; served 1914–17 in 1/1 Hunts Cyclist Batt., and with 33rd Brigade on Somme. *Publications:* War Time Sermons; The Huntingdon Children's Service and Prayer Book; King's School Ely, Prayer Book; Kimbolton School Prayer Book; Huntingdon Grammar School Prayer Book. *Recreation:* Worcester College Eight (rowing). *Address:* Diddington Vicarage, Buckden, Hunts. *T:* Buckden 215.

Died 9 Dec. 1944.

KNOWLES, Mabel Winifred, (May Wynne); Church Worker in charge of St Luke's Mission Church, connected with the parish of St Luke's, Victoria Docks; *b* 1 Jan. 1875; 2nd *d* of William and Letitia Knowles; father senior partner Knowles & Foster, merchants and bankers of Moorgate Street. *Publications:* some twenty-five novels, chiefly historical; best known—Henry of Navarre, Witch-finder, Marcel of the Zephyrs, The Terror of the Moor; Red Fruit; Whither; Little Brown Tala (broadcast in Children's Hour); Big Money; Education of Nicky (both filmed); many books for girls and boys; serial and short story writer. *Recreations:* none. *Address:* Tyne House, 93 Maplin Road, Custom House, E16. *T:* Albert Dock 2480.

Died 29 Nov. 1949.

KNOWLES, (Mary Hannah) Frances Ivens, CBE 1929; Chevalier de la Légion d'Honneur, Croix de Guerre (avec palme), Médaille d'Honneur des Epidémies en or; MB, MS Lond.; ChM Liverpool (Hon.); FRCOG; County Medical Officer BRCS Cornwall; *m* 1930, C. M. Knowles, Barrister-at-Law. *Educ:* University Scholar and Gold Medallist in Obstetric Medicine, 1900; studied at Royal Free Hospital, London; Dublin, Vienna. Late Clinical Lecturer in Midwifery and Gynæcology, University of Liverpool; Hon. Consulting Gynæcological Surgeon, Stanley Hospital; Hon. Consulting Surgeon, Liverpool Maternity Hospital; Ex-President, Federation of Medical Women; Member of Consultative Council on Medical and Allied Sciences, Ministry of Health; Surgeon-in-Charge, Scottish Women's Hospitals, Royaumont and Villers Cotterets, France, 1914–19. *Recreation:* gardening. *Address:* Killagorden, Truro. *T:* Truro 2255.

Died 6 Feb. 1944.

KNOWLES, William Henry; *b* 14 May 1857; FSA, FSA Scot.; FRIBA (retd); *m* 1890, Jessie (*d* 1925), 6th *d* of late John Benson, Newcastle; one *s*. Member of the Architectural Committee of the Victoria Histories for the Counties of England; Past Pres., Bristol and Gloucestershire Archæological Society and of Worcestershire Archæological Society; Hon. Member Newcastle Soc. of Antiquaries; Chairman Gloucester Roman Research Committee; Local Secretary for Worcestershire of the Society of Antiquaries; Member of Central Council for the care of churches; of Worcestershire branch of CPRE; of the committee of the Northumberland County History; with R. H. Forster directed and reported on the Excavations of the Romano-British site of Corstopitum, 1907–14. *Publications:* Vestiges of Old Newcastle and Gateshead, 1890; The Romano-British Site of Corstopitum, 1909; Tynemouth Priory, 1910; numerous papers on archæological subjects in transactions of various societies. *Address:* Chesfield, Malvern. *T:* 18. *Club:* Royal Societies.

Died 18 Jan. 1943.

KNOWLSON, Thomas Sharper; *b* Bilton Park, Knaresbro', 1867; 2nd *s* of late William Knowlson. *Educ:* Victoria Park School, Harrogate; Richmond College, Surrey. Lecturer on Applied Psychology; special lecturer on Business Psychology at the University of Wisconsin, 1910; for many years was Director of Instruction at the Pelman Institute and is the principal author and editor of the Pelman course. *Publications:* edited G. H. Lewes' Principles of Success in Literature, 1898; The Art of Thinking, 1899; How to Write a Novel, 1900; The Art of Success, 1903; Business, 1909; The Education of the Will, 1909; The Origins of Superstitions, 1910; Efficiency, 1914; Originality: A Popular Study of the Creative Mind, 1917; A Thought-Book on the Socratic Method, 1920; The Secret of Concentration, 1931;

Selling Your Ability (USA), 1933, English ed., 1943; Think for Yourself, 1934; Brain Building for Success (with W. J. Ennever), 1939 (condensed edition, Your Mind and How to Use It, 1943); Put on Your Thinking Cap, 1944; Creating New Ideas, 1945. *Address:* Swingle Swangle, Matfield, Kent.

Died 2 July 1947.

KNOX, Alfred Dilwyn, CMG 1943; 2nd *s* of late Rt Rev. E. A. Knox, DD, and Ellen Penelope, *d* of Dr Valpy French, Bishop of Lahore. *Educ:* Eton; King's College, Cambridge (Scholar). Fellow of King's College, Cambridge, 1910–22.

Died 27 Feb. 1943.

KNOX, Brig. Sir Errol (Galbraith), Kt 1949; MBE 1918; Managing Director since 1940 The Argus and Australasian Ltd, Melbourne; *b* 25 June 1889; *s* of late Joseph Knox; *m* 1919, Gertrude Mary, *y d* of late George Millbank Coore, sometime Director of Education, London; one *s* two *d. Educ:* Fort St School; Sydney Univ. Sub-Editor Sunday Times, Sydney; private Australian Expeditionary Force, 1915, served France, 1916–19, rank of Major Air Staff, RAF, loaned from Australian Flying Corps (despatches twice); News Editor Daily Telegraph, Sydney; Managing Editor Evening News, Sydney; Director Associated Newspapers Limited; Treas. Empire Press Union (Australian Section), 1923–29 and since 1939; Pres. Australian Newspapers Conference, 1940; Pres. Australian Newspaper Proprietors Assoc. 1941–42; Managing Editor the Argus and Australasian Ltd, Melbourne, 1937; Director-General of Public Relations Dept of the Army, 1942–44 (honorary); recalled from retired list and Brig. 1942. *Recreation:* farming. *Address:* The Argus and Australasian Ltd, Melbourne, Australia; 285 Walsh Street, South Yarra. *Clubs:* Melbourne, Navy, Army and Air Force (Melbourne).

Died 17 Oct. 1949.

KNOX, Lt-Col George Stuart, CMG 1919; late RE; *b* 4 Sept. 1871; *s* of late Major James Knox, 19th Foot, sometime Governor of HM's Prison at Wandsworth, and *e d* of late Charles Ross; *m* Clara, *d* of late Finlay Campbell, DL, of Brantridge Park, Sussex. *Educ:* Cheltenham College; RMA, Woolwich. Sometime Assistant Surveyor-General Federated Malay States, and Director of Surveys British East Africa; served European War, 1914–19 (despatches, CMG). *Address:* c/o Lloyds Bank, 6 Pall Mall, SW1.

Died 15 Oct. 1945.

KNOX, Rev. Wilfred Lawrence, MA; DD; FBA; Fellow and Hon. Chaplain, Pembroke College, Cambridge; Hon. Canon of Ely since 1933; *s* of late Rt Rev. E. A. Knox. *Educ:* Rugby; Trinity College, Oxford. Warden, Trinity Coll. Mission Settlement, Stratford, E; Junior Examiner in the Board of Education; Assistant Priest, St Mary's, Graham Street, SW, and St Saviour's, Hoxton, N; Priest of the Oratory of the Good Shepherd since 1920. *Publications:* The Catholic Movement in the Church of England; St Paul and the Church of Jerusalem; Meditation and Mental Prayer; The Church in Crisis; (with Rev. E. Milner-White) One God and Father of All; Life of St Paul; St Paul and the Church of the Gentiles, 1939; (with Rev. A. R. Vidler) The Development of Modern Catholicism; and The Gospel of God and the Authority of the Church; Some Hellenistic Elements in Primitive Christianity (The Schweich Lectures 1942); The Acts of the Apostles, 1948. *Recreation:* fishing. *Address:* Pembroke College, Cambridge.

Died 9 Feb. 1950.

KNUDSEN, Martin; Dr phil *hc* Lund (Sweden); Professor of Physics, University of Copenhagen, 1912–41; *b* 15 Feb. 1871; *s* of Jørgen Knudsen, farmer, and Stine Knudsen; *m* 1903, Ellen Ursin; three *s* two *d. Educ:* Odense and Copenhagen. Docent in Physics,

University of Copenhagen, 1901. Rector of the University, 1927–28; Sec. Royal Danish Academy, 1917–46; Danish Delegate, International Council for the Exploration of the Sea, 1902–48, Vice-Pres., 1933–48; President Internat. Assoc. of Physical Oceanography, 1930–36; Vice-Pres. Internat. Union of Pure and Applied Physics, 1923–34; Member of various foreign societies; H. C. Ørsted Medal, 1916; Agassiz Medal, 1936. *Publications:* several publications on physical and hydrographical subjects. *Address:* Höghsmindevej 58, Gentofte, Denmark. *T:* Ge 4047.

Died 27 May 1949.

KOE, Brig.-Gen. Lancelot Charles, CBE 1919; retired; *e s* of Stephen Lancelot Koe; *m* 1st, 1902, Florence Cecilia (*d* 1936), *y d* of late Maj.-Gen. D. E. Hoste, CB, RA, 23 Sussex Square, Brighton; 2nd, 1937, Violet, *widow* of Capt. A. R. Raby, RN. *Educ:* Charterhouse; France; Germany; RMC, Sandhurst. Joined the Royal Irish Regiment, 1882; served Soudan Expedition, 1884–85; the Nile and desert march; Hazara Expedition, 1888; Benin Expedition, 1897 (severely wounded); served on Boundary Commission, German Cameroons; Royal Garrison Regt, 1901–05; Staff Officer to Ceylon Volunteer Forces, 1906–09; commanded International Legation Guards, Peking, 1910–14; served European War, 1914–16; Commanded District of Southern Command till 1919; retired, 1919. *Recreations:* outdoor games and sports. *Address:* Uplands, East Grinstead, Sussex. *Club:* United Service.

Died 17 Feb. 1941.

KOOP, Albert James, BA (Camb.); retired Civil Servant; *b* Brighton, 4 Oct. 1877; *e s* of A. H. M. Koop, Brighton; *m* 1906, Inez Gertrude, *d* of late Sir Caspar Purdon Clarke, CIE; two *s. Educ:* Brighton College; Pembroke College, Cambridge. Assistant, Victoria and Albert Museum, 1900; Keeper, Dept of Metalwork, 1935–37; Hon. Member, Japan Society, Editor of Transactions since 1920; Fourth Class, Order of Rising Sun, Japan. *Publications:* Japanese Names and how to Read them (Meiji Benran), 1923; Early Chinese Bronzes, 1924; numerous contributions to art periodicals and official publications. *Recreations:* Philately, Japanese studies. *Address:* 6 Napier Avenue, SW6. *T:* Renown 3522.

Died 8 Feb. 1945.

KORTRIGHT, Henry Somers, RBA; artist; *b* Southampton, 6 July 1870; *s* of Captain John S. Kortright, Indian Navy, and Matilda Rebecca Kortright; *m* 1907, Primrose Margaret, *d* of H. J. Harvey, Paymaster-in-Chief, RN; two *s* one *d.* Pupil of Prof. Hubert v. Herkomer, RA, CVO. Has exhibited for many years at Royal Academy, Paris Salon, and other exhibitions. *Pictures:* The Peaceful Hour; Nearing Fourscore Years; An Old Garden; The Dutch Garden (purchased by King Edward VII, 1906); The Moat Wall (hon. mention, Salon, 1907); The Cottage Border; Bluebells and Campion; The Beeches of Knole; The Court Room, Bank of England; Father Thames, etc. *Address:* Grenville Lodge, De La Warr Road, Bexhill-on-Sea; 23 Cedars Road, Clapham Common, SW. *T:* Macaulay 1686.

Died 25 April 1942.

KOTAH, Lt-Col HH Maharajahdiraj Maharaj Mahimahendra Maharaorajaji Shri Sir Umed Singh Bahadur, GCSI 1911; GCIE 1907; GBE 1918; KCSI 1900; Hon. Colonel in Army; *b* 1873; *S* 1889; *m* 1908; one *s. Educ:* Mayo College, Ajmer. State has area of 5684 square miles, and population of 685,804, the Maharao receiving salute of 19 guns. His administration is progressive; the most important events of his rule have been the restoration, on the deposition of the late Ruler of the Jhalawar State, of 15 out of 17 districts which had been ceded in 1838 to form that principality, and remittance of all arrears of land revenue, amounting to 50 lakhs of rupees on the occasion of the Coronation of King Edward. *Address:* Kotah, Rajputana.

Died March 1941.

KOTEWALL, Sir Robert Hormus, Kt 1938; CMG 1927; LLD (Hon.) Hongkong, 1926; JP 1918; unofficial member Legislative Council representing the Chinese; *b* Hongkong, 1880; *e s* of late H. R. Kotewall, merchant; *m* Edith, *e d* of late Henry Lowcock, Shanghai; one *s* eight *d. Educ:* Queen's College and Diocesan Boys School, Hongkong. Entered Hongkong Civil Service, 1896; acting 1st Clerk Magistracy and official JP, 1913; 1st Clerk Colonial Secretary's Office, 1916; resigned Civil Service, 1916; acting member, Hongkong Executive Council, 1929; Principal, R. H. Kotewall & Co.; Director, Chinese Estates, Ltd and other companies; Hon. Director, Ching Siong Land Investment Co., Ltd; President, Hongkong Boy Scouts Association; member Court and Council, Hongkong Univ.; Chairman Board of Control, Morrison Hall, Hongkong Univ.; member, Executive Committee, Chinese General Chamber of Commerce; member, Standing Law Committee; Vice-Chairman, Public Dispensaries Committee; Vice-Chairman, Society for Protection of Women and Children; V-P Society for Protection of Children; Patron, Ching Woo Athletic Association; Patron, South China Athletic Association. *Publications:* Government in its Relation to National Welfare; Forestry; two Chinese plays, Uncle Kin and The Maid of the Hill. *Recreations:* reading, photography, riding, and yachting. *Address:* Hatton House, Kotewall Road, Hongkong. *TA:* Kotewall, Hongkong. *Clubs:* Chinese; Chinese Merchants (Hongkong).

Died 23 May 1949.

KREYER, Brig. Hubert Stanley, DSO 1914; OBE 1923; *b* 4 July 1890; *s* of late Lt-Col F. A. C. Kreyer, Indian Army; *m* 1918, Alice Leonie, 2nd *d* of late Capt. J. H. H. Berkeley, 83rd Regt. *Educ:* Victoria College, Jersey; Sandhurst. Entered army, 1911; served European War, 1914–18 (despatches, DSO, Croix de Guerre); Brevet Major, 1919; Major, 1929; Lt-Col, 1935; Col, 1939; commanded 1st Battalion The Green Howards, 1935–39; Commander 150th (York and Durham) Infantry Brigade, TA, 1939; retired pay, 1941. *Address:* c/o Glyn Mills & Co., Holt's Branch, Whitehall, SW1. *Club:* Naval and Military.

Died 14 Aug. 1949.

KROGH, August, PhD, Hon. LLD Edinburgh; Hon. MD Budapest, Lund; Hon. ScD Harvard, Rutgers, Oxford; Hon. PhD Oslo; Emeritus Professor of Zoophysiology, Copenhagen University, since 1945; *b* 15 Nov. 1874; *e s* of shipwright V. Krogh, in Grenaa; *m* 1905, Marie (born Jörgensen), MD (*d* 1943); one *s* three *d. Educ:* Aarhus Cathedral School; Copenhagen University. Magister sc. (Zoology), 1899; Assistant at University Physiological Laboratory, under Chr. Bohr. 1899–1908; Lecturer in Zoophysiology, 1908; Prof. 1916; member of Danish Royal Soc. of Science, 1916–49; Nobel Prize in Physiology and Medicine, 1920; Foreign Member Royal Society, Nat. Acad. Washington, K. Svenska Vetensk. Akad., Stockholm, Norske Videnskapselsk, Roy. Soc. Edinburgh, Indian Acad. of Sci., etc.; Associate Member Société de Biologie, Paris, etc. Baly Medal, Croonian Lecture Roy. Soc. 1945. *Publications:* Records of Research (chiefly physiological) in Skand. Arch. Physiol. Journal of Physiology and other journals; The Respiratory Exchange of Animals and Man, 1916 (Monographs on Biochemistry); The Anatomy and Physiology of Capillaries, Silliman Lectures, Yale University, 1922; second edition revised and enlarged, 1928; Osmotic Regulation in Aquatic Animals, 1939; The Comparative Physiol. of Resp. Mech., 1940. *Address:* Laboratoriet, Sobredden 24, Gentofte, Denmark. *T:* GE 4690.

Died 13 Sept. 1949.

KUTCH, HH Maharaja Dhiraj Mirzan Maharao Shri Khengarji Sawai Bahadur Maharao of, GCSI 1917; GCIE 1887; *b* 23 Aug. 1866; *S* 1875; *m* 1884; two *s* two *d.* Represented India, Imperial Conference, 1921; received freedom of City of London, 1921. The State has an area of 8249 square miles, and a population of nearly 514,307. Undertook to give £3000 (sterling) monthly for support of Indian Regiment during European War, 1915; represented India, League of Nations, 1921; received Freedom of the City of Bath, 1921. *Address:* The Palace, Bhuj, Kutch, Western India.

Died 15 Jan. 1942.

KUTCH, Maharao of; Lt-Col HH Maharaja Dhiraj Mirza Maharao Shri Sir Vijayaraji, Savai Bahadur, GBE 1945; Ruler of Kutch; *b* 1885; *e s* of His Late Highness Maharaja Dhiraj Mirza Maharao Shri Khengarji, Savai Bahadur, GCSI, GCIE; *m* 1907, Maharaj Kunvari Shri Padmakunvar Ba Sahiba of Sirohi; three *s* three *d. Educ:* privately under European and Indian tutors. Has widely travelled in Europe and parts of India; is putting into practice his schemes for the betterment of his people in all directions by developing the State's possibilities, notably in irrigation. Has instituted an independent High Court, a legislature and Village Councils. In spite of several years of deficient rainfall has contributed munificently to the War Effort and worked in full co-operation with the Govt of India for the safety and tranquility of India; was a member of the National Defence Council of India, 1944–45. *Recreations:* in his earlier days was a great tennis player—his favourite sports being cricket, football, tennis, shikar and sculling; takes keen interest in botany and bird-life. *Address:* The Palace, Bhuj (Kutch) India. *TA:* Bhuj (Kutch) (India).

Died 26 Feb. 1948.

KYFFIN-TAYLOR, Brig.-Gen. Gerald; *see* Taylor.

KYLE, Lt-Col Robert, CMG 1919; DSO 1918; JP; *b* 1862. Formerly Lieut-Col Highland Light Infantry. Served European War, 1914–18 (despatches, DSO, CMG, Legion of Honour, Belgian Croix de Guerre with palm). *Address:* Southview, Milngavie, Dumbartonshire.

Died 17 Feb. 1942.

KYNOCH, Sir John Wheen, Kt 1939; Director of G. and G. Kynoch, Ltd, Tweed Manufacturers, Keith; *b* 26 Sept. 1878; *s* of late George Kynoch, Keith, and late Edith Wheen, Wanstead, Essex; *m* 1900, Mary Percival Marriott (*d* 1937); two *s* one *d. Educ:* Uppingham; Leeds University. DL, JP, and Hon. Sheriff Substitute for Banffshire; Provost of Keith, 1919–25, and afterwards served for several years on Banffshire County Council; Chairman of Banffshire Unionist Association. *Address:* Isla Bank, Keith. *Clubs:* Constitutional; Scottish Conservative, Edinburgh.

Died 8 Feb. 1946.

KYTE, George William; KC 1907; Member of International Joint Commission; *b* St Peter's, Nova Scotia, 10 July 1864; *m* 1st, 1893, Tena (*d* 1932), *d* of Valentine and Lydia Chisholm, Heatherton, Nova Scotia; two *s* nine *d*; 2nd, 1933, Mrs Emma M. Bissett, St Peter's, NS. *Educ:* St Francis Xavier University, Antigonish. Studied law and admitted to Bar of Nova Scotia 1891; Clerk Assistant Legislative Assembly of Nova Scotia, 1892, 1894, 1897, and 1901; Chief Clerk, 1903; MP Richmond County, Nova Scotia, 1908 and 1911; MP for Electoral District, Richmond-South, Cape Breton, 1917–25; Liberal Whip, 1910; Chief Government Whip in the House of Commons, 1922; Canadian Commissioner to the British Empire Exhibition at Wembley, London, 1924; Member of the International Joint Commission to adjust matters in controversy between Canada and the United States, July 25, 1928; Roman Catholic; Liberal. *Address:* St Peter's, Nova Scotia.

Died 16 Nov. 1940.

L

LA BROOY, Justin Theodore, CB 1916; *b* Kalutara, Ceylon, Oct. 1857; 2nd *s* of Francis Frederick Theodore La Brooy and Amelia Sophia Meynert; *m* 1885, Amelia Fanny, 2nd *d* of Robert Johnston, Sidcup, Kent; one *s* three *d. Educ:* Corpus Christi College, Cambridge. Entered Higher Division of Civil Service after open competition, 1881; Civil Assistant to Chief Superintendent, Royal Ordnance Factories, Woolwich, 1900; Liquidator of Ordnance Factory Contracts, 1918; retired, 1920; has received letters of thanks for services on committees from three Secretaries of State for War; Chairman of Governing Body of the Woolwich Polytechnic, 1914–18. *Recreations:* educational work and reading. *Address:* Fernleigh, Manor Road, Whitstable, Kent. *T:* Whitstable 2365.

Died 10 Dec. 1944.

LABY, Thomas Howell, FRS 1931; Professor of Natural Philosophy University of Melbourne, 1915–February 1944; *b* Victoria, 1880; *m* 1914, B. Littlejohn; two *d. Educ:* University of Sydney; Emmanuel College, Cambridge, (Research Exhibitioner and Prizeman); MA, ScD, MA (Melbourne). Demonstrator of Chemistry, University of Sydney, 1900–05; Exhibition of 1851 Scholar; Joule Student of the Royal Society; Professor of Physics, Wellington, New Zealand, 1909–15; designed with others by end June 1915, anti-gas box respirator; adviser to Australian Government on X-rays and radium, 1928–37; President for 1911 and 1928, Section A, Australasian Association Advancement of Science; Assessor for Federal Arbitration Court, 1918; Hon. Member, Ralegh Club, Oxford; President, Institute of Physics, Australia, 1939–41; Member, Radio Research Board, 1928–40; Chairman, Optical Munitions Panel of Australia. *Publications:* (with late Dr Kaye) Physical and Chemical Constants, 9th ed.; Editor (with A. B. Edge), Principles and Practice Geophysical Surveying; papers on heat, X-rays, reflection atmospherics by ionosphere, precision measurements of fundamental constants of physics, etc. *Address:* 551 Toorak Rd, Melbourne, SE2, Australia.

Died 21 June 1946.

LACEY, Sir Francis Eden, Kt 1926; BA; Barrister-at-law; *b* Wareham, Dorsetshire, 19 Oct. 1859; *y s* of late W. C. Lacey; *m* 1st, Lady Helen Carnegie (*d* 1908), *d* of 9th Earl of Northesk; 2nd, Mary Marshall, *widow* of J. Campbell Walker, and *d* of Robert Ramsay, Melbourne, Australia. *Educ:* Sherborne School; Caius College, Cambridge. Played for Hants and Cambridge; Secretary to the Marylebone Cricket Club, 1898–1926. *Address:* Sutton Veny House, nr Warminster, Wilts. *T:* Sutton Veny 7.

Died 26 May 1946.

LACHANCE, Arthur, advocate; KC 1903; BL, LLD; Ex-Chief Justice of the Court of Sessions of the Peace, city and district of Quebec; Crown Attorney, 1905–20; Professor of Criminal Law at Laval University, Quebec, 1920–29; Member House of Commons for Quebec Centre, 1905–17; *b* 22 June 1868; *m* 1903; no *c. Educ:* Seminary and Laval University, Quebec. Called to Bar, province of Quebec, 1894; has practised since in Quebec; in his youth was engaged in journalism; in politics since 1894; a Roman Catholic; a Liberal. *Recreations:* reading and music. *Address:* Appt 3, 6 Moncton Avenue, Quebec. *T:* 5784.

Died 1 March 1945.

LACK, Harry Lambert, MD, FRCS; retired; Consulting Aural Surgeon, London Hospital; Consulting Surgeon, Hospital for Diseases of Throat, Golden Square; *b* 1867; *m* 1909, Kathleen Frances, *e d* of Col McNeill Rind, late Sussex Regt; three *s* one *d. Educ:* King's College London. *Publications:* The Pathology, Diagnosis, and Treatment of Inflammatory Affections of the Nose and its Accessory Sinuses and Air-cells (Jacksonian Prize Essay RCS, 1899); The Diseases of the Nose, 1906, and numerous papers in scientific journals. *Address:* 71 Marlborough Place, NW8. *T:* Maida Vale 2219.

Died 14 Feb. 1943.

LACKIE, William Walker, CBE 1919; *b* July 1869; *s* of David Lackie, Montrose; *m* 1900, Anne Robson, of Tarset House, Northumberland; two *s* one *d. Educ:* Montrose Academy; Grammar School, Aberdeen; University College, Dundee; Glasgow University. Served with Mavor and Coulson, Electrical Engineers, Glasgow, 1888–92; Mains Superintendent, Glasgow Corporation, 1892–96; Chief Assistant to Electrical Engineer, Glasgow Corporation, 1897–1902; Chief Engineer and Manager to Electricity Department, Glasgow Corporation, 1902–20; one of the Technical Commissioners under Electricity (Supply) Act, 1919, 1920–34; retired, 1934. *Publications:* various contributions to proceedings of Institution of Electrical Engineers; Institution of Engineers and Shipbuilders in Scotland; Incorp. Municipal Electrical Association; Glasgow University, Engineering Society, etc. *Recreations:* golf and photography. *Address:* Kielder, Burwood, Walton-on-Thames Surrey. *T:* Walton-on-Thames 1580.

Died 10 Feb. 1945.

LACON, Sir George Haworth Ussher, 6th Bt *cr* 1818; DSO 1918; Royal Warwickshire Regiment; retired with rank of Lt-Col; *b* 15 March 1881; *s* of Thomas B. U. Lacon and Florence, *d* of R. G. Banks of Toronto; *S* brother, 1911; *m* 1907, *c* Vere Valerie Florence Eleanore (*d* 1916), *o d* of late H. S. H. Lacon, Ormesby Hall, Norfolk; one *s* one *d. Educ:* Eton. Served S African War, 1899–1901 (Queen's medal 3 clasps); European War, 1914–18 (wounded, DSO). *Heir: s* George Vere Francis [*b* 25 Feb. 1909; *m* 1935, Hilary Blanche, *yr d* of C. J. Scott, Adyar, Walberswick; two *s*]. *Address:* Sheringham, Norfolk.

Died 21 March 1950.

LACY, Captain Ernest Edward, CB 1918; RN, retired; *b* 12 April 1865; *s* of late Vice-Adm. E. Lacy; *m* 1900, Hilda Marguerite, (*d* 1937), *d* of T. Robertson, Sydney, NSW; one *s*. Midshipman HMS Inconstant; Egyptian War, 1882 (medal, bronze star); served Mombasa, landing for capture of M'weli's stronghold, 1895 (medal); King's Harbour-Master, Queenstown, 1912–19; United States DSM, 1919. *Address:* c/o Westminster Bank, Ltd, Sidmouth.

Died 1 April 1946.

LAFERLA, Albert Victor, LLD, CBE 1942; Director of Education, Malta; *b* 18 June 1887; *s* of William Laferla; *m* 1915, Blanche Reynaud; two *d. Educ:* Flores' College, Malta; Malta University. *Publications:* Story of Man in Malta, 1935; British Malta, 1938. *Address:* 20 Scots Street, Valletta, Malta.

Died 7 Jan. 1943.

LAFONTAINE, Henri Marie; Attorney-at-Law; Professor of International Law; Lecturer at the Institute of High Studies of Belgium; former Senator (1894–1936) and Vice-President of the Senate; former Delegate of Belgium at the Assembly of the League of Nations (1920, 1921); Secretary-General of the Union of International Associations; Director of the International Bibliographical Institute, Brussels; President of the International Peace Bureau; member of the Interparliamentary Council (1927–32); *b* Brussels, 22 April 1854; *m* 1903, Mathilde Lhoest. Nobel Peace Prize, 1913. *Publications:* Les droits et les obligations des entrepreneurs des travaux publics; Traité de la Contrefaçon; Pasicrisie Internationale; Bibliographie de la Paix et de l'Arbitrage; The Great Solution (Magnissima Charta); Editor of the magazine La Vie Internationale, Annuaire de la Vie Internationale, Code des Vœux des Congrès Internationaux, Classification décimale universelle. *Address:* Square Vergote 9, Brussels.
Died 14 May 1943.

LaGUARDIA, Fiorello Henry; Director General UNRRA, April–Dec. 1946; *b* New York City, 11 Dec. 1882; *m* 1929, Marie Fisher; one *s* one *d. Educ:* public and high school, Prescott, Arizona. LLB New York Univ. 1910; LLD New York Univ. 1938; St Lawrence Univ. 1938; Yale Univ. 1940; Washington and Jefferson College, 1942. Served in American Consular Service, Budapest, Hungary, and Trieste, Austria, 1901–04; Am. Consular Agent at Fiume, Hungary, 1904–06; returned to NY City; interpreter in Immigration Service at Ellis Island, 1907–10, studying law evenings at New York Univ.; Deputy Attorney-General, State of New York, 1915–17; Rep. 14th District New York City 65th and 66th Congresses, 1917–19; during European War absented himself from House of Representatives; 1st Lt USA Air Service, 1917, promoted to rank of Capt. and later to that of Major; commanded US air forces on Italian-Austrian front. President Board of Aldermen, New York City, 1920–21; Rep. 20th District New York City, 68th-72nd Congresses, 1923–33. Mayor of City of New York, 1934–45. US Delegate Inter-parliamentary Conference, Berlin 1928, London 1930. President US Conference of Mayors, 1936–45. US Director Office of Civilian Defense, 1941–42. Chairman US Section Permanent Joint Board on Defense United States and Canada since 1940; American Delegate International Civil Aviation Conference, Chicago, Ill, 1944. Special Ambassador US to Brazil, 1946. Knight Commander Order of Crown of Italy; Order of Redeemer (Greece); Order of St Olav (Norway); Commander Legion of Honor (France); and many other decorations. *Address:* 5020 Goodridge Avenue, New York City 63; 30 Rockefeller Plaza, New York City 20. *Clubs:* Engineers', Advertising, New York.
Died 20 Sept. 1947.

LAHEJ, Sultan of, Sir Abdul Karim Fadthli Bin Ali. Hon. KCMG, 1935; Hon. KCMG, 1918. *Address:* Lahej, Aden.
Died 18 June 1947.

LAIDLAW, Rt Hon. Thomas Kennedy; PC Ireland, 1922; High Sheriff of County Dublin, 1919; *b* 8 Nov. 1864; 2nd *s* of late Robert Laidlaw of Glasgow and Balmory, Bute, and Christina, *d* of Thomas Kennedy of Glasgow; *m* 1896, Elizabeth Balfour (*d* 1928), *d* of late William Clark of Newark, New Jersey, USA, and Curling Hall, Largs, Ayrshire, and Margaret Russell, *d* of John Macalister Symington of Paisley; one *s* two *d. Educ:* Park School and Glasgow University. *Address:* Somerton, Castleknock, County Dublin. *Clubs:* Marlborough; Royal Yacht Squadron, Cowes; Kildare Street, Dublin; Western, Glasgow; Jockey, Newmarket.
Died 9 Sept. 1943.

LAILEY, His Honour Barnard; KC 1914; *e s* of late James Lailey, Hambleden, Bucks; *m* Catherine, *e d* of late John Lillywhite of Lyewood, Hants; one *s.* Called to Bar, Middle Temple, 1890; practised at Common Law and Parliamentary Bar; South Eastern Circuit; CC Judge Circuit 7 (No. Cheshire, etc.), 1916–17; Circuit 51 (Hampshire), 1917–39; retired 1939; Member CC Rule Committee; President Council CC Judges, 1932; Chairman Hampshire Quarter Sessions and County Rating and Appeals Committees, 1932–38; Commissioner of Assize S Wales and Chester Circuit, 1924; 1st prize Council of Legal Education, Common Law, and Equity, 1890; Chairman Banstead Commons Conservators, 1910–12; Examiner in Law, Surveyors' Institution, 1915; JP Hants, Surrey, Cheshire, and Lancs; actively engaged in voluntary war work (Harrogate Inquiry, etc.), 1914–18. *Publications:* Extraordinary Traffic on Highways, 1912; Jottings from a Fee Book, 1932. *Recreations:* shooting, golf. *Address:* The Cottage, Swanmore, Hants. *TA:* Swanmore. *T:* Bishops Waltham 121. *Clubs:* Constitutional; Hampshire; Royal Naval, Portsmouth; Royal Southern Yacht.
Died 9 Feb. 1944.

LAILEY, Guy Patrick Barnard; Recorder of Wenlock since 1928; *b* 1888; *s* of late His Honour Barnard Lailey, KC; *m* 1917, Joan Mary, *d* of E. H. Lailey, Watford; two *d. Educ:* Winchester; Exeter College, Oxford. Called to Bar, Middle Temple, 1912; served European War, 1914–19. *Recreations:* lawn tennis, golf. *Address:* Avoncliff, Chalk Hill, Watford. *T:* Watford 2677.
Died 7 Jan. 1946.

LAINE, Sir Abraham James, KCIE 1935; CIE 1930; BA; Indian Civil Service, retired; *b* 26 Aug. 1876; *s* of late Abraham Lainé, Rue Piette, Castel, Guernsey, CI; *m* Maud Elizabeth, *d* of P. D. Ozanne, Les Pelleys, Castel, Guernsey, CI; two *s* two *d. Educ:* Elizabeth College, Guernsey; Pembroke College, Oxford. Entered Indian Civil Service, 1900; Member of Assam Executive Council, 1930–35; acting Governor of Assam, 1935; retired 1935; Jurat of the Royal Court, Guernsey, 1938. *Address:* Thistlewood, Les Gravées, Guernsey, CI.
Died 22 Feb. 1948.

LAING, Alfred Martin; *b* Dunphail, 12 June 1875; 6th *s* of late Robert Laing, Tomnamoon, Dunphail, and Mary Cruickshank; *m* Norah Mary (*d* 1945), *yr d* of Alfred Wright, Shrewsbury; 1947, Esther Bartholdy Kapel, Helsingör, Denmark. *Educ:* Forres Academy; Robert Gordon's College, Aberdeen; MA (Aberdeen University) 1900; Grierson Law Bursar (Edin. Univ.) 1900–03; LLB (Edin. Univ.) 1903. Called to Scottish Bar, 1904; External Examiner in Law for Aberdeen University, 1913–14 and 1919–22; served in Gallipoli, attached 1st Essex, 88th Brigade, 29th Division, invalided Oct. 1918; Sheriff Court Advocate Depute, 1919–21; Sheriff-Substitute of Caithness, Orkney and Zetland, at Kirkwall, 1921–26; Sheriff-Substitute of Ayrshire at Kilmarnock, 1926–42. *Recreations:* fishing, shooting, golf, tennis. *Address:* 26 Learmonth Terrace, Edinburgh 4. *Clubs:* Royal Automobile; Western Meeting (Ayr); Scottish Arts (Edinburgh).
Died 14 Oct. 1949.

LAIRD, John, FBA, MA, Hon. DLit (Belfast), LLD (Edin.); Regius Professor of Moral Philosophy, University of Aberdeen; *b* Durris, Kincardineshire, 17 May 1887; *e s* of Rev. D. M. W. Laird; *m* 1919, Helen Ritchie, *e d* of John Forbes, Belfast. *Educ:* Aberdeen Grammar School; Edinburgh University (graduated MA 1908, with first-class honours in Philosophy; Shaw Fellow); Heidelberg; Trinity College, Cambridge University (Scholar). BA 1911; MA 1920; First Class in both parts of Moral Sciences Tripos. Assist at St Andrews, 1911; Professor of Philosophy in Dalhousie University, Halifax, NS, 1912; Professor of Logic and Metaphysics, Queen's University, Belfast, 1913–24;

Gifford Lecturer, Glasgow University, 1939–40; Mills Lecturer, University of California, 1923–24. *Publications:* Problems of the Self, 1917; A Study in Realism, 1920; The Idea of the Soul, 1924; Our Minds and their Bodies, 1925; A Study in Moral Theory, 1926; Modern Problems in Philosophy, 1928; The Idea of Value, 1929; Knowledge, Belief, and Opinion, 1930; Morals and Western Religion, 1931; Hume's Philosophy of Human Nature, 1932; Hobbes, 1934; An Enquiry into Moral Notions, 1935; Recent Philosophy, 1936; (Editor) S. Alexander's Philosophical and Literary Pieces, 1939; Theism and Cosmology, 1940; Mind & Deity, 1941; The Device of Government, 1944. *Address:* Powis Lodge, Old Aberdeen.

Died 5 Aug. 1946.

LAKE, Col Ernest Atwell Winter, CBE 1944; DL Essex; County Commandant, Essex, Army Cadet Force; *b* 5 Aug. 1886; *s* of late W. A. E. Lake, Indian Police; *m* 1924, Phyllis Marjorie Silcock; two *s. Educ:* Clifton College; RMC, Sandhurst. Indian Army, 127th Queen Mary's Own Baluch LI and 2nd Bn Baluch Regt Sector Comdr Home Guard (CBE). *Recreations:* sailing, fishing. *Address:* Titbeech House, Hatfield Peverel, Essex. *T:* Hatfield Peverel 50. *Clubs:* United Service; Royal Corinthian Yacht, Burnham-on-Crouch.

Died 7 Dec. 1945.

LAKE, Kirsopp; Professor Emeritus, Harvard University; FAAS; *b* Southampton, 7 April 1872; *s* of Dr G. A. K. Lake and Isabel Clark; *m* 1st, Helen Courthope Forman; 2nd, Silva Tipple New; two *s* one *d. Educ:* St Paul's School; Lincoln College, Oxford (Exhibitioner); 2nd class Hons Theol. 1895; BA 1895; MA 1897; Hon. DD St Andrews, 1911; Leiden, 1922; Hon. DLitt, Michigan, 1926; Hon. PhD, Heidelberg, 1936; Arnold Essay Prizeman, 1902; Medal of British Academy for Biblical Studies, 1936. Hon. Fellow of Lincoln College, Oxford, 1941; Curate of Lumley, Durham, 1895; Curate of St Mary the Virgin, Oxford, 1897–1904; Cataloguer of Greek MSS in Bodley's Library, 1903–04; Prof. of Theology at Leiden, 1904–14; Professor of Early Christian Literature, 1914–19; Winn Professor of Ecclesiastical History, 1919–32; Professor of History, Univ. of Harvard, 1932–38; organised expedition to excavate Samaria, 1929–34; organised excavation at Van, 1938–39; Lecturer in NT Union Theological Seminary, NY, 1915–19; Haskell Lecturer at Oberlin College, 1919; Ingersoll Lecturer for 1922 in Harvard Univ.; Ichabod Spencer Lecturer at Union College, Schenectady, 1923; Flexner Lecturer in Bryn Mawr College, 1932. *Publications:* The Text of the New Testament, 1900; Texts from Mt Athos, 1902; Codex 1 and its allies, 1902; The Athos leaves of Cod. H-Paul, 1904; The Athos Leaves of the Shepherd of Hermas, 1907; The Historical Evidence for the Resurrection of Jesus Christ, 1907; Professor von Soden's Treatment of the Text of the Gospels, 1909; The Early Days of Monasticism on Mt Athos, 1909; The Codex Sinaiticus, 1911; The Earlier Epistles of St Paul, their Motive and Origin, 1911; The Apostolic Fathers, 1912; The Stewardship of Faith, 1915; The Beginnings of Christianity, the Acts of the Apostles, vol. i 1920; vol. ii 1922; vol. iii 1926; vols iv and v 1932; Landmarks in Early Christian History, 1920; The Codex Sinaiticus, part ii 1922; Immortality and the Modern Mind, 1922; Religion Yesterday and To-morrow, 1925; The Cæsarean Text of Mark, 1927 (with R. P. Blake and Silva New); Six Collations of New Testament Manuscripts, 1932 (with Silva New); Paul: His Heritage and Legacy, 1934; An Introduction to the New Testament, 1937; *Dated Greek Minuscule Manuscripts* with Silva Lake, Fasc. i and ii 1935; Fasc. iii and iv 1935; Fasc. v and vi 1936; Fasc. vii and viii 1937; Fasc. viii and ix 1939; Fasc. x 1940; Indices to vols i-x, 1945; Editor with Silva Lake of *Studies and Documents,* vols i-xvi published

since 1936. *Recreations:* golf, chess, croquet. *Address:* 1825 Diamond Avenue, South Pasadena, Calif, USA. *Clubs:* Century, New York; University, Pasadena.

Died 10 Nov. 1946.

LAKE, Lt-Col Morice Challoner, CMG 1936; British Council Representative Arabia and Persian Gulf since 1940; *b* 28 May 1885; *s* of Herbert John Lake, Barrister-at-law. *Educ:* Wellington College; RMC Sandhurst. Commissioned, 1904; Indian Army, 1905–37, 24th Punjabis and 109th Infantry; served European War, 1914–19 (despatches); raised and commanded 1st Yemen Infantry in Aden, 1918–25; raised and commanded Aden Protectorate Levies, 1928; Macgregor Memorial Medallist, 1927; Political Officer Aden, 1928–34; Political Secretary Aden, 1934–40; Acting Resident and C-in-C, Aden, May–Oct. 1935 and 1936; Acting Governor, Oct. 1937–Feb. 1938, Aug.–Dec. 1938, Sept. 1939; retired 1940; apptd Hon. Col Aden Protectorate Levies. Star of Ethiopia, 1933. *Recreations:* golf, cricket. *Address:* Aden; c/o Grindlay and Co., 54 Parliament Street, SW1. *Clubs:* Naval and Military, Junior United Service.

Died 25 July 1943.

LAKE, Richard, FRCS; retired; *b* 14 Dec. 1861; *s* of Thomas Lake, Cheekes Court, Sittingbourne, Kent; *m* 1st, Mildred, *d* of Justinian Pelly; one *d*; 2nd, 1918, Ellen, *d* of George Sapsworth, of Steyning. Surgeon, National Aid Soc. (British Red Cross), Soudan Campaign, 1885 (medal and clasp and star); Servo-Bulgarian War, 1885–86 (Order of Red Cross of Bulgaria and medal, 4th class, Order of St Sava); Surgeon Laryngologist, Mount Vernon Hospital for Consumption, 1897–1904; Consulting Surgeon, Diseases Ear, Nose, and Throat, University Coll. Hospital; Royal Ear Hospital; Seamen's Hospital; Geoffrey E. Duveen Lecturer on Otology, University of London, 1924–28; Surgeon to the Royal Ear Hospital (Throat, Nose, and Ear Department, University College Hospital), 1898–1926; President, West London Medico-Chirurgical Society, 1907–08; President, Otological Section Royal Society of Medicine, 1913–14; Capt. 2nd Middlesex Vol. Artillery. *Publications:* Laryngeal Phthisis; Handbook of Diseases of the Ear (5th edition, with A. E. Peters); Neuman's Cerebellar Abscess (trans.); International Directory, Laryngologists and Otologists (2nd edition); Contributions to Art and Science of Otology; Fishing Memories; The Grayling. *Address:* The Rise, Bradford-on-Avon.

Died 1 Nov. 1949.

LAKE, Sir Richard (Stuart), KCMG 1918; *b* Preston, 10 July 1860; 3rd *s* of late Lt-Col P. G. B. Lake and Margaret Phillips of Quebec; *m* 1910, Dorothy, *y d* of late James Fletcher, LLD; four *s* one *d. Educ:* Heversham Grammar School. In British Civil Service, Admiralty and Cyprus, 1878–83; went to Canada, 1883; Member of Legislative Assembly, North-West Territories 1898–1904; MP for Qu'Appelle 1904–11; Lt-Governor of Saskatchewan, 1915–21. *Recreation:* golf. *Address:* 1280 Newport Avenue, Victoria, BC, Canada. *Club:* Union (Victoria).

Died 23 April 1950.

LAKER, Albert; *b* 14 Feb. 1875; *y s* of late Edward Laker; *m* 1898, Thirza, *y d* of late John Spencer. Several years private secretary to Edmund Yates, founder and editor of The World; subsequently manager, managing-editor and principal proprietor of that journal; last editor of the Gentleman's Magazine and first editor of The Patrician; later manager and director of The Globe; joined The Referee 1921, and managing editor until 1931; Director, Everyman, 1932–33; Chairman and Managing Director of The Municipal Journal, Municipal Year Book, etc. *Address:* 6 Dealtry Road, Putney, SW15. *T:* Putney 0369.

Died 24 March 1948.

LAKIN, Cyril Harry Alfred; journalist, Barrister-at-law, Inner Temple; *b* 29 Dec. 1893; *e s* of Harry Lakin, Highlight, near Barry; *m* 1926, Vera, *o d* of late F. B. Savill; one *d. Educ:* St John's College, Oxford, MA. Joined S Wales Borderers 1914, served in France and Salonika, 1915–17; Assistant Divisional Commissioner, Ministry of Food, 1918; Assistant Editor, Daily Telegraph, 1929–33; Literary Editor Sunday Times and Daily Telegraph, 1933–37; Asst Editor and Lit. Ed., Sunday Times, 1937–45; broadcast talks and commentaries BBC and to Empire and USA MP (Nat. U) Llandaff and Barry Division, Glamorgan, 1942–45. *Address:* 154 Chiltern Court, NW1. *T:* Welbeck 5544; Highlight Barry. *T:* 157. *Clubs:* Athenæum; Cardiff and County (Cardiff).

Died 23 June 1948.

LAKIN, Maj.-Gen. John Henry Foster, CB 1933; CSI 1921; *b* 1878; *o s* of late Lieut-Colonel E. Lakin, 32nd Foot; *m* 1914, Helen Dorothea, *d* of late Col A. W. Baird, CSI, FRS; one *s* one *d. Educ:* Haileybury; Royal Military College, Sandhurst. DA and QMG, Eastern Command, India, 1928. Commander, Delhi Independent Brigade Area 1929–33; ADC to the King 1931–33; Maj.-Gen. 1933; Colonel of 4th Battalion (PWO) 8th Punjab Regiment, 1933; Colonel of 7th Gurkha Rifles, 1937; Order of Lion and Sun, Persia; Order of Crown of Roumania; FRGS; FRHS; retired 1936. *Address:* Spynie House, nr Elgin, Scotland. *T:* Elgin 7174. *Club:* Army and Navy.

Died 3 Feb. 1943.

LAL, Kanhaiya Lal, MA; LLD; *b* 17 July 1866; *s* of Pandit Govind Ramji and Shrimati Kunnan Devi. *Educ:* The Muir Central College, Allahabad. Entered the Provincal Judicial Service, United Provinces, 1891; officiated as subordinate Judge, 1906; Assistant Sessions Judge, 1908; Rai Bahadur, 1911; District and Sessions Judge, 1911; Additional Judicial Commissioner, 1912; Judicial Commissioner, 1922; acted as Officiating Judge of the High Court at Allahabad, 1920; Judge, High Court of Judicature, Allahabad, 1924; retired, 1926; Member, Executive Council and Court, Lucknow University, 1922–24; Member, Court and Council, Benares Hindu University since 1924; Honorary Treasurer, Member Executive Council and Court, Allahabad University, since 1927; Vice-Chairman, Age of Consent Committee, 1928–29; Member Religious Endowments Committee, United Provinces, 1927–29. *Publications:* Elementary History of India; Dharma Shiksha, or Moral Culture; A Note on the Reorganisation of the Judicial Staff. *Recreations:* tennis, study. *Address:* 9 Elgin Road, Allahabad, United Provinces, India.

Died 14 Sept. 1945.

LAL, Rt Hon. Sir Shadi; *see* Shadi Lal.

LAMB, Major Algernon Joseph Rutherfurd, DSO 1914; late The Queen's Bays (2nd Dragoon Guards); District Commissioner, The Boy Scouts Association; Fellow, Institute of Horse and Pony Club; Director, The Stella Coal Co., Ltd; *b* 4 Oct. 1891; *s* of W. R. Lamb, JP, of Ryton Hall, Co. Durham; *m* 1st, 1921, Grace Galloway Frances (marr. diss. 1939), 3rd *d* of late Sir Francis Denys-Burton, 3rd Bt, and late Lady Denys-Burton of Draycott Hall, Yorks, and Pollacton, Carlow, Ireland; two *s*; 2nd, 1940, Philippa, Lady Hulse, *d* of late A. J. Taylor, Strensham Court, Worcestershire. *Educ:* Eton; Sandhurst. Entered army, 1911; served European War as Machine Gun Officer, 1914–15 (DSO); DAAG Egyptian Army Headquarters, Khartoum, 1919–21; retired pay, 1935; Administrative Officer of 50th (Northamptonshire Regt) AA Battalion RE (TA) Feb. 1939; Légion d'Honneur (Croix de Chevalier); 1914 Star; Order of the Nile, 4th Class; Sudan general service medal, 1910, 2 clasps. *Publications:* Horse Facts, 1936; The Story of the Horse, 1938. *Address:* Silverstone House, Towcester. *T:* Silverstone 235. *Club:* Cavalry.

Died 18 Dec. 1941.

LAMB, Arthur Moore; DL; JP Co. Lancaster; High Sheriff, 1924–25; *b* 12 Feb. 1873; *s* of late William James Lamb, JP, of Eskdale, Birkdale. *Educ:* Repton; Wigan Mining School (Gold Medallist). Director of the Wigan Coal and Iron Co., Ltd; President, Lancashire and Cheshire Miners' Permanent Relief Society; Member of Committee to report to the Royal Commission of Mines on means of preventing accidents from falls of ground, on the haulage, and in shafts, 1907; Pres., Lancashire and Cheshire Coal Association, 1908; English Juror on Mining Exhibition at Brussels International Exhibition, 1910; Member of Home Office Committee on Mining, 1912. *Recreation:* shooting. *Address:* Eskdale, Birkdale. *T:* Birkdale 66269. *Club:* Junior Carlton.

Died 29 June 1946.

LAMB, Col Sir Charles Anthony, 4th Bt *cr* 1795; CMG 1918; MVO 1903; late Rifle Brigade; *b* 21 March 1857; *g s* of 2nd Bt and *s* of late C. J. S. Montgomerie Lamb; S brother, 1921; *m* 1886, Leila Frances, *d* of W. Rushton Adamson of Rushton Park, Battle, Sussex. *Educ:* Cheltenham; Royal Military College, Sandhurst. Served in South African War; military attaché at Rome and Berne, 1901–06; at Rome, 1915–18; Commander of Order of St Maurice and St Lazarus, and of Order of the Crown of Italy; Croce di Guerra (Italy); Lt-Col, Brevet Col, retired pay. *Heir:* none. *Address:* Hazeley House, Hartley Wintney, Basingstoke, Hants. *Club:* Naval and Military.

Died 28 July 1948 (ext).

LAMB, Col David Ogilvy Wight, CBE 1939; OBE 1919; *b* 29 Jan. 1885; 3rd *s* of late David I. Lamb; *m* 1921, Theana, *o surv. c* of A. B. Stewart; two *s. Educ:* Trinity College, Glenalmond; RMC Sandhurst (honours). 2nd Lieut 1904; joined 10th Lancers (Hodson's Horse), 1905; psc, 1920; Commanded Hodson's Horse, 1930–34; active service: Mesopotamia, Mahsud, Afghanistan, Waziristan. *Recreations:* polo, shooting, fishing, and golf. *Address:* c/o Lloyds Bank, 6 Pall Mall, SW1. *Club:* Cavalry.

Died 3 July 1942.

LAMB, Ernest Horace, DSC, DSc, AMInstCE, MIMechE; *b* Adelaide, S Australia, 5 May 1878; *e s* of late Sir Horace Lamb, FRS; *m* 1907, Lilian, 2nd *d* of late Rev. G. H. Brierley; one *s. Educ:* Manchester Grammar School, and Owens Coll., Manchester (Victoria Univ.). BSc 1899; DSc 1933. Lt RM 1914; Capt., 1915; served with the Divisional Engineers, Royal Naval Division in Gallipoli Campaign, 29 April 1915–23 Jan. 1916, at both Anzac and Cape Helles positions; transferred to Lieut RNVR and appointed to HMS Vernon, 1916; Telford Gold Medal, InstCE, 1924; University Professor of Civil and Mechanical Engineering and Vice-Principal Queen Mary College (University of London), 1913–45; Dean of the Faculty of Engineering, London University, 1924–28; Member of Senate, London University, 1929–34; Emeritus Prof. Univ. of London, 1946. *Publications:* miscellaneous papers in scientific and engineering journals. *Address:* 1 Cranmer Road, Cambridge.

Died 12 Oct. 1946.

LAMB, Sir Harry Harling, GBE 1923; KCMG 1919 (CMG 1910); *b* 15 Sept. 1857; *s* of late Henry William Lamb, Sidmouth; *m* Sabina (*d* 1948), *d* of Commendatore Felice Maissa. *Educ:* Uppingham; W. B. Scoones'. Vice-Consul, Van (Acting), 1885; Mossoul, 1886; Scutari, 1886–94; Consul, Suakin, 1894; Erzeroum, 1899; Chief Dragoman to HBM's Embassy, Constantinople, 1903–07; Consul-General at Salonica, 1907–13; British Delegate, International Commission of Control for Albania, 1913; employed Foreign Office,

1914–18; attached British Mission in Bulgaria, 1919, and British High Commission, Constantinople, 1920; Consul-General, Smyrna, 1921–23; retired, 1923. *Address:* 2 Rosemount Flats, Sidmouth, Devon.

Died 22 Dec. 1948.

LAMB, Sir Joseph Quinton, Kt 1929; Chairman of Co. Agricultural Education Committee and of Groundslow Sanatorium; *b* 2 May 1873; *s* of late Joseph Lamb, Hanley, Staffs; *m* 1912, Alice Mary, *d* of Thomas Vaughan Salt, Derby. *Educ:* Tattenhall. Retired farmer; MP (U) Stone Division of Staffs, 1922–45; a JP and County Alderman for Staffordshire; a Member of National Farmers' Union (Chairman, 1921), of Staffordshire Education Committee, Vice-Chairman of Staffordshire, Wolverhampton, and Dudley Joint Committee for Tuberculosis, and Chairman of Staffs Joint Mental Hosp. Board; Member of Council Mental Hospital Assoc.; a Governor of the Harper Adams Agricultural College, Newport; and of Royal Veterinary College; Vice-Chairman, Staffordshire CC; Vice-Chairman County Council Assoc. (E and W), 1941; Chairman, 1945; Vice-Pres. Catchment Boards Assoc. 1943; Mayor of Newcastle-under-Lyme, 1932; Freeman of the Borough, 1934; contested Stone, 1918. *Address:* Oaklands, Eccleshall, Staffordshire. *T:* Eccleshall 251.

Died 20 Nov. 1949.

LAMB, Sir Thomas, Kt 1939. Senior Director, Begg, Dunlop and Co., Calcutta; Member Bengal Legislative Council. *Address:* Begg, Dunlop and Co., 2 Hare Street, Calcutta, India.

Died 10 Feb. 1943.

LAMBARDE, Brig.-Gen. Francis Fane, CMG 1919; DSO 1915; late RA; *b* 24 Dec. 1868; *s* of Francis Lambarde of Sevenoaks, Kent; *m* Marian Ethel, 3rd *d* of Joseph Hinks, JP, of Bournemouth; no *c.* Entered Army, 1888; Major, 1908; retired, 1910; served South Africa, 1901–02 (Queen's medal, 4 clasps); European War, 1914–19 (despatches, CMG, DSO, Chevalier, de la Légion d'Honneur, Croix de Guerre of France and Belgium); FSA. *Address:* Ledbury, Park Lane, Sevenoaks.

Died 21 Feb. 1948.

LAMBERT, Sir Arthur William, Kt 1930; MC, DL, JP; Director of Companies; *b* Newcastle, 17 July 1876; *m* 1905, Ethel May Amers. *Educ:* Royal Grammar School, Newcastle. City Councillor, 1910–44; Sheriff of Newcastle-upon-Tyne, 1924–25; Lord Mayor, 1926–27 and 1928–29; Alderman, 1930; Governor Royal Grammar Sch., Newcastle; Pres., British Legion, Newcastle Branch, 1921–46; Northern Regional Comr for Civil Defence, 1939–45; Active Service with Northumberland Fusiliers, 1916–19 (MC); Chm. NE Coast Exhibition, 1929; Pres. Northumberland Golf Union, 1932. Life Governor, Royal Victoria Infirmary; Member of Council, King's College, Durham University. Knight of St Olav, First Class, 1930. *Recreations:* music, fishing, watching cricket and golf, gardening and log-cutting. *Address:* 10 Kensington Terrace, Newcastle-upon-Tyne. *T:* 21231; Leam Cottage, West Woodburn, Northumberland. *T:* West Woodburn 216. *Club:* Northern Conservative (Newcastle-upon-Tyne).

Died 29 Oct. 1948.

LAMBERT, Sir George Bancroft, KCSI 1929; CSI 1922; ICS retired; Chief Warden, ARP Eastbourne, and Member of Eastbourne Town Council; *b* 28 Oct. 1873; *m* 1902, Ann, *d* of Rev. Rutland Spooner; one *s. Educ:* Kingswood; Magdalen College, Oxford. Joined ICS 1897; district officer, UP, 1907–17; Inspector General of Registration, UP, 1918; Financial Secretary to Govt, UP, 1919; Chief Secretary to Government United Provinces, India, 1921–27; Finance Member of Executive Council, United Provinces, 1928–30, and

1931; Acting Governor, UP, Dec. 1928–April 1929; Governor Oct. 1930–April 1931; retired 1932. *Address:* Priors Down, Edensor Road, Eastbourne.

Died 14 Nov. 1945.

LAMBERT, Rear-Adm. Robert Cathcart Kemble, DSO 1919; *b* 1874; *m* 1st, 1910, Isabel (*d* 1937), *d* of Ralph Nevile, Wellingore, Lincs; 2nd, 1945, Sophie, *widow* of Comdr G. P. Hunter-Blair, RN, and *e d* of late Prince Alexis Koudacheff. Joined RN 1887; Capt. 1914; retired, 1923; Rear-Adm. 1924; served European War, 1914–19 (DSO); JP parts of Kesteven (Lincs). *Address:* Wellhead, Nocton, Lincoln. *Club:* United Service.

Died 31 Oct. 1950.

LAMBERT, Brig.-Gen. Walter John, DSO 1917; Royal Deccan Horse, retd; *b* 1876; *o s* of late Sir John Lambert, KCIE; *m* 1921, Mabel Janetta, *widow* of Capt. Sir Montague Cholmeley, Bt, Easton Hall, Grantham, and *e d* of late Montagu Walter Sibthorp, JP, of Canwick Hall, Lincoln. *Educ:* Brighton College; Sherborne School; RMC, Sandhurst, Gazetted, 2nd East Lancs Regt 1894. Joined Indian Cavalry, 1898; Brigade Major, Cavalry Brigade, Bangalore, 1911; Inspecting Officer, Hyderabad and Mysore Imperial Service Troops, 1911; joined Indian Cavalry in France, March 1915; commanded a Service Batt., 14th King's Liverpool Regiment, Salonica, Sept. 1915; joined Salonica Force, Nov. 1915 (despatches five times, DSO and two bars); joined Egyptian Expeditionary Force, 1917; commanded a Cavalry Regiment and a Cavalry Brigade; retired, 1924. *Recreations:* cricket, polo, and big-game shooting, especially in India. *Address:* 9 Cadogan Gardens, SW3. *T:* Sloane 6136. *Clubs:* Cavalry, Hurlingham, MCC.

Died 28 July 1944.

LAMBORN, Edmund Arnold Greening, Hon. MA Oxon; Schoolmaster, Antiquary, and Man of Letters; late Headmaster, The East Oxford School; Occasional Inspector, Board of Education; late Lecturer in English, War Office Training School for Officers, and Assistant Master of Method, Oxford University Day Training College; Co-Examiner in English Poetics, University of London Diploma in Dramatic Art, 1927, 1928–29, 1935–37; *b* 19 Nov. 1877; *s* of Arnold Edwin Lamborn, Oxford, and Susanna, *d* of Richard Greening, Cowley, Oxon. *Educ:* by books, buildings, and the companionship of wild creatures. Worked 1892–1944 as pupil-teacher, assistant-master and headmaster, in public elementary schools. *Publications:* Articles in educational journals; A History of Berkshire, 1908; Stories from the History of Berkshire, 1909; A Perspective of History, 1910; Architecture in Oxford Stone, 1912; The Rudiments of Criticism, 1916; Selections from Longfellow, 1917; The Teaching of Literature (in the Modern Teacher), 1920; Expression in Speech and Writing; Shakespeare, the Man and his Stage (with G. B. Harrison); Towns and Town Planning (with T. H. Hughes), 1923; articles on Ecclesiastical Architecture and Military Architecture in Barnard's Mediæval England, 1924; Poetic Values, a Guide to the Appreciation of the Golden Treasury; Present Day Prose; Oxford: A Short Historical Guide, 1928; The English Parish Church, its Architecture and Antiquities, 1929; Reason in Arithmetic, 1930; Architecture, in Handbook to the University of Oxford, 1932; History of Headington Quarry and Shotover, 1933; Introduction to Wells's Charm of Oxford, 1934; The Shrine of St Edburg, 1935; The Churches of Bix (in the first No. of Oxoniensia, 1936); The Arms of Oxford, 1938; Painted Glass in Oxford, 1939; The Chaucer Tombs; Armorial Glass in the Oxford Diocese, 1940; The Armorial Fonts of the Oxford Diocese, 1941; Historical Notes on Wytham and Seacourt, 1943; The Ancestry of Mr Winston Churchill, and other Genealogical Studies, 1944; A Parliament Roll of 1512; The Armorial Glass at Lacock Abbey, 1945; Sir Walter's Heraldry; The Oxford Country, 1946; The Golden Cross and its Guests: Seven Centuries of an

Oxford Inn, 1947. *Recreations:* heraldry, topography, bird song, and the education of education officials. *Address:* Littlemore, Oxford.

Died 24 Aug. 1950.

LAMBTON, Viscount; John Roderick Geoffrey Francis Edward Lambton; *b* 6 Sept. 1920; *e s* of 5th Earl of Durham.

Died 4 Feb. 1941.

LAMBTON, Brig.-Gen. Hon. Charles, DSO 1898; late Lieut-Col 5th Fusiliers; *b* 3 Nov. 1857; 4th *s* of 2nd Earl of Durham; *m* 1912, Marion, *d* of William H. Garforth; one *s* one *d. Educ:* Eton. Received commission, 1876. Joined 5th Fusiliers, 1877; served in India, 1880–83; ADC to Viceroy of Ireland, 1886–89; Straits Settlements, 1895–96; Egypt, 1898; Soudan Expedition (DSO and medals); South Africa, 1899–1902 (despatches, Queen's medal 4 clasps, King's medal 4 clasps, Brevet Col); commanded 2nd Battalion 5th Fusiliers, 1900–04; Brig.-Gen. (temp.), 1914–15, Commanding a Brigade; Temp. Lt-Col and Commandant Durham Vol. Regt, 1917–20; Member of The Jockey Club. *Recreations:* various. *Address:* Mortimer Hill, Mortimer, Berks. *Club:* Turf.

Died 5 Dec. 1949.

LAMBTON, Hon. George; *b* 23 Nov. 1860; 5th *s* of 2nd Earl of Durham; *m* 1908, Cecily, *d* of late Sir J. Horner, KCVO; one *s* one *d. Educ:* Eton; Trinity College, Cambridge. Formerly Lieut Derbys Militia. *Publication:* Men and Horses I have Known, 1924. *Address:* Mesnil Warren, Newmarket. *Club:* Turf.

Died 23 July 1945.

LAMMIE, Col (temp. Maj.-Gen.) George, CBE 1941; MC; ADC to the King since 1945; *b* 10 Dec. 1891; *s* of John Lammie, Glasgow; *m* 1918, Annie Ferguson, *er d* of Sommerville Grieve Edinburgh; no *c. Educ:* George Watson's College, Edinburgh. Gazetted from London Scottish to The Royal Scots, 1914; Bt Major, 1929; Major The Seaforth Highlanders, 1930; Bt Lt-Col, 1932; Lt-Col and Col, 1938; temp. Maj.-Gen., 1942; served European War, France and Flanders, 1914–18 (despatches, MC); Palestine, 1936–37 (despatches); GSO2 Southern Command, 1933–35; GSO1 War Office, 1938–39; Commander 147 Inf. Bde, 1940–41; Director of Quartering, War Office, 1941–44; Comdr 3 District CMF, 1944–45. *Address:* Conway, Rectory Road, Farnborough, Hants. *T:* 686. *Clubs:* United Service, Caledonian.

Died 17 June 1946.

LAMOND, Frederic; pianist and composer; Professor at Scottish National Academy of Music since 1939; *b* Glasgow, 28 Jan. 1868. *Educ:* Glasgow; Frankfort; also had lessons from von Bülow and Liszt. First appeared in 1885 at Berlin and at Vienna; made London début 1886; spent several years in Germany. *Compositions:* a symphony, overtures, trios, sonatas, etc. *Address:* Scottish National Academy of Music, Glasgow.

Died 21 Feb. 1948.

LAMONT, Very Rev. Prof. Daniel, MA, BD, DD; native of Bute. *Educ:* Hutcheson's School, Glasgow; Glasgow University. Minister at Kilmarnock, Edinburgh, Glasgow, and Helensburgh; Moderator of the General Assembly of the Church of Scotland, 1936; Professor of Practical Theology in New College, Edinburgh, 1927–45; Prof. of Christian Ethics and Practical Theology, University of Edinburgh, 1939–45. *Publications:* The Church and the Creeds; The Creative Work of Jesus; Christ and the World of Thought; The Anchorage of Life. *Recreation:* music. *Address:* 27 Cluny Gardens, Edinburgh.

Died 4 May 1950.

LAMONT, Lt-Col John Charles, CIE 1919; Indian Medical Service (retd); *b* 1 July 1864; *s* of Charles Gordon Lamont, Liverpool; *m* Eveline (*d* 1935), *y d* of Stephen Adam, Edinburgh; no *c. Educ:* Liverpool College; University of Edinburgh. MB and CM, with First-Class Honours, 1885. Demonstrator of Anatomy, University of Edinburgh, 1886–87; entered Indian Medical Service, 1887; saw active service Chin-Lushai Expedition, 1889–90 (medal); Manipur Expedition, 1891 (clasp); Professor of Anatomy, Lahore, and Examiner in Anatomy, Punjab University, 1894–1906 and 1915–19; Fellow of the Punjab University, 1898; Lt-Col 1907; retired, 1908; Lecturer in Anatomy, University College, Dundee (University of St Andrews, 1906–14; Examiner in Anatomy, Royal College of Physicians, Edinburgh, 1911–14; volunteered for service 1914, and re-employed by the Government of India, 1915–19; Fellow of Royal Society of Edinburgh, 1920. *Publications:* contributions to Journal of Anatomy, vols xxi, xxx, xlii, xliv. *Recreations:* fishing, golf. *Address:* 7 Merchiston Park, Edinburgh. *T:* 51608. *Clubs:* Caledonian United Service, Edinburgh.

Died 19 June 1945.

LAMONT, Sir Norman, 2nd Bt *cr* 1910; DL, JP, FSA (Scot.); *b* 1869; *o surv. s* of 1st Bt and Adelaide, 2nd *d* of Sir G. Denys, 2nd Bt; *S* father, 1913. *Educ:* Winchester; College of Agriculture, Downton (certificate 1890). Parliamentary Private Secretary (unpaid) to Prime Minister, Sir H. Campbell-Bannerman, 1906–08; to President of Board of Trade, Mr Churchill, 1909; Hon. Sec. of Scottish Liberal Association, 1904–08; MP (L) Buteshire, 1905–10; contested Buteshire (L), 1900 and 1910; Member of Departmental Committee on Agricultural Education, 1907–08; Chairman of Departmental Committee on Labour Exchanges, 1909; Member of Legislative Council of Trinidad, 1915–23; a Governor of the Imperial College of Tropical Agriculture, 1921–45. Chairman of West India Assoc. of Glasgow. Chairman of Third Mile, Tangga Bat, and Glen Rubber Cos. Owns 8000 acres. *Publications:* Problems of the Antilles, 1912; Inventory of Lamont Papers, 1914; (jointly) a Catalogue of Trinidad Moths, 1927; Problems of Trinidad, 1933; Gleanings, 1946. *Heir:* none. *Address:* Knockdow, Toward, Argyll; Palmiste, Trinidad, BWI. *Club:* Royal Automobile.

Died 3 Sept. 1949 (ext).

LAMONT, Thomas William; Chairman of Board J. P. Morgan and Co., Inc., New York; Director of various American industrial corporations; *b* Claverack, New York, 30 Sept. 1870; *s* of Thomas Lamont and Caroline Deuel Jayne; *m* 1895, Florence Haskell Corliss; two *s* one *d. Educ:* The Phillips Exeter Acad., Exeter, New Hampshire; Harvard Univ., Cambridge, Mass (AB). Representative of the US Treasury on American Commission to Negotiate Peace, Paris, 1919; Chairman of the American Group, International Consortium for Assistance of China; Chairman of International Committee of Bankers for Adjustment of Mexican Foreign Debts; LLD Union College 1921; Rochester Univ., 1929, Harvard University, 1931, Columbia University, 1932, New York University, 1934; Officier de l'Ordre National de la Légion d'Honneur; Cross of Commander of Royal Order of George the First (Greece); Commendatore del Ordine della Coronne d'Italia (Italy); Grand Officier de l'Ordre de la Couronne (Belgium); Commander of Order of Saints Mauritius and Lazarus (Italy); Grand Cross of Saint Gregory Magno (Vatican); Heraldic Order of Cristobal Colon (Dominican Republic). *Publications:* Henry P. Davison: The Record of a Useful Life, 1933; My Boyhood in a Parsonage, 1946; various papers and addresses on international and educational subjects. *Recreations:* golf, fishing, yachting. *Address:* 23 Wall Street, New York City; 107 E 70th Street, New York City; Torrey Cliff, Palisades, Rockland County, New York. *TA:* Lamont, Care Morgan, New York. *T:* Hanover 2–2323,

Butterfield 8–0064. *Clubs:* Harvard, University, Union League, Metropolitan, Century, Down Town, Links, Union. New York Yacht (New York), etc.

Died 2 Feb. 1948.

LA MOTHE, Frederick Malcolm; late First Deemster and Clerk of the Rolls for the Isle of Man; retired 1934; *b* 22 Nov. 1864; *m* Edith Rose (*d* 1933); one *d. Educ:* King William's College, IOM. *Address:* Mona Lodge, Ramsey, Isle of Man. *T:* Ramsey 2171.

Died 22 Feb. 1947.

LAMPEN, Rev. Charles Dudley; Canon of Nassau; *b* 23 Jan. 1859; *s* of Rev. S. P. Lampen, Rector of Tempsford, Beds; *m* Harriet Isobel (*d* 1940); two *s* five *d.* Formerly Rector of Cathedral, Nassau and Vicar of Eastry, Kent; Rector of Newchurch, Kent, 1920–40. *Publications:* Theological Works, Novels, and Stories; Composer of Oratorios, Christus Rex; The Coming of the Lord; The Incarnation; The Kingdom of God; The Holy Rood; St Augustine of Canterbury; Chœur Seraphique; and Church music. *Address:* Leybourne Rectory, West Malling, Kent.

Died 27 July 1943.

LAMPEN, Rev. Canon Herbert Dudley; Rector of St Margaret of Antioch, Toppesfield, since 1926; Canon of Chelmsford Cathedral, 1925; *b* 19 April 1868; *s* of Rev. Stephen Pering Lampen, MA, Rector of Tempsford, Beds; *m* Anna Elizabeth, *d* of H. G. Barkley, Maghera, Co. Derry; three *s* two *d. Educ:* Woodbridge Grammar School; Corpus Christi College, Cambridge (Spencer Scholar); 2nd Class Theo. Tripos, 1st Class Camb. TE; Ridley Hall. Curate, St Peter, Islington; St Matthew, Red Hill; Secretary, CPAS for NW District; Vicar St John's, Upper Holloway, 1901; Walthamstow, 1907–26, and Rural Dean, 1919–26; Proctor in Convocation, 1922; Chaplain to Bishop of Barking, 1919; Chaplain 7th Batt. Essex Regt 1913. *Publication:* Short stories in the Captain, Boys' Own Paper, etc. *Recreation:* travel. *Address:* Toppesfield Rectory, Yeldham, Essex. *T:* 224 Great Yeldham. *Club:* Oxford and Cambridge.

Died 14 May 1941.

LAMPEN, Lt-Gen. Lewis Charles; Royal Marines, retired 1934; *b* 23 July 1878; *s* of Major-General John Lampen ISC; *m* 1906, Cecily Mary, *d* of R. H. Hughes, MA, MB, Plymouth; one *s. Educ:* Alton School, Plymouth; Kelly College, Tavistock. Joined Royal Marines as 2nd Lieut 1897; served in HM Ships Trafalgar, Ocean, Sutlej, Hawke, Queen Elizabeth (Legion of Honour and Commander of Crown of Italy); Commanded Depôt RM Deal 1930–31; ADC to the King 1930–31; JP. *Recreations:* gardening and golf. *Address:* Chollacott Lane House, Whitchurch, Tavistock. *T:* Tavistock 275.

Died 8 Oct. 1946.

LAMPSON, Rt Hon. Godfrey (Lampson Tennyson) L.; *see* Locker-Lampson.

LANCASHIRE, George Herbert, MRCS, LRCP, MD (Brux.); Hon. Consulting Physician Manchester and Salford Hospital for Skin Diseases, 1905; Hon. Dermatologist Royal Deaf and Dumb Schools; late Lecturer on Dermatology, Manchester University; *b* 1866; *s* of Joseph Lancashire, Middleton; *m* 1904, Amy, *d* of William Ruttenau, Manchester; one *s* two *d. Educ:* Manchester Grammar School; Owen's College, Manchester. Qualified, 1890. Assistant Medical Officer to Manchester and Salford Hospital for Skin Diseases, 1895; spent a period of study in Vienna, 1900; passed MD Brux., 1901; became member of the Dermatological Society of London, 1902; engaged in private practice in Dermatology exclusively from 1895; Retired from Practice. *Publications:* Translation of Freund's Radio-Therapy from the German, 1904; numerous articles on dermatological subjects in the

medical journals. *Recreations:* music, fishing. *Address:* Lower Lynton, Alderley Edge, Cheshire. *T:* Alderley 3327.

Died 20 Nov. 1945.

LANCASTER, Percy, RI, ARE, RBA, RCA, RBC, Lic. RIBA; painter and etcher; *b* Manchester, 28 Nov. 1878; *s* of Frederick and Emily Lancaster; *m* 1906, Florence, *d* of John Waite of Shepton Mallet, Somerset; one *d. Educ:* trained as an architect, but later turned to an artistic career; studied at the Southport School of Art. Member of Manchester Academy; represented by works in the Public Collections of South Kensington, Manchester, Hull, Leicester, Liverpool, Oldham, Huddersfield, Southport, Birkenhead, Bristol, Preston, Los Angeles. *Recreations:* motoring and gardening. *Address:* 166 Liverpool Rd, Southport.

Died 26 Nov. 1950.

LANCASTER, Sir Robert Fisher, Kt 1945; Secretary and Executive Officer Co-operative Wholesale Society Ltd and Secretary Co-operative Insurance Society Ltd since 1923; *b* 5 Sept. 1885; *s* of Thomas and Mary Lancaster; *m* 1918, Dora Mary Watson; two *d. Educ:* Kendal School, Westmorland. Solicitor, 1908; served as managing clerk with Botterell Roche & Temperley, Newcastle-on-Tyne; Solicitor to Co-operative Wholesale Society Limited, 1917. *Address:* 32 Lancaster Road, Birkdale. *T:* Birkdale 6466.

Died 4 Dec. 1945.

LANCASTER-JONES, Ernest; Keeper, Science Museum, S Kensington, SW7; *b* 8 Nov. 1891; *s* of Peter Jones and Elizabeth Anne Haslam, Radcliffe, Lancs; *m* Geraldine Hilda Anne (*d* 1942), *d* of R. F. A. Farnham Burnham-on-Sea; one *s* one *d. Educ:* Bury Grammar Sch.; Christ's Coll., Cambridge. BA 1914. Commissioned East Lancashire Regiment, 1915; Royal Military Academy, 1916; Commissioned Royal Engineers, 1916; served in Greece, Macedonia, Egypt, 1917–19; Assistant Keeper, Science Museum, 1920. *Publications:* Catalogue of the Geodesy and Surveying Collections, Science Museum; various papers on Applied Geophysics. *Recreations:* walking, chess. *Address:* Windymeads, Courthouse Road, Maidenhead, Berks.

Died 9 Sept. 1945.

LANCELOT, Rev. John Bennett; Vicar, St James, Birkdale, since 1917; Hon. Canon, Liverpool; Examining Chaplain to Bishop of Liverpool; *b* Gresford, Denbighshire, 1864; *m* 1893, Agnes, *d* of Dr Heathcote; one *s* two *d. Educ:* King's School, Chester; Jesus College, Oxford (Scholar); 1st class Classical Mods 1885; 2nd class Lit.Hum. 1887. Assistant Master, Manchester Grammar School, 1887–93; Curate of Northenden, 1888–89; Curate of Christ Church, Didsbury, 1890–93; Headmaster, King's School, Rochester, 1893–1900; Principal Liverpool College, 1900–17; Rural Dean of North Meols, 1929–34. *Publications:* Essentials of Faith and Prayer: Guidance from the Mount; Have we a Case?; Francis James Chavasse; The Religion of the Collects; The Transfiguration; Parables of Judgement. *Address:* St James's Vicarage, Birkdale.

Died 3 Dec. 1944.

LANCHESTER, Frederick William, FRS, LLD; Hon. MIMechE; Hon. Fellow, Royal Aeronautical Society; Hon. M and Past President InstAE, Consulting Engineer; *b* 23 Oct. 1868; *s* of Henry Jones Lanchester; *m* 1919, Dorothea, *d* of Rev. Thomas Cooper of Field Broughton, Newton-in-Cartmel. *Educ:* private; Royal College of Science. Designed and built first British petrol automobile, 1895–96; founded Lanchester Company 1899, Manager, 1899–1904; designer and technical adviser, 1904–14; Consultant and technical adviser to Daimler and BSA Companies, 1910–30; Consulting Engineer to Beardmore (Diesel Dept), 1928–30; member of Advisory Committee for Aeronautics, 1909–20. Daniel Guggenheim Gold Medal (USA),

1931; Alfred Ewing Gold Medal, 1941; James Watt Gold Medal, 1945. *Publications:* Aerial Flight, 1907; Aircraft in Warfare, 1914; The Flying Machine from an Engineering Standpoint, 1916; Relativity, 1935; The Theory of Dimensions and its Application; for Engineers, 1936; A Concise System and Table of Logarithms, 1938; numerous scientific and engineering papers, lectures, etc. *Address:* Dyott End, Oxford Road, Moseley, Birmingham. *T:* South 1282.

Died 8 March 1946.

LANCTOT, Charles; KC; *b* Laplaine Que., 19 Oct. 1863; *s* of Edmond Lanctot and Elizabeth Roy; *m* Donalda Sariol (*d* 1926). *Educ:* Ste Marie College; private tutors; Laval University. Admitted to Bar, 1885; practised law in Montreal until appointed Special Law Officer of the Crown, 1891; Deputy Attorney-General and Law Clerk of the Province of Quebec, 1905–36; Member of the Commission for the Revision of the Code of Civil Procedure of the Province of Quebec; President of the Commission for the Consolidation of the Statutes of the Province of Quebec; President of the Civil Service Commission of the Province of Quebec. *Publications:* Theory and Practice of Criminal Law; Manual for JPs; Annotated Criminal Code of Canada. *Recreations:* fishing, shooting, riding, motoring. *Address:* 9 Haldimand Street, Quebec. *TA:* Lanctot, Quebec. *T:* 2–1079 Quebec. *Clubs:* Garrison, Quebec; University, Montreal.

Died 10 Dec. 1946.

LANDAU, Dorothea, (Mrs Da Fano); Member of the Graphic Society; formerly of the RIO (resigned 1920) and the Royal Society of British Artists (resigned 1930); *m* 1915, C. Da Fano, MD, FLS, FRMS (*d* 1927); one *s* one *d*.

Died 16 Nov. 1941.

LANDER, Cecil Howard, CBE 1928; DSc, MInstCE, MIMechE, FInstP; FInstF; Dean of Military College of Science; Emeritus Professor of Engineering, Imperial College and University of London; *b* 1881; *s* of E. H. Lander, Stockport; *m* 1906, Beatrice, *d* of late T. Whalley, Stockport; two *d*. *Educ:* private schools; University of Manchester. Engineer with Manchester Ship Canal Company, Hopkinsons and Talbot, Heenan and Froude; Consulting Engineer to Industrial firms; Lecturer in Engineering, Manchester Univ.; Engineer to Home Office Humidity Committee, 1910–11, 1912–13; Asst to Director of Fuel Research, 1920; Deputy Director, 1922; Director of Fuel Research, 1923–31; London University Professor of Engineering at Imperial College, 1931–46. Vice-Chairman British National Committee of the World Power Conference; Member of Mines Department Coal Advisory Committee and other Government Committees; Assessor to Royal Commission on the Coal Industry, 1925; Pres. Institute of Fuel, 1946–48; was Lieut RNVR in War of 1939–45 was Chairman of Committees under Ministry of Aircraft Production and Petroleum Warfare Dept. Melchett Medal of Institute of Fuel, 1945. *Publications:* Humidity and Ventilation in Cotton Factories; Low Temperature Carbonisation; Scientific and Technical Papers in Proceedings of Royal Society; Institution of Civil Engineers; Home Office Reports; BA Reports, Phil. Mag.; Reports of the Director of Fuel Research, etc. *Recreations:* music and motor cruising. *Address:* The Sundial, Dunally Park, Shepperton, Mx. *T:* Walton on Thames 1318. *Club:* Athenæum.

Died 17 March 1949.

LANDON, Maj.-Gen. Herman James Shelley, CB 1911; CMG 1919; retired; *b* 1859; *s* of late James Landon; *m* 1903, Christian, *d* of late William Sharp; one *d*. *Educ:* Harrow; Sandhurst. Joined 1st Batt. 6th Royal Regt 1879; Lt-Col Royal Warwickshire Regt, 1902; Colonel, 1907; Brig.-Gen. 3rd Inf. Brigade, 1910–14; Major-Gen. 1914; served Soudan, 1898; present at battles of Atbara and Khartoum (despatches, Queen's medal, Khedive's medal 2 clasps); South Africa, 1900; in command of 2nd Bt Royal Warwickshire Regt; present at Sand River, Vet River, Johannesburg, Diamond Hill, and Belfast, and operations in Orange Free State (despatches, Bt Lt-Col, medal and 5 clasps); commanded 1st Royal Warwickshire Regt 1902–06; Inspector of Gymnasia in India, 1906–10; served European War, 1914–18; in command of 3rd Brigade, 1st Div., 9th, 33rd, 35th and 64th Division (promoted Major-Gen.; despatches thrice; CMG). *Address:* Scottow, Norfolk.

Died 16 Oct. 1948.

LANDSTEINER, Karl, MD; Member Rockefeller Institute for Medical Research; *b* Vienna, 14 June 1868; *s* of Leopold Landsteiner and Fanny Hess; *m* 1916, Helene Wlasto; one *s*. *Educ:* University of Vienna. Pathologist, Vienna, The Hague; Nobel Prize for Medicine, 1930; DSc University of Chicago, 1927; Paul Ehrlich Medal, 1930; Dutch Red Cross Medal, 1933; Cameron Prize, 1938. Member of the Royal Swedish Academy of Sciences; Royal Danish Academy of Sciences; Hon. Fellow Royal Society of Medicine; National Academy of Sciences; R. Accademia di Scienze, Lettere ed Arti, Modena; American Association of Immunologists (President, 1929); Swedish Medical Society; Hon. member Vienna Medical Society; Hon. member Pathological Society, Philadelphia; Harvard Society; Hon. DSc, Cambridge; Hon. DSc Harvard; Hon. Member Pathological Society of Great Britain and Ireland; Hon. DM, Univ. Libre de Bruxelles; Membre associé, Société Belge de Biologie, Bruxelles; Corresponding Member Medico-Chirurgical Society of Edinburgh; Member American Philosophical Society, Philadelphia; Member Deutsche Akademie der Naturforscher, Halle; Foreign Member of Royal Society; Chevalier Legion of Honour. *Publications:* Papers on immunology and bacteriology, particularly on human blood groups; chemistry of immune reactions; aetiology of poliomyelitis; aetiology of paroxysmal haemoglobinuria; serological reactions in syphilis. *Address:* Rockefeller Institute for Medical Research, 66th Street and York Avenue, New York.

Died 26 June 1943.

LANE, Sir Arbuthnot; see Lane, Sir W. A.

LANE, Rear-Adm. Henry Gerald Elliot, CBE 1919; *b* 27 March 1875; *s* of late Henry Alexander Lane. Lieut 1897; Com. 1908; Capt. 1915; retired, 1922; served European War, 1914–19 (CBE). *Address:* c/o Lloyds Bank, 399 Oxford Street, W1.

Died 26 Jan. 1946.

LANE, Brig.-Gen. Herbert Edward Bruce, CMG 1917; *b* 29 Sept. 1862. Entered RA 1882; Capt. 1891; Major, 1900; Lt-Col 1910; Col 1913; Brig.-Gen. 1920; Adjutant Militia, 1893–98; served Burma, 1885–87 and 1887–89 (medal 2 clasps); European War, 1914–18 (CMG). *Address:* c/o Lloyds Bank Ltd, Cox's and King's Branch, 6 Pall Mall, SW1.

Died 9 Dec. 1950.

LANE, Col Samuel Willington, CBE 1919; *b* 1860; *m* 1st, Mary Elizabeth (*d* 1922), *d* of Henry William Watson, of Burnopfield, Co. Durham; 2nd, 1924, Sarah (*d* 1948), *d* of John Unwin, Eastcliffe, Southport. Served NW Frontier of India, 1897–98 (medal with clasp); S Africa, 1900–02 (despatches, Bt Lt-Col Queen's medal with three clasps, King's medal with two clasps); European War, 1914–19 (despatches, CBE). *Address:* Elmshurst, Catisfield, Hants.

Died 9 Dec. 1948.

LANE, Sir (William) Arbuthnot, 1st Bt *cr* 1913; CB 1917; MB, MS Lond. FRSC Eng.; Chevalier de la Légion d'Honneur; Consulting Surgeon to Guy's Hospital and to the Hospital for Sick Children, Great Ormond Street, and to the French Hospital; President of the New Health Society; *b* Fort George, Scotland, 4 July 1856; *e s* of Brigade Surgeon B. Lane, MS; *m* 1st 1884, Charlotte (*d* 1935), *γ d* of J. Briscoe, Tinvane, Kilkenny, Tipperary; one *s* three *d*; 2nd, 1935, Jane, *d* of late Nathan Mutch, Rochdale. *Educ:* Stanley House, Bridge of Allan; Guy's Hospital. *Publications:* New Health for Everyman, 1932; numerous papers on surgery and anatomy; books on operative treatment of fractures, cleft palate, etc. *Heir: s* William Arbuthnot [*b* 7 June 1897; *m* 1937, Fritzi, *yr d* of Col Hanns Markus; one *d*]. *Address:* 46 Westbourne Terrace, W2. *T:* Paddington 5954. *Club:* Athenæum.

Died 16 Jan. 1943.

LANE, Lt-Col William Byam, CIE, 1918; CBE 1919; IMS, retired; *b* Antigua, 8 Feb. 1866; *s* of Edgar Henry Lane; *m* 1896, Edith Kate Westlake Reindorp; two *s* one *d*. *Educ:* Christ's Hospital, London; Neuenheim College, Heidelberg; St Bart's, London. MRCS, Eng., LRCP Lond. 1888; Hazara Expedition, 1891 (medal with clasp); Waziristan, 1894–95 (clasp); Chitral Relief Force, 1895 (medal with clasp). Inspector-General of Prisons, Central Provinces, India, 1905–16; Inspector of Disciplinary Labour Corps, Mesopotamia Expeditionary Force, Oct. 1916–Feb. 1920; Inspector-General, Civil Jails, Mesopotamia, Feb. 1920–April 1921; Acting Director of Health Services, Mesopotamia, July 1919–Feb. 1921; retired from IMS 8 Feb. 1921; Master Mercers' Company, 1925–26. *Address:* 146 King Henry's Road, NW3. *T:* Primrose 0306.

Died 20 Nov. 1945.

LANESBOROUGH, 8th Earl of, *cr* 1756; **Henry Cavendish Butler;** Baron of Newtown-Butler, 1715; Viscount Lanesborough, 1728; *b* 2 June 1868; 2nd *s* of 6th Earl and Anne, *d* of Rev. John Dixon Clark, Belford Hall, Northumberland; *S* brother, 1929; *m* 1st, 1894, Isabel (*d* 1905), *d* of R. A. Daniell; two *d*; 2nd, 1917, Grace Lilian, *d* of late Sir Anthony Abdy, 3rd Bt; one *s*. *Heir: s* Lord Newtown-Butler. *Address:* Swithland Hall, Loughborough. *T:* Rothley 1. *Club:* Curzon.

Died 22 Aug. 1950.

LANG OF LAMBETH, 1st Baron *cr* 1942, of Lambeth, co. Surrey; **Most Rev. and Rt Hon. Cosmo Gordon Lang,** PC 1909; GCVO 1937; Royal Victorian Chain, 1923; Lord High Almoner to the King, since 1933; Prelate of the Order of St John of Jerusalem; DD, DCL, LLD, DLitt; a Trustee of the British Museum, 1928–42 and since 1942; Fellow of All Souls College, Oxford, 1889–93, 1897–1928, Hon. Fellow, since 1942; Hon. Fellow of Magdalen College; Hon. Fellow, Balliol College; *b* 31 Oct. 1864; *s* of late Very Rev. John Marshall Lang, DD, CVO. *Educ:* Glasgow University; Balliol College, Oxford. Scholar, 1882; 2nd class Lit. Hum. 1885; 1st class Mod. Hist. 1886. Student of the Inner Temple, London, 1883–89. Curate of Leeds, 1890–93; Fellow and Dean of Divinity, Magdalen College, Oxford, 1893–96; Vicar of St Mary's, Oxford (the University Church), 1894–96; Vicar of Portsea, 1896–1901; Bishop of Stepney, 1901–08; Canon of St Paul's, 1901–08; Archbishop of York, 1908–28; Archbishop of Canterbury, 1928–42; Hon. Chaplain to late Queen Victoria; visited USA, 1918. *Publications:* The Miracles of Jesus, as Marks of the Way of Life, 1900; The Parables of Jesus, 1906; The Opportunity of the Church of England, 1906. *Address:* The King's Cottage, Kew Green, Richmond, Surrey.

Died 5 Dec. 1945 (ext).

LANG, (Alexander) Matheson; actor-manager; *b* Montreal, Canada; *s* of Rev. Gavin Lang, Mayfield, Inverness, Scotland; *m* Nellie Hutin Britton. *Educ:* Inverness College; St Andrews University. Commenced stage career with Mr Louis Calvert's repertory company on tour; spent four years with Sir Frank Benson's Shakespearian company; visited America as leading actor with Mrs Langtry; then played Benedick to the Beatrice of Miss Ellen Terry in her revival of that play, 1904; played with Sir George Alexander and with Mr and Mrs Oscar Asche; appeared as Hamlet and Romeo, 1909, also as Pete in Pete and John Storm in The Christian, and as the Devil's Disciple; appeared as Charles Surface, New York, 1910; visited Australia and South Africa with his own company, also including brief visits to India and China; on his return in 1913, appeared as Charles Surface; then produced and appeared in a dramatisation of Kingsley's Westward Ho!; The Barrier and Mr Wu; appeared as Hotspur in revival of Henry IV, and later revived Pete; produced The Merchant of Venice and played Shylock, Under Cover; adapted The Purple Mask from the French; part adapter of Carnival, 1919; produced Othello and played the part of Othello, 1919; produced The Wandering Jew, 1920; Christopher Sly, 1922; Blood and Sand, The Bad Man, The Tyrant, The Chinese Bungalow, Such Men are Dangerous, and Jew Süss; toured in Canada, 1926–27; also has appeared in a number of films of his productions, such as Carnival, The Wandering Jew, Mr Wu, The Chinese Bungalow. *Publication:* Mr Wu Looks Back, 1940. *Recreations:* golf, yachting, tennis. *Address:* 11 Redington Road, Hampstead, NW3.

Died 11 April 1948.

LANG, Sir William Biggart, Kt 1937; Chairman of John Lang and Sons Ltd, Lathe Manufacturers, Johnstone, near Glasgow; *b* Johnstone, 19 Sept. 1868; *s* of John Lang, Johnstone; *m* 1897, Agnes Barr; three *d*. *Educ:* Paisley Grammar School. Director of John Lang and Sons Ltd in 1895; Chairman of Machine Tool Committee of Ministry of Munitions, 1915–18; President North West Engineering Association, 1921 and 1922; Member Management Board of Engineering and National Employers Federation, 1921–24; Member of Johnstone Town Council, 1908–23 and Provost of Johnstone, 1914–23; JP Renfrewshire; President of Johnstone YMCA since 1911. *Recreations:* golf, curling and billiards. *Address:* The Grange, Johnstone, near Glasgow. *TA:* Lang, Grange, Johnstone. *T:* Johnstone 142. *Clubs:* Royal Automobile; Royal Scottish Automobile, Glasgow.

Died 17 Feb. 1942.

LANG-COATH, Howell Lang, CBE 1941; JP Monmouthshire; formerly Town Clerk, Clerk of the Peace, Air Raid Precautions Controller, Clerk to Port Health Authority, etc., Swansea; *b* 28 June 1878; *s* of late Major J. C. Coath, Bridgend, Glamorgan, and Martha, *d* of late John Howell, Porthcawl, Glamorgan; *m* 1904, Bertha Halstead, *d* of late Thomas Allison, Springbank, Huddersfield. *Educ:* privately; Hereford School. Solicitor, Huddersfield Corporation; Chief Solicitor Sheffield Corporation; Past Pres. Society of City and Borough Clerks of the Peace; Member, Royal Agricultural Society of England and Royal Welsh Agricultural Society; Member of Hunters' Improvement and National Light Horse Breeding Society; Vice-Pres. of Masters of Foxhounds Assoc.; Master of the Llangibby Hounds. *Recreations:* hunting, riding, and golf. *Address:* Ty Gwilym, Llangibby, Usk, Mon. *T:* Tredunnock 253. *Clubs:* Monmouthshire County, Newport, Mon.

Died 1 Oct. 1949.

LANGDALE, Lt-Col Philip Joseph, OBE; JP; DL; TFR, late 8th Hussars; 3rd *s* of late Charles Joseph Langdale, *s* of Hon. Charles Joseph Stourton, who assumed in 1814 the surname of Langdale only, in compliance with the testamentary injunction of his cousin, Philip Langdale of Houghton, Co. York; the head of the senior branch of the family of Lord Langdale; *m* 1895, Gertrude Lysley (*d* 1939), *d* of Admiral Samuel Hoskins Derriman, CB, of Uplands, Sussex, and 52 Queen's Gate, SW, and Gertrude, *d* of Gerard Lysley, MP, of Pewsham, Wilts; Mimwood, Herts; Mirfield, Yorks; and 23 Prince's Gardens, SW; three *d*. *Educ:* Stonyhurst College; RMC, Sandhurst. Joined 8th

Hussars, 1883; commanded East Riding Yeomanry. *Address:* Houghton Hall, Sancton, Yorkshire. *T:* Market Weighton 34. *Clubs:* Boodle's; Yorkshire (York).
Died 15 April 1950.

LANGDON, Adolph Max; KC; *m* Amy, *d* of late Fred. Lewis, Barrister-at-law; two *s* one *d. Educ:* Manchester Grammar School; Pembroke College, Oxford. Late Hon. Sec. Manchester Jewish Board of Guardians; Commissioner of Assize, 1923 and 1924; Recorder, Burnley, 1909–15; Recorder of Salford, 1915–41; Head of the Inns of Court School of Law and Director of Legal Studies, 1925–39; Treasurer of the Inner Temple, 1934–35; Member of Royal Commission for Awards to Inventors, 1924–35. *Address:* 47 Victoria Road, Kensington, W8. *T:* Western 0414. *Club:* Reform.
Died 1 March 1949.

LANGDON-BROWN, Sir Walter, Kt 1935; MA, MD Cantab; Hon. DSc Oxon; FRCP; Hon. FRCPI; Hon. LLD (Dalhousie and NUI); Emeritus Professor of Physic, University of Cambridge; Fellow of Corpus Christi College; Consulting Physician, St Bartholomew's Hospital and Metropolitan Hospital; Senior Medical Officer Provident Mutual Life Assurance Assoc.; Member of Council, Pharmaceutical Society; Hon. FFR; Hon. Fellow Royal Society of Medicine; Hon. Freeman, Society of Apothecaries; Hon. Fellow Hunterian Society and Harveian Society; *b* Bedford, 13 Aug. 1870; *e s* of Rev. Dr Brown, the biographer of Bunyan; *m* 1st, Eileen Presland; 2nd, Freda, *o c* of Henry Bishop Hurry. *Educ:* Bedford School; St John's College, Cambridge (Scholar, Hutchinson Research Student and Raymond Horton-Smith prize); St Bartholomew's Hospital (Scholar). Senior Physician to Imperial Yeomanry Hospital, Pretoria, 1900; formerly President Section of Medicine, British Medical Assoc.; Croonian Lecturer, and Senior Censor Royal College of Physicians; Harveian Orator Royal College of Physicians; Linacre Lecturer; Member of General Medical Council. *Publications:* Thus We are Men; Physiological Principles in Treatment, 8th edition, 1943; Sympathetic Nervous System in Disease, 2nd edition, 1921; The Endocrines in General Medicine, 1927; and other medical works. *Address:* 12 Madingley Road, Cambridge. *T:* 56763. *Clubs:* Athenæum, Lansdowne.
Died 3 Oct. 1946.

LANGHAM, Sir Cyril (Leigh Macrae), Kt 1946; *b* 13 April 1885; *s* of Rev. Preb. J. J. Langham, Weston-super-Mare; *m* 1919, Elsie Violet, *d* of Rev. William Stone; no *c. Educ:* Merchant Taylors' School. Admitted Solicitor, 1907; in practice as solicitor, 1909–15, member of firm of Langhams, Bartlett's Buildings, Holborn Circus; Lieut RASC, 1915–19, served in France; Inland Revenue, Junior Legal Assistant, 1920; Ministry of Labour, Senior Legal Assistant, 1924; Assistant Solicitor, 1934; Solicitor, 1943–49; retired, 1949. *Address:* 9a Wimborne Road, Bournemouth. *Club:* Bournemouth (Bournemouth).
Died 11 Oct. 1950.

LANGHAM, Col Frederick George, CMG 1915; late 5th Royal Sussex Regt (TF); Solicitor; Clerk to the Justices, Hastings and Bexhill; *b* 22 July 1863; *s* of Frederick Adolphus Langham; *m* 1890, Frances Mary Ashbee (*d* 1927); three *s* one *d. Educ:* Tonbridge School; Trinity Hall, Cambridge, MA, LLB. Served European War, 1914–18 (despatches, CMG, VD). *Address:* Half Acre, Starrs Green, Battle. *Club:* East Sussex.
Died 29 Sept. 1946.

LANGHORNE, Maj.-Gen. Algernon Philip Yorke, CB 1937; DSO 1908; MC; *b* 18 July 1882; *s* of late Rev. J. Langhorne; *m* 1920, Joan, *o d* of late Col J. Hill, CB, Wollaston Hall, and Mrs Hill, 6 South Street, W1, *widow* of Capt. J. B. Jenkinson, Rifle Brigade. *Educ:* Marlborough. Cork Artillery, 1900–02; served Zakka Khel expedition, 1908, as ADC to GO commanding

forces (despatches); Mohmand expedition, 1908 (despatches, medal with clasp, DSO); European War 1914–18 (despatches); Lt-Col 1929; Col 1931; Brigadier Royal Artillery, Aldershot Command 1934–36; Maj.-Gen. 1935; Inspector of RA, War Office, 1936–39; retired pay, 1939. *Club:* Army and Navy.
Died 28 Nov. 1945.

LANGHORNE, Brig. James Archibald Dunboyne, CBE 1936; DSO 1915; late RA; *b* 1879; *s* of late Rev. John Langhorne, Vicar of Lamberhurst; *m* 1914, Constance Phyllis (*d* 1937), *e d* of late Henry Grant Madan Conybeare, JP, Gunfield, Ingatestone, Essex; one *s. Educ:* Tonbridge School; RMA, Woolwich. Entered RA 1898; Capt. 1904; Major, 1914; served European War, 1914–18 (wounded, despatches, DSO, Brevet Lt-Col); Lt-Col 1923; Col 1927; Member of Balfour Mission to USA 1919; Member Inter-Allied Control Commission, Germany, 1920–26; Col Royal Artillery, Western Command, 1927–31; Inspector-Gen. of West Indian Local Forces and Officer Comdg the Troops, Jamaica, 1932–36; retired pay, 1936. *Address:* c/o Lloyds Bank, Cox's Branch, 6 Pall Mall, SW1.
Died 11 May 1950.

LANGLEY, Frederick Oswald, MC, LLB, BA; Metropolitan Police Magistrate since 1932; Chancellor of the Diocese of Lichfield since 1928; Chancellor of Diocese of Ripon since 1932; *b* 9 May 1883; *s* of late Frederick T. Langley, Wolverhampton; *m* 1912, Muriel Janet, *d* of late Rowland Lewis, JP, of Penn; one *s* one *d. Educ:* Uppingham; Caius Coll., Cambridge. Barrister, Inner Temple, 1907; served European War, 1914–18; to France with 6th South Staffordshire Bn, March 1915; Third and Fourth AHQ, Aug. 1915; GSO3 (Intelligence) 1917 (despatches twice); Assistant Military Attaché, British Legation, Berne, 1918–20; Legion of Honour; Law Officer, Singapore, Straits Settlements, 1921–23; Recorder of Oswestry, 1926–32. *Publications:* Singapore to Shoreditch; and odds and ends of verse and prose in Punch, 1906–1922, including The Watchdogs (1914–1918). *Address:* Old Street Magistrate's Court, EC1; Alderton, Woodbridge, Suffolk. *TA:* Alderton (Suffolk). *T:* Bawdsey 228. *Club:* Brooks's.
Died 22 Jan. 1947.

LANGMAN, Sir Archibald Lawrence, 2nd Bt *cr* 1906; CMG 1902; DL, JP; late Major, North Somerset Yeomanry; Hon. Associate Order of St John of Jerusalem; *b* 2 Sept. 1872; *o s* of Sir John L. Langman, 1st Bt, and Mary (*d* 1904), *d* of James Marks; *S* father, 1928; *m* 1904, Eleanor Katherine, 2nd *d* of 1st Baron Lyell; one *s* two *d*. Served S Africa with Langman Field Hospital, 1900 (despatches, CMG, medal with 3 clasps); High Sheriff of Somerset, 1938. *Heir: s* John Lyell, [*b* 9 Sept. 1912; *m* 1936, Pamela Gaskell, *o d* of Capt. Spencer Kennard; two *d*]. *Address:* North Cadbury Court, Somerset. *T:* North Cadbury 202; Balintore, Kirriemuir, Angus. *Clubs:* Cavalry, Lansdowne, Royal Automobile.
Died 9 Dec. 1949.

LANGRISHE, Comdr Sir Hercules Robert, 5th Bt; 1775; RNVR; DL, JP; *b* 27 June 1859; *e s* of 4th Bt and Adela, *d* of Thomas de Blois Eccles, Charlemont, Staffs; *S* father, 1910; *m* 1887, Helen, *d* of Rt Hon. Fitzwilliam Hume-Dick, Humewood, Co. Wicklow; one *s. Educ:* Malvern. *Recreations:* hunting, yachting, shooting, ex-MFH. *Heir: s* Terence Hume [late Lieut Irish Guards and Royal Air Force; *b* 9 Dec. 1895; *m* 1926, Joan, *e d* of Major Ralph Grigg, late 18th Hussars; three *s*]. *Address:* Knocktopher Abbey, Co. Kilkenny. *Clubs:* Marlborough, Carlton; Royal Yacht Squadron, Cowes; Kildare Street, Dublin.
Died 23 Oct. 1943.

LANGTON, Sir George Philip, Kt 1930; OBE 1917; KC 1925; BA Oxon; **Hon. Mr Justice Langton;** Judge of the High Court of Justice since 1930; *b* 1881; *s* of F. R. Langton of Danganmore, Kilkenny, and Margaret

Tobin of Halifax, Nova Scotia; *m* 1919, *d* of D. F. Leahy, JP, DL, of Shanakiel, Cork; one *d*. *Educ:* Beaumont College, Old Windsor; New College, Oxford. Called to Bar, Inner Temple, 1905; served European War, Lieut and Capt RGA Garrison Adjutant, Queenstown Harbour, 1915; War Office, Intelligence, 1915–16; Ministry of Munitions, Director Labour Department and Commissioner Labour Disputes, 1916–18; Ministry of Labour Controller Demobilisation Department, 1918–19; English Member Comité Maritime International; Vice-Chairman of Council of Legal Education and Chairman of the Board of Studies. *Recreations:* golf and lawn tennis; member of Working GC and All England LTC (Wimbledon). *Address:* 51 Draycott Place, SW3; Royal Courts of Justice, Probate Division, WC. *T:* Kensington 8570. *Clubs:* Athenæum, Beefsteak.

Died 9 Aug. 1942.

LANKESTER, Herbert, MD Lond.; Diocesan Lay Reader for Diocese of London; *b* 20 March 1862; *e s* of Henry Lankester, MRCS, Leicester; *m* 1883, Gertrude (*d* 1932), *d* of late Colonel J. S. W. H. Farrer, Coldstream Guards; one *s* two *d*. *Educ:* Tettenhall Coll., Wolverhampton; St Thomas' Hospital. Hon. Secretary CMS Medical Mission Auxiliary, 1891; Secretary Medical Mission Fund, and Physician to church Missionary Society, 1894–1903; Home Secretary, CMS, 1903–10; Financial Secretary, 1910–23; General Secretary, 1923–26; Treasurer, Conference of British Missionary Societies, 1924–31. *Recreation:* golf. *Address:* 9 Eversfield Road, Eastbourne. *T:* and *TA:* Eastbourne 796.

Died 30 Jan. 1947.

LANMAN, Charles Rockwell, Orientalist; Professor of Sanskrit, Harvard University, 1880–1936; LLD (Yale, Aberdeen); *b* Norwich, Connecticut, 8 July 1850; *m* Mary Hinckley; one *s* four *d*. *Educ:* Yale College; University of Tübingen; University of Berlin; University of Leipzig. Called to Johns Hopkins University, Baltimore, 1876; travelled in India, 1889, and acquired about 500 MSS, Sanskrit and Prākrit, for Harvard; Percy Turnbull Lecturer on Poetry of India, Baltimore, 1898; Lecturer, Lowell Institute, Boston, 1898; Secretary and Editor, Transactions and Proceedings (5 vols), 1879–84, President, 1890, American Philological Association; Corresponding Secretary, American Oriental Society, 1884–94 (Vice-President 1897–1907, President 1907, 1919); Joint-editor of its Journal and Proceedings about 15 years; Fellow American Academy Arts and Sciences; Member American Philosophical Society, Société de Linguistique; Hon. Member Royal Asiatic Soc., Asiatic Society of Bengal, Société Asiatique, German Oriental Soc., Bihar and Orissa Research Society, India, and French School of Far East, Indo-China; Foreign Member Bohemian Soc. of Sciences, Prague; Corresponding Member Society of Sciences of Göttingen, Oriental Institute, Czechoslovakia, Institute of Bologna, Russian Academy of Sciences, British Academy, and Academy of Inscriptions and Belles-Lettres of Institute of France. *Publications:* Nouninflection in the Veda, 1880; Sanskrit Reader, 1888; Hindu Pantheism, 1890; Rājaçekhara's Karpūra-Mañjarī, a Prākrit play, 1900; Whitney's Atharva-Veda, translated (with Comment), revised and completed by Lanman, 1905; edits, with co-operation of various scholars, Harvard Oriental Series; Jātaka-Mālā, Buddhist Stories; Vijñāna-Bhikshu's Sankhya Philosophy; Brihad Devatā, Deities and Myths of Rig-Veda; Little Clay Cart, Skt play transl.; Vedic Concordance; Buddhism in Translations; Panchatantra, Hindu Tales; Bhāravi; Yoga-Bhāshya; Veda of Black Yajus School; Vedic Repetitions; Bhavabhūti; Vikrama's Adventures; Buddhist Legends; Kālidāsa's Shakoontala; Rigveda Brāhmanas; Religion of Veda; Rig-Veda translated, with Commentary; Buddha's Teachings; Buddhaghosa's

Visuddhimagga; 40 vols. *Recreations:* has rowed some 10,000 miles on Charles River, mostly in narrow shell; continued into 88th year. *Address:* 9 Farrar Street, Cambridge, Mass. *TA:* Indiaman, Boston.

Died 20 Feb. 1941.

LANSDOWNE, 7th Marquess of, *cr* 1784 (GB); **Charles Hope Fitzmaurice;** 28th Baron of Kerry and Lixnaw, 1181; Baron Nairne, 1681; Earl of Kerry, Viscount Clanmauriee, 1723; Viscount Fitz-Maurice and Baron Dunkeron, 1751; Earl of Shelburne, 1753; Baron Wycombe, 1760; Earl of Wycombe and Viscount Calen, 1784; Captain, Royal Wiltshire Yeomanry; *b* 9 Jan. 1917; *e surv. s* of the 6th Marquess and Elizabeth (who *m* 2nd, 1940, Lord Colum Crichton-Stuart), *d* of late Sir E. S. Hope, KCB; *S* father 1936. *Educ:* Eton; Balliol College, Oxford. Served War of 1939–45 (prisoner). *Heir: cousin* Capt. George John Charles Mercer Mercer-Nairne, Royal Scots Greys, *b* 1912. *Address:* Bowood, Calne, Wiltshire. *T:* Calne 43; Derreen, Kenmare, Co. Kerry.

Died 20 Aug. 1944.

LAPAGE, Charles Paget, MD (Manchester), FRCP (London); Physician for Children St Mary's Hospital, Manchester; Reader in Diseases of Children, Manchester University; *b* Nantwich, 1879; *s* of late C. C. Lapage, MD, Nantwich; *m* 1915, Hilda, *d* of Dr Alexander Macdonald, Kirkoswald; two *s* one *d*. *Educ:* Epsom College; Manchester University. Major RAMCT (ret.) (despatches). *Publications:* Indigestion in Older Children, 1944; Infant Mortality Causes and Remedies, 1944; articles in Parsons and Barling's Diseases of Children, 1933; Treatment of Asthma in Children, 1947. *Recreations:* mountaineering, etc. *Address:* 20 St John Street, Manchester 3; Barton House, Didsbury Park. *TA:* St John Street, Manchester. *T:* Blackfriars 2524 and Didsbury 3333. *Clubs:* Union, Manchester.

Died 23 Sept. 1947.

LAPOINTE, Rt Hon. Ernest, PC 1937; PC Canada, 1921; MP, Quebec East, since 1919; KC 1908; BA, LLB (Laval); LLD (Cambridge, Montreal, Laval, McGill, Toronto); Minister of Justice for Canada, 1924–30 and since 1935; also Attorney-General since 1935; *b* 6 Oct. 1876; *s* of late Sifroi Lapointe and late Adele Lavoie, both French-Canadians; *m* 1904, Emma, *d* of J. A. Pratte, Riviere-du-Loup; one *s* one *d*. *Educ:* Rimouski College and Laval University, Quebec. Called to Bar, 1898; practised law at Riviere-du-Loup, District of Kamouraska, and Quebec City; Member House of Commons for the County of Kamouraska, 1904–19; Minister of Marine and Fisheries, 1921; Canadian Delegate at League of Nations in Geneva, 1922; negotiated and signed with Hon. Mr Fielding a Treaty with France in 1922; negotiated and signed on behalf of Canada a Treaty with the United States regarding the Pacific Fisheries, being the first Treaty signed by a Canadian alone and with full powers from the King; signed four other Treaties with the United States; was Leader of the Government in the House of Commons during session of 1926; represented Canada in Australia at the inauguration of the new Capital at Canberra, May 1927; was the Canadian Plenipotentiary at the Naval Conference in Geneva, June–July 1927; Head Canadian Delegate to Imperial Conference, 1929, on Imperial and Dominion legislation; Canadian Delegate to unveiling of Vimy Memorial, France, 1936; member Canadian Delegation to Coronation of King George VI, 1937, and to Imperial Conference, London, 1937. A Barrister; Liberal; Roman Catholic. *Recreations:* reading, golf. *Address:* The Claridge, Quebec, Canada; The Roxborough, Ottawa. *Clubs:* Rideau, Country, Ottawa; Garrison, Quebec; Cercle Universitaire, Montreal; Cercle Interalliée, Paris.

Died 26 Nov. 1941.

LAPWORTH, Arthur, DSc, LLD (St Andrews and Birmingham), MSc (Manchester), BSc (Birmingham), FRS; Professor Emeritus in Manchester University; *s* of late Professor Charles Lapworth, FRS; *m. Educ:* Mason Science College (now the University of Birmingham); Central Technical College, South Kensington. Lecturer and Demonstrator in Chemistry, School of Pharmacy, Bloomsbury Square, WC; Lecturer in Chemistry, Goldsmiths' College, New Cross, SE; awarded Davy Medal of Royal Society, 1931. *Publications:* numerous original papers on chemistry. *Address:* 26 Broadway, Withington, Manchester.
Died 5 April 1941.

LARCOM, Sir Thomas Perceval, 3rd Bt *cr* 1868; DSO 1918; Major, late RHA; FRGS; *b* Ireland, 5 Oct. 1882; *e s* of 2nd Bt and Jeanie, *e d* of Alex. Perceval, Temple House, Co. Sligo; *S* father, 1892. *Educ:* Eton. Entered RA 1902; Capt. 1914; Major, 1916; served European War, 1914–18 (DSO); retired pay, 1928. Lt-Col (HG) 1946. *Recreations:* sport, travel. *Heir: b* Philip [late Lieut RNVR, *b* 13 Sept. 1887; *m* 1920, Aileen Monica Royds, *d* of Rev. A. G. Colbeck, Rector of Easton, Wickham Market; one *s* one *d*]. *Address:* Brandeston, Woodbridge, Suffolk. *T:* Earl Soham 242. *Club:* Travellers'.
Died 30 Oct. 1950.

LARCOMBE, Dudley Thomas Reynolds; late Secretary and Manager, All England Lawn Tennis Club, Wimbledon; *b* 1879; *s* of Thomas Larcombe ISO; *m* 1906, Ethel Warneford, *d* of Herbert Warneford Thomson, MD; no *c. Educ:* King's College School. Held Commission in Royal Guernsey Light Infantry, 1907–13; RAPC 1914–19; retired with rank of Major; Member of the Council of the Lawn Tennis Association since 1925; played hockey for Middlesex for several seasons. *Recreations:* lawn tennis, cricket, golf, and hockey. *Address:* Shene, Budleigh Salterton, Devon. *Club:* Junior Army and Navy.
Died 3 Dec. 1944.

LARKIN, Herbert Benjamin George, CBE 1920; Joint Assistant Manager P. & OSN Co.; Director AUSN Co. Ltd; Director Aberdeen and Commonwealth Line Ltd; *b* 1872; *s* of George Edward Larkin; *m* 1894, Annie Mary Frances (*d* 1936), *d* of P. McHugh. Chairman of Australian Commonwealth Shipping Board, 1923–28.
Died 15 Sept. 1944.

LARKING, Lt-Col Reginald Nesbitt Wingfield, CBE 1919; late Scots Guards; Hon. Colonel Kent Cadet Regt RA; *b* 5 Dec. 1868; *s* of late Colonel Cuthbert Larking, JP; *m* 1st, 1899, Violet Campbell (marr. diss.), *d* of late William Macbean Rankine, Dudhope, Forfarshire; 2nd, 1926, Helen Nusha, *d* of late John B. King, San Francisco. Entered Army, 1891; retired pay, 1907; served S Africa, 1899–1900 (Queen's medal and two clasps); European War, 1914–19 (CBE, Order of Star of Roumania with Swords, Order of Crown of Belgium, Legion of Honour, etc.). *Address:* Nincot, Ninhams Wood, Farnborough, Kent. *T:* Farnborough, Kent, 363. *Club:* Brooks's.
Died 10 May 1943.

LARMOR, Sir Joseph, Kt 1909; FRS; MA (Camb.), DSc (Lond.), Hon. ScD (Camb. Oxf., Queen's, and Dub.), LLD (Glas., Aber., Birm., St Andr.), DCL (Durh.), LLD Lond. Centenary, Hon. FRS Edin., Hon. Member Royal Irish Academy; FRAS; Fellow of St John's College, Cambridge, since 1880; *b* Magheragall, Co. Antrim, 11 July 1857; *e s* of Hugh Larmor and Anna, *d* of Joseph Wright of Stoneyford. *Educ:* Royal Belfast Academical Institution; Queen's College, Belfast; St John's College, Cambridge. Professor of Natural Philosophy, Queen's College, Galway, and in the Queen's University in Ireland, 1880–85; Lecturer in Mathematics, Cambridge University, 1885–1903;

Lucasian Professor of Mathematics, 1903–32; formerly Examiner in Mathematics and Natural Philosophy in the Univ. of Lond.; past President (Hopkins Prize, 1897), Cambridge Philosophical Society; Secretary of the Royal Society, 1901–12, Vice-President, 1912–14; MP (U) Cambridge University, 1911–22; Treasurer London Mathematical Society, 1892–1913 (De Morgan Medal, 1914), President 1914–15; Hon. Member American Academy of Arts and Sciences, Boston, Literary and Philosophical Society (Wilde Medal) Manchester, Asiatic Society of Bengal, Calcutta Mathematical Society, R. Cornwall Polytechnical Society; Foreign Member American Philosophical Society of Philadelphia, Société Hollandaise des Sciences, Washington Academy; Foreign Associate, US National Academy of Sciences, R. Accad. dei Lincei, Rome; Correspondant of the Institute of France (Prix Poncelet, 1918); Corr. Mem. Inst. di Bologna; Royal Society's Royal Medal, 1915, Copley Medal, 1921; Hon. Freeman, City of Belfast. *Publications:* Æther and Matter, 1900; memoirs on mathematics and physics, republished in two vols with extensive additions, 1927–1929; has completed the Collected Editions of the memoirs and correspondence of Sir G. G. Stokes, Lord Kelvin, James Thomson, J. Clerk Maxwell, G. F. FitzGerald, H. Cavendish. *Address:* St John's College, Cambridge; Holywood, Co. Down. *Club:* Athenæum.
Died 19 May 1942.

LARNDER, Col Eugene William, CBE 1920; late Army Veterinary Service; *b* 23 Dec. 1864; *s* of late G. R. Larnder; *m* 1889, Mary (*d* 1936), *o d* of Dr John Brake Marshall; one *s* killed in action 1917, two *d. Educ:* privately; Royal Veterinary College, London. Served in Methuen's Horse in the Bechuanaland Expedition, 1884–85; First Commission, 1888; served in India, 1889–96; South African War, 1899–1901; South Africa, 1908–10; European War, with the Salonika Force as ADVS, and in France as DDVS (despatches); proceeded to India, Nov. 1918 and served as DDVS in the Afghan War, 1919 (despatches, CBE); awarded the Royal Humane Society's Certificate on vellum for saving life at Cape Town, 1897. *Recreation:* yachting. *Address:* Croy Lodge, Paignton, S Devon. *Clubs:* Junior United Service; Royal Torbay Yacht.
Died 13 April 1941.

LARYMORE, Major Henry Douglas, CMG, 1896; late Royal Artillery; *b* 16 Sept. 1867; *e s* of A. D. Larymore, late Deputy Inspector-General of Jails, Bengal; *m* 1897, Constance, *y d* of late Rev. A. H. Belcher, BA, Rector of St Andrews, Fasque, Kincardineshire; two *s. Educ:* Westminster School. Joined Army, 1886; employed in W Africa, 1891–97; and in India, 1897–1901; served with Jebu Expedition as Staff Officer (despatches, medal with clasp, thanked by Government and Executive and Legislative Councils of Lagos), 1892; employed on various political missions to Hinterland of Gold Coast; ADC Ashanti Expedition (despatches, bronze star), 1895–96; acted as British Resident at Kumassi; Haùsa Scholar, Christ's College, Cambridge, 1903; rejoined Royal Artillery on Inspection Staff, Jan. 1915, and proceeded USA in charge Explosives Section Munitions Commission; Resident Northern Nigeria. *Recreations:* polo, shooting, fishing, golf.
Died 30 Jan. 1946.

LASHMORE, Engr Rear-Adm. Harry, CB 1915; DSO 1915; *b* 16 Nov. 1868; *s* of late Henry Lashmore, Gayhurst, Portswood Road, Southampton; *m* 1900, Beatrice, *d* of late John Evans, Cardiff. Promoted to Engr-Commander for Special Service, 1907; served European War, HMS Inflexible, 1914–15 (despatches, CB, DSO, Order of the Nile); retired list, 1925. *Address:* 31 Meadway Court, NW11.
Died 8 Nov. 1945.

LASKER, Emanuel; PhilD (Erlangen), 1900; *b* Berlinchen (Germany), 24 Dec. 1868; *m* L. Marco, novelist. *Educ:* University of Berlin; University of Göttingen; University of Heidelberg. Studied mathematics from March 1888 to March 1891, and from May 1896 to Oct. 1897. Won chess championship of England, 1892; of America, 1893; of the world, 1894— return match, 1896; first prize in the chess tournaments of London, March, 1892, April 1892; New York, 1893; St Petersburg, 1895; Nuremberg, 1896; London, 1899; Paris, 1900; St Petersburg, 1914; New York, 1924; lost championship, 1921. *Publications:* About a certain Class of Curved Lines (Nature, 17 Oct. 1895); Metrical Relations (Nature, 8 Aug. 1895); Common Sense in Chess, 1896; An Essay on the Geometrical Calculus (Proceedings of Lond. Math. Socs Nov. 1896 and May 1897); Über Reihen auf der Convergenzgrenze (Proceedings of Royal Society), 1901; Zur Theorie der Moduln und Ideale (Mathem. Annalen), 1904; Lasker's Chess Magazine, founded 1904; Struggle, 1806; Das Begreifen der Welt (Cosmos under the aspect of comprehension), 1913; Die Philosophie des Unvollendbar (the philosophy of the Unattainable), 1919; Lasker's Manual of Chess, 1927; Die Kultur in Gefahr (culture endangered), 1928; Das verständige Kartenspiel; Brettspiele der Völker, 1929; Schachfibel, 1930; Bridgefibel, 1931; Skatfibel, 1931. *Recreation:* lawn tennis.

Died 11 Jan. 1941.

LASKI, Harold J.; Professor of Political Science, University of London, since 1926; *b* Manchester, 30 June 1893; 2nd *s* of late N. Laski, Manchester; *m* Frida, *er d* of F. J. Kerry of Acton Hall, Suffolk; one *d. Educ:* Manchester Grammar School; New College, Oxford (Hon. Exhibitioner). Beit Essay Prize, 1913; 1st Class Honour School of Mod. Hist., 1914. Lecturer in History at McGill University, 1914–16; at Harvard University, 1916–20; Harvard Lecturer at Yale Univ., 1919–20; Henry Ward Beecher Lecturer at Amherst College, 1917; Storrs Lecturer in Yale University, 1933; Donnellun Lecturer at Trinity College, Dublin, 1936; connected with London School of Economics since 1920; Visiting Professor at Yale University, 1931; Vice-Chairman of the British Institute of Adult Education, 1921–30; Hon. LLD University of Athens, 1937; Member of the Fabian Society Executive, 1922; 1936; Member of the Executive Committee of the Labour Party, 1936–49, Chairman, 1945–46; Member of the Industrial Court since 1926; Member of the Lord Chancellor's Committee on Delegated Legislation, 1929; Member of the Departmental Committee on Local Government, 1931; on Legal Education, 1932; Member of Council of Institute of Public Administration; Lecturer in Political Science at Magdalene College, Cambridge, 1922–25. *Publications:* The Problem of Sovereignty, 1917; Authority in the Modern State, 1919; Political Thought from Locke to Bentham, 1920; Foundations of Sovereignty, 1921; Letters of Burke (ed.), 1922; The Defence of Liberty against Tyrants (ed.), 1924; Autobiography of J. S. Mill (ed.), 1924; A Grammar of Politics, 1925; Communism, 1927; Liberty in the Modern State, 1930; The Dangers of Obedience, 1930; An Introduction to Politics, 1931; Studies in Law and Politics, 1932; The Crisis and the Constitution. 1932; Democracy in Crisis, 1933; The State in Theory and Practice, 1935; The Rise of European Liberalism, 1936; Parliamentary Government in England, 1938; The American Presidency, 1940; Reflections on the Revolution of Our Time, 1943; Faith, Reason, Civilisation, 1944; The American Democracy, 1948; and many articles in the New Republic, Harvard Law Review, the Nation, Manchester Guardian, etc. *Recreation:* book collecting. *Address:* Devon Lodge, Addison Bridge Place, W14. *T:* Fulham 2444.

Died 24 March 1950.

LASKI, Nathan, MA Hon. Manchester Univ; JP; Chairman Manchester Jewish Hospital and Manchester and Salford Jewish Council; Chairman Jewish Board of Guardians, etc.; Member of War Pensions Committee; *b* 24 June 1863; *s* of Naphtali and Esther Laski; *m* 1889, Sarah Frankenstein; two *s* one *d. Educ:* Private School, Middlesbrough. Indian merchant for over 50 years; retired 1930 and devoted himself to Social work. *Publications:* A Week in Palestine, 1924; India as I know it, 1928. *Recreation:* reading. *Address:* Smedley House, Cheetham, Manchester. *T:* Collyhurst 1920. *Club:* Reform.

Died 21 Oct. 1941.

LATHAN, George; JP; MP (Lab) Park Division, Sheffield, 1929–31 and since 1935; *b* 5 Aug. 1875; *e s* of George and Sarah Ann Lathan, Norwich; *m* Gertrude Alice, 2nd *d* of Francis Everett, Norwich; one *d. Educ:* Council Schools; evening classes; private study. Entered service M & GN Railway as clerk at Norwich, 1889; various positions in service till 1912; actively interested from youth onwards in trade union, co-operative and political questions; Member Board of Management of Railway Clearing System Superannuation Fund Corporation, 1906–12; President Norwich Co-operative Society, 1906–12; President RCA 1908–12; Chief Assistant Secretary Railway Clerks Association, 1912–37; Member National Wages Board for Railways, 1921–34; President National Federation of Professional Workers, 1921–37, now Hon. Parliamentary Adviser; Member Council of International Confederation of Intellectual Workers (Paris), and member of Advisory Committee, International Labour Office, Geneva, 1923–37; Member National Executive Committee and Treasurer of Labour Party (Chairman, 1931–32); Member National Council of Labour; Member National Council of Labour; Member of Executive Committee of British Council, 1941. *Publications:* sundry articles on railway and political questions, etc. *Address:* Earlham, 24 Osidge Lane, N14. *T:* Enterprise 2428.

Died 14 June 1942.

LATIMER, Sir Courtenay, KCIE 1935; CSI 1931; CIE 1920; ICS; an Adviser to the Secretary of State for India since 1940; *b* 22 Sept. 1880; *s* of late Alfred Latimer, Plymouth; *m* 1910, Primrose, *d* of late Sir Robert Aikman, Kt, Puisne Judge of High Court of Judicature, Allahabad; two *s. Educ:* St Paul's School; Christ Church, Oxford. Entered ICS, 1903; transferred to Political Department, 1908; Assistant to AGG Central India, 1908; Assistant Secretary to the Govt of India Foreign and Political Dept, 1909; Census Superintendent North-West Frontier Province, 1910; Assistant Secretary to Chief Commissioner, NWFP, 1913–17; Deputy Commissioner, Dera Ismail Khan, 1918–21; Secretary to Chief Commissioner NWFP, 1921; Deputy-Secretary to the Govt of India, Foreign and Political Department, 1923–24; Political Agent Malakand, 1927; Revenue Commissioner, NWFP, 1929; Resident in Kashmir, 1931; AGG in the States of Western India, 1932; Additional Secretary Political Dept, 1937; Secretary to HE the Crown Representative, 1938–40. *Publication:* Report on Census of NW Frontier Province, 1911. *Address:* 72 Courtfield Gardens, SW5. *Clubs:* East India and Sports, Leander.

Died 14 June 1944.

LATOUR, Comte de Henry B.; *see* Baillet-Latour.

LATROBE, William Sanderson, CBE 1938; retired Civil Servant, Dominion of New Zealand; *b* 15 Oct. 1870; *s* of Samuel La Trobe; *m* 1909, Ina Mary Roberts; three *d. Educ:* Auckland University College; St John's College, Cambridge (senior scholar and Wright's Prizeman). MA, NZ University; MA Camb. Junior lecturer Engineering School, Cambridge Univ., 1898–1904; Director Wellington (NZ) Technical College, 1904–18; established first Technical High

School in New Zealand, 1905; Superintendent of Technical Education, Education Dept, New Zealand, 1918–38. *Address:* 310 Riddell Road, St Heliers, Auckland, E1, New Zealand.

Died 27 Sept. 1943.

LATTA, Sir John, 1st Bt *cr* 1920; Chairman Lawther, Latta & Co., shipowners and merchants, Baltic Exchange Chambers, 28 St Mary Axe, EC3; *b* 9 May 1867; *s* of William Latta of Darmalloch, Old Cumnock, J. P., Ayrshire; *m* 1896, Ada May, *d* of J. Y. Short of Ashbrooke Hall, Sunderland; two *d. Educ:* Ayr Academy. Chairman, Nitrate Producers Steamship Co. Ltd; included amongst those chosen for presentation to King Edward VII, Nov. 1904, in recognition of services rendered during South African war; rendered services in connection with sea transport in Great European War. *Heir:* none. *Address:* Lowndes House, Lowndes Place, SW1. *Clubs:* City of London, Constitutional, Hurlingham.

Died 5 Dec. 1946 (ext).

LATTA, Hon. Samuel John; Commissioner of Libraries, Archives and Publications, Province of Saskatchewan, since 193; *b* London, Ont, 3 April 1866; *s* of John Latta, Canadian, and Eliza Barrell, English; *m* 1887, Agnes Annie (*d* 1934), *d* of Capt. James Boyland, London, England; one *s* one *d. Educ:* London Collegiate Institute; St Mary's Collegiate Institute; Ottawa Normal School; Public School of Huron Co. Was Councillor and Secretary-Treasurer of Rural Municipality of Last Mountain Valley; Hay Township Clerk in Ontario for 5 years; taught school at Wingham, Exeter, Zurich, and London in Ontario, 1883–1906; Principal of Colbourne St School in London when he left for the West in 1905; publisher Prairie News, 1907–27; elected to represent Last Mountain in Saskatchewan Legislature, 1912; Minister of Highways, 1917–21; Education, 1921–27; Provincial Secretary and Minister Municipal Affairs, 1927–29; charge of Bureau of Publications and Government Printer, 1917–29; Director of Publicity World's Grain Exhibition and Conference, 1930–33; Hon. Provincial Commissioner Boy Scouts Association, and awarded Silver Wolf; Freemason; Liberal; United Church. *Publications:* Latta's Drawing Book, 1900; Call of the Sunset (novel), 1936. *Recreations:* hunting, fishing, golf, bowling, billiards. *Address:* 2051 Cameron St, Regina, Sask. *Clubs:* Assiniboia, Regina.

Died 22 March 1946.

LATTER, Algernon, MA; *b* Bromley, Kent, 26 Nov. 1870; *s* of Robinson Latter, solicitor. *Educ:* King's School, Canterbury; Trinity College, Oxford. Assistant Master, Felsted School, 1893–97; King's School, Canterbury, 1897–1908; Headmaster, Junior King's School, 1908–16; Headmaster, King's School, Canterbury, 1916–27. *Recreations:* Rugby football— Oxford University, Blackheath, South of England; Cricket—Band of Brothers, Oxford University Authentics, Bickley Park, St Lawrence; Golf, Rochester, and Cobham Park. *Address:* Danes Place, Cobham, Kent. *T:* Cobham, Kent 3122. *Club:* Bromley and County.

Died 23 Jan. 1944.

LATTER, Oswald Hawkins, MA (Oxon); *b* Fulham, 7 Aug. 1864; 2nd *s* of late Rev. Arthur S. Latter and Susanna Stilwell, *d* of William Hawkins; *m* Ada Elizabeth (*d* 1933), 3rd *d* of T. Garneys Wales of Downham Market, 1890; one *s* two *d. Educ:* Charterhouse School, 1878–83; Keble College, Oxford, 1883–87. 1st class Natural Science (Animal Morphology), Oxford, 1887. Berkeley Fellow of Owens College, Manchester, Jan.–July 1888. Senior Demonstrator to Linacre Professor, Oxford, July 1888–May 1890; Tutor of Keble College, Oxford, 1889–90; senior Science Master at Charterhouse School, 1890–1926; retired. *Publications:* The Natural History of some Common Animals; Practical Nature Study for Schools; Bees and Wasps;

Studies of Living Things; Elementary Zoology; Biology; Readable School Biology. *Recreations:* entomology, botany, gardening. *Address:* The Elms, Charterhouse Road, Godalming, Surrey.

Died 11 Oct. 1948.

LATYMER, 6th Baron *cr* 1431; **Hugh Burdett Money-Coutts;** *b* 13 Aug. 1876; *s* of 5th Baron and Edith Ellen (*d* 1942), *e d* of late Charles Churchill, Weybridge Park; *S* father, 1923; *m* 1900, Hester Frances, 4th *d* of late Maj.-Gen. John Cecil Russell, CVO; three *s* one *d. Publications:* Chances and Changes, 1931; Stalking in Scotland and New Zealand, 1935. *Heir: s* Hon. Thomas Burdett Money-Coutts. *Address:* Shipton Lodge, Shipton under Wychwood, Oxon. *Clubs:* Oxford and Cambridge, Beefsteak, MCC, Leander.

Died 23 Nov. 1949.

LAUDER, Sir Harry (MacLennan), Kt 1919; *b* Portobello, 4 Aug. 1870; *m* 1890, Annie (*d* 1927), *d* of late James Vallance. *Educ:* by Stumpy Bell as a half-timer in Arbroath. Career varied; first mill boy in flax-spinning mill, Arbroath, then a miner; now is what the people have made him; first on stage at Arbroath. *Publications:* Harry Lauder at Home and on Tour; Harry Lauder's Logic, 1917; has written a Scottish comedy; composes his own songs and writes his own music: A Minstrel in France, 1918; Roamin' in the Gloamin', 1928; Wee Drappies, 1931. *Recreations:* trying to hit a wee gutty ba', trying to catch salmon and trout, motoring, shooting. *Address:* Lauder Ha, Strathaven, Lanarkshire. *Club:* Kirn Golf.

Died 26 Feb. 1950.

LAUGHLIN, Irwin; Representative for the United States on the International Commission for the Advancement of Peace set up by the Treaty of 1914 between the United States and Denmark; Member of the Board of Regents of the Smithsonian Institution, 1923–35; *b* Pittsburgh, 26 April 1871; *e s* of Major George M. Laughlin and Isabel, *d* of Hon. William M'Kennan, Judge of the US Circuit Court for Pennsylvania, New Jersey, and Delaware; *m* 1912, Thérèse, *e d* of Adrian Iselin of New Rochelle and New York; one *d. Educ:* St Paul's School, Concord; Yale Univ., BA 1893. Private Secretary to American Minister to Japan, 1903; 2nd Secretary of Legation at Tokyo, 1905; Secretary of Legation and Consul-General at Bangkok, 1906; 2nd Secretary of Legation at Peking, 1907; of Embassy at St Petersburg, 1907–08; Secretary of Legation at Athens, 1908; 2nd Secretary of Embassy at Paris, 1909; Secretary and Councillor of Embassy at Berlin, 1910; Councillor of Embassy in London, 1912–19; has acted repeatedly as Chargé d'Affaires at Berlin and in London, and was Secretary of Special Embassy to Sultan of Turkey, Oct. 1910; Secretary for the Conference on the Limitation of Armament to the Hon. Henry Cabot Lodge, member of the American Delegation to that Conference; Envoy Extraordinary and Minister Plenipotentiary of the United States to the Hellenic Republic, 1924–26; US Ambassador to Spain, 1929–33. *Recreation:* riding. *Address:* Meridian House, Crescent Place, Washington, USA. *TA:* Merhouse, Washington. *Clubs:* St James's, Burlington Fine Arts; Knickerbocker, University, New York; Metropolitan, Washington; Pittsburgh, Pittsburgh.

Died 18 April 1941.

LAUGHTON, Major Joseph Vinters, CBE 1919; late 21st Lancers; *b* 1862. Served Nile Expedition, 1898 (medal); European War, 1914–19 (despatches, CBE). *Address:* 7 Bellevue Terrace, Waterford, Ireland.

Died 10 Nov. 1948.

LAURIE, Arthur Pillans, MA Cantab; DSc Edin.; FRSE; Hon. RSA; FCS; LLD Edin; *b* 6 Nov. 1861; *e s* of Prof. S. S. Laurie; *m*; one *d. Educ:* Edinburgh Academy and University; University of Cambridge. First-Class Science Tripos, Cambridge, 1884;

subsequently Fellow of King's College. Cantor Lecturer, 1891; Member of the Home Office Departmental Committee on Pottery Manufacture, 1893; Lecturer in Physics and Chemistry at St Mary's Hospital Medical School, 1895, and Gilchrist Lecturer; Examiner in Chemistry to the Royal College of Physicians, London, 1898; Examiner in Oils and Colours to the City and Guilds Institute, 1898; Assistant Commissioner to the Royal Commission on Secondary Education, 1895; Professor of Chemistry to Royal Academy of Arts, 1912; Member of Chemical Products Supply Committee, Board of Trade, 1914; Member of Panel of Scientific Experts, and Chairman of Chemical Inventions Committee, Munitions Inventions Department of Ministry of Munitions, 1915, and of Chemical Waste Products and Building Materials Committees, 1918; Member of Building Research Board Committee of Department of Scientific and Industrial Research; Principal of the Heriot-Watt College, Edinburgh, 1900–28. *Publications:* Scientific Investigations in Physico-Chemistry; The Food of Plants, 1893; Processes, Pigments, and Vehicles—a Manual for Art Students, 1895; Greek and Roman Methods of Painting, 1910; Materials used in the Painter's Craft, from the Earliest Times to the End of the 17th Century, 1911; The Pigments and Mediums of the Old Masters, 1914; The Painter's Methods and Materials, 1926; A Study of Rembrandt, and His School, 1929; The Brushwork of Rembrandt and his School, 1932; Simple Rules for Painting in Oils; Pictures and Politics, 1934; New Light on Old Masters, 1935; The Technique of the Great Painters, 1949. *Club:* Athenæum.

Died 7 Oct. 1949.

LAURVIG, Count Preben Ferdinand A.; *see* Ahlefeldt-Laurvig.

LAVAL, Pierre; *b* 1883; *m. Educ:* Docteur en droit. Socialist Deputy for the Seine, 1914; Independent Senator for the Seine, 1926; Minister of Public Works, 1925; Minister of Justice, 1926; Minister of Labour, 1930 and 1932; Prime Minister and Foreign Minister, 1931–32; Minister of Colonies, 1934; Foreign Minister, 1934–35; Prime Minister and Foreign Minister, 1935–36; Deputy Prime Minister and Minister of Information, 1940; Foreign Minister, 1940; Prime Minister, Foreign Minister, Minister of the Interior and Minister of Information and Propaganda, France, 1942.

Died 15 Oct. 1945.

LAVER, Prof. William Adolphus; Examiner for the Universities of Melbourne, Adelaide, Hobart, for the Australian Music Examination Board, and for Royal College of Music, London; Chairman Australian Music Examinations Board, 1938; *b* 20 Aug. 1866; parents both English; *m* 1894, Agnes Robertson, niece of Sir John McIntyre; three *s* one *d. Educ:* Dr Hoch's Conservatorium, Frankfurt-on-Main. Studied Germany, 1881–89, under Prof. Dr Scholz, Ivan Knorr, James Kwast, Prof. Bernhard Cossmann, Prof. Magnus Boehme, Prof. Hugo Heermann. Ormond Professor of Music and Director Conservatorium, University of Melbourne, 1915–26; Acting Ormond Professor and Director University Conservatorium, Melbourne, for 1938; Dean of Faculty of Music, University of Melbourne, 1938; Representative University Conservatorium, Melbourne, at International Educational Research Conference in 1937; connected with University of Melbourne and the University Conservatorium ever since its foundation; Hon. Member Royal college of Music, London, 1937. *Publications:* many compositions, songs, pianoforte, chamber music and orchestral, and editions of works of Bach, Beethoven, etc. *Recreations:* walking tours in the country, very fond of animals and bird life. *Address:* Eothen, Kinglake, Victoria, Australia.

Died 1 July 1940.

LAVERY, Sir John, Kt 1918; LLD; RA 1921; RSA; RHA; HROI; Corresponding Member of the Institute of France; Chevalier of the Crown of Italy and of Leopold of Belgium; President Royal Society of Portrait Painters since 1932; Member Royal Acads of Antwerp, Milan, Rome, Brussels and Stockholm, and Société Nationale des Beaux-Arts, Paris; the Sécessions of Berlin, Munich, and Vienna, and the Society of Spanish Artists, Madrid; Hon. LLD Belfast; Hon. Freeman of the City of Belfast; and of City of Dublin, 1935; Hon. LLD of Trinity College, Dublin, 1936; painter; *b* Belfast, March 1856; *m* 1st, 1890, Kathleen (*d* 1891), *o d* of James MacDermott; 2nd, 1910, Hazel (*d* 1935), *d* of Edward Jenner Martyn. *Educ:* Studied Glasgow, London, and Paris. Pictures in many public galleries in Europe and America. *Publication:* Autobiography: The Life of a Painter, 1940. *Address:* 5 Cromwell Place, SW7. *T:* Kensington 1020. *Club:* Chelsea Arts.

Died 10 Jan. 1941.

LAW, Sir Algernon, KCMG 1916; CB 1908; *b* 7 Aug. 1856; *γ s* of Hon. William Law; *m* 1st, Constance Mary (*d* 1909), *d* of late Rev. Charles Bagot, Rector of Castle Rising; one *s*; 2nd, 1912, Hon. Catherine Hozier (*d* 1930), *d* of 1st Lord Newlands. Assistant Under Secretary of State for Foreign Affairs, 1914–16; Controller of Commercial and Consular Affairs, Foreign Office, 1912; Acting Counsellor in the Diplomatic Service; formerly British Delegate to International Sugar Commission at Brussels, and Member of the Royal Commissions on Imperial Copyright, and on the International Exhibitions at Brussels, Turin, and Rome, and of the Commercial Intelligence Committee. *Publication:* (editor) India under Lord Ellenborough, 1926. *Address:* The Dene, Oval Way, Gerrard's Cross.

Died 27 Oct. 1943.

LAW, Herbert Henry, CB 1917; MICE; *b* 1862; *e s* of Henry Law, MICE; *m* 1st, 1889, Annie Christine (*d* 1926), 2nd *d* of late Rev. Canon Cross, DD; 2nd, 1931, Dorothy Grace, *d* of late W. H. W. Poole, MA. Assistant Engineer, Delagoa Bay Railway, 1886; State Railways, Straits Settlements, 1889; Chief Engineering Inspector, Local Government Board, Whitehall, 1913–21. *Address:* Hernewood, Chalfont St Giles, Bucks.

Died 15 Jan. 1943.

LAW, Hugh Alexander; Knight of Grace of the Sovereign and Military Order of Malta; 2nd *s* of late Rt Hon. Hugh Law, Lord Chancellor of Ireland, and Helen Mary, *d* of William White of Shrubs, Co. Dublin; *m* Charlotte, *d* of Rev. Alexander George Stuart of Bogay, Co. Donegal; one *s* three *d. Educ:* Rugby; University College, Oxford. MP (N) West Donegal, 1902–18; served in Ministry of Munitions (secretariat), 1915–16, and in News Department of Foreign Office, 1916–18; on Advisory Council of Ministry of Reconstruction, 1918; member of the Bars of England and Ireland; member of the Congested Districts Board for Ireland, 1919, and of the Housing Committee, Local Government Board for Ireland, 1919–22; Member of the Irish Free State Parliament, 1927–32. *Publications:* Anglo-Irish Literature; part author of History of Ireland in Nations of To-day series. *Recreations:* riding, fishing. *Address:* Marble Hill, Ballymore, Co. Donegal. *Clubs:* Stephen's Green, Dublin.

Died 2 April 1943.

LAW, Brig.-Gen. Robert Theophilus Hewitt, CB 1917; retired; *b* 13 Oct. 1855; *o s* of Col Robert Law, 31st Regt; *m* Mary Isobel (*d* 1945), *d* of John Thom, JP, Birkacre, Chorley; no *c. Educ:* private school; Sandhurst. Joined 77th DCO Regt 1875; served Zulu War (medal and clasp); in S Africa, India, and Burma till 1885; joined Army Ordnance Department, and was on the Staff at Mauritius, Gibraltar, S Africa; served S African War, 1900 (medal, clasp); Aldershot; Brig.-Gen. and Inspector

Ordnance Services. WO, 1913; served European War 1917–19 (despatches twice, CB). *Recreations:* shooting, fishing. *Club:* Army and Navy.

Died 3 July 1949.

LAW, Samuel Horace, MD, FRCSI; Surgeon to the Throat, Nose and Ear Department of the Adelaide Hospital; Consulting Laryngologist to Mercers Charitable Hospital; Hon. Throat and Ear Surgeon, Stewart Institution; Fellow Royal Society of Medicine; *b* 22 Oct. 1873; *e s* of T. Pakenham Law, KC, and Amy, *d* of Horace Rochfort, Clogenane, Carlow; *m* 1905, Sybil Mary, *d* of Sir George Clay, 3rd Bt; three *s* one *d*. *Educ:* Monkton Combe School; Trinity College, Dublin; Vienna; Hudson Scholar, Adelaide Hospital. *Publications:* various Monographs on Nose, Throat and Ear. *Recreations:* yachting, motoring, etc. *Address:* 46 Merrion Square, Dublin. *T:* 61386, Dublin; San Elmo, Dalkey. *Clubs:* Kildare Street, Dublin; Royal St George Yacht.

Died 27 Feb. 1940.

LAW, Sir Sydney, Kt 1938; JP County of Worcester; Manufacturer; *b* 28 Sept. 1861; *s* of Samuel and Mary Ann Law; *m* 1885, Laura Williams Palmer (*d* 1939); one *s*. *Educ:* Wolverhampton Grammar School. *Address:* Woodthorpe, near Stourbridge, Worcs. *T:* Lye 56.

Died 27 Nov. 1949.

LAWRENCE, 3rd Baron *cr* 1869; **Alexander Graham Lawrence;** Bt 1858; *b* 29 March 1878; *s* of 2nd Baron and Mary, (*d* 1938), *o c* of Richard Campbell, Glencarradie and Auchinbreck, Argyllshire; *S* father, 1913; *m* 1st, 1907, Dorothy Helen, CBE (*d* 1935), *d* of late A. Pemberton-Hobson; one *s* four *d*; 2nd, 1935, Jessie (*d* 1936), *d* of late Col Byron Gordon Daniels and *widow* of W. F. Lawrence; 3rd, 1938, Mrs W. Burnet Craigie, *widow* of William Burnet Craigie. *Educ:* Eton; Worcester College, Oxford. Capt. 3rd Battalion Bedfords. Regiment; Major 11th London; DL, JP Middlesex. *Recreation:* hunting. *Heir: s* Hon. John Anthony Edward [*b* 16 Oct. 1908; *m* 1936, Margaret Jean, *d* of Arthur Downer, Rotherfield, Kent; one *s*]. *Club:* Carlton.

Died 24 June 1947.

LAWRENCE, (Arabella) Susan; *b* 1871; *d* of Nathaniel Tertius Lawrence. *Educ:* Newnham College, Cambridge. MP (Lab) East Ham North, 1923–24, and 1926–31; Parliamentary Secretary, Ministry of Health, 1929–31; Chairman of Labour Party 1930; Member of London School Board, 1900; London County Council, 1910–12, and 1912–28; Poplar Borough Council, 1919–24; National Federation of Women Workers, 1912–21; Deputy Chairman LCC, 1925–26. *Address:* 28 Bramham Gardens, SW5.

Died 25 Oct. 1947.

LAWRENCE, Lt-Col Bryan Turner Tom, VC 1901; *b* 1873; *s* of late John Turner Lawrence, Lower Park House, Bewdley, Worcs; *m* 1936, Nancy Mary (*d* 1944), *d* of late James Manfield, Weston Favell House, Northampton, second wife and widow of Carl F. Leijel. *Educ:* King Charles First's School, Kidderminster. Joined 17th Lancers, 1894; Promoted 18th Royal Hussars, 1904; served S African War (VC); European War (Brev. Major); Kurdistan (Lieutenant-Colonel); dangerously wounded BEF 1914; served on the General Staff EEF 1917–19; and on the General Staff Iraq Levies, 1923–24; Commanded a mobile column in operations in E Kurdistan, 1925–26; served in present war, 1939–42; a Military Knight of Windsor, 1934–38. Member: English riding team, Olympic Games, Stockholm; British Team, Internat. Horse Show, Olympia for several years. *Publication:* (under pseudonym Pegasus) Horse Talks. *Recreations:* riding and yachting. *Address:* Avebury Cottage, Londiani, Kenya Colony. *Club:* United Service.

Died 6 June 1949.

LAWRENCE, Lt-Col Henry Rundle, CIE 1925; Indian Army, retired; *b* 20 July 1878; *s* of late Lt-Col H. J. Lawrence, Indian Army; *m* 1st, Mary Gertrude (*d* 1927), *d* of late F. Adams, Cardiff; 2nd, 1928, Maud Geraldine, *o d* of late Lt-Col Alick Currie, 9th Norfolk Regt, and *widow* of Major Edgar Brandreth, Indian Cavalry. *Educ:* Winchester; Pembroke College, Cambridge. Entered RFA 1900, Indian Army, 1903; Government of India Political Dept 1904; served East Africa, 1916–17 (despatches twice); Secretary to Resident, Hyderabad, 1919; Political Agent, Haraoti and Tonk, 1921; Additional Commissioner, Ajmer-Merwara, 1926; President, Council of State, Jaipur, 1927; retired, 1930. *Address:* Leominster, Herefordshire.

Died 4 Feb. 1949.

LAWRENCE, Sir Henry Staveley, KCSI 1926 (CSI 1918); *b* Co. Donegal, 20 Oct. 1870; *y s* of late George Henry Lawrence, Bengal Civil Service; *m* 1st, 1899, Phyllis Louise Napier (*d* 1912); two *s* one *d*; 2nd, 1914, Rosamond, *d* of Col E. Napier, late Carabineers; one *s*. *Educ:* Haileybury College; Magdalen College, Oxford. Entered Indian Civil Service, 1890. Plague duty, Sind, 1896; initiated evacuation policy; Kaiser-i-Hind medal, 1900; Secretariat of Bombay Govt, 1897–1901; Director of Agriculture, 1902–06; Founded College of Agriculture in Poona, 1906; medal of RSA for address on Indian Agriculture, 1908; District work in Sind, 1908–13; before Royal Commission on Indian Services advocated higher scope for Indians, 1913; Commissioner in Sind, 1916–20; Finance Member of Council, 1921–26; Act. Governor of Bombay, 1926; Member Royal Commission on Agriculture in India, 1926–28; Member Imperial Conf. on Agriculture, 1927. Tour in Canada for National Education Society on Indian Reforms, 1932; addressed Houses of Parliament in Ottawa; addressed Conservative Party in House of Commons on Indian Reforms, 1934. *Publications:* The Indian White Paper, 1934; Freedom from Fear and Want, 1942; The Inspiration of Shakespeare, 1948. *Address:* Greenheys, Boars Hill, Oxford. *T:* Oxford 85112. *Club:* East India and Sports.

Died 29 June 1949.

LAWRENCE, Gen. Hon. Sir Herbert (Alexander), GCB 1926; KCB 1917; CB 1916; Chairman and Managing Director of Glyn, Mills & Co; *b* 8 Aug. 1861; *s* of 1st Lord Lawrence; *m* 1892, Hon. Isabel Mary Mills (*d* 1941), *e d* of 1st Lord Hillingdon; (two *s* killed in action), one *d*. Formerly Major and Bt Lt-Col 17th Lancers; late Colonel, 17th/21st Lancers, and Manchester Regt; formerly Lt-Col Commanding and Hon. Col King's Colonials Yeomanry; served South Africa, 1899–1902 (despatches, Queen's medal 6 clasps, King's medal 2 clasps, Bt Lt-Col); Dardanelles, 1915 (prom. Major-General, CB); Egypt, 1916; France, 1917–19; Chief of Staff, Headquarters, British Armies in France, from Jan. 1918; Lieut-Gen. 1918; General, 1919; retired pay, 1922; Member, Royal Commission on Coal Industry, 1925; Governor of Wellington College; Hon. LLD University of St Andrews; Hon. DCL University of Oxford; Commander, Legion of Honour, 1916; 2nd class Serbian Order, Karageorge, 1916; Grand Officer Legion of Honour, 1918; Croix de Guerre, French; Grand Cordon Crown of Belgium; Belgian Croix de Guerre, 1918; American Distinguished Service Order, 1918; Grand Cross St Benedict of Aviz, 1918; Grand Cross Crown of Roumania, 1918; 1st Class Rising Sun, Japan. *Address:* Woodcock, Little Berkhamsted, nr Hertford. *Clubs:* Brooks's, Naval and Military.

Died 17 Jan. 1943.

LAWRENCE, Col Hugh Duncan, CMG 1919; retired pay; *b* 19 July 1862; *e s* of H. M. Lawrence, GPO; *m* 1st, 1888, Flora Macdonald (*d* 1896), *widow* of C. R. Gilson of Dedham, Essex, 2nd *d* of James Robertson of Struan House, Launceston, Tasmania; one *s*; 2nd, 1901, Mary Alice Maude, *e d* of late Col S. Maunsell, RAMC; two *d*.

Educ: Blackheath Proprietary School. Entered Army, East Surrey Regiment, 1882; served in Gibraltar, 1882–84; to India, 1884; at Staff College, 1889 and 1890; to India, 1891; Adjt 3rd Battalion, 1897–1902; served South Africa, 1901–02 (despatches, medal, 3 clasps); to India, 1903; Brigade Major, India, 1905–09; commanded 2nd Battalion, 1911–15; AAG War Office, 1915–16; AAG Northern Command, 1916–19 (despatches). *Address:* Thorpes, Hawkhurst, Kent. *Club:* United Service.

Died 25 June 1946.

LAWRENCE, Sir (James) Taylor, Kt 1942; MA (Aberdeen), BA (Cantab); Chief Justice, Colony and Aden, since 1937; Lt-Col (local), OC Aden Home Guard, 1942; *b* Edzell, Angus, 28 Jan. 1888; *s* of Rev. W. Gordon Lawrence and Margaret Taylor; *m* 1915, Gladys Irene Parsons; no *c. Educ:* King Edward's School, Birmingham; Aberdeen University (Simpson Prizeman, Greig Prizeman, Lyon Prizeman, Dr David Rennet Gold Medal, Fullerton Scholar); Trinity College, Cambridge (Exhibitioner, First Class Mathematical Tripos, Pts I & II); University College, London. Ferguson Scholar (Scotland). Indian Civil Service, 1911–33; Assistant Collector and Magistrate, Bombay Presidency, 1912–19; mentioned in despatches, 1919; Assistant Judge, 1919–22; District and Sessions Judge, 1923–27; Agent to the Sardars in the Deccan, 1926; Judicial Assistant to the Resident, Aden, 1927–31; Deputy Secretary, Finance Dept, Govt of Bombay, 1924–26; Lecturer in Mathematics, Aberdeen University, 1931–36; special duty, Colonial Office, 1936–37. *Recreations:* various. *Address:* c/o Grindlay & Co., 54 Parliament Street, SW1.

Died 1 Aug. 1944.

LAWRENCE, Lt-Col Sir (Percy) Roland (Bradford), 2nd Bt *cr* 1906; MC; late Coldstream Guards; *b* 9 April 1886; *s* of Sir Walter Lawrence, 1st Bt, and Lilian Gertrude (*d* 1929), *d* of John Gwynne James, Hereford; *S* father, 1940; *m* 1925, Susan, 3rd *d* of late Sir Charles Addis, KCMG; two *s* two *d. Educ:* Eton; RMC, Sandhurst. Served European War, 1914–16 (despatches twice, MC). *Heir: s* David Roland Walter, *b* 1929. *Address:* Oak Walk, St Peter, Jersey. *T:* Western 572. *Clubs:* Guards', Boodle's, Royal Automobile.

Died 16 May 1950.

LAWRENCE, Susan; *see* Lawrence, A. S.

LAWRENCE, Sir Taylor; *see* Lawrence, Sir J. T.

LAWRENCE, Rt Rev. William, DD, STD, LLD; *b* Boston, Mass, 30 May 1850; *s* of Amos A. and Sarah Elizabeth (Appleton) Lawrence; *m* 1874, Julia Cunningham (*d* 1927); two *s* five *d. Educ:* Harvard University (AB); Episcopal Theological School, Cambridge (BD). Rector, Grace Church, Lawrence, Mass, 1876–84; Professor of Homiletics and Pastoral Care, Episcopal Theological School, Cambridge, 1884–89; Dean, 1889–93; Bishop of Massachusetts, 1893–1927; Fellow of Harvard University, 1913–31; Preacher to Harvard University, 1888–91, 1910–13; Overseer of Harvard University, 1894–1906, 1907–13; President of Board of Trustees of Groton and St Mark's Schools, 1917; President of Church War Commission, and Vice-Chairman Gen. War Time Commission; Member Mass Historical Society and Fellow American Academy of Arts and Sciences. *Publications:* Life of Amos A. Lawrence; Visions and Service; Life of Roger Wolcott; Sketch of Phillips Brooks; The American Cathedral; Fifty Years; Biographical Sketch of Senator Cabot Henry Lodge; Memories of a Happy Life; The New American; Life of Phillip Brooks; A Harvest of Happy Years. *Recreations:* Summer Cottage, Bar Harbor, Me. *Address:* 122 Commonwealth Avenue, Boston. *T:* Commonwealth 0912, Boston; (Spring and Autumn) Milton, Mass, USA. *Clubs:* Union, Harvard, Boston; Harvard, New York.

Died 6 Nov. 1941.

LAWRENCE-ARCHER, Col James Henry, CIE 1919; late RA; *b* 1871; *s* of Major J. H. Lawrence-Archer. Served North-West Frontier of India, 1897–98 (medal with two clasps); European War (medal). *Address:* Rio, Keymer Crescent, Goring-by-Sea, Sussex.

Died 29 Aug. 1948.

LAWS, Bernard Courtney, ARCSc (Lond.) in Physics and Mechanics; DSc (Lond.) in Engineering; Dr-ès-Sc (Paris); Fellow Institute of Physics; Member of the Institute of Naval Architects; Member of the London Mathematical Society; Consulting Naval Architect and Engineer; *m* 1900, Eugénie Miller, *d* of late John Miller Watson, Engineer, RN; one *s. Educ:* private school; HM Dockyard, Portsmouth; Admiralty Experimental Tank, Haslar; Royal Coll. of Science, London. Whitworth Exhibition; National Scholar, George Stephenson Gold Medal, Institution of Civil Engineers. Apprenticeship in HM Dockyard, Portsmouth; charge of Designing Office, Fairfield Company; Naval Architect to Le Chantier Naval de Nicolaieff, Russia; Special Surveyor for Research to Lloyds Register, later Consultant for Research to Lloyds Register of Shipping; Consultant to Tungum Alloy Cos.; many years examiner in Shipbuilding subjects to City and Guilds of London Institute; sometime examiner to Institution of Civil Engineers; President Lloyds Technical Association; Inventor of Instruments for measuring and recording strains in structures. *Publications:* Answers to questions in Naval Architecture; Stability and equilibrium of Floating Bodies, translated into Russian by order of the Imperial Academy, St Petersburg; various papers on Scientific and Engineering subjects in Proceeding Inst Civil Engineers; Report of British Association; Transactions Inst. Naval Architects; Transactions North-East Coast Institution of Engineers and Shipbuilders; American Society of Architects and Marine Engineers; Philosophical Magazine; The Shipbuilder and Marine Engine Builder; Cassier's Magazine. *Address:* Claverton, 60 Cheam Road, Sutton, Surrey. *T:* Vigilant 2133.

Died 17 Sept. 1947.

LAWSON, Sir Arnold, KBE 1920; FRCS Eng., MD Brux, LRCP Lond.; Ophthalmic Consultant to Royal Navy; Consulting Ophthalmic Surgeon, Middlesex Hospital; Consulting Surgeon to the Royal London Ophthalmic Hospital; Consulting Ophthalmic Surgeon to the Royal Hospital and Home for Incurables, Putney, and to the Royal Medical Benevolent College, Epsom; President Royal Medical Benevolent Fund; Chairman Ophthalmic Advisory Board, St Dunstan's Hostel; FRSM; late President Ophthalmological Section, RSM and Hon. Treasurer of the Ophthalmological Society of the UK; *b* 4 Dec. 1867; 4th *s* of George Lawson, FRCS, Surgeon Oculist to Queen Victoria; *m* 1904, Helen Hargreaves (*d* 1944), *e d* of Andrew Clark, FRCS, Eng.; Hon. Surgeon to HM George V; two *s* one *d. Educ:* Merchant Taylors' School. Entered Middlesex Hospital as Senior Entrance Scholar, 1886; Hetley Scholarship in 1890; Senior Broderip Scholarship, 1891; MRCS, LRCP, 1891; FRCS Eng., 1893; Ophthalmic Surgeon to the Children's Hospital, Paddington, 1896; Assistant Surgeon to the Royal London Ophthalmic Hospital, 1900, Surgeon, 1907–14; Assistant Ophthalmic Surgeon, Middlesex Hospital, 1910, Surgeon, 1914–32; late Ophthalmic Surgeon St John and St Elizabeth's Hospital; Ophthalmic Surgeon, St Dunstan's Hostel for Blinded Sailors and Soldiers, 1915–20; and to King Edward VII Hospital for Officers, 1914–19. *Publications:* Editor and part author of Lawson's Diseases of the Eye (6th edition); War Blind at St Dunstan's; articles on Diseases of the Iris and Ciliary Body, Sympathetic Ophthalmitis and Cataract in Latham and English's System of Treatment; The Treatment of Eye Disease by Radium (with Sir J. Mackenzie Davidson); many papers to Trans. Ophthalmological Society of the UK, BMJ, Lancet,

Practitioner, and Oxford Medical Publications. *Address:* 12 Harley Street, W1. *T:* Langham 1232. *Clubs:* Garrick, Royal Automobile.

Died 19 Jan. 1947.

LAWSON, Sir Henry Joseph; 3rd Bt *cr* 1841; *b* 25 Dec. 1877; *o s* of 2nd Bt and Agnes (*d* 1945), *e d* of Edmund Molyneux Seel; *S* father, 1910; *m* Ursula Mary, *o c* of late Philip John Canning Howard, Corby Castle, Carlisle; two *s* two *d*. *Educ:* Stonyhurst. Owns about 2700 acres. *Heir: s* Ralph Henry [*b* 27 Sept. 1905; *m* 1935, Lilyan Mary, *e d* of late Sir Edmund Chaytor, 6th Bt, and of Mrs Burton Fiske]. *Address:* Wood House, Catterick, Yorks.

Died 21 Oct. 1947.

LAWSON, Hon. James Earl; PC Canada, 1935; KC, 1931; Barrister; Director of Buscombe and Dodds Limited; Viceroy Manufacturing Co., Ltd; Burry Biscuit Corp. of New Jersey; President and Managing Director, Odeon theatres of Canada Ltd; President, Eagle Lion Films of Canada Ltd; Director; Gaumont Kalee Ltd; Director: Monogram Pictures Ltd; J. Arthur Rank 16 Ltd; National General Insurance Co. Ltd; People's Credit Jewellers Ltd; Holden Mfg. Co. Ltd; *b* Hamilton, Ontario, 21 Oct. 1891; *s* of James and Jenny Lawson; *m* 1915, Anita Blanche, *d* of Lewis James Bateman, Toronto; one *s* one *d*. *Educ:* Hamilton and Ottawa Public Schools; Ottawa Collegiate; Osgoode Hall. Admitted to Bar, 1916; MP York, South, Canadian House of Commons, 1928–40; Minister of National Revenue in Mr Bennett's Cabinet, Aug.–Oct. 1935; Member Liberal-Conservative Business Men's Club; Conservative; United Church of Canada. *Recreations:* golf, handball. *Address:* 372 Bay Street, Toronto, Ont; 3 Rosemary Lane, Forest Hill Village, Toronto, Ont. *T:* Adelaide 0323, Orchard 7101. *Clubs:* Albany, Granite, Mississauga Golf (Toronto); Rideau (Ottawa).

Died 13 May 1950.

LAWSON, Rear-Adm. Robert Neale, CB 1918; *b* 8 March 1873; *s* of Rev. Robert Lawson; *m* Malvina Felton of Stanley, Falkland Islands; two *s* four *d*. Served Naval Expedition on the Benin River, 1894 (medal and clasp); in Naval Intelligence Dept, 1905–07; Navigator of Flag-ships, 1907–13; Captain, 1913; Flag-Captain to Commander-in-Chief, Home Fleets, 1913–15; Captain of Chester, 1916–19 (despatches, Battle of Jutland); retired, 1919; Rear-Adm., retired, 1923. *Publications:* Novels: Beloved Shipmates, 1924; Happy Anchorage, 1925; Monograph: A Plan for the Organisation of a European Air Service, 1935. *Recreations:* gardening, camping. *Address:* Lower Bridmore Farm, Berwick St John, Shaftesbury.

Died 11 Aug. 1945.

LAWSON-TANCRED, Major Sir Thomas (Selby), 9th Bt *cr* 1662; late Indian Army; *b* 14 May 1870; *e s* of 8th Bt and Mary Harriett, *d* of late Col George Willoughby Hemans, Queen's Square, Westminster; *S* father, 1910; *m* 1912, Margery Elinor, *d* of late A. S. Lawson, Aldborough Manor; two *s* two *d*. *Educ:* Eton; RMC Sandhurst. Took the name of Lawson in addition to Tancred, 1914. Served Miranaiz Expedition, 1891 (medal with clasp); European War, 1914–18. *Publication:* Records of a Yorkshire Manor, 1937. *Heir: s* Henry, *b* 1924. *Address:* Aldborough Manor, Boroughbridge. *Clubs:* Junior United Service; Yorkshire, York.

Died 15 Dec. 1945.

LAYARD, Raymond de Burgh Money, CMG 1913; late HBM Consul-General, Kobé, Japan; *b* Bhaugulpore, Bengal Presidency, 30 Sept. 1859; *o surv. s* of General F. P. Layard, and *nephew* of Sir Henry Austen Layard; *m* 1892, Isabel (*d* 1928), *sister* of late General Sir Henry Scobell, KCVO; two *d*. *Educ:* Wellington College. Entered Consular Service for Japan, 1881, as Student Interpreter; after being Acting Consul at various places in Japan, was Consul at Hakodate, Tamsui (Formosa),

Nagasaki, Honolulu (Hawaii); promoted Consul-General, 1908, served as such at Manila and Kobé; Coronation Medal, 1911; retired, 1913. *Recreations:* shooting, boating, etc. *Address:* 22 Campden Grove, Kensington, W8. *T:* Western 5587. *Club:* Thatched House.

Died 19 Sept. 1941.

LAYTON, Captain Perceval Norman, CBE 1918; RD, RN Reserve; lately an Elder Brother of Trinity House; Director London Assurance; *b* 26 Dec. 1872; *s* of late James Norman Layton; *m* 1937, Pauline Mary Scott-Wicher. *Address:* Patch Cottage, Coombe Hill, Surrey. *T:* Kingston 0948.

Died 16 Oct. 1943.

LAYTON, William Grazebrook, CBE 1930; *b* Queensland, Australia, 1868; *m* 1898, Rosalie, *d* of William Deane, solicitor, Sydney; one *s* one *d*. *Educ:* Brisbane Grammar School. Joined the service of the Municipal Council of Sydney as a junior clerk, 1885; Town Clerk of the City of Sydney, 1924–31. *Address:* Boonah, Blaxland, Blue Mountains, NSW.

Died 20 Aug. 1949.

LAZARUS-BARLOW, Walter Sydney, BA, BC; MD Camb.; FRCP Lond.; Grand Council British Empire Cancer Campaign; Departmental Editor for Medical Sciences, Encyclopædia Britannica, 14th ed.; late Professor of Experimental Pathology, Middlesex Hospital Medical School, Univ. of London; late Member of Cancer Committee Ministry of Health; late Director of the Cancer Research Laboratories, Middlesex Hospital; late Captain RAMC (TC). *Educ:* City of London School; Downing College, Cambridge (scholar and prizeman); St George's Hospital (exhibitioner). *Publications:* A Manual of General Pathology, 2nd ed. 1903; Elements of Pathological Anatomy and Histology for Students, 1903. *Address:* Coverdale, West Mersea, Essex. *T:* West Mersea 106.

Died 15 Jan. 1950.

LAZENBY, Frederick George, CBE; Secretary and House Governor of Saint Monica's Home of Rest, Westbury-on-Trym, Bristol; *b* Alton, Hampshire, 1876; *s* of Francis Lazenby; unmarried. *Educ:* Queen's School. Admitted Solicitor 1899; practised in Bristol; retired, 1924. War work; Enquiry Department, Red Cross; voluntary work in connection with 2nd Southern—3rd Western—the Beaufort War and Auxiliary Hospitals; Recruiting and National Service and other Committees; Chairman of Committee under the Southern Command for vocational training of wounded in Hospital Orthopaedic Workshops. *Address:* 3 Upper Belgrave Road, Clifton, Bristol. *T:* Bristol 34602. *Club:* Constitutional.

Died 23 May 1943.

LEA, Lt-Col Percy Gerald Parker, CMG 1918; DSO 1916; late Royal Army Service Corps; *b* 28 March 1875; *s* of late Col Samuel Job Lea, CB; *m* 1911, Elsie Grant, *y d* of Frederick Spencer, JP, DL, of Oakhill, Somerset. Entered Army (33rd Duke of Wellington Regt). 1895; ASC 1899; Capt. 1901; Major, 1913; served South African War, 1899–1902 (despatches, Queen's medal 5 clasps, King's medal 2 clasps); European War, 1914–18 (despatches four times, DSO, CMG); retired pay, 1922. *Club:* United Service.

Died 27 Sept. 1945.

LEA, Sir (Thomas) Sydney, 2nd Bt *cr* 1892; JP Worcestershire; *b* 28 Jan. 1867; *s* of 1st Bt, and Louey, *d* of late William Birch; *S* father, 1902; *m* 1896, Mary Ophelia (*d* 1933), *d* of Robert Woodward of Arley Castle, near Bewdley; three *s* one *d*. *Educ:* Charterhouse; Clare Coll., Cambridge. BA 1888; LLB 1889; MA 1892. *Heir: s* Thomas Claude Harris, Lt-Comdr RNVR [*b* 13 April 1901; *m* 1924, Barbara Katharine (*d* 1945), *d* of late

Albert J. Pell; one *s* (Thomas Julian, *b* 18 Nov. 1934) four *d*]. *Address:* Dunley Hall, Stourport, Worcs. *TA:* Lea Dunley, Stourport. *T:* Stourport 40.

Died 18 Nov. 1946.

LEACH, Henry, FRGS; *b* Chorley, Lancs, 19 Nov. 1874. *Educ:* privately. Associated with daily newspapers at Hanley, Scarborough, and Nottingham, 1892–98; Editor, Nottingham Evening News, 1897; came to London at invitation of Alfred Harmsworth (Lord Northcliffe); Evening News, 1898; Daily Mail, 1898–1903; first editor of Caxton Magazine, 1901; wrote much on golf for the Daily chronicle, Evening News, Daily Mail, and Daily Telegraph, visiting the American Championships for the Times and Daily Mail; editor Golf Illustrated 1905–06, and founder and editor of The Golfer; has travelled extensively and spent long periods in Spain and North Africa, especially Morocco, and explored the Riff in 1927; for many years Spanish correspondent to leading American journals, and has lectured on Spain and Morocco, and acted as special correspondent to the Manchester Guardian and other leading newspapers; has written monthly causerie, The Heart of Things, in Chambers's Journal since 1907. *Publications:* The Duke of Devonshire, a personal and political biography, 1904; The Complete Golfer (with Harry Vardon), 1905; Fleet Street from Within, 1905; The Spirit of the Links, 1907; Letters of a Modern Golfer, 1910; The Happy Golfer, 1914; Spanish Morocco, with the Riff, 1928; etc. *Recreations:* golf, motoring, water-colour sketching. *Address:* 5 Queen Anne Row, Walmer, Kent. *Clubs:* Savage, Spanish, Royal Automobile.

Died 17 June 1942.

LEACH, Captain John Catterall, DSO 1941; MVO 1927; HMS Prince of Wales; Director of Naval Ordnance, 1939; *b* 1894; *s* of Charles Rothwell Leach; *m* 1916, Evelyn Burrell, *o d* of R. H. Lee; two *s*. Served European War; Lieutenant-Com. of HMS Renown during the Duke and Duchess of York's tour in Australia and New Zealand, 1927 (MVO). *Address:* Yarner, Bovey-Tracey, South Devon. *T:* Bovey-Tracey 4. *Club:* United Service.

Died 10 Dec. 1941.

LEACH, William; Member Bradford City Council, 1907–13, 1919–23 and since 1925; worsted manufacturer, retired; *b* Bradford, 1870. *Educ:* Bradford Grammar School. Contested Central Bradford, 1918; MP (Lab) Central Bradford, 1922–24, 1929–31 and 1935–45. Under-Sec. for Air, 1924. *Address:* 16 Haslingden Drive, Bradford.

Died 21 Nov. 1949.

LEACOCK, Stephen Butler, BA, PhD, LittD; LLD; DCL; Professor Emeritus, McGill University, Montreal; *b* Swanmoor, Hants, 30 Dec. 1869; *s* of W. P. Leacock of Oak Hill, IW, and Agnes, *d* of Rev. Stephen Butler; *m* 1900, Beatrix (*d* 1925), *d* of Col Hamilton, Toronto; one *s*. *Educ:* Upper Canada; College; University of Toronto, BA; University of Chicago, PhD. On the Staff of Upper Canada College, 1891–99; in Graduate School Univ. of Chicago, 1899–1903; on the Staff of McGill University, Montreal, 1901–36; Head of Department of Economics, 1908–36; made of tour of the Empire, 1907–08, giving lectures on Imperial Organisation under the auspices of the Cecil Rhodes Trust. *Publications:* Elements of Political Science, 1906; Baldwin and La Fontaine (Makers of Canada Series), 1907; Literary Lapses, 1910; Nonsense Novels, 1911; Sunshine Sketches of a Little Town, 1912; Behind the Beyond, 1913; Arcadian Adventures with the Idle Rich, 1914; Moonbeams from the Larger Lunacy, 1915; Essays and Literary Studies, 1916; Further Foolishness, 1916; Frenzied Fiction, 1917; The Hohenzollerns in America, 1919; The Unsolved Riddle of Social Justice, 1920; Winsome Winnie, 1920; My Discovery of England,

1922; Over the Footlights, 1923; College Days, 1923; The Garden of Folly, 1924; Winnowed Wisdom, 1926; Short Circuits, 1928; The Iron Man, The Tin Woman, 1929; Economic Prosperity in the British Empire, 1930; Back to Prosperity, 1931; Afternoons in Utopia, 1932; Mark Twain, 1932; Charles Dickens, 1933; Lincoln Frees the Slaves, 1934; Humour: Its Theory and Technique, 1935; Greatest Pages of Charles Dickens, 1935; Greatest Pages of American Humour, 1936; Hellements of Hickonomics, 1936; Funny Pieces, 1936; My Discovery of the West; Humour and Humanity; Here are My Lectures, 1937; Model Memoirs and Other Sketches from Simple to Serious, 1939; Too Much College, 1939; Our British Empire, 1940; My Remarkable Uncle, 1942; Our Heritage of Liberty, 1942; Montreal: Seaport and City, 1942; Canada, 1942; How to Write, 1943; Happy Stories, 1945. *Recreations:* fishing, carpentering, and gardening. *Address:* McGill University, Montreal, Canada; The Old Brewery Bay, Orillia. *Clubs:* University, Montreal.

Died 28 March 1944.

LEAD, Major Sir William Chollerton, KCMG 1941; Kt 1935; MC. Member Legislative Council of Tanganyika. *Address:* Mazinde, Tanganyika.

Died 21 Jan. 1942.

LEAHY, Brig. Thomas Bernard Arthur, CMG 1919; DSO 1917; late Royal Army Ordnance Corps; *b* 13 June 1878; 7th *s* of late Col Arthur Leahy, Royal Engineers, 7th *s* of late John Leahy of Southill, Killarney, County Kerry; *m* 1904, Agnes Wentworth (*d* 1943), *o d* of Mordaunt Stevens, Nice; one *s* two *d*. *Educ:* Stubbington House, Fareham; Cheltenham College. 2nd Lieut Royal Marine Artillery, 1896; Captain, 1903; passed Ordnance Course, 1905; transferred to AOD 1913; China, 1900; European War, 1914–18 (DSO, CMG); ADOS 1929–32; AAG War Office, 1931–32; Deputy Director of Ordnance Services, 1932–35; retired pay, 1935. *Club:* Army and Navy.

Died 21 Nov. 1947.

LEAHY, Major Thomas Joseph Carroll, DSO 1919; MC; late Royal Northumberland Fusiliers; *b* 12 Feb. 1889; *e s* of late Thomas J. Carroll-Leahy, yr; *m* 1927, Vera, *o d* of late Colonel Eden Vansittart, DSO. *Educ:* Beaumont College, Old Windsor; Royal Military College, Sandhurst. Joined 2nd Batt. the Royal Dublin Fusiliers, 1909; remained on home service until sailing with that battalion for France, Aug. 1914; saw continuous service on the Western Front through European War as a Regimental and Staff Officer, and, after a Staff appointment, with a Division in the Army of Occupation on the Rhine; returned as Adjutant, 1st Batt. the Royal Dublin Fusiliers, at home, 1919; transferred to Northumberland Fusiliers, 1922; joined 1st Bn with Rhine Army of Occupation; Staff Captain, Headquarters, Southern Command, Salisbury, 1922–26; served in India and China with 2nd Bn, 1927–31, and in Jamaica (BWI) Bermuda and Egypt with 1st Bn, 1932–35; Transferred to Home Establishment, 1935; retired to Army Reserve, 1936; re-employed on Staff of HQ of an AP Div., 1939, and appointed to command a Sub-Area in the rank of Temp. Colonel, 1940. *Recreations:* hunting, polo. *Clubs:* Army and Navy; Kildare Street, Dublin.

Died 5 Dec. 1942.

LEAKE, Percy Dewe, FCA, FSS, FREconS, FZS; founder and senior partner of P. D. Leake & Co; *s* of late John Knight Leake; *m* Désirée (*d* 1937), *d* of late Captain John George Image. In practice as a chartered accountant; has written and lectured extensively on accountancy subjects; was retained by the PMG and gave evidence in the well-known case of The National Telephone Co. Ltd v. HM Postmaster-General; has visited USA and Canada and studied their methods of cost accounting; Member of the Board of Trustees,

Albany, Piccadilly, W1. *Publications:* Depreciation and Wasting Assets and their Treatment in computing Annual Profit and Loss, 5th ed., 1948; The Question of Depreciation and the Measurement of Expired Outlay on Productive Plant, a Plea for the Study and Use of Better Methods; Leake's Register of Industrial Plant for the Measurement of Depreciation, with Introductory Notes, 2nd ed. 1946; The Need of Present Accounting for past Unexpired Capital Outlay; Can the Annual Assessment of Industrial Profit and Loss be raised to an exact Science?; The Use and Mis-use of the Sinking Fund; Commercial Goodwill, its History, Value, and Treatment in Accounts, 4th ed. 1948; Balance Sheet Values, 4th ed. 1946; Capital: Adam Smith: Karl Marx, 1933; Inflated Industrial Share Capital, 1936; etc. *Recreations:* walking, shooting, fishing, mountaineering, boating, squash rackets, lawn tennis. *Address:* K1, Albany, Piccadilly, W1; 3 Whitehall Court, SW1. *Clubs:* Authors', Gresham.

Died 27 Nov. 1949.

LEARMONTH, Adm. Sir Frederick Charles, KBE 1925; CB 1917; CBE 1919; ADC to the King, 1917; Commander French Legion of Honour, 1919; *b* 14 Jan. 1866; *y s* of Colonel Alexander Learmonth of Dean, MP. Entered Royal Navy, 1879; promoted to Lieutenant from Royal Yacht Victoria and Albert, 1887; Commander, 1900; Captain, 1906; Rear-Adm., 1918, attached to Hydrographic Service, 1891; surveys in all parts of the world; Superintendent of Charts, Admiralty, 1908; Author of MS publications on surveying subjects; received the thanks of the Lords Commissioners of the Admiralty when in command of HMS Goldfinch, 1904; Egeria, 1907; Endeavour, 1913, for Hydrographic Surveys conducted in WC Africa and Newfoundland, British Columbia and Alaska, and North Sea respectively; served at Admiralty as Director of Fixed Defences, 1918–19; Hydrographer of the Navy, 1919–24; Chairman of various technical Committees relating to Territorial Waters, Load Line; retired, 1921; Admiralty Representative on Port of London Authority, 1925; Nautical Assessor to the House of Lords, 1925–33; acting Conservator of the River Mersey, 1930–33. *Address:* 87 Victoria Street, SW1. *Clubs:* United Service, Junior Constitutional.

Died 3 June 1941.

LEARMONTH, Frederick Valiant Cotton L.; *see* Livingstone-Learmonth.

LEAROYD-COCKBURN, Col Charles Douglas, CBE; late RE; *b* 23 Oct. 1859; *m* Mary Clayton (*d* 1932), *d* of W. Y. Cockburn, JP, DL; two *s*. Served in Suakim campaign, 1885; Burma, 1885–86 (despatches); South Africa, 1900–02 (despatches, Brevet Lt-Col). *Address:* Syresham House, Brackley, Northants. *Clubs:* Naval and Military, MCC.

Died 29 Dec. 1946.

LEBRUN, Albert, GCB (Hon.) 1938; *b* Mercy-le-Haut (Meurthe-et-Moselle) le 29 août 1871; *m* Marguerite Nivoit (*d* 1947). *Educ:* École Polytechnique. École Supérieure des Mines. Ingénieur au Corps des Mines; Conseiller Général du Canton d'Audun-le-Roman, 1898; Député de Meurthe-et-Moselle, 1900; Ministre des Colonies, 1911–13; Ministre de la Guerre, 1913; Ministre des Colonies, 1913–14; Président de la Commission du Budget de la Chambre; Ministre du Blocus et des Régions Libérées, 1917–19; Sénateur de Meurthe-et-Moselle, 1920; Président du Conseil d'Administration de la Caisse autonome d'Amortissement, 1926–31; Vice-Président du Sénat, 1925–29; Président du Sénat, 1931–32; Président de la République Française, 1932–40. *Address:* Vizille, nr Grenoble, France.

Died 6 March 1950.

LE BRUN, Paymaster Captain William Henry, CBE 1919; Royal Navy, retired; *m* Elise Eleonore Neel (*d* 1935). *Address:* Sans Ennui, St Aubin, Jersey.

Died 23 Jan. 1942.

LECKIE, Col John Edwards, CMG 1917; CBE 1919; DSO 1900; Mining Engineer; *b* Canada, 19 Feb. 1872; *s* of late Major R. G. Leckie; unmarried. *Educ:* Bishops College School, Lennoxville. Graduated from Royal Military Coll. after four years' course; post-graduate course at King's Coll., BSc. Served first with Lord Strathcona's Horse, then as Capt. 2nd Canadian Mounted Rifles in S Africa, 1900–02 (despatches, Queen's medal 5 clasps, DSO); Mining Engineer; Member Can. Inst. Mining and Metallurgy; Major 72nd Seaforth Highlanders of Canada; served European War, 1914–19 (despatches, CMG); Commandant 16th Batt. The Canadian Scottish, 1915–18; commanded Forward Area, Murman Coast, NREF, 1918–19 (despatches, CBE, St Vladimir, White Eagle, Serbia, Croix de Guerre, France); exploring in Mexico, 1920; Venezuela, 1927–28; Hudson's Bay, 1928–29; Cocos Island, 1932–33. *Address:* Vancouver, BC, Canada. *Clubs:* Vancouver (Vancouver); Union (Victoria).

Died 7 Aug. 1950.

le COUTEUR, Frank; *o s* of late Francis Edward le Couteur, Jersey; *m* 1913, Hilda May (*d* 1935), *o c* of Canon R. J. Campbell, DD; two *d*; 1946, Sylvia, *o c* of H. H. Lloyd. *Educ:* Victoria College, Jersey. Reporter, Sub-Editor, Chief Sub-Editor, Picture Editor, Evening News, 1905–22; Daily Express, 1922–24; Editor, The Graphic, 1924–26; Assistant Editor, Sunday Express, 1927–28; Daily Express, 1929, retired 1948. *Publications:* contributions to Punch, etc. *Address:* L'Écluse, Vallée des Vaux, Jersey, CI. *T:* Sion 175.

Died 11 Dec. 1950.

LEDGARD, Sir Henry, Kt 1915; retired; *b* 20 Dec. 1853; *y s* of late Henry Ledgard of Teddington; *m* 1st, 1881, Florence Robertson (*d* 1918); four *d*; 2nd, 1922, Margaret Helen, *d* of Armitage Ledgard, Manor House, Thorner, Yorks. Ten years in a London office; 8 years Secretary and Manager, the Muir Mills Co., Ltd, Cawnpore; 29 years with Cooper, Allen & Co., Ltd, Cawnpore, as partner, Managing Director, and Advisory Director; President of the Upper India Chamber of Commerce, Cawnpore, 1901, 1912, 1913, 1914, and 1915, and represented that body on the Legislative Council of the United Provinces, India, 1912–15; Member of the Board of Industries of the UP, 1914 and 1915; President of the Cawnpore Expansion Committee, 1913–15; Honorary Adviser to the Government of India on Boot Production, 1919–20; Member Indian Postal Enquiry Committee, 1920; Member Indian Railways Committee, 1921. *Club:* Oriental.

Died 16 Oct. 1946.

LEDGARD, Reginald Armitage, CBE 1939 (OBE 1918); *b* 22 May 1883; *s* of William Edward Ledgard, Surgeon, Kirkby Lonsdale, and Lavinia, *d* of William Hanchett, Ickleton, Co. Cambs; *m* 1935, Phyllis Debenham, *er d* of late Rev. Percy James Debenham Johnson; two *d*. *Educ:* Pocklington School. ACA 1907. Assistant to Comptroller Port of London Authority, 1910; Auditor, National Insurance Audit Dept, 1911; Seconded to Exchequer and Audit Dept, 1915; Director of Accounts, National Service Dept, 1916; Director of Accounts and subsequently Director of Establishments, Ministry of National Service, 1917; Director of Accounts, Ministry of Pensions, 1919; Accountant General, Ministry of Pensions, 1934–47; retired, 1947. *Recreations:* sports generally and local historical research. *Address:* The Old Rectory, Bygrave, Baldock, Herts. *T:* Baldock 45.

Died 29 May 1949.

LEDINGHAM, Sir John C. G., Kt 1937; CMG 1918; FRS 1921; MB, FRCP, DSc, MA; Hon. LLD (Aber.), 1935; Hon. ScD (Dublin, Leeds); *b* Boyndie, Banffshire, 1875; *s* of Rev. James Ledingham, MA, Minister of Boyndie, and Isabella, *d* of Rev. James Gardiner, Minister of Rathven; *m* 1913, Barbara, *d* of David Fowler, Broomieknowe, Midlothian; one *s* one *d. Educ:* Boyndie Public School; Banff Academy; University of Aberdeen. MA 1895; First Class Hons in Mathematics and Physics; Simpson Math. Prizeman; Arnott Prizeman; BSc 1900 (with Distinction); MB (1902) with Honours; Fife-Jamieson and Struthers Gold Medallist in Anatomy; Anderson Scholar, 1902–04; post-graduate study University of Leipzig, 1902–03, and London Hospital, 1904–05. Assistant Bacteriologist, Lister Institute, London, 1905–08; Chief Bacteriologist, Lister Institute, 1908–30; Director, Lister Institute, 1931–43; late Prof. of Bacteriology, Univ. of London, Emeritus Prof., 1943; in charge of Bacteriological Dept, King George Hospital, Waterloo, SE, 1915; Lt-Col RAMC, 1915; Member of Medical Advisory Committee in the Mediterranean; Consulting Bacteriologist, Mesopotamia, 1917; Harben Lecturer, London, 1924; Herter Lecturer, Baltimore, 1934; Member of Medical Research Council, 1934–38; President 2nd International Congress for Microbiology, London, 1936; Hon. Pres. 3rd Internat. Congress for Microbiology, New York, 1939. *Publications:* with J. A. Arkwright, Carrier Problem in Infectious Diseases, 1912; numerous contributions to Pathology, Bacteriology, and Immunity in English and Foreign Journals. *Address:* Meadows, Hillview Road, Mill Hill, NW7. *T:* Mill Hill 4860. *Club:* Athenæum.

Died 4 Oct. 1944.

LEDÓCHOWSKI, Wlodimir Halka, Count; General of the Society of Jesus since 1915; *b* Loosdorf, Lower Austria, 7 Oct. 1866; *s* of Anthony Halka, Count Ledóchowski, and Josephine, Countess Salis Zizers; nephew of late Cardinal Ledóchowski. *Educ:* The Theresianum, Vienna. Studied law at the Cracovian University, 1885; philosophy and theology in the Seminary at Tarnov, and at the Gregorian University in Rome, 1887–89. Entered the noviciate of the Galician Province of the Society of Jesus, 1889; priest, 1894; after a short period of literary and pastoral activity, he was nominated Provincial of the Galician Province, 1901; Assistant of the German Assistancy, 1906. *Address:* Borgo S Spirito 5, Rome 113. *TA:* Gisa, Rome.

Died 13 Dec. 1942.

LEE OF FAREHAM, of Bridport, 1st Viscount *cr* 1922; Baron *cr* 1918; **Arthur Hamilton Lee,** PC 1919; GCB 1929; GCSI 1925; GBE 1918; KCB 1916; KJStJ; Hon. LLD (Cambridge); FSA; FRIBA (Hon.); JP; *b* Bridport, 8 Nov. 1868; *s* of Rev. Melville Lee; *m* 1899, Ruth, Lady of Grace of St John of Jerusalem, *e d* of J. G. Moore of New York. *Educ:* Cheltenham; Woolwich. Entered Royal Artillery 1888; Adjt Hong-Kong Volunteers, 1889–90; Adjt RA Isle of Wight, 1891–93; Capt., 1898; Bt-Major, 1900; Lt-Col, retired, 1900; Prof. of Strategy and Tactics, RMC, Canada, 1893–98; organised Military Survey of the Canadian Frontier, 1894–96; Special Correspondent Daily Chronicle, Klondyke Gold Rush, 1896; British Military Attaché with the US Army during Spanish-American war, 1898 (medal); Hon. Member 1st US Vol. Cavalry (Roosevelt's Rough Riders); Military Attaché, Washington, 1899, with rank of Lieut-Col; European War, 1914; rejoined Army as Colonel on the Staff, and detailed for special service with the Expeditionary Force (despatches twice, 1914 Star with clasp); Colonel in Army, 1917; Governor of Christ's Hospital; President of Cheltenham College, 1917–40; Chairman of Inter-Departmental Committee on the Humane Slaughtering of Animals, 1904; Chairman Parliamentary Aerial Defence Committee, 1910–14; Civil Lord of Admiralty, 1903–05; introduced and piloted through Parliament White Slave Traffic Act, 1912; Parliamentary Military Secretary, Ministry of Munitions, 1915–16; Personal Military Secretary to the Secretary of State for War (Mr Lloyd George), July–Dec. 1916; Director-General of Food Production, 1917–18; MP (C) South or Fareham Division of Hampshire, 1900–18; Minister of Agriculture and Fisheries with seat in Cabinet, Aug. 1919–Feb. 1921; First Lord of the Admiralty, Feb. 1921–Nov. 1922; Member of Imperial Cabinet, 1921; second British Delegate to the Washington Conference, Nov. 1921–Feb. 1922; Chairman of Royal Commission on the Public Services in India, 1923–24; Chairman of Committee on Police Pay and Pensions, 1925; Chairman of Royal Commission on Cross-river Traffic, 1926; Chairman of Royal Commission on Police Powers and Procedure, 1928; Chairman Radium Commission and Trustee of National Radium Fund 1929–33; Chairman Sulgrave Manor Board, 1925–37; Joint Editor the English Heritage Series; organised Exhibition of British Primitive Painting at Burlington House, 1923; Trustee of the Wallace Collection since 1924, of National Gallery, 1926–33 and since 1941 (Chairman 1931 and 1932); Member of Royal Fine Art Commission since 1926 and Deputy Chairman since 1940; Member, Executive Committee of National Art Collections Fund; Chairman Management Committee Courtauld Institute of Art, 1932–37; Chm. Warburg Library and Institute, 1933–45; Silvanus Thompson Lecturer and Medallist of Röntgen Society, 1932; admitted as Citizen and Goldsmith of London, 1924; Ex-Chairman of Trustees Haig Memorial Homes; Vice-Pres. of Star and Garter Home, Richmond; President, Royal Hospital and Home for Incurables, Putney, 1928–39; gave the Chequers Estate to the Nation, 1921. *Publications:* A Good Innings, 1868–1940; Letters that Remain (both privately printed); articles on various subjects in Edinburgh Review, Scribner's, Burlington Magazine, Apollo, etc. *Heir:* none. *Address:* Old Quarries, Avening, Glos. *T:* Nailsworth 201. *Clubs:* Athenæum, Travellers', Burlington Fine Arts; Royal Yacht Squadron (hon.), Cowes.

Died 21 July 1947 (ext).

LEE, Auriol; Independent Producer; *b* London, Sept. 1880; *d* of Dr Robert and Katharine Lee; *m* 1911 (divorced 1922); no *c. Educ:* Abroad. Actress; Stockbroker; Stage Director. *Recreations:* travelling, reading. *Address:* Savoy Hotel, Strand, WC2. *T:* Temple Bar 4343.

Died 2 July 1941.

LEE, Edward Owen, CIE 1944; MA; *b* 3 Nov. 1891; *s* of Harry Lee, ICS, and Alice Anderton, *d* of General H. S. Obbard, IA. *Educ:* Malvern; King's College, Cambridge. Porson Prize, 1913; BA 1st Class Honours, Classical, 1913; MA 1948. Entered Indian Civil Service, 1915; District Magistrate, 1922; Chairman Assam Labour Board, 1933; Controller of Emigrant Labour, 1933; Commissioner of Excise, 1936; Commissioner Chota Nagpur Division, 1939; Commissioner Bhagalpur Division, 1942; Member, Board of Revenue, Bihar, 1944–47; retired from ICS, 1947. *Recreation:* bridge. *Address:* Fairmead Court Hotel, Rondebosch, Cape Province, S Africa. *Clubs:* East India and Sports; Civil Service (Cape Town).

Died 23 Oct. 1950.

LEE, Rev. Canon Edwin Maywood O'Hara, BA, Vicar of S Katharine, Rotherhithe, SE 16, 1899–1938; Hon. Canon of Southwark, 1931–38, Canon Emeritus since 1938; *b* London, 1859; *e s* of late Benjamin Bass Browne Lee, HM Civil Servant in charge of RN Victualling Yard, Malta, and Elizabeth Maria, *d* of late William Russell Harrison, BNC, Oxford, Surgeon. *Educ:* Malta; University College, Durham. Ordained and became Curate of S John, Horsleydown, 1883; of S Katharine, Rotherhithe, 1887; Borough Councillor, Chairman of Dispensary Committee and Guardian of the Poor for Bermondsey for many years; Mayor's Chaplain,

1909, 1913; platoon commander in the 2nd Battalion South London Volunteer Regiment, 1916; Local LCC School Manager; Member of the Anglican and Eastern Churches Association. *Recreations:* reading and nature study. *Address:* 12 Hillcrest Road, Sydenham, SE26. *T:* Sydenham 5477.

Died 29 Jan. 1942.

LEE, Frank; MP (Lab) NE Division of Derbyshire, 1922–31 and since 1935; Assistant-Secretary to the Derbyshire Miners' Association; *b* 1867. *Address:* 9 Tennyson Avenue, Chesterfield. *T:* 193.

Died 21 Dec. 1941.

LEE, Lennox B.; Chairman, Calico Printers' Association, 1909–47; and other Public Limited Companies; *b* 7 Nov. 1864; *e s* of late Sir J. C. Lee; *m* 1892, Edith, *d* of Malcolm McLellan; one *s* one *d*. *Educ:* Eton. Entered Sherwood Foresters, 1884–88; travelled widely over North-West Africa, 1885–89; JP Herefordshire, 1905; High Sheriff, Herefordshire, 1915; President, Federation of British Industries, 1929; late member of the Finance and Industry Committee; member of the Selection Committee, DOT; member of the Advisory Council Board of Trade; FRGS. *Address:* How Caple Court, Herefordshire. *TA:* Howcaple. *T:* Howcaple 202. *Clubs:* Marlborough-Windham, Leander.

Died 14 Dec. 1949.

LEE, Sydney, RA 1930 (ARA 1922); RE 1915; RWS 1945 (ARWS 1942); Treasurer, 1932–40, and Trustee RA, since 1932; Chairman Smith Bequest, Southampton, 1932; Board of Trade Council of Art and Industry, 1934; artist, painter, etcher, wood engraver; *b* 1866; *m* 1893, Edith, *d* of Frederick Elgar. *Educ:* Studied Manchester School of Art and Atelier Colarossi, Paris. Exhibitor at leading London Exhibitions, Paris Salon, and International Exhibitions; European Delegate International Jury Carnegie Inst., Pittsburg, USA, 1938; gold medal awarded at Dresden International Exhibition, 1901; gold medal Milan International, 1906, and Barcelona, 1907; two pictures (Among the Dolomites and Top of the St Gothard) purchased by Chantrey Fund for National Collection, 1924 and 1942, also by Manchester Corporation (The Top of the Pass), 1924; Walker Art Gallery, Liverpool, Theatre Marcellus, 1927; The Gallery, Glasgow Corporation, Hamilton Bequest, 1929; The House with the closed shutters purchased by the Royal Academy, 1943; wood engraving, Ponte Paradiso and other prints, purchased Contemporary Art Society, also aquatint, The Mountain Fortress; RA Diploma work, The Red Tower, 1930; works at permanent collections, Corporations of Hull, Rochdale, Southampton, British Museum, South Kensington Museum; Posters for L & NER Representative exhibition of 90 engravings at Colnaghi's Gallery, 1937, etching, wood engraving, aquatint, mezzotint. *Address:* 26 Holland Park Rd, Kensington, W14. *Clubs:* Athenæum, Arts.

Died 31 Oct. 1949.

LEE, Rt Rev. William, MBE 1920; Bishop of Clifton (RC), 1932–48; *b* Michelstown, Co. Cork, 1875. *Educ:* St Colman's, Fermoy; St John's, Waterford; Oscott. Priest, 1901; Canon of Clifton, 1910; Domestic Prelate, 1926; Provost, 1928–32; Vicar General, 1929; Vicar Capitular, 1931; Chevalier of the Crown-of-Belgium. *Address:* St Ambrose, Leigh Woods, Bristol.

Died 21 Sept. 1948.

LEECH, Ernest Bosdin, MA, MD (Cantab); FRCP (Lond.); Hon. MA (Manch.); Hon. Consulting Physician, Manchester Royal Infirmary; Ex-President, Manchester Medical Society; *b* 9 April 1875; *s* of Sir Bosdin T. Leech, Timperley, Cheshire; *m* Mary, *d* of Rev. H. Walder of Walderston, Jamaica; two *d*. *Educ:* Cheltenham College; Christ's College, Cambridge; Manchester University. *Publications:* Medicine in the

Provinces in England; Picturesque Episodes of Manchester Medical History; Early Medicine and Quackery in Lancashire. *Address:* Chadlington House, Victoria Park, Manchester, 14. *T:* Rusholme 1059.

Died 19 Sept. 1950.

LEECH, John, KC 1910; MA, LLB; *b* 1857; *s* of late Charles Leech, QC; *m* Sarah Frances (*d* 1931), *d* of late Major George Hudson Greaves. *Educ:* Trinity College, Dublin. Irish Barr, 1881; Bencher, King's Inns, 1938; Senior Crown Counsel for County Longford, 1920; Bencher Inn of Court of Northern Ireland, 1925; Barr Middle Temple, 1927; Sometimes Judge of Recorder's Court of Belfast and of County Court of Antrim. *Address:* Westview, 19 Beulah Hill, Upper Norwood, SE19. *T:* Livingstone 2067.

Died 24 July 1942.

LEEDHAM, Air Cdre Hugh, CB 1942; OBE 1930; late RAF; Managing Director Ericsson Telephones Ltd since 1945; *b* 3 May 1889. *Educ:* Birmingham University. Served European War, 1914–18; Group Capt. 1938; Air Commodore, 1940. In War of 1939–45; Director of Radio Production, Ministry of Aircraft Production, 1939–43; Director of Radio Research and Development, MAP, 1943–45; retired, 1945. *Address:* Ericsson Telephones Ltd, 56 Kingsway, WC2.

Died 5 Nov. 1947.

LEEKE, Col Ralph; DL, JP; retired pay; *b* 25 Dec. 1849; *e s* of late R. M. Leeke and Lady Hester Urania Fellowes, 2nd *d* of 4th Earl of Portsmouth; *m* 1881, Hon. Mary Theresa Manners, 2nd *d* of 2nd Baron Manners. *Educ:* Harrow; Christ Church, Oxford. Entered Army, 1870; Col 1889, late Grenadier Guards. *Address:* Aston Hall, Newport, Salop. *T:* Newport, Salop 62.

Died 30 Oct. 1943.

LEEN, Very Rev. Edward; Rector since Sept. 1939, Professor of Philosophy since 1931 at the House of Studies, Kimmage Manor, Dublin; *b* 1885. *Educ:* Rockwell College, Cashel; Gregorian University, Rome. Ordained Priest, 1914; Doctorate in Theology, 1916; MA National University, Ireland, 1917; Professor of Philosophy, 1917–18; DLittNUI 1940; Secretary to Most Rev. Dr Shanahan, Vicar Apostolic, S Nigeria, 1920–21; Dean of Studies, Blackrock, 1922–25; President of Blackrock College, 1925–31. *Publications:* Progress through Mental Prayer, 1935; In the Likeness of Christ, 1936; The Holy Ghost, and His Work in Souls, 1936; The True Vine and Its Branches, 1938; Why the Cross?, 1938; The Church before Pilate, 1939; What is Education?, 1943; Pamphlet on Catholic Education and various articles in Irish Ecclesiastical Record and in Studies. *Address:* Kimmage Manor, Dublin. *T:* Dublin 95151.

Died 10 Nov. 1944.

LEEN, Rt Rev. James; Archbishop-Bishop of Port Louis, Mauritius, since 1926; *b* Abbeyfeale, Ireland, 1 Jan. 1888. *Educ:* Rockwell College, Cashel. BA National University, 1913; Gregorian University, Rome, 1916–22; Doctorate in Philosophy, 1917; Doctorate in Theology, 1921. Professor of Philosophy, Seminaire Français, Rome, 1922–23; Professor of Theology in Blackrock, 1924 and 1925; Titular Archbishop of Phasis ad personam 1933. *Address:* Port Louis, Mauritius.

Died 19 Dec. 1949.

LEEPER, Rev. Canon Arthur Lindsay, MA, Hon. CF; Vicar of Huddersfield since 1935 and Rural Dean since 1940; Canon of Wakefield; Chaplain to the King since 1939; *b* 19 May 1883; *s* of Charles and Annie Dora Leeper; *m* 1912, Ellen Gladys Melly (decd); two *c*. *Educ:* St Stephens Green School; Trinity College, Dublin. Ordained 1908 to Ballyshannon, Co. Donegal; Asst Sec. CMS, 1910–11; TCF, 1918–19; CF, TA, 1919–29;

Vicar of St Jude, Hull, 1919; Vicar of Hutton Rudby, Yorks, 1927. *Recreation:* golf. *Address:* The Vicarage, Huddersfield, Yorks. *T:* Huddersfield 3640.

Died 16 Feb. 1942.

LEES, Sir Arthur Henry James, 5th Bt *cr* 1804; *b* 18 Jan. 1863; *s* of 4th Bt and Charlotte, *d* of W. M'Taggart; *S* father, 1917; *m* 1927, Helen Agnes Marion Gibb, *d* of late Charles C. Chittick and Mrs Chittick of Belle Vue, Nevis, and *widow* of Thomas Orr Gibb; one *d*. Fellow of the Royal Empire Society. *Address:* Farrer & Co., 66 Lincoln's Inn Fields, WC2; Nevis, BWI.

Died 10 March 1949.

LEES, Charles Archibald, CBE 1919; Lt-Col, RAMC, TA (retd); MRCS Eng., LRCP Lond., 1894; *b* 1869; *s* of Archibald R. R. Lees and Katherine St Quintin; *m* Mary Juliet, *d* of Edward Rhodes Harrison; two *s* one *d*. *Educ:* St Mary's Hospital. Practised in Huntingdonshire and in London; served in Volunteer and Territorial Forces, 1901–11; European War, 1914–19 (despatches, bt promotion, CBE); commanded 2nd London General Hosp., 1917–21; Superintendent Grangethorpe Hosp. (Ministry of Pensions) and Medical Assessor, 1920–23; Member House of Lords Pension Appeal Tribunals, 1923–24; at sea, 1924–30. *Address:* 61 Forest Road, Broadwater, Worthing, Sussex. *T:* Worthing 1959.

Died 3 Sept. 1943.

LEES, Col Charles Henry Brownlow, CMG 1917; *b* 1871. Served NW Frontier of India, 1897–98 (medal with clasp); European War, 1914–18 (despatches, CMG, French Croix de Guerre). *Address:* Beechwood Corner, Albert Road, Deal, Kent.

Died 1 March 1941.

LEES, Rev. George Robinson, MA; FRGS; *b* 1860; *m* 1st, Edith Annie, *d* of George Clark, Masboro; 2nd, Alice Sharrer, *d* of Rev. Canon Kelk of Jerusalem; three *s* three *d*. *Educ:* Bede College; Durham University. Engaged in scholastic work; Head Master of LJS School, Jerusalem (6 years); travelled in Eastern Palestine and Syria; lectured on people and customs of the East in England and America; Curate of St Mark's, Tollington Park, N, 1897–99; St Mary's, Finchley, N, 1890–1900; Vicar of St Andrew, Lambeth, 1900–15; St Saviour, Brixton Hill, SW, 1915–24; Blean, 1924–34. *Publications:* The Life of Christ; Jerusalem Illustrated; Jerusalem and its People; Village Life in Palestine; Life and Adventure beyond Jordan; The Witness of the Wilderness; Bedawin Life in the Desert; article on Asia Minor, Palestine, and Syria, in Customs of the World; contributed paper to Royal Geographical Society Across Southern Bashan; various articles in magazines on Eastern Life and Customs.

Died 2 March 1944.

LEES, Jack; an official of Northumberland Miners' Association; West Rainton, Durham. MP (Lab) Belper Division of Derby, 1929–31.

Died 11 Aug. 1940.

LEES, Oswald Campbell, CSI 1912; *b* March 1857; *s* of Sir John Campbell Lees; *m* Ethel, *e d* of late J. B. Worgan, ICS; one *s* one *d*. PWD, India, 1878; Under-Secretary to Government of India, 1897–1901; transferred to Burma, 1906; Chief Engineer and Secretary to Government of Burma, 1909; retired on pension, 1912; recalled subsequently by Government of India to report on possible development of Bengal waterways, and submitted plans and estimate for Grand Trunk Canal project, 1913; served with REs, 1915–18, and with RAF, 1918–22. *Address:* 24 Argyll Road, Kensington, W8. *T:* Western 0662.

Died 11 March 1945.

LEES-SMITH, Rt Hon. Hastings Bertrand, PC 1931; MP (Labour) Keighley Division of Yorkshire, 1922–23, 1924–31 and since 1935; MA, DSc London; *b* India, 1878; 2nd *s* of late Major H. Lees Smith, RA; *m* 1915, Joyce, 2nd *d* of S. H. Holman; two *s*. *Educ:* Aldenham School. Educated for army and obtained cadetship at Royal Military Academy, Woolwich, 1895. Resigned Woolwich cadetship and went up to Queen's College, Oxford, MA; associated with Ruskin College, Oxford, from its foundation in 1899; Chairman of Executive Committee of Ruskin College, 1907–09; MP (L) Northampton, 1910–18; contested Don Valley Division of Yorkshire as Independent Radical, 1918; joined Labour Party, 1919; Postmaster-General, 1929–31; President of Board of Education, 1931; Acting Chairman of Parliamentary Labour Party since 1940. *Publications:* Studies in Indian Economics, published by Government of Bombay; India and the Tariff Problem, 1909; Second Chambers in Theory and Practice, 1923; Guide to Parliamentary Papers, 1924. *Address:* 77 Corringham Road, NW11. *T:* Speedwell 1000. *Club:* Athenæum.

Died 18 Dec. 1941.

LEETE, Frederick Alexander, CIE 1923; late India Forest Department. Joined India Forest Dept, 1891; on deputation to Canada and United States, 1918; Chief Conservator, Burma, 1920; retired, 1925. *Address:* Naini, Wrecclesham, Farnham, Surrey.

Died 11 Dec. 1941.

LE FANU, Most Rev. Henry Frewen; Archbishop of Perth since 1929 and Primate of Australia since 1935; *b* 1 April 1870; *s* of W. R. Le Fanu, Commissioner of Public Works, Ireland; *m* 1904, Margery Annette Ingle (*d* 1926), *d* of Rev. J. N. Dredge; three *s* three *d*. *Educ:* Haileybury; Keble College, Oxford, MA (2nd Class Honours School of History); DD (Lambeth); Wells College. Ordained, 1894; Curate of Poplar, 1894–99; resident Chaplain to Bishop of Rochester, 1899–1901; Chaplain, Guy's Hospital, 1902–04; Archdeacon and Canon Residentiary of St John's Cathedral, Brisbane, 1905–15; Coadjutor Bishop of Brisbane, 1915–29; sub-prelate, Order of St John of Jerusalem. *Address:* Church Office, Perth, W Australia. *Clubs:* Weld, Perth, WA.

Died 9 Sept. 1946.

LE FANU, Thomas Philip, CB 1913; Commissioner of Public Works, Ireland, 1913–26; *b* 9 Dec. 1858; *e s* of W. R. Le Fanu and Henrietta, *d* of Sir Matthew Barrington, Bart; *m* 1890, Florence (*d* 1941), *d* of Rev. James Sullivan, Rector of Askeaton; one *s* one *d*. *Educ:* Haileybury; Trinity College, Cambridge. Entered Public Record Office, Ireland, 1881; Chief Secretary's Office, 1884; Private Secretary to Rt Hon. A. Birrell, 1910–13; Vice-President, Royal Irish Academy, 1918–20, 1925–30; President Royal Society of Antiquaries of Ireland, 1933–36. *Publications:* Memoir of the Le Fanu Family, 1924; some papers in the Proceedings of the Royal Irish Academy, the Huguenot Society, the Journal of the Royal Society of Antiquaries of Ireland, etc. *Address:* Abington, Bray, Co. Wicklow. *T:* Bray 106. *Clubs:* Kildare Street, Dublin.

Died 21 Oct. 1945.

LE FLEMING, Sir (Ernest) Kaye, Kt 1937; MA, MB, BC Cantab; MD (Hon.) Dublin, 1932, Melbourne, 1935; MRCS, LRCP, FSA; Vice-President British Medical Association; *b* 1872; 5th *s* of John Le Fleming, MA, and Hariet Mary Neville, Tonbridge, Kent; *m* 1901, Florence Murton, *d* of A. T. Beeching, JP County of Kent; two *s*. *Educ:* Tonbridge School (Judde Exhibitioner); Clare College, Cambridge; St George's Hospital. Played golf for Cambridge *versus* Oxford, 1894–95; Direct Representative General Medical Council since 1929; Chairman of Council BMA, 1934–39; Gold Medallist, 1941; Chairman British Medical Association Report on Nutrition, 1935, and Report on Physical Education, 1936; Chairman Annual

Representative Meeting British Medical Association, 1931–34; Member National Advisory Committee, Physical Fitness, and Central Council Physical Recreation; Vice-President School MO Association; Hon. Sec. Dorset County, London Society of Antiquaries; Medical Officer Canford School. *Publications:* An Introduction to General Practice, 1936; numerous articles on Medico-Political Subjects in Lancet, British Medical Journal, etc. *Recreations:* golf, antiquarian research. *Address:* St Margarets, Wimborne, Dorset. *T:* Wimborne 33. *Club:* Royal Societies.

Died 16 July 1946.

LE FLEMING, Sir William Hudleston, 9th Bt *cr* 1705; *b* 1861; *s* of William Le Fleming, 2nd *s* of 6th Bt, and Mary, *e d* of Thomas Wilson of Windermere; *S* cousin, 1925; *m* 1885, Martha, *d* of John Kelland, Crwys Morchard, Devon; two *s* three *d. Heir: s* Frank Thomas [*b* 27 Dec. 1888; *m* 1921, Isabella Annie Fraser, *d* of James Craig, Taranaki, NZ; three *s*]. *Address:* Rydal Manor, Vogeltown, New Plymouth, New Zealand.

Died 31 Oct. 1945.

LE GALLIENNE, Richard; man of letters and journalist; *b* Liverpool, 20 Jan. 1866; *e s* of John Le Gallienne, engaged in business in that city; *m* 1st, 1891, Mildred Lee (*d* 1894); 2nd, 1897, Julie Norregard; 3rd, 1911, Irma Hinton Perry. *Educ:* Liverpool College. Served articles to firm of chartered accountants for seven years; abandoned business for literature; for a few months Private Secretary to Wilson Barrett; literary critic for the Star, 1891; finally settled in London. *Publications:* My Ladies' Sonnets (privately printed), 1887; Volumes in Folio, 1888; George Meredith, 1890; The Book-Bills of Narcissus, 1891; English Poems, 1892; The Religion of a Literary Man, 1893; Prose Fancies, 1st series, 1894; Robert Louis Stevenson and other Poems, 1895; Retrospective Reviews, 1896; Prose Fancies, 2nd series, 1896; The Quest of the Golden Girl, 1896; If I were God, 1897. Editor of an edition of Isaak Walton, The Compleat Angler, and of a verse translation of edition of Omar Khayyám; The Romance of Zion Chapel, 1898; Young Lives, 1899; Worshipper of the Image; Travels in England; The Beautiful Lie of Rome; The Life Romantic, 1900; Sleeping Beauty, 1900; An Old Country House, 1902; Painted Shadows, 1907; Little Dinners with the Sphinx, 1909; Vanishing Roads and other Essays, 1915; Pieces of Eight, 1918; The Romantic '90's, 1926; The Magic Seas, 1930; From a Paris Garret, 1943. *Recreations:* walking and swimming.

Died 15 Sept. 1947.

LEGGE, Lt-Gen. James Gordon, CB 1917; CMG 1912; MA, LLD, Barrister-at-law; *b* 15 Aug. 1863; *s* of late J. H. Legge of Gosford, NSW; *m* Annie Frances, *d* of late G. Ferguson of Sydney, NSW; two *s. Educ:* Cranleigh School, Surrey; Sydney Univ. Lieut 1st Infantry Regt (Militia), NSW, 1887; Capt., Permanent Staff, NSW, 1894; Major, CMF, 1902; Lt-Col, 1909; Col 1914; Maj.-Gen. 1915; DAAG, NSW, 1904–08; Military Secretary, HQ, 1908–09; QMG, Australia, 1909–12; ADC to Governor-General, 1904–09; served S Africa, 1899–1902; Representative of Australia on Imperial General Staff, War Office, 1912–14; commanded 1st, and afterwards 2nd, Australian Division in Egypt, Gallipoli, and France, 1915–16; Chief of the General Staff, Australia, 1914–20; Commandant Royal Military College, 1920–22; retired, 1922; holds Order of Danilo (Montenegro), 2nd Class, 1917; Legion of Honour. *Publications:* Australian Military Law; Select Cases from Supreme Court of NSW, 1824–1862; Manœuvre Orders; Lectures on Universal Training in Australia. *Address:* Weetangera, ACT, Australia.

Died 18 Sept. 1947.

LEGGE, Brig.-Gen. William Kaye, CMG 1918; DSO 1917; retired; *b* Woodsome Hall, nr Huddersfield, 13 June 1869; *s* of Hon. Charles G. Legge, HM Inspector of Constabulary; *m* Constance Adeline, *d* of J. D. Palmer; two *s. Educ:* Bedford School. Joined Essex Regiment, 1889; Adjt 2nd Essex Regt, 1895–99; served S African War, 1899–1902 (despatches twice); PSC, 1905; on staff—Dublin 1906–10; S Africa, 1912–13; Gibraltar, 1914; Queenstown (Ireland), 1914; European War since Jan. 1915; DAA and QMG, AA and QMG, DA and QMG (despatches six times; Bt of Lt-Col; DSO, CMG, Bt of Col); promoted to the command of 2nd Essex Regt, Feb. 1916; DA and QMG 1916–19, temporary rank of Brigadier-General; Col 1920; AA and QMG 2nd Division, 1920–24; commanded the 163rd (Norfolk and Suffolk) Infantry Brigade TA, 1924–26; retired pay, 1926. *Recreations:* golf, fishing, shooting. *Address:* c/o Lloyds Bank, 6 Pall Mall, SW.

Died 29 March 1946.

LEGGETT, Major Sir Edward Humphrey Manisty, Kt 1920; DSO 1900; late RE; *b* 7 Dec. 1871; *s* of late Major G. E. Leggett, 77th Regiment; *m* 1907, Ada, *d* of John Dyson of Merriott, Crewkerne. *Educ:* Clifton College; RMA, Woolwich (Pollock gold medallist, 1900), and on staff of London and NW Railway. Was Board of Trade (British) Delegate to International Railway Congress, 1895. Served South African War on Headquarters Staff, 1899–1902, (Queen's SA medal with 4 clasps and King's SA medal with 2 clasps, despatches, DSO, and brevet of Major); Director of Burgher Camps and Settlements, Transvaal, 1902–05; lent to Colonial Office for special duty in East Africa and Uganda, 1907–10; Member of Legislative Council of British East Africa, 1908–09; attached to Belgian War Office, 1914–18 (Order of the Crown of Belgium); Chairman East African Section, London Chamber of Commerce, 1919–30; A Vice-President, Royal Society of Arts, and Chairman, Dominions and Colonies Committee of the Society, 1925–31. *Address:* 11 Elvaston Place, Queen's Gate, SW7. *Club:* Reform.

Died 17 May 1947.

LEGGETT, Henry Aufrere, CB 1928; CBE 1920 (OBE 1918); *b* 3 June 1874; *s* of late Major G. E. Leggett, Middx. Regt, and *d* of late Sir Henry Manistry, Judge of the High Court; *m* 1915, Catherine Marjorie, *d* of late Sir Cecil Coward; one *s* one *d. Educ:* Clifton; University College, Oxford. Honours Classical Moderations and History Final Schools. Entered Local Govt Board, 1897; Assistant Private Secretary to Rt Hon. John Burns, MP, President Local Govt Board, and Private Secretary to Rt Hon. Walter Runciman and Rt Hon. Dr Macnamara; Assistant Director of Establishments Ministry of Health, 1919–24; Director of Establishments, Ministry of Health, 1924–37 and Chief General Inspector, 1934–37; Commander Belgian Order of the Crown, 1919. *Address:* Pinecote, Marsham Way, Gerrards Cross, Bucks. *T:* Gerrards Cross 2517. *Club:* Reform.

Died 4 Sept. 1950.

LEGGETT, Vice-Adm. Oliver Elles, CB 1919; RN; JP Portsmouth; *b* 1876; *s* of late Captain R. A. Leggett, 69th Regiment; *m* 1st, 1900, Maud (*d* 1931), *d* of F. Andrew, Manchester; no *c*; 2nd, 1934, Ethel, *widow* of Commander J. F. H. Cole, RN. Served European War, 1914–19 (despatches, CB; Legion of Honour; 2nd class Order of St Anne of Russia); Flag-Capt. to Admiral of the Fleet Viscount Jellicoe's Naval Mission to Overseas Dominions, 1919; a Naval ADC to the King, 1926; Rear-Adm. 1926; retired list, 1926; Vice-Adm., retired, 1931; served at Admiralty, 1941–45. *Address:* Apple Tree Farm, Prinsted, near Emsworth, Hants. *T:* Emsworth 501. *Club:* United Service.

Died 18 March 1946.

LEGH, Edmund Willoughby, CIE 1924; Secretary CMS and CEZMS, Madras; *b* 1874; *m* 1914, Baroness Elisabeth von Engelhardt. *Educ:* Malvern; University College, Oxford. Entered ICS, 1896; Second Secretary to Government of Madras, 1925; retired, 1926. *Address:* c/o National Bank of India, 26 Bishopsgate, EC2.

Died 24 July 1943.

LE GRICE, Charles Henry, CBE 1939; *b* 1870; *o s* of C. D. N. Le Grice, Trereife; *m* 1907, Dorothy I., *yr d* of Colonel Downes, RA, Donnington, Newbury; one *s*. *Educ:* Royal Agricultural College, Cirencester (MRAC). Fellow of Land Agents Society. Late Agent to late P. Wroughton, MP, and A. K. Loyd, MP; JP Berkshire and Cornwall; High Sheriff for Cornwall, 1937–38; Alderman of Cornwall County Council; President Royal Geological Society of Cornwall; President St Ives and Penzance Conservative Association. *Publications:* short articles on Farming and Estate Management. *Recreation:* shooting. *Address:* Trereife, Penzance. *T:* Penzance 178. *Clubs:* Carlton; Cornish.

Died 8 Jan. 1942.

LEHAR, Franz; composer; *b* Komarom, Hungary, 30 April 1870. *Educ:* Academy of Music, Prague. *Works:* The Merry Widow; The Count of Luxembourg; Gipsy Love; Eva; Die Ideale Gattin; Endlich Allein; Frasquita; Frederica; The Land of Smiles; Giuditta; Paganini; Blaue Mazur; Gottergatte; Schöne ist die Welt, Zarewitsch, Libellentanze, Cloclo (Lolotte), Wiener Frauen, Wo die Lerche Singt, Tatjana, Die Tangokönigin, Der Sterngucker, Peter und Paul im Schlaraffenland, Mitislaw der Moderne, Die Gelbe Jacke, Frühling. *Address:* Hotel Baur au Lac, Zürich, Switzerland.

Died 24 Oct. 1948.

LEICESTER, 3rd Earl of, *cr* 1837; **Thomas William Coke;** Viscount Coke, 1837, GCVO 1908; KCVO 1906; CMG 1902; CVO 1905; MVO 1901; *b* 20 July 1848; *s* of 2nd Earl and *e d* of Samuel Charles Whitbread, Cardington, Bedfordshire; *S* father, 1909; *m* 1879, Hon. Alice White, DBE (*d* 1936), *d* of 2nd Lord Annaly; two *s* two *d*. *Educ:* Harrow. Late Col Scots Guards, late Lt-Col Norfolk Artillery Militia; served in Egyptian Campaign, 1882; Suakim Expedition, 1885; retired, 1894; served Boer War, 1901–02; Lord-Lieut Norfolk, 1906–29. Owns about 40,000 acres. *Heir: s* Viscount Coke. *Address:* Holkham Hall, Wells, Norfolk. *Clubs:* Guards', Turf, Marlborough.

Died 19 Nov. 1941.

LEICESTER, 4th Earl of, *cr* 1837; **Thomas William Coke;** Viscount Coke, 1837; Major, late Scots Guards; Lord Lieutenant of Norfolk since 1944; *b* 9 July 1880; *e s* of 3rd Earl and Hon. Alice White, DBE (*d* 1936), *d* of 2nd Lord Annaly; *S* father, 1941; *m* 1905, Marion Gertrude, *d* of late Col Hon. W. R. Trefusis; one *s* two *d*. *Educ:* Eton. Reserve; served in Boer War and European War, 1914–19. *Heir: s* Viscount Coke, MVO. *Address:* Holkham Hall, Wells, Norfolk.

Died 21 Aug. 1949.

LEICESTER, Lt-Col John Cyril Holdich, CIE 1927; Indian Medical Service (retired); late Hon. Surgeon to Viceroy of India; late Acting Surgeon-General, Bengal, and Professor of Obstetrics and Gynecology, Medical College, Calcutta, and Surgeon to the Eden Hospital for Women, Calcutta; *b* 1872; *er s* of late Rev. John Augustus Leicester; *m* 1907, Queenie, *o d* of late Lt-Col E. Dobson, IMS; no *c*. *Educ:* Dulwich College; University; College and Hospital, London. MD, BS, BSc, FRCP, FRCS. Late Examiner in Midwifery and Gynecology and Fellow of Calcutta University; Fellow of the Royal Society of Medicine; qualified 1896; passed first into the Indian Medical Service, 1898; retired, 1927; served China, 1900 (medal); European War, 1914–18 (despatches, Bt Lt-Col, 1914–15 Star, Victory and Allied medals); Afghan War, 1919 (medal). *Publications:* contributions in Midwifery and Gynecology to The

Lancet, Journal of Obstetrics, Surgery Gynecology and Obstetrics, and other journals. *Recreations:* photography, motoring, scouting, etc. *Address:* Clare Cottage, Cold Ash, Newbury, Berks. *TA:* Cold Ash. *T:* Thatcham 3281. *Club:* Army and Navy.

Died 19 May 1949.

LEICESTER, Sir Peter Fleming Frederic, 8th Bt *cr* 1671; Capt. 51st King's Own Light Infantry (retired); *b* 25 Jan. 1863; *e s* of Rev. Frederic Leicester (*g s* of 4th Bt) and 2nd wife, Amelia, *d* of Lieut-Col John Campbell; *S* cousin, John, 3rd Baron (ext) de Tabley, 1895; *m* 1st, 1904, Kate Patten (*d* 1928), *e d* of late Edward M. Warden, USA; 2nd, 1930, Marthe, *er d* of Louis de Miéville de Rossens, Switzerland. *Heir: cousin* Charles Byrne Warren [*b* 30 March 1896. Radley. Served European War, 1914–18].

Died 12 Jan. 1945.

LEIGH, Col Oswald Mosley, JP, TD; late M. F. H. Fitzwilliam and Island, Wexford; *b* 30 Aug. 1864; *e s* of Oswald Peter Leigh (*d* 1876) and Frances, *o d* of Rev. George Ayton Whitaker, MA, Knoddishall, Suffolk; *m* 1889, Florence Louisa (*d* 1915), 2nd *d* of J. Edward Reiss, of Jodrell Hall, Cheshire; one *s* one *d*. *Educ:* Eton. Hon. Lt-Col Earl of Chester's Imperial Yeomanry; served South African War; Hon. Capt. Regular Army; served European War from 1914 in West Kent Yeo.; and then, 1915, commanding RE Kent Mounted Rifles; served on 19 Corps' Staff, 1917–June 1919. *Address:* Belmont Hall, Northwich, Cheshire. *T:* Comberbach 35. *Club:* Bachelors'.

Died 26 Feb. 1949.

LEIGH, His Honour Thomas Bowes; *b* 1867; *s* of William Leigh, JP; *m* 1897, Martha, *d* of H. Podeus; three *s* two *d*. *Educ:* Manchester Grammar School; Victoria University of Manchester; Dalton Mathematical Exhibitioner, 1883; BSc 1885. Called to the Bar (Middle Temple), 1901; Northern Circuit; Recorder of Burnley, 1921–25; Judge of County Courts on Circuit No. 8 (Manchester, etc.), 1925–42; First President Manchester and District Medico Legal Society, 1937–41; a Vice-President British and Foreign Bible Society, 1938; Chairman, Inland Fish Distribution Committee, Manchester, 1942; Chm., Manchester Tribunal Furnished Houses (Rent Control) Act, 1946. JP Lancashire; Hon. LLD Manchester. *Address:* Wilmslow, Cheshire.

Died 29 July 1947.

LEIGH-HUNT, Gerard, RCA; *b* London, 1873; 2nd *s* of late Walter Leigh-Hunt, 7 Stanhope Place, W, and *g g s* of Leigh Hunt; *m* 1907, Thyra, *d* of late Albert Steven Hatchett-Jones, Solicitor; one *s* one *d*. *Educ:* St John's Wood Art Schools; Royal Academy Schools. Articled to a Civil Engineer, with whom travelled in Mexico and United States; later took up art, entering RA schools when 19; gained Silver Medal drawing of a head from the life; served in Yeomanry South African War, (Queen's medal, three clasps); on return resumed painting portraits, one-figure subjects and landscape; has exhibited at Royal Academy, Royal Cambrian Academy, the Walker Art Gallery, Liverpool, Royal West of England, The Paris Salon, Royal Society of Artists, Birmingham; also at Hull, Doncaster, etc.; joined up Royal Naval Volunteer Reserve, 1915 (British War Medal); later Inns of Court OTC, receiving commission. *Recreations:* billiards, travel, motoring. *Address:* Verulam, Canford Cliffs, Dorset. *T:* Canford Cliffs 454.

Died 7 Jan. 1945.

LEIGH-MALLORY, Rev. Herbert Leigh, MA; Hon. Canon of Chester, Canon Emeritus since 1940; *b* the Manor House, Mobberley, Cheshire, 26 July 1856; *s* of Rev. George Mallory, MA, of the Manor House, Mobberley, Rector of Mobberley, and 2nd wife, Henrietta, *d* of Trafford Trafford of Oughtrington Park, Cheshire; *m* 1882, Annie Beridge, *d* of Rev. John Jebb,

MA, of Walton Lodge, Chesterfield, and Rector of Brampton; two s two d. *Educ:* King William's College, Isle of Man; Trinity College, Cambridge. Curate of St Andrew the Less, Cambridge; Curate-in-Charge of the Abbey Church, Cambridge; Curate of Great Haseley, Oxon; Rector of Mobberley, 1885–1904; Vicar of St John the Evangelist, Birkenhead, 1904–27; Rector of Dodleston, Cheshire, 1927–40; took name of Leigh-Mallory by Royal assent, 1914. *Address:* 3 Abbots Hayes, Chester.

Died 13 Aug. 1943.

LEIGH-MALLORY, Air Chief Marshal Sir Trafford Leigh, KCB 1943; CB 1940; DSO 1919; RAF; Allied Air C-in-C South-East Asia since 1944; *b* 1892; *yr s* of late Rev. H. L. Leigh-Mallory; *m* 1915, Doris Jean, 2nd *d* of late Edmund Stratton Sawyer; one *s* one *d*. *Educ:* Haileybury; Magdalene College, Cambridge, LLB. Served European War, 1914–19 (despatches, DSO); Comdt, School of Army Co-operation, 1927–30; Instructor at the Staff College, Camberley, 1930–31; Deputy Director of Staff Duties at the Air Ministry, 1931–34; at Imperial Defence College, 1934; commanded No. 2 Flying Training School, Digby, Lincoln, 1935; Senior Air Staff Officer, Iraq, 1936–37; AOC No. 12 Fighter Group, 1937–40; AOC No. 11 Fighter Group, 1940–42; Air Officer Commanding-in-Chief, Fighter Command, 1942; Air C-in-C Allied Expeditionary Air Force, 1943–44. *Club:* United Service.

Died 14 Nov. 1944.

LEIGH-WOOD, Lt-Col Sir James, KBE 1919; CB 1918; CMG 1902; a Governor of Christ's Hospital; Vice-President Royal Empire Society; Chairman British Empire Games Federation; Vice-Pres. Boy Scouts Association; Vice-President, Gordon Boys School; Governor, St Bartholomew's Hospital; Knight of Grace of Order of St John of Jerusalem; one of HM Lieutenants for the City of London; a liveryman of the Goldsmiths' Company; South African War (despatches twice, Queen's medal, CMG); European War, General Staff, War Office, 1916–19 (despatches, KBE, CB, Commander of Order of Leopold II). *Address:* 32 Upper Brook Street, W1. *Clubs:* Brooks, Oriental, City of London.

Died 21 March 1949.

LEIGHTON, Captain John Albert, CBE 1919; DSO 1918; late RNR; *b* 1881. Served European War, 1914–18 (despatches, DSO, Order of Crown of Belgium). *Address:* 456 Upper Richmond Road, Putney, SW15. *T:* Prospect 3179.

Died 22 Oct. 1945.

LEIGHTON, Marie Connor; novelist; *b* Clifton; *d* of James Nenon Connor, Capt. 87th Foot; *m* Robert Leighton (*d* 1934); one *s* one *d*. *Educ:* mainly in France. *Publications:* A Morganatic Marriage; Husband and Wife; The Heart's Awakening; The Harvest of Sin, Convict 99, Michael Dred, Detective, In God's Good Time, A Napoleon of the Press, Hush Money, 1901; Vengeance is Mine, 1902; Was She Worth It? 1902; The Amazing Verdict, 1904; An Eye for an Eye; Sealed Lips; Her Ladyship's Silence, 1907; Money, 1909; Joan Mar, Detective; Convict 413 L, 1910; Justice; Greed; Builders of Ships, Her Convict Husband, 1911; The Triangle, 1911; The Missing Miss Randolph, 1912; Black Silence, 1913; Under the Broad Arrow, 1914; The Fires of Love, 1915; The Man who Knew All; Human Nature; The Story of a Great Sin; The Mystery of the Three Fingers; Dark Peril; Boy of My Heart (published anonymously), 1916; The Baked Bread (anonymously), 1917; The Shame of Silence, 1917; The Letters of an Expectant Grandmother (anonymously), 1918; The Stolen Honeymoon, 1920; Lady Highmoor's Secret; The Crooked Cat; The Mystery of the Torry Diamonds; The

Silence of Dr Duveen. *Recreation:* indefinite. *Address:* Berryfield, Princess Risborough, Bucks. *Club:* The After Dinner.

Died 28 Jan. 1941.

LEISK, James Rankine, CMG 1914; Member of South African Board of Barclays Bank (Dominion, Colonial and Overseas); *b* 25 May 1876; *s* of late David Drever Leisk, Glasgow; widower; one *d*. *Educ:* Glasgow Academy. Secretary to Treasury, Transvaal, 1903–09; Secretary for Finance, Union of South Africa, 1910–17; South African Director, Central Mining and Investment Corpn, Ltd, 1919–21; Chairman and Managing Director of National Bank of South Africa, Limited, 1922–25; served South African War, Highland Light Infantry; European War, South African Infantry (Croix de Guerre, despatches). *Address:* 283 Celliers Street, Pretoria, South Africa. *Clubs:* Pretoria (Pretoria); Rand (Johannesburg).

Died 2 Aug. 1948.

LEITCH, Sir Walter, Kt 1933; CBE 1918; Director G. J. Coles & Co. Ltd, Victoria Palace, Ltd, Eagle Star Insurance Co. Ltd, Swallow & Ariell, Ltd, Robertson & Mullens, Ltd; *b* 1867; *s* of George Leitch, Roxburghshire; *m* Dr Bertha Main, MB, BCh (Melbourne); no *c*. *Educ:* Morebattle Public School. A Commissioner of the State Savings Bank of Victoria, 1935–39; was a Director of Baker Perkins, Ltd (engineers), London, Peterbro', and Baker Perkins Inc., New York; Director of Munitions for Commonwealth of Australia, 1915–19; Member of Commonwealth Tariff Boards, 1922–29; Agent-General for Victoria, Australia, 1929–33; President Melbourne Dental Hospital and Victoria Baby Health Centre Association, 1933–45; resided in USA three years, and has travelled extensively in North, Central, and South America and South Africa. *Recreations:* golf, motoring. *Address:* 4 Bank Place, Melbourne, C1, Victoria, Australia. *TA:* Watleitch, Melbourne. *Clubs:* Australian, Athenæum, Royal Melbourne Golf, Royal Automobile of Victoria, Commercial Travellers' of Victoria, Melbourne.

Died 9 July 1945.

LEITH, Captain George Piercy, CBE 1919; RN, retired; *b* 1877; *s* of Frederick Leith, Walmer Court, Kent; *m* 1917, Ethel May, *d* of F. A. Hooper, Dunedin, NZ. Served European War, 1914–19 (despatches, CBE).

Died 31 Aug. 1945.

LEITH, Gordon, CB 1917; CBE 1919; *b* 10 March 1879; *y s* of late Walter Leith of the Manor House, Ashby-de-la-Zouch, Leicestershire; *m* 1923, Gladys Bellville, *d* of late Arthur Chester-Master and *g d* of Thomas William Chester-Master of the Abbey, Cirencester, and of Knole Park, Almondsbury, Glos. *Educ:* Harrow; Trinity College, Cambridge. Entered the banking firm of Speyer Brothers, 1900; a partner, 1911–19, when retired; senior partner of Gordon Leith & Co., Bankers, 1923–27; London Partner of Kuhn Loeb & Co., Bankers, New York, and Chairman and Managing Director of European Merchant Banking Company, Limited, 1927–30; now carrying on business as banker (Gordon Leith and Co.), at 2 Crosby Square, EC3; Director of various Companies; rejoined Northumberland Yeomanry as 2nd Lieut on outbreak of war; Captain, 1914; Major, 1916; Lt-Col 1917; Col 1918; called to War Office, QMG's Department, July 1915; Chairman of the Board of Management, Navy and Army Canteen Board, 1916–17; Chairman South Paddington Conservative and Empire Association. *Address:* 14a Manchester Square, W1; The Grove, Seal, Sevenoaks. *T:* Seal 49; Seawall Cottage, The Parade, Sandgate, Kent. *T:* Sandgate 78502. *Clubs:* Marlborough, White's, Carlton.

Died 2 April 1941.

LELAND, Col Francis William George, CBE 1919; DSO 1917; late RASC; *b* 20 Aug. 1877; 2nd *s* of late John Leland, Beltichburne, Drogheda; *m* 1st, Ellen Adelaide (*d* 1941), *y d* of Thomas Payne James; one *s*; 2nd, 1942, Ella Houston, 2nd *d* of Rev. John M'Ilrath, Ulsterville Avenue, Belfast, N Ireland. *Educ:* Drogheda Grammar School; King's School, Warwick; Neuenheim College, Heidelberg; Trinity College, Dublin, BA. Served South African War, 1901–02 (Queen's medal and four clasps); European War, 1914–19 (CBE, DSO, despatches, Bt Lt-Col). Assistant Director of Supplies and Transport, Eastern Command, 1928–31; retired pay, 1931; OC RASC Portsmouth and later CRASC Hampshire Division, 1939–41. *Publication:* With the MT in Mesopotamia. *Recreations:* rowing, tennis, golf, hunting, etc. *Address:* 158 Donaghadee Road, Bangor, Co. Down, N Ireland.

Died 22 Sept. 1943.

LELEUX, Sydney Wallis; *b* 1862; *s* of Alexander L. Leleux, Brixton Hill, London (*d* 1914); *m* 1st, Margaret Maude (*d* 1911), *d* of late Sir Thomas Skinner, 1st Bt; one *d*; 2nd, 1912, Doris Ashley Eileen, MR1, RMS (exhibited at the Royal Academy Exhibitions of 1929–32 inclusive, and 1936; Paris Salon in 1932–34; she died 1941); *d* of late F. W. Goodman; one *s*. *Educ:* private schools; Albert College, Framlingham. In 1878 joined the staff of Thomas Skinner, and association continued to the end of 1915, for several years as partner. *Address:* c/o Midland Bank, Ltd, Threadneedle Street, EC2.

Died 12 Sept. 1941.

LEMAIRE, Ernest Joseph, CMG 1934; Clerk of the Privy Council for Canada, 1923–39, retired 1 Jan. 1940; *b* 22 Oct. 1874; *s* of Theodore Lemaire and Marie Berthiaume; *m* 1895, Clara, *e d* of Nazaire Têtu, Ottawa; one *s*. *Educ:* St Charles College, Sherbrooke, Quebec. Entered Privy Council Office, Canada, 1894; Private Secretary to Rt Hon. Sir Wilfrid Laurier, Prime Minister, 1904–12; Post Office Department 1912–23; Catholic. *Address:* Montreal and Hudson Heights, Province of Quebec, Canada. *Clubs:* Canadian, Montreal; Univ., Ottawa.

Died 6 Oct. 1945.

LE MARCHANT, Adm. Evelyn Robert, DSO 1918; *m* 1905, Edith Anne, *yr d* of Arthur Crocker; one *s* one *d*. Served at the Messina Earthquake, 1909 (Italian Order—St Maurice and St Lazarus); European War (DSO); retired list. *Address:* Forest Edge, Woodgreen, Fordingbridge, Hants. *Club:* Army and Navy.

Died 12 Feb. 1949.

LE MESURIER, Wing-Comdr Eric Clive, DSO 1941; DFC; RAF; *b* 24 May 1915; *s* of Major F. H. S. Le Mesurier (originally an Alderney family). *Educ:* Weymouth College. Left school at age of 17 to study Equitation; obtained Institute of the Horse Instructors Certificate in 1934 and taught in England and in the Channel Islands; spent one year in racing stables in 1935 and joined RAF on a short service commission in the GD Branch in 1936; served at home before the war and went out to France with BEF at end of Sept. 1939 (despatches, DFC, DSO). *Recreations:* hunting, tennis, swimming, cross-country running. *Address:* The Bungalow, Melcombe Avenue, Weymouth, Dorset. *T:* Weymouth 1309.

Died 23 Dec. 1943.

LEMIEUX, Hon. Dr Louis Joseph, MD; *b* Montreal, Canada, 11 April 1870; 5th *s* of H. A. Lemieux and Marie Anne Bisaillon; *m* 1st, 1893, Alice Henriette (*d* 1930), *d* of Senator L. O. David, Historian of Canada; one *d*; 2nd, 1932, Suzanne, *o d* of Dr Fernand de Munter, Brussels. *Educ:* St Mary's College, Montreal. Doctor of Medicine, Laval University, Montreal; studied medicine in Paris, 1900. Physician to Notre Dame Hospital, Montreal; Professor History of Medicine, Laval University; Member of Quebec Legislative Assembly for Gaspé County, 1903–10; Sheriff of Montreal, 1910–25; while occupying that position was Organiser and Administrator of the Archives Department for the district of Montreal, the Juvenile Court of Montreal, the Medico-Legal Department of the Province of Quebec, also the Quebec Board of Censors, of which he was President; Medical Adviser for the Canadian Pacific Railway in Montreal and also the Canadian Government Intercolonial Railway; President Europa Biological Corporation; delegated by the Canadian Government to supervise the Election Law in France in respect to the voting of the Canadian Troops during the election of 1917; Agent General for the Province of Quebec in London, 1925–36; Officier d'Académie, 1911; Officier d'Instruction Publique, 1912; proprietor and publisher monthly journal Quebec (London), 1925–37; Roman Catholic. *Publication:* Biographies of The Governors-General of Canada, 1931. *Recreations:* reading and golf. *Clubs:* Canada, Overseas League, Junior Carlton, Royal Automobile.

Deceased.

LEMONIUS, Lt-Col Gerard Maclean, CBE 1919; *b* Lancashire, of British parents; *m* Gertrude Jane, *d* of David William Jenkins, JP, Caerleon, Mon; two *s*. *Educ:* Rugby School. *Address:* c/o Martins Bank, Ltd, 68 Lombard Street, EC3.

Died 3 June 1950.

LENFESTEY, Giffard Hocart, RBA; landscape painter; *b* Faversham, 6 Sept. 1872; *e s* of late W. Giffard Lenfestey, chemist; *m* Lilian (*d* 1916), *d* of late J. B. Manning. *Educ:* Royal College of Art; studied in Paris under Raphael Collin, and in Florence. Member of the Council of the Royal Society of British Artists, and exhibits principally at these galleries, the RA, and the principal provincial exhibitions.

Died 22 Dec. 1943.

LENFESTEY, Col Leopold d'Estreville, CIE 1927; Indian Army (retd); *b* 1875; *m* 1910, Kathleen, *d* of Henry Frederick Meredith; two *s* one *d*. *Educ:* Crediton; London University. Royal Artillery, 1900–26; Asst Ordnance Consulting Officer for India, 1914–15; Supt rifle factory, India, 1920–26; Director of Disposals, India, 1926–30; late Col Indian Army Ordnance Corps, retired 1932; Director of Contracts, Army Headquarters, India, 1930–34. *Address:* Brynhir, Effingham, Surrey. *T:* Bookham 358.

Died 10 July 1948.

LENNOX; *see* Gordon-Lennox.

LENTON, Mrs Babington; *see* Pope, Jessie.

LENY, Brevet Lt-Col R. L. Macalpine-, DSO 1918; farmer, Kenya Colony; *b* 11 Feb. 1870; *e s* of late W. Macalpine-Leny, of Dalswinton, Dumfriesshire; *m* Nellie Violet (*d* 1935), 2nd *d* of late Major-General A. H. Murray, RA; one *s* one *d*. *Educ:* Eton; Royal Military College, Sandhurst. Army; served 16th Lancers in Boer War, and on staff in the Great War. *Recreation:* played polo when a Cornet for 16th Lancers and for his club in Kenya Colony. *Address:* Nanyuki, Kenya Colony. *Club:* Naval and Military.

Died 11 Feb. 1941.

LEON, Sir George Edward, 2nd Bt *cr* 1911; JP; *b* 7 May 1875; *s* of 1st Bt and Esther (*d* 1875), 2nd *d* of late Edward Henry Beddington; *S* father, 1926; *m* 1st, 1899, Mildred Ethel, *d* of late L. J. Jennings, MP; one *s* one *d*; 2nd, 1928, Mrs Dorothy Gordon-Lennox. *Educ:* Eton. Barrister, Lincoln's Inn, 1898. *Heir: s* Ronald George [*b* 22 Oct. 1902; *m* 1st, 1924, Rosemary Armstrong; one *d*; 2nd, 1932, Dorothy Katharine, *d* of late Sir Guy Standing, KBE; two *s*]. *Address:* Warfield House, Bracknell, Berks. *T:* Winkfield Row 14.

Died 14 May 1947.

LEONARD, George Hare, MA Cantab; MA, Bristol; Professor Emeritus in the University of Bristol; *b* 1863; 3rd *s* of George Hare Leonard, JP; *m* Mary, *d* of Robert Hall Warren, FSA. *Educ:* Mill Hill School; Clare College, Cambridge. Lecturer for the University Extension Lecture Syndicate, Cambridge, 1884–91; Warden of the Broad Plain House Settlement, Bristol, 1891–1900; Lecturer at University College, Bristol, in History and Literature, 1901; Professor of History, 1905. *Publications:* various papers on the War and historical, social, and religious subjects. *Recreation:* miniature gardening. *Address:* 1 Prince's Buildings, Clifton, Bristol. *T:* Bristol 35885.

Died 31 Jan. 1941.

LEONI, Franco; composer; *b* Milan, 24 Oct. 1864; *o s* of Alberto Leoni; *m* 1898, Evelyn Parker; one *d. Educ:* Royal Conservatoire of Music, Milan, under Ponchielli (Diploma d'onore). First opera produced in Italy at the age of 21. *Publications:* Ib and Little Christine; Tzigane; Francesca da Rimini; Oracolo; Rip Van Winkle; Mazzemarello; Sun-girl; Countess Cathleen; The Land of Heart's Desire; Baruffe Chiozzotte; Golgotha; cantatas, chamber music, and songs. *Recreations:* bicycling, riding, rowing. *Address:* 16 Arkwright Mansions, NW3. *T:* Hampstead 1589.

Died 8 Feb. 1949.

LE PELLEY, Lt-Col Edward Carey, DSO 1919; late RA; *b* 1870; *s* of Colonel Ernest le Pelley and Frances Carey; *m* Hilda, 3rd *d* of Colonel T. C. McKenzie; one *d. Educ:* Elizabeth College, Guernsey; RMA Woolwich. Served European War, 1914–19 (despatches, DSO). *Address:* Wyncourt, Barnhorn Road, Bexhill, Sussex.

Died 24 Nov. 1942.

LE POER TRENCH, Lt-Col Frederick Amelius, CB 1900; CBE 1919; *b* 6 July 1857; *y s* of late Rev. F. W. Le Poer Trench; *m* 1st, 1883, Mary Gertrude (*d* 1928), *d* of C. W. Roberts of Radstock; 2nd, 1929, Frances Lee (*d* 1937), *d* of late T. J. Bryant, Brighton. Retired; late officer commanding ASC Gibraltar; entered army, 1876; Colonel, 1903; served South Africa, 1899–1902 (despatches, Queen's medal 4 clasps, King's medal 2 clasps, CB); retired, 1905. *Address:* 12 Pembroke Vale, Clifton, Bristol.

Died 4 Jan. 1942.

LE QUESNE, Ferdinand Simeon, VC; Lt-Col Royal Army Medical Corps (retired); *b* Jersey, 25 Dec. 1863; 3rd *s* of late Lieut-Col Giffard N. Le Quesne, Royal Jersey Artillery, and late Augusta W., *d* of Rear-Admiral Charles Simeon; unmarried. *Educ:* In Channel Islands; King's Coll. Hosp., London. Major Royal Army Medical Corps, 1898; Burma Expedition, 1889; Operations against the Chins (severely wounded, medal with clasp, VC); Chin-Lushai field force, 1890 (clasp); Wunthoo field force, 1891 (clasp); South African war (Queen's medal, Cape Colony, 1901, 1902, clasps); Lieut-Col 1906. *Address:* c/o Glyn, Mills & Co., Whitehall, SW1.

Died 14 April 1950.

LE ROSSIGNOL, Walter Aubin; lately Senior Puisne Judge, High Court, Lahore; *s* of late J. M. Le Rossignol of St Heliers, Jersey. *Educ:* Victoria College, Jersey; Exeter College, Oxford. Entered ICS 1891; retired, 1926. *Recreation:* golf. *Address:* c/o Grindlay & Co., Ltd, 54 Parliament St, SW1.

Died 11 Aug. 1945.

LESLIE, Henrietta, (Mrs Harrie Schütze); author; *o c* of Arthur L. Raphael, 42 Portland Place, W1; *m* 1913, Dr H. Schütze, MD; no *c. Publications:* The Straight Road; The Roundabout; Parentage; Where Runs the River?; A Mouse with Wings; Conflict; Belsavage; Other People's Property; Dedication; Hirelle; The Road to Damascus; Who are You?; After Eight O'clock; Mrs Fischer's War; Naomi's Child; Mother of Five;

Daughters Defiant; Martin, Come Back!; And Both he Loved; No Spring Till Now; Good Neighbours; Mistress of Merle; Mother of Pearl; Can this be I?: Emily in Arlington Street; Martha Plover; Young Sam, etc. *Plays:* The Palace of Cards; The Loving Heart (with John Dymock); Mrs Fischer's War (with Joan Temple); Coffee for Two; When the Bough Breaks (with Laurier Lister); The Tree (with Laurier Lister). *Travel:* Where East is West, Life in Bulgaria; Harlequin Set. *Autobiography:* More Ha'pence than Kicks. *Recreation:* travelling. *Address:* Glebe House, Glebe Place, Chelsea, SW3. *T:* Flaxman 6303.

Died 19 July 1946.

LESLIE, Rt Hon. James Graham; PC 1942; HM Lieut and Custos Rotulorum County Antrim, 1945; Senator of the Parliament of Northern Ireland since 1921; *b* 1868; *e s* of late Seymour Montague Leslie and first wife, Louisa, *y d* of Wm Graham, of Fitzharris, Berks; *m* 1901, Grace, *o d* of late J. L. Brodie; one *s* two *d. Educ:* privately. Barrister-at-law, Gray's Inn, 1896; High Sheriff, Co. Antrim, 1907; County Councillor, 1919–24; Foreman of the Grand Jury, 1921–47. *Recreation:* shooting. *Address:* Leslie Hill, Ballymoney, Co. Antrim. *T:* Ballymoney 109. *Club:* Ulster (Belfast).

Died 16 May 1949.

LESLIE, Col Sir John, 2nd Bt *cr* 1876; CBE 1919; DL; late Comdg 12th Batt. R. Inniskilling Fusiliers; Lieutenant for Co. Monaghan, 1921; *b* 7 Aug. 1857; *s* of 1st Bt and Lady Constance Damer, *sister* of 5th Earl of Portarlington; *S* father, 1916; *m* 1884, Léonie Blanche (*d* 1943), *d* of Leonard Jerome of New York; three *s. Educ:* Eton. Entered army, Grenadier Guards, 1877; retired as Lieut 1888; served Egypt (Tel-el-Kebir), 1882; *S* Africa, 1900; Commanded 5th Batt. R. Irish Fusiliers until retired as Colonel, 1908. *Recreation:* shooting. *Heir: s* (John R.) Shane. *Address:* Glaslough, Co. Monaghan. *Club:* Turf.

Died 25 Jan. 1944.

LESLIE, John D.; *see* Dean-Leslie.

LESLIE, Lt-Col John Henry; DL; *b* 1858; *e s* of late Henry Leslie of Bryn Tanat, Mont; *m* 1886, Alice Maud (*d* 1924), *y d* of late Maj.-General S. F. Graham, BSC; two *s* three *d. Educ:* Shrewsbury; Royal Military Academy, Woolwich. Lieutenant RA, 1877; Major, 1895; ret. pay, 1897; Bt Lieut-Col, 1918. *Publications:* History of Stewart Lodge, No. 1960, 1896; The History of Landguard Fort, 1898; A List of Officers of the Madras Artillery, 1748 to 1861, 1900; Services of the RA in the Peninsular War, 1808 to 1814, 1908; The Story of a British Flag, Captured by the French at Quatre Bras 1815, 1911; Tradition in the Royal Artillery, 1913; The Centenary of the Battle of Waterloo, 1916. *Recreations:* music and the stage; the study of Regimental history and of British War Medals. *Address:* 97 Marsh Road, Pinner, Middlesex. *T:* Pinner 2190. *Clubs:* Army and Navy, Savage; Bath and County.

Died 8 Jan. 1943.

LESLIE, Col John Robert Sloan, CB 1941; TD; DL, JP; Welfare Officer, Scottish Command; Chairman, Glasgow Territorial Army and Air Force Association; Chairman, Glasgow Branch British Red Cross Society; *b* Glasgow, 30 July 1871; *s* of Thomas Leslie and Margaret Wallace. *Educ:* Glasgow. Engaged in Coal Trade as Shipper and Contractor; Territorial Army, 1891–1939; The Cameronians, ranks, 1891–1901; Lieut, 1901–06; Captain, 1906–11; Major, 1915; Lt-Col, 1916; Hon. Colonel, 1934–39; served in France, 1916–18. Chairman Coal Trade Benevolent Society of Scotland, 1925; Deacon of Incorporation of Coopers, Glasgow, 1931–35; Preses Weavers' Society of Anderston, 1936–37; Governor of Victoria Infirmary since 1936; Member of Executive Committee of Princess Louise

Hosp. for Limbless Soldiers and Sailors. *Recreations:* golf, fishing. *Address:* 68 Gordon Street, Glasgow. *Clubs:* New, Glasgow; New, Edinburgh.

Died 4 Oct. 1943.

LESLIE, Sir Norman Alexander, KBE 1919; CBE 1918; Order of the Crown of Italy; FICS; partner in firm of Law, Leslie & Co., c/o The Baltic Exchange, St Mary Axe, EC; Director of George Thompson and Co., Ltd; *b* 1870; *s* of late John Leslie; *m* 1898, Mimy Muriel (*d* 1934), *d* of late James Gambier; three *d*. *Educ:* Sherborne School. Voluntary service at Admiralty in requisitioning branch of Transport department, 1915–16; transferred to newly formed Ministry of Shipping, where with Commander R. G. H. Henderson, RN, inaugurated the convoy system in 1917. In 1919 wrote The System of Convoys for Merchant Shipping 1917 and 1918, a government record. *Address:* Birchwood, West Byfleet, Surrey. *T:* Byfleet 195.

Died 23 Oct. 1945.

LESLIE, Gen. Sir Walter Stewart, KCB 1931; KBE 1921; CB 1920; CMG 1919; DSO 1917; Colonel of the 16th Punjab Regiment since 1945; *b* 23 March 1876; 3rd *s* of late Lieutenant-Colonel A. Y. Leslie, of Kininvie, Banffshire; *m* 1911, Lora Mary, 2nd *d* of late James Corballis, JP, of Ratoath Manor, Co. Meath. *Educ:* RMC, Sandhurst. Commissioned 1st Bn Royal West Kent Regt, 1896; joined 40th Pathans, 1898; 31st Punjabis, 1900; psc 1912; after the Armistice commanded the troops in Cilicia; BGGS North Force, Syria, 1919; served Malakand and Buner Campaign, 1897–98; European War, 1914–18; France, Mesopotamia, and Palestine (despatches several times, CMG, DSO, Brevet Lt-Col and Col, Order of the White Eagle, Order of the Nile); Afghan War, 1919; Mahsud Campaign, 1919 (CB); commanded the Wana Column operating against the Wazirs, Nov. 1920–March 1921 (KBE); ADC to the King, 1922–24; Maj.-Gen., 1924; Lt-Gen. 1930; Deputy Adjt-Gen. Army Headquarters, India, 1924–27; DQMG and DMQ, AHQ, India, 1927–28; commanded Lahore District 1928–31; Adjutant-General in India 1932–36; General 1935; ADC General to the King 1935–36; retired 1936. *Recreations:* shooting, fishing, golf.

Died 9 Aug. 1947.

LESLIE-JONES, Frederick Archibald, CBE, MA; *b* 9 July 1874; *s* of late H. Leslie-Jones, MD, FRCS; *m* 1904, Christiana Mary, *e d* of late Rev. J. G. K. Baskett, of Donhead, Salisbury; two *s* three *d*. *Educ:* Bromsgrove School; Lincoln College, Oxford (Exhibitioner). BA, 2nd Class Classical Mods and 2nd Class Lit.Hum., 1897; MA, 1900. Certificate in Teaching, Oxford, 1899; Oxford Univ. Rugby Football XV, 1894–97; Captain, 1896–97; English International, Rugby, 1895. Assistant Master, Marlborough College, 1897–1904; Principal, Aitchison College, Lahore, 1904–17; Principal, Mayo College, Ajmer, India, 1917–28; Assistant Master, Malvern College, 1928–31; sometime Lieut-Col, 1st Punjab Rifles; Indian Defence Force, 1914–19; President, Publicity Board, Ajmer-Merwara, during the War; Hon. Magistrate; Special Constable, 1938–43. *Publication:* A View of English History. *Address:* White House, Malvern Link.

Died 24 Jan. 1946.

LESLIE-ROBERTS, H(ugh); *see* Roberts.

LESSLIE, Brig.-Gen. William Breck, CB 1919; CMG 1915; late RE; *b* 4 Nov. 1868; *s* of William Lesslie, Kingston, Ontario, Canada; *m* 1896, Edith Lucy Blyth. Entered RE 1888; Capt. 1899; Major, 1904; Lt-Col 1916; served East Africa, 1902–04 (despatches, Bt Maj., medal with clasp); European War (Dardanelles, France, and Flanders), 1914–18 (despatches, CB, CMG, Bt Lt-Col and Col); retired, 1925. *Address:* Monktons, Mortimer, Berks.

Died 23 Nov. 1942.

LESSORE, Thérèse; painter; *m* 1926, Walter R. Sickert (*d* 1942). *Address:* 10 Landsdowne Road, W11.

Died 10 Dec. 1945.

LESTER-GARLAND, Lester V., MA, FLS. *Educ:* Sherborne School; Magdalen Coll., Oxford (Demy). Assistant Master at St Edward's School, Oxford, 1883–86; Fellow of St John's College, Oxford, 1886–89; Lecturer, 1886–96; Principal of Victoria College, Jersey, 1896–1911. *Publications:* Memoir of H. D. Harper, 1896; Flora of Jersey, 1903; The Religious Philosophy of Baron F. von Hügel, 1933; The Idea of the Supernatural, 1934. *Address:* Bathford House, Bathford, Somerset.

Died 23 March 1944.

LETHBRIDGE, Col Ernest Astley Edmund, CMG 1916; DSO 1900; commanded 1st Batt. Oxfordshire and Buckinghamshire LI; *b* 26 Dec. 1864; 2nd *s* of Sir Wroth A. Lethbridge, 4th Bart; *m* 1919, Ruth Mary, *yr d* of late Hon. E. A. Holmes-à-Court, and *widow* of Major Charles E. Forrest, DSO; one *d*. *Educ:* Eton; Royal Military Coll., Sandhurst. Entered army, 1885; served S Africa, 1899–1902 (despatches twice, Queen's medal three clasps, King's medal two clasps, DSO); European War (Mesopotamia), 1914–16 (despatches thrice, CMG, Bt Col, Croix de Guerre with Palms). *Address:* The Firs, Headington Hill, Oxford. *T:* Oxford 6340. *Club:* Carlton.

Died 29 April 1943.

LETHBRIDGE, Sir Wroth (Periam Christopher), 5th Bt *cr* 1804; Chairman and President, 1026 Ormskirk and District Squadron of Air Training Corps; *b* Brighton, 19 Dec. 1863; *e s* of Sir Wroth Acland Lethbridge, 4th Bart, and Annie, *d* of T. Benyon, The Gleddowe, Leeds; *m* 1st, 1892, Alianore (who obtained a divorce, 1911), *y d* of late Edward Chandos Pole, Raebourne Hall, Derby, and Lady Anne Chandos Pole, *d* of 5th Earl of Harrington; one *s* two *d*; 2nd, 1911, Kathleen (who obtained a divorce, 1928), *o c* of late Robert O'Hara; 3rd, 1928, Hilda, *y d* of late Canon Blundell, Halsall. *Educ:* Eton. Joined 3rd Batt. Princess of Wales' Own West Yorkshire Regt, 1892; transferred 1st Batt. Leicestershire Regt, 1885; 3rd Batt. Grenadier Guards, 1885; Capt. 1898; retired 1903; Deputy Censor, Lines of Communication, to Expeditionary Force, Oct. 1914; reinstated to Grenadier Guards as Captain, Dec. 1914; employed special duty, Guards' Division, Base Depot, BEF, since Feb. 1916; Egyptian Expeditionary Force, 1917; Special Military Mission, USA, 1918; Special Constable during Strike, 1926; joined Home Guard, 1940. *Publications:* various magazine articles. *Recreations:* shooting, fishing, and other amusements. *Heir: s* Capt. Hector Wroth Lethbridge [*b* 26 Aug. 1898; *m* 1946, Diana, *widow* of Major John Vivian Bailey, The Royal Scots Fusiliers, and *er d* of Lt-Col Frank Noel, Hopton Hall, Great Yarmouth; one *d*. Served in last war in Rifle Brig. and on W Coast of Africa in 1943]. *Address:* 29 Cheyne Walk, SW. *T:* Flaxman 5406; La Mancha Hall, Halsall, Ormskirk. *T:* Halsall 13. *Clubs:* Army and Navy, Athenæum.

Died 20 Feb. 1950.

LETOURNEAU, Séverin; KC 1906; Chief Justice of the Court of King's Bench of the Province of Quebec (Appeal Division) and of the Province of Quebec; *b* St Constant, Co. of Laprairie, Que., 23 May 1871; *m* 1896, Antonine, *d* of A. Lanctôt, merchant. *Educ:* Graduated at the Jacques-Cartier Normal School, Montreal, 1891; Laval University, law BA, 1895. Called to Bar, 1895; began law practice with C. Pelletier; Chief Organiser of the Liberal Party for the Montreal district, 1911; member of the county Montreal-Hochelaga for the Local Parliament, 1912 and 1916; Legislative Councillor, 1919; life-member of the Notre-Dame Hospital, of Le Cercle

Universitaire of Montreal and Chapleau Club. Catholic in religion and Liberal in politics. *Address:* 421 Argyle Avenue, Montreal, Canada.

Died 17 Dec. 1949.

LETT, Eva, MA (Med. and Mod. Lang. Tripos); Principal of the Diocesan Training College, Ripon, since 1930; *y d* of late R. A. Lett, BA, MD. *Educ:* Wakefield; Paris; Newnham College, Cambridge. Principal of the Bergman Osterberg College, Dartford, 1922–30; Member of the Ripon Diocesan Conference; Member, Diocesan Education Council; Governor of Skellfield School. *Address:* Training College, Ripon. *T:* 9.

Died 30 Nov. 1945.

LETTON, Charles Thomas, CIE 1935; MBE 1919; *b* 25 March 1878; *s* of late Charles William Letton; *m* 1904, Maude Annie, *d* of Edward Barnes; one *s* two *d*. Entered Govt of India Printing and Stationery Dept, 1907; Controller of Printing and Stationery, India, 1930–35; retired, 1935. *Address:* Dakuria, 71 Goldstone Crescent, Hove, Sussex. *T:* Preston 4217.

Died 18 March 1949.

LEUBA, Prof. James Henri, PhD, Professor Emeritus, Bryn Mawr College, USA since 1933; *b* Neuchatel, Switzerland, 9 April 1868; *s* of Henri Leuba and Cecile Sandoz; *m* 1896, Berthe Schopfer; one *s* one *d*. *Educ:* BS University of Neuchatel, 1887; PhD Clark University, USA 1895. Went to US 1888; Lecturer in Psychology; Professor and Head of the Department of Psychology at Bryn Mawr College, USA. *Publications:* A Psychological Study of Religion, its Origin, Nature, and Future, 1912, translated into French and Japanese; The Belief in God and Immortality, 1916; The Psychology of Religious Mysticism, 1925, translated into French and German; God or Man? A Study of the value of God to Man, 1933. *Address:* Bryn Mawr, Pa, USA.

Died 10 Dec. 1946.

LEVEN, 13th Earl of, *cr* 1641, **AND MELVILLE,** 12th Earl of, *cr* 1690; **Archibald Alexander Leslie-Melville,** KT 1934; Baron Melville, 1616; Baron Balgomie, 1641; Viscount Kirkcaldie, 1690; Representative Peer for Scotland; Lord Lieutenant of Nairnshire since 1935; Bt Col late commanding Lovat Scouts; *b* 6 Aug. 1890; *s* of 11th Earl and Hon. Emma Selina Portman (*d* 1941), *e d* of 2nd Viscount Portman; *S* brother, 1913; *m* 1918, Lady Rosamond Sylvia Diana Mary Foljambe, *d* of 1st Earl of Liverpool; four *s* one *d*. *Educ:* Eton; Sandhurst. Served European War with Scots Greys, 1914 (dangerously wounded, taken prisoner and escaped). *Heir: s* Lord Balgonie. *Address:* Glenferness, Nairn. *Club:* Carlton.

Died 15 Jan. 1947.

LEVER, Sir (Samuel) Hardman, 1st Bt *cr* 1920; KCB 1917; *b* 18 April 1869; *m* 1900, Edythe, *d* of Matthew Hamilton Gault, Montreal. Assistant Financial Secretary Ministry of Munitions, 1915–16, in charge of Contracts and Finance; Financial Secretary to the Treasury, 1917–21; an assistant Commissioner for Finance, USA, 1917–18; Treasury Representative at Ministry of Transport, 1919–21; Member of Weir Committee on Electricity (Grid); Chairman of Telegraph Committee Enquiry; headed Air Missions to Canada, 1938, and to Australia and New Zealand, 1939; has Legion of Honour and Order of Crown of Italy. *Address:* 64 Eaton Square, SW1; Northlands, Winchester. *T:* Winchester 2532.

Died 1 July 1947 (ext).

LEVERHULME, 2nd Viscount *cr* 1922, of the Western Isles; **William Hulme Lever;** Baron *cr* 1917; Bt *cr* 1911, Governor of Lever Brothers and Unilever Ltd; Chairman of Knowles Ltd, Cotton Spinners, Bolton; Hon. Col 4th AA Divisional RASC; *b* Bolton, 25 March 1888; *s* of 1st Viscount and Elizabeth Ellen (*d* 1913), *d* of Crompton Hulme of Bolton; *S* father, 1925; *m* 1st, 1912, Marion (marr. diss. 1936), *d* of late Bryce Smith of Manchester;

one *s* two *d*; 2nd, 1937, Winifred Agnes, *d* of late Lt-Col J. E. Lloyd, Bidston, Cheshire. *Educ:* Eton; Trinity College, Cambridge (MA). High Sheriff of Cheshire, 1923; DL; JP Cheshire; Charter Mayor of Bebington 1937, and first Freeman of the Borough, 1945; President of: London Chamber of Commerce, 1931–34; of Advertising Association, 1931; of Institution of Chemical Engineers, 1932–34; of Royal Warrant Holders' Association, 1933; of Society of Chemical Industry, 1936–38; of Epsom College, of Caterham School, the Royal Commercial Travellers' Schools, and Chairman of the Governors of Bolton School; a Pro-Chancellor of Liverpool University, 1932–36; Hon. LLD (Liverpool), 1937; Knight of Justice of Order of St John of Jerusalem; Grand Officer of Order of Leopold II of Belgium; Officer of the Legion of Honour. *Publication:* Viscount Leverhulme, by his son, 1927. *Recreations:* golf and shooting. *Heir: s* Hon. Philip William Bryce Lever [*b* 1 July 1915; *m* 1937, Margaret Ann, *o c* of John Moon, Tiverton; three *d*]. *Address:* Thornton Manor, Thornton Hough, Cheshire. *T:* Thornton Hough 234. *Clubs:* Arts, Reform.

Died 27 May 1949.

LEVERSON, Col Julian John, CB 1918; CMG, 1897; retired, RE; *b* London, 16 May 1853; 2nd *s* of G. B. C. Leverson and Henrietta, *d* of David Johnasson, Usworth Hall, Durham; unmarried. *Educ:* privately; University College School; RMA, Woolwich; Staff College, Sandhurst. Served in Egyptian Campaign, 1882; Bechuanaland Expedition, 1884–85; DAAG Intelligence Division of War Office, 1886–91; Secretary of Mr Stanhope's Committee on Fortification and Armament of our Military and Home Mercantile Ports, 1888; Assistant Commissioner Delimitation Russo-Turkish Frontier, 1880; Turco-Greek Frontier, 1881; Commissioner for the Settlement of Claims to Land in British Bechuanaland, 1885–86; Anglo-Portuguese Frontiers in East Africa, 1891–93; British Representative at Manica Land Boundary Arbitration, 1896; Commissioner Barué Delimitation Commission, 1898; Military Censor at the Press Bureau, 1914–18. *Address:* Flat 31, 20 Grosvenor Square, W1. *T:* Mayfair 3101. *Clubs:* Army and Navy, Naval and Military.

Died 19 July 1941.

LEVESON GOWER, Granville Charles Gresham; JP, DL; *b* 1865; *e s* of late Granville William Gresham Leveson Gower of Titsey Place, and Hon. Sophia, *y d* of 1st Lord Leigh; *m* 1894, Evelyn, 2nd *d* of late Henry A. Brassey of Preston Hall, Aylesford; three *s*. *Educ:* Eton; Balliol Coll., Oxford (BA 1889, MA 1894). Late Lieut Hampshire Carabineers YC; Major Commanding 3/1st West Kent Yeomanry; Lord of the Manors of Titsey, Limpsfield, and Tatsfield, and Patron of three livings. *Heir:* Richard Henry Gresham, *b* 27 Nov. 1894. *Address:* Titsey Place, Limpsfield. *Club:* Travellers'.

Died 4 Dec. 1948.

LEVETT, Major Berkeley John Talbot, CVO 1926; late Scots Guards; *b* 1863; *s* of late Col Theophilus John Levett, MP, of Wychnor Park, Staffordshire; *m* 1900, Sibell Lucia, *d* of late Hamar Alfred Bass, MP. A Gentleman Usher to HM, 1919–31; an Extra Gentleman Usher since 1931; an Extra Equerry to Duke of Connaught, 1922. *Address:* Cottington, Sidmouth.

Died 1 Nov. 1941.

LEVINE, Abraham, MA, FIA; *b* 14 July 1870; 2nd *s* of late Rev. J. Levine, Glasgow; *m* 1899, Maria, *er d* of Sydney Myer, Hereford; one *s*. *Educ:* Glasgow University (Ferguson Mathematical Scholar, 1890–92); Jesus College, Cambridge (Scholar and Fellow). Chairman of Life Offices Association, 1921–22; President of the Institute of Actuaries, 1928–30; President of Chartered Insurance Institute 1936–37; Assistant Actuary to National Mutual, 1900; Actuary to Alliance, 1906–29; General Manager, Alliance Assurance

Co., Ltd, 1929–39. *Recreation:* music. *Address:* 11 St Mary Abbott's Place, Kensington, W8. *T:* Western 0341.

Died 12 Feb. 1949.

LEVY, Hermann; Dr rer. pol, former Professor of Economics; writer and lecturer; *b* 22 May 1881; *m* Margarethe Schlegel; one *s*. *Educ:* Berlin and Munich. Lecturer at University of Halle, 1905–07, Professor at University of Heidelberg, 1907–18; Professor at Technische Hochschule, Berlin-Charlottenburg, 1918–33; lectured at King's College, Cambridge, in 1934; gave Sidney Ball lecture at Oxford, 1935. *Publications:* Large and Small Farms, 1911; Economic Liberalism, 1913; Monopolies, Cartels and Trusts in British Industry, 2nd ed. 1927; Industrial Germany, 1935; The New Industrial System, 1936; Retail Trade Associations, 1942; National Health Insurance, 1944; The Shops of Britain, 1948; England and Germany, 1949; (with Sir Arnold Wilson, MP) Industrial Assurance, 1937; Burial Reform and Funeral Costs, 1938; Workmen's Compensation 1939 and 1941 (two vols). *Recreations:* music, novel writing (ps. Hermann Lint). *Address:* 149 Lichfield Court, Richmond, Surrey. *T:* Richmond 4420.

Died 16 Jan. 1949.

LEVY, J. Langley; author; Editor of Sunday Times, Johannesburg, 1910–42; Médaille du roi Albert; Trustee Johannesburg Municipal Library; Chairman Public Library Consultative Committee; Hon. Vice-President Johannesburg Publicity Association; Council National Cancer Association of South Africa and Chairman Publicity Committee; Johannesburg Archives Committee; Hon. Member Critics' Circle, London; Hon. President, Transvaal Magicians' Circle; Hon. Vice-President Johannesburg Repertory Players; *b* Liverpool, 25 May 1870; *s* of John L. Levy, London, and Esther, *d* of Joseph Levy, London; *m* 1897, late Mabel Ada, *d* of late Edward Rushton, RAM Corps; one *s* three *d*. *Educ:* Liverpool Institute. Studied art under John Finnie, Robert Anning Bell, and modelling under C. J. Allen; was associated for some years with Clayton and Bell of London. Drifted into journalism by contributing a series of articles on The Jew in Liverpool to the Liverpool Review 1899; Sub-Editor of the Review, 1899; Editor, 1902; relinquished position in 1903 to make trip through Europe, Australia, and South Africa; resumed editorship, 1904; joined editorial staff, London Daily Express, 1905; officiated as Art Critic, Standard, Evening Standard, and Daily Express. *Publications:* The Secret of Strathburn House; In the Name of Love; The Princess and the Mountebank, published serially in Daily Express; numerous short stories in the Pall Mall, Windsor, Royal, and Novel magazines. *Plays:* The School of Athens; The Charm of Iamblichus; East Lynne in Essence; Hamlet, translated from Danish into American; Oom Jan; part author of Ta Ta, Darling!; The Man who Went to the Front. *Film Scenarios:* Gloria; The Liquor Seller; The Gun Runners; And Then—! *Recreations:* Elizabethan literature and the modern drama. *Address:* Carlton Hotel, Johannesburg, S Africa. *Clubs:* Savage, Authors'.

Died 11 May 1945.

LEWER, Mrs Ethel; late Editor of The Feathered World; *b* Dum-Dum, India, 1861; *d* of Major N. D. Garrett, RA; *m* 1st, 1886, Alexander Comyns, BA, LLD (*d* 1890); (one *s* killed, Messines, 1914) one *d*; 2nd, 1896, S. H. Lewer, JP, publisher and editor. *Educ:* privately. In conjunction with Mrs Marshall opened first typewriting office in London, 1884; on death of first husband took over editorship of The Feathered World, being the first woman to own, edit, and publish her own paper; retired, 1935. *Publications:* books connected with birds generally. *Recreation:* gardening. *Address:* Longcroft, Aldeburgh, Suffolk. *T:* Aldeburgh 25. *Club:* Aldeburgh Golf.

Died 8 Feb. 1946.

LEWES, Col Price Kinnear, CMG 1919; DSO 1916; late RA; JP for Co. Cardigan; *b* 1870; *s* of late Major Price Lewes, late RA, of Tyglyn Aeron, Ciliau Aeron, Cardiganshire, and Florence, *d* of late T. C. Kinnear, of Halifax, NS; *m* 1st, 1894, Ethel Georgiana Murray Prust; one *s*; 2nd, 1914, Ellen Elizabeth Vezey Jones (*d* 1937); 3rd, 1939, Dorothy Agnes, *widow* of F. P. Gravelle, Ardmore, USA, and *d* of C. A. Jones-Parry, JP, Tyllwyd, Cardiganshire. *Educ:* Charterhouse. 2nd Lieut RA 1890; Captain RGA 1899; Major, 1910; Lt-Col 1917; Col 1921; served European War (CMG, DSO); Assistant Director of Artillery, War Office, 1918–21; Member, Ordnance Committee, 1921–24; retired pay, 1924. *Address:* 45 Hawke Road, Norwood, SE19.

Died 9 Jan. 1943.

LEWIN, Maj.-Gen. Ernest Ord, CB 1920; CMG 1918; DSO 1916; late RA; *b* 1879; 3rd *s* of late F. A. Lewin, barrister; *m* 1920, Anne Elizabeth Henderson, *e d* of late Robert Slack, Derwent Hill, Keswick; one *s* one *d*. *Educ:* Winchester; King's Coll., Cambridge (BA with honours). Joined the RA 1900; served 10 years in India, 4 years of which in N Battery Royal Horse Artillery; Staff Officer to Inspector of RH and RFA in India, 1912 1914; Adjutant RHA Woolwich, 1914; served European War 1914–18 (despatches four times, DSO, Bt Lt-Col, CMG); Brigadier, Royal Artillery, Headquarters, Aldershot Command, 1927–31; Maj.-Gen. 1932; General Officer Comdg, Malaya, 1934–35; Commander 55th (West Lancashire) Division TA, 1935–38; retired, 1938; on outbreak of war GOC Portsmouth Area; Maj.-Gen. i/c of Administration, Southern Command, 1940–41. *Address:* Winson House, Winson, Cirencester. *T:* Fossebridge 213. *Club:* Lansdowne.

Died 10 May 1950.

LEWIN, George Arthur, CMG 1935; JP; *b* 23 Jan. 1867; *s* of James and Martha Lewin; *m* 1890, Mary Elizabeth Turpin; one *s* one *d*. *Educ:* Lyttelton, New Zealand. Served on the literary staff of Lyttelton Times for a number of years; Town Clerk, Lyttelton, 1900; Town Clerk of City of Dunedin, New Zealand, 1911–37; Member Local Government Loans Board; Member Board of Management State Advances Corporation. *Recreations:* rowing, cricket. *Address:* 452 Highgate, Roslyn, Dunedin, NW1, New Zealand.

Died 25 June 1941.

LEWIN, Brig.-Gen. Henry Frederick Elliott, CB 1929; CMG 1916; late RA; *b* 26 Dec. 1872; *e s* of late Commander W. H. Lewin, RN; *m* 1913, Countess Roberts; (one *s* killed in action (Irish Guards), 1940). Entered Army, 1894; Captain, 1900; Major, 1911; Lt-Col 1916; Bt Col 1919; Col 1921; employed with Egyptian army, 1901–11; served European War, 1914–18 (despatches, CMG, Chevalier Légion d'honneur); Brig.-Gen. 1917–19; Assistant Adjt-Gen., RA, WO, 1922–25; commanded R. Artillery, Northern Command, 1925–29; retired pay, 1929; Comptroller to Princess Royal, 1930–32; DL Wilts, 1942; JP Wilts, 1936; Commanded 9th Bn, Wiltshire Home Guard, 1940–42. *Address:* The Camp, Ascot, Berks. *Clubs:* Army and Navy, Cavalry.

Died 1 Dec. 1946.

LEWIS, Cyril Arthur Liddon, CBE 1934; BA; *b* 27 Sept. 1873; *s* of late Rev. Thomas Curling Lewis; *m* 1904, Hilda, *e d* of late H. Percy Boulnois, MInstCE; one *s* one *d*. *Educ:* Radley; Brasenose College, Oxford. Barrister-at-Law, Lincoln's Inn, 1900; HM Land Registry 1904; Registrar, HM Land Registry, 1923; served European War, 1914–16, Flanders and France, 4th Royal Berks Regt (severely wounded); retired, Major. *Address:* Tylers, Cuckfield, Sussex.

Died 18 Feb. 1943.

LEWIS, Maj.-Gen. Edward Mann, Hon. KCMG 1919; LLD; US Army; retired; b New Albany, Indiana, 10 Dec. 1863; s of William Henry and Julia Frances Snively Lewis; m 1888, Harriet Russell Balding Wisconsin; two s one d. Educ: US Military Academy; De Pauw University and University of California. 2nd Lieut 11th Infantry, 1886; 1st Lieut 20th Infantry, 1893; Capt. 1899; transferred to 8th Infantry, 1908; Major, 16th Infantry, 1909; to 19th Infantry, 1912; Lieut-Col 1915; Col 1917; Brig.-Gen. NG in Federal service, 1916; Brig.-Gen. NA 1917; Maj.-Gen. USA 1918; Brig.-Gen. Regular Army, 1920; Major-General Regular Army, 1922; Prof. Military Science and Tactics, De Pauw University, Greencastle, Ind, 1892–96; served in Cuba, Spanish-Am. War, 1898; Philippine Insurrection, 1899–1901; duty San Francisco, following earthquake and fire, 1906; Professor Military Science and Tactics, University of California, 1908–12; with expedition to Vera Cruz, 1914, commanding 19th Infantry; Senior Insp.-Instr, Illinois, NG, 1915–17; Officer-in-Charge Militia Affairs at Headquarters, North-Eastern Department, Boston, 1917; Comdr 13th Provisional Division Llano Grande, Texas, 1916; Commanded 76th Infantry Brigade, NG, 1917; US Troops in Paris, 1917–18; Third Brigade Second Div., 1918; 30th Div. 1918; 3rd Div., 1920–21; 2nd Div., 1922; VIII Corps Area, 1923; Hawaiian Division, 1924; Hawaiian Dept, 1925; retired from Active Service, 1927; Member SR Soc. Army Santiago de Cuba, Phi Beta Kappa; Distinguished Service Medal, US; KCMG; Commandeur Legion of Honour; Commandeur Order of Leopold; Grand Officer Order of Danilo (Montenegran); Croix de Guerre (French) two Palms; Croix de Guerre (Belgian). Clubs: Army and Navy (Washington); Union League (San Francisco).

Died 27 July 1949.

LEWIS, Sir George James Ernest, 3rd Bt cr 1902; Temp. Lieut-Comdr RNVR; Member of the firm of Lewis and Lewis, and Gisborne & Co., Solicitors, 10, 11, and 12 Ely Place, Holborn, EC1; b 25 Feb. 1910; s of 2nd Bt and Marie, d of Emil Hirsch; S father, 1927. Educ: Eton. Heir: none. Clubs: Bath, Garrick.

Died 2 Jan. 1945.

LEWIS, Gilbert Newton; Professor of Chemistry, University of California, Berkeley, since 1912; b Weymouth, Mass, 23 Oct. 1875; s of Frank W. Lewis and Mary B. White; m 1912, Mary Hinckley Sheldon, Cambridge, Mass; two s one d. Educ: Univ. of Nebraska; Harvard (AB 1896, PhD 1899); University of Leipzig and University of Göttingen. Instr. Chemistry, Harvard 1899–1900, 1901–06 (on leave of absence, in charge weights and measures, Philippine Islands, 1904–05); Asst Prof. of Chemistry, 1907–08, Assoc. Prof., 1908–11, Prof., 1911–12, Mass Inst. Technology; Silliman Lecturer, Yale, 1925; Maj. USA, 1918; Lt-Col, 1919; Chief of Defence Div. Gas Service, AEF. Publications: Thermodynamics and the Free Energy of Chemical Substances (with M. Randall), 1923; Valence and the Structure of Atoms and Molecules, 1923; The Anatomy of Science, 1926.

Died 24 March 1946.

LEWIS, Maj.-Gen. Harold Victor, CB 1940; CIE 1939; DSO 1917; MC; Col 4/10th Baluch Regt since 1940; late 4/10th Baluch Regt and Royal Garhwal Rifles; b 1887; s of late Rev. V. A. N. Lewis; m 1924, Joyce Bailey; one s one d. Educ: Uppingham. Served European War, 1914–18 (despatches) four times; MC with bar, DSO); Afghan War, 1919; Waziristan and Mahsud Expeditions, 1919–20 (despatches); Operations, NWF, 1930; Operations in Waziristan, 1937–38 (CIE); psc; Bt Lt-Col 1930; Lt-Col 1932; Comdt 4th Bn 19th Hyderabad Regiment, 1932–33; Deputy Director of Staff Duties, AHQ, India, 1933–35; Bt Col 1933; Col, 1934; AA and QMG Peshawar, 1935–37; Col (Temp. Brig.) 1937; Commander Razmak Brigade, 1937–40;

Commander Jullundur Area, Feb.–June, 1940; Maj.-Gen. 1940; Divisional Commander, India, 1941; retired, 1942. Club: United Service.

Died 20 Sept. 1945.

LEWIS, Rev. Canon James Abraham, BA; Canon Precentor of Llandaff Cathedral since 1930; Vicar of Cardiff since 1931; b 20 Oct. 1874; s of John Lewis, Schoolmaster, Bettws, Carmarthenshire; m 1911, Winifred, y d of Evan Lewis, JP, Llandaff; five d. Educ: Llandovery School; St David's College, Lampeter (Scholar and Prizeman). Ordained 1898; served curacies at Llwynypia and Llandrindod Wells; Minor Canon of Llandaff, 1907–14; Vicar and Rural Dean of Aberdare, 1914–31; Canon Residentiary of Llandaff, 1928; Member of Governing Body and Representative Body, Church in Wales; Member of Standing Committee of National Society; Chaplain Order of St John of Jerusalem. Recreation: music. Address: The Vicarage, Cathedral Road, Cardiff.

Died 8 Jan. 1946.

LEWIS, John, CBE 1919; JP; b 1851; m 1882, Anne, d of Samuel Williams. Address: Meiros Hall, Defrach, Henllan, Cardiganshire.

Died Jan. 1943.

LEWIS, Sir Thomas, Kt 1921; CBE 1920; FRS; MD, FRCP, DSc, LLD; Physician, University College Hospital; Hon. Consulting Physician, Ministry of Pensions; b 26 Dec. 1881; s of Henry Lewis, Tynant, Cardiff; m 1916, Lorna, d of Frank Treharne James, Merthyr Tydfil; one s two d. Educ: University College, Cardiff; Univ. Coll. Hospital, London. Fellow of Univ. Coll., London. Croonian Lecturer, Royal Society, 1917; Royal Medal, 1927; Copley Medal, 1941; Oliver-Sharpey, Linacre, Harveian, Huxley Lecturer; Consulting Physician City of London Hospital; formerly Consulting Physician on Diseases of the Heart, Eastern Command; Member, Medical Research Council, 1933–37. Publications: Mechanism of the Heart Beat, 1911; Clinical Disorders of the Heart Beat, 1912; Clinical Electro-Cardiography, 1913; Lectures on the Heart, 1915; The Soldier's Heart and the Effort Syndrome, 1940; Bloodvessels of the Human Skin 1927; Diseases of the Heart, 1932; Clinical Science, 1934; Vascular Disorders of the Limbs, 1936; Pain, 1942; articles to Scientific Journals; late Editor of Heart; Editor of Clinical Science. Address: University College Hospital Medical School, Gower Street, WC. Club: Athenæum.

Died 17 March 1945.

LEWIS, Vernon Arthur, CMG 1946; MC; Chief Justice, Southern Rhodesia, since 1950; b Capetown; 5th s of Dr C. F. Lewis. Educ: The South African College; New College, Oxford (Rhodes Scholar). Served European War, 1914–18, battery commander (MC). Called to the Bar, Inner Temple, 1910; formerly Puisne Judge of the High Court, Southern Rhodesia; Member Rhodesian Parlt and Minister of Justice, Defence, and Internal Affairs, 1934. Address: High Court, Salisbury, Southern Rhodesia.

Died 22 May 1950.

LEWIS, Sir Wilfrid Hubert Poyer, OBE; DL Pembrokeshire; JP; MA, Oxon; Hon. Mr Justice Lewis; Justice of High Court of Justice, King's Bench Division, since 1935; Chairman Pembrokeshire Quarter Sessions; Fellow of Eton College; Hon. Fellow of University College, Oxford; b 1881; e s of late Arthur Griffith Poyer Lewis, MA, JP, of Henllan, Narberth, Pembrokeshire, and g s of Rt Rev. Lewis, Lord Bishop of Llandaff, DD; m 1st, 1908, Margaret Annie (d 1932), e d of late Rt Hon. Sir John Eldon Bankes, GCB, of Soughton Hall, Northop, Flintshire; one s three d; 2nd, 1934, Elizabeth, e d of Dr David Barty King, 6 Devonshire Street, W1; two s. Educ: Eton; Univ. College, Oxford. Barrister, Inner Temple, 1908; Bencher, 1929; Chancellor of Diocese of Llandaff,

1914–35; of Monmouth, 1921–35; of Manchester and of Blackburn, 1929–35; of Worcester, 1930–35; Junior Counsel to the Treasury (Common Law); served European War, 1914–19, Lieut (Captain, 1916) Glamorgan Yeomanry. *Address:* Henllan, Narberth, Pembrokeshire; 31 Campden Hill Road, W8; 3 Hare Court, Temple, EC. *T:* Central 3171.

Died 15 March 1950.

LEWIS, William Henry; High Sheriff of Montgomeryshire, 1935–36; *b* 1866; *s* of Richard and Jane Ryder Lewis; *m* 1914, Edith Mary Lewis. *Educ:* Oswestry; Edinburgh University. MB, CM, 1887; BSc 1888. JP and Ex-Alderman CC Montgomeryshire; Vice-President NW Blind Society. *Recreation:* wood carving. *Address:* Cae Hywel, Llansantffraid, Montgomeryshire.

Died 24 Sept. 1948.

LEWIS, Sir Willmott Harsant, KBE 1931; Correspondent of The Times in Washington, USA, 1920–48; *b* Cardiff, 18 June 1877; *s* of James Oliver, and Marion Harsant Lewis; *m* 1st, late Lina Jessie Ringer; 2nd, 1926, Ethel, *d* of Frank Brett and Janet Newbold Noyes, Washington; one *s* two *d*; 3rd, 1939, Norma, *d* of Col T. F. Bowler, Okemah, Okla. *Educ:* Eastbourne; Continent of Europe. Worked as journalist in England, France, China, Japan, Korea, Philippine Islands, and United States; was in Far East through period which included abolition of exterritoriality in Japan, Boxer Rebellion, announcement of Anglo-Japanese Alliance, and Russo-Japanese War; served European War in France, 1917–19; joined staff of The Times, 1919. *Address:* 2356 Massachusetts Avenue, Washington, USA. *TA:* Lontimes Washington. *T:* North 8219. *Club:* Devonshire.

Died 4 Jan. 1950.

LEWISHAM, Viscount; William Legge; Lt Staffordshire Yeomanry; *b* 23 Jan. 1913; *o s* of 7th Earl of Dartmouth, GCVO. *Educ:* Eton; Hertford College, Oxford.

Died Oct. 1942.

LEY, Sir (Henry) Gordon, 2nd Bt *cr* 1905; JP; Governing Director Ley's Malleable Castings Co. Ltd, Derby; *b* 12 March 1874; *s* of 1st Bt and Georgina Townsend (*d* 1886), *d* of late Capt. George Willis of Aislaby Hall, Yorks; *S* father, 1916; *m* 1st, 1899, Rhoda (who obtained a divorce, 1927 and *d* 1935), *d* of Herbert Prodgers, JP, of Kington St Michael, Wilts; two *s* one *d*; 2nd, 1927, Mabel Annie (who obtained a divorce, 1939), *d* of late Sir Philip Brocklehurst, Bt, of Swythamley Park, Macclesfield; 3rd, 1939, Dorothea Gertrude Borwick, *d* of late Charles Grey. *Educ:* Repton. Late Major 1st South Notts Hussars Yeomanry; Lord of Manors of Kirkoswald, Lazonby, Staffield and Glassonby in Cumberland. *Heir:* *s* Gerald Gordon. *Clubs:* Flyfishers', Royal Automobile.

Died 27 Sept. 1944.

LEY, Adm. James Clement, CB 1918; CVO 1916; *b* 1869; *m* 1906, Judith, *d* of late Rev. Evelyn Boothby. Served European War (despatches, CB, CVO); retired list, 1923; Russian Order of St Anne; Japanese Rising Sun, 2nd Class. *Address:* Almeley, Boxford, Newbury.

Died 15 July 1946.

LEY, James William Thomas; journalist; Editorial representative at Newport of the Western Mail; *b* Bristol; *m* 1912, Florence Madeleine, *e d* of late John Westcott, of Hatherleigh, North Devon; one *s*. *Educ:* Bristol Grammar School. Articled to journalism at Bristol Mercury; subsequently became a reporter on the Mercury Staff; assistant editor, The Easy Chair, 1904; later editor; founded Bristol and Clifton Dickens Society, 1902; Hon. Sec. and Treas. till 1904; Hon. General Secretary Dickens Fellowship, 1904–09; Vice-Pres. since 1920; one of founders of The Dickensian; rejoined Bristol Mercury Staff, 1909; later on staffs of Bath

Herald, Monmouthshire Post, Newport, and Evening Express, Cardiff; Assistant Editor Monmouthshire Post, 1919–21; joined Editorial Staff Evening Express 1921 as Man in the Street; a co-opted member of the Newport Boro. Free Libraries, Museum and Art Gallery Committee, 1930–37 and since 1942; Vice-Pres. National Union of Journalists, 1938–39, Pres. 1939–40. *Publications:* The Boz Birthday Book, 1905; Christmas in Dickens Land, 1905; The Drood Trial, 1914; The Dickens Circle, 1918; First annotated edition of John Forster's Life of Charles Dickens, 1928; (with Walter Dexter) The Origin of Pickwick, 1936; contributed Essay on Mr Tupman to A Pickwick Portrait Gallery, 1936. *Recreations:* literature and Dickensiana. *Address:* Hatherleigh, 2 Allt-yr-yn Road, Newport, Monmouthshire. *T:* Newport 3676.

Died 21 Aug. 1943.

LEYS, Sir (William) Cecil, Kt 1931; President of Leys Institute; *b* Auckland, 27 Feb. 1877; *s* of late Thomson Wilson Leys, LLD, Auckland, NZ; *m* 1921, Hilary, *d* of P. A. Vaile, barrister-at-law, Auckland, NZ; one *s*. *Educ:* Auckland Grammar School. Served European War, 1915–18, Balkans with Red Cross, and Mesopotamia with RNVR; Chairman of United Press Assoc., 1938–39, 1944–47. Chairman NZ Section Empire Press Union, 1941–46; Trustee of Reuters Ltd. *Address:* 24 Victoria Av., Remuera, Auckland, SE2, NZ.

Died 22 June 1950.

LIAKAT ALI, Sir Syed, Kt 1934; MA, LLB; *b* 1 July 1878; *s* of Syed Hamid Ali; widower; no *c*. *Educ:* Bareilly; Allahabad. Enrolled as an advocate of Allahabad High Court entered Bhopal State Service, 1903; held various appointments till 1922; Chief Justice, Bhopal High Court, 1922–27; Minister in attendance to HH The Ruler of Bhopal State, 1927–34; President of The State Legislative and Judicial Councils, 1927–36; member Bhopal State Cabinet, 1939–45; member Delhi University (formerly) and Aligarh Muslim University Courts. *Recreation:* motoring. *Address:* Bhopal, Central India.

Died 30 March 1947.

LIAQAT HYAT KHAN, Nawab Sir, KBE 1939 (OBE 1923); Kt 1933; Khan Bahadur; Political Adviser to the Ruler of Bhopal; *b* 1 Feb. 1887; *s* of Hon. Nawab Mohammed Hyat Khan, CSI; *m*; four *s* six *d*. *Educ:* privately. Deputy Superintendent, Punjab Police, 1909; Superintendent in charge of a District, 1919; King's Police Medal, 1916; served as Officer in charge Shahi Mela at the time of Prince of Wales's visit to Lahore, 1922; services lent to Patiala State as Home Secretary, 1923; Home Minister in Patiala State; resigned from Punjab Police, 1930; Prime Minister, Patiala State, 1930–40; retired from Patiala State Service, 1940; represented the Patiala State twice at the Round Table Conference in 1931 and 1932, and at the Joint Parliamentary Committee in 1933; also served on the Consultative Committee in India in connection with the Indian Reforms in 1932. *Recreation:* tennis. *Address:* Lakeview, Bhopal, India.

Died 9 July 1948.

LIAS, William John; Judge of County Court No. 59 (Plymouth) District, 1930–40; late Professor of International Law, Sheffield University; *s* of late Rev. John James Lias, Chancellor of Llandaff Cathedral, and Edith Susan Attenborough; *m* 1923, Winifred Marion Nickels, 3rd *d* of J. H. Beazley, Oak Dene, Noctorum, nr Birkenhead; one *s* one *d*. *Educ:* Haileybury Coll. (Exhibitioner); Jesus College, Cambridge (Scholar); 2nd Class Classical Tripos, 1889. Editor Cambridge Review, 1890–91; Headmaster Downs School, Clifton, Bristol, 1894–99; called to Bar, Lincoln's Inn, 1901; practised at Liverpool; Sub-Lieutenant and Lieutenant, RNVR, 1904–12; contested (L) West Derby Division, Liverpool, Jan. and Dec. 1910; Capt. in Lancashire Fusiliers, 1915;

transferred to RE 1917; served in France, 1916–19; OC Gas School, Rouen, 1917 (despatches). *Address:* Lumsholme, Middle Warberry, Torquay.

Died 20 July 1941.

LIDBURY, Ernest Alan, CBE 1924; *b* 1862. Formerly Assistant Secretary, Board of Customs and Excise. *Address:* 30 Highland Heath, Putney, SW15.

Died 29 Feb. 1948.

LIDDELL, Sir Frederick Francis, KCB 1916 (CB 1911); KC 1929; *b* 7 June 1865; *s* of Very Rev. H. G. Liddell, Dean of Christ Church, Oxford; *m* 1901, Mabel, *d* of Arthur Magniac, The Hermitage, Ascot; two *s* one *d* (and one *s* decd). *Educ:* Eton; Christ Church, Oxford, 1888 (first class Lit. Hum.). Private secretary to Lord Stanmore (then Sir Arthur Gordon), Governor of Ceylon, 1888–90; Fellow of All Souls College, Oxford, 1891–1906; Eldon Scholar, 1892; called to the Bar, 1894; 1st Parliamentary Counsel, 1917–28; Counsel to the Speaker, 1928–43; an Ecclesiastical Commissioner for England, 1944–48. *Publication:* edited Manual of Military Law. *Address:* Caesar's Camp, Sandy, Beds. *T:* Sandy 156.

Died 19 March 1950.

LIDDELL, Lionel Charles, MVO 1908; Consul at Copenhagen, retired 1911; *b* 22 May 1868; 3rd *s* of Very Rev. H. G. Liddell, Dean of Christ Church; *m* 1902, Florence (*d* 1942), *d* of Arthur Magniac; two *s* one *d*. *Educ:* Winchester; Christ Church, Oxford. Vice-Consul, Soulina, 1894; Galatz, 1897; Consul at Lyons, 1902; 4th Class Order of Dannebrog; Secretary Grand Committee on War Trade, 1914–18. *Recreations:* golf, fencing.

Died 21 March 1942.

LIDDELL, Maj.-Gen. Sir William Andrew, KCMG 1919; CB 1916; late RE; retired; *b* 26 Dec. 1865; *s* of late W. B. Liddell, Madras; *m* 1st, 1894, Ada Lilian Livesey (*d* 1915); one *d*; 2nd, 1921, Helen Gladys, *y d* of late Charles Townshend Murdoch, Buckhurst, Wokingham, and *widow* of Brig.-Gen. J. A. Tanner. *Educ:* Clifton College; RMA, Woolwich. Assistant and Deputy Secretary to Government of India, Military Department, 1900–06; Director of Fortifications and Works, War Office, 1920–24; served Operations of Zhob Field Force, 1890; European War, 1914–18 (despatches seven times, KCMG, CB, Officer Legion of Honour, Commander Order of the Crown, prom. Maj.-Gen.); retired pay, 1924; Director of Works and Buildings, Air Ministry, 1924–28; Col Comdt RE, 1933–35. *Address:* Manor House, Finchampstead, Berks. *Club:* United Service.

Died 17 Nov. 1949.

LIDIARD, Sir Herbert, Kt 1923; *b* Sept. 1864; *s* of late John Lidiard, JP, Clapham Common, first Mayor of Wandsworth; *m* 1st Kate Mary Lina (*d* 1924), *o d* of late Col A. R. Fuller, RA; one *s* one *d*; 2nd, 1931, Alex, *widow* of J. Wilson-Moore. Several times Mayor of Paddington; ten years member for Paddington on the LCC; many years Chairman South Paddington Conservative Association; Ruling Counsellor Paddington Habitations Primrose League; contested S Paddington parliamentary election, 1930. *Address:* 47 South Street, W1. *T:* Grosvenor 3317; 7 Great James Street, Bedford Row, WC1. *T:* Holborn 9140; Birchington, Kent.

Died 14 July 1941.

LIEBLING, Dr George; MusDoc (University of S California); concert-pianist and composer; *b* Berlin; American citizen, 1931; *s* of Jacob Liebling and Henriette Mosler; *m* Alice Goldberger. *Educ:* High School, Berlin, and Kullak's Academy of Music; studied later with Liszt. Played in Berlin at age of 11; concert tours in Europe, in Africa, and since 1924 in America; appeared as soloist with Sir Henry Wood, Sir Fred. Cowen, Sir Charles Villiers Stanford, Koussevitsky in Boston, Alfred Hertz in San Francisco, Art. Rodzinski in Los Angeles; Royal Court Pianist to Duke Alfred of Saxe-Coburg; commanded to play to Queen Victoria at Osborne, 1898; Order of Double Dragon, China; Lion and Sun, Persia; Cross of King Ludwig III of Bavaria; Gold Medal by Pope Pius X. *Works:* Dramatic-Musical Legend of St Catherine, 1906; opera: The Wager, 1912; opera; Chula, 1934; Concerto for piano with orchestra, 1925; Concerto for violin, 1924; about 200 works of every form and type for orchestra, suites, symphonic poem, piano, violin, cello, songs; Mass of Life, for four solo voices, chorus, orchestra, and organ, 1931; Lecturer and writer on musical subjects; Contributor to musical magazines; music to two of Shakespeare's poems: The Clown's Song Nr 4 from Twelfth Night, Foresters Song from As You Like It. *Recreation:* studying Shakespeare and books of philosophy. *Address:* c/o Musical Courier, 119 W 57th Street, New York City.

Died 7 Feb. 1946.

LIGHTLEY, Rev. John W., MA, BD, DLit; Minister of Methodist Church; Chairman of the Leeds District, 1915–30; President of the Conference, 1928–29; *b* Simonside, South Shields, 24 June 1867; *s* of Wm Lightley. *Educ:* Wesleyan Schools at East Jarrow and Castleford; Didsbury Coll., Manchester; Paris, at the Faculty of Protestant Theology and the Sorbonne; Leipzig, at the University. Intended for the teaching profession, but left this for the Ministry, entering the Theological College, 1889; held pastorates at Alnmouth (Northumb.), Newcastle-on-Tyne, Bolton, Paris (English), Harrogate (twice), and Headingley (twice); Tutor in OT subjects at Headingley College until the war broke out and led to the temporary closing of the College; Fernley Lecturer, 1919; elected to the Legal Hundred, 1921; Principal of Wesley College, Headingley, 1930–36. *Publications:* Les Scribes (a thesis for the BD, Paris), 1905; Jewish Sects and Parties in the time of Christ, 1925. *Address:* 49 West Park Crescent, Roundhay, Leeds 8. *T:* Leeds 68331.

Died 14 June 1948.

LIGHTSTONE, Herbert, DSO 1917; MC, FD, MD, CM; Deputy Director-General Medical Services, Ministry of Pensions, since 1933; Director-General Acting since 1938; *b* 27 Oct. 1878; *s* of Michael and Fanny Lightstone, Montreal; *m* 1912, Doris Eva Joseph (*d* 1927), of 66 Porchester Terrace, W2; two *d*. *Educ:* Montreal High School; Bishop University; McGill University, Montreal. Medical Superintendent, Women's Hospital, Montreal; Demonstrator of Anatomy, Bishop University, Montreal; Clinical Assistant, Aural Dept, London Hospital; Registrar, London Throat Hospital; served Spanish-American War with American Red Cross in Cuba, 1898; South African War with Canadian Field Artillery, 1899–1901 (Queen's medal 3 clasps); European War, 1914–19, France, Belgium, Germany, and North Russia; Lt 6th Cavalry Field Ambulance; MO Headquarters, 4th Army Command, 47 Casualty Clearing Station; MO Headquarters, North Russia (DSO, MC, FD, despatches 6 times). *Recreations:* travelling, golf. *Address:* 49 Lowndes Square, SW1. *T:* Sloane 3567; Brownleas, Aldwick, Sussex. *T:* Bognor 733. *Clubs:* Savage, Royal Automobile.

Died 12 Feb. 1942.

LILFORD, 5th Baron *cr* 1797; **John Powys;** JP; *b* 12 Jan. 1863; *s* of 4th Baron and *d* of Robert William Brandling, Low Gosford, Northumberland; *S* father, 1896; *m* 1894, Milly (*d* 1940), *d* of George Soltau-Symons, Chaddlewood, Plympton. *Educ:* Harrow; Brasenose College, Oxford (BA). Captain 3rd Batt. Northants Regt. Owns about 15,600 acres. *Recreations:* cricket, shooting, well-known breeder of shorthorn cattle. *Heir:* *b* Hon. Stephen Powys. *Address:* Lilford Hall, Oundle; Bank Hall, Preston. *Clubs:* Carlton, Travellers'.

Died 17 Dec. 1945.

LILFORD, 6th Baron *cr* 1797; **Stephen Powys;** *b* 8 March 1869; *e surv. s* of 4th Baron and Emma Elizabeth, *d* of Robert William Brandling, Low Gosford, Northumberland; *S* brother, 1945. *Educ:* Harrow, Trinity College, Cambridge. *Address:* Lilford Hall, Oundle, Peterborough. *Club:* Travellers'.

Died 19 Sept. 1949.

LILLEY, Canon Alfred Leslie; Canon Emeritus of Hereford; *b* 14 Aug. 1860; *e surv. s* of Joseph Lilley of Balleer, Co. Armagh; *m* 1st, 1895, Mary Leslie (*d* 1937), *e surv. d* of Major John Blackburn of 17 Ashley Gardens, Westminster; two *d*; 2nd, 1938, Winifred Eleanor, *e d* of F. E. G. Badger, Hodnet and Liverpool. *Educ:* Royal School, Armagh; Trinity College, Dublin. Moderator and Medallist in Modern Literature; Gold Medallist in Composition and Oratory of the University Philosophical Society; Medallist in Composition and Oratory of the College Theological Society. Downes Divinity Premium; Private Tutor at Trinity College, Dublin, 1886–89; Curate of Glendermott, Derry, 1889–91; Holy Trinity, Sloane Street, 1891–1900; Vicar of St Mary's, Paddington, 1900–12; Canon Residentiary of Hereford Cathedral, 1911–36; Prælector, 1911–39 and Chancellor, 1922–36, of Hereford; Archdeacon of Ludlow, 1913–28. *Publications:* Sir Joshua Fitch: his Life and Work, 1906; Adventus Regni, 1907; Modernism, 1908; What We Want (trans from Italian), 1907; Programme of Modernism (introduction), 1908; The Soul of St Paul, 1909; The Religion of Life, 1910; Nature and Super-nature, 1911; The Nation in Judgment, 1911; Prayer in Christian Theology, 1924; Worship; Its Necessity, Nature, and Expression, 1926; Sacraments, their Meaning for Christian Worship, 1928; Religion and Revelation, 1932; contributor to A Lent in London, Lombard Street Sermons, Prophets of the Century, Good Citizenship, Practical Questions, New Century Problems, Hastings' Encyclopædia of Religion and Ethics; Social Discipline in the Christian Community; Social and Political Thinkers of the Sixteenth and Seventeenth Centuries. *Address:* 25 Norham Road, Oxford.

Died 31 Jan. 1948.

LILLEY, Ernest Lewis, MB, BS Lond., FRCS Eng.; Consulting Surgeon to Leicester and Leicestershire Maternity Hospital; *b* 30 May 1876; *s* of Samuel John Lilley; *m* 1913, Margaret Nora, *y d* of late Dr Richard Wood, Llanbedr; no *c. Educ:* Wyggeston School; Charing Cross Hospital. Late Member of Council, BMA; Member of Council, Medical Defence Union; Chairman of National Service Recruiting Board; President of Leicester Public Medical Service; Member of Council, University College, Leicester; Organist of Great Meeting; late Captain RAMC (T); ex-Pres. Leicester Literary and Philosophical Soc. and Leicester Medical Soc. Member Therapeutic Substances and National War Formulary Committees, Ministry of Health. Author National Formulary, in Rolleston and Moncrieff's Favourite prescriptions. *Recreation:* music. *Address:* Waterloo Gates, 86 New Walk, Leicester; Delapré, Scraptoft, Leicestershire. *T:* Leicester 22471.

Died 22 Nov. 1948.

LILLICO, William Lionel James, CBE 1920; a partner in William Lillico & Son, corn and seed merchants, 6 Cherry Orchard Road, Croydon; *b* 1880; *s* of late William Lillico, Coombe Hill House, Croydon; *m* 1915, Florence, *d* of George E. Goldsmith; one *d.* Director of Feeding Stuffs Supplies, Ministry of Food during the European War. *Address:* Hillcrest, Brownlow Road, Croydon. *T:* Croydon 5767.

Died 18 Oct. 1948.

LILLINGSTON, Rev. Canon Arthur Blackwell Goulburn, MA; Canon Residentiary of Durham, 1914–42; Canon Emeritus, 1942; Sub-Dean, 1927; Rural Dean of Durham, 1924; *b* 12 Nov. 1864; 2nd *s* of late Rev. F. A. C. Lillingston, at one time Archdeacon of Yass, NSW; *m* 1st, 1895, Mabel Mary (*d* 1922), *e d* of late G. W. Campbell, 22 Queen's Gate Gardens, SW; one *s* (*yr s* killed in Libya in Nov. 1941); 2nd, 1926, Margaret Milora (*d* 1928), 3rd *d* of late William Cross of Minterne, Dorset; 3rd, 1931, Margaret Helen, *d* of Rev. C. F. Bickmore. *Educ:* Queens' College, Cambridge. Ordained 1887; Curate of St Paul, Onslow Square, 1887–95; Vicar of Christ Church, Blackburn, 1895–99; St Margaret, Ipswich, 1899–1904; Holy Trinity, Hull, 1904–14; Hon. Canon of York Minster, 1913; Vicar of St John's, Paddington, 1914; Examining Chaplain for the Bishop of Durham, 1914–20, and since 1934. *Publication:* Thoughts on Evangelism, 1918. *Recreations:* golf, motoring, fishing. *Address:* The College, Durham. *T:* Durham 44.

Died 20 April 1943.

LIMERICK, May, Countess of; Mary Imelda Josephine, CBE 1920; *d* of late Joseph Burke Irwin; *m* 1890, 4th Earl of Limerick (*d* 1929). *Address:* Hall Place, Bexley, Kent.

Died 11 March 1943.

LINCOLN, Joseph; *b* 13 Feb. 1870; *m* 1897, Florence E. Sargent, Chelsea; one *s. Publications:* Cape Cod Ballads, 1902; Cap'n Eri, 1904; The Old Home House, 1905; Partners of the Tide, 1905; Mr Pratt, 1906; Cy Whittaker's Place, 1907; Keziah Coffin, 1908; Our Village, 1909; The Depot Master, 1910; The Woman-Haters, 1911; Cap'n Warren's Wards, 1911; The Postmaster, 1912; The Rise of Roscoe Paine, 1912; Mr Pratt's Patients, 1913; Cap'n Dan's Daughter, 1914; Kent Knowles; Quahaug, 1914; Thankfuls Inheritance, 1915; Mary-'Gusta, 1916; Extricating Obadiah, 1917, Shavings, 1919; Portygee, 1920; Galusha the Magnificent, 1921; Fair Harbor, 1922–1923; Doctor Nye, 1923–1924; Rugged Water, 1924–1925; Queer Judson, 1925–1926; Big Mogul, 1926; The Aristocratic Miss Brewster, 1927; Silas Bradford's Boy, 1928; Blowing Clear, 1929; All Alongshore, 1931; Head Tide, 1932; Back Numbers, 1933; Blair's Attic, 1929 (with J. Freeman Lincoln). *Address:* Chatham, Mass, USA. *Clubs:* Dutch Treat, New York; Art, Franklin Inn, Philadelphia.

Died 10 March 1944.

LINDLEY, Rt Hon. Sir Francis (Oswald), PC 1929; GCMG 1931; KCMG 1926); CB 1919; CBE 1917; JP 1934; Official Verderer to the New Forest since 1943; *b* 12 June 1872; 4th *s* of late Lord Lindley; *m* 1903, Hon. Etheldreda Mary Fraser (*d* 1949), 3rd *d* of 13th Lord Lovat; four *d. Educ:* Winchester; Magdalen College, Oxford. Attaché, 1896; Clerk, FO, 1897; Acting Third Secretary, Vienna, 1899; Tehran, 1900–01; Second Secretary, Diplomatic Service, 1902; served under the Egyptian Government, 1902–04; in HM Agency, Cairo, 1904–06; Tokyo, 1906–08; Foreign Office, 1908–09; promoted First Secretary, Diplomatic Service, 1909; Sofia, 1909–11; Christiania, 1912; Counsellor of Embassy at Petrograd, Nov. 1915; HM Commissioner in Russia June 1918; HM Consul-General in Russia, 1919; High Commissioner, Vienna, 1919–20; Envoy Extraordinary and Minister Plenipotentiary to Republic of Austria, 1920; at Athens, 1922–23; Oslo, 1923–29; Ambassador to Portugal, 1929–31; Ambassador Extraordinary and Plenipotentiary to Japan, 1931–34; retired, 1934; holds War Medals, Jubilee Medal, 1935, and Coronation medals of 1902, 1911, and 1937; has received allowances for knowledge of International Law, Persian, and Arabic; is Chairman of Meux's Brewery Co. and of the Sena Sugar Estates, Limited, and a Director of the Imperial Continental Gas Association and the Anglo-Portuguese Bank; a County Alderman for Hampshire; is a member of Council and Hon. Treasurer of Zoological Society of London; Chairman Test and Itchen Fishing Association; Home Office Advisory Committee on interned Aliens since 1939. *Publications:* A Diplomat off

Duty, 1928; Life of Lord Lovat, 1935. *Address:* The Weir House, Alresford, Hants. *T:* Alresford 59. *Clubs:* Turf, Brooks's.

Died 17 Aug. 1950.

LINDLEY, Hon. Walter Barry; JP Barrister-at-law; *b* 1861; 2nd and *e surv. s* of late Baron Lindley; *m* 1908, Hilda Mary, *o d* of Capt. C. M. Fox, late Border Regt, and Mrs Fox of Corfe House, Taunton. *Educ:* Winchester; University College, Oxford (MA); Lincoln's Inn. CC Judge, Derbyshire, 1902–12; Chairman, Quarter Sessions, Derbyshire, 1909–12. Judge of County Courts in Devon and Somerset (Circuit 57) 1912–34; Deputy Chairman of Quarter Sessions (Somersetshire) 1914–20; Chairman, 1920–31. *Address:* Corfe House, Taunton. *Clubs:* Athenæum; County, Taunton.

Died 29 March 1944.

LINDNER, Peter Moffat, RWS, ROI, RWA, RBC; landscape and sea painter; *b* Birmingham, 12 Feb. 1852; *s* of late Maximilian Lindner; *m* Augusta Katherine Baird, *d* of late Capt. F. M. Smith, RA; one *d*. *Educ:* Proprietary School, Edgbaston. Studied at Slade School and Heatherley's. Exhibitor for many years at New English Art Club, Grosvenor, New Gallery, Royal Academy, and Continental galleries; represented in State Collections and Permanent Galleries at Wellington (NZ), Auckland (NZ), Blackpool, Barcelona, Rome, Liverpool, Bradford, Oldham, Hull, Dublin, Huddersfield, Doncaster, Cheltenham, and Brighton; Bronze Medal Paris International Exhibition, 1900; Gold Medal, Barcelona International Exhibition, 1911; Medal, SA International Exhibition, 1892. *Recreations:* fly-fishing, golf. *Address:* Chy-an-Porth, St Ives, Cornwall. *Club:* Arts.

Died 19 Sept. 1949.

LINDOW, Lt-Col Isaac William B.; *see* Burns-Lindow.

LINDSAY, 13th Earl of, *cr* 1633; **Archibald Lionel Lindesay;** Lord Lindsay of The Byres, 1445; Baron Parbroath, 1633; Viscount Garnock; Baron Kilbirny, Kingsburne and Drumry, 1703; *b* 14 Aug. 1872; *s* of 11th Earl of Lindsay and Emily Marian, *d* of Robert Crosse, *widow* of Capt. E. C. Barnes, 91st Regt; *S* brother, 1939; *m* 1900, Ethel (*d* 1942), *d* of W. Austin Tucker, Boston, USA; one *s*. Heir: *s* Viscount Garnock. *Address:* Manchester-by-Sea, Mass, US.

Died 15 Oct. 1943.

LINDSAY, Col Creighton Hutchinson, CMG 1915; DSO 1918; MD, MB, BCh Edin.; DPh Cantab; Col AMS Territorial Army; retired; *b* 25 April 1877; *e s* of Stewart Lindsay, Islandburn, Ballaghy, Londonderry; *m* 1906, Margaret Hélène Swenarton; one *s* two *d*. *Educ:* University, Dublin and University, Edinburgh. Served in Edinburgh City Volunteer Artillery, 1897–1901; Lieutenant, RAMC (Vol.), 1907; transferred to Territorial Force, 1908; Captain, 1911; Major, 1914; temp. Lt-Col 1915; temp. Col 1917; left England, March 1915, with 29th Division; was senior medical officer in charge of landing at Y Beach, Gallipoli, on 25 April 1915; commanded 87th Field Ambulance since the landing (despatches eight times, DSO). *Address:* Wentworth, Dene Road, Northwood, Middlesex.

Died 21 Feb. 1941.

LINDSAY, Sir Darcy, Kt 1925; CBE 1919; *b* Duns, 14 Nov. 1865; *s* of David Baird Lindsay of Dowhill; unmarried. *Educ:* abroad. Late Secretary, Royal Insurance Company, Ltd, Calcutta; Kaisar-i-Hind Gold Medal, 1911. *Address:* 26 and 27 Dalhousie Square, Calcutta, India. *Clubs:* East India and Sports; Bengal, New, Calcutta.

Died 17 April 1941.

LINDSAY, Ernest Charles, CBE, 1919, MB, BS (Lond.), FRCS; Surgeon, London Hospital; Consulting Surgeon Poplar Hospital; Surgeon, Royal Masonic Hospital; Fellow Association of Surgeons of Great Britain and Royal Society of Medicine; *b* 24 April 1883; *s* of late Rev. George Lindsay, Christchurch, NZ; *m* 1921, Mrs Mae C. Davis, Undercliff, St Margaret's Bay. *Educ:* Otago University. *Address:* 149 Harley Street, W1.

Died 23 Oct. 1943.

LINDSAY, John Allan, CBE 1937; DL; JP; Chairman Leith Dock Commission and Leith Employment Committee; *b* 1865; *s* of late Thomas Lindsay, Shipowner, Leith; *m* 1901, Lillias Catherine, *d* of late Robert Cairns, Shipowner, Leith; one *s* and *d*. *Educ:* Edinburgh Institution. Leith Town Council, 1904–20; Provost of Leith, 1916–20; Leith Hospital Board for 25 years, President for 12 years. *Address:* Gleniffer, Trinity, Edinburgh. *T:* 83151.

Died 21 April 1942.

LINDSAY, Leonard Cecil Colin, FSA, FSA Scot; Private Chamberlain to Pope Pius XII and formerly to Popes Leo XIII, Pius X, Benedict XV and Pius XI; formerly Secretary of the New Gallery; Treasurer of the Catholic Record Society; *b* 23 June 1857; 4th *s* of late Hon. Colin Lindsay of Deer Park, Honiton, and Lady Frances Howard, *d* and *co-heiress* of 4th Earl of Wicklow; *m* 1902, Clare, *e d* of Col Francis Baynham Vaughan of Courtfield, Herefordshire. *Educ:* Oscott Coll., Birmingham. Private Sec. to the Earl Marshal for the Coronation, 1901–02; Member of the Special Embassy sent to Madrd by HH Pius X for the marriage of King Alphonso (Commander of the Order of Isabel the Catholic); Albert Medal for work for Belgians during the late War. *Address:* 15 Morpeth Mansions, Morpeth Terrace, SW1; 29 Plemont Gardens, Bexhill. *Clubs:* Windham, Burlington Fine Arts; Devon and Exeter, Exeter.

Died 15 Oct. 1941.

LINDSAY, Lionel Arthur, MVO 1912; OBE 1920; late Chief Constable of Glamorganshire; *b* 1861. Adjutant, Major and Inspector of Egyptian Gendarmerie. *Address:* Canton, Cardiff. *Clubs:* Bath, Royal Automobile; Cardiff and County, Cardiff.

Died 15 April 1945.

LINDSAY, Rt Hon. Sir Ronald (Charles), PC 1925; GCB 1939; GCMG 1926; KCB 1929; KCMG 1925; CB 1922; CVO 1919; MVO 1908; *b* 3 May 1877; 5th *s* of 26th Earl of Crawford; *m* 1st, 1909, Martha (*d* 1918), *d* of ex-Senator J. Donald Cameron, Pennsylvania; 2nd, 1924, Elizabeth Sherman, *d* of late Colgate Hoyt, New York. Attaché, 1898; 2nd Secretary, 1904; at St Petersburg, 1899–1903; Tehran, 1903–05; Washington, 1905–07; Paris, 1907–08; Foreign Office, 1908–11; The Hague, 1911–13; Secretary to British Representatives, International Opium Conference, 1911; Grand Officer, Order of the Nile, 1915; Under-Secretary of State for Finance to Egyptian Government, 1913–19; Counsellor of Embassy at Washington, 1919–20; Minister Plenipotentiary at Paris, 1920–21; Under-Secretary (addl) at the Foreign Office, 1921–24; HM Representative, Constantinople, 1924–25; Ambassador, 1925–26; British Ambassador at Berlin, 1926–28; Permanent Under-Sec. of State, Foreign Office, 1928–30; British Ambassador at Washington, 1930–39. *Address:* Stapleton House, Blandford. *Club:* Travellers'.

Died 21 Aug. 1945.

LINDSAY, Ven. Thomas Enraght, MA; Archdeacon of Cleveland, 1907–38, Emeritus since 1938; Canon of York since 1918; Examining Chaplain to Archbishop of York since 1907; *s* of late Rev. Thomas Lindsay; *m* 1892, Marie Isobel (*d* 1938), *d* of late Captain G. K. S. Massy Dawson, JP, DL, Ballincourte, Ireland. *Educ:* Manchester Grammar School; Sidney Sussex Coll., Camb. (Scholar). Ordained 1886; Chaplain Epsom College, 1886–88;

Curate of Doncaster, 1889–93; Vicar of Loversal, Yorks, 1891–92; St Paul's, Middlesbrough, 1893–1905; Scarborough, 1905–13; Saltburn-by-the-Sea, 1913–25; Rector of Stokesley, 1925–36. *Address:* St Ovin, Lastingham, York.

Died 7 Sept. 1947.

LING, George Herbert; Professor of Mathematics; Director of the Summer School; Dean of the Faculty of Arts and Science, University of Saskatchewan; Acting-President, 1919–20; *b* Wallacetown, Ontario, 15 Jan. 1874; *m* 1906, Effie, *d* of George J. Sherry, Peterboro, Ontario; one *s. Educ:* University of Toronto (BA 1893), LLD (Hon.), 1927; University of Chicago; Columbia University (PhD 1896). Instructor in Mathematics, Wesleyan University, Middletown, Connecticut, 1896–1901; Tutor, Instructor and Adjunct Professor, Columbia University, 1901–09; Instructor in Mathematics (summer session), University of Cincinnati, 1900; University of California, 1906; New York University, 1912; Columbia University, 1918; Member, Council of the American Mathematical Society, 1916–19; Secretary-Treasurer, National Conference of Canadian Universities, 1923–28; President, 1928–29. *Publications:* On Tidal Theory; On Simple Groups of Order, 1093–2000 (with G. A. Miller); Elements of Projective Geometry (with G. Wentworth and D. E. Smith). *Address:* Saskatoon, Canada. *Clubs:* University of Toronto, New York; Saskatoon, Saskatoon.

Died 21 Oct. 1942.

LINNELL, Air Marshal (temp.) Sir Francis John, KBE 1943; CB 1941; OBE 1923; Deputy AOC-in-C, RAF, Middle East, 1943–44; *b* 1892; *m* 1917, Margaret Christabel, *d* of R. A. Carpenter, St Leonards. *Educ:* Bloxham. Served in European War in RNAS and RAF (despatches thrice); Air Commodore, 1939; Air Vice-Marshal, 1939. *Address:* HQ, RAF Middle East.

Died 3 Nov. 1944.

LION, Leon M.; actor, playwright and play producer; Chevalier Legion of Honour, 1928; *b* London, 12 March 1879; *m* 1907, Kathleen Crighton Symington (who obtained a divorce, 1925). *Educ:* Private School, Hampstead. First appeared as actor in London in True Blue at Olympic Theatre, 1895; toured with Forbes Robertson, Martin Harvey, Fred Terry, George Edwardes, etc.; Scarlet Pimpernel, 1905; Title role in New Boy revival, 1907; Asticot in Beloved Vagabond, 1908; Merchant of Venice, False Gods, etc., 1909–10; Aristide Pujol, Typhoon, Within the Law, 1912–13; produced Ghosts, Monna Vanna, Three Daughters of Dupont, 1913–15 (first performances in England); Management at New Theatre with the Chinese Puzzle, Jack o' Jingles, Time to Wake Up, 1918–19; Right to Strike, Brown Sugar, Count X, 1920–21; Araminta. The Faithful Heart, Other People's Worries, 1922; Galsworthy Cycle and Windows; Mid-Channel; Sweet Lavender; The Outsider; Coming of Gabrielle, 1923; Lord of Creation, Blinkers, Tiger Cats, In the Snare, 1924; S African tour, 1924–25, returning Aug. 1925 with No. 17; Cristilinda, The Godless, Enchantress, 1926; Escape, Riceyman Steps, The Fanatics, The One Eyed Herring, The Lady in Law, The Way of the World, 1927; Two White Arms, The Man They Buried, Many Waters, Listeners, Justice, Loyalties, The Love Lorn Lady, The Stranger in the House, The Unknown Warrior, To What Red Hell, Napoleon's Josephine, Holding out the Apple, 1928; Living Together, The Skin Game, Mariners, Exiled, 1929; This Way to Paradise, 1930; Money Money, The World of Light, Black Magic, The Immortal Lady, Champion North, 1931; While Parents Sleep, Man Overboard, Hocus Pocus, 1932; The Bear Dances, a Cup of Happiness, The Holmeses or Baker Street, Beggars in Hell, 1933; So Good! So Kind!!, Night Club Queen, 1933; Libel!, CID, Hurricane, The Big House, 1934; Galsworthy Festival Season, 1935; My Son's My Son, 1936; Ibsen Festival,

1936; The Five Ways, 1937; Land's End (with Anmer Hall), 1938; Trumpeter, Play!, 1938; Hundreds and Thousands, 1939. *Plays:* Co-author (with Tom Gallon) of The Man Who Stole the Castle, 1900–02, The Fairy Uncle, 1906, The Touch of the Child, The Naked Man; (with Malcolm Cherry) of Mr Jarvis, 1911, Jack o' Jingles, 1919; (with Marian Bower) of The Chinese Puzzle and Altar of Liberty, 1918–19; (with Austin Philips) Playing the Game, Promotion, 1912; (with H. A. Vachell) Blinkers, 1923; (with Rafael Sabatini) In The Snare; (with Basil Mitchell) The Five Ways, 1937; (with Sarah Benedict Tapping) Hundreds and Thousands, 1939; (with L. A. Jones) No Name in the Visitors Book, 1941; (with May Edginton) Danger, 1943; (with Clifford Bax) Hemlock for Eight, 1943. *Publications:* The Chinese Puzzle (with Marian Bower), Novel, 1919; The King who had Nothing to Learn; The Mobs-woman; The Touch of the Child. *Recreations:* poetry, motoring. *Club:* Savage.

Died 27 March 1947.

LIPATTI, Dinu; Pianiste et Compositeur; Professeur de virtuosité au Conservatoire de Genève (Suisse); *b* Bucarest, 19 March 1917; de père roumain et mère roumaine. *Educ:* Bucarest and Paris. Elève de Paul Dukas, Alfred Cortot et Nadia Boulanger; filleul et disciple de Georges Enesco; brillante carrière de pianiste dans tous les pays d'Europe. De nombreux concerts et enrégistrements (Columbia Graphophone Company) en Angleterre. *Publication:* Concertino en style classique op. 3 pour piano et orchestre de chambre (édité par Universal Édition), 1936. *Recreation:* lecture. *Address:* 7 Rue des Chaudronniers, Geneva, Switzerland. *TA:* Lipatti Geneva. *T:* 4–55–01.

Died 3 Dec. 1950.

LISTER, Col James Fraser, CMG 1918; MIEE; Director Spencers (Melksham), Ltd; *s* of late W. J. Lister of Dursley, Glos; unmarried. *Educ:* Dean Close, Cheltenham. Raised and commanded the Southern Telegraph Cos RE on formation of TF, 1908; served European War, 1914–18 (promoted full Colonel, CMG). *Recreations:* golf, fishing, and shooting. *Address:* 12 All Saints Road, Clifton, Bristol.

Died 30 March 1944.

LISTER, Tom, CIE 1932; *b* 10 May 1887. *Educ:* Wheelwright Grammar School, Dewsbury; St John's College, Cambridge. Entered ICS, 1910; retired, 1937. *Address:* Bramhope Hall, Bramhope, nr Leeds, Yorkshire.

Died 26 March 1945.

LISTER, Sir William Tindall, KCMG 1919; KCVO 1934; CMG 1916; MA, MD, FRCS; Consulting Surgeon-Oculist to the King; Consulting Ophthalmic Surgeon, London Hospital; Consulting Surgeon, Royal London Ophthalmic Hospital; *b* 4 Nov. 1868; *y s* of late Arthur Lister, FRS; *m* 1894, Grace, 4th *d* of Wm Cleverly Alexander; four *s. Educ:* Oliver's Mount School, Scarborough; Trinity College, Cambridge. Surgeon Oculist to HM Household, 1919–36; late Consulting Ophthalmic Surgeon, Expeditionary Force; Ophthalmic Surgeon to the London Hospital; Ophthalmic Surgeon Hospital for Sick Children, Great Ormond Street, and Assistant Surgeon Central London Ophthalmic Hospital; served European War, 1914–19 (despatches, KCMG, CMG). *Publications:* contributions to ophthalmic literature. *Address:* The Old House, Bledlow Ridge, High Wycombe, Bucks. *Clubs:* Leander, Alpine.

Died 7 July 1944.

LISTON, Lt-Col William Glen, CIE 1913; MD, DPH; *b* 30 July 1873. Entered IMS 1898; Captain, 1901; Major, 1910; entered Bacteriological Department, 1908; Director of the Bacteriological Laboratory, Parel, and Senior Member of the Plague Research Commission, 1911; retired, 1924; Bacteriologist Royal College of

Physicians, Edinburgh, 1925–47; Consulting Physician to Colonial Office, 1926–47. *Address:* Garramore, Morar, Inverness-shire.

Died 18 Oct. 1950.

LITTLE, Andrew George, MA; DLitt; *b* 1863; *s* of Rev. Thomas Little, Rector of Princes Risborough; *m* 1893, Alice Jane, *d* of late William Hart, Fingrith Hall, Blackmore. *Educ:* Clifton College; Balliol College, Oxford; Göttingen University. 1st Class Modern History, Oxford, 1886. Professor of History, University College, Cardiff, 1892–1901; Reader in Palæography, University of Manchester, 1904–28; Examiner in Modern History at Oxford, 1904–06, and in University of Wales, 1907–08; Chm. of British Society of Franciscan Studies, 1906–37; Member of Council of Canterbury and York Society since 1910, Chairman, 1927; Ford's Lecturer in English History at Oxford, 1915–16; War Trade Intelligence Department, 1916–18; FBA, 1922; Vice-President, R. Historical Society, 1923–26, 1928, Hon. Vice-President, 1940; President of the Historical Association, 1926–29; Hon. DLitt Oxford, 1928; Hon. LittD Manchester, 1935. *Publications:* Grey Friars in Oxford, 1892; Mediæval Wales, 1902; Description du MS Canonici Misc., 525, 1903; Initia Operum Latinorum, 1904; Tractatus from Thomae de Eccleston, 1904; Liber Exemplorum, 1908; Tractatus Jo. Pecham, 1909; Opus Tertium of Roger Bacon, 1912; Roger Bacon Commemoration Essays, 1914; Collectanea Franciscana, 1914; Studies in English Franciscan History, 1917; Un nouveau manuscrit Franciscain, 1919; A Guide to Franciscan Studies, 1920; History of the Franciscan Province of Ireland, 1920; Studies in the History of Political Philosophy by the late Professor C. E. Vaughan (edited with Memoir), 2 vols, 1925; Mediæval Studies presented to Professor Tout (edited in conjunction with Professor Powicke), 1925; Some recently discovered Franciscan documents and their relations to Celano and Speculum Perfectionis, 1926; Franciscans and Dominicans of Exeter (with R. Easterling), 1928; Roger Bacon, De retardatione senectutis, etc. (edited with E. Withington), 1928; Sabatier's Speculum Perfectionis, Tome II, Etude Critique (edited), 1931; Oxford Theology and Theologians ad 1282–1302 (with F. Pelster, SJ), 1934; Franciscan History and Legend in English Mediæval Art, 1937; Franciscan Papers, Lists and Documents, 1943; contributions to historical journals; Cambridge Mediæval History, vol. vi. *Address:* Risborough, Sevenoaks. *Club:* Athenæum.

Died 22 Oct. 1945.

LITTLE, Gen. Arthur Greenway, CMG 1918; Royal Marines, retired; *b* 1875; *s* of G. G. Little, District Judge, Jamaica; *m* 1906, Phyllis Dorothy, *d* of late Charles H. Beloe, MICE, Liverpool; one *s. Educ:* United Service College, Westward Ho! Joined Royal Marines, 1894; Director of Naval Recruiting, 1924–27; Marine ADC to the King, 1928–29; Commandant Portsmouth Division Royal Marines, 1927–29; retired list 1932. *Address:* South Down, Tavistock, Devon. *Club:* United Service.

Died 9 Nov. 1948.

LITTLE, David, CBE 1936; JP; Director; *b* 20 June 1867; *s* of Andrew and Anne Little; *m* 1897, Mary (*d* 1945); three *s* one *d. Educ:* Leeds Modern School. *Recreations:* yachting, golf, curling. *Address:* 21 Wetherby Road, Roundhay, Leeds. *TA:* David Leeds. *T:* Leeds 66472. *Clubs:* National Liberal; Leeds.

Died 4 March 1947.

LITTLE, Sir Ernest Gordon Graham-, Kt 1931; BA Cape Univ.; MD Lond.; FRCP Lond.; MRCS Eng.; Physician in charge of the Skin Department, St Mary's Hospital, 1902–34 and 1940–41; Consulting Physician, East London Hospital for Children; Member of the Senate, 1906–50; Chairman of the Council for External Students, 1922, retd 1946; Member of the Court since its inception, 1929, retd 1947; Member of other principal Committees, University of London; Consulting Dermatologist to the Benevolent Funds of the NUT, Concert Artistes Association, and Officers of Local Government Board; *s* of Michael Little, JP, ICS, and Anna, *d* of Alexander English of Cape Town; *m* Sarah Helen, *d* of Maurice Kendall (one *d* drowned at sea 1932; one *s* killed on active service, RAFVR 1942). *Educ:* South African College, Cape University (Gold Medallist, Porter Scholar). Studied medicine at Guy's Hospital and St George's Hospital, London University; Rotunda Hospital, Dublin; and University of Paris; represented University of London at Tercentenary of University of Hungary, 1935. Rep. Royal Society of Medicine at Pasteur centenary celebrations at Universities of Paris and Strasbourg; Hon. Pres. 9th International Dermatological Congress, 1935; during World War, Consulting Dermatologist to the Military Hospitals in London; late Pres.-elect, Dermatological Society of Great Britain; Vice-President, Harveian Society; Past President of British Assoc. of Dermatology and Syphilology; Past Pres. of Dermatological Sections of RSM and BMA; Hon. Mem. American Dermatological Assoc. and the Dermatological Societies of France, Italy, Hungary, Spain, Austria, Poland, Denmark, and Argentina. Hon. Mem. Royal Academy of Medicine, Rome; Royal Soc. Physicians, Budapest; Norwegian Medical Soc.; Member of Council and Governor, London School of Hygiene and Tropical Medicine; Governor Royal Veterinary College; MP (Ind) University of London, 1924–50; late Chm. Civil Service Cttee and Founder and First Chm. University Members' Committee, House of Commons; Pres. University of London Graduates' Assoc. since 1922; Member of Council: Brit. Chess Fed.; London Soc.; Footpaths Preservation Soc.; Soc. of Individualists; League for European Freedom; Fighting Fund for Freedom, etc. *Publications:* articles in Nineteenth Century, Contemporary Reviews, Empire Review, Edinburgh Review, etc. on Voluntary Hospitals, General Medical Council, Emergency Medical Service, Radium and the Public, British Empire and Backward Races, Wholemeal Bread, etc., and articles on Medical subjects in Journal of the American Medical Assoc., British Journal of Dermatology, Lancet, etc. Frequent contributor political and educational subjects, London Daily Press and periodicals, educational and scientific journals Great Britain, Europe and USA. *Address:* 19 Upper Wimpole St, W1; Wimpole Lodge, Epsom, Surrey. *T:* Epsom 2080. *Clubs:* Athenæum, Knights of the Round Table, Casual.

Died 6 Oct. 1950.

LITTLE, George Leon; landscape and animal painter; *b* London; *y s* of Thomas Little; *m* 1st, Emma Harvey (*d* 1918), *d* of George Smith of The Luham, Edenhall; 2nd, Elma Mary, *d* of J. J. Curtis of Horley; one *s* one *d. Recreation:* lecture-recitals on Dickens. *Address:* Wraycot, Lower Kingswood, Surrey. *TA:* Lower Kingswood. *T:* Reigate 2511.

Died 13 May 1941.

LITTLE, Rev. James, BA, BD, STD; Minister of Castlereagh Presbyterian Church since 1915; MP (U) Co. Down since 1939 (Ind U since 1945); *b* Oct. 1868; *s* of Francis Little, and Eleanor Kennedy; *m* 1903, Jane Graham, *e d* of late Rev. Hugh Hastings; two *s* five *d. Educ:* Queen's University, Belfast; Royal University, Dublin; Presbyterian College, Belfast. Minister of Dundrod Presbyterian Church, 1900–10; of Knoxland Parish, Dumbarton, 1910–15; Member of Dumbarton School Board, 1911–14; Life Governor Royal Victoria Hospital, Belfast; Grand Chaplain of Loyal Orange Institution in Ireland, 1938; Member of Executive of Bible Society and of Portstewart Convention Committee. *Publications:* The Cross in Holy Scripture, 1911; The Cross In Human Life, 1912; A Plea For The Preaching of The Cross, 1918; In Touch With The Throne, 1919; Light For Dark Days, 1924; The Story of

An Historic Church, 1935; The Bible in Life and Character, also booklets and brochures. *Recreations:* walking and gardening. *Address:* Castlereagh Manse, Co. Down. *TA:* Castlereagh, Belfast. *T:* Belfast 57804.

Died 31 March 1946.

LITTLE, Robert, RWS, RSW, FSA Scot; *b* Greenock; *s* of Robert Little, shipowner, and Annie Pitcairn; *m* Ada L. M. Bogle (*d* 1934); one *s* one *d*. *Educ:* Academy, and Avenue Park School, Greenock; Edinburgh Academy; Glasgow University. Student of the Royal Scottish Academy, 1876–81; British Academy, Rome, 1882; Paris, 1886. Elected Member, Royal Scottish Water-Colour Society, 1886; Hon. retired member, 1936; Associate, Royal Society of Painters in Water-Colours, London, 1892; Member, 1899; Vice-President, 1913–16, Hon. retired member, 1934; awarded Paris Salon Diploma, 1898; Paris International Exhibition, bronze medal, 1900; examples of work in Manchester, Huddersfield, and Ipswich Art Galleries, Watt Institution, Greenock, in the Guildhall Art Gallery, London, and in Argentina, Canada, Australia, etc. *Address:* 2B Clanricarde Gardens, Tunbridge Wells. *T:* Tunbridge Wells 2350.

Died 18 Oct. 1944.

LITTLEHAILES, Richard, CIE 1927; MA; *b* 14 Feb. 1878; 2nd *s* of late John Littlehailes, Sunderland; *m* Roberta May (*d* 1941), *o d* of J. Rutherford, Sunderland; one *s* one *d*. *Educ:* Bede School, Sunderland; Balliol College, Oxford; Kiel University. Demonstrator and Lecturer, Clarendon Laboratory, Oxford, 1902; Indian Educational Service, 1903; Director of Public Instruction, Madras, 1919; Educational Commissioner with the Government of India, 1927; Educational Adviser, Baroda State, 1933; Vice-Chancellor Madras University, 1934–37; retired. *Publications:* The Duration of School Life; Reports on Public Instruction. *Recreations:* apiculture, gardening and bridge. *Address:* Longstile, Connaught Road, Fleet, Hants. *T:* Fleet 817.

Died 16 Dec. 1950.

LITTLER, Rev. Harold Davies, MA; Vicar of the Collegiate Church of S Mary, Warwick, since 1945; Hon. Canon of Coventry Cathedral since 1944; Examining Chaplain to Bishop of Coventry, 1943; Proctor in Convocation of Canterbury, 1944, and Member of Church Assembly; *b* 1887; *s* of John Littler; *m* 1913, Marian, *o d* of John Phethean Monks, Bolton, Lancs; no *c*. *Educ:* Rossall School (Scholar); Jesus College, Oxford (Scholar); 2nd Class Mod. Hist., 1910; FRHistS 1911; FSA 1946. Assistant Master at Pocklington School, 1910–11; House Master at Liverpool College, 1911–19; Curate of Christ Church, Linnet Lane, Liverpool, 1914–18; Chaplain St Mary's Church, for the Blind, Liverpool, 1918–19; Headmaster of Coatham School, Redcar, 1919–41; Rector of Shipston-on-Stour, 1941–45; Clerical Secretary Coventry Diocesan Conference 1946. Select Preacher at Oxford (Latin Sermon), 1947; Chaplain to the High Sheriff of Warwickshire, 1947–48. *Publication:* School Sermons. *Recreations:* travel, fishing. *Address:* The Old Deanery, Warwick. *TA:* Littler, Warwick. *T:* Warwick 392. *Clubs:* Royal Societies; Warwick County (Warwick).

Died 3 Jan. 1948.

LITTLETON, Hon. Charles Christopher Josceline, DSO 1918; Lt-Col retired; *b* 18 July 1872; 3rd *s* of 3rd Baron Hatherton; *m* 1st, 1903, Aline Beatrix (*d* 1919), 2nd *d* of late Sir Frederick Hervey Bathurst, 4th Bt; one *s*; 2nd, 1922, Lettice Mina, *widow* of Lieut-Col R. P. H. Bernard, *d* of late Gerald Paget. Served European War (DSO, despatches thrice); High Sheriff of Radnorshire, 1937–38; Arabian Order of the Nahda, 4th Class. *Address:* Bridge Cottage, Sheepwash, Beaworthy, Devon. *Club:* Lansdowne.

Died 12 March 1950.

LIVERPOOL, Earl of, 5th holder of title and 2nd of revived title; **Arthur William de Brito Savile Foljambe,** GCB 1920; PC 1917; GCMG 1914; GBE 1918; KCMG 1912, and a Knight of Justice of the Order of St John of Jerusalem; Viscount Hawkesbury of Kirkham, Co. Yorks, and Mansfield, Co. Notts; *cr* of earldom, 1796; revived, 1905; also Baron Hawkesbury of Haselbech, Northamptonshire, and of Ollerton, Sherwood Forest, Nottinghamshire *cr* 1786; title revived, 1893; MVO 1900; Governor of New Zealand, 1912–17; Governor-General, 1917–20; *b* 27 May 1870; *s* of the Earl of Liverpool, Lord Steward, 1905–07, and Louisa Blanche, *e d* of Frederick John Howard (*brother-in-law* of 7th Duke of Devonshire); *S* father 1907; *m* 1897, Hon. Annette Louise Monck, GBE, *d* of 5th Viscount Monck. *Educ:* Eton; RMC, Sandhurst. 2nd Lt Rifle Brigade, 1891; Lt 1893; Captain, 1897; ADC to Earl Cadogan, KG, Lord Lt of Ireland, 1898–1900; formerly Major, The Rifle Brigade (Prince Consort's Own); Staff Captain, Dublin District, July 1900 to Dec. 1901; served South Africa, 1901–02; Major, 1907; State Steward and Chamberlain to the Earl of Aberdeen, KT, Lord Lieut of Ireland, 1906–08. Owns estates in Lincolnshire. *Recreations:* hunting, shooting, cricket, and racquets. *Heir:* *b* Hon. Gerald W. F. Savile-Foljambe, DSO. *Address:* Canwick Hall, Lincoln. *Club:* Naval and Military.

Died 15 May 1941.

LIVESAY, Brig.-Gen. Robert O'Hara, CMG 1919; DSO 1902; *b* 27 June 1876; *o s* of late Col R. A. Livesay, RE; *m* 1917, Margaret, *o d* of William Pretyman. *Educ:* Wellington College; Sandhurst; Staff College. Entered Army, 1896; served South Africa, 1899–1902 (despatches, Queen's medal 5 clasps, King's medal 2 clasps, DSO); left army Feb. 1914; called up Aug. 1914; appointed GSO, 2nd grade; re-gazetted regular army Oct. 1915, as junior Capt. in The Queen's (his old) regiment; European War, 1914–18 (despatches, prom. Bt Major, Lt-Col and Col CMG); 1st Infantry Brigade, Aldershot; retired with rank of Brig.-General, 1920; American DSM; Legion of Honour. *Recreations:* English International Rugby Football, Kent County Cricket. *Address:* c/o Coutts & Co., 440 Strand, WC2; The Manor House, Magham Down, near Hailsham, Sussex. *T:* Herstmonceux 3258.

Died 23 March 1946.

LIVINGSTON, Brig.-Gen. Guy, CMG 1917; FRGS; late Royal Air Force; *b* 1881; *m* 1st, Ethel Dalgetty Tatlow; 2nd, 1922, Mrs Diva Amelia Primrose (*d* 1933); 3rd, 1934, Anne Hamilton (whom he divorced 1940). *Educ:* St Paul's School. Director of Air Organisation in War Office, 1917; Deputy Master-General of Personnel, Air Ministry, 1918; lent USA Govt to organise American Military Air Service, 1918; Aeronautical Correspondent The Times, 1919; served South African War, 1902 (Queen's medal with three clasps); European War, 1914–18 (CMG, despatches four times, Orders of Crown of Italy, St Stanislas of Russia). *Publication:* Hot Air in Cold Blood, 1933. *Club:* Royal Air Force.

Died 10 May 1950.

LIVINGSTONE, Sir Alexander Mackenzie, Kt 1933; Director of Steel and Building Companies; Member of the London Tribunal for hearing the cases of Conscientious Objectors, 1940; *b* 18 Oct. 1880; *s* of late Duncan Livingstone of Applecross, Ross-shire, and Catherine, *d* of Alexander Mackenzie, Dingwall; *m* 1905, Mary, (*d* 1946), *d* of Donald M. MacAskill, Montreal; four *s*; *m* 1947, Maggie Clark, *d* of late Robert Murray, Stornoway. MP (L) Inverness, Western Isles Division, 1923–29; Contested Dover, 1918; Inverness, 1922 (twice); Whip, Radical Parliamentary Group, formed in opposition to the leadership of Mr Lloyd George; declared himself unable to endorse the Liberal Unemployment Pledge, and consequently withdrew in 1929 as Liberal candidate for the Western Isles; joined

Labour Party, 1930; JP County of London. *Address:* 2 St Albans Road, NW5. *T:* Gulliver 3831. *Clubs:* National Liberal; Royal and Ancient (St Andrews).

Died 24 Sept. 1950.

LIVINGSTONE-LEARMONTH, Frederick Valiant Cotton, DSO 1900; late Lieut NSW Mounted Rifles; Director of Bank of Australasia; Australian Agricultural Co.; Peel River Land Co; *b* Ercildoune, Victoria, 6 June 1862; 3rd *s* of Thomas Livingstone-Learmonth, Park Hall, Stirlingshire, Scotland; *m* 1901, Rin, *o d* of Rev. Canon Carlisle of Melbourne; two *d. Educ:* Westminster; Pembroke Coll., Camb. (MA). At age of 21 went out to Australia and took up squatting pursuits; went to South Africa with 2nd Contingent NSW Mounted Rifles, Jan. 1900; took part in engagements at Osfontein and Driefontein, and made the general advance to Pretoria under Lt-Col De Lisle in Gen. Ian Hamilton's column; with De Lisle at Diamond Hill; was there for two months under Lt-Col Hickman, and subsequently and up to April 1901, served continuously with Lt-Col De Lisle in his operations in the ORC and Cape Colony. *Address:* Corner House, South Stoke, via Reading.

Died 12 July 1945.

LLEWELLIN, George Herbert, CBE 1922; JP; *b* 1871; 2nd *s* of late Alderman John Llewellin, JP, CC; *m* 1895, Alice Maude Mary, *e d* of Morgan Jones, Delbury, Shropshire; five *s* four *d. Educ:* Haverfordwest Grammar School; Wellington College. Three times Mayor of Haverfordwest, 1911–17–1918; High Sheriff of Town and County of Haverfordwest, 1922; Chairman of Roose Bench and Governing Body of Haverfordwest Grammar School; Trustee Local Charities; Ministry's Nominee of Pembrokeshire Agricultural Committee. *Recreations:* farming, motoring. *Address:* Red Hill, Haverfordwest, Pembrokeshire. *T:* 169.

Died 30 May 1946.

LLEWELLYN, Brig.-Gen. Evan Henry, DSO 1918; JP; *b* 31 July 1871; *s* of Llewellyn and Rose Mary Llewellyn; *m* 1913, Clara Maude, MBE, *d* of Charles Ross, Oaken Holt, Oxford; two *s* two *d. Educ:* Wellington College; Sandhurst. *Address:* Nethway House, Kingswear, Devon. *T:* Kingswear 207.

Died 19 Oct. 1948.

LLEWELLYN, Col Sir Hoel, Kt 1943; DSO 1900; DL; Chief-Constable, Wilts, since 1908; *b* 24 Nov. 1871; *s* of late Colonel Evan Henry Llewellyn, MP; *m* 1st, 1902, Winifred (*d* 1931), *y d* of late Alexander Berens; 2nd, 1933, Mary Constance, *d* of Walter Sandeman, Morden House, Cambridgeshire. *Educ:* Royal Navy. As midshipman saw active service, East Coast of Africa, 1888–90 (despatches); artillery officer, Matabele War, 1893–94 (despatches); commanding artillery, 2nd Matabele War, 1896–97 (recommended for VC by General Commanding); Captain BSA Police and JP Matabeleland, 1896; served throughout S African War; commanded armoured trains N of Mafeking and artillery of General Plumer's Column (despatches four times); transferred to SA Constabulary, 1901; Comdt Lichtenburg District and JP Transvaal Colony, 1902; served with the Mediterranean Expeditionary Forces, 1914–15 (wounded); promoted to the rank of Colonel, graded as AAG on the General Headquarter Staff, and appointed Provost Marshal of Egypt and the British Mediterranean Expeditionary Force; served in France, Tank Corps) despatches 3 times). *Address:* Caen Hill House, Devizes. *TA:* Police Devizes. *T:* Devizes 39. *Club:* White's.

Died 2 April 1945.

LLEWELLYN, Lt-Col John Malet, CBE 1924; 3rd *s* of late Llewellyn Llewellyn of Nethway, Kingswear, S Devon; *m* 1939, Margaret, *e d* of late Canon Parry Pughe. *Educ:* Malvern College. Joined the Devonshire Regiment, 1904; served European War in East Africa and France (twice wounded, despatches); was in charge of the administration of the Northern Frontier Province, and later OC Troops, Kenya; retired pay, 1925; unofficial member Legislative Council, Tanganyika, 1929–34. Secretary Lansdowne Club, London W1, 1936–45.

Died 8 Dec. 1945.

LLEWELLYN, Sir William, GCVO 1931; KCVO 1918; RA 1920; ARA 1912; RI; Member of Royal West of England Academy; Hon. Member of the Royal Scottish Academy; Hon. Member of the Royal Hibernian Academy; Hon. Member of the Royal Institute of Oil Painters; Hon. Fellow of the Society of Painter Etchers; Hon. Fellow Royal Institute of British Architects; Hon. Fellow of the Institute of British Decorators; Hon. Corresponding member of the National Academy of Design, New York; once a member of The New English Art Club, The Royal Society of British Artists, Royal Society of Portrait Painters, and Royal British Colonial Society of Artists—since resigned; Grand Officer of the Order of Orange Nassau, Holland; Grand Cross of the Crown of Italy; Commander of the Legion of Honour; Albert Medal, Royal Society of Arts; *b* Dec. 1863; *m* 1893, Marion (*d* 1926), *d* of T. M. Meates, Wimbledon; one *d. Educ:* South Kensington under Sir E. Poynter; Paris under Ferdinand Cormon, Lefebvre and Ferrier. President of the Royal Academy, 1928–38; Trustee of National Gallery, 1933–40; Painter of many portraits—including the State portrait of Queen Mary, the United Services Club portrait and others of Her Majesty. *Address:* Little Blundell House, Campden Hill, Kensington, W8. *T:* Park 8807. *Clubs:* Athenæum, Arts, Savage.

Died 28 Jan. 1941.

LLEWELLYN-JONES, Frederick; HM Coroner for Flintshire; *b* Bethesda, Caernarvonshire, 18 April 1866; *e s* of Humphrey Bradley Jones and Lucy A. George; *m* 1892, Elizabeth, *y d* of late Edward Roberts, Ruthin; three *s* two *d. Educ:* Friar's School, Bangor; Bala College; University College of Wales, Aberystwyth; BA (Wales and London); LLB (London); Dr Sc. Pol (Hon.) University of Pécs, Hungary. Member Royal Hungarian Order of Merit; Admitted Solicitor, 1891; associated with Educational and Health Administration in Wales; Chairman, Holywell School Board, 1898–1904; Member of Flintshire Joint Education Committee; Member of Court of Governors of University College of Wales, Aberystwyth and University College of North Wales, Bangor; formerly Member Welsh University Court and Court of Governors of Welsh National Library and of Welsh National Museum; MP (L) Flintshire 1929–35; Chairman, Flintshire Insurance Committee, 1912–40; First President, and President, 1937–38, Assoc. of Welsh Insurance Committees; President of Federation of English, Scottish, and Welsh Insurance Committees, 1924–26, 1929–31, and 1934–37; appointed by National Insurance Commissioners and Ministry of Health Member of successive Advisory Committees and Welsh Consultative Health Council; Member of Central Council for Health Education, 1923–40; Fellow of the Royal Empire Society; Associate of the Institute of Public Administration; has taken an active part in connection with World Peace and International Politics; President of the Welsh League of Nations Union, 1933; Member International Law Association, 1912–39; Grotius Society of London, 1915–39; Royal Institute of International Affairs; American Society of International Law, and other English and foreign Peace and International Law Societies; Society of Comparative Legislation; Société de Législation Comparée, Paris; Medico-Legal Society of London, 1915–38; Member of the Cymmrodorion Society and of the Gorsedd of the Welsh National Eisteddfod. *Publications:* The Road Traffic Act, 1930; Contributions to Transactions of Grotius Society and Medico-Legal Society; articles on International Law and

Comparative Law in various periodicals. *Recreation:* walking. *Address:* Isfryn, Mold, Flintshire. *TA:* Coroner Mold. *T:* Mold 18 and 99.

Died 11 Jan. 1941.

LLEWELYN-WILLIAMS, Dr David, CBE 1935; MC; FRCS (E); LLD (hc, Univ. of Wales); *b* 3 Feb. 1870; *s* of Rev. John Williams, Presbyterian Minister; *m* 1906, Margaret A. Price; two *s* one *d. Educ:* Llandudno Collegiate School; Edinburgh. Entered Public Health Service in 1904, as Assistant MO of H for Leith, 1906; DPH 1906; Medical Officer of Health for Wrexham and District, 1910; for the County of Denbigh, 1912; Medical Officer to National Health Insurance Commission (Wales); joined the RAMC 1914 and served in France until 1919 (MC). Granted by the French President, for help rendered to Civilians in the war area, the Médaille de la Reconnaissance Française, and the Médaille d'Honneur des Epidémies; Medical Member of the Welsh Board of Health, 1920–35; Vice-Chairman of the Council of the Welsh National School of Medicine. *Publications:* several booklets and pamphlets on public health subjects. *Address:* Bwlchgwyn, 16 Min-y-Don Avenue, Old Colwyn, N Wales. *T:* Old Colwyn 5689.

Died 12 May 1949.

LLOYD, 1st Baron *cr* 1925, of Dolobran; **George Ambrose Lloyd,** PC 1924; GCSI 1924; GCIE 1918; CIE 1917; DSO 1917; FRGS; Secretary of State for the Colonies since 1940; Captain late Warwickshire Yeomanry; *b* 19 Sept. 1879; *s* of S. S. Lloyd of The Priory, Warwick, and Dolobran, Montgomeryshire, Wales; *g s* of S. Lloyd, MP Rugby Division of Warwick, and also Plymouth; *m* 1911, Hon. Blanche (late Maid of Honour to Queen Alexandra), *d* of late Hon. F. C. Lascelles; one *s. Educ:* Eton; Cambridge. Student Eastern Politics. Travelled extensively in Burmah, India, Little Thibet, the Himalayas, Egypt, Morocco, and Asia Minor; afterwards appointed Hon. Attaché to HM Embassy at Constantinople; Special Commissioner for HMG to inquire into and report upon the future of British trade in Turkey and Mesopotamia and Persian Gulf, 1908; served European War in Egypt, Gallipoli, Mesopotamia, and the Hedjaz, 1914–18 (despatches six times); MP (U) West Staffordshire, 1910–18; Governor of Bombay, 1918–23; MP (C) Eastbourne, 1924–25; High Commissioner for Egypt and the Sudan, 1925–29; President of Navy League, 1930; President Seamen's Hospitals, President Royal Central Asian Society; Chairman British Council, 1936; Star of the Nile; St Ann of Russia, of the Hedjaz. *Publications:* The Great Opportunity, 1919; Egypt since Cromer, vol. i, 1933, vol. ii, 1934; The British Case, 1940. *Heir: s* Hon. Alexander David Frederick Lloyd [*b* 30 Sept. 1912. Eton; Cambridge]. *Address:* 11 Morpeth Mansions, SW1. *T:* Victoria 5111; Cloud's Hill, Offley, Hitchin. *Clubs:* Carlton, Garrick, Bath; Royal Yacht Squadron, Cowes.

Died 4 Feb. 1941.

LLOYD, Sir Alan Hubert, Kt 1939; CSI 1934; CIE 1928; Indian Civil Service (retired); *b* 30 Aug. 1883; *s* of late John Lloyd, Cheadle Hulme, Cheshire; *m* 1923, Violet Mary Orrock; no *c. Educ:* King William's College, Isle of Man; Gonville and Caius College, Cambridge; Members' Prize for Latin Essay; Bhavnagar Medal. Joined Indian Civil Service in Burma, 1907; served in Customs Department, 1910–23; Member Central Board of Revenue, India, 1923–38; Secretary, Commerce Dept, Govt of India, 1939–42; finally retired, after temporary re-employment, 1947. *Address:* c/o National Bank of India, Ltd, Delhi. *Club:* East India and Sports.

Died 9 May 1948.

LLOYD, Rev. Albert Henry, CBE 1919; Rector of St Giles-in-the-Fields since 1929. *Educ:* King's College, London. Was Secretary of the Church Army, Naval and Military War Work, 1914–18. *Address:* St Giles School House, Endell Street, WC2.

Died 29 June 1941.

LLOYD, Brig.-Gen. Arthur Henry Orlando, CB 1919; CMG 1917; MVO 1901; late Lt-Col Shropshire Yeo., and Capt. retd Grenadier Guards; JP, DL County Salop; *b* 31 May 1864; *o s* of late Arthur Philip Lloyd of Leaton Knolls and Leila K. S., *d* of late Vice-Admiral Hon. C. O. Bridgeman; *m* 1893, Anna Maria Heywood (*d* 1935), *d* of Arthur Pemberton Heywood Lonsdale of Shavington and Cloverley, Co. Shropshire; one *s* one *d. Educ:* Eton. Served in Grenadier Guards, 1884–97; Adjutant 2nd Batt. Grenadier Guards, 1889–93; Suakim Campaign, 1885 (medal and clasp, Khedive's Star); European War (CB, CMG); JP, DL Co. Salop; Alderman Salop CC; Director (local) Alliance Assurance Co. *Address:* Leaton Knolls, near Shrewsbury. *T:* Bomere Heath 24. *Clubs:* Guards', Carlton.

Died 24 Oct. 1944.

LLOYD, Bertram Arthur; Emeritus Professor of Forensic Medicine, University of Birmingham; Consulting Surgeon, Birmingham United Hospital, Children's Hospital, Birmingham, and Smallwood Hospital, Redditch; *b* Birmingham, 1884; *s* of Walter John Lloyd and Elizabeth Bolton, Birmingham; *m* 1930, Hilda Nora Shufflebotham, MRCS, LRCP; no *c. Educ:* King Edward's High School, Birmingham; Birmingham Univ.; London Hospital. MRCS, LRCP, 1908; MB, BS Lond., 1909; FRCS Eng., 1911. ChM Birm., 1933; late House Surgeon, Hospital for Sick Children, Great Ormond Street and Resident Medical Officer Charing Cross Hospital; Capt. RAMCT, 1915–19, attached to 1st Southern and Second 1st Southern General Hospital; President University Graduates' Club, Birmingham, 1935; President University of Birmingham Medical Society, 1935–36. *Recreations:* foreign travel, mountaineering, music. *Address:* 40 Harborne Road, Edgbaston, Birmingham. *T:* Edgbaston 2270; Spadesbourne, Mearse Lane, Barnt Green, Worcs. *T:* Hillside 1358. *Club:* Union (Birmingham).

Died 22 Jan. 1948.

LLOYD, Dorothy, J.; *see* Jordan Lloyd.

LLOYD, Comdr Edward William, CB 1911; RN; *b* 26 June 1855; *s* of W. Butler Lloyd, Preston, Montford Hall, Shropshire; *m* 1st, 1883, Charlotte McCrea (*d* 1938), *d* of Rev. H. A. Taylor; two *s* one *d*; 2nd, 1938, Bertha, *d* of Richmond Tupper, Coggeshall, Essex. *Educ:* Foster's School, Stubbington; HMS Britannia. Passed into the Navy, 1868; served in the Mediterranean and Pacific; Sub-Lieut 1877; three first-class certificates; Lieut 1877; served in HMS Temeraire in expedition to Sea of Marmora, 1878; First-Class gunnery Lieut 1880; served on the gunnery staff of HMS Excellent; in HMS Inflexible, 1881–85; present during bombardment of Alexandria and subsequent proceedings on the coast of Egypt; (medal, clasp, and Egyptian star); served on senior staff, HMS Excellent, 1885–88; on staff of the Director of Naval Ordnance, Admiralty, 1889; Commander, 1889; resigned, 1889; joined Sir W. G. Armstrong, Whitworth & Co.; Emergency List of Naval Officers, 1901; Order of Rising Sun, Fourth Class, 1904, for services to the Japanese Government; Commander Tyneside Division RNVR 1904–14; served with Ministry of Munitions, Oct. 1915–Feb. 1919. *Publication:* (joint) Artillery, its Progress and Present Position. *Recreations:* shooting, fishing, croquet, and motoring. *Address:* Monkmoor, Beechwood Avenue, Weybridge. *TA:* Lloyd, Monkmoor, Weybridge. *T:* Walton-on-Thames 546.

Died 22 Sept. 1945.

LLOYD, Ernest Sampson, CSI 1924; ICS (retired); JP; Chairman, Worcestershire Agricultural Wages Committee and Worcestershire War Agricultural Committee, Cottage Panel; *b* 1870; 2nd *s* of Sampson Zachary Lloyd of Areley Hall, Stourport, Worcestershire; *m* 1899, Mary, *d* of William Young, St Peter's Manor, Droitwich; three *s*. *Educ:* Clifton College; Lincoln College, Oxford. Indian Civil Service in the Madras Presidency, 1894–1923; Collector and District Magistrate; President of the Madras Corporation, 1906–10; Revenue Secretary; Financial Secretary; Acting Chief Secretary, 1923. *Recreation:* gardening. *Address:* The Lower House, Areley Kings, Stourport, Worcestershire. *T:* Stourport 88.

Died 7 Aug. 1945.

LLOYD, Francis Ernest, BA, MA, DSc (Hon.) Univ. of Wales and Masaryk Univ; FRSC (President 1933); FLS; Emeritus Professor of Botany, McGill University, Montreal; *b* Manchester, 4 Oct. 1868; *s* of Edward Lloyd, Aberystwith, and Leah Pierce, Denbigh; *m* 1903, Mary Elizabeth, *d* of late Thomas Hart, Northfield, Mass; two *s*. *Educ:* Liverpool Institute; Lafayette College; Princeton University; University of Bonn and University of Munich. Instructor in Biology, Williams College, Mass, 1891; Professor, Biology and Geology, Pacific University, Oregon, 1892; Adjunct Professor Biology, Teachers College, Columbia University, NY, 1897; Investigator, Carnegie Institute of Washington (Desert Laboratory), 1906; Cytologist, Arizona Agricultural Experimental Station, 1907; Director, Dept of Investigation, Continental-Mexican Rubber Co., 1907; Professor, Botany, Alabama Polytechnic Institute, 1908; Macdonald Professor of Botany, McGill University, 1912–34; Explorations, etc. Lumholtz Expedition to Mexico, 1890; Columbia Univ. Expedition to Puget Sound and Alaska, 1896; New York Botanical Garden Expedition to Dominica, BWI, 1903; Rubber Investigation in Java, Sumatra and Malaya, 1919; member of numerous foreign societies; President Section K, BAAS, 1933; Alpha Omega Alpha; Sigma XI (Member Executive Committee). *Publications:* Botany in the Teaching of Biology in the Secondary Schools, 1904; Comparative Embryology of the Rubiaceae, 1902; Physiology of Stomata, 1908; Guayule, a Rubber Plant of the Chihuahuan Desert, 1911; Elementary Course in General Physiology (with G. W. Scarth), 1930; The Carnivorous Plants, 1942; and other contributions to botanical literature. *Recreation:* travel. *Address:* Carmel, California, USA; McGill University, Montreal, Canada.

Died 17 Oct. 1947.

LLOYD, Sir Idwal Geoffrey, Kt 1937; CSI 1933; Indian Civil Service (retired); *b* 13 Jan. 1878; *s* of late John Lloyd Cheadle Hulme, Cheshire; *m* 1910, Georgette Helena Grant; three *d*. *Educ:* King William's College, Isle of Man; Gonville and Caius Coll., Cambridge (Bhavnagar Medal, 1902). Joined the ICS in Burma, 1902; served as Assistant Commissioner; Under-Secretary to the Government of India, 1909–10; Deputy Commissioner in Burma, 1916; Commissioner, 1927; Financial Commissioner, 1930–35; Temporary member of Governor's Council, 1930–31 and 1932; member of Governor's Council (Finance and Revenue Depts), 1935–37; (late) Major, Rangoon Batt., Indian Defence Force. *Club:* East India and Sports.

Died 6 March 1946.

LLOYD, Sir John Edward, Kt 1934; MA, DLitt (Oxon), Hon. DLitt (Wales), Hon. DLitt (Manchester), FBA; Emeritus Professor of History, University College of North Wales, Bangor; *b* 5 May 1861; *s* of Edward Lloyd, linen draper, Liverpool; *m* 1893, Clementina Miller of Aberdeen; one *s* one *d*. *Educ:* University College of Wales, Aberystwyth; Lincoln College, Oxford. First Class in Classical Moderations, 1883; First Class in Honours School of Modern History and BA 1885.

Lecturer in Welsh and History at the University College of Wales, Aberystwyth, 1885–92; Secretary and Registrar and Lecturer in Welsh History at the University College of North Wales, Bangor, 1892; Professor of History, 1899–1930; Warden of Guild of Graduates of University of Wales, 1899–1901; Member of Council of University College of North Wales; Extern Examiner in History for the National Univ. of Ireland, 1916–20; Ford's Lecturer in the University of Oxford, 1919–20; Sir John Rhys Memorial Lecturer, 1928; Chairman of the Ancient Monuments Board for Wales; FSA; President of the Welsh Language Society; of the Cambrian Archæological Association, 1923 and 1937; Vice-Pres. Royal Historical Society; Member of the Royal Commission on Ancient Monuments in Wales; of Royal Commission on Tithe Rent Charge; Medallist and Vice-Pres. of the Hon. Society of Cymmrodorion; Member of the Council of the National Library of Wales and of the National Museum of Wales; Chairman of the Union of Welsh Independents, 1934–35; received Freedom of the City of Bangor, 1941. *Publications:* A History of Wales to the Edwardian Conquest, 1911; editor of Hubert Lewis's Ancient Laws of Wales; contributor of articles on Welsh worthies to the Dictionary of National Biography; three school text-books on the History of Wales to 1282; the Cambridge County Geography of Carnarvonshire, 1911; Hywel Dda Millenary Handbook, 1928; The Welsh Chronicles (Proceedings of the British Academy, xiv); A History of Wales, 1930 (Welsh translation, 1943); Owen Glendower, 1931; Sir Harry Reichel (a memorial volume), 1934; editor and contributor, A History of Carmarthenshire, Vol. I, 1935; Vol. II, 1939; The Story of Ceredigion, 1937. *Address:* Gwaen Deg, Bangor, North Wales. *T:* 233.

Died 20 June 1947.

LLOYD, Brig. Gen. John Henry, DSO 1917; JP; High Sheriff of Flintshire, 1934–35; *b* 1872; *s* of late Major J. H. Lloyd, RA; *m* 1900, Amy Oliver, *d* of late Sir Thomas Jackson, Bt; two *s* one *d*. *Educ:* Wellington; RMC, Sandhurst. Served King's Own Royal Regt, 1892–1913; European War, 1914–19 (DSO); retired with rank of Brig. Gen., 1919. *Address:* Queensbridge, Ellesmere, Salop. *T:* Overton 3.

Died 5 Nov. 1941.

LLOYD, Maj.-Gen. Sir Owen Edward Pennefather, VC; KCB 1923; CB 1910; *b* 1 Jan. 1854; *s* of late Major M. Pennefather Lloyd, 59th Regt, of Co. Roscommon; *m* Florence (*d* 1938), *d* of late Captain and Lady Louisa Morgan, of Bridestown House, Co. Cork, and *g d* of 3rd Earl of Mount Cashel; one *s* one *d*. *Educ:* Fermoy College and Queen's University, Cork. Member of the Royal Irish University; LRCS; LRCP; LM Edin. Joined Army Medical Service, 1878; went through Zulu War, 1879; was present at the attack and capture of Sekukunni's stronghold as Assist Instructor to Bearer Column, Transvaal War, 1881–82; in Standerton during siege; Kachin Expedition, 1892–93; attack on Fort Siva; given the VC for conspicuous bravery during the attack; took command of fort after death of Capt. Morton, officer commanding; was medical officer to the Franco-British Boundary Commission to the Mekong River, 1894–95; Medical Officer to British-Chinese Boundary Commission on Burma Frontier, 1898–99; acted as HBM's Commissioner during absence of Sir G. Scott; PMO Bareilly Brigades, India, and Hon. Surg. to Viceroy; PMO S Africa; served European War (despatches); retired, 1913; Colonel Commandant, RAMC, 1922–24. *Recreations:* all kinds of field sports, especially big-game shooting; well known as a shikari in Burmah, killing, in the year 1897, 150 head of big game, including six tusker elephants.

Died 5 July 1941.

LLOYD, Lt-Col Thomas Owen, CMG 1916; DL, JP Argyllshire; late The Black Watch; *b* 30 Sept. 1866; *s* of late Thomas Lloyd of Minard, Co. Argyll; *m* 1902, Mabel (*d* 1941), 3rd *d* of late Bayly Collyns; two *s* one *d*. Served S African War, 1901–02 (Queen's medal 4 clasps); European War, 1914–16 (despatches, CMG). *Address:* Minard Castle, Argyll.

Died 17 March 1945.

LLOYD, Maj.-Gen. Wilfrid Lewis, CBE 1941; DSO 1941; MC; Divisional Commander, India, since 1942; *b* York, 1 March 1896; *s* of E. T. Lloyd, ICS Shrewsbury; *m* 1922, Phyllis Janet Turner; one *s* one *d*. *Educ:* Shrewsbury School; Trinity College, Dublin. Commissioned, 1914, 7th KSLI; served European War, France, 1915–17 (MC); transferred to Indian Army, 1917, 1st Kumaon Rifles; served NWF, India, 1919–20; attended Staff College, Camberley, 1927–28; Brigade Major, 1930–33; Commanded 4/19 Hyderabad Regt, 1936–39; Colonel and GSO1 of a Div., 1939; Bde Commander, 1940; served Middle East, 1939–41 (CBE, DSO and bar); acting Major-Gen., 1941; Director of Military Training, GHQ, Delhi, 1941–42; Temp. Maj.-Gen., 1942. *Recreations:* tennis, shooting, fishing, ornithology. *Address:* c/o Lloyd's Bank, 6 Pall Mall, SW1.

Died 22 Jan. 1944.

LLOYD, William, FRSM; FFSc; Aural and Laryngeal Surgeon to Music Hall Benevolent Home; late House Surgeon, London Throat Hospital; late Surgeon in charge of the Nose, Ear, and Throat Department, Kensington General Hospital and St Pancras and Great Northern Dispensary; late Senior Clinical Assistant Nose, Ear, and Throat Department London Hospital, E; late Hon. Aural and Laryngeal Surgeon, Music Hall Artistes Benevolent Home, and Eccentric Club Hostels for limbless soldiers, etc; *b* 1874. *Educ:* University College of Wales; London Hospital. Laryngologist to Signor Caruso for 15 years; to the Magic Circle; stopped whistling for cabs; brought first and successful action at Marlboro Street station against Claridge's Hotel. Hon. Member of Inner Magic Circle. *Publications:* Hay Fever and Hay Asthma, its Causes, Diagnosis, and Treatment, 3rd edition, 1931; articles in various medical journals. *Address:* 58 Brook Street, Grosvenor Square, W1. *T:* Mayfair 3085. *Clubs:* Royal Automobile, National Sporting.

Died 11 June 1948.

LLOYD GEORGE OF DWYFOR, 1st Earl *cr* 1945; **David Lloyd George,** PC 1905; OM 1919; Viscount Gwynedd of Dwyfor, 1945; DCL (hon.) Oxon; LLD Wales, 1908; Hon. LLD Edin., 1918; Hon. LLD Sheffield, 1919; Grand Cordon of the Legion of Honour, 1920; MP (L) Caernarvon 1890–1931, (Ind L) since 1931; Solicitor; Prior of the Priory for Wales, Order of St John of Jerusalem, since 1943; *b* Manchester, 17 Jan. 1863; *s* of late William George, Master of Hope Street, Unitarian Schools, Liverpool; *m* 1st, 1888, Margaret (GBE 1920) (*d* 1941), *d* of Richard Owen, Mynyddednyfed, Criccieth; two *s* two *d*; 2nd, 1943, Frances Louise Stevenson. *Educ:* Llanystumdwy Church School and privately. Solicitor, 1884; President of the Board of Trade, 1905–08; Chancellor of the Exchequer, 1908–15; Minister of Munitions, 1915–16; Secretary of State for War, 1916; Prime Minister and First Lord of the Treasury, 1916–22; Chairman Cærnarvonshire Quarter Sessions, 1929–38. *Publications:* War Memoirs (6 vols), 1933–1936; The Truth about the Peace Treaty (2 vols), 1938. *Heir:* *s* Viscount Gwynedd. *Address:* Bron-y-de-Churt, Surrey; Ty Newydd, Llanystumdwy, Caernarvonshire. *Clubs:* National Liberal, Reform.

Died 26 March 1945.

LLOYD JAMES, Arthur, MA; University Professor of Phonetics, School of Oriental and African Studies, London, 1933–41; formerly; Linguistic Adviser to BBC, Secretary of BBC Advisory Committee on Spoken English, Phonetic Adviser to Linguaphone Institute, London and Adviser on Radio Telephone Speech to RAF; *b* 21 June 1884; *s* of late William James, Mining Engineer, Penrhiwceiber, S Wales, and Rachel Jones; *m* Elsie (Fellow Royal Academy Music) (*d* 1941), *d* of late Luther Owen, Llanelly; one *s*. *Educ:* Llanelly; University College, Cardiff; Trinity College, Cambridge. Lecturer in Phonetics, Islington Training College, 1910–14; served European War, Royal Engineers, 1916–19; Lecturer in Phonetics, University College, London, 1920–27; Royal Academy of Dramatic Art, 1924–33; School of Oriental Studies, London, 1927; University Reader in Phonetics, 1930; associated with broadcasting, and speech problems involved, from 1924; has broadcast on speech and language in England, on the Continent, in USA and Canada; Member of Philological Society, Modern Language Association, International Phonetic Association. *Publications:* Historical Introduction to French Phonetics; English Conversation Course; Literary Phonetic Reader; English Speech; Bible Readings; Broadcast English Handbooks; 1. Words of Doubtful Pronunciation, 2. English Place Names, 3. Scottish Place Names, 4. Welsh Place Names, 5. Place Names of Northern Ireland, 6. Foreign Place Names, 7. British Family Names and Titles; The Broadcast Word; A Basic Phonetic Reader; Our Spoken Language; Speech Signals in Telephony; articles on African and Asiatic Languages in School of Oriental Studies Bulletin, and Africa; articles on Broadcast Speech in Radio Times, Listener, American Speech, etc.; article on Pronunciation in Encyclopædia Britannica, 14th ed. Talking Films on Speech; King's English.

Died 24 March 1943.

LOCH, 2nd Baron *cr* 1895; **Edward Douglas Loch,** CB 1918; CMG 1915; DSO 1898; MVO 4th Cl.; DL and JP Suffolk; late Grenadier Guards; *b* 4 April 1873; *o s* of 1st Baron and Elizabeth (*d* 1938), *d* of Hon. E. E. Villiers, *niece* of 4th Earl of Clarendon; *S* father, 1900; *m* 1905, Lady Margaret Compton, *o d* of 5th Marquess of Northampton; two *s* three *d*. Entered army, 1893; Brigade Major, 3rd Infantry Brigade, 1910–11; Bt Lt-Col, 1913; temp. Brig.-Gen., 1915–18; retired pay, 1922; served Soudan, 1898, including Khartoum (despatches, DSO, British medal, Khedive's medal with clasp); Divisional Signalling Officer, S African Field Force, 1900–02 (despatches, Bt-Maj.); European War, 1914–18 (despatches five times, CMG, Bt Col, CB, Maj. Gen.); Lord-in-Waiting to HM, 1913–14; Captain of the King's Bodyguard of the Yeomen of the Guard, 1924, and 1929–31; Alderman W Suffolk County Council; Chairman United Service Fund; Chairman of Governors, Dulwich College; Chairman Greyhound Racing Trust and Assoc.; Joint Treasurer University College, University of London. *Heir:* *s* Hon. George Henry Compton Loch, Lieut 11th Hussars, *b* 3 Feb. 1916. *Address:* 51 Lennox Gardens, SW1. *T:* Sloane 2028; Stoke College, Stoke by Clare, Suffolk. *T:* Clare 244. *Clubs:* Guards', Travellers'.

Died 14 Aug. 1942.

LOCH, Maj.-Gen. Granville George, CB 1925; CMG 1916; CBE 1923; DSO 1918; *b* 22 July 1870; *s* of General Francis Adam Ellis Loch, CB, Bombay Staff Corps, and Katherine Reid; *m* Edith, *er d* of late Joseph Samuel Armstrong, ICS; one *d*. Served European War, 1914–18 (despatches, CMG, DSO, Bt Lt-Col and Col); Waziristan, 1920–21 (despatches, CBE); commanding 1st Indian Infantry Brigade, 1922–26; Inspector-General Iraq Army, 1927–30; Maj.-Gen. 1927; retired pay, 1930; Colonel The Royal Scots, 1935–40. *Address:* 48 Morpeth Mansions, Westminster, SW1. *Club:* United Service.

Died 25 Nov. 1950.

LOCK, Flight Lt Eric Stanley, DSO, DFC and Bar, 1940; RAF; *b* 19 April 1919; *s* of C. E. Lock, Bayston Hill, Shrewsbury; *m* 1940, M. V. Meyers. *Educ:* Prestefelde, Shrewsbury. Farmer; served war of 1939–41 (despatches). *Address:* Bayston Hill, Shrewsbury. *TA:* Bayston Hill. *T:* Bayston Hill 25.

Died 3 Aug. 1942.

LOCK, Brig.-Gen. Frederic Robert Edward, DSO 1917; (retired) Indian Army; *b* 21 April 1867; *e s* of late Colonel E. S. Lock, 2nd South Lancashire Regt, of Headington, Oxford, and West Monkton, Somerset, and Caroline Louisa Cardew; *m* 1914, *y d* of late E. F. Duncanson of Nutwood, Bickley, Kent; one *s* (*yr s* killed in action March 1945), one *d. Educ:* Warrington Grammar School; Sandhurst. Commissioned to 2nd Gloucester Regt, 1886; transferred to Indian Army, 1889; transferred to Pension Establishment, 1919; served Aden operations in the interior, 1903–04; North-West Frontier, 1915; Mesopotamian Expeditionary Force, 1915–18 (despatches 3 times, DSO): GOC Euphrates L of C Defences, Mesopotamian Expeditionary Force, 1916–18; commanded 112th Infantry, Indian Army, 1911–16. *Address:* Wakehill, near Ilminster, Somerset. *T:* Ilminster 63. *TA:* Ilminster. *Club:* United Service.

Died 23 June 1945.

LOCKER-LAMPSON, Rt Hon. Godfrey (Lampson Tennyson); PC 1928; *b* 19 June 1875; *e s* of Frederick Locker-Lampson and Jane Hannah, *d* of Sir Curtis Lampson, 1st Bt; *m* 1st, Sophy Felicité (*d* 1935), *d* and *heir* of William Hatfield de Rodes; three *d*; 2nd, 1937, Barbara Hermione, *yr d* of Oswald Best Green, Walton-on-the-Hill, Surrey. *Educ:* Eton; Trinity College, Cambridge. Served four years in the Foreign Office and Diplomatic Service at the Hague and St Petersburg; called to Bar, 1906; contested Chesterfield Division of Derbyshire, 1906; MP (U) Salisbury, 1910–18; Wood Green, 1918–35; Royal Wiltshire Yeomanry, 1914–15; ADC 4th Corps, 1916; Parliamentary Private Secretary to Home Secretary, 1917, and to Assistant Foreign Secretary, 1918; a Charity Commissioner, 1922–23; Under-Secretary of State to the Home Office, 1923–24, and Nov. 1924–Dec. 1925; Under-Secretary of State for Foreign Affairs, 1925–29; Member of British Delegation to League of Nations, Geneva, 1928; represented Office of Works in House of Commons, 1925. *Publications:* An Appendix to the Catalogue of the Rowfant Library, 1900; On Freedom—a Metaphysical Study, 1911; Ancient Greek Coins (collected by GLL, catalogued by ESG Robinson), 1923; A Consideration of the State of Ireland in the Nineteenth Century, 1907; Financial Procedure in the House of Commons, 1924; A Soldier's Book of Love Poems—an Anthology, 1917; Oratory British and Irish, the Great Age, 1918; Thoughts in Middle Life, 1919; The Country Gentleman and other Essays, 1932; A Tale in Everything, 1934; A Few Italian Pictures Collected by GLL (described by R. Langton Douglas); Peep Show, 1937; Poems to Baa, 1941; Songs of the Heart, 1942; Love Lyrics and Other Melic Numbers, 1943; Mellow Notes, 1945; Sun and Shadow, collected Love Lyrics and other Poems, 1945; Disappearance of the English Country Squire, 1946. *Address:* Rowfant Cottage, Crawley, Sussex. *T:* Turners Hill 302. *Clubs:* Curzon House; Bembridge Sailing.

Died 1 May 1946.

LOCKHART, Sir Robert Cook, Kt 1914; linen manufacturer; Ex-Provost of Kirkcaldy; Chairman Kirkcaldy and Dysart Water Commission, 1914–19; Past President Kirkcaldy Rotary Club; Chairman Over-Seas League, Kirkcaldy Centre; Chairman Mutual Service Association Unemployed Centre; Chairman Kirkcaldy Ice Rink Ltd; Vice-Chairman Kirkcaldy National Service Committee; *b* 29 Aug. 1861; *s* of Robert Lockhart, Edinburgh, linen manufacturer at Kirkcaldy, and Margaret Alexander, *d* of Captain Cook, Leith; *m* 1891, Jeanette Sutherland Davidson. *Educ:* Edinburgh

Collegiate School; private tutors abroad. Joined firm of N. Lockhart and Sons, founded by grandfather in 1797, 1881; took keen interest in politics; was for some years Secretary of Kirkcaldy Liberal Association, of which Vice-President or President, 1888–1924; Chairman of Local Employment Committee since its formation; was President of Young Scots; Chairman Chamber of Commerce, 1900 and 1916; President of Royal National Lifeboat Institution in Kirkcaldy since its inception; Ex-President YMCA; Ex-President of PSA Brotherhood; Elder in St Brycedale UF Church; JP and Honorary Sheriff-Substitute for Fifeshire; Ex-Chairman Liberal Club; represented Kirkcaldy Burghs on Executive of Scottish Liberal Association, 1897–1928; Pres. Operatic Society; Ex-Major Commanding 1st Batt. Fifeshire Volunteer Regt; Ex-Chairman Eastern Division Scottish Liberal Federation; President Royal Caledonian Curling Club, 1931–32. *Recreations:* curling, bowling, motoring. *Address:* Allanbank, Kirkcaldy. *T:* Kirkcaldy 2177. *Clubs:* Scottish Liberal, Edinburgh.

Died 23 April 1943.

LOCKYER, Captain Hughes Campbell, CB 1916; *b* 4 March 1866; 3rd *s* of late Sir J. Norman Lockyer, KCB; *m* 1901, Geraldine Louise, *y d* of John F. Stairs, Halifax, NS; one *s. Educ:* Merchant Taylors' School; Royal Academy, Gosport. Served Egyptian War, 1882 (medal, bronze star); Lieut of Stork, surveying vessel, 1888–91; Navigating Officer of Fearless, 1891–93 (thanks of Admiralty); of Cordelia, 1895–98 (thanks of Admiralty); of Hood, 1899–1900 (thanks of Admiralty); Irresistible, 1902; Commander, 1902; Navigating Officer of Bulwark, 1903–05; Assist to Capt. of Devonport Dockyard, 1905; King's Harbourmaster, Plymouth Sound, 1906; Capt. and King's Harbour Master, Malta, 1909–12; Captain, Implacable, 1913–17; served Gallipoli, 1915 (CB); Commander of Order of Crown of Italy, 1916; retired, 1918. *Publications:* Reference Chart of the English Channel; The Tragedy of the Battle of the Beaches Cape Helles, Gallipoli, 1915, 1936. *Recreation:* angling. *Address:* Riversleigh House, Langport, Somerset. *T:* Langport 10.

Died 22 June 1941.

LODGE, Frank Adrian, CIE 1913; JP, Naivasha; *b* Liverpool, 4 Nov. 1861; *s* of Henry Lodge; *m* 1887, Catherine, *d* of James Butcher; one *s* one *d. Educ:* Eton. Entered Indian Forest Service, 1883 Conservator, 1906–14; retired, 1914; Inspector General of Forests, Hyderabad (Deccan), 1914–21. *Address:* Rivelyn, Naivasha, Kenya, East Africa.

Died 13 April 1947.

LOFTING, Hugh John; children's writer; *b* 14 Jan. 1886; *s* of John Brien Lofting and Elizabeth Agnes Lofting; *m* 1st, 1911, Flora W. Small, New York; one *s* one *d*; 2nd, 1928; Katherine Harrower-Peters (*d* 1929); 3rd, 1935, Josephine Fricker, Toronto; one *s. Educ:* Mount St Mary's College, Chesterfield, Derbyshire. Prospecting and surveying in Canada, 1908; civil engineer in West Africa, 1910–11; with Lagos Railway; in Cuba, 1912; with United Railways of Havana; with Irish Guards in Flanders, France (wounded); with British Ministry of Information in New York; writing and drawing. *Publications:* The Story of Mrs Tubbs; The Story of Dr Dolittle; The Voyages of Dr Dolittle; Dr Dolittle's Post Office; Dr Dolittle's Circus; Dr Dolittle's Zoo; Dr Dolittle's Caravan; Doctor Dolittle's Garden; Doctor Dolittle in the Moon; Doctor Dolittle's Return; Porridge Poetry; Noisy Nora; The Twilight of Magic; Gub Gub's Book; Tommy, Tilly, and Mrs Tubbs; Victory for the Slain, 1942; (posthumous) Doctor Dolittle and the Secret Lake, 1949; awarded Newbery Medal for 1922. *Recreations:* fishing, mountain climbing, skiing, golf. *Address:* c/o J. B. Lippincott Co., Washington Square, Philadelphia. *Clubs:* Players', Dutch Treat, New York.

Died 26 Sept. 1947.

LOFTUS, Cissie; *see* M'Carthy, M. C.

LOGAN, Sir Ewen Reginald, Kt 1928; JP; MA; *b* 1868; *s* of Francis Logan, Cliffe Side, Bournemouth; *m* 1903, Edith Frances, *e d* of late Captain W. F. Molony, RIC, Farnham; two *s*. *Educ:* Charterhouse; Exeter College, Oxford (MA). Student Inner Temple. Called to Bar, 1899; joined Middlesex and North London Sessions, 1900; 2nd Lieut Imperial Yeomanry, 1901; entered Mines Dept, Transvaal Government, 1901; served Boer War, 1901 (Queen's medal 4 clasps), Assistant Resident Magistrate, Transvaal, 1902–04; Magistrate East Africa Protectorate, 1905–14; Chief Justice of Supreme Court, Seychelles, 1914–20; administered Government of Seychelles, 23 July 1916 to 8 March 1917, and 13 May to 7 Oct. 1918; a Puisne Judge of the Supreme Court of the Gold Coast, 1920–25; Chief Justice of the Supreme Court of the Bahamas, West Indies, 1925–27; Judge of High Court, Northern Rhodesia, 1927–31. *Recreations:* rowing, lawn-tennis, riding, photography. *Address:* 60 Troy Court, Kensington, W8. *T:* Western 3396. *Club:* Athenæum.

Died 16 Sept. 1945.

LOGAN, Brig.-Gen. Francis Douglas, CB 1930; CMG 1918; DSO 1917; late RA; *b* 31 July 1875; *y s* of late David Logan, Chief Engineer S Indian Railway; *m* Alice Maude, *y d* of late Capt. A. W. Chitty, CIE, late Indian Navy; two *d*. *Educ:* Charterhouse; Royal Military Academy, Woolwich. Commission R. Artillery, 1895; served Omdurman Campaign, 1898; Adjutant Artillery Volunteers, 1901–04; passed Staff College, 1908–09; Staff Capt. Southern Command, 1910–11; DAAG Scottish Command, 1912–13; DAA and QMG 2nd Mounted Div. Sept. 1914; DAA and QMG 8th Div., Feb. 1915; AQMG Third Army, Aug. 1915–18; DA and QMG L of C June 1918; Base Comt, Calais, April 1919 (despatches four times, Bt Lt-Col, DSO, Croix d'Officier Légion d'Honneur, CMG, Bt Col); AQMG N Command, 1920–24; AA and QMG 1st Division, 1924–27; Brigadier in charge of Administration Egypt, 1927–31; retired pay, 1931; ARP, 1939–40; Lieut Home Guard, 1940–41; Civil Defence, 1942. *Recreation:* golf. *Address:* c/o Lloyds Bank, 6 Pall Mall, SW1.

Died 30 April 1947.

LOGAN, Hon. Hance James; KC 1912; Barrister; *b* Amherst Point, NS, 26 April 1869; *s* of James Archibald Logan; *m* 1st, 1892, Eleanor L. Kinder (*d* 1899); (*o s* died from being gassed in European War); 2nd, 1921, Anna Blanche Mackenna (*d* 1937). *Educ:* Model School, Truro; Pictou Academy; Dalhousie University. Called to Bar of Nova Scotia, 1892; elected to Parliament of Canada for Cumberland County, 1896, 1900, 1904, 1921; Chairman of Committee on Public Accounts; pressed upon Parliament the policy of confining British preference to Canadian ports; a strong advocate of rights of maritime provinces; President, Maritime Board of Trade, for two terms; Commissioner from Canadian Government to West Indies and South American Republics to inquire into possibilities of closer trade relations of these countries with Canada, 1924; one of the Members of Parliament who negotiated the Canada-British West Indies Trade Agreement of 1925; went to West Indies as one of the official party on the initial voyage of the Lady Nelson, the first of the ships provided under the terms of the agreement, 1928; Director of the Canadian National Railways, 1928; called to Senate of Canada, 1929. *Address:* Glenlands, Parrsboro, NS.

Died 26 Dec. 1944.

LOGSDAIL, William, RBC; RP; *b* Lincoln, 25 May 1859. *Educ:* Grammar School and School of Art, Lincoln. Gold medals for oil and water colour in National Competition 1875–76; first in Concours Internationale, Antwerp Academy, 1880. Exhibitor at Royal Academy since 1877. Principal pictures: The Antwerp Fish Market (purchased by Queen Victoria); La Piazza di San Marco; A Venetian Festa; St Paul's and Ludgate Hill (purchased by King Umberto of Italy); St Martin in the Fields (purchased by the Chantrey Fund); The Lord Mayor's Show; A Venetian Interior, Eighteenth Century, etc.; exclusively portraits since 1903; medals Paris, Chicago, Calcutta. *Address:* The Manor House, Noke, Oxford.

Died 3 Sept. 1944.

LOMAS, Ernest Gabriel, OBE 1923; *b* London, 23 Jan. 1878; *s* of late John Lomas and Maria T. Gabriel; *m* 1914, E. Violet, *d* of late G. H. Fernau; two *s*. *Educ:* Bradfield College; St John's College, Oxford (Exhibitioner); Trinity College, Cambridge. Student Interpreter (Levant) Consular Service, 1902; Assistant, 1904; Acting 3rd Dragoman British Embassy Constantinople, 1903–04; Acting Vice-Consul, Constantinople, 1905; Casablanca, 1906–08; Vice-Consul Casablanca, 1909; Acting Consul, Casablanca, each year 1909–14; transferred to Rabat, 1914; Consul at Fez, 1920; transferred to Rabat, 1921; Transferred to Cairo, 1924; Consul General at Tunis, 1930; HM Consul General, Salonica, 1934; retired, 1938. *Recreations:* rowing, sailing, tennis, rifle shooting. *Address:* St Jean, Territet, Switzerland. *Clubs:* Overseas, Royal Automobile.

Died 18 May 1947.

LONDON, Sir (Edgar) Stanford, Kt 1921; CBE 1918; Barrister-at-law; *b* 5 Feb. 1861; *s* of late Thomas London, Gloucester; *m* 1883, Marion Fanny Pinnell, *d* of late Septimus Luff, Parkstone, Dorset; one *s* two *d*. *Educ:* King's School, Gloucester. Entered the Inland Revenue Department, 1881; Chief Inspector, 1920–22; Member of Committee on the Administration of Unemployment Insurance, 1911; Member of Committee to Consolidate the Income Tax Acts, 1916–17; called to Bar, Gray's Inn, 1893; Member of Middle Temple, 1922; Chairman St Paul's Hospital, 1923–33, and President, 1928–33; Vice-President All Saints Hospital since 1933; Master Glaziers' Coy 1930–31; Fellow of Institute of Linguists. *Address:* Craigdarragh, 10 Briar Walk, Putney, SW15. *TA:* Craigdarragh, Putney. *T:* Putney 2386. *Clubs:* Roehampton, Royal Thames Yacht.

Died 19 April 1943.

LONDONDERRY, 7th Marquess of, *cr* 1816; **Charles Stewart Henry Vane-Tempest-Stewart,** KG 1919; PC 1925; Privy Councillor Northern Ireland 1921, PC Ire. 1918; MVO 1903; Baron Londonderry, 1789; Viscount Castlereagh, 1795; Earl of Londonderry, 1796; Baron Stewart, 1814; Earl Vane, Viscount Seaham, 1823; sits under creations 1814 and 1823; Chancellor of the Queen's University, Belfast, since 1923; Chancellor of Durham University since 1931; Lord Lieutenant of Co. Durham since 1928; Chief Commissioner, Civil Air Guard, since 1938; HM Lieut Co. Down; Major (Brev. Lt-Col) Royal Horse Guards; Hon. Air Commodore 502 Sq. RAF; Regional Comdt ATC, Northern Ireland; *b* 13 May 1878; *e s* of 6th Marquess of Londonderry and Lady Theresa Susy Helen Chetwynd Talbot, *e d* of 19th Earl of Shrewsbury; *S* father, 1915; *m* 1899, Hon. Edith Chaplin, DBE (author of Henry Chaplin; A Memoir, 1926; The Magic Inkpot, 1928; Retrospect, 1938), *d* of 1st Viscount Chaplin; one *s* three *d*. *Educ:* Eton; RMC, Sandhurst. MP (C) Maidstone; 1906–15; Under-Secretary for Air, 1920–21; Minister of Education, and Leader of the Senate, Government of Northern Ireland, 1921–26; First Commissioner of Works, 1928–29 and Aug.–Oct. 1931; Secretary of State for Air, 1931–35; Lord Privy Seal and Leader of House of Lords, 1935; served European War, ADC to Lt-Gen. Sir W. Pulteney, 5 Aug. 1914–19 Aug. 1915; 2nd in command RH Guards, Aug. 1915 (despatches twice); Mayor of Durham, 1936–37. Hon. Air Commodore 607 Squadron, 1935–40. *Publications:* Ourselves and Germany, 1938; Wings of Destiny, 1943. *Heir:* *s* Viscount Castlereagh. *Address:* Londonderry House, Park Lane, W1. *T:* Grosvenor 1616; Wynyard Park,

Billingham-on-Tees; Mount Stewart, Newtownards, Co. Down. *Clubs:* Carlton; Royal Yacht Squadron, Cowes.

Died 11 Feb. 1949.

LONG, 2nd Viscount *cr* 1921, of Wraxall; **Walter Francis David Long;** Maj. Coldstream Guards, RARO; Director of the Ocean Trust Co. Ltd; *b* 14 Sept. 1911; *o s* of late Brig.-Gen. Walter Long, CMG, DSO and Sibell, *d* of 2nd Baron Derwent (she *m* 2nd, 1921, Major Sir Ralph Glyn); *S* grandfather, 1924; *m* 1933, Laura (who obtained a divorce, 1943; she *m* 2nd, 1943, Earl of Dudley), 2nd *d* of Hon. Guy Charteris; one *d. Educ:* Eton; Sandhurst. ADC to the Governor-General of New Zealand, 1934. *Heir: uncle* Hon. Richard Eric Onslow Long. *Address:* 6a Montagu Place, W1; South Wraxall Manor, Bradford-on-Avon, Wilts. *Clubs:* White's, Beefsteak.

Died 23 Sept. 1944.

LONG, Brig.-Gen. Sir Arthur, KBE 1919; CB 1917; CMG 1916; DSO 1900; *b* 26 Feb. 1866; *s* of James and Elizabeth Long, Henlow, Beds; *m* 1893, Maud Eleanor, 2nd *d* of Rev. Canon James Davenport Kelly, of Manchester. *Educ:* Modern School, Bedford. 1st Batt. Leinster Regiment, 1887–90; Army Service Corps since 1890; served in defence of Ladysmith, Dec. 1898–March 1900 (special service); on Staff Gen. Hunter's Division; Gen. Ian Hamilton's Division (despatches twice, Queen's medal 4 clasps, King's medal 2 clasps, DSO); commanding ASC, Egypt; Assist Director Supplies, Army Headquarters, 1901–02; Assist Director, Transport, S Africa, 1903–04; European War, 1914–19 (despatches six times, KBE, CB, CMG); Director of Supplies and Transport, British Army, in Macedonia and Black Sea, Jan. 1916; retired, 1919. *Club:* United Service.

Died 15 Nov. 1941.

LONG, Arthur Tilney, CBE 1919; *b* 1871; *s* of J. W. Long and Sarah Devereux; *m* 1911, Kathleen, *d* of F. Cliffe, Barrister-at-law of the Middle Temple; one *s* two *d.* Served South African War (medal four clasps); late British Consul; Agent of the Union of South Africa; retired 1928. *Address:* Glenduan, The Glen, Wakapuaka, Nelson, NZ.

Died 14 Nov. 1946.

LONG, Basil Kellett; MP (United Party) Gardens, South Africa, since 1938; *b* 1878; *e s* of Rev. E. H. K. Long, late Rector of Newton Flotman, Norwich; *m* Mary Elizabeth, *d* of John Cave; two *s* two *d. Educ:* Norwich School; Brasenose, Oxford; 2nd Classical Mods, 1st Final History. Went to Cape Town to read for Cape Bar, 1902; called, 1905; elected as one of Representatives of Woodstock in Cape Parliament, 1908; Editor, the State, 1909–12; a Law Adviser to South African National Convention, 1909; elected as Member of House of Assembly for Liesbeek in first Parliament of Union of South Africa, 1910; resigned to become Dominions Editor of the Times, 1913; Foreign and Dominions Editor, 1920–21; Editor the Cape Times, 1921–35; retired. *Publications:* (with Sir Arthur Willert and H. V. Hodson) The Empire in the World, 1937; Drummond Chaplin; His Life and Times in Africa, 1941. *Recreation:* golf. *Address:* Houses of Parliament, Cape Town, South Africa. *Clubs:* Athenæum; Civil Service, Cape Town; Royal Cape Golf.

Died 2 Jan. 1944.

LONG, Captain Eustace Ruffel Drake, CBE 1937; RN; Chief Inspector of Naval Ordnance since 1936; *b* 3 Aug. 1883; *y s* of late Rev. David Long; *m* 1925, Sylvia Augusta, *d* of Sir John R. Starkey, Bt; one *s* one *d. Educ:* Weymouth College; Stubbington House; HMS Britannia. Lieutenant, 1905; served in HMS Achilles in European War (despatches); Commander, 1917; Naval Ordnance Inspection Department, 1919; Ordnance Committee, 1934. *Address:* 9 Culford Mansions, SW3. *T:* Kensington 9781. *Club:* United Service.

Died 30 June 1941.

LONG, Lt-Col William Hoare Bourchier; Director, Mann, Egerton & Co., Ltd; *b* Cannes, 22 March 1868; *y s* of late Richard P. Long of Rood Ashton and Charlotte A. (L), *d* of Rt Hon. W. W. F. Hume-Dick, and *y brother* of first Viscount Long of Wraxall; *m* 1911, Vera Cecily Marchant, *o d* of J. A. Oliver of Wootton Court, Kent, and Folkestone; one *s. Educ:* Harrow; Oxford. Joined the Queen's Own (R. West Kent), 1889; served with Mounted Infantry in South Africa (medal and clasps); transferred to Irish Guards, 1900; retired, illhealth; during War Commandant Ulster and other Base Depôts, France; commanded 12th London Regt (Rangers), 1922–24; Master, Dunston Harriers, 1905–10. *Recreations:* all sports, painting, etc. *Address:* Villa Vera, Bordighera, Italy. *T:* 22.59. *Clubs:* Guards', Royal Automobile, I Zingari.

Died 17 July 1943.

LONG INNES, Hon. Reginald Heath; *b* Sydney, 17 Nov. 1869; *s* of late Sir J. George Long Innes, Judge of Supreme Court of NSW; *m* 1905, Mary Louise, *y d* of late Denis McCartie (one *s* killed 26 Feb. 1942 in air operations over Kiel, RAAF) three *d. Educ:* Malvern College; New College, Oxford (BA, 2nd Class Honours Jurisprudence; BCL, 2nd Class Honours); Lincoln's Inn (Open Inns of Court Studentship, and Lincoln's Inn Studentship). Called to English Bar, 1893; KC (New South Wales), 1916; Puisne Judge of Supreme Court of NSW, and Judge in Bankruptcy, 1925–40; Chief Judge in Equity, New South Wales, 1935–40; retired, 1940; 1st Lieut 21st Battalion (afterwards 6th Batt. 1st Regiment) AMF, Senior Cadets; home service only, 1916–19. *Recreations:* cricket, tennis, golf, swimming. *Address:* Woodlands, Medlow Bath, NSW.

Died 26 May 1947.

LONGBOTTOM, Arthur William; Railway Townsman; *b* 25 May 1883; *s* of John David Longbottom; *m* 1906, Beatrice, *d* of William E. Kaye, Wakefield; two *d. Educ:* All Saints National School; Halifax Technical College. Railway Clerk since 1898; MP (Socialist), Halifax, 1928–31; Councillor, Halifax County Borough, 1912; Alderman, 1924; Mayor, 1923–24; Magistrate, 1924. *Recreation:* gardening. *Address:* 19 St Annes Road, Halifax.

Died 12 Sept. 1943.

LONGHURST, Cyril, CB 1917; Assistant Secretary, Committee of Imperial Defence; *b* 1879; 4th *s* of late A. E. T. Longhurst, MD, Chandler's Ford, Hants; *m* 1906, 2nd *d* of late Admiral Fox-Boxer.

Died 22 April 1948.

LONGHURST, Rev. William Henry Roberts, MA; Hon. Canon of Worcester, 1910–36, Canon Emeritus since 1936; *b* 11 Sept. 1838. *Educ:* Pembroke College, Oxford. Ordained 1865; Curate of Christ Church, Savernake, 1865–67; Rawmarsh, 1867–69; Lillington 1869–71; Vicar of Holy Trinity, Worcester, 1871–79; Kempsey, 1879–92; Queenhill, 1892–1918. *Address:* Sea Haven, Budleigh Salterton.

Died 3 Sept. 1943.

LONGMUIR, Robert Findlay, CBE 1928; JP, FICS; *b* Irvine, 3 Aug. 1864; *s* of Alexander Longmuir, JP, Roseholm, Irvine; *m* Marion R. B. Marr; two *s. Educ:* Irvine Royal Academy; Gymnasium, Old Aberdeen. Ship and Insurance Broker, Irvine; JP Ayr; Elder, Established Church of Scotland. *Address:* Roseville, Irvine, Ayrshire. *T:* 3363.

Died 25 Aug. 1942.

LONGSON, His Honour Judge Edward Harold; Judge of County Courts Circuit No. 19; *b* 1872; *e s* of late James Edward Longson, Bowdon, Cheshire; *m* 1908, Hannah Elizabeth, *d* of John Fletcher Haworth, Hale, Cheshire; one *s* two *d. Educ:* privately; New College, Oxford. Inner Temple, called 1895; practised in the Chancery Palatine Court, Manchester. *Recreations:* cricket and golf. *Address:* Lady Grove, Two Dales, Derbyshire.

Died 21 March 1941.

LONGSTAFF, Cedric Llewellyn, CBE 1938; TD, JP and DL Staffs; MA (Oxon); FRGS; *b* 17 Feb. 1876; 2nd *s* of late L. W. Longstaff, OBE, Wimbledon; *m* 1st, 1903, Lilias Marow (*d* 1942), *er d* of Sir Thomas W. P. Blomefield, 4th Bt, CB; two *s* (and one killed in action at El Alamein) one *d*; 2nd, 1944, Queen Maud, *er d* of Mrs Warwick Pengelly. *Educ:* Eton; Christ Church, Oxford. BA 1897; MA 1901. Deputy Registrar of Diocese of Lichfield and of its Archdeaconries, 1903–10; Chairman of Blundell, Spence and Co. Ltd of Hull and London and of its subsidiaries; commanded Volunteer Service Co. East Surrey Regiment in South Africa 1900–01 (Queen's medal with 5 clasps); served European War, 6th N Staffs, in France and Belgium as Capt. and Major (1915 Star, Victory and Allies medals); Sheriff of Lichfield, 1918; Home Guard from its formation; Hon. Colonel 7th North Staffs Regiment, 1939–47; Major (retired). *Recreations:* rifle shooting, fishing, shooting, golf; shot for Eton, Oxford University, Surrey and Staffordshire, and has been Captain of Staffordshire County Teams. *Address:* Whittington Lodge, near Lichfield, Staffs. *T:* Whittington 249. *Club:* English-Speaking Union.

Died 1 March 1950.

LONGSTAFF, Sir John, Kt 1928; RPS, RBC; Trustee of the Melbourne National Gallery; First President of Australian Academy of Art, since 1938; *b* Clunes, Victoria, Australia, 10 March 1862; *s* of Ralph Longstaff and Jessie, *d* of late John Campbell; *m* Rosa (*d* 1939), *d* of late Henry Crocker; four *s* one *d. Educ:* Grammar School, Clunes; Melbourne National Gallery Art Schools under G. F. Folingsby. Secured the first Government Travelling Scholarship, 1887; same year went to Paris, studying painting under F. Cormon; awarded Mention Honorable at the Salon for the picture The Young Mother, 1891. Exhibited numerous portraits, including Lady in Black, Salon 1892 and Royal Academy 1894; principal pictures are in Melbourne and Sydney Galleries; these include The Sirens, Burke and Wills at Cooper's Creek, Bush Fires at Gippsland, Portraits of King Edward VII and Queen Alexandra, Henry Lawson, etc. *Address:* 118 Wellington Parade, East Melbourne, C2, Victoria, Australia; 16 Marlborough Hill, St John's Wood, NW8. *Clubs:* St John's Wood Arts, Chelsea Arts; Yorick, Naval and Military, Melbourne.

Died 1 Oct. 1941.

LONSDALE, 5th Earl of, *cr* 1807 (UK); **Col Hugh Cecil Lowther,** KG 1928; GCVO 1925; DL; Bart 1764; Viscount and Baron Lowther, 1797; Lord Lieutenant Cumberland and Custos Rotulorum, 1917; Hereditary Admiral of Coasts of Cumberland, Westmorland, and Lord Warden of the West Marches; Hon. Col 1st Cumberland Vol. Artillery since 1884; Hon. Col 3rd Batt. Border Regt since 1891; late Hon. Colonel 51st (Westmorland and Cumberland) Field Brigade; RA, TA; *b* 25 Jan. 1857; *s* of 3rd Earl and Emily, *e d* of St George Caulfeild of Donamon Castle, Co. Roscommon; *S* brother 1882; *m* 1878, Lady Grace Cecilie Gordon, CBE (*d* 1941), *d* of Charles, 10th Marquis of Huntly. *Educ:* Eton. Mayor of Whitehaven, 1894–96; DAAG for Imperial Yeomanry in S Africa, 1900; Chevalier Legion of Honour; Chairman of the Cumberland and Westmorland Joint Territorial Force Associations;

Chairman of the Westmorland Quarter Sessions, 1909–36; Hon. Colonel 2nd King Edward's Horse; JP Westmorland and Rutland; late Master of the Woodland Pytchley, Blankney, Cottesmore, Quorn, and again Cottesmore Hounds. Owns about 175,000 acres. *Heir: b* Hon. Lancelot E. Lowther. *Address:* The Carlton Hotel, SW1; Lowther Castle, Penrith; The Stud House, Barley Thorpe, Oakham. *Clubs:* Jockey, Turf, Royal Automobile, Orleans, National Sporting.

Died 13 April 1944.

LONSDALE, John Pemberton Heywood H.; *see* Heywood-Lonsdale.

LORAM, Charles Templeman, BA (Univ. of Cape of Good Hope); MA, LLB (Cambridge); MA (Yale); PhD (Columbia, USA); Hon. EdD (Univ. of Colorado); Sterling Professor of Education, Yale University since 1931, and Chairman and Director of Studies, Department of Culture Contacts and Race Relations, Graduate School, Yale University, since 1933; *b* Pietermaritzburg, South Africa, 10 May 1879; 2nd *s* of Albert Edmund and Alice Loram; *m* 1910, Hilda Vautier, *d* of Dr Joseph Amy; one *s* four *d. Educ:* Pietermaritzburg College; King's College, Cambridge; Columbia University. Teacher, Pietermaritzburg College, 1896–1900; Leys School, Cambridge, 1905–06; Inspector of Schools, Natal, 1906–17; Chief Inspector of Native Education, 1917–20; Member Native Affairs Commission 1920–29; Chief Inspector of Schools, 1929–30; Supt of Education, Natal, 1930–31; Member Commission of Enquiry into causes of Bondelzwarts Rebellion, SW Africa, 1920; Member Phelps Stokes Fund Educational Commissions to Africa, 1921 and 1924; Chairman Commission of Enquiry into training of Natives in Medicine and Public Health, Univ. of S Africa, 1927; Trustee Yale-in-China and American Colonization Society since 1933; Summer Session Lecturer at Columbia University and Universities of Hawaii, Colorado, California; Phelps Stokes Fund, 1939; Fellow, Silliman Coll., Yale Univ., 1939. *Publications:* Education of the S African Native; (Joint) The Navy's Problem; article in Internat. Review of Missions, School and Society, Reports of SA Association for Advct. of Science, and Educational journals; Educational Year Book, 1931, 1933. *Recreations:* music, drama, touring, motoring. *Address:* 1030 Whitney Avenue, Hamden, Conn, USA. *TA:* Yale University, New Haven. *T:* 8.5936.

Died 9 July 1940.

LORD, Col John Ernest Cecil, CMG 1919; DSO 1917; VD; *b* Tasmania, 8 May 1870; *m* 1901, Hannah M., *d* of late William Henry Smith; five *c.* Tasmanian Civil Service; Commissioner of Police, Tasmania, 1906–40; served European War, 1916–19, in command of 40th Batt. Australian Imperial Force (CMG, DSO, Croix de Guerre, despatches); Hon. ADC to the Governor-General of Australia, 1920–23; Officer Order St John of Jerusalem. *Address:* Cygnet, nr Hobart, Tasmania. *Clubs:* Tasmanian, Naval and Military (Hobart).

Died 29 Oct. 1949.

LORD, Sir Walter G.; *see* Greaves-Lord.

LORDEN, Sir John William, Kt 1925; JP; *b* Colchester, 15 July 1862; *m* 1st, 1883, Ellen Mary (*d* 1923), *d* of Matthew Garrod, Wandsworth Common; one *s* two *d*; 2nd, 1924, Emma Sarah, *widow* of Robert Sawyer, *o d* of late John Lord, Rochdale. *Educ:* privately. Member of Wandsworth Borough Council, 1900–21; Mayor, 1903–04, and 1907–08; Alderman, 1906–21; member London County Council, 1909–12; MP (U) North St Pancras, 1918–23. *Address:* Little Ratton, Willingdon, Eastbourne. *T:* Hampden Park 25. *Clubs:* Carlton, Constitutional.

Died 21 April 1944.

LORIMER, Emily Overend, (Mrs D. L. R. Lorimer), OBE, MA (Oxon); *b* 1881; *er d* of late Judge T. G. Overend, KC; Recorder and County Court Judge of Londonderry; *m* 1910, Lt-Col D. L. R. Lorimer, CIE; one *d* (adopted). *Educ:* Alexandra Coll., Dublin; Somerville Coll., Oxford; Univ. of Munich. BA Royal Univ. of Ireland, 1st Place and 1st Cl. Hons Mod. Languages, 1904; 1st Class Oxf. Final Sch. Mod. Langs (German) 1906. Tutor in Germanic Philology, Somerville College, Oxford, 1907–10; MA Oxford (retrospectively open to women), 1926; Director Red Cross Missing and Wounded Enquiries in Egypt, 1915; Editor and Manager, Basrah Times under Political Dept IEF 'D.,' 1916 and 1917 (OBE, despatches); District Commissioner Welwyn Garden City Girl Guides, 1926–30; Acting Warden Bedford College House, Univ. of London, 1930–31; Linguistic-anthropological expedition with husband to Hunza in the Karakoram, Times Correspondent, 1934–35. *Publications:* Persian Tales (with husband) 1919; What Hitler Wants (Penguin Special) 1939; Language Hunting in the Karakoram, 1939; What the German Needs, 1942; Translations from the German; Ernst Kantorovicz; Frederick II 1194–1250, 1931; Joachim von Kürenberg, His Excellency the Spectre, Life of Fritz von Holstein, 1933; Moeller van den Bruck, Germany's Third, Empire, 1934; Gustav Krist, Alone through the Forbidden Land, also Prisoner in the Forbidden Land, 1938; Hans Roger Madol, Christian IX of Denmark, 1939; Wilhelm Filchner, a Scientist in Tartary, 1939. From the French: Jérôme Carcopino, Daily Life in Rome at the Zenith of the Empire, 1939; Beljame, Men of Letters and the English Public in the 18th Century, edited by Professor Bonamy Dobrée, 1946; René Maunier, The Sociology of Colonies, 1948. *Address:* 32 Parkway, Welwyn Garden City, Herts. *T:* Welwyn Garden 696. *Club:* University Women's.

Died 10 June 1949.

LORIMER, Norma; author; *b* Auchterarder, Perthshire; *d* of late T. W. Lorimer and Elizabeth Palmer. *Educ:* High School, Castletown, Isle of Man. Lived fifteen years in the Isle of Man; spent three years in the United States, Canada, China, and Japan; has visited Italy and Sicily many times. *Publications:* A Sweet Disorder; Josiah's Wife; Mirry-Ann; By the Waters of Sicily, 1901; Catherine Sterling, 1903; On Etna, 1904; By the Waters of Carthage, 1906; (and with Douglas Sladen) More Queer Things about Japan, 1904; Queer Things about Sicily, 1905; The Pagan Woman, 1907; By the Waters of Egypt, 1909; By the Waters of Italy, 1910; The Second Woman, 1911; A Wife out of Egypt, 1913; By the Waters of Germany, 1914; On Desert Altars, 1915; The Gods' Carnival, 1916; By the Waters of Africa (with R. E. Keefer), 1917; There was a King in Egypt, 1918; With Other Eyes, 1919; A Mender of Images, 1920; Path of Love, 1921; The False Dawn, 1923; The Shadow of Egypt, 1924; The White Sanctuary, 1925; Alec's Mother, 1926; The Yoke of Affection, 1926; The Mediterranean and Beyond, 1927; The End of the Matter, 1928; Moslem Jane, 1929; Alone, 1931; Millstones, 1932; False Value, 1933; The Story of Isobel Lennox, 1935; Where Ignorance is Bliss, 1938. *Address:* 7 Pitcullen Terrace, Perth, Scotland.

Died 14 Feb. 1948.

LORING, Vice-Adm. Ernest Kindersley, CB 1919; *b* 1869; *s* of Rev. E. H. Loring; *m* 1897, Ottilie (*d* 1945), *e d* of L. Messel, of Nymans, Handcross, Sussex; one *s* two *d*. *Educ:* HMS Britannia. Midshipman, 1885; Captain, 1910; Naval Transport Officer at Anzac, Gallipoli, April 1915 (despatches); commanded HMS Albion, 1915; Naval Assistant to Third Sea Lord, 1916; subsequently commanded HMS Indomitable and Warspite in Grand Fleet; CB and Officer Legion of Honour for war services; ADC to the King, 1920; Rear-Admiral, 1921; retired, 1923; Vice-Admiral, 1926.

Address: Court House, Rusper, Sussex. *Clubs:* United Service, Royal Automobile; Royal Yacht Squadron (Hon.).

Died 24 Dec. 1945.

LOUDON, Sir John, Kt 1948; *b* 15 Sept. 1881; *s* of John Loudon, Birkwood, Kirkmuirhill, Lanarkshire; *m* 1911, Rosalind, *d* of J. B. Harrison, Tillsonburg, Ontario, Canada; one *s* one *d*. *Educ:* Glasgow High School. Gov. Director, John London & Co., Ltd, Provision and Produce Importers, London Bridge House, SE1; Director, Bacon and Ham, Ministry of Food. Commissioner of Income Tax, 1935–. Served S Africa, 1899–1902, with Imperial Yeo. Sharpshooters. *Recreations:* golf, shooting. *Address:* Roseberry, 128 Hempstead Road, Watford, Herts. *T:* Watford 2568. *Clubs:* Royal Automobile; West Herts (Hendon).

Died 22 May 1948.

LOUGHNANE, Farquhar McGillivray, FRCS; Senior Hon. Surgeon, St Mary's Hospital, Plaistow; Hon. Surgeon, All Saints' Hospital; Urological Surgeon, London County Council; Consulting Surgeon, Hampton Cottage Hospital; Surgeon EMS; Assistant Urological Surgeon, Prince of Wales's Hospital; *b* 1885; *m* 1927, Blanca Keatinge. *Educ:* Clapham Coll.; King's Coll.; St Thomas's Hospital (Entrance Science and Peacock Scholarships and Treasurer's Gold Medal). House Surgeon and CO St Thomas's; House Surgeon, Royal Sea-bathing Hospital, Margate; RMO, Camberwell Infirmary; RSO, Salford; Senior House Surgeon, Royal Infirmary, Leicester; Surgeon, BRX, France; Capt. RAMC, Mesopotamia. *Publications:* Spinal Tuberculosis Treatment by Bone-graft; Frost Bite; Renal Sarcoma of Infants; Case of Von Recklinghausen's Disease; Circumcision; Urethral Stricture; Handbook of Renal Surgery; Cystitis; Differential diagnosis of hæmaturia; Re-appearance of prostate after Prostatectomy; A new operation for genital tuberculosis; Per-Urethral Treatment of Enlarged Prostate; Retention of Urine; Urethroscopy; Endoscopic Resection for Enlarged Prostate; Prostatic Obstruction and its Treatment; A Case of Renal Aneurysm; Transplantation of the Gracilis muscle to cure Stress Incontinence in Women; Care of patients after Trans-urethral Prostatectomy; Present Position of Trans-urethral Prostatectomy; Stricture of the Urethra; Genital Tuberculosis. *Recreations:* golf and gardening. *Address:* 29 Devonshire Place, W1. *T:* Welbeck 2489. *Club:* Royal Empire Society.

Died 14 July 1948.

LOUIS, Sir Charles, 5th Bt *cr* 1806; Captain of the Mercantile Marine, retired; Treasurer and Co-Trustee of the National Union of Masters and Mates; *b* 9 April 1859; *s* of 4th Bt and Jane, *d* of J. M'Kay; *S* father, 1900; *m* 1st, 1887, Florence Alice (*d* 1933), *d* of John Lawford; 2nd, 1935, Mrs Alice Mary Semmens Dupen, Taplow Court, Torquay *widow* of G. Semmens Dupen. *Heir:* none. *Address:* Taplow Court, Torquay.

Died 27 July 1949 (ext).

LOUTH, 14th Baron *cr* 1541; **Randal Pilgrim Ralph Plunkett;** DL; JP Co. Louth; Major Westminster Dragoons, 1914; *b* on board yacht 'Pilgrim', near Dieppe, 24 Sept. 1868; *o s* of 13th Baron and Anna, *d* of late Walter M'Geough Bond, Drumsill, and the Argory, Co. Armagh; *S* father, 1883; *m* 1st, 1890, Eugénie de Miarritze (marr. diss. 1912), *d* of Edmond Hooke Wilson Bellairs; one *s* one *d*; 2nd, 1913, Dorothy Lettice (*d* 1923), *d* of late Col T. L. Hampton Lewis, 5th Dragoon Guards Henllys and Bodiar, Anglesey; 3rd, 1926, Marie Ethel (*d* 1941), *widow* of Sir John Prichard-Jones, Bart. *Educ:* Oscott Coll., Birmingham; Woburn Park, Weybridge. Roman Catholic; Conservative; late 3rd Batt. Wiltshire Regt; served in European War, 1914–18. Owns about 5000 acres. *Recreations:* hunting, shooting, fishing. *Heir: s* Hon. Otway Plunkett. *Address:* 3 Grosvenor Square, W1; Louth Hall, Ardee, Co. Louth. *Club:* Travellers'.

Died 28 Oct. 1941.

LOUTH, 15th Baron *cr* 1541; **Otway Randal Percy Oliver Plunkett;** *b* 26 April 1892; *o s* of 14th Baron and Eugénie de Miarritze (*d* 1947), *d* of Edmond Hooke Wilson Bellairs; *S* father, 1941; *m* 1928, Ethel Molly Gallichen; one *s. Educ:* Downside. *Heir: s* Hon. Otway Michael James Oliver Plunkett, *b* 19 Aug. 1929.

Died 3 Feb. 1950.

LOVE, James Kerr, MD; (Hon.) FRFPS (Glas.); Hon. Fellow, 1933; LLD (Glas.), 1930; Hon. Aural Surgeon, Glasgow Royal Infirmary; formerly Lecturer on Aural Surgery, University of Glasgow; Aurist, Glasgow Institution for the Deaf and Dumb; Examiner on Physiology, National Association of Teachers of the Deaf; Hon. Fellow American Laryngological, Rhinological, and Otological Society; National Bureau Lecturer on the prevention of Deafness, 1912; Major RAMC (T), 4th Scottish General Hospital; ex-President Section of Otology, Royal Society of Medicine, 1924–25; *b* Beith, Ayrshire, 1858; *s* of James Love, Townhead, Beith; *m* 1887, Jane, *e d* of Joseph Corbett, DD, Camphill Church, Glasgow; three *d. Educ:* Beith Academy; Glasgow High School and University. *Publications:* Deaf-Mutism, a Clinical and Pathological Study, 1896; Diseases of the Ear for Practitioners and Students, 1904; The Deaf Child: A Manual for Teachers and School Doctors, 1911; Diseases of the Ear in School Children: An Essay on the Prevention of Deafness, 1919; editor, with introduction, Helen Keller in Scotland, 1933. *Recreations:* photography, golf, motoring. *Address:* 5 Newton Place, Glasgow. *T:* Douglas 5497; Sunnyside, West Kilbride, Ayrshire. *T:* West Kilbride 2120.

Died 30 May 1942.

LOVE, Richard Archibald, CBE; JP Co. Lancaster; *b* 18 Oct. 1873; *s* of late Rev. Robert Love, MA, Vicar of Great Crosby, Lancashire; *m* 1925, Vera Hamilton, *yr d* of Robert Hamilton Carling, Tynemouth, Northumberland; one *s. Educ:* Merchant Taylors' School. President, Liverpool Corn Trade Association, 1914–15; Member of the Royal Commission on Wheat Supplies, London; Resident Commissioner in Australia for the Royal Commission on Wheat Supplies, 1917–19; Resident Commissioner in charge of the Liverpool and North of England Branch of the Commission, 1919–22. *Address:* Greetby Hill, Ormskirk, Lancs. *T:* Ormskirk, Liverpool 185.

Died 29 June 1941.

LOVEDAY, Rev. Eric Stephen, MA (Oxon); BA (Wales); Vicar of St Martin-in-the-Fields since 1941; Chaplain in Ordinary to the King; *b* 27 July 1904; *o s* of Peter Bremner and Helen Mabel Loveday, Aberystwyth, Cardiganshire; *m* 1932, Millicent, *d* of Christina and Edward Newman. *Educ:* Llandovery College; University College of Wales, Aberystwyth; Jesus College, Oxford; Ripon Hall, Oxford. Deacon, 1928; Priest, 1929; Curate Handsworth Parish Church, 1928–32; Perpetual Curate St Mark, Londonderry Diocese of Birmingham, 1932–34; Rector St Peter, Bristol, 1934–41. Select Preacher, Univ. of Cambridge, 1944. *Publications:* Three Trees (A broadcast sermon), 1938; The Rising Waters (A book for Lent reading), 1940; God's Week and Ours (Broadcast sermons), 1941. *Recreations:* golf, the theatre, water-colour sketching. *Address:* 5 St Martin's Place, WC2. *T:* Temple Bar 1684. *Club:* Athenæum.

Died 10 July 1947.

LOVELACE, Mary Caroline, Countess of; *e d* of Rt Hon. James Archibald Stuart Wortley; *m* 2nd Earl of Lovelace, 1880. *Publications:* Zelinda and the Monster, 1896; Ralph, Earl of Lovelace: a Memoir, 1920. *Address:* Wentworth House, Swan Walk, Chelsea, SW3. *T:* Flaxman 2126; Ockham Park, Ripley, Surrey.

Died 18 April 1941.

LOVELL, William George, CBE 1920; Chairman of Lovell & Christmas (Limited), and Hodgson's Kingston Brewery Co. Limited; *b* 1868; *s* of John Cary Lovell; *m* 1891, Kate (*d* 1939), and 1942, Mabel, *d* of late G. A. Ring. Director of Butter and Cheese Supplies Ministry of Food, during European War. *Address:* 144 Tulse Hill, SW2. *T:* Tulse Hill 4700.

Died 7 Jan. 1944.

LOVERIDGE, Walter David, CMG 1930; *b* 1867. Entered NSW Public Service, 1884; a Public Service Commissioner for NSW, 1918–24; President Sydney Harbour Trust, 1924–30. *Address:* 86 Northwood Road, Northwood, Sydney, NSW.

Died 6 May 1940.

LOVETT, Sir (Harrington) Verney, KCSI 1916; CSI 1911; MA Oxon; *b* 29 April 1864; *s* of late Rev. Robert Lovett and Elizabeth, *d* of Hugh Lumsden, Pitcaple Castle, Aberdeenshire; *m* 1893, Clara Crofton, OBE, *d* of late Major C. Jamieson, BSC; one *d. Educ:* Sherborne School; Balliol College, Oxford. Entered Indian Civil Service, 1884; has served in the United Provinces of Agra and Oudh; Kaiser-i-Hind gold medal, 1901, for anti-plague services; Delhi Durbar Coronation medal, 1911; Member Board of Revenue United Provinces, of three Committees specially appointed by the Government of India, and of the Imperial Legislative Council of the Viceroy; retired from the ICS, 1919; Reader in Indian History Oxford University 1920–32; FRHS. *Publications:* A History of the Indian Nationalist Movement; India (Nations of To-Day Series); articles in the Quarterly Review; ten chapters in the Cambridge History of India, vol. vi. *Address:* 11 Linton Road, Oxford.

Died 22 March 1945.

LOW, Alexander, MA, MD (Aber.); LLD; Emeritus Regius Professor of Anatomy, Aberdeen University; *b* Oldmachar, Aberdeenshire, 1868; *s* of Alexander Low, farmer, Cothill, Oldmachar, Aberdeenshire. *Educ:* Aberdeen Grammar School; Aberdeen University; Freiburg; Vienna; Zürich. *Publications:* papers on Anatomical, Anthropological, and Embryological Subjects in Scientific Journals. *Recreation:* photography. *Address:* 144 Blenheim Place, Aberdeen. *T:* Aberdeen 23592.

Died 15 Nov. 1950.

LOW, Sir Charles Ernest, KCIE 1919; CIE 1909; BA; Indian Civil Service, retired; *b* 1869; *s* of Rev. C. Low, MA; *m* 1897, May (whom he divorced 1920), *d* of J. R. Porter, St Lawrence Thanet; two *d*; 2nd, 1921, Helen Ada, 2nd *d* of late Capt. E. K. E. Spence, Bengal Staff Corps. *Educ:* Rugby; Wadham College, Oxford. Entered ICS 1893; retired 1922; Kaisar-i-hind Medal, 1901. *Publications:* Gazetteer of the Baloghet District; Manual of Mining Rules for the Central Provinces. *Recreation:* University trial eights 1892 and 1893.

Died 4 Feb. 1941.

LOW, Robert Cranston, MD, FRCPE, FRSE; Consulting Physician to the Skin Department, Royal Infirmary, Edinburgh; late Lecturer on Diseases of the Skin, Edinburgh University; *b* Edinburgh, 1879; 2nd *s* of late Thomas Low; *m* 1st, 1914, Evelyn Frances, *d* of late W. Glen Henderson, Glasgow; 2nd, 1922, Alice Armstrong, *d* of late Wm Grant, Edinburgh; one *s. Educ:* Merchiston Castle School and University, Edinburgh; Medical Schools of Breslau, Hamburg, Vienna and Paris. MB, ChB, Edinburgh University, 1902; MRCP 1904;

FRCPE 1906; MD (gold medal for thesis, Edin. Univ. 1924). Resident Physician, Royal Maternity Hospital, Edinburgh, 1902–03; Royal Infirmary, Edinburgh, 1903; Royal Edinburgh Hospital for Sick Children, 1903–04; Clinical Assistant, Skin Dept, Royal Infirmary, 1904–05; studied diseases of skin in Breslau, Vienna, Hamburg, Paris, during 1905–06; Assistant Physician to Skin Dept, Royal Infirmary, Edinburgh, 1906. *Publications:* Carbonic Acid Snow as an aid to Diagnosis and Treatment of Diseases of the Skin, 1911; Anaphylaxis and Sensitisation, with special reference to the Skin and its Diseases, 1924; The Common Diseases of the Skin, 3rd edition 1938; numerous articles on dermatology in various medical journals. *Recreations:* gardening, golf and sketching. *Address:* Pathhead, 37 Oxgangs Road, Fairmilehead, Edinburgh. *T:* Edinburgh 71360.

Died 3 Feb. 1949.

LOW, Col Stuart, DSO 1917; *b* 1888; *s* of Sir Austin Low, CIE; *m* 1913, Hon. Lucy Gwen Atkin (who obtained a divorce, 1929), *d* of Baron Atkin, PC. *Educ:* Winchester. Served European War, 1914–18 (wounded, despatches twice, DSO).

Died 7 Dec. 1942.

LOW, Vincent Warren, CB, MD, BS, FRCS; Vice-President and Consulting Surgeon, St Mary's Hospital; Late Chief Consulting Surgeon to London, Midland and Scottish Railway Co.; Member of Council, King Edward's Hospital Fund for London; late President, Royal Society of Medicine; late Vice-President, Royal College of Surgeons; late Surgeon to St Mary's Hospital; late Member of Court of Examiners, Royal College of Surgeons; late Examiner in Surgery, London, Cambridge, and Liverpool Universities and Queen's University, Belfast; Civil Surgeon, South African War, 1900–02 (Queen's medal and 7 clasps); Colonel AMS; late Consulting Surgeon to HM troops in Mediterranean; *m* 1902, Mabel, *e d* of John Ashby, JP, of The Close, Staines; four *s* two *d. Address:* 76 Harley Street, W1. *T:* Langham 1786.

Died 2 Sept. 1942.

LOWE, David; *b* Leslie, Fifeshire, 1868; 4th *s* of Joseph Garland Lowe; *m* Margaret Irving Alston. *Educ:* Leslie Public School; Dundee College. *Publications:* Gift of the Night (poems), 1898. A Scots Wanderjahre (essays), 1900; A Man of Leisure (play), 1902; Burns's Passionate Pilgrimage, 1904; Farthing Joe, 1904; Sonnets of Sweet Sorrow, 1905; Ballad of a Great City, 1908; Burns; Poet of Peace and War, John Barlas, 1915; Souvenirs of Scottish Labour, 1919; From Pit to Parliament, the Story of the Early Life of James Keir Hardie, 1923; contributor to Critic, English Illustrated, Pearson's, etc. *Address:* 157 Crofthill Road, Croftfoot, Cathcart.

Died 18 Nov. 1947.

LOWE, Rev. Herbert Hampson, MA; Prebendary of St Paul's, 1931; *b* June 1865; *s* of Canon Joseph Lowe, late of Haltwhistle, Northumberland; *m* 1897, Dorothy Frances, *d* of John Hopgood, Clapham Park; three *s. Educ:* Uppingham; Trinity College, Cambridge. Assistant Curate, St John's, Battersea, 1889–93, St Gabriel's, Pimlico, 1895, 1897, and Kensington, 1897–1905; Vicar, St Barnabas', Kensington, 1905–26; Rural Dean of Kensington, 1926–39. *Recreation:* golf (Mid Surrey, Royal Ashdown Forest). *Address:* Sycamore Cottage, Forest Row, Sussex. *T:* Forest Row 140.

Died 24 July 1945.

LOWE, Percy Roycroft, OBE, BA; MB; BC Cantab; late President, British Ornithologists' Union; Chairman, European and British Sections International Committee for Preservation of Birds; *b* 2 Jan. 1870; *s* of John Rooe Lowe, Stamford, Lincolnshire; *m* Harriette Dorothy, *d* of E. G. B. Meade-Waldo; one *d. Educ:* private; Jesus College, Cambridge; Guy's Hospital, London. Held appointments at Leicester General Infirmary and Derby County Infirmary (Senior House Surgeon); has never engaged in civil practice; Civil Surgeon in charge HRH Princess Christian's Hospital Train, South African War, 1899–1901; Relief of Ladysmith; in medical charge of Earl of Dunraven's Hospital Yacht for Officers in Great War, operations in Mediterranean; subsequently joined RAMC with rank of Captain and again appointed to command of HRH Princess Christian's new Hospital Train (despatches, OBE); made six yachting voyages with Sir Frederic Johnston, Bt, 1903–09, making extensive collections of island forms of birds (now preserved in the British Museum); Keeper in charge of Ornithology (British Museum of Natural History, 1918); is a member of the Advisory Committee for Ornithology to the Home Office; Member Council of RSPB, etc.; represented HM Govt, at International Ornithological Congress, Rouen, 1938, and has represented the Home Office at various other Ornithological Congresses on the Continent; Hon. Member of various foreign ornithological institutions; Verner von Heidenstan Gold Medal, Royal Swedish Academy of Science; Salvin-Godman medal, BOU, 1946. *Publications:* A Naturalist on Desert Islands; many scientific publications on Anatomy and Classification of Birds, published in scientific journals. *Recreations:* golf, dry fly fishing, shooting. *Address:* Hugo House, 178 Sloane Street, SW1; Parkland, Burley, Ringwood, Hants. *Club:* Athenæum.

Died 18 Aug. 1948.

LOWE, Vice-Adm. Sidney Robert D.; *see* Drury-Lowe.

LOWE, Maj.-Gen. William Henry Muir, CB 1906; retired; *b* 20 Oct. 1861; *s* of late W. H. Lowe, ICS; *m* 1895, Frances (*d* 1942), *widow* of Capt. R. Johnson; one *s* one *d. Educ:* RMC Sandhurst. Entered 7th Dragoon Guards, 1881; Capt. 1887; Major, 1892; Lt-Col 1899; Bt Col 1900; Col 1903; retired, 1908; served Egyptian Expedition, 1882; present at battle of Tel-el-Kebir (medal and clasp, Khedive's star); Burmese Expedition, 1886–89 (medal and two clasps); South African War, 1900–02 (despatches twice, Queen's medal with five clasps, King's medal with two clasps, Brevet Col); AQMG 2nd Army Corps, 1903–05; Colonel in charge of Cavalry Records, Northern Command, 1905–07; Inspector of Cavalry, 1914; Brigade Commander with rank of Brig.-Gen. 1915; late Col in charge, Cavalry Records, and Staff Officer for Imperial Yeomanry.

Died 7 Feb. 1944.

LOWELL, Abbott Lawrence; President of Harvard University, 1909–33; President-Emeritus since 1933; *b* Boston, 13 Dec. 1856; *s* of Augustus Lowell and Katharine Bigeiow Lawrence; *m* Anna Parker Lowell (*d* 1930). *Educ:* Harvard University. Graduated with highest honours in mathematics, 1877; Harvard Law School, 1880; practised Law in Boston, 1880–97. Lecturer at Harvard, 1897–99; Prof. Science of Government, Harvard, 1900–09; Trustee of the Lowell Institute of Boston since 1900; Hon. PhD Berlin, 1910; LLD University of Louvain, 1909, University of Strasbourg, 1919, Cambridge University, 1920, Victoria University of Manchester, 1920; LittD Oxford University, 1920; Doctor of Political Science University of Leiden, 1920; Docteur (Hon.) University of Paris, 1921, University of Edinburgh, 1930, and several American Universities; Corresponding Fellow of the British Academy; Honorary Member of the Irish Academy; Foreign Member of the Academy of Arts and Sciences of the University of Utrecht; Grand Officer Legion of Honour; Commander of the Order of the Crown (Belgium). *Publications:* Transfer of Stock in Corporations (with Judge Francis C. Lowell), 1884; Essays on Government, 1889; Governments and Parties in Continental Europe, 1895; Colonial Civil Service (with Prof. H. Morse Stephens), 1900; The Influence of Party on Legislation in England and America, 1902; The Government of England, 1908; Public Opinion and Popular

Government, 1913; The Governments of France, Italy and Germany, 1914; Greater European Governments, 1918; Public Opinion in War and Peace, 1923; Conflicts of Principle, 1932; At War with Academic Traditions, 1934; Biography of Percival Lowell, 1935; What a College President has Learned, 1938. *Address:* 171 Marlborough Street, Boston, Mass, USA.

Died 6 Jan. 1943.

LOWES, John Livingston, AM, PhD (Harvard), MA (Oxford), Hon. LLD (Washington and Jefferson College, McGill Univ.), Hon. LittD (Univ. of Maine, Yale Univ., Brown Univ., Harvard Univ.), Hon. LHD (Tufts College), Hon. DLitt (Oxford); sometime Fellow of Balliol, Corr. FBA, FAAS, and other learned societies; Professor of English, Harvard University, 1918–30; Francis Lee Higginson Professor of English Literature, 1930–39, Emeritus since 1939; Senior Fellow, Society of Fellows, since 1933; first George Eastman Visiting Professor, Oxford, 1930–31; *b* 20 Dec. 1867; *s* of Abram Brower Lowes and Mary Bella Elliott; *m* 1897, Mary Cornett; one *s*. *Educ:* Jefferson Academy; Washington and Jefferson College (AB 1888); University of Leipzig and University of Berlin; Harvard University. Adjunct Professor of Mathematics, Washington and Jefferson College, 1888–91; Prof. of English, Hanover College, 1895–1902, and Swarthmore College, 1905–09; Prof. of English, 1909–18, Dean of the College, 1913–14, Washington University; Dean of the Graduate School of Arts and Sciences, Harvard University, 1924–25; Lecturer, Universities of Cincinnati, California and Texas, Univ. College of Wales, Brooklyn Institute of Arts and Sciences, Northwestern University (Harris Foundation), Swarthmore College (Cooper Foundation), Lowell Institute, etc. *Publications:* Convention and Revolt in Poetry, 1919; The Road to Xanadu, 1927; Of Reading Books, 1929; Of Reading Books and other Essays, 1930; The Art of Geoffrey Chaucer, 1931; Geoffrey Chaucer, 1934; Essays in Appreciation, 1936; The Noblest Monument of English Prose, 1937; articles, especially on Chaucerian subjects and Keats, in American and foreign philological and literary journals; Editor (with George Lyman Kittredge) of synonyms in New International Dictionary; Editor of All's Well that Ends Well and Hamlet, and of The Selected Poems of Amy Lowell. *Address:* 984 Memorial Drive, Cambridge, Mass, USA. *Clubs:* Faculty, Cambridge; Odd Volumes, Harvard, Saturday, Boston; Harvard, New York; Elizabethan (Hon.), New Haven.

Died 15 Aug. 1945.

LOWINSKY, Thomas Esmond; painter; *b* London, 2 March 1892; *e s* of late T. H. Lowinsky of Tittenhurst, Sunninghill, Berks; *m* Ruth, *d* of Leopold Hirsch; one *s* (*er s* killed in action, 1944) two *d*. *Educ:* Eton; Trinity College, Oxford; Slade School of Art. Enlisted in the Inns of Court OTC, Aug. 1914; commissioned Queen's Own (Royal West Kent Regiment); transferred the Scots Guards; active service France; Army of Occupation at Cologne; demobilised April 1919; exhibition of painting and drawings Leicester Galleries, London, Feb. 1926; works acquired by The Chantrey Bequest, 1939; The Tate Gallery; The National Gallery of Wales, Cardiff; The British Museum; The Victoria and Albert Museum; The Duveen Fund; The Fitzwilliam Museum, Cambridge; Sheffield Art Gallery; Municipal Gallery, Carlisle; Wolverhampton Art Gallery; Member Advisory Council Victoria and Albert Museum; Exec. Committee Contemporary Art Soc. *Publications:* Illustrations: Sidonia the Sorceress, by William Meinhold; Elegy on Dead Fashion, by Edith Sitwell; Doctor Donne and Gargantua, by Sacheverell Sitwell; Exalt the Eglantine, by Sacheverell Sitwell; The Princess of Babylon; Plutarch's Lives; The School for Scandal; Modern Nymphs, a book of drawings with an essay on clothes by Raymond Mortimer; etc. *Address:* The Old Rectory, Aldbourne, Wilts. *T:* Aldbourne 36. *Club:* Guards'.

Died 24 April 1947.

LOWIS, Cecil Champain; Indian Civil Service (retired); *b* 31 Jan. 1866; *s* of Edmund Elliot Lowis and Susan Mary Currie; *m* 1894; three *d*. *Educ:* Newton College; Germany; Corpus Christi College, Cambridge. Appointed after examination of 1885; Assist Commissioner, Burma; Deputy Commissioner; Officiating Chief Secretary to Government, 1903 and 1904; lent to Government of Egypt as Director-General of Egyptian Census, 1906–08; Commissioner and Superintendent of Ethnography, Burma, 1908; retired, 1912; served in France during the war in command of an Indian Labour Company, 1917–18. *Publications:* Novels: Fascination; Four Blind Mice; The Runagate; The Grass Spinster; Green Sandals; The Penal Settlement; The Huntress; The Dripping Tamarinds; The Green Tunnel; Prodigal's Portion, 1936, etc. *Address:* Elm House, Marshall Rd, Godalming. *T:* Godalming 180.

Died 9 Oct. 1948.

LOWNDES, Rt Hon. Sir George Rivers, PC 1929; KCSI 1918; KC 1917; a Bencher of Lincoln's Inn; *b* 1862; 3rd *s* of Rev. Canon Lowndes; *m* 1896, Hilda (*d* 1941), 2nd *d* of Bt-Maj. Lachlan Forbes, late 31st Regt; three *s* one *d*. *Educ:* Winchester; New College, Oxford. Called to Bar, 1892; late Legal Member of the Viceroy of India's Executive Council; Member of the Judicial Committee of the Privy Council since 1929. *Address:* Gaddens Close, Ringwood. *Club:* Fly-Fishers'.

Died 18 Sept. 1943.

LOWNDES, Mary E.; *b* 1863; *d* of Richard Lowndes, author of works upon Philosophy and upon Marine Insurance and General Average. *Educ:* Girton College, Cambridge, MA Cambridge; LittD Trinity College, Dublin, 1907. Head-Mistress, Rosemary Hall School, Greenwich, Conn, USA; retired, 1938. *Publications:* Translation of Höffding's Outlines of Psychology, 1889; Michel de Montaigne, 1898; The Nuns of Port Royal, 1909. *Address:* Greenwich, Conn, USA. *Clubs:* Cosmopolitan, New York.

Died 19 March 1947.

LOWRY, Rt Hon. William; PC (N Ire.) 1943; KC 1926; Judge of High Court of Justice, N Ireland, 1947–49; retd 1949. *Educ:* Queen's Univ., Belfast (MA, LLB). Called to Bar, King's Inns, 1907; MP Londonderry City, Parliament of Northern Ireland, 1939–47; Parliamentary Secretary to Ministry of Home Affairs, 1940–43; Minister of Home Affairs, 1943–44; Attorney-General, Northern Ireland, 1944–47. *Address:* 97 Osborne Park, Belfast.

Died 14 Dec. 1949.

LOWSON, James Gray Flowerdew, PhD; Owner of Quarwood; interested in landscape gardening and preservation of the countryside; *b* 7 July 1860; *y s* of William Lowson, DL, JP, of Balthayock, Perthshire, and Helen Flowerdew; *m* 1890, Adelaide, *d* of Colonel Courtenay Scott; one *s* one *d*, *er s* (Rifle Brigade) killed in War. *Educ:* University, Edinburgh and University, Heidelberg. Three years Heidelberg under Professor Bunsen studying chemistry; graduated PhD summa cum laude, 1880. After one year at Sorbonne in Paris worked for three years as an ordinary workman in Scotland while studying the practical application of science to industry, principally in connection with paper-making materials—working hours then twelve-hour shifts without any interval for meals, and every second week all night in place of day, and no one appeared any the worse; thereafter invited by an owner to report and advise generally on his works and subsequently to undertake entire control, which he did personally for three years; thereafter invited to take a supervisory control of various other important concerns, which he did for many years; has also made many examinations and reports for Banking and other interests in various parts of the world, involving large outlays, the employment of many work-people, and the selection of men for many important technical positions, both here and abroad, under his control; during the war was a member of several Government Committees connected with industrial matters and trench warfare questions; in younger days was a Member of the Midlothian County Council; served as Lieut in Midlothian Coast Artillery Volunteers, and later as Captain of 9th (Highland Batt.) Royal Scots; a Member of King's Bodyguard (Royal Company of Archers) for Scotland; the first District Commissioner of Boy Scouts for the Stratford-on-Avon Division of Warwickshire, a Life Governor of University College, Dundee, and a Governor of the Shakespeare Memorial Theatre. *Recreations:* shooting, Alpine climbing, foxhunting. *Address:* Quarwood, Stow-on-the-Wold, Glos. *T:* Stow-on-the-Wold, 14. *Club:* Union.

Died 16 Sept. 1942.

LOWTHER, Viscount; Anthony Edward Lowther; JP Westmorland; DL Westmorland and Cumberland; Hon. Col 4th Bn Border Regt (T), 1932; *b* 1896; *s* of 6th Earl of Lonsdale; *m* 1922, Muriel Frances, 2nd *d* of late Sir George Farrar, Bt, DSO, and Lady Farrar of Chicheley Hall, Newport Pagnell, Bucks; two *s* one *d*. *Educ:* Wellington. Late 10th Hussars Hon. Capt.; High Sheriff Westmorland, 1930; Lord Lieutenant of Westmorland, 1939–45. *Address:* Askham Hall, Penrith, Cumberland. *T:* Pooley Bridge 226. *Clubs:* Turf, White's.

Died 6 Oct. 1949.

LOWTHER, Lt-Col Sir Charles Bingham, 4th Bt *cr* 1824; CB 1948; DSO 1917; CStJ 1947; late 8th Hussars and Northamptonshire Yeomanry; JP Denbighshire; DL Denbighshire, 1947; *b* 22 July 1880; *s* of late George William Lowther, *e s* of 3rd Bart and Mary Francis Alice (*d* 1921), *e d* of late Col Charles Bingham, RA; *S* grandfather, 1894; *m* 1st, 1909, Marjorie Noel (*d* 1925), *d* of late Thomas Fielden, MP, of Grimston, Yorks; one *s* one *d*; 2nd, 1936, Ruth Kynaston, *d* of Major C. F. K. Mainwaring. *Educ:* Winchester; RMC, Sandhurst. Served South Africa, 1900–01; European War, 1914–19 (despatches, DSO, Bt-Col); High-Sheriff of Northants, 1926–27. *Heir: s* William Guy, Major 8th Hussars [*b* 9 Oct. 1912; *m* 1939, Grania Suzanne, *y d* of late Major Douglas Campbell, of Blythswood, and the Hon. Mrs Douglas Campbell, Toad Hall, Firmley, Hants; one *s* (Charles Douglas, *b* 22 Jan. 1946)]. *Address:* Erbistock Hall, Overton Bridge, Wrexham. *Clubs:* Cavalry, Boodle's.

Died 22 Jan. 1949.

LOWTHER, John Arthur, MVO 1937; Private Secretary to Duke of Kent; *b* 13 Oct. 1910; *s* of Hon. C. W. Lowther and Lady George Cholmondeley; *g s* and heir of 1st Viscount Ullswater, PC; *m* 1937, Priscilla, 2nd *d* of Reginald Lambert; one *s* one *d*. *Educ:* Eton. Temp. Lt, RNVR, 1939. *Address:* 9 Motcomb Street, SW1. *Club:* Bath.

Died 25 Aug. 1942.

LOWTHER-CROFTON, Vice-Adm. Edward George, DSO 1900; *b* 9 Aug. 1873; *s* of late Major Lowther-Crofton; *m* 1st, 1911, Magdalen, *d* of Duncan Anderson; 2nd, 1931, Mabel Eaton. Entered Navy, 1886; served China, 1900 (DSO); Commanded 9th Destroyer Flotilla; Assistant to Admiral of Patrols; Rear-Adm. retired, 1920. *Club:* Army and Navy.

Died 19 July 1942.

LOWTHIAN, Caroline; *see* Prescott, Mrs Cyril.

LOYD, Arthur Thomas, OBE, DL, JP, MA; Lord Lieutenant of County of Berks, since 1935; an Ecclesiastical Commissioner for England, 1923; Warden of Bradfield College; Hon. Col 80th AA Regt (TA); Hon. Fellow, Hertford College, 1941; a Trustee, Wallace Collection, 1942; *b* 19 April 1882; 2nd *s* of late Rev. Lewis Haig Loyd; *m* 1911, Dorothy, *d* of late P. F. Willert, of Headington, Oxford; one *s* three *d*. *Educ:*

Eton; Hertford College, Oxford. MP (Conservative) Abingdon Division of Berks, 1921–23; for a time in the Egyptian Public Service; High Sheriff, Berks, 1927; Chairman Berks CC 1938–44. *Address:* Lockinge House, Wantage, Berks. *T:* Wantage 63. *Club:* Travellers'.

Died 8 Nov. 1944.

LUARD, Maj.-Gen. Charles Camac, CB 1919; CMG 1918; Colonel of Durham Light Infantry, 1934–37; *b* 1867; *s* of late Lieut-General R. G. A Luard, CB; *m* 1909, Catherine Isabel Hammond, *d* of late H. R. Solly, Serge Hill, King's Langley; one *d*. *Educ:* Clifton College; RMC, Canada. Served South African War, 1900–02 (Queen's medal and 4 clasps, King's medal and 2 clasps, Bt Major); European War, 1914–18 (despatches, CB, CMG); GOC Forces in South China, 1925–29; retired pay, 1929. *Address:* Birches, Yateley, Hants.

Died 28 June 1947.

LUARD, Lowes Dalbiac. Painter, Etcher, Draughtsman; Occasional writer and lecturer on art. *Address:* 10 Hall Road, NW8. *T:* Maida Vale 6274. *Club:* Arts.

Died 20 Sept. 1944.

LUBBOCK, Basil; author; *b* 9 Sept. 1876; *s* of Alfred Lubbock, *brother* of 1st Lord Avebury; *m* 1912, Dorothy Mary, *widow* of Commander T. U. Thynne, RN, and *d* of late Charles Warner, CB. *Educ:* Eton. Went to Canada, 1897; went over Chilcoot Trail into Klondyke in second year of the gold excitement; on leaving Klondyke shipped on a four-mast barque as ordinary seaman and came home round the Horn; during Boer War held a commission in Menne's scouts, a South African corps (despatches for helping to save life under fire); served European War; Territorial Commission 1/3 Wessex Brigade RFA, Oct. 1914–April 1919 (India and France, MC); Member of Nautical Research Society. *Publications:* Round the Horn before the Mast; Jack Derringer; Deep Sea Warriors; The China Clippers, 1914; The Colonial Clippers, 1921; The Blackwall Frigates, 1922; The Log of the Cutty Sark, 1924; Western Ocean Packets; Adventures by Sea from Art of Old Time, 1925; The Last of the Windjammers, 2 vol.; Sail, 3 vol.; The Down Easters, 1929; Bully Hayes, South Sea Pirate, 1931; The Nitrate Clippers, 1932; The Opium Clippers, 1933; Barlows Journal, 2 vol. transcribed and edited, 1934; Coolie Ships and Oil Sailors, 1935; The Arctic Whalers, 1937. *Recreations:* yachting and boating, hunting, cricket (Eton eleven, 1894, 1895). *Address:* Monks Orchard, Seaford, Sussex. *Clubs:* Royal Automobile; Royal Yacht Squadron, Cowes.

Died 3 Sept. 1944.

LUBBOCK, Lady Sybil Marjorie; *b* 1879; *yr d* of 5th Earl of Desart, KP, PC, KCB; *m* 1st, 1901, William Bayard Cutting (*d* 1910); one *d*; 2nd, 1918, Geoffrey Scott; 3rd, 1926, Percy Lubbock. *Publications:* A Book of the Sea, 1918; Four Tales by Zélide, 1925; On Ancient Ways: A Winter Journey, 1928; A Page from the Past: Memories of the Earl of Desart, 1936; The Child in the Crystal, 1939. *Address:* Villa Medici, Fiesole, Florence, Italy.

Died 31 Dec. 1943.

LUBITSCH, Ernst; Producer-Director 20th Century-Fox Studio, Los Angeles, California; *b* 29 Jan. 1892; *s* of Simon Lubitsch and Anna Lindenstedt; one *d*. *Educ:* Sophien Gymnasium, Berlin. Actor with Max Reinhardt; Motion Picture actor and director, Berlin, later Hollywood, Calif. Chief European Productions: Madame Dubarry, One Arabian Night, Deception (Henry VIII), Montmartre (Carmen); Chief American Productions: Marriage Circle, Forbidden Paradise, Lady Windermere's Fan, The Patriot, The Love Parade, Monte Carlo, The Man I Killed, Trouble in Paradise, Design for Living, Merry Widow, Bluebeard's Eighth Wife, Ninotchka, Shop Around the Corner, To Be or Not to Be, Heaven Can Wait, Cluny Brown. *Recreations:*

sports and reading. *Address:* 20th Century-Fox Studio, Los Angeles, California, USA. *TA:* Lubitsch Hollywood, Calif.

Died 30 Nov. 1947.

LUCAN, 5th Earl of, *cr* 1795; **George Charles Bingham;** Bt 1632; Baron Lucan, 1776; Baron Bingham, UK, 1934, PC 1938; GCVO 1939; KBE 1920; CB 1919; TD 1920; Hon. Brig.-General since 1917; Irish Representative Peer since 1914; *b* 13 Dec. 1860; *e s* of 4th Earl and Lady Cecilia Catherine Gordon-Lennox (*d* 1910), *γ d* of 5th Duke of Richmond, KG; *S* father, 1914; *m* 1896, Violet, OBE, 1920, *d* of J. Spender Clay, Ford Manor, Lingfield; two *s* two *d. Educ:* Harrow; RMC Sandhurst. Late Rifle Brigade, 1881–96; served Bechuanaland Expedition, 1884–85; European War, 1914–16; DL, JP Middlesex; High Sheriff, Co. May, 1902; Lt-Col commanding 1st London Vol. Rifle Corps, 1901–08; 5th City of London Rifles (London Rifle Brigade), 1908–12; Colonel (temp. Brig.-General) commanding 1st London Infantry Brigade, 1912–16; Hon. Col London Rifle Brigade, 1923–46. MP (C) Chertsey Div., Surrey 1904–06; Chairman, City of London TF Association, 1912–41; ADC to the King, 1920–28; a Lord-in-Waiting to the King, 1920–24, and 1924–29; Captain of the Hon. Corps of Gentlemen-at-Arms, Jan.–June 1929 and 1931–40; holds Order of St Stanislaus of Russia (2nd Class), Order of the Nile, 3rd Class, 1916. *Heir: s* Lord Bingham. *Address:* 19 Orchard Court, W1. *T:* Welbeck 6030. *Club:* Carlton.

Died 20 April 1949.

LUCAS, Col Alfred George, CB 1902; MVO 1901; VD; JP Herts and Suffolk; late Colonel Com. Suffolk Imperial Yeomanry; DAG Imperial Yeomanry; *b* 26 Oct. 1854; 2nd *s* of C. T. Lucas of Warnham Court, Sussex, and Charlotte Emma, *d* of C. Tiffin; *m* 1st, Edith Hamilton (*d* 1925), *d* of late W. Hamilton Crake; two *s* three *d*; 2nd, 1932, Catherine Monie, *d* of late Fergus McCallum, Girvan, Ayrshire. *Educ:* privately. Partner till 1895 in the firm of Lucas Bros and Lucas and Aird; Director E. Lacon and Co.'s Brewery, Great Yarmouth since 1895; Director Law Union and Rock Life Assurance Co., The San Paulo Coffee Estates Company; Director County Fishing Co., Ltd; Lieut 17th Suffolk Rifle Volunteers, 1873–75, 1st Suffolk Artillery Volunteers, 1875–82; Suffolk Yeomanry, LSH, 1883–1906; Lieut-Col Commanding, 1891; hon. Col, 1897; Chairman IY Committee and DAG Imp. Yeo., 1900; hon. Col in Army, 1903; Mayor of Lowestoft, 1896 and 1898; High Sheriff, 1904; served S Africa, 1900 (despatches); Commandant B Group Norfolk Volunteers, 1917–18. *Recreations:* cricket, played for Suffolk and Herts Counties; hunting, shooting, fishing, golf, etc. *Address:* 47 Wilbury Road, Hove, Sussex. *T:* Hove 3833. *Clubs:* Junior Carlton; Royal Norfolk and Suffolk Yacht.

Died 4 May 1941.

LUCAS, Captain Armytage Anthony, CBE 1919; RN, retired; *m* 1923, Phyllis Katherine, 3rd *d* of late George John Coldham, Solicitor, of 3 and 4 Clement's Inn, and Mrs Coldham, of Ormond Lodge, Weston Road, Bath; one *d. Address:* Seerscroft, Faygate, Sussex.

Died 21 Feb. 1950.

LUCAS, Hon. Sir Edward, Kt 1921; *b* 14 Feb. 1857; *s* of Adams Lucas, Galonetra, Co. Cavan; *nephew* of late Leonard Lucas, MD, Inspector-General, RN; *m* 1890, Mabel Florence, *d* of John Brock, JP, Tanunda, South Australia; two *d. Educ:* Bailieboro. Arrived in South Australia, 1878; engaged in mercantile pursuits; owned businesses in Adelaide, Gawler, Hamley Bridge, Balaklava; JP South Australia; Mayor of Gawler two years; Member Legislative Council, 1900–18; Leader and Chairman of Liberal Party; Agent-General for South Australia, 1918–25; has acted as Agent General for

Tasmania; member of State War Council; Vice-Chairman of State Recruiting Committee; Chairman and Member of several Commissions; Member of Committee Prince Alfred College, Methodist Ladies College, Memorial Hospital, Mount Barker Rest Home, and Aborigines Friends Association (10 years); Pres., Navy League, SA Branch; President and Life Member Prisoners' Aid Association; Life Member, District Trained Nursing Association. *Address:* Galonetra, Robe Terrace, Medindie, South Australia.

Died 4 July 1950.

LUCAS, Henry Frederick Lucas; *b* Louth, Lincolnshire; *s* of late St John Welles Lucas, MRCS, and Louisa, *d* of Capt. J. I. W. Bazalgette, RN, *sister* of Sir Joseph Bazalgette, CB, and of Helen, Lady Twysden; *m* 1st, 1877, Sarah Blanche, *d* of Rev. Louis Henry Mordacque, JP, Vicar of Haslingden, Lancashire; one *s*; 2nd, 1890, Kathleen Liffie, *d* of Rev. Leonard Browne Beatson of The Hall, Pinchbeck, Spalding, Linc.; three *s*. Came to Rugby, 1878; had a studio there since that date; work consisting chiefly painting portraits of horses and hounds; has painted a large number of noted race-horses—The Bard, Bendigo, Isinglass, Galtee More, Father O'Flynn, Come Away, The Tetrach; four winners of the Italian Derby—Hira, Dedalo, Belbuc, and Sansonetto, and many others at home and abroad, besides many equestrian portraits.

Died 20 June 1943.

LUCAS, Rt Rev. William Vincent, MA, Bishop of Masasi, 1926–44; *b* 20 June 1883; *s* of Rev. Vincent William Lucas, MA; unmarried. *Educ:* Magdalen College School; St Catherine's Society, University of Oxford; Theological College, St Stephen's House, Oxford. Deacon, 1906; priest, 1907; Curate of St Michael, Shepton Beauchamp, 1906–09; UMCA Missionary at Kiungani, 1909–12; Masasi, 1912–26; Chaplain East African Force, 1917–19; Provost and Sub-dean of Masasi Collegiate Church and Canon of Zanzibar, 1922–26. *Publication:* Essay on The Christian Approach to Non-Christian Customs, in Essays Catholic and Missionary, 1928.

Died 8 July 1945.

LUCE, Morton; *b* High Wycombe, Bucks, 7 May 1849; *e s* of Rev. E. J. Luce. *Educ:* Oundle; private study. Some time Assistant Lecturer, Bristol University. *Publications:* Guide to Parsing and Analysis, 1882; New Studies in Tennyson, 1892; A Handbook to the Works of Tennyson, 1895; Shakespeare's Tempest, 1902; Introduction to Tennyson (Temple Primers), 1902; A Handbook to the Works of Shakespeare, 1905; Shakespeare's Twelfth Night, 1905; Thysia, an Elegy, 1908; Rich's Apolonius and Silla, 1910; edited The False One (Beaumont and Fletcher), 1910; Threnodies, Sketches, and other Poems, 1910; Idyllia, 1911; Thysia, American edition, enlarged, 1911; Shakespeare, the Man and his Work, 1913; enlarged Handbook to Tennyson (7th edition), 1914; revised and enlarged editions of The Tempest and Twelfth Night, 1918; New Idyllia; Sketches of a Stream, 1923; The Tempest, 5th ed. 1938; Twelfth Night, 5th ed. 1938 (Arden Series); Man and Nature or Essays and Sketches, 1935; The Real Mary Webb and other Essays; articles in The Nineteenth Century, Fortnightly, Contemporary, Hibbert Journal, and other reviews. *Address:* 30 Nithsdale Road, Weston-super-Mare.

Died 4 Jan. 1943.

LUCIE-SMITH, Sir Alfred van W., Kt 1911; *b* 9 Jan. 1854; *s* of Sir John Lucie-Smith, late Chief Justice of Jamaica; *m* 1st, Alice, *d* of Leopold Aves; 2nd, Meta, *d* of late Sir David Palmer Ross; six *s* one *d. Educ:* Rugby. Solicitor, 1877; called to Bar, Middle Temple, 1881; Acting Solicitor-General, British Guiana, 1882–87; President District Court, Cyprus, 1887; Acting Consular Judge, Constantinople, 1896; Resident Magistrate,

Kingston, Jamaica, 1896; Puisne Judge, British Guiana, 1898; Chief Justice of Trinidad and Tobago, 1908–24; retired, 1924.

Died 3 June 1947.

LUCK, Col Brian John Michael, CMG 1918; DSO 1917; *b* 1874; *s* of Frederick Locke, DL, JP, of Dane House, Hartlip, Kent; *m* 1901, Mary Ann, *d* of late J. R. Haig, DL, JP, of Blairhill, Scotland, and Highfields Park, Sussex; one *s*. Served European War, 1914–19; Lt-Col RA 1917; Col 1921; employed on Inter-allied Commission of Control in Germany, 1921–23; Col R. A. Eastern Command Headquarters, 1924; CRA Gibraltar, 1925–26; retired, 1926; JP Kent. *Address:* Cade House, West Malling, Kent. *Club:* United Service.

Died 26 Sept. 1948.

LUCK, Captain Cyril Montagu, CMG 1918; DSO 1916; late RIM; Hon. Brigadier-General; *b* 12 Jan. 1872; 4th *surv. s* of late Frederick Locke, JP, DL, Kent; *m* 1920, Joyce, Gwendolen, 4th *d* of Lt-Col A. A. Ruck, late 8th (The King's) Regt of Esgair, Machynlleth; two *d*. Entered Royal Indian Marine, 1892; served Persian Gulf, 1909–11 (medal and clasp); retired, 1912; served European War, 1914–19; granted temp. commission, 3 Sept. 1914; Commander, Royal Navy, 1915; lent to War Office as Temporary Major, RE, Deputy Assistant Director Inland Water Transport, BEF; Promoted T/Lt-Col, Col, and T. Brig.-General in 1917 (despatches six times, CMG, DSO, Commandeur de l'Ordre de la Couronne, and the Belgian Croix de Guerre, 1918; Officier de l'Ordre National de la Légion d'Honneur, 1919; Knight of Grace of the Order of St John of Jerusalem in England, 1918); Director of Inland Water Transport, France, 1917–19. *Address:* Whiteholme, Selsey, Sussex.

Died 2 Oct. 1944.

LUCKOCK, Maj.-Gen. Russell Mortimer, CB 1934; CMG 1918; DSO 1915; Fellow of Lancing College; Vice-President Army Rifle Association since 1949; *b* 1877; *s* of late Very Rev. H. M. Luckock, Dean of Lichfield; *m* 1903, Mabel Thorne (*d* 1949), *d* of late S. L. Seckham, DL, of Whittington, Lichfield. *Educ:* Harrow; Trinity College, Cambridge; BA 1899, MA 1929. Joined King's Own Regt 1900; served South African War, 1899–1902 (Queen's medal and 3 clasps, King's medal and 2 clasps); Assistant Instructor, School of Musketry, 1908–11; passed Staff College, 1913–14; European War, 1914–18; Brigade Major, 24th Inf. Brigade, 1915; GSO 17 Div. 1915; GSO 4th Army, 1916–18 (despatches, CMG, DSO, Bt Lieut-Col Legion of Honour, Croix de Guerre); GSO Staff Coll., Camberley, 1919–21; GSO to Lord Rawlinson in N Russia, 1919; GSO, AHQ India, 1921; Col 1922; Commandant, Small Arms Schools, India, 1922–25; OC 163rd Infantry Brigade, TA, 1926–28; Brigadier, General Staff, Southern Command, Salisbury, 1928–32; Maj. Gen. 1932; Commander 54th (East Anglian) Division, TA, 1934–38; retired pay, 1938; Hon. Col Cambridgeshire Regt, 1929–46; Hon. Col East Anglian Divl Signals, 1938–47; Hon. Col 54th (E Anglian) Div. RASC, 1939–47; Col The King's Own Royal Regt, 1945–47. *Address:* Husvig, Lymington, Hants. *T:* 648. *Club:* Royal Automobile.

Died 1 Jan. 1950.

LUCY, Sir Henry William Cameron-Ramsay-F.; *see* Fairfax-Lucy.

LUDBY, Max, RI 1891; artist; *b* London, 4 Nov. 1858; *m* 1894, Helen Cotter Morison (*d* 1939), *d* of late James Cotter Morison; one *d. Educ:* Essex. Studied at Antwerp, 1882–84. *Pictures:* A Berkshire Common, RA, 1888; One of the Flock, RI, 1891; An Old Shepherd, RI, 1893; From Oxford to Greenwich, a series of 82 Water-colour Drawings exhibited at Dowdeswells, 1893; Some Sketches of Venice, a series of 60 Watercolour Drawings

exhibited at Dickinson and Foster's, 1897. *Address:* Deerholm, Normandy, nr Guildford, Surrey. *T:* Normandy 40.

Died 18 March 1943.

LUDLOW, Lady; Alice Sedgwick; *d* of James Mankiewicz, Pembridge Square, W; *m* 1st, 1888, Sir Julius Charles Wernher, 1st Bt (*d* 1912); two *s* (and one *s* killed in the last War, 1916); 2nd, 1919, 2nd Baron Ludlow (*d* 1922). Lady of Grace, St John of Jerusalem; JP. *Address:* Bath House, Piccadilly, W1. *T:* Grosvenor 2443.

Died 30 Nov. 1945.

LUDLOW, Brig.-Gen. Sir Walter Robert, KCB 1936; CB 1911; CB (Mil.) 1918; DL; VD, TD; *b* 1857; *e s* of Joseph Ludlow, Solihull; *m* 1883, Helen Florence (*d* 1940), 3rd *d* of late Charles Hart, Harborne Hall, Staffs; one *s* (and one killed in action on the Somme, 1916) four *d. Educ:* Malvern College. Is a surveyor and valuer; Fellow of Surveyors' Institution, 1890; Surveyor to Board of Trade, 1895; JP Birmingham and County Warwick; Colonel Commandant of Cadets for the County of Warwick, 1913–26; late Lieut-Colonel commanding 8th Batt. Royal Warwickshire Regiment, which he raised 1908 on formation of Territorial Force and now Hon. Col; joined Birmingham Volunteers, 1874; Lieut-Colonel, 1901; Col commanding No. 2 Batt. Volunteers (now 6th Batt. Royal Warwickshire Regt), 1901–08; commanding 184th Inf. Brigade, 1915–16; Area Commandant, British Expeditionary Force, Flanders, 1917–18. *Publication:* Zululand and Cetewayo, 1882. *Address:* Lovelace Hill, Solihull, Warwickshire. *TA:* Solihull. *T:* Solihull 0029. *Clubs:* Union, Conservative, Birmingham.

Died 14 Oct. 1941.

LUDWIG, Emil; *b* 25 Jan. 1881; *m* Elga Wolff; two *s. Educ:* Breslau; Heidelberg. Began as a dramatist; wrote twelve years only plays, nearly all in verse; began after thirty with psychological essays and lives; calls himself a portrait painter; lives since his twenty-sixth year independently in the country in Tessin, Switzerland. Since 1932 Swiss Citizen. *Publications:* Lives of Jesus, Goethe, Napoleon, Bismarck, William II, Lincoln, two volumes with different portraits; Cleopatra, 1937; Roosevelt, 1938; Schlieman of Troy, 1931; July 1914, 1929; Gifts of Life: A retrospect, 1931; Talks with Mussolini, 1932; Talks with Masaryk; Leaders of Europe, 1934; Hindenburg, 1935; Masaryk Speaks, 1936; The Nile, 1936; The Nile in Egypt, 1937; A New Holy Alliance, 1938; The Germans, 1942; Stalin, 1942; The Mediterranean, 1943; How to Treat the Germans, 1944; Beethoven, Life of a Conqueror, 1945; History of Cuba, 1946; Of Life and Love, 1946; Othello, 1947; also three novels and twelve theatre-pieces, including Versailles, produced in London, 1932. *Address:* Ascona, Switzerland. *T:* Locarno 72240.

Died 17 Sept. 1948.

LUGARD, 1st Baron *cr* 1928, of Abinger; **Frederick Dealtry Lugard,** PC 1920; GCMG 1911; KCMG 1901; CB 1895; DSO 1887; Hon. DCL (Oxon) and Durham; Hon. LLD Cambridge, Glasgow, and Hong-Kong; Commander Legion of Honour, 1917; Grand Cross of Order of Leopold II of Belgium; Gold Medallist, RGS; *b* 22 Jan. 1858; *s* of Rev. F. G. Lugard; *m* 1902, Flora Louise, DBE (*d* 1929), *d* of late Gen. Shaw, CB. *Educ:* Rossall; Sandhurst. Served Afghan War, 1879–80 (medal); Sudan Campaign, 1885 (despatches, medal and two clasps, bronze star); Burma Campaign, 1886–87 (despatches thrice, DSO, medal with two clasps); commanded expedition against slave traders on Lake Nyasa, 1888 (severely wounded); served under East African Chartered Company in command of Expedition and as Administrator of Uganda, 1889–92 (medal); also under Royal Niger Company for Borgu treaties, 1894–95 (medal); also for British West

Charterland to Lake Ngami, 1896–97; HM Commissioner Hinterland of Nigeria and Lagos, and Commandant of West African Frontier Force (which he raised), with rank of Brigadier-General, 1897–99 (medal); High Commissioner and Commander-in-Chief of Northern Nigeria, 1900–06; Governor and Commander-in-Chief of Hong-Kong, 1907–12; Governor and Commander-in-Chief of Northern Nigeria and Southern Nigeria (simultaneously), 1912–13; Governor-General of Nigeria, 1914–19; British Member of Permanent Mandates Commission League of Nations, 1922–36; Director of Barclays Bank (DC and O). *Publications:* Our East African Empire, 1893; The Dual Mandate in British Tropical Africa, 1922 (awarded RCI gold medal). *Address:* Little Parkhurst, Abinger Common, Surrey. *TA:* Abinger-Common, Surrey. *T:* Abinger 79. *Club:* Athenæum.

Died 11 April 1945.

LUKE, 1st Baron *cr* 1929, of Pavenham; **George Lawson Johnston,** KBE 1920; JP; Lord Lieutenant of Bedfordshire since 1936; High Sheriff of Bedfordshire, 1924; Member of the Post Office Advisory Council since 1922; Member of Council London Chamber of Commerce; an Hon. Secretary King Edward's Hospital Fund for London; Chairman Revenue Committee King Edward's Hospital Fund for London and Member of Committee since 1901; Hon. Secretary, Thankoffering for the King's Recovery, 1929; Hon. Treasurer Royal Northern Hospital, 1909–23; Chairman, Ministry of Information's Advisory Committee on the Appointment of Advertising Agents; Chairman, Executive Committee Hospitals of London Combined Appeal, 1922; Chairman, British Charities Association; Treasurer County of London Red Cross; Chairman of British National Committee of the International Chamber of Commerce; Chairman, Committee on Nutrition, Ministry of Health; Chairman of Oakley Hunt Committee; Director of Daily Express from its foundation till 1917; Chairman Bovril, Ltd; Director Australian Mercantile, Land and Finance, Ltd; Lloyds Bank; Vice-Chairman Ashanti Goldfields Corporation; Vice-President British and Foreign Bible Society; moved the Hospital Payment Amendment to Third Party Risks section of Traffic Act, House of Lords, Dec. 1929 and 1933; introduced Voluntary Hospitals (Paying Patients) Bill, 1935; also reintroduced when it became law, 1936; *b* 9 Sept. 1873; *s* of late John and Elizabeth Lawson Johnston, of Kingswood, Kent; *m* 1902, Hon. Edith Laura St John (Order of Mercy with bar; a Lady Pres. of League of Mercy; Co. Commissioner Girl Guides, Bedfordshire, 1916–37; Correspondent for British Girl Guides of South America; Member of Bedfordshire CC Education Committee; Pres. S. and SFA City of London Division, 1914–18 and County Beds, 1936–39; she died 1941), 5th *d* of 16th Baron St John of Bletsoe; two *s* four *d. Educ:* privately (in Canada); Dulwich College; Blair Lodge, Scotland. During the War, Chairman, Section B2 (of Raw Materials) under Surveyor-General of Supply (War Office); Chairman, East India Kip Committee (Raw Materials) War Office; Member King Edward VII's Coronation Gift Committee, 1901–02; Governor Polytechnic (Regent St); one of the Managers Royal Institution, 1925 and 1932. Has travelled a good deal, especially in Colonies and South America. Owns 3,000 acres in North Beds. *Recreations:* hunting, travelling. *Heir: s* Lt-Col Hon. Ian St John Lawson Johnston, MA. *Address:* Pavenham Bury, near Bedford; Odell Castle, Bedfordshire. *T:* Oakley 269. *TA:* Pavenham. *Clubs:* Bath, Carlton, City of London, Hurlingham.

Died 23 Feb. 1943.

LUKE, Sir Charles Manley, Kt 1939, JP; retired engineer and shipbuilder; *b* 4 Feb. 1857; *s* of Samuel and Ann Luke; *m* 1880, Annie Pinny; four *s* one *d. Educ:* Wesleyan Day School and Continuation School, Penzance. Lived first 17 years in Penzance; left for New Zealand in sailing ship, 1874; went into business, 1876;

Mayor of Wellington, 1895; member of Legislative Council for seven years and of Education Board, College Board of Governors, Harbour Board, Royal Commission on Federation with Australia, 1901, executive of New Zealand Exhibition, 1885, War Relief, War Funds Council; Chairman Chamber of Commerce, President of Manufacturers and Industrial Assoc. and various sports bodies; member and chairman for fifty years of Hospital Trustees and Board; last President Primitive Methodist Connexion in New Zealand and first Vice-President of United Church. *Publications:* in local and Methodist Church papers. *Recreations:* cricket when young, bowler for 46 years. *Address:* Wellington, New Zealand. *T:* 40.852. *Clubs:* English Speaking Union; New Zealand, Wellington.

Died 19 April 1941.

LUKER, Col Roland, CMG 1919; MC; DL (Lincolnshire); late Lancashire Fusiliers; *b* 1 July 1878; 2nd *s* of late Henry Luker; *m* Aileen (*d* 1944), *yr d* of late Major S. Phillips, DL, of Gaile House, County Tipperary; one *d. Educ:* Aldenham School; Pembroke College, Cambridge; Staff College, Camberley. Served South African War, 1900–02; European War, 1914–18, in France and Flanders with Regt and on Staff (MC, Brevet Lieut-Col, CMG, Officer Crown of Rumania, despatches six times); Commanded 1st Batt. Lancashire Fusiliers, 1928–30; Col 1930 (1922); War Office 1930–34; ADC to the King, 1933–34; retired, 1934; Home Guard Zone Commander (Holland), 1940–43; County Cadet Commandant (Lincolnshire), 1944. *Address:* Uffington Cottage, Stamford. *Club:* Army and Navy.

Died 23 July 1947.

LUKIN, Hon. Lionel Oscar; Judge of Federal Arbitration Court, 1926–43; Judge of the Federal Bankruptcy Court for Australia, presiding in Sydney and Melbourne, 1930–43; also sole Justice of the Supreme Court of the Australian Capital Territory and presiding at Canberra, 1934–43; *b* 4 Jan. 1868; *s* of George Lionel Lukin; *m* Catharine Alicia Rennick (*d* 1934); two *s* two *d. Educ:* Brisbane Grammar School. Called to Bar, 1890; Puisne Justice of the Supreme Court of Queensland, 1910–26. *Address:* High Court Buildings, Melbourne, Australia. *Clubs:* Australian, Melbourne; Australian, Sydney; Queensland, Brisbane.

Died 1 June 1944.

LUMBY, Lt-Col Arthur Friedrich Rawson, CIE 1927; OBE 1923; Indian Army, retired; Personal Assistant to Military Secretary, India Office; *b* 1890; *s* of late Prof. J. R. Lumby, Cambridge; *m* 1916, Lettice Mary, *d* of Rev. F. K. Hodgkinson; one *s. Educ:* Rugby; Christ's College, Cambridge. Served European War, 1914–19 (wounded, despatches); retired from Indian Army, 1937. *Club:* Junior Army and Navy.

Died 28 July 1943.

LUMBY, John Henry, MA. *Educ:* Elementary School; University College, Liverpool. Assistant Master in Birkenhead and Liverpool, 1895–1924; Secretary to the Education Committees, National Union of Teachers, 1924–27; Editor, The Schoolmaster and Woman Teacher's Chronicle, 1927–33; sometime Charles Beard Historical Research Exhibitioner, University of Liverpool. *Publications:* Contributions to the Transactions of the Historic Society of Lancashire and Cheshire; Calendar of the de Hoghton deeds and papers; Calendar of the Norris deeds. *Address:* 82 Sheil Road, Liverpool 6.

Died 23 Nov. 1948.

LUMIÈRE, Louis; Membre de l'Institut de France; Conseiller technique; *b* 5 Oct. 1864; *s* of Antoine Lumière et Joséphine Costille; *m* 1893; two *d.* Créateur de l'Usine Lumière Plaques photographiques; Inventeur des Plaques Autochromes pour la photographie directe des Couleurs; Inventeur du Photorama, de la photo-stéréo-synthèse, des rechauds catalytiques pour nacelles d'avions; Inventeur de diffuseurs acoustiques appliqués d'abord aux machines parlantes puis aux haut-parleurs de TSF; Des centaines de mille ont été construits etc.; Ecrans colorés permettant la réalisation du cinématographe Stéréoscopique; Inventeur du cinématographe, 1894–95, etc.; Grand Cross Legion of Honour, 1939. *Publications:* nombreuses communications aux Sociétés scientifiques et photographiques soit seul soit en collaboration. *Address:* Villa Lumen, Bandol, (Var), France. *T:* 14.

Died 6 June 1948.

LUMLEY, Lyulph, (Druso); *b* London. *Educ:* University College School; privately. After some years of journalistic work became unexpectedly an editor. Editor of the Court Journal, 1892–1903. *Publications:* Plays: The Golf Match; My Lady's Bonnet; and short stories, humorous sketches, and dialogues in various publications. *Recreations:* violin-playing, golf, collecting china.

Died 14 May 1944.

LUMSDEN, E. S., RSA 1933; painter and etcher; *b* London, 22 Dec. 1883; *s* of late S. M. Lumsden and *g s* of Rev. R. Comyn Lumsden; *m* twice; one *d. Educ:* Health broke down while in HMS Worcester; studied Art at Reading under Morley-Fletcher and in Paris; ARE, 1909; RE 1915; ARSA 1923. Pres. Society of Artist Print-makers, Glasgow, 1929–47; Librarian, Royal Scottish Academy, 1945; RBA 1946; Vice-Pres. Sheffield Print Club; Hon. Member Scottish Print Club; Hon. Member Scottish Print Club; up to 1939 had produced 340 etchings of many countries including France, Spain, British-Columbia, Japan, China, Korea, Burma, India, and Ladak; present work principally portraiture; works purchased by the following corporations:—Victoria and Albert Museum; Canadian National Gallery; National Gallery of New Zealand; National Museum, Copenhagen; Contemporary Art Society (both painting and etchings); Modern Arts Association, Edinburgh; Library of Congress (Washington); Royal Scottish Academy (Thorburn-Ross Bequest); Municipal Galleries of Liverpool, Manchester, Glasgow, Birkenhead, Aberdeen, Paisley, Cork, Belfast, Dunedin, NZ, Johannesburg, and Toronto, etc. *Publications:* The Art of Etching, 1925; The Etchings of Clerk of Eldin, etc. *Address:* 42 York Place, Edinburgh. *T:* 24937.

Died 29 Sept. 1948.

LUMSDEN, Maj.-Gen. Herbert, CB 1945; DSO 1940; MC; special representative with Gen. MacArthur since 1943; *b* 8 April 1897; *s* of John Lumsden; *m* 1923, Alice Mary, *yr d* of George Roddick, JP; two *s. Educ:* RMA, Woolwich. 2nd Lt RA, 1915; served European War, 1915–18 (MC); Lt 12th Royal Lancers, 1925; commanded 12th Royal Lancers, 1938–40; Colonel, 1940; Temp. Maj.-Gen. 1942, War Subs. 1943; Temp. Lt-Gen. 1943; Maj.-Gen. 1944; served war of 1939–45; commanded 10th Corps, 8th Army 1942–43 (despatches twice, DSO and Bar, wounded). *Recreation:* racing. *Address:* Radcot House, Clanfield, Oxfordshire.

Died 6 Jan. 1945.

LUMSDEN, Sir John, KBE 1918; DL (County of Dublin); MD (Univ. Dublin); Knight of Justice, Order of St John of Jerusalem; *b* 14 Nov. 1869; *s* of John Lumsden, Leeson Park, Dublin; *m* 1896, Caro F., *y d* of late Major Fitzhardinge Kingscote (Rifle Bde) of Furbo, Galway; one *s* five *d. Educ:* Taunton; Dublin University. Chairman Joint Committee British Red Cross Society and Order of St John for Eire; Commissioner Éire District St John Ambulance Brigade; temp. Major, RAMC, 1917–18; attached 83 General Hospital, BEF; Physician to the Household of the Lord Lieutenant of Ireland, 1921–22; granted Silver Life-saving Medal Order of St John of Jerusalem, 1916, and British Red Cross Society Medal for special services, 1916; organised

Red Cross and Auxiliary Hospitals, Southern Ireland, 1914–18; Consulting Physician Irish Counties and Dublin Castle War Hospitals, 1915–18; Fellow Royal Academy of Medicine, Ireland; A Governor of Rotunda Hospital, Royal Hospital for Incurables and St Patrick's Mental Hospital; Chief Medical Officer, Guinness's Brewery, Dublin; Ex-Senior Visiting Physician and Lecturer in Clinical Medicine, Mercer's Hospital, Dublin; Ex-External Examiner in Medicine National University, Ireland; Consulting Physician, Royal National Hospital for Consumption, Newcastle. *Publications:* various medical to journals; author of treatises on Infant Feeding, Medical Examination in Life Insurance, Investigations of Budgets Workmen's Families, Dublin. *Recreations:* fishing, shooting, and golf. *Address:* 4 Fitzwilliam Place, Dublin; Earlscliff, Howth, Co. Dublin. *TA:* First Aid, Dublin. *T:* Dublin 61354, Sutton 119.

Died 3 Sept. 1944.

LUMSDEN, Rear-Adm. Walter, CIE 1915; CVO 1912; RN, retired; DL, JP; *b* 16 April 1865; *e surv. s* of late Henry Lumsden, FRGS, Pitcaple Castle, Aberdeenshire, and Edith Jane, *d* of Rev. R. S. Battiscombe, MA; *m* 1903, Ethel Flora, *d* of late Sir Thomas Naghten Fitz-Gerard, CB, FRCSI; one *d. Educ:* HMS Britannia; to sea as Naval Cadet, 1880. Midshipman, 1880; served on board HMS Invincible at bombardment of Alexandria, 1882 (slightly wounded, medal clasp and Khedive's star); Sub-Lieut, 1885; Lieut, 1888; Commander, 1900; Captain, 1906; Director Royal Indian Marine, and Hon. ADC to Viceroy of India, 1909–17; retired from Royal Navy, 1909; retired Rear-Adm. 1917; from outbreak of War in Aug. 1914 was Principal Naval Transport Officer and Naval Intelligence Officer in India; also Senior Naval Officer, Bombay, 1915–17; also Manager for the Government of all enemy merchant ships captured in Indian waters. War of 1939–45 served as Head Observer in ROC, Sept. 1939–Feb. 1943. *Address:* Pitcaple Castle, Aberdeenshire. *TA:* Pitcaple. *T:* Pitcaple 204. *Club:* Army and Navy.

Died 22 Nov. 1947.

LUNDGREN, Captain Albert Edvin, CBE 1922; Representative and Marine Superintendent of the Transatlantic Steamship Co. of Gothenburg; *b* Onsala, Sweden, 9 June 1878; *s* of Alexander Edvin Lundgren, Coastguard Officer of the Royal Swedish Customs; *m* 1906, Anna-Lisa, *d* of Captain John Edward Ryberg, Gothenburg; two *d. Educ:* Sweden. After serving his apprenticeship in the Swedish Navy to obtain his commission as an Officer of the Reserve, joined the Transatlantic Steamship Co. Ltd, 1903; as a Commander of several of the Company's ships became well known in the Swedish-Australian trade route; was appointed to superintend their shipbuilding, etc., in the United States of America, 1916; in Dec. the same year transferred to London to represent the company there; representative in London of the Swedish Shipping Commission, 1918–19; then requested by the company to go to Java and investigate certain matters there, and since Aug. 1920 has had his headquarters in Sydney as Representative and Marine Superintendent of the Transatlantic Steamship Company; was elected President of the Swedish Chamber of Commerce for Australasia and South Sea Islands (Incorporated). *Address:* 4 Bridge Street, Sydney, Australia. *TA:* Trans. *T:* BW 1421. *Clubs:* Royal Sydney Yacht, Royal Automobile, Sydney.

Died May 1942.

LUNN, Hugh Kingsmill; *see* Kingsmill, H.

LUNN, William; MP (Lab) Rothwell Division of Yorks, since Dec. 1918; *b* 1 Nov. 1872. *Educ:* Rothwell Board School. A check-weighman; started work in the pit at 12 years of age; contested Holmfirth Division, 1912; Parliamentary Secretary to Department of Overseas Trade, 1924; Parliamentary Under-Secretary for the

Colonies, 1929; Parliamentary Under-Secretary of State, Dominions Office, 1929–31; Chairman of Overseas Settlement Committee, 1929. *Address:* 206 Wood Lane, Rothwell, Yorks.

Died 17 May 1942.

LUNT, Rt Rev. Geoffrey Charles Lester, DD 1936; MA, MC; Bishop of Salisbury since 1946; *m* 1912, Lilias Marjorie Sherbrooke; one *s* one *d*. *Educ:* Sherborne School; Exeter College, Oxford. Ordained, 1909; Assistant Curate at Christ Church, Clifton, Bristol, 1909–11; Secretary of Church Missionary Society for Public Schools and Young People's Work, 1911–14; Vicar of St Paul's, Bedminster, Bristol, 1914–19; Chaplain to the Forces in France, 1917 (MC); Vicar of All Saints, Northampton, 1919–26; Archdeacon of Egypt and Sub-Dean of Cairo, 1926–28; Vicar of St Mary's, Portsea, 1928–34; Hon. Canon of Portsmouth, 1931–34; Proctor in Convocation for the Diocese of Portsmouth, 1931–34; Bishop of Ripon, 1935–46. Commissary to the Bishop of Egypt and Sudan since 1928. *Recreations:* golf, tennis. *Address:* Bishop's House, The Close, Salisbury. *Clubs:* United Sports, Royal Empire Society.

Died 17 Dec. 1948.

LUPTON, Arthur Sinclair, CBE 1931; MA; *b* 1877; *y s* of late Rev. Joseph Hirst Lupton, DD; *m* 1921, Mollie Ross, *e d* of J. Richmond-Bryce, MD; no *c*. *Educ:* St Paul's School; St John's College, Cambridge. Barrister Gray's Inn, 1905; Vice-Principal of Working Men's College, London until 1921; Assistant Secretary to the Commissioners of HM Customs and Excise until 1937; contributor to Encyclopaedia of The Laws of England, and other publications. *Address:* Ross Lynn, Windermere Road, Kendal, Westmorland. *T:* Kendal 743.

Died 9 Jan. 1949.

LUPTON, John, MA; *b* 23 April 1869; 2nd *s* of late Rev. Joseph Hirst Lupton, DD, surmaster of St Paul's School and Preacher of Gray's Inn; *m* 1905, Nora, 2nd *d* of I. A. Hattersley; one *s* three *d*. *Educ:* St Paul's School; St John's College, Cambridge (Foundation Scholar). 1st class, Classical Tripos, part i 1891; 1st class, part ii 1892; 2nd class, Theological Tripos, part ii 1893; Naden Divinity Student; Fellow of St John's College, 1896–1901. Assistant Master at St Paul's School, 1896–1910, and Hon. Librarian, 1909–10; Headmaster of King Henry VIII School, Coventry to 1931. *Recreations:* captain of Cambridge University Lacrosse Club; international cap (lacrosse) v. Ireland, 1896 and 1898; played for St John's at Rugby football, lawn tennis, and fives. *Address:* Poplars Farm, Tansor, Peterborough, Northants. *T:* Cotterstock 242.

Died 9 July 1946.

LUSH-WILSON, His Honour Sir Herbert W., Kt 1923; KC; JP (Co. Hereford); Common Law Bar; County Court Judge on Circuit 59, 1920–22; of the Exeter and Plymouth County Courts, 1901–20; *b* 2 April 1850; 2nd and *e surv. s* of late Right Hon. Lord-Justice Lush; *m* 1876, Rose Frances Wilson (*d* 1890), *o c* of late William Wilson of Pyon House, Canon Pyon, Herefordshire. *Educ:* Westminster; Trinity Hall, Cambridge. Passed 2nd in 1st class Law special in 1872. Barrister, 1873; QC 1895; Conservative candidate for East Northamptonshire, 1895; selected Conservative candidate, 1896, for Burton-on-Trent, but resigned. *Publication:* edited, in association with M. D. Chalmers, member of the Council of India, 3rd edition of Wilson's Jurisdiction Acts. *Recreations:* shooting, rowing, cycling, riding. *Address:* 88 St James's Street, SW; 2 Paper Bldgs, Temple, EC. *Clubs:* Carlton, Athenæum, Reform.

Died 19 Nov. 1941.

LUSHINGTON, Rev. Franklyn de Winton, MA; HCF; *b* 29 March 1868; 5th *s* of late Franklyn Lushington, ICS, Accountant-General of Madras; *m* 1899, Monica Sydney (*d* 1934), *d* of late Rev. Lancelot

Sanderson, MA, Headmaster of Elstree School; one *d*. *Educ:* Clare College, Cambridge. Scholar and Prizeman, 1887; BA; 2nd class Class. Tripos, 1890; MA 1895. Ordained deacon, 1893; priest, 1894; assistant master at Elstree School, 1892–99; assistant chaplain, Montreux, 1899–1901; curate, St James, Bury St Edmunds, 1901; chaplain, St Paul's, Valetta, Malta, 1901–03; Archdeacon of Malta, 1902–03; Headmaster of Elstree School, 1903–10; of Dover College, 1911–15; CF, BEF, 1914–18; Vicar of Danehill, 1918–21; First Headmaster of Chillon College, Montreux, 1921–23; Preacher and Lecturer in USA and Europe, 1923–28; Vicar of King's Langley, Herts, 1928–34; Temporary Diocesan Missioner, St Albans Diocese. *Publications:* Sermons to Young Boys, 1898, 3rd ed. 1911; The Character of the Saint, 2nd ed. 1911; On Personal Service; Christ's Way and Modern Problems. *Recreation:* golf. *Club:* Authors'.

Died 30 March 1941.

LUSK, William C.; Managing Director and Deputy Chairman Associated Electrical Industries Ltd; Chairman British Thomson Houston Co. Ltd; Deputy Chairman Metropolitan Vickers Electrical Co. Ltd; Director, Power Securities Corporation Ltd; and Lancashire Electric Light & Power Co. Ltd; *b* Nashville, Tennessee, USA, 10 Sept. 1875; *s* of Alfred Hume and Elizabeth Clardy Lusk; *m* 1926, Mrs Louise M. Casler, New York; no *c*. *Educ:* Yale University (BSc). Joined General Electric Co. of Schenectady, NY, 1897; represented that Company in India for 3 years, 1901–04; joined London office of same company, 1904; later joined British Thomson Houston Co. Ltd, London, becoming Managing Director of that Company, 1922. Became naturalised British subject Oct. 1938. *Recreations:* golf, shooting, swimming. *Address:* Crown House, Aldwych, WC2; Soames House, Coombe Hill Road, Kingston Hill, Surrey. *Clubs:* Bath; Sunningdale, Swinley Forest and Coombe Hill Golf; University, New York.

Died 25 Feb. 1944.

LUTTRELL, Alexander Fownes; JP, DL; *b* 1 June 1855; *e s* of George Fownes Luttrell and Ann Elizabeth, *y d* of Sir Alexander Hood, 2nd Bt; *m* 1886, Alice Edwina (*d* 1912), *e d* of late Col Munro Ferguson of Raith and Nóvar; two *s*. Late Grenadier Guards; served Soudan, 1885. Patron of 4 Livings. *Address:* Court House, East Quantoxhead, Bridgwater. *TA:* Kilve. *T:* Holford 242. *Club:* Brooks's.

Died 2 Dec. 1944.

LUTYENS, Sir Edwin L., OM 1942; KCIE 1930; Kt 1918; RA 1920; ARA 1913; DCL Oxford, 1934; Hon. LLD Liverpool, 1928; Officier Légion d'Honneur, 1932; FSA; architect and artist; Member of the Royal Fine Art Commission since 1924; Hon. Member of the Royal Scottish Academy; President of the Royal Academy since 1938; *b* London, 29 March 1869; *s* of Charles Lutyens; *m* 1897, Lady Emily Lytton, *d* of 1st Earl of Lytton; one *s* four *d*. *Educ:* privately. Member of Committee to advise Government of India as to site of Delhi, 1912; architect for Government House, Imperial Delhi; works include Whitehall Cenotaph; British School of Art, Rome; British Pavilion, Paris, 1900; British Art Exhibition Building, Rome; Picture Gallery and South African War Memorial, Johannesburg; Head Offices of the Anglo-Persian Oil Company, Limited; New British Embassy, Washington; one of the principal Architects for the Imperial War Graves Commission. *Address:* 13 Mansfield Street, W1. *TA:* Aedificavi, London. *T:* Langham 1838. *Clubs:* Athenæum, Burlington, Arts, Garrick, Beefsteak, Savage.

Died 1 Jan. 1944.

LUXMOORE, Rt Hon. Sir (Arthur) Fairfax (Charles Coryndon), Kt 1929; PC 1938; **Rt Hon. Lord Justice Luxmoore;** KC 1919; JP; a Lord Justice of Appeal, since 1938; *b* 1876; *e s* of late Arthur Coryndon Hansler Luxmoore, Danescliffe, St Lawrence, Thanet; *m* 1907,

Dorothea Tunder, 4th *d* of late T. P. Royle, Hough Green House, Chester; three *d*. *Educ:* King's School, Canterbury; Jesus College, Cambridge (BA, Hon. Fellow, 1938). Barrister-at-law, Lincoln's Inn, 1899; Bencher, 1923; General Council of Bar; Judge of Chancery Division, High Court, 1929–38; Chairman East Kent Quarter Sessions, 1931–40; Chairman Rating Appeal Committee for East Kent, 1929–40; Mayor of New Romney, 1920–26; contested (L) Isle of Thanet Division of Kent, 1924. Chairman of Departmental Cttee on Post-War Agricultural Educn, 1941–43. *Recreations:* cricket, shooting, and golf; Cambridge University Rugby Football XV, 1896, 1897; English Rugby Football XV, 1900–01. *Address:* Bilsington Priory, nr Ashford, Kent. *T:* Aldington 252. *Clubs:* Athenæum, Oxford and Cambridge.

Died 25 Sept. 1944.

LYALL, Dame Beatrix Margaret, DBE 1924; CBE 1920; JP London, 1920; *d* of late Simpson Rostron, Beddington, Surrey, and Mrs Rostron, South Warnborough Manor, Hants; *m* 1899, George Hudson Lyall (*d* 1938); one *s*. *Educ:* home. Social worker for many years; public speaker on National, social and religious questions; Member East Fulham on London County Council, 1919–34 and 1935–36; Vice-Chairman LCC, 1932; Chairman Parks Committee LCC, 1925–26; Chairman Parliamentary Committee, 1929–30–1931; Life Vice-President Mothers' Union; Vice-President Primrose League; Member Conservative & Unionist Council; Member London Diocesan Conf. European War, 1914–18, was voluntary speaker for several Government Departments as well as privately; Head of Hospital Supplies, S London, 1939–45. *Publications:* numerous pamphlets and newspaper articles. *Address:* Prince of Wales Hotel, De Vere Gardens, W8.

Died 8 May 1948.

LYALL, Charles Elliott, OBE 1919; *b* Simla, India, 1 Sept. 1877; *s* of late Sir C. J. Lyall, KCSI; *m* Marjorie Helen Smith. *Educ:* Winchester College; Balliol College, Oxford. Joined Sudan Political Service as Deputy Inspector, 1901; Junior Inspector, 1905; Senior Inspector, 1909; Governor Halfa Province, 1914; Governor, Kassala Province, Sudan, 1917; Civil Secretary, Sudan Government, 1921–26; retired, 1926; 4th class Osmania, 1913; 3rd class Order of the Nile, 1917. *Recreations:* golf, shooting, fishing. *Address:* Home Close, Green Lane, Burnham, Bucks. *T:* Burnham 242. *Club:* Travellers'.

Died 28 Dec. 1942.

LYALL, Frank Frederick, CIE 1914; ICS, retired; *b* 12 June 1872; *s* of late D. R. Lyall, CSI; *m* 1906, Ina Kathleen, 3rd *d* of late A. M. Markham, ICS; no *c*. *Educ:* Edinburgh Academy; Balliol College, Oxford. Entered ICS, 1891; Joint Magistrate and Deputy Collector, 1899; Magistrate and Collector, 1906; Committee on Co-operative Credit in India, 1914–15; Ministry of Munitions (London), 1916–19; Commissioner, 1919; retired, 1926; General Manager Kassim Bazar Raj, 1923–29; Kaiser-i-Hind Medal, 1911. *Recreations:* polo, hunting, big and small game shooting, tennis, racquets, motoring. *Address:* c/o P. and O. Banking Corporation, EC.

Died 7 July 1950.

LYALL, Col Graham Thomson, VC 1918; Managing Director, Aerocrete (Scotland), Ltd, Victoria Works, Airdrie, Lanarkshire; *b* Manchester, 8 March 1892; *s* of Rev. Robert Henry Lyall, Darwen, and late Agnes Lisette Wells; *m* Elizabeth Moffat Scotland, *e d* of late Provost Frew, Meadowside House, Airdrie, Lanarkshire. *Educ:* Nelson Municipal Secondary School; Naval Engineering College; Toronto University. Mechanical Engineer; went to Canada, 1911; connected with Canadian Steel Foundries, Welland, Ontario, latterly with Canadian Niagara Power Co., Niagara Falls; joined 19th Lincoln Regt Aug. 1914; went with 81st Batt. to France, 1916; joined 4th Canadian Mounted Rifles, 1916; received commission on the field for bravery in action, 1917 (VC for operations at Bourlon Wood); retired, 1919; member of Institute of British Engineers. *Recreations:* swimming, tennis, boating, motoring, cricket, hockey, billiards, golf and shooting. *Address:* Forest Park, Airdrie, Lanarkshire. *T:* Airdrie 3359.

Died 28 Nov. 1941.

LYALL, Lt-Col Robert Adolphus, DSO 1917; retired; *b* 21 Oct. 1876; *s* of late Rt Hon. Sir A. C. Lyall; *m* 1924, Catharine Broadwood, *d* of late George Wilmot Rivaz; two *s*. *Educ:* Eton; Sandhurst. 32nd Sikh Pioneers; Political Department Government of India; active service North-West Frontier, China, East Africa, Palestine; HBM's Consul-General Chinese Turkistan, 1924–25; High Sheriff of Bedfordshire, 1944; DL Beds. *Address:* Flitwick Manor, Flitwick, Beds. *Club:* Garrick.

Died 5 Sept. 1948.

LYDDON, Col William George, CMG 1917; late Royal Artillery; *b* 1871; *m* 1909, Mary Helen (*d* 1926), *d* of Major David Steuart of Steuart Hall, Stirling. *Educ:* RM Academy, Woolwich. Entered RA, 1890; Captain, 1899; Major, 1911; Lt-Col, 1917; Col, 1921; served South African War, 1900–01 (Queen's medal 4 clasps); Seconded to Army Ordnance Corps, 1907–13; Inspection Staff, 1914–20; Deputy Director of Munitions Inspection in USA, 1916–19 (CMG); Inspector of Steel, Sheffield, 1919–20; Inter-Allied Commission of Control in Germany, 1920–22. *Publication:* British War Missions to the United States, 1914–1918, 1938. *Address:* c/o Lloyds Bank, 6 Pall Mall, SW1. *Club:* United Service.

Died 7 May 1944.

LYDE, Lionel William, MA (Oxon), FRGS, FRSGS; *b* 1863; *s* of late Canon Lyde, MA, Queens' Coll., Camb.; *m* 1896, Lily, *d* of Major-General Gildea, CB; two *s*. *Educ:* Sedbergh School; Queen's College, Oxford (Classical Exhibition and Modern History Essay prize). Senior English Master, Merchiston Castle School, Edinburgh, 1887–90; Headmaster of English Department in Glasgow Academy, 1890–99; Headmaster of Bolton Grammar School, 1899–1903; Professor of Geography in the University of London, 1903–28; Emeritus Professor since 1928. *Publications:* The Continent of Europe; The Continent of Asia; Man in Many Lands; Contexts in Pindar, 1935; The Golden Lady, 1937, etc. *Address:* The Old House, Cirencester. *T:* Cirencester 62.

Died 24 Jan. 1947.

LYELL, 2nd Baron *cr* 1914, of Kinnordy; **Charles Antony Lyell,** VC 1943; Bt *cr* 1894; Capt. Scots Guards; *b* 14 June 1913; *o s* of late Hon. C. H. Lyell, MP, and Rosalind Margaret, *e d* of Vernon J. Watney, of Cornbury Park, Charlbury, Oxon; *S* grandfather, 1926; *m* 1938, Sophie, 2nd *d* of Major S. W. Trafford; one *s*. *Educ:* Eton; Christ Church, Oxford, BA. County Councillor for Angus. *Recreations:* stalking, shooting. *Heir: s* Hon. Charles Lyell, *b* 27 March 1939. *Address:* 37 Eaton Place, SW1; Kinnordy, Kirriemuir, Angus. *T:* Sloane 4417. *Clubs:* Guards', Boodle's.

Died 27 April 1943.

LYELL, Denis David; author; has specialised in making drawings of game spoor; *b* Calcutta, 6 Feb. 1871; *e s* of late James Carmichael Lyell and Kate Harriette Latham; *m* 1914, Marion, *o d* of late W. A. Brown, Dundee. Formerly tea-planter in East India, later a hunter and field-naturalist in south Central Africa; served Boer and European Wars, (Medals). *Publications:* Hunting Trips in Northern Rhodesia, 1910; Nyasaland for the Hunter and Settler, 1912; Wild Life in Central Africa, 1913; Memories of an African Hunter, 1923; The African Elephant and its Hunters, 1924; The Hunting and Spoor of Central African Game, 1929; contributed to Big-

Game Shooting in Africa (Lonsdale Library, vol. xiv., 1932); African Adventure—Letters from Famous Big-Game Hunters, 1935; (with late Major C. H. Stigand) Central African Game and its Spoor, 1906. *Address:* The Briars, Peebles. *Club:* Shikar.

Died 23 Sept. 1946.

LYLE, Sir Archibald Moir Park, 2nd Bt *cr* 1929; MC, TD, JP, MA; Vice-Lieutenant, County of Perth; Member of Royal Archers, King's Bodyguard for Scotland; *b* 1884; *o s* of Sir Alexander Lyle, 1st Bt, and G. Eleanora (*d* 1918), *d* of Archibald Moir, JP, banker, Alloa; *S* father, 1933; *m* 1908, Dorothy, *e d* of Sir James de Hoghton, 11th Bt; one *s* one *d*. *Educ:* Fettes College, Edinburgh; Trinity College, Oxford (double blue). Served European War in Scottish Horse, 1914–18 (despatches, MC). *Heir: g s* Gavin Archibald [*b* 1941, *s* of late Ian Archibald de Hoghton Lyle and of Hon. Lydia Yarde-Buller, *d* of 3rd Baron Churston]. *Address:* Glendelvine, Murthly, Perthshire; A. 14 Albany, W1.

Died 4 Dec. 1946.

LYLE, Col Hugh Thomas, CBE 1919; DSO 1887; retired; *b* 24 April 1858; *e s* of John Lyle of Knocktarna; *m* 1886, Alice Fanny, 2nd *d* of late Sir Warren Hastings D'Oyly, 10th Bt; one *s* one *d*. *Educ:* Uppingham; Sandhurst. Entered army, 1879; Major, 1895; served Burma, 1885–86 (severely wounded, despatches, DSO, medal with clasp); Hazara, 1891 (despatches, clasp); South Africa, 1899–1902 (despatches twice, Brevet Lieut-Col, Queen's medal 3 clasps, King's medal 2 clasps); commanded 2nd Royal Welsh Fusiliers, 1904–08; commanded 8th Batt. RI Rifles, Sept. 1914–Sept. 1915; 17th RI Rifles, Nov. 1915–May 1918, when Ulster Division was disbanded (CBE); DL Co. Londonderry. *Address:* Knocktarna, Coleraine, Co. Londonderry.

Died 24 Jan. 1942.

LYLE, John Cromie, CVO 1911; *b* 1862; *s* of late Rev. John Lyle; *m* 1895, Emily Frances, *d* of late Col Merrick; one *s* two *d*. *Educ:* Haileybury; RIE College. Assistant Engineer, India, PWD, 1885; Executive Engineer, 1896; Deputy Consulting Engineer for Railways, Calcutta, 1895; Superintending Engineer, 1910–13; Engineer in Chief, Delhi Durbar Railways; retired 1913. *Address:* Strathroy, Portrush, Co. Antrim. *T:* Portrush 148.

Died 24 Sept. 1947.

LYLE, Robert Charles; Racing Correspondent since 1921 and Sporting Editor since 1919 of the Times; now War Correspondent of the Times; *b* Dunmow, Essex, 25 Jan. 1887; 2nd *s* of Robert Charles and Ann Lyle, Dunmow, Essex; *m* 1913, Daisy, 2nd *d* of John Square and Alice Brunskill, Bishops Stortford, Hertfordshire; three *s* three *d*. *Educ:* Felsted; Corpus Christi College, Cambridge. Joined reporting staff of Daily Express, London, 1909; afterwards wrote for a number of papers principally Observer and Pall Mall Gazette; served European War with RASC, attached for the last three years to Headquarters Third Cavalry Division with BEF in France (MC and bar); has done many broadcasts on the Derby, Grand National, St Leger and other important races. *Publications:* Brown Jack; Hockey; The Aga Khan's Horses, 1938. *Recreations:* racing and golf. *Address:* Woodview, Lower Green Road, Esher. *T:* Emberbrook 1062.

Died 27 Sept. 1943.

LYLE, Robert Patton Ranken, MA, MD, FCOG, LRCPI; Emeritus Professor of Midwifery and Gynæcology, Durham University; President, Princess Mary Maternity Hospital Newcastle; *b* Coleraine, 1870. *Educ:* Trinity Coll, Dublin; Middlesex Hosp.; Paris. Late Assistant Master, Rotunda Hospital, Dublin. *Publications:* papers in medical journals. *Address:* Brightside, 16 Granville Road, Newcastle-on-Tyne, 2.

Died 1 Feb. 1950.

LYLE, Samuel, CBE 1919; MB, ChB. *Educ:* Edinburgh University. Commissioner Medical Services, Ministry of National Service during European War. *Address:* 1 West End Terrace, Stockton-on-Tees.

Died Aug. 1941.

LYLE, Sir Thomas Ranken, Kt 1922; FRS 1912; MA, DSc; *b* Coleraine, 26 Aug. 1860; *s* of Hugh Lyle; *m* 1892, Clare, CBE, *d* of late Thomas Millear; one *s* three *d*. *Educ:* Coleraine Academical Institution; Dublin University; graduated in 1883 in Mathematics and Mathematical Physics and in Experimental Physics and Chemistry, obtaining First Senior Moderatorship with large Gold Medal in each; University Studentship, 1883; McCullagh Prize, 1884; Madden Prize, 1888. Lecturer in Mathematics, Catholic University College, Dublin; represented the Irish Board of Lights at the experiments on lighthouse illuminants, South Foreland, 1884–85; Professor of Natural Philosophy, Melbourne University, Victoria, 1889–1915, now Emeritus Professor; reported to Government of Victoria on Technical Schools in the British Isles and United States of America; Chairman of Board of Visitors of Melbourne Observatory; Member of State Electricity Commission of Victoria, 1917–37; Chairman, 1917–19; Member of Council of Education, Victoria; played in the Irish International Rugby Football Team, 1885–86–1887. *Publications:* various scientific memoirs. *Address:* 225 Walsh Street, South Yarra, Melbourne, Australia. *Club:* Melbourne.

Died 31 March 1944.

LYLE, William, MB, BCh; MP Queen's University, N Ire. Parliament, 1942–45, and since 1949; President (formerly County Director), Belfast Branch BRCS; *b* 30 March 1871; *s* of Rev. Leslie A. Lyle, BA, and Emily Mary Scott; *m* 1897, Sara Helena Fitzgerald; three *s* two *d*. *Educ:* Queen's Univ., Belfast. Formerly Poor Law Medical Officer and MOH, Newton-stewart, Co. Tyrone; member Tyrone County Council and Pres. North of Ireland Branch BMA (now Hon. Treasurer). *Address:* Moyle, Belmont Road, Belfast. *T:* Belfast 63129.

Died 2 Aug. 1949.

LYLE-SAMUEL, Alexander; *b* 10 Aug. 1883; *s* of late Rev. George Samuel, of Christ Church, Aston, Birmingham; assumed additional name of Lyle by deed poll upon marriage with Julia G. Lyle, of Springwood, Tenafly, NJ; one *s* one *d*. *Educ:* King Edward's School, Birmingham; Trinity Hall, Cambridge. Member of the Hon. Society of the Middle Temple; travelled extensively in America, residing there 1913–15, when came home to serve in European War; was rejected several times, then was Lieutenant until 1917, when was invalided out; MP (L) Eye Division of Suffolk, Dec. 1918–23. *Recreations:* reading, swimming, politics.

Died Nov. 1942.

LYNAM, Edward William O'Flaherty, DLitt (NUI); MRIA; FSA; FRGS; Superintendent of the Map Room, British Museum, WC1; *b* London; *e* twin *s* of J. P. D. Lynam, MA, Inspector of Schools, Ireland, and Agnes O'Flaherty; *m* Martha, *y d* of James Perry, MICE; one *s* one *d*. *Educ:* Clongowes Wood, Ireland; Univ. College, Cork; Royal University of Ireland; Université de Besançon; Univ. of London. Served Artists' Rifles and Royal Irish Regt, 1914–19; Capt. 1918; invalided out; Middlesex Home Guard, 1940–43. President, Hakluyt Society, 1945–49, Vice-Pres. 1949–; Vice-Pres., Viking Society. Co-editor, Imago Mundi; Member of: Ancient Maps Cttee of The Internat. Geographical Union; of Council, Royal Geographical Society; of Commission de Bibliographie, Union Internationale d'Histoire des Sciences, and of other academic cttees. *Publications:* Many monographs, articles, reviews on the history of cartography, of exploration, of Ireland and of Scandinavia; Maps of the Fenlands, 1934; The First Engraved Atlas of the World, 1941; British Maps and

Map Makers, 1944; The Character of England in Maps, 1945; Period Ornament, Symbols and Lettering on Maps, 1946; Richard Hakluyt and his Successors (editor), 1947; The Carta Marina of Alaus Magnus, 1949. *Recreations:* photography, music, various games. *Address:* 62 Shepherd's Hill, Highgate, N6. *T:* Mountview 6904. *Club:* English-Speaking Union.

Died 29 Jan. 1950.

LYNCH, Col David A., CBE 1918; *b* Sept. 1880; *s* of late David Lynch, QC, and Elizabeth White; *g s* of late Hon. David Lynch, one of HM Judges in Ireland; *m* 1913, Doris Alberta, *d* of late Admiral Savory, MVO, RN, and Miss Gregory, New York; one *d. Educ:* Oratory School, Edgbaston; Trinity College, Dublin. Entered Army, 1899; Captain, 1906; served South African War, 1900–02; invalided from the Army, 1912; rejoined, European War, 5 Aug. 1914 till Jan. 1920 (despatches, Brevet-Major, Brevet-Lt-Col, CBE); Gold Staff Officer at Coronation of King George V and King George VI; Private Chamberlain of Sword and Cape to HH the Pope. *Recreations:* hunting, polo, shooting. *Address:* 74 Gloucester Place, Portman Square, W1. *T:* Welbeck 3095. *Clubs:* Carlton, Hurlingham.

Died 7 Feb. 1944.

LYNCH, Patrick; KC; Attorney-General for Eire, 1937–40. *Educ:* Royal University of Ireland (BA). Irish Bar, 1888; Inner Bar, 1906. LLD *Hons Causa* NUI. *Address:* St Ann's Hill Hydro, Blarney, Co. Cork.

Died 9 Dec. 1947.

LYNCH, Hon. Patrick Joseph; *b* Newcastle, Co. Meath, May 1867; *s* of Michael Lynch, Farmer; *m* 1st, Annie Cleary; 2nd, 1933, Mary, *d* of Michael Brown, Father of Narrogin, WA; three *c. Educ:* Model School, Baileborough, Co. Cavan. After his arrival in Australia followed varied occupations on land and sea; holder Award Royal Humane Society; Member of Boulder, WA, Council, 1901–04; Gen. Secretary Goldfields Enginemen's Association, 1897–1904; MLA, WA, for Mount Leonora, 1904–06, resigned; Minister of Public Works, June–Aug. 1905; Senator for WA 1906–38 (Nationalist); President The Senate, Commonwealth of Australia, 1932–38; Member Royal Commission on Fruit Industry, 1912–14; Vice-Chairman of Standing Committee on Public Works, 1914–16; First Chairman River Murray Commission in which the four Governments of the Commonwealth, NSW, Victoria, and SA are concerned; Minister of Works and Railways, 1916–17; member Joint Committee on Public Works, 1923–26; member Select Committee on Standing Committees, Sydney, 1929–30. *Recreation:* bowls. *Address:* Mt Leonora Farm, Three Springs, W Australia. *Clubs:* Western Australia, Perth.

Died 15 Jan. 1944.

LYND, Robert, Hon. DLitt Queen's University, Belfast, 1946; on staff of the News, Chronicle; 'John o' London' in John o' London's Weekly; *b* Belfast, 20 April 1879; *s* of Rev. R. J. Lynd, DD, and Sarah Rentoul; *m* 1909, Sylvia Lynd. *Educ:* Royal Academical Inst., Belfast; Queen's Coll., Belfast (BA 1899). *Publications:* Irish and English: Portraits and Impressions, 1908; Home Life in Ireland, 1909; Rambles in Ireland, 1912; The Book of This and That, 1915; If the Germans conquered England, and other Essays, 1917; Old and New Masters; Ireland a Nation, 1919; The Passion of Labour, 1920; The Art of Letters, 1921; The Pleasure of Ignorance, 1921; The Sporting Life, 1922; Books and Authors, 1922; Solomon in all his Glory, 1922; The Blue Lion, 1923; The Peal of Bells, 1924; The Money-Box, 1925; The Orange Tree, 1926; The Little Angel, 1926; The Goldfish, 1927; Dr Johnson & Company, 1928; The Green Man, 1928; It's a Fine World, 1930; Rain, Rain, Go to Spain, 1931; The Cockleshell, 1933; Both Sides of the Road, 1934; I Tremble to Think, 1936; In Defence

of Pink, 1937; Searchlights and Nightingales, 1939; Life's Little Oddities, 1941; Things One Hears, 1945. *Address:* 5 Keats Grove NW3.

Died 6 Oct. 1949.

LYNDEN-BELL, Maj.-Gen. Sir Arthur Lynden, KCB 1919; KCMG 1917; CB 1915; CMG 1905; *b* Brookhill House, Co. Wexford, Ireland, 2 Jan. 1867; 3rd *s* of Major-Gen. Lynden-Bell; *m* 1905, Bertha Marion, *d* of 1st Viscount Chilston. *Educ:* Clifton College; RMC, Sandhurst. Joined the Buffs, 1885; Captain, 1894; Major, 1902; Lt-Col 1908; Colonel, 1912; served Chitral Campaign as Adjutant of the Buffs; passed Staff College, 1898–99; sent on Special Service to S Africa; served as Adjutant of MI Batt. (severely wounded); served at War Office as Staff Captain Intelligence Department, and subsequently as DAQMG Intelligence Department, 1900–05; General Staff, Southern Command, 1907–11; General Staff, Lowland Division, 1911–14; served European War, 1914–17 (despatches ten times, CB, promoted Maj.-Gen. KCMG); Director on Staff Duties, 1918–21; retired pay, 1924; Colonel of The Buffs (Royal East Kent Regiment), 1929–37; Hon. MA Oxford and Cambridge; DL, JP Kent. *Address:* Stone Ridge, Platt, near Sevenoaks. *T:* Boro' Green 53. *Club:* Naval and Military.

Died 14 Feb. 1943.

LYNES, Rear-Adm. Hubert, CB 1918; CMG 1917; *b* 27 Nov. 1874; unmarried. *Educ:* Stubbington House. Entered Navy, 1887; in Naval Ordnance Dept, 1903–05; at Whale Island for experimental work, 1908–10; commanded Cadmus, China, 1910–11 (prom. Capt.); commanded Admiralty Yacht Enchantress, 1912–13; commanded HMS Penelope, 1914–17 (CMG); Commodore, Dunkerque, in command of Allied Naval and Royal Marine Forces, Flanders, June 1917–June 1918; commanded the Ostend Forces at Admiral Keyes' Blocking of Zeebrugge, April 1918 (Croix de Guerre with Palme); organised and commanded the Blocking of Ostend, May 1918 (CB, Commander Legion of Honour, Commander Order of Leopold); commanded HMS Warspite, June 1918–Jan. 1919, present at the Surrender of German Fleet; retired at own request, 1919; Rear-Adm., retired, 1922; MBOU (Godman-Salvin Medal, 1936), FRGS, FZS; Member South African Ornithological Soc.; Corr. Fellow American Ornithol Union and German Ornithol Soc.; Mem. d'Hon. Cercle Zool. Congolais; Hon. Mem. Royal Hungarian Ornithol Inst.; Mem. Soc. Sciences Nat. du Maroc. *Publications:* papers on ornithological subjects in Ibis and other periodicals. *Recreation:* Natural History. *Address:* 57 Victoria Road, S Kensington, SW7. *Club:* United Service.

Died 10 Nov. 1942.

LYNHAM, John E. A., BA, MB, BCh, BAO, RUI, MD Belfast; MRCP London; DMRE Cambridge; Physician; Visiting Radiologist at the Queen Mary's (Roehampton) Hospital; Consultant Radiologist to the LCC; Radiologist to the Woolwich and District War Memorial Hospital; *b* 1882; *s* of late Prof. J. I. Lynham, MD, MCh, MAO, FRUI; *m* 1912, Harriet Maud, *d* of late W. J. F. Hopkins, Magistrate and District Commissioner, Fiji; one *s* one *d. Educ:* Queen's Colleges, Galway and Belfast; St Bart's and Middlesex Hospital. RMO Woolwich Infirmary, 1909–11; Assistant in the Electrical and Radio Therapeutic Department, Cancer Hospital; Fellow, and late President Electro-Therapeutic Section, Royal Society of Medicine; Member of British Institute of Radiology; Fellow of the Medical Society of London; Member of British Medical Association; President, Irish Medical Schools and Graduates Association, 1936. *Publications:* various essays and papers chiefly relating to the Radiological Aspects of Tuberculosis and Cancer. *Address:* 11 Portsmouth Road, Kingston-on-Thames.

Died 14 Dec. 1946.

LYNN, Sir Robert, Kt 1924; MP (U) West Belfast in Ulster Parliament, 1921–29, North Antrim, since 1929; Chairman of Ways and Means and Deputy Speaker since 1937; was Chairman of Education Committee in Northern Ireland; Chairman of the Advisory Educational Council; *b* Co. Antrim, 1873; *m* 1896, Florence, *d* of William Moss, Belfast; one *s*. *Educ:* privately. Has been in journalism since 1893; leader writer Northern Whig, 1903; Assistant Editor, 1911; Editor Northern Whig 1913–28; MP (U) Woodvale, Belfast, in Imperial Parliament, Dec. 1918–22, West Belfast, Nov. 1922–May 1929. *Address:* Ardmore, Holywood, Co. Down.

Died 5 Aug. 1945.

LYNX, Larry; *see* Sarl, A. J.

LYON, Lt-Col Charles; late Royal Artillery; owner of land in Cheshire and Lancashire; JP, DL Cheshire; *b* 7 April 1865; *s* of late Colonel Francis Lyon, RA, and of late Hon. Flora Lyon, sister of 11th Viscount Valentia; *m* 1st, 1894, Rachel (*d* 1926), *d* of late Sir Arthur Elibank Havelock, GCSI, GCMG; one *d*; 2nd, 1927, Gladys, *widow* of Major Arthur Lyon, Border Regt. *Educ:* Wellington College; RM Academy, Woolwich. First commissioned in Royal Artillery, 1884; to retired pay as Major, 1908; Lt-Col Territorial Force, 1909–13; commanded 2nd Wessex (How) Brigade RFA; rejoined Aug. 1914 as Major RFA; served in France, 1915–16, Lieut-Col comdg 151st Brigade RFA (despatches, granted rank of Lt-Col); High Sheriff, Cheshire, 1924–25. *Address:* 26 Lowndes Street, SW1. *Club:* United Service.

Died 29 Feb. 1944.

LYON, Hon. Francis B.; *see* Bowes-Lyon.

LYON, Adm. Sir George Hamilton D'Oyly, KCB 1940; CB 1936; *b* 3 Oct. 1883; *s* of late George Kenneth Lyon, Bengal Civil Service, and Mrs F. G. Swayne, 3rd *d* of late Sir Warren Hastings D'Oyly, Bart; *m* 1912, Helenora Mary, *d* of late J. C. H. Pierson and Mary Pierson; two *s* (and one killed in action near Dunkirk, May 1940). *Educ:* King's School, Bruton; HMS Britannia. Commander, 1916; Captain, 1922; Rear-Admiral, 1934; Vice-Admiral, 1938; Admiral, 1942; served in HMS Monarch, Grand Fleet, throughout European War, and was present at Battle of Jutland; Head of British Naval Mission to Greece, 1929–31; Commodore (D) Commanding Home Fleet Destroyers, 1932–34; Rear-Admiral Commanding Third Cruiser Squadron, 1935–37; Commander-in-Chief Africa Station, 1938–40; Commander-in-Chief The Nore, 1941–43. Commander Order of the Redeemer of Greece; Greek Medal of Military Merit 1st Class; Grand Cross Order of Aviz of Portugal. *Recreations:* Rugby football; played full back for England, 1908, cricket, Hampshire and Royal Navy, golf, tennis. *Address:* Ramley Cottage, Pennington, nr Lymington, Hants. *Club:* Junior United Service.

Died 20 Aug. 1947.

LYON, Thomas Stewart; *b* Port Glasgow, Scotland, 22 Sept. 1866; *s* of Thomas Stewart Lyon and Isabella Dalgarno Gossip; *m* 1st, 1890, Josephine (*d* 1923), *d* of late Robert Dwyer, Sandhill, Ontario; 2nd, 1925, Renée Grant Fischer, Bradford, Ontario. *Educ:* Parochial and Public Schools. Left Scotland early manhood; lived various places Canada and United States; became interested in questions of social reform; Associate Editor of Labour Reformer, Toronto, 1888; joined staff Toronto Globe, of which he was successively City Editor, Parliamentary Correspondent, News Editor, and Associate Editor; Editor, 1915–26; a Liberal; President of Toronto Young Men's Liberal Club, 1894–95; President, Ontario Federation of Liberal Clubs, 1895–96; at the front with the Canadian Corps as correspondent of the Canadian daily press, 1917;

Chairman Hydro-Electric Power Commission of Ontario, 1934–37. *Address:* 20 Willcocks Street, Toronto, Canada. *Clubs:* Ontario, Toronto.

Died 1 June 1946.

LYONS, Col Sir Henry George, Kt 1926; Hon. DSc Oxon; Hon. ScD Dublin; FRS; Grand Cordon Medjidieh, 2nd class Osmanieh; *b* London, 11 Oct. 1864; *s* of Gen. T. C. Lyons, CB; *m* 1896, Helen Julia, *e d* of late Philip Charles Hardwick; one *s* one *d*. *Educ:* Wellington College. Lieut RE, 1884; retd 1901; Director-General Geological Survey, Egypt, 1896–98; of Survey Dept, Egypt, 1898–1909; Victoria Research Medal, RGS, 1911; European War, 1914–19; Commandant Army Meteorological Services; Director Meteorological Office; Director and Secretary of the Science Museum, 1920–33; Treasurer Royal Society, 1929–39; Colonel, 1918; Symons Medallist Royal Meteorological Society, 1922. *Publications:* Report on the Island and Temples of Philæ; Physiography of the Nile; The Cadastral Survey of Egypt; The Royal Society, 1660–1940, 1944. *Address:* Picketts Field, Great Missenden, Bucks. *T:* Great Missenden 408. *Club:* Athenæum.

Died 10 Aug. 1944.

LYONS, Most Rev. Patrick; Bishop of Kilmore, (RC), since 1937; *b* Co. Louth, 1875. *Educ:* Maynooth. Administrator, Dundalk, 1910; Parish Priest of St Peter's, Drogheda, Vicar-General and Archdeacon of Armagh, 1934–37. *Address:* Bishop's House, Cullis, Cavan, Ireland.

Died 27 April 1949.

LYS, Rev. Francis John, MA; Hon. DCL, Fellow of Worcester College, Oxford; *b* 13 July 1863; *e s* of late F. D. Lys, Highclere, Weymouth, formerly Bere Regis; *m* 1st, 1894, Elisabeth (*d* 1930), *e d* of late Jonathan Hopkinson, Frant, Sussex; 2nd, 1931, Muriel Baines, *yr d* of late Hon. Theodore Bruce, MLC Adelaide. *Educ:* Sherborne School; Worcester College, Oxford (Scholar); 1st Class in Class. Hon. Mods 1884; Chancellor's Prize for Latin Verse 1885, 2nd Class in Lit. Hum. 1886. Assistant Master at Radley College, 1887–88; Lecturer, 1889, and later Fellow, Tutor, Senior Tutor, Bursar of Worcester College, Provost, 1919–46; Moderator (Classical Honours), 1899, 1900; Senior Proctor, 1917–18; Statutory Commissioner for University of Oxford, 1923; Vice-Chancellor Oxford University, 1932–35. *Publications:* various articles, chiefly on educational subjects. *Recreation:* gardening. *Address:* Pullen's Gate, Headington, Oxford. *T:* Oxford 6870.

Died 30 Sept. 1947.

LYSAGHT, Sidney Royse; author; *e s* of late T. Royse Lysaght of Mintinna, Co. Cork, and *g s* of late William Lysaght of Hazlewood, Co. Cork; *m* Kathrine, *d* of late J. Clarke of Waddington, Lincolnshire; one *s*. *Publications:* The Marplot, 1893; One of the Grenvilles, 1899; Poems of the Unknown Way, 1901; Her Majesty's Rebels, 1907; Horizons and Landmarks, 1911; My Tower in Desmond, 1925; The Immortal Jew, a drama, 1931; A Reading of Poetry, 1934; A Reading of Life, 1936. *Address:* Hazlewood, Mallow, Co. Cork. *Club:* Savile.

Died 20 Aug. 1941.

LYSAGHT, William Royse, CBE 1918; JP, DL Monmouthshire; High Sheriff of Monmouthshire, 1915; *b* 1858; *s* of Thomas Royse Lysaght of Clifton and Mintinna, Co. Cork; *m* 1890, Elizabeth, *d* of Rev. J. E. Gladstone, MA, of Braunton, N Devon; one *s* two *d*. *Educ:* privately. Honorary Freeman of the County Borough of Newport, Mon. *Recreations:* shooting, racing, gardening. *Address:* Castleford, Chepstow, Mon. *Club:* Carlton.

Died 27 April 1945.

LYTTELTON, Hon. Mrs Alfred, (Dame Edith Lyttelton), GBE 1929; DBE 1917; *d* of late Archibald Balfour; *m* 1892, Rt Hon. Alfred Lyttelton, PC (*d* 1913); one *s* one *d*. *Educ:* privately. Member of Council, Soc. for Psychical Research (President, 1933–34); Member Joint Council of Vic.-Wells and National Theatre; Governor Stratford Memorial Theatre; War Refugees Committee, 1914–18; Deputy Director of Women's Branch of Ministry of Agriculture, 1917–19; British Substitute Delegate to the League of Nations Assembly, 1923, 1926, 1927, 1928 and 1931, at Geneva. *Publications: Plays:* Warp and Woof; Peter's Chance; various small plays; *Books:* Memoir of Alfred Lyttelton; The Faculty of Communion; Our Superconscious Mind, 1931; Some cases of Prediction, 1937. *Recreations:* reading, drama. *Address:* 18 Great College Street, Westminster, SW1. *T:* Whitehall 7460.

Died 2 Sept. 1948.

LYTTELTON, Rev. Hon. Edward, MA, DD, DCL; Hon. Canon of Norwich since 1931; late Dean of Whitelands College, Chelsea; *b* London, 23 July 1855; 7th *s* of 4th Lord Lyttelton and Mary, *d* of Sir S. Glynne; *m* 1888, Caroline (*d* 1919), *d* of Very Rev. John West, DD, Dean of St Patrick's, Dublin; two *d*. *Educ:* Eton; Trinity College, Cambridge (Foundation Scholar). BA 1878; MA 1881; 2nd class Classical Tripos, 1878. Assistant Master Wellington Coll., 1880; Eton, *m*1882; Chairman of Council of Teachers' Guild, 1891–1903; Headmaster, Haileybury, 1890–1905; of Eton College, 1905–16; Rector of Sidestrand, Norfolk, 1918–20; Chaplain to Bishop of St Albans, 1892; member of Commission on Secondary Education, 1894; Hon. Canon of St Albans, 1895–1905; Member of Consultative Committee to the Board of Education, 1900. *Publications:* Cricket, 1890; Mothers and Sons, 1892; Are we to go on with Latin Verses? 1897; Training for the Young in the Laws of Sex, 1900; Studies in the Sermon on the Mount, 1905; Schoolboys and Schoolwork, 1909; Character and Religion, 1912; The Corner Stone of Education, 1914; The Dedicated Life, 1917; Letters on Education, 1922; Memories and Hopes, 1925; The Christian and Birth Control, 1929; Whither? A Study of Shams and Safeguards, 1931. *Recreations:* scenery, music. *Address:* Grangegorman, Overstrand, Norfolk.

Died 26 Jan. 1942.

LYTTON, 2nd Earl of, *cr* 1880; **Victor Alexander George Robert Lytton,** KG 1933; PC 1919; GCSI 1925; GCIE 1922; Grand Cross Order of Crown of Belgium *cr* 1926; Bailiff Grand Cross, Order of St John of Jerusalem, 1945; Hon. LLD University of Manchester, 1933; DL, JP Hertfordshire; Baronet, 1838; Baron Lytton, 1866; Viscount Knebworth, 1880; *b* Simla, 9 Aug. 1876; *s* of 1st Earl and Edith, *d* of Hon. Edward Villiers, *niece* of 4th Earl of Clarendon; *S* father, 1891; *m* 1902, Pamela, CI 1927, *d* of late Sir Trevor Chichele-Plowden; (eldest *s* killed in flying accident, 1933, younger *s* killed in action, 1942) two *d*. *Educ:* Eton; Trinity College, Cambridge. Chairman of the Royal Commission for the Brussels, Rome, and Turin Exhibitions, 1910, 1911; Civil Lord of the Admiralty, 1916; Additional Parliamentary Secretary to the Admiralty, 1917; British Commissioner for Propaganda in France, 1918; Civil Lord of the Admiralty, 1919–20; Under-Secretary of State for India, 1920–22; Governor of Bengal, 1922–27; Viceroy and Acting Governor-General of India, 10 April–9 Aug. 1925; Leader of Indian delegation to the 8th and 9th Assemblies of the League of Nations at Geneva, 1927 and 1928; Chairman: Palestine Potash Ltd; Central London Electricity Ltd; London Power Company; Hampstead Garden Suburb Trust, Ltd; League of Nations Mission to Manchuria, Jan. 1932; Permanent Cttee of Conciliation and Arbitration between Holland and Turkey, created 1935; Council of Aliens, 1939–41 (Foreign Office); Entertainments National Service Cttee, 1942–45 (Ministry of Labour); Pres. Royal Society of Literature; Pres. Garden Cities and Town Planning Assoc.; Chm. of the Old Vic; Pres. of the Central School of Speech training and Dramatic Art; Pres. of UNA. A British delegate to the League of Nations, Sept. 1931; owns about 600 acres. *Publications:* Life of Edward Bulwer, First Lord Lytton, 1913; Old Treasure, 1934; New Treasure, 1934; Antony Viscount Knebworth—A Record of Youth, 1935; The Web of Life, 1938; Pundits and Elephants, 1942; Love Incarnate, 1945. *Recreations:* shooting, fishing, skating, and ski-ing. *Heir: b* Hon. Neville (Stephen) Lytton, OBE. *Address:* Knebworth House, Knebworth. *T:* Knebworth 2310; 18 Chester Street, SW1. *T:* Sloane 8810. *Club:* Athenæum.

Died 25 Oct. 1947.

M

McADOO, William Gibbs, AM, LLD; lawyer; Chairman of Board of Directors of American President Lines, Ltd; Senator of United States, 1932–38; *b* 1863; *m* 1st, 1885, Sarah Houstoun Fleming, Chattanooga, Tenn (*d* 1912); 2nd, 1914, Eleanor Randolph, *d* of President Woodrow Wilson; 3rd, Doris Cross. *Educ:* University of Tennessee. Admitted to Bar, 1885; originated the Hudson River Tunnel System; President and Director Hudson and Manhattan Railroad Company, 1902–13; Delegate Democratic National Convention, 1912; Secretary of the Treasury, 1913–18; Director General of Railroads, 1917–18; Chairman California delegation to Democratic National Convention, 1932; President, National Aeronautic Association, 1934–35. *Publications:* The Challenge: Liquor and Lawlessness *versus* Constitutional Government, 1928; Crowded Years (autobiography), 1931. *Address:* 311 California Street, San Francisco, Calif, USA.

Died 1 Feb. 1941.

McALEER, Hugh K.; MP Mid-Tyrone, Northern Ireland; Member of Tyrone County Council, and other Local Boards and Committees; *b* Beragh, Co. Tyrone; *s* of late John McAleer and late Ellen Kelly; *m* Kate Donnelly; no *c*. *Educ:* Beragh Public Elementary School. Did press work after leaving school; principal teacher of Clogherney Upper National School, 1886; in a like position in Aughnaglea National School and Moneydarragh Male School; retired from teaching, 1899; started general business in Sixmilecross, 1899, subsequently adding auctioneering to other activities; took a prominent part in politics; was a supporter of the Constitutional Policy as advocated by Redmond, Dillon, and Devlin; Member of the National Board (Ancient Order of Hibernians). *Recreation:* antiquarian pursuits. *Address:* Sixmilecross, Co. Tyrone.

Died 13 May 1941.

MACALISTER, Charles John, MD (Edin.); FRCP (Lond.); TD; retired; Hon. Consulting Physician, Royal Liverpool Hospital for Children, Liverpool Royal Southern Hospital; formerly Hon. Physician to the Leasowe Hospital for Children; Consulting Physician, Liverpool Home for Incurables and Schools for the Deaf and Dumb, Bourton-on-the-Water Cottage Hospital; Ex-President, Liverpool Medical Institution and Liverpool Biological Society, and of the Adult Deaf and Dumb Benevolent Institution; late Lecturer on Clinical Medicine, University of Liverpool; late Surg.-Major Liverpool Scottish Regt; 3rd *s* of late William Boyd Macalister of Liverpool; *m* 1st, (*d* 1915), *d* of William Carter, MD, FRCP, of Liverpool; one *s* four *d*; 2nd, 1918, Mary Leslie, 4th *d* of late Rev. James Stalker, DD; two *d*. *Educ:* Liverpool Institute High School; University of Edinburgh. Pathologist Royal Southern Hospital, 1887; Medical Tutor and Lecturer on Practical Medicine, 1892; one of the founders of the Royal Liverpool Country Hospital for Children, 1898. *Publications:* A Research concerning The Symphytum Officinale and its contained Allantoin, 1936; History of the Liverpool Royal Southern Hospital, 1936; History of Royal Liverpool Country Hospital for Children, 1930; and many papers to medical journals. *Address:* The Gorse, Bourton-on-the-Water, Glos.

Died 25 Oct. 1943.

MACALISTER, Robert Alexander Stewart, LittD (Cambridge, Dublin, and University of Wales); LLD (Glasgow); FSA, ARCO; Professor of Celtic Archæology, University College, Dublin, 1909–43; Organist and Choirmaster, Adelaide Road Church, Dublin, 1920–27; President, Royal Irish Academy,

1926–31; President, RSAI, 1925–28; President, Cambrian Archaeological Association, 1932–33, 1934–35; Chairman, Ancient Monuments Advisory Council, IFS; Member, IFS Historical MSS Commission; *b* Dublin, 8 July 1870; *s* of Professor Alexander Macalister. *Educ:* Rathmines Sch., Dublin; private study in Germany; Cambridge Univ. Director of Excavations, Palestine Exploration Fund, 1900–09 and 1923–24. *Publications:* Studies in Irish Epigraphy, 3 vols, 1897–1907; Excavations in Palestine (with Dr F. J. Bliss), 1902; The Vision of Merlino, 1903; Bible Sidelights from the Mound of Gezer, 1906; Two Irish Arthurian Romances, 1908; Memorial Slabs of Clonmacnoise, 1909; A History of Civilization in Palestine, 1912, 2nd ed. 1921; The Excavation of Gezer, 3 vols, 1912; The Philistines, Their History and Civilization, 1913; A Grammar of the Nuri Language, 1914; Muiredach, Abbot of Monasterboice, His Life and Surroundings, 1914; The History and Antiquities of Inis Cealtra, 1916; Leabhar Gabhala (with Prof. MacNeill), 1916; The Life of Ciaran of Clonmacnois, 1921; A Text-book of European Archæology, 1921; Ireland in Pre-Celtic Times, 1921; Report on the Excavation of the Hill of Ophel, Jerusalem, 1925; A Century of Excavation in Palestine, 1925; 2nd edn, 1930; The Archæology of Ireland, 1927, 2nd edn, 1944; Suite in D Minor, for piano and violin, 1927; A [school] History of Western Europe, 1928; The Excavation of Uisneach (with Dr R. Ll. Praeger), 1929; Tara, a Pagan Sanctuary of Ancient Ireland, 1931; Ancient Ireland, 1935; The Secret Languages of Ireland, 1936; Translation of Dr R. R. Schmidt's Der Geist der Vorzeit, 1936; The Book on the Taking of Ireland vol. i 1938, vol. ii, 1939, vol. iii 1940, vol. iv, 1941; The Book of Fermoy, 1939; Corpus Inscriptionum Celticarum, 1945; The Book of Ui Maine, 1943; Monasterboice, its history and monuments, 1946. *Address:* Barrmore, Lady Margaret Road, Cambridge.

Died 26 April 1950.

McALLISTER, Alister; *see* Wharton, A.

McALPINE, Sir Alfred (David), Kt 1932; JP; public works contractor; member of the firm Sir Robert McAlpine & Sons, 50 Pall Mall, SW1; *b* 6 Nov. 1881; *s* of Sir Robert McAlpine, 1st Bart; *m* 1907, Ethel May, *d* of late James Williams, Aboyne, Aberdeenshire; one *s* two *d*. *Educ:* Kelvinside Academy; privately. Has been Chairman of the Wrexham Division of the Conservative Party, and is Hon. Treasurer of North Wales Division of National Union of Conservative and Unionist Associations; High Sheriff of Denbighshire, 1923; Life Governor of Wrexham War Memorial Infirmary. *Recreations:* keen sportsman—racing, cricket, and shooting. *Address:* Marchwiel Hall, Wrexham. *T:* Wrexham 212. *Club:* Conservative.

Died 25 May 1944.

MACALPINE-LENY, Brevet Lt-Col R. L.; *see* Leny.

MACAN, Reginald Walter, DLitt Oxon, Hon. LittD, TCD; FRSL; *b* Dublin, 1848; 3rd *s* of John Macan, QC, Judge Court of Bankruptcy, Ireland; *m* 1881, Mildred E., *o surv. d* of R. Healey, Liverpool; three *d*. *Educ:* St Columba's College, Dublin; Charterhouse; University of Oxford (1st Class Mods 1869, 1st Class Lit.Hum. 1871); University of Jena; University of Zürich. Senior Student of Christ Church, 1872. Tutor, 1876–82; Hibbert Travelling Scholar, 1873; Lecturer BNC, 1883–90; Fellow and Tutor of University, 1884–1906; Master of University College, Oxford, 1906–23; University Reader in Ancient History, 1890–1910; member of

Hebdomadal Council, 1892–1914; member of Governing Body, Charterhouse School, 1895–1928. *Publications:* The Resurrection of Jesus Christ, 1877; The Fourth, Fifth, and Sixth Books of Herodotus, 2 vols 1895; The Seventh, Eighth, and Ninth Books, 3 vols 1908; The Collects rendered into Latin Verse, 1928; and numerous articles. *Address:* Broom Hill House, Boars Hill, Berks, Oxford.

Died 23 March 1941.

MACANN, Lt-Col Arthur Ernest Henry; Counsellor, British Embassy, Tehran, Iran since 1943; *b* 19 Feb. 1898; *s* of Dr Macann; *m* Cécile Rosemary Stallard; two *s. Educ:* Brighton College. Indian Army, 1917–24; served Persia, 1918; Afghan War, 1919; joined Indian Political Service, 1924; Vice-Consul Zahidan, Iran, 1926–28; Secretary British Legation, Kabul, Afghanistan, 1930–32; Secretary to Govt, NW Frontier Province, 1933–36; Counsellor British Legation, Kabul, 1936–38; Secretary to the Resident in Mysore, 1940–42; Consul-General, Ahwaz, Iran, 1942–43. *Recreations:* tennis, squash, ski-ing. *Address:* c/o External Affairs Dept, Govt of India, New Delhi. *Club:* United Service.

Died 16 June 1944.

McARA, Sir Thomas W., Kt 1932; JP; late Secretary and Technical Adviser to London Newspaper Proprietors Association; *b* 8 Jan. 1864; *s* of Daniel McAra, Crieff, Perthshire; *m* 1891, Florence E. Borrowman; two *s* three *d. Educ:* National School. Apprenticed Compositor and served House of Cassell as Printers' Overseer; Chairman London Society of Compositors, 1909–18; Chairman St Bride's Printing School Committee, 1919–20; Chairman Governors St Bride Foundation, 1927–28; Freeman and Liveryman Stationers' Company; Member of Board and Chairman House Committee, Royal Free Hospital; represents LCC on London School of Printing. *Recreation:* gardening. *Address:* Lee-of-the-Hill, Edneys Hill, Wokingham, Berks. *T:* Wokingham 166. *Club:* Press.

Died 10 Dec. 1942.

McARTHUR, William Lyon, CBE 1920; retired Civil Servant; *b* Scotland, 3 Dec. 1870; *m* Beatrice Helen, *d* of Charles Edward Turle. *Educ:* Worcester College, Oxford. Joined the War Office as First Division Clerk, 1894. *Address:* 46 St Ann Street, Salisbury, Wilts. *T:* Salisbury 2957.

Died 12 July 1946.

MACARTHUR-ONSLOW, Maj.-Gen. Hon. James William, VD, BA, LLB; Chairman Camden Park Estate, Ltd, NSW; *b* 7 Nov. 1867; *e s* of late Captain Hon. A. A. W. Onslow, RN, MLC, and Elizabeth S., *d* of late Hon. James Macarthur of Camden Park, NSW; *m* 1897, Enid, *d* of late A. H. Macarthur; one *s* two *d. Educ:* Sydney Grammar School; Trinity College, Cambridge. Joined NSW Mounted Rifles (now 6th Australian Light Horse), 1891; subsequently commanded the regiment, and later 1st Light Horse Brigade Commonwealth Military Forces; served S African War, and in Relief of Chitral attached to 1st Batt. KRR; in European War served in AIF Overseas Transport Service; retired with rank Major-General in Australian Military Force, 1924; Member NSW Legislative Assembly, 1907–22; Member Legislative Council of NSW 1922–34; was Hon. ADC to Governor-General of Australia. *Recreations:* gardening, motoring, fly-fishing. *Address:* Camden Park, Menangle, NSW. *T:* Camden 117. *Clubs:* Travellers'; Australian, Australasian Pioneers', Sydney.

Died Nov. 1946.

MACARTNEY, Sir George, KCIE 1913; CIE 1900; *b* Nankin (China), 19 Jan. 1867; *s* of late Sir Halliday Macartney, KCMG; *m* 1898, Catherina Theodora, *d* of James Borland; two *s* one *d. Educ:* Dulwich College; France. Bachelier ès Lettres of the Université de France. Entered service of Govt of India, 1889; on Special Duty

with Sikkim Field Force, 1889–90; Special Duty in Chinese Turkestan, 1890–93; received, 1896, the thanks of HM's Government for his services on the Anglo-Russian Pamir Boundary Commission; received, 1897, the thanks of the Kashmir Durbar for his work in Chinese Turkestan in connection with the release of about 600 slaves of Kashmiri origin; received thanks of Government of India, 1906, for acquiring certain ancient Central Asian manuscripts; British Consul-General at Kashgar, Chinese Turkestan, 1910–18; retired. *Address:* 4 Overseas, St Luke's, Jersey, CI.

Died 19 May 1945.

MACARTNEY, Sir William Isaac, 4th Bt *cr* 1799; *b* 13 Oct. 1867; *s* of 3rd Bt and Catherine (*d* 1904), *d* of A. Miller, Merindindi, Victoria; *S* father, 1911. *Heir: b* Alexander Miller, *b* 24 July 1869. *Address:* Jolimont, Port Mackay, Queensland, Australia.

Died April 1942.

MACASSEY, Rev. Ernest Livingston, DD (Lambeth) 1935; MA; TD; Vicar of Mapledurham, Oxon, since 1935; 3rd *s* of late L. L. Macassey, MInstCE, Holywood, Co. Down; *m* 1911; one *s. Educ:* Upper Sullivan School, Holywood; Elstow, Bedford; Hertford College, Oxford (MA, BD). 2nd Lieut KSLI 1907–10; Ordained 1910. Worked in London Diocese for 25 years in poor parishes; Vicar of East Grinstead, 1924–25; Chaplain Territorial Army, 1911–32; Senior Chaplain, Home Counties Division, 1922–32; served European War, 1914–19. Formerly paragraphist and special writer Evening Standard, Sunday Dispatch. *Publications:* Lenten Readings, 1935; Peter (joint), 1935; Selected Carols for a Village Choir, 1939; A Hymn for the Home Front (10th impression); A Victory Thanksgiving Service, 1945 (2nd impression); special articles Daily Express, Daily Mail, Daily Telegraph, etc. *Address:* The Vicarage, Mapledurham, Oxon. *T:* Kidmore End 2271. *Club:* Carlton.

Died 28 Aug. 1947.

MACAULAY, Rev. Alexander Beith, DD (Edin.); Professor (Emeritus) Apologetics and Systematic Theology, Trinity College (Church of Scotland), Glasgow; late external Examiner to the Universities of St Andrews, Aberdeen, Glasgow, and Edinburgh; *b* 1871; *m*; six *d. Publications:* The Word of the Cross; An Edition of the Vulgate Psalter; The Death of Jesus, 1938, etc. *Recreations:* fishing and golf. *Address:* 3 Corrennie Drive, Edinburgh 10.

Died 25 March 1950.

MACAULAY, Thomas Bassett, LLD, Edinburgh, Aberdeen, and McGill; *b* Hamilton, Ontario, 6 June 1860; two *s* three *d. Educ:* Hamilton; Montreal. Entered service of the Sun Life Assur. Company of Canada, 1877; Actuary, 1880; Secretary, 1889; Director, 1896; Managing Director, 1906; President, 1915; Chairman of the Board, 1934; Chairman Emeritus, 1935; Fellow Institute of Actuaries of Great Britain; Charter Member, Actuarial Society of America, and President for two terms; represented Actuaries of the United States and Canada at International Congresses at Paris, 1900, Berlin, 1906, being elected Vice-Pres. on both occasions; Ex-Pres., The Canadian Life Insurance Officers' Assoc.; Represented Leeward Islands at Canadian West Indian Trade Conference, Ottawa, 1925; Pres. Canadian West Indian League; Hon. Pres. Navy League of Canada; Dominion Chairman of the National Committee on Food Resources, 1917; Governor, Montreal General Hosp., and Fraser Inst. Public Library; Founded Macaulay Inst. for Soil Research, Aberdeen, Scotland, 1930; also experimental farm for utilization of peat land, Stornoway, Hebrides; identified with many philanthropic movements; conducts an extensive private experimental farm at Hudson Heights, specialising in the breeding of Holstein-Friesian cattle, and developments of hardy strains of maize and soya beans. Hon. freeman of the burgh of Stornoway. *Address:* Hudson Heights, PQ, Canada.

Died 3 April 1942.

McAVITY, Lt-Col Thomas Malcolm, CBE 1919, DSO 1916; President, Consolidation Coal Co. (USA) and Chairman of Board of Empire-Hanna Coal Co., Canada, since 1941; *b* 14 March 1889; *s* of late John A. McAvity of T. McAvity & Sons, Ltd, New Brunswick; *m* 1915, Frances (decd), *d* of late Hon. Sir Douglas Hazen, PC, Canada, KCMG; three *s*; 1939, Frances Bergen. *Educ:* Rothesay Collegiate School, NB; Royal Military College, Canada, Graduate. General Staff Canadian Army Corps, BEF, France, 1915–19 (despatches four times, DSO, CBE); Malcolm McAvity & Co., London and Montreal, 1919–26; President Rochester and Pittsburgh Coal Co., Canada, 1926–29; Vice-President Rochester and Pittsburgh Coal Co., USA, 1929–32; President Empire Coal Co., Canada, 1932–39; Vice-President Consolidation Coal Co. and President Empire-Hanna Coal Co. of Canada, 1939–41. *Address:* Rockwood, Calhoun Drive, Greenwich, Conn, USA; 30 Rockefeller Plaza, New York, NY. *Clubs:* Canadian, New York.

Died 30 April 1944.

MACBEAN, Reginald Gambier, MVO 1909; *b* 1 Aug. 1859; 2nd *s* of late Alex. Macbean, formerly HBM's Consul at Leghorn and Rome, and Margaret, *d* of late Rev. George Home Robertson, of Ladykirk, Berwickshire. *Educ:* Eton. Formerly in business as banker and merchant in Leghorn and Rome; Vice-Consul, Genoa, 1897, where he was Acting Consul in each year from 1898–1900, and Acting Consul-General in each year from 1901–08; Secretary to British Chamber of Commerce for Italy (Genoa) from its foundation, 1904, until his promotion to Palermo; HBM's Consul for Sicily and the Sicilian Islands, 1909; retired, 1924. *Address:* c/o Mrs C. A. Macbean, Red Brae, Beaconsfield, Bucks.

Died 23 Dec. 1942.

MACBETH-RAEBURN, Henry Raeburn; *see* Raeburn.

M'BRIDE, Peter, MD, FRCP Edin.; FRSE; retired from practice, 1910; *b* 1854; *s* of late James M'Bride. *Educ:* Clifton College; Edinburgh University. MB, CM, 1876. Was Clinical Resident Physician Royal Infirmary; went to Vienna to study otology and laryngology; was Surgeon to Edinburgh Ear Dispensary; appointed to new department for Ear and Throat Diseases in Edinburgh Royal Infirmary, 1883; held this position for twenty years, during the last five of which was University Lecturer on Otology, Laryngology, and Rhinology; twice President of combined section of Otology and Laryngology, British Medical Association; during 1903 and 1904 was President of the Laryngological Society of London; Vice-President of the Otological Society of the United Kingdom and President of the Otological Section of the Royal Society of Medicine, 1907–09; Semon Lecturer in Laryngology, Univ. of London, 1913; Hon. Member Scot. Ot. and Lar. Soc.; Corr. Member the Berlin Laryngological, the Viennese Laryngological, and French Otological, Rhinological, and Laryngological Societies; Corr. Fellow of the American Laryngological Assoc. *Publications:* A Guide to the Study of Ear Disease, 1884; translation of Gottstein's Diseases of the Larynx, 1885; Diseases of the Throat, Nose, and Ear, 3rd edition, 1900; and numerous papers on affections of the ear, nose, and throat in various medical journals; Philosophy of Daily Life (published under pseudo initials E. C. M.); Psycho-Analysts Analysed, 1924; The Riddle of Personality, 1926; The Philosophy of Sport, 1932; Doctors and Patients, 1933. *Address:* 3 St Peter's Grove, York. *Clubs:* Union; University, Edinburgh; Harrogate; Yorkshire, York.

Died 16 June 1946.

McBRIDE, Wilbert George; Professor of Mining Engineering, McGill University, since 1927; *b* Ontario, 9 Feb. 1879; *y s* of William McBride and Mary Ann McComb, BSc, McGill University, 1902. Mining Engineer with the Copper Queen Mine, Bisbee, Arizona, 1902–03; Chief Engineer of this Company, spending a large proportion of time examining prospects and mines in Mexico and the South-Western States, 1903–07; Superintendent, Sierra de Cobre Mines, Cananea, Sonora, Mexico, 1907–09; General Superintendent, Great Western Copper Co., Courtland, Arizona, 1909–16; Assistant General Manager, Morenci Branch, Phelps-Dodge Corporation, Morenci, Arizona, 1916–17; General Manager The Old Dominion Co., Globe, Arizona, 1917–27; Past Chairman, Arizona Section, American Institute of Mining and Metallurgical Engineers; Past President McGill Chapter Sigma Xi; Director United Gold Equities of Canada; Chromite Ltd; member of Inst. of Mining and Metallurgy, Canadian Inst. of Mining and Metallurgy (Pres. 1941–42), and American Institute of Mining and Metallurgical Engineers; Sigma Xi; The Engineering Institute of Canada. *Publications:* several papers for technical societies and journals. *Recreations:* fishing and shooting. *Address:* McGill University, Montreal, Canada. *Clubs:* Faculty, Montreal.

Died June 1943.

McCALLUM, Colin Whitton; *see* Coborn, Charles.

MACCALLUM, Sir Mungo (William), KCMG 1926; MA, LLD, DLitt; *b* Scotland, 1854; *y s* of M. MacCallum, Glasgow; *m* 1882, Dorette Margarethe Peters, Hanover; one *s*. *Educ:* Glasgow High School; University of Glasgow; University of Leipzig; University of Berlin. Professor of English Literature and History, University College of Wales, 1879; Professor of Modern Literature, University of Sydney, 1887–1920; Professor Emeritus, 1921; Acting Warden of the University of Sydney, 1923; Warden, 1924; Vice-Chancellor, 1925–27; Deputy Chancellor of the University of Sydney, 1928–34; Chancellor, University of Sydney, 1934–36. *Publications:* Studies in Low German and High German Literature, 1884; Tennyson's Idylls of the King, and Arthurian Story from the Sixteenth Century, 1894; Shakespeare's Roman Plays, 1910; Albert Bythesea Weigall, 1913; The Dramatic Monologue, Warton Lecture before the British Academy, 1925; Queen Jezebel, 1930; Sir Walter Scott's Equipment, 1932; Chaucer's Debt to Italy, 1933. *Address:* Tmara, 225 New South Head Road, Sydney, Edgecliff, NSW. *Clubs:* Australian, University, Sydney.

Died 3 Sept. 1942.

McCANDLISH, Lt-Col Patrick Dalmahoy, CBE 1919; DSO 1918; JP, DL, West Lothian; *b* 6 June 1871; *y s* of late John MacGregor McCandlish and Mary, *e d* of late Patrick Dalmahoy of Bourhouses; unmarried. *Educ:* Loretto; Trinity College, Cambridge. Joined Argyll and Sutherland Highlanders, 1894; retired as Captain, 1913; served European War (Brevets of Major and Lieut-Colonel, CBE, DSO, despatches). *Address:* Muiredge, Bo'ness, West Lothian. *Clubs:* New, Edinburgh.

Died 22 Dec. 1942.

McCANN, Frederick John, MD (Honours), Edin.; MB, CM (Honours), FRCS Eng.; FRCOG; MRCP Lond.; Consulting Surgeon, Samaritan Free Hospital for Women, Marylebone Road, NW; President League of National Life; Vice-President Ligue Internationale pour la Vie et la Famille; Vice-President Medico Legal Society; Ex-President Chelsea Clinical Society; late Lecturer on Gynæcology, Medical Graduates' College and Polyclinic; Consulting Gynæcologist, West End Hospital for Diseases of the Nervous System; Consulting Gynæcologist, Cray Valley Cottage Hospital and Harrow Cottage Hospital; late President, West London Medico-Chirurgical Society; Fellow, Royal Society of Medicine and Medical Society; Hon. President, section of Obstetrics and Gynæcology XVth International Medical Congress, Lisbon. *Educ:* Edinburgh University; King's College, London; Berlin; Dresden. Formerly House Surgeon, Children's Hospital, Gt Ormond Street; Resident Medical Officer, Queen Charlotte's Lying-in Hospital; Resident Medical Officer, Belgrave Hospital for Children; Senior House Surgeon, West London Hospital; Demonstrator of Anatomy, Univ. of Edinburgh; has visited the Medical Schools of Paris, Berlin, Leipzig, Vienna, Munich, Buda Pest, and Lisbon. *Publications:* The Treatment of Common Female Ailments, 3rd edition; Cancer of the Womb, its Symptoms, Diagnosis, Prognosis, and Treatment; Treatment of Puerperal Infection; The Surgical Treatment of Female Sterility; Gonorrhœal Infection in the Female (Encyclopædia Medica); Diseases of Vagina, Diseases of Vulva (Encyclopædia of Medicine and Surgery); The Technique of the more extensive operations for Cancer of the Womb, etc. *Recreations:* music, golf, swimming. *Address:* 11 Upper Wimpole Street, W1. *T:* Welbeck 1124.

Died 28 March 1941.

M'CANN, Thomas S., BA Trin. Coll., Dublin; KC 1908; *b* 1868; *s* of late Thomas S. M'Cann, Dublin; *m* 1894, Alice, *d* of late John Baldwin Murphy, QC; three *s* two *d*. *Educ:* Beaumont College; Trinity College, Dublin. Called to Bar in Ireland, 1892. *Address:* Frankfield, Foxrock, Co. Dublin. *T:* Foxrock 43. *Clubs:* Stephen's Green, Royal Irish Yacht.

Died 1 Feb. 1942.

McCARTHY, Dame (Emma) Maud, GBE 1918; RRC and bar, Legion of Honour (Chevalier), France; Lady of Grace, Order of St John of Jerusalem, Médaille de la Reine Elizabeth avec Croix Rouge, Belgium, Médaille Épidémies en Vermeille and American Red Cross Medal, Florence Nightingale Medal; *b* 22 Sept. 1858; *d* of late William Frederick McCarthy; Deepdene, Sydney, NSW. *Educ:* privately. Trained London Hospital, 1889–99; served South African war, 1899–1902; Matron Queen Alexandra's Imperial Military Nursing Service, 1903–10; Principal Matron QAIMNS, War Office, 1910–14; Matron in Chief, QAIMNS, British Armies in France, 1914–19; Matron in Chief, Territorial Army Nursing Service, 1920–25; visited the United States as a guest of the American Army Nursing Service, 1924; visited Canada as the guest of the Canadian Nursing Services to be present at the unveiling of the memorial to the Canadian nurses who gave their lives in the European War erected in the Federal Parliament Buildings in Ottawa, 1926. *Address:* 6 St Luke St, SW3. *Clubs:* United Nursing Services, The Victoria League, Cowdray.

Died 1 April 1949.

McCARTHY, Rt Rev. James W., DD; RC; Bishop of Galloway since 1914; *b* 1853. *Educ:* Blairs College; Scots College, Valladolid; St Peter's, Glasgow. Ordained priest, 1879; served missions at Port Glasgow and Pollokshaws; was member of Port Glasgow, Eastwood, and Glasgow School Boards, Glasgow Secondary Education Committee, West of Scotland Provincial Committee for the Training of Teachers, Downhill Training College, Board of Education of the Archdiocese of Glasgow, Catholic Education Council for Scotland, Chapter of Archdiocese of Glasgow, Administrator of St Andrew's Glasgow Cathedral, 1900–14. *Address:* Candida Casa, Maxwelltown, Dumfries.

Died Dec. 1943.

McCARTHY, Most Rev. John, DD; Bishop of Sandhurst, (RC), since 1917; Assistant at the Pontifical Throne, 1929; *b* Ballyvaughan, Co. Clare, 1858. *Educ:* St Flannan's College, Ennis; Irish College, Paris. Priest, 1883; Vicar-Gen. of Melbourne, 1913. *Address:* St Kilians', Bendigo, Australia.

Died 18 Aug. 1950.

M'CARTHY, Marie Cecilia; (known professionally as Cissie Loftus); mimic; *b* Glasgow, 22 Oct. 1876; *m* 1st, 1894, Justin Huntly M'Carthy (*d* 1936); 2nd, 1909, Dr A. H. Waterman, Chicago. *Educ:* Convent of the Holy Child, Blackpool. Passed examination Royal Academy of Music; first appearance as mimic, Oxford Music Hall, July 1893; since played in London, Gaiety Theatre, Palace, Alhambra, and Coliseum; also Marguerite in Faust, with Sir Henry Irving; Peter Pan; and in America Ophelia, with E. H. Sothern; also leading parts in If I were King; appeared in Comedy with Mme Modjeska; starred in Zangwill's Serio-Comic Governess; played Viola in Twelfth Night, produced for her by Mme Modjeska. *Publications:* First Verses; Three Short Stories; Jim's Ida; Buttonhead's Brother; A Tiny Tragedy; about a dozen songs, including—My Bed is like a little Boat, words by Robert Louis Stevenson; Shadow Song, sung in Peter Pan, by R. L. Stevenson; Can't live widout ye any more; If I were you. *Recreations:* swimming, hobbies—collecting autographs and photographs.

Died July 1943.

McCARTHY, Dame Maud; *see* McCarthy, Dame E. M.

McCARTHY-O'LEARY, Brig. Heffernan William Denis; *see* O'Leary.

McCAW, George Tyrrell, MA, CMG 1936; OBE 1927; Hon. Member, Institution of Royal Engineers; Editor, Empire Survey Review; *b* 1870; *s* of Robert McCaw and Mary Elizabeth Lester. *Educ:* Lurgan College; Trinity College, Dublin. General Valuation and Boundary Survey, Ireland, 1893–1903; Geodetic Survey of North Eastern Rhodesia, 1903–06; Arc of Meridian in Uganda, 1908–09; Officer i/c Trigonometrical Survey of Fiji, 1911–15; Served European War, Lieut RE and Capt. GS, RE, 1918–19; War Office, 1918–36; formerly Secretary, Air Survey Committee and Joint Secretary, Colonial Survey and Geophysical Committee. *Publications:* Various Official Reports and Pamphlets; Photogrammetry (trans. from German). *Address:* Taghnevan House, Lurgan, NI; The Library, Colonial Office, SW1. *Club:* Royal Empire Society.

Died 17 Oct. 1942.

McCAY, Lt-Col David; IMS (retired); Fellow of Asiatic Society of Bengal; Fellow of Calcutta University; *b* 6 Feb. 1873; *s* of Rev. Wm McCay, Garvagh, Co. Derry; *m* Florence Howard, *d* of late Capt. Hixson, RN, Sydney, Australia; three *s* two *d*. *Educ:* Academical Institution, Coleraine; Queen's Colleges, Cork and Belfast; RUI; MB, BCh, BAO, 1898. Entered IMS 1899; China War, 1900–01; Prof. of Physiology, Medical College, Calcutta, 1903–18; Professor of Materia Medica, Therapeutics, Professor of Clinical Medicine, Medical College, Calcutta, and physician Medical College Hospital, Calcutta, 1919–25; MRCP (Lond.), 1911; MD (Gold Medal), 1914, Belfast University; Research Work: Foods of India, their chemical and nutritive value, 1906–10; the protein requirements of Indians, 1912–14; the causes of the prevalence of Diabetes in India; its chemical pathology and treatment, 1915–18; the chemical condition of the blood in the terminal stages of diabetes and in different forms of nephritis, 1917–19; Editor, Indian Medical Gazette, 1918–21; officiating Surgeon-General with the Government of Bengal, 1923. *Publications:* Scientific Memoirs of the Government of India (new series); three memoirs dealing with the food-stuffs of India, and the metabolism of Indians; the Protein Element in Nutrition (International monograph series); five papers on Diabetes in Journal of Medical Research, India; numerous papers on medical subjects. *Recreations:* tennis, golf, motoring. *Address:* Downside, Woking, Surrey. *T:* Woking 739; Kriegerspoort, Hanover, CP, South Africa. *Club:* Oriental.

Died 13 July 1948.

MccGWIRE, Lt-Col John Edward, CBE 1919; CStJ; *e s* of J. F. Kane MccGwire and Juliet, 2nd *d* of W. P. Metchim, Petersham, Surrey; *m* 1909, Jean Elizabeth, *o d* of Col H. B. N. Adair, RE; one *d* (*er s* died as result of war wounds, *yr s* killed on active service, 1941). *Educ:* privately. Studied Law at the Middle Temple. Called to the Bar, 1917. 2nd Lt 5th Battalion The Royal Fusiliers (Militia); served S African War, 1901–02 (Queen's SA Medal and 5 clasps). Transferred to Army Service Corps, 1903. Served European War in France, Belgium (1914 Star and Clasp, War Medal and Victory Medal, Communiques thrice). After holding several Regimental Commands and Staff Appointments retired 1933 with rank of Lt-Col. Re-employed Regimentally and in Command of Troops during 1939–41 (War Medal), reverting to Retired List, 1941. *Recreations:* usual. *Address:* 32 Audley Road, Folkestone, Kent. *Club:* Army and Navy.

Died 7 Oct. 1950.

McCLAUGHRY, Air Vice-Marshal Wilfred Ashton, CB 1942; DSO 1919; MC, DFC, psc; RAF; AOC in Egypt since 1942; *b* 26 Nov. 1894; *s* of James Kingston McClaughry, Adelaide. *Educ:* Queen's College, North Adelaide; Adelaide University; Adelaide School of Mines. Left Australia 1914 with 9th Australian Light Horse Regiment and served in Egypt and Gallipoli (twice wounded); seconded to RFC and served in No. 50 (Home Defence) Squadron then No. 100 Night Bombing Squadron, later as a Flight Commander in No. 2 Australian Squadron and commanded No. 4 Australian Squadron until the end of the war (in France), (despatches thrice, DSO, MC, DFC); since 1918 graduated at RAF Staff College and Imperial Defence College; served abroad in Iraq, Egypt, Palestine, Aden, and Somaliland; Air Officer Commanding British Forces in Aden, 1936–38; Director of Training Air Ministry, 1938–40; Commanded No. 9 Fighter Group. *Recreations:* squash racquets, cricket, tennis, ski-ing. *Club:* Royal Air Force.

Died 4 Jan. 1943.

McCLEAN, Rev. Richard Arthur, CBE 1922; LLD; *b* 1862; *m* 1912, Mary Louise, 3rd *d* of late Capt. Dovaston. *Educ:* Trinity College Dublin (LLD). Ordained, 1892; Curate of St John, Sligo, 1892–95; Rector of Carnarvon, W Australia, 1895–96; Swan, 1896–99; Curate of Ballymacarett, 1900–01; Rathkeale, 1901–05; Incumbent of Rathkeale, 1905–25; Invalided from Church, 1925; Canon of Limerick, also Chaplain to the Lord Lieutenant, 1907–11. Served European War, 1914–18 (despatches thrice, OBE, CBE, Serbian Order of St Sava, Ribbon for Valour); Senior Church of England Chaplain, 10th Irish Division, Gallipoli and Serbia; invalided from Army, 1918. *Club:* University (Dublin).

Died 16 June 1948.

McCLELLAN, John William Tyndale, CMG 1919; *b* 1865; *s* of late Rev. J. B. McClellan; *m* 1908, Edith Doyle, *d* of late Rev. H. D. Sewell. Senior Commissioner, Kenya Colony; retired, 1922. *Address:* The Cottage, Horsmonden, Kent.

Died 28 Nov. 1948.

McCLENAGHAN, Ven. Henry St George; retired; *b* 24 Sept. 1865; *s* of Canon George McClenaghan, Athlone; *m* 1895, Constance M. L. Warren; two *s*. *Educ:* Ranelagh School, Athlone; Foyle College Derry; Trinity College, Dublin, BA and MA. Curate of Glendermott, 1891; Curate of Christ Church, Derry 1894; Rector of Killaghtee, 1894–1919; Canon of Raphoe, 1917; Rector of Conwall Union and Archdeacon of Raphoe, 1919–38. *Address:* Upton, Willow Bank, Dun Laoghaire, Co. Dublin. *T:* Dun Laoghaire 83526.

Died 10 March 1950.

McCLINTOCK, Lt-Col Robert Lyle, CMG 1919; DSO 1900; late RE; *b* 26 March 1874; *s* of late Col W. McClintock, RA, of Dunmore, County Donegal; *m* 1908, Jennie (*d* 1938), *d* of late Sir G. Casson Walker, KCSI. *Educ:* Wellington College. Entered Army, 1893; retired, 1923; served Niger Expeditionary Force, 1898 (medal and two clasps, despatches, brevet of Major); South African War, 1899–1902 (despatches, DSO, medal with three clasps); East Africa, 1914–18 (Brevet Lt-Col, CMG). *Address:* Lloyds Bank, Ltd, Cox's Branch, 6 Pall Mall, SW1.

Died 11 July 1943.

McCLOY, John Moorcroft, MD, DPH; Hon. Physician to the King since 1941; Chief Medical Officer, Ministry of Home Affairs, Northern Ireland; Chairman, Joint Nursing and Midwives Council, Northern Ireland; *b* Philadelphia, 1874; *er s* of James McCloy and Elizabeth Gray, Belfast; *m* 1918, Kathleen Theodora, *d* of Robert Alexander Kyle, Belfast; one *d*. *Educ:* Queen's College, Belfast. Medical Inspector, Local Government Board of Ireland; Past-President, Ulster Medical Society; late Examiner in Public Health, Queen's University of Belfast; Member of several Government Commissions; Temp. Captain RAMC France, 1915–19. *Recreations:* fishing and travelling. *Address:* 17 Wellington Park, Belfast; Stormont, Belfast. *T:* Belfast 66030, Belfast 63210.

Died 27 May 1943.

McCLURE, Samuel S.; editor and publisher; *b* Frocess, Co. Antrim, Ireland, 17 Feb. 1857; of Scotch-French parentage; *m* Harriet Hurd (*d* 1929); one *s* three *d*. *Educ:* Knox College (AM), Galesburg, Ill, USA 1882. Editor The Wheelman, Boston, Mass, USA; 1884, with the Century Company, NY; Nov. 1884, established McClure's Newspaper Syndicate; founder, McClure's Magazine, which he established in 1893; trustee of Knox College, Galesburg, Ill, USA; has made close studies in many directions of nations and forces of modern civilisation; spent 2 years in Italy, studying Fascism. *Publications:* My Autobiography; Obstacles to Peace, 1917; The Science of Political and Industrial Self-Organization, and The Influence of Human Organization upon History, 1934; The Achievements of Liberty, 1935. *Recreation:* travel. *Address:* 38 East 37th Street, New York City. *TA:* Aiddecamp, New York. *Clubs:* British Empire; Union League (New York); Cosmos (Washington).

Died 22 March 1949.

McCLYMONT, Lt-Col Robert Arthur, CBE 1919; DSO 1916; late RFA; *b* 14 Sept. 1874. Employed with King's African Rifles, 1903–07; Egyptian Army, 1911–13; served South African War, 1902 (Queen's medal four clasps); Somaliland, 1904 (medal, two clasps); European War, 1914–17 (despatches, DSO).

Died 2 March 1949.

MACCOLL, Dugald Sutherland, DLitt Oxon; MA London; LLD Glasgow; Fellow of University College, London; Member of Council of School of Rome, 1925; Hon. Associate, RIBA; *b* Glasgow, 1859; *s* of Rev. Dugald MacColl; *m* 1897, Andree (*d* 1945), *d* of Dr Emile Zabé; two *s*. *Educ:* Glasgow Academy; University College School and College, London; Lincoln College Oxford (Scholar, and Newdigate Prizeman). Hon. Member of English and Scottish Royal Watercolour Societies, New English Art Club and Art Workers' Guild. Works in British and Dominions Galleries. Successively art-critic of Spectator, of Saturday Review and Week-end Review, editor of Architectural Review and of Artwork, and Lecturer on the History of Art at University College, London; Keeper of Tate Gallery, 1906–11; Keeper of the Wallace Collection, 1911–24; Trustee of the Tate Gallery, 1917–27; Member of Royal Fine Arts Commission, 1925–29; took initiative in foundation of National Art Collections Fund and Contemporary Art Society. *Publications:* (with Miss Jane

Harrison) Greek Vase Paintings; Nineteenth Century Art, The Administration of the Chantrey Bequest, Rhythm in English Verse, Prose, and Speech (in Essays and Studies by Members of the English Association, 1914) 'Bull,' and other War Verses, 1919; Confessions of a Keeper, and other Papers, 1931; Poems 1940; Life, Works and Setting of Philip Wilson Steer, 1945. *Address:* 1 Hampstead Way, NW11. *Club:* Athenæum.

Died 21 Dec. 1948.

McCONAGHY, Hugh, CBE 1935; Director, Australian Industries Protection League; *b* Binalong, NSW, 11 Aug. 1877; *s* of David McConaghy and Mary Parke Simpson; *m* 1901, Ruby, *d* of Thomas William Henry; two *s* one *d*. *Educ:* Superior Public School. Cootamundra, NSW. Early years in Railways and Postal Services; Australian Customs 30 years; Collector of Customs, State of Victoria, 1924; Deputy Comptroller-General of Customs for Commonwealth, 1927; Chairman, Tariff Board, Commonwealth of Australia, 1927–42. *Recreations:* golf, shooting. *Address:* Temple Court, Melbourne, C1, Australia; 21 Parlington Street, Canterbury, E7, Victoria, Australia. *T:* MU2085, WF5940. *Club:* RACV Melbourne.

Died 24 Aug. 1943.

McCONAGHY, Col John Gerald, CB 1931; DSO 1916; MVO 1920; Indian Army, retired; *b* 19 April 1879; *s* of late Surgeon-General William McConaghy, IMS, and Mary Broderick, *d* of General C. Birdwood, IA; *m* 1919, Frances Lucy Alice, *e d* of W. H. M. Lattey; two *s*. *Educ:* United Services College, Westward Ho!; Sandhurst. Entered Army, 1898; Poona Horse, Indian Army, 1899; 25th Cavalry FF, 1903; 20th Lancers, 1923; joined Australian and New Zealand Army Corps as Camp Commandant, Nov. 1914; DAA and QMG of Australian and NZ Army Corps, Aug. 1915; served European War, 1914–17 (despatches, DSO, Serbian White Eagle, 4th Class); Afghan War, 1919, served as AA and QMG of the 2nd Indian Division (despatches); retired 1932. *Clubs:* Naval and Military; United Service, Simla, India.

Died 12 March 1942.

McCONNELL, Sir Joseph, 2nd Bt *cr* 1900; DL for Belfast; MP (U) Co. Antrim since 1929; *b* 17 Sept. 1877; *s* of 1st Bt and Mary (*d* 1896), *d* of Charles Smylie; *S* father, 1927; *m* 1900, Lisa, *d* of late Jackson McGown; two *s* one *d*. *Heir: s* Lieut-Commander Robert Melville Terence McConnell, RNVR [*b* 7 Feb. 1902; *m* 1928, Rosamond Mary Elizabeth, *d* of James Stewart Reade, Clonmore, Lisburn, Co. Antrim; three *s* one *d*]. *Address:* Glen Dhu, Strandtown, Belfast.

Died 27 Aug. 1942.

M'CONNELL, Robert; General Manager of the Royal Insurance Co. Ltd and of the Liverpool and London and Globe Insurance Co. Ltd, 1929–31. Entered service of Sun Fire Office, 1885; chief of the Fire Dept of the Royal, 1896, becoming in 1901 manager in Manchester; London manager, 1907; President London Insurance Institute, 1915–16; Member of the Advisory Committee appointed under the Munitions (Liability for Explosions) Act, 1916; also a member of a non-statutory committee to which the more difficult claims were submitted; Member of the Unemployment Insurance Board, 1921–29; Chairman London Salvage Corps, 1922–24; Member of Royal Commission on Fire Brigades and Fire Prevention, 1922–23; Fellow of the Chartered Insurance Institute, President, 1926–27; President Insurance Officials Society, 1928–39; Hon. Member Insurance Institute of America since 1927; Master of the Worshipful Company of Farriers, 1914–17 and 1932; Member of Council of the Metropolitan Hospital Sunday Fund, the Royal Surgical Aid Society and the Royal London Ophthalmic Hospital. *Club:* Reform.

Died 18 June 1942.

MACCORMAC, Henry, CBE 1919, MD, FRCP; Consulting Physician, Skin Department and Lecturer on Dermatology, Middlesex Hospital; Membre Correspondent étranger, Société Française de Dermatologie; Corresponding Member, American, Danish, and Belgian Dermatological Societies; *s* of late John MacCormac, Belfast, and Lucie, *d* of C. De Lacherois Purdon; *m* 1931, Marion Maud, *e d* of Dr Broomhall, Tai Yuan Fu, China; one *s*. *Educ:* Edinburgh University; London, Paris. Fellow Royal Society of Medicine, Past-President, Dermatological Section; late Assistant Bacteriologist Medical Registrar and Physician to out-patients, Middlesex Hospital; Specialist Medical Referee for Industrial Dermatitis. Served European War, 1915–19; late Lt-Col RAMC, and Consulting Dermatologist, BEF France (despatches twice, CBE); Médaille d'Honneur de l'Assistance Publique en Argent. *Publications:* various articles on Dermatology and Pathology. *Recreation:* golf. *Address:* 23 Wimpole Street, W1. *Clubs:* Athenæum, Savile.

Died 12 Dec. 1950.

McCORMACK, John, Count; singer; *b* Athlone, Ireland, 14 June 1884; *m* 1906, Lily Foley, Dublin. *Educ:* Milan, under Signor Sabatini. Made début at Covent Garden 1907 as Turiddu in Cavalleria Rusticana; at New York, 1909; has sung in every country in the world except Russia and South America; naturalized American citizen, 1919; LittD Holy Cross College, Worcester, Massachusetts, 1917; Decorated by H. H. Benedict XV with Commander of Order of St Gregory, also Commander of Holy Sepulchre, 1921, Grand Cross, 1931; Doctor of Music National University of Ireland, 1927; raised to Papal peerage by H. H. Pius XI, 1928; Chevalier of Legion of Honour, 1924; made Freeman of City of Dublin, 1923; Knight Commander of Malta, 1932; Chamberlain of the Cape and Sword to His Holiness the Pope, 1933.

Died 16 Sept. 1945.

McCORMACK, Hon. William; *b* 1879; *s* of Patrick McCormack. MLA, 1912–30; Speaker, 1915–19; Home Secretary, 1919–23; Secretary for Public Lands, 1923–25; Premier, Chief Secretary, and Treasurer, Queensland, 1925–29.

Died 19 Nov. 1947.

MACCORMICK, Sir Alexander, KCMG 1926; Kt 1913; MD; Hon. FRCS Eng. and Edin.; Hon. Consulting Surgeon to Royal Prince Alfred Hospital, Sydney; late Hon. Surgeon, St Vincent's Hospital, Sydney; late Consulting Surgeon at St Vincent Hospital and the Coast Hospital, Little Bay; *b* Taynish, Argyllshire, 31 July 1856; *m* 1895, Ada Fanny, *d* of Charles Cropper, Yamma, NSW; one *s* two *d*. *Educ:* Edinburgh University. Went to Australia, 1883; was Demonstrator of Physiology, Edinburgh University, and Demonstrator of Anatomy and Physiology, Sydney University; late House Surgeon, Liverpool Royal Infirmary; Consulting Surgeon, with hon. rank of Major, with British Army, S African War, 1900 (despatches); Consulting Surgeon with the Army in France, 1914, 1915 and 1917 (Colonel). *Recreation:* yachting. *Address:* (temp. International Sportsmen's Club, Upper Grosvenor St, W1); Le Val, St Brelade, Jersey. *TA:* Craignish, London; Kilmory, Point Piper, Sydney. *Clubs:* Royal Thames Yacht, Royal Cruising Royal Yacht Squadron (Cowes); Victoria (Jersey); Royal Northern Yacht, Royal Clyde Yacht (Glasgow); Prince Edward Yacht, Royal Sydney Yacht Squadron, Imperial Service (Sydney).

Died 25 Oct. 1947.

McCORMICK, Lt-Col Andrew Louis Charles, CIE 1919; late Royal Engineers; *b* 1869; *s* of Andrew Gemmell McCormick, Ayr; *m* 1895, Winifred, *e d* of Deputy-Surgeon General J. Fairweather, IMS; two *d*.

Educ: Jersey; RMA, Woolwich. Joined RE, 1888; served Tirah Campaign; late Senior Master of the Mint, Calcutta; retired, 1923.

Died 2 May 1943.

M'CORMICK, Arthur David, RI, FRGS; artist; *b* Coleraine, 14 Oct. 1860; *y s* of late Arthur M'Cormick, Coleraine. *Educ:* Coleraine and Belfast. Studied South Kensington Art Schools, 1883–86. Artist with Sir Martin Conway's Expedition to Karakoram, Himalayas, 1892–93; with Clinton T. Dent in Central Caucasus, 1895. *Publication:* An Artist in the Himalayas, 1895. *Recreations:* mountaineering, yachting. *Address:* 53 Colet Gardens, Barons Court, W14. *T:* Riverside 3569. *Clubs:* Arts, Authors.

Died 12 March 1943.

McCORMICK, Rt Rev. John Newton, DD; *b* Richmond, Virginia, 1 Feb. 1863; *s* of John M'Cormick and Virginia Newton; *m* 1889, Bessie Chapman Tucker, Baltimore, Maryland; four *s* one *d. Educ:* Stuart Hall; BA Randolph-Macon College; Post Graduate Johns Hopkins University. Missionary Diocese of Southern Virginia, 1892–93; Rector, St Paul's, Suffolk, 1893–95; St Luke's, Atlanta, Georgia, 1895–98; St Mark's, Grand Rapids, Michigan, 1898–1906; Bishop Coadjutor of Western Michigan, 1906–09; Bishop of Western Michigan, 1909–37; holds Commission as Chaplain, USA (Officer Reserve Corps), with rank of Lt-Col; had charge of overseas work, War Commission Episcopal Church; also served as Chief of Hospital Chaplains in France, American Red Cross, with assimilated rank of Major, USA; Lt-Col Officers Reserve Corps USA; Bishop in charge of the American Churches in Europe, 1923. *Publications:* Distinctive Marks of the Episcopal Church, 1902; The Litany and the Life, 1904; Pain and Sympathy, 1908; Good News from a Far Country, 1910; A Small Part, Reminiscences; various charges, addresses, etc. *Recreation:* golf. *Address:* 1630 Lake Drive, Grand Rapids, Michigan. *Clubs:* Peninsular, Kent Country, Army and Navy, Grand Rapids.

Died 26 Nov. 1939.

McCOURT, William Rupert, CMG 1937; Clerk of Legislative Assembly, New South Wales, since 1930; *b* New South Wales, Feb. 1884; *s* of Hon. William McCourt; one *d. Educ:* Newington College, Sydney. Entered New South Wales Parliamentary Service, 1901. *Address:* Parliament House, Sydney, New South Wales.

Died 16 Feb. 1947.

McCOWEN, Oliver Hill, LLB, CBE 1918; Associate National Secretary YMCA, retired; *b* Tralee, Ireland, 16 May 1870; *s* of Robert McCowen, JP; *m* Elizabeth, *d* of John Prentiss, MD, Baltimore, Maryland, USA. *Educ:* Belfast and Dublin, BA (1893), LLB (1895). Entered the Legal Profession, 1893; practised as a Solicitor until 1898; Organising Secretary YMCA for Burma, 1898–1914; Chief Secretary YMCA War Work, France, 1914–19; Kaiser-i-Hind medal, 1907, and Delhi Durbar medal in 1911; a Chevalier of the Order of the Crown of Belgium. *Address:* Ashbury Lodge, Wallace Avenue, West Worthing.

Died 12 Aug. 1942.

McCRACKEN, Lt-Gen. Sir Frederick William Nicholas, KCB 1917; CB 1910; DSO 1902; late 2nd Batt. Royal Berkshire Regiment; *b* 18 Aug. 1859; *y s* of late R. de Crez McCracken of Blackheath, Kent; *m* 1887, Ann Liston (*d* 1923), *d* of late T. C. Glover of Mount Grange, Edinburgh, and Earlsferry House, Elie, Fife; two *d. Educ:* Sandhurst. 2nd Lieutenant 49th Foot, 1879; Lieut, 1880; Capt., 1884; Major, 1897; Lt-Col, 1903; Brevet Col, 1905; Major-Gen., 1914; Adjt, 1st Berks Regt, 1883–85; Commanded 7th Infantry Brigade, 1912–14; 15th Scottish Division, 1915; Commanded Army Corps, 1917–18; Commander-in-Chief, Scottish Command, 1918–19; served Egyptian

Campaign, 1882 (medal and Khedive's star), Suakin, 1885, M'Neil's Zeriba (despatches, brevet of Major, 2 clasps); Egyptian Frontier, 1885–86; action of Giniss; served throughout the campaign in S Africa (despatches, brevet of Lt-Col, DSO, Queen's medal with 3 clasps, King's medal with 2 clasps); European War, 1914–18 (despatches seven times, promoted Maj.-Gen., and Lt-Gen. KCB); retd pay, 1922. *Club:* United Service.

Died 8 Aug. 1949.

McCRACKEN, William, FRSA, FRSE, FHAS, FRPS, FSI, FLAS; Agent for The Marquess of Crewe, KG, since 1890; *e s* of James McCracken, Black Hall, Northumberland; unmarried. *Educ:* University of Edinburgh. Held Chair of Agriculture and Rural Economy, Royal Agricultural College, 1885–90; subsequently Hon. Professor and Examiner of RAC; Examiner, 5 years for Agricultural Department, Cambridge University; 21 years for NDA Joint Examination Board; 5 years for SE Agricultural College; 19 years for Fellowship of Surveyors' Institution, and for other Examining Bodies; County Alderman, 1899; JP for County of Chester, 1908; Chairman of Small Holdings and of Agricultural Education Committees of Cheshire CC; Chairman of General Purposes and Works Committee of River Weaver Catchment Board; served in war time on committees of Ministry of Agriculture and Fisheries on the Production and Distribution of Milk, and on the Agricultural Education of Women, and as Ministry Representative upon Appeal tribunal; Commission in Cheshire Volunteer Regt; during the Armistice upon Civilian Advisory Board of Army in France and Belgium; Member of Council of Agriculture for England; Member of County Councils Association; formerly interested in farm live stock as breeder, exhibitor, and judge. *Publications:* on Small Holdings, Drainage, and other agricultural subjects. *Recreations:* shooting, golf, formerly hunting. *Address:* Englesea House, Crewe. *T:* Crewe 2000.

Died 12 Sept. 1948.

McCREA, Brig.-Gen. Alfred Coryton, CMG 1916; late 37th Dogras, Indian Army; Colonel of 1st Battalion (PWO) 17th Dogra Regiment since 1933; *b* 6 Sept. 1864; *s* of Rear-Admiral John Dobrée McCrea. *Educ:* Haileybury. 2nd Lieut Royal Irish Fusiliers, 1887; Captain Indian Army, 1898; Major, 1905; Lieut-Col, 1912; served Hazara, 1891 (medal with clasp); Burma, 1892–93 (clasp); Chitral, 1895 (medal with clasp); European War, Mesopotamia, 1914–17 (CMG); Col, 1918; retired, 1920; RHS Bronze Medal, 1905. *Address:* Kilcarron, Srinagar, Kashmir.

Died 8 Aug. 1942.

McCREA, Hugh Moreland, OBE, MD, BCh, BAO; Physician; Major Home Guard, Medical Service; *b* Belfast; *s* of John McCrea, MA, MD; *m* Kate Rose, *d* of Charles Hannen, late Chinese Customs; two *d. Educ:* Royal Academical Institution, Belfast; Queen's College, Belfast (science scholar, Malcolm Exhibition in Medicine and Coulter Clinical Scholarship); Royal University of Ireland and Queen's University, Belfast. Late Assistant Physician to out-patients, Children's Hospital, Paddington Green; Fellow of the Royal Society of Medicine and of the Medical Society of London; Member of the British Medical Association; late Physician to the City of London Military Hospital; late permanent Assessor and President of No. 2 Final Appeal Medical Board Compulsory Service Act; late House Physician and House Surgeon Royal Victoria Hospital, Belfast. *Publications:* numerous in medical journals. *Recreations:* golf, tennis, fishing, and skating. *Address:* 149 Harley Street, W1. *T:* Welbeck 4444. *Clubs:* Conservative; Wentworth, Virginia Water; Phyllis Court, Henley.

Died 8 Nov. 1941.

McCREADY, Hugh Latimer, CBE 1937; DL; MA; Chairman, William Ewart and Son, Ltd; *b* 12 Oct. 1876; *s* of Rev. E. M. McCready, BA, MB, Rector of Magheradroll, Co. Down, and Marian, *d* of Sir William Ewart, Bt, MP, Glenmachan, Belfast; *m* 1911, Frances Esther Blair, MA; three *s* two *d. Educ:* Trinity College, Dublin. Member Senate, Queen's University, Belfast; President Belfast Chamber of Commerce, 1927; Chairman Linen Industry Research Assoc., 1930–39; Chairman Loans Advisory Committee for Northern Ireland, 1929–39; Chairman Linen Industry Post-War Planning Committee, 1943–44; Chairman, Central Council Linen Industry, 1946–. *Address:* 64 Myrtlefield Park, Belfast. *T:* Belfast 65361. *Clubs:* Ulster (Belfast); University (Dublin).

Died 10 April 1950.

McCULLAGH, Rt Hon. Sir Crawford, 1st Bt *cr* 1935; Kt 1915; PC (N Ireland) 1941; Director of Gibson & Co. Ltd, Classic Cinemas Ltd, Maguire & Patterson Ltd; *b* 1868; *s* of Robert McCullagh of Fortland, Aghalee; *m* 1896, Margaret Craig, CBE (*d* 1944), *d* of William Brodie, Bolton-le-Moors; one *s* two *d.* Lord Mayor of Belfast, 1914–16, 1931–41, and 1943–46; DL, JP Belfast; Freeman of the City of Belfast; Alderman for Woodvale Ward; High Sheriff, 1911; MP South Belfast, Parliament of Northern Ireland, 1921–25; Member of Senate, Northern Ireland, 1931–42, 1943–46. *Heir: s* Joseph Crawford, *b* 1907. *Address:* Lismara, Whiteabbey, Co. Antrim. *Clubs:* Constitutional; Ulster Reform, Union, Belfast.

Died 13 April 1948.

MACCULLOCH, Rev. Canon John Arnott, Hon. DD (St Andrews); Hon. Canon, Cumbrae Cathedral; Canon of St Ninian's Cathedral, Perth, 1928–45; Examining Chaplain to Bishop of St Andrews, 1915–45; *b* 22 July 1868; *e s* of John MacCulloch, Edinburgh; *m* 1891, Mary Julia, *d* of Rev. William Crawford, Edinburgh; one *s* two *d. Educ:* Merchant Company's School, Edinburgh; Theological College, Edinburgh. Luscombe Scholarship and Urquhart Greek Prize, 1891. Ordained, 1891; Vice-Principal, Edinburgh Theological College, 1895; Rector of St Columba's, Portree, Isle of Skye, 1897–1911; Rector, St Saviour's, Bridge of Allan, 1911–45; represented the Episcopal Church in Scotland on the Mission of the Christian Churches to Germany, 1909; Bell Lecturer Theological Coll., Edinburgh, 1912–14; Member Council, Scottish Anthropological and Folk-Lore Society, 1947, Vice-Pres., 1948, Diploma of Fellowship for work in Anthropology and Folk-lore, 1949; Vice-Pres. Section H (Anthropology). British Assoc., 1947. *Publications:* Comparative Theology, 1902; Religion, its Origin and Forms, 1904; The Misty Isle of Skye, 1905; revised edn, 1948; The Childhood of Fiction, a Study of Folk-Tales and Primitive Thought, 1905; The Religion of the Ancient Celts, 1911; Early Christian Visions of the Other World, 1912; Celtic Mythology, 1917; Die Kelten, in Chantepie de la Saussaye's Lehrbuch der Religionsgeschichte, 4th ed., 1925; R. L. Stevenson and the Bridge of Allan, with other Stevenson Essays, 1927; Eddic Mythology, 1930; The Harrowing of Hell: A Comparative Study of an Early Christian Doctrine, 1930; Medieval Faith and Fable, 1932; The Celtic and Scandinavian Religions, 1949; Editor of the Scottish Churchman, 1933–1946. *Address:* 19 Merchiston Avenue, Edinburgh 10. *T:* 54688.

Died 8 Sept. 1950.

McCULLOCH, Brig.-Gen. Robert Henry Frederick, CMG 1918; DSO 1897; JP, County of Southampton; late RA; *b* Bath, 21 Oct. 1869; *o surv. s* of late Robert McCulloch, of Hymenstown House, Cahir, Co. Tipperary; *m* 1922, Louise Angela Eunice, *y d* of late Major-Gen. Sir Francis de Winton, GCMG, CB, and *widow* of Capt. W. M. Meredith, the King's Regiment. *Educ:* Eastman's Royal Naval Academy; Bath College;

Royal Military Academy, Woolwich. Joined RA 27 July 1888; served in Matabeleland in command of a section of the 10th Mtn Battery RA 1896 (slightly wounded, despatches, DSO medal); DAAG, Lines of Communication, S Africa, 1900–01 (Queen's SA medal 2 clasps); European War, 1914–18 (Officer Legion of Honour, 1914 Star, French Croix de Guerre, CMG, Officer Maurice and Lazarus, Italy, British War and Victory medal); retd pay 1921. *Address:* Cupola House, Hayling Island, Hants. *T:* Hayling Island 77830.

Died 16 Oct. 1946.

MacCUNN, Captain Fergus; Chief Secretary, Royal Society for the Prevention of Cruelty to Animals since 1934; *b* 19 April 1890; *s* of late Hamish MacCunn, Scottish composer, and Alison, *d* of John Pettie, RA; *m* Maude, *d* of Major Richard Scott, Cranleigh, Surrey; one *s. Educ:* tutor; private schools. Actively interested in Animal Welfare Work for the past 30 years; Chief Accountant, RSPCA, 1919; Assistant Secretary, 1924; late London Scottish and King's Own Yorkshire Light Infantry; served European War overseas, 1914; wounded, 1915, severely wounded, 1917; afterwards serving in Ireland; speaker and lecturer on animals subjects; Vice-Pres., Society for the Protection of Animals in North Africa; British delegate to Washington (USA) Convention, 1935; Hon. Member American Humane Association, 1935; Vice-Pres. American Humane Education Soc.; Hon. Member Massachusetts SPCA, 1936; Medal of Honour, Foreningen Til Dyrenes Beskyttelse, 1936; Organised Veterinary Unit Italo-Ethiopian War, 1936; Hon. Member Latvian SPCA, 1938; organised Finnish War Animals Fund, 1940, Finnish-Russia War; re-opened British Sick and Wounded Horses Fund (1914–18) recognised by Army Council as sole channel for voluntary assistance to Veterinary Forces of the Crown; holds position on executive of many animal welfare bodies. *Publications:* Country Friends; Pets for Young People (with Wellesley Pain). *Recreations:* swimming, tennis, gardening. *Address:* Beech Croft, Cranleigh, Surrey. *T:* Cranleigh 115.

Died 18 May 1941.

McCURDY, Rt Hon. Charles Albert; PC 1920; KC 1919, Midland Circuit; MP (L) Northampton, 1910–23; Chairman, 1925–27, of the United Newspapers (1918), Ltd; Director of London Express Newspapers, Ltd; Chairman of Trust of Insurance Shares, and Bedford General Insurance, Ltd; *b* 13 March 1870; *er s* of Rev. Alexander McCurdy, Loughborough, Leicestershire; *m* 1893, Louise Ellen, *d* of Frederick Parker, Cambridge. *Educ:* Loughborough Grammar School; Pembroke College, Cambridge. Called to Bar, 1896; Parliamentary Secretary, Ministry of Food, 1919–20; Food Controller, 1920–21; Joint Parliamentary Secretary to the Treasury, Coalition Liberal Chief Whip, 1921–22; Chairman, Central Committee Profiteering Act, 1919–20; Member of Royal Wheat Commission, 1920–21; a founder of the League of Nations Union. *Publication:* Empire Free Trade, 1930. *Address:* 30 Cornhill, EC3. *Clubs:* Reform, Bath, Oriental.

Died 10 Nov. 1941.

MacCURDY, John Thomson, ScD (Cantab); Lecturer Psychopathology, Cambridge University; Fellow Corpus Christi College, Cambridge; *b* Toronto, Canada, 1886; *s* of late Prof. J. F. McCurdy; *m* 1914, Winifred, *d* of David B. Jones, Chicago; one *s* one *d. Educ:* University of Toronto; Johns Hopkins University. BA Toronto (Biology), 1908; MD Johns Hopkins, 1911; Fellow Pathology Johns Hopkins and Research in Munich and Breslau, 1911–12. Lecturer Medical Psychology, Cornell University, and Assistant Psychiatric Institute, New York, 1913–22; Captain, Medical Corps AEF, 1917–18; President, American Psychopathological Association, 1922; MA Cambridge, 1923. *Publications:* Psychology of War, 1917; War Neuroses, 1918; (Editor) Hoch's Benign Stupors, 1921; Dynamic Psychology, 1922;

Psychology of Emotion, 1925; Common Principles in Psychology and Physiology, 1928; Mind and Money, 1932; Structure of Morale, 1943; Germany, Russia and the Future, 1944; various papers on Mental Diseases and Psychological subjects. *Recreations:* golf, tennis. *Address:* Corpus Christi College, Cambridge. *TA:* Corpus, Cambridge. *T:* Cambridge 5018.

Died 1 July 1947.

MACDERMOT, The, (Charles Edward); styled Prince of Coolavin; Barr-at-law; retired; Vice-Chairman, General Prisons Board, Ireland; JP, DL, Co. Sligo; High Sheriff, 1909; *b* 29 Dec. 1862; *e s* of Rt Hon. Hugh The MacDermot, ex-Attorney-General for Ireland; *m* Caroline, *d* of John J. Whyte, DL, of Loughbrickland, Co. Down; two *s* two *d. Educ:* Downside Coll., nr Bath; Dublin University. *Heir: s* Charles MacDermot, *b* 20 Feb. 1890. *Address:* Coolavin Monasteraden, Co. Sligo.

Died 8 May 1947.

MACDERMOTT, Patrick; MP (N) Co. Kilkenny, N, 1891–1902; *b* 1859; *s* of late J. Macdermott, Woodford, Co. Galway; *m* Helena Beatrice, *d* of late Arthur Pearson, Betchworth House, Highgate, N. *Club:* National Liberal.

Died Sept. 1942.

MACDIARMID, Sir Allan Campbell, Kt 1945; Chairman and Managing Director, Stewart's and Lloyds, Ltd; *b* 18 Aug. 1880; *y s* of late Allan Macdiarmid and Elizabeth, *d* of Rev. Wm Tulloch; *m* 1910, Grace Buchanan, *d* of late J. H. McClure; three *s* two *d. Educ:* Kelvinside Academy, Glasgow; Uppingham. Qualified as Chartered Accountant; joined the firm of Stewart's and Lloyds, Ltd, as Secretary, 1909. *Address:* Kingshill House, Berkhamsted, Hertfordshire. *T:* Berkhamsted 75; 3 Stanmore Court, St James's Street, SW1. *T:* Abbey 3130. *Clubs:* Caledonian, East India and Sports.

Died 14 Aug. 1945.

MACDONAGH, Michael; author and journalist; *b* Limerick, 1860; *m* 1888, Mary (*d* 1924), *d* of John Govan, Dublin; one *s. Educ:* Christian Brothers' Schools. Became a reporter on a local paper at an early age. In his 22nd year joined the Freeman's Journal, Dublin, and for eight years was one of its special correspondents in Ireland and in the Houses of Parliament. Joined The Times parliamentary and reporting staff 1894. Has contributed articles on Ireland, Irish literature, and parliamentary history and custom to the magazines. Fellow Institute of Journalists; Pres. Irish Literary Society of London. *Publications:* Bishop Doyle; The Book of Parliament; Irish Life and Character; Parliament: its Romance, its Comedy, its Pathos; The Life of Daniel O'Connell; The Viceroy's Post-bag; The Reporters' Gallery; The Speaker of the House; The Irish at the Front; The Irish on the Somme; The Home Rule Movement; The Pageant of Parliament; The Life of William O'Brien, 1928; The English King, 1929; Daniel O'Connell and the Story of Catholic Emancipation, 1929; In London during the Great War: The Diary of a Journalist, 1935. *Recreation:* country walks. *Address:* 133 Copse Hill, SW20. *T:* Wimbledon 1748.

Died 27 Feb. 1946.

MACDONALD, 6th Baron *cr* 1776; **Ronald Archibald Macdonald;** Bt 1625; *b* 9 June 1853; *y s* of 4th Baron and Maria, *d* of George Thomas Wyndham, Cromer Hall, Norfolk; *S brother* 1874; *m* 1875, *cousin* Louisa (*d* 1922), 2nd *d* of Col George William Holmes Ross, Cromarty; one *d.* Owns about 100,000 acres. *Heir: g s* Alexander Godfrey Macdonald. *Address:* Armadale Castle, Isle of Skye. *Clubs:* Carlton; Scottish Conservative, Edinburgh.

Died 20 Jan. 1947.

MACDONALD, Most Rev. Alexander, DD; Titular Archbishop of Hebron; *b* Nova Scotia, 18 Feb. 1858. *Educ:* St Francis Xavier's Coll., Antigonish; Propaganda, Rome. Ordained 1884; Professor of Latin and Philosophy, St Francis Xavier's College, 1884–1903; Parish Priest of St Andrew's, Antigonish, 1903–08; Bishop of Victoria, 1908–23. *Publications:* The Apostles' Creed; Religious Questions of the Day (4 vols); The Sacrifice of the Mass; It is the Mass that Matters; The Primacy of Thought in Poetry; The Mass Explained, 1930; The Continued Sacrifice and several other pamphlets on the Mass, 1930–1936; Evolution in the Light of Reason and Revelation, 1934; etc. *Address:* University of St Francis Xavier's College, Antigonish, Nova Scotia.

Died 24 Feb. 1941.

McDONALD, Most Rev. Andrew Joseph, OSB; Archbishop of St Andrews and Edinburgh, (RC), since 1929; *b* 1871; *s* of late D. P. McDonald, of Invernevis, Fort William. *Educ:* Fort Augustus Abbey School. Abbot of Fort Augustus Abbey, 1919–29. *Address:* 42 Greenhill Gardens, Edinburgh. *T:* 53337.

Died 22 May 1950.

MACDONALD, Angus Roderick; 23rd Chief of Clanranald; *b* 29 April 1858; 2nd *s* of Admiral Sir Reginald Macdonald, KCB, KCSI, 21st Chief, and Hon. Adelaide Louisa Vernon, 2nd *d* of 5th Baron Vernon; *S* brother, 1908; *m* 1884, Leucolene Helen, *d* of late Rev. Henry Clarke, The Côte, Torquay, and Kirkland Hall and Beaumont Côte, Lancashire; no *c. Educ:* Clifton College; RI Engineering College, Coopers Hill. As a Civil Engineer in the Indian Public Works Department, 1879; services lent by the Govt to the Gwalior (Native) State, 1887–90; lent to Alwar State, 1890, where he was State Engineer till 1902; retd 1904; since then lived mostly at St Jean-de-Luz, south of France; finally left France in 1936 and came to Torquay. *Address:* Tirrim, Lincombe Hill Road, Torquay. *T:* Torquay 2409. *Club:* 1900.

Died 17 March 1944.

MACDONALD, Col Charles Joseph, CMG 1918; MD; late AMS; *b* 1862; *s* of Charles MacDonald of Britfieldstown House, Co. Cork; *m* 1906, Emma Geraldine, *d* of Lieut-Col J. F. Brodie, Maryville, Kilworth, Co. Cork; one *s* two *d. Educ:* Queen's College, Cork; Charing Cross Hospital. Served European War, 1914–18 (CMG). *Address:* Castlemahon, Blackrock, Co. Cork.

Died 1947.

MACDONALD, Rev. Duncan, MA, Moderator of the General Assembly of the Free Church of Scotland, 1934; Minister of Milton Free Church, Glasgow, since 1919; Lecturer in Religious Instruction to Free Church Students attending Glasgow Provincial College for Training of Teachers; *b* 1 June 1885; *s* of Hugh MacDonald and Barbara Hendry; *m* 1931, Flora Agnes, *d* of Archibald MacNeilage, late editor of Scottish Farmer. *Educ:* Glen Urquhart; Aberdeen University. Ordained in 1910 Free Church minister of Duthil, Inverness-shire; Chaplain to the Forces, 1917–19 (France). *Publications:* articles to religious magazines. *Address:* 18 Newton Terrace, Glasgow, C3.

Died 18 Feb. 1941.

MACDONALD, Rev. Duncan Black, MA, DD, DHL; Professor of Semitic Languages in the Hartford Theological Seminary, 1892–1931; Professor Emeritus since 1933; Head Mohammedan Department, Kennedy School of Missions, Hartford, 1911–25; Hon. Consulting Professor, 1933; *b* Glasgow, 9 April 1863; *s* of Thomas Logie and Margaret Macdonald; *m* 1898, Mary Leeds Bartlett (*d* 1929), Hartford, USA; no *c. Educ:* University of Glasgow (MA 1885, BD 1888, sometime Scholar and Fellow); University of Berlin, 1890–91, 1893. Haskell Lecturer on Comparative Religion,

University of Chicago, 1906; Special Lecturer, Wellesley College, 1907, 1909, 1912; American Lecturer on Mohammedanism at the Congress of Arts and Science, St Louis Exposition, 1904; Lamson Lecturer on Mohammedanism, Hartford, 1909; Lecturer on Mohammedanism at the Episcopal Theological School, Cambridge, USA, 1912; Haskell Lecturer, Oberlin, Ohio, for 1914, on Light cast by Arabic literature on OT; Lecturer on OT, Berkeley Divinity School, 1917–18; travelled Egypt, Syria, Turkey, 1907–08; DD, Trinity College, USA, 1909; Glasgow, 1920; Dr of Hebrew Letters, Jewish Theological Seminary of America, 1937. *Publications:* Development of Muslim Theology, Jurisprudence and Constitutional Theory, 1903; Selections from Ibn Khaldun, 1905; Religious Attitude and Life in Islam, 1909; Aspects of Islam, 1911; Hebrew Literary Genius, an interpretation, 1933; Hebrew Philosophical Genius, a Vindication, 1935; contributor on Muslim Theology, Law and Constitution to 11th ed. of Encyclopedia Britannica, to the Leyden Encyclopedia of Islam, to Hastings' Encyclopedia of Religion and Ethics, and to many journals and reviews. *Societies:* Royal Asiatic (hon.), American Oriental. *Recreations:* Arabian Nights and storyology, especially Oriental; psychical research. *Address:* 233 Tryon Street, South Glastonbury, Conn.

Died 6 Sept. 1943.

MACDONALD, Dame Ethel, DBE 1935; *d* of late Major W. Cairns Armstrong; *m* 1st, P. Craigie Robertson; 2nd, 1892, Col Rt Hon. Sir Claude Maxwell Macdonald, PC, GCMG, GCVO, KCB (*d* 1915). *Address:* Royal Cottage, Kew, Surrey.

Died 20 March 1941.

MACDONALD, Greville, MD; Consulting Physician to King's College Hospital (retired); Fellow and Emeritus Professor of King's College, 1905; *b* Manchester, 20 Jan. 1856; *e s* of late George MacDonald; *m* Phoebe Winn (*d* 1927). *Educ:* King's Coll. School and Hospital. Resident Medical Officer to Hospital for Diseases of Throat, 1886; Hon. Physician, 1887; Throat Physician and Lecturer on Diseases of Throat and Nose to King's College Hospital, 1893; Consulting Physician to King's College Hospital, 1906; Corresp. Fell. American Laryngological Assoc. *Publications:* On the Respiratory Functions of the Nose, 1888; Board School Laryngitis; A Treatise on Diseases of the Nose and its Accessory Cavities, 2nd ed. 1892; Hay Fever and Asthma, 1893; The Religious Sense in its Scientific Aspect, 1903; The Tree in the Midst, 1904; The Ethics of Revolt, 1907; The Sanity of William Blake, 1908; the Child's Inheritance, 1910; The Magic Crook, 1911; Trystie's Quest, 1912; Jack and Jill, 1913; How Jonas found his Enemy: a Romance of the South Downs, 1916; The North Door: a Cornish Romance, 1920; Billy Barnicoat, 1922; George MacDonald and his Wife, 1924; Count Billy, 1928; Reminiscences of a Specialist, 1932; The Wonderful Goat-Skin, 1943. *Address:* Wildwood, Haslemere. *T:* Haslemere 138.

Died 3 Nov. 1944.

McDONALD, Brig.-Gen. Harold French, CMG 1917; DSO 1916; Chairman Canadian Pension Commission since 1936; *b* Fort Qu'Appelle, Sask, 22 Nov. 1885; *y s* of late Archibald McDonald, Chief Factor, Hudson Bay Coy; *m* 1917, Marjorie, 2nd *d* of T. H. Gilmour, KC, Winnipeg. *Educ:* Upper Canada College, Toronto; McGill University, Montreal (BSc 1907). Civil Engineer and Land Surveyor, Winnipeg; Member of the Dominion Alberta, Manitoba, and Saskatchewan Associations of Land Surveyors; Member of Council Manitoba Land Surveyors' Association, 1913–14; Lieut 16th Canadian Batt. (Canadian Scottish), Aug. 1914; Capt. Sept. 1914; seriously wounded, St Julien, April 1915; Major, Jan. 1916; seriously wounded, Pozieres, Sept. 1916 (CMG, DSO, despatches twice); Order of St Anne, 2nd Class, with Swords; Lieut-Col Dec. 1916; Brig.-Gen. Dec. 1917; General Officer

Commanding Military District No. 13, 1919; retired, 1920. *Address:* Ottawa, Ontario; Banff, Alberta. *Clubs:* Vancouver, University, Ottawa.

Died Aug. 1943.

MACDONALD, Hon. James Alexander; *b* 1858; *m* Mary, *d* of Henry Richardson, Stratford, Ont. *Educ:* Toronto Univ.; Osgoode Hall. Barrister, 1889; KC, 1905; Chief Justice, Court of Appeal, British Columbia, 1909–37. *Address:* Victoria, BC. *Clubs:* Union, Victoria.

Died 20 Dec. 1939.

McDONALD, Sir James Gordon, KBE 1937; Kt 1929; Beit Railway Trustee, etc; *b* Aberdeenshire, 1867; *s* of Hugh McDonald, Ellon, Aberdeenshire. *Educ:* Grammar School, Aberdeen. A pioneer of Rhodesia, 1890; engaged in gold mining since 1890; closely associated with Cecil Rhodes. *Publications:* Rhodes: A Life; Rhodes: A Heritage, 1943. *Clubs:* Bath, Windham; Bulawayo, Rhodesia.

Died Dec. 1942.

MACDONALD, John Smyth, FRS 1917; *b* Dublin, 1867; *s* of George Macdonald; *m* Katherine Mary Stewart of Holm, Stornoway, NB; three *s* four *d*. *Educ:* King's School, Chester; Emmanuel College, Cambridge, etc. (BA Mathematical Tripos, 1889); Liverpool University; Holt Fellow, Physiology, 1891; Research Scholar, British Medical Association, 1899–1901. Teaching posts in the Physiological laboratories of Liverpool University, Dundee (St Andrews University), and Sheffield. President, Section I of British Association, Portsmouth, 1911, and of Section of Physiology, British Medical Association, Liverpool, 1912; Professor of Physiology, Sheffield University, 1903–14; Holt Professor of Physiology, Liverpool University, 1914–32; Professor Emeritus since 1932. *Publications:* Structure and Function of Nerve Fibres in the Proc. Roy. Soc.; The Structure and Function of Striated Muscle, Quarterly Journal of Experimental Physiology, etc., etc. *Address:* St Helen's, Bridge of Allan, Stirling. *Clubs:* University, Liverpool.

Died 29 March 1941.

MACDONALD, Mrs L. M., (L. M. Montgomery), OBE; FRSA; *b* Clifton, PEI, 1874; *d* of Hugh John Montgomery and Clara Woolner Macneill; *m* 1911, Rev. Ewan Macdonald, Presbyterian clergyman; two *s*. *Educ:* Prince of Wales College; Dalhousie College. Lived till her marriage on a PE Island farm; taught in school for three years, and wrote for periodical publications for several years; moved to Ontario, 1911. *Publications:* Anne of Green Gables, 1909; Anne of Avonlea; Anne of the Island; Anne's House of Dreams; Chronicles of Avonlea; Kilmeny of the Orchard; The Story Girl; The Golden Road; Rainbow Valley; The Watchman (poems); Rilla of Ingleside; Emily of New Moon; Emily Climbs; The Blue Castle; Emily's Quest; Magic for Marigold; Aunt Becky Began It; Pat of Silver Bush; Mistress Pat; Anne of Windy Willows; Jane of Lantern Hill; Anne of Ingleside. *Recreations:* reading, walking, and motoring. *Address:* 210a Riverside Drive, Toronto, Ontario, Canada. *Clubs:* Royal Society of Arts; Canadian Authors' Association, Montreal; Canadian Women's Press, Toronto.

Died 24 April 1942.

MACDONALD, Col Norman, JP Renfrew; TD; advocate; Sheriff-Substitute of The Lothians and Peebles since 1946; *b* 2 Nov. 1890; *e s* of Norman D. Macdonald; *m* 1925, Agnes Mundell, 2nd *d* of Dr J. V. Paterson; two *s* one *d*. *Educ:* Edinburgh Academy. 2/Lt 9th Bn (Highlanders) The Royal Scots, 1911; Lt-Col, 1930; served European War, 1914–19; Lt-Col, commanding 9th Bn (Highlanders) The Royal Scots, 1930; called to Scots Bar, 1919; Sheriff-Substitute of Caithness, Orkney and Zetland at Wick, 1932–36; of Renfrew and Bute at Greenock, 1936–40; of Lanarkshire at Glasgow, 1940–46; Hon. Sheriff-Substitute of Angus and Selkirk. *Address:* 23 Belhaven Terrace, Glasgow. *T:* West. 6833.

Died 24 July 1948.

MACDONALD, Percy Stuart, CIE, 1941; SSC; Secretary of Thomas Duff & Co. Ltd, and Associated Companies, 64 Reform Street, Dundee; *b* 1890; *s* of late Rev. J. S. Macdonald, Leith; *m* 1927, Alice Mary, *d* of late John Galloway of Tayport, Fife. Chairman Indian Jute Mills Association, 1938 and 1939; Vice-Pres. Indian Central Jute Committee, 1938 and 1939; Jute Controller, India, 1939–40; Member Ministry of Supply Mission to India, S Africa, Australia, New Zealand, Hong Kong, Burma, and Malay States, 1940–41; Member Eastern Group Conference, 1940. *Address:* Balcairn, Blackness Road, Dundee. *T:* 67511. *Clubs:* Oriental, Bengal, Calcutta.

Died 1 Jan. 1945.

MacDONALD, Pirie; photographer; *b* Chicago, 27 Jan. 1867; *s* of Dr George MacDonald and Margaret Reilly; *m* 1890, Emilie Van Deusen, Hudson, NY. Engaged as photographer since 1883; since 1900 exclusively of men; has been awarded Cramer grand prize cup, grand prize for portraiture, diamond decoration, the laurel wreath, and 7 gold and 2 silver medals by Photographers' Association of America; bronze trophy Boston; special silver medal and later gold medal Indianapolis; diamond medal Omaha; gold medal, Philadelphia; gold medal, St Louis Exposition; and medals in London, Birmingham, Belfast, Frankfort, Trier, Amsterdam, Brussels, Nancy, and Paris; first and third President Professional Photographers Society of New York; member Chambre Syndicale Française de la Photographie; Officer d'Académie, 1906; Palme Académique, 1st class 1920; Hon. Fellow Royal Photographic Society (Great Britain); Member Council of London Salon of Photography; Member Iona Society, St Andrews Society. *Address:* 576 Fifth Avenue, New York. *Clubs:* Pilgrims, Rotary, Professional Photographers, New York.

Died 22 April 1942.

MacDONALD, Sydney Gray, MA, MB, BC Cantab; FRCS; Consulting Surgeon; Specialty, Diseases of the Urinary Organs; Consulting Genito-Urinary Surgeon, West London Hospital; Genito-Urinary Surgeon, Royal Masonic Hospital, and Chelsea Hospital for Women; late Surgeon, King George Vth Hospital; and late Temporary Captain, RAMC; *b* 1879; *e s* of Eben. MacDonald, Sydney, New South Wales; *m* 1919, Mary Martineau, 3rd *d* of late Major-General F. H. B. Marsh; one *d. Educ:* privately; St John's College, Cambridge; St Thomas's Hospital, London. Fellow of the Association of Surgeons of Great Britain and Ireland. Ex-President of Urological Section of Royal Society of Medicine and Fellow of the Medical Society of London; Member of the British Medical Association, and of the Association Internationale d'Urologie. *Publications:* contributions to the Surgery of the Urinary Organs in books and in various medical journals. *Recreations:* golf and shooting. *Address:* 1 Welbeck House, Welbeck Street, W1. *T:* Welbeck 6748; Edgehill, Wadhurst, Sussex. *T:* Wadhurst 108. *Clubs:* Oxford and Cambridge; Royal Wimbledon Golf; Royal and Ancient, St Andrews.

Died 20 Feb. 1946.

McDONELL, Æneas Ranald, CBE 1920; Hon. Major; 21st Chief of Glengarry; *b* 8 Aug. 1875; *e s* of Æneas Ranald W. McDonell, 20th of Glengarry (*d* 1901), and Catherine Frances, *d* of Henry Herries Creed; *m* 1909, Dora Edith (*d* 1935), 2nd *d* of late Dr H. W. Hartford, Christchurch, Hants; two *s. Educ:* St Paul's School. Served with North Persian forces and in Russia, 1916–18 (despatches, CBE). *Address:* Swanage, Dorset.

Died 10 May 1941.

MACDONELL, Lt-Gen. Sir Archibald Cameron, KCB 1919; CB 1917; CMG 1916; DSO 1901; ED; LLD (Hon.), Queen's University, 1922; late Commandant, The Royal Military College of Canada; *b* Windsor, Ontario, 6 Oct. 1864; *s* of S. S. Macdonell, QC, DCL, Lt-Col 1st Essex Regiment; *m* 1890, Mary Maud Flora (*d* 1936), 3rd *d* of late Lt-Col J. T. Campbell, 72nd Highlanders and Royal Fusiliers; one *d. Educ:* Trin. Coll. School, Port Hope, Ontario; Royal Military Coll., Kingston. Lieutenant Canadian Mounted Infantry, Permanent Corps, 1888; Adjutant and Quartermaster, 1888; exchanged into North-West Mounted Police, 1889; volunteered into 2nd Batt. Canadian Mounted Rifles, for service in South Africa (dangerously wounded, despatches, S African medal 4 clasps, DSO); commanded Depot, and 'C' Division Royal North-West Mounted Police, Canada, and Battleford District; commanded Lord Strathcona's Horse and Royal School of Instruction, Winnipeg; European War, 1914–18 (despatches seven times, CB, KCB, CMG, Legion of Honour, Croix de Guerre, French, wounded); retired. *Address:* 22 Collingwood Street, Kingston, Ontario, Canada. *Clubs:* Toronto, Toronto; Ranchman's.

Died 23 Dec. 1941.

MACDONELL, Archibald Gordon; author and journalist; *b* 3 Nov. 1895; *s* of William Robert Macdonell, LLD and Alice Elizabeth White. *Educ:* Winchester. Lieut RFA 51st Highland Division (TF) 1916–18; Headquarters Staff of League of Nations Union, 1922–27; contested (L) Lincoln, 1923 and 1924. *Publications:* England Their England; Napoleon and His Marshals; How Like an Angel; A Visit to America; Lords and Masters; My Scotland; Autobiography of a Cad; The Spanish Pistol; What Next, Baby?; Flight from a Lady, 1939; The Crew of the Anaconda, 1940. *Recreations:* golf, cricket, tennis. *Address:* 10 Markham Street, SW3.

Died 16 Jan. 1941.

MACDONNELL, Mervyn Sorley, OBE; JP; *b* 24 July 1880; *s* of H. MacDonnell, MD; *m* Ethel Gladys, *d* of J. S. Jameson (*d* 1888) and Countess Contardon Pes di Villamarina (*d* 1933); three *d. Educ:* Elstree; Cheltenham Coll.; Trinity Coll., Dublin. Sudan Civil Service, 1905–12; Egyptian Civil Service, 1912–23; High Commissioner, Free City of Danzig, 1923–26; General Staff, EEF, 1915–19; Governor Western Desert Province, Egypt, 1920–23; Special Commissioner for Transjordan Frontier Settlement, 1931; Commissioner for Transitional Payments, County Durham, 1932–34; BBC representative for Saar Plebiscite, 1934. *Address:* The Hermitage, St Catherine, Bath.

Died 22 March 1949.

MACDONOGH, Lt-Gen. Sir George Mark Watson, GBE 1925; KCB 1920; KCMG 1917; CB 1915; Knight of Grace, Order of St John of Jerusalem; Col Comdt Royal Engineers, 1924; an Imperial War Graves Commissioner; Member, Central Committee for Regulation of Prices, 1939–41; Member, Finnish Aid Bureau, 1940; a Member of Council and Vice-President, 1941–42, Zoological Society of London, 1934–38 and 1939–41; President, China Association, 1930–35; President, Federation of British Industries, 1933–34; Member, War Emergency Committee FBI; President, Anglo-Finnish Society; Vice-President, Finland Fund; President, Institute of Exports, 1938; Vice-President, Japan Society; Chairman, Hospital St John and St Elizabeth, NW8; Member, Royal Commission on Local Government, 1923–29; Member of Council, London Chamber of Commerce, 1936–41; Vice-President and Member, Executive Council, International Law Association; Member Council, Royal Institute of International Affairs, 1928–41; Fellow, Institute of Bankers; Barrister-at-law, Lincoln's Inn, 1897; Member, London Committee, Hong-Kong and Shanghai Bank; Chairman, International Paint and Compositions Co.; Chairman, Watts Fincham (1932), Ltd; Chairman,

Scammell Lorries, Ltd; Director, Venezuelan Oil Concessions, Ltd, Director, National Provident Institution; *b* 4 March 1865; *m* Aline, *d* of late Emil Borgström, Helsingfors, Finland. Entered Army, 1884; Captain, 1892; Major, 1901; Lt-Col, 1909; Colonel, 1912; Maj.-Gen., 1916; Lieut.-Gen., 1919; retired pay, 1925; psc; Gen. Staff Officer, 1st Grade, War Office, 1912; Adjt-General to the Forces, 1918–22; served European War, France, 1914–16; Director of Military Intelligence, 1916–18 (despatches, CB, prom. Maj.-Gen. for distinguished service in the field, Commander Legion of Honour, Commander Crown Belgium, Grand Crosses (both with and without swords) St Stanislaus, Russia, Grand Cross Sacred Treasure, Japan, Grand Officer Crown of Italy, Grand Officer Rising Sun, Japan, Grand Officer White Elephant, Siam, Grand Officer White Eagle, Serbia, Grand Officer Excellent Crop, China, Grand Cross White Rose (Finland), French and Belgian Croix de Guerre, Distinguished Service Medal, USA, Commander St Olav, Norway, Isabel the Catholic, Spain, 2nd Class Military Merit, Spain, Grand Cross Cruz Roja (Cuba); Knight Commander St Silvester (Holy See); Knight of Magistral Grace Sovereign Order of Malta; Coronation, 1911, Silver Jubilee, 1935, and Coronation, 1937, Medals). *Address:* Martello House, Cliff Road, Folkestone. *T:* Folkestone 3534; Lensbury Club, Teddington. *Clubs:* Army and Navy, Travellers'.

Died 10 July 1942.

McDOUALL, Brig.-Gen. Robert, CB 1919; CMG 1917; CBE 1920; DSO 1900; Kt Dannebrog Order, 1906; late The Buffs; *b* 3 Nov. 1871; *s* of late John McDouall, Stranraer, Wigtownshire; *m* 1902, Mabel Constance, *d* of late Gen. Sir C. R. Pennington, KCB; one *s* one *d*. *Educ:* Felsted School; RMC, Sandhurst. Entered army, 1892; Captain, 1899; served Chitral Relief Force, 1895 (medal with clasp); South Africa, 1899–1902 (despatches twice; Queen's medal 4 clasps, King's medal 2 clasps, DSO); European War, 1914–18 (despatches seven times, Bt Lt-Col, CMG, CB, 1914 Star, GS Medal and Victory Medal; Officer Légion d'Honneur, 1920); retired pay, 1924. *Address:* c/o Lloyds Bank, Canterbury.

Died 31 May 1941.

McDOUGALL, Dugald Gordon, MA, BCL Oxford; MA, LLD 1909, Melbourne; Emeritus Professor of Law, University of Tasmania; *b* Hawthorn, Melbourne, 28 March 1867; 2nd *s* of late Dugald McDougall, formerly head of Sands and McDougall, printers and stationers, of London, Melbourne, etc; *m* 1901, Helen Ione, *d* of James Reibey Atkinson, surveyor, Ipswich, Queensland; six *s*. *Educ:* private school, St Leonards-on-Sea, England; Hawthorn Grammar School, Melbourne; Trinity College, Melbourne University; Balliol College, Oxford. Wyselaskie Scholarship in Modern Languages, 1886; Final Scholarships in Classics and in Modern Languages, 1888; Williams Exhibition (at Balliol), 1888; 1st class Classical Moderations, 1890; 1st class Final School of Jurisprudence, 1892; 1st class Examination for BCL, 1894. Called to English Bar at Inner Temple, 1892; admitted to Victorian Bar, 1895; practised 1895–1900; Professor of Law and Modern History in Tasmania, 1901–33. *Publications:* Self-Governing Colonies, 1905; Commonwealth and States, 1907. *Recreations:* formerly lawn tennis, golf, royal tennis, billiards; championship in latter at Oxford, 1892.

Died 21 June 1944.

MACDOUGALL, Gordon Walters, BCL; KC; late Professor of Private International Law, McGill University; *m* 1906, Hilda Beatrix, 2nd *d* of W. de M. Marler. *Educ:* McGill University. Advocate, 1894; KC 1906. *Clubs:* Mount Royal, St James's, Montreal (Montreal).

Died Aug. 1947.

MACDOUGALL, Margaret; (writes under name of Margaret Armour); poet; novelist; translator; *b* Philpstoun House, West Lothian; *e d* of late Alexander Henderson Harry and Christina Stewart Armour; *m* 1895, W. B. Macdougall (*d* 1936); no *c*. *Educ:* George Watson's Ladies' College, Edinburgh (Dux, Gold Medallist; Winner of Leaving Scholarship; University of Edinburgh Local Exam. Scholarship); Munich; Paris. *Publications:* Essays, short stories, poems; contributed to various magazines. Publications in book form: Home and Early Haunts of Stevenson, 1895; Songs of Love and Death, 1896; The Fall of the Nibelungs (done into English), 1897; Thames Sonnets and Semblances, 1897; The Shadow of Love, 1898 (the above five volumes illustrated and decorated by W. B. Macdougall); translations into English verse of Heine's New Poems, 1904; Germany and Romancero, Books I and II, 1905; Romancero, Book III and Last Poems, 1905; Agnes of Edinburgh, 1909; translation of Wagner's Ring of the Nibelung; The Rhinegold and the Valkyrie, 1910; Siegfried and the Twilight of the Gods, 1911; The Fall of the Nibelungs; Gudrun (done into English), 1928; The Impostor and the Poodle, 1939. *Recreations:* sailing, motoring. *Address:* 28 Chalmers Street, Edinburgh 3, Scotland. *Clubs:* Overseas, Edinburgh.

Died 13 Oct. 1943.

MacDOUGALL, Sir Raibeart MacIntyre, KCMG 1945; CIE 1935; *b* 30 April 1892; *s* of John Maclean MacDougall, MD, CM, Greenock; *m* 1917, Agnes, *d* of Edward McGuire, Glasgow; one *s* four *d*. *Educ:* Greenock Academy; Glasgow University, MA. Entered Indian Civil Service, 1915. Counsellor to Governor of Burma, 1941–47; retired, 1947. *Address:* 28 Winchester Road, Worthing. *Club:* Oriental.

Died 2 Nov. 1949.

MACDOUGALL, Robert Stewart, MA (Hons), DSc, Hon. LLD (Edin.), FRES, FRSE; retired; late Steven Lecturer in Agricultural Entomology and Reader in Agricultural Entomoloty and Reader in Agricultural Zoology and Forest Zoology, University of Edinburgh; late Adviser in Biology to Board of Agriculture in Scotland; late Member of Committee Imperial Bureau of Entomology; late Member of the Scientific and Technical Commission for Plant Diseases and Pests of the International Institute of Agriculture, Rome; late Consulting Zoologist to Highland and Agricultural Society; Professor Emeritus of Biology Royal (Dick) Veterinary College, Edinburgh; late a Governor of the George Heriot Trust and a Governor of the Heriot-Watt College; *b* 5 June 1862; *m* Lily (*d* 1930), *d* of D. R. W. Huie, Edinburgh; 1936, Kathleen, *d* of late Capt. Walter Sussan. *Educ:* George Heriot's School, Edinburgh; University of Edinburgh and University of Munich. Acted as Technical Adviser in Zoology, Board of Agriculture and Fisheries, 1904–13; President Botanical Society of Edinburgh, 1913–15. *Address:* Linkfield House, Greenhill Gardens, Edinburgh. *T:* 55669. *Clubs:* National Liberal; University, Edinburgh.

Died 28 March 1947.

M'DOWALL, Rev. Charles Robert Loraine, MA; *b* 9 June 1872; *e s* of late Rev. Charles M'Dowall, DD, Headmaster of Highgate School, Prebendary of St Paul's; *m* 1902, Beatrice Mary, *e d* of Rev. W. J. Burdett; two *s* two *d*. *Educ:* Marlborough; Exeter College, Oxford (Scholar). Ordained, 1899. Assistant Master, Wellington College, 1896–1902; Eton Coll., 1902–10; Headmaster, King's School, Canterbury, 1910–16; Assist Curate, Parish Church, Croydon, 1916–17; Assist-Master, Eton Coll., 1917–30; Vicar of Brabourne, Kent, 1931–45. *Address:* Clare Cottage, Dunmow, Essex.

Died 14 Oct. 1950.

McDOWELL, Lt-Col Arnott Edward Connell, CIE 1937; Inspector General of Police and Police Adviser to the Residents, Eastern States; *b* 13 March 1883; *s* of late Edward Howard McDowell; *m* 1904, Mary Gabriel

Finucane; three *s* three *d. Educ:* Wimbledon College (SJ); Royal Military College, Sandhurst. Served in S African War, Cheshire Regt, 1901–02; joined Indian Army, 1904; served European War on the North West Frontier of India and in Mesopotamia, 1914–18; in 1918 raised and commanded the 1/133rd Infantry in India; Deputy Inspector General of Police 1923 and as such several years in charge of the Provincial CID; Inspector General of Police, Bihar, 1933–38. *Recreations:* shooting and tennis. *Address:* Patna, EIR, India. *TA:* Eaststates, Calcutta. *Club:* East India and Sports.

Died 1 Jan. 1944.

McEACHERN, Malcolm; International bass singer; *b* Albury, NSW, Australia, of British parentage; *m* Hazel Doyle, pianist, Sydney, NSW; one *s. Educ:* Public School, Albury. Soloist with Dame Nellie Melba on Australian Tour; Celebrity Concerts in England; has sung all over the British Isles and in principal London Concert Halls, and is now equally well-known as Mr Jetsam of the entertainers, Mr Flotsam and Mr Jetsam; Records for Columbia. *Recreations:* golf, boxing, cricket, and Rugby football, billiards and snooker. *Address:* 50 Foscote Road, Hendon, NW4. *T:* Hendon 1786. *Club:* Savage.

Died 17 Jan. 1945.

M'ELDERRY, Robert Knox, MA; Emeritus Professor of Greek in the Queen's University of Belfast; Librarian Presbyterian College, Belfast; *b* Ballymoney, County Antrim, 7 July 1869; *s* of John M'Elderry, JP for the Co. of Antrim, and Matilda, *d* of Robert Knox, Springfield; *m* Margaret, *d* of Very Rev. J. Courtenay Clarke, DD; two *s* one *d. Educ:* Academical Institution, Coleraine; Queen's College Belfast; St John's College, Cambridge. In the Royal University of Ireland—BA with First-Class Honours (First Place) in Ancient Classics, 1891; MA with First-Class Honours and Studentship, 1893; Jun. Fellow in Ancient Classics, 1896; Fellow, 1905. In Cambridge Univ.—First Class, Second Division, Classical Tripos Part I, 1894; First Class, with asterisk for special distinction in Ancient History, Classical Tripos Part II, 1895; Members' Prizeman, 1895, for Latin Essay on Θαλαττοκρατια Britannica; Scholar, and Wright's and Hughes' Prizeman, St John's College; Fellow of St John's College, 1897. Senior Classical Master in Campbell College, Belfast, 1896–1902; Professor of Greek, Queen's College (now University College), Galway, 1902–16; Professor of Ancient Classics, 1916–24; sometime Member of Council of Society for Promotion of Roman Studies. *Publications:* papers on Roman History in Classical Review, Classical Quarterly, and Journal of Roman Studies. *Address:* Glenside, 34 Sans Souci Park, Belfast.

Died 10 July 1949.

McELLIGOTT, Edward John; KC; Circuit Judge for the Counties of Kerry, Limerick and Clare; 4th *s* of late Gerald McElligott, Mount Rivers, Listowel, Kerry; *m* 1912, Margaret Hilda, *e d* of Col J. Nugent Cahill, Ballyconra House, Ballyragget; one *s. Educ:* St Vincent's College, Castleknock; Trinity College, Dublin. Called to Irish Bar, 1896; Inner Bar, 1911; Senior Crown Prosecutor for Cork, 1913; Treasury Counsel (Valuation Department), 1914; Chairman Munitions Tribunal, Ireland, 1915; Extern Examiner in Real Property, National University, 1920. *Recreation:* gardening. *Address:* Temple Mungret, Limerick.

Died 15 Aug. 1946.

MACEWEN, Sir Alexander Malcolm, Kt 1932; BL; Solicitor, senior partner Stewart Rule & Co., Inverness; *b* Calcutta, 10 Jan. 1875; *s* of Robert Sutherland Taylor MacEwen, Barrister, Recorder of Rangoon, and Annie Gordon, *d* of Sheriff-Substitute R. Sutherland Taylor; *m* 1906, Mary Beatrice, *er d* of late Surgeon Major George Henderson, IMS; three *s* two *d. Educ:* Clifton College; Edinburgh University. Qualified Solicitor, 1901 and subsequently joined firm of Stewart Rule & Co.,

Inverness; entered Town Council of Inverness, 1908; Provost, 1925–31; Chairman, Education Committee, Inverness-shire, since 1930; Chairman, Royal Northern Infirmary, 1925–34; taken a leading part in local government and other public work in the Highlands; Secretary, Highlands Reconstruction Association; Member of Scottish National Development Council; worked on behalf of Belgian refugees during the War (médaille du Roi Albert); Chairman, Highland Transport Co. Ltd; Deltenne (Ceylon) Tea Estates Ltd and other companies. *Publications:* The Thistle and the Rose, 1932; Scotland at School, 1938; Towards Freedom, 1938. *Address:* Kessock House, Kessock, Ross-shire.

Died 29 June 1941.

MACEWEN, Alexander Robert, CSI 1946; CIE 1938; MC; ICS; Member Board of Revenue, Madras; *b* 8 Aug. 1894; *s* of Rev. Professor A. R. MacEwen, DD, New College, Edinburgh; *m* 1925, Christina Katherine Macnish; one *d. Educ:* Edinburgh Academy; Lincoln College, Oxford. Served European War, with 1/5th Highland Light Infantry, 1914–19; passed into ICS, 1919; Revenue Settlement Officer, 1923–30; Secretary to Board of Revenue, Madras, 1930–33; Collector and District Magistrate, Malabar, 1934–38; Secretary to Government of Madras, Home Dept, 1938. *Recreations:* golf, tennis. *Address:* Kintyre, Adyar, Madras, India. *T:* Madras 86198. *Clubs:* Caledonian United Service, Edinburgh: Madras, Madras.

Died 16 Feb. 1946.

MACEWEN, Brig.-Gen. Douglas Lilburn, CB 1915; CMG 1918; DL, JP; *b* 19 Nov. 1867; *e s* of William L. MacEwen and Jane Glen Walker, of Glenlora, Renfrewshire; *m* 1st, Sophie, *y d* of Sir John Millais, 1st Bart; one *d*; 2nd, 1909, Mary, *d* of late Lewis Edwards, New York. Entered Army, Cameron Highlanders, 1889; Captain, 1897; Major, 1904; Lt-Col 1912; Brig.-Gen., 1916; General Staff Officer, 2nd Grade, War Office, 1910–12; General Staff Officer, 1st Grade, War Office, 1914; served South African War, 1899–1900 (Queen's medal 5 clasps); European War, 1914–16 (severely wounded, despatches, CB, Commander Legion of Honour); retired pay, 1923; member of King's Bodyguard, Scotland. *Address:* Corsock, Castle Douglas, Kirkcudbrightshire.

Died 3 Jan. 1941.

MACEWEN, John A. C., MB, CM, BSc; FRFPS. Hon. Consulting Surgeon and Manager, Royal Infirmary, Glasgow and Erskine Hospital for the Limbless; Professor of Surgery, St Mungo's College, Glasgow; County Councillor, Bute. *Publications:* Surgical Anatomy; Fractures, Dislocations, and Artificial Limbs; Text-book of Surgery, etc. *Address:* 3 Woodside Crescent, Glasgow. *T:* Douglas 5194; Garrachty, Isle of Bute. *T:* Kilchattan Bay 31. *Clubs:* Royal Scottish Automobile, Glasgow.

Died 12 Jan. 1944.

McEWEN, Sir John (Blackwood), Kt 1931; MA, LLD, Glasgow, Mus. Doc. Oxon; FRAM; *b* Hawick, 13 April 1868. *Educ:* Royal Academy of Music. Was Professor of pianoforte, harmony, and composition, Glasgow; Professor of harmony and composition, Royal Academy of Music, 1898–1924; Principal of Royal Academy of Music, 1924–36.

Died 14 June 1948.

MACEWEN, Brig.-Gen. Maurice Lilburn, CB 1915; late 16th Lancers; *b* 13 April 1869; *m* 1897, Margaret, *d* of late Sir John Woodbourne, KCSI. Entered army, 1890; Capt. 1897; Major, 1903; Lt-Col 1910; Colonel, 1914; Adjutant, Imperial Yeomanry, 1901–03; served S African War, 1900–01 (despatches, Bt Major, Queen's medal 6 clasps); European War, 1914–16 (despatches, CB, Commander Legion of Honour).

Died 6 Oct. 1943.

McFADYEAN, Sir John, Kt 1905; MB, BSc, Edinburgh; Hon. LLD Aberdeen; MRCVS; *b* 17 June 1853; 2nd *s* of Andrew McFadyean of Barrachan, Wigtownshire; *m* 1883, Mara Eleanor (*d* 1929), *d* of Thomas Walley; three *s* two *d*. *Educ:* Ewart Institute; Edinburgh University; Edinburgh Veterinary College. *Address:* Highlands House, Leatherhead.

Died 1 Feb. 1941.

MACFARLANE, Donald, CIE 1937; *b* Haulbowline, Co. Cork, Ireland, 3 Aug. 1882; *s* of late D. Macfarlane, MICE, Superintending Engineer, Admiralty; *m* 1909, Aylmer, *d* of late H. H. Lake, MICE, Superintending Engineer, Gwalior, C India; one *s* one *d*. *Educ:* Weymouth College; RIEC, Coopers Hill. PWD India, 1903; Under Secretary, Punjab PWD, 1916; Military Railways, Mesopotamia, 1917–18; Director of Works Sudan Govt (on loan), 1923–26; Superintending Engineer Punjab PWD, 1927; Chief Engineer, 1932; retired 1937; Technical Adviser, Ministry of Home Security, 1939; Deputy Principal Officer, Civil Defence 12th Region, Tunbridge Wells, 1941–42. *Address:* Little Hadlow, Hadlow Down, Sussex. *T:* 269.

Died 30 May 1946.

MACFARLANE, Brig.-Gen. Duncan Alwyn, CB 1915; DSO 1900; late KOSB; Inspector of Infantry, 1915–18; *b* 19 Nov. 1857; *s* of late Rev. J. D. Macfarlane, MA; *m* 1913, Edith Lavinia, *d* of late Rear-Admiral Hon. Richard Bingham; one *d*. *Educ:* Radley; Magdalen College, Oxford, BA. Entered army, 1882; Captain, 1888; Major, 1900; served Suakim Field Force, 1888 (medal with clasp, Khedive's star); Soudan Frontier, 1889; Chitral Relief Force, 1889 (dangerously wounded, medal with clasp); North-West Frontier, India, 1897–98 (despatches, brevet of Major, two clasps); South Africa, 1900–02 (despatches twice, DSO, brevet of Lieut-Col, Queen's medal three clasps, King's medal two clasps); European War, 1914–19, Comdr 1st Bn KOSB, 1905–09; Comdr Seaforth and Cameron Bde (TF), 1911–14; Cmdr 81 Infantry Bde, 1914–15; Inspector Infantry, 1915–18; Col KOSB, 1928–38; DL Inverness, 1936. *Address:* Dunain Park, Inverness. *T:* 512. *Club:* Naval and Military.

Died April 1941.

MACFARLANE, Sir James, Kt 1932; LLD Glasgow University, 1922; *b* 1857; *s* of John Macfarlane, Glasgow; *m* 1882, Catherine (*d* 1936), *d* of Robert French, Glasgow; two *s* three *d*. *Educ:* Larchfield Academy, Helensburgh; Glasgow High School and Glasgow University. Joined his father in the business of Macfarlane Lang and Co., Ltd, Bread and Biscuit Manufacturers (founded in 1817 by his Grand Uncle) in 1878, and of which he has been Chairman since 1908; interested in philanthropic work and was a member of the Board of Managers of the Glasgow Royal Infirmary, 1899–1939, Chairman, 1914–39, and has devoted much time to other philanthropic interests connected with Glasgow; is a Member of six of the Glasgow Trade Incorporations; Deacon Convener of the Trades House of Glasgow, 1899; DL of the County of the City of Glasgow and has been a JP since 1900. *Address:* 2 Cleveden Crescent, Glasgow, W2. *T:* Western 159. *Clubs:* Carlton, Constitutional; Conservative, Edinburgh; New, Art, Glasgow.

Died 26 Jan. 1944.

McFARLANE, Brig. Percy Muir, CBE 1936; served with AIF Australia and Middle East; now Retired List, Australian Staff Corps; *b* 10 Jan. 1880; *s* of Lieut John Muir McFarlane and Sarah Elizabeth Close; unmarried. *Educ:* privately. Served S Africa, 1899–1902 (Queen's medal with three clasps, King's medal with two clasps); European War, 1914–18, in Gallipoli (wounded despatches, Brevets Major and Lt-Col, 1914–15 Star, two medals); psc Camberley 1920; Exchange duty with Army in India, 1923–25; acting Military Commandant, New South Wales, 1934–35; Military Commandant,

South Australia, 1935; Military Commandant, Western Australia, 1935; Military Commandant, Western Australia, 1936–39. *Address:* The Glen, Minns Road, Gordon, Sydney, NSW, Australia. *Clubs:* Athenæum, Melbourne; Australian, Sydney.

Died 2 Aug. 1946.

MACFIE, John William Scott, MA (Cantab); MB, ChB (Edin.); DSc (Edin.); DTM (Liverpool); *b* 1879; *o surv. s* of late J. W. Macfie, of Rowton Hall, Chester, and Dreghorn Castle, Midlothian. *Educ:* Oundle; Gonville and Caius College, Cambridge (Foundation Scholar and Frank Smart Prizeman); Edinburgh University; Radcliffe Infirmary and County Hospital, Oxford. West African Medical Staff, 1910–23; Northern and Southern Nigeria and Gold Coast. Acting Director, Medical Research Institute, Lagos, 1913; Director Medical Research Institute, Accra, 1914–23; War Office Malaria Investigation, Liverpool, 1917–19; Mary Kingsley Medal, Liverpool School of Tropical Medicine, 1919; Lecturer on Protozoology, Liverpool School of Tropical Medicine, 1923–25; Medical Research Council Investigation on Chemotherapy of Malaria (London School of Hygiene and Tropical Medicine), 1927–31; British Ambulance Service in Ethiopia (British Red Cross) 1935–36; Emergency Officer, St Pancras Medical War Committee, 1939–41; Temp. Major, RAMC, 1941–43, Malariologist, Nos 3 and 8 Malaria Field Laboratories, Egypt, Palestine, and Syria. *Publications:* An Ethiopian Diary, 1936; John Macfie of Edinburgh and his family, 1938; researches on tropical diseases and parasitology, especially on malaria and trypanozomiasis; also contributions to Entomology, particularly reports with descriptions of new species, on Ceratopogonidæ (Biting Midges), Mosquitoes, and tse-tse flies. *Address:* No. 42 Filsham Road, St Leonards-on-Sea. *Clubs:* Reform, Royal Empire Society; East Sussex (St Leonards).

Died 11 Oct. 1948.

McGANN, Lt-Col H. H., CIE 1930; retired; *s* of Col T. J. McGann, IMS, retired; unmarried. *Educ:* private; RMC, Sandhurst. Entered Indian Army, 1902; Deputy Inspector General of Military Police, Burma, 1923–31; served European War (despatches). *Recreation:* golf. *Address:* High View, Mysore, India. *Club:* East India and Sports.

Died 20 June 1943.

McGEER, Gerald Grattan; KC; Member House of Commons; Practising Barrister; *b* Winnipeg, 6 Jan. 1888; *s* of James McGeer, Co. Wicklow, and Emily Cooke McGeer, St Helens, Lancashire; *m* 1917, Charlotte Emma Spencer; one *s* one *d*. *Educ:* Vancouver; Dalhousie Law School, Halifax. Iron moulder by trade, Active in Labour circles; In law, conducted the Western freight rate cases, 1921–28, which resulted in the establishment of Western grain trade to Vancouver; Mayor of the City of Vancouver, 1935–36; Prominent in Provincial and Federal politics. *Publications:* The Conquest of Poverty, or Money, Humanity and Christianity; pamphlets: Is Canada Under-Currencied?; Money and Credit and Its Management; Managed Empire Money is Empire Economic Power; The Conquest of Poverty, and magazine articles. *Recreations:* Gymnasium work, travel, public speaking and reading. *Address:* 4812 Belmont Avenue, Vancouver, BC, Canada. *Cable Address:* McGeer. *T:* Seymour 1263 and Point Grey 109. *Clubs:* Vancouver, Point Grey, Golf and Country, Vancouver.

Died Aug. 1947.

MACGEOUGH BOND, Sir Walter Adrian, Kt 1917; JP, DL; BA; *b* 1857; *e s* of Joshua M. Bond, MP, Drumsill, Co. Armagh, and Albertine, *o d* of late Frederick Shanahan, Barrister, King's Inn, Dublin; *m* 1901, Ada Nichols of Kilbrack House, Doneraile; one *s*. *Educ:* Christ Church, Oxford; Germany; Bachelier ès Lettres and licentiate in law, Paris. Bar, Inner Temple,

1884; practised as Advocate in Egypt; Judge of Cairo Court of Appeal, 1888; Vice-President, 1899; retired, 1916; holds 2nd class Medjidie and 2nd class Osmanieh, 2nd Star of the Nile. *Recreations:* now, classical Greek; in early life, riding, shooting, golf, mountain-walking. *Club:* Travellers'.

Died 21 Nov. 1945.

MACGILLIVRAY of MacGillivray, Angus, CM, MD, DSc, LLD, FRSE, FSA Scot., JP; TD; Commander of the Grand Priory in the British Realm of the Venerable Order of the Hospital of St John of Jerusalem; formerly Reader in Ophthalmology, St Andrews University; Hon. Consulting Ophthalmic Surgeon, Dundee Royal Infirmary; Consulting Surgeon, Dundee Eye Institution; Consulting Surgeon, Royal Orphanage, and Royal Dundee Institution for the Blind; late Consulting Ophthalmic Surgeon, St Andrews Provincial Training College; Ophthalmic Specialist, Angus County Council; formerly Ophthalmic Specialist Dundee and Fifeshire Education Authorities; formerly Consulting Ophthalmic Surgeon, Tay Defences and Dundee War Hospital and Red Cross Hospitals, Eastern Central District of Scotland; b Abriachan, Inverness, 13 May 1865; 2nd s of Angus MacGillivray; m 1st, Elizabeth M. (decd), 2nd d of Alex. Middleton of Belmont, JP, Aberdeen; two s; 2nd, Gertrude A., y d of late John Hall, JP, CC, Scarborough. *Educ:* Abriachan; Fordyce Acad.; Aberdeen Univ.; Birmingham; London. Honours graduate in Medicine of University of Aberdeen; Struthers' Gold Medallist in Anatomy. VP Section of Ophthalmology, BMA, 1902, RSM, 1916–18; Major, RAMC TA, retired; Chief, Dundee Highland Society, 1912–39; First Pres. Dundee, Aberdeen, Banff, and Kincardine Association; Member University Court, St Andrews University; Member of Board of St Andrews Provincial Training College; ex-President Forfarshire Medical Association and ex-President Dundee Branch BMA; ex-President Caledonian Medical Society; County Controller and County Director for the City of Dundee Branch of BRCS, 1926–39; formerly Chairman Dundee Educational Trust; formerly Demonstrator of Anatomy and Assistant to the Professor of Physiology, Aberdeen University; Capt. 1st Forfarshire RGA Volunteers; formerly Research Fellow in Science, St Andrews University. *Publications:* numerous papers, abstracts, monographs, and reviews on ophthalmology in various medical journals; Our Gaelic Proverbs, A Mirror of the Past; The Highland Dress. *Recreations:* fine arts and archæological (Celtic) pursuits, gardening, and motoring. *Address:* Chattan Croft, Crail, Fife. *T:* Crail 316.

Died 15 Oct. 1947.

McGILLYCUDDY, Lt-Col Ross Kinloch, (The McGillycuddy of the Reeks), DSO 1916; late 5th Lancers and 4th Royal Irish Dragoon Guards; b 26 Oct. 1882; m 1908, Helen Grace, y d of Edward Courage of Shenfield Place, Essex; two s one d. *Educ:* Fettes College, Edinburgh. RMA, Woolwich. Entered Army, RA; 1902; Lieut 1905; RHA 1907; 4th Dragoon Guards, 1909; Captain, 1912; served European War, 1914–19 (despatches seven times, DSO, Bt Major, Bt Lt-Col, Legion of Honour); retired pay, 1922; re-employed GS, 1940–42; Member of the Senate of Eire, 1929–43. *Heir:* s John Patrick. Capt. late Northamptonshire Yeomanry [b 1909; m 1945, Elizabeth Margaret (Betty), e d of Major John E. Otto, Astrop Grange, King's Sutton, Banbury; one s (b 4 Oct. 1948) one d]. *Address:* The Reeks, Beaufort, Co. Kerry. *T:* Beaufort 4. *Club:* Kildare Street (Dublin).

Died 28 April 1950.

McGIRR, John Joseph Gregory; b Parkes, NSW, 11 Oct. 1879; s of John Patrick McGirr of Westport, Ireland, and Mary Sullivan of Limerick, Ireland; m Rachel Miler-Hermes, BA, of Sydney University; three s five d. *Educ:* St Stanislaus' College, Bathurst; St Joseph's Convent, Parkes. Entered politics at the age of 22 years;

one of Labour's first bunch for the Australian Senate; Mem. for Yass, 1912–20, Cootamundra, 1920–22; Member for the City of Sydney, 1922–25; was then chosen as the first Minister for Motherhood in the world in the NSW State Parliament, also Minister for Health afterwards, elected also as Minister for Labour and Industry, NSW; introduced a Bill to fix the basic wage by Act of Parliament, and the Motherhood Endowment Bill; afterwards resigned from Labour Party; now out of politics and attends to his grazing and real estate interests throughout NSW. *Publication:* a book on Motherhood Endowment. *Recreation:* general sports. *Address:* Sunray, North Sydney, NSW.

Died 23 March 1949.

MACGLASHAN, John, CIE 1929; MInstCE; MIE (Ind.); b 1874; s of John MacGlashan and Jean Polson; m 1907, Grace Isobel Fraser, Inverness; two s two d. *Educ:* Gordon's College, Aberdeen; Aberdeen University. Trained as a Dock Engineer pupil at Aberdeen Harbour; Assistant Engineer to the Bombay Port Trust; Resident Engineer to the Calcutta Port Trust; District Engineer, 1909; Deputy Chief Engineer, 1912; Engineer-in-chief, 1918; retired after the completion of the new King George's Dock, 1930; ex-Chairman, Bengal Association of Engineers; Viceroy's Prizeman, Institute of Engineers, India. *Publication:* Dock and Harbour Engineering Lectures at the Bengal Engineering College, Calcutta. *Address:* The White Cottage, Hatfield Peverel, Essex. *T:* Hatfield Peverel, 49. *Clubs:* Bengal, Royal Calcutta Turf (Calcutta).

Died 21 April 1948.

McGLINN, Brig.-Gen. John Patrick, CMG 1916; CBE 1919; VD; b 11 April 1869. Joined 4th NSW Infantry, 1889; served S African War, 1900–01 (Queen's medal six clasps); Australian Imperial Force, European War, 1914–20 (despatches, CMG, CBE); Chairman Sir Samuel McCaughey AIF Bequest; Member War Veterans' Homes Trust, Victoria; Member of Board of Commissioners Commonwealth Public Service, 1923–30; State War Council of Victoria, 1935–42. JP, NSW and Victoria. *Address:* 26 Studley Avenue, Kew, Melbourne, E4, Australia. *Clubs:* Navy, Army and Air Force, Melbourne.

Died 7 July 1946.

McGONIGAL, His Honour Judge John; KC; County Court Judge of Tyrone, since 1939; b 20 Jan. 1870; s of Michael McGonigal of Sydenham, County Down; m 1901, Margaret, e d of Richard Davoren of Friarsland, Roebuck, County Dublin; three s four d. *Educ:* St Malachy's College, Belfast; The French College, Blackrock, Dublin. Called to Irish Bar, 1892; Member of the North-East Circuit; Professor of the Law of Personal Property, Contracts and Torts at King's Inns, Dublin, 1910–13; called to Inner Bar, 1911; Senior Crown Prosecutor for the City of Belfast, 1917; Bencher of the Inn of Court of Northern Ireland. *Recreations:* golf, tennis. *Address:* 6 Windsor Gardens, Malone Road, Belfast. *T:* Belfast 66990.

Died 24 July 1943.

McGOWAN, Rt Rev. Henry, MA; Bishop of Wakefield since 1946; b Bristol, 1891; e s of Henry McGowan; m 1918, Nora Heath, d of Edward William Godwin; two s. *Educ:* Bristol Grammar School; St Catharine's College, Cambridge (Scholar, Stewart of Rannoch Scholar); Ridley Hall. BA (2nd Class Classical Tripos), 1913; MA 1921. Curate of Cheltenham, 1914–16; St Michael's, Bournemouth, 1916–23; Chaplain, 4th Div., BEF, 1918–19; Vicar of St Mark, Birmingham, 1923–25; Emmanuel, Southport, 1925–31; Vicar of Aston, 1931–45; Archdeacon of Aston, and Hon. Canon of Birmingham, 1938–45; Hon. Association Padre of Toc H, 1930; Choirmaster and Organist of College of Cantors in Liverpool Cathedral, 1927–31; Bishop's Messenger, Diocese of Liverpool, 1928–31; Lecturer, St Aidan's Theological College, Birkenhead, 1928–31;

Director of Music to Cromer Convention, 1928–38; Rural Dean of Aston, 1931–38; Chaplain Territorial Army, attached to 8th Battalion The Royal Warwicks Regt 1935–40; Proctor in Convocation and Member of the National Church Assembly since 1936; Chairman Anglican Evangelical Group Movement, 1937–38; Chairman Birmingham Youth Committee, 1941–45; Member Education and Reconstruction Committees, City of Birmingham, 1942–45; Life Governor, Birmingham Univ.; Hon. Fellow, St Catharine's College, Cambridge, 1946; DD (Lambeth), 1947. *Publications:* Various articles and reviews on religious and musical topics; Communion Service, 1930; Te Deum, 1938. *Recreations:* music and drama, walking, motoring, squash rackets, etc. *Address:* Bishop's Lodge, Woodthorpe, Wakefield. *Club:* Junior United Service.

Died 8 Sept. 1948.

MACGRANAHAN, Very Rev. James, DD; Ex-Moderator of the Presbyterian Church in Ireland; Senior Minister of First Presbyterian Church, Londonderry; *b* Castlederg, Co. Tyrone, 1855; *s* of Benson MacGranahan, Principal of the Edwards' Endowed School; *m* 1887, May, 2nd *d* of John Glover, solicitor, Magherafelt; three *s* one *d. Educ:* Queen's Colleges, Galway and Belfast. Ordained, 1885; held pastorates in Magherafelt, Larne, Belfast, and Londonderry; retd 1927. *Publications:* occasional articles contributed to magazines. *Recreation:* golf. *Address:* 98 Balmoral Avenue, Belfast. *T:* Belfast 65918. *Club:* Malone Golf.

Died 5 April 1940.

McGRATH, Temp. Captain William, DSO 1940; Royal Engineers; *b* 8 July 1917; *s* of late James McGrath and Mrs E. D. McGrath. *Educ:* Coleraine AI (Northern Ireland); RMA Woolwich; Pembroke College, Cambridge. Entered RMA Woolwich, 1936; Commissioned Royal Engineers, 1938; served European War, France, 1940; evacuated from St Valery en Caux, June 12, 1940. *Recreations:* Rugby football, rowing, swimming. *Address:* Mountsandel, Coleraine, Co. Derry, N Ireland. *T:* Coleraine 310.

Died Feb. 1942.

MACGREGOR, Sir (Alasdair Duncan) Atholl, Kt 1935; Chief Justice of the Supreme Court of Hong Kong since 1934; *b* 4 June 1883; *s* of Robert Roy MacGregor ISO and Henrietta Davidson; *m* 1919, Gertrude Mary, *y d* of late R. Branton Tasker, Marino, Caernarvon; no *c. Educ:* George Watson's College, Edinburgh; Edinburgh University; Lincoln College, Oxford. MA (Edin.) 1902, BA (Oxon) 1905, Called to Bar at Lincoln's Inn, 1908; KC (Trinidad and Tobago) 1927; Assistant District Commissioner Southern Nigeria, 1912; Police Magistrate, Lagos, 1914–22; Crown Counsel, Nigeria, 1922; Solicitor General, Nigeria, 1923; Attorney General, Trinidad and Tobago, 1926; Attorney General, Kenya, 1929; Chairman Malayan Temporary Allowances Committee, 1937. *Recreations:* golf and walking. *Address:* Marino, Caernarvon, North Wales; Supreme Court, Hong Kong. *Club:* Royal Empire Society.

Died 30 Oct. 1945.

McGREGOR, Hon. Alexander John; *b* Robertson (Cape), 1864; *s* of Rev. Andrew McGregor; *m* 1891, Betty, *d* of late Pres. Brand; (one *s* killed on active service, 1916) three *d. Educ:* South African College, Cape Town; Oriel College, Oxford. President Oxford Union Society; Barrister, Inner Temple; admitted Cape Bar, 1889; State-Attorney, OFS, 1889; on Bench at Bloemfontein, 1892–95; resigned 1895, and resumed practice, Cape Town; Law Lecturer, South African College, 1896–98; KC, 1907; acted on the Bench at Kimberley and Grahamstown, 1910 and Capetown, 1912; went on Bench, Grahamstown, 1913; Bloemfontein, 1915; Judge of the Supreme Court, South Africa, Orange Free State Prov. Div.; retired, 1929. *Publications:* Translation of Voct on Fideicommissa, with

annotations, 1897; compiled Digest of Laws affecting Natives for the South African Native Affairs Commission (Bluebook), 1904; A. W. McGregor—A Memoir, 1917. *Address:* Ravensnest, Waterkloof, Pretoria, S Africa. *Clubs:* Civil Service, Cape Town; Pretoria, Pretoria; Bloemfontein, Bloemfontein.

Died 28 Nov. 1946.

MACGREGOR, Sir Atholl; *see* Macgregor, Sir A. D. A.

MACGREGOR, Rev. Duncan Campbell, DD; *b* 24 April 1858; *er s* of late Rev. Duncan Macgregor; *m* 1888, Christina (*d* 1938), *e surv. d* of William Ranken Fortune of Muircambus, Fife; one *s. Educ:* Dundee High School; Edinburgh University (MA 1877); Free Church College, Glasgow. Minister (Free Church of Scotland) at Elie, Fife, 1882–95; Minister of Trinity Presbyterian Church, Wimbledon, 1895–1930; Editor of Presbyterian, 1904–06; Convener of Publications Committee, Presbyterian Church of England, 1906–16, and of Foreign Mission Committee, 1917–27; Moderator of his Church, 1920–21; DD Edinburgh University, 1921; retired, 1930. *Publications:* Life of G. H. C. Macgregor; a number of sermons and articles in magazines. *Address:* 23 York Avenue, Sheen Lane, SW14. *T:* Prospect 5775.

Died 9 Aug. 1943.

MACGREGOR, Eric Dickson, CB 1946; *b* 29 Dec. 1886; *s* of George Macgregor, MA, teacher; *m* 1911, Maisie, *d* of Dr James Stevenson; no *c. Educ:* Glasgow High School; University, Glasgow and University, Oxford. Entered Civil Service, 1911. Local Government Board; Assistant Secretary, Ministry of Health; Director of Establishments, Ministry of Health, 1939–47. *Recreation:* walking. *Address:* 63 York Mansions, Battersea Park, SW11. *T:* Macaulay 1989. *Club:* Reform.

Died 11 Jan. 1950.

MACGREGOR, James Cochran Stevenson; Head of Staff Training, BBC, since 1948; *b* Glasgow, 29 May 1897; *y s* of late Very Rev. W. M. Macgregor, DD; *m* 1921, Mary Katharine, *e d* of Rev. Arthur Herbert Gray; four *d. Educ:* Bootham School, York; Edinburgh University; Trinity College, Oxford (BA 1920). Served European War, Royal Artillery, 1915–18; administrative staff, English Electric Co., 1920; joined BBC, 1925; first Editor, Empire News Service, 1934; Empire Programme Director, 1936; seconded to Ministry of Information, 1939; Director of Broadcasting Division, 1941; Assistant Controller, Deputy Editor, and Acting Editor (News) of BBC, 1942–48. *Address:* 5 Fordington Road, N6. *T:* Tudor 1464. *Club:* Oxford and Cambridge.

Died 30 Aug. 1949.

MACGREGOR, John Julius, CBE 1920; *b* 1869. Was Chairman of Directing Board of Gloucester Filling Factory, Ministry of Munitions, during European War. *Address:* c/o Midland Bank, Porthcawl, Glam.

Died 4 April 1948.

MACGREGOR, Robert Menzies, CMG 1929; *b* 24 July 1882; *s* of late Atholl MacGregor, Madras Civil Service. *Educ:* Glenalmond; King's College School; RIE College, Coopers Hill. Assistant Engineer PWD, Punjab, 1903; Executive Engineer, 1911; Superintending Engineer, 1926; services lent to the Sudan Government, 1923; retired from Indian Service, 1929; retired from Sudan Service, 1937; Nile, 2nd Class, 1932; Commander, Hungarian Order of Merit, 1936. *Clubs:* Caledonian, Travellers'.

Died 8 Jan. 1946.

MACGREGOR, Very Rev. Dr William Malcolm, DD, LLD; *b* Glasgow, 1861; *m* Amy, *d* of J. C. Stevenson, MP; one *s* two *d. Educ:* Edinburgh University; Free Church College, Glasgow. Minister in Troon, Glasgow, and Edinburgh; Moderator, United Free Church of Scotland, 1919; Baird Lecturer, 1913; Warrack Lecturer, 1942; Professor of NT Exegesis, Trinity College, Glasgow, 1919–35, Principal, 1928–38.

Publications: Jesus Christ the Son of God; Christian Freedom; Repentance unto Life; Some of God's Ministries; For Christ and the Kingdom; Christ and the Church; Persons and Ideals. *Address:* 8 Braid Avenue, Edinburgh.

Died 12 July 1944.

McGRIGOR, Lt-Col Sir Charles Colquhoun, 4th Bt *cr* 1831; OBE 1921; late 2nd Battalion Rifle Brigade; *b* 26 April 1893; *s* of 3rd Bt and Helen, *s* of J. G. Meiggs, an American; *S* father, 1924; *m* 1919, Amabel, *o d* of late E. L. Somers Cocks, 47 Wilton Crescent, and Bake, St Germans, Cornwall; one *s. Educ:* Eton; Sandhurst. *Recreations:* shooting, fishing. *Heir: s* Charles Edward, *b* 1922. *Club:* Army and Navy.

Died 28 Oct. 1946.

MACHEN, Arthur; author; *b* 1863. *Publications:* Eleusinia: The Anatomy of Tobacco; The Chronicle of Clemendy; The Great God Pan; The Three Impostors; The Hill of Dreams; The House of Souls; Dr Stiggins; Hieroglyphics; The Bowmen; The Great Return; The Terror; War and the Christian Faith; The Secret Glory; Far Off Things; Things Near and Far; The Shining Pyramid; Dog and Duck: a London Calendar; Strange Roads; Ornaments in Jade; The London Adventure; The Canning Wonder; Dreads and Drolls; The Green Round; The Cosy Room; The Children of the Pool, 1936; A Handy Dickens, 1941; Holy Terrors, 1946. *Recreation:* Dog and Duck. *Address:* Amersham, Bucks.

Died 15 Dec. 1947.

MACHRAY, Robert, BA; author, journalist, writer on Foreign Affairs; formerly Canon of St John's Cathedral, Winnipeg, and Professor of Ecclesiastical History, Lecturer in English Literature, etc., St John's College, University of Manitoba, Canada; *b* Fyvie, Aberdeenshire, 1857; *s* of late W. Forsyth Machray, JP; *m* 1886, Kathleen Beatrice, *d* of S. J. Vankoughnet, KC, Toronto; one *d. Educ:* St John's Coll. School, Winnipeg; Univ. of Manitoba (1st Medallist), Winnipeg; Sidney Sussex, Cambridge (Scholar). Ordained, 1883; served under his uncle, the first Archbishop of Rupert's Land, till 1889, when continued throat-affection compelled him to resign; has travelled extensively; first novel published, 1898; has written for many Brit. and USA magazines and journals; specialises Middle East subjects and Central and South-Eastern Europe generally; War Editor of the Daily Mail, 1904–05; Foreign Affairs Critic, Saturday Review, 1921–24. *Publications:* Poland, 1914–1931; The Little Entente to 1929; The Poland of Pilsudski, 1914–1936; The Struggle for the Danube and the Little Entente, 1929–1938; The Eastern Question Revived, 1939; The Polish-German Problem, 1941; East Prussia, 1943; The Problem of Upper Silesia, 1945; Life of Archbishop Machray; Grace O'Malley, Princess and Pirate; The Vision Splendid (with Miss Florence Bright); Sir Hector; A Blow over the Heart; The Night Side of London (illustrated by Tom Browne); The Mystery of Lincoln's Inn; The Ambassador's Glove; The Private Detective; Her Honour; The Mystery of the Middle Temple; The Disappearance of Lady Diana; Sentenced to Death; The Woman Wins; Her Secret Life; The Stanhope Gate Mystery. *Address:* Tudor Court Hotel, Cromwell Road, SW7.

Died 24 Jan. 1946.

MACILREITH, R. T.; KC Canada. Chairman NS Board of Commissioners of Public Utilities; late Mayor of Halifax, Nova Scotia. *Address:* Halifax, NS.

Died 13 July 1943.

MACILWAINE, Dr Alexander Gillilan Johnson, CIE 1916; late Major RAMC; *b* 4 Jan. 1887; *s* of late Edward Nangle MacIlwaine, Belfast; *m* Adela Rose, *d* of Alex. Taylor, Belfast; one *s* one *d. Educ:* Roy. Belfast Academical Institution; Royal School, Armagh; Queen's Univ., Belfast, LRCSI, LRCPI; Post Graduate London and Middlesex Hospitals. Hon. Surgeon to the Viceroy

in India, 1915–20; Embarkation, DADMS, Bombay; served European War, Mesopotamia (despatches, Bt Major); services acknowledged by Mesopotamia Sanitary Commission; Officer of St John of Jerusalem; retired, 1922. *Address:* 57 and 74 Chesterfield House, Chesterfield Gardens, Curzon St, W1. *T:* Mayfair 6740.

Died 3 March 1942.

MACILWAINE, John Bedell Stanford, RHA 1911; ARHA 1893; *b* Dublin, 21 April 1857. *Educ:* High School, Dublin. Studied architecture under late Sir Thomas Drew, PRHA; afterwards attended the Schools of the Royal Hibernian Academy to study painting. Rarely paints anything but Irish landscapes; interested in submarine devices; acted as Engineer for the Conan Submarine Fuze from the initial to final stage; made the first accurate and reliable fuze for exploding depth charges, principle established at Woolwich Arsenal in March 1913, tested officially at Lydd following Sept., each shot marked correct; purchase ordered by Ordnance Board; invented the automatic aeroplane range-finder and many tools in connection with fuzes; universal hopper (adjustable); was one of those kidnapped into Free States in 1922; appointed a member of Fine Art Committee in connection with Ulster Pavilion at Wembley Exhibition, 1924–25; one of the Founder Members of the Irish Arts Club, and Imperial Three Arts Club. *Publications:* matters relating to art; numismatics; gardening; poultry; spiritism; Practical Poultry Keeping for Women; How England played the Game; Tales Retold, Facts and Faries; Sketching from Nature with Oil Colours; MDCCLVII and After. *Recreations:* numismatics, angling, shooting, gardening. *Address:* Annaghroe House, Caledon, Co. Tyrone. *TA:* Caledon. *Club:* Imperial Three Arts.

Died 14 Jan. 1945.

McILWAINE, Hon. Sir Robert, Kt 1939; KC; MA; LLB; *b* 1871; *s* of late Henry McIlwaine, Larne, Ireland; *m* 1902, Sophia Mary, *d* of late George Hanna, Ballymena; three *s* two *d. Educ:* Queen's Colleges, Belfast and Galway. Joined Civil Service of Cape Colony, 1895; transferred to Rhodesian Service, 1898; held many offices, e.g. Magistrate, Inspector of Schools, Master of High Court, High Sheriff, Solicitor-General, official member Legislative Council, Water Court Judge and Judge of High Court from which latter position retired in 1898; Chairman National Resources Board, 1941; has acted as Chairman of several Commissions. *Recreations:* arboriculture and horticulture. *Address:* Salisbury Club, S Rhodesia.

Died Oct. 1943.

McILWRAITH, Sir Malcolm, KCMG 1905; CMG 1904; KC 1914; *b* London, 18 July 1865; *o s* of late Robert M'Ilwraith of 35 Hans Place, S.W., and formerly of Bombay, and Mary, *d* of William Greenwood, FRCS, of Huddersfield; *m* 1900, Evelyn Sydney (*d* 1921), 2nd *d* of Sir Richard Douglas Powell, 1st Bt, MD; one *s* one *d. Educ:* Marlborough; Berlin University; Paris School of Law. Licencié en droit de la Faculté de Paris, 1887 (Honours); called to Bar, Lincoln's Inn, 1890; Bencher, 1922; Judicial Adviser to the Egyptian Government, 1898–1916; instituted Criminal Assize Courts in Egypt, 1905; holds Grand Cordon of Order of Medjidieh, and Grand Cordon Order of the Nile. *Publications:* articles in the Fortnightly, XIXth Century, Law Quarterly, and other Reviews. *Address:* 36 Stanhope Gardens, SW7. *T:* Kensington 6783. *Clubs:* Brooks's, Garrick.

Died 18 March 1941.

McINTOSH, Alexander Morrison, CMG 1919; TD; MB, ChB; FRCSE; Senior Regional Medical Officer, retired, Department of Health for Scotland; *b* 3 March 1877; *s* of David McIntosh, hosiery manufacturer, Edinburgh and Galashiels; *m* Janet, *d* of late Rev. G. W. Strang, Cambeltown; three *d. Educ:* George Watson's College, Edinburgh; Edinburgh University. Demonstrator in Anatomy and Pathology; House

Surgeon, Royal Infirmary, Edinburgh; House Surgeon, Royal Hospital for Sick Children, Edinburgh; Physician, Cowgate Dispensary, Edinburgh; Physician, Cowgate Dispensary, Edinburgh; Surgeon, Ponton Street Dispensary, Edinburgh; Clinical Tutor to Professor of Clinical Surgery, Edinburgh University; House Surgeon and Clinical Assistant, Ear, Nose and Throat Department, Royal Infirmary, Edinburgh; Clinical Assistant, Lock Wards, Royal Infirmary, Edinburgh; Assistant Director of Medical Services, 52nd Division, 65th Division and 67th Division; Acting Deputy Director of Medical Services, 8th Corps, Egyptian Expeditionary Force. *Recreations:* golf, motoring. *Address:* 1 Relugas Road, Edinburgh. *T:* Edinburgh 42790.
Died 19 March 1944.

McINTOSH, George, CBE 1944; ED 1937; Manager Hantapara Tea Estate; Chairman, Dooars Planters' Association, 1939–44; *b* 18 Jan. 1889; *m* 1919, Katherine Bennett Mitchell; three *s* one *d. Educ:* Harris Academy and Dundee Technical College, Dundee, Scotland. Tea Planter since 1910; Manager since 1918; Member District Board, Jalpaiguri, since 1924; Second-in-Command, Northern Bengal Mounted Rifles, 1937–39; Vice-Chairman, Dooars Planters' Assoc. 1938. *Recreations:* hill climbing, shooting. *Address:* Hantapara Tea Estate, Hantupara PO (Jalpaiguri) Dooars, Bengal, India. *Clubs:* Bengal, Bengal United Service (Calcutta).
Died 24 Oct. 1949.

McINTOSH, Hon. Hugh Donald; JP; Associate Member of Academie Diplomatique Internationale; *b* Sydney, NSW, 10 Sept. 1876; *s* of Hugh McIntosh, 42nd Highlanders; *m* 1897, Marion Catherine Backhouse, *d* of Thomas Backhouse, JP, of Sydney; no *c.* Past President of the British Empire League in Australia; Life Governor of Sydney Hospital, Prince Alfred Hospital, Royal Alexandra Hospital for Women, St Austin Home for Incurables, Victoria, New South Wales Benevolent Society and National Advertising Benevolent Society; Founder and Member of The Australia Day Committee; Founder of Australasian Branch of the Egypt Exploration Society; Patron and Past President Returned Soldiers' Association, New South Wales; Life Member Australian Historical Society, Sydney Cenotaph Permanent Committee and Sydney Citizens Committee; Fellow Royal Empire Society; recipient of illuminated address and public presentation from the forty-two surviving Australian holders of the Victoria Cross; recipient of address of thanks from Returned Soldiers' Association upon resigning presidency; Member of Allies Day Committee; Chairman and Treasurer of the Anzac Day Memorial Committee; President of the Anzac Returned Soldiers' Band; Founder and Past President of Milk Bar Association of Great Britain and Ireland; Organising Secretary of Timber Building Manufacturers' Association of Great Britain, Ltd. *Recreation:* active interest in sport in all its branches. *Address:* Taurmead, Lock Avenue, Maidenhead. *T:* Maidenhead 1237. *Clubs:* Royal Automobile, British Sportsman's; Phyllis Court, Henley; National, National Sporting of Australasia, Sydney.
Died 2 Feb. 1942.

MacINTYRE, Ian, MA, LLB, WS; *b* Greenock, 27 Nov. 1869; *s* of late Duncan MacIntyre, shipowner, Edinburgh; *m* 1st, 1896, Ida (*d* 1942), *e d* of Charles Van der Gucht; one *s* three *d;* 2nd, 1942, Gwendoline Maude, *d* of Henry Coates, Newcastle. *Educ:* Fettes College and University, Edinburgh. Writer to the Signet since 1893; MP (U) West Edinburgh, 1924–29; Member of Edinburgh Town Council, 1918–20; Member RCA. *Recreations:* golf, shooting, formerly Rugby football; Scottish International XV 1890 and 1891. *Address:* 32 Ormidale Terrace, Murrayfield, Edinburgh. *T:* Edinburgh Central 61973. *Clubs:* Conservative; University, Edinburgh.
Died 29 June 1946.

McINTYRE, Air Vice-Marshal Sir John, KBE 1935; CB 1932; MC, MA, MB, BCh. *Educ:* King's College, Cambridge (Vintner Exhibition); 1st Class Natural Science Tripos, 1902; St Mary's Hospital. Late House Surgeon and House Physician, St Mary's Hospital; Director of RAF Medical Services, 1930–35; retired list, 1935; re-employed, RAF as Group Capt., 1939–45; late Hon. Surgeon to the King. *Club:* Caledonian.
Died 7 Oct. 1950.

MACINTYRE, Margaret; *d* of late Lieut-Gen. Macintyre, RA. *Educ:* Received musical training at Dr Wylde's London Academy of Music under Signor Garcia, brother of Mme Malibran and Mme Viardot Garcia. Toured through Russia and on other parts of the Continent, as well as South Africa and America; was prima donna at La Scala, Milan, Petrograd, Moscow, etc.
Died April 1943.

MACIVER, David R.; *see* Randall-Maciver.

MACK, Rear-Adm. Philip John, DSO 1940; RN; *b* 6 Oct. 1892; *s* of Major Paston Mack, 12th Lancers, of Paston Hall, Norwich; *m* 1930, Elizabeth, *d* of Cecil Percy Dawson, Shanghai, China. *Educ:* RN Colleges, Osborne and Dartmouth. Joined RN 1905; served European War, 1914–19; Capt. 1934; Naval Attaché S America, 1936–39; War of 1939–45 (DSO and Bar). *Address:* Paston Hall, Norwich. *T:* Mundesley 79. *Club:* United Service.
Died 29 April 1943.

MACKAIL, John William, OM 1935; MA, LLD (Edinburgh, St Andrews, and Adelaide), LittD (Cambridge), DLitt (Oxford), DLit (London and Queen's University, Belfast), FBA, Hon. ARIBA, FRSL; Professor of Ancient Literature in the Royal Academy; Professor of Poetry, Oxford University, 1906–11; President of the Classical Association, 1922–23; of the English Association, 1929–30; of the British Academy, 1932–36; Hon. Fellow (formerly Scholar and Fellow) of Balliol College, Oxford; Examiner and Assistant Secretary, Board of Education, 1885–1919; *b* 1859; *m* 1888, Margaret, *o d* of Sir Edward Burne-Jones, 1st Bt; one *s* two *d. Publications:* Select Epigrams from the Greek Anthology, 1890; Latin Literature, 1895; Life of William Morris, 1899; The Springs of Helicon, 1909; Lectures on Greek Poetry, 1910; Lectures on Poetry, 1911; Life of George Wyndham, 1925; Classical Studies, 1925; JL Strachan-Davidson, a Memoir, 1926; Studies of English Poets, 1926; The Aeneid of Virgil, 1930; The Approach to Shakespeare, 1930; The Odyssey in English Verse, 1932; Studies in Humanism, 1938; The Sayings of Christ, 1938. *Address:* 6 Pembroke Gardens, Kensington, W8. *T:* Western 5139. *Club:* Athenæum.
Died 13 Dec. 1945.

MACKAY, Ernest John Henry, MA, DLitt, FSA; Archæologist; Air Raid Warden, Kensington, since 1940; *b* 5 July 1880; *s* of Richard Cockrill Mackay and Mary Dermott Thomas; *m* 1912, Dorothy Mary Simmons, BA, BSc; one *s. Educ:* Bristol Grammar School; Bristol University. Archæological excavations in Egypt, 1907–12; Excavations and photographic survey of Theban Tombs, 1913–16; war service in Egypt and Palestine (Capt., RASC), 1916–19; Member Army Commission for Survey of Ancient Monuments in Palestine and Syria, 1919–20; Custodian of Antiquities, Palestine Government, 1919–22; Field Director of Oxford Univ. and Field Museum, Chicago, Archæological Expedition to Mesopotamia, 1922–26; Director of Excavations at Bahrein, Persian Gulf, for the British School of Archæology in Egypt, 1925; Special Officer for Exploration, Archæological Survey of India, 1926–31; Director of Expedition of American School of Indic and Iranian Studies and Boston Museum of Fine Arts to Chanhudaro, India, 1935–36. *Publications:* Contributions to reports of British School of

Archæology in Egypt, 1910–1915; Hébron, Le Haram el Khalil (with Père L. H. Vincent), 1923; The 'A' Cemetery at Kish, 1925; A Sumerian Palace and the 'A' Cemetery at Kish, 1926; Bahrein and Hemamieh, 1929; Excavations at Jemdet Nasr, Iraq, 1930; Mohenjodaro, and the Indus Civilization (with Sir John Marshall and others), 1931; The Indus Civilization, 1935; Further Excavations at Mohenjo-daro (1927–1931), 1938; Chanhu-daro Excavations, 1941; and numerous contributions to archæological journals. *Recreations:* archery, metal-work, and travel.

Died 2 Oct. 1943.

MACKAY, George, MD, FRCSE, MRCS Eng., MRCSE; Member of the Royal Company of Archers, King's Bodyguard for Scotland; *e s* of late Deputy-Surg.-Gen. George Mackay, Madras Army, and Ellen Rose Robertson, *d* of late Arthur J. Robertson of Inches, Inverness-shire; *m* 1896, Elise Marjorie, *d* of late Lt-Col Sir Alexander Burness M'Hardy, KCB, RE; three *s*. *Educ:* Clifton College; Inverness College; Univ. of Edinburgh; Vienna; London, etc. Formerly Lecturer on Diseases of the Eye, Univ. of Edinburgh; President Royal College of Surgeons, Edinburgh, 1919–21; Vice-President Ophthalmological Society of United Kingdom; President Caledonian Medical Society; late Ophthalmic Medical Referee under the Workmen's Compensation Act; late Consulting Ophthalmic Surgeon to the Royal Infirmary, Deaconess Hospital, Royal Blind Asylum, and Deaf and Dumb Inst. *Publications:* contributions to ophthalmic literature and antiquarian notes. *Recreations:* golf, fishing; Seanachaidh and Hon. Librarian to the Clan Mackay Society. *Address:* 9 Belford Avenue, Edinburgh 4. *T:* 24929. *Club:* University Union (Edinburgh).

Died 8 May 1949.

McKAY, Ven. John; *b* 1870; *s* of John McKay, Brydekirk, Dumfries, and Woburn, Beds; *m* 1900, S. C. Grover; one *s* one *d*. *Educ:* Howard House School, Thame; Church Missionary College, Islington. Seven years training as an Architect; to Nigeria as a layman under the CMS 1893; ordained 1904; Pioneer work at Oshogbo, Nigeria, 1900–18; Rector of Norton-sub-Hamdon, Somerset, 1919–25; returned to Nigeria 1925 as Archdeacon of the Yoruba Country and Secretary of the Mission; Examiner in the Yoruba language to the Nigerian Govt and to the CMS; retired from CMS 1929; Rector of Swithland, Leicestershire, 1931–40; Examiner in Yoruba to the Universities of London, Oxford, Cambridge and Glasgow. *Publications:* Ifarapa Aisan (a small booklet on simple treatment of Tropical Diseases written for African Teachers); Life of Bishop Crowther (for African boys). *Recreation:* lawn tennis. *Address:* Brydekirk, Rothley Plain, nr Leicester. *T:* Rothley 264.

Died 14 March 1942.

McKECHNIE, Sir William Wallace, KBE 1935; CB 1930; MA (Edin.), BA (Oxon); LLD (Edin.); *e s* of late William McKechnie, Edinburgh; *m* 1905, Elizabeth, *e d* of late James Coutts, SSC, Edinburgh; one *s* two *d*. *Educ:* Daniel Stewart's College, Edinburgh; Edinburgh University (Ferguson Scholar, 1895); Trinity College, Oxford (1st Classical Moderations, 1896; 1st Literæ Humaniores, 1898); studied in France. Assistant in Greek, University of Edinburgh, 1898–99; Lecturer in Humanity, University of Glasgow, 1899–1901; Junior Inspector of Schools, 1901–03; HM Inspector of Schools, 1903–22; Permanent Secretary, Scottish Education Department; retired 1936; Member of: Departmental Committee on Sexual Offences against Children in Scotland, 1924–26; Departmental Committee on Young Offenders in Scotland, 1925–28; Departmental Committee on Examinations of Masters and Mates, 1927–28; Scottish Committee of the Board of Trade Council for Art and Industry, 1934–35; Home Office Committee on Corporal Punishment, 1937–38;

Scottish Council Physical Fitness, 1937–38; Special Committee on Grants to Scottish Universities, 1937–38; Hon. Fellow Educational Institute of Scotland, 1935; Hon. Member, Edinburgh Company of Merchants, 1936; Member of Edinburgh Town Council since 1937, Bailie 1944. *Publication:* edition of Baudelaire's Scarabée d'Or. *Address:* 9 Canaan Lane, Edinburgh 10. *Clubs:* Scottish Conservative, Edinburgh.

Died 23 Aug. 1947.

McKEE, Col Samuel Hanford, CMG 1916; BA, MD, CM; FRCS (C); Oculist to the Montreal General Hospital; *b* Fredericton, NB, Canada, 11 Oct. 1875; *s* of Samuel H. McKee, manufacturer, and Jean Armour; *m* 1906, Shirley Britton, *d* of Mrs D. Colin Cowan, of Gananoque, Ontario, Canada. *Educ:* Model School, Fredericton, Governor-General's Medal; University of New Brunswick, BA 1896, Douglas Gold Medal; MD McGill 1900; Freiburg, Baden, 1903–05. House Surgeon, Royal Victoria Hospital, 1900–03; Oculist to Montreal Maternity Hospital, 1907; Secretary to Montreal Medico-Chirurgical Society later President; Oculist to Alexandra Hospital; Demonstrator and Lecturer in Bacteriology, and later Professor of Ophthalmology, McGill, 1939; Colonel CAMC Dec. 1917; served European War (despatches, CMG); Member of American Association of Pathologists, American Academy of Ophthalmology and Oto-Laryngology (Pres. 1932), American Ophthalmological Society, Oxford Ophthalmological Congress. *Publications:* (papers) Ueber Dionin; The Bacteriology of Conjunctivitis; Meningococcus Conjunctivitis; A New Pathogenic Micro-organism of the Conjunctiva; Morax Axenfeld Conjunctivitis, The Bacteriology of the Eye, for The Encyclopedia of Ophthalmology; The Nature of Trachoma Bodies (with Dr S. B. Wolbach), and numerous other articles. *Recreations:* fishing, golf, badminton; President, Canadian Badminton Association, 1920–32. *Address:* 1528 Crescent Street, Montreal. *Clubs:* Mount Royal, University, Royal Montreal Golf, Badminton and Squash, Montreal.

Died 25 Nov. 1942.

MACKEITH, Malcolm Henry, DM (Oxon), MRCP (London); Dean of the British Postgraduate Medical School since 1934; *b* 14 April 1895; *s* of Alexander Arthur Mackeith, MB, CM, and Alice, *e d* of Henry Gadd, Exeter; *m* 1925, Joan Parr, *o d* of Ernest Mallam, DM (Oxon); two *s* one *d*. *Educ:* King Edward VI School, Southampton; Queen's College, Oxford (Southampton Exhibitioner); Guy's Hospital (Entrance Scholarship). 27th Field Ambulance, 9th (Scottish) Division, 1914–17; Theodore Williams Scholarship in Physiology, Oxford, 1st Class Honours Final Honour School of Natural Science (Physiology), Oxford, 1919; BM, BCh Oxford; Lecturer Magdalen College, Oxford, 1921; Fellow and Tutor in Medicine, Magdalen College, 1922–33; Home Bursar, 1926–30, Dean of the Medical School, Oxford, 1930–33; University Demonstrator in Pharmacology, 1923–33; Recorder of Section I (Physiology) British Association for the Advancement of Science, 1926–31; Secretary of British Pharmacological Society from foundation, 1931. *Publications:* papers in scientific journals.

Died 5 Feb. 1942.

McKENNA, Harold; a Metropolitan Police Magistrate, 1927–46; formerly at Greenwich, Lambeth, and Marylebone Courts; Bow Street, 1936–46; *b* 1879; *e s* of late Leopold and Ellen McKenna of Honeys, Waltham St Lawrence, Berks; *m* Gwladys, *y d* of late Martin Edwards of Beech Hill, Usk, Mon; one *d*. *Educ:* Westminster; Christ Church, Oxford; MA. Called to Bar, Inner Temple, 1903; joined Oxford Circuit; several times a Commissioner under the Municipal Corporations Acts for the preparation of Schemes for Ward Boundaries; was a Referee under the Contributory Pensions Act;

Chairman Berks Quarter Sessions, 1945–46; JP. *Address:* Fairfield, Burnham, Bucks. *T:* Burnham 100. *Clubs:* Reform; Berkshire Reading.

Died 19 Dec. 1946.

McKENNA, Brig. James Charles, CB 1936; DSO 1916; Indian Army retired; *b* 4 Aug. 1879. 2nd Lieut, Border Regt, 1898; Lieut, Indian Army, 1901; Capt. 1907; Major, 1915; Lt-Col, 1921; Col, 1927; retired, 1936.

Died 23 Sept. 1943.

McKENNA, Rt Rev. Patrick; RC Bishop of Clogher since 1909; *b* 1869. *Educ:* Monaghan; Maynooth. Ordained 1894; Professor at St Kieran's College, Kilkenny, 1897–1901; Professor; Maynooth, 1904–09. *Publication:* one of the founders Irish Theological Quarterly. *Address:* The Palace, Monaghan.

Died 7 Feb. 1942.

McKENNA, Rt Hon. Reginald; PC 1907; Chairman Midland Bank, Limited, since 1919; *b* London, 6 July 1863; *y s* of late Wm Columban McKenna; *m* 1908, Pamela, *d* of late Sir Herbert Jekyll, KCMG; one *s. Educ:* privately; King's Coll., London; Trinity Hall, Cambridge (Scholar and Hons in Mathematics, Hon. Fellow, 1916). Contested Clapham, 1892; Barr 1887; practised till election to Parliament; MP (L) N Monmouthshire, 1895–1918; Financial Secretary to the Treasury, 1905; President of Board of Education, 1907–08; First Lord of the Admiralty, 1908–11; Home Secretary, 1911–15; Chancellor of the Exchequer, 1915–16. *Publication:* Post-War Banking Policy, 1928. *Recreations:* bow, Cambridge University Eight, 1887; winner of the Grand and Steward's Cups at Henley. *Address:* 70 Pall Mall, SW1. *T:* Whitehall 2633; Halnaker Park, Chichester, Sussex. *Club:* Brooks's.

Died 6 Sept. 1943.

MACKENNAL, Ven. William Leavers, MA; Archdeacon of Ely since 1942; *b* 2 Feb. 1881; *s* of Alexander Mackennal, BA, DD, and Fanny Mackennal, BA, DD, and Fanny Mackennal; *m* 1913, Gladys Hope Whitworth; no *c. Educ:* Rugby; Trinity College, Cambridge; Bishop's Hostel, Farnham. Deacon, 1907; Priest, 1908; Asst Curate Great St Mary's, Cambridge, 1907; Chaplain Westcott House, Cambridge, 1908; Curate of Dunster, 1909–13; CF, 1915–18; Rector of Compton Martin, 1914–19; Vicar of Chesterton, Cambridge, 1919–33; Kirkby Lonsdale, 1933–37; Hitchin, 1937–42; Select Preacher Cambridge University, 1910 and 1943. *Publication:* Life of Major John Haworth Whitworth, 1918. *Address:* Boxmoor Cottage, Cambridge.

Died 20 June 1947.

MACKENZIE, Alastair Oswald Morison; KC Scotland; *b* 1858; 4th *s* of Lord Mackenzie, one of the Senators of the Scottish College of Justice; *m* 1903, Isabella Rose Forbes (*d* 1913), *d* of Lt-Col A. Forbes Mackay; one *d. Educ:* Loretto; Brasenose College, Oxford. Called to Scottish Bar, 1885; Advocate Depute, 1900–02; Sheriff-Substitute of Lanarkshire, 1902–12; Sheriff of Inverness, Elgin, and Nairn, 1912–17; Renfrewshire, 1917; Lanarkshire, 1917–33. *Recreations:* golf, fishing. *Address:* Noble Tree Cross, Hildenborough, Kent.

Died 28 Aug. 1949.

MACKENZIE, Sir Alexander, KBE 1919; Director Brazilian Traction, Light and Power Co; *b* 30 June 1860; *m* 1908, May, MBE (*d* 1937), *d* of late S. H. Blake, KC, Toronto. Called to Bar, Toronto, 1883. *Address:* Villa Benivieni, Florence, Italy; 25 King Street West, Toronto 2, Canada. *Clubs:* Brooks's; Toronto, York, Toronto.

Died 12 July 1943.

MACKENZIE, Col Edward Leslie, CIE 1919; DSO 1900; *b* 6 May 1870; *s* of late Major C. G. Mackenzie, 28th Rgt; *g s* of Admiral James George Mackenzie of Forret, Fife; *m* 1920, Irene, *widow* of Francis Ware, *er d* of late James McGean. Entered army, 1890; Capt. 1899; Major, 1907; Lt-Col 1915; Col 1919; served South Africa, 1900 and 1902 (severely wounded, despatches, Queen's medal 4 clasps, King's medal 2 clasps, DSO); West Indian Frontier, 1918–19; retired pay, 1922. *Address:* Herne Lodge, Tunbridge Wells.

Died 2 June 1947.

MACKENZIE, George, FRGS; Editor, Northern Chronicle, Inverness; *b* Cromarty, 25 Nov. 1881; *y s* of late A. H. Mackenzie, Registrar, etc; *m* Florence, *y d* of Wm Bell, Middlesbro'; one *d. Educ:* Cromarty Higher Grade School. Working journalist since 1900; chief reporter, Daily Chronicle, British Guiana, 1908–11; Assistant Literary Editor, Timehri, a Guiana magazine devoted to discovery, research, and sociology; Hon. Secretary, British Guiana Museum, and Hon. Secretary, Scientific and Literary Sub-Committees of Royal Agricultural and Commercial Society, British Guiana. *Recreations:* photography and angling. *Address:* The Sutors, 28 Broadstone Park, Inverness. *T:* 717.

Died 20 Jan. 1950.

MACKENZIE, H. Millicent, MA; Professor of Education, University College, S Wales, and Monmouthshire, 1904–15; Hon. Dean of Education as National Service Training Scheme, 1916–22; *b* 1863; *d* of late W. W. Hughes of Clifton, Bristol; *m* 1898, J. Stuart Mackenzie (*d* 1935). *Educ:* schools in Clifton and in Switzerland; University College, Bristol; Cambridge Training College. First appointed Lecturer in Education, 1891; has travelled inspecting schools and lecturing in India, Burmah and Ceylon, Germany, Switzerland, and United States. *Publications:* Training of Teachers in the United States; Hegel's Theory and Practice of Education; Freedom in Education; John Stuart Mackenzie (an edited Autobiography); various pamphlets and papers on educational subjects. *Address:* Upfield Cottage and Upcot, Brockweir, Mon. *T:* Tintern 263.

Died 10 Dec. 1942.

MACKENZIE, Col Harry Malcolm, CIE 1932; MB, ChB, DPH, Cambridge; IMS (retd); *s* of late Alexander Mackenzie, MA; *m* 1907, Elfreda, *d* of late A. A. Hudson, KC; one *s* one *d. Educ:* Larchfield School, Helensburgh; Royal High School, Edinburgh; Edinburgh University. Indian service, mainly in NW Frontier Province and Punjab; served European War, 1914–18 (1914 star, two medals). *Publications:* various contributions to Lancet and British Medical Journal. *Recreations:* golf, fishing, shooting. *Address:* Redgates, Fleet, Hants. *Club:* North Hants Golf.

Died 25 Feb. 1947.

M'KENZIE, Rev. Harry Ward, MA; *b* St Albans, 10 Dec. 1850; *m* 1889, Maude (*d* 1940), *e d* of Rev. H. G. Merriman, DD; one *s. Educ:* Keble College, Oxford. 2nd class Lit. Hum., 1874. Assistant master at Loretto School and at St Paul's College, Stony Stratford; tutor and bursar, Wellington College; headmaster, Lancing College, 1889–94; 2nd master, Durham School, 1894; headmaster, Durham School, 1905–07; Uppingham School, 1907–15; member of Classical Association. *Address:* 25 Winchester Road, Oxford. *Clubs:* National Liberal, MCC, Surrey County CC.

Died 17 April 1941.

MACKENZIE, Lt-Col Herbert John, DSO 1917; late (PWO) 12th Frontier Force Regt; *b* 19 Sept. 1878; *e s* of late P. W. J. Mackenzie; *m* 1917, Vere, *d* of Colonel C. ff. Churchill; one *s* one *d. Educ:* Dover College 2nd Batt. King's Own Scottish Borderers; served S Africa, 1900–01 (medal and 4 clasps); North-West Frontier of India, 1908 (medal and clasp); European War, 1914–18 (despatches, DSO); retired, 1928; Albanian Gendarmerie; Commander of the Order of Skanderbeg, 1930. *Address:* c/o Grindlay & Co., 54 Parliament Street, SW1. *Club:* United Service.

Died 4 Aug. 1941.

M'KENZIE, Hon. Hugh; JP, Victoria and New South Wales; *b* Highlands of Scotland, 1853; *m* 1878; four *s* two *d. Educ:* Scotch College, Melbourne. Came to Australia with parents, 1855; went into business at the age of 21; entered municipal life as a member of the Borough Council of Echuca, 1882; twice Mayor of Echuca; retired from municipal life, 1904; Minister for Lands, 1909–13; Commissioner of Crown Lands and Survey, State of Victoria, Australia, 1909–13; Member for Rodney, 1904–17; Minister for Railways and Water-Supply, Victoria, 1915–17. *Address:* Echuca, Victoria, Australia.

Died 4 Aug. 1942.

MACKENZIE, Rt Hon. Ian Alistair, PC 1947; KC; MA, LLB; Member of Canadian Senate since 1948; *b* Assynt, Scotland, 27 July 1890; *s* of George Mackenzie and Anne Macrae; *m* 1947, Helen Mary McRae, Winnipeg, Manitoba. *Educ:* Edin. Univ., MA (Hons Classics), LLB (Summa cum laude); specialized in Celtic languages; two years research work in Ireland. Came to Canada, 1914; Barrister; Pres. Vancouver GWVA; Provincial Executive, 1920; Dominion Executive, 1921; BC Legislative Assembly, 1920, 1924 and 1928; Prov. Sec. of BC, 1928; MP (Liberal) Vancouver-Centre, BC, 1930; resigned from BC Legislature and appt. Minister of Immigration in Mr Mackenzie King's Cabinet, 1930; Minister of National Defence, Canada, 1935–39; Minister of Pensions and National Health, 1939–44; Minister of Veterans Affairs, 1944–48; a Presbyterian. *Recreations:* yachting, golfing, reading. *Address:* Mayfair Apts, Ottawa, Ontario, Canada. *Clubs:* Caledonian; Vancouver, Capilano Golf and Country, Royal Vancouver Yacht (Vancouver, BC); Ottawa Country, Royal Ottawa Golf (Ottawa).

Died 2 Sept. 1949.

MacKENZIE, Brig. James Dunbar, CIE 1943; Indian Army, retired; *b* 19 July 1889; *s* of late Nicol Finlayson MacKenzie, MA, FRGS, MInstCE; *m* 1921, Phyllis (KIH medal, 1944), *d* of late Prof. Arthur Thomson, MA, FRCS, MB; one *s* one *d. Educ:* Nairn Academy; Cheltenham College; RMC Sandhurst; Staff Coll., Quetta. 2nd Lt East Surrey Regt 1909; Lt Indian Army, 1914; Capt. 1915; Maj. 1925; Bt Lt-Col 1933; Lt-Col 1935; Col 1937; Temp. Brig. 1941. Served European War, 1914–19 (1914 Star, GS and Vic. Medals); NWF India, 1920, Wana Column (Medal and clasp, despatches); NWF India, 1937–40 (Medal and clasp). Area Comdr India, 1941–44; retired, 1944; Hon. Brig. 1944. *Recreations:* fishing, sailing. *Address:* 185 Woodstock Road, Oxford. *T:* Oxford 59712. *Clubs:* Royal Bombay Yacht, Bombay.

Died 4 Aug. 1947.

MACKENZIE, Lt-Col John, CIE 1911; CBE 1927; Indian Army, retired 1927; *b* 21 Sept. 1876; *e s* of late Surgeon-Major G. P. Mackenzie, IMS; *m* 1908, Dorothy Helen, *o d* of late Col W. G. Massy, CMG; one *s* one *d. Educ:* Merchiston Castle School, Edin.; RMC, Sandhurst. 35th Sikhs, 1897; Comptroller of the Household to the following Viceroys of India: The Earl of Minto, 1907–10; Lord Hardinge, 1910–16; Lord Chelmsford, 1916–21; Military Sec. to the Earl of Lytton, Governor of Bengal, 1922–27; Commandeur, Ordre de la Couronne, Belgium, 1926. *Address:* c/o Grindlay's Bank, 54 Parliament St, SW1.

Died 9 Dec. 1949.

MACKENZIE, Rt Rev. Kenneth, DD; *b* Edinburgh, 10 June 1863; γ *s* of late Lord Mackenzie, Senator of the College of Justice, Scotland; *m* 1897, Alice (*d* 1944), 5th *d* of late James Farquhar White of Balruddery,

Forfarshire; two *s* four *d. Educ:* Loretto; Keble College, Oxford; Cuddesdon Theological College. BA 1887, 2nd class Mods, 3rd class Modern History; MA, 1895; DD, 1907; Knight of the Holy Sepulchre, 1929; Sepulchre, 1929. Deacon, 1890; Priest, 1891; Curate of St Mary Redcliffe, Bristol, 1890–95; St Paul's, Dundee, 1895–1900; Rector, 1900–07; Provost of Cathedral of St Paul, Dundee, 1905–07; Bishop of Argyll and the Isles, 1907–42. *Recreations:* golf, fishing. *Address:* Caberfeidh Cottage, Oban, Argyll.

Died 20 April 1945.

MACKENZIE, Michael Alexander, MA, LLD, FIA; Professor Emeritus at University of Toronto; President, Penny Bank of Ontario, 1926; Director, Traders' Finance Corporation; Director, Toronto General Insurance; Director, Canadian General Investment Trust; Vice-President, Teachers' Insurance and Annuity Association of America from its inception to 1937; Consultant to numerous Institutions and Municipalities on Pension matters; *b* Ingersoll Ontario, 28 Feb. 1866; *s* of Archdeacon G. C. Mackenzie, Brantford, Ontario, and Helen Boomer, Galt, Ontario; *m* 1895, Elizabeth Maud, *d* of Richard Niven, Chrome Hill, Lisburn, Ireland; one *s* three *d. Educ:* Trinity College School, Port Hope; Trinity College, Toronto; Selwyn College, Cambridge. *Publications:* Interest and Bond Values, 1912; Elements of Theory of Life Contingencies, 1932. *Recreation:* yachting. *Address:* Oakville, Ontario, Canada. *T:* 286. *Clubs:* Arts and Letters, Royal Canadian Yacht (Toronto).

Died 5 July 1949.

MacKENZIE, Nicol Finlayson, MInstCE; FRGS; Hon. MA (Oxon); *b* Nairn, 23 Feb. 1857; γ *s* of Lt Roderick MacKenzie, Indian Navy; *m* 1888, Isobel (*d* 1932), *d* of J. D. Lamb of Nairn; one *s. Educ:* Edinburgh Institution; Edinburgh University; Royal Indian Engineering College, Coopers Hill. Served 24 years in the Indian Public Works Department; Under-Secretary for Irrigation to Government of India, 1894–97; Sanitary Engineer to Government United Provinces, 1901–02; retired, 1902; received thanks of Local Government for services on construction of the Nadrai Aqueduct; Senior Instructor in Surveying RIE College, Coopers Hill, 1902–06; Instructor in Surveying in the Schools of Engineering, Forestry, and Geography, Oxford University, 1906–27; Special Lecturer on Irrigation, King's College, London, 1908–20; Assistant Inspector Munitions Areas, Sheffield, and Lancaster, 1916–19. *Publications:* Methods of Surveying; Notes on Irrigation Works; contributions on professional and technical subjects. *Recreations:* fishing, golf, lawn tennis. *Address:* 185 Woodstock Road, Oxford. *T:* Oxford 59712.

Died 18 April 1943.

MACKENZIE, Col Sir Robert Campbell, of Edinbarnet; KBE 1919; CB 1911; VD; TD; DL, JP, Co. of City of Glasgow; DL, JP Dumbartonshire; Colonel in the Territorial Army; retired; Hon. Colonel 5th Bn HLI; Income Tax Commissioner and Member of Licensing Appeal Courts in the county of Dumbarton; *b* 12 Jan. 1856; *s* of late Walter Mackenzie, JP, CA, of Law and Edinbarnet, and Elizabeth, *d* of Alex. Campbell, of Barnhill, Dumbartonshire; *m* 1st, 1884, Katherine Ellis (*d* 1885), *d* of David Richardson, of Hartfield; 2nd, 1896, Henrietta Mary (*d* 1930), OBE, *d* of Rev. Alex. Macquisten, DD; one *s* one *d. Educ:* Glasgow Acad.; Uppingham School; Glasgow University. In business as a chartered accountant; Director Scottish Board Liverpool and London Globe Insurance Co., William Dixon, Ltd, etc.; served Lt and Captain Glasgow Highland Regt Volunteers, 1875–89; Lt-Col and CO 1st Vol. Batt. HLI, 1889–1906; Col commanding HLI Brigade, 1906–11; 3rd Line Group Lowland Division, 1915. *Recreations:* shooting, fishing, curling, etc. *Address:* Edinbarnet,

Duntocher, Dumbartonshire. *T:* Douglas, Glasgow 6301; Bearsden, Glasgow 0259. *Clubs:* Bath; Western, Glasgow.

Died 26 May 1945.

MACKENZIE, Col Sir Victor Audley Falconer, 3rd Bt *cr* 1890, of Glen-Muick; DSO 1916; MVO 1906; late Scots Guards; Extra Groom-in-Waiting to the King since 1936; *b* 15 Dec. 1882; *s* of 2nd Bt and Lucy, *d* of Duncan Davidson of Tulloch; *S* father, 1906. *Educ:* Eton; Sandhurst. Owns about 42,000 acres. Served European War, 1914–18 (DSO, twice wounded); temp. Lt-Col commanding 1st Bn Scots Guards, Feb. 1918 till end of war; Commandant of Guards' Depôt, 1923–24; commanded 2nd Batt. Scots Guards, 1924–28; Commander, 153rd (Black Watch and Gordon) Infantry Brigade, TA, 1930–32; retired pay, 1932. *Heir: nephew* Alexander George Anthony Allan [*b* 4 Jan. 1913; *s* of late Capt. Allan Keith Mackenzie and Hon. Louvima, *o d* of 1st Viscount Knollys (she *m* 2nd, 1922, Richard Henry Spencer Checkley)]. *Address:* Glen-Muick, Ballater, Aberdeenshire. *Clubs:* Turf, Guards'.

Died 18 April 1944.

MACKENZIE, William Andrew; *b* Invergordon, Ross-shire, 14 Aug. 1870; *e* and *o surv. s* of late Andrew Mackenzie; *m* 1897, Annie, *e d* of late John Webster, Aberdeen. *Educ:* Alness Public School; Tain Royal Academy; Grammar School, Aberdeen. Studied medicine at the Marischal College, Aberdeen, 1887–90. Edited Bon-Accord, Aberdeen, 1891–93; joined the staff of Mr James Henderson, Red Lion House, contributing much anonymous work to the Sketch, Pall Mall Gazette, etc., 1893–97; editor Black and White, 1897–1900; editor, Burns and Oates, publishers, 1919; Secretary-General of the Save the Children International Union (Union International de Secours aux Enfants), Geneva, 1920–40; Knight of Saint Gregory, 1922; Gold Cross for Distinguished Service, Austrian Republic, 1927; President, Cercle Catholique de Genève, 1928; Vice-President, Caritas Catholica, 1930. *Publications:* Poems, 1893; privately, Rosemary, 1894; Hogmanay, 1895; The Wind Bloweth where it Listeth, 1896; This Year of Grace, 1897; Rowton House Rhymes, 1912; novels: The Glittering Road; His Majesty's Peacock; The Bite of the Leech; In the House of the Eye; The Drexel Dream; The Black Butterfly; The Red Star of Night; The Flower o' the Peach; and many serials. *Address:* Château d'Hermance, Geneva.

Died 18 Nov. 1942.

MACKENZIE, Col William Shand, CBE 1934; late Royal Army Pay Corps; *b* 5 Sept. 1876; *s* of John Mackenzie, Solicitor, Inverness; *m* 1905, Coralie Mabel, *d* of Captain G. E. Lloyd-Williams, 24th Regt; one *s* one *d. Educ:* George Watson's College, Edinburgh; Glasgow University. 2nd Lt Gloucester Regt 1899; transferred to APD 1904; served S African War (Queen's Medal and 3 clasps); European War (despatches twice, Brevet Lt-Col, 1914–15 Star, British War Medal, Victory Medal); retired pay, 1936. *Address:* Kandy, Gally Hill Road, Church Crookham, Hants. *T:* Fleet 463.

Died 19 Dec. 1944.

McKERGOW, Lt-Col Robert Wilson, OBE; DL; TD; *b* 1866; *o s* of late R. McKergow of Dunkeld House, Burgess Hill, Sussex; *m* 1894; two *s* one *d. Educ:* Downing College, Cambridge. Farms own land in Sussex; Master of Southdown Foxhounds, 1903–08; helped to raise Sussex Yeomanry, 1901, and commanded 3rd Line Sussex Yeomanry during the war; afterwards commanded 4th Reserve Battalion Royal West Kent Regiment till dismissed on account of ill health; High Sheriff for Sussex, 1933–34; Joint Master of Crawley and Horsham Foxhounds, 1912–14; Master of the Crawley and Horsham Foxhounds, 1919–33; shooting big game,

British East Africa, 1911. *Recreations:* shooting, polo, and hunting. *Address:* Twineham Grange, Twineham. *Clubs:* Union, Brighton.

Died 21 Oct. 1947.

MACKEURTAN, Harold Graham, LLB (Cantab); KC; Advocate, Supreme Court of South Africa; *b* Durban, 26 Feb. 1884; *e s* of George Monach Mackeurtan, Banker, and E. M. L. Birt; *m* 1913, Patricia Willis, *d* of W. D. Fraser, Captain, Mercantile Marine (retd); two *s* one *d. Educ:* Durban High School; Trinity College, Cambridge. Barrister-at-Law, Inner Temple, 1906; Advocate, Supreme Court of Natal, 1906; KC Union of South Africa, 1919; MP Union Parliament, 1921–24. *Publications:* Law of Sale in S Africa, 1921; Cradle Days of Natal, 1930. *Recreations:* old Natal History, gardening. *Address:* Inchmahome House, Prospect, Durban North; 4 Temple Chambers, Durban, SA. *Club:* United University.

Died 18 Dec. 1942.

McKEW, Rev. Robert, DD; CBE 1919; *e surv. s* of John McKew, Valencia, Kerry; *m* 1909, Maude Normand Newall; one *d. Educ:* Trinity College, Dublin. Chaplain in HM Navy, 1902; served in following ships—HMS Hyacinth, Berwick, King Edward VII, Venerable, Hercules, King George V; during the War in HMS Cornwall, 1914–17; HMS Collingwood, 1917–19 (Chevalier of Legion of Honour, CBE); Chaplain of the Fleet, 1924–29; Hon. Chaplain to the King, 1925–29; Archdeacon of the Isle of Wight, 1929–36. *Recreations:* tennis and golf. *Address:* Danecourt, Shanklin, IOW. *T:* Shanklin 283.

Died 11 Oct. 1944.

McKIBBIN, Major Thomas, CBE 1919; OBE 1918; MD; Medical Officer of Health for Otago and Southland; *b* March 1879. Served European War, 1915–18 (despatches, OBE, CBE, 1914–15 star, two medals); Director of Division of Public Hygiene, Department of Health, New Zealand, 1924. *Address:* Post Office Building, Princess Street, Dunedin, New Zealand.

Died 3 Nov. 1943.

MACKIE, Charles; journalist; contributor of articles on literature, sport, the drama, Old English country life, etc., Yorkshire Herald; *e s* of late Thomas Mackie, formerly of Forres, Morayshire; *m* 1891, Helen Castle, 3rd *d* of late Thomas Castle, Berners Street, WC; one *s* one *d. Educ:* privately. Formerly editor of Norfolk Chronicle and Norwich Gazette; for fifteen years Hon. Secretary of the Scots Society of St Andrew, Norwich; editor of Dumfries and Galloway Courier and Herald, 1909–13; editorial staff of Yorkshire Herald, 1914–17, and since 1924; editor of the Southern Reporter, Selkirk, 1917–24; elected to Selkirk Town Council and appointed a burgh representative to Selkirk County Council, 1920; member of County Board of Appeal, 1922. *Publications:* Norfolk Annals, 1901; The High Road—Where are We?; edited for fourteen years Norfolk and Norwich Notes and Queries; numerous articles on popular antiquities, sports, drama, etc.; writer of the daily literary feature in the Yorkshire Evening Press. *Recreation:* tramps in unfrequented districts, preferably by himself. *Address:* 10 Wentworth Road, York.

Died 23 Oct. 1940.

MACKIE, Brevet Col (Frederick) Percival, CSI 1932; OBE; MD, ChB, MSc, DPH (Bristol), FRCS, FRCP; late KHS, IMS (retired); Chief Medical Officer, British Overseas Airways Corp.; late Pathologist to the Hospital for Tropical Diseases, London; *b* 19 Feb. 1875; *s* of Rev. John Mackie, Rector of Fylton, Glos; *m* 1st, 1913, Gladys May, *d* of W. J. Ball, Clifton; one *s*; 2nd, 1926, Mary Elizabeth, *d* of late W. Haddon Owen, Louth, Lincs; two *s. Educ:* Dean Close School, Cheltenham; Bristol University; St Bartholomew's Hospital. Entered

Indian Medical Service (1st place, Scholarship in Surgery, Gold Medal in Medicine), 1902; Younghusband Mission to Thibet, 1903; Assistant Director, Plague Research Laboratory, Bombay, 1905; Royal Society's Sleeping Sickness Commission, Uganda, 1908; Special Research Officer (Government of India) on Kala-azar, 1911; Military Service in Baluchistan, France, and Mesopotamia, 1914–19 (despatches twice, OBE); Professor of Pathology, Calcutta University, 1920; Director of the Pasteur Institute, Shillong, Assam, 1921; Director of the Haffkine Institute, Bombay, 1923; Chairman of the Plague Expert Committee of the League of Nations, 1928–31; Officiating Public Health Commissioner, Government of India, 1928; Officiating Surgeon-General with the Government of Bombay, 1929; Officiating Director of the Pasteur Institute and Research Laboratory, Shillong, Assam, 1931. *Publications:* contributions to Literature mainly in Tropical Diseases. *Recreations:* sport, travel. *Address:* 3 Goldney Avenue, Bristol, 8. *Club:* Royal Empire.

Died 15 July 1944.

MACKIE, Col Tom Darke, CMG 1919; OBE 1918; MIMechE; RAF; Directorate of Works and Buildings, Air Ministry; *b* Sedbergh, Yorkshire, 1880; *o s* of late Rev. John Henry Mackie, MA, Rector of Filton, Gloucestershire; *m* 1908, Constance, *e d* of Walter Kilminster, of Wells, Somerset; one *s* two *d. Educ:* Sedbergh Grammar School; Bristol University. Apprenticed Barrow Hæmatite Steel Company; Mechanical Engineer under Sir John Dewrance; served European War; Flight Lieut, RNAS 1914; Flight Commander, 1915; Squadron Commander, 1916; Wing Commander, 1917; transferred to RAF as Lieut-Colonel, promoted Colonel, 1918; served in Belgium, Dardanelles, and France; first Battle of Ypres (1914 Star and bar); in command of Air Construction Service, 1917; Director of Air Construction Service, 1918 and 1919. *Recreations:* motoring, music, and reading. *Address:* 2 Harrington Road, Brighton. *Club:* Savile.

Died 13 Oct. 1941.

MACKINDER, Rt Hon. Sir Halford John, PC 1926; Kt 1920; *b* Gainsborough, 15 Feb. 1861; *e s* of late Draper Mackinder, MD; *m* Emilie Catherine, 2nd *d* of late Christian D. Ginsburg, LLD (her address, Villa Tragara, Capri, Italy). *Educ:* Gainsborough Grammar School; Epsom College; Christ Church, Oxford. President of Oxford Union Soc., 1883; Barr Inner Temple, 1886; Reader in Geography, Oxford University, 1887–1905; Reader and afterwards Professor of Geography in the University of London, 1900–25; Principal of University College, Reading, 1892–1903; Student of Christ Church, Oxford, 1892–1905; President of Geographical Section, British Association, 1895 and 1931; made first ascent of Mount Kenya, 1899; contested Warwick (L), 1900; the Director of London School of Economics and Political Science, 1903–08; Senator of London University, 1904–08; medallist Royal Scottish Geographical Society, 1903; contested Hawick Burghs (LU), 1909; MP (U) Camlachie Division, Glasgow, Jan. 1910–22; British High Commissioner for South Russia, 1919–20; Chairman of the Imperial Shipping Committee, 1920–45; and of the Imperial Economic Committee, 1926–31; was member of Royal Commissions on Income Tax (1919), Awards to Inventors (1919), Food Prices (1925), and of the Montagu War Savings Committee (1916); Officier de l'Instruction Publique de France (1901); Commander of the Crown of Roumania (1921); Vice-President of Royal Geographical Society, 1933–36; Hon. Member of Berlin (1903) and Hungarian (1922) Geographical Societies. Daly Gold Medallist of American Geog. Soc. of New York, 1943; and Patron's Gold Medallist, Royal Geog. Soc. of London, 1945. *Publications:* Britain and the British Seas, 2nd edition, 1907; The Rhine, its Valley and History, 1908; Elementary Studies in Geography, 18th edition, 1930; Eight Lectures on India, 1910;

Democratic Ideals and Reality, 1919. *Address:* Elville, Kimberley Road, Parkstone, Dorset. *Clubs:* Athenæum, Alpine.

Died 6 March 1947.

McKINLAY, Adam Storey. MP (Lab) County of Dumbarton 1941–50; West Dunbartonshire, Feb.–March 1950; Vice-Chairman Scottish Parliamentary Labour group; a woodworker. MP (Lab) Partick Division of Glasgow, 1929–31. JP Glasgow. *Address:* 149 Kestrel Road, Glasgow, W3.

Died 17 March 1950.

McKINNELL, James Jesse, CBE 1935; JP; *b* 11 Jan. 1869; *s* of James Jesse McKinnell and Clara Whiteman; *m* 1894, Grace Eldridge (*d* 1947); one *s* one *d. Educ:* Rugby School. In business at Rugby for many years; Chairman of Rugby UDC, 1914–19; First Mayor of Rugby, 1932–34; JP County of Warwick since 1917; CC, 1917–21. *Recreation:* gardening. *Address:* 20a Clifton Road, Rugby. *TA:* McKinnell, Clifton Rd, Rugby. *T:* 3202.

Died 15 April 1950.

MACKINNEY, Frederick Walker, CBE 1931; *b* 25 Jan. 1871; *m* Minnie Louise Brenchley (*d* 1940); two *s. Educ:* St Marylebone Grammar School. In service of London County Council, 1889–1934; Chief Officer of Supplies, 1909–34; Member of the Managing Committee of the Franklands Village Housing Society, Ltd, etc. and formerly member of the Food Council (Vice-Chairman 1935–39) and Marketing Committee of the late Empire Marketing Board, and Cuckfield Urban District Council (Chairman 1938–39). *Address:* Wayside, West Common, Haywards Heath, Sussex. *T:* Lindfield 168.

Died 12 July 1950.

MACKINNON, Lt-Col Alexander Charles Broughton, CBE 1926; Indian Army (retired) 2nd KEO VII Gurkha Rifles; *b* 1 Feb. 1878; *s* of Colonel Walter Carr Mackinnon, late 87th Royal Irish Fusiliers and 3rd Buffs; *m* 1921, Dorothy Constance, *d* of late Sir Murray Hammick, KCSI, CIE; one *d.* Entered Northamptonshire Regt, 1898; transferred to Indian Army, 9th Gurkha Rifles, 1901; Capt., 1907; Lt-Col, 1922; retired, 1927; served European War, France, 1914–15 (despatches); Mesopotamia, 1915–16 (despatches); Afghan War, 1919 (despatches); Operations in Malabar, 1921–22; 4th Order of the White Eagle of Serbia, with Swords, 1917. *Address:* c/o Lloyds Bank, Cox and King's Branch, 6 Pall Mall, SW1. *Club:* United Service.

Died 6 May 1942.

MacKINNON, Rt Hon. Sir Frank Douglas, Kt 1924; PC 1937; **Rt Hon. Lord Justice MacKinnon;** a Lord Justice of Appeal since 1937; *b* 1871; *e s* of late B. T. MacKinnon of Lloyd's and of Lingfield, Surrey; *m* Frances, *e d* of W. H. Massey of Twyford, Berks; one *s. Educ:* Highgate School; Trinity College, Oxford (Hon. Fellow, 1931). Barrister, Inner Temple, 1897; KC 1914; Bencher, 1923; Reader, 1944; Treasurer, 1945; Judge of the King's Bench Division of High Court of Justice, 1924–37; ex officio Railway Commissioner, 1928–37; President of Johnson Society of Lichfield, 1933; Chairman of Association of Average Adjusters, 1935; President of Pegasus Club, 1939; Chairman of Bucks Quarter Sessions; President of Bucks Archæological Society; Member of Historical MSS Commission; FSA. *Publications:* Annotations on Lamb's Old Benchers of the Inner Temple, 1927; Annotated edition of Fanny Burney's Evelina, 1930; The Murder in the Temple, 1935; Grand Larceny, 1937; On Circuit, 1940; (posthumous) Inner Temple Papers, 1948. *Address:* Royal Courts of Justice, Strand; Clover, Aldeburgh, Suffolk. *T:* Aldeburgh 172. *Club:* Athenæum.

Died 23 Jan. 1946.

MACKINNON, James, MA, PhD, DD, DTheol, LLD, FRSE; *b* Turriff, Aberdeenshire, 1860; *m* 1886, Pauline Klein; one *s. Educ:* University of Edinburgh; University of Bonn; University of Heidelberg. For some time Lecturer in History in Queen Margaret College, University of Glasgow; for three years Examiner in History, University of Edinburgh; Lecturer in History, University of St Andrews, 1896–1908; Professor of Ecclesiastical History, University of Edinburgh, 1908–30; has devoted himself to historic research as well as the academic teaching of History; has taken active part in educational administration as member of Edinburgh Provincial Committee for training of Teachers and as Convener of Education Committee of Edinburgh Royal Blind School; President of the Carlyle Society of Scotland. *Publications:* Culture in Early Scotland, 1892; The Union of England and Scotland, 1896, 2nd edition, 1907; The History of Edward III, 1900; The Growth and Decline of the French Monarchy, 1902; A History of Modern Liberty (vols I to III), 1906–1908, (vol. IV), 1941, (vol. V), 1945; The Social and Industrial History of Scotland to 1700, 1920; from 1700–1920, 1921; Constitutional History of Scotland to the Reformation, 1924; Luther and the Reformation (vol. i), 1925; (vol. ii), 1928; (vol. iii), 1929, (vol. iv), 1930; The Historic Jesus, 1931; The Gospel in the Early Church, 1933; From Christ to Constantine, 1936; Calvin and the Reformation, 1936; The Origins of the Reformation, 1939. *Recreations:* golf, curling, gardening. *Address:* 12 Lygon Road, Edinburgh. *T:* 42437.

Died 12 July 1945.

MACKINNON, Vice-Adm. Lachlan Donald Ian, CB 1936; CVO 1935; *b* 2 Dec. 1882; *s* of Rev. Donald Hilaro Ousely Dimsdale MacKinnon and Jemima Macalpine-Leny; *m* 1912, Imogen Lorna Sayers Lee; one *s* two *d. Educ:* HMS Britannia. Midshipman RN, 1898; Commander, 1916; Captain, 1923; Rear-Adm., 1935; Vice-Adm., 1938; served in HMS Crescent, Commanded by the late King George V, 1898; Dido, Boxer War, 1899–1901 (China Medal); Lent as Instructor to Turkish Navy, 1910–12; European War, 1914–18, HMS Indomitable and Barham; Bombardment of Dardanelles Forts, 1914; Dogger Bank, 1915; Jutland, 1916; Commanded HMS Assistance and Danae, 1924–27; Captain of the Fleet to C in C Mediterranean, 1930–32; Commanded HMS Warspite, 1932–33; Chief of Staff of C in C Portsmouth, 1933–36; ADC to the King, 1934; Rear-Admiral 2nd Battle Squadron, 1937–39; retd list, 1939; Sept. 1939, Commodore RNR for charge of Convoys. *Recreations:* usual. *Address:* c/o Lloyds Bank, 16 St James's St, SW1. *Club:* United Service.

Died 11 Oct. 1948.

MACKINNON, Murdoch; *b* 16 March 1865; *s* of Lauchlin MacKinnon and Mary MacDonald, Inverness-shire; *m* 1914, Perle B., *d* of late Francis P. Taylor; one *s. Educ:* Prince of Wales College. Elected to the local Legislature, 1897; sat continuously until 1919; Provincial Secretary and Commissioner of Agriculture, 1911–19; Lieut-Gov. of Prince Edward Island, 1919–24. *Address:* 61 Grafton Street, Charlottetown, Prince Edward Island, Canada.

Died 12 Oct. 1944.

MACKINNON of MACKINNON, Francis Alexander; 35th Chief of the clan MacKinnon; DL; JP; *b* 9 April 1848; *e s* of late W. A. Mackinnon of MacKinnon, of Acryse Park, Kent, MP; *m* 1888, Hon. Emily Isabel Hood (*d* 1934), *e d* of Adm. 1st Baron Hood of Avalon, GCB; one *s* one *d. Educ:* Harrow; St John's College, Cambridge. Late Major, RE Kent Yeomanry. *Address:* Drumduan, Forres, Morayshire. *Club:* Union.

Died 27 Feb. 1947.

McKINSTRY, Captain Edward Robert, CBE 1919; RD, RNR; *b* 1861; *s* of late Col Alexander McKinstry; *m* 1887, Bessie (*d* 1939), *d* of late Charles Waterman. *Educ:* School Ship, Conway. Served European War, 1914–19 (despatches, CBE); Younger Brother Trinity House; Member of Hon. Company of Master Mariners. *Address:* Daneby, Farnham Common, Bucks.

Died 1 Jan. 1943.

MACKINTOSH, Sir Alexander, Kt 1932; late Parliamentary Correspondent; *b* 3 Feb. 1858; *m* 1884, Annie, *d* of Andrew Bannerman, Bendigo, Victoria; one *s* one *d*. In press gallery 57 years; has been Chairman of Parliamentary Lobby Journalists and also of Press Gallery. *Publications:* Joseph Chamberlain: An Honest Biography, 1906, new edition, 1914; From Gladstone to Lloyd George, 1921; Echoes of Big Ben, 1945; and numerous articles in magazines; assisted the Earl of Oxford and Asquith in the preparation of his books. *Recreations:* reading and walking. *Address:* 57 Union Road, SW4. *Club:* National Liberal.

Died 15 April 1948.

MACKINTOSH, Most Rev. Donald; RC Archbishop of Glasgow since 1922. *Educ:* Blairs; Notre Dame Des Champs, Paris; Scots College, Rome. Ordained, 1900; Vice-Rector, Scots College, Rome, 1901–13; Rector, 1913–22. *Address:* Archbishop's House, Bearsden, Glasgow.

Died 8 Dec. 1943.

MACKINTOSH, Donald James, CB 1917; MVO 1902, MB, LLD, FRSE; DL; JP, County of the City of Glasgow; *b* Shotts, Lanarkshire, 13 Jan. 1862; *s* of late Donald Mackintosh; *m* 1894, Margaret, *d* of late Thomas Fullarton, of Redstone, Perthshire; one *d. Educ:* Dykehead School, Shotts; Madras College, St Andrews; Univ. of Glasgow (MB, CM 1884). Resident Surgeon to the Glasgow Eye Infirmary, 1884; one of the RMO, City of Glasgow Fever Hospital, Belvidere, 1886, and for some time Senior RMO there; Medical Superintendent of the Victoria Infirmary, Glasgow, 1890; of the Western Infirmary, Glasgow, 1892–1937; retired 1937; KGStJ; Chairman of Council and VP, St Andrews Ambulance Assoc.; Colonel AMS (TF), from 1912, retired; formerly Member of Council BMA; a Vice-President British Hospitals Association; was ADMS (Lowland Division); Chairman Glasgow and West of Scotland Branch of the BMA, 1912–16; was a Member of Consultative Council on Medical and Allied Services, Scottish Board of Health; Vice-Chm. of Council, Scottish Nursing Council; was a Member of the Council, Royal Coll. of Nursing, Limited, and Chairman of Scottish Board; Member of Voluntary Hospitals Commission, 1937. *Publications:* Skiagraphic Atlas; The Construction, Equipment, and Management of a General Hospital, 1909, 2nd edition 1916; papers to medical journals on medical subjects, chiefly on hospital construction and administration. *Address:* 3 Kirklee Gardens, Glasgow, W2. *Clubs:* Automobile, Glasgow.

Died 12 June 1947.

MACKINTOSH, James, KC Scot, LLD; advocate; Professor of Civil Law, Edinburgh University, 1893–1938, now Emeritus; Sheriff of Ross, Cromarty and Sutherland, 1912–40; Dean of Faculty of Law, Edinburgh, 1910–38; Tagore Professor, University of Calcutta, 1933; *b* 22 Feb. 1858; *m* 1894, Anna Robina (*d* 1940), *d* of J. Giddings, Deputy-Controller of Legacy Duty for Scotland; one *s. Educ:* Grammar School, Old Aberdeen; St Andrews (MA); Exeter College, Oxford (BA). Scotch Bar, 1886. *Publications:* The Roman Law of Sale, 1892. One of the Editors of Burge's Foreign and Colonial Laws; Roman Law in Modern Practice (Tagore Lectures), 1934. *Recreation:* golf. *Address:* 6 Clarendon Crescent, Edinburgh. *Clubs:* University, Edinburgh.

Died 3 May 1944.

MACKLIN, Sir (Albert) Noel (Campbell), Kt 1944; Chairman and Managing Director of Fairmile Marine Co. Ltd; *s* of Charles Campbell Macklin, Barrister; *m* Leslie Cordery; one *s* two *d*. *Educ:* Eton. Served European War, France, 1914–15, Capt. RHA (invalided); Lieut RNVR 1916–18. Director of Small Craft Disposals, Admiralty, 1945–46. *Address:* The Cottage, Fairmile, Cobham, Surrey.
Died 10 Nov. 1946.

MACKLIN, Sir James, Kt 1920; JP, DL; *b* 23 Sept. 1864; *m* 1890, Barbara Emly, MBE, *d* of A. M. Main, Salisbury. Mayor of Salisbury for six years; granted freedom of the city, 1921. *Address:* Harnham Lodge, Salisbury.
Died 19 April 1944.

MACKLIN, Sir Noel; *see* Macklin, Sir A. N. C.

MACKLIN, T. Eyre, RBA; painter and sculptor; *b* Newcastle-on-Tyne, 1867; *o s* of John Eyre Macklin, journalist; *m* 1893, Alys Philpott, journalist, *d* of J. E. Philpott, London; one *s*. *Educ:* privately; Art education, Royal Academy Schools and Paris (silver medal at Academy, 1888). Exhibitor at Academy since 1889, and at Salon, Champs Elysées; special artist Pall Mall Budget, 1888–92; has illustrated numerous books; drawings for magazines, and poster designs; lived in France many years painting portraits and plein-air figure subjects, the latter frequently reproduced, several bought for foreign galleries; has painted many of the magistrates for the Public Gallery and Town Hall, Newcastle-on-Tyne; numbers of presentation portraits; has also been occupied with sculpture the last few years; chief works: the Northumberland War Memorial, Newcastle-on-Tyne; War Memorial at Auckland, New Zealand; Bangor War Memorial, Co. Down; at present painting portraits in London. *Recreations:* shooting, motoring. *Clubs:* Savage, London Sketch.
Died 1 Aug. 1943.

MACKWORTH, Sir Humphrey, 7th Bt *cr* 1776; JP; *b* 11 July 1871; *e surv. s* of 6th Bt, and Alice, *d* of Joseph Cubitt, CE; *S* father, 1914; *m* 2nd, 1923, Dorothy Cecil Cleeves Llewellyn. Served South Africa, 1902; late Lieut 3rd Batt. RW Surrey Regt; Remount Dept during European War; MFH Llangibby, 1908–20; late Capt. Royal Monmouthshire RE. *Heir: b* Harry Llewellyn. *Address:* Beech Hill, Usk, Mon.
Died 2 May 1948.

MACLACHLAN OF MACLACHLAN, John; 23rd Chief of Clan in direct descent, JP, DL; Vice-Lieutenant of the County of Argyll; Royal Company of Archers, King's Bodyguard for Scotland; Major comdg 1st Batt. Argyllshire Volunteer Regiment, 1916–19; *b* 3 Jan. 1859; 2nd *s* of George Maclachlan of Maclachlan; *m* 1919, Marjorie, *d* of late A. C. Macpherson of Cluny, and *widow* of D. N. Nicol, of Ardmarnock; three *d*. *Educ:* Clifton College. *Recreations:* shooting, golf, curling. *Address:* Castle Lachlan, Strathlachlan, Argyllshire. *TA:* Strathlachlan. *Clubs:* New, Edinburgh.
Died 18 Sept. 1942.

MACLACHLAN, Sir T. J. Leigh, Kt 1927; *b* Barrhead, Renfrewshire, 1864; *s* of Rev. Ivie M. Maclachlan, BA; *m* Edith Osborne; two *d*. *Educ:* Ayr Academy; University, Glasgow and University, Edinburgh. Joined Staff Liberal Unionist Association, 1887; representative for South Wales, 1888–89; district agent Lancashire, Cheshire and Cumberland, 1890–1905; agent superintendent, Liberal Unionist Council, 1905–12; visiting agent, Conservative Central Office, 1912–20; chief organiser Conservative Party, 1921–26; Principal Agent of the Conservative Party, 1927–28. *Recreations:* lawn tennis, swimming. *Address:* 23 Princes Avenue, N10. *T:* Tudor 1779.
Died 1 March 1946.

MACLAGAN, Maj.-Gen. Ewen George S.; *see* Sinclair-Maclagan.

MACLAREN, Archibald Campbell; *b* Manchester, 1 Dec. 1871; 2nd *s* of James Maclaren and Emily Carver; *m* 1898, Kathleen Maud Power, Myrnong, Toorak, Melbourne; two *s*. *Educ:* Elstree and Harrow Schools. Harrow XI. Played for England in Australia, 1894–95, 1897–98, 1901–02; captained teams, 1897–98, 1901–02; and for England against Australia, 1896, 1899, 1902, 1905, 1909, captaining teams, 1899, 1902, 1909, capt. of Lancashire; maker of record score in cricket; commissioned RASC Dec. 1914; invalided out with rank of Captain, Oct. 1917; captained MCC team to Australia and New Zealand, 1922–23. *Publication:* Cricket, Old and New, 1924. *Recreations:* cricket, coursing, shooting, motoring, racing. *Address:* Warfield Park, Bracknell, Berks.
Died 17 Nov. 1944.

McLAREN, Henry, DSO 1919; MC; TD; MIMechE; Engineer; *b* 1883; *o s* of late Sir John McLaren, KBE; *m* 1919, Edith, *o d* of late Walter Beverley, Barrister-at-law; one *d*. *Educ:* Mill Hill School. Bt Col Royal Corps of Signals (TA); served European War, 1915–19, in Gallipoli, Sinai, Palestine, and Syria (despatches, DSO, MC, 3rd Class Order of the Nile). *Address:* Rossefield, Bramley, Yorks.
Died 23 April 1943.

MACLAREN, Col the Hon. Murray, PC Can; CMG 1916; BA, MD, CM, LLD; MRCS, FACS; *b* 1861; *s* of late Dr Laurence MacLaren; *m* 1888, Olivia Mary Nicholson (*d* 1936); two *s* two *d*. *Educ:* University of New Brunswick, LLD; University of Edinburgh, LLD; LLD Dalhousie University. Senior Consulting Surgeon, St John General Public Hospital; formerly Member of Senate of University of New Brunswick; President of Canadian Medical Assoc., 1914; formerly PMO Military District No. 8, Canada (long service decoration); Officer commanding No. 1 Canadian General Hospital, First Canadian Expeditionary Force, Sept. 1914–April 1916; Deputy Director, Medical Services, Canadian Contingents, London (despatches, CMG, 1914–15 Star, General Service and Victory Medals, Commander of the Order of Avis); Minister of Pensions and National Health, Canada, 1930–34; MP for St John City and St John and Albert Counties, New Brunswick, 1921–34; Lieut-Governor of New Brunswick, 1935–40; Knight of Grace, Order St John of Jerusalem; Fellow American Surgical Assoc.; Fellow American College of Surgeons; FRCS Canada; Jubilee Medal, 1935; Coronation Medal, 1937. *Recreations:* fishing, golf. *Address:* 75 Coburg Street, St John, New Brunswick, Canada. *Clubs:* Union, St John.
Died Dec. 1942.

McLARTY, Hon. Norman Alexander, PC Canada, 1939; KC, BA; Secretary of State of Canada, Dec. 1941–April 1945; MP (L) Essex West, Ontario, since 1935; *b* St Thomas, Ontario, 18 Feb. 1889; *s* of Duncan McLarty, MD, and Hattie Allan, both Canadians; *m* 1914, Dorothy M., *d* of J. B. McColl, Toronto, Ontario; two *d*. *Educ:* University of Toronto; Osgoode Hall, Toronto. Barrister; Postmaster General of Canada, Jan.–Sept. 1939; Minister of Labour, 1939–41. *Recreation:* golf. *Address:* 153 Gilmour St, Ottawa, Canada. *T:* 2–8034. *Clubs:* Essex Golf; Windsor; Royal Ottawa Golf, Country, Rideau, Ottawa.
Died 17 Sept. 1945.

M'LAUGHLIN, Andrew Cunningham; Professor of History, University of Chicago, 1906–29; Professor Emeritus since 1929; Member of American Historical Association; *b* 14 Feb. 1861; *s* of David and Isabella Campbell M'Laughlin; *m* 1890, Lois Angell; one *s* three *d*. *Educ:* University of Michigan. AB 1882; LLB 1885; AM 1895; LLD 1912. Instructor in Latin, University of Michigan, 1886–87; Professor of American History, University of Michigan, 1891–1906; Director of Bureau of Historical Research of Carnegie Institution, Washington, DC, 1903–05; associate editor of American

Historical Review, 1898–1914; managing editor same journal, 1901–05. *Publications:* Lewis Cass (in American Statesmen series), 1891; A History of the American Nation, 1898; The Confederation and the Constitution, 1905; The Courts, the Constitution and Parties, 1912; America and Britain, 1919; Steps in the Development of American Democracy, 1920; Foundations of American Constitutionalism, 1932; A Constitutional History of the United States, 1935. *Recreations:* walking, golf. *Address:* University of Chicago, Chicago, Illinois.

Died 24 Sept. 1947.

MACLEAN, Sir Alexander, Kt 1939; retired; *b* 16 June 1872; *s* of late Neil Maclean. Auckland, NZ; *m* Elsie Fanny, *d* of Henry Searle, Oxford; three *s* two *d*. *Educ:* Grammar School, Auckland, New Zealand. Founder of Macleans, Ltd; on Council The Citizen Service League; Vice-Pres. Empire Rheumatism Council, etc; Trustee of Lord Mayor Treloar Hospital and Coll.; patrn., Bournemouth Old People's Welfare hostels. *Recreations:* music, gardening and travel. *Address:* Strathavon, West Overcliff Drive, Bournemouth. *T:* Bournemouth 5670. *Clubs:* Caledonian, Devonshire.

Died 13 Feb. 1948.

MACLEAN, Surg. Rear-Adm. Alexander, CB 1925; DSO 1916; *b* 1868; *m* 1912; one *s*. *Educ:* Edinburgh Univ. (MB and CM with 1st Class Honours, 1889). Served at Battle of Jutland, 1916 (despatches, DSO, Russian Order of St Stanislas); in charge of the Royal Hospital at Haslar, 1923–26; retired list, 1926; Honorary Surgeon to the King, 1925. *Address:* Struan, Bell Hill, Petersfield, Hants. *T:* Petersfield 712.

Died 13 April 1945.

MACLEAN, Angus, BSc; CE; retired; *b* Kilcalmonell, Argyll, 16 Nov. 1863; 3rd *s* of Hugh MacLean, Tarbert, Argyll; *m* 1898, Maud, *d* of William Pagan, Comptroller of Money Order and PO Savings Bank Departments for New Zealand; one *d*. *Educ:* University of Glasgow. Graduated BSc (Glasgow) and BSc (London); Walker Prizeman and George Harvey Prizeman, Glasgow University; Neil Arnott Exhibitioner, London University. Assistant in Glasgow University Observatory, 1886; Assistant to Professor of Natural Philosophy and subsequently Lecturer in Experimental Physics, Royal Technical College, 1888; Secretary to Glasgow Royal Philosophical Society till 1899; Principal of Paisley Technical College 1899–1929; Convener of Coats' Observatory, Paisley, till 1924; President of Paisley Philosophical Institution, 1922–25; Occasional Inspector in Science, Scottish Education Dept till 1939. *Publications:* Text-Book on Practical Physics; edited Handbook on West of Scotland Industries, British Association Meeting, 1901. *Recreations:* mineralogy, boating. *Address:* Brecklarach, Tarbert, Argyll.

Died 6 Nov. 1948.

MACLEAN, Angus Alexander, KC Canada; LLB; *b* Belfast, PEI, 17 Dec. 1854; *m* 1st, 1882, Leah (*d* 1897), *d* of late John Yeo, Charlottetown; 2nd, 1898, Frances, *d* of late Henry Longworth; two *s*. *Educ:* Prince of Wales College, Charlottetown; Harvard Law School. Barrister; QC 1894; Member of House of Commons, 1904–17; Comptroller Royal Canadian Mounted Police, Ottawa, Ontario, 1917–28. *Address:* Charlottetown, Prince Edward Island.

Died 3 April 1943.

MACLEAN, Most Rev. Arthur John, DD; Bishop of Moray, Ross and Caithness since 1904; Primus of Episcopal Church in Scotland, 1935–43; Hon. Canon of Cumbrae since 1883, and of Edinburgh Cathedral since 1905; *b* 1858; *s* of late Rev. A. J. Macleane, editor of Horace; *m* 1894, Eva, *d* of late John Maclean, MD. *Educ:* Eton; King's Coll. Camb. (Jeremie Prize, 9th Wrangler). Ordained 1882; head of Archbishop's Assyrian Mission, 1886–91; Rector of Portree, 1891–97; Dean of Argyll and the Isles, 1892–97; Rector of Selkirk, 1897–1903;

Principal of Scottish Episcopal Theological College, Pantonian Professor and Canon of Edinburgh Cathedral, 1903–05. *Publications:* Grammar of Vernacular Syriac in English, 1895; Dictionary of Vernacular Syriac, 1901; Recent Discoveries illustrating Early Christian Life Worship, 1904; The Ancient Church Orders (Cambridge Handbooks of Liturgical Study), 1910; editor East Syrian Liturgies, 1890 and 1892; Old and New Syriac Grammars, 1890; Modern Syriac and English Verb Vocabulary, 1891; The Didache, 1922; joint author, The Catholicos of the East and his People, 1892; translator, East Syrian Daily Offices, 1894; East Syrian Epiphany Rites, 1905; joint translator, The Testament of Our Lord, a 4th Century Church Order, 1902. *Address:* Eden Court, Inverness. *Clubs:* Scottish Conservative, Edinburgh.

Died 24 Feb. 1943.

MACLEAN, Brig.-Gen. Charles Alexander Hugh, DSO 1918; Legion of Honour; retired Army Officer; *b* Pennycross, Isle of Mull, Argyllshire, 21 Nov. 1874; *s* of late A. J. Maclean of Pennycross, Isle of Mull; *m* 1st, Mabel Julia, *d* of Maclaine of Lochbuie; one *s* one *d*; 2nd, 1927, Dorothy Mary Hermione, 3rd *d* of late Charles Henry Alston, MBE. *Educ:* Edinburgh; Bonn; RMC, Kingston, Canada. Joined 48th Highlanders, Toronto, 1892; transferred to Argyll and Sutherland Highlanders, 1895; Adjt Volunteers, 1901–06; District Signalling Officer, South Africa, 1906–09; DAA and QMG 52nd (Lowland) Division, 1910–14; AA and QMG 52nd Division in Gallipoli, 1915–17; Brig.-General 234 Brigade in Palestine, 1917; Vice-President Mull and Iona Association; Chieftain of Clan Maclean Association; Scottish Pipers Society; the Piobaireachd Society. *Publication:* Songs and Bagpipe Music. *Recreations:* shooting, fishing, golf. *Address:* Elmscroft, Sidmouth, Devonshire. *Clubs:* Royal Highland Yacht, Oban.

Died 19 Sept. 1947.

McLEAN, Lieut-Colonel Charles Herbert, DSO 1919; VD; Barrister; *b* 16 May 1877; *s* of Laughlin and Sophia McLean; unmarried. *Educ:* Kings College, Nova Scotia, BCL. Admitted to New Brunswick Bar, 1911; Barrister at Law, 1912; served Spanish American War with 1st Ohio Cavalry; Lieutenant 8th Princess Louise Hussars, 1909; Major 28th New Brunswick Dragoons, 1911; Lieut-Colonel commanding 28th NB Dragoons Overseas; Organised 'B' Squadron of the 28th NB Dragoons, and appointed Major in command of that Squadron, 1915; with the 6th Canadian Mounted Rifles Canadian Expeditionary Force, England July 1915, France Oct. 1915, on re-organization of the CMR Brigade in France was transferred with 'B' Squadron to 4th CMR's in command of 'D' Company; served in France Oct. 1915 to Armistice, being demobilized with 3rd Division (Despatches twice, DSO); Unit Service Officer for NB Depts. Soldiers Civil Re-establishments 1919–20; Acting ADC to Lieut-Governor since 1932. *Recreations:* golf, horse-back riding. *Clubs:* Union, St John.

Died Nov. 1940.

McLEAN, Edward B.; *s* of late John Roll McLean, owner of the Washington Post and the Cincinnati Enquirer; *m d* of late Thomas F. Walsh, owner of the Camp Bird Mine, Colorado; two *s* one *d*. *Clubs:* Chevy Chase, Metropolitan, Washington.

Died July 1941.

MACLEAN, Gordon Thompson, CMG 1941; Inspector General of Consular Establishments, Foreign Office, since 1930; *b* 17 Sept. 1884; *s* of Captain Thompson Maclean, RN, and Frances Hodder Lee; *m* 1918, Gertrude Elizabeth, *d* of Walter Wilkinson, Chilwell, Notts; two *d*. *Educ:* Royal Naval School, Eltham; Trinity College, Dublin (BA and Moderator silver medallist in History and Political Science). Vice-Consul Boston, 1909; transferred to La Paz, 1912; employed at Rotterdam, 1914; Consul at Zagreb, 1920;

Addis Ababa, 1926; Nantes, 1929; in charge of the Consulate at Madrid, 1930; Silver Jubilee Medal, 1935; Coronation Medal, 1937. *Address:* The Clock House, Weybridge Park, Weybridge, Surrey. *T:* Weybridge 1120. *Clubs:* Royal Automobile, Royal Empire Society.

Died 1 June 1943.

MACLEAN, Ida Smedley, DSc (Lond.); *d* of W. T. Smedley; *m* 1913, Dr Hugh MacLean; one *s* one *d*. *Educ:* King Edward's High School, Birmingham; Newnham College, Camb. Member of Staff of Lister Institute of Preventive Medicine; President, British Federation of University Women, 1929–35; Beit Memorial Research Fellow, 1910–14. *Publications:* The Metabolism of Fat, 1943; communications in Journals of Chemical, Physiological, and Biochemical Societies. *Recreation:* golf. *Address:* 2 Elm Park Gardens, SW10. *T:* Flaxman 6382.

Died 2 March 1944.

MACLEAN, James A., PhD, LLD; *b* Mayfair, Ontario, 2 Aug. 1868; *s* of Alexander MacLean and Hannah Bateman; *m* 1907, Mary V. Robinson; six *s*. *Educ:* Strathroy Collegiate Institute; University of Toronto; Columbia University, NY. Professor of Political Science, University of Colorado 1894–1900; President University of Idaho, 1900–12; President University of Manitoba, 1912–34. *Publications:* educational papers and addresses. *Address:* Glencoe, Ontario, Canada.

Died 18 Jan. 1945.

MACLEAN, Lt-Col John Bayne, VD; LLD; journalist; publisher; Founder and Chairman of the Board, MacLean-Hunter Publishing Co., Ltd; Chairman, The MacLean-Hunter Ltd, London, Eng., etc; *b* The Manse, Crieff, Ont, 1862; *s* of Rev. Andrew Maclean and Katherine Cameron, both of Inverness-shire, Scotland; *m* 1900, Anna (*d* 1949), *d* of Prof. Denison D. Slade, Harvard. *Educ:* Toronto; Royal School Artillery, Kingston. Over 50 years Canadian Militia, 10th Roy. Grenadiers and 17th Duke of York's Roy. Canadian Hussars; Officer, Order of St John of Jerusalem, 1898; Hon. Counsellor, Canadian Red Cross Society; Comdr of the Military Order of Christ, Portugal; Financial Editor, Toronto Mail and of Empire, 1884–93; started series of business and other national newspapers and magazines, 1887; now has 36 publications in Canada, US and Great Britain, including The Financial Post and Maclean's Magazine; specialising in commerce, industry, politics, and finance. *Address:* 481 University Avenue, Toronto 2. *T:* Ad.: 5981; Sun Life of Canada Bldg, Trafalgar Sq., SW1. *Clubs:* York, Toronto, Toronto Hunt (Toronto); St Maurice, La Tuque (Que.); Everglades, Palm Beach (Florida).

Died 25 Sept. 1950.

MacLEAN, Hon. John Duncan, CBE 1946; MD, CM; Commissioner of Canadian Farm Loan Board, 1929–47; *b* 8 Dec. 1873; *s* of Roderick MacLean; *m* 1911, Mary Gertrude, *d* of Joseph Watson, Owen Sound, Ontario; three *s* three *d*. *Educ:* McGill Univ., Montreal. MPP British Columbia, 1916–28; Provincial Secretary and Minister of Education, 1916; Premier of British Columbia, 1927–28; President of the Council, Minister of Education, Finance and Industries; Hon. LLD, University of British Columbia, 1926. *Recreations:* golf, curling. *Address:* 188 Carling Avenue, Ottawa, Canada.

Died 28 March 1948.

McLEAN, Miss Mary, CBE 1928. *Educ:* Canterbury College, Christchurch, NZ, MA. Principal of Wellington Girls' College, NZ, 1901–26. *Address:* 56 Mulgrave Street, Wellington, New Zealand.

Died 9 Feb. 1949.

MacLEAN, Neil Adam; KC 1934; Sheriff-Substitute of Fife and Kinross at Dunfermline since 1940; *b* 13 Dec. 1885; *s* of Rev. Hector MacLean, BD, Gorebridge, Mid-Lothian, and Catherine Barr; *m* 1918, Rhoda, *d* of Rev. Joseph Gardner, MA, Macduff, Banffshire; one *s*. *Educ:*

George Watson's College and University of Edinburgh (MA, LLB). Admitted to Faculty of Advocates, 1911; Sheriff-Substitute of Argyll at Dunoon and of Bute at Rothesay, 1937–40. *Recreation:* fishing. *Address:* 3 Dalrymple Crescent, Edinburgh 9.

Died 6 July 1944.

M'LEAN, Norman, MA, Edin. and Cant.; DLitt, LLD, FBA, Fellow of Christ's College, Cambridge; engaged (with late Rev. Dr A. E. Brooke) in preparing larger Cambridge edition of the Septuagint; *b* Lanark, 2 Oct. 1865; *e s* of late Rev. Daniel M'Lean, Lanark; *m* 1896, Mary Grace (*d* 1905), *o d* of Col C. R. Luce, JP, DL, Malmesbury. *Educ:* Edinburgh High School; Edinburgh Univ.; Christ's Coll., Camb. Tyrwhitt Hebrew Scholarship and Mason Prize, Camb., 1891; Jeremie Septuagint Prize, Camb., 1890; Master of Christ's College, Cambridge, 1927–36; examiner in Classics at Edin. Univ. 1891, 1894. Examiner for Oriental Languages Tripos, 1895–96, 1899–1900, 1909–11, and for Theological Tripos, 1896–97, 1901–02, 1908–09, 1911–12. *Publications:* Ecclesiastical History of Eusebius in Syriac, edited with the late Professor Wright; vol. i (Genesis-Ruth), and vol. ii (Later Historical Books), of the larger Cambridge Septuagint, edited with late Rev. Dr A. E. Brooke. *Address:* 12 Cranmer Road, Cambridge. *T:* 5225.

Died 20 Aug. 1947.

M'LEAN, Simon James, CMG 1935; Member Board of Railway Commissioners for Canada, 1908; Assistant Chief Commissioner, 1919–38; Chairman Royal Commission on Lake Grain Rates and Insurance, 1923; *b* 14 June 1871; *s* of James and Mary M'Lean; *m* 1899, Helen Baillie, BA, *d* of J. Lorn M'Dougall, CMG; one *s* two *d*. *Educ:* Ottawa Collegiate Institute; University of Toronto, BA 1894, LLB 1895, LLD 1931; Columbia Univ., MA 1896; Univ. of Chicago, PhD 1897. Professor of Economics and Sociology, University of Arkansas, 1897–1902; Expert on Railway Commission Legislation and Special Commissioner on Railway Rate Investigation for Department of Railways and Canals, Canada, 1899–1902. Associate Professor of Economics and Social Science, Leland Stanford Jr University, California, 1902–05; Expert in charge of Railway Valuation in the Rocky Mountain States for Bureau of Census and Interstate Commerce Commission, 1903–04; Chairman, Transportation section of Commonwealth Club, San Francisco, 1905; Associate Professor of Political Economy, University of Toronto, 1906–08; Chairman, Board of Conciliation and Investigation, Temiskaming and Cobalt Central Mines, Cobalt, Ontario, 1908; Barrister-at-law, Ontario, 1916; Member (Vice-Chairman), Board of Trustees, Ottawa Collegiate Institute, 1919–33; Pres. Canadian Political Science Association, 1931–32. *Publications:* Tariff History of Canada, University of Toronto Series, 1895; History of Transportation Ways Overland in Canada and its Provinces, 1913; Traffic, with special reference to Canadian Conditions, in the Modern Business Series of the Alex. Hamilton Institute, Canadian edition, 1929; articles on railway and business economics. *Address:* Board of Railway Commissioners for Canada, Ottawa. *Clubs:* Rideau, Country (Ottawa).

Died 5 Nov. 1946.

MACLEAY, Sir (James William) Ronald, GCMG 1932; KCMG 1922; CMG 1918; *b* 1870; *o s* of late Col A. C. Macleay, CB, 3rd Batt. Seaforth Highlanders, and Mabel, *d* of late Col W. Anderson, CB, Royal Bengal Artillery; *m* 1901, Evelyn Emily, 2nd *d* of late Rt Hon. Sir Robert Peel, 2nd Bart, PC, GCB, and Lady Emily, *d* of Marquess of Tweeddale. *Educ:* Charterhouse; Balliol College, Oxford. Attaché in the Diplomatic Service, 1895; has served in different capacities in Washington, Copenhagen, Brussels, Madrid, Constantinople, Belgrade, Mexico, the Foreign Office, and again in Brussels, where he represented HM Government at the

2nd Conference for the Unification of Commercial Statistics; Counsellor of Embassy to HM Legation at Peking, 1914; Envoy Extraordinary and Minister Plenipotentiary to the Argentine Republic, 1919–22; British Minister to China, 1922–26; to Czechoslovakia, 1927–29; British Ambassador to the Argentine Republic, 1930–33; Chairman of the Lord Mayor's Committee, in Prague, for Czech Refugees, 1938–39. *Recreations:* golf and shooting. *Address:* 49 Upper Brook Street, W1. *Clubs:* St James's, Travellers', Beefsteak.

Died 5 March 1943.

MACLEHOSE, James, MA, LLD, FSA, FSA Scot; *b* Glasgow, 9 April 1857; 2nd *s* of James MacLehose, publisher and bookseller to the University of Glasgow; *m* 1896, Mary, *y d* of Alexander Macmillan, publisher; one *s* two *d. Educ:* University of Glasgow. JP Upper Ward of Lanarkshire. Chairman and a Managing Director of Robert MacLehose & Co. Ltd, printers to the University of Glasgow; President of the Federation of Master Printers and Allied Trades of Great Britain, 1921–22; Chairman of the Joint Industrial Council of Printing and Allied Trades of United Kingdom, 1921–22; Member King's Bodyguard for Scotland, Royal Company of Archers; Trustee of the National Library of Scotland; Member, Board of Referees (Finance Acts); Member Advisory Council Science Museum. *Publications:* The Glasgow University Press, 1638–1931; edited several volumes on Scottish History and Archæology; editor of Scottish Historical Review, 1903–1928. *Address:* 5 Heriot Row, Edinburgh. *Clubs:* Athenæum; New, Edinburgh.

Died 14 Dec. 1943.

MACLELLAN, William Turner, CBE 1918; Officier of the Legion of Honour, and of the Order of Leopold, and of the Crown of Italy; Assistant Controller of Iron and Steel Production; *y s* of late Walter MacLellan of Blairvaddick, Dumbartonshire, and Thomasina Turner; *m* Lilias Mabel, *d* of J. Wyllie Guild, CA, Glasgow; no *c. Educ:* Larchfield, Helensburgh; Glasgow University. Has carried out important engineering contracts at home and abroad, including large wharves at Puerto Mexico, Manaos, Assiout Dam regulators, etc. *Recreation:* golf. *Address:* 23 Bryanston Court, W1. *TA:* MacLellan, London.

Died 3 May 1945.

MACLEOD, Maj.-Gen. Charles William, CB 1935; CMG 1919; DSO 1915; Colonel Commandant RASC since 1938; *b* 25 May 1881; *m* 1914, Jean Hewat, *d* of late Dr Lorraine, Hawick; two *d.* Entered army, 1900; Captain, 1904; Adjt, 1913–14; Major, 1914; Lieut-Col, 1921; Bt Col, 1922; Col, 1923; Maj.-Gen., 1934; served S Africa, 1900–02 (Queen's medal 2 clasps, King's medal 2 clasps); European War, 1914–18 (DSO, CMG, Bt Lt-Col, Legion of Honour); Inspector of RASC, 1929–33; ADC, 1928–34; Director of Supplies and Transport, War Office, 1933–37; retired pay, 1937; Area Officer in Scotland and London to Department of Director-General of Munitions Production, 1937–39; re-employed 1939 as Deputy Director of Supplies and Transport, War Office; reverted to retired pay, 1944. *Club:* United Service.

Died 18 Oct. 1944.

MacLEOD, Duncan, CBE 1943; *b* 14 Oct. 1876; *m* 1901; three *s* three *d.* Distiller and Whisky Broker. *Address:* Skeabost, Isle of Skye. *TA:* Macleod, Skeabostbridge. *T:* Skeabostbridge 2. *Club:* Caledonian.

Died 9 Jan. 1949.

McLEOD, George William Buckham, CBE 1927; Member of the Central Valuation Committee, 1926–38; formerly Statistical Officer and Deputy Accountant General, Ministry of Health; *b* 1868; *m* 1907, Cicely (now a JP), *d* of late J. Dunham Massey; one *d.* Called to Bar, Middle Temple, 1909. *Address:* Iona, Camborne Road, Sutton, Surrey. *T:* Vigilant 1425.

Died 5 Feb. 1947.

MacLEOD, Captain Sir Ian Francis Norman, 3rd Bt *cr* 1924; Intelligence Corps; *b* 25 Sept. 1921; *s* of Sir Norman MacLeod, 2nd Bt, and Isa, *d* of Francesco Brusati, Milan; *S* father 1939. *Educ:* Winchester. *Heir:* uncle Rev. George F. *Address:* 4 Park Circus Place, Glasgow.

Died 28 April 1944.

MACLEOD, Sir James MacIver, KBE 1929; CMG 1912; Chevalier of the Legion of Honour, 1916; *b* Glasgow, 25 April 1866; *s* of late William Lorimer MacLeod, W African merchant; *m* 1st, 1904, Elizabeth Agnes (*d* 1932), 2nd *d* of William Brown, MD, of Old Hall, Kilmacolm; two *d*; 2nd, 1938, May Elizabeth Bradfute, *d* of late Rev. David Scott, DD, Dalziel. *Educ:* Cardross, NB; Dollar. Unpaid Vice-Consul, Fez, 1892; Secretary Interpreter, Sir E. Satow's Mission to Moorish Court, 1894–95; HBM's Vice-Consul for Fez, 1896; HBM's Consul for Eastern Morocco, to reside at Fez, 1907; HBM's Consul for Morocco, to reside at Fez, 1908; present at post during siege of Fez by Moorish rebels and subsequent occupation by French troops, 1911; present at post during mutiny, massacre of certain Europeans, and insurrection at Fez, and during attacks on Fez, and later hostilities, 1912; was also in charge of Portuguese interests, and temporarily of American interest at Fez; employed at Foreign Office, Aug. 1917–April 1919; HBM's Consul-General in Chile, 1919–23; Tunis, 1923–30; retired, 1930. *Publication:* English Edition of Lerchundi's Grammar of Moorish Arabic. *Address:* Bankend, New Galloway, Kirkcudbrightshire. *T:* New Galloway 262. *Club:* Royal Societies.

Died 6 Nov. 1944.

MacLEOD, Sir John Lorne, GBE 1920; Kt 1917; LLD Edin. University; DL and JP City of Edinburgh; JP Argyll; *b* Inveraray, Argyll, 1873; unmarried. *Educ:* Arts and Law Classes at Edinburgh University. Admitted member of Society of Solicitors, Supreme Courts of Scotland, 1895, Member of Edinburgh Town Council for Canongate Ward, 1905–19; City Treasurer, 1912–14; Lord Provost of Edinburgh and Lord Lieutenant of the County of the City, 1916–19; upon cessation of War activities, initiated and promoted proceedings, which led to adoption by Town Council of Provisional Order for amalgamation and extension of City boundaries, and was leading witness for Corporation in the Parliamentary proceedings, which resulted in creation of Greater Edinburgh in 1920; Food Commissioner for Scotland, 1920–21; Member Royal Commission on Food Prices, 1924–25, and served on several Departmental Committees; Chairman, Jute Trade Board for Great Britain, 1924–29; Chairman, Executive Scottish Travel Association, 1930–33; Member, appointed by Privy Council, General Nursing Council for Scotland, and Chairman since 1921; Chief Gaelic Society of Inverness, 1923–24; Pres., Clan MacLeod Society; Chairman, Royal Celtic Society; Chairman, Highlands and Islands Fund; Director of the Scottish Life Assurance Co., Ltd and Chairman since 1925. *Address:* 72 Great King Street, Edinburgh.

Died 7 Sept. 1946.

MACLEOD, Lewis Rose; Editor, Rand Daily Mail, Johannesburg, since 1924; *b* Oamaru, New Zealand, 6 Aug. 1875; *y s* of Donald Archibald Macleod of Skye and Margaret Rose of Tain, Scotland; *m* Beatrice Louise, 2nd *d* of William Moneur Wallis of Young, New South Wales; two *d. Educ:* Moore College Grammar School, New South Wales. Entered journalism in Australia at age of twenty, contributed extensively in prose and verse to Australian publications, and later was for a time editor of a goldfield newspaper in New South Wales backblocks;

went to South Africa in 1905 and became first editor Sunday Times, Johannesburg, where he wrote libretto first South African musical comedy, The Girl from Springfontein; went to London, 1916; literary editor of The Daily Mail, 1916–24; Member 1st Committee PEN Club; Chairman S African Branch Empire Press Union, 1939. *Publications:* several one-act plays and two musical comedies. *Address:* PO Box 1138, Johannesburg, SA. *Clubs:* Savage; Rand, Country, Johannesburg; Pretoria, Pretoria; Civil Service, Capetown.

Died 7 March 1941.

McLEOD, Sir Murdoch Campbell, 2nd Bt *cr* 1925; retired East India merchant; *b* Calcutta, 17 July 1893; *s* of Sir Charles Campbell McLeod, 1st Bt, and Mary Louisa, *e d* of Surgeon-General Henry Cayley, IMS, CMG; *S* father, 1936; *m* 1920, Annette Susan Mary, *d* of Henry Whitehead, JP, 26 Pelham Crescent, SW7; one *s* (*er s* Roderick Campbell McLeod, Lt Scots Guards, killed in action at Salerno, Sept. 1943). *Educ:* Winchester. Served European War, Seaforth Highlanders and General Staff, 1914–18; FLS; Fellow of Royal Entomological Society. *Recreations:* entomology, shooting, golf. *Heir: s* Charles Henry [*b* 1924; Winchester]. *Address:* Culverlea House, Pennington, Lymington, Hants. *T:* Lymington 203. *Clubs:* Royal Societies, MCC.

Died 21 April 1950.

MACLEOD, Sir Norman (Cranstoun), Kt 1919; *b* 10 July 1866; 3rd *s* of late R. B. Æ. Macleod, of Cadboll, Ross-shire; *m* Anna Augusta (*d* 1945), *d* of Charles Hormann, and *widow* of Richard Morris. *Educ:* Wellington College; New College, Oxford. Called to Bar, 1890; Official Assignee, Bombay, 1900; Member of Legislative Council of India, 1908; Puisne Judge of Bombay, 1910–19; Chief Justice, High Court, Bombay, 1919–26. *Address:* Pyports, Cobham, Surrey.

Died 5 July 1945.

MACLEOD, Col Robert Lockhart Ross, CB 1917; CBE 1919; MB; DPH; *b* 20 Sept. 1863. Major RAMC 1897; Lt-Col 1905; Col 1915; served S Africa, 1901–02 (Queen's medal 4 clasps); European War, 1914–17 (despatches thrice, CB); Deputy Director Medical Services, 1915; retired, 1919. *Address:* 67 Park Road, Chiswick, W4. *Club:* Junior Army and Navy.

Died 19 Dec. 1943.

McLINTOCK, Sir William, 1st Bt *cr* 1934; GBE 1929; KBE 1922; CVO 1922; Member of the Glasgow Institute of Accountants and Actuaries; *b* Glasgow, 26 Sept. 1873; *e s* of Thomson McLintock, chartered accountant, Glasgow; *m* 1901, Margaret, *d* of Henry Lyons, Sligo; one *s* three *d. Educ:* Dumfries Academy; Glasgow High School. Senior partner of Thomson McLintock & Co., Chartered Accountants, London, Glasgow, and other towns in Great Britain; Member of the Broadcasting Committee, 1935; served on financial Risks Committee; Royal Commission on Income Tax; National Debt and Taxation Committee; Company Law Amendment and Unemployment Insurance Committees; acted as one of the Financial Advisers to the Imperial Wireless and Cable Conferences; Member Board of Referees; Industrial Arbitration Court; Racecourse Betting Control Board, 1928–33; Development (Public Utility) Advisory Committee; Economic Advisory Council, 1929; Sub-Committee of Committee of Civil Research to enquire into Cotton Industry; Committee on the Electrification of Railway Systems of Great Britain; Member of Committee on Cement Production; Member of Appeal Tribunal of Further Education and Training Scheme. *Recreations:* golf, shooting. *Heir: s* Thomson [*b* 1905; *m* 1929, Jean, *d* of late R. T. D. Aitken, Newcastle, NB, Canada]. *Address:* No. 2, 86 Portland Place, W1; Granite House, Cannon Street, EC4. *TA:* c/o Teemakell, Cannon, London. *Clubs:* Bath, Caledonian, City of London, Gresham.

Died 8 May 1947.

McLOUGHLIN, Maj.-Gen. George Somers, CMG 1915; DSO 1899; late RAMC; *b* 13 May 1867; 2nd *s* of late Lieut-Col J. McLoughlin; *m* 1901, Audrey Katharine (*d* 1927), *d* of Rev. A. H. Harrison. Entered Army, 1890; Major, 1902; Lt-Col 1912; Maj.-Gen. 1922; served Uganda, 1897–98 (despatches, DSO, 3rd class Brilliant Star of Zanzibar, medal with 2 clasps); South Africa, 1900–01 (Queen's medal 4 clasps); European War, 1914–17 (despatches, CMG); retired pay, 1922. *Club:* Army and Navy.

Died 27 Dec. 1943.

McMAHON, Col Sir (Arthur) Henry, GCMG 1916; GCVO 1911; KCIE 1906; CSI 1897; FZS (Council and Ex-Chairman); FGS, FRGS; KJStJ; *b* 28 Nov. 1862; *e surv. s* of Lt-Gen. C. A. McMahon, FRS, and Elisabeth, *d* of late Lt-Col C. F. Head, 93rd Highlanders; *m* 1886, Mary Evelyn, DGStJ, *d* of late F. Christopher Bland, Derryquin Castle, Co. Kerry; two *d. Educ:* Haileybury; RMC, Sandhurst (Sword of Honour, 1882). Joined 8th (The King's) Regt, 1883; entered ISC and joined 1st Sikhs, Punjab Frontier Force, 1885; entered Punjab Commission, 1887; joined Indian Political Department, 1890; accompanied Kundar and Sherani Expeditions as Political Officer; Pol Agent, Zhob, 1891 and 1893; Pol Agent, Thulchotiali, 1892; accompanied Durand Mission to Cabul as Pol Officer, 1893 (CIE); as British Commissioner demarcated boundary between Beluchistan and Afghanistan, 1894–95–1896 (CSI); Pol Agent, Gilgit, 1897–98; Pol Agent, Dir, Swat, and Chitral, 1899–1901; Revenue and Judicial Commissioner, Baluchistan, 1901–02; HBM's Arbitrator on boundary between Persia and Afghanistan in Seistan, and as such British Commissioner Seistan Mission, 1903–05 (KCIE); Chief Officer in charge of the visit of the Amir of Afghanistan to India, 1907; created an Afghan Sardar of the First Class, 1907; Agent to the Governor-General and Chief Commissioner of Beluchistan, 1905–11; Foreign Secretary to the Government of India, 1911–14; appointed Master of Ceremonies to His Majesty the King during the Royal visit to India (GCVO); British Plenipotentiary for Treaty regarding Tibet between England, China, and Tibet, 1913–14; First High Commissioner Egypt (British Protectorate), 1914–16 (GCMG); Grand Comm. of Egyptian Order of Mahomed Ali; British Commissioner on Middle East International Commission (Peace Conference), 1919; created officer of the first class of the Order of El Nahda by the King of the Hedjaz, 1920; Chairman of Management Committee and Member of Board of British Empire Exhibition, 1920–25; Chairman of Fellowship of British Empire, 1923–27; President of English National Council of YMCA, 1923–47; ex-Chairman of London Foot Hospital; President of Liverpool and Manchester Foot Hospitals. *Recreations:* fishing, yachting. *Address:* Cadogan Hotel, Sloane Street, SW1. *T:* Sloane 7141. *Clubs:* United Service, Garrick, Beefsteak; Royal Yacht Squadron (Cowes).

Died 29 Dec. 1949.

McMAHON, Gregan, CBE 1938; Director, Gregan McMahon Players, Melbourne Repertory Theatre; *b* 2 March 1874; *m* 1900, Mary Hungerford; one *s* one *d. Educ:* St Ignatius College, Riverview, Sydney, NSW; Sydney University. After graduating Sydney Univ. Classical Honourman, studied Law but took up theatrical career; first engagement under Robert Brough, thence William F. Hawtrey and firm of J. C. Williamson; founded first Repertory Theatres, Sydney and Melbourne; producer for many years to the J. C. Williamson Firm; first to exploit in Australia plays of G. Bernard Shaw, John Galsworthy, Granville Barker, Pirandello, Tchekhov, John Drinkwater and other literary dramatists; has produced over 300 plays; also successful as actor. *Address:* c/o J. C. Williamson, Comedy Theatre, Melbourne, Victoria. *TA:* c/o Musette Melbourne.

Died 30 Aug. 1941.

McMAHON, Col Sir Henry; see McMahon, Col Sir A. H.

MACMANAWAY, Rt Rev. James, DD. *Educ:* Trinity Coll., Dublin. Ordained 1888; Curate of Clanabogan, 1888–90; Rector of Termonmaguirke, 1890–91; Rector of Five Mile Town, 1891–1910; Canon of St Patrick's Cathedral, Dublin, 1912; Examining Chaplain to Bishop of Clogher, 1914; Member of Representative Church Body since 1910; Rector of Monaghan, 1910; Canon of Clogher, 1905; Archdeacon of Clogher, 1917–23; Rector of Enniskillen, 1919–23; Bishop of Clogher, 1923–43. *Address:* Aghavea House, Brookeborough, Co. Fermanagh.

Died 29 Nov. 1947.

MACMICHAEL, Neil, CSI 1926; *b* 23 July 1871; *s* of late Rev. N. Macmichael, Craignish, Argyllshire; *m* 1919, Margaret, *d* of late Hugh Macnish, Greenwood, Assam; two *d. Educ:* Royal High School, Edinburgh; Edinburgh University; Balliol College, Oxford. First Class Honours in Mathematics, 1893. Entered ICS, 1893; Special Settlement Officer, 1900–04; Secretary, Board of Revenue, 1904–05; Collector and District Magistrate, 1908–18; Member Board of Revenue, 1921; First Member Board of Revenue, Madras 1926; Temporary Member, Executive Council, Madras, 1927; retired, 1929. *Recreation:* gardening. *Address:* Ivybank, Campbeltown, Argyll.

Died 28 April 1949.

McMICKING, Major Gilbert, CMG 1900; *b* 24 March 1862; 3rd *s* of Gilbert McMicking of Miltonise, and Helen, *d* of Alexander MacFarlane of Thornhill; *m* 1st, 1893, Gertrude Rosabel (*d* 1920), *y d* of late Nathaniel Gore; two *s*; 2nd, 1921, Ethel, *y d* of late Binny Douglas and Mrs Douglas, formerly of 108 Oakley Street, Chelsea, SW. *Educ:* Cheltenham College; Wimbledon School; RM Academy, Woolwich. Captain, RA, retired; commanded CIV Battery, South Africa, 1900 (despatches, Queen's medal 3 clasps, CMG, Hon. Major in Army); Temp. Major, RFA, Oct. 1914; Temp. Lt-Col RFA, Feb.–Oct. 1915 (1914–15 Star, General Service, Victory Medal); MP (L). Stewartry of Kirkcudbright, 1906–10 and 1910–18; Galloway, 1918–22; Parliamentary Private Secretary to Secretary of State for War, 1908–10. *Address:* 26 Carlyle Square, Chelsea, SW3. *T:* Flaxman 4344; Miltonise, Glenwhilly, via Newton-Stewart, Wigtownshire. *Club:* Reform.

Died 15 Nov. 1942.

McMICKING, Col Harry, CB 1922; DSO 1902; psc; late Royal Scots (Lothian Regt); *b* 28 Oct. 1867; *y s* of late G. McMicking of Miltonise, Wigtownshire; *m* 1907, Gertrude (*d* 1939), *o d* of 4th Duke de Stacpoole; two *s*. Joined Regt 1887; Colonel, 1919; served S Africa, 1899–1902, on Staff Mounted Infantry and later as column commander (despatches twice, Queen's medal 6 clasps, King's medal 2 clasps, DSO), including Modder River, Paardeberg Bloemfontein, etc.; European War, 1914 (despatches, Bt Col, 1914 Star, wounded); retired pay, 1923. *Address:* Northcote, Witley, Surrey. *Club:* Naval and Military.

Died 30 April 1944.

MACMILLAN, Very Rev. Ebenezer, MA; DD (Hon. Glas.) 1931; Minister of St Andrew's Church, Pretoria, SA; seconded as Liaison Officer between S African Air Force and RAF, with rank of Major; Former Head of Department of the Philosophy of Religion in the University of Pretoria, 1920–34; *b* Ullapool, Ross-shire, Scotland, 9 June 1881; 4th *s* of Reverend John Macmillan, United Free Church Minister of Lochbroom, and of Sarah Boyd; *m* 1917, Everild Delscey Wier, *o d* of late Sir Arthur Wier Mason, Judge President of the Transvaal; one *s* one *d. Educ:* Hutcheson's Grammar School, Glasgow; Glasgow University; Marburg, Germany. MA 1903; BD 1907. Ordained and inducted to South Church, Bearsden, Scotland, 1907; St Andrew's, Pretoria, 1911; twice Moderator of Presbyterian Church of South Africa, 1923–24 and 1935–36. *Publications:* The Service Book and Ordinal of the Presbyterian Church of South Africa, 1920; Seeking and Finding, Oxford Group Sermons, 1932; Finding and Following, A Book of the Oxford Group, 1935. *Recreation:* fishing. *Address:* The Manse, Pretoria. *TA:* Presbyterian, Pretoria. *Clubs:* Authors'; Pretoria, Pretoria.

Died 30 Oct. 1944.

McMILLAN, Prof. W. H., BSc, MIMinE, FInstF, FInstPet, FRSE; James A. Hood Professor of Mining in the University of Edinburgh and the Heriot-Watt College, Edinburgh, since 1936; released temp. since 1940 to undertake duties of Regional Mining Supplies Officer for Scottish Region under Ministry of Fuel and Power; *m*; two *d. Educ:* Stirling High School; St Andrews University; Glasgow University. Practical Experience in Stirlingshire, Lanarkshire and Fifeshire; Colliery Managers Certificate, 1911; Assistant Professor of Mining, Glasgow University, 1908–11; Professor of Mining, University College, Nottingham, 1911–36; Past President Midland Branch National Assoc. of Colliery Managers; during 1914–18 War, held a Commission on unattached list of Territorial Force; Member of numerous Technical Institutions and Associations, including National Association of Colliery Managers, Association of Mining Electrical Engineers, Institution of Mining Engineers, Special Lighting Committee Institution of Mining Engineers. *Publications:* numerous papers on various mining subjects including 22 original investigations on Mine Illumination problems. *Recreations:* golf, motoring. *Address:* The Mining Laboratories, Grassmarket, Edinburgh. *T:* 23915, (home) 42121.

Died June 1947.

McMORDIE, Mrs Julia, CBE 1919; JP; Hon. LLD (Belfast); High Sheriff of Belfast, 1928; Lady of Grace of St John of Jerusalem; late Alderman Belfast Corporation; *b* Hartlepool; 5th *d* of late Sir Wm Gray, DL; *m* 1885, late R. J. McMordie, MA, MP East Belfast, five times Lord Mayor of Belfast; one *s* one *d. Educ:* Chislehurst. MP (Northern Ireland) for South Belfast, 1921–25. *Address:* East Cliff, Budleigh Salterton, Devon.

Died 12 April 1942.

McMULLAN, Sir Thomas Wallace, Kt 1929; DL Co. Down; *b* 3 Oct. 1864; *s* of Thomas McMullan, Belfast; *m* 1892, Florence Henrietta (*d* 1931), *d* of S. R. MacLean, Rye, New York; one *s. Educ:* Methodist College, Belfast; Queen's University, Belfast. Belfast Harbour Commissioner; MP (Unionist) County Down, Northern Parliament, 1921–29. *Address:* Stoneleigh, Bangor, Co. Down. *T:* Bangor 47. *Clubs:* Ulster Reform, Union, Belfast; Royal Ulster Yacht; Royal Co. Down Golf.

Died 20 Jan. 1945.

MACMULLEN, Gen. Sir (Cyril) Norman, GCB 1935; KCB 1930; CB 1921; CMG 1919; CIE 1920; DSO 1915; *b* 1877; *s* of Col F. W. Macmullen; *m* 1905, Maud, *d* of Col MacIver-Campbell, CB, of Ashwick; two *d.* Served NW Frontier, 1897–98 (medal and clasp); Tibet Expedition, 1903–04 (medal); European War, 1914–19 (despatches, CMG, DSO, Brevets Lt-Col and Col, Legion of Honour, Order of Crown of Belgium, Croix de Guerre, French and Belgian); Afghan War, 1919 (CIE); DQMG, Army Headquarters, India, 1924–27; Lt-Gen. 1928; GOC Rawalpindi District, 1927–29; Adjutant General in India, 1930–32; General, 1931; ADC General to HM, 1931–35; GOC in C, Eastern Command, India, 1932–36; retired 1937. *Club:* United Service.

Died 12 Nov. 1944.

MacMULLEN, Maj.-Gen. Hugh Tennent, CB 1943; CBE 1942; MC; *b* 11 Feb. 1892; *s* of W. F. MacMullen, Cork, Ireland; *m* 1927, Olive M. Webb-Bowen; one *s* one *d*. *Educ:* Clifton College; RMC, Sandhurst. Gazetted East Lancashire Regt, 1912; Capt., 1915; Major, 1927; Lt-Col, 1937; Col, 1939; Brig., 1940; Temp. Maj.-Gen., 1942; Instructor RMC Sandhurst, 1923–27; Commanded 1/-East Lancashire Regt, 1937–39; served European War (1914 Star, British War and British Victory Medals, MC, Belgian War Cross); War of 1939–45 (CBE, Hon. MA Oxon); retired pay, 1945. *Publication:* East Lancashire Regiment in the Great War, 1936. *Address:* c/o Lloyds Bank, 6 Pall Mall, SW1. *Club:* Army and Navy.

Died 23 Oct. 1946.

MACMULLEN, Gen. Sir Norman; *see* Macmullen, Gen. Sir C. N.

McMULLEN, Lt-Col Osmond Robert, CMG 1917; TD; DL Herts; Chairman McMullen & Son, Ltd, The Brewery, Hertford; *s* of late O. H. McMullen, of Westfield, Hertford; *m* 1903, Winifred, *d* of H. Algernon Taylor, The Retreat, Bishop Stortford; two *s* one *d*. *Educ:* Rugby. RFA (TF). Served European War, 1914–19 (twice mentioned, CMG); retired with permission to retain rank of Lieut-Colonel; JP Herts, 1925; High Sheriff, 1927. *Recreations:* hunting, shooting, lawn tennis. *Address:* Presdales Hall, Ware, Herts. *T:* Ware 34.

Died 13 Jan. 1946.

McMUNN, Maj.-Gen. James Robert, CB 1919, CMG 1916; AMS; *b* 10 July 1866; *y s* of late Dr Samuel McMunn, Ballymote, Co. Sligo, and Catherine Margaret, *d* of late James Powell, Cuilmore, Gurteen, Co. Sligo; unmarried. *Educ:* privately; Royal College of Surgeons, Dublin. Commission in RAMC, 1893; Captain, 1896; Major, 1905; Lt-Col, 1915; Col, 1917; Maj.-Gen., 1923; served in India, 1895–1901; Tirah Campaign, 1897–98 with 2nd R. Inniskilling Fusiliers and No. 24 British Field Hospital (medal with 3 clasps); South African Campaign (Queen's medal 4 clasps); Staff Officer to PMO SA 1906–10; Registrar Royal Victoria Hospital, Netley, 1910–13; European War, OC No. 11 Stationary Hospital, Aug.–Sept. 1914; OC No. 4 Cavalry Field Ambulance, 1st Cavalry Div., 1914; No. 11 Stationary Hospital, 1914–15; special duty, 1915 (despatches, promoted Lt-Col, CMG); OC 39 General Hospital, 1915–18; ADMS Base, BEF 1918; retired pay, 1926; mentioned for valuable services in connection with the War, 1919. *Recreation:* shooting. *Club:* Junior United Service.

Died 15 Sept. 1945.

McMURRAY, James Hamish, CBE 1920 (OBE 1919); FRSA; MRAS; late Chief Manager, now a Director, Imperial Bank of Iran. *Address:* Dewhurst Lodge, Wadhurst, Sussex.

Died 19 Sept. 1950.

McMURRAY, Thomas Porter, CBE 1946; MB, MCh Belfast, FRCS (Edinburgh); Emeritus-Professor of Orthopædic Surgery, Liverpool University; Consulting Orthopædic Surgeon, David Lewis Northern Hospital; Consulting Orthopædic Surgeon, Royal Liverpool Children's Hospital; Visiting Surgeon, Alder Hey Children's Hospital; Consulting Surgeon to Ministry of Pensions Hospital, Childwall; Hon. Consulting Orthopædic Surgeon, Army; Hon. Consulting Orthopædic Surgeon, Orthopædic Hospital, Hartshill, Stoke-on-Trent; *b* Belfast, 5 Dec. 1887; *s* of Samuel McMurray and Elizabeth Boden; *m* 1915, Dorothy (*d* 1936), *d* of Squire Hill, Jordanstown; one *s* one *d*; 1944, Winefred Nora, *d* of Ernest Evershed, Brighton. *Educ:* Royal Academy, Belfast; Queen's University, Belfast. Capt. RAMC; Inspector of Orthopædic Hospitals in Ireland; Surgeon to Military Orthopædic Hosp., Alder Hey; Ex-Pres. of British Orthopædic Assoc.; Pres.-Elect,

BMA, for 1950. *Publications:* Diagnosis of Internal Derangements of the Knee, 1928; Certain Injuries of the Knee Joint, 1934; The Life of Hugh Owen Thomas, 1935; Osteoarthritis of the Hip Joint, 1935; Un-united Fractures of the Neck of the Femur, 1936; Treatment of Hallux Valgus and Rigidus, 1936; A Practice of Orthopædic Surgery, 1937 (3rd ed., 1949); Treatment of Tuberculous Arthritis of the Hip Joint, 1937; Fracture of the Neck of the Femur treated by Oblique Osteotomy, 1938; Tuberculosis of the Hip Joint, 1938; Fractures of the Shaft and Sub-capital Region of the Humerus, 1938; Slipping of the Upper Femoral Epiphysis and its Treatment, 1938; Osteoarthritis of the Hip Joint, 1939; Notes on the Life of Sir Robert Jones, 1939; Surgery of Deformities resulting from War Injuries of the Extremities, 1940; The Diagnosis and Treatment of Fractures and Dislocations of the Pelvis and Hip Joint, 1940; The Use of the Thomas Splint, 1941; Delay in the Union of Fractures, 1942; Uses and Abuses of Splints and other Instruments in the Treatment of Nerve Lesions, 1942; Conservatism in Orthopædic Surgery, 1942; The Semilunar Cartilages, 1942; Thomas and his Splint, 1946; etc. *Recreations:* golf, shooting. *Address:* Ystrad Cottage, Denbigh. *T:* Denbigh 182; 28 Rodney Street, Liverpool, 1. *Clubs:* University, Racquet (Liverpool).

Died 16 Nov. 1949.

McMURTRIE, Francis Edwin; AINA; author and journalist; Naval and Shipping Correspondent, Sunday Express; Editor of Jane's Fighting Ships since 1923; *b* London, 8 April 1884; *s* of James McMurtrie and Blanche, *d* of Rev. Joseph Harrison; *m* 1911, Grace Eleanor, *y d* of late H. J. P. Trudgett. *Educ:* Salway College. Contributor to general and technical press since 1904; associated with Jane's Fighting Ships during same period; Naval and Shipping Correspondent Daily News and News Chronicle, 1928–40, Daily Telegraph, 1940–42; Member of Council of Navy Records Society, and of Viking Society for Northern Research; a founder and Hon. Sec. of The Anchorites dining club (established 1919); Hon. Secretary, Old Salways Association. Pres. and Hon. Sec., The Press Gang. *Publications:* Ships of the Royal Navy; The World's Warships; The Cruise of the Bismarck; The Great Pacific War (with late H. C. Bywater); The Romance of Navigation (with late W. B. Whall); Modern Naval Strategy (with Adm. Sir Reginald Bacon). *Recreations:* seagoing, walking, philately. *Address:* Mandeville, Hoddesdon, Herts. *T:* Hoddesdon 2464. *Clubs:* Royal Thames Yacht, Garrick, Press, Norwegian.

Died 22 Feb. 1949.

MACNAB, Col Allan James, CB 1918; CMG 1919; FRCS, Eng.; Indian Medical Service, retired; *b* 1864; *s* of late Alex. Macnab, CE; *m* 1895, Honoria, (*d* 1942), *d* of late Lieut-General Sir Lewis Dening, KCB, DSO; one *s* two *d*. *Educ:* Winchester; King's Coll. Late House Surgeon, King's College Hospital; entered Indian Medical Service 1890; Montefiore Gold Medal in Military Surgery, Netley; in medical charge QO Corps of Guides, 1891–1903; Surgeon to the Viceroy of India, 1904–05; Civil Surgeon, Simla, 1905–08; Residency Surgeon in Kashmir, 1910–14; ADMS of a Division in France and Palestine, 1916–18 (despatches 3 times), Bt-Col, CB); DDMS of an Army Corps in Palestine and Syria, 1919; DDMS Army Headquarters in India, 1920–21; retired, 1921. *Address:* Hedges, Park Road, Winchester. *T:* Winchester 2843.

Died 20 May 1947.

McNAB, Hon. Archibald Peter; Lieutenant-Governor of Saskatchewan, 1936–45; Commissioner on Local Government Board, 1926; President of Soo Line Milling Co., Weyburn; President of McNab Milling Co., Humboldt; President of Neelan Live Stock Co., Saskatoon; *b* Glengarry, Ont, 29 May 1864; *s* of Malcolm McNab and Margaret McCrimmon, both Scotch; *m* 1892, Edith Todd; four *s* two *d*. *Educ:* public school,

Glengarry. MPP Saskatchewan, 1908–27; Minister of Public Works and Telephones, 1908–26. *Address:* Government House, Regina, Sask, Canada.

Died 29 April 1945.

MACNAB, William, CBE 1920; FIC; MIChemE; Consulting Chemist; *b* 1858; *s* of late William Macnab, shipbuilder and engineer, Greenock; *m* 1889, Jane (*d* 1932), *d* of J. Reid, Glasgow. *Educ:* Greenock Academy; Edin. Institution; Glasgow Univ. Travelled in America, Canada, Siberia, India and Africa. Hon. Sec. Seventh International Congress Applied Chemistry, 1909; Member of Jury Brussels Exhibition, 1910; Turin, 1911; Member of Lord Moulton's Committee on Explosives, 1914; Technical Adviser Ministry Munitions during the War (Dept Explosives Supply). *Publications:* Scientific papers; Translator (with C. N. Hake) of Berthelot's Sur la force des Matières Explosifs; Compiler of Technical Records of Explosives Supply, 1915–1919. *Address:* 58 West Cromwell Road, SW5. *T:* Western 1923.

Died 2 Sept. 1941.

MACNAGHTEN, Brig.-Gen. Ernest Brander, CMG 1917; DSO 1915; RA (retired); *b* 11 Sept. 1872; *s* of late Col W. H. Macnaghten, CB, and Alice Ellen, *d* of Lt-Gen. M. J. Brander, ISC; *m* 1906, Yvonne Marie, *d* of late Surg.-Col J. S. Forester, Royal Horse Guards; one *s* four *d.* Entered army, 1892; Captain, 1900; Major, 1909; Lt-Col 1915; Brigade Major, RA, India, 1908–10; Instructor, 1st Class, School of Gunnery, 1912; served W Africa, 1898 (medal with clasp); S African War, 1899–1902 (Queen's medal 4 clasps, King's medal 2 clasps); E Africa, 1902–04 (despatches twice, medal with clasp); European War, 1914–18 (Bt Lt-Col, DSO, CMG, Bt Col, Croix de Guerre, despatches eight times); ADC to the King, 1920. Late Chairman Shanghai Municipal Council. *Address:* Oberis, Finchampstead, Berkshire. *T:* Eversley 2270. *Club:* United Service.

Died 21 Nov. 1948.

MACNAGHTEN, Sir Henry, Kt 1923; partner, Wallace & Co., Bombay; *b* 4 Sept. 1880; *s* of late Canon H. A. Macnaghten; *m* 1919, Frances, *d* of late Rev. James Cropper; two *s* one *d. Educ:* Eton; King's College, Cambridge. 1st class Classical Tripos, 1902. East India merchant, 1903; Chairman, Bombay Chamber of Commerce, 1921–22; Lieutenant-Colonel Bombay Battalion AFI, 1922–26; Member Legislative Council, Bombay, 1920–23. *Recreations:* won 3 miles Cambridge v. Oxford, 1903; cricket, shooting, fishing. *Address:* Brookfield, Lyminster, Sussex. *T:* Arundel 3205. *Club:* Oriental.

Died 29 May 1949.

MACNAGHTEN, Terence Charles, CMG 1923; CBE 1918; *b* 1872; *s* of late Elliot Macnaghten and Jane Maria, *d* of late T. G. Vibart, BCS. *Educ:* Charterhouse; Hertford College, Oxford. Administrator of St Kitts (St Christopher) and Nevis, 1929–31; late Assistant Secretary Dominions Office, and Vice-Chairman of the Oversea Settlement Committee. *Address:* 36 Chapel Street, Belgrave Square, SW1. *Clubs:* Reform, Brooks's.

Died 30 June 1944.

MACNAIR, Mrs Harley Farnsworth; *see* Ayscough, Florence.

McNAMARA, Lt-Gen. Sir Arthur Edward, KCB 1939; CB 1928; CMG 1918; DSO 1916; The Queen's Royal Regiment; *b* 13 Feb. 1877; *γ s* of late William McNamara of Dundanion, Blackrock, Co. Cork; unmarried. *Educ:* Oratory School, Birmingham. Served South Africa, 1899–1902 (Queen's and King's medals with seven clasps, wounded, despatches); European War, 1914–18 (wounded, despatches 6 times, CMG, DSO, Bt Lt-Col, Bt Col, Belgian Croix de Guerre); GSO1 4th Division, 1919–23; commanded 19th Indian Infantry Brigade, Lucknow, 1923–26; Commandant Small Arms School, 1926–29; Brigadier, General Staff Eastern Command, 1929–31; Commander 42nd (East Lancs) Division TA, 1933; Director of Military Training, War Office, 1933–36; retired pay 1938. *Address:* Dundanion, Blackrock, Co. Cork. *Clubs:* Army and Navy, Boodle's.

Died 26 March 1949.

MACNAMARA, Col John Robert Jermain; MP (U) for Chelmsford since 1935; London Irish Rifles, Royal Ulster Rifles; *b* 11 Oct. 1905; *s* of John Radley Macnamara and Natalie Maud Jermain. *Educ:* Cheam; Haileybury. Served in Royal Fusiliers (mainly in India), 1927–33; joined London Irish Rifles, 1934; contested Upton Division of West Ham, 1934; widely travelled. *Publication:* The Whistle Blows, 1938. *Recreation:* travel. *Address:* 25 Palace Street, SW1. *Club:* Athenæum.

Died 22 Dec. 1944.

MACNAUGHTON, Rev. John, MA, LLD; late Professor of Classics, McGill University, and Professor of Latin, Toronto University, Toronto, Canada; *b* Scotland, 1858; *m. Educ:* Grammar School and University, Aberdeen; Cambridge; Edinburgh Theological College; University of Heidelberg and University of Berlin. Went to Canada, 1900.

Died 5 Feb. 1943.

MACNAUGHTON-JONES, Rev. William Hudson, MA, Hon. Canon of Norwich since 1931; *b* Cork; *s* of late H. Macnaughton-Jones, MD, FRCS; *m* Mabel Kate, *d* of W. R. Cooper, Mayfield, Norwich; two *s* two *d. Educ:* Cork Grammar School; Heidelberg College; Paris; Peterhouse, Cambridge. Curate, Holy Trinity, Norwich and Eaton, Norwich; Vicar, Lakenham, Trowse and Arminghall, 1899–1911; East Dereham, with Hoe, 1911–33; Sedgeford with Southmere, 1933–38. *Address:* Highfield, Brundall, Norfolk. *T:* Brundall 200.

Died 1 Feb. 1941.

McNEICE, Rt Rev. John Frederick, DD. *Educ:* Trinity College, Dublin. Deacon, 1895; priest, 1897; Curate of Cappoquin, 1895–99; Holy Trinity, Belfast, 1899–1900; St Clement's, Belfast, 1901–02; Incumbent, 1902–03; Incumbent of Holy Trinity, Belfast, 1903–08; Incumbent of Carrickfergus, 1908–31; Precentor and Canon of Connor Cathedral, 1921–26; Archdeacon of Connor, 1926–31; Bishop of Cashel and Waterford, 1931–34; Bishop of Down and Connor and Dromore, 1935–42; Examining Chaplain to Bishop of Down, 1927; Canon of St Patrick's Cathedral, Dublin, 1930. *Publications:* Carrickfergus and its Contacts, 1928; Reunion: the Open Door, 1929; The Church of Ireland in Belfast, 1778–1931, 1931; Spiritual Rebirth, 1932; Some Northern Churchmen, 1934; Our First Loyalty, 1937.

Died 14 April 1942.

M'NEILL, Brig.-Gen. Angus John, CB 1922; CBE 1925; DSO 1918; TD 1926; late Seaforth Highlanders; *b* 1874; *s* of Captain Duncan M'Neill (of Colonsay), late Scots Greys, and Fanny, *d* of Admiral Sir Charles Talbot, KCB; *m* 1907, Lilian (*d* 1949), *widow* of Captain Charles Findlay, Queen's Own Cameron Highlanders, *o d* of late Maj.-Gen. Sir Harry Barron, KCMG; one *s. Educ:* Harrow. Joined 1st Battalion Seaforth Highlanders, 1895; Crete, 1897; Soudan, 1898 (despatches); South Africa, 1899–1900; commanded Montmorency's Scouts (despatches twice, brevet of Major); ADC to GOC, Eastern Command, 1901–03; on the Staff of the School of Instruction for Mounted Infantry, Longmoor Camp, 1904–08; retired, 1910; joined the Lovat Scouts Yeomanry; European War, 1914–18; Brig.-Gen., 1917 (despatches five times, DSO Serbian Order Karageorge with swords, Order of the Nile, 1914–15 Star); Commanded Norfolk and Suffolk Infantry Brigade (TA), 1920–22. Raised and Commanded British Gendarmerie of Palestine, 1922–26; Chief Stockbreeding Officer to Government of Palestine, 1926–31. *Address:* Mazraa, Acre, Israel. *Club:* Army and Navy.

Died 22 June 1950.

MACNEILL, John, (Eoin); Professor of Early History in the University College of the National University of Ireland; b Glenarm, Co. Antrim, 1867; m Agnes, d of James Moore, Solicitor, Ballymena. Minister of Education and Member of Executive Council, Irish Free State, 1922–26; Speaker of Dail Eireann, 1921–22; Member Dail Eireann for National University, 1921–23, for Co. Clare, 1923–27; MP (SF) National University, Ireland, and for Londonderry City, 1918–22. Address: 13 Hatch Street, Dublin.

Died 15 Oct. 1945.

McNERNEY, Joshua William; London Editor, Irish Independent and its associated newspapers since 1905; b Dublin, 2 Jan. 1872; 2nd s of late Joshua McNerney; m 1926, Eileen Mary, e d of late John Sherlock, BA, Official Debates Staff, House of Commons; one s. Educ: Catholic University School, Dublin. Reporter on Dublin Evening Mail, 1891, and afterwards on Dublin Daily Express; joined reporting staff of Independent Newspapers, 1897; later chief reporter; Member of Press Gallery since 1902; a Lobby Journalist since 1906; Doyen of Lobby Journalists; completed in 1941 fifty years in daily journalism; Fellow of Institute of Journalists; called to Bar, Middle Temple, 1924; member of Council of Guild of St Francis of Sales. Recreations: walking and photography. Address: 56 Rodenhurst Road, Clapham Park, SW4. T: Tulse Hill 5185. Club: National Liberal.

Died 2 Jan. 1944.

McNICOLL, Brig.-Gen. Sir Walter Ramsay, KBE 1937; CB 1919; CMG 1918; DSO 1915; VD; b South Melbourne, Victoria, Australia, 27 May 1877; s of late William Walter Alexander McNicoll, New South Wales and Ellen Ramsay; m 1905, Hildur Marschalck, d of late Baron Oscar Severin Wedel-Jarlsberg; four s. Educ: Melbourne University, BA, Diploma of Education. Senior Master, Melbourne High School, 1905–11; Headmaster Geelong High School, 1911–14; served European War, Dardanelles, 1914–18, the landing at Anzac (wounded, despatches five times, DSO); commanded 10th Australian Infantry Brig. (Victoria and Tasmania), 1916 (CMG, CB, Belgian Croix de Guerre); Director of Education, AIF; Principal, Presbyterian Ladies College, Goulburn, NSW, 1921–32; ADC to Governor-General of Commonwealth, 1931–35; Member Commonwealth House of Representatives for Werriwa, NSW, 1931–34; Administrator of New Guinea, 1934–43; Hon. Conductor Goulburn Liedertafel, 1922–34. Publications: Report on Non-Military Employment in the Australian Imperial Force; Report to Education Dept, Victoria, on Secondary Education in England; press articles on public affairs. Recreations: tennis, golf, music. Address: 78 Salisbury Road, Rose Bay, NSW. T: FM 1663. Clubs: Navy, Army, and Air Force (Melbourne); Imperial Service (Sydney).

Died 24 Dec. 1947.

McNISH, Col George, CBE 1919; TD; DL; JP; merchant; b Glasgow, 10 Sept. 1866; s of Robert McNish of Ardenlea, West Kilbride, Ayrshire, JP; m 1901, Margaret, e d of Wm Frew, Inspector to the Northern Lighthouse Commissioners; two d. Educ: Hutcheson's Grammar School and High School, Glasgow. Joined the Volunteer Force, 1893; and continued with the Territorial Force, Battalion 7th Highland Light Infantry; mobilised Aug. 1914 and served continuously during European War (CBE); late Officer in Charge of Labour Corps Record Office. Address: 9 Cleveden Gardens, Kelvinside, Glasgow. Clubs: Royal Scottish Automobile, Glasgow.

Died 18 Sept. 1943.

McNULTY, Rt Rev. John, DD, MA, Bishop of Nottingham since 1932; b Manchester, 11 Aug. 1879, of Irish parents. Educ: St Bede's College, Manchester; Benedictine College, Douai; Ushaw College, Durham; Cambridge University (BA honours); University of

Fribourg (Switzerland). In business in Manchester, 1894–97; Priest, 1911, and appointed to staff of St Bede's College, Manchester; Master of St Edmund's House, Cambridge, 1921; Parish Priest and Dean of St Anne's, Ancoats, Manchester, 1929. Recreation: music. Address: Bishop's House, The Park, Nottingham. T: Nottingham 44786.

Died 8 June 1943.

MACNUTT, Rev. Canon Frederick Brodie, MA; Canon Residentiary of Canterbury, 1938–45; Emeritus since 1945; Chaplain to the King since 1931; Examining Chaplain to the Bishop of Leicester; b 26 Sept. 1873; s of late Dr G. A. Macnutt; m 1st, Hettie Sina (d 1945), d of late Rev. Charles Bullock, BD; one s; 2nd, 1946, Evelyn May, d of Col Sir Frederick Oliver, TD, DL, JP, and Lady Oliver, CBE. Educ: S Paul's School; Scotch College, Melbourne; Trinity College, Cambridge (Sizar); Ridley Hall, Cambridge. Ordained, 1898; Curate of Holy Trinity, Beckenham, 1898–1900; Preacher and Assistant of S James's, Piccadilly, 1901; Curate-in-Charge of Christ Church, Wimbledon, 1902–03; Vicar of S John's, Cheltenham, 1904–07; S Matthew's, Surbiton, 1907–18; Canon Residentiary of Southwark Cathedral, 1909–18; Vicar of S Martin's, Leicester, 1918–38; Provost of Leicester, 1927–38; Sub-Dean of the Collegiate Church of S Martin, Leicester, 1922–26; Archdeacon of Leicester, 1920–38; Fellow of the Royal Historical Society, 1926; Chaplain with the Brit. Expeditionary Force in Flanders and France, 1915–18; Hon. Chaplain to the Forces, 1921. Publications: The Inevitable Christ: Sermons preached in Southwark Cathedral, 1911; Advent Certainties, Cathedral Sermons, 1913; Preparation for Confirmation, 1910; The Reproach of War, 1914; Editor of The Church in the Furnace—Essays by seventeen Temporary Church of England Chaplains on Active Service in France and Flanders, 1917; Classics of the Inner Life, 1924; The Early Diocese of Leicester, 1926; From Chaos to God, Post-War Sermons and Addresses, 1929; (with Rt Rev. E. S. Woods) Theodore, Bishop of Winchester, 1933; A War Primer, an Anthology of War Prayers, Intercessions, Prayers of Devotion, 1939; Four Freedoms, Atlantic and Christian, 1943. Recreation: was athletic Blue at Cambridge. Address: Fircroft, Salisbury Road, Tower Hill, Horsham. T: Horsham 222.

Died 17 July 1949.

MACONCHY, Brig.-Gen. Ernest William Stuart King, CB 1911; CMG 1917; CIE 1909; DSO 1891; b 18 June 1860; s of late George Maconchy of Rathmore, Co. Longford; m 1895, Caroline Agnes, d of Alexander H. Campbell, JP, DL, of 8 Cornwall Gardens, SW; one s (killed in action) one d. Entered army, 1882; Bt Major, 1898; Major, 1901; Lieut-Col 1904; Col 1907; Brig.-Gen. 1916; served Hazara Expedition, 1888 (medal with clasp); Hazara, 1891 (wounded, despatches, clasp, DSO); Izazai expedition, 1892; Chitral Relief Force, 1895 (medal with clasp); North-West Frontier of India, 1897–98 (despatches, brevet of Major, three clasps); Waziristan, 1901 (clasp); AQMG Intelligence, India, 1903; Commanding 51st Sikhs Frontier Force, 1904; Secretary Government of India, Department of Military Supply, 1906–09; retired, 1914; Commanding 178th Brigade, Sherwood Foresters, 1915; Hon. Brig.-General, 1917. Address: Edenmore, Hook, Hants. T: Hook 135.

Died 1 Sept. 1945.

MACONCHY, Captain Frederick Campbell, DSO 1900; East Yorks Regt; b 22 Aug. 1868; 4th s of late George Maconchy of Rathmore, Longford; m 1st, 1899, Maud Elinor, d of G. A. Thompson of Terrington Hall, Cork; 2nd, 1901, Eleanor Mary (d 1936), d of Major Robert Beaton of Nydie, Fife. Entered army, 1889; Captain, 1899; Adjutant, 1900–02; served South Africa, 1900–01 (despatches, Queen's medal 3 clasps DSO); retired, 1906.

Died 30 Aug. 1943.

M'OWAN, Islay, CMG 1929; *b* 4 April 1871; *m* Christine, *e d* of late G. L. Griffiths of Fiji; one *d. Educ:* Melbourne Grammar School. Joined Fiji Civil Service, 1892, and was attached to Secretariat, being successively Magistrate, Governor's Commissioner, Member of the Legislative Council, and Inspector-General of Constabulary and Prisons; British Agent and Consul, Tonga Islands, 1917–26; Secretary Native Affairs, Fiji, and Member of Executive and Legislative Councils, 1926; Governor's Deputy, 1926 and 1928; Acting Colonial Sec., 1930; Officer Administering the Government, June 1930; retired, 1932. *Address:* 8 Hampden Avenue, Cremorne, Sydney, NSW.

Died 4 April 1948.

MACPHAIL, Col Alexander, CMG 1919; DSO 1915; LLD McGill, Queen's; late Head of Civil Engineering Department, Queen's University, Kingston, Canada; retired 1939; *b* 1870; *s* of late William Macphail and Catherine Moore Smith; *m* Agnes Mary (*d* 1946), *d* of late Ven. J. Macmorine, Archdeacon of Ontario; one *s*. Served European War, 1914–18; Commanded 1st Canadian Division Engineers, BEF (despatches, DSO). *Address:* 50 Clergy Street, Kingston, Ontario.

Died 13 Jan. 1949.

McPHAIL, Walter; JP of the City of Edinburgh; Managing Editor Edinburgh Evening News; *s* of Sergt C. McPhail, 71st Highland Light Infantry; *m* Mary, *d* of late James Brydon. *Educ:* Edinburgh Castle School and George Watson's College, Edinburgh. Began as apprentice in Courant, 1881; entered Evening News Office after Edinburgh Courant ceased publication, 1886; Leader-writer and later Editor of Edinburgh Evening News since 1913; organised News Shilling Fund in aid of Edinburgh Royal Infirmary Extension Appeal, and helped to raise over 1,060,000 shillings (£53,000). *Publication:* Edinburgh Street Studies. *Recreations:* reading, speaking, watching sporting attractions, and dodging bores. *Address:* Edinburgh Evening News Office, 18 Market St, Edinburgh. *T:* Edinburgh 27011 and 43098.

Died 29 Aug. 1941.

MACPHERSON, Brig.-Gen. Alexander Duncan, CB 1931; CMG 1918; DSO 1916; DL and JP County of Inverness; late Queen's Own Cameron Highlanders; *b* 10 Dec. 1877; *m* 1918, Kathleen, *y d* of late J. Stewart Oxley, CBE; one *d*. Retired pay, 1931. *Address:* Holme House, Inverness. *Club:* Royal Automobile.

Died 22 May 1944.

MACPHERSON, Arthur George Holdsworth; Lieut RNVR; *b* 1873; *s* of late Sir William Macpherson, Judge of the High Court, Calcutta. *Educ:* Cheltenham College. Formed the Macpherson Collection of old prints and paintings, totalling, 12,000 items, and featuring every phase of the sea history of the English-speaking race; the collection was acquired in June 1928 by Sir James Caird, Bart, and presented by him to the Trustees of The National Maritime Museum, Greenwich; Takes an active interest in ocean cruising, and from 1932–38 sailed 46,000 miles to various parts of the world in his 8–ton cutter Driac II; Commodore Portsmouth Sailing Club. *Clubs:* Oriental, Royal Cruising; Royal Albert Yacht.

Died 10 Sept. 1942.

MACPHERSON, Ewan Francis, CB 1918; BA; *y s* of late Allan Macpherson, Blairgowrie, Perthshire; *m* Agnes, 2nd *d* of late William Young of Stanhill Court, Charlwood, Surrey; one *s* one *d. Educ:* Winchester; Brasenose College, Oxford (scholar and Hulmeian Exhibitioner), first class Classical Moderations, second class Greats and Law. Called to Scottish Bar, 1890; Legal Secretary to the Lord Advocate, 1901–04; Legal Member of the Scottish Board of Health, 1904–22; Chairman of the Board, 1922–28. *Recreations:* fishing, shooting, golf, ski-ing. *Address:* Southfield, Ockley, Surrey. *T:* Capel 83. *Clubs:* New, Edinburgh.

Died 28 April 1941.

MACPHERSON, Sir John, Kt 1922; CB 1917; MD, FRCPE; Emeritus Professor of Psychiatry, University of Sydney; *b* Dores, Inverness-shire, 17 Nov. 1857; *s* of late Rev. Allan Macpherson; *m* Rachel Annie, 2nd *d* of late David Wallace, Balgrummo, Fife; two *d. Educ:* Edinburgh University. MB 1882; MD (Gold Medal), 1896. Medical Superintendent Stirling District Asylum, 1889–90; Lecturer on Mental Diseases, Edinburgh Royal Colleges, 1895–99; Commissioner in Lunacy for Scotland, 1899–1921; Morison Lecturer, 1904–05; President of the Medico-Psychological Association of Great Britain and Ireland, 1910–11; Maudsley Lecturer, 1928. *Publications:* Mental Affections; articles to the Encyclopædia Britannica (11th ed.), the Dictionary of the Bible and Ethics, Green's Encyclopædia of Medicine, and various medical journals. *Address:* Hillside, Cleeve, Somerset.

Died 14 Aug. 1942.

MACPHERSON, Sir Norman Macgregor, Kt 1930; Solicitor Supreme Courts of Scotland; Solicitor in Scotland to the Treasury, Lords Commissioners of the Admiralty, War Department and Air Ministry; *s* of Rev. Finlay Macpherson, Larbert, Stirlingshire; *m* 1903, Jean (*d* 1939), *d* of late R. Hunter Craig, MP, of Knock Castle, Ayrshire; one *s* one *d. Educ:* Stirling High School; Edinburgh University. Secretary Edinburgh Territorial Army Association, 1914–18; Secretary of War Office Committee of Institution of Civil Engineers, 1915–18; Secretary of Special Arbitration Tribunal on Wages of Women Munition Workers, 1917–18; Secretary of Commission to enquire into and report on State purchase of Liquor Trade, 1917; Secretary of Treasury Committee of Inquiry into Accounts of Aerodrome Construction Works, 1919; Secretary of Court of Inquiry into claims and conditions of labour of dockers in United Kingdom, 1920; Secretary of Commission appointed by British Government and Provisional Government of Ireland to assess and apportion losses by destruction of property in Ireland, 1922; Solicitor for Lord Advocate on Commission dealing with claims of Irish Deportees, 1923; Solicitor for Inland Revenue Officers in Scotland at introduction of de-rating scheme, 1930. *Address:* Viewfield House, 12 Tipperlinn Road, Edinburgh. *Club:* Union.

Died 16 Oct. 1947.

MACPHERSON, Stewart; *b* Liverpool; *e s* of late Henry C. Macpherson; *m* Leonora Frances, *d* of late W. G. Kemp, MD, Wellington, NZ; two *s* one *d. Educ:* City of London School; Royal Academy of Music, London. Fellow and (until 1931) Professor of Harmony and Composition, Examiner, Lecturer and Member of Committee of Management, Royal Academy of Music; Hon. Member of the Royal College of Music; Member of Governing Body of the Associated Board of Royal Schools of Music, London; Dean of the Faculty of Music in the University of London, 1924–27; Prof. of Musical Composition, Royal Normal College for the Blind, 1903–21; Conductor of the Westminster Orchestral Society, 1885–1902; Extern Examiner (1912, 1913, and 1914) for musical degrees, National University of Ireland; Founder and first Chairman of Music Teachers' Association (now Vice-President); for some years a Director of the Royal Philharmonic Society; has lectured at Royal Institution of Great Britain, RAM, and to many Societies throughout the country; has taken a prominent part in modern movements in musical education; is an Hon. Member of several musical and educational societies. *Publications:* Practical Harmony; Appendix to ditto; Practical Counterpoint; Rudiments of Music; 350 Exercises in Harmony, Counterpoint and Modulation; Questions and Exercises on the Rudiments of Music;

Form in Music, 1908; Music and its Appreciation, 1910; The Appreciative Aspect of Music-study, 1910; Studies in Phrasing and Form, 1911; Aural Culture based upon Musical Appreciation (with Ernest Read); The Musical Education of the Child, 1915; Melody and Harmony, 1920; The Appreciation Class, 1923; Studies in the Art of Counterpoint, including Canon and Fugue, 1928; A Simple Introduction to the Principles of Tonality, 1929; A Commentary on Bach's Wohltemperites Klavier, 1933 and 1935; First Steps in Musicianship (with Hilda Collens), 1934; Cameos of Musical History, 1937; Published compositions include Mass in D for chorus and orchestra; Notturno for orchestra; Ballade for orchestra; Iroquois melodies for voice and pianoforte; short anthem composed for the RAM Centenary Service in St Paul's Cathedral, 1922; songs, pianoforte pieces, services, etc.; several compositions still in MS including a Concerto for Violin and Orchestra, first produced in 1904 by Sir Henry Wood; has brought out an Analytical edition of the whole of the Pianoforte Sonatas of Beethoven. *Recreations:* walking, reading of many kinds, and the study of paintings. *Address:* c/o Westminster Bank, Notting Hill Gate, W11.

Died 27 March 1941.

MACPHERSON, Sir Stewart; *see* Macpherson, Sir T. S.

McPHERSON, Sir Thomas, Kt 1947; MBE. Director and General Manager, Wallsend Slipway and Engineering Co., Ltd. *Address:* 27 Percy Gardens, Tynemouth, Northumberland.

Died 19 May 1947.

MACPHERSON, Sir (Thomas) Stewart, Kt 1933; CIE 1922; LLD (Edin.); JP, CC, Inverness-shire; *b* 21 Aug. 1876; *e s* of James Macpherson, JP, Newtonmore, and Anne, *d* of Jas Stewart; *m* Helen (MA; Kaisar-i-Hind Gold Medal), *e d* of Rev. A. B. Cameron, DD, Edinburgh; five *s* two *d. Educ:* George Watson's College; Edinburgh Univ. (MA first class honours Classics); Trinity College, Oxford (Exhibitioner). Barrister-at-law, Middle Temple. Entered Indian Civil Service, 1899; served in Bengal as Magistrate and as Settlement Officer; and in Bihar and Orissa as District and Sessions Judge, and as Supt and Remembrancer of Legal Affairs, and Secretary to the Legislative Council (1916–20); Member Legislative Council, 1917–20; Registrar (1920–23) and then Puisne Judge of the High Court of Judicature, Patna; retired, 1936. Vice-Chancellor, (Hon.) of Patna University, 1930–33. *Publications:* Settlement Report of Porahat; (jointly) Ranchi District Gazetteer. *Recreations:* golf, fishing. *Address:* Newtonmore, Inverness-shire. *Clubs:* United Service, Calcutta; Highland (Inverness).

Died 6 Aug. 1949.

McQUARRIE, Mr Justice William Garland; Justice, Court of Appeal of British Columbia since 1933; *b* Ottawa, Ont, 26 July 1876; *s* of Lachlan and Mary McKinnon McQuarrie; *m* 1907, Elsie Owen Macgowan; one *s* one *d. Educ:* Winnipeg; New Westminster; Osgoode Hall, Toronto. Called to British Columbia Bar 1900; Practised at New Westminster and Vancouver, BC; Lieut DCOR, 1916; Lt-Col FVR Bn; member (Conservative) for New Westminster 1917–30; KC (British Columbia) 1919; member of Canadian Bar Assoc. since 1920; Member Empire Parliamentary Association, Canadian Branch, and in 1924 was one of Canada's delegates on Association's tour of South Africa; Past President and Hon. Life Member New Westminster Board of Trade. *Recreations:* fishing and golf. *Address:* 1876 King Edward Avenue, Vancouver, British Columbia, Canada. *Clubs:* Westminster; Union, Victoria; Jericho Country, Vancouver, Vancouver.

Died 30 May 1943.

McQUESTEN, Hon. Thomas Baker, BA, LLB; KC; Minister of Highways, Province of Ontario; *b* 30 June 1882; *s* of Isaac McQuesten and Mary Baker; unmarried. *Educ:* Hamilton Public Schools and Collegiate Institute; University of Toronto and Osgoode Hall, Toronto. *Recreations:* walking and fishing. *Address:* 41 Jackson Street West, Hamilton, Ontario, Canada. *T:* 2–2340 (Hamilton); Adelaide 1211 (Toronto). *Clubs:* Hamilton, University, Toronto.

Died 13 Jan. 1948.

McQUIBBAN, Lewis, CB 1928; CBE 1923; *b* 31 July 1866; *m* 1897, Constance, *e d* of late Arthur Lowd Jeffries, London; one *s* one *d.* Head of Secondary Schools Branch of Scottish Education Department till 1913; Secretary to Highlands and Islands Medical Service Board, 1913; Assistant Secretary to Scottish Board of Health, 1919–21; Permanent Secretary, Ministry of Education for Northern Ireland, Belfast, 1921–27, and Civil Service Commissioner for Northern Ireland; retired, 1927. *Address:* Sycamore House, Amersham-on-the-Hill, Bucks.

Died 19 Nov. 1944.

MACQUOID, Brig.-Gen. Charles Edward Every Francis Kirwan, CIE 1920; DSO 1898; *b* 2 Aug. 1869; *e s* of Col R. K. Macquoid and Frances Every, *d* of General Alfred Cooper; *m* 1931, Sylvia Margaret, *o d* of late Lt-Col L. N. Hughes D'Aeth, OBE, DL, JP. *Educ:* Dover College. 2nd Lt 8th The King's Regt, 1888; Lieut 3rd Infantry, HC, 1888; exchanged to 20th Deccan Horse; Commandant 4th Cavalry, 1916–19; served in Military operations North East Frontier, India, 1895–96; Tirah, 1897–98; operations against Khani Khel Chamkanis; North-West Frontier; Mohmand expedition; Samana (medal with 3 clasps, despatches twice, DSO). South Africa, 1900 (medal with clasp); European War, France, Egypt and Mesopotamia, 1914–18; Brig.-General, 1918; GOC Kuki Punitive Measures, 1918 (despatches CIE); GOC Brigade Afghan Frontier, 1919; Col 1920. *Publication:* Strategy, illustrated by British Campaigns, 1905. *Address:* Marlborough Hotel, Tunbridge Wells. *Club:* United Service.

Died 11 April 1945.

McRAE, Maj.-Gen. Hon. Alexander Duncan, CB 1917; retired; Member of Canadian Senate since 1931; *b* Glencoe, Ont, 17 Nov. 1874; *m* 1900, Blanche Latimer Howe; three *d. Educ:* High School, Glencoe; London College, Ont. Seven years in banking business, USA; five years in emigration and land business, Winnipeg; since timber business; served European War, 1915–17 (CB); former Quartermaster-General Overseas Canadian Forces; Director of Organization of Ministry of Information, Great Britain; Chairman, Organization Committee, National Liberal Conservative Convention and Chief Whip, 1926–30; elected to House of Commons, 1926; Conservative; Presbyterian. *Address:* 1489 McRae Avenue, Vancouver BC, Canada. *Clubs:* Vancouver, Vancouver; Rideau, Ottawa; Manitoba, Winnipeg.

Died 26 June 1946.

MACRAE, Very Rev. John Eric, MA; Dean of Brechin since 1936; Rector of All Souls Church, Invergowrie, since 1924; *b* 1870; *s* of A. E. MacRae, MD; *m* 1900, Ethelwyn Marjorie (*d* 1940), *d* of John Simpson, CE, London; one *s* one *d. Educ:* Grammar School, Aberdeen; University of St Andrews. Deacon 1894; Priest, 1895; Curate of St Pauls Cathedral Church, Dundee, 1894–96; St Saviour, Pimlico, 1896–99; Chaplain of St Mary's Cathedral, Edinburgh, 1899–1901; Senior Curate Christ Church, Albany Street, London, 1901–04; Rector of St Clement's, Salford, 1904–10, and of All Saints, Worcester, 1910–20; Organiser of Clergy Fund for Episcopal Church in Scotland, 1920–24; CF (BEF) 1915–17 (Belgian Croix de Guerre); Editor, Scottish Chronicle, 1925–28, Scottish Guardian, 1929–35; JP Perthshire, 1939. *Publications:* Scottish Churchman's

Tracts, 1925–1926; Origins of Presbyterian Ministry, 1930; Editor 3rd edition of Bishop A. Mitchell's Scotland's Church, 1933; Editor Scottish Episcopal Year Book since 1928. *Recreation:* angling and motor-boating on West Coast of Scotland. *Address:* The Rectory, Invergowrie, Dundee. *T:* Invergowrie 245; Carnmore, Kyle of Lochalsh, Ross-shire. *Clubs:* Scottish Conservative, Edinburgh.

Died 12 March 1947.

MACREADY, Gen. Rt Hon. Sir (Cecil Frederick) Nevil, 1st Bt *cr* 1923; PC (Ire.) 1920; GCMG 1918; KCB 1912; KCMG 1915; CB 1906 and 1911; LLD (Hon.) Aberdeen; *b* 7 May 1862; *s* of William Charles Macready; *m* 1886, Sophia Geraldine (*d* 1931), *y d* of Maurice Uniacke Atkin, late of Ledington, Co. Cork; one *s* two *d*. *Educ:* Marlborough; Cheltenham. Lt Gordon Highlanders, 1881; Capt. 1891; Major, 1899; Lieut-Col 1900; Colonel, 1903; Major-Gen., 1910; Lt-Gen. 1918; served Egypt, 1882 (medal with clasp, bronze star); S Africa, 1899–1902 (despatches twice, Brevet Lieut-Col, Queen's medal 6 clasps, King's medal 2 clasps); European War, 1914–16 (despatches four times, GCMG); AAG Cape Colony, 1902–05; AQMG Cape Colony, 1905–06; AAG Headquarters of Army, 1907–09; commanding 2nd Infantry Brigade, 1909–10; Director of Personal Services, 1910–14; Adjutant-General, BEF, France, 1914–16; Adjutant-General to the Forces, 1916–18; Commissioner of Metropolitan Police, 1918–20; GOC in C. Forces in Ireland, 1920–22; retired pay, 1923; Member of Army Council, 1916; JP, Co. London; Grand Officer, Legion of Honour, 1915; Crown of Belgium, Sacred Treasure of Japan, Crown of Italy. *Publication:* Annals of an Active Life, 1924. *Heir: s* Maj.-Gen. Sir Gordon N. Macready, KBE. *Address:* 78 Park Mansions, Knightsbridge, SW1.

Died 9 Jan. 1946.

MacROBERT, Sir Iain Workman, 4th Bt *cr* 1922; Pilot Officer RAF; *b* 9 April 1917; 3rd *s* of Sir Alexander MacRobert, 1st Bt, KBE, LLD, VD, and Rachel, JP, BSc, etc., *d* of late Dr William Hunter Workman; *S* brother, 1941. *Heir:* none. *Address:* Douneside, Tarland, Aberdeenshire.

Died 30 June 1941 (ext).

MacROBERT, Sir Roderic Alan, 3rd Bt *cr* 1922; Flight Lieut RAF; *b* 8 May 1915; 2nd *s* of Sir Alexander MacRobert, 1st Bt, KBE, LLD, VD, and Rachel, JP, BSc, etc., *d* of late Dr William Hunter Workman; *S* brother, 1938. *Educ:* Cranleigh; St John's College, Cambridge. *Recreations:* ice hockey, shooting. *Heir: b* Iain Workman MacRobert, *b* 1917. *Address:* Douneside, Tarland, Aberdeenshire.

Died 22 May 1941.

MACRORIE, Vice-Adm. Arthur Kenneth, CMG 1919; MVO 1913; Royal Navy; *b* 6 June 1874; 2nd *s* of late Rt Rev. W. K. Macrorie, DD, DCL, Bishop of Maritzburg; *m* 1902, Edith Frances Grey, *o d* of Col R. O. Vyvyan, late Indian Army, and *niece* of Sir Vyell Vyvyan, 9th Bt of Trelowarren, Cornwall. *Educ:* HMS Britannia. Entered Navy, Jan. 1888; Midshipman, 1890; Lieutenant, 1896; Commander, 1907; Captain, 1914; Rear-Adm., 1924; retired list, 1924; Vice-Adm., retired, 1929; served Dardanelles, 1914–15 (despatches); commanded HM Yacht Victoria and Albert, 1911–14; Signal School at Portsmouth, 1918–20; HMS Emperor of India, 1922–24; ADC to the King, 1924; awarded a good service pension, 1923; JP for West Sussex; Order of Danebrog, Legion of Honour, Sacred Treasure (Japan), Redeemer (Greece). *Recreations:* golf, tennis, shooting. *Address:* Norton Glebe, Aldingbourne, Sussex. *Club:* Junior United Service.

Died 25 Nov. 1947.

MacRORY, His Eminence Cardinal Joseph, DD; RC Cardinal Archbishop of Armagh since 1928; *b* Ballygawley, Co. Tyrone, 1861. *Educ:* Armagh; Maynooth. Priest, 1885; First President of Dungannon Academy; Professor of Moral Theology and S. Scripture at Olton College, Birmingham, 1887–89; Professor of S. Scripture and Oriental Languages, Maynooth, 1889–1905; Professor of Hermeneutics and NT Exegesis, 1905–15; Vice-Pres. Maynooth College, 1912–15; Bishop of Down and Connor, 1915–28; Member of the Irish Convention, 1917–18; Cardinal, 1929; Papal Legate at laying of Foundation Stone of Liverpool Cathedral in June 1933; and at the National Eucharistic Congress in Melbourne, Dec. 1934. *Publications:* The Gospel of St John; The First and Second Epistles to the Corinthians; The New Testament and Divorce; Co-editor of The Irish Theological Quarterly, which he helped to found; contributor to the IT Quarterly, the Irish Ecclesiastical Record, the Catholic University Bulletin of America, etc. *Address:* Ara Coeli, Armagh.

Died 13 Oct. 1945.

McSWINEY, Bryan Austin, FRS 1944; BA, ScD, MB, BCh; BAO; Dean St Thomas's Hospital Medical School since 1940; Professor of Physiology, Sherrington School of Physiology, St Thomas's Hospital, SE1, since 1936; Member of the Senate, University of London, 1946; *b* Chicago, 20 May 1894; *m* Mabel Marie, *y d* of late W. B. Law, CI, RIC; three *s* two *d*. *Educ:* Clongowes Wood College; Trinity College, Dublin (Reuben Harvey Scholar). Assistant to Scientific Adviser, Ministry of Food, 1917; Assistant to Professor Institutes of Medicine School of Physic, TCD; Lecturer in Experimental Physiology, University of Leeds, 1919; Lecturer in Experimental Physiology, University of Manchester, 1920–26; tutor and secretary, Faculty of Medicine, University of Manchester, 1923–26; Professor of Physiology, University of Leeds, 1926–36; John Mallet Purser Lecturer, Trinity College, Dublin, 1945; surgeon sub-lieut, RNVR, 1915–16; Lieutenant, RAMC, 1918; Hon. Treasurer Physiological Society, 1935–45. *Publications:* papers in scientific journals. *Recreations:* tennis, walking, gardening. *Address:* 61 Hampstead Way, NW11. *T:* Speedwell 6382. *Club:* Athenæum.

Died 8 March 1947.

MACTAGGART-STEWART, Sir Edward Orde; *see* Stewart, Sir E. O. M.

McVITTIE, Col Robert Henry, CB 1927; CMG 1917; CBE 1919; *b* Jaina, 28 July 1872; 2nd *s* of late Surgeon-Gen. C. E. McVittie, IMS, Hon. Physician to HM; *m* Elsie Vernon (*d* 1944), *d* of late A. S. Urquhart, Behar; two *s*; 1944, Nona, *d* of late Dr Harry Gage Moore. *Educ:* Bedford Gram. School; RMA, Woolwich. 2nd Lieut RA 1892; Capt. 1900; Army Ordnance Department, 1906; Major, 1913; Adjutant Indian Volunteers, 1899–1904; served NW Frontier, India, 1897–98 (medal two clasps); European War 1914–18 (CMG, Bt Lieut-Col); Bt Col 1921; Colonel, 1924; ADOS Scottish Command, 1922; ADOS, Egypt, 1923–27; ADOS, Headquarters, Eastern Command, 1928–29; retired pay, 1929; rejoined the Army, 1940; retired, 1942; Ministry of Supply, 1942–45. *Recreations:* shot for Ireland four years at Bisley; selected for Army VIII 1910; member Kent Co. Rugby team; member Association Indian Football Council, 1894–95; boxing: won heavy-weight, RMA. *Address:* 25 Putnoe Lane, Bedford. *T:* Bedford 5017.

Died 11 May 1949.

MACWATT, Maj.-Gen. Sir (Robert) Charles, Kt 1925; CIE 1916; MB, BSc, FRCPE, FRCS, FRGS, FZS; *b* 22 Jan. 1865; *m* 1st, Blanche Mathilde (*d* 1924), *d* of late Lieut-General S. F. Blyth, CB; two *s*; 2nd, 1944, Marguerite, *widow* of Lt-Col Richard Chapman Wilson. Captain IMS 1887; Major, 1899; Lt-Col 1907; Col 1918; Maj.-Gen. 1923; served Hazara Expedition, 1888 (medal with clasp); Lushai, 1889 (clasp); Hazara, 1891 (clasp); 2nd Miranzai Expedition, 1891 (clasp); Director-General, Indian Medical Service, 1922–26; retired, 1926; late Hon. Surgeon to the King; Kaiser-i-Hind Medal First Class. *Address*: c/o Lloyds Bank, Ltd, Cox and King's Branch, PO Box 48, Bombay, and 6 Pall Mall, SW1. *Clubs*: Royal Thames Yacht, Lansdowne.

Died 14 April 1945.

McWHAN, John, MA, PhD, FRSE; Lecturer in Mathematics in the University of Glasgow; *b* 1885; 2nd *s* of late John McWhan, Headmaster, Cambuslang School; *m* 1926, Winifred, 4th *d* of late George Douglas Stevens, MBE, Chilworth, Surrey, and Mrs Stevens, 64 Lovelace Gardens, Southend-on-Sea; one *s*. *Educ*: University of Glasgow and University of Göttingen. Geo. A. Clark Scholar, Glasgow, 1907–11. Lecturer in Mathematics, and Internal Examiner for degree of BSc (Eng.), since 1913; Member, Edinburgh Mathematical Society, The Mathematical Association, etc. *Publications*: original papers contributed to Proceedings Royal Society of Edinburgh, Proceedings Edin. Math. Soc., Mathematical Notes, and elsewhere. *Recreation*: golf. *Address*: 37 Airthrey Avenue, Jordanhill, Glasgow, W.4. *T*: Scotstoun, 1360.

Died 14 July 1943.

MADDICK, George John; *b* 1849; *m* 1875, Kate (*d* 1919), *y d* of late Samuel Nicholson, Belton Lodge, Clapham; one *s*. *Educ*: High Cross Coll., Tottenham. Art Editor of Illustrated Sporting and Dramatic News; Director of The Sporting and Dramatic News Publishing Co. Ltd; Managing Director Illustrated London News and Sketch Publishing Co. Ltd; Chairman Bassano, Ltd; Managing Director Lascelles, Ltd; after 57 years of being Managing Director of Sporting and Dramatic News and 36 years Director and Managing Director of the Illustrated London News and Sketch, retired 30 Dec. 1933 from the Newspaper World. *Recreations*: golf, shooting, racing. *Address*: Kells, Devenish Road, Sunningdale, Berks. *Club*: Devonshire.

Died 20 Dec. 1942.

MADDOX, Stuart Lockwood, CSI 1912; JP; MA; *b* 3 June 1866; *s* of late Rev. R. H. Maddox, BD, Rector of Kirkheaton, Yorks; *m* Violet, *d* of late Brig.-Surg. Col Meadows, IMS. *Educ*: Fettes College; Worcester College, Oxford. Entered Indian Civil Service, 1887; Settlement Officer of Orissa, 1892–99; Director of Land Records and Agriculture, Bengal, 1903–05; Secretary of the Board of Revenue, Bengal, 1905–09; Chairman of the Corporation of Calcutta, 1910–13; retired, 1914; MLC, 1907–08, 1910–13. *Address*: Newlands, Crawley Ridge, Camberley. *T*: Camberley 278.

Died 29 Aug. 1942.

MADGAVKAR, Sir Govind Dinanath, Kt 1931; BA; ICS (retired); *b* 21 May 1871; *m* Bhadrabai, *d* of late Shankar Pandurang Pandit, Oriental Translator to the Government of Bombay; two *s* one *d*. *Educ*: St Xavier's and Elphinstone College, Bombay; Balliol College, Oxford. Assistant Commissioner, Burma; Assist Collector; Assistant Judge; District and Sessions Judge; Judicial Commissioner, Sind; Puisne Judge of High Court, Bombay; Acting Chief Justice, 1930; retired, 1931; Adviser to the Holkar State, 1933–34; Privy Councillor, Baroda, 1938; President Bombay Revenue Tribunal, 1939; Judge, Supreme Court, Kolhapur, 1942–43. *Address*: 118 Koregaon Park, Poona, India. *T*: 295. *Clubs*: National Liberal; Mahableshwar, Bombay.

Died 18 April 1948.

MADHAVA, RAO, V. P., CIE 1899; Kaiser-i-Hind Gold Medal, 1900. For 36 years in the service of Mysore State in important capacities; Inspector-General of Police, the first Indian to be appointed, 1892; Plague Commissioner, 1898; Member of the Council of Regency, 1898–1902, when the present Maharajah received full governing powers, and then appointed a

Member of the Executive Council and Revenue Commissioner; Dewan of Travancore, 1904–06; Dewan of Mysore, 1906–09; BA and Fellow of the Madras University; Dewan of Baroda, 1914–16; went to England on Congress deputation in 1919 to give evidence on Indian reforms before the Parliamentary Committee; has presided over a number of conferences (political, social, industrial, etc.); now lives in retirement. *Recreations*: golf, riding, motor, and gardening. *Address*: Baroda Villa, Tanjore, India.

Died 1 Dec. 1934.

MADIGAN, Cecil Thomas, MA, DSc (Oxon) BE (Ad.); FGS; Lecturer in Geology, University of Adelaide; *b* Renmark, S Australia, 15 Oct. 1889; *e s* of late Thomas Madigan; *m* 1915, Wynnis Knight, *e d* of late T. C. Wollaston, Adelaide; three *s* two *d*. *Educ*: University of Adelaide; Magdalen College, Oxford. Diploma in Mining Engineering of University of Adelaide and Fellowship SA School of Mines, 1911, surrendered for BE 1932; Rhodes Scholar for South Australia, 1910. Member Australasian Antarctic Expedition, 1911–14; leader Eastern sledging party, King George V Land, 1912–13; leader relief party, 1913; King's Polar Medal, 1914; Commission in RE, Sept. 1914; BEF France, 1915–18; Captain, 1916; demobilized, 1919 (despatches, twice wounded); BA first class honours nat. sci. (geology), Oxford, 1919; MA, 1922; DSc, 1933; Sudan Civil Service, 1920; Lecturer in Geology in the University of Adelaide, 1922–40; carried out aerial reconnaissance of unknown portions of Central Australia, 1929; leader of expedition to Lake Eyre, South Australia, 1929; Pres., Royal Society of South Australia, 1935; President, Section of Geography and Oceanography, Australian and New Zealand Association for the Advancement of Science, 1937; President Legacy Club of Adelaide, 1938; Clarke Memorial Lecturer, Royal Society of NSW, 1938; Leader Simpson Desert Expedition, 1939. First Chief Instructor, School of Military Engineering (Field), Liverpool, NSW, 1940–42; Major, RAE, 1940; Lieut-Col 1941; Murchison Grant of RGS 1941; retired from Army 1943 and returned to duties at University of Adelaide. *Publications*: The Meteorology of Cape Denison, Adelie Land, 1929; Central Australia, 1936, rev. ed. 1944; Crossing the Dead Heart, 1946; various papers in the proceedings of the learned societies. *Recreation*: Geological exploration. *Address*: Bernafay, Blackwood, South Australia.

Died 14 Jan. 1947.

MADOCKS, Brig.-Gen. William Robarts Napier, CB 1919; CMG 1916; DSO 1917; late RA; JP; *b* 1871; 2nd *s* of late Henry Robarts Madocks, Glanywern, Denbigh, and Hon. Anne Amelia, *d* of 1st Baron Napier of Magdala; *m* 1903, Laura (*d* 1934), *d* of late Sir Walter Buller, KCMG, FRS; one *d*. *Educ*: RMA, Woolwich. Joined RFA in India, 1891; Staff Officer New Zealand Defence Forces, 1896–99; served in SA War with New Zealand Mounted Rifles, 1899–1900, also as ADC to GOC Mounted Infantry, 1900–01, and DAAG 1901–02 (despatches, Bt Major); entered Staff College, 1905; on Gen. Staff Southern Coast Defences, 1907; Military Secretary to Inspector-General Oversea Forces, 1910–13; commanded a battery in European War, Aug. 1914 to Feb. 1915 (wounded, despatches, CMG); General Staff British Expeditionary Force, 1915–17; Brig.-Gen. RA 1917–19 (DSO, CB, despatches, Croix de Guerre, with palm); Commandant N Wales Infantry Brigade TA 1920–24; Colonel on the Staff, Malta, 1924–27; retired with rank of Brigadier-General, 1927. *Recreation*: all field sports. *Address*: Old Basing House, Basingstoke. *Clubs*: Flyfishers', Royal Automobile.

Died 27 Oct. 1946.

MAETERLINCK, Count Maurice; Belgian author; *b* 29 Aug. 1862; *m* Renée Dahon. *Publications*: Serres chaudes; Les aveugles; La princesse Maleine, 1890 (English, 1892); Les sept princesses; Pelléas et Mélisande,

1892 (English 1892, 1894); Alladine et Palomides, 1894 (English, 1898); Aglavaine et Sélysette, 1896 (English, 1897); Douze chansons, 1896; Le trésor des humbles (English, 1897); Intérieur; La mort de Tintagiles: L'intruse; La sagesse et la destinée (English, 1898); La Vie des Abeilles (English, 1901); Le Temple Enseveli, 1902; Monna Vanna (play); Joyzelle (play), 1903; The Double Garden, 1904; L'intelligence des fleurs, 1907; The Blue Bird, 1909; La Mort, 1913; various translations of other authors, with prefaces: two small dramas. Ariane et Barbebleue and Sœur Béatrice, 1899; Mary Magdalene (play), 1910; The Death of Tintagiles (play), 1913; The Unknown Guest; The Wrack of the Storm, 1916; Betrothal, 1918; The Burgomaster of Stilemonde, 1918; Les Sentiers dans la Montayne, 1919; The Great Secret; The Life of the White Ant, 1926; The Life of Space, 1927; The Magic of the Stars, 1930; The Life of the Ant, 1931; L'Araignée de Verre, 1932; La Grande Loi, 1933; Avant le Grand Silence, 1934; Pigeons and Spiders, 1935; The Hour-Glass, 1936; L'ombre des Ailes, 1936; Devant Dieu, 1937; The Abbot of Setubal (play), 1940. *Recreations:* bee-keeping, canoeing, skating, bicycling, motoring, etc.

Died 6 May 1949.

MAGENNIS, William, MA; Hon. DLitt; KCSS; Barrister-at-law; Professor of Metaphysics, University College, Dublin; Commissioner of Intermediate Education (Ireland); Commissioner of National Education; Professor, Carysfort Training College since 1889; Member Governing Body University College, and Member of Senate, National, University of Ireland; late Member of Dail Eireann (TD) for the University; Member of Senate of Eire; Governor National Gallery of Ireland; *b* 1869. *Educ:* Christian Schools, Belfast; Belvedere College and University College, Dublin. 1st class Honours and 1st class Exhibition BA, RUI; 1st class Honours MA; Studentship in Philosophy; Fellow, Royal University of Ireland. Called to Bar, King's Inns, Dublin, 1893; Examiner to the Board of Intermediate Education, 1893; First Advising Examiner in English, 1900; Editor of Lyceum, 1890–92; of New Ireland Review, 1893. *Publications:* Irish Democracy; Blind Bartimeus, and other Poems; editions of English Classics; Lectures on Poetry and Criticism, Ethics and Art, etc.; articles on Literary and Philosophical topics in Irish and American periodicals since 1888. *Recreations:* photography, art. *Address:* University College, Dublin.

Died 30 March 1946.

MAGHERAMORNE, 3rd Baron *cr* 1887; **Dudley Stuart McGarel-Hogg;** *b* 3 Dec. 1863; *s* of 1st Baron and Caroline, *d* of 1st Lord Penrhyn; *S* brother, 1903. *Recreations:* riding and shooting. *Heir:* *b* Hon. Ronald T. McGarel-Hogg. *Address:* 37 Knyveton Road, Bournemouth.

Died 14 March 1946.

MAGILL, Andrew Philip, CB 1919; LLB; late Assistant Secretary, Ministry of Home Affairs for Northern Ireland; 2nd *s* of late Charles Magill, Upton Lodge, Drumdoncra, Dublin; *m* 1920, Mabella Edith, *e d* of late James MacTier, Vernant Lodge, Belfast, Ireland. *Address:* 47 Knock Road, Belfast. *T:* Belfast 53133.

Died 21 April 1941.

MAGILL, Walter Alexander, CBE 1937; ISO; retired Civil Servant; *b* 3 April 1879; *s* of Charles Magill, Dublin and Dromore, Co. Down, and Marie Spengler, Lausanne, Switzerland; *m* 1st, 1909, Emma Azile Doake (decd); 2nd, 1919, Margaret Elizabeth Mathews; one *s*. *Educ:* private schools; Trinity College, Dublin (Mod. BA). Boy Clerk Irish Land Commission and Office of Public Works, Dublin, 1895–97; 2nd Division Clerk, Education Office, Dublin and DMP Office, Dublin, 1898–1908; Secretary and Accountant DMP Office, 1908; Ministry of Home Affairs, Northern Ireland, 1921;

Principal Officer, Asst Secretary, Permanent Secretary, 1935–39, in that Ministry. *Recreation:* golf. *Address:* Islandderry, Massey Avenue, Belfast. *T:* Belfast 63311.

Died 31 March 1950.

MAGLIONE, His Eminence Cardinal Luigi, PhD, STD, JCD; Secretary of State to His Holiness since 1939; *b* Casoria, 2 March 1877; *s* of Nicholas Maglione and Maria Gaetana Cortese. *Educ:* Capranica College; Gregorian University; Apollinare Atheneum; Academy for Noble Ecclesiastics. Priest, 1901; Official of the Secretariate of State, 1908–18; Prof. of Ecclesiastical Diplomacy, Academy for Noble Ecclesiastics, 1912–18; Tutor in Theology, Leonine College, 1910–13; Spiritual Director, Capranica College, 1912–18; Private Chamberlain to His Holiness, 1910; Domestic Prelate to His Holiness, 1918; Representative of the Holy See in Switzerland, 1918–20; Titular Archbishop of Caesaria in Palestine, 1920; Nuncio Apostolic to Switzerland, 1920–26; Nuncio Apostolic to France, 1926–36; Cardinal, 1935, and assigned the Titular Church of St Prudentiana; Prefect of the Sacred Congregation of the Council, 1938–39. *Address:* The Vatican, Vatican City.

Died 22 Aug. 1944.

MAGNAY, Thomas; JP; Accountant; *b* 1876; *s* of late George Magnay; *m* 1899, Mary, *d* of John Fittes Smith; four *c*. *Educ:* Elswick Works Technical Schools, Newcastle-on-Tyne. MP (National Liberal) Gateshead, 1931–45. Contested Blaydon Division 1929, Gateshead 1945. *Address:* Crosslands, Durham Rd, Low Fell, Gateshead.

Died 3 Nov. 1949.

MAGNES, Judah Leon, PhD; President, Hebrew University, Jerusalem; *b* San Francisco, California, 5 July 1877; *s* of David Magnes and Sophie Abrahamson; *m* 1908, Beatrice Lowenstein; three *s*. *Educ:* Oakland, California; Cincinnati; Berlin and Heidelberg. Instructor and Librarian, Hebrew Union College, Cincinnati; Rabbi, Temple Emanuel, New York; Chm., Jewish Community, New York; Executive Committee, American Civil Liberties Union. *Address:* Jerusalem, Palestine.

Died 27 Oct. 1948.

MAGRATH, Charles Alexander, LLD; FRSC; *b* North Augusta, Ontario, 22 April 1860; *s* of Bolton Magrath and Laura M'Phee; *m* 1st, 1887, Margaret Holmes Mair (*d* 1892); one *s*; 2nd, 1899, Mabel Lilias, *d* of late Sir A. T. Galt, GCMG; two *d*. *Educ:* private tuition. Went to Canadian West, 1878; engaged in irrigation and other development work in Southern Alberta; represented Lethbridge in North-West Assembly for several years, finally becoming member in Haultain Cabinet; elected as Liberal-Conservative in 1908 to House of Commons for Medicine Hat constituency; defeated, 1911; Member Canadian Section International Joint Commission, 1911–15, and Chairman, 1915–36; Fuel Controller, Canada, 1917–20; chairman of temporary Commission created in 1913 by Ontario to investigate and report on comprehensive system of highways for that province; President, Victorian Order of Nurses, 1922–28; Member, Federal Advisory Fuel Committee, 1922–25; Chairman Hydro-Electric Power Commission of Ontario, 1925–31; Member Newfoundland Royal Commission, 1933. *Address:* 841 St Charles Street, Victoria, BC. *Clubs:* Union (Victoria, BC).

Died 30 Oct. 1949.

MAGUIRE, Sir Alexander Herbert, Kt 1917; Chairman and Managing Director of Maguire & Paterson, Ltd, Dublin, and of Maguire & Paterson (NI), Ltd, match manufacturers; Privy Chamberlain of the Sword and Cape to the Pope; *b* 18 May 1876; *s* of late John Thomas Maguire, Liverpool; *m* 1902, Isabel Mary, *d* of late Hugh William Todd, Liverpool; one *s* two *d*. *Educ:* Waterloo College, Liverpool. Initiated movement which led to prohibition of use of white phosphorus in match manufacture, and was responsible for passing of the White Phosphorus Match Prohibition Act. *Address:* Ardmulchan, Navan, Co. Meath. *Clubs:* Royal Automobile; Ulster Yacht, Belfast.

Died 20 Jan. 1947.

MAHAFFY, Robert Pentland; barrister; *b* Dublin, 1871; 2nd *s* of late Sir J. P. Mahaffy, GBE, DCL, etc. Provost of Trinity College, Dublin; *m* 1919, Hon. Evelina Viscount, *d* of late Hon. Conrad Dillon and sister of 19th Viscount Dillon; two *s*. *Educ:* Foundation Scholar of Marlborough College and King's College, Cambridge; First Class in History Tripos, 1893; Whewell Scholar, 1894; Prince Consort's Prizeman and Worts' Travelling Scholar, 1896. One of the editors of the Calendar of State Papers, 1896–1914; called to the Bar, 1901; Inns of Court OTC, 1898–1914; Captain, Devon Regiment, 1914; severely wounded, 1 July 1916; Egyptian Army, 1917–19; civilly employed as Judge of Blue Nile and Kordofan Provinces; Assist Legal Adviser Rhineland High Commission, 1919; Major, Royal Fusiliers (TF), 1920; Legal Adviser to the Governor of Malta, 1921–29. *Publications:* Life of the Emperor Francis Joseph, 1908 (2nd ed. 1914); Law relating to Motor Cars, 1910 (3rd ed. 1929); The Road Traffic Act, 1930 (2nd ed. 1936); The Statute of Westminster (1931), 1932; several volumes of the Calender of State Papers. *Recreations:* shooting, golf, rowing. *Address:* 3 Essex Court, Temple, EC4. *T:* Central 3808; Greatash, Chislehurst. *T:* Chislehurst 61. *Clubs:* United University, Leander.

Died 8 May 1943.

MAHAIM, Ernest A. J.; *b* 27 April 1865; *s* of Aime Mahaim and Ernestine Squelard; *m* 1892; one *s* one *d*. *Educ:* Athenée and University, Liège. During the war, Director for the Province of Liège of the Belgian National Committee; Minister of Industry and Labour, 1921; Delegate of the Belgian Government to the International Labour Conferences and to the governing body of ILO (Geneva); President of the Conference, 1930, and of the governing body, 1931–32; Professor at the University of Liège, 1892–1935; Professor Emeritus, 1935; Director of the Solvay Institute of Sociology, Brussels, 1923–35; Hon. Director, 1935; Member of the Belgian Royal Academy, of the Institute of International Law, of the International Institute of Statistics; Correspondent of the Institut de France, of the Royal Economic Society, London, of the Academia of Madrid, etc.; Hon. LLD Universities of Glasgow and Geneva. *Publications:* Études sur l'Association professionelle, 1891; Les Abonnements d'ouvriers sur les chemins de fer et leurs effets sociaux, 1910; Le Droit International Ouvrier, 1913; La Belgique Restaurée, 1925; Le Secours Chômage en Belgique, 1925; L'Organisation Internationale de Travail, 1925; contributions to many reviews. *Recreation:* tennis. *Address:* 9 Avenue du Hêtre, Cointe, Liège, Belgium. *TA:* Cointe, Liège. *T:* 135.43. *Clubs:* Fondation Universitaire, Brussels.

Died 1 Dec. 1938.

MAHON, Lt-Col Bryan MacMahon, CIE 1942; DSO 1917; MC 1916; Indian Cavalry (retired); *b* 18 Feb. 1890; *s* of William Henry Cortlandt Mahon and Mary Caroline Elliot; *m* Adeline Mary, *d* of late Albert Farquhar, of Woodnesborough Grange, Sandwich, Kent, and Aboyne, Aberdeenshire; one *d*. *Educ:* Dulwich College. Joined The Honourable Society of Lincoln's Inn, 1910; called to Bar, 1918; 2nd Lieutenant in 18th London Regiment, Aug. 1914; served in France and Belgium, 1915–17 (wounded, despatches thrice, MC, DSO); joined Indian Cavalry, 1918; served on North-West Frontier with Frontier Irregular Corps (Indian General Service Medal and Clasp Waziristan, 1922–24); Commandant the Kurram Militia, Kurram Valley, NWFP, 1931–34; Commandant, The Scinde Horse, 1937–39; Military Secretary to the Viceroy of India, 1939–42; Adviser to the Heir-Apparent of the Maharaja

of Jodhpur, 1942–45; Brevet Major, 1930; Brevet Lieutenant-Colonel, 1936; Lieut-Colonel, 1937. *Publications:* Trench Warfare in France, Journal of the United Service Institution of India, Jan. 1919; Hermoso Toros, Cavalry Journal, Oct. 1931; Cavalry i Kurram and Khost, Cavalry Journal, Oct. 1933. *Recreations:* sport and travel. *Address:* Woodnesborough House, near Sandwich, Kent. *Clubs:* Cavalry, Royal Automobile; Royal St George's Golf (Sandwich).

Died 16 Sept. 1949.

MAHON, John FitzGerald; *b* 20 Jan. 1858; 3rd *s* of Sir William Vesey Ross Mahon, 4th Bart; *m* 1898, Lady Alice Evelyn, 5th *d* of 5th Marquess of Sligo; one *s*. *Address:* 33 Cadogan Square, SW1. *T:* Sloane 7311. *Club:* Carlton.

Died 5 Nov. 1942.

MAHONEY, Merchant Michael, CBE 1935; First Secretary Canadian Legation Washington DC, USA, 1927–38, Commercial Counsellor, 1938, Counsellor of Legation and Embassy since 1941; *b* 17 July 1886; *s* of Michael Mahoney and Mary Brennan; *m* 1st, 1915, Loretto De Rochie (*d* 1934); one *s* one *d*; 2nd, 1935, Mary Frances Moloney. Served with Imperial Munitions Board, 1916–18; with Canadian War Mission at Washington, USA, 1918–21; Representative Department External Affairs of Canada at Washington, USA 1921–27. *Recreations:* golf and fishing. *Address:* Canadian Embassy, Washington, DC, USA. *T:* Decatur 1011.

Died 4 May 1946.

MAHOOD, James, CBE 1938; ISO 1930; *b* 8 Sept. 1876; *s* of Thomas and Jane Mahood, Portaferry, Co. Down; *m* 1907, Violet Maud (*d* 1949), *d* of George Daintry, Folkestone; two *d*. *Educ:* privately. Entered Paymaster General's Office, 1896; Senior Examiner, 1919; Head of Division, 1923; Principal Clerk, 1927; Asst Paymaster General, 1935–38; retired, 1938; re-employed as Chief Accountant, Ministry of Supply, 1939–41; Chairman Chiswick Ground Executive Civil Service Sports Council, Ltd 1939–40; Hon. Sec. Merton Park (Wimbledon) Golf Club, Ltd, and Morden Park Golf Club, Morden, Surrey, 1939–40; Hon. Sec. Coombe Wood Golf Club, Kingston Hill, 1948. Runner-up British Chess Championship, 1913; Winner of Hampstead Chess Championship, 1904 and Civil Service Chess Championship, 1928–29–1930; NRA Recruits Silver Medallist, 1904 and NRA Bronze Medallist (Middlesex Rifle Assoc.), 1906. *Recreations:* golf, sea fishing, wild-fowling. *Address:* Mapledor, 16 Regent Road, Surbiton Hill, Surrey. *T:* Elmbridge 2593.

Died 14 March 1950.

MAILLOL, Aristide; sculptor; *b* Banyuls, Eastern Pyrenees, 1861. *Educ:* École des Beaux Arts under Cabanel. *Address:* Marlyle-Roi, Seine et Oise, 15 rue Thibaud; Banyuls, Eastern Pyrenees, France.

Died Sept. 1944.

MAIN, Rev. Archibald; Chaplain to the King since 1925; *b* Partick, Glasgow, Dec. 1876; *m* 1907, Mary Jardine, *d* of Andrew Giffen, Glasgow; one *d*. *Educ:* Garnethill School, Glasgow; University of Glasgow and University of Oxford; MA (Glasgow), 1899; Snell Exhibitioner; BA (Oxon), 1903; Stanhope Historical Prize; DLitt (Glasgow), 1912, for thesis on Life and Times of Ralph Cudworth. Examiner for MA Degree of St Andrews University in Political Economy, 1906–08; in Modern History and Political Economy, 1912–14; Minister of the parish of St Madoes, Perthshire, 1904–12; of Old Kilpatrick, 1912–15; Professor of Ecclesiastical History, St Andrews, 1915–22; Regius Professor of Ecclesiastical History in the University of Glasgow, 1922–42; Minister of Kirkbean, Dumfries, 1942–46; Chaplain to the Forces (overseas) 1918–19; Examiner in Political Economy at Glasgow University 1921; DD

(Glasgow) 1921; Cunningham Lecturer, 1925–26; editor of The Man's own Paper, 1926; Examiner in Church History at Belfast and at St Andrews Univ.; Lee Lecturer, 1933; represented the Church of Scotland in Canada, 1925, Argentina, 1929 and Victoria, Australia, 1934; Baird Lecturer, 1935–36; Moderator of General Assembly of Church of Scotland, 1939–40; LLD (Glasgow), 1943. *Publications:* The Emperor Sigismund, 1903; articles in Hastings' Dictionaries; reviews in Review of Theology and Philosophy; contributed to The Outline of Christianity, vol. iii, and to the History of Christianity in the Light of Modern Knowledge; articles and reviews in the Scottish Historical Review and other periodicals. *Recreations:* golf and curling. *Address:* Ardgour, Stoneykirk, Stranraer. *T:* Sandhead 211. *Clubs:* Overseas League; Royal and Ancient, St Andrews.

Died 14 March 1947.

MAIN, David, CB 1932; VD; Solicitor; Lt-Col and Hon. Col RA (TA); retired; Chairman Cumberland Territorial Army Association, 1922–37; Chairman of Joint Committee of Cumberland and Westmorland Territorial Army Association, 1927–37; *b* Whithorn, Wigtownshire, 2 Feb. 1861; *s* of George Agnew Main, Carlisle; unmarried. *Educ:* Dollar Academy; privately. Admitted Solicitor, 1884; Commanded 1st Cumberland Royal Garrison Artillery (Vols), 1905–08; Commanded 4th East Lancs (Howitzer) Brigade RFA (TA), 1908–10; retired on completion of Command, 1910; rejoined 1915 for War Service and demobilised 1919; Original Military Member of Cumberland (TA) Association. *Recreations:* formerly rugby football, cricket and tennis. *Address:* 3 Eden Mount, Stanwix, Carlisle. *T:* 872. *Clubs:* Constitutional; County, Carlisle.

Died 11 June 1941.

MAIN, Henry, CBE 1943; Commander, Order of Orange-Nassau; JP; Managing Director Caledon Shipbuilding & Engineering Co. Ltd, Dundee, Angus; *b* 31 Oct. 1888; *o s* of Thomas Edward Main and Catherine Cameron; *m* 1915, Catherine Gunn Miller; four *d*. *Educ:* Fairfield Secondary School, Glasgow; Royal Technical College, Glasgow. Director Sir W. G. Armstrong Whitworth & Co. (Shipbuilders) Ltd, Newcastle-on-Tyne; National Shipbuilders Security Ltd; President Shipbuilding Employers' Federation, 1939–40; Freeman City of London; Liveryman Worshipful Company of Shipwrights; Member Technical Committee of Lloyd's Register of Shipping London; Member Glasgow Committee of Lloyd's Register of Shipping; Member Dundee Harbour Board; Regional Director for East of Scotland, Admiralty (MS & R); Panel Member Nat. Arbitration Tribunal; Member of Council, British Shipbuilding Research Association. *Recreation:* golf. *Address:* Hamewith, Glamis Road, Dundee, Angus. *TA:* Main Caledon, Dundee. *T:* Dundee 68395. *Clubs:* Royal Automobile; Eastern (Dundee); Panmure Golf (Barry).

Died 8 April 1949.

MAINDS, Allan Douglass, ARSA; Professor of Fine Art and Director King Edward VII School of Art, King's College, Durham University, since 1931; *b* Helensburgh, Dumbartonshire, 1881; *y s* of William Reid Mainds and Catherine Gilfillan; *m* Mary, *yr d* of George Hogg, Old Kilpatrick, Dumbartonshire; one *s* one *d*. *Educ:* Haldane Academy; Glasgow School of Art. Haldane Travelling Scholar, 1907–08; studied under Professor Jean Delville of Brussels, and at Rome. Member of Staff of Life School and Lecturer in Art History at Glasgow School of Art, 1909–31; served with Royal Field Artillery in France; elected a Painter Associate of the Royal Scottish Academy, 1929. *Recreation:* travelling. *Address:* Elmfield Road, Gosforth, Northumberland. *T:* Newcastle 51101. *Clubs:* Glasgow Art; Pen and Palette, Newcastle.

Died 4 July 1945.

MAINWARING, Albert James, CIE 1934; BA; ICS; Magistrate and Collector, Bihar and Orissa, since 1933; *b* 30 Nov. 1891. *Educ:* King's School, Worcester; Pembroke College, Oxford. Entered ICS, 1914; military service, 1916–19. *Address:* Monghyr, Bihar and Orissa, India.

Died 30 Nov. 1941.

MAINWARING, Charles Francis Kynaston; JP, DL; *b* 17 Dec. 1871; *e s* of Salusbury Kynaston Mainwaring (*d* 1895), and Edith Sarah, 2nd *d* of Sir Hugh Williams, 3rd Bart, of Bodelwyddan, Flintshire; *m* 1903, Mary Sybil, 3rd *d* of Sir James Rankin, 1st Bart; one *s* four *d*. *Educ:* Eton; Trinity Hall, Cambridge. High Sheriff, Shropshire, 1907; a Capt. and Hon. Major late 3rd Batt. Oxfordshire LI; Patron of 2 livings. *Address:* Seven Sisters, Ellesmere, Salop. *T:* Ellesmere 123. *Club:* Junior Carlton.

Died 30 Jan. 1949.

MAINWARING, Col Sir Watkin Randle Kynaston, Kt 1933; CB 1939; CBE 1919; DL, JP Co. Flint; Hon. Col 60th Royal Welch Fusiliers A-TR since 1937; *b* 1875; 2nd *s* of late Salusbury Kynaston Mainwaring of Oteley, Ellesmere; *m* 1903, Violet Frances, *y d* of late Sir A. de Rutzen, Chief Metropolitan Magistrate; one *s* one *d*. *Educ:* Eton; Christ Church, Oxford. Private Secretary, unpaid, to Rt Hon. W. H. Long at Local Govt Board and Irish Office; Assistant Quartermaster-General at General Headquarters, Egypt, 1916–19 (Servian Order of the White Eagle, Order of El Nadjha Hedjaz and Order of the Nile, CBE, despatches four times); High Sheriff, Co. Flint, 1924; a Director Gillett Brothers' Discount Co. Ltd. *Recreation:* agriculture. *Address:* Hafod y Coed, St Asaph, N Wales. *TA:* Hafod y Coed, Tremeirchion. *T:* Trefnant 322. *Clubs:* Oxford and Cambridge, Junior Carlton.

Died 14 July 1944.

MAIR, Brig.-Gen. George Tagore, CMG 1919; DSO 1906; *b* 28 April 1873; *s* of late Robert Slater Mair, MD; *m* 1931, Elaine Catherine, *d* of late Clifford R. Pease. *Educ:* Epsom. Entered army (RA) 1893; Capt., 1900; Major, 1910; Lt-Col 1915; Col 1919; retired, 1928; served S Africa, 1900 (severely wounded, Queen's medal 3 clasps); W Africa 1903 and 1906 (despatches, DSO, WA medal). *Address:* Enton Hatch, Godalming. *Club:* Army and Navy.

Died 25 Nov. 1941.

MAIR, Dame Sarah Elizabeth Siddons, DBE 1931; LLD; *b* 23 Sept. 1846; *d* of Major Arthur Mair, 62nd Light Infantry and Elizabeth Harriot Siddons; *g d* of Sarah Siddons; unmarried. Voluntary worker. *Recreations:* archery, chess. *Address:* 5 Chester Street, Edinburgh. *T:* 22003.

Died 13 Feb. 1941.

MAITLAND, Viscount; Ivor Colin James Maitland; Lieut Lothian and Border Horse; *b* 24 Aug. 1915; *o s* of 15th Earl of Lauderdale; *m* 1936, Helena Ruth, *yr d* of late Col Sir Herbert Perrott; three *d*. *Educ:* Stowe.

Died 18 Jan. 1943.

MAITLAND, Sir Adam, Kt 1939; late Chairman of Directors, The Pall Mall Gazette and Globe; Chairman of the Berry Hill Collieries, Ltd, and of the Berry Hill Brickworks, Ltd; Director of the London Board of the Royal Exchange Assurance; MP (C) Faversham Division, 1928–45; JP Henley-on-Thames; Chairman of Departmental Committee on Costs and Maintenance of Hospitals, Sanatoria and other Municipal Buildings; Member of Joint Select Committee on Water Resources of the Country; Committee Chairman, House of Commons; Member of Select Committee on National Expenditure; Former Member of Surrey County Council and Vice-Chairman, Coulsdon and Purley Urban District Council; Vice-President, Association of Municipal Corporations; Vice-President, National Association of Building Societies; President National

Fire Brigades' Association; *b* Bury, Lancs, 25 May 1885; *s* of late Joseph Maitland, Aberdeenshire; *m* Nancy Helen, *d* of H. Chadwick, Bury; one *d*. *Educ:* Manchester Central School; private tuition. FSAA; in 1914–18 War in hon. capacity rendered service to Financial Section of Ministry of Food; as a member of Trade Committees dealing with Rolling Stock and Transport, rendered assistance to the Ministry of Munitions and the Board of Trade; took active part in promoting and maintaining War Savings Associations; interested himself in several local associations in Lancashire dealing with disabled and wounded soldiers and their dependants; Order of the Three Stars of the Republic of Latvia. *Recreations:* golf and tennis. *Address:* Beechlands, Henley-on-Thames, Oxon. *Clubs:* Carlton, Constitutional, MCC.

Died 5 Oct. 1949.

MAITLAND, Sir John, 6th Bt *cr* 1818; TD; Assistant Master, Alleyn's School, Dulwich, 1920–49; *b* 25 Nov. 1879; *e s* of Sir John Nisbet Maitland, 5th Bt and Florence (*d* 1899), *d* of Philip Rickman of Twickenham; *S* father 1936; *m* 1915, Kathleen Offley, 2nd *d* of H. T. Keates, Petersfield; one *d*. *Educ:* Haileybury; Trinity College, Cambridge (MA, LLB). Barrister, Inner Temple; late Lieut RGA (SR) and Capt. OTC; served European War, 1916–19 (despatches). *Recreation:* reading. *Heir: b* Lieut-Col G. R. Maitland, DSO. *Address:* 62 Holmdene Avenue, Herne Hill, SE24. *T:* Brixton 2168. *Club:* East India and Sports.

Died 27 Nov. 1949.

MAITLAND, Thomas Gwynne, MA, BSc, MD, ChB, DPhil; Medical Superintendent, Cunard White Star Co. Ltd; *m* Gwynneth Kathleen, *d* of Frederick Wood; one *s* one *d*. *Educ:* University College School, London; private; University of Edinburgh (Distinction for Thesis in MD); University of Manchester (Honours Philosophy); and University of Paris. Late Resident Physician, Brompton Hospital; One time editor of Manchester Medical Gazette; Demonstrator of Physiology at Manchester; Lecturer on Physiology at Universities of Wales, Birmingham, and Manchester; Honorary Physician of Walsall and District Hospital; Lecturer on Psychology at the Midland Institute; Co-editor of the Midland Medical Review: Director of Typhus Colony, Skopelj, Serbia; late Honorary Lieut-Col in Serbian Army. *Publications:* Examination of the Basis of Personality; Hysteria, a Psychological Study; numerous other publications. *Recreations:* lawn tennis, ski-ing, and curling. *Address:* Hatchmere Wood, Norley, Cheshire. *T:* Liverpool Central 9201. *Clubs:* Bath, Queen's.

Died 10 Aug. 1948.

MAITLAND, Victor Kennard, CSI 1947; MC 1918; MA; Forestry and Soil Conservation Adviser, British Middle East Office of Foreign Office since 1947; *b* 12 June 1897; 2nd *s* of George Arthur and Mabel Katherine Maitland; *m* 1927, Louise Marie, *d* of late William Gaedke, Chicago, USA; no *c*. *Educ:* St Olave's Grammar School; Queen's College, Oxford. Served European War, 1914–18, Capt. Royal Tank Corps, France, Belgium, Germany (wounded twice, MC), 1916–19; MA (Oxford); Diploma of Forestry; joined Indian Forest Service, Dec. 1921; served CP, India, as Asst Conservator, Dep. Conservator, Conservator, 1939, Chief Conservator, 1946; Research Officer, 1923–26; Secretary Forest Cttee, etc., 1928–; various special duties in connection with aboriginal tribes; Major AIRO, Royal Tank Corps, 1935; Director Forest School, 1937–39; Special Magistrate 1st Class; assisted training of 1st Wingate expedition; organised war supplies of timber, 1940–45, and CP post-war forest planning; interested in rural uplift, agricultural and health development and land use planning; retires from Indian Forest Service, July 1949. *Publications:* various technical publications, Forest Research Institute, Dehra Dun,

Indian Forester, and CP Govt Press. *Recreations:* sailing, ski-ing, shooting. *Address:* c/o Lloyds Bank, 6 Pall Mall, SW1. *Clubs:* Little Ship; Gezira Sporting (Cairo).

Died 25 April 1950.

MAJOR, Alfred George; *b* Barrow-in-Furness, Aug. 1879; *s* of S. E. Major, Solicitor; *m* 1909, Amy Blanche Compson; one *s*. *Educ:* St John's School, Leatherhead. Appointed Student Interpreter in HM Consular Service in China, 1901; Vice-Consul, 1917; Consul 1923; Consul-General, 1931; served at Peking, Canton, Wuchow, Macao, Shanghai, Hankow, Hangchow, Swatow, Pakhoi, Hoihow, Chungking, Tsingtao, Harbin, Tsinanfu, and Mukden; transferred to the General Consular Service, 1935; HM Consul-General at Genoa, 1935–39. *Publication:* Instructions to HM Consular Officers in China 1915 and 1927. *Recreation:* motoring.

Died 16 June 1940.

MAJOR, Ernest Harry, FRIBA; *b* 30 June 1876; 4th *s* of Henry Major, Lisburn, and *brother* to Edith Major, CBE; *m* Leila Mary, *d* of late Herbert Bennett; one *s* one *d*. *Educ:* Royal Academical Institution, Belfast. Articled to A. T. Jackson, Belfast; came to London and studied in the offices of Rowland Plumbe and F. W. Tasker; joined the firm of H. F. Tasker; general and domestic practice. *Recreations:* now restricted to watching other people playing football, cricket and golf. *Address:* Queen Anne's Mansions, SW1. *T:* Whitehall 6262; Fridays, Ockley, Surrey.

Died 13 Feb. 1941.

MAKGILL, Robert Haldane, CBE 1919; Medical Officer, Government Health Department, New Zealand, 1901–38; *b* 24 May 1870; *s* of Captain Sir John Makgill, RE, of Kemback, Fifeshire; unmarried. *Educ:* Edinburgh University. MBCM (Edin.), 1893; MD (Edin.), 1899; DPH (Camb.), 1901. Served in South African War as Civil Surgeon Natal Field Force, 1900; European War in RAMC in Egyptian Expeditionary Force (Sanitary Branch), 1915–16; ADMS (San.) New Zealand EF, 1916–18.

Died 3 Oct. 1946.

MAKINO, Nobuaki, Count; late Grand Keeper of the Imperial Seals; *b* 22 Oct. 1861; *s* of Marquis Okubo; *m* Miné, *d* of Viscount Mishima; one *s* one *d*. *Educ:* Tokio University; England. Was Japanese Minister in Rome and Vienna; Minister of Education, Agriculture, Commerce, and Foreign Affairs; one of the representatives of Japan at the Peace Conference, 1919. *Address:* Tokio, Japan.

Died 25 Jan. 1949.

MAKOWER, Ernest Samuel, FSA; *b* London, 5 March 1876; 3rd *s* of late Moritz Makower; *m* Rachel, 2nd *d* of J. Caro, Norwich; one *s* one *d*. *Educ:* University College School; France; Germany. Chairman, M. Makower & Co., Ltd; Chairman, Makower McBeath Propy., Australia, Makower McBeath, Ltd, New Zealand, and 1919 Australian Imperial Forces Disposal Board; Vice-President of Overseas League Council of Rayon and Silk Assoc. and of the London Society; Chairman of Silk Section of Chamber of Commerce; gave Essex Ring to Westminster Abbey; formed Prime Ministers' Room, London Museum; Trustee of London Museum; Director Royal Academy of Music; Member Financial Executive British Council. *Recreations:* art, music, museums, riding, racing. *Address:* Holmwood, Binfield Heath, Oxon. *T:* Sonning 2161. *Clubs:* Savile, Athenæum, Burlington Fine Arts; Newmarket.

Died 2 May 1946.

MAKOWER, Dr Walter, OBE 1934; Member of the Board of Management of the Research Association of British Rubber Manufacturers; *b* London, 1879; *s* of Louis Makower, merchant; *m* 1911, Dorothy Lois Drey, Manchester; one *s* two *d*. *Educ:* University College

School; University College, London; Trinity College, Cambridge. BSc (London), 1900; DSc (London), 1909; Fellow of University College, London, 1913; Cavendish Laboratory, Cambridge, 1902–04; BA (Camb.), 1904; MA (Camb.), 1909; John Harling Fellow, University of Manchester, 1904–06. Lecturer and Demonstrator, Physics University of Manchester, and subsequently Assistant Director of Physical Laboratories, 1906–17; Lieut RNVR and Capt. RAF, 1917–19; Chief Physicist Dunlop Rubber Co., Ltd, 1920; Professor of Science, Royal Military Academy, Woolwich, 1925–38. *Publications:* Radio-Active Substances, 1907; Practical Measurements in Radio-Activity, 1913; various papers on Radio-Activity, and other papers in Proceedings of Royal Society, Physical Society, Royal Meteorological Society, Philosophical Magazine. *Address:* 153 Eglinton Hill, SE18. *T:* Woolwich 1049.

Died 7 July 1945.

MALAN, Rt Hon. François Stephanus, PC 1920; RA, LLD, (Univ. of S Africa) DEduc (Univ. of Stellenbosch); Member of Union Senate since 1927; President of Senate since 1940; *b* 12 March 1871; *m* 1st, 1897, Johanna Brummer; two *s* two *d*; 2nd, 1928, Mrs A. E. Attwell. *Educ:* Victoria College, Stellenbosch; Cambridge University (LLB); Cape University (BA). Advocate, Supreme Court, Cape Colony, 1895; Editor, Ons Land, 1895–1908; Minister of Agriculture, 1908–10; Minister of Education, United South Africa, 1910–21; MLA, Malmesbury, 1900–24; Minister of Mines and Industries, 1912–24; acting Prime Minister, 1918–19; Member of National Convention, 1908; Delegate to Imperial Conference, 1911. *Publications:* Biography: Marie Koofmans de Wet, 1925; 'n Ideale Huwelik, 1928; Ons Kerk en Prof. Du Plessis, 1933. *Address:* Mount Pleasant, Belmont Avenue, Oranjezicht, Cape Town. *T:* 2.2073. *Clubs:* City, Cape Town.

Died 31 Dec. 1941.

MALAVIYA, Pandit Madan Mohan; Rector, Benares Hindu University, since 1940; President, Indian National Congress, 1909; *b* Allahabad, 25 Dec. 1861; *m*; four *s* three *d*. *Educ:* in Hindi and Sanskrit; Dharmajyanopadesha Pathasala; in English Dist School; Muir Cen. Coll., Allahabad. Edited The Hindustan, 1887–89; The Indian Union, 1889–92; The Abhyudaya, 1907–09; BA Calcutta Univ., 1884; LLB Allahabad University, 1892; Vakil of the High Court at Allahabad; was Senior Vice-Chairman of the Local Municipal Board; Member Provincial Legislative Council, 1902–12; Member Imperial Legislative Council, 1910–20; Hon. Fellow Allahabad University; Member Indian Industrial Commission, 1916–18; President Indian National Congress, 1918; Vice-Chancellor Benares Hindu University, 1919–40; Member Indian Legislative Assembly since 1924; President, Hindu Mahasabha, 1923–25; President Sanatan Dharma Mahasabha since 1928; President Seva Samiti, India, since 1914; Chief Scout Seva Samiti Boy Scouts Assoc., India, 1919–39. *Address:* Hindu University, Benares, India.

Died 12 Nov. 1946.

MALBRÁN, Dr Manuel E., GBE; Ambassador Extraordinary and Plenipotentiary of the Argentine Republic to Italy since 1938; *b* Cordoba, Argentina, 1876; *s* of Tristan A. Malbrán, owner of estates in the Argentine and prominent in Argentine politics; *m* Maria Luisa, *d* of Isauro de la Lastra; one *s* two *d*. *Educ:* Buenos Aires University. Lawyer; Legal Adviser to the National Council of Public Health; Member of the National University of Buenos Aires; Doctor (Hon.) National University of Mexico; Minister Plenipotentiary in Venezuela, Colombia, Cuba and Mexico; Ambassador Extraordinary and Plenipotentiary in Chile, Washington

and London; Delegate to various international conferences. *Publications:* monographs, etc. *Address:* Argentine Embassy, Rome. *Clubs:* Travellers', Hanworth, Argentine.

Died 12 Nov. 1942.

MALCOLM, Charles Adolf, CIE 1931; *b* 27 Aug. 1879; *e s* of late Rear-Admiral George John Malcolm, RN; *m* 1926, Doris Mary, *y d* of late William Moxon Browne, Barrister-at-Law; one *d*. *Educ:* Abroad; RIEC, Cooper's Hill. Appointed to the Indian Forest Service, 1902; Dep. Conservator, 1905; Dep. Controller, Indian Munitions Board, Bombay, 1918; Conservator of Forests, 1920; Chief Conservator of Forests, Central Provinces, India, 1928–34; retired, 1934. *Address:* 7 Egliston Road, SW15. *T:* Putney 3675.

Died 8 June 1948.

MALCOLM, George, CBE 1918; *b* 1876; *s* of late J. Malcolm, Blairgowrie; *m* 1913, Mary Sophia Lowden, *d* of J. K. Allan. A Controller at War Office and Ministry of Munitions during European War; Director of Ralli Bros Ltd, London. *Address:* Little Court, Crockham Hill, Edenbridge, Kent.

Died 30 Jan. 1941.

MALCOLM, Sir Ian (Zachary), of Poltalloch; KCMG 1919; JP; British Government Representative on the Suez Canal Board, 1919–39; *b* Quebec, 3 Sept. 1868; *e s* of late Col E. D. Malcolm, CB; *m* 1902, Jeanne Marie, *d* of late Mrs Langtry [Lady de Bathe]; three *s* one *d*. *Educ:* Eton; New College, Oxford. Hon. Attaché British Embassy, Berlin, 1891–93; transferred to Paris, 1893; attached to Embassy at St Petersburg for coronation of Emperor, 1896; Secretary to the Prince of Wales Hospital Fund, 1897 and 1898; MP Stowmarket Div. NW Suffolk, 1895–1906; Assistant Private Secretary to Lord Salisbury 1895–1900; Parliamentary Private Secretary to the Chief Secretary for Ireland, 1901–03; Secretary Union Defence League, 1906–10; contested (C) North Salford, 1910; MP (C) Croydon, 1910–19; British Red Cross Officer in France, Switzerland, Russia, North America, 1914–17; accompanied Mr Balfour's War Commission to the United States, 1917; Private Secretary to Mr Balfour at Peace Conference, Paris, 1919; Principal British Delegate to the International Congress of Navigation at Cairo, 1926, and Venice, 1931; Grand Cordon of the Nile, 1926; Commander of the Legion of Honour, 1927. *Publications:* Indian Pictures and Problems, 1907; The Calendar of Empire; Considerations, 1913; War Pictures behind the Lines, 1915; Stuff and Nonsense, 1919; Poets at Play, 1925; A Persian Pastoral, 1926; Lord Balfour, 1930; Trodden Ways, 1895–1930, 1930; Vacant Thrones: A Parliamentary Sketch Book, 1895–1931, 1931; Highland Lore and Legend, 1938; magazine articles. *Heir: e s* Lt-Col George Ian Malcolm, Argyll and Sutherland Highlanders [*m* 1929, Enid, *o d* of Maj.-Gen. H. S. Gaskell, CB]. *Address:* Poltalloch, Kilmartin, Argyllshire. *Clubs:* Carlton, MCC; New, Edinburgh.

Died 28 Dec. 1944.

MALCOLM, Robert Carmichael, MA, LLB; Sheriff-Substitute of Forfarshire at Dundee since 1921; *b* Invergarry, Inverness-shire, 30 Jan. 1868; *s* of late George Malcolm, Factor, Invergarry; *m* 1903, Norah, *d* of late William M'Keown, Land Surveyor, Edinburgh; one *s* one *d*. *Educ:* Invergarry School; George Watson's College, Edinburgh; Edinburgh University. Called to Scottish Bar, 1892; Sheriff-Substitute of Inverness, Elgin and Nairn, and also of Argyll at Fort William, 1912–21. *Recreations:* shooting, fishing, golf, photography, etc. *Address:* Thorngarth, Broughty Ferry W, Dundee. *T:* Broughty Ferry 7452. *Clubs:* Eastern, Dundee.

Died 17 Aug. 1941.

MALCOLM, Ronald; Chairman of Coutts & Co., 1931–46, now director; Director, National Provincial Bank Ltd; *s* of late W. R. Malcolm; *m* Isabel, *d* of late Sir Robert Duff, GCMG; three *s* one *d*. *Educ:* Eton. *Address:* 3 Mulberry Walk, SW3. *T:* Flaxman 9072; Walton Manor, Tadworth, Surrey. *Club:* Travellers'.

Died 3 Nov. 1949.

MALCOLMSON, Vernon Austen, MA, JP, Lord of the Manor of Aston; Patron of the Living of St Mary's, Aston cum Shephall; Member of the Stock Exchange; *b* 15 Oct. 1872; *er s* of George Forbes Malcolmson and Katherine Annesley Austen; *m* 1901, Hon. Lilian Strutt, 2nd *d* of 2nd Baron Belper, PC and *g d* of 2nd Earl of Leicester; one *s* one *d*. *Educ:* Eton; Trinity Coll., Cambridge, MA, History and Political Economy. Co-Founder, British Empire Producers' Organisation; Federation of British Industries; Empire Industries Assoc.; Empire Economic Union; British Sugar Beet Society; Industrial Peace Union; Member of HM Ministry of Labour Commission on the Employment of Ex-Officers, 1919; Assistant Organiser British Red Cross Missing and Wounded Dept, 1915–16; Rep. at Imperial Conf. Ottawa nominated by Central and Associated Chambers of Agriculture, 1932; Chairman, Westminster Housing Trust; Co-Founder and Director, Scottish Flax Co. Member of House of Laity, Church Assembly. *Publications:* The Place of Agriculture in the life of a Nation, and other publications in connection with Agriculture and Imperial Development; The Old Testament and Apocrypha—for Every Day. *Recreations:* hunting, fishing, shooting, and all forms of sport and games. *Address:* Aston Bury, Stevenage, Herts. *Clubs:* Brooks's, MCC, Farmers.

Died 23 Nov. 1947.

MALER KOTLA, Nawab of; Lt-Col HH Nawab Sir Ahmad Ali Khan, Bahadur, KCSI 1915; KCIE 1921; *b* 10 Sept. 1881; *S* 1908. *Address:* Maler Kotla, Punjab, India.

Died 16 Oct. 1947.

MALET de CARTERET, Captain Charles Edward. Solicitor-General, Jersey, 1912; Attorney-General, 1925–31; Bailifi of Jersey, 1931–35. *Clubs:* Victoria, Jersey.

Died 28 Jan. 1942.

MALIK MOHAMMED UMAR HAYAT KHAN (TIWANA), Maj.-Gen. Hon. Sir, GBE 1934; KCIE 1916; CIE 1906; CBE 1919; MVO 1911; Nawab (Hereditary 1929); Hon. ADC to the King (Extra) since 1936; Member of Council of the Secretary of State for India, 1929–34; Member of Governor-General's Imperial Council since 1910; an elected Member of the Council of State; Hon. Lieut-Col in Army, 1920; Col 1930; Maj.-Gen. 1935; attached to 19th King George's Own Lancers; Hereditary Provincial Durbari; Hon. Magistrate (1st class); *b* 1874; *s* of late Malik Sahib Khan, KB, CSI; *m*; one *s*. *Educ:* Chiefs' College, Lahore, India. One of the largest landholders in the Punjab; in possession of Delhi Durbar medal, 1903; served Somaliland War, 1902–04 (Jidballi medal and clasp); Tibet Expedition, 1903–04; European War, 1914–15 (Star 1914, despatches six times, KCIE); Afghan War, 1919 (Hon. Lt-Col); a Member of the Punjab Legislative Council for two terms; an Attaché to HM the Amir, 1907; sent as Head Indian, London Coronation, medal 1911; Deputy Herald, Delhi Durbar, 1911; Delhi Durbar medal, 1911; Hon. ADC to the King, 1930; was invited to Silver Jubilee as ADC to HM 1935; performed Haj Pilgrimage, 1935; Pres. Falconers' Club, England; Member Kennel Club, India. *Publications:* various pamphlets. *Recreations:* motoring, polo, pig-sticking, riding, shooting, athletics, hawking, coursing. *Heir: s* Major Malik Mohammed Khizar Hyat Khan. *Address:* Kalra, Shahpur, Punjab, India. *Club:* Carlton.

Died 24 March 1944.

MALINOWSKI, Bronislaw; Professor of Anthropology in the University of London, tenable at the London School of Economics since 1927; on leave for duration of hostilities since Oct. 1939; Visiting Professor of Anthropology at Yale since 1939; Fieldwork in Valley of Oaxaca, Mexico, 1940, 1941; *b* 7 April 1884; parentage on both sides Polish szlachta (landed gentry and nobility); *m* 1919, Elsie Rosaline (*d* 1935), *y d* of late Sir David Masson, KBE, FRS; three *d*; 1940, Anna Valetta Hayman-Joyce. *Educ:* King Jan Sobieski Public School; Polish Univ. Cracow. PhD 1908 with the highest honours in the Austrian Emp. (Sub auspiciis Imperatoris); did research at the British Museum and the London School of Economics from 1910. Went with the Robert Mond Anthropological Expedition to New Guinea and NW Melanesia, 1914, returning in 1918 to Australia, and in 1920 to Europe; Journey to USA and Mexico by invitation of Laura Spelman Rockefeller Memorial, visiting Universities and Pueblo Indians (1926); Trip to S and E Africa, survey work among Bantu tribes (Swazi, Bemba, Chagga, Bantu Kavirondo), 1934; Delegate of London University to Harvard Tercentenary; Hon. DSc (Harvard), 1936; Lecturer at Oslo Instituttet for Kulturforskning, 1936; Reader in Social Anthropology in the University of London, 1924; Corresponding Member of Polish Academy of Science, 1930; Correspondent of Italian Committee for Study of Population Problems, 1932; Member of Royal Academy of Science of Netherlands, 1933; Messenger Lecturer at Cornell University, 1933; Hon. Member of Royal Society of New Zealand, 1936; Correspondent of Institute for Comparative Study of Cultures, Oslo, 1936. *Publications:* The Family among the Australian Aborigines, 1913; Primitive Religion and Social Differentiation (in Polish), 1915; The Natives of Mailu, in Trans. of the RS of S Austr., 1915; Baloma: the Spirits of the Dead in the Trobriand Islands, in Jl of R. Anthrop. Inst., 1916; Argonauts of the Western Pacific, 1922; Magic Science and Religion, in Science, Religion and Reality, 1926; Crime and Custom in Savage Society, 1926; articles Anthropology in Ency. Brit., 1926 (13th ed.); Social Anthropology, Kinship, Marriage in 14th ed. 1929; Myth in Primitive Psychology, 1926 (Chinese transl. 1935); The Father in Primitive Psychology, 1927; Sex and Repression in Savage Society, 1927 (Chinese transl. 1937); The Sexual Life of Savages in NW Melanesia, 1929 (translated since into French, German, Spanish Polish and Italian); Coral Gardens and their Magic, 2 vols, 1935; The Foundations of Faith and Morals (Riddell Memorial Lectures 1934–1935), 1936; articles in Nature, Psyche, Journal of the Royal Anthropological Institute, Man, Atlantic Monthly; etc. *Address:* 128 Hall of Graduate Studies, Yale Univ., New Haven, Conn, USA.

Died 16 May 1942.

MALKIN, Sir (Herbert) William, GCMG 1937; KCMG 1930; CB 1923; CMG 1918; KC 1931; Legal Adviser to Foreign Office since 1929; *b* 17 April 1883; *o s* of late H. C. Malkin, of Corrybrough, Inverness-shire; *m* 1913, Margaret, *o c* of R. Burnet Morris. *Educ:* Charterhouse; Trinity College, Cambridge. Called to Bar, Inner Temple, 1907; bencher, 1941; employed in Foreign Office since 1911; Assistant Legal Adviser, 1914–25; Second Legal Adviser, 1925–29. *Address:* Foreign Office, SW1; The Barton, Gerrard's Cross, Bucks. *T:* Gerrard's Cross 3373; Corrybrough, Inverness-shire. *T:* Tomatin 206. *Clubs:* Athenæum, United University.

Died 4 July 1945.

MALLABY, Col (temp. Brig.) Aubertin Walter Sothern, CIE 1945; OBE 1941; Commander 49th Indian Infantry Brigade since Sept. 1944; *b* 12 Dec. 1899; *s* of William Calthorpe Mallaby and Katharine Mary Frances, *d* of George Miller, CB; *m* 1935, Margaret Catherine, *o d* of Maj.-Gen. Leslie Cockburn Jones, CB; two *s* one *d*. *Educ:* Brighton College. 2nd Lt Indian

Army, Oct. 1918; served with 1/67th Punjabis, later 1st Bn 2nd Punjab Regt, in the Black Sea Army, 1919–20, and India, 1920–29; Staff College, Camberley, 1930–31; Staff employment interspersed with regimental service, 1932–37; War Office, 1938–42 (Deputy Director of Military Operations, 1941–42); Regimental service in Bengal and Assam, 1942, with 2nd Punjab Regt and 19th Hyderabad Regt; Director of Military Operations, GHQ India, March 1943–Sept. 1944 with rank of Maj.-Gen. *Address:* c/o Grindlay & Co. Ltd, 54 Parliament St, SW1; c/o Grindlay & Co., Bombay.

Died 30 Oct. 1945.

MALLABY-DEELEY, Sir Guy Meyrick Mallaby, 2nd Bt *cr* 1922; Company Director; late Lieut 5th Dragoon Guards; *b* Park Place, Mitcham, Surrey, 23 May 1897; *o s* of Sir Harry Mallaby-Deeley, 1st Bt and Julia Jane (*d* 1933), *d* of late John Parson-Smith, of Abbotsmead, nr Shrewsbury; *S* father, 1937; *m* 1920, Marjorie Constance Lucy, *o d* of late James Ernest Peat, of Cranmer, Mitcham, Surrey; one *s* two *d. Educ:* Trinity College, Cambridge; RMC Sandhurst. Served European War with 5th Dragoon Guards, France and Belgium; Army of Occupation on Rhine; Reserve of Officers. *Heir: s* Anthony Meyrick, *b* 30 May, 1923. *Address:* Slater's Oak, Effingham, Surrey. *T:* Bookham 193.

Died 21 Jan. 1946.

MALLADRA, Prof. Alessandro; Doct. in Sciences; Director of Royal Vesuvius Observatory, 1926–35; Hon. Director since 1935; *b* Turin, 10 April 1868; *s* of Secundus and Camilla Simondetti; unmarried. *Educ:* Collegio Rosmini of Domodossola, Laureate in Natur. and Phys. Sciences at R. University of Turin, 1890. Professor of Nat. and Physic. Sciences in Lyceum, Gimnasium of Domodossola, 1890–1910; Director of Geophysical Observatory of Domodossola, 1898–1910; geologist of Simplon Tunnel Comp., 1898–1906; Assistant and Conservator of R. Vesuvius Observatory, 1910–26; President and General Secretary of Association of Volcanology of Geodetic and Geophysical International Union since 1919; member of many Italian and foreign Academies and Scientific Societies. *Publications:* Notes and memoirs (about 200) on Alpine Glaciers and Geology, of Simplon Tunnel, on Vesuvius and volcanic activity and product; Manager of Annali del R. Osservatorio Vesuviano, annual; Bulletin Volcanologique, Trimestral. *Address:* Verona, Corso V. Em. 79, Italy. *Clubs:* Alpino ital.; Touring ital.; Excursionist Neapolitains; Lega navale ital.; Croce Rossa ital.; Aerotecnica.

Died 10 July 1944.

MALLESON, Maj.-Gen. Sir Wilfrid, KCIE 1920; CB 1916; CIE 1910; *b* 8 Sept. 1866; *s* of Rev. E. Malleson, Rector of Great Bookham, Surrey; *m. Educ:* Wimbledon; RMA, Woolwich. Joined Royal Artillery, 1886; transferred to Indian Army, 1904; was for six years on the staff of Lord Kitchener as head of the Intelligence Branch, Indian Army Headquarters; accompanied the Mission to Kabul under Sir Louis Dane, 1904–05; served on General Staff, India, until Jan. 1914; Chief Censor in India, Aug.–Oct. 1914; Inspector-General Communications British East Africa, Oct. 14–Jan. 1915; on special mission to Belgian Congo Jan.–April 1915; commanding Brigade and (temp.) Division, British East Africa, 1915–16 (despatches); Head of British Mil. Mission to Turkistan, 1918–20 (despatches); served Afghan War, 1919 (KCIE); retired, 1920; Foreign decorations—Russia, Bokhara, Afghanistan. *Address:* c/o Lloyds Bank, 6 Pall Mall, SW1.

Died 24 Jan. 1946.

MALLET, Sir Charles Edward, Kt 1917; *b* Dec. 1862; *o s* of Charles Mallet and Louisa, *d* of George Udny; *m* 1895, Margaret (*d* 1938), *e d* of Rt Hon. Sir H. E. Roscoe; two *s. Educ:* Harrow; Balliol College, Oxford (1st class History, 1885). Called to Bar, Middle Temple, 1889; contested West Salford, 1900; North Salford,

1917; South Aberdeen, 1922 and 1923; JP Hants, 1906; MP (L) Plymouth, 1906–10; Financial Secretary to War Office, 1910–11; Sec. for Indian Students at the India Office, 1912–16; Chairman of Council of Charity Organisation Society, 1928–31; Hon. DLitt Oxon, 1935. *Publications:* A History of the Univ. of Oxford, 1924; Mr Lloyd George, a Study, 1930; Lord Cave, a Memoir, 1931; Herbert Gladstone, a Memoir, 1932; Anthony Hope and His Books, 1935, etc. *Recreations:* usual. *Club:* Athenæum.

Died 21 Nov. 1947.

MALLET, Sir Claude Coventry, Kt 1911; CMG 1902; *b* 20 April 1860; 3rd *s* of late Hugh Mallet (4th Light Dragoons and 16th Lancers), of Ash, Co. Devon, and Georgina, *d* of late Venerable Henry Bathurst, Archdeacon of Norwich; *m* 1892, Dona Matilde, CBE, *d* of Don G. de Obarrio and Dona Rita de Vallarino; one *s* one *d. Educ:* Brighton College. Vice-Consul at Panama, 1884; Colon, 1885; Consul at Colon, 1888; and for the Departments of Panama, Cauca, Bolivar, and Magdalena, 1891; Chargé d'Affaires at Lima, 1894; Quito, 1894–95; Bogotá, 1902–03; Minister Res., Panama and Costa Rica, 1908–14, and Minister Plenipotentiary, 1914–19; Envoy Extraordinary and Minister Plenipotentiary at Buenos Aires, 1919–20 and 1922; Envoy Extraordinary and Minister Plenipotentiary to Uruguay, 1919–25; Special Ambassador on the occasion of the inauguration of the President of the Argentine Republic, 1922; Ditto, Uruguayan Republic, 1923; retired, 1925; received the thanks of HM's Government for valuable services to the nation. *Publications:* reports on commercial subjects and the Panama Canal. *Recreations:* fishing, yachting. *Club:* Argentine.

Died 25 April 1941.

MALLETT, Edward, DSc, MInstCE, MIEE, FInstP; Fellow of University College, London; Principal, Woolwich Polytechnic; *b* 6 May 1888; *s* of John Edward Mallett and Jenny Croft; *m* Helen Wright Brow; one *s* one *d. Educ:* Southend High School; Univ. College, London. Apprenticeship at Cromptons', Chelmsford; Engineer in Post Office Engineering Dept; Assistant Professor of Electrical Engineering at City and Guilds (Engr.) College, SW7; during war Lieut and Captain in 52nd and 74th Divisional Signal Companies. *Publications:* Text-Books on Telegraphy and Telephony, Vectors for Electrical Engineers; Foundations of Technical Electricity (with T. B. Vinycomb); papers on Electrical Engineering subjects. *Recreation:* farming. *Address:* King's Court, Writtle, Essex.

Died 10 Dec. 1950.

MALLETT, Sir Rowland, Kt 1934; MD, LRCP and S (Edin.); retired; Hon. Cons. Surgeon Bolton Royal Infirmary; *b* 18 July 1869; *s* of Frederic Blakesley Mallett and Mary Frances Kearsley; *m* 1901, Mary Constance, *d* of Charles William Dixon, Westhoughton; one *s* three *d. Educ:* Rossall; Edinburgh University. Started practice, 1891; Hon. Surgeon Bolton Royal Infirmary, 1893–1929; MO Post Office, Medical Referee Workmen's Compensation Act; during the war Hon. Secretary Local Medical War Committee; entered Town Council, 1921; Vice-Chairman Watch Committee; Chairman Conservative Association, 1924–34; Chairman British Red Cross Society (Bolton Div.); Deputy President Bolton Conservative Association; Deputy Leader Conservative Party Bolton Town Council; Chairman Local Medical and Panel Committee; Vice-Chairman District Nurses Association. *Recreations:* golf and lawn tennis. *Address:* The Gables, Minchinhampton, Stroud, Glos.

Died 29 Oct. 1947.

MALLIK, Devendra Nath, BA (Cantab), ScD (Dub.), FRSE; late Principal, Carmichael College, Rangpur, N Bengal; retired 1941; *b* Bengal, 1866; *m* 1896; two *s* two *d. Educ:* St Xavier's College, Calcutta; University College, London; Peterhouse, Cambridge. Gilchrist

Scholar, 1887–93; Clothworkers' Exhibitioner and Prizeman in Physics, Medallist in Chemistry, University College, London, 1888; BSc London, 1889; Foundation Scholar and Prizeman, Peterhouse, Cambridge, 1889–93; BA (Cantab.), Mathematical Tripos, Part I, 1st Class 1892; Part II Class II, 1893. Professor of Mathematics and Physics, Patna College, Bengal, 1893–1908; Prof. of Mathematics, Presidency College, Bengal, 1908–21; Professor of Physics, Muslim Univ., Aligarh, 1922–26; University Reader in Physics, Calcutta University, 1911; ScD (Dub.), FRSE 1908; Director of Public Instruction, Jammu and Kashmere State, 1928–29. *Publications:* Algebra, part ii; Elements of Geometry; Elements of Dynamics, including Statics; Todhunter's Mensuration for Indian Schools; Optical Theories, 1918; Elements of Astronomy, 1921; various papers in the Philosophical Magazine. *Address:* 10 New Road, Alipore, Calcutta; Carmichael College, Rangpur.

Died 8 Dec. 1941.

MALLINSON, Albert; Song-composer; *b* Leeds, 1870; *s* of James and Harriet Ann Mallinson; *m* Anna Steinhauer, Danish soprano. *Educ:* Studied under Dr W. Creser (late organist Chapel Royal, St James's). Has held several important posts as organist; went to Australia, 1891, for health, and remained four years; subsequently became private organist to Viscount Portman; chiefly known as a song-writer; has composed over 400 songs, of which 300 are published; other compositions include chamber, orchestral, and church music; he and his wife have toured Germany, Scandinavian countries, Australasia (twice), and S Africa, giving recitals entirely devoted to his compositions; resided at Dresden, 1904–14. *Recreation:* literature. *Address:* Flynderborg, Elsinore, Denmark.

Died 5 April 1946.

MALLINSON, Sir William James, 2nd Bt *cr* 1935; JP Surrey; DL Co. London; *b* 25 July 1879; *s* of Sir William Mallinson, 1st Bt; *S* father 1936; *m* 1905, Mabel, *d* of J. W. Rush, Tunbridge Wells; one *s*. Sheriff of Surrey, 1933. *Heir:* *s* William End, *b* 1909. *Address:* Pine End, Reigate, Surrey. *T:* Reigate 3016. *Clubs:* Royal Thames Yacht, Royal Automobile.

Died 26 Feb. 1944.

MALLORY; *see* Leigh-Mallory.

MALMESBURY, 5th Earl of, *cr* 1800; **James Edward Harris;** DL, JP; Baron Malmesbury, 1788; Viscount FitzHarris, 1800; a Lord in Waiting to King George V, 1922–24; Provincial Grand Master (Masonic) of Hampshire and the Isle of Wight since 1923; a County Alderman of Hampshire County Council since 1906, and Chairman, 1927–38; President of County Councils' Association 1931–33; Hon. Treasurer Anti-Socialist Union since 1917; *b* Ballyedmond Castle, Co. Down, 18 Dec. 1872; *e s* of 4th Earl and Sylvia Georgina (*d* 1934), *d* of late A. Stewart of Ballyedmond Castle, Co. Down; *S* father, 1899; *m* 1905, Hon. Dorothy Gough-Calthorpe, CBE (Lady of Grace, Order of St John of Jerusalem, Order of Mercy, with bar), *y d* of 6th Lord Calthorpe; one *s* one *d*. *Educ:* Christ Church, Oxford (BA, Modern History, Honours, 1895) MA 1913. Lt Hants Yeomanry Cavalry, 1892–95; Lt 3rd Batt. (Mil.) Hampshire Regt, 1895–99; Captain 3rd Batt. (Mil.) Hampshire Regt, 1899–1902; Major (retired) 3rd (Special Reserve) Batt. Hampshire Regt; served European War, 1914–19; Assist Priv. Sec. (unpaid) to Under-Sec. of State for Colonies (Earl of Onslow), 1901; Pres. Home Counties Division of Nat. Union, 1903–04; London County Councillor (Stepney Division), 1904–05, Moderate and Conservative; Senior Grand Warden of English Freemasons, 1904 and 1905; Chairman of London Hospital Saturday Fund, 1921–38; Pres. of the Library Assoc., 1913. Owns about 4000 acres. Pictures at Hurn Court, notably Romneys, Canalettos, and Sir Joshua Reynolds. *Publications:* contributed to Ancestor, antiquarian and heraldic

publications; Editor and contributor New Order; volume of Political Essays, 1908. *Heir:* *s* Viscount FitzHarris. *Address:* Amyand House, Park Road, Winchester, Hants. *Clubs:* Carlton, Brooks's, Bath, Conservative, Royal Automobile.

Died 12 June 1950.

MALORY, Shaun; *see* Russell, R. J. K.

MAMHEAD, 1st Baron *cr* 1931, of Exeter; **Robert Hunt Stapylton Dudley Lydston Newman;** 4th Bt *cr* 1836; JP, DL; *b* 27 Oct. 1871; *o s* of 3rd Bt and Emma, *d* of Field Dudley; *S* to father's baronetcy 1892. MP (U) Exeter, 1918–29; (Ind) 1929–31. Owns about 2000 acres. *Heir:* to baronetcy: *cousin* Ralph Alured Newman, *b* 23 April 1902. *Address:* Mamhead Park, Kenton, Exeter. *T:* Mamhead 28.

Died 2 Nov. 1945.

MANCHESTER, 9th Duke of, *cr* 1719; **William Angus Drogo Montagu;** PC 1906; Earl of Manchester, 1626; Viscount Mandeville, Baron Montague of Kimbolton, 1620; formerly Captain 6th Battalion Lancashire Fusiliers; 5th Batt. KRR, and subsequently Captain His Majesty's Bodyguard, The Yeomen of the Guard, 1906; RND 1914–15; *b* London, 3 March 1877; *s* of 8th Duke and Consuelo, *d* of Antonio Yznagz de Valle, Ravenswood, Louisiana; *S* father 1892; *m* 1st, 1900, Helena, (who obtained a divorce, 1931 and *m* 1937, 11th Earl of Kintore), *d* of late Eugene Zimmerman, USA; two *s* two *d*; 2nd, 1931, Kathleen Dawes. *Educ:* Eton; Trinity, Cambridge. Protestant, Unionist. Owns about 4000 acres; possesses pictures by Vandyke, Titian, Holbein, Reynolds, Rubens, Lely, Lawrence, etc.; Kimbolton Castle containing many relics of residence and death of Catherine of Aragon. *Publication:* My Candid Recollections, 1932. *Recreations:* all outdoor recreations, especially hunting and shooting. *Heir:* *s* Viscount Mandeville. *Address:* Kimbolton Castle, St Neots; Tanderagee Castle, Co. Armagh; Brampton Park, Huntingdon; Kylemore Castle, Connemara.

Died 9 Feb. 1947.

MANCROFT, 1st Baron *cr* 1937, of Mancroft in the City of Norwich; **Arthur Michael Samuel;** 1st Bt *cr* 1932, of Mancroft in the City of Norwich; MP (U) Farnham Division of Surrey, 1918–37; Parliamentary Under-Secretary to the Secretary of State for Foreign Affairs, Parliamentary Secretary to the Board of Trade and Minister for Department of Overseas Trade, 1924–27; Financial Secretary to HM Treasury, 1927–29; Lord Mayor of Norwich, 1912–13; received the Honorary Freedom of the City of Norwich, 1928; *b* Norwich, 6 Dec. 1872; *e s* of Benjamin Samuel of Norwich and Rosetta, *e d* of Philip Haldinstein of Norwich; *m* 1912, Phoebe, 2nd *d* of Alfred Chune Fletcher, MRCS; one *s* two *d*. *Educ:* Norwich Grammar School. Manufacturer, retired; Chairman of House of Commons Select Committee of Public Accounts, 1930 and 1931; Member of Joint Committee of House of Lords and House of Commons on Water Resources, 1935–36; Member of Council of the Association of British Chambers of Commerce, 1915–24; Hon. Treasurer since 1929; Chairman of Governors of the Imperial Institute, 1924–27; Assist to Director of Army Contracts at War Office, 1914–15; Staff Assistant, Ministry of Munitions, 1915–16; Member of the Trade Organisation Committee (Whitley Councils) of the Ministry of Reconstruction and Training Committee for Ex-Officers, Ministry of Labour; Member of the (1919) Board of Trade Consultative Council and of House of Commons (1920) Select Committee on National Expenditure; Chairman, Ministry of Munitions Investigations Committee, 1920; Member of House of Commons Select Committee on Estimates, 1921–24 and of Board of Trade 1924 Committee to review the (1914) Bankruptcy Act. *Publications:* Life of Giovanni Battista Piranesi; The Working of the Bill of Exchange with an Explanation of the Overseas Trade Balance; The

Herring: its Effect on the History of Britain; The Mancroft Essays. *Heir: s* Hon. Stormont M. S. Mancroft, Capt. RA, *b* 27 July 1914. *Address:* 48 Montagu Square, W1. *T:* Paddington 2580. *Club:* Carlton.

Died 17 Aug. 1942.

MANDER, Lionel Henry Miles; author, actor, radio commentator; *b* 14 May 1888; 2nd *s* of S. T. Mander, Wightwick Manor, nr Wolverhampton, and Flora St Clair, *d* of H. N. Paint, MP, Cape Breton, NS; *m* Kathleen Bernadette, *d* of W. G. French, Sydney, NSW (marr. diss. 1936); one *s*. *Educ:* Harrow; McGill Univ., Montreal. Sheep farmer, New Zealand, 1908; started flying (Bleriot), 1909, at Pau; Cup for first official flight, Brooklands, 1910; acquired and built with C. Grahame-White, Hendon airdrome, 1910; free ballooning, 1912; aero certificate 31. Served 4½ years European war. Entered film business, 1920, and has written, directed, and/or acted in over one hundred pictures in Europe, Australia, and USA; was first to apply motion picture technique to talking screen, 1926. Labour candidate for Putney, 1934. Conducted own radio programme in USA 1938–41, answering questions regarding British Empire customs, politics, and history, then joined Blue networks radio Round Table representing Britain. Member Fabian Society. *Plays produced:* Common People, 1926; It's a Pity about Humanity, 1931; Blessed are the Rich, 1944. *Publications:* Albania Today, 1925; Oasis, 1926; Gentleman by Birth, 1930; To My Son in Confidence, 1935; also many short stories and pamphlets. *Recreations:* debate, travel, and music. *Address:* 7231 Pacific View Drive, Los Angles 28, California. *TA:* Los Angeles, Calif. *T:* Hempstead LA 5057. *Clubs:* Bath; Zeta Psi, New York.

Died Feb. 1946.

MANDLIK, Sir Narayan Vishvanath, Kt 1937; BA; LLB (Bombay); Advocate, High Court, Bombay; *b* 6 Sept. 1870; adopted *s* of late Rao Saheb V. N. Mandlik, CSI and late Annapurnabai; *m* 1881, Indirabai (decd), *d* of late G. Y. Jog; no *c*. *Educ:* Elphinstone High School; Elphinstone Coll., Bombay. Pleader, 1905; Advocate, 1929; served on Bombay Presidency War Relief Committee, 1914–18, also on other similar Committees; Honorary Presidency Magistrate, Bombay, 1904; member of Bombay Municipal Corporation, 1904–26; Chairman, Municipal Standing Committee, 1915–16; Fellow of Bombay University, 1932; Sheriff of Bombay, 1928; Freemason; member or Trustee of several Public Bodies; member of East India Association, London; Silver Durbar Medal, 1911; Silver Jubilee Medal, 1935; Coronation Medal, 1937. *Religion:* Hindu, Chitpavan Brahmin. *Recreations:* fond of riding and tennis in younger days. *Address:* Hermitage, Pedder Road, Bombay, India; Murud in Taluka, Dapoli, District Ratnagiri; Sunny Lodge, Mahableshwar. *Clubs:* Willingdon Sports, Orient, Hindu Gymkhana, Royal Western India Turf (Bombay); Ladies (Poona).

Died 20 Jan. 1948.

MANGIAGALLI, Riccardo P.; *see* Pick-Mangiagalli.

MANGIN, Ven. Robert Rattray, MA Oxford; Archdeacon of Lindisfarne since 1924; Hon. Canon of Newcastle Cathedral; Vicar and Rural Dean of Alnwick since 1906; *b* 1 Oct. 1863; *s* of Rev. Edward Nangreave Mangin; *m* 1893, Rosa E. L. (*d* 1940), *d* of Capt. Orde of Shorestone Hall, Northumberland; one *s* one *d*. *Educ:* Marlborough Coll.; New College, Oxford; Leeds Clergy School. Curate of Newburn-on-Tyne, 1887–92; Alnwick, 1892–95; Vicar of Ashington, 1895–99; Vicar, Benwell, 1899–1906. *Recreations:* representative Oxford University in Rugby football; fishing, lawn tennis, etc. *Address:* Alnwick Vicarage, Northumberland.

Died 27 June 1944.

MANGIN, Sir Thorleif Rattray Orde, Kt 1949; CMG 1943; Chief Commissioner of Gold Coast Colony, since 1945; *b* 27 Sept. 1896; *s* of late Ven. R. R. Mangin; *m* 1926, Mary Eliot; one *s* one *d*. *Educ:* Marlborough College. Served European War, 1915–19, Sub-Lieut RNVR; entered Colonial Civil Service, 1919; Assistant District Commissioner, 1919–24; Dist Comr, 1924–33; Dep. Provincial Comr, 1933–39, Prov. Comr, 1939–44; Sec. for Native Affairs, 1944–45; administered Govt of the Gold Coast, Oct.–Dec. 1946, March–June 1949. *Recreation:* golf. *Address:* Government Lodge, Cape Coast, Gold Coast. *Club:* Royal Aero.

Died 29 Sept. 1950.

MANGLES, Brig.-Gen. Roland Henry, CB 1924; CMG 1919; DSO 1902; late The Queen's Royal Regt; *b* 9 Feb. 1874; *m* 1909, Sylvia Amy Rhys, *d* of late Rev. W. Hand; two *s*. *Educ:* Marlborough. Entered army, 1894; Captain, 1902; served West Africa, 1897–98 (despatches, medal with clasp); South Africa, 1899–1902 (wounded, Queen's medal with 5 clasps, King's medal 2 clasps, DSO); European War, 1914–18 (despatches, Bt-Maj., Lt-Col, and Col); commanded Cairo Infantry Brigade; retired pay, 1927. *Address:* East House, Dedham, Essex.

Died 29 Sept. 1948.

MANION, Hon. Dr Robert James; Director of Civil ARP for Canada; *b* 19 Nov. 1881; *s* of P. J. Manion and Mary O'Brien; *m* 1906, Yvonne Desaulniers, Ottawa, Canada; three *s*. *Educ:* Toronto; Edinburgh. Graduated in Medicine at Toronto University, 1904; MD, CM Edinburgh, LRCP and S 1906. Practised medicine till 1915, when served in France with French Army; in 1916 and 1917 served at front with Canadian Army (MC); Member House of Commons of Canada, 1917–35; MP London, Ont, 1938–40; in Cabinet, Sept.–Dec. 1921, July–Sept. 1926; Minister for Railways, Canada, 1930–35; Leader of Conservative Party, Canada, 1938–40. *Publications:* A Surgeon in Arms; Life is an Adventure. *Clubs:* Rideau, Ottawa; Thunder Bay Country; Kaministikwia.

Died 3 July 1943.

MANIPUR, HH Sir Chura Chand Singh Maharajah of, KCSI 1934; CBE 1917; *b* 1886; *S* 1891; *m*; five *s* six *d*. The State has an area of 8638 square miles and a population of 445,606. Salute, 11 guns. *Address:* Manipur, Assam.

Died 7 Nov. 1941.

MANN, Sir Duncombe; *see* Mann, Sir T. D.

MANN, Sir Edward, 1st Bt *cr* 1905; JP; Chairman of Mann, Crossman & Paulin, Brandon's Putney Brewery, and Daniel Watney & Co. Ltd; *b* 2 March 1854; 2nd *s* of late Thomas Mann; *m* 1882, Anna Jane (*d* 1928), *d* of Paul Bell of Stiffkey, Norfolk, Mayor of Stepney, 1900–01, and 1901–02; three *s* one *d*. *Heir: s* Edward John. *Address:* Thelveton Hall, Scole, Norfolk. *Clubs:* Junior Carlton; Norfolk County, Norwich.

Died 29 Sept. 1943.

MANN, Heinrich; late President of Prussian Academy of Arts; *b* Lübeck, 27 March 1871; *m* 1914; one *d*; *m* 1939, Emmy Kroeger, Niendorf; one *d*. *Educ:* Berlin. *Publications:* English Editions: Berlin, 1931; The Goddess, or the Three Romances of the Duchess d'Assy; The Patrioteer, 1918; The Poor, 1917; The Chief, 1925; Mother Mary; The Royal Woman, 1930; The Little Town, 1931; The Blue Angel, 1932; The Hill of Lies, 1935; The Youth of King Henry IV, 1936; Henri IV, King of France, 1938. *Plays:* Madame Legros, etc. *Address:* 2145 Montana Ave, Santa Monica, California, USA.

Died 12 March 1950.

MANN, Jacob, MA, DLit (London); Professor of Talmud and Jewish History, Hebrew Union College, Cincinnati, Ohio, USA, since 1922; b Przemysl, Galicia, 26 Aug. 1888; s of Nisan Mann and Mindel Eichbaum; m 1928, Margit Klein, Breslau; two s. Educ: Jews' College and University College, London. Came to London, 1908; passed BA Examination of London University with First Class Honours, 1913; qualified for the Jewish Ministry at Jews' College, 1914; MA London University, with a mark of distinction, 1915; DLit London University, 1920; came to United States, 1920. Instructor of Bible, Talmud, and Jewish History at Baltimore Hebrew College and Teachers' Training School, 1921–22; Visiting Professor at Hebrew University, Jerusalem, 1927–28. Publications: The Jews in Egypt and in Palestine under the Fatimid Caliphs, Vol. I 1920, Vol. II 1922; Texts and Studies in Jewish History and Literature, Vol. I 1931; Vol. II 1935; The Bible as read and preached in the Old Synagogue, Vol. I, 1940; numerous scientific articles in Jewish Review, Jewish Quarterly Review, Revue des Études Juives, Journal Royal Asiatic Society, American Journal of Theology, Expository Times, Hebrew Union College Annual, Hazofeh, Tarbiz and other periodicals. Address: 671 Gholson Avenue, Avondale, Cincinnati, Ohio, USA.

Died 23 Oct. 1940.

MANN, James Scrimgeour, RI, President, Royal Cambrian Academy of Art; marine painter; b Dundee, 1883; s of Captain J. S. Mann and Marjorie Peter; m 1917, Catherine Mary Allen Pengelly. Educ: Harris Academy; abroad. Studied at Liverpool School of Art. Member of the Liverpool Academy of Arts; Member of Court of Governors, National Museum of Wales; Exhibitor at principal Exhibitions; served European War with Scottish Horse and 5th Battalion The King's Regiment (severely wounded). Address: The Four Winds, Thorsway, Caldy, Cheshire. T: Hoylake 1819.

Died 1 June 1946.

MANN, Sir (Thomas) Duncombe, Kt 1915; b 16 Oct. 1857; m 1st, 1880, Marie Blanche (d 1926), o d of David Keigwin, of Merton, Surrey; two s; 2nd, 1926, Janet Elliot (d 1941), 2nd d of James Jeffery, of Clonakilty, Co. Cork. Educ: Eastbourne; London University. Barrister-at-law, Gray's Inn, 1886; Officer l'Ordre de Léopold, Belgium, 1919. Address: The Brown House, Bexhill-on-Sea, Sussex. T: Bexhill 112.

Died 27 Nov. 1949.

MANN, Tom; b Foleshill, Warwickshire (mining district), 15 April 1856. Worked on farm from age of 9 to 11; down mine and on pit bank, 11 to 14; served 7 years engineering in Birmingham; settled in London, 1877; worked as journeyman engineer; joined Amalgamated Society of Engineers, 1881 (General Secretary, 1918–21); been closely connected with Trade Union movement since 1881; joined Socialists, 1885; first Secretary of London Reform Union; has stood as Parliamentary candidate four times; first secretary of the National Democratic League. Publications: pamphlets on the Eight Hours Movement; A Socialist's View of Religion; The Programme of the ILP and the Unemployed; The Dockers and Sailors in 1897; The International Socialist Movement; Why I joined the NDL; From Single Tax to Syndicalism; Russia in 1921; Tom Mann's Memoirs; What I Saw in China, 1927. Address: Norfolk Crescent, Sidcup, Kent.

Died 13 March 1941.

MANNERS, Lord Cecil (Reginald John); b 4 Feb. 1868; 3rd s of 7th Duke of Rutland. Educ: Charterhouse; Trinity Hall, Cambridge. Formerly an assistant private secretary to Secretary of State for India, Viscount Cross; MP (C) East or Melton Division of Leicestershire, 1900–06. Club: Turf.

Died 8 Sept. 1945.

MANNERS, Ernest John; Director, Bass, Ratcliff & Gretton Ltd and Worthington & Co. Ltd; b 14 Feb. 1877; 2nd s of late W. P. Manners, Burton-on-Trent; m 1st; one d; 2nd, 1918, Ada Mary, γ d of late John Kendrick, Brundall, Norwich. JP Burton-on-Trent, 1926, Derbyshire, 1935; High Sheriff of Derbyshire, 1943. Address: The Old Hall, Netherseale, Burton-on-Trent; Dove Cottage, Alstonfield, Derbyshire. TA: Netherseal. T: Overseal 58. Clubs: Royal Thames Yacht; Burton, Abbey, Burton-on-Trent; County, Derby.

Died 31 May 1944.

MANNERS-SMITH, Francis St George, CIE 1907; s of Surgeon-Gen. C. Manners-Smith; m 1884, Caroline (d 1939), d of Thomas Ashby, Staines. Educ: Clifton College; RIE College, Coopers Hill. Entered PWD, India, 1879; retired as Chief Engineer and Secretary to Government, Burmah, 1913; Kaiser-i-Hind Medal, 1900. Address: Yewdale, Budleigh Salterton.

Died 22 March 1941.

MANNHEIM, Karl; Dr Phil; Professor of Education, University of London, since 1945; Editor, International Library of Sociology and Social Reconstruction (London, New York); b Budapest, 27 March 1893; s of Gustav Manheim and Rosa Eylenburg; m 1921, Dr Julia Lang. Educ: University of Budapest; University of Berlin; University of Paris; University of Freiburg i/Br.; University of Heidelberg. Lecturer (Privatdozent) in Sociology, Univ. of Heidelberg, 1926–30; Professor of Sociology and Head of the Dept of Sociology, Univ. of Frankfurt am Main, 1930–33; lecturing engagements at the Universities of Leiden, Amsterdam, Groningen, Utrecht, 1933; Lecturer in Sociology at London School of Economics (University of London), 1933–45. Publications: Strukturanalyse der Erkenntnistheorie (Patterns of Epistemology), Berlin, 1922; Das Konservative Denken (Conservative Thought) in Archiv für Sozialwissenschaft, Tübingen, 1927; Die Gegenwartsaufgaben der Soziologie (The Task of Sociology in our Time), Tübingen, 1932; Rational and Irrational Elements in Contemporary Society, Hobhouse Memorial Lecture, London, 1934; Ideology and Utopia: An Introduction to the Sociology of Knowledge, London-New York, 1936, 3rd ed. 1945; Man and Society in an Age of Reconstruction, London-New York, 1940, 4th ed. 1945; Diagnosis of our Time, London-New York, 1943, 3rd ed. 1945; articles in English, French, German, Spanish, Hungarian, Polish, Chinese, Japanese books and periodicals. Address: 5 The Park, NW11. T: Speedwell 0375. Club: Athenæum.

Died 9 Jan. 1947.

MANNING, Bernard Lord; Fellow, Senior Tutor, and Lecturer of Jesus College, Cambridge; b 31 Dec. 1892; s of late Rev. George Manning, Ravenstonedale, Westmorland; unmarried. Educ: Caistor Grammar School; Jesus College, Cambridge (Foundation Scholar). Lightfoot Scholar in the University of Cambridge; First Class in Historical Tripos, Parts I and II, 1915; Thirlwall Prizeman, 1917. Editor the Cambridge Review, 1916–18; Donaldson Bye-Fellow of Magdalene College, Cambridge, 1916–18; Educational Adviser to Indian Students in the University of Cambridge, 1919–21; Bursar of Jesus College, 1920–33. Publications: The People's Faith in the Time of Wyclif; The Making of Modern English Religion; Essays in Orthodox Dissent; contributions to the Cambridge Medieval History. Address: Jesus College, Cambridge. Clubs: Athenæum, United University.

Died 8 Dec. 1941.

MANNING, Rt Rev. William Thomas; Bishop of New York, 1921–46; retired, 1946; b Northampton, 1866. Educ: Northampton Grammar School; University of the South, Sewanee, Tennessee. Took orders, 1891; was Professor of Dogmatic Theology in the University of the South; Rector of Trinity Parish, New York, 1908–21. *Address:* 8 Washington Mews, New York, USA.

Died 18 Nov. 1949.

MANOHAR LAL, Hon. Sir, Kt 1941; MA (Punjab); BA (Camb.); Barrister-at-Law; Finance Minister, Punjab, since 1937; *b* 1 Jan. 1880. *Educ:* Punjab University; St John's College, Cambridge (Double 1st Class Hons, Philosophy and Economics; Foundation Scholar and McMahon Law Student, Brotherton Sanskrit Scholar Cobden Prize). Whewell Scholar in International Law, 1904–05. Principal, Randhir College, Kapurthala, 1906–09; Minto Prof. of Economics, Calcutta Univ., 1909–12; Advocate, High Court, Lahore; Fellow and Syndic, Punjab Univ., since 1915; Member, Punjab Council and Assembly for Punjab Univ., 1921–23 and since 1927; Minister of Education, Punjab Govt, 1927–30; Pres., All-India Economic Conference (Dacca), 1935. *Publications:* articles on economic subjects. *Address:* Club Road, Lahore, Pakistan.

Died 1 May 1949.

MANSEL, Sir John Philip Ferdinand, 14th Bt *cr* 1621; *b* 22 Aug. 1910; *e s* of 13th Bt and Mary Philippa Agnes Germaine, *d* of Frederick Littlewood; *S* father, 1933; *m* 1940, Hannah, *d* of Ben Rees. *Heir: b* Rauf, *b* 30 Aug. 1915. *Address:* Maesycrugiau Manor, Carmarthenshire.

Died 6 April 1947.

MANSEL-JONES, Col Conwyn, VC 1900; CMG 1918; DSO 1915; a Gentleman at Arms since 1920; Col retired pay; West Yorks Regiment; Barrister, Lincoln's Inn, 1914; *b* 1871; *s* of late Herbert Riversdale Mansel-Jones, Judge of County Courts; *m* 1913, Marion, *d* of late William Barton-Wright. *Educ:* Haileybury; RMC, Sandhurst. Entered army, 1890; Captain, 1899; retired, 1910; Bt Major, 1916; Bt Lt-Col, 1917; DAAG for Recruiting Headquarters, 1901; Recruiting Staff Officer, London Area, 1906; DAAG 1914; AAG, with rank of Lieut-Col, 1915; served Ashanti, 1895–96 (bronze star); served BCA 1898–99 (Africa General Service Medal, 1899); S Africa, 1899–1902 (severely wounded, despatches, Queen's medal 2 clasps, VC for bravery at assault of Terrace Hill, Tugela); served European War, 1914–18 (despatches seven times, DSO, Officer Legion of Honour). *Address:* Weirs End, Brockenhurst, Hants. *Club:* Junior United Service.

Died 29 May 1942.

MANSELL, Air Vice-Marshal Reginald Baynes, CB 1944; CBE 1942; British Air Commission, Washington, USA, since 1943; *b* 22 May 1896; *s* of late A. E. Mansell, Clifton, Bristol; *m* 1925, Mabel Lucie, *d* of H. J. Pugh, Westbury-on-Trym, Bristol; two *s. Educ:* Bristol Grammar School. Commissioned 4th (City of Bristol) Bn Gloster Regt 1914; BEF France, 1915; transferred RFC 1915; BEF with RFC 1916; various appointments with RFC and RAF home and abroad, 1916–38; Sqdn Leader, 1926; Wing Comdr 1934; Group Capt. 1938; Air Commodore, 1940; Air Vice-Marshal, 1943. Chief Overseer, Air Ministry, 1938–40; Director of Operational Requirements, Air Ministry, 1940–41; Commandant Aircraft and Armament Experimental Establishment, 1942–43. *Address:* The Old House, Grateley, Andover, Hants. *T:* Grateley 23. *Club:* Army and Navy.

Died 22 Jan. 1945.

MANSERGH, Mrs Southcote; *see* Moody, Mme Fanny.

MANSFIELD, F. J.; President of the National Union of Journalists, 1918–19; editorial staff of The Times 1914–34; Lecturer and Examiner in Practical Journalism, University of London 1925–34; *b* 1872; *m*; three *s* one *d.* Formerly on staffs of Western Morning News and the Standard; member of Lord Chancellor's Committee on Law of Defamation, 1939, and Home Office Advisory Committee, Defence Regulations 18B, 1940–41; lay preacher, Methodist Church, since 1898; President, Worthing Free Church Federal Council, 1944–45. *Publications:* The Complete Journalist, a study of the principles and practice of Newspaper Making, 1935; Sub-editing, a book mainly for young journalists, 1932; Gentlemen, the Press!, the Official History of the National Union of Journalists, 1943; Inside a Newspaper Office, a Chapter in Inside Information, 1944; book reviews in the Journalist; magazine articles. *Recreations:* browsing in history and technique of journalism, and gardening. *Address:* 50 St Lawrence Avenue, Worthing, Sussex. *T:* Worthing 3551.

Died 21 Dec. 1946.

MANSFIELD, Vice-Adm. Sir John Maurice, KCB 1948; CB 1945; DSO 1945; DSC; Flag Officer (Submarines) since 1946; *b* 22 Dec. 1893; 2nd *s* of Edward Dillon Mansfield, MA, and Muriel Edith Campbell Mansfield; *m* 1916, Alice Talbot Napier; one *s* one *d. Educ:* Lambrook, Bracknell, Berks; RN Colleges, Osborne and Dartmouth. Training Cruiser HMS Cornwall, 1910; Courses at Whale Island, Vernon and Navigation School, 1914; HMS Warrior, 1914–15; HM Submarines C2, H8, H10, G9, 1915–17; C20 and H42 (in command), 1917–21; HMS Barham, President, Ramillies, Columbine, Royal Sovereign, Cairo, 1921–29; HM Yacht Enchantress, 1929; Comdr 1929; HMS Viceroy (Med. Fleet), 1930; RN Staff College, Greenwich, 1931; Staff College, Andover, 1932; HMS Courageous (as Exec. Officer), 1933–34; Capt. 1934; Directing Staff, RN War College, Greenwich, 1934–37; Flag Capt. HMS Norfolk (East Indies), 1937–39; HMS Devonshire, 1939–40; COS to C-in-C, WA, 1941–43 (despatches twice); Rear-Adm. 1943; commanded 15th Cruiser Squadron, 1944–45. DSO for Invasion of South France, 1944; Assistant Chief of Naval Staff, U-boat Warfare and Trade, 1945; Flag Officer, Ceylon, 1945–46; Vice-Adm. 1946. *Recreations:* fishing, shooting, tennis, squash racquets. *Address:* Magnolia Cottage, Lower Woodford, Salisbury, Wilts. *TA:* Middle Woodford, Wilts. *T:* Middle Woodford 4. *Clubs:* United Service, Curzon House.

Died 4 Feb. 1949.

MANSFIELD, Alderman William Thomas; JP; an organiser for the National Union of General and Municipal Workers; *b* South Bank, Yorkshire; *m* 1910; one *s. Educ:* Easington and Staithes Elementary School. Commenced work at Grinkle Mines at the age of 13; check-weighman at Grinkle Mines, 1908; MP (Lab) Cleveland Division of North Riding, 1929–31; a member of the North Riding County Council, 1919; also served as a member of the Hinderwell Urban District Council, 1911–20; General Secretary, Cleveland Miners' and Quarrymen's Association, 1920–34. *Recreations:* books, football, cricket. *Address:* Melrose, 40 Hilda Place, Saltburn-by-the-Sea, Yorks. *T:* Saltburn 64.

Died 19 March 1939.

MANSION, John Edmond, Hon. MA Oxon; Director George G. Harrap & Co. Ltd; *b* 18 Oct. 1870; *s* of Horace Mansion and Sarah Douglas; *m* 1901, Annie Ramsay (*d* 1940), *d* of late Samuel Murdoch Crosbie; one *s* one *d. Educ:* Dreux (France); Edinburgh; Marburg. Head of Modern Language Department at Dollar Academy, Royal Belfast Academical Institution, and George Watson's College, Edinburgh; joined firm of G. G. Harrap & Co., 1914. *Publications:* Author and editor of numerous modern language text-books; editor of Harrap's Standard French and English Dictionary (Part I 1934, Part II 1939). *Recreations:* philology, motoring. *Address:* 20 Sudbrooke Road, SW12. *T:* Battersea 1380. *Club:* Authors'.

Died 9 June 1942.

MANSON, James Bolivar; *b* 26 June 1879; *e s* of James Alexander Manson; *m* 1903, Lilian Laugher; two *d. Educ:* Alleyn's School, Dulwich; Heatherley's and Lambeth School of Art; Académie Julian, Paris, under Jean-Paul Laurens. Corresponding member of the Académie Septentrionale; Exhibitor at International Society, New English Art Club (Member); one-man shows at the Leicester Galleries, London; Galerie Balzac, Paris; Alex. Reid's Gallery, Glasgow; Art Critic, successively on the Outlook, Daily Herald, and Evening News; Assistant at National Gallery, Millbank, 1912; Assistant Keeper, 1917–30; Director Tate Gallery, Millbank, 1930–38; has pictures in Tate Gallery and Manchester, Belfast, Aberdeen, Birmingham, Bristol, Southampton, Bradford, Newcastle-on-Tyne Art Galleries, Hull, Salford, Musée Royal, Brussels, Belgrade, Luxembourg, Paris; National Gallery of South Africa, Cape Town; Secretary of Camden Town Group; 1st Secretary London Group; Secretary of Monarro Group; Chairman, Selecting Committee, French Exhibition, 1932; Chairman Empire Art Loan Collections Society; formerly Chairman Standing Advisory Committee on Fine Arts. *Publications:* Rembrandt, 1923; translated Cézanne, by T. Klingsor, 1924; Hours in the Tate Gallery, 1926; Degas, 1927; English Oil colour Painters, 1930; The Tate Gallery, 1930; Ernest Biéler, peintre Suisse, 1936; Dutch Painting, 1945; Modern Painting (Ency. Brit., 14th ed.); articles on Art in magazines. *Recreation:* reading. *Address:* 6 Carlyle Studios, 296 King's Road, Chelsea, SW3. *Clubs:* Savage, Burlington Fine Arts, Arts, PEN; Savage (Bristol).

Died 3 July 1945.

MANT, Sir Reginald Arthur, KCSI 1933; KCIE 1924; CSI 1919; late ICS; *b* 27 Sept. 1870; *s* of George Mant, Gigoomgan, Queensland; *m* 1905, Eileen Gertrude, *d* of Col E. O. Tandy, IMS; one *s* one *d. Educ:* Maryborough Grammar School, Queensland; Trinity College, Oxford. Appointed to the ICS after the examination of 1893 and posted to the Punjab; Under-Secretary to Government, Punjab, 1899; Under-Secretary to the Government of India (Finance Department), 1901; Deputy Secretary, 1904; Joint Secretary to the Government of India (Military Finance), 1908; Financial Secretary to the Government of the Punjab, 1910–15; Secretary to the Government of India (Department of Revenue and Agriculture), 1916–20; temporary Member of the Council of the Governor-General, 1919; Member of the Indian Fiscal Commission, 1921–22; Finance Member (temporary) of Council of Punjab, 1923; Member Council of India, 1924–34; Member of Royal Commission on Indian Currency and Finance, 1925–26; Member of East Africa Commission, 1927–28; Vice-President Royal Society of Arts, 1929; Member of Gold Delegation of Financial Committee of League of Nations, 1929–32; Director, Union Corporation, Ltd. *Recreations:* shooting, golf. *Address:* c/o Lloyds Bank Ltd, 6 Pall Mall, SW1. *Clubs:* Oriental, Walton Heath.

Died 30 March 1942.

MAPPIN, Sir Charles Thomas Hewitt, 4th Bt *cr* 1886; *b* 7 March 1909; *s* of late Thomas Wilson Mappin, *s* of 3rd Bt and Violet Maud, *d* of late Joseph C. Mappin; *S* grandfather, 1925; *m* 1930, Ruby Joy (who obtained a decree nisi, 1941), *o d* of Capt. Gordon Duff, late RGA. *Educ:* Wellington College; Sandhurst. *Heir: great uncle* Samuel Wilson, *b* 20 Oct. 1854.

Died 8 Nov. 1941.

MAPPIN, Sir Samuel Wilson, 5th Bt *cr* 1886; *b* 20 Oct. 1854; *s* of Sir Frederick Thorpe Mappin, 1st Bt; *S* great nephew, 1941; *m* 1881, Laura (*d* 1937), *d* of William Morton; two *s* one *d. Educ:* Trinity College, Cambridge. BA 1877. *Heir: s* Frank Crossley [*b* 1884; *m* 1909, Ruby, *d* of George Lamberton Thomson, Auckland, NZ; three *d*]. *[Baronetcy not claimed.]*

Died 12 Dec. 1942.

MAR, Helen; concert artist; *m* Rohan Clensy (*d* 1919). *Address:* 35 Great Queen Street, Kingsway, WC2. *T:* Holborn 0743.

Died Nov. 1940.

MARAIS, Colin B.; *see* Bain-Marais.

MARCHAMLEY, 2nd Baron *cr* 1908, of Hawkstone; **William Tattersall Whiteley;** late Lieutenant Commander RNVR and Major RAF; Pilot Officer RAFVR 1939, Flight Lt 1940; *b* 22 Nov. 1886; *e s* of 1st Baron and Alice (*d* 1913), *d* of W. Tattersall, Quarry Bank, Blackburn; *S* father, 1925; *m* 1911, Margaret Clara, *d* of Thomas Scott Johnston of Glenmark, Waipara, New Zealand; one *s* one *d. Educ:* Eton; Hertford College, Oxford. High Sheriff County of Southampton, 1921; contested South-East Leeds, Parliamentary Elections, 1923 and 1924. *Heir: s* Hon. John William Tattersall Whiteley, Capt. Armoured Corps, 1944, *b* 24 April 1922. *Address:* 2a Whitehall Court, SW1. *Club:* Golfers'.

Died 17 Nov. 1949.

MARCHANT, Bessie, (Mrs J. A. Comfort); author; *b* 12 Dec. 1862; *d* of William Marchant and Jane Goucher; *m* 1889, Rev. Jabez Ambrose Comfort; one *d. Educ:* privately. Writer of books for young people. *Publications:* more than one hundred and fifty books, also many serials and short stories. *Recreation:* gardening. *Address:* Gothic House, Charlbury, Oxon.

Died 10 Nov. 1941.

MARCHANT, Sir Stanley, Kt 1943; CVO 1935; MA, DMus (Oxon), FSA, FRAM, FRCM, FRCO; Principal of Royal Academy of Music since 1936; Hon. Fellow of Pembroke College, Oxford, since 1946; Organist Emeritus of St Paul's Cathedral since 1936; Chairman of Council of Royal School of Church Music since 1947; Master of Worshipful Company of Musicians, 1948; *b* London, 15 May 1883; *m* Hilda Constance, *d* of late E. Holyman; one *s* one *d. Educ:* Royal Academy of Music (Goss Scholar). Organist of Kemsing Parish Church, Kent, 1899–1903; Christ Church, Newgate Street, EC, 1903–13; St Peter's, Eaton Square, SW, 1913–21; Sub-Organist of St Paul's Cathedral, 1916–27; Organist of St Paul's Cathedral, 1927–36; Organist at Silver Jubilee Thanksgiving Service of King George V and Queen Mary, St Paul's Cathedral, 6 May 1935 (CVO); Professor at Royal Academy of Music, 1913–36; Warden of Royal Academy of Music, 1934–36; Alsop Lecturer in Music, Univ. of Liverpool, 1936–37; King Edward Prof. of Music in the Univ. of London, 1937–48, now Emeritus; Member: of Senate, Univ. of London, 1938–48; of Board of Studies in Music, Univ. of Oxford, 1941–44; MA Oxon (by Decree of Convocation), 1942; quondam Examiner in Music, Univs of Durham and London; President of Royal College of Organists, 1930–32, of Incorporated Association of Organists, 1933–36, of Incorporated Society of Musicians, 1935–36; Member of Court of Assistants of Royal Society of Musicians; Chairman Schubert Society; Member Arts Council of Great Britain, Chairman of Music Panel; Chairman of Goldsmith's College (University of London), 1944; Member of Council of Queen's College, Harley Street, and of Royal College of Art, 1942; Trustee of Royal Opera House, Covent Garden, 1946; Governor of Old Vic and Sadler's Wells, 1946; Commissioner of Crown Estate Paving Commission; Visiting Music Master, Wycombe Abbey School, 1926–36; Fellow of the College of St Nicolas (Royal School of Church Music); Musical Adviser to the College of the Sea, 1946; served European War, 1917–19. *Publications:* Editor (with Rev. M. F. Foxell, MVO) of the St Paul's Cathedral Psalter, 1934; composer of church music, school songs, etc. *Recreation:* water-colour painting. *Address:* Royal Academy of Music, Marylebone Road, NW1. *Club:* Athenæum.

Died 28 Feb. 1949.

MARCHBANK, John; Director British Airways Overseas Corporation, 1943; *b* Lambfoot, Dumfries, 1883. Worked as a shepherd until he was fourteen, then as a cattleman and dairyman; entered service of Caledonian Railway Co. as a porter at Beattock Station at age of eighteen; joined Dumfries Constabulary; re-entered service of Caledonian Railway as a shunter at Buchanan Street Station, Glasgow; joined Amalgamated Society of Railway Servants, 1906; a member of Executive Committee of NUR, 1916–18; President, 1922–24; Assistant General Secretary, 1925; General Secretary, 1934–42; Vice-Pres. International Transport Workers Federation since 1935. *Address:* 63 Rosebery Road, N10. *T:* Tudor 5237.

Died 23 March 1946.

MARCHBANKS, James, CMG 1933; MICE; *b* Dunedin, NZ, 1862. Chief Engineer, Wellington Harbour Board, 1909–32; retired, 1932. *Address:* The Buckrig, Heretaunga, NZ. *Clubs:* Wellington, Wellington, NZ.

Died 6 April 1947.

MARESCAUX, Captain Alfred Edward Hay, CMG 1917; RN (retired); *o s* of late Captain Alfred Marescaux, RN (retired), Nice; *m* Evelyn, *d* of late Major-General French, CB. Naval Cadet in Achilles, Egyptian War, 1882 (medal, bronze star); served China in Champion, 1884; received thanks of Italian Government for services at wreck of Utopia, Gibraltar, 1891. *Address:* Villa Nicole, Beaulieu-sur-Mer, AM, France.

Died 4 Oct. 1942.

MARETT, Robert Ranulph, FBA; MA, DSc, Hon. DLitt (Oxon), LLD (St Andrews), FRAI; Rector of Exeter College, Oxford, since 1928; Corresponding member, Ecole d'Anthropologie; Fellow Royal Society of Letters, Lund; *b* Jersey, 13 June 1866; *o s* of Sir Robert Marett, Kt, Bailiff of Jersey; *m* 1898, Nora, *d* of late Sir John Kirk, GCMG, KCB; one *s* two *d*. *Educ:* Victoria College, Jersey; Balliol College, Oxford (Senior Exhibitioner). First classes in Classical Moderations and Literæ Humaniores; Chancellor's Prize (Latin Verse), 1887; Green Prize (Essay on Primitive Ethics), 1893. Member of Inner Temple, and called to Jersey Bar; formerly held Commission in Royal Jersey Militia, and has also served in University Corps; Fellow of Exeter College and Tutor in Philosophy, 1891–1928; Sub-Rector, 1893–98; Examiner in Literæ Humaniores, 1905–08; Proctor, 1918–19; President of the Folklore Society, 1913–18; President of Section H. (Anthropology) of the British Association, Newcastle, 1916; President of the Sociological Institute, 1932–35; Frazer Lecturer, Cambridge, 1927; Andrew Lang Lecturer, St Andrews, 1928; Lowell Lecturer, Boston, USA, 1930; Thomson Lecturer, Aberdeen, 1931; Gifford Lecturer, St Andrews, 1931–33; Donellan Lecturer, TCD, 1933; late University Reader in Social Anthropology at Oxford; Huxley Medal, R. Anthrop. Inst., 1939; President British Speleological Association. *Publications:* Essay on Origin and Validity in Ethics in Personal Idealism, 1902; Oxford editor of Anthropological Essays in honour of E. B. Tylor, 1908; editor of Anthropology and the Classics, 1908; The Threshold of Religion, 1909; The Birth of Humility, 1910; Anthropology, 1912; Psychology and Folklore, 1920; The Diffusion of Culture, 1927; Man in the Making, 1928; The Raw Material of Religion, 1929; Faith, Hope, and Charity in Primitive Religion, 1932; Sacraments of Simple Folk, 1933; Head, Heart and Hands in Human Evolution, 1935; Tylor, 1936; A Jerseyman at Oxford, 1941; various papers in philosophic and scientific periodicals; articles in Ency. Brit. (14th ed.), British Year Book, Hastings' Dictionary of Religion and Ethics, etc. *Address:* Exeter College, Oxford; La Haule Manor, Jersey.

Died 18 Feb. 1943.

MARGESSON, Col Evelyn William, CMG 1918; retired pay; Norfolk Regt; *b* 16 May 1865. *Educ:* Eton; Sandhurst. Entered Army, 1885; retired, 1906; served Chitral Relief, 1895 (medal and clasp); Tirah, 1897–98 (severely wounded); South Africa, 1900–02 (despatches, Bt Major Queen's and King's medals 2 clasps); European War, 1914–18 (despatches, CMG).

Died 9 March 1944.

MARGESSON, Sir Mortimer R., Kt 1928; JP; *b* 16 March 1861; *e s* of late Rev. R. W. Margesson, Rector of Blendworth, Hants; *m* 1886, Lady Isabel Augusta Hobart-Hampden (*d* 1946), *sister* of 7th Earl of Buckinghamshire; two *s*. *Educ:* Harrow. Private Secretary to Earl of Plymouth since 1900. *Address:* 27 Ashley Gardens, SW1. *T:* Victoria 5722. *Club:* Junior Carlton.

Died 6 April 1947.

MARGESSON, Captain Wentworth Henry Davies, CB 1919; late RN; *b* 1869; *s* of late W. G. Margesson, Findon Place, Sussex; *m* 1908, Gwendolen Agnes, *d* of C. E. Thornycroft, Thornycroft Hall, Cheshire; two *s* one *d*. *Educ:* Stubbington; HMS Britannia. *Address:* Machiti, Trelawney, Southern Rhodesia.

Died 8 Nov. 1950.

MARGETSON, Alfred James, MSc, MIMechE; HM Inspector of Schools (Engineering), 1921–37, and formerly Professor of Civil and Mechanical Engineering at the Technical College, Finsbury, of the City and Guilds of London Institute; *b* 7 March 1877; *s* of Alfred George and Emily Margetson, Clifton, Bristol; *m* 1914, Joyce Althea Mary Newman, Bath; one *d*. *Educ:* private schools; a City of Bristol Technical Scholarship at the Merchant Venturers Technical College, Bristol (now the Faculty of Engineering of the Univ. of Bristol); MSc Univ. of Bristol; BSc Engineering of the Univ. of London; Medals for engineering and railway design. Six years as Assist in Railway Wagon and Carriage Works Co. Ltd, Bristol; five years Lecturer in Engineering at the Merchant Venturers Technical College, Bristol; London University Demonstrator in Engineering at the City and Guilds Central Technical College; Assistant Professor in Engineering, Imperial College of Science and Technology, South Kensington; Member of the Institution of Mechanical Engineers. *Publications:* Experiments for the Electrical Laboratory; Technical Reviews and Papers; Engineering Primers. *Recreation:* golf. *Address:* The Cottage, Boro'bridge Road, Knaresborough, Yorks, WR. *T:* Knaresborough 3124.

Died 3 May 1944.

MARGETSON, Very Rev. William James; Provost of St Mary's Cathedral, Edinburgh, 1925–38, Provost Emeritus since 1938; Prebendary of Trehaverock since 1939; *b* 29 March 1874; *s* of Alfred George and Emily Margetson, of Bristol; *m* 1st, 1923, Marion Constance Lillian (*d* 1937), 2nd *d* of F. A. Jenoure, of Boston, Jamaica; two *s*; 2nd, 1938, Charlotte Edith (*d* 1945), 2nd *d* of Dr A. H. F. Barbour, Edinburgh. *Educ:* Oxford University; BA 1896; MA 1907. Deacon, 1897; priest, 1898; Rector of St Petroc Minor, Cornwall, 1901–09; Vicar of Holy Trinity, South Wimbledon, 1910–18; St Mark, Surbiton, 1918–22; Rector of Newington, 1922–25. *Address:* Barrymore Cottage, Newquay Cornwall. *T:* Newquay 2551.

Died 30 March 1946.

MARGRETT, Charles Henry, CBE 1923; JP; *b* 1863; *s* of late Charles Margrett, Cheltenham; *m* 1888, Anne A., *d* of William Page, Southam, Gloucestershire. *Address:* Sandford House, Cheltenham.

Died 22 Nov. 1941.

MARINDIN, Maj.-Gen. Arthur Henry, CB 1919; DSO 1918; Hon. Col 1st Tay Cadet Bn, Black Watch; *b* 1868; *s* of Henry Colvile Marindin, *s* of Samuel Marindin, of Chesterton, Salop, and Isabella Colvile, of

Craigflower, Fife, and Mary Elizabeth, d of J. G. Watkins, of Woodfield; m Gertrude Florence Evelyn, MBE, d of late Edward Robert Erskine Wilmot-Chetwode, of Woodbrook, Queen's County; one s three d. Educ: Eton; King's College, London (Applied Science); New College, Oxford (BA); RMC, Sandhurst. Gazetted to 42nd Royal Highlanders (The Black Watch), 1891, and to command 2nd Bn The Black Watch, 1919; passed Staff College and served in various Staff appointments; served South African War, 1900–02 (medal and clasps, despatches); European War, 1914–18, on Staff, in command of 105th Infantry Brigade, 1916–18, and as temporary Major-General in command of 35th Division, 1918–19 (1915 Star, General Service Medal, Victory Medal, CB, DSO, two Brevet promotions, Legion of Honour, French Croix de Guerre with palm, Commander of Belgian Order of La Couronne, Belgian Croix de Guerre with two palms); Commanded 12th Infantry Brigade and Dover Sub-Area, 1919–23; retired, 1925; Hon. Col 6/7th Black Watch, 1932–38. Recreations: outdoor sports and games. Address: Fordel, Glenfarg, Perthshire. Clubs: Naval and Military; New, Edinburgh.

Died 28 June 1947.

MARK, J. M. A Solicitor. MP (U) Londonderry County and City, 1921–29, North Derry, 1929–33; Resident Magistrate, 1933–43, retd 1943. Address: Banks, Limavady, N Ireland.

Died 5 Jan. 1948.

MARKHAM, Rt Rev. Algernon A., MA; Bishop Suffragan of Grantham since 1937; Dean of Stamford since 1936; Rector of Stoke, Lincs, since 1933; b Saxby Rectory, Lincs, 15 May 1869; 4th s of Rev. Charles Warren Markham and Margaret, d of late J. W. Barton of Stapleton Park, Yorks, and Saxby Hall, Lincs; m 1908, Winifred Edith, 2nd d of late Col F. St J. Barne of Sotterley and Dunwich, Co. Suffolk, and Lady Constance Barne, sister of 5th Marquis of Hertford; one s four d. Educ: Westminster; Trinity College, Cambridge. Deacon, 1892; Priest, 1893; Curate of Warrington Parish Church, 1892–99; Vicar of S Jude's, Liverpool, 1899–1908; of Grimsby, 1908–28; of Grantham, 1928–33; Prebendary of Brampton in Lincoln Cathedral, 1912. Address: Stoke Rectory, Grantham.

Died 27 June 1949.

MARKHAM, Sir Henry Vaughan, KCB 1941; MC; JP; Permanent Secretary, Admiralty, since 1940; b 4 Feb. 1897; e s of late John Markham and Elizabeth Vaughan. Educ: Repton School; Corpus Christi College, Oxford. Served RGA, European War, Western Front (despatches, MC); Home Civil Service (Admiralty), 1921; Principal Priv. Sec. to First Lords (Sir Samuel Hoare and Mr Duff Cooper), 1936–38. Recreation: walking. Address: Admiralty, Whitehall, SW1. Club: United University.

Died 14 Dec. 1946.

MARKS, Ernest Samuel, CBE 1938; JP; Alderman City of Sydney and Chairman of its Health and Recreation Committee; Chairman, British Empire Games Committee (Australian Division); President Noise Abatement League of NS Wales; Chairman United Charities of New South Wales; Deputy Chairman of Australian Red Cross (NSW Division); Chairman, NSW Rugby Football Union; b West Maitland, NSW, 1872; s of Joseph Marks, JP, and Elizabeth Benjamin; unmarried. Educ: Royston College, Sydney. Lord Mayor of Sydney, 1930 (first after the re-establishment of the City Council); Member for North Sydney in NSW Parliament, 1927–30; President of NSW Sports Club for twenty-five years; actively connected with, and held executive office in, NSW Rugby Union, Amateur Athletic Association, Amateur Swimming Association,

Coursing Association, Boxing and Wrestling Association and other Sporting bodies; Honorary Secretary, Amateur Athletic Union of Australia 1896–1933; Director National (Political) Club; appointed by Government on various Royal Commissions; Chairman Recreation and Travel Panel, Australian Commission for Wembley Exhibition; Hon. Treasurer War Service Committee; Member State Recruiting Committee; Joint Organiser Sportsman's Unit, and other activities during European War, 1914–18; has travelled extensively in Europe, America, and the Far East; connected with the wool and produce trade for thirty years. Publications: various articles on amateur sport and municipal government. Recreations: fishing, surfing, athletics, and travel. Address: Manor, 42 Macleay Street, Sydney, NSW. Clubs: Sports, National, Tattersall's (Sydney).

Died 2 Dec. 1947.

MARKS, Fredrick William, CBE 1939; FCA (Aust.); Consulting Accountant; Trustee Australian Museum; Chairman of Directors Prince Henry Hospital; Vice-President Central District Ambulance; Chairman Metropolitan Meat Industry Advisory Council and Theatres and Films Commission; Member NSW Government Taxation Board; Member of Board of Control of United Dental Hospital of Sydney; Member of Committee of Investigation Hospitals Control and Finance; b 20 April 1886; s of late M. Marks, Neutral Bay, Sydney; m 1909, Viva, d of late A. L. Stinson; one s four d. Educ: Fairlawn Grammar School; public schools. Member NSW Government Budget Committee, 1932; Chairman of Committee of Management Metropolitan Meat Industry Board, Sydney, 1932; Royal Commissioner enquiry relating to Metropolitan Board of Water Sewerage and Drainage, 1932–33; Commissioned by NSW Government to enquire into Poultry Industry, 1933; Commissioned by Government to enquire into Film Industry 1934; Member of Theatres and Public Halls Investigation Committee, 1938; Chairman NSW Government Films Advisory Committee, 1935–39; was for some years a Director of Royal North Shore Hospital. Recreation: golf. Address: Keith House, Bradley's Head Road, Mosman, NSW; Old Meadows, Burradoo, NSW. T: XM 1121. Clubs: University, Sydney; Manly and Australian Golf.

Died 14 Aug. 1942.

MARLOW, Col Benjamin William, CSI 1917; CIE; b 1 Dec. 1863. Educ: Clifton College. Entered army, 1884; Captain, ISC, 1895; Major, Indian Army, 1902; Lt-Col 1904; Col 1908; Military Accountant-General, Army Headquarters, Simla, 1908–19; retired, April 1920; served Burma, 1886 (medal with clasp); expedition to Dongola, 1896 (medal, Egyptian medal). Address: c/o Lloyds Bank, 6 Pall Mall, SW1.

Died 20 April 1943.

MARLOW, Sydney Raymond, CMG 1943; Financial Secretary, Tanganyika Territory, since 1942; b 17 Dec. 1896; s of late John Marlow, Northampton; m 1932, Marjorie, d of A. W. Frost, Birmingham; two s. Educ: Northampton Town and County School. Lt 4th Northants, 1915; Capt. Nigeria Regt, West African FF, 1918; Asst Treasurer, Nigeria, 1919; Deputy Treasurer, 1935; Deputy Financial Secretary, 1937. Recreations: golf, violin, MBOU. Address: Inglenook, Dallington, Northampton.

Died 12 July 1945.

MARNHAM, Francis John; JP; b 1853; s of John Marnham, JP of Boxmoor, Herts; m 1881, Gertrude, d of R. Drury Lown; one s two d. Educ: privately. Formerly Member Stock Exchange; JP Borough of Torquay; MP (L) Chertsey Div. Surrey, 1906–10; Mayor of Torquay, 1926–27; a Baptist. Address: Meadfort Rock, Torquay, Devon. Club: National Liberal.

Died 18 Jan. 1941.

MARR, Francis Alleyne, DSO 1918, MC; Geologist, Burmah Oil Co. since 1919; *b* 9 Nov. 1894; *s* of late Prof. J. E. Marr, ScD, FRS, and A. Birkett Stubbs; *m* 1931, Margaret Cantrell. *Educ:* Oundle; St John's College, Cambridge. Served in France and Flanders, 1914–19 (despatches, DSO, MC); Capt. 1st Camb. Regt; Brigade Major 118th Infantry Brigade. *Recreations:* squash and tennis. *Clubs:* Junior Army and Navy, United University.

Died Nov. 1942.

MARRIAGE, Herbert James; Consulting Aural Surgeon, St Thomas's Hospital since 1932; Aural Surgeon, St Thomas's Hospital, 1904–32; Clinical Teacher in Otology and Rhinology at Royal Army Medical College; *b* 17 Jan. 1872; *s* of James Marriage of Beckenham; *m* 1910, Amy Grace, *d* of E. W. Richardson, Eastbourne; two *s* one *d*. *Educ:* City of London School; St Thomas's Hospital; MRCS Eng.; LRCP Lond., 1897; MB Lond., 1899; BS, 1901; FRCS Eng., 1902. House Surgeon, House Physician and Surgical Registrar, St Thomas's Hospital, and Surgical Tutor at St Thomas's Hospital Medical School; subsequently studied Otology and Rhinology at Halle, Vienna, and Berlin; Fellow of Royal Society of Medicine (late President of Otological Section). *Publications:* (with Sir Cuthbert Wallace) Case of Attempted Division of Eighth Nerve within the Skull for the Relief of Tinnitus, Lancet, 1904; Case of Cerebellar Abscess, Operation, during the Performance of Artificial Respiration, Trans. Otol. Soc., vol. vii; Skin-Grafting in Mastoid Operations, Proc. Roy. Soc. Med., 1915; War Injuries and Neuroses of Otological Interest, Journal of Laryng. Rhinol. and Otol., 1917. *Recreations:* lawn tennis, golf. *Address:* Woldingham House, Woldingham, Surrey. *T:* Woldingham 3202.

Died 12 Jan. 1946.

MARRINER, Lt-Col Bryan Lister, DSO 1918; late RA; *b* 22 April 1888; *s* of late W. H. L. Marriner and F. Foster; *m* 1918, Evelyn May Ilieve; one *d*. *Educ:* Cheltenham College; RMA, Woolwich. Served European War, France and Belgium Sept. 1914–June 1918 (DSO, despatches twice); Afghanistan and NWF, India, June–Dec. 1919; Khajuri Operations Oct. 1930–Feb. 1931 (despatches); GSW in hand at Givenchy in March 1915; Lt-Col 1935; retired pay, 1936. *Address:* 18 Poole Road, Bournemouth.

Died 15 April 1943.

MARRIOTT; *see* Smith-Marriott.

MARRIOTT, Col Alfred Sinclair, CBE 1928; late Indian Army; *b* 3 July 1876; *s* of late Alfred Barrow Marriott, Indian Police; *m* 1914, Violet Mary, *d* of late Ambrose More O'Ferrall, Co. Kildare; no *c*. *Educ:* Blundell's School, Tiverton; Sandhurst. Gazetted Bedfordshire Regt 1897; transferred to Indian Army, 1900; Director Military Farms Dept, 1921–29; retired 1929. *Clubs:* Naval and Military, Kennel.

Died 2 Jan. 1943.

MARRIOTT, Charles Bertrand; KC 1926; Recorder of Northampton since 1928; Chairman of Quarter Sessions, Rutland; Deputy Chairman of Quarter Sessions, Northants and Leicestershire; *b* 1868; *s* of late Sir Charles Hayes Marriott, FRCS, MD Lond., JP, DL for Leicestershire, of Harcourt House, Kibworth, near Leicester; *m* 1922, Frances Pendlebury Worsley (*d* 1945), *widow* of Richard Worsley of Broxmead, Cuckfield, Sussex. *Educ:* Uppingham; Trinity College, Oxford. BA (Honours in History). Called to the Bar, Inner Temple, 1892; Bencher, 1934; Member of Midland Circuit; Counsel to Port of London Authority and Thames Conservancy. *Recreations:* golf, shooting. *Address:* 1 Paper Buildings, Temple, EC4; The Old Hall, Wing, nr Oakham, Rutland. *T:* Central 0165, Manton 216. *Clubs:* Carlton, MCC; Leicester County; Northampton.

Died 11 May 1946.

MARRIOTT, Eric Llewellyn, CIE 1934; *b* 28 May 1888. Joined Indian Police, 1907; Supt, 1917; Deputy Inspector-General of Police, Bihar, 1934–38; retired, 1938.

Died 22 March 1945.

MARRIOTT, Frederick, RE, ARCA; RBC; painter and etcher; *b* 20 Oct. 1860. *Educ:* Royal College of Art. *Address:* 6a Netherton Grove, Chelsea, SW10. *T:* Flaxman 7229. *Club:* Chelsea Arts.

Died 2 Oct. 1941.

MARRIOTT, Sir John Arthur Ransome, Kt 1924; MA; Hon. Fellow, formerly Fellow and Lecturer of Worcester College, Oxford; *b* 1859; *e s* of Francis Marriott of Bowdon and Hayfield, Derbyshire; *m* 1891, Henrietta, *d* of Rev. W. P. Robinson, DD, Warden of Glenalmond; one *d*. *Educ:* Repton; New College, Oxford. Lecturer of New College, 1884; Dunkin Lecturer in Sociology, 1903–04; Secretary to Oxford Univ. Extension Delegacy, 1895–1920; contested (C) Rochdale, 1886; MP (C) Oxford City, 1917–22; York, 1923–29. Served on Select Committee on National Expenditure (Sessions 1917–18–1919–20), Member of Second Chamber Conference, 1917–18; Chairman of Select Committee on Estimates, 1924 and 1925; Director of Great Northern Railway, 1919–23. *Publications:* Makers of Modern Italy, 1889 (revised and enlarged edition, 1931); George Canning and his Times, 1903; The Life and Times of Lucius Cary, Viscount Falkland, 1907; The Remaking of Modern Europe, 1909; Second Chambers, 1910; English Political Institutions, 1910; The French Revolution of 1848 (ed.), 1913; England since Waterloo, 1913; The English Land System, 1914; The Evolution of Prussia, 1915 (with C. G. Robertson); The Eastern Question: a Study in European Diplomacy, 1917; English History in Shakspeare, 1918; The European Commonwealth, 1918; The Right to Work, 1919; Syndicalism: Economic and Political, 1921; Europe and beyond, 1921; England under the Tudors, 1922; Economics and Ethics, 1923; Our Own Times (in These Eventful Years), 1924; The Mechanism of the Modern State (2 vols), 1927; Empire Settlement, 1927; How we are Governed, 1928; The Crisis of English Liberty, 1930; How We Live, 1930; A History of Europe from 1815 to 1923, 1931; The English in India, 1932; Evolution of Modern Europe, 1453–1923, 1932; Oxford: Its Place in National History, 1933; The Life of John Colet, 1933; Queen Victoria and her Ministers, 1933; Modern England: A History of My Own Times, 1934; Twenty-five Years of the Reign of King George V, 1935; Dictatorship and Democracy, 1935; Life of Castlereagh, 1936; Commonwealth or Anarchy, 1937; This Realm of England, 1938; The Evolution of the British Empire and Commonwealth, 1939; English History in English Fiction, 1940; The Tragedy of Europe, 1941; A Short History of France, 1942; Federalism and the Problem of the Small State, 1943; Anglo-Russian Relations, 1944; Memories of Four Score Years, 1946; lectures; contrib. to Quarterly Review, Edinburgh, Fortnightly, Nineteenth Century, Hibbert Journal, etc. *Recreations:* talking and writing. *Address:* Worcester College, Oxford.

Died 6 June 1945.

MARRIS, Sir William Sinclair, KCSI 1921; KCIE 1919; CIE 1914; Hon. DLitt (Durham), 1929; Hon. LittD (NZ), 1941; Grand Officier de l'Ordre de Léopold, 1926; Life Member of Council, Cheltenham College; Trustee, Royal Holloway College; Governor, Royal Agricultural College, Cirencester; Chairman, Assistance Advisory Committee, Gloucester; Member, Gloucestershire Education Committee; *b* 9 Oct. 1873; *s* of Charles Marris; *m* 1st, 1905, Eleanor Mary Fergusson (*d* 1906); one *s*; 2nd, 1934, Elizabeth Wilford Good. *Educ:* Wanganui, NZ; Canterbury College, NZ; Christ Church, Oxford. Passed first in ICS open, 1895. Assistant Magistrate, UP, 1896; Under Secretary to

Govt, UP, 1899; Under-Secretary to Govt of India, 1901; Deputy Secretary to Govt of India, 1904; services lent to Transvaal Govt 1906; Civil Service Commissioner, Transvaal, 1907; Deputy Chairman of Commission on Central South African Railways, 1907; Magistrate and Collector, Aligarh, UP, 1910; Member of Executive Committee, Coronation Durbar, 1912; Acting Sec. to Government of India, Home Department, 1913; Inspector-Gen. of Police, UP, 1916; Joint Sec. to Govt of India, 1917; Home Sec., Govt of India, 1919–21; Reforms Commissioner, 1919–20; Governor of Assam, 1921–22; Governor of the United Provinces, 1922–28; Member of the Council of India, 1928–29; Principal of Armstrong College, 1929–37; Vice-Chancellor, Durham University, 1932–34; Pro-Vice-Chancellor, 1929–32, 1934–37. *Publications:* The Odes of Horace, Catullus, Homer's Odyssey, Homer's Iliad, in English Verse; articles in reviews. *Address:* Dollar House, Cirencester. *T:* Cirencester 280.

Died 12 Dec. 1945.

MARSDEN, Sir John Denton, 1st Bt *cr* 1924; JP; Chairman and Managing Director of Consolidated Fisheries, Ltd, Grimsby, Swansea, Lowestoft; Member of the Advisory Committee on Fishery Research, Development Commission; *b* Huddersfield, Yorks, 9 Nov. 1873; *m* 1911, Agnes Mary, *d* of Thomas Robert Ronald of Little Danson, Welling, Kent; one *s* one *d*. President of the British Trawlers' Federation, 1925–33 and 1939–43; High Sheriff of Lincolnshire, 1942–43. *Heir: s* John Denton Marsden [*b* 25 Aug. 1913; *m* 1939, Hope, *yr d* of late G. E. Llewelyn; one *s* one *d*]. *Address:* Panton Hall, Lincoln. *T:* Wragby 214.

Died 26 April 1944.

MARSDEN, Wilfred Alexander, CB 1943; MA; Keeper of Printed Books, British Museum, 1930–43; *b* 16 May 1878; *y s* of late Lt-Col William Marsden, Cedar Court, Farnham, Surrey, and Katharine, *d* of late B. Rigby Murray, DL of Parton, Kirkcudbrightshire; *m* 1910, Gwladys, *d* of late William Keown-Boyd, of Downpatrick; one *s* one *d*. *Educ:* Wellington College; University College, Oxford. Assistant in Department of Printed Books British Museum, 1903; Deputy Keeper, 1924; Hon. Member, Spalding Gentlemen's Society; Hon. Life Member, Friends of the National Libraries. *Address:* Pound Hall, Long Melford, Suffolk.

Died 13 Dec. 1949.

MARSH, Col Frank, CBE 1919; MB, MCh, FRCS (Eng.), etc.; RAMC (T); Knight of Grace of Order of St John of Jerusalem in England; DL Warwickshire; late Hon. Col RAMC Units, 48th (SM) Div. (TA); Consulting Surgeon, Birmingham United Hospital; Associate King's College, London; Ex-Vice-Chairman Warwickshire Territorial Army Association and Chairman Recruiting Committee; Ex-President Birmingham Medical Institute; Birmingham Medical Benevolent Society; Midland Medical Society; and Birmingham Branch of British Medical Association; *b* Tillington, near Stafford, 1855; *s* of late Edward Marsh; *m* 1886, Annie Constance, *d* of late Wm Hooper, Beechwood, Clapham Common, SW; two *s* two *d*. *Educ:* King's College and Hospital, London. Surgeon Imperial Ottoman Army, Turco-Russian War, 1877–78 (War Medal); House Surgeon, Stafford County Infirmary; Medical Officer of Health, Stafford; Surgeon, Queen's Hospital, Birmingham, 1886–1903; Ingleby Lecturer, Birmingham University, 1902; Surgeon, Birmingham and Midland Ear and Throat Hospital, 1896–1903; Lecturer on ⌄ Surgery, Dental Dept, Birmingham University; OC 1st Southern General Hospital, RAMC (T), 1912–17 (despatches, Brevet Colonel); ADMS Birmingham District, June 1917–Sept. 1919; Territorial Efficiency Decoration, 1935; Silver Jubilee Medal, 1935; Coronation Medal, 1937. *Publications:* many contributions to current medical and

surgical Literature. *Recreation:* salmon and trout fishing. *Address:* c/o Lloyds and Nat. Prov. Foreign Bank Ltd, Monte Carlo, Monaco. *T:* 015.94 Monaco.

Died 12 Sept. 1943.

MARSH, Frank Burr, PhD, FRHistS; Professor of Ancient History, University of Texas, since 1926; *b* 4 March 1880; *s* of Edwin J. Marsh and Alma L. Burr. *Educ:* University of Michigan. Instructor, University of Michigan, 1903–10; University of Texas since 1910. *Publications:* English Rule in Gascony (1199–1259), 1912; The Founding of the Roman Empire, 1st Ed., 1922, 2nd revised edition, 1927; The Reign of Tiberius, 1931; A History of the Roman World from 146 to 30 BC, 1935; Editor with H. J. Leon of Tacitus, Selections from his Works, 1936. *Address:* University of Texas, Austin, Texas, USA.

Died 31 May 1940.

MARSH, Lt-Col Jeremy-Taylor, CMG 1915; OBE 1932; late RASC; *b* 16 Dec. 1872; *e surv. s* of late Col J. T. Marsh, RE, of West Jerpoint, Kilkenny; *m* 1906, Constance Mary, *o d* of A. H. Robinson; one *s.* 2nd Lt 4th (RI) Dragoon Guards from Militia, 1894; transferred Indian Army, 9th Bengal Lancers, 1897; exchanged British Service, Army Service Corps, 1906; Special appointment to Australian Commonwealth, 1912, to reorganise Australian Army Service Corps; served Tirah, 1897–98 (medal two clasps); European War (Dardanelles), 1914–18 (despatches, CMG, Bt Lt-Col); retired pay, 1922; re-employed Barrack Dept RASC 1923; retired 1934. *Address:* Vyne Lodge Farm, Bramley, Basingstoke, Hants. *T:* Bramley Green 233.

Died 15 March 1944.

MARSH, Margaret Munnerlyn Mitchell, (Mrs J. R. Marsh), Hon. MA Smith College, 1939; *b* Atlanta, Georgia, USA; *o d* of late Eugene Muse Mitchell and late Maybelle Stephens Mitchell; *m* 1925, John Robert Marsh; no *c.* *Educ:* Washington Seminary, Atlanta, Georgia; Smith College, Northampton, Mass. *Publication:* (as Margaret Mitchell) Gone with the Wind, a novel (winner of 1936 Pulitzer Award). *Address:* 1268 Piedmont Avenue, North East, Atlanta, Zone 5, Georgia, USA.

Died 16 Aug. 1949.

MARSHALL, Hon. Duncan M'Lean, DSc; Member of Senate of Canada since 1938; Agricultural Counsel, Cockfield Brown and Co., Toronto, Canada; Member, National Live Stock Records Executive; *b* 24 Sept. 1872; *m* Tena M'Isaac, Charlottetown, PEI; three *s.* Editor and manager of the Daily Bulletin, Edmonton; MPP (L) Olds, 1909; Minister of Agriculture, Alberta, 1909–21; Commissioner of Agriculture for Canada, 1922–24; Minister of Agriculture, Ontario, 1934–37; breeder of shorthorn cattle; Hon. Doctor of Agriculture, Iowa State College of Agriculture, 1935. *Publications:* Field and Farmyard, textbook on farming and live stock; Weed Control; Thieves in the Fields; Shorthorn Cattle in Canada. *Address:* Toronto, Canada.

Died 16 Jan. 1946.

MARSHALL, Francis Hugh Adam, CBE 1933; ScD (Cantab), DSc (Edin.), Hon. DSc (Manch.), Hon. LLD (Edin.), FRS, FRSE; Fellow of Christ's College, Cambridge; *b* High Wycombe, 11 July 1878; *y s* of late Thos Marshall, JP, and Mary Lucas of High Wycombe, and afterwards of Freshwater, Isle of Wight. *Educ:* St Mark's School, Windsor; privately; University College, London; Christ's College, Cambridge. Research Student, University of Edinburgh, 1900; Carnegie Fellow, 1904–07. Lecturer on the Physiology of Reproduction, Edinburgh, 1905–08; Lecturer on Agricultural Physiology, Cambridge, 1908–19; Reader, 1919–43; Proctor, Cambridge, 1911–12; Fellow of Christ's College, 1909; Tutor, 1912–23; Dean, 1926–46; Vice-Master, 1939–42; Director of the Animal Nutrition Institute, Cambridge, 1930–33; Council of Senate,

1914–18; Council of Royal Society, 1933–35; sent to Algeria on a Delegation by the Ministry of Agriculture to report upon Dr Voronoff's gland-grafting experiments, 1927; Baly medal, Royal College of Physicians, 1935; Croonian Lecturer, RS, 1936; Royal Medal of Royal Society, 1940. *Publications:* The Physiology of Reproduction, 1910, 3rd edition, 1949; Physiology of Farm Animals, 1920, 4th edition (with E. T. Halnan), 1946; an Introduction to Sexual Physiology, 1925; Fertility and Animal Breeding (with J. Hammond), 1925, 6th edition, 1945; and other scientific publications. *Recreation:* ornithology. *Address:* Christ's College, Cambridge. *T:* Cambridge 5094. *Club:* Athenæum.

Died 5 Feb. 1949.

MARSHALL, Maj.-Gen. Francis James, CB 1919; CMG 1918; DSO 1917; *b* 20 Aug. 1876; *s* of late James Marshall, Advocate of Duncrievie, Glenfarg, and Margaret, *d* of Rev. J. Champion of Edale, Derbyshire; *m* 1906, Alice Maude, *e d* of late W. Horn, Advocate, of Woodcote, Blackshiels; one *s* four *d*. *Educ:* Rugby; RMC, Sandhurst. Joined Seaforth Highlanders, 1895; served in India, Mediterranean, Egypt, and S Africa; passed through Staff College, 1907; served on the staff in West Indies and at home; occupation of Crete, 1897; Soudanese Campaign, 1898; S Africa, 1901–02; European War, 1914–18 (CB, CMG, DSO); Director of Military Training, India, 1920–23; late Brigade Commander 11th Infantry Brigade; Assistant Director of Territorial Army, 1928–29; ADC to the King, 1926–29; Major-General, 1929; Commander 54th (East Anglian) Division TA, 1930–34; retired pay, 1934; Commander 1st Inverness (East and Nairnshire) Bn Home Guard, 1940. *Recreations:* fishing, shooting. *Address:* Hilton House, Inverness. *T:* Inverness 252.

Died 22 May 1942.

MARSHALL, Frank James; Chess Champion, United States, 1909–36; *b* New York City, 10 Aug. 1877; *s* of Alfred G. Marshall, Bristol, and Sarah Graham, Ireland; *m* 1905, Caroline Dorothea Krauss; one *s*. *Educ:* Canada. Chess: won first Prize, London, 1899; Cambridge Springs, Pa, 1904; Nuremburg, 1906; Dusseldorf, 1907; Havana, 1913; Chicago, 1925; World's Record, 156 games simultaneously, Montreal, 7 hours 20 minutes; lost 7, drew 14; Captain US Team which won Hamilton Russell Cup, Prague, 1931, Folkestone, 1933, Warsaw, Poland, 1935, Stockholm, 1937. *Publications:* Chess Openings; Chess Swindles; Modern Chess; Chess in Championship Play; Chess, Step by Step; Chess Masterpieces; Comparative Chess; Chess in an Hour; My Fifty Years of Chess. *Recreation:* bridge. *Address:* 23 West 10th Street, New York. *T:* Gramercy 7–3716. *Clubs:* Marshall Chess, New York.

Died 9 Nov. 1944.

MARSHALL, Col Hannath Douglas, CIE 1927; OBE; VD; *b* Bengeo, Herts, 29 July 1872; 3rd *s* of Rev. C. J. Marshall. *Educ:* Bengeo; Rugby. Tea planter, 1890–1926; Commandant Surma Valley Light Horse (Assam, India), 1924; retired; Superintendent Scottpore Tea Co. and Bhubandhar Tea Co. in Surma Valley, Assam. *Recreations:* polo, tennis, golf, field sports. *Address:* Maryknoll, Church Streton, Shropshire. *Club:* Golfers'.

Died 23 Oct. 1944.

MARSHALL, Horace, MA; Stipendiary Magistrate for the City of Leeds since 1910; *s* of late Thomas Marshall, MA, Registrar in Bankruptcy and District Registrar, Leeds; *m* 1923, Millicent, *d* of T. Elliot, and *widow of* Bryan Cookson, Oakwood, Wylam; one *s* one *d*. *Educ:* Eton; Trinity College, Oxon (1st open Exhibition); 2nd class classical moderations and Lit. Hum. Called to Bar, Inner Temple, 1894; went NE Circuit. *Recreations:* shooting, fishing, golf. *Address:* Grimston Lodge, Tadcaster. *T:* Tadcaster 3112.

Died 6 May 1944.

MARSHALL, Hugh John Cole, CBE 1934; Secretary, Royal Literary Fund, 1919–45; *b* 2 June 1873; *s* of James Cutcliffe Marshall and Mary Cole; *m* 1909, Bessie Yule. *Educ:* Dr Osmond's School, Hanley; High School, Newcastle under Lyme. Employed by Richard Bentley and Sons (Publishers), 1889–99; commission in RE 46th (N Midland) division (TF), 1915; Captain RE 1917; Adjutant RE 46th Division, 1917; Major RE 1919 (despatches thrice, OBE, Croix de Guerre). *Recreations:* reading and fishing. *Address:* Ash Tree Cottage, Broxbourne.

Died 2 Dec. 1947.

MARSHALL, Brig.-Gen. Hugh John Miles, CB 1919; CMG 1916; RE; *b* Mussorie, India, 5 Sept. 1867; *s* of Maj.-Gen. W. E. Marshall, Indian Staff Corps; *m* 1909, Sarah Katherine (*d* 1938), *d* of John Gillam of Penrhyn, Stourbridge, Worcestershire; one *s*. *Educ:* Wellington Coll.; RMA, Woolwich. Entered Army, 1887; Capt. 1897; Major, 1905; Lieut-Col 1914; Col 1918; temp. Col on the Staff, 1921; Chief Engineer, Western Command, India, 1921–24; retired, 1924; served India, Burma, and China; Chin Lushai Expedition, 1889–90 (medal with clasp); European War, 1914–19; France, Belgium and Italy (despatches, CB, CMG, Italian Order of St Maurice and Lazarus, French Croix de Guerre). *Recreation:* golf. *Address:* c/o Lloyds Bank, Ltd, Cox's Branch, 6 Pall Mall, SW1.

Died 25 Aug. 1946.

MARSHALL, John Frederick, CBE 1936; MA; Director, British Mosquito Control Institute, Hayling Island; *b* 5 Sept. 1874; *s* of late Charles Marshall, Huntingdon; *m* 1902, Blanche Gray; one *d*. *Educ:* Rugby (Cricket XI, 1892–93; Rackets, 1892–93); King's College, Cambridge (Entrance and Undergraduate Scholar). First Class Mechanical Sciences Tripos, Part I. 1896, and Part II (with special distinction), 1898. Called to Bar, Inner Temple, 1902; has since been engaged in scientific research; Fellow of the Royal Society of Tropical Medicine and Hygiene; represented Cambridge University at real tennis, 1897, and won MCC Gold Tennis Prize, 1914; organized 1920, scheme for mosquito control of Hayling Island; built and equipped the British Mosquito Control Institute (Hayling Island), 1925. *Publications:* Unofficial Mosquito Control in England, 1922; Coastal Mosquitoes and their Control (British Association Address), 1925; Principles and Practice of Mosquito Control, 1927; The Organization of Mosquito Control Work (Presidential Address in Zoology Section, South-Eastern Union of Scientific Societies, Portsmouth Congress, 1930); The British Mosquitoes, 1938; The Morphology and Biology of Culex molestus, 1944; various contributions to scientific journals. *Address:* c/o British Mosquito Control Institute, Hayling Island, Hants. *Club:* Royal Automobile.

Died 5 Dec. 1949.

MARSHALL, Maj.-Gen. John Stuart, CB 1935; DSO 1917; OBE 1924; *b* 1883; 2nd *s* of late J. J. Marshall, Yelverton, Devon; *m* 1920, Alice Deborah, *o d* of late Major-General Gerald Cree, CB, CMG; one *d*. *Educ:* US College, Westward Ho! Served South African War, 1902 (Queen's medal and two clasps); European War (East Africa), 1914–18 (despatches, DSO, Bt Major); Waziristan, 1922–24 (despatches); operation North-West Frontier, India, 1930–31 (bar to DSO, despatches); Chitral Reliefs, 1932 (despatches); operations against Upper Mohmands, 1933 (despatches); retired, 1940. *Address:* c/o Lloyd's Bank, Pall Mall, SW1. *Club:* United Service.

Died 5 May 1944.

MARSHALL, Lumley Arnold; ISO 1912; *b* 1852; 2nd *s* of late General Hubert Marshall, Madras; *m* 1st, 1877, Martha Ellen (*d* 1902), 4th *d* of late Slaney Jones; 2nd, 1908, Emily (*d* 1930), *y d* of late Slaney Jones. *Educ:*

Edinburgh Academy. Entered the Civil Service, Class I open competition, 1873; Assistant Sec., General Post Office, 1912; retired, 1914.

Died 29 Nov. 1942.

MARSHALL, Brig. Norman, DSO 1917; MC; *b* 1886; *s* of late Rev. Alexander Marshall, DD, formerly Minister of Scots Church, Melbourne; *m* 1917, Kathleen, *d* of A. G. Black, Melbourne. Served European War, 1915–18 (despatches, MC, DSO with two bars). *Address:* Mount Malakoff, Stanthorpe, Queensland.

Died 12 Sept. 1942.

MARSHALL, Brig.-Gen. Thomas Edward, CB 1919; CMG 1917; *b* Hartford, Cheshire, 1865; *s* of late Sir T. H. Marshall; *m* 1919, 2nd *d* of late W. Shimeld, of Lowdham Grange, Notts. *Educ:* Eton; RMA, Woolwich. Entered Army, 1885; served in Burma, India, Mediterranean; served Manipur Expedition, 1891; Wuntho (Burma) Expedition, 1891; N Chin Hills Expedition, 1892–93 (Indian medal 3 clasps, despatches); European War in France, 1915–18 (CB, CMG, despatches four times). *Recreations:* played for RMA, Woolwich, cricket and Association football, shooting. *Address:* Bryn-y-Coed, Bangor, N Wales.

Died 13 Feb. 1946.

MARSTON, Sir Charles, Kt 1926; JP; FSA; Chairman of the Villiers Engineering Co. Ltd; President of the Victoria Institute; KJStJ; *b* 6 April 1867; *e s* of late John Marston, JP, Freeman of the Borough of Wolverhampton, and late Ellen, *d* of Charles Edge, architect, Birmingham; *m* 1st, 1895, Louise Isabel (*d* 1921), *o d* of William Gordon Johnson, Ithaca, NY; two *d*; 2nd, 1922, Ruth (*d* 1934), *d* of W. H. Miller, Ithaca, New York; 3rd, 1935, Mary Battey, *widow* of George Bonney, New York. *Educ:* Wolverhampton School; Mason College (now Birmingham University). *Manufacturer, Politician, Traveller, Biblical Archæologist. Publications:* The Christian Faith and Industry; The New Knowledge about the Old Testament, 1933; New Bible Evidence, 1934; The Bible is True, 1934; The Bible Comes Alive, 1937; Essays on Economic and Religious Questions. *Address:* 124 Tettenhall Road, Wolverhampton; Green Pastures, Tiddington Road, Stratford-on-Avon; Longville, Perton, Compton, Wolverhampton. *Clubs:* Carlton, National, Royal Automobile.

Died 21 May 1946.

MARSTON, Freda, ROI 1929; RBA 1924; ARBC 1929; painter; *b* Hampstead, 24 Oct. 1895; 2nd *d* of late George Clulow; *m* 1922, St Clair Marston, ROI, RBA, ARBC (*d* 1943). *Educ:* Clapham High School; Art School, Regent Street Polytechnic; studied in Italy. Work represented in the Towner Art Gallery, Eastbourne; Prince of Wales Museum, Bombay; Leamington Art Gallery; Stoke-on-Trent. *Address:* 13 Langham Road, Robertsbridge, Sussex.

Died 27 March 1949.

MARSTON, Reginald St Clair, ROI 1923; RBA 1923; ARBC 1933; *b* Willenhall, 1886; 7th *s* of late Edmund Dunton Marston; *m* 1922, Freda Clulow (Freda Marston, ROI). *Educ:* Birmingham; Paris; Munich. Pictures in Whitworth Gallery, Manchester; Towner Gallery, Eastbourne; Wolverhampton Art Gallery; and Salisbury Gallery, Rhodesia. *Address:* Moorfields Cottage, Langport, Somerset.

Died 26 Feb. 1943.

MARTEL, Brig.-Gen. Sir Charles Philip, Kt 1921; CB, 1916; late RA; late Chief Superintendent, Ordnance Factories, 1917–21; Superintendent, Royal Gun and Carriage Factory, 1912–17; Member of Ordnance Board, 1911–12; Military Assistant to Chief Superintendent, Ordnance Factories, Woolwich, 1907–11; Secretary to the Ordnance Committee,

Woolwich, 1901–04; Professor of Artillery, Ordnance College, and Principal Experimental Officer, 1904–05; *b* 3 Feb. 1861; *m* 1884, Lilian Mary, *y d* of W. H. Mackintosh, MD; one *s* one *d*. Retired with rank of Brig.-Gen. 1920. *Address:* Queenswood, Cranford Avenue, Exmouth, S Devon. *Club:* Army and Navy.

Died 19 July 1945.

MARTEN, Sir (Clarence) Henry (Kennett), KCVO 1945; Provost of Eton College since 1945; *b* 28 Oct. 1872; 2nd *s* of late Sir Alfred Marten, KC, MP. *Educ:* Eton College; Balliol College, Oxford (1st Class, Modern History). Assistant Master at Eton since 1896; House Master, 1907–27; Lower Master, 1926–29; Vice-Provost, 1930–45; President of the Historical Association, 1929–31. *Publications:* Ground-work of British History (with late Townsend Warner of Harrow), Histories (with E. H. Carter and Laurence Housman); On the Teaching of History and Other Addresses; contributor to Prime Ministers of the Nineteenth Century, etc. *Address:* The Lodge, Eton College, Windsor. *T:* Windsor 304. *Club:* Athenæum.

Died 11 Dec. 1948.

MARTEN, Eric Charles; Hon. Mr Justice Marten; Judge High Court of Judicature, Lahore, Punjab, India, from 1944; *b* 14 Feb. 1899; *s* of J. T. Marten, CSI, ICS, and Agatha Templeman; *m* 1925, Louie Joan Unwin; two *s* one *d*. *Educ:* Uppingham; RM College, Sandhurst. Indian Army (Cavalry), 1918–21; Indian Civil Service (Punjab), 1923; Judge High Court (additional), 1942. *Recreations:* riding, shooting, golf. *Clubs:* Army and Navy; Punjab, Lahore.

Died 21 June 1948.

MARTEN, Vice-Adm. Sir Francis Arthur, KBE 1944; CB 1923; CMG 1919; CVO 1920; *b* 1879; *s* of late G. N. Marten of Marshals Wick, St Albans; *m* Phyllis Raby, *d* of W. Morgan; two *s*. Served European War, 1914–20 (despatches, promoted Captain, CMG, CVO); commanded Royal Naval College, Osborne, 1920–21; Royal Naval College, Dartmouth, 1921–22; Captain of the Fleet, Atlantic Fleet, 1923–25; retired list, 1928; Vice-Adm. retired, 1932; Commander of the Order of Dannebrog (1st class); Joint Master, Cotswold Hounds, 1928–34. *Address:* Puck bridge, Whittington, Andoversford, Glos. *Clubs:* United Service, MCC.

Died 14 March 1950.

MARTEN, Sir Henry; *see* Marten, Sir C. H. K.

MARTIN, Alderman Sir Albert, Kt 1938; JP. *Address:* Belgrave, The Cliffs, Southend.

Died 4 Oct. 1943.

MARTIN, Very Rev. Alexander, DD, LLD; Principal Emeritus of New College, Edinburgh; Chaplain to the King in Scotland since 1929; Professor of Apologetics and Practical Theology, New College, Edin., 1897–1927; Principal, 1918–35; Moderator of General Assembly United Free Church of Scotland, 1920 and 1929; Freedom of the City of Edinburgh, 1929; *b* 1857; *s* of Rev. Hugh Martin, DD, Free Church minister of Panbride, afterwards of Edinburgh, author of various theological works; *m* 1887, Jane Thorburn, *d* of Rev. Thomas Addis, DD, of Morningside Free Church, Edinburgh; two *s* two *d*. *Educ:* Watson's Coll., Edin.; Edin. Univ.; New College (Theological Hall), Edin. Medallist and Bruce Prizeman in classes of Mental Philosophy; Rhind Scholarship; Bruce of Grangehill Scholarship; Ferguson Scholarship (open to the Scottish Universities); Hamilton Fellowship; graduated MA, with a 1st class in Philosophy, 1880; Cunningham Fellowship on leaving New College, 1883. Assistant to Professor of Moral Philosophy, Edinburgh Univ., 1880–83; Examiner in Mental Philosophy at Edin. University, 1886–88; minister of Morningside Free Church, Edinburgh. *Publications:* Winning the Soul, 1897; The Present Position of Apologetics, 1897; The Finality of

Jesus for Faith, 1933; and various reviews and articles. *Address:* 17 Grange Terrace, Edinburgh. *T:* Central 43107. *Clubs:* University, Edinburgh.

Died 14 June 1946.

MARTIN, Hon. Archer; *b* 6 May 1865; 2nd *s* of Edward Martin, QC, DCL, of Ballinahinch, Hamilton, Ontario, Canada, and *g g s* of Richard (' Humanity') Martin, MP (author of Martin's Act for Prevention of Cruelty to Animals, and principal founder of the RSPCA), of Ballinahinch Castle, Co. Galway; *m* 1889, Emily Mary, 2nd *d* of John Breakenridge Read, Barr.-at-law, of Osgoode Hall, Toronto; two *s. Educ:* Trin. Coll. Sch., Port Hope, Ontario; Ghent, Belgium. Bar, 1887; appointed Counsel for Dominion Govt and Representative of Minister of Justice in Vancouver Island, 1896; special commissioner to inquire into and report upon affairs of BC Crown Timber Lands Agency, 1897; a Puisne Judge of Supreme Court of British Columbia, 1898; Deputy Judge in Admiralty for British Columbia, 1899; special commissioner to settle mining disputes in the Porcupine District, arising out of British and United States Treaty on the Canada-Alaskan boundary, 1900; Judge in Admiralty for BC, 1902; a Justice of Appeal, 1909; Chief Justice of British Columbia, 1937–40. *Publications:* Genealogy of Martin of Ballinahinch Castle; The Hudson's Bay Company's Land Tenures; Chart of the Judges of Vancouver Island and British Columbia; Martin's Mining Cases, vols i and ii. *Recreations:* golf, gardening, swimming. *Address:* Ballinahinch, Victoria, British Columbia, Canada. *Clubs:* Union, Victoria.

Died 1 Sept. 1941.

MARTIN, Arthur John, CBE 1942; BA Lond.; HBM Consul-General, Chungking, China since 1940; *b* 23 June 1883; *s* of Thomas Pearce and Nancy Tremills Martin; *m* 1924, Mary Erwin, *d* of Leopold Anthony and Anna de Camp Camacho, Staten Island, New York, and cousin of late Admiral William Snowden Sims; two *s. Educ:* private school; King's College, London. Called to Bar, Middle Temple 1919; Student Interpreter in China 1907; served at Swatow, Hankow, and Peking 1909–12; on active service with Inns of Court OTC and Yorkshire Hussars Yeomanry 1914–15; Vice-Consul at Batavia and Acting Consul-General 1915–18; served in Hangchow, Wenchow, Ningpo, Peking, Kansu, Tientsin, and Mukden, 1919–22; Assessor in Mixed Court at Shanghai and Deputy in Provisional Court, 1923–27; Registrar of Supreme Court at Shanghai 1928–29; Consul at Foochow and Amoy 1929–37; Consul-General, Tsingtao, 1938–40. *Recreations:* polo, shooting, etc. and collecting Chinese pottery and porcelain. *Address:* British Consulate-General, Chung king, China. *Clubs:* Thatched House, Royal Automobile.

Died 6 April 1942.

MARTIN, Col Claude Buist, CMG 1919; late RAMC; *b* 1869; *m* 1903, Mary, *d* of J. L. Thomas, Southampton; one *s* one *d. Educ:* Edinburgh University, MB, CM. Late Commandant Royal Army Medical College; served Chitral, 1895 (medal with clasp); S Africa, 1899–1902 (despatches twice, Queen's medal with five clasps, King's medal with two clasps); European War, 1914–19 (despatches twice, Order of St Sava, CMG); retired pay, 1924.

Died 27 Dec. 1950.

MARTIN, Cyril Hubert; ISO 1922; Assistant Secretary, Government of India, Department of Revenue and Agriculture (retired); *b* 1 July 1867; 2nd *s* of late John Charles and Phillipina Rose Martin; *m* 1898, Katherine Mary, *e d* of late Henry Twidale of the Calcutta High Court of Judicature. *Educ:* St Xavier's College, Calcutta. Entered the service of the Govt of India in the Dept of Revenue and Agriculture, 1887; KSG 1930. *Recreation:* literary. *Address:* Ensham, Catholic Club, Simla, India.

Died 30 Nov. 1940.

MARTIN, Brig.-Gen. Edward Fowell, CB 1919; CMG 1918; DSO 1917; VD; Sergeant at Arms, Legislative Assembly, W Australia, 1932–50; *b* 22 Aug. 1875; *s* of Edward Martin, Droubalgie Station, Forbes, NS Wales. *Educ:* King's College, Goulburn. Served European War, 1914–19 (despatches, DSO, CMG, CB). *Address:* Legislative Assembly, Perth, W Australia.

Died 22 Sept. 1950.

MARTIN, Frederick, CBE 1942; DL Aberdeenshire, 1949; Convener Aberdeenshire County Council since 1949; *b* Peterhead, 23 Oct. 1882; 3rd *s* of William Martin and Agnes Clark; *m* Flora, *d* of late J. C. Rennie of Milladen, Aberdeenshire; two *d. Educ:* Peterhead Acad. Journalist on staff of Aberdeen Free Press and Morning Post till 1914; served as 2nd Lieut in 5th Gordon Highlanders, T, 1914–15; became blind during period of training, and afterwards passed through St Dunstan's Hostel for Blinded Soldiers and Sailors; MP (L) East Aberdeenshire, Nov. 1922–Oct. 1924; contested (L) Central Aberdeenshire, 1929, and (Lab) East Aberdeenshire, 1931 and 1935; joined Labour Party, 1929; Vice-Chairman Aberdeenshire Education Authority, 1925–30; CC 1929; Chairman Public Health Committee, 1932–45; Chairman Education Committee, 1946–47; Vice-Convener of County, 1946–49. Grand-President Bolton Unity of Oddfellows, 1925–26. *Recreation:* angling. *Address:* St Dunstan's, Mintlaw, Aberdeenshire. *TA:* Frederick Martin, Mintlaw. *T:* Mintlaw 229. *Clubs:* Royal Northern (Aberdeen); Scottish Liberal (Edinburgh).

Died 18 Jan. 1950.

MARTIN, Granville Edward B.; *see* Bromley-Martin.

MARTIN, Henry Robert Charles, FSA 1929; Richmond Herald since 1928; Captain (retired) East Lancashire Regiment; *b* 1889; *e s* of late Henry Thomas Martin, of South Kensington and of Ceylon; *m* 1914, Mary Gladys, *y d* of late Rev. J. W. St Quintin, Rector of Hatley St George, Co. Cambridge; three *d. Educ:* Bedford School; Lincoln College, Oxford. Admitted member of the Middle Temple, 1912; served European War, 1914–18, with 3rd (Special Reserve) Bn East Lancashire Regiment; Captain, 1917; Rouge Croix Pursuivant of Arms, 1922–28. *Recreations:* lawn tennis, hockey, and badminton. *Address:* College of Arms, EC4. *T:* City 2762. *Club:* Windham.

Died 23 July 1942.

MARTIN, John; retired at the end of 1924 after 48 years' service on the Editorial Staff of the Daily Telegraph and 62 years active work as a journalist; *b* Petrockstow, Devon, 2 Oct. 1847; *m* 1871, Emma Jones, Exeter; three *d. Educ:* Devonport Mathematical School. Began journalism on Western Daily Mercury, 1863; joined Central Press, London, 1870; only man surviving who reported the Tichborne trial-at-bar, 1872–74; entered Press Gallery of the House of Commons, 1871; appointed to Parliamentary Staff of the Daily Telegraph, 1877; Chief of Staff, 1890–92; Political Correspondent, 1892–1919; after 42 years' service in the Gallery and Lobby, transferred to Staff in Fleet Street. Chairman, Lobby Committee several years in succession; Chairman, Gallery Committee, 1917–18, being then Father of the Gallery; Hon. Treasurer of Press Club, 1886–88; Chairman of London district of Institute of Journalists, 1896–97, Vice President, 1897, Fellow, 1898. PM and DC Gallery Lodge of Freemasons; Member of Grand Lodge of England, since 1912; Vice-Patron, Royal Masonic Benevolent Institution and Royal Masonic Institution for Boys; Vice-President, Royal Masonic Institution for Girls; Life Governor, Royal Masonic Hospital and Nursing Home; subscriber to the Masonic Memorial Million Fund. Founder, 1888, and for ten years, Hon. Sec., Devonians in London; Vice-President, London Devonian Association. Winner, Challenge Cup, value 100 guineas, London Press Billiard Handicap, 1899. *Address:* 9 Clifton Estate, Colebrook, Plympton, S Devon.

Died 17 Aug. 1944.

MARTIN, John; Chairman of Argus Newspaper Group in South Africa; *b* Stirling, Scotland, 1884; *m* 1911, Elinore Mary Scott-Waring Green; one *s* two *d.* Director, Bank of England, 1936–46; one of HM Lieutenants of the City of London; President, Transvaal Chamber of Mines, 1929, 1932, 1934; Vice-President 1927, '30, '31, '33, '35 and 1937; Chm. Argus South African Newspapers; The Argus Printing and Publishing Company Ltd, and the Rhodesian Printing and Publishing Company Ltd; Member of the South African Economic and Wage Commission, 1926; Chairman, Southern Rhodesia Railway Enquiry, 1929. Head of Union Government Supply Mission, Washington, 1942. *Address:* The Star Office, Johannesburg; The Thatched House, Riviera, Johannesburg.

Died 28 March 1949.

MARTIN, Percy F., FRGS; author and journalist; retired, 1933; *b* 30 March 1861. *Educ:* University College, London; abroad. Specialist Writer: Pall Mall Gazette, 1885–88; Evening News, 1886–88; London Financial Editor The Freeman's Journal, 1887–89; Correspondent in Mexico of the Times, the Tribune, and the Glasgow Herald, and in India of the Times (Engineering Supplement) and the Evening Standard; Special Correspondent of the Financial News, Financial Times, and The Engineer in South and Central America; contributor to the Times Trade Supplement, the Times Engineering Supplement, the Times Educational Supplement, The Daily Graphic, The Britannica Year-Book, and the Economist; Peoples of all Nations; Countries of the World, Business Encyclopædia; Chief Correspondent in Italy for the New York Journal of Commerce; Travelling Correspondent Reuter's Trade Service. *Publications:* Through Five Republics of South America, 1905; Mexico's Treasure House, 1906; Mexico of the XX Century, 1907; Handbook to Latin-American Investments; El Salvador of the Twentieth Century, 1911; Peru of the Twentieth Century, 1911; Greece of the Twentieth Century, 1912; Maximilian in Mexico, 1913; The Sudan in Evolution, 1921; Egypt, Old and New, 1923. *Recreations:* travel, motoring, driving. *Address:* c/o Coutts & Co., 440 Strand, WC2.

Died 1 June 1941.

MARTIN, Robert M. Holland, CB 1911; FSA; Director Martin's Bank, Ltd (Chairman, London Board), Union Discount Co. of London, Ltd, Gas Light and Coke Co., Southern Railway (Chairman), Alliance Assurance Co; *b* 10 Oct. 1872; *s* of Rev. Frederick Whitmore Holland and Penelope, *d* of Robert Martin of Overbury Court, Tewkesbury; took surname of Martin in addition to that of Holland by Royal licence dated 14 Aug. 1917; *m* 1897, Eleanor Mary, *d* of G. E. Martin of Ham Court, Upton-on-Severn; six *s.* *Educ:* Eton; Trinity College, Oxford. Chairman County of London Territorial Army and Air Force Association, 1925–32; Hon. Sec. Bankers' Clearing House, 1905–35; High Sheriff of Worcestershire, 1938. *Address:* Overbury Court, Tewkesbury. *T:* Overbury 2. *Clubs:* Savile, Burlington Fine Arts, Athenæum.

Died 27 Jan. 1944.

MARTIN, Very Rev. Thomas, DD; Parish Minister of Peebles, retired; Home Mission Convener of Church of Scotland, and Moderator of the General Assembly of the Church of Scotland for the year 1920–21; *b* Scone, Perthshire, 14 April 1856; *s* of Hugh Martin, farmer; *m* Christian I. Robertson, London; one *s* one *d. Educ:* St Martin's Parish School; University, Edinburgh and University St Andrews. Parish Minister at Perth; Forgan; Cramond; St Mary's, Edinburgh; The Barony, Glasgow; and Peebles; Lecturer in Pastoral Theology for two years

at the four Scottish Universities. *Recreation:* golf. *Address:* Neidpath, Davidson's Mains, Edinburgh. *T:* Edinburgh 77195.

Died 7 Jan. 1942.

MARTIN, Paymaster Rear-Adm. William Ernest Russell, CMG 1917; RN (retired); *b* 20 May 1867; *o s* of late Paymaster-in-Chief W. H. Martin, RN, and Florence Eugenia, *d* of late Hon. S. S. Ingham, Speaker of the House of Assembly, Bermuda; *m* 1894, Annie Josephine, *y d* of late Brigade Surgeon W. Langworthy Baker and Betsy Heaward, *d* of late Dr Walter Yarde Bond, Newton Abbot; one *s*, Fairlie Russell, 2nd Lt 1st Royal Scots Fusiliers attached RFC; killed near Ypres, aged 19. *Educ:* privately. Joined Royal Navy, 1884; served Alexandra, flag of Admiral Lord John Hay, Mediterranean; Orion (specially commissioned at Malta in Russian War scare, 1885); Northampton, flag of Admiral Lyons, N America and WI; Shannon, west coast of Ireland; Aurora, cruiser; Orontes and Tamar, Imperial Troopships; Wildfire, flag of Admiral Heneage, The Nore; Pembroke, as Secretary to Admirals Morant and Andoe, at Chatham; served as Secretary to Admiral Sir Edmund S. Poë, GCVO, KCB, in all his commands, namely: Training Squadron, 1897–1900; Home Fleet, 1904; First Cruiser Squadron, 1905; East Indies, 1905–07; Cape, 1907–08; and Mediterranean, 1910–12; also as Paymaster of Pallas, Hibernia, Hannibal, Majestic (1914), Harwich Coastguard, Impregnable and Vivid I.; acted as Special Correspondent for Daily Mail during the volcanic eruptions at Martinique and St Vincent in 1902; served on Staff of Principal Naval Transport Officer, France, 1914–17 (despatches twice); retired voluntarily, 1 June 1922; President Fellowship of Freedom and Reform, Plymouth Branch; acted as Editor Italian Mail at Florence, 1926; Hon. President of British Friends of Italy, Milan, 1935. *Publication:* The Adventures of a Naval Paymaster. *Recreations:* fishing, sailing. *Address:* Mabruk, 4 Essa Road, Saltash, Cornwall.

Died 17 June 1946.

MARTIN, William Henry Blyth, CBE 1934; JP, DL; Hon. Sheriff Substitute for Forfarshire; *b* 2 Oct. 1862; *s* of James Martin and Agnes Hutcheson; *m* 1899, Lizzie Allardyce Middleton; three *s* one *d. Educ:* Dundee Institution; Edinburgh University. Practised as a Solicitor in Dundee; Town Clerk of Dundee, 1903–36. *Address:* Taymount, Dundee.

Died 15 Dec. 1946.

MARTIN, Hon. William Lee; MLC, New Zealand, 1946; MP for Raglan; *b* Oamaru, New Zealand, 1870; 2nd *s* of Joseph Martin and Susan Allworthy; *m* 1894, Harriet Wilhelmina, *d* of James and Annie Warnes, Greymouth, NZ; three *s* three *d. Educ:* Waimate High School; Sydenham, Christchurch. Some years officer in Salvation Army; Secretary Painters Union Wanganui; Member Board Governors Wanganui Technical College; started farming Waikato, 1912; President Waikato sub-Province Farmers Union; Member Central Waikato Power Bd; Chairman Tamahere Road Board; Minister of Agriculture, New Zealand, 1935–41; Past Grand President United Ancient Order of Druids; Member Repatriation Board (Hamilton); local preacher Methodist Church. *Recreations:* brass bands, bowling, cricket, football. *Address:* Ingleton Terrace, Hamilton, NZ; Parliament Buildings, Wellington, NZ.

Died 21 Dec. 1950.

MARTIN-HARVEY, Sir John; *see* Harvey, Sir J. M.

MARTIN-HURST, William, MA, FRGS; Managing Editor Exclusive News Agency since 1904; *b* Bradford, 16 July 1876; *m* Eda Mary (*d* 1941), *o d* of William Forrest, Rockwood, Blackburn; two *s* two *d. Educ:* Marlborough; Giggleswick; France, Germany, Canada. Descriptive writer, Montreal Star, 1896–98; Daily Mail, 1898–1902, travelling correspondent, Bulgaria, Serbia, Greece, Russia, Turkey. *Publications:* Many articles, mainly travel, in national press; contributor to British and foreign geographical and educational works and encyclopædias; writer on Oriental ceramics of the Yung Chêng and Ch'ien Lung periods. Collaborated with Dr G. C. Williamson in 'Book of Famille Rose,' 1925. *Recreations:* collecting porcelain and postage stamps, gastronomy, travel. *Address:* The End House, Roehampton. *TA:* Martinhurst, Roehampton. *T:* Putney 0363. *Club:* Authors' (Member of General Council).

Died 4 April 1941.

MARTIN-JONES, Rev. S., MA; Rector of Haslemere, Surrey, since 1932; *b* Forest Hill, Kent, 8 Sept. 1872; *s of* Thomas and Sarah Clement Jones; *m* 1st, Rose Alyce, *d* of Frederick Jones, Sydenham; three *s* one *d*; 2nd, Winifred, *d* of Stanley Jones, Bromley, Kent. *Educ:* Dulwich College; Emmanuel College, Cambridge; Clergy Training School, Cambridge; Oxford House, Bethnal Green. Curate St Paul's Middlesbro', 1896; Parish Church, Walsall, 1901; founded Walsall Brotherhood and floated Walsall Brotherhood Social Club Ltd; Vicar All Saints, Necton, Norfolk, 1904; Diocesan Inspector of Schools, Norwich Diocese, 1906–10; Vicar of Wymondham, 1911; Rural Dean of Hingham, 1921, Hon. Canon Norwich Cathedral; Secretary, Diocesan Retreat House, 1912; Proctor in Convocation for Norwich Diocese, 1929, for Guildford Diocese, 1935. *Publications:* Comfort and Consolation; Wymondham and its Abbey. *Recreations:* played for Cambridge against Oxford at lawn tennis, Secretary, Varsity Tennis team, 1894, played for Kent, Staffordshire and Norfolk. *Address:* Haslemere Rectory, Haslemere, Surrey. *T:* 616.

Died 7 Feb. 1941.

MARTINDALE, Sir Arthur Henry Temple, KCSI 1904; CSI 1900; *b* 13 March 1854; *e s* of late Colonel B. H. Martindale, CB; *m* 1st, 1877, Isabella Marion Mackenzie (*d* 1879); one *s*; 2nd, 1886, Clara, *e d* of late William Hudleston, CSI, of Hutton John, Cumberland; two *d*. *Educ:* Cheltenham Coll. Entered India Civil Service, 1875; Foreign Dept 1877; Political Agent, Quetta, 1887; Commissioner, Ajmer-Merwara, 1894; Resident, Western States, Rajputana, 1895; Chief Commissioner, Ajmer-Merwara, 1898; Agent to the Viceroy and Governor-Gen. of India for the province of Rajputana in India, 1898–1905; retired, 1905; Knight of Grace, Order of St John of Jerusalem. *Address:* Church House, Merrow, nr Guildford, Surrey. *T:* Guildford 614.

Died 25 Jan. 1942.

MARTINDALE, Ven. Henry, MA; Rector of Ashwell, nr Baldock, since 1941; *b* 1879; *s* of late Robert Benson Martindale and Mary Agnes, *d* of Thomas Crewdson; *m* 1926, Augusta Celia, *d* of late Very Rev. A. E. Burn, DD, Dean of Salisbury; one *s* two *d*. *Educ:* Friends School, Kendal; Heversham Grammar School; Keble College, Oxford; Lincoln Theological College. Bank of Liverpool, 1895–1906; served South African War, 1900 (attached St John Ambulance Brigade); graduated, Oxford 3rd cl. Th. Hon. 1909; Deacon, 1910; Priest, 1911; Curate of Kentish Town Parish Church, 1910; St Martin's, Lower Edmonton, 1911–13; Chaplain of Parel, Bombay, 1913–15; Bombay Ecclesiastical Establishment, 1915; Chaplain to the Forces, Mesopotamia, 1916–19 (despatches); Archdeacon of Bombay, 1927–33; Rector of East Barnet, 1933–37; Vicar of Woburn, Beds, 1937–41; RD of Fleete, 1938–41. *Address:* The Rectory, Ashwell, near Baldock.

Died 10 April 1946.

MARTINEAU, Sir Philip Hubert, Kt 1933; Solicitor; *b* 28 Oct. 1862; *s* of Hubert Martineau and Elizabeth Mary Alston; *m* 1888, Alice Margaret, *d* of His Hon. Judge Robert Vaughan Williams; three *s. Educ:* Harrow; Trinity College, Cambridge. President of the Law Society, 1931–32; Member of the Inspection Committee of the Trustees Savings Banks; Director Guardian

Assurance Company, Ltd. *Recreations:* shooting, fishing, golf. *Address:* Watermartins, Sunningdale, Berks. *T:* Ascot 72. *Club:* Oxford and Cambridge.

Died 7 Oct. 1944.

MARTINEAU, Sir William, Kt 1935; JP; Chairman Martineau's Ltd, Sugar Refiners, London; late President Ross and Cromarty Unionist Association; *b* 8 Dec. 1865; *s* of George Martineau, CB; *m* 1895, Ann Duncan Kilgour (*d* 1946); two *s. Educ:* Uppingham; Cambridge. *Recreations:* shooting, fishing, and golf. *Address:* Kincraig, Invergordon, Ross-shire; 4 Sloane Court, SW3. *T:* Sloane 8435. *Clubs:* Carlton, Oxford and Cambridge.

Died 29 May 1950.

MARTON, Lt-Col Richard Oliver, CMG 1916; DSO 1900; late Royal Garrison Artillery; *b* 19 Aug. 1872; *s* of late Col G. B. H. Marton; *m* 1899, Margaret Elizabeth, *d* of late Egerton Leigh of Jodrel Hall, Cheshire; one *s*. Entered army, 1892; Captain, 1899; served S Africa, 1899–1902 (despatches, Queen's medal four clasps, King's medal two clasps, DSO); European War (despatches, 1914 Star, CMG). *Address:* Capernwray, Carnforth, Lancashire; Seafield House, New Romney, Kent.

Died 12 May 1945.

MARTYN, Brig.-Gen. Arundel, CB 1919; CMG 1918; *b* 1868; *s* of late Col Anthony Martyn, of Buckingham Lodge, Exmouth, Devon; *m* Theodora, *d* of late E. P. Barlow, JP, Kearsney Court, Dover; one *s. Educ:* Marlborough Coll. Joined 4th Batt. Devon Regt, 1886; R W Kent Regt, 1888; served South African War, 1900–01; on staff (Brevet-Major, despatches); in Macedonian Gendarmerie (Chief Executive Officer, 1904–07); served European War, commanded 1 RW Kent Regt Aug.–Oct. 1914; afterwards served in France as Brig. cmdg Brigade, 1914–15; Salonica, 1916; France, 1917 (despatches five times, Brevet Colonel, CB, CMG); Comdr Order of the Crown of Belgium; comdg S African Military Command, 1918. *Recreations:* cricket, football, lawn-tennis, golf. *Address:* Hart's Delyte, Budleigh Salterton, Devon.

Died 15 July 1945.

MARTYN, Sir Henry Linnington, KCVO 1931; CVO 1927; MVO 1923; MB, BS (Lond.), FRCS (Eng.); late Surgeon Apothecary to HM Household at Windsor; Consulting Surgeon, Ear, Nose and Throat Department, King Edward VII Hospital, Windsor; Consulting Aural Surgeon Maidenhead Hospital, Staines, Chalfont, Windlesham and Iver Cottage Hospitals; *b* London, 1888; *s* of Henry Matthews Martyn of Broadclyst, Devon, and Helena Sarah Martyn of Peel, Isle of Man; *m* 1st 1913, Nora Mary (marr. diss. 1939), *o d* of Paul and Mary Addington of Wimbledon; one *d*; 2nd, 1939, Dr Freda Kelly, *er d* of W. B. Kelly, Hatch End, Middlesex. *Educ:* King's College School, Wimbledon; King's College Hosp., London. MRCS (Eng.), LRCP (Lond.), 1910, MB, BS (Lond.), 1911 with Honours in Surgery, Medicine, and Forensic Medicine, and University Gold Medal; FRCS (Eng.), 1913. House Surgeon, King's Coll. Hosp., 1911; temporary Lieut RAMC, Aug. 1914–Aug. 1915; temporary Capt. RAMC, May 1917–Jan. 1919; Surgical Specialist, No. 10 Gen. Hosp., BEF; invalided as result of sickness contracted on Active Service with Hon. rank Capt., Jan. 1919 (1914 Star, General Service and Victory medals). *Recreations:* yachting, painting. *Address:* Tudor Cottage, The Lane, Dittisham, near Dartmouth, Devon. *T:* Dittisham 54.

Died 7 Jan. 1947.

MARVIN, Francis Sydney, MA; FRHistS; Staff Inspector, Board of Education, until 1924; *b* City of London, 6 Aug. 1863; *m* 1904, Edith Mary Deverell; two *s. Educ:* Merchant Taylors' School; St John's College, Oxford (Senior Scholar; 1st in Mods., 1st in Greats, 2nd in Modern History). For a time teacher in elementary schools and extension lecturer; Inspector,

1890; in Lancashire, West Cornwall, Westmorland and Cumberland, West Ham; Divisional Inspector and Inspector of Training Colleges in Yorkshire, 1903–13; East Central Division, 1914; organiser of courses and lectures for teachers and others in modern languages, history, and educational science, especially of Unity History Schools, since 1915; Professor of Modern History in the University of Egypt, 1929–30. *Publications:* The Living Past, 1913; The Unity of Western Civilization (editor), 1915; Progress and History (editor), 1916; The Century of Hope, 1919; Recent Developments of European Thought, 1920 (editor); The Evolution of World Peace (editor), 1921; Western Races and the World (editor), 1922; Science and Civilisation (Editor), 1923; England and the World (editor), 1925; India and the West, 1927; Art and Civilization (editor), 1928; The Modern World, 1929; The New World Order (editor), 1932; The Nation at School, 1933; Old and New, 1935; Auguste Comte (series of Modern Sociologists), 1936; The New Vision of Man, 1938; joint author of versions of Iliad and Odyssey, and The Making of the Western Mind, 1923; articles on education, history, and philosophy. *Recreations:* tennis, swimming, music. *Address:* Pantiles, Welwyn Garden City. *T:* Welwyn Garden 981.

Died 14 Nov. 1943.

MARYON-WILSON, Sir Spencer Pocklington Maryon M.; *see* Wilson, Sir S. P. M. M.

MASARYK, Jan Garrigue, CBE (Hon.); LLD; Minister of Foreign Affairs, Czechoslovak Government, since 1940; Deputy Prime Minister, 1941–45; *b* 1886; *s* of late T. G. Masaryk. Czechoslovak Minister to Great Britain, 1925–38; resigned. Leader Czechoslovak Delegation, Paris Peace Conference. *Address:* Prague. *Clubs:* St James's, Beefsteak.

Died 10 March 1948.

MASCAGNI, Pietro; composer; *b* Leghorn, 7 Sept. 1863. *Educ:* Milan Conservatoire. *Publications:* La Cavalleria Rusticana, 1890; L'Amico Fritz, 1891; Les Rantzau, 1893; Ratcliff, 1895; Iris, 1898; Isabeau, 1911; Parisina, 1913; Nero, 1935.

Died 2 Aug. 1945.

MASON, Alfred Edward Woodley, FRGS; author; *b* 7 May 1865; *y s* of late William Woodley Mason, Everleigh, Dulwich. *Educ:* Dulwich College; Trinity Coll., Oxford; MA. Capt., Manchester Regt, 1914; Major, RMLI, 1917; MP (L) Coventry, 1906–10; Hon. Fellow Trinity College, 1943. *Publications:* A Romance of Wastdale, 1895; The Courtship of Morrice Buckler, 1896; The Philanderers, 1897; Lawrence Clavering, 1897; Parson Kelly (with Mr Andrew Lang), 1899; Miranda of the Balcony, 1899 (produced as a play, New York, 1901); The Watchers, 1899; Ensign Knightley; Clementina, 1901; The Four Feathers, 1902; The Truants, 1904; Running Water, 1907; The Broken Road, 1907; Col Smith (Comedy), 1909; At the Villa Rose, 1910; The Witness for the Defence (Play), 1911; The Turnstile, 1912; Open Windows (Play), 1913; The Four Corners of the World (Stories), 1917; The Summons, 1920; At The Villa Rose (Play), 1921; Running Water (Play), 1922; The Winding Stair, 1923; The House of the Arrow, 1924; No Other Tiger, 1927; The Prisoner in the Opal, 1929; The Dean's Elbow, 1930; The Three Gentlemen, 1932; The Sapphire, 1933; A Present from Margate (with Ian Hay—Play), 1933; Dilemmas, 1934; Sir George Alexander and the St James' Theatre; The Wouldn't be Chessmen, 1935; Fire Over England, 1936; The Drum (film), 1937; Königsmark, 1938; The Life of Francis Drake, 1941; Musk and Amber, 1942; The House in Lordship Lane, 1946. *Recreations:* mountain climbing, boat-sailing. *Address:* 51 South Street, W1. *Clubs:* St James', Alpine; Royal Yacht Squadron (Cowes).

Died 22 Nov. 1948.

MASON, David Marshall; Associate of the Institute of Bankers; Founder and Chairman Executive Committee Sound Currency Association; *b* 7 Dec. 1865; *e s* of Stephen Mason, MP Mid-Lanarkshire and Martha, *d* of late John Marshall, Machan, Lanarkshire; *m* Mary, 3rd *d* of Hon. George W. Crouse, Akron, Ohio, USA, formerly Member of Congress; two *s* five *d*. *Educ:* Partick and Kelvinside Academies, Glasgow; Craigmount, Edinburgh; Glasgow University; Germany. Contested (L) Tradeston Division of Glasgow 1906 and 1910; MP (L) Coventry, 1910–18; Edinburgh, East, 1931–35; joined Liberal National Party, 1939; contested (L) Chislehurst Division of Kent, 1918, Romford Division of Essex, 1922 and 1923, Barnstaple Div. of North Devon, 1929. *Publications:* Six Years of Politics; Monetary Policy, 1914–1928; various pamphlets on political and financial subjects. *Recreations:* reading, golf, fishing, and shooting. *Address:* 34 Queen's Gate Gardens, SW7. *T:* Western 0099. *Clubs:* Reform, Bath, National Liberal.

Died 19 March 1945.

MASON, Rev. Richard Swann S.; *see* Swann-Mason.

MASSINGBERD, Field Marshal Sir Archibald Armar M.; *see* Montgomery-Massingberd.

MASSON, Rosaline; author; historian; *d* of late Prof. David Masson, LLD, Historiographer Royal for Scotland, and Emily Rosaline Orme. *Publications:* My Poor Niece, 1894; Use and Abuse of English, 1896 (5th, revised, ed. 1929); Lives of Robert Pollock and of W. E. Aytoun (Famous Scots Series), 1897; A Departure from Tradition, 1898; The Transgressors, 1899; In Our Town, 1901; Leslie Farquhar, 1902; Edinburgh (illustrated by John Fulleylove, RI), 1904; new editions 1925 and (enlarged) 1931; Our Bye-Election, 1908; Edinburgh (Peeps at Many Lands Series), 1910; Nina, 1911; In Praise of Edinburgh (Anthology), 1912; Wordsworth (People's Books Series), 1913; R. L. Stevenson (People's Book Series), 1914; edited Shakespeare Personally, by David Masson, 1914; edited I Can Remember Robert Louis Stevenson, 1922 (2nd, enlarged, edition 1925); Life of Robert Louis Stevenson, 1923 (2nd ed., 1924); Scotia's Darling Seat (History of the Cockburn Association), 1926; A Better Man, 1928; Poets, Patriots, and Lovers, 1933; Scotland the Nation (History of Scotland), 1934; Short History of Scotland the Nation, with translations into Polish, Norwegian, Dutch, and other languages of British Allies, 1941; literary and historic articles in various periodicals. *Address:* 20 Ann Street, Edinburgh. *T:* 26942.

Died 7 Dec. 1949.

MASSY, Brig.-Gen. Edward Charles, CB 1918; CMG 1919; DSO 1917; Royal Artillery; late Hon. Col 92nd Brigade RA (5th London) TA; *b* 5 Oct. 1868; *m* 1903, Grace Mary, *y d* of late Henry Adrian Burrowes of Dangan Castle, Co. Meath; one *s* one *d*. *Educ:* Cheltenham; RMA, Woolwich. Entered Royal Artillery, 1888; Capt. 1898; Major, 1904; Lt-Col 1914; served Tirah Campaign, 1895; was in command of 5th London Territorial Artillery when war broke out; took them out to France, March 1915, and was with them at Festubert, Loos, Somme, etc., till promoted temp. Brig.-Gen. March 1917; proceeded to Palestine and commanded artillery of 52nd Division and 7th Indian Division in Palestine (DSO, CB, CMG, despatches 6 times); retired, 1920. *Address:* c/o Lloyds Bank, Cox & King's Branch, 6 Pall Mall, SW1.

Died 26 May 1946.

MASSY, Col Godfrey, CMG 1918; late the Norfolk Regiment; *b* 1863; *s* of Hugh Deane Massy, of Stagdale, County Limerick; *m* 1889, Margaret Frances (*d* 1928), *d* of C. Dodd; one *d*. Served European War, 1914–19 (despatches twice, CMG). *Address:* Peacocks, Midhurst, Sussex.

Died 18 March 1944.

MASSY, Col William George, CMG 1917; (late) Royal Horse and Field Artillery; *b* Canterbury, 31 May 1857; *s* of Surg.-Gen. H. H. Massy, CB; *m* 1882, Harriet Teresa Battersby (*d* 1932); one *s* one *d*. *Educ:* privately. Commission, Royal Artillery, 1877; served S African War (Queen's medal and 2 clasps, King's medal and 2 clasps); passed Staff Coll.; held various regimental and staff employments; retired, 1907; re-employed CRA East Anglian Division, 1908–12; served European War, 1914–17 (despatches twice, CMG). *Recreation:* all kinds of sport.

Died 16 April 1941.

MASTER, Lt-Col Arthur Gilbert, DSO 1915; late RASC; *b* 6 June 1867; *m* 1897, Elizabeth (*d* 1940), 2nd *d* of late Edward Hotham Newton of Fulford Park, York; one *s* two *d*. *Educ:* Exeter Coll., Oxford; BA 1889; MA 1906. Entered army (W India Regt), 1891; Capt. ASC, 1898; Major, 1904; Lt-Col, 1913; served S African War, 1899–1902 (Queen's medal 4 clasps, King's medal 2 clasps); European War, with BEF, France, 1914–18 (DSO). *Address:* Fulford Park, York. *Clubs:* United Service; Yorkshire, York.

Died 11 March 1942.

MASTER, Rev. Harold C.; *see* Chester-Master.

MASTERMAN, Arthur Thomas, FRS, DSc (St Andrews and London), MA, FRSE; *b* Tunbridge Wells, 1869; 3rd *s* of late Thomas W. Masterman, Rotherfield Hall, Sussex; *m* Caroline (*d* 1933), *o d* of late Rev. S. T. Notcutt, of Bristol; one *s* one *d*. *Educ:* University School, Hastings; Weymouth; Christ's College, Cambridge (Scholar). Assistant Professor Natural History, St Andrews University, 1893–99; Lecturer in Comparative Embryology, and Fellow of University of St Andrews, 1897–99; Lecturer in Biology and Zoology, School of Medicine of the Royal Colleges, Edinburgh, 1900–03; Lecturer in Zoology, Church of Scotland Training College, Edinburgh, 1900–03; Lecturer in Zoology, Cambridge University Extension Society; Examiner to Royal College of Physicians, Edinburgh, 1899–1903, to University of St Andrews, 1902, University of Durham, 1908; Superintending Inspector (Director of Fishery Investigations) HM Board of Agriculture and Fisheries, 1903–20; British Government Expert to International Council for the Exploration of the Sea, 1905–14; Secretary to HM Treasury Committee on Fishery Investigation, 1908–09; Technical Dept, Air Ministry, 1917; National Salvage Council, 1918; Gold Medallist (Macdougall-Brisbane) Royal Society, Edinburgh, 1902. *Publications:* (joint with Prof. W. C. M'Intosh), Life Histories of British Marine Food Fishes, 1897; Elementary Text-book of Zoology, 1901–1902, numerous researches on zoological and fishery subjects. *Recreations:* formerly football, swimming, water polo, golf; President, Cambridge Univ. Swimming Club, 1892–93; captained first water polo team v. Oxford Univ. SC, 1892. *Address:* 50 Ebury Street, SW1; 38 Kedale Road, Seaford. *Clubs:* Athenæum, Royal Automobile.

Died 10 Feb. 1941.

MASTERS, Edgar Lee; writer; *b* Garnett, Kansas, 23 Aug. 1869; *s* of Hardin Wallace Masters and Emma J. Dexter; *m* 1898, Helen M., *d* of Robert E. Jenkins, Chicago. *Educ:* High School and Knox College. Admitted to Bar, 1891; Democrat. *Publications:* A Book of Verses, 1898; Maximilian (drama in blank verse), 1902; The New Star Chamber and other Essays, 1904; Spoon River Anthology, 1915; Songs and Satires, 1916; The Great Valley, 1916; Toward the Gulf (poems), 1918; Starved Rock (poems), 1919; Domesday Book, 1920; The Open Sea, 1921; Children of the Market Place, 1923; The New Spoon River, 1925; Jack Kelso, 1927; The Fate of the Jury, 1929; Lincoln: The Man, 1931; The Tale of Chicago, 1933; The Serpent in the Wilderness, 1933; Dramatic Duologues, 1934; Vachel Lindsay, 1935; Invisible Landscapes, 1935; The Golden Fleece of California, 1936; Poems of People, 1936; Whitman, 1937; The New World, 1937; The Tide of Time, 1937; Mark Twain, 1938. *Address:* Hotel Chelsea, NYC, USA.

Died 5 March 1950.

MASTERS, Sir Frederick, Kt 1939; Member Advisory Committee for Appointment of Justices for County of London since 1933; *b* 3 July 1872; *s* of Frederick Thomas and Elizabeth Masters; *m* 1894, Emily Maud Lewis; no *c*. *Educ:* Littlehampton Grammar School; Protestant School, Dieppe, France. Member Stepney Borough Council, 1904–12; JP, County of London, 1933. *Recreations:* golf, fishing. *Address:* Nuneham, Garrads Road, Streatham, SW16. *T:* Streatham 1239. *Club:* Sudbury Golf (Wembley).

Died 8 Nov. 1947.

MASTERS, Rev. Canon James Herbert, MA; Hon. Canon of Rochester Cathedral, 1926–40, Canon Emeritus since 1940; Hon. Chaplain to Bishop of Rochester since 1940; *b* 2 Dec. 1863; *e s* of Canon James Hoare Masters, Residentiary Canon of Chichester Cathedral; *m* 1906, Henrietta Lowe, *widow* of W. S. Warner, New York; no *c*. *Educ:* Charterhouse; Trinity College, Cambridge. Deacon, 1893; Priest, 1894; Curate of Frant, Sussex; Curate of Speldhurst in charge of St John's, Groombridge, 1896; Rector of Speldhurst-with-Groombridge, 1911–30; Rural Dean of Tunbridge Wells, 1930–32; Surrogate in Diocese of Rochester, 1930–40. *Recreation:* golf. *Address:* Beeding, Tunbridge Wells. *T:* Tunbridge Wells 547. *Clubs:* Oxford and Cambridge; Royal Ashdown Forest Golf (President, 1939).

Died 3 Feb. 1942.

MATHER-JACKSON, Sir Henry; *see* Jackson.

MATHERS, Frederick Francis, Hon. LLB 1892; KC 1909; *b* St John, NB, 17 Oct. 1871; *s* of I. H. Mathers, Halifax, NS, formerly of Newry, Ireland, and Kathleen, *d* of late Robert M'Donnell of The Grove, Stillorgan, Ireland; *m* 1899, Ethel, *d* of Howard Bligh, Halifax; one *d*. *Educ:* Halifax Schools; Dalhousie Univ. Law School; Harvard Univ. Law School. Called to Bar, 1892; practised profession at Halifax, 1893–1902; Deputy Provincial Secretary and Clerk of the Executive Council, 1902–18; Registrar of Joint Stock Companies, 1910–18; Deputy Attorney-General, 1918–40; Lieutenant-Governor of Nova Scotia, 1940–42; President Nova Scotia Barristers Society, 1929 and 1930. Hon. Col Halifax Rifles. *Address:* 376 South Street, Halifax, Nova Scotia.

Died April 1947.

MATHESON, Cdre Sir Charles George, Kt 1937; DSO 1917; RD; RNR, retd; *b* 1876; *s* of Major Robert Ross Matheson; *m* 1st, 1911, Olive Beryl (*d* 1943), *d* of Ricardo Palmer, Ivy House, Bushey; three *s*; 2nd, 1946, Mrs Scott, *widow* of Major Robert Scott. Served European War, 1914–18 (despatches, DSO); retired from Orient Line, 1938; ADC to King George V, 1931. *Publication:* Fifty Years of Ocean Hazard, 1939. *Address:* Westminster Bank, Ltd, Henley-on-Thames.

Died 24 May 1948.

MATHESON, Prof. Donald Capell, FRCVS, DVSM (Vict.), FRSE; Professor of Pathology, Bacteriology, and Meat Inspection, the Royal (Dick) Veterinary College, Edinburgh, 1913–46; Acting Principal, 1945–46; *b* 1880; *e s* of late Donald Fraser Matheson and Janet Matheson, London; *m* 1908, Mary Beatrice, *yr d* of late Thomas Bryant and Mary Sophia Bryant, Hastings. *Educ:* Royal Veterinary College, London; Victoria University of Manchester. Demonstrator in Comparative Pathology, etc., University of Liverpool, 1907–12; Member of Committee on Standards Public Health (Meat) Regulations, Scot., 1924; Mem. of Committee, Scottish Egg-laying Tests, 1924–39; Fellow of the Royal Physical

Society, Edinburgh. *Publications:* various papers in British and Indian Veterinary Journals. *Address:* 3 Lockharton Crescent, Edinburgh.

Died 8 March 1948.

MATHESON, Very Rev. Frederick William, MA Oxon; Hon. DD Glasgow, 1935; Dean of Carlisle since 1938; *b* 29 July 1882; *e s* of late Rev. John Matheson of Strathnairn, Inverness, and Susan Ewen, *d* of Captain George Arbuthnot of Peterhead, Aberdeenshire; unmarried. *Educ:* Trinity College, Glenalmond; Keble College, Oxford (Stevenson Scholar); Cuddesdon Theological College. Lecturer at Keble College, 1908–09; Tutor, 1909–21; Dean, 1914–21; Member of College Council, 1921; Canon Residentiary of Carlisle Cathedral, 1921–23; Warden of Trinity College, Glenalmond, 1923–38; Canon of St Ninian's Cathedral, Perth, 1924–38; Member of Glenalmond Council, 1914–23; served 22 years in Volunteers and TF; Lieutenant-Colonel Oxford University OTC, resigned 1921, TD; served during war as Captain and Major Officers Schools and No. 4 Officer Cadet Battalion, 1914–19 (MBE); Select Preacher, Oxford, 1931–33. *Address:* The Deanery, Carlisle. *T:* 681. *Club:* Athenæum.

Died 1 July 1942.

MATHESON, John, MA; Professor of Mathematics since 1911 and Dean of Faculty of Arts since 1924, Queen's University, Kingston; *b* Kincardine, Ontario, 1873; parents were Scotch pioneers; *m* 1903, May Davy, of Newburgh, Ontario; two *s* one *d*. *Educ:* Kincardine High School; Queen's University; University of Chicago. Taught in Ontario High Schools for seven years; Lecturer in Mathematics in Queen's University, 1902; Assistant Professor, 1906; Associate Professor, 1908. *Address:* Queen's University, Kingston, Canada.

Died 24 Jan. 1944.

MATHESON, Rt Rev. John A., DD; Bishop of Aberdeen (RC), since 1947; *b* Tomintoul, Banffshire, 28 April 1901; *s* of John Matheson. *Educ:* Blairs College, Aberdeen; Scots College, Rome. Curate at St Mary's Cathedral, Aberdeen, 1925–27; Parish priest at Sacred Heart Church, Torry, Aberdeen, 1927–30; Parish priest at St Nathalan's Church, Ballater, 1930–43; Parish priest of St Mary's Church, Dufftown, 1943–47. *Recreation:* golf. *Address:* 19 Golden Square, Aberdeen. *T:* Aberdeen 766.

Died 5 July 1950.

MATHESON, M. Cecile; formerly Member of the Industrial Court and Member of Trade Bds; Ex-Lecturer in Social Economics (Delegacies for Extra-Mural Studies, Cambridge, Oxford and London); Ex-recording Secretary, International Council of Women. *Educ:* private schools; Bedford College, London. Warden Birmingham Women's Settlement, 1906–16; Member of Women's Advisory Committee Board of (Liquor) Control, 1915; Member of Departmental Cttee on Old Age Pensions, 1919; Cutlery Safeguarding Enquiry (Board of Trade), 1925, etc. Research, etc., in England, America, India, and on the Continent in connection with the Board of Education and various Government and private inquiries. *Publications:* (Part) Women's Work and Wages; Teaching of Domestic Science in Switzerland; Domestic Training of Girls in Germany and Austria (Special Reports on Educational Subjects, Vols 16 and 19); Citizenship (Student Christian Movement); Indian Industry: Yesterday, To-day, and To-morrow. *Address:* 14 Moreland Court, NW2. *T:* Hampstead 3561.

Died 28 April 1950.

MATHESON, Percy Ewing, MBE MA; Hon. Fellow of New College and Fellow of Winchester College; formerly Oxford Secretary of Oxford and Cambridge Schools Examination Board; *b* 23 Jan. 1859; 3rd *s* of Rev. James Matheson of Nottingham; *m* 1896, the Hon. Elizabeth Fox Bruce (*d* 1935), *d* of 1st Baron Aberdare.

Educ: Nottingham High School, 1868–74; City of London School, 1875–77; Balliol College, 1877–81 (Scholar); 1st class in Classical Moderations, 1878; 1st class in Final Classical School. Elected Fellow of New College, 1881; assistant-master at Fettes College, 1881–82; assisted in classical teaching at Balliol and University Colleges; editor of Oxford Mag. 1884–85; Lecturer of New College, 1884; Dean 1889–1903; Senior Tutor, 1921–26; secretary to the Delegacy for the Inspection and Examination of Schools, 1887–1920; Governor of the Royal Holloway College, 1894–1925; Chairman, 1920–25; Senior Proctor, 1895–96; Member of the Hebdomadal Council, 1896–1914; Delegate of University Press, 1907–32; Guardian of the Poor, 1888–1905; Member of Royal Commission on the Civil Service, 1912–15; temporary appointment in Ministry of Munitions (Wages Section), Nov. 1916–Dec. 1918; Member of the Secondary Schools Examination Council, 1917–24; Member of Statutory Commission for University of Oxford; President of the New College Society, 1939–40. *Publications:* A Skeleton Outline of Roman History; The Life of Hastings Rashdall, 1928; Bluntschli's Theory of the State (translated with R. Lodge and D. G. Ritchie); Demosthenes' Orations against Philip, 2 vols, and Demosthenes' Oration on the Crown, edited with Evelyn Abbott; translation of the Discourses and Manual of Epictetus, 2 vols; Education To-day and To-morrow; Holy Russia and other Poems translated from the Russian; The Growth of Rome; Selections from Bacon, edited with E. F. Matheson; Moritz's Travels of a German in England in 1782, edited with Introduction; translation of Moritz's Anton Reiser, with Introduction; Taylorian Lecture on German Travellers in England, 1770–1795. *Address:* 3 Brookside, Headington, Oxford.

Died 11 May 1946.

MATHESON, Sir Roderick Mackenzie Chisholm, 4th Bt *cr* 1882, of Lochalsh; *b* 26 Dec. 1861; *s* of 1st Bt; *S* brother, 1929; *m* 1st, 1883, Jane Clark (*d* 1895), *d* of late John Grant; one *d*; 2nd, 1899, Emma Frances (*d* 1929), *d* of late James A. Croft; 3rd, 1931, Cecil, *d* of late Sir Chas. Lyall, KCIE, and *widow* of William A. Fleet, Grenadier Guards. Heir: *b* General Sir Torquhil G. Matheson, KCB. *Address:* 28 Fairacres, Roehampton Lane, SW15. *Club:* Royal Automobile.

Died 24 July 1944.

MATHESON, Most Rev. Samuel Pritchard, DD; *b* Manitoba (then Red River Settlement), 20 Sept. 1852; *s* of John Matheson and Catherine Pritchard; *m* 1st, 1879; Seraphine Marie Fortin (*d* 1893); two *s* three *d*; 2nd, 1906, Alice E. Talbot; two *d*. *Educ:* St John's College School and St John's College, Winnipeg (BD 1882). Ordained Deacon, 1875; Priest, 1876; Master, St John's College School; Professor of Exegetical Theology, St John's College; Canon of St John's Cathedral; Dean of St John's Cathedral; Deputy Headmaster and subsequently Headmaster, St John's College School; Deputy Warden and subsequently Warden and Chancellor of St John's College; Chancellor of the Provincial University of Manitoba, 1900–34; Grand Master of Grand Lodge of Manitoba, AF and AM; Secretary of Provincial Synod of Rupert's Land; and subsequently Prolocutor of same; Prolocutor of General Synod of Canada, 1902; Archbishop of Rupert's Land, 1905–31; Primate of all Canada, 1909–31; retired, 1931. *Publications:* nothing but official addresses. *Recreations:* fond of gun, and horseback riding, and used to do a good deal of grouse shooting. *Address:* 91 Kingway, Winnipeg, Canada.

Died 19 May 1942.

MATHEWS, Gregory Macalister, CBE 1939; FRSE; *b* Biamble, NSW, 10 Sept. 1876; *s* of late Robert H. Mathews; *m* Marian (*d* 1938), 2nd *d* of late Henry Charles White, Mudgee; one *s*. *Educ:* The King's School, Parramatta, NSW. Custodian of drinking cup made from skull of St Teilo, originally reliquary presented as heirloom to Sir David Mathew, 1450. Engaged in pastoral pursuits in North Queensland for some years; has travelled round the world, obtaining material information in ornithology; a member of the leading ornithological societies of the world; Delegate for Australia for the 5th International Ornithological Congress, Berlin, 1910; 6th Copenhagen, 1926; 7th, Amsterdam, 1930; 8th Oxford, 1934; 9th Rouen, 1938; Member International Ornithological Committee; Vice-President British Ornithological Union, 1924; Assistant Editor Ibis, 1931–41; Chairman British Ornithologists Club, 1935–38; presented to Australian Commonwealth, his unique Australian Ornithological Library, 1939. *Publications:* Hand List of the Birds of Australia, 1908; Birds of Australia, twelve folio volumes, 1910–1927; editor of the Austral Avian Record since 1912; a Reference List of the Birds of Australia, 1912; a Reference List of the Birds of New Zealand, 1913; a List of the Birds of Australia, 1913; Check List of the Birds of Australia, Part I 1920, Part II 1923, Part III 1924; Manual of Birds of Australia, 1921; Birds of Norfolk and Lord Howe Islands, 1928; Systema Avium Australasianarum, Vol. I 1927, Vol. II 1930; Supplement to the Birds of Australia and of New Zealand, 1936; Books and Birds, 1942; Notes on Order of Petrels, 1943; Working List of Australian Birds, 1946. *Recreations:* hunting, shooting, travelling. *Address:* Meadway, Saint Cross, Winchester, Hants. *T:* 4198. *Club:* Hampshire (Winchester).

Died 27 March 1949.

MATHEWS, Henry Edmund, OBE 1919; TD; HML; FRIBA; FRSanI; *b* Highbury, N, 22 May 1868; *e s* of late J. Douglass Mathews, FRIBA, FSI, and *g s* of Henry Mathews, Architect, of London, and E. F. Law, JP, FRIBA, Architect, of Northampton; *m* 1898, Florence Mabel, *y d* of late H. Jefferiss of Sydenham; one *s* one *d*. *Educ:* Merchant Taylors' School. Articled to his father, after having had a technical training at the City and Guilds of London Technical College; commenced practice on his own account at East Grinstead, Sussex, 1890, and afterwards entered into partnership with late father as J. Douglass Mathews & Son, of 11 Dowgate Hill, EC; Architect and Surveyor to the London Estate and Hospital of St Bartholomew, Smithfield, 1913–39, and the Worshipful Company of Tallow Chandlers; Member of Court of Common Council (City of London), 1922–32; senior partner of the firm of J. Douglass Mathews & Partners; Assistant GS of Works, 1939; Grand Steward, 1937; LRPPG St Bearer, Sussex; late Major 4th Royal Sussex Regiment; Embodied Service 4 Aug. 1914 to March 1919. *Address:* 3 Ebury Street, SW1. *T:* Victoria 6223; Stack House, Oxted, Surrey. *T:* Oxted, 337.

Died 3 Feb. 1947.

MATHEWS, Henry Montague Segundo, CSI 1911; JP; Burma Commission, retired; *b* Ordunia, Spain, 24 Sept. 1860; *s* of late Henry Montague Mathews, CIE, formerly Chief Engineer, Public Works Department, Burma; *m* 1902, Nina Margaret Tilly (*d* 1936); two *s* two *d*. *Educ:* Medical College, Epsom; Royal Indian Engineering College, Coopers Hill. Assistant Superintendent Indian Government Telegraph Department, 1879–86; in charge Government Telegraphs in third Burmese War of 1885–86 (war medal); Assistant Commissioner, Burma, 1886; Settlement Officer, 1888; Deputy Commissioner, 1898; Revenue Secretary to Government of Burma, 1899; Member of Legislative Council of Burma, 1900–02; Commissioner of Division, 1906–07; Commissioner of Settlement and Land Records, Burma, 1907–15. *Address:* Clover Bank, Northam, N Devon.

Died 25 Oct. 1941.

MATHEWS, Shailer; Professor of Historical and Comparative Theology, University of Chicago, 1904; Dean, Divinity School, 1908; Emeritus, 1933; *b* Portland, Maine, USA, 26 May 1863; *m* 1890, Mary

Philbrick Elden; one *s* two *d*. *Educ:* AB Colby College, 1884; AM 1887; DD 1902; LLD 1934; DD Oberlin Univ., 1908; Brown University, 1915; Miami Univ., 1922; University of Glasgow, 1928; Chicago Theological Seminary, 1933; Docteur en Théologie, Faculté Libre de Théologie Protestante de Paris, 1929; LLD Pennsylvania College, 1915; University of Rochester, 1926; Colby College, 1934; Graduate, Newton Theological Institution, 1887. Associate Professor, Rhetoric and Elocution, Colby College, 1887–89; University of Berlin, 1890–91; Professor of History, Colby College, 1889–94; Lecturer in New Testament Literature, Newton Theological Institution, 1888–89; Associate Professor of New Testament History, University of Chicago, 1894–97; Professor, 1897–1904; Junior Dean Divinity School, 1899–1908; President, Western Economic Society, 1911–20; President, Federal Council of the Churches of Christ in America, 1912–16; President Northern Baptist Convention, 1915–16; President Phi Beta Kappa Association Chicago Area, 1934–40; Director Religious Work Department, Chautauqua Institution (NY), 1912–33; Secretary and Vice-Director US War Savings Committee for Illinois, 1917–19; Pres. Chicago Church Federation, 1929–32; Lecturer, Haverford College Library Foundation, 1908; Earle Foundation (Pacific School of Religion), 1913; William Belden Noble Lectures (Harvard Univ.), 1916; McNair Lectures (Univ. of North Carolina), 1918; Bennett Lectures (Wesleyan University), 1921; Gates Lectures (Grinnell College), 1923; Alden Lectures (Washburn College), 1926; Cole Lectures (Vanderbilt University), 1926, 1934; Ingersoll (Harvard University), 1933; Barrows Lectures in India (University of Chicago), 1933–34; Trustee Church Peace Union; President Kobe College Corporation; Editor of The World To-Day, 1903–11; Biblical World, 1913–21; Editor New Testament Handbooks, Bible for Home and School, Woman Citizen's Library, Social Betterment Series, Handbooks of Religion and Ethics. *Publications:* Select Mediæval Documents, 1892; 2nd ed. 1900; Social Teaching of Jesus, 1897; History of New Testament Times in Palestine, 1899; revised and enlarged ed. 1933; The French Revolution, 1900 (revised and enlarged edition, 1924); Constructive Studies in the Life of Christ (with Prof. E. D. Burton), 1901, revised 1927; Principles and Ideals for the Sunday School (with Prof. E. D. Burton), 1903; The Messianic Hope in the New Testament, 1905; The Church and the Changing Order, 1907; The Social Gospel, 1910; The Gospel and the Modern Man, 1910; Scientific Management in the Churches, 1912; The Making of To-morrow, 1913; The Individual and the Social Gospel, 1914; The Spiritual Interpretation of History, 1916; Patriotism and Religion, 1918; Dictionary of Religion and Ethics (with G. B. Smith), 1921; The Validity of American Ideals, 1922; The Faith of Modernism, 1924; The Contributions of Science to Religion (with the co-operation of thirteen scientists), 1924; Outline of Christianity, vol. iii (General Editor), 1926; The Student's Gospels (with E. J. Goodspeed); Jesus on Social Institutions, 1928; The Atonement and the Social Process, 1930; Growth of the Idea of God, 1931; Immortality and the Cosmic Process, 1933; Christianity and Social Process, 1934; Creative Christianity, 1935; New Faith for Old: an autobiography, 1936; The Church and the Christian, 1938; Is God Emeritus?, 1940. *Recreation:* apple orchard. *Address:* Divinity School, University of Chicago, Chicago. *TA:* Woodlawn Av. 5736. *T:* Hyde Park 1286. *Clubs:* Quadrangle (Pres. 1902–03), University, Chicago.

Died 23 Oct. 1941.

MATHIAS, Charles Ronald; *b* 20 Sept. 1877; *s* of late Charles Mathias; *m* Shelah Natalie Farewell Fynn, Fox Hill, South Africa; one *s* (and one, Pilot Officer RAF, killed in action over Holland, 11 July 1940). *Educ:* Cheltenham College. Natal Police, 1901–13; served

Boer War; Zulu Rebellion, 1906; High Sheriff for Pembrokeshire, 1937; Chairman Pembrokeshire County Council, 1938–39. *Address:* Lamphey Court, Lamphey, Pembrokeshire. *TA:* Lamphey, Pembroke. *Club:* County.

Died 28 Feb. 1949.

MATHIAS, Lewis James, CBE 1920; JP, DL; senior partner in firm of J. Mathias & Sons, shipowners; *b* 1864; *e s* of late John Mathias and Jane, *d* of late Richard Davies, Llanbadarnfawr, Cardiganshire; *m* 1900, Elsie (*d* 1921), 4th *d* of Edward Hooper, manufacturer, Birmingham; one *s* two *d*. *Educ:* Ardwyn School, Aberystwyth. Late officer commanding Cardiganshire Battery RFA, 2nd Welsh Brigade; during the war was attached to the Staff at Brecon; Life Governor and Councillor of the National Library of Wales, Aberystwyth; Governor and Councillor of the University College of Wales, Aberystwyth; High Sheriff for the county of Cardigan, 1922–23; contested (L) Cheltenham, 1911; member of Cardiganshire Territorial Association. *Recreations:* fishing, shooting, golf, and motoring. *Address:* Bronpadarn, nr Aberystwyth. *TA:* Mathias, Aberystwyth. *T:* Aberystwyth 604.

Died 24 Oct. 1945.

MATHIAS, Sir Richard, 1st Bt *cr* 1917; Kt 1913; JP; *b* 1 June 1863; *y s* of late John Mathias, Aberystwyth, and Jane (*d* 1896), *e d* of late Richard Davies, of Llanbadarnfawr, Cardiganshire; *m* 1899, Annie, *y d* of Evan Hughes, Cardiff; one *s*. *Educ:* Ardwyn School, Aberystwyth. Called to Bar, Lincoln's Inn, 1896; High Sheriff of Monmouthshire, 1923; Life Member of the Institute of Directors; a Life Member of the Monmouthshire Chamber of Agriculture; MP (L) Cheltenham, 1910–11. *Recreation:* motoring. *Heir: s* Richard Hughes Mathias, *b* 6 April 1905. *Address:* Wellpools, Charlwood, near Horley, Surrey.

Died 26 Oct. 1942.

MATHIESON, Hon. John A.; KC; Chief Justice Supreme Court, Prince Edward Island, 1917–43; Administrator of the Government, 1919; *b* 19 May 1863; *m* 1896; one *s* three *d*. *Educ:* Prince of Wales College. Teacher; Barrister; Member Legislature since 1900; Leader of Conservative Opposition, 1903; Prime Minister and Attorney-General, Prince Edward Island, 1911; Administrator of the Government of Prince Edward Island 1919, 1923, 1931, 1933, 1936, 1937. *Address:* Charlottetown, PE Island.

Died 7 Jan. 1947.

MATLEY, Charles Alfred, DSc (Lond.), FGS; retired civil servant; *b* 4 Feb. 1866; *e s* of Charles Edward and Georgina Matley; *m* 1891, Annie Loach (*d* 1942); one *s*. *Educ:* King Edward VI's School, Birmingham; Mason College. Varied career in Government Service; GPO 1884–90; War Dept and War Office (Finance Branch) 1890–1913; Indian Finance Dept 1913–21; retired 1921; Lecturer in Geology, Birmingham and Midland Institute, 1898–1902; Government Geologist for Jamaica, 1921–24; Murchison Medal of Geological Society of London, 1929, for geological researches in various parts of British Empire; leader of Percy Sladen Trust Expedition to India in search of remains of Dinosaurs, 1932–33. *Publications:* Many papers and memoirs, 1897–1946, on regional geology, dealing with researches in England, Wales, Scotland, Ireland, India, West Indies and Fiji; some palæontological papers. *Recreations:* geological mapping, travel. *Address:* 10 Milverton Terrace, Leamington Spa. *Club:* Athenæum.

Died 7 Aug. 1947.

MATSUDAIRA, Tsuneo; President of House of Councillors of Japan, 1947; *b* Tokyo, Japan, 17 April 1877; *s* of late Katamori Matsudaira (Lord of Aizu); *m* 1906, Nobu, *d* of late Marquis Nabeshima; two *s* two *d*. *Educ:* graduated at College of Law, Imperial University, Tokyo, 1902; LLD Lafayette College, Rutgers

University and University of Missouri. Attaché of Japanese Embassy, London, 1902; later 3rd Secretary and 2nd Secretary; on Staff, Treaty Revision, 1911; 2nd Secretary Legation, Peking, 1912–14; Consul-General at Tientsin, 1914; Chief of Diplomatic Mission in Siberia, 1918; Member Inter-Allied Railway Commission, Siberia, 1919; Chief of European and American Dept of Foreign Office, 1920; Secretary-General to Japanese Delegation to Disarmament Conference, Washington DC, 1921; Vice-Minister for Foreign Affairs, 1923; Ambassador to United States, 1925–28; Japanese Ambassador at the Court of St James, 1929–36; Minister of the Imperial Household, Japan, 1936–45; Member of Privy Council, 1946–49; Japanese delegate to general assembly, League of Nations 1929 and 1930; Japanese delegate to the London Naval Conference, 1930; Chief Japanese Delegate to Disarmament Conference, Geneva, 1932; Japanese Delegate to Monetary and Economic Conference, London, 1933; 1st Class Order of Sacred Treasure, 1924; 1st Class Rising Sun, 1931. *Recreations:* golf, fishing, shooting. *Address:* Shinagawaku, Ebara Nanachome, 524 Tokio, Japan. *Club:* Tokyo.

Died 14 Nov. 1949.

MATSUI, Rt Rev. Peter Yonetaro, DD; *b* in a Buddhist family, 1869; *m* 1897; two *s* one *d*. *Educ:* Trinity Divinity College, Osaka; Wycliffe College, Toronto. Deacon, 1898; Priest, 1902; visited the USA, 1905; England, 1906; Professor in Trinity College, Osaka, 1900–14; Pastor of St Paul's Church, Tokyo, 1914–28; Bishop of Tokyo, 1928–43; Chairman of the Standing Committee of the Diocese of Tokyo, 1923–28; Examining Chaplain to Bishop Foss (Osaka), Bishop Hamilton (Nagoya), Bishop Basil (Kobe), and Bishop Motoda (Tokyo). *Publications:* How we got our Bible (translation); Life of Christ; Nippon Seihokwai; Jesus Christ. *Address:* c/o Bishop's Office, 10 Sakae Cho, Shiba, Tokyo, Japan.

Died 16 Nov. 1946.

MATT, Albert E.; Professor, Trinity College and Royal Academy; *b* Ipswich, 20 June 1864; *s* of Elijah Matt; *m*; one *s* two *d*. *Educ:* Ipswich. Began in Covent Garden Orchestra, 1881; travelled with Royal English Opera Company through Britain and part of Ireland; in 1891 began to compose orchestral pieces. *Publications:* Dawn; Sunset; Rural Scenes; Norwegian Scenes; Angelus and Carnival; Devotion Rustique; Promenade Au Soir; Grand March, etc.; several Salon pieces. *Recreation:* topography. *Address:* 15 Berkhamsted Avenue, Wembley Hill, Middlesex. *T:* Wembley 4919.

Died 7 Dec. 1941.

MATTHAI, George, MA (Cantab), ScD (Cantab), FRSE, FZS, FLS; Indian Educational Service; Professor of Zoology in the Government College, Lahore and in the University of the Punjab; *b* 13 Nov. 1887; *s* of late Thomas Matthai; *m* 1924, Mary (*d* 1931), 2nd *d* of K. Chandy, Bangalore. *Educ:* Madras University (MA). Sometime Research Student of Emmanuel College, Cambridge; Mackinnon Research Student of the Royal Society, 1914–17. *Address:* Lahore, Punjab, India. *Club:* Royal Societies.

Died 25 June 1947.

MATTHAY, Tobias, FRAM, FRCM; Principal of the Tobias Matthay Pianoforte School, Ltd; *b* London, 1858; *m* 1893, Jessie Kennedy (*d* 1937), reciter and singer, *y d* of late David Kennedy, the Scottish singer; no *c*. *Educ:* privately. Entered Royal Academy of Music, 1871; Pianoforte Prof., 1880–1925; has written many books on Interpretation and Piano Technique, piano music, songs and orchestral and chamber works; has lectured and initiated the lecture-class lesson form of instruction for teachers and others. *Publications:* Act of Touch; First Principles; Relaxation Studies; Musical Interpretation; Child's First Steps; Foreign Rotation; Pianist's First Music Making; On Method; On Memorizing; The Slur or Couplet of Notes, The Visible and Invisible in Piano

Technique; An Epitome and Summary of Piano Technique; On Musical Concentration; Colouring v. Inflection; Fallacies of to-day; Psychology Lectures, etc.; Approach to Music; First Lights on Piano-playing, 1942. *Music:* Symphonie Overture, In May; Concerto in one movement; Overture: Reminiscences of Country Life; Piano Quartet in one movement; Prize Quartet; Ballade for 'Cello and Piano, op. 40; 31 Variations; Love phases; Mono-themes; Two Sketch Books; Moods of a Moment; Lyrics; On Surrey Hills; Summer Twilights, Three Lyric Studies; Stray Fancies; Seven Historiettes; Five Miniatures; Four Daily Exercises for advanced players; number of smaller pieces for Piano, Elves, Romanesque, Toccatas, Prelude, Bravura, Mood Phantasy, Cameos, Playthings for Little Players, 3 vols; 1st Solo Book; etc.; also songs; Gramophone Record: Columbia DX 444. *Recreations:* walking, motoring, gardening. *Address:* High Marley, Haslemere. *T:* Haslemere 304.

Died 14 Dec. 1945.

MATTHEW, Edwin, MA, MD, MB, CM, FRCP (Ed.); Consulting Physician, Leith Hospital. *Educ:* Edinburgh University. Professor of Clinical Medicine, Edinburgh University, 1935–36. *Address:* 9 Walker Street, Edinburgh.

Died 7 July 1950.

MATTHEW, John Godfrey, CMG 1930; OBE 1920; MA; late Sudan Political Service; *b* 14 March 1881; *s* of John William Matthew; *m* 1912, Sibyl (*d* 1932), *d* of Captain H. Pearson, RN; two *d. Educ:* Charterhouse (scholar, Head of School); Wadham College, Oxford (exhibitioner). Joined Sudan Political Service, 1905; served Sennar and Red Sea Provinces; Acting Governor, Red Sea Province, 1917–20; Assistant Financial Secretary, 1920–27; Secretary for Education and Health (Director of Education), Sudan Government, and member Governor-General's Council, 1927–32; Secretary, Jerusalem and the East Mission; Governor of the Charterhouse and of Charterhouse School; Executive Committee, Gordon Memorial College; 2nd Class Order of the Nile, 1929; 3rd Class Order of the Nahda (Hedjaz), 1920. *Recreations:* golf, fishing. *Address:* Sandpits, Kingsgate Road, Winchester. *T:* 4312. *Clubs:* Athenæum; Hampshire, Winchester.

Died 3 June 1947.

MATTHEWS, Major Durham, OBE, JP; *b* 15 Jan. 1876; *s* of Thomas Bright Matthews of Thorparch Hall, Yorkshire, and Adeline Simpson; *m* 1902, Eileen Talbot, *o d* of late Sir John Talbot Power, Bt (one *s* killed 1940). *Educ:* Eton College. Joined 17th Lancers, 1898; served South African War, 1900–01; Staff, 1901–03; Adjt South Irish Horse, 1906–11; served European War, 1914–18 (OBE, despatches twice). High Sheriff of Suffolk, 1944–45. *Address:* 39 Hill Street, Berkeley Square, W1; Lanwades Park, Newmarket. *T:* Kentford 15. *Clubs:* Cavalry; Jockey (Newmarket); Irish Turf, Kildare Street (Dublin).

Died 16 Dec. 1950.

MATTHEWS, Edith Marcia, MA; *b* 1883; *d* of late Rev. J. H. D. Matthews. *Educ:* Godolphin School, Salisbury; Newnham College, Cambridge. Private teaching; Assistant Mistress, S Margaret's School, Bushey, 1908–15. Headmistress, S Mary's School, Calne, 1915–45. JP Wilts. *Address:* The White Cottage, Wilcot, Marlborough. *T:* Pewsey 2186.

Died 13 Oct. 1946.

MATTHEWS, Ernest Lewis, CMG, 1914; KC; retired Judge of the Supreme Court of South Africa (Natal Provincial Division); formerly Law Adviser to Government of Union of South Africa; *b* Gloucester, 12 April 1871; *s* of late J. A. Matthews, JP, Lewishurst, The Spa, Gloucester; *m* Ethel Mary Tebbs, *e d* of late Rev. Wm Tebbs, Vicar of St John's Caterham Valley, Surrey; one *s* one *d. Educ:* King's College, London; Baliol

College, Oxford. Called to Bar, Inner Temple, 1895; Oxford Circuit; became a Legal Adviser to Transvaal Government, 1902; Legal Adviser to High Commissioner for South Africa, 1904–07; Acting Attorney-General of Transvaal, 1910. *Address:* c/o Standard Bank of S Africa, Pietermaritzburg, Natal. *Clubs:* Victoria, Pietermaritzburg.

Died 22 Dec. 1941.

MATTHEWS, Harry G.; *see* Grindell-Matthews.

MATTHEWS, John Charles, BA, MB, BC (Camb.); Assistant, Inoculation Department, St Mary's Hospital; Hon. Bacteriologist Star and Garter; *b* Newton-by-Castleacre, Norfolk, 1872; *s* of late Thomas Matthews, of Sporle, Norfolk; *m* 1912, Florence Ethel, *widow* of F. E. Collingwood, New York. *Educ:* Grantham Grammar School; Thames Nautical Training College, HMS Worcester; Cambridge University, Honours Nat. Science; St Mary's Hospital. Apprenticed to Shaw, Saville & Albion Co., and served two years at sea before taking degree at Cambridge; after qualifying, House Physician at St Mary's Hospital, and subsequently attached as Civil Surgeon to Army of Occupation, Egypt, 1900–03; Examiner Materia Medica and Pharmacology, Kasr-el-Aini, Cairo; has been one of Sir Almroth Wright's assistants at Inoculation Department, St Mary's Hospital, since 1906. *Publications:* Articles on Bacteriology Immunity and Vaccine Therapy, Oxford Practice of Medicine; a few contributions to Medical publications on vaccine therapy, and a communication on a new method of growing Pfeiffer's influenza bacillus, Lancet, July 1918. *Recreations:* golf, fishing, etc. *Address:* 20 Wimpole Street, W1. *T:* Langham 1118. *Club:* Fly Fisher's.

Died 25 May 1946.

MATTHEWS, Julia B., (Mrs Fairfax Ivimey), RI; *m* Lieutenant Fairfax Ivimey, RNVR, Lord of the Manor of Treverbyn, Cornwall. *Educ:* self-taught. Has exhibited at Royal Academy, Royal Institute, Society of British Artists, Royal Hibernian Academy, Paris Salon, etc. *Address:* The Fort, Newquay, Cornwall.

Died 8 Feb. 1948.

MATTHEWS, Robert Lee, CBE 1928; *b* 1876; *s* of late William Matthews, Leeds; *m* 1903, Ada, *d* of late John Parkinson, Leeds; one *s* one *d. Educ:* Central High School, Leeds. Chief Constable of Leeds, 1923–37; retired, 1937; President, Chief Constables Association, 1931; Officer of Order of St John of Jerusalem, 1930. *Address:* Spe-Cott, Ancaster Road, Leeds 6. *T:* Leeds 51542.

Died 10 Aug. 1950.

MATTINSON, Sir Miles, Kt 1922; KC; *b* 26 Dec. 1854; *s* of Thomas Mattinson of Newcastle-on-Tyne; *m* 1st, 1879, Lizzie (*d* 1934), *d* of late Mark Dearden, Manchester; two *s* one *d*; 2nd, 1934, Jessie De Lisle, *e d* of late Frank Mortimer, Chiswick. *Educ:* Gray's Inn. Bacon Scholarship, 1874; 1st class Studentship, 1875; Certificate of Honour, 1876. Bar, 1877; practised on Northern Circuit; contested (C) Carlisle, 1880; Dumfries Burghs, 1885 and 1886; MP Walton Division of Liverpool, 1888–92; contested Bolton, 1910; Recorder of Blackburn, 1886–1922; QC 1897; a Bencher of Gray's Inn. *Publications:* The Law of Corrupt Practices at Elections; Selection of Precedents in Pleading. *Address:* Monk's Path, Warwicks Bench, Guildford, Surrey. *Club:* Carlton.

Died 29 Feb. 1944.

MAUBERT, Louis; Chevalier de la Légion d'Honneur, Officier d'Académie, Officier de Danebrogue; Officier de Vasa, Suède; Ordre de St Charles, Monaco; sculptor, ceramist; *b* Paris, 1875; *m* 1916; one *d. Educ:* École de Beaux Arts, Paris; Atelier de Falguière. Mobilisé Armée Auxiliaire chef du Service Radiologique à Marseille; Vice-Hôpital Franco-Britannique, Menton. Sculptor of many busts, monuments, and statues. *Publication:* Traité d'Anatomie Artistique with ninety-two plates according to Nature. *Recreations:* hunting, fishing, aviation. *Address:* Nice, 160 B^d de Cessole. *Club:* Artistique (Nice).

Died 1949.

MAUCHLINE, Baron; Ian Huddleston Abney-Hastings; *b* 23 March 1918; *s* of Countess of Loudoun. *Address:* Loudoun Castle, Galston, Ayrshire.

Died 11 July 1944.

MAUD, Col Harry, CBE 1920; DSO 1917; with Pure Oil Co. of America; *b* 31 Jan. 1867; *s* of late Rev. H. Landon Maud. *Educ:* Leamington College; University College, Oxford. Served in France under DST, 1914; Major on General List, 1915; Col and ADQMG 1918 (despatches, DSO, CBE, American DSM and French Legion of Honour). *Address:* 20 Elm Park Rd, SW.

Died 19 Jan. 1948.

MAUD, Brig.-Gen. Philip, CMG 1903; CBE 1920; *b* 8 Aug. 1870; *s* of late Rev. H. Landon Maud; *m* 1st, 1907, Dorothy (*d* 1920), *y d* of late Rev. J. M. Braithwaite; one *s* two *d*; 2nd, 1922, Hyacinthe Mary, *e d* of late Courtenay Wellesley, formerly of Bletchingley, Surrey. *Educ:* Leamington College; RMA, Woolwich. Gazetted to Royal Engineers, 1889; served NW Frontier, India, 1897–98 (medal with clasp). In charge of British East Africa and Abyssinia boundary survey in 1902–03 (CMG); passed Staff College, 1906; General Staff Officer at Headquarters, 1907–10; retired, 1910; Chief Officer of LCC Parks, Dept 1911–35; Mobilised, General Staff, Aug. 1914; Bt Lieut-Colonel, 1916; General Staff Officer, 1st Grade, 1916; Bt Col 1918; Brigadier-General, 1918; demobilised Oct. 1919. *Address:* 20 Elm Park Road, Chelsea, SW3. *T:* Flaxman 8991.

Died 28 Feb. 1947.

MAUD, Lt-Col William Hartley, CMG 1908; DL, JP Somerset; *b* 10 Oct. 1868; *e s* of late Lt-Col W. S. Maud, RE; *m* 1906, Isabella Lucy (*d* 1935), *d* of Henry Byne, Satterleigh, North Devon, and *widow* of Wilfred Marshall, of Norton Manor, Taunton. *Educ:* Wellington; Sandhurst. Somerset Light Infantry, 1888; Capt. 1898; served NW Frontier, India, 1897–98 (medal with clasp); N Nigeria, 1902–03 (despatches, medal with clasp); Staff Officer to Insp.-Gen., W African Frontier Force, 1903–07 (CMG); retired, 1908; War Office Staff Captain and DAAG, Aug. 1914–19 (despatches, Brevet Lt-Col, White Eagle, 4th Class); High Sheriff of Somerset, 1933. *Address:* Periton Mead, Minehead. *Club:* United Service.

Died 12 May 1948.

MAUDE, Sir Walter, KCIE 1920; CSI 1914; *b* 1862; *m* 1892, Carrie Maude, *d* of late E. F. T. Atkinson, ICS. *Educ:* Highgate School; Balliol College, Oxford. Entered ICS 1881; Settlement Officer, Orissa, 1892; Magistrate and Collector, 1895; Commissioner, 1905; Member Board of Revenue, Bihar and Orissa, 1912; Member, Executive Council, 1917; President Bihar and Orissa Provincial Legislature, 1921; retired, 1921. *Address:* Petit Tor, St Martins, Guernsey.

Died 2 May 1943.

MAUDSLAY, Algernon, CBE 1917; *b* 1873; 3rd *s* of late Herbert Charles Maudslay, of Upton Grove, Tetbury, Glos, and of Sea View, Isle of Wight; unmarried. *Educ:* privately. No official position until 1914; Hon. Secretary War Refugees Committee, 1914–19; Hon. Secretary Anglo-Belgian Union; Hon. Director-General British Committee of the Russian Red Cross Society, 1920–24; Chairman of the Exhibition of Flemish and Belgian Art, 1927; British Representative on the International Relief Union Executive Committee, 1933; Member of Council British Red Cross; Order of the Commander of the Crown of Belgium, 1919; Order of St Sava IV of Serbia, 1919; Order of Royal Red Cross of Serbia, 1919; Grand Officer Order Leopold II, 1925. *Recreations:*

hunting, yachting (Hon. Treasurer Yacht Racing Association since 1927), shooting. *Address:* The Down House, Itchen Abbas, nr Winchester, Hants. *T:* Itchen Abbas 252. *Clubs:* Marlborough-Windham, Royal Thames Yacht; Royal Yacht Squadron, Royal London Yacht (Cowes); Hampshire County (Winchester).

Died 2 March 1948.

MAUDSLEY, Sir Henry Carr, KCMG 1919; CMG 1916; CBE 1919; MD London; FRCP London; Consulting Physician to the Royal Melbourne Hospital and to St Vincent's Hospital; formerly Lecturer on Medicine, Melbourne University and on Clinical Medicine, Royal Melbourne Hospital; *b* 25 April 1859; *e s* of late Thomas Maudsley, Stainforth, Settle, Yorkshire; *m* 1890, Grace Elizabeth (*d* 1933) *y d* of Rev. Canon Stretch; one *s* one *d*. *Educ:* University College, London. Formerly Resident Medical Officer, University College Hospital, London; Physician and Pathologist to Alfred Hospital; served European War (despatches, CMG). *Address:* 8 Collins Street, Melbourne, C1, Australia. *Clubs:* Melbourne, Melbourne.

Died 5 March 1944.

MAUFE, Herbert Brantwood, MA, FGS, MIMM; *b* 27 Aug. 1879; *e s* of late Henry Maufe, Ilkley, Yorks; *m* Doris, *e d* of late W. E. L. Thompson; one *s*. *Educ:* Bradford School; Christ's College, Cambridge (Exhibitioner and Scholar). Geological Survey of Scotland, 1901–10, with service on Geological Survey of Ireland in 1903 and 1904 and in British East Africa for the Colonial Office in 1905–06; Director Geological Survey of Southern Rhodesia, 1910–34; awarded Lyell Medal, 1930; Draper Medal, 1934. *Publications:* reports in official publications; papers in scientific journals and proceedings of societies. *Address:* PO Box 733, Salisbury, Southern Rhodesia. *Clubs:* Athenæum, Union; Salisbury.

Died 8 May 1946.

MAUFE, Captain T. Harold Broadbent, VC 1917; MA Cantab; Director; *b* 6 May 1898; *yr s* of late Frederic B. Maufe, St John's Wood, NW; *m* 1932, Mary Gwendolen, *d* of George Carr, Low Wood, Ben Rhydding, Yorkshire; one *s* one *d*. *Educ:* Uppingham; Royal Military Academy, Woolwich; Clare College, Cambridge; Royal School of Mines, South Kensington. 2nd Lt RGA 10 May 1916; joined BEF France, July 1916 (VC); under intense artillery fire repaired Telephone line between rear and forward positions on his own initiative, also extinguished fire in an ammunition dump regardless of risk. *Address:* Whitehorn, Myddelton, Ilkley Yorkshire. *T:* Ilkley 758.

Died 28 March 1942.

MAULA BAKHSH, Nawab Maula Bakhsh Khan Bahadur of Batala, CIE 1919; *b* 7 May 1862; *m* 2nd *d* of Haji Mirza Abbas Kahn, CMG, CIE, British Agent, Khurasan, Persia; two *s* five *d*. Joined Punjab Postal Dept, 1880; Manager Dead Letter Office and Postal Stock Depot, Karachi 1881; joined Imperial Circle, Public Works Dept, Simla, 1882; services placed at disposal of Foreign and Political Dept, 1887; on special duty, North-Eastern Persia, 1887–88; Attaché, Hashtadan Perso-Afghan Boundary Commission, 1888–89; Attaché to Agent Governor-General and HBM's Consul-General, Khurasan and Seistan, 1890–93; Assistant Agent Governor-General, Meshed, 1894; British Vice-Consul, Khurasan and Seistan, 1896–98; on special Political duty in Kain, Seistan and Baluchistan, 1898; on special duty in Intelligence Branch, Quarter-Master General's Dept, Simla, for revising Gazetteer of Persia, 1898–99; Assist District Supt of Police in charge Nushki District, Baluchistan, 1900; Extra Assist Commissioner and Magistrate, Punjab, 1900–01; Personal Assist to Chief Commissioner, Baluchistan, 1901–02; on special duty with Amir of Seistan, 1901; Attaché Seistan Boundary Commission, 1902–04; Oriental Secretary Kabul Political Mission,

1904–05; Attaché Foreign and Political Department Government of India, 1905–19; Chief Indian Political Officer with HM Amir Habibullah Khan of Afghanistan, during HM's Indian tour, 1906–07; Political Officer North-West Afghan Frontier Field Force, 1919; Secretary, Indo-Afghan Peace Conference, Rawalpindi, 1919; Home Minister, Jammu and Kashmir State, 1919–22; Member for Commerce and Industries, Jammu and Kashmir State Council, 1922–23; Chief Minister, Bahawalpur State, 1925–28. *Address:* c/o Political Department, New Delhi, India.

Died 27 April 1949.

MAUND, Air Vice-Marshal Arthur Clinton, CB, 1941; CBE 1920; DSO 1918; *b* 30 July 1891; *s* of late Edward Arthur Maund; *m* Marguerite Hill; one *d*. *Educ:* St Paul's School. Served European War, 1914–18 (despatches, DSO, Croix de guerre with star, 2nd class Russian Order of St Stanislas with swords, 4th class Russian Order of Vladimir with swords and ribbon); Commanded RAF at Archangel, N Russia, 1918; RAF Mission in S Russia with General Denikin, 1919; served in India, 1922–23; RAF Staff College, Andover, 1924–25; Air Staff, Air Ministry, 1930–33; commanded, Aeroplane and Armament Experimental Establishment, 1933–37; Air Officer in charge of Administration, Fighter Command, RAF, Bentley Priory, Stanmore, 1937. *Club:* Royal Empire Society.

Died 13 Dec. 1942.

MAUNDER, Annie Scott Dill, (Mrs Walter Maunder); *b* Strabane, co. Tyrone, 14 April 1868; *d* of late Rev. W. A. Russell; *m* 1895, (Edward) Walter Maunder, FRAS (*d* 1928). *Educ:* home; Victoria College, Belfast; Girton College, Cambridge. Senior Optime, Mathematical Tripos, 1889; elected Pfeiffer Student for Research, Girton College, 1897–98; Computer at the Royal Observatory, Greenwich, 1891–95, and 1915–20; Editor of the Journal of the British Astronomical Association, 1894–96 and 1917–30; Vice-President BAA, 1896–99, 1900–03, 1942; represented Astronomy at Women's International Congress, London, 1899. *Publications:* Catalogue of Recurrent groups of Sunspots; also various researches in astronomy, published with her husband in the Proc. Roy. Soc. Lond.; Monthly Notices of the Roy. Ast. Soc.; and Journal BAA; Astronomical Allusions in the Sacred Books of the East; Early Hindu Astronomy, Astronomy and Meteorology of the Rigveda Hymns (Journals of the Victoria Institute, April 1915, April 1934, April 1939); Iranian Migrations Before History (Scientia, Feb. 1916); Origin of the Planetary Symbols; Origin of the Constellations (Observatory Magazine, Aug. 1934 and Dec. 1936); Astronomical Appendix to the Travels of Peter Mundy, Vol. V 1650–1667, Hakluyt Society, 1936. *Eclipse Expeditions:* Lapland, 1896; India, 1898, where she secured the longest coronal extensions yet photographed; Algiers, 1900; Mauritius, 1901; and Labrador, 1905. *Address:* 52 Elms Crescent, Clapham, SW4.

Died 15 Sept. 1947.

MAUNSELL, Richard Edward Lloyd, CBE 1918; *b* Raheny, Co. Dublin; 7th *s* of John Maunsell of Edenmore, Raheny; *m* 1896, Edith Annie, 2nd *d* of Thos Pearson of Crompton Fold, nr Bolton, Lancs; one *d*. *Educ:* Armagh Royal School; Trinity College, Dublin (MA). Asst Loco. Engineer GS & W Railway of Ireland, 1896–1911; Chief Mechanical Engineer, 1911–13; Chief Mechanical Engineer, SE and C. Railway, 1913–23; Chief Mechanical Engineer Southern Railway, 1923–37. *Club:* Constitutional.

Died 7 March 1944.

MAUNY-TALVANDE, Countess de; Lady Mary Elizabeth Agnes Byng; *d* of 4th Earl of Strafford; *m* 1898, Count de Mauny-Talvande (*d* 1941); one *s*, Victor Alexander Christian Henry George [Commander RN; served European War; also serving in War of 1939–45; for whom Queen Victoria, Princess Christian of

Schleswig-Holstein and Princess Victoria of Wales were sponsors] one *d* (for whom Queen Alexandra stood sponsor). Maid of Honour to Queen Victoria, 1894–98. *Address:* Sandelheath, Fordingbridge, Hants.

Died 18 Feb. 1946.

MAURICE, Lt-Col Albert Jafa, TD; LDS, RCS Ed.; Fellow of the Royal Society of Medicine; Consulting Dental Surgeon to St Pancras Dispensary; *b* 1864; *s* of late Samuel Maurice, Chester; *m* 1890, Matilda (*d* 1939), *d* of late Edwin Sykes, Holly Grove, Huddersfield; one *s*. *Educ:* King's School, Chester; Liverpool University. Formerly Assistant Demonstrator of Anatomy in University College, Liverpool; Dental Surgeon to the Belgrave Hospital for Children, and to the London Lock Hospital; Editor of The Dental Surgeon, 1926–32; sometime Captain and Instructor of Musketry, 1st VB Royal Welch Fusiliers; then in RASC, Territorial Army; served in France and Salonika; Commanded 56th Divisional Train. *Publications:* remarks on the use of anæsthetics in dental surgery. *Recreations:* archæology, croquet. *Address:* 21 College Crescent, NW3. *T:* Primrose 2700. *Club:* Royal Societies.

Died 8 Jan. 1943.

MAURICE, Col George Thelwall Kindersley, CMG 1915; CBE 1920, late RAMC; *b* 23 March 1867; *m* 1905, Olive (*d* 1949), *d* of late Sir H. C. Burdett, KCB, KCVO; one *s*. *Educ:* Marlborough Coll.; St Mary's Hosp. Entered army, 1895; Capt., 1898; Major, 1907; Lt-Col 1915; Bt Col June 1917; Col Dec. 1917; served European War, 1914–18 (despatches, CMG); Afghan War, 1919 (CBE); retired pay, 1921; JP Wilts. *Publications:* Birth Control and Population; Observations and Reflections on Wild Creatures. *Recreations:* sport and natural history. *Address:* Marlborough, Wilts. *T:* Marlborough 119.

Died 8 March 1950.

MAURICE, Col Godfrey Kindersley, DSO 1919; MC; MRCS and LRCP; RAMC (retd); *b* 15 Jan. 1887; *s* of late James Blake Maurice, MD, FRCS, and late Mary Agnes Maurice; unmarried. *Educ:* Marlborough. Qualified MRCS, LRCP (St Mary's), 1910; Territorial RAMC, 1912; commissioned Regular Army, 1915; served European War, 1914–18 (despatches, DSO, MC); seconded to Egyptian Army, 1921; Principal Medical Officer, Sudan Defence Force and Assistant Director, Sudan Medical Service, 1928; retired from British Army, 1931. Served War of 1939–45, N Africa, Italy (despatches). *Recreations:* fishing, shooting. *Address:* Manton Weir House, Marlborough. *T:* Marlborough 214.

Died 19 June 1949.

MAURICE, Henry Gascoyen, CB 1916; Cross of Chevalier of the Belgian Order of the Crown, 1919; BA Oxon; Barrister-at-law; Secretary, Society for the Preservation of the Fauna of the Empire; *b* 24 May 1874; 6th *s* of late James Blake Maurice, MD, FRCS, JP, of Lloran House, Marlborough; *m* 1913, Ruth, *o d* of late Edward Spencer, MA, of Bella Vista, Blackrock, Co. Dublin; one *s*. *Educ:* Marlborough; Lincoln College, Oxford (Scholar). BA 1897; 2nd Hon. Mods; 2nd Lit. Hum. After a period of private coaching and travel, called to Bar, Lincoln's Inn, 1904; Assistant to Director of Education for Wilts, 1904–05; attached to Board of Education Legal Branch, 1905–07, when became private secretary to Sir Robert Morant; private secretary to Mr Walter Runciman, MP, 1909–12, first at Board of Education, and then at Board of Agriculture and Fisheries; in charge of the Fisheries Department, 1912–38; President Zoological Society of London, 1942–48 (Gold Medal, 1949); late Fisheries Secretary, Ministry of Agriculture and Fisheries; President of the International Council for the Exploration of the Sea, 1920–38, and, now, Président d'Honneur; gold medal of the Johannes Schmidt Foundation for Oceanographical Research, 1937. *Publications:* Sometimes an Angler; The

Wisdom of the Ass; and many articles on Natural History and analogous subjects. *Recreations:* fishing and natural history. *Address:* 6 St Mark's Sq., Regent's Park, NW1. *Club:* Oxford and Cambridge.

Died 12 May 1950.

MAW, William Nawton, CIE 1916; ICS, retired; *b* 1 Aug. 1869; *s* of Nawton Maw, Rosedale Abbey, Yorks; *m* 1st, 1898, Una Agnes, *d* of Col W. Brooke-Meares; no *c*; 2nd, 1942, Elizabeth Mabel Bourne, *widow* of J. G. Bourne, ICS. *Educ:* Wesley Coll., Sheffield; St John's Coll., Cambridge (BA). Entered ICS, 1893; Commissioner of Nerbadda Division, 1923; retired 1928. *Club:* East India and Sports.

Died 13 June 1946.

MAWER, Sir Allen, Kt 1937; MA, LittD, FBA; Provost of University College, London, since 1930; *b* 8 May 1879; *s* of late George Henry Mawer, South Hackney; *m* 1909, Lettice, *d* of late Rev. C. Heath, Wellesley Court, Cheltenham; four *d*. *Educ:* Coopers Company's Grammar School; University College, London; Gonville and Cains College, Cambridge. BA, University of London, First Class, Exhibitioner; Morley Medallist, University College; Foundation Scholar of Gonville and Caius College; First Class with double distinction in English sections of Mediæval and Modern Languages Tripos; Fellow of Gonville and Caius College, 1905–11. Hon. Fellow, 1935; Lecturer in English in the University of Sheffield, 1905–08; Joseph Cowen Professor of English Language and Literature, Armstrong College, Newcastle, 1908–21; Baines Prof. of English Language, Liverpool, 1921–29; Hon. Foreign Member of the Royal Flemish Academy; President of the Modern Language Association, 1932–39; President of the Philogical Society, 1936; Hon. DCL (Durham), 1937; VP of Viking Society; Director of Survey of English Place-Names. *Publications:* The Vikings (Cambridge Manuals); Place Names of Northumberland and Durham; The Chief Elements in English Place Names; Place Names of Buckinghamshire; The Place Names of Beds and Hunts; The Place Names of Worcestershire; The Place Names of Sussex (joint author); The Place Names of Devon, 1932; The Place Names of Northants, 1933; The Place Names of Surrey, 1934; The Place Names of Warwickshire, 1936; The Place Names of Hertfordshire, 1939 (joint author); Problems of Place Name Study, 1929; contributions on Anglo-Saxon and Scandinavian subjects to Encyclopædia Britannica (new edition); English Historical and Modern Language Reviews, etc. *Recreations:* cycling and walking tours. *Address:* 12 Abingdon Gardens, W8. *T:* Western 7611. *Clubs:* Athenæum, University of London.

Died 22 July 1942.

MAWSON, Cecil Allerton Greville; *b* 22 Feb. 1876; *s* of Lt-Col W. Willmott Mawson. *Educ:* Eton College. High Sheriff of Rutland, 1944–45. *Address:* Westbourne House, Belton, nr Uppingham, Rutland. *T:* Belton 204.

Died 4 May 1950.

MAX-MULLER, Sir William Grenfell, GBE 1928; KCMG 1922; CB 1911; MVO 1908; Chairman of Bagdad Light and Power Co. since 1934; Member of Council of Foreign Bondholders; *b* 9 June 1867; *s* of late Right Hon. Professor Max-Müller and late Mrs Max-Müller; *m* 1908, Wanda Maria, *d* of late Professor Heiberg, Christiania; two *s*. *Educ:* Eton; University College, Oxford. Attache, 1892; 3rd Secretary, 1894; 2nd Secretary 1897; 1st Secretary, 1904; Councillor of Embassy, 1909; Minister Plenipotentiary, 1918; has served in Constantinople, The Hague, Washington, Madrid, Mexico, Christiania, and Peking; employed in the Foreign Office, 1902–05, 1911–12, and 1914–20; HM Consul-General at Budapest, 1913–14; Minister to Poland, 1920–28. *Address:* 93 Gloucester Place, W1. *T:* Welbeck, 3800. *Clubs:* St James's, Turf.

Died 10 May 1945.

MAXSE, Ernest George Berkeley, CMG 1899; FRGS; *b* 18 Nov. 1863; *e s* of late Lieut-Col Sir Henry Fitzhardinge Maxse, KCMG; is in remainder to Barony of Berkeley; *m* 1st, 188, Sarah Alice (*d* 1908), *o d* of T. Nottage Miller of Bishop's Stortford; one *s* one *d*; 2nd, 1914, Mary Louisa, *d* of Dr Turle of Avon, Swanage. *Educ:* Harrow. Served for some time in 1st Hanoverian Lancers; Vice-Consul at Algiers, 1890–94; Consul for Continental Greece, 1894–97; Consul and Deputy Commissioner for Samoa, 1897–99; Consul at Bilbao, 1899; was in charge of British interests at Samoa during disturbances in 1899; was a Special Judicial Commissioner for Western Pacific; served as volunteer with Naval Brigade in all engagements (despatches, CMG); in charge of Armenian relief work at Piræus, 1896; temporarily employed at Foreign Office, 1904; HM Consul for the Island of Réunion, 1900–12, and 1913; Consul-General, Chile, 1912–14; Consul-General in Holland and Admiralty Convoy Officer at Rotterdam, 1914–19; also in charge of propaganda and Passport and Military Control Officer (thanks of Admiralty, Home Office, and other Departments); HM Consul-General at Zürich, and for Principality of Lichtenstein, 1919; retired, 1924. *Address:* 18 Cherry Garden Avenue, Folkestone. *Clubs:* Travellers'; Radnor, Folkestone.

Died 13 March 1943.

MAXTON, James; MP (Lab) Bridgeton Div. of Glasgow since 1922; a teacher; *b* 22 June 1885; *m* 1st, 1919, Sissie Whitehead (*d* 1922); one *s*; 2nd, 1935, Madeleine Glasier. *Educ:* Grahamston School, Barrhead; Hutcheson's Grammar School, Glasgow; Glasgow University, MA. Organiser in Scotland for Glasgow Federation of ILP, 1919–22; Member of Glasgow Education Authority, 1919–22; Chairman of Independent Labour Party, 1926–31 and 1934–39. *Publications:* Lenin, 1932; If I were Dictator, 1935. *Address:* Beechwood, Barrhead, Renfrewshire. *T:* Barrhead 141.

Died 23 July 1946.

MAXWELL, Brig.-Gen. James McCall, CB 1915; DSO 1918; late RA; *b* 26 Jan. 1865; *s* of Gen. A. Maxwell, CB; *m* 1913, Dorothy Frances, *d* of late Baron von Notting. *Educ:* Cheltenham College; RMA, Woolwich. Entered army, 1884; retired pay, 1920; Captain, 1893; Major, 1900; Lt-Col 1910; served European War, 1914–18 (despatches, CB). *Address:* Daldowie, Camberley, Surrey. *Club:* Royal Automobile.

Died 30 May 1945.

MAXWELL, Sir John, Kt 1930; CMG 1921; Chairman Traffic Commissioners, Northern Area Scotland, 1931–32, Northern Area of England since 1932, and Licensing Authority under Road and Rail Traffic Act, 1933; Regional War Transport Commissioner; late Chief Commissioner of Ashanti; *b* 6 Sept. 1875; *s* of John Maxwell, Maxwelltown, Kirkcudbrightshire; *m* 1st, Marion, *d* of Herbert and Elizabeth Tallent, Westacre, Norfolk; 2nd, Helen Hood, *er d* of William K. and Margaret Findlay, Warren Drive, Wallasey, and Barncailzie Hall, Kirkcudbrightshire; one *d*. *Educ:* Dumfries Academy; Glasgow University. Served articles as a solicitor with Walker & Sharpe, Maxwelltown, Dumfries; studied law at Glasgow University, 1896–98; qualified as a Solicitor, 1899; Assistant District Commissioner, Gold Coast, 1902; Travelling Commissioner, 1905; Provincial Commissioner, 1907; Secretary for Native Affairs, 1923; has acted Governor (twice), Colonial Secretary, Attorney-General, and Solicitor-General; Chairman of numerous Committees, including the Reorganisation of Municipal Government on the Gold Coast; Pres. Newcastle Battalion Boys Brigade; Pres. Newcastle and Tyneside Burns Club. *Publication:* The Gold Coast Handbook, 1st, 2nd, and 3rd editions. *Recreations:* golfing, motoring, shooting. *Address:* 41 Grey Street, Newcastle-upon-Tyne; 26 Westfield Drive, Gosforth, Newcastle-upon-Tyne;

Belmont, Dumfries. *TA:* Transco, Newcastle-upon-Tyne. *T:* Gosforth 52245. *Clubs:* Royal Societies, Royal Empire Society; Conservative, Newcastle-upon-Tyne.

Died 31 March 1946.

MAXWELL, Hon. Somerset Arthur; MP (U) King's Lynn Div. of Norfolk since 1935; *b* 20 Jan. 1905; *o s* of 11th Baron Farnham, DSO; *m* 1930, Susan, *d* of late Capt. Marshall O. Roberts, 15 Grosvenor Square, W, and of Mrs Irene Roberts, Lightwater Manor, Surrey; two *s* one *d. Educ:* Harrow. Capt. Middlesex Yeomanry, 1931; Parliamentary Private Secretary, 1937, to Sir Victor Warrender, Financial Secretary to the War Office, 1938–39, to Rt Hon. L. Hore-Belisha, Secretary of State for War. Served War of 1939–45 (wounded). *Recreations:* hunting, shooting, ski-ing, golf. *Heir: s* Barry Owen Somerset, *b* 7th July 1931. *Address:* 21 Cambridge Square, W2. *T:* Ambassador 2121; Fring Hall, Docking, Norfolk. *Clubs:* Turf, Buck's.

Died Dec. 1942.

MAXWELL, Thomas Doveton; *s* of late Maj.-Gen. William Maxwell, R (Bengal) Art; unmarried. *Educ:* Blundell's School, Tiverton; Balliol College, Oxford. BA. Barrister-at-law, Gray's Inn; Civil Service, Nigeria, 1902–17; Puisne Judge, Kenya Colony, 1917–24; Puisne Judge, Nigeria, 1924; retired, 1928. *Club:* Union.

Died 8 Nov. 1946.

MAXWELL, Sir William, KCIE 1915; CIE 1909; MVO 1911; *b* 3 Jan. 1870; *m* 1894, Elizabeth, *d* of D. Harper; one *d. Educ:* Queen's College, Belfast, Trinity College, Dublin. Entered ICS 1889; served in Bengal till 1900; Postmaster-General, Bombay, 1901; Deputy Director-General, Post Office, India, 1903; acted as Secretary to the Government of India Commerce and Industry Department, 1910; Director-General of Posts and Telegraphs, India; Additional Member of the Gov.-General's Council; retired, 1918. *Club:* East India and Sports.

Died 15 Feb. 1947.

MAXWELL, Sir William, Kt 1928; JP County of the City of Aberdeen; Director, Aberdeen Journals, Limited, 1928; Editor, Aberdeen Journal and Aberdeen Press and Journal, 1910–27; previously on the literary staffs of the London Standard, Pall Mall Gazette and St James's Gazette, and the Scotsman; President, Scottish Unionist Association, 1935–36; *b* Castle-Douglas, Galloway. *Address:* 4 Bon Accord Square, Aberdeen. *Clubs:* Scottish Conservative, Edinburgh.

Died 20 May 1947.

MAXWELL-SCOTT, Rear-Adm. Malcolm M.; *see* Scott.

MAXWELL-WILLSHIRE, Sir Gerard Arthur; *see* Willshire.

MAXWELL STUART, Arthur Constable; *b* 31 May 1845; *s* of Hon. Henry Constable Maxwell Stuart of Traquair, Peebleshire, and Terregles House, Kirkcudbrightshire. *Educ:* Stonyhurst College. *Address:* Traquair, Innerleithen, Peebleshire; Scarthingwell Hall, Tadcaster, Yorks. *Clubs:* Junior Carlton; Yorkshire, York.

Died 7 Nov. 1942.

MAY, 1st Baron *cr* 1935, of Weybridge; **George Ernest May;** 1st Bt *cr* 1931, KBE 1918; FIA; Chairman, Import Duties Advisory Committee since 1932; late Secretary to the Prudential Assurance Co; *b* 1871; *s* of William C. May; *m* 1903, Lily Julia, OBE, *d* of G. Strauss; two *s* one *d.* Entered Prudential Assurance Co., 1887; Manager of the American Dollar Securities Committee, 1916–18; DQMG Canteens, War Office, 1917–19; Chairman Economy Committee, 1931; Director British Overseas

Bank till 1931. *Heir: er s* Hon. John Lawrence May, *b* Aug. 1904. *Address:* Eyot House, Weybridge. *T:* Weybridge 43; 42 Orchard Court, W1.

Died 10 April 1946.

MAY, 2nd Baron *cr* 1935, of Weybridge; **John Lawrence May;** 2nd Bt *cr* 1931; engineer; *b* 15 Aug. 1904; *s* of 1st Baron and Lily Julia, OBE, *d* of G. Strauss; *S* father 1946; *m* 1929, Roberta Thoms; one *s* one *d. Educ:* Wellington College, Berks. *Recreation:* anything to do with motors. *Heir: s* Hon. Michael St John May, *b* 1931. *Address:* c/o Lily, Lady May, 42 Orchard Court, W1.

Died 9 March 1950.

MAY, Captain Arthur Dekewer Livius, CBE 1919; retired, 1919; *b* 28 May 1875; *yr s* of late J. C. Frampton May, Curvalion, Creech St Michael, Taunton; *m* Henrietta, *y d* of late William Bowley. *Address:* Langaller, Catisfield, Fareham, Hants. *Club:* Naval and Military.

Died 12 June 1943.

MAY, Aylmer William, CMG 1924; MA, MD; late Principal Medical Officer Rhodesia Railways; *b* 1874; *s* of late Dr Walter May, Kilmoganny, Co. Kilkenny; *m* 1913, Dulcie, *d* of late H. Hughes, Johannesburg; one *s* two *d. Educ:* Trinity College, Dublin. Govt Bacteriologist Transvaal, 1907–08; late Member of Executive and Legislative Councils, Northern Rhodesia. Served S Africa, 1900–02; European War, 1914–19; Principal Medical Officer, N Rhodesia, 1908–28. *Publications:* various papers on tropical diseases. *Address:* Bulawayo Club, Bulawayo, Southern Rhodesia.

Died 2 April 1950.

MAY, Barry, CMG 1916; CBE 1920; *b* Southsea, 24 June 1869; *e s* of late Staff-Commander D. J. May, RN, and M, *d* of late Thomas Barry of Cape Colony; *m* 1901, Florence Thomson; one *s* one *d. Educ:* St Saviour's Grammar School, and the Diocesan College, Rondebosch. Joined service of Crown Colony of British Bechuanaland, 1888; on annexation of British Bechuanaland to Cape Colony in 1895 was specially selected for service in the Bechuanaland Protectorate; Government Secretary, 1902, and acted as Resident Commissioner on various occasions; Deputy Resident Commissioner and Treasurer of Basutoland, 1912–16; Deputy Resident Commissioner, Bechuanaland Protectorate, 1916; seconded for special duty in 1916 as Imperial Controller in South Africa in connection with expenditure by Union Government. *Recreations:* shooting and golf.

Died 7 June 1948.

MAY, Sir Gould, Kt 1923; MD; *s* of late Right Hon. George A. C. May, Lord Chief Justice of Ireland; unmarried. *Educ:* Rugby; Trinity College, Cambridge. MA, MD (Cantab); MRCP (London). Consulting Gynæcologist, Grosvenor Hospital for Women, SW; Consulting Physician to other medical charities; Knight of Grace of St John of Jerusalem. *Recreations:* fishing, shooting. *Address:* Clare Hall, Clare, Suffolk; 10 Chapel Street, SW1. *T:* Sloane 8441. *Club:* Oxford and Cambridge.

Died 12 Feb. 1944.

MAY, Lt-Col John Cyril, DSO 1900; late East Surrey Regt; *b* 1 April 1874; *e s* of late J. C. Frampton May of Creech St Michael, Taunton; *m* 1st, 1907, Edith Margaret (*d* 1925), *y d* of late Colonel S. E. Maunsell, RAMC; one *s*; 2nd, 1929, Annie Louise, *er d* of late Lt-Gen. Philip Story, Indian Army, of The Hill, Stowmarket. *Educ:* Bradfield College. Entered army, 1895; served South Africa, 1899–1902 (despatches four times, Queen's medal 5 clasps, King's medal 2 clasps, DSO); European War, France and Belgium, 1915–16; retired pay, 1922. *Address:* Trimley House, Trimley St Mary, Suffolk.

Died 29 May 1943.

MAY, Otto, MA, MD (Cantab), FRCP (Lond.); Chairman, British Social Hygiene Council; Hon. Member, Association of Life Ass. Med. Directors of America; late Principal Medical Officer, Prudential Assurance Co.; 2nd *s* of late Wm May and Emma May; *m* Gertrude Mabel, 2nd *d* of late T. H. Rose, JP; two *s*. *Educ:* privately; St John's Coll., Cambridge (Foundation Scholar); first-class Nat. Science Tripos, Parts I and II. Demonstrator of Physiology, Cambridge Univ.; Liston Gold Medal, Univ. College, London; Aitchison Scholar, University College Hospital; Research Scholar, British Medical Association; Beit Research Fellow; Medical Registrar, Middlesex Hospital; Physician, Evelina Hospital. *Publications:* The Prevention of Venereal Diseases; numerous papers in medical and scientific journals. *Address:* Wellside, Well Walk, Hampstead, NW3. *T:* Hampstead 3249. *Clubs:* Oxford and Cambridge, Hampstead Golf.

Died 15 Aug. 1946.

MAYBIN, Sir John Alexander, KCMG 1939; CMG 1935; MA; Governor and Commander-in-Chief of Northern Rhodesia since 1938; *b* 5 Aug. 1889; *s* of William Maybin, MA, Ayr; unmarried. *Educ:* Edinburgh University. Cadet Ceylon, Civil Service, 1914; Police Magistrate, Panadura 1916; Chief Secretary, Nigeria, 1934–38. *Recreations:* golf, fishing, stamp collecting. *Address:* Government House, Lusaka, Northern Rhodesia. *Club:* East India and Sports.

Died 9 April 1941.

MAYBURY, Brig.-Gen. Sir Henry (Percy), GBE 1928; KCMG 1919; CB 1917; CMG 1919; RE; MInstCE; JP Kent; Consulting Civil Engineer; *b* 1864; *m* 1885, Elizabeth (*d* 1929), *d* of late Thomas Sheldon, Ludlow; one *s* two *d*; 1942, Katharine Mary, *o d* of S. W. Pring, Winchester. Served European War, France and Flanders (KCMG, CB); retired, 1919; Dir-Gen. of Roads, Ministry of Transport, 1919–28; Consulting Engineer and Adviser to the Minister of Transport on Road and Traffic questions, 1928–32; Chairman of London and Home Counties Traffic Advisory Committee, 1924–33; Member of the London Passenger Transport Board, and of the London and Home Counties Traffic Advisory Committee, 1933–42; President of the Institute of Transport, 1921–22; President of the Institution of Civil Engineers, 1933–34. *Address:* Bush House, Aldwych, WC2. *T:* Temple Bar 7461; Four Winds, Mousecroft Lane, Shrewsbury, Shropshire. *Club:* Athenæum.

Died 7 Jan. 1943.

MAYEDA, Marquis Toshinari; General (posthumous promotion) Japanese Army; member House of Peers; *b* 5 June 1885; *s* of Viscount Mayeda; *S* 15th Marquis Mayeda, feudal Lord of Kaga; *m* 1st, 1906, Namiko Mayeda (*d* 1923), *d* of Marquis Toshitsugu Mayeda; one *s* three *d*; 2nd, 1925, Kikuko Sakai, *sister* of Count Sakai; one *s* three *d*. *Educ:* The Japanese Peers School; The Imperial Military Academy; The Imperial Staff College. 2nd Lieut Imperial Japanese Army, 1905; after graduating at the Staff College, attached to the Imperial General Staff, 1912; studied in Germany, 1913; Attached to the British Expeditionary Force in France, 1914–16; visited England for the second time, 1918, as one of the suite of the Imperial Japanese Prince who conveyed the Sword of a Japanese Field-Marshal to the King of England; Instruction Officer at Staff College, 1919; stayed in Paris as a Japanese Military Delegate concerning the Peace Treaty; fixed the frontier between Germany and Denmark, Germany and Belgium, 1920–23; Guard Battalion Commander, 1923; Instruction Officer at the Staff College, 1924; Military Attache to Imperial Japanese Embassy in London, 1927–30; Guard Regiment Commander, 1931; Tokio Brigade Commander, 1933; Director of 4th Section General Staff, 1935; commandant of the Staff College, 1936; Commander of the 8th Division, Hirosaki, 1937;

Supreme Comdr, N Borneo Garrison, 1942. President, Japan-Denmark Society, and Japan-Poland Society; Order of Sacred Treasure 2nd class, Rising Sun 3rd class, Japan; Commander of Legion of Honour; France Commander of Polish Restitution, with Star, Poland; Officier de Couronne, Italy; Officier de l'ordre de Leopold, Belgium; Commander de Danebrog, Denmark. *Address:* Komaba, Tokio.

Died 5 Sept. 1942.

MAYER, Sylvain, KC 1913, BA, PhD; *b* 9 Aug. 1863; *s* of late M. L. Mayer; *m* 1891, Lilian Mary Blakeway (*d* 1945); one *s* three *d*; *m* 1946, Mrs Gladys Marion Millicent Cooper. *Educ:* University College School; University College (Andrews Scholar); Heidelberg University. BA with Honours at London University, 1882; Doctor of Philosophy, Heidelberg University, 1884. Called to Bar, Middle Temple, 1887; also a Member of Gray's Inn and the Northern Circuit; contested North Hackney, 1895; Fulham, Dec. 1910; Woodbridge, 1924; shortly after the outbreak of the Great War he and Mr C. H. Phillips organised and bore all expenses of a committee for supplying comforts to the Russian army, which continued to operate until the Russian Revolution broke out in 1917. *Publications:* Comedies: Papa's Honeymoon, Criterion Theatre, 1890; A Gay Widower, Vaudeville Theatre, 1892. Novel: Captured in Court. Code of Law of Rating (three editions); Law of Agricultural Holdings (six editions); Law of Compensation; French Code of Commerce; The Representation of the People Act, 1918; Reminiscences of a KC, Theatrical and Legal, 1924; Funeral Oration of Pericles, 1926; Press articles on Economic subjects. *Recreations:* golf, chess. *Address:* 18 Lexham Gardens, W8; 1 Garden Court, Temple, EC4. *Club:* Savage.

Died 13 Sept. 1948.

MAYHEW, Arthur Innes, CMG 1936; CIE 1919; Temporary Principal, Colonial Office; *b* 1878; *s* of Rev. A. L. Mayhew, Chaplain, Wadham College, Oxford; *m* May Catherine, *d* of late Sir James Davies, Kt; two *s* one *d*. *Educ:* Winchester (Scholar); New College, Oxford (Scholar); First-Class in Classical Moderations and Literæ Humaniores. Entered Indian Educational Service, 1903; resigned, 1922, after holding posts of Director Public Instruction, Central Provinces, and Education Commissioner, Govt of India; Master at Eton College, 1922–28; Secretary, Education Committee, Colonial Office, 1929–39. *Publications:* The Education of India, 1926; Christianity and the Government of India, 1929; Education in the Colonial Empire, 1938; The English Bible, 1939. *Address:* Normanhurst, Datchet, near Slough, Bucks.

Died 16 March 1948.

MAYNARD, Maj.-Gen. Sir Charles Clarkson Martin, KCB 1919; CB 1918; CMG 1918; DSO 1900; Colonel, The Devonshire Regt, 1930–43; *b* 15 Sept. 1870; *y s* of late Forster Fowler Martin Maynard, LRCP, MRCS; *m* 1909, Dorothy Agnes, *e d* of late Arthur Davidson; one *s* one *d*. *Educ:* St Paul's School; RMC, Sandhurst. Junior and Senior Foundation Scholar at St Paul's School; honours and prize-winner at Sandhurst. Joined Devonshire Regiment, 1890; served in Burmah campaign (medal and clasp), 1889–92; appointed Superintendent of Gymnasia, Malta, 1894; served in Tirah campaign, 1897 (medal and 2 clasps); held appointments of Railway Transport Officer, Punjaub, and Station Staff-Officer, Mian Mir, 1898–99; served in South African campaign, 1899–1902 (Queen's medal and 6 clasps, King's medal and 2 clasps; despatches 3 times, DSO); European War, 1914–18 (despatches 7 times, Lt-Col, Col, KCB, CB, CMG); 2nd in Command of Imperial Light Infantry, S Africa, 1900–01; Staff Officer, Zululand, 1902; graduated at the Staff College, 1903–04; Brigade Major of 7th Infantry Brigade, Southern Command, 1905–07; General Staff at Army

Headquarters, 1907–09 and 1910–14; various Staff appointments during European War, including Brigade Commander, 1915–17, GOC in C Allied Forces, Murmansk, 1918–19 (1914 Star, General Service medal, Victory medal, Légion d'Honneur, France, Grand Cordon St Anne, Russia, White Eagle, Serbia); Brig.-Gen. in charge Administration, Western Command, 1920; Major-General, 1923; retired pay, 1925. *Publication:* The Murmansk Venture, 1928. *Address:* Glassenbury Cottage, Bexhill-on-Sea.

Died 28 June 1945.

MAYNARD, Dudley Christopher, OBE, ARIBA; partner in the firm of Hayward & Maynard, Architects and Surveyors, 14 John Street, Adelphi, WC2; *b* 27 Nov. 1874; *s* of C. D. Maynard, LRCS, and Emily McAdam; *m* 1906, Mary Gertrude, *d* of Robert Cockell, Cheltenham; two *s* one *d*. *Educ:* privately at Cambridge and Lausanne. Architect in partnership with A. B. Hayward since 1900; agents for the Adelphi Estate; Architect to the British Red Cross; built Queen Mary's Hospital at Frognal, Sidcup, for Facial Cases, and Roehampton Hospital for Limbless Men during the War; also the Little Theatre, besides town and country houses, etc. *Publications:* The Old Inns of Kent, besides numerous pamphlets and newspaper articles. *Recreations:* golf, photography, and chess. *Address:* Ballochmorrie, Coulsdon. *T:* Purley 1713. *Clubs:* Constitutional; Kingswood Golf.

Died 29 March 1941.

MAYNARD, Sir (Herbert) John, KCIE 1920; CSI 1915; Hon. DLitt (Punjab), 1925; ICS; retired, 1927; Vice-Chancellor Punjab University, 1917; Member of Executive Council of Governor, Punjab, 1921–26; *b* 12 July 1865; *s* of Frederick Waite Maynard; *m* 1896, Alfreda Horner, *d* of Richard Eppes, Appomattox, City Point, Virginia; one *s* three *d*. *Educ:* Merchant Taylors' School; St John's College, Oxford (classical scholar). Stanhope Prize Essay, 1885; first class Modern History, 1886. Entered ICS 1883; Deputy Commissioner, 1889; Counsellor to Raja of Mandi, 1889–90; Judicial Secretary to Govt, Punjab, 1896–99; Commissioner of Excise, 1903–06; Commissioner, Multan, 1906–11; Rawalpindi, 1911–13; Financial Commissioner, Punjab, 1913–20; Parliamentary Candidate (Lab), King's Lynn, 1929, Stroud, Glos, 1931, East Fulham, 1931. *Publications:* Russia in Flux; before October; The Russian Peasant and other studies, 1942. *Recreations:* golf, member of the Fabian Society. *Address:* 18 Gilston Road, SW. *T:* Kensington 7191.

Died 6 Dec. 1943.

MAYNE, Arthur Brinley; *b* 9 Jan. 1893; 4th *s* of late J. M. Mayne, Swansea; *m* 1926, Dorothy, *e d* of late Rev. Dr H. A. Watson, and formerly the first Headmistress of the Atherley School for Girls, Southampton; two *s*. *Educ:* Llandovery College (open Scholar); Balliol College (open Mathematical Scholar). 1st Class Mathematical Moderations and Goldsmiths Exhibition, 1911; Junior University Mathematical Scholarship, 1912; 1st Class Final Honour School of Mathematics and Physics, 1913; King Edward VII Research Studentship, 1914. Senior Maths Master and Housemaster, Taunton School, Taunton, 1917–19; Second Master, Senior Maths Master and Senior Housemaster, Cathedral School, Hereford, 1920–22; Headmaster Cambridge and County High School for Boys, Jan. 1923–Dec. 1945; Member of Committee of Headmasters' Conference, 1933; considerable experience as Examiner in Mathematics for various Examinations. *Publications:* The Essentials of School Geometry, 1933; Scottish Edition, 1934; The Essentials of School Algebra, 1938; The Essentials of School Arithmetic, 1947. *Recreations:* various. *Address:* 10 Eversley Road, Sketty, Swansea.

Died 7 June 1948.

MAYNE, Brig.-Gen. Charles (Robert Graham), CMG 1919; DSO 1902; late Highland Light Infantry; *b* 10 Sept. 1874; *o s* of late Major R. G. Mayne; *m* 1913, Elsie Bertha, *y d* of late W. B. Huntington, DL, of Blackmore Park, Worcester, and 143 Piccadilly, W. Entered army, 1895; Capt. 1901; Major, 1915; served Ashanti, 1900; Northern Nigeria, 1901; Southern Nigeria, 1902; Egyptian Army, 1903–13; Military Secretary to Sirdar and Governor-General, 1910; Blue Nile Expedition, 1903; European War, 1914–17 (despatches, wounded twice, Bt Lt-Col, Bt Col, CMG, Croix de Guerre); Assistant Military Secretary, War Office, 1919; Deputy Military Secretary, War Office, 1921–23; retd pay, 1923; ADC to the King, 1921–23. *Address:* Charlton House, Radstock, Somerset. *Club:* United Service.

Died 7 April 1944.

MAYNE, Ethel Colburn; *d* of late Charles E. B. Mayne, sometime of the Royal Irish Constabulary and the Irish Resident Magistracy, and Charlotte Emily Henrietta (Emily), *d* of Captain William Sweetman, 16th Lancers. *Educ:* private schools in Ireland. Published her first short story in The Yellow Book, 1895, under pseudonym Frances E. Huntly, which was dropped on publication of first volume of stories, 1898; contributed stories to Yellow Book and Chapman's Magazine, still under pseudonym, 1895–96; has reviewed much fiction in The Nation and Daily News, written many articles in Daily Chronicle and Yorkshire Post, and translated much from French and German for various publishers. *Publications:* The Clearer Vision (stories), 1898; Jessie Vandeleur (novel), The Fourth Ship, Gold Lace, One of our Grandmothers (novels), and Things that No One Tells, Come in; Blindman (short stories); Nine of Hearts, 1923; Inner Circle, 1925; other works: Enchanters of Men; Byron (2 vols), The Romance of Monaco, Browning's Heroines; The Life and Letters of Anne Isabella, Lady Noel Byron, 1929; A Regency Chapter, 1939; Marcelle Tinayre's Study of Madame de Pompadour (translation), 1925; Emil Ludwig's Wilhelm der Zweite (translation), 1926; Emil Ludwig's Goethe, 1928; Haller's Philip Eulenburg: the Kaiser's Friend (translation), 1930; Du Bos's Byron (translation), 1932. *Recreations:* walking, reading, patience. *Address:* 25 The Avenue, St Margaret's, Middlesex.

Died 30 April 1941.

MAYO, Rev. John Augustus; Rector of Whitechapel since 1916; Prebendary of St Paul's since 1935. *Educ:* University of Durham, LTh. Deacon, 1888; Priest, 1889; Vicar of St Anne, Holloway, 1898–1916. *Address:* Rectory, Whitechapel, E1. *T:* Bishopsgate 6163.

Died 12 Nov. 1941.

MAYOR, Robert John Grote, CB 1919; MA; *b* 1869; *s* of late Rev. Joseph Bickersteth Mayor; *m* 1912, Beatrice, *d* of late Daniel Meinertzhagen; one *s* two *d*. *Educ:* Eton; King's College, Cambridge (Fellow). Education Department, 1896; Assistant Secretary, Board of Education, 1907–19; Principal Assistant Secretary, 1919–26; Chairman of Committee on Co-operation between Universities and Training Colleges, 1926–28; and of Central Advisory Committee for Certification of Teachers, 1930–35. *Address:* 26 Addison Avenue, W11. *Clubs:* United University, Alpine.

Died 19 June 1947.

MEAD, Frederick; Barrister-at-law; *b* 22 July 1847; *s* of George Edward Mead, solicitor, Chelsea; *m* 1878, Sophia (*d* 1944), *d* of R. H. Poland, Blackheath; three *s*. *Educ:* King's College, London (Fellow). Barr. Middle Temple, 1869; Counsel to the Treasury, Middlesex Sessions, 1879–86; Central Criminal Court, 1886–89; Metropolitan Magistrate, 1889–1933; Marlborough Street Police Court, 1907–33; on committee Marine

Society since 1894, past Chairman. *Address:* 4 Eliot Place, Blackheath, SE3. *T:* Lee Green 0895. *Club:* Junior Carlton.

Died 14 Dec. 1945.

MEAD, Maj.-Gen. Owen Herbert, CBE 1940; DSO 1919; General Officer Commanding 3rd Division Pacific Section, 2nd NZEF; *b* 24 Jan. 1892; *s* of Edward Mead and Flora Williams; *m* 1926, Barbara, *d* of C. A. Loughnan; two *d*. *Educ:* Marlborough College. Joined NZ Expeditionary Force, 8 Aug. 1914 as 2/Lieut; served Egypt and Gallipoli (wounded); Capt., 16 March 1916; served in France until wounded, Somme, Sept. 1916 (despatches); Major, March 1917; served in France; Lt-Col 15 Sept. 1917; commanded a battalion until end of war (despatches twice, DSO); joined NZ Staff Corps as Capt., 1919; Staff Officer i/c No. 6 Regimental District, Palmerston North, 1920–24; No. 5 Regimental District, Wellington, 1925–26; Major 1925; attended Staff College, 1927 and 1928; attached to War Office, 1929; Staff Officer i/c No. 11 Regimental District, Dunedin, 1930–35; Lt-Col, 1935; Adjutant-General, NZ Military Forces, 1935–37; Col, 1937; Adjutant and QMG, 1937–38; Officer Comdg Northern Military District, NZ, 1938–39; Adjutant-General, GHQ, 1939–40; Officer Commanding Southern Military District, NZ, 1940; Brigadier, 1940; Major-General, 1942. *Recreations:* golf, tennis, cricket, fishing. *Address:* c/o Army HQ, Wellington, NZ.

Died 25 July 1942.

MEADEN, Surg. Captain Edward Henry, CMG 1918; Royal Navy (retired); *b* Warminster, Wiltshire, Feb. 1864; *y s* of late Martin Meaden, of Clydesdale, Clifton, Gloster; *m* 1891, Lillian Atthill, *e d* of late Captain Atthill, 89th Regiment; one *d*. *Educ:* Bath College. Entered Royal Navy, 1886; served on the China station in HMS Alacrity, 1891–94; volunteered his services to the Hong-Kong Colonial Government during the summer of 1893 on the outbreak of plague (letter of thanks from the Government for his services); served on the Mediterranean station and in the Red Sea during Soudan War of 1908; Principal Medical Officer of the Naval Division, European War; afterwards Senior Medical Officer of HMS Inflexible; present at battle of the Falkland Islands, 8 Dec. 1914, and the following year served in the same ship during the naval operations in the Dardanelles (despatches, CMG); retired invalided, 14 Jan. 1918. *Address:* Hazeldene, Denvilles, Havant, Hants.

Died 23 Jan. 1943.

MEADUS, Engr Captain William Henry, CBE 1919; RN ret; *b* 1862; *s* of Capt. John Howard Meadus, Poole, Dorset; *m*; three *d*. Entered Navy, 1877; served in HMS Dart which was reported to be lost off coast of New Zealand, and on arriving at Sydney had unique experience of reading own obituary, 1889, spent three years in her surveying South Sea Islands; in Destroyer Ardent, taking part throughout Cretean Rebellion, 1896; HMS Bonaventure, which was reported lost off South American Coast whilst proceeding to Pacific Station, 1903; afterwards proceeded to China and remained during Russo-Japanese War; RN Barracks, Portsmouth, for mechanical training of seamen, 1906; Engineer Commander D of 6th Flotilla, Portsmouth, 1910; served throughout European War in charge of repairs for HM Ships, Mersey District. *Recreation:* golf. *Address:* Cumberland Court, Craneswater, Southsea.

Died 22 March 1947.

MEARES, John Willoughby, CIE, 1922; FRAS, MInstCE, MIEE, MIE (Ind.); Consulting Engineer (retired); late Electrical Adviser to the Government of India and late Chief Engineer Hydro-Electric Survey of India; *b* 1871; 3rd *s* of late Thomas Meares of Clive Hall, Shrewsbury; *m* 1st, 1898, Frances Helen (*d* 1929), *d* of late A. M. Curteis, JP of Godalming; one *s*; 2nd, 1930, Margaret Helen Lane; one *s*. *Educ:* Winchester;

University College, London. Trained as an electrical engineer at the works of Cromptom and Co., Llanelly and Chelmsford; went to India, 1896, to carry out hydro-electric installation at Darjeeling; electrical engineer to Bengal Government, 1898; officiating Controller of Patents (India), 1910 and 1914. *Publications:* The Indian Electricity Act, 1903; The Law relating to Electrical Energy in India and Burma, 1911–1922, 1929, 1933, 1937, and 1940; Electrical Engineering in India, 1914; Electrical Engineering Practice, 1916 (3 vols), 5th ed. 1942; Hydro-Electric Developments, 1920; Water Power, 1934; Contract Bridge in a Nuttshelle, 1937, 1939, 1942, 1943; Company Drill in a Nutshell, 1939, 1940, 1941; Rules, Decisions, Etiquette of Golf in a Nutshell, 1943. *Address:* 86 Lowther Road, Bournemouth. *T:* 1725.

Died 11 Jan. 1946.

MEATH, 13th Earl of, *cr* 1627; **Reginald Le Normand Brabazon,** CB 1915; CBE 1919; Baron Ardee, Ireland, 1616; Baron Chaworth, of Eaton Hall, Co. Hereford, UK, 1831; *b* 24 Nov. 1869; *e s* of 12th Earl and Lady Mary Jane Maitland (*d* 1918), *o surv. d* of 11th Earl of Lauderdale; *S* father, 1929; *m* 1908, Lady Aileen Wyndham-Quin, *o c* of 4th Earl of Dunraven; one *s* two *d*. *Educ:* Wellington College. Entered Army, Grenadier Guards, 1889; Captain, 1899; Major, 1906; Lt-Col 1912; Lt-Col Irish Guards, 1914; Brig.-Gen. 1918; served S Africa, 1900–02 (Queen's medal 3 clasps, King's medal 2 clasps); European War, 1914–18 (CB); Colonel, Irish Guards, 1916. *Heir:* *s* Lord Ardee. *Address:* Kilruddery, Bray, Co. Wicklow.

Died 10 March 1949.

MECHAN, Sir Henry, Kt 1927; LLD; DL; *b* Glasgow; *s* of Arthur Mechan; *m* Jane, *d* of Andrew Blackwood Stewart; no *c*. *Educ:* Glasgow; privately. Captain in Volunteer Regiment; contested (C) West Renfrewshire; founded Chair of Public Health in Glasgow University; on board of several Glasgow Hospitals and other public bodies. *Recreations:* motoring, golf, music. *Address:* Sundown, Kelvinside, Glasgow. *TA:* Nautical, Glasgow. *T:* Western 1358, Glasgow. *Club:* Carlton.

Died 11 June 1943.

MEDLICOTT, Col Henry Edward, DSO 1918; Deputy Director Anglo-Iranian Oil Co. Ltd since 1926; retired Indian Army and RFA; *b* 24 July 1882; *s* of late H. E. Medlicott, of Sandfield, Potterne, Wilts; *m* 1910, Clare Charlotte Margorie Gabrielle, 2nd *d* of late Sir Martin Gosselin, GCVO, and Hon. Lady Gosselin; one *s* three *d*. *Educ:* Cheltenham College; Royal Military Academy, Woolwich. Joined Royal Field Artillery, 1900; served South African War with Irish Horse; transferred to 3rd Bengal Cavalry, 1907; ADC to C-in-C in India, 1909–10; served European War in France, 1914–18 (despatches, DSO, French and Belgian Croix de Guerre); Afghan War, 1919 (despatches); served in War of 1939–45 with BEF in France 1940 and Petroleum Warfare Department, 1940–43. *Address:* 15 Hay Hill, Berkeley Square, W1. *TA:* Tocildem Piccy, London. *T:* Regent 7449. *Clubs:* Buck's, Whit's.

Died 11 April 1948.

MEDLICOTT, Rev. Canon Robert Sumner, MA; Hon. Canon of Winchester; *e s* of late Rev. Walter Medlicott, Vicar of Swanmore, Hants, and Edith Louisa Sumner; *m* 1905, Ellen Douglas, *d* of John James Irvine of Waterford, Kubusi, S Africa; one *s* two *d*. *Educ:* Winchester; Magdalen College, Oxford; Wells Theological College. Served curacies at Derby and Leeds Parish Church; Vicar of St Thomas of Canterbury, Portsmouth, 1903–15; Rector of Burghclere with Newtown, Hants, 1915–37. *Address:* Diplands, St Mary Bourne, Andover, Hants. *T:* St Mary Bourne 235. *Clubs:* United University, Leander.

Died 8 Jan. 1941.

MEE, Arthur; Editor of The Children's Newspaper; *b* Stapleford, Notts, 21 July 1875; *s* of Henry Mee, Nottingham; *m* 1897, Amy Fratson, of East Cottingwith, Yorks; one *d. Educ:* Stapleford. Entered journalism on the Nottingham Evening News at 20; joined editorial staff of Sir George Newnes at 21; started Obiter Scripta in St James's Gazette, Nov. 1900, and Men and Women column in same newspaper, Oct. 1902, continuing both daily until May 1903; editor of Black and White (1901–03); Literary Editor, Daily Mail, 1903–05; editor of Harmsworth Self-Educator, 1906; Harmsworth History of the World, 1907; The Children's Encyclopedia, 1908 (continued for 25 years as a monthly under name of My Magazine); The World's Great Books, 1909; Harmsworth Natural History, 1911; Harmsworth Popular Science, 1912; The Children's Treasure-House, 1921; I See All, the first Picture Encyclopedia, 1929; Arthur Mee's Thousand Heroes, 1933. *Publications:* Joseph Chamberlain, 1900; King and Emperor, 1901; Lord Salisbury, 1901; England's Mission, by England's Statesmen; Defeat or Victory? The Fiddlers, The Parasite, SOS, the books of the Prohibition Crusade, of which a million and a half were sold in 1917–1918; Arthur Mee's Gift Book, 1917; Little Treasure Island, 1920; Every Child's Creed, 1921; Arthur Mee's Hero Book, 1921; Arthur Mee's Golden Year, 1922; Arthur Mee's Wonderful Day, 1923; The Children's Bible, 1924; One Thousand Beautiful Things, 1925; Talks to Boys, Talks to Girls, 1925; (edited) The Children's Life of Jesus, 1926; The Children's Shakespeare, 1926; Book of Everlasting Things, 1927; The Children's Hour, 1928; The Loveliest Stories in the World, 1929; The Children's Bunyan, 1929; Arthur Mee's Story Book, 1930; Jesus Said, 1931; God Knows, 1935; Salute the King, 1937; One Thousand Famous Things, 1937; The Rainbow Books (eight small volumes), 1939; Why we had to go to War, 1939; The Blackout Book, 1939; Nineteen-Forty: Our Finest Hour, 1941; Book of the Flag, 1941; Call the Witnesses, 1941; Immortal Dawn, 1942; Wonderful Year, 1943; The King's England, a Survey of 10,000 towns and villages; introductory vol. (Enchanted Land) and 37 county vols, 1936–1943. *Address:* Eynsford Hill, Kent; John Carpenter House, Whitefriars, EC4. *T:* Farningham 27, Central 8080. *Club:* Reform.

Died 27 May 1943.

MEEHAN, Francis Edward, MBE; JP; merchant and farmer; *b* 17 Sept. 1868; *s* of Laurence and Jane Meehan of Manorhamilton; *m* Molly, *d* of George and Catherine Hamilton, Dowra, Co. Cavan. *Educ:* at the local intermediate school. Took a prominent part in politics from an early age, and always advocated the rights and national demands of Ireland; MP (N) Leitrim, 1908–18. *Recreations:* cricket, horses, dogs, and birds. *Address:* Manorhamilton, Ireland.

Died 22 Dec. 1946.

MEEK, Alexander, DSc, FZS; *b* Broughty Ferry, 7 April 1865. *Educ:* Broughty Ferry; Royal College of Science; University of St Andrews; University of Freiburg. Graduated (BSc), St Andrews, 1889; MSc (Dun.), 1896; Hon. DSc (Dun.), 1921. Worked at St Andrews Marine Laboratory, 1889–91; Lecturer in Agricultural Zoology in County of Aberdeen, 1891–94; Lecturer in Zoology, Armstrong College, 1894–1906; Professor of Zoology, Armstrong College, now King's College, in the University of Durham, 1906–32 (now Emeritus Professor), and Director, Dove Marine Laboratory, Cullercoats, Northumberland, 1897–1932. *Publications:* Migrations of Fish, 1916; Fishes of Northumberland; Fishes of Durham, in Victoria County Histories; History of Fisheries, in Northumberland County History, vol. vii; Essentials of Zoology; The Progress of Life; numerous papers on growth, embryology, and general and marine zoology; Editor of Reports of Dove Marine

Laboratory to 1932. *Recreations:* golf, painting. *Address:* Gunton Dell, Lowestoft, Suffolk. *Club:* Royal Northumberland Yacht (Blyth).

Died 2 Nov. 1949.

MEGAW, Robert Dick; Puisne Judge, High Court of Justice in Northern Ireland (Chancery Judge), 1932–43; *e s* of John Megaw, JP, Ballyboyland, Ballymoney, Co. Antrim; *m;* two *s* five *d. Educ:* Ballymoney Intermediate School; Royal Academical Institution, Belfast; Queen's College, Belfast; Inns of Court (Middle Temple). BA, MA, and LLB in the Royal University of Ireland, Certificate of Honour and Special Prize for Constitutional Law and History, Inns of Court, 1893. Called to Irish Bar, 1893; KC 1921; Professor of Common Law, King's Inns, Dublin, 1912–14; KC 1921; MP Co. Antrim in Parliament of NI, 1921–25; Parliamentary Secretary of Ministry of Home Affairs, Northern Ireland, 1921–25; Member of Senate of the Queen's University of Belfast; Commissioner appointed by Ministry of Home Affairs, NI, to inquire into the administration of the Housing Acts by the Belfast Corporation, 1925–26; Judicial Commissioner of the Land Purchase Commission of Northern Ireland, 1927–37; Bencher of the Honourable Society of the Inn of Court of Northern Ireland. *Address:* Brekagh, Malone Road, Belfast. *Clubs:* Ulster, Belfast.

Died 2 May 1947.

MEHTA, Hon. Sir Homi, KCIE 1946; KBE 1941; Kt 1933; JP; *b* 1 April 1871; *s* of Maneckjee Framjee Mehta and Avanbai; *m;* three *s* two *d. Educ:* Bombay. Banker, merchant, and millowner; Managing Director and Chairman, British India General Insurance Co., Ltd, Zenith Life Assurance Co., Ltd, Gaekwar Mills Co., Ltd, Navsari Cotton and Silk Mills Ltd, Kemp and Co., Ltd, Dhrangadhra Chemical Works, Ltd, Raza Sugar Co., Ltd, Buland Sugar Co., Ltd; Governing Director of H. M. Mehta & Co. Ltd; Homi Mehta & Sons, Ltd; H. M. Mehta & Sons, Ltd; Director, Central Board Reserve Bank of India. Chairman of Bombay War Gift Fund, Red Cross Fund, and Pres. of Victory Thanks-giving Fund. *Publications:* Financial Control during this War and the last War, 1940; The Future of Cotton, 1941; Possible Effects of Post War Currency Plans on India, 1943. *Address:* Goolita, Worli Sea Face, Worli, Bombay, India. *Clubs:* National Liberal, Royal Automobile; Willingdon, Orient, Ripon (Bombay); Roshanhara (Delhi); Western India Turf (Bombay and Poona).

Died 15 April 1948.

MEHTA, Sir Mangaldas Vijbhukandas, Kt 1936; OBE; LM and S; MRCP; FRCP; FCPS; FRCOG. *Address:* St Vincents, Ridge Road, Malabar Hill, Bombay 6, India.

Died 27 June 1945.

MEHTA, Sir Manubhai Nandshankar, Kt 1922; CSI 1919; MA, LLB; Foreign and Political Minister, Gwalior, since 1940; Chairman Committee of Ministers, Chamber of Princes, since 1944; *b* 22 July 1868; *s* of late Rao Bahadur Nandshankar Tuljashanker (author of Gujarati Historical Novel—Karen Ghelo); *m;* four *s* six *d. Educ:* Elphinstone College, Bombay. Honours in History and Political Economy. Logic and Moral Philosophy; Senior Fellow, 1888–90; Elphinstone Prize, Ellis Scholarship, Homeji Cursetji Dady Prize, and the Arnould Scholarship. Professor of Logic and Philosophy, and Law Lecturer, Baroda College, 1891–99; Private Secretary to HH Maharaja Gaekwar, 1899–1905; accompanied HH to England, France, Germany, Switzerland, and Italy; late Famine Commissioner, High Court Judge, Naib Diwan and Legal Remembrancer, 1911–14; Revenue Minister and First Counsellor, 1914–16; Diwan (Prime Minister) of Baroda, 1916–27; Prime Minister, Bikaner, Rajputana, 1927–34; Home Minister, Gwalior, 1937; attended the Indian Round Table Conference in 1930–31, 1931 and 1932; served on the Consultative Committee of the Viceroy in India,

1932; attended the Joint Parliamentary Committee on Indian Reforms, 1933. *Publications:* The Hind Rajasthan—or Annals of Native States of India; Principles of Law of Evidence (in Gujarati), three volumes. *Recreations:* tennis, badminton. *Address:* Gwalior, India.

Died 14 Oct. 1946.

MEHTA SHUJA-UL-MULK, Sir, KCIE 1919. *Address:* Chitral, NW Frontier Province, India.

Died 13 Oct. 1936.

MEIGHEN, Maj.-Gen. Frank Stephen, CMG 1917; *b* 1870; *s* of late Robert Meighen, Montreal; *m* 1913, Gwyneth, *d* of Col G. Allen Jones, Quebec. *Educ:* High School, Montreal; McGill University, BA. A Director of Canadian Pacific Railway Co. and Bank of Toronto; President Lake of the Woods Milling Co., and New Brunswick Railway Co.; served European War, 1914–18 (despatches twice, CMG, Légion d'Honneur). *Address:* 3465 Drummond Street, Montreal; Bourlon House, St Genevieve de Pierrefonds, Canada. *Clubs:* Mount Royal, St James's, Montreal; York, Toronto.

Died 19 Jan. 1946.

MEIKLE, Lt-Col James Hamilton, DSO 1919; *b* 1876; *e s* of late John Meikle, JP, of Barskimming and Lochlibo; *m* 1903, Janet Armour, *d* of William Young Fleming, JP, of Elmhurst, Langbank; four *s*. *Educ:* privately. Served South Africa, 1900–01, in the ranks of the Imperial Yeomanry, and present at operations in Orange River Colony, including actions of Biddulphsberg and Wittebergen and operations in Cape Colony and Transvaal (Queen's medal with 4 clasps); appointed to command Ayrshire RHA 1913; Lt-Col 1917; European War, 1915–19—in Egypt and Palestine, commanding 18th RHA Brigade, present at Gaza, Beersheba, and Jaffa, and in France and Belgium commanding 256th (2nd Highland Brigade, RFA), 51st Division (despatches twice, DSO, French Croix de Guerre avec palm); appointed to command 187th Brigade, RFA, Rhine Army; is a Member of the King's Bodyguard for Scotland; Hon. Secretary for the Clackmannan and Kinross Branch of the Scottish Branch British Red Cross Society; JP; DL County of Clackmannan, 1939. *Recreations:* shooting, fishing. *Address:* Brankstone, Bogside Station, by Alloa, Clackmannanshire. *T:* Newmills 34.

Died 5 Feb. 1941.

MELCHETT, 2nd Baron *cr* 1928, of Landford; **Henry Mond;** Bt *cr* 1910, Hon. Colonel 27th Regiment RA; Director of International Nickel Company of Canada, Ltd, etc.; Trustee of the Ramsay Memorial Fellowship; *b* London, 10 May 1898; *o s* of 1st Baron and Violet (DBE 1920) (*d* 1945), *d* of James Henry Goetze, and *g d* of late John Bentley; S father, 1930; *m* 1920, Amy Gwen Wilson, Klerksdorp, Transvaal; one *s* one *d*. *Educ:* Winchester. Served in South Wales Borderers in France, 1915–18 (wounded, 1916); MP (L) Isle of Ely, 1923–24; (C) East Toxteth Division of Liverpool, 1929–30; Deputy Chm. Imperial Chemical Industries, Ltd, 1940–47. *Publications:* Why the Crisis, 1931; Modern Money, 1932; Thy Neighbour, 1936. *Recreations:* hunting and polo. *Heir: s* Hon. Julian Edward Alfred Mond, Sub-Lieut RNVR [*b* 9 Jan. 1925; *m* 1947, Sonia Elizabeth, *er d* of Lt-Col R. H. Graham, 21 Emperor's Gate, SW; one *s* (*b* 24 Feb. 1948). Eton]. *Address:* 50 Grosvenor Square, W1. *TA:* Mondenry Parl, London. *T:* Grosvenor 4377. *Club:* Carlton.

Died 22 Jan. 1949.

MELCHETT, Violet, Lady, DBE 1920; *d* of late James Henry Goetze, and *g d* of late John Bentley; *m* 1894, 1st Baron Melchett of Landford (*d* 1930); one *s* two *d*. Interested in politics, first Liberal, and since 1928, when her husband joined the Conservative party she became a Conservative; a pioneer in Welfare work in Wales;

Chairman of the Chelsea Health Society, and now Chairman of the Violet Melchett Infant Welfare Centre, which combines an Infant Welfare Centre, Day Nursery, and Mothercraft Home in one building, which, with the land, was the gift of Lord Melchett; Chairman of the Ladies Association of the Infants' Hospital; Chairman of Ladies' Association of St George's Hospital; Vice-President of the Sun Babies Nursery, Hoxton; a President of Queen Mary's London Needlework Guild; Lady President of the Chelsea Branch of the League of Mercy; Freeman of the Borough of Chelsea; Member of the Executive of the Mothercraft Training Society, Highgate; Governor of St George's Hospital and Governor of the Infants' Hospital, Vincent Square; President of a War Supply Depot at 35 Lowndes Square, SW, since 1939; Sister Commander of St John of Jerusalem. *Address:* 35 Lowndes Square, SW1. *T:* Sloane 4973. *Clubs:* Ladies' Carlton, Forum.

Died 25 Sept. 1945.

MELDON, Lt-Col Philip Albert, DSO 1916; late RFA; Chairman and Managing Director, Burns, Oates & Washbourne, 1932–39; Senior Intelligence Officer Home Office, 1940; Special Employment Foreign Office, 1940; *b* 1874; *e s* of late Sir Albert Meldon, DL; *m* 1925, Hon. Albreda Bewicke-Copley, *sister* of 5th Baron Cromwell. *Educ:* Beaumont College; Dublin University, MA. Joined RFA, 1900; served South African War, 1900–02 (Queen's medal 2 clasps, King's medal 2 clasps); Prof. of Artillery and Tactics at Royal Military College, Canada, 1913–14; served European War in France, the Dardanelles and Egypt (wounded thrice, despatches, DSO); served with Inter-Allied Commission of Control, Germany, 1919–24; Commandant RA Training Centre, India, 1927–28; retired pay, 1929; represented Ireland at football and cricket. *Address:* 20 Grosvenor Square, W1. *Clubs:* Naval and Military, MCC.

Died 8 April 1942.

MELHUISH, Alderman Sir Charles W., Kt 1936; JP; retired builder and contractor; *b* 18 June 1860; *s* of William and Jane Melhuish; *m* 1937, Mrs E. M. Moore (*d* 1939). *Educ:* Canton Church Schools and Science and Art Schools, Cardiff. Apprenticed in Building Trade, 1876, and engaged in it until 1894, when opened up on own account; retired in 1929; held office in Cardiff Conservative Association since 1886; Member of Cardiff Board of Guardians, 1901 till their ceasing in 1930; Member of Cardiff City Council since 1916; Alderman since 1922; Deputy Lord Mayor, 1925–26; Lord Mayor, 1931–32. *Recreations:* none at present, Rugby football in younger days. *Address:* 35 Teilo Street, Cardiff. *Club:* Riverside Conservative Cardiff.

Died 17 April 1946.

MELLOR, Sir Frank, Kt 1936; BA; LLB; *b* 15 April 1863; 5th *s* of late Wright Mellor, DL, JP, of Cote Royd, Huddersfield; *m* 4th *d* of William Camac, Philadelphia, USA; three *s* one *d*. *Educ:* St John's College, Cambridge (Exhibitioner). Called to Bar, Inner Temple, 1886; joined North Eastern Circuit and West Riding Yorkshire Sessions; Registrar in Bankruptcy of the High Court of Justice, 1917–36. *Address:* 53 Victoria Road, Kensington, W8. *T:* Western 5017. *Club:* Reform.

Died 2 Feb. 1941.

MELLOR, Sir George, Kt 1921; JP. Chairman, Central Fund, King's Lancashire 1915–19; Military Convalescent Hospital; Chairman of the County Fund, King's Lancashire Convalescent Centre; has devoted himself to the development of hospital work, particularly in regard to ex-Service men; Hon. Life Governor Royal National Life Boat Institution; President St Anne's-on-Sea War Memorial Hospital, etc. *Address:* Grand Hotel, St Anne's-on-Sea.

Died 24 Feb. 1947.

MELLOR, Brig.-Gen. Sir Gilbert, KBE 1923, CB 1918; CMG 1916; KC 1920; *b* 1872; *e s* of late Sir James Mellor; *m* 1911, Isabel, *d* of late Henry F. Makins. *Educ:* Charterhouse; Trinity Hall, Cambridge (Scholar, BA, LLB). Barrister-at-law; served S African War, 1900; European War, 1914–18 (despatches, CMG, CB, Chevalier, Legion of Honour); Sec., Royal Commission Martial Law in S Africa, 1902; British Agent, Venezuelan Claims Commission, 1903; Deputy Judge Advocate-General, 1914–32; JP, Kent (Chairman, Bearsted Bench); Deputy Chairman West Kent Quarter Sessions since 1944. *Address:* Ulcombe Place, Maidstone. *T:* Ulcombe 232. *Clubs:* United University, MCC.

Died 16 April 1947.

MELLOR, Wing-Comdr Harry Manners, MVO 1936; Staff College, Camberley; *b* 30 March 1903; 2nd *s* of late Salisbury Manners Mellor, St Helens House, St Helens, Isle of Wight; *m* 1935, Diana Marian Wyld; one *s* one *d*. *Educ:* Rugby School; RAF College, Cranwell. Pilot Officer, 1923; Squadron-Leader, 1936; at Air Ministry, 1930–33; Air Equerry to Prince of Wales, 1933–36; Officer Commanding 810 (TSR) Squadron, 1936–39. *Recreations:* sailing, squash rackets (Manager of US and Canadian tour of Jester Club), Hon. Secretary RAF Squash Rackets, 1929–36; shooting, golf. *Address:* White Cottage, Eversley, Hants. *Clubs:* RAF; Bembridge Sailing; Island Sailing.

Died 26 May 1940.

MELLOR, William; Member Daily Herald Staff; *b* Crewe, 20 July 1888; *s* of William Mellor, Unitarian Minister; *m* 1919, Helen Edna Thomson; one *s*. *Educ:* Elementary School; Willaston School; Exeter College, Oxford. Secretary of the Fabian Research Department, 1913; joined staff of then Daily Herald, 1913; served on the paper when it became a weekly during the war as Industrial Correspondent; then employed on post-war Daily Herald in various capacities; Editor, 1926–31; Assistant Managing Editor Odhams Press, Ltd, 1931–36; Editor, The Tribune, 1937–38; Editor, Town and County Councillor, 1936–40. *Publications:* Direct Action; The Meaning of Industrial Freedom (with G. D. H. Cole); The Claim of the Unemployed; The Cooperative Movement and the Fight for Socialism; Workers' Control in Industry (ed. with G. D. H. Cole). *Recreations:* cricket-watching and walking. *Address:* 5 The Croft, Primrose Gardens, NW3. *T:* Primrose 0488. *Club:* Trade Union.

Died 8 June 1942.

MELVILLE, Col Charles Henderson, CMG 1918; MB, CM Edinburgh, DPH London; *b* 20 May 1863; *s* of Swinton S. Melville, BCS, and Charlotte, *d* of Robert Cadell, of Ratho, Midlothian; *m* 1st, 1893, Anne Cecilia, *d* of W. E. Musson, MD, Clitheroe; 2nd, 1901, Margaret, *d* of Rev. G. Dickson, Coulsdon; one *d*; 3rd, 1908, Ruth, *d* of Charles Pearce Serocold, Taplow; three *s* one *d*. *Educ:* Uppingham; Edinburgh University. Joined Army Medical Service, 1886; served in India till 1906; served Hazara campaign, 1888 (medal with clasp); Sanitary Officer, Madras Command and Burma, 1902; Sanitary Officer, Army Headquarters, India, 1905; Sanitary Expert, Army Medical Advisory Board, War Office, 1906; Professor Military Hygiene, Royal Army Medical College, 1908; Assistant Director Medical Services 1st Army Central Force (Home Defence), 1915; Sanitary Adviser to Principal Director Medical Services, MEF, 1915–16; ADMS (Sanitary) EEF, 1916; Sanitary Officer, Aldershot Command, 1917; retired, 1919. *Publications:* Military Hygiene and Sanitation, 1912; Handbook of Hygiene (Davies and Melville), 1913; Historical Section, System of Syphilis, vol. vi; The Life of Gen. the Rt Hon. Sir Redvers Buller, VC, 1923. *Recreations:* fishing, geology, archæology. *Address:* c/o Holt and Co., Kirkland House, Whitehall, SW1.

Died 8 June 1943.

MELVILLE, Maj.-Gen. Charles William Francis, CB 1935; MB, ChB (Edin.); FRCS (Edin.); IMS, retired; *b* 27 March 1877; 8th *c* of late Francis S. Melville, Edinburgh; unmarried. *Educ:* Edinburgh Collegiate School; Edinburgh University. First Commission in the Indian Medical Service, 1901; Medical Officer of the 9th Bengal Lancers (Hodson's Horse), 1904–14; during this period held officiating appointments in the Lahore Medical College (1907 and 1908); Staff Surgeon to Force H. Quarters during the Abor Expedition, 1911–12 (despatches); during European War, 1914–18 was at Army Headquarters, India, and later joined the Egyptian Expeditionary Force, commanding a Field Ambulance, with the 53rd Division; substantive Colonel, 1929, ADMS, Kohat District, 1929–32; Hon. Physician to the King, 1931; DDMS Army Headquarters, India, 1932–33; Major-General, 1933; DDMS Eastern Command, India, 1933–37; retired 1937. *Address:* c/o Grindlay's Bank, 54 Parliament Street, SW1; 41 Putney Hill, SW15. *T:* Putney 6095. *Club:* Naval and Military.

Died 14 April 1949.

MELVIN, George Spencer, MD; Professor of Physiology and Dean of Medical Faculty, Queen's University, Kingston, Ont, since 1919; *b* Montrose, Scotland, 7 Oct. 1887; *s* of William Fothringham Melvin and Jane Brownlee; *m* 1919, Isabel, *d* of Rev. J. S. Stewart, Aberdeen; one *s* one *d*. *Educ:* Montrose Academy; Aberdeen University; MB (Hons), 1909; John Murray Medallist; MD (Hons), 1912. Lecturer Experimental Physiology, University, Aberdeen, 1909–14; Major, RAMC (T) with 51st Division France, 1914–19; Lecturer Experimental Physiology, Aberdeen, 1919. *Publications:* numerous articles on Blood Pressure. *Recreations:* golf, skiing, motoring. *Address:* 127 King Street W, Kingston, Ont. *T:* 95 F. *Club:* Cataraqui Golf (Kingston).

Died 14 Sept. 1949.

MENARY, Surg. Captain John, CB 1917; RN, retired, 1919; MD, MCh, RUI; *b* 12 Jan. 1865; *e s* of late John Menary, Co. Armagh; *m* Constance, *y d* of late James Bell, Leeson Park, Dublin. Staff-Surgeon, 1898; Fleet-Surgeon, 1902. *Recreations:* golfing, fishing, walking. *Address:* Fareham, Hants.

Died 10 Dec. 1941.

MENDL, Sir Sigismund Ferdinand, KBE 1918; Chairman of the National Discount Co. and Director of the London Life Association, etc; *b* 2 Dec. 1866; *e s* of late Ferdinand Mendl; *m* 1888, Frances (*d* 1943), *d* of late A. H. Moses; two *s*. *Educ:* Harrow; University College, Oxford. BA 1887; 2nd class Honours Jurisprudence; MA 1890. Barr Inner Temple; President of the London Corn Trade Association, 1909–12 and 1915–19; Member of the War Office Advisory Committee on Army Contracts, 1915–18; of the Royal Commission on Wheat Supplies until 1920; contested Isle of Wight *versus* Sir R. Webster, 1892; and Plymouth, 1895; MP Plymouth, 1898–1900. *Address:* 2 Weymouth Street, W1. *Club:* Oxford and Cambridge.

Died 17 July 1945.

MENINSKY, Bernard; Instructor in Drawing, LCC Central School of Arts and Crafts; formerly at Westminster School of Art, and Oxford City School of Art; *b* 25 July 1891; *s* of Isaac and Ann Meninsky; *m* 1927, Nora Barczinsky; two *s*. *Educ:* St Simon's School, Liverpool; Liverpool School of Art; Slade School of Art, London. Paintings and drawings in Tate Gallery, British Museum, National Gallery, Dublin, Manchester Art Gallery, Bradford, Aberdeen and other provincial Art Galleries, National Galleries of Adelaide and Melbourne, Australia, and in Minnesota, Mass, USA Official War Artist in European War, 1914–18. Represented in many international art exhibitions in Europe and America.

Publications: Drawings of Mother and Child, 1920; Illustrations to Milton, 1947. *Recreation:* music. *Address:* 63 Canfield Gardens, NW6. *T:* Maida Vale 2555.

Died 12 Feb. 1950.

MENON, Sir Konkoth R.; *see* Ramunni Menon.

MENZIES, Alexander John Pople, OBE 1918; Advocate; *b* Dumbartonshire, 6 July 1863; *m* 1889, Elizabeth Bannerman (*d* 1938) 4th *d* of John Davidson, Ravenswood, Inverness. *Educ:* Inverness Academy; University of Edinburgh; University of London; University of Brussels. Admitted a Member of the Faculty of Advocates, 1886; Sheriff-Substitute of Caithness, Orkney, and Zetland at Lerwick, 1914–19; Stirling, Dumbarton and Clackmannan at Dumbarton, 1919–34. *Publications:* Local Government Act 1889, 1889; 1st volume of the Law of Scotland affecting Trustees, 1891; 2nd volume, 1897; 2nd edition in one volume, 1913. *Address:* Highwood, Frogston Road West, Edinburgh 10. *T:* 71373. *Clubs:* Scottish Liberal, Edinburgh.

Died 3 April 1943.

MENZIES, Col Charles T.; formerly commanding the South-East of Scotland RGA (Berwickshire Militia); commanded 2/7th Argyll and Sutherland Highlanders, and subsequently on service in France; DL; JP Berwickshire; *b* 1858; *y s* of late John Menzies, Edinburgh; *m* 1900, Helen Frances, *d* of late John Aitken of Gartcows; one *s* one *d. Educ:* Edinburgh. Formerly Master Berwickshire Foxhounds; a Director of John Menzies & Co., Ltd, Edinburgh. *Recreation:* field sports. *Address:* Kames, Duns, Berwickshire. *TA:* Leitholm. *Clubs:* Boodle's; New, Edinburgh.

Died 15 Sept. 1943.

MENZIES, Sir Frederick Norton Kay, KBE 1932; Hon. LLD (Edin.), 1933; MD, FRCP (Edin. and London); DPH, FRSE; KHP 1937–41; KGStJ; late MOH and School MO, LCC; *b* 2 Nov. 1875; 2nd *s* of late John Menzies, CE, of Menaibank, Carnarvon, N Wales; *m* Harriet May, *e d* of late E. Honoratus Lloyd, KC; one *s* one *d. Educ:* University, Edinburgh; University, Vienna; and University, Berlin. Resident House Physician at the Royal Infirmary, Edinburgh; The Hospital for Consumption, Brompton; The Children's Hospital, Great Ormond Street; The Western Fever Hospital, Fulham, etc. Demonstrator and Lecturer, Public Health Department, University College, London; Examiner, Public Health and State Medicine, London Conjoint Colleges and Liverpool University, etc.; late Medical Adviser, United Services Fund; late Director of the Hospital and Medical Services Department; Joint Council of the Order of St John of Jerusalem and British Red Cross Society; Member of the Voluntary Hospital Commission; Representative of the Ministry of Health, Central Midwives Board; Member of the Council of the National Association for the Prevention of Tuberculosis; Member of the Trevethin Committee of Inquiry on Venereal Diseases, 1922–23; Member of Departmental Committee (Ministry of Health on Training and Employment of Midwives), 1927–28; Member of Advisory Committee (Home Office) on Scientific Investigation of Crime, 1935–36; Member of the Inter. Dept Committee of Enquiry into the Nursing Services, 1937–38–1939; of General Nursing Council, 1937–42; Rep. for N Wales of War Organisation of the BRCS and Order of St John, 1940–45; late Chairman, Central Council for Maternity and Child Welfare; Member: Council of King Edward's Hosp. Fund; Governing Body British Postgrad. Med. Federation and Postgrad. Med. Sch., Hammersmith; Medical Advisory Council, Nuffield Provincial Hospitals Trust, since 1940; Cttees of Florence Nightingale School of Nursing and St Giles's Hospital for British Lepers; Chairman: Queen Mary's Hosp., Roehampton; British Hosp., Port Said, and Home Ambulance Service Cttee of BRCS and St John; FRSM; Fellow of the Society of MOH; FRSanI; Cullen

Prize, RCP, Edinburgh, 1934; Bisset-Hawkins Gold Medal, RCP, London, 1941. *Publications:* numerous reports and papers upon Public Health Problems and the Voluntary Hospitals of Great Britain; Annual Reports to LCC on Public Health of London, 1925–1940. *Address:* 41 Melbury Court, W8. *Clubs:* Athenæum, Hurlingham, Roehampton; Royal Welsh Yacht.

Died 14 May 1949.

MENZIES, William George S.; *see* Steuart-Menzies.

MERCER, Alexander Warren, CBE 1924; *b* 1871; retired Indian Imperial Police Service; *e s* of late Warren Herklots Mercer and *g s* of late Maj.-Gen. Thomas Warren Mercer, BS Corps; *m* Justina (Dorothy) Christie (*d* 1939). *Educ:* Aldenham School. Entered Indian Police, 1892; Officiating Political Officer Wana, Waziristan, 1895–98; Political Assistant, Kohat, and Commandant Samana Rifles, 1908; Principal, Police Training School, 1911; Superintendent Police CID (Political) Punjab, 1916; Lieut-Col Commanding 4/30th Punjabis, 1916; Deputy-Inspector General Police, 1920; King's Police Medal, 1916. *Publication:* The War-Game Bellum, Adopted by AHQ India and approved by War Office, London. *Address:* Aldie, Elmsleigh Park, Paignton, S Devon. *T:* 5229. *Club:* Paignton.

Died 13 Nov. 1943.

MERCER, Col Herbert; *b* Sandling Place, Maidstone, Jan. 1862; *s* of Richard Mercer of Sandling Place and East Farleigh, Kent, and Madeline, *d* of Major Castle; *m* Elizabeth (*d* 1929), *d* of Thos Bower of Stradishall Place, Suffolk. *Educ:* Harrow; Trinity Coll., Cambridge. Joined 3rd Dragoon Guards, 1884; completed command, 1908; served S Africa; European War. MP (U) Sudbury Division of West Suffolk, 1922–23. *Club:* Cavalry.

Died 8 Feb. 1944.

MERCER, John Swan, OBE 1920; KC, Scotland, 1933; Sheriff of Lanarkshire, 1933–37; *b* 26 Aug. 1867; *s* of late James Mercer, JP, farmer, of Southfield, Dalkeith, Midlothian; *m* 1907, Emily Maud, *d* of late James Maclean, Solicitor and County Clerk of Wigtown. *Educ:* Royal High School and University, Edinburgh. BL Edinburgh. Advocate, Scotland, 1899; appointed Counsel for Crown as *Ultimus Haeres*, 1911; Sheriff-Substitute of Caithness, Orkney and Shetland at Kirkwall, 1912–21; of Renfrew and Bute at Greenock, 1921–24; of Lanarkshire, 1924–33. *Address:* 34 Lygon Road, Edinburgh. *T:* 44579.

Died 7 Oct. 1947.

MERCER, Stephen Pascal, OBE 1943; BSc, NDA; Professor of Agricultural Botany, The Queen's University, Belfast, since 1924; Senior Technical Research Officer, Ministry of Agriculture, Northern Ireland, since 1928; *b* 1891; *y s* of Fred Mercer, landscape painter; *m* 1919, Constance, *d* of Rev. A. L. Davidson, Crailing. *Educ:* Brewood; Harper Adams. Lecturer in Agricultural Botany, Armstrong College, University of Durham, 1916; Assistant Director, Official Seed Testing Station for England and Wales, 1919; Head of Seed Testing and Plant Disease Division, Ministry of Agriculture, Northern Ireland, 1922. *Publications:* Survey of Seed Growing in England and Wales; Farm and Garden Seeds; pamphlets and articles. *Recreations:* gardening, ski-running. *Address:* Hanging Leaves, Carrickfergus, Co. Antrim. *T:* Carrickfergus 2237. *Club:* Farmers'.

Died 18 Aug. 1944.

MEREDITH, Hon. Mr Justice James Creed, KC, MA, LittD, MRIA; Judge of Supreme Court, Eire, since 1936; *s* of late Sir James C. Meredith, LLD; *m* Lorraine, *d* of Charles Percy, Weredale Park, Montreal; two *d. Educ:* Trinity College, Dublin (First Senior Moderator and large gold medallist). Judge of High Court, Irish Free State, 1924–36; Vice-President of the Supreme Saar Plebiscite Tribunal, 1934–35. *Publications:* Kant's

Critique of Æsthetic Judgment, 1912; Kant's Critique of Teleological Judgment, 1919; The Rainbow in the Valley, 1939. *Address:* Hopeton, Rathgar, Co. Dublin. *T:* Terenure, Dublin 95301. *Clubs:* Royal Irish Yacht, Kingstown.

Died 14 Aug. 1942.

MEREDYTH, Paymaster Rear-Adm. Charles Edward Hughes, CBE 1919; RN (retired); *b* 20 May 1861; *s* of Rev. T. E. Meredyth, Shropshire; *m* Eveline Violet (*d* 1948), *d* of Leslie Crawford, Bombay; one *s*. *Educ:* Atherstone; Denstone. Served European War, 1914–18 (despatches, CBE). *Address:* Greenways, Rowlands Castle, Hants. *T:* Rowlands Castle 273.

Died 15 March 1949.

MEREWETHER, Lt-Col John Walter Beresford, CIE 1916; Indian Army, retired; late Political Department, India; *b* 24 June 1867; *s* of late Col G. L. C. Merewether, RE; *m* 1924, Lylie Evelyn, *widow* of Major Hector Corbyn, and *d* of Mrs Aitchison, 80 Brook Street, W. *Educ:* Marlborough; Sandhurst. Entered Leinster Regiment, 1886; 43rd Gurkha Rifles, 1893; has been Resident at Aden and Kolhapur; served East Africa, 1901 (medal with clasp); Aden, 1903–04; European War, 1914–16 (CIE). *Publication:* (with the Earl of Birkenhead) The Indian Corps in France. *Recreations:* riding, shooting, billiards, cricket, etc. *Club:* Naval and Military.

Died 3 May 1942.

MERRETT, Sir Charles Edward, Kt 1934; CBE, 1929; VD, JP; Managing Director, Welch, Perrin and Co. Pty Ltd, Melbourne since 1915; Director of Temperance & General Mutual Life Assurance Society Ltd; Scottish Union & National Insurance Co.; O. Gilpin Ltd; Fowler Road Maintenance Co. Pty Ltd; *b* South Yarra, Vic., 1863; *s* of Samuel Headen and Sarah Ashton Merrett; *m* Annie Florence Slocombe; one *s* one *d*. *Educ:* Church of England Grammar School, Melbourne. Joined Welch Perrin and Co., 1880; partner 1890; retained at Head Quarters, Australian Army during War; has been Commanding Officer 10th, 11th, and 29th Light Horse Regiments; retired rank of Col; Pres. (32 years) Royal Agricultural Society, Victoria, from 1915; Vice-Pres. Nat. Rifle Assoc. England. Canned Fruits Board; Member State Employment Council; Commandant, Australian Rifle Team to Bisley, 1914, 1928 and 1937. *Address:* Welch Perrin and Co. Pty Ltd, Melbourne, Australia. *Clubs:* Athenæum, Naval and Military (Melbourne).

Died 11 Nov. 1948.

MERRIAM, John Campbell; President, Carnegie Institution of Washington, 1921–38, President Emeritus since 1939; palæontologist, educator, administrator; *b* Hopkinton, Ia, 20 Oct. 1869; *s* of Charles Edward Merriam and Margaret Campbell Kirkwood; *m* 1st, 1896, Ada Gertrude Little (*d* 1940), of Berkeley, Calif; three *s*; 2nd, 1941, Margaret Louise Webb. *Educ:* BS Lenox College, Ia; PhD, University of Munich, 1893; ScD Columbia Univ. 1921; Princeton University, 1922; Yale University, 1922; University of Pennsylvania, 1936; University of State of New York, 1937; Oregon State College, 1939; LLD Wesleyan University, 1922; University of California, 1924; New York University, 1926; University of Michigan, 1933; Harvard University, 1935; George Washington University, 1937; University of Oregon, 1939. Instructor Palæontology and Hist. Geology, 1894–99; Assistant Professor, 1899–1905; Associate Professor, 1905–12; Prof., 1912–20; Dean of the Faculties, 1920, University of Calif; Chairman National Research Council, 1919; Regent, Smithsonian Institution; Fellow, AAAS (Pres. Pacific Div., 1919–20); Geological Society of America (Pres. 1920); Am. Palæontological Society (Pres. 1917); Member numerous Academies of Sciences, etc.; Chairman Research Committee, California State Council of Defence, 1917–20; Commission du Parc National Albert; President Executive Committee Pan-

American Institute of Geog. and History, 1935–38; Congregationalist; Republican. *Publications:* many palæontological and other scientific papers since 1904. *Address:* Carnegie Institution of Washington, Washington, DC. *Clubs:* Cosmos, Washington; Century Association, New York; Commonwealth Club of California, San Francisco.

Died 30 Oct. 1945.

MERRIFIELD, Leonard Stanford, FRBS; sculptor; *b* Wyck Rissington, Gloucester, 1880; *s* of Thomas Merrifield and Isabella Matilda Stanford; *m* Catherine Muriel, *d* of late Colonel Sir Howard Melliss, KCSI; one *s*. *Educ:* at home; Cheltenham School of Art; City Guilds of London School of Art, Kennington; Royal Academy Schools (Landseer Scholarship and Armitage Prize); Mention Honorable Paris Salon. Has exhibited in the Royal Academy, Paris Salon, and other exhibitions since 1906. *Principal Works:* life-sized marble statue of Williams Pantycelyn (Cardiff City Hall); heroic bronze statue of Richard Trevithick Camborne; Monument including Colossal Statue of Lord Carson at Stormont, Belfast; memorials to Bishop Blunt in Scarborough and Hessle Parish Churches, to Mrs Studholme at York Minster, Hedd Wynn, Trawsfynydd; Charles Frohman; Memorial Fountain, Marlow; War Memorials at Merthyr Tydfil, Burnham, Tadcaster, Holywood, Comber, and Lurgan, also Northern Circuit War Memorial; War Memorial Panels at Newlyn and Merthyr Tydfil; many portrait busts and reliefs; is also a medallist; Regt Memorials to DCLI, Bodmin, and Royal Garhwal Rifles, India; Statuettes and Challenge Trophies, HAC, Royal Garhwal Rifles, etc. *Address:* 48 Glebe Place, Chelsea, SW3. *T:* Flaxman 8528. *Club:* Chelsea Arts.

Died 25 April 1943.

MERRIMAN, P. J., MA, LLD; President University College, Cork, since 1919; *b* 1877. Professor of History, 1909–19, and Registrar, 1915–19, University College, Cork; Pro-Vice-Chancellor, National University of Ireland. *Address:* University College, Cork.

Died Sept. 1943.

MERRIMAN, Roger Bigelow; Gurney Professor of History and Political Science, and Master Emeritus of Eliot House, Harvard University; *b* Boston, Mass, 24 May 1876; *s* of Daniel and Helen Bigelow Merriman; *m* 1904, Dorothea, *y d* of Henry W. and Frances Eliot Foote; two *s* two *d*. *Educ:* Harvard University (AB 1896, AM 1897, PhD 1902); Balliol college, Oxford (BLitt 1899, DLitt 1922); LLD (hon.) Glasgow, 1929; DLitt (Hon.) Cambridge, 1935; LHD (Hon.), Hobart College, Geneva, NY, 1942; Berlin and Paris. Harvard Lecturer at the French Provincial Universities, 1915; Assist Professor, 1908–18, Professor of History, Harvard University, 1918–29; Harvard Exchange Professor at the University of Paris, 1926; President of the Harvard (Alpha) chapter of the Phi Beta Kappa, 1927–28; David Murray Lecturer at University of Glasgow, 1937; Vice-Pres. of Massachusetts Historical Society; Chevalier de la Légion d'Honneur. *Publications:* Life and Letters of Thomas Cromwell, 1902; (ed.) Annals of the Emperor Charles V by Francisco López de Gómara, with an English translation, 1912; The Rise of the Spanish Empire, vols i and ii, 1918, vol iii, 1925, vol iv, 1934; Six Contemporaneous Revolutions, 1938; Suleiman the Magnificent, 1944. *Address:* 175 Brattle Street, Cambridge, Mass, USA. *T:* Tro. 0170. *Clubs:* Athenæum; Somerset, Boston.

Died 8 Sept. 1945.

MERRY DEL VAL, Marquis de, GCVO; Hon. LLD Cambridge; Fellow King's College, London; Hon. DCL Oxford; Hon. LLD Liverpool; GC Charles III, GG Isabella the Catholic, Crown of Belgium; Hafidian Order of Morocco; medals of Coronation of Alfonso XIII, Regency of Maria Cristina, and Queen Victoria's Diamond Jubilee; Corresponding Member of the Royal Academy of History, Madrid; *cr* Marquis by Royal decree of 9 July 1925; *b* London, 1864; *e s* of late Don Rafael Merry del Val, formerly Secretary of Legation in London, Ambassador in Vienna and to the Holy See, and Josephine de Zulueta, *d* of 2nd Count de Torre Diaz; *m* 1901, Maria de Alzola y Gonzalez de Castejon, *d* of HE Don Pablo de Alzola, Chamberlain to the King of Spain, Member of Spanish Senate, etc.; two *s*. *Educ:* Beaumont College; Saint Michel, Brussels; Louvain University. Entered Spanish Diplomatic Service, 1882; Attaché and Secretary of Embassy in Brussels, London, Vienna, Rome, and Foreign Office, Madrid; Assistant Private Secretary to the King of Spain; Minister Resident, Chief of the Commercial Department, Spanish Foreign Office; Envoy Extraordinary and Minister Plenipotentiary in Tangier and Brussels; Member of Special Missions to Vienna, 1895; Moscow, 1896, and London, 1897; Spanish Ambassador in London, 1913–31; was Chamberlain to the King of Spain. *Recreations:* riding, lawn-tennis.

Died 26 May 1943.

MESS, Henry Adolphus, BA, PhD; Reader in Sociology in the University of London since 1935; Director of Studies to National Council of Social Service since 1942; *b* 9 June 1884; *s* of Henry Adolphus Mess and Mary Ann Thornton; *m* 1920, Sofie, *d* of Captain H. N. Hansen; two *s* one *d*. *Educ:* Bancroft's School, Woodford; Birkbeck and King's Colleges; Research Scholar of London School of Economics. Secretary of Mansfield House University Settlement, 1912–19; Social Study Secretary of Student Christian Movement, 1919–24; Lecturer in Social Science to Lancashire and Yorkshire Congregational Unions, 1924–25; Director of Bureau of Social Research for Tyneside, 1925–29; Director of Tyneside Council of Social Service, 1929–35. *Publications:* Casual Labour at the Docks, 1916; The Facts of Poverty, 1920; Studies in the Christian Gospel for Society, 1923; Factory Legislation and its Administration, 1926; Industrial Tyneside, 1928; Social Groups in Modern England, 1939; Social Structure, 1942. *Address:* Bedford College for Women (Wartime Address: Cambridge).

Died 23 Jan. 1944.

MESTON, 1st Baron *cr* 1919, of Agra and Dunottar; **James Scorgie Meston,** KCSI 1911; CSI 1908; LLD (Aberdeen), 1913 (Edinburgh), 1933; Rede Lecturer, Cambridge, 1920; MD hon., Zürich, 1929; VD 1914; Chancellor of Aberdeen Uniersity, 1928; Hon. Fellow of University College, London; FRSL; *b* Old Aberdeen, 12 June 1865; *m* 1891, Jeanie, CBE (a Dame of Grace, St John of Jerusalem), *o d* of late James M'Donald; one *s*. *Educ:* Grammar School and University, Aberdeen; Balliol College, Oxford. Entered ICS 1885; Financial Secretary to Government, United Provinces, 1899–1903; Adviser to Governments of Cape Colony and Transvaal on civil service reform, 1904–06; Secretary to Finance Dept, Government of India, 1906–12; Lieut-Governor, United Provinces, Agra and Oudh, 1912–18; a representative of India, Imperial War Cabinet and Conference, 1917; Finance Member of Governor-General's Council, 1919; retired, 1919; formerly Vice-Chairman of the Supervisory Commission, League of Nations; Knight of Grace, St John of Jerusalem, 1916; President Royal Statistical Society, 1932; Pres. Liberal Party Organisation, since 1936; Received freedom of the cities of London, 1917, Manchester, 1917, Aberdeen, 1935. *Publication:* Nationhood for India, 1931. *Heir: s* Hon. Dougall Meston. *Address:* Hurst Place, Cookham Dene, Berks. *T:* Bourne End 162. *Clubs:* Athenæum, Reform, National Liberal.

Died 7 Oct. 1943.

METCALFE, Rev. Edmund Lionel; Rector of St Vedast, Foster Lane, since 1935; Prebendary of St Paul's, 1923. *Educ:* Eton; Christ Church, Oxford; Leeds Clergy School. Curate of Holy Trinity, Leeds, 1893–96; Eton

Mission, Hackney Wick, 1896–1900; Vicar, 1900–06; Vicar of St Pancras, 1906–35, and Rural Dean. *Address:* 16 Brunswick Gardens, Kensington, W8. *T:* Bayswater 2250.

Died 26 June 1941.

METCALFE, Brig.-Gen. Sydney Fortescue, CMG 1918; DSO 1915; RFA retired; *b* 1 April 1870; *m* 1921, Kathleen, 4th *d* of late Samuel Perry, JP, DL, of Woodrooff, Clonmel. Entered Army, 1889; Captain, 1900; Major, 1906; Lt-Col 1914; Instructor, 1st class, School of Gunnery, 1908–12; served S African War, 1899–1900 (Queen's medal 4 clasps); European War, 1914–18 (wounded 1914, despatches four times, DSO, Bt Col, CMG, Chevalier Legion of Honour); temp. Brig.-Gen. June 1916; retired pay, 1923.

Died 9 May 1948.

METCALFE, Sir Theophilus John Massie, 7th Bt *cr* 1802; *b* 19 June 1866; *s* of late Charles Theophilus Metcalfe, CSI, and Ellen Georgina Babington, *d* of late Rev. Benjamin Peile; *S* cousin, 1928; *m* 1925, Evna Vivyenne Celia (Suzanne), *d* of W. M. Wright, NZ; no *c*. *Educ:* Eton; Royal Agricultural College, Cirencester, MRAC. Civil Service, Andaman Isles and Burma. *Heir: nephew* Theophilus John [*b* 15 Oct. 1916; *s* of late Lt-Col E. D. T. Metcalfe, OBE, MC, Indian Army]. *Club:* Royal Automobile.

Died 11 Sept. 1950.

METCALFE-SMITH, Lt-Col Bertram, CBE 1919; *b* 1863. Served South Africa, 1900–02 (Queen's medal with two clasps, King's medal with two clasps); European War, 1914–19 (despatches, CBE). *Address:* Shore House, Swanage.

Died 25 Nov. 1944.

METFORD, Col Sir Francis Killigrew Seymour, KCB 1938; CB 1934; OBE 1919; VD, TD; DL, JP, Chairman Gloucestershire Territorial Association, 1927–38; late Hon. Colonel 66th Brigade RA, TA; Chairman Priday Metford and Co. Ltd, Millers; *b* 19 Feb. 1863; *s* of Dr Joseph Seymour Metford and Emily Francis Wait; *m* 1889, Agnes Howard *d* of Rev. H. Tripp, Rector of Winford, Somerset; one *s* two *d*. *Educ:* Royal Naval College, Southsea; Clifton College. *Recreations:* hunting till recently, golf. *Address:* Fox Elms, Robinswood Hill, Gloucester. *T:* Gloucester 3300. *Clubs:* County, Gloucester.

Died 29 Jan. 1946.

MEWS, Arthur, CMG 1918; JP; Member and Secretary, Board of Governors, Memorial University College, St John's, 1936 (Secretary only, since 1946); *b* St John's, 8 April 1864; *s* of George W. Mews and Frances Catherine Kelson; *m* 1892, Mabel (*d* 1945), *d* of Hon. J. B. Woods, PMG; one *s* three *d*. *Educ:* Methodist College, St John's. Thirteen years with J. & W. Stewart, general merchants, of Greenock, Scotland; Accountant in Government Telegraphs, 1893; Clerk to the Government Financial Secretary, 1894; Financial Clerk, Colonial Secretary's Office, 1895; Deputy Colonial Secretary, 1898; Registrar of Joint-Stock Companies, 1899; Censor of Telegraph Cables and Wireless Stations for duration of the War; Member of St John's Defence Committee, 1915; Deputy Clerk to Executive Council, 1921; Deputy Secretary of State since 1931; Deputy Press Censor, 1915; Member of the Rhodes Scholarship Selection Committee, 1919, 1929 and since 1930; Secretary for Home Affairs, St John's, 1934; retired, 1935; Secretary, Fisheries Enquiry Commission, 1935; Chairman of Executive Board of Governors, United Church and Presbyterian College; Member of the Methodist Conference; Member of Conference and of Board of Foreign Missions and Board of Publications of the United Church of Canada; Chairman of Educational Advisory Council of the Newfoundland Conference of the United Church of Canada; Organist, Cochrane Street Centennial Church, St John's, since 1883; Past

Grand Director of Music (Hon. SC, Masonic); Grand Organist of District Grand Lodge, NF (Masonic). *Recreations:* fishing, music, golf. *Address:* 50 Rennie's Mill Road, St John's, Newfoundland; Cherry Row, Manuels, CB. *Clubs:* Rotary, Round Table, Masonic (St John's, Newfoundland).

Died 26 Dec. 1947.

MEXBOROUGH, 6th Earl of, *cr* 1766; **John Henry Savile;** DL, JP; Baron Pollington, 1753; Viscount Pollington, 1766; *b* 27 Sept. 1868; *s* of 4th Earl and Agnes Louisa Elizabeth, *d* of John Raphael; *S half-brother* 1916; *m* 1905, Hon. Marjorie Knatchbull-Hugessen, *d* of 2nd Baron Brabourne; one *s* four *d. Educ:* Eton. Captain, Remounts, with BEF in France; late 2nd Lieut 2nd Life Guards. *Heir: s* Viscount Pollington. *Address:* Arden Hall, Helmsley, Yorks; Methley Park, Leeds. *Club:* Travellers'.

Died 16 Sept. 1945.

MEXBOROUGH, Anne, Countess of; *d* of late Rev. A. H. Belcher of Fasque, Kincardineshire; *m* 1st, 1900, G. B. Ritchie (from whom she obtained a divorce); 2nd, 1916, 5th Earl of Mexborough (*d* 1916). *Address:* 10 Hans Place, SW1.

Died 11 Feb. 1943.

MEYER, Lt-Col Charles Hardwick Louw; Indian Medical Service (retd); *b* Grahamstown, South Africa, 19 Nov. 1859; *m* 1898, Mary Scott (*d* 1928), *d* of T. M. Cotgrave; two *s. Educ:* Grahamstown, Queenstown, and Bloemfontein, South Africa; Guy's Hospital, SE MD, BS (London), with honours; MRCS; 1st place in competitive examination for the Indian Medical Service, Feb. 1887; 1st place in examination at the Army Medical School, Netley, July 1887—winning Herbert Prize and Ranald Martin Memorial Gold Medal. Special recommendation from Secretary of State for India to the Government of India; at different periods Professor of Physiology, Hygiene, Pathology, and Medicine, Grant Medical College, Bombay; late Principal, Grant Medical College, Bombay; 2nd in Command Lady Hardinge Hospital for Indian Soldiers, Brockenhurst, Hants, 1914–16; Surgeon, Gouldas Tejpal Hospital, Bombay, 1916–17; Consulting Physician, Waziristan Field Force, 1917; Consulting Physician, War Hospitals, Southern Army, India, 1917–19; Member of Medical Board, India Office, London, 1921. *Publications:* several minor papers on medical subjects. *Address:* c/o Thos Cook & Son (Bankers Ltd), Berkeley Street, W1. *Clubs:* Oriental; Byculla, Bombay.

Died 30 Aug. 1942.

MEYERSTEIN, Sir Edward William, Kt 1938; JP; retired Stockbroker; Member of London Stock Exchange; *b* 17 Oct. 1863; *s* of William and Henrietta Meyerstein; *m* 1886, Jessy Louise Solomon (*d* 1940); one *s. Educ:* University College School. High Sheriff of Kent, 1937–38 and 1941–42. *Recreations:* golf, shooting, fishing. *Address:* Morant's Court, Sevenoaks, Kent. *T:* Sevenoaks 986. *Club:* MCC.

Died 1 Feb. 1942.

MEYNELL, Francis Hugo Lindley, DSO 1917; JP; DL; *b* 14 April 1880; *s* of late Hon. Frederick Meynell (Wood) and Lady Mary Meynell (author of Sunshine and Shadows over a Long Life, 1933); *m* Lady Dorothy Legge, *e d* of 6th Earl of Dartmouth, PC, GCVO; two *s* two *d. Educ:* Eton. Twice contested borough of Barrow-in-Furness in Unionist interest; served European War, 1914–17 (DSO, wounded). *Recreations:* golf, shooting, and fishing. *Address:* Hoar Cross, Burton-on-Trent. *TA:* Hoarcross. *Clubs:* Brooks's, Bath.

Died 16 Dec. 1941.

MEYNELL, Brig.-Gen. Godfrey, CMG 1918; late commanding 2nd King's Shropshire Light Infantry; *b* 19 Aug. 1870; *m* Violet, *e d* of George Cammell, Brookfield, Hathersage; one *s* three *d. Educ:* Winchester; Sandhurst. Served in Tirah Campaign, 1897–98; Staff

College, 1901–02; European War, 1914–18 (wounded, despatches four times); Brig.-Gen. commanding 171st Infantry Brig. (CMG); AAG British Army of the Rhine, 1924–26; retired pay, 1926. *Address:* Meynell Langley, Derby. *T:* Kirk Langley 207. *Clubs:* Army and Navy; Derbyshire County, Derby.

Died 1 Feb. 1943.

MEYNELL, Wilfrid, CBE 1943; author; *b* 1852; *m* 1877, Alice Thompson (*d* 1922), poet and essayist. *Publications:* Journals and Journalism (under *nom de plume* John Oldcastle); Benjamin Disraeli: an Unconventional Biography, republished as The New Disraeli; Come and See; Aunt Sarah and the War; Who Goes There?; Verses and Reverses; Rhymes with Reason; editor of the collected Works of Francis Thompson and of Alice Meynell; formerly contributor to Nineteenth Century, Contemporary Review, Athenæum, Academy, Saturday Review. *Recreation:* serendipity. *Address:* 47 Palace Court, W2. *T:* Bayswater 2847; Greatham, Pulborough, Sussex.

Died 20 Oct. 1948.

MEYRICK, Rev. Frederick J., MA; Prebendary of Chichester Cathedral since 1931; Proctor in the Lower House of Convocation (Canterbury) since 1919; *b* 11 Dec. 1871; *s* of Rev. F. Meyrick, Rector of Blickling and Hon. Canon of Lincoln Cathedral; *m* 1902, Helen (*d* 1940), *d* of late Sir William Richmond, KCB, RA; four *d. Educ:* Felsted; New College, Oxford; Salisbury Theological College. Deacon, 1895; Priest, 1896; Assistant Curate, St Mary's, Woolwich, 1895–1901; Vicar of St Peter Mancroft, Norwich, 1901–29; Rural Dean of Norwich, 1912–29; Vicar and Rural Dean of Hove, 1929–43; Hon. Canon of Norwich Cathedral, 1915–30; Chairman of the Norwich Bd of Guardians, 1904–08; for many years regular contributor to the press. *Publications:* Fifteenth-Century Glass in St Peter Mancroft, Norwich, 1911; Pathos and Humour in a Great Window, 1920; Round about Norfolk and Suffolk, 1925; Hove and the Parish Church, 1933; Life in the Bush 1840–1847, 1939. *Recreation:* gardening. *Address:* 2 Pembroke Avenue, Hove.

Died 10 Jan. 1945.

MEYRICK, Walter Henry, CBE 1942; late Secretary Behar Planters' Association Ltd and Manager Estates; *b* 7 Nov. 1880; *s* of J. Meyrick and A. Huthwaite; *m* Ailsa Margaret France Mackenzie; one *d* (one *s* killed on active service, RN, 1941). *Educ:* Tonbridge. Indigo Planter; retired, 1946. *Address:* PO Box 265, Umtali, Southern Rhodesia.

Died 25 Aug. 1950.

MEYSEY-THOMPSON, Ernest Claude; JP; MP (U) Handsworth Div. Staffs, 1906–22; *b* 1859; 6th *s* of Sir H. S. Meysey-Thompson, 1st Bt; *m* 1894, Alice, 2nd *d* and co-heir of late Col J. Joicey of Newton Hall, Northumberland; one *s* one *d. Educ:* Eton; Trinity College, Cambridge. Formerly Major, Yorks Hussars, Territorial Army; raised the 161st, 164th, and 168th Brigades RFA in Yorkshire; the 176th in Leicester, and the 175th in Staffordshire; gazetted temp. Lieut-Colonel and appointed to command the 175th (Staffordshire) Brigade RFA, 24 June 1915; attached to a Brigade, RFA, Aug. 1915, at Armentières; returned to complete the training of the 175th Brigade RFA, and then raised the 144th, 147th, 148th, 149th, 150th, and 157th Heavy Batteries RGA; appointed to command the 5th Divisional Ammunition Column, BEF, 1 Oct. 1915; spent several years in New Zealand; is deeply interested in politics; an authority on Imperial and Colonial questions; has devoted much time to the study and improvement of agriculture, especially improvement of grass land, and to horse and cattle breeding; Chairman of Private Committee in House of Commons on Remounts before and during War; has travelled widely on the continents of Europe, Asia, Africa, and N America, as well as in Australia and New Zealand.

Publications: India of To-day; A Treatise on Grassland. *Recreations:* hunting, shooting, and all country pursuits. *Address:* Spellow Hill, Knaresborough. *Clubs:* Carlton; Yorkshire, York.

Died 28 Feb. 1944.

MICHELIN, William Plunkett; *b* 15 March 1872; *e s* of late William Michelin, Bristol, landowner in Jamaica, West Indies, and Letitia Jane, *d* of late Rook Clark Plunkett, and *g d* of late Dominic Plunkett, Co. Roscommon. Barrister-at-law, Middle Temple, 1905; entered Colonial Service, 1890; Judicial Department, Jamaica, 1891–1906; District Commissioner, Gold Coast Colony, 1906–11; acted as Solicitor-General on several occasions, 1908–11; Police Magistrate, Coomassie, 1911–13; acted as Circuit Judge, Sierra Leone, Jan.–April 1913; Police Magistrate and Coroner, Gibraltar, 1913–19; acted as Attorney-General on numerous occasions, 1913–19; 2nd Puisne Judge, Leeward Islands, 1919; first Puisne Judge, 1920; acted as Chief Justice of the Leeward Islands, Oct. 1920–March 1921, Dec. 1922–March 1923, and of the Gold Coast Colony May–Sept. 1925, Feb.–April 1927, Oct.–Nov.1929 and April–Sept., 1933; Puisne Judge of the Gold Coast Colony, 1923–34; retired, 1934. *Publication:* Revised Edition of the Statutes of St Christopher and Nevis (Leeward Islands), 1922. *Club:* Royal Societies.

Died 2 July 1943.

MICHIE, James, CBE 1920; retired Marine Engineer; *b* 1867; *s* of late James Michie, Banff; *m* 1894, Louisa (*d* 1941), *d* of Joseph Monro, Aberdeen. *Address:* 3 Alloa Road, Goodmayes, Essex.

Died 14 Oct. 1943.

MICHIE, Prof. John Lundie, MA, LLD (Queensland); Professor of Classics in the University of Queensland since 1910; *b* 4 June 1882; *s* of late Charles Michie, Crathie, Aberdeenshire; *m* 1926, Isabel Harriet, *d* of late T. S. Sword, Member of Land Court of Queensland; two *d. Educ:* Aberdeen University; Trinity College, Cambridge. Junior Assistant in Humanity in Aberdeen University, 1908–09; Senior Assistant in Humanity and Lecturer in Roman History in Aberdeen University, 1909. *Address:* University of Queensland, Brisbane, Australia. *TA:* University, Queensland. *Clubs:* Queensland, Brisbane.

Died 23 June 1946.

MICKLETHWAIT, Frances Mary Gore, MBE, FIC, ARCSc (Lond.); *b* 7 March 1867; *e d* of late J. P. Micklethwait, JP, Penhein, Chepstow, Mon. *Educ:* privately; Swanley Horticultural College; Royal College of Science, London. Chemical Research, 1902–13; Beit Memorial Fellowship for Medical research, 1914; Various technical positions in Ministry of Munitions, 1914–18; with Boots Pure Drug Co., 1919; Principal, Horticultural College, Swanley, Kent, 1920–21. *Publications:* in collaboration with various eminent men in the chemical world, about 30 papers. *Address:* c/o Midland Bank Ltd, Gerrards Cross, Bucks.

Died 25 March 1950.

MIDDLEBRO, William Sora; KC 1910; Member of Parliament of Dominion of Canada 1908–21; Chairman Special Government investigating Army Contracts *re* boots; Chief Government Whip and Chairman, Public Accounts Committee; *b* Orangeville, Ontario, 17 Oct. 1868; *s* of John and Margaret Middlebro (English); *m* 1st, 1903, Laura J. Trethewey (*d* 1907); no *c*; 2nd, 1913, Pearl Irene, *d* of G. B. Ryan, Guelph, Ont; (one *s* killed 17 July 1940, the first overseas casualty in the RCAF). *Educ:* Owen Sound Collegiate Institute; Osgoode Hall Law School, Toronto. Mayor of City of Owen Sound, Ontario, 1899 and 1900; a Bencher of Law Society of Ontario since 1926; now a Life Bencher of Law Society of Upper Canada. *Address:* Owen Sound, Ont. *T:* Owen Sound 1. *Clubs:* Sydenham, Golf and Country (Owen Sound); Albany (Toronto).

Died 17 Nov. 1948.

MIDDLEMISS, Charles Stewart, CIE 1916; FRS 1921; BA, FGS, FASB; *b* 1859; *s* of late Robert Middlemiss of Hull; *m* Martha Frances, *d* of late Major-Gen. F. Wheeler, Bengal Staff Corps; one *s* one *d. Educ:* Caistor; St John's College, Cambridge. Geological Survey of India, 1883–1917; Superintendent, 1895; retired, 1917; Superintendent Mineral Survey of Kashmir, 1917–30; retired, 1930. *Publications:* in the Survey Memoirs and Records. *Recreations:* sketching, music. *Address:* Aviemore, Crowborough.

Died 11 June 1945.

MIDDLETON, A. Safroni; novelist, composer and dramatist; *s* of Charles S. Middleton, Author of the first Shelley Biography, Lives of England's Self-made Men, etc; *m cousin,* Alice Elizabetta St John, *niece* of Sir Spencer St John, GCMG; one *s* three *d.* Apprenticed White Star Clipper ships; studied music on voyages; 1st violin, HM Theatre, New South Wales, and the Carl Rosa Opera Company; exploration in Borneo, Papua and Malay States. *Compositions:* numerous military band marches, entr'actes, waltzes, songs, etc. *Publications:* Sestrina; No Extradition; Child of the Forest; Island Princess, Ragged Romance; Gabrielle of the Lagoon; South Sea Foam; Tropic Shadows; Two Faces in Borneo; Australian Bush Lyrics; Musical Plays: La Foresta; Gabrielle; Rhymes from the Bush, the Sea and Mountain; Sestrina (Lyrical Drama); The Ships Figurehead; L'Odissea Immortale; The Dreaming Skull (Novel); A Symphony in Trees (Poems); Deep Moving Waters (Poems); Torn Sails and Sunset (Poems); Subconscious Philosophy (Essay); The Pagan; Love's Parliament; The Two Shelleys (Interpretation); The Forest Lovers (Father Damien's Protégés). *Recreation:* astronomy. *Address:* c/o Boosey & Co., 295 Regent Street, W1.

Died 7 Nov. 1950.

MIDDLETON, Sir Charles Arthur, 8th Bt *cr* 1662; *b* 22 Oct. 1873; *o surv. s* of Sir Arthur Edward Middleton, 7th Bt and Lady Constance Amherst (*d* 1879), *d* of 2nd Earl Amherst; *S* father 1933. *Heir: nephew* Stephen Hugh, *b* 20 June 1909. *Address:* Belsay Castle, Northumberland.

Died 22 Feb. 1942.

MIDDLETON, Lambert William; *b* 29 April 1877; *s* of late Henry N. Middleton, JP, DL, Northumberland, and Sophia, *d* of Sir Wm Meredith, Chief Justice of Quebec; *m* 1922, Lady Sybil Grey, 2nd *d* of 4th Earl Grey; one *s* one *d. Educ:* Eton; New College, Oxford. Called to the Bar, 1900; entered the private banking partnership of Lambton & Co. in Northumberland, which was subsequently amalgamated with Lloyds Bank; A Director of the National Bank of Scotland. *Recreations:* shooting, fishing. *Address:* Lowood, Melrose, Scotland. *T:* Melrose 89. *Clubs:* Travellers'; New, Edinburgh.

Died 10 Dec. 1941.

MIDDLETON, Sir Thomas, KCIE 1929; KBE 1918; CB 1913; LLD (Aberdeen, Edin., Wales); DSc (Reading); FRS 1936; Chairman Agricultural Research Council since 1938; *b* Cromarty, 31 Aug. 1863; *s* of Alexander A. Middleton, JP; *m* 1890, Lydia Miller (*d* 1934), *d* of Prof. Davidson, Adelaide, SA, and *g d* of Hugh Miller; one *s* one *d. Educ:* Merchiston Castle School, Edinburgh; Glasgow University; Edinburgh University. Professor of Agriculture, Baroda College, India, 1889–96; Lecturer in Agriculture, University College of Wales, Aberystwyth, 1896–99; Professor of Agriculture, Durham College of Science, 1899–1902; Professor of Agriculture, Cambridge, 1902–07; Assistant Secretary, Board of Agriculture, 1906–19; Deputy Director-General, Food Production Department, 1917–19; Commissioner under Development and Road

Improvement Funds Acts, 1919–41; Vice-Chairman, 1929–41; Member of the Royal Commission on Agriculture in India, 1926–28; Gold Medallist and Hon. Member, Royal Agricultural Society; Hon. Member Highland and Agricultural Society. *Address:* Agricultural Research Council, Dean's Yard, SW1; Whyte House, Strawberry Vale, Twickenham.

Died 14 May 1943.

MIDLETON, 1st Earl of, *cr* 1920; **William St John Fremantle Brodrick,** KP 1915; PC 1897; JP, DL; Viscount, Midleton *cr* 1717, Midleton, Ireland; Viscount Dunsford of Dunsford, Surrey, 1920; Baron Brodrick, Midleton, Ireland, 1715; Baron Brodrick, Peper Harow, 1796; High Steward of Kingston-upon-Thames since 1930; *b* 14 Dec. 1856; *e s* of 8th Viscount Midleton and Hon. Augusta Mary Fremantle, 3rd *d* of 1st Baron Cottesloe; *S* to father's Viscounty, 1907; *m* 1st, 1880, Lady Hilda Charteris (*d* 1901), *d* of 10th Earl of Wemyss; one *s* four *d*; 2nd, 1903, Madeleine, *d* of late Col Hon. J. Stanley; two *s*; Conservative. *Educ:* Eton; Balliol Coll., Oxford. President of the Union; Financial Secretary to War Office, 1886–92; Under-Secretary of State for War, 1895–98; for Foreign Affairs, 1898–1900; Sec. of State for War, 1900–03; for India, 1903–05; MP (C) W Surrey, 1880–85, Guildford Division, Surrey, 1885–1906; Alderman London County Council, 1907–13; served on Irish Convention, 1917–18; LLD Trinity College, Dublin, 1922. Owns about 5000 acres. *Publications:* Ireland, Dupe or Heroine, 1932; Records and Reactions, 1856–1939, 1939. *Heir: s* Viscount Dunsford. *Address:* Peper Harow, Godalming; 34 Portland Place, W1. *T:* Langham 2944; Midleton, Ireland. *Clubs:* Carlton; Kildare Street, Dublin.

Died 13 Feb. 1942.

MIDWINTER, Captain Sir Edward Colpoys, KBE 1927; CB 1912; CMG 1911; CBE 1919; DSO 1898; Controller Sudan Government London Office 1925–32; General Manager of Sudan Government Railways and Steamers, 1906–25; Member Governor-General's Council, 1913–25; *b* 1 Nov. 1872; *s* of late Rev. E. A. Midwinter. *Educ:* St Paul's School; RMA, Woolwich. Entered RE 1892; Capt. 1903; served Nile, including battle of Omdurman, 1897–98 (despatches, DSO, 2nd Class Nile, 3rd Class Osmanie, 4th Class Medjidie, Sudan medal, Egyptian medal 2 clasps); resigned RE 1907; formerly El Lewa Pasha in Egyptian Army. *Address:* 9 Belvedere Grove, Wimbledon. *Club:* National.

Died 17 Jan. 1947.

MIDWOOD, Lt-Col Harrison, CBE 1919; late Highland Light Infantry; *b* 14 Dec. 1857; *o s* of late Captain William Bellhouse Midwood, Heron House, Richmond; *m* 1st, 1885, Annie Louisa Chester, *o d* of late W. F. Brooks, Chester House, Southsea; no *c*; 2nd, 1922, Muriel Elizabeth Stuart, 4th *d* of late Alexander Campbell of Auchanross, Isle of Bute; no *c*. *Educ:* Cheltenham; Hanover. Entered Army, 1876; Lt-Col 1903; retired, 1907; served Egyptian Campaign, 1882 (severely wounded, medal with clasp and Bronze Star); Indian Frontier Malakand Field Force (medal and clasps); European War, Commandant on the lines of communication (CBE, 1914 Star, British War Medal and Victory Medal); retired list. *Recreations:* shooting, cricket, and fishing. *Club:* Army and Navy.

Died 3 Jan. 1944.

MIERS, Sir Henry (Alexander), Kt 1912; DSc, MA, Hon. DCL (Oxford); Hon. PhD (Christiania); Hon. DSc (Manchester, Sheffield), Hon. LLD (Liverpool, Michigan); FRS, FGS, FCS; Fellow of Magdalen College, Oxford; Hon. Fellow, Trinity College, Oxford; *b* Rio de Janeiro, 25 May 1858; *s* of Francis C. Miers, CE. *Educ:* Eton College; Trinity College, Oxford. Assistant in the British Museum, 1882–95; instructor in Crystallography at the Central Technical College, S Kensington, 1886–95; editor of the Mineralogical

Magazine, 1891–1900; Waynflete Professor of Mineralogy, Oxford, 1895–1908; Principal of the University of London, 1908–15; Vice-Chancellor of the University of Manchester and Professor of Crystallography, 1915–26; Fellow of Eton College, 1903–34; formerly Secretary to the Delegates of the University Museum, Delegate of the University Press, and Member of the Hebdomadal Council, Oxford; Vice-President of the Chemical Society, 1901–04; of the Geological Society, 1902–04; of the Royal Society of Arts, 1913; President Mineralogical Society, 1904–09; President Geological Section, British Association, 1905, Educational Section, 1910; President Museums Association, 1928–33; Library Association, 1932; Council of the Royal Society, 1901–03; Member Advisory Council Dept Sci. and Ind. Research, 1919–26; Trustee of the British Museum, 1926–39; Member Standing Commission on Museums and Galleries; Chairman of John Rylands Library, 1920–26; Honorary Member Acad. Wiss. Munich; Accad. Acireale; Soc. Linn. Normandie; Royal Cornwall Polytech. Society; Geologists' Association; Manch. Lit. and Phil. Soc.; Russian Min. Soc.; German Min. Soc.; Museums Association; American Association of Museums; Wollaston Medal of Geological Society, 1934. *Publications:* numerous scientific papers; The Soil in Relation to Health (with Dr R. Crosskey), 1893; Mineralogy, 1902; A Visit to the Yukon Gold Fields, 1901; Report on Public Museums, 1928; Reports (with S. F. Markham) on Museums of Canada, 1932; of Africa, 1933. *Address:* 18 Aberdare Gardens, West Hampstead, NW6. *T:* Maida Vale 2975.

Died 10 Dec. 1942.

MIFSUD, Hon. Sir Ugo Pasquale, Kt 1927; LLD, BLit; MLA Valletta, 1921–33; Head of the National Party and formerly Prime Minister, Malta; *b* Valletta, Malta, 12 Sept. 1889; *s* of late Judge G. B. Mifsud and late Marianne Muscat; *g s* of late Judge Pasquale Mifsud and late Hon. C. M. Muscat; *m* 1927, Blanche, *d* of late Col J. L. Francia, MVO. *Educ:* private tuition; Malta University. Bachelor in Literature, 1906; Doctor of Laws, 1910. President University Students Representative Committee, 1906–10; had extensive practice in Prize and Commercial cases; Secretary National Assembly, 1919; Senator, 1927, but declared preference for Legislative Assembly; Minister for Industry and Commerce, 1921–24; Minister for the Treasury, 1924–26; Minister for Justice, 1926–27 and 1932–33; Leader of the House, 1921–23 and 1924–27 and 1932–33; Head of the Ministry, 1924–27 and 1932–33; Leader of the Opposition in the Legislative Assembly, 1927–30; directed Malta's participation at British Empire Exhibition at Wembley in 1924; was on literary staff of International Law Notes; is member of International Law Association and a writer on International Law; attended Warsaw Conference of International Law Association as Chairman of Aviation and Radio Committee, 1928, the Oxford Conference of International Law in 1932 as one of the Chairman on the British Delegation, and in 1934 Budapest International Law Conference as Chairman on Trade Marks Committee; represented Malta Parliament on Delegation to Canada in 1928; travelled extensively on European Cont., also in North Africa and North America; was Vice-President Malta Branch of Empire Parliamentary Association. *Recreation:* travelling. *Address:* 5 Victoria Avenue, Sliema, Malta. *TA:* Ugo Mifsud, Malta. *Clubs:* Maltese della Borsa, Malta.

Died 11 Feb. 1942.

MIGNAULT, Pierre Basile; Consulting Counsel, 507 Place d'Armes, Montreal; *b* Worcester, Massachusetts, 30 Sept. 1854; *s* of Pierre Basile Mignault, MD, and Catherine O'Callaghan; *m* 1888, Marie Elizabeth Henrietta Branchaud of Beauharnois, Quebec; two *s* one *d*. *Educ:* St Mary's College, Montreal; McGill University. Called to Bar, 1878; KC 1893; Batonnier (President) of

Montreal Bar, 1906–07; Puisne Justice of the Supreme Court of Canada, 1918–29; a Member of the International Joint Commission (between Canada and the United States), 1914; FRS Canada; was a Vice-President of the Canadian Bar Association; was Professor of Civil Law at McGill University; BCL McGill; LLD Laval, McGill, Montreal and Paris. *Publications:* Manuel de Droit Parlementaire, 1888; Code de Procédure Civile Annoté, 1891; Le Droit Paroissial, 1893; Le Droit Civil Canadien, 1895–1916; Joint Editor of the Quebec Official Law Reports, 1891–1905. *Recreation:* golf. *Address:* Gleneagles, Côte des Neiges Road, Montreal; Golf Avenue, Pointe Claire, Quebec.

Died 15 Oct. 1945.

MILBANKE, Sir John Charles Peniston, 11th Bt *cr* 1661; Wing Comdr (temp.) RAF Regt AAF; *b* 9 Jan. 1902; *s* of Lt-Col Sir John Peniston Milbanke, VC, 10th Bt (killed in action Gallipoli), and Leila, *d* of Colonel Hon. Charles Crichton, Grenadier Guards; *S* father, 1915; *m* 1928, Lady Loughborough, Sheila, *d* of late Harry Chisholm, Sydney, NSW. *Educ:* Harrow; Trinity College, Cambridge. *Heir:* *b* Ralph Mark, MC, Temp. Capt. R of O, RAC (Hussars), *b* 11 April 1907. *Clubs:* White's, Hurlingham, Turf; Kildare Street, Dublin; Traveller's, Paris.

Died 1 June 1947.

MILBANKE, Sir Ralph Mark, 12th Bt *cr* 1661; MC 1940; *b* 11 April 1907; 2nd *s* of Lt-Col Sir John Peniston Milbanke, VC, 10th Bt (killed in action, Gallipoli) and Leila, *d* of Col Hon. Charles Crichton, Grenadier Gds; *S* brother, 1947. *Educ:* Harrow; RMC, Sandhurst. *Address:* Arlington House, W1. *T:* Regent 3749. *Clubs:* White's, Cavalry; Kildare Street (Dublin); Travellers' (Paris).

Died 24 Nov. 1949.

MILBORNE-SWINNERTON-PILKINGTON, Sir Thomas Edward; *see* Pilkington.

MILBURN, Captain Booker, DSO 1916; MC; late Coldstream Guards; *b* 7 Sept. 1888; 2nd *s* of late Wm Milburn and Mrs Milburn of 22 Lennox Gardens, SW1; *m* 1st, 1924, Violet Alice (by whom he was divorced), *er d* of late Admiral Hon. Sir Victor Stanley, KCB; 2nd, Betty, *d* of Capt. W. H. Calthrop Calthrop, AM, RN, retd; two *s. Educ:* Malvern; Jesus College, Cambridge. Served European War, 1914–18 (DSO, MC, despatches); 1st Herts Regt 1914–16; entered Coldstream Guards, 1916; Adjt 2nd Batt. 1919–22; retired, 1926. *Recreations:* golf, fishing. *Address:* Allt Mhuilinn, Dornoch, Sutherland. *Club:* Guards'.

Died 11 March 1941.

MILBURN, Charles Henry, OBE (Mil.); MB, MS (Dunelm); DL, JP; Esq. Order of Hospital of St John of Jerusalem in England; medal, Ambulance Dept, 1901; Special South African Medal of the Order of St John, 1902; VD 1906; Consulting Surgeon, Victoria Hospital, Hull; Consulting Surgeon, Hull and Sculcoates Dispensary; Life Governor, Epsom College; Vice-President, Kipling Society; Member (President, Harrogate Victory Branch) British Legion; Lieut-Col (Hon. Col), 2nd Northumbrian Brigade RFA (TF) 1908–11; *b* 1860; *s* of late Rev. J. C. Milburn, Birmingham; *m* 1890, Edith, *e d* of late Lieut-Col H. Cooper Gleadow (*d* 1941); one *d. Educ:* privately; Durham College of Science; University of Durham College of Medicine, Newcastle-on-Tyne. Tulloch Scholar, 1879; Prizeman (medallist) in Anatomy, Physiology, Practical Physiology, Public Health, and Surgery. House Surg. Durham County Hospital, 1882–84; Consulting Surgeon, Hull Lying-In Charity, 1886–99. Life Member (Central Council 1899–1918; Constitution Cttees 1900–02; Army Medical Reform Cttee, 1896–98; Vice-Pres. Navy, Army and Ambulance Section, Annual Meeting, 1913) BMA Chm., Local Med. War Cttee, 1914–15; served as Surgeon to No. 2 British Red Cross Hospital, France, Dec. 1915–Feb.

1917; and in Ambulance Train, France, 1917–18; temp. and Hon. Major RAMC, Jan. 1916–Feb. 1917; Dep. Commissioner of Medical Services, Headquarters, Ministry of National Service, 1918–19; Commissioner of Medical Services, and Deputy Regional Director, Yorkshire Region, Ministry of Pensions, 1919–20; Divisional Medical Officer, North-Eastern Division, Ministry of Health, 1920–25. *Publications:* papers in BMJ, etc.; Epitaphs, by Rudyard Kipling, in Kipling Journal, 1936; The Homes of Rudyard Kipling, in Kipling Journal, 1940–1941; Some Kipling Parodies, 1942; The Seven 'Cleopatras' in the British Navy (1779–1943). *Address:* 9 South Drive, Harrogate.

Died 27 Oct. 1948.

MILDMAY OF FLETE, 1st Baron *cr* 1922, of Totnes; **Francis Bingham Mildmay;** PC 1916; DL, JP Devon; Lt-Col West Kent Imp. Yeomanry; President of the Royal Agricultural Society of England, 1932, 1941–43; and of Veterinary Committee of the same; Member of Executive Council of the Royal Veterinary College; extensive breeder and exhibitor of S Devon cattle; President, Hunters Improvement and Light Horse Breeding Society, 1922 and 1937; *b* London, 26 April 1861; *e s* of late H. B. Mildmay, Shoreham, Kent, and Flete, Devon, and Georgiana Frances, *d* of J. Bulteel and Lady Elizabeth, *d* of Earl Grey, the Prime Minister; *m* 1906, Alice, *d* of late Seymour Grenfell; one *s* one *d. Educ:* Eton; Trin. Coll., Cambridge (BA 1884). Director of Great Western Railway Co., 1915–45; Member of Managing Board of Middlesex Hospital; Member of the Council of King Edward's Hospital Fund for London, and the Revenue Committee of the same; late Member and Treasurer of the Medical Research Council; Member of Council of Lister Institute of Preventive Medicine; introduced and carried second reading of Agricultural Produce Marks Bill; proposed in the House of Commons the election as Speaker of Mr Speakers Lowther and Whitley; served with squadron of Imperial Yeomanry in South Africa; European War, 1914–19 (despatches four times); Member of the Civil List Committees at the Accessions respectively of King Edward VII and King George V; MP (U) Totnes Div. Devonshire, 1885–1922; one of the original Liberal Unionists who combined to oppose the Home Rule Bill of the 1885 Parliament; one of the three Members of the Committee of the Privy Council appointed by the Prime Minister to scrutinise the list of Political Honours before it is submitted to His Majesty, 1923–24; Lord Lieutenant of Devon, 1928–36; Member Executive Committee and President National Unionist Association, 1922 London and 1923 Plymouth; member of National Hunt Committee, 1937. *Recreations:* polo, hunting, shooting, played polo for Cambridge, 1881–83; member of Sussex team which won champion polo cup, Hurlingham, 5 years; won House of Commons' steeplechase, 1892. *Heir:* *s* Capt. Hon. Anthony Bingham Mildmay, Welsh Guards, *b* 14 April 1909. *Address:* 46 Berkeley Square, W1. *T:* Grosvenor 2134; Shoreham Place, Sevenoaks, Kent; Flete, Ivybridge, Devon; Mothecombe House, Holbeton, Plymouth. *Clubs:* Turf, Brooks's, I Zingari.

Died 8 Feb. 1947.

MILDMAY OF FLETE, 2nd Baron *cr* 1922, of Totnes; **Anthony Bingham Mildmay;** *b* 14 April 1909; *s* of 1st Baron Mildmay of Flete, PC; *S* father, 1947. *Educ:* Eton; Trinity College, Cambridge. Served War of 1939–45, with Welsh Guards in NW Europe (despatches). A Governor of Royal Veterinary College; Representative (elected) for Devon on Council of Royal Agric. Soc. of England; Member of National Hunt Cttee Amateur Steeplechase Jockey; headed list of Amateur riders in NH season, 1946–47, with 32 winners; has ridden over 100 winners. *Recreations:* hunting, shooting, racing. *Heir:* none. *Address:* Mothecombe, Holbeton, S Devon. *T:* Holbeton 24; 9 North Audley Street, W1. *T:* Mayfair 0382. *Clubs:* Turf. White's, Buck's.

Died 12 May 1950 (ext).

MILDMAY, Sir Anthony St John-, 8th Bt cr 1772; MC; late Captain Grenadier Guards; b 13 Aug. 1894; s of 7th Bt and Isabel Emily, 2nd d of Rev. C. A. St John-Mildmay of Hazelgrove; S father, 1929; m 1st, 1920, Violet (who obtained a divorce, 1933). 2nd d of Col A. W. H. Hay-Drummond; one s; 2nd, 1934, Beatrice May Dickeson, née Bowles (who obtained a decree nisi, 1942). Educ: Eton; RMC, Sandhurst. Owns about 10,900 acres. Heir: s Henry Gerald, 2nd Lt Grenadier Guards, b 17 April 1926.

Died 3 Oct. 1947.

MILDMAY, Sir Henry Gerald St John-, 9th Bt cr 1772; late Lt Grenadier Guards; b 17 April 1926; s of 8th Bt and Violet (who obtained a divorce, 1933). 2nd d of Col A. W. H. Hay-Drummond; S father, 1947. Educ: Eton. Served War of 1939–45, Grenadier Guards, 1944–45. Heir: kinsman Rev. Aubrey Neville St John-Mildmay, b 14 Feb. 1865. Address: Fulford House, Culworth, Banbury, Oxon. T: Sulgrave 355.

Died 4 Nov. 1949.

MILDREN, Col (Hon. Brig.-Gen.) William Frederick, CB 1919; CMG 1916; DSO 1917; Hon. Colonel 6th City of London Rifles; a Director of the Amalgamated Press, Ltd, and the Imperial Papers Mills, Ltd; b 1874; s of William Williams Mildren of Hayle, Cornwall. Served European War, in command of 6th City of London Rifles and 141st Infantry Brigade, 1914–19 (despatches 7 times, CB, CMG, DSO, Croix de Guerre with Palm). Address: The Fleetway House, Farringdon Street, EC4.

Died 23 May 1948.

MILES, Eustace, MA; Founder of the Normal Physical School; Tripos (Hons) Coach at Cambridge University, and Lecturer to University Board of Civil Service Studies; b West End House, Hampstead, 22 Sept. 1868; s of W. H. Miles (of Simpkin, Marshall & Co.) and Mary M'Connell; m 1906, Hallie (author), y d of late Rev. R. H. Killick, Rector of St Clement Danes, Strand. Educ: Heath Mount, Hampstead; Eastbourne College; Marlborough; King's College, Cambridge (Entrance and Undergraduate Scholar); 1st class Classical Tripos, 1890; Hon. Men, for Chancellor's Classical Medals, 1891. Assist Master at Rugby School; Amateur Champion of America at Racquets and Tennis, 1900; Amateur Champion of England at Racquets, 1902; Singles and Doubles; Doubles, 1904, 1905, 1906; at Tennis, 1898 to 1903, 1905, 1906, 1909, 1910; winner of Gold Prize, 1897, 1898, 1899, 1901 to 1906, 1908 to 1912; Amateur Champion of World at Racquets, 1902, and at Tennis, 1898–1903, and 1905. Publications: Lawn-tennis Lessons (new ed.); Better Food for Boys; The Teaching of Jesus To-day; Mathematical Law in the Spiritual World; A Boy's Control and Self-Expression; Racquets, Tennis, and Squash; The Power of Concentration; Let's Play the Game; Wanted, Men; Economy of Energy; Through the Day; 150 Milestones Booklets on Health and Efficiency; Life After Life; Keep Happy; How to Prepare Essays, etc.; How to Remember; How to learn Philology; several English and foreign language textbooks; numerous books on health and fitness. Recreations: tennis, racquets, lawn tennis, walking, punning and riddle-making, patience. Address: 66 York Mansions, SW11.

Died 20 Dec. 1948.

MILES, George Edward, MVO 1904, 4th class, 1924; b 1852; e s of William Miles; m 1880, Harriet (d 1913), d of James Wagstaff; no c. Educ: St Mark's and Brunswick House Schools, Windsor. Entered Lord Chamberlain's Department, Windsor Castle; Inspector of the Palace, Windsor Castle, 1901–24; Chief Officer of Windsor Castle Salvage Corps since its formation, 1906–24; Pres. of Windsor and Eton Scientific and Archæological Society, 1901; Hon. Librarian, Royal Albert Institute, Windsor, 1906–13; received 1887 Jubilee medal and 1897 bar; King Edward's and King George's Coronation medals, several foreign Orders, etc. Recreations: country walking, reading, archæology. Address: Essendon, 66 Frances Road, Windsor, Berks.

Died 25 March 1942.

MILES, Brig.-Gen. Philip John, CB 1918; CMG 1919; FRGS; b 23 Dec. 1864; s of Rev. P. E. Miles and Elinor, d of Rev. R. F. Jex-Blake; m d of Col F. N. Miles, Bengal Staff Corps; one s three d. Educ: Shrewsbury School. Joined Royal Marine Light Infantry, 1885; transferred to Indian Army, 1887; served in 45th Sikhs, 57th Wilde's Rifles FF, 53rd Sikhs FF, and commanded 51st Sikhs FF, 1909–14; also served on special duty in Gilgit Agency and in Chinese Turkistan; Col 1913; temp. Brig.-Gen. 1914; served NWF India Hazara Expedition, 1888 (medal with clasp); Miranzai Expedition (1st expedition), 1891; China, 1900 (medal); NW Frontier, India, 1908 (despatches, medal with clasp, Bt Lt-Col); European War commanded 47th Infantry Brigade in France, Dec. 1915–Jan. 1916; returned India, 1917; commanded column Marri Punitive Force, 1918 (despatches, CMG); commanded Multan Brigade, 1918–19 (thanked by Govt of India); commanded Brigade Waziristan Field Force, 1919 (despatches, 1914–15 Star, British War and Victory medals, Afghan medal); retired Dec. 1919 with honorary rank of Brigadier-General. Address: 3 Ryeworth Road, Charlton Kings, Glos. T: 52256.

Died 26 Dec. 1948.

MILES, Brig. Reginald, CBE 1943; DSO 1918; MC; idc, psc; b Springston, New Zealand, 10 Dec. 1892; s of late William Miles and Mary Margaret Restell; m 1st; four d; 2nd, 1940. Educ: Royal Military College, Duntroon, Australia. Served European War, 1914–19, Gallipoli, France, and Belgium (despatches, DSO, MC); commanded 15th Battery, 1916–17; Bde Major, NZ Div. Artillery, 1918; Staff Officer, Coast Defence, Wellington, 1920–22; Adjt Field Arty Bde, Christchurch, 1923; Staff College, Camberley, 1924–25; attached War Office, 1926; Artillery Staff Officer, Northern Command, Auckland, 1927–31; GSO1 Northern Command, 1931–36; OC Northern Military District, 1937; Imperial Defence College, 1938; late 3rd Military Member, Army Board, Wellington, New Zealand; Comdr, Headquarters, Divisional Artillery, 1st Echelon, 2nd NZ Expeditionary Force, 1939 (Bar to DSO, CBE). Recreation: golf. Address: 7 Pencarrow Avenue, Mt Eden, Auckland, NZ. Clubs: United Services, Auckland.

Died 26 Oct. 1943.

MILES, William Ernest, TD, FRCS Eng., LRCP Lond., Hon. FACS, Hon. FRCSI; Consulting Surgeon (late Emeritus) Royal Cancer Hospital, London; Surgeon, Gordon Hospital for Diseases of the Rectum; Consulting Surgeon, Royal Hospital, Richmond, and West Herts Hospital; Fellow of the Association of Surgeons of Great Britain and Ireland; Fellow of Royal Society of Medicine and Medical Society of London; late Member of the National Radium Commission; Hon. Fellow, American Proctological Society; Consulting Proctologist to Queen Alexandra's Military Hospital, Millbank; Foreign Associate of French Academy of Surgery; b 1869; o s of William Miles, BA Oxon, JP; m 1944, Janet Mary, d of Ernest Robert Loxton. Educ: Queen's Royal College, Trinidad; St Bartholomew's Hospital Coll. (Univ. of London). Demonstrator of Anatomy, St Bartholomew's Hosp., 1896–99; late Pres., Sect. of Proctology, RSM; Lt-Col RAMC (TA) retired; served BEF (France and Belgium), 1914–19; commanded No. 7 Red Cross Hospital for Officers, 1914–15; DADMS 58 Division, 1916–17; commanded 56 General Hospital, 1918–19; consulting surgeon to Etaples Area, 1919 (Mons Star, British War Medal, Victory Medal); Lettsomian Lecturer, Medical Society of London, 1923. Publications: Diseases of the Rectum, Cancer of the Rectum, Rectal

Surgery, and numerous articles in the various surgical journals. *Recreations:* tennis, golf, shooting. *Address:* 82 Harley Street, W1. *T:* Langham 2260.

Died 24 Sept. 1947.

MILFORD, Brig. Ernest William, CBE 1943; MC; Brigadier (late The Lincolnshire Regt); *b* 22 April 1898; *o s* of William and Amelia Milford, Clifton, Bristol. *Educ:* Colston's School. Commissioned in Lincolnshire Regt, 1915; served European War, 1914-18 (severely wounded, despatches, MC); graduated at Staff College; Instructor at Senior Officers' School and Staff College; War of 1939-45 GSO2; AA and QMG 52nd Div.; AQMG (Operations) Southern Command; Brigadier i/c Administration 12 Corps; DQMG General Headquarters. *Recreations:* yachting, photography, bibliography. *Address:* 41 Durdham Park, Bristol. *T:* 34105. *Club:* United Service.

Died 23 July 1944.

MILL, Hugh Robert, DSc (Edinburgh, 1886); LLD (St Andrews, 1900); Geographer and Meteorologist; *b* Thurso, 28 May 1861; *s* of Dr James Mill; *m* 1st, 1889, Frances (*d* 1929), *d* of Dr F. R. MacDonald, Inveraray; 2nd, 1937, Alfreda, *d* of Frederick Dransfield, Darton, Yorks. *Educ:* Edinburgh University. Chemist and Physicist to Scottish Marine Station, 1884-87; University Extension Lecturer, 1887-1900; Recorder of Section E, British Association, 1893-99; President, Section E, 1901; Hon. Secretary Royal Meteorological Society, 1902-06; President, 1907-08; one of the British representatives on International Council for the Study of the Sea, 1901-08; Member of Board of Trade Committee on Water Power of British Isles, 1918-21; Librarian Royal Geographical Society, 1892-1900; Vice-President, 1927-31; Chairman of Trustees and Director of British Rainfall Organization, and editor of British Rainfall and Symons's Meteorological Magazine, 1901-19; presented to Trustees for the nation the accumulated records of rainfall in the British Isles since 1677, 1910; Rainfall Expert to Metropolitan Water Board, 1906-19; President of the Geographical Association, 1932; Hon. Member of several foreign Societies. Awarded Makdougal-Brisbane Medal, RSE, 1894; Victoria Research Medal, RGS, 1915; Symons Medal, RMetS, 1918; gold medal RSGS, 1923; Cullum Medal of American Geographical Society, New York, 1930; Commander Norwegian Order of St Olav, 1932. *Publications:* Realm of Nature, new ed. 1913; The Clyde Sea Area: The English Lakes, 1895; Hints on the Choice of Geographical Books, 1897; New Lands, 1900; The Siege of the South Pole, 1905; Historical Introduction to Sir Ernest Shackleton's Heart of the Antarctic, 1909; The Life of Sir Ernest Shackleton, 1923; Record of Royal Geographical Society, 1930; many papers in the Encyclopædia Britannica and in scientific journals since 1882; Introduction to J. Rymill's Southern Lights, 1938; Life Interests of a Geographer (Autobiography, privately produced, 1945); edited Report of Sixth International Geographical Congress, 1896; The International Geography, new ed. 1911. *Recreations:* gardening, travel. *Address:* Hill Crest, Dormans Park, East Grinstead, Sussex. *T:* Dormans Park 219.

Died 5 April 1950.

MILL, Thomas, CMG 1918; CBE 1919; MB, BS (Ed.); FRCS (Ed.); FRACS; late Colonel, NZ, MC (Ret.); Consulting Ear, Nose and Throat Surgeon; Hon. Surgeon, Ear, Nose, and Throat Department, North Canterbury Hospital, Christchurch, NZ; *b* 12 Nov. 1878; *y s* of John Mill, Port Chalmers, NZ. *Educ:* Port Chalmers District High School; Otago Boys High School; University, Otago; University, Edinburgh; Royal College, Edinburgh; and Royal College, Dublin. Formerly RMO Cumberland Infirmary, Carlisle; Hon. Physician, Hospital, Christchurch, NZ; Chief Resident Surgeon, Beaufort War Hospital, Bristol (Major

RAMC); Surgeon, NZ Military Hospital, Walton-on-Thames; Officer Commanding, No. 2 NZ General Hospital, Walton-on-Thames; Rotorua Military Hospital, NZ; Trentham Military Hospital; Auckland Military Hospital; Orthopædic Surgeon Defence Dept, NZ; Hon. Assistant-Surgeon, Throat Hospital, Golden Square, London; Clinical Assistant, Ear, Nose, and Throat Dept St George's Hospital, London; served European War, 1915-18 (CMG and CBE, despatches twice); President NZ Branch British Medical Association, 1930. *Address:* c/o Bank of New Zealand, 1 Queen Victoria Street, EC.

Died 8 Oct. 1941.

MILLAIS, Sir Geoffroy William, 4th Bt *cr* 1885; *b* 18 Sept. 1863; *s* of 1st Bt and Euphemia Chalmers, *e d* of George Gray; *S* nephew, 1920; *m* 1901, Madeleine Campbell, *d* of Col C. H. Grace; two *s* one *d*. Heir: *s* Ralph Regnault, Squad. Leader RAFVR [*b* 4 March 1905; *m* 1939, Felicity, *d* of Brig.-Gen. W. W. Warner, CMG; one *d*. Trinity College, Cambridge, BA]. *Address:* Spreakfield, Frensham, Surrey.

Died 7 Nov. 1941.

MILLAR, Alexander, CBE 1928; *b* 1867; 3rd *s* of Alexander Millar; *m* 1895, Florence, *d* of Thomas Weir, Coatbridge, Scotland; one *d*. Wholly in the public service; formerly Accountant to Antrim County Council and Secretary until 1941. *Address:* 23 University Square, Belfast. *T:* Belfast 24061.

Died 16 April 1944.

MILLARD, Evelyn; actress; *b* London; *d* of late John Millard, Professor of Elocution at the Royal Academy and Royal College of Music; *m* 1900, Robert Porter Coulter (*d* 1915); one *d. Educ:* privately. Made first appearance in Miss Sarah Thorne's stock company at Margate, 1891; played Juliet, Hero, Julia in The Hunchback, etc.; joined Mr Fred Thorne's Repertoire Company, 1891, playing Sophia, Fanny Goodwill in Joseph's Sweetheart, Clara Douglas in Money, and Miss Tomboy; Adelphi, 1891-93, playing Constance in The Trumpet Call, Alice Lee in The White Rose, Sybil Garfield in The Lights of Home, Polly Fletcher in The Lost Paradise, Lady Mildred Dashwood in The Black Domino; Mr Comyns Carr's Company, 1894, played Rosamund in Sowing the Wind; St James's Theatre, 1894-96, played Dulcie Larondie in The Masqueraders, Cecily Cardew in The Importance of Being Ernest, Mrs Tanqueray, Lady Harding in The Idler, Blanche Chilworth in Liberty Hall, Lois in The Divided Way, and Princess Flavia in The Prisoner of Zenda; in 1897 created the part of Mdlle. de Belle-Isle in The Silver Key at Her Majesty's Theatre; also played Portia in Mr Tree's production of Julius Cæsar, 1898; Lady Ursula in The Adventure of Lady Ursula, 1898; Glory Quayle in The Christian, 1899; Miss Hobbs and Madame Butterfly, 1900; Francesca in Paolo and Francesca, and Mildred in The Unforeseen, 1902; joined Mr Lewis Waller's Company at Imperial Theatre in Sept. 1904; played Lettice in His Majesty's Servant, Juliet in Romeo and Juliet, Lady Mary in Monsieur Beaucaire, Mildred in The Perfect Lover, Sept. 1905; Columbina in The Harlequin King, Countess de Roquelaine in Brigadier Gerard, at the Lyric Theatre, Desdemona in Othello, Maid Marian in Robin Hood, Oct. 1906; Anne Churchill in The Little Admiral, and Lady Clancarty.

Died 9 March 1941.

MILLARD, Col Reginald Jeffery, CMG, 1917; CBE 1919; Hon. Consulting Physician Prince Henry Hospital, Sydney; *b* 1868; *m* 1898, Margaret Alice Millard. *Educ:* Sydney University; University College, London. Served European War, 1915-17 (despatches, CMG, CBE, 1914-15 Star, two medals). *Address:* 135 Macquarie Street, Sydney, NSW.

Died 14 Nov. 1943.

MILLAY, Edna St Vincent, LittD, LHD; Poet; Member of American Academy of Arts and Letters; Member of American Society of Composers, Authors and Publishers; *b* Rockland, Me, 22 Feb. 1892; *d* of Henry Tolman Millay and Cora Buzzell; *m* 1923, Eugen Jan Boissevain. *Educ:* Vassar. LittD Tufts, Russell Sage Foundation Coll., Colby Coll., Univ. of Wis; LHD NY Univ. *Publications:* Renascence and other Poems, 1917; Figs from Thistles, 1920; Second April 1921; Aria da Capo, 1921; The Lamp and the Bell, 1921; Two Slatterns and a King, 1921; The Harp-Weaver, and other Poems, 1923; The King's Henchman, 1927; The Buck in the Snow, 1928; Poems, 1929; Fatal Interview, 1931; The Princess marries the Page, 1932; Wine from these Grapes, 1934; Flowers of Evil, from the French of Charles Baudelaire (with George Dillon), 1936; Conversation at Midnight, 1937; Huntsman, What Quarry? 1939; Make Bright the Arrows, 1940; Collected Sonnets, 1941; Collected Lyrics, 1943; winner, Pulitzer prize, 1922, for best volume of verse. *Address:* Austerlitz, NY, USA.

Died 19 Oct. 1950.

MILLBOURN, Sir Ralph, Kt 1934; Member of London Stock Exchange since 1927; *b* 27 Sept. 1862; *s* of late James and late Mary Millbourn; *m* 1892 Alice S. Jones (decd); no *c. Educ:* Private School, High Wycombe. Became associated with John Barker and Co. Ltd 1885; Vice-Chairman 1915; retired from the Company 1927; Chairman of Ex-Service Welfare Society for Mentally disabled neurasthenic Ex-Service men for about 8 years; Liveryman of the Merchant Taylors' Company; Freeman of City of London.

Died 27 Aug. 1942.

MILLER, Alexander Thomas; KC 1919; *b* 14 Oct. 1875; *s* of Alexander Allen and Mary Ellen Miller; *m* 1st, Ruth Barrett; three *s* one *d*; 2nd, Harrie Cooper; one *s* one *d. Educ:* Brighton College; Liverpool University. *Address:* 2 Essex Court, Temple, EC4. *T:* Central 8374. *Club:* Garrick.

Died 1 March 1942.

MILLER, Maj.-Gen. Austin T., CB 1942; MC; *b* 28 July 1888; *s* of Joseph Miller, JP, of Bedford, Beds; *m* 1916, Eileen, *d* of Col Sir Edward Cole, CB; one *d. Educ:* Bedford School; Caius College, Cambridge. Entered Indian Army, 10th Bengal Lancers, 1910; transferred to Sherwood Foresters, 1914; Staff College, Camberley, 1921–22; commanded 1st Bn Sherwood Foresters; commanded 164th Infantry Brigade; Maj.-Gen. in charge of Administration, Scottish Command; retired pay, 1945. *Address:* c/o Grindlay & Co., 54 Parliament Street, SW1. *Club:* Junior United Service.

Died 16 May 1947.

MILLER, Sir Dawson, Kt 1918; KC 1912; *b* Dec. 1867; 2nd *s* of Thos R. Miller, London; *m* 1894, Effie Thérèse, *d* of John Mill Frodsham, MD, JP; two *d. Educ:* Durham School; Trinity College, Oxford; BA 1890. Bar, Inner Temple, 1891; Chief Justice of the High Court, Patna, India, 1917–28. *Address:* 19 Tite Street, Chelsea, SW3. *T:* Sloane 0507; The Pines, Bembridge, IOW. *T:* Bembridge 124. *Club:* United University.

Died 3 Oct. 1942.

MILLER, Sir Francis N.; *see* Norie-Miller.

MILLER, Gray; Chairman, British American Tobacco Co. Ltd; Vice-Chairman Tobacco Securities Trust; *b* 8 May 1885; *s* of Henry R. Miller and Jeannie Dabney Gray; *m* 1945, Noreen, *d* of William Barraclough. Was Chairman Imperial Tobacco Co. of Canada—residing at Montreal. *Recreations:* fishing, shooting. *Address:* Bridley Manor, Worplesdon, Surrey. *T:* Worplesdon 65.

Died 11 May 1947.

MILLER, Harold Tibbatts, CBE 1935; *b* 17 March 1873; *y s* of Henry Miller and Margaret Hack; *m* 1902, Ethel Amy, *o c* of Alfred Armfield, Bermondsey and Hove; four *s* one *d. Educ:* Alleyn's School, Dulwich. Entered Trinity House Service, 1889; Chief Accountant, 1921; Assistant Secretary, 1929; Sec. 1932; retired 1935; Liveryman of Ship wrights Company; Hon. Visitor, King George's Fund for Sailors; Member of Council, Children's Aid Society, and Tower Hill Improvement Scheme; Hon. Sec. and Treas., Seamark Club for Junior Officers of the Merchant Navy. *Recreation:* golf. *Address:* 86 Portsea Hall, Portsea Place, W2. *T:* Paddington 0671; Seamark Club, 7 The Crescent, Minories, EC3. *T:* Royal 5200.

Died 10 May 1948.

MILLER, James, RSA 1930; ARSA 1900; FRIBA; FRSE; Architect (retd). *Educ:* Perth Academy. Member of Royal Fine Art Commission for Scotland since 1932; Member of Scottish Architectural Advisory Committee, 1935. *Principal works:* Glasgow International Exhibition Buildings, 1901; Glasgow Royal Infirmary Reconstruction; New Medical School, Glasgow Univ.; New Natural Philosophy Buildings, Glasgow Univ.; Clyde-bank Burgh Buildings and Town Hall; Turnberry Hotel, Ayrshire; Glasgow Central Station Hotel Extension; Perth Royal Infirmary; Institution of Civil Engineers, Westminster; Extensions and alterations to Institution of Mechanical Engineers, Storey's Gate, Westminster; Hotel-Hydro, Peebles; new Head Office for the Union Bank of Scotland, Ltd, Glasgow; Commercial Bank of Scotland, West George Street, Glasgow; Commercial Bank, Bothwell St, Glasgow; Welfare Buildings for Cadbury Bros, Bournville; Royal Scottish Automobile Club, Glasgow; Commercial College, Glasgow; Stirling New Royal Infirmary; new Head Offices for Nairn & Co., Kirkcaldy; Reconstruction of Broadway House, Westminster; Restoration of the Church of the Holy Rude, Stirling. *Address:* Randolphfield, Stirling. *Clubs:* Art, Royal Scottish Automobile (Glasgow).

Died 28 Nov. 1947.

MILLER, James Gordon; Vice-President of West India Committee since 1947; *b* 9 Aug. 1874; *m* 1909, Elizabeth Helen Cameron; no *c. Educ:* City Public School and the Athenæum College, Glasgow. A Governor of Imperial Coll. of Tropical Agriculture and Member of Finance Cttee; Dep. Chm. of West India Cttee, 1936–45, Chm. 1945–47; Chm. Caroni Ltd; Director of various companies. *Address:* Frithbie, Annan, Dumfriesshire. *T:* Annan 116. *Clubs:* West Indian (Vice-Pres.); Royal Clyde Yacht, Royal Scottish Automobile (Glasgow).

Died 11 Sept. 1950.

MILLER, Sir John Ontario, KCSI 1911; CSI 1901; Hon. LLD (Aberdeen); *b* Toronto, Canada, 7 Aug. 1857; *m* 1888, Mary Evelina, *d* of late Sir Alfred Lyall; one *s* (and one killed European War, 1914). *Educ:* King's College, Aberdeen. Chief Secretary to Government NW Provinces and Oudh, 1898–1902; Secretary Government of India, Revenue Department, 1902–03; Chief Commissioner Central Provinces, India, 1905–07; Ordinary Member of Council of Governor-General of India, 1907–10; Member of the Port of London Authority, 1917–25; Assistant Secretary in Ministry of Food; has written pamphlets and articles on currency questions. *Address:* Robson's Orchard, Mid Lavant, Sussex. *T:* Lavant 137.

Died 19 Jan. 1943.

MILLER, Reginald Henry, MD, FRCP; Consulting Physician, St Mary's Hospital Paddington, W2; Consulting Physician, Paddington Green Children's Hospital, W2; *s* of Dr Andrew Miller, Hampstead; *m. Educ:* Charterhouse; St Mary's Hospital; London University. *Publications:* medical. *Address:* Park Prewett EMS Hospital, Basingstoke.

Died 23 Dec. 1948.

MILLER, William; author and newspaper correspondent; b Wigton, Cumberland, 8 Dec. 1864; s of William Miller, mine-owner; m 1895, Ada Mary, d of Major T. P. Wright. Educ: Rugby; Hertford College, Oxford. MA (1st class Classical Moderations; 1st class Literae Humaniores). Called to the Bar, Inner Temple, 1889; entering journalism, contributed to Cosmopolis, The Quarterly Review, The Contemporary Review, The English Historical Review (since 1892), History, The Journal of Hellenic Studies, Foreign Affairs, etc; correspondent of the Morning Post in Rome and Athens, 1903–37; for the last forty years has also been occupied in studying Medieval and modern Greek and Balkan history; FBA; FRHistS; Hon. LLD National University of Athens; Hon. Student of British Archæological School at Athens; Corr. Member, Historical and Ethnological Society of Greece and of Academy of Athens. Publications: The Latins in the Levant (1204–1566); Essays on the Latin Orient; The Ottoman Empire and its Successors (1801–1936); A History of the Greek People (1821–1921); Trebizond, the last Greek Empire; The Balkans; Travels and Politics in the Near East; The Latin Orient; The English in Athens before 1821; The Early Years of Modern Athens; The Turkish Restoration in Greece, 1718–1797; Greek Life in Town and Country; Greece, 1928; also the chapters on Medieval Greece and the Balkans in the Cambridge Medieval History. Recreation: swimming. Address: Ocean View Hotel, Durban, South Africa.

Died 23 Oct. 1945.

MILLER, Sir William (Frederic), 5th Bt cr 1788; b 7 April 1868; S father, 1875; m 1890, Mary Augusta, d of late Charles John Manning, niece of Cardinal Manning; one s one d. 3rd Batt. Princess of Wales's Own Yorkshire Regt, retired, 1887; served South Africa (Imperial Yeomanry), 1900–01; served as Capt. on the Staff of 17th Corps with the BEF (wounded 29 Sept. 1918). Owns about 4500 acres. Recreation: hunting. Heir: s Alastair George Lionel Joseph, late Capt. Irish Guards and Flight Comdr RAF [b 5 March 1893; m 1st, 1919, Kathleen, y d of late Major Stephen Howard, CBE; one s; 2nd, 1927, Margaret May, d of Frederick Shotter; two d]. Club: Marlborough-Windham.

Died 20 Dec. 1948.

MILLER, Col William Miles, CBE 1941; MC; b Montreal, Canada, 12 Sept. 1891; s of Frederick Fraser Miller, Civil Engineer, and Mary Sophie Bertha Smith; m 1926, Marion Gooderham Huestis, Toronto, Canada; one s one d. Educ: Royal Military College of Canada. Commissioned Royal Canadian Engineers, 1912; Royal Engineers, 1914; Royal Signals, 1921; served European War, France, 1914–19 (MC, despatches thrice); Canada, 1919–21; England, 1921–27; India, 1927–39; Chief Signal Officer Burma for Burma Rebellion, 1931–32 (despatches); OC Peshawar District Signals, 1932–36; NW Frontier Operations, 1933 (despatches); Chief Signal Officer, British Troops in Egypt, 1939–41 (CBE), East Africa Command, 1941–44; retired pay, 1944. Address: c/o R. Sec., Lloyds Bank Ltd, 6 Pall Mall, SW1. Club: Army and Navy.

Died 30 Sept. 1946.

MILLER-CUNNINGHAM, Sir George, of Leithenhopes, KBE 1921; CB 1914; DL, JP, Peeblesshire; BA (Oxon); b 27 Jan. 1867; assumed additional name of Miller-on succeeding to Leithenhopes Estate; 2nd s of late George Miller-Cunningham, FRSE, JP, DL, Leithenhopes, Peeblesshire; m 1897, Georgiana Justina Elizabeth Lucy (d 1937), o d of late Captain George Gordon Macpherson of Cluny, Coldstream Guards; one s. Educ: Shrewsbury School; Brasenose College, Oxford. Admitted to the Scottish Bar, 1892; Assistant Private Secretary to the First Lord of the Admiralty (Lord Tweedmouth), 1906–08; to the Secretary of State for the Colonies (Earl of Crewe) 1908–10; Private Secretary to

the Lords President of the Council (Viscount Wolverhampton, Earl Beauchamp, and Viscount Morley, Marquess of Crewe, Earl Curzon), 1910–19; Personal Private Sec. to the Secretary of State for Foreign Affairs and Leader of the House of Lords (Earl Curzon), 1919–20. Recreation: fishing. Address: Leithen Lodge, Innerleithen, Peeblesshire. Clubs: Royal Automobile; New, Edinburgh.

Died 11 July 1945.

MILLER-JONES, Sir Thomas, Kt 1937; Chairman, Thomas Hill-Jones Limited and Frazzi Limited; b 26 April 1874; s of late Thomas Hill-Jones; m 1903, Bessie Kate, d of late George Miller, Southsea; one s one d. Educ: Uxbridge. Contested (C) Limehouse Division of Stepney, 1923 and 1924; Member of London Hospital House Committee; Member Grand Council of Federation of British Industries. Recreations: yachting, golf. Address: Mayes Park, Warnham, Sussex; Bou-Saada, East Beach, Selsey, Sussex. Clubs: Constitutional, Royal Corinthian Yacht, Chemical.

Died 15 Sept. 1944.

MILLERAND, Alexandre; de l'Institut; b Paris, 1859; m; two s two d. Educ: Lycée Michelet à Vanves (Seine); Lycée Henri IV à Paris. Avocat à la Cour d'Appel de Paris depuis 1881; Conseiller municipal de Paris (1884–85); Député de Paris, 1885–1920; Ministre du Commerce, 1899–1902; Ministre des Travaux publics, 1909–10; Ministre de la Guerre 1912–13, et d'Août 1914 à Novembre 1915; Commissaire général de la République d'Alsace et de Lorraine, 1919–20; President du Conseil, Ministre des Affaires Etrangères, Janvier 1920; President of the French Republic, 1920–24; Member of Senate, 1925–27, and since 1927. Publications: Socialisme réformiste en France 1903; Travail et travailleurs, 1906; Politique de réalisations, 1911; Pour la défense nationale, 1913; La Guerre liberatrice, 1918. Recreation: bon marcheur. Address: 10 rue Mansart, Versailles; 94 Avenue Kléber, Paris, XVIᵉ.

Died 6 April 1943.

MILLETT, George Prideaux, CIE 1915; Conservator of Forests, Bombay Presidency, retired; b Longford, near Gloucester, 23 March 1863; s of J. C. Millett, Penzance; m 1896, Saidé Russet, d of late Charles Gibson Millar, CE, Melbourne, Victoria; three s four d. Entered Indian Imperial Forest Service, 1884; Senior Conservator of Forests, 1911; retired, 1918; Additional Member of Bombay Legislative Council, 1911–12, and 1914; King-Emperor's Durbar Medal, Delhi, 1911; Captain Cheshire Regt (TF), 1915; TFR 1917; Timber Supply Dept, Board of Trade, 1917–21. Address: 21 Holland Villas Road, Kensington, W14.

Died 29 Dec. 1950.

MILLS, Alderman Sir Ernest Arnold, Kt 1938; Freeman of Lambeth; m; three s one d. Late Alderman and Mayor of Lambeth; Member Lambeth Borough Council for over 40 years; formerly Member Metropolitan Water Board. Address: The Crest, Gloucester Road, Tankerton-on-Sea, Kent; 4 St Saviours Road, SW2.

Died 15 Dec. 1949.

MILLS, Rev. Canon Henry Holroyd, MA, FZS; Canon Residentiary and Treasurer of Truro Cathedral, 1925–44; Hon. Canon of the Stall of St Uni in Truro Cathedral, 1915; b 20 Sept. 1860; s of late Major-General Henry Mills, Bengal Staff Corps, and Mary Anne Mills, d of George Chaplain Holroyd; m 1888, Edith Annie (d 1927), d of Rev. G. Davey Symonds; no c. Educ: Harrow; Pembroke College, Cambridge; Leeds Clergy School. Deacon, 1883; Priest, 1885; Curate of Longton, Staffs, 1883–85; Burford, Salop, 1885–88; Curate-in-charge of Tichborne, Hants, 1888–94; Vicar of Treslothan, Cornwall, 1894–1906; Rector of St Stephen-in-Brannel, Cornwall, 1906–25; Rural Dean of St Austell, 1911–25; Vice-President of the Royal

Institution of Cornwall (President, 1920–21). Awarded the Henwood Gold Medal for articles on Old West Country Goldsmiths, 1923; Silver Medal of Royal Cornwall Polytechnic Society for Photographs of Bird Life. Collection of photographs of the Celtic Crosses of Cornwall presented to the Royal Institution of Cornwall. *Address:* Petherton, Truro. *T:* Truro 2866.

Died 6 Jan. 1947.

MILLS, Stephen, CMG 1920; *b* Sydney, NSW, 1857; *s* of late John and Emily Mills, Ashfield, NSW; *m* Alice Maude, *d* of William Hudson, Roslyn House, Croydon; two *s. Educ:* private schools. Member Public Service, NSW, 1880; Surveyor and Engineer; admitted to the Bar, NSW, 1903; joined Commonwealth Service, 1904; Comptroller General of Customs, 1913; Deputy Commissioner, Inter-State Commission, 1917. *Publication:* Taxation in Australia, 1925. *Recreations:* walking, reading. *Address:* Valency Road, Malvern, Melbourne, SE6, Australia.

Died 1 Nov. 1948.

MILMAN, Sir Francis, 5th Bt *cr* 1800; *b* 27 Oct. 1872; *s* of 4th Bt and Katharine, *d* of Stephen C. Moore, DL, JP, Barne, Clonmel; *S* father, 1922; *m* 1898, Georgina Maude Emma, *o c* of late Thomas Ripon Wallis. *Heir: b* William Ernest, *b* 11 Aug. 1875. *Address:* La Rinconada, Doblas FCS, Pampa Central, Argentina.

Died 10 Oct. 1946.

MILNE, 1st Baron *cr* 1933, of Salonika and of Rubislaw, Co. Aberdeen; **George Francis Milne,** GCB 1927; GCMG 1919; KCB 1918; KCMG 1919; CB 1912; DSO 1902; DCL; LLD; KGStJ; Grand Cross of several foreign orders; Master Gunner, St James's Park, 1929–46; Col Comdt RA since 1918 and Pioneer Corps, 1940–45; *b* 5 Nov. 1866; *s* of late George Milne of Westwood, Aberdeen; *m* 1905, Claire Marjoribanks, MBE, DGStJ, *d* of Sir John N. Maitland, 5th Bt; one *s* one *d.* Entered army, 1885; Captain, 1895; Major, 1900; Lt-Colonel, 1902; Col, 1905; Brig.-Gen. commanding 4th Divisional Artillery, 1913–14; Maj.-Gen. 1915; temp. Lt-Gen. 15 Dec. 1915; General, 1920; Field-Marshal, 1928; served Soudan, 1898, including Khartoum (British and Khedive's medals with clasp); South Africa (1899–1902, despatches, DSO, Brevet of Lieut-Col, medal and four clasps, King's medal two clasps); European War, 1914–18 (despatches, Maj.-Gen., Lt-Gen., General, KCB, KCMG, GCMG), Chief Staff Officer, 3rd Corps Headquarters Staff, 2nd Army; Commanded 27th Division and 16th Army Corps; British Salonica Force and Army of Black Sea; Lieutenant of the Tower of London, 1920–23; ADC to the King, 1923; GOC-in-C Eastern Command, 1923–26; Chief of Imperial General Staff, 1926–33; Governor and Constable of Tower of London, 1933–38. *Heir: s* Major Hon. George Douglass Milne, RA [*b* 10 Feb. 1909; *m* 1940, Cicely, 3rd *d* of Ronald Leslie, 8 Sloane Gardens, SW1; one *s* one *d.* Served war of 1939–45 (wounded and prisoner)]. *Address:* 66 Exeter House, Putney Heath, SW15. *Club:* Army and Navy.

Died 23 March 1948.

MILNE, Arthur; *see* Milne, E. A.

MILNE, Christian Hoyer Millar, MA, DLitt (Aber.), 1926; DPhil (Oxon), 1941; FRSE 1905; *b* Montrose, 18 Sept. 1870; *s* of late Fraser Gordon Milne and Jane Eliza Cruickshank; unmarried. *Educ:* Grammar School and University of Aberdeen. Graduated in Arts, 1891, with first-class honours in Philosophy. One of the Masters in George Watson's College for Boys, Edinburgh, 1892–1900; Rector, The High School, Arbroath, 1900–11; Headmaster, Daniel Stewart's College, Edinburgh, 1911–35. *Publication:* A Reconstruction of Augustine's Gospels, 1926. *Recreations:* cycling and golf. *Address:* 19 Merchiston Gardens, Edinburgh 10. *T:* Edin. 63545. *Clubs:* Stewart's College, Edinburgh.

Died 7 Nov. 1945.

MILNE, Rev. Edgar Astley, MA; JP; Rector of Compton Valence, Dorchester, since 1933; *b* 1862; *s* of late Alfred Milne, Chiddingfold, Surrey; *m* Amy Elizabeth (*d* 1934), *d* of Thomas Starling, Higham Ferrars, Northamptonshire; three *d. Educ:* Charterhouse; Trinity College, Cambridge; Leeds Clergy School. Master Trinity Beagles, 1883–85; curate of Ashtead, Surrey, 1886; Rector of Shenley, Bucks, 1890–1900; farmed own glebe, Master of North Bucks Harriers, 1895–1900; Master Cattistock Foxhounds, 1900–31; Chaplain West Somerset Yeomanry since 1912; Chaplain, 2nd South-Western Mounted Brigade, 1914. *Recreations:* foxhunting and gardening. *Address:* The Rectory, Compton Valence, Dorchester. *TA:* Compton Valence.

Died 29 Jan. 1945.

MILNE, (Edward) Arthur, MBE; FRS 1926; MA (Camb., Oxford), MSc (Manchester), DSc (Oxford), Hon. DSc (Amsterdam), FRAS, FRMetSoc, FInstP; Rouse Ball Professor of Mathematics and Fellow of Wadham College, Oxford University, since 1928; *b* Hull, 14 Feb. 1896; *s* of late Sidney Arthur Milne, Hessle, E Yorks; *m* 1st, 1928, Margaret Scott (*d* 1938), *d* of Hugh Fraser Campbell, of Dornoch, Sutherland; one *s* two *d;* 2nd, 1940, Beatrice Brevoort (*d* 1945), *d* of late William Whetten Renwick, New York; one *d. Educ:* Hymers College, Hull; Trinity College, Cambridge (Entrance Scholar and Senior Scholar). Attached Anti-Aircraft Experimental Section Munitions Inventions Department, 1916–19; Lieut RNVR, 1917–19; Fellow of Trinity Coll., 1919–25; Smith's Prizeman, 1922; Assistant Director of the Solar Physics Observatory, Cambridge, 1920–24; Lecturer, Trinity College, Cambridge, 1924–25; University Lecturer in Astrophysics, Cambridge, 1922–25; Beyer Professor of Applied Mathematics, Manchester University, 1924–28; served Ordnance Board, Ministry of Supply, 1939–44; Bakerian Lecturer, 1929; Lecturer, Summer School, University of Michigan, 1929; Johnson Memorial Prize, 1931; Halley Lecturer, 1932; special lecturer, Univ. College of Wales, Aberystwyth, 1933; Joule Lecturer (Manchester), 1934; Gold Medal, Royal Astronomical Society, 1935; President, London Mathematical Society, 1937–39; Royal Medal of Royal Society, 1941; James Scott Lecturer, Royal Soc. of Edinburgh, 1943; Pres. R. Astronomical Soc., 1943–45. Bruce Medal, Astronomical Society of the Pacific, 1945; Hopkins Prize, Camb. Phil. Soc., 1946; Hon. Mem., Amer. Astronom. Soc., 1947; For. Hon. Mem., Amer. Acad. Arts and Sciences, 1947; Hon. Mem. Calcutta Math. Soc., 1948. *Publications:* Thermodynamics of the Stars (Handbuch der Astrophysik, 1930); The White Dwarf Stars, 1932; Relativity, Gravitation and World-Structure, 1935; Vectorial Mechanics, 1948; Kinematic Relativity 1948; paper, on mathematical physics, relativity, and astrophysics. *Address:* Wadham College, Oxford; 19 Northmoor Road, Oxford.

Died 21 Sept. 1950.

MILNE, George Torrance, CBE 1923; *b* 1862; *m* 1904, Bessie, *γ d* of John Golby. *Educ:* Edinburgh University. Senior Trade Commissioner in Canada, 1918–19 and 1921–23. *Address:* Lansdowne House, Holly Walk, Leamington Spa.

Died 6 Feb. 1943.

MILNE-REDHEAD, Lt-Col Richard Henry, CMG 1900; *b* 1862; *e s* of Richard Milne-Redhead; *m* 1888, Kathleen Mary (*d* 1937), *e d* of Surg.-Major Kiernan; two *d. Educ:* Eton. Late 3rd Batt. East Lancashire Regiment; served South Africa (despatches, Queen's medal four clasps, CMG). *Address:* Whitegates, Copythorne Road, Brixham, S Devon.

Died 7 Jan. 1944.

MILNE-THOMSON, Col Alexander, CMG 1916; *m* 1st, Eva Mary (*d* 1922), *d* of late Rev. J. Milne; 2nd, 1925, Else *d* of late Burgomaster Karl Fromknecht, Goslar, Germany; two *s* one *d*. *Educ:* Edinburgh University. Served S Africa 1902 (Queen's medal with two clasps); European War, 1914–18 (despatches twice, CMG, 1914 Star, French Croix de Guerre with Silver Star). *Address:* Wairoa, Stockland, Honiton, Devon. *T:* Stockland 227.

Died 17 Oct. 1944.

MILNE-WATSON, Sir David, 1st Bt *cr* 1937; Kt 1927; TD; MA, LLB, LLD (Hon.), DL; Hon. Col The Rangers, King's Royal Rifle Corps; Governor of the Gas Light and Coke Co.; *s* of David Watson and Anne Carnegie Milne; has assumed the additional surname of Milne; *m* Olga Cecily, *d* of Rev. George Herbert; two *s* one *d*. *Educ:* Merchiston Castle and University, Edinburgh; Paris; Marburg University; Balliol College, Oxford. Barrister Middle Temple, 1896; contested SE Essex, 1895; Past President of the National Gas Council; Past Chairman, Federation of Gas Employers; Past Chairman, Joint Industrial Council for the Gas Industry; President British Gas Federation; awarded Birmingham medal of Institution of Gas Engineers, 1938; Chairman of the British Gas Engineers, 1938; past Chairman British Sulphate of Ammonia Federation; Chairman of National Benzole Association; Member of National Fuel and Power Committee; past Member of Government Department of Scientific and Industrial Research; Chairman of the Government Market Supply Committee; DL County of London; Member of National Defence Public Interest Committee; Governor of Imperial College; Pres. Dorset County Hospital, 1939; Member of the Territorial Force Association of the County of London, and during War, 1914–18, was Chm. the Hospital Supplies Committee; was member of Govt Committee on Housing. Chief of the Scottish Clans Association of London, 1936–37. *Recreations:* fishing, shooting, gardening. *Heir: s* David Ronald [*b* 15 July 1904. Trinity College, Glenalmond; Balliol College, Oxford]. *Address:* Ashley Chase, Abbotsbury, Dorset. *Clubs:* Athenæum, Flyfishers'.

Died 3 Oct. 1945.

MILNER, Frank, CMG 1925; MA; Headmaster Waitaki High School, Oamaru, NZ, since 1906; *b* Nelson, NZ, 7 Nov. 1875; *s* of late Wm Milner of 102 Nile Street E, Nelson, NZ; *m* 1907, Florence Violet, *e d* of W. Harrison George, Melbourne; three *s* one *d*. *Educ:* Nelson College; Canterbury University College. Junior and Senior Scholar of University of New Zealand; Classical exhibitioner; MA, 1896, with first-class honours. Assistant Master at Nelson College, 1897–1906; President NZ Secondary Schools Association, 1920, 1930–32; NZ Representative at Pan-Pacific Educational Conference, 1921, at Vancouver Conference of Canadian Council of Education, 1929, and at Boston World Rotary Conference, 1933; Member of National Council of Education; Overseas Member of English Headmasters' Conference; Member NZ University Senate, 1927–29; Member NZ Council Boy Scouts Association; Member NZ Council for Educational Research; President, NZ Federation of Teachers, 1930; Fellow and North Otago Representative of Royal Empire Society. *Recreations:* tennis, swimming, tramping. *Address:* Waitaki High School, Oamaru, New Zealand.

Died 9 Dec. 1944.

MILNER, Frank Leopold; KC 1914; *b* 14 Aug. 1870; *s* of late P. W. Milner, of Yorkshire ancestry, and Elizabeth, *d* of late Caleb Hammond; *m* 1st, Hannah Sarah (*d* 1926), *d* of late Adam Esson Dechman of Sherbrooke, NS; 2nd, 1928, Una Eliza, *d* of late Rev. John Cameron, Bridgetown, NS. *Educ:* lPublic School. Taught in public schools a few years; admitted to the Nova Scotia Bar, 1895; Recorder and Town Clerk of

Bridgetown, NS, a number of years until he removed to Amherst, 1910; Mayor of Amherst, 1918; Member of the Nova Scotia Board of Commissioners for the Promotion of Uniformity of Provincial Legislation in Canada, 1927; Chairman of the Workmen's Compensation Board of Nova Scotia, 1928–38; Special Lecturer for several years in Dalhousie University Law School in Conveyancing. *Publications:* articles in law magazines. *Recreation:* reading. *Address:* Amherst, Nova Scotia. *TA:* Milner. *T:* 2818.

Died 10 Feb. 1946.

MILNER-JONES, Edward William; Recorder of Swansea since 1930; *b* 1853; *e s* of Edward Jones of Velindre, Llandovery; *m* Isabel, *d* of the late Rev. H. Hayter-Hames, Rector of Chagford, Devon. Called to Bar, Lincoln's Inn, 1881; Recorder of Carmarthen, 1905–17; of Merthyr Tydvil, 1917–30. *Address:* Chisbury, Christchurch Road, SW14.

Died 19 March 1942.

MILROY, Thomas Hugh, MD, DSc, FRSE; Hon. LLD Edin.; Hon. DSc Nat. Univ. Ireland; Hon. MD (Dublin Univ.); Hon. DSc (Belfast); formerly Professor of Physiology, Queen's University, Belfast, now Emeritus Professor; *b* Wigtownshire, 1869; *e s* of late John Milroy of Kirkcowan, Wigtownshire. *Educ:* University of Edinburgh; University of Berlin; University of Marburg. Formerly Assistant Professor and Lecturer Edinburgh University. *Publications:* A Text-book of Practical Physiological Chemistry (with late Dr J. A. Milroy); papers on various physiological subjects, published chiefly in the Journal of Physiology. *Address:* Woodville, North Berwick. *T:* North Berwick 387.

Died 20 March 1950.

MINCHIN, Lt-Col Charles Frederick, DSO 1900; *b* 22 Sept. 1862; *e s* of Charles Nicholls Minchin and Mary Jane Lugard; *m* 1905, Violet Winifred (*d* 1936), *d* of Henry Ellis of Charters House, Branksome Park, Bournemouth; one *d*. *Educ:* Cheltenham College; United Services College, Westward Ho!; Royal Military College, Sandhurst. Lieut Bedfordshire Regt, 1882; joined Indian Army, 1885; 1st (Prince Albert Victor's Own) Punjab Cavalry, 1886; Indian Political Dept 1891; served as Attaché, Calcutta; Assistant Political Officer, Khyber, Chitral, and Gilgit; Political Agent, Bikanir, 1902; Consul-General, Khorassan and Seistan, 1904; Superintendent of Gazetteer revision, Baluchistan, 1906; Political Agent Dir, Swat, Chitral, North-West Frontier Province, 1907; Political Agent Baghelkhand, 1908; Deputy Commissioner, Bannu, 1909–10; Divisional and Sessions, Judge Derajat, 1911; retired, 1921; served, 1897, as 2nd in command of an expedition sent by British West Charterland Co., London, to Lake Ngami Country in S Africa; served with S African Field Force, 1899–1902; first with Thorneycroft's Mounted Infantry, and later as Lieut-Col commanding 18th Battalion Imperial Yeomanry, and a mobile column. *Decorations:* Hazara Campaign, 1895 (medal with clasp); S African Campaign, 1899–1902 (despatches twice, DSO, 2 medals with 8 clasps). *Address:* 5 Selsey Avenue, Southsea. *T:* Portsmouth 31659.

Died 7 Dec. 1943.

MINCHIN, Harry Christopher, MA; engaged in literary and educational work; *b* 1861; 3rd *s* of Rev. Henry Charles Minchin, MA; *m* 1904, Olivia, *e d* of Rear-Admiral Reginald Yorke. *Educ:* Malvern College; Wadham College, Oxford, 1st class Mods; 2nd Lit. Hum. An assistant master till the age of forty; grew weary of being a whetstone to the wits of others, and took the plunge of independence; has since contributed to the leading newspapers, reviews, and magazines; was for fourteen years a reviewer of current literature in the Sunday Times; has published fugitive verses in English and in Latin; talked himself out on the wireless in 1925. *Publications:* The Arcadians (while at Bradfield); A Little Gallery of English Poets; Simples from Sir Thomas Browne's Garden; Oxford (with Robert Peel); The Life of Robert Browning (with late W. Hall Griffin), revised edition, 1938; Talks and Traits; Walter Savage Landor, Last Days, Letters and Conversations, 1934; Frensham Then and Now (with H. J. Baker), 1938. *Recreations:* walking, reading, thinking, hoping. *Address:* Gorsedene Cottage, Farnham, Surrey. *T:* Frensham 121.

Died 1 Nov. 1941.

MINFORD, Hugh. MP (U) Antrim, Parliament of Northern Ireland, since 1929; JP Co. Antrim. *Address:* Park View, Park Gate, Co. Antrim, Northern Ireland; Parliament Buildings, Belfast.

Died 18 Dec. 1950.

MINOT, George Richards, AB, MD, SD, FRCP (Edin.); FRCP (Lond.); Fellow, American Academy Arts and Sciences, American Philosophical Society, Royal Society of Medicine, etc.; Member, National Academy of Sciences of United States; Professor of Medicine, Harvard University, 1928-48, Emeritus, since 1948; Hon. Member (formerly Director) Thorndike Memorial Laboratory; Visiting Physician, Boston City Hospital, 1928-49, retired; Member Board of Consultation, Massachusetts General Hospital; Consulting Physician Peter Bent Brigham since 1928, and Beth Israel Hospital, Boston, since 1929; *b* Boston, 2 Dec. 1885; *s* of James Jackson Minot, MD, and Elizabeth Whitney; *m* 1915, Marian Linzee Weld; one *s* two *d*. *Educ:* Harvard University, AB 1908, MD 1912, SD 1928. Formerly Member Cancer Commission of Harvard Univ.; Vice-Pres. Harvard Alumni Assoc., 1947-48. Consulting Physiologist of the US Bureau of Mines, 1919; President American Climatological and Clinical Association, 1931-32; President Assoc. of Amer. Physicians, 1937-38; Vice-Pres., étranger, Société Française D'Hematologie, 1938-39; Chairman Section Practice of Medicine, Amer. Med. Assoc. 1935; Member of numerous scientific and medical organisations and received various awards. The most recent are Moxon medal of the Royal College of Physicians, London, 1933; The John Scott Medal of the Board of Directors of the City Trusts, City of Philadelphia, 1933; Nobel Laureate in Physiology and Medicine, 1934 (jointly with George Hoyt Whipple and William Parry Murphy for their discoveries concerning the liver treatment of the anæmias); Gold Medal of Massachusetts Humane Society, 1935; Gordon Wilson lecturer and medal of Amer. Clin. and Climat. Assoc. 1939. *Publications:* about 180 papers and articles in books on medical topics especially concerning the blood and its disorders. *Recreations:* gardening, cruising, golf, old books, natural history. *Address:* 311 Beacon St, Boston, Mass; 71 Sears Road, Brookline, Mass, USA. *Clubs:* Brookline Country; Tavern, Harvard, Saturday (Boston).

Died 25 Feb. 1950.

MINSHULL-FORD, Maj.-Gen. John Randle; *see* Ford.

MITCHELL, Alan Alexander McCaskill, CIE 1936; Commissioner, Lahore Division, Punjab; *b* 24 Nov. 1882; *s* of Hugh Mitchell, Barrister-at-Law, formerly Captain RE and Mary Catherine Edwards Creswell; *m* 1908, Mary Maclaurin (*d* 1932), *d* of James Drew of Craigencallie, Kirkcudbrightshire; one *s* one *d*. *Educ:* St Paul's School; Peterhouse, Cambridge. Entered Indian Civil Service, 1906. *Address:* Lahore, Punjab, India; c/o Grindlay and Co., 54 Parliament Street, SW1. *Clubs:* East India United Service; Punjab, Lahore; United Service, Simla.

Died 25 Nov. 1941.

MITCHELL, Arnold; Architect; *m* Edith Devitt; one *s* two *d*. *Educ:* privately. Soane medallist, foreign travelling student and medallist of the Royal Institute of British Architects; medallist of the Arch. Assoc. *Works:* Brook House, Agricultural Buildings for Cambridge University, University College School, Frognal, Thos Cook's Head Office, Berkeley Street, and Schools and Houses at home and abroad. *Recreation:* sketching. *Address:* Library Cottage, The Walk, Lyme-Regis. *T:* Lyme-Regis 124.

Died 2 Nov. 1944.

MITCHELL, Arthur Brownlow, OBE 1919; DL; Member Senate Queen's University, Member Parliament Queen's University since 1935; Chairman on Board-of-Management Royal Victoria Hospital, Belfast; *b* 24 Oct. 1865; *s* of Walter Mitchell and Annie Brownlow; *m* 1898, Mabel Christina Crouch; two *s* (*e s* killed in action) one *d*. *Educ:* Blue Coat School, Dublin; Royal Academical Institution, Belfast; Queen's University, Belfast. MB 1890, FRCSI 1900 (1st place). Surgeon Ulster Hospital, Children and Women; Surgeon Royal Victoria Hospital; Lieut-Col RAMC; Hon. Member of Army Medical Consultants Council, 1917-19. *Publications:* numerous articles in British Medical Journal, Trans Roy. Academy Med. of Ireland and Ulster Medical Society, Spiral Fractures, Sir Robt Jones Birthday Book, Surgical Articles Whitlas Dict. of Treatment. *Recreations:* cricket, golf. *Address:* 18 Derryvolgie Avenue, Belfast. *T:* 65111. *Clubs:* Ulster Reform, Belfast; Royal Co. Down Golf, etc.

Died 4 Sept. 1942.

MITCHELL, Charles Ainsworth; scientific author and forensic chemist; Editor of The Analyst; *b* Thetford, Norfolk, 20 Nov. 1867; 3rd *s* of Thomas Robinson Mitchell, MD, FRCS, and Sarah, *d* of Houghton Ainsworth; *m* Edith, *d* of Thomas Southwell Keely. *Educ:* King William's College, Isle of Man; Exeter College, Oxford (MA, DSc). Fellow Royal Institute of Chemistry, 1897. Vice-President, 1937-40; President of the Medico-Legal Society, 1935-37; Hon. Vice-President, Medico-Legal Society of France, 1937. *Publications:* Science and the Criminal, 1911; The Evidence of the Casket Letters, 1929; The Scientific Detective and The Expert Witness, 1931; Inks (4th ed.), 1937; several other scientific books; Flower Cameos (nom de plume, Michael Fancourt), 1939; A Scientist in the Criminal Courts, 1945; contributor of scientific or literary articles or verse to Discovery, Chambers's Journal, Illustrated London News, Art Worker's Quarterly, Windsor, etc. *Recreations:* photography and archæology. *Address:* 16 Blomfield Road, W9.

Died 5 Jan. 1948.

MITCHELL, Brig.-Gen. Charles Hamilton, CB 1918; CMG 1917; DSO 1916; MInstCE, MEngInstCan; MAmSocCE; Consulting Engineer and Dean of Faculty of Applied Science and Engineering, University of Toronto, 1919-41; *b* Canada, 1872; *s* of Rev. G. A. Mitchell, BA; *m* 1901, Myra E. Stanton; no *c*. *Educ:* Univ. of Toronto (BASc and CE); Hon. Degrees LLD and DEng.; Educated as Civil Engineer. City Engineer Niagara Falls, 1894-1901; Asst Engineer Ontario Power Co. of Niagara Falls, 1901-05; Consulting Engineer since 1906 on many Canadian hydroelectric projects and for Governments of Dominion of Canada and various Canadian Provinces on water power; served on numerous arbitrations and Royal Commission on Ontario Hydro-Radial Railways, and in 1924 appointed by Canadian Government to International Joint Board of Engineers on St Lawrence Waterway Project; President, Engineering Institute of Canada, 1929; Pres., Prof. Engineers' Assoc., Ontario, 1922; President, Toronto Board of Trade, 1927 and 1933; President, Empire Club of Canada, 1921; Officer in Militia Service of Canada since 1899; served European War, 1914-19, as General Staff Officer (Intelligence) with 1st Canadian Division, Canadian Corps, 2nd (Imperial) Army, and GHQ British Forces in Italy and at War Office (despatches seven times, DSO, CMG, CB); Officier Légion d'Honneur, France, 1916, Officer Order of Leopold, Belgium, 1917; Croix de Guerre, Belgium and Italy; Order of Crown of Italy. *Publications:* several technical works in book and pamphlet form on Hydro-Electric Power and Canadian

Economic subjects. *Recreations:* golf, walking, mountaineering (Alpine Club of Canada, Swiss Alpine Club). *Address:* University of Toronto, Toronto, Canada. *Clubs:* Athenæum; National (Pres. 1933 and 1934), York, Royal Canadian Yacht, Rosedale Golf, Murray Bay Golf, Military Institute, Toronto.

Died 26 Aug. 1941.

MITCHELL, Hon. Charles Richmond; a Justice of the Supreme Court of Alberta, Appellate Division, 1926; Chief Justice Trial Division since 1936; *b* 20 Nov. 1872; *s* of late James Mitchell, New Brunswick; *m*; two *s* one *d.* *Educ:* Newcastle, NB; University of New Brunswick, BA; King's Coll., Windsor, NS, BCL 1897. District Court Bench for Judicial District of Calgary, 1907–10; represented the Provincial constituency of Medicine Hat, 1910–13 and of Bow Valley, 1913–26; Attorney-General and Minister of Education, 1910–12; Minister of Public Works, 1913; Provincial Treasurer, 1913–21; Minister of Municipal Affairs and Health, 1920–21; KC 1917. *Address:* Court House, Edmonton, Alberta; 10018–114th Street, Edmonton, Alberta.

Died 16 Aug. 1942.

MITCHELL, Sir Edward Fancourt, KCMG 1918; KC, MA, LLB Camb.; Barrister; Member of Inner Temple; Member of the Bar in the States of Victoria and NSW; late Leader of the Bar in the State of Victoria; Chancellor of Archdiocese of Melbourne; President Melbourne Cricket Club; Hon. Member BMA; *b* 1855; *s* of late Sir William Mitchell, President of Legislative Council, Victoria; *m* Eliza Fraser, *d* of late Dr Morrison, Scotch College, Melbourne; four *d.* *Recreations:* watching high class cricket and football. *Address:* Equity Chambers, Bourke Street, Melbourne, Victoria, Australia. *Clubs:* Australian, Melbourne, Melbourne.

Died 7 May 1941.

MITCHELL, Adm. Francis Herbert, CB 1924; DSO 1915; *b* 1876; *s* of Col Herbert Leonard Mitchell, 28 Cornwall Gardens, SW; *m* 1901, Marion, *d* of Henry Russell, Quebec; two *s.* Entered RN, 1889; Lieut, 1895; Commander, 1905; Captain, 1913; Rear-Admiral, 1924; Vice-Adm., 1929; Admiral, 1933; served in Gallipoli, 1915 (despatches four times, DSO, Legion of Honour); was Naval Adviser to Commander-in-Chief of the Forces, Egypt, up to 1916 (despatches twice, 3rd class Order of the Nile); Rear-Adm. in 2nd Battle Squadron Atlantic Fleet, 1925–26; Vice-Admiral in charge and Admiral Superintendent Malta Dockyard, 1928–31; retired list, 1933. *Address:* 20 Hyde Park Place, W2. *T:* Paddington 2584. *Club:* United Service.

Died 7 March 1946.

MITCHELL, Sir George Arthur, Kt 1935; MA, LLD, FRSE, MIMinE; DL; JP; Chairman and Director of several colliery companies; *b* 1860; *s* of Alexander Moncrieff and Elizabeth Mitchell; unmarried. *Educ:* Glasgow Univ. Pres.: Mining Institute of Scotland, 1894–98, Federated Institution of Mining Engineers, 1895–96, Lanarkshire Coalmasters' Assoc., 1901–08, and Mining Association of Great Britain, 1906–07; Vice-President, Institution of Engineers and Shipbuilders in Scotland, 1919–22; Member of Standing Committee of Iron and Steel Manufacturers for many years; Deacon of Incorporation of Hammermen in Glasgow, 1922–23; President, Glasgow Chamber of Commerce, 1923–25; Association of British Chambers of Commerce, 1928–29, and Royal Philosophical Society of Glasgow, 1928–31; Dean of Guild of Glasgow, 1932–34; Member of Scottish Committee on Iron and Steel Production under Ministry of Munitions during the war; Member of the Board of Trade Advisory Committee, 1928–30; British Delegate to Economic Consultative Committee at Geneva 1928, to International Statistical Convention at Geneva 1928; Chairman of Committee on Obsolete Tonnage, 1931; Member of 1930 Census of Production Committee. *Publications:* papers and addresses on Mining

and on Industrial and Commercial Subjects to Mining Institutions, Philosophical Society, Chambers of Commerce. *Address:* Park of Drumquhassle, Drymen. *T:* Drymen 12. *Clubs:* Western, New, Scottish Automobile (Glasgow).

Died 16 Feb. 1948.

MITCHELL, Harold John, CMG 1939; Member Overseas Settlement Board since 1936; *b* 1877; *s* of John Edmund Mitchell; *m* 1900, Clara Maud, *d* of Thomas Mortlock Powell; one *s* two *d.* *Address:* Friston Down, near Eastbourne.

Died 22 July 1941.

MITCHELL, Henry Tai, CMG 1939; JP; Chairman, Arawa Trust Board; Councillor, Rotorua Borough; Member of National Patriotic Fund Board (New Zealand), NZ Anglican Mission Trust Board and Board of Governors, Rotorua High School; *b* 5 May 1877; *s* of Henry Walker Mitchell, Dollar, near Edinburgh, and Whakarato Taiehu, Ohinemutu, Rotorua, NZ; *m* 1900, Te Aomihi Mere Konui; two *s* nine *d.* *Educ:* Public Schools; Three Kings' College, Auckland. Took up farming at Matata then served with his father who was one of the first licensed surveyors appointed in New Zealand; joined Lands and Survey Department in 1894; Assistant Surveyor, then District Surveyor, then Director of Native Surveys in Bay of Plenty District; resigned from Civil Service in 1914 and entered private practice as surveyor and engineer for 12 years; joined Native Department in 1926; declined Judgeship for Cook Islands in 1938. *Recreations:* President Rotorua Rugby Union and NZ Maori Lawn Tennis Assoc.; Hon. Surveyor Rotorua Racing Club. *Address:* Arawa Street, Rotorua, NZ. *T:* 102.

Died May 1944.

MITCHELL, Henry Thomas; retired; *b* 1870; *e s* of late Henry Mitchell, Acton, W; *m* 1900, Catharine Senior, *d* of late William Henry Wormsley, Penang; one *s.* *Educ:* Ealing College. Formerly with London and South-Western Bank, Limited; General Manager, Barclays Bank, 1925–33. *Recreation:* motoring. *Address:* 52 Castelnau, Barnes, SW13. *T:* Riverside 2198.

Died 14 Jan. 1946.

MITCHELL, James, CBE 1927; JP; *b* Aberdeen, 20 March 1865; *s* of James Mitchell, Cruden, Aberdeenshire; *m* 1908, Martha A. Buckle, Sydney; one *s* one *d.* *Educ:* Aberdeen. Joined New South Wales Police Service, 1884; passed through every phase of police work until attaining rank of Superintendent, 1908; visited police centres in Great Britain and continent, 1904, 1925 and 1930; responsible for present system of police training in New South Wales; Commissioner of Police for New South Wales, 1914–30; retired, 1930. *Recreations:* bowls and golf. *Address:* Cruden, 607 New South Head Road, Rose Bay, Sydney, New South Wales. *TA:* Nemesis, Sydney. *T:* FM 1840.

Died 27 Oct. 1941.

MITCHELL, Rev. John Thomas, MA Oxford, BD (TCD); Residentiary Canon of Liverpool Cathedral, 1933; Canon Emeritus since 1938; Rector of Wavertree since 1894; Vice-Chairman, Diocesan Board of Education since 1944; Member Diocesan Reorganisation Committee and of Board of Supervision of Church of England Training Colleges; Hon. Secretary Warrington Training College; Proctor and Assessor in Convocation; formerly Member Commission on Parochial Endowments; Chairman of the Northern Provincial Council for the Protection of Churches; *s* of Thomas Mitchell; *m* Isabella Caroline, *d* of John Bingham; one *d.* *Educ:* Loretto School; Corpus Christi College, Oxford; Leeds Clergy School. Ordained, 1888; Curate at West Ham Parish Church, Bexley, Kent, and Leeds Parish Church; Hon. Canon of Liverpool

1914–33. *Address:* Wavertree Rectory, Liverpool. *T:* Wavertree 98. *Clubs:* Athenæum; University, Athenæum, Liverpool.

Died 6 Aug. 1947.

MITCHELL, Margaret; *see* Marsh, M. M. M.

MITCHELL, Sir Peter Chalmers, Kt 1929; CBE 1918; FRS 1906; FZS, DSc, LLD; Hon. Student of Christ Church, Oxford; *b* Dunfermline, 23 Nov. 1864; *e s* of late Rev. Alex. Mitchell, DD; *m* Lilian, *y d* of late Rev. Charles Pritchard, DD, FRS, Savilian Professor of Astronomy in the University of Oxford. *Educ:* Aberdeen University (MA); Christ Church, Oxford (Exhibitioner); Berlin and Leipzig; honours in Mental Philosophy; University medallist in Literature; 1st class in Final Honour School of Natural Science; MA. University demonstrator in Comparative Anatomy, and assistant to Linacre Professor at Oxford, 1888–91; organising secretary for Technical Instruction to Oxfordshire County Council, 1891–93; lecturer on Biology at Charing Cross Hospital, 1892–94; at London Hospital, 1894; examiner in Biology to the Royal College of Physicians, 1892–96, 1901–03; Secretary to Zoological Society of London, 1903–35; examiner in Zoology to the University of London, 1903; member of Mr Tennant's Committee on Fishery Investigations and of Mr Harcourt's Committee on Sleeping Sickness; Captain, attached to Imperial General Staff, 1916–19; Liaison Officer War Office and British War Mission, 1918; Vice-Pres., Cremation Society; Hon. Vice-President Zoological Society; ARP Warden. *Publications:* Outlines of Biology, 1894; The Biological Problem of To-day (translated), 1896; Thomas Henry Huxley, 1900; The Nature of Man (translated), 1903; The Childhood of Animals, 1912; Evolution and the War, 1915; Report on the Propaganda Library in Intelligence Division of War Office, 1917; Centenary History of the Zoological Society of London, 1929; Materialism and Vitalism in Biology, 1930; The Seven Pillars (novel by W. F. Florez translated); Seven Red Sundays, 1936, Mr Witt Among the Rebels, 1936, and The War in Spain, 1937 (from Spanish of Ramón Sender); My Fill of Days: Reminiscences, 1937; My House in Málaga, 1938; The Forge (from Spanish of Arturo Barea), 1941; various scientific memoirs in the Anatomical Journal, Quarterly Journal of Microscopical Science, Proceedings of the Zoological Society, etc. *Address:* 44 Courtfield Gardens, SW5. *Clubs:* Savile, Athenæum.

Died 2 July 1945.

MITCHELL, Very Rev. Robert Andrew; Dean of Lincoln, since 1930; *s* of John Harper Mitchell, JP. *Educ:* Magdalen College, Oxford. Vicar of Highfield, Southampton, 1903–20; Vicar of St Michael, Chester Square, SW, 1920–30; Hon. Canon of Winchester, 1914–30; a Chaplain to the King, 1929–30. *Address:* The Deanery, Lincoln. *Club:* United University.

Died 13 July 1949.

MITCHELL, Thomas Walker, MD; Editor of the British Journal of Medical Psychology, 1920–35; *b* 18 Jan. 1869; *y s* of Robert Mitchell, Avoch, Ross-shire; *m* 1931, Henrietta Violet, *y d* of late Thomas George Kerans, Cheltenham. *Educ:* Fortrose Academy; University of Edinburgh. Graduated MB, CM, 1890; MD, 1906. Has been closely connected with the revival of psycho-therapeutics in England from the beginning in 1906–07, when a Society for the Study of Suggestive Therapeutics (afterwards the Psycho-Medical Soc.) was founded; Pres., Psycho-Medical Soc., 1911; Hon. Sec. of the Medical Section of the Society for Psychical Research, 1911–18; Pres. of the Society for Psychical Research, 1922; Fellow of the British Psychological Society (Chm. of the Medical Section, 1924); FRSM; Member of the British Psycho-Analytical Society; Frederic W. H. Myers Memorial Lecturer, 1931. *Publications:* The Psychology of Medicine, 1921; Medical Psychology and Psychical Research, 1922; Psychology

and Psychical Research (in Psychology and the Sciences, edited by Wm Brown), 1924; Problems in Psychopathology, 1927; Beneath the Threshold (The Myers Memorial Lecture), 1931; articles in the Proceedings of the Society for Psychical Research, the British Journal of Psychology, the British Medical Journal, and other periodicals. *Recreations:* cricket, shooting, fishing, chess, billiards. *Address:* Wayside, Fordcombe, near Tunbridge Wells. *T:* Fordcombe 83.

Died 19 Dec. 1944.

MITCHELL, Sir William Foot, Kt 1929; Lord of the Manor of Quendon; JP Essex; *b* 26 June 1859; *s* of W. S. Mitchell, Glasgow, and Harriet Foot, London; *m* 1886, Elsie (*d* 1937), *d* of Leonard J. Hadley, Gloucester; one *d.* *Educ:* privately; London, Glasgow, and Paris. Resided 14 years in the East as a merchant, mostly in China and Japan; retired, 1906; formerly a Director of the Shell Transport and Trading Co., Ltd, and the Chartered Bank of India, etc.; MP (C), Dartford Division of Kent, 1910, Saffron Walden Division of Essex, 1922–29. *Recreations:* riding and shooting. *Address:* Quendon Hall, Essex. *Club:* Carlton.

Died 31 July 1947.

MITCHELL, Air Chief Marshal Sir William Gore Sutherland, KCB 1938; CB 1935; CBE 1924; DSO 1918; MC, AFC; Gentleman Usher of the Black Rod, House of Lords, since 1941; Commandant, London Command, ATC, since 1942; *b* Sydney, Australia, 8 March 1888; *s* of W. B. Mitchell; *m* 1919, Essy, *y d* of Lt-Col W. Plant, Indian Army. *Educ:* Wellington College. Highland Light Infantry, 1909; seconded to Royal Flying Corps, 1913; transferred to Royal Air Force, 1919; served European War, 1914–19 (despatches, MC, DSO, AFC); Waziristan, 1919–20, 1922–23 (despatches, CBE); Director of Training, Air Ministry, 1929–33; Commandant, RAF College, Cranwell, 1933–35; Air Officer Commanding British Forces in Iraq, 1935–37; Air Member for Personnel on Air Council, 1937–39; Air Officer Commanding-in-Chief, Royal Air Force, Middle East, 1939–40; Inspector-General of RAF, 1940–41. *Address:* 14 Eresby House, Rutland Gate, SW1. *Club:* Army and Navy.

Died 15 Aug. 1944.

MITCHELL-INNES, Alfred; *b* 30 June 1864; *y s* of Alexander Mitchell-Innes, Ayton Castle and Whitehall, Berwickshire; *m* 1919, Evelyn (*d* 1946), *d* of Sir William Miller, Bt, Manderston, Berwickshire, and *widow* of Richard Hunter, Thurston, E Lothian. *Educ:* privately. Entered the Diplomatic Service, 1890; appointed to Cairo, 1891; Financial Adviser of the King of Siam, 1896; Under-Secretary of State for Finance in Egypt, 1899; Councillor of British Embassy, Washington, 1908–13; Minister to Uruguay, 1913–19; retired, 1919; Bedford Town Council, 1921–31, and 1934–47; retired, 1947; Grand Cross of the Medjidieh. *Publications:* Love and The Law, Hibbert Journal, Jan. 1913; Essays on Money and Credit in the Banking Law Journal of New York, 1913; Martyrdom in our Times, 1932. *Address:* 11 Goldington Road, Bedford. *T:* Bedford 61003.

Died 13 Feb. 1950.

MITCHELL-INNES, Captain Cecil, CBE 1920; King's Police Medal, 1916; *b* 1866; 6th *s* of late Gilbert Mitchell-Innes of Edinburgh; *m* 1892, Sarah Etheldreda, 2nd *d* of late Colonel James Le Geyt Daniell; one *s* one *d.* *Educ:* Cheam School, Surrey; Fettes College, Edinburgh; Royal Military College, Sandhurst. Captain, Leinster Regiment, 1893–98; Queen's Own Cameron Highlanders, 1898–1903; Chief Constable of Lincolnshire, 1903–31. *Address:* 5 Cadogan Street, SW3.

Died 14 Feb. 1949.

MITCHELSON, Sir Archibald, 1st Bt *cr* 1920; Chairman of Mitchelson Partners, Ltd, Investment Bankers, 27 Old Broad Street, EC2 and of J. Samuel White & Co. Ltd; Chairman of Kamunting Tin

Dredging, Ltd, Great Universal Stores Ltd; *b* 1878; *s* of Thomas Mitchelson and Anne Sargent Mitchelson; *m* 1903, Mary (*d* 1940); one *d. Heir:* none. *Address:* 27 Old Broad Street, EC2. *TA:* Chelsonmit, Stock, London. *T:* London Wall 3143 and 1638; Edmundsbury, Beverley Lane, Coombe Lane, Kingston on Thames, Surrey. *T:* Kingston 0907.

Died 30 Dec. 1945 (ext).

MITFORD, Major Hon. Thomas David Freeman-; KRRC; *b* 3 Jan. 1909; *o s* of 2nd Baron Redesdale. *Educ:* Eton. Called to Bar, Inner Temple, 1932; Second Deputy Judge Advocate, Judge Advocate General's Office, 1938–39. *Clubs:* Brooks's, Pratt's.

Died March 1945.

MITFORD, Col William Kenyon, CMG 1900; CVO 1937; DL, JP Sussex; *b* 7 Oct. 1857; *e s* of late William Townley Mitford, MP, and Hon. Margaret Emma, *d* of 3rd Lord Kenyon; *m* 1886, Cicely Maud, *d* of late Wyndham Slade, of Montys Court, Somerset; two *s. Educ:* Eton; Sandhurst. Lt-Col and Hon. Col Middlesex Yeomanry, 1892–1903; late Capt. 8th Hussars; served Afghan War, 1879 (medal); South African campaign, 1899–1900 (despatches, Queen's medal two clasps, CMG); European War (1914–15 Star, General Service and Victory medals); one of HM's Hon. Corps of Gentlemen-at-Arms, 1900–39; Knight of Grace of Order of St John of Jerusalem; ADC to King Edward VII 1904–10; ADC to King George V 1910–24. *Address:* Pitshill, Petworth. *Clubs:* Cavalry, Carlton.

Died 20 Sept. 1943.

MITTER, Sir Brojendra Lal, KCSI 1932; Kt 1928; *b* 1875; *m* 1908, *d* of P. N. Bose of Ranchi; one *s* one *d. Educ:* Presidency Coll., Calcutta; Lincoln's Inn, London. MA and BL, Calcutta University. Called to Bar, Lincoln's Inn, 1904; practised in the Calcutta High Court; Standing Counsel to the Government of India, 1922; Advocate-General, Bengal, 1925–28; Law Member of Executive Council of Governor-General of India, 1928–34; Vice-President, 1932; led Indian Delegation to League of Nations, 1931 and 1933; Member Bengal Executive Council, 1934–37; Advocate-General of India, 1937–45; Dewan of Baroda, 1945–47 acting Governor of West Bengal, 1947. *Recreation:* gardening. *Address:* Alipore, Calcutta. *Clubs:* Calcutta, Royal Calcutta Turf (Calcutta).

Died Feb. 1950.

MITTON, Col George J.; *see* Jones Mitton.

MITTON, H. Eustace, MembInstCE, FSI, FInstFuel; JP; Director and Mining Consultant, the Butterley Co., Ltd, and Director of other companies; *b* Bishop Auckland, 1871; 3rd *s* of Rev. Henry A. Mitton, Sherburn, Durham; *m* 1906, Augusta E., *y d* of H. M. Bazeley, Bideford; three *s* two *d. Educ:* Private School, St Albans, Herts; Durham School. Prospected on Yukon, 1891; youngest white man to penetrate as far as Forty Mile Creek; mineral referee for all England, 1912, 1913; President, Institution Mining Engineers, 1929–30 and 1931; gold medal list of the Institution, 1934; Member Council Mining Research Association, Great Britain and many other committees associated with same. Brother Officer Order of St John of Jerusalem. *Publications:* various papers on Mining in Transactions; introduced Rheolaveur system of washing coal in this country and published Treatise on same. *Recreations:* fishing, reading lives of prominent men. *Address:* Appletreewick, Beckwell Valley, Sidmouth, S Devon. *T:* Sidmouth 4. *Club:* Constitutional.

Died 7 Sept. 1946.

MOBERLY, Brig. Hugh Stephenson, CB 1926; *b* 25 Aug. 1873; *y s* of late Col Charles Morris Moberly, Indian Army; *m* 1924, Norah Mary, *o d* of late John James Marsland. *Educ:* Malvern College; RMC, Sandhurst; Staff College, Quetta. Served China

Expedition, 1900; European Great War, 1914–18; IEF 'D' (Brevet Lieut-Col); Indian Frontier, Waziristan, 1919; retired, 1928. *Recreation:* games. *Address:* Bybrook Cottage, Easebourne, Midhurst, Sussex. *T:* Midhurst 265.

Died 9 Sept. 1947.

MOCKFORD, Julian; Public Relations Director of S African High Commissioner, London, since 1942; *b* Montreal, Canada, 25 Jan. 1898; *y s* of Herbert and Lina Mockford, Pietersburg, Transvaal; *m* 1923, Mabel Beverley Clapham, Johannesburg; (*o s* killed in bombing operations, Austria, 1944); *m* 1940, Lettice Mary Bond (born Rees). *Educ:* Milton High School, Bulawayo; South African College High School, Cape Town; Witwatersrand University, Johannesburg. Served European War with South African Infantry Brigade, France (wounded, prisoner). Joined The Star-Johannesburg, 1919, doing variety of editorial jobs for that journal and associated Argus group until 1942. Gen. Sec. S African Soc. of Journalists, 1927–29; edited The Springbok, organ of British Empire Service League in S Africa, 1932–34; special correspondent The Times and S African Newspaper Press Union with Prince George (late Duke of Kent) on his African journey, 1934; edited The Pretoria News, 1935; S African Argus group's Fleet St office, 1937–42; war correspondent BEF, France, 1939, and British Army, Navy and Air Force, Great Britain, 1940–42; member Dominions committee, Royal Society of Arts, 1943–49, chairman United Nations Information Organisation, 1945; member of S African Delegation, Paris Peace Conf., 1946; Union Government Press Officer, Royal Visit to S Africa, 1947. *Publications:* Biography: Khama, King of the Bamangwato, 1931. History: Here are South Africans, 1944. War effort: South Africa To-Day, 1944. Educational: Union of South Africa, 1945. Travel: The Golden Land, 1949; Pursuit of an Island, 1950 (posthumous). *Address:* 152 Chiltern Court, Regent's Park, NW1. *T:* Welbeck 5544. *Clubs:* Royal Empire Society, Royal Automobile.

Died 4 April 1950.

MOERAN, Ernest John; *b* Heston, Middlesex, 31 Dec. 1894; *s* of Joseph William Wright Moeran, Irish, Co. Cork, and Ada Esther Whall, Norfolk; *m* 1945, Peers Coetmore, cellist. *Educ:* Uppingham School; Royal College of Music. Served European War, 1914–18 (wounded). Studied composition with John Ireland, 1920–23; gave series of chamber concerts. Wigmore Hall, 1925; first opportunity of getting orchestral works produced came through late Sir Hamilton Harty who played his 1st Rhapsody with the Hallé orchestra in Manchester in 1924. *Publications:* String Quartet, 1921; 1st Orchestral Rhapsody, 1922; Violin Sonata, 1923; numerous songs, choral pieces, and folk-song arrangements, 1923–1930; string trio and sonata for 2 violins, 1931; 2 pieces for small orchestra, 1931; Nocturne for Baritone, Chorus, and Orchestra, 1934; Symphony in G minor, 1938; Choral Suite, Phyllida and Corydon, 1939; Violin Concerto, 1942; Rhapsody for piano and orchestra, 1943; Overture for a Masque, 1944; Cello Concerto, 1945; Sinfonietta for orchestra, 1945; Oboe Quartet, 1946; Cello Sonata, 1947. *Recreations:* walking the countryside, billiards, croquet, and swimming. *Address:* c/o Novello & Co. Ltd, 160 Wardour Street, W1.

Died 1 Dec. 1950.

MOFFAT, Alfred; composer and editor of old music; *b* Edinburgh, 4 Dec. 1868. *Educ:* Edinburgh Collegiate School. Studied musical composition in Berlin for five years under Prof. Ludwig Bussler. Remained in Germany for another six years writing for German music-publishing firms; came to London about the end of the century. *Works:* Meisterschule der Alten Zeit, which began with 24 sonatas, and now comprises 42 violin sonatas, 18 violoncello sonatas, 22 trio sonatas, contains a number of sonatas by hitherto unknown 18th-century English composers for the violin; 4 trio sonatas by Purcell (g minor), Handel and Leclair (2); Kammersonaten, 35 violin sonatas; Old English Violin Music; French Violin Music of the 18th century, 24 numbers; English Music of the 18th century, 35 numbers; Old Keyboard Music (with Harold Craxton); volumes of folk-songs, each containing 200 songs with piano accompaniment, and many supplied with historical notes—Minstrelsy of England, Minstrelsy of Scotland, Minstrelsy of Ireland, Minstrelsy of Wales, Minstrelsy of the Scottish Highlands (with Gaelic and English words), Songs of the Georgian Period, Characteristic Songs and Dances of all Nations (with the late J. D. Brown), A Garland of English Folk-songs, Folk-songs of the North Countrie (the two last with Frank Kidson), English Peasant Songs (with Ethel Kidson); Melodious Scotland, 18 numbers, Old Master-songs; many arrangements of songs, duets, etc., by Purcell. *Recreations:* collecting early musical works; Member of the Court of Assistants of the Royal Society of Musicians. *Address:* 132b Elgin Avenue, W9. *T:* Cunningham 1392.

Died 9 June 1950.

MOFFAT, Robert Unwin, CMG 1899; Colonial Medical Service, retired; *b* Kuruman, South Africa, 1866; 3rd *s* of late Rev. J. S. Moffat, CMG; *m* 1st, 1899, Hilda (*d* 1912), *y d* of J. Vavasseur; one *d*; 2nd, 1925, Alice Loeffier. *Educ:* St Andrew's Coll., Grahamstown, S Africa; Edinburgh Univ. Bachelor of Medicine and Master of Surgery, Edinburgh, 1890; Doctor of Medicine, 1907. Entered British East Africa Company's service, 1891; accompanied Sir Gerald Portal's expedition to Uganda, 1893; first Principal Medical Officer of the Uganda Protectorate, 1898; retired, 1906. Decorated for services in Uganda Mutiny. *Publication:* John Smith Moffat, CMG, 1921.

Died 15 Nov. 1947.

MOFFATT, Rev. James, BD; DLitt; Hon. MA (Oxon); DD (St Andrews, Oxford); *b* Glasgow, 4 July 1870; *s* of late George Moffatt, CA, Glasgow; *m* 1896, Mary, *e d* of late Dr Arch. Reith, Aberdeen; two *s* one *d*. *Educ:* Academy, University, and Free Church College, Glasgow. MA (Classical Honours) and John Clark Fellow (Classics), Glasgow Univ.; Stevenson Scholar Freeland Scholar (Hebrew), Joshua Paterson Fellow, FC College, Glasgow. Ordained, 1896; Jowett Lecturer, London, 1907; Hibbert Lecturer, Yates Professor of Greek and New Testament Exegesis, Mansfield College, Oxford, 1911–15; Professor of Church History, UF College, Glasgow, 1915–27; Washburn Prof. of Church History in Union Theological Seminary, New York, 1927–39. *Publications:* The Historical New Testament; English edit. and trans of Harnack's Ausbreitung des Christentums; The Golden Book of Owen: Literary Illustrations of the Bible; Primer to Novels of George Meredith; Editions of Thessalonians and Revelation in Expositor's Greek Testament; Paul and Paulinism; Critical Introduction to New Testament Literature; Theology of the Gospels; New Translation of New Testament; The Approach to the New Testament (Hibbert Lectures); Epistle to the Hebrews (International Critical Commentary); The Old Testament, a New Translation; The Bible in Scots Literature; Everyman's Life of Jesus; the Expositor's Yearbook; The Golden Book of Tillotson; The Presbyterian Churches; Love in the New Testament; The Day Before Yesterday; Grace in the New Testament; His Gifts and Promises (sermons); He and She; He and She, the Second; The First Five Centuries of the Church; First Corinthians; The Books of the Prophets; Jesus Christ the Same. *Address:* 445 Riverside Drive, New York.

Died 27 June 1944.

MOGG, Lt-Col Graham Beauchamp Coxeter R.; *see* Rees-Mogg.

MOGGRIDGE, Adm. Arthur Yerbury; retired; *b* 20 Sept. 1858. Entered Navy, 1872; Commander, 1895; Capt., 1900; served Egyptian War, 1882 (medal, bronze star); ADC to the King, 1908–09; Rear-Adm., 1909; commanded Home Fleet, Portsmouth Division, 1912; Vice-Adm., 1915. *Address:* Park Hotel, Exeter Road, Exmouth.

Died 13 Nov. 1946.

MOIR, Vice-Adm. Dashwood Fowler, DSO 1918; RN; *b* 1880; *s* of late Dr John Moir, St Andrews, Fife; *m* Ada, *d* of late Dr W. M. Muirhead; two *s* one *d*. Served South Africa, 1901; Aro Expedition, 1902 (despatches); European War, 1914–19 (despatches, DSO); ADC to the King, 1931; Rear-Adm. and retired list, 1931; Vice-Adm., retired, 1936. *Address:* Brimpton House, Brimpton, Reading. *T:* Woolhampton 72.

Died Aug. 1942.

MOIR, James Reid, FRS 1937; archæologist; President, Ipswich Museum; Fellow, Royal Anthropological Institute; Hon. Member Institute of Palæontology of Man, Brno, Czechoslovakia; Vice-President, Suffolk Institute of Archæology and Natural History; Hon. Member, Prehistoric Society of East Anglia; *b* Hitchin, 13 June 1879; *s* of Lewis Moir, JP; *m* 1909, Mary Frances, *d* of Rev. R. G. Penny. *Educ:* Northgate School, Ipswich. *Discoveries:* flint implements below Red Crag of Suffolk, proving existence of Man in Pliocene period; two occupation-levels in Red Crag at Foxhall, Suffolk; the experimental fracture of flint and conclusions arising therefrom; Palæolithic flint implements in glacial deposits of East Anglia; early Palæolithic-Chellean implements in the Cromer Forest Bed of Norfolk; Upper Palæolithic occupation-levels at Ipswich; the manner of evolution of the Rostro-carinate Implements into the Palæolithic hand-axes; the characteristics of striations upon flint surfaces; the succession and Inter-glacial age of implements from deposits at Hoxne, Suffolk; Upper Palæolthic flint implements in brown boulder clay, Hunstanton, Norfolk; the separation of the Sub-Crag implements into five groups of different ages, and (1941) those from the later Cromer Forest Bed into seven groups, thus greatly extending the antiquity of man; has for many years carried out archæological diggings in East Anglia, closely associated with late Sir Ray Lankester in scientific work. *Publications:* Monograph on Evolution of Flint Implements (Phil. Trans), 1920; Pre-Palæolithic Man, 1919; The Great Flint Implements of Cromer, Norfolk, 1923; The Antiquity of Man in East Anglia, 1927; Prehistoric Archæology and Sir Ray Lankester 1935; Hux. Mem. Lecture, 1939; and numerous scientific papers. *Recreations:* cycling, walking. *Address:* The Mill House, Flatford, Suffolk. *T:* East Bergholt 33.

Died 24 Feb. 1944.

MOIR, Rear-Adm. William Mitchell, CBE 1919; retired; *b* 12 Dec. 1873; *yr s* of late James Moir, Grange Place, Alloa; *m* 1903, Edith Ogston, *y d* of late John Ashbury Bailey, JP, Alloa; one *s*. *Educ:* Cargilfield, Edinburgh; HMS Britannia. Joined HM Navy, 1888; Lieutenant, 1894; Commander, 1907; Captain, 1915; Rear-Admiral (Retired List), 1926. *Recreations:* golf and tennis. *Address:* 19 Lowndes Square, SW1. *T:* Sloane 7826. *Club:* United Service.

Died 7 March 1942.

MOK, Rt Rev. Shau Tsang; Bishop of Canton (Assistant Bishop, Diocese of Victoria, Hong Kong) since 1935; *b* Tsang Shing district of Kwangtung province, 1866; *s* of Mok Wai Chung, a non-Christian, but mother was converted to Christianity late in life; *m*; three *s* five *d*. *Educ:* CMS Theological College, Hong Kong. Ordained priest 1903; priest-in-charge of churches in Delta, 1903–22; Pastor of Church of Our Saviour, Canton, 1922–33; Archdeacon, 1928. *Address:* Holy Trinity College, Tung Sha Road, Canton, S China.

Died May 1943.

MOLE, Brig. Gerard Herbert Leo, DSO 1940; MC; 129 Infantry-Brigade Home Forces; *b* 24 Oct. 1897; *s* of Philip Charles Mole and Nina O'Dea; *m* 1924, Claire Marie Kassapian; three *s* two *d. Educ:* St Xavier's College, Calcutta; Mount St Mary's College, Spinkhill, Derbyshire. Joined R Irish Rifles, 1916; Seconded MGC 1916 till end of War; served in France and N Russia (MC, General Service and British War Medals); West Africa with WAFF in Northern Nigeria till 1923; served in Cologne with R Ulster Rifles and thence to India till 1933; served at Home till outbreak of war: went to France with BEF; also served NW Europe (despatches, DSO and Bar). *Recreations:* golf, shooting, travel. *Address:* c/o Lloyds Bank Ltd, 6 Pall Mall, SW1.

Died 14 Nov. 1944.

MOLESWORTH, 9th Viscount *cr* 1716; **George Bagot Molesworth;** Baron of Philipstown, 1716; late Capt. Duke of Cornwall's LI; *b* 6 June 1867; *e s* of 8th Viscount Molesworth and Georgina, *d* of George Bagot Gosset, 4th Dragoon Guards; *S* father 1906; *m* 1894, Nina Alida, *y d* of late Col H. D. Faulkner; two *d.* Served Tirah, 1897–98 (medal with 2 clasps). *Heir: b* Hon. Charles Richard Molesworth. *Address:* Wellfend, Chorley Wood, Herts. *T:* Chorley Wood 118. *Club:* Naval and Military.

Died 20 March 1947.

MOLESWORTH, Brig.-Gen. Edward Hogarth, CB 1907; *b* 2 May 1854. Entered army, 1872; Capt. 1885; Major, 1893; Lt-Col 1899; Colonel, 1908; AAG Lucknow Division, India, 1902; served Afghan War, 1879–80 (medal); Zaimusht Expedition; Akha, 1883–84 (despatches); Abor, 1894; Mishmi Expedition, 1900–01; Brigade Commander 8th Lucknow Div., 1906–09; retired, 1911; served European War (Secretary of State's Despatch). *Address:* Elstree House, Lambridge, Bath. *Club:* United Service.

Died 17 March 1943.

MOLESWORTH, Col Herbert Ellicombe, CMG 1919; DSO 1917; *b* Bishop's Teignton, S Devon, 15 Dec. 1872; *s* of late Maj.-Gen. H. T. Molesworth, RA; *m* 1914, Eileen Mary Renny-Tailyour; two *d. Educ:* US College; Westward Ho!; RM Academy, Woolwich. Commissioned in RA 1891; Capt. 1899; Major, 1912; temp. Lt-Col 1916; Col 1921; served European War (despatches four times, DSO); retired pay, 1922. *Recreations:* golf, shooting. *Address:* Naseby, Lydford, Devon. *Club:* United Service.

Died 24 Dec. 1941.

MOLESWORTH, Col Richard Pigot, CMG 1919; RA; *b* 25 Jan. 1868; *s* of late Maj.-Gen. H. T. Molesworth, RA; *m* 1904, Madeleine, *d* of late Dr O. Galgey, Co. Cork; one *s. Educ:* US College, Westward Ho!; RM Academy, Woolwich. Entered RA 1887; served in India, 1888–98; Waziristan Expedition, 1894 (medal and clasp); NW Frontier, 1897 (medal and clasp); Captain, 1897; Major, 1906; Lieut-Colonel, 1914; retired 1920; served in Bermuda and West Indies, 1902–06; Portsmouth, 1907–08; India, 1908–14; Mesopotamia, 1915, actions of Shaiba, Amara, and Kut-el-Amara (despatches, Bt Col); France in Command of an Artillery Brigade, 1916–19, operations on the Somme, 1916–17, the battle of Arras, 1917, Passchendaele, 1917, La Bassee front, advance and occupation of Lille, 1918 (despatches, CMG, Officer Legion of Honour); on retired pay, 1920. *Address:* c/o Lloyds Bank, Ltd, 6 Pall Mall, SW1.

Died 24 Feb. 1946.

MOLESWORTH-ST AUBYN, Sir Hugh, 13th Bt *cr* 1689; *b* 3 Jan. 1865; *s* of 12th Bt and Caroline, 3rd *d* of Rev. Charles Wheler of Ledston Hall, Yorks, and Otterden Place, Kent; *S* father, 1913; *m* 1894, Emma Sybil (*d* 1929), *d* of Adm. Charles Wake; three *s* one *d. Educ:* Charterhouse; Church Church, Oxford, BA. Formerly Captain Duke of Cornwall's Light Infantry;

served European War, 1915–18, at Bodmin with Depôt DCLI; Member of Cornwall County Council, 1910–19; High Sheriff, 1922–23; JP for County of Cornwall since 1903. *Recreations:* formerly hunting and shooting. *Heir: s* John [*b* 12 Jan. 1899; *m* 1926, Celia Marjorie, *e d* of Lt-Col Valentine Vivian, CMG; one *s* two *d*]. *Address:* Pencarrow, Washaway, Bodmin, Cornwall. *T:* St Mabyn 21. *Club:* Oxford and Cambridge.

Died 5 Jan. 1942.

MOLONY, Edmund Alexander, CBE; Pensioned Officer of Indian Civil Service; *b* 17 Jan. 1866; *s* of late Edmund Weldon Molony, Indian Civil Service; *m* 1898, Ethel Blanche, *d* of late Herbert John Smith, Barla; no *c. Educ:* Marlborough College, Emmanuel College, Cambridge (Scholar). Member of the Indian Civil Service, 1886–1919; held various positions including the commissionerships of Benares, Gorakhpore and Agra; Member of the Legislative Council of the United Provinces of Agra and Oudh. *Publications:* Several articles on irrigation from wells and the subsoil water, including Manual of Irrigation Wells; also Salients from the History of Kashmir. *Address:* 28 Charlbury Road, Oxford. *T:* Summertown 5724.

Died 5 Oct. 1942.

MOLONY, Rt Hon. Sir Thomas Francis, 1st Bt *cr* 1925; PC Ireland, 1913; KC; MA, LLD; Vice-Chancellor, University of Dublin, since 1931; *b* 31 Jan. 1865; *y s* of James Molony, Harcourt Street, Dublin; *m* 1899, Pauline, *o d* of Bernard Rispin, Eccles Street, Dublin; two *s* three *d. Educ:* Trinity Coll., Dublin. Prizeman in Roman Law, 1884; in Feudal and English Law, 1885; in Jurisprudence and International Law, 1886; Senior Moderator and Gold Medallist in History and Political Science, 1886; obtained Exhibition, King's Inns, Dublin, 1887; obtained Common Law Scholarship Middle Temple, 1889. Called to Irish Bar, 1887; QC 1899; called to English Bar, 1900; Crown Counsel for Co. Carlow, 1906–12; County and City of Dublin, 1907–12; A Commissioner of Education in Ireland, 1907–24; Extern. Examiner in Law, National University of Ireland, 1910–12; contested West Toxteth Division of Liverpool, Dec. 1910; Bencher, King's Inns, 1911; HM's Second Serjeant-at-Law, 1911; Solicitor-General for Ireland, 1912–13; Attorney-General, 1913; a Judge of the High Court of Justice in Ireland (King's Bench Division), 1913–15; a Lord Justice of Appeal in Ireland, 1915–18; Lord Chief Justice of Ireland, 1918–24; Member of the Intermediate Education Board for Ireland, 1914; Member of the Royal Commission on Disturbances in Dublin, 1914; Member of the Royal Commission on certain Shootings during the Sinn Fein Rising, 1916; Chairman of Irish Association of Volunteer Training Corps, 1916; Chairman, Vice-Regal Committee on Intermediate Education in Ireland, 1918; Visitor TCD, 1918–31; KGStJ, 1920; President Statistical and Social Inquiry Society of Ireland, 1920; Chairman of the Home Office Committee on the treatment of juvenile offenders, 1925; Director of the National Bank, Limited, 1925; Bencher of the Inn of Northern Ireland, 1926; of the Middle Temple, 1933; President City of Dublin Corps St John's Ambulance Brigade and Irish Centre, St John's Ambulance Association, 1930; Chairman Universities China Committee in London and of the Departmental Committee on Veterinary Education, 1936. *Heir: s* Hugh Francis, *b* 2 Sept. 1900. *Address:* Shanganagh, The Drive, Wimbledon, SW20. *T:* Wimbledon 2023. *Clubs:* Reform, National Liberal; St Stephen's Green (Dublin).

Died 3 Sept. 1949.

MOLYNEUX, Rt Rev. Frederick Merivale, MBE 1917; MA (Oxon); Hon. CF 1919; *b* 10 May 1885; *s* of late Rev. F. E. Molyneux; *g s* of Echlin Molyneux, QC. *Educ:* Rossall School; Keble College, Oxford; Cuddesdon College. Ordained, 1909; Curate All Souls', Leeds, 1909–13; Chaplain Cuddesdon College,

1913–20; Vicar of High Wycombe, 1920–25; CF Mesopotamia, 1916–19 (despatches); Assistant Bishop of Melanesia, 1925–28; Bishop, 1928–32. *Address:* Stuckton, Fordingbridge, Hants.

Died 20 Nov. 1948.

MOMIN, Khan Bahadur Mohammad Abdul, CIE 1935; Member Legislative Council; Commissioner of Wakfs, Bengal, since 1936; *b* 28 July 1876; *s* of Nawab Abdul Jabbar, Khan Bahadur, CIE; *m* 1894; two *s* one *d*. *Educ:* Presidency College, Calcutta. Belongs to the Moslim Aristocracy of Bengal; Grandfather and father served Govt in the highest positions open to Indians; father after retirement from Govt served was Prime Minister of Bhopal State; graduated 1896; joined Govt Service as Sub-Deputy Collector 1897; Provincial service 1905; worked as Settlement Officer for many years; Under-secretary Revenue, 1916–18; Press Censor during war; District Collector and Magistrate of Jessore, Nadia and Noakhali; Director of Land Records, 1927–29; Commissioner Chittagong Division, 1929–31; retired from Govt Service, 1931; was Member of the Legislative Assembly of India as Govt Representative, 1924–25; Revenue expert of Govt; Member Bengal Tenancy Bill Committee; Jail Committee; President of Moslim Education Advisory Committee. *Publications:* Final Settlement Report of Jessore; Report on Progress of Moslim Education. *Recreations:* polo and tennis. *Address:* Hamida Hall, Tallyganj, Calcutta, India. *T:* South 1319. *Club:* Calcutta.

Died 18 June 1946.

MONAHAN, Rt Rev. Alfred Edwin, DD; Bishop of Monmouth since 1940; *b* 1877; *s* of William Beattie Monahan and Mary Hepworth; *m* Margaret Amos, St Ibbs, Hitchin; one *s* two *d*. *Educ:* St Andrew's College; Dublin Univ. (TCD), 2nd Honours and 1st Respondent; Ely Theological College. Deacon, 1904; Priest, 1905; Assistant Missioner, Wellington College Mission, Walworth, 1904–06; Curate of St Swithun and Old St Martin, Worcester, 1906–12; Vicar of Monmouth, 1912–40; Archdeacon and Canon of Monmouth, 1930–40; Member of the Representative Body and Governing Body of the Church in Wales; Judge of the Provincial Court of the Church in Wales; Member of the Continuation Committee of Faith and Order. *Recreations:* rowing, Rugby football. *Address:* Bishopstow, Newport, Mon.

Died 10 Aug. 1945.

MONAHAN, George Henry, CMG; *b* 30 Dec. 1873; *s* of Joseph and Isabella Jane Monahan; *m* 1908, Eleanor Maltby Robinson; two *s*. *Educ:* Public Schools and High School, Sydney. Joined the Staff of the Legislative Assembly of New South Wales, 1890; transferred to Staff of the Senate of the Commonwealth, 1901; Clerk of the Senate, 1920–38; retired, 1938. *Recreations:* tennis, bowls. *Address:* Mugga Way, Red Hill, Canberra, Australia.

Died 13 Sept. 1944.

MONAHAN, Most Rev. Peter Joseph; Archbishop of Regina since 1935; *b* 1882. *Educ:* Grand Seminary, Montreal. Priest, 1909; Pastor of St Patrick's, Fort William, 1924–32; Bishop of Calgary, 1922–35. *Address:* Archbishop's House, 2522 Retallack Street, Regina, Saskatchewan.

Died 1 May 1947.

MONCREIFF, 4th Baron *cr* 1873; **James Arthur Fitz-Herbert Moncreiff;** *b* 19 July 1872; *s* of 3rd Baron and Florence Kate, *d* of Col R. H. Fitz-Herbert; *S* father, 1913; *m* 1909, Lucy Vida, *e d* of David Lechmere-Anderson, LRCP, Inveresk, Doncaster; three *s* four *d*. *Educ:* Repton School; New College, Oxford. *Recreations:* cricket, golf, billiards. *Heir: s* Capt. Hon. Harry Robert Wellwood Moncreiff, RASC, *b* 4 Feb. 1915. *Address:* Tullibole Castle, Kinross.

Died 8 Dec. 1942.

MONCRIEFF, Rt Hon. Lord; Alexander Moncrieff; PC 1947; 3rd *s* of late Alexander Moncrieff, Advocate, and Sheriff of Ross and Cromarty; *m*; two *s* one *d*. *Educ:* privately; Glasgow University; Edinburgh University. Called to Bar, 1894; KC Scotland, 1912; one of the Senators of the College of Justice in Scotland, 1926–47; Lord Justice Clerk of Scotland, Feb. to Oct. 1947; FRSE; Hon. Pres. Newman Assoc., 1947–49. *Address:* 8 Abbotsford Crescent, Edinburgh; Cairnbank, North Berwick. *Club:* New (Edinburgh).

Died 5 Aug. 1949.

MONCUR, George, BSc, MInstCE; Emeritus Professor of Civil Engineering, Royal Technical College, Glasgow; *b* 1868; *s* of late John Muir Moncur, Coupar Angus; *m* 1907, Annie G. Stewart, Glasgow; no *c*. *Educ:* Madras Academy, Cupar, Fife; Dundee University College; Edinburgh University. Pupillage under late Robert Blacadder, CE, Dundee. Chiefly engaged Sewerage and Water Works, 1886–90; Location and Construction of new Railways under the Chief Engineer Caledonian Railway, 1892–97; Permanent Way, Equipment, and Railway Maintenance, Wharves, and Piers, 1897–1900, Steel Construction in renewal of Bridges and Railway Stations, and new Locomotive Shops for Great North of Scotland Railway, 1900–05; Lecturer on Civil Engineering, Royal Technical College, Glasgow, 1905; retired 1933. *Publications:* Editor of the Glasgow Series of Civil Engineering Text Books. *Recreations:* angling and golf. *Address:* Marlee, Seamill, West Kilbride, Ayrshire.

Died 5 Feb. 1946.

MONEY, Sir Leo (George) Chiozza, Kt 1915; author and journalist; *b* Genoa, 13 June 1870; *s* of late Joseph A. Chiozza and Fawnia, *d* of late Edward Allwright; assumed additional surname of Money in 1903; *m* 1892, Gwendolen, *d* of late George Elliot Stevenson; one *d*. *Educ:* privately. Managing editor of Commercial Intelligence, 1898–1903; brought about complete revision of the Board of Trade Returns, 1903; was a witness before the Select Committee on Income Tax, 1906; member of Select Committee on Home Work, 1907–08; member of the Restriction of Enemy's Supplies Committee, 1914–15; member of the War Trade Advisory Committee, 1915–18; Parliamentary Private Secretary (unpaid) to Mr Lloyd George when Minister of Munitions, 1915–16; MP (L) North Paddington, 1906–10; (L) East Northants, 1910–18; defeated as Labour candidate for S Tottenham, 1918; Parliamentary Secretary to the Ministry of Pensions, in which capacity he drafted the new Pensions Scheme of 1917; Parliamentary Secretary to the Ministry of Shipping, 1916–18, when he proposed the successful Atlantic concentration of shipping convoys against the submarines, 1917; resigned and joined the Labour Party; Chairman of the Tonnage Priority Committee, 1917–18; Chairman of the National Maritime Board, 1917–18; Ex-officio Member of Shipping Control Committee, 1916–18; Member of the Royal Commission on the Coal Industry, 1919; member of the Committee on Withheld Pay of Naval Officers, 1924; Editor Economic, Financial, Industrial, Engineering, and Sociological Sections of Encyclopædia Britannica, 14th edition, 1929. *Publications:* British Trade and the Zollverein Issue, 1902; Riches and Poverty, 1905; The Great State (in collaboration), 1912; The Nation's Wealth, 1914; The Triumph of Nationalization, 1920; The Immortal Purpose, and other Poems, 1924; The Peril of the White, 1925; Can War be Averted? 1931; Sonnets of Life, 1932; Product Money, 1933. *Address:* The Old Quarry, Bramley, Surrey. *T:* Bramley 3276. *Club:* Royal Societies.

Died 25 Sept. 1944.

MONEY, Brig.-Gen. Noel (Ernest), CMG 1919; DSO 1900; *b* 17 March 1867; *e s* of Captain Albert William Money; *m* 1903, Maud Boileau (*d* 1939), 2nd *d* of Edward Wood of Culmington Manor, Shropshire; one *s* one *d*. *Educ:* Radley; Christ Church, Oxford. Served with Shropshire Imperial Yeomanry in South African War, 1900–01; with South African Constabulary, 1901 to end of war (wounded, despatches, DSO, Queen's medal and 3 clasps, King's medal and 2 clasps); European War, Major Shropshire Yeomanry, Lt-Col West Kent Regt (wounded, despatches, CMG, bar to DSO) Commanded 159th Infantry Brigade in the 53rd Welsh Division in Palestine. *Address:* Qualicum Beach, Vancouver Island, British Columbia. *Club:* White's.
Died 30 May 1941.

MONIE, Rev. Peter William, CSI 1920; Rector, Old St Paul's Church, Edinburgh; *b* 30 March 1877; *s* of late P. Monie, Rothesay, Bute; *m* Ursula Winifred (*d* 1935), *d* of late Rev. H. S. K. Bellairs; two *s*. *Educ:* Irvine Royal Academy; Glasgow Univ.; Balliol Coll., Oxford. Indian Civil Service, Bombay Presidency, 1900; served as Assistant Collector and Assistant-Judge; Under-Secretary to Govt of Bombay, 1905; to Govt of India (Home Department), 1907; acting Collector, Nawabshah Sind, 1913; Secretary to the Govt of Bombay, 1915; Municipal Commissioner for the City of Bombay, 1916; Deputy Director of Development, Bombay, 1920; retired, 1925; Hon. Administrator Toc H, 1925–35; ordained deacon, priest; hon. asst curate, St Mary's Cathedral, Glasgow, 1936. *Address:* Lauder House, Jeffrey Street, Edinburgh.
Died 10 Dec. 1946.

MONOD, Wilfred; ancien pasteur de l'Eglise réformée à l'Oratoire du Louvre, Paris; professeur honoraire à la Faculté libre de théologie protestante de Paris; président d'honneur de l'ancien Comité général de l'Union nationale des Eglises réformées de France; president d'honneur du Comité française de l'Alliance universelle pour l'amitié internationale par les Eglises; ancien membre du Comité exécutif du Mouvement Life and Work (Stockholm, 1925); Membre du Comité de Continuation du Mouvement Faith and Order (Lausanne, 1927); *b* Paris, 24 Nov. 1867; *s* of late Théodore Monod; *m* Dorina Monod; three *s*. *Educ:* Bachelier ès lettres, licencié en philosophie, docteur en théologie; Doctor (Hon.) University of Edinburgh. *Publications: Volumes de sermons—*1ere série: Il a souffert, Il règnera, Il vit; 2e série: L'Evangile du Royaume, Sur la Terre, Vers la justice; 3e série: Certitudes; Délivrances; Pour la reconstruction; Aux chercheurs; Je suis la Vie; Les Béatitudes; Les Anges; Notre Culte; La Tentation; Les bras étendus; L'amour imperissable; Monte plus haut!; Cakya Mouni et Jésus; Jésus admira; Trois fois le jour; Le Buisson ardent; L'avoir du chrétien; Les eaux de Mara; 'Tonnerre' ou 'Ange'?; Voir Jésus. *Volumes de Méditations—*Le problème de la mort, Silence et Prière (English translation, 1931: Silence and Prayer), Prière et Silence, Pour communier, Vers l'Evangile sous la nuée de guerre, Courts sermons pour culte sans pasteur; Bible et Prière. *Volumes de Conférences—*Peut-on rester chrétien? La fin d'un christianisme; Aux croyants et aux athées; Jésus ou Barabbas. *Théologie:* Les bases psychologiques du dogme de la Rédemption; L'Espérance Chrétienne (2 vols); Du Protestantisme; La nuée de témoins: histoire de l' Eglise (2 vols); Le Problème du Bien (3 vols). *Chosesvues:* Echos et reflets; A Paris et ailleurs; Après la Journée (1867–1937). *Catéchismes:* 1. Venez à moi, 2. Vers Dieu (The Road to God, English translation, 1928); 3. Viens et vois! *Pour les pasteurs:* Vade mecum pastoral; L'esprit du ministère; Textes liturgiques pour la Cène. *Editeur* du Bulletin Veillez! organe du Tiers Ordre Protestant. *Address:* 6 Square de Port Royal, Paris (xiii).
Died 2 May 1943.

MONRO, Sir Horace Cecil, KCB 1911; CB 1902; *b* 1861; *e s* of late Rev. H. G. Monro. *Educ:* Repton; Clare College, Cambridge (Scholar, 1881; BA, Classical Tripos, 1883). Entered the Local Government Board, 1884; was private secretary to Sir Hugh Owen, KCB, permanent secretary of the Local Government Board, 1889–92, and to Mr Ritchie, Mr Fowler, Mr Shaw Lefevre, and Mr Chaplin, successive Presidents of the Local Government Board, 1892–97; Barrister, Middle Temple, 1900; Assistant Secretary, Local Government Board, 1897–1910; Permanent Secretary, 1910–19; Commander Order of Leopold, Belgium. *Club:* Oxford and Cambridge.
Died 23 April 1949.

MONROE, James Harvey, (Hon. Mr Justice); Judge High Court of Judicature at Lahore, 1931–44; Lt-Col (Hon. Col) Commanding Punjab Contingent AF (I); Honorary ADC to the Viceroy of India; Hon. Bencher of the Inn of Court of Northern Ireland; *b* 7 April 1884; *o s* of Samuel Holmes Monroe, MA, Solicitor, of Armagh, and Mary Elizabeth, *d* of E. Fullerton; *m* Margaret Adeline, *o d* of Andrew McClelland of Banbridge; one *s* three *d*. *Educ:* Armagh Royal School; Trinity College, Dublin. Foundation Scholar and Exhibitioner, BA, LLB; Senior Moderator, TCD; Auditor, and Gold Medallist in Oratory. Vice-President, College Historical Society; called to Irish Bar, 1909; Lieutenant, RNVR; KC 1920; Judge, Native Courts, Egypt (resigned, 1923); Bencher of the Inn of Court of Northern Ireland, 1926–31; Sometime Special Law Lecturer, Queen's University, Belfast. *Recreations:* lawn tennis, golf. *Clubs:* Ulster, Belfast; University, Dublin.
Died 21 May 1944.

MONROE, Paul, PhD, LLD, LittD; Barnard Professor of Education, Columbia University, 1925; Director, International Institute of Teachers College, Columbia University, 1923; President, Robert College and Constantinople College for Women, 1932–35; *b* N Madison, Ind, 7 June 1869; *s* of Rev. Wm Y. Monroe and Juliet Williams; *m* 1891, Emma Ellis, Franklin, Ind; one *s* one *d*. *Educ:* B. S. Franklin (Ind) College, 1890; PhD Univ. of Chicago, 1897; Student University of Heidelberg, 1901; LLD Univ. of Peking, 1913; Franklin College, 1918; Univ. of Brazil, 1939; LittD Columbia Univ., 1929, Dublin, 1933; Fellow of Sociology, University of Chicago, 1895–97; Hon. Fellow, Educational Institute of Scotland, 1925; Hon. Fellow, Hungarian Academy of Science, 1930. Instructor, History, 1897–99; adjunct Professor, History of Education, 1899–1902; Professor, 1902, Director School of Education, 1915–23, Teachers' College, Columbia University; Lecturer in Education, University of California, 1905; Yale University, 1906–07; Survey Educational System of Philippine Islands, 1913 and 1925, of Porto Rico, 1926; of Iraq, 1931; Member Board of Trustees, China Foundation, Peiping, China; China Institute, New York; American Foundation, New York; Institute of International Education, New York; American School of Sofia, Bulgaria: Trustee, Lingnan University, Canton, China; President, World Federation of Educational Associations, 1931–33, 1935–37, 1937–39, 1939–45; Director, Carnegie Corporation International Conferences on Examinations, Eastbourne, 1931; London, 1933; Folkestone, 1935; Dinard, France, 1938; Member Administrative Committee American University Union in London and in Paris. *Publications:* Source Book in the History of Education for the Greek and Roman Period, 1901; Thomas Platter and the Educational Renaissance of the Sixteenth Century, 1904; a Text-Book in the History of Education, 1905; Brief Course in the History of Education, 1907; Principles of Secondary Education, 1914; China: A Nation in Evolution, 1928; Comparative Essays, Vol. I, 1930, Vol. II, 1932; Founding American Public School System. Vol. 1, 1940; educational articles in technical publications; Editor, Dept of Education, International

Encyclopædia; International Year Book and Nelson's Encyclopædia; Editor in chief Cyclopædia of Education, 1910–1913; Editor Brief Course of Educl Texts; Home and School Series, 1914; Technical Art Series, 1914; Editor, International Education Review, Cologne. *Address:* Garrison-on-Hudson, NY, USA. *Clubs:* Century, New York.

Died 6 Dec. 1947.

MONROE, Will S.; author, and Professor of Psychology in the Normal College at Montclair, New Jersey, USA, 1909–25; retired, 1925; *b* 22 March 1863. *Educ:* Stanford University (BA); University of Jena; University of Leipzig; University of Paris; and University of Grenoble. Principal and Superintendent of schools in Pennsylvania and California, 1881–92; Professor Normal College, Westfield, Mass, 1896–1908; sometime Lecturer at Columbia University, the University of Illinois, the University of Vermont, and University of Chicago; gave lectures at the University of Sofia, Bulgaria, and the American University at Beirût, Syria, 1926–27; member of Jury, International Exposition at St Louis, 1903; delegate of the United States to the International Exposition and Congress, Liége, 1905; Milan, 1906, and Brussels, 1910; Member of the Special Commission of the US to prepare for the Peace Conference, 1918–19; Builder of the Monroe Skyline Trail, a part of the Long Trail of the Green Mt Club of Vermont; Fellow American Association Advancement of Science; President of the Great Pyrenees Dog Club of America; Hon. President of the Pyrenees Mt Dog Club of Great Britain. *Publications:* Educational Labors of Henry Barnard, 1893; Comenius' School of Infancy, 1896; Bibliography of Education, 1897; Entwickelung des sozialen Bewustseins des Kindes, 1899 the same translated in Swedish, Bulgarians (and Flemish); Comenius and the Beginning, of Educational Reform, 1900; History of the Pestalozzian Movement, 1905; Turkey and the Turks, 1907; In Viking Land, 1908; Sicily, the Garden of the Mediterranean, 1909; Bohemia and the Czechs, 1910; Our Country and its People (with Anna Buckbee), 1911; Europe and its People, 1912; Bulgaria and her People, 1914; Spell of Bohemia, 1929; A Visit to Walt Whitman, 1934; Associate Editor of Monroe's Cyclopædia of Education, 1911–1913; and contributor to American, German, and French educational reviews. *Recreations:* gardening, dogs, and general reading. *Address:* Couching Lion Farm, Waterbury, Vermont, USA. *Clubs:* Authors'; Authors', New York; Anglicky Kroužek, Prague; English, Sofia.

Died 29 Jan. 1939.

MONTAGU, Col Edward, CBE 1919; late 1st and 2nd Battalions Suffolk Regt; *b* Valletta, Malta, 23 Nov. 1861; *e surv. s* of late General Sir Horace Wm Montagu, KCB, Colonel Commandant Royal Engineers, and late Catherine Frances, *d* of General P. V. England, RA Colonel Commandant, RA; *m* 1894, Charlotte Eva, *d* of late Edward Kemble, formerly a Judge of Supreme Court, Jamaica; one *s*. *Educ:* Wellington College; Royal Military College, Sandhurst. Graduate of Staff Coll., Camberley. Over thirty years in 1st and 2nd Batts Suffolk Regt; commanded 1st Suffolk Regt, 1908–12; served Hazara Expedition, India, 1888; Chin-Lushai Expedition, Burma, 1889–90; European War, 1914–18; served abroad in Malta, Egypt, Aden, India, and Burmah; held Staff appointments in Egypt, Plymouth, and France; retired Dec. 1918. *Recreations:* usual. *Address:* Holmwood, Swaffham, Norfolk. *TA:* Swaffham, Norfolk. *T:* Swaffham 317.

Died 14 Jan. 1941.

MONTAGU-DOUGLAS-SCOTT; *see* Scott.

MONTEAGLE OF BRANDON, 5th Baron *cr* 1839; **Charles Spring Rice;** *b* 28 Jan. 1887; *o s* of 4th Baron and Elisabeth Ann FitzGerald, *d* of 19th Knight of Kerry; *S* father 1937; *m* 1925, Emilie de Kosenko, *d* of Mrs Edward Brooks, Philadelphia, USA; two *s* one *d*. *Educ:*

Harrow; Trinity College, Cambridge. Special Reserve of Officers, RASC, 1909; served European War; Regular Army Reserve of Officers, 1921. *Recreations:* golf, shooting, sailing. *Heir:* *s* Hon. Gerald Spring Rice, Lt Irish Guards, *b* 5 July 1926. *Address:* Glanleam, Valencia, Co. Kerry. *TA:* Valencia 11. *Clubs:* Boodle's, MCC, Royal Automobile; Kildare Street, Dublin.

Died 9 Dec. 1946.

MONTEATH, Sir Ruthven Grey, Kt 1915; late partner Mackinnon, Mackenzie & Co., Calcutta, Bombay, and Karachi; *b* Calcutta, 1864; 2nd *s* of late Alexander MacLaurin Monteath, CSI, ICS; *m* 1908, Mabel Minnie, *e d* of late W. J. Jones, Cheznous, Guernsey; three *s*. *Educ:* Old Trafford School, Manchester. Went to India, 1887; Chairman Bombay Chamber of Commerce, 1910; President Bengal Chamber of Commerce, 1914; Additional Member Viceroy's Legislative Council, 1910 and 1914. *Address:* Duchally, Auchterarder, Perthshire. *T:* Auchterarder 55.

Died 23 April 1949.

MONTEITH, Nelson, BSA; *b* Downie Township, Perth Co., 21 Nov. 1862; *s* of Samuel Monteith and Annie Jane Nelson, both Irish; *m* 1894, Ida M. Lupton. two *s* seven *d*. *Educ:* Public School; Commercial Coll.; Ontario Agricultural Coll.; Degree from Toronto University. Has been Councillor Deputy Reeve, and Reeve of Downie Tp.; also Warden of Perth County; elected at by-election, 1899; defeated at General Election, 1902; elected 1905; Minister of Agriculture, Province of Ontario, 1905–08; defeated 1908; an Episcopalian; Conservative; a farmer by profession. Chairman of Stratford Suburban Road Commission; President of British Mortgage and Trust Corporation of Ontario for past 24 years. *Address:* Stratford, Canada.

Died 18 Oct. 1949.

MONTGOMERY, Sir (Charles) Hubert, KCMG 1927; KCVO 1930; CB 1920; CVO 1911; Grand Officer of the Order of the Nile; Officer of the Legion of Honour; *b* 24 Aug. 1876; 4th *s* of late Rt Hon. Hugh de F. Montgomery, PC, of Blessingbourne; *m* 1914, Grace Victoria, *d* of Hon. Hungerford T. Boddam, Judge of High Court, Madras (Hon. Mrs Geoffrey Mills); two *s*. Entered Foreign Office, 1900; Private Secretary to successive Under-Secretaries of State for Foreign Affairs, 1904–07; Précis-Writer to Secretary of State for Foreign Affairs, 1907; Assistant Private Secretary to Prime Minister (Campbell-Bannerman), 1908; again Précis-Writer, 1908–10; Secretary of Earl Marshal's Office for the Coronation of King George, 1911; Marshal of the Ceremonies, 1913 (title changed to Vice-Marshal of the Diplomatic Corps in 1920); attached to staff of Earl of Reading, High Commissioner and Special Ambassador to the United States, 1918; Chief Clerk and Assistant Secretary in the Foreign Office, 1919; Assistant Under-Secretary of State, 1922; Deputy Under-Secretary of State, 1930; British Minister at the Hague, 1933–38; holds Coronation medals of King Edward VII, King George V and King George VI; Jubilee Medal, 1935. *Address:* Highclere, Sevenoaks, Kent.

Died 2 Dec. 1942.

MONTGOMERY, Sir Henry James Purvis-Russell-Hamilton-Montgomery, 7th Bt *cr* 1801; of Stanhope; JP, DL; *b* 1859; *e s* of late Thomas Henry Montgomery, and Hon. Anna Maria, *sister* of 15th Lord Elphinstone; *S* cousin, 1930; *m* 1882, Mary Maud, MBE, *o c* of Thomas Purvis Russell of Warroch, Kinrossshire; two *s* two *d*. *Educ:* Trinity College, Glenalmond; Jesus College, Cambridge. Assumed prefix surnames Purvis-Russell, 1907; Convener of Kinross-shire. *Heir:* *s* Basil Russell Purvis-Russell [*b* 1884; *m* 1915, Amelia A. Richards; two *d*]. *Address:* Hattonburn, Milnathort, Scotland.

Died 6 Aug. 1947.

MONTGOMERY, Sir Hubert; *see* Montgomery, Sir C. H.

MONTGOMERY, L. M.; *see* Macdonald, Mrs L. M.

MONTGOMERY, Robert Mortimer; KC 1914; Recorder of Chester since 1926; *s* of Rev. J. K. Montgomery, Unitarian Minister, Chester, and Mary M'Alister of Holywood, near Belfast; *m* 1st, 1900, Mabel (*d* 1927), *d* of late Francis Ayrton, Chester; one *s* one *d*; 2nd, 1932, Zilla Mary, *d* of late Captain E. T. Stevenson, Bombay; two *s*. *Educ:* King's School, Chester; St Catherine's Soc., Oxford. MA. Called to Bar, Inner Temple, 1893; Bencher, 1923; Treasurer, 1944; Liberal candidate for Crewe Division of Cheshire, 1923. Independent Member of Committee on Holidays with Pay, 1938. *Publications:* Licensing Practice, 1st edn, 1895, 7th edn 1914; Excess Profits Duty, 1st edn 1916; 2nd edn 1919; The War Damage Act, 1941; The War Damage Act, 1943. *Recreations:* played Association football for Oxford University against Cambridge 1890, 1891, and 1892 (half-back). *Address:* 3 Paper Buildings, Temple, EC4. *T:* Central 4488; 5 Fitzwarren Gardens, Highgate, N19. *T:* Archway 2460.

Died 31 Dec. 1948.

MONTGOMERY-CUNINGHAME, Sir Thomas Andrew Alexander; *see* Cuninghame.

MONTGOMERY-MASSINGBERD, Field-Marshal Sir Archibald (Armar), GCB 1934; KCB 1925; KCMG 1919; LLD (Queen's University, Belfast), 1934; Vice-Lieutenant of Lincolnshire, 1940–46; *b* 6 Dec. 1871; 2nd *s* of late Rt Hon. Hugh de F. Montgomery, PC; assumed name of Montgomery-Massingberd, 1926; *m* 1896, Diana, *y d* of late Edmund Langton; no *c*. *Educ:* Charterhouse; Royal Military Acad., Woolwich. Served S African War, 1899–1902 (despatches, Queen's medal four clasps, King's medal two clasps, wounded); European War, 1914–18 (despatches nine times, Bt Lt-Col, Bt-Col, Maj.-Gen., CB, KCMG; Commander Legion d'Honneur, Croix de Guerre, American DSM); Deputy Chief of General Staff, India, 1920–22; commanded 53rd Welsh Division, TF, 1922–23; commanded 1st Division, 1923–26; Lieut-Gen. 1926; Col-Commandant RA 1927–41; General Officer Commanding-in-Chief, Southern Command, 1928–31; General, 1930; Adjutant-General to the Forces, 1931–33; ADC General to the King, 1931–35; Field-Marshal, 1935; Chief of Imperial General Staff, 1933–36; Col Comdt Royal Tank Corps, 1934–39; Col Comdt 20th Burma Rifles, 1935; Col Comdt Royal Malta Artillery, 1937–41; Hon. Col 46th (Lincoln Regt) Anti-Aircraft Bn, 1937. *Address:* Gunby Hall, Spilsby, Lincs. *Club:* Naval and Military.

Died 13 Oct. 1947.

MOODY, Madame Fanny, (Mrs Southcote Mansergh); Prima Donna Royal Italian Opera, Covent Garden; *b* Redruth, Cornwall, 1866; *d* of James Moody, photographer in that town; *m* Southcote Mansergh ('Charles Manners') (*d* 1935), oratorio, Italian and English Grand Opera and concert singer. *Educ:* Girls' High School, Redruth. Studied singing for four years with Madame Sainton Dolby. Three years Prima Donna under late Carl Rosa; four consecutive years Prima Donna Royal Italian Opera under the late Sir Augustus Harris, and has sung with all the principal choral societies throughout Great Britain, America, Canada, and South Africa, and has since 1897 sung with her husband in their own Company (the Moody-Manners Opera Co.) at Covent Garden and throughout Great Britain. *Recreations:* croquet and motoring. *Address:* The Hermitage, Dundrum, Co. Dublin.

Died 21 July 1945.

MOON, Col Alfred, CMG 1916; OBE 1919; VD; *b* Manchester, 25 March 1861; *s* of late W. H. Moon, Sheffield; *m* 1906, Christina Elsie, 4th *d* of Kenneth McLennan, Brisbane; no *c*. *Educ:* Farnsworth's Grammar School, Sheffield. Went to Australia, 1883; established

wholesale business, Brisbane, 1897; became commissioned officer Queensland Rifles, 1898, and a year later organised Queensland Rifles Cycle Corps for service in South Africa; in 1901, in command of a unit from Queensland in conjunction with troops from all parts of the Commonwealth, attended the ceremonies connected with the opening, by King George V, of the First Federal Parliament in Melbourne; the same year appointed Staff Officer for Supplies and Transport, 1st Military District, at a later date organising and commanding the Australian Army Service Corps, 1st Military District; for several years Alderman of the City of Brisbane, and also Chairman of the Finance Committee; on the outbreak of War, 1914, became Asst Director of Transport and Supply, 1st Military District, and a month later proceeded to Melbourne and organised the 1st Australian Division Supply Column, arriving with it in England, Feb. 1915; went to France as Divisional Supply Column to 17th Division, transferring to 1st Australian Division on its arrival in France, April 1916; Fellow Royal Empire Society. *Recreations:* gymnastics, sculling. *Address:* Beckingham, 34 Cranbrook Road, Rose Bay, NSW, Australia.

Died 28 April 1943.

MOON, Edward Robert Pacy; *b* 1858; *s* of Robert Moon; *m* 1900, Frideswide, *y d* of late Right Hon. Mr Justice Kekewich. *Educ:* Winchester (Senior Co. Prae, 1875–77); New College, Oxford, 1st Class Classical Moderations, 2nd Class Lit. Hum.; MA. Barrister, Inner Temple, 1884; contested N St Pancras, 1892, 1895, 1900, 1906; MP (C) St Pancras, N, 1895–1906; House of Laymen (Canterbury), Representative Church Council 1910–20; Poor Law Guardian for Kensington, 1907–19; a Member of the Kensington Borough Council, 1913–31; a VP of the Central Asian Society to 1928; VP CEMS; VP Bible Society; Fellow of the Royal Empire Society and Statistical Society; Chairman of Council of Garden City Association, 1906–10; Member London Chamber of Commerce. *Publication:* Four Weeks as Acting Commandant at the Belgian Field Hospital, 1915. *Recreations:* travelled regularly, except for one year during the War, 1877–1928. *Address:* 201 Coleherne Court, SW5.

Died 11 Sept. 1949.

MOONEY, Herbert C., MB, BCh, FRCSI; late Surgeon Oculist to the Lord-Lieutenant; Ophthalmic and Aural Surgeon, St Vincent's Hospital; Consulting Ophthalmic Surgeon, Dublin Skin and Cancer Hospital, Hume Street. *Address:* St Vincent's Hospital, Dublin.

Died 21 May 1948.

MOORCROFT, William, FRSA, Potter to Her Majesty Queen Mary; *b* 27 March 1872; *s* of Thomas Moorcroft; *m* 1st, Florence Norah Fleay, *d* of late V. L. Lovibond, The Hermitage, Fulham, SW; one *s* one *d*; 2nd, Marian Hazel, *d* of L. S. Lasenby, Warberry House, Surbiton, Surrey; one *s*. *Educ:* privately; South Kensington; Paris. Spent greater part of life in originating and developing Moorcroft Pottery; Fellow of British Institute of Industrial Art; Royal College of Art (medallist) 1899; Gold Medal, St Louis, 1904; Gold Medal, Brussels, 1910; Gold Medal, Ghent, 1913; Gold Medal, Paris, 1925; Grand Prix, Antwerp, 1930; Grand Diploma of Honour International Exhibition of Modern Decorative and Industrial Arts, Milan, 1933; Diplôme Commémoratif, Paris, 1937; Diploma of Honour (issued in appreciation of services rendered in contributing to the representation of the Arts, Science, and Industry of the British Empire), British Empire Exhibition; Principal works, The Museum of Fine Arts, Syracuse, State of New York, Permanent Collection Toronto Art Gallery, Deutsches Museum, Munich. *Publications:* contributed articles to various magazines on the science and art of Pottery-making. *Recreation:* golf. *Address:* Trentham,

Staffordshire. *TA:* Moorcroft, Trentham. *T:* Trentham 49058. *Clubs:* Royal Societies, British Empire; Trentham Golf.

Died 14 Oct. 1945.

MOORE, Ven. Alexander Duff; Rector of Kilbride (Bray) Diocese of Glendalough since 1937; Archdeacon of Glendalough since 1937; *b* 1872; *s* of Canon Courtenay Moore, Rector of Mitchelstown, Diocese Cloyne; *m* Harriet Nina, *d* of Henry James Bourchier of Baggotstown House, Co. Limerick. *Educ:* Haileybury College; Trinity College, Dublin; BA 1897, Div. Test 1898, MA 1909. Deacon, 1897; Priest, 1898; Curate of Castlerickard, 1897–98; Killoughey, 1898–1901; Rector of Bally-common and Killaderry, 1901–06; Rector of Killiskey, Diocese of Glendalough, 1906–34; Rector of Tullow, Diocese of Dublin, 1934–37; Rural Dean of Wicklow, 1916; Select Preacher, Dublin University, 1927; Canon of Christ Church Cathedral, Dublin, since 1923; Prebendary of St Michael's, 1936; Warden of Alexander College, Dublin, 1941. *Recreations:* field sports and lawn tennis. *Address:* Kilbride Rectory, Bray, Co. Wicklow. *Clubs:* Royal Irish Automobile, Dublin.

Died 18 Oct. 1942.

MOORE, Captain Alldin Usborne, CMG 1919; RN (retired); *b* 2 Dec. 1878; *s* of Vice-Admiral W. Usborne Moore; *m* 1907, Muriel Frances Sara Burnyeat; two *d.* *Educ:* Pinewood, Farnborough. Entered Navy, 1891; Assistant Transport Officer at Taku during Boxer Rebellion, 1900; Commander, 1909; Captain, 1915; retired, 1922; French Croix de Guerre with palm, 1916. *Address:* 19 Gwendolen Avenue, Putney, SW15. *T:* Putney 1938.

Died 15 Aug. 1942.

MOORE, Col Arthur Trevelyan, CBE 1919; late RE; *s* of Sir William J. Moore KCIE; *m* Constance (*d* 1946), *g d* of Sir Edward Kennedy, Bt; two *d.* *Educ:* United Services College, Westward Ho. Lieutenant 1885; Colonel, 1914; retired 1920; served Isazai Expedition, 1892; European War, 1914–18 (despatches, CBE); Secretary Institution of RE and Ed. RE Jl, 1902–07. *Recreations:* usual. *Address:* Binfield Lodge, Binfield, Berks. *Club:* Junior United Service.

Died 13 Jan. 1948.

MOORE, Col Charles Hesketh Grant, CMG 1915; DSO 1904; late Indian Army; *b* 5 July 1868; *m* 1899, Cecil Louise, *d* of Major C. Murphy, RA; two *s.* *Educ:* Dulwich College; abroad. Entered army, 1888; Captain, 1899. Served NW Frontier, India, 1897–98 (despatches, medal with clasp); Thibet, 1903–04 (despatches, DSO); NW Frontier of India, 1908 (despatches, medal); European War, 1914–17 (despatches, CMG); Assistant Director of Supplies and Transport, Indian Cavalry Corps, 1915; Deputy Director, Transport, AHQ, India, 1918; Deputy Director Supplies and Transport, Southern Command, 1918–20; Colonel, 1920; retired, 1920. *Address:* Lingfield, Surrey.

Died 3 Jan. 1942.

MOORE, Sir Charles James S.; *see* Stevenson-Moore.

MOORE, Rt Rev. Edward Alfred Livingstone; Vicar of Horspath, Oxford, since 1938; *b* Oxford, 13 Nov. 1870; *s* of late Rev. Edward Moore, DD, sometime Principal of St Edmund Hall, Oxford, and Canon of Canterbury; unmarried. *Educ:* Marlborough; Oriel College, Oxford (Scholar); BA; 1st class Classical Mods, 2nd class Lit. Hum., 2nd class Theology. Deacon, 1894; priest, 1895; Curate of Aston, Birmingham, 1894–96; Missionary of the CMS, S India, since 1896; Principal CMS Divinity School, Madras, 1904–14; Chairman of the Tinnevelly CMS Church Council, 1915–24; Bishop of Travancore, 1925–37. *Address:* Horspath Vicarage, Oxford.

Died 22 Sept. 1944.

MOORE, Eric Olawolu, CBE 1937; Barrister-at-Law; Un-official Member of Legislative Council of Nigeria since 1923; *b* 6 Nov. 1878; *s* of Hon. Cornielius B. Moore, Merchant and Treasurer of the Egba United Government; *m* 1904, Vaughan Aida Ibiremi; one *s* three *d.* *Educ:* Lagos Grammar School; Sierra Leone Grammar School; Monkton Combe School, near Bath. Called to Bar, Middle Temple; nominated Member of Legislative Council of Nigeria, 1917. *Recreation:* riding. *Address:* Ijemo House, Lagos. *TA:* Moore, Lagos. *T:* 025. *Club:* Royal Empire Society.

Died 10 Jan. 1944.

MOORE, Frederick Craven, MSc, MD (Manch.), FRCP; Emeritus Professor of Systematic Medicine in the Victoria University of Manchester; Hon. Consulting Physician Manchester Royal Infirmary, and Hon. Consulting Physician to the Ancoats Hospital, Manchester; *b* Manchester, 1871; *m* 1929, Marjory, 2nd *d* of late Sir Edward Holt, Bart. *Educ:* The Owens College, Manchester. Graduated in Medicine with 1st Class Honours; was awarded Gold Medal for MD dissertation; Dauntesey Scholar and University Scholar in Medicine; Agnew Scholar in Diseases of Children. Engaged in the study and teaching of Pathology to 1901; since then Consulting Physician; Fellow of the Royal Society of Medicine; Member of the Pathological Society of Great Britain and Ireland; Member of the Association of Physicians of Great Britain and Ireland; Member of the Royal Institution; ex-President of the Manchester Pathological Society and Manchester Clinical Society. *Publications:* various papers on Pathological subjects and more recently on Investigations into Disorders of Digestion. *Recreations:* golf, horticulture, Oriental art. *Address:* Duckyls, nr East Grinstead, Sussex. *T:* Sharpthorne 52. *Club:* Athenæum.

Died 18 Nov. 1943.

MOORE, Sir Frederick William, Kt 1911; MRIA; FLS; MA; DSc; Trustee National Library; ex-President Royal Zoological Society of Ireland; Commissioner of Irish Lights Board; *b* 1857; *m* 1901, Phyllis, *d* of Robert Paul, of Broomhill, Co. Dublin; one *s.* Keeper, Royal Botanic Gardens, Glasnevin, Dublin, 1879–1922; ex-President Royal Horticultural Society of Ireland. Victoria Medal of Honour. *Address:* Willbrook House, Rathfarnham, Co. Dublin. *Club:* Friendly Brothers of St Patrick (Dublin).

Died 23 Aug. 1949.

MOORE, Grace; *see* Parera, Grace Moore.

MOORE, Col Harold Arthur, CBE 1919; MC; TD; JP; Managing Director H. A. Moore & Co., Ltd, and National Meter Co., Ltd; *b* Toronto, Canada, 19 June 1880; *s* of Alfonso Matthew Moore, Toronto, *s* of C. F. Moore, London, Canada, and Emily Ruth, *d* of Wm Westlake, Plymouth, Devon; *m;* one *s* two *d.* *Educ:* Toronto; Washington High School; London University. Interested in manufacturing and commercial businesses; formerly Lieut-Col RAF and Lieut-Col 3rd Batt. London Regt (TA); served European War, 1914–19 (despatches, MC, CBE); Hon. Col 69th Searchlight Regt RA. *Address:* Beechwood, Cookham Dean, Berks. *TA:* Multifacio, London. *T:* Marlow 110. *Clubs:* Sports, Royal Air Force; Temple Golf, etc.

Died 25 Oct. 1945.

MOORE, Rev. Henry Kingsmill, DD; FLS; Canon of St Patrick's National Cathedral, 1914–34; Principal of Church of Ireland Training College, 1884–1927; *s* of Rev. Canon Moore, LLD; *m* Constance, *d* of John Turpin, Youngrove, Co. Cork; one *s.* *Educ:* Midleton College, Co. Cork; Balliol College, Oxford. Deacon, 1879; Priest, 1880; Diocesan Inspector, Cork, Cloyne, and Ross, 1881; Chaplain to late Lord Lieutenant of Ireland; member of the General Synod, 1889–1931; member of the Standing Committee of the General Synod, 1889–1931; Governor King's Hospital, the

Incorporated Society, the Erasmus Smith Board; Chairman of High School Committee; Chairman of Islands and Coasts Society; Vice-President of Sunday School Society for Ireland; member, on nomination of Archbishop of Canterbury, of Inner Committee of nine appointed at request of Lambeth Conference for the improvement and development of Sunday School Teaching; Fellow of Linnean Society and of Royal Society of Antiquaries of Ireland; member of National Programme Conference, 1925–26, nominated to represent the Church of Ireland; member of Committee appointed by Government, 1926–27, to report on the present system of inspection of National Schools, invited to act by the Ministry. *Publications:* Class Teaching for Sunday School Teachers; Fundamental Principles of Education; An Unwritten Chapter in the History of Education; Lessons in Bible Teaching; The Way to Teach the Bible; The Training of Infants; The Centenary Book of the Church of Ireland Training College; Irish History for Young Readers; Reminiscences and Reflections, 1930; Joys of the Garden, 1936; The Sphere of a Bishop, 1936; Ireland and her Church, 1937; The Work of the Incorporated Society for Promoting Protestant Schools in Ireland, 1938; Our Lord's Teaching with Reference to Finance, 1942; Organisation, 1943. *Recreations:* cycling, gardening, and music. *Address:* Cedar Mount, Dundrum, Co. Dublin. *T:* Dundrum 96312.

Died 1 Dec. 1943.

MOORE, John Bassett; Judge of the Permanent Court of International Justice, The Hague, Holland, 1921–28; *b* Smyrna, Delaware, 3 Dec. 1860; *s* of Dr John A. Moore and Martha A. Ferguson; *m* 1890, Helen Frances Toland; three *d. Educ:* University of Virginia. Studied law, Wilmington, Delaware, 1880–83. Admitted to Bar there, 1883; entered the Dept of State, at Washington, as law clerk, under civil service rules, 1885; third Assistant Secretary of State, 1886; Secretary to Fisheries Conference, 1887–88; to Conference on Samoan Affairs, 1887; Assistant Secretary of State, 1898; Secretary and Counsel to the American Peace Commission at Paris; Agent of the United States before the United States and Dominican Mixed Commission, 1903–04; US Delegate to 4th International American Conference, Buenos Aires, 1910; Minister Plenipotentiary to the Centenario, Chile, 1910; US Delegate, International Commission of Jurists, Rio de Janeiro, 1912; Counsellor of the Department of State with power to act as Secretary of State, 1913–14; Member Permanent Court of Arbitration at The Hague, 1913–38; US Member and Pres., with the rank of Ambassador, of Commission of Jurists to consider Amendment of the Laws of War, 1922–23; Prof. of International Law and Diplomacy, Columbia University, New York, 1891–1924; President American Political Science Association, 1914; President Lake Mohonk Conference on International Arbitration, 1914, 1915; Member of Pan-American Financial Conference, Washington, and of Inter-American High Commission organised by it, 1915; Director, and Member Executive Committee, Equitable Life Assurance Society of the US since 1925; Incorporator, American National Red Cross; Hon. Pres., formerly Pres., Pan-American Society of the US, 1915–22; Hon. Pres. Hispanic Soc. of America; LLD of Yale University, 1901, University of Chile, Brown University, 1914, Columbian University, Delaware College, University of State of New York, University of Pennsylvania, McGill University, Columbia University, Washington College; awarded Roosevelt Distinguished Service Medal, 1927. *Publications:* Report on Extraterritorial Crime, 1887; Report on Extradition, 1890; Treatise on Extradition and Interstate Rendition (2 vols), 1891; American Notes on the Conflict of Laws, 1896; History and Digest of International Arbitrations (6 vols), 1898; American Diplomacy, its Spirit and Achievements, 1905; Digest of International Law (8 vols), 1906; Works of James Buchanan (12 vols), 1908; Four Phases of American

Development: Federalism, Democracy Imperialism, Expansion, 1911; The Principles of American Diplomacy, 1918; International Law and some Current Illusions, and other Essays, 1924; International Adjudications, Ancient and Modern; Modern Series vols 1–6, 1929–1933; Ancient Series, vol. 2, 1936. *Address:* Columbia University, New York. *Clubs:* Authors'; Century, Bar Association, New York; Cosmos, Metropolitan, Washington.

Died 12 Nov. 1947.

MOORE, Sir Leopold Frank, Kt 1937; Proprietor Livingstone Mail; Chemist, etc; *b* London, 1868; *e s* of Benjamin Moore and Fanny May; *m* 1894, Katherine Maud; *d* of A. Tait; no *c. Educ:* Wyggeston School, Leicester. Apprenticed to a Leicester chemist, assistant London till 1892 (passed exam.); migrated to S Africa, in business Mafeking, Bulawayo, finally Livingstone, 1904; started Livingstone Mail, 1906; participated public affairs, notable opposition to recruitment Chinese Labour for S Rhodesia Mines, 1899; Advisory Council N Rhodesia, 1918; re-elected till 1941; one of two unofficial delegates to Coronation for Northern Rhodesia. *Recreations:* none. *Address:* Box 5, Livingstone, Northern Rhodesia. *TA:* Mail, Livingstone. *T:* 251. *Club:* Livingstone.

Died 15 May 1945.

MOORE, Col Maxtone, CMG 1919; DSO 1916; *b* 7 Feb. 1876; *m* 1909, Louisa Chichester Hart; two *s.* Served South African War, 1899–1902 (Queen's medal and six clasps, King's medal and two clasps); European War, 1914–18 (despatches, DSO, 1914 Star, British War Medal, Victory Medal); retired pay, 1925. *Address:* c/o Lloyd's Bank, 6 Pall Mall, SW1. *Club:* Flyfishers'.

Died 16 June 1950.

MOORE, Pierce Langrishe, CIE 1912; ICS, retired; *b* 1873; *m* 1904, Muriel, *d* of Lumisden Strange; two *s* one *d. Educ:* Cheltenham; Christ Church, Oxford (Scholar). Entered ICS, 1896; District Magistrate, Bangalore, 1904; Head Assist Magistrate and Collector, 1909; Sub-Collector and Joint-Magistrate, 1910; President Madras Corporation, 1909–14; Inspector-General of Police, Madras, 1914–19; Secretary to Government of Madras, 1923; Board of Revenue, Madras, 1927; retired 1930.

Died 7 March 1944.

MOORE, Col Robert Reginald Heber, CBE 1919; MD; RAMC ret; *b* 1858; *s* of late Rev. Canon Thomas Moore, Midleton College, Co. Cork; *m* 1st, 1884, *d* of R. J. Glass, Portaferry; 2nd, 1920, Christina Turnbull, MBE, RRC, *d* of Lewis Bilton, WS, Edinburgh. *Educ:* Dublin University (MD, BCh). Served European War, 1914–19 (despatches, CBE). *Publications:* Pruning in Summer; An Unorthodox Method of Growing Apples and Pears for Amateurs, Women and Men, 1933. *Address:* Painswick Lodge, Cheltenham.

Died 27 Sept. 1942.

MOORE, Mrs Stuart; *see* Underhill, Evelyn.

MOORE, Thomas Sturge; author and wood engraver; Member of the Academic Committee of the Royal Society of Literature; *b* 4 March 1870; *e s* of Dr D. Moore and Henrietta Sturge; *m* 1903, Marie, *d* of Rev. George Appia, Lutheran Pastor, Paris; one *s* one *d. Publications:* (Poetry) The Vinedresser and other Poems, 1899; Aphrodite against Artemis, 1901; Absalom, 1903; Danaë, 1903; The Little School, 1905; Poems, 1906; Mariamne, 1911; The Sicilian Idyll and Judith, 1911; The Sea is Kind, 1914; The Little School (Enlarged), 1917; The Powers of the Air, 1920; Tragic Mothers, 1920; Judas, 1923; Mystery and Tragedy, 1930; Poems (Collected Edition), 4 vols, 1932–1933; Selected Poems, 1934; The Unknown Known and a dozen odd poems, 1939; (Prose) The Centaur and the Bacchant, from the French by Maurice de Guerin, 1899; Altdorfer, 1900; Durer, 1904; Correggio, 1906; Art and Life, 1910; Hark to these Three, 1915; Some Soldier Poets, 1919; Armour for Aphrodite, 1929; Charles Ricketts, RA; Editor (with D. C. Sturge Moore) Works and Days from the journal of Michael Field, 1933. *Address:* 40 Well Walk, NW3.

Died 18 July 1944.

MOORE, Rt Hon. Sir William, 1st Bt *cr* 1932; PC Ireland, 1921; *b* 22 Nov. 1864; *e s* of late William Moore, Moore Lodge, Ballymoney, Hon. Physician in Ireland to Queen Victoria, and Sidney Blanche, *o d* of Captain Abraham Fuller, King's County; *m* 1888, Helen Gertrude (*d* 1944), *y d* of Joseph Wilson, DL, Co. Armagh; two *s* one *d*. *Educ:* Marlborough; Trinity College, Dublin (BA, MA and LLD (jure dig.) Honours in classics, modern history Vice-Chancellor's Prizeman English Composition, President Univ. Phil. Soc., first Gold Medallist in Oratory). LLD (hon.) Queen's University, Belfast, 1926. Called to Irish Bar, 1887; joined NE Circuit; called to English Bar, 1899; QC (Ireland), 1899; a Bencher of the King's Inns; a Bencher of the Inn of Court of Northern Ireland; Bencher (Honorary) Inner Temple (1926); Senior Crown Prosecutor for City of Belfast, 1915–17; Judge of King's Bench Div., Ireland, 1917–21; Lord Justice of Appeal in Supreme Court of Northern Ireland, 1921–25; Lord Chief Justice of Northern Ireland, 1925–37; took prominent part in debates in House on Devolution and Home Rule; member of a Plantation family in N Antrim; JP, DL Co. Antrim; a member of Co. Antrim Grand Jury; one of the founders of the Ulster Council; one of the first to sell estates under the Act of 1903; Chancellor Diocese of Down, Church of Ireland; MP (C) N Antrim, 1899–1906, North Armagh, 1906–17. *Recreations:* country life, salmon-fishing, and usual pursuits. *Heir: s* William Samson. *Address:* Moore Lodge, Kilrea, NI. *Clubs:* Ulster, Belfast.

Died 28 Nov. 1944.

MOORE, Rev. Canon William; JP; *y s* of late Robert Moore, Bourton, Dorset; *m* B. E. Rosenthal (Beatrice Rosenthal); one *s* one *d*. *Educ:* City of London School; King's College, London, AKC. Curate St James', Hereford, 1896–1900; St Paul's, Portman Square, 1900–06; Vicar of Wragby, Panton, and Gotho, Lincs, 1906–38; Rector of Colsterworth, near Grantham, 1938–42; Surrogate, 1908; Salonika, 1917; Hon. CF; Prebendary of Dunholme in Lincoln Cathedral, 1931. *Address:* Austral House, Stanhope Avenue, Woodhall Spa, Lincs.

Died 31 Dec. 1943.

MOORE-SALVIN, John Edmund Shorrock, ARCS; *b* 1873; *o s* of Henry Moore; *m* 1904, Heloise (*d* 1927), 2nd *d* of late Osbert Salvin, FRS, of Hawksfold, Fernhurst, Sussex; one *s*. *Educ:* Tonbridge Sch. Marshall Scholar, Royal Coll. Science, London; Associate in Biology, Royal College Science, London; studied at Marine Biological Station, Naples, 1895; Leader of First Tanganyika Expedition, 1896; Leader of Second Tanganyika Expedition, 1899, traversing the continent from Zambesi to Nile; during this journey the Snows of the Mountains of the Moon were reached for the first time; Huxley Gold Medal for Research given by Royal College of Science, 1900; Demonstrator of Zoology in Royal College of Science, 1900; Acting Professor of Zoology, 1903, 1905. Professor of Experimental and Pathological Cytology, and Director Cancer Research Laboratories, University of Liverpool, 1906–08, and Internal Examiner in Zoology, University of London; retired after death of his father, 1908. *Publications:* To the Mountains of the Moon; The Tanganyika Problem, being an Account of Researches undertaken during the above two African expeditions; Five Foolish Virgins, stories, 1934; numerous special memoirs relating to general biology and cytological matters. *Recreations:* mountaineering, rough travel, tennis, shooting. *Club:* Authors'.

Died 15 Jan. 1947.

MOORES, Maj.-Gen. Sir Guise G.; *see* Guise-Moores.

MORANT, Brig.-Gen. Hubert Horatio Shirley, DSO 1917; *b* 27 Dec. 1870; *y s* of late Lt-Gen. H. H. Morant and Katherine Selina, *o d* of Francis Locke, of Rowdeford, Wilts; *m* 1914, Helen Isabella, 2nd *d* of late John Coppin Straker; one *s* two *d*. *Educ:* Charterhouse; RMC, Sandhurst. Egyptian Army, 1898–1908; served Nile, 1898 (two medals and clasp, 4th class Osmanieh and Medjidieh); European War, 1914–18 (DSO, and bar, wounded four times); raised and commanded 10th DLI; commanded 3rd and 147th Infantry Brigades; commanded 1st Bn DLI, 1919–23; commanded Northumberland Infantry Brigade (TA), 1924–27; retired pay, 1927; Col of Durham LI, 1937–40. *Address:* The Hermitage, Hexham.

Died 20 Sept. 1946.

MORAY, 18th Earl of, *cr* 1561; **Francis Douglas Stuart,** MC; MA; Lord Abernethy and Strathearn, 1562; Lord Doune, 1581; Baron of St Colme, 1611; Baron Stuart (G. Brit.), 1796; late Captain Scottish Horse (Yeomanry) and RAF; Lord Lieutenant of County of Moray since 1935; Forestry Commissioner since 1942; Chairman Police Committee Moray and Nairn County Council since 1934; *b* 10 July 1892; *e s* of 17th Earl and Edith Douglas, *d* of late Rear-Admiral George Palmer; *S* father, 1930; *m* 1924, Barbara, *d* of J. Archibald Murray, New York; three *d*. *Educ:* Eton; Trinity College, Cambridge. Served European War, 1914–18 (despatches, Military Cross for bringing down a Fokker). *Heir: b* Lieut-Commander Hon. Archibald John Morton Stuart, *b* 14 Nov. 1894. *Address:* 1 Hans Place, SW1. *T:* Kensington 9595; Donibristle Park, Aberdour, Fife; Castle Stuart, Inverness-shire; Darnaway Castle, Forres, Morayshire; Doune Lodge, Doune, Perthshire. *Clubs:* Turf, Royal Air Force; New, Edinburgh.

Died 9 July 1943.

MORDAUNT, Elinor; *b* Cotgrove Place, Notts; *e d* of St John Legh Clowes and Hon. Mrs Clowes. *Educ:* at home. Went out to Mauritius, 1897, and married there; the Island of Mauritius, under the name of Terracine, has formed the scene for several books and a number of short stories, including the book of short stories The Island; returned to England, 1899; went to Australia, 1902, on a sailing ship, from which her book The Ship of Solace is taken; took up decorative painting and gardening; returned to England in 1908, and went round the world in 1923 on sailing and cargo boats for the Daily News, paying particular attention to the New Guinea Isles and small islands of the Dutch East Indies; since then travelled in East Africa, Siam, Malay States and Central America. *Publications:* The Garden of Contentment; The Ship of Solace; The Cost of It; Lu of the Ranges; Bellamy Simpson; The Family; The Rose of Youth; The Park Wall; Before Midnight; The Pendulum; The Processionals, 1918; The Little Soul; Laura Crichton, 1921; Alas, That Spring, 1922; Reputation, 1923; People, Houses and Ships, 1924; Shoe and Stocking Stories, 1926; The Dark Fire, 1927; And Then, 1927; Father and Daughter, 1928; Full Circle, 1931; Cross Winds, 1932; Purely for Pleasure, 1932; Mrs Van Kleek, 1933; Traveller's Pack, 1933; The Family, 1934; These Generations (dramatised as The Lady of La Paz); Prelude to Death, 1936; Sindbada, 1937; Pity of the World, 1938; Royals Free; Roses in December, 1939; Death It Is, 1939; Judge Not, 1940; Tropic Heat; Blitz Kids, 1941. *Recreation:* being at sea. *Address:* 43 Daver Court, Manor Street, Chelsea.

Died 25 June 1942.

MORE-O'FERRALL, Dominic; *see* O'Ferrall.

MORELAND, Rt Rev. William Hall, DD; Acting Rector, St Paul's Church, Delray, Florida; *b* Charleston, South Carolina, 9 April 1861; *s* of E. M. Moreland, banker, Charleston, SC, of Co. Antrim, Ireland, and Caroline Hall, of English extraction; *m* Harriett E. Slason of New Hampshire; three *s* three *d*. *Educ:* private schools in SC; University of the South, Sewanee, Tenn;

Berkeley Divinity School, Middletown, Conn; BA, BS, BLt, MA, University of the South; DD from Berkeley; STD from University of the South. Priest, 1885; Rector at Hartford, Conn, Nashua, NH, San Francisco, Calif; Bishop of Sacramento, 1899–1934. *Publication:* What is Christianity? The Church or the Churches, Which? *Recreations:* tennis, fishing, hunting. *Address:* Delray, Florida, USA. *Clubs:* Elks, Rotary, Sacramento.

Died 27 Oct. 1946.

MORELL, Sir Stephen Joseph, Kt 1927; *b* 1869; *m* 1901, Elizabeth Rutherford, *d* of late George Watson Telford; three *s* one *d. Educ:* Scotch College, Melbourne. Lord Mayor of Melbourne, 1926–28; Director of Carlton and United Breweries Ltd, Melbourne Cooperative Brewery Coy. Ltd, Victoria Insurance Coy. Ltd, Equity Trustees Coy. Ltd; Member of Melbourne and Metropolitan Tramways Board. *Address:* Avoca St, S Yarra, Melbourne. *Club:* Athenæum (Melb.).

Died 6 July 1944.

MORFORD, Maj.-Gen. Albert Clarence St. C.; *see* St Clair-Morford.

MORGAN, Alexander, OBE 1931; MA, DSc, LLD, FRSE; Director of Studies, Edinburgh Provincial Training College, 1920–25; *b* 21 Aug. 1860; 2nd *s* of William Morgan, Leith; *m* 1888, Isobel, *e d* of John Duthie, Aberdeen; two *s. Educ:* North Parish School, Aberdeen; Grammar School, Old Aberdeen; University of Edinburgh. MA 1886, with First Class Honours in Mathematics and Natural Philosophy (gained Sir David Baxter Scholarship in Mathematics, and Neil Arnott Bursary as most distinguished student of year in Physical Laboratory); DSc 1897, for original investigation in Mathematics. Lecturer in Mathematics in Edinburgh Church of Scotland Training College, 1886; Rector, 1903; Director of Studies, Provincial Committee, 1920; President of Educational Institute of Scotland, 1912; Chairman, Scottish Education Reform Committee, 1916–17. *Publications:* The Geometrical Representation of Elliptic Integrals of the First Kind, 1897; Elementary Physiography, 1898; Advanced Physiography, 1901; The Training and Status of Primary and Secondary Teachers in Switzerland, 1902; Psychology Past and Present, 1907; Education and Social Progress, 1916; Rise and Progress of Scottish Education, 1927; Makers of Scottish Education, 1929; Scottish University Studies, 1933; Charters and Statutes of Edinburgh University, 1937. *Clubs:* Scottish Liberal, Edinburgh.

Died 17 March 1946.

MORGAN, Major Sir David Hughes-, 1st Bt *cr* 1925; Kt 1920; late 3rd South Wales Borderers; Chairman of Western Mail and Echo, Cardiff; Chairman Chepstow Race Club; Mayor of Tenby for eight years; *b* 16 Aug. 1871; *e s* of late David Morgan, Henllys, Llandovery; *m* 1896, Blanche Elizabeth Wedge, *e d* of late James Buckley, Bryncaeran, Llanelly; two *s* two *d. Educ:* private school; Queen's Coll., Oxford. High Sheriff of Breconshire, 1899; JP Borough and County of Brecon and Borough and County of Pembroke; drove one of the Daimler cars in the Herkomer Trophy in Germany, 1906; Captain of College Football and Cricket XIs; prospective Unionist candidate for Pembroke Boroughs, 1911–18, when the seat was merged into the county. *Recreations:* motoring, cricket, golf, shooting, fishing. *Heir: s* John Vernon [*b* 12 Aug. 1900; *m* 1923, Lucie Margaret, *d* of late Thomas Jones Parry, Llwyn-Onn Hall, Denbighshire; three *s*]. *Address:* Penally House, Penally, Pembrokeshire; Manasein, Brecon. *Clubs:* Junior Carlton, Royal Automobile, MCC.

Died 16 March 1941.

MORGAN, Rev. G. Campbell, DD (Chicago Theol. Semin.); Preacher and Lecturer Westminster Chapel, 1933–34; minister, 1935–43; emeritus since 1943; *b* Tetbury, Glos, 9 Dec. 1863; *s* of Rev. George Morgan; *m* 1888, Annie, *d* of William Morgan of Staunton, Glos;

four *s* two *d. Educ:* The Douglas School, Cheltenham. Master in Jewish Collegiate School, Birmingham, 1883–86; Mission Preacher, 1886–88; ordained to Congregational ministry 1889; Pastorates at Stone, Staffs, 1889–91; Rugeley, Staffs, 1891–93; Westminster Road, Birmingham, 1893–97; New Court, Tollington Park, London, 1897–1901; Northfield Bible Conference Extension Lecturer, 1901–04; Westminster Congregational Church, Buckingham Gate, London, 1904–17; YMCA Work, 1918; Highbury Quadrant Congregational Church, 1918–19; Bible Lecturer, USA, 1919–29; Extension Lecturer and Member of the Faculty of Los Angeles Bible Institute, 1927–28; Pastor Tabernacle Presbyterian Church Philadelphia, 1929–32; Bible Lecturer Gordon Coll. of Theology and Missions, Boston, 1930–31. *Publications:* Discipleship; The Hidden Years at Nazareth; God's Methods with Man; Wherein?; Life Problems; The Ten Commandments; God's Perfect Will; The Spirit of God; The True Estimate of Life; The Crises of the Christ; A First Century Message to Twentieth Century Christians; The Christ of To-day; The Practice of Prayer; Simple Things of the Christian Life; Parables of the Kingdom; The Analysed Bible (10 vols); Christian Principles; The Missionary Manifesto; The Bible and the Cross; Evangelism; The Life of the Christian; The Teaching of the Lesson; The Study and Teaching of the English Bible; Messages of the Books of the Bible; The Teaching of Christ; The Ministry of the Word; The Acts of the Apostles; The Graded Bible; Searchlights from the Word; The Gospel according to Mark; The Gospel according to Matthew; Categorical Imperatives of the Christian Faith; Studies in the Prophecy of Jeremiah; The Gospel according to Luke; The Gospel according to John; The Heart and Holiness of God; Great Chapters of the Bible; God's final Word to Man; The Great Physician; Voices of 12 Hebrew Prophets; The Bible in 400 years; The Fulfilment of Life; Triumphs of Faith; Parables and Metaphors of Our Lord; To Die is Gain; Enoch; The Bible and the Child; The Voice of the Devil; and other booklets. *Address:* 345 St Ermin's, SW1. *T:* Whitehall 3176.

Died 16 May 1945.

MORGAN, George, CBE 1919; ISO 1911; Chevalier de l'Ordre de Léopold, 1919. Entered Post Office Engineering Department, 1871; Controller, Post Office Stores Department, 1908–19; acquired control of Post Office Factories and of Stamps, 1912; Member of Fair Wages Advisory Committee until 1919; Official Adviser to Central Committee on Women's Employment, 1914–19; *b* 15 April 1853; *m* 1880, Annie Eliza, *d* of Joseph Feltham. *Address:* Downings, Wallington, Surrey. *T:* Wallington, 3101.

Died 18 Dec. 1943.

MORGAN, Rev. Harold Dunbar, MA, LLD; Rector of Stockport, Cheshire, since 1939; Hon. Canon of Chester, since 1939; *e s* of late Thomas Morgan (sometime Chief Warehouse Manager, Mersey Docks and Harbour Board) and late Ruth Morgan; *m* 1909, Agnes Maude, 2nd *d* of H. F. Jensen; two *s* three *d. Educ:* Wallasey Grammar School (Head of the School); Trinity College, Dublin (Senior Moderator). Deacon, 1906; Priest, 1907; Assistant Curate, St Luke's, Bold Street, Liverpool, 1906–11; St Cyprian's, Edgehill, Liverpool, 1911–13; Vicar of St James's, Toxteth Park, Liverpool, 1913–17; St Cyprian's, Edgehill, Liverpool, 1917–29; Vicar and Lecturer of Rotherham, Yorks, 1929–39; Rural Dean of Liverpool South, 1922–29; Rural Dean of Rotherham, 1929–39; Hon. Canon of Liverpool Cathedral, 1925–29; Hon. Canon of Sheffield Cathedral, 1929–36; Canon Residentiary of Sheffield Cathedral, 1936–39; Proctor in Convocation, 1935–39; Warden of Lay Readers' Association, Diocese of Sheffield, 1930–39; Chaplain of Royal Southern Hospital, Liverpool, 1913–20. *Address:* The Rectory, Stockport, Cheshire.

Died 8 Dec. 1945.

MORGAN, Ven. Harry J., MA, Archdeacon of Bangor since 1937; Rural Dean of Tyndaothwy, Anglesey, 1927; Surrogate Diocese Bangor 1928; Canon Residentiary, Bangor Cathedral 1930; Prebendary of Penmynydd, 1933; Chancellor since 1934; *b* 16 Nov. 1871; *s* of Rev. John Morgan, Rector of Edern, Carnarvonshire, and Brynymor, Aberystwyth, and Anne Morgan; *m* Edith Winifred, *d* of Harry Clegg, JP, DL, Plas Llanfair, Llanfair PG, Anglesey; one *d. Educ:* Christ College, Brecon; Brasenose College, Oxford. Curate of Llanfair PG, Anglesey 1899–1901; Beaumaris, 1901–06; Rector of Llanaber-w-Barmouth, 1906; Rector of Llandegfan-w-Beaumaris, Anglesey, 1907–37. *Address:* Gadlys, Llansadwrn, Anglesey. *Club:* Royal Anglesey Yacht.
Died 30 Oct. 1947.

MORGAN, Henry; President, Association of British Chambers of Commerce, 1942–44; Senior Partner, Henry Morgan & Co., Incorporated Accountants, 1 Great Winchester St, EC2; *b* 15 Sept. 1875; *s* of Henry Morgan; *m* 1928, Daphne Margaret Dickson-Hill; two *d. Educ:* privately. High Sheriff of Montgomeryshire, 1942; Chairman of the Council London Chamber of Commerce, 1938–41; President, Society of Incorporated Accountants and Auditors, 1929–32; Member, Board of Referees, 1928; Member, German Debts Committee, 1935, and Enemy Trade Debts Committee, 1940. *Recreations:* angling, golf. *Address:* Melvin, Green Lane, Burnham, Bucks. *T:* Burnham 390, Hounslow 6211. *Clubs:* Junior Carlton, Portland.
Died 3 Nov. 1944.

MORGAN, His Honour John Lloyd; KC 1906; *b* 13 Feb. 1861; *y s* of late Rev. William Morgan, Prof. of Theology, Presbyterian College, Carmarthen. *Educ:* Tettenhall College, Staffordshire; Owens College, Manchester; Trinity Hall, Cambridge (BA). Barr. Inner Temple, 1884; MP (L) W Carmarthenshire, 1889–1910; Recorder of Swansea, 1908–10; CC Judge Carmarthen, 1910–26; retired, 1926. *Address:* 11 Penllwyn Park, Carmarthen. *Club:* Reform.
Died 17 May 1944.

MORGAN, John Pierpont; Chairman of J. P. Morgan and Co., Inc., New York; Morgan, Grenfell and Co., London; Drexel and Co., Philadelphia; Morgan et Cie, Paris; *b* New York, 1867; *s* of late J. Pierpont Morgan; *m* 1890, Jane Norton Grew (*d* 1925); two *s* two *d. Educ:* St Paul's School, Concord; Harvard. Trustee Metropolitan Museum of Art; Vice-Pres. American Museum of Natural History; Governor Peabody Donation Fund; Trustee New York Public Library; Trustee Cooper Union, New York; LLD Trinity College, Hartford, Conn, 1918; LLD Cambridge University, England, 1919; DCSc. New York University, 1922; LLD Harvard University, 1923; LLD Princeton University, 1929; DCL Oxford, 1930; Officer Legion of Honour, 1919; Commander, 1920; Grand Order of Leopold II (Belgium), 1920; Grand Officer of Order of Leopold (Belgium), 1930; First Order of Sacred Treasure (Japan) 1927; Grand Cross of the Order of St Gregory the Great, 1938; Honorary Freedom of Goldsmiths Company, 1919. *Recreations:* yachting, shooting. *Address:* 12 Grosvenor Square, W1. *T:* Mayfair 6844; Wall Hall, Watford, Herts; 231 Madison Avenue, New York; Matinicock Point, Glencove, Long Island. *Clubs:* Athenæum (hon.), White's, Garrick, City of London; Metropolitan, Union, New York Yacht, University, Century, Racquet, New York; Metropolitan, Washington.
Died 13 March 1943.

MORGAN, Lt-Gen. Reginald Hallward, CBE 1922; late Royal Marines; *b* Stoke, Devonport, 25 May 1871; *s* of late Charles Greensill Morgan, HM Civil Service; *m* 1901, Sarah Muriel (*d* 1938), *d* of late Paymaster-in-Chief William Horniman, RN; three *d. Educ:* King's School, Rochester; Portsmouth Grammar School. Joined RMLI 1890; served South African War,

1899–1900; Commandant of Ascension Island, 1905–08; Instructor of Gunnery, Chatham Division, 1908–10; Senior Naval Intelligence Officer, China, 1911–16; General Staff Officer, 1st Grade, Hong Kong, 1916–18; Director of Naval Recruiting, 1921–24; Colonel Commandant Chatham Division Royal Marines, 1924–26; ADC to the King, 1924; Maj.-Gen. 1926; Lieut-General, 1928; retired list, 1929. *Recreations:* cricket, tennis, golf, and fishing. *Address:* c/o Westminster Bank Ltd, 26 Haymarket, SW1.
Died 30 April 1948.

MORGAN, Brig.-Gen. Rosslewin Westropp, CMG 1919; DSO 1916; *b* 17 Oct. 1879; *s* of late Westropp Thomas Morgan, Lieut-Col KOSB, and Mary Morgan; *m* 1920, Maud Esther Nathan, 13 Neville Court, St John's Wood, NW; one *s. Educ:* Wellington; Sandhurst. Joined 1st Batt. S Staffordshire Regt, 1899; Temp. Brig.-General, 1916; served South African War, 1900–02 (Queen's medal 3 clasps, King's medal 2 clasps); joined 2nd Batt. in France, Dec. 1914; Adjutant; served European War, 1914–17 (wounded near Richebourg, despatches, DSO and bar, Bt Lt-Col, CMG); commanded 157th (Highland) Infantry Brigade TA, 1926–29; Officer i/c Infantry Record and Pay Office, Warley, 1929–33; retired pay, 1933. *Recreations:* golf, amateur acting.
Died 11 Feb. 1947.

MORGAN, Thomas Hunt, PhD, LLD, ScD, Professor of Biology, Emeritus, California Institute of Technology; *b* 1866. Foreign Member Royal Society (Darwin medal, 1924, Copley Medal, 1939); President National Academy of Science, 1927–31; BS Univ. of Kentucky, 1886; MS 1888; PhD, LLD Johns Hopkins Univ.; LLD Univ. of Kentucky, McGill Univ., Montreal, University of Edinburgh and University of California; DSc University of Michigan; Dr hc, University of Paris; PhD (Dr of Nat. Phil.) Heidelberg University, 1931; Professor of Biology, Bryn Mawr College, 1891–1904; Professor of Experimental Zoology, Columbia University, 1904–28; Pres. AAAS 1930; Member various American and foreign learned societies. Nobel Prize for Medicine, 1933. *Address:* California Institute of Technology, Pasadena, California, USA.
Died 4 Dec. 1945.

MORGAN, William; Emeritus Professor of Automobile Engineering, Merchant Venturers' College, University of Bristol, Professor 1909–36; BSc Lond.; Member, Institute of Automobile Engineers; *b* 8 Nov. 1870; *m* 1897; one *s* one *d. Educ:* Geo. Dixon School, Birmingham; University, London. Teacher of Chemistry and Physics at Bablake School, Coventry; Lecturer in Mathematics and Chemistry at Technical Inst., Coventry; Manager of Pupils Department, Daimler Works, Coventry; Managing Director Wessex Engineering Co., Bristol; General Manager Mills Munitions Co., Birmingham; Pres. of the Institution of Automobile Engineers, 1929–30. *Publications:* technical papers. *Recreation:* gardening. *Address:* Mayfield, Uplands Road, Saltford, Bristol. *T:* Saltford 117.
Died 29 May 1945.

MORGENTHAU, Henry, GBE 1920; *b* Mannheim, 26 April 1856; *s* of Lazarus Morgenheim and Babette Guggenheim; came to United States, 1865; *m* 1883, Josephine Sykes, New York; one *s* three *d. Educ:* Public School No. 14 and Coll. City of New York; LLB Columbia, 1877; LLD Constantinople College for Girls, of Oberlin University, Temple University, University of Athens, and University of Syracuse. Member law firm Lachman, Morgenthau & Goldsmith, New York, 1879–99; President Central Realty Bond and Trust Co., 1899–1905; Henry Morgenthau Co., 1905–13; Chairman Finance Committee Dem. Nat. Com., Campaign, 1912 and 1916; Ambassador to Turkey, 1913–16; in charge of interests in Turkey of Great Britain, France, Italy, Russia, Belgium, Montenegro, San

Marino, Servia, Switzerland during the War; Head of American Commission to investigate Conditions in Poland; Chairman of Greek Refugee Settlement Commission; Grand Officer of Legion of Honour. *Publications:* Secrets of the Bosphorus, 1919; All in a Life-Time, 1922; An International Drama, 1930; My Trip Around the World, for private circulation. *Address:* 1133 Fifth Avenue, New York. *Clubs:* Century, Bankers' Harmonie, Economic, Country, New York.

Died 25 Nov. 1946.

MORIARTY, Rt Rev. Ambrose James, DD; Bishop of Shrewsbury, (RC), since 1934; *b* Stockport, 7 Aug. 1870; *nephew* of Rt Rev. S. W. Allen, fourth Bishop of Shrewsbury. *Educ:* Cotton; Oscott; English College, Rome. Priest, 1894; Curate, Shrewsbury Cathedral, 1894–97; Priest-in-Charge, 1897–1932; Canon Theologian, 1910; Vicar-General, 1925, and Provost to Cathedral Chapter, 1927; Titular Bishop of Miletopolis and Coadjutor of Bishop of Shrewsbury, 1932–34; Assistant to the Pontifical Throne, 1944. Served on Shrewsbury School Board, 1898, then on Local Education Committee and Vice-Chairman; Poor Law Guardian, 1898; Member of Council of Shropshire Archæological Society. *Recreation:* fishing. *Address:* The Council House, Shrewsbury. *T:* 3513.

Died 3 June 1949.

MORIN, Leopold Frédéric Germain; bénédictin de l'Abbaye de Maredsous, Belgique; *b* Caen, 6 Nov. 1861. *Educ:* autodidacte. Hon. LittD Université d'Oxford; Dr theol. de Zürich, Fribourg en Br. et Budapest; FRSL. Membre corr. de l'Académie des sciences de Bavière, membre d'honneur de l'Académie d'Archéol. Chrét. de Rome. A retrouvé récemment les œuvres du fameux moine Gottschalk du IXᵉ siècle; Auteur de nombreux travaux sur l'ancienne littérature chrétienne, spécialement du IVᵉ au XIIᵉ siècle, publiés pour la plupart dans la Revue Bénédictine de Maredsons, de 1884 jusque maintenant; éditeur de la collection des Anecdota Maredsolana (3 vol. 4to); 2ᵉ série, Etudes, Textes, Découvertes, avec autobibliographie de l'auteur, 1913; S Augustini Tractatus sive sermones inediti, 1917; S Augustini sermones post Maurinos reperti, nunc primum disquisiti, in unum collecti, et codicum fide instaurati, Romæ 1930; Découvertes principales: Version latine très ancienne de l'Épître de Clément de Rome; Commentarioli et Tractatus de s. Jérôme sur les Psaumes; Lectionnaire wisigothique de Tolède du VIIᵉ siècle; l'Auteur du Te Deum, Niceta de Remesiana; ouvrages inédits d'Arnobe le Jeune, et autres; édition princeps des Œuvres de s. Césaire d'Arles, 1937–43; Règle de S Benoît, trad. française avec notes explicatives, 1943. *Address:* Fribourg en Suisse, Couvent des Cordeliers.

Died 11 Feb. 1946.

MORINE, Sir Alfred Bishop, Kt 1928; KC 1898; *b* 31 March 1857; *s* of Alfred and mary Morine; *m* 1884, Alice Mason; one *s* one *d. Educ:* Dalhousie Law School, Halifax, NS. Editor newspapers, 1878–94; called to Bar, Nova Scotia, 1894; Newfoundland, 1894; called to Bar, Ontario, 1906; Member of House of Assembly, 1886–1906; 1914–19; Colonial Secretary, Newfoundland, 1894; Minister Finance and Customs, 1898; Minister of Justice and Attorney-General, 1919; Leader of Legislative Council, Newfoundland, 1924–28; lived in St John's, 1883–1906; Toronto, 1906–12; St John's, 1912–27. *Publications:* Mining Law of Ontario; Canadian Notes to Russell on Crimes; Consulting Editor Dominion (Canada) Law Reports. *Recreation:* angling. *Address:* 114 Belsize Drive, Toronto, Canada.

Died 18 Dec. 1944.

MORISON, Rt Hon. Lord; Thomas Brash Morison; PC 1920; KC 1906; *b* Edinburgh; *s* of late P. Morison, SSC, Edinburgh; *m* 1st, 1899, Isabel Elizabeth (*d* 1934), 2nd *d* of late Andrew Hendry, solicitor, Dundee; two *s* one *d*; 2nd, 1935, Georgina Morgan, *d* of late William

Mitchell, Levenbank, Markinch. *Educ:* Edinburgh University (MA, LLD). Called to Scottish Bar, 1891; and to English Bar, 1899; KC 1906; Senior Advocate Depute, 1908–10; Sheriff of Fife and Kinross, 1910–13; Solicitor-General for Scotland, 1913–20; Lord Advocate, Scotland, 1920–22; Bencher, Gray's Inn, 1920; Treasurer, 1938; MP (CL) Inverness, 1917–22; one of the Senators of the College of Justice in Scotland, 1922–37; retired, 1937. *Address:* 30 Inverleith Place, Edinburgh. *Club:* New Edinburgh.

Died 28 July 1945.

MORLEY, Arthur, OBE; KC 1933; MA; Chairman Middlesex Quarter Sessions since April 1945; Chancellor, Diocese of Bradford, since 1941; JP Sussex; *b* 19 Nov. 1881; 4th *s* of late William James Morley, Heaton, Bradford, and Annie, *d* of Richard Brook; *m* 1908, Dorothy Innes Murray, *o d* of late William Forrest; one *s* one *d. Educ:* Bradford; Christ Church, Oxford. Called to Bar, Middle Temple, 1913; Bencher, 1938; joined North-Eastern Circuit; received the OBE and thanks of the Army Council for hospital services during War of 1914–18; for 17 years Member of the General Council of the Bar; Recorder of Richmond, Yorks, 1928, of Huddersfield, 1928–34; of Sheffield, 1934–41; of Leeds, 1940–43; Metropolitan Magistrate, 1943–44; Deputy Chairman Middlesex Quarter Sessions, Jan. 1945. *Recreation:* golf. *Address:* Oakwood Mansions, W14. *T:* Western, 6836; Wickham Farm, Haywards Heath, Sussex. *T:* Haywards Heath 371. *Club:* Union.

Died 11 Jan. 1946.

MORLEY, Sir George, Kt 1937; CBE 1920; BCL; Chief Constable of Durham County since 1922; *b* 1873; *s* of William James Morley of Heaton, Bradford, and Annie, *d* of Richard Brook; *m* Agnes, *d* of Joseph Tetley Milnes of Hillside House, Bradford, and Bishop's Lydeard. *Educ:* Bradford; Worcester College, Oxford. Lt Harwich Militia Division, RE, 1897–98; Royal Irish Constabulary, 1898; Chief Constable of Hull, 1910; commanded 12th East Yorks Batt. for a short time in 1914; Chairman of Committee of Management of Hull Savings Bank, 1921; a Governor of Hymer's College, Hull, 1912–22. *Address:* Chief Constable's Office, Durham; West House, Durham. *Clubs:* Oxford and Cambridge, Royal Automobile; Durham County, Durham.

Died 13 Oct. 1942.

MORLEY, Harry, ARA 1936; RWS 1931, Vice-President, 1937; RE 1931; RP 1936; *b* Leicester, 1881; *s* of Thomas Morley, Leicester; *m* 1911, Lilias Helen Swain; two *d. Educ:* Ald. Newton's School, Leicester; The School of Art, Leicester; Royal College of Art, London. Studied for an architect, holding travelling scholarships at Royal College of Art in Architecture, and Owen Jones studentship of Royal Institute of British Architects. Turned painter; studied London, Paris, and Italy; regular exhibitor, Royal Academy, since 1909, and London Exhibitions; picture in Tate Gallery, Apollo and Marsyas, bought by Chantrey Bequest, 1924; pictures in permanent collections at Leeds, Manchester, Bradford, Leicester, Bath, Reading, Durban SA, etc.; appointed to Faculty of Engraving, British School at Rome, 1931; Master of the Art Workers Guild, 1936; Pres. Leicester Society of Artists, 1940. *Address:* 4 Pembroke Road, Kensington, W8. *T:* Western 1691.

Died 18 Sept. 1943.

MORLEY, Henry Forster, MA, DSc (Lond.), FCS, FIC; late Director of the International Catalogue of Scientific Literature; late Director, Royal Society's Catalogue of Scientific Papers; late Lecturer, Charing Cross Hospital Medical School; *b* 1855; *s* of Henry Morley, Professor of English Literature; *m* 1893, Ida Rose (*d* 1943), *d* of Stephen Seaward Tayler; one *s. Educ:* Univ. Coll. School, Univ. Coll., London; University of Bonn; University of Munich; University of Berlin; University of Paris. Graduated MA (mathematics), 1877;

DSc (organic chemistry), 1883. Assistant Professor of Chemistry at University College, London, 1883–87; Professor of Chemistry at Queen's College, 1888–1901. *Publications:* Outlines of Organic Chemistry, 1883; joint-editor of Watts' Dictionary of Chemistry; scientific papers in Journal of the Chemical Society and elsewhere. *Address:* 5 Lyndhurst Road, NW3; Church Hill House, Midhurst, Sussex. *T:* Midhurst 232.

Died 3 April 1943.

MORLEY, Robert, RBA 1889; *b* 20 July 1857; *s* of late Prof. Henry Morley, LLD. *Educ:* The Slade School, University College, under Professors Poynter and Legros, and afterwards at Munich and Rome. Was Slade Scholar and Painting medallist. Until 1888 exhibited chiefly figure pictures, but afterwards turned to animal painting and landscape; was Hon. Sec. RBA and subsequently Hon. Treasurer, 1890–96. *Recreation:* natural history. *Address:* The Knapp, Elcombe, Stroud, Glos.

Died 3 April 1941.

MORPHEW, Col Edward Maudsley, CMG 1918, DSO 1917, MRCS, LRCP Lond.; late RAMC; retired pay, 1921; *b* 28 July 1867; *s* of Surgeon Major A. Morphew; *m* 1st; one *s* two *d*; 2nd, 1939, Margaret Audrey Hudson. *Educ:* University College, London. Served NW Frontier (Tiran), 1897–98; S African War, 1899–1902 (Queen's medal with 4 clasps, King's medal with 2 clasps); European War, 1914–19 (despatches, CMG, DSO). *Address:* Home Close, Mundesley, Norfolk.

Died 8 March 1947.

MORRELL, Philip; *b* 4 June 1870; *o surv. s* of the late Frederic Morrell of Black Hall, Oxford, and Harriette Anne, *d* of Rev. Philip Wynter, DD, President of St John's College, Oxford; *m* 1902, Lady Ottoline Bentinck (*d* 1938), half-sister of 6th Duke of Portland, KG; one *d*. *Educ:* Eton; Balliol College, Oxford. MP (L) South Oxfordshire, 1906–10; Burnley, 1910–18; JP; MA. *Publication:* Leaves from the Greville Diary. *Address:* 10 Gower Street, WC1. *Clubs:* Reform, Savile.

Died 5 Feb. 1943.

MORRIS, Alfred; JP; ACP; *b* 18 June 1874; *s* of Henry Morris, Dorset; *m* 1896, Lily Elliott, Derby; one *d*. *Educ:* Cheltenham. Pupil Teacher, Cheltenham, 1893–94; First Assistant Master, Brighton Road C School, Derby, 1895–97; Headmaster Margam, Port Talbot, 1897–1905; Headmaster Saiyingpum School, Hong Kong, 1905–26; Headmaster King's College, Hong Kong, 1926–34; Tutor in English, Hong Kong University, 1917–22; Master of Method, 1922–33; President, St David's Society; Em. Pr. Provincial Priory of China; Deputy District Grand Master, District Grand Lodge of Mark Master Masons of Hong Kong and South China; retired Commissioner and Director of Ambulance, St John Ambulance Assoc. and Brigade; Commander Venerable Order St John of Jerusalem; Provincial Prior of China; Past Grand Deacon, Grand Lodge of England; Past District Grand Warden, District Grand Secretary, and DG Scribe E, DG Chapter of Hong Kong, South China, 1915–39; Retired from Government Service, 1934. *Recreations:* golf, tennis, swimming. *Address:* St John Ambulance Headquarters, Hong Kong. *Clubs:* Sports; Hong Kong, Hong Kong Race. *[Interned in Hong Kong.]*

Died 8 July 1945.

MORRIS, Col Arthur Hugh, CIE 1921; CBE 1919; MRCS (Eng.), LRCP (Lond.); late RAMC; *b* 26 Feb. 1872. Entered Army 1896; served European War, 1914–15 (despatches, CBE); Mesopotamia, 1919–21 (CIE); retired pay 1922.

Died 6 July 1941.

MORRIS, Charles Arthur, CVO 1901; MA, MB, MC Camb.; FRCS England; *b* Guntoor, Madras Presidency; *s* of late Fred. W. Morris, ICS; *m* 1893, Ethel, *d* of late Samuel Seldon, CB, of HM Customs. *Educ:* Caius College, Camb. (Natural Science Honours); St Bartholomew's Hospital, London. Late House Surgeon at St Bartholomew's Hospital, and late Resident Medical Officer at Royal Infirmary, Liverpool; Consulting Surgeon to Grosvenor Hospital for Women and Children; Medical Officer, King Edward VII Hospital for Officers. Decorated for gratuitous services to sick and wounded officers; late Major RAMC (T). *Address:* 11 Carlisle Mansions, SW1. *T:* Victoria 3638.

Died 25 Feb. 1942.

MORRIS, Charles Sculthorpe, CVO 1943; MRCS; LRCP, LDS; Sergeant Surgeon-Dentist to the King; formerly Surgeon-Dentist to the King; *b* 1875; *s* of late George Bentham Morris, Capt. RMLI, Tauranga, NZ, member Legislative Council of NZ; *m* 1914, Frances Mary Alicia, *d* of late William Fitzwilliam Burton, Burton Hall, Co. Carlow and Goltho, Lincs; (son, killed on active service); two *d*. *Educ:* Tauranga, NZ, and Guy's Hospital. *Recreations:* golf, beekeeping. *Address:* 77 Albert Hall Mansions, SW7. *T:* Kensington 1925. *Club:* Savile.

Died 19 Dec. 1949.

MORRIS, Major Cyril Clarke Boville, CBE 1938; MC; MIMechE; *b* Spalding, Lincolnshire, 8 Feb. 1882; *s* of late Charles K. Morris, MRCS, JP, Blackheath, SE; *m* 1909, Anita Jeanette, *d* of Annie O'Flanagan; one *s* one *d*. *Educ:* Haileybury College. Pupil at Great Eastern Railway Locomotive Works, Stratford; three years Engineer in charge of GE Railway Motor Department; Assistant Divisional Officer, London Fire Brigade, 1908; Chief Officer of the London Fire Brigade, 1933–38; Director of Training, Fire Brigades Division, Home Office, 1939; Regional Controller, Ministry of Supply, Cambridge, 1939–42; King's Police Medal, 1923; Deputy Assistant Director of Transport, 1917; served in France Oct. 1914–July 1917 (MC, 1914 Star with Bar, Royal Humane Society's Bronze Medal, 22 Oct. 1914, despatches twice). *Publications:* The Organization and Mechanical Appliances of the London Fire Brigade (Institution of Mechanical Engineers); Fire: An Autobiography, 1940. *Address:* c/o National Provincial Bank, Torrington, Devon.

Died 31 Oct. 1950.

MORRIS, Edward Gilbert, OBE; Director of Education, Colony and Protectorate of Nigeria, since 1938; *b* 15 July 1884; *s* of William Morris, MICE, and Norah Charles; *m* 1911, Mary Grave Morris; three *d* one *s*. *Educ:* Bedford School; Hertford College, Oxford. Uganda Administrative Service, 1908; Lt Unattached List, 1914–15; Capt. Uganda Transport Corps, 1916–18; Political Officer, Tanganyika, 1919; Resigned from Colonial Service, 1920; Managing Director, Bantu Trading and Developments Ltd 1920–23; rejoined Uganda Administration, 1924; Labour Commissioner, 1925; Inspector of Schools, 1925–29; Deputy Director of Education, 1929; Director of Education, 1929–34; Director of Education, Kenya Colony, 1934–38. *Publications:* (With R. A. Snoxall) Luganda-Swahili Handbook; Elimu ya Kiswahili. *Recreations:* Oxford University Rugby XV 1904–05, swimming, water polo 1903–06; golf. *Address:* c/o Westminster Bank, Deptford, SE. *Club:* United Empire.

Died 11 May 1943.

MORRIS, Sir Francis, Kt 1928; JP London; *b* 1859; 3rd *s* of late Francis Morris; *m* 1894, Edith, *d* of late E. H. Rhodes, Land Revenue Record Office; three *s* one *d*. Engaged during working life in various forms of social work, both voluntary and statutory; Chairman of Children's Country Holidays Fund, 1912–38; Chairman of Metropolitan Asylums Board, 1924–28; Vice-Chairman of Public Assistance Committee of the

London County Council, 1930–33; Chairman of Administrative Committee of Charity Organisation Society, 1913–34. *Recreation:* walking. *Address:* 26 Loudoun Road, NW8.

Died 3 May 1944.

MORRIS, Sir George Cecil, 6th Bt *cr* 1806; *b* 10 April 1852; *s* of Sir John Armine Morris, 3rd Bt; *S nephew,* 1937; *m;* one *d.* Heir: *nephew* Herbert Edward, *b* 4 July 1884. *Address:* Monavale, New South Wales.

Died 17 July 1940.

MORRIS, Sir George Lockwood, 8th Bt *cr* 1806; retired engineer; *b* 29 Jan. 1859; *s* of George Byng Morris (2nd *s* of 2nd Bt); *S* kinsman, 1947; *m* 1889, Wilhelmina Cory; one *s* one *d. Educ:* Clifton College. Formerly Lieut Royal Monmouthshire Engineers Militia. *Recreations:* hunting, shooting. *Heir:* s Cedric Lockwood Morris. *Address:* Yew Tree Cottage, Henley-on-Thames. *T:* Henley 806.

Died 23 Nov. 1947.

MORRIS, Harrison Smith; Commissioner General from the United States to the Roman Art Exposition commemorating United Italy, 1911 (Commendatore Crown of Italy); President of Wharton Steel Company, 1910–17; *b* Philadelphia, Pa, USA, 4 Oct. 1856; *s* of George W. Morris and Catharine (Harris) Morris; *m* Anna Wharton, 1896; one *d. Educ:* private and public schools in Philadelphia. Hon. member Phi Beta Kappa, Univ. of Pennsylvania; Ex-Chairman, Committee on Ways and Means, and Fellow of the National Academy of Design of New York; One of Incorporators American Academy in Rome; Pres. Emeritus, Newport (RI) Art Assoc.; in Treasury Department, Philadelphia and Reading Coal and Iron Company, 1873–92; Managing Director of the Pennsylvania Academy of the Fine Arts, 1892–1905; Editor of *Lippincott's Magazine,* 1899–1905; Art Editor, *Ladies' Home Journal,* 1905–08. *Publications:* A Duet in Lyrics (with John Arthur Henry); A Mosaic, edited, 1891; Where Meadows meet the Sea, edited, 1892; In the Yule-Log Glow, edited and original, 1892; Tales from Ten Poets, 1893; Tales from Shakespeare, a continuation of Lamb's, 1893; Madonna and other Poems, 1894; Lyrics and Landscapes, 1908; Masterpieces of the Sea, Biography of William T. Richards, 1912; Hannah Bye, a novel, 1920; The Landlord's Daughter, a novel, 1923; Martial Notes (poems), 1929; Confessions in Art, 1930; Walt Whitman, a Brief Biography with Reminiscences, 1929; Odes, 1938. *Address:* 1600 Chelten Avenue, Philadelphia 26, Pa. *TA:* Philadelphia. *T:* Waverly 1982; Horsehead, Jamestown, Rhode Island. *T:* Jamestown 103. *Clubs:* Franklin Inn, Sketch, Corinthian Yacht (Philadelphia); The Players', Salmagundi (New York).

Died 12 April 1948.

MORRIS, Sir Herbert Edward, 7th Bt *cr* 1806; *b* 4 July 1884; *s* of late Herbert Morris, 5th *s* of 3rd Bt; *S* uncle, 1940; *m* 1938, Olive Irene Griffiths; no *c. Educ:* mainly Military. Has served in many parts of the world. Heir: *kinsman* George Lockwood [*b* 29 Jan. 1859; *m* 1889, Wilhelmina, *d* of Thomas Cory; one *s* one *d*]. *Address:* Chestnuts, 29 Bellevue Road, West Cross, Mumbles, Swansea.

Died 15 Aug. 1947.

MORRIS, Herbert Picton, MA, LLM; *b* 4 April 1856; *y s* of late John Grant Morris of Allerton Priory, near Liverpool; *m* 1882, Alice, *y d* of late Thomas Russell, CMG, of Normanswood, Farnham, Surrey; one *d. Educ:* Eton; Trinity College, Cambridge. Law Tripos, 1878 (bracketed senior in First Class). Called to Bar, Inner Temple, 1880; Legal Clerkship in Charity Commission, 1886; Private Secretary to late Sir Henry Longley, KCB, and late Sir Charles Alderson, KCB 1891–1900; a Principal Clerk in the Charity Commission, 1900–05; an Assistant Charity Commissioner for England and Wales,

1905–16; Second Charity Commissioner, and Secretary of the Charity Commission, 1916–19; Chief Charity Commissioner, 1919–21; Member Metropolitan Asylums Board, 1923–30. *Recreations:* School Wall Eleven, and Oppidan Wall Eleven, Eton, 1874. *Address:* 61 Pont Street, SW1. *T:* Kensington 2236. *Club:* Oxford and Cambridge University.

Died 12 Feb. 1946.

MORRIS, Ira Nelson; Diplomatist, writer, capitalist; *m;* one *s* one *d. Educ:* Yale University. Commissioner General to Italy on behalf of Panama-Pacific National Exposition, 1913; United States Minister to Sweden, 1914–23; Member of the American Museum of Natural History; President American Scandinavian Foundation, Chicago Chapter; Chairman International Radio Forum; Grand Officer, Legion of Honor; Grand Cross, Victor Emmanuel III; Grand Cross, Royal Order of the Northern Star, Gustaf; Grand Cross, Ferdinand, Roumania; Sanct Olav's Order, Haakon VI; Grand Cross, Finnish White Rose; Grand Star of Persia; Grand Cordon, Nishan Iftquor, Kapurthala. *Publications:* With the Trade Winds, 1897; From an American Legation, 1923; former publisher, Public Affairs, monthly magazine, Washington. *Address:* Continental Illinois Bank Building, Chicago, Ill. *TA:* Imor, Chicago; Eaglehead, Manchester, Mass. *Clubs:* Army and Navy, Yale, New York; University, Washington; Union Interalliée, American, Paris.

Died Jan. 1942.

MORRIS, James Archibald, RSA 1931; ARSA 1916; FRIBA, FRSE, FSA Scot.; Member of Royal Commission on Historical Monuments (Scotland); Art Workers' Guild; *b* Ayr, 14 Jan. 1857; *s* of late Archibald Morris and Ann Watson, Ayr; *m* Elizabeth (*d* 1935), *d* of Charles Forgan, Towerhill, Kilmaurs, Ayrshire; two *s* one *d. Educ:* Ayr Academy; Glasgow School of Art; Slade School, Univ. Coll., London; Royal Academy Schools. Travelled Italy, France, Germany; works: mainly domestic in England and Scotland, and a few churches; preservative work: Crosraguel Abbey, Auld Brig of Ayr, and others. *Publications:* Crosraguel Abbey, 1886; The Brig of Ayr, 1910; Ayrshire white Needlework, 1916; (Joint) Lister and the Lister Ward, 1927; Auld Toon o' Ayr, 1928; Alloway: The Protection and Preservation of its Memorials of Robert Burns, 1930; John Callaghan, Poet and Tutor, 1933; A Romance of Industrial Engineering, 1939; lectures and pamphlets. *Recreations:* golf and photography. *Address:* Wellington Chambers, and Savoy Croft, Ayr. *T:* 2841. *Clubs:* Prestwick Golf; Glasgow Art.

Died 18 Nov. 1942.

MORRIS, Noah, MD, ChB, DSc, DPH, FRCP, FRFPSG; Regius Professor of Materia Medica and Therapeutics, University of Glasgow, since 1937; *m* 1921, Hattie, 2nd *d* of late P. Michaelis, London; one *s* one *d. Educ:* The High School, Glasgow; Glasgow University. BSc with special distinction, 1913; MB, ChB with commendation, 1915; DPH (Liverpool), 1917; FRFPS Glasgow, 1921; MD (Hons), Glasgow, 1921, Bellahouston gold medal; DSc Glasgow; 1934; MRCP (Lond.), 1938; FRCP (Lond.), 1943. Capt. RAMC; served in France and Italy; Lecturer in Pathological Biochemistry, Glasgow Univ., and Biochemist to Royal Hospital for Sick Children, Glasgow; Prof. of Physiology, The Anderson College of Medicine; Assistant to Regius Professor of Physiology, Glasgow University; Muirhead Demonstrator in Physiology, Glasgow University. *Publications:* Acidosis and Alkalosis (with S. G. Graham), 1933; Chapters on Deficiency Diseases and Diseases of the Ductless Glands in Text-book of Medical Treatment, 1939; Carbohydrate Metabolism in Coeliac Disease, Quarterly Journal of Medicine (April 1936); The Plasma Phosphatase in

Disease, Quarterly Journal of Medicine (April 1937), etc. *Address:* Barone, 7 West Chapelton Crescent, Bearsden, by Glasgow. *T:* Bearsden 2453.

Died 1 June 1947.

MORRIS, Reginald Owen, DMus (Oxon); FRCM; Teaching staff, Royal College of Music; *b* York, 1886. *Educ:* Harrow; New College, Oxford; Royal College of Music. *Publications:* Contrapuntal Technique in the XVI Century, 1922; The Structure of Music, 1935; Introduction to Counterpoint, 1943; The Oxford Harmony, Vol. I, 1946; etc.; also various musical compositions. *Clubs:* Oxford and Cambridge, Savile.

Died 15 Dec. 1948.

MORRISON, Alexander; Solicitor (retired); formerly Town Clerk of Bridge of Allan, JP Stirlingshire, and Hon. Sheriff-Substitute for the Counties of Stirling, Dumbarton and Clackmannan; *b* 12 March 1868; *s* of late Alexander Morrison; *m* 1897, Emma Brown, *d* of late John Martin. *Educ:* Stirling High School; Glasgow Univ. Initiated and carried through movement for the raising of the status of the Secretary for Scotland; has taken a prominent part in the work of the Convention of Royal Burghs, in the Scottish Housing movement and in the restoration to Scotland of the ancient Scottish Records removed to London by Edward I in 1296. *Publications:* local historical papers; Memoranda on Burghal Finance and Administration. *Address:* Ranworth, Doune, Perthshire.

Died 3 April 1941.

MORRISON, Archibald Cameron, OBE 1919; MA, LLB, LLD; Advocate in Aberdeen; Professor of Conveyancing (Hugh McLennan chair) Aberdeen University, 1927, now Professor Emeritus; Clerk of the Peace for the County of Aberdeen since 1925; Honorary Sheriff Substitute of Aberdeenshire since 1925; *b* Logie Pert, Angus, 29 July 1870; 4th *s* of John Morrison, Parish Schoolmaster, Logie Pert, and Elizabeth Paterson Cameron; *m* 1901, Agnes Sproul, 4th *d* of John Nicolson, Paisley; no *c*. *Educ:* Logie Pert School; Royal High School, Edinburgh; St Andrews University (MA); Glasgow University (LLB). Began practice in Aberdeen, 1899; Member of Society of Advocates in Aberdeen, 1899, Pres. 1942; Law Examiner for Scotland under Solicitors Act 1933, 1934–44; 2nd Lieut Gordon Highlanders, 1915; Appeal Military Representative for 75th Recruiting Area (Aberdeen, Kincardine and Banff), 1916; retired with honorary rank of Lieutenant, 1917; Lecturer on Conveyancing, Aberdeen University, 1919; took close interest in politics as Unionist, ultimately becoming Honorary Secretary South Aberdeen Unionist Association; Member of Aberdeen University Court, 1935–39. *Publications:* Brochure in two editions on Emergency War Legislation relating to Houses and Mortgages; Contributions to Scottish Journal of Agriculture on Simplicity and Economy in Transfer of Land and on State Intervention in Agriculture from 15th to 20th Century; Articles in Encyclopedia of the Laws of Scotland on The Law of Leases, Registration and the Records of Scotland, Searches. *Recreation:* golf. *Address:* 18 Bon Accord Crescent, Aberdeen; 54 Rubislawden North, Aberdeen. *TA:* Fideliter Aberdeen. *T:* Aberdeen 4730 and 2181. *Club:* University (Aberdeen).

Died 4 Nov. 1948.

MORRISON, Arthur; novelist, dramatist, and writer on oriental art; formerly journalist; Fellow and member of Council, Royal Society of Literature; *b* 1863; *m* 1892, Adelaide, *d* of late Frederick Thatcher of Dover (one *s* decd as result of Service in 1914–18 War). On staff of National Observer throughout Henley's editorship. *Publications:* Tales of Mean Streets, 1894; Martin Hewitt, Investigator, 1894; Chronicles of Martin Hewitt, 1895; Adventures of Martin Hewitt, 1896; A Child of the Jago, 1896; The Dorrington Deed-Box, 1897; To London Town, 1899; Cunning Murrell, 1900; The Hole in the Wall, 1902; The Red Triangle, 1903; The Green Eye of Goona, 1904; Divers Vanities, 1905; Green Ginger, 1909; The Painters of Japan, 1911; volume in series, Short Stories of To-day and Yesterday, 1929; Fiddle o'Dreams, 1933. *Plays,* That Brute Simmons (with Herbert C. Sargent), 1904; The Dumb Cake (with Richard Pryce), 1907; A Stroke of Business (with Horace Newte), 1907; besides many articles, etc., in various publications. *Recreations:* collector of pictures and other objects of art; formed well-known collections of paintings by Chinese and Japanese old masters, now in British Museum; has collection of works of all the chief English masters and some others. *Address:* High Barn, Chalfont St Peter, Bucks. *T:* Chalfont St Giles 170. *Club:* Savage.

Died 4 Dec. 1945.

MORRISON, Hon. Aulay MacAulay; Chief Justice of the Supreme Court of British Columbia since 1929; *b* Baddeck, Nova Scotia, 15 June 1863; 5th *s* of Christopher Morrison and Flora MacAulay of Harris, Scotland; *m* 1900, Elizabeth, *d* of James Livingston, MP, Ontario; one *s* one *d*. *Educ:* Sydney and Pictou Academies; Dalhousie University (LLD). Admitted to Bar of Nova Scotia, 1888; British Columbia, 1890; MP New Westminster, 1896 and 1904. *Clubs:* Vancouver, Union, Victoria.

Died 27 Feb. 1942.

MORRISON, Most Rev. James, PhD, DD, LLD; Archbishop of Nova Scotia, (RC), since 1944; *b* St Andrews, Prince Edward Island, 1861; *s* of Donald Morrison and Elizabeth Campbell. *Educ:* St Dunstan's College, Charlottetown, PEI; College of the Propaganda, Rome. Ordained 1889; Curate at St Dunstan's Cathedral, Charlottetown, 1890; Professor of Philosophy in St Dunstan's College, Charlottetown, 1891; President of the College, 1892–95; Rector of the Cathedral, 1895–1907; Vicar-General of the Diocese, 1904; Pastor of the parish of Vernon River, PEI, 1907; Apostolic Administrator of the diocese of Charlottetown, 1911; Bishop of Antigonish, 1912–44. *Address:* Antigonish, Nova Scotia.

Died 13 April 1950.

MORRISON, Mrs Julia Minnie, CBE 1920; *d* of John Hamilton Whitcroft; *m* 1890, Beamish Morrison. Organiser of Free Buffet for Soldiers, Kingstown Pier, Dublin. *Address:* 3 Arkendale Road, Kingstown, Ireland.

Died 22 Dec. 1942.

MORRISON, Sir Murray; *see* Morrison, Sir W. M.

MORRISON, Rev. William Douglas, LLD; *b* 1852; *s* of R. Morrison, Newtown; Kirriemuir, NB; *m* Alice, *d* of J. Butler, 14 New Burlington St, W, and Hollywood, Wimbledon; one *s* one *d*. *Educ:* Glenalmond; St Andrews (LLD). Ordained by Bishop of Ripon, 1877; Chaplain in HM Prison Service, 1883–98; Rector of St Marylebone, 1908–41. *Publications:* The Jews under the Roman Empire, 1889; Crime and its Causes, 1890; Juvenile Offenders, 1896, etc. *Address:* 9 Clarendon House, 6 Strathearn Place, Hyde Park Square, W2. *T:* Paddington 1705; Sandbanks, New Romney, Kent. *T:* Littlestone 104. *Club:* Reform.

Died 13 Dec. 1943.

MORRISON, Sir (William) Murray, Kt 1943; MInstCE; MIEE; FInstMet; FInstP; *b* 7 Oct. 1873; *s* of William and Marjory Morrison, Birchwood, Inverness-shire; *m* 1913, Marie Vera, *d* of K. E. Markel, PhD; one *d*. *Educ:* Inverness College; Edinburgh University; Glasgow and West of Scotland Technical College. Pioneered establishment of aluminium industry in Great Britain and hydro-electric development in Highlands of Scotland; joint Technical Adviser to British Aluminium Co. Ltd with late Lord Kelvin; General Manager, 1910; Director, 1927; Deputy Chairman, 1934–47, and Managing Director 1930–45 British Aluminium Co. Ltd, North British Aluminium Co. Ltd, and Lochaber

Power Co.; Pioneer of production of aluminium in Norway commencing in 1907; Commander of Order of St Olav, 1933; Past Member of Council Inst. of Electrical Engineers; Past Member of Council and Vice-Pres. Institute of Metals and of Faraday Soc.; Past Vice-Chm. British Non-Ferrous Metals Research Assoc. Platinum medal of Institute of Metals, 1942. *Publications:* various communications to scientific societies. *Recreations:* stalking, tennis, skating, curling. *Address:* 29 Bramham Gardens, SW5. *T:* Frobisher 5421; Kirby House, Kirby Bedon, Norfolk. *Clubs:* Marlborough-Windham, City of London, Royal Automobile; Norfolk (Norwich); Highland (Inverness).

Died 21 May 1948.

MORRISON-BELL, Sir Claude William Hedley, 2nd Bt *cr* 1905; JP, Northumberland; formerly Capt. Arg. and Suth. Highlanders; *b* 5 May 1867; *s* of 1st Bt and Louisa Maria, *d* of W. H. Dawes, JP, of The Hall, Kenilworth; *S* father, 1914; *m* 1903, Frances Isabel, *d* of Lieut-Col C. A. Logan; one *s* three *d*. *Heir: s* Charles Reginald Francis, *b* 26 June 1915. *Address:* Highgreen, Tarset, Northumberland; Glendon, Corfe Mullen, Wimborne. *Clubs:* Army and Navy, Royal Automobile; Northern Counties, Newcastle.

Died 22 Nov. 1943.

MORRISON-BELL, Lt-Col Eustace Widdrington; *b* 10 Feb. 1874; 4th *s* of late Sir Charles Morrison-Bell, 1st Bt; *m* 1914, Hon. Harriet Trefusis, *d* of 20th Baron Clinton; one *s* two *d*. *Educ:* Eton; Sandhurst. Joined Rifle Brigade, 1892; served Indian Frontier, 1899; S Africa, 1901–02; European War (despatches); Member of LCC for Marylebone, 1912–20. *Recreations:* shooting, polo, yachting. *Clubs:* Royal Yacht Squadron, Cowes.

Died 13 Dec. 1947.

MORRISROE, Rt Rev. Patrick, DD; Bishop of Achonry, (RC), since 1911; *b* Charlestown, Co. Mayo, 1869. *Educ:* Ballaghadereen; Maynooth. A Dean of Maynooth, 1902–11. *Address:* The Abbey, Ballaghadereen, Ireland.

Died 27 May 1946.

MORROW, Forbes St John, LLD, Police Magistrate, West Ham, 1925–43; *b* 1860; 2nd *s* of late Forbes Morrow, Bettyville, Raheny, Co. Dublin; *m* Ellen Welsford, (*d* 1933), *e d* of late John Wilson, Carnsampson, Co., Antrim; no *c*. *Educ:* Bective College; Trinity College, Dublin, LLD 1892. Called to Bar, Inner Temple, 1894; South-Eastern Circuit; Herts and Essex Quarter Sessions and CCC; for seven years Vacation Judge at the County of London Sessions; contested (U) Dewsbury, 1900; Ilkeston, 1910; Member of London County Council as Municipal Reformer, 1907; Chairman of Works Committee, LCC, 1908; Chairman of Parliamentary Committee of the LCC, 1913, 1914, and 1915; retired, 1922. *Publications:* Morrow's Building Cases; occasional articles in Fortnightly, Macmillan's, National, etc. *Recreations:* fishing, travelling. *Address:* 19 Wetherby Mansions, SW5. *Clubs:* United, 1900, Junior Carlton.

Died 23 March 1949.

MORROW, Very Rev. William Edward Reginald, MA; late Provost (Emeritus) Chelmsford Cathedral; Rector of St Mary the Virgin, Chelmsford, 1935; Prov. Chelmsford Cath., 1929; Hon. Canon of Chelmsford, 1914; Proctor in Convocation, 1929; *b* 5 March 1869; *y s* of late Forbes Morrow of Raheny, Co. Dublin, and Wellington Road, Dublin; *m* 1918, Lucy Matilda (*d* 1923), *e d* of late Norman Watney, DL, of Valence, Westerham. *Educ:* Dublin Univ. Ordained, 1894, for the Curacy of West Ham Parish Church, where he remained as Senior Curate until 1904; interested himself in Friendly Societies, becoming a Forester and Good Templar, and inaugurating Friendly Societies Services; Vicar of North Woolwich, 1904; All Saints', Forest Gate, 1909–19; Clifton, Bristol, 1919–25; Vicar of

Wandsworth (All Saints with Holy Trinity, West Hill), Surrey, 1925–29; chosen to be one of the Mission of Help to the Prairie Dioceses of Canada, 1912; Chaplain to The Rangers (12th County of London Regt), 1912; Chaplain to High Sheriff of Essex, 1943; Past Grand Chaplain (Eng.); Past Grand N. in the Royal Arch Chapter; Past Grand Chaplain (Eng.) Mark Masonry; Past Great Prelate, Order of Knights Templars. *Publications:* several articles in church papers; Christ Magnified; The Catholic Church of the Future; The Moral Battlefields of Missionary Enterprise, and other sermons. *Recreations:* an old Rugby football three-quarter back; has run with the University Harriers and played most games; golf, tennis; Alpine climbing. *Address:* Highcote, Sutton Valence, near Maidstone, Kent. *T:* Sutton Valence 3288.

Died 11 Feb. 1950.

MORSE, Charles; Registrar Exchequer Court of Canada, 1912–32; now practising as Counsel in Dominion Courts; *b* 24 Dec. 1860; 3rd *s* of late Charles Morse, QC, Judge of Probate for Queen's County, NS, and Margaret Henderson; *m* 1885, Susan Mary, *e d* of W. Tyng Peters of St John, NB; two *s* one *d*. *Educ:* Liverpool (NS) Academy; Dalhousie University, Halifax. LLB 1885; BCL (*ad eund.*) Trinity University, Toronto, 1899; DCL 1900. Called to Bar of Nova Scotia, 1885; KC 1908; Deputy-Registrar Exchequer Court of Canada, 1904; for some years Examiner in Law at Trinity University; Member of Corporation of Trinity College; Member of Senate of University of Toronto, 1931–36; Edited the Canadian Bar Review from its foundation until 1935; now Consulting Editor. *Publications:* Apices Juris: A Collection of Legal Essays, 1906; Law Reports of Exchequer Court of Canada, vols i to xiii; founded (with C. H. Masters, KC) Canadian Annual Digest, 1896; assisted E. R. Cameron, KC, in preparation of Canadian Cases Judicially Noticed, 1912; Provincial and Municipal Government in the Atlantic Provinces, forming part of volume xiv of Canada and its Provinces, 1914; Digest of Exchequer Court Cases, 1924. *Recreations:* golf and fishing. *Address:* 44 M'Leod Street, Ottawa, Canada. *Clubs:* Authors'; University, Ottawa.

Died 3 Nov. 1945.

MORTIMER, Francis James, CBE 1942; Hon. FRPS, FRSA; Editor of The Amateur Photographer and Cinematographer; Past President of Royal Photographic Society; *b* 1875; *s* of F. C. Mortimer, dental surgeon, Portsmouth; *m* 1st, 1905; two *d*; 2nd, 1931, Lucy Embling, *o d* of J. Embling Dart, Ashley Manor, near Winchester. *Educ:* Portsmouth Grammar School. Articled to Albert Besant (brother of Sir Walter Besant), solicitor, 1891; after passing Law Societies' Examinations adopted a journalistic career; with special application to art, poster designing, press and pictorial photography; awarded over 400 medals and other awards for photographic work at leading exhibitions in all parts of the world, and also silver and bronze medals for poster designs at the Crystal Palace Exhibitions, 1899 and 1900; has specialised in marine photography for many years; President of the Photographic Convention of the United Kingdom, 1913–14; Judge at International Photographic Exhibitions in all parts of the country; represented Great Britain in photography and acted on Board of Judges at the Century of Progress World's Fair, Chicago, 1933; President of The Camera Club, London; Hon. Secretary of the London Salon of Photography; Hon. Fellow of the Royal Photographic Society. *Publications:* Marine and Surf Photography; Magnesium Light Photography; Photography of the Sea; The Oil and Bromoil Processes; Photography for the Press, etc.; numerous articles on photographic processes and art in the photographic press, magazines, newspapers, etc.; Editor of Photograms of the Year, of the Year-Book of Photography, and of the Dictionary of Photography; Joint-Editor of British Journal of Photography, 1904–1905; Editor of the Photographic News, 1906–1907; Editor of Amateur

Photographer, 1908–1918; Art Editor, The Amateur Photographer and Photography, 1918–1925. *Recreations:* sketching, painting, photography, sailing, motoring, swimming, collector of Japanese prints and curios; broadcasts frequently on photographic subjects. *Address:* Dorset House, Stamford Street, SE1. *T:* Waterloo 3333. *TA:* Amaphot, Sedist, London. *Clubs:* Camera, Press, Royal Automobile, Savage.

Died 26 July 1944.

MORTIMER, John Desmond, MB Lond., FRCS Eng.; *s* of late Capt. C. E. Mortimer; *m* Catherine, *d* of late Alex. Crowe of Woodcote Grove, Epsom; two *d.* Held appointments at Great Ormond Street Hospital, Bethlem Royal Hospital (Gold Medallist Medico-Psychological Association), etc.; now Consulting Anæsthetist, Golden Square and Central London Throat Hospitals, Royal National Orthopædic Hospital, etc. *Publications:* Anæsthesia and Analgesia; and articles on this subject in The Lancet and other medical journals. *Address:* The Gray Bungalow, Stodmarsh Road, Canterbury.

Died 20 March 1942.

MORTLOCK, Rev. Canon E., MA; Canon Residentiary of Chichester; Precentor of Chichester Cathedral since 1937; Commissioner Ecclesiastical Duties Measure; *b* 30 Sept. 1859; *s* of Rev. E. T. Mortlock, Rector of Snailwell, Newmarket; *m* 1900, Katharine Daniell Cuddy (*d* 1939); no *c. Educ:* Haileybury; Trinity College, Cambridge; Wells Theological College. Assistant Curate of Godalming, 1882–87; S Peter's, Bexhill, 1887–91; Vicar of S Barnabas, Bexhill, 1891–1926; Prebendary and Canon of Chichester, 1921; Rural Dean of Hastings, 1922–26. *Address:* The Treasury, Chichester.

Died 6 Aug. 1945.

MORTON, Brig.-Gen. Edward, CBE 1919; retired; Commandant General Legion of Frontiersmen since 1933; *b* 28 April 1871; *s* of late Col Robert Morton, RA; *m* 1905, Adeline Louise (*d* 1948), *d* of Rev. Thomas Wall Langshaw, Rector of West Grinstead; two *d. Educ:* privately. Served in NWM Police, Canada, 1889–93; British Army, 1894–1922; Regiments 5th Fusiliers, York and Lancaster Regiment and Cheshire Regt; Nile Expedition, 1898 (Queen's medal, Khedive's medal); South Africa, 1899–1902 (Queen's medal 4 clasps, King's medal 2 clasps); European War (Bt Lt-Col-CBE). *Address:* The Croft, Bourn, Cambridge. *T:* Caxton 270.

Died 21 Dec. 1949.

MORTON, Edward Reginald, MD, CM, FRCS Ed; *b* 14 Oct. 1867; 3rd *s* of Edward Deane Morton, MB, of Barrie, Ontario, Canada; *m* 1898, Margaret, 2nd *d* of J. B. Handyside, of Fenton, Drem, East Lothian; one *s. Educ:* Barrie; Toronto; Edinburgh. Graduated at Trinity University, Toronto, 1890; passed necessary qualifying examinations in Edinburgh, 1891; Fellow of Royal College of Surgeons of Edinburgh, 1893. Accompanied Lord Brassey to Melbourne in the Sunbeam RYS, 1895; returned to England and commenced practice in Taunton, Somerset, 1897; in charge of X-ray and Electrical Departments of the London Hospital, 1903–09; in charge of the X-ray Department of the West London Hospital, 1903–26. *Publications:* Medical Electricity and Radiography, 1914; A Text-book of Radiology, 2nd ed. 1919; various contributions to Medical Annual and medical and scientific journals. *Recreations:* golf, horticulture, mechanics. *Address:* Westbourne, Gullane, East Lothian. *T:* Gullane 2172. *Club:* Bath.

Died 21 Jan. 1944.

MORTON, Hugh, MD, FRFPSG; JP; late Professor of Medicine, Anderson College; Visiting Physician, Western Infirmary, Glasgow; Lecturer and Examiner in Clinical Medicine, Glasgow University; *b* 8 Aug. 1883; *s* of late Robert Morton, Pollokshields; *m* Janette Torrance, *o d* of late John Herbertson, Newlands; one *s.*

Educ: Glasgow University; Berlin and Paris. Consulting physician, specialising in diseases of the stomach and bowels. *Publications:* Biochemistry of the Cerebro-spinal Fluid; Diseases of Stomach and Duodenum, Green's Encyclopædia of Medicine; The Etiology and Treatment of Gastric and Duodenal Ulcers; A Theory on the Etiology of Cancer; Catarrhal Duodenitis; Recent Researches on Syphilis (with Browning and McKenzie); Diseases of the Stomach, 1931. *Recreation:* motoring. *Address:* 4 Newton Place, Glasgow, C3. *TA: and T:* Douglas 4675, Glasgow. *Clubs:* Royal Scottish Automobile, Literary, Glasgow.

Died 10 Dec. 1941.

MORTON, Col Hugh Murray, CBE 1919; DSO 1917; late RAMC; *b* 1873; *s* of late John Morton, Longtown, Cumberland; *m* Helen, *d* of late George Carruthers, Ranbeck, Cumberland; one *s. Educ:* Grosvenor College, Carlisle; Edinburgh University (MB and CM). Assistant House Surgeon, Cumberland Infirmary, Carlisle, 1897–98. Served S Africa; 1899–1902 (Queen's medal with five clasps). Tugela Heights, Relief of Ladysmith, Laing's Nek, Orange River Colony, Transvaal (King's medal with two clasps); European War, Gallipoli, 1915, Landing and Evacuation at Suvla Bay; Egypt, 1916; Mesopotamia, 1916–19 as ADMS 13th Division (despatches, DSO, 1915 Star, British and Allied War Medals); retired pay, 1924; re-employed during present war, Sept. 1939–Jan. 1940; Sheriff of Berwick upon Tweed, 1943–44. *Address:* Kirkland, Berwick-on-Tweed. *T:* Berwick 6196.

Died 7 Aug. 1946.

MORTON, Sir James, Kt 1936; LLD (St Andrews); AssocMCT; Chairman of Morton Sundour Fabrics, Ltd; Standfast Dyers and Printers, Ltd; Founder of Scottish Dyes, Ltd, now incorporated in Imperial Chemical Industries; *b* 24 March 1867; *s* of Alexander Morton, JP, and Jean Wiseman, Darvel, Ayrshire; *m* 1901, Beatrice Emily, *e d* of late Major-General W. T. Fagan, Bengal Staff Corps; two *s* four *d.* First to produce fabrics specially dyed and guaranteed against action of sun and water; at outbreak of war, started first manufacture in Britain for production of anthraquinone vat dyestuffs which led to foundation of Scottish Dyes, Ltd; was first recipient of Faraday Centennial Medal 'in special recognition of signal service rendered to Chemical Science and Industry in this country during last ten years, by developing and extending manufacture of anthracene dyestuffs, and more recently by extending their application to silk and wool'; awarded Medal of Royal Society of Arts for lecture delivered on History of Fast Dyes, 1929; Member of Committee on New Industrial Development, 1931–32; Member of the Dyestuffs Industry Development Committee (Advisory to Board of Trade), 1921–34; Member of the original Council of the Design & Industries Association; Inventor of improvements in the arts of weaving, dyeing and printing. *Publications:* William Morris—An Appreciation; To Young Weavers; History of the Development of Fast Dyeing, and Dyes; Papers on Technical Subjects. *Recreations:* study of the native textiles of many nationalities ancient and modern, private collection. *Address:* Dalston Hall, by Carlisle.

Died 22 Aug. 1943.

MORTON, William Blair, MA; DSc, MRIA; Emeritus Professor of Physics, Queen's University, Belfast; *b* 1868. *Educ:* Queen's Coll., Belfast; St John's Coll., Cambridge. Assistant in Natural Philosophy at Queen's College, Belfast, 1892–97; Professor, 1897–1933. *Publications:* papers in Phil. Mag., Proc. of Physical Soc., and of RIA. *Address:* Queen's University, Belfast.

Died 12 Aug. 1949.

MOSES, James J. H., JP; Alderman Plymouth City Council, 1940–45; shipwright; *b* Dartmouth, 14 Aug. 1873; *s* of James J. H. Moses, shipwright, and Susannah L. Peek; *m* 1897, Agnes Ferris; no *c. Educ:* Board School, Dartmouth. Started work part time at age of nine as newspaper boy; became full-time errand boy at thirteen years of age; apprenticed to trade of shipwright at fifteen; entered HM Dockyard, Devonport, 1895; Member of Borough Council, Devonport, 1911; Council of Greater Plymouth, 1914; Alderman, 1921; Borough Magistrate, 1918; Mayor of Plymouth, 1926–27; Devon County Magistrate, 1927; Member of the Executive Committee of the Ship Contractors and Shipwrights' Association; contested Drake Division of Plymouth, 1923 and 1924; MP (Lab) Drake Division of Plymouth 1929–31; Prospective Labour Candidate for Camborne Division, Cornwall; local preacher and temperance worker, Methodist Church since 1891. *Address:* 95 Alexandra Road, Devonport. *T:* Devonport 655. *Club:* Labour.

Died 28 May 1946.

MOSLEY, Rt Rev. Henry, DD; *b* 1868; *m* 1908, Mildred, *d* of Rev. E. Willis, Horsham, Sussex; one *d*. *Educ:* Keble College, Oxford. Ordained to Curacy of St Andrew, Bethnal Green, 1893; joined Trinity College, Oxford, Mission at Stratford, 1897; Rector of All Saints, Poplar, 1902; St John's, Hackney, 1911; Rural Dean of Hackney, Stoke Newington; Rector of St Margaret's, Lothbury, 1921–28; Bishop of Stepney, 1919–28; Bishop of Southwell, 1928–41. *Address:* Standen, Hannington, nr Basingstoke, Hants. *Club:* United University.

Died 20 Jan. 1948.

MOSS, Kenneth Neville, OBE; MSc; MInstMinE; FInstF, FGS; MInstCE; Professor of Mining, Birmingham University, since 1922 and Dean of the Faculty of Science, 1935–40; *b* 30 May 1881; *e s* of William Moss of Penns, Warwickshire; *m* Dorothy, *d* of late Professor R. Warington, FRS, MA; four *d*. *Educ:* Queen Mary's School, Walsall; Birmingham University. Practical mining experience gained in the Cannock Chase, South Yorkshire, and North Staffordshire coalfields; served in the army as Adjutant to the 59th Divisional Royal Engineers, 1915–19 (despatches twice, OBE); for one year was Organiser of Mining Instruction for the county of Derbyshire; Assistant Professor of Mining, Birmingham University, 1920–22; Chairman of Advisory Committee on Coal and Petroleum of Mineral Resources Department of the Imperial Institute; Member of a Departmental Committee on juvenile recruitment to the Mining Industry; Member of the Research Committee of the Council of the Institution of Civil Engineers; Past-President of the National Association of Colliery Managers; Past Pres., South Staffs and Warwickshire Institute of Mining Engineers; interested in several Mining and Engineering Students Societies; studied mining conditions in France, Germany, Belgium, Holland, Czecho-Slovakia, Rumania, Canada, USA, South Africa, Northern and Southern Rhodesia. *Publications:* Gases, Dust and Heat in Mines; Some Effect of High Air Temperatures and Muscular Exertion upon Colliers, in the Proceedings of the Royal Society; several papers in Mining Journals; editor and part author of Historical Review of Coal Mining. *Recreations:* yachting, tennis. *Address:* 22 Vernon Road, Edgbaston, Birmingham. *T:* Edgbaston 775. *Clubs:* Athenæum; Royal Temple Yacht, Ramsgate.

Died 20 Oct. 1942.

MOSS, Hon. Matthew Lewis; KC; West Australian Bar; Legal Adviser in London to the Government of Western Australia; *b* 1 Dec. 1863; *e s* of late Joseph Moss, Dunedin, New Zealand, and Esther Moss; *m* Katherine Lyons Moss (*d* 1936); two *s*. *Educ:* Dunedin. Admitted as a Barrister and Solicitor in New Zealand, 1886; admitted to West Australian Bar, 1892; Member of Legislative Assembly, West Australia, for North Fremantle, 1895–96; West Province in Legislative Council, West Australia, 1900–14; Colonial Secretary, 1901; Hon. Minister, 1902; Attorney-General, 1905; left West Australia, 1913; since then has acted as Legal Adviser to Government of West Australia, and on two occasions has

acted as Agent-General for Western Australia. *Address:* 308 Carrington House, Hertford Street, W1. *T:* Mayfair 1431. *Clubs:* Constitutional, Royal Automobile.

Died 26 Feb. 1946.

MOSS-BLUNDELL, Henry Seymour; *see* Blundell.

MOSSCOCKLE, Rita Francis; widow; *d* of late Henry Sparrow, Himley House, Himley, Staffordshire; *m* 1883, Charles Mosscockle, formerly a Solicitor and Commissioner for Queensland, who was educated at King's College, London, and Trinity College, Cambridge. *Publications:* Fantasias; The Golden Quest; The Four Ages; Poems and Collected Poems (2nd issue). *Recreations:* music, singing, and literature, motoring and dogs of which many are kept. *Address:* Clewer Park, Clewer, Berkshire. *T:* Windsor 11; 26 Hertford Street, Mayfair, W1. *T:* Grosvenor 2370. *Clubs:* Wentworth, Virginia Water.

Died 30 July 1943.

MOSSE, Lt-Col Arthur Henry Eyre, CIE 1933; late Indian Army; *b* 28 Sept. 1877; *s* of Deputy Surgeon General C. B. Mosse, CIE, AMS; *m* 1918, Grace Maude Cruickshank; one *s* one *d*. *Educ:* King's School, Canterbury; Bedford School; RM College, Sandhurst. Various appointments in the Indian Political Department; served European War as a Political Officer in Aden, 1914–15, Mesopotamia, 1915–18 (despatches); Vice-President, Council of Administration, Bhavnagar State, 1927–31; Resident 2nd Class, 1929; Officiating Agent to the Governor General States of Western India, 1931; retired, 1932. *Publications:* My Somali Book; occasional articles on sport and natural history. *Recreations:* natural history, shooting, golf. *Address:* c/o Lloyds Bank, Ltd (Dept G 2), 6 Pall Mall, SW1.

Died 21 April 1943.

MOSSES, William, OBE 1918; JP; General Secretary, United Patternmakers Association, 1884–1917; General Secretary, Federation of Engineering and Shipbuilding Trades, since 1890; late Director of Labour Enlistment Complaints Section of the Ministry of Munitions; retired from the Industrial Relations Department of the Ministry of Labour, 1925; *b* Newcastle-on-Tyne, 1858; *m* 1883; three *d*. *Educ:* various schools in Newcastle-on-Tyne. Served apprenticeship as a patternmaker at Elswick Engine Works, and worked as a journeyman at trade in various works until 1884; has been a delegate to the Trade Union Congress, 1885–1917, and a member of the Parliamentary Committee, 1907–17; represented the Congress at the Pittsburg Convention of the American Federation of Labour, 1905; acted as Secretary to the Industrial Commissioner which toured the United States, Feb.–April 1918, and was technical adviser to the Daily Mail Industrial Mission to the United States in 1926; Member of the Greenwich Board of Guardians. *Recreations:* swimming, golf. *Address:* 19 Hervey Road, Blackheath, SW3. *T:* Greenwich 2474.

Died 17 May 1943.

MOSTYN-OWEN, Lt-Col Roger Arthur; *see* Owen.

MOTHERWELL, Hon. William Richard, LLD, FBSA; *b* Perth, Ontario, 6 Jan. 1860; *m* 1st, 1884, Adeline Rogers (*d* 1905), New Boyne, Ontario; one *s* one *d*; 2nd, 1908, Catherine Gillespie, File Hills, Sask. *Educ:* Perth Collegiate Institute; Guelph Agricultural College. MLA Qu'Appelle, 1905–08; Humboldt, 1908–12; Kindersley, 1912–19; MP Regina City, 1921–25; Melville since 1925; Minister of Agriculture for Saskatchewan, 1905–18; Minister of Agriculture for Canada, 1921–26, and 1926–30; has owned and managed 640–acre farm at Abernethy, Sask, since 1882; Hon. Fellow of the British Society of Aviculture, 1927; LLD University of Saskatchewan, 1928; awarded Order of Agricultural Merit (Commander) by Quebec Government, 1928. *Address:* Ottawa, Canada.

Died 25 May 1943.

MOTILAL, Raja Bahadur Sir Bansilal, Kt, 1933. banker. *Address:* Hyderabad, Deccan, India.

Died 4 March 1935.

MOTION, Robert Russa, LLD Virginia Union University, 1916, Oberlin College, 1916, Wilberforce University, 1916; Williams College, 1920; LitD Lincoln University, 1920; AM Harvard, 1929; LLD, Howard University, 1930; President-Emeritus, Tuskegee Normal and Industrial Institute; *b* Amelia County, Va, 26 Aug. 1867; *s* of Booker Moton and Emily Brown; *m* 1st, 1905, Elizabeth Hunt Harris (*d* 1906) of Williamsburg, Va.; 2nd, 1908, Jennie Dee Booth of Gloucester, Va; two *s* three *d*. *Educ:* Hampton Institute, 1890. Organizer and 1st President of Negro Organization Society of Virginia since 1912; Trustee People's Village School (Mt Meigs, Ala), Phelps-Stokes Fund, Negro Reform School for Boys (Hanover, Va), Fisk University (Nashville, Tenn), Hampton Institute (Hampton, Va); President National Negro Business League since 1919; Member of US Flag Association; Member of Executive Committee of Permanent Roosevelt Memorial, National Child Welfare Association; Charter Member, Southern Commission on Inter-racial Co-operation; Chairman, President Hoover's Educational Commission to Haiti, 1930; Recipient of Harmon Award for Promotion of Inter-racial Amity, 1930; Spingarn Medal, 1932; Member, Phi Beta Sigma. *Publications:* Racial Good-Will, 1916; Finding a Way Out, autobiography, 1921; What the Negro Thinks, 1929; magazine articles. *Recreations:* fishing and hunting. *Address:* Capahosic, Virginia, USA.

Died 31 May 1940.

MOTION, Major Thomas Augustus; MFH; JP; 3rd *s* of Richard William Motion, London, High Sheriff of Warwickshire; *m* 1927, Lady Elizabeth Hesketh-Prichard, *d* of 3rd Earl of Verulam; one *d*. Major, Warwickshire Yeomanry, 1915. *Address:* Serge Hill, Abbots Langley. *Club:* Carlton.

Died 20 Feb. 1942.

MOTTISTONE, 1st Baron *cr* 1933, of Mottistone; **Maj.-Gen. John Edward Bernard Seely,** PC 1909; CB 1916; CMG 1918; DSO 1900; KStJ 1947; Chairman of National Savings Committee, 1926–43, Vice-President since 1918; Lord Lieutenant of Hants and Isle of Wight since 1918; *b* 31 May 1868; *y s* of Sir Charles Seely, 1st Bt; *m* 1st, 1895, Emily Florence (*d* 1913), *d* of late Col Hon. Sir H. G. L. Crichton; two *s* four *d*; 2nd, Hon. Evelyn Izmé Murray, *y d* of 10th Baron and 1st Viscount Elibank and *widow* of Capt. George C. N. Nicholson, RFC; one *s*. *Educ:* Harrow; Trinity College, Cambridge. Called to Bar, Inner Temple, 1897; late Col commanding Hampshire Carabineers; served with Imperial Yeomanry in South Africa, 1900–01 (despatches, Queen's medal 5 clasps, DSO); European War, 1914–18 (despatches five times, CB, CMG); MP (L) for Isle of Wight, 1900–06, and Dec. 1923–Oct. 1924; Under-Secretary for the Colonies, 1908–10; Under-Secretary of State for War, 1911; MP (L) Abercromby Division, Liverpool, 1906–10; Secretary of State for War, 1912–14; Under-Secretary of State for Air and President of Air Council, Jan.–Nov. 1919; Parliamentary Under-Secretary Ministry of Munitions and Deputy Minister of Munitions, 1918; MP (L) Ilkeston Division, Derby, 1910–22; Maj.-Gen., 1918–19; Col and Hon. Major-Gen. TF Res.; Hon Air Commodore until 1946; gold medal (French Government) for saving life at sea, 1891. *Publications:* Adventure, 1930; Fear and Be Slain, 1931; Launch, 1932; For Ever England, 1932; My Horse Warrior, 1934; Paths of Happiness, 1938. *Heir:* s Hon. (Henry) John (Alexander) Seely. *Address:* Mottistone Manor, Isle of Wight. *T:* Brighstone 22; 34 Tufton Court, Westminster, SW1. *T:* Abbey 1677. *Clubs:* Brooks's, Athenæum, Beefsteak; Royal Yacht Squadron (Cowes).

Died 7 Nov. 1947.

MOTTRAM, James Cecil, MB, MRCS, LRCP, DPH; Director Research Laboratory, Mount Vernon Hospital, Northwood; *b* Stody Lodge, Holt, Norfolk, 1880; *o s* of James Mottram; *m* Rhoda, *o d* of Prof. Pritchard of Royal Veterinary College; two *s* one *d*. *Educ:* The Beacon, Sevenoaks; University College and Hospital, London; St John's College, Cambridge. First Assistant, Cancer Research laboratories, Middlesex Hospital. *Publications:* Controlled Natural Selection; Flyfishing: Some New Arts and Mysteries; Sea Trout and other Fishing Studies; Trout Fisheries: Their Care and Preservation, 1928; numerous communications to Royal Society, Royal Society of Medicine, Zoological Society, Linnean Society, Pathological Society on Cancer, Radiology and Animal Coloration. *Recreation:* fishing. *Address:* 78a Green Lane, Northwood, Middlesex. *Club:* Flyfishers'.

Died 4 Oct. 1945.

MOULE, Edward Christopher; Assistant master, Sherborne School, since 1940; *b* Hangchow, China, 12 Feb. 1902; *s* of Rev. H. W. Moule and L. C. Pope; *m* 1929, Arthurina Elizabeth Anderson; three *s* one *d*. *Educ:* Weymouth College; Emmanuel College, Cambridge (Scholar). Davison Scholar at Yale University. Assistant Master, Bradfield College, 1925–37; House Master, 1933–37; Headmaster of Weymouth College, 1937–40. *Recreations:* walking, books, swimming. *Address:* Sherborne School, Dorset.

Died 12 Jan. 1945.

MOULE, Ven. Walter Stephen, MA; *s* of late Arthur Evans Moule, DD, Archdeacon in Mid-China, and Eliza Agnes Bernau; *m* 1894, Agnes Lucy (*d* 1936), *d* of late Rev. Henry Wright, Hon. Sec. of CMS; no *c*. *Educ:* Monkton Combe School; Corpus Christi Coll. and Ridley Hall, Camb. Graduated in Math. Honours, 1st Sen. Opt., 1886; 1st Class Camb. Prelim. Theol. Exam. Deacon, 1887; Priest, 1889; Missionary of CMS; Vice-Principal Trinity College, Ningpo, 1888; Principal, 1897; President, 1919; Archdeacon in Chekiang, 1911–25; Vicar of Abbotsbury, Dorset, 1925–42. *Publications:* (in English) Holy Communion: or the Supper of the Lord, 1902; The Offerings made like unto the Son of God, 1914; The Bible, its Contents and Message, 1944; Abbotsbury, 1946; (in Chinese) Expository Comm. on Genesis, Exodus, Leviticus, Numbers, Messianic Psalms, Isaiah, Romans, Ephesians, Hebrews, James, Pastoral Epistles, Comm. on the Apostles' Creed and Thirty-nine Articles, etc. *Address:* Swallowcliffe, Cliff Drive, Southbourne, Hants.

Died 25 Aug. 1949.

MOULSDALE, Rev. Stephen Richard Platt, MA, BD, Hon. DCL 1937; Rector of Hintlesham with Chattisham, Ipswich, since 1936; *b* 18 Aug. 1872; *e s* of Rev. Thomas Henry Platt Moulsdale, Rector of Ballysumaghan, Co. Sligo; *m* 1908, Mary Frideswide (*d* 1933), *o d* of late Rev. Clement Thomas Hales, Headmaster of Aysgarth School, Yorks; no *c*. *Educ:* Primrose Grange, Sligo; Bishop Hatfield's Hall, Durham; St Aidan's Theological College. Deacon, 1896; Priest, 1897; Curate of St Chad's, Liverpool, 1896–1903; Principal of St Chad's College, Durham, 1904–36; BA Durham, 1900; MA 1903; BD 1907; Member of Senate, University of Durham, 1908; Junior Proctor, 1911–13; Senior Proctor, 1913–14; Secretary, Council of Durham Colleges, 1915–19; Lecturer in Christian Worship, 1920–36; Dean of the Faculty of Arts, 1921; JP Durham City, 1921–37; Examining Chaplain to the Lord Bishop of Durham, 1920–36; Proctor in Convocation for the Archdeaconry of Durham, 1921–31; Pro-Vice-Chancellor, University of Durham, 1932–33 and 1936–37; Vice-Chancellor, 1934–36. *Recreations:* motoring, swimming. *Address:* Hintlesham Rectory, Ipswich. *T:* Hintlesham 258.

Died 25 Oct. 1944.

MOUNT EDGCUMBE, 5th Earl of, *cr* 1789; **Piers Alexander Hamilton Edgcumbe;** Viscount Mount Edgcumbe and Valletort, 1781; Baron Edgcumbe of Mount Edgcumbe, Co. Cornwall (UK), 1742; late Col commanding 3rd Batt. Duke of Cornwall's LI; JP, DL Cornwall; DL Devon; a Deputy Warden of the Stannaries; *b* 2 July 1865; *o s* of 4th Earl of Mount Edgcumbe and Lady Katherine Elizabeth Hamilton (*d* 1874), 4th *d* of 1st Duke of Abercorn; *S* father, 1917; *m* 1911, Lady Edith Villiers (*d* 1935), *o d* of 5th Earl of Clarendon; no *c.* Served in South African War. *Heir: cousin* Kenelm William Edward Edgcumbe. *Address:* 47 Belgrave Square, SW1; Mount Edgcumbe, Plymouth; Cotehele House, St Dominick, RSO, Cornwall. *T:* Sloane 8773. *Clubs:* Carlton, Marlborough, Turf.
Died 18 April 1944.

MOUNTAIN, Sir Edward Mortimer, 1st Bt *cr* 1922; Kt 1918; Chairman and Managing Director of the Eagle, Star Insurance Co., Ltd; Chairman Philip Hill & Partners and Philip Hill Investment Trust; *b* 24 Nov. 1872; *s* of Henry Stanford Mountain and Louisa, *d* of Henry Eve; *m* 1897, Ellen Evelyn, *d* of A. Sieglè; one *s. Educ:* Dulwich College. *Recreations:* shooting, fishing, golf. *Heir: s* Brian Edward Stanley [*b* 22 Aug. 1899; *m* 1926, Doris Elsie, *e d* of E. C. E. Lamb, 2 Queen Street; Mayfair, W; two *s* one *d*]. *Address:* 70 Arlington House, Arlington St, W1. *T:* Regent 0648; Fairmile Hatch, Cobham, Surrey. *T:* Cobham 2488; Dunkeld House, Dunkeld, Perthshire. *T:* Dunkeld 243; Pier House, Seaview, I of W. *T:* Seaview 2266.
Died 22 June 1948.

MOUNTFORD, Lewis James, CBE 1918; late Indian Civil Service; *b* 1 Aug. 1871; *s* of Henry Mountford, West Dulwich, SE. *Educ:* Dulwich College; Pembroke College, Cambridge. Entered Indian Civil Service, Bombay Presidency, 1892; Additional Member of Viceroy's Council, 1919; Commissioner in Sind, 1923; retired 1926. *Publication:* Relations between Debtor and Creditor in Sind. *Recreation:* field sports. *Address:* c/o Coutts & Co., 440 Strand, WC2. *Clubs:* Royal Automobile; Royal Bombay Yacht.
Died 17 Dec. 1944.

MOUNTSTEPHEN, Sir William H., Kt 1933; JP; Leather Merchant; *b* 8 Nov. 1868; *s* of G. Mounstephen and Sarah Levass Libby; *m* 1896; two *d. Educ:* Devonport Public School. Hon. Secretary Devonport Mercantile Association since 1905 (Chairman 1926); Chairman Devonport and Western Counties Home for the Blind; served on Devonport County Borough Council; President and Chairman Devonport Liberal Association; Governor of Union Savings Bank; filled every office open to a Layman in the Methodist Church. *Recreations:* public work, gardening. *Address:* Leigh Grange, South Brent, Devon. *T:* South Brent 3132.
Died 9 May 1946.

MOWAT, Robert Balmain, MA, DLitt; Professor of History in the University of Bristol since 1928; Hon. Fellow of Corpus Christi College, Oxford; *b* Edinburgh, 26 Sept. 1883; 2nd *s* of late Robert Mowat, partner in the publishing house of W. & R. Chambers; *m* 1910, Mary, *d* of Sir C. S. Loch; five *s* one *d. Educ:* George Watson's College, Merchiston Castle School, and University of Edinburgh; Balliol Coll., Oxford. 1st Class Final Honours, School of Literæ Humaniores, 1905; 1st Class Modern History, 1906; Arnold Prize, 1908 (bracketed equal). Assistant Master, Eton College, 1906–07; Fellow and Tutor of Corpus Christi College, Oxford, 1907–28; Naval Intelligence Department, 1916–18; engaged in Secretariat of the War Cabinet, 1918–19; Conference of Paris in suite of General Smuts, 1919; Member of Board of Education Committees on investigation of Secondary Schools' Examinations, 1921 and 1925; Professor of History in the University of Wisconsin, 1925–26; Member of the Council of Cheltenham Ladies' College and of Clifton High School; Member of the Phi Beta Kappa Society; Carnegie Visiting Professor, USA, 1940–41. *Publications:* The Wars of the Roses, 1913; Einhardi Vita Caroli Magni (with H. W. Garrod), 1915; Select Treaties and Documents to illustrate the European States System, 1915; The Later Middle Ages, 1916; The Great European Treaties of the Nineteenth Century (with Sir A. Oakes), 1918; The Life of Henry V, 1920; A History of Great Britain, 1920–1921; A History of European Diplomacy in the Nineteenth Century, 1922; A Hundred and Sixty Years of British History, 1923; Contemporary Europe, 1924; The Diplomacy of Napoleon, 1924; The Diplomatic Relations of Great Britain and the United States, 1925; A History of European Diplomacy, 1914–1925, 1927; A History of European Diplomacy, 1450–1789, 1928; The Life of Lord Pauncefote, 1929; The Concert of Europe, 1930; International Relations, 1931; The States of Europe, 1815–1871, 1932; England in the Eighteenth Century, 1932; Problems of the Nations, 1933; Public and Private Morality, 1933; The Age of Reason, 1934; Revolution and Recovery, 1934; The Americans in England, 1935; Diplomacy and Peace, 1935; Gibbon, 1936; Europe in Crisis, 1936; The Romantic Age, 1937; A Chronicle of Kingship, 1066 to 1937 (with J. D. Griffith Davies), 1937; The Fight for Peace, 1937; The United States of America, 1938; Jean-Jacques Rousseau, 1938; The American Entente, 1939. *Recreations:* gardening, walking. *Address:* Corpus Christi College, Oxford; The University, Bristol.
Died 1 Sept. 1941.

MOWATT, Lt-Col Charles Ryder John, DSO 1916; *b* 1872. Entered Northamptonshire Regt 1894; served S African War, 1899–1902 (Queen's medal with 4 clasps, King's medal with 2 clasps); European War, 1914–19 (despatches, DSO); Commandant of an Instructional School, 1918. *Address:* Hereweare, Silvermere, Cobham, Surrey. *Club:* Army and Navy.
Died 9 Dec. 1943.

MOWBRAY, Robert, CIE 1945; *b* 31 March 1877; *s* of Henry Mowbray; *m* 1914, Lucy Turner; one *s* three *d. Educ:* Manchester Grammar School; Brasenose College, Oxford. Served in India Office from 1900. Green (Moral Philosophy) Prize, Oxford, 1905; Government Director of Indian Railway Companies, 1931–46. *Address:* 37 Gloucester Road, New Barnet, Herts. *T:* Barnet 6388.
Died 23 March 1947.

MOXON, Sir John, Kt 1938; OBE; member of firm Moxon & Petty, solicitors, 4–5 Commercial Street, Newport, Mon; Director of Piccadilly Hotel, Ltd and R. E. Jones, Ltd; *m*; one *s. Address:* The Lodge, Malpas, Newport, Mon.
Died 23 Dec. 1943.

MOXON, Canon Reginald Stewart, DD; Hon. Canon of Portsmouth since 1935; Examining Chaplain to the Bishop of Portsmouth; Proctor in Convocation since 1935; *s* of George Moxon, Wakefield; *m* Ina Mary, *d* of Richard Whitlock Rowson, Warrington; two *s* one *d. Educ:* Manchester Grammar School; Caius College, Cambridge (Scholar). First Class Classical Tripos, 1897; Second Class Theological Tripos, Pt II, 1899; Steele Studentship in Theology, 1898. Second Master at Warrington Grammar School, 1899–1905; Sixth Form Master at King's School, Canterbury, 1905–11; Headmaster of Lincoln School, 1911–29; Vicar of East Cowes, 1929–37; Vicar of Ryde, 1937–46; MA 1901; BD 1908; DD 1922. *Publications:* The Apocryphal Gospels, 1905; Contributor to Smith's Concise Dictionary of the Bible, 1908; Vincentius of Lerins, 1915; The Doctrine of Sin, 1922; Modernism and Orthodoxy, 1924. *Recreations:* tennis, golf, and motoring. *Address:* Dunraven, Trinity Street, Ryde, Isle of Wight.
Died 29 Jan. 1950.

MOXON, Rev. Prebendary Thomas Allen; Rector of Blymhill, Staffs, since 1941; Prebendary of Lichfield Cathedral since 1934; *b* 9 Nov. 1877; *s* of George Moxon and Martha Johnson; *m* Evelyn Goodwin, *d* of L. S. Stroyan, JP, Alfreton, Derbyshire; two *s* one *d*. *Educ:* Manchester Grammar School; St John's College, Cambridge (scholar and Nadin Divinity Student), 1st Class Classical Tripos, 1899; 2nd Class Historical Tripos, 1900. Deacon, 1901; Priest, 1902; Classical Sixth Master, Nottingham, 1902–05; Curate of St Anne's, Soho, 1905–07; Vicar of Alfreton, Derbyshire, 1907–16; Rural Dean of Alfreton, 1910–16; on active service in France under BRCS, 1916–17; Classical Sixth Form Master and Housemaster at Shrewsbury School, 1917–31; Headmaster of Denstone College, 1931–41. *Publications:* St Chrysostom on the Priesthood; Tennyson's In Memoriam; contributor to Hastings' Dictionary of Christ and the Gospels and Hastings' Dictionary of the Bible. *Address:* Blymhill Rectory, near Shifnal, Salop.
Died 15 Sept. 1943.

MOYNE, 1st Baron *cr* 1932, of Bury St Edmunds; **Walter Edward Guinness,** PC 1924; DSO 1917; Lieut-Colonel formerly DYO Loyal Suffolk Hussars; Resident Minister in Cairo since 1944; *b* Dublin, 1880; 3rd *s* of 1st Earl of Iveagh; *m* 1903, Lady Evelyn Erskine (*d* 1939), 3rd *d* of 14th Earl of Buchan; two *s* one *d*. *Educ:* Eton. Served South Africa, 1900–01 (wounded, despatches, Queen's medal 4 clasps); contested (C) Stowmarket Division of Suffolk, 1906; MP (U) Bury St Edmunds, 1907–31; Member LCC North Paddington, 1907; European War, 1914–18; in command of Batt. as Brigade-Major and GSO2 (DSO, despatches thrice, bar to DSO 1918); Under-Secretary of State for War, 1922–23; Financial Secretary to Treasury, 1923–24, and Nov. 1924–25; Minister of Agriculture and Fisheries Nov. 1925–June 1929; Financial Mission to Kenya, 1932; Chairman Departmental Committee on Housing, 1933; Chm. Royal Commission on University of Durham, 1934; Chairman Departmental Committee Cinematograph Films Act, 1936; Chairman West Indies Royal Commission, 1938–39; Joint Parliamentary Secretary, Ministry of Agriculture, 1940–41; Secretary of State for the Colonies, 1941–42; Leader of the House of Lords, 1941–42; Deputy Minister of State, Cairo, 1942–44. *Publications:* Walkabout, 1936; Atlantic Circle, 1938. *Recreation:* rowed 3 years in Eton eight, and was Captain of the Boats. *Heir: s* Hon. Bryan Walter Guinness. *Address:* 10 Grosvenor Place, SW1; Knockmaroon, Castleknock, Co. Dublin; Bailiffscourt, Littlehampton. *T:* Sloane 8291. *Clubs:* Turf, Athenæum, Carlton; Royal Yacht Squadron, Cowes.
Died 6 Nov. 1944.

MOZLEY, Lt-Col Edward Newman, DSO 1916; RE, retired; *b* 21 May 1875; *s* of John Rickards and Edith Merivale Mozley; *m* 1908, Annie Campbell Scott; one *s* one *d*. *Educ:* Eton; Woolwich. In RE, 1894–1919; served South African War with Field Troop RE; Professor of Military Engineering, Royal Military College of Canada, 1904–09; employed on Ordnance Survey, 1909–14; European War, Gallipoli, Egypt and France (DSO, Bt Lt-Col, despatches thrice); Housing Commissioner for South Western Counties of England (under Ministry of Health), 1919–21; Former President Yorks Branch Mathematical Assoc. *Publications:* The Housing Question; Graduated Exercises on Elementary Mathematics; Guide to the Old Testament; articles in periodicals. *Address:* 10 Melville Crescent, Edinburgh.
Died 19 June 1950.

MOZLEY, Rev. John Kenneth, DD; Lecturer of Leeds Parish Church since 1945; *b* 8 Jan. 1883; 3rd *s* of late Rickards Mozley, sometime Fellow of King's College, Cambridge, and one of HM Inspectors of Workhouse Schools; *m* 1910, Mary Geraldine (*d* 1941), *d* of John William Nutt, sometime Fellow of All Souls' College, Oxford; no *c*. *Educ:* Malvern College; Leeds Grammar School; Pembroke College, Cambridge (Scholar), 1st Class Classical Tripos, Part I 1905; President Cambridge Union, 1905; 1st Class Theological Tripos, Part II with distinction, and George Williams Prize, 1906; Crosse Scholarship, 1906; Allen Scholarship, 1907; Norrisian Prize, 1909; Fellow of Pembroke College, 1907–19. Principal of Leeds Clergy School, 1920–25; Lecturer of Leeds Parish Church, 1920–30; Warden of St Augustine's House, Reading, 1926–30; Canon and Chancellor of St Paul's Cathedral, 1930–41; Preacher of Lincoln's Inn, 1937–44; Examining Chaplain to the Bishop of Ripon, 1911–25; to the Bishop of Oxford, 1925–37; to the Archbishop of York, 1935–42; to the Bishop of Hereford, 1941; Select Preacher, Oxford, 1917–19, 1942–44; Cambridge, 1918, 1921, 1923, 1926, 1933, 1943, Hulsean Preacher, 1939. *Publications:* Ritschlianism; Christian Belief; The Doctrine of the Atonement; The Heart of the Gospel; The Achievements of Christianity; Historic Christianity and the Apostles' Creed; The Impassibility of God; The Doctrine of God; The Beginnings of Christian Theology; The Gospel Sacraments; The Doctrine of the Incarnation. *Recreation:* chess. *Address:* 3 Woodland Place, Bathwick Hill, Bath. *T:* Bath 3180. *Club:* Athenæum.
Died 23 Nov. 1946.

MUDIE, Brig. Thomas Couper, DSO 1919; psc; Barrister-at-law, Inner Temple; *b* 8 Oct. 1880; *s* of late James Mudie, Broughty Ferry; *m* 1916, Phyllis Marion Bell Curror; two *s* (and one killed in action in war of 1939–45) one *d*. *Educ:* Fettes College, Edinburgh. Served South African War, 1899–1902; European War, 1914–19 (despatches, DSO); late Comdt of the Royal Tank Corps Centre; AA and QMG in charge of Administration, Malta, 1927–31; retired pay, 1932. Secretary, 1932–44, Director, 1944–47, Scottish Branch, British Red Cross Society. *Address:* 11 Hillhead Street, Glasgow, W2. *T:* Glasgow Western 3888.
Died 29 Sept. 1948.

MUECKE, Francis Frederick, CBE 1919; FRCS, MB, BS; Consulting Surgeon Ear, Nose and Throat Department, London Hospital; late Aural Surgeon Maida Vale and Golden Square Hospitals; Lt-Col RAF; *b* Adelaide, Australia, 1879; *s* of Hon. H. C. E. Muecke, Adelaide; *m* 1st, 1905, Ada Crossley (*d* 1929); no *c*; 2nd, 1930, Jean McMurtrie, *d* of late James Henderson, Cumnock, Ayrshire. *Educ:* Prince Alfred College and Adelaide University. Represented University in cricket, lawn tennis, lacrosse, and rowing; arrived in England 1903 and joined the London Hospital; elected to the Staff, 1909; joined the Army as Lt 1914; was present at the Suvla landing and took part in the following offensives; Somme Ancre, Arras, and Paschendaele (despatches); transferred to RAF as Lt-Col (CBE); Platoon Officer and Company MO Surrey Home Guard, 1940–44; practising as Specialist in Ear, Nose, and Throat. *Publications:* Nasal Septum and its Abnormalities; Vocal Irregularities; Colds in the Head; Tempero-sphenoidal Abscess; Aural Meningitis. *Recreation:* golf. *Address:* The Greenings, Charlwood, Surrey. *T:* Norwood Hill 74. *Clubs:* Conservative, Princes.
Died 13 April 1945.

MUGGERIDGE, Henry Thomas; JP; Secretary to a Public Company; *b* 26 June 1864; *s* of Henry Ambrose Muggeridge, Penge; *m* 1893; four *s*. *Educ:* St John's School, Penge. Joined Fabian Society, 1892; in business in the City for fifty years; lectured and wrote for many years; elected to Croydon Borough Council, 1911; Chairman of Croydon Electricity Committee, 1927–30; Chairman of Croydon Libraries Committee; Member Management Committee of Workers' Travel Association since 1925; contested S Croydon, 1918, 1922, 1923, and 1924; MP (Lab) Romford, 1929–31. *Publications:* many pamphlets and articles in newspapers and reviews, a booklet The Labour Pilgrim's Progress. *Recreations:* walking, music, literature. *Address:* 22 Haling Park Road, South Croydon. *T:* Croydon 5843. *Club:* Fabian Society.

Died March 1942.

MUIR, Col Archibald Huleatt Huntly, CIE 1935; OBE 1919; *b* 20 April 1886; *s* of Colonel Archibald Mungo Muir and Frances Emma Huleatt; *m* 1st 1913, Dorothy *d* of late K. L. Turton-Smith; one *s*; 2nd 1921; May, *d* of late Luke Hansard. *Educ:* Wellington; Sandhurst. Entered Army, 1905, attached R. Irish Fusiliers; Indian Army, 15th Sikhs, 1906; served with Indian Expeditionary in France, 1914–15; Iraq, 1916–17; Instructor Cadet College, Quetta, 1918; DAQMG in Afghan War, 1919; Staff College, Camberley, 1921–22; GSO II War Office, 1923–27; Imperial Defence College, 1930; Commandant 2nd Battalion 11th Sikh Regt, 1930–32; Military Secretary to the Earl of Willingdon, 1933–36; retired from Indian Army, 1937. *Recreations:* Racquets, tennis, golf. *Club:* Army and Navy.

Died 27 Sept. 1948.

MUIR, James, DSc, MA; FInstP; *b* 1875; 2nd *s* of Allan Muir, Glasgow; unmarried. *Educ:* University of Glasgow; Trinity Coll., Cambridge. Two years' business training; BSc (Engineering), Glasgow, 1896; 1851 Exhibition Science Research Scholar, 1897–1900; BA (Research), Cambridge, 1899; DSc (Glasgow), 1902; MA (Cambridge) 1904. Lecturer and Demonstrator at the Technical College and University of Glasgow, 1900–06; Professor of Natural Philosophy at the Royal Technical College, Glasgow, 1906–38. *Publications:* On the Recovery of Iron from Overstrain, and On the Tempering of Iron Hardened by Overstrain, Phil. Trans., 1899, 1902; On Changes produced by Quenching Metals, and On the Overstraining of Iron by Tension and Compression, Proc. Roy. Soc. 1902, 1906; etc. *Address:* 35 Queen Mary Avenue, Glasgow, S2.

Died 17 Feb. 1945.

MUIR, Ramsay, LittD; *b* 1872. *Educ:* University College, Liverpool; Scholar of Balliol; 1st Lit.Hum. 1898; 1st Modern History 1899. Lecturer in Modern History at Owens College, Manchester; Lecturer at University of Liverpool, 1900–06; Professor, 1906–13; Professor of Modern History in the University of Manchester, 1913–21; Member of the Calcutta University Commission, 1917–19; MP (L) Rochdale, 1923–24; Chairman of the Organisation Committee of the Liberal Party, 1930–31; Chairman National Liberal Federation, 1931–33; President of National Liberal Federation, 1933–36; Vice-President Liberal Party Organisation, 1936. *Publications:* History of Municipal Government in Liverpool, 1906 (in collaboration); History of Liverpool, 1907; Peers and Bureaucrats, 1910; Atlas of Modern History, 1911; Britain's Case against Germany; Making of British India, 1915; Nationalism and Internationalism, 1916; The Expansion of Europe, 1917; National Self-Government, 1918; History of the British Commonwealth, vol i, 1920, vol ii, 1922; Liberalism and Industry, 1920; Politics and Progress, 1923; America the Golden, 1927; British History, 1928; Roham the Great, 1929; How Britain is Governed, 1930; Political Consequences of the Great War, 1931; The Interdependent World, and its Problems, 1933; A Brief History of Our Own Times, 1934; The Record of the National Government, 1936; Civilization and Liberty, 1940; Ramsay Muir: An Autobiography and some Essays, edited by Stuart Hodgson, 1944. *Address:* 7 Regents Court, Park Road, NW1. *Clubs:* Reform, National Liberal; University, Liverpool.

Died 4 May 1941.

MUKERJI, Sir Lal Gopal, Kt 1932; BA, LLB; Rai Bahadur; *b* 29 July 1874; *s* of A. K. Mukerji, Pleader, Ghazipur, United Provinces; *m* 1893, Srimati Nalini Devi, *d* of P. N. Banerji, Provincial Service, UP; three *s*

five *d. Educ:* Victoria High School, Ghazipur; Muir Central College, Allahabad; University of Allahabad. Practised at the Ghazipur District Bar, 1896–1902; entered Judicial Service, 1902; Munsif, 1902–13; Subordinate Judge, Subordinate and Sessions Judge, and District and Sessions Judge, 1914–23; was on deputation with the Government of India as a Special Officer in the Legislative Department, to revise the Transfer of Property Act, 1921–22; Additional Puisne Judge, High Court, 1923–26; Puisne Judge, High Court of Judicature, Allahabad, 1926–34; retired 1934; Judicial Minister Kashmir and Jammu State, 1936–38; Pres. Board of Judicial Advisers since 1940; Rai Bahadur as a personal distinction, 1922. *Publications:* Law of Transfer of Property in British India, 1925; 2nd ed., 1931. *Recreations:* walking, tennis, gardening. *Address:* Allahabad, India.

Died 9 Aug. 1942.

MUKERJI, Sir Manmatha Nath, Kt 1935; MA; BL; *b* 28 Oct. 1874; *s* of late Unadi Nath Mukerji, Engineer E. B. Railway (Bengal); *m* Sm. Sureswari Debi, *d* of late Sir Gooroo Dass Banerji, Kt; six *s* three *d. Educ:* The Albert Collegiate School; the Albert College; the Presidency College, and the Ripon College, Calcutta. Practised as a Vakil of the Calcutta High Court, 1898–1923; Judge High Court, Calcutta, 1924–36; Acting Chief Justice of Bengal, July–Aug., 1934, and Nov.–Dec., 1935; Acting Law Member, the Viceroy's Executive Council, June–Nov., 1938. *Address:* 8/1 Harsi Street, Calcutta, India.

Died 6 Dec. 1942.

MULHERN, Most Rev. Edward C.; Bishop of Dromore, (RC), since 1916; *b* 1863. *Educ:* St Macartan's Seminary, Monaghan; Maynooth. *Address:* Bishop's House, Newry.

Died 12 Aug. 1943.

MULHOLLAND, Gp Captain Denis Osmond, CBE 1943; AFC 1919; Company Director; *b* Sept. 1891; *s* of J. H. Mulholland, JP, Donaghadee, Co. Down; *m* 1929, Félice Grant McConnell, *née* McIntyre; no *c. Educ:* Campbell College, Belfast. Connaught Rangers, 1914–18; seconded RFC 1915 (despatches, AFC); transferred to RAF 1919; served Palestine 1936 (despatches); War of 1939–45 (despatches, CBE); retired list, 1946. *Address:* The Lodge, California Lane, Bushey Heath. *T:* Bushey Heath 1231. *Clubs:* Royal Automobile, Belfry.

Died 12 April 1949.

MULHOLLAND, Hon. (Godfrey) John (Arthur Murray Lyle), MC; Partner Edward de Stein and Co., merchants; Vice-Chairman Legal and General Assurance Society Ltd; Director Westminster Bank Ltd and other companies; *b* 3 Oct. 1892; 3rd *surv. s* of late 2nd Baron Dunleath; *m* 1923, Hon. Olivia Vernon Harcourt, 2nd *d* of 1st Visc. Harcourt; one *s* two *d. Educ:* Eton; Trinity College, Cambridge. Served European War as Capt. RASC, 1915–19 (MC, despatches). *Recreations:* cricket, golf, shooting. *Address:* Langhurst Manor, Chiddingfold, Surrey. *T:* Chiddingfold 20. *Club:* Turf.

Died 1 March 1948.

MULLEN, Lt-Col Leslie Miltiades, CMG 1934; DSO 1917; VD; Governor HM Gaol, Hobart, Tasmania, since 1928; *b* 15 Aug. 1882; *s* of William Rowland and Caroline Mullen; *m* 1910, Alma Hoper Langeveldt; one *s* one *d. Educ:* Queen's College, Maryborough, Vic. Served with 5th Victorian Mounted Rifles South African War (Queen's Medal 5 clasps); 12th Battalion AIF European War joined as Lieutenant and promoted Lieut-Colonel and to command 9th Battalion AIF served 5 years (DSO, Belgian Croix de Guerre, Colonial Auxiliary Force Officer Decoration VD, 1914–15 Star, General Service Medal and Victory Medal, despatches twice); State President, Tasmania Returned Soldiers and Sailors Imperial League of Australia since 1922;

Represented Australia at BESL Conference in Canada, 1931. *Recreations:* cricket and golf. *Address:* 1 Melville Street, Hobart, Tasmania. *Clubs:* Naval and Military, Athenæum, Auto Car, Hobart.

Died 18 March 1943.

MULLENEUX, Captain Hugh Bowring, CBE 1919; RN retired; *b* 1878; *s* of late Hugh Mulleneux, Liverpool; *m* 1910, Mabel Josephine, *d* of late Joseph Hubback, Liverpool; one *s.* Served European War, 1914–19 (despatches, American DSC); European War, 1939–45, on staff of Commander-in-Chief, Plymouth; Polish Order of Polonia Restituta. *Address:* Beachcroft, Budleigh Salterton, Devon.

Died 4 Feb. 1947.

MULLER, Lt-Col John, DSO 1919, MC, retired; Temp. Lt-Col Somerset Light Infantry, 1941; *b* 7 July 1883; *s* of George Herbert Muller, CBE, VD, and Josephine Wadsworth; *m* 1917, Clarrie, *d* of E. A. Matthews, Eastburn, Cross Hills Keighley; one *d. Educ:* Ilkley Grammar School. Vol. and TA, 1900–16, 6th Bn West Yorks Regt, Regular Army, 1916–19, Welch Regt; served European War, 1914–18 (DSO, MC, despatches, Belgian Croix de Guerre). *Recreations:* fishing, hunting. *Address:* Oaklands, South Petherton, Somerset. *T:* South Petherton 272.

Died 23 June 1942.

MULLER, Sir William Grenfell M.; *see* Max-Muller.

MULLINER, Ven. Harold George, MA; Archdeacon of Westmorland, Hon. Canon of Carlisle, Vicar of Winster, Director of Religious Education in Diocese of Carlisle, since 1944; *b* 18 Sept. 1897; *s* of late Augustus Greville Mulliner and Edith Sarah Wall, Liverpool; *m* 1926, Kathleen Grace, *d* of Anthony Waldegrave Carter, Caversham, Reading; no *c. Educ:* Birkenhead School; Hertford College, Oxford; Ripon Hall, Oxford. Held commission in King's Liverpool Regiment, 1918–19 and wounded in France; 1st Class Hon. Modern History, 1922; Deacon, 1924; Priest, 1925; Curate of Caversham, 1924–25, of Garston, 1925–28, of Holy Trinity, Southport, 1928–29; Vicar of North Stainley, Ripon, 1929–37; Domestic Chaplain to Bishop of Ripon, 1929–35; Residentiary Canon and Chancellor of Truro Cathedral, 1937–44; Examining Chaplain to Bishop of Ripon, 1935–37, to Bishop of Truro, 1937–44, to Bishop of Carlisle since 1944; Director of Religious Education in Diocese of Truro, 1937–44; Cornwall Education Committee, 1943–44, Westmorland Education Committee since 1945; Cornwall Civil Defence, County Equipment Officer, 1940–42; Select Preacher, University of Cambridge, 1939. *Publication:* Arthur Burroughs: A Memoir. *Recreations:* cricket and tennis. *Address:* Winster Vicarage, Windermere. *T:* Windermere 536.

Died 1 July 1946.

MULLINS, Gen. George James Herbert, CB 1919; *s* of Rev. George Henry Mullins, late of Uppingham School and Gt Billing, Northants, and J. M., *e d* of T. Mallam, Oxford; *m* Katharine L., *e d* of Thos Leah, MRCS, of Stonehouse, Plymouth. *Educ:* King's School, Canterbury; Keble College, Oxford. 2nd Lieut Royal Marine Light Infantry, 1889; served South African War, 1899, and Boxer Rising, 1900 (medals and clasps); European War (despatches, 3 medals, Croix de Guerre avec Palme, CB); Col Commandant Plymouth Div. RM 1921–24; Lt-Gen. 1926; Gen. 1928; retired list, 1928. *Recreations:* boating, sailing and fishing. *Address:* c/o Lloyds Bank, Ltd, 28 George Street, Plymouth. *Club:* United Service.

Died 26 June 1943.

MULOCK, Rt Hon. Sir William, PC 1925; KCMG 1902; KC; MA, LLD; *b* Bond Head, Canada, 19 Jan. 1844; *s* of Thomas Homan Mulock, MD; *m* 1870, Sarah Ellen (*d* 1912), *d* of James Crowther, barrister, Toronto;

two *d. Educ:* Newmarket Grammar School; University of Toronto. Graduated in Arts, 1863. Barr 1868; QC 1888; first elected to Parliament of Canada, 1882; re-elected 1887, 1891, 1896, 1900, and 1904; Vice-Chancellor of University of Toronto on death of Chief Justice Moss, 1881, and was continuously re-elected until 1900, when he resigned in consequence of the extent of his other public duties; Postmaster-General of Canada, 1896–1905, and Minister of Labour, 1900–05; Chief Justice Exchequer Div. of the Supreme Court of Ontario, 1905–23; Chief Justice of Second Division, 1923; Chief Justice of Ontario, 1923–36; Chancellor of the University of Toronto since 1924; on his motion, the Inter-Imperial Postal Conference adopted Penny Postage within the Empire, 1898; introduced and carried through House of Commons a bill establishing the Department of Labour, 1900; for some years was Lecturer on Equity and Law Examiner for the Law Society of Upper Canada; Representative of Government, Dominion of Canada, at inauguration of Federal Parliament of Australia. *Address:* Toronto, Ontario, Canada. *Clubs:* York, University, Toronto.

Died 1 Oct. 1944.

MULVANY, Charles Mathew, MA; BLitt (Oxon); *b* Dunville, Canada, 28 Aug. 1867; *e s* of late Fleet Surgeon John Mulvany. *Educ:* Portsmouth Grammar School; St Paul's, London; Magdalen, Oxford; Bonn, Leipzig, Jena; 1st Class Mod. 1888; Craven Scholar, 1888; 1st Lit. Hum. 1890. Fellow of Magdalen College, 1891–1908. Professor (Indian Educational Service) Queen's College, Benares, 1897–1922; retired, 1922; some time Fellow University of Allahabad; member Classical Association; Society for promotion of Hellenic Studies. *Publications:* Translation from Urdu, 1901; Our Common Inheritance I The Indo-European Language, 1911; articles in Classical Review, etc. *Address:* Benares Cantonments.

Died 11 June 1945.

MULVANY, Most Rev. Thomas. Bishop of Meath, (RC), since 1929. *Address:* The Palace, Mullingar, Ireland.

Died 16 June 1943.

MUMFORD, Henry Plevy; *b* Antigua, West Indies, 26 July 1862; father missionary; *m* 1895, Ethel Foskett; three *s* two *d* (*e s* fell at Arras, 1917). *Educ:* Fulneck; the Moravian College, Fairfield, Manchester; New College, Edinburgh. Master at Gracehill, Fulneck, and at Neuwied on the Rhine, 1883–88; ordained, 1891; Minister at Brockweir on the Wye, 1892–95; Belfast, 1895–1906; London, Fetter Lane and Hornsey, and Upton Manor, 1906–18; began Moravian Missions Magazine, 1902; Minister of Baildon Moravian Church, Yorkshire, 1918–29; Editor of the Messenger, 1900–16; retired from active service, 1929. *Address:* Torridon, Somers Road, Reigate, Surrey.

Died 15 March 1941.

MUNDAY, Charles Frederick, CB 1925; *b* 1868; *s* of Charles Frederick Munday; *m* 1919, Louisa, *d* of William Sherrin Rees. Deputy Director of Naval Construction, Admiralty, 1924–28. *Address:* The Toft House, Bournemouth, Hants.

Died 29 Feb. 1948.

MUNN, Lt-Col Reginald George, CMG 1919; FRGS; *e s* of late Rev. G. S. Munn, MA, JP, Rector, Madresfield, Worcestershire; *m* 1906, Helen Muriel (*d* 1943), *e d* of late H. C. Jeddere-Fisher, Wilderwick, Surrey; two *s* one *d. Educ:* Haileybury; RMC Sandhurst. 2nd Lieut, 2nd Derbyshire Regt, 1889; trans 36th Sikhs, IA, 1891; Captain, 1900; Major, 1907; Lieut-Colonel, 1915; NWF, Hazara, 1891 (medal and clasp); Relief of Chitral, 1895 (medal and clasp); Samana, 1897 (despatches, clasp); NWF, 1897 (despatches, clasp); Tirah, 1897 (despatches, clasp, severely wounded); Waziristan, 1900–02, HQ Staff (despatches, clasp); Kabul

Khel Wazirs, 1902 (C-in-C India's despatch); Somaliland as ADC to GOC in C, 1903–04, etc. (despatches, medal and clasp); special mission to Abyssinian Ogaden Tribes; HQ Staff, India, 1904–06; Chief Instructor Musketry, and DAAG Imperial Service Troops, 1908–13; Indian Coronation Medal, 1911; European War, Tsingtao, 1914 (severely wounded); Admiralty, 1915–16; India Office, 1916; Military Secretary to the Governor of Madras, 1916–17; DAAG, War Office, 1917–19 (CMG 1914–15 Star, GS Medal, Victory Medal with Palm); retired (invalided), 1920; Director Fertilizer Sales Ltd, 1925–30; inventor and copatentee, Bell-Munn Flame Proof Gauntlet. *Address:* Turley Cottage, East Grinstead. *Club:* MCC.

Died 12 April 1947.

MUNRO, Sir George Hamilton, 12th Bt *cr* 1634; *b* 10 May 1864; *e s* of late Harry Munro, 2nd *s* of 9th Bart; *S* cousin 1935; *m* 1891, Amelia Sarah, *d* of John Chapple, Peckham, Surrey; no *c*. *Educ:* privately. *Publications:* verses in magazines. *Recreation:* walking. *Heir: b* Arthur Talbot, *b* 1866. *Address:* The Cliffe, Portsmouth Road, Guildford, Surrey.

Died 2 May 1945.

MUNRO, John Arthur Ruskin, MA; Rector of Lincoln College, Oxford; *b* 24 Feb. 1864; *er s* of Alexander Munro, sculptor; *m* Margaret Caroline Neaves, 2nd *d* of Rev. C. H. Parez; one *s* four *d*. *Educ:* Charterhouse; Exeter College, Oxford. 1st Class Mods, 1883; 1st Class Lit. Hum. 1886; Fellow of Lincoln College, 1888. Examiner in Lit. Hum. 1894–96; Junior Proctor, 1900; Bursar of Lincoln College, 1904–19; Hon. Fellow, Exeter College, 1929. *Publications:* numerous articles on Ancient History, Archæology, and Geography. *Address:* Lincoln College, Oxford.

Died 18 Feb. 1944.

MUNRO, Patrick; MP (U) Llandaff and Barry, Glamorgan, since 1931; Junior Lord of the Treasury, 1937–42; *b* 9 Oct. 1883; 5th *s* of late Patrick Munro and Mary Helen Catherine Dormond; *m* 1911, Jessie Margaret, *d* of late E. P. Martin. *Educ:* Leeds Grammar School; Christ Church, Oxford (Open History Scholarship), 2nd class Honours School of History, MA. President Vincents Club Oxford, 1906–07. Joined Sudan Political Service, 1907; Governor Darfur Province, 1923–24; Governor Khartoum Province, 1925–29; mentioned in despatches, 1919; Order of the Nile (3rd class), 1929; Parliamentary Private Secretary to Capt. Euan Wallace when Under-Sec. of State, Home Office 1935, and when Sec. of Overseas Trade Dept 1935; Assistant Whip (unpaid) 1937; Member of British Delegation to Capitulations Conference, Montreux, 1937. *Recreations:* football, polo and fishing; Rugby Blue, Oxford, 1903, 1904, 1905; Captain, 1905; Rugby International for Scotland, 1905, 1906, 1907, 1911; Captain 1907 and 1911; President Scottish Rugby Union, 1939; Half Blue for High Jump, Oxford, 1906. *Address:* Cathedine Cottage, Bwlch, Breconshire. *T:* Bwlch 16. *Club:* Carlton.

Died 3 May 1942.

MUNRO, William Thow, CBE 1936; Director in many textile companies; *b* 9 May 1884; 2nd *s* of William Munro; *m* 1910, Christina, *y d* of John Forbes Orr, Wellington, New Zealand; two *d*. *Educ:* George Watson's College, Edinburgh; Leeds University. After school, trained for woollen trade; farmed in New Zealand for 3 years; since then travelled extensively; Member of Govt Delegations to USA, Canada and Europe; Member of Overseas Development Council; Chairman for 4 years of British Textile Council for BIF. *Recreations:* golf, tennis. *Address:* Muirhouse, Davidson's Mains, Edinburgh, 4. *T:* 77430. *Clubs:* Constitutional; Scottish Conservative (Edinburgh).

Died 24 Oct. 1948.

MUNROE, Lt-Col Hon. Hugh Edwin, OBE, VD, MD, CM, FACS, LRCP and S Edin.; FRCS (Can.); LLD (McGill University); *b* Glengarry Co., Ontario, Canada, 1879; *s* of Wm Munroe, Inverness, and Jenett McEwen, Perth; *m* 1904, Myrtle Brown, Bowdon, Man; one *s* one *d*. *Educ:* McGill University (LLD); Edinburgh Univ. Practised surgery in Saskatoon for 25 years; Father of city Hospitals and Chairman of its board of Governors for ten years; Lieut-Governor of the Province of Saskatchewan, 1931–36; President of Saskatchewan Medical Association (Past); Past President of Saskatchewan Conservative Association; rejected Conservative candidate, 1905 and 1912; Alderman first city council; four years' active service (despatches 3 times, France, Dardanelles etc. OBE). *Publications:* articles to Medical journals on war and civil surgery, etc. BMJ and journals. *Recreations:* golf and riding. *Address:* Manitou Beach, Watrous, Sask. *Club:* Saskatoon.

Died 12 March 1947.

MUNTHE, Axel, CVO; MD, Paris; *b* Sweden, Nov. 1857; *m*; two *s* of British nationality served with British Army. *Educ:* University of Uppsala, Sweden. For many years physician to the Queen of Sweden; now retired from practice. *Publications:* The Story of San Michele; Red Cross and Iron Cross; Memories and Vagaries; Letters from a Mourning City. *Address:* Torre di Materita, Anacapri, Bay of Naples; c/o John Murray, 50 Albemarle Street, W1. *Club:* St James's.

Died 11 Feb. 1949.

MUNTZ, Sir Gerard Philip Graves, 3rd Bt *cr* 1902; Lieutenant, RN; *b* 13 June 1917; *s* of 2nd Bt and Henrietta Winifred, 3rd *d* of late Lt-Col F. L. Graves, RA; *S* father, 1927. *Heir:* none. *Address:* Apley House, Sparsholt, nr Winchester.

Died 6 Dec. 1940 (ext).

MURDOCH, John Smith, CMG 1927; FRIBA; late Director-General of Works and Chief Government Architect Commonwealth of Australia; *b* 1863; *s* of late John Murdoch, Cassisford, Morayshire. *Educ:* Forres Academy; Rafford School.

Died 21 May 1945.

MURDOCH, Hon. Thomas, CMG 1943; President of Legislative Council in Tasmania since 1937; member of State Parliament since 1914; *b* 15 March 1868; 4th *s* of John and Margaret Murdoch; *m* 1907, Lesley Tope, Melbourne; one *s* one *d*. *Educ:* Hutchins School, Hobart. Chieftain of Tasmanian Caledonian Society; President of Hobart Chamber of Commerce four times; Belgium Consul in the State. Chevalier of the Order of Leopold II; Chevalier of the Crown of Belgium. *Address:* Hobart, Tasmania. *TA:* Sunbeam, Hobart, Tasmania. *T:* 4302, 4303, 3612. *Clubs:* Australasian Pioneers, Sydney.

Died 30 June 1946.

MURDOCH, William; pianist; *b* Bendigo, Australia, 1888; *s* of Andrew Murdoch; *m* Antonia Dorothea, *y d* of late Henry Simon, Manchester; two *s* two *d*. *Educ:* Melbourne University; Royal College of Music, London. Left Australia at the age of 17, having won the Clarke Scholarship to the Royal College of Music, and has made his home in England ever since; has played many times with all the leading British orchestras, and has also devoted much time to the playing of chamber-music; has toured extensively in most European countries, also USA, Canada, S Africa, Australia and New Zealand. *Publications:* Brahms, with an Analytical Study of the complete Pianoforte Works, 1933; Chopin: his Life, 1934; A number of songs and pianoforte pieces; also many arrangements for piano of the organ works of Bach. *Recreations:* golf, billiards. *Address:* High Lawns, Holmbury St Mary, Dorking. *T:* Abinger 206; 120 Wigmore Street, W1. *T:* Welbeck 2714. *Club:* Savage.

Died 9 Sept. 1942.

MURISON, Sir (James) William, Kt 1919; *b* Aberdeen, 23 March 1872; *γ s* of Prof. A. F. Murison, KC; *m* 1904, Mabel (*d* 1938), 2nd *d* of John Paterson; one *s* one *d.* *Educ:* BA, LLB Trinity Hall, Cambridge (honours in Classics and Law). Barrister-at-law, Middle Temple; late Chief Justice of HBM Court, Zanzibar; and Judge of Court of Appeal for Eastern Africa; Acting Colonial Secretary Straits Settlements, June 1920; Governor's Deputy, 26 July–Sept. 1920; KC (Straits Settlements), 1924; Attorney-General, 1919–25; Chief Justice, 1925–33; Chairman of Commission, Dec. 1933 to enquire into Arab-Jewish Riots in Palestine; a Chairman of War Pension Tribunals, 1944. *Recreations:* tennis, golf. *Clubs:* Athenæum, East India and Sports; Huntercombe and Royal Jersey Golf.

Died 28 Aug. 1945.

MURPHY, Hon. Denis; retired Judge of the Supreme Court of British Columbia; *b* 20 June 1870; *m* 1900, C. Maude, *d* of A. C. Cameron, Cornwall, Ontario; three *s* two *d.* *Educ:* Ottawa University. *Address:* 4350 Marguerite Ave, Vancouver, BC.

Died 1 May 1947.

MURPHY, Rt Hon. Edward Sullivan; PC (Northern Ireland), 1939; KC 1918; **Lord Justice Murphy;** Lord Justice of Appeal, Supreme Court of Northern Ireland, since 1939; *b* 3 Feb. 1880; 4th *s* of late Rt Hon. Mr Justice Murphy; *m* 1st, 1905, Alice Louisa (*d* 1942), *y d* of Rt Hon. Lord Justice Holmes; no *c*; 2nd, 1943, Mary Craig, 3rd *d* of late John Buchanan, Kilmarnock. *Educ:* Charterhouse (Scholar and School Exhibitioner); Trinity College, Dublin (Classical Scholar, Senior Moderator, Classics and Logics and Ethics); University Student, Vice-Chancellor's Prizeman, MA (Gold Medallist, College Historical Society). Called to Irish Bar, 1903; Inner Temple, 1921; Bencher, King's Inns, 1921; Bencher, Inn of Court of Northern Ireland; MP Derry City, Northern Ireland: MP Derry City, Northern Ireland Parliament, 1929–39; Attorney-General for Northern Ireland, 1937–39. *Address:* 30 Windsor Park, Belfast. *Clubs:* Ulster, Belfast; Northern Counties, Londonderry; Friendly Brother House, Dublin.

Died 3 Dec. 1945.

MURPHY, Hon. Frank; Associate Justice of the Supreme Court of the United States since 1940; *b* Harbor Beach, Mich, 13 April 1890; *s* of John F. Murphy and Mary Brennan. *Educ:* University of Michigan (AB 1912, LLB 1914); graduate studies at Lincoln's Inn, London and Trinity College, Dublin, 1919. Hon. LLD Univ. of Santo Thomas, Manila, PI, 1934; Fordham Univ., 1935, and from many other universities. Admitted to Michigan Bar, 1914; law clerk with Monaghan and Monaghan, Detroit, and night school teacher, 1914–17; 1st Lieut and Capt. of Infantry, AEF, serving also with Army of Occupation, German Rhineland; Chief Assistant US District Attorney, Detroit, 1919–20; in private practice, 1920–23; Instructor in Law, Univ. of Detroit, 1922–27; Judge, Recorders Court, Detroit, 1923–30; Mayor of Detroit, 1930–33; first President of the US Assoc. of Mayors, 1933; last Governor-General of Philippine Islands, 1933, and first US High Commissioner to Philippines, 1935; Governor of Michigan, Nov. 1936; Attorney-General of the United States, 1939. *Address:* US Supreme Court, Washington, DC, USA.

Died 19 July 1949.

MURPHY, Harold Lawson, KC 1936; MA; *b* 1882; *s* of Rt Hon. Mr Justice Murphy and Mary, *d* of Rt Hon. Mr Justice Keogh; *m* Elsie (*d* 1931), *d* of Rt Hon. Lord Justice Holmes. *Educ:* Charterhouse School; Trinity College, Dublin. Entered Dublin Univ., 1900; Littledale Prizeman (English Literature), 1901; Clough Memorial Prizeman, 1902; BA 1903; 1st of First Class and large Gold Medallist (Modern History and Political Economy); Helen Blake Scholarship (History Research),

1904; Gold Medallist in Oratory (Historical Society), 1905; Auditor of College Historical Society Session, 1905–06; Barrington Lecturer in Political Economy, 1910. *Address:* 6 Stanley Crescent, W11. *T:* Park 8107. *Club:* Royal Air Force.

Died 5 Jan. 1942.

MURPHY, James Francis, CMG 1937; Chairman, Australian Wool Realization Commission, Commonwealth Wool Adviser, and Economic Adviser to the Minister for Commerce and Agriculture, since 1945; *b* Carlton, Victoria, 12 March 1893; *s* of Peter and Mary Winifred Murphy, Irish; *m* 1922, Beatrice Emily McClounan; two *s* two *d.* *Educ:* Christian Brothers Colleges, South and East Melbourne; Melbourne University. Joined Commonwealth Civil Service, 1910; served in External Affairs, Home Territories, and Prime Minister's Departments up to 1931; Secretary and Adviser to Australian Delegation to Ottawa Conference, 1932; Assistant Secretary Commerce Department, 1933; Secretary Dept of Commerce and Agriculture, 1934–45; Commonwealth Food Controller, 1943–45. *Recreations:* gardening, walking. *Address:* Australian Wool Realization Commission, Melbourne, Australia. *TA:* Cenwool, Melbourne. *T:* Melbourne MU9261.

Died 17 Jan. 1949.

MURPHY, John; late Member Kerry County Council; *b* Killarney, 1871; *m* 1895, Annie, *d* of E. M'Carthy, Kilbrean. *Educ:* Presentation Monastery, Killarney. MP (N) for East Kerry, 1900–10. *Address:* Park Place Hotel, Killarney.

Died 17 April 1930.

MURPHY, Rev. John, MA, BD, DLitt, DD (Glasgow), MA (Manchester); Emeritus Professor of Comparative Religion in Manchester University, and Tutor in Lancashire Independent College, Manchester; *b* Lanark, 13 March 1876; *s* of Henry Murphy, JP, and Elizabeth Smith; *m* Isabella, *d* of Prof. A. F. Simpson, MA, Edinburgh; no *c.* *Educ:* Glasgow University; Scottish Congregational College, Edinburgh; Berlin; Heidelberg. Minister of Congregational Church at Dumfries, 1901–07; Albany Street, Edinburgh, 1907–12; Hamilton, 1912–21; Dennistoun, Glasgow, 1921–30; Lecturer Scottish Congregational College, 1919 and 1921. *Publications:* Primitive Man; His Essential Quest, 1927; Lamps of Anthropology, 1943; The Origins and History of Religions, 1948; contributions to Mélanges Franz Cumont, Expository Times, Storia Delle Religioni, Man, Hibbert Journal, etc. *Address:* 118 Davyhulme Road, Davyhulme, Manchester.

Died 28 July 1949.

MURPHY, Sir Stephen James, Kt 1935; *s* of Lt-Col P. Murphy, IMS, and Helen, *d* of Surgeon J. McCraith, RN; *m* 1st, Mary Macleod, Ballarat (*d* 1910); 2nd, Emily Alice, *d* of William Denis Browne, Lynnwood, Leamington Spa; one *s* one *d.* *Educ:* Framlingham College; University College, London. Appointed to the Indian Civil Service after the examination of 1898 on the Bombay Establishment, and served in Bombay Presidency as Assistant Collector and Magistrate, Assistant Judge and Additional Sessions Judge, District and Sessions Judge, Remembrancer of Legal Affairs and Legal Secretary to Government, 1922; Judicial Commissioner in the States of Western India; Acting Judge, High Court, Bombay, 1928; Puisne Judge, High Court, Bombay, 1929–35; retired, 1935. *Address:* Kyrenia, Cyprus.

Died 21 Oct. 1950.

MURPHY, Rev. William, CBE 1919; in Holy Orders of Church of Rome; (retired); 1st class Chaplain to the Forces; *b* 1872. Served European War, 1914–19 (despatches, CBE, 1914–15 star, two medals); retired pay, 1928. *Address:* Borris, Co. Carlow.

Died 5 Feb. 1943.

MURPHY, William Lombard, MA; MD; BCh Camb.; FRCSI; LRCP and SI; MSc (hon. causa) National University of Ireland; *b* Dublin; *s* of late Wm Martin Murphy of Dublin, and Mary *d* of James Fitzgerald Lombard. *Educ:* Clongowes Wood College; Feldkirch, Austria; St John's College, Cambridge. Formerly Surgeon in charge of Throat and Nose Department, St Vincent's Hospital, Dublin; Captain RAMC (TF), resigned 1920; served in Macedonia (despatches, Chevalier of the Legion of Honour, French Croix de Guerre, Serbian Order of St Sava, Greek Order of the Redeemer); Chairman of Board of Directors Independent Newspapers; Director Great Southern Railways Co. (Amalgamated Railways of Eire); Director of Dublin United Tramways Co.; President Dublin Chamber of Commerce, 1924; delegate representing Employers, Irish Free State, International Labour Conference, 1928, 1930, and 1931. *Publications:* papers on medical subjects. *Recreations:* lawn tennis, golf, travel. *Address:* Dartry, Upper Rathmines, Dublin. *Clubs:* Reform; University, Dublin.

Died 9 Jan. 1943.

MURRAY, Alma; Actress; *b* London, 21 Nov. 1854; *d* of Leigh Murray, actor; *m* 1876, Alfred Forman (*d* 1925), translator of Wagner's Nibelung's Ring, Tristan and Isolde, Parsifal, Tannhäuser; one *d. Educ:* privately. First appeared when a child at Olympic Theatre; at the Lyceum, 1879–81; at chief West End theatres, 1882–97; principal actress in Shelley and Browning performances, including Beatrice in the Cenci; first appearance as Rosalind in As You Like It, April 1897, at the Metropole Theatre, Camberwell; Criterion Theatre, Jan. to April 1902, as Clarissa, in Mr L. N. Parker's 'The Sequel'; Pavilion Theatre as Marion Grey in G. R. Sims's Woman from Gaol, 1903; with Mr Tree as Mrs Maylie in Oliver Twist, 1905; suburban tour of Hall Caine's Prodigal Son as Anna, 1906; provincial tour of same, 1906; Aldwych Theatre as Jane in Jerome K. Jerome's Fanny and the Servant Problem, 1908; Garrick Theatre as Blind Kerry in Hall Caine's The Bishop's Son, 1910; Lyceum Theatre as Queen in Pelleas and Melisande, 1911; His Majesty's Theatre as Mrs Maylie in the revival of Oliver Twist, 1912; Court and Prince of Wales' Theatres as Lady Dedmond in Galsworthy's The Fugitive, 1913; His Majesty's Theatre as Mrs Eynsford-Hill in Shaw's Pygmalion, 1914; St James's Theatre as Baroness de Lisle in Besier's Kings and Queens, and His Majesty's Theatre as Mrs Maylie in revival of Oliver Twist, 1915. *Recreations:* reading, country walks, observing character. *Address:* c/o Miss Elsa Forman, 63 Rowan Road, W6.

Died 3 July 1945.

MURRAY, Gen. Sir Archibald (James), GCB 1928; GCMG 1917; KCB 1911; KCMG 1915; CB 1904; CVO 1907; DSO 1902; *b* 21 April 1860; *s* of late Charles Murray, of Woodhouse, near Kingsclere, Hants; *m* 1st, 1890, Caroline Helen (*d* 1910), *e d* of late Lt-Col Henry Baker Sweet, of Hillersdon, Tiverton; one *s*; 2nd, 1912, Mildred Georgina, *d* of late Col W. Toke Dooner, CBE, Ditton Place, Maidstone. *Educ:* Cheltenham College; Sandhurst. Entered 27th Regiment, 1879; became Capt. Royal Inniskilling Fusiliers, 1887; Major, 1898; Lt-Col 1900; Col 1902; Maj.-Gen. 1910; Lt-Gen. 1915; served Zululand, 1888; South Africa, 1899, 1900, and 1902 (dangerously wounded, despatches several times, Queen's medal 5 clasps, King's medal 2 clasps, DSO); European War, 1914–18 (despatches, KCMG, now Gen.); Director of Military Training, Headquarters, 1907–12; Inspector of Infantry, 1912–14; Deputy-Chief of the Imperial General Staff, then Chief of the Imperial General Staff, 1915; General Officer Commanding, 1st Class, Egypt, 1916–17; Colonel Royal Inniskilling Fusiliers; GOC in C. Aldershot, 1917–19; retired pay, 1922; Grand Officer Legion of Honour; Grand Officier SS Maurice and Lazarus, Italy; Grand Cross White Eagle, Serbia, 1917; Grand Cross Order of the Nile, 1916;

Grand Cordon of Sacred Treasure of Japan. *Address:* Makepeace, Park Lane, Reigate, Surrey. *T:* Reigate 2773. *Club:* Travellers'.

Died 23 Jan. 1945.

MURRAY, Lt-Col Arthur E.; *see* Erskine-Murray.

MURRAY, Charles, CMG 1922; LLD (Aberdeen); AMICE; *b* Alford, Aberdeenshire, 28 Sept. 1864; *m* Edith, *e d* of late W. H. Rogers, Canonteigne, Cape Town and Kimberley; one *s* two *d.* Manager York Gold Mining Company Ltd, 1899; Boer War (Lieut Railway Pioneer Regiment), 1900; Deputy Inspector of Mines, Transvaal, 1901; Registrar of Crown Titles, 1902; Under-Secretary for Public Works, 1905; Chief Engineer and Secretary for Public Works, Transvaal, 1907; Secretary for Public Works, Union of South Africa, 1910; retired, 1924; Director of Works (Lieut-Col), SA Defence Force, 1917. *Publications:* Hamewith, 1900; A Sough of War, 1917; In the Country Places, 1920; Collected edition of Hamewith, etc., 1927. *Recreations:* golf and trout fishing. *Address:* The Lythe, Banchory, Kincardineshire. *T:* Banchory 120. *Clubs:* Rand, Johannesburg; Civil Service, Cape Town.

Died 12 April 1941.

MURRAY, Rt Rev. Charles Herbert; Bishop of Riverina, NSW since 1944; *b* 21 Sept. 1899; *s* of Charles Herbert and Edith Jane Murray; *m* 1931, Cynthia Fane Wheeler; two *s. Educ:* Wesley College, Melbourne; Trinity College, University of Melbourne; Christ Church, Oxford. Deacon, 1922; Priest, 1923; Rector, Christ Church, North Adelaide, 1933–38; Vicar, Christ Church, South Yarra, 1938–44; Canon, St Paul's Cathedral, Melbourne, 1940–44. RAAF Chaplain (part time), 1940–43. *Recreation:* golf. *Address:* Bishop's Lodge, Hay, NSW. *TA:* Hay, NSW. *T:* Hay 112. *Clubs:* Savage (Melbourne); University (Sydney).

Died 26 June 1950.

MURRAY, Charles Wadsworth; *b* 1894; *o surv. s* of late Charles James Murray and late Lady Anne, *o d* of 6th Earl of Aylesford; *m* 1924, Elizabeth, *d* of Frank Grant, Knockie, Inverness; one *d. Educ:* Eton; Trinity College, Cambridge. *Address:* Couldoran Kishorn, Strathcarron, Ross-shire.

Died 22 May 1945.

MURRAY, Col Donald Norman Watson, CMG 1918; DSO 1917; MD; FRACP, New Zealand Medical Corps; *b* New Zealand, 1876; *s* of B. M. Murray, Scotland; married. *Educ:* Auckland College and Grammar School; Edinburgh University; Graduated 1902; MD 1904. Served South African War, 1900 (RAMC); European War, 1914–19; New Zealand Expeditionary Force, operations on Suez Canal, 1915; Gallipoli, 1915; France, 1916 (DSO); Senior House Surgeon, Leicester Royal Infirmary, 1904; House Physician, 1903. *Recreation:* motoring. *Address:* 19 Tuhimata Street, St Heliers Bay, Auckland, E1, NZ. *T:* 42–389. *Clubs:* Northern, Auckland.

Died 4 Sept. 1945.

MURRAY, Sir Evelyn; *see* Murray, Sir G. E. P.

MURRAY, Sir George, KBE 1920; Statistical Branch, War Office, 1917–20; *b* 12 Aug. 1865; 4th *s* of Lieut-Colonel Charles Murray, 42nd Royal Highlanders (Black Watch); *m* 1891, Lily Gwendoline (*d* 1929), twin *d* of Walter Mayhew, Duxbury Park, Chorley, Lancashire. *Address:* 37 Kensington Park Gardens, W11. *T:* Park 6961. *Club:* Junior Carlton.

Died 2 Feb. 1942.

MURRAY, Sir (George) Evelyn (Pemberton), KCB 1919; CB 1916; *b* 25 July 1880; *s* of late Rt Hon. Sir George H. Murray, GCB, GCVO; *heir-pres.* to 9th Duke of Atholl; *m* 1906, Muriel, *d* of late Philip Beresford Hope. *Educ:* Eton; Christ Church, Oxford. Entered Civil Service, 1903; Private Secretary to President,

Board of Education, 1905–09; late Commissioner of Customs and Excise; Secretary to the Post Office, 1914–34; Chairman of the Board of Custom and Excise, 1934–40. *Publication:* The Post Office, 1927. *Club:* Brooks's.

Died 30 March 1947.

MURRAY, Hon. Sir George John Robert, KCMG 1917; BA, LLM; Chief Justice of the Supreme Court of South Australia and Lieutenant-Governor since 1916; *b* 27 Sept. 1863; *s* of late Alexander Borthwick Murray. *Educ:* High School, Edinburgh; St Peter's Collegiate School and University, Adelaide (won Scholarship which required him to go to Europe for four years); Trinity College, Cambridge (bracketed Senior in Law Tripos). Won Inns of Court Studentship. Called to Bar, Inner Temple, 1888; South Australia, 1889; New South Wales and Victoria, 1890; KC 1906; Judge of the Supreme Court, 1912; Member of Council, Adelaide University, since 1891; Vice-Chancellor, 1915; Chancellor since 1916; Commander of St John of Jerusalem, 1933. *Address:* Murray Park, Magill, South Australia. *Clubs:* Athenæum, Oxford and Cambridge; Adelaide, Adelaide.

Died 18 Feb. 1942.

MURRAY, Sir Hugh, Kt 1924; CIE 1911; CBE 1918; JP Hants; *b* 27 April 1861; *s* of late Lt-Col Chas Murray, 42nd R. Highlanders; *m* 1st, Gwendoline Mabel Langridge; one *s*; 2nd, Dorothy Christine, *d* of late Rt Hon. Sir William Mather; one *s* one *d. Educ:* Trent College. Entered Imperial Forest Service, 1882; Senior Conservator of Forests, Bombay, and Additional Member of the Bombay Legislative Council; retired, 1911; employed at the War Office, Nov. 1914–May 1917; Deputy Controller of Timber Supplies, June 1917; Assistant Forestry Commissioner for England and Wales, 1918; Forestry Commissioner, 1924–34. *Address:* Bramble Hill Lodge, Lyndhurst, Hants. *Club:* Brooks's.

Died 9 Feb. 1941.

MURRAY, James Alexander, FRS 1925; BSc, MD; *b* 1873; *y s* of late W. Murray, Cramond, Midlothian; *m* 1927, Ethel Emily, *d* of late L. Beere, London; no *c. Educ:* Heriots; Edinburgh; Würzburg; Freiburg i/Br. Assistant Imperial Cancer Research Fund, 1903; Director, Imperial Cancer Research Fund, 8–11 Queen Square, London WC1, 1915–35. *Publications:* papers on Cancer and allied subjects. *Address:* c/o Westminster Bank, 74 Kilburn High Rd, NW6.

Died 20 Nov. 1950.

MURRAY, James Whiteford; DL; Director of Ker, Bolton & Co., Ltd, London; *s* of late James Murray, Catter House, Drymen; unmarried. *Educ:* privately. President of Glasgow Chamber of Commerce, 1915–18; a member of a number of Government Committees before and during the War; an original member of the Imperial Shipping Committee until resignation, 1932. *Recreations:* shooting and golf. *Address:* Pirniehall, Drymen Station, Stirlingshire. *Clubs:* Western, Glasgow.

Died 19 March 1941.

MURRAY, John, MB, BCh Dublin University; FRCS England; Consulting Surgeon to the Middlesex Hospital; Consulting Surgeon to Paddington Green Children's Hospital and to St Saviour's Hospital; late Examiner in Surgery, Royal Naval Medical Service; late External Examiner in Surgery, Birmingham University; Captain RAMC (TF), retired, 3rd London General Hospital, Wandsworth; *b* Monkstown, Co. Dublin, 16 June 1863; *s* of late John Murray, of Dublin, solicitor; *m* 1st, 1898, Bertha Marion (*d* 1905), *y d* of late Rt Hon. Sir Alfred Wills; 2nd, 1906, Gertrude Margaret, *y d* of late W. Mills-Baker; one *s* one *d. Educ:* Repton School; Dublin University. BA 1884; MB BCh 1886. FRCS England 1890. House Surgeon, London Temperance Hospital, 1887–88; Casualty Surgical Officer, Middlesex Hospital, 1890–93; Surgical Registrar, 1893–96; Assistant

Surgeon, 1896–1903; Surgeon to Out-Patients, 1903–07; Surgeon, 1907–28; Dean, 1902–08; Lecturer on Practical and Operative Surgery, 1900–08; Lecturer on Surgery, 1908–28; Surgical Tutor, 1897–1900; Consulting Surgeon to the Hospital for Hip Disease, Sevenoaks, and to the Cottage Hospital. Member, Court of Examiners, Royal College of Surgeons, 1915–25. *Publications:* Middlesex Hospital Reports, 1894–95–96; Surgery of the Thorax; International Text-book of Surgery; contributions to medical journals. *Address:* c/o Coutts & Co., 440 Strand, WC2.

Died 16 Aug. 1943.

MURRAY, Engr Captain John Adam, CBE, 1919; RN Retired; *b* Leeds, 5 Sept. 1860; *s* of David T. Murray; *m* Mary Ann Ellington, New Brompton, Kent; one *s. Educ:* Leeds Modern School; Chatham Dockyard School; RN College, Greenwich. Assistant Engineer of HMS Constance in Pacific, 1882–86; subsequently served as Assistant and Engineer in Hero, Calypso, Sparrow on West and East Coasts of Africa, 1890–93; Sheldrake in North Sea; Iphigenia in China, 1897–1900; Engineer Commander of Good Hope, when the late Mr J. Chamberlain was taking passage to S Africa, and as escorting flagship of Cruiser Squadron to the late King Edward round Ireland; Engineer Commander of Boscawen II at Portland for training boys, 1904–05; Engineer Commander of Victorious, flagship of Atlantic Fleet, 1905–08; Engineer Commander Chatham Dockyard, 1908–11, when retired as Engineer Captain; in service of Lloyd's Register of Shipping, 1913–14; served during the War as Engineer Captain for overseeing duties in Newcastle, Fleetwood and Aberdeen (CBE); awarded Greenwich Hospital Pension, 1929. *Recreations:* bowling and philately. *Address:* Craig-y-don, 59 Evington Drive, Leicester.

Died 2 March 1948.

MURRAY, Rev. John Oswald, MA, DD; *b* Ballymena, Ireland, 4 Jan. 1869; *s* of Very Rev. J. W. Murray, LLD, Dean of Connor, and Margaret Moyers; *m* 1st, 1902, Ada, *d* of John Marwood, RN; one *d*; 2nd, 1927, Lilian Athalie, *widow* of Edmund Ashdown. *Educ:* Diocesan School, Ballymena; Trinity College, Dublin; First Classical Scholar and Vice-Chancellor's Gold Medallist. President, University Philosophical Soc., Dublin, 1892–93; Curate of St Martin-in-the-Fields, London, 1896–1902; Canon of St John's Cathedral, Winnipeg, and Professor of Systematic Theology in St John's College, 1902–20, and since 1926; Vice-Chairman Irish Literary Society of London, 1898–1902; Chaplain Canadian Overseas Forces, 1916–19; Diocesan Curate, Diocese of Meath, 1924–26; Commissary to the Archbishop of Rupert's Land, 1920; DD St John's Coll., Winnipeg, 1920. *Publication:* Christianity and Human Thought, 1909. *Recreations:* walking, cycling, reading. *Address:* 239 Polson Avenue, Winnipeg, Canada.

Died 25 Oct. 1943.

MURRAY, Rev. John Owen Farquhar; Fellow of Selwyn College, Cambridge, since 1928; Hon. Canon Ely Cathedral, 1918; *s* of late Surg.-Gen. J. Murray; *m* 1902, Frances Margaret, *d* of late Rev. R. B. Somerset, formerly Fellow of Trin. Coll., Cambridge; one *s* one *d. Educ:* Harrow; Trin. Coll., Camb. (2nd Class Classical Tripos; Crosse Univ. Scholar, and Carus Greek Testament Prize; Hebrew and Scholefield Prize; 1st Class Theological Tripos). Ordained, 1883; Dean of Emmanuel Coll. Cambridge, 1884–1903; Six Preacher of Canterbury Cathedral, 1903–08; Hon. Canon, 1908–09; Warden of St Augustine's Coll., Canterbury, 1903–09; Hulsean Lecturer, Cambridge, 1917–18; Master of Selwyn College, 1909–28. *Publications:* The Revelation of the Lamb; The Courage of Hope; Cambridge Greek Testament: The Epistle to the Ephesians; Studies in the Temptation of the Son of God; The Christian Armour; The Goodness and Severity of God; Du Bose as a Prophet of Unity; Asking God; The

Magnet of the Cross; The Obedience of the Cross; Jesus according to St John. *Recreations:* Association football, played for Cambridge against Oxford, 1880. *Address:* 15 Selwyn Gardens, Cambridge. *T:* Cambridge 4634. *Club:* Sheringham Golf.

Died 29 Nov. 1944.

MURRAY, Col Kenelm Digby Bold, CB 1933; DSO 1917; IA retired; Director in Military Studies, Cambridge University, since 1933; commanded Cambridge University OTC, 1934–45; *b* 1879; 2nd *s* of late Col Kenelm Digby Murray, DSO; *m* 1911, Gwendolen, *d* of late Thomas Andrew de Wolf, Sydney, NSW; one *s* one *d*. *Educ:* Haileybury. Served European War, 1914–17 (wounded, DSO). *Address:* c/o Holt & Co., Kirkland House, Whitehall, SW1.

Died 3 Feb. 1947.

MURRAY, Robert; JP; retired Director, Scottish Co-operative Wholesale Society; *b* 1870. MP (Lab) Western Division of Renfrew, 1922–24; formerly journalist, and has written extensively on social, literary and political topics. *Address:* Arlan-Rhu, Carlibar Road, Barrhead, Renfrew. *T:* Barrhead 1268.

Died 9 Aug. 1950.

MURRAY, Rev. Canon Robert Henry, MA, LittD, MRIA 1910; Hon. Canon of Worcester Cathedral, 1933–40; late Director of Clerical Studies in diocese of Worcester; late Diocesan Warden of the Central Society of Sacred Study; Examiner in History to the Civil Service Commission, London, and Senior Examiner in History to the Board of Intermediate Education, Belfast; Supervisor of Historical Studies in Oxford University; Governor of Birmingham University; *o s* of William and Margaret Murray; *m* 1st, 1910; May, *y d* of Rt Hon. Sir Frederick R. Falkiner, KC; 2nd, 1939, Margaret Ellen, *e d* of R. A. Gardner, MA (Cantab). *Educ:* Queen's College, Belfast; Trinity College, Dublin. BA, 1896; MA, 1899 (RUI); entereo TCD, 1904; BA, 1906; 1st of 1st Class (gold medal) Final Honour Schools, History and Political Science; 1st Vice-Chancellor's Prize in English Prose, 1905; University Prizeman in Political Economy, 1907; Helen Blake Scholar in History, 1908; Elrington Essay, 1909; LittD, 1909; Whately Memorial Prize, 1917 and 1922. Minor Canon, St Patrick's Cathedral, Killala, 1902–04; Chaplain of the Royal Hibernian Military School, Dublin, 1904–11; Chaplain to the Forces, 1914–16; Ministry of Information, 1914–18; Ministry of Food, 1916–18; Rector of the Magdalen Church and Examining Chaplain to the Archbishop of Dublin, 1919–22; expelled by Sinn Fein from Ireland, 1922, whose followers destroyed the MS of 'A History of the Growth of Toleration,' 4 volumes, which Professor Bury had read and approved; Rector of Broughton, Huntingdon, 1922–28; Vicar of Pershore and Wick, 1928–38; Rural Dean of Pershore, 1929–38; Foreign Office Research Dept, 1939; Lecturer in History, Trinity College, Dublin, 1921–22; Select Preacher, Dublin University, 1921–22; Cambridge University, 1926. *Publications:* Revolutionary Ireland and its Settlement, 1911; (editor) The Journal of John Stevens 1912; The Public Record Office, Dublin, 1919; Erasmus and Luther: their Attitude to Toleration, 1920; A Short Guide to some MSS in the Library of Trinity College, Dublin, 1920; Ireland, 1494–1829, 1920; Dublin University and the New World, 1921; Science and Scientists in the Nineteenth Century, 1925; The Political Consequences of the Reformation, 1926; The History of Political Science from Plato to the Present, 1926; The Hereafter and the Undying Hope, 1926; The History of the 8th Hussars, 2 vols 1928; Studies in the English Social and Political Thinkers of the Nineteenth Century, 2 vols, 1929; The Life of Edmund Burke, 1931; The Life of Archbishop Bernard, 1931; Group Movements Throughout the Ages, 1936; The King's Crowning, 1936; The Individual and the State, 1946; Inspiration, Human and Divine, 1948; (editor) J. B.

Bury's History of the Papacy in the Nineteenth Century, 1929; (joint) Anglican Essays, 1923; Ireland, 1924; The Victoria History of the Counties of England, 1925; The Oxford Convention of the Clergy of the Diocese of Worcester, 1936; Written for our Learning, 1938; Harmsworth's Universal History; contributor to Hastings' Encyclopædia of Ethics and Religion, the Encyclopædia Britannica, the Dictionary of National Biography, and to Encyclopædia of the Social Sciences; contributor to reviews. *Recreations:* collector of books on history, especially those relating to the growth of toleration and the letters of Edmund Burke; motoring, lawn tennis. *Address:* Grove House, The Icknield Way, Goring-on-Thames.

Died 2 Nov. 1947.

MURRAY, Brig.-Gen. Sir Valentine, KBE 1919; CB 1918; CMG 1915; Royal Engineers; retired; late of Indian State Railways; *b* 13 Feb. 1867; *s* of George Murray, Barrister-at-law, of 19 Old Square, Lincoln's Inn; *m* 1909, Flora Constance, *e d* of Ralph Entwistle Peters of Eastington, Gloucestershire. *Educ:* Malvern College; RMA Woolwich. Lieut Royal Engineers, 1886; Capt., 1896; Bt Major, 1900; Major, 1904; Lieut-Col, 1912; Colonel, 1916; temporary Brig.-Gen., 1917–19; served S African War, 1899–1902 (despatches, Bt Major, Queen's medal with 3 clasps; King's medal with 2 clasps); European War in France, 1914–19 (despatches five times, CMG, CB, 1914 Star, Commandeur, Legion of Honour). *Address:* Summerholm, Bourne End, Bucks. *Club:* United Service.

Died 8 April 1942.

MURRAY, Walter Charles, MA, LLD, DCL; *b* 1866; *e s* of Charles Murray, MD, and Elizabeth Mackenzie; *m* 1895, Christina Cameron; three *d*. *Educ:* Fredericton Collegiate School; University of New Brunswick (BA); University of Edinburgh (MA Honours in Philosophy); Berlin, Canadian Gilchrist Scholar, 1887–90. Professor of Philosophy, University of New Brunswick, 1891; Munro Professor of Philosophy, Dalhousie University, 1892–1908; President of the Univ. of Saskatchewan, 1908–37; LLD (Hon.) Queen's, 1904; Alberta, 1915; McGill, 1921; McMaster, 1923; Manitoba, 1928; Wisconsin, 1928; Dalhousie, 1938; DCL (Hon.), Saskatchewan, 1938; FRSC; Member of Halifax City Council, 1905–08; Member of National Research Council, Canada, 1917–31; Member of University Commissions, British Columbia 1911, Alberta 1915, Manitoba 1924; Member Dominion Commission *re* Property of Presbyterian Church in Canada, 1926; Trustee of Carnegie Foundation for Teaching, 1920–38; Member of Commission *re* Dominion Civil Service, 1929; Royal Commission on Transportation, 1931; Manitoba University Commission, 1932; National Film Board, 1939–41. *Publications:* educational and historical pamphlets. *Recreation:* curling. *Address:* Saskatoon, Saskatchewan.

Died 23 March 1946.

MURRAY-SMITH, Lt-Col Arthur, CBE 1919; Royal Artillery, retired; *b* 25 April 1868; *s* of Rev. I. Gregory Smith, LLD, and Agnes Augusta Murray; *m* 1899; one *s* one *d*. *Educ:* Marlborough; RM Academy, Woolwich. Served Hazara Field Force, 1891; Isazai Field Force, 1892; Chitral Relief Field Force, 1895; European War, 1914–18 (Brevet Lt-Col, CBE). *Address:* c/o Winter & Co. (Solicitors), 16 Bedford Row, WC1.

Died 3 Aug. 1943.

MURRAY-THREIPLAND, Col William, DSO 1916; of Dale and Toftingall, Caithness; DL, JP, Caithness; DL, Glamorgan; Colonel Welsh Guards since 1937; late commanding Welsh Guards and Regimental District; commanded 4th (the Border) Battalion King's Own Scottish Borderers; late Major Grenadier Guards; *b* 1866; 2nd *s* of late Wm Scott-Kerr, JP, DL, of Chatto, Roxburghshire; succeeded to the estates above-mentioned from his cousin-german Sir Patrick Murray-Threipland, 5th Bart of Fingask and Kinnaird; *m* 1899, Charlotte Eleanor, *y d* and *co-heiress* of William Wyndham Lewis, DL, JP, of The Heath and New House, Glamorgan; one *s* [*m* 1st, 1933, Marged, *o d* of Sir Stafford Howard and Lady Howard-Stepney of Cilymaenllwyd, Llanelly and Woodend, Ascot; 2nd, 1938, Margaret, *d* of R. F. McNair Scott, 44 Queen's Gate Gardens, SW]. *Educ:* Fettes College, Edinburgh. Lieut 3rd Batt. Royal Highlanders, Militia, 1885; 2nd Lieut Grenadier Guards, 1887; served in Soudan Campaign, 1898 (Khartoum, Queen's and Khedive's medals and clasp); served S Africa, 1900–02 (King's and Queen's medals with 5 clasps) European War, 1914–18 (DSO); retired as Captain 1902, and as Colonel, 1921. *Address:* Dale House, Halkirk, Caithness. *T:* Westerdale 201; New House, Llanishen, Glamorgan. *T:* Llanishen 80; Dryburgh Abbey, St Boswells, Roxburghshire. *T:* St Boswells 2120. *Clubs:* Guards'; New, Edinburgh.

Died 24 June 1942.

MUSPRATT, Brig.-Gen. Francis Clifton, CB 1918; CMG 1916; Indian Army, retired; Col of 1/XVI Punjabis; *b* 21 Feb. 1864; *s* of late H. Muspratt, ICS. Served Isazai Expedition, 1892–Chitral, 1895 (medal with clasp); Tirah, 1897–98 (clasp); European War, 1914–16 (despatches, CMG). *Address:* 44 Lansdowne Road, Bournemouth, Hants.

Died 14 April 1944.

MUSSOLINI, Benito; *b* Predappio (Forli) il 29 luglio 1883; *m* Signora Rachele Guidi; four *c*. *Educ:* Scuole Normali di Forlimpopoli; Università di Losanna. Nel giornalismo; redattore, con Cesare Battisti, del giornale Il Popolo di Trento; direttore della Lotta di Classe, organo della Federazione Socialista Forlivese, 1911; direttore dell'Avanti fino al settembre 1914; fondatore del Popolo d'Italia nel 1914; partecipò alla guerra come militare di truppa nel corpo dei bersaglieri, ferito nel febbraio 1917; eletto deputato di Milano e Ferrara nel maggio, 1921; Presidente del Consiglio dei Ministri, 1922–26; Ministro degli Affari Esteri, 1924–29 e 1932–36; Ministro delle Corporazioni, 1926–29 e 1932–36; Ministro delle Colonie, 1928–29; Capo del Governo, Primo Ministro, Segretario di Stato, 1926–43; Ministro dell'Interno, 1922–24 e 1926–43; Ministro della Guerra, 1926–29 e 1933–43; Ministro della Marina e per l'Aeronautica, 1933–43; Ministro Segretario de Stato per gli Affari Esteri, 1943. *Publications:* Il Trentino visto da un socialista; Diario di guerra; Discorsi politici; Diuturna; Roma antica sul mare; My Autobiography, 1928; (with G. Forzano) Campo di Maggio and Villafranca, plays. *Recreations:* violino, equitazione, scherma, automobilismo, aviazione.

Died 28 April 1945.

MUTTER, Rev. Cecil G., LTh Dunelm; *b* Jan. 1876; *y s* of William and Mary Mutter. *Educ:* Canterbury. Ordained at Salisbury; served curacy at Wellington, NZ; Chaplain to Archbishop of New Zealand, Diocesan Missioner and Canon of Christchurch, NZ, 1914; Vicar of Sydenham, NZ and Chaplain in Ordinary to the Bishop of Christchurch, NZ, 1923; Warden, Community of the Sacred Name; Vicar of Hartlip near Sittingbourne, 1931–38. *Address:* Roseneath, Hartlip, near Sittingbourne. *T:* Newington 25.

Died 23 Aug. 1942.

MYDDELTON, Robert Edward, JP, DL; TD; *b* 1866; *e s* of late R. Myddelton, Chirk Castle, and Catherine, 3rd *d* of Edward Gyles Howard; *m* 1898, Lady Violet (*d* 1901), *d* of 1st Marquess of Abergavenny; one *s* [Lt-Col Ririd Myddelton, MVO 1945, Coldstream Guards; *m* 1931, Lady Margaret Mercer Nairne, *o d* of Lady Violet Astor and late Lord Charles Mercer Nairne; two *s* one *d*] one *d*. Colonel RFA, TA. *Address:* 44 Clarges Street, W1. *T:* Grosvenor 2762; Chirk Castle, North Wales. *Clubs:* Orleans, Turf.

Died 12 Aug. 1949.

MYERS, Rev. Canon Charles, MA; Canon Emeritus of Salisbury Cathedral, since 1937; *b* 17 Dec. 1856; *s* of late Charles Myers, of Swanmore House, Bishop's Waltham, Hants. *Educ:* Eton; Balliol College, Oxford; Cuddesdon College. Assistant Curate, Wantage, 1881–85; Principal of St Stephen's House, Oxford, 1885–88; Vicar of Lyme Regis, 1888–94; Chaplain to the late Bishop (Wordsworth) of Salisbury, 1886–1911; Rector of St Martin's, Salisbury, 1894–1915; Prebendary of Durnford, 1905–26; Hon. Chaplain to late Bishop (Ridgeway) of Salisbury, 1911–21; Rural Dean of Wilton, 1914–19; Sub-Dean, 1919–26; Canon Residentiary in Salisbury Cathedral, 1915–27; Hon. Chaplain to late Bishop (Donaldson) of Salisbury, 1922–35; Prebendary of Calne and Treasurer of Salisbury Cathedral, 1926–37. *Address:* Ledenhall, The Close Salisbury.

Died 13 Feb. 1948.

MYERS, Charles Samuel, CBE 1919; FRS; MA, MD, ScD (Camb.), Hon. DSc (Manch.); Hon. LLD (Calcutta); Hon. DSc (Pennsylv.); Hon. Fellow (formerly Fellow) of Gonville and Caius College, Cambridge; Hon. Sci. Adviser (late Principal) of National Institute of Industrial Psychology; Member of Advisory Committee, War Office, on Personnel Selection; formerly Director of the Psychological Laboratory, and Reader in Experimental Psychology, University of Cambridge; Lieut-Col late RAMC; Consulting Psychologist, British Armies in France, 1914–19; *b* 13 March 1873; *e s* of W. Myers, London; *m* Edith, *y d* of I. Seligman; two *s* three *d*. *Educ:* City of London School; Gonville and Caius College, Cambridge; St Bartholomew's Hospital, London. 1st class Natural Sciences Tripos, Parts I (1893) and II (1895), and Arnold Gerstenberg Student, 1896, University of Cambridge. Member of Cambridge Anthropological Expedition to Torres Straits and Sarawak, 1898–99; House Physician, St Bartholomew's Hospital, 1899–1900; Professor of Psychology, King's College, London, 1906–09; Editor of the British Journal of Psychology, 1911–24; first President, British Psychological Society; President, Section J. British Assoc., 1922, 1931; President, International Congress of Psychology, 1923; Herbert Spencer Lecturer, Oxford, 1929; Hobhouse Memorial Lecturer, London, 1932; Joule Memorial Lecturer, Manchester, 1933; Bradshaw Lecturer, Royal College of Physicians, 1933; James Forrest Lecturer, Inst. of Civil Engineers, 1942; late Member of Home Office Factory Lighting Com. and of Industrial Health Research Board. *Publications:* An Introduction to Experimental Psychology; A Text-Book of Experimental Psychology; Present-day Applications of Psychology; Mind and Work; Industrial Psychology in Great Britain; Business Rationalisation, 1932; A Psychologist's Point of View, 1933; In the Realm of Mind, 1937; Shell Shock in France 1914–1918, 1940; (with Henry J. Welch) Ten Years of Industrial Psychology; contributions to various medical journals. *Recreations:* travelling, music, walking. *Address:* Winsford, near Minehead, Somerset. *Clubs:* Athenæum, Alpine.

Died 12 Oct. 1946.

MYERS, Sir Dudley Borron, Kt 1933; OBE 1918; *b* 23 Feb. 1861; *s* of Thomas Borron Myers, JP, of Porters Park, Shenley, Herts. and Margaret Storie, *d* of Rev. Canon Henry Melvill, of St Paul's Cathedral; *m* 1891, Anna Frances, *d* of late Major Thomas William Hilton, Indian Army. *Educ:* Eton; privately. In business in Calcutta, 1882–1912; afterwards devoted himself to voluntary public service; organised the European Association (of India) on an All-India basis, 1912–14; First President of the Association, 1913–14; war work in England, 1914–20; attached to the Government Commission for providing occupation for Belgian Refugees (awarded King Albert's medal), 1915: Hon. Secretary, Employment Bureau, Queen Mary's Convalescent Auxiliary Hospital for the Limbless,

Roehampton, 1915–19; Committee Queen Mary's Workshop, Pavilion Military Hospital, Brighton; attached to the United Services Fund, 1919; attached to the Conservative and Unionist Central Office, 1923–33; Joint Hon. Secretary, Conservative India Parliamentary Committee, 1924–32; Hon. Member of the Committee since 1932; Adviser on Indian Affairs to the Conservative Central Office to date of retirement in 1933. *Publications:* Spirit Guidance (published anonymously), 1934; Spiritual Forces, 1939. *Address:* c/o Lloyds Bank Ltd, 16 St James's Street, SW1. *Club:* Carlton.

Died 15 Jan. 1944.

MYERS, Leo Hamilton; novelist; *b* Cambridge, 1881; *e s* of F. W. H. Myers and Eveleen, *d* of Charles Tennant; *m* 1908, Elsie, *d* of late General William J. Palmer, Colorado Springs, Colorado, USA; two *d*. *Educ:* Eton; Trinity College, Cambridge. *Publications:* The Orissers, 1923; The Clio, 1925; The Near and the Far, 1927; Prince Jali, 1930; The Root and the Flower, 1935 (James Tait Black Memorial Prize, and Femina Vie Heureuse Prize); Strange Glory, 1936; The Pool of Vishnu, 1940. *Address:* Tilecotes, Marlow, Bucks. *T:* Marlow 626. *Club:* Union.

Died 8 April 1944.

MYERS, Rt Hon. Sir Michael, GCMG 1937 (KCMG 1930); PC 1931; KC 1922; Chief Justice of New Zealand, 1929–46; *b* Motucka NZ, 7 Sept. 1873; *s* of Judah Myers; *m* 1899, Estelle, *d* of Hon. Maurice Salom, MLC, Adelaide, SA; two *s*. *Educ:* Thorndon School, Wellington; Wellington College, NZ; Canterbury College (LLB 1897). Formerly: member of legal firm of Bell, Gully, Myers and O'Leary; Crown Prosecutor, Wellington; Administrator of Govt of NZ Hon. Bencher Inner Temple, 1944. Represented NZ on United Nations Committee of Jurists at Washington and at San

Francisco Conference, 1945. *Recreation:* golf. *Address:* 7 Upland Road, Wellington, W1, NZ. *Club:* Wellington (Wellington).

Died 8 April 1950.

MYERS, Tom; JP; Ministry of Health representative on local Committee for Administration of National Health Service Act; *b* 15 Feb. 1872; parentage very humble; *m* 1904; two *s* two *d*. *Educ:* Elementary school up to twelve years of age; three years of that period half-time. Member of Thornhill Urban District Council, 1904–10, Dewsbury County Borough, 1910–20 and 1935–43; Mayor of Dewsbury, 1940–41; MP (Lab) Spen Valley Division, Yorkshire, 1920–22; working life: factory, coal pit, and glass-bottle works, the latter for fifteen years; through the various stages of the trade. *Publications:* Housing and Health; pamphlets, Co-operation and Coal Supply; The Capital Levy, Liberalism and Socialism; Labour and Education; Coal under Capitalism; Trade in Armaments; Facts of the Cotton Trade; Who Pays for War?; The Economic Outlook; regular contributor to local Press and occasionally to the wider publications. *Address:* Thornhill Lees, Dewsbury, Yorks.

Died 21 Dec. 1949.

MYLNE, Rev. Alan Moultrie; *b* 2 Jan. 1886; *s* of Bishop Louis George Mylne, of Bombay, and Amy Frederica Moultrie; *m* 1922, Dorothy, *d* of Rev. J. B. Gray, DD, Crick Rectory, Rugby; no *c*. *Educ:* Marlborough; Keble College, Oxford; Cuddesdon Theological College. Lay Reader, Cathcart, Cape Colony, 1908–10; Curate, Rawmarsh (Yorks), 1912–13; The Lickey (Worcs), 1913–14; Alvechurch (Worcs), 1914–17; 3rd Class Chaplain to the Forces, 1917–19; Curate, Malvern Priory (Worcs), 1919–20; Vicar, St George's, Worcester, 1920–28; Rector of Bulawayo, 1928–36; Rector of St Cuthbert's, Port Elizabeth, 1936–39; Archdeacon of Matabeleland, 1928–36. *Recreation:* carpentering.

Died 5 March 1944.

N

NAEGELI, Otto, Hon. LLD Edin. 1927. Professor of Medicine, University of Zürich; Director of Medical Clinic at Zürich. *Address:* The University, Zürich.

Died 11 March 1938.

NAIDU, Madame Sarojini, Hon. DLit Allahabad, 1938; Chancellor of the University of Allahabad; Fellow of the Royal Society of Literature in 1914; *b* Hyderabad; *e c* of Dr Aghorenath Chattopadhyay, educationalist; of Bengali Brahmin extraction; *m* 1898, Dr M. G. Naidu, Principal Medical Officer of HH the Nizam's service; two *s* two *d*. *Educ:* Hyderabad; King's College, London; Girton College, Cambridge. Spent a year on the Continent; published three volumes of poetry in English, which have been translated into all the Indian vernaculars, and some into other European languages; also been set to music; delivered lectures and addresses in all the chief cities of India on questions of social, religious, and educational and national progress; decorated by King Edward with the Gold Kaiser-i-Hind medal for organising flood relief work in Hyderabad; specially connected with the Women's Movement in India, and the welfare of Indian students; Member of the Bombay Municipality, 1923–29; one of the leaders of a recent political movement for the freedom of India; elected first Indian Woman President of the Indian National Congress, 1925; delivered Convocation Addresses at some of the leading Universities of India; travelled throughout East Africa and South Africa on a political mission on behalf of the Indian settlers in 1924; lecture tour in the United States and Canada, 1928–29; represented India at important international gatherings; Delegate Indian Round Table Conference in London in 1931; Member of Govt of India Deputation to S Africa in 1932; Acting Governor of United Provinces, 1947; had Freedom of the Cities of Madras, Calcutta, Karachi, and others. *Publications:* Poetry—The Golden Threshold with a preface by Arthur Symons; The Bird of Time, with a preface by Edmund Gosse, CB; The Broken Wing; stories and articles in English and Indian journals. *Recreations:* motoring, gardening. *Address:* The Golden Threshold, Hyderabad, Deccan, India. *Club:* Lyceum.

Died 2 March 1949.

NAIRNE, Sir (John) Gordon, 1st Bt *cr* 1917; Kt 1914; formerly Comptroller, and late a Director, of the Bank of England; one of HM Lieutenants for the City of London; *b* 4 Jan. 1861; *o s* of late Andrew Nairne, Castle Douglas, Kirkcudbrightshire; *m* 1894, Narciza, 5th *d* of late Baron de Costa Ricci; one *d*. Officier Légion d'Honneur (France), 1918; Officier Order of the Crown (Belgium), 1919; etc. *Heir:* none. *Address:* Furlongs, Tring, Herts. *T:* Tring 2352. *Club:* Conservative.

Died 9 Feb. 1945.

NANCE, Rev. James Trengove; Hon. Canon of Peterborough, 1911–37, Canon Emeritus since 1937; *b* 5 April 1852; 3rd *s* of James Nance, surgeon, of Eccleshall, Staffs; *m* 1887, Mary Ethel, *d* of Edwin Ball of Pershore; no *c*. *Educ:* Winchester College (Scholar); New College, Oxford (Scholar). 1st Class Moderations, 1872; 1st Class Literæ Humaniores, 1874. Assistant Master, Haileybury College, 1876; Fellow of St John's College, Oxford, 1876–87; Tutor, 1878–86; BA, 1875; MA, 1877; BD, 1881; Deacon, 1877; Priest, 1880; Rector of Polstead, Suffolk, 1886–95; East Farndon, Northants, 1895–1905; Rural Dean of Rothwell (Third Portion), 1903–05; Rector of Cranham, Essex, 1905–08; Vicar of St Mary's, Leicester, 1908–16; Rural Dean of Christianity or Leicester, 1910–15; Rector of Wheathampstead, Herts, 1916–21; Rector of Peakirk, 1921–32. *Address:* 6 St Helen's Cres., Hastings. *T:* Hastings 2611.

Died 19 Nov. 1942.

NANTEL, Hon. Wilfrid Bruno; KC; *b* St Jérôme, 7 Nov. 1857; *s* of Guillaume Nantel and Adelaide Desjardins, French-Canadians; *m* 1885, Georgianna Gauthier (*d* 1930); three *s* one *d*. *Educ:* Ste Thérèse Seminary; Laval University (LLD). Alderman of the town of St Jérôme, PQ, during 10 years, and Mayor of same town for 6 years; elected for House of Commons, 1908 and 1911; Minister of Inland Revenue, 1912–14; Deputy Chief of the Railway Commission for Canada, 1914. *Address:* St Jérôme, County of Terrebonne, PQ, Canada.

Died 23 May 1940.

NAPER, Captain William Lenox, MC; *b* 1879; *o s* of James Lenox Naper (*d* 1901), and Hon. Katherine Frances (*d* 1879), *d* of 3rd Lord Langford; *m* 1902, Adela Mary Charlotte, *e d* of late Col Hon. Walter Rodolph Trefusis. *Educ:* Eton. Captain Royal Horse Guards, 1906–08; DL, JP, Co. Meath; High Sheriff, 1911; served European War, 1914–19 (France, Egypt, Palestine); ADC, C in C Egyptian Expeditionary Force, 1917–19; MFH Ballymacad, 1919–29; 4th Nile (Egypt), Alexander 1st, Greece. *Address:* Loughcrew, Oldcastle, SO, Co. Meath. *Clubs:* Kildare Street, Dublin.

Died 25 Oct. 1942.

NAPIER, 12th Lord *cr* 1627, **AND ETTRICK,** 3rd Baron *cr* 1872; **Francis Edward Basil Napier;** a Baronet, 1666; *b* 19 Nov. 1876; *e s* of 11th Baron Napier and Ettrick and Harriet, *d* of late Edward Lumb, Wallington Lodge, Surrey; *S* father, 1913; *m* 1899, Hon. Clarice Hamilton, 3rd *d* of 9th Baron Belhaven and Stenton; three *s* one *d*. Is a member of Royal Company of Archers (King's Bodyguard for Scotland); formerly Lieut 60th Rifles; Captain, 7th King's Royal Rifle Corps, during European War, 1914; Equipment Officer Royal Air Force, 1917; JP Selkirkshire. *Recreations:* shooting and yachting. *Heir: s* Master of Napier. *Address:* Thirlestane Castle, Ettrick, Selkirk. *T:* Ettrick 2. *Club:* Royal Forth Yacht.

Died 22 March 1941.

NAPIER OF MAGDALA, 4th Baron *cr* 1868 (UK); **Edward Herbert Scott Napier,** MInstCE; Indian State Railways; retired; *b* 16 Dec. 1861; 4th *s* of Field-Marshal Lord Napier of Magdala, 1st Baron, and 2nd wife Mary Cecilia C. I., *d* of Maj.-Gen. Edward William Smyth Scott; *S* half-brother, 1935; *m* 1900, Florence Martha (*d* 1946), *d* of General John Maxwell Perceval, CB; one *s* three *d*. *Educ:* RIE College, Coopers Hill. Entered Indian Public Works Service, 1883; retired 1909. *Heir: s* Lt-Col Hon. Robert John Napier, RE [*b* 16 June 1904; *m* 1939, Elizabeth Marian, *y d* of E. H. Hunt, FRCS; two *s* two *d*]. *Address:* PO Box 529, Nairobi, Kenya Colony.

Died 20 July 1948.

NAPIER, Col (temp. Maj.-Gen.) Charles Scott, CB 1945; CBE 1944; *b* 3 Feb. 1899; *s* of Archibald Scott Napier and Katherine Edith Liveing; *m* Ada Kathleen Douetil; one *s*. *Educ:* Wellington College; RMA, Woolwich. Royal Engineers, 1916–43; Col 1943. *Recreations:* art, literature, history. *Address:* c/o Lloyds Bank, Ltd, 6 Pall Mall, SW1. *Club:* United Service.

Died 16 June 1946.

NAPIER, Lt-Col Hon. Henry Dundas, CMG 1907; late Scottish Borderers and Central India Horse; *b* 16 Feb. 1864; 5th *s* of 1st Lord Napier of Magdala; *m* 1897, Sybil, *d* of John Gurney of Sprowston Hall, Norwich; one *s* one *d. Educ:* Harrow. Was Military Attaché at Teheran, 1901–02, at St Petersburg, 1903–07, and Sofia and Belgrade, 1908–11. Entered Army, 1884; Captain, 1895; Brevet Major, 1900; Lt-Colonel, 1910; retired, 1912; reappointed Military Attaché at Sofia on outbreak of War, 1914, and also at Bucharest, 1915; was captured by a German submarine in the Adriatic, 1915, and remained a prisoner of war for two years in Austria; British Military Representative at Sofia, 1918–19. *Publications:* Experiences of a Military Attaché in the Balkans; Field-Marshal Lord Napier of Magdala, GCB, GCSI, 1927; Letters of Field-Marshal Lord Napier of Magdala, 1936. *Address:* Scutts Farm, Hartley Wintney, Hants.

Died 13 Nov. 1941.

NAPIER, Sir Walter John, Kt 1909; DCL; Barrister-at-law; JP Cheshire; *b* 10 July 1857; *s* of late George W. Napier, Alderley Edge, Cheshire; *m*; one *d. Educ:* Rugby School; Corpus Christi College, Oxford; 1st class School of Jurisprudence; Lincoln's Inn; Studentship, Inns of Court. After practising in Vice-Chancellor's Court of County Palatine of Lancaster and on Northern Circuit commenced practice in Singapore, 1889; acted as an unofficial MLC, 1896–97, unofficial MLC, 1900–07; Member of Commissions on Education, and on Shipping Conference and of Committees to draft Courts and Civil and Criminal Procedure Codes; Attorney-General, Straits Settlements, 1907–09; Member of West African Land Committee, 1912; Member Surrey County Council, 1920–25; Chairman Minorities Committee and Member Executive Committee, League of Nations Union, 1925–35. District Grand Master Eastern Archipelago, 1903–09. *Publication:* Introduction to the Study of Law as administered in the Colony of the Straits Settlements. *Recreation:* gardening. *Address:* Chinton Hanger, Churt, Farnham.

Died 14 Feb. 1945.

NARBETH, John Harper, CB 1923; CBE 1920; MVO 1906; *b* Pembroke Dock, S Wales, 26 May 1863; *s* of a Methodist local preacher; *m* Aquila Elizabeth (*d* 1931), *d* of W. J. Anstey, Portsmouth; two *s*. Entered HM Dockyard, Pembroke Dock, 1877; Royal Naval College, Greenwich, 1882; Assistant Constructor, Portsmouth Yard, 1885; Secretary to Committee on Sheathing HM Ships, 1891; served at Admiralty, 1887–1923; employed chiefly on battleship designs; prepared original design of Dreadnought, 1906; responsible for several improvements which combined to make Dreadnought possible; Constructor, 1901; Chief Constructor, 1911; Assistant Director of Naval Construction, 1919–23; originated design of Ark Royal, pioneer aircraft carrier (reconstructed merchant ship, 1913), vessel renamed Pegasus, 1935; during war had charge of design and construction of immense numbers of oil tank steamers, mine-sweeping vessels, and aircraft carriers; since the war responsible under Sir Eustace d'Eyncourt for completion of cruisers Dragon, Emerald, Hawkins classes, and for re-designing and reconstruction of the aircraft carrier HMS Furious; Chairman of Joint Technical Committee on Aviation Arrangements in HM Ships (Admiralty and Air Ministry), 1918–23; designed (for Air Ministry) unique and successful craft as combined repair vessel and floating dock for flying boats; MINA since 1887; Adviser on Shipbuilding Timber Fireproofing Co., 1926; Technical Adviser to Chilean Naval Commission, 1927; actively engaged in social, temperance, and religious work; retired, 1923, but still interested in all technical and scientific progress. *Publications:* Three Steps in Naval Construction; King Edward VII, Lord Nelson, Dreadnought; A Proposed Aircraft-carrying Mail Steamer (jointly with Sir Eustace d'Eyncourt); History of Internal Combustion Engines and Development of Motor Ships; 100 Years Warship Building; Can Wood be Rendered Fire-proof; various articles in technical journals on Oil, Engineering, Flying Boats; Biographies of distinguished Naval Architects and Engineers, etc. *Address:* 63 Elmbridge Road, Gloucester.

Died 19 May 1944.

NARES, Maj.-Gen. Eric Paytherus, CB 1947; CBE 1941; MC; Commanding British Troops in Berlin since Aug. 1945; *b* 9 July 1892; 3rd *s* of Ramsay Nares, Kingston-on-Thames; *m* 1931; Jeanne (*d* 1936), *d* of Mrs J. H. Meyers, The Hague, Holland; no *c. Educ:* Marlborough College; RMC, Sandhurst. Cheshire Regiment, 1911; served European War, France and Belgium (wounded twice, despatches thrice, MC and Bar); Bt Major, 1919; psc 1928; Major, 1927; Lt-Col 1936; Col 1938; Maj.-Gen. 1943; Palestine, 1936–39, AA and QMG, 8th Div. (despatches twice). War of 1939–45, Middle East, Temp. Brig., 1940 (CBE, despatches thrice); North Africa and Central Mediterranean (despatches twice). Commander Legion of Merit, 1946. *Recreations:* golf, fishing. *Address:* c/o Lloyds Bank, Ltd, Cox & King's Branch, 6 Pall Mall, SW1. *Club:* Army and Navy.

Died 18 June 1947.

NARES, Owen Ramsay; actor-manager; *b* Maiden Erleigh, Berks; *s* of late W. O. Nares and Sophie Marguerite, *d* of late W. R. Beverley, artist; *m* Marie (actress), *d* of G. M. Polini; one *s. Educ:* Reading School. After contemplating a business career, persuaded by mother to try stage; trained for this profession with Miss Rosina Filippi for some time in 1908 and obtained first engagement at Haymarket Theatre in 1909; subsequently toured provinces for two years before a serious break-down in health necessitated a year's rest; after appeared in London continuously for eleven years before again touring provinces with own companies; toured South Africa early 1926. *Publication:* Myself and Some Others, short biographical sketch, 1925. *Recreations:* golf and most games; water-colour sketching. *Clubs:* Garrick, Bath.

Died 31 July 1943.

NASH, Prof. Alfred William, MSc, FCS, FIF, MIChemE, MI MechE; Professor of Petroleum, Science and Technology, University of Birmingham, since 1924; *b* 1886; *e s* of William J. Nash, CE, Ongar, Essex; *m* 1912, Betty, 2nd *d* of David Maurice Booker, Horsham, Sussex; one *s* two *d*. President of the Institute of Petroleum. *Publications:* The Principles and Practice of Lubrication; The Principles of Motor Fuel Preparation and Application; Editor of Contributions, The Science of Petroleum; numerous papers to scientific societies on petroleum. *Recreations:* shooting, fishing, riding, motoring. *Address:* Hapri, Solihull, Warwickshire. *T:* Solihull 0146.

Died 14 March 1942.

NASH, George Howard, CBE 1918; MIEE, MRI, FAIEE; *b* 1881; *s* of George Nash and Mahala Elizabeth Sarah Kent, of Lee, Kent; *m* Florence Clarice (*d* 1936), *d* of late Edward Mills, Mus. Bac.; one *s*; 1949, Monica Enid, *widow* of R. B. Macfie, OBE, FRCS. *Educ:* Grocers School; Northampton Polytechnic; London Univ. Apprenticed late National Telephone Co., Ltd, then with various electrical engineering firms till 1905, when joined the engineering staff of the Western Electric Co. Ltd, which Company later joined the Standard Group; Chief Engineer of Standard Telephones and Cables Limited, 1911–28; Assistant European Chief Engineer of International Standard Electric Corporation, 1920–28; European Chief Engineer International Standard Electric Corporation, 1928–29; Executive Vice-President of International Telephone and Telegraph Laboratories Inc., 1929–33; Vice-President of International Standard Electric Corporation, 1930–33; Vice-President of Mexican Telephone and Telegraph Co. 1929–33; on Board of Directors of International

Telegraph and Telephone Company, Ltd, 1928–33; on Board of Directors of Standard Telephones and Cables, Ltd, 1927–38; Chairman International Marine Radio Corporation, 1930–34; Technical Consultant International Standard Electric Corporation, 1933–38; Deputy Director, Ministry of Aircraft Production, 1942–45. During European War, 1914–18, carried out special work of research and invention, as follows:— Siesmophone, 1916; Nash fish hydrophone, 1917; Technical Adviser Admiralty Experimental Station, Portland, 1918–19; Member IEE, 1919; Fellow American IEE, 1919. *Address:* 1 Barons Keep, Barons Court, W14.

Died 7 April 1950.

NASH, Brig.-Gen. Henry Edmund Palmer, DSO 1918; *b* 6 March 1869; *s* of late Canon James Palmer Nash; *m* 1903, Diana Isabel Armitage (*d* 1943); no *c. Educ:* Charterhouse. Joined The Royal Scots 1891; Captain, 1897; Major, 1910; Lt-Col 1920; retired, 1923; served South African War (Queen's medal and five clasps); European War France and Belgium (DSO with Bar, Bt Lt-Col, despatches, Brigade Commander). *Address:* Ventura, Fleet, Hants.

Died 22 April 1949.

NASH, Rt Rev. James Okey, CR, MA and Hon. DD Oxford; MA, *ad eund.* University of South Africa; *b* 1862; *s* of Thomas Nash and Amelia Stewart; unmarried. *Educ:* King William's College, Isle of Man; Hertford College, Oxford (Scholar), 1st Class Mods and 2nd Class Lit. Hum.; Cuddesdon Theological College. Curate St Andrews, Bethnal Green, 1886–89; Resident Pusey House, Oxford, 1889–92; one of original members Community of the Resurrection; Vicar of Radley, 1895–98, Chaplain London Deaconess Institute, 1893–98; Resident Westminster Abbey and Mirfield, 1898–1902; came to South Africa, 1902; Head of C. R. House, Johannesburg; Examining Chaplain Bishop of Pretoria; Headmaster St John's College, Johannesburg, 1906–17; Coadjutor Bishop of Capetown, 1917–30; Member Lambeth Conference, 1920 and 1930; SA representative, Faith and Order Conference, Lausanne, 1927; and Edinburgh, 1937; resigned, 1930. *Publications:* The Victory of Faith, 1933; Joint Editor with Charles Gore, William Law's Defence of Church Principles. *Address:* House of Resurrection, Mirfield, Yorks.

Died 7 April 1943.

NASH, Paul; painter and designer; *b* London, 11 May 1889; *e s* of late William Harry Nash, Recorder of Abingdon, and Caroline Maude, *e d* of Capt. Milbourne Jackson, RN; *m* 1914, Margaret Theodosia, *o d* of Rev. N. Odeh, late Chaplain to the Bishop in Jerusalem; no *c. Educ:* St Paul's; The Slade School. First exhibited group of drawings Carfax Gallery, 1912; Exhibition with John Nash, Dorien Leigh Gallery, 1913; enlisted Artists' Rifles, 1914; later gazetted Hampshire Regiment; injured Ypres salient, 1917; returned to England; one of the official artists Western Front, autumn 1917; Exhibition of war paintings and drawings, Leicester Galleries, 1918; Exhibition of recent paintings and drawings, Leicester Galleries, 1924; Instructor in design, Royal College of Art, 1924–25; Exhibition of drawings and water-colours, Mayor Gallery, 1925; Warren Gallery, 1927; Exhibition of Wood Engravings, Redfern Gallery, 1928; Exhibition of Paintings, Leicester Gallery, 1928; British Representative Carnegie International Exhibition Jury of Award, 1931; Exhibition of Water Colours, Leicester Galleries, 1932, Redfern Gallery, 1935, 1937, and 1942; exhibited International Surrealist Exhibitions, London, 1936, and Paris, 1938; Exhibition of recent work, Leicester Galleries, 1938; exhibited room of paintings, English Pavilion, Venice Biennale, 1938. At outbreak of War organised Arts Bureau in Oxford for War Service; Official War Artist to Air Ministry, 1940; Official War Artist, Ministry of Information, 1941. Exhibition of applied design (1907–43) touring under auspices of CEMA opened

Ashmolean Museum, Oxford, 1943. Retrospective exhibition of paintings and drawings (1912–43), Temple Newsam, Leeds, 1943. Exhibition of paintings, drawings and designs, Cheltenham Public Art Gallery, 1945. *Publications:* Places, Prose Poems and Wood-engravings, 1922; Genesis, 12 engravings on wood, 1924; Room and Book (Essays on Decoration), 1932; Monographs in Contemporary British Artists Series, 1923, British Artist Series, The Fleuron, 1927, Contemporary British Painters, Soho Gallery, 1937, and Penguin Modern Painters, 1944; (posthumous) Outline, 1949. *Address:* 106 Banbury Road, Oxford. *T:* Oxford 59750; c/o Arthur Tooth & Son, 31 Bruton Street, W1.

Died 11 July 1946.

NASH, Sir Vincent, Kt 1902; created Knight Commander of the Order of St Gregory the Great by His Holiness Pius the X 1909; High Sheriff of Limerick 1902; received Coronation Medal, 1902; JP, DL; late temporary Major and Registrar of Queen Mary's Military Hospital, Whalley, Lancashire; *b* Jan. 1865; *s* of late James Nash, JP, Limerich; *m* 1896, Agnes, *e d* of late James Haran, JP, Limerick. *Address:* Shannon View House, Kilmurry, Co. Limerick. *Clubs:* County, Limerick.

Died 4 Feb. 1942.

NASIM ALI, Sir Syed, Kt 1945; **Hon. Mr Justice Nasim Ali;** MA; BL; Puisne Judge High Court of Judicature, Calcutta, since 1936. Additional Judge High Court, Calcutta, 1933. *Address:* High Court of Judicature, Fort William, Bengal, India.

Died 28 Sept. 1946.

NATHAN, Charles, CB 1944; *b* 23 Oct. 1891; *s* of Benjamin Arthur and Rosina Nathan; *m* 1921, Constance Marion, *yr d* of late Frank Chitham; two *d. Educ:* Rossall School; Brasenose College, Oxford. Entered Ministry of Agriculture, 1915; Deputy Secretary, Ministry of Agriculture and Fisheries, 1945–47. Served overseas with Wiltshire Regt 1916–19. *Address:* The Boot, Chearsley, Bucks. *T:* Long Crendon 293. *Clubs:* United University, Farmers'.

Died 10 April 1949.

NATHAN, Manfred, KC 1919; MA, LLD; Médaille du Roi Albert; Corresponding Member of the Institut International Intermédiaire; President, Income Tax Appeal Court, S Africa; member of Grotius Society; *b* Hanover, Cape Colony, 18 Nov. 1875; *e s* of late Carl Nathan, JP, and Cecilie, *d* of Dr Edward Nathan, PhD Hamburg; *m* 1903, Mina Florence, *d* of late E. J. Sessel, London; one *s* one *d. Educ:* Public School, Hanover; Gill College; Cape University, BA (lit. and phil. hons), 1894; LLB, 1897; LLD (by exam.), 1901; MA (hist.), 1910. Called, Cape Bar, 1897; Transvaal Bar, 1897; Barrister, Middle Temple; was junior counsel for Sir John Kotze in Edgar case, one of contributing causes of Boer War; represented German companies before South-West Africa Concessions Commission, 1920; Counsel for Delegation of Swazi Nation to Colonial Office, 1922–23; several times Chairman Johannesburg Bar Council; three years Chairman of Johannesburg School Board; a founder of the University of the Witwatersrand; member Transvaal Provincial Council, 1917–20; member Union Govt Flag Commission, 1926–27, and other Government Commissions; acting Judge, Supreme Court, South Africa, 1928, 1930; Vice-President SA Zionist Federation, 1901–06; King's Jubilee Medal, 1935; Coronation Medal, 1937. *Publications:* The Common Law of South Africa, 1904; 2nd edition 1912; Company Law of South Africa (3rd ed., 1939); Private Companies (2nd ed. 1938); various other works on South African law; The Renascence of International Law, 1924; The South African Commonwealth, 1919; South African Literature, 1925; South Africa from Within, 1926; Empire Government, 1928; (with Sir E. N. Thornton) Public Health Law of South Africa (3rd ed., 1941); Law of Damages in South Africa, 1930; Libel and Slander in SA 1933; Land and Mining Title in S Africa; Workmen's Compensation in SA; Finance and Revenue Laws of SA 1936; The Voortrekkers of SA, 1937; Sarie Marais (novel), 1938; The Huguenots in South Africa, 1939; Paul Kruger, 4th ed., 1944; Hire-Purchase, 1942; Not Heaven Itself (autob.), 1944. *Recreations:* walking, gardening, scribbling, travel. *Address:* Inland Revenue, Pretoria, SA. *T:* Johannesburg, 22.6829. *Clubs:* Authors'; Rand, Country, Johannesburg; Phyllis Court, Henley-on-Thames.

Died 12 July 1945.

NATION, Brig.-Gen. John James Henry, CVO 1917; DSO 1917; late RE; *b* 5 Dec. 1874; *s* of late General Sir John L. Nation, KCB; *m* 1932, Olive Elizabeth, *widow* of Capt. Walter Rubens. *Educ:* Royal Military Academy, Woolwich. Entered Royal Engineers, 1895; Captain, 1904; Major, 1914; Bt Lt-Col 1917; Lt-Col 1921; Col 1921; Instructor RMA, Woolwich, 1903–08; Staff-Captain War Office, 1911–14; Brigade-Major, SME 1915; AAG, GHQ France, 1916–18; Brigadier-General GHQ France, 1918; DA and QMG Marshal Foch's HQ, 1918–19; AAG War Office, 1921–27; Military Attaché, Rome, 1927–31, and to Durazzo in addition, 1928–31; retired pay, 1931; MP (U), East Hull, 1931–35; lent for service under the Persian Government under the terms of the Anglo-Persian Agreement, 1919; served South African War, 1899–1902 (despatches); European War, 1914–18 (despatches six times, CVO, DSO, Brevet Lieutenant-Colonel, Commander Légion d'Honneur, French Croix de Guerre, Officer of Order of Leopold of Belgium, Belgian Croix de Guerre); operations in NW Persia, 1919 accompanied Italian Military Operations in Tripolitania and Cyrenaica, 1928; sent on Military Mission to Italian Somaliland, Eritrea, and Abyssinia, 1928; retired with rank of Brig. Gen., 1931; Member of the Oversea Settlement Board, 1936–37; War of 1939–45 as War Correspondent; with BEF till April 1940; Zone Commander, Home Guard, 1940–42. FRGS. *Address:* Petersham Lodge, Petersham, Surrey. *Club:* Turf.

Died 5 Nov. 1946.

NAUGHTON, Most Rev. James; Bishop of Killala, (RC), since 1911; *b* Ballina, Co. Mayo, 1864. *Educ:* Maynooth. Priest, 1889; Administrator of the Cathedral, Ballina, 1891–1906; President of St Muredach's Diocesan College, Ballina, 1906–11; Assistant at Papal Throne, 1939. *Address:* St Muredach's, Ballina, Co. Mayo.

Died 16 Feb. 1950.

NAYLOR, Henry Darnley, MA Cantab; Emeritus Professor of Classics in the University of Adelaide, South Australia; *b* Scarborough, England, 21 Feb. 1872; *s* of John Naylor, Mus. Doc., organist of York Minster; *m* 1st, 1898, Jessie Cairns (*d* 1913), *e d* of late John C. Lloyd of Melbourne; one *d*; 2nd, 1916, Ethel Richman, *e d* of late Alex. McK. Wilson of Adelaide; one *s*. *Educ:* St Peter's School, York; Trinity College, Cambridge. First Class in Classical Tripos, 1894, and Walker Prize in Classics. Lecturer and tutor at Ormond College, University of Melbourne, 1895–1906; Vice-Master of Ormond, 1903–06; Vice-President of the British Classical Association, 1913; member of the Adelaide University Council; Governor of the Public Library of S Australia; member of the Council of St Mark's College (University), and Chairman of the Scotch College; contested (L) Whitehaven Division, 1929, and elected Governor of Keswick School. *Publications:* Latin and English Idiom, 1909; Short Parallel Syntax, 1910; More Latin and English Idiom, 1915; Horace, Odes and Epodes: a study in poetic wordorder, 1921; 365 short quotations from Horace with varied metrical versions, 1935; frequent contributor to the Classical Review and Classical Quarterly; also contributed to the Encyclopædia

Britannica of 1929. *Recreations:* bridge, addressing League of Nations meetings. *Address:* Oxenhope, Portinscale, Keswick, Cumberland. *T:* Keswick 201.

Died 8 Dec. 1945.

NEAL, Mary C. S., CBE 1937; *b* Edgbaston, Birmingham. *Educ:* High School. *Publications:* Editor, Espérance Morris Book, 2 vols; The Shakespeare Revival (with R. Buckley); English Folk Song and Folk Dance (with F. Kidson). *Recreation:* drama. *Address:* Green Bushes, Littlehampton, Sussex.

Died 22 June 1944.

NEAL, Sir (William) Phené, 1st Bt *cr* 1931; Kt 1930; solicitor, Bevois House, 27/30 Basinghall Street, EC2; Alderman, Ward of Lime Street, 1922–38, of Bridge Without, 1938–42; *b* 22 Oct. 1860; *o s* of William Neal, solicitor; *g s* of Samuel Neal, solicitor; *m* 1889, Eleanor Vise (*d* 1935), *d* of late T. G. Beatley, CC; no *c*. *Educ:* University College School. Admitted solicitor, 1888; elected Member of Ward of Broad Street for the Corporation of the City of London, 1893; Senior Sheriff, City of London, 1929–30; Lord Mayor of London, 1930–31; one of HM's Lieuts. for the City of London; Governor and member of the House Committee and special building committee of St Bartholomew's Hospital; Governor and Almoner of Christ's Hospital; Governor of St Thomas's Hospital; Past Master Bakers' Company; Past Master Horners' Company and Paviors' Company; Member of Livery Loriners' Company, etc. *Recreation:* shooting. *Heir:* none. *Address:* 3 Hyde Park Chambers, 159 Knightsbridge, SW1. *T:* Kensington 7719.

Died 7 July 1942 (ext).

NEALE, Edward A.; late General Manager Great Southern and Western Railway; Lieut-Col Engineer and Railway Staff Corps, Royal Engineers, (T); *b* Oct. 1858; *m* 1st, 1882; 2nd, 1906; two *s* one *d*. Entered Great Southern and Western Service, 1878; General Manager, Waterford and Central Ireland Railway, 1895; subsequently Traffic Manager, G. S & W Railway. *Recreation:* golf. *Address:* Athassel, Silchester Road, Dun Laoghaire, Co. Dublin. *T:* Dunlaoghaire 339. *Clubs:* National Yacht, Dunlaoghaire.

Died 8 Feb. 1943.

NEAME, Lt-Col Arthur Laurence Cecil, OBE 1920; JP, Kent; Chairman Faversham County Bench, 1939–45; High Sheriff of Kent, 1936–37; *b* 3 April 1883; *e s* of late Arthur Neame of Woodlands, Selling, Kent; *m* 1917, Hon. Dorothy Dewar, 3rd *d* of 1st Baron Forteviot of Dupplin, Perthshire; one *s* two *d*. *Educ:* Uppingham School; RM Acad., Woolwich. 2nd Lieut Royal Engineers, 1902; Captain, 1913; Major, 1917; served European War, 1914–18 (despatches twice, promoted temporary Lt-Col, OBE); retired, 1920, with rank of Lieut-Col; re-employed, 1941–45. *Clubs:* United Service, White's.

Died 23 April 1948.

NEAT, Captain (S) Edward Hugh, CMG 1919; *b* 12 April 1864; *s* of Rev. J. W. Neat, MA; widower; one *s*. *Educ:* Kelly College, Tavistock, Devon. RN, 1881–1910, retired. Secretary to Admiral Powlett, to Commodore Beaumont, to Naval Transport Officer, France, 1914–19 (despatches 4 times, CMG). Hon. Asst Sec. to Medical War Cttee, Oxford, during War of 1939–45. *Recreations:* were cricket and golf. *Address:* 41 Five Mile Drive, Oxford. *T:* Oxford 58525.

Died 6 July 1948.

NEATHERCOAT, Ernest Tom, CBE 1923; DL Sussex; JP; FCS; Chairman of Savory and Moore, Ltd, J. E. Hanger and Co. Ltd, Artificial Limbmakers Ltd, Pharmaceutical Products, Ltd, Laurence Press Ltd, John Kay Ltd, Moore's Stores, Ltd, Metcalfe's Stores, Ltd, Kemp's Stores Ltd, E. B. Jones & Co. Ltd, Hay's Grocery Stores Ltd, William Martindale Wholesale Ltd; Governing Director of G. S. Mascall Son & Co., Ltd;

Managing Director of Knoll, Ltd; Chairman of Prince of Wales's General Hospital, N London; FZS; FRGS; *b* Ely, Cambridge, 7 Aug. 1880; *m* 1904, Ada Jackson, Great Saxham, Suffolk; one *s*. *Educ:* Soham School. Pharmaceutical chemist and manufacturer; Chairman Weybridge Council, 1914–20; Chairman Pharmacy Board of Examiners, 1919–24; President Pharmaceutical Society of Great Britain, 1919–24; President International Pharmaceutical Conference, Diamond Jubilee Meeting, London, 1923; contested (C) Gower Glamorgan, 1924, and Cardiff South Division, 1929; Member of NE Metropolitan Regional Hosp. Board; Governor of St Bartholomew's Hosp.; Member of West Sussex County Council; Master of the Livery of the Farriers' Company; Governor of the Royal Agricultural Society of England and of the Royal Veterinary College. *Address:* Holbrook Park, Horsham, Sussex. *T:* Horsham 466. *Clubs:* Carlton, Athenæum, Devonshire, City Livery.

Died 28 July 1950.

NEEDHAM, Alicia Adelaide, ARAM, ARCM, LRAM, composer and pianist; *b* Co. Meath; *d* of J. W. Montgomery; *m* 1892, Dr Joseph Needham (*d* 1920); one *s*. *Educ:* Victoria Coll., Londonderry; Royal Academy of Music, London; studied pianoforte under Arthur O'Leary, and harmony and counterpoint under Prof. Prout and Mr F. Davenport. Ovate Bardess of the Welsh Gorsedd (title Telyn-yr-Iwerdon—Harp of Ireland). Hon. Member of the Irish Literary Society, London; Chairman first meeting of Pan-Celtic Association, Belfast, 1898; Associate of Philharmonic Society, 1902; prize-winner (six successive years) for the best original songs, etc., Feis Ceoil, Irish Musical Festival; winner of the £100 prize (Earl of Mar's Committee) for the best Coronation Song, 1902—words by Harold Begbie—entitled The Seventh English Edward; first and only Lady President Royal National Eisteddfod of Wales, 1906; during 1914–19 Searcher for the Wounded and Missing, B. Red Cross; on Roll of Honour St James's Palace. *Publications:* about 400 songs (including Husheen and the Fairy's Lullaby); My Dark Rosaleen, piano solos, duets, quartettes, Evening Service, and hymns; 12 Hush Songs, 1899; 12 Ballads for Bairns, 1900; 12 Lyrics for Lovers, 1902; Seven Songs for Soldiers, including Who Carries the Gun? and Who's that Calling? the words specially written by Sir Conan Doyle; 3 Dialect Songs, 3 Sacred Songs, 3 Love Songs—Arabic, Irish, Connaught; 6 new Soldiers' Songs—Bad Luck to their Marching, Might I March through Life Again, The Gordons, Ballad of the Victoria Cross, Passing Thro', My Dear and Only Love; Irish Song-Cycle—A Bunch of Shamrocks; 12 Small Songs for Small People; 100 Songs for the American Public Schools; Scottish Song-Cycle—A Bunch of Heather; and The Little Drummer, 1907; 50 French Songs, 1908; Numerous new songs and hymns, 1909; Army and Navy Song-Cycle, Red, White and Blue, 1912; Irish Song-Cycle—A Branch of Arbutus, 1914; 50 Christmas Carols, etc.

Died 24 Dec. 1945.

NEEDHAM, Sir Christopher Thomas, Kt 1919; LLD Manchester University; DL, JP for Lancashire; Chairman of National Boiler & General Insurance Co. Ltd; Director of District Bank, Ltd (Chairman, 1922–36), London & North-Eastern Railway Co., Manchester Ship Canal Co.; and of Alliance Assurance Co. Ltd; *b* 30 Aug. 1866; *e s* of John Needham, Eccles, Lancs; *m* 1902, Florence White (*d* 1905); one *d*. *Educ:* Manchester Grammar School; University of Manchester, BA. Chairman of Council, Manchester University, 1934–41, a Governor since 1908, Chairman of Union, 1892, of Convocation, 1911–14, and Treasurer, 1921–24; Pres. Lancashire Cricket Club, 1941–43; Member of Council of East Lancashire Territorial Army and Air Force Association; Trustee and Deputy Chairman of John Rylands Library; Member of Council of British Empire

Cotton Growing Corporation; Member of Manchester, Salford, and Stretford Joint Hospitals Advisory Board; Member of Manchester Civic Advisory Committee; President of Manchester Ear Hospital; of Proctor Gymnasium & Hulme Lads' Club, 1913–43; Vice-Pres. of Lancashire Playing Fields Association and of Manchester National Saving Movement; MP (L) South-West Manchester, 1910–18; Hon. Secretary Association of Chambers of Commerce, 1913–16; Director Manchester Chamber of Commerce, 1914–16; Member of Govt Committees on War Loans for Small Investors, 1916; on Reorganisation of Board of Trade, 1917; of Advisory Council of Ministry of Reconstruction, 1918; of Treasury Committee on Fresh Issues of Capital, 1918; of Company Law Amendment Committee, 1918; of Indian Currency Committee, 1919; of Advisory Committee, Chinese Indemnity Fund; of Royal Commission on the Civil Service, 1929–31; President of Manchester Statistical Society, 1919–21; President of Manchester Bankers' Institute, 1923. *Address:* Fair Oak, West Didsbury, Manchester, 20. *T:* Didsbury 1106. *Clubs:* Reform; Reform, Union, Manchester.

Died 29 April 1944.

NEEDHAM, Rev. Canon John Stafford; Chairman, Australian Board of Missions, since 1922; Chairman, National Missionary Council of Australia; Hon. Canon, St Andrew's Cathedral, Sydney; Lecturer, St Andrew's Cathedral, Sydney; Commissary for Bishops of New Guinea, Polynesia and Bunbury; *b* 2 Feb. 1875; *s* of Samuel Pascal Brasch Needham and Catherine Haynes; *m* 1904; six *s* one *d*. *Educ:* Grammar School, Fremantle; All Saints' Grammar School, Melbourne; St John's Theological College, Perth. Clerk employed by Felton and Grimwade, Melbourne; Civil Servant in Western Australia; Parishes in Western Australia and Queensland; Missionary to the Aborigines in Queensland. *Publications:* Report on Aborigines; Editor of White and Black in Australia. *Recreation:* reading. *Address:* Queen's Road, Westmead, NSW. *T:* UW 9585.

Died 26 Feb. 1942.

NEEDHAM, Bt Col Sir Richard Arthur, Kt 1932; CIE 1919; DSO 1916; *b* 1877; 4th *s* of late John Needham, Eccles; *m* 1925, Harriet Ellen, *d* of late Lt-Col R. Dewar, RA. *Educ:* Manchester University. MD; DPH; FRCS (Eng.); FRCP (Edin.). Entered Indian Medical Service in 1903; Bt Col, 1924; served N China, 1905–08; special duty with mission for repatriation of Chinese troops from Tibet, 1912; European War (France), 1914–16 (despatches three times, DSO); India, 1917–19 (despatches, CIE); Deputy Director-General Indian Medical Service, 1918–24; special duty, Organisation of State Medical Services, Railway Dept, India, 1925–26; Delegate of India at Office Internationale d'Hygiène publique, Paris, 1923 and 1927; Visitor of Medical Colls in India approved by the General Medical Council, 1923–30; retired from IMS, 1930; Visitor on behalf of General Medical Council to Medical Colleges, Rangoon, Ceylon, Singapore and Hong Kong, 1932–39; Visitor on behalf of Colonial Office to Medical Schools of Nigeria and Uganda, 1939–40; Member of Council British Medical Association, 1932–38; Commissioner, Indian Red Cross War Organisation, Middle East, CMF, Italy, 1940–45. Knight, Order of St John of Jerusalem. *Address:* c/o District Bank Ltd, 47 Old Bond Street, W1; Grosvenor House, W1. *Clubs:* Oriental, East India and Sports.

Died 24 Oct. 1949.

NEELD, Lt-Col Sir Audley (Dallas), 3rd Bt *cr* 1859; CB 1901; MVO 1901; DL, JP Wilts and Berks; retired; late commdg 2nd Life Guards; *b* Holt, Wilts, 23 Jan. 1849; 3rd *s* of Sir John Neeld, 1st Bt, and Eliza Harriet, *d* of Major-General Dickson, CB; *S* brother, 1900; *m* 1873, Hon. Edith Vivian (*d* 1926), *y d* of 2nd Baron Vivian. *Educ:* Harrow; Brasenose College, Oxford. Cornet and Sub-Lieutenant 2nd Life Guards, 1871; Captain, 1881; Major, 1889; Lieut-Colonel, 1899;

commanded Household Cavalry Regiment, South Africa, 1899–1900 (despatches); High Sheriff of Wilts, 1905. Owns about 10,000 acres. *Recreations:* hunting, shooting, etc. *Heir:* none. *Address:* Grittleton, Chippenham. *T:* Grittleton 2. *TA:* Grittleton. *Club:* Carlton.

Died 1 May 1941 (ext).

NEFF, Erroll Aubrey, CMG 1939; MD; DPH; Director of Medical Services, Cyprus, since 1934; *b* 1887. *Educ:* High School, Ingersoll, Ont; Toronto University; Western University. Served European War, 1914–19. *Address:* Medical Dept, Nicosia, Cyprus.

Died 28 Aug. 1942.

NEILANS, Alison R. N.; General Secretary, Association for Moral and Social Hygiene since 1913; Editor of The Shield (the British Review of Moral and Social Hygiene) since 1916; *b* 1884; *d* of Robert Neilans, Coldstream-on-Tweed, and Alison Ferguson Noble. *Educ:* private school (Langley House, Dulwich). Suffrage organiser in the Women's Movement, 1907–12; Honorary posts: Executive Member Internat. Council of Women, Internat. Alliance of Women for Suffrage and Equal Citizenship; Chairman of 2 International Committees dealing with Traffic in Women and Moral Welfare work; Member of Committee on Woman Power. *Publications:* Author of section Changes in Sex Morality, in book Our Freedom and Its Results, 1936; Are Moral Standards Necessary? 1935; other articles on sex problems. *Recreations:* mountain walking, gardening and all open air activities. *Address:* Livingstone House, Broadway, Westminster, SW1. *T:* Whitehall 4651.

Died 17 July 1942.

NEILD, Rev. Canon Alfred; Chaplain of Hukarere School, Napier, 1933; *b* 1865; 2nd *s* of Alfred Neild, Manchester; *m* 1899, Anne Meta, *d* of Major W. G. Stack; four *s* two *d*. *Educ:* Pembroke College, Cambridge (MA, Classical and Theological honours). Ordained, 1888; Curate of St James', Collyhurst, 1888–90, Grappenhall, 1891–93; Bebington, 1893–96; Vicar of Pohangina, NZ, 1897–1900; Warden of Selwyn College, Dunedin, 1900–05; Canon, Dunedin Cathedral, 1906–08; editor, NZ Guardian, 1904; Vicar of St Mary's, Mornington, 1906–13; Archdeacon of Dunedin, 1907–13; Chaplain, Te Aute College, 1922–33; Canon of Napier Cathedral, 1930; editor of Waiapu Church Gazette, 1935. *Recreation:* chess. *Address:* Diocesan Office, Napier, NZ.

Died 8 Dec. 1941.

NEILSON, Henry John, CBE 1918; MD; *b* 30 Dec. 1862; *s* of M. G. Neilson, Glasgow; *m* 1889, Ann Keil (*d* 1943), *d* of John Tullis, Glasgow; two *s*. *Educ:* Glasgow High School; University of Glasgow; Vienna and Berlin. House Physician and House Surgeon, Glasgow Royal Infirmary. In practice in Nottingham, 1888–1915; ex-President Nottingham MC; Major RAMC, 1915–17; Deputy Chief Commissioner of Medical Services, Ministry of National Service; Chief Commissioner of Medical Service, Ministry of Pensions; Divisional Medical Officer, South-western Division, Ministry of Health. *Publications:* Need for Statutory Revaccination; Observation of Pupil as a Guide in Administration of Chloroform, Journal of Anatomy and Physiology. *Recreation:* golf. *Address:* Heriot House, Woking, Surrey. *TA:* Neilson, Woking. *T:* Woking 339. *Club:* Royal Automobile Royal Clyde Yacht (Glasgow).

Died 13 April 1949.

NEILSON, John Shaw; Poet; Attendant Country Roads Board, Melbourne; *b* Penola, 1872; *s* of John Neilson and Margaret McKinnon; unmarried. *Educ:* State School, Penola, South Australia, State School, Ninimay, Victoria. First verse accepted by the Australasian, 1893; started to write for Bulletin, Sydney, about 1900; The Book-fellow, 1907; engaged in farming with his two brothers, 1902–16. *Publications:* Heart of Spring, 1919;

Ballad and Lyrical Poems, 1923; New Poems, 1927; Collected Works, 1934. *Address:* 160 Gordon Street, Footscray, Victoria, Australia.

Died 12 May 1942.

NEILSON, William Allan, MA, LLD (Edin.), PhD, LLD (Harvard); LLD (Amherst, Brown, Dartmouth, Princeton, Oberlin, McGill, Mt Holyoke, Middlebury, Vermont, Smith), LHD (Williams, Kenyon), DLitt (Yale); Commander of the Order of Alfonso XII (Spain); Chevalier de la Legion d'Honneur; *b* Doune, Scotland, 28 March 1869; *s* of David Neilson and Mary Allan; *m* 1906, Elisabeth Muser; two *d*. *Educ:* Edinburgh University; Harvard University. English Master, Upper Canada College, Toronto, 1891–95; Associate in English, Bryn Mawr College, 1898–1900; Instructor, Harvard, 1900–04; Adjunct Professor and Prof., Columbia, 1904–06; Prof., Harvard, 1906–17; President of Smith College, Northampton, Mass, 1917–39; Exchange Professor University of Paris, 1914–15. *Publications:* Origins and Sources of the Court of Love; Essentials of Poetry; Robert Burns; Intellectual Honesty; Edition of Shakespeare (Cambridge Poets); (Collaborated) Facts about Shakespeare, Tudor Shakespeare, History of English Literature; Associate Editor Harvard Classics; Editor Roads to Knowledge; We Escaped; Editor-in-Chief, Webster's New International Dictionary, 2nd edn. *Address:* Brinton Hill, Falls Village, Conn, USA. *T:* Lakeville, Conn 14–2. *Clubs:* Tavern, Boston; Century, Harvard, Town Hall New York.

Died 13 Feb. 1946.

NELSON, 4th Earl *cr* 1805; **Thomas Horatio Nelson;** Baron Nelson of the Nile and Hilborough, 1798; Visc. Merton of Trafalgar and Merton, 1801; *b* 21 Dec. 1857; *s* of 3rd Earl and Lady Mary Jane Diana Agar (*d* 1904), *o d* of 2nd Earl of Normanton. *Heir:* *b* Hon. Edward Agar Horatio Nelson [*b* 10 Aug. 1860; *m* 1889, Geraldine, *d* of Henry H. Cave, Rugby; five *s* three *d* Late Lt 3rd Bt Wiltshire Regt]. *Address:* Trafalgar House, Salisbury.

Died 30 Sept. 1947.

NELSON, Sir Amos, Kt 1922; JP; Head of J. Nelson & Sons, cotton manufacturers and doublers; *b* 31 Jan. 1860; *m* 1st, 1879, Mary (*d* 1931), *d* of Henry Driver, of Winewall; four *s* two *d*; 2nd, 1931, Harriet, *yr d* of W. Hargraves, West Marton; one *s*. Mayor of Nelson, 1903–06. *Address:* Gledstone, Skipton.

Died 13 Aug. 1947.

NELSON, Sir Arthur Edward, KCIE 1932 (CIE 1923); Kt 1929; OBE 1919; JP Oxford City; *b* 17 April 1875; *s* of H. Nelson, Uttoxeter, Staffs; *m* Sarah McLachlan; two *d*. *Educ:* Newcastle High School; Magdalen College, Oxford. Served in Central Provinces, India, as Assistant Commissioner, Deputy Commissioner, Excise Commissioner, Chief Secretary to Government; Member of Executive Council of the Governor of the Central Provinces, India, 1928–32; Acting Governor, Central Provinces, 1932. *Recreation:* golf. *Address:* 7 Brookside, Headington, Oxford. *Club:* East India and Sports.

Died 19 April 1950.

NELSON, Gp Captain Hugh, CBE 1944; MBE 1928; American Legion of Merit (Officer) 1946; AMIMarE; AFRAeS; retired from RAF 1945; was Deputy Director of Technical Training, Air Ministry; *b* 28 May 1890; *s* of late William Henry Nelson, Coventry; *m* 1919, Marjorie Douglas; one *s* one *d*. *Educ:* Bablake School, Coventry. Royal Naval Artificer Apprentice, 1905–09; Royal Naval Engine Room Artificer, 1909–11; Royal Naval Air Service, 1911–18; RAF 1918–45; Aviator's Certificate, 675 dated 1 Nov. 1913; European War, 1914–18 (despatches 4 times, 1914 Star and 2 medals). Royal Humane Society Testimonial for saving life at sea. *Publications:* Aero Engineering, 1937; Aeronautics, 1938;

Dictionary of Aeronautical Terms, 1946. *Recreation:* fencing. *Address:* Lynthorne, Normandy, nr Guildford, Surrey. *T:* Normandy 3161.

Died 1 July 1948.

NELSON, Captain Maurice Henry Horatio, CBE 1919; RN (retired); *b* 1864; *s* of Rear-Admiral Hon. Maurice Horatio Nelson; unmarried. *Educ:* Royal Academy, Gosport. Entered Navy, 1878; Lieut 1887; Commander, 1902; retired, 1919. *Recreations:* yachting, racing in Solent Handicap, Q class. *Address:* Summer House, Hamble, nr Southampton. *Clubs:* Royal South Western Yacht, Castle Yacht, Hamble River Sailing, Saltash Sailing; Royal Southern Yacht, Southampton.

Died 23 Dec. 1942.

NELSON, William Henry, CSI 1938; *b* 1880; *s* of David Nelson, Rosewell, Midlothian; *m* 1915, Iris, *d* of R. G. Walters, Calcutta; one *s* one *d*. *Educ:* George Watson's College; Edinburgh University; Balliol College, Oxford. Entered Indian Civil Service, 1904; Assistant Magistrate, 1905; Magistrate and Collector, 1911; Settlement Officer, Rajshahi, 1912; Deputy Commissioner, Jalpaiguri, 1920; Secretary to Govt of Bengal in the Revenue Dept 1928; Commissioner, 1930; Member Board of Revenue, Bengal, 1937; retired, 1940. *Recreations:* golf, fishing. *Address:* Derrybawn, Fleet, Hants. *T:* Fleet 250. *Clubs:* United Service, Calcutta.

Died 17 Jan. 1948.

NESBITT, Robert Chancellor; Chairman, National Mutual Life Association of Australasia Board for Great Britain since 1915; Deputy Chairman, British Law Insurance Co.; Director, Union Bank of Australia; Chairman, London Diocesan Fund; Member, The House of Laity; Member of Central Board of Finance; Member, Church Assembly Committee to consider Penalties of Præmunire; Treasurer of London Diocesan Conference; Chairman, Incorporated Church Building Society; a Governor of Guy's Hospital; Member, Executive Council, Hospital Saving Association; *e s* of Robt Henry Nesbitt, MA Oxon; *m* 1895, Lilian Mary (*d* 1942), 4th *d* of Edward Ellis, Shadingfield Hall, Suffolk; one *s* two *d*. Solicitor; former senior partner in firm of Markby, Stewart & Wadesons; Advocate of the Shanghai Bar; acted for the Welsh Church in the proceedings whereby the Royal Charter and Statutes now governing the Disestablished Church were granted; member of Council of the Law Society, 1909–26; Director, Solicitor's Benevolent Association, since 1917; Chairman 1936–37; Member of the Lord Chancellor's Committee on Supreme Court Fees, 1920; Chairman, Special Training Grants Committee, Ministry of Labour, 1921; Member of the Lord Chancellor's Committee on Circuit arrangements, 1922; Chairman, Ministry of Labour (Irish Court-Martial Officers) Committee, 1922; Vice-Chairman Rochester Diocesan Board of Finance, 1914–24; FSAScot; MP (U) Chislehurst Division of Kent, 1922–24. *Publications:* Trustee Companies, 1903; Church Finance in London, 1917; Three Strenuous Weeks, 1922; Reform of the Church Courts, 1934 and 1935; The Tithe Settlement Reviewed, 1936; Montrose, 1936; Nisbet of that ilk, 1942. *Recreations:* golf, travel, chess. *Address:* 87 Cadogan Gardens, SW3. *T:* Kensington 0626. *Clubs:* Athenæum, City of London; New, Edinburgh; Royal and Ancient, St Andrews.

Died 27 Jan. 1944.

NETTLETON, Wing-Comdr John Dering, VC 1942; Commanding a Rhodesian Bomber Squadron since 1943; Pilot RAF; *b* 28 June 1917; *s* of John Hennah Nettleton and Ethel Maud Barker; *m* 1942, Betty, *d* of Capt. G. Havelock, Paignton; one *s* (posthumous). *Educ:* Stansburys', Cape Town. South African Training Ship General Botha for 2½ years; Merchant Service 1½ years; joined Training Ship at 13 years old; Merchant Service at 16 years old; left Merchant Service at 17½ years and started Civil Engineering with Cape Divisional Council; joined RAF as Acting Pilot Officer, 1938; daylight attack on Augsburg, 1942 (VC). *Recreations:* cricket, tennis, Rugby. *Address:* RAF Station, Waddington, Lincs. *T:* Waddington 46.

Died 13 July 1943.

NEVE, Ernest Frederic, MD, CM; FRCS Edin.; FRCS Eng.; Consulting Surgeon, Kashmir Mission Hospital; Founder Kashmir State Leper Hospital; Vice-President Church Missionary Society; President Kashmir Medical Association; Foundation Member Himalayan Club; *b* Brighton, 1861; *s* of David and Mary Jane Neve; *m* 1915; Jean Sophia, *d* late T. G. C. Browne, Director of Guardian Assurance Society. *Educ:* Brighton Grammar School; Edinburgh University (MD with gold medal, 1885, Goodsir Prize, 1885, Gunning Lister Prize, 1889); Kaisar-i-Hind gold medal of first class for public service in India, 1918. *Publications:* Beyond the Pir Panjal; A Crusader in Kashmir; Things Seen in Kashmir; Kashmiri made easy; Eng.-Kashmiri Vocabulary; numerous articles to medical journals. *Recreation:* Himalayan climbing; first ascent of Mt Kolahoi and other Kashmir peaks. *Address:* Sonawar Bagh, Srinagar, Kashmir.

Died 6 Feb. 1946.

NEVILLE, Arthur William, CB 1942; Principal Assistant Secretary, Ministry of Health, 1938–46; *b* 8 Feb. 1884; *s* of late James Henry Neville, Kensington; *m* 1910, Ethel Louise, *d* of late Charles Yeatman Pannett; one *s* one *d*. *Educ:* Westminster City School; Jesus College, Cambridge. BA Hons London; BA, LLB and Lightfoot Univ. Schol, Cambridge. Barrister-at-law, Middle Temple; HM Inspector of Factories and Private Secretary to Chief Inspector, 1907; Inspector, National Health Insurance Commission, 1912; Insurance Dept, Ministry of Health, 1919; Asst Secretary, 1934. *Address:* Ottery, Highwood Hill, NW7. *T:* Mill Hill 2182. *Club:* Oxford and Cambridge.

Died 18 June 1948.

NEVILLE, Sir Reginald James Neville, 1st Bt *cr* 1927; JP Norfolk, and a Chairman of Quarter Sessions; Trustee of City of London Parochial Charities; *b* Bombay, 22 Feb. 1863; *e s* of late Mr Justice James Sewell Neville (Inner Temple), High Court, Calcutta, of Sloley Hall, Norfolk; *m* 1st, 1890, Ida (*d* 1913), 4th *d* of late Sir Edmund Henderson, RE, KCB; one *s* two *d*; 2nd, 1920, Violet Sophia Mary, *e d* of Lt-Col C. J. Baines, Gloucester Regiment; one *s*. *Educ:* Charterhouse (Scholar), Trinity College, Cambridge; Winchester Reading Prizeman. Barrister (Inner Temple), 1887; Recorder of Bury St Edmunds, 1905–43; Master Bowyers Company, 1929–30; MP (C) Wigan, 1910–18; Norfolk E, 1924–29; contested South Leeds, 1892 (and Bye), 1895, 1900, 1908 (Bye), and 1923; Wigan, Jan. 1910, Dec. 1918; Norfolk East, 1929. *Heir: er s* James Edmund Henderson, MC [*b* 1897; *m* 1932, Marie Louise, *o d* of C. E. Pierson, Flesk, Burnham, Somerset. Eton; RMC, Sandhurst. Served European War, 1914–19 (wounded, MC)]. *Address:* Sloley Hall, near Norwich, Norfolk. *T:* Swanton Abbot 36. *Clubs:* Carlton, United University; Norfolk County (Norwich).

Died 28 April 1950.

NEVINSON, Christopher Richard Wynne, Chevalier of the Legion of Honour; ARA 1939; RBA, 1932; NEAC; *b* Hampstead, 13 Aug. 1889; *s* of late Henry Woodd Nevinson, and late Margaret Wynne Nevinson; *m* 1915, Kathleen Mary, *d* of C. C. Knowlman. *Educ:* Uppingham; St John's Wood School of Art; Slade School; Julien's; Paris. Exhibited first work in London, 1910, since which date has exhibited continuously, London, Paris, New York City, Washington, Chicago; was in Flanders, 1914–15; discharged from Army, 1916 (Mons Star); first Exhibition of War Paintings, Leicester Galleries, 1916; appointed an Official Artist, 1917, and returned to France; ten Works purchased by the Imperial War Museum, five by the Canadian War Memorials Fund, Ottawa; series of drawings, etchings, and lithographs acquired by the British Museum,

Luxemburg, and Petit Palais, Paris, Harvard University, USA, National Gallery of Canada, Ottawa, National Gallery, Brussels; 1941, Fire of London, purchased by National War Records, Ministry of Information; other pictures at National Gallery of British Art (the Tate Gallery), Metropolitan Museum, NY, National Gallery of Wales Fitzwilliam Museum, Cambridge, Manchester, Walker Art Gallery, Liverpool; Dublin, Birmingham, Aberdeen, Cartwright Memorial Museum, Bradford, Northampton, Leeds, Belfast, Leicester, London Museum, Strass Museum, Zagreb, Newcastle upon Tyne City Art Galleries, Rochdale Art Gallery, Contemporary Art Society, Glasgow Art Gallery; invited by Czecho-Slovak Republic officially to represent British Art at Prague, 1920. *Publications:* Modern War; British Artists at the Front; The Great War; Fourth Year; C. R. W. Nevinson, Contemporary British Artists Series; Masters of Etching Series, The Studio Publications; Paint and Prejudice, 1937. *Recreations:* motor-caravanning, journalism. *Address:* 1 Steele's Studios, Haverstock Hill, NW3. *T:* Primrose Hill 1677. *Clubs:* Arts, New English Art, Royal British Artist.

Died 7 Oct. 1946.

NEVINSON, Henry Woodd, LLD Liverpool, 1935; LittD Dublin, 1936; Hon. Student of Christ Church, Oxford, 1940; *b* Leicester, 1856; *m* 1st, Margaret Wynne Jones; 2nd, 1933, Evelyn Sharp. *Educ:* Shrewsbury School; Christ Church, Oxford. Correspondent of the Daily Chronicle during Greek and Turkish War, 1897; in Crete, 1897; in Spain, 1898; and in Natal and Transvaal during the Boer War, 1899–1902; Representative of the Macedonian Relief Committee in the Monastir Vilayet, 1903; visited Central Africa, 1904–05, and exposed the Portuguese slave trade in Angola and the Islands of San Thomé and Principe; was in Russia during 1905–06; present at the street fighting in Moscow; was appointed to take the English Address to the President of the first Duma, 1906; travelled in the Caucasus and devastated provinces of Georgia, 1906–07; was in India as correspondent for the Manchester Guardian, 1907–08; at Barcelona during the outbreak of 1909, and at Melila for the Spanish Campaign in Morocco, as correspondent of the Daily News; in Albania for the Relief Fund, 1911; correspondent of Daily Chronicle with the Bulgarian army, 1912, and in Albania, 1913; was in Berlin for the Daily News at Outbreak of War, Aug. 1914, afterwards in northern France; helped to organise the Friends' Ambulance Unit between Dunkirk and Ypres; accredited by War Office as correspondent in Dardanelles for the Manchester Guardian and provincial papers; present at landing and evacuation Suvla Bay, 1915; wounded during attack on Scimitar Hill in Aug.; accredited as correspondent with British army at Salonika and in Egypt, 1916; and in France and Germany, 1918–19; leader-writer, Daily Chronicle, 1897–1903; Daily News, 1908–09; on staff of The Nation from its origin, 1907, to Massingham's resignation, 1923; writer for the Daily Herald; represented the Manchester Guardian at the Washington Conference, 1921–22; invited to accompany Captain Amundsen to North Pole, but reluctantly refused, 1925; Special Correspondent for the Manchester Guardian in Syria and Palestine, and Iraq, 1926, at the Naval Conference, Geneva, 1927, and at the meetings between Prime Minister Mr Ramsay Macdonald and President Hoover in Washington, 1929; President of the London PEN Club, 1938; President of the Council for the Defence of Civil Liberties, 1939. *Publications:* Neighbours of Ours, 1895; In the Valley of Tophet, 1896; The Thirty Days' War, 1898; Ladysmith, 1900; The Plea of Pan, 1901; Between the Acts, 1903; Chapters on France in Mr Hallam Murray's On the Old Road, 1904; Books and Personalities, 1905; A Modern Slavery, 1906; The Dawn in Russia, 1906; series of articles on the Caucasus in Harper's Monthly, 1907; The New Spirit in India, 1908; Essays in Freedom, 1909; Peace and War in the Balance (the Moncure Conway

Lecture), 1911; The Growth of Freedom, 1912; Essays in Rebellion, 1913; The Dardanelles Campaign, 1918; Lines of Life, 1920; Original Sinners, 1920; Essays in Freedom and Rebellion, 1921; Changes and Chances (autobiography), 1923; More Changes More Chances, 1925; Last Changes Last Chances, 1928; The English, 1929; England's Voice of Freedom, 1929; Rough Islanders, or the Natives of England, 1930; Goethe: Man and Poet, 1931; In the Dark backward, 1934; Fire of Life, 1935; Running Accompaniments, 1936; Between the Wars, 1936; Films of Time, 1938; Thomas Hardy, 1941; (posthumous) Visions and Memories, 1944. *Recreations:* in the past, walking, riding, rowing. *Address:* 4 Downside Crescent, Hampstead, NW3. *T:* Primrose 3794. *Clubs:* Athenæum, National Liberal (both hon.).

Died 9 Nov. 1941.

NEWALL, Hugh Frank, FRS, MA, Hon. DSc (Durham); Emeritus Professor of Astrophysics, Cambridge; Astronomer formerly engaged in astrophysical research at the Observatory, Cambridge, in connection with the large equatorial presented to the University by his father; *b* Gateshead-on-Tyne, 21 June 1857; *y s* of late Robert Stirling Newall, FRS, and Mary, *d* of Hugh Lee Pattinson, FRS; *m* 1st, 1881, Margaret (*d* 1930), *d* of late Rev. C. T. Arnold; 2nd, 1931, Dame Bertha Surtees Phillpotts, DBE, MA, LittD (*d* 1932). *Educ:* Rugby; Trinity College, Cambridge. Formerly Assistant to the Cavendish Professor of Physics, Cambridge, and Demonstrator in Experimental Physics, Cavendish Laboratory, 1886–90; Director of the Solar Physics Observatory, 1913–28; Professor of Astrophysics, 1909–28; Fellow of Trinity College, Cambridge; President of Royal Astronomical Society, 1907–09; President of the Cambridge Philosophical Society, 1914–16; Foreign Member of the Spectroscopisti Italiani; Vice-President of International Astronomical Union, 1925. *Publications:* papers on physical and astrophysical subjects. *Address:* Madingley Rise, Cambridge. *Club:* Athenæum.

Died 22 Feb. 1944.

NEWBERRY, Percy Edward, MA; OBE; Honorary Reader in Egyptian Art at the University of Liverpool; Fellow of King's College, London; *b* 23 April 1869; *y s* of late H. J. Newberry of Ealing; *m* 1907, Essie Winifred, *y d* of William Johnston of Bromborough, Cheshire. *Educ:* King's College School, and King's College, London. Began the study of Egyptology, 1884; Officer in charge of the Archæological Survey of Egypt of the Egypt Exploration Fund, 1890; undertook a survey of the Necropolis at Thebes, 1895–1901; on the staff of the Catalogue Général of the Services des Antiquities of the Cairo Museum, 1902; Brunner Prof. of Egyptology in the Univ. of Liverpool, 1906; resigned, 1919; President of Anthropological Section, British Association, 1923; Vice-Pres. Royal Anthropological Institute, 1926–27; Professor of Ancient Egyptian History and Archæology in the University of Egypt, Cairo, 1929–33; explored Gebel Elba region of the Red Sea Province of the Sudan, 1927–28; during the war engaged in gauge-making, and later Assistant Secretary London and South-Eastern Region Ministry of National Service. *Publications:* Thomas Carlyle on the Repeal of the Union, 1888; Rescued Essays of Thomas Carlyle, 1890; The Season's Work at Ahnas and Beni Hasan, 1891; Beni Hasan, 2 vols, 1892–1893; El Bersheh, 2 vols, 1893–1894; The Amherst Papyri, 1900; The Life of Rekhmara, 1900; The Tomb of Thoutmosis IV, 1904; Scarabs, 1905; Scarab-shaped Seals, 1907; Funerary Statuettes (Shawabti Figures), 1929, forming volumes of the Catalogue Général of the Cairo Museum; The Timins Collection, 1908; Dives Pragmaticus, 1910; in collaboration with Prof. Flinders Petrie, Hawara, Biahmu, and Arsinoe, 1889; and Illahun, Kahun, and Gurob, 1890; with Misses Benson and Gourlay, The Temple of Mut, 1898; with John Garstang, El Arabeh, 1902; and A Short History of Ancient Egypt, 1904; with Professor Maspero and

Theodore M. Davis, The Tomb of Iouiya and Toiyou, 1907; with the Marquis of Northampton and Professor Spiegelberg, The Theban Necropolis, 1908; with the Earl of Carnarvon and Howard Carter, Five Years' Explorations at Thebes, 1912; Burlington Fine Arts Club, Exhibition of Ancient Egyptian Art Catalogue (with H. R. Hall); The Floral Wreaths, in Howard Carter's Tutankhamen, vol. ii; (with Prof. Peet) Handbook to the Egyptian Collection of the Liverpool Museum, 1923; also numerous contributions to English, French, and German scientific journals. *Address:* Winkworth Hill, Hascombe, near Godalming, Surrey. *T:* Hascombe 48. *Clubs:* Constitutional, Burlington Fine Arts.

Died 7 Aug. 1949.

NEWBERY, Francis H., Cavaliere Ufficiale of the Order of the Crown of Italy; Member Internat. Soc. SPG; RWA; ARCA; Emeritus Director of the Glasgow School of Art; *b* Membury, Devon; *m* Jessie, *e d* of William Rowat, Paisley; two *d. Educ:* Art Schools, Bridport and South Kensington. Art Master, Middle Class Corporation Schools, Cowper Street, City; same at Grocers' Company's Schools, Hackney Downs; Art Examiner to local Trusts; Higher Inspection Scotch Education Department. *Publications:* Pictures purchased for the Public Galleries of Venice, Udine, Turin, Magdeburg, Munich, Santiago, Paisley, Exeter, Newcastle-on-Tyne. Medals: Brussels, Santiago. Diploma of Honour, Turin. *Address:* Corfe Castle, Dorset.

Died 18 Dec. 1946.

NEWBOLD, Lt-Col Charles Joseph, DSO 1916; BA; Managing Director A. Guinness, Son & Co., Ltd; Chairman Brewers Society; 2nd *s* of late William Newbold and late Eleanor Newbold, East Grinstead; *m* 1924, Daphne, *d* of late Algernon Perssé and late Hon. Mrs Perssé of Creg Clare, Co. Galway; one *s. Educ:* Uppingham (Scholar and Exhibitioner); Caius College, Cambridge (Scholar, Honours Nat. Sci. Tripos). Served in France with Royal Engineers, 1914–18 (Lieut-Colonel, DSO, despatches three times). *Recreations:* Rugby football, Cambridge Blue, English International. *Address:* Said House, Chiswick Mall, W4. *Clubs:* Carlton; Royal St George Yacht; Kildare Street, Dublin.

Died 26 Oct. 1946.

NEWBOLD, Sir Douglas, KBE 1944; CBE 1938; OBE 1933; Civil Secretary, Anglo-Egyptian Sudan, since 1939; *b* 13 Aug. 1894; 7th *s* of late W. Newbold, 7 Broadwater Down, Tunbridge Wells, and of late Mrs E. I. Newbold, Imberley Lodge, East Grinstead. *Educ:* Uppingham (Scholar and Exhibitioner); Oriel College, Oxford (Classical Scholar). Enlisted West Kent Yeomanry, 1914; commissioned Dorset Yeomanry, 1915; served European War with Dorset Yeomanry and Cavalry Machine Gun Corps, in Mudros, Egypt and Palestine, 1915–18; took part in Senussi Campaign battles of Gaza, and advance on Jerusalem (wounded); joined Sudan Political Service, 1920; took part in expeditions into Libyan Desert by camel and car, 1923, 1927 and 1930; Governor Kordofan Province, 1932–38; Order of Nile, 3rd class, 1935. *Publications:* various articles on archæology and exploration, in Geographical Journal, Antiquity, and Sudan Notes and Records. *Recreations:* archæology and squash racquets. *Address:* c/o Mrs T. G. H. Burton, Burr Hill, East Grinstead; Civil Secretary, Khartum. *T:* East Grinstead 490. *Clubs:* Conservative; Sudan, Khartum.

Died 23 March 1945.

NEWBOLD, John Turner Walton, MA; FRSA 1936; *b* Culcheth, Lancashire, 8 May 1888; *s* of Thos R. Newbold and Elizabeth, *d* of Jackson Turner, of Tunstall House, Kirkby Lonsdale; widower. *Educ:* Buxton College; University of Manchester. Joined Fabian Society, 1908; Independent Labour Party, 1910; left to join Communist Party of Great Britain, 1921; joined Plebs League for Independent Working Class Education, 1917; Member of Executive thereof, 1918, 1919, 1923; Member of Executive Labour Research Department, 1922–26; Member of Executive of the Communist Party of Great Britain, as also of the Communist International, 1922–23; engaged since leaving University in 1912 in industrial and economic research, lecturing in history and politics. Contested (Lab) Motherwell, Dec. 1918; MP (Communist) Motherwell and Wishaw Division of Lanark Nov. 1922–Dec. 1923; resigned from Communist Party and Communist International, 1924; contested (Lab) Epping, May 1929; Member of the Macmillan Committee on Finance and Industry, 1929–31; resigned from Labour Party, 1931. *Publications:* How Europe Armed for War (1871–1914); Politics of Capitalism; Capitalism and the War; Railways, 1825–1925; Democracy, Debts and Disarmament. *Address:* c/o Overseas League, 24 Royal Exchange Square, Glasgow, C1. *Clubs:* Overseas; University Union, Manchester.

Died Feb. 1943.

NEWBURGH, 10th Earl of, *cr* 1660; **Charles Bandini;** Viscount Kynnaird, Baron Livingstone, 1660; Prince, Marquis Bandini, Lord of Varano in the Roman States, Duke of Mondragone and Count of Carinola in late Kingdom of Naples; *b* Rome, 1 Jan. 1862; *s* of 9th Earl and Maria, *d* of Cavaliere Giuseppe Maria Massani of Rome; *S* father, 1908; *m* 1885, Donna Maria, *d* of Prince di Trabia e di Butera, Palermo; one *d. Heir: d* Lady Maria Sofia Giuseppina [*b* 1889; *m* 1922, Count Manfredi Gravina (*d* 1932)]. *Address:* 1 Via Virginio Orsini, Rome.

Died 14 June 1941.

NEWCASTLE, 8th Duke of, *cr* 1756; **Henry Francis Hope Pelham-Clinton-Hope;** Earl of Lincoln, 1572; [assumed additional name of Hope by Royal Licence, 1887]; *b* 3 Feb. 1866; *s* of 6th Duke and Adela, *d* of late Henry Thomas Hope of Deepdene, Surrey; *S* brother, 1928; *m* 1st, 1894, Mary Augusta (May Yohe), *d* of William Yohe (whom he divorced 1902); 2nd, 1904, Olive Muriel (*d* 1912), *d* of George Horatio Thompson, banker, Melbourne, formerly wife of Richard Owen; one *s* two *d.* Late Lt Nottinghamshire Yeomanry Cavalry (Sherwood Rangers). Owns about 35,600 acres. *Heir: s* Earl of Lincoln. *Address:* Harrowlands, Dorking; Castle Blayney, Ireland.

Died 20 April 1941.

NEWCOMBE, Major Edward Osborn Armstrong, DSO 1917; *b* 1874; *s* of late Edward Newcombe, MICE; *m* 1909, Anna Maria Laura (Nita), *d* of late Hon. Hugh Leslie Courtenay; one *d. Educ:* Bath College; Royal Military Academy, Woolwich. Commission Royal Engineers, 1893; served in Egyptian Army, 1896–99; Sudan Campaign, 1896–98 (despatches, Orders of Osmanieh, Medjidieh, British and Egyptian medals two claps); S African War, 1899–1902, on staff (despatches, Queen's medal with four clasps, King's medal with two clasps); European War, 1914–17, with Egyptian Army (despatches, DSO, Order of Nile); retired from active list, April 1912; Traffic Manager, Sudan Govt Railways. *Recreation:* golf. *Club:* Army and Navy.

Died 15 May 1941.

NEWDIGATE, Bernard Henry; author; retired publisher and printer; *b* 12 April 1869; 3rd *s* of late Alfred Newdigate; *m* 1919, Ada (*d* 1942), *d* of late J. H. Monahan, QC; no *c. Educ:* Stonyhurst Coll., BA Lond., 1887. Formerly Director, Art and Book Co. Ltd and Arden Press Co. Ltd; appointed by Board of Education to assist HM Inspectors in inspection of printing classes, 1913. Lieut, 8th R. Warwickshire Regt, 1914; Capt., 1916. Director, Shakespeare Head Press Ltd, 1921–42. *Publications:* St Augustine and His Companions (from the French), 1897; (edited) A Kempis, De Imitatione Christi in Latin and English, 1933; (ed.) The Poems of Ben Jonson, 1936; (ed.) The Phœnix and Turtle, by Shakespeare, Ben Jonson, etc., 1937; The Art of the

Book (Studio Special number), 1938; Michael Drayton and His Circle, 1941; joint editor of The Works of Michael Drayton, Vol. V, 1941; contributor on literary and typographical subjects to Times Literary Supplement, London Mercury, Tablet, etc. *Address:* Foxcombe Heath, Boars Hill, Oxford. *T:* Oxford 85142.

Died 24 May 1944.

NEWELL, Hugh Hamilton, CBE 1936; MInstCE; MIEA; Commissioner for Main Roads, New South Wales, controlling also Sydney Harbour Bridge since 1932; *b* Belfast, Ireland, 29 April 1878; *s* of John Newell and Margaret Shaw; *m* 1903, Ethel, *d* of John Holmes Reid, Tenterfield, NSW; one *s* three *d*. *Educ:* No. 6 District School, Erie, Pa, USA; Fort Street Model School, Sydney. Entered Public Works Department, Sydney, as Engineering Cadet, 1894; Asst Engineer in various country centres, 1897–1907; in charge of National Works District of Newcastle, 1907–12; District Engineer, Bathurst, 1912, Lismore, 1915; Head Office of PWD, in charge of sub-branch of National and Local Govt Works Section, 1917; District Engineer, Wollongong and Manager of Port Kembla Shipping, Electricity Power Supply and Harbour Works, 1924; Engineering Member of Main Roads Board of New South Wales, 1925, Deputy President, 1928, President, 1932; Transport Commissioner, Highway and Roads Transportation, 1932; Member of Council of Scots College, 1929, Chairman since 1937; Member of Council of Ulster Association of New South Wales, 1929, President, 1935–36; Member of New South Wales Advisory Committee of Institution of Civil Engineers (London), 1929, Chairman of the Committee, 1939; Member of Council of St Columba Grammar School, 1930. *Publication:* Road Engineering and its Development in Australia 1938. *Recreations:* gardening, model making, motoring. *Address:* Morambro, 89 Cabramatta Road, Mosman, New South Wales, Australia. *T:* XM3073.

Died 15 March 1941.

NEWLAND, Maj.-Gen. Sir Foster (Reuss), KCMG 1919; CB 1918; CMG 1917; AMS; MB, BCh Dub.; MD (Hon.) Univ. Dub.; *b* 10 Jan. 1862; *s* of Dr Foster Newland; *m* 1918, Donna Nennella Salazar y Mûnatones (who obtained a divorce, 1928), *d* of late Count Michele Salazar, Lieut-General Italian Army; one *d*. *Educ:* Shrewsbury School. Entered RAMC 1886; served in India; South African War (medal with five clasps); European War, France, 1914–17 (despatches seven times, KCMG, CB, Commander of the Order of St Maurice and St Lazarus, Italy, KG St John); DMS Italy, 1917–18; DMS Egypt, 1918–22; retired pay, 1922. *Club:* Army and Navy.

Died 24 Dec. 1943.

NEWLAND-PEDLEY, Frederick, FRCS Eng., LDSE; Consulting Dental Surgeon to Guy's Hospital, and for many years Lecturer in Dental Surgery there; Founder of the Dental School of Guy's Hospital; Not in practice; *m* 1916, Octavie Gertrude Bernardine Thérèse, *d* of Nicolas and Octavie Gathy, of Liége, Belgium; no *c*. *Educ:* Dulwich College; Guy's Hospital; Royal Dental Hospital. Formerly Dental Surgeon to Evelina Hospital for Sick Children, and the North-West London Hospital; Dental Surgeon to the Imperial Yeomanry Hospital, South African War (medal); volunteer Dental Surgeon to troops in France, 1914, and worked at No. 2 British Red Cross Hospital in Rouen. *Publications:* various contributions to the medical and dental press. *Recreation:* golf; twice winner of Open Championship of Belgium. *Address:* Heath-View, 22 Willow Road, Hampstead, NW3.

Died 4 May 1944.

NEWMAN, Edward, CMG 1923; JP; *b* 1858; *γ s* of Edward Newman, MD, Fleet Surgeon Royal Navy, of Craig Ailey, Cove, Dunbartonshire; *m* Katharine Anne Wilson; one *d*. *Educ:* privately. Came to NZ in early 'eighties and bought large block of unimproved land in Turakina Valley; improved and eventually subdivided and sold this in 1906; entered Parliament as supporter of Reform Party, 1908; retired 1922; Member, Legislative Council, NZ, 1923–30. Member, New Zealand Railways Board, 1931–36. Founder, NZ Sheepowners' Acknowledgment of Debt to British Seamen's Fund, by which about £250,000 was collected for benefit of dependants of seamen of RN and Mercantile Marine killed or wounded at sea during World War. *Address:* Dunsinane, Marton, NZ. *TA:* Marton, NZ. *T:* 84.

Died 24 April 1946.

NEWMAN, Captain Edward John Kendall, CBE 1919; RN, retired; *b* 1860; *s* of John Manby and Eliza Jenifer Newman. *Educ:* privately; HMS Worcester. Master, Mercantile Marine; Royal Navy; Benin Expedition, 1897; Boer War, 1899–1901; Admiralty Transport Officer, London and Rotterdam, 1914.

Died 17 Dec. 1941.

NEWMAN, Lt-Col Ernest Alan Robert, CIE 1918; MD; IMS, retired; Consulting Ophthalmic Surgeon Rutland Co. Council; *b* 1867; *m* 1901, Lilian Duggan, *d* of Lt-Col J. Young; one *s* one *d*. *Educ:* Haileybury; Caius Coll., Cambridge; St Bartholomew's Hospital. Superintendent Medical School, and Civil Surgeon, Dacca, Bengal; retired, 1923. *Address:* Ramna, N Luffenham, Oakham, Rutland. *T:* 207.

Died 2 March 1943.

NEWMAN, Frank Herbert; *b* Lucknow, India, 1875; 4th *s* of F. A. Newman, ICS; *m* 1907, Muriel, *e d* of E. C. Cadle; one *s* three *d*. *Educ:* The Royal College of Science, London; University of Bonn; University of Leipzig; the Sorbonne, Paris. Visited United States to study Educational Conditions, 1900; Director of Technical Instruction, Carlisle, 1901; appointed to organise Higher Education in Norwich, 1903; Educational Adviser, Durham Council, 1904; Educational Adviser to the North Riding (Yorks) County Council, 1907; Principal of Battersea Polytechnic, 1915–19. *Publications:* Report on Higher Education in the county of Durham; various contributions to Nature and Educational Journals. *Recreations:* walking, gardening. *Address:* Deep Cut, Frimley, Surrey.

Died 27 Nov. 1948.

NEWMAN, Sir George, GBE 1935; KCB 1918; Kt 1911; MD (Edin.); Hon. DCL (Durham); Hon. LLD (London, Edin., McGill, Toronto, Glasgow, Leeds); Hon. DSc (Oxford); Hon. FRCS Eng.; FRSE; DPH (Cambridge); FRCP (Lond.); Hon. Freeman Society of Apothecaries of London; Hon. Member of Public Health Association of Australasia; Hon. Fellow, New York Academy of Medicine and Fellow of King's College, London; Fothergill Gold Medal, 1935; Bisset-Hawkins Gold Medal, RCP, 1935; Formerly Crown Nominee and Treasurer General Medical Council; *b* 23 Oct. 1870; *m* 1898, Adelaide Constance (*d* 1946), *d* of Samuel Thorp, Alderley Edge. *Educ:* Univ. of Edinburgh; King's College, London. Senior Demonstrator of Bacteriology and Infective Diseases in King's College, London, 1896–1900; Emeritus Lecturer on Public Health, St Bartholomew's Hospital, University of London; late Medical Officer of Finsbury and Bedfordshire County; Chief Medical Officer Ministry of Health, 1919–35 and Board of Education, 1907–35; Chairman of Health of Munition Workers Committee; Medical Member of Central Control Board (Liquor Traffic), 1915–19, and Member of Inter-Departmental Committees on Playgrounds, Reformatories, Tuberculosis, Medical Research, Production and Distribution of Milk, Dental Registration, Post-Graduate Medical Education, Maternal Mortality, etc.; Chairman of Trustees of Dartford Physical Training College; Yale Lecturer, 1927; Linacre, 1928; Gresham, 1929; Halley Stewart, 1930; Heath Clark, 1931. *Publications:* Bacteriology of Milk,

1903 (joint author); Bacteriology and the Public Health 1904; Hygiene and Public Health, 1917; Infant Mortality, 1906; An Outline of the Practice of Preventive Medicine, 1919; Recent Advances in Medical Education in England, 1923; Interpreters of Nature, 1927; Yale Lecturers on Citizenship, 1928; Halley Stewart Lectures on Health and Social Evolution, 1930; Rise of Preventive Medicine, 1932; The Building of a Nation's Health, 1939; official Reports, 1908–1935. *Address:* Grims Wood, Harrow Weald, Middlesex. *T:* Hatch End 79. *Club:* Athenæum.

Died 26 May 1948.

NEWMAN, Harold Lancelot, CIE 1930; *b* 5 Aug. 1878; *s* of late C. P. Newman, Lloyds Bank, Ltd; *m* 1905, May, *d* of Professor T. A. Hearson, MICE; three *d*. *Educ:* Marlborough; RIEC, Coopers Hill. Indian Forest Service, entered as Assistant Conservator of Forests, 1901; Conservator of Forests, 1922; Chief Conservator of Forests, Bombay Presidency, 1928; retired 1933. *Recreations:* shooting, golf, bridge. *Address:* 51 Redcliffe Gdns, SW10. *T:* Fremantle 7911. *Club:* East India and Sports.

Died 12 Feb. 1949.

NEWMAN, Sir John Robert Pretyman, Kt 1924; JP, DL; late Major, Middlesex Regiment; *b* 22 Aug. 1871; *s* of late John A. R. Newman, JP, DL, of Newberry Manor, Co. Cork, and Matilde, *d* of Col Bramston-Smith, JP, DL, of Pencraig, Anglesea; *m* 1st, 1895, Olive (*d* 1896), *d* of Lord Plunket, DD, Archbishop of Dublin; 2nd, 1898, Ina (*d* 1935), *o c* of late Col Wm Pretyman, 60th Rifles; 3rd, 1945, Ethel, *y d* of late Thomas Dainty, Geddington, Northants. *Educ:* Charterhouse; Trinity College, Cambridge; BA, 1893. Succeeded to estates on death of his father, 1893; contested (C) SE Division of Essex, 1906; MP (U) Enfield Div. Middlesex, 1910; Finchley Division, Middlesex, Dec. 1918–23; served as Captain in 5th Batt. (Militia) Royal Munster Fusiliers, and in European War in France as Major in 17th Battalion (Footballers) Middlesex Regiment. *Recreations:* hunting, shooting. *Clubs:* Carlton, Royal Automobile; Kildare Street, Dublin.

Died 12 March 1947.

NEWMAN, William Henry, CBE 1939; Ship-Broker; Senior Partner of W. H. Newman and Son since 1927; *b* 3 Feb. 1865; *m* 1897, Mary Jane Weiss, British Born Subject; (son, Pilot Officer Newman, killed on active service 28 May 1940). one *d*. *Educ:* Gravesend, Kent. Seven years in Coal Merchant's Office, London; proceeded to Antwerp 1889; engaged in Ship-Broker's Office 18 years; commenced business on own account 1907, as Ship-Broker, Chartering and Forwarding Agent; President British Chamber of Commerce in Belgium for five years, 1928–32. Officier de L'Ordre de Leopold; King Albert's Medal. *Recreations:* golf, music. *Address:* 4 Avenue Marie Thérèse, Antwerp. *TA:* Newman Antwerp. *T:* 28985. *Club:* Constitutional.

Died 13 April 1947.

NEWNHAM, Ernest Percy, CIE 1919; *b* 1870; *m* Alice Edith (*d* 1934). Chief Instructor, Royal Indian Marine Dockyard, Bombay. *Address:* South Logan, Devonshire Road, Sutton. *T:* Sutton 1744.

Died 26 Dec. 1943.

NEWNHAM, Rt Rev. Jervois Arthur, MA, DD Hon.; LLD Hon.; *b* 1852; *s* of Rev. G. W. Newnham, Vicar of Combe Down, Bath, and Catherine Penneck Read; *m* 1892, Letitia Agnes, *d* of Rev. W. Henderson, DD, Principal of Montreal Diocesan Theological College; five *d*. *Educ:* Bath College; private tutors; McGill University, Montreal; Diocesan Theological College. Incumbent of Onslow, Montreal Diocese; Curate Christ Church Cathedral, Montreal; Rector St Matthias, Montreal; Missionary, Moosonee; Bishop of Moosonee,

1893–1904; of Saskatchewan, 1904–21; Rector of Clifton, Bedfordshire, 1921–25. *Address:* 6 Rockwood Place, Hamilton, Ont, Canada.

Died 12 Jan. 1941.

NEWNHAM, William Harry Christopher, MA (Cantab), MB (Cantab), MRCS (Eng.); Gynæcologist to the Bristol General Hospital; *b* 1859; *s* of Dr Newnham of Wolverhampton; *m* Kathleen Mervyn (*d* 1923), 2nd *d* of late W. C. Beloe; two *d*. *Educ:* Wolverhampton; Caius College, Cambridge. House Surgeon, House Physician, and Resident Obstetric, Guy's Hospital; Resident Medical Officer at the Evelina Hospital for Sick Children; House Surgeon at the Bristol General Hospital. *Publications:* Hysterectomy for Malignant Disease; Intra-peritoneal Hysterectomy; Ruptured Tubal Pregnancy; Removal of Fibro-Myoma, 18 Ibs. 11 ounces. *Address:* Cambridge House, 16–17 Royal York Crescent, Clifton, Bristol, 8. *T:* 1342 Bristol. *Club:* Clifton.

Died 11 Jan. 1941.

NEWPORT, Surg. Captain Alexander Charles William, CVO 1922; MVO 1920; RN, retired; *b* 1874; *m* 1907, Florence Mabel (*d* 1934), *d* of late Capt. H. T. Anley, The Buffs. *Educ:* Dover College. Served European War 1914–19. *Address:* 17 Cousins Grove, Southsea.

Died 19 April 1948.

NEWSHOLME, Sir Arthur, KCB 1917; CB 1912; MD Lond. (qual. for gold medal), 1881; MB (Univ. Schol. in Med.), 1880; FRCP Lond. 1898, M 1893 (St Thos); late Principal Medical Officer, Local Government Board; *b* 1857; *s* of Robert Newsholme, Haworth, Yorks; *m* 1881, Sara (*d* 1933), *d* of William Mansford, Marlborough, Lincoln. Pres. Society Medical Officers of Health, 1900–01; late Medical Officer of Health, Brighton; late Examiner in Public Health to the University, Cambridge, Examiner in State Medicine, University, London, and Examiner in Preventive Medicine, University, Oxford; Milroy Lect. RCP 1895; late Consulting Medical Officer Westminster and Battersea Training Colls, and Medical Officer Health, Clapham and Brighton; Member of Inter. Department Committees on Tuberculosis, Dental Registration, etc.; of the Army Sanitary Committee; Lieut-Col RAMC (T); late Lecturer on Public Health, Johns Hopkins Univ. *Publications:* The Ministry of Health, 1925; Evolution of Preventive Medicine, 1927; The Story of Modern Preventive Medicine, 1929; International Studies on the Relation between the Private and Official Practice of Medicine, 1931, Volumes I–III, 1931–1932; Medicine and the State, 1932; (with J. A. Kingsbury) Red Medicine, 1934; Fifty Years in Public Health, 1935; The Last Thirty Years in Public Health, 1936; various reports on Child Mortality, etc., to the Local Government Board; Elements of Vital Statistics, 1889, 1924; The Brighton Life Tables, 1881–1890 and 1891–1923; Natural History and Affinities of Rheumatic Fever (Milroy Lecture), 1895; Epidemic Diphtheria: a Research on the Origin and Spread of the Disease from an International Standpoint, 1898; The Prevention of Tuberculosis, 1908; contrib. 'Vital Statistics of Peabody Buildings,' Jl Stat. Soc., 1891; 'A National System of Notification and Registration of Sickness,' ibid. 1895; 'The Alleged Increase of Cancer' (with G. King, FIA), Proc. Roy. Soc. 1895; 'The Spread of Enteric Fever by means of Sewage-contaminated Shellfish,' Jl Sanit. Inst. 1896, etc.; The Prevention of Phthisis, with special reference to its Notification to the Med. Off. Health, 1899; 'An Inquiry into the Principal Causes of the Reduction of the Death-Rate from Phthisis,' Jl Hyg., 1906; American Addresses on Health and Insurance, 1920. *Address:* The White House, Durrington Hill, Worthing.

Died 17 May 1943.

NEWSON, Sir Percy Wilson, 1st Bt *cr* 1921; Kt 1920; Director of East Indian Coal Company Ltd; *b* 4 April 1874; *y s* of late William Henry Newson, Suffolk; *m* 1908, Helena, *er d* of late Lt-Col Denham Franklin, Co. Cork; two *d*. President of the Bank of Bengal, 1920; a Governor of the Imperial Bank of India, 1921; MP (C) Tamworth Division of Warwickshire, 1922–23. *Heir:* none. *Address:* Kingsclear, Camberley, Surrey. *T:* Camberley 300. *Club:* Carlton.

Died 17 May 1950 (ext).

NEWSTEAD, Robert, FRS 1912; JP (Chester); MSc; Emeritus Professor of Entomology, Liverpool University; Tutor of Rural Economy, The College, Chester, 1929–31; Associate Linnæan Society; Fellow Entomological Society; Hon. Member Royal Horticultural Society; Hon. Curator and Chairman Chester and North Wales Archæological Society; Grosvenor Museum, Chester; Hon. Freedom City of Chester, 1936; *b* 11 Sept. 1859; *m*. Acted as assistant to late Miss Ormerod; Pres. N Western Federation of Museums and Art Galleries, 1938; Pres. Assoc. of Economic Biologists, 1912–13, President Chester Society of Natural Science, Literature and Art, 1912–14, 1929–31; member Imperial Bureau of Entomology; member of the Big Game and Sleeping Sickness Committee; member of Committee for the Economic Preservation of Birds. *Publications:* Monograph of the Coccidæ of the British Isles; a Guide to the Study of the Tsetse-flies; various papers on Economic Entomology and Pathogenic Animals, Archæology, etc. *Address:* St Mary's Cottage, 67 Handbridge, Chester.

Died 16 Feb. 1947.

NEWSUM, Sir Clement Henry, Kt 1935; JP, DL; *b* 1865; *m* 1891, Alice Maude, (*d* 1946), *d* of Alderman George Neill, JP, Rotherham, Yorks. High Sheriff, Lincolnshire, 1924. *Address:* Eastwood House, Greetwell Road, Lincoln.

Died 17 Nov. 1947.

NEWTE, Horace Wykeham Can; author and playwright; 3rd *s* of late Frederic Charles and Louisa Newte; *m* 1898, Vera Irene, *d* of late Baron von Rasch. *Educ:* Christ's Hospital. *Publications:* The Red Rosette; The Wife; The Square Mile; Sparrows; The Lonely Lovers; Calico Jack; The Sins of the Children; The Socialist Countess; The Ealing Miracle; Living Pictures; Pansy Meares; The Home of the Seven Devils; A Young Lady; A Pillar of Salt; Salvation Sal; Sidelights, 1916; Ruth, the Woman Who Loved, 1916; He whom I Follow, 1917; The House that Fell, 1917; The Experiment; A Good Time, 1919; The Rogue's Progress; The Gentle Bigamist, 1920; The Extra Lady, 1922; Treasure Upon Earth, 1923; The Triumph, 1924; Whither, 1925; House Sinister, 1930; 14 one-act plays produced in London and provinces; over ninety short stories in magazines and London and provincial newspapers and over a thousand special articles in London and provincial newspapers. *Address:* c/o Barclays Bank, 191 Earls Court Rd, SW5.

Died 25 Dec. 1949.

NEWTON, 2nd Baron *cr* 1892; **Thomas Wodehouse Legh;** PC 1915; JP; DL; *b* 19 March 1857; *e s* of 1st Baron Newton and Emily, *d* of late Ven. C. Wodehouse, Archdeacon of Norwich; *S* father, 1899; *m* 1880, Evelyn ((*d* 1931) author of The House of Lyme, 1917; Lyme Letters, 1660–1760, 1925), *d* of late W. Bromley-Davenport; two *s* three *d*. *Educ:* Eton; Christ Church, Oxford. Diplomatic Service, 1880–86; Major, Imperial Yeomanry; MP (C) Newton, Lancashire, 1886–99; Paymaster-General, 1915–16; Assistant Under-Secretary of State for Foreign Affairs (unpaid), 1916; Controller of Prisoners of War Dept, 1916–19. *Publications:* Lord Lyons: A Record of British Diplomacy, 1913; Lord Lansdowne: A Biography, 1929; Retrospection, 1941.

Heir: s Hon. Richard W. D. Legh. *Address:* 75 Eaton Square, SW1. *T:* Sloane 4624. *Clubs:* Travellers', Carlton.

Died 21 March 1942.

NEWTON, Sir Alan; *see* Newton, Sir H. A. S.

NEWTON, Arthur; *b* 1 Jan. 1858; unmarried. *Educ:* British School, Battersea. Was for 44 years connected with the Water Supply of London; for many years Accountant to the Southwark and Vauxhall Water Company and later became the Accountant and Chief Financial Officer to the Metropolitan Water Board, retiring in 1922; actively interested in Religious and Philanthropic Work; President of the Baptist Union of Great Britain and Ireland, 1930–31; Treasurer of the London Baptist Association; Director of Baptist Union Corporation, Ltd, and the London Baptist Property Board, Ltd; President of the London SW Band of Hope Union. *Recreations:* travel and music. *Address:* Woodlands Park Hotel, Cobham. *Club:* National Liberal.

Died 3 April 1942.

NEWTON, Arthur Percival, CBE 1941; MA, DLit, BSc, FSA; Emeritus Professor of Imperial History in University of London; *b* Birmingham, 23 July 1873; *e s* of Rupert Edward Newton, Birmingham; *m* 1st, 1899, Lily (*d* 1919), *d* of late Henry Denby; 2nd, 1920, Maud Muriel, *d* of Thomas Moody, FSI, of Cleeve House, Barton, Hants; two *d*. *Educ:* King Edward's School, Birmingham; Mason College, Birmingham (open Scholar); King's College, London (Fellow); BSc (Lond.); BA (Lond.), First Class Honours in Hist.; MA (Lond.), with distinction; DLit (Lond.). College, London, 1895–1913. Assistant Lecturer in Physics, King's College; Lecturer in American and Colonial History, 1914–18; University and King's College, Rhodes Lecturer, 1914–18; Secretary of Imperial Studies Committee, University of London, 1914–18; Organiser of Imperial Studies Committee, Royal Empire Society, since 1914; Vice-Pres. of Historical Association since 1924; Vice-Pres. Royal Historical Society; Vice-President of Commission Internationale d'Historie Coloniale; Membre effectif de l'Institut Colonial International; Foreign Member of Académie des Sciences Coloniales, Paris; Medal of the Académie, 1936; Foreign Member Academia Portuguesa da Historia; Gold Medal of Royal Empire Society, 1938; Member of Council of the Hakluyt Society; Joint Editor of the Cambridge History of the British Empire; visited Universities of United States and the British Dominions under auspices of Universities Bureau of Empire and Inst. of International Education, 1919–20; Visiting Professor in the University of the Punjab and Reader in the University of Calcutta, 1928–29; member of Governing Committee of Institute of Historical Research, University of London, since 1921. *Publications:* The Colonising Activities of the English Puritans, 1913; The Empire and the Future (Editor), 1915; The Old Empire and the New, 1917; editor of Imperial Studies Series; An Introduction to the Study of Colonial History, 1919; Select Bibliography of Colonial History, 1919; Chapters on Anglo-American Relations in Camb. Hist. of Brit. Foreign Policy, 1923; Federal and Unified Constitutions, 1923; The Unification of South Africa, 1924; The Universities and Educational Systems of the British Empire, 1924; Travel and Travellers of the Middle Ages (ed.), 1925; Thomas Gage, the English American, 1928; The Development of the British Empire, 1929; The Great Age of Discovery, 1932; The European Nations in the West Indies, 1933; One Hundred Years of the British Empire, 1940; The King's Chamber under the Early Tudors, and other contributions in Eng. Hist. Rev. and Amer. Hist. Rev.; The Foundation of the Great Farm of the English Customs, in Trans R. Hist. Soc.; Editor of the Sackville

MSS for the Historical MSS Commission and of the Calendar of State Papers, Colonial. *Address:* 99 Kingsley Way, N2.

Died 12 Aug. 1942.

NEWTON, Sir Francis James, KCMG 1919; CMG 1892; CVO 1911; *b* West Indies, 13 Sept. 1857; 3rd *s* of late F. R. Newton, of S. Cruz, WI; *m* 1889, Henrietta S. (*d* 1930), *e d* of D. Cloete of Newlands, Cape of Good Hope. *Educ:* Rugby; University College, Oxford (MA). Barrister, Inner Temple; ADC and Private Sec. to late Sir Hercules Robinson (High Commn), 1880–89; Adm. Govt British Bechuanaland, 1888; Col Sec. British Bechuanaland, 1890–95; adm. Govt British Bechuanaland, 1892 and 1894–95; Special Commn Matabeleland, 1894; Resident Comr Bechuanaland Protectorate, 1895–97; Colonial Secretary, British Honduras, 1898–1901; Colonial Secretary, Barbados, 1901–02; Treasurer British S Africa, Coy, 1902–19; administered Government NW Rhodesia during 1906, and S Rhodesia on various occasions; Colonial Secretary on Grant of Government to S Rhodesia, 1923; High Commissioner for Southern Rhodesia, 1924–30; Chairman Rhodesian Committee of Barclay's Bank (DC and O), 1930–38. *Address:* Salisbury, Southern Rhodesia. *Club:* Carlton.

Died 9 May 1948.

NEWTON, Rt Rev. Henry; Canon of Cathedral of St Peter and St Paul, Dogura, since 1937; *b* Victoria, 5 Jan. 1866; *m* 1903, Sara, *d* of Captain Sully of Brisbane. *Educ:* St Paul's College, Sydney; Merton College, Oxford, DD Hon. 1920. Ordained, 1891; Curate St John, Hackney, 1891–93; Esk, Queensland, 1893–98; Missionary, Diocese of New Guinea, 1899; Vicar-General, New Guinea, 1908–10; Bishop of Carpentaria, 1915–22; Bishop of New Guinea, 1922–36. *Address:* Dogura, Samarai, Papua.

Died 25 Sept. 1947.

NEWTON, Sir (Hibbert) Alan (Stephen), Kt 1936; Consulting Surgeon, Royal Melbourne Hospital; Member of Council, University of Melbourne; Past-President, Royal Australasian College of Surgeons; *b* 30 April 1887; *s* of late Hibbert Henry Newton, JP, Clerk of Parliaments, Victoria, and Clara Violet (*d* 1935), *d* of William Ravenscroft Stephen; *m* 1919, Mary Cicely, *d* of J. Hartley Wicksteed, JP, Weetwood, Headingley, Yorkshire; one *s* one *d*. *Educ:* Haileybury College, Melbourne; University of Melbourne. Graduated, 1909; MS Melbourne, 1912; FRCS Eng., 1919; Hon. Fellow British Assoc. of Surgeons; Hon. FRSM; Foundation Fellow, Royal Australasian College of Surgeons; Fellow American College of Surgeons. Served European War, Captain AAMC, 1916; Temporary Major, 1919; Colonel AAMC, 1940; Chairman Medical Equipment Control Committee of Commonwealth of Australia, 1940–45; Member of Faculty of Medicine and Stewart Lecturer in Surgery, Univ. of Melbourne; Director, National Mutual Life Assoc. of Australasia Ltd, Fourth Victorian Permanent Building Soc., Trustees Executors and Agency Co., Ltd; Member Medical Board of Victoria; President Board W. & E. Hall Inst. Med. Research. *Publications:* numerous papers in surgical journals. *Recreation:* golf. *Address:* 272 Domain Road, South Yarra, Melbourne, SE1, Australia. *T:* Windsor 4924. *Clubs:* Marlborough-Windham; Melbourne (Melbourne); Union (Sydney).

Died 4 Aug. 1949.

NEWTON, Rev. Joseph Fort, DLitt; DD; DHL; LLD, Rector of St Luke and the Epiphany, Philadelphia, since 1938; *b* Decatur, Texas, 21 July 1880; *s* of Lee Newton and Sue G. Battle; *m* 1900, Jennie Mai Deatherage of Sanders, Carroll Co., Kentucky; one *s* one *d*. *Educ:* Hardy Institute; Southern Baptist Theological Seminary, Louisville. Baptist Minister, 1893; pastor 1st Baptist Church, Paris, Texas, 1897–98; founder and pastor, People's Church, Dixon, Ill, 1901–08; pastor Liberal

Christian Church. Cedar Rapids, Ia, 1908–16; Pastor, City Temple, 1916–19, Church of the Divine Paternity, New York, 1920–25; Rector Memorial Church of St Paul, Overbrook, Philadelphia, 1925–30; Co-Rector, St James's Church, Philadelphia, 1930–36; Church of St Luke and Epiphany, 1937. *Publications:* David Swing, Poet-Preacher, 1909; Abraham Lincoln, 1910; Lincoln and Herndon, 1910; The Builders, 1911; The Eternal Christ, 1912; Sermons and Lecturers, 1912; The Mercy of Hell, 1917; The Sword of the Spirit, 1918; Preaching in London, 1922; Preaching in New York, 1923; The Truth and the Life, 1925; God and the Golden Rule, 1927; The Religion of Masonry, 1927; Altar Stairs, a Book of Prayers, 1928; The New Preaching, 1929; Things I Know in Religion, 1930; The Angel in the Soul, 1932; If I had only one Sermon to Prepare, 1932; Living Everyday, 1937; We Here Highly Resolve, 1939; The Stuff of Life, 1939; His Cross and Ours, 1941; Living Up to Life, 1941; Live, Learn and Love, 1943; Where Are We in Religion?, 1944; River of Years, Autobiography, 1946; The One Great Church, 1947; Life Victorious, a Testament of Faith, 1948. *Address:* 330 S 13th Street, Philadelphia, USA.

Died 25 Jan. 1950.

NEWTON, Col Sir Louis (Arthur), 1st Bt *cr* 1924; Kt 1917; *b* London, 17 Dec. 1867; *s* of late Reuben Newton, Macclesfield; *m* 1st, 1891, Eleanor Jane (*d* 1929), *d* of George Faulder; two *s* two *d*; 2nd, 1930, Mrs Florence E. H. Wheatley, *o d* of William Yates Baker, Streatham. A Lieutenant and Alderman of the City of London (Senior Sheriff, 1917); Lord Mayor of London, 1924; Governor of the Honourable The Irish Society, 1928–33; High Sheriff of Kent, 1940; Gov. of the Royal Hospitals; Chairman of the Crystal Palace Trustees, and Almoner of Christ's Hosp.; Commissioner of Income Tax for the City of London; Chairman of Trustees of Morden College, Blackheath; Member of the London County Council 1931–34; Hon. Fellow of the Auctioneers Institute; formerly Hon. Col 56th (1st London) Divisional Train, RASC; Member of the Coal Mines National Industrial Board; Past Grand Warden, Grand Lodge of English Freemasons; Past Master of the Loriners', Feltmakers' and Needlemakers' Companies; Grand Cordon of the Order of the Star of Rumania; Grand Officier of the Orders of Crown of Italy, The White Lion of Czechoslovakia, and Leopold II of Belgium. *Heir: s* Edgar Henry [*b* 6 May 1893; *m* 1917, Gladys Maud, *d* of James Wilson Garner; one *s* one *d*]. *Address:* 169 Queen's Gate, SW7. *T:* Kensington 9176. *Club:* Constitutional.

Died 17 April 1945.

NEWTON, Robert Henry, CBE 1920; retired master mariner; *b* Liverpool, 1864; *s* of Captain Robert and Caroline Newton; *m* 1st, 1889, Annie Colquitt; 2nd, 1898, Catherine Jones; one *s* one *d*. *Educ:* Northern Institute, Liverpool. Went to sea at age of 13; joined City of Dublin Steam Packet Co., 1886; appointed to command, 1903; continued in command of their mail steamers until 1920. *Address:* Homelea, Walthew Avenue, Holyhead.

Died 24 April 1943.

NEWTON, William Godfrey, MC; JP Wilts; MA (Oxon), FRIBA; Chartered Architect; *b* 1 Dec. 1885; *y s* of late Ernest Newton, RA; *m* 1926, Dagmar, *o d* of Rev. Canon R. E. Broughton; two *s* two *d*. *Educ:* Marlborough; Oriel College, Oxford; Royal College of Art, South Kensington. *Architectural Works:* Housing Scheme, Otford; Country Houses; Memorial Hall, Garden and Science Building, 10 Classrooms, Marlborough College; Hall and 20 Classrooms, and Boarding House, Uppingham School; Housing at Woolwich; Town Plan and Housing at Shirehampton; County Fire Office; Braydon Hall; Church at Alassio; Convent Chapel, Bournemouth; Classrooms, Bradfield College; Nurses' Home, Savernake Hospital; Merchant Taylors' Company School at Sandy Lodge; Hospital at

Devizes; Radley College Science Block; Territorial Headquarters in Albany Street, and the White City; Chapel for Aldenham School; Buildings for Worcester College, Oxford; Senior School for W Riding; Head Office Croydon Gas Co.; Development Scheme for Makerere College, Uganda, and for Gordon College, Khartoum; served World War (MC) Artists and 1/23rd Batt. London Regt, 1914–17; ADC/CGS at General Headquarters, 1917; commanded 1/21st Battalion London Regiment, 1918; Lieut-Col, 1919; member of Council, RIBA, 1920, 1921, 1923, 1949; Pres. Architectural Association, 1921; late Editor of Architectural Review; Lecturer on Architecture at University of Oxford, 1924; late Professor of Architecture, Royal College of Art. Pres. Wessex Society of Architects, 1948. *Publications:* The Architectural Contribution of Imperial Rome, 1912; Military Landscape Sketching, 1916; Prelude to Architecture, 1925; The Work of Ernest Newton, RA, 1925. *Recreation:* enjoying the infinite variety of things and people. *Address:* 4 Raymond Buildings, Gray's Inn, WC. *T:* Chancery 7684; Old Rectory, Manningford Abbas, Wilts. *Club:* Athenæum.

Died 11 Jan. 1949.

NEWTON, William Henry; Professor of Physiology, University of Edinburgh, since 1948; *b* 24 April 1904; *s* of Rev. J. T. Newton; *m* 1931, Stella, *d* of Roger Reynolds; two *d*. *Educ:* Ashville College, Harrogate; Manchester University. BSc 1st Cl. Hons, Platt Physiol. and Graduate Schol., 1925; MSc, Grad. Entr. Schol. in Medicine, 1926; MB, ChB, House Phys. Manch. Royal Infirmary, 1929; MD (Manch.), 1934; DSc (Lond.), 1939. Sharpey Scholar, 1930. Lecturer, 1930, Senior Lecturer, 1933, and Reader, 1936, in Physiology, Univ. Coll., London. Visiting Lecturer St George's Hosp. (Applied Physiology), 1933–37, and Chelsea Polytechnic, 1933–36. Rockefeller Foundation Fellow, Yale, Univ., 1937–38. Sub-Dean Faculty of Medical Sciences, 1939–43, and acting-Head Physiology Dept 1939–44, Univ. Coll.; George Holt Prof. of Physiology, Liverpool Univ., 1944–48. Editor, Quarterly Journal of Experimental Physiology; Mem. Cttee of Physiol. Soc. (Sec., 1942–47); Fellow Roy. Soc. Med. *Publications:* Evans' Recent Advances in Physiology, 1936, 1939, 1949; Introduction to Physiology, 1948; Chapters in text-books and scientific contributions since 1927 to Brit. and Am. physiolog. journals. *Recreation:* painting. *Address:* 14 Pentland Avenue, Edinburgh 13. *T:* 87086.

Died 20 Dec. 1949.

NEYLAN, Sir Daniel, Kt 1922; CBE 1918; late Joint Secretary Disposal and Liquidation Commission, and Secretary, Surplus Stores, etc., Liquidation Department HM Treasury; retired, 1927; *b* 1866; *s* of late James Neylan, Dysart, Co. Clare; *m* Alice Campbell (*d* 1938). Was Financial Adviser to Salonika Expeditionary Force. *Address:* 36 Shirley Drive, Hove.

Died 29 Nov. 1943.

NGATA, Hon. Sir Apirana Turupa, Kt 1927; LLB; *b* Kawakawa, Te Araroa, New Zealand, 3 July 1874; *m* Arihia (*d* 1929), *d* of Tuta Tamati, Whareponga, NZ; four *s* six *d*. *Educ:* Waiomatatini Native Village School; Te Aute College; Canterbury University College. BA 1893; MA 1894; LLB 1896. Barrister and solicitor, 1897; Travelling Secretary Te Aute Students' Association, 1899; Organising Inspector for Maori Councils, 1902–04; member House of Representatives for Eastern Maori, 1905–43; Royal Commissioner under Native Land Act, 1904–05; Stout-Ngata Commission, 1907–09; Chairman of Directors, Waiapu Farmers' Co-op. Co. since 1912, and of the Ngatiporou Co-op. Dairy Co. since 1925; member of Executive Council, 1909–12; Minister for Native Affairs and Cook Islands, and State Fire and Government Life Insurance Departments, New Zealand, 1928–34; Acting Attorney-General, 1930–31; a Director of the Tokomaru Co-op. Freezing Co.; member of the Maori Purposes Board, the Board of

Maori Ethnological Research up to Dec. 1928, Chairman of those Boards to Oct. 1934; member Board of Maori Arts and Crafts; Chairman: Native Land Purchase Board; Native Trust Investment Board; Maori (Football) Advisory Board; member Senate NZ Univ. since 1929; Pres. Council Polynesian Soc., 1939; Member: NZ Geographia Board, 1938; Maori Recruiting Committee since Sept. 1939; NZ Centennial Celebrations Council, 1939–40. *Address:* The Bungalow, Waiomatatini, NZ.

Died 14 July 1950.

NICHOL, Robert John. Director of R. Hood Haggie and Son, Ltd, Rope Manufacturers, Newcastle. *Address:* Cranford, Stocksfield, Northumberland. *T:* Stocksfield 3106.

Died 9 Jan. 1946.

NICHOLAS, Col Stephen Henry Edmund, CIE 1926; Indian Army (retired); *b* 1870; *s* of late Prebendary E. P. Nicholas, Vicar of Worfield, Shropshire, and of Wombourne, Staffordshire; *m* 1896, Maud Lane Plews (*d* 1933), *g d* of John Plews, civil engineer, of London; no *c*. *Educ:* Swansea; RMC, Sandhurst. First Commission, 1890, joining the 1st Battalion East Surrey Regiment; Indian Army, 1892; served NW Frontier of India, 1897–98; European War, 1916, in Mesopotamia; employed in the Judge Advocate-General's Department in India, 1912–26; Judge Advocate-General in India, 1923–26; Colonel, 1920. *Address:* 11 Darlington Place, Bath. *T:* Bath 5521. *Club:* Junior Army and Navy.

Died 6 Feb. 1948.

NICHOLL, Sir Allan Hume, Kt 1938; CBE 1920; DL; brewer; *b* Usk, Mon; *s* of late Captain Hume Nicholl; 1st Royal Dragoons; *m* 1891, Rosalie (*d* 1937), *d* of late Dr Thornton, JP Margate; two *d*. *Educ:* Cordwallis, Maidenhead; King's College, London. Mayor of Lewisham during European War; Deputy Assistant Commissioner City of London Police Reserve; Lt-Colonel commanding 1st Cadet Battalion 20th Co. of London Regiment; Vice-President, late Chairman, of London Safety First Council; Hon. Treasurer, and Chairman of Executive Committee of National Safety First Council; Chairman of Lewisham War Pensions Com.; Member of War Pensions Advisory Committee; Chairman, Sydenham Infant Welfare; Chairman, Lewisham Parochial Charities; Trustee Crystal Palace; Member of Grand Lodge of England; Member of British Red Cross Society; FZS; FRGS; Member of Royal United Service Institution. *Recreations:* fishing, shooting. *Address:* The Hawthorns, Sylvan Hill, Upper Norwood, SE. *T:* Livingstone 2670. *Club:* Junior Carlton.

Died 8 July 1941.

NICHOLLS, Albert George, MA; MD; DSc; FRSC; FRCP (C); Fellow Royal Institute Public Health; Consulting Editor, Canadian Medical Assoc. Journal; late Professor of Pathology, Dalhousie University, Halifax, NS; Major CAMC, retired; during European War was DADMS, Sanitation, MD No. 6; *b* Shotley Bridge, Co., Durham, 1870; *s* of late Rev. John Nicholls and late Mary Elizabeth Harland; *m* 1907, Lucia Pomeroy Van Vliet of Lacolle, Quebec; three *s*. *Educ:* Montreal High School; McGill University; Erlangen; Prague; and Vienna. Graduated Dux of the Montreal High and Grammar School, with Davidson Gold Medal for Classics, and Lansdowne Silver Medal for History and Literature; Chapman Gold Medal for Classics at McGill University; Final Prize in the Faculty of Medicine; BA 1890; MA 1893; MD, CM 1894; DSc 1909; FRSC, 1908; FRCP (C), 1931. Church of England; on Teaching Staff of McGill University, 1897–1914; King George V Silver Jubilee Medal; King George VI Coronation Medal. *Publications:* upwards of fifty monographs and other publications on medical subjects; chief among them are: Multiple Progressive Hyaloserositis; The Dust-bodies of the Blood; The Aetiology of Chronic Bright's Disease; Immunity in

Tuberculosis; A Textbook, Principles of Pathology (with Prof. Adami). *Recreations:* motoring, photography. *Address:* 2174 Sherbrooke Street, West, Montreal, Que. *T:* Wilbank 9237. *Clubs:* Authors; University (Montreal).

Died 3 March 1946.

NICHOLLS, George, OBE, JP; *b* 25 June 1864. Pastor Evangelist Congregational Church, Chatteris, Cambs, 1894–1902; afterwards Congregational Churches at Silverdale and Chesterton, Staffs; MP (L) North Northants, 1906–10; contested Faversham Division, Kent, 1910; elected to Peterborough Town Council, 1912; Mayor, 1916–18; chief organiser for Agricultural Organisation Society on the Allotment and Small Holdings Section; member of the Agricultural Wages Board, of the recent Royal Commission on Agriculture, of the Central Agricultural Council, of the Soke of Peterborough Small Holdings Committee, and of Peterborough United Charities. *Address:* Kimberley Lodge, 162 Lincoln Road, Peterborough. *Club:* National Liberal.

Died 30 Nov. 1943.

NICHOLLS, Richard Howell, CBE 1920; *b* 1868; *s* of Richard Nicholls, Grays, Essex. Superintendent of the Line, Great Western Railway, 1919–32; late Lieut-Col Engineer and Railway Staff Corps; Member Institute of Transport. *Address:* Belhurst, Eldorado Crescent, Cheltenham. *T:* Cheltenham 52454.

Died 13 Oct. 1946.

NICHOLLS, Lt-Col William Ashley, DSO 1917; late RA; *b* 14 Dec. 1883; *o s* of late Gen. Sir W. C. Nicholls, KCB; *m* 1922, Hilda Evelyn, *y d* of Brig.-Gen. J. R. Gaussen, CMG; one *s* two *d*. *Educ:* Cheltenham Coll.; RMA, Woolwich. Second Lieut RA 1901; Capt. 1914; Major, 1916; Lt-Col 1930. Served European War, 1914–19 (despatches 4 times, DSO); Iraq, 1920; retired pay, 1934. *Address:* East Dean, nr Salisbury.

Died 25 June 1941.

NICHOLS, Robert Malise Bowyer; *b* 6 Sept. 1893; *e s* of late John Bowyer Buchanan Nichols and Katherine (*née* Pusey), of Lawford Hall, Manningtree, Essex; *m* 1922, Norah, *e d* of Frederick and Maud Denny, Horwood House, Winslow, Bucks. *Educ:* Winchester; Trinity College, Oxford. Second Lieut RFA, Oct. 1914–Aug. 1916; served on Western Front; British Mission (Ministry of Information) to the US, 1918; Professor of English Literature in the Imperial University, Tokio (chair of Lafcadio Hearn), 1921–24. *Publications:* Invocation (poems), 1915; Ardours and Endurances (poems), 1917; Aurelia (poems), 1920; Guilty Souls (drama, with preface), 1922; Fantastica (romances of idea, with preface and epilogue), 1923; Under the Yew (novelette), 1927; Wings over Europe (drama with Maurice Browne), 1929; Fisbo, a satirical poem, 1934; Such was my Singing (poems), 1942. *Recreations:* conversation, music. *Address:* c/o Barclay's Bank, Vere Street, W1.

Died 17 Dec. 1944.

NICHOLSON, Bertram, CMG 1932; CBE 1924; DSO 1902; MC; *b* 14 Jan. 1875; *s* of late William Nicholson, JP, Richmond, Natal; *m* 1st, 1904, Adelaide Marion, *d* of late Alexander Stewart, Glasgow; 2nd, 1940, Marianne, *yr d* of late J. C. Sutherland. *Educ:* Pietermaritzburg College, Natal. Natal Civil Service, 1894–99; served South Africa with 2nd Imperial Light Horse, 1899–1902 (despatches twice, DSO); Sub-native Commissioner, Hlatikulu, Swaziland, 1902–04; Member Special Criminal Court, 1904; Assistant Resident Magistrate, 1904–07; Assistant Commissioner, 1907; served European War, 1914–15, with Imperial Light Horse, and later Intelligence Officer, Central Force, German South-West Africa (despatches, MC); Government Secretary and Deputy Resident Commissioner, Swaziland, 1917; Chairman of British Members of the Swaziland

Boundary Commission to inquire into disputed boundary between the Swaziland Protectorate and Portuguese Territory, 1920; acted as Resident Commissioner, 1922, 1923, 1928 and 1931; retired on pension, 1933. *Address:* Mbabane, Swaziland. *Clubs:* Transvaal Automobile, Johannesburg.

Died 25 July 1943.

NICHOLSON, Sir Charles, 2nd Bt *cr* 1859; MA; FRIBA; *b* 27 April 1867; *s* of late Sir C. Nicholson of Totteridge, Herts, formerly Speaker of the House of Assembly at Sydney and Chancellor of Sydney University; *m* 1st, 1895, Evelyn Louise (*d* 1927), *d* of Rev. H. Olivier; one *s* two *d*; 2nd, 1931, Catherine Maud, *y d* of late L. Warren, Winchfield. *Educ:* Rugby; New College, Oxford. Architect; pupil of J. D. Sedding; Consulting Architect for Wells, Lichfield, Llandaff, Portsmouth, Sheffield, Belfast Cathedrals; Diocesan Architect to Wakefield, Winchester, Portsmouth and Chelmsford. *Recreation:* travel. *Heir: s* John Charles [*b* 10 Jan. 1904; *m* 1928, Caroline Elizabeth, *d* of late Rt Rev. John Frederick McNeice]. *Address:* Church House, Headington, Oxford; 2 New Square, Lincoln's Inn, WC2.

Died 4 March 1949.

NICHOLSON, Adm. Sir Douglas Romilly Lothian, KCMG 1919; KCVO 1919; *b* 4 March 1867; *s* of late Gen. Sir Lothian Nicholson, KCB, and Hon. Mary Romilly, *d* of 1st Lord Romilly; *m* 1907, Sybil Edith Mary, *o d* of late Hon. Edward Romilly. Served Egyptian War, 1882 (medal, bronze star); Commodore HM's Yachts, 1913–14; served in the Grand Fleet as a Captain and Rear-Admiral during the War, 1914–18 (KCMG, KCVO, Commander of the Legion of Honour, Order of the Rising Sun, 2nd class); Vice-Admiral commanding Reserve Fleet, 1922–23; Admiral, 1925; retired list, 1926. *Address:* The Castle, Bude Haven, Cornwall.

Died 8 Feb. 1946.

NICHOLSON, George Gibb, CBE 1920; Chevalier de la Legion d'honneur, 1934; MA (Syd.), BCL (Oxon); McCaughey Professor of French, University of Sydney, 1921–45; Emeritus Professor, 1946; *b* Chorltoncum-Hardy, England, 20 Sept. 1875; *s* of late Donald Nicholson, bank manager; *m* 1905, Marguerite Marie Danuser; one *s* one *d*. *Educ:* University of Sydney (Lithgow Scholar, James King of Irrawang Travelling Scholar); Balliol College, Oxford; University of Paris. Assistant Lecturer in French and German, University of Sydney, 1903–12; and concurrently (1904–05) Tutor in Philosophy, St Andrew's College; Assistant Professor, 1913–20; Assistant Censor, 1914–15; Censor in chief control of Press, Cable, and Postal Censorship of NSW, 1916–19; District Censor in chief control of Press, Radio, Cable, and Postal Censorship of NSW, Sept.–Nov. 1939. *Publications:* A Practical Introduction to French Phonetics, 1909; Passages for Translation into French and German (with C. J. Brennan), 1914; Recherches philologiques romanes, 1921; Un nouveau principe d'étymologie romane, 1936; various articles in Romania (Paris), Revue de linguistique romane (Paris), Revista de filología española (Madrid), Zeitschrift für romanische Philologie (Halle), and Hispanic Review (Philadelphia). *Address:* Chesentrys, Mount Street, Hunter's Hill, Sydney, NSW. *T:* Hunter 305. *Club:* University (Sydney).

Died 22 Dec. 1948.

NICHOLSON, Brig.-Gen. George Harvey, CB 1916; CMG 1919; JP Hants; *b* 5 Dec. 1862; *s* of W. S. Nicholson, JP, Eastmore, Isle of Wight; *m* 1892, Blanche, *d* of Capt. F. C. Annesley, 28th Regt; one *s*. *Educ:* Charterhouse. Hampshire Regt, 1882–1913; commanded 2nd Bn 1909–13; commanded Hampshire Brigade TF, 1914; served Burmese War, 1887–89 (medal with clasp); European War, 1914–18 (CB, CMG, despatches thrice). *Recreations:* yachting, fishing, shooting. *Address:* Novar, Winchester. *Clubs:* Army and Navy, Constitutional; Solent Yacht.

Died 13 June 1942.

NICHOLSON, Brig.-Gen. Graham Henry Whalley, CB 1922; CMG 1915; late RA; *b* Chatham, 30 Aug. 1869; *o s* of late Captain H. W. Nicholson, 82nd Foot (S Lancashire Regt); *m* 1897, Helen Isobel, *d* of late Dr W. Eagleson Gordon, Bridge of Allan, Stirlingshire; two *s*. *Educ:* Portsmouth; Royal Military Academy, Woolwich. Passed into Woolwich, 1886; Commissioned 2nd Lieut RA 1888; Lieut 1891; Captain, 1898; Bvt Major, 1900; Major, 1904; Lt-Col 1914; Col 1918; Brig.-Gen. 1915; Garrison-Adjutant, Egypt, 1896–98; Adjutant, 1902–03; Staff Captain, Scotland, 1903–04; Instructor in Gunnery, RH and RFA, 1904–08; served Egypt, 1898 (despatches, 4th class Medjidie, medal, Egyptian medal with clasp); South African War, 1899–1902 (despatches twice, Bt Major, Queen's medal 6 clasps, King's medal 2 clasps); European War, 1914–18 (wounded Battle of Aisne, despatches six times, CMG, Bt Col); retired pay, 1924. *Address:* c/o Lloyds Bank, Ltd, Cox's Branch, 6 Pall Mall, SW1.

Died 1 Feb. 1946.

NICHOLSON, Harold, MA Cantab; *b* 29 Sept. 1883; *s* of George Nicholson and Esther Rice; *m* 1914, May Parrott; two *s* one *d*. *Educ:* Merchant Taylors' School, Crosby; King's College, Cambridge. Assistant Master, Merchiston Castle, Edinburgh, 1906–07; Manchester Grammar School, 1907–14; Headmaster, Watford Grammar School, 1914–22; Headmaster of Taunton School, 1922–36. *Publications:* Edited Langlais, La Chasse de Sarcey, Laboulaye, Contes Bleus; Heyse, Die Dichterin von Carcassonne; Taunton School Addresses; The Legend of the Horseshoe; Legends, Stories and Fables from the French. *Recreations:* music and golf. *Address:* Stratford Lodge, N Warnborough, Odiham, Hants. *T:* Odiham 142.

Died 13 March 1949.

NICHOLSON, Harry Oliphant, MD Aberdeen (Highest Honours and Strathcona Prize), 1901; MB, CM (Aberdeen) 1891, FRCP Edinburgh; Examiner Scottish Midwives' Board; Ex-President, Edinburgh Obstetrical Society; *b* 13 March 1870; *s* of late Henry Alleyne Nicholson, MD, DSc, FRS, Professor of Natural History in the University of Aberdeen; *m* 1899, Euphemia, 4th *d* of Sir Michael Nairn, 1st Bt; two *s* one *d*. *Educ:* University of Aberdeen and University of Edinburgh; Berlin. After graduation, House Physician and Surgeon, Royal Hospital for Sick Children, Aberdeen; in medical practice at Kirkcaldy, Fifeshire, 1891–99; in private practice in Edinburgh since 1900, and has acted as Clinical Assistant for Medical Out-patients, Royal Infirmary, Edinburgh, 1901; Physician, New Town Dispensary, 1902; Physician-Accoucheur, New Town Dispensary, 1903–07; Senior Assistant Physician, Royal Maternity Hospital, Edinburgh, 1904–24; University Lecturer on Clinical Obstetrics; Examiner in Midwifery in the University of Aberdeen, 1911–13; Examiner in Midwifery and Gynæcology, Royal Coll. of Physicians, Edinburgh; Membre Corr. Soc. des Sciences Méd. d'Angers. *Publications:* article Pulse, Encyclopædia Medica, 1902; article Eclampsia, Index of Treatment, 1931; Obstetrics, Oxford Index of Therapeutics, 1931; Eclampsia and the Thyroid Gland; numerous other contributions relating to Medicine, Obstetrics, and Diseases of Children. *Recreations:* geology, motoring, and travelling. *Address:* 20 Manor Place, Edinburgh. *T:* Central 22460.

Died 26 May 1941.

NICHOLSON, John Wilfred, CIE 1942; IFS, retd; *b* 13 Jan. 1893; *m* 1922, Cicely Mary Luscombe Whyte; one *s* two *d*. *Educ:* Merchiston Castle School, Edinburgh; Wadham College, Oxford. Joined Indian Forest Service in Bihar and Orissa, 1916; military service, 1916–19; on deputation to East Africa as Forest Adviser to Govts of Kenya and Uganda, 1927–30; Conservator of Forests, Orissa, 1936; now retd. *Publication:* Bihar and Orissa. The Forests from Within, 1926. *Recreations:* golf and gardening. *Address:* Somerset West, CP, S Africa. *Clubs:* Mahanadi; Ranchi.

Died 24 April 1949.

NICHOLSON, Meredith; US Minister to Nicaragua, 1938–40; *b* Crawfordsville, Indiana, 9 Dec. 1866; *m* 1st, 1896, Eugenie Kountze; two *s* one *d*; 2nd, 1933, Dorothy Lannon. US Minister to Paraguay, 1933–35; to Venezuela, 1935–38. *Publications:* The House of a Thousand Candles, 1905; Port of Missing Men, 1907; Siege of the Seven Suitors, 1910; A Hoosier Chronicle, 1912; Otherwise Phyllis, 1913; Broken Barriers, 1922; Hope of Happiness, 1923; And They Lived Happily Ever After, 1925; The Cavalier of Tennessee, 1928; and various volumes of essays and addresses.

Died 21 Dec. 1947.

NICHOLSON, Reginald, MBE; JP; *b* 15 July 1869; *s* of late W. N. Nicholson, senior Master in Lunacy; *m* 1915, Natalie, *d* of Dr F. S. Pearson, New York. *Educ:* Charterhouse. Assistant Traffic Manager, Bengal Nagpur Railway, 1894; Manager of The Times, 1911–15; MP (Co. L) Doncaster Division of Yorks Dec. 1918–22. *Address:* Meadow Barn, Godalming, Surrey. *T:* Godalming 16. *Club:* Royal Automobile.

Died 27 April 1946.

NICHOLSON, Reginald Popham, CMG 1914; CBE 1939; BA Cantab, Hon. Life Member Royal African Society; *b* 1874; *m* 1928, Mary Elinor, *d* of late A. G. Rickards, KC, VD. *Educ:* Clifton; Christ's College, Cambridge. Private Secretary to Sir F. Lugard, High Commissioner of Northern Nigeria, 1900, and subsequently a Political Officer until 1906; served Sokoto Kano Campaign, 1903 (medal and clasp), and minor operations, 1903–05; attached to Colonial Office, East African Dept, 1906–08. Colonial Secretary and Registrar-General, Bermuda, 1908–15; Administrator of St Vincent, 1915–22; acted as Administrator of St Lucia, March 1917–Dec. 1918; Col Secretary British Guiana, 1922–25; Colonial Secretary of Cyprus, 1926–29; represented Cyprus at 1st Colonial Office Conference, 1927; acting Gov. of Br. Guiana and of Cyprus for over 2 years in all; retired, 1929; Secretary R. African Society and Editor of its Journal, 1932–38; Empire Division, Ministry of Information, March–Dec. 1940; Red Cross Foreign Relations Department, 1941–43; has exhibited drawings at the N English Art Club, etc. Chairman, Surrey County Cttee, Citizens Advice Bureaux. *Address:* Tallboys, Abinger Hammer, Surrey. *Club:* Brooks's.

Died 15 March 1950.

NICHOLSON, Reynold Alleyne, MA; LittD; Hon. LLD (Aberdeen); FBA; Emeritus Professor of Arabic; Fellow of Trinity College, Cambridge; Associate Member of Persian Academy; Gold Medallist of Royal Asiatic Society; *b* 19 Aug. 1868; *s* of late Henry Alleyne Nicholson, MD, FRS, Professor of Natural History in the University of Aberdeen; *m* 1903, Cecilia, *d* of late Thomas Varty of Stagstones, Penrith. *Educ:* University of Aberdeen; Trinity College, Cambridge. Porson Prize for Greek verse, 1888 and 1890; first class, Classical Tripos, 1890; first class, Indian Languages Tripos, 1892; Fellow of Trinity College, Cambridge, 1893; studied Arabic under Professor Robertson Smith; also at Strassburg and Leyden. Examiner in Classics to the University of Aberdeen, 1897; Professor of Persian, University Coll., London, 1901; Lecturer in Persian in the Univ. of Cambridge, 1902–26; Sir Thomas Adams's Professor of Arabic, 1926–33. *Publications:* Selected Poems from the Divani Shamsi Tabriz, 1898; Tadhkirat-ul-Awliya (Memoirs of the Saints), Part I, the Persian text edited with variants and indices, 1905; Part II, 1907; A Literary History of the Arabs, 1907; (with late F. Du Pre Thornton) Elementary Arabic, First Reading-Book,

1907; Second Reading-Book, 1909; Third Reading-Book, 1911; Introduction and Notes to FitzGerald's Omar Khayyám, 1909; Translation of the Kashf-al-Mahjub, 1911; The Tarjuman-al-Ashwaq (mystical poems) of Ibn-al-Arabi, with translation and commentary, 1911; The Don and the Dervish (a book of verse, original and translated), 1911; The Mystics of Islam, 1914; The Kitab al-Luma, an Arabic treatise on mysticism, edited with abstract of contents in English, 1915; The Secrets of the Self, from the Persian of Iqbal, 1920; Studies in Islamic Poetry, 1921; Studies in Islamic Mysticism, 1921; with G. le Strange, the Farsnama (Persian text), 1921; Translations of Eastern Poetry and Prose, 1922; The Idea of Personality in Sufism, 1923; The Mathnawi of Jalalu'ddin Rumi, edited with translation and commentary, vols i–viii; 1925–1940; Stories from the Mathnawi, 1931; articles in the Journal of the Royal Asiatic Society and elsewhere. *Recreation:* golf.

Died 27 Aug. 1945.

NICHOLSON, Sir Sydney Hugo, Kt 1938; MVO 1926; MA, MusBac Oxon; FRCO; Doctor of Music, Canterbury, 1928; Founder and Director of the Royal School of Church Music since 1927; *b* 9 Feb. 1875; *y s* of late Sir Charles Nicholson, 1st Bt, DCL, LLD; unmarried. *Educ:* Rugby; New College, Oxford. Organist of Barnet Parish Church, 1898; Organist Lower Chapel, Eton College, 1903; Acting Organist Carlisle Cathedral, 1904; Manchester Cathedral, 1908–18; Organist of Westminster Abbey, 1918–27; Warden of St Nicholas College, Chislehurst, 1928–39. *Publications:* Quires and Places where they Sing, 1933; Peter, the Adventures of a Chorister; Church Music; British Songs for British Boys; Cantatas, Light Operas, Songs, and much Church Music. *Address:* (temp.): Myrtle Cottage, Woodchurch, Ashford, Kent. *Club:* Athenæum.

Died 30 May 1947.

NICHOLSON, Sir Walter (Frederic), KCB 1922; CB 1916; *b* 22 July 1876; *s* of late P. E. Nicholson; *m* 1939, Dorothy, *y d* of late Horace Lamb, DSc, FRS, and *widow* of Sir John Reeve Brooke, CB. *Educ:* St Paul's School; Balliol College, Oxford. Civil Servant, Admiralty, 1899–1920; Secretary of the Air Ministry, 1920–30; A director of Imperial Airways (Government nominee), 1931–37. *Address:* 4 Whitehall Court, SW1. *T:* Whitehall 3160. *Club:* Reform.

Died 28 Feb. 1946.

NICHOLSON, Sir William, Kt 1934; Managing Director of Messrs W. Nicholson and Son, Leeds, Governing Director Summerstone Estate Co; *b* Crown Point House, Leeds, May 1865; *s* of William Nicholson, Leeds, and Emily Elizabeth Briggs, Lincoln; *m* 1898, Anne Cawthra (*d* 1942), Horlon Hall, Bradford, *widow* of John Cawthra; no *c*. *Educ:* Leeds Grammar School; privately. Director of the Builders Accident London Insurance Co. and South Market Co. Leeds; Chairman Leeds Highways and Lord Mayor of Leeds, 1911–12; President Leeds Conservative Association, Boy Scouts, Balfour Club and Hunslet Cricket and Football Club; Member of Lord Roberts National League Executive in London; Parliamentary Candidate South Leeds, 1910; President and Treasurer National Federation Building Trade Employers, 1907. *Recreations:* travel, golf, grouse, shooting, fishing. *Address:* Hellifield Peel, Hellifield, Yorks; Summerstone Lodge, Middlesmoor, Yorks. *T:* 22 Hellifield. *Clubs:* Carlton, Junior Carlton; Leeds.

Died 29 Feb. 1944.

NICHOLSON, Rt Hon. William Graham; PC 1925; JP; Alderman, Co. Southampton; late Lt-Col and Hon. Col commg 3rd Batt. Hants Regt; *b* 11 March 1862; *e s* of William Nicholson, JP, DL, Basing Park, Hants; *m* 1890, Alice Margaret (*d* 1935), *d* of late Rt Hon. William Wither Bramston Beach, MP, Oakley Hall, Basingstoke, and Keevil House, Wilts; two *s*. *Educ:* Harrow; Trinity College, Cambridge. BA 1884. MP (C) Petersfield

Division, Hants, 1897–1935; retired, 1935. *Recreations:* yachting, shooting, hunting. *Address:* 2 South Audley Street, W1. *T:* Grosvenor 1350; Basing Park, Alton, Hants. *Clubs:* Carlton; Royal Yacht Squadron, Cowes.

Died 29 July 1942.

NICHOLSON, Sir William (Newzam Prior), Kt 1936; painter; *b* Newark-on-Trent, 1872; *s* of late William Newzam Nicholson, MP, and Annie Elizabeth Prior, Newark-on-Trent; *m* 1st, 1893, Mabel, *d* of David Pryde, LLD, of Edinburgh; 2nd, 1919, Edith, *d* of Sir Lionel Phillips, 1st Bt; one *d*. *Educ:* The Magnus School, Newark-on-Trent. Trustee of Tate Gallery, 1934–39; Designed and executed stained glass window for parish church at Mells, 1932; Woodcuts: including Queen Victoria; Portraits: including W. E. Henley (Tate), Miss Jekyll (Tate), George Saintsbury (Merton), Walter Greaves (Manchester), The Girl with the Tattered Gloves (Fitzwilliam), The Rt Hon. the Earl of Harewood, Lord Horder; Landscapes: Malaga Bull Ring, La Ropa; Still Life: including The Hundred Jugs. *Publications:* An Alphabet, 1898; An Almanac of Twelve Sports (with Rudyard Kipling), 1898; London Types (with W. E. Henley), 1898; Characters of Romance, 1900; Clever Bill, 1926; The Pirate Twins, 1929; A Book of Blokes, 1930. *Recreations:* boomerang, bilboquet. *Address:* Little Triton, Blewbury, Berks. *T:* Blewbury 294. *Club:* Savile.

Died 16 May 1949.

NICHOLSON, Adm. Wilmot Stuart, CB 1917; *b* 1872; *s* of Maj.-Gen. Stuart Nicholson CB, Col Commandant, RA; *m* 1934, Christabel Sybil, *d* of late Rev. Dr P. D. Eyre, DD. Midshipman of Calliope at Samoa, 1889; Lieutenant, 1893; Commander, 1903; Captain, 1909; Captain-Superintendent of Destroyers being built by contract, 1910–12; Captain D (X), Harwich Force, 1915–16; Captain HMS Furious, Chief of Staff to Admiral Commanding Aircraft, 1917–18; Captain (Aircraft) Atlantic Fleet, 1919; Rear-Adm. 1920; Vice-Adm. 1925; commanded Second Light Cruiser Squadron, 1921–23; Chief of Submarine Service, 1923–25; retired list, 1927; Adm., retired, 1930; Officer Legion of Honour. *Address:* 8 Ashburn Gardens, SW7. *Club:* United Service.

Died 9 June 1947.

NICKSON, Rt Rev. George, DD (Camb.), LLD (TCD); Hon. DD (Durham), Hon. LLD (Bristol); *b* 9 May 1864; *e s* of John Nickson, Cefn Isaf, Tal-y-Cafn, N Wales; *m* 1891, Ada T. (*d* 1937), *y d* of James E. Phenix, Greenfield, Kilternan, Co. Dublin; two *d*. *Educ:* Southport; Trinity College, Dublin; Corpus Christi College, Cambridge. First Class Theol. Tripos, 1887. Deacon, 1888; Priest, 1889; Tutor and Bursar of Ridley Hall, Cambridge, 1888–97; Lecturer in Divinity at Selwyn Coll., Cambridge, 1895–97; Curate of Holy Trinity, Cambridge, 1888–90; Vicar of St Benedict, Cambridge, 1891–94; Fairfield, Liverpool, 1897–1905; St Andrew's, Southport, 1905–06; Examining Chaplain to Bishop of Durham, 1901–08; Rural Dean of West Derby, 1902–05; Select Preacher, Cambridge, 1893–96, 1915 and 1920; Oxford, 1915–17; Proctor in Convocation, 1906; Bishop-Suffragan of Jarrow, 1906–14, Canon of Durham Cathedral; Bishop of Bristol, 1914–33; President of the Council of Durham Colleges in University of Durham, 1910; Pro-Chancellor of University of Bristol, 1922–33; Lady Margaret Preacher, Cambridge, 1923; Sub-Prelate of the Order of St John of Jerusalem, 1931. *Recreations:* fishing, cabinet-making, silver work. *Address:* Lis Escop, Church Stretton, Shropshire.

Died 23 Feb. 1949.

NICOLL, James Gibson; JP; General Manager, 1925–38, Scottish Union and National Insurance Co., Edinburgh (now retired); *b* 19 Oct. 1870; *m* 1893; three *d*. *Educ:* High School, Dundee. Glasgow Secretary of the Scottish Union and National, 1904–08; Assistant

Secretary at Head Office of the Scottish Union and National, 1908–10; London Secretary of the Scottish Union and National, 1910–25; Chairman Associated Scottish Life Offices, 1934–36; President Chartered Insurance Institute of Great Britain and Ireland, 1928–29, Fellow since 1912; President of London Insurance Offices Football Association, 1919–25; Past President of the Insurance Society of Edinburgh. *Recreation:* golf. *Address:* c/o Drummonds Branch, Royal Bank of Scotland, 49 Charing Cross, SW1. *Club:* Caledonian.

Died 22 July 1949.

NICOLL, Lt-Col Peter Strachan, CB 1934; CBE 1919; TD; DL, JP; Chairman, City of Dundee Territorial Army Association, 1922, retired 1934; *b* Dundee, 1864; *s* of Robert Nicoll and Isabella Strachan; *m* 1889; one *s* two *d. Educ:* Dundee High School. Engaged in coal and shipping business; Lord Dean of Guild, Dundee, 1913–14 and 1920; DL and JP County of the City of Dundee; Chairman, Territorial Association, 1922; Chairman, Dundee Business Club, 1921; Vice-President, 1922–23; Hon. Vice-President Dundee Area Council of British Legion, comprising Forfarshire and Perthshire; 50 years Volunteer and Territorial; Regiment, The Black Watch; European War, 1914–18 (CBE, despatches thrice, Order of the Nile third class); Member of Dundee Baker Incorporation, Bonnetmaker Incorporation, Dundee Guildry Incorporation; President, The Black Watch Association (Dundee Branch). *Recreations:* golf, bowling, curling. *Address:* Hazel Bank, Kirriemuir, Angus.

Died 28 May 1942.

NICOLSON, Wing-Comdr James Brindley, VC 1940; DFC 1944; RAF; now serving abroad; *b* 29 April 1917; *er s* of Leslie Gibson Nicolson and Dorathea Hilda Brindley, Shoreham-by-Sea; *m* 1939, Muriel Caroline Kendall; one *s. Educ:* Tonbridge School. Experimental Engineering at Ricardo's Works, Shoreham, 1935 and 1936; joined RAF (Short Service Commission), 1936; completed training 1937 and posted to 72 (Fighter) Squadron; posted to 249 (Fighter) Squadron, 1940. *Recreations:* cricket, tennis, squash, Rugby, hockey.

Died May 1945.

NISBET, Robert Buchan, RSA, Hon. RSW; Hon. Member Royal Belgian Water Colour Society; landscape painter; *b* Edinburgh, 1 July 1857; *s* of John Nisbet, decorator, Edinburgh; *m* Margaret, *d* of Duncan F. Dempster, Greenock, 1895. *Educ:* Edinburgh Institution; diploma, Dresden International Exhibition, 1892; medal Antwerp International Exhibition, 1894; medal Vienna International, 1898. *Pictures:* Evening Stillness (purchased by Chantrey Bequest, 1890); Thundery Weather (Dresden); Harrowing (Vienna); Brown Autumn (Berlin National Gallery); Ploughing (Munich); A Scottish Moorland (Petrograd); Evening (Leeds Permanent Gallery); Waiting for the Tide, 1898; Between Showers (Reims Gallery), 1898; Summer in Surrey (Durban Gallery), 1898; Nov. Evening (Adelaide Gallery), 1899; A Fishing Village (Huddersfield Gallery), 1900; A Landscape, Carnegie Art Gallery, Pittsburg; Ferryden, Auckland Art Gallery, NZ. *Recreations:* golf, fishing, bicycling, stamp collecting. *Address:* Bardon, Ferntower Road, Crieff. *T:* Crieff 65. *Club:* Scottish Arts.

Died 15 Aug. 1942.

NISSE, Bertram Sydney, MD, MRCP; Hon. Physician British Red Cross Society's Clinic for Rheumatism; *er s* of G. H. and Rebecca Nissé; *m* 1932, Hélèna, *d* of D. I. Jacobs, Newcastle; one *s* one *d. Educ:* St Olave's; London Hospital (Buxton Entrance Scholarship in Arts). University Gold Medal, London MD Examination. Held various appointments at the London Hospital; Chief Assistant, formerly Resident Medical Officer, National Heart Hospital; Fellow Royal Society of Medicine; Vice-President, recently Hon. Secretary, Section of Physical Medicine; Fellow Medical Society of London and Hunterian Society; Member International Society Medical Hydrology. *Publications:* Rheumatism, 1938; contributions and papers dealing mainly with cardiology and rheumatism to various medical journals, including Proceedings Royal Society of Medicine, Annals of Eugenics, American Heart Journal, Clinical Journal, International Journal of Medicine and Surgery, etc. *Recreations:* walking, and the theatre. *Address:* 59 Harley Street, W1. *T:* Langham 4088.

Died 14 Aug. 1946.

NIVEN, Frederick John; author; *b* Valparaiso, Chile, 31 March 1878; *y s* of late John Niven, Glasgow; *m* 1911, Mary Pauline Thorne-Quelch. *Educ:* Hutchesons' Grammar School, Glasgow; Glasgow School of Art. Varied career; somewhat of a rolling stone; during War of 1914–18, Ministry of Information. *Publications:* The Lost Cabin Mine, 1908; The Island Providence, 1910; A Wilderness of Monkeys, 1911; Above Your Heads, 1911; Dead Men's Bells, 1912; The Porcelain Lady, 1913; Ellen Adair, 1913; Justice of the Peace, 1914; The SS Glory, 1915; Hands Up! 1915; Two Generations, 1916; Cinderella of Skookum Creek, 1916; Maple-Leaf Songs, 1917; Sage-Brush Stories, 1917; Penny Scot's Treasure, 1918; The Lady of the Crossing, 1919; A Tale that is Told, 1920; The Wolfer, 1923; Treasure Trail, 1923; Justice of the Peace, an American edition, with prefaces by Hugh Walpole and Christopher Morley, 1923; A Lover of the Land, and other poems, 1925; Ellen Adair, American edition, 1925; Queer Fellows, in America entitled Wild Honey, 1927; Canada West (in Outward Bound Library), 1930; The Three Marys, 1930; The Paisley Shawl, 1931; The Rich Wife, 1932; Mrs Barry, 1933; Triumph, 1934; The Flying Years, 1935; Old Soldier, 1936; The Staff at Simson's, 1937; Colour in the Canadian Rockies, 1937; Coloured Spectacles, 1938; The Story of Their Days, 1939; Mine Inheritance, 1940; Brothers in Arms, 1942; Under which King? 1943; wrote article on Canada for Peoples of All Nations. *Recreations:* mostly walking, but keen on all methods of travel, seeing new places and revisiting remembered ones. *Address:* c/o A. P. Watt & Son, Hastings House, 10 Norfolk Street, WC2.

Died 30 Jan. 1944.

NIVEN, Sir John, Kt 1937; Shipowner; late Director of Commercial Services, Ministry of Shipping; partner in firm of Andrew Weir and Co., 21 Bury Street, EC3; *b* Scotland, 7th Jan. 1877; *m* 1910, Annie Marguerite Nathan; no *c. Educ:* Glasgow High School. Started with Andrew Weir and Co., 1892; Chairman of Baltic Mercantile Shipping Exchange, 1935–37; Member of Council of Chamber of Shipping; was on Ships Replacement Committee under Shipping Replacement Act. *Recreation:* golf. *Address:* 28 Kepplestone, Eastbourne. *T:* Eastbourne 3681.

Died 20 Jan. 1947.

NIXON, Sir Christopher (William), 2nd Bt *cr* 1906; DSO 1918; Major, late RA; DL; *b* 19 Nov. 1877; *s* of 1st Bt and Mary Agnes, *d* of Dominick Edward Blake; *S* father, 1914; *m* Louise, *y d* of Robert Clery, JP, The Glebe, Athlacca, Limerick; three *s* one *d. Educ:* Beaumont; Trinity College, Dublin; RUI—MA (Hon.). Barrister-at-Law, King's Inns; entered army, 1900; Captain, 1909; Major, 1914; served European War, 1914–18 (DSO); retired pay, 1924. *Heir: s* Christopher John Louis Joseph, *b* 21 March 1918.

Died 23 April 1945.

NIXON, Alderman John William, MBE; MP (Ind U) Woodvale Division of Belfast, Parliament of Northern Ireland, since 1929; Graddum, Co. Cavan. Alderman for Court Ward Belfast City, 1924. *Address:* Woodvale House, Ballygomartin Road, Belfast.

Died 11 May 1949.

NIXON, Rev. Leigh Hunter, MVO 1934; MA; Rector of Tydd St Mary, Wisbech since 1933; Hon. Priest to the King since 1934; Fellow of Lancing College, 1925; Chairman Hurstpierpoint School Committee, 1926; *b* Madras, 22 Sept. 1871; *e s* of Robert Bell Nixon and Margaret Selina, *d* of Surgeon-Major Hunter (Madras Army); *m* 1905, Harrie, *d* of Alexander Millar, Hollyhurst, Clapham Common; two *s* one *d. Educ:* Hurstpierpoint; Keble College, Oxford, BA 1895; MA 1900; Oxford University Cross-Country Team, 1894; Ely Theological College, 1896. Deacon, 1897; Priest, 1898; Assistant Curate of Clapham, 1897; Curate in charge of St Saviour's, Clapham, and Deputy Minor Canon of Westminster, 1903; Minor Canon, 1906; Librarian, 1909; Precentor of Westminster Abbey, 1912; Diocesan Inspector of Schools, London Diocese, 1907–31; Secretary, London Diocesan Church Schools Association, 1910–18; Chaplain, Cutlers' Company, 1913–15; Acting Chaplain to the Forces, 1915–18; Deputy Priest-in-Ordinary to the King, 1919; Priest-in-Ordinary to the King, 1920–34. *Recreation:* music. *Address:* Rectory, Tydd St Mary, Wisbech; The Beacon, Mundesley, Norfolk.

Died 25 Aug. 1941.

NOAD, Lewis; KC 1933; Practising Barrister in Admiralty and Commercial Courts; Arbitrator to Lloyds; *b* 8 Oct. 1865; *s* of William John Noad and Mary Anne Belcher; *m* Carlotta (*d* 1945), *d* of Thomas Tottman, Tamworth, Staffs; no *c. Educ:* St Mary's Coll. Went to sea at 15 years of age trading round Cape Horn and on West Coast of S America for two years in small sailing vessel, (Barque Hugh Fortescue) afterwards in large Calcutta sailing clipper Benvenue (lost off Sandgate); afterwards in Anglo-Australasian Companies Port Darwin, Port Fairy, Port Pirie, and P. & OSN Cos. Rome, Brindisi, Massilia; Master Mariner; called to Bar, Lincoln's Inn, 1896; Bencher Lincoln's Inn, 1935. *Recreations:* golf, music, the microscope. *Address:* 7 King's Bench Walk, Temple, EC. *T:* Museum 0244, Central 9789. *Clubs:* Reform, Eighty: Coombe Hill; Moray Golf.

Died 17 Dec. 1950.

NOAKES, Ven. Edward Spencer, LLD, Trinity College, Dublin; Archdeacon of Derby, 1909–43, Archdeacon Emeritus since 1943; Hon. Canon of Derby, 1928; *m* Georgina Alethea (*d* 1936); one *s* one *d. Educ:* St Catharine's College, Cambridge (MA, 2nd class Theological Tripos). Ordained, 1889; Master, Perse School, Cambridge, 1889–94; Curate of St Andrew's, Cambridge, 1890–92; Headmaster Newark Grammar School, 1894–1904; Vicar of Edale, 1905–08; Rural Dean of Eyam, 1907–08; Vicar of St John's, Derby, 1908–14; Vicar of St Matthew, Darley Abbey, 1914–30; Examining Chaplain to the Lord Bishop of Southwell, 1909–27; Rural Dean of Derby, 1910–12; Examining Chaplain to the Bishop of Derby, 1928; Hon. Chaplain VF, 1917–20. *Address:* 13 Vernon Street, Derby. *Club:* Derby County.

Died 30 Dec. 1944.

NOAL, Comdr Richard John, CBE 1920 (OBE 1918); RNR retired; *b* 1870; *s* of William Noal; *m* 1896, Edith Hannah Harkness (*d* 1943); one *s* one *d.* Rendered services to Ministry of Shipping during European War. *Address:* Sherwood, 19 Brampton Grove, Hendon, NW4. *T:* Hendon 2388.

Died 12 July 1950.

NOBLE, Edward; novelist, Master Mariner; *b* 9 March 1857; *m* 1885, Alice Willcox (*d* 1922); *brother* of Dr T. Tertius Noble; one *d. Educ:* privately. Twenty odd years wandering, and on the seven seas—in sailing and tramp and mail ship; dabbling in engineering, in paint, in work that is unclassified as well as in that which generally is understood to be part and parcel of the business known as sailorising, both ashore and afloat. *Publications:* The Edge of Circumstance; Waves of Fate; The Lady Navigators; Fisherman's Gat; The Grain Carriers; Lords of the Sea; Chains; The Vicar of Normanton; Lifted Curtains; Dust from the Loom; The Bottle-Fillers; Outposts of the Fleet; The Naval Side; The Mandarin's Bell; The Fire of Spring; Moving Waters; The Pulse of Darkness. *Address:* c/o Barclays Bank, Ltd, Carshalton, Surrey.

Died 12 May 1941.

NOBLE, Sir Saxton William Armstrong, 3rd Bt *cr* 1902; MInstCE; FSA; Sacred Treasure of Japan (Second Class), Rising Sun (Fourth Class); a Director of the Royal Academy of Music; formerly a Director of Mond Nickel Co. and The Whitehead Torpedo Coys and a Managing Director of Sir W. G. Armstrong Whitworth & Co. Ltd; *b* 13 Feb. 1863; 2nd *s* of late Sir Andrew Noble Bt, KCB, FRS, and Margery, *d* of A. Campbell, Quebec; *S* brother 1937; *m* 1891, Celia Brunel (author of The Brunels, Father and Son, 1938), *d* of Arthur James of Eton College; one *s* two *d. Educ:* Winchester. *Recreations:* shooting, fishing, music. *Heir: s* Humphrey Brunel Noble, MC [*b* 1892, *m* 1926, Celia, *d* of late Capt. Stewart Cormac Weigall, RN; two *s* one *d*]. *Address:* 23 Royal Crescent, Bath. *T:* 3878; Kent House, Knightsbridge, London SW7. *T:* Kensington 0808. *Clubs:* Athenæum, Burlington Fine Arts, Garrick, Royal Automobile, Beefsteak.

Died 12 Oct. 1942.

NOBLE, Sir William, Kt 1920; MIEE; Director, General Electric Co; *b* Aberdeen, 22 April 1861; *m* 1st, 1885, Mima (*d* 1916), *d* of William Macdonald, Aberdeen; one *s* two *d*; 2nd, 1918, Marion (*d* 1926), *widow* of J. Galloway Weir, MP; 3rd, 1935, Elsie Ethel Rae. *Educ:* Public School and Gordon's College, Aberdeen. PO Engineer at Aberdeen; then successively Technical Officer, GPO, London; Superintending Engineer, London; Engineer-in-Chief. Chevalier de la Croix Belgique. *Recreation:* golf. *Address:* The Chase, Blackdown, Leamington Spa; 60 Park Lane, W1. *Clubs:* Devonshire, Royal Automobile, City Livery.

Died 10 Nov. 1943.

NOBLETT, Bt Lt-Col Louis Hemington, CBE 1919; JP; *b* 15 Jan. 1869; *s* of Henry Sutton Noblett, solicitor, Cork; *m* Edith Mary, *d* of George Bennett of Little Rissington Manor, Glos; two *d. Educ:* Bath College. Joined 1st Royal Irish Rifles, 1888; served with them in Ireland, England, S Africa, and India; served with and commanded a company in Lumsden's Horse during SA War, 1900 (despatches, Bt Major); retired, 1913; served as Embarkation Staff Officer at Liverpool and Folkestone, 1914–19 (despatches, Bt Lt-Col, CBE, Chevalier de l'Ordre de la Couronne). *Recreations:* cricket, polo, hunting. *Address:* Ashton, Chaffcombe, Chard. *T:* Chard 3228.

Died 4 April 1948.

NOEL, Hon. Charles (Hubert Francis), OBE 1918; Major Coldstream Guards; retired; *b* 22 Oct. 1885; 2nd *s* of 3rd Earl of Gainsborough; *m* May, *e d* and heiress of late Brig.-Gen. Archibald Campbell Douglas-Dick, CB, of Pitkerro; four *s* two *d.* Served European War with BEF, 1914–18; served also 1939–42, Home Forces. County Colonel Commandant for Angus Army Cadet Force, 1943–46. *Address:* Moreland House, Cleish, Kinross-shire.

Died 26 April 1947.

NOEL, Rev. Conrad le Despenser Roden; Vicar of Thaxted since 1910; *b* 12 July 1869; *s* of Hon. Roden Noel, poet and Alice de Broë; *m* 1895, Miriam Greenwood; one *d. Educ:* Wellington; Cheltenham; Corpus Christi, Cambridge; Chichester Theological College; London Doss Houses, and Portsmouth slums with Father Dolling. Various assistant curacies, the last two being St Mary's, Paddington Green, with Rev. A. E. Lilley as Vicar and St Mary's, Primrose Hill, with Rev. Percy Dearmer; during the London period on the literary staff of The Daily News and contributor to The Daily Chronicle and weekly and monthly journals; Lecturer for various Socialist bodies, especially in the North and Midlands, Scotland and Wales; arrested for free speech in Manchester. *Publications:* Day of the Sun, 1901; The Labour Party, 1906; Socialism and Church History, 1910; Byways of Belief, 1912; Uplifting the Son of Man, 1919; Battle of the Flags, 1922; Life of Jesus, 1937; Jesus the Heretic, 1939; also various pamphlets, joint publications and contributions. *Recreations:* in earlier life, longdistance running, swimming, chess, debating and discussion; later, political and theological controversy. *Address:* The Vicarage, Thaxted, Dunmow, Essex. *T:* Thaxted 221.

Died 22 July 1942.

NOEL, Bt Col Harold Ernest, DSO 1918; TD; DL; *b* 30 Sept. 1884; *s* of Byron Noel, Ockham, Surrey; *m* 1914, Isabella Bruce Baird, *d* of G. H. Blunt, Leicester; no *c. Educ:* private. Trained as Land Agent and practising as such. Served European War, 1914–18 (despatches, two medals, DSO). *Address:* Blaby Hill, Leicester. *T:* Leicester 89469.

Died 26 Nov. 1941.

NOEL-BUXTON, 1st Baron *cr* 1930, of Aylsham; **Noel Edward Noel-Buxton;** PC 1924; *b* 1869; 2nd *s* of Sir T. Fowell Buxton, 3rd Bt; *m* 1914; Lucy Edith (Lady Noel-Buxton, MP), *e d* of late Major Henry Pelham Burn; two *s* three *d. Educ:* Harrow; Trinity College, Cambridge (History Honours, 1889; MA 1894). Was Major 2nd Tower Hamlets RV; ADC in S Australia to his father (the Governor), 1896; served on Whitechapel Board of Guardians and Central Unemployment Body; was Member of Home Office Departmental Committee on Lead Poisoning; wounded by political assassin, Oct. 1914, while on mission to secure adhesion of Balkan States in the War; MP (L) Whitby, 1905–06; MP N Norfolk (L) 1910–18 (Lab), 1922–30; Minister of Agriculture and Fisheries, Jan.–Nov. 1924 and 1929–30; contested Ipswich, 1900; Pres. of the National Gardens Guild, the Save the Children Fund, National Laymen's Missionary Movement, and (joint) The Anti-Slavery Soc.; Chm. of the Miners' Welfare Committee, 1931–34. *Publications:* Europe and the Turks; With the Bulgarian Staff; Travels and Reflections, 1929; part-author of The Heart of the Empire, Travel and Politics in Armenia, The War and the Balkans, Balkan Problems and European Peace, Oppressed Peoples and the League of Nations. *Recreations:* gardening, travel. *Heir: s* Hon. Rufus Alexander Buxton [*b* 13 Jan. 1917; *m* 1939, Nancy, *yr d* of Col K. H. M. Connal, CB; two *s*; assumed names of Rufus Alexander Buxton in lieu of those of Noel Alexander Noel-Buxton, 1944]. *Address:* 11 Wilton Place, SW1. *Club:* Athenæum.

Died 12 Sept. 1948.

NOKES, George Augustus; *see* Sekon, G. A.

NOLAN, Michael James, LRCSI, L & LMRCPI, CPM; JP Co. Down; Consulting Visitor in Lunacy to Lord Chief Justice, Northern Ireland, and to the Chief Justice, Irish Free State; late Resident Medical Superintendent, Down County Mental Hospital, Downpatrick, N Ireland; *b* 29 Sept. 1859; 2nd *s* of James Nolan, The Crescent, Limerick; *m* 1st, 1886, Kathleen Mary (*d* 1930), *e d* of late Thomas Greene, JP, Green Lawn, Ennis; one *s*; 2nd, 1934, Kathleen Alice, *widow* of E. Maziere Courtenay, MB, and *y d* of late Canon R. W. Whelan. *Educ:* Crescent College, Limerick; Royal College of Surgeons. President of the Ulster Medical Society, 1926–27; Hon. Member and President Royal Medico-Psychological Association of Great Britain and Ireland, 1924–25; previously private practice and Deputy RMS, Richmond Asylum, Dublin; Fellow Royal Soc. of Medicine; Fellow of the Royal Academy of Medicine Ire.; Regional Delegate (N Ireland) of the National Council for Mental Hygiene; Member of the Advisory

Committee on Appointments of Queen's Univ. of Belfast. *Publications:* Co-Editor Handbook for Mental Nurses, seventh Edition; many contributions to professional journals. *Recreations:* reading, gardening, motoring. *Address:* 3 The Crescent, Newcastle, Co. Down.

Died 27 Dec. 1944.

NOLLET, Edouard; Général d'Armée; Grand Chanceller de la Légion d'Honneur; *b* 28 Janvier 1865; *s* of Paul Nollet et Henriette d'Anget; *m* 1901, Marie Vigan; one *s* three *d. Educ:* Divers Lycées; École Polytechnique; École Supérieure de Guerre. Sous Lieut d'artillerie, 1884; Capitaine, 1892; breveté d'État Major, 1898; Colonel, 1911; Général de brigade, 1914; Général de Division, 1916; Membre du Conseil Supérieur de la guerre, 1921; *avant la guerre*, Rapporteur de la Commission Centrale de réception des Poudres de guerre, Professeur adjoint de tactique générale et de stratégie à l'École Supérieure de guerre, Directeur du Cours de tir d'artillerie de campagne; *pendant la guerre* Commandant l'artillerie d'un Corps d'Armée, une brigade d'infanterie, une division d'infanterie, une division de chasseurs alpins (diables bleus) et successivement deux Corps d'Armée; *après la guerre*, Président de la Commission Militaire Interalliée de Contrôle en Allemagne, Ministre de la Guerre; Membre du Conseil Supérieur de la guerre; Grand Chancelier de la Légion d'Honneur; Grand Croix de la Légion d'Honneur, Médaille Militaire; KCMG et nombreux ordres étrangers. *Publications:* Une expérience de désarmement (5 ans de Contrôle Militaire en Allemagne); articles de revue. *Address:* Grande Chancellerie de la Légion d'Honneur, 64 Rue de Lille, Paris.

Died Jan. 1941.

NOON, Nawab Sir Malik Mohamed Hayat, Kt 1935; CSI 1931; a Member of the Council of State; late Commissioner, Lahore; *b* June 1875; *o s* of Malik Fateh Khan Noon; *m*; three *s* one *d. Educ:* Chiefs' College, Lahore. Worked as extra Assistant Commissioner, 1901–15; extra Assistant Settlement Officer and Settlement Officer in Ambala and Montgomery districts and as Deputy Commissioner in Jhang, Montgomery, Rohtak, Gujranwala and Lyallpur districts; was Commissioner of Ambala and Lahore Divisions for sixteen months; landowner; Provincial Durbar, sword of honour for recruiting services during war. *Address:* Village Nurpur Noon, District Shahpur, Punjab, India.

Died 16 March 1941.

NOPS, Sir Wilfrid Walter, Kt 1947; LLB (Lond.); Clerk of the Central Criminal Court; Clerk of the Peace of City of London; *b* 7 May 1884; *s* of late Walter Nops, ISO, and late Elizabeth Moule; *m* 1912, Helen Lilian Jennings; one *s* two *d. Educ:* Quernmore, Bromley, Kent; King's College, London. Secretary's Office, GPO, 1902–09; Officer of Central Criminal Court, 1909–; Barrister-at-Law, 1912; Past Master of Worshipful Company of Gold and Silver Wyre Drawers, 1946. *Recreations:* tennis, golf, photography, microscopy. *Address:* Broomfield House, Herne, Kent. *Clubs:* Reform, City Livery.

Died 30 Dec. 1948.

NORBURY, 4th Earl of, *cr* 1827; **William Brabazon Lindsay Graham-Toler;** Baron Norwood, 1797; Baron Norbury, 1800; Viscount Glandine, 1827; *b* 2 July 1862; *o s* of 3rd Earl and Lady Steuart Lindsay Bethune, *d* of 9th Earl of Lindsay; *S* father, 1873; *m* 1908, Lucy Henrietta Katharine (author of Summers of Yesterday, 1934), *e d* of late Hon. and Rev. William Charles Ellis. *Educ:* Harrow; Christ Church, Oxford. *Heir: cousin* Capt. Ronald Ian Montague Graham-Toler. *Address:* Green Wood Gate, Withyham, Sussex. *T:* Crowborough 197.

Died 20 April 1943.

NORBURY, Sir Henry Frederick Oswald, Kt 1937; Registrar Probate, Divorce, and Admiralty Division, High Court of Justice, 1923–35, Senior Registrar of Principal Probate Registry since 1935; *b* 27 July 1880; *s* of late Inspector-General of Hospitals and Fleets Sir Henry Frederick Norbury, KCB, KHS, RN; *m* 1911, Esmé Frances, *d* of late John Bradford of Hartleymere, Ealing Common, W; one *s* two *d. Educ:* Merchant Taylors' School, London; St John's College, Oxford (Scholar) (2nd Class Mods; Aegrotat Lit. Hum.); BA, 1903; MA, 1905; BCL, 1908. Barrister-at-Law, Inner Temple, 1907; Past-Master of the Merchant Taylors' Company; a Vice-Pres. British Records' Soc. *Address:* Principal Probate Registry, Somerset House, WC2. *Club:* United University.

Died 15 Dec. 1948.

NORIE-MILLER, Sir Francis, 1st Bt *cr* 1936; JP County Perth; Chairman of the General Life Assurance Company, Aldwych, WC; Governor General Accident, Fire and Life Assurance Corporation, Ltd, Perth and London; *b* 11 March 1859; *s* of Henry Miller, Chief of Statistical Dept of HM Customs, London; *m* 1st, Grace Harvey (*d* 1931), *d* of Rev. H. J. Day, Vicar of Cheshunt, Herts; one *s* (and one killed in War of 1917) one *d*; 2nd, 1934, Florence Jean Belfrage, 4th *d* of late William McKim, Scone, Perthshire. *Educ:* privately. Trained for law and joined Insurance Company; for 57 years Chief Officer of the General Companies; MP (LNat) Perth, 1935; for over 21 years Chairman of the School Board of Perth or Perth County Education Authority; and for 32 Director (15 years Chairman) of County and City of Perth Royal Infirmary. *Recreation:* golf. *Address:* Cleeve, Perth, Scotland; 5 Orme Court, W2. *Club:* Reform.

Died 4 July 1947.

NORMAN, 1st Baron *cr* 1944, of St Clere; **Montagu Collet Norman,** PC 1923; DSO 1901; late the Beds Regt, 4th Batt.; Governor, Bank of England, 1920–44; Lieut City of London; *b* 1871; *e s* of late F. H. Norman, Moor Place, Much Hadham, Herts; *m* 1933, Priscilla, *d* of late Major Robert Reynties, Belgian Artillery, and Lady Alice Josephine, *d* of 7th Earl of Abingdon. *Educ:* Eton; King's College, Cambridge. Served South Africa, 1900–01 (despatches, Queen's medal 4 clasps, DSO). *Address:* Thorpe Lodge, Campden Hill, W8. *T:* Park 6266. *Club:* Athenæum.

Died 4 Feb. 1950 (ext).

NORMAN, Sir (Henry) Nigel St Valery, 2nd Bt *cr* 1915; CBE 1943; Aeronautical Consultant; Chairman, Airwork Ltd, Heston; Partner, Norman, and Dawbarn, Aeronautical Consulting Engineers and Architects; Fellow, Royal Aeronautical Society; Group Captain, Auxiliary Air Force Reserve; *b* 21 May 1897; *s* of Rt Hon. Sir Henry Norman, 1st Bt, and Ménie Muriel Dowie; *S* father, 1939; *m* 1926, Patricia Moyra, *e d* of late Lt-Col J. H. A. Annesley, DSO, CMG; three *s. Educ:* Winchester; Royal Military Acad., Woolwich; Trinity College, Cambridge, MA. Served France, in RGA and RE, 1916–19; Metropolitan Railway, 1922–28; Private Aeroplane owner since 1926; with F. A. I. Muntz founded Airwork Ltd to construct and develop Heston Airport, 1928; Commanded No. 601 (County of London) Squadron, AAF; in course of professional work has flown extensively over Europe, North America, Africa and India; in partnership has specialized in planning of major airports in United Kingdom and abroad. *Publications:* papers read before Institute of Town Planning, Royal Aeronautical Society, Architectural Assoc., London Society, Chartered Surveyors' Institution, etc. *Recreations:* flying, shooting, fishing. *Heir: s* Mark Annesley, *b* 8 Feb. 1927. *Address:* Clifferdine House, Rendcombe, Cirencester, Glos. *Clubs:* Oxford and Cambridge, MCC.

Died 19 May 1943.

NORMAND, Captain Patrick Hill, DSO 1900; *b* 20 Feb. 1876; 3rd *s* of late Patrick Hill Normand; *m* 1st, 1907, Matilda M. Marsh; three *s*; 2nd, 1921, Agnes Dorothy, *widow* of Captain R. W. Harding, London Regiment; one *s. Educ:* Fettes College, Edinburgh. Took part in Jameson Raid, taken prisoner at Dornkop, and deported, 1895; joined Imperial Light Horse as Lieut 1899, at Maritzburg, Natal, and helped to form regiment; present at battle of Elandslaagte (wounded); in siege of Ladysmith, wounded at Waggon Hill (despatches); went with General Mahon's column to relief of Mafeking; advance on Barberton with General French's Division (despatches); Deputy Governor Transvaal Prisons Department, 1903; Governor, 1908; served with Expeditionary Force in France from May 1917 to March 1919, as Deputy Assistant Provost-Marshal; retired from Prisons Service, Feb. 1931. *Address:* Brookside, Fovant, Wilts.

Died 27 March 1943.

NORRIS, Charles Arthur, CBE 1937; OBE 1935; Actuary and General Manager since 1935, The National Mutual Life Association of Australasia Ltd Melbourne, Australia; Commissioner State Electricity Commission of Victoria, Australia since 1934; Member of National Security (Capital Issues) Advisory Board; Member of the Board of Trustees of the AIF Canteens Trust and Sir Samuel McCaughey Bequest; *b* Melbourne, 6 Sept. 1874; *s* of late William Norris, Cambridge, England; *m* 1900, Rose Maud Annie, *d* of Rev. Stephen Howard; one *d. Educ:* Carlton College, Melbourne. FIA Lond. 1903. General Secretary 1910, The National Mutual Life Association of Australasia Ltd; Chairman of Transport Regulation Enquiry Board, Victoria, Australia, 1932; Commonwealth Representative on Employment Council State of Victoria since 1932; at various times Member of different Financial and Economic Committees advising Governments; Edited Financial Section Melbourne Punch, 1903–05. *Publications:* Sundry Papers and Articles on Financial, Economic and Allied Subjects; Report on Transport Regulation in Victoria. *Recreations:* nothing particular; walking, reading (scientific), high fidelity reproduction recorded music. *Address:* 3 Marshall Avenue, Kew, Melbourne, E4. *TA:* Sirron Melbourne. *T:* Hawthorn 3326. *Clubs:* Melbourne, Melbourne.

Died 30 Sept. 1941.

NORRIS, Charles Gilman; author; *b* Chicago, Ill, USA; *s* of Benjamin Franklin Norris and Gertrude G. Doggett; *m* Kathleen Norris, author; one *s. Educ:* University of California. Connected editorially with Country Life in America, American Magazine, Sunset Magazine, Christian Herald; Major of Infantry, retired; Member of the Military Order of Foreign Wars of the US. *Publications:* The Amateur, 1915; Salt, 1919; Brass, 1921; The Rout of the Philistines, Poetical Drama 1922; Bread, 1923; Pig Iron, 1925; Zelda Marsh, 1927; A Gest of Robin Hood, drama, 1929; Seed, 1930; Zest, 1933; Hands, 1935; Bricks without Straw, 1938. *Address:* La Estancia, Saratoga, California, USA. *Clubs:* Bohemian, San Francisco; Menlo Country, Menlo; The Players, The Dutch Treat, New York City.

Died 25 July 1945.

NORRIS, Rt Rev. Francis Lushington, DD; *b* 1 Sept. 1864; 4th *s* of Ven. J. P. Norris, DD, Archdeacon of Bristol (*d* 1891), and Edith (*d* 1928), *d* of Rt Hon. Stephen Lushington, Judge of the Admiralty. *Educ:* Winchester (Scholar); Trinity College, Cambridge; Wells Theological College. Ordained 1887; Curate at Tewkesbury, 1887–89; went to Peking as SPG missionary, 1889; Bishop of China (North), 1914–40; Chairman of the House of Bishops, Chung Hua Sheng Kung Hui, 1931–40. *Publications:* China (in Mowbray's series on Church Expansion); Concerning

Confirmation. *Address:* Peking, China, via Siberia. *TA:* Anlikan, Peking. *Clubs:* Church Imperial, Church House.

Died 2 July 1945.

NORRIS, Herbert; costume architect and archæologist; *s* of Arthur and Susan Norris; *m* Alice Maud, *o c* of C. Corbett-Blades, MD; one *d. Educ:* privately; Royal College of Art. Served articles as architect, but specialised in historical and theatrical costume, and in stage-setting; a pupil of, and asst to, late C. Willhelm, 1896–1920; has designed settings and costumes for over 100 plays in London, the Provinces and America; for a number of British films, and for pageants at Bury St Edmunds 1907, Winchester 1908, Festival of Empire, Crystal Palace, 1910, Abergavenny 1913, Harlech 1920 and 1922, Wembley 1924, and Shakespeare's England, Earl's Court, 1912; responsible for principal groups at Shakespeare Ball, 1911; Hundred Year's Ago Ball, 1912; Versailles Ball, 1913, and for costumes at Elizabethan Fête, Royal Palace, Stockholm, 1912; on the YMCA and member of modelling staff Imperial War Museum during European War, 1914–18; Lecturer on Historical Costume and Stagecraft to Students for University of London's Diploma in Dramatic Art; Lecturer on Historical Costume at the East London College, University of London, for the Board of Education and the Central School of Speech Training, Royal Albert Hall, 1919–39; retained to design and supervise Historical Sections, Madame Tussaud's Exhibition, 1928–31. All Costumes, etc., for Stratford-on-Avon Memorial Theatre Productions, 1919, 1920, 1921, 1922; Costumes and Settings for Henry V, 1937, Henry VIII, 1938, Richard III, 1939, Richard II, 1944. Period Expert to the Gaumont-British Picture Corporation Ltd Drawings of Military Equipment for 'The King's Armies' in dioramas representing landing of Romans, 55 bc, Battles of Hastings, 1066, and of Crécy, 1346, exhibited in RUSI Museum, 1936. *Publications:* Costume and Fashion, vol. i, 1924; vol. ii, 1927; vol. iii, The Tudors, 1938; vol. vi, The Nineteenth Century, 1934; Church Vestments, their Origin and Development, 1949; series of articles in The Art Record on The Evolution of Costume, 1902. *Address:* Godbegot, Thame, Oxon.

Died 7 Nov. 1950.

NORRIS, Acting Captain Stephen Hugh, DSO 1940 (and Bar, 1955); DSC; RN; *b* 9 Sept. 1903; *s* of Hugh L. Norris; *m* 1930, Nancy Anderson; three *s. Educ:* Osborne and Dartmouth. Midshipman, HMS Malaya, 1921; Sub-Lieut, 1924; Lieutenant, 1926; Lieut-Comdr, 1934; HMS Firedrake, 1938–42 (DSC and Bar, DSO); Comdr 1942. *Address:* East Farleigh House, Maidstone.

Died 13 Nov. 1944.

NORTH, 13th Baron *cr* 1554; **John Dudley North,** Lieut RN; *b* 7 June 1917; *o s* of late Hon. Dudley William John North, MC, and Dorothy, *d* of late Captain J. P. Donne; *S* grandfather, 1938; *m* 1940, Margaret, *d* of R. W. H. Glennie, Cape Province, S Africa. *Educ:* RN College, Dartmouth. *Heirs:* sisters Dorothy Ann (Mrs Clive Graham) and Susan Silence. *Address:* Kirtling Tower, Newmarket.

Died 19 Dec. 1941.

NORTH, Lt-Col Edward Bunbury, CMG 1919; DSO 1917; late Commanding 3rd Royal Fusiliers; *b* 28 March 1869; 2nd *surv. s* of late North North of Thurland Castle and Newton Hall, Lancs; *m* 1899, Margaret, *d* of late Hon. J. Dundas, MP; one *s* two *d.* Served with Egyptian Army, 1898–99 (despatches, 4th Class Medjidie); campaigns in Soudan; with Royal Fusiliers in S Africa, 1899–1900; attached Imperial Japanese Army, 1907–09; served European War, 1915–18, BEF, as Brigade-Major in West Riding Brigade, 147th Infantry Brigade, 124th Infantry Brigade, commanding 4th Royal Fusiliers, 1916–17, 10th Bn The Queens, 1918; 123 Infantry

Brigade, Army of the Rhine; 3rd Royal Fusiliers, 1919–21 (CMG, DSO, despatches thrice, wounded); retired pay, 1923. *Address:* Summerdale House, Holme, Carnforth, Lancashire. *T:* Crooklands 210.

Died 23 July 1944.

NORTH, Major Edward Tempest Tunstall; JP; *b* 1900; *s* of Brig.-Gen. Bordugge North North, CB, MVO, Newton Hall, Kirkby Lonsdale; *m* 1928, Mary Scott, *d* of Thomas William Wilkinson, Curwen Woods, Carnforth; one *s* one *d. Educ:* Eton; Trinity College, Cambridge. JP Westmorland, 1925, Lancs, 1935; Capt. Yorkshire Hussars, 1931; Major, 1939; MP (Con.) Warwickshire (Nuneaton Division), 1931–35. *Address:* Newton Hall, Whittington, Carnforth. *T:* Kirkby Lonsdale 232. *Club:* Windham.

Died 1 Jan. 1942.

NORTH, Worshipful Frederick Keppel; Barrister-at-law; Chancellor of the Dioceses of Norwich and of St Edmundsbury and Ipswich; *b* 7 May 1860; *e s* of late Charles North and Augusta, *e d* of Hon. and Rev. Thomas R. Keppel, Rector of North Creake, Norfolk; *m* 1898, Grace (*d* 1946), *d* of Gen. Hon. Sir Percy Robert Basil and Lady Louisa Feilding; two *s. Educ:* Eton; Trinity College, Cambridge (BA, LLB). Called to Bar, Inner Temple, 1884; South-Eastern Circuit; Chairman of the Norfolk Quarter Sessions; Vice-President of Society of Chairmen of Quarter Sessions; Patron of the Living of Rougham. *Recreations:* cottage improvement, tree planting, and watching cricket. *Address:* Rougham Hall, King's Lynn. *T:* Weasenham 230. *Clubs:* Church House; Norfolk (Norwich).

Died 24 March 1948.

NORTH, Herbert L., BA, ARIBA; architect; *b* Leicester, 1871; *s* of Thomas North, Antiquary and Campanologist, and Fanny North; *m* 1897, Ida Maude Davies; one *d. Educ:* Uppingham; Jesus College, Cambridge. Church Work and House Work (twice illustrated in Country Life) at Llanfairfechan, also in N and S Wales, Midlands, Lake District, and elsewhere. *Publications:* Old Churches of Arllechwedd; Old Cottages of Snowdonia, with Harold Hughes, FSA, ARIBA, and Old Churches of Snowdonia. *Recreation:* gardening. *Address:* Wern Isaf, Llanfairfechan, N Wales. *T:* Llanfairfechan 4.

Died 9 Feb. 1941.

NORTH, William Albert; JP, High Sheriff for County of Leicester, 1935; *b* 1881; *s* of late Sir Jonathan North; *m* 1905, Mabel Creswell, *d* of W. H. Turner, Leicester; three *s* four *d. Educ:* privately. *Address:* Keythorpe Hall, Leicestershire. *TA:* Keythorpe, East Norton. *T:* Tugby 220. *Clubs:* Reform; Leicester County, Leicester.

Died 22 Dec. 1946.

NORTHBROOK, 4th Baron *cr* 1866; **Francis Arthur Baring;** Bart 1793; *b* 20 July 1882; *s* of late Hon. Francis Henry Baring, 2nd *s* of 1st Baron Northbrook and Lady Grace Elizabeth Boyle, 2nd *d* of 9th Earl of Cork; *S cousin*, 2nd Earl of Northbrook, 1929; *m* 1st, 1914, Evelyn Gladys Isabel (*d* 1919), *d* of J. G. Charles, 39 St George's Road, SW; one *s* one *d*; 2nd, 1941, Constance Maud, *o d* of late Frank Griffin, Kew. *Educ:* Eton; Trinity College, Oxford. JP Hants. *Heir:* *s* Hon. Francis John Baring, *b* 31 May 1915. *Address:* Woodlands Farm, Bramdean, Alresford, Hants. *T:* Bramdean 202.

Died 15 Dec. 1947.

NORTHBROOK, Countess of; Florence Anita Eyre, CBE 1920; *d* of late Eyre Coote, West Park, Hants; *m* 1st, 1883, Sir Robert John Abercromby, 7th Bt (*d* 1895); two *s*; 2nd, 1899, 2nd and last Earl of Northbrook (*d* 1929). *Address:* Abbots Worthy House, Kingsworthy, Winchester. *T:* Winchester 4110.

Died 4 Dec. 1946.

NORTHCOTE, Rev. Hon. Arthur Francis; Hon. Canon of St Edmundsbury and Ipswich, 1922–32; Canon Emeritus since 1932; *b* 2 Nov. 1852; 4th *s* of 1st Earl of Iddesleigh; *m* 1st, 1877, Alice Caroline (*d* 1878), *d* of E. R. Owen, Oxford; one *d*; 2nd, 1880, Mary Arabella (*d* 1888), *d* of S. Bush Toller, QC, Hampstead; one *s* three *d*; 3rd, 1892, Emily Catherine (*d* 1931), *d* of Col Kekewich, 5th Northumb. Fusiliers, Tiverton, Devon; one *d*. *Educ:* Rugby; New College, Oxford; MA. Rector of Dodbrooke, Devon, 1881–84; Washfield, Devon, 1884–90; Vicar of St Gregory, Canterbury, 1890–1900; Rector of Monks' Eleigh, Suffolk, 1900–32; Rural Dean of Lavenham, 1919–27; was an Alderman of the County Council and Chairman of the West Suffolk Education Committee. *Address:* Parklands, Bradninch, Exeter. *T:* Hele 220.

Died 30 Aug. 1943.

NORTHCOTE, Sir Geoffry Alexander Stafford, KCMG 1935 (CMG 1931); MA; Knight of Grace, Order of St John of Jerusalem; *b* 9 Feb. 1881; *s* of late Rev. Canon Hon. Arthur Francis Northcote; *m* Edith Juliet Mary, *d* of Rev. J. W. Adams, VC; two *s*. *Educ:* Blundell's School, Tiverton; Balliol College, Oxford. Entered the Colonial Service, 1904; Kenya (formerly East African Protectorate), 1904–27; Chief Secretary, Northern Rhodesia, 1928–30; Colonial Secretary, Gold Coast, 1930–34; Governor and C-in-C British Guiana, 1935–36; Governor and C-in-C Hong-Kong, 1937–41. *Club:* Marlborough-Windham.

Died 10 July 1948.

NORTHCOTE, Lady Rosalind Lucy Stafford; *e d* of 2nd Earl of Iddesleigh. *Publications:* The Book of Herbs, 1904; Devon: its Moorlands, Streams, and Coasts, 1908. *Address:* Pynes, Exeter.

Died 31 Dec. 1950.

NORTON, 4th Baron *cr* 1878; **Ronald Wolston Fleetwood Adderley;** *b* 15 Oct. 1885; *s* of 2nd Baron and Caroline Dixie, *d* of Sir Alexander Dixie, 10th Bart; *S* brother, 1933; *m* 1931, Hylda, *d* of Robert William Tovey, Cheltenham, and *widow* of Hilary George Dunbar. *Heir: uncle* Hon. (Henry) Arden Adderley. *Address:* 7 Lansdowne Crescent, Cheltenham.

Died 4 Jan. 1944.

NORTON, 5th Baron *cr* 1878; **Henry Arden Adderley;** DL, JP; late Capt. Warwickshire Yeomanry Cavalry; Member of Territorial Force Association, Co. Warwick; rejoined Yeomanry April 1915 as Capt; *b* 26 Sept. 1854; 2nd *s* of 1st Baron; *S nephew*, 1944; *m* 1881, Grace Stopford Sackville (*d* 1944), *y d* of William Bruce Stopford Sackville of Drayton, Northants; one *s* four *d*. *Educ:* Eton; Christ Church, Oxford; BA 1879. Called to Bar, Inner Temple, 1880; JP Co. Warwick, 1879. *Publications:* History of Warwickshire Yeomanry Cavalry, 1896; Warwickshire Yeomanry in the Great War, 1922. *Heir: s* Hon. Hubert Bowyer Arden Adderley [*b* 1886; *m* 1912, Elizabeth, *d* of W. J. Birkbeck; two *s* three *d*]. *Address:* Fillongley Hall, Coventry. *T:* Fillongley 303. *Club:* Windham.

Died 1 Jan. 1945.

NORTON, Charles William, RI 1935; ARWA, RCA; figure and landscape painter in oils and water colour; *b* Beverley, Yorks, 1870; *m* Gertrude, *d* of William Ward Beverley; one *s* two *d*. *Educ:* Studied at Regent Street Polytechnic Art School and Julians, Paris. Exhibited RA, Paris Salon, etc. *Recreations:* gardening and fishing. *Address:* 68 Malden Road, Cheam, Surrey. *Club:* London Sketch.

Died 21 Nov. 1946.

NORTON, David Evans, MA; *b* 4 Jan. 1863; 2nd *s* of late Rev. D. E. Norton, formerly Rector of Maperton, Somerset; *m* 1893, Maud, *y d* of Rev. A. Y. Bazett, formerly Rector of Quedgeley, Gloucestershire. *Educ:* King's School, Bruton; Keble College, Oxford. Assistant Master, Brighton College, 1887–90; Headmaster, King's

School, Bruton, 1890–1916; Assistant Master, Winchester College, 1916–19; Lecturer at Keble College and St Hugh's College, Oxford, 1921–22; Member Cheltenham College Council, 1919–29; Governor of King's School, Bruton, 1924. *Address:* Wansdyke Cottage, Claverton Down, Bath.

Died 7 March 1946.

NORTON, George Frederic; composer; *b* Manchester; unmarried. *Educ:* Manchester Grammar School, etc. On leaving school entered insurance office in Manchester; abandoned business career and studied singing with Tosti and others; appeared several times with Carl Rosa Opera Company as Valentine in Faust and Devilshoof in Bohemian Girl; toured in La Poupée as Father Maxime; afterwards settled down to composition; wrote the music of Pinkie and the Fairies, Pamela, and Chu Chin Chow, etc. *Recreations:* lawn tennis, golf, and billiards. *Address:* Holford, near Bridgwater, Somerset. *Clubs:* Beefsteak, St John's Wood Arts.

Died 15 Dec. 1946.

NORWOOD, William Stuart; KC (Irish Bar); Barrister, Irish and English Bars; formerly Bencher of King's Inns, Dublin, and JP Co. Cork; *o s* of late William Norwood of Ballyhalwick, Dunmanway, Co. Cork; *m* 1919, Phyllis, *d* of G. C. A. Hasloch, Broomclose, Cobham, Surrey. *Address:* 14 Wetherby Gardens, SW5; 16 Old Buildings, Lincoln's Inn, WC2. *T:* Holborn 2214.

Died 11 March 1944.

NOSWORTHY, Richard, CMG 1926; *b* Cheshire, 13 May 1860; *s* of Charles P. Nosworthy; *m* Beatrice (*d* 1939), *d* of late William Michelin; three *s* (and one killed in the War) one *d*. *Educ:* in England. Entered Jamaica Civil Service, 1880; held appointments in various Departments; 1st class Clerk Colonial Secretariat, 1905; Secretary of Board of Supervision for Poor Relief, 1905–09; Supervisor of Revenue and Valuation Commissioner, 1907–18; Assistant Colonial Secretary, 1918; Acting Colonial Secretary in 1921; Island Treasurer and Manager of the Government Savings Bank, 1921; Collector General, Jamaica, 1924–28; Chairman of the Agricultural Loan Board; Chairman of the Currency Commissioners; Collector General and Controller of the Widows' and Orphans' Fund; Chairman of the Marine Board, 1924; Manager of the Civil Service Guarantee Association; sent to America to conclude purchase of Jamaica Government Railway Bonds, 1912, and as a member of the Banana Commission, 1915; Censor, 1915–19; Acting Administrator of Dominica, 1922; Delegate to Ottawa to effect Trade Treaty between Canada and West Indies, 1925. *Recreations:* tennis, golf. *Address:* c/o Bank of Nova Scotia, 108 Broad Street, EC. *Club:* West Indian.

Died 29 March 1946.

NOSWORTHY, Hon. Sir William, KCMG 1929; sheep farmer; *b* 18 Oct. 1867; *s* of late Stephen Nosworthy, St Alban's, Christchurch; *m* 1909, Lilian Kate, 2nd *d* of late E. G. Wright, ex-MP for Ashburton, and Mrs H. Myra Wright, Windermere, Ashburton; no *c. Educ:* Cook's Private School and Boys' High School, Christchurch. Member of Parliament for Ashburton, 1908–28; Government Whip, 1912–19; Minister of Agriculture, 1919–25; Minister of Immigration and Minister for Tourist and Health Resorts, 1919–28; Minister of Finance, 1925–26; Minister of External Affairs, and Postmaster-General and Minister of Telegraphs, 1926–28; Delegate to Empire Parliamentary Association Gathering in Canada in 1928. *Address:* Walnut Avenue, Ashburton, NZ. *Clubs:* County, Ashburton.

Died 26 Sept. 1946.

NOTT, Frederic Trevor, MA, TD; Headmaster, King Edward VIth School, Stafford, 1924–46; *b* 5 Oct. 1885; *s* of Rev. Frederick George Nott, MA, Oxon, and Maria, *d* of Ellis Powell-Jones, JP; *m* 1914, Brenda Winifred

Tranter; one *d. Educ:* Hereford Cathedral School; Brasenose College, Oxford. Assistant Master, Giggleswick School, 1909–10; Cheltenham College, 1911; VIth Form Master Cranleigh School, 1912; served European War, 1914–19; Adjutant 1st Bn Herefordshire Regiment (TF); severely wounded at Suvla Bay Landing, 1915; Acting Major, 1916; Staff Captain at Leeds, 1917; served with the 1st KSLI and 1st Bn Herefordshire Regiment in France, and on the Rhine from winter of 1917 till demobilized, 1919; Major the Herefordshire Regiment; returned to Cranleigh and commanded the OTC Contingent, 1920–24; served on 5th Div. Staff, 1941–43, in Ireland, India, and Iran: DAAG Xth Army, Iran, 1943; invalided; 1944; returned to King Edward VIth School, May 1944; member of Headmasters' Conference, 1932. *Recreations:* hockey (Brasenose College XI), tennis, gardening, fishing, golf, etc. *Address:* Park End, Aylestone Hill, Hereford. *Club:* Naval and Military.

Died 30 April 1950.

NOVAR, Viscountess; Helen Hermione, GBE 1918; LLD; *b* 1865; *d* of 1st Marquis of Dufferin and Ava and Dowager Marchioness of Dufferin and Ava, DBE, VA, CI (*d* 1936); *m* 1889, Ronald Munro Ferguson, Viscount Novar, KT, GCMG, PC (*d* 1934). *Educ:* home. *Address:* Raith, Kirkcaldy, Fife; Novar, Evanton, Ross-shire.

Died 9 April 1941.

NOWELL-ROSTRON, Rev. Sydney, MA, BD; Hon. CF, OCF; Rector of Marston Morteyne, Bedfordshire, since 1944; *b* 10 Aug. 1883; *s* of Rev. I. Rostron, MA, Vicar of St Barnabas, Douglas, Isle of Man; *m* Ella Vivian, *d* of Henry Vivian Davies, Port Elizabeth, South Africa. *Educ:* Liverpool College; St John's College, Cambridge (Sizar Exhibitioner, Scholar, MA); Ridley Hall, Cambridge. 1st class Theological Tripos 1905; Naden Divinity Student, 1905; Hulsean Prize, 1906. Curate of St George's, Hulme, Manchester, 1906–09; Lecturer at the Scholae Episcopi, Manchester, 1907–09; Principal of St John's Hall, Durham, 1909–12; Vicar of St Lawrence, Kirkdale, Liverpool, 1912–14; Vicar of St Andrew's, Sefton Park, Liverpool, 1914–18; Chaplain to the Forces (BEF, France), 1916–17; Secretary of British and Foreign Bible Society 1918–22; Vicar of St Matthew's, Bayswater, W2, 1922–32; Whitehead Professor of Pastoralia at London College of Divinity, 1928–42; Rector of Bradfield, Berks, 1932–35; Vicar of Paddington, and Chaplain of St Mary's Hospital, 1935; 1941; Vicar of St Stephen's, Lansdown, Bath, 1941–44. *Publications:* The Christology of St Paul (in the Library of Historic Theology), Commentary on I and II Corinthians; Commentary on Job; The Challenge of Calamity. *Recreations:* golf, walking, tennis. *Address:* The Rectory, Marston Morteyne, Bedfordshire. *T:* Lower Shelton 48. *Club:* National.

Died 17 March 1948.

NOXON, William Courtland; *b* Ingersoll, Ontario, Canada; *s* of James Noxon and Margaret Jane McDonald; *m* Georgina Elizabeth Furby; three *s* one *d. Educ:* Pickering and Upper Canada Colleges. Manufacturer, banker, and broker; Agent-General for Province of Ontario in British Isles, 1921–34. *Recreation:* gardening. *Address:* 136 Lyndhurst Avenue, Toronto, Canada.

Died 22 Dec. 1943.

NOYCE, Sir Frank, KCSI 1934; Kt 1929; CSI 1924; CBE 1919; *b* 4 June 1878; *e s* of Alfred Noyce of Dean House, Alderholt, Salisbury; *m* 1911, Enid Isabel (Kaisar-i-Hind Medal, 1st Class 1937), *yr d* of W. M. Kirkus, Garsdale, Sefton Park Road, Liverpool; two *s* one *d. Educ:* Bishop Wordsworth's School, Salisbury, and Salisbury School; St Catharine's College, Cambridge (Honorary Fellow). Le Bas University Essay Prize, 1902; Hon. LLD Aligarh Muslim University; Hon. DLitt Delhi University. Entered Indian Civil Service, 1902, and served in Madras as Assistant Collector and Magistrate;

Special Assistant Settlement Officer, 1906–08; Assistant Secretary to the Government of Madras, 1909; Under-Secretary, 1910; Under-Secretary to the Government of India Department of Revenue and Agriculture, 1912; Officiating Secretary, 1915–16; Secretary Indian Cotton Committee, July 1917; Controller of Cotton Cloth, Sept. 1918; Vice-President, and subsequently President, Indian Sugar Committee, 1919; Member Burma Land Revenue Committee, Dec. 1920; Indian Trade Commissioner in London, 1922; Secretary, Law and Development Departments of the Madras Government, 1923; President, Indian Coal Committee, 1924; Commissioner of Labour, Madras, 1925; Secretary Local Self-Government Department of the Madras Government, 1926; President Indian Tariff Board (Cotton Textile Industry Enquiry), 1926; Attached Officer and Assistant Commissioner, Royal Commission on Indian Agriculture, 1927; Secretary to the Government of India Department of Education, Health, and Lands, 1929–32; Member of Governor-General's Executive Council in charge of Industries and Labour Department, 1932–37; Director Mysore Gold Mining Co. and of East Indian Railway Co. *Publications:* England, India, and Afghanistan (Le Bas University Essay), 1902; contributor to Studies in Indian Co-operation, edited by R. B. Ewbank, 1919, to Social Service in India, edited by Sir Edward Blunt, 1938, and to British Commonwealth Objectives, edited by Sir Harry Lindsay, 1946. *Recreation:* book collecting. *Address:* Grayshott House, Grayshott, Hindhead, Surrey. *T:* Hindhead 628. *Club:* Athenæum.

Died 7 Oct. 1948.

NOYES, Gen. Sir Cyril Dupré, KCSI 1943; CB 1939; CIE 1937; MC; *b* 3 Feb. 1885; 3rd *s* of late Rev. H. E. Noyes, DD; *m* 1918, Violet Maud Edith, *d* of late Col H. C. Lucas; no *c. Educ:* St Lawrence College, Isle of Thanet; RMA, Woolwich. Joined Royal Artillery, 1904; transferred to Indian Army (2nd QVO Rajput LI) 1907; Commandant, 2/2nd Punjab Regt 1930–32; Graduate of Staff College, Quetta, and of Imperial Defence College, London; General Staff, Baluchistan District; Instructor (GSO1) Staff College, Quetta; Commander 2nd Indian Infantry Brigade; Rawalpindi, 1935–38; Deputy Quartermaster-General and Director of Movements and Quartering, Army Headquarters, India, 1939–40; District Commander, India, 1940–41; Quartermaster-General, India, 1941; GOC, in-C, Northern Army, India, 1942; General, 1942; retired, 1943; served Naval Operations. Persian Gulf, 1912–13; European War, 1914–18; Suez Canal, Mesopotamia (MC, despatches); 3rd Afghan War; Mohmand Operations, 1935 (despatches); Waziristan Operations, 1936–37 (despatches, CIE). *Address:* Broomdowns, Wateringbury, Kent. *Club:* United Service.

Died 11 March 1946.

NUGENT, Brig. Gen. Frank B.; *see* Burnell-Nugent.

NUGENT of Clonlost, Guy Patrick Douglas John; 6th Baron Nugent; Lieut 1st Bn The Royal Sussex Regt; *b* 1 July 1915; Head of Cadet branch of family of Westmeath; *s* of 5th Baron Nugent (Austrian title, conferred in 1836, Royal Warrant granted by King Edward VII in 1908 for use of title in British Isles) and of Frances Every Douglas, *d* of Lieut Robert Douglas Campbell-Douglas of Blythswood; *S* father, 1938. *Educ:* Stowe School. Profession: actor. *Recreations:* fencing, shooting, golf, tennis, squash racquets. *Heir:* *b* Baron David James Douglas Nugent. *Address:* 63 Wick Hall, Hove, Sussex. *T:* Hove 2007.

Died 6 Sept. 1944.

NUNN, Sir Percy, Kt 1930; MA, DSc (Lond.); Hon. LittD (Liverpool and Dublin), Hon. LLD (St Andrews); Director, University of London Institute of Education (formerly London Day Training College), 1922–36 (Vice-Principal, 1905–22); Professor of Education, 1913–36; Emeritus Professor since 1937; *b* 1870; *s* of E.

S. Nunn, MA, LLD, of Weston-super-Mare; *m* 1894, Ethel Hart; one *d*. *Educ:* University College, Bristol. Master in various secondary schools, 1891–1905; Examiner in Education, Philosophy, and Psychology in various Universities; Pres. of Training College Association, 1915; President of Mathematical Association, 1917–18; President of Section L, British Association, 1923; President of Aristotelian Society, 1923–24; Chairman Ed. Section of Br. Psychological Society, 1919; Visiting Professor, Columbia University, 1925; Member Teachers' Registration Council (repr. Univ. of London); Member Advisory Committee of Colonial Office on Education; Statutory Commissioner under University of London Act, 1926; Senator, University of London, 1929–36. *Publications:* Aims of Scientific Method, 1907; Board of Education Report on Training of Teachers of Mathematics, 1912; The Teaching of Algebra, 1914; Exercises in Algebra, 1913–1914; Education: Its Data and First Principles, 1920; Relativity and Gravitation, 1923; Chapters in Adamson's Practice of Instruction, 1907, Hodson's Broad Lines in Science Teaching, 1909, Education Reform, 1917, Adams's The New Teaching, 1918; articles in Teacher's Encyclopædia, 1911, and Encyclopædia Britannica, 1926; Chapters in International Year Book of Education (Columbia University), 1924–1927; Anthropomorphism and Physics (Annual Phil. Lecture, British Academy), 1927; various papers in Proceedings of the Aristotelian Society; articles and reviews in Nature, Mind, Hibbert Journal, British Journal of Psychology, Mathematical Gazette, Experimental Pedagogy and the educational journals. *Club:* Athenæum.

Died 12 Dec. 1944.

NURSE, George Edward, VC 1899; late Lieut RA; *b* London, 1873. Served S Africa with RA, 1899–1902 (VC); European War, 1914–16. *Address:* 15 Crosfield Road, Liverpool 7.

Died 25 Nov. 1945.

NUSSEY, Col Albert Henry Mortimer, CBE 1919; DSO 1916; Permanent Force (Staff), Union of S Africa Defence Forces; *b* 11 July 1880; *m* 1913, *e d* of T. Kelly, Bloemfontein. *Educ:* public schools and private tuition. Joined the OFS Civil Service, 1897; served with Boer forces, 1899–1902, on Gen. De Wet's Staff, 1900; attended Peace Convention as Staff Officer; Private Secretary to Minister for Agriculture (Gen. De Wet); Adjutant, Military District No. 11, 1913; Major and District Staff Officer, Kroonstad, 1914; served German South-West campaign, 1915 (Bt Lt-Col, CBE), German East Africa, 1915; Chief of Staff, Second Division, 1 April 1916 (wounded); Brig.-Gen. commanding First SAM Brigade, 8 Aug. 1916 (DSO, despatches thrice, and once especially by Gen. Smuts); present rank, Lt-Col in Union Defence Forces; Hon. Brig.-General Imperial Army. *Address:* c/o Dept of Defence, Pretoria, South Africa; Defence Headquarters, Military District No. 4, Johaunesburg. *Clubs:* Potchofstroom, Potchefstroom.

Died 8 June 1944.

NUSSEY, Sir Willans, 1st Bt *cr* 1909; JP, DL; *b* 12 Oct. 1868; *s* of late Thomas Nussey, Bramley Grange, York; *m* 1st, 1897, Edith (*d* 1934), *d* of E. M. Daniel, MD, Fleetwood, and Mrs Daniel, Saxefield, Scarborough; one *s*; 2nd, 1935, Edith Maud Cliff, OBE, 3rd *d* of late William Dewhirst and Elizabeth Cliff, JP, Meanwood Towers, nr Leeds. *Educ:* Trinity Hall, Cambridge. Barr Inner Temple, 1893; contested Maidstone, 1892; MP (R) Pontefract, 1893–1910; Chairman Appeal Committee, NR Yorkshire. *Heir: s* Thomas Moore Nussey, JP [*b* 19 July 1898. Eton; RMC, Sandhurst King's College, Cambridge. Late Lieut 17th Lancers. Crosby House, Londonderry, Northallerton. Brooks's]. *Address:* Little Rushwood, Sutton Howgrave, Bedale, Yorkshire. *Club:* Brooks's.

Died 12 Oct. 1947.

NUTHALL, Brig.-Gen. Charles Edwin, CB 1916; CMG 1918; *b* 1862; *s* of late G. W. Nuthall, Down Hall, Kingston-on-Thames; *m* 1886, *o d* of A. W. Ayers, JP, Dover; one *d*. *Educ:* King's College School. Entered RAVC 1884; Lt-Col 1904; Col 1910; Hon. Brig.-General (retired), 1919; Inspecting VO, Madras, 1904–08; DVS E Command and London district, 1909–13; South Africa, 1913–14; Aldershot, 1914; Deputy DG, AVS, War Office, 1914–17; DVS, India, 1918–19. *Address:* 32 Creffield Road, W5. *T:* Acorn 0348.

Died 6 April 1943.

NUTTALL, Lt-Col Sir (Edmund) Keith, 2nd Bt *cr* 1922; RE; Chairman of the firm of Edmund Nuttall, Sons & Co. Ltd, Civil Engineering Contractors, of Trafford Park, Manchester and 22 Grosvenor Gardens, SW1; *b* 27 March 1901; *s* of 1st Bt and Ethel Christine, 2nd *d* of Rev. Frederick Lillington, MA Oxon; S father, 1923; *m* 1925, Gytha Primrose Harrison, *e d* of Sidney H. Burgess, of Heathfield, Bowdon, Cheshire; one *s*. *Educ:* Brighton College; Clare College, Cambridge. Served war of 1939–45, France (despatches). *Recreation:* hunting. *Heir: s* Nicholas Keith, *b* 21 Sept. 1933. *Address:* Lowesby Hall, Leicestershire; 5 Chesterfield Street, W1.

Died 31 Aug. 1941.

NUTTALL, Rev. Frank; *b* Ilkeston, Derbyshire, 24 Sept. 1870; *s* of Percival and Cordelia Nuttall; *m* 1st, 1900, Violet Pusey Fernihough (*d* 1932); one *s* one *d*; 2nd, 1933, Margaret Kellock, *widow*, 2 Upper Wimpole Street, W. *Educ:* Oakham School; Sidney Sussex College, Cambridge. Ordained, 1896; Curate at St Peter's, Hunslet Moor, Leeds, and St James', New Brighton, Cheshire; Indian Chaplain, Madras Ecclesiastical Establishment, 1900–25; Archdeacon of Madras, 1922; Vicar of Chevithorne, Tiverton, 1924–29; retired, 1929. *Address:* The Gateway, Langport, Somerset. *T:* Langport, 65.

Died 7 Aug. 1943.

O

OAKELEY, Hilda Diana, MA (Oxon), MA (McGill), DLit (London); writer; *b* Durham, Oct. 1867; *d* of late Sir H. E. and Caroline Howley Oakeley. *Educ:* Ellerslie School, Manchester; Somerville College, Oxford. First Class Lit. Hum. 1898. First Warden of Royal Victoria College, McGill University, Montreal, and Lecturer in Philosophy, 1899–1905; Tutor for Women Students, Warden of Ashburne House, and Lecturer in Philosophy, University of Manchester, 1905–07; Warden of King's College for Women, and Lecturer in Philosophy, 1907–15; Warden of Passmore Edwards Settlement, 1915–20; University Reader in Philosophy, 1921–31; Head of the Department, King's College London, 1930–31 (Acting Head from 1925); Chairman, Board of Studies in Philosophy, University of London, 1923–26, 1929–31; Chairman, Board of Examiners in Philosophy, 1929–31; Vice-President Mary Ward Settlement; Governor North London Collegiate and Camden Schools for Girls, 1934–50; President Aristotelian Society, 1940–41. *Publications:* History and Progress, and other Essays and Addresses, 1923; Greek Ethical Thought, 1925; A Study in the Philosophy of Personality, 1928; History and the Self, 1934; The False State, 1937; My Adventures in Education 1939; Should Nations Survive?, 1942; articles and reviews in Proceedings of the Aristotelian Society, Mind, Church Quarterly, Hibbert Journal, American Philosophical Review, International Journal of Ethics, Philosophy, Contemporary Review, Journal of International Affairs, etc.; contribution Personality, Encyclopædia Britannica, 1929. *Recreations:* talk with friends; visits to picture galleries. *Address:* 22 Tufton Court, Westminster, SW1. *T:* Abbey 5994.

Died 7 Oct. 1950.

OAKES, Sir Harry, 1st Bt *cr* 1939; JP retired; *b* 23 Dec. 1874; *s* of William Pitt Oakes, Sangerville, Maine, USA; *m* 1923, Eunice Myrtle McIntyre, Sydney, Australia; three *s* two *d. Educ:* Bowdoin College, Brunswick, Maine, USA. Prospecting and Mining; Former President Lake Shere Mines, Ontario. *Recreations:* golf, polo. *Address:* Caves Point, Nassau, Bahamas; 15a Kensington Palace Gardens, W8. *Clubs:* Carlton; City, Nassau, Bahamas; York, Toronto; Gulf Stream, Palm Beach, Fla.

Died 8 July 1943.

OAKES, Col Richard, CB 1931; CBE 1919; *b* 12 March 1876; *s* of Col R. F. Oakes, Springhead, Sandhurst Road, Tunbridge Wells; *m* 1st, Mabel (*d* 1904), *d* of Charles Trubshaw, Derby; 2nd, Audrey, *d* of F. J. Hawksworth, Natal; one *s* one *d. Educ:* Harrow; RMA Woolwich. 2nd Lieut RE 1896; Capt. 1905; Major 1914; Bt Lt-Col 1915; Lt-Col 1922; Col 1919; served S Africa, 1899–1902 (despatches twice); CSA Railways, 1902–08; European War, 1914–19 (Bt Lt-Col, despatches twice, CBE); Chief Mechanical Engineer, War Office, 1917; Deputy Director of Railways, Mesopotamia, 1917–20; Deputy Engineer-in-Chief, India, 1922–25; Assistant Director of Transportation, War Office, 1925–29; President Royal Engineer Board, 1929–31; retired, 1931. *Address:* Conzella, 6 Kelvin Grove, Hook Road, Surbiton. *T:* Elmbridge 1579.

Died 14 July 1944.

OAKLEY, Harry Ekermans, CBE 1924; OBE 1918; a Civil Engineer; *b* 1866; *s* of Harry Oakley; *m* 1905, Alice Isobel, *d* of Dr Samuel Woodman, Ramsgate. Entered Works Department of the Admiralty, 1890; transferred to Air Ministry, 1918; Deputy Director of Works and Buildings; retired. *Address:* Stonycroft, Shrublands Road, Berkhamsted, Herts.

Died 6 Jan. 1943.

OAKLEY, Lt-Col and Bt-Col Henry John Percy, MC; TD; Actuary, North British and Mercantile Insurance Co., Ltd; President Insurance Officials' Society, 1939; *b* 22 Sept. 1878; *s* of late William Oakley; *m* 1904, Lilian Beatrice, *d* of late James Tinsley; one *s* one *d. Educ:* The Birkbeck School. Fellow, Institute of Actuaries, 1905, Hon. Secretary, 1927–29, Vice-President, 1929–33, Hon. Treasurer, 1936–38, President, 1938–40; Chairman (previously Hon. Treas.), The Actuaries' Club, 1933–38, and Hon. Treasurer, National Artillery Association; Chairman, The Life Offices Assoc., 1937–39; Mobilised with City of London Brigade RFA; served in France, 1915–19; Adjt, 1915–16; Staff Captain, 1918–19, 40 Division RA (MC, despatches); Commanded 90th (City of London) Field Brigade RA (TA), 1927–33, Hon. Colonel since 1938; Governor of St Bartholomew's, Metropolitan, Royal Northern, and Royal Free Hospitals; Member of Governing Body, City of London College; Hon. Fellowship, Actuarial Society of America, 1939; Fellow American Institute of Actuaries, 1939; Fellow Royal Statistical Soc.; Fellow Inst. of Arbitrators; Freeman of City of London and Liveryman of Dyers Company; Military Member of Council and Chairman, Finance Committee, City of London TA, Association. *Publications:* The Annuity Business of British Offices and other papers Journal of Institute of Actuaries and Journal of Faculty of Actuaries; The Mortality of Annuitants (with Sir William Palin Elderton) and other papers. *Recreations:* riding, horticulture. *Address:* Little Waltham Lodge, near Chelmsford. *T:* Little Waltham 227, London Wall 2320.

Died 3 Feb. 1942.

OAKLEY, John. Editor-in-Chief, Telegraph and Independent, Sheffield; Member of the Sheffield Education Committee, 1918; JP 1922; member of Court of Governors and the Council of Sheffield University, of the Council of Sheffield Chamber of Commerce, and of Executive Committee of Council of Social Service. *Publications:* (with Nancy Oakley) The Clevedon Case; The Lint House Mystery. *Address:* Thornsett House, Thornsett Road, Sheffield.

Died 15 Jan. 1945.

OAKLEY, Sir John Hubert, GBE 1928; Kt 1919; Practising Surveyor and head of the firm of D. Smith, Oakley and Garrard, 32 St James's Street, SW1; *b* 1867; *e s* of late Christopher Oakley, Chislehurst, Kent; *m* 1891, Ida, only *d* of late Daniel Watney of Brittleware, Croydon; one *d. Educ:* Uppingham; Royal Agricultural College, Cirencester. Served on the Council of the Surveyors' Institution for twelve years, and elected President for its jubilee year, 1918–19; served on Royal commission, Oxford and Cambridge University (Estates), 1919–21; Committee on Crown and Government Lands, 1921–22; Royal Commission on Compensation for suffering and damage caused by enemy action, 1922–24; River Ouse Drainage Commission, 1925–26; Irish Grants Committee, 1926–29. *Recreations:* fishing and shooting. *Address:* 32 St James's Street, SW1. *T:* Whitehall 9385. *Club:* Conservative.

Died 5 Dec. 1946.

OATES, Lt-Col William Coape, DSO 1918; DL; retired Army Officer; JP and County Alderman for Notts; *b* 7 July 1862; *er s* of Wm Henry Coape Oates, of Langford Hall, Newark; *m* Louise Mary Kerr (marr. diss. 1912); one *s* one *d. Educ:* Harrow; RMC Sandhurst. Served with Royal Munster Fusiliers in Burmese War, 1885 (medal and 2 clasps); S African War, 1900–01 (severely wounded, medal and 2 clasps); Commanded 2/8th Sherwood Foresters in France and Belgium, European War (wounded, DSO, despatches twice); Chairman, Notts Rural Community Council and Notts Playing Fields Association, in both cases since their inception. *Publications:* Wild Ducks, which appeared serially in the Field; 2/8th Sherwood Foresters in Great War. *Recreations:* cricket, was Captain RMC Sandhurst in 1882 and got 131 v. RMA Woolwich, elected member of MCC, 6 June 1881; shooting especially, formerly fishing and hunting. *Address:* Besthorpe, nr Newark on Trent. *TA:* Colonel Oates, Collingham, Notts. *Clubs:* Nottinghamshire, Nottingham.

Died 20 Feb. 1942.

OATLEY, Sir George Herbert, Kt 1925; Hon. LLD; RWA, FRIBA; Chartered architect; *b* 3 Jan. 1863; *e s* of George Oatley of Sandown, IW; *m* 2nd *d* of W. F. Lawrence of Clifton; one *s* one *d.* Architect of Bristol University, and of many buildings, including churches, residences, hospitals, asylums, commercial and other. *Address:* 12 Great George Street, Bristol 1. *T:* Bristol 21241. *Club:* Athenæum.

Died 12 May 1950.

O'BRIAIN, Art Patrick; Director and Deputy-Chairman Minerals Exploration and Development Co., Ltd; *b* 1872. *Educ:* St Charles College, London. Followed profession of engineering up to 1918; Irish Republican Official Envoy and Representative in Great Britain, 1919–24; Managing Director G. D. Ernest and Co. Ltd, Publishers, and Managing Editor Music Trades Review, 1924–35; Irish Minister Plenipotentiary to France and to Belgium, 1935–38; President of Gaelic League of London, 1914–35; Sinn Fein Council of Great Britain, 1916–23; Irish Self-Determination League of Great Britain, 1919–25; several times imprisoned for political activities; deported 1923. *Publication:* A Handbook of Irish Dances (with J. G. O'Keeffe). *Address:* c/o Dept External Affairs, Dublin.

Died 12 Aug. 1949.

O'BRIEN, His Honour Judge Daniel Joseph; KC; *s* of Michael O'Brien, Kingstown; *m* 1903, Mary Bertha, *d* of Thomas Fullerton, Kingstown; two *s* three *d. Educ:* Christian Brothers; St Stainlaus College (SJ), Tullamore; University College, Dublin. Victoria Prizeman King's Inns, Dublin, 1898. Called to the Irish Bar, 1898; Inner Bar, 1914; Revising Barrister, Limerick, 1911; Antrim, 1912; Crown Prosecutor, County Carlow, 1912; Senior Crown Prosecutor, County and City of Kilkenny, 1917; Standing Counsel to the General Post Office in Ireland, 1918; County Court Judge for County and City of Waterford, County and City of Kilkenny, and Queen's County, 1920–24; Chairman of Railway Tribunal, Eire, 1924–44. *Address:* 26 Merlyn Park, Dublin. *Club:* St Stephen's Green (Dublin).

Died 30 Nov. 1949.

O'BRIEN, Dermod, Hon. RA 1911; Hon-RSA 1912; DL and Freeman, Limerick; President Royal Hibernian Academy of Arts since 1910; Governor and Guardian National Gallery, Ireland; *b* 10 June 1865; *e s* of late E. W. O'Brien; *m* 1902, Mabel (*d* 1942), 2nd *d* of late Sir Philip Smyly; three *s* two *d. Educ:* Harrow; Trinity College, Cambridge; Antwerp, Paris, and Slade. Went to Rome and started art education at Antwerp, silver medal, under Chas. Verlat, 1887; Paris, Julian's Studio, 1890; settled in London, Trafalgar Studios, Chelsea, 1893; moved to Dublin, 1901; has exhibited at RA, New Gallery, NEAC, Liverpool, RHA, etc.; ARHA 1905; RHA 1907; served on Vice-Regal Milk Commission, Ireland, and Milk Distribution Committee, 1915–16; organised an Irish Conference Committee from which came the Irish Convention; on Committee of Irish Dominion League, Proportional Representation for Ireland, Co-operative Organisation, etc., Art Lectures,

etc. *Recreation:* painting. *Address:* 65 Fitzwilliam Square, Dublin. *T:* 62234. *Clubs:* Chelsea Arts, Farmers': Kildare Street, United Arts, Dublin.

Died 3 Oct. 1945.

O'BRIEN, Brig.-Gen. Edmund Donough John, CB 1911; CBE 1919; JP; *b* Peshawur, 19 Aug. 1858; *s* of late Col Sir Terence O'Brien, KCMG, sometime Governor of Heligoland and Newfoundland; *m* 1890, Florence Harriet, *d* of Frederick Wheeler, of Worcester Park, Surrey; one *d. Educ:* RM College, Sandhurst. 2nd Lieut 40th Foot, 1878; Capt. 3rd Dragoons, 1888; Major 14th Hussars, 1896; Lt-Col 1903; Col, 1907; commanding 14th Hussars, 1901–07; served Afghan War, 1879–80, attached 1st Punjab Cavalry; present at march Kabul to Kandahar, temporarily with 15th Sikhs, and battle (despatches, medal with clasp, bronze star); South Africa with 14th Hussars; present at Relief of Ladysmith, and operations on Tugela Heights, Diamond Hill (despatches, Queen's medal 5 clasps, King's medal 2 clasps, Brevet Lt-Col); DAAG Bengal, 1894–97; Assistant Director Remounts SA, 1907–10; commanded Potchefstroom District, 1910–14; retired, 1914; commanded Mounted Brig., 1915–17; commanding a Labour Group in France, 1917–19. *Address:* Abbotswood, Buxted, Sussex. *TA:* Buxted, 233.

Died 21 July 1945.

O'BRIEN, Edward Joseph Harrington; writer and editor; European Story Editor Metro-Goldwyn-Mayer British Studios, Ltd; *b* Boston, Mass, USA, 10 Dec. 1890; *s* of Michael Francis and Minna Gertrude O'Brien; *m* 1st, 1923, Romer Wilson (*d* 1930); 2nd, 1932, Ruth Gorgel; one *s* two *d. Educ:* Boston College; Harvard University. Associate Editor, The Poetry Journal, 1912–15, and of Poet Lore, 1914–15; Editor and Founder, New Stories, 1933–35. *Publications:* White Fountains, 1917; The Forgotten Threshold, 1919; Distant Music, 1921; The Advance of the American Short Story, 1923; Hard Sayings, 1927; The Dance of the Machines, 1929; Son of the Morning, 1932; The Guest Book, 1935; The Short Story Case Book, 1935; Editor of: The Best Short Stories (26 annual Vols), 1915–1940; The Best British Short Stories (19 annual vols), 1921–1940; The Masque of Poets, 1918; The Great Modern English Stories, 1919; Modern English Short Stories, 1930; The Twenty Five Finest Short Stories, 1931; Modern American Short Stories, 1932; New English Short Stories, 1935; Elizabethan Tales, 1937; The Best American Short Stories of 25 Years, 1939; Selected English Short Stories, 1940. *Recreations:* walking, travel, book collecting. *Address:* Latchmoor House, The Common, Gerrards Cross, Bucks. *TA:* Obrien, Metrobrit Denham. *T:* Gerrards Cross 2254. *Clubs:* Savage; Harvard, New York.

Died 24 Feb. 1941.

O'BRIEN, Sir Timothy Carew, 3rd Bt *cr* 1849; JP and DL, Co. Cork; late Capt. 5th Batt. Royal Irish Fusiliers; Lieut Derbyshire Yeomanry Cavalry; served in the Remounts during War of 1914–18 (despatches); Hon. Major in Army; *b* Nov. 1861; *S uncle* 1895; *m* 1885, Gundrede, *d* of Sir Humphrey De Trafford, 2nd Bt; one *s* five *d. Educ:* Downside; St Charles College; New Inn Hall, Oxford. *Recreations:* was a leading member of Middlesex XI and Oxford Cricket XI, has played in all principal matches; hunting. *Heir: e surv. s* Robert Rollo Gillespie, [*b* 9 June 1901; *m* 1925, Esther Ethel, *d* of Norman Coghill, Almington Hall, Market Drayton; three *d*]. *Clubs:* Bath, Carlton; Kildare Street (Dublin).

Died 9 Dec. 1948.

O'CALLAGHAN-WESTROPP, Col George, (The O'Callaghan); ADC to the King; late Colonel Reserve of Officers; a Senator for Southern Ireland, 1921–22; JP Co. Clare; High Sheriff, 1919; *b* Attyflin Park, Co. Limerick, 18 Feb. 1864; *o s* of Col John O'Callaghan, DL, JP, of Maryfort (Lismehane), Co. Clare, and Mary Johnson, *e d* of John Westropp of Attyflin Park; *m* 1st,

1895, Henrietta Cecilia Rose (*d* 1929), *o d* of late Capt. G. A. B. Godbold, 27th Inniskilling Fusiliers; one *s* three *d*; 2nd, 1937, Muriel Haidee Westropp, *o d* of late Major Charles Wilson Battley and of Mrs D'Oyly Battley, Belvedere Hall, Bray, Co. Wicklow. *Educ:* Cheltenham College; RMC, Sandhurst. Lieut, 1st Batt. Royal Irish Rifles, 1882; Captain, 1888; retired, 1889, on appointment as Captain to Clare Artillery, commanded from 1898 until disbanded in 1909; in 1885 by Royal Licence assumed the name and arms of Westropp in addition to those of O'Callaghan, in compliance with the will of his maternal uncle, Captain Ralph Westropp of Coolreagh, Co. Clare, to whose estates he had succeeded in 1883; Member of Royal Commission on the Militia and Volunteers, 1903–04; Ammunition Column Committee, 1906; second Esher Committee (Territorial Forces), 1906; ADC to King Edward VII, 1905; to King George V, 1910; to King Edward VIII, 1936. *Publications:* various on Military, Political, Irish Land and Agricultural Questions. *Recreations:* shooting, fishing, cricket. *Address:* Lismehane, O'Callaghan's Mills, Co. Clare; 52a Lansdowne Road, Dublin. *Clubs:* Kildare Street, Dublin.

Died 28 July 1944.

O'CARROLL, Joseph Francis, MD, RUI; FRCPI; late Physician to Richmond, Whitworth, and Hardwicke (Government) Hospitals, Dublin; late Professor of Medicine, University College, Dublin; *b* 29 April 1855; *s* of late P. F. O'Carroll, Dublin, and Katherine Garvey, Dublin; *m* Frances, 2nd *d* of late Joseph MacLoone, JP, Donegal; one *s* three *d*. *Educ:* Dublin Royal Univ.; Vienna. *Publications:* several papers on medical subjects, mainly heart disease and diseases of nervous system. *Address:* Lynwood, Dundrum, Co. Dublin. *T:* 96378.

Died 18 Feb. 1942.

OCHTERLONY, Sir Matthew Montgomerie, 4th Bt *cr* 1823; ARSA 1939; FRIBA; FRIAS; Firm of H. O. Tarbolton and Sir Matthew M. Ochterlony, Bt, FFRIBA; *b* 28 Feb. 1880; *s* of Sir David F. Ochterlony, 3rd Bart, and Somerville (*d* 1930), *d* of Barron Grahame, of Morphie, Kincardineshire; *S* father, 1931; *m* 1st, 1921, Eleanor Mary Lawrie (*d* 1938), *e d* of late David F. L. Row Fogo of Row, Perthshire; 2nd, 1942, Mary Alfreda, *d* of John Meiklejon, Westlands House, Dalkeith. *Recreations:* motoring and photography. *Heir: b* Charles Francis, *b* 27 June 1891. *Address:* Spylaw Cottage, Colinton, Edinburgh 13. *T:* Edinburgh 27442, Colinton 87585. *Clubs:* Caledonian United Service, Edinburgh.

Died 4 Oct. 1946.

O'CONNELL, Rev. Sir John Robert, Kt 1914; MA; LLD; FSA Ire.; FRGS; FRHistS; *b* 12 Feb. 1868; *o s* of Thomas Francis O'Connell, 10 Mountjoy Square, Dublin, and Maria, *o d* of Robert Francis Stein of Woodview, Blackrock, Co. Dublin; *m* 1901, Mary (*d* 1925), *e d* of Thomas Scally of Deepwell, Blackrock, Co. Dublin. *Educ:* Belvedere College, SJ, Dublin; Trinity College, Dublin. BA, 1889; MA, LLD, 1894. Formerly solicitor and head of Thomas F. O'Connell & Son, Solicitors, Dublin; Director of the National Bank; Member of Senate of University of Dublin; member of the Governing Body of University College, Cork; Fellow of Royal Society of Antiquaries of Ireland; Member of the Royal Irish Academy; a Vice-President Statistical and Social Enquiry Society of Ireland, Member of Board of Superintendence of Dublin Hospitals; JP Co. Cork; Vice-President Incorporated Law Society of Ireland, 1924; Solicitor to the Dublin and South-Eastern Railway Company of Ireland; Knight Commander of Order of St Gregory the Great, 1924; Chairman of the Association for the Housing of the Very Poor of Dublin; Knight Grand Cross of the Order of the Holy Sepulchre; Chaplain Magistral Obedience Order of Malta; President Lingard Society, 1938–39; has travelled extensively in the East; ordained priest by Cardinal Bourne in Westminster Cathedral, 1929; LLD (Hon.) NUI 1930. *Publications:* The Collegiate Chapel, Cork, its ideals and its aims; Lyra Martyrum, 1525–1681, an anthology of the poetry of the English Martyrs; Life of St Thomas More, 1935; various papers and addresses on philanthropic, literary, biographical and social subjects and historical studies. *Address:* Artillery Mansions, 75 Victoria Street, SW1. *T:* Abbey 1773. *Club:* Reform.

Died 28 Dec. 1943.

O'CONNELL, Captain Sir Maurice (James Arthur), 5th Bt *cr* 1869; late Royal Fusiliers; Lord of the Manor of Ballycarbery; Cavaliere di Onore e di Devozione del Sovrano Militare Ordine di Malta; *b* 24 Dec. 1889; *s* of 4th Bt and Mary Pauline (*d* 1934), *d* of Lt-Col J. F. Hickie, of Slevoyre, Co. Tipperary; *S* father, 1919; *m* 1920, Margaret Mary, *d* of late Matthew J. Purcell, Burton Park, Buttevant; one *s* one *d*. Served European War (despatches twice, MC). *Heir: s* Morgan Donal Conail [*b* 29 Jan. 1923. Served War of 1939–45, Royal Signals, 1943–46]. *Address:* Lakeview, Killarney, Co. Kerry.

Died 15 Sept. 1949.

O'CONNELL, His Eminence William Henry; Cardinal, 1911; Archbishop of Boston since 1907; *b* Lowell, Mass, 8 Dec. 1859; *s* of John O'Connell and Bridget Farley. *Educ:* Boston College, AB 1881; North American College, Rome. Ordained Priest, Rome, 1884; Rector of North American College, Rome, 1895; Domestic Prelate, 1897; Bishop of Portland, Me, 1901; Assistant at Pontifical Throne, 1905; Special Papal Envoy to the Emperor of Japan, 1905; given Grand Cordon of the Sacred Treasure by Mikado, 1905; Archbishop of Constance and Coadjutor with succession of Boston, 1906; Grand Cross Corona d'Italia, Malta; St John of Jerusalem; Grand Cross of the Order of Malta; Grand Cordon of the Sacred Treasure (Japanese); Grand Cross of the Crown of Italy; Grand Cross of the Constantinian Order of St George; Grand Cross of the Holy Sepulchre; Grand Cross of the Legion of Honor (France); Gold Medal of Merit from the Republic of Lebanon. *Publications:* Sermons and Addresses, twelve volumes; Recollections of Seventy Years. *Address:* Lake Street, Brighton, Mass, USA.

Died 22 April 1944.

O'CONNOR, Lt-Col Sir Frederick; see O'Connor, Lt-Col Sir W. F. T.

O'CONNOR, Thomas Arthur Leslie S.; *see* Scott O'Connor.

O'CONNOR, Vincent Clarence Scott, FRGS; *e s* of Thomas Ablett O'Connor and Emma Lavinia Scott; *g s* of Mark Miall O'Connor of Claremorris, Co. Mayo, and Wallace Scott, Edinburgh; *m* 1st, Dora Georgiana (*d* 1930), *y d* of Rev. Edward Mansfield, of Highnam, Glos; one *s*; 2nd, Muriel, *d* of Clement McNeale, Hampstead. *Educ:* privately. Entered Financial Department, Government of India, as Assistant Accountant-General; retired as Accountant-General, Government of India, and Finance Adviser for Railways; held commission for three years in Volunteer Artillery; trained with RA 1917; Trooper in Light Horse in India, 1917–18; during 1916 was present at the fighting fronts in France, Italy, Macedonia, and Sinai Peninsula; travelled across Mediterranean as guest of French Admiralty; made a ten months' voyage round the world, on the invitation of the Admiralty, in HMS Hood, 1923–24, and travelled 16,000 miles overland in South and East Africa, Malaya, Australia, New Zealand, and Canada; Has twice visited the United States; Believes in the British Empire. *Publications:* The Silken East, a record of Life and Travel in Burma, 1904; new ed. 1928; Mandalay and other old Cities of Burma, 1907; Travels in the Pyrenees, 1912; The Scene of War, 1917; An Eastern Library, 1920; The Charm of Kashmir, 1920; A Vision of Morocco, 1923;

The Empire Cruise, 1925; Isles of the Ægean, 1929. *Address:* c/o Lloyds Bank, 6 Pall Mall, SW1. *Clubs:* Authors', Pilgrims; Interallie, Paris.

Died 21 March 1945.

O'CONNOR, Lt-Col Sir (William) Frederick (Travers), Kt 1925; CSI 1924; CIE 1904; CVO 1922; RA; Indian Political Department; retired, 1925; *b* 30 July 1870; *e s* of Matthew Weld O'Connor and Harriette Georgina, *d* of Anthony O'Reilly, of Baltrasna, Co. Meath. *Educ:* Charterhouse; Woolwich. Royal Artillery, and Indian Political Department, 1905; served in Swat Valley and Tirah Campaigns, 1897–98 (medal and 3 clasps); Kashmir Imperial Service Troops, Gilgit, 1899–1903; Secretary and Interpreter to the Mission to Lhasa, 1903–04 (medal and clasp, severely wounded, CIE); entered army, 1890; Captain, 1899; Major, 1908; Lt-Col, 1916; British Trade Agent at Gyantse, Tibet, 1904–08; Consul in Seistan, 1909–12; Consul-General and Agent to the Governor-General in India in Khorasan, April–Nov. 1910; Consul, Shiraz, Persia, 1912–15; Swedish Order of the Sword, 1909; prisoner of war in Persia, Nov. 1915–Aug. 1916; on special duty in Siberia, April–Oct. 1918; Resident in Nepal, 1918–20; British Envoy in Nepal, 1921–25; negotiated and signed a new Treaty between Great Britain and Nepal, Dec. 1923; Order of the Star of Nepal, 1933. *Publications:* Folk Tales from Tibet, 1906; On the Frontier and Beyond, 1931; Things Mortal, 1940. Songs: (words and music) The Old House; Quietude, etc. *Address:* 56 Glebe Place, SW3. *Clubs:* Royal Thames Yacht, Royal Automobile.

Died 14 Dec. 1943.

O'CONOR DON, Owen Phelim O'Conor; *b* 10 Dec. 1870; *s* of late Rt Hon. Charles Owen O'Conor Don and Georgina, *d* of T. A. Perry, Bitham House, Warwickshire; *S* brother, 1917; *m* 1st, 1913, Mary (*d* 1916), *d* of F. C. McLaughlin, Detroit; one *d*; 2nd, 1919, Gwendoline, *o surv. c* of Charles M. O'Conor, Mount Druid, Castlerea. *Address:* Clonalis, Castlerea, Co. Roscommon.

Died 1 March 1943.

ODHAMS, Ernest Lynch; *b* 28 March 1880; *e s* of John Lynch Odhams and Kate, 3rd *d* of W. E. Bridges; *m* 1905, Frances Louise, 3rd *d* of Lancelot Crozier, Delhi, India; one *s* two *d*. *Educ:* Preparatory School, Ramsgate; King's College School, London. Secretary (15 years) and Director (10 years) Odhams, Ltd; journalistic work in India, leader-writer in Oriental Review, etc.; book-reviewing for English Journals; joined BBC 1923, Station Director of Newcastle; returned to London, 1925 to start World-Radio (then Radio Supplement), BBC's Foreign Journal; Editor of it, 1925–39; retired from BBC, 1940. *Address:* Elmer Beach House, Middleton-on-Sea, Sussex. *T:* Middleton-on-Sea 382. *Club:* Authors'.

Died 13 April 1947.

O'DONNELL, Maj.-Gen. Eric Hugh, CBE 1943; *b* Dublin, 11 March 1893; *s* of late Bryan Louis O'Donnell, MA, Ballingaddy, Co. Limerick, and late Lucinda Egan; *m* 1919, Mabel Mary Elizabeth, 2nd *d* of late Joseph Charles Dunbar, Cork and Ceylon; one *d*. *Educ:* St George's College, Woburn Park, Weybridge. 2nd Lieut RFA (TA) Aug. 1914; Regular Commission RFA 1915; served France and Flanders, 1–16159 (wounded); Macedonia and Caucasus, 1917–19 (despatches); called to Bar (Inner Temple), 1925; retired from Army, 1926. Practised SE Circuit and London; a Chairman of Courts of Referees under National Unemployment Insurance Acts, 1928, and sat as Arbitrator under Ministry of Agriculture Marketing Schemes until 1939; mobilised Aug. 1939; Staff Captain AG1, War Office; DAAG 1939; AAG 1940; Col 1941; Brig. 1941; Maj.-Gen. 1945 (Director of Public Relations), War Office; reverted to Reserve, Oct. 1946; a Master of the Supreme Court (King's Bench Division) 1946–50, resigned 1950. *Recreations:* tennis, golf,

shooting. *Address:* Greenacre, Merstham, Surrey; 4 Paper Buildings, Temple, EC4. *T:* Merstham 143. *Club:* Army and Navy.

Died 4 July 1950.

O'DONNELL, Rev. Michael J., DD; *b* Kilraine, Glenties, Co. Donegal, 10 Feb. 1881. *Educ:* St Eunan's Seminary, Letterkenny (exhibitions and distinctions in all the intermediate grades); Maynooth College; Royal University of Ireland (exhibitions); University of Strasburg and University of Munich. Degree in Mental and Moral Philosophy, Royal University, 1906; DD Maynooth College, 1907. Professor of Theology, Maynooth, 1909–14; Professor of Senior Moral Theology, 1914–21; Professor at Letterkenny College, 1922–26; pastoral work in Ardara and in Burtonport until 1932; retired, 1932. *Publications:* Penance in the Early Church, 1907; one of the editors of the Irish Theological Quarterly since 1910; Correspondent in Canon Law and Theology to the Irish Ecclesiastical Record since 1910; contributor to several other publications. *Address:* Dun Laoghaire, Co. Dublin.

Died 6 Feb. 1944.

O'DONNELL, Sir Samuel Perry, KCSI 1927; KCIE 1925; CSI 1923; CIE 1918; *b* 16 Dec. 1874; *s* of Robert Edmund O'Donnell and Margaret Bennett; *m* 1909, Edith d'Arcy Paton (*d* 1945). *Educ:* Brighton College; Repton; London University. Appointed to ICS, 1897; Secretary to Local Govt United Provinces, 1912–17; Chief Secretary to Local Govt, UP, 1917–19; Secretary to Reforms Office, 1920; Secretary to Govt of India, Home Dept, 1921–22; Member of the Executive Council, UP, 1923–28. *Recreations:* tennis and golf. *Address:* 22 Palace Court, W2.

Died 24 March 1946.

O'DONNELL, Thomas; Circuit Court Judge of Kerry, Limerick, and Clare since 1941; *b* 1872. *Educ:* Farranakilla NS (First Reid Prize, 1890); Training College, Marlborough Street. MP (N) West Kerry, 1900–18; Called to Irish Bar, 1905; Called Inner Bar, 1933; Chairman Tralee and Dingle Railway, 1905–18. *Address:* 27 Raglan Road, Dublin. *T:* Ballsbridge 64512.

Died 11 June 1943.

O'DONNELL, Maj.-Gen. Sir Thomas Joseph, KCIE 1919; CB 1916; DSO 1900; RAMC; late Director of Medical Services, India; *b* 18 Jan. 1858; 3rd *s* of late P. O'Donnell, High Constable of the Barony of Glenquin, of Killeedy, Ballagh, County Limerick; *m* 1919, Marion, *widow* of Capt. W. L. Graham of Carfin, Lanarkshire. *Educ:* St Stanislaus College, Tullabeg, King's County; Fellow Royal Institute of Public Health. Served with Field Artillery, Egypt, 1881–82 (medal, Khedi ve's star); served with Kimberley Light Horse under Sir C. Warren, Bechuanaland Expedition, 1885–86; with Inniskilling Dragoons, operations in Zululand, 1887–88; with 3rd Batt. Rifle Brigade, Tirah campaign, 1897–98 (medal and clasp); with 12th Royal Lancers, South Africa, 1899–1901 (despatches twice, medal, 6 clasps, DSO); European War, 1914–18 (despatches five times). *Recreations:* hunting, fishing, shooting; rode many winners in South Africa and India. *Address:* Old Castle, Ledbury. *T:* Trumpet 73; Killeedy, Ballagh, County Limerick. *Club:* Junior United Service.

Died 10 Nov. 1947.

O'DONOGHUE, Col Montague Ernest, CBE 1919; Indian Army, retired; *b* 16 Feb. 1859; 2nd *s* of late Colonel Charles O'Donoghue, 76th Foot (Duke of Wellington's Regiment); *m* Edith, *d* of late Major W. Fuller, ISC; one *s*. *Educ:* Bath; RMC Sandhurst. Entered 67th Foot, 1878; Indian Army, 1884; served Afghan War, 1879–80 (medal); Burma War, 1885–87 (medal); Commanded Battalion IA 1900–07; served European War, 1914 to Armistice 1918 (medal, despatches, CBE). *Address:* c/o Grindlay & Co., 54 Parliament Street, SW1.

Died 26 June 1943.

O'DUFFY, Gen. Eoin; President, National Athletic and Cycling Association of Ireland; *b* near Castleblayney, Co. Monaghan, 30 Oct. 1892. District Surveyor to Monaghan County, 1913; engineer and architect to Cootehill Rural Council, 1918; to Clones Rural Council, 1919; TD for Monaghan, 1918–22; Deputy Chief of Staff, GHQ, 1921; Chief of Staff, 1921–22; GOC the Forces, IFS, 1924–25; Chief Commissioner of Civic Guard, 1922–33; organised and led Irish Brigade to Spain to fight on the side of General Franco, 1936–37; Brigadier-General in Spanish Army. *Publications:* Crusade in Spain; The History of the Garda Siochana (Irish Police Force); articles on police duty and sport. *Address:* Farney, Merrion Park, Blackrock, Co. Dublin. *T:* 82445. *Clubs:* United Arts, 1916–21, Dublin.

Died 30 Nov. 1944.

O'DWYER, Robert; *b* Bristol, 1862, of Irish parents. Organist in Bristol, 1879–91; joined Carl Rosa Opera Co. 1891; conductor Rousbey Opera, 1896; Organist Rathmines, Dublin and St Francis Xavier S. J.; Professor of Irish Music, University College, Dublin (National University of Ireland), 1914–39; Director, University College, Dublin, Musical Society. *Publications:* Irish Opera; Eithne (Gaiety Theatre, Dublin), 1910; Irish Hymn Book Danta Dé, 1929; Irish opera in one act, Cleopatra; Book of six Gaelic songs for school children's use, 1928; 3 String Quartettes, MSS. played at 2 RV Dublin Broadcast Station, and other original compositions, since 1928; several songs, some organ and church music, and many arrangements of Irish melody. *Address:* 7 Wellington Place, Clyde Road, Dublin.

Died 6 Jan. 1949.

OESTERLEY, Rev. William O. E., MA; DD; LittD; retired from St Mary, Aldermary, EC4; Professor, Hebrew and Old Testament Exegesis at King's College, University of London, 1926–36; Emeritus Professor, 1936; Fellow, 1929; Prebendary of St Paul's Cathedral, 1936; Examining Chaplain to Bishop of London; Warburton Lecturer in Lincoln's Inn Chapel; *b* Calcutta, 1866; *s* of E. Oesterley, Calcutta and London; *m* Mabel Fanny, *d* of G. H. Page, of Hay, Breconshire; two *d*. *Educ:* Brighton College; Jesus College, Cambridge; Wells Theological College. Curacies in Houghton-le-Spring, Co. Durham, St Botolph's, Colchester, St Nicholas, Brighton; Vicar of St Alban's, Bedford Park, W, 1914–23; Rector of St Mary, Aldermary, 1923, retd; Examiner in Hebrew in the Universities of Cambridge, Durham, London, Bristol, Wales, Liverpool. *Publications:* Studies in Greek and Latin Versions; The Old Latin Texts of the Minor Prophets; Codex Taurinensis; The Religion and Worship of the Synagogue; The Evolution of the Messianic Idea; The Books of the Apocrypha: their Origin, Contents, and Teaching; The Literature of Rabbinical and Mediæval Judaism; Immortality and the Unseen World; A Study in Old Testament Religion; The Sacred Dance; The Jewish Background of the Christian Liturgy; The Wisdom of Egypt and the Old Testament; Proverbs, in Westminster Commentaries; (with T. H. Robinson) Hebrew Religion, 1930; (with T. H. Robinson) A History of Israel, (2 vols); (with T. H. Robinson) An Introduction to the Books of the Old Testament, 1934; An Introduction to the Books of the Apocrypha, 1935; The Gospel Parables in the Light of their Jewish Background; The Song of Songs, metrical translation with introduction and notes; Roses of Sharon; A New Approach to the Psalms; Readings from the Apocrypha; The Psalms, translated with text-critical and exegetical notes; The Jews and Judaism during the Greek Period; the Background of Christianity, 1941, and many other works. *Recreations:* music, gardening. *Address:* 21 Heathgate, NW11.

Died 10 Jan. 1950.

O'FERRALL, Dominic More-; DL; *b* 1854; *o s* of late Edward More-O'Ferrall, of Kildangan, and Susan, *d* of late Dominick O'Reilly, of Kildangan; *m* 1898, Annie, *d* of late Lt-Col Francis McDonnell, CB, of Plâs Newydd, Monmouthshire; three *s*. High Sheriff, Kildare, 1879. *Address:* Kildangan, Co. Kildare.

Died 18 Feb. 1942.

OGILVIE, Lt-Col Duncan, CIE 1919; RE (retired); *b* 1873; *s* of late Lt-Col A. J. Ogilvie, RHA; *m* 1899, A. M. E., *e d* of late Admiral F. H. Smith, RN. Served European War, 1914–19 (despatches twice, two medals); Afghan War, 1919 (CIE, medal with clasp). *Address:* 7 Victoria Park, Dover. *T:* Dover 447.

Died 22 Dec. 1941.

OGILVIE, Col Edward Collingwood, CMG 1917; CBE 1919; late RE; JP, Hants; *b* 2 Dec. 1867; *s* of late Lt-Col A. J. Ogilvie, RA, and Emily Collingwood Fitzwilliams; *m* 1901, K. M., 3rd *d* of late Col R. E. Home, CIE, RE; no *c*. *Educ:* Cheltenham College; RMA, Woolwich. Sword of Merit. 2nd Lieut RE 1887; India, 1889; Bombay Sappers and Miners, Kirkee; Indian Telegraph Dept and Military Works Services; served Miranzai Expedition, 1892 (medal and clasp); Chitral Relief Force, 1895 (medal and clasp); Capt. 1897; Major, 1905; Lieutenant-Colonel, 1913; CRE, 12th Division, Mesopotamia, Sept. 1915; (despatches; promoted Bt Col 1916; services especially brought to notice by Gen. Maude, CMG; served as Dy Director of Works, and officiated as Director of Works, MEF (despatches); invalided to India, Feb. 1918; retired pay, 1921. *Address:* Branxholm, Fleet, Hants. *T:* Fleet 303. *Club:* United Service.

Died 4 April 1950.

OGILVIE, Sir Frederick (Wolff), Kt 1942; Hon. LLD (Dubl. and Belf.); Principal of Jesus College, Oxford, since 1944; *b* 7 Feb. 1893; *y s* of W. M. Ogilvie, Valparaiso and Harrow Weald; *m* 1922, Mary Helen, *e d* of Rev. A. B. Macaulay, DD; two *s*. *Educ:* Packwood Haugh; Clifton College; Balliol College, Oxford. 1st Class Classical Mods, 1913; MA (Oxon), 1919. Served in 4th Bedfordshire Regt (captain), 1914–19; Fellow and Lecturer, Trinity College, Oxford, 1920–26; Professor of Political Economy, University of Edinburgh, 1926–34; President and Vice-Chancellor of Queen's University, Belfast, 1934–38; Director-General British Broadcasting Corporation, 1938–42; Member of Edinburgh Univ. Court, 1932–34; Member of Trade Boards, 1927–34 and 1943–45; Chairman Joint Advisory Committee on Adult Education for SE Scotland, 1930–34; Member of National Advisory Council for Juvenile Employment (Scotland), 1931–34; Member of Food Council (Great Britain) and of Consumers Committee for Scotland (Agricultural Marketing Acts), 1933–34; Chairman of Ministry of Labour, Northern Ireland, Committee for Instruction of Unemployed Juveniles, 1936–38; Member of Art Advisory Council of Northern Ireland, 1936–38; Member of Economics Committee of Agricultural Research Council, 1932–40; Member of Staff of British Council, 1943–45; Chairman of Tin Box Wages Council since 1945; Fellow of Royal Society of Edinburgh; Member of Royal Irish Academy. *Publications:* The Tourist Movement, an Economic Study, 1933; contributions to Economic Journal, Giornale degli Economisti, Encyclopædia of the Social Sciences, Dictionary of National Biography, Scottish Historical Review, Quarterly Review, etc. *Address:* Jesus College, Oxford. *Club:* Athenæum.

Died 10 June 1949.

OGILVIE, Col Thomas, CB 1919; CMG 1915; TD; DL of the County of the City of Aberdeen; JP City of Aberdeen; *b* 1871; *m* 1896, Jessie, *d* of James Henderson, JP, manufacturer, Hawick; two *s* one *d*. *Educ:* Merchiston Castle, Edinburgh. Served European War, 1914–19 (CB, CMG, despatches 6 times); Hon. Col 8th Bn The Gordon Highlanders. *Address:* Fernbank,

Banchory, Kincardineshire. *T:* 68. *Clubs:* Scottish Conservative, Edinburgh, Edinburgh; Royal Northern Aberdeen.

Died 17 April 1944.

OGILVY, Brig. David, CIE 1935; DSO; OBE; *b* 1881; *m* 1906, Vere Grace, *d* of late Sir Henry Fawcett, KCMG; one *d. Educ:* Trinity College, Glenalmond; RMA, Woolwich. Served S Africa, 1899–1902; Somaliland, 1903–04; European War, 1914–19 (wounded, despatches, DSO, Bt Lt-Col); Afghan War, 1919; Waziristan, 1923; Chief Engineer Eastern Command, India, 1928–32; retired 1934. *Address:* Linton House, Cluny, Aberdeenshire.

Died 2 June 1949.

O'GORMAN, Lt-Col Patrick Wilkins, CMG 1918; MD Brux., MRCP Ed., LRCS and LM Ed., LRFP and S Glas., DPH Cantab; Papal Cross Pro Ecclesia et Pontifice, 1927; Indian Medical Service retired; Editor, The Catholic Medical Guardian (Journal of Medico-Moral Jurisprudence and Deontology), 1923–34; *b* 1860; *s* of Major Cornelius Calinan O'Gorman, ACD, Limerick; unmarried. *Educ:* Edinburgh University; RCP and S Ed.; King's College, London, etc. Lt-Col 1909; served in 1st and 2nd Miranzai campaigns, NW Frontier, India, 1891 (medal and clasp); NW Frontier, India, 1914–17, and German East Africa (Administrative Medical Officer, Lindi Force), 1917–18 (CMG, despatches, 3 medals), invalided, 1919; served 42 years in Military and Civil Indian Medical Services. For several years member Council and Executive Committee Anglo-Indian Temperance Association, London; co-founder British Empire Medical Guild of Sts Luke, Cosmas, and Damian. London, 1910; Member Council Association Propagation Faith, London and Member Medical Mission Board, 1921–36; Lecturer Catholic Evidence Guild, London, 26 years to Oct. 1947; Member of Council of the Indian Empire Society and of the late India Defence League; co-founder of the Indian Catholic Truth Society, 1918; Founder and Life Hon. Master Catholic Pharmaceutical Guild; Co-reviver of Catholic Nurses Guild, etc; Lecturer on Tropical Hygiene and Sanitation for Missionaries, St Charles's College, N Kensington, 1933–39. *Publications:* Scientific Valuation of Alcohol in Health, 1900, etc.; Rational Therapeutics, and other papers; Sterilisation of the Unfit, 1923 and What are Life, Soul, and Memory? 1924 (Catholic Medical Guardian); (invented for Army) New Method of Sick Transport, 1925 (idem); Catholic Associations and Federations: their Social, Moral, and Civic Value, 1913, etc.; The Errors of Rome, a Reply, 1914 (2nd ed. 1919); A Scheme for the Catholic Federal Union of the East Indies, 1919; Indian Prisons and the Indian Prison Committee (Jl East India Assoc., 1924), etc. *Address:* 3 St John's Road, Harrow-on-the-Hill, Middlesex.

Died 22 Sept. 1950.

O'GOWAN, Maj.-Gen. Robert W.; *see* Wanless-O'Gowan.

O'GRADY, Donald de Courcy, DSO 1919; medical practitioner; *b* 31 May 1881; *s* of Captain Standish de Courcy and Isobel Beatrice O'Grady; *m* 1929, Lilian; no *c. Educ:* Naval College, Eltham. Royal Army Medical Corps; Lt-Col retired; served NWF India Mohmand Expedition, 1908 (medal and clasp); European War, 1914–19 (despatches, DSO, Croix de Guerre). *Recreations:* fishing, shooting, cricket. *Address:* 38 Jodrell Road, Victoria Park, E3.

Died 28 Jan. 1943.

O'GRADY, Brig.-Gen. Henry de Courcy, CIE 1919; Indian Army (retired); *b* 1873; *s* of Captain Standish de Courcy O'Grady; *m* 1908, Sybil, *d* of Colonel D. Macpherson, formerly Indian Army. *Educ:* Tonbridge. Served NW Frontier of India, 1902 and 1908 (despatches, medal with clasp); European War, 1914–19

(despatches, CIE, Brevets Lt-Col and Col, Officer of Legion of Honour); Afghanistan, 1919 (despatches, clasp). *Address:* c/o Lloyds Bank, 6 Pall Mall, SW1. *Club:* United Service.

Died 23 Feb. 1949.

OGSTON, Brig.-Gen. Charles, CB 1920; CMG 1918; DSO 1915; late Gordon Highlanders; *b* 14 Sept. 1877; 2nd *s* of late Alexander Milne Ogston, DL, Ardoe, Kincardine. Entered army, 1897; Capt. 1902; Major, 1915; Lt-Col 1920; Col 1923; Adjutant, 1906–09; DAA and QMG 1912; AQMG 1916; DA and QMG 1918; served NW Frontier, India, 1897–98 (medal with clasp); South Africa, 1899–1902 (Queen's medal 4 clasps, King's medal 2 clasps); European War, 1914–18 (despatches, DSO, CMG, Bt Lt-Col); Deputy Director of Organisation, War Office, 1924–25; retired pay, 1925. *Address:* Kildrummy Castle, Mossat, Aberdeenshire. *Clubs:* Naval and Military; Royal Northern, Aberdeen.

Died 10 Nov. 1944.

O'HARA, Major Charles Kean, OBE 1920; *b* 10 Dec. 1860; *e s* of C. W. O'Hara, DL, JP, of Annaghmore and Coopershill, and Annie C. Streatfield, of The Rocks, Uckfield; unmarried. *Educ:* Eton College. Joined Sligo Militia, 1880; joined 3rd West York Militia, afterwards York and Lancaster, 1881; contested (Unionist) Co. Sligo, 1883; High Sheriff, Co. Sligo, 1886; HM's Lieutenant of Co. Sligo and Custos Rotulorum, 1902; Peace Commissioner (PC) to Saorstat Eireann, 1924. *Recreations:* hunting, polo, racing, shooting, fishing, tennis, driving, etc., cricket, football (keeps a private pack of harriers). *Address:* Annaghmore, Collooney, Co. Sligo. *Clubs:* Kildare Street, Dublin; Royal St George Yacht, Kingstown; Constitutional, County, Sligo.

Died 4 Aug. 1947.

O'HARA, Valentine J.; *b* 1875; *s* of late Thomas O'Hara, Portarlington; *m* Florence, *d* of late William Butt, Ampthill, Beds. *Educ:* Abroad; Stonyhurst; Queen's College, Galway (Royal University of Ireland.). Long resident in the old Russian Empire; served on the Anglo-Russian Committee Petrograd and the Inter-Allied Trade Commission, Stockholm; imprisoned under the Bolshevik regime; on return to England joined the Middlesex Regiment for the North Russian Expedition; demobilized 1919 at the request of the Foreign Office and appointed Member of Political Mission for the Baltic States (Estonia, Latvia and Lithuania). *Publications:* Poland (1861–1923) in Story of the Nation series; Russia, in Modern World Series, 1925 (with N. Makeev); Anthony O'Hara, Knight of Malta (a Memoir); contributions to the foreign Press, to Nineteenth Century, Fortnightly Review, National Review, Review of Reviews, Studio, etc.; translation and adaptation of Russian Plays into English. *Club:* Royal Empire Society.

Died 8 Oct. 1941.

O'KEEFE, Hon. David John, CMG, 1941; MHA, Tasmania, since 1934; Speaker, 1934–42; *b* 21 Aug. 1864; *s* of David O'Keefe, farmer, and Mary Ann McCullagh; *m* 1st, 1897, Sara Wilson (*d* 1921); one *s* three *d*; 2nd, 1924, Agnes Hughes, *widow. Educ:* private and State schools. Left school at thirteen years of age; worked on farms and at various labouring occupations for five years; worked in mines and quartz-crushing and gold-saving mills for five years; began journalistic work at 23 years; studied mining and mineralogy; filled positions on several newspapers, including editorship of Herald at Zeehan, Tasmania, for five years; and special services reporting on mines in several parts of Australia for Argus of Melbourne; Senator for Tasmania in the Parliament of the Commonwealth of Australia, 1901–06 and 1910–20; Member House of Representatives for Denison, 1922–24. *Publications:* a number of special articles on gold, copper, and silver-lead mining.

Recreations: walking, shooting (field and rifle), fishing, swimming. *Address:* 111 Cameron Street, Launceston, Tasmania.

Died 21 July 1943.

O'KEEFFE, Maj.-Gen. Sir Menus William, KCMG 1918; CB 1915; MD; LLD; AMS; Col Comdt RAMC 1927–29; *b* 3 Aug. 1859; *s* of late Wm O'Keeffe, MD, of Mount Keeffe, Newmarket, Co. Cork; *m* Janetta Canning, *d* of late William S. Baird, JP, Belfast; one *d.* *Educ:* Queen's University, Ireland. Major, 1893; Lt-Col 1901; Colonel, 1910; Surg.-Gen. 1915; Inspector of Medical Services, War Office, 1910; served Egypt 1882, including actions at Kassassin, Tel-el-Kebir (medal with clasp; bronze star); Tirah, 1897–98; Mohmand Campaign, NW Frontier, 1908: European War, 1914–17 (despatches seven times, CB, KCMG, Legion of Honour, 1st Class Order of St Anne with swords); LLD Queen's University, Ireland, 1918. *Address:* Abbeywood, Camberley. *T:* Camberley 177.

Died 29 Nov. 1944.

O'KEEFFE, Stephen Martin Lanigan, CMG 1935; *b* 1878; *s* of Stephen Charles Martin Lanigan O'Keeffe, DL, JP, of Glenaguile House, Co. Tipperary and of Delville House, Glasnevin, Co. Dublin; *m* 1914, Marjorie Isabella, *d* of J. H. Humphreys, Montevideo. Formerly MLA, Southern Rhodesia, also Minister of Internal Affairs, Minister of Justice and Minister of Defence; High Commissioner in London for S Rhodesia, 1935–46. *Address:* PO Box 588, Bulawayo, S Rhodesia.

Died 1 Dec. 1948.

OKELL, Rt Rev. Frank Jackson; Suffragan Bishop of Stockport since 1949; Archdeacon of Macclesfield since 1941; Rector of Astbury since 1944; *b* 3 Feb. 1887; *γ s* of late George Okell, The Manor House, Barrow, Cheshire; *m* 1917, Gertrude Emily Carrington Houghton; one *s* (and one killed in action, 1942) four *d.* *Educ:* Rugby; Trinity College, Oxford. Curate of Bolsterstone, Yorks, 1914–15; Curate of Sheffield Cathedral, 1915–20; temp. CF, 1915–19; Rector of Bangor Monachorum, Flints, 1920–25; Rector of Eccleston, Cheshire, 1925–36; Rector of Malpas, 1936–44; Rural Dean of Malpas, 1936–41. *Recreations:* cricket and golf. *Address:* The Rectory, Astbury, nr Congleton, Cheshire. *Club:* Grosvenor (Chester).

Died 7 Oct. 1950.

OKYAR, Bay Fethi; Minister of Justice, Turkey, 1939–41; Deputy to the Kamutay for Bolu since 1938. Après être sorti de l'École de Guerre, avec le grade de capitaine d'État-Major, il fut attaché à l'armée de Macédoine, et très vite il devint un des chefs les plus écoutés du parti jeune-turc qui devait mettre fin au régime hamidien, par la proclamation de la Constitution. Il fut nommé, dans la suite, attaché militaire à Paris; lors de la guerre italo-turque, il se signala par son admirable énergie dans la défense de la Tripolitaine; il quitta l'armée pour la Politique et devint Secrétaire Général du Comité Union et Progrès; Après la signature du traité de paix entre la Turquie et la Bulgarie à la suite de la guerre balkanique il assuma, avec autorité, le poste délicat de Ministre à Sofia. Il prit une part active aux derniers événements qui se sont déroulés en Anatolie et il fut un des plus grands promoteurs du mouvement national. Successivement Ministre de l'Intérieur, délégué plénipotentiaire dans maintes négociations, Président de la Grande Assemblée Nationale, deux fois président du Conseil des Ministres; Ambassadeur à Paris, 1925–30, date à laquelle il resilia ses fonctions pour jouer de nouveau un rôle politique en Turquie par la création d'un nouveau parti qui fut le Parti Libéral; Ambassadeur de la République Turque à Londres, 1934–39. *Address:* 34 Ruméli Sokagi, Nichantache, Istanbul.

Died 7 May 1943.

OLDCASTLE, John; *see* Meynell, Wilfred.

OLDFIELD, Col Christopher George, CMG 1916; CBE 1918; retired; *b* 28 Feb. 1863; *s* of late Sir Richard Oldfield, ICS; *m* 1887, Margaret Elizabeth Cortlandt (*d* 1941), *d* of late Joshua Le Bailly of Rockmount, Jersey; one *d.* *Educ:* Haileybury; Woolwich. Joined the Royal Artillery, 1883; retired, 1914; volunteered for service in European War and served throughout in the Royal Army Ordnance Corps (CMG, CBE, despatches thrice). *Recreations:* golf, painting. *Address:* Highbridge, Deepcut, Surrey.

Died 19 Sept. 1944.

OLDFIELD, Maj.-Gen. Sir Louis, KBE 1934; CB 1919; CMG 1919; DSO 1915; late RA; *b* 3 Feb. 1872; 3rd *s* of Col F. J. Oldfield, 3rd Bombay Light Cavalry; *m* Millicent (*d* 1949), *d* of Lt-Col E. G. Bredin, RA; one *d.* *Educ:* Clifton College. Entered army, 1892; Captain, 1900; Adjutant, 1906–09; Major, 1909; Lieut-Col 1915; Major-General, 1926; Adjutant, Volunteers, 1902–05; served European War, 1914–18, France and Flanders (DSO, CB, CMG, despatches, Bt Col); Chief Instructor in Gunnery, School of Artillery, 1924–25; commanded 47th (2nd London) Division, TA, 1927–30; General Officer Commanding Malaya, 1931–34; retired pay, 1934; ADC to the King, 1924; Col Commandant RA, 1938–42. *Address:* Lockerley Manor, near Romsey, Hants. *Clubs:* United Service, Roehampton.

Died 8 Jan. 1949.

OLDHAM, Charles Evelyn Arbuthnot William, CSI 1918; FRGS, Hon. Vice-President RAS; ICS (retired); *b* 15 Sept. 1869; *s* of Charles Æmilius Oldham. *Educ:* Galway Grammar School; private tuition; Balliol College, Oxford. *Address:* 21 Courtfield Rd, SW7.

Died 18 Nov. 1949.

OLDMAN, Maj.-Gen. Richard Deare Furley, CB 1923; CMG 1917; DSO 1905; late Norfolk and Wilts Regts; *b* 17 June 1877; *m* 1912, Helen Marie, *d* of Walter Pigot, Dundrum; three *s* one *d.* Entered army, 1897; Captain, 1905; Major, 1915; Colonel, 1919; Maj.-Gen. 1930; served West Africa, 1905–08, N Nigeria (DSO); European War, 1914–18 (despatches, Bt Colonel, Bt Lt-Col, CMG); Inspector-General of West African Frontier Force, 1924–26; commanded 6th Infantry Brigade, 1926–30; ADC to the King, 1927–30; Commander 47th (2nd London) Division TA 1931–34; retired pay, 1935. *Address:* Firholt, Crowthorne, Berks. *Club:* United Service.

Died 11 Nov. 1943.

OLDMEADOW, Ernest James; author; *b* Chester, 31 Oct. 1867; 3rd *s* of George Edward Oldmeadow; *m* 1897, Annie Cecilia, *d* of Rev. Joseph Dawson. *Educ:* King's School, Chester. Editor of The Dome, 1897–1900; music-critic of The Outlook, 1900–04; contributor to the Standard, Westminster Gazette, Nineteenth Century and After, Saturday Review, Morning Post, etc.; Editor of the Tablet, 1923–36; member of Westminster City Council; Knight Comm. of Order of St Gregory the Great, 1934. *Publications:* Lady Lohengrin, 1896; The Little Christian Year, 1898; Schumann; Chopin, 1905; The North Sea Bubble, 1906; Susan; The Scoundrel, 1907; Great Musicians; Apollonius of Tyana (with Dr F. W. Groves Campbell); Aunt Maud, 1908; Antonio, 1909; A Babe Unborn, 1911; Home Cookery in War Time, 1915; Coggin, 1919; The Hare, 1920; Wildfang, 1922; Miss Watts, 1923; In Town To-morrow, 1937; A Layman's Christian Year, 1938; Francis Cardinal Bourne, Vol. I, 1940, Vol. II, 1944; Potatoes: To Know Them and Serve Them, 1943; The Lilies of the Kitchen, 1943. His books have appeared in French, German, and Norwegian translations. *Recreation:* Ecclesiology. *Address:* 20 Temple Fortune Lane, NW11. *T:* Speedwell 1434.

Died 11 Sept. 1949.

O'LEARY, Brig. Heffernan William Denis McCarthy-, DSO 1918; MC; *b* 1885; 2nd *s* of late Lieut-Col William McCarthy-O'Leary of Coomlagane, Co. Cork. *Educ:* Stonyhurst. Served European War (wounded, despatches, DSO, MC); Major and Bt Lieut-Col 1925; Lt-Col 1929; Col 1933; commanded Royal Irish Fusiliers, 1929–33; commanded 158th (Royal Welch) Infantry Brigade TA, 1933–37; retired pay, 1937.

Died 23 Feb. 1948.

OLIVE, Sir James William, KBE 1924; CBE 1920; *b* 1856. Assistant Commissioner Metropolitan Police, 1920–22; Deputy Commissioner of Police, 1922–26; retired, 1926. *Address:* 9 Brooksville Avenue, NW6. *T:* Willesden 1087.

Died 13 Jan. 1942.

OLIVER, Rev. Arthur West, MA; Vicar of King Charles the Martyr, Tunbridge Wells, 1902–30, retired; Rural Dean of Tunbridge Wells, 1925–30; Hon. Canon, Rochester, 1919; Canon Emeritus since 1934; Member of National Assembly, Proctor in Convocation, 1921–29; Licensed Preacher, Salisbury Diocese, 1930; *b* New Orleans, USA, July 1858; *s* of G. W. Oliver and A. D. Hill; *m* Louisa (*d* 1922), *e d* of Edward H. Harrison, Plymyard, Eastham, Cheshire; one *s* three *d*. *Educ:* privately; Queen's College, Oxford. Five years in commercial life; Curate of Milton, next Sittingbourne, Kent; Walton on the Hill, with charge of Mission District, St Matthew's, Bootle; Vicar of St Matthew's, Bootle. *Recreations:* golf, boating, tennis. *Address:* Downside, Warminster, Wilts. *T:* Warminster 182.

Died 2 May 1941.

OLIVER, Charles A., CBE 1919; *b* 1861; *y s* of late Admiral R. A. Oliver; *m* 1911, Hilda, *d* of late Lt-Col Woollcombe-Adams, of Anstey Hall, Warwickshire. *Educ:* Winchester. Entered Admiralty, 1885; Assistant Director of Navy Contracts, 1904; retired, 1921; during War of 1914–18 was a member of La Commission Internationale de Ravitaillement, Salvage, and Disposal Boards (CBE). *Address:* 1 Addison Gardens, W14. *T:* Park 6123. *Clubs:* Athenæum, Union.

Died 30 March 1945.

OLIVER, Edwin; *y s* of William Oliver, artist; *m* Gertrude Kent, *d* of late Riley Carr; one *s* two *d*. Editor of Atalanta and the Idler, 1895–99; staff of Standard, 1900–06; Assistant Editor of Outlook, 1907; Editor of The Outlook, 1910–17.

Died 29 Sept. 1950.

OLIVER, Francis Alfred, CMG 1930; CBE 1926; *b* London, 15 Dec. 1866; *s* of late Henry Oliver, Harrogate, and late A. M. Jones; *m* 1st, 1900, Marion Alexandrina Winton Forrester (*d* 1927); one *d*; 2nd, 1932, Margaret, *d* of late A. J. Holiday, Featherstone Hall, Pontefract, and *widow* of W. T. Oliver. *Educ:* privately; London University. Acting Consul, Guatemala, 1893; Vice-Consul, Bremerhaven, 1902; Hamburg, 1906; Acting Consul-General, Hamburg, 1907, 1908, 1909 and 1910; Berlin, 1910; Consul and First Secretary in Diplomatic Service (local rank) and Chargé d'Affaires in Paraguay, 1911–19; Consul at Madrid, 1919–21; Consul-General at Hamburg, 1921–30; British Delegate on International Commission for delimitation of Czechoslovak port zones in Germany, 1929; retired, 1930; employed at Home Office, 1938–41; at Foreign Relations Dept, War Organisation of British Red Cross and St John of Jerusalem since 1942. *Address:* c/o Drummond's Branch, Royal Bank of Scotland, Charing Cross, SW1.

Died 3 Oct. 1944.

OLIVER, James, MD, MCh, FRS (Edin.); Consulting Physician, The Hospital for Women, and Consulting Gynæcologist, King George Hospital, Ilford, Essex; *b* Ayr, 18 Nov. 1857; 3rd *s* of James Oliver, Ayr; *m* Mary Jane (*d* 1933), *d* of George Younger of Warkworth; two *s* one *d*. *Educ:* Ayr Academy; Glasgow University; Edinburgh University; University College Hospital, London. Formerly Senior Physician, Farringdon General Dispensary; House Surgeon, Alnwick Infirmary and Durham County Hospital, House Physician, Queen's Hospital, Birmingham; The National Hospital for Epilepsy and Paralysis, Queen's Square, London and the Hospital for Women, London. *Publications:* Diseases of Women; Manual of Diseases of Women; Abdominal Tumours and Abdominal Dropsy in Women; various writings on Health and Standard of Purity of Foods. *Recreations:* golf, fishing. *Address:* 5 Tankerville Terrace, Newcastle-upon-Tyne.

Died 13 Jan. 1941.

OLIVER, John Rathbone, MD, PhD; Associate in History of Medicine, Johns Hopkins University, since 1930; Professor of History of Medicine, Medical School, University of Maryland since 1928; *b* Albany, NY, 4 Jan. 1872; *s* of Gen. Robert Shaw Oliver and Marion Lucy Rathbone; unmarried. *Educ:* AB Harvard, 1894; grad. Gen. Theol. Sem., 1900; MD, Univ. of Innsbruck, 1910; PhD, Johns Hopkins, 1927. Master at St Paul's School, Concord, NH, 1894–97; Priest Episcopal (Anglican) Church, 1900; Curate St Mark's Church, Philadelphia, 1900–03 (resigned; restored to Orders, 1927); Surgeon, Austrian Army, 1914–15; Psychiatrist, Johns Hopkins Hospital, 1915–17; Chief Medical Officer to Supreme Bench of Baltimore, 1917–30; private practice as psychiatrist; Warden Alumni Memorial Hall, Johns Hopkins Univ. until 1936; Member Medical ORC Trustee Prisoners' Aid Society; Member AMA, American Psychiatric Association, Royal Society Medicine (British); Phi Beta Kappa; Republican; Episcopalian. *Publications:* The Good Shepherd, 1915, rev. ed. 1932; The Six-Pointed Cross in the Dust, 1917; Fear, 1927; Victim and Victor, 1928; Foursquare, 1929; Rock and Sand, 1930; Article 32, 1931; To-morrow's Faith, 1932; Pastoral Psychiatry and Mental Health, 1932; Priest or Pagan, 1933; The Ordinary Difficulties of Everyday People, 1935; Greater Love, 1936; Contributor to Journal Criminal Law, International Clinics, John Hopkins Bulletin, etc. *Recreations:* book-collecting, golf. *Address:* The Charles Apartments, 3333 North Charles Street, Baltimore, Md, USA. *Clubs:* Savile; University, Charcoal, Press, Baltimore; Harvard, New York.

Died 21 Jan. 1943.

OLIVER, Lady Mary Louise, CBE 1929; JP, City of Leicester; *b* 1868; *d* of late Joseph Danolds, Northampton; *m* 1896, Lt-Col Sir (Charles) Frederick Oliver (*d* 1939); three *s* one *d*. President of Central Council of Leicester Women's Conservative Association; Officer of Order of St John and Vice-Pres. of Leicestershire. *Address:* The Firs, Leicester.

Died 3 July 1950.

OLIVER, Rev. Richard John Deane, CBE 1919; late Royal Army Chaplains Department; *yr s* of Richard Charles Deane Oliver, JP, Rockmills House, Co. Cork. *Educ:* College of St Columba, Co. Dublin; Trinity Coll., Dublin, MA. Private Secretary to Lord Plunket, Archbishop of Dublin, 1886; Domestic Chaplain, 1888; Chaplain HM Forces Dublin, 1892; Senior Chaplain, Orange River Colony, 1900 (despatches, specially promoted); Senior Chaplain, Colchester, 1905; Senior Chaplain, Shorncliffe, 1912; Assistant Chaplain-General, Eastern Command, 1915–20 (three times brought to notice of Secretary of State for valuable services); retired, 1920; Chaplain at St Maxime, 1924, Capri, 1924–25, and Grasse, AM, France, seasons 1925–39. *Address:* c/o Lloyds Bank, Sandgate, Folkestone, Kent. *Clubs:* Church Imperial, Overseas League.

Died 27 April 1942.

OLIVER, Sir Thomas, Kt 1908; MD; Hon. LLD Glasgow; Hon. DSc University of Sheffield, 1908; DSc (hon.) Danzig, 1934; Hon. DCL University of Durham, 1921; FRCP; DL Northumberland; JP for city and county Newcastle-upon-Tyne; with aid of Local Committee raised in 1914 the Tyneside Scottish Brigade (20th-23rd Battalions Northumberland Fusiliers); Consulting Physician, Royal Victoria Infirmary, Newcastle; Ex-President of University of Durham College of Medicine, Newcastle; Knight of Grace Order St John of Jerusalem, 1924; Chevalier Legion of Honour, 1929; gold medal Ministry of Public Assistance, France, 1924; late Professor of Physiology, Durham; Emeritus Professor of Medicine, University of Durham; late Medical Expert, Dangerous Trades Committee, Home Office; Hon. President, International Congress of Accidents and Industrial Diseases, Geneva, 1931; *b* St Quivox, Ayrshire, 2 March 1853; 2nd *s* of James Oliver, Ayr; *m* 1st, 1881, Edith (*d* 1888), *e d* of William Jenkins, Consett Hall, Co. Durham; 2nd, 1893, Emma (*d* 1912), *d* of John Woods, Benton Hall, Newcastle; one *s* three *d*. *Educ:* Ayr Academy; Glasgow Univ.; Paris. Practised in Preston, Lancashire, 1875–79; since 1879 a consulting physician in Newcastle; Goulstonian Lecturer, Royal College Physicians, 1891; Member 'White Lead' Commission, Home Office, 1892–93; Representative of Home Office at Madrid International Congress on Hygiene, 1898; Medical Expert Home Office Special Enquiry Lucifer Matches and Potteries; Harben Lecturer Royal Institute Public Health, 1905; Hon. Corr. Mem. Med. Phys. Soc. Amsterdam, 1905; Hon. Corr. Mem. Soc. Med. des Hôpitaux de Paris, 1906; Medal of Honour, Univ. of Brussels, 1920; Delegate of the Australian Commonwealth International Labour Conference, League of Nations, Geneva, 1921; received Freedom City of Boston, Mass, 1923; Vice-Chancellor, Durham University, 1928–30. *Publications:* Lead Poisoning, 1892; translator and editor Bouchard's Auto-intoxication, 1894; Industrial Diseases, Allbutt's System of Medicine, vol. ii, 1897; Metallic and other forms of Poisoning, Gibson's System of Medicine, 1901; Diseases of Occupation, 1908; Lead Poisoning, 1914; Occupations, 1916; The Health of the Workers; articles in Encyclopædia Medica, Ency. Brit. and papers on Heart and Lung Diseases, etc., medical journals; editor Dangerous Trades, 1902. *Recreations:* fishing, shooting. *Address:* 7 Ellison Place, Newcastle-upon-Tyne. *T:* 22861. *Clubs:* Athenæum, Authors'.

Died 15 May 1942.

OLIVER, Thomas, DSc Edin., BSc Lond.; Principal-emeritus of the Scottish Woollen Technical College (retired, 1931); *b* 1871. *Educ:* attended Kirkton Parish School. Shepherd's Assistant: twelve years in woollen mills; appointed Textile Teacher, 1898; BSc London., 1901; BSc Edin., 1904; Carnegie Research Fellow, 1905; DSc Edin., 1908; life-long efforts mainly directed to the development of technique in Scottish woollen trade; Mather Lecturer (Textile Institute), 1933. *Publications:* Weaving and Designing, Weaving Problems, Setting and Costing, textile works; Wool Technology; Scotch Tweed Journal. *Address:* 90 Channel St, Galashiels.

Died 12 Sept. 1946.

OLIVIER, 1st Baron *cr* 1924, of Ramsden; **Sydney Olivier,** PC 1924; KCMG 1907; CB 1917; CMG 1898; BA; LLD; *b* 1859; 2nd *s* of Rev. H. A. Olivier, Winchfield; *m* 1885, Margaret, *e d* of Homersham Cox, Judge of County Courts, E Kent; four *d*. *Educ:* Lausanne; Kineton School; Tonbridge School; Corpus Christi College, Oxford; Germany. Entered Colonial Office (heading open competition), 1882; Secretary Fabian Society, 1886–90; Acting Colonial Secretary, British Honduras, 1890–91; Auditor-General Leeward Islands, 1895–96 (special appointment to examine and reorganise accounts and finances); private secretary to Earl of Selborne, 1896–97; secretary West India Royal Commission, 1897; sent to Washington, 1898, to assist in reciprocity negotiations on behalf of W Indian Colonies; Colonial Secretary, Jamaica, 1899–1904, and Acting Governor, 1900, 1902, and 1904; Principal Clerk W African and W Indian Departments Colonial Office, 1904–07; Governor of Jamaica, 1907–13; Permanent Secretary of the Board of Agriculture and Fisheries, 1913–17; Assistant Comptroller and Auditor of the Exchequer, 1917; retired, 1920; West Indian Sugar Commission, 1929–30; Secretary for India, 1924; JP Oxon. *Publications:* Poems and Parodies, 1881; Dictionary of Oxford (Dickens); White Capital and Coloured Labour; The Anatomy of African Misery; The Empire Builder; The Myth of Governor Eyre, 1933; Jamaica: The Blessed Island, 1936; contributor to Fabian Essays and Fabian Tracts; magazine and review articles on Socialism, Economics, Art, etc.; occasional verse, sundry official reports. *Recreations:* the normal forms of loafing and dilettantism. *Address:* Wychwood, Selsey Avenue, Bognor Regis. *T:* Bognor Regis 1346. *Club:* West Indian.

Died 15 Feb. 1943 (ext).

OLIVIER, C. F.; KC Canada. Ex-Mayor of Sherbrooke, Quebec. *Address:* 197 Quebec Street, Sherbrooke, Quebec.

Died 31 Dec. 1940.

OLIVIER, Edith, MBE; *d* of Rev. Dacres Olivier, Rector of Wilton, Wilts. *Educ:* home; St Hugh's College, Oxford. Mayor of Wilton, 1938–39, 1939–40, and 1940–41. *Publications:* The Love Child; As far as Jane's Grandmothers; The Triumphant Footman; Dwarf's Blood; The Seraphim Room; The Eccentric Life of Alexander Cruden; Life of Mary Magdalen; Without Knowing Mr Walkley; Country Moods and Tenses; Night Thoughts of a Country Landlady; Four Victorian Ladies of Wiltshire; etc. *Address:* Daye House, Quidhampton, Salisbury.

Died 10 May 1948.

OLLARD, Rev. Sidney Leslie, FSA 1946; Canon of St George's Chapel, Windsor, 1936–48; Hon. Fellow of St Edmund Hall, Oxford 1938; *b* 1875; *e surv. s* of late Sidney Ollard, Solicitor, Wisbech, Cambs; *m* 1914, Mary, *e d* of late Rev. T. C. Ward; four *s*. *Educ:* Aldenham School; St John's College, Oxford; Casberd Scholar, 1896; BA 2nd Class Mod. Hist. 1896; MA 1899; DLitt 1946; Ely Theological College. Deacon, 1899; Priest, 1900; Curate of Holy Trinity, Hastings, 1899–1902; Christ Church (Oxford) Mission, Poplar, 1902–03, Examining Chaplain to Bishop (Lloyd) of Newcastle-on-Tyne, 1904–07; Vice-Principal and Tutor of St Edmund Hall, Oxford, 1903–13; Rector of Dunsfold, 1914–15; Rector of Bainton, Yorks, 1915–36; Hon. Canon of Worcester, 1911–35; Prebendary of York Minster, 1935–36; Proctor in Convocation for Diocese of York, 1921–36; Examining Chaplain to Bishop of Worcester, 1907–16; to Archbishops Lang and Temple of York, 1916–38; to the Bishops (Fisher and Douglas) of Nyasaland, 1917–36. *Publications:* The Oxford Movement, 1909; The Six Students of St Edmund Hall, 1911; ed. Dictionary of English Church History, 1912, 3rd ed. 1948; ed. Wakeman's History of the Church of England, 1914; 11th ed. 1926; Short History of the Oxford Movement, 1915, 3rd ed. 1933; ed. (with Bishop F. C. N. Hicks) Holden's Anglican Claim, 1916; Dunsfold and its Rectors, 1919; A Forty Years' Friendship, 1919; Reunion, 1919; The Anglo-Catholic Revival 1925; edited with Rev. P. C. Walker, Visitation Returns of Abp Herring, 1743 (vol. i 1928, vol. ii 1929, vols iii and iv 1930, vol. v 1931); contributed to vol. xii of Cambridge History of English Literature, to Dict. of Nat. Biog. 1912–1921 (1927) and 1922–1930 (1937), and to Confirmation, vol. i; ed. Historical Monographs relating to St George's Chapel, Windsor Castle, first 3 vols, 1939. *Address:* 1 Queens Road, Datchet, Bucks.

Died 28 Feb. 1949.

OLLERENSHAW, Robert, MD, ChB (Vict.), FRCS (Eng.), LRCP (Lond.); Casualty Orthopædic Surgeon, Royal Manchester Children's Hospital; Hon. Casualty Surgeon, Orthopædic Department, Salford Royal Hospital; Clinical Lecturer in Orthopædic Surgery, Manchester University; Consulting Surgeon, Manchester Crippled Children's Society, etc; *b* 4 Sept. 1882; *s* of George Ollerenshaw, JP, Glossop, Derbyshire; *m* 1911, Florence Eleanor (*d* 1933), 2nd *d* of late Hon. Robert Watson, Ottawa, Canada; two *s*. *Educ:* Manchester Grammar School; Manchester University; London Hospital; Berlin. Late House Surgeon, Surgical Registrar, Manchester Royal Infirmary; House Surgeon, Liverpool Children's Hospital; served with 2nd Western General Hospital, and with 57th General Hospital, France, 1914–18, Major RAMC; FRSM (President of Orthopædic Section); Vice-President of British Orthopædic Association; Vice-President Orthopædic Section, British Medical Association, 1929–30; Member of Manchester Medical and Pathological Societies; President Manchester Surgical Society; Fellow of International Society of Orthopædic Surgery; Hon. Fellow of French Orthopædic Association. *Publications:* Causation and Treatment of Coxa Vara, 1912; Sacro-Coccygeal Tumours, 1913; Recurrent Dislocation of the Shoulder, 1919; Rotation Dislocation of Astragalus, 1921; Cysts of the Semilunar Cartilages, 1920; Treatment of Fractures, 1921; Tendon Transplantation, 1922; Giant-celled Tumours of Tendons, 1923; Congenital Deficiency of the Tibiæ, 1923; Surgical Treatment of Infantile Paralysis, 1926; Fractures of the Ankle, 1929; Fractures involving the knee joint, 1930; Manipulative Methods, 1930; Cysts of the Semilunar Cartilages, 1935; Infantile Coxa Vara, 1939; Slipped Epiphysis of the Femur, 1939; Section on Wounds of Knee Joint, in Bailey's Surgery of Modern Warfare, 1942. *Address:* 21 St John Street, Manchester. *T:* Blackfriars 0280; Broome House, Didsbury, Manchester. *T:* Didsbury 1121. *Clubs:* Royal Automobile; Clarendon, Manchester.

Died 19 May 1948.

O'LONDON, John; *see* Whitten, Wilfred.

OLSSON, Julius, RA 1920; ARA 1914; JP; marine painter; *b* London, 1864; *m* 1925, Edith Mary Ellison. Served European War, Lieut RNVR; President Royal Institute Oil-Painters; Medallist and hors concours Paris Salon. *Recreations:* yachting, golf. *Address:* St Helier's, Dalkey, Dublin. *Club:* Arts.

Died 8 Sept. 1942.

O'MALLEY, Lewis Sydney Steward, CIE 1919; *b* 1874; *s* of late Rev. Bryan O'Malley, and Frances, *d* of Rev. Hon. Thomas Robert Keppel; *m* 1900, Ida, *d* of W. S. Prichard; four *d*. *Educ:* Norwich Grammar School; Hertford College, Oxford (Scholar). Joined Indian Civil Service, 1898; Under-Secretary, Government of Bengal, 1903–05; Superintendent, Gazetteer Revision, Bengal, 1905–09; Census Superintendent, Bengal, 1909–12; Secretary to the Government of Bengal, 1916–21; retired ICS, 1924. *Publications:* The Indian Civil Service, 1601–1930, 1931; Indian Caste Customs, 1932; India's Social Heritage, 1934; Popular Hinduism, 1935. *Address:* Cornerways, Deepdene, Dorking.

Died 10 May 1941.

OMAN, Sir Charles (William Chadwick), KBE 1920; Knight of the Order of St Sava, 1920; FSA; Hon. DCL and MA Oxon; Hon. LLD Cambridge and Edinburgh; Fellow of All Souls College, Oxford, since 1883; Chichele Professor of Modern History, Oxford, 1905; Fellow of British Academy, 1905; President Royal Historical Society, 1917–21, Royal Numismatic Society, 1919–30; and Royal Archæological Institute, 1927–37; Corresp. Member of La Real Academia de la Historia of Madrid, and of the Academies of Lisbon, Aix, and San Luis of Saragossa; Hon. Fellow of New College, Oxford, 1936; *b* Mozufferpore, 12 Jan. 1860; *o c* of Charles Philip

Austin Oman, planter, and Anne Chadwick; *m* Mary, *d* of Gen. R. Maclagan, RE, 1892; one *s* two *d*. Senior Scholar of Winchester, 1877; Senior Scholar of New College, Oxford, 1878; 1st class Final Classical Schools, 1882; 1st class Modern History School, 1883; Lothian Prizeman, 1884; Gold Medallist of the Royal United Service, Institution, 1911; Creighton Lecturer, University of London, 1922; MP (C) Oxford University, 1919–35. *Publications:* A History of Greece, 1888; Warwick the Kingmaker, 1891; Short History of the Byzantine Empire, 1892; A History of Europe 476–918, 1893; A Short History of England, 1895; A History of the Art of War in the Middle Ages, 1898, 2nd edition 1924; A History of the Peninsular War, vols i ii iii iv v vi vii, 1807–1814, 1902–1930; Seven Roman Statesmen, 1902, The Great Revolt of 1381, 1906; A History of England before the Norman Conquest, 1910, 8th edition, 1937; Wellington's Army, 1912; The Unfortunate Colonel Despard, 1922; Castles, 1926; Napoleonic Studies, 1929; The Coinage of England, 1931; Things I Have Seen, 1933; Sixteenth Century Studies, 1936; The Art of War in the Sixteenth Century, 1937; On the Writing of History, 1939; Memories of Victorian Oxford, 1941; The Lyons Mail, 1945. *Address:* All Souls College, and Frewin Hall, Oxford. *Clubs:* Athenæum, Burlington Fine Arts.

Died 23 June 1946.

O'MEAGHER, Col John Kevin, CBE 1919; late General Reserve of Officers; *b* 24 June 1866; *s* of late J. C. O'Meagher, MRIA, officier d'Académie Française. *Educ:* Prior Park College, Bath; Royal University of Ireland (BA 1886); Sandhurst. Joined the Royal Munster Fusiliers, 1888; served South African War, 1899–1902 (despatches, Brevet Major, Queen's medal three clasps, King's medal two clasps); Mohmand Campaign, 1908 (subsidiary despatches, medal and clasp); appointed to command 2nd Royal Munster Fusiliers, 1913; European War, 1914–18 (despatches, CBE, 1914 Star, General Service medal, Victory medal); granted rank of Col on retirement. *Address:* 25 Wellington Rd, Dublin.

Died 29 April 1946.

O'MEARA, Francis; HM Consular Service; Consul at Lyons, 1937–40; *b* 1886; *s* of late T. F. O'Meara, MInstCE, of the Indian, later Natal Government Railways, formerly of Ormond (Nenagh) Castle, Co. Tipperary; *m* 1928, Helen, *d* of late John Frost, Highbury, and widow of N. A. Rodulfo, Exmouth. *Educ:* Clongowes; England, Belgium, and Germany. Passed a competitive examination and appointed Vice-Consul in the Consular Service, 1913; acting Consul-General at Boston, 1914; Vice-Consul at Colon, Panama, 1915–16; at Quito, Ecuador, 1917–19; in charge of Legation there, Nov. 1917; Vice-Consul at Genoa, 1919–21; employed in the foreign office, 1921–23; Chargé d'Affaires and Consul-General at Monrovia, 1923–26; transferred to Liège, 1926; acted as temporary Head of the American Section, Dept of Overseas Trade, 1929–30; transferred to Santiago de Cuba, 1930; Chargé d'Affaires at Havana, July–Dec. 1930; Consul at Havre, 1932–34; Consul-General at Loanda, 1934–37. *Publication:* A New Light on Napoleon's Captivity at St Helena. *Recreations:* swimming, rowing.

Died 2 Dec. 1941.

OMONT, Henri; de l'Institut; Inspecteur general des bibliothèques, Conservateur des Manuscrits de la Bibliothèque Nationale; *b* Evreux, Eure, 15 Sept. 1857; *m* Fernande de Fresquet; trois *s*. *Educ:* Lycée d'Evreux; École des Chartes. Bibliothécaire universitaire, 1879; Archiviste paléographe, 1881; Surnuméraire au Dépt des MSS. de le Bibl. Nat., 1881; Conservateur du même département, 1900; Président du Conseil de perfectionnement de l'École des Chartes et du Comité des travaux historiques, membre des Commissions supérieures des Bibliothèques et des Archives, et de la Commission supérieure des Archives diplomatiques,

Membre et ancien président des Sociétés des Antiquaires de France, et de Normandie, de l'Association des études grecques, de la Société des Anciens Textes français, etc.; Docteur ès lettres de l'Université d'Oxford, associé de la British Academy et des Académies de Copenhague, Cracovie, Dublin, Munich, etc. *Publications:* Catalogues des manuscrits grecs de la Bibliothèque Nationale (4 vols), 1886–1898; des MSS hagiographiques grecs, 1896; des nouv. acq. lat. et franç. 1891–1931; de la Collection Moreau, 1891; des manuscrits français (15 vols), 1895–1921; des MSS Phillipps, etc.; Anciens Inventaires de la Bibl. Nat. (6 vols), 1889–1920; Reproductions de MSS grecs, latins et français (Démosthène, Dioscoride, Platon, Ptolémée, Fabliaux, etc.) (36 vols), 1887–1931; Fac-similés des MSS grecs datés et des miniatures des MSS grecs du VIᵉ au XIVᵉ siècle de la Bibl. Nat., 1891–1929; Athènes au XVIIᵉ siécle, Sculptures du Parthénon, 1897; Missions archéologiques en Orient aux XVIIᵉ et XVIIIᵉ siècles, 1902, etc. *Recreation:* walking. *Address:* 45 rue St Ferdinand, XVIIᵉ, Paris.

Died 9 Dec. 1940.

O'NEILL, 3rd Baron *cr* 1868; **Shane Edward Robert O'Neill;** late Lieut 8th Hussars; *b* 6 Feb. 1907; *s* of late Hon. Arthur O'Neill (*e s* of 2nd Baron) and Lady Annabel Crewe-Milnes, *e d* of 1st Marquess of Crewe, KG, PC (she *m* 2nd, Major J. H. H. Dodds, CMG); *S* grandfather, 1928; *m* 1932, Anne Geraldine, *e d* of Hon. Guy Charteris; one *s* one *d*. *Educ:* Eton; RMC, Sandhurst. *Heir: s* Hon. Raymond Arthur Clanaboy O'Neill, *b* 1 Sept. 1933. *Address:* 35 Montagu Square, W1. *T:* Paddington 5401; Shane's Castle, Antrim, Ireland. *T:* Antrim 7. *Clubs:* Cavalry, Turf.

Died 24 Oct. 1944.

O'NEILL, Sir Arthur Eugene, KBE 1920 (CBE 1918); Director Frank C. Strick & Co., Ltd, shipowners; *b* 17 Dec. 1877; *m* Edith Frances Tomson (*d* 1945); one *s* one *d*. *Educ:* St Edmund's College; Old Hall, Ware. Received KBE for services, Transport Dept, Admiralty, European War. *Address:* White Cliffe, Spencer Road, Birchington, Kent. *Club:* Junior Carlton.

Died 2 July 1950.

O'NEILL, Rev. George, SJ, MA; Emeritus Professor of English Language at University College, Dublin; Professor of Modern Languages and Church History at Corpus Christi College, Melbourne; *b* Dungannon, 1863; *s* of George F. O'Neill, LLB. *Educ:* St Stanislaus Coll., Tullamore; Milltown Park; University of Prague and University of Paris. MA with Hons of Royal University of Ireland, 1891; Fellow, 1900. *Publications:* Could Bacon have written the Plays? 1907; The Clouds around Shakespeare, 1911; Blessed Mary of the Angels, 1910; many articles in Irish and American periodicals; Blaise Pascal and other pamphlets for CTS, etc.; Five Centuries of English Poetry, 1912; The Golden Legend (selections), 1914; Essays on Poetry, 1920; Readings from Newman, 1923; Scripture Readings for Times of Retreat, 1926; Life of the Rev. J. T. Woods, 1928; Life of Mother Mary of the Cross, 1931; The Servant of the Sacred Heart, 1933; Golden Years on the Paraguay, 1934; The Psalms (translation and commentary), 1937; Book of Job (translation and commentary), 1938. *Address:* Corpus Christi College, Melbourne, Australia.

Died 19 July 1947.

O'NEILL, Rev. John, DPh; Professor of Philosophy at Maynooth since 1908; *b* Tipperary, 1880. *Educ:* Rockwell, Thurles, Maynooth. Ordained, 1903; Bachelorships in Theology and in Canon Law, 1903; studied Philosophy at the University of Louvain, 1903–05 (Doctorate in Philosophy, 1905); Professor of Sacred Scripture and of Philosophy at St Patrick's College, Carlow, 1905–08; studied, 1911–12, at Universities of Fribourg (Switzerland) and of Munich; Canon of the Archdiocese of Cashel and Emly, 1924. *Publications:* The Cosmology of the Greeks and Aristotelian Schoolmen, 1924; contributor on philosophical subjects to the Irish Ecclesiastical Record and to the Irish Theological Quarterly. *Address:* Maynooth, Ireland.

Died 9 May 1947.

ONSLOW, 5th Earl of, *cr* 1801; **Richard William Alan Onslow,** PC 1926; GBE *cr* 1938; Bart 1660; Baron Onslow, 1716; Baron Cranley, 1776; Viscount Cranley, 1801, PC 1926; GBE 1938; Chairman of Committees and Deputy Speaker House of Lords, 1931–44; President, Society for Empire Fauna Protection; Colonel in Army (Retired); President, General Lying In Hospital; Central National Service Committee, 1939; President, Council of Albert Hall, 1934–43; Trustee, Beit Memorial Fellowships, since 1928; *b* 23 Aug. 1876; *e s* of 4th Earl of Onslow and Hon. Florence Coulston Gardner (*d* 1934), *d* of 3rd Lord Gardner; *S* father, 1911; *m* 1906, Hon. Violet Marcia Catherine Warwick Bampfylde, CBE, ARRC, GCStJ, *d* of 3rd Lord Poltimore; one *s* one *d*. *Educ:* Eton; New College, Oxford. MA 1909. Attaché HM Diplomatic Service, 1901; appointed Madrid, 1902; Tangier, 1903; 3rd Sec. Petrograd, Private Secretary to Ambassador, 1904–06; 2nd Sec. Berlin, 1907; Commercial Sec. Berlin, 1908; Assistant Private Secretary to Sir Edward Grey, 1909; Private Secretary to the Permanent Under-Secretary, 1911–13; Assistant Clerk, Foreign Office, 1913–14; Lt in Army, 1915; served European War (despatches thrice, 1914–15 Star, General and Victory Medals, OBE, Commander Legion of Honour); Captain, 1916; GSO, 2nd Grade, 1916; Major, 1918; Colonel Assistant Director Staff Duties, BEF, France, 1918; British War Mission, Paris, 1918–19; Lord-in-Waiting, 1919–20; Special Representative of King at funeral of Crown Princess of Sweden, Stockholm, 1920; Civil Lord of the Admiralty, 1920–21; Civil Commissioner Bristol during strike, 1921, and S Wales 1926; Parliamentary Secretary, Board of Agriculture, and afterwards Ministry of Health, 1921–23, and Board of Education, 1923–24; Under-Secretary for War, 1924–28; Paymaster-General, 1928–29, British Delegate, Arms Traffic Conference, Geneva, 1925, Nature Protection Congress, Paris, 1931; African Fauna Conferences, London, 1933 and 1938; Chairman, Metropolitan Police Housing Committee, 1920; Voluntary Hospitals Commission, 1921; Rent Restriction Committee, 1922; Royal Commission on Local Government, 1923; Joint Committee on East Africa, 1931; Chairman Burnham Committee on Teachers' Salaries, 1934–43; Council of Morocco Association, 1917–21, 1924, and 1938; Knight Grand Cross, Order of St John of Jerusalem. *Publications:* The Empress Maud, 1940; 63 Years, an Autobiography, 1944; Magazine and Newspaper articles. *Heir: s* Viscount Cranley, MC. *Address:* Clandon Park, Guildford; St Agnes, Scilly. *Clubs:* Carlton, Beefsteak, Turf, Travellers', MCC; Guildford County.

Died 9 June 1945.

ONSLOW, Maj-Gen. Hon. James William M.; *see* Macarthur-Onslow.

ONSLOW, Captain Richard Francis John, MVO 1937; DSC; Royal Navy; *e s* of late Rev. M. R. S. Onslow, Chaplain RN, and Fanny Harriet Green; *g s* of late Sir Matthew Onslow, Bt, Hengar, Cornwall; *m* 1st, 1920, Sylvia Rachel Green Price (*d* 1933); one *s* one *d*; 2nd, 1939, Betty, *d* of Brig.-Gen. R. A. Gillam, CMG. *Educ:* RN Colleges, Osborne and Dartmouth. Served European war, 1914–18, North Sea, Dover Patrol and Belgian Coast; Caspian Naval Force, 1919; Naval Mission to Persia, 1920; Commander RN College, Dartmouth, 1934–35; HM Yacht Victoria and Albert, 1936–37; HMS Coventry, 1938–40.

Died 9 April 1942.

ONSLOW, Sibella Macarthur, CBE 1930; *b* 4 June 1871; *d* of late Capt. A. A. W. Onslow, RN, and Elizabeth Macarthur, who after her husband's death took the name of Macarthur Onslow. Country life and travelling. *Publication:* Some Early Records of Macarthurs of Camden. *Recreations:* riding, gardening. *Address:* Gilbulla, Menangle, NSW. *T:* Menangle 2. *Clubs:* Ladies' Empire; Queen's, Sydney.

Died 16 July 1943.

OPPENHEIM, E(dward) Phillips; author; *b* 1866; *m* 1891, Elsie, *d* of A. Hopkins, Boston, USA; one *d. Educ:* Wyggeston Grammar School, Leicester. *Publications:* The Master Mummer; Anna the Adventuress; Mysterious Mr Sabin; A Man and his Kingdom; The Survivor; The Traitors; A Prince of Sinners; Mr Wingrave, Millionaire; A Maker of History; The Secret; Conspirators; The Missioner; Jeanne of the Marshes; The Illustrious Prince. The Missing Delora; The Falling Star; Havoc; Double Four; Peter Ruff; The Lighted Way, 1912; The Mischief Maker, 1913; The Way of these Women; The Amazing Partnership; The Game of Liberty; A People's Man; Mr Grex of Monte Carlo; The Double Traitor; The Kingdom of the Blind, 1917; The Other Romilly; Mr Lessingham Goes Home; The Great Impersonation, etc., 1920; The Great Prince Shan, 1922; The Inevitable Millionaires, 1923; Nobody's Man, 1923; The Evil Shepherd, 1923; The Mystery Road, 1924; The Wrath to Come, 1924; Gabriel Samara, 1925; The Golden Beast, 1926; Prodigals of Monte Carlo, 1926; Miss Brown of Xyo, 1927; The Light Beyond, 1928; Chronicles of Melhampton, 1928; Pudgy Pete and Co.; The Fortunate Wayfarer; Matorni's Vineyard, 1928; Jennerton and Co.; The Treasure House of Martin Hews; The Human Chase, 1929; Happenings to Forrester; The Million Pound Deposit, 1930; The Lion and the Lamb; Up the Ladder of Gold; Slane's Long Shots; Inspector Dickens Retires; Simple Peter Cradd, 1931; Sinners Beware, 1931; Moran Chambers Smiled, 1932; The Ostrekoff Jewels, 1932; Murder at Monte Carlo, 1932; The Gallows of Chance, 1934; The Bank Manager; The Strange Boarders of Palace Crescent, 1934; The Spy Paramount; General Besserley's Puzzle Box; Advice Limited; Battle of Basinghall Street, 1935; The Bird of Paradise; Ask Miss Mott, 1936; The Dumb Gods Speak; Envoy Extraordinary, 1937; Curious Happenings to the Rooke Legatees, 1937; The Colossus of Arcadia, 1938; And Still I Cheat the Gallows, 1938; The Spymaster, 1938; Sir Adam Disappeared, 1939; The Last Train Out, 1941; The Pool of Memory, 1941; The Shy Plutocrat, 1941; Mr Mirakel, 1942; and many other novels and volumes of short stories, including The Mystery of Mr Bernard Brown; The Long Arm of Mannister; The Adventures of Aron Rod; The Adventures of Ernest Bliss; Judy of Bunter's Buildings; The Double Life of Mr Alfred Burton. *Recreations:* yachting, shooting, golf, and usual country sports. *Address:* Le Vauquiédor, Guernsey, CI; c/o Barclays Bank Ltd, 160 Piccadilly, W1. *Clubs:* Savage, Authors', Garrick.

Died 3 Feb. 1946.

OPPENHEIMER, Albert Martin, CBE 1927; Hon. Secretary First Aid and Life Saving Congress, Frankfurt a/Main, 1908, and Vienna, 1913; *b* 10 April 1872; *s* of Sir Charles Oppenheimer, HBM's Consul-General at Frankfurt; *m* 1906, Lucy Esther (*d* 1935), *d* of late Alexander Meyer-Cohn, Berlin. *Educ:* Lycée, Frankfurt a/M. Three war medals, Queen Victoria Coronation Medal, King Edward Coronation Medal, Knight Commander Crown of Italy, Hungarian Order of Merit, Red Eagle of Prussia. *Publications:* First Aid Dictionary in six languages, 1913; translations of a number of legal works on the Peace Treaty and others, and essays on various subjects on International Law and in respect to the Treaty of Peace; lectured at Berlin, Budapest, Zürich, and elsewhere. *Recreations:* golf, chess, and collecting objets d'art. *Address:* 23 Bury Walk, Chelsea, SW3. *T:* Kensington 4348. *Clubs:* Constitutional, Gresham (Hon.).

Died 25 July 1945.

OPPER, Frederick Burr; artist; *b* Madison, Lake Co., Ohio, 2 Jan. 1857; *s* of Lewis Opper and Aurelia Burr; *m* 1882, Nellie Barnett. An artist of Puck for 18 years; with Hearst's New York Journal, 1899; has retired from active work. *Publications:* The Folks in Funnyville; Our Antediluvian Ancestors, 1902; Happy Hooligan, 1902; Alphonse and Gaston, 1902; John Bull, 1903; Happy Hooligan Home Again, 1907; Maud the Matchless, 1907; also illustrated Bill Nye's History of the United States, Mother Goose, Mark Twain's Sketches, and other humorous books. *Address:* 62 Circuit Road, New Rochelle, NY, USA.

Died 29 Aug. 1937.

ORAM, Dame (Sarah) Elizabeth, DBE 1919; RRC 1896; Principal Matron, QAIMNS (retired); *b* 25 Dec. 1860; *d* of late Samuel Thomas Oram, Thirsk, Yorks. Joined Army Nursing Service, 1886; transferred to QAIMNS, 1903; Matron-in-Chief, Egypt, 1915–19 (despatches three times, bar to RRC); served in Egypt, 1892–96; S African War, 1900–03. *Address:* 30 Aubrey Walk, W8. *T:* Park 9740. *Club:* United Nursing Services.

Died 26 June 1946.

ORCHARD, Hon. Richard Beaumont, CBE 1920; *b* 14 Oct. 1871. Member Australian Broadcasting Commission; Pres. of Kuringai Chase Trust, NSW; Member of Commonwealth House of Representatives, 1913–19; Hon. Minister in charge of Recruiting, Commonwealth of Australia, during European War; an Australian Commissioner to British Empire Exhibition, 1924. *Address:* 101 Yarranabbe Road, Darling Point, Sydney, NSW.

Died 24 July 1942.

ORCZY, Baroness, (Mrs Montague Barstow); playwright and novelist; *b* Tarnaörs, Hungary; *o c* of late Baron Felix Orczy and late Emma, *née* Comtesse Wass; *m* Montague (*d* 1943), *s* of late Rev. M. W. Barstow, MA, of Thornton Watlass Rectory, Yorkshire; one *s. Educ:* Brussels; Paris; studied painting at the Heatherley School of Art, exhibited Royal Academy. Began writing, 1900; first important work was detective stories known as The Old Man in the Corner series, Royal Magazine. *Plays:* The Scarlet Pimpernel, 1905, written in collaboration with her husband; The Sin of William Jackson, 1906; Beau Brocade, 1910; The Legion of Honour, 1918. *Publications:* The Emperor's Candlesticks; The Scarlet Pimpernel, 1905; By the Gods Beloved; A Son of the People, 1906; I Will Repay, 1906; The Tangled Skein, 1907; Beau Brocade, 1908; The Elusive Pimpernel, 1908; Petticoat Government, 1910; A True Woman, 1911; Fire in Stubble, 1912; Eldorado, 1913; Unto Cæsar; The Laughing Cavalier, 1914; A Bride of the Plains, The Bronze Eagle, 1915; Leather Face, 1916; A Sheaf of Blue Bells; Lord Tony's Wife, 1917; The Man in Grey; Flower o' the Lily, 1918; The League of the Scarlet Pimpernel, 1919; His Majesty's Well-Beloved, 1919; The First Sir Percy, 1920; Castles in the Air, 1921; Nicolette, 1923; The Triumph of the Scarlet Pimpernel, 1922; The Honourable Jim, 1924; Pimpernel and Rosemary, 1924; Unravelled Knots, 1925; The Celestial City, 1926; Sir Percy Hits Back, 1927; Blue Eyes and Grey, 1928; Skin o' my Tooth, 1928; Adventures of the Scarlet Pimpernel, 1929; Marivosa, 1930; A Child of the Revolution, 1932; A Joyous Adventure, 1932; The Way of the Scarlet Pimpernel, 1933; The Scarlet Pimpernel Looks at the World (essays), 1933; A Spy of Napoleon, 1934; The Uncrowned King, 1935; The Turbulent Duchess, 1935; The Divine Folly, 1937; No Greater Love, 1938; Mam'zelle Guillotine, 1940; Links in the Chain of Life (Memoirs), 1946; Will-o'-the-Wisp, 1946. *Address:* c/o Swiss Bank Corporation, 11c Regent Street, SW1.

Died 12 Nov. 1947.

ORDE, Roden Horace Powlett, OBE 1938; Director, Central Bureau of Hospital Information, 12 Grosvenor Crescent, SW1; Hon. Secretary, British Hospitals Association; *b* 1867; 3rd *s* of late Captain Henry Powlett Shafto Orde, Shoreston Hall, Northumberland, and Rosa Anne Elizabeth Saga Repp; *m* 1910, Augusta Isobel Amelia, *d* of late Thomas Graves Law, LLD, Woodlands, Duddingston, Edinburgh; five *s* four *d. Educ:* Richmond School, Yorkshire; Trinity College, Cambridge (BA 1889). Engaged in Hospital Administration since 1898; has been a member of several commissions connected with hospitals and has visited officially many hospitals at home and abroad; editor of Hospitals Year Book; rowed in the Inter Varsity Boat Race for Cambridge in 1888 and 1889. *Address:* 63 Twyford Avenue, Ealing, W3. *T:* Acorn 4519. *Club:* Royal Empire Society.

Died 24 May 1941.

ORDE BROWNE, Sir Granville St John, Kt 1947; CMG 1942; Substitute Member of Committee of Experts on Native Labour, International Labour Office, since 1934; Adviser on Colonial Labour to Secretary of State for the Colonies since 1938; *b* Woolwich, Kent, 26 Oct. 1883; *o s* of late Capt. Charles Orde Browne, late Royal Artillery, and Annie Maria Michell; *m* 1923, Margaret Florence, *o d* of Rev. H. Fearnley-Whittingstall; three *d. Educ:* Wellington College; Royal Military Academy, Woolwich. Commissioned in Royal Artillery, 1902; served in Zulu Rising, 1906; Asst District Commissioner East African Protectorate, 1909; re-commissioned in Royal Artillery, 1915; served throughout East African campaign (OBE, despatches four times); retired with rank of Major, 1920; Senior Commissioner, Tanganyika Territory, 1921; Labour Commissioner, Tanganyika, 1926; retired, 1931; undertook special investigation of Labour in Northern Rhodesia, 1937, in West Indies, 1938, West Africa, 1939, Far East, 1941. *Publications:* Vanishing Tribes of Kenya; The African Labourer; Africans learn to be French (in collaboration); Here's How; numerous official publications, and also contributions to scientific journals. *Recreations:* carpentry, music. *Address:* The White House, Widmer End, High Wycombe, England. *TA:* and *T:* Holmer Green 21.

Died 12 May 1947.

O'REILLY, Sir Lennox (Arthur Patrick), Kt 1936; KC 1920; *b* 24 July 1880; *m* Laurie, 4th *d* of late Alexander Clavier; two *d.* Admitted to the Bar of St Lucia, BWI, 1902; admitted to the English Bar (Lincoln's Inn), 1908; practising in Trinidad since 1912. *Recreation:* bridge. *Address:* 52a Jerningham Avenue, Port of Spain, Trinidad. *Clubs:* West Indian, Reform, National Liberal, Royal Automobile; Union (Port of Spain).

Died 17 March 1949.

ORIEL, George Harold, MA, MDBCh (Cantab); late Anderson Demonstrator of Clinical Chemistry, Guy's Hospital; *b* Bath, 12 June 1894; *s* of Rev. B. Oriel, Swansea; *m* 1920, Muriel J. Robson; one *s. Educ:* Taunton School; Sidney Sussex College, Cambridge (Scholar, Natural Science); Guy's Hospital. Natural Science Tripos, 1915; MA, MB, BCh (Cantab), 1920; MD (Cantab), 1925. Assistant Surgeon, Royal Albert Hospital, Devonport, 1923–25; Parsons Research Fellow, Guy's Hospital, 1928; War service in RN Hospitals. *Publications:* A Study in Allergy, Lancet, 1928; Observations on the Biochemistry of Asthma, 1929; A Protease in the Urine, Lancet, 1930; Allergy, 1932; Further Observations on the Biochemistry of Asthmatic Conditions, 1933; Allergy in The British Encyclopædia of Medicine, 1936. *Recreation:* yachting. *Address:* 143 Harley Street, W1. *T:* Welbeck 2277.

Died 2 May 1939.

O'RIORDAN, Conal Holmes O'Connell, FRSL; known from 1891 until 1920 by nom-de-guerre Norreys Connell; Man of Letters; represents RSL on Council of National Book League; President Ealing Branch National Book League; Co-founder with R. A. Scott-James and late Edward Garnett of the Square Club, 1907; *b* Dublin, 29 April 1874; *y s* of late Daniel O'Connell O'Riordan, QC, and his first cousin Kate O'Riordan; *m*; two *s* two *d. Educ:* by Jesuits in Ireland, but left school at age most boys begin, and studied for army. At sixteen fall from horse developed spinal trouble and wrecked career. At seventeen went on stage, eighteen played Engstrand in Ghosts to Alving of Lewis Waller, nineteen began writing; succeeded J. M. Synge as Director of Abbey Theatre, Dublin, 1909; has had many activities away from art; rejected for the army in 1914, eventually found way to the front as Head of YMCA Rest Hut; invalided home two days after armistice; served continuously London Civil Defence, 1940–45. President Irish Lit. Soc., 1937–39; Shute Lecturer, Liverpool Univ. on the Art of the Theatre, 1933–34; Tredegar Memorial lecturer, RSL, 1946. *Publications:* Adam of Dublin, 1920; Adam and Caroline, 1921; In London, 1922; Rowena Barnes, 1923; Married Life, 1924; His Majesty's Pleasure (a play), 1925; The Age of Miracles, 1925; Young Lady Dazincourt, 1926; Soldier Born, 1927; Soldier of Waterloo, 1928; The King's Wooing (a Play), 1929; Napoleon Passes (a commentary), 1933; Soldier's Wife, 1935; Captain Falstaff and other Plays, 1936; Soldier's End, 1938; Judith Quinn, 1939; Judith's Love, 1940, etc. *Recreation:* sleep. *Address:* 106 Meadvale Road, W5. *T:* Perivale 2136.

Died 18 June 1948.

ORMANDY, William Reginald, DSc; Consulting and Research Chemist; *b* 25 Oct. 1870; *s* of W. Ormandy, Chorley; *m* 1899, Maud Houghton, Newton le Willows; no *c. Educ:* Wigan Grammar School; School of Mines, Wigan (Hewlett Prize); Owens College, Victoria University, Manchester (Hon. Research Scholarship, Hon. Research Fellowship, Bishop Berkeley Fellowship); Tübingen University; Fellow of the Institute of Fuels. Member of the Institution of Chemical Engineers; Member of Institute of Petroleum; Member of Institute, Automobile Engineers; Member of Institute of Metals; Member of Ceramic Society; FCS; Silver Medal Royal Society of Arts; specially interested in Liquid Fuels and Electro-Osmotic treatment of Refractories; Member of Inter-Departmental Committee on Alcoholic Fuel; Member of Imperial Motor Transport Fuel Committee; Fellow of the Institute of Chemistry; Member of the Empire Fuel Committee; Past President I Aut. Eng. *Publications:* Scientific Papers in the following Journals:—Chemical Society of London; Ceramic Society Petroleum Technologists; Automobile Engineers. *Recreations:* motoring and yachting. *Address:* Bell Moor, NW3. *T:* Hampstead 4840. *Club:* Chemical Industry.

Died 11 Sept. 1941.

ORMATHWAITE, 4th Baron *cr* 1868; **George Harry William Walsh;** Bt 1804, MVO 1905; DL; JP Radnorshire; *b* 3 Dec. 1863; 3rd *s* of 2nd Baron Ormathwaite and Lady Emily Somerset, *d* of 7th Duke of Beaufort; *S* brother, 1937. *Educ:* Wellington. Late Lieut Grenadier Guards; served with Imperial Yeomanry, South Africa, 1899–1901. *Heir: b* Hon. Reginald Walsh, MVO. *Address:* Barland Cottage, Presteign, Radnorshire. *T:* Presteign 72. *Club:* Pratt's.

Died 27 Oct. 1943.

ORMATHWAITE, 5th Baron *cr* 1868; **Reginald Walsh;** Bt 1804, MVO 1906; British Consul at New York, 1908–11; late British Consul at the Piræus and then at Dunkirk; *b* 17 July 1868; 7th *s* of 2nd Baron Ormathwaite; *S* brother 1943; *m* 1908, Lady Margaret Jane Douglas Home, *d* of 12th Earl of Home; one *s* two *d. Heir: s* John Arthur Charles, *b* 25 Dec. 1912. *Address:* Pen-y-bont Hall, Pen-y-bont, Radnorshire. *Club:* Travellers'.

Died 13 Feb. 1944.

ORME, Gilbert Edward, MA, MB, ChB Cantab; MRCS Eng., LRCP Lond.; Physician; *b* 28 March 1874; *e s* of late Edward Collier Orme, Sydney, Australia; *m* 1904, Katharine Beatrice, *d* of Dr J. J. Fraser, Clitheroe, Lancs; one *d. Educ:* King's School, Parramatta NSW; Gonville and Caius College, Cambridge. Late Chairman Lancashire and Cheshire Branch, Blackburn, Westminster and Holborn Division BMA; late President Harveian Society of London; Member Council King Edward's Hospital Fund for London; Hon. Sec. League of Mercy; Member Interdepartmental Committee on Nursing Services; Chairman Local War Emergency Committee, Westminster and Holborn Division BMA; Member Council of Queen's Institute of District Nursing; late Medical Officer, Stonyhurst College, Blackburn; JP Lancs (retired); Order of Mercy, 1933; Hon. Surgeon, Associate St John's Ambulance Assoc. *Publication:* Article on Stigmatism, Medical Press and Circular, 1937. *Recreations:* fishing, shooting, yachting. *Address:* 23 Gilbert Street, Grosvenor Square, W1. *T:* Grosvenor 2801. *Clubs:* Junior Carlton, Leander; University Cruising, Cambridge.

Died 7 April 1945.

ORMIDALE, Hon. Lord; George Lewis Macfarlane; one of the Senators of the College of Justice in Scotland, 1910–32; retired 1 Oct. 1932; *b* Edinburgh, 22 March 1854; *γ s* of late Robert Macfarlane, a Senator of the College of Justice in Scotland with the judicial title of Lord Ormidale, and Grace, *d* of James Greig, WS, of Eccles House, Berwickshire; *m* 1891, Mary Crichton (*d* 1936), *γ d* of James Hunter, 49 Moray Place, Edinburgh; one *s* one *d. Educ:* Edinburgh Academy; St John's College, Oxford (BA 1876); Edinburgh University. Scots Bar, 1878; KC 1903; Sheriff of Fife and Kinross, 1909; Commissioner of Lunacy for Scotland, 1909; Commissioner of Northern Lights, 1909. Member of the King's Bodyguard for Scotland. *Recreations:* fishing, shooting. *Address:* 3 St Colme Street, Edinburgh. *T:* 24003. *Clubs:* New, Edinburgh.

Died 21 April 1941.

ORMONDE, 4th Marquess of, *cr* 1825; **James Arthur Wellington Foley Butler;** 22nd Earl of Ormonde (*cr* 1328); Earl of Ossory, 1526; Viscount Thurles, 1537; Baron Ormonde (UK), 1821; 28th Hereditary Chief Butler of Ireland; *b* 23 Sept. 1849; *s* of 2nd Marquess and Frances Jane, *e d* of Sir Edward Paget; *S* brother, 1919; *m* 1887, Ellen, *d* of Gen. Anson Stager, US Army; two *s* two *d.* State Steward to Earl of Carnarvon when Viceroy of Ireland. *Heir: s* Earl of Ossory. *Address:* Gennings, Maidstone, Kent.

Died 4 July 1943.

ORMONDE, 5th Marquess of, *cr* 1825; **James George Anson Butler;** Earl of Ormonde (*cr* 1328); Earl of Ossory, 1526; Viscount Thurles, 1537; Baron Ormonde (UK), 1821; 29th Hereditary Chief Butler of Ireland; Major 1st Life Guards, retired, 1920; *b* 18 April 1890; *s* of 4th Marquess and Ellen, *d* of Gen. Anson Stager, US Army; *S* father, 1943; *m* 1915, Hon. Sybil Inna Fellowes (*d* 1948), *d* of 2nd Baron De Ramsey; one *d. Educ:* Harrow; RMC Sandhurst. DL for Co. Kilkenny. European War, 1914–19, France and Belgium (wounded). *Heir: b* Lt-Col Lord Arthur Butler, MC. *Address:* 53 Orchard Court, Portman Square, W1. *T:* Welbeck 3074.

Died 21 June 1949.

ORMSBY, Lt-Gen. Robert Daly, CBE 1924; Royal Marines, retired; *b* 9 Oct. 1879; *s* of late R. D. Ormsby, Director of Public Works, Hong Kong and of P. W. D., Ceylon; *m* Emily Dorothy, *d* of late F. H. Grinlinton, CMG; one *s* two *d. Educ:* Felsted School. 2nd Lt RM

1898; Major, 1916; Bt Lt-Col 1919; Lt-Col 1927; Col Comdt 1931; Maj.-Gen. 1933; Lt-Gen. 1935; DAAG at RM HQ, 1921–26; a Royal Marine ADC to the King, 1932–33; retired list, 1936. *Club:* United Service.

Died 7 Feb. 1946.

ORMSBY, Rev. Thomas, DSO 1916; Lieut-Colonel, retired pay; late Army Pay Department; *b* Castleneynoe, Co. Sligo, 30 May 1871; *γ s* of late John Yeadon Ormsby of Ballinamore, Co. Mayo; *m* Lucy Mary, *d* of Captain Colin H. Thomson (74th Highlanders) of Salruck, Co. Galway; one *d. Educ:* St Columba's College, Sherborne. 2nd Lieut 3rd Batt. Connaught Rangers, 1888; joined 2nd Batt. South Stafford Regt from Militia, 1891; Capt. Army Pay Dept 1899; Major, 1911; Lt-Col, 1918; served European War, Mediterranean Expeditionary Force, Feb.–Nov. 1915, including service in Egypt, Gallipoli, and the islands, and with the Salonika Army, 1915–16 (DSO); retired pay, 1920; Deacon, 1922; Priest, 1923; Curate, St Nicholas Collegiate Church, Galway; Rector, Oughterard, Co. Galway, 1929–36. *Publications:* Army Finance as a Military Science; various articles on Army Organisation, etc. *Recreations:* fishing, shooting. *Address:* Milford, Cloghan's Hill, Tuam, Eire. *Clubs:* Royal Irish Automobile, Dublin.

Died 14 March 1942.

ORMSBY-GORE, Hon. Seymour Fitzroy; late senior partner in firm of Gore & Co., stockbrokers; late captain 3rd Kent Artillery Volunteers; *b* 1863; 3rd *s* of 2nd Baron Harlech. *Educ:* Eton; Brasenose College, Oxford. MA, 1889. Late Lieut Oxfordshire Militia; formerly connected with shipping interests, and a frequent contributor to magazines on Irish political subjects; MP (C) for West Lindsey or Gainsborough Div. of Lincolnshire, 1900–06; contributor to fiction under nom de plume of Simon Carne; assistant cable censor, 1914; draft conducting officer (temp. Capt.) the 3rd Battalion Lincolnshire Regt 1915–16 also Draft-Conducting Officer, Thames and Medway Garrison, 1917; alternate Chairman, 1923–31, of Grand Trunk Junior Stocks; has travelled in most countries of Europe, Morocco, South Africa, United States, and through South America and West Indies. *Recreations:* hunting, fencing, and lawn tennis. *Club:* Turf.

Died 19 Nov. 1950.

ORPEN, Major Redmond Newenham Morris, CMG 1901; FRES; *b* 22 May 1864; *m* 1906, Dora Agnes, *d* of late Abraham Difford. Commanded Orpen's Horse and Border Scouts; served South Africa, 1900–02 (despatches, two medals and clasps). *Address:* c/o PO Box 206, Cape Town, South Africa.

Died 9 Oct. 1940.

ORPEN-PALMER, Brig.-Gen. Harold Bland Herbert, CMG 1919; DSO 1918; late The Royal Irish Fusiliers; *b* 1876; *s* of late Rev. Abraham Henry Herbert Orpen-Palmer, of Killowen, Kenmare, Co. Kerry; *m* Mary, *d* of late Maj.-Gen. W. W. Pemberton, IA; one *s. Educ:* Cheltenham College; Pembroke College, Cambridge; BA. Served S Africa, 1899–1902 (despatches, Queen's medal with three clasps, King's medal with two clasps); European War, 1914–19 (despatches, DSO, CMG, Russian Order of St Stanislas); Military Attaché, Peking, 1920–24; commanded 147th (2nd West Riding) Infantry Brigade, TA, 1926–28; Commanded Shanghai Volunteer Corps, 1928–31; retired pay, 1931. *Address:* Turnpike Field, Hartley Wintney, Hants.

Died 18 Oct. 1941.

ORPEN-PALMER, Col Reginald Arthur Herbert, DSO 1916; late E Surrey and Leinster Regiments; *b* Monkstown, Co. Dublin, 26 Dec. 1877; *o surv. s* of late Rev. Abraham Herbert Orpen-Palmer, Killowen, Kenmare, Co. Kerry; *m* Lilian, *d* of John Leland, Drogheda, and *widow* of late C. B. Irwin. *Educ:* Cheltenham College; Clare College, Cambridge.

Entered Army, 1898; served S African War, 1899–1902 (Queen's medal and four clasps), King's medals and two clasps); European War, 1914–16 (wounded, DSO, despatches); officer commanding the Record and Pay Office, Hounslow, 1927–31, retired pay, 1931. *Address:* The Bridge House, Lexden, Colchester.

Died 22 March 1943.

ORR, Arthur A.; artist; *s* of Thomas and Emily Orr; *g s* of William Somerville Orr, publisher, one of the original proprietors of Punch. *Educ:* Dublin; Westminster School of Art and Royal College of Art. Exhibitor at Royal Academy from 1899, New Gallery, Grosvenor, Walker Gallery, Liverpool, etc. *Works:* windows in several English and Colonial Cathedrals; Te Deum Window at Christchurch, Eaton, Norwich; four windows and large west window SS. Peter and Paul, Ilford, Essex; two East windows and Great West window also smaller one SS Mary and Michael, Commercial Road, E; War Memorial Window Chesterfield Parish Church; Public Memorial Window to Canon English, and window commissioned by His late Majesty King Manoel at St James, Twickenham; Cardinal Bourne Memorial, Harpenden Catholic Church, and three other windows there; designed Ecclesiastical work at Derry, Chester, Rangoon, Christ Church, Dublin Cathedrals, and Plymouth Catholic Cathedral; Dame Mary Scharlieb, MD, memorial at St Mary Magdalene Church, Osnaburgh Street, NW1; all windows in St Thomas's Church, Westminster Bridge Road, SE, and Lewisham, SE, Catholic Church, etc. *Recreations:* Rugby and Association football, and cricket. *Address:* 63 Moat Drive, Harrow, Middlesex.

Died 9 Nov. 1949.

ORR, Sir Charles (William James), KCMG 1928 (CMG 1921); *b* 20 Sept. 1870; *y s* of late Major A. Orr, Coleraine, Co. Derry; *m* 1911, Dorothy, *o d* of late W. Mark Ashton, Heyscroft, West Didsbury, Manchester; two *d*. *Educ:* Bath College; Royal Military Academy, Woolwich. Entered Royal Artillery, 1889; Captain, 1899; retired, 1908; Major (retired), 1919; served in Chitral Relief Expedition, 1895 (medal with clasp); Indian Frontier, 1897 (clasp); Tirah Expedition, 1897–99 (clasp); South African War, 1899–1902 (medal, 2 clasps); China War, 1900–01 (medal); Resident in Northern Nigeria, 1903; acted as Secretary to the Administration, 1909; Member of Committee appointed by Colonial Office on Land Tenure in West Africa; Chief Secretary, Cyprus, 1911; acted as High Commissioner on several occasions; invalided, 1917; attached Intelligence Branch, War Office, 1918–19; Colonial Secretary, Gibraltar, 1919–26; acted as Governor on several occasions; Governor and Commander-in-Chief of the Bahamas, 1926–31; retired, 1931. *Publications:* The Making of Northern Nigeria, 1911; Cyprus under British Rule, 1918. *Address:* Grangeside, Bramley, Surrey. *Clubs:* Army and Navy, Hurlingham.

Died 18 April 1945.

ORR, Major Frank George, CBE 1919; late RFA; *b* 1881; *s* of John Orr, JP; *m* Janie, *d* of William Brown, CBE. Served European War, 1914–19 (despatches, CBE). *Address:* 3 Hatfield Drive, Glasgow, W.

Died 8 March 1945.

ORR, James Peter, CSI 1911; CBE 1919; BA (Cantab); *b* 20 Jan. 1867; *s* of James Edward Orr; *m* 1898, Amy, *d* of Henry Ryan of Ootacamund, India; one *s* two *d*; 1940, Ada, *widow* of A. G. Edie, Indian Forest Service. *Educ:* St John's College, Hurstpierpoint; Caius College, Cambridge (scholar). Mathematical Tripos, 1889. Indian Civil Service, 1888–1919; Junior Collector and Magistrate, 1905; Senior Collector, Bombay, 1909; Chairman, City Improvement Trust, Bombay, 1909–19; Director of Housing, London County Council, 1919–21; Chairman Local Employment Committee,

Acton, 1922–30; Member of the Overseas League. *Address:* Ravenscroft, 2 Cannongate Avenue, Hythe, Kent.

Died 8 Jan. 1949.

ORR, John Charles; Editor of Londonderry Sentinel 1893 until he retired in 1931 (chief reporter, 1883–93); *b* 13 Dec. 1858; *e s* of late John Orr, stockbroker, Belfast; *m* 1887, Lily, *y d* of late James McCleery, Belfast; two *s* two *d*. *Educ:* Royal Academical Institution, Belfast. Joined the staff of Belfast News Letter, 1878; Fellow and Past Vice-President, Institute of Journalists; Past Chairman, Ulster District of same; life member Newspaper Press Fund. *Address:* 17 Bawnmore Road, Belfast. *T:* Belfast 67221.

Died 1 Dec. 1941.

ORR, Robert Low, KC, MA, LLB; *b* Glasgow, 15 Dec. 1854; *s* of Robert Orr, JP; *m* 1891, Euphemia, *d* of late John Millar, MD, Edinburgh; one *d*. *Educ:* Elgin Academy; George Watson's College (first dux), and University, Edinburgh; Göttingen University; 1st Class Honours (Classics); Greek Travelling Fellowship and John Edward Baxter Classical Scholarship; First Prizeman Scots Law Class Forensic Prize. Advocate, 1881; Sheriff Court Depute, 1892; Extra Advocate-Depute, 1892–95; Junior Counsel for United Free Church in litigations arising out of Church Union, 1900; edited official report of these cases, 'The Free Church of Scotland Appeals, 1903–04'; Advocate-Depute, 1905; KC 1905; Senior Advocate-Depute, 1906; Sheriff-Substitute of the Lothians and Peebles, 1908–38. *Publications:* Alexander Henderson, Churchman and Statesman, 1919; Lord Guthrie: A Memoir, 1923. *Address:* 73 Great King Street, Edinburgh. *T:* Central 20969. *Clubs:* Scottish Liberal, Edinburgh.

Died 23 March 1944.

ORTON, Charles William P.; *see* Previté-Orton.

ORTON, George Harrison, MA, MD, BC (Camb.), MRCS (Eng.), LRCP (Lond.) DMRE (Camb.); Consulting Radiologist, St Mary's Hospital; late Radiologist, King George V Military Hospital; Consulting Radiologist, Graylingwell Military Hospital, Chichester, and National Hospital for Diseases of the Heart; Secretary, Section of Radiology XVII International Congress of Medicine, London, 1913; Member of Council, Medical Society of London; President, Electrotherapeutic Section, Royal Society of Medicine; *b* 1873; *e s* of late George Hunt Orton, FRCS; *m* 1909, Elise Marie, 2nd *d* of Henry Zimmermann of Manchester. *Educ:* Charterhouse School; Trinity College, Cambridge; St Bartholomew's Hospital. Formerly Chief Assistant in the Electrical Department, St Bartholomew's Hospital; Medical Officer in charge of X-Ray Department, Cheyne Hospital for Sick Children; The Royal Free Hospital and Mount Vernon Hospital for Diseases of the Chest. *Publications:* The Röntgen Rays in the Diagnosis of Diseases of the Chest; The X-Ray Diagnosis of Renal and Ureteral Calculi; numerous papers on X-Ray subjects in the Medical Journals. etc. *Recreations:* fishing, shooting, sailing, motoring. *Address:* Roughdown, Chalfont St Giles, Bucks. *T:* Chalfont St Giles 85.

Died 18 April 1947.

ORWELL, George; (pseudonym of Eric Blair); author; *b* 25 June 1903; *m* 1933, Eileen O'Shaughnessy (*d* 1945); 1949, Sonia Mary Brownell. *Educ:* Eton (scholar). *Publications:* Burmese Days, 1934; The Road to Wigan Pier, 1937; Homage to Catalonia, 1938; Coming Up for Air, 1939; Animal Farm, 1945; Critical Essays, 1946; The English People, 1947; Nineteen-Eighty Four, 1949, etc.; (posthumous) Shooting an Elephant (essays), 1950. *Address:* c/o Messrs Secker & Warburg, Ltd, 7 John Street, Bloomsbury, WC1.

Died 21 Jan. 1950.

OSBORN, Sir Algernon Kerr Butler, 7th Bt *cr* 1662; JP; Major (retired) 3rd Batt. Bedfordshire Regt; *b* 8 Aug. 1870; *o s* of Henry John Robert Osborn and Emily, 3rd *d* of Thomas St Quintin of Hatley Park, Cambridgeshire; *S* grandfather, 1892; *m* 1903, Beatrice Elliot Kennard, *d* of W. Bunce Greenfield of Haynes Park, near Bedford, and 35 Gloucester Square, W; one *s* (elder son killed in action, 1944) one *d*. Heir: *s* Danvers Lionel Rouse [*b* 31 Jan. 1916; *m* 1943, Constance Violette, *d* of Major Leonard F. Rooke]. *Address:* North Lodge, Sheringham, Norfolk.

Died 19 July 1948.

OSBORNE, Captain F. Creagh-, CB 1918; RN; *s* of late General C. Creagh-Osborne, CB; *m* 1st, 1902, Adelina (*d* 1925), *d* of late Colonel M. Hancock; one *d*; 2nd, 1926, Mabel Frances Taylor, MBE; two *s*. *Educ:* Britannia. Served on board Dido during China War, 1900 (medal); Director Admiralty Compass Department, 1912–26; Imperial Russian Order of St Anne, 2nd class, 1917. *Publications:* various service text-books. *Address:* 2 Grove Flats, Lymington, Hants. *Clubs:* Royal Yacht Squadron (Hon.), Cowes.

Died 1 Sept. 1943.

OSBORNE, Sir Francis, 15th Bt *cr* 1629; *b* 1 Nov. 1856; *S* cousin, 1879; *m* Kathleen, *d* of late George Whitfield, 3 Cornwall Gardens, SW, and Modreeny, Co. Tipperary, 1890; one *s* three *d*. *Educ:* Lancing. Heir: *s* George Francis, MC [Major Royal Sussex Regt; *b* 27 July 1894. Repton; Sandhurst]. *Address:* The Grange, Framfield, Sussex.

Died 23 Oct. 1948.

OSBORNE, Col Henry Campbell, CMG 1918; CBE 1935; VD; Secretary-General, Canadian Agency Imperial War Graves Commission, National Defence HQ, Ottawa; *b* 1874; *s* of late James Kerr Osborne of Toronto; *m* 1902, Marian (*d* 1931), *d* of late George Grant Francis, Toronto, and *widow* of Charles Lambeth Bath, Swansea; no *c*. *Educ:* Trinity College School, Port Hope; Trinity College, University of Toronto (MA). Bar, Canada; Colonel, Canadian Reserve of Officers, formerly Permanent Staff. *Address:* 222 Daly Avenue, Ottawa, Canada. *Clubs:* Junior Carlton; Toronto (Toronto); Rideau (Ottawa); University (Montreal).

Died 20 April 1949.

OSBOURNE, Brig.-Gen. George Nowell Thomas S.; *see* Smyth-Osbourne.

OSBOURNE, Lloyd; *b* San Francisco, 7 April 1868; *s* of Samuel Osbourne and Fanny Van de Grift (who afterwards married Robert Louis Stevenson); *m* Katherine Durham, 1896. *Educ:* tutors; private schools; Edinburgh University. United States Vice-Consul-General, Samoa and Friendly Islands, to 1897. *Publications:* In collaboration with Robert Louis Stevenson—The Wrong Box, 1889; The Wrecker, 1892; The Ebb Tide, 1894. By himself—The Queen versus Billy; Love, the Fiddler; The Motor Maniacs; Baby Bullet, the Motor of Destiny; Three Speeds Forward; The Tin Diskers; Schmidt; Harm's Way; The Kingdoms of the World; The Adventurer; Wild Justice, 1922; The Grierson Mystery, 1928; Peril, 1929; The Little Father of the Wilderness and The Exile—plays (both in collaboration with Austin Strong); and many stories in the magazines. *Recreations:* boxing, sailing, riding, motoring. *Address:* (winter) Lambs'. *Club:* New York City.

Died 23 May 1947.

O'SHEE, James John; solicitor since 1890; MP (N) for West Waterford, 1895–December 1918; *b* Tipperary, 3 Nov. 1866; 4th *s* of John Shee, Newtown, Carrick-on-Suir, and Mary Britton; *m* 1921, Nancy, *d* of T. R. Naughton, Killaghy Castle, Co. Tipperary; two *s* four *d*.

Educ: Rockwell College, Cashel; University College, Dublin. *Address:* Oakville, Clonmel. *TA:* O'Shee, Oakville, Clonmel. *T:* Clonmel 56.

Died 1 Jan. 1946.

O'SHEE, Lt-Col Richard Alfred Poer, CMG 1911; *b* 6 Aug. 1867; *e s* of late Nicholas Power O'Shee, of Gardenmorris, and Lady Gwendoline, 4th *d* of 1st Earl of Lichfield. Entered Royal Engineers, 1887; Captain, 1897; Major, 1905; employed Niger Coast Protectorate, 1897; Gold Coast, 1897–98; Anglo-Portuguese Boundary Commission, East Africa, 1904–06; Anglo-French Boundary Commission, Niger and Lake Chad, 1909; Boundary Delimitation Commission, Bolivia, 1910; retired pay, 1911; served Benin, 1897 (despatches, Brevet Major, medal with clasp); West Africa, 1897–98 (clasp). *Address:* Gardenmorris, Kilmacthomas, Co. Waterford. *Club:* Army and Navy.

Died 28 Jan. 1942.

OSMASTON, Col Cecil Alvend FitzHerbert, CB 1916; CBE 1919; RMA; retired, 1920; *b* 24 July 1866; 4th *s* of late John Osmaston, of Osmaston Manor, Derby, and Florence Mary Rice; *m* Minnie Buckley, *d* of late General Sir Henry B. Tuson; three *s* one *d*. *Educ:* Winchester. Adjutant Royal Marine Artillery, 1894–99; Adjutant Sligo R. Garrison Artillery Militia, 1899–1905; Instructor of Gunnery, 1908–10; Member of Ordnance Board, 1910–13; served European War, France, 1914–16 (CB); Member of Ordnance Committee, 1916–17; Assistant Controller, Munitions Inventions Department, 1917–19. *Address:* Mockbeggars, Fittleworth, Sussex.

Died 12 Aug. 1949.

OSMOND, Wing-Comdr Edward, CBE 1919; late RAF; *b* 1890; *m* 1915. Served European War, 1914–19 (despatches, CBE, French Croix de Guerre with palms, Officer of Order of Crown of Belgium); retired list, 1937.

Died 7 May 1946.

OSTBERG, Ragnar, Hon. RA 1930; Architect; Professor at the Royal Art Academy in Stockholm; *b* 14 July 1866. *Educ:* Royal Gold Medallist Royal Institute of British Architects, 1926. *Works:* Stockholm Town Hall: the Östermalm School, the Royal Patent and Registration Office, Thorsten Laurins Villa, Gebers Villa, Bonnier's House at Djurgäden, Jonas C'son Kjellberg's House at Lidingön; The Kelmar Public School; Old Upsala Castle (Restoration); The Helsingborg Crematorium; The Stockholm Marinmuseum; Gold Medallist American Institute of Architects, 1934, etc. *Address:* Stockholm.

Died 6 Feb. 1945.

OSTLER, Hon. Sir Henry Hubert, Kt 1939; KC 1924, LLB; *b* Timaru, NZ, 2 July 1876; *s* of William Henry Ostler, JP, Ben Ohau station, Canterbury, and Emma Brignell Roberts; *m* 1911, Lucilla Berneice, *d* of James Duigan, journalist, Wanganui; one *s* two *d*. *Educ:* Christ's Hospital, London; Victoria University College, Wellington, NZ. Farming in Levin District, 1892–1900; Associate to the Rt Hon. Sir Robert Stout, 1903–07; Founder and Editor of Spike the Victoria University College Magazine; Editor NZ Law Reports and of Digests, 1907–10; Crown Prosecutor, Wellington, and First Assistant Law Officer, Crown Law Office, 1910–15; Partner in legal firm of Jackson, Russell, Tunks & Ostler, Auckland, 1915–24; Judge of Supreme Court and Court of Appeal of New Zealand, 1925–43; Chairman of NZ Prisons Board, 1938–43; Member of Victoria University College Council, 1911–15 and since 1932, and Chairman, 1913 and 1914; Member of NZ University Senate, 1915–19; Examiner in law for NZ University for many years; Member of Wellington Licensing Committee, 1911–14; Life Member of Wellington Acclimatisation Society, and member of Council for many years; Chairman and Life Member of Auckland Acclimatisation Society. *Recreations:* fishing, shooting, deer-stalking, big game hunting. *Address:* 27 Talavera Terrace, Wellington, C1, NZ. *Clubs:* Wellington, NZ; Auckland.

Died 23 Feb. 1944.

O'SULLIVAN, Eugene; MP (IN) East Kerry, 1910; Auditor to Kerry County Council over County Guaranteed Railways; Managing Director Killarney Mineral Water Manufacturing Co. Ltd; *b* Firies Castle, 1879; *s* of Marcus O'Sullivan and Nora M'Mahon-Reardon; unmarried. *Educ:* Firies Public School; The Seminary, Killarney. Started commercial life with an uncle in drapery trade; found it uncongenial; abandoned it after a few years; took up appointments above, and has since lived mostly at his home in the country; has taken for 10 years a prominent part in public affairs; contested East Kerry, 1906. *Publications:* written and spoken a great deal on Irish Land Question, especially the Land Purchase side. *Recreations:* shooting, rowing, football, billiards, cycling. *Address:* Firies Castle, Farranfore, Co. Kerry. *T:* 20 Y Killarney. *Clubs:* Central, Killarney.

Died 19 May 1942.

O'SULLIVAN, John M., MA, DPhil; Professor of History, University College, Dublin; Member of Dail Eireann for Kerry, 1923–43; Member of the Senate, National University and of the Governing Body University College, Dublin; *b* Killarney, 18 Feb. 1881; 2nd *s* of late M. O'Sullivan, JP; *m* Agnes, 3rd *d* of John Crotty, JP, Lismore; two *s* two *d*. *Educ:* St Brendan's, Killarney; Clongowes Wood College; University College, Dublin; University of Bonn and University of Heidelberg. Sometime Fellow in Philosophy in the RUI. Parliamentary Secretary to the Minister for Finance, 1924–26; Minister for Education, and Member of Executive Council, Irish Free State, 1926–32; Delegate to the Assembly of League of Nations, 1924, 1928, 1929, 1930; rapporteur on Public Health, 1928; President of the Fifth Commission, 1929. *Publications:* Vergleich der Methoden Kants und Hegels auf Grund ihrer Behandlung der Kategorie der Quantität; Old Criticism and New Pragmatism, Dublin, 1909; articles on Philosophy and History in various periodicals.

Died 9 Feb. 1948.

O'SULLIVAN, Timothy. MP (N) East Kerry 1910–18; on Central Council of Land and Labour Association. *Address:* Main Street, Killarney, Ireland.

Died 15 Aug. 1950.

OULTON, William Harold Stowe, JP; MA, LLM; *b* 1 Feb. 1869; *s* of late W. Oulton, LLD, JP, Liverpool, and Emily Stowe; *m* 1897, Kate, *d* of Mrs J. P. Brunner; three *s*. *Educ:* Leys School; Christ's College, Cambridge. Revising Barrister; Assistant Recorder of Liverpool; Deputy Stipendiary of Liverpool; Metropolitan Magistrate, 1925; retired, 1940. *Recreations:* motoring and fishing. *Address:* Stoneleigh, Tower Hill, Horsham. *Clubs:* Garrick, Carlton.

Died 25 July 1941.

OUTRAM, Major Sir Francis Davidson, 4th Bt *cr* 1858; OBE; *b* 4 Aug. 1867; *s* of 2nd Bt and Jane Anne (*d* 1903), *e d* of late P. Davidson, Inchmarlo, Kincardineshire; *S* brother, 1925; *m* 1st, 1893, Maud Charlotte (*d* 1913), *d* of late J. P. Kitchin, The Manor House, Hampton; one *d*; 2nd, 1915, Isabel Mary, *d* of late H. C. Berry. *Educ:* Haileybury; RIEC, Coopers Hill. 2nd Lt Royal Engineers, 1889; Bt Major, 1918. *Heir:* great-nephew, Alan James Outram, *b* 15 May 1937. *Address:* c/o Lloyds Bank, 6 Pall Mall, SW1.

Died 30 June 1945.

OUTRAM, Lt-Col Harold William Sydney, CBE 1919; TD; Director-General of Aeronautical Inspection, Ministry of Aircraft Production, since 1943; Deputy Director-General, 1941–43. *Educ:* Royal School of Mines, S Kensington. ARSM, AMIEE, FRAeS, MIEI.

Served European War, 1914–19 (despatches, CBE); Director of Aeronautical Inspection, Air Ministry, 1923; Director of Aircraft Production, 1938. *Club:* Royal Air Force.

Died 31 May 1944.

OVANS, Major Hugh Lambert, CBE 1920; late Northumberland Fusiliers; *b* 1881; *s* of late J. L. Ovans, East Sheen; *m* 1907, Marjorie Cecil, *o c* of late Sir Cecil Michael Wilford Brett, CSI. *Educ:* Marlborough College. Served European War, 1914–19 (wounded, despatches, star); Head of Release from Colours Branch, Ministry of National Service, 1917–18, and in Ministry of Labour, 1918–19; Director of Military Prisons and Detention Barracks in India, 1929–33; retired from Army, 1931. *Recreations:* reading and riding. *Address:* Laverton House, Laverton, nr Bath. *T:* Beckington 50. *Club:* Naval and Military.

Died 26 April 1946.

OVENS, Col (Brig.-Gen.) Robert Montgomery, CMG 1915; JP; *b* 3 July 1868; 2nd *s* of late John Coote Ovens, JP, Aughnagaddy House, and Killybegs, Co. Donegal; *m* 1910, Beatrice, *d* of William Clibborn, Liverpool; three *d*. *Educ:* Westward Ho; RMC Sandhurst. Entered army, 1889; Capt. 1896; Major, 1907; Lt-Col commanding 1st South Staffordshire Regiment 1913; Colonel, 1917; DAAG Musketry, India; Station Staff Officer 1st Class, India; Brigade-Major, India; temp. Brig.-General, 1916–19; served European War, 1914–18 (wounded, despatches thrice, CMG, Order of St Stanislas of Russia (3rd class). *Recreations:* shooting, fishing, and hunting. *Address:* Mytchett Heath, Mytchett, Aldershot. *T:* Farnborough 611; Aughnagaddy House, Ramelton, Co. Donegal. *TA:* Ramelton, Co. Donegal.

Died 20 Dec. 1950.

OVERTON, George Leonard; *b* Coventry, 18 May 1875; *s* of John Overton; *m* 1903, Florence, *d* of Benjamin Hird, Bradford; one *s* one *d*. *Educ:* Bradford Technical College; Royal College of Science, London. ARCS (Physics) 1897; Assistant, Astronomical Department of the Royal College of Science, 1897–1908; appointed to Science Museum, 1898; Keeper of Water and Air Transport Division, 1926–35; served with Electrical Engineers (RE) Volunteers in South Africa, 1901–02; Fellow of the British Horological Institute. *Publications:* Clocks and Watches, 1922; various official publications of the Science Museum. *Address:* 25 Ellerby Street, Fulham, SW6.

Died 15 May 1948.

OVEY, Lt-Col Richard Lockhart, DSO 1916; TD; DL, JP; *b* 1878; *e s* of late Richard Ovey, DL, JP, Badgemore, Henley-on-Thames; *m* 1903, Rachel Emma, *d* of late Capt. A. H. Chapman, 19th Hussars; one *s* two *d*. *Educ:* Eton; Magdalen College, Oxford. Lieut-Col (TD) Oxfordshire and Buckinghamshire LI (TA); retd 1921; formerly Lieut 52nd Light Infantry; served European War, 1914–18 (despatches, DSO); County Alderman, Oxon; High Sheriff, 1927. *Recreations:* shooting and fishing. *Address:* Hernes, Rotherfield Greys, Henley-on-Thames. *T:* Henley-on-Thames 245. *Club:* Junior United Service.

Died 9 July 1946.

OWEN; *see* Cunliffe-Owen.

OWEN, Col Arthur Lewis S.; *see* Scott-Owen.

OWEN, Basil Wilberforce Longmore, MVO; Commander Royal Navy (retired); *e s* of late Very Rev. Dr C. Mansfield Owen, Dean of Ripon; *m* 1914, Evelyn Mary, *o d* of Alfred Taylor, JP, CC, Norfolk, of Starston Place, Harleston, Norfolk; two *s*. *Educ:* Milford-on-Sea; Dartmouth. Commanded the following of HM Ships during the War: HMD Stour, HMS Vixen, HMS

Nessus, HMS Ruby, HMS Onslaught, HMS Mameluke, HMS Sirdar; retired at own request, 1927. *Address:* Rysa Lodge, Seething, Norwich. *Club:* United Service.

Died 2 July 1943.

OWEN, Sir David John, Kt 1931; Chairman of Anglesey and Caernarvonshire Agricultural Wages Committee; Member of Central Advisory Water Committee; *b* Liverpool, 8 March 1874; *s* of Rev. R. Ceinwenydd Owen, and Elizabeth Jane Jones; *m* 1st, 1899, Mary Elizabeth (*d* 1906), *d* of late Capt. William Owen, Carnarvon; 2nd, 1908, Marian Maud, *widow* of late J. H. Thomas, Carmarthen, and *d* of late Alderman William Williams, JP, Haverfordwest; no *c. Educ:* Liverpool Institute. In the service of the Mersey Docks and Harbour Board, Liverpool, for 13 years; Manager and Secretary to Paul Bros, Flour Millers, Liverpool and Birkenhead, 1904; Assistant Manager of Goole Docks, 1908; Manager, 1915; General Manager and Secretary to the Belfast Harbour Commissioners, 1915; General Manager to the Port of London Authority, 1922–38; Past President of National Confederation of Employers' Organisations; Past Pres. of the Institute of Transport; Member of Royal Commission on Lotteries and Betting, 1932–33; member of Holidays with Pay Committee, 1937; Chairman of Merchant Shipping Reserve Advisory Committee (Board of Trade), 1939. *Publications:* A Short History of the Port of Belfast, 1917; History of Belfast, 1921; The Port of London Yesterday and To-day, 1927; The Origin and Development of the Ports of the United Kingdom, 1939. *Address:* Llanfair, Park Road, Beckenham, Kent. *T:* Beckenham 2564; Bryn Maelog, Rhosneigr, Anglesey. *T:* Rhosneigr 287. *Club:* Reform.

Died 17 May 1941.

OWEN, Most Rev. Derwyn Trevor, DD; Archbishop of Toronto, and Primate of Church of England in Canada since 1934; *b* Twickenham, England, 29 July 1876; *s* of Trevor Randulph Owen, formerly of the 11th Hussars, and Florence, *d* of late Surgeon-General Paynter, CB, of Tenby, S Wales; *m* 1904, Nora Grier Jellett, *y d* of late Judge Jellett of Picton, Ontario; three *s* two *d. Educ:* Eastbourne; Toronto Church School; Trinity University, Toronto. Deacon, 1900; Priest, 1901; Curate, St John's Church, Toronto; in England 1901–02, serving in temporary positions in All Hallows, Barking, EC; St Mary's, Huntingdon, etc.; Curate, St James' Cathedral, Toronto, 1902–08; Assistant Rector, Holy Trinity Church, Toronto, 1908–10; Rector, 1910–14; Rector of Christ's Church Cathedral, Hamilton, Ontario, Canada, 1914–25; Dean of Niagara, 1915–25; Bishop of Niagara, 1925–32; of Toronto from 1932; DD Trinity University, Toronto, Jure Dignitatus, 1916; DCL Hon. Bishop's University, Lennoxville, Quebec, 1928; Hon. DD, Wycliffe College, Toronto, 1931; King's College, Halifax, NS, 1937; Hon. STD Columbia University, New York; Hon. LLD, Occidental College, California, 1946. *Address:* Synod House, 135 Adelaide Street East, Toronto. *T:* Adelaide 7479.

Died 9 April 1947.

OWEN, Dr Gwilym, MA, DSc; FInstP; Professor of Physics, Aberystwyth University College, 1919–38; Acting-Principal, 1934; Vice-Principal, 1935; *b* Denbigh, 1880; *s* of Rev. W. Owen, Liverpool. *Educ:* Ruthin Grammar School; University College, Liverpool; Gilchrist Scholar of the Victoria University, 1898; 1851 Exhibition Scholar of University of Liverpool, 1901; Christ's College, Cambridge, 1901–04. Research student at Cavendish laboratory under Professor Sir J. J. Thomson, 1901–04. Lecturer and Demonstrator of Physics at Liverpool University, 1904–13; Professor Auckland University College, New Zealand, 1913–19. *Publications:* papers in Philosophical magazine on thermionics and condensation nuclei; (in Welsh); Athroniaeth Pethau Cyffredin, 1907; Cwrr y

Llen, 1914; Rhyfeddodau'r Cread, 1933; Mawr a Bach, 1936. *Address:* c/o University College, Aberystwyth, Wales.

Died 9 Nov. 1940.

OWEN, Rev. Ithel George, MA; Rector of Bradwell-on-Sea, Essex, 1921–38; Rural Dean of Dengie; Surrogate for Diocese of Chelmsford; *b* 6 March 1863; *s* of late Rev. Edward Owen, MA, Rector of Bradwell-on-Sea, Essex; JP Bucks; *m* 1893, Mary Georgina Eardley, *o d* of William Henry Childers, Lt-Com. RN; one *s* two *d. Educ:* privately; Corpus Christi College, Cambridge. Curate of Hallow, Worcester, 1886; Rector of St Andrews Church, St Andrews, Fife, 1893–99; Rural Dean of Swinford, 1907–18; Chaplain to the High Sheriff of Worcestershire, 1905; to the High Sheriff of Staffordshire, 1913; Surrogate for the Diocese of Worcester; Hon. Canon of Worcester Cathedral, 1917–36, Canon Emeritus since 1936; Rector of Old Swinford, Worcestershire, 1899–1921. *Recreations:* formerly cricket and football. *Address:* The Hill House, Ewelme, Oxford.

Died 5 Jan. 1941.

OWEN, John; novelist; *b* Liverpool. HM Forces, 1915–19. *Publications:* The Cotton Broker, 1921; The Idealist, 1922; Robert Gregory, the History of a Little Soul, 1922; The Hoarding, 1923; The Glory of Going On, 1924; The Giant of Oldborne, 1926; The Shepherd and the Child, 1929; Many Captives, 1930; The Running Footman, 1931; Everard Bringle, 1933; The Road and the Wood, 1936; The Blind for Sacrifice, 1937; The Beauty of the Ships, 1940; The Traitor, 1941; Blitz Hero, 1942; The Burden, 1943; Wind in the Sky, 1944; Suffolk Madman, 1946; Home Sweet Home, 1948. *Recreations:* swimming, cycling walking. *Address:* The White House, Felixtowe.

Died 2 Jan. 1949.

OWEN, Rt Rev. Leslie, BD, MA; Bishop of Lincoln since 1946; Hon. CF; *b* 4 Feb. 1886; *e s* of Alfred William and Mary Owen; *m* 1920, Iris Marjorie, *y d* of late Walter John Lawrance, Dean of St Albans; one *s* one *d. Educ:* Merchant Taylors' School, London; St John's College, Oxford (Scholar and Exhibitioner); Pusey and Ellerton Hebrew Scholar; Houghton Septuagint Prize and 2nd Class Theol. School, Ely Theological College. Deacon, 1911; Priest, 1912; Curate of Ashford, Kent, 1911–14; Curate of the Parish Church, Folkestone, 1914–19; temporary Chaplain to HM Forces, 1916–19; Lecturer and Vice-Principal of Bishop's College, Cheshunt, 1919–22; Secretary of Central Candidates Committee, 1922–24, and General Sec. of Central Advisory Council of Training for the Ministry, 1924; Chaplain to the Duke of Portland at Welbeck, 1924–28; Warden of Scholar Cancellarii, Lincoln, 1928–36; Prebendery of Welton Beckhall and Canon in Lincoln Cathedral, 1933–36; Examining Chaplain to the Bishop of Southwell, 1927–36, and to the Bishop of Lincoln, 1933–36; Archdeacon of Auckland, Canon Residentiary of Durham Cathedral, and Examining Chaplain to the Bishop of Durham, 1936; Bishop Suffragan of Jarrow, 1939–44; Bishop Suffragan of Maidstone, 1944–46; Select Preacher to the University of Cambridge, 1935 and 1945; to the University of Oxford, 1940–42. *Recreation:* fishing. *Address:* Bishop's House, Eastgate, Lincoln.

Died 2 March 1947.

OWEN, Lt-Col Lindsay Cunliffe, DSO 1918; late RE; *s* of late Col H. O. B. Owen, late RA; *m* 1916, Eglantyne Mary, *d* of late Capt. J. W. Osborne, CBE, RN. *Educ:* Wellington College; RMA, Woolwich. Commission in the Royal Engineers, 1907; served European War in France and Belgium, 1914–18 (DSO, Bt Majority, despatches four times); retired pay, 1936. *Recreation:* all sports. *Address:* The Glen, Upper Hale, Farnham, Surrey. *Club:* Junior United Service.

Died 4 Feb. 1941.

OWEN, Lt-Col Roger Arthur Mostyn-, DSO 1918; late the Rifle Brigade; *b* 1888; *s* of late Lt-Col Charles Roger Mostyn-Owen, of Erway, Ellesmere, Shropshire; *m* 1922, Margaret Eva, *d* of late George Littleton Dewhurst and late Mrs Walter Jones, Aberuchill, Perthshire, and Hurlingham Lodge, SW; one *s* one *d*. *Educ:* Eton; Sandhurst. Served European War, 1914–18 (despatches 3 times, wounded, DSO); Sheriff of Shropshire 1941. *Address:* Woodhouse, Oswestry, Salop. *Clubs:* Buck's, Cavalry.

Died 25 June 1947.

OWEN, Lt-Col Roger Carmichael Robert, CMG 1906; OBE 1919; *b* 2 March 1866; *s* of late Rev. Loftus Owen. *Educ:* Rossall. Entered 3rd King's Shropshire LI Aug. 1884; Oxfordshire Light Infantry, 1888; Captain, 1898; retired pay, 1906; Major, 1915; Lt-Col 1918; Major-Gen. and Pasha in Egyptian Army, 1916; retired from Egyptian Army with rank of Pasha, 1918; employed with King's African Rifles, 1899–1902; appointed to Egyptian Army, 1902; Director of Intelligence Department, Egyptian War Office and Sudan Agent, Cairo, 1905–08; Governor and OC Military District, Mongalla Province, Sudan, 1908–18; Governor of Eastern and Southern Deserts Prov., Egypt, 1918–20; served Manipur Expedition, 1891 (medal, clasp); Wuntho Expedition, Upper Burmah, 1891 (clasp), in both as Superintendent of Army Signalling; Mohmand Expedition, 1897–98 (medal with clasp); Tirah Expedition, 1897–98, including operations in Bara Valley and Khyber Pass (severely wounded, clasp); Political Officer, Southern Column, Beir Expedition, 1912 (medal with clasp); served with Expeditionary Force, Lafite and Lokoia Mountains, Southern Soudan (clasp); Senior Member, Sinai Boundary Commission, 1906; holds 3rd class Medjidie; Grand Officer order of Nile; mentioned in despatches twice, Oct. 1916, July 1919; FRGS. *Publication:* Bari Grammars and Vocabulary. *Recreations:* polo, big game shooting and fishing. *Clubs:* Naval and Military; Turf, Cairo.

Died 1 Aug. 1941.

OWEN, Ven. Walter Edwin; Archdeacon of Kavirondo, Kenya Colony, 1918–45, Archdeacon Emeritus, 1945; *b* 1879; *s* of John Simpson and Caroline Isabel Owen; *m* 1911, Lucy Olive, *d* of Rev. Octavius F. and Amy Walton (the latter authoress of Christy's Old Organ, Peep Behind the Scenes, etc.); three *s*. *Educ:* St Enoch's, Belfast; Islington Theological College. Intended for business profession, but in 1901 offered as missionary to Church Missionary Society; ordained, 1904; priest, 1905; short curacy, St John's, Reading, 1904; rural Dean of Budu, Uganda, 1915; Chaplain to Forces, German East Africa Campaign, 1916. *Publications:* articles on native questions in East African Standard and in Manchester Guardian; published results of Miocene discoveries, 1934; translational work in 3 Bantu languages, Lunyankole, Lutoro, and Lukonjo and in Nilotic language Dholus. *Recreation:* archæology. *Address:* Ngiya, Yala, Kenya Colony; Stocks Green, Hildenborough, Tonbridge.

Died 18 Sept. 1945.

OXENHAM, John; writer; *m* Margery (*d* 1925), *d* of William Anderson, Greenock; two *s* four *d*. *Educ:* Old Trafford School; Victoria University, Manchester. Went into business and lived for some years in France and United States; travelled over greater part of Europe and Canada; visited Southern States with view to orange-growing or sheepfarming; decided against them and came home; took to writing as alleviative and alternative from business, found it much more enjoyable than business, so dropped business and stuck to writing. *Publications:* God's Prisoner, 1898; Rising Fortunes, 1899; A Princess of Vascovy, 1900; Our Lady of Deliverance, 1901; John of Gerisau, 1902; Under the Iron Flail, 1902; Bondman Free; Mr Joseph Scorer; Barbe of Grand Bayou, 1903; A Weaver of Webs; Hearts in Exile, 1904; The Gate of the Desert; White Fire, Fire, 1905; Giant Circumstance; Profit and Loss, 1906; The Long Road; Carette of Sark, 1907; Pearl of Pearl Island; The Song of Hyacinth, 1908; My Lady of Shadows; Great-Heart Gillian, 1909; A Maid of the Silver Sea; Lauristons, 1910; The Coil of Carne; Their High Adventure, 1911; Queen of the Guarded Mounts; Mr Cherry; The Quest of the Golden Rose, 1912; Mary All-Alone; Red Wrath; Bees in Amber (Verse), 1913; Maid of the Mist; Broken Shackles, 1914; Flower of the Dust; Everywoman and War; Hymn, For the Men at the Front; All's Well!, (Verse); Corner Island; My Lady of the Moor; The King's High Way (Verse); '1914,' 1916; The Vision Splendid (Verse), 1917; The Fiery Cross (Verse), 1917; High Altars; Hearts Courageous (Verse), 1918; All Clear! (Verse); Winds of the Dawn (Essays), 1919; Gentlemen—The King! (Verse), 1920; A Hazard in The Blue, 1923; The Wonder of Lourdes; The Perilous Lovers; Chaperon to Cupid, 1924; The Cedar Box, 1924; Selected Poems, in one vol.; Scala Sancta; The Hidden Years, 1925; The Recollections of Roderic Fyfe; The Man who would Save the World, 1927; The Hawk of Como, 1928; God's Candle, 1929; The Splendour of the Dawn; Cross Roads, 1930; A Saint in the Making; The Hidden Years, illustrated by Margaret W. Tarrant, 1931; Anno Domini, 1932; God and Lady Margaret, 1933; Christ and the Third Wise Man, 1934; Wide Horizons (Verse), 1940. *Recreations:* Alpine walking, rowing. *Address:* c/o Christy and Moore, 222 Strand, WC2.

Died 23 Jan. 1941.

OXFORD AND ASQUITH, Countess of; Emma Alice Margaret, (Margot); *b* 2 Feb. 1864; 6th *d* of Sir Charles Tennant, 1st Bt; *m* 1894, 1st Earl of Oxford and Asquith (*d* 1928); one *s* one *d*. *Publications:* The Autobiography of Margot Asquith, 1922; Places and Persons, 1925; Lay Sermons, 1927; Octavia, 1928; More Memories, 1933; (Editor) Myself when Young, 1938; Off the Record, 1944. *Address:* 14 Kensington Square, W8.

Died 28 July 1945.

OXLEY, Sir Alfred James R.; *see* Rice-Oxley.

P

PACK-BERESFORD, Denis R., OBE 1918; JP; DL, Co. Carlow; Member Royal Irish Academy; *b* 23 March 1864; *e s* of Denis W. Pack-Beresford, DL MP for Co. Carlow; *m* 1891, Alice (*d* 1918), *o d* of James Acheson Lyle of Glandore, Kilrea, Co. Derry. *Educ:* Rugby; Christ Church, Oxford (BA 1887). High Sheriff, Co. Carlow, 1890. *Recreations:* natural history, fishing. *Address:* Fenagh House, Bagnalstown, Co. Carlow. *T:* Fenagh 3; The Tansey, Baily, Co. Dublin. *T:* Sutton 122. *Clubs:* Travellers'; Irish Automobile, Kildare Street, Dublin.

Died 6 March 1942.

PACKE, Sir Edward Hussey, KBE 1920; JP, DL, CC, Leicestershire; *b* 6 Jan. 1878; *o surv. s* of late Hussey Packe and late Lady Alice Wodehouse, *e d* of 1st Earl of Kimberley; *m* 1909, Hon. Mary Sydney Colebrooke, *d* of 1st Lord Colebrooke; two *d*. *Educ:* Eton. Assistant Private Secretary to the Marquis of Lansdowne at the War Office, 1900; Assistant Private Secretary to the Earl of Selborne at the Admiralty, 1901–05, to Lord Cawdor, 1905, to Mr Balfour, 1916, to Sir Edward Carson, 1916–17; Private Secretary to Sir Eric Geddes, 1917–19, and to Mr Walter Long, 1919; attached to Admiralty Staff 1914–19; High Sheriff of Leicestershire, 1911; a Government Director Anglo-Persian Oil Company; served as a Gold Staff Officer at the Coronations of TM Edward VII, George V, and George VI; has the Legion of Honour and the Order of the Crown of Italy. *Address:* Prestwold Hall, Loughborough. *T:* Wyneswold 236. *Club:* Brooks's.

Died 11 May 1946.

PACKER, Col Harry Dixon, CIE 1920; MRCS, LRCP; late RAMC; *b* 1872; *s* of late S. Gilbert Packer, Nottingham; *m* 1907, Gertrude Ivy, *d* of late A. Briggs, Bournemouth, Hants; one *d*. *Educ:* University School, Nottingham; Guy's Hospital. Entered RAMC, 1899; served S African War, 1899–1902 (Queen's medal with 4 clasps, King's medal with 2 clasps); European War, 1914–18, in India and Mesopotamia; 3rd Afghanistan War (CIE); AD of MS Home Counties, 1923–27; retired, 1927. *Address:* c/o Glyn Mills & Co., Holt's Branch, Whitehall, SW1.

Died 26 June 1947.

PADEREWSKI, Ignace Jean, GBE 1925; Hon. MusD Cambridge, 1926; pianist, composer; President of the Polish National Council, 1940; *b* Province of Podolia, Russian Poland, 6 Nov. 1860; *m* 1st, Antonina Korsak (*d* 1881); one *s*; 2nd 1899, Baroness de Rosen (*d* 1934). *Educ:* Began to learn the piano at three, and at seven was placed under teacher; studied at the Conservatory of Warsaw under Janotha and Roguski, and later, at Berlin, composition under Friedrich Kiel. First concert tour in Poland and Russia; became teacher at the Conservatory at Warsaw at the age of 18; went to Vienna in the autumn of 1884 to study piano under Theodore Leschetizky; in 1885–86, professor of piano and counter-point at the Conservatory of Strasbourg (Alsace); studied again a few months with Leschetizky, 1887; début Vienna 1887, Paris 1889, London 1890, New York 1891; since then eighteen tours in the United States; played in almost all the leading cities of Europe, North and South America, Australia, New Zealand, and South Africa. Composer: Manru opera produced Dresden, Cologne, Bonn, Prague, Lwow, Cracow, 1901; New York, Chicago, Boston, Warsaw, etc., 1902; symphony, concerto for piano and orchestra, fantasia, sonatas, variations, and many pieces and songs. During World War, devoted time mainly to concertising for the benefit of Polish war sufferers and to public speaking on behalf of Poland; organised in the US, 1917, an army of Polish volunteers known as the Polish army in France; officially recognised representative of Polish people, 1917–18; at Washington; led in organising Polish republic, 1918–19; Premier of Poland, 1919; Member of the Peace Conference at Paris; first delegate of Poland to the Council of Ambassadors and to the League of Nations, 1920; Member of the Royal Academy of Santa Cecilia, Rome, 1897; Member of the Institut de France, 1926; Member of the American Academy for Arts and Letters, 1930; Hon. Member of Royal Academy of Music; Hon. PhD of the University of Lwow, 1911; Hon. MusDoc. Yale, 1917; PhD University, Cracow, 1919; CLD University, Oxford, 1920; CLD University, Columbia, 1922; CLD University of Southern California, 1923; PhD University of Poznan, 1924; LLD University of Glasgow, 1925; PhD University of Warsaw, 1931; MusDoc New York, 1933; Doc. of Letters, University of Lausanne, 1933; Grand Cross of the British Empire (GBE); Grand Cross of the Order of Leopold of Belgium; Grand Cross of St Maurice et Lazare of Italy; Grand Cross of the White Eagle of Poland; Grand Cross of Polonia Restituta; Grand Cross of the Legion of Honour, France. *Publication:* The Paderewski Memoirs (with Mary Lawton), 1939.

Died 29 June 1941.

PADWICK, Francis Herbert, CBE 1917; JP; *b* 21 March 1856; *s* of late Frederick Padwick, of West Thorney Manor Sussex; *m* 1882, Mary Grace, *y d* of late Rev. Dr T. P. Boultbee; one *s* four *d*. *Educ:* Tonbridge School; Corpus Christi College, Cambridge, MA. Bar, Inner Temple, 1882; Chairman Committee of Agricultural Education for Women, 1915; a member of Committee on Settlement Employment of Discharged Sailors and Soldiers, 1916; of Agricultural Advisory Committee, 1917; of Central Agricultural Advisory Committee to Food Controller and Board of Agriculture, 1918; and of Council of Agriculture for England, 1920; President National Farmers' Union, 1919. Alderman of West Sussex County Council, 1921, and Chairman of its Agricultural Education Sub-Committee, 1910–32. *Address:* The Red House, West Ashling, Chichester. *TA:* West Ashling. *T:* West Ashling 207. *Club:* Farmers' (Chairman 1929).

Died 24 Feb. 1945.

PAE, David; *b* New Pentland, Midlothian, 1864; *m* 1908, Margaret Small, *y d* of late John Galloway, Dundee; one *s* one *d*. *Educ:* General Gibsone's School, Pentland; Newport Public School; University College, Dundee. Served apprenticeship to journalism on the staff of the People's Journal; editor People's Friend, Dundee, 1900–38; has written numerous popular serial stories and books of Scottish sketches. [His father, also editor of People's Friend, was author of many serials, and founder of the system of serial publication in newspapers]. *Recreations:* walking, gardening, botany, reading, photography. *Address:* Craigmount, Newport, Fife. *T:* Newport (Fife) 2217.

Died 9 May 1948.

PAGAN, Brig.-Gen. Alexander William, DSO 1915; *b* 1878. Entered Gloucestershire Regt 1899; Capt. 1906; Major, 1915; Brevet Lt-Col 1917; Col 1921; served S African War, 1900–02; European War, 1914–18 (wounded, despatches, DSO, Brevet Lt-Col, Croix de Guerre); Assistant Commandant, Small Arms School, Hythe, 1925–29; commanded 10th (Jubbulpore)

Infantry Brigade in India, 1929; retired pay, 1929; Colonel of Gloucestershire Regt, 1931–47. *Address:* Upton Knoll, Upton St Leonards, Glos.

Died 4 Aug. 1949.

PAGDEN, Arthur Sampson, CMG 1917; BA, Honours, Cantab, 1881; *b* 9 Sept. 1858; *s* of Robert Pagden, late of Woodcote, Epsom; *m* 1900, Frances Emma Beatrice, *d* of Kenneth Haweis James, late of 23 Pembridge Square, W; no *c. Educ:* Wellington College (Scholar); King's College, Cambridge (Scholar). Eighth in First Class Classical Tripos, 1881; University shooting eight, Wimbledon, 1881. Ceylon Civil Service since 1881; Chairman Municipal Council, Colombo, 1901–05; Principal Assistant Colonial Secretary, 1905–06; Postmaster-General, 1907–13; Controller of Revenue, Member of Legislative and Executive Councils, Ceylon, 1913; acted as Colonial Secretary, 1916, 1918, and 1919; retired on pension, 1920. *Recreations:* golf, motoring, music. *Address:* c/o Westminster Bank, Hanover Square, W1. *Clubs:* Oriental, Hurlingham.

Died 16 July 1942.

PAGE, Sir Archibald, Kt 1930; MInstCE, Hon. MIEE; *b* Alloa, Scotland, 1875; *s* of late John Page, Alloa; *m* 1906, Anne, *d* of late John Forsyth, Clackmannan; one *s* three *d. Educ:* Dollar Academy; Heriot-Watt College, Edinburgh; Royal Technical College, Glasgow. Deputy City Electrical Engineer, Glasgow, 1905–17; General Manager Clyde Valley Electric Power Company, 1917–20; Electricity Commissioner, 1920–25; Director and General Manager County of London Electric Supply Co., Ltd, 1925–27; General Manager Central Electricity Board, 1927–35, Chairman, 1935–44; Past President Institution of Electrical Engineers; Faraday Medallist, 1943. *Address:* Haworth, 1 West Hill, Sanderstead, Surrey. *T:* Sanderstead 1250. *Club:* St Stephen's.

Died 7 March 1949.

PAGE, Very Rev. Arnold Henry; *b* Carlisle, 1 March 1851; 3rd *s* of William Bousfield Page, FRCS Eng., JP Cumberland, and Anne Ferguson, *d* of William Nanson, Town-Clerk of Carlisle; *m* 1889, Blanche Cecilia (*d* 1938), *d* of Colonel C. Grantham, 9th and 89th Regiments, and Adeline, *d* of Col Johnson, 5th Fusiliers. *Educ:* Repton School; Balliol College, Oxford (BA 1875; MA 1877). Called to Bar, Inner Temple, 1878; Deacon, 1882; Priest, 1883; Curate St Mary's, Bryanston Square, W, 1882–83; St Botolph's, Bishopsgate, 1883–86; Rector of Tendring, 1886–1908; Dean of Peterborough, 1908–28; JP Essex, 1894, and Liberty of Peterborough, 1911 (Chairman, 1924–28); represented Brightlingsea on Essex County Council, 1892–95; Chairman, Tendring Union Guardians, District Council and Assessment Committee, 1899–1908; of the Tendring Parish Council from its formation till 1908, and of Tendring School Board from its formation in 1893 till its extinction; a Member of the Advisory Committee for elementary and higher education under Essex County Council in East Essex districts till 1908; President Harwich Division Liberal Association, 1891–1908; Hon. Freeman of Peterborough, 1928. *Address:* 102 Elm Park Gardens, SW10.

Died 10 Nov. 1943.

PAGE, Major Harold Hillis, DSO 1919; MC; Government Secretary Territory of New Guinea; Senior Member (Official) Legislative Council since 1933; *b* Grafton, New S Wales, 8 Aug. 1888; *s* of late Charles Page; *m* Anne Miller Brewster, LAB, of Scone, Perthshire; one *s* three *d. Educ:* Public School, Grafton, NSW; Sydney University (BA). State School Teacher, 1904–13; Commonwealth Public Service, 1913–21; New Guinea Public Service since 1921. Enlisted AIF, 1915 (promoted Lieut, Captain, Major on field, MC, DSO, despatches thrice, wounded thrice); termination of War 2nd in Command 25th Bn AIF; demobilised, 1919;

Major Reserve of Officers. *Address:* Lae, Territory of New Guinea. *Clubs:* Imperial Service, Sydney, NSW; Rabaul, Rabaul, TNG.

Died 1 July 1942.

PAGE, Harry Marmaduke, FRCS; Consulting Anæsthetist to the West London Hospital; Fellow of the Royal Society Medicine and the West London Medico-Chirurgical Society; *b* 1860; *s* of late W. E. Page, MA, MD (Oxon), FRCP, and Julia Catherine, *d* of Robert Keate, PRCS, Serjeant-Surgeon to Queen Victoria; unmarried. *Educ:* Charterhouse; St George's Hospital. Late Hon. Anæsthetist to the King George and other Red Cross Hospitals; Late Hon. Anæsthetist to Guy's Hospital and Hon. Anæsthetist to the Dental School; Hon. Anæsthetist to the Belgrave Hospital for Children; Vice-President of the West London Medico-Chirurgical Society; retired. *Publications:* papers on anæsthetic subjects in the Transactions of the 17th International Congress of Medicine, 1913; Royal Society of Medicine; West London Medico-Chirurgical Societies, Lancet, and British Medical Journal. *Address:* 5 Hurlingham Court, Ranelagh Gardens, SW6.

Died 2 June 1942.

PAGE, Maj.-Gen. Lionel Frank, CB 1943; DSO 1917; GOC-in-C Atlantic Command since July 1943; *b* Frodingham, Driffield, Yorks, 17 Dec. 1884; *s* of H. J. Page, *s* of J. Page, JP, of Southminster, Essex, and A. E., *d* of Capt. Winchester Jones, 60th Rifles; *m* 1915, Rose Laura Whitehouse; one *s* one *d. Educ:* Berkhamsted School. Went to Canada, 1903; farming, later brokerage; held a commission in 35th Central Alberta Horse previous to outbreak of War; joined 5th Canadian Batt. Aug. 1914; went to France, Feb. 1915; served continuously as Lieut, Capt., and Major (2nd in command) of 5th Batt.; given command of 50th Can. Batt. March 1917 (DSO and two bars); commanded Canadian Troops in Iceland, June 1940; Canadian Base Units in England, Nov. 1940; Maj.-Gen. and commanded 4th Canadian Div. June 1941; Canadian Troops in Newfoundland, Dec. 1941–July 1943. *Address:* HQ Atlantic Command, Halifax, NS.

Died 26 Aug. 1944.

PAGE, Robert Palgrave, CBE 1920; MBE 1917; *b* 1867; *s* of late Samuel Page, Surbiton. *Educ:* Harrow; Trinity Hall, Cambridge. Was Civil Assistant at War Office. *Recreations:* foreign travel, shooting and fishing. *Clubs:* Travellers', Orleans.

Died 30 April 1947.

PAGE, William Morton, CBE 1918; lately Air Commodore, RAFVR (Administrative and Special Duties Section); *b* 1883; *s* of George Charles Page of Ashby-de-la-Zouch; *m* 1st, 1911, Nora Margaret (*d* 1924), *d* of W. H. Harsant, Clifton; one *s* two *d*; 2nd, 1926, Ada Margaret Leech, *o d* of late C. O. Harvey, Clifton, Bristol. *Educ:* Ashby-de-la-Zouch Grammar School; King's College, Cambridge (Eighth Wrangler, 1905, Class I Div. I Maths Tripos Part II, 1906; Smith's Prizeman, 1907); Fellow of King's College, Cambridge, and MA 1908. HM Inspector of Schools, 1908–28; Director of Educational Services, Air Ministry, 1929–44; an Officer of Order of St Maurice and St Lazarus of Italy, and Chevalier of Legion of Honour; Assistant Secretary for Requirements and Statistics, Ministry of Munitions, 1917; Fellow of the Royal Astronomical Society. *Address:* 16 Lansdowne Road, SW20. *T:* Wimbledon 2877. *Clubs:* Oxford and Cambridge; Royal Western Yacht (Plymouth).

Died 12 Dec. 1950.

PAGE-HENDERSON, Lt-Col Henry Cockcroft; JP North Riding Yorks; *b* 1856; *e s* of Robert Henry Page-Henderson; *m* 1st, 1890, Frances Millicent Mary (*d* 1898), *d* of late J. C. Evans; 2nd, 1900, May (*d* 1942), *d* of late J. Paterson, Kinburn House, St Andrews, NB. *Educ:* Harrow. Entered 6th (Inniskilling) Dragoons,

1878; Lieut-Col 1899; served Boer War, 1881; Bechuanaland Expedition, 1884–85; South Africa, 1899–1900; retired, 1905. *Address:* Middle Moor, Minehead, Somerset. *T:* Minehead 125.

Died 27 Nov. 1942.

PAGET, Dame Rosalind, DBE 1935; ARRC; *b* 1855; *d* of John Paget, Metropolitan Police Magistrate. First Inspector Queen's District Nurses; Founder Midwives' Institute (now College of Midwives); Editor of Nursing Notes. *Address:* Colwood Park, Bolney, Sussex.

Died 19 Aug. 1948.

PAINE, Lt-Col Albert Ingraham, CMG 1916; DSO 1902; *b* 12 Jan. 1874; *s* of Hammon Paine, Folkestone; *m* 1906, Elsie Caroline, 4th *d* of Philip J. D. Wykeham of Tythrop House, Thame; two *d.* Served S Africa, 1899–1902 (despatches twice, DSO); European War, 1914–18 (despatches twice, CMG); JP Gloucestershire. *Address:* Bledington, Kingham, Oxon.

Died 29 June 1949.

PAINE, William Worship; *b* 2 Nov. 1861; *γ s* of late Sir Thomas Paine; *m* 1888, Helen Edith Mary, *d* of late William Worship; one *s* one *d. Educ:* Temple Grove, East Sheen; Rugby; New Coll., Oxford. Graduated with first-class Honours in Law Final School; articled to the firm of Paine, Son & Pollock, 1884. Partner, 1888; senior partner, 1898; a General Manager of Lloyds Bank, 1918; retired, 1925; a witness before the War Wealth Committee in 1920 and the Colwyn Committee, 1925, on the proposal for a Capital Levy. *Publications:* Banking; The Menace of Socialism; many articles and letters in the Times and other periodicals on the Capital Levy, the Nationalisation of Industry, and other economic subjects. *Recreations:* music, golf, tennis, bowls, and gardening, foreign travel; played racquets, single and double, for Oxford v. Cambridge in 1884. *Address:* Mill Lawn, Reigate, Surrey. *T:* Redhill 461.

Died 25 Dec. 1946.

PAINTER, Brig.-Gen. Arnaud Clarke, CMG 1918; *b* 27 Sept. 1863; *e s* of Richard Painter, Ryde, IW; *m* 1st, 1886, Amy Caroline (*d* 1895), *y d* of late Thomas Whistler Smith, Glenrock, Sydney, NSW; one *s* one *d*; 2nd, 1905, Harriet Katherine Theresa, *d* of late Colonel Henry Fyers Turner, CB, Royal Engineers. *Educ:* Clifton College; Royal Military Academy, Woolwich. Lieut in Royal Engineers, 1883; Capt. 1891; Major, 1900; Lt-Col 1907; Colonel, 1911; Brig.-Gen. 1915; retired, 1919; in India, China, Japan, Mediterranean; employed in Ordnance Survey of Great Britain, 1896–1903; Chief Engineer Coast Defences, Southern Command, 1914; Chief Engineer, Malta Command, 1915–19; served in European War (Dardanelles), 1915; Serbian Order of the White Eagle. *Address:* c/o Lloyds Bank Ltd, 6 Pall Mall, SW1.

Died 23 Nov. 1945.

PAKEMAN, Sir John, Kt 1927; CBE 1919; CC, Solicitor; *b* 22 July 1860; *m* 1881, Florence, *d* of Major Thomas Drever; three *d. Educ:* privately. Admitted solicitor, 1883; elected a member of the Corporation of London, 1900; Chairman of the Board of Income Tax Commissioners (City of London); late Chairman of the Special Committee of the Corporation; a member of the Traffic Advisory Committee; a member of the London Court of Arbitration; past Chief Commoner; past Chairman of The Bridge House Estates Committee, the Law and City Courts Committee, the Port of London Sanitary Authority, and other Committees and authorities; served on British War Mission to America; Chairman of Sect. II of the Appeal Tribunal of Military Service Acts and other voluntary war work; masonry, PGD. *Publications:* contributions to newspapers, journals, etc. *Recreations:* music, golf, tennis, etc. *Clubs:* Constitutional Guildhall, Royal Automobile, etc.

Died 7 Sept. 1946.

PALÉOLOGUE, Maurice; de l'Académie française; Ambassadeur de france; *b* Paris, 13 Jan. 1859. Diplomatist and writer. *Publications:* Romans: Sur les ruines, Le cilice, etc.; Critique littéraire: Vauvenargues, Alfred de Vigny, Dante, etc.; Histoire: Talleyrand, Metternich et Chateaubriand, Cavour, La Russie des Tsars, Les Entretiens de l'Impératrice Eugénie; The Turning Point, 1935; The Enigmatic Czar, 1938; Les Précurseurs de Lénine, 1939; etc. *Address:* 1 rue de Téhéran, Paris, viii°.

Died 21 Nov. 1944.

PALEY, Col Alan Thomas, CMG 1918; DSO 1915; *b* 11 May 1876; *s* of late Col Edward Paley. Gazetted Rifle Brigade, 1897; Captain, 1902; Adjutant, 1905–07; Major, 1914; Lt-Col 1919; Col 1919; Officer, Company Cadets, RMC 1907–10; General Staff Officer, 3rd Grade, 1913; 2nd Grade, 1915; 1st Grade, 1916; passed Staff College; Assist Commandant RMC, 1918; served NW Frontier, India, 1897–98 (medal with clasp); S Africa, 1902 (Queen's medal 4 clasps); European War, 1914–18 (despatches five times, Bt Lt-Col, Bt Col, DSO, CMG); Iraq, 1920 (despatches, medal with clasp); Brigadier-Gen.; Commanded 143rd Infantry Brigade, 1924–25; retired, 1925; Chevalier Legion of Honour, 1917; appointed a Gentleman-at-Arms in His Majesty's Body Guard, 1925; commanded London Rifle Brigade, 1929–33. *Address:* Coxwell House, Cirencester. *Clubs:* Army and Navy, Travellers'.

Died 4 Sept. 1950.

PALIN, Col Gilbert Walter, CB 1914; CIE 1911; Indian Army; *b* 29 Sept. 1862; 2nd *s* of late Lt-Gen. C. T. Palin, Bombay Staff Corps; *m* 1889, Florence (*d* 1942), *e d* of Colonel C. Swinhoe, Bombay Staff Corps; two *s* one *d. Educ:* Clifton College. 2nd Lieut Royal Denbigh and Merioneth Rifles (3rd Batt. the Royal Welsh Fusiliers), 1880–83; 2nd Batt. North Staffordshire Regt, 1883–85; Indian Army, 1885; joined the Bombay Commissariat Department, 1886; Director of Army Clothing Department, 1906–10; Captain, 1894; Major, 1901; Lieut-Col, 1905; Brevet-Col, 1909; Colonel, 1911; served Zhob Valley Expedition, 1884; Isazai Field Force, 1892; Suakim Force (Indian Brigade), 1896 (Queen's Soudan Medal, Khedive's medal); Tirah (Afridi War), 1897–98 (despatches, Indian medal); Director Supply and Transport Rawalpindi Concentration and Manœuvres for Prince of Wales, 1905; and for Coronation Durbar, Delhi, 1911 (CIE Durbar medal); European War 1914–18 (medal); retired from Army, 1919; an Air Warden, 1938; Good Service Pension, 1932. *Recreations:* fishing, painting. *Address:* c/o National Provincial Bank, Henley-on-Thames, Oxon.

Died 31 Dec. 1946.

PALIN, Lt-Col Randle Harry, CIE 1929; OBE 1919; Kaiser-i-hind medal, 1915; *b* 20 Feb. 1873; 4th *s* of late Lieut General C. T. Palin; *m* 1908, Hilda Mary (*d* 1944), *d* of Francis Kidd; two *d. Educ:* Clifton College; RMC Sandhurst. Commissioned, 1893; joined 2nd Bn KOYLI; appointed to the Indian Army in King George's Own 130th Baluch Infantry, 1894; Cantonment Magistrate of Quetta, 1905; served NW Frontier of India, China 1900–02, and European War (despatches, OBE); Director of Military Lands and Cantonments in the Govt of India, 1924; retired, 1930. Home Guard, 1940–45 (Defence Medal). *Address:* Mount Langton, Rodwell, Weymouth.

Died 20 April 1950.

PALIN, William Mainwaring; *b* Hanley, Staffordshire, 1862; *s* of William Palin, engraver; *m* 1st, 1901, Amy Frances (*d* 1906), *d* of James Mansergh, FRS, PICE; 2nd, Jennie, *γ d* of late Henry Dale of Cobridge, Staffs; one *s* one *d. Educ:* Cobridge Collegiate, Stoke-on-Trent. Apprenticed five years to Josiah Wedgwood & Sons, Etruria, Staffs; at eighteen obtained a National Art Training Scholarship at the Royal College of Art; two years following was in Italy; studied 2 years in Paris under Lefebvre and Boulanger. Principal works: Orphans, RA

1892, Chicago, 1893, Salon, 1894 (purchased by the French Government with diploma), decoration of the M'Ewan Hall, Edinburgh University, 1893–95; The Artist's Mother, RA 1898; decoration of St Clement's Church, Bradford, Yorks, 1900; The Light that Never Fails, RA 1901; A Summer Afternoon, RA 1904; An Idyll Twilight, RBA 1905; Morning Sunshine, Caudebec-en-Caux, RA 1910; Rome International, 1911; Chums, RA 1915. *Address:* 88 Edge Hill, Wimbledon, SW19. *T:* 4527.

Died 23 July 1947.

PALMER; *see* Orpen-Palmer.

PALMER, 1st Baron *cr* 1933, of Reading (this constitutes the first Peerage that has been conferred for services to Music); **Samuel Ernest Palmer;** 1st Bt *cr* 1916; High Sheriff for the County of London, 1924–25; JP 1902; one of HM Lieutenants for City of London; *b* 28 March 1858; *e s* of late Samuel Palmer of Northcourt, Hampstead (one of the founders of Huntley & Palmers); *m* 1881, Amy (*d* 1947), *o d* of Alderman Nottage; two *s.* *Educ:* Malvern College; privately abroad. Director of Huntley & Palmers; Deputy Chairman Great Western Railway, 1906–48; a Vice-President and Member of the Council of the Royal College of Music; and elected 1st Fellow; presented with the Honorary Freedom of the Worshipful Company of Musicians in recognition of the services he has rendered to Music; Founder of the Royal College of Music Patrons' Fund, and the Ernest Palmer Fund for opera study, as well as the Berkshire Scholarship at the same institution, also of two scholarships at the Guildhall School of Music, besides many other gifts towards the encouragement of British Musical Composers and British Executive Artists; a Vice-President Royal College of Organists; Member of Royal Choral Society Committee of Management. *Heir: s* Hon. Ernest Cecil Nottage Palmer. *Address:* 10 Grosvenor Crescent, SW1. *Clubs:* Athenæum, Carlton; Berks County (Reading).

Died 8 Dec. 1948.

PALMER, 2nd Baron *cr* 1933, of Reading; **Ernest Cecil Nottage Palmer;** Bt *cr* 1916; Deputy Chairman, Huntley and Palmers Ltd; Deputy Chairman Huntley, Boorne and Stevens Ltd, Reading; Vice-Chairman Associated Biscuit Manufacturers Ltd; Chartered Accountant; *b* 9 June 1882; *er s* of 1st Baron Palmer and Amy (*d* 1947), *o d* of Alderman Nottage; *g s* of Samuel Palmer of Northcourt, Hampstead (one of founders of Huntley and Palmers); *S* father, 1948; *m* 1909, Marguerite, *d* of William McKinley Osborne, USA Consul-General to Great Britain; two *s* one *d. Educ:* Winchester; Oriel College, Oxford, BA. *Heir: s* Hon. Raymond Cecil Palmer [*b* 24 June 1916; *m* 1941, Victoria Ellen, *o d* of late Captain J. A. R. Weston-Stevens, Maidenhead; one *d.* Harrow; University College, Oxford. Sometime Lieut Grenadier Guards (invalided)]. *Address:* Fernhurst, Pinkney's Green, Berks. *Club:* Oxford and Cambridge.

Died 6 June 1950.

PALMER, Sir Anthony Frederick Mark, 4th Bt *cr* 1886; acting Major RA; late Lieut Royal Northumberland Fusiliers; now on Headquarters Staff, Middle East; *b* 29 Aug. 1914; *s* of late Frederick Charles Palmer, *o s* of 3rd Bt and Mabel, *d* of late Norton J. Hughes-Hallett, OBE, DL, of Lovat House, Cheltenham; *S* grandfather, 1935; *m* 1939, Henriette, *d* of Comdr Francis Cadogan; one *s* one *d. Educ:* Marlborough College; Sandhurst. *Recreations:* athletics (won Army long jump, 1937), tennis, cricket. *Heir: s* Charles Mark, *b* 21 Nov. 1941. *Address:* Shurdington Court, Cheltenham. *T:* Witcombe (Glos) 32. *Club:* Naval and Military.

Died 18 May 1941.

PALMER, Sir (Charles) Eric, Kt 1946; DL; JP; *e s* of late Charles H. Palmer, JP, Bozedown House, Whitchurch, Oxon; *m* Gwenllian Salier, 2nd *d* of David Jones of Melbourne, Australia; one *s* one *d. Educ:* Harrow; Exeter College, Oxford. Chairman of Huntley & Palmers, Ltd; Chairman of Huntley Boorne & Stevens, Ltd; Chairman of Associated Biscuit Manufacturers, Ltd; Pres. of the National Assoc. of Biscuit Manufacturers; Chm. (Independent) Cake and Biscuit War-Time Alliance. High Sheriff of Berkshire, 1926–27; MFH South Berkshire Foxhounds, 1914–16; served European War with 1st Life Guards in France. *Recreations:* hunting, shooting. *Address:* Shinfield Grange, near Reading, Berkshire. *T:* Spencers Wood 83226. *Clubs:* Boodle's; Berks County (Reading).

Died 16 Dec. 1948.

PALMER, Lt-Col Claude Bowes, CBE 1918; DL, JP County Durham; Commanded Northumberland RAMC (V); Hon. Lieut-Col in the Army; formerly County Director of Northumberland and Durham Voluntary Aid Detachments; late Commissioner St John Ambulance Brigade; Knight of Justice Order of St John of Jerusalem; King George Coronation Medal; European War-Victory and British War Medals; *b* London, 29 March 1868; 5th (but *o* surv.) *s* of late Sir Charles Mark Palmer, 1st Bart, MP, and (second wife) Augusta Mary, *d* of late Alfred Lambert of Paris and Massa-di-Carrara; *heir-pres.* to 5th Bt; *m* 1897, Marian (OBE Royal Red Cross (2nd Class), Dame of Grace Order of St John of Jerusalem, Medal of Belgian Order of Elizabeth, despatches European War), *d* of late Edward Charlton Ramsey, S Shields. *Educ:* Cheltenham College; Royal Mining Academy, Freiberg, Saxony. Mining Engineer; formerly Member of Durham Territorial Army Association; Lieutenant late Army Motor Reserve. *Recreations:* motoring (has motored through Algeria and Tunisia), travelling (Far East, Australasia, United States, West Indies, Central America). *Address:* The Spinneys, St Leonard's Hill, Windsor. *T:* Windsor 1155.

Died 7 April 1949.

PALMER, Clement Charlton, MusD Oxon; FRCO; *b* Barton-under-Needwood, Staffs, 1871; *s* of Clement Palmer, JP. *Educ:* Repton. Organist and Choirmaster St Leonard's, Wichnor, 1887–88; Organist St Andrew's, Pau, 1888–89; Assistant Organist Lichfield Cathedral, 1890–97; Organist and Choirmaster Holy Trinity, Burton-on-Trent, 1891–97; Parish Church, Ludlow, 1897–1908; Organist and Master of the Choristers, Canterbury Cathedral, 1908–36; Conductor Ludlow Choral Society, 1897; Presteigne Choral Society, 1899; Leominster Choral Society, 1902; Canterbury Cathedral Musical Society. *Compositions:* Pieces for Organ, Organ Arrangements: Morning, Communion, and Evening Service in E Flat; Evening Service in F Minor; Evening Service in B Flat; Morning and Evening Service in F (men's voices). *Address:* 51 Old Dover Road, Canterbury.

Died 13 Aug. 1944.

PALMER, Edward Timothy; *b* Croydon, 1878. Contested Canterbury, 1918; Greenwich, 1922; MP (Lab) Greenwich, 1923–24 and 1929–31; Secretary Prudential Staff Union; retired, 1934. Essex County Councillor, 1946. *Address:* Cintra, Thundersley Park Road, South Benfleet, Essex. *T:* S Benfleet 2257.

Died 22 April 1947.

PALMER, Sir Eric; *see* Palmer, Sir C. E.

PALMER, Frederick Bernard; Chairman of G. J. Palmer and Sons, Ltd, Proprietors of the Church Times; *b* 1862; *s* of George Josiah Palmer, founder of the Church Times; *m* Ethel Agnes, *e d* of late Sir Thomas Stevenson, MD; one *s. Educ:* Bloxham School. Formerly business manager, and subsequently sole proprietor of the Church Times; Chairman of the governing committee of Bloxham School, Fellow of the Society of SS Mary and Nicholas, Lancing. *Recreations:* riding, travel. *Address:* 7 Portugal Street, WC2.

Died 30 Jan. 1947.

PALMER, Lt-Col Frederick Carey Stuckley S.; *see* Samborne-Palmer.

PALMER, George Henry, FSA; *b* Rochester, 9 March 1871; *s* of late Edward Palmer, Wandsworth; unmarried. *Educ:* King's School, Rochester. Assistant, Victoria and Albert Museum, 1889; Assistant Keeper, 1892; Keeper of the Library, Victoria and Albert Museum, 1897–1931; served European War, Suvla Bay, landing to evacuation, in 2/4 Royal West Kent; afterwards AESO Alexandria, ESO Haifa and Suez (despatches twice); Local Army Welfare Officer, Surrey, since 1940. *Publications:* Rochester Cathedral, in Bell's Cathedral Series; translated Dr P. J. Ree's Nuremberg; contributions to official publications of Victoria and Albert Museum, to the Uses of Libraries, edited by Dr E. A. Baker, and to art magazines. *Address:* 18 Beauchamp Road, East Molesey, Surrey. *T:* Molesey 1822.

Died 2 July 1945.

PALMER, Col Henry Ingham Evered, CMG 1916; *b* Lincoln, 5 April 1862; *s* of Canon G. T. Palmer, Rector of St Mary's Newington; *m* Mary Adelaide (*d* 1942), *y d* of late Major-General R. Murray, CSI, Director of Telegraphs, India. Joined 1st Batt. Worcestershire Regiment, 1883; Indian Army, 1886; commanded the 25th Cavalry Frontier Force, 1910–14; served Miranzaic, 1891 (medal with clasp); Chitral, 1895 (medal with clasp); NW Frontier, India, 1897–98 (wounded, 2 clasps); Waziristan, 1901–02 (clasp); joined Remount Service, Aug. 1914; appointed Deputy Director of Remounts Second Army, France, 1915 (despatches, CMG); Deputy Director of Remounts, Italian Expeditionary Force, 1917 (despatches twice, Commander Crown of Italy). *Address:* c/o Manager, Lloyds Bank, 6 Pall Mall, SW1. *Club:* United Service.

Died 17 Nov. 1943.

PALMER, James Lynwood; *b* Linwood, Market Raison, Lincolnshire; *y s* of late Canon Palmer, Rochester; *m;* no *c. Educ:* King's College, London. Student of no Art School; his pictures have never been shown at any public Exhibition, but he has painted for King George V and the majority of the owners of the most celebrated race-horses of the century in America, France, and Germany, besides hunting and coaching pictures, etc.; painted King George V's horse, Limelight, for the Jockey Club's Jubilee Gift; contributor of sporting articles Morning Post, Evening Standard, English Life, etc. *Recreations:* coaching, hunting, and horses in any form. *Address:* The White House, Heston, Hounslow. *T:* Hounslow 0048. *Clubs:* Boodle's, Chelsea Arts.

Died 22 June 1941.

PALMER, John Leslie; author; *b* 1885; *m* 1911, Mildred Hodson Woodfield; one *s* one *d. Educ:* Balliol College, Oxford (Brackenbury Scholar). Dramatic Critic and Assistant Editor of The Saturday Review, 1910–15; Dramatic Critic of The Evening Standard, 1916–19; War Trade Intelligence Department, 1915–19; Member of the British Delegation of the Peace Conference, Paris, 1919; Permanent Secretariat of the League of Nations, 1920–39; British Broadcasting Corporation, 1939. *Publications:* The Censor and the Theatres, 1912; The Comedy of Manners, 1913; The Future of the Theatre, 1913; Peter Paragon, 1915; The King's Men, 1916; The Happy Fool, 1922; Looking after Joan, 1923; Jennifer, 1926; Studies in the Contemporary Theatre, 1927; Molière, 1930; Timothy, 1931; Ben Jonson, 1934; The Hesperides, 1936; Under the Long Barrow, 1939; Mandragora, 1940. *Recreation:* music. *Address:* 45 Hampstead Way, NW11. *Clubs:* Garrick, Junior Carlton.

Died 5 Aug. 1944.

PALMER, Ven. Joseph John Beauchamp, MA; Vicar of Mudford, Yeovil, since 1921; *b* Wells, Somerset, 10 Feb. 1866; *e s* of late Rev. Joseph Palmer, Rector of West Camel, Somersets, and Elizabeth Harriott Wood, *d* of late John Beauchamp, of Wells, Somersets. *Educ:* Wells Grammar School; privately; St John's College, Camb. (Sizar, Exhibitioner, Scholar, and Naden Divinity Student); BA, 10th Wrangler, 1888; 2nd class Theo. tripos, 1890; MA 1902. Curate of Horningsea, Cambridgeshire, 1889; Missionary CMS, 1891; Principal, Cambridge Nicholson Institution, Kottayam, 1894–1919; Senior Tutor and Dean, London College of Divinity, 1902–03; Examining Chaplain to Bishop in Travancore and Cochin, 1905; Surrogate, 1908; Commissary to Bishop in Travancore and Cochin, 1906; in charge, Lympsham, Blackford and Theale, Dio. Bath and Wells, 1911–12; Archdeacon of Kottayam, 1906–21; in charge St Mark's, Leamington, 1920; East Lydford and Wheathill, 1921. *Recreations:* music and gardening. *Address:* Mudford Vicarage, Yeovil. *TA:* Mudford, Som.

Died 16 Feb. 1942.

PALMOUR, Sir Charles (John Geoffrey), Kt 1946; Senior Partner, Whinney Smith & Whinney; *b* 16 Aug. 1877; *m* 1923, Rose Margaret Campbell. *Educ:* privately. Chartered Accountant; President Institute of Chartered Accountants in England and Wales, 1938–44. *Recreations:* shooting, golf. *Address:* 26 Orchard Court, Portman Square, W1. *Clubs:* Carlton, Thatched House.

Died 20 April 1948.

PANCKRIDGE, Sir Hugh Rahere, Kt 1939; Puisne Judge High Court of Judicature, Calcutta, since 1930; *b* London, 2 Oct. 1885; *o s* of late Rev. Wm Panckridge, MA, Rector St Bartholomew the Great, Smithfield, EC; *m* 1940, Hylda, *widow* of John Arthur Laing Swan, CSI, CIE, ICS. *Educ:* Winchester Coll. (Scholar); Oriel Coll., Oxford (Exhibitioner); 2nd Honour Moderations, 2nd Literæ Humaniores, BA, 1908; MA, 1934. Called to Bar, Inner Temple, 1909; Advocate Calcutta High Court, 1910; 2nd Lieut Indian Army Reserve of Officers, 1914; Lieut, 1916; Captain, 1918; served France and Palestine (despatches); Standing Counsel, Bengal, 1926; Officiating Judge High Court, 1929; Additional Judge High Court, 1929. *Publication:* A Short History of the Bengal Club, 1928. *Recreations:* golf, lawn tennis. *Address:* High Court, Calcutta, India. *Clubs:* Oxford and Cambridge, Oriental; Bengal, Calcutta.

Died 23 Aug. 1942.

PANDYA, Jagannath Bhavanishanker, CBE 1941; Member of Executive Council, Kenya, since 1935; Member of Legislative Council, Kenya, 1925–28 and since 1934; Governing Director of 12 private limited liabilities Companies established in Kenya, Uganda, and Tanganyika, and has business interests in India also; also Governing Director of The Kenya Daily Mail, a daily and weekly paper published in English and Gujrati, the only Indian paper in Kenya and Uganda; *b* 12 Jan. 1891; *m* 1909, Bhagirathi; two *s* two *d. Educ:* Bhavnagar; Kathiawar, India. Arrived in Kenya, 1907; started the business of Pandya and Co., Ltd in 1917; joined public life in 1920; President of Eastern Africa Indian National Congress in 1934 and led Congress deputations to India twice; Founder of Federation of Indian Chambers of Commerce and Industries of Eastern Africa and three times its President; Chairman of Indian Elected Members' Organisation and member of numerous standing committees and Boards for wartime work; Chairman of Indian Man-power Committee; worked as a member of various important Commissions many times; member of East African Delegation to Eastern Group Conference, Delhi, 1940. *Recreation:* gardening. *Address:* PO Box 135, Mombasa, Kenya. *TA:* Pandyaco, Mombasa. *T:* 863. *Clubs:* Indian Sports, Mombasa.

Died 3 Aug. 1942.

PANET, Brig.-Gen. Alphonse Eugene, CB 1919; CMG 1916; DSO 1917; late RE; *b* Quebec, 13 Dec. 1867; *s* of late Col C. E. Panet; *m* 1895, Corinne (*d* 1936), *d* of late Sir H. E. Taschereau, PC; one *s* one *d*. *Educ:* RMC, Kingston, Canada. Entered Army, 1888; India and Burma, 1890–1924; served Waziristan 1894–95 (medal with clasp); European War, 1915–19 (despatches, CB, CMG, DSO, Belgian Croix de Guerre, Bt Col 1918; French Croix de Guerre); retired list, 1924. *Address:* Crumlin Lodge, Crowthorne, Berks. *T:* Crowthorne 126. *Club:* Junior United Service.

Died 30 March 1950.

PANTON, Sir Philip Noel, Kt 1946; MA, MB, BCh Cantab; late Consultant Adviser in Pathology to the Ministry of Health; *b* Wareham, Dorset; *s* of late James and Mrs J. E. Panton. *Educ:* Harrow; Trinity College, Cambridge. Late Clinical Pathologist and Director of the Hospital Laboratories, The London Hospital. *Publications:* Clinical Pathology; papers in medical and scientific journals. *Recreation:* fly fishing. *Address:* Otter's Pool, Bourne End, Bucks.

Died 27 Dec. 1950.

PARDOE, Col Frank Lionel, DSO 1914; DL for Counties of Gloucestershire and Bristol; Vice-Chairman, Gloucestershire Territorial Association, since 1938; Deputy County Army Welfare Officer, Gloucestershire and Bristol, since 1939; Chairman, Gloucestershire County Cadet Committee, since 1947; late 60th Rifles; *b* 26 Feb. 1880; *s* of late Rev. John Pardoe of Leyton, Essex, and Graveley, Herts; *m* 1911, Sybil Margaret, *d* of Captain Clayton Mitchell, RN, of West Highlands, Winchester, and *widow* of C. D. Eyre, 60th Rifles, of Middleton-Tyas, Yorkshire; one *s* one *d*. *Educ:* Eton; Sandhurst. Entered Army, 1900; Captain, 1908; Major, 1915; Lt-Col, 1928; Bt Colonel, 1938; served South Africa, 1899–1902 (Queen's medal 2 clasps, King's medal 2 clasps, wounded); European War, 1914–18 (wounded thrice, despatches four times, DSO); commanded 1st Batt. 60th Rifles, 1928–30; retired pay, 1930; commanded 5th Bn Gloucestershire Regt (TA), 1934–38. OStJ 1947; Defence Medal. *Recreations:* shooting, fishing. *Address:* Bartonbury, Cirencester, Glos. *T:* 289. *Club:* Army and Navy.

Died 10 Aug. 1948.

PARENT, Hon. George; KC; Senator, Barrister; *b* 15 Dec. 1879; *s* of Hon. S. N. Parent and Clara Gendron; *m* Kathleen Grenier; two *s*. *Educ:* Ste Anne de la Pocatière; St Dunstan College PEI; Laval University, Quebec. Politician; Member for Montmorency, 1904–11; Quebec West, 1917–30; President, Citadel Brick, Ltd; Director, Southern Canada; Quebec Power; Liberal Senator for the division of Kennebec. *Recreations:* golf, fishing, curling. *Address:* Battlesfield Park, and 70 St Paul, Quebec. *TA:* Fitpartar. *T:* 5034 and 2–5665. *Clubs:* Quebec Garrison, Kent and Quebec Golf, Quebec; Montreal Reform; Country, Ottawa.

Died 14 Dec. 1942.

PARERA, Grace Moore; Prima Donna of Opera, Concerts, Radio, and Motion Pictures; *m* 1931, Valentin Parera. *Educ:* Ward-Belmont College, Nashville, Tenn; Wilson-Greene School of Music, Washington, DC; in Studios of the outstanding musical maestros of Europe. Debut, Metropolitan Opera in La Bohème, Feb. 1928; Opera Comique in Manon, Paris, Sept. 1928; debut Motion Pictures in the sensational pioneer film featuring grand opera, One Night of Love, in 1933; debut Covent Garden London Opera, May 1935, in La Bohème; Decorations from the Kings of Sweden, Denmark, and Norway, and The American Academy of Arts and Sciences in America. *Publication:* Autobiography, You're Only Human Once, 1944. *Recreations:* golf, tennis, swimming, and writing. *Address:* Far Away Meadows, Sandy Hook, Conn. *Cable Address:* MOPA, New York.

Died 26 Jan. 1947.

PARES, Surg. Lt-Col Basil, CMG 1916; DSO 1915; late Royal Horse Guards; *b* 24 April 1869; *s* of late John Pares; *m* Evelyn, *d* of G. Lambert Whistler; two *s* three *d*. *Educ:* Lancing College; Emmanuel College, Cambridge; St Mary's Hospital, London. Served S Africa, 1899–1901 (Queen's medal 5 clasps); European War, 1914–18 (DSO, CMG); retired pay, 1922. *Address:* Postford, St John's, Woking.

Died 17 Nov. 1943.

PARES, Sir Bernard, KBE 1919; DCL (Toronto); Lecturer on Russian history; FKC London; *b* 1 March 1867; *s* of late John Pares; *m* 1901, Margaret Ellis, 2nd *d* of E. A. Dixon, Colchester; three *s* two *d*. *Educ:* Harrow; Trinity College, Cambridge. University Extension Lecturer, London, Cambridge, Oxford and Liverpool; Reader in Modern Russian History, Liverpool, 1906–08; Secretary to the School of Russian Studies at the University of Liverpool, 1907–17; Professor of Russian History, Language, and Literature, University of Liverpool, 1908–17, and in University of London, 1919–38; Director of the School of Slavonic and East European Studies, 1922–39; Editor of the Russian Review, 1912–14; Secretary to the Anglo-Russian Committee in London, 1909–14; attached to the Russian Army, 1914–17; Russian Red Cross; Soldier's Cross and Medal of St George, 1915–16; attached to HM Ambassador in Petrograd, 1917; White Lion of Czechoslovakia, 3rd class, 1927; several visits to Soviet Russia; temporary Civil Servant, 1939–40; lectured in England on Russia, 1940–42; lectured in USA for the Ministry of Information, and taught in American Universities, 1942–44. *Publications:* Russia and Reform, 1907; Chapters on Russia in the Cambridge Modern History, vol. xii, 1910; Day by Day with the Russian Army, 1915; Letters of the Tsaritsa to the Tsar (Introduction), 1924; The Mischief of being Clever (from Russian of A. Griboyedov), 1925; A History of Russia, 1926; Fables of Krylov (verse translation), 1926 (Penguin ed. 1942); My Russian Memoirs, 1931; Moscow admits a Critic, 1936; The Fall of the Russian Monarchy, 1939; Russia, Penguin Series, 1940, further eds 1941, American eds 1943–1944; Russia and the Peace (America and England), 1944. *Address:* c/o British Consulate-General, 25 Broadway, New York City, USA. *Club:* Athenæum.

Died 17 April 1949.

PARISH, Arthur John, CB 1911; CBE 1919; Instructor Capt. RN (retired); MA; *b* 1861; 2nd *s* of Rev. W. S. Parish, late Rector of Freckenham; *m* 1911, Helen Mary, 2nd *d* of W. Griffiths, CE, 61 Sinclair Road, W; two *d*. *Educ:* King's School, Ely; St Peter's College, Cambridge. *Address:* Afton Lodge, Freshwater, Isle of Wight.

Died 19 Jan. 1942.

PARK, James, Hon. MInstMM; FGS; Emeritus Professor; *b* Thanestone Hall, near Aberdeen, 2 July 1857; 3rd *s* of J. Elphinstone Park; *m* 1st, Frances, *o d* of Capt. W. Rogers, Surrey; three *s* seven *d*; 2nd, Janie, *d* of Jas Gray, St Clair. *Educ:* Church School; Royal College Science, London. Assist Geologist to New Zealand Geological Department, 1878–89; Director Thames School of Mines, 1889–94; Superintendent of group of Thames Mines, 1894–1901; and Consulting Engineer for Anglo-Continental Mining Syndicate; Chairman University Research Board; Professor of Mining and Mining Geology, and Dean of the Mining Faculty, Otago University, 1901–32; retired, 1932; sometime President NZ Institution of Mining Engineers and Otago Institute; sometime Governor NZ Royal Society; President Dominion Mining Congress, 1925–26. *Publications:* Geology of New Zealand; Text-book of Mining Geology, 5th edn; Text-book of Theodolite Surveying, 6th edn; Text-book of Cyanide Process of Gold Extraction, ten edns in New Zealand, England, and Germany; Text-book of Geology, 2nd edn; Assaying and Practical Chemistry, 5th edn; Text-book of Practical Hydraulics, 2nd edn; Official Memoirs on Geology of

Alexandra District; Geology of Cromwell District; Geology of Queenstown District; Geology of Oamaru District and Subdivision of NZ Middle Cainozoic; Geology and Mineral Resources of Western Southland; Alfred Domett's Romance; Recollections of Sir George Grey; Pioneering Days in NZ; over one hundred papers on original research, mostly on Geological subjects, contributed to learned societies. *Recreations:* cricket and mountaineering. *Address:* Otago University, Dunedin, New Zealand. *Club:* Authors'.

Died 28 July 1946.

PARKE, Ernest; JP Warwickshire; Director Northern Newspaper Company, Limited, Darlington; *b* 1860; *s* of Fenning Plowman Parke, Stratford-on-Avon; *m* 1884, Sarah Elizabeth (*d* 1937), *d* of Joseph Blain, Manchester; one *s. Educ:* Stratford-on-Avon Grammar School. *Recreation:* farming. *Address:* Moorlands, Kineton. *T:* Kineton 45. *Club:* National Liberal.

Died 21 June 1944.

PARKER, Brig.-Gen. Arthur, CMG 1915; late 5th (Royal Irish) Lancers; *b* 14 Jan. 1867; 2nd *s* of Lieut-Col C. J. B. Parker, Stonebridge, Grantham, Lincs; *m* 1891, Eleanor Augusta, *d* of Rev. A. D. Hilton, Vicar of Uxbridge Moor; one *d.* Entered army, 1887; Capt. 1894; Maj. 1903; Lt-Col 1913; served S African War, 1899–1902 (despatches twice, Queen's medal 5 clasps, King's medal 2 clasps); European War, 1914–18 (despatches, CMG); retired pay, 1919. *Address:* Love Hill, Langley, Bucks. *Club:* Cavalry.

Died 28 Jan. 1941.

PARKER, Charles Thomas, CBE 1920; JP; Alderman City Council; now Chairman of the Education Committee; *b* 1859; *s* of John Francis Parker, Osbournby, Lincolnshire; *m* 1881, Mary Ann, *d* of Charles Hunt; four *d. Educ:* The Village School, Osbournby. In business as grocer and provision merchant; Mayor City of Lincoln, 1909, 1915, 1916, 1917, and 1918. *Recreation:* gardening. *Address:* Osbournby House, Cross o'th Cliff, Lincoln. *T:* 571.

Died 16 Aug. 1944.

PARKER, Hon. Edmund William; Director of Spassky Copper Mine, Ltd; *b* 2 March 1857; 8th *s* of 6th Earl of Macclesfield; *m* 1883, Fanny Emma (*d* 1942), *d* of Capt. Baldwin of Dunedin, NZ; one *s. Educ:* Eton. Was for 4½ years in Child's Bank; emigrated to New Zealand, 1881; joined the firm of Dalgety & Co. in Dunedin; was with them for 17 years as Manager; and later Superintendent of their NZ branches; returned to England, 1898. *Address:* 51 South Street, Park Lane, W1. *Club:* Boodle's.

Died 27 March 1943.

PARKER, Rev. Ernest Julius, MA (Ex-Archdeacon of Salisbury, S Rhodesia); Rector of Winwick, PO Rugby; *b* 20 Oct. 1872; *s* of late Rev. A. W. Parker, Rowledge Vicarage, Farnham; *m* 1908, May Ford; one *s* four *d. Educ:* Marlborough College; Brasenose College, Oxford (Scholar). Curate of Westbourne, Sussex, 1895–98; St John's, Stamford Hill, N London, 1898–1902; Railway Chaplain, S Rhodesia, 1902–04; Salisbury Cathedral, 1904–32; assistant priest or priest in charge, 1904–13; Rector of Cathedral, 1913–28; native mission work, 1928–32. *Publication:* The People's Chant Book. *Address:* Winwick Rectory, West Haddon, Rugby.

Died 31 Jan. 1942.

PARKER, Col Frederic James, CB 1918; retired; *b* London, 6 April 1861; 4th *s* of Lieut-Col William Parker, JP, DL, Co. Lincoln, of Hanthorpe House, Bourn, Lincolnshire; *m* 1907, Emily Margaret Joan (Daisie), *d* of Henry Bullock, of Radwinter, and late of Faulkbourn Hall, Essex, and *g d* of James Augustus Shiel Bouverie, of Delapre Abbey, Northampton; two *s. Educ:* Tonbridge; Sandhurst. Late commanding 1st Batt. Northamptonshire Regt (old 48th Foot); entered Army, 1882; Adjutant 1st Batt. 1899–1902; served European

War, 1914–18 (despatches three times, CB); special appointment on staff as Commandant on Lines of Communication, graded as an AAG at the War Office. *Recreations:* shooting and fishing. *Address:* Highbridge, Bishopstoke, Hants. *Club:* Junior Constitutional.

Died 8 July 1944.

PARKER, Sir George Phillips, Kt 1919; OBE; Knight Royal Order of Danebrog, 1914; *b* 16 Nov. 1863; *s* of late George Phillips Parker and late Charlotte, *d* of William Brownfield; *m* Aida Maria Mercedes, *d* of Feliz Lassaletta de Vergara; two *s* two *d. Educ:* privately. Admitted solicitor, 1884 (Honours); became partner in Woodcock, Ryland & Parker, 1889; Vice-Chairman of former Board of Guardians of St George's and St Giles', and Member of Holborn Board of Guardians'; Mayor of Holborn, 1913–19; Chairman of Holborn Division of Red Cross Society; Founder of Holborn Red Cross Hospital for discharged Soldiers' and Sailors' Shell-shock Cases, Roehampton, subscribed for by subscriptions of citizens of Holborn; Chairman of Holborn Tribunal, 1916–19; Chairman of War Savings Association, Holborn, etc.; Freemason; Grand Officer, Grand Lodge of Freemasons, Grand Lodge of Master Masons, and Great Priory of Knight Templars. *Publications:* Pamphlets on National Service, and other war work. *Club:* Eccentric.

Died 26 Dec. 1943.

PARKER, Col Henry William Manwaring, CMG 1917, (late) RA; *s* of Captain G. F. Hastings Parker, RN, and Susan, *d* of William Rolles Fryer, and *g s* of Captain Henry Parker, RN, and Lady Frances Parker; *m* 1905, Beatrice Mary (*d* 1944), *d* of W. A. Chaplin, Wyndham Lodge, Melton Mowbray; no *c. Educ:* Charterhouse; RMA, Woolwich. Entered Royal Artillery, 1888; served Isazai Expedition, 1892; NW Frontier of India, 1897–98 (medal and clasp); Waziristan, 1901–02 (despatches, clasp); retired as Major, 1914; served European War, 1914–18; to Belgium with Heavy Artillery of 7th Division, 1914 (despatches, promoted Lieut-Colonel, CMG, Col); JP Hants. *Recreations:* fishing, shooting. *Address:* Rosecroft, Chapel Road, Curdridge, Southampton. *Club:* Army and Navy.

Died 9 Jan. 1948.

PARKER, James, CH 1918; *b* Awthorpe, Lincs, 1863; *m* 1887, Clara Oram, Halifax. *Educ:* Wesleyan School, Louth. Nine years a member Halifax County Borough Council; President Trades Council and member of Chamber of Commerce, 1895–1906; contested Halifax, 1900; MP (Lab) Halifax, 1906–18; Cannock Div. of Staffs, 1918–22; a Lord Commissioner of the Treasury, 1917–22. *Address:* Burnleigh, Chester Road, Halifax.

Died 11 Feb. 1948.

PARKER, James Gordon, PhD, FRIC, FRMS, DSc; late Principal of Leather-sellers Technical College, SE1; *b* Newport, Fife, 1869; *s* of Edward Parker of The Cliff, Newport; *m* 1898, Florence (*d* 1947), *d* of Farnham Budgett; one *s* one *d. Educ:* Madras Coll., St Andrews; Owens Coll., Manchester; Universities of Heidelberg, Göttingen, Strassburg and Paris. Founder and Hon. Secretary of International Association of Leather Trades Chemists, 1897–1912; President, 1912–14 and 1920–21; President of Society of Leather Trades Chemists, 1918–20; member of Supplies Committee (Leather) at War Office, 1914–18, also Allies Commission of Supplies; Order of Leopold, 2nd Class; Crown of Italy, 2nd Class; Medallist, Royal Society of Arts for Research on Decay of Bookbinding Leather. *Publications:* Bookbinding Leather, its Preservation; Value of Tanning Materials; Analytical Methods, Valonia Industry; various Technical Publications on Leather. *Recreations:* golf, motoring. *Address:* Scotscraig, Blackheath, SE3. *T:* Greenwich 0618.

Died 30 April 1948.

PARKER, Louis N., FRAM, FRHistS; Officier de l'Instruction Publique; Hon. Life Governor Royal National Life Boat Institution; dramatist, composer; *b* Calvados, France, 21 Oct. 1852; *o s* of Chas. Albert Parker; *m* Georgiana Bessie (*d* 1919), *e d* of Charles Calder, Sherborne, 1878; two *d. Educ:* abroad. Royal Academy of Music (Fellow, 1898). Upon leaving Royal Academy of Music appointed Director of Music in Sherborne School, 1873, and remained there 19 years. *Publications:* Silvia, The 23rd Psalm, Young Tamlane, and Belle Margaret, all cantatas for solo, chorus, and orchestra; songs; part-songs, etc. *Plays produced,* either alone, as translations, or in collaboration—A Buried Talent; Chris; Taunton Vale; The Love-Knot; Love in a Mist; Rosmersholm; The Bohemians; The Sequel; David; Gudgeons; Once upon a Time; The Blue Boar; The Mayflower; Love-in-Idleness; Rosemary; The Man in the Street; The Spell-bound Garden; Magda; Change Alley; The Vagabond King; The Happy Life; Ragged Robin; The Termagant; The Jest; Man and his Makers; The Sacrament of Judas; Captain Burchell's Luck; The Bugle Call; Cyrano de Bergerac; The Masque of War and Peace, 1900; The Swashbuckler; The Cardinal; L'Aiglon; The Heel of Achilles; The Twin Sister; The House of Burnside; The Optimist; Agatha; The Monkey's Paw; The Sorceress; Beauty and the Barge; Everybody's Secret; The Creole; The Sherborne Pageant; Harlequin; The Duel; The Lady of Dreams; The Warwick Pageant; Jemmy; Mr George; Bury St Edmunds Pageant; Masque of Life; Last Days of St Benet's Abbey; Illusions; The Lady of the Manor; The Dover Pageant; Peter; The Colchester Pageant; The York Pageant; Beethoven; The White Sister; Chanticleer; Sire; Drake; Pomander Walk; The Minuet; Disraeli; Lady of Coventry; Paper Chase; Joseph and his Brethren; David Copperfield; Bluff King Hal; The Masque of War and Peace, 1915; Mavourneen, 1916; Follow the Drum; The Women's Tribute; An English Nosegay; The Aristocrat; Moonshine; The Pageant of Fair Women, 1917; The Treasures of Britain; The Pageant of Freedom, 1918; The Great Day, 1919; Summer is a-comin in, 1919; Typho, Lourdes, 1921; Mr Garrick; A Wreath of a Hundred Roses, 1922; The Golden Triangle; The Lord of Death; Queen Victoria, 1923; Monsieur D'Artagnan; The Right Hand of the Prince; Our Nell, 1924; The Lost Duchess, 1925; A Venetian Wedding, 1926; Marjolaine, 1928; Several of my Lives (autobiography), 1928; Several of my Lives (autobiography), 1928; Their Business in Great Waters; The Bridge; The Invincible Lovers, 1929; Disraeli (novel); The Abyss, 1930; The Walled Garden, 1932; The King of Elba, 1933; A Rogue's Wife, 1934; Le Lys de France (Nancy), 1936; The Pageant of Kenilworth (with Anthony Parker), 1939; Shocks (BBC with A. Blackwood), 1941. *Recreations:* music, remembering. *Address:* Inverteign, Bishopsteignton, S Devon. *T:* 314. *Club:* Garrick.

Died 21 Sept. 1944.

PARKER, Vice-Adm. Patrick Edward, DSO 1919; RN; *b* 1881; *s* of James Edward Parker; *m* 1917, Violet Swinden; one *s.* Served European War, 1914–18 (despatches, DSO, Officer of Crown of Belgium). Assistant Director of Naval Equipment, Admiralty, 1928–30; Naval ADC to the King, 1929–30; Rear-Adm. and retired list, 1930; Vice-Adm., retired, 1935; employed as Commodore RNR from outbreak of hostilities, 1939. *Club:* Hurlingham.

Died Aug. 1941.

PARKER, Hon. Reginald; *b* 1854; *s* of 6th Earl of Macclesfield; *m* 1876, Katharine Mary Linden (*d* 1939), *d* of Henry Ames, Northumberland; three *d. Educ:* Eton. Seven years in a bank, since when a director of companies. *Address:* 103 Rivermead Court, Hurlingham, SW6. *T:* Renown 2872. *Clubs:* Boodle's, St James's.

Died 23 March 1942.

PARKER, Captain Reginald Francis, CB 1919; CMG 1917; RN (retired); serving in Royal Observer Corps on Dartmoor; *b* 1871; *s* of Captain G. F. Hastings Parker, RN; *widower,* one *s* one *d. Educ:* Stubbington House, Fareham. Served in Naval Intelligence Department, 1906–08; retired Captain, 1910; Admiralty Transport Officer at Southampton, 1912–14; Principal Naval Transport Officer, South Wales, 1914–17; served at Admiralty, 1917–19. *Address:* Tristis Cottage, Harford, Ivybridge, S Devon. *T:* Ivybridge 169. *Club:* United Service.

Died 23 Feb. 1946.

PARKER, Richard Barry, JP; FRIBA (retired), PPTPI; architect; *s* of Robert Parker, Buxton; *m* Constance Mabel, *d* of Robert Burton, Norwich; two *s. Publications:* (with Sir Raymond Unwin, PPRIBA) The Art of Building a Home; many papers, etc., on Town Planning. *Address:* Norton Way, Letchworth. *T:* Letchworth 149.

Died 21 Feb. 1947.

PARKER, Robert Lewis, CMG 1930; Associate of Arts; *b* 22 Oct. 1862; *s* of Robert John Parker, late of Launceston; *m* 1st, 1887, Aimée Josephine (*d* 1933), *d* of Hon. Joseph Archer, JP, Panshanger; one *d*; 2nd, 1934, Janet Marion Swaine, Frome, Somerset, England. *Educ:* Launceston Church of England Grammar School. Admitted to Bar, 1884; a founder of and Trustee, Toosey Memorial Hospital, Longford, resigned; Chairman (resigned) of Trustees of Anzac Memorial Hostel, 1919–36; late Trustee of Christ's College, and Trustee of Church property in Tasmania; Chairman Equity Trustee Co. of Tasmania, resigned; Commissioner of Sinking Funds of City of Launceston, resigned; Life Member and Vice-Pres. Launceston Public Library, now taken over by City Council; a Life Fellow of the Royal Empire Society; one of the founders of the Navy League in Launceston; was Chairman of the Tasmanian Flood Relief Committee; Associate Commissioner, Hydro-Electric Department of Government of Tasmania until 1936; Certificate of Merit and Badge, Returned Sailors and Soldiers Imperial League of Australia, 1935; Jubilee Medal, 1935. *Recreations:* golf, photography, philately. *Address:* 18 Adelaide Street, Tasmania.

Died 3 Nov. 1948.

PARKER, Brig.-Gen. St John William Topp, CB 1916; CMG 1918; *b* Passage West, Co. Cork; *m;* one *s* two *d. Educ:* Oxford Military College, Cowley. Joined the 56th (the Pompadours); served for three years at Malta and Cyprus; transferred to the Army Service Corps; served Kareene Expedition and Hut Tax Rebellion in West Africa, 1897–98; Lagos Hinterland, 1898 (West African medal, 2 clasps); volunteered for immediate service in South Africa and left England, 1899; invalided, 1901 (medal, 6 clasps); held administrative billets in Scottish and Western Commands and on promotion to Substantive Colonel was appointed Assist Director of Supplies, War Office; Deputy Director of Supplies and Transport to one of the Armies in France, 1914; Brig.-Gen. 1917 (CMG); retired pay, 1919. *Address:* (temp.): 26 Harcourt Terrace, Earl's Court, SW10.

Died 24 April 1943.

PARKER, Engr Captain William Ramsey, CBE 1919; RN retired; *b* 1862. Chief of Repair Work, NE Coast of Scotland, 1914–19. *Address:* 99 Wick Hall, Hove, Sussex.

Died 1 Dec. 1943.

PARKES, Ernest William, CMG 1935; *b* 23 March 1873; *e s* of William and Annie Parkes, Dublin; *m* 1st, 1902, late Susannah Ellen, 2nd *d* of late James Stimpson Hall, Goorambat, Victoria; two *s*; 2nd, 1928, late Eliza Kate (widow), 3rd *d* of George Keane, Benalla, Victoria. *Educ:* State Schools, Melbourne. Appointed to Government Printing Office, Melbourne, 1887; transferred to Legislative Council Staff of Victoria, 1895;

Junior Officer to first Staff of House of Representatives, Commonwealth of Australia, 1901; Clerk of the House of Representatives, Canberra, 1927–37; Retired from Public Service, 1937. *Recreation:* bowls. *Address:* Huntingdon, Canberra, ACT, Australia. *T:* B 232.

Died 20 April 1941.

PARKES, Louis C., MD; DPH. Late Medical Officer of Health, Chelsea, London; late Consulting Sanitary Adviser to HM's Board of Works. *Address:* Holmbury St Mary, Surrey.

Died 11 Oct. 1942.

PARKHILL, Hon. Sir (Robert) Archdale, KCMG 1936; *b* Paddington, Sydney, NSW, 27 Aug. 1879; *s* of Robert Parkhill and Isabella Chisholm; *m* 1906, Florence Ruth, *d* of John Watts; one *s* one *d. Educ:* Waverley and Paddington Public Schools. MP Warringah in Commonwealth Parliament, 1927–37; Minister for Home Affairs and Minister for Transport of the Commonwealth, Jan.–May, 1932; Minister for the Interior, May–Oct. 1932; Postmaster-General, 1932–34; Minister for Defence, 1934–37; Delegate for Commonwealth of Australia to International Postal Congress, Cairo, 1934; Delegate to Imperial Conference, 1937; Member of Liberal Party. *Recreation:* reading. *Address:* 77 King Street, Sydney, NSW, Australia; 3 Fairfax Road, Bellevue, NSW.

Died 2 Oct. 1947.

PARKINGTON, Thomas Robert, FRSA; Hon. MJI; *b* Ipswich, 1866; *m* Florence Ellen Barratt. *Educ:* British School, and School of Art, Ipswich. Indentured building trade; joined (1886) Sir Gordon Sprigg (formerly of Ipswich), Prime Minister of Cape Colony, in S Africa; engaged for several years in Swaziland and Transvaal erecting milling and gold quartz mining plants; constructed first plant in South Africa for treating quartz mill tailings by cyanide of potassium; returned to Ipswich, and for 34 years public works contractor; also carried out model housing schemes and developed his own estates; served 18 years on Ipswich Dock Commission and Board of Management; Alderman of Ipswich Town Council; active supporter of ambulance work, life member of Suffolk Institute of Archæology, and presented numerous works of art and objects of archæological interest to Victoria and Albert, Colchester and Ipswich Museums, and Christchurch Mansion (Ipswich) collection; 1926–28 saved, restored, furnished, etc., Flatford Mill, Mill House, Willy Lott's Cottage and surrounding estate, and presented them in national trust in memory of John Constable, RA, and for perpetual service of the arts; Officer of the Grand Priory in the British Realm of the Venerable Order of the Hospital of St John of Jerusalem; endowed bed in East Suffolk and Ipswich Hospital; built 50 houses for occupation by ex-Servicemen, 1918–19. *Publications:* My Visit to the Holy Land; South Africa, Recollections of a Pioneer. *Recreations:* art, music, and all kinds of sport. *Address:* Pykenham House, Northgate, Ipswich. *TA:* Parkington's, Ipswich. *T:* 3330. *Club:* Conservative.

Died 26 June 1942.

PARKINSON, Frank; Chairman: Crompton Parkinson Ltd, British Electric Transformer Co. Ltd, and Derby Cables Ltd; *b* 1887; *s* of Joseph Parkinson, Guiseley, nr Leeds; *m* 1st, 1914, Gertrude Elizabeth, *d* of George Hull, Guiseley; 2nd, 1936, Mrs Doris Burke, *d* of J. W. Macduff and of Lady Forrest, Sheffield; one *s. Educ:* Guiseley Day School; Leeds University. *Recreations:* golf and farming. *Address:* Electra House, Victoria Embankment, WC2; Charters, Sunninghill, Berks. *T:* Temple Bar 5911, Ascot 902. *Club:* Union.

Died 28 Jan. 1946.

PARKINSON, Hargreaves; Editor of The Financial News, 1938–45, and of The Financial Times (incorporating The Financial News), Oct. 1945–49; *b* 3 June 1896; *s* of John and Mary Parkinson, Fleetwood; *m*

1924, Constance Purton; one *s* one *d. Educ:* Blackpool Grammar School; King's College, London; London School of Economics. Served European War, France, 1916–19, 235 Siege Battery, RGA; War Trade Intelligence Dept, 1919; Dept of Overseas Trade, 1919–22; National Savings Committee (Asst Press Officer), 1922–23; The Economist, 1923–38 (City Editor, 1928, Associate Editor, 1935). *Publications:* The ABC of Stocks and Shares, 1925; The Small Investor, 1930; Scientific Investment, 1933; Ordinary Shares, 1944; The Hatch System, 1946; Advanced Hatch, 1949. *Recreations:* music, walking, reading about Antarctic exploration. *Address:* Pines Crest, Pelhams Walk, Esher. *T:* Esher 1247. *Club:* Reform.

Died 23 May 1950.

PARKINSON, John, MA, ScD (Cantab), FGS, FRGS; *b* London, 1872; *m* 1897, Eleanor F. Whitlock; one *s* one *d. Educ:* University College, London; St John's College, Cambridge. Granted British Association Table in Zoology (research on variations of Mollusca) at Naples, 1897–98. Lecturer in Geology and Geography, Harrow, 1902–03; Principal, Mineral Survey, Southern Nigeria, 1903–06; Geologist to Liberian Development Co., WCA, 1906–07, travelling principally along lower and middle reaches of the St Paul River; subsequently engaged in economic geology, largely work connected with petroleum in West Africa, Kenya, Trinidad (Chief of Geological Staff); Venezuela (Chief of Geological Staff); India and Burma and Tanganyika Territory; Leader, British Museum (Nat. Hist.) Expedition to East Africa, 1927–28; conducted Water Reconnaissance for Colonial Office (Northern Frontier District) Kenya and Jubaland, travelling up to Abyssinian Frontier, 1914–15; awarded Lyell Fund Geological Society, 1915; Geologist to Water Supply Development Scheme in British Somaliland, 1931–32; temporarily attached to Mining and Geological Department, Kenya Colony, 1940; later to Ministry of Economic Warfare; left through illness, 1942. For geological study has visited Ceylon and Canada. *Publications:* The Dinosaur in East Africa, 1930; two novels: A Reformer by Proxy, 1909, and Other Laws, 1911; about 40 papers in scientific periodicals on Geological and Geographical subjects, also occasional short articles, reviews, etc. *Recreation:* writing. *Address:* 144 Bishop's Mansions, SW6.

Died 19 July 1947.

PARKINSON, John Allen, CBE 1931; MP (Lab) Wigan since Dec. 1918; *b* Hindley Green, Lancashire, 15 Oct. 1870; *m* 1st, Alice (*d* 1904), *d* of J. Pilkington; 2nd, 1905, Ida Alice, *d* of W. Atkinson. Checkweigher, 1906; a member of Abram UD Council, 1908; JP Lancaster, 1908; Member of the Lancashire County Council, 1915–19; Miners' Agent Lancashire and Cheshire Miners' Federation, 1917; Comptroller of the King's Household, 1924; a Lord Commissioner of the Treasury, 1929–31; Parliamentary Secretary, Ministry of Transport, 1931; a Labour Whip, 1924; Member of Mine Managers Examination Board, 1928–29; Member of Standing Joint Committee, Lancashire County Council, 1936. *Address:* Glenthorne, Orrell Mount, N Wigan, Lancashire.

Died 7 Dec. 1941.

PARKYN, William Samuel, ARCA; ARWA; SMA; marine and landscape artist; member of Pastel Society; *b* 14 July 1875; *e s* of Col G. J. Parkyn, late RASC; *m* 1913, Margaret, *e d* of Rev. Benjamin William Day; Rector St Peter's, Sandwich (retd). *Educ:* Blackheath; Rochester. Studied Art, Blackburn School, London, and under Mr Louis Grier at St Ives. Started painting as a profession at 22; makes special study of ships, Naval and Merchant Service also sand-dunes; exhibits in Royal Institute, Royal Academy, and other Exhibitions. *Recreation:* walking. *Address:* Pentire, The Lizard, Cornwall. *T:* Lizard 258. *Club:* St Ives Arts.

Died 7 Oct. 1949.

PARLETT, Sir Harold George, Kt 1924; CMG 1921; *b* 2 Nov. 1869; *s* of G. W. Parlett; *m* Ethel, *d* of Gordon Malzard, Jersey; two *s* one *d. Educ:* privately. Junior Clerk in the Ecclesiastical Commission, 1889–90; resigned; Student Interpreter in Japan, 1890; Acting Registrar of HM Court in Yokohama, 1898–99; Assistant Japanese Secretary at HM Legation in Tokyo, 1899–1904; Acting Consul at Nagasaki, 1905–06; Vice-Consul at Dairen, 1907; Vice-Consul at Hakodate, 1908; Consul at Dairen, 1910; seconded for service with the late Ministry of Information, 1918–19; Japanese Counsellor of HM Embassy in Tokyo, 1919–27; retired, 1927; employed temporarily by the Foreign Office, 1928–35, by the Ministry of Information in 1940, and again by the Foreign Office from 1941. *Publications:* A Brief Accountant of Diplomatic Events in Manchuria, 1929; joint compiler with E. M. Hobart-Hampden of An English-Japanese Dictionary of the Spoken Language. *Recreations:* shooting, fishing. *Address:* Heian, Sway Road, Lymington, Hants.

Died 28 June 1945.

PARMOOR, 1st Baron *cr* 1914 of Frieth; **Charles Alfred Cripps;** PC 1914; KCVO 1908; KC 1890; MA; Lord President of the Council, 1924 and 1929–31; British Representative on the Council of the League of Nations, Geneva, and Delegate of the British Empire to the Assembly, 1924; Leader of the House of Lords, 1929–31; Member of the Judicial Committee of the Privy Council, specially appointed, 1914; *b* 3 Oct. 1852; *s* of Henry William Cripps, QC; *m* 1st, 1881, Theresa (*d* 1893), *d* of Richard Potter; four *s* one *d*; 2nd, 1919, Marian Emily, *d* of late Rt Hon. J. E. Ellis and Mrs Ellis, Wrea Head, Scalby, Yorks. *Educ:* Winchester (scholar); New College, Oxford. 1st Class Math. Mods., 1872; 1st Class History, 1874; 1st Class Law, 1875; 1st Class BCL, 1876; Senior Studentship Inns of Court, 1877; Fellow of St John's College, Oxford, and Winchester College. Hon. Fellow, New College, Oxford; Attorney-General to the Prince of Wales, 1895; reappointed 1901 and 1912; Chairman of Canterbury House of Laymen; First Chairman House of Laity in Church Assembly; MP (C) Stroud Division of Gloucestershire, 1895–1900; Stretford Division of Lancs, 1901–06; (U) Wycombe Division, Bucks, 1910–14; Vicar-General of Canterbury, 1902–24; Chancellor and Vicar-General of York, 1900; Chairman and Vice-Chairman of Quarter Sessions in Bucks, 1899–1925. *Publications:* Principles of Compensation; A Retrospect, 1936; editor, Laws of the Church and Clergy. *Recreations:* football Capt. Winchester; Soccer Oxford Blue, Soccer Cup, 1873; farming. *Heir: s* Hon. Alfred Henry Seddon Cripps. *Address:* Parmoor, Henley-on-Thames.

Died 30 June 1941.

PARNWELL, Sidney Arthur; *b* 1880; 3rd *s* of late J. Parnwell, Brampton, Huntingdon; *m*; one *s*. Articled to Daniel Watney & Sons, Land Agents and Surveyors; after qualifying as a Fellow of the Surveyors' Institution entered the Great Northern Railway (Surveyors' Department); Land Agent to G. E. Railway, 1909; Assistant to the General Manager, 1915; Secretary to the Company, 1916; Acting General Manager, 1918; Assistant General Manager, 1919; Divisional General Manager, Southern Area L. and NE Railway, 1922; now retired, and practising as a Surveyor in partnership with Daniel Watney and Sons, 4a Fredericks Place, Old Jewry, London EC2. *T:* Kelvin 1400; (temp): The Hyde, Gt Missenden Bucks.

Died 26 Nov. 1944.

PARODI, Ernest Victor; *b* 1870; *s* of late Richard E. Parodi, Gibraltar; *m* 1910, Cleo, *e d* of late William John Peacock, Gibraltar. *Educ:* Stonyhurst. Called to Bar, Inner Temple, 1893; Solicitor-General of Northern Nigeria, 1903; Judge of Supreme Court, Northern Nigeria, 1910–13; a Judge of the Supreme Court of Sierra Leone and Judge of the Circuit Court of the Protectorate, 1913; acted on various occasions as Attorney-General, Northern Nigeria, 1903–08; as Chief Justice, Northern Nigeria, 1908–12; and as Chief Justice of Sierra Leone, 1913–21.

Died 9 Aug. 1944.

PARR, Cecil William Chase, CMG 1923; OBE; *s* of late Harington Welford Parr, Colonial Civil Service, of Titchfield, Hants. Entered Federated Malay Civil States Service, 1889; Acting Agent, Malay States Information Agency, 1912; Governor of British North Borneo, 1913–15; British Resident, Pahang, 1916; Perak, FMS, 1921; served with Remounts in France, 1915; Major in Malay States Volunteers; raised and trained a corps (OBE). *Recreations:* riding, polo, shooting.

Died 26 May 1943.

PARR, Hon. Sir (Christopher) James, GCMG 1935; KCMG 1925; CMG 1914; Barrister; *b* 18 May 1869; *s* of late Reuben Parr, Waikato, NZ; *m* 1st, 1895, Ethel Clara Haszard (*d* 1933); four *d*; 2nd, 1938, Barbara Mary Whitworth, widow. *Educ:* primary schools; Auckland Grammar School and University. Member Auckland University Council and Auckland Grammar School Board; Mayor of Auckland, 1911–15; MP Eden, Auckland, 1914–26; Minister of Public Health, 1920–23; Minister of Justice, New Zealand, 1923–26; Postmaster-General, 1925–26, and Minister of Education, 1920–26; High Commissioner in London for the Dominion of New Zealand, 1926–29 and second term, 1934–36; Member and Leader of Legislative Council of New Zealand, 1931–33; Member of NZ Parliamentary Commission and Visit France and Great Britain, 1916; Representative of New Zealand at League of Nations, 1926, 1927, 1928, 1929, and 1934; Member of Imperial Defence Committee, 1928; Member of Imperial Economic Committee, 1934. *Recreation:* yachting. *Address:* New Zealand House, 415 Strand, WC2. *Clubs:* Travellers'; Northern, Auckland; Wellington, Wellington.

Died 2 May 1941.

PARRY, Very Rev. Albert William, MA, DSc (Lond.); Dean of St David's 1940–49; Canon of St David's Cathedral, 1921; Treasurer, 1930; *s* of late J. Parry, Beechcroft, Rhyl; *m* Katie, *d* of late Rev. T. Mortimer Green, Registrar of University College, Aberystwyth. *Educ:* University College, Aberystwyth; St Michael's College, Llandaff. Honours in English Language and Literature at BA exam.; Honours in Economics and Political Science at BSc exam. Curate of St John's Church, Cardiff, 1900–01; Lecturer and Tutor at St Luke's College, Exeter, 1901–02; Headmaster, All Saints School, Clifton, 1902–03; Professor of Education, University College, Exeter, 1903–08; Principal, Trinity College, Carmarthen, 1908–40; Chaplain to the Forces, attached South Wales Infantry Brigade, 1915–19; Hon. Chaplain Forces, 1934; formerly Editor Llan and Church News, the Organ of the Church in Wales. *Publication:* Education in England in the Middle Ages. *Recreations:* golf, tennis.

Died 18 Sept. 1950.

PARRY, Charles de Courcy, CBE 1920; *b* 1869; *y s* of Capt. F. J. Parry (RMLI), late HM Inspector of Constabulary; *m* 1895, Gwendoline Mary, *e d* of late G. W. Wilkinson, J. P. Risca, Monmouthshire; one *s. Educ:* Repton School. Chief Constable of Cumberland and Westmorland, 1902–20; served also in the following Police Forces: Derbyshire, Bristol, Monmouthshire, Kent (Deputy Chief Constable), Bath (Chief Constable); and Cumberland and Westmorland (Chief Constable), 1902–20; one of HM's Inspectors of Constabulary, 1927–30; JP Worcestershire, 1924; JP Gloucestershire, 1933. *Address:* Glebe Cottage, Ross-on-Wye. *Club:* Junior Carlton.

Died 19 Nov. 1948.

PARRY, His Honour Sir Edward Abbott, Kt 1927; *b* 2 Oct. 1863; *s* of John Humffreys Parry, Serjeant-at-Law; *m* 1st, Helen (*d* 1932), *d* of Thomas Hart, FGS, Grange-over-Sands; one *s* two *d*; 2nd, 1936, Ellen Ann Page. Barrister Middle Temple, 1885; County Court Judge, Manchester, 1894–1911; Chairman West Kent Appeal Tribunal, 1916; Industrial Unrest Commissioner NW Area, 1917; President Pensions Appeal Tribunal, 1917–18; Judge of County Court, Lambeth, 1911–27. *Publications:* Letters from Dorothy Osborne to Sir William Temple, 1887; Life of Macklin, 1890; Katawampus, 1895; Butter-scotia, 1896; Katawampus Kanticles, 1896; The First Book of Krab, 1897; The Scarlet Herring, 1899; The Story of Don Quixote, 1900; Pater's Book of Rhymes, 1901; England's Elizabeth (with Louis Calvert), produced Theatre Royal, Manchester, April, 1901; Katawampus, Children's Play (with Louis Calvert), produced Dec. 1901, Prince of Wales's Theatre; revised edition Dorothy Osborne's Letters, 1903; with Fred. Mouillot, What the Butler Saw, Wyndham's Theatre, 1905; Judgments in Vacation, 1911; What the Judge Saw, 1912; The Law and the Poor, 1914; The Law and the Woman, 1916; with Lt-General Sir A. E. Codrington; Pensions; Past and Present, 1918; What the Judge Thought, 1922; The Drama of the Law, 1924; The Overbury Mystery, 1925; Vagabonds All, 1926; Berrington, and The Gospel and the Law, 1928; The Bloody Assize, 1929; Concerning Many Things, 1929; Queen Caroline, 1930; The Persecution of Mary Stewart, 1931; My Own Way, 1932. *Address:* Clarendon, Sevenoaks. *T:* Sevenoaks 233. *Clubs:* Garrick, Green Room, Reform.

Died 1 Dec. 1943.

PARRY, Most Rev. Edward Archibald, DD; *e s* of Edward Parry, Suffragan Bishop of Dover (*s* of Admiral Sir William Edward Parry, Kt, the Arctic Navigator), and Matilda, *d* of Benjamin Williams of Hillingdon, Middlesex; *godson* of Archbishop Tait. *Educ:* Winchester; Oriel College, Oxford (2nd class Theology); read for Holy Orders with Dean Vaughan at the Temple and at Llandaff. Ordained, 1883; Assistant Curate of St Mary, Acton, Middlesex, 1883–88; Resident Chaplain to Bishop (Thorold) of Rochester, 1889–1990; Rector of Sundridge, Kent, 1890–98; Vicar of St Mark, New Milverton, Leamington, 1898–1900; Bishop of Guiana, 1900–21; Archbishop of West Indies, 1917–21. *Recreations:* books, travel. *Address:* Deanery, Port of Spain, Trinidad. *Club:* Athenæum.

Died 1 Jan. 1943.

PARRY, Sir (Frederick) Sydney, KBE 1925; CB 1902; *b* 5 June 1861; *s* of Right Rev. Edward Parry, Bishop Suffragan of Dover (*d* 1890); *m* 1891, Anna Mary, *d* of late Very Rev. Hon. W. H. Fremantle, Dean of Ripon; one *s* one *d*. *Educ:* Winchester; Balliol College, Oxford. Appointed to Board of Trade, 1885; Treasury, 1886; Assistant Private Secretary to Chancellor of Exchequer, 1888–92; Private Secretary to First Lord of the Treasury, 1897–1902; Deputy Chairman of Board of Customs, 1904–09, and of Board of Customs and Excise, 1909–25. *Address:* Hooke Hall, Uckfield, Sussex. *Club:* Athenæum.

Died 22 May 1941.

PARRY, Lt-Col Henry Jules, CBE 1919; DSO 1900; MB, RAMC; retired, 1910; *b* 5 Feb. 1867; *m* 1899, Helen Dorothea Elizabeth Cockburn, *d* of late Robert Pitcairn, Barrister-at-law. Served South Africa, 1899–1902 (despatches, Queen's medal 5 clasps, King's medal 2 clasps, DSO); European War, 1914–19 (Bt Lt-Col). *Address:* Trebarwith, 2 Keswick Road, Boscombe. *Club:* Boscombe.

Died 23 Feb. 1944.

PARRY, Sir Sydney; *see* Parry, Sir F. S.

PARSONS, Hon. Sir Angas; *see* Parsons, Hon. Sir H. A.

PARSONS, Lt-Col Durie, CMG 1919; DSO 1917; *b* 1872; *m* 1915, Frances May (*d* 1926), *d* of Captain R. B. Needham, RN; one *d*. Served West Africa, 1898 (medal and clasp); South African War, 1899–1902 (Queen's medal and six clasps, King's medal and two clasps); European War, 1914–18 (despatches four times, CMG, DSO, Bt Lieut-Colonel); retired pay, 1920. *Address:* St George's Hill Golf Club, Weybridge. *T:* Weybridge 406.

Died 3 Aug. 1945.

PARSONS, Major Edward Howard Thornbrough, CBE 1918; DL, JP; *b* 12 March 1868; *s* of late Capt. Edward Thornbrough Parsons, RN; *m* 1913, M. M. Winifred Glen, *d* of Sir Thomas Glen-Coats, 1st Bart; two *s*. *Educ:* Clifton; Royal Military Academy, Woolwich. Royal Artillery, 1888; RFA; and RHA in S African War, 1899–1900 (severely wounded, despatches twice); Chief Constable Metropolitan Police, 1903–23; is a Knight of Grace of the Order of St John of Jerusalem. *Address:* Fordbank, Milliken Park, Renfrewshire; Carskiey, Southend, Argyll. *Clubs:* Army and Navy; Royal Northern Yacht.

Died 24 Aug. 1946.

PARSONS, Frank Bett, MA, MD (Cantab), FRCP (Lond.), Physician; Physician to Addenbrooke's Hospital, Cambridge and Papworth Village Settlement; *b* 29 Oct. 1902; *s* of Stephen Parsons, Chatteris, Cambs; *m* 1927, E. W. Sabberton; one *s* one *d*. *Educ:* Wellingborough Downing College, Cambridge; St Bartholomew's Hospital. Resident Medical Officer, Maida Vale Hospital; Hon. Secretary Section of Anæsthesia, British Medical Association 1930 and 1932; Fellow Royal Society of Medicine. *Publications:* various papers in medical and scientific journals. *Recreation:* travel. *Address:* 56 Trumpington Street, Cambridge; 77 Grange Road, Cambridge. *T:* Cambridge 2769.

Died 4 Dec. 1948.

PARSONS, Frederick Gymer, DSc Lond., FRCS, FSA; Research Fellow in Anthropology at St Thomas's Hospital; late Professor of Anatomy, University of London; Lecturer at St Thomas's Hospital and at Bethlem Royal Hospital; *b* 1863; *m* Mary Parker (*d* 1915); two *s*. *Educ:* St Thomas's Hospital. Demonstrator and Lecturer at St Thomas's Hospital; Lecturer at London School of Medicine for Women; Hunterian Professor at Royal College of Surgeons; Senior Warden, Apothecaries' Hall; Examiner at the University of Oxford, Cambridge, Aberdeen, London, Birmingham, National University of Ireland, University of Wales, Royal College of Physicians, Royal College of Surgeons, Apothecaries' Hall, and other bodies; President Anatomical Society; Vice-Pres. Royal Anthropological Institute; President Section H British Association. *Publications:* Practical Anatomy, 1912; The Earlier Inhabitants of London, 1927; The History of St Thomas's Hospital, vol. i 1932; vol. ii 1934; vol. iii 1936; thirty articles in Encyclopædia Britannica; over sixty papers on anatomical, anthropological, and zoological subjects. *Recreation:* gardening. *Address:* Orchard Cross, Whiteleaf, Bucks. *Club:* Athenæum.

Died 11 March 1943.

PARSONS, Godfrey Valentine Hope; Barrister-at-law; Stipendiary Magistrate for the City of Cardiff since 1946; *b* 24 Sept. 1894; *s* of His Honour late Judge Albert Parsons, KC, and Ada Julia Harrison; unmarried. *Educ:* Clifton College, Bristol. Captain and Adjutant 15th Brigade, Royal Horse Artillery, 29th Division, 1914–18, and ADC to the CRA, Army of the Rhine, 1918–19; called to Bar, Middle Temple, 1922; Marshal to the Lord Chancellor (Viscount Sankey); practised on Northern Circuit and South Wales Circuit, 1922–46. *Recreations:* riding, fishing, golf. *Address:* The Law Courts, Cardiff. *T:* Cardiff 938.

Died 16 March 1948.

PARSONS, Hon. Sir (Herbert) Angas, KBE 1945; Kt 1936; Judge of Supreme Court of S Australia, 1921–45; Senior Puisne Judge, 1927–45; Order of Merit of the Rising Sun (Japan) 1921; KC 1916; *b* North Adelaide, 23 May 1872; *e s* of late Hon. John Langdon Parsons, formerly Minister of Education of South Australia, Government Resident of Northern Territory and Member of Parliament of South Australia, and Rosetta, *g d* of George Fife Angas, Father and Founder of South Australia; *m* 1900, Mary Elsie, *e d* of late Hon. Sir Langdon Bonython, KCMG; two *s. Educ:* Private Alfred College; Roseworthy Agricultural College; University of Adelaide (LLB, 1897). Barrister, South Australia, 1897; Attorney-General of South Australia, 1897; Attorney-General of South Australia and Minister of Education, 1914; Member South Australian House of Assembly, 1912–14, 1918–20; Acting Chief Justice, 1935–36; Vice-Chancellor, Warden of the Senate and Member of the Council of the University of Adelaide; President Royal Society of St George (South Australian Branch), 1922–25; Commissioner representing SA at the Franco-British Exhibition, London, 1908; sometime Member of the Council of the South Australian Law Society; President of the Automobile Association of SA, 1910–21; President of the Good Roads Association of SA, 1913–21; President League of Empire (South Australian Branch), 1920–21; Hon. Consul for Japan in SA, 1903–21. *Address:* Bonython, East Terrace, Adelaide, Australia. *Club:* Adelaide.

Died 2 Nov. 1945.

PARSONS, Sir Leonard Gregory, Kt 1946; FRS; MD, FRCP; FRCOG; FFR; Dean of Faculty of Medicine and Emeritus Professor of Paediatrics, University of Birmingham; Consulting Physician United Birmingham Hospitals; member of Gen. Medical Council; *b* 25 Nov. 1879; *s* of T. L. Parsons, Four Oaks, Birmingham; *m* 1908, Ethel May Mantle; one *s* one *d. Educ:* King Edward's School, Aston; Univ. of Birmingham. Arris and Gale Lecturer, Royal College of Surgeons, 1912; Capt. RAMC (TF), 1914–23; temp. Major RAMC, 1916–19; Officer in charge Medical Division 36th General Hospital, British Salonica Force attached to Royal Serbian Army, 1916–18; Officer in charge Medical Division, 48th General Hospital, British Salonica Force, 1918–19; Order of St Sava of Serbia, 1917; Goulstonian Lecturer, Royal College of Physicians, 1924; Ingelby Lecturer, University of Birmingham, 1928; Vice-President International Congress of Pædiatrics, Stockholm, 1930; Rachford Memorial Lecturer, University of Cincinnati, 1931; President Children's Section, Royal Society of Medicine, 1932–33; Withering Lecturer University of Birmingham, 1937; Schorstein Memorial Lecturer, London Hospital, 1938; President British Pædiatric Assoc. 1942–45; Moxon Medal, RCP, 1942; Charles West Lecturer, RCP, 1943; Blair Bell Lecturer RCOG, 1945; Blackader Lecturer Canadian Medical Association, 1946; Harveian Orator, RCP, 1950; Harben Lecturer, The Royal Inst. of Public Health and Hygiene, 1950; Hospital Officer (No. 9 Region), Ministry of Health, 1941–45. *Publications:* various contributions to medical journals. *Address:* 58 Calthorpe Road, Edgbaston, Birmingham. *T:* Edgbaston 0904; Hillfield, Four Oaks, Warwickshire. *T:* Four Oaks 69.

Died 17 Dec. 1950.

PARSONS, Rt Rev. Richard Godfrey, DD; Bishop of Hereford since 1941; *b* Pendleton, Lancs, 12 Nov. 1882; *o s* of late Wm Parsons of Abingdon, formerly Secretary of Bengal Chamber of Commerce, and Bertha, *d* of Wm Waddelow Best, MD, of Thetford; *m* 1912, Dorothy, *o d* of late Francis Gales Streeter of Littlehampton and Dunsfold; one *s. Educ:* Durham School; Magdalen College, Oxford (Classical Demy); Cuddesdon College; 2nd Class Moderations, 1903; 1st Class Lit.Hum., 1905; 1st Class Hon. Theology, 1906; BA, 1905; Liddon

Theological Student, 1906; MA, 1908; BD and DD, 1924; Hon. DD Prague (John Hus Faculty), 1946. Deacon and Priest, 1907; Curate of Hampstead Parish Church, 1907; Fellow, Praelector, and Chaplain of University Coll., Oxford, 1907–11; Examining Chaplain to Bishops Ryle and Talbot of Winchester, 1909–24, to Bishops Knox and Temple of Manchester, 1919–26; Principal of Wells Theological College and Prebendary of S Decuman's in Wells Cathedral, 1911–16; Chaplain to the Forces, 1916–17; Vicar of Poynton, Cheshire, 1916–19; Rector of Birch in Rusholme, Manchester, 1919–31; Suffragan Bishop of Middleton, 1927–32; Hon. Canon of Manchester Cathedral, 1926–30; Canon Residentiary and Subdean of Manchester Cathedral, 1931–32; Bishop of Southwark, 1932–41; Select Preacher, Cambridge, 1928; Oxford, 1937 and 1939; Dean of the Faculty of Theology in the Univ. of Manchester, 1929–30; Hon. Fellow of Univ. College, Oxford, 1942. Visitor of S Michael's College, Tenbury. *Publications:* Essay on Interpretation of Christ in 'Foundations,' 1912; Joint Editor of the Outline of Christianity, 1926. *Address:* The Palace, Hereford. *Club:* Travellers'.

Died 26 Dec. 1948.

PARTRIDGE, Sir Bernard, Kt 1925; artist; principal cartoonist, Punch; *b* London, 11 Oct. 1861; *γ s* of late Professor Richard Partridge, FRS, President Coll. of Surgeons, Prof. of Anatomy to Royal Academy, etc., whose brother, John Partridge, was Portrait Painter Extraordinary to Queen Victoria; *m* 1897, Lydia Faith Harvey. *Educ:* Stonyhurst Coll. Stained-glass designing and decorative painting, 1880–84; worked for press and book illustration from 1884 to present time; joined staff of Punch, 1891. Paints occasionally in oil, water, and pastel; ex-member of Royal Institute of Painters in Water-Colours and the New English Art Club; was at one time on the stage. *Recreation:* golf. *Address:* 10 Holland Park Road, Kensington, W14. *T:* Western 5808. *Club:* Athenæum.

Died 9 Aug. 1945.

PARTRIDGE, Rt Rev. Frank, DD (Lamb.), Hon. DD (Lond.), BA; Bishop of Portsmouth since 1936; late Secretary of Corporation of the Church House; Hon. Secretary of the Queen Victoria Clergy Fund; *b* 31 Dec. 1877; *s* of John Wood Partridge, formerly of St John, Newfoundland; *m* 1910, Elizabeth M., *γ d* of late William Barton, Whitby; two *s* one *d. Educ:* privately; University of London; Cuddesdon. Assistant Curate of Hawarden, 1906–10; Secretary of Bishop of Chichester's Fund, 1910–18; Chichester Diocesan Board of Finance, 1912–18; Editor, Chichester Diocesan Kalendar, 1914–19; Chichester Diocesan Gazette, 1915–19; Secretary, Chichester Diocesan Synod, 1914–19; Chaplain to the Bishop of Chichester, 1913–19; Financial Secretary of the National Assembly of the Church of England, 1921–34; Sec. of the Central Church Fund, 1918–34; Secretary of the Legal Board of the Church Assembly, 1924–33; Secretary of the Press and Publications Board, 1923–33. Canon and Prebendary of Sidlesham in Chichester Cathedral, 1918–34; Archdeacon of Oakham and Canon Residentiary of Peterborough Cathedral, 1934–36; Chaplain to the King, 1934–36; Examining Chaplain to Bishop of Peterborough, 1935–36. Proctor in Convocation for the Diocese of Chichester, 1921–34. *Publications:* The Roffensian Register (2nd edition), 1908; The Soul of Wealth, 1918; TAB; A Memoir of Thomas Allnutt, 2nd Earl Brassey, 1921; Disestablishment, 1929; The Church Assembly and the Church, 1930; many articles in reviews and newspapers. *Recreations:* cricket, classical literature. *Address:* Bishopswood, Fareham, Hants; Church House, Westminster, SW1. *T:* Fareham 3247. *Clubs:* Athenæum; Royal Naval, Portsmouth.

Died 1 Oct. 1941.

PASCOE, Sir Edwin Hall, Kt 1928; MA, ScD (Cantab); DSc (London); FGS; Fellow, Royal Asiatic Society, Bengal; *b* 17 Feb. 1878; *e s* of late Edwin Pascoe of Montague House, Barnet, Hertfordshire; *m* Mia, *d* of James MacLean of Beauly, Inverness; no *c. Educ:* St John's College, Cambridge (Foundation Scholar). Joined the Geological Survey of India, 1905; Kangra Earthquake Investigation, 1905; Survey of the Burma Oilfields, 1905–09; NE Assam, 1910; accompanied the Makwari Punitive Expedition, Naga Hills, 1910; NE Assam, Punjab, and NW Frontier, 1912; deputed to the Persian Gulf, Arabian Coast, and W Persia, 1913; accompanied the Slade Oilfields Commission in Persia and the Persian Gulf, 1913–14; Punjab and NW Frontier, 1914–15; Lieut Indian Army, Reserve of Officers, 1915, attached 32nd Sikh Pioneers; attached 128th Pioneers, on active service, Mesopotamia, 1916: Superintendent Geological Survey of India, 1917; on Deputation to Mesopotamia, 1918–19; Director, Geological Survey of India, and Editor of the Memoirs and the Records, 1921–32; President of the Governing Body, Indian School of Mining and Geology; Pres. Mining and Geological Institute of India, 1924, and Treasurer and Editor of the Transactions from 1920–30; Vice-President, Asiatic Society of Bengal, 1928–30; Delegate, Imperial Economic Conference, London, 1931; Geological Survey Board, 1934; Geological Advisory Panel, Anglo-Iranian Oil Co., since 1935; Home Guard, 1942. *Publications:* The Oilfields of Burma; The Petroleum Occurrences of Assam and Bengal; Petroleum in the Punjab and North-West Frontier Province; Geological Notes on Mesopotamia, with special reference to Occurrences of Petroleum; several shorter papers in the Records, Geological Survey of India, and elsewhere; Manual of the Geology of India, 3rd Edit. *Address:* St Nicholas' Lodge, Harpenden, Herts. *Clubs:* Authors'; Himalayan.

Died 5 July 1949.

PASKE-SMITH, Montague Bentley Talbot, CMG 1941; CBE 1923; OBE 1920; FRGS; *b* Calgary, Canada; *y s* of late Rev. Edward Paske-Smith, Vicar of Newton-on-Ouse, York; *m* 1912, Maria Teresa Bertran de Lis, 3rd *d* of Alvaro Bertran de Lis, Madrid; two *d. Educ:* Elizabeth College, Guernsey. A Student Interpreter in Japan, 1907; Acting Vice-Consul, Manila, 1909–10; Acting Consul, Shimonoseki, 1914; Acting Vice-Consul, Manila, 1915–18; Vice-Consul, Manila, 1918; Acting Consul-General, 1919–20 and 1921; Vice-Consul, Osaka, 1919; Acting Consul-General, Kobé, 1921–22; Consul, Nagasaki, 1924; Osaka, 1927; acting Consul-General, Manila, 1930; Consul, Dairen, 1931; Honolulu, 1932–34; Madrid, 1934–36; Minister at Bogota, 1936–41. *Publications:* England and Japan; Western Barbarians in Japan and Formosa in Tokugawa Days; Japanese Traditions of Christianity. *Recreation:* tennis. *Address:* 24 Lowndes St, SW1.

Died 10 Jan. 1946.

PASLEY, Major Sir Thomas (Edward Sabine); 3rd Bt *cr* 1794; late 2nd Royal Berkshire Regiment; *b* Bowness, Windermere, 12 Nov. 1863; *e s* of late Captain T. M. S. Pasley and Emma, *d* of John Losh of Trinidad; *S* grandfather, 1884; *m* 1890, Lady Constance Wilmot Annie Hastings (*d* 1922), *e d* of 13th Earl of Huntingdon; two *d. Educ:* Marlborough; Cavendish Coll. Camb. (BA); Sandhurst. Was ADC to Gen. Officer commanding Western District, 1895; served South Africa, 1899–1900 (despatches); European War, 1914–17; retired pay, 1904; Commandant, Gordon Boys' Home, 1918–31. *Heir: b* Malcolm Pasley [*b* 17 April 1870; *m* 1897, Nona Marion, *d* of late J. M. Paine of Coombe Lands, Addlestone; one *s.* Commander RN, retired]. *Address:* (temp.): Almonds, Old Marston, Oxford. *Club:* Army and Navy.

Died 7 April 1947.

PASSFIELD, 1st Baron *cr* 1929, of Passfield Corner; **Sidney James Webb,** PC 1924; OM 1944; LLB; Hon. DSc (Econ.), London; LittD Wales; Hon.D. in Political Economy (Munich); *b* London, 13 July 1859; 2nd *s* of Charles Webb; *m* 1892, Beatrice (*d* 1943), 8th *d* of Richard Potter. *Educ:* private schools, London; Switzerland; Mecklenburg-Schwerin; Birkbeck Institute; City of London Coll. Clerk in Col Broker's office, London, 1875–78; War Office (Low. Div.), by open competition, 1878–79; Surveyor of Taxes, by open competition (Class I), 1879–81; Colonial Office (Class I), by open competition, 1881–91; resigned 1891, for County Council; sometime (honorary) Lecturer on Political Economy at City of London College and Working Men's College, and then (hon.) Professor of Public Administration, University of London (London School of Economics), 1912–27; MP (Lab) Seaham Division Co. Durham, 1922–29. Barrister (Gray's Inn), 1885; Member of Faculty and Board of Studies in Economics, London University; Member (unpaid) of Royal Commission under Development Act, 1910–22; President of the Board of Trade, Jan.–Nov. 1924; Secretary of State for Dominion Affairs, 1929–30, and for the Colonies, 1929–31; served on Royal Commission on Trade Union Law, 1903–06, on Coal Industry Commission, 1919, and on Departmental Committees on Technological Institute at S Kensington, 1904–05; Agricultural Settlements and Emigration, 1905–06; Territorial Army, 1906–07; Census of Production, 1907–08; Intelligence as to Distress in London, 1914–15; Economic Conditions of Industrial Discovery, 1915–16; Railways, 1917–18; Trusts, 1918–20; Fertilisers, 1919–20; Central Committee of Profiteering Act, 1919–20; Member of LCC (for Deptford), 1892–1910; Member of Senate, London University, 1900–09. *Publications:* Socialism in England, 1890; The Eight Hours Day, 1891, in conjunction with Harold Cox; The London Programme, 1892; Labour in the Longest Reign, 1897; London Education, 1904; Grants in Aid, 1911; Towards Social Democracy?, 1916; The Works Manager To-day, 1917; Story of the Durham Miners, 1921; edited How to Pay for the War, 1916; Fabian Essays, edition of 1920; and author of the following in conjunction with his wife—The History of Trade Unionism, 1894; Industrial Democracy, 1897; Problems of Modern Industry, 1898; History of Liquor Licensing, 1903; English Local Government (The Parish and the County, 1906; The Manor and the Borough, 1908; Statutory Authorities, 1922; The Story of the King's Highway, 1913; English Prisons under Local Government, 1922); English Poor Law Policy, 1910; The State and the Doctor, 1910; The Prevention of Destitution, 1911; A Constitution for the Socialist Commonwealth of Great Britain, 1920; Consumers' Co-operative Movement, 1921; Decay of Capitalist Civilisation, 1923; English Poor Law History, Vol. I, The Old Poor Law 1927; Vols II and III, The Last Hundred Years, 1929; Methods of Social Study, 1932; Soviet Communism: A New Civilisation?, 1935, 4th edition, 1945; The Truth about Soviet Russia, 1942; joint editors of The Break-up of the Poor Law and the Public Organization of the Labour Market, being the Minority Report of the Poor Law Commission, 1909. *Recreation:* walking. *Address:* Passfield Corner, Liphook, Hants. *TA:* Passfield. *T:* Passfield 206. *Clubs:* Athenæum, Fabian Society.

Died 13 Oct. 1947 (ext).

PASSFIELD, Lady; *see* Webb, Mrs Sidney.

PASTEUR, William, CB 1919; CMG 1918; MD, FRCP, MRCS; late temp. Col AMS; Consultant-Physician to the British Armies in France; Col retd RAMC (T); Consulting Physician to the Middlesex Hospital and to the Queen's Hospital for Children; late House Physician, University College Hospital; *m* 1890, Violet Mabel, *y d* of late Col R. Sellon, RE; two *d. Educ:* The Philberds, Maidenhead; University College,

London; Vienna. Served European War, 1914–18 (despatches, CB, CMG). *Address:* Brendon, Warwick Park, Tunbridge Wells. *T:* Tunbridge Wells 704. *Club:* Alpine.

Died 1 Sept. 1943.

PASTON-BEDINGFELD, Sir Henry Edward, 8th Bt *cr* 1660; JP for Norfolk; late Major, 3rd Battalion The King's (Liverpool Regiment); *b* 29 Aug. 1860; *s* of 7th Bt, and Augusta, *o c* of E. Clavering of Callaly Castle, Northumberland; *S* father, 1902; *m* 1904, Sybil, *e d* of late H. Lyne Stephens of Grove House, Roehampton; one *s* two *d. Heir: s* Edmund George Felix, *b* 2 June 1915. *Address:* Oxburgh, King's Lynn, Norfolk. *TA:* Oxborough. *Club:* Junior United Service.

Died 18 May 1941.

PASTON-COOPER, Sir Charles Naunton Paston, 4th Bt *cr* 1821; composer of songs; *b* Gadebridge Park, Hemel-Hempstead, Hertfordshire, 27 Sept. 1867; *o surv. s* of Sir A. P. Paston-Cooper, 3rd Bart, and the late Etheldreda, *d* of late S. Onslow-Newton; *S* father, 1904; *m* Tatiana, *o c* of Prince and Princess Dmitri Dolgorouky of Russia, 1899. *Publications:* Just for your Sake; We are not Sure of Sorrow; In what Far Land; Ave Maria; A Leavetaking; I Love you So. *Heir: cousin* Henry Lovick, *b* 1875.

Died 4 Dec. 1941.

PATCH, Lt-Gen. Alexander McCarrell; US Army; commanding Seventh Army; *b* Fort Huachuca, Arizona, 23 Nov. 1889; *s* of Capt. Alexander M. Patch; *m* 1916; one *d. Educ:* Military Academy, West Point, NY; Command and General Staff School; Army War College. Served European War, 1917–18, in France; Member of Infantry Board at Fort Benning, Georgia, 1936; commanded Infantry Replacement Training Center, Camp Croft, South Carolina, 1941; in command of US troops co-operating with French Forces in defence of New Caledonia, 1942; Commander of ground forces at Guadalcanal, 1943 (Navy's Distinguished Service Medal).

Died 21 Nov. 1945.

PATCH, Brig.-Gen. Francis Robert, CB 1922; CMG 1918; DSO 1917; late RA; *b* 1868; *s* of late Col Robert Patch, CB; *m* Mary Isabel, *d* of late A. Vereker Smyth; one *d.* Served Miranzai (despatches, wounded), Isazai, and Chitral Expeditions; *S* Africa, 1899–1902 (despatches thrice, Bt Major, Queen's and King's medals 8 clasps); European War (Mesopotamia), 1915–18 (despatches, CMG, DSO); retired pay, 1923. *Address:* Westminster Bank Ltd, Haymarket, SW1.

Died 14 March 1947.

PATE, Henry Reginald, CIE 1931; *b* 10 Aug. 1880; *s* of late Rev. H. W. Pate, MA; *m* 1924, Ethel Blanche, *widow* of Capt. Claude Bignell, 4th Rajputs, and *d* of late Henry Villiers Margary; no *c. Educ:* Clifton; King's College, Cambridge (Classical Scholar, Bell Scholar); 1st Class Classical Tripos, 1902. Appointed to ICS, 1904; posted to Madras Presidency; Settlement Officer Tinnevelly and Ramnad districts, 1911–13; Secretary, Board of Revenue, Madras, 1916–20; Deputy Secretary, Govt of India, Army Department, 1921–24; Officiating Secretary, Government of India, Army Department, 1924; Collector and District Magistrate of Malabar, 1925–28; Secretary to the Government of Madras, Revenue Department, and Member, Legislative Council, Madras, 1928–31; retired from ICS, 1934. *Publication:* A Gazetteer of the Tinnevelly District, Madras Government Press, 1917. *Address:* Habyn Hill, Rogate, Sussex. *T:* Rogate 9.

Died 21 June 1942.

PATERSON, A.; *b* 1865; *m* 1911, M. Walker, Ham Common, Surrey. *Educ:* High School of Glasgow; Univ. of Glasgow. Editor, Yorkshire Evening Post; Editor, Daily Dispatch; Managing Editor and Director of E. Hulton & Co., Ltd, 1906–24; retired, 1924. Managing Editor and Director of Allied Newspapers in Manchester, 1924 till retirement with a seat on the Board, 1932; Director, Allied Newspapers, Ltd, 1924–39. *Address:* 20 Edge Lane, Chorlton, Manchester 21. *T:* Chorlton 3548.

Died 22 Dec. 1944.

PATERSON, Sir Alexander, Kt 1947; MA (Oxon); MC; HM Comr of Prisons and Director of Convict Prisons, 1922–47; *b* 20 Nov. 1884; *m* 1927, Frances Margaret, *er d* of J. Bernard Baker, of Oxford; one *d. Educ:* Bowdon College, Cheshire; University College, Oxford. Private Secretary, Irish Office; Elementary School teacher in Bermondsey; Assistant Director of Borstal Association, etc.; Lecturer at London School of Economics, etc.; enlisted in Bermondsey Battalion at outbreak of war; Captain in same unit; served European War, 1914–19 (despatches, MC); principal officer Ministry of Labour, 1919–22; visited Burma to advise the Government of Burma on penal questions, 1925–26; visited the United States to study their penal systems, 1931; visited Bermuda and West Indian Colonies at request of Colonial Office, also Penal Settlement in French Guiana, 1937; visited East Africa, Somaliland and Aden at request of Colonial Office, 1939; Vice-President of International Penal and Penitentiary Commission, 1938 and as such attended American Prison Congress at New York in 1939; appointed by Home Secretary to visit Internment Camps in Canada, 1940–41, and to be Director of Czech Trust, 1941; sent by Colonial Office on special missions to West Coast of Africa, 1943–44, and to Malta and Gibraltar, 1944. Hon. Fellow of University College, Oxford, 1944. *Publications:* Across the Bridges; Paterson on Prisons, 1950 (posthumous). *Recreations:* reading, digging, singing. *Club:* Oxford and Cambridge.

Died 7 Nov. 1947.

PATERSON, Alexander Nisbet, MA; ARSA, RSW; FRIBA, retired; architect; *b* Glasgow, 1862; *s* of Andrew Paterson, manufacturer, and Margaret Hunter; *m* 1897, Maggie Hamilton, Helensburgh; one *s* one *d. Educ:* Glasgow Academy and Univ.; Ecole des Beaux Arts, Paris; offices of late Sir John Burnet, RA, etc., R. W. Edis, FSA, and Sir Aston Webb, RA. After obtaining experience, together with travel for study in France, Holland, Italy, home countries, and (as Godwin Bursar, RIBA) in United States, commenced practice in Glasgow, 1891–92; principal buildings designed and erected there: University Press Offices; The National Bank of Scotland, St Enoch Sq.; Clubhouse for Liberal Club, since remodelled for the Scottish National Academy of Music; the Carnegie Aquarium, the Scottish Zoological Park, Edinburgh; with domestic work and decoration throughout west of Scotland and in Edinburgh; painter in water-colour, and exhibited in Salon, Royal Academy, New English Art Club, RSA, R Glasgow Institute, and RSW; Member of HM Ancient Monuments Board for Scotland. *Publications:* various lectures to RIBA, London, and elsewhere; and papers in professional journals. *Address:* The Long Croft, Helensburgh. *T:* Helensburgh 187. *Clubs:* Glasgow Art, Glasgow Literary.

Died 10 July 1947.

PATERSON, Andrew Barton, CBE 1939; journalist; *b* 17 Feb. 1864; *s* of Andrew Bogle Paterson, grazier, and Rose Isabella Barton; *m* Alice Emily, *d* of W. H. Walker of Tenterfield Station, grazier; one *s* one *d. Educ:* Sydney Grammar School. Educated for the law. Admitted Solicitor, Supreme Court of NS Wales; practised law till Boer War; went to Boer War as representative of Sydney Morning Herald and Melbourne Argus, and was on staff of Reuter's Agency; visited Philippines as correspondent SM Herald during Philippines-America War; visited China at end of Boxer rebellion; represented SM Herald in early part of war of 1914; ambulance driver, Australian Hospital, Boulogne, 1914–15; joined Australian Remount Service, 1915, as second lieutenant; in Egypt and Palestine with remounts till end of war; promoted to rank of Major. *Publications:* Man from Snowy River, and other verses; Rio Grande's Last Race, and other verses; Saltbush Bill, JP, and other verses; An Outback Marriage (novel); Three Elephant Power (tales and sketches); Old Bush Songs (collection); Australian Song, Waltzing Matilda; The Animals Noah Forgot (children's verses), 1933; Happy Despatches (personal recollections of world-famous people), 1934; The Shearer's Colt (racing story), 1936. *Recreations:* lawn tennis, polo. *Address:* 19 South Street, Double Bay, Sydney, Australia. *Clubs:* Australian, Sydney.

Died 5 Feb. 1941.

PATERSON, Sir Clifford Copland, Kt 1946; OBE 1919; DSc; FRS 1942; Founder, 1919 and Director since 1919 of Research Laboratories of General Electric Co. Ltd, Wembley; *b* 17 Oct. 1879; *s* of late Frederick and Janette Paterson; *m* 1905, Eleanor Daisy Ogden; two *s* one *d. Educ:* Mill Hill School; Faraday House. National Physical Laboratory, 1901–18 (Principal Assistant); President, Institution of Electrical Engineers, 1930–31; and Faraday Medallist, 1945; President Illumination Commission, 1928–31; President Institute of Physics, 1937–38; Pres. Electrical Research Assoc., 1938–39; Pres. Junior Inst. of Engineers, 1934–35; Pres. Illuminating Engineering Soc., 1928 Chairman DSIR Cttee on the Lighting of Buildings; Chairman General Council of Brit. Standards Inst.; Member, Advisory Council of DSIR, Ministry of Transport Cttee on Street Lighting; Home Office Cttee on Factory Lighting; Board of Trade Cttee on Ships Navigation Lights; Engineering Adv. Cttee of Min. of Production; Master Worshipful Comp. of Tallow Chandlers, 1939–41. *Publications:* numerous papers. *Recreations:* yachting and horticulture. *Address:* Waldringfield, Green Lane, Oxhey, Herts; Research Laboratories of GEC Ltd, Wembley. *TA:* Research-phone-Wembley. *T:* Watford 4064, Arnold 4321. *Club:* Athenæum.

Died 26 July 1948.

PATERSON, Brig.-Gen. Ewing, DSO 1901; late Inniskilling Dragoons; *b* 8 June 1873; last *surv. s* of late John Paterson of Kinburn and Langraw, St Andrews, Fife; *m* 1907, Jessy, *widow* of W. E. Rigden; three *d.* 6th Dragoons, 1893; served South Africa, 1899–1900; Gen. French's columns to Pretoria, Diamond Hill, Middleburg, Barbeton, Carolina, Bethel, Ermelo, wounded, and invalided home (despatches, DSO and bar); Adjutant Devon Yeomanry Brigade, 1901–05; Lt-Colonel, 1916; Colonel, 1920; commanded the Inniskilling Dragoons in France, 1915–18; 6th Cavalry Brigade, 1918 to end of War (despatches five times, Brevet Colonel); Commandant Cavalry School, 1920–22; retired pay, 1923; Master Dundalk Harriers, 1896–97; N Devon Harriers, 1901; Barnstaple Staghounds, 1901–03. *Address:* The Golden Farm, Cirencester.

Died 8 Dec. 1950.

PATERSON, Col George Fredrick Joseph, CIE 1937; OBE 1926; MC; *b* 26 March 1885; *s* of Colonel H. Paterson, 23rd Punjab Pioneers, Indian Staff Corps; *m* 1914, Xenia J. A. C., *d* of D. A. Beaver, HMB Consul, Santos, Brazil; one *s* one *d. Educ:* Oratory School, Birmingham; RMC Sandhurst. 1st Commission, 1904; joined 34th Sikh Pioneers Indian Army, 1905; served European War, France, 1914–15; Mesopotamia, 1916–19 (despatches twice, MC); transferred to Cantonments Department, 1919; Director, Military Lands and Cantonments, Defence Dept Government of India, 1935; retired from Indian Army, 1942. *Club:* Junior United Service.

Died 25 Dec. 1949.

PATERSON, Lt-Col Henry Francis William, CIE 1936; IA, retired; *b* 1880; *m* 1912, Ruth Amy, *d* of W. S. Stacey; one *s.* Retired from Indian Army, 1935. *Address:* Huntly, Hawksdown, Walmer, Kent.

Died 27 Dec. 1943.

PATERSON, James Veitch, MA; MB, CM, FRCS Edin.; Consulting Ophthalmic Surgeon, Royal Infirmary, Edinburgh; *b* Dumfriesshire, 1866; *m* 1895, Susanna Ann, *d* of late John Robert Aitchison, India Office, London; two *s* three *d. Educ:* Edinburgh Academy and University; Vienna. *Publications:* contributions to ophthalmic literature. *Recreations:* fishing, curling. *Address:* Tweedbank, Peebles. *T:* 182.

Died 10 May 1943.

PATERSON, Mary Muirhead, CBE 1920; JP; retired Civil Servant. *Address:* Craufurd, Lasswade, Midlothian. *T:* Lasswade 2372. *Clubs:* Queen's, Edinburgh.

Died 10 June 1941.

PATERSON, Gen. Robert Ormiston, OBE 1918; Royal Marines, retired; *b* 20 May 1878; 2nd *s* of Robert Ormiston Paterson, Civil Engineer of Cheltenham and Weston-super-Mare; *m* 1912, Mary Elizabeth, *d* of Robert Main Wilson, Fodbank, nr Dunfermline; one *s. Educ:* Cheltenham Grammar School. Joined Royal Marine Light Infantry, 1895; transferred to Royal Marine Artillery, 1896; Captain, 1900; Major, 1913; Lieut-Colonel, 1921; Colonel, 1922; Colonel Commandant, 1926; Major-General, 1928; Lieut-General, 1929; General, 1930; ADC to the King, 1927–28; served during war, Coast Defences, Cromarty; HMS Lion; in command of RM Expeditionary Force, N Russia, and Base Commandant, Murmansk; retired list, 1931; President Bideford Branch, British Legion; Member Devon County Committee, British Legion. *Recreations:* golf and motoring. *Address:* Dunedin, Orchard Hill, Bideford. *T:* Bideford 149. *Clubs:* United Service; Royal North Devon Golf, Westward Ho!; Phyllis Court, Henley-on-Thames.

Died 6 Sept. 1941.

PATERSON, Col Stanley, CBE 1919; JP; retired pay; landowner, Kenya Colony; *b* 13 Feb. 1860; *yr s* of D. A. Paterson, JP, of Dalnaglar and Toinloid, Perthshire; *m* 1901, Constance, *o d* of R. Brettell, JP, of the Grange, Chertsey, Surrey; one *d. Educ:* privately. Joined Highland Light Infantry Militia, 1877; transferred to Argyll and Sutherland Highlanders, 1879; commanded 2nd Battalion, 1903–07; served South Africa, China, and India; commanded No. 2 (South of Scotland) District, 1912–18; European War (despatches, CBE); acquired considerable estates and settled in Kenya Colony, 1919; is a Fellow of the Royal Geographical Society and of the Royal Empire Society. *Publications:* several stories of travel and sport in Chambers's Journal. *Recreations:* shooting, fishing, farming. *Address:* The Brass Mill Newent, Glos; Melangini, Gilgil, Kenya Colony. *Club:* Naval and Military.

Died 21 Aug. 1950.

PATERSON, Maj.-Gen. Thomas George Ferguson, CB 1935; DSO 1917; BA, MB, BCh, BAO; Indian Medical Service, retired; *b* 6 Dec. 1876; *m* 1908, Edith Marion Irene (*d* 1939), *d* of Frederick Powell Moore; one *s* two *d. Educ:* private; Trinity Coll., Dublin. Entered IMS, 1902; Capt., 1905; Major, 1913; Bt Lt-Col, 1919; Lt-Col, 1921; Bt Col, 1928; Col, 1930; Maj.-Gen., 1932; KHP, 1928–35; served European War (Mesopotamia), 1914–18 (despatches, DSO, Bt Lt-Col); retired, 1935. *Recreation:* outdoor sports.

Died 7 July 1942.

PATESHALL, Col Henry Evan Pateshall, CB 1942; DSO 1918; TD 1942; JP; DL; *b* 20 July 1879; *s* of late Lt-Col H. E. P. Pateshall, late commanding East Yorkshire Regt; *m* 1910, Edith Ruth Phyllis, *d* of late Rev. William Jebb Few, Guildford, Surrey; no *c. Educ:* Rugby School; RMC, Sandhurst. Gazetted the East

Yorkshire Regt, 1899; retired, 1914; gazetted to the Herefordshire Regt, 1914; served South Africa, 1900–02 (King's and Queen's medals); European War, employed on Staff, Gallipoli, Egypt, Palestine (DSO, 1915 Star, Allies' Medal, General Service Medal); commanded the Herefordshire Regt TA, 1920–26; Hon. Col 2nd Bn Herefordshire Regt, 1939–47; High Sheriff of Herefordshire, 1931. Home Guard, Herefordshire County Organiser, Battalion and Group Commander, 1940–44. *Recreations:* shooting and all out-door recreations. *Address:* Allensmore Court, Hereford. *TA:* Pateshall, Allensmore. *T:* Belmont 226. *Club:* County (Hereford).

Died 18 Oct. 1948.

PATON, James Bowie; KC; MA, LLB; Clerk of Justiciary. *Address:* 55 Great King Street, Edinburgh.
Died 25 May 1940.

PATON, Sir James Wallace, Kt 1919; *b* 15 Jan. 1863; *m* 1893, Kate, *d* of George Calvert, Southport; three *s* one *d.* Mayor of Southport, 1908–09; JP Co. Lancaster. *Address:* Gold Rill, Grasmere, Westmorland.
Died 12 Aug. 1948.

PATON, Maj.-Gen. John, CB 1916; CMG 1918; VD; *b* Nov. 1867; *s* of Capt. J. Paton, Newcastle, NSW; *m* 1896, *d* of S. A. Donelly, Ex-MP; one *s. Educ:* private; High School, Newcastle, NSW. Trained in a mercantile house; now Managing Director of R. Hall & Son, Ltd, general merchants of Sydney and Newcastle, and other towns in Australia; Alderman for three years and JP for NSW; President Newcastle Chamber of Commerce, 1920–23 (4 years); served thirty years in the NSW Citizen Forces; Commander of 2nd Division (NSW) Commonwealth Military Forces, 1926; retired as Hon. Maj.-Gen., 1926; at the outbreak of War went with the Naval and Military Expeditionary Force which captured the German Islands in the Western Pacific; commanded the mixed force of 600 at the capture of Rabaul, the capital of German New Guinea, and commanded the garrison there for five months; commanded small party which captured the German gunboat Komet (complimented by Admiralty); joined 7th Brigade AIF; served in Gallipoli, Sept.–Dec. 1915, in command of Rear Party at evacuation; France, since March 1916 (Brig.-Gen. 1 Jan. 1916; despatches, CB). *Recreations:* golf, champion, Newcastle Golf Club, three years. *Address:* Newcastle, NSW. *Clubs:* Australian, Sydney; Newcastle, Newcastle, NSW.

Died 21 Nov. 1943.

PATON, John Lewis, MA; *b* Sheffield, 13 Aug. 1863; *s* of late Rev. Dr J. B. Paton of Nottingham. *Educ:* Gymnasium, Halle; Nottingham High School; Shrewsbury School (Head boy); St John's College, Cambridge (Fellow, 1887). Bracketed 1st in Classical Tripos, Pt i, 1886; 1st class in Classical Tripos, Pt ii, 1887, with special distinctions in Language and History; Junior Chancellor's Medallist for Classics, 1887. One year Assistant Master at Leys School, Cambridge; and ten years Sixth Form Master at Rugby School; late Headmaster of University Coll. School; Special Lecturer, Education, Victoria Univ.; President of Teachers' Guild, 1907–08; Consultative Committee of Board of Education, 1907–15; Examiner in Education, Manchester University, 1906–07, Oxford Univ., 1908, 1922–23, Cambridge, 1910–11; Pres. Modern Language Association, 1911; High Master Manchester Grammar School, 1903–24; Lectured for National Council of Education in Canada, 1924–25; President of Memorial University College, St John's, Newfoundland, 1925–33. *Publications:* Chapters on the Aims and Practice of Teaching, 1896; Essay on Teaching of Latin; The Public Schools from Within, 1906; On Discipline; The Secondary Education of the Working Classes, 1909; On the Teaching of Classics in Prussian Secondary Schools (Special Reports of the Board of Education), 1907; Life

of John Brown Paton, DD, 1914; Cambridge Essays on Education, 1917; Vocation, 1919. *Recreation:* gardening. *Address:* Chalkway, Kemsing, nr Sevenoaks.
Died 28 April 1946.

PATON, Leslie, MA, MB (Cantab), FRCS; Vice-President and Consulting Ophthalmic Surgeon, St Mary's Hospital, Paddington; Consulting Ophthalmic Surgeon, National Hospital for Diseases of the Nervous System, Queen Square, WC; Hon. Ophthalmic Surgeon to Royal Caledonian Asylum, to Royal Scottish Hospital, and to Royal Academy of Dramatic Art; Past President, Ophthalmological Society of United Kingdom; Past President, Neurological Section Royal Society of Medicine; Past President, Ophthalmic Section, British Medical Association; Membre d'Honneur, Société Franç. d'Ophtal.; Hon. Member of the International Ophthalmological Council and of various foreign ophthalmological societies; late Chairman of Council, British Ophthalmologists; late Chairman and Managing Director, British Journal of Ophthalmology; Hon. Fellow, American Medical Association; *b* Edinburgh, 1872; 2nd *s* of late James Paton, FLS; *m* 1906, May, *d* of late R. Reid Kirkwood; two *d. Educ:* Glasgow, Cambridge, London, and Bonn. *Publications:* contributions on ophthalmic subjects in medical papers and journals. *Address:* 29 Harley Street, W1. *T:* Langham 1708.

Died 15 May 1943.

PATON, Rev. William; Secretary, International Missionary Council and Editor, The International Review of Missions since 1927; Joint General Secretary, Provisional Committee of World Council of Churches, since 1938; *b* London, 13 Nov. 1886; *o s* of James and Elizabeth Paton; *m* Grace Mackenzie, *e d* of Rev. David Macdonald, BD, and Mrs K. E. S. Macdonald; four *s* two *d. Educ:* Whitgift School; Pembroke College, Oxford; Westminster College, Cambridge. 2nd Cl. Hon. Classical Mods, 1906, 2nd cl. Lit. Hum., 1908; Dr Williams scholar, 1910; MA 1911; Hon. DD (Edin.), 1939. Missionary Secretary, Student Christian Movement, 1911–21; General Secretary, National Christian Council of India, Burmah and Ceylon, 1922–27. *Publications:* Jesus Christ and the World's Religions, 1916; Social Ideals in India, 1919; The Highway of God (with K. Harnett), 1920; Alexander Duff, 1922; A Faith for the World, 1929; The Faiths of Mankind, 1932; Christianity in the Eastern Conflicts, 1937; World Community, 1938; The White Man's Burden, 1939; The Message of the Worldwide Church, 1940; The Church and the New Order, 1941. *Recreations:* walking and golf. *Address:* 27 Beaconsfield Road, St Albans, Herts. *T:* St Albans 984. *Club:* United University.

Died 21 Aug. 1943.

PATRICK, (Colin) Mark; MP (C) Tavistock Division since 1931; *b* 21 Oct. 1893; *s* of late Colin Grant Patrick, Longparish, Hampshire; *m* 1st, Mary, *d* of late Col H. Mulliner; 2nd, Lady Evelyn Graham, *d* of 3rd Earl of Lovelace; one *s* two *d. Educ:* Eton; Christ Church, Oxford. Served European War with 16th Lancers, 1914–19 (wounded Ypres 1915, despatches); entered HM Diplomatic Service, 1919; served in Foreign Office, Cairo, The Hague, Berne, Moscow, etc.; acted as Chargé d'affaires in Holland and Switzerland; resigned, 1930; Parliamentary Private Secretary to the Under Secretary of State for Foreign Affairs, 1932; to the Secretary of State for India, 1933–34; and to Secretary of State for Foreign Affairs, 1935; a Director of Carreras, Ltd; rejoined 16th Lancers, 1940. *Publication:* Hammer and Sickle, 1933. *Recreations:* various. *Address:* 15 South Street, Park Lane, W1. *T:* Grosvenor 1466; Warrens Cross, Whitchurch, nr Tavistock. *T:* Sampford Spiney 32. *Clubs:* Travellers', Buck's.

Died 7 Jan. 1942.

PATRICK, Herbert Lindsay F.; *see* Fitz Patrick.

PATRO GARU, Rao Bahadur Sir Annepu Parasuramadas, KCIE 1935; Kt 1924; Member of the Council of State (Central) India since 1937; Agriculturist; High Court Vakil Ganjam; landholder; Delegate to the Round Table Conference, London, 1930; Delegate to the RDC, 1929–32 and Delegate to the Joint Parliamentary Committee on Indian Reforms, 1933; Indian Delegate to the League of Nations, Geneva, 1931; *b* 1875; widower; one *s* one *d. Educ:* Madras Christian College; Law College, Madras; Madras University. Connected with Administration of Local Self-Government for twenty years as President and Chairman of Local Boards and Municipality; sits on several committees of Government and Legislature; Member of the Madras Legislative Council, 1920–36; Minister of Education, Public Works, and Excise, 1921–27; as Minister of Education, author of Madras University Reorganisation Act and Andhra Univ. Act; President of the All-Parties Conference held in Delhi in 1930 to solve the Communal problems and Minorities problem in India; President of the All-India Committee of the Justice movement (non-Brahmin). *Publications:* Rural Economics, a Study of Rural Conditions in the Madras Presidency; Studies in Local Self-Government. *Recreations:* hockey and football. *Club:* Cosmopolitan (Madras).

Died 26 May 1946.

PATTEN, Charles J., MA, MD, ScD; FRAI; Emeritus Professor of Anatomy, University of Sheffield; formerly Examiner in Anatomy, University of Birmingham; formerly Examiner in Anatomy, Morphology, and Anthropology, University of Wales, Queen's University, Belfast, and Universities of Leeds and Manchester; Honorary Associate of the Rationalist Press Association and Hon. President of the Glasgow Division; Corresponding Member of the Royal Zoological Society, Ireland; Fellow of the Royal Society for Protection of Birds; Fellow of the Royal Anthropological Institute; *b* Ballybrack, Co. Dublin, 1870; *er s* of Richard Patten, MA of the Court of Exchequer, Ireland, and Elizabeth Victoria Mongan; *m* Mabel Elizabeth, *e d* of late Rev. Canon W. J. King, formerly of Kilcoleman Rectory, Miltown, Co. Kerry; one *s* one *d. Educ:* Trinity College, Dublin; Triple First of the First Honors and First Senior Moderator and Gold Medallist in Natural Science, Dublin University. *Publications:* The Aquatic Birds of Great Britain and Ireland; The Passing of the Phantoms; The Memory Factory in Biology; The Story of the Birds; Triumphs in Bird-Life, etc.; contributor of many papers on Anatomy, Evolutionary Topics and Ornithology (especially on Bird-Migration) to various scientific and popular journals. *Recreations:* boating, fishing, shooting, and expeditionary field-natural history. *Address:* Leyton House, Hale Rd, Farnham, Surrey. *T:* Farnham 681–90.

Died 13 June 1948.

PATTERSON, Rev. Alexander Hamilton, MA Cambridge; MA (*ad eundem*) Durham; Hon. Canon of Durham; Hon. Secretary Durham Diocesan Readers' Board and Bede College, Durham; Officiating Chaplain to the Forces, 1915–18; *b* 1851; *s* of Alexander Patterson of Liverpool; *m* Lucy (*d* 1940), *d* of Rev. Edward Marston, Rector of Holy Trinity, Chester. *Educ:* The Liverpool Institute; St Catharine's College, Cambridge (Scholar); 2nd class, Classical Tripos, 1874. Curate of Bywell, St Andrew, 1874–77; Diocesan Inspector of Schools, 1877–94; Vicar of St Helen's, Gateshead, 1894–1927; Vicar of Aycliffe, Darlington, 1927–36. *Address:* Middleton One Row, Darlington.

Died 15 Oct. 1943.

PATTERSON, David Clarke; late Indian Civil Service; *b* 5 May 1879; *s* of late David Clarke Patterson, Holywood, Co. Down, and Isabelle Patterson, Annadale, Belfast; *m* 1907, Marguerite Mather Atkinson, Warrenpoint, Co. Down; two *s* two *d. Educ:* Oundle School; Christ's College, Cambridge. Honours Degree in Mathematics, 1901. Appointed to ICS, 1902; joined first appointment in India, 1903; held various executive and judicial appointments in Bengal, Behar and Assam, 1903–31; Puisne Judge, High Court of Judicature, Calcutta, 1931–39; retired, 1939. *Address:* Hotel Bonivard, Territet, nr Montreux, Switzerland.

Died 16 Jan. 1948.

PATTERSON, Rev. Melville Watson, MA; Emeritus Fellow of Trinity College, Oxford; *b* 12 Oct. 1873; 3rd *s* of W. Patterson, Birkenhead; *m* 1905, Clara Burdett Money-Coutts, *e d* of 5th Baron Latymer; three *d. Educ:* Winchester College; New College, Oxford (Scholar). 1st class Honour Moderations, 1894; Hall Greek Testament Prize, 1895; 1st class Literæ Humaniores, 1896; 1st class Modern History, 1897. Fellow of Trinity College, and Lecturer in Modern History, 1897; afterwards Vice-President, and Senior Tutor, Trinity College till 1938; Deacon, 1899; Priest, 1903; Junior Proctor of Oxford University, 1910–11; Examining Chaplain to Bishop Robertson (of Exeter) till his retirement from the See, 1903–16; Member of the Governing Body of Radley College. *Publications:* A History of the Church of England, 1909; The Life and Times of Sir Francis Burdett, 5th Bart, 1931; Translation of De Tocqueville's Ancien Régime, 1933. *Recreation:* golf. *Address:* Bramcote, Boars Hill, Oxford. *T:* Oxford 85384.

Died 19 Jan. 1944.

PATTERSON, Norman, MB, BCh Edin; FRCS; late Surgeon to the Throat Hospital, Golden Square; Surgeon, Throat, Nose and Ear Department, London Hospital; *b* 1877; *s* of Rev. James Patterson, Ancrum, Roxburghshire; *m* Winifred Dorothea Crockford; (one *s* killed Dec. 1944) one *d. Educ:* Melville College; Edin. University; King's College and London Hospital. Has held various appointments at the London Hospital and elsewhere. *Publications:* Throat and Ear section Choyce's System of Surgery; contributions to medical journals. *Address:* Nobs Crook, Ashridge Park, Berkhamstead, Herts. *T:* Little Gaddesden 3123.

Died 16 Jan. 1950.

PATTERSON, Lt-Col Sir Stewart Blakeley Agnew, KCVO 1933; CSI 1927; CIE 1922; Knight of 1st class of Order of Sword of Sweden, 1909; Indian Army; Political Department, retired; *b* India, 18 March 1872; *s* of late Alexander Blakeley Patterson, CIE, Indian Civil Service, of Ballymena, Co. Antrim, and Charlotte Maria, *d* of late John Black, JP, of Annaskea House, Co. Louth; *m* 1907, Augusta Rachel, *d* of late General Robert Bruce, CB, of Glendouglie, Perthshire; no *c. Educ:* Marlborough College; RMC, Sandhurst. Entered The Queen's Royal Regt (West Surrey), 1892; 38th Dogras, 1894; served in Waziristan Expedition, 1894–95 (medal and clasp); North-West Frontier, Malakand, Chakdara, Mamand Valley, 1897–98 (medal and 2 clasps); during European War in Adjutant-General's Branch AHQ (medal); Political Depart, Govt of India, 1898; served in NW Frontier, Rajputana, Foreign Office, and Kashmir; held posts of Political Agent, Wana, Comr Ajmer, Resident at Jaipur, and Sec. to Govt of India Political Dept; Member of the Council of State and Legislative Assembly, 1925; retired as Agent to Governor-General in Rajputana and Chief Comr, Ajmer-Merwara, 1927; Political ADC to Secretary of State for India, 1928–33. *Recreations:* golf, lawn tennis, shooting, fishing. *Address:* Daneswood, Dover Park Drive, Roehampton, SW15. *T:* Putney 3070. *Clubs:* Naval and Military, Roehampton.

Died 17 March 1942.

PATTERSON, Thomas Stewart, DSc (Lond. and Glas.), PhD (Heidelberg); LLD (Glas.); Emeritus Gardiner Professor of Organic Chemistry, University of Glasgow (Professor, 1919–42); Member, University Court, 1933–41; *b* 1872; *e s* of T. L. Patterson, Greenock; *m* 1905, Lizzie Paterson, *e d* of Rev. M. P. Johnstone, Greenock; one *s. Educ:* Greenock Academy; Merchiston Castle School, Edinburgh; Glasgow

Technical College; Heidelberg University; Mason Univ. College, Birmingham (Priestley Scholar). Demonstrator, and later Assistant Lecturer at the Yorkshire College, Leeds, 1896–1904; Waltonian Lecturer and Lecturer in Organic Chemistry, Glasgow, to 1919; a Governor of Merchiston Castle School, 1934–42. *Publications:* papers in various journals, chiefly on optical activity, optical superposition, rate of transformation of certain organic compounds, and on chemico-historical subjects: John Mayow (Isis, 1931) and Jean Beguin (Annals of Science, 1937). *Recreations:* yachting, golf, photography. *Address:* 89 Oakfield Avenue, Glasgow, W2. *T:* Western 4238.

Died 14 Feb. 1949.

PATTINSON, Samuel; JP; *b* 1870; *s* of William Pattinson, JP, Ruskington; *m* 1897, Betsy Sharpley, *d* of late G. Bainbridge, JP, Lincoln; one *s* one *d*. *Educ:* Abingdon House, Northampton. Director of Pattinson & Co. Ltd, Sleaford, and Bainbridges, Ltd, Lincoln; contested Horncastle, 1918 and 1920; an Alderman of the County Council for Kesteven, Lincs, being Chairman of the Finance Committee of the County; MP (L) Horncastle Division of Lindsey, 1922–24. *Address:* Westholme, Sleaford, Lincs. *T:* Sleaford 40. *Clubs:* National Liberal, Devonshire.

Died Nov. 1942.

PATTON, Gen. George S., CB (Hon.) 1944; Commanding US Fifteenth Army since 1945; *b* 1885. *Educ:* Virginia Military Institute; Military Academy, West Point, NY (graduated 1909). Served European War, 1917–18 (DSC). Commanded US Seventh Army, 1943–44; Commanded US Third Army, 1944–45; General, 1945.

Died 21 Dec. 1945.

PATTON, Rt Rev. Henry Edmund, DD; Bishop of Killaloe since 1924; *b* Dublin, 1 July 1867; *m* 1909, Kathleen, *d* of J. R. Stewart; one *d*. *Educ:* St Columba's College; Dublin University. Ordained 1892; Rector of Donaghpatrick, 1905; of All Saints, Blackrock, 1908; of Birr, 1914. *Publications:* History of the Church of Ireland; Methods of Appointment to the Episcopate; Fifty Years of Disestablishment. *Address:* Clarisford, Killaloe, Ireland.

Died 28 April 1943.

PAUER, Max; pianist; *b* London, 31 Oct. 1866; *s* of late Ernst Pauer. *Educ:* Studied under his father and V. Lachner. Teacher at Cologne Conservatory, 1887–97; Stuttgart Conservatory, 1897; Principal of same Institution, 1909; Principal, Leipzig Conservatory, 1924–32. *Address:* Haus Sonneck, Jugenheim ad B, Germany.

Died 12 May 1945.

PAUL, Col Denis, CB 1920; CMG 1916; CBE 1918; late Royal Army Ordnance Corps; *b* 13 Dec. 1865. Commissioned Lieutenant Royal Artillery, 1891; transferred to AOD, 1896; served S African War, 1899–1902 (despatches, Queen's medal 2 clasps, King's medal 2 clasps); European War, 1914–17; Principal Inspector Ordnance Machinery, France (despatches, CMG, CBE); retired pay, 1922; British Vice-Consul, Lugano, 1926–28. *Address:* c/o Westminster Bank, Charing Cross.

Died 28 Feb. 1944.

PAUL, Rev. Prof. F. J., MA, BD (London); DD (Glasgow); DD (Queen's University, Belfast); Professor of Church History, The Presbyterian College, Belfast, since 1922, and Principal since 1923; *m* 1903, Ann Edina Hately, *o d* of late Rev. J. Wilson and Mrs MacIntosh, Evelaw, Polwarth Terrace, Edinburgh; three *s*. *Educ:* Queen's College, Belfast; Scholar in Classics, Royal University of Ireland, 1894; Literary Scholar (first place), Queen's College, Belfast, 1894–97; Porter Scholar, 1897; Senior Scholar in Classics, 1898. Smyth Lecturer, 1914; New College and University, Edinburgh; University of Leipzig. Ordained in Bushmills Presbyterian Church, 1902; Prof. of Church History,

Magee College, Londonderry, 1911–22; Extern Examiner for DLitt, University of Edinburgh and for PhD, University of Aberdeen; Cunningham Lecturer, University of Edinburgh, 1938. *Address:* Presbyterian College, Belfast. *Club:* Univ. of London.

Died 3 July 1941.

PAUL, Frank Thomas, DSc, ChM Liverpool, FRCS Eng.; Professor Emeritus, Liverpool University; Major, RAMC (T) (retired); Surgeon Hoylake and West Kirby Cottage Hospital, retired; *b* 3 Dec. 1851; *s* of Thomas Paul, Ashwood Lodge, Pentney, Norfolk; *m* 1888, Geraldine, *d* of Eustace Greg; four *d*. *Educ:* Yarmouth Grammar School; Guy's Hospital Medical School. Entered Guy's, 1869; House Surgeon, 1874; Liverpool Royal Infirmary, 1875; Surgeon, Stanley and Royal Southern Hospitals, 1878–91; since Royal Infirmary, Teaching appointments at Medical School; Demonstrator of Physiology, Pathologist, Lecturer in Dental Anatomy, Lecturer and later Professor in Medical Jurisprudence since 1878; for seven years Dean of the Medical Faculty; Member of various societies; President Liverpool Medical Institution, British Medical Association, Pathological and Clinical Societies of London, etc. *Publications:* Selected Papers, Surgical and Pathological, 1925; article on Intestinal Obstruction, Binnie's Surgery, NSA; Text-book in Domestic Economy; address in Surgery, British Medical Association, 1912; various medical papers on Surgical, Pathological, and Dental subjects. *Address:* Cloudeslee, Headley Road, Grayshott, Surrey. *T:* Headley Down 154.

Died 17 Jan. 1941.

PAUL, Maurice Eden, MD (Brux.), MRCS, LRCP; Medical Practitioner (retired), and author; *b* Sturminster Marshall, Dorset, 1865; *s* of late Charles Kegan Paul, clergyman, publisher, and author, and Margaret Agnes Colvile, novelist. *Educ:* University College School; University Coll., London; London Hospital. Tutor in Japanese provincial University, 1892–94; Times correspondent with northern Japanese army in China-Japan war, 1895; practised medicine in Japan, China, Perak, Singapore, Alderney, and England, 1895–1912; founder and editor of Nagasaki Press, 1897–99; Paris correspondent of Daily Citizen, 1912–14; on tramp from Paris to Vienna when war began, and spent first three months of war in Vienna; since then has lived chiefly in London. *Publications:* Socialism and Science, 1909; Karl Marx and Modern Socialism, 1910; Psychical Research and Thought Transference, 1911; Socialism and Eugenics, 1911; The Sexual Life of the Child, 1921; Steinach's Rejuvenation Experiments, 1923; Chronos, or the future of the family, 1930. (With Cedar Paul): The Appreciation of Poetry, 1920; Creative Revolution, 1920; Proletcult, 1921; Communism, 1921. As Editor: H. G. Sutton's Lectures on Pathology, 1891; and jointly with Cedar Paul, Population and Birth Control, a Symposium, 1921; W. J. Robinson's A Doctor's Views on Life, 1927. Translations: Lagrange's Physiology of Bodily Exercise, 1888; and several medical and scientific works. Many translations made jointly with Cedar Paul, including from the French: Baudouin's Studies in Psychoanalysis (1922); Berthoud's The New Theories of Matter and the Atom, 1924; Guyon's Sexual Freedom, 1939; from the Russian: Buharin and Preobrazhensky's The ABC of Communism, 1922; The Restoration of Agriculture in the Famine Area of Russia, 1922; Stalin's Leninism, 1928; Ryazanoff's Communist Manifesto, 1930; from the Italian: Michel's Sexual Ethics, 1914; Loria's Karl Marx, 1920; from the German: Engels' The Elements of Child Protection, 1912; Marx's The Socialist Programme, 1919; Rathenau's In Days to Come, 1921; Rosa Luxemburg's Letters from Prison, 1923; Marx's Eighteenth Brumaire of Louis Bonaparte, 1926; Bauer's Woman and Love, 1927; Lange Eichbaum, The Problem of Genius, 1931; Fülöp-Miller, Leaders, Dreamers, and Rebels, 1935; Triumph over

Pain, 1938; Arnold Zweig, Truth about the German Jews, 1937; Strasser's Germany To-morrow, 1940; Treitschke's Origins of Prussianism, 1941; Stechert's Thrice against England, 1945. *Recreations:* psychology, study of languages. *Address:* c/o Lloyds Bank, 263 Tottenham Court Road, W1.

Died 1 Dec. 1944.

PAVRY, Faredun Cursetji, CIE 1930; *b* June 1877; *m* Kathleen McCarthy; two *s. Educ:* Cooper's Hill (Fellow). Chief Engineer, Indian State Railways, 1926–32; sometime Member Railway Board, India. *Address:* Mayfield, Millbrook, Jersey.

Died 17 Dec. 1943.

PAYEN-PAYNE, de Vincheles; *b* 1866; *s* of James Bertrand Payen-Payne; *m* Marguerite Berthe, *d* of Alfred Coudere; one *s. Educ:* Lycée St Louis, Paris; University College, London. Assist Master King's College School, 1893–98; Principal of Kensington Coaching College, 1898–1936; retired in 1940; formerly Assistant Examiner to University of London and Civil Service Commission; Chairman of Jersey Society, 1920–35. *Publications:* French Idioms and Proverbs, 1893; trans Memoirs of Bertrand Barère, 1896; trans into French of Art of P. A. de Laszlo; Wace and the Roman de Rou, 1913; editor French Lyrics by Swinburne, 1919; French Poems of To-Day (in collaboration), 1924; French Test Book, 1932; Some Henley Letters, 1933; A Little Book of French Verse, 1935; Traps in French for the Unwary, 1939; editor of many school editions of French authors. *Recreations:* reading, travel. *Address:* 48 Palace Mansions, Addison Road Bridge, W14.

Died 6 Aug. 1945.

PAYNE, Col Alexander Vaughan, CMG 1918; 1st Wilts Regt; *b* Devon, 31 Aug. 1857; *e s* of late Rev. John Vaughan Payne, MA, of Musbury; *m* 1886, Janet, MBE, *d* of late Joseph George Medlicott, IGS; one *d. Educ:* Sandhurst. Entered Army, 1878; ADC to late Gen. Sir Hugh Gough, VC, GCB; commanded 2nd Wiltshire Regt; served throughout Zulu Campaign, 1879; Defence of Ekowe (medal with clasp); South African War, 1901–02; in command Mounted Infantry Batt., and on Staff (medal with 5 clasps); throughout European War on Staff (despatches three times, CMG, Serbian White Eagle, Officier Légion d'Honneur, Officier St Maurice and St Lazarre, Italy, Queen Victoria's Jubilee Medal). Lord of the Manor of Musbury; patron of one living. *Recreations:* hunting, shooting, fishing. *Address:* The Lodge, Sidmouth, Devon. *T:* Sidmouth 80. *Club:* Naval and Military.

Died 9 May 1943.

PAYNE, Charles, CBE 1920; DL; JP Belfast; shipbuilder; retired Director, Harland & Wolff, Ltd; *b* 1871; 4th *s* of William Payne, Stockton-on-Tees; *m* 1901, Grace Agnes, *d* of Andrew Browne, Galwally, Belfast; one *s. Educ:* privately. Managing Director National Shipyards, 1918–19. *Address:* 94 Sydenham Avenue, Strandtown, Belfast.

Died 6 June 1948.

PAYNE, Charles Robert Salusbury; JP Beds; Lieut-Commander RN (retired); *b* 1859; *m* 1893, Aline, *d* of James Henry Murray; two *d. Address:* Hollybank, Emsworth, Hants. *Club:* Union.

Died 16 Oct. 1942.

PAYNE, de Vincheles P.; *see* Payen-Payne.

PAYNE, Col Edward Henry, CIE 1921; Indian Army; retired; *b* Witney, Oxfordshire, 24 Dec. 1868; *er s* of late Rev. J. Payne, DCL; *m* 1894, Hariet Mary (*d* 1930), *e d* of late G. W. L. Ricketts, Inspector-General of Police and Forests, Mysore, India; one *s. Educ:* Continent; Sandhurst. Commissioned in the Oxfordshire Light Infantry, 1889; transferred to the Indian Army (1st Infantry, Hyderabad Contingent); joined the Military

Accounts Dept 1897; retired, 1923; served Afghan Campaign, 1919; Mahsud and Waziristan Campaigns, 1919–21 (despatches). *Club:* Junior United Service.

Died 19 Sept. 1941.

PAYNE, Henry, MInstCE, MIMechE; Hon. FRAeS; Emeritus Professor, University of Melbourne, formerly Dean of the Faculty of Engineering; *b* Calcutta, 3 March 1871; *e s* of late Rev. James E. Payne of London Missionary Society; *m* 1900, Charlotte Wilson, 2nd *d* of late Henry Thompson, of Deal. *Educ:* Modern School, Bedford; SSM, Blackheath; City and Guilds' Technical College, Finsbury, London. Lecturer in Engineering and Applied Mathematics Depts, University Coll., London, 1898–1903; first occupant of the Corporation Chair of Engineering, South African College, Cape Town, 1903–05, and 1906–09 first occupant of the Corporation Chair of Civil Engineering at the same college. Organised and carried out large extensions to the Engineering School of the Melbourne University, where he was Professor of Engineering, 1910–32. *Publications:* papers on engineering subjects in the Proceedings of the Cape (now South African) Society of Civil Engineers, and of (professional) societies in Victoria. *Recreations:* gardening, walking, chess. *Address:* Courthill, Healesville West, Victoria, Australia.

Died 28 March 1945.

PAYNE, Col Herbert Chidgey Brine, CMG 1917; CBE 1919; late RAPC; *b* 1862; *s* of late Lt-Col J. Payne; *m* 1921, Mildred, *y d* of late Rev. Canon J. Lightfoot. *Educ:* Harrow. Joined 1st Batt. N Staffs Regt 1885; served through Zulu Rebellion, 1888; Boer War, 1899–1902 (despatches, Queen's medal 4 clasps, King's medal 2 clasps); European War, 1914–18, as Chief Paymaster of the British Army in Macedonia and Black Sea (CMG, CBE, 3rd class Order of St Sava); transferred to Army Pay Dept 1895. retired pay, 1922. *Address:* Grange Cottage, Watts Lane, Eastbourne.

Died 8 Feb. 1945.

PAYNE, Hon. Herbert James Mockford; Senator in Commonwealth Parliament, 1920–38; *b* Hobart, Tasmania, 17 Aug. 1866; 2nd *s* of Henry and Hannah Payne, Hobart; *m* 1st, Annie, *e d* of Joshua Stones, Ludfordville, Ulverstone, Tasmania; one *s* two *d*; 2nd, 1938, Constance Evelyn, *y d* of Robert Rogers, St Mervyns, Coburg, Victoria. *Educ:* Central State School, Hobart. Entered Parliament as Member for Burnie, 1903; re-elected, 1906; Member for Darwin, 1909–19; Chairman of Committees, 1909–12; Treasurer, Minister of Agriculture and Railways, Tasmania, 1912–14; JP Tasmania; many years actively engaged in Friendly Society's work; is PPGM of Manchester Unity, IOOF. *Recreations:* bowling, gardening, motoring. *Address:* 101 The Grove, Coburg, Vic.

Died 26 Feb. 1944.

PAYNE, Lt-Col Leslie Herbert, DSO 1917; VD; Superintendent and Secretary, Tasmanian Institution for the Blind, Deaf and Dumb; JP, Hobart; *b* Burnie, Tasmania, 5 Nov. 1888; *e s* of Hon. H. J. M. Payne; *m* Ruby, *e d* of late Andrew Bessell, Railway Department, Tasmania; three *s* one *d*. Served European War with Australian Imperial Forces, France (despatches twice, DSO); Member for Denison in Tasmanian House of Assembly, 1924–25; Lt-Col commanding 40th Battalion Infantry Australian Military Forces, 1922–27; Unattached List, Australian Military Forces, 1927; Reserve of Officers, AMF, 1932. *Address:* Gordon Avenue, New Town, Hobart, Tasmania. *Clubs:* Naval and Military, Hobart.

Died 22 Dec. 1942.

PAYNE, Major Robert Leslie, DSO 1915; late 1st Batt. the Connaught Rangers; *b* 7 May 1880; *m* 1914, Lilian Mary, *d* of Thomas Duncan. Entered army, 1899; Captain, 1906; Major, 1916; served South African War,

1899–1902 (Queen's medal 4 clasps, King's medal 2 clasps); European War, 1914–17 (despatches, DSO); retired pay, 1921. *Address:* Ardnageena, Broadstairs.
Died 22 Dec. 1942.

PAYNE, Walter, OBE; *b* London; *s* of late George Adney Payne; *m* 1933, Claire Beatrice, *d* of late Ida and Mor Wisinger, Budapest. *Educ:* City of London School; Heidelberg University. Barrister, Middle Temple; Chartered Accountant; Chairman and Managing Director, London Pavilion, Ltd; Variety Theatres Consolidated, Ltd, Director of Moss Empires, Ltd; Victoria Palace Ltd; Vice-President Society of West End Theatre Managers (previously President, 21 years); Director Outside Organisation and Munitions' Tribunals, Ministry of Munitions, 1915–18; Chief Resettlement Officer, London and South of England Demobilisation and Resettlement Department, 1918–19; Deputy-Controller, Civil Liabilities (Military Service) Dept, 1919–20. *Recreations:* reading, the theatre. *Address:* 7 Cleveland Row, St James's, SW1. *T:* Whitehall 4870. *Clubs:* Savile, Bath, Garrick.
Died 30 Oct. 1949.

PAYNTER, Col Camborne Haweis; *b* 1864; *m* 1904, Ethel (*d* 1933), *o d* of late Sir Edgcombe Venning; one *d.* High Sheriff of Cornwall, 1929; Capt. 5th Dragoon Guards, 1889–90; Major 6th Dragoons, 1899–1901. *Address:* Boskenna, St Buryan, Cornwall. *Club:* Army and Navy.
Died 11 Jan. 1949.

PAYNTER, Brig.-Gen. Sir George Camborne Beauclerk, KCVO 1950; CMG 1919; CVO 1930; DSO 1914; a Groom-in-Waiting to the King, since 1933; an Equerry in Ordinary to the King, 1927–30; an Extra Equerry since 1930; Lord Lieutenant of County Sutherland since 1945; *b* 2 Aug. 1880; *m* 1921, Alba, MBE 1941, *d* of late Major Sir Philip Hunloke, GCVO; one *s* two *d. Educ:* Eton. Entered Scots Guards, 1899; Captain, 1904; Major, 1915; Col 1922; served South Africa, 1899–1900 (Queen's medal 3 clasps, King's medal 2 clasps); European War, 1914–18 (despatches 8 times, CMG, DSO and bar, Bt Lt-Col, Croix de Guerre); Cmd. Scots Guards and Regimental Dist and 167th (London) Infantry Brigade, 1923–27; retired pay, 1929; King's Messenger since Sept. 1939; GSO 1 Home Guard North Midland District, 1940–43; assistant Director, Ministry of Fuel and Power, 1943. Order of St Anne, 3rd Class; Croix de Guerre; winner Grand Military Gold Cup, 1907 and 1914. *Address:* Eaton Grange, Grantham. *TA:* Knipton 43; Suisgill, Kildonan, Sutherland. *Clubs:* Turf, Bath.
Died 15 Aug. 1950.

PEACH, Adm. Charles William K.; *see* Keighly-Peach.

PEACOCK, Rev. Charles Alfred, CBE 1919; MA; *b* 1868; *s* of late Rev. Edwin Peacock, Vicar of Netherexe, Devon; *m* 1900, Annie Kathleen, *d* of late Capt. W. Edgecumbe-Rendle (10th Regt); one *s* one *d. Educ:* Oxford. Ordained 1894; Curate of Henley-on-Thames, 1894–97; Vicar of Netherexe, 1897–99; Acting Chaplain Forces, Aldershot, 1899; S Africa, 1901–03 (medal and 5 clasps); SCF 1st Division, SAFF, Garrison Chaplain, Pretoria, SCF Orange River Colony; Chaplain, Brigade of Guards, Wellington Barracks, 1903–08; Malta, 1908–12; Woolwich, 1912–17 (SCF Woolwich District); Assistant Chaplain-General Irish Command, 1917; Chaplain to Lord-Lieutenant of Ireland, 1919; Assistant Chap.-Gen. Western Command and Northern Ireland District, 1922–24; retired pay, 1924; Rector of Stoke Dry, 1924; Rector of St Peter's with All Saints', Stamford, 1929–35; Vicar of West Tisted, 1935–37. *Recreations:* cricket, fishing. *Address:* Roxburgh Cottage, 8 Westonville Avenue, Margate. *Clubs:* Phyllis Court, Henley.
Died 2 Dec. 1944.

PEACOCK, Lady Millie; Member for Allandale, Victoria Legislative Assembly, 1933–35; *d* of J. B. Holden; *m* 1901, Hon. Sir Alexander Peacock, KCMG (*d* 1933). *Address:* Creswick, Victoria, Australia.
Died 8 Feb. 1948.

PEACOCK, Sir Peter, Kt 1918; JP; *b* 13 April 1872; *s* of Jesse and Susan Peacock; *m* 1893, Maria Timmins; four *s* one *d. Educ:* Warrington. First entered Council, 1903; Mayor, 1913 (only Mayor of Warrington elected for six years); Alderman, 1914; a Liveryman of the City of London Feltmakers' Guild, 1918; Hon. Freeman of the County Borough of Warrington, 1918; Chairman of Committee under Lord Derby's Recruiting Scheme; Member of Appeal Tribunal for West Lancashire; Ex-Chairman of the Health Insurance Committee; Chairman of Warrington Savings Bank Trustees; a prominent Mason and Past Worshipful Master of Lodge of Lights; a Governor of the Masonic Institution for Boys, and a Member of the Royal Arch Chapter and the Mark. *Address:* Warrington.
Died 22 July 1948.

PEACOCK, Ralph; portrait painter; *m* Edith (*d* 1945), *d* of James Brignall; two *s. Educ:* Royal Academy Schools (gold medal, Creswick, and other prizes). Exhibited at Royal Academy. Works at permanent exhibitions: Tate Gallery, Walker Art Gallery, Liverpool, National Galleries of Perth, Adelaide, and Durban: medals at Paris and Vienna. *Address:* The Gate House, Ellerton Road, Wimbledon, SW20. *T:* Wimbledon 1546. *Club:* Arts.
Died 17 Jan. 1946.

PEACOCK, William Henry, CBE 1934; MB, BS Durh.; LRCP Lond.; MRCS Eng.; DPH Camb.; DTM and HEng; *b* 9 Feb. 1881; *s* of William and Margaret Peacock; *m* 1911, Mary Hamilton, *d* of Dr Ernest Tredinnick, Craven Arms, Shropshire; one *d. Educ:* Darlington Grammar School; University of Durham College of Medicine, Newcastle-on-Tyne. West African Medical Staff (Southern Nigeria), 1910; Temporary Captain in Army (General List), 1915–16; seconded as Temporary Lieutenant RAMC 1916; Capt. 1917; Acting Major, 1918–19; Active service in Cameroons and with British Salonika Force, 80th Field Ambulance 26th Division (despatches twice, Order of St Sava, Fifth Class); Senior Sanitary Officer, Sierra Leone, 1919; Deputy Director of Sanitary Service, Sierra Leone, 1926; Deputy Director of Health Service, Nigeria, 1930; retired, 1935. *Publications:* Fracture of the Os Calcis, 1909; (with D. B. Blacklock) Destruction of Rats by Exhaust Gas (Lancet, 1924). *Recreation:* golf. *Address:* West Leigh, Church Stretton, Shropshire. *T:* Church Stretton 178.
Died 22 Oct. 1946.

PEAKE, George Herbert; JP; *b* 1859; *s* of late Henry Peake, of Westholme, Sleaford, Lincs, and Eliza, *d* of late Charles Kirk; *m* 1895, Evelyn Mary (*d* 1945), *e d* of Hon. John Charles Dundas; three *s* one *d. Educ:* Trinity Hall, Cambridge (LLB, MA). Called to Bar, Lincoln's Inn, 1887; Major Territorial Force Reserve; late temp. Major (previously Major) Nottinghamshire) Sherwood Rangers) Yeomanry. DL Notts. *Heir: s* Rt Hon. Osbert Peake, PC. *Address:* Sutton Hall, Thirsk, Yorkshire. *T:* Sutton Thirsk 200.
Died 11 Oct. 1950.

PEAKE, Harold John Edward, MA, FSA; Vice-President of the Royal Anthropological Institute; President of the Newbury District Field Club; President of the Newbury District Hospital; Chairman of the Governors of the Newbury Grammar School; Corresponding Fellow of the Societa Romana di Antropologia; *b* 27 Sept. 1867; *e s* of late Rev. John Peake, Vicar of Ellesmere; *m* 1897, Charlotte Mary Augusta (*d* 1934), *e d* of late Captain Richard Lane Bayliff; no *c.* Member Berkshire Education Committee, 1919–43; President of the Anthropological Section of the British Association for the Advancement of Science, 1922; President of the Royal Anthropological Institute, 1926–28; Member of Council of the Society of Antiquaries, 1928–30; Huxley Memorial Lecturer and Medal list (RAI), 1940. *Publications:* The English Village, 1922; The Bronze Age and the Celtic World, 1922; (with Prof. H. J. Fleure) The Corridors of Time, 1927–1936; The Origins of Agriculture, 1928; The Flood, 1930; The Archæology of Berkshire, 1931; Early Steps in Human Progress, 1933; Papers in the Journal of the Anthropological Institute, the Antiquaries Journal, Man, etc. *Address:* Westbrook House, Newbury. *TA:* Boxford, Berks. *T:* Boxford 204. *Clubs:* Athenæum; Berkshire.

Died 22 Sept. 1946.

PEAKE, Thomas; DL; Alderman and JP for Isle of Ely; *b* 1868; *s* of Thomas Peake, King's Lynn; *m* 1892, A. A. Canham, Littleport; one *s* four *d. Educ:* King's Lynn Private School. Corn Merchant; Member of Parish Council, 43 years; Capt. 3rd Batt. Cambs V Regiment; Member Isle of Ely County Council since 1904; Alderman, 1925; Member of Ely Rural District Council, 1913–; High Sheriff for Cambridgeshire and Hunts, 1937–38; Chairman of the Isle of Ely Liberal Association. *Recreations:* golf and shooting. *Address:* Littleport. *T:* Littleport 17. *Club:* National Liberal.

Died 27 June 1945.

PEAKER, Frederick; journalist; former Labour and Educational Correspondent of the Morning Post, and later Consultant and Adviser; *b* 20 Feb. 1867; *e s* of Alfred Peaker, Leeds; *m* 1895, Eveline (JP, County of London) (*d* 1939), *y d* of E. Pearson, of Holmfirth, Yorks; one *s* two *d. Educ:* St John's College, York. Taught in Leeds Schools, 1886–94; Secretary of Leeds Teachers' Association and Member of the Leeds School Board, 1894–1903; Member of the Leeds City Council, 1903–04; Member of the Executive of the National Union of Teachers, 1891–1904; Editor of the School Manager, 1904–05; on the editorial staff of the Tribune, 1906–07; joined the editorial staff of the Morning Post, 1908; Editor of Schoolmaster, 1924–26; Member of the Journalism Committee of the University of London and External Examiner in Practical Journalism; MA (Hon.) University of Leeds; Fellow of Educational Institute of Scotland; President of the Institute of Journalists, 1923, 1924, and 1925; Trustee of T. P. O'Connor Fund for Sick and Aged Journalists; Freeman and Liveryman City of London (Stationers and Newspaper Makers' Co.); PM Alfred Robbins Lodge of Freemasons; PZ of the Gallery Chapter. *Publications:* British Citizenship; its Rights and its Duties; many special articles on Labour and Education. *Recreations:* walking, motoring. *Address:* Priory Cottage, Guisborough. *T:* Guisborough 44. *Clubs:* National Liberal; Cleveland.

Died 14 July 1942.

PEARCE, Col Cyril Harvey, CBE 1919; TD; DL, East Riding of County of York; solicitor; *b* 19 July 1878; *s* of Thomas and Sarah Elizabeth Pearce; *m* 1904, Martha Cross; three *c. Educ:* Denstone College. Commanded 5th Yorkshire Regt during European War, now 5th Green Howards (wounded, CBE, TD); Hon. Colonel 5th Green Howards. *Recreations:* Rugby football (Yorkshire County), golf. *Address:* 11 Parliament Street, Hull. *T:* Central 36769.

Died 13 Feb. 1943.

PEARCE, Ernest Alfred John, CBE 1925; OBE 1918; *b* 1868; *s* of late John Pearce, Surveyor of Stores, Chatham Dockyard; *m* 1903, Alice Pearson (*d* 1940), *d* of late Henry Hastrick, Chatham Dockyard. Late Director of Warship Production Royal Corps of Naval Constructors at the Admiralty. *Address:* 7 The Avenue, Tiverton, Devon.

Died 28 Dec. 1943.

PEARCE, Sir Frank James, Kt 1939; LDS, RCS Eng., DDS Penn; Consulting Dental Surgeon, Guy's Hospital; *b* 1878; *s* of late Rev. James Pearce; *m* 1921, Phyllis Crome, *d* of Mark Verden; three *d. Educ:* Kingswood School, Bath; Guy's Hospital; University of Penn. Travelling Dental Scholarship Guy's Hospital, 1900; various appointments Guy's Dental School, including Lecturerships on Materia Medica and Operative Dental Surgery; Dental Surgeon to Guy's Hospital; Hon. Sec. British Dental Association, 1912–17; Pres. 1936; Pres. 1st Empire Dental Meeting, 1936; FRSM; Pres. Section Odontology, RSM 1937. *Recreation:* golf. *Address:* 57a Wimpole Street, W1. *T:* Welbeck 6465.

Died 12 Nov. 1946.

PEARCE, Sir (Standen) Leonard, Kt 1935; CBE 1919; DSc; MInstCE; MIEE; MIMechE; FAmerIEE; FCGI; Engineer-in-Chief of the London Power Company, Horseferry Road, SW, since 1926; *b* Crewkerne, Somerset, 28 Sept. 1873; *s* of late Rev. Standen Pearce; *m* 1901, Susie Kate (*d* 1938), *d* of late G. R. Cockhead, Crouch End, London; one *d. Educ:* Bishops Stortford College; Finsbury Technical College. Apprenticeship with the Electrical Engineering Corporation of West Drayton and Richardsons, Westgarth of Hartlepool; subsequent positions held with the British India Steam Navigation Co., the Metro-Elec. Supply Co., the British Thomson-Houston Co.; the Central London Railway Co.; Deputy-Chief Electrical Engineer, Manchester, 1901; Chief Electrical Engineer and Consulting Engineer and Manager Electricity Department, 1904–25; an Electricity Commissioner, Savoy Court, London, 1925–26 and again 1940–45; Past President Incorporated Municipal Electrical Association; Past Chairman Institution of Electrical Engineers, Manchester Section; Past Chm. Institution of Civil Engineers, Manchester Section; Past President Junior Institution of Engineers; Thomas Hawksley Lecturer, Institution of Mechanical Engineers, 1940. *Publications:* several Technical Papers before the Institution of Electrical Engineers, the Institution of Civil Engineers, and Incorporated Municipal Electrical Association. *Recreations:* tennis, golf, mountaineering. *Address:* 8 Park Hill, Bickley, Kent. *T:* Imperial 1069. *Clubs:* Athenæum, Alpine; Engineers (Manchester).

Died 20 Oct. 1947.

PEARCE, Thomas Ernest; JP, Senior Partner, John D. Hutchison and Co., Hongkong; MLC Hongkong; Chairman, Hongkong Jockey Club; *b* 19 Feb. 1883; British; *m* 1910, Evelyn Rodger; two *s. Educ:* Blackheath. 37 years business in Hongkong. Directorships: Hongkong and Shanghai Banking Corporation; Canton Insurance Office Ltd; Hongkong Fire Insurance Co. Ltd; Hongkong Electric Co. Ltd; Dairy Farm Ice and Cold Storage Co., Ltd; Hongkong Tramways Co., Ltd; Green Island Cement Co., Ltd; Hongkong Realty and Trust Co., Ltd; Hongkong and Canton Ice Co., Ltd; Hongkong Land Investment and Agency Co., Ltd. *Recreations:* racing, cricket, golf. *Address:* 299 The Peak, Hongkong. *TA:* Spero. *Clubs:* Thatched House; Hongkong, etc.

Died Dec. 1941.

PEARL, Raymond; Professor of Biology, School of Hygiene, Johns Hopkins University, since 1930; *b* Farmington, New Hampshire, USA, 3 June 1879; *s* of Frank Pearl and Ida May McDuffie; *m* 1903, Maud Mary De Witt; two *d. Educ:* Dartmouth College, AB, 1899; Hon. ScD, 1919; University of Michigan, PhD, 1902; Special Student, University of Leipzig, 1905; University College, London, 1905–06; LLD, University of Maine, 1919; LittD St John's College in Annapolis, 1935. Assistant and Instructor in Zoology, University of Michigan, 1899–1906; Instructor in Zoology, University of Pennsylvania, 1906–07; Biologist and head of Dept of Biology, Maine Agricultural Experiment Station, 1907–18; Professor of Biometry and Vital Statistics, School of Hygiene, Johns Hopkins University, 1918–25;

Research Professor, 1925–30; Professor of Biology, School of Medicine, Johns Hopkins University, since 1923; Director of the Institute of Biological Research, Johns Hopkins University, 1925–30; Statistician, Johns Hopkins Hospital, 1919–35; Lowell Lecturer, Boston, Mass, 1920; Special Lecturer, University of London, 1927; Heath Clark Lecturer, University of London, 1937; Patten Foundation Lecturer, Indiana University, 1938; Chief of Statistical Division, US Food Administration, 1917–19; Member National Academy of Sciences; American Philosophical Society; American Society of Zoologists; Institut Internationale de Statistique, etc.; Fellow: American Academy of Arts and Sciences; American Statistical Association, etc.; President of the International Union for the Scientific Investigation of Population Problems, 1928–31; Pres. American Assoc. of Physical Anthropologists, 1934–36; Pres. of American Statistical Association, 1939; Hon. FSS, London; Knight (1920) and Officer (1929) of the Crown of Italy; Trustee; St John's College, Annapolis, 1928–34; Science Service, Washington, 1929–35. *Publications:* Modes of Research in Genetics, 1915; Diseases of Poultry, 1915; The Nation's Food, 1919; The Biology of Death, 1922; Introduction to Medical Biometry and Statistics, 1923 (Rev. ed. 1930); Studies in Human Biology, 1924; The Biology of Population Growth, 1925; Alcohol and Longevity, 1926; To Begin With, 1927 (rev. ed. 1930); The Rate of Living, 1928; Constitution and Health, 1933; The Ancestry of the Long-Lived, 1934; The Natural History of Population, 1939; numerous contributions to scientific journals. *Recreation:* music. *Address:* Johns Hopkins University, Baltimore, Maryland, USA. *Clubs:* University, Baltimore; Dartmouth, New York.

Died 17 Nov. 1940.

PEARS, Adm. Sir Edmund Radcliffe, KBE 1919; CB 1917; *b* Ootacamund, India, 25 April 1862; *s* of late Lt-Col A. C. Pears of Charlcombe, Bath; *m* 1890, Jeanie Mayhew, *d* of late J. H. Innes, Vancouver Island; one *s*. *Educ:* Clifton Coll. Entered RN 1875; Acting Sub-Lt of Ruby during Egyptian War, 1882, and landed with Naval Bde at Suez (Egyptian medal and Khedive's star); First Lieutenant of Mohawk during disturbances at Bluefields, Nicaragua, 1894, and landed with armed party for protection of British subjects; First Lieut of Forte during Benin Expedition, 1897, and was present at capture of Benin City (Benin medal); Commander in command of Perseus on Somali coast during expeditions against Mad Mullah, 1902–03 (Somaliland medal); commanded Blenheim, 1905–06; Arrogant, 1906–08; Triumph, 1908–09; Agamemnon, 1910–11; Commodore of Training Service, 1912–14; Commanded 10th Cruiser Squadron in Naval Manœuvres, 1913; in command of a Naval Base, 1914–19; Vice-Admiral, 1919; retired, 1920; Admiral, 1924. *Address:* c/o Glyn Mills & Co. (Holt's Branch), Whitehall, SW1.

Died 21 June 1941.

PEARSE, Sir John Slocombe, Kt 1935; *b* 1870; *s* of John Pearse, Plymouth; *m* 1904, Helena Mary, *d* of James Masters; one *d*. *Educ:* Plymouth Grammar School. Member Common Council, City of London since 1922; Sheriff, 1934–35; Deputy for the Ward of Cripplegate Within; one of His Majesty's Lieutenants for the City of London, 1937. *Clubs:* Constitutional, City Livery Royal Automobile.

Died 15 March 1949.

PEARSE, Rev. Thomas Northmore Hart S.; *see* Smith-Pearse.

PEARSE, Brig.-Gen. Tom Harry Finch, CMG 1915; *b* 15 Sept. 1864; *m* 1892, Mabel Catherine, *d* of late John Colquhoun of Castletown House, Strabane, Tyrone; one *d*. Entered army, East Lancs Regiment, 1885; Captain, 1893; Major, 1906; Lt-Col Cheshire Regiment, 1912; Col 1916; Brig.-Gen. 1915; retired,

1919; served European War, 1914–18 (despatches, CMG). *Address:* c/o F. Branch, Lloyds Bank, Ltd, 6 Pall Mall, SW1.

Died 16 Sept. 1947.

PEARSON, Charles Yelverton, MD, MCh, FRCS Eng.; Professor of Surgery, University College, Cork (formerly Queen's), 1900–28, now Emeritus; *b* Kilworth, Co. Cork, 27 Aug. 1857; 4th *s* of William W. Pearson, MD; *m* 1st, 1881, Christiana Dorothea, *e d* of Dr Tuckey of Bantry, Co. Cork; two *s* one *d*; 2nd, 1924, May Clemence, *er d* of Lawson L. Ferguson, Glen View, Co, Wicklow; two *d*. *Educ:* at the Model and Messrs Perrotts' Schools, Cork; obtained numerous scholarships, exhibitions, and prizes in Queen's College, Cork, and graduated MD with 1st honours and gold medal in the Queen's Univ., 1878. Appointed Senior Demonstrator of Anatomy in Queen's College, 1878; Professor of Materia Medica, 1884; obtained the Fellowship of the Royal Coll. of Surgeons of England, 1886, by examination; Consulting Surgeon to North Charitable Infirmary, and Surgeon to County and City of Cork Victoria Hospital for Women and Children; Hon. Obstetric Surgeon to County and City of Cork Lying-in Hospital; life hon. member of the Austin Flint Medical Association of Iowa, USA, 1900; appointed Surgical Fellow of the Royal University of Ireland, 1903; Senator of the National University of Ireland, 1908; Examiner in Surgery for IMS, 1912; Hon. Surgeon to the King in Ireland, 1916; holds several other medical appointments. *Publications:* Modern Surgical Technique, 1906; has made numerous contributions to medical and surgical literature, etc. *Recreations:* yachting, salmon and trout-fishing, shooting, motoring. *Address:* Knockrea Park, Cork. *T:* 1613.

Died 13 May 1947.

PEARSON, George Sherwin Hooke, CMG 1917; JP; *b* 1875; *s* of Capt. G. J. H. Pearson, JP; *m* 1st, 1904, Adeline Percy (*d* 1927), *d* of late Admiral Sir H. F. Woods, KCVO; two *s* one *d*; 2nd, 1928, Alice C. Stace. *Educ:* Eton; Magdalen College, Oxford. *Address:* Baynton House, East Coulston, Westbury, Wilts. *T:* Bratton 241.

Died 26 Jan. 1941.

PEARSON, Col George Thomson, CBE 1919; *b* 1876; *m* 1905. Served European War, 1914–19 (despatches, CBE). *Address:* Crosby Court, Northallerton, Yorkshire.

Died 9 July 1946.

PEARSON, Sir Louis Frederick, Kt 1923; CBE 1919; JP Notts; *b* 1863; *m* Gertrude (*d* 1936), *yr d* of late Thomas Potter of Trowell and Bramcote, Notts; one *s* two *d*. *Educ:* Grosvenor Sch., Nottingham. Chairman of the Rushcliffe Division Conservative Association, 1911–33; Chairman Nottingham General Hospital; High Sheriff of Nottinghamshire, 1934–35. *Address:* Lenton Grove, Nottingham; The White Cottage, Brailsford, Derby. *Clubs:* Carlton; Notts County, Nottingham.

Died 5 Nov. 1943.

PEARSON, Sidney Vere, MA, MD, Cambridge; MRCP London; *b* 1875; *s* of Rev. S. Pearson and Bertha E., *d* of William Crosfield, Liverpool; *m* 1916, May Elizabeth, *d* of James Earl, Norwich; one *s* one *d*. *Educ:* Highgate; Manchester Grammar School; Emmanuel College, Cambridge; St George's Hospital. Formerly Assistant Physician East London Children's Hospital, President Society of Superintendents of Tuberculosis Institutions, Ex-Chairman Joint Tuberculosis Council; Physician, Mundesley Sanatorium, 1905–49. *Publications:* The State Provision of Sanatoriums, 1913; The Growth and Distribution of Population, 1934; London's Overgrowth, 1939; Men, Medicine and Myself, 1946; Contributions to medical journals. *Recreations:* rowed Cambridge Univ. Eight, 1898; Sociology and

Economics; water colours, walking, travel. *Address:* Rillbank, Mundeslev, Norfolk. *Clubs:* Athenæum, English Speaking Union.

Died 18 March 1950.

PEART, Joseph Norriss, DSO 1942; BA (NZ), MA (Cantab); Headmaster, King's College, Auckland, NZ, since 1936; serving, Major, with NZEF in Egypt, commanding HQ Co. 18 Bn; *b* 12 Feb. 1900; *s* of Alfred Peart and Selina Tunnicliffe; *m* 1930, Anne, *o d* of Dr C. H. Phillips, Norbury, London; one *s* two *d. Educ:* Auckland Grammar School, NZ; Auckland University College (Scholar); Emmanuel College, Cambridge. Asst Master Nelson College, NZ, 1922–24; Asst Master Epsom College, Surrey, 1926–35, Second Master, 1933–35. *Recreations:* Rugby Football (University, Nelson Province, and All Blacks Trial XVs), lawn tennis, golf, squash rackets. *Address:* King's College, Middlemore, Auckland, SE7, New Zealand. *T:* Otahuhu 56. *Clubs:* Middlemore Golf; English Public Schools, Auckland.

Died 8 Sept. 1942.

PEASE, Col Henry Thomas, CIE 1907; VD, AVS; *b* 20 July 1862; *s* of F. R. Pease of Rusholme Hall, Yorkshire; *m* 1901, Leila Marion, *d* of late Colonel W. H. J. Stopford, Indian Army; one *s* two *d. Educ:* St Edmund's College, Old Hall Green, Ware. Army Veterinary Dept, 1884; Major, 1902; Colonel, 1907; Inspector-General, Civil Veterinary Department, Simla, Punjab, 1907–12; Principal, Veterinary College, Punjab, 1912–19; Commandant Punjab Light Horse, 1912–19; Hon. ADC to C in C; retired, 1919. *Publications:* numerous scientific, some in Urdu.

Died 12 April 1943.

PEAT, Sir George, Kt 1943; Deputy Director, Liner Division, Ministry of War Transport; Partner of P. Henderson & Co., 95 Bothwell Street, Glasgow, C2; *b* 1893; *s* of George Peat, Shipowner, Strathallan, Uddingston, Scotland; *m* 1919, Elizabeth Lorimer. *Address:* Liner Division, Ministry of War Transport, Berkeley Square House, Berkeley Square, W1; 4 Beaumont Gate, Glasgow, W. *T:* Glasgow West 3453.

Died 28 June 1945.

PECK, Maj.-Gen. Arthur Wharton, CB 1919; CMG 1918; late Indian Cavalry; Colonel of Sam Browne's Cavalry, 1931–45; *b* 1869; *m* Kathleen Halima (*d* 1946), *d* of late Colonel W. L. Chester; two *s. Educ:* Clifton College; RMC, Sandhurst. Served Waziristan, 1894 (medal and clasp); S African War (Queen's medal, three claps); NW Frontier, 1908 (medal with clasp); European War, 1914–18 (despatches, CB, CMG); retired, 1921. *Address:* 28 The Parks, Minehead.

Died 16 Sept. 1948.

PECK, Maj.-Gen. Sydney Capel, CB 1927; DSO 1917; Past President, Institution of Automobile Engineers; *b* 1871; unmarried. *Educ:* The Perse School; Sidney Sussex Coll., Cambridge (MA). Member Council Institution Automobile Engineers; served N Nigeria, 1902–03 (medal with clasp); European War, 1914–18 (despatches, DSO, Bt Lt-Col); Head of British Mission, Fiume, 1919; British Commissioner and President, Klagenfurt Interallied Plebiscite Commission (S Austria), 1920–21; Director of Artillery, 1924; Director of Mechanization, War Office, 1927; retired pay, 1933. *Clubs:* Army and Navy, Carlton, Royal Automobile.

Died 25 June 1949.

PEDDIE, Coventry Dick, CBE 1930; Advocate; *b* 2 Dec. 1863; 4th *s* of late John Dick Peddie, RSA, MP; *m* 1902, Margaret, *d* of late A. Peddie Waddell, WS, and Mrs Ralston Peddie Waddell of Balquhatstone and Glenelrig, Stirlingshire; one *s* (one *d* decd). *Educ:* Edinburgh Academy; Fettes College; Edinburgh University, MA, LLB. Called to Scottish Bar, 1889;

Secretary to Commissioners of Northern Lighthouses, 1901–29. *Address:* 15 Clarendon Crescent, Edinburgh; Balquhatstone, Slamannan, Stirlingshire.

Died 3 May 1950.

PEDDIE, John Taylor; monetary specialist, economist, philosopher and theologian; *b* Glasgow, 27 June 1879; *s* of William Peddie and Jeanie McNee Harper; *m* 1911, Maud Kathleen, *d* of late Col Charles P. Costello, IMS; one *s* one *d.* Fellow, R. Economic Soc., 1918; first to capture Palma Trophy from the United States with own selected team of Canadian Riflemen, Sea Girt, New Jersey, 1901; has shot for Great Britain at Bisley on Palma and Kalapore Teams; for Scotland at Bisley on Mackinnon and Scottish Twenty Teams; winner of Ontario Championship (Gold Medal, 1902) and Middlesex Championship (Gold Medal, 1906); St George's and King's Badges; originator of War Office Miniature Rifle. *Publications:* First Principles of Production, 1915; Flaw in the Economic System, 1928; Dual System of Stabilisation, 1931; The Crisis of the £, 1932; The Economic Mechanism of Scripture (two volumes), 1934, 1935; Farming and Money (with Jorian E. F. Jenks), 1935; The Rule of Equity, 1940; The Wealth Standard, 1947; Pamphlets: Charter of Economic Equity, 1943; ABC of Economic Equity, 1944; A Criticism of the Bretton Woods Proposals, 1944. *Recreation:* golf. *Address:* 26 Stafford Court, Kensington, W8.

Died 24 Sept. 1947.

PEDDIE, Dr William, LD, DSc, FRSE; Harris Professor of Physics, University College, Dundee, University of St Andrews, 1907–42; *b* Orkney, 1861; *m* 1891, Jessie Isabella Dott. *Educ:* Orkney, Edinburgh. Formerly Lecturer in Natural Philosophy, Edinburgh University. *Publications:* Manual of Physics; Elementary Dynamics of Solids and Fluids; Colour Vision; Molecular Magnetism; numerous scientific papers. *Address:* The Weisha, Ninewells, Dundee.

Died 2 June 1946.

PEDEN, Hon. Sir John Beverley, KCMG 1930; KC, 1923; BA, LLB; MLC New South Wales since 1917, President since 1929; Fellow of the Senate, Sydney University, 1910–41; Chairman of Board of Trustees of Sydney Grammar School since 1932; President of the Trustees of Captain Cook's Landing Place, 1934–41; President Boys' Brigade, Sydney, since 1939; *b* 1871; *s* of late Magnus Jackson Peden, Randwick, NSW; *m* 1904, Margaret Ethel (*d* 1928), *d* of John Charles Maynard; two *d. Educ:* Sydney Gram. School; Sydney University, BA, 1892, LLB, 1898. Fellow of St Paul's College, Sydney, 1898–1928. Called to NSW Bar, 1898; Challis Professor of Law and Dean of Faculty of Law, Sydney Univ., 1910–41; member of Royal Commission on Greater Sydney, 1913; Chairman Commonwealth Constitution Commission, 1927. *Address:* Illawambra, Chatswood, Sydney, NSW. *Clubs:* Australian, University, Sydney.

Died 31 May 1946.

PEDLER, Margaret; authoress; *γ d* of late Thomas Bass, Teignmouth, Devon; *m* W. G. Q. Pedler (*d* 1929), JP, Bow, Devon. Studied music (singing and pianoforte) at Royal Academy of Music, and has published several songs of which she is the author of both words and music; her first novel, The Splendid Folly, was published in 1918, and from that time onward she has devoted herself entirely to literature. *Publications:* The Splendid Folly; The Hermit of Far End; The House of Dreams-Come-True; The Lamp of Fate; The Moon out of Reach; The Vision of Desire; The Barbarian Lover; Waves of Destiny; Red Ashes; Tomorrow's Tangle; Yesterday's Harvest; Bitter Heritage; The Guarded Halo; Fire of Youth; Kindled Flame; Many Ways; Desert Sand; Pitiless Choice; Green Judgment; Checkered Paths; The Shining Cloud; Flame in the Wind; No Armour Against Fate; Blind Loyalty; Not Heaven Itself; Then Came the Test; No Gifts from Chance; Unless Two be Agreed.

Recreations: tennis, music, swimming, etc. *Address:* 43 Kingston House, Princes Gate, SW7. *T:* Kensington 0243. *Club:* Hurlingham.

Died 28 Dec. 1948.

PEDLEY, Arthur Charles, CB 1920; ISO 1905; *b* July 1859; *s* of late Matthew Pedley of Chatteris, Cambs, and Elizabeth Wayman, *d* of Richard Amory of Haddenham, Cambs; *m* 1886, Elizabeth Mary (*d* 1932), *d* of late C. H. Woodcraft; one *d*. *Educ:* Bedford Modern School. Appointed to Local Government Board, Dublin, 1877; to War Office, 1879; acting assistant principal, 1900; clerk to the Commissioners of Income Duty for army, 1901–02; Assistant Principal, 1902; acting Principal, 1904; Principal, 1913; retd 1919. *Address:* The Woodlands, Spinney Walk, Anlaby Park, Hull.

Died 16 Dec. 1943.

PEDLEY, Frederick N.; *see* Newland-Pedley.

PEEL, Rev. Albert, MA, LittD Leeds; BLitt Oxford; LLD (Rockford, Ill); DD (Carleton); Editor, (1922–45) of The Congregational Quarterly and of the Transactions of the Congregational Historical Society; joint-editor of the Congregational Church Monthly; Chairman Congregational Union of England and Wales, 1940–41; *b* Gomersal, near Leeds, 20 March 1887; *e s* of Rawson and Louisa Peel; *m* 1913, Ethel Constance, *e d* of Rev. W. Harrop; one *d*. *Educ:* Leeds and Oxford, 1st Class Hons Hist. BA and Univ. Scholar (Leeds). Fellow of Royal Historical Society. Minister, Great Harwood Congregational Church, Lancs, 1913–22; Clapton Park Congregational Church, London, 1922–34. *Publications:* The Seconde Parte of a Register, 1915; The Brownists in Norfolk and Norwich, 1920; The First Congregational Churches, 1920; Q: The Earliest Gospel? 1923; Oliver Cromwell, England's Uncrowned King, 1924; The Free Churches, 1903–1926 1927; A Hundred Eminent Congregationalists, 1530–1924, 1927; Letters to a Victorian Editor, 1929; These Hundred Years, 1931; A Brief History of English Congregationalism, 1931; Essays Congregational and Catholic, 1931; Robert Forman Horton, 1937; Inevitable Congregationalism, 1937; Thirty-Five to Fifty, 1938; Christian Freedom, 1938; The Savoy Declaration, 1939; Journal, 1940, 1941; The Christian Basis of Democracy, 1943; The Notebook of John Penry, 1593, 1944, Reconciling the World, 1946; The Noble Army of Congregational Martyrs, 1948; The Congregational Two Hundred, 1948; International Congregationalism, 1949. *Recreations:* cricket, walking, historical research. *Address:* 35 Memorial Hall, EC4.

Died 3 Nov. 1949.

PEEL, Major Hugh Edmund Ethelston; late Welsh Horse; *b* 1871; *e s* of Edmund Peel, Brynypys, Flints, DL, JP; *m* 1892, Gwladys (*d* 1931), *d* of Capt. C. G. H. Rowley Conwy of Bodrhyddan, Flints, DL, JP; one *s*. *Educ:* Eton. DL, JP Flints; JP Denbighshire. High Sheriff of Montgomeryshire, 1907; Lieut King's Shropshire Light Infantry (Militia), 1888–93; Montgomeryshire Yeomanry, 1893–98; Captain, Remount Service, Oct. 1914–Dec. 1914; Welsh Horse, Dec. 1914; Major, 1 March 1915 Chairman, Flintshire County Council, 1924. *Address:* Bryn-y-pys, Overton, Wrexham; Llandrinio Hall, Llanymynech, Montgomeryshire. *Club:* Orleans.

Died 25 June 1950.

PEEL, Sir Robert, 6th Bt *cr* 1800; *b* 11 Dec. 1920; *s* of 5th Bt and Beatrice Lillie; *S* father, 1934. *Heir: cousin* 2nd Earl Peel.

Died 10 April 1942.

PEEL, Roland Tennyson, CBE 1939; MC; Assistant Secretary India Office; *b* 9 Oct. 1892; 4th *s* of late Edward Lennox Peel; *m* 1931, Marjorie Lilian, *d* of late Lionel G. Thomas; one *s*. *Educ:* Bedford School; Hertford College, Oxford. Military Service Aug. 1914–Dec. 1918; served in France with 6th Bn Seaforth Highlanders (TF), 1915–17; Captain (MC, despatches);

Civil Service, 1919, and posted to India Office; Assistant Secretary, 1931; External Secretary, 1938. *Recreations:* golf, tennis, fishing. *Address:* Cranford, Aviary Road, Pyrford, Surrey. *Clubs:* United University, MCC.

Died 4 July 1945.

PEEL, Walter, CBE 1923; OBE 1920; (hon.) LLM Liverpool Univ.; JP County of Chester; Chairman Wirral Petty Sessional Division, 1935–46; Deputy Chairman Cheshire Quarter Sessions, 1935–42; Chairman, Cheshire County Licensing Committee; District Registrar of High Court of Justice, Liverpool, 1919–42; *b* 7 Sept. 1868; 2nd *s* of Edmund Richard Peel, Rock Ferry, Cheshire; *m* 1896, Helen Margaret (*d* 1897), *d* of John Henry Hubback, New Ferry, Cheshire; one *s*. *Educ:* Malvern. Admitted solicitor, 1891; Registrar, Liverpool Court of Passage, 1903–19; was a representative of the diocese of Chester in the York House of Laymen and Representative Church Council, 1904–18, and member of Central Board of Church Finance; Vice-Chairman of South-West Lancashire War Pensions Committee to 1945, and on committee of various organisations in Liverpool dealing with ex-service men; has served on Departmental Committees of Ministry of Pensions. *Publication:* The Jurisdiction and Practice of the Court of Passage. *Recreations:* bridge, philately. *Address:* 68 Watergate St, Chester. *T:* Chester 3174. *Clubs:* Flyfishers'; Grosvenor (Chester); Athenæum (Liverpool).

Died 27 Aug. 1949.

PEEL, Sir William, KCMG 1931; KBE 1928; CMG 1926; Kt of Grace of the Order of St John of Jerusalem, 1931; *b* 27 Feb. 1875; *s* of late Rev. W. E. Peel, Boston Spa, Yorkshire; *m* 1911, Violet Mary Drake, *d* of late W. D. Laing; two *s*. *Educ:* Silcoates School; Queens' College, Cambridge (11th Wrangler, 1896; BA 1896; MA 1931, Hon. Fellow); Hon. LLD Hong Kong. Cadet, Malayan Civil Service, 1897; President, Municipal Commissioners, Penang, 1911; President, Municipal Commissioners, Singapore, 1918; Joint Passage Controller, Malaya, 1919; Food Controller, 1919; Controller of Labour, 1920; British Adviser to the Government of Kedah, 1922; Resident Councillor, Penang, 1925; Chief Secretary to Government, Federated Malay States, 1926–30; Officer Administering the Government and High Commissioner, Malay States, May–June 1927; Governor and Commander-in-Chief, Hong-Kong, 1930–35. *Recreations:* riding, golf. *Address:* Weydown, Little Common, Bexhill. *T:* Cooden 166. *Club:* Oxford and Cambridge.

Died 24 Feb. 1945.

PEGRAM, A. Bertram, RBS; *b* 1873; *m* Mary Constance Buzzard; one *s* one *d*. *Educ:* Art Education; Royal Academy Schools (2 medals) and Paris (medal) travelling scholarship. Frequent exhibitor London and Provinces; numerous works, decorative and monumental, in Great Britain; portrait memorials of Abraham Lincoln, General Armstrong, Robert Curtis Ogden, Senator Platt, and others, in USA. *Recreations:* reading, waking, etc. *Address:* 10 Primrose Gardens, Hampstead, NW3.

Died 14 Jan. 1941.

PEGRAM, Vice-Adm. Frank Henderson, CB 1943; DSO 1940; 4th Sea Lord since 1943; *b* 25 Feb. 1890; *s* of Thomas Pegram, The Grange, Hoylake; *m* 1922, Benoni, *d* of Walter Addison, Natal; one *d*. *Educ:* Mostyn House, Parkgate; HMS Britannia. Joined RN, 1905; served European War, 1914–18, Lieut, HMS Hibernia (Grand Fleet, Gallipoli); HMS Lion, 1917; HMS General Crauford, 1918 (on Belgian Coast as executive and gunnery officer, Belgian Croix de Guerre); Lieut Commander, 1919; Commander, 1926; in charge of British Naval Mission to Chile, 1928–30; Capt., 1932; Deputy Director, Staff College, 1937–39; War of 1939–45, HMS Glasgow in command, 1939–40 (DSO Norway); Commodore Cmdg S America Div., 1940;

Rear-Adm., 1941; Flag Officer Cmdg. West Africa, 1942–43; Vice-Adm., 1943. *Address:* Catherington Cottage, Horndean, Hants. *T:* Horndean 3132. *Club:* United Service.

Died 8 March 1944.

PEIRS, Hugh John Chevallier, CMG 1919; DSO 1916; Solicitor, 1913; *b* 1 Feb. 1886; *o s* of late Hugh Vaughan Peirs, Queen's Well, Carshalton, and *g s* of Rev. S. A. Pears, DD, Headmaster of Repton School; changed spelling of name from Pears to Peirs, 1909; *m* 1922, Eirene Helen Frances, *e d* of John Barrington Chevallier, JP, Aspall Hall, Suffolk; one *d. Educ:* Charterhouse; New College, Oxford. Honours, Law Final, 1909, BA. Charterhouse Football XI, 1905; OUAF XI, 1909; 2nd Lieut 3rd Batt. The Queen's (Royal West Surrey Regt), 1906; served European War, 1914–18; demobilised with rank of Lt-Col, 1919, from command of 8th Batt. The Queen's (Royal West Surrey Regiment) (CMG, DSO and 2 bars, despatches 6 times). *Address:* St Germains, St Albans, Herts; 17 Albemarle Street, W1. *T:* Regent 0077. *Club:* United University.

Died 10 June 1943.

PEIRSE, Maj. Sir Henry Bernard de la Poer B.; *see* Beresford-Peirse.

PELHAM, Sir (Edward) Henry, KCB 1933 (CB 1921); JP (Kent); *b* 1876; *s* of late Professor Henry F. Pelham, President of Trinity College, Oxford, and Laural *d* of late Sir E. N. Buxton, Bart; *m* 1905, Hon. Irene Lubbock, *y d* of 1st Baron Avebury; one *s* three *d. Educ:* Harrow; Balliol College, Oxford. Entered Board of Education, 1900; Principal Assistant Secretary, 1920; Deputy Secretary, 1929–31; Permanent Secretary, Board of Education, 1931–37; Chairman, Grants Committee, under Government Physical Recreation Scheme, 1937–39. *Recreations:* golf, walking. *Address:* Currant Hill, Westerham, Kent. *T:* Westerham 271. *Clubs:* Athenæum, Brooks's.

Died 18 Dec. 1949.

PELHAM, Rt Rev. Herbert S.; Bishop of Barrow-in-Furness since 1926; Suffragan Bishop in Diocese of Carlisle; Rector of Aldingham since 1926; Hon. Canon of Carlisle since 1937; *b* 1881; *s* of late Professor Pelham, President of Trinity College, Oxford. *Educ:* Harrow; University College, Oxford; MA. Head of the Oxford Mission in Bermondsey, 1905–07; Head of Birmingham Street Children's Union, 1907–12; Domestic Chaplain to the Bishop of Birmingham (Dr Russell Wakefield), 1912–14; Head of the Harrow Mission and Vicar of Holy Trinity, Latimer Road, 1914–16; Vicar of Barking (nominated by All Souls College, Oxford), 1916–26. *Publication:* The Training of a Working Boy. *Recreation:* golf. *Address:* Aldingham Rectory, Ulverston. *T:* Bardsea 215. *Club:* Athenæum.

Died 11 March 1944.

PELHAM, James T.; *see* Thursby-Pelham.

PELHAM, Rev. John Barrington; *b* 7 Jan. 1848; 2nd *s* of Bishop Pelham of Norwich; *m* 1884, Caroline, *d* of Rev. William Buller, Lanreath, Cornwall. *Educ:* Trinity College, Cambridge (MA). Curate of St Margaret's, Lowestoft, 1871–75; Southwold, 1878–79; St John the Evangelist, Lowestoft, 1879–82; Vicar, 1882–84; St Philip's, Heigham, 1884–88; Higham, 1889–1908; Thundridge, 1908–14; Hon. Canon, Norwich, 1906. *Recreations:* bowls, riding his tricycle. *Address:* Stanmer, Albury Road, Guildford.

Died 10 Jan. 1941.

PELLIOT, Paul; Professor at the Collège de France; Member of the French Institute (Académie des Inscriptions et Belles-Lettres); *b* 1878. Went to Indo-China, 1899; reached Pekin, 1900, and went through the siege of the Legations; appointed by Geographical Society and the Academy to conduct an archæological exploration of Chinese Turkestan, 1906–09; has valuable collection of Eastern inscriptions, etc. *Publications:* Tcheou Ta-Kouan, Mémoires sur les coutumes du Cambodge, 1902; Deux Itinéraires de Chine en Inde, 1904; Un traité manichéen, 1911–1913; Les Mongols et la Papauté, 1921; Les grands voyages maritimes chinois, 1933; Marco Polo; The Description of the World, vols I and II, 1939. *Address:* 59 Avenue Foch, Paris. *T:* Passy 0419.

Died 29 Oct. 1945.

PELLY, Rev. Douglas Raymond, DSO 1918; HCF; MA; VD; *b* 20 Feb. 1865; *s* of late Canon R. P. Pelly; *m* 1898, Verena Noélie, *d* of Rev. G. W. Herbert; three *s* one *d. Educ:* Harrow; Emmanuel College, Cambridge. Missionary in S Africa; founded St Augustine's College, Penhalonga; Curate in charge of Feckenham, nr Redditch; Vicar of Buckley, nr Hawarden; Commissary to Bishop of Southern Rhodesia; Chaplain of the Forces for the duration of the war; Corps Chaplain of XII Corps, Salonica Force; Rector of Woolbeding. *Publication:* Translation of Hymns and Gospel of St John into Chizwina. *Address:* The Manor, Wyke Champflower, Bruton.

Died 14 March 1943.

PELLY, Sir Harold, 4th Bt *cr* 1840; JP; Capt. demobilised, 1st Vol. Bn Dorset Regt; *b* 28 Feb. 1863; 4th *s* of 2nd Bart and 2nd wife Blanche Elizabeth, *d* of Sir Frederick Vincent, 11th Bart; *S half-brother* 1877; *m* 1889, Anna (*d* 1939), *d* of Robert Poore, Old Lodge, Salisbury; two *s* three *d. Educ:* Harrow; Christ Church, Oxford (BA). *Heir: s* Major Harold Alwyne Pelly, MC. *Address:* Post Green, Lytchett Minster, Dorset. *T:* Lytchett Minster 219.

Died 3 Nov. 1950.

PELLY, Adm. Sir Henry Bertram, KCVO 1923; CB 1916; MVO 1901; *b* 9 Sept. 1867; 6th *s* of late Captain Richard Wilson Pelly, RN; *m* 1904, Lilian, *e d* of Sir William Vincent, 12th Bt; two *s* two *d. Educ:* Brighton; HMS Britannia. Joined navy as naval cadet, 1881; lieutenant, 1891; promoted Commander, 1901, for service in Royal Yachts; 4th class MVO for service at the funeral of Queen Victoria, 1901; Captain, 1906; Vice-Adm., 1922; commanded HMS Tiger in actions off Dogger Bank and Jutland Battle, and in North Sea, 1914–16 (despatches, CB); Rear-Adm. of Egypt and Red Sea Station, 1919–20; Rear-Admiral, Gibraltar, 1921–23; retired list, 1925; Admiral, 1926; a Younger Brother of the Trinity House. *Publication:* 300,000 Sea Miles, An Autobiography, 1938. *Recreations:* golf, shooting. *Address:* Romany Cottage, Churchill, Axminster, Devon.

Died 27 Dec. 1942.

PELLY, Captain John Noel, CBE 1942; RN (ret.); Commanding Officer, HMS King Alfred; *b* 15 June 1888; *s* of Edmund N. Pelly, Witham Lodge, Essex; *m* 1924, Rosalind, *d* of R. G. Gatehouse, Abbots Grange, Bebington, Cheshire; one *s* one *d. Educ:* HMS Britannia. European War, 1914–18, HMS Queen Elizabeth and Ramillies; China, HMS Cornflower in Command, 1928–29; Maintenance Commander, Devonport, 1929–31; Younger Brother of Trinity House, retired 1934. *Recreations:* cricket, shooting, and farming. *Address:* Witham Lodge, Essex. *TA:* Witham Essex. *T:* Witham 94. *Clubs:* United Service, MCC.

Died 6 June 1945.

PEMBERTON, Sir Max, Kt 1928; author; JP; *b* Birmingham, 19 June 1863; *s* of late Thomas Josnua Pemberton, Beech Mount, Liverpool. *Educ:* Merchant Taylors' School; Caius College, Cambridge (MA). Published first novel, The Diary of a Scoundrel, 1891; editor of Chums, 1892–93; editor of Cassell's Magazine, 1896–1906; Director Northcliffe Newspapers. *Publications:* The Iron Pirate, 1893; The Sea Wolves, 1894; Jewel Mysteries I have known, 1894; The Impregnable City, 1895; The Little Huguenot, 1895; A

Puritan's Wife, 1896; A Gentleman's Gentleman, 1896; Christine of the Hills, 1897; Queen of the Jesters, 1897; The Garden of Swords, 1899 Signors of the Night, 1899; Feci, 1900; Pro Patria, 1901; The Giant's Gate, 1901; The House under the Sea, 1902; The Gold Wolf, 1903; Dr Xavier, 1903; Red Morn, 1904; Beatrice of Venice, 1904; Mid the Thick Arrows, 1905; The Hundred Days, 1905; My Sword for Lafayette, 1906; The Diamond Ship, 1907; The Lodestar, 1907; Wheels of Anarchy, 1908; Sir Richard Escombe, 1908; The Show Girl, 1909; The White Walls, 1910; Captain Black, 1911; War and the Woman, 1912; Prince of the Palais Royal, 1921; Paulma, 1922; Lord Northcliffe; a Memoir, 1922; The Mad King Dies, 1928; The Life of Sir Henry Royce, 1934; Sixty Years Ago and After, 1936. *Revues:* Hullo, Ragtime; Come Over Here. *Plays:* The Dancing Master; The Finishing School; Lights Out; The Bells of St Valoir; My Lady Frayle (part author). *Recreations:* motoring, rowing, golf. *Clubs:* Garrick, Leander.

Died 22 Feb. 1950.

PENDENYS, Arthur; *see* Humphreys, A. L.

PENDER, 1st Baron *cr* 1937, of Porthcurnow; **John Cuthbert Denison-Pender;** *b* 1882; *e s* of late Sir John Denison-Pender, GBE, KCMG; *m* 1906, Irene (*d* 1943), *o c* of Sir Ernest de la Rue, KCVO; two *s* one *d*. *Educ:* Eton. Entered service of The Eastern Telegraph Co., and passed through its numerous branches, including important cable-laying operations. Formerly Director of Eastern Telegraph Co. and its associated companies; Cable and Wireless Ltd (Man. Dir 1928–36, Chm. 1932–36); Governor and Joint Managing Director of Cable and Wireless (Holding) Ltd (retired from all the foregoing, 1945, after 45 years' service in the telegraph industry). LCC South St Pancras, 1910–19; MP Newmarket Division, 1913–18; served European War, France and Belgium, Sept. 1914–July 1917, then WO to end of war; temp. Capt. Jan. 1915; MP (U) Balham and Tooting Division of Wandsworth, 1918–22; late Hon. Col City of London Signals, TA; Commander of Royal Danish Order of the Dannebrog. *Recreations:* racing, shooting. *Heir: s* Hon. John Jocelyn Denison-Pender, CBE. *Address:* 18 Basil Mansions, Basil Street, SW3. *Club:* White's.

Died 4 Dec. 1949.

PENDER, Brevet Col William Stanhope, CIE 1936; MBE 1919; Indian Army, retired; *b* Rushworth, Victoria, Australia, 1889; *s* of William Pender; *m* 1921, Phyllis, *d* of John Bradburne Dodds, Newcastle-on-Tyne; one *d*. *Educ:* Camberwell Grammar School, Victoria, Australia. Farming in Australia to 1914; joined Australian Expeditionary Force and transferred to the Indian Army in 1917; retired, 1943. *Recreation:* golf. *Address:* 2 Pannells, Freshwater Bay, IOW.

Died 1 May 1948.

PENDERED, Mary Lucy; *b* London, 1858; *d* of late Thomas Pendered; unmarried. *Educ:* Wellingborough. Went to Wellingborough, 1865, and lived there till 1906 and since 1916; after short stories she made her debut in a Yorkshire paper with a serial based upon Mark Melford's melodrama, 'Sins of the Father'; since then she has had published a number of novels, two biographies, John Martin, Painter, 1923, and The Fair Quaker (standard work on Hannah Lightfoot), 1910, two books of essays, short stories and articles. *Publications:* Anonymous, The Truth about Man, Memoirs of Mimosa, Star of the Morning, All We, Like Sheep; in collaboration; Skirts of Eden, His Absolute Shall, The Champion; two children's books; two Anthologies; Dust and Laurels, 1893; A Pastoral Played Out, 1895; An Englishman, 1899; Musk of Roses, 1903; The Fair Quaker, 1910; The Secret of the Dragon, 1911; Daisy, the Minx, 1911; At Lavender Cottage and Lily Magic, 1912–1914; Plain Jill, The Secret Sympathy, The Silent Battlefield, 1915–1918; The Book of Common Joys, 1916; Land of Moonshine, 1922; Corisande, 1926; The

Uncanny House, 1927; Amber Rose, 1928; Mortmain, 1928; A Heart Call, 1929; The Forsaken House at Misty Vale, 1932; Herriot of Wellinborrow, 1934. *Plays:* William Penn; Diana Dines Out; The Quaker; Banish the Bogie, 1932; Princess or Pretender? (with Justinian Mallett), Biography, 1939. *Recreations:* music, reading, interested in public work. *Address:* The Spinney, Gt Addington, Kettering. *T:* Cranford 229.

Died 19 Dec. 1940.

PENDLEBURY, Charles, MA, FRAS; Senior Mathematical Master of St Paul's School, 1877–1910; Hon. Secretary of the Mathematical Association, 1886–1936; Member Brentford Board of Guardians, 1913–30, Chiswick Education Committee since 1914, Chiswick Urban District Council, 1916–27; Brentford and Chiswick Urban District Council, 1927–30; Council, College of Preceptors, since 1908; Hon. Treasurer, Society of Schoolmasters since 1921; Member of Fulham Vestry and Borough Council, 1895–1909; *b* Liverpool, 5 July 1854; *y s* of late J. Pendlebury; *m* 1882, Emily (*d* 1933), *e d* of late W. P. Coleburn of Liverpool. *Educ:* Liverpool College; St John's College, Cambridge (scholar). *Publications:* Lenses and Systems of Lenses, treated after the manner of Gauss, 1884; Arithmetic for Schools, 1886 (Key, 1892); Examples in Arithmetic, 1888; Examination Papers in Arithmetic, 1889 (Key, 1889); Elementary Arithmetic, 1890; Arithmetic for Indian Schools (with T. S. Tait), 1894; Arithmetic for the Standards (with W. S. Beard), 1895; Elementary Trigonometry, 1895; Commercial Arithmetic (with W. S. Beard), 1898; Graduated Arithmetic, 1898; Shilling Arithmetic (with W. S. Beard), 1899; Short Course of Plane Trigonometry, 1900; Arithmetic for the Standards (Scheme B), 1903; New School Arithmetic (with F. E. Robinson), 1904 (Key, 1905); New Examples in Arithmetic, 1904; Junior Arithmetic, 1906; New Shilling Arithmetic (with F. E. Robinson), 1906. Examination Papers in Arithmetic, Mensuration and Logarithms, 1910 (Key, 1915); Preparatory Arithmetic, 1912 (enlarged, 1924); New Concrete Arithmetic (with H. Leather), 1914; Revision Papers in Arithmetic, 1916; Business Arithmetic (with W. S. Beard), 1920. *Recreations:* country rambles and whist. *Address:* Arlington House, 39 Burlington Road, Chiswick, W4. *T:* Chiswick 0361. *Club:* Savage.

Died 18 Aug. 1941.

PENDLEBURY, John Devitt Stringfellow, MA; FSA; FRSA; Captain General List, 1941; *b* London, 12 Oct. 1904; *e s* of Herbert Stringfellow Pendlebury, and Lilian Dorothea, *d* of Sir Thomas Lane Devitt, 1st Bt; *m* 1928, Hilda Winifred, *y d* of late Edmund D. White, Caldy, Cheshire; one *s* one *d*. *Educ:* Winchester College; Pembroke College, Cambridge. Exhibitioner, Shoolbred Scholar, Beatson Scholar, 1st class Classical Tripos, 1927 with distinction in Archæology; Athletic Blue and International (High Jump), 1926–27; Cambridge University student to British school of Archæology at Athens, 1927–28; Macmillan Student, 1928–29; Member of Archæological Expeditions in Macedonia, 1928, Armant and Tell el Amarna, 1928–29, Curator at Knossos, 1930–34; Director of Excavations Tell el Amarna, 1930–36; directed excavations on Mount Dikte since 1936; British Vice Consul, Candia, Crete, 1941. *Publications:* Aegyptiaca, a Catalogue of Egyptian objects in the Aegean Area, 1930; A Handbook to the Palace of Minos, 1933; City of Akhenaten II, 1933; Tell el Amarna, 1935; The Archæology of Crete, 1939; various papers to Archæological journals. *Recreations:* cricket, tennis, hockey, golf, walking in Greece. *Address:* 31 Barrow Road, Cambridge. *Clubs:* Oxford and Cambridge; Turf, Cairo.

Died 22 May 1941.

PENNELL, Kenneth Eustace Lee, CIE 1944; MC; *b* 26 July 1890; *s* of Lt Col R. and Mrs J. C. Pennell; *m* 1920, Elizabeth Payne Danby; two *s*. *Educ:* Kelly College, Tavistock; Jesus College, Cambridge. BA Mechanical

Sciences Tripos, 1911. Joined Indian Service of Engineers, 1912; Assistant Chief Engineer and Under-Secretary to Government, Public Works Dept, Assam, 1934; Superintending Engineer, 1936; Chief Engineer and Secretary, Public Works Dept, 1938–43; retired 1945. *Address:* Little Gable, Woodmancote, Henfield, Sussex.

Died 29 Sept. 1948.

PENNEY, Rev. William Campbell, BA, MA. *Educ:* Sherborne School; Hertford Coll., Oxford (Scholar); First-Class Honour Mods (Classics), 1884; Second-Class Lit. Hum., 1886. Assistant Master Cheltenham College, 1886; Assistant Master, Blundell's School, Tiverton, 1886–89; Headmaster, Elizabeth College, Guernsey, 1889–1924; Life Member of Education Guild of Great Britain and Ireland; Examiner in the History, Theory, and Practice of Education, Oxford, 1903; Diocesan Inspector of Schools, Heytesbury Deanery, Sarum, 1925; Vicar of Norton Bavant, Wilts, 1924–38. *Address:* 374 Franklands Village, Haywards Heath, Sussex.

Died 8 March 1945.

PENNINGTON, Lt-Col Hubert Stanley Whitmore, CMG 1919; DSO 1917; late RASC. Served European War, 1914–19 (despatches, DSO, CMG).

Died 17 Aug. 1949.

PENNINGTON, Hon. John Warburton, CBE 1926; *b* 1870; *s* of Daniel Pennington; *m* 1894, Ellen S. Tantau, of St Arnaud, Victoria, Australia. MLA Victoria, 1913–35; Hon. Minister, 1920–21 and 1921–23; Victorian Representative at British Empire Exhibition, 1924–25; Minister of Agriculture, Forests, Markets, and Migration, 1928–29; Minister of Education, Victoria, 1932–35. *Address:* Bealiba, Victoria, Australia.

Died 5 April 1945.

PENNYMAN, Preb. William Geoffrey, MA; Rector of St Mary-le-Bow, etc. since 1938; Prebendary of St Paul's Cathedral since 1934; *y s* of late James Stovin Pennyman, Ormesby Hall, Yorkshire; *m* Beatrix, *d* of late Sir James Walker, 2nd Bart, of Sand Hutton; two *d.* *Educ:* Charterhouse; Brasenose College, Oxford. Private Secretary to late Sir Robert Duff, Governor of New South Wales, 1892–94; Ordained Curate, St Mary Abbotts, Kensington; Private Chaplain to Archbishop Maclagan (York), 1898; Curate, Holy Trinity, Chelsea, 1901; Vicar of Bishopthorpe, York, and Hon. Chaplain to Archbishop of York, 1905–15; Vicar, St Mary the Virgin, Shrewsbury, 1910; Vicar of St Mark's, North Audley Street, W1, 1918–38. *Publications:* The War's Challenge to the Church; The Collapse of Convention. *Address:* 226 Cranmer Court, Chelsea, SW3. *T:* Kensington 3775. *Clubs:* Athenæum Yorkshire, York.

Died 12 March 1942.

PENNYMORE, Lt-Col Percy George, DSO 1916; TD; late 2nd Batt. Monmouthshire Regt, TF; *b* 7 Dec. 1869; 2nd *s* of late Colonel Philip George Pennymore, JP, VD, Usk, Monmouthshire; *m* 1897, Mabel Fowler, Blaenavon, Monmouthshire; no *c.* Served European War, 1914–16 (DSO). *Address:* Wheelergate, Stourbridge, Worcestershire. *TA:* Pennymore Stourbridge. *T:* Stourbridge 5514.

Died 4 Aug. 1940.

PENRHYN, 4th Baron *cr* 1866; **Hugh Napier Douglas-Pennant;** *b* 6 Aug. 1894; *o surv. s* of 3rd Baron and Hon. Blanche Georgiana Fitzroy (*d* 1944), *d* of 3rd Lord Southampton; *S* father, 1927; *m* 1922, Hon. Sybil Hardinge (who obtained a divorce 1941), *yr d* of 3rd Viscount Hardinge. *Educ:* Eton; RMC. Late Lieut 2nd Dragoons; Lord Lieutenant of Caernarvonshire, 1933–41. *Heir:* Lt-Col Frank Douglas-Pennant. *Address:* 11 Orchard Court, Portman Square, W1; Penrhyn Castle, Bangor; Wicken Park, Stony Stratford. *Club:* Jockey (Newmarket).

Died 26 June 1949.

PENROSE, Dame Emily, DBE 1927; OBE 1918; MA; DCL Oxford; Hon. LLD Sheffield; Hon. Fellow, Somerville College, Oxford; *b* London, 18 Sept. 1858; *e d* of late F. C. Penrose, FRS, architect, Surveyor of St Paul's Cathedral, Hon. Fellow Magdalene College, Cambridge. *Educ:* Somerville College, Oxford; 1st class Lit. Hum. 1892. University Extension Lecturer; lectured at British Museum and South Kensington Museum; Principal of Bedford College, London, 1893; Professor of Ancient History at Bedford College, 1893; Principal of the Royal Holloway College, 1898–1907; Principal of Somerville College, Oxford, 1907–26; Member of the Senate of London University, 1900–07; Member of Advisory Committee on University Grants, 1911–19; Member of Royal Commission on University Education in Wales, 1916; Member of Royal Commission on the Universities of Oxford and Cambridge, 1919; University of Oxford Commissioner, 1923; Member of the Oxford Society; Member of the British Empire Shakespeare Society. *Address:* Woodbury, 11 Grove Road, Bournemouth. *Club:* Albemarle.

Died 26 Jan. 1942.

PERAK, Sultan of, since 1939; **HH Paduka Sri Sultan Abdul Aziz Al'Muktassim Bil'lah Shah,** KCMG (Hon.) 1939; KBE (Hon.) 1937; CMG (Hon.) 1924; *b* 14 Nov. 1887; *o s* of Raja Musa bin Sultan Jaffar; *m* 1911; one *s.* *Educ:* Anglo-Chinese School, Ipoh; Central School, Taiping; Malay College, Kuala Kangsar. Joined State Secretariat as a Malay Probationer, 1908; transferred to Krian Land Office as General Assistant, 1909; Upper Perak as Asst District Officer, Lenggong, 1911; Matang as Asst District Officer, Larut and Matang, 1912; Krian as Inspector of Padi, 1914; Lenggong as Asst Dist Officer, 1915; Raja Muda, 1919. Vice-President, Perak State Council; President of Council of Chiefs and Ulamas (Committee of State Council dealing with Customs and Islamic Religion); Member of Federal Council, Federated Malay States, 1933–35; Member of State Finance Committee, Perak; Standing Committee of Perak State Council; Advisory Committee of Malay Regiment; Commission to inquire into the condition of coconut and other vegetable oil producing industries in Malaya, 1934; joined Malayan Volunteer Infantry, Perak Battalion, as a private, 1920; Later promoted to 2nd Lt, Lt, Capt. and Company Commander; left Active Service, 1935; transferred to Reserve of Officers. *Recreations:* golf and tennis. *Address:* Perak, Federated Malay States. *Clubs:* Lower Perak. Lower Perak Malay, Dew Recreation (Teluk Anson); Perak, New (Taiping); Krian (Parit Buntar); Idris, Iskandar Polo (Kuala Kangsar); Penang Turf (Penang), etc.

Died 29 March 1948.

PERCIVAL, Col Sir Harold Franz Passawer, KCMG 1921; CMG 1917; CBE 1919; DSO 1902; MA; Steward of Christ Church, Oxford, since 1928, Student since 1929; Member of Hebdomadal Council and Curator of University Chest; Delegate for Military Instruction; Member of Territorial Force Association; Governor of St Edward's School; *b* London, 12 Feb. 1876; *s* of E. P. Percival, LLD; *m* 1904, Constance Lilian, *d* of J. Meyrick; two *d.* *Educ:* Christ Church, Oxford. 2nd Lieut Derbyshire Regiment (Sherwood Foresters), 1898; Lieut, 1900; transferred to ASC 1902; Adjutant, 1905–08; Adjutant E Anglian Division at T and S Column, 1909; Staff Captain War Office, 1909–12; Instructor Staff Coll., Camberley, 1912–14; DAQMG British Expeditionary Force, France, 1914–15; AQMG British Military Mission, Berlin, 1918–19; British Commissioner in Allied Administration for the Plebiscite of Upper Silesia, 1919–21 (KCMG); Lt-Col, 1921; temporary command of King's Own Malta Regiment, 1925; Col 1925; Assistant Director of Supplies and Transport, and Embarkation Staff Officer, Fortress Headquarters, Malta, 1926–28; retired pay, 1929; served Boer War, 1899–1902 (despatches, Queen's medal 3 clasps, King's medal 2 clasps, DSO), commanded Section of muzzle-loading guns and employed with Mounted Infantry; European War, 1914–16; Assistant Director of Supplies, War Office, 1915–17; Deputy Director, War Office, 1917–18 (despatches, CMG, CBE, Bt Lieut-Col, 1914 Star, General Service and Allied medals, Officer Legion of Honour, 4th Class White Eagle of Serbia, Officer of Order of Crown of Italy, Commander of Order of Leopold II of Belgium). *Address:* Christ Church, Oxford. *Club:* United Service.

Died 28 April 1944.

PERCIVAL, John, MA, ScD Cantab; Emeritus Professor of Agricultural Botany, University of Reading; *m* Ethel, *d* of Rev. E. M. Johnstone, MA, Naval Chaplain; one *s*. *Educ:* St John's College, Cambridge. Natural Sciences Tripos, Pts I and II, 1887–88. Junior Demonstrator, Cambridge Univ. Chemical Laboratory 1891; Professor of Botany, Agricultural College, Wye, Kent, 1894–1903; Professor of Agricultural Botany, University College, Reading, 1903–32; Vice-President, Linnean Society, 1926–27. *Publications:* The Wheat Plant; Text-books of Agricultural Botany (8th edition) and Agricultural Bacteriology (2nd edition); Wheat in Great Britain. *Recreations:* fly-fishing, sketching, climbing. *Address:* Leighton, Shinfield Green, Reading, Berks.

Died 26 Jan. 1949.

PERCIVAL, Prebendary Launcelot Jefferson, KCVO 1936; CVO 1926; MA; Domestic Chaplain to the King; Precentor of His Majesty's Chapels Royal; Deputy Clerk of the Closet since 1931; Prebendary of St Paul's Cathedral; Sub-Almoner to the King; Chaplain of the Order of John of Jerusalem; *b* 22 May 1869; *s* of John Percival, late Bishop of Hereford; *m* Margaret Douglas, *d* of Thomas Pilkington, JP, DL, of Sanside, Caithness; three *s* one *d*. *Educ:* Clifton Coll.; Trinity College, Oxford; Leeds Clergy School. Curate of St Mary Abbotts, Kensington, 1895–97 and 1901–04; Domestic Chaplain to Bishop of London, 1897–1901; Vicar of St James's, Fulham, 1904–10; Rector of St Mary, Bryanston Square, 1910–26; Rural Dean of St Marylebone, 1912–26; Priest in Ordinary to Queen Victoria, Edward VII, George V and Edward VIII. *Recreations:* Oxford University Rugby XV 1889–92; Captain Trinity College Cricket XI; Hereford County Cricket XI; English Rugby XV 1890–92. *Address:* St James's Palace, SW1. *T:* Whitehall 1162. *Clubs:* Athenæum, MCC, I Zingari; Royal and Ancient, St Andrews.

Died 22 June 1941.

PEREIRA, Maj.-Gen. Sir Cecil (Edward), KCB 1919; CB 1918; CMG 1917; Coldstream Guards; *b* 24 July 1869; *s* of Edward and Hon. Mrs Pereira; *m* 1903, Helen, *d* of George Lane-Fox; two *s* three *d*. *Educ:* Oratory School. Served Niger Territory, 1896–97; Uganda, 1897–98; South African War; European War (despatches, Bt Colonel, Major-General, CMG, KCB); commanded 56th (London) Division Territorial Army; retired pay, 1923. *Address:* 26 Egerton Gardens, SW3. *Club:* Guards'.

Died 26 Oct. 1942.

PERKINS, Walter Frank; *b* 3 May 1865; *o s* of Walter Perkins, Southampton; *m* Elizabeth, *e d* of Robert Dempster, Vale Royal, Hartford, Cheshire. *Educ:* Forest School, Essex; Royal Agricultural College, Cirencester. MP (U) New Forest, 1910–22. *Publications:* New Forest Bibliography, 2nd Ed., 1935; British Writers on Agriculture, 3rd Ed., 1939. *Address:* Boldre Bridge House, Lymington, Hants. *T:* Lymington 63; Duntisbourne House, Cirencester.

Died 17 March 1946.

PERKS, Sydney, FSA; late Architect and Surveyor to the Corporation of the City of London; retired, 1931; *y s* of late C. Perks and Mrs Perks, of Claridge House, Sevenoaks; unmarried. *Educ:* King's College School. Articled to late Thomas Henry Watson, FRIBA. Elected a Professional Associate of Surveyors' Institution, 1887;

Fellow, 1913; ARIBA 1887; FRIBA 1903; for several years Member of Council, RIBA; exhibited at Royal Academy, 1897, 1899, 1902, 1903, 1908, 1910, 1911, 1912, 1914, 1915, 1918, 1926, 1928 and 1929; Designed bronze Memorial in Cornhill to the poet Gray; and to John Howard the Prison Reformer at the Central Criminal Court; Silver Medal of Royal Society of Arts for the paper on his discoveries and restoration of the Guildhall. Principal Works: St Mary's Institute, Putney, a church near Horsham, several blocks of residential flats, Gresham Coll. (joint architect), Weights and Measures Offices, Housing Schemes at Ilford, Lambeth, Camberwell, Stepney, and Shadwell; Residences for Married Constables, Brixton, Nurses' Home Stone Asylum, Rating Offices Law Court, Committee Rooms, etc., Guildhall, Snow Hill Police Buildings, Spitalfields Market, Police, Chief Office, Old Jewry, Restoration Scheme for the Guildhall; Restoration Scheme for the Mansion House for the Corporation of London. *Publications:* The History of the Mansion House, 1922; Essays on Old London, 1927; The Water Line of the City of London after the Great Fire, 1936; Residential Flats of all Classes; Dilapidations; Party Structures, London Building Act, 1894. *Recreations:* gardening and long walks. *Address:* Claridge House, Sevenoaks. *T:* Sevenoaks 113.

Died 2 Nov. 1944.

PERLO, Rt Rev. G. O. Filippo, OBE 1918; DD; LLD; Commander of Order of the Crown of Italy; Vicar-Apostolic of Kenya and Titular Bishop of Maronia, 1910; *b* Turin, 1873. *Educ:* University of Turin. *Address:* Scalea, Ugo Bassi, 19, Rome.

Died 4 Nov. 1948.

PERLO, Rt Rev. P. G. Gabriele, DD; Commander of the Crown of Italy and of the Star of Italy; *b* Fossano, Piedmont, Italy, 1879. *Educ:* University of Turin. Priest 1902; left for Africa as missionary, 1902. Titular Bishop of Amizona, and Vicar-Apostolic of Italian Somaliland, 1928–30. *Address:* Scalea, Ugo Bassi, 19, Roma (144).

Died 26 Sept. 1948.

PEROWNE, Rt Rev. Arthur William Thomson; *b* 13 June 1867; 4th *s* of John James Stewart Perowne DD, Bishop of Worcester (*d* 1904), and Anna Maria Woolrych; *m* 1st, 1895, Helena Frances Oldnall-Russell (*d* 1922); three *s*; 2nd, 1926, Mabel (lately CMS Missionary, Nasik, India), 2nd *d* of Thomas Henry Bailey, MICE, FSI. *Educ:* Haileybury College; King's College, Cambridge; BA 1889; MA 1891; DD 1920. Deacon, 1893; Priest, 1894; Curate of Hartlebury and Chaplain to Bishop of Worcester, 1893–1901; Vicar of Hallow, Worcester, 1901–04; St George's Edgbaston, 1904–13; Rural Dean of Edgbaston, 1905–13; Hon. Canon of Birmingham, 1912–13; Vicar of St Andrew's, Plymouth, 1913–20; Prebendary of Exeter, 1917; Archdeacon of Plymouth, 1918–20; Bishop of Bradford, 1920–31; Bishop of Worcester, 1931–41; Chaplain to HM, 1918. *Recreations:* golf, fishing. *Address:* 13 Pitt Street, Gloucester.

Died 9 April 1948.

PERRAULT, Hon. Joseph Edouard; KC and member of International Joint Commission, Ottawa, Canada; *b* Murray Bay, 30 July 1874; *s* of Joseph Stanislas Perrault, KC, lawyer of Murray Bay (Quebec), and Louisa Brault; *m* 1908, Madeleine Richard, Montreal. *Educ:* The Seminary of Quebec; Laval University. Admitted to the Bar, 1898; batonnier of the Province of Quebec Bar, 1921; Liberal candidate in the bye-election of Drummond-Arthabaska, but was defeated on the Navy issue; was later elected at the General Provincial election of 1916; re-elected 1919, 1923, 1927, 1931, and 1935; Minister of Colonisation, Mines and Fisheries, 1919–29; Minister of Highways and Mines, 1929–36, also Minister of Colonization, 1935–36; Attorney-General 1936; Doctor in Law, Laval University, 1925; Doctor in Law, Bishop University, 1932; Commandeur du Mérite

Agricole, Sept. 1925; Commandeur de l'Ordre de la Couronne de Belgique, 1926; Chevalier de la Légion d'honneur, 1928; ministre du conseil du patronage de l'École des Hautes Études commerciales de Montréal. *Recreations:* golf, fishing. *Address:* 511 Place D'Armes, Montreal, PQ, Canada. *Clubs:* Golf, University, Cercle Universitaire, Montreal.

Died 13 June 1948.

PERREE, Walter Francis, CIE 1919; *b* 3 May 1871; *s* of Francis Perrée, Jersey; *m* 1898, Mabel E., *d* of G. C. Godfray, Jersey; no *c. Educ:* Victoria College, Jersey; RIEC Coopers Hill. Joined the Indian Forest Service, 1893; served in Bengal, Burma, Assam, and the United Provinces; Assistant Inspector-General of Forests, 1907–09; Conservator of Forests, 1912–19; Chief Conservator and President, Forest Research Institute and College, Dehra Dun, 1919–25; retired, 1926. *Address:* c/o Lloyds Bank, St Helier, Jersey.

Died 6 Dec. 1950.

PERRIN, Harold Ernest, CBE 1936; Secretary Royal Aero Club, 1903–December 1945; *b* 23 Nov. 1877; *m* 1910, Dorothy Leslie; one *s* one *d. Educ:* Bromsgrove. *Recreations:* golf, fishing. *Address:* 186 Rivermead Court, Hurlingham, SW. *T:* Renown 2793. *Clubs:* Royal Automobile, Royal Aero, Royal Wimbledon.

Died 9 April 1948.

PERRING, Engr Rear-Adm. Harold Hepworth, CB 1938; CBE 1945; Director of J. Samuel White & Co., Ltd, Cowes; *b* Devonport, 11 Nov. 1885; *s* of George Perring, Dittisham, Devon and Devonport; *m* 1915, Florence Lucy Bale; one *s* one *d. Educ:* Royal Naval Engineering College, Keyham; Royal Naval College, Greenwich. Engr Sub. Lieut 1905; Engineer Commander, 1920; Engineer Captain, 1930; Engineer Rear-Admiral, 1936; ADC to the King, 1936; retired list, 1938. *Recreations:* golf and bridge. *Address:* Yonder, 95 Ember Lane, Esher Surrey. *Club:* Army and Navy.

Died 1 July 1949.

PERRING, Col Sir John, Kt 1934; DL London and Middlesex; JP; Chairman John Perring Ltd and Jackaman Ltd; *b* 16 Jan. 1870; *s* of Henry and Elizabeth Perring; *m* 1897, Florence, (OSJ), *d* of Charles Higginson; two *s* two *d. Educ:* London. KGStJ; Army Welfare Officer, Middlesex; Hon. Colonel 36th (Middlesex) Anti-Aircraft Searchlight Bn RA (T); President of Conservative Association Balham and Tooting; Member of Middlesex County Territorial Army and Air Force Association; Member LCC, 1922–37; Chairman of Establishment Committee (LCC) for eight years (staff and buildings); Standing Joint Cttee London Sessions; Chm. of Justices Wandsworth and Battersea Division; served on Metropolitan Water Board; Past Master of the Worshipful Company of Tin Plate Workers, 1934; Vice-Chairman County of Middlesex Territorial Cadet Association. *Address:* London Road, Twickenham; 49 Exeter House, Putney Heath, SW15; Pointed Gable, 35 West Parade, Worthing. *Clubs:* Constitutional, Royal Automobile London Magistrates.

Died 23 March 1948.

PERRY, Rt Rev. James De Wolf, DD, STD, LLD; Bishop of Rhode Island, 1911 to Oct. 1946; Presiding Bishop of the Protestant Episcopal Church in the United States of America, 1930–37; *b* 3 Oct. 1871; *s* of Rev. James De Wolf Perry, DD, and Elizabeth Russell Tyson; *m* 1908, Edith Dean Weir, New Haven; two *s. Educ:* Germantown Academy, Philadelphia; University of Pennsylvania, AB 1891, STD 1911, LLD 1931; Harvard, AB 1892; Episcopal Theological School, Cambridge, Mass, BD 1895. DD Brown University, 1912, Trinity College, Hartford. Connecticut, 1932, Univ. of South, Tennessee, 1933; STD General Theological Seminary, New York, 1931, Columbia University, 1931. Deacon, 1895; Priest, 1896; Assistant Minister, Christ Church, Springfield, Mass, 1895–97; Rector, Christ Church,

Fitchburg, Mass, 1897–1904; Rector, St Paul's Church, New Haven, Conn, 1904–11; Chaplain 6th Mass Infantry, 1898–1904; Senior Red Cross Chaplain, 1918–19, AEF; Vice-President, Pilgrims of US; Chaplain General Society of Cincinnati; Overseer Harvard College; Member Phi Kappa Sigma; Légion d'Honneur, France. *Address:* Bishop's House, 10 Brown Street, Providence, Rhode Island, USA. *Clubs:* Authors'; Art, University, Providence; Century, New York.

Died 20 March 1947.

PERRY, Robert Grosvenor, CBE 1917; JP; *b* 1873; 4th *s* of late Henry Bracey Perry of Ley Hall, Handsworth; *m* 1st, Ethel Constance (*d* 1938), *y d* of late Colonel Stanley Arnold, CB, of Barton House, Warwickshire, and of Dungallon, Oban, NB; one *s* one *d*; 2nd, 1938, Sybil, *widow* of F. M. May. *Educ:* privately. Head of His Majesty's Factory, Oldbury, 1914–19. High Sheriff of Warwickshire, 1947–48. *Recreations:* hunting, yachting, and in early life athletics. *Address:* Barton House, Moreton-in-Marsh, Glos. *T:* Barton-on-the-Heath 22. *Clubs:* Boodle's, Bath; Bembridge Sailing (Bembridge IOW); Solent Yacht (Yarmouth IOW).

Died 3 May 1949.

PERRY, Rev. Stephen Nugent, TD, MA; Surrogate; Hon. Canon of Manchester; *b* Dublin, 30 Sept. 1861; *s* of William Perry; *m* 1st, 1889, Catherine Jane Halliday, Leeds; 2nd, 1906, Mrs L. G. Baynton; one *s* five *d. Educ:* Trinity College, Dublin. Deacon, 1885; Priest, 1887; Curate of Hunslet Parish Church, Leeds, 1885–88; Parish Church, Preston, Lancs, 1888–92; Rector of St Mark's, Holland Street, Manchester, 1892–1905; Rector of St James's, Higher Broughton, 1905–37; Hon. Chaplain, 1st class, TA, 1922; formerly Chaplain East Lancs RE and Acting Chaplain to the Leeds Rifles (3rd West York Volunteers). *Recreation:* golf. *Address:* 45 Parsonage Road, Heaton Moor, Stockport. *T:* Heaton Moor 2909. *Clubs:* Old Rectory, Manchester.

Died 26 April 1941.

PERRY, Rev. William, MA, BD, DD; *m* Jessie Harvey (*d* 1938), *d* of late Sir H. Littlejohn; one *d. Educ:* Aberdeen University; Edinburgh Theo. College. Ordained, 1893; Curate of Greenock, 1893; Old St Paul, Edinburgh, 1895–97; Vice-Principal the College, 1897–99; Rector of St John, Alloa, 1899–1903; Holy Trinity, Stirling, 1903–05; St John's, Selkirk, 1906–10; St Andrew, Aberdeen, 1910–12; Principal, College of Scottish Episcopal Church; Dean of Edinburgh and Rector of Colinton, 1929–39; Rector of Buckland, Worcs, 1939–40; Canon, St Mary's Cathedral, Edinburgh, 1912; Chancellor, 1916; Hon. Canon in Residence, St Mary's Cathedral, Edin., 1940–47; Lecturer, Edinburgh University, 1921; Select Preacher, Univ. of Oxford, 1925–27, and Cambridge, 1931; Theol. Examiner Aberdeen University, 1924. *Publications:* The Scottish Liturgy: its Value and History, 1918; 2nd ed. 1921; Providence and Life, 1919; Anthony Mitchell, Bishop of Aberdeen, 1920; George Hay Forbes, a Romance in Scholarship, 1927; The Scottish Prayer Book, 1929; The Oxford Movement in Scotland; Alexander Penrose Forbes, the first Tractarian Bishop, 1939; Scottish Communicants Manual, 1939; Guide to the Scottish Prayer Book, 1941. *Address:* 28 Spylaw Bank Road, Colinton, Edinburgh.

Died 30 April 1948.

PERRY, William James, MA; DSc; late Reader in Cultural Anthropology, University of London; *s* of Rev. Dr Perry, late Headmaster of St Anne's Schools, Redhill; *m* 1915, Gwynllyan Lilian, *d* of late D. Wykeham-Williams; one *d. Educ:* City of London School; Selwyn College, Cambridge. Reader in Comparative Religion in the University of Manchester, 1919–23; Upton Lecturer in the History of Religions, Manchester College, Oxford, 1924–27. *Publications:* The Megalithic Culture of Indonesia, 1918; The Children of the Sun, 1923; The Origin of Magic and Religion, 1923; The

Growth of Civilisation, 1924; Gods and Men, 1927; The Primordial Ocean, 1935. *Address:* Tyler's Cross, Royden-by-Ware, Herts. *T:* 3103.

Died 29 April 1949.

PERSHING, Gen. John Joseph, GCB 1918; General of the Armies of the United States, retired; *b* Linn County, Missouri, 13 Sept. 1860; *m* 1905, Frances, *d* of Senator Francis E. Warren, Cheyenne, Wyoming; one *s* (wife and 3 daughters lost their lives in the burning of their quarters at the Presidio, 27 Aug. 1915). *Educ:* Kirksville Normal School; US Military Academy. 2nd Lieut 6th US Cavalry, 1886; 1st Lieut 10th Cavalry, 1892; Capt. 15th US Cavalry, 1901; served Apache Indian Campaign, 1886; Sioux Campaign, 1890–91; Military Instructor, University of Nebraska, 1891–95; Instructor in Tactics, US Military Academy, 1897–98; served in Santiago Campaign, 1898; Chief Bureau of Insular Affairs, War Department, 1898–99; Philippine Islands, 1899–1903; Moro Campaigns, 1902–03; General Staff, 1903–06; Military Attaché, Tokio, 1905–06; was with Kuroki's Army in Manchuria, 1905; appointed General Officer in 1906; in Philippine Islands, 1909–13, as Military Governor Moro Province; command of 8th Brigade, Presidio, California, 1914; commanded border districts, 1914–16; in command of US troops sent into Mexico in pursuit of Villa, 1916–17; Commander-in-Chief American Expeditionary Forces in Europe, June 1917–Sept. 1919 (Grand Cross Legion of Honour); Chief of Staff, United States Army, 1921–24; has many decorations and hon. degrees. *Publication:* My Experiences in the World War, 1931. *Address:* Washington, DC, USA. *Clubs:* Army and Navy, New York; Army and Navy, Metropolitan, Washington.

Died 15 July 1948.

PERUGINI, Mark Edward; author-journalist; *b* London, of British parents, both on London stage, 1865–79; *m* 1st, 1913, Violet de Montravel, (*d* 1920); 2nd, 1930, Irene Rose Dale, *née* Mawer. *Educ:* City of London School. Early years in commercial life, relinquished for journalism; became Private Sec. to late Justin McCarthy; joined Editorial staff of Lady's Pictorial, subsequently Editor for some years; ex-Lieut RNVR (ID). Has contributed to many leading journals, British and American. *Publications:* Selections from William Blake; The Flame; The Drum; Mime; Poems by C. and M. Lamb; Victorian Days and Ways; The Omnibus-Box; A Pageant of the Dance and Ballet. *Address:* 9 Montpellier Spa Road, Cheltenham, Glos.

Died 15 Oct. 1948.

PETAVEL, James William; on Educational Colonies research Work of Hyderabad State Co-operation Department; *b* 10 Jan. 1870; *s* of Rev. W. Petavel, London and Neuchatel; *m* 1896; two *s* three *d*. *Educ:* HM School Ship Conway, Liverpool; Royal Military Academy, Woolwich. Received commission in Royal Engineers, 1889; served on Bombay defences, Indian Public Works Dept, Queen's Own Sappers and Miners; Adjutant on return home 1895 to 1st West Yorks RE (Terr.); retired, 1900; then coach in military subjects for Staff College and Promotion Exams, at the Cavalry School, Netheravon; founder, 1911, and Hon. Secretary with J. B. Pennington, ICS; retired, of the Educational Colonies Association; Principal, Maharajah of Cossimbazar's Polytechnic Institute, 1916–28; Holder of a special Lectureship on the Poverty Problem in Calcutta University, 1920–28; President, Indian Match Manufacturers' Association, 1923–28; Editor of Bread and Freedom. *Publications:* A Coming Revolution; Christianity and Progress; Administrative Efficiency and What it Might Give Us; The Other Great Illusion; The Folly of Class War; Man and Machine Power in War and Reconstruction; Self-Government and the Bread Problem (two editions); Unemployment (two eds); The Plan of the Educational Colonies Association; The Coming Triumph of Christian Civilization, 1912; Rien Ne Vous Serait Impossible (in French); joint translator

with Kiran Chandra Sen, of Behula, The Indian Pilgrim's Progress; joint author with the same, of books on match manufacturing in India; The Wonderful Opportunity in India, second edition, 1930; The Colony Solution, 1933; A Labour Army Plan for India's Youths (2 editions), 1934; United Communities Socialism and Education, paper read to All India Educational Conference, Delhi, 1934; The Coming Great Change in Education, Mysore State Commerce and Industries Department; Good Employment for the Educated Classes, Hyderabad State Co-operation Department; Some Facts Relating to Educational Employment, Baroda State Education Department, 1937; Reports to the Hyderabad State Department of Co-operation on educational colony established and others projected; Is Socialism India's Hope? (reprint from the Maharatta). *Recreations:* riding and sailing. *Address:* Hyderabad, Deccan, India.

Died 29 Aug. 1945.

PETERS, Rev. Canon Arthur E. G.; Prebendary of Durnford, and Canon of Salisbury Cathedral, 1930–42; Emeritus since 1942; *b* 12 Feb. 1866; *s* of Rev. Thomas Peters, Vicar (formerly) of Burstock, Dorset, and Mary Ann Rudge, of Ewelme; *m* Jessie Catherine Loftus (*d* 1942), Croydon; one *s*. *Educ:* Christ's Hospital; Worcester College, Oxford. Curate of Gillingham, Dorset, 1891–95; St Alban's, Fulham, 1895–98; Member (and later Warden) of St Andrew's Society, 1898–1906; Chaplain (domestic) to the Bishop of Salisbury, 1901; (hon.) 1906–11; Vicar of St Mary's, Marlborough, 1906–17; Rural Dean of Marlborough, 1912–17; Vicar of Bremhill, with Foxham and Highway, 1917–39; Rural Dean of Avebury, 1925–39. *Address:* 54 Newbridge Hill, Bath. *T:* Bath 7775.

Died 20 Jan. 1943.

PETERS, Edwin Arthur, BA, MD, FRCS; Consulting Surgeon to the Nose, Throat, and Ear Department, University College Hospital, and Bolingbroke Hospital, London; *m* M. R. A. Mains; one *s* three *d*. *Educ:* Charterhouse; Cambridge; Heidelberg; Guy's Hospital. Capt. RAMC, 1914–19. *Publications:* Diseases of the Ear; Tonsils and Nasopharyngeal Sepsis. *Address:* 12 Inverness Terrace, W2. *T:* Bayswater 3616; Ingleside, Netley Abbey. *Club:* Savile.

Died 29 Jan. 1945.

PETERS, Acting Captain Frederic Thornton, VC 1943; DSO 1915; DSC 1917; RN, retired list. Served European War, 1914–18 (despatches, DSO, DSC); War of 1939–45 (Bar to DSC, VC, DSC from USA). *Club:* United Service.

Died Nov. 1942.

PETHERICK, Captain Cyril Hamley, CBE 1943; OBE 1923; Second Secretary, Ministry of Finance, Northern Ireland, since 1944; *b* 8 Jan. 1893; 4th *s* of late W. W. Petherick of N Cornwall; *m* 1915, Irena May Mellon, Rathgar, Co. Dublin; two *s* one *d*. *Educ:* West Buckland School, N Devon. Entered Imperial Civil Service, 1912; served European War, Captain, 1915, Gallipoli and Balkan Campaigns, Staff, 1917 (despatches); General Army R of O, 1921; Asst Principal, Chief Secretary's Office, Ireland, 1920; Principal Officer, Ministry of Finance, Northern Ireland, 1921; Asst Secretary, 1935; Principal Asst Sec., 1939–44. *Address:* Ardbraccan House, Bangor, Co. Down. *Clubs:* Royal Ulster Yacht, Bangor.

Died 23 Dec. 1944.

PETIGARA, Khan Bahadur Kavasji Jamshedji, CIE 1933; OBE 1931; ISO 1926; JP; IP; retired, 1936; Estate Manager of Prince Aly Khan, Aga Khan Building, Dalal Street, Fort, Bombay; *b* 24 Nov. 1877; *s* of Jamshedji Nusserwanji Petigara and Dhunbaiji Bastavalla; *m* Avanbai, *d* of Jehangirshaw Ardeshir Taleyarkhan; one *s*. *Educ:* Surat; Bombay. Started career as a Sub Inspector of Police in the Bombay City CID, and gradually went through all the grades; promoted to the Indian Police Service, 1928. *Address:* Dhun Villa, 21 Palli Hill, Bandra, Bombay, India. *Clubs:* Orient, City Police, Bombay.

Died 28 March 1941.

PETIT, Rev. Paul, MA; Hon. Canon of Canterbury Cathedral since 1904; General Licence Diocese London since 1890; *b* 25 Dec. 1856. *Educ:* Corpus Christi College, Cambridge. BA Theological Honours, 1882; MA 1885. Deacon, 1882; Priest, 1883; Curate of St Luke, Cambridge, 1882–84; Aylesford, Kent, 1884–85; Manchester Cathedral, 1885–87; Priest-Vicar Lichfield Cathedral, and Chaplain and Lecturer Lichfield Theological College, 1887–89; 1st Warden of the Training College for Lay Workers under the Society for Promoting Christian Knowledge, 1889–93; Chief Secretary, Additional Curates Society, 1893–1932; Member Archbishops' Committee on Church Finance, 1909–14; Member Central Board of Finance, 1915–21; Member Central Advisory Council of Training for the Ministry, 1913–27. *Address:* 121 St George's Square, SW1.

Died 7 Sept. 1941.

PETO, Sir Basil, 1st Bt *cr* 1927; *b* 13 Aug. 1862; *s* of Sir S. Morton Peto, 1st Bart; *m* 1892, Mary Matilda Annie (*d* 1931), *d* of late Captain T. C. Baird; three *s*. *Educ:* Harrow. Building contractor; partner Peto Brothers, Pimlico, 1884–91; Director Morgan Crucible Co., Ltd, 1892–1904; works managing director and engaged in mining and buying Plumbago; spent nearly a year in the United States and Canada, 1884; twice visited since; four times visited India and Ceylon. Chief Commissioner (unpaid) Belgian Refugee Affairs, 1916; MP (C) Devizes Division, Wilts, Jan. 1910–Dec. 1918; Barnstaple Division of Devon, 1922–23 and 1924–35. *Recreations:* shooting, fishing, golf. *Heir: s* Lieut-Col (James) Michael Peto. *Address:* Gatehouse, Iford, Bradford-on-Avon. *T:* Bradford-on-Avon 2228.

Died 28 Jan. 1945.

PETRE, Major Edward Henry; late Suffolk Regt; *b* 1881; *s* of late Francis William Petre and Margaret, *e d* of E. Bowes Cargill of Dunedin, NZ; *g g s* of 11th and *c* and *heir-pres.* of 17th Baron Petre.

Died 26 Dec. 1941.

PETRE, Maud D. M.; *d* of Hon. Arthur Petre and Lady Catherine Howard. *Educ:* at home. Began writing at nineteen; did various religious works, in particular Ethiopium Servus; a study of the life of St Peter Claver and Where Saints have trod; entered into the Modernist movement; has nursed a good deal in France and England during War; resided a part of the year at the Abbaye de Pontigny (Youne) where she assisted in the direction of a centre of intellectual and international relations. *Publications:* The Soul's Orbit; Catholicism and Independence; Life of George Tyrrell (whose executor she is); Modernism—its Failure and its Fruits; Reflections of a Non-Combatant; Democracy at the Cross Roads; National Morality and the League of Nations; The Two Cities; Biography of the Ninth Lord Petre and history of English Catholics of His Time; My Way of Faith; Von Hügel and Tyrrell; The Story of a Friendship; a volume on Alfred Loisy, 1942; various articles in Hibbert Journal, Nineteenth Century, Dublin Review and Ricerche Religiose (Rome). *Address:* 15 Campden Grove, W8.

Died 16 Dec. 1942.

PETRE, Lt-Col Oswald Henry Philip T.; *see* Turville-Petre.

PETRE, Rear-Adm. Walter Reginald Glynn, DSO 1917; late RN; *b* Dec. 1873; *y s* of late Sir George Glynn Petre, KCMG, CB; *m* 1906, Agnes Marie, *γ d* of late Captain Eugene Cadic of Rennes, France; four *s* three *d*. *Educ:* Royal Naval Academy, Gosport. Joined HMS Britannia, 1887; Midshipman, 1889; Sub-Lieut 1894; Lieut 1896; Commander, 1907; Captain, June 1915;

served Persian Gulf, 1897 (thanks of Indian Govt); served in boat expedition to capture pirates in Persian Gulf for pearl trade; Commander of Leviathan, which escorted South African troops home; European War (despatches twice, DSO); Command of Minelayers in North Sea; Senior Officer of Minelayers in the Mediterranean after evacuation of Gallipoli for mining operations; British Captain of the Port, Constantinople, 1921–22; retired list, 1923; Senior Allied Captain of the Port at Constantinople under the Allied occupation, 1921–23; retired March 1923 at his own request. *Address:* Pinecroft, St George's Road, Weybridge, Surrey. *Club:* Naval and Military.

Died 26 Dec. 1942.

PETRIE, Ven. Alan Julian; Vicar of St Mary's, Merivale, Christchurch, since 1940, and Archdeacon of Rangiora and Westland, NZ, since 1944; *b* 30 May 1888; *s* of James Andrew Petrie and Rosalie Miriam Brooke Hickson; *m* 1916, Gladys Muriel Parkinson; one *d*. *Educ:* Selwyn College, Dunedin, NZ; LTh Durham. Deacon, 1912; Priest, 1913; Priest-in-charge Owaka, 1913–14; Curate, St Matthew's, Dunedin, 1914–17; Chaplain to the Forces, 1917–18; Vicar of Mount Somers, 1919–21; Vicar of Lyttelton, 1921–28; of Ashburton, 1928–37; of Akaroa, 1937–40; Archdeacon of Akaroa and Ashburton, 1934–44; Chaplain 2nd Class (Lt-Col), 1933. *Address:* St Mary's Vicarage, Merivale, Christchurch, NZ.

Died 3 Sept. 1947.

PETRIE, Sir Flinders; *see* Petrie, Sir W. M. F.

PETRIE, Ven. Frederick Herbert; Archdeacon of Rangitikei, NZ since 1934; Examining Chaplain to Bishop of Wellington, 1940; Vicar General, 1944; Archbishop of New Zealand's Commissary, 1946; *b* 30 March 1875; *s* of Canon James Petrie; *m* 1900, Jane Moore; one *d*. *Educ:* Grammar School, Aberdeen; Aberdeen University; Edinburgh Theological College; MA King's College, Aberdeen University, 1895; Walker Bursar (First) Edin. Theological College, 1896; Jameson Bursar and Urquhart Greek Prize (First) 1897; 1st Class Prelim. Theol. Exam. 1897. Deacon, 1898; Priest, 1899; Assistant Curate, Holy Trinity, Stirling, 1898–1900; Arbroath, 1900; Rector of Monymusk, 1900–04; St Alban's, Perth, WA 1904–07; Missionary in Melanesia, 1907–09; Vicar of Porirua, NZ, 1909–11; Johnsonville, NZ 1911–19; Roseneath, 1919–21; Vicar of Feilding, NZ, 1921–46; Hon. Canon of Wellington, NZ 1925; Member of Standing Committee and Board of Nomination, Wellington, NZ. *Recreations:* cricket, fishing and bowling, also rose-growing. *Address:* 11 York Street, Feilding, NZ. *Club:* Feilding.

Died 8 July 1948.

PETRIE, Sir (William Matthew) Flinders, Kt 1923; FRS, FBA, DCL, LittD, LLD, DLit, DSc, PhD; Edwards Professor of Egyptology, University College, London, 1892–1933, Emeritus Professor since 1933; *b* Charlton, 3 June 1853; *o c* of William Petrie, CE, and Anne, *d* of Captain Matthew Flinders, RN, Australian explorer; *m* 1897, Hilda, *d* of Denny Urlin of Rustington Grange; one *s* one *d*. *Educ:* privately. Surveying British remains, 1875–80; excavating in Egypt, 1880–1924 (principal discoveries: Greek settlements at Naukratis and Daphnæ, prehistoric Egyptian at Koptos and at Naqada, inscription of Israelite war at Thebes; Kings of the earliest Dynasties at Abydos; Hyksos camp; city of Onias and palaces of Memphis, Tarkhan, Treasure of Lahun); excavating in Palestine, 1926–38; founded Egyptian Research Account, 1894, enlarged as the British School of Archæology in Egypt, 1905. *Publications:* Inductive Metrology, 1875; Stonehenge, 1880; Pyramids and Temples of Gizeh, 1883; Tanis I, 1885; Naukratis I, 1886; Tanis II, 1887; Season in Egypt, 1888; Racial Portraits, 1888; Historical Scarabs, 1889; Hawara, 1889; Kahun, 1890; Lachish (T. Hesy), 1891; Illahun, 1891; Medum, 1892; Ten Years' Digging, 1893; History of

Egypt, 3 vols, 1894–1923; Tell el Amarna, 1895; Koptos, 1896; Naqada, 1896; Egyptian Tales, 2 vols, 1895; Decorative Art, 1895; Six Temples at Thebes, 1897; Deshasheh, 1897; Religion and Conscience in Ancient Egypt, 1898; Syria and Egypt, 1898; Dendereh, 1900; Diospolis, 1901; Royal Tombs of the First Dynasty, 1900; Hierakonpolis I, 1900; Royal Tombs of the Earliest Dynasties, 1901; Abydos I, 1902; Abydos II, 1903, etc., Ehnasya, 1904; Roman Ehnasya, 1904; Methods and Aims in Archæology, 1904; Researches in Sinai, 1906; Hyksos and Israelite Cities, 1906; Migrations, 1906; Religion of Ancient Egypt, 1906; Gizeh and Rifeh, 1907; Janus in Modern Life, 1907; Athribis, 1908; Personal Religion in Egypt, 1908; Memphis I, 1909; Qurneh, 1909; The Palace of Apries, 1909; Arts and Crafts in Egypt, 1909; The Growth of the Gospels, 1910; Meydum and Memphis, 1910; Historical Studies, 1910; Egypt and Israel, 1910; Revolutions of Civilisation, 1911; Roman Portraits, 1912; The Labyrinth, 1912; The Formation of the Alphabet, 1912; The Hawara Portfolio, 1913; Tarkhan I, 1913; Tarkhan II, 1914; Riqqeh, 1914; Lahun I, 1914; Amulets, 1914; Heliopolis, 1914; Scarabs, 1917; Tools and Weapons, 1917; Corpus of Prehistoric Pottery, 1918; Eastern Exploration, 1919; Some Sources of Human History, 1919; Prehistoric Egypt, 1920; Status of the Jews in Egypt, 1922; Social Life in Ancient Egypt, 1923; Lahun II, 1923; Religious Life in Ancient Egypt, 1924; Sedment I, II, 1924; Tombs of the Courtiers 1924; Buttons and Design Scarabs, 1925; Ancient Weights and Measures, 1926; Glass Stamps and Weights, 1926; Descriptive Sociology of Ancient Egypt, 1926; Hill Figures of England, 1926; Objects of Daily Use, 1927; Gerar, 1928; Bahrein and Hemamieh, 1929; Corpus of Palestinian Pottery, 1930; Antæopolis, 1930; Bethpelet I, 1930; Decorative Patterns, 1930; Ancient Gaza, 5 vols, 1931–1938; Seventy Years in Archæology, 1931; Palestine and Israel, 1934; Measures and Weights, Shabtis, 1935, Anthedon, Sinai, 1937; Funeral Furniture and Stone and Metal Vases, 1937; Egyptian Architecture, 1938; Making of Egypt, 1939; Wisdom of the Egyptians, 1940. *Recreations:* excavating, collecting antiquities, photographing. *Address:* c/o American School of Research, Jerusalem.

Died 28 July 1942.

PETTIGREW, Sir Andrew Hislop, Kt 1913; LLD; JP; Chairman Campbells and Stewart & M'Donald, Ltd, Glasgow; Director of the Scottish Temperance Life Assurance Company, Limited; *b* New Lanark, 14 April 1857; *s* of John Pettigrew and Agnes Hislop; *m* 1st, 1881, Amelia Kirkwood, *d* of late Alexander M'Naughton, Glasgow; 2nd, 1919, Annie A. (*d* 1937), *d* of Angus Macleod, Glasgow, formerly Cape Town; 3rd, 1938, Joan, 2nd *d* of H. R. Cottam, Rondebosch, South Africa. *Educ:* Lanark. Came to Glasgow in 1875 and rapidly filled increasingly important positions; started firm of Pettigrew & Stephens, 1888; eight years later his partner Mr W. H. Stephen died; the business grew rapidly, and was formed into a Limited Co., 1904; invited to assume management of Stewart & M'Donald, Limited, Glasgow, 1908; Chairman of Executive, Scottish History Exhibition, 1911; DL, JP County of City of Glasgow; LLD Glasgow University; has served on Town Council of the city; has been a Deacon of one of the incorporations and a member of the Trades House; Liberal. *Recreation:* motoring. *Address:* 7 University Garden, Glasgow. *T:* Glasgow 4275 Western. *TA:* Ingram, Glasgow. *Clubs:* Glasgow Liberal, Scottish Automobile, Glasgow.

Died 15 July 1942.

PEYTON, Guy Wynne Alfred, CBE 1920 (MBE 1917); *b* 2 June 1862; *e s* of late Colonel John Peyton, 7th Dragoon Guards; *m* 1948, Letitia Lovell, Wynthrop, Rickmansworth. *Educ:* Wellington College; Brighton College. For many years engaged in pastoral pursuits in Queensland; JP, Queensland; Private Secretary to Sir

Henry Sclater, GCB, Adjutant-General, War Office, 1914–15; Private Secretary successively to Mr Tennant, Lord Derby, and Lord Strathcarron, Under-Secretaries of State for War, at War Office, 1916–19. *Address:* Wynthrop, Chorleywood Rd, Rickmansworth, Herts. *Club:* Boodle's.

Died 28 July 1950.

PHELPS, William Lyon, BA; PhD Yale; MA Harvard; LittD Brown, Colgate, McMaster and Lafayette Coll., Columbia and Univ. of Vermont, 1941; LHD New York Univ. and Muhlenberg; LLD Kalamazoo, Yale, Clark, Denison, 1931, Miami, 1933; DD, Tusculum Coll., 1928; DST Syracuse, 1930; DCL Jefferson Medical Coll., Pennsylvania Military Coll., Hahnemann Medical Coll., 1940; Lampson Professor of English Literature, Yale, 1901–33; late Public Orator, Yale University; Member of American Academy of Arts and Letters; Member of American Philosophical Society; Fellow American Academy of Arts and Sciences; Fellow American Geographical Society; *b* New Haven, Conn, 2 Jan. 1865; *y s* of late Rev. Dr S. Dryden Phelps and Sophia Emilia Linsley; *m* 1892, Annabel Hubbard (*d* 1939), Michigan. *Educ:* Yale; Harvard; Paris; Munich. Formerly Morgan Fellow and Instructor at Harvard; Gold Medal National Institute of Social Sciences. *Publications:* The Beginnings of the English Romantic Movement, 1893; Essays on Modern Novelists, 1910; Essays on Russian Novelists, 1911; Teaching in School and College, 1912; Essays on Books, 1914; Browning, 1915; The Advance of the English Novel, 1916; The Advance of English Poetry, 1918; The Twentieth Century Theatre, 1918; Reading the Bible, 1919; Essays on Modern Dramatists, 1920; Human Nature in the Bible, 1922; As I Like It, 1923; Some Makers of American Literature, 1923; Human Nature and the Gospel, 1925; Howells, James, Bryant, and other Essays, 1924; Adventures and Confessions, 1926; Autobiography with Letters, 1939; Marriage, 1940; A Mothers' Anthology, 1940; Children's Anthology, 1941; Christ or Cæsar; Music; Essays on Things. *Recreations:* golf, whist. *Address:* Yale University, New Haven, USA. *TA:* New Haven, Ct. *Club:* Athenæum.

Died Aug. 1943.

PHELPS, William Peyton, MA, FIA; late Director, formerly Manager and Secretary, Equity and Law Life Assurance Society; late Director, formerly Actuary and Manager, Law Reversionary Interest Society, Limited; *b* 22 April 1865; 2nd *s* of late Col Peyton Phelps, late Royal (Bombay) Engineers. *Educ:* City of London School; Gonville and Caius College, Cambridge. Fellow of the Institute of Actuaries, 1891. A Vice-President 1912–15; President, 1922–24; Chairman, Life Offices' Association, 1916–18; Member of Council, Royal Patriotic Fund Corporation, 1922–24; Member of Board of Trade Departmental Committee for amending the Assurance Companies Act, 1909. *Address:* 19 Ormonde Gate, Chelsea, SW3. *T:* Flaxman 2904. *Club:* Conservative.

Died 14 March 1942.

PHILBRICK, Arthur James, CBE 1923; *b* 1866; *s* of F. A. Philbrick, KC, County Court Judge; *m* 1898, Sybil Chermside; one *s* one *d*. *Educ:* Rugby; Trinity College, Cambridge. BA, LLB, 1887. Called to Bar, Middle Temple, 1889; entered Colonial Service, 1901; served on Gold Coast, 1901–24; Chief Commissioner, Northern Territories, Gold Coast, 1921–24; retired, 1924. *Recreations:* golf and fishing. *Club:* Oxford and Cambridge.

Died 30 Jan. 1941.

PHILIP, Very Rev. Adam, DD; Moderator United Free Church General Assembly, 1921; Minister at Longforgan 1881–1932; *b* Glasgow, 1856; *s* of Rev. George Philip, DD, St John's Free Church, Edinburgh; *m* Mary Nicol, *d* of James Couper, glass manufacturer, Glasgow; two *s*. *Educ:* Glasgow Academy; Royal High School,

Edinburgh; Univ. of Edinburgh, Honours in philosophy; New College, Edinburgh; Leipzig. Ordained, 1881; travelled in Europe and Palestine, etc.; Warrack Lecturer, 1930. *Publications:* The Evangel in Gowrie; Songs and Sayings of Gowrie; Father's Hand; Ancestry of the Archbishop of Canterbury; Devotional Literature of Scotland; Parish of Longforgan; Thomas Chalmers; Thoughts on Worship and Preaching, Lingering in the Sanctuary, 1936, etc. *Address:* 19 Greenhill Gardens, Edinburgh.

Died 18 Nov. 1945.

PHILIP, James Charles, OBE 1918; FRS 1921; DSc; Professor Emeritus of Physical Chemistry; *b* Fordoun, Kincardineshire, 12 Feb. 1873; *y s* of late Rev. John Philip, DD; *m* Jane, *e d* of late William Henderson, Aberdeen; one *s* one *d*. *Educ:* Fordoun Public School; Aberdeen Grammar School; Aberdeen University; Göttingen University. Town Council Gold Medallist, King's College, Aberdeen, 1893; Murray Scholar, 1895. Assistant to C. T. Heycock and F. H. Neville of Cambridge, 1898; Demonstrator and Lecturer, Royal College of Science, 1900; Assistant Professor of Chemistry in the Imperial College, 1909–13; Professor of Physical Chemistry, 1913–38; Sec. Chemical Society, 1913–24, Pres. since 1941; Chairman Bureau of Chemical Abstracts, 1923–32; Member of Senate, University of London, 1932–38; President Section B (Chemistry) Brit. Assoc., 1936; President Society of Chemical Industry, 1939–41. *Publications:* Romance of Modern Chemistry, 1909; Physical Chemistry; its Bearing on Biology, 1910; Achievements of Chemical Science, 1913; articles on physico-chemical subjects in Thorpe's Dictionary of Applied Chemistry; original papers, mostly in the Journal of the Chemical Society. *Recreations:* music, lawn-tennis, golf. *Address:* 63 Madeley Road, Ealing, W5. *T:* Perivale 6094.

Died 6 Aug. 1941.

PHILIPP, Prof. John; painter and etcher; *b* 8 June 1869; *s* of Eli Philipp, banker; *m* Clara Frank. *Educ:* Hamburg; Munich; Paris. *Works:* Auguste Rodin; Prince Regent Luitpold of Bavaria; Professor von Neumayer; Adolphe von Menzel; Friederich Spielhagen; Otto Ernst; Detlev von Liliencron; Arthur Nikisch; Pope Benedict XV; Sigmund Freud; Dr Karl Muck; Eugen d'Albert; Albert Einstein (etching bought by the British Museum); Pope Pius XI; Mussolini. *Publications:* Rodin; Menzel as a Model; How I Painted Pope Pius XI etc.

Died 15 Oct. 1938.

PHILIPPS, Sir John Erasmus Gwynne Alexander, 3rd Bt *cr* 1887; *b* 11 Sept. 1915; *o s* of Capt. Sir Henry Erasmus Edward Philipps, 2nd Bt, of Picton Castle, and Victoria Gladys Elizabeth (*d* 1939), *o c* of late John William Gwynne-Hughes of Tregeyb, Llandilo, Lord-Lieutenant of Carmarthenshire; *S* father, 1938. *Educ:* Eton; Cambridge; Royal Agricultural College, Cirencester. Member of Inner Temple; Sheriff of Pembrokeshire, 1942; Chairman Pembrokeshire RSPCA; Member Executive Committee Pembrokeshire Central Landowners' Association and NFU; OStJ. *Heir:* cousin Richard Foley Foley-Philipps, *b* 24 Aug. 1920. *Address:* Picton Castle, Haverfordwest, Pembrokeshire, S Wales. *T:* Haverfordwest, 42; L6 Albany, Piccadilly, W1. *Clubs:* St James', Bachelors'.

Died 27 Nov. 1948.

PHILIPS, John Austin Drury; author (as Austin Philips); *b* 4 Nov. 1875; *e s* of late John Philips, Postmaster and Surveyor of Manchester, and Alice Maud, *e d* of Charles Austin; *m* Mary Iris, *d* of Hubert and E. Nesbit Bland, Well Hall, Eltham, Kent. *Educ:* Malvern College. Entered Post Office as Sorting Clerk and Telegraphist, Leicester, 1893; Surveyor's Department, GPO, and Investigation Branch, GPO; lent to PMG's Dept, Pietermaritzburg for special Survey Duties, 1902–03; Postmaster of Droitwich, 1905; began literary career by writing verses for magazines and journals; turned to short

story-writing; has written a large number of stories dealing with Post Office crime and other Civil Service subjects; resigned from Civil Service in order to devote himself wholly to literature; has dramatised a number of his short stories (in collaboration with Leon M. Lion and others), while some of his short stories have been filmed; Clerical work with Home Guard, 1940–41; Civil Defence Service, 1942; Fire Guard Area Officer, 1943–45. *Publications:* Poems; The Heart of a Boy (as Paul Wingate), 1940; Songs of Love and Youth (Collected Early Poems), 1935; Red Tape; A Budget of Tares; Battles of Life; A Colombo Night and Others (all collections of short stories); The Common Touch; Pariah and Brahmin; Were They Justified?; The Furnace of Adversity; The Man in the Night Mail Train; That Girl Out in Corsica; The Boy at the Bank; The Unknown Goddess; Give All to Love!; The Real Thing; Somewhere in Sark, 1935 (all novels); The Fourth Man; Playing the Game; Promotion (all one-act plays). *Recreations:* cricket, beagling, walking—but his work first. *Address:* c/o A. P. Watt & Son, Hastings House, 10 Norfolk Street, WC2.

Died 2 Sept. 1947.

PHILIPSON, Hilton; *b* Tynemouth, Northumberland, 5 Nov. 1892; *e s* of late Roland Philipson, Director of NER, etc; *m* 1917, Mabel Russell; two *s* one *d*. *Educ:* Eton; Oxford. Served in Scots Guards as Lieut 1914–19; adopted as candidate—in National Liberal interest—for Berwick-on-Tweed, 1921; MP (NL) Berwick-upon-Tweed Division of Northumberland, Nov. 1922. *Recreations:* golf, tennis, motoring. *Address:* 62 Green Street, Park Lane, W1. *Clubs:* Bachelors', Bath.

Died 12 April 1941.

PHILIPSON-STOW, Robert Frederic; *see* Stow.

PHILLIMORE, 2nd Baron *cr* 1918, of Shiplake in County of Oxford; **Godfrey Walter Phillimore;** 3rd Bt *cr* 1881; DL Oxon; late Capt. Highland LI; *b* 29 Dec. 1879; *e surv. s* of 1st Baron and Agnes (*d* 1929), *d* of Charles Manners Lushington, MP; *S* father, 1929; *m* 1st, 1905, Dorothy Barbara (*d* 1915), *e d* of late Lt-Col A. B. Haig, CMG, CVO, and Frances, *d* of 3rd Baron Harris; three *s* one *d*; 2nd, 1923, Marion, *d* of late Maj.-Gen. Ives and Susan, *e d* of 4th Baron Talbot de Malahide. *Educ:* Christ Church, Oxford; MA. Served European War, 1914–16 (wounded, prisoner, MC). *Publication:* Recollections of a Prisoner of War, 1930. *Heir:* *g s* Robert Godfrey Phillimore [*b* 1939; *s* of late Capt. Hon. Anthony Francis Phillimore, 9th Queen's Royal Lancers and Anne, 2nd *d* of Maj.-Gen. Sir Cecil Pereira, KCB]. *Address:* Coppid Hall, Henley-on-Thames. *Clubs:* Athenæum, Carlton.

Died 28 Nov. 1947.

PHILLIMORE, Captain Valentine Egerton Bagot, CBE 1920; DSO 1900; late RN; *b* 14 Feb. 1875; *s* of late Admiral Sir A. Phillimore, KCB; *m* 1st, 1908, Mary Kathleen (*d* 1909), *d* of George Robinson of Overdale, Yorks; 2nd, 1910, the Noble Inés Sceberras-D'Amico, *d* of 16th Baron of Castel Cicciano. *Educ:* HMS Britannia. Entered Navy, 1888; served China, 1900 (DSO, despatches naval and military, letter of thanks from senior American officer for services during attack on Tientsin Native City); served in command of HMS Alsatian and HMS Motagua in Northern Patrol, 1914–15; in command of Auxiliary Patrol Area, 1915–16; Senior Naval Officer, West Coast of Africa, 1916–18; Senior Naval Officer, Genoa, 1918–19; Naval Adviser to British Military Mission, South Russia, 1920 (CBE); Head of British Section, Naval Inter-Allied Commission of Control, Turkey, 1920–21; retired list, 1922; an Alderman of the Borough of Ryde, 1933–39. *Address:* Fishbourne, Isle of Wight. *Clubs:* Royal Victoria Yacht, Ryde.

Died 24 Oct. 1945.

PHILLIPS, Alison; *see* Phillips, W. A.

PHILLIPS, Sir Frederick, GCMG 1942; KCMG 1933; CB 1927; Joint Second Secretary HM Treasury; Chairman of the Financial Committee of the League of Nations; *b* 1884; *s* of late E. R. Phillips. *Educ:* Aske's School; Emmanuel College, Cambridge. First Class Mathematical Tripos, 1906; First Class Natural Sciences Tripos, 1907. Entered HM Treasury, first place in Civil Service Class I Examination, 1908; Assistant Secretary, 1919; Principal Assistant Secretary, 1927; Under Secretary, 1932; represented HM Treasury in USA, 1940–43. *Address:* 7 Glenesk Road, Eltham, SE9. *T:* Eltham 1730. *Clubs:* Reform, United University.

Died 14 Aug. 1943.

PHILLIPS, George; Barrister-at-Law; *b* 22 Feb. 1876; 3rd *s* of John Phillips, Swansea; *m* Winifred Adelene, *d* of Edward Arr Jones, Swansea; one *d*. *Educ:* Swansea. High Sheriff of Carmarthenshire, 1938; called to Bar, Lincoln's Inn, 1938; member of South Wales Circuit, 1939. *Recreations:* farming, genealogy and travel. *Address:* No. 8 Old Square, Lincoln's Inn, WC2; Cilyblaidd Pencarreg, Carmarthenshire. *Clubs:* Farmers'; Carmarthen and County (Carmarthen).

Died 30 Dec. 1948.

PHILLIPS, His Honour Harold Ernest; ISO 1933; Commissioner and Judge of the Turks and Caicos Islands, 1923–33; *b* 15 Sept. 1877; 3rd *s* of late Joseph Henry Phillips, CMG, Senior Non-Official Member of the Executive Council of British Honduras; *m* 1899, Claudia, *d* of John Alexander MacDonald of British Honduras; one *s* one *d*. *Educ:* privately in London. Entered British Honduras Civil Service, 1893; held various offices; acted as Colonial Secretary and Governor's Deputy on several occasions; represented British Honduras at the Canada-West Indies Conference at Ottawa, June 1920; Fellow of the Royal Empire Society. *Recreations:* walking, music. *Address:* c/o Royal Empire Society, Northumberland Avenue, WC2.

Died 20 June 1941.

PHILLIPS, Henry Bettesworth, CBE 1948; Managing Director Carl Rosa Opera Co; *b* 23 Dec. 1866. *Educ:* Foyle College, Londonderry. Impresario, Phillips' Dublin, Belfast and Irish Provincial Concerts, 1890–1914; Managing Owner Carl Rosa Opera Co., 1918–. *Recreation:* work. *Address:* 2 Campden House Terrace, Kensington Church Street, W8. *T:* Park 7998.

Died 19 March 1950.

PHILLIPS, John George P.; *see* Porter-Phillips.

PHILLIPS, Very Rev. John Leoline, DD; Dean Emeritus of Monmouth; *b* 2 Aug. 1879; *s* of Rev. D. Phillips, Rector of Radyr; *m* Gwenda, *d* of C. Marment, Llandaff; two *s*. *Educ:* Christ College, Brecon; Keble College, Oxford (Classical Scholar). St Paul's School, 1905–21. Served RAOC 1915–19; Reader of Gray's Inn Chapel, 1911–20; Headmaster of Christ College, Brecon, 1921–31. Dean of Monmouth, 1931–46. *Recreations:* none. *Address:* St Nicholas Cottage, Caldicot, Mon. *T:* Caldicot 327.

Died 31 March 1947.

PHILLIPS, Sir John Randal, Kt 1930; OBE 1927; MB 1882; *b* 26 April 1857; *s* of John Randal Phillips; *m* 1883, Julietta, *d* of T. B. Evelyn, Wotton; one *d*. *Educ:* Lodge School; Codrington College; Edinburgh University. *Address:* Barrack Hill, Barbados.

Died 9 Dec. 1945.

PHILLIPS, Rev. Lawrence Arthur, MA; Rector of Walton, Street, Somerset, since 1931; *b* 1870; *s* of Arthur Phillips, Barrister-at-law, Middle Temple, formerly Standing Council to the Government of India; *m* 1904, Mary Ethel, *d* of Thomas Nickels, Woodlands House, Rockferry. *Educ:* Charterhouse; Trin. College, Oxford. Fellow and Dean of Pembroke College, Oxford, 1895; Rector of Sibson, Leicester, 1899; Principal of Lichfield

Theological College, 1910–31; Prebendary of Lichfield, 1914–35; Rural Dean of Glastonbury, 1935–42. *Address:* Walton Rectory, Street, Somerset. *T:* Street 44.

Died 12 Feb. 1949.

PHILLIPS, Captain Sir Lionel Francis, 2nd Bt *cr* 1912; RA; *b* 1914; *s* of late Harold Lionel Phillips and Hilda Wildman, *d* of late Frank Hills, JP, Hamilton, Canada; S grandfather, 1936; *m* 1939, Camila Mary, *er d* of Hugh Parker, 22 Chapel Street, Belgrave Square, SW1; one *s*. *Educ:* Eton College. *Heir: s* Robin Francis, *b* 29 July 1940. *Club:* Bachelors'.

Died 6 July 1944.

PHILLIPS, Sir Lionel Lawson Faudel F.; *see* Faudel-Phillips.

PHILLIPS, Rev. Theodore Evelyn Reece, MA, FRAS; FRMetSoc; Secretary Royal Astronomical Society, 1919–26; President, 1927 and 1928; *b* 28 March 1868; *s* of late Rev. Abel Phillips, Vicar of Holy Trinity, Yeovil; *m* 1906, M. H. Kynaston, Croydon; one *s*. *Educ:* Yeovil Grammar School; private tutors; St Edmund Hall, Oxford. Ordained, 1891; First Curacy at Holy Trinity Taunton; later curacies at Holy Trinity, Yeovil; St Saviour's, Croydon; and Ashtead, Surrey; Rector of Headley, Epsom, 1916–41; University Extension Lecturer, 1903–22; Lecturer under the Gilchrist Educational Trust since 1935; Director of the Jupiter Section of the British Astronomical Association, 1901–33; Director of Saturn Section, 1935–40; President of that Association, 1914–16; has his own private observatory; his astronomical work is mainly concerned with the planets, double stars, and variable stars (Jackson-Gwilt medal and gift of the Royal Astronomical Society, 1918; Walter Goodacre medal and gift of the British Astronomical Association, 1930); President of Commission 16 of the International Astronomical Union, 1925–35; President Newcastle-upon-Tyne Astronomical Society; has always been interested in meteorology; was Member of League of Nations Committee on Calendar Reform. *Publications:* numerous papers in astronomical publications; Joint Editor of the Splendour of the Heavens; Editor of Sir R. Ball's Popular Guide to the Heavens, 4th edition; some articles on Planets in Encyclopædia Britannica. *Recreations:* was fond of cricket; is much interested in Alpine and British Flora. *Address:* Westways, Sandlands Road, Walton-on-the-Hill, Surrey.

Died 13 May 1942.

PHILLIPS, Adm. (Acting) Sir Tom Spencer Vaughan, KCB 1941; CB 1937; C-in-C Eastern Fleet since 1941; Lord Commissioner of the Admiralty and Vice Chief of Naval Staff, 1939–41; *b* 19 Feb. 1888; *s* of late Colonel T. V. W. Phillips, Royal Artillery; *g s* of late Admiral Sir Algernon F. R. de Horsey, KCB; *m* 1919, Gladys Metcalfe, *d* of late Captain F. G. Griffith-Griffin, DCLI; one *s*. *Educ:* Stubbington House, Fareham; HMS Britannia. Entered Navy, 1903; Commander, 1921; Captain, 1927; served European War, 1914–19, Acting Captain, 1917; Staff College, 1919–20; served on Permanent Advisory Commission for Naval, Military, and Air Questions, Geneva, 1920–22; Assistant Director of Plans, Admiralty, 1930–32; Chief of Staff and Flag Captain to Commander-in-Chief, East Indies, 1932–35; Director of Plans, Admiralty, 1935–38; Commodore Commanding the Home Fleet Destroyer Flotillas, 1938–39; ADC to the King, 1938–39; Rear-Admiral, 1939. *Address:* Binton Corner, Seale, Surrey. *Clubs:* United Service, Royal Cruising; Royal Western Yacht, Plymouth; Royal Yacht Squadron, Cowes (Hon.).

Died 10 Dec. 1941.

PHILLIPS, (Walter) Alison, MA, LittD; Hon. Fellow of Merton College, Oxford, since 1938; *b* 21 Oct. 1864; *m* 1906, Catherine Beatrice Sennett. *Educ:* Weimar; Merchant Taylors' School; Merton Coll., Oxford; Senior Scholar of St John's College, 1886. President of the Union Society, 1887. Chief assistant editor of the Encyclopædia Britannica (11th ed.) 1903–11; Special Correspondent of The Times in South America, 1912; on the staff of The Times, 1913; Lecky Professor of Modern History, University of Dublin, 1914–39. *Publications:* Selected Poems of Walter von der Vogelweide, translated from the Middle High German, 1896; The War of Greek Independence, 1897; Modern Europe, 1901, 5th ed. 1905; George Canning, 1902; three chapters in vol. x of the Cambridge Modern History, 1907; The Confederation of Europe, 1914; (2nd enlarged edition, 1919); Poland, 1915, revised ed., 1928; Diplomacy, and many other articles in the Ency. Brit. (11th ed.), 1911; History of Ireland, 1909–1921; Diplomacy, Self-Determination, in Ency. Brit. (12th ed.), 1921; chapter 1, vol. ii of Cambridge History of British Foreign Policy, 1922; The Revolution in Ireland, 1923 (2nd corrected and enlarged edition, 1925); What Happened at the Reformation, 1926; War of the Creeds; Thirty Years' War, in Harmsworth's Universal History, 1928; translation, with introduction, of Gratz and Schüller's Economic History of Austria-Hungary during the War, 1928; Diplomacy, Treaties, in Ency. Brit. (14th ed.), 1929; French Revolution (Benn's Sixpenny Library), 1929; translation, with introduction, of Gaxotte's French Revolution, 1932; ed. History of the Church of Ireland, 3 vols, 1933–1934; The Belligerents and Neutral Commerce during the Revolutionary and Napoleonic Wars, Vol. II of Neutrality, 1936; Lecky: Centenary Lecture at Trinity College, Dublin 1938. *Club:* Savile.

Died 28 Oct. 1950.

PHILLIPS, William, MA; Professor of Education, and Head of the Men's Training Department at the University College of South Wales and Monmouthshire, 1905–32; Emeritus Professor, since 1932; *b* 15 April 1867; *m* 1903, Elizabeth Jones, Cardiff; three *c.* Taught for some years in Board Schools; entered University College, Cardiff, 1897; BA with honours in latin and Greek, 1900; MA for a Thesis, 1903. *Publications:* Studies in Questions relating to Eye-Training, 1914; The Theory and Practice of teaching Welsh to English-speaking Children without the aid of English, 1921; Y Porth i'r Gymraeg (The Gate into Welsh); The General Influence of Studies, Brit. Journal of Educ. Psych., 1938; S. R. a Rhyddhau'r Caéthion, Y Traethodydd, 1938. *Address:* 4 Ninian Road, Roath Park, Cardiff.

Died 16 Dec. 1941.

PHILLPOTTS, Sir Ralegh Buller, Kt 1946; Chairman British Tabulating Machine Co; *b* 22 Oct. 1871; *o s* of William Francis Phillpotts of Lincoln's Inn, Barrister, and Gertrude Caroline Buller, Strete Ralegh, Whimple, Devon; *m* 1898, Jean, *γ d* of late Alan Stewart, Kinloch Rannoch, Perthshire; two *s* one *d. Educ:* Winchester; Balliol College, Oxford. 1st class Jur. 1893. Called to Bar, Linc. Inn, 1894; Secretary and legal adviser, British Westinghouse Electric and Manufacturing Co., 1901–04; similar position with Speyer Bros, Merchant Bankers, 1904–07; admitted Solicitor, 1907; partner Surtees Phillpotts & Co. (later amalgamated with Linklaters & Paines) Member Council Law Society, 1911. Served with Devon Yeomanry, European War, 1914–18; retired from practice, 1920; a JP for Devon, 1927; Joint Chairman Devon Quarter Sessions, 1934–38; Deputy Chairman, 1938–44; a Governor of Seale Hayne Agric. Coll.; Chairman Exec. Cttee, Council for Preservation of Rural England, Devon Branch. *Publication:* Asst Editor, White and Tudor, Leading Equity Cases, Ed. vii, 1901. *Recreations:* all field sports, gardening. *Address:* Rora House, Liverton, Newton Abbot, Devon. *T:* Bickington 202. *Clubs:* Brooks's; Devon and Exeter (Exeter).

Died 1 Oct. 1950.

PHIPPS, Lt-Col Charles Edward, CB 1916; *b* 3 April 1864; *m* 1901, Elizabeth Henrietta Garde, Timoleague, Co. Cork; one *s* two *d.* Entered RA, 1886; Captain, 1896; Major, 1904; Lieutenant-Colonel, 1914; Assist Inspector, Army Ordnance Department, 1898–1902; Chief Instructor, Ordnance College, 1904–05 and 1907; Professor, 1907–14. Deputy Chief Inspector USA, 1914–16; RGA Inspection Staff, Royal Arsenal, 1914; Director of Safety of Factories Branch, Ministry of Munitions, 1916–20. *Address:* 21 Chesterton Grove, Cirencester.

Died 22 Jan. 1946.

PHIPPS, Sir Edmund (Bampfylde), Kt 1917; CB 1916; *b* 29 Dec. 1869; *s* of Col Ramsay Weston Phipps, RA, and Ann Elizabeth Foskett Bampfylde, *d* of Dr John Bampfylde Daniell; *m* 1906, Margaret Percy (Mayor of Chelsea, 1929–30, 1930–31; she died 1944), *d* of late William Wilton Phipps and Dame Jessie Phipps; two *s* one *d. Educ:* Winchester; New College, Oxford. Tutor to children of Duke and Duchess of Connaught, 1893–96; Assist Sec., Girls' Public Day School Co., Ltd, 1897–1901; entered the office of the Board of Education, 1901; Private Sec. to Sir Robert Morant; Principal Assistant Secretary for Elementary Education, 1912–26; Deputy Sec., 1926–29; General Secretary of the Ministry of Munitions, 1916–17; Member of Council of GPDS Trust and of the Council of the College of St Mark and John, Chelsea. *Address:* 21 Carlyle Square, Chelsea, SW3. *Club:* Windham.

Died 13 Jan. 1947.

PHIPPS, Rt Hon. Sir Eric (Clare Edmund), PC 1933; GCB 1941; GCMG 1934; GCVO 1939; KCMG 1927; CMG 1920; CVO 1922; Grand Cross of the Legion of Honour; Commander of the Ordre de Léopold; *b* 27 Oct. 1875; *o s* of late Sir Constantine Phipps, HM Minister at Brussels, 1900–06; *m* 1st, 1907, Yvonne (*d* 1909), *γ d* of late Comte de Louvencourt; 2nd, 1911, Frances, *γ d* of late Herbert Ward, 105 Avenue Malakoff, Paris; four *s* two *d. Educ:* King's College, Cambridge. Passed competitive examination, 1899. Attaché to HM Embassy at Paris, then to Constantinople, Rome, and to Paris again in 1909, where he was for three years private secretary to HM Ambassador the Rt Hon. Sir F. Bertie (afterwards Lord Bertie); First Secretary of HBM Embassy, Petrograd, 1912; to Madrid, 1913; to Paris, 1916; British Secretary to the Paris Peace Congress, 1919; Assistant Secretary at the Foreign Office, 1919–20; Counsellor of HM Embassy, Brussels, 1920–22; Minister Plenipotentiary at Paris, 1922–28; Envoy Extraordinary and Minister Plenipotentiary at Vienna, 1928–33; Ambassador Extraordinary and Plenipotentiary in Berlin, 1933–37; in Paris, 1937–39; attached to the British Delegation at The Hague Reparations Conferences, Aug. 1929 and Jan. 1930; is a Director of Midland Bank and member of the Council of Foreign Bondholders. High Sheriff for Wiltshire, 1943–44. *Address:* West Stowell House, Marlborough. *Clubs:* White's, St James's, Turf, Beefsteak.

Died 13 Aug. 1945.

PICARD, Émile; Membre de l'Académie Française; Secrétaire perpétuel de l'Académie des Sciences; Membre du Bureau des Longitudes; Professeur hon. à l'Université de Paris; et à l'Ecole Centrale des Arts et Manufactures; le 24 juillet 1856. Membre de la Société Royale de Londres, de la Société Royale d'Edinbourg et de l'Académie Royale d'Irlande; Docteur des Universités de Cambridge, de Glasgow, de Berlin, de Louvain, de Liège; Membre d'honneur de la Société Mathématique de Londres; Membre des Académies des Sciences de Rome, de Berlin, de St-Petersbourg, de Copenhague, de Lisbonne, de Bruxelles, de Turin, de Bologne, de Milan, de Christiania, d'Upsal, de Helsingfors, de Washington, de Boston, Liège, Prague, Bucarest, Göttingen, Athènes, Buda-Pesth, etc. Ancien élève de l'Ecole Normale Supérieure, 1874; Ancien Professeur à l'Université de Toulouse, 1879–81; Maître de Conférences à l'Ecole

Normale Supérieure, 1882–86; Professeur d'Analyse Supérieure à la Faculté des Sciences de l'Université de Paris, 1886; Professeur de Mécanique Générale à l'Ecole Centrale des Arts et Manufactures, 1894. *Publications:* Nombreux mémoires sur les mathématiques pures et appliquées dans un grand nombre de périodiques; Traité d'Analyse; Théorie des fonctions algébriques de deux variables indépendantes; La science moderne et son état actuel-Discours et mélanges, 1922; Mélanges de mathématiques et de physique, 1924; Un coup d'œil sur l'histoire des sciences et des théories physiques, 1930; Eloges et Discours Académiques, 1931; Notices et discours, 1936. Conférences faites en Amérique, etc. *Address:* Institut de France, 25 Quai Conti, Paris (VI).

Died 11 Dec. 1941.

PICK, Frank; *b* Spalding, Lincs, 23 Nov. 1878; *m* Mabel Mary Caroline Woodhouse. *Educ:* St Peter's School, York. Articled to a solicitor, George Crombie, of York; qualified 2nd Class Hons; LLB of Lond. University with Honours; joined the railway service under Sir George Gibb on the old North Eastern Railway; came to London with him to join the Underground Group, 1906; transferred to serve under Lord Ashfield and continued with him as Managing Director to the Underground Group of Companies until their transfer to the London Passenger Transport Board; Vice-Chairman of the Board, 1933–40; Member of the London and Home Counties Traffic Advisory Committee; Member of Crown Lands Advisory Committee; Hon. Member RIBA; Member of Royal Commission on Police Powers and Procedure; late Chm. of the Council for Art and Industry of the Board of Trade. *Recreations:* the wider aspects of transport and seeing the world. *Address:* 15 Wildwood Road, Golders Green, NW11. *T:* Speedwell 1929. *Club:* Reform.

Died 7 Nov. 1941.

PICK-MANGIAGALLI, Riccardo; Italian-Bohemian pianist and composer; Direttore del R. Conservatorio G. Verdi di Milano, 1936; *b* Strakonitz, 1882. *Educ:* Milan Conservatory. *Works:* Numerosi pezzi per pianoforte, canto, violino, etc. Musica da camera: Sonata op. 8 per pianoforte e violino; Quartetto op. 18 per archi; Pianoforte e orchestra: Humoresque, op. 35; Pianoforte Orch. Trois Miniatures op. 4; Sortilegi, op. 39 (poema sinfonico). Grande orchestra: Notturno e Rondo fantastico, op. 28 Voci e ombre del vespero-Marosi, op. 42; Quattro poemi, op. 45; Piccola suite; Preludio e fuga, op. 47, per Orchestra; J. S. Bach, Due Preludi; Chopin, Polonaise in A flat, op. 53; (Quartetto d'archi) Tre fugue per quartetto; (Pianof. e orchestra) Concerto in sol magg. per pianof. e orchestra; (Grande orchestra) Scene Carnavalesche; Preludio e Scherzo sinfonica; Rapsodia epica. Teatro: La Berceuse (Balletto); Il salice d'oro (favola musicale), 1914; Il Carillon magico (commedia mimo-sinfonica), 1918; Sumitra (leggendo monomimica), 1922; Mahit (commedia mimo-sinfonica), 1923; Basi e Bote (commedia lirica), 1927; Casanova a Venezia (azione coreografica, 1929); L'ospite inatteso (gioco lirico, 1934); Variasioni Coreografiche Scala, 1935; Notturno Romantico (opera lirica in un atto e due quadri) Roma, 1936; Visioni (Balletto) su musiche di Chopin, Milano, Scala, 1942; (Teatro) Evocazioni (balletto), Scala 1947. *Address:* via Bigli 28, Milano, Italy.

Died 8 July 1949.

PICKARD, Gp Captain Percy Charles, DSO 1941; DFC; *b* 16 May 1915; *m* 1939, Dorothy, *d* of Colonel Hodgkin, DSO, Irish Guards; one *s. Educ:* Framlingham College. Five years farming in Kenya; joined RAF 1936; served in Bomber Command, then ADC to Air Marshal Baldwin; returned to Bomber Command at outbreak of war; since served in six night bomber squadrons (DFC, DSO, and two bars). *Recreations:* hunting, shooting. *Club:* RAF.

Died 18 Feb. 1944.

PICKARD, Sir Robert (Howson), Kt 1937; FRS, DSc (Lond.), PhD (Munich), FRIC; Consultant to British Leather Manufacturers Research Association; *b* 1874; *s* of late Joseph Henry Pickard, Edgbaston; *m* 1901, Ethel Marian Wood (*d* 1944); one *s* one *d. Educ:* King Edward School, Camp Hill; Mason Univ. Coll.; Univ. of Munich. Principal, Technical School, Blackburn, 1907–19; Principal Battersea Polytechnic, 1920–27; Director British Cotton Industry Research Association 1927–43; Member of Senate, University of London, since 1926, Vice-Chancellor, 1937–39, Chairman of Convocation, 1948. Member of Council of Chemical Society, 1916–20, 1926–28, Vice-President, 1931–34 and 1937–40; Vice-President Institute of Chemistry, 1927–30 and 1939–43; President, 1936–39; Chm. Chemical Council, 1936–38; Past President Society of Chemical Industry, Society's Medallist, 1941; Member of Consultative Committee of Board of Education, 1920–23, of the Warble Fly Committee of Board of Agriculture, 1922–24, and of Departmental Committee of Home Office on Dust in Cardrooms, 1927; Chairman Roedean School Council; Member of the Courts of Universities of Birmingham and Manchester. Hon. Liveryman Leathersellers Co.; Hon. Member Soc. Public Analysts; Past President Assoc. Technical Institutions. *Publications:* numerous original papers on chemical subjects in Trans. Chem. Soc. *Address:* Tumber House, Headley, Surrey. *T:* Headley 21. *Club:* Athenæum.

Died 18 Oct. 1949.

PICKERING, Bt Col Emil William, DSO 1917; TD; JP; DL West Riding of Yorkshire; additional Deputy Regional Commissioner, Northern Region, since 1941; *b* 3 Jan. 1882; *m* 1919, Evelyn Joyce Morton, *e d* of John E. Shaw of Brooklands, near Halifax, Yorkshire; two *s.* Served European War (despatches, DSO); MP (Co. U) Dewsbury, Dec. 1918–22. *Recreation:* shooting. *Address:* Netherton Hall, nr Wakefield, Yorkshire. *T:* Horbury 69.

Died 14 March 1942.

PICKFORD, Sir Alfred Donald, Kt 1921; OBE 1946; Kaisar-i-Hind gold medal; Partner, Begg Roberts & Co., London; Chairman, International Tea Market Expansion Board; *b* 20 May 1872; *s* of Charles Hampden Pickford and Isabella Horne; unmarried. *Educ:* George Watson's College and Fettes College, Edinburgh. Sheriff of Calcutta, 1920; Member Indian Legislative Assembly, 1921. *Clubs:* Oriental, Athenæum; Bengal, Royal Turf, Calcutta.

Died 7 Oct. 1947.

PICKLES, Edward Llewellyn, CB 1945; OBE 1933; LLB; Chairman of Power Jets (R. & D.) Ltd; *b* 8 March 1884; *s* of Rev. Isaac Pickles; *m* Maggie Turner (*d* 1948); two *s* one *d. Educ:* University, Leeds and University, London (King's College). HM Patent Office, 1905. Various appointments in Admiralty, Air Ministry; Director of Contracts, Ministry of Aircraft Production; Under-Secretary, Ministry of Supply, retired. *Address:* 14 Lancaster Avenue, Hadley Wood.

Died 14 Sept. 1949.

PICKMERE, Edward Ralph, MA, JP; *s* of J. R. Pickmere, Warrington; *m* Edith May, *d* of W. Oliver, London; three *s* one *d. Educ:* Boteler Grammar School, Warrington; Exeter College, Oxford. BA 1878; MA 1881. Articled to late Edw. Whitley, MP, 1879; Town Clerk and Prosecuting Solicitor Liverpool, 1899–1920; JP Montgomeryshire, 1906. *Address:* Mount Hall, Llanfair, Welshpool. *T:* Llanfaircaereinion 18.

Died 13 Oct. 1941.

PICKTHALL, Col (temp. Brig.) Wallace Edward Colin, CBE 1941; OBE 1929; Deputy Director of Ordnance Services, Scottish Command; *b* 9 Nov. 1891; *m* 1924, Ellen Eva, *d* of Commander F. Pierce, RN; one *s. Educ:* Elstow School; RMC, Sandhurst. 2nd Lt West Yorkshire Regt, 1913. Transferred to RAOC, 1920,

1939, 1945. Director of Ordnance Services BNAF and MEF, Deputy Director Northern and South-Eastern Commands and 3rd Corps. *Recreations:* cricket, golf, fishing. *Address:* c/o Lloyds Bank Ltd, Cox and King's Branch, 6 Pall Mall, SW1. *Clubs:* Junior United Service, MCC.

Died 19 Sept. 1948.

PIDDINGTON, Albert Bathurst; KC; Barrister (formerly Mr Justice Piddington); *b* Bathurst, NSW, 9 Sept. 1862; *s* of late Archdeacon Piddington, of Tamworth, NSW; *m* 1896, Marion Louisa, *d* of late Canon O'Reilly; one *s. Educ:* Sydney Grammar School; Sydney University (various scholarships; BA 1883; gold medal in classics). Vice-Warden of St Paul's College, 1884; visited Europe, 1887; Lecturer in English Literature, Sydney Univ., 1889–94; and was Examiner in German, French, History, and English; Associate to late Mr Justice Windeyer, 1889; called to Bar, 1890; Member Legislative Assembly for Tamworth, 1895; took an active part in the federal controversies in 1897 and 1898; elected in 1910 and 1913 to Sydney University Senate; a delegate to the Congress of Universities of the Empire at London, 1912; a Royal Commissioner on Shortage of Labour and Factory Employment, 1911; a Justice of the High Court, 1913, resigned; Chief Commissioner of the Inter-State Commission, Commonwealth of Australia, 1913–20; Industrial Commissioner of New S Wales, 1926–27; President Industrial Commission of New South Wales, 1927–32; Chairman Basic Wage Commission, 1919–21; a Royal Commissioner to enquire into industrial arbitration in NSW, 1913; MA (special grace), Melbourne, 1913; Member Advisory Council of Science and Industry Executive, 1916–21; President Modern Languages Association since 1925; Chairman Queensland Govt Committee on Child Endowment Act; Pres. Fellowship of Australian Writers, 1939; Chairman, Board of Official Visitors to Mental Hospitals, Sydney, 1942. *Publications:* edited Sir Roger de Coverley (selections from the Spectator), 1893, and selections from Paradise Lost, 1894; Spanish Sketches, 1916; Young Italy (translated drama), 1916; Report on Queensland Productivity and Remuneration of Labour, 1925; Worshipful Masters, 1929; Bapu Ghandi, 1930; Shakespeare and the Idea of Beauty, 1930; The King and the People and the Severing of their Unity; a Study of the 1932 Constitutional Crisis in New South Wales, 1932; The United States of Europe, 1940. *Address:* Breffny, Glenbrook, NSW.

Died 6 June 1945.

PIENAAR, Maj.-Gen. Daniel Hermanus, CB 1942; DSO 1941; commanding 1st S African Division in Libya; *b* Ladybrand, Orange Free State, 1893; *m.* Joined Dept of Defence, 1911; served European War, 1914–19 (despatches); War of 1939–45 (despatches, DSO and Bar, CB).

Died 19 Dec. 1942.

PIERCE, Sir John, Kt 1939; *b* 1863; *s* of Joseph Pierce, Birmingham; *m* 1887, Harriet (*d* 1943), *d* of William Howarth, Manchester; one *d.* Ex-Deputy Chairman Pearl Assurance Company, Ltd; Director, People's Land, Buildings and Dwellings Company, Ltd. *Address:* White Ledges, St Stephen's Rd, Ealing, W13; Pearl Assurance Co., Ltd, High Holborn, WC1.

Died 14 March 1949.

PIERCY, Benjamin Herbert; *b* 1870; *s* of late Benjamin Piercy of Marchwiel Hall, Denbighshire; *m* 1st Mildreda, *d* of late J. Sawrey-Cookson of Neasham Hall, Darlington; 2nd, Daphne, *d* of Hardwicke Lloyd Hardwicke of Tytherington Grange, Gloucestershire; two *s* one *d.* Served for some years in XII Royal Lancers, later commanded a company of Imperial Yeomanry in South African War (despatches); 2nd in Command in 2nd South Notts Hussars, Home Defence, European War; chiefly resides on his estate in Sardinia, where he is interested in agriculture. *Recreations:* shooting, yachting. *Address:* Macomer, Sardinia. *Clubs:* Naval and Military; Royal Yacht Squadron, Cowes.

Died 15 Dec. 1941.

PIERS, Sir Charles Pigott, 9th Bt *cr* 1660; *b* 27 June 1870; *s* of 8th Bt and Rose, *d* of Charles Saunders, Fulwood Park, Liverpool; *S* father, 1913; *m* 1902, Hester Constance (Stella) (*d* 1936), *e d* of late S. R. Brewis of Ibstone House, Ibstone; one *s. Educ:* Eton; Trinity Hall, Cambridge. Late Hon. Major 4th Batt. Sherwood Foresters; served S Africa, 1900–01; European War, 1915–19, as Maj. 29th (Vancouver) Batt. Canadian Forces; also served as a General Staff Officer on the Canadian Corps Staff, and with the Canadian Section of the General Headquarter Staff, 3rd Echelon. *Publication:* Sport and Life in British Columbia. *Heir: s* Charles Robert Fitzmaurice [*b* 30 Aug. 1903; *m* 1936, Ann Blanche Scott, *o d* of late Capt. Thomas Ferguson (The Royal Highlanders); one *d.* Cadet, RN Colleges, Osborne and Dartmouth]. *Address:* Union Club of BC, Victoria, BC.

Died 27 June 1945.

PIERSON, Reginald Kirshaw, CBE 1943; BSc; AMICE; FRAeS; Chief Designer Vickers Armstrongs Ltd (Aircraft Section) since 1917; *b* 9 Feb. 1891; *s* of Rev. K. T. Pierson; *m* 1917, Dora Llewellyn-Jones; one *s* one *d. Educ:* Felsted. Served pupil apprenticeship, 1908–11 with Vickers Ltd; joined newly formed aircraft section, 1911; gained pilot's certificate No. 688 in 1913. *Recreations:* shooting, fishing, tennis. *Address:* Manor Cottage, Smithwood Common, Cranleigh. *T:* Cranleigh 497.

Died 10 Jan. 1948.

PIGGOTT, Sir Theodore Caro, Kt 1924; BA; *b* Padua, Italy, 26 Oct. 1867; *s* of Rev. H. J. Piggott, Rome; *m* 1891, Eleanor Mildred (*d* 1942), *d* of Walter Tschudi Lyall; two *d. Educ:* Kingswood School, Bath; Christ Church, Oxford. Passed into the Indian Civil Service, 1886; Assistant Magistrate and Collector, United Provinces, 1888; acting Additional Judge of Aligarh, 1895–96; acting Deputy Commissioner of Bahraich, 1897–99; Deputy Commissioner, 1900; District and Sessions Judge, Moradabad, 1900–03; Special Judge under the Bundelkhand Encumbered Estates Act, 1903–06; acting Additional Judicial Commissioner of Oudh, 1908, confirmed, 1909; Judicial Commissioner, 1911; Delhi Durbar, 1911; Chairman of Committee on Primary Education, 1913; confirmed as Puisne Judge of the Allahabad High Court in 1914, having acted in previous years; served on Committee for revising Code of Criminal Procedure, 1916; Vice-Chancellor, Allahabad University, 1919–20; Puisne Judge, Allahabad, 1914–25; retired, 1925. *Publication:* Outlaws I have Known, 1930. *Recreation:* golf. *Club:* East India and Sports.

Died 3 July 1944.

PIGGOTT, Rev. William Charter; *s* of W. F. Piggott, Leighton Buzzard, Bedfordshire; *m* Elizabeth Annie, *d* of E. A. Fry, Finchley; two *s. Educ:* Huddersfield College; Headingley Wesleyan College. After leaving Methodism organised Brotherhood Church, Harrow Road, 1896–1900; Congregational Church, Greville Place, Kilburn, 1901–04; Bunyan Meeting, Bedford, 1905–12; Whitefield's Central Mission, Tottenham Court Road, as co-superintendent with late Rev. C. Silvester Horne, MP, 1912–14; sole superintendent, 1914–17; Minister of Streatham Congregational Church, 1917–37; retired 1937; Chairman of the London Missionary Society, 1930; Chairman of the Congregational Union of England and Wales, 1931–32. *Publications:* The Christ Imperative; The Imperishable Word; John Bunyan; Pioneers of Freedom; The Shepherds' Wonder. *Recreation:* golf. *Address:* 20 Waterloo Road, Bedford.

Died 5 Nov. 1943.

PIGOTT, Lt-Col Grenville Edmund, CMG 1916; DSO 1898; late Royal Army Service Corps; *b* 18 Feb. 1870; *m* 1902, Alice Molesworth (*d* 1919), *o d* of Lieut-Col A. J. Ogilvie. *Educ:* Harrow; Corpus Christi Coll., Camb. Entered army, 1892; Capt., 1899; Major, 1906; Lt-Col, 1914; served Nile Expedition, 1898, including Atbara, Khartoum (despatches, DSO); South Africa, 1899–1902 (despatches, Queen's and King's medals with 7 clasps); served Somaliland Expedition, 1909–10, as Director of Supplies and Transport (despatches, thanks of Colonial Office, medal, and clasp); European War, 1914–18 (despatches twice, 1914 Star, CMG); retired pay, 1920.

Died 2 July 1942.

PIGOTT, Col Robert Edward Pemberton, CIE 1911; VD 1905; MIEE; late Chief Electrical Engineer, Bombay, Baroda, and Central India Railway, India; Lt-Col and Hon. Col Auxiliary Force (India) (retired); *b* 6 Oct. 1866; *s* of late Col E. C. Pemberton-Pigott, of the Essex (44th) Regt; *m* 1893, Maude Alice, *d* of late A. T. Wilkinson, CE. *Educ:* Trent College, Nottingham. Represented Corps at Delhi Durbar (medal), 1903; temp. Major 12th Battalion Essex Regt, 25 Jan. 1915–28 July 1915; Lt-Col commanding 12th (Service) Bn Suffolk Regt, 29 July 1915–16 Sept. 1916; Hon. Lieut-Col in the Army, 16 Sept. 1916; attended Coronation Durbar (medal), 1911. *Club:* East India and Sports.

Died 20 Nov. 1943.

PIGOTT, William; *see* Wales, Hubert.

PIGOTT-BROWN, Captain Sir John Hargreaves, 2nd Bt *cr* 1902; Coldstream Guards; *b* 16 Aug. 1913; *s* of late Capt. Gordon Hargreaves Brown, Coldstream Guards, and Editha, *d* of late Admiral W. H. Pigott; *S* grandfather, 1922; *m* 1940, Helen, *o d* of Major Gilbert Egerton Cotton, Priestland, Tarporley, Cheshire; one *s.* Assumed by Royal Licence, 1925, the additional surname and arms of Pigott. Served War of 1939 (wounded). *Heir: s* William Brian, *b* 20 Jan. 1941. *Address:* Broome Hall, Dorking, Surrey.

Died 25 Dec. 1942.

PIKE, Lt-Col Cuthbert Joseph, CBE 1919; DL; *b* 1868; *s* of late Walter Pike of Camborne, Cornwall; *m* 1901, Dorothy Margaret Mary (*d* 1933), *y d* of late Daniel O'Connell, MP; four *s* four *d. Educ:* Oscott College; Germany. Served in South African and European Wars. *Address:* The Cottage, Hook, Basingstoke, Hants. *T:* Hook 99. *Club:* Royal Automobile.

Died 17 Jan. 1947.

PIKE, John Milton; KC 1908; FRSA; Member Wilson, Pike, Stewart & Lewes, Barrister and Solicitors; *b* Raleigh, Ont, 9 Nov. 1872; *s* of John B. Pike, President, Detroit Dredging Co., and Annie McIntyre; *m* 1st, 1895, Mrs Lucy Alberta Heyward (*d* 1924), *d* of James Reeve, Chatham; 2nd, 1928, Alma MacPherson, *d* of Joseph Vipond and Janet Cameron; one *d. Educ:* Chatham Collegiate Institute (1st class honours in modern languages, winning the Craddock silver medal for general proficiency. Called to Ontario Bar, 1893; President Kent Law Association, 1908–09; one of Ontario Government Crown Prosecutors; practises before the Judicial Committee of the Privy Council; President West Kent Conservative Association, 1906; Lieutenant 24th Kent Regiment since 1907; now on reserve list; Conservative; Anglican; Past Preceptor Kent Preceptory, No. 20, Knights Templar; Past Grand Pursuivant Sovereign, Great Priory of Canada. *Publications:* Pike's Canadian Municipal Law, 1929; Annotations on Drainage Law, and on Trustees and Executors, Life Tenants and Remaindermen in Dominion Law Reports. *Recreations:* yachting, walking. *Address:* Murray Street, Chatham, Ontario. *T:* 386. *Clubs:* British Empire, Royal Societies; Maple City, Chatham; Albany Canadian Military Institute, Toronto.

Died 16 May 1940.

PIKE, Maj.-Gen. Sir William Watson, KCMG 1919; CMG 1918; DSO 1900; FRCSI; late AMS; *b* 10 March 1860; *s* of late William Pike, JP, of Glendarary; *m* 1886, Sarah Louisa (*d* 1918), *d* of E. Wheatley. Entered army, 1882; Surgeon-Major, 1894; Lt-Col 1902; Col 1911; served South Africa, 1899–1902 (despatches twice, Queen's medal 5 clasps, King's medal 2 clasps, DSO); Director of Medical Services, First Army, BEF, European War, 1914–17 (despatches, CMG, promoted Surg.-Gen. 1917); Special Commissions East Africa, 1917–18, and India, 1918–19; Major-General, 1918; retired, 1920. *Recreations:* Rugby International, Ireland, 1879–83; Hockey Interprovincial, Ireland, 1898. *Address:* c/o Glyn, Mills & Co., 22 Whitehall, SW1.

Died 26 June 1941.

PILCHER, Maj.-Gen. Edgar Montagu, CB 1918; CBE 1919; DSO 1900; MA, MB, and BC (Cantab), 1890; FRCS Eng. 1905; late AMS; late Consulting Surgeon to British Army; Hon. Surgeon to the King; *b* 25 April 1865; *m* 1st, 1899, Lilias Mary (*d* 1940), *e d* of late Capt. Henri Campbell, ISC; 2nd, 1940, Brenda Georgiana, *yr d* of late A. F. Warr, MP. Served North-West Frontier, India, 1897–98 (medal with 2 clasps); South Africa, 1899–1902 (despatches, DSO, Queen's medal with 5 clasps, King's medal with 2 clasps); European War (despatches, CB, CBE); retired pay, 1924. *Address:* Thirty Trees, Ashtead, Surrey.

Died 26 Dec. 1947.

PILDITCH, Sir Philip (Edward), 1st Bt *cr* 1929; Kt 1918; JP County of London; *b* Compton, near Plymouth, 12 Aug. 1861; *e s* of late Philip John Pilditch, Plymouth; *m* 1888, Emily Mary, *e d* of John Lewis of National Provincial Bank, Threadneedle Street and Richmond; two *s* one *d. Educ:* Cheveley Hall, Mannamead; King's College. Contested (U) Western (St Ives) Division, Cornwall, 1906; East Islington, Dec. 1910; MP (U) Spelthorne Division of Middlesex, Dec. 1918–31; Member LCC, East Islington and Strand, 1907–19; Vice-Chairman of Council, 1913–14; Chairman Parliamentary and Local Govt Committees; taken considerable part in Poor Law, Taxation, Economy, and Housing Reform; Member Estimates, Exports Credits and Indian Committees, House of Commons, and of all committees concerning Law of Landlord and Tenant, Town Planning, etc. between 1915 and 1932; has been Governor King's College, Northern Polytechnic; Chairman Middlesex County Conservative Organisation, 1925–26; has taken part in preservation of Elizabethan Plymouth, since 1926; and in preservation of Hadrian's Wall and the passage of the Ancient Monuments Act, 1930–31; President Old Plymouth Society; Member Council English Speaking Union; London Society; head of firm of Pilditch, Chadwick & Co., Architects and Surveyors; Captain (retired) 1st Sussex V Artillery; Founder Battalion Funds in 50 Battalions of the New Army in Surrey, Middlesex, and London during war. *Publications:* professional, literary, and historical papers; Retrenchment, 1923; The Eighties and Today, 1927; Elizabethan Plymouth, 1929; Old Thurlestone, 1939. *Heir: s* Philip Harold, *b* 1890. *Address:* Old Bond Street House, W1. *T:* Regent 1604; Bartropps, Weybridge Heath, Surrey. *T:* Weybridge 260. *Clubs:* Sunningdale Golf (Sunningdale); St George's Hill Golf (Weybridge).

Died 17 Dec. 1948.

PILDITCH, Sir Philip Harold, 2nd Bt *cr* 1929; *b* 30 Oct. 1890; *s* of Sir Philip Edward Pilditch, 1st Bt; *S* father 1948; *m* 1st, 1918, Frances Isabella, *d* of J. G. Weeks, JP, Bedlington, Northumberland; two *s*; 2nd, 1936, Patricia Marcia Muriel, *d* of Alexander Whittet, Weybridge, Surrey; one *d. Educ:* Winchester College; Pembroke College, Cambridge. BA History and Architecture. Served European War, 1914–19, RA (TF); Major 1918 (despatches); re-employed with Heavy AA, 1940–41. Partner Pilditch, Chadwick & Co., Architects and Surveyors, 1919–45; FRIBA, FRICS. *Publications:*

Barbarian, a tale of Hadrian's Wall, 1932; Uphill Journey, 1938; The War Diary of an Artillery Officer, 1939; Alpine Memoirs, 1949; articles and stories in Chambers's Journal, 1925–1935. *Recreation:* mountaineering. *Heir: s* Philip John Frederick, [*b* 10 Aug. 1919; *m* 1948, Phyllis Jean, *d* of D. C. Stewart-Smith]. *Address:* 6 Old Bond Street, W1; Abbotswood, Oakfield Glade, Weybridge, Surrey. *Clubs:* Alpine, Junior Carlton, Junior United Service.

Died 6 Dec. 1949.

PILE, Sir George Laurie, Kt 1939; CBE 1937; President Legislative Council, Barbados; *b* 1857; *s* of late Sir George Clarke Pile, Barbados; *m* 1881, Emily Elizabeth Lyall. *Educ:* Clifton College; Oxford University, BA. *Address:* Bulkeley, Barbados.

Died 15 March 1948.

PILGRIM, Guy Ellcock, FRS 1943; FGS; FASB; Supernumerary Staff, Department of Geology, British Museum (Natural History); *b* Barbados, W Indies, 1875; *s* of Henry Ellcock Pilgrim; *m* Beatrice Lucy Wrenford; one *s*. *Educ:* Harrison College, Barbados; University College, WC BSc London, 1901; DSc, 1908. Appointed to the Geological Survey of India, 1902; Superintendent, Geological Survey of India, 1920; retired, 1930; Corresponding Member of the Palæontological Society of America, 1923; attached as 2nd Lieut to 125th Napier's Rifles, 1915; war medals for service in Mesopotamia and Persia, 1916–19; Fellow of the Asiatic Society of Bengal, 1925; President of the Geological Section of the Indian Science Congress for 1925. *Publications:* Two Memoirs on the Geology of Persia and the Persian Gulf; (with W. D. West) on the Geology of the Simla Hills; Studies on the Fossil Primates of India; Memoirs on the Fossil Giraffidæ, the Fossil Suidæ, the Fossil Carnivora and the Fossil Bovidæ of India; numerous papers in the Pal. Indica. and Records of the Geological Survey of India and in English and foreign journals dealing with stratigraphy and vertebrate palæontology; British Museum Catalogues of Pontian Bovidæ and Carnivora. *Recreations:* lawn tennis, golf, and bridge. *Address:* Upton, near Didcot, Berkshire. *T:* Blewbury 268. *Clubs:* United Service, Calcutta.

Died 15 Sept. 1943.

PILKINGTON, Robert Rivington, KC 1906; BA; *y s* of late Henry Mulock Pilkington, QC, LLD, DL, of Tore, Tyrrellspass, Co. Westmeath; *m* 1899, Ethel (*d* 1920), *d* of Captain Longworth Dames of Greenhill, Edenberry, King's Co.; one *d*. *Educ:* Uppingham (Scholar); Pembroke College, Cambridge (Scholar). Called to English Bar, Lincoln's Inn, 1893; admitted legal practitioner in Western Australia, 1894, where practised profession until 1921; MLA Perth, 1917–21; contested Dundee as Independent Liberal, 1922; MP (L) Keighley Division of Yorks, 1923–24. *Address:* 2 Langham Mansions, Earl's Court Square, SW5. *Clubs:* Weld, Perth.

Died 30 June 1942.

PILKINGTON, Sir Thomas Edward Milborne-Swinnerton-, 12th Bt *cr* 1635; *b* 9 Dec. 1857; *s* of 11th Bt and Isabella Georgiana Elizabeth, *d* of late Rev. Charles R. Kinleside; *S* father, 1901; *m* 1895, Lady Kathleen Mary A. Cuffe (*d* 1938), *o c* of 4th Earl of Desart; two *s* one *d*. *Educ:* Eton; Christ Church, Oxford (MA). Served S Africa, 1880–81; Egypt, Tel-el-Kebir in 60th Rifles, 1882–84; Lieutenant-Colonel commanded 7th Batt. King's Royal Rifle Corps, 1903–08; 14th Reserve Batt. KRR, 1914–16; Special Service, France and Germany, 1917–19. High Sheriff of Yorkshire, 1911–12. *Heir: s* Bt Major Arthur William Milborne-Swinnerton-Pilkington, MC. *Address:* Chevet Park, Wakefield. *Club:* Carlton.

Died 17 Feb. 1944.

PIM, Rt Hon. Jonathan; PC; Justice of the King's Bench Division of the High Court of Justice, Ireland, 1915–24; Attorney-General for Ireland, 1914–15; Solicitor-General for Ireland, 1913–14; Commissioner of Charitable Donations and Bequests; *b* 1858; *s* of late Thomas Pim, Greenbank, Monkstown, Co. Dublin. *Educ:* Trinity College, Dublin. *Address:* 4 Burlington Road, Dublin. *Clubs:* Reform, Royal Societies; University, Royal Irish Yacht (Dublin).

Died 22 April 1949.

PINCHOT, Gifford; Forester; *b* Simsbury, Connecticut, 11 Aug. 1865; *s* of James W. Pinchot and Mary Eno; *m* 1914, Cornelia E., *d* of General Lloyd S. Bryce, New York; one *s*. *Educ:* Yale; studied forestry in Germany, France, Switzerland, and Austria. First American professional forester. Began first systematic forestry in US, 1892. United States Forester, 1898–1910; Chairman National Conservation Commission, 1908–09; Professor of Forestry, Yale, 1903–36, Emeritus since 1936; Commissioner of Forestry of Pennsylvania, 1920–22; Governor of Pennsylvania, 1923–27 and 1931–35. Discovered fish juice for castaways at sea, 1942. Secured placing fishing tackle on all American lifeboats, 1943. *Publications:* (with H. S. Graves) The White Pine, 1896; The Adirondack Spruce, 1898; A Primer of Forestry, 1899 and 1905; The Fight for Conservation, 1910; (with C. O. Gill) The Country Church, 1913; The Training of a Forester, 1914, 1937; (with C. O. Gill) Six Thousand Country Churches, 1919; To the South Seas, 1930; Just Fishing Talk, 1936; Breaking New Ground, 1946. *Recreation:* fishing. *Address:* Milford, Pa, USA. *Clubs:* Century, Explorers, New York; Cosmos, Washington.

Died 4 Oct. 1946.

PINCKARD, George Henry, MA, JP; 4th *s* of J. Coles, JP, and Amelia, *d* of F. Lermitte, and *grand-nephew* of late George Henry Pinckard, whose name and Combe Court estate he assumed in 1893; *m* 1909, Ruby, *e d* of Rev. Charles Fryer Eastburn, RD, late Rector of Medbourne-cum-Holt, Leicestershire; two *d*. *Educ:* Marlborough; Jesus College, Cambridge; Royal Agricultural College, Cirencester. Called to Bar, Lincoln's Inn, 1895; President of Guildford and West Surrey Agricultural Association, 1908; Lord of the Manor of Witley; Master of Chiddingfold Hounds for eight years; and supervised Remount Depôt on part of his estate presented to the War Office by him in 1911. Proprietor Yachting Monthly and Motor Cruising Magazine. *Clubs:* Carlton, MCC.

Died 7 Sept. 1950.

PINNEY, Charles Robert, MC; *b* 18 Nov. 1883; *s* of late Henry Edward Pinney and Mary Jane Long; *m* 1918, Mary Desmond, *o d* of late Sir Hubert Murray, KCMG; one *s* one *d*. *Educ:* Essendon Grammar School, and tutor. Appointed to Papuan Civil Service, 1906; enlisted as trooper in 4th AL Horse, 1914; wounded Lone Pine, Gallipoli, 1915; commission in 6th Bn AIF, appointed MG and Intelligence Officer, 1915; appointed to Brigade Staff as Intelligence Officer, 1916; promoted Captain and appointed OC of D Company, 6th Bn, 1917 (despatches, MC); gazetted Captain in Commonwealth Military Forces, Reserve of Officers, 1920; returned to duty in Papuan Civil Service, 1920; Chief Draughtsman, 1920; Staff Surveyor in addition, 1924; Commissioner for Lands, Director of Mines and Agriculture, Member of the Executive and Legislative Councils, 1930; Administrator of Territory of Norfolk Island, 1932–37. *Recreations:* riding, tennis, golf. *Address:* Bucklebury, Burradoo Road, Burradoo, NSW. *T:* Bowral 234. *Clubs:* Imperial Service, Pacific Islands, Sydney.

Died 18 Nov. 1945.

PINNEY, Maj.-Gen. Sir Reginald (John), KCB 1918; CB 1917; Legion of Honour, 1917; JP, DL, High Sheriff, Dorset, 1923; Colonel of the Royal Fusiliers (City of London Regiment), 1924–33; Hon. Colonel of

Dorset Coast, Brig. RA 1921–28, and of 4th Dorset Regt, 1928; retired pay; *b* 2 Aug. 1863; *e s* of Rev. J. C. Pinney, Vicar of Coleshill, Warwickshire (*d* 1911), and Harriett Margaretta (*d* 1877), 3rd *d* of late Rev. John Digby Wingfield-Digby, Vicar of Coleshill; *m* 1900, Hester, *o d* of Henry Head, JP, of Buckingham, Shoreham, Sussex; two *s* (and *e s* killed in Lybia, 1941) three *d*. *Educ*: Winchester; Royal Military College, Sandhurst. Joined the Royal Fusiliers, 1884; passed the Staff College, 1890; served on the Staff in India; served South African War, 1901–02; commanded 4th Batt. Royal Fusiliers, 1903–07; Bt Col 1906; AAG Egypt, 1909–13; commanded the Devon and Cornwall Infantry Brigade, 1913–14, and 23rd Infantry Brigade at the War, 1914–15; Maj.-Gen. 1915; commanded 35th Division, Jan. to Sept. 1916, and 33rd Division, Sept. 1916 to Feb. 1919, in France and Belgium (KCB). Lord of the Manor of Broadwindsor. *Address*: Racedown, near Bridport. *T*: Broadwindsor 222. *Club*: Travellers'.

Died 18 Feb. 1943.

PINSENT, Dame Ellen Frances, DBE 1937; CBE 1925; Hon. MA Birmingham; *b* 1866; *d* of late Rev. Richard Parker, Claxby Rectory, Lincolnshire; *m* 1888, Hume Chancellor Pinsent (*d* 1920); (two *s* killed in War, 1914–18) one *d*. Member of Royal Commission on Care and Control of Feebleminded, 1904–08; was a Member of Birmingham City Council; late one of the Senior Commissioners of Board of Control. *Publications*: The Mental Health Services, Oxford and Berks. Four novels: Jenny's Case; Children of this World; No Place for Repentance; Job Hildred. *Address*: Rough Lee, Boars Hill, Oxford. *Club*: University Women's.

Died 10 Oct. 1949.

PINSENT, Sir Richard Alfred, 1st Bt *cr* 1938; Hon. LLD Birmingham; MA; partner in Pinsent & Co. since 1877; *b* Devonport, 3 Aug. 1852; *m* 1878, Laura Proctor (*d* 1931), *d* of Thomas Ryland; three *s* (and two killed in war). *Educ*: Amersham Hall, Reading; Edinburgh Academy. Admitted a solicitor, 1873; President Birmingham Law Society, 1901–03 and 1926; President of the Law Society, 1918–19, and now senior Member of the Council and Chairman of the Statutory Discipline Committee. *Heir*: *s* Roy, *b* July 1883. *Address*: Selly Wick, Birmingham. *Clubs*: Union, Birmingham.

Died 2 Oct. 1948.

PIPER, Henry Mansell, CBE 1945; Secretary, British Employers' Confederation since 1928; *b* 28 July 1890; *s* of late William Henry Piper; *m* 1918, Ivy Minnie Olive Taperell; one *s*. Served RFC and RAF, 1915–19; Assistant Secretary, British Employers' Confederation, 1921–28. *Address*: Belvedere, Higher Drive, Banstead, Surrey. *T*: Ewell 2088. *Club*: Junior Carlton.

Died 7 Jan. 1949.

PIRIE, Alexander Howard, MD, ChB, BSc; Consultant, Royal Victoria Hospital, Montreal, Canada; Consultant Radiologist to Department of Pensions and National Health, Canada; President, American Röntgen Ray Society, 1927–28; *b* 25 Dec. 1875; *s* of George Clarke Pirie, MD, physician, Dundee, Scotland, and Helen Johnson of Berwickshire; *m* 1st, 1903, Ethel (*d* 1938), *d* of Caleb Martin, MD, physician, Toronto, Canada; no *c*; 2nd, 1939, Mary Sager, Montreal. *Educ*: University, St Andrews; University, Edinburgh; Sorbonne, Paris. Gained five medals at Universities; MB 1897; practised at 7 Harley Street, London; held appointments in London Hospital, St Bartholomew's, and Univ. College. Secretary of Röntgen Society of London; invited to Montreal by Governors of Royal Victoria Hospital, 1911; Chairman of X-Ray Section of Canadian Medical Association at London, Ontario, 1913, and at St John, New Brunswick, 1914; 1st (Volunteer) Batt. Royal Highlanders, 1892–95; Royal Scots and 1st Queen's Royal Volunteer Batt., 1895–97; Medical Officer to London Scottish, 1901–11; Canadian Expeditionary Force in France and England, 1915–19;

Major, retired; retired Lecturer on X-rays at McGill University; Delegate from Canada to International Congress, 1925 and 1928; Ex-Mayor of Baie d'Urfee; awarded gold medal of the Am. Röntgen Ray Society 1932. *Publications*: A New Meter for X-Rays; Treatment of Skin Diseases and other Affections by X-Rays; A New Rotating Stereoscopic Fluoroscope; (joint) The Students' Surgery, etc. *Recreations*: gardening, sculpture, painting, astronomy. *Address*: Pirie House, Alstonvale, Hudson Heights, PQ, Canada; Malabar, Florida, USA. *Clubs*: Faculty Club of M'Gill University, Montreal.

Died 15 Nov. 1944.

PIRIE, Sir George, Kt 1937; MA; LLD; RSA 1923; Pres. RSA 1933–44; *b* Campbeltown, Argyllshire, 1863; *s* of John Pirie, MD; *m* Jean S., *d* of John Wingate, manufacturer, Glasgow; two *s* one *d*. *Educ*: Glasgow Academy and University. Studied art in Paris under Boulanger and Lefebvre and E. Fremiet; subjects of pictures are chiefly animals and birds. Served in RAMC 1915–19; ARSA 1913. *Address*: Wardend, Torrance, Stirlingshire. *T*: Balmore 251. *Clubs*: Chelsea Arts; Glasgow Art; Scottish Arts, Edinburgh.

Died 17 Feb. 1946.

PIRRIE, Col Francis William, CMG, 1918; CIE 1917; Indian Army, retired; *b* 1867; *m* 1899, Alice Edith Elfreda, *d* of late Lieut A. G. S. de Salis, 95th Regt; one *s* one *d*. *Educ*: Cheltenham; RMC Sandhurst. Served Chitral Relief Force, 1895 (medal and clasp); NW Frontier of India, 1897–98 (clasp); European War (Mesopotamia), 1914–18 (despatches six times, Bt Col, CMG, CIE); retired, 1922. *Address*: c/o Lloyds Bank, 6 Pall Mall, SW1.

Died 30 Sept. 1948.

PISSARRO, Lucien; artist, landscape painter, wood engraver, designer, and printer of books (Eragny Press); *b* Paris, 20 Feb. 1863; *e s* of Camille Pissarro, the French impressionniste painter; *m* Esther L. Bensusan; one *d*. *Educ*: France. Studied under Camille Pissarro. Came to England, 1890; met Ch. Ricketts and Ch. Shannon and contributed wood engravings to the Dial; started the Eragny Press, 1894, and published the Queen of the Fishes, after which 15 books were printed with the Vale type; in 1902 designed the Brook type, and subsequently designed, printed, and published 16 books; painted landscapes in England and France; member New English Art Club; pictures bought by the Chantrey Bequest, by the Ministre des Beaux Arts, Paris, Contemporary Art Society, and galleries of Manchester, Leeds, Liverpool, Belfast, etc.; naturalised British subject, 1916. *Address*: The Brook, Stamford Brook, W6. *T*: Riverside 2333.

Died 10 July 1944.

PITCHER, Air Cdre Duncan le Geyt, CMG 1918; CBE 1919; DSO 1919; *b* Naini-Tal, UP, India, 31 Aug. 1877; 2nd *s* of late Col D. G. Pitcher; *m* 1921, Frances Evelyn (*d* 1932), *d* of Mrs Barnes, 14 Buckingham Street, Adelphi, WC. *Educ*: Sedbergh School; Geneva University; Sandhurst. 2nd Lieut 24th Regt (South Wales Borderers), 1898; transferred to 11th Rajputs, 1901; to 2nd Central India Horse, 1901; Royal Humane Society Bronze Medal, 1903; Adjutant 1904; Personal Assistant to the Agent in Central India, 1907; Tutor to the Maharajah of Holkar, 1908; Captain, 1909; Assistant Inspector, Imperial Service Troops, Central India, 1910–11; Pilot's Certificate, Royal Aero Club, No. 125, 1911; served with Central India Horse in Central Persia, 1911–13; joined Central Flying School, 1914; attached to Royal Flying Corps, and posted to BEF, France, Aug. 1914; Temp. Major, Jan. 1915; Temp. Lieut-Col April 1915; Assistant Commandant, CFS, April 1915; Commandant, Dec. 1915; Wing Commander, BEF, France, March 1916; Major, Indian Army, 1916 (despatches, Bt Lt-Col Dec. 1916, Mons star, CMG); Controller of Technical Design to the Air Board; Director of Equipment, Air Ministry, 1922–25; commanding 22nd Group RAF, 1926–29; retired, 1929;

Officier of the Order of St Maurice and St Lazarus; Officier of the Légion d'Honneur. *Recreations:* polo, shooting, and mechanics. *Club:* Army and Navy.

Died 1 Sept. 1944.

PITE, William Alfred, FRIBA; Architect, retd 1938; *b* 4 Aug. 1860; *e s* of Alfred R. Pite, architect, London; *m* 1891, Ethel Clara, 2nd *d* of Septimus W. Sibley, FRCS, Harley Street; one *s* (2nd *s* killed in action Palestine, 1918) two *d*. *Educ:* King's College School, London; National Art Training School, S Kensington; Univ. College, London. Articled to his father, 1876; also with J. Oldrid Scott, FRIBA, 1881; obtained Travelling Studentship, Architectural Association, 1882; Pugin Studentship, 1883; Vice-Pres. Architectural Association, 1900–01, 1902–03; member of RIBA Council and Board of Examiners; has erected churches, public and private buildings, in London and country; architect of King's College Hospital, Denmark Hill, SE, Nurses' Home, Royal Infirmary. Bradford, London Homœopathic Hospital and Institute, New Royal Victoria Hospital, Bournemouth, St Giles Infirmary, Edward VII National Memorial of Wales Tubercular Hosp., Sully, Glam. Girls Hospital, Barkingside, Boys Garden City, Woodford Bridge, for Barnardo's Homes, Perceval Memorial Church of All Saints, Ealing, St James', Alperton, St Peter's, Acton, houses at Hindhead Haslemere, Ealing, etc. (In collaboration) Royal Infirmary, Doncaster. Woolwich Memorial, Sevenoaks, Saffron Walden, Miller General, Greenwich and Deptford, Walsall and West Bromwich, Sutton, Epsom College, Penzance Hospitals, etc.; Institutes for RNM Deep Sea Fishermen, Aberdeen, Grimsby. Fleetwood, Padstow, etc.; Consulting Architects to Royal Infirmary, Aberdeen, All Saints, Ealing, St James', Alperton, St Andrew, Hampstead, St Jude's Church, Thornton Heath, St John, Baptist, Beckenham, etc. *Address:* 13 Old Orchard Road, Eastbourne. *T:* 591.

Died 16 Aug. 1949.

PITKEATHLY, Sir James Scott, KCIE 1939; Kt 1933, CMG 1930; CIE 1920; CVO 1911; CBE 1919; DSO 1918; *b* 1882; *s* of James Pitkeathly; *m* 1913, Eleanor Mary (*d* 1938), *d* of late Henry Haines of Astley, Worcs, and Tipton, Staffs; 1945, Mrs Ellen Allen Klokow, Beresford House, St James's Place, SW1, *d* of late Francis Moir Stuart; one *s*. Electrical Inspector for United Provinces, India, 1903–12; Electrical Engineer, Delhi Durbar camp, 1911; Imperial Works, Delhi, 1912; Chief Controller of Stores, Indian Stores Dept, 1922–39; Officer on Special Duty Defence Co- ordination Department, Simla and New Delhi; retired, 1940. Served European War, 1915–18 (CBE, DSO); Afghan War, 1919 (CIE). *Clubs:* Thatched House, Oriental; Bengal (Calcutta).

Died 26 June 1949.

PITMAN, Hon. Lord; James Campbell Pitman; KC; *b* 1864; *s* of late Frederick Pitman, WS, Edinburgh, and Anna, *d* of John Tait, Sheriff of Perth, Perthshire; *m* 1891, Jemima Helen, *d* of late Edward Chancellor; one *s* one *d*. *Educ:* Eton; New College, Oxford. Called to Scottish Bar, 1889; Standing Counsel in Scotland to the Commissioners of Woods and Forests, the Board of Trade and the Postmaster-General, 1903–20; Sheriff of Caithness Orkney, Zetland, 1920–28; one of the Senators of the College of Justice in Scotland, 1928–39. *Address:* 1 Glenfinlas Street, Edinburgh. *Clubs:* New, Edinburgh.

Died 10 Feb. 1941.

PITMAN, His Honour Charles Murray; KC 1925; JP Berkshire; *b* 8 Jan. 1872; 7th *s* of late Frederick Pitman, WS, Edinburgh; *m* 1909, Hilda Mary, *d* of A. E. Donkin, Rugby. *Educ:* Eton; New College Oxford. Rowed in Eton Eight, 1890 and 1891; rowed in Oxford Eight, 1892, 1893, 1894, 1895. Called to Bar, 1897; Judge Advocate of the Fleet, 1924–33; Recorder of Rochester, 1924–33; Official Referee of Supreme Court of

Judicature, 1933–45; Bencher of the Inner Temple, 1926; Chairman Berkshire Quarter Sessions, 1927–45. *Publications:* (with R. P. P. Rowe) Badminton Library volume on Rowing, 1898; Record of University Boat Race, 1909. *Address:* Remenham Lodge, Henley-on-Thames. *T:* Henley 151.

Died 13 Oct. 1948.

PITMAN, Frederick Islay, MA; retired stockbroker; Chairman Henley Royal Regatta; *b* 18 April 1863; third *s* of late Frederick Pitman, WS, Edinburgh; *m* Helen Isabel Auldjo-Jamieson; two *d*. *Educ:* Eton; Trinity College, Cambridge. Rowed Eton eight, 1881 and 1882; Cambridge, 1884–85–1886; won Diamond Challenge Sculls, 1886; Wingfield Sculls, 1886. *Recreations:* in the past: rowing, hunting. *Address:* Scarletts, Twyford, Berks. *TA:* Scarletts, Kiln-Green. *T:* Wargrave 108. *Clubs:* City University, Leander.

Died 22 Jan. 1942.

PITMAN, Maj.-Gen. Thomas Tait, CB 1915; CMG 1918; *b* 22 Dec. 1868; 6th *s* of late Frederick Pitman, WS, Edinburgh; *m* 1920, Violet Mary, *d* of Sir Michael Lakin, 1st Bt. Entered Army, 1889; Captain, 1895; Major, 1905; Lt-Col, 1912; Col, 1916; Maj.-Gen., 1923; served NW Frontier, India, 1897–98 (medal with clasp); S African War, 1899–1902 (despatches, Queen's medal 5 clasps); European War, 1914–18, commanded 4th Cavalry Brigade, 1915–18; 2nd Cavalry Division, 1918–19 (despatches, CB, CMG, Commander Legion of Honour, Croix de Guerre); commanded Rhine Cavalry Brigade, 1919; 2nd Cavalry Brigade, Tidworth, 1920–23; 48th South Midland Division TA, 1926–30; retired pay, 1930; late Col 11th Hussars; late JP Co. Hereford. *Address:* Brobury House, Letton, Hereford. *Club:* Cavalry.

Died 8 March 1941.

PITT-TAYLOR, Gen. Sir Walter William, KCB 1936 (CB 1919); CMG 1918; DSO 1902; late Rifle Brigade; *b* 30 Aug. 1878; *s* of late Charles Pitt Taylor; *m* 1920, Daphne (*d* 1945), *d* of Rt Hon. Sir James Stronge, 5th Bt. *Educ:* Eton. Entered army, 1899; Capt., 1905; Major, 1915; Lt-Col, 1917; Maj.-Gen., 1929; Lt-Gen., 1934; General, 1938; served South Africa, 1899–1902 (Queen's and King's medals with 6 clasps, despatches, DSO); European War, 1914–18 (despatches nine times, Bt Maj., Lt-Col and Col, CMG, CB); Officer, Legion of Honour, Croix de Guerre; Silver Medal for Valour and Croix de Guerre, Italy; commanded 17th Indian Infantry Brigade, 1923–25; commanded 5th Inf. Brig., Aldershot, 1925–28; ADC to King George V, 1926–28; Director of Recruiting and Organisation, War Office, 1929–32; Commander of 3rd Division, 1932–34; Lieutenant of Tower of London, 1935; General Officer Commanding-in-Chief, Western Command, India, 1936–38; retired pay, 1939. *Address:* Barscobe, Balmaclellan, Kirkcudbrightshire. *Club:* Naval and Military.

Died 22 Nov. 1950.

PITTAR, Barry, RBA, RWA 1919; FZS; SGA; put down Studios for Fine Porcelain and Fine Earthenware at Markyate and the Whipsnade Zoo for particularly modelling animals in Glazed ware Electric Furnaces and Plant, 1932; *b* 1880; *s* of Sir Thomas J. Pittar, KCB, CMG; *m* Edith Nina Davies, Shropshire. Oil and Water Colour painter, Architect and Plastic Artist, Etcher, Poster Artist and Ceramist; Technical Adviser to the Fire Clay Co., S Africa, London Art and Colour Co. *Educ:* City of London School, St John's Wood, RCA Gold Medallist; studied under Sir George Frampton. Exhibits in Paris Salon; became chief Architectural Artist to the Royal Doulton Potteries at Lambeth; Illustrator for Graphic, Illustrated London News, Christian Science Monitor; official purchasers: Durban Municipality. Australia, Hull Corporation, Victoria and Albert Museum, Bethnal Green Museum; Principal Works: Doorway Chartres Cathedral, Sir William Garforth of Pontifex Hall, portrait of Moor, St Maria Della Salute;

one-man Exhibitions at Fine Art Society, Ryman & Co., and Ackermann, New York. *Publications:* London in Colour; Sir Lionel Phillips Magazine, S Africa, Cape Town. *Recreations:* gardening, chemistry. *Address:* Little Cheverells, Markyate, near Dunstable. *T:* Markyate 226.

Died 23 June 1948.

PLANCK, Prof. Dr Max; Geheimer Regierungsrat; Ehrenpräsident der Kaiser Wilhelm-Gesellschaft; *b* 23 April 1858; *s* of Johann Julius Wilhelm Planck and Emma Patzig; *m* 1st, 1887; 2nd, 1911; one *s* (und zwei Söhne, 1914 u. 1945 gefallen). *Educ:* München. Privatdozent in München. Professor in Kiel und in Berlin. Sekretar der Preussischen Akademie der Wissenschaften, 1912–43; Präsident der Kaiser Wilhelm-Gesellschaft, 1930–37; Kanzler des Ordens Pour le mérite seit 1930; Nobelpreis, 1918. Foreign Member der Royal Society, London, und Ehren-Mitglied vieler anderer Gesellschaften; Schöpfer der Quanten-Theorie, 1900. *Publications:* Thermodynamik; Einführung id Theoretische Physik; Wege zur Physikalischen Erkenntnis; (posthumous) A Scientific Autobiography and Other Papers. *Address:* Göttingen, Merkelstr. 12.

Died 4 Oct. 1947.

PLANT, Maj.-Gen. Eric Clive Pegus, CB 1945; DSO 1917; OBE 1919; OStJ 1947; psc; *b* 23 April 1890; *y s* of Lt-Col C. F. Plant, Brisbane; *m* 1918, Oona, 2nd *d* of late J. Hunter Brown; two *s.* Served European War, 1914–18 (DSO and bar, OBE, Croix de Guerre); GSO2, War Office, 1927–29; GSO1, 1st Cavalry Division, 1929–33; GSO1, 1st Military District, 1933–37; Director of Military Training, 1937–39; Commandant, RMC, Duntroon, 1939; Commanded an Infantry Brigade, AIF, in Middle East, 1940–41; GOC Western Command, 1942; GOC Vic. L of C Area, 1943; GOC, NSW L of C Area, 1944–46; ADC to the King, 1939–46, retd. *Address:* Bay View Rd, Bay-View, NSW, Australia.

Died 18 May 1950.

PLANTE, Monseigneur J. Omer; Evêque titulaire de Dobero, Auxiliaire de Quebec; *b* St Michel de Bellechasse, 2 Jan. 1867; *s* of de Célestin Plante et de Mary-Ann Laverty- Chamberland. *Educ:* Séminaire de Quebec; Université Laval. Professeur d'histoire au séminaire de Quebec, 1893–99; Vicaire à Montmagny, 1899; Aumonier de Spencerwood, 1899–1900; En Europe, 1900–01; Aumonier de Merici, 1903–10; curé de L'Ange Gardien, 1910–20; curé de Beauport, 1920–25; Notre Dame de Levis, 1926–27; Evêque-auxiliaire de S. É. le Cardinal Rouleau, 1927; de S. E. le Cardinal JMR Villeneuve, archevêque de Quebec, 1932; Assistant au trône pontifical, 1938.

Died 5 April 1948.

PLASKETT, John Stanley, CBE 1935; FRS 1923; BA, DSc, FRASC 1907; FRSC 1910; Director, Dominion Astrophysical Observatory, Victoria, BC, 1917–35; *b* near Woodstock, Ont, 17 Nov. 1865; *s* of Joseph and Annie Plaskett; *m* 1892, Rebecca Hope Hemley; two *s.* *Educ:* Woodstock, Ont, High School; Toronto University. Engineering at Woodstock and in Edison El. Co. at Schenectady, 1885–89; Assistant Physics, Univ. Toronto, 1890–1903; BA 1899; appointment to Astronomical Branch Dep. of Interior, Ottawa, 1903; Astronomer, Dominion Observatory, Ottawa, 1905; charge of observations, Can. Eclipse Expedition to Labrador, 1905; initiation radial velocity observations, Ottawa, 1906; spectroscopic observation Solar rotation, 1910; initiation of project large Canadian reflector, 1911; successful completion of negotiations and award of contract for 72–inch reflecting telescope, 1913; Hon. DSc Pittsburg; supervision construction and erection of 72–inch telescope; testing and installation of 72–inch mirror, 1914–18; organisation of Dominion Astrophysical Observatory at Victoria, BC, 1917; Hon. DSc Univ. of Toronto, 1923; Fellow American Association Advancement of Science, 1923; Canadian Representative, Cambridge Meeting of the International

Astronomical Union, 1925, and of the Leiden Meeting, 1928; Hon. LLD University of British Columbia, 1925; Foreign Member American Philosophical Society, 1930; Recipient of Rumford Premium of American Academy of Arts and Sciences, 1930; George Darwin Lecturer and Gold Medallist of the Royal Astronomical Society, 1930; Bruce Medallist, Astronomical Society of the Pacific, 1932; Flavelle Medallist, Royal Society of Canada, 1932; Hon. LLD McGill University, 1932; Hon. LLD, Queens University, 1934; Draper Medallist, National Academy of Sciences, 1935; Halley Lecturer, 1935. *Publications:* over 100 papers on optics of telescope and spectroscope, and on numerous phases of Astronomical Spectroscopy in Jl RASC, Ap. J, Pub. ASP, Pub. Dom. Obs., Pub. Dom. Apl. Obs., and others; Principal Papers—Star Image in Spectroscopic Work; Design of Spectroscopes; Solar Rotation, 1911–1914; Radial Velocity 594 Stars; H and K lines of Calcium in O-Type Stars; Dimensions of Eclipsing Variables; The O-Type Stars; The Rotation of the Galaxy; The B-Type Stars; Diffuse Matter in Interstellar Space. *Recreations:* landscape photography, golf. *Address:* 318 Armit Road, Victoria, BC Canada. *TA:* Victoria. *T:* Empire 6354. *Clubs:* Union, Victoria Golf, Victoria.

Died 17 Oct. 1941.

PLATT, Major Eric James Walter; JP Anglesey and Caernarvonshire; DL Caernarvonshire; Vice Lieutenant for Caernarvonshire since 1940; *b* 15 Nov. 1871; *s* of late Col Henry Platt, CB, and late Eleanor Sykes; *m* 1895, Florence Grace, 5th *d* of late Samuel Perry, Woodroff, Co. Tipperary; one *d. Educ:* Eton; Trinity Hall, Cambridge. Lieut 4th Batt. RWF; Major Denbighshire IY; served as Remount Officer, 1914–18; Member of National Hunt Committee. *Recreations:* shooting, fishing, racing. *Address:* Gorddinog, Llanfairfechan, N Wales. *T:* Llanfairfechan 5. *Clubs:* Junior Carlton, Thatched House.

Died 13 Oct. 1946.

PLATT, Comdr Francis Cuthbert, DSO 1918; RN; *b* 13 Aug. 1885; *m* 1926, Frances, MB, DPH, *er d* of Charles Heron-Watson, Airleywight, Bankfoot, Perthshire. Served European War, 1914–18, Anti-submarines (despatches, DSO). *Address:* Penny Cottage, Hinton Martel, Wimborne, Dorset. *T:* Witchampton 75. *Club:* Junior United Service.

Died 15 Feb. 1941.

PLATTS, Frederick William, CMG 1921; *b* Melbourne, Victoria, 1865; 3rd *s* of Rev. F. C. Platts, MA; *m* 1908, Barbara Maud, *d* of late Edwin Charles Morris of Warren House, Southbourne, Hants; two *s* one *d. Educ:* Church of England Grammar School, Melbourne; Otago Boys' High School, Dunedin; LLB Univ. of NZ. Called to the Bar, 1895; Resident Commissioner and Chief Judge of the High Court of the Cook Islands, 1915–21; Stipendiary Magistrate, Hamilton, New Zealand, 1921–34. *Address:* 1 Joffre Street, Hamilton, NZ.

Died 24 May 1941.

PLATTS, W. Carter; author and journalist; *b* Huddersfield, 5 Aug. 1864; *o s* of late William Platts, Huddersfield; *m* 1889, Ellen, *d* of late George Savile, Huddersfield; one *s* one *d. Educ:* Huddersfield College. First engaged in woollen cloth manufacture, but abandoned commerce for literature and journalism about 1890, since which, besides publishing novels and volumes of humorous fiction, has written extensively on outdoor topics and country life, especially angling; a contributor of photographically illustrated articles to the Field, Sporting and Dramatic News, Salmon and Trout Magazine, Country Life, Ladies' Field, etc.; Angling Editor, Yorkshire Post. *Publications:* The Tuttlebury Tales; The Tuttlebury Troubles; Whims of Erasmus; Papa (Limited); Betwixt the Ling and the Lowland; Chiefly Uncle Parker; Angling Done Here; A Few Smiles; Light Lines and Tight Lines; The Million-Heiress and John; Timmins of Crickleton; The Crickleton Chronicles; Bunkumelli; Up-to-To-morrow; More Tuttlebury Tales; Nan of the B—B; The Mystery of the House that Wasn't There; He and She on the B-bar-B; Trout Streams; Their Management and Improvement; The Jedburgh Way; Trout Streams and Salmon Rivers; Modern Trout Fishing; Grayling Fishing; The Young Angler, etc. *Recreation:* fishing. *Address:* Bright Street, Skipton, Yorks. *TA:* Carter Platts, Skipton.

Died 7 April 1944.

PLAYNE, Air Cdre Basil Alfred, DSO 1915; MB, ChB, MRCS; Royal Air Force, retired; re-employed with rank of Group Captain since 1939; *b* 1885; *y s* of late Edward Playne, Minchinhampton; *m* 1913, Margaret Lowther, *d* of late Thomas Fisher, Cambridge; no *c. Educ:* Clifton College; Pembroke College, Cambridge (Exhibitioner); St Bartholomew's Hospital. Temporary Surgeon, RN, 1914–18; served European War, 1915 (despatches, DSO); PMO, Aden Command, 1931–32; Iraq Command, 1932–34; Halton Command, 1934–35; Headquarters Coastal Command, 1935–38; retired list, 1938. *Recreations:* sailing; shooting. *Address:* Spring Cottage, Minchinhampton, Stroud, Glos. *T:* Nailsworth 248. *Clubs:* Royal Air Force, Cruising Association; RAF Yacht.

Died 6 Feb. 1944.

PLENDER, 1st Baron *cr* 1931, of Sundridge, Co. Kent; **William Plender;** Bt *cr* 1923, GBE 1918; Kt 1911; Hon. LLD (Birmingham); High Sheriff of Kent, 1928–29, and JP; Lieut City of London; High Sheriff, County of London, 1927–28 and DL; KJStJ; Order of Mercy with bar; Hon. MInstCE; President, Institute of Chartered Accountants, 1910–11, 1911–12, and 1929–30; *b* 20 Aug. 1861; *e s* of William Plender (*d* 1911); *m* 1st, 1891, Marian Elizabeth (*d* 1930), DGStJ, *d* of late John Channon; no *c*; 2nd, 1932, Mabel Agnes, DStJ, *d* of Peter George Laurie and *widow* of George Norton Stevens, 7 Hyde Park Gardens. Senior partner since 1904, Deloitte, Plender, Griffiths & Co., London, United States, Canada, Argentine, Mexico, Cuba, Brazil, and South Africa; has been engaged on Government and public inquiries at home and abroad; served on Royal Commissions and Departmental Committees; acted for the Metropolitan Water Board on acquisition in 1903 of London Water Companies; advised the Government in connection with the Port of London Bill, 1908; President Chartered Accountants' Students Society of London, 1909–38; Member of Committee on Irish Finance, 1911; Investigator appointed in 1912 to enquire into existing conditions of medical work and remuneration under the National Insurance Act, 1911; Member Royal Commission on Railways, 1913; Commissioner (unpaid) under the Welsh Church Act, 1914–42; Treasury Controller, German, Austrian, and Turkish Banks, 1914–18; Member of Foreign Trade Debts Committee, 1914; of Committee appointed in 1914 by Postmaster-General to consider organization of the Telegraph Service; of Liquor Trade Finance Committee (England and Wales), 1915; Government Representative on Metropolitan Munitions Committee, 1915–18; of Clerical and Commercial Employments Committee, 1915; of Advisory Committee and Chairman of Panel Military Service (Civil Liabilities) Committee, 1916; of Enemy Debts Committee, 1916; Chairman City of London War Savings Association, 1916–41 (Vice-President, 1941); Member of the Liquor Trade Finance (England and Wales) Committee, 1917; of the Surplus Government Property Disposal Board, 1918; of the Company Law Amendment Committee, 1918; Chairman Civil Liabilities (Demobilization) Committee, 1918; Nominated Director United Services Trustee, 1918; Hon. Financial Adviser to the Board of Trade, 1918; Chairman of Panel Ministry of Labour Grants Committee, 1919; Member of Committee Public Trustee Organization Inquiry, 1919; Chairman Advisory

Committee of the Clearing Office (Enemy Debts), 1920; Member of Tribunal on Ministry of Munitions, 1921; Member of Lord Chancellor's Committee Remuneration of Solicitors, 1921; Commissioner (unpaid) Railways Amalgamation Tribunal, 1921; First Independent Chairman (unpaid), National Board for the Coal Industry, 1921–25; Chairman of Advisory Committee, Trade Facilities Act, 1921; Member of Commission on Property and Finances of Church of England, 1923; Independent Chairman Durham Coal Industry, 1927; Member Royal Commission on Cross-river Traffic in London, 1926; Member Export Credits Guarantee Committee of Enquiry, 1928; Member of Iron and Steel Committee—Economic Advisory Council, 1929; Member of Committee on National Expenditure, 1931; Independent Chairman Northumberland Minimum Wage Board, 1931; Member Post Office Committee of Enquiry, 1932; President Kent County Cricket Club, 1932; Pres. 4th International Congress on Accounting, London, 1933; Chairman Governing Body, City of London College, 1935–41 (President 1941); Chairman German Debts Committee, 1935; Hon. Treas., RGS, since 1936; a Governor of King's School, Canterbury, since 1936; Member Coal Mining Royalties Tribunal, 1937; Hon. MIJ; Hon. Treasurer Royal Society of Painter-Etchers and Engravers; Vice-President Poplar Hospital for Accidents; Governor St Thomas's Hospital; Member of many Masonic Lodges; PGW England. *Heir:* none. *Address:* 5 London Wall Buildings, EC2. *T:* London Wall 3232; Claridges, Brook St, W1. *Clubs:* Athenæum, Beefsteak, Brooks's, City of London, Reform.

Died 19 Jan. 1946.

PLESS, HSH Daisy, Princess of, (Mary Theresa Olivia); Dame of the Orders of St Theresa of Bavaria and of Isabella the Catholic of Spain, German Red Cross Medal, etc; *d* of late Col W. Cornwallis-West, of Ruthin Castle, Denbighshire, and Newlands Manor, Hants; *m* 1891, HSH Hans Heinrich, 15th Prince of Pless (whom she divorced 1922; he *d* 1938); three *s. Publications:* My Garden at Furstenstein, 1912; Daisy, Princess of Pless, by Herself (translated into German as Tanz auf dem Vulkan; also into Swedish and Hungarian); More about Myself and Friends, 1930; From My Private Diary, 1931; What I Left Unsaid, 1936. *Recreations:* travelling, gardening, writing. *Address:* La Napoule, Cannes, AM, France.

Died July 1943.

PLEYDELL-BOUVERIE, Col Hon. Stuart, DSO 1917; OBE 1926; TD; late commanding 52nd AA Brigade RA, TA; Director Phœnix Assurance Co., Ltd, London Guarantee and Accident Co. Ltd, British Tyre and Rubber Co. Ltd, Metropolitan Industrial Dwellings Ltd; *b* 1877; *y s* of 5th Earl of Radnor; *m* 1900, Edith Dorothy, *d* of Albert Vickers; four *s. Educ:* Harrow. Engineer; served European War, 1914–17 (DSO, despatches thrice). *Address:* High Barn, Godalming. *TA:* Bouverie Godalming. *T:* Hascombe 47. *Clubs:* Junior Carlton, Beefsteak, MCC.

Died 6 April 1947.

PLOWDEN, Cecil Ward Chicheley, CIE 1909; *b* 18 Oct. 1864; 2nd *s* of late Maj.-Gen. G. W. C. Plowden; *m* 1908, Sylvia Jessie, *y d* of Capt. Keeble; one *s.* Joined Bengal Police Department, 1884; Inspector-General of Police, Bengal, 1916; retired, 1919.

Died 22 Sept. 1944.

PLOWDEN, Rear-Adm. Richard Anthony Aston, DSO 1919; RN, retd. Served European War, 1914–19 (despatches, DSO); Captain (D), of the Nore Destroyer Flotilla, 1926–28; Captain of the Dockyard, Malta, 1928–30; commanded HMS Centurion, 1931–32; Rear-Adm. and retired list, 1933. *Address:* c/o Admiralty, SW1.

Died 24 Feb. 1941.

PLOWDEN, Roger Edmund Joseph; JP; *b* 1879; *s* of late William Francis Plowden and Lady Mary, *sister* of 1st Marquis of Zetland; *m* 1918, Mary Florence (*d* 1930), *e d* of Reginald H. Cholmondeley; one *s* three *d*. *Educ:* Beaumont College. Served with the Shropshire Yeomanry during European War in Egypt, Palestine and France. *Recreation:* all sports. *Address:* Plowden Hall, Lydbury North, Shropshire. *T:* Lydbury North 6. *TA:* Lydbury North. *Club:* Boodle's.

Died 22 May 1946.

PLOWMAN, Clifford Henry Fitzherbert, CMG 1937; OBE 1928; JP Beds 1941; *b* 23 July 1889; *o s* of late Rev. H. W. T. Plowman, MA, Bengal Ecclesiastical Establishment; *m* 1924, Nora Margaret Pottinger, *o d* of late G. A. Tweedy, ICS; one *s* two *d*. *Educ:* Kings' School, Ely; Trinity College, Cambridge; BA (Classical Tripos); FZS; FRES. Entered Colonial Civil Service as Assistant District Commissioner, E Africa Protectorate, 1912; Political Officer, Turkana Expedition, 1915 (Africa General Service medal and clasp); Acting Officer in charge, Northern Frontier District, 1919–20; seconded to Foreign Office as HM Vice-Consul, Harar, Ethiopia, 1920; transferred to Somaliland as HM Consul, Harar, 1922; HM Chargé d'Affaires, Addis Ababa, 1925–26; Political Officer and Assistant Commissioner, British Somaliland-Ethiopia Boundary Commission, 1931–33; Secretary to the Govt of Somaliland, 1933–40; Administered Government of Somaliland on several occasions, 1934–39; retired, 1940; employed in Civil Defence, Beds (ARPS), 1940–41; attached General Staff, War Office, 1941–43; Home Guard (Capt.), 1940–44; Oriental Secretary, Addis Ababa, 1945–47; Silver Jubilee medal, 1935; Coronation medal, 1937; Order of the Star of Ethiopia (2nd Class), 1930. *Address:* 2 Lansdowne Road, Bedford. *T:* Bedford 5028. *Club:* Travellers'.

Died 25 Oct. 1948.

PLOWMAN, Sir George Thomas, Kt 1923; CMG 1908; JP; *b* 1858; *s* of Thomas Plowman, of Boston, England; *m* 1883, Harriott Ann, *d* of Thomas Tribe, of New Barnet, Herts. Entered Colonial Secretary's Office, Natal, 1889; Chief Clerk, 1894; Secretary to Prime Minister and Secretary Lands and Works, 1901–10; Member of Civil Service Board, 1901; Joint Secretary, S African National Convention, 1908; Provincial Secretary of Natal, 1910–17; Deputy Administrator, 1917; Administrator of Natal, 1918–28. *Address:* 380 Musgrave Road, Durban, Natal. *Club:* Durban.

Died 29 June 1943.

PLOWMAN, Mark, (Max); Editor, The Adelphi since 1938; *b* Northumberland Park, Tottenham, N, 1 Sept. 1883; 4th *s* of Mark Plowman and Anna Maria Hunt; *m* 1914, Dorothy Lloyd Sulman; one *s*. *Educ:* various inferior private schools. Secretary Peace Pledge Union, 1937–38. *Publications:* four books of Verse, and War and the Creative Impulse, 1919; Introduction to Study of Blake, 1927; A Subaltern on the Somme (By Mark VII), 1928; The Faith called Pacifism, 1936. *Address:* The Adelphi Centre, The Oaks, Langham, near Colchester. *T:* Boxted 200.

Died 3 June 1941.

PLUMER, 2nd Viscount *cr* 1929, of Messines and of Bilton, Yorkshire; Baron *cr* 1919; **Thomas Hall Rokeby Plumer,** MC; *b* 17 May 1890; *s* of 1st Viscount and Annie Constance (*d* 1941), OBE, Lady of Grace, St John of Jerusalem, *y d* of George Goss; *S* father 1932; *m* 1919, Monica, *o d* of late Brig.-Gen. Henry Tempest-Hicks, CB; three *d*. *Educ:* Eton. Served European War, 1914–19. *Heir:* none. *Address:* St Audreys, Hatfield, Herts. *Clubs:* Carlton, Junior Carlton.

Died 24 Feb. 1944.

PLUMMER, Charles Henry Scott, CB 1944; *b* 18 Oct. 1859; *e s* of late Charles Scott Plummer of Sunderland Hall, Selkirk, and Sophia, *d* of Joseph Goff of Hale Park, Hants; *m* 1908, Muriel Grace, *d* of A. H. Johnstone

Douglas; one *s* two *d*. *Educ:* Eton. Joined 86th Regt 1878; retired, 1883; afterwards served in the KOSB Militia, the Border Mounted Rifles, and Lothians and Border Horse; succeeded to the entailed estates of Sunderland Hall and Middlestead on the death of his father, 1880; is Lord-Lieutenant of the County of Selkirk. *Address:* Sunderland Hall, Galashiels, Scotland. *Club:* Army and Navy.

Died 26 June 1948.

PLUMMER, Henry Crozier, MA, FRS, FRAS, MRIA; *b* Oxford, 24 Oct. 1875; *e s* of W. E. Plummer; *m* 1924, Beatrice Howard (*d* 1946), *d* of Henry Howard Hayward, MRCS. *Educ:* St Edward's School; Hertford College, Oxford. Open Mathematical Scholar; first classes in Mathematical Moderations and Final School, and second class in Natural Science (Physics). Assistant Lecturer in Mathematics, Owens College, Manchester, 1899–1900; Assistant Demonstrator in Clarendon Laboratory, Oxford, 1900–01; Assistant in University Observatory, Oxford, 1901–12; Fellow at the Lick Observatory, University of California, 1907–08; Andrews Professor of Astronomy in the University of Dublin and Royal Astronomer of Ireland, 1912–21; Professor of Mathematics in Military College of Science, Woolwich, 1921–40; Pres. Royal Astronomical Society, 1939–41; Halley Lecturer, 1942. *Publications:* An Introductory Treatise on Dynamical Astronomy, 1918; The Principles of Mechanics, 1929; Probability and Frequency, 1939; Four figure Tables with Mathematical formulae, 1941. *Address:* 3 Canterbury Road, Oxford. *T:* 2608. *Club:* Athenæum.

Died 30 Sept. 1946.

PLUMMER, John Archibald Temple; JP; *b* near Ipswich, Suffolk, 10 Aug. 1877; *o s* of late John Isaac Plummer, MA, FRAS of Orwell Park Observatory, and Royal Observatory, Hong Kong; *m* 1902, Marion Alma Hendley (*d* 1939); two *s*. *Educ:* Ipswich. Joined the old China firm of Bradley and Co. 1893; has resided in the Far East ever since, chiefly in Hong Kong and Shanghai; retired from business, 1936. *Recreations:* golf and horticulture. *Address:* Byways, Ferndown, Dorset. *Clubs:* Thatched House; Hong Kong, Royal Hong Kong Golf, Shanghai.

Died 19 June 1943.

PLUMPTRE, Adelaide M., (Mrs H. P. Plumptre), CBE 1943; Vice-President, Canadian Red Cross Society, since 1939; Hon. Director, Canadian Red Cross Prisoner of War Bureau; Hon. National Commandant, Red Cross Corps; *d* of late Rev. William Wynne Willson, Rector, Hanborough, Oxford; *m* 1901, Canon H. P. Plumptre, formerly Rector of St James' Cathedral, Toronto; one *s* one *d*. *Educ:* Lansdowne School, Weymouth; Somerville College, Oxford. Charter member, Canadian Girl Guides; Hon. Secretary National Council of Women of Canada; Superintendent of Supplies and Hon. Secretary Canadian Red Cross Society, 1914–19; Toronto Board of Education: Member and Chairman, 1933; Alderman, Toronto City Council, 1936–40. Founder and first National Commandant, Canadian Red Cross Corps, 1939–41. *Publications:* Editor, Canadian Red Cross Despatch, 1940; magazine articles. *Club:* University Women's (Toronto).

Died 4 Sept. 1948.

PLUNKET, Hon. and Most Rev. Benjamin J., MA, DD; *b* Bray, 1 Aug. 1870; 2nd *s* of 4th Baron Plunket, Archbishop of Dublin, and Annie Lee, *d* of late Sir Benjamin Guinness, Bt, MP; *m* 1904, Dorothea Hester (*d* 1936), 3rd *d* of Sir Thomas Butler, 10th Bt; two *s* two *d*. *Educ:* Harrow; Corpus Christi College, Cambridge. Ordained, 1896; Curate, St Peter, Dublin, 1896–1902; Rector of Aghade with Ardoyne, 1902–07; Vicar of St Ann's, Dublin, 1907–13; Treasurer and Canon of St Patrick's Cathedral, Dublin, 1911–13; Domestic Chaplain to the Archbishop of Dublin, 1911–13;

Chaplain to the Lord-Lieutenant of Ireland, 1904–13; Bishop of Tuam, Killala, and Achonry, 1913–19; Bishop of Meath, 1919–25. *Address:* Sybil Hill, Raheny, Co. Dublin. *T:* Dublin 35238. *Clubs:* Kildare Street, University, Irish Automobile, Dublin; Royal St George Yacht, Kingstown.

Died 26 Jan. 1947.

PLUNKETT, George Noble, Count (Papal hereditary), President, Academy of Christian Art; Vice-Pres. Catholic Poetry Society; MRIA; ex-President RSAI; Hon. Assoc. RIBA; Barr.-at-law; Director of National Museum of Science and Art, Dublin, 1907–16; *b* Dublin, 3 Dec. 1851; *e surv. s* of late P. J. Plunkett, UDC, Rathmines; *m* 1884, Josephine, *d* of P. Cranny, Muckross Park; one *s* two *d. Educ:* Nice; Clongowes College; Dublin University. Prizeman in French language and literature, TCD; Vice-Pres. of Royal Irish Academy, 1907–08 and 1911–14, and representative of Academy on Nobel Prize Committee for Literature; Hon. Member and Medallist of Hispanic Society of America; Foundation Member, National Academy; President Society for Preservation of the Irish Language; Vice-Pres. of National Literary Society, Classical Assoc. of Ireland, Celtic Congress (Brussels), the International Art Congress, etc.; Commander of Order of the Holy Sepulchre; Cross of St John of Lateran; Grand Cross of SS Cyril and Methodius, Bulgaria (Holy See); he has helped to found many Societies for the promotion of education and the special study of art, literature, music, and science; MP for N Roscommon, 1917–22, and Co. Roscommon to 1927; has been Minister for Foreign Affairs and of Fine Arts under the Dail; received Freedom of Sligo and Kilkenny. *Publications:* Sandro Botticelli, 1900; co-editor with Rev. Dr Hogan, FRUI, of The Jacobite War in Ireland, 1894; editor of M. Stokes' Early Christian Art in Ireland, 1911–1915; Pinelli, 1904, for the Dante Society; Architecture of Dublin (British Assoc. HB, 1908); Arrows, 1921; Echoes, 1928; poems; Introduction to Church Symbolism, 1932; Art lectures and addresses, 1929–1941; many contributions to Irish literary collections and leading Irish journals and magazines; edited Hibernia, a review of literature and art, Dublin, 1882–1883. *Recreation:* has travelled throughout Europe and America. *Address:* 42 Upper Mount St, Dublin.

Died 12 March 1948.

PLYMOUTH, 2nd Earl of, *cr* 1905; **Ivor Miles Windsor-Clive;** PC 1929; Viscount Windsor (UK 1905); 15th Baron Windsor (Eng. *cr* 1529); Lord-Lieutenant of Glamorgan, 1923; DL Cos. Worcester and Salop; Sub-Prior, Order of St John of Jerusalem, 1943; *b* 4 Feb. 1889; 2nd and *o surv. s* of 1st Earl and Alberta, *d* of Rt Hon. Sir Augustus Berkeley Paget; *S* father, 1923; *m* 1921, Lady Irene Charteris, *d* of 11th Earl of Wemyss; three *s* three *d. Educ:* Eton; Trinity College, Cambridge. Member for West St Pancras on LCC, 1913–19; MP (Cons.) Ludlow Division of Shropshire, Jan. 1922–March 1923; Captain of the Gentlemen-at-Arms, 1925–29; Parliamentary Under-Secretary for Dominion Affairs, Jan.–June 1929; Parliamentary Sec., Ministry of Transport, 1931–32; Parliamentary Under Secretary of State, Foreign Office, 1936–39; Hon. freedom of Cardiff, 1936; Past Pres. National Museum of Wales; Pro-Chancellor, University of Wales, 1941. Owns about 30,500 acres. *Heir: s* Viscount Windsor. *Address:* Hewell Grange, Redditch; St Fagans Castle, Cardiff. *Clubs:* Carlton, Bachelors', Travellers'.

Died 1 Oct. 1943.

PO, Sir San Crombie, Kt 1933; CBE 1925; MD; medical practitioner; (Nominated) Senator, Burma Government, since 1937; Hon. Major 11th Bn The Burma Rifles, 1938; *b* 4 Oct. 1870; *s* of Saw Aungnyo and Naw Bwewah of Kozu Village, near Bassein, Burma; *m* 1895, Amy Loonee; five *s* two *d. Educ:* Burma; 8 years in Hamilton and Albany, NY, USA. Returned to Burma, 1894; joined Government Service, 1895;

Resident Medical Officer, 5½ years; officiated Civil Surgeon, 1½ years; resigned Government Service, 1902; Municipal Commissioner, 1912–20; Vice-President, 1921; a Member of Burma Legislative Council, 1917–23 and 1923–24; President of Karen National Association, 1925; Layman Missionary in charge of Bassein-Myaungmya Sgaw-Karen Baptist Churches, 1933. *Publications:* First Aid to the Injured Burmese; Burma and the Karens, 1928; a pamphlet on the Care of Infants and Mothers in Burmese. *Address:* Bassein, Burma. *T:* 32. *Clubs:* Cosmopolitan, Karen Social Society (Bassein).

Died 7 June 1946.

POCKLEY, Francis Antill, MD Edin., 1st class honours; MD Sydney; MRCS Eng.; FRACS; retd; Emeritus Lecturer on Ophthalmology, University of Sydney; Hon. Consulting Ophthalmic Surgeon, Royal Prince Alfred Hospital, Sydney; Hon. Consulting Surgeon Royal North Shore Hospital, Sydney; President Australasian Medical Congress, 1911; Past President, NSW Branch British Medical Association; Past President Ophthalmological Society of New South Wales; President Soldiers' Club; *b* 28 April 1857; *s* of Robert Francis Pockley and Selnia Antill; *m* Helen Clara Hooke (decd); one *s* (two *s* killed in Great War) one *d. Educ:* Sydney Grammar School; University of Edinburgh; Vienna. *Publications:* numerous in medical and ophthalmic journals. *Recreations:* exploring, motoring, fishing, gardening, reading. *Address:* Graystanes, Wahroonga, Sydney, NSW. *T:* Wahroonga 22. *Clubs:* Union, Australasian Pioneers, Royal Automobile of Australia, Sydney.

Died 3 July 1941.

POCOCK, Col Herbert Innes, CMG 1917; AMS, retired; MRCS, LRCP Lond.; Specialist in Dental Surgery, Aldershot Army Corps; Hon. Fellow, Royal Institute of Public Health; *b* 2 June 1861; 3rd *s* of Rev. Nicholas Pocock; *m* Edith Shepard Platts; three *s* one *d. Educ:* Lancing College; Bristol. Entered army, 1887; served European War, 1914–18 (CMG, despatches twice). *Recreations:* played football, Gloucester County, 1886, Captain Medical Staff Corps football team, 1888, Aldershot. *Address:* The Bungalow, St Rumons, Newquay, Cornwall. *T:* Newquay 2162.

Died 21 Aug. 1947.

POCOCK, Brig. Philip Frederick, CB 1924; DSO 1918; Indian Army, retired; *b* 1871; *m* Ethel Mary (Jo), (*d* 1941); no *c. Educ:* Bedford School; Sandhurst. Served Chitral Relief Force, 1895 (medal with clasp); Mesopotamia, 1914–18 (despatches, DSO, French Croix de Guerre); Afghanistan, 1919 (despatches, medal with clasp); Mahsud, 1919–20 (despatches, clasp); Waziristan, 1919–21 (despatches, clasp); Waziristan, 1921–24 (clasp). *Address:* White Lodge, Cambridge Road, Stansted, Essex. *Club:* United Service.

Died 9 Nov. 1941.

POCOCK, Reginald Innes, FRS 1911; FLS; FZS; FRAI; Temporary Assistant in the Zoological Department of the British Museum since 1923; *b* Clifton, Bristol, 4 March 1863; 4th *s* of late Rev. Nicholas Pocock, MA, and Edith, *d* of James Cowles Prichard, MD, FRS, the ethnologist; *m* 1889, Constance (*d* 1942), *d* of Thomas Osborne; one *s. Educ:* Frank Townsend's School, Clifton; St Edward's School, Oxford; University College, Bristol. Junior and Senior Assistant in the Zoological Department of the British Museum in charge of the collections of Arachnida and Myriopoda, 1885–1903; Superintendent, Zoological Society's Gardens, Regent's Park, 1904–23. *Publications:* Arachnida of British India and Mammalia of British India, Vols I, II, 1939–1941; many papers on anatomy, classification, bionomics, and palæontology of arthropoda and mammalia in scientific journals and Encyclop. Britannica. *Recreations:* formerly athletics generally, especially Rugby football, running, and lawn tennis; field natural history and zoology always. *Address:*

The Natural History Museum, S Kensington, SW; 33 Torrington Square, Bloomsbury, WC1; The Guard House, Chideock, Dorset.

Died 9 Aug. 1947.

POCOCK, Captain Roger; *b* 1865; *s* of late Commander Pocock, RN. *Educ:* Wellesley training ship; Ludlow Grammar School. Served in Royal NW Mounted Police during 2nd Riel Rebellion; frozen and pensioned; afterwards missionary in New Caledonia; seaman with the Yokohama pirates, and in some thirty other trades of wild life; rode along Rocky Mountains from Canada to City of Mexico, 1899; scout in SA Field Force, 1901; travelled in Greenland, and founded the Legion of Frontiersmen, 1904; enlisted, 1914; Captain, May 1915; research with deep sea fisheries, 1919–21; Oxford expedition to Spitsbergen; Geographer to sea expedition in SY Frontiersmen, 1923; admitted to Charterhouse, 1928; working as sculptor. *Publications:* A Frontiersman (autobiography); Curly; Jesse of Cariboo; The Splendid Blackguard; Horses; The Wolf Trail, etc.; Chorus to Adventurers (2nd autobiography), 1931; ed. Frontiersman's Pocket Book; Plays and adaptations: The Celluloid Cat; Crime and Punishment; Dr Jekyll and Mr Hyde. *Recreations:* painting and travel. *Address:* c/o Lady Simson, Ponders, Chieveley, Newbury. *Club:* Savage.

Died 12 Nov. 1941.

POE, Col John, CMG 1919; DSO 1915; MB; late RAMC; *b* 24 Sept. 1873; *m* 1st, 1899, Katherine (*d* 1918), *d* of R. J. Goff, Piercetown, Newbridge, Co. Kildare; 2nd, 1922, Mary, *widow* of Captain H. de L. Walters. Entered RAMC, 1897; Captain, 1900; Major, 1909; served European War, 1914–18 (despatches, DSO, CMG, Bt Col); retired pay, 1924. *Address:* c/o Glyn, Mills & Co., Whitehall, SW1.

Died 12 May 1941.

POIRET, Paul; artiste; *b* 20 Avril 1879; divorcé; one *s* two *d.* Couturier, établi en 1903 à Paris dans les affaires de couture jusqu'en 1925, et de nouveau en 1931 sous le numéro Passy 10–17. *Publications:* Popolôrepô; 107 recettes et curiosités culinaires; En habillant l'Époque; Revenez-y; Art et Phynance; Ballet Italien. *Recreations:* yachting, propriétaire du côtre M. Dumollet.

Died 30 April 1944.

POLE, Sir Cecil Pery Van Notten-, 4th Bt *cr* 1791; DL, JP; *b* 30 March 1863; *S* grandfather, 1887; *m* 1894, Freda (*d* 1940), *d* of Sir Thomas Freake, 2nd Bt. Late Lieut 2nd Batt. Roy. Fusiliers; Capt. Royal Gloucester Hussars; Major 23rd Batt. London Regiment. *Heir: kinsman* Peter van Notten, *b* 6 Nov. 1921. *Address:* Todenham House, Moreton in Marsh, Gloucestershire. *TA:* Todenham. *Clubs:* Arthur's, White's.

Died 21 May 1948.

POLK, Hon. Frank L.; Partner, Davis Polk Wardell Gardiner and Reed, 15 Broad Street, New York; Director, Northern Pacific Rly Co.; Trustee, Bowery Savings Bank, Mutual Life Insurance Co., US Trust Co; *b* New York, 13 Sept. 1871; *s* of Ida Asche Lyon and William Mecklenburg Polk; *m* 1908; three *s* two *d. Educ:* Groton School; Yale University, BA, Hon. MA; Columbia Law School, LLB. Pres. Municipal Civil Service Commission, 1908–09; Corporation Counsel, NY, 1914–15; Counsellor Dept of State, 1915–19; Under-Secretary of State, 1919–20; Commissioner Plenipotentiary of US to negotiate peace and head American Delegation of Peace Conference, Paris, July–Dec., 1919; Capt. USV Spanish Amer. War, 1898; Pres. New York Public Library; Grand Cross Legion of Honour, France; Grand Commander Order of Leopold, Belgium; First Class Poland Restituta; Grand Cross Order of Crown, Roumania; Hon. Degrees: DCL University of the South, 1928; LLD Rollins College, New York University, 1935. *Address:* 15 Broad Street,

New York, NY, USA. *TA:* Polkton. *T:* Hanover 2.-3400. *Clubs:* Century Assoc., Knickerbocker, Racquet and Tennis, Piping Rock, New York.

Died 7 Feb. 1943.

POLLARD, Alan Faraday Campbell, DSc (Eng.); ARCS; FInstP; AMIEE; Professor Emeritus, Imperial College, University of London; Fellow, Physical Society; Director, Daniel Varney Ltd; Vice-President, British Society for International Bibliography; *b* 30 Nov. 1877; *s* of Lt-Col B. H. Pollard, Indian Staff Corps; *m* 1915, Mildred Gabrielle, *d* of Frederick Urwick; one *s* one *d. Educ:* Cheltenham College; University College, London; St Bartholomew's Hospital; King's College, London. On Technical Staff of Siemens Bros Dynamo Works, Ltd; Managing Director of the Hanway Engineering Co., Ltd; Chief Physicist Nobel's Explosives Co., Ltd; Captain RAF; Sub-Section Director of development of Aircraft Instruments, Air Ministry. Professor of Instrument Design, University of London; Hon. Secretary of Optical Society, London; President of Fédération Internationale de Documentation, 1928–31; appointed by the Minister of Pensions as Technical Expert on Williamson Committee. *Publications:* An Experimental Study of the Stresses in Masonry Dams; The Decimal Bibliographical Classification of the Institut International de Bibliographie; The Kinematical Design of Couplings in Instrument Mechanisms; etc. *Address:* Rythe Lawn, Angel Road, Thames Ditton, Surrey. *T:* Emberbrook 2254.

Died 15 Aug. 1948.

POLLARD, Albert Frederick, MA; Member of Royal Historical MSS Commission; Hon. LittD, Manchester; Hon. DLit (London); Hon. DLitt (Oxford); Hon. Fellow of Jesus College; Fellow of All Souls College, Oxford 1908–36; Hon. VP, Royal Historical Society; FBA; Professor of Constitutional History, etc., University of London, 1903–31; Founder of the Historical Association, 1906, and Editor of History, 1916–22, and of the Bulletin of the Institute of Historical Research, 1923–39; Founder and Chairman of Institute of Historical Research, 1920–39; Corresponding Member (1930) of the Académie des Inscr. et Belles Lettres (Inst. de France); *b* Ryde, 16 Dec. 1869; *e surv. s* of Henry Hindes Pollard, JP, of Ryde; *m* 1st, 1894, Catherine Susanna (*d* 1934), *e d* of William Lucy, Oxford; one *s* one *d*; 2nd, 1942, Marjorie, *e d* of late Thomas Orchardson. *Educ:* Portsmouth Grammar School; Felsted School; Jesus Coll., Oxford. 1st class honours, Modern History, 1891; Lothian prize, 1892; Arnold prize, 1898. Assistant editor, Dictionary Nat. Biogr., Jan. 1893 to completion of 1st Supplement, Sept. 1901; Chairman of the Board of Studies in History in London University, 1910–23, and Member of Senate, 1910–15; President of Historical Association, 1912–15; first Goldwin Smith Lecturer, Cornell University, 1913; Creighton Lecturer, University of London, 1916; Member of Government Committees on the League of Nations, 1918, the University of London (1924–25) and Parliamentary Records (1929); contested Parliamentary representation of the University of London, 1922–23–1924; Sir George Watson Lecturer in American History, 1924; Professor *pro tem.* Columbia University, 1924–25; Ford's Lecturer in the University of Oxford, 1927–28; David Murray Lecturer in the University of Glasgow, 1936. *Publications:* 500 articles (one vol.) in Dict. Nat. Biogr.; The Jesuits in Poland, 1892; Political Pamphlets (ed.), 1897; England under Protector Somerset, 1900; Henry VIII (Goupil Series), 1902, new edition 1905, 1913; Tudor Tracts (ed.), 1903; five chapters in Cambridge Modern History, vol. ii, 1904, one in vol. x, 1907; A Life of Thomas Cranmer, 1904 (2nd edition, 1926); Factors in Modern History, 1907 (3rd edition, 1932); The British Empire (ed.), 1909; vol. vi (1547–1603) 7th impression, 1934, in Political History of England, 1910; A History of England (Home University Library), 1912; The Reign of Henry

VII from contemporary sources, 3 vols, 1913–1914; The Commonwealth at War, 1917; The League of Nations: an Historical Argument, 1918; A Short History of the Great War, 1920; The Evolution of Parliament, 1920 (4th ed. 1938); Factors in American History, 1925; Wolsey, 1929. *Address:* Brierfield, Milford-on-Sea, Hants.

Died 3 Aug. 1948.

POLLARD, Alfred William, CB 1922; FBA 1922; MA Oxford; Hon. DLit Durham, 1921; Hon. DLitt Cambridge, 1934; Fellow of King's College, London, 1907; Hon. Fellow St John's College, Oxford, 1923; Hon. Secretary, Bibliographical Society, 1893–1934; Editor of The Library, 1903–34 (1903–19 with Sir J. Y. W. MacAlister); Hon. Librarian of the Central Library for Students, 1920–26; Hon. Treasurer, 1918–19 and 1927–29; Chairman of Finance Committee, 1930–36; Director, Early English Text Society, 1930–37; *b* London, 14 Aug. 1859; *s* of E. W. Pollard, MRCS; *m* 1887, Alice England (*d* 1926), Newnham College, Cambridge; one *d*. *Educ:* King's College School, London; St John's College, Oxford. 1st Class Classical Mods and Final School. Assistant in Department of Printed Books in the British Museum, 1883; Assistant-Keeper, 1909; Keeper, 1919–24; Sandars Reader in Bibliography, University of Cambridge, 1915; Professor of English Bibliography, King's College, University of London, 1919–32. *Publications:* edited English Miracle Plays, 1890; Herrick, 1891; Books about Books, 1893; Bibliographica, 1894–1896; 'Globe' Chaucer, 1898; English Bookman's Library and Macmillan's Library of English Classics, 1900; The Castell of Labour, 1905; Catalogue of Early Printed Books in the possession of J. P. Morgan, 1907; Records of the English Bible, 1911; On Active Service, Letters of G. B. Pollard, RFA, 1915; A New Shakespeare Quarto (Richard II 1598), 1916, etc.; author of a Chaucer Primer, 1893; Early Illustrated Books, 1893; Italian Book Illustrations, 1894; Old Picture Books, 1902; An Essay on Colophons, 1905; Shakespeare's Folios and Quartos, 1909; Catalogue of Books of the First Printers collected by Rush C. Hawkins, 1910; Life, Love, and Light; Practical Morality for Men and Women, 1911; Fine Books, 1912; Italian Book-Illustrations and Early Printing (Dyson Perrins collection), 1914; A Census of Shakespeare Quartos (with Miss H. C. Bartlett), 1916; Two Brothers, 1916; Shakespeare's Fight with the Pirates, 1917; St Catharine of Siena, 1919; The Foundations of Shakespeare's Text (The British Academy Annual Shakespeare Lecture), 1923; Shakespeare's Hand in the Play of Sir Thomas More, 1923 (with others); A Short Title Catalogue of English Books (1475–1640), with G. R. Redgrave and others, 1926; Chapter on Shakespeare's Text in the Cambridge Companion to Shakespeare Studies, 1934. *Recreation:* gardening. *Address:* 40 Murray Road, Wimbledon, SW19. *Clubs:* Athenæum; Grolier, New York (Hon. Foreign Corresponding Member); Odd Volumes, Boston (Hon. Member).

Died 8 March 1944.

POLLARD, Maj.-Gen. James Hawkins-Whitshed, CB 1918; CMG 1915; DSO 1919; late Royal Scots Fusiliers; *b* 13 May 1866; *er s* of late Rear-Admiral Pollard; *m* 1st, 1899, Clare Evelyn (*d* 1917), *d* of George H. Low, Canadian Rifles; three *s*; 2nd, 1927, Adelaide Thérèse Jane Staunton Leechman, *née* Bagot; two *s*. *Educ:* Repton; Sandhurst. Entered army, 1886; Captain, 1895; Major, R Scots Fusiliers, 1906; Lieut-Col 1915; Major-Gen. 1923; served Burma, 1887–89 (medal with clasp); Chin-Lushai Expedition, 1890 (clasp); Isazai Expedition, 1892; Waziristan, 1894–95 (clasp); Chitral, 1895 (medal with clasp); S Africa, 1899–1902 (despatches, Queen's medal 4 clasps, King's medal 2 clasps); Somaliland, 1902–04 (despatches, medal with clasp); European War, 1914–18 (despatches seven times, promoted Col, CMG, CB, DSO); retired pay, 1925. *Club:* United Service.

Died 18 Feb. 1942.

POLLEN, Captain Francis Gabriel Hungerford, CBE 1919; RN (retired); *b* 25 March 1862; 4th *s* of late John Hungerford Pollen, FSA, and Maria Margaret, 2nd *d* of Rev. Charles John La Primaudaye; *m* 1890, Flora Mary (*d* 1936), *o d* of late James Logan Dunolly; one *s* two *d*. Served Soudan 1884–85 (medal and clasp); European War 1914.

Died 28 April 1944.

POLLITT, Gerald Paton, LDS, RCS Eng., DDS Penna; late Hon. Dental Surgeon, London Hospital; and Lecturer, London Hospital Dental School; late Hon. Consultant in Dental Surgery, Military Hospitals in London, and Assistant Dental Surgeon, King George Hospital; late Hon. Dental Surgeon, Paddington Green Children's Hospital; Fellow Royal Society of Medicine; Member of British Dental Association, of Society for Study of Orthodontics, and of School Dentists' Society; late President American Dental Society of London; *b* Manchester, 18 Jan. 1877; *e s* of late J. S. and C. Pollitt; *m* 1913, Dora, *y d* of late H. P. Potter, MD, FRCS; two *s*. *Educ:* abroad; Guy's Hospital; University of Pennsylvania. *Publications:* article in English System of Dental Surgery and contributions to Dental Journals. *Recreations:* golf, shooting, fishing. *Address:* 99 Park West, Marble Arch, W2. *T:* Langham 1573. *Club:* Royal Thames Yacht.

Died 15 Dec. 1943.

POLLITZER, Sir Frank Joseph Coleman, Kt 1937; JP; Alderman and Sheriff, 1936–37, City of London; *b* 1869; *m* 1900; two *s* one *d*. *Educ:* Philological Grammar School. Head of Messrs Beck and Pollitzer, Transport Contractors, until 1931, when retired. *Recreation:* actively interested in all athletics and sport. *Address:* 32 Grosvenor Street, W1. *T:* Mayfair 1703. *Club:* Constitutional.

Died 7 Nov. 1944.

POLLOCK, Sir Adrian Donald Wilde, KCMG 1938; Kt 1921; City Chamberlain and Treasurer since 1912; *b* 24 Sept. 1867; 2nd *s* of late Major-General Sir R. Pollock, KCSI, and Adriana, *d* of late Sir Harris Nicholas, GCMG; *m* 1894, Hon. Mary Honora Rhoda Gully, 3rd *d* of 1st Viscount Selby; two *d*. *Educ:* Wellington. Admitted Solicitor, 1890; Remembrancer, City of London, 1903–12. *Recreations:* golf and tennis. *Address:* 20 The Grove, Boltons, SW10. *T:* Flaxman 7536. *Club:* Brooks's.

Died 21 Aug. 1943.

POLLOCK, Rt Rev. Bertram, KCVO 1921; CVO 1909; DD; *b* 6 Dec. 1863; *y s* of late G. F. Pollock, formerly Senior Master of the Supreme Court and the Queen's and the King's Remembrancer, and *g s* of late Rt Hon. Sir F. Pollock, Bt, Lord Chief Baron; *m* 1928, Joan Florence Helena, *d* of Rev. A. C. D. Ryder; one *d*. *Educ:* Charterhouse (Scholar); Trinity College Camb. (Scholar), BA 1885; BD 1902; DD 1903. Assistant Master at Marlborough Coll., 1886–93; ordained at Salisbury, 1890; Master of Wellington College, 1893–1910; Bishop of Norwich, 1910–42; Chaplain-in-Ordinary to King Edward VII and Examining Chaplain to Bishop of Lichfield. *Publications:* Good Men Without Faith, 1923; The Church and English Life, 1932; The Nation and the Nation's Worship, 1933; Church and State, 1936. *Recreation:* represented Cambridge in the Quarter Mile *versus* Oxford, 1886. *Club:* Athenæum.

Died 17 Oct. 1943.

POLLOCK, Rev. Charles Archibald Edmund, MA; *b* 1858; *e s* of late A. A. Pollock; *m* 1895, Grace Isabella, 3rd *d* of late Rev. G. B. Blenkin; two *s* two *d*. *Educ:* Highgate School; King's College, London; Trinity College, Cambridge (Scholar 1877), BA (6th Wrangler),

1881; Fellow of Corpus Christi College, 1882; MA, 1883. Mathematical Lecturer, 1883–1919; Dean, 1895–1901; President, 1921–28, and Bursar, 1913–28, of Corpus Christi College, Cambridge; Deacon, 1887; Priest, 1888; Senior Proctor, Camb. Univ., 1911. *Recreation:* travel. *Address:* Harefield, Chaucer Road, Cambridge. *T:* Cambridge 5140.

Died 13 Aug. 1944.

POLLOCK, Courtenay Edward Maxwell; sculptor, inventor, and writer; *b* Birmingham; *s* of late Robert Pollock and Eliza Selina Hollins; step *s* of late Prof. Arthur Foxwell, MD, FRCP; *m* 1910, Mary Beatrice (operatic singer known in Europe as Beatrice Lamotte), *d* of late Richard Mott, Torquay; five *s* two *d*. *Educ:* Ilkley College; Birmingham University; Birmingham School of Art; scholar Royal College of Art, London. Taught at Jewellers' School of Art, Birmingham, five years; collections of his work exhibited, London, 1903 and 1909; New York, 1910; Boston, Mass, 1911; Birmingham, 1911; Exhibition of his film sets, London, 1936, and of his sculptured portraits, London, 1937; Member of Royal Society of British Artists, 1904; resigned, 1921; Fellow of Royal Society of Literature, 1921; Member Royal West of England Academy, 1921; works include Foxwell Memorial, Birmingham; Draper Memorial, Hopedale, Mass; bust of Sir Hubert Parry, in Royal College of Music; Spring, bronze statue exhibited Rome, 1911; Study in Light, statue exhibited Coronation Exhibition, Shepherd's Bush, 1911; bust of late Sir Henry Irving, at Garrick Club, a second version purchased for permanent collection by Bristol Art Gallery, another in permanent collection, Bournemouth Museum; Henry Irving, in Empire Theatre, New York; busts of Mr Joseph Chamberlain, Royal Academy, 1912, and Birmingham, 1914; copy of latest version in Birmingham Municipal Gas Department, 1925; Miss Margaret Elwes, 1928; Mr T. H. Perkins, 1932; Mr and Mrs Van der Elst; Mr and Mrs Harold Tippets; Mr Stanley Tippetts and Miss Nina Clifford, 1934; Miss Marlene Dietrich, 1936; Miss Edna Best, Miss Betty Stockfeld, Miss Elizabeth Allen, Viscountess Elibank, King George VI, Mrs William Le Marchant, Miss M. Lindsay Williams and others, 1937; memorial to late Walter Maclaren, MP; statue Lorelei, Royal Academy, 1914; marble bust of Mrs John Jarvis, Royal Academy, 1914; bronze bust of Rt Hon. Sir T. Vezey Strong, Royal Academy, 1915, now in Guildhall, London; bust of Viscount Northcliffe, Royal Academy, 1920; bust of Viscount Rothermere; Physical Fitness, war memorial trophy for Cape Town, 1920; bronze portraits of The Maharaja Gaekwar of Baroda, 1923, 1924; executed many War Memorials; early in the War joined the British Motor Service V. Corps and subsequently RAF; during War responsible for certain aircraft inventions and engaged in aeroplane construction. *Publications:* various articles and treatises on sculpture; Sculpture section of Ency. Brit.; Harmsworth Popular Self Educator; Children's Encyclopædia; Biographical Dictionary, etc.; some novels, poems, short stories, and essays; invented and published, 1916, the war game which bears his name; produced in 1934 an electrical contrivance known as the Mobile Heads, an invention which exactly simulates the actions and expression changes in the human face and body; recently engaged in stage and screen plays and on Film Art Direction. *Recreations:* swimming and travel. *Address:* 16 Denbigh Road, W13. *Club:* London Sketch.

Died 7 June 1943.

POLLOCK, Lt-Col John Alsager, DSO 1919; Oxfordshire and Bucks LI retired; *b* 1882; *s* of late Lieutenant-Colonel A. W. A. Pollock; *m* 1917, Gladys Violet, *d* of late Capt. H. W. Nevill. *Educ:* Wellington College. Served South Africa, 1899–1902 (Queen's medal with two clasps, King's medal with two clasps); Sudan, 1914 (medal with clasp, 4th Class Order of the Nile); European War, 1914–19 (despatches, DSO);

Egyptian Army, 1908–16; drove a car from London to Cape Town, 1931–32. *Recreations:* hunting, shooting. *Address:* Hamble House, Thruxton, Hants. *Club:* Army and Navy.

Died 22 Sept. 1941.

POLLOCK, Maj.-Gen. John Archibald Henry, CB 1903; *b* 1 Dec. 1856; 2nd *s* of late Archibald R. S. Pollock, Bengal CS; *m* 1898, Lilian Forrester, *d* of John Fortune of Bengairn, Kirkcudbrightshire; one *s* two *d*. *Educ:* Haileybury; RMC, Sandhurst. Entered Army, 1874; Captain, 1885; Major, 1894; Lt-Col 1900; served Jowaki-Afridi Expedition, 1877–78 (medal with clasp); Afghan War, 1878–79 (medal with clasp, despatches); Mahsud Wuzeree Expedition, 1881 (despatches); NW Frontier, India, Waziristan, 1894–95 (clasp); Tochi, 1897–98 (despatches, medal with clasp); China Expeditionary Force, 1900, including relief of Peking (despatches, medal and clasp, Brevet Col); Brig.-Gen. 1904; Maj.-Gen. 1906; retired, 1911; Colonel 1/12th PWO Sikhs, FF; JP Stewartry of Kirkcudbright. *Address:* Bengairn, Castle Douglas, Kirkcudbrightshire.

Died 27 Feb. 1949.

POLSON, Col Sir Thomas Andrew, KBE 1919; CMG 1918; TD; Chairman of Butlin's Ltd, Duffield Iron Corporation, Ltd, James Walker, Goldsmith and Silversmith, Ltd; Pye Ltd and Rolls Razor Ltd; Director of Cairnton Trust and Finance Co. Ltd; MP (Ind) Dover, 1921–22; late Chief Inspector of Clothing, Royal Army Clothing Department (despatches); formerly Major Commanding A Squadron, City of London Yeomanry, Rough Riders; qualified Q Army List; commanded depôt of the regiment; lent to Air Ministry as personal assistant to late Lord Rothermere (First Secretary of State), and represented the Ministry on Army Agricultural Committee; served on Expenditure of Stores and Supplies Committee; Hon. Treasurer Anti-Waste League; Chairman and Chief Organizer United Empire Party; *b* Tuam, Co. Galway, 28 Aug. 1865; *e surv. s* of late Thomas Andrew Polson of Dublin and Tuam, and Catherine, *d* of late Joseph Potter of Dublin; *m* 1st, 1886, Rachel, *widow* of Col William Denny; one *s* two *d*; 2nd, 1918, Elizabeth (*d* 1945), *d* of John Lindsay of Edinburgh, and *widow* of F. A. Lindsay-Smith, JP CC. *Educ:* Dublin. *Publication:* Horses and Horsemastership, 1909. *Club:* Cavalry.

Died 22 Aug. 1946.

POLWARTH, 9th Baron *cr* 1690; **Walter George Hepburne-Scott,** CBE; VD; LLD; Representative Peer for Scotland since 1929; Lord Lieutenant of East Lothian, 1937–44; *b* 7 Feb. 1864; *e s* of 8th Baron Polwarth and Lady Mary Hamilton Gordon (*d* 1914), *d* of 5th Earl of Aberdeen; *m* 1888, Edith Frances (*d* 1930), *e d* of Sir T. Fowell and Lady Victoria Buxton; four *d*. *Educ:* Eton; Trinity College, Cambridge. Contested South Edinburgh, 1886; East Lothian, 1892 and 1895; Chairman of Board of Lunacy for Scotland, 1897–1909; Chairman of Prison Commissioners, Scotland, 1909–29; JP, DL East Lothian; late Hon. Col of 8th Royal Scots (Territorial Army). *Heir:* *g s* Master of Polwarth. *Address:* Humbie House, Humbie, East Lothian. *T:* Humbie 5. *Clubs:* National; New, Edinburgh.

Died 24 Aug. 1944.

POLWARTH; Master of; Hon. Walter Thomas Hepburne-Scott; DL, JP; sheep-farming; Chairman, Association for the Preservation of Rural Scotland; Director, Highland and Agricultural Society of Scotland; County Councillor for Roxburghshire; Chairman, Central National Service Committee for Scotland, 1939; *b* 1890; *s* of 9th Baron Polwarth, CBE; *m* 1914, Elspeth Glencairn Campbell, 2nd *d* of late Rt Rev. A. E. Campbell, Bishop of Glasgow; two *s*. *Educ:* Rugby; Trinity College, Cambridge, BA. Late Capt. Lothians and Border Horse Yeo. and Lothian and Border

Armoured Car Co.; Lieut-Col Home Guard, 1941. *Recreations:* hunting and shooting. *Address:* Harden, Hawick, Scotland. *Clubs:* New, Edinburgh.

Died 7 Sept. 1942.

PONCE, Don Ignacio; *see* Gutierrez-Ponce.

PONSONBY OF SHULBREDE, 1st Baron *cr* 1930, of Shulbrede, Sussex; **Arthur Augustus William Harry Ponsonby;** *b* 16 Feb. 1871; 3rd *s* of late Gen. the Right Hon. Sir Henry Ponsonby and the Hon. Lady Ponsonby, *g d* of Earl Grey, the Prime Minister; *m* 1898, Dorothea, *d* of Sir Hubert Parry, 1st Bart, and Lady Maud Parry; one *s*. *Educ:* Eton; Balliol College, Oxford. Page of Honour to Queen Victoria, 1882–87; served in the Diplomatic Service at Constantinople, 1894–97, Copenhagen, 1898–99; Foreign Office, 1900–02; contested (L) Taunton, 1906; principal private secretary to Prime Minister (late Sir Henry Campbell-Bannerman), 1906–08; MP (L) Stirling Burghs, 1908–18; contested Dunfermline Burghs, 1918; MP (Lab) Brightside Division of Sheffield, 1922–30; Under-Secretary of State for Foreign Affairs, 1924; Parliamentary Under-Secretary for Dominions, June–Dec., 1929; Parliamentary Secretary, Ministry of Transport, 1929–31; Chancellor of Duchy of Lancaster, 1931; Leader of the Opposition in the House of Lords, 1931–35; JP Sussex; Member of Council of Roy. College of Music. *Publications:* The Camel and the Needle's Eye, 1909; The Decline of Aristocracy, 1912; Democracy and Diplomacy, 1915; Wars and Treaties (1815–1914), 1917; (with Dorothea Ponsonby) Rebels and Reformers, 1917; Religion in Politics, 1921; English Diaries, 1923; More English Diaries, Scottish and Irish Diaries, 1927; Now is the Time, 1925; Samuel Pepys, 1928; Casual Observations, 1929; Queen Victoria, 1933; John Evelyn, 1934; Life Here and Now, 1936; Henry Ponsonby (his life from his letters), 1942. *Heir: s* Hon. Matthew Henry Hubert Ponsonby [*b* 28 July 1904; *m* 1929, Hon. Elizabeth Bigham, *o d* of 2nd Viscount Mersey, CMG, CBE; two *s* three *d*]. *Address:* Shulbrede Priory, Lynchmere, near Haslemere. *TA:* Shulbrede, Fernhurst; 17 Kensington Square, W8.

Died 23 March 1946.

PONSONBY, Rev. Maurice George Jesser, MC; MA; *b* 1880; 2nd *s* of Hon. E. C. W. Ponsonby; *m* 1918, Lady Phyllis Sydney, OBE (*d* 1942), *e d* of 1st Earl Buxton, PC, GCMG; one *s* three *d*. *Educ:* Trinity College, Oxford. Dean of Johannesburg, 1923; Rector of St Mary's Pro-Cathedral, Johannesburg, 1923; Canon Missioner to Bishop of St Albans, 1924; Rector of Much Hadham, 1930–39. *Address:* Old Vicarage, Forest Hill, Oxford. *T:* Stanton St John 34.

Died 27 Feb. 1943.

PONSONBY, Thomas Brabazon; *e s* of late Chambre Brabazon Ponsonby; *m* 1909, Frances May, *d* of late Major George Paynter; three *s* one *d*. *Educ:* Eton; Oxford. Served South African War with 10th Royal Hussars; JP and DL Co Tipperary; High Sheriff, Co. Kilkenny, 1906; late Commissioner of Forestry; Member Agricultural Wages Board for Ireland. *Publication:* Agricultural Labour. *Recreations:* hunting, agriculture, forestry. *Address:* Kilcooley Abbey, Thurles, Co. Tipperary. *Club:* Carlton.

Died 17 Nov. 1946.

PONTOPPIDAN, Henrik; Danish novelist; *b* 24 July 1857. Bourgeois Honoraire; Nobel prize in Literature, 1917; doctor of honour, member of honour of the Danish Society of Novelists, and member of honour of the London PEN Club. *Publications:* Village Tales, 1883; From the Huts; Lykke Per, etc. *Address:* Holmegaardsvej 2 Charlottenlund, pr. Copenhagen.

Died 21 Aug. 1943.

POOLE, Sir Reginald Ward Edward Lane, KCVO 1934; Kt 1928; Solicitor, Lewis & Lewis, 10–11 and 12 Ely Place, EC; *b* 23 Nov. 1864; *s* of late Professor Reginald Stuart Poole, LLD, of the British Museum; *m* Michelle (*d* 1934), *d* of late Henry Peveril Le Mesurier, CMG; two *d*. *Educ:* Bedford School; London University. Articled to the late Sir George Lewis (first baronet); admitted as a solicitor, 1891; member of the firm since 1894; member Council Law Society, 1919–40; President, 1933–34; Chairman of the Discipline Committee; member of Royal Commission on Police Powers and Procedure, 1929; member of Committee appointed by British Hospitals' association to consider and report on the present position of the Voluntary Hospitals of the country, 1937; Member of Committee appointed by the Lord Chancellor to consider the Law of Defamation, 1939. *Recreation:* golf. *Address:* Bucklerswood, Beaulieu, Hants. *T:* Beaulieu 33. *Clubs:* Garrick, Pratt's.

Died 11 Aug. 1941.

POPE, Rev. Hugh, OP, STM, DSS; Vicar of St Albert's, Edinburgh, since 1942; *b* Kenilworth, 6 Aug. 1869; *s* of Richard Vercoe Pope. *Educ:* The Oratory School, Birmingham; studied medicine at Queen's College, Birmingham, 1888–91. Entered the Order of Preachers, Dominicans, or Blackfriars, 1891; ordained, 1896; took degree of Lector in Theology, Louvain, 1898; professor at Hawkesyard, Rugeley, 1898–1909; took the Licentiate in Holy Scripture, Rome, 1908; took Doctorate in Holy Scripture, Rome, 1909; created Master in Theology, 1911; Professor of New Testament Exegesis at the Dominican Collegio Angelico, Rome, 1909–13; Prior of the Dominican Novitiate House, Woodchester, Glos, 1914–20; Regent of Studies in the Dominican House of Studies at Hawkesyard, Rugeley, 1920; and at the House of Theological Studies, Oxford, 1929–32; Prior of Hawkesyard, 1935–41. *Publications:* Life of Fr Thos Burke, OP, 1895; The Date of Deuteronomy, 1909; The Church and the Bible, 1928; A History of the English Versions of the Bible, 1946; St Augustine: On the Unity of the Church, English translation with Introduction and Notes, 1946; various translations; also papers in the Theological and Biblical Reviews. *Address:* St Albert's Priory, 24 George Square, Edinburgh.

Died 23 Nov. 1946.

POPE, Jessie, (Mrs Babington Lenton); writer of light verse and fiction; *b* Leicester; *d* of Richard George Pope and Elizabeth Windover. *Educ:* Craven House, Leicester; North London Collegiate School. Has contributed some 200 poems and articles to Punch; has written humorous fiction, verse, and articles for the leading magazines, weekly illustrated papers, and daily newspapers; edited The Ragged Trousered Philanthropists. *Publications:* Paper Pellets, Airy Nothings, and Hits and Misses (light verse); The Tracy Tubbses; The Shy Age; Love on Leave (fiction); three volumes of War Poems; How England Grew Up (history), and many books for children. *Address:* Ivy House, Fritton, nr Gt Yarmouth. *T:* Fritton 14.

Died 14 Dec. 1941.

POPE, Maj.-Gen. Vyvyan Vavasour, CBE 1940; DSO 1916; MC; late Royal Tank Corps; *b* 30 Sept. 1891; *s* of late James Pope and Blanche Holmwood Langdale; *m* 1926, Sybil, *o d* of late C. E. Moore; one *s*. *Educ:* Lancing Coll. Commissioned North Stafford Regt, 1912; served in France, 1914–18 (wounded thrice, despatches five times, DSO, MC, Brevet Major); North Russia, 1919 (despatches); Staff College, 1924–25; Brigade Major, RTC Centre, 1926–27; GSO2 Southern Command, 1928–29; GSO2 War Office, 1931–33; Imperial Defence College, 1934; GSO1 War Office, 1936–37; Brigadier, General Staff, Southern Command, 1938. *Address:* c/o Lloyds Bank, Ltd, 6 Pall Mall, SW1. *Club:* Junior United Service.

Died 5 Oct. 1941.

POPE-HENNESSY, Maj.-Gen. Ladislaus Herbert Richard, CB 1928; DSO 1908; *b* 1875; *e s* of late Sir John Pope-Hennessy, KCMG, MP, of Rostellan Castle, Co. Cork, and Catherine, *o d* of Sir Hugh Low, GCMG; *m* 1910, Una Birch, (Dame Una Pope-Hennessy, DBE); two *s*. *Educ*: Beaumont. Oxford Light Infantry, 1895; West African Frontier Force, 1898–99; attached to King's African Rifles, 1899–1908; Commandant of 4th King's African Rifles, 1906; Staff Officer to IGKA Rifles, 1907–08; Lt-Col 2nd Batt. Oxford and Bucks Light Infantry, 1919–20; AAG War Office, 1920–24; AA and QMG Military Inter-Allied Commission of Control, Berlin, 1924–26; Military Attaché, Washington, 1927–30; Commander 50th (Northumbrian) Division and Area, 1931–35; retired pay, 1935; served West Africa, 1898 (medal); East Africa, 1900–01, operations against Ogaden Somalis (medal); Somaliland, 1902–03 (clasp, despatches); East Africa, 1905; operations in Sotik (clasp, despatches, DSO); operations in Nandi, 1905–06 (clasp, despatches, Bt Maj.); operations in Somaliland, 1909–10 (clasp, despatches); European War, 1914–18 (despatches four times, Bt Lt-Col and Bt Col Chevalier of Legion of Honour); GSO3 and GSO2 in France, 1915–16; commanded 1st Oxf. and Bucks Lt Inf. in Mesopotamia, 1916–17; GSO1 3rd Indian Div. 1917; BGGS 1st Indian Army Corps, 1917–19; psc; G. District Warden, Hampstead ARP. *Publications*: The Irish Dominion: a Method of Approach to a Settlement; articles on military subjects to the Edinburgh Review and Quarterly Review; translator of Colin: Transformations of War. *Address*: 74 Avenue Road, Regent's Park, NW8. *T*: Primrose 0507. *Club*: Brooks's.

Died 1 March 1942.

POPE-HENNESSY, Dame Una, DBE 1920; Lady of Grace of St John of Jerusalem, 1919; *o d* of late Sir Arthur Birch, KCMG; *m* 1910, Maj.-Gen. Ladislaus Herbert Richard Pope-Hennessy, CB, DSO (*d* 1942); two *s*. *Publications*: Three English Women in America, 1929; The Aristocratic Journey, 1931; The Laird of Abbotsford, 1932; Early Chinese Jades; Edgar Allan Poe: a Critical Biography, 1934; The Closed City (Leningrad), 1938; Agnes Strickland: Biographer of the Queens of England, 1940; Durham Company, 1941; Charles Dickens, 1945; A Czarina's Story, 1948; Canon Charles Kingsley, 1948. *Address*: 28 Lansdowne Road, W11. *T*: Park 6160.

Died 17 Aug. 1949.

POPHAM, Sir Henry Bradshaw, KCMG 1938; CMG 1935; MBE 1918; *b* 1 Aug. 1881; *s* of Thomas Dalton Popham and Annie Emma West; *m* 1st, Irene Millicent (*d* 1930), *d* of late H. C. Collyer, The Grange, Seaton, Devon; one *s*; 2nd, 1933, Dorothy Jessie, *d* of late A. E. Dyer, Mus. Doc., Cheltenham. *Educ*: Tonbridge. Joined Somerset Lt Infantry, 1900; served South African War (2 medals); West African Frontier Force, 1906–10; Colonial Administrative Service (Gold Coast), 1910; Political Officer, Togoland, 1914–20; Senior Assistant Colonial Secretary, 1921; Provincial Commissioner and Member of Gold Coast Legislature, 1922–23; invalided from Service, 1923; on staff Wembley Exhibition, 1924–25; Commissioner in Cyprus, 1925; Administrator, Dominica, 1933–37; Governor and Commander-in-Chief, Windward Islands, 1937–42. *Publications*: various articles, etc. on West African Affairs. *Recreations*: sailing and fishing. *Address*: Villa Point, St Vincent, BWI. *Club*: Royal Automobile.

Died 15 April 1947.

POPHAM, Col Robert Stewart, CMG 1919; DSO 1902; late Sherwood Foresters; *b* 27 July 1876; *s* of Benjamin Popham of Kinsale, Cork; *m* 1907, Mildred Mary Stewart, *d* of late Major A. J. Roberts, 44th Regiment; one *s*. Entered army, 1899; served S Africa, 1899–1902 (despatches, DSO, medal with four clasps, King's medal two clasps); European War (Bt Lt-Col, despatches, CMG, wounded); Captain, 1906; Major,

1915; Lt-Col 1922; Col 1926; half-pay, 1926; Brigade Commander 143rd Warwickshire Infantry Brigade, 1927–31; retired pay, 1931. *Address*: c/o Lloyds Bank, 6 Pall Mall, SW1.

Died 23 May 1949.

PORRITT, Arthur; *b* Warrington, Lancs, 29 May 1872; *m* 1898, Madeleine (*d* 1942), *d* of Mrs Frank Day; two *s*; *m* 1945, Harriet Ingersoll, Seasalter, Kent. *Educ*: People's College, Warrington; privately. Parliamentary Staff of Manchester Examiner, 1890–92; Managing Editor of the Independent and Nonconformist, 1895–99; joined the Christian World, 1899; resigned Editorship, 1936. *Publications*: (with W. G. Grace) W. G. Cricketing Reminiscences; The Strategy of Life; The Best I Remember: Life of Dr J. H. Jowett; The Causes of War (edited); J. D. Jones of Bournemouth—A Memoir; More and More of Memories, 1946; many booklets and pamphlets on religious and missionary subjects. *Recreations*: reading, gardening, bowls, travelling. *Address*: Ranmora, Leatherhead Road, Great Bookham. *T*: Bookham 87. *Club*: National Liberal.

Died 24 Jan. 1947.

PORTAL, 1st Viscount *cr* 1945, of Laverstoke; **Wyndham Raymond Portal;** PC 1942; 3rd Bt *cr* 1901, GCMG 1949; DSO 1918; MVO 1918; Lord Lieutenant of County of Hampshire and of Southampton; JP; late Life Guards; Chairman of Portals, Ltd; Trustee of Lord Nuffield's scheme for assistance of Special Areas since 1936; *b* 9 April 1885; *e s* of Sir W. W. Portal, 2nd Bt, and Florence, CBE, *d* of Hon. St Leger Glyn, 2nd *s* of 1st Baron Wolverton; *S* to father's baronetcy, 1931; *m* 1909, Lady Louise Rosemary Kathleen Virginia Cairns, MBE, *o c* of 2nd Earl Cairns. *Educ*: Eton; Christ Church, Oxford. Served European War, 1914–18 (DSO, Bt Major); Regional Commissioner for Wales under Civil Defence Scheme, 1939; Additional Parly Sec. to Ministry of Supply, 1940–42; Minister of Works and Planning and First Comr of Works and Public Buildings, 1942–44. Late Chairman: Bacon Development Board; Coal Production Council. President of Olympic Games, 1948. *Heir*: (to Baronetcy only): *uncle* Sir Spencer John Portal. *Address*: Laverstoke House, Whitchurch, Hants. *T*: Overton 245. *Clubs*: Turf; Royal Yacht Squadron.

Died 6 May 1949 (ext).

PORTAL, Brig.-Gen. Sir Bertram Percy, KCB 1937; CB 1917; DSO 1902; *b* 10 Jan. 1866; 3rd *s* of late Sir Wyndham Portal, 1st Bart; *m* 1899, Hon. Margaret Louisa Littleton (*d* 1945), *e d* of 3rd Baron Hatherton; one *s* five *d*. *Educ*: Wellington College; Sandhurst. Joined 17th Lancers, 1885; ADC to Governor of Madras (Sir Arthur Havelock), 1896–98; served S Africa, 1900–02 (S African medal 3 clasps, King's medal 2 clasps, despatches, DSO); commanded 17th Lancers, 1903–07; retired, 1907; commanded Reserve Cavalry Regt, 1914–16; commanded Cavalry Brigade in France, 1916–18; Chairman of Hampshire and Isle of Wight Territorial Army Association, 1925–38; DL, JP, Hants; Vice-Lieutenant, 1932–42; CC Hants, 1932; County Alderman, 1943; Governor of Wellington College, 1934–44. *Address*: Southington House, Overton, Hants. *T*: Overton 288. *Club*: Naval and Military.

Died 7 Feb. 1949.

PORTEOUS, Lt-Col John James, CMG 1918; late RA (1876–96); *b* 1857; 3rd *s* of Alexander Porteous of Lauriston, Kincardineshire; *m* 1st, 1882, Nelly Isabella Macdonald (*d* 1921), *o d* of Percy Morris of The Hall, Uttoxeter; 2nd, 1923, Mrs J. W. Bouch (*d* 1942), Ashorne, Warwick. *Educ*: Harrow; RMA Woolwich. Served Afghan War, 1879–80 (despatches, medal, severely wounded); Remount Department, 1900, 1914–19 (Bt Lt-Col, CMG). *Address*: Ashorne, Warwick. *Club*: Naval and Military.

Died 17 March 1948.

PORTER, Col Geoffrey M., RE; formerly Master of His Majesty's Mints, Calcutta and Bombay; *b* Madras, 10 Oct. 1854; *s* of late Robert Tindal Porter, Madras Civil Service; *m* F. L. Minchin; one *d. Educ:* Cheltenham College; RMA, Woolwich. Joined Royal Engineers, 1873; attached Bengal Sappers and Miners, 1877; service with Kabul Field Force, 1879 (medal); Military Works Department in India till 1897, during which he was employed on defence and other works, and on the design and construction of wet and dry docks in Bombay; officiated as Mint Master of the Calcutta and Bombay Mints; Senior Mint Master, 1904; deputed on special duty to USA, 1905, to study modern developments in coining machinery and appliances; since engaged in connection with introduction of bronze and nickel coinages into India; retired, 1909; re-employed on Lines of Communication in France, 1914–17; Fellow of the Royal Empire Society. *Address:* Tenterden, Kent. *T:* Tenterden 253.

Died 24 Oct. 1944.

PORTER, Sir Haldane; *see* Porter, Sir W. H.

PORTER, Sir (Harry Edwin) Bruce B.; *see* Bruce-Porter.

PORTER, Major Herbert Alfred, DSO 1905; late 19th Hussars and West African Frontier Force; *b* 15 Jan. 1872; *m* 1913, Rachel, *d* of late Arthur Edwards, Liverpool. Entered army, 1894; Captain, 1903; served W Africa, 1898 (medal with clasp); S Africa, 1900; W Africa (N Nigeria), 1900–01, 1902–03 (despatches thrice, Brevet Major, medal, two clasps, DSO); retired, 1910; served European War, 1914–17.

Died 22 June 1939.

PORTER, John Bonsall, EM, PhD, DSc; Professor Emeritus McGill University; until 1927 Director of Mining Department and Chairman of Faculty of Engineering McGill University; Organising Hon. Secretary, Canadian Engineering Standards Committee, 1917 and Vice-Chairman, 1922–36; Chairman Canadian Advisory Committee InstCE, 1921–31 and Member Council, 1923–26; Past Corr. Member Council InstMM; Past President, Mining Section, Canadian Society of Civil Engineers; Vice-President Canadian Mining Institute, 1907–09; Past President Sigma Xi Society McGill University; *b* 1 Oct. 1861; British subject; *e s* of late John H. Porter and Lydia, *d* of late Chas. Bonsall; *m* Ethel Hardinge, *d* of late Chas. H. Going of Altavilla, Cahir, Tipperary, Ireland; one *d. Educ:* private; Columbia University, New York. Geological and mining investigations in Canada and Southern US, Instructor in Mining in Univ. of Cincinnati, 1882–84; professional work in engineering of railways and mineral properties chiefly in US, 1884–96; consulting practice since 1896; in charge of Dom. Govt investigation of coal resources of Canada, 1906–12; in charge Sphagnum Dressings Department, Canadian Red Cross, 1915–19. *Publications:* The Coals of Canada, 6 vols, 1911; The Weathering of Coal, 1914; numerous technical papers on engineering and educational subjects in journals and transactions; also various papers on sphagnum dressings and allied Red Cross war supplies. *Recreations:* yachting, fishing, shooting. *Address:* 3600 M'Tavish Street, Montreal; Long Beach Farm, Guysboro', Nova Scotia. *TA:* Retrop, Montreal. *Clubs:* Royal Societies; Royal Nova Scotia Yacht Squadron, Halifax; University, Faculty, Montreal.

Died 17 March 1944.

PORTER, Sir (William) Haldane, Kt 1926; CB 1917; *b* 1867; *s* of late Rev. J. Leslie Porter, DD, President, Queen's College, Belfast; *m* 1906, Sybil Osborne Pochin (*d* 1941); one *s* one *d. Educ:* Queen's College, Belfast; Oxford (BA 1891). Called to Bar, 1895; HM Inspector under the Aliens Act, Home Office, 1905; HM Chief Inspector, Aliens Branch, Home Office, 1919–30;

Assistant Managing Director, Arthur Guinness Son & Co. Ltd, 1930–44. *Recreations:* gardening and golf. *Address:* 98 James's Street, Dublin. *Clubs:* Travellers'; Kildare Street, Dublin.

Died 12 Sept. 1944.

PORTER-PHILLIPS, John George, MD (Lond.), BS, FRCP (Lond.), MRCS; late Physician Superintendent of Bethlem Royal Hospital; Consulting Physician and late Physician for and Lecturer in Psychological Medicine at St Bartholomew's Hospital; Examiner in Mental Diseases to the Royal College of Physicians, London; Lecturer in Mental Pathology at London (Royal Free Hospital) School of Medicine for Women; Physician at the Hospital for Nervous Diseases, Lambeth Road, SE1; Principal Medical Officer at King Edward's School, Witley; Examiner in Mental Diseases at the RAM College; Fellow of the Royal Society of Medicine; Member of the British Medical Association; late examiner in Psychological Medicine and Mental Diseases, and Educational Secretary of the Royal Medico-Psychological Association; *b* Darjeeling, India; *s* of late Robert Phillips; *m* Kathleen Phyllis, *d* of late Leader Stevenson, MD; one *s* two *d. Educ:* Brighton; University College, London; Guy's Hospital. Gaskell Gold Medal and Prize in Psychological Medicine. *Publications:* various articles and papers on nervous and mental diseases. *Recreations:* golf, fishing, natural history and art. *Address:* The Dower House, Monks Orchard, Beckenham, Kent. *T:* Spring Park 1298; 19 Cavendish Square, W1. *T:* Langham 2230. *Clubs:* Athenæum, Savage.

Died 24 Feb. 1946.

PORTEUS, Rev. Canon Thomas Cruddas, MA, BD; FRHistS; Vicar of St George's, Chorley, 1934–47; Canon of Blackburn Cathedral since 1942; *b* Netherton, Worcs, 1876; *s* of Rev. T. Porteus; *m* 1906, Beatrice G. P. Hadfield; one *s* one *d. Educ:* Owens College, Manchester. Vicar of St John the Divine, Coppull, Lancs, 1912–34; President, Chorley Historical Society; President of Lancashire Authors Assoc., 1938–45, President, Lancs and Cheshire Antiquarian Soc. 1940–43. *Publications:* Captain Myles Standish, 1920; New Light on Mab's Cross, 1923; Astley Hall, 1923; Cottonopolis, 1923; Life of James Darlington, 1926; History of Standish, 1927; Lancashire School Founders, 1929; Leyland Hundred, 1931; Calendar of Standish Deeds, 1933; The Jacobite Plot of 1692, 1936; Life of Roger Haydock, 1938; Mab's Cross Legend and History, 1941; Memories of an Antiquary, 1942; The Mysterious Murder of Sir William de Bradshaigh, 1944; History of Chorley Parish Church, 1945; Contributions to Manchester University Verses, 1913, A Lancashire Anthology, 1923, Lancashire in Prose and Verse, 1930, Enc. Brit., 15th Ed. *Address:* Summer Hill, Bolton Road, Chorley. *T:* Chorley 2786.

Died 2 July 1948.

PORTLAND, 6th Duke of, *cr* 1716; **William John Arthur Charles James Cavendish-Bentinck,** KG 1900, PC, GCVO 1896; Royal Victorian Chain, 1932; Chancellor of the Order of the Garter, 1937; DL, JP; Earl of Portland, Viscount Woodstock, and Baron of Cirencester, 1689; Marquess of Titchfield, 1716; Baron Bolsover, 1880; Master of the Horse, 1886–92, and 1895–1905; Lord-Lieutenant of Caithness, 1889–1919; Lord-Lieutenant of Nottingham, 1898–1939; Lieut Coldstream Guards, retired 1880; Lt-Col Hon. Artillery Co., 1881–88; Hon. Col 4th Batt. Sherwood Foresters since 1889; appoints two Family Trustees of British Museum; Provincial Grand Master Notts Freemasons, 1898–1933; *b* 28 Dec. 1857; *s* of late Lieut-Gen. Arthur Cavendish-Bentinck, *g s* of 3rd Duke, and Elizabeth Sophia, *d* of Sir St Vincent Hawkins Whitshed, Bt; *S* cousin, 1879, and stepmother in Barony of Bolsover, 1893; *m* 1889, Winifred (DBE 1935), *d* of late Thomas Yorke Dallas-Yorke; two *s* one *d. Publications:* Fifty Years and More of Sport in Scotland, 1933; Memories of

Racing and Hunting, 1935; Men, Women and Things, 1937. *Heir: s* Marquis of Titchfield, MP. *Address:* 17 Hill Street, W1. *T:* Mayfair 0830; Welbeck Abbey, Worksop; Langwell, Berriedale, Caithness-shire. *Clubs:* Carlton, Guards', Turf, Marlborough.

Died 26 April 1943.

PORTMAN, 5th Viscount (UK) *cr* 1873; **Edward Claud Berkeley Portman;** late MFH Taunton Vale; late joint MFH Warwickshire; *b* 1898; *o s* of 4th Viscount Portman and Harriette Mary (*d* 1939), *d* of William Stevenson; *S* father, 1929; *m* Hon. Sybil Mary Douglas-Pennant, *y d* of 3rd Baron Penrhyn; two *d. Educ:* Eton; RMC, Sandhurst. Lieut 1st Life Guards Res. Served European War, 1914–19. *Heir: uncle* Hon. Seymour Berkeley Portman, *b* 1868. *Address:* Staple Fitzpaine Manor, Taunton.

Died 14 July 1942.

PORTMAN, 6th Viscount (UK) *cr* 1873; **Seymour Berkeley Portman;** *b* 19 Feb. 1868; *s* of 2nd Viscount Portman; *S* nephew, 1942. *Heir: b* Capt. Hon. Gerald Berkeley Portman. *Address:* Durweston, Blandford, Dorset.

Died 2 Nov. 1946.

PORTMAN, 7th Viscount (UK) *cr* 1873; **Gerald Berkeley Portman;** *b* 23 Jan. 1875; 6th *s* of 2nd Viscount; *S* brother 1946; *m* 1902, Dorothy Marie Isolde, *d* of Sir Robert Sheffield, 5th Bt; two *s* one *d. Educ:* Eton; RMC, Sandhurst. Late 10th Hussars; ADC to Viceroy of India, 1901; Capt. 10th Hussars, 1901; served European War, 1914–19; MFH Portman Hounds, 1932–40. *Heir: s* Hon. Gerald William Berkeley Portman [*b* 20 Aug. 1903; *m* 1st, 1926, Marjorie Bentley, *d* of George Bentley, Gerrard, Montreal, Canada; 2nd, 1946, Nancy Maureen, 4th *d* of Capt. Percy Herbert Franklin, RN, retd]. *Address:* The Manor, Healing, Lincolnshire; Inverinate, Kyle of Loch Alsh, Ross-shire. *Club:* Orleans.

Died 3 Sept. 1948.

PORTSEA, 1st Baron *cr* 1934, of Portsmouth; **Bertram Godfray Falle;** 1st Bt *cr* 1916; *b* 1860; *o s* of J. G. Falle, one of the Judges of the Royal Court of Jersey, of Hambie, etc., and Mary *d* and *co-heiress* of F. Godfray, Barrister-at-law, of Bagatelle, Jersey; *m* 1906, Mary (*d* 1942), *d* of Russell Sturgis and *widow* of Lieut-Col L. R. Seymour. *Educ:* Victoria College, Jersey; privately; Pembroke College, Cambridge (Honours Mathematics and Law); University of Paris (B. en Droit). Advocate Royal Court of Jersey; called to Bar, Inner Temple, 1885; Enroller Deeds HM Office of Works; Judge Native Tribunal, Cairo; contested (LU) East Somerset, 1906; MP (U) Portsmouth, 1910; Portsmouth (N), 1918–34; served as Temp.-Major RFA, at home and in France, 1914–18. *Recreations:* shooting, fishing, driving, and riding. *Heir:* none. *Club:* Brooks's.

Died 1 Nov. 1948 (ext).

PORTSMOUTH, 8th Earl of, *cr* 1743; **Oliver Henry Wallop;** Viscount Lymington, Baron Wallop, 1720; Hereditary Bailiff of Burley, New Forest; *b* 13 Jan. 1861; 3rd *s* of 5th Earl and Lady Eveline Alicia Juliana Herbert, *d* of 3rd Earl of Carnarvon; *S* brother, 1925; *m* 1897, Marguerite (*d* 1938), *d* of S. W. Walker, Kentucky; two *s. Educ:* Eton; Balliol College, Oxford. *Heir: s* Viscount Lymington. *Address:* Farleigh Wallop, Basingstoke, Hants.

Died 9 Feb. 1943.

POSKITT, Rt Rev. **Henry John,** DD, MA; Bishop of Leeds, (RC), since 1936; *b* Birkin, Yorks, 6 Sept. 1888. *Educ:* Corpus Christi College, Cambridge, MA; Ely Theological College. Took Anglican Orders, 1911; curate St Hilda's, Leeds, 1911–15; received into Roman Catholic Church, 1915; studied in Rome, 1915–21, and Paris, 1921–22; priest, 1917; Curate at St Peter's Scarborough, 1922–25; Parish Priest and Rural Dean of

Bedale, 1925–32; Rector of Leeds Diocesan Seminary, 1932–36. *Address:* Bishop's House, Weetwood Lane, Leeds 6. *T:* 51996.

Died 19 Feb. 1950.

POTT, Francis Lister Hawks, LittB, BD, DD; STD; President Emeritus, St John's University, Shanghai, China; *b* New York City, 22 Feb. 1864; *s* of James Pott and Josephine Hawks, both of New York City; *m* 1st, 1888; three *s* one *d;* 2nd, 1919. *Educ:* Trinity School, New York City; Columbia University; General Theological Seminary, New York City. Came to China, 1886; head of St John's College, 1888–1941; has spent all his time in educational work and work of a literary character; hon. DD, Trinity College, USA, 1900; University of Edinburgh, 1910; Hon. STD Columbia University, 1929; elected Missionary Bishop of Diocese of Wuhu, China, 1910; declined; received Third Class Decoration Chiao Ho from President of Chinese Republic, 1921; Second Class, 1925; Chairman of the North China Branch of Royal Asiatic Society, Shanghai, 1932. *Publications:* The Causes of the Outbreak in China, 1900; Sketch of Chinese History, 1907; Lessons on Shanghai Vernacular, 1908; The Emergency in China, 1912; A Short History of Shanghai, 1928; Revised and Enlarged Edition of Sketch of Chinese History, 1936; on Committee for translation of Prayer Book into Chinese; translator of some theological books. *Recreation:* golf. *Address:* St John's University, Shanghai, China.

Died 8 March 1947.

POTT, Rear-Adm. Herbert, MVO 1928; Royal Navy, retired; Naval Attaché, Washington, USA, since 1940; *b* 1886; *s* of late Col William Pott, Steyning, Sussex; *m* 1931, Mary, 3rd *d* of F. M. S. Grant, Knockie Lodge, Inverness. *Educ:* HMS Britannia. Entered Navy, 1901; served European War; Commander HMY Victoria and Albert, 1926–28; Naval Attaché at Rome, 1934–36; commanded HMS London, 1937–39; Rear-Adm., 1939; retired list, 1939. *Address:* Newton Lees, Kelso. *Club:* Junior United Service.

Died 4 Aug. 1945.

POTTER, Albert Knight, MA; Professor of English in Brown University since 1898, Emeritus, 1935; *b* Berwick, Maine, 2 Nov. 1864; *s* of late Rev. Albert K. Potter; *m* 1894, Mabel, *d* of late John B. Palmer; one *d. Educ:* Brown University; Leipzig; Berlin. Principal, High School, Middleboro, Mass, 1887–90; Classical Master, High School, Springfield, Mass, 1890–97; studied at Oxford, 1906–07. *Publications:* contributions, chiefly to professional journals, etc. *Recreations:* golf, billiards. *Address:* 212 Waterman Street, Providence, Rhode Island, USA. *Clubs:* Authors'; University, Art, Agawam Hunt (Providence).

Died 17 Nov. 1948.

POTTER, Cyril H.; *b* 16 Nov. 1877; 2nd *s* of E. S. Potter of Fullwood Park, Cheltenham; *m* 1st, Ida, *y d* of Colonel C. H. T. Marshall; one *s* two *d;* 2nd, 1933, Joanna, *widow* of Captain Douglas Reid and *y d* of J. C. Bridge. *Educ:* Eton. Served in 4th Batt. Royal Welsh Fusiliers, 1895–99; 10th Hussars, 1899–1905; South African War (medal with 4 clasps); Capt. 5th Batt. King's Royal Rifles, 1909–13; Capt. 10th Hussars (SR), 4 Aug. 1914; ADC to Lt-Gen. Sir C. M. Kavanagh, KCB, 9 Sept. 1914; Assistant Military Secretary Cavalry Corps, Feb. 1917 (despatches thrice, Croix de Chevalier 5th class Legion of Honour, 1914 Star with clasp, Brevet Major, 1919, OBE, General Service Medal and Victory Medal with palm); contested (C) Middleton Division, Lancs, 1906; Prestwich Division, Lancs, 1910, and North Salford, 1910; appointed to HM Corps of Gentlemen-at-arms, 1919; Area Meat and Livestock Officer, South Western Area, Sept. 1939. *Recreations:* yachting, shooting, cricket. *Address:* Playford Hall, Ipswich. *Clubs:* Orleans, Army and Navy, MCC; Royal Yacht Squadron, Cowes; Royal Lymington Yacht (Admiral).

Died 6 Aug. 1941.

POTTER, Rev. Michael Cressé, ScD, MA, Cantab et Dunelm; Emeritus Professor of Botany in University of Durham, 1925; *b* 7 Sept. 1858; *s* of Rev. R. Potter, MA, Rector of Corley, Warwickshire, and *nephew* of late Professor R. Potter, MA Cantab, University College, London; *m* Norah Helen (*d* 1942), *e d* of late William Silburn, solicitor, Yorks. *Educ:* St Edward's School, Oxford; Perse School, Cambridge; St Peter's College, Cambridge. Mathematical and Natural Sciences Triposes; Wort's Travelling Scholar for Botanical Research in Portugal, 1886, and for the study of a Tropical Flora in Ceylon, 1888–89. Assistant Curator of the Cambridge Univ. Herbarium; a Lecturer on Botany, Cambridge Univ., 1883–89; initiated courses of lectures upon the Geographical Distribution of Plants (ecology); with Dr Walter Gardiner re-instituted the University Botanical Museum founded by Prof. Henslow; established bacterial plant diseases; Hon. Consulting Botanist, Newcastle Farmers' Club; Pres. of British Mycological Society, 1909; Chairman of British Assoc. (1916) Committee to consider Organisation of Research in Plant Pathology; President, Bournemouth Natural Science Society, 1941; inventor of the fermentation or organic cell, a primary non-metallic voltaic cell, and designed experiments which show that a correction in the Mechanical theory may be expected to include electricity. *Publications:* Elementary Text-book of Agricultural Botany; translator and editor of Dr E. Warming's Haandbog i den systematiske Botanik; Bio-Electric Potentials; numerous original papers dealing chiefly with investigations in Plant Pathology and Electro-Physiology, in the Proc. Royal Society, etc. *Recreations:* walking, cycling, gardening, bellringing, dowsing. *Address:* Corley Croft, New Milton, Hants. *T:* New Milton 775. *Club:* Organon.

Died 9 March 1948.

POTTER, Rev. Reginald Joseph William Henry, MA; Rector of Ickham Canterbury, since 1934; Hon. Canon of Canterbury since 1933; *b* 16 March 1877; *s* of late William and Ellen Potter; *m* Frances Amy, *d* of late Frederick Michael and Anna Rice; two *s*. *Educ:* Cathedral Choir School, Exter; King's College (Choral Scholar) and Westcott House, Cambridge. Deacon 1904; Priest 1905; Curate of Dewsbury Parish Church 1904–09; Minor Canon of Canterbury, 1909–34; Sacrist 1911–21; Chaplain, Canterbury Mental Hospital, 1909–34; Lecturer in Elocution and Voice Production, St Augustine's College, Canterbury, since 1911; Secretary Canterbury Diocesan Board of Finance, 1914–34; Secretary Canterbury Dilapidations Board, 1923–34; Hon. Treasurer Canterbury Diocesan Conference since 1923, and Hon. Secretary since 1932; Hon. Secretary Canterbury Clerical Registry, 1927–34; Member Canterbury Diocesan Board of Finance and Dilapidations Board, 1934; Proctor in Convocation; Chairman Canterbury Diocesan Choral Union, 1939. *Recreations:* music and golf. *Address:* Ickham Rectory, Canterbury. *TA:* Ickham Rectory, Wickhambreaux. *T:* Littlebourne 73.

Died 6 Oct. 1941.

POTTINGER, Lt-Col Robert Southey; Indian Army (retired); JP Devon; *b* 31 Jan. 1870; *s* of late Lieut-General B. H. Pottinger, RA; *m* 1st, Ada Katherine Mayers; 2nd, Muriel Robertson, *d* of Dr F. C. H. Piggott, MD, Teignmouth; two *s* three *d*. *Educ:* Cheltenham College; RMA, Woolwich. Entered Royal Artillery, 1889; served in Field Battery in India; joined Indian Army, 1892, and entered Political Department; served as Political Agent in Aden, Cutch, Kathiawar, Mahi Kantha and Savantvadi, and Resident at Kolhapur. *Address:* West Hill, Teignmouth, Devon. *T:* Teignmouth 70.

Died 1 March 1943.

POTTS, Lt-Col Edmund Thurlow, CMG 1918; DSO 1915; MD; late RAMC; *b* 8 June 1878; *m* 1921, Blanche, *d* of late Thomas Beardsall. *Educ:* Edinburgh University. Physician and Surgeon Royal Hospital, Chelsea, 1922–27; Entered army, 1905; Captain, 1909; Major, 1915; Bt Lieut-Colonel, 1928; Lt-Col, 1930; served European War, 1914–18, ADMS of an Army (despatches, DSO, CMG; Chevalier Légion d'Honneur). ADMS (Pers.), India, 1929–32; retired pay, 1933; Medical Officer HM Tower of London, 1933–39; Ministry of Health, 1939–44. *Address:* Lauriston, Wych Hill, Woking.

Died 25 Sept. 1948.

POTTS, Brig.-Gen. Frederick, CB 1918; CMG 1915; late RA; *b* 31 Jan. 1866; unmarried. Entered army, 1885; Captain, 1895; Major, 1900; Lt-Col 1912; Adjutant Volunteers, 1894; served Zululand, 1888; European War, 1914–18 (despatches seven times, CMG, CB).

Died 19 Aug. 1945.

POTTS, George, BSc (Dunelm), PhD (Halle-a-Saale), NDA, NDD, FHAS (Agric. and Forestry); *b* Northallerton, 1877; *e s* of late George Atkinson Potts, Whitehurworth, Trimdon; *m* 1st, 1910, Sallie (*d* 1918), 3rd *d* of late W. Burge, Worcester; no *c*; 2nd, 1929, Elsie, *d* of late S. Strapp, Bethlehem, S Africa. *Educ:* Hartlepool; Catterick; British Dairy Institute, Reading; Armstrong College, Newcastle-on-Tyne; Halle University. Holder of Durham Senior Exhibition, 1899–1902; Assistant Lecturer in Agriculture, Armstrong College, Newcastle, 1902–05; Professor of Botany, University College of the Orange Free State, Bloemfontein, 1905–38, now Professor Emeritus; Botanist in charge of the Botanical Survey Central Area of the Union of South Africa, 1918–38; President of Section C, South African Association for the Advancement of Science, 1914; Member of OFS Commission on Rural Education, 1914–16. *Publications:* several articles on Botany and Agriculture including Hay Fever, as caused by the Pepper Tree (Schinus), Finger and Toe, and Vegetation of Orange Free State. *Address:* 27 Park Road, Bloemfontein, SA.

Died 11 July 1948.

POULTON, Sir Edward Bagnall, Kt 1935; FRS; Hon. LLD Princeton; Hon. DSc Durham, Dublin, Reading; DSc Sydney; Hope Professor of Zoology in the University, 1893–1933; Fellow of Jesus College, Oxford, since 1898; *b* Reading, 27 Jan. 1856; *o s* of William Ford Poulton, Reading, architect; *m* 1881, Emily (*d* 1939), *e d* of the late George Palmer, formerly MP, Reading; one *d*. *Educ:* private school; Jesus College, Oxford (Scholar), MA; 1st class Nat. Science School, 1876; DSc 1900. Librarian Oxford Union Society, 1877–78; Pres. 1879; Burdett-Coutts Univ. Scholar, 1878; Demonstrator in Comparative Anatomical Department of Univ. Museum, 1877–79; Lecturer in Natural Science, and tutor of Keble College, Oxford, 1880–89; Lecturer in Natural Science, Jesus College, Oxford, 1880–88; Member of Council of Royal Society, 1897–99, 1908–10; Vice-President, 1909–10; Darwin Medallist, 1914; Member of Hebdomadal Council of Oxford University, 1898–1905; President of the Royal Entomological Society of London, 1903–04, 1925–26, and the centenary year 1933, when elected Hon. Life President; President of the Linnean Society of London, 1912–16; Linnean Medallist, 1922; President of 2nd International Entomological Congress, Oxford, 1912; Romanes Lecturer, Oxford, 1915; President British Association, 1937; member several foreign scientific societies; Commander (Class II), Swedish Order of the Pole Star. *Publications:* The Colours of Animals, etc., International Sci. Series, London, 1890; Charles Darwin and the Theory of Natural Selection, 1896; Essays on Evolution, Oxford, 1908; Charles Darwin and the Origin of Species, 1909; Viriamu Jones, and other Oxford Memories, 1911; Life of Ronald Poulton, 1919; editor of vols i–xx of Hope Reports, 1897–1933 (for private circulation); editor (with others) of the English translation of Weismann's Essays on Heredity, etc., 1889; editor of Shelford's Naturalist in Borneo, 1916; author of many Memoirs on zoological subjects in the Proceedings and Transactions of the Royal, Linnean, Zoological, and Royal Entomological Societies. *Recreations:* gardening, carpentering, and various building operations. *Address:* Wykeham House, Oxford. *TA:* and *T:* 2015; St Helens Cottage, St Helens, Isle of Wight. *Club:* Athenæum.

Died 20 Nov. 1943.

POULTON, Elgan Nathaniel George, CBE 1938; JP; Private Secretary Minister of Internal Affairs and Social Security, NZ; *b* 7 Dec. 1881; *er s* of George Henry Ralph Greville Poulton; *m* 1906, Alexina, 2nd *d* of Captain Benjamin Bern, Dunedin, New Zealand; four *s*. *Educ:* Terrace School; Cornford's Private College. Commenced career in journalism, serving on the staffs Evening Post, Wellington; New Zealand Herald, Auckland; New Zealand Times, Wellington; subsequently, in 1902, joined the Seddon Government as Private Secretary, serving in that capacity, Ministers of successive Governments. *Publications:* short stories for New Zealand and Australian periodicals. *Address:* Parliament House, Wellington, NZ; 60 Glenmore Road, Wellington, NZ. *T:* (Official) 44–666, (Private) 26–538.

Died 25 Sept. 1944.

POUND, Adm. of the Fleet Sir (Alfred) Dudley (Pickman Rogers), GCB 1939; OM 1943; GCVO 1937; KCB 1933; CB 1919; First Sea Lord and Chief of Naval Staff, 1939–43; First and Principal Naval ADC to the King since 1941; *b* 29 Aug. 1877; *s* of Alfred John Pound and Elizabeth Pickman Rogers, Boston, USA; *m* 1908, Bessie Caroline Grace Whitehead (*d* 1943); two *s* one *d. Educ:* Fonthill, East Grinstead; The Limes, Greenwich; HMS Britannia, etc. In command of HMS Colossus at Battle of Jutland, 31 May 1916 (despatches); Royal Humane Society's Bronze Medal; officier of Legion of Honour; Rising Sun 3rd class (Japan); American DSM; Director of Plans Division, Admiralty, 1922–25; Chief of Staff of Admiral Sir Roger Keyes, Commander-in-Chief, Mediterranean, 1925–27; Rear-Adm., 1926; a Lord Commissioner of the Admiralty and Assistant Chief of the Naval Staff, 1927–29; Rear-Adm. commanding Battle Cruiser Squadron, 1929–31; Vice-Adm., 1930; Admiralty Representative on League of Nations Advisory Commission, 1932; Second Sea Lord and Chief of Naval Personnel at the Admiralty, 1932–35; Adm., 1935; temp. Chief of Staff, Mediterranean, 1935–36; Commander-in-Chief, Mediterranean, 1936–39; Admiral of the Fleet, 1939. Grand Cross of Royal Order of St Olav; Order of Polonia Restituta. *Clubs:* Athenæum, United Service.

Died 21 Oct. 1943.

POWELL; *see* Baden-Powell.

POWELL, Sir Allan; *see* Powell, Sir G. A.

POWELL, Col Atherton Ffolliott, DSO 1900; late Royal Artillery; *b* 6 Jan. 1858; *s* of Capt. Thomas Ffolliott Powell, formerly of the 16th Lancers, and HM's Commissioner of Prisons for Scotland; *m* 1904, Alice, *d* of Maj. S. H. Powell of Park Hill, King's Lynn; one *s* one *d. Educ:* Cheltenham. Entered army, 1878; Capt., 1886; Major, 1896; served Egyptian Frontier Field Force, 1885–86 (despatches, medal, Khedive's star); North-West Frontier India, 1897–98 (medal 3 clasps); S Africa, 1899–1902 (despatches, Queen's medal 4 clasps, King's medal 2 clasps, DSO); commanded Heavy Brigade at Plymouth, 1906–10; retired, 1909; rejoined Army for temporary service, 7 Oct. 1914. *Address:* The Upper House, Wickham, Hants. *T:* Wickham 2168. *Club:* Army and Navy.

Died 23 Sept. 1941.

POWELL, Maj.-Gen. Sir Charles Herbert, KCB 1917; CB 1908; *b* 23 Oct. 1857; *s* of Capt. W. Wellington Powell, late 9th Foot; *m* 1889, Alice (*d* 1917), *d* of late James Mackenzie of Auchenheglish, Dumbartonshire. *Educ:* private school. Entered army, 1876; Captain, Indian Army, 1887; Maj., 1896; Lt-Col, 1902; Colonel, 1907; Maj.-Gen., 1907; retired, 1919; DAQMG Malakand Field Force, 1897–98; Buner Field Force, 1898; Staff-Officer, China, 1900–01; Brigade Commander, India, 1907–12; raised and commanded Ulster Division of New Army, 1914–15; Commander British Red Cross in Serbia, 1918–19; served Waziristan, 1894–95 (despatches, medal with clasp); NW Frontier, India, 1897–98 (despatches twice, brevet Lt-Col, medal with clasp); China, 1900 (medal). *Address:* The Lower House, Wickham, Hants. *Club:* Army and Navy.

Died 23 Oct. 1943.

POWELL, Brig. Donald, DSO 1938; Indian Army; *b* 21 Oct. 1896; *s* of late Richard John Powell and Alice Alethea Powell, Bellevue, Bedford; unmarried. *Educ:* Bedford School; RMC, Sandhurst. Served North-West Frontier, 1915–16; East Africa, 1916–17 (twice wounded, French Croix de Guerre); North-West Frontier, 1937–39 (despatches, DSO); Brevet Major, 1929; ADC to Governor of Madras, 1919–22; General Staff Officer, India Office, 1932; commanded 1st Battalion 16th Punjab Regiment, 1937–39. *Address:* c/o Grindlay and Co., PO Box No. 93, Bombay. *Club:* Naval and Military.

Died 8 Aug. 1942.

POWELL, Sir (George) Allan, GBE 1944; Kt 1927; CBE 1920; DL; *s* of late R. D. Powell; *m* Jeannie Jack, *d* of Dr W. Marshall of Innellan; one *s. Educ:* Bancroft's School; King's College, London. Barrister-at-law, Gray's Inn; Resident Officer-in-Charge of the Government War Refugees Camp, Earl's Court, with 4000 beds for soldiers and civilians of allied nationalities, 1914–18; Clerk to the Metropolitan Asylums Board 1922–30, organised new Department of Public Assistance for the London County Council, 1930–32; Member Import Duties Advisory Committee, 1932–39; Chairman British Broadcasting Corporation, 1939–46; Member Royal Commission on Food Prices, 1924–25; Night Baking Committee, 1925; Vice-Chairman of the Food Council and Chairman of its Executive Committee, 1925–29; Chairman of the Food Council, 1929–32; Member Committee on Key Industries Duties, 1935; Committee on Industrial Alcohol, 1943; Pres. State Medicine and Industrial Hygiene Section, Public Health Congress, 1933; Chairman Institute of Public Administration Confs., 1934, 1944 and 1946; Chairman, Radio and Cinema Section, British Association Conference, 1943; Mayor of Kensington, 1937–39; Chairman, Briggs Motor Bodies, Ltd; Vice-Pres. Royal Sanitary Institute; Honorary Fellow American Public Health Association; has Orders of Leopold of Belgium, White Eagle of Serbia, and the Médaille de la Reconnaissance Francaise. *Publications:* Four Years in a Refugee Camp; The MAB and its Work, 1867–1930; various addresses and papers for international and national Congresses. *Address:* 34 Kensington Square, W8; Mead Cottage, Ridgeway, Gerrards Cross, Bucks. *Club:* Athenæum.

Died 24 Jan. 1948.

POWELL, Rt Rev. Grandage Edwards, MA Oxon; Assistant Bishop, Diocese of Carlisle, since 1944; *b* 20 Nov. 1882; *s* of Rev. Astell Drayner Powell, Hon. Canon of Manchester, and Annie Edwards; *m* 1913, Madeline Mary Allen; two *s. Educ:* Rugby; University College, Oxford. Curate of Fallow-field, 1906–12; Blackburn Parish Church, 1912–15; Vicar of St Matthew's, W Kensington, 1915–24; Vicar of St Peter's, Leicester, 1924–34; Canon of St Martin's Collegiate Church, Leicester, 1924–26; Hon. Canon of Leicester Cathedral, 1927–34; Rural Dean of Leicester, 1931–34;

Archdeacon of Carlisle and Canon of Carlisle Cathedral, 1934–44; Suffragan Bishop of Penrith, 1939–44. *Address:* The Plains, Wetheral, Carlisle. *T:* Wetheral 159.

Died 5 March 1948.

POWELL, Helena Langhorne; *b* 25 Sept. 1862; *d* of William Powell, Yorkshire and London. *Educ:* Clapham High School; Newnham College, Cambridge. 1st Class Historical Tripos, Cambridge, 1884. Assistant Mistress, Oxford High School, 1885–92; Headmistress, Leeds Girls' High School, 1892–1903; Principal of the Cambridge Training College, 1903–08; Principal of St Mary's College, Paddington, 1909–26; Fellow of the Royal Historical Society. *Publications:* History in Biography Series—James I—James II; Religious Teaching in Secular Schools; Editor of the Bede Histories; Writer of Tudors and Stuarts, vol. iii of series ii in the Bede Histories. *Address:* 127 Vassall Road, SW9.

Died 4 June 1942.

POWELL, Henry Arthur, CMG 1917; MB, ChB, Adelaide; JP; late Commanding Officer No. 2 Australian General Hospital, Wimereux, France; *b* Kadina, South Australia, 31 Jan. 1868; *s* of Charles Bendin Powell of Malvern, SA; *m* 1897, Katie Frances Smith of Yalumba, SA; no *c*. *Educ:* Glenelg Grammar School; Adelaide University. Graduated 1891. Three years surgeon to Adelaide General and Adelaide Children's Hospitals; general practice in Kadina and Wallaroo district for seventeen years; a year in Adelaide; came to Europe with the first hospital units of the Australian Imperial Force, served nearly two years in Egypt, Lemnos and Gallipoli, since then in England and France; Member of the Council of the SA Branch British Medical Association; twice Mayor of Kadina, etc. *Recreations:* tennis, golf, shooting, etc. *Clubs:* Adelaide, Adelaide.

Died June 1944.

POWELL, Col Henry Lloyd, DSO 1919; DL, JP Hants; Colonel Royal Artillery, retired; *b* 1866; *s* of Thomas Powell, Coldra, Newport, Mon; *m* 1889, Mildred Eileen, *d* of Lt-Col P. Paget, Scots Guards of Brightwell, Farnham, Surrey; one *s* two *d*. *Educ:* Harrow. Lieut RA, 1885; served South African War, 1900 (medal 4 clasps, despatches); European War, 1914–18 (DSO and three medals, despatches 3 times); retired from RA, 1902; commanded a TFA Brigade, 1913–19; served in India and Mesopotamia; India, 1914–16; Mesopotamia, 1916–19; retired, 1919. *Recreation:* shooting. *Address:* Valetta, Emsworth, Hants. *T:* Emsworth 86. *Club:* Army and Navy.

Died 29 Aug. 1941.

POWELL, Gp Captain (temp.) John Alexander, DSO 1941; OBE 1941; Royal Air Force; *b* Maidstone, 1 July 1909; *s* of Captain W. B. Powell, now of St Andrews, Jamaica; *m* 1935, Mary Felicity, *d* of late Colonel L. T. Ashworth, Hambleton Hall, Oakham; one *s* one *d*. *Educ:* abroad; privately; RAF College, Cranwell. Cranwell, 1927–28; Flying Officer, 1931; Flight Lieut, 1935; Squadron Leader, 1938; Wing Commander, 1940; temp. Group Captain, 1942; loaned to Govt of S Rhodesia, 1937–40; served War of 1939–45 (despatches). *Recreations:* hunting, squash, polo. *Address:* Beggars' Bush, South Brent, Devon. *Club:* Royal Air Force.

Died 18 Aug. 1944.

POWELL, Rev. Morgan Jones, DD; Canon of Llandaff, 1922; *b* 27 June 1863; *s* of late Alderman Thomas Powell, The Elms, Swansea; *m* Enid Annie, *d* of late Robert Margrave, Llanelly, Carms.; no *c*. *Educ:* Bishop Gore's Grammar School, Swansea; Balliol College, Oxford. Deacon, 1887; Priest, 1888; served Curacies in Tredegar, Mon, Brecon, and Llanelly; Rector of Llanfrynach, Breconshire, 1901–08; Vicar of Aberystwyth, Cardiganshire, 1908–18; Vicar of Cardiff, 1918–31; Rector of Peterston-super-Ely, 1931–38; Rural Dean of Cardiff, 1919–31; Rural Dean of Llanbadarnfawr, 1909–18; Proctor in Convocation for

Diocese of St David's, 1907–18; Member of Governing Body, Church in Wales; Member of Court of Governors of University College of South Wales and Monmouthshire; Representative of Province of Wales on British Council of the World Alliance for promoting International Friendship through the Churches, 1928–35. *Recreations:* fishing, bicycling. *Address:* 30 Goring Road, Llanelly, Carmarthenshire.

Died 16 March 1947.

POWELL, Maj.-Gen. Sidney Henry, CB 1915; *b* 1 June 1866; *s* of Vice-Admiral R. A. Powell, CB; *m* 1919, Mary Alison, *widow* of Maj. Edward Molyneux, CIE, DSO, *d* of T. H. W. Knolles of Oatlands, Co. Cork; one *d*. Entered RE 1884; Col 1913; employed with Egyptian Army, 1901–03; General Staff Officer, 1st grade, India, 1910; served 1st and 2nd Miranzai Expeditions, 1891 (despatches; medal with clasp); NW Frontier, India, 1897–98 (medal with clasp); European War, France, in charge of signals Indian Corps, 1914; in charge of signals 1st Army, 1915; Chief Engineer XIII Corps, 1916; Chief Engineer GHQ Home Forces, 1918–19 (despatches, CB); retired, 1923, with hon. rank of Maj.-Gen.; Col Comdt of Indian Signal Corps, 1934–36. *Address:* Garth House, 17 The Beach, Walmer, Kent. *T:* Deal 277.

Died 15 Dec. 1945.

POWER, Albert G., RHA; *b* 1883; *s* of Mary Atkins and Henry Power, Dublin; *m* 1904, Agnes, 2nd *d* of James and Ann Kelly, Dublin; five *s* three *d*. *Works:* Busts of Lord Mayor McSwiney, President Griffiths, James Stephens, W. B. Yeats; marble bust of Dr Mannix, Archbishop of Melbourne; recumbent figure of late Most Rev. Dr Walsh, Archbishop of Dublin; commissioned to do bust of late Sir Hugh Lane, and figure of Padraic O'Conaire, poet. *Recreation:* angling. *Address:* 18 Geraldine Street, Dublin.

Died 10 July 1945.

POWER, Sir D'Arcy, KBE 1919; Consulting Surgeon and Archivist to St Bartholomew's Hospital; Hunterian Trustee Royal College of Surgeons of England; Hon. Librarian Royal College of Surgeons of England; Foreign Corresponding Member of Academy of Medicine, Paris; Hon. Fellow of American Surgical Association, and of Medical and Chirurgical Society of Buda-Pesth; Hon. Fellow Interstate Postgraduate Medical Association of North America; Corresponding Member of the Dutch Association for the History of Medicine, Physics and Mathematics; President of the Bibliographical Society, 1926–28; The Samuel Pepys Club, 1925–28; President of the Section of Comparative Medicine, Royal Society of Medicine, 1926–28; President of the Section of Surgery, the British Medical Association, 1926–27; President d'honneur at Geneva Congress of International Society of the History of Medicine and of Société Internationale de Chirurgie, 1940; Visiting Lecturer at the Johns Hopkins University, Baltimore, 1930–31; a Manager of the Metropolitan Asylums Board (Min. H), 1922–27; Lieutenant-Colonel RAMC (T); *b* London, 11 Nov. 1855; *e s* of Henry Power, FRCS (Eng.); *m* 1883, Eleanor (*d* 1923), *y d* of George Haynes Fosbroke of Bidford, Warwickshire; one *s*. *Educ:* Merchant Taylors' School, London; New and Exeter Colleges, Oxford. BA with 1st class honours in Natural Science, 1878; MA 1881; MB 1882; FRCS (Eng.), 1883; Hon. FRFPS Glasgow, 1932; Hon. Fellow Royal Australasian College of Surgeons, 1935; Hon. Fellow Royal Society of Medicine, 1937. Formerly Examiner in Surgery, RAMC, and at Univs of Oxford, Cambridge, Durham, Belfast, Nat. Univ. of Ireland, and at the RCS (Eng.); Hunterian Orator RCS (1924); Mitchell Banks Memorial Lecturer (Liverpool), 1933; formerly Member of Council of Society of Antiquaries; Member of the Executive Committee of the Imperial Cancer Research Fund; Ex-President of the Medical Society of London, of the Harveian Soc. of London, and of the Section of the History of Medicine, Royal Society of Medicine. *Publications:* A Mirror for Surgeons, 1940;

Selected Writings, 1931; various contributions on war surgery, syphilis, cancer, intestinal obstruction, the surgical diseases of children and the History of Medicine. *Address:* 10a Chandos Street, Cavendish Square, W1. *T:* Langham 4040. *Club:* Oxford and Cambridge.

Died 18 May 1941.

POWER, Sir John (Cecil), 1st Bt *cr* 1924; *b* 21 Dec. 1870; *y s* of late William Taylor Power, Eldon, Co. Down; *m* Mabel Katherine Louisa (*d* 1945), *d* of late J. Hartley Perks, JP, Bramham Gardens, SW; two *s* three *d*. MP (C) Wimbledon, 1924–45. Founder Institute of Historical Research; Founder Royal Institute of International Affairs and Hon. Treasurer, 1920–43; Hon. Treasurer British Council; Director Royal Insurance Company, 1934–49; Member of Cttee Royal Humane Soc.; Member of Executive, Travel and Industrial Development Assoc of Great Britain and Ireland. *Publications:* articles on politics, foreign affairs and travel. *Recreations:* golf, music. *Heir: s* Ivan McLannahan Cecil Power, *b* 29 Nov. 1903. *Address:* Yeatton House, Hordle, Hants. *T:* Milford-on-Sea 358; Villa Fressinet, Grasse (AM), France. *Clubs:* Carlton, Bath.

Died 5 June 1950.

POWER, Mrs (John) Wyse; *b* Baltinglass, Co. Wicklow; *d* of Eamonn ō Toole and Mary Norton; *m* John Wyse Power, journalist; one *s* one *d*. In elected public positions since 1902; Poor Law Guardian, Governor Mental Hospital, Councillor of Dublin's Corporation and Chairman of its Committee of Public Health and Finance; Member of Senate of Saorstát Eireann, 1922–36. *Address:* 15 Eailsfort Terrace, Dublin.

Died 5 Jan. 1941.

POWER, Sir William (Richard), Kt 1937; *b* 8 Feb. 1861; *s* of Joseph Power, South Hackney and Colyton, Devon; *m* 1886, Cornelia Frances (*d* 1944), *e d* of William Clarke Ellison, Walthamstow; no *c*. *Educ:* Richmond House School, Hackney. Mayor of Hackney, 1928–29. *Address:* York House, Buckden, Hunts.

Died 10 June 1945.

POWER, Mrs Wyse; *see* Power, Mrs J. W.

POWERSCOURT, 8th Viscount *cr* 1743; **Mervyn Richard Wingfield,** KP 1916; MVO 1902; Baron Wingfield, 1743; Baron Powerscourt, (UK), 1885; late Irish Guards; HML Co. Wicklow, 1910; JP Co. Dublin; *b* 16 July 1880; *e s* of 7th Viscount Powerscourt and Lady Julia Coke (*d* 1931), *e d* of 2nd Earl of Leicester, KG; *S* father, 1904; *m* 1903, Sybil (*d* 1946), 2nd *d* of Walter Pleydell-Bouverie; one *s* one *d*. Protestant. Liberal Unionist. Owns 38,725 acres, Co. Wicklow; at Powerscourt, pictures by Mireveldt; Philippe de Champaigne; Morland; C. Jansens; Mytens; Wright of Derby, etc. *Recreations:* mechanics, sporting trophies, etc. *Heir: s* Hon. Mervyn Patrick Wingfield. *Address:* Powerscourt, Enniskerry, Co. Wicklow, Ireland. *Clubs:* White's; Royal Yacht Squadron, Cowes.

Died 21 March 1947.

POWLES, Lewis Charles, MA, RBA; landscape and portrait painter; *b* 1860; 2nd *s* of Rev. H. C. Powles, MA, Rector of Ashleworth, Gloucestershire, and Emily, *d* of Rev. Allen Cooper, MA, Vicar of St Mark's, N Audley Street; *m* 1905, Isabel Grace, *y d* of late Rev. Harry Wingfield, Rutland; two *d*. *Educ:* Haileybury; Christ Church, Oxon. Has exhibited pictures in the various International Exhibitions, Royal Academy, etc.; represented in the permanent collections at the Victoria and Albert Museum, Imperial War Museum, Hull, Huddersfield, Brighton, Hastings, Eastbourne, etc.; Member of the Society for Psychical Research since 1890 and actively interested in the subject. *Recreation:* formerly fencing. *Address:* Little Cliff, Rye, Sussex. *T:* Rye 19. *Club:* Authors'.

Died 6 July 1942.

POYNDER, Lt-Col Frederic Sinclair, DSO 1938; MVO 1921; OBE 1922; MC; late 9th Gurkha Rifles; *b* 1893; *s* of Major C. E. Poynder; *m* 1930, Grace Muriel, *y d* of J. F. Campbell, late Master of the Royal Mint, Perth, Western Australia; one *s*. *Educ:* Wellington College. Served European War, 1914–19 (wounded, despatches twice); Afghanistan, 1919 (MC); Waziristan, 1923; NWF India, 1930; Waziristan, 1937 (DSO); ADC to Duke of Connaught on his visit to India, 1921 (MVO); to Prince of Wales on his visit to India, 1921–22 (OBE); retired, 1938; 1st class Chevalier of Order of Sword of Sweden. *Club:* United Service.

Died 23 March 1943.

POYNTON, Arthur Blackburne, MA; Hon. DLit; *b* 28 June 1867; 4th *s* of late Rev. F. J. Poynton, MA, Rector of Kelston, Bath; *m* 1896, Mary, *e d* of late J. Y. Sargent, MA, Fellow of Hertford College; two *s* three *d*. *Educ:* Marlborough College; Balliol College, Oxford (Scholar). Hertford and Craven Scholar; Fellow of Hertford College, 1889–94; Fellow of University College, Oxford, 1894–1935, Bursar, 1900–35, Master, 1935–37, Hon. Fellow, 1937. Senior Proctor, 1902; Curator of Bodleian Library, 1912–37; Public Orator in the University of Oxford, 1925–32; Chevalier of the Legion of Honour; Order of Astaur (Afghanistan), Third Class. *Publications:* Cicero, Pro Milone, 2nd ed. 1902; Flosculi Græci, 1920; Flosculi Latini, 1922; Isocrates; a public lecture in Greek, 1928. *Address:* 1 Polstead Road, Oxford.

Died 8 Oct. 1944.

POYNTON, Frederic John, MD, FRCP London; Consulting Physician to University College Hospital and to the Hospital for Sick Children, Great Ormond Street; Capt. (retired) RAMC (T); Fellow of the Philharmonic Society; Member of Council of Marlborough College; *b* 1869; *s* of the late Rev. F. J. Poynton, Rector of Kelston, Bath; *m* 1904, Alice Constance, *y d* of Sir John W. P. Campbell-Orde, 3rd Bart; one *s* one *d*. *Educ:* Marlborough Coll.; University College, Bristol; St Mary's Hospital, London (scholar). Consulting Physician to Heart Hospital, West Wickham; Heart Hospital, Lancing and Winford Orthopædic Hospital; National Children Adoption Assoc.; Dawson Williams Prize for advance of study of children's diseases in the British Empire, 1930; Hon. Member Cardiological Society of Great Britain and Ireland; Hon. Fellow Royal Institute of Public Health and Hygiene; President British Pædiatric Association, 1931; Senior Censor, RCP, 1930; Bradshaw, Lettsomian and Harben lecturer upon Rheumatism in the young and its prevention. *Publications:* Researches on Rheumatism; Heart Disease and Aneurysm; Heart Disease in Childhood; Recent Advances in the Study of Rheumatism; Report to International League against Rheumatism on the Social factors in the Causation of Rheumatism in Great Britain, 1938; Kelston: a village in Somerset. *Recreations:* cricket (Marlborough XI, 1886; Somerset XI, 1891–96); hockey (Middlesex County XI, 1894). *Address:* 24 Combe Park, Weston, Bath. *T:* Bath 7517.

Died 29 Oct. 1943.

POYSER, Sir Kenneth Elliston, Kt 1941; DSO 1917; Legal Adviser in Dominions Office and Colonial Office since 1941; *s* of late A. S. Poyser, Barrister-at-law; *m* 1918, E. May, *d* of H. M. Robinson, Penkull, Stoke-on-Trent; one *d*. Served European War, 1914–18 (despatches, DSO); Attorney-General, Uganda, 1928–33; Puisne Judge, Ceylon, 1933–39; Chief Justice, Federated Malay States, 1939–41. *Address:* Westwood, Haslemere, Surrey. *Clubs:* Travellers', Thatched House.

Died 6 June 1943.

PRADHAN, Sir Govindrao Balwantrao, Kt 1931; BA, LLB, JP; *b* May 1874; *s* of Mr Balwant Atmaram Pradhan; *m* Ramabai, *d* of Mr P. B. Pradhan, retired, Assistant Engineer. *Educ:* BJ School, Thana; Elphinstone College and Government Law College, Bombay.

Practised as lawyer at Thana; Public Prosecutor, Kolaba, 1907; resigned, 1920: for twenty years a member of the Thana Municipality, for several years its Vice-President, and for seven years its elected President: member of District Local Board, Thana, for three years: was one of the Directors of the Thana District Cooperative Bank; President, Thana District Boy Scouts; elected to the Bombay Legislative Council in 1923, and re-elected in 1926 by the Thana and Bombay Suburban Districts Non-Mahomedan Rural Constituency; Minister, Government of Bombay, 1927; Finance Member of the Government of Bombay, 1928. *Address:* Balwant Bag, Thana, India.

Died 7 March 1943.

PRAGA, Alfred, RBA, late President Society of Miniaturists; late Member of Council, Royal Society of British Artists; a Vice President The Imperial Arts League; *b* Liverpool; *m* 1891, Teresa (*d* 1920), *g d* of late Sir Francis Knowles, Bt; one *s*. *Educ:* Art School in connection with the Science and Art Department of South Kensington; Antwerp and Paris. Was instrumental in reviving the art of miniature painting in England, and in conjunction with the late Lord Ronald Gower and Dr Lumsden Propert, founded the first Society for the promotion of Miniature Painting in 1895. *Works:* Father, I have Sinned, 1893; The Heiress, 1895; A Favourite of the Sultan, 1894; Sorrow and Sun, 1894; portraits of Mdme Sarah Grand and Dr J. Lumsden Propert, 1896; portrait of Li Hung Chang, 1898. Miniatures and small portraits:—Portraits of Princess Henry of Pless, The Earl and Countess of Egmont, The late Lady Glenesk, Sir Henry Irving, Earl Spencer, Lord Alverstone, 1902, Bishop of Nottingham, 1903; Portrait of King Edward VII, commissioned by Sir William Treloar for the Savage Club, 1910, Princess Beatrice (RA 1912); Lady Lavery (Royal Academy, 1922); Princess Marie Louise, 1923 (for the Queen's Doll's House); Miss Evelyn Laye as Mdme de Pompadour (RA 1924); Lady Lavery and Miss Barbara Hoffe (Paris Salon, 1924); Madame Sarah Grand (Mayoress of Bath), painted in 1896 and purchased by the Mayor of Bath in 1928 for the city; The Marchesa Malacrida, Royal Academy, 1928; Portrait of Anna Pavlova for Scala Museum, Milan; Ruby, Royal Academy, 1932. *Publications:* The Renaissance of Miniature Painting (Magazine of Art); Phil May as I knew him (Art Chronicle); Art Editor Literary Pageant 1911; occasional contributor to other periodicals. *Address:* Flat 4, 3 Roland Gardens, S Kensington, SW7. *T:* Kensington 7689. *Clubs:* Savage, Chelsea Arts.

Died 25 Feb. 1949.

PRAIN, Lt-Col Sir David, Kt 1912; CMG 1912; CIE 1906; MA, MB, LLD, FRSE, FLS, FRS, FZS, Hon. MRIA; Carnegie Trustee for Universities of Scotland since 1917; *b* Scotland, 11 July 1857; *m* 1887, Margaret (*d* 1942), *d* of Rev. W. Thomson, MA, Belhelvie. *Educ:* Parish School, Fettercairn; Grammar School, Aberdeen; University, Aberdeen and University, Edinburgh. Demonstrator of Anatomy, College of Surgeons, Edinburgh, 1882–83, and University of Aberdeen, 1883–84; entered Indian Medical Service, 1884; Curator, Calcutta Herbarium, 1887–98; Professor of Botany, Medical College, Calcutta, 1895–1905; Director Botanical Survey of India and Superintendent Royal Botanic Garden, Calcutta, 1898–1905; Director of Royal Botanic Gardens, Kew, 1905–22; Director of Forest Products Research, 1922–25; Chairman Advisory Council, Plant and Animal Products, Imperial Institute, 1926–35; Trustee of the Indian Museum, 1898–1907 and of the British Museum, 1924–36; Secretary Board of Scientific Advice for India, 1903–04; Fellow University of Calcutta, 1900–05; Council Asiatic Society of Bengal, vice-pres., 1904; Council Linnean Society, vice-pres., 1906–10, president, 1916–19; Council British Association, 1907–14; vice-president, 1931; president Botanical Section, 1909, President Conference of Delegates, 1932; Council Royal Society, 1908–10;

treasurer, 1919–29; Council John Innes Horticultural Institution, chairman, 1909–43; Council Royal Horticultural Society, 1916–18, vice-president, 1919–43; Council Ray Society, 1916–30, vice-president, 1917–20, 1924–27, 1930–31, 1937–38, treasurer, 1932–37; Council Zoological Society, 1923–27, 1928–32; Barclay Medal Asiatic Society of Bengal, 1909 and 1942; Victoria Medal, Royal Society of Arts, 1925; Veitch Medal, Royal Horticultural Society, 1912; Albert Medal, Royal Society of Arts, 1925; Veitch Medal, Royal Horticultural Society, 1932; Linnean Medal, Linnean Society, 1935; Bruhl Medal, Asiatic Society of Bengal, 1939; pres. Association of Economic Biologists, 1919–21; Gilbert White Fellowship, 1921–24; Imperial Botanical Conference, 1924; Hon. Life-President, Imperial College of Tropical Agriculture, Trinidad, 1938. *Publications:* numerous monographs and papers, mainly botanical. *Address:* The Well Farm, Whyteleafe, Surrey. *Club:* Athenæum.

Died 16 March 1944.

PRANCE, Basil Camden, CIE 1935; OBE; *b* 23 Jan. 1884; *s* of late Rev. L. N. Prance, Rector of Stapleford Tawney, Essex; *m* 1935, Margaret Hope, *d* of late John Tolmie, Edinburgh; one *s* two *d*. *Educ:* Rugby; Christ Church, Oxford. Indian Civil Service, 1907–24. *Address:* Wood End, Toddington, nr Winchcombe, Glos. *T:* Toddington 48.

Died 5 July 1948.

PRATT, Edward Millard; late ICS; *b* 29 Aug. 1865; *s* of late Edward Pratt, Bombay; *m* 1913, Gertrude, *d* of James Lord; one *s*. *Educ:* Dulwich College; University College, London. Entered ICS, 1886; Assist Collector and Magistrate, 1887; Judicial Assist to Political Agent, Kathiawar, 1895; Judge and Sessions Judge, 1896; Remembrancer of Legal Affairs, 1905; Judicial Commissioner of Sind, 1910; Puisne Judge, High Court, Bombay, 1918–25; retired, 1925. *Publications:* Joint author Mulla and Pratt's Indian Stamp Act; editor Mulla's Civil Procedure Code, Mulla's Transfer of Property Act and Mulla's Registration Act. *Recreation:* reading. *Address:* Greenhedges, Maidenhead. *T:* Maidenhead 1667.

Died 28 June 1949.

PRATT, Frederick Greville, CSI 1925; *b* 4 Dec. 1869; 4th *s* of late Edward Pratt, of Indian Salt Revenue Service; *m* 1903, Enid Blanche Malet St Lo; three *s* one *d*. *Educ:* Dulwich College; Hertford College, Oxford. Entered Indian Civil Service, 1890; Collector and District Magistrate in various districts of the Bombay Presidency; Settlement Commissioner and Director of Land Records, 1909; Commissioner, Northern Division Bombay Presidency, and Member, Bombay Legislative Council, 1915–25. *Address:* 26 Forest View Road, E Grinstead, Sussex. *T:* E Grinstead 468.

Died 6 Oct. 1949.

PREECE, Engr Vice-Adm. Sir George, KCB 1938; CB 1933; *m* 1910, Dorothy Mary Lord. Served European War, 1914–16 (despatches); Professor of Marine Engineering, RN College, Greenwich, 1923–27; Fleet Engineer Officer, HMS Nelson, 1927–28; Eng. Rear-Admiral, 1930; Engineer Vice-Admiral, 1936; Engineer-in-Chief of the Fleet, Admiralty, 1936–42; retired, 1942. *Address:* 11 Stratheden Road, Blackheath, SE3.

Died 5 Jan. 1945.

PREEDY, His Honour Judge Digby C.; *see* Cotes-Preedy.

PREEDY, Kenelm; Recorder of Shrewsbury since 1935; Barrister-at-Law; 2nd *s* of late Rev. Digby H. Cotes-Preedy, Vicar of King's Norton, sometime Minor Canon of Worcester; *m* Irene, *d* of Vincent Robinson, Newark, Notts; one *s*. Called to Bar, Middle Temple, 1904; Bencher, 1940; Oxford Circuit; served European War, 1915–18; represented Government of Palestine in enquiry into Palestine Riots, 1929. *Recreations:* fishing, shooting, and golf. *Address:* 6 Queens' Gate Gardens, SW7. *T:* Western 0129; Bradstone Manor, Bradstone, Devon; 1 Hare Court, EC4. *T:* Central 7731.

Died 4 May 1945.

PRENDERGAST, Hon. James Emile Pierre, MA, LLD; *b* Quebec City, 22 March 1858; *s* of James Prendergast, Barrister, and Emelie Gauvreau; *m* 1886, Olivina, *d* of late François Mondar, Joliette, PQ; four *s* seven *d*. *Educ:* Quebec Seminary; Laval Univ. Advocate, 1881; MPP La Verandeye, 1885–86–1888; Woodlands, 1889; St Boniface, 1892–96; Provincial Secretary, 1888–89; County Court Judge, Winnipeg, 1897–1902; Judge, Supreme Court, North-Western Territory, 1902; Judge, Supreme Court, Saskatchewan, 1907; Judge, Court of King's Bench, Manitoba, 1910; Puisne Judge, Court of Appeal, Manitoba, 1922–30; Chief Justice of Manitoba, 1930–44. Roman Catholic. *Address:* Winnipeg, Manitoba.

Died 18 April 1945.

PRENDERGAST, Adm. Sir Robert (John), KCB 1920; CB 1919; *b* 9 July 1864; *m* 1905, Bertha Janet, *o c* of late Capt. John Binnie Mackenzie, 1st Royal Scots Regt. Entered RN 1877; Capt. 1903; Rear-Admiral, 1914; Vice-Admiral, 1920; ADC to the King, 1913–14; served European War, 1914–18; Rear-Adm., Scapa (Orkneys), 1916–19; Vice-Adm. commanding Orkneys and Shetlands, 1919–20; retired, 1919; Admiral, 1924. *Address:* Meads House, Eastbourne. *T:* Eastbourne 271. *Clubs:* (Hon.) Royal Yacht Squadron, Cowes.

Died 14 May 1946.

PRESCOTT, Charles John, MA (Oxon); DD (Emory, US); Minister of the Methodist Church of Australasia; retired; *b* Bridport, Dorset, 9 June 1857; *s* of Rev. J. J. Prescott; *m* Annie Elizabeth, *d* of W. P. Price, Cardiff; two *s* two *d*. *Educ:* Kingswood School, Bath; Worcester Coll., Oxford (Exhibitioner); Handsworth Theological Institution, Birmingham. Entered ministry of Australian Methodist Church, 1882; minister at Parramatta, NSW, and tutor to theological students, 1883–85; Headmaster of Burwood Ladies' College, 1886–99; Headmaster of Newington College, Stanmore, Sydney, 1900–31; Acting Master Wesley College, Sydney University, 1935; Acting Principal Annesley Girls' College, 1937; President of NSW Methodist Conference, 1910; President at various times of Teachers' Guild of NSW, Headmasters' Association of NSW and Teachers' Central Registry; Chaplain to Australian Forces, 1914–33; Acting Senior Chaplain for Methodist Church, NSW, 1914–19 (home duties); Member of Bursary Endowment Board, 1915–45; Advocate of Church Re-union; Member of Executive Committee (4) of Joint Australian Council of Churches contemplating Reunion; Member of Council of Royal Empire Society (Sydney Branch). *Publications:* Official Addresses; The Romance of School; Matters for Methodists; Methodist Churchmanship; contributor to local Press. *Address:* Exminster, Victoria Square, Ashfield, Sydney, NSW, Australia. *T:* UA 2444.

Died 13 June 1946.

PRESCOTT, Mrs Cyril, (Caroline Lowthian); *b* Penrith; *d* of late Isaac Lowthian; *m* 1889, Cyril Arthur Prescott, *y s* of late Chancellor of Carlisle; three *s*. *Educ:* at home; studied music under Oscar Beringer for a time. First valse Marguerite; made name with Venetia and Myosotis valses; latest valse, Skating; best known song, Gates of the West; last song, By Celia's Arbour. *Publications:* Bittersweet, Lullaby; Auf Wiedersehen and Saionara; Beauty's Daughters, and many others; Mother Hubbard; Black and Tan Polkas; La Contadina; Cobwebs; Alfresco; In the Moonlight (dances), etc. etc. *Address:* 29 Cholmeley Park, Highgate, N6. *T:* Mountview 1377.

Died 5 Sept. 1943.

PRESCOTT, Sir George (Lionel Lawson Bagot), 5th Bt *cr* 1794; late Capt. 2nd Life Guards; *b* 5 Oct. 1875; *e s* of 4th Bt and Louisa Franklyn, *d* of Lionel Lawson; *S* father, 1894; *m* 1932, Mrs Elizabeth Hughes Melcer. Served South African War, 1900; European War, 1914; Military Secretary to Lord Lieutenant of Ireland, 1916; served Northern Russian Expeditionary Force, 1918. Owns about 4000 acres. *Heir: b* Charles William Beeston, OBE, *b* 8 April 1877. *Address:* 3 Mansfield Street, W1. *T:* Langham 4233. *Clubs:* Turf, St James's.

Died 20 June 1942.

PRESCOTT, Col Sir William (Henry), 1st Bt *cr* 1938; Kt 1922; CBE 1920; DL; MInstCE; MIMechE; Hon. Col 1st AA Divisional Signals (TA) RCS; Barrister-at-law (Gray's Inn); Fellow of the Royal Society of Arts; Chairman, Metropolitan Water Board, 1928–40; Chairman, Lee Conservancy Board; Chairman, Lee Conservancy Catchment Board; Member of the Lee Valley Drainage Commission; Past President British Waterworks Association (Inc.); Member, Government Water Advisory Committee to the Ministry of Health; Member Government Roads Advisory Committee to the Ministry of Transport; Past Grand Deacon, United Grand Lodge of England; Past Master, Worshipful Company of Paviors: Liveryman, Worshipful Company of Glaziers; Freeman of the City of London; High Sheriff of Middlesex, 1929; and of Cambridgeshire and Huntingdonshire, 1938; Alderman of the Middlesex County Council, Chairman, 1936–37; Chairman of the East Middlesex Drainage Committee; Represents Middlesex County Council on the Metropolitan Water Board; Chairman, Edmonton Petty Sessional Division of County of Middlesex, 1936–42; Governor, Tottenham Grammar School; Governor of the Prince of Wales' General Hospital (Tottenham); Past Chairman of Tottenham Polytechnic, Girls' High School, County School, and Grammar School; MP (CU) North Tottenham, Dec. 1918–22; Consulting Civil Engineer; *b* 1874; *s* of John Prescott; *m* 1898, Bessie Smith (*d* 1940), *d* of late Mark Stanley, of Ambleside; two *s* two *d*. *Educ:* privately. Commanded the 222nd Field Co. RE (33rd Division RE), BEF (European War); invalided home, 1915. *Heir: s* Richard Stanley, *b* 26 Jan. 1899. *Address:* The Chestnuts, Godmanchester, Hunts. *T:* Huntingdon 175.

Died 15 June 1945.

PRESTON, Arthur, CBE 1919; *b* 18 Dec. 1864; *γ s* of late Joseph Thomas Preston, Finchley; *m* 1910, Sylvia Mary (*d* 1944), *d* of Col Augustus Le Messurier, CIE, RE; one *s* one *d*. *Educ:* Caversham. Went into business in London, Alex. Lawrie and Co., East India Merchants, 1882; went to Calcutta, Balmer Lawrie and Co. 1885; became a partner and retired in 1913; Hon. Secretary, Indian Soldiers' Fund, London, 1916–18; Hon. Secretary, Royal Surrey County Hospital, Guildford, 1916–30. *Recreations:* golf, music. *Address:* Barmoor, 18 Poyle Rd, Guildford. *T:* Guildford 5121.

Died 9 Dec. 1948.

PRESTON, Sir Frederick George Panizzi, KBE 1918; JP; *e s* of late R. T. Preston and Mrs Preston of Hayes Court, Kent; *m* Ethel Mary (*d* 1941), *d* of Rev. Thomas Peters, MA; one *s* one *d*. Executed special Mission for HM Government in Italy and Spain, 1917; High Sheriff for the County of Wilts, 1921; Patron of one living. *Address:* Landford Manor, Salisbury. *TA:* Landford. *T:* Earldoms 226. *Clubs:* Carlton, Athenæum; Royal Yacht Squadron (Cowes).

Died 18 July 1949.

PRESTON, Sir Walter Reuben, Kt 1921; Chairman of Platt Bros and Co. (Holdings) Ltd and of Stone-Platt Engineering Company; President of Textile Machinery Makers Ltd; Director of Midland Bank Ltd; *b* 20 Sept. 1875; *s* of late R. T. Preston and of Mrs Preston of Hayes Court, Kent; *m* 1900, Ella Margaret, *e d* of Huson Morris; three *s*. *Educ:* Bedford Grammar School. Master of Avon Vale Foxhounds, 1914–18; largely interested in engineering; contested (U) East St Pancras, Jan. 1910, and Stepney, Dec. 1910; MP (U) Mile End, 1918–23; Cheltenham, 1928–37. *Recreations:* yachting and hunting. *Address:* Tetbury, Glos. *Clubs:* Turf, Carlton; Royal Yacht Squadron, Cowes.

Died 6 July 1946.

PRESTON, William; JP for Borough of Walsall; Managing Director of William Sanders & Co., Wednesbury Ltd, Manufacturing Electrical Engineers; *b* Feb. 1874; *m* 1907, Lilly Swinfen Sanders. *Educ:* Walsall Grammar School; Weston School, Bath. MP (U) Walsall, 1924–29. *Recreations:* golf, cricket, and interested in all sports. *Address:* Gorway, Walsall. *T:* Walsall 3990. *Club:* Constitutional.

Died 22 Nov. 1941.

PRESTON, Lt-Col William John Phaelim, DSO 1916; OBE 1919; late 97th Deccan Infantry, Indian Army; *b* 11 June 1873; *s* of late Surg.-Gen. A. F. Preston, KHP, AMS of Co. Meath; *m* 1912, Ina, *e surv. d* of late Rt Hon. Sir Christopher Nixon, 1st Bt, PC, MD, Vice-Chancellor of the National University of Ireland; one *s.* *Educ:* St Helen's College, Southsea; RMC, Sandhurst. Gazetted to 2nd Batt. Middlesex Regt 1892; Kalat Expedition, 1893; joined Indian Army, 1896; served European War in Mesopotamia in temporary and full command of the 97th Deccan Infantry (severely wounded, despatches, DSO); Afghanistan and Indian Frontier, 1919; with Baluchistan Field Force; retired from the Service, 1922. *Recreations:* music, tennis, golf. *Address:* C/o Lloyds Bank, King's Branch, 6 Pall Mall, SW1. *Club:* Roehampton.

Died 18 Jan. 1943.

PRETORIUS, Major Philip Jacobus, CMG 1918; DSO 1916; late MLA, South Africa. Served East Africa, 1914–18 (despatches, DSO CMG).

Died 24 Nov. 1945.

PREVITÉ-ORTON, Charles William, LittD, FBA 1929; Fellow of St John's College, Cambridge; *b* 16 Jan. 1877; *s* of late Rev. William Previté Orton; *m* 1913, Ellery Swaffield, *o d* of late Rev. J. S. Orton; one *d.* *Educ:* Stoneygate School, Leicester; St John's College, Cambridge. BA 1908; MA 1912; LittD 1928; First Class, Historical Tripos, Part I, 1907, Part II, 1908; Gladstone Prizeman, 1907; Members' Prizeman (English Essay), 1909; Scholar of St John's College, 1907–09; Fellow of St John's College, 1911–17 and 1925. Librarian of St John's College till 1937; FRHistS; Joint Editor of Cambridge Medieval History; Joint Editor of the English Historical Review, 1925–26; Editor, 1926–38; Prof. of Medieval Hist., Cambridge Univ., 1937–42. *Publications:* Political Satire in English Poetry; Early History of the House of Savoy; Outlines of Medieval History; The Defensor Pacis of Marsilius of Padua; Opera Inedita TL de Frulovisiis; History of Europe, 1198–1378; contributions to the Cambridge History of English Literature, The Cambridge Medieval History, Proc. British Academy, and the English Historical Review, etc. *Address:* 55 Bateman Street, and St John's College, Cambridge. *T:* Cambridge 3766.

Died 11 March 1947.

PREVOST, Francis; *see* Battersby, H. F. P.

PREVOST, Marcel; Member, French Academy, 1909; Grand Officier de la Légion d'Honneur; Croix de guerre; *b* Paris, 1862. *Educ:* Seminary, Orleans; Mgr Dupanloup; Jesuit Schools; Bordeaux and Paris. Entered Ecole Polytechnic, 1882; civil engineer in State tobacco factories to 1890. *Publications:* Le Scorpion; Chonchette; Confession d'un Amant, 1890; Les Demi-Vierges; Le Jardin Secret; Les Vierges Fortes: Frédérique; Lea; Lettres de Femmes; Lettres à Françoise; La Princesse d'Erininge; L'accordeur aveugle; Monsieur et Madame Moloch; La Fausse Bourgeoise; Les Anges gardiens, 1913, etc.

Produced on the stage: Les Demi-Vierges (3 acts), L'Abbé Pierre (1 act); La Plus Faible (4 acts), Pierre et Thérèse (4 acts); Les Anges gardiens (4 acts); L'Adjudant Benôit; D'un Poste de Commandement, 1918; La Nuit finira, Mon cher Tommy; Nouvelles Lettres à Françoise; Sa Maîtresse et Moi; La Retraite ardente; Voici ton Maître; L'Américain; Marie-des-Angoisses; Fébronie; Clarisse et sa fille; la Mort des Ormeaux; l'homme Vierge, 1929. *Address:* 49 rue Vineuse, Paris. *T:* Passy 85.08; Château de la Roche, par Vianne (Lot-et-Garonne); Villa Angustias, Aix-les-Thermes (Ariège).

Died 8 April 1941.

PRICE, Hon. Brig.-Gen. Bartholomew George, CB 1918; CMG 1917; DSO 1900; *b* 7 May 1870; *s* of Dr Bartholomew Price, Master of Pembroke, Oxon; *m* 1919, Joan, *d* of late Sir Walter Mytton Colvin; one *s.* *Educ:* Winchester; Christ Church, Oxford. Entered Army, 1892; Capt. 1899; served S Africa, 1899–1902 (despatches, Queen's medal 5 clasps, King's medal 2 clasps, DSO); European War, 1914–19 (despatches, Bt Lieut-Col and Colonel, CMG, CB); late Commandant, York and Durham Infantry Brigade; retired, 1925. *Club:* Army and Navy.

Died 30 Nov. 1947.

PRICE, Brig.-Gen. Charles Henry Uvedale, CB 1914; DSO 1899; Indian Army, retired; *b* 16 June 1862; 3rd *s* of Gen. G. Uvedale Price; *m* 1889, Ada Mary, *d* of John O. H. N. Oliver, CSI. Lieut Welsh Regt, 1881; ISC, 1883; Captain, 1892; Major, 1901; Lieut-Col, 1905; Col, 1908; DAAG India, 1900–05; served Burmah, 1886–88 (medal with two clasps, severely wounded); Uganda, 1897–98 (despatches, brevet-majority, DSO, medal with two clasps); GOC Aden, 1915–16; retired, 1920. *Address:* c/o National Bank of India, EC.

Died 22 Feb. 1942.

PRICE, Rev. Cyril, MA; *s* of Rev. Thomas Price; *m* Cordelia Elizabeth, *d* of late Rev. Duke Yonge of Puslinch, Devonshire. *Educ:* King Edward's School, Birmingham; Worcester Coll., Oxford. Deacon, 1890; Priest, 1891; Curate of Stratford-on-Avon, 1890–92; Curate of Alcester, 1892–97; Chaplain on HM's Indian Ecclesiastical Establishment, 1897; served at Calcutta, Cuttack, Kamptee, Sabathu, Umballa, Kasauli, Dinapore, Mhow, Ranikhet, Nagpur, Jubbulpore; Senior Chaplain, 1910; Archdeacon of Nagpur, 1910–19; Vicar of Eldersfield, 1920–25; Rector of Nafford with Birlingham, 1925–36. *Address:* The Orchard, Eckington, Pershore.

Died 29 Aug. 1943.

PRICE, Sir Francis (Caradoc Rose), 5th Bt *cr* 1815; Major late Glamorgans, Yeomanry; *b* 29 June 1880; *s* of 3rd Bt and Isabella, *d* of J. W. Tarleton, Killeigh, King's Co.; *S* brother, 1901; *m* 1909, Marjorie, *d* of Sir W. Russell Russell, Hawkes Bay, NZ; three *s* three *d.* 2nd Lt 1st Batt. Royal Welsh Fusiliers; entered Army, 1900; served S Africa, 1900. *Heir: s* Rose Francis, *b* 15 March 1910. *Address:* Ashleworth, Gloucester.

Died 24 Feb. 1949.

PRICE, Brig.-Gen. George Dominic, CMG 1918; late W Yorks Regt; *b* 1867; *e s* of late Sir Frederick Price, KCSI; *m* 1918, Alice (*d* 1930), *widow* of Vice-Admiral F. C. B. Robinson, and *d* of late Col Cyril Blackburne Tew. Served West Coast of Africa, 1893–94; European War, 1914–19; Chevalier Legion of Honour; Order of White Eagle (Serbia), St Stanislaus (Russia), St Vladimir (Russia); retired pay, 1924. *Address:* Inchcoulter, Exmouth. *Club:* Naval and Military.

Died 26 Feb. 1943.

PRICE, H. L., MA (Oxon); Headmaster of Bishop's Stortford College since 1932; *b* 1899. *Educ:* Bishop's Stortford College; Corpus Christi College, Oxford. Assistant master at Uppingham, 1922–24; Christ's

Hospital, 1925–31, housemaster, 1929–31. *Recreations:* cricket, golf. *Address:* The College, Bishop's Stortford, Herts.

Died 18 July 1943.

PRICE, Harry; psychist; Honorary Secretary and Editor, University of London Council for Psychical Investigation (formerly National Laboratory of Psychical Research, of which he was Founder and Director, 1925–34); Chairman, National Film Library (British Film Institute), 1935–41; Member of Council, Shakespeare Film Society; *b* 17 Jan. 1881; *o s* of late Edward Ditcher Price, Shrewsbury and late Emma Randall Meech; *m* 1908, Constance Mary, *o d* of late Robert Hastings Knight. *Educ:* London; Shropshire. Devoted life to study of the abnormal and formation of library (now the Harry Price Library of Magical Literature, in the University of London; 20,000 vols) of works on psychical research, magic and collateral subjects; Lecture tours, Scandinavia, 1925 and 1927; represented British psychical research, International Psychic Exhibition, Copenhagen, 1925; founded and equipped (at S Kensington) first laboratory in Great Britain for the scientific examination of alleged abnormal phenomena, 1925; Foreign Research Officer, American Society for Psychical Research, New York, 1925–31; solved mystery of fire-walking in first British experiments, 1935–37; investigated claims of principal mediums in Great Britain and several European countries, Broadcasting since 1935. *Publications:* The Sceptic (psychic play), 1898; Coins of Kent and Kentish Tokens, 1902; Shropshire Tokens and Mints, 1902; Joint Editor, Revelations of a Spirit Medium, 1922; Cold Light on Spiritualistic Phenomena, 1922; Stella C.; An Account of Some Original Experiments in Psychical Research, 1925; Short-Title Catalogue of Works on Psychical Research, Spiritualism, Magic, etc. 1929; Rudi Schneider: A Scientific Examination of His Mediumship, 1930; Regurgitation and the Duncan Mediumship, 1931; An Account of Some Further Experiments with Rudi Schneider, 1933; Leaves from a Psychist's Case-book, 1933; Psychical Research (talking film), 1935; Confessions of a Ghost-Hunter, 1936; Faith and Fire-Walking, article in Encyclopædia Britannica, 1936; A Report on Two Experimental Fire-Walks, 1936; The Haunting of Cashen's Gap (with R. S. Lambert), 1936; Fifty Years of Psychical Research, 1939; The Most Haunted House in England: Ten Years' Investigation of Borley Rectory, 1940; Search for Truth: My Life for Psychical Research, 1942; Poltergeist over England, 1945; The End of Borley Rectory, 1946; film scenario of Borley hauntings (with Upton Sinclair), 1948; Works translated into eight languages; numerous pamphlets and contributions to British and foreign periodical literature. *Recreations:* collecting rare works on magic; foreign travel; cinematography; numismatics. *Address:* Arun Bank, Pulborough, Sussex. *T:* Pulborough 21. *Clubs:* Reform; Oxford Union, Oxford.

Died 29 March 1948.

PRICE, Rt Rev. Horace MacCartie Eyre, DD; Assistant Bishop and Archdeacon (since 1919) of Ely and Canon Residentiary (since 1921) of Ely Cathedral; *b* Malvern, 3 Aug. 1863; *s* of Rev. W. Salter Price (*d* 1911); *m* 1890, Alice G., *d* of Lionel and Elizabeth Millard, of Bungay, Suffolk; two *s* two *d*. *Educ:* Rossall; Trinity Coll., Camb. (3rd Class Classical Tripos). Ordained 1886; CMS Missionary and Vice-Principal Fourah Bay Coll., Sierra Leone, 1886–89; Curate of Wingfield, Suffolk, 1889–90; Principal of CMS Boys' School, Osaka, Japan, 1890–97; Acting Secretary CMS, Osaka CMS, 1897–98; Secretary CMS, Osaka, 1899–1904; Central Japan, 1904–06; Principal CMS Divinity School, Osaka, 1900–03; Archdeacon of Osaka, 1901–06; Bishop in Fuh-Kien, 1906–18; served as CF Mediterranean Expeditionary Force, 1915–16; British

Salonika Force and Egyptian Expeditionary Force, 1918–19; Vicar of Pampisford, 1919–21. *Address:* The College, Ely. *Club:* Cambridge County.

Died 21 Nov. 1941.

PRICE, John Lloyd; JP; MP; Member for Boothby, Federal House of Representatives, since 1928; Member Commonwealth Parliamentary Standing Committee on Public Works; Deputy Chairman of Committees, Federal House Representatives; Secretary of the Federal Parliamentary United Australia Party and Deputy Government Whip; *b* Everton, Liverpool, 14 Feb. 1882; *s* of late Hon. Thomas Price, MP, ex-Premier South Australia; *m* Elsie, *e d* of R. M. McBride, JP, Tarmoola Station, Leonora, Western Australia; one *s* one *d*. *Educ:* Mitcham and Unley Public Schools; Adelaide School of Mines; Adelaide Shorthand and Business Training College. Commenced work Civil Service, South Australia, 1898; rose to important position in Office of Crown; resigned Service to contest seat in Parliament, March 1915, and was elected for District of Port Adelaide, which seat he held until appointed Agent-General in 1925; Agent-General for South Australia in England, 1925–28. *Recreations:* golf, tennis, cricket. *Address:* 102 Cross Roads, Highgate, South Australia; Federa Members Rooms, Canberra, ACT, Australia.

Died 23 April 1941.

PRICE, Langford Lovell F. R., MA (Oxford), Hon. LLD (Leeds); *b* London, 20 July 1862; *γ s* of late Rev. Aubrey Charles Price, Clapham, Surrey, and Camilla, *d* of Langford Lovell Hodge, Antigua; unmarried. *Educ:* Dulwich; Trinity Coll. Oxford (Scholar). 1st class Mods 1882; 1st class Lit. Hum. 1885. Fellow and Treasurer of Oriel College, Oxford, 1888–1918; re-elected Fellow, 1918–23, elected Emeritus Fellow, 1944; Proctor, 1896–97; Lecturer to the Toynbee Trust, 1886–87; Newmarch Lecturer in Statistics, Univ. Coll. Lond. 1895–96; Reader in Economic History in the University of Oxford, 1909–21; Examiner in Moral Sciences Tripos, 1898, Historical Tripos, 1906, and Economics Tripos, 1919, Cambridge; Victoria Univ. 1898; Univ. of Wales, 1903; Univ. of Liverpool, 1908; Univ. of Birmingham, 1913 and 1919; Royal Society of Arts, 1913–29; Univ. of Bristol, 1920; University College, Nottingham, 1922; University of Leeds, 1923; Hon. Sec. of Royal Economic Soc.; Member of Intern. Statistical Institute. *Publications:* Industrial Peace: its Advantages, Methods, and Difficulties, 1887; West Barbary: or Notes on the System of Work and Wages in the Cornish Mines, 1891; A Short History of Political Economy in England, 1891 (new issue with additional part on recent writing, 1931); Money and its Relations to Prices, 1896 (new issue with Epilogue on movements of Prices in the 20th Century, 1929); Economic Science and Practice, 1896; A Short History of English Commerce and Industry, 1900; The Present Position and Future Prospects of the Study of Economic History, 1908; Co-operation and Co-partnership, 1914; English edition of Ely and Wicker's Elementary Principles of Economics, 1915. *Address:* 39 Preston Drove, Brighton.

Died 26 Feb. 1950.

PRICE, Marjorie Muriel; novelist; *b* 15 March 1907; *d* of Edward Harold Price and Muriel Page; *m* 1934, F. C. V. Brightman, Lt-Comdr RN; one *d*. *Educ:* Channing School, Highgate. Published first novel, 1930. *Publications:* The Mantle of Saltash; Sequence; The Happy Kingdom; We Deceive Ourselves; Pandora Dances; They Were Young; The Continuous Star; The Woman Sunday; We go Round; Family Pride; Marriage Vow; Second Summer; The Blithe Spirit; Woman for Sale; Singing Glory; Colour Bar; Trial by Gunfire; Triple Star. Also, under name of Victoria Rhys: The Angels Fell; Be Thyself Once More. *Recreations:* golf, motoring, and reading. *Address:* c/o Collins, 48 Pall Mall, SW1.

Died 3 April 1946.

PRICE, Col Sir Rhys Howell, KBE 1918; CMG 1900; CBE 1917; VD; *b* 1872; *s* of late Sir Thomas Price, KCMG, and Mary, *d* of Matthias Howell, Neath; *m* 1902, Constance Mary, 2nd *d* of Hon. John M. Peacock, Queenstown, Cape Colony; one *s* one *d*. Served S Africa, 1899–1902; Kaffrarian Rifles and commanding a column (wounded, despatches thrice, Queen's medal 4 clasps, King's medal 2 clasps, Union medal, CMG); Officer Commanding Union Expeditionary Base, Capetown and Durban, 1914–15; Director of War Recruiting, Nov. 1916; QMG Union Defence Forces, 1918–19; Chairman, Unionist and Conservative Assoc., Eastern Division of Surrey; Past Chairman East London (SA) Chamber of Commerce Inc. and S African Section London Chamber of Commerce Inc. *Address:* Highlands, Purley Downs, Surrey. *T:* Sanderstead 1287. *Clubs:* Conservative, Royal Automobile.

Died 27 Sept. 1943.

PRICE, S. Warren, FGS, MIME; late Professor of Mining, University of Wales; Assoc. Royal School of Mines. *Address:* Brynderi, Peterston-Super-Ely, nr Cardiff.

Died 8 Jan. 1944.

PRICE, Brig.-Gen. Thomas Herbert Francis, CMG 1918; DSO 1917; late Duke of Cornwall's Light Infantry; *b* 1869; *y s* of late Sir Frederick Price, KCS1; *m* 1919, Surline May, *d* of Hon. Henry Moses, MLC, Sydney, NSW, and *widow* of Major J. A. Higgon, Pembrokeshire Yeomanry and Royal Welch Fusiliers. Served Tirah Expedition, 1898; S African War, 1902; European War, 1914–18 (despatches, Bt Lt-Col, CMG, DSO); retired pay, 1921. *Address:* The Old Rectory, Twyford, Hants. *T:* Twyford 2213. *Club:* Army and Navy.

Died 12 Feb. 1945.

PRICE, Brig.-Gen. Thomas Rose Caradoc, CMG 1919; DSO 1917; Chevalier Légion d'Honneur, 1917; late Probyn's Horse and Welsh Guards; *b* 2 Aug. 1875; *s* of late Colonel T. Price, CB; *m* 1911, Dorothy, *d* of late Sir Henry Verey; two *s* one *d*. *Educ:* Melbourne; RMC; psc. ADC to GOC Aldershot Comd., 1911; General Staff, Army HQ, India, 1913–14; served NW Frontier, Malakand Field Force, 1897–98; Selstan Boundary Commission, 1903; Thibet, 1903–04; European War in France; on General Staff (HQ's 55th Division and Third Army); with 1st Batt. Welsh Guards: and as GOC 114th Infantry Brigade, 38th Welsh Div., 1914–19; OC Welsh Guards and 142nd Inf. Brigade (TA), 1924–28; Commandant, Hythe Wing, Small Arms School, 1928–31; retired 1931; Brigadier Commanding, North London Sub-Area and Docks, 1939–41, retired 1941; ARP Warden, Westminster, 1941–45. *Address:* Madron House, Hythe, Kent. *Club:* Guards'.

Died 20 Oct. 1949.

PRICE, Thomas Slater, OBE; FRS 1924; PhD (Leipzig); FRIC; DSc (Lond. and Birmingham); FRSE 1932; Professor of Chemistry at the Heriot-Watt College, Edinburgh, 1931–40, Professor Emeritus since 1940; *b* Wednesbury, Staffs, 24 Aug. 1875; *e s* of late Thomas Price and Mary Ann Slater, Wednesbury; *m* 1904, Florence, *e d* of late Stephen Beardmore, Wednesbury; one *s* two *d*. *Educ:* King Edward's High School, Birmingham; Mason College, Birmingham (Priestley Scholar); BSc (Lond.), with 1st Class Hons in Chemistry and Physics; 1851 Exhibitioner University of Leipzig; MA, PhD, Leipzig; 1851 Exhibitioner University of Stockholm. Lecturer in Chemistry, Firth College, Sheffield, 1900–01; Senior Lecturer in Chemistry, University of Birmingham, 1901–03; Head of Chemical Dept, Technical College, Birmingham, 1903–20; Director of Research to the British Photographic Research Association, 1920–30; Examiner in Physical Chemistry to Institute of Chemistry, 1907–11; Member of Council of Institute of Chemistry, 1911–14, 1921–24, Vice-President, 1924–27; Member of Council of Chemical Society, 1921–24; Senior Honorary Secretary, 1924–28; Hon. Treasurer, 1928–31; Vice-President 1931–34; Member of Council of Royal Photographic Society, 1922–31; Vice-President, 1926–29; Membre d'Honneur de la Societé Française de Photographie; Lieut-Comdr RNVR, 1916–19; Naval Representative on the Chemical Warfare Committee. *Publications:* Practical Organic Chemistry (with D. F. Twiss); Per-acids and their Salts; numerous papers on chemistry in various scientific journals. *Address:* Heriot-Watt College, Edinburgh; 2 Cluny Drive, Edinburgh 10.

Died 29 Oct. 1949.

PRICE HUGHES, Mary Katherine H., CBE 1938; formerly Head of West London Mission Sisterhood; *b* 3 April 1853; 4th *d* of late Rev. Alfred Barrett; *m* 1873, Rev. Hugh Price Hughes, MA (*d* 1902); two *s* one *d*. *Educ:* Laleham, Clapham Park. Church work in connection with husband's Ministry and an active participation in social work for 50 years in connection with the West London Mission. *Recreations:* reading and foreign travel. *Address:* 38 Circus Road Mansions, St John's Wood, NW8. *T:* Cunningham 4386.

Died 13 Jan. 1948.

PRICHARD, Rev. Alfred George; LCC; Congregational Minister (retired); *b* Blackfriars, 12 June 1869; *s* of late Councillor George Prichard and Ellen Mollett, *d* of late Rev. G. M. Murphy; *m* 1893, Elizabeth Margaret, *d* of E. R. Taylor; two *s*. *Educ:* Elementary School; Pupil Teachers Centre; private theological training. Pastor of Congregational Church, Denton, Norfolk, 1893–97; Pastor (and founder) of Little Ilford Congregational Church, 1897–1907; Minister (and founder) of Battersea Free Church, 1908–38; Director of London Missionary Society; Mayor of Battersea, and JP, County of London, 1929–30; Governor of Battersea Polytechnic and Sir Walter St Johns School Trust; Vice-Chairman Representative Managers of Lond. Elementary Schools; Vice-Chairman and Deputy Chairman of Metropolitan Boroughs Standing Joint Committee and Chairman of its General Purposes Committee; Member of Royal Commission on London Squares; Member of Departmental Committee of Ministry of Health on Public Cleansing in London; of Metropolitan Asylums Board; of Central Unemployed Body for London; of LCC (West Islington) since 1928, and Chairman or Vice-Chm. of various of its committees and Sub-Committees; Parliamentary-Candidate for Chelsea, 1929. *Publications:* various articles, including series on religious and social conditions in Norfolk, and on theological and general correspondence with Right Hon. W. E. Gladstone; Fifty Plain Pacifist Points (2nd ed.) 1937. *Recreation:* cricket. *Address:* 66 Prince of Wales' Mansions, Battersea, SW11. *Clubs:* National Liberal, Surrey County Cricket.

Died 8 Dec. 1945.

PRICHARD, Brig.-Gen. Charles Stewart, CB 1915; DSO 1902; late 58th (Northamptonshire Regt); *b* 20 Oct. 1861. *Educ:* Marlborough. Entered army, 1882; Captain, 1889; Major, 1901; Lt-Col 1911; Col 1915; served South Africa, 1899–1902 (despatches twice, Queen's medal 4 clasps, King's medal 2 clasps, DSO); European War, 1914–16 (despatches, CB); Brig.-General on retirement in 1918. *Address:* Parslow's Hillock, Princes Risborough. *T:* Hampden-Row 27.

Died 17 June 1942.

PRICHARD, Harold Arthur, LLD Aberdeen; Professor Emeritus, Oxford; Hon. Fellow of Corpus Christi College, Oxford, 1937; Fellow of the British Academy; *b* 30 Oct. 1871; *s* of W. S. Prichard; *m* 1899, Mabel H. Ross; two *s* one *d*. *Educ:* Clifton; New College, Oxford. Fellow of Hertford College, Oxford, 1895–98. Fellow and afterwards Tutor of Trinity College, Oxford, 1898–1924; White's Professor of Moral Philosophy,

Oxford, 1928–37. *Publications:* Kant's Theory of Knowledge; Articles in *Mind*. *Address:* 6 Linton Road, Oxford.

Died 29 Dec. 1947.

PRICHARD, Lt-Col Hubert Cecil, CBE 1918; DL for County of Glamorgan; landowner, JP, District Councillor; *b* 6 Feb. 1865; *e surv. s* of late C. J. C. Prichard and Mary Anna Thomas, of Pwllywrach; *m* 1905, Nora Diana, *er d* of A. Piers of Estrelle, Boscombe; two *s* one *d. Educ:* Clifton College; Magdalene College, Cambridge; Royal Military College, Sandhurst. 2nd Lieut East Yorkshire Regt, 1888; retired as Captain, 1897; joined Glamorgan Imperial Yeomanry as Major, 1900; retired as Lt-Colonel, 1907; rejoined in European War and commanded 3rd Line South Wales Mounted Brigade, and afterwards commanded Prisoners of War Camps in Scotland. *Recreations:* shooting, cricket, etc. *Address:* Pwllywrach, Cowbridge, Glamorgan. *T:* Cowbridge 256.

Died 12 Nov. 1942.

PRIDMORE, Walter George, CMG 1915; MB, BS (Dunelm); MRCS; late Honorary Surgeon to the King; *b* 23 Sept. 1864; 3rd *s* of late Thomas Whitaker Pridmore (Civil Service); *m* 1st, 1892, Emily Cecilia Kayes (*d* 1935) of Queen Alexandra Indian Nursing Service; one *d*; 2nd, 1936, Margaret, *d* of Edward Murray, Civil Engineer. *Educ:* Sir Roger Cholmeley's School, Highgate; Middlesex Hospital; Durham University. MRCS (Eng.), 1886; MB, MS (Durham), 1887. House Surgeon to J. W. Hulke, Middlesex Hospital, and House Physician to Dr W. Cayley at the same Hospital; entered Indian Medical Service, 1891; Surgeon, 1891; in India, 1891–1914; served Chin Lushai Expedition with Tashon Column, 1892; held civil appointments in Burma, and was Ophthalmic Surgeon in Rangoon General Hospital, 1910–14; on active service with No. 5 Indian General Hospital, Egypt Expeditionary Force, 1914–18 (CMG); Colonel, 1918; retired, 1923. *Publications:* Contributions to Medical Journals; Dysentery with Intussusception; Dengue Fever, etc. *Recreations:* tennis and motoring; played forward in Middlesex Hospital Rugby Football XV, and for Durham University. *Address:* c/o Grindlay & Co., 54 Parliament Street, SW1. *T:* St Alban's 648.

Died 24 March 1943.

PRIESTLEY, Lt-Col Harold Edgar, CMG 1916; late RAMC; MRCS, LRCP (Lond.); MRCP (Edin.); *m*; two *s. Educ:* Germany; St George's Hospital. Served European War, 1914–16; CMG in recognition of his distinguished service and devotion to duty at the camp at Wittenberg, Germany, during the typhus epidemic which prevailed there from Feb. to June 1915; retired pay, 1932; holds Gold Medal of the Order of St John of Jerusalem. *Address:* c/o Glyn Mills, Holt and Co., Whitehall, SW1.

Died 16 March 1941.

PRIESTLEY, Herbert Ingram; Professor of History since 1917, and Director since 1940, of the Bancroft Library, University of California; Director Institute International Relations, 1930; *b* Fairfield, Michigan, 2 Jan. 1875; *s* of John Stanley Priestley and Sarah Parker, Lincolnshire; *m* 1901, Bessie B. Snodgrass; one *s* one *d. Educ:* PhB, University of Southern California, 1900; MA 1907; PhD, University of California, 1917. Instructor, University of Southern California, 1899–1900; Teacher, Los Angeles Military Academy, 1900–01; Teacher and Superintendent, Schools, Naga, Luzon, 1901–04; Principal, Wilmington School, 1904–07; Teacher of Spanish, Riverside California High School, 1907–10; Superintendent, Corona, California Schools, 1910–12; Assistant Curator, Bancroft Library University, California, 1912–20; Librarian, 1920–40; Hon. Prof. Mexican National Museum of Archæology and History, since 1933; Member American and S American historical

societies. Mason. *Publications:* José de Gálvez, Visitor General of New Spain, 1765–1771, 1916; The Mexican Nation, a History, 1923; Spanish Colonial Municipalities, 1921; The Luna Papers, 2 vols 1928; The Coming of the White Man (vol. i A History of American Life), 1929; France Overseas, A Study of Modern Imperialism, 1938; France Overseas through the Old Regime, 1939; Some Mexican Problems (joint author), 1926; Modern Mexican History, a Syllabus, 1920; California, the Name (joint author), 1917; Tristan de Luna, Conquistador, 1936; Pedro Fages' Description of California, 1937; numerous articles in reviews, translations and book reviews; Member Bd of Editors, The American Archivist. *Recreations:* gardening, travel in Orient, Mexico, Canada, Alaska, USA, Europe and North Africa. *Address:* Bancroft Library, University of California, Berkeley, California, USA. *Clubs:* Faculty, California.

Died 6 Feb. 1944.

PRIESTLEY, Sir Joseph Child, Kt 1927; KC 1903; *b* 1862; 2nd *s* of late Sir William Overend Priestley, MD, MP Edinburgh and St Andrews Universities, and late Lady Priestley, *d* of late Dr Robert Chambers of Edinburgh; *m* 1891, Annette Maud Warner, *d* of Ralph George Price, 26 Hyde Park Gardens, W2; one *d. Educ:* Marlborough; Pembroke College, Cambridge. Called to Bar, 1888; practised latterly entirely in Probate and Divorce Court; Bencher Inner Temple, 1917; DL, JP Herts, 1906; late Chairman of Herts County Council; Chairman of Herts Quarter Sessions. *Recreations:* shooting and fishing. *Address:* 5 Crown Office Row, Temple, EC4; Tatmore Place, Hitchin, Herts. *T:* Hitchin 148. *Club:* Oxford and Cambridge.

Died 9 June 1941.

PRIESTLEY, Joseph Hubert, DSO 1917; BSc (Lond.), FLS; Professor of Botany, University of Leeds, since 1911; *b* Tewkesbury, 5 Oct. 1883; *s* of J. E. Priestley, Headmaster of Tewkesbury Grammar School; *m* 1911, Marion E. Young, Cotham, Bristol; two *d. Educ:* Tewkesbury Grammar School; Univ. College, Bristol. Head of Botanical Department and Lecturer in Botany, University College, Bristol, 1905–11; Consulting Botanist to Bath and West and Southern Counties Society, 1910–11; President of Section K of the British Association for Advancement of Science, 1932; Pro-Vice-Chancellor, University of Leeds, 1935–39; Aug. 1914 with BEF as Captain TF Unattached List; disembodied Jan. 1919; on General Staff (Intelligence), Aug. 1915 until date of disembodiment (despatches twice, DSO, Croix de Chevalier de la Couronne (Belgium). *Publications:* papers in various scientific journals, mainly on plant physiology and developmental anatomy. *Address:* 12 Weetwood Road, West Park, Leeds, 6. *T:* Leeds 51926.

Died 31 Oct. 1944.

PRIESTMAN, Sir John, 1st Bt *cr* 1934; Kt 1923; sole proprietor of shipbuilding firm of John Priestman & Co; *b* Bishop Auckland; *m* S. Marie du T., *d* of late Dr Pownall of Manchester; one *d. Educ:* Bishop Auckland. Served apprenticeship to shipbuilding; acted as Chief Draughtsman for two important Wear firms; founded firm of John Priestman & Co., 1882; Chairman of Enfield Steamship Co., Sunderland, Cliffside SS Co. Ltd, Newcastle, and the Brinkburn Steamship Co. Ltd, Sunderland, and largely interested in many commercial undertakings; County Magistrate for Durham; was for twenty years Chairman of Urban District Council of Southwick on Wear; received freedom of Sunderland 1933. *Address:* Cliffside, Roker. *T:* 5040; Tyringham, Rutland Road, Harrogate.

Died 5 Aug. 1941 (ext).

PRIME-STEVENSON, Edward Irenæus; *see* Stevenson.

PRIMROSE, Alexander, CB 1918; MB, CM Edin.; FRCS Eng.; LLD Edin. and Dalhousie; Dean of the Faculty of Medicine, 1920–32, and Emeritus Professor of Clinical Surgery, University of Toronto; Consulting Surgeon, Toronto General Hospital and Hospital for Sick Children; *b* Pictou, Nova Scotia, 5 April 1861; *e s* of Howard Primrose and Olivia, *d* of late Hon. Alexander Campbell; *m* 1889, Clara Christine, *d* of late George Ewart, Toronto, Canada; three *d* (one *s* killed in action, 1916); 2nd, 1921, Elizabeth, *d* of late Mr Justice Britton and *widow* of late Major Charles A. Moss. *Educ:* Pictou Academy; Edinburgh University; Middlesex Hospital, London. President, 1931, of the American Surgical Association; Regent (1919–24), American College of Surgeons; Pathologist and Chloroformist, Paddington Green Children's Hospital London, 1888; Assistant Demonstrator of Anatomy, Surgeons' Hall, Edinburgh, 1885; Prosector in Anatomy, RCS 1887; Demonstrator of Anatomy, 1889; Professor of Anatomy, 1896–1909, Univ. of Toronto; Pres. Pathological Society of Toronto, 1898; Toronto Medical Society, 1900; Toronto Academy of Medicine, 1918; Canadian Medical Association, 1932; member Examining Board, Ontario College of Physicians and Surgeons, 1889–1902; Surg., No. 4 Canadian General Hospital, Salonika, 1915–16, with rank of Lieut-Colonel in Canadian Expeditionary Force; Consulting Surgeon, Canadian Forces in England, with the rank of Colonel, 1917. *Publications:* The Anatomy of the Orang-Outang, 1898–1899; Tuberculous Disease of the Bones and Joints; The American Practice of Surgery, vol. iii, 1907; papers in scientific journals. *Recreation:* golf. *Address:* Medical Arts Building, Toronto. *T:* Midway 6800. *Clubs:* British Empire; York, Toronto Golf, Toronto; Royal Canadian Yacht.

Died 8 Feb. 1944.

PRINCE, John Dyneley, BA, PhD; Professor Emeritus, Columbia University, New York; *b* New York, 17 April 1868; *e s* of late John Dyneley Prince; *m* Adeline E., *d* of late Alfred L. Loomis, MD, LLD; one *s*. *Educ:* private schools and tutors; Columbia University, New York (BA 1888). Representative of Columbia University on the expedition to Southern Babylonia sent out by the University of Pennsylvania, 1888–89; Berlin University, 1889–90; PhD Johns Hopkins Univ. 1892; Prof. of Semitic Languages at the New York University 1892–1902; at Columbia Univ., 1902–15; Dean of New York Univ. Graduate School, 1895–1902; Speaker New Jersey Legislature, 1909; President New Jersey Senate, 1912; Acting Governor of New Jersey, 1912; President NJ Civil Service Commission, 1917–21; Professor of Slavonic Languages at Columbia University, New York, 1915–35; Director East European Languages at Columbia University, 1935–37; American Minister to Denmark, 1921–26; to Yugoslavia, 1926–33; St Sava (Serbia), Grand Officer, 1912; Grand Officer Polonia Restituta, 1922; Grand Cordon Yugoslavian Crown, 1933; Grand Cross of Dannebrog, 1933. *Publications:* Mene Mene Tekel Upharsin, Baltimore, 1893; A Critical Commentary on the Book of Daniel, Leipzig, 1899; articles in Encyclopædia Biblica, 1902–1903; Kulóskap the Master (Algonkin poems), with Charles G. Leland, 1902; Materials for a Sumerian Lexicon, 1908; articles in Ency. Britannica and in Hastings' Dictionary of Religions; Assyrian Primer, 1909; Russian Grammar, 1920; Practical Grammar of the Lettish Language, London, 1925; Practical Grammar of the Serbo-Croatian Language, 1929; Fragments from Babel, 1939; American-Danish-Greenland Commissioner, 1940; papers to learned societies. *Address:* East European Dept, Columbia University, NY.

Died 11 Oct. 1945.

PRINCE, Lt-Col Robert, CIE 1937; OBE 1922; retired; *s* of Thomas Tennant Prince, Laurel Lodge, Barnet, Herts; *m* 1906; five *s* two *d*. *Educ:* Malvern College. First Commission, The King's Regt, 1899; Military Accounts

Dept, 1907; Military Accountant General, India, 1931–36; served South African War, 1899–1902; European War, 1914–18; Waziristan, 1922. *Address:* The Grange, Ash, nr Martock, Somerset. *T:* Martock 144.

Died 2 Nov. 1945.

PRINGLE, Lt-Col David, CBE 1919; VD. Served European War, 1915–19 (despatches, CBE).

Died 15 July 1936.

PRINGLE, Brig. Hall Grant, DSO 1917; late RFA; *b* 1876; *m* 1918, Mrs Ridley, Knorren, Brampton, Cumberland, *widow* of Capt. C. N. Ridley, Yeomanry, of Park End, Northumberland; one *d*. Served China, 1900; N Nigeria, 1901–02 (medal and clasp); European War, 1914–17 (despatches, DSO, Order of Aviz of Portugal, Rising Sun of Japan); Inspector of the West Indian Local Forces and Officer Commanding troops in Jamaica, 1922–25; retired pay, 1925.

Died 22 Dec. 1942.

PRINGLE, James Hogarth, MB, CM, FRCS; late Examiner in Surgery, Universities of Edinburgh and Durham; Major, IV Scottish Base Hospital Territorial Forces; Consulting Surgeon, Royal Infirmary, Glasgow; *b* Parramatta, New South Wales; *s* of late G. Hogarth Pringle, MD, FRCS. *Educ:* Sedbergh School; University of Edinburgh; University of Vienna; University of Berlin. *Publications:* Fractures and their Treatment; numerous articles on surgical subjects. *Address:* Whiteflat, Killearn, Stirlingshire. *T:* Killearn 42.

Died 24 April 1941.

PRINSEP, Anthony Leyland; Chevalier of the Legion of Honour; Theatrical Manager; *b* London, 1888; *s* of late Val Prinsep, RA, and Florence Leyland; *m* 1st, Marie Löhr (marr. diss.); one *d*; 2nd, Margaret Bannerman (from whom he obtained a divorce, 1939). *Educ:* Eton; Trinity College, Cambridge. Played lawn-tennis for Cambridge against Oxford, 1909–10–1911; became a Lloyd's underwriter; during the war Lieut RNVR; Manager Globe Theatre, London, 1918–28; produced among others following plays; Nurse Benson, Victory, Voice from the Minaret, L'Aiglon, Our Betters, Blue Beard's Eighth Wife, Lullaby, Prisoner of Zenda, Italian Season for Ruggero Ruggeri. *Recreations:* tennis and lawn-tennis. *Address:* 2 Ulster Terrace, Regent's Park, NW1. *Clubs:* Arts, Green Room, All England Lawn Tennis.

Died 26 Oct. 1942.

PRITCHARD, Brig.-Gen. Aubrey Gordon, CMG 1916; Indian Army, retired; *b* 8 Oct. 1869; *s* of late Lieut-Gen. Sir Gordon Pritchard, KCB; *m* 1922, Hilda, *yr d* of William Whitworth, JP, Barrister-at-law, 18 Essex Villas, W8. *Educ:* Wellington. Entered army, Connaught Rangers, 1889; Lieut, ISC 1891; Captain, Indian Army, 1900; Major, 1907. Served European War, 1914–17 (CMG, Bt-Col); retired, 1921. *Recreations:* pig-sticking, big-game shooting, polo. *Address:* Hill House, Higham, near Colchester. *Club:* Army and Navy.

Died 12 March 1943.

PRITCHARD, Brig.-Gen. Clive Gordon, CMG 1919; DSO 1917; late RGA; *b* Mussoorie, 10 Aug. 1871; *s* of late Lieut-Gen. Sir Gordon Douglas Pritchard, KCB, Col Commandant RE, and late Agnes Maria, *d* of W. H. Cox, JP; *m* 1901, Edith, *d* of Rev. J. Ellershaw, Clifton, Bristol; one *d*. *Educ:* Temple Grove, East Sheen; Malvern College; Royal Military Academy, Woolwich. First Commission, Royal Artillery, 1891; Capt. 1899; Commanded Hong-Kong Volunteers under Colonial Government with local rank of Major, 1902–07; Major, 1911; commanding a Garrison Artillery Company in Hong-Kong on outbreak of war; arrived home, March 1915, and trained a new Heavy Battery (No. 16), and took it to France 10 July 1915; temp. Lt-Col May 1916, and commanded a Heavy Artillery Group throughout Battle of the Somme; Counter Battery Staff Officer, 1 Sept. 1916–17 (DSO, CMG, despatches twice); Lt-Col

1917; Bt Col Jan. 1918); Temp. Brig.-Gen. commanding Corps Heavy Artillery, July 1917; Brig.-Gen. RA, GHQ, France, April 1918–Dec. 1918; GOC RA XI Corps, Jan. 1919; Commander of the Belgian Order of the Crown and Belgian Croix de Guerre, 1917; American Distinguished Service Medal, 1918; Colonel, 1920; CRGA Aldershot Command, 1920–22; retired pay, 1922; Secretary Cooden Beach Golf Club 1927–36. *Address:* 5 Manor Road, Bexhill-on-Sea. *T:* Bexhill 1216. *Club:* English-Speaking Union.

Died 31 Aug. 1948.

PRITCHARD, (George) Eric (Campbell), MA, MD (Oxon), FRCP (London); Consulting Physician; Consulting Pædiatrician to Queen Charlotte's Maternity Hospital; Consulting Physician, Queen's Hospital for Children; Hon. Consulting Physician for Infant Consultations, St Marylebone and Western General Dispensary; Hon. Consulting Physician, Sunshine Homes for Blind Babies, National Association for the Blind; Hon. Consulting Physician Wellgarth Nursery Training College; *s* of Charles Pritchard, DD, Savilian Professor of Astronomy, Oxford; *m* 1st, 1894, Marian Elizabeth, *d* of Walter M. Westropp Dawson, DL, JP, Ferns, Ireland; one *s*; 2nd, Ellen Beatrice, *y d* of William Foster, Hove. *Educ:* Clifton; Oxford; St Mary's Hospital, London; Berlin. First Class Honours, final schools, Natural Science, Oxford, 1887; University scholarship, St Mary's Hospital, London. Medical Director Infants Hospital, Vincent Square, 1922–36; late Physician, City of London Hospital for Diseases of the Heart and Lungs; Fellow Royal Society Medicine; late President Section for Study of Disease in Children; late President British Pædiatric Association; Vice-Pres. Child Study Society; founder and first Chairman Society of Infant Consultations; late Hon. Secretary National League for Health, Maternity and Child Welfare; Joint Hon. Secretary National Association for the Prevention of Infant Mortality and for the Welfare of Infancy; Chairman Association of Infant Consultations and Schools for Mothers; Chm. Executive Cttee Nat. Council for Baby Week, 1917–38; Chairman Children's Jewel Fund. *Publications:* The Infant; Handbook of Modern Treatment, 1938; Physiological Feeding of Infants and Children, 4th edition; Infant Education; The New-born Infant; Translator Professor Mary's Movement; Regulation and Control of the Manufacture and Sale of Drugs and Foods for Infants; and various on Infant Mortality. *Address:* c/o National Bank, 274 Oxford St, W1.

Died 20 Oct. 1943.

PRITCHETT, John Suckling, MA, BCL; Recorder of Lincoln since 1920. *Educ:* King Edward's School, Birmingham; Balliol College, Oxford. Called to Bar, Inner Temple, 1881; Alderman of the City of Birmingham, 1911; Bailiff of King Edward's School, 1931; Hon. Legal Adviser to the Library Association. *Address:* Hill Top, Kings Norton, Birmingham, 30.

Died 18 Jan. 1941.

PROBY, Granville, CB 1947; DL, JP, MA, FSA, FRHistS; Lord Lieutenant of Huntingdonshire since 1946; Clerk in House of Lords, 1907–44; Principal Clerk, 1941–44; *b* 1883; *e s* of late Col Douglas James Proby and Lady Margaret F., 2nd *d* of 4th Earl of Donoughmore. *Educ:* Eton; Trinity College, Oxford. Barrister, Inner Temple, 1920; High Sheriff of Cambs and Hunts, 1935; Chairman of Hunts Quarter Sessions, 1941; Joint Editor of Victoria County History of Huntingdon, 1926–35. *Address:* Elton Hall, Peterborough. *T:* Elton 258. *Clubs:* Travellers', Athenæum, United University, Farmers, Roxburghe, Royal Automobile; Kildare Street, Dublin; Hunts County.

Died 9 March 1947.

PROCTOR, Col Alfred Henry, DSO 1917; *s* of late C. S. Proctor, Newcastle-on-Tyne; *m* Dorothy, *d* of late George Rome; two *s*. *Educ:* Rutherford College; Durham University. MB, BS 1902; MS 1904; MD 1905, Gold Medal; FRCSE 1923; Charltou Scholar in Med. Entered Indian Medical Service, 1904; Capt. 1907; Major 1915; Temp. Lieut-Col 1917; Lieut-Col 1924; Col 1933; served in S African War; European War, 1914–20, France, Egypt, Mesopotamia (despatches twice, DSO); Resident Surgeon Medical College Hospital, Calcutta; Resident Surgeon, Presidency General Hospital, Calcutta; Surgeon-Superintendent, 1923–33; Surgeon General, Govt of Bengal, 1933; Inspector General, Civil Hospitals, United Provinces, 1933–35; Honorary Surgeon to Viceroy; retired 1935; Medical Superintendent Southport EMS Hospital; Emeritus Dean, British Postgraduate Medical School; Member, Services Cttee; Colonial Medical Advisory Cttee. *Address:* 4 Tynedale Villas, Hexham, Northumberland. *Club:* Oriental.

Died 23 March 1950.

PROCTOR-SIMS, Ernest William; *see* Sims.

PROSSER, Rt Rev. David Lewis, DD, MA; Bishop of St David's since 1927. *Educ:* Llandovery; Keble College, Oxford (Mod. Hist. Scholar). Hon. Fellow of Keble College, 1949. Deacon, 1892; Priest 1893; Assistant Curate of Holy Trinity, Aberystwyth, 1892; Christ Church, Swansea, 1896; Vicar of Pembroke Dock, 1909–27; Archdeacon of St David's, 1920–27; Archbishop of Wales, 1944–49, resigned. Hon. LLD (Wales), 1949. *Publications:* Thoughts at the Preparation for Holy Communion; The Fulness of God; Addresses at Parade Services; Holy Worship. *Address:* The Palace, Abergwili, Carmarthenshire. *T:* Carmarthen 597.

Died 28 Feb. 1950.

PROSSER, Sir John, Kt 1927; CVO 1928; LLD Edin., 1932; Writer to the Signet, Edinburgh; *b* 1857; *s* of David Prosser, Bridge of Cally, Perthshire, and Mary Lawrie; *m* 1886, Mary Anne (*d* 1915), *d* of John Taylor, Elgin; one *s* two *d*. *Educ:* Local schools in Perthshire; Edinburgh University. Passed Solicitor, 1879; admitted to SSC Society, 1883; Writer to the Signet, 1898; member of various Commissions and Departmental Committees; JP for Dundee, 1894; member of the General Board of Control for Scotland, 1918–25; Crown Agent in Scotland and a Prison Commissioner, 1919–20. *Address:* 19 York Place, Edinburgh. *Clubs:* Northern, Edinburgh.

Died 16 June 1945.

PROSSER, Seward; Chairman of the Board, Bankers Trust Co; 16 Wall Street, New York, USA; Director, Barden Copper Co., International Nickel Co. of Canada, Ltd, Kennecott Copper Corporation, Utah Copper Corporation and many other companies; *b* Buffalo, New York, 1 May 1871; *s* of Henry Wilbur Prosser and Anna Fay; *m* 1902, Constance Barber, Englewood, NJ; three *d*. *Educ:* Public Schools; Englewood School for Boys. Began active career with Equitable Life Assurance Society of the US, later member firm Prosser and Homans, representing same, VP Astor Trust Company, 1907–12; President Liberty National Bank, 1912–14; President Bankers Trust Company, 1914–23. *Recreations:* yachting, owner of schooner Constance. *Address:* Palisade Avenue East, Englewood, NJ. *T:* Englewood 3–3050. *Clubs:* University, New York; Englewood, Englewood, NJ; Rolling Rock, Ligonier, Pa; Woods Hole Golf, Woods Hole, Mass; Quissett Yacht, Quissett, Mass; Porcupine, Nassau, Bahamas.

Died 1 Oct. 1942.

PROVIS, Edward, MA; *b* 1849; 3rd *s* of Samuel and Mary Provis of Bemerton, Wilts; *m* 1886, Margaret Blanche (*d* 1936), *y d* of Maj. Manley, of 32nd Madras Native Infantry; two *d*. *Educ:* King's College, London;

Clare College, Cambridge. BA (13th Wrangler), 1872; MA 1876. Assistant Master Friars School, Bangor, 1873–75, Bromsgrove School, 1875–81; Blackheath School, 1882–1905; Headmaster of Blackheath School, 1905–07. *Address:* 10 The Paragon, Blackheath, SE.

Died March 1941.

PROWDE, Oswald Longstaff, CMG 1926; MInstCE; 3rd Class Order of Ismail, 3rd Nile, 4th Medjidieh; Civil Engineer; *b* Melsonby, Yorks, 22 May 1882; *s* of late Edwin Longstaff Prowde, MA, MD, Sunderland. *Educ:* Pocklington School, Yorks; St John's Coll., Cambridge, BA Egyptian Govt. Irrigation Service, 1905–25. *Address:* 41 Harlow Moor Drive, Harrogate. *T:* Harrogate 5839.

Died 5 Nov. 1949.

PROWSE, Richard Orton, MA; novelist; *b* Woodbridge, Suffolk, 22 July 1862; *e s* of late Rev. R. H. Prowse, Rector of Framingham, Norfolk. *Educ:* Cheltenham; Balliol Coll., Oxford, MA. *Publications:* The Poison of Asps, 1892; A Fatal Reservation, 1895; Voysey, 1901; Ina, play in four acts, produced by Stage Society, 1904; James Hurd, 1913; A Gift of the Dusk, 1920; The Prophet's Wife, 1929; Proud Ashes, 1934. *Recreation:* travelling. *Address:* 47 St Quintin's Avenue, W10.

Died 25 May 1949.

PRYCE, Richard; novelist; *b* Boulogne; 2nd *s* of late Col Pryce, Gunley, Montgomeryshire, and Sarah, *d* of General Christopher Hamilton, CB, and Hon. Mrs Hamilton, *d* of 2nd Lord Castlemaine. *Educ:* Leamington. *Publications:* An Evil Spirit, 1887; The Ugly Story of Miss Wetherby, 1889; Just Impediment, 1890; The Quiet Mrs Fleming, 1890; Miss Maxwell's Affections, 1891; Deck-chair Stories, 1891; Time and the Woman, 1892; Winifred Mount, 1894; The Burden of a Woman, 1895; Elementary Jane, 1897; Jezebel, 1900; The Successor, 1904; Towing-path Bess, 1907; Christopher, 1911; David Penstephen, 1915; The Statue in the Wood, 1918; Romance and Jane Weston, 1924; Morgan's Yard, 1932. *Plays:* Little Mrs Cummin, comedy in 3 acts, 1909; The Visit, 1909 (from stories by Mary E. Mann); Helen with the High Hand, play in 3 acts (from Arnold Bennett's novel), 1914; The Old House, play in 3 acts (based on Candlelight, Mrs Dudeney's novel), 1920; Thunder on the Left, play in three acts (from Christopher Morley's novel), 1928; Frolic Wind (from R. Oke's novel), 1935; part author of Saturday to Monday; comedy in three acts, 'Op o' me Thumb, A Privy Council, The Love Child, The Dumb-Cake, etc. *Address:* The Cottage, Groom Place, Belgrave Square, SW1. *Club:* Royal Aero.

Died 30 May 1942.

PRYDE, James; *b* 30 March 1869; *s* of late David Pryde, MA, LLD, St Andrews; *m* 1899. *Educ:* Paris (Atelier Julien, under Bouguereau). Member of the International Society of Sculptors, Painters, and Gravers; Hon. Member of Czechoslovakian Academy. *Works:* exhibited at Grosvenor Gallery, Grafton Galleries, New Gallery; International Exhibitions at Knightsbridge and Piccadilly, Munich Secessionist Exposition, Berlin, Dresden, St Louis, Pittsburgh, etc.; represented in the National (Tate) Gallery of British Art, Aberdeen National Gallery, Liverpool Corporation Gallery, Corporation Galleries, Glasgow, and Johannesburg Collection; Edinburgh National Gallery, Luxembourg, Manchester, Bradford, Leeds, Aberdeen, Wales. *Address:* 3 Lansdowne House, Holland Park, W11.

Died 24 Feb. 1941.

PRYER, Major Alfred Amos, DSO 1917; late Royal Army Veterinary Corps; *b* 22 May 1891; *o s* of late Amos Pryer, Thornfields, Bishop Stortford, Hertfordshire; *m* 1923, Phyllis Margaret Charlotte Mary, *o d* of late William Simpson, Newton Abbot, Devon, and *niece* of Madame Fanny Moody-Manners; three *s* one *d*. *Educ:* Bishop Stortford College. House Surgeon, Royal

Veterinary College, London, 1913; first Commission, 1914; Major, 1925; served European War, France, 1914–19 (DSO, Chevalier, Portuguese Order of Aviz, Brevet-Majority, despatches thrice); India, 1920, 1922–25; Mesopotamia, 1920–21; Anatolia, 1922; retired pay, 1937. *Recreations:* hunting, racing, motoring, golf.

Died 13 June 1943.

PRYN, Surg. Rear-Adm. Sir William Wenmoth, KBE 1919; CB 1918; Surgeon Rear-Admiral, retired; *b* Tredown, Saltash, 21 Oct. 1859; *s* of William Pryn; *m* 1891, Isabella Kate, *d* of Major John Cotter, The Buffs; two *s* two *d*. *Educ:* College House Schools, Saltash; Blundell's School, Tiverton; Guy's Hospital, London (Gold Medallist in Surgery, 1880). House Surgeon and Resident Obstetric, Guy's; joined Navy, 1886; Assistant to Medical Director-General, 1906–10; Fleet-Surgeon, Haslar; Deputy Surgeon-General, Chatham, Gibraltar, and Plymouth Hospitals; Surgeon Rear-Admiral, Plymouth, 1917–19. *Publications:* Common Infectious Diseases in Communities at Susceptible Ages, Health of Navy, 1903; Tuberculosis in the Navy, 1860–1906; its influence on Invaliding and the Death-rate, British Journal of Tuberculosis, 1908; Tests for Colour Vision, British Medical Journal, 1910. *Address:* Roborough, Christchurch Road, Sidcup, Kent.

Died 20 Feb. 1942.

PRYOR, Grafton Deen, TD; JP Suffolk; Recorder of Ipswich since 1937; Chairman, Newmarket (Suffolk) Divisional Justices, 1940; JP Cambridgeshire, 1941; Chairman Cambridgeshire Quarter Sessions, 1941; Deputy Chairman of Corset, Perambulator and Invalid Carriage Trade Wages Councils; Chairman, Ministry of Agriculture Dispossession Appeal Tribunal; *b* 1 April 1883; *s* of late J. V. Pryor, Milton Hall, nr Cambridge, and Elizabeth Fanny, JP, *d* of late G. Hawson, Workshop, Notts; *m* 1913, Elsie, *d* of late John Lane, Newmarket; no *c*. *Educ:* Haileybury; Pembroke College, Cambridge (MA). Called to Bar, Inner Temple, 1909; served European War, 1914–19; Major, Cambridgeshire Regt (Retired); Chairman Cambridgeshire and Isle of Ely Court of Referees, 1925–45; Chm. Military Service (Hardship) Cttee for Cambridgeshire and Isle of Ely, 1938–45; Military Member Cambridgeshire and Isle of Ely Territorial Army Assoc. (Vice-Chm., 1943–44); Deputy Regional Transport Comr, Eastern Region, 1942–45; County Alderman for West Suffolk. *Recreations:* shooting, fishing, walking. *Address:* Peel House, Newmarket. *T:* Newmarket 261; 4 Paper Buildings, Temple, EC4. *T:* Central 0196. *Clubs:* Oxford and Cambridge; County, Ipswich; County, Bury St Edmunds.

Died 7 March 1947.

PRYSE, Sir Lewes Thomas Loveden, 3rd Bt *cr* 1866; *b* 5 Feb. 1864; 3rd *s* of 1st Bt and Louisa Joan, *d* of Capt. John Lewes, Llanlear, Cardiganshire; S brother, 1918; *m* 1st, 1894, Florence Madeline (from whom he obtained a divorce, 1938, for desertion), *d* of Col F. Howell of Trewellwell, Co. Pembroke; 2nd, 1938, G. Marjorie Howell. *Recreations:* hunting, shooting, fishing. *Heir: b* George Rice Pryse-Saunders [*b* 20 Feb. 1870; *m* 1895, Geraldine Mabel, *d* of late C. M. Abadam; one *s* one *d*]. *Address:* Gogerddan, Bow Street, RSO, Cardiganshire.

Died 23 May 1946.

PRYSE-RICE, Dame Margaret Ker, DBE 1918; *y d* of late Capt. James Stewart, of Alltyrodyn, Cardigans; *m* J. C. P. Vaughan Pryse-Rice (*d* 1937); one *s*. *Recreation:* gardening. *Address:* Ystrad, near Llandovery, Wales. *T:* Llandovery 75.

Died 1 June 1948.

PRYSE-SAUNDERS, Sir George Rice, 4th Bt *cr* 1866; landowner; *b* 19 Feb. 1870; 5th *s* of Sir Pryse Pryse, 1st Bt, and Louisa Joan, *d* of Capt. John Lewes, Llanlear, Cardiganshire; S brother, 1946; assumed additl surname of Saunders, 1932; *m* 1895, Geraldine Mabel, *d* of late Conrade Abadam, Middleton Hall, Carmarthenshire; one *s* one *d*. *Educ:* Brighton; HMS Worcester; Polytechnic College, Zürich. Formerly engaged in civil engineering; Asst Inspector, Board of Agriculture; Estate Agent. European War, 1914–18, Welsh Horse Yeomanry; War of 1939–45, Commandant Special Constabulary, Cardiganshire. JP and DL, Cardiganshire. *Recreations:* fishing, shooting and hunting. *Heir: s* Pryse Loveden [*b* 12 Nov. 1896; *m* 1938, Emily Georgiana Harriet, *d* of late Capt. Henry Compton Frederick Cavendish, RN]. *Address:* Ty Mawr, Ciliau Aeron, Lampeter, Cardiganshire. *TA:* Ty Mawr, Cilcennin. *T:* Aeron 28. *Club:* Royal Automobile.

Died 9 Sept. 1948.

PUDDESTER, Sir John Charles, Kt 1939; Commissioner of Government for Newfoundland and Vice-Chairman; *b* 4 Oct. 1881; *s* of Mark and Sarah B. Puddester; *m* 1902, Mary E. Moores; four *s* five *d*. *Educ:* Methodist School and College, Newfoundland. Schoolmaster, 1899–1903; Accountant Reid Newfoundland Co., 1903–16; Managing Director Robinson Co. Ltd, Printers and Publishers, 1916–32; Member House of Assembly Newfoundland, 1924–33; Secretary of State, 1932–34; Commissioner of Public Health and Welfare, and War Pensions in present Commission of Government. *Recreation:* motoring. *Address:* St Johns, Newfoundland. *Clubs:* Masonic, Murray's Pond Country, Avalon Yachting, St Johns.

Died 22 April 1947.

PUDSEY, Lt-Col Denison, DSO 1918; farming, Kenya Colony; *b* 1876; *s* of Col Henry Fawcett Pudsey and Clara Denison; unmarried. *Educ:* Repton School. Joined the Army, 1896; served British Legation Guard and attached British Legation, Peking, 1904–11; interpreter in Chinese; served European War, Tsingtau, France, Salonika, Italy (despatches three times, DSO, Military Order of the Tiger, China); served Military Inter-Allied Commission of Control, Germany, 1919–24; Director for the Trans Nzoia of the Kenya Farmers Association Ltd. *Address:* St Michaels Mount, Kitale, Kenya Colony. *Club:* Junior United Service.

Died 18 Nov. 1940.

PUECH, Denys; sculptor; *b* Gavernac, Aveyron, Nov. 1854; *m* 1906, Princesse Anina Gagarine-Stourdza (decd). Gained the Prix de Rome, 1884; member of the Beaux-Arts Academy, 1905; Directeur de l'Académie ès France à Rome, 1921–33; Commandeur de Légion d'honneur; Grand Croix l'ordre de St Stanislas de Russie et Grand Officier de Medjidie. *Principal works:* La Seine; Muse de Chenier; La Sirène; Dream of St Antony of Padua; Bust of a Child; La Musique; L'Enfant au Poisson; monuments—Jules Simon, Lecomte de Lisle, Mariette Pacha, Caire; busts—President Loubet, Emperor Nicolas II, Jules Ferry, Sainte-Beuve, President Deschanel, President G. Doumergue, Pope Benoit XV, Jeune Romain; Statue of Prince Albert I, in Oceanographical Museum, Monaco; Cannes Memorial Statue to King Edward VII. *Address:* Palais de l'Institut, Paris; 5 Boulevard Denys Puech, à Rodez, Aveyron.

Died 9 Dec. 1942.

PUGH, Ven. Edward William Wynn. *Educ:* Selwyn College, Cambridge (MA); St Michael's College, Aberdare. Curate of Usk, 1898–1902; Missionary to Indians, Lytton, BC, 1902–09; Archdeacon of Yale, 1909–14; Superintendent of Indian Missions, New Westminster, and Archdeacon of Lytton, 1914–27. *Address:* Lillooet, British Columbia.

Died 19 May 1950.

PUGH, William Thomas Gordon; Hon. Consultant Surgeon, King Edward VII Welsh National Memorial; late Chief Medical Superintendent, Children's and Surgical Tuberculosis Services, London County Council; Medical Superintendent, Queen Mary's

Hospital for Children, Carshalton, Surrey; *b* Hodley, Montgomeryshire, 9 April 1872; *s* of late William H. Pugh, HM Civil Service; *m* 1909, Elaine, *o d* of late David Edmond Hobson of Shaftesbury, Fort Beaufort, and St Lawrence, Adelaide, South Africa, one *s* one *d*. *Educ:* University College of Wales; Middlesex Hospital Medical School; London University. Senior Broderip Scholar, 1894; MD Lond.; FRCS Eng. Fellow of the Royal Society of Medicine and late President of the Orthopædic Section. *Publications:* Practical Nursing, 15th ed. 1945; reports and contributions to medical journals on subjects connected with surgical tuberculosis and infectious diseases. *Recreation:* travel. *Address:* Greyholme, 6 Browning Avenue, Boscombe, Bournemouth. *T:* Boscombe 1237.

Died 22 July 1945.

PULFORD, Air Vice-Marshal Conway Walter Heath, CB 1941; OBE 1919; AFC; Director Volunteer Reserve expansion, 1938–41; Air Vice-Marshal, 1939; Air Officer Commanding Far East, 1941; *s* of Russell Richard Pulford and Lucy Anne Pulford. *[Reported missing in Far East on 12 Feb. 1942.]*

Died 10 March 1942.

PULLEIN, John; Fellow of the Royal College of Organists; Organist and Choirmaster, Woodside Parish Church, Glasgow, since 1946; *b* Lincoln; *s* of William and Hannah Pullein. *Educ:* Lincoln Cathedral Choir School (Choir boy, Lincoln Cathedral); pupil of Dr G. J. Bennett. Organist and Choirmaster, Parish Church, Willingham-by-Stow; St Swithin's, Lincoln; St Peter's, Harrogate; Organist and Choirmaster, St Mary's Cathedral, Glasgow, 1917–40; Organist and Choirmaster, Bonhill Old Church, Vale of Leven, 1941–43; Conductor, Glasgow and Galloway Diocesan Choral Association; Member of Council, Royal College of Organists. *Publications:* Part-Songs; Church Music; Organ Music; Organ Arrangements. *Recreations:* reading, walking. *Address:* 52 Carrington Street, Glasgow, C4. *Clubs:* Society of Musicians, Art (Glasgow).

Died 9 Dec. 1948.

PULLEY, Sir Charles Thornton, Kt 1922; DL, JP; *b* 24 July 1864; *er s* of Charles Oldaker Pulley (*d* 1873), and nephew of Sir Joseph Pulley, 1st and last baronet (*d* 1901); *S* uncle, 1901; *m* 1906, Irva (*d* 1942), *d* of Peter M. Keenan, Washington, USA; no *c*. *Educ:* King's College School and King's College, London. Member of the London Stock Exchange; High Sheriff for Co. Hereford, 1912–13; MP (Coal.), South Hereford Div. May 1918; Herefordshire (Hereford Division), 1919–20; presented an Art Gallery to the City of Hereford, 1912; President of the Herefordshire General Hospital, 1912, and the Herefordshire and Worcestershire Agricultural Society, 1913; was President of the Hereford Division Unionist Association and Chairman of that Association for many years; Chairman of Hereford Bankers War Savings Committee, 1940; breeder of thoroughbred bloodstock; Member of Council of Thoroughbred Breeders Associations since its inception in 1917. *Address:* Lower Eaton, Hereford. *Clubs:* Carlton, Naval and Military.

Died 5 April 1947.

PULLING, Alexander, CB 1912; *b* 23 Sept. 1857; *e s* of late Alexander Pulling, Serjeant-at-Law of Newark Park, Gloucestershire; *m* 1891, Margaret Ellen, 4th *d* of late S. Bealey of Canterbury, New Zealand; two *s* four *d*. *Educ:* Harrow; Trinity College, Cambridge. BA 1880. Barrister-at-law, Inner Temple, 1881; Originator and, till 1895, Editor for Council of Law Reporting of the cumulative system of Law Report Digests; originated 1887–90 the systematic publication and co-ordination of Delegated Legislation (Statutory Rules); Counsel to Board of Trade on Merchant Shipping Bills, 1893 and 1894; Counsel, 1895–1918, to Board of Trade on Tramways and Light Railways; Editor from the outbreak of war till 1918 for Government Departments of all the

Manuals of Emergency Legislation and War Legislation Codes; Official Editor to HM's Treasury of Revised Statutes, Statutory Rules and Orders and connected publications till retirement, 1923. *Publications:* Index to London Gazette, 1830–1883 (1886); The Sin of Witchcraft, 1902; Handbook for County Authorities, 1888; Pulling's Shipping Code, 1894; Delegated Legislation; Proclamation, Railways and all the articles on Dominions and Protectorates, in Encyclopædia of the Laws of England, 1904–1908; Light Railway Model Forms (published officially), 1911; Disqualifications for and Vacation of Seats in House of Commons (privately printed), 1922. *Recreations:* gardening, sport, natural history, study of comparative mythology, heraldry, topography, genealogy. *Address:* Whitestone House, Whitestone, nr Exeter. *T:* Longdown 24.

Died 13 Jan. 1942.

PULLINGER, Thomas Charles Willis, CBE 1920; OBE 1918; JP; *b* 1867; *s* of Fleet-Paymaster Thomas Penford Pullinger, RN, Wyvenhoe, Dartford; *m* 1893, Aurélie Berenice Sitwell, of St Nicholas, D'Aliermont, Seine Inférieur, France; four *s* six *d*. *Educ:* Dartford Grammar School. *Recreations:* farming, yachting. *Address:* The Brae, St Brelade, Jersey. *TA:* Pullinger, St Brelade, Jersey. *T:* St Aubins, Jersey 198. *Clubs:* Royal Automobile; Royal Scottish Automobile, Royal Clyde Yacht, Glasgow; United, Jersey.

Died 19 July 1945.

PULLMAN, Major Alfred Hopewell, DSO 1915; Reserve of Officers, Queen's Own (Royal West Kent Regiment), retired; *m* Emilie Louisa Outram Marshal; one *s* one *d*. Served S Africa, 1901–02 (Queen's medal five clasps); European War, 1914–18 (despatches twice, DSO, wounded); Commandant NCO's School of Instruction, Eastern Command, 1917; NCO's School of Instruction, Aldershot Command, 1918; invalided from service on account of wounds on active service, 21 March 1918. *Address:* San Remo, Effingham Road, Surbiton, Surrey.

Died 22 April 1942.

PULTENEY, Lt-Gen. Sir William Pulteney, GCVO 1930; KCB 1915; KCMG 1917; KCVO 1918; CB 1905; DSO 1896; Gentleman Usher of Black Rod to House of Lords since 1920; *b* 18 May 1861; *y s* of late Rev. R. T. Pulteney of Ashley, Market Harboro';; *m* 1917, Jessie Alexandra, *d* of Sir John Arnott, 1st Bt. *Educ:* Eton. Joined the Scots Guards, 1881; served Egypt, 1882; present at action of Mahuta and battle of Tel-el-Kebir; employed under the Foreign Office in Uganda, 1895–97; served in Unyoro Expedition, 1895; Nandi Expedition, 1895–96 (despatches, DSO); South Africa, 1899–1902 (despatches thrice, Brevet-Col, Queen's medal 6 clasps, King's medal 2 clasps); European War, 1914–15 (despatches, KCB); Grand Officer Legion of Honour; commanded 16th Infantry Brigade, 1908–09; 6th Div., the Irish Command, 1910–14; commanded 3rd Army Corps, BEF, 1914–Feb. 1918; 23rd Army Corps in Great Britain; Mission to Japan, 1918, with Prince Arthur of Connaught; JP; Vice-Consul to the Congo Independent Free State, 1899. *Publication:* The Immortal Salient, 1925. *Recreations:* shooting, fishing; had considerable experience in big game shooting in East Africa. *Address:* 3 Fitzhardinge Street, Portman Square, W1. *T:* Welbeck 3456. *TA:* Pulteney, London. *Clubs:* Guards', Turf.

Died 14 May 1941.

PURBRICK, Reginald; *b* Melbourne, Feb. 1877; *m* 1st, 1902, Dorothy Stevens (marr. diss. 1932); two *s*; 2nd, 1939, Mme Gisele Bertha Melanie Camille Mouton Castermans (*d* 1942), formerly Baronne de Vivario. *Educ:* St Kilda Grammar School, Melbourne. Qualified for entrance to Melbourne University, but took up a commercial career which extended throughout Australia and many of the principal commercial centres of the Empire and the world generally; retired, 1921; MP (U)

Walton Division of Liverpool, 1929–45; widely travelled on business and pleasure; qualified as Chartered Accountant in Australia, but has never practised professionally. *Recreations:* golf and tennis; greatly interested in athletics; as a young man in Australia was amateur champion in walking and boxing; wrestling, fencing, running, swimming, rowing, etc. *Club:* Carlton.

Died 6 Nov. 1950.

PURCHASE, Henry George, LLD; *b* 1873; *e s* of George Henry Purchase and Victoria, *d* of David Meade, Weymouth; *m* 1902, Kathleen (*d* 1910), *y d* of Charles Roberts, JP, Holybrook, Co. Cork. Barrister-at-law; Member of Middle Temple and Northern Circuit; localised at Liverpool; LLD (London); Hon. Secretary of Cromwell Tercentenary Celebration, 1899; Assistant Hon. Secretary, New Reform Club, 1900; Parliamentary Private Secretary (unpaid) to the Chairman of National Health Insurance Committee, 1919; MP (CL) Kennington Division of Lambeth, 1918–22; Hon. Secretary of Committee of London Liberal MPs, 1918–22; of Parliamentary Committee dealing with Coastwise Traffic, 1918; special mission to France to reorganise English and American Hospital at Neuilly, 1915; assisted in Organisation of Enforcement Branch, Ministry of Food, 1918; subsequently Assistant Director of the Ministry of Food, 1942–43; contested Kennington, 1922; Kidderminster, 1923 and 1924; Leicester, 1929; Gainsborough, 1931; Blackpool, 1935; Member of the Bar delegation to Canada and the United States, 1930. *Publications:* The Law relating to Documents of Title to Goods; Occasional Papers. *Recreations:* golf, chess, tennis, and travelling. *Address:* 2 Paper Buildings, Temple, EC4. *T:* Central 0169. *Club:* National Liberal.

Died Sept. 1945.

PURCHON, William Sydney, MA, FRIBA; Head of the Welsh School of Architecture, the Technical College, Cardiff, since 1920; *b* 1879; *s* of William Smith Purchon and Martha Isabella Hunter; *m* Eleanor Maud, *d* of Alfred Strong; one *s* two *d*. *Educ:* Royal Academy Schools, etc. Articled to Brodrick, Lowther & Walker, Architects, Hull, 1893–98; Assistant to W. W. Gwyther, Architect, London, 1898–99; Architectural Assistant in Admiralty Works Dept, 1899–1907; Lecturer in charge of Department of Architecture, the University of Sheffield, 1907–20; Architect to Thos Firth & Sons and John Brown & Sons, 1915–19; Member of RIBA Council, 1934–37; Examiner in Architecture to University of Manchester and Central Welsh Board; Member of Board of Examiners, RIBA; Member of Board of Architectural Education; President, South Wales Institute of Architects, 1935–37; acting Principal Cardiff Technical College, 1941. *Publications:* Lethaby's Architecture (Revised Edition); numerous essays on Architectural subjects. *Address:* The Technical College, Cardiff. *T:* Cardiff 6813. *Club:* Connaught.

Died 9 Dec. 1942.

PURDON, Maj.-Gen. William Brooke, DSO 1917; OBE 1922, MC; DPH; QUB; MB; BCh; BAO, RUI; Ulster Agent in London from May 1946; late Medical Superintendent, Queen Mary's Hospital, Roehampton; *s* of late Richard Purdon, Belfast; *m* Dorothy Myrtle, *d* of William Coates, Belfast; one *s* one *d*. *Educ:* Queen's College, Belfast. Served European War, 1914–17 (despatches, DSO, MC); Assistant Director of Hygiene. War Office, 1930–34, British Troops in Egypt, 1934–35; Prof. of Hygiene, Royal Army Medical Coll., 1935–38; Commandant and Director of Studies, Royal Army Medical College, 1938–40; DMS, BEF, June 1940; Hon. Surgeon to the King, 1938–41; DDMS Western Command, 1940–41; retired pay, 1941. Médaille d'Honneur du Service de Santé Militaire en Vermeil; Légion d'Honneur. *Recreations:* Rugby football (Ireland and Army), shooting, fishing. *Clubs:* Army and Navy; Ulster, Union, Royal Ulster Yacht (Belfast).

Died 1 Dec. 1950.

PUREFOY, Adm. Richard Purefoy FitzGerald, CBE 1919; MVO 1902; DL, JP; *b* 26 May 1862; *e s* of Richard Purefoy FitzGerald of North Hall, Preston Candover, Hants, and Henrietta Mary, *o c* of Rev. Anthony Chester of Chicheley, Bucks; *m* 1895, Mary Lillias, *e d* of late Rev. Francis G. Sandys Lumsdaine of Lumsdaine; one *d*. [Assumed name of Purefoy, 1899]. Served Eastern Soudan, 1884; landed with Naval Brigade for protection of Suakim (medal, Bronze Star); Commander of HM Yacht, 1899–1902 (prom. Captain, MVO); Naval Adviser to Army Council, 1904; Assistant to Admiral Commanding Coastguard, 1909–11; retired, 1916; European War, 1914–18; Naval Attaché, The Hague, 1916–18. *Address:* Shalstone Manor, Buckingham. *T:* Finmere 212. *Club:* Army and Navy.

Died 19 Dec. 1943.

PURNELL, Charlotte, OBE 1933; MB, BS Durham; MS; Surgeon English Mission Hospital, Amman. *Educ:* London School of Medicine for Women; Newcastle-upon-Tyne. Late Senior House Surgeon, Bolton Infirmary; in charge of Military Hospital in Lancashire during European War. *Address:* English Hospital, Amman, Transjordania.

Died 20 June 1944.

PURSE, Benjamin Ormond; Statistical Research Department, National Institute for the Blind, 224 Great Portland Street, W1; *b* 29 Aug. 1876. *Educ:* Henshaw's Institution for the Blind; various University courses. Sociologist; gave evidence before Royal Commission on Poor Law, 1907; member of Interdepartmental Committee on the Welfare of the Blind, 1914; on Advisory Committee for the Welfare of the Blind since 1917; Vice-Pres. Henshaw's Institution for the Blind; Board of Management, Assoc. for Promoting the General Welfare of the Blind. *Publications:* The Economics of Industry; Some Commercial Aspects of Craft Instruction; The Censorship of Charities; Home Teaching and Visiting of the Adult Blind; The British Blind; Moods and Melodies (poems); regular contributor to New Beacon since 1916. *Address:* c/o National Institute for the Blind, 224 Great Portland Street, W1.

Died 31 March 1950.

PURUCKER, (Hobart Lorenz) Gottfried von; Theosophical Leader; *b* Suffern, NY, 15 Jan. 1874; *s* of Gustaf Adolf Heinrich Edmund Friedrich and Juliana Smyth; unmarried. *Educ:* Geneva, Switzerland. When 18 years of age went to USA, settling for several years in California, spending a certain time, for experience, on different ranches; in 1897–98 travelled extensively in South America; returned to New York early in 1899, thence to Geneva; spent several years in Paris; again went to USA in 1903, and after some weeks of travel took up permanent residence at the International Theosophical Headquarters at Point Loma, California; accompanied Katherine Tingley on her second world-tour, 1903–04; again accompanied Katherine Tingley to Europe, 1908 and 1912; Professor of Sanskrit and Hebrew, Theosophical University, Point Loma, 1919; DLitt 1921; succeeded Katherine Tingley as leader of the Theosophical Society, 1929; in 1930 inaugurated world-wide Theosophical Fraternization-Movement; lecture-tours, 1931, USA, England, Holland, Sweden, Finland, Germany, Switzerland; established temporary International Theosophical Headquarters, for a year, at Oakley House, Bromley Common, Kent, 1932–33; returning with staff to Point Loma, California, in Oct. 1933; in June 1942 transferred them to near Covina, California; Editor-in-Chief The Theosophical Forum. *Publications:* Theosophy and Modern Science, 1929 (revised in 1941 as Man in Evolution); H. P. Blavatsky, the Mystery (with Katherine Tingley), 1929; Questions we all ask (2 Vols), 1930; Golden Precepts of Esotericism, 1931; Fundamentals of the Esoteric Philosophy, 1932; Occult Glossary, Compendium of Oriental and Theosophical Terms, 1933; The Esoteric Tradition (2 Vols), 1935; The Story of Jesus, 1938; The Masters and the Path of Occultism, 1939. *Address:* International Theosophical Headquarters, Covina, California. *TA:* Purucker Covinacalif.

Died 27 Sept. 1942.

PURVES, Robert Egerton, CIE 1916; Public Works Department, retired; *b* 1859; European parentage; *m* 1899, Sybil Marguerite Clague; two *s* one *d*. *Educ:* Thomson College. Apprenticed engineer, 1881; Assistant Engineer, 1882; Executive Engineer, 1895; Superintendent Engineer, 1907; Chief Engineer and Secretary to Govt, Punjab, Irrigation Branch, 1913–14; retired, 1914; since practising as Hydraulic Engineer and Irrigation Expert. *Address:* 21 Elmwood Avenue, Kenton, near Harrow.

Died 16 Dec. 1943.

PURVES, Col Sir Thomas Fortune, Kt 1929; OBE, MIEE; President, Institution of Electrical Engineers, 1929–30 (elected Hon. Member, 1948); President, Institution of Post Office Electrical Engineers, 1922–33; Chairman, Engineering Joint Council, 1930–31; President, Burns Club of London, 1931–32; President, Border Counties Association of London, 1933–46; Member of General Board, National Physical Laboratory, 1929–37, Assessor to Advisory Council, Department of Scientific and Industrial Research, 1920–33; Hon. Member, Electro-technische Verein, 1930–39; Member of General Council and of Engineering Divisional Council, British Standards Institution, 1934–42; Member, Board of Managers, Royal Institution, 1935–39; Member, Grand Council of Federation of British Industries, 1942–48; Member of Council, British Electrical Industries Research Association, 1937–48; *b* Blackadder Mount, Berwickshire, 31 Dec. 1871; *s* of Andrew Purves and Jane Fortune, both of Berwickshire; *m* 1906, Euphemia Hill, *d* of late John Bertram, Apse Manor, Isle of Wight; one *s* two *d*. *Educ:* Duns Academy, Berwickshire; Heriot-Watt College, Edinburgh; Edinburgh University. Entered Civil Service by open competition, 1889; Engineering Department of Post Office, 1892; Technical Officer, 1900; Assist Superintending Engineer, 1903; Staff Engineer, 1907; Assist Engineer-in-Chief, 1919; Engineer-in-Chief of the British Post Office, 1922–32; retired, 1932; Managing Director, United Telephone Cables Ltd, 1932–36; Director of the Cable Makers' Association, 1936–48; retired Dec. 1948. Served during European War, 1914–18, as Major, RE, in Army Signal Service; Hon. Col London Home Counties Division, Royal Corps of Signals, 1923–28; has represented the British Government abroad with plenary powers at many international technical conferences and on special delegations. *Publications:* various books and articles on electrical communications engineering. *Address:* 37 Baskerville Road, Wandsworth Common, SW18.

Died 29 Jan. 1950.

PURVES-STEWART, Sir James; *see* Stewart.

PURVIS, Rt Hon. Arthur Blaikie; PC 1940; Chairman British Supply Council in North America since 1941; *b* London, England, 31 March 1890; *s* of William Blaikie Purvis, Perth, Scotland, and Annie Marie Baker, London, England; *m* 1918, Margaret, *d* of Cyrus Emory Jones, Jamestown, NY; one *s*. Junior with Lynch Brothers, London, 1905; held various positions with Nobel Explosives Company Limited, Glasgow (now Imperial Chemical Industries Ltd, London), 1910–24; President and Managing Director Canadian Industries Ltd, manufacturers of chemicals, Montreal, 1925; Director, Bank of Montreal; Bell Telephone Company of Canada; British American Oil Company, Limited; Canadian Investment Fund Ltd; Canadian Lastex Ltd; Canadian Pacific Railway Company; Canadian Safety Fuse Company, Ltd (President also); Consolidated Mining and Smelting Company of Canada Ltd; Consolidated Paper Corporation; Dunlop Tyre and Rubber Goods Company, Ltd (Vice-Chairman);

Liverpool and London and Globe Insurance Company, Ltd; North American Telegraph Company, Ltd; Northern Electric Company, Ltd; Royal Trust Company; Steel Company of Canada, and Sun Life Assurance Company of Canada; Chairman, National Employment Commission, 1936–38; Director-General, British Purchasing Commission, 1939–40; Chairman, Anglo-French Purchasing Board, Dec. 1939–June 1940; Governor, McGill Univ.; Trustee Member, Royal Institute for the Advancement of Learning; Board of Governors, Frontier College; President of Quebec Provincial Council of St John Ambulance Association, 1939. *Address:* 1020 Pine Avenue West, Montreal, Quebec. *Clubs:* Bath; St James's, Mount Royal, Mount Bruno, Forest and Stream, Montreal; Rideau, Ottawa; York, Toronto; The Century Association, New York, NY.

Died 14 Aug. 1941.

PURVIS, Adm. Sir Charles Edward K.; *see* Kennedy-Purvis.

PYCRAFT, W. P.; late Assistant-Keeper in charge of Osteological Collections, including Anthropology, British Museum (Natural History); *b* Great Yarmouth, 1868; *m* 1899, Lucy Agnes, *d* of Dunlay Shee; two *d.* Assistant Linacre Professor Comparative Anatomy, Oxford, 1892–98; Fellow Linnean Soc.; Hon. Fellow Zoological Soc.; Hon. Member Amer. Ornithologists' Union; Member Royal Anthropological Institute; Member Eugenics Society. *Publications:* A History of Birds; Random Gleanings from Nature's Fields; The Sea-Shore; British Birds and their Natural History; The Infancy of Animals; The Courtship of Animals; Camouflage in Nature; Birds of Great Britain, 1934, etc.; numerous Memoirs in publications of various Scientific Societies. *Recreation:* study of Natural History. *Address:* Little Paddock, Longcross, Chertsey. *T:* Longcross 310.

Died 1 May 1942.

PYE, Col William Edmund, CIE 1917; Indian Army (retired); *b* 29 April 1872; *s* of late Capt. Kellow C. Pye, RE; *m* 1903, Kitty (*d* 1938), *y d* of Col Hamilton; one *s.* *Educ:* Wellington; Sandhurst. Entered Derbyshire Regt 1892; Captain Indian Army, 1901; Major 1910; Col 1922; served Tirah, 1897–98 (medal two clasps); China, 1900 (medal); European War, operations in Persia, commanded Seistan Area (two medals); Afghanistan & NWF, 1919 (despatches); Persia, 1919–20 (medal and clasp); retired, 1924. *Address:* Kilpeck, Crowborough, Sussex.

Died 30 Aug. 1949.

PYM, Col Frederick Harry Norris, CMG 1918; Retired Pay, AOD; *b* 17 Nov. 1868. Entered Army, 1886; retired, 1906.

Died 17 June 1944.

PYM, Leslie Ruthven; DL, JP, MP (U) Monmouth since 1939; *b* 24 May 1884; *s* of late Rt Rev. Walter Ruthven Pym, Bishop of Bombay; *m* 1914, Iris, *d* of Charles Orde, Hopton House, Great Yarmouth; one *s* three *d. Educ:* Bedford; Magdalene College, Cambridge. Parliamentary Private Secretary to Parliamentary Secretary, Ministry of Food, 1940–42; Junior Lord of the Treasury 1942; Comptroller of HM's Household, May 1945. President Land Agents Society, 1936. *Address:* Penpergwm Lodge, Abergavenny, Monmouthshire. *T:* Gobion 208; Hasells Hall Sandy Bedfordshire; 2 Halkin Place, SW1. *Clubs:* Travellers', Carlton.

Died 17 July 1945.

PYM, Rev. Thomas Wentworth, DSO 1917; retd; *b* 1885; *s* of late Rt Rev. Walter Ruthven Pym, Bishop of Bombay; *m* 1918, Dora Olive, *d* of late William Ivens of Harboro' Parva, Rugby; two *s* two *d. Educ:* Bedford School; Trinity College, Cambridge, MA. Formerly Chaplain at Trinity College, Cambridge, and Assistant Chaplain-General to the Third Army in France; served European War, 1914–19 (DSO, despatches three times); Head of Cambridge House, Camberwell, 1919–25; Rural Dean of Camberwell, 1922–25; Diocesan Missioner and Canon of Southwark, 1925–29; Chaplain and Fellow of Balliol College, Oxford, 1932–38; a Proctor of Convocation, Southwark, 1926; Chaplain to HM, 1922–37; Canon Residentiary of Bristol, 1929–32; Diocesan Missioner, 1932–41 and Hon. Canon of Bristol, 1932. *Publications:* (Joint) Papers from Picardy, 1917; Mark's Account of Jesus; Psychology and the Christian Life, 1921; More Psychology and the Christian Life, 1925; Spiritual Direction, 1928; The Place of Sex in Life, 1928; A Parson's Dilemmas, 1930; Sharing, 1933; Conduct, 1933; Our Personal Ministry; Sex and Sense, 1938. *Address:* 10 Downfield Road, Clifton, Bristol, 8.

Died 20 July 1945.

PYMAN, Frank Lee, FRS; DSc (Vict.); PhD (Basle); FIC; Research Director, Boots Pure Drug Co. Ltd; *b* Malvern, 9 April 1882; *e s* of Frank Pyman, MA, LLB, of London, and Florence, *d* of late Henry Lee, JP; *m* 1907, Ida Catrine, *e d* of George Lowry, Putney; three *s* two *d. Educ:* Dover College; Victoria University of Manchester; Zurich Polytechnic. Late Professor of Technological Chemistry, Municipal College of Technology, University of Manchester; formerly Director of the Welcome Chemical Research Laboratories. *Publications:* contributions to the Journal of the Chemical Society. *Address:* Manor House, Radcliffe-on-Trent, Notts. *T:* Radcliffe-on-Trent 110. *Club:* Devonshire.

Died 1 Jan. 1944.

PYNE, Brig. Henry George, CB 1944; MC 1916; Chief Engineer, Southern Command, since 1943; *b* 23 Aug. 1887; *s* of G. M. Pyne and Fanny Dwyer; *m* 1924, Betty M. Martin (*née* Calthrop); one *s* one *d. Educ:* Bedford; RMA, Woolwich. Commission, 1908. European War, 1914–18, Western front (MC, despatches, wounded); Egyptian Army, 1919–22; CRE Delhi (India), 1926–30; CRE Gibraltar, 1933–37; Deputy Chief Engineer Southern Command, 1938–39; Chief Engineer Western Command (India), 1939; Chief Engineer 4th Corps, Norway, 1940; Chief Engineer 5th Corps, 1940; ADFW War Office, 1941–43. Retired 1945. *Recreations:* riding, shooting, and fishing. *Address:* Ballyvolane, Fermoy, Ireland. *Club:* United Service.

Died 26 Dec. 1945.

Q

QUARMBY, Sir John, Kt 1934; Alderman, West Riding County Council; Vice-Chairman, 1939; *b* 3 May 1868; *s* of James Quarmby and Betsy Sykes; *m*; one *s*. *Educ:* Longwood Grammar School. Chairman of Directors Quarmby and Sykes, Ltd, Meltham, Huddersfield; JP West Riding Yorkshire, 1921. *Recreation:* hunting. *Address:* Stocksmoor, Huddersfield. *T:* Kirkburton 114.

Died 4 Jan. 1943.

QUAYLE-JONES, Brig.-Gen. Morey, CB 1898; CMG 1917; CBE 1920; DL, JP Warwickshire; *b* Pakenham, Suffolk, 8 March 1855; *s* of late Rev. Charles William Jones, Vicar of Pakenham; *m* 1888, Isabel (*d* 1945), *d* of Maitland Dashwood; one *d*. *Educ:* Wellington College. Barrister-at-law, Middle Temple, 1890. Major, 4th Pioneers, Bechuanaland Expedition, 1884–85; Lieut-Col 1898; Commanded 1st Batt. the Royal Warwickshire Regiment, Nile Expedition, 1898 (CB, despatches, Soudan medal and clasp, and English medal); 2nd Batt.; South African War, 1899–1901 (Queen's medal four clasps); Commanded 6th Regimental District, 1901–04; Brig.-Gen. 17th Infantry Brigade, Irish Command, 1905–09; retired, 1909; rejoined Army, 1914, as Brig.-Gen. Commanding 104th Infantry Brigade, 4th Army, 1914–15; 11th Reserve Brigade, 1915–16 (medal, despatches, CMG); National Service Sub-Commissioner, 1917. *Address:* Barton Mere, Great Barton, nr Bury St Edmunds. *Club:* Army and Navy.

Died 3 Jan. 1946.

QUEENBOROUGH, 1st Baron *cr* 1918; **Almeric Hugh Paget,** GBE 1926; JP Suffolk and London; Knight of Justice of St John of Jerusalem; President, National Union of Conservative and Unionist Associations, 1928–29, 1940, and 1941, and of Eastern Provincial Division, 1909–46; Parliamentary Provincial Whip for Eastern and Home Counties since 1911; Hon. Fellow, Corpus Christi College, Cambridge; Governor, Guy's Hospital; President, Miller General Hospital of Greenwich until 1948; late: Member of Council, Zoological Society of London, Treasurer, League of Nations Union, Joint Hon. Treasurer, London School of Hygiene and Tropical Medicine; *b* 14 March 1861; *y s* of late Gen. Lord Alfred Henry Paget, CB, 5th *s* of Field-Marshal 1st Marquis of Anglesey; *m* 1st 1895, Pauline (*d* 1916), *d* of late Hon. Wm C. Whitney, Secretary of State for Navy, US America; two *d*; 2nd, 1921, Edith (*d* 1933) *d* of Wm Starr Miller, New York; three *d*. *Educ:* Harrow. Lived many years in United States of America, ranching and farming in North-West; later in New York; director of various large commercial undertakings there, and President Chihuahua and Pacific Railroad; Member of the Government Committee on Detention and Delay at Ports of Neutral Shipping; Member Executive Committee Tariff Reform League and Central Land Association; President Royal Society of St George, Director Canadian Gen. Investment Trust Ltd, Chicago Gaika Development Trust, and Third Canadian Investment Trust; contested Cambridge, 1906; High Sheriff, Suffolk, 1909; Member Council, Yacht Racing Assoc.; MP (U) Cambridge, 1910–17; resigned, 1917. *Recreations:* yacht racing, shooting, travel. *Heir:* none. *Address:* Camfield Place, Hatfield. *T:* Essendon 226. *Clubs:* Carlton, Turf, St Stephen's, Bath, Royal Thames Yacht (Vice-Commodore); Royal Yacht Squadron (Cowes).

Died 22 Sept. 1949 (ext).

QUEKETT, Sir Arthur Scott, Kt 1923; Parliamentary Counsel to Government of Northern Ireland, 1921–45; *b* London, 27 Aug. 1881; *e s* of late Arthur Edwin Quekett, MA Oxon, and Marion, *d* of late J. P. Adams; *m* 1914, Edith Blanche, *y d* of late Francis Quekett Louch, solicitor, Newbury, Berks; three *s*. *Educ:* Merchant Taylors' School, London; Trinity College, Dublin; Littledale Prize, 1903; BA, 1905; LLB 1909; LLD 1918; King's Inns, Dublin, Victoria Prize. Barrister-at-law, 1909; KC (Northern Ireland) 1923; Legal Assistant Local Government Board for Ireland, 1912–21; Inspector of Local Acts, Local Government Board for Ireland, 1919–21. *Publications:* contributions to Journal of Comparative Legislation and other legal periodicals; The Constitution of Northern Ireland, Part I 1928; Part II 1933. *Recreations:* golf, lawn tennis, music. *Address:* 43 Earlswood Road, Belfast. *T:* Belfast 55195. *Clubs:* Constitutional; Ulster, Belfast.

Died 2 Oct. 1945.

QUICK, Rev. Oliver Chase, MA; DD, Oxon, 1939; Hon. DD St Andrews, 1928, Durham, 1941; Canon of Christ Church and Regius Professor of Divinity in the University of Oxford, 1939–43; a Chaplain to the King since 1933; *b* Sedbergh, Yorks, 1885; *o s* of late Rev. Robert Hebert Quick (educationalist and author of Educational Reformers); *m* 1917, Frances Winifred, *d* of Hugh W. Pearson, Malton, Yorks; two *s* two *d*. *Educ:* Harrow School; Corpus Christi College, Oxford, Ellerton Prize, 1911; Bishop's Hostel, Farnham, 1909–11. Deacon, 1911; Priest, 1912; Curate of St Paul's, Beckenham, 1911–12; Vice-Principal of Leeds Clergy School, 1912–14; Curate of St Martin's-in-the-Fields, 1914–15; Resident Chaplain to Archbishop of Canterbury, 1915–17; temp. CF 1917–18; Vicar of Kenley, Surrey, 1918–20; Canon Residentiary of Newcastle Cathedral, 1920–23; of Carlisle, 1923–30; Canon and Precentor of St Paul's Cathedral, 1930–34; Canon of Durham Cathedral and Professor of Divinity and Ecclesiastical History in University of Durham, 1934–39. *Publications:* Modern Philosophy and the Incarnation, 1915; Essays in Orthodoxy, 1916; The Testing of Church Principles, 1919; Liberalism, Modernism and Tradition, Paddock Lectures, 1922; Christian Beliefs and Modern Questions, 1923; Catholic and Protestant Elements in Christianity, 1924; The Christian Sacraments, 1927; The Realism of Christ's Parables, 1929; The Ground of Faith and the Chaos of Thought, 1931; The Gospel of Divine Action, 1933; Doctrines of the Creed, 1938; Christianity and Justice, 1940. *Address:* Christ Church, Oxford.

Died 21 Jan. 1944.

QUICKE, Captain Noel Arthur Godolphin; *b* 27 Dec. 1888; 2nd *s* of E. H. G. Quicke, Newton House, Newton St Cyres, Devon; *m* 1921, Constance May, 2nd *d* of Sir John Shelley, 9th Bt; two *s* one *d*. *Educ:* Clifton College; RMC Sandhurst. Duke of Cornwall's LI, 1909–20 (despatches); JP Devon, 1927; County Commandant Special Constabulary, 1939; High Sheriff of Devon, 1939. *Recreation:* shooting. *Address:* Newton House, Newton St Cyres, nr Exeter. *T:* Newton St Cyres 22. *Club:* Bath.

Died 16 Dec. 1943.

QUIDDE, Ludwig; writer; refugee pacifist; *b* Bremen, 23 March 1858; *m* Margarethe Jacobson. *Educ:* Gymnasium, Bremen; University of Strasburg and University of Göttingen. Secretary of the Prussian Hist. Inst at Rome, 1890; Member of the Academy of Science at Munich, 1892; Municipal Council of Munich, 1901; Bavarian

Second Chamber, 1907; Interparl. Union, 1908; permanent member, 1921; Vice-Chairman Bavarian Provisional Council, 1918; National Assembly of Weimar, 1919; founded Munich Peace Society, 1894; a Member of the International Peace Council since 1901; Vice-President since 1920; Editor of the Zeitschrift für Geschichtswissenschaft, 1889–95; Editor of the Deutsche Reichstagsakten (14th and 15th century), 1882–1936; Nobel Peace Prize, 1927. *Publications:* historical and political (especially pacifist) subjects. *Address:* München, Ohmstrasse 17, Germany. *T:* 30643; Geneva, 8 Avenue Blanc, Switzerland.

Died 4 March 1941.

QUIGLEY, Arthur Grainger; *b* Birkenhead; *m* Lottie Houghey, *d* of late John P. Forster of Little Sutton, Cheshire; one *d*. *Educ:* Birkenhead. Studied drawing and painting at Birkenhead School of Art and later at the City School of Art, Liverpool. Assistant Curator, Walker Art Gallery, 1898–1920; Director, 1920–31; retired, 1931. *Recreation:* painting. *Address:* 14 Sea View Terrace, St Ives, Cornwall.

Died 16 Dec. 1945.

QUILLER-COUCH, Sir Arthur Thomas, Kt 1910; JP Cornwall; MA Oxford; MA Cambridge; LittD Bristol; LLD Aberdeen; LLD Edinburgh; FRSL; Member of Academic Committee; King Edward VII Professor of English Literature, Cambridge University, since 1912; Fellow Jesus College, Cambridge; Hon. Fellow of Trinity College, Oxford; is a Freeman of Bodmin, Fowey, and Truro; *b* Cornwall, 21 Nov. 1863; *e s* of late Thomas Quiller-Couch; *g s* of Jonathan Couch, Polperro, the ichthyologist; *m* 1889, Louisa Amelia, *d* of late John Hicks, of Fowey; one *d*. *Educ:* Newton Abbot College; Clifton College; Trinity College, Oxford. Lecturer Classics Trin. Coll., Oxford, 1886–87; removed to London; was connected with the Speaker from its commencement until autumn of 1899; in 1891 left London for his native county, where he has since resided; Mayor of Fowey, 1937. *Publications:* Dead Man's Rock, 1887; Troy Town, 1888; The Splendid Spur, 1889; Noughts and Crosses, 1891; The Blue Pavilions, 1891; I Saw Three Ships, 1892; The Warwickshire Avon, 1892; The Delectable Duchy, 1893; Green Bays: Verses and Parodies, 1893; Wandering Heath, 1895; The Golden Pomp, 1895; Ia, 1896; Adventures in Criticism, 1896; Poems and Ballads, 1896; The Ship of Stars, 1899; Old Fires and Profitable Ghosts, 1900; The Oxford Book of English Verse, 1900; The Laird's Luck, 1901; The Westcotes, 1902; The White Wolf, 1902; The Adventures of Harry Revel, 1903; Hetty Wesley, 1903; Two Sides of the Face, 1903; Fort Amity, 1904; Shining Ferry, 1905; Shakespeare's Christmas, 1905; From a Cornish Window, 1906; Sir John Constantine, 1906; Poison Island, 1907; Merry Garden, 1907; Major Vigoureux, 1907; True Tilda, 1909; Lady Good-for-Nothing; Corporal Sam and other Stories; The Oxford Book of Ballads, 1910; Brother Copas, 1911; The Oxford Book of Victorian Verse; Hocken and Hunken, 1912; The Vigil of Venus and other Poems, 1912; News from the Duchy; Nicky-Nan Reservist, 1915; On the Art of Writing, 1916; Memoir of Arthur John Butler, 1917; Mortallone and Aunt Trinidad, 1917; Foe-Farrell; Shakespeare's Workmanship; Studies in Literature, 1918, second series, 1922, third series, 1929; On the Art of Reading, 1920; Charles Dickens and other Victorians,

1925; The Poet as Citizen, 1934; Q's Mystery Stories, 1937; Memories and Opinions, 1944; Editor, Oxford Book of Prose, 1925; Co-editor of The New Shakespeare. *Recreations:* yachting, rowing. *Address:* The Haven, Fowey, Cornwall; Jesus College, Cambridge. *Clubs:* Royal Thames Yacht; Royal Fowey Yacht (Commodore); Cambridge University Cruising (President).

Died 12 May 1944.

QUIN, Sir Stephen, Kt 1918; DL, JP; *b* 26 Dec. 1860; *s* of John Quin, DL, Limerick; *m* 1886, Emma Mary, *d* of Michael Theobald Crean, Barrister-at-law and Irish Land Commission, Dublin; two *s*. *Educ:* Ushaw College, Durham. High Sheriff Limerick City, 1897–98; Mayor of Limerick, 1916–17; Member of Irish Convention, 1917–18; DL, JP Co. and City of Limerick; Queen Victoria's Jubilee Medal, 1897. *Address:* Swinley Wood, South Ascot, Berks. *T:* Ascot 721. *Clubs:* United Service, Dublin; County, Limerick.

Died 11 May 1944.

QUINAN, Kenneth Bingham, CH 1917; consulting chemical engineer, special work in connection with explosives, Supply Department, Ministry of Munitions; *b* 1878. *Address:* Bizweni, Somerset West, Cape Province, S Africa.

Died 26 Jan. 1948.

QUIRK, Lt-Col Douglas, CMG 1919; DSO 1917; Italian Croce di Guerra, 1918; late Commanding 8th Service Battalion, The King's Own Yorkshire Light Infantry (in France and Italy); *b* 24 March 1887; *s* of late Rev. Canon James Francis Quirk; *m* 1918, Ella Gladstone, *y d* of late G. R. Leyland of Grassendale, Liverpool, and Mrs Leyland of Oxton, Birkenhead. *Educ:* Pocklington School, East Yorkshire. Land Agent and Farmer in civil life; 2nd Lieut in 8th (S) Batt. York and Lancaster Regt 1914; Adjutant, 1914–16; went through all grades and took over present command on 1 March 1917; previously commanded temporarily the 9th (S) Batt. The York and Lancaster Regt, 11th (S) Batt. The Notts and Derby Regt; Commandant of the 23rd Divisional School; went out to France, 27 Sept. 1915; served European War, 1914–19 (DSO, CMG, despatches four times); demobilised as from 30 March 1919; assumed appointment as District Commissioner under Ministry of Agriculture and Fisheries, on 31 March 1919, for Counties of Yorkshire and Durham. *Recreations:* shooting, hunting, and tennis. *Address:* St John's Avenue, Thorner, near Leeds.

Died 13 June 1941.

QUIRK, Rev. Canon Robert; Canon Residentiary since 1939, Treasurer since 1938 and Librarian since 1940 of Salisbury Cathedral; *b* 18 Jan. 1883; *s* of John Nathaniel Quirk, Bishop Suffragan of Sheffield and later of Jarrow; *m* 1908, Anna Diana (Stella) Sedgwick; one *s* two *d*. *Educ:* Eton (Kings' Scholar, Newcastle Scholar); King's College, Cambridge, 1st Class Classics. Assistant Master, Winchester College, 1905–38; Chaplain, 1912–38; Housemaster, 1919–36; TCF 1917–18, Hon. CF 1919. *Recreations:* gardening, walking. *Address:* 54 The Close, Salisbury. *T:* Salisbury 2996. *Clubs:* Athenæum, English-Speaking Union.

Died 12 March 1949.

R

RABINO, H. Louis, CMG 1937; OBE; *b* 27 July 1877; *s* of Joseph Rabino di Borgomale; *m* M. Paule (*d* 1947), *d* of Col R. J. Pagès des Huttes; one *s. Educ:* privately. Acting Consul, Kermanshah, 1904 and 1905; Vice-Consul at Resht, 1906–12; Mogador, 1912–16; Acting Consul and then Consul at Casablanca, 1915–22; Consul at Cairo, 1922–24; negotiated with the French Protectorate authorities in Morocco the settlement of the question of Crown and mosque property in British hands, 1917–19; HBM Consul-General, Smyrna, 1924–28; Salonika, 1928–29; Cairo, 1929–37; Consul-General in North Africa and President of Naval Courts, 1943–45; and in France, 1945. Counsellor at the Embassy, Paris, in charge of War Claims Department, 1945–47. *Publications:* Le Guilan; Mazandaran and Astarabad; Le Monastère de Sainte-Catherine (Mont-Sinai); Coins, Medals and Seals of the Shahs of Iram, 1501–1943; Essai d'un Armorial de l'ancien Comté de Nice et de la Principauté de Monaco; numerous papers on Persia and Morocco, and genealogical studies. *Address:* c/o Westminster Foreign Bank Ltd, 18 Place Vendôme, Paris 1.

Died 26 Sept. 1950.

RACHMANINOFF, Sergei Vassilievitch; pianist and composer; *b* Novgorod, Russia, 2 April 1873; *m*; two *d. Educ:* Moscow and Petrograd Conservatories. Has appeared in Europe and America with leading orchestras as pianist and as conductor of his own works; written two Operas, four Symphonies, four Pianoforte Concertos; a large number of Pianoforte pieces and songs. *Publication:* Recollections, 1934. *Address:* c/o Ibbs and Tillett, 124 Wigmore Street, W1.

Died 28 March 1943.

RACKHAM, Harris, MA; Fellow of Christ's College, Cambridge; *b* 22 Dec. 1868; *s* of late Alfred Thomas Rackham, Admiralty Marshal; *m* 1901, Clara Dorothea, *d* of Henry Tabor. *Educ:* City of London School; Christ's College, Camb. (Scholar); BA 1890; Fellow, 1894. Classical Tutor, 1898–1911; Senior Tutor, 1911–14; Tutor, 1919–23; Lecturer, 1898–1915 and 1919–38; Lecturer, Newnham College, 1893–1910; University Lecturer, 1926–34; temporary Assistant Master, Winchester College, 1891–92 and 1915–17; Intelligence Department, Admiralty, 1917–18; Treasury, 1918–19; late Cambridge Secretary for Toynbee Hall; temporary Lecturer, Emmanuel College, 1939–40. *Publications:* edition of Prometheus Vinctus of Æschylus; translations of Cicero's De Finibus, Academica, De Natura Deorum and (with E. W. Sutton) De Oratore of Aristotle's Ethics, Politics, Athenian Constitution, Eudemian Ethics and Rhetoric to Alexander, and of Pliny's Natural History, Vols I–IV, in Loeb series; Early Statues of Christ's College; This Way and That (translations into and out of Greek and Latin verse and prose); Aristotle's Ethics for English Readers; edited Antiquities of Christ's College (from Christ's College, Magazine) and Memoir of Thomas Cecil Fitzpatrick. *Address:* 9 Park Terrace, Cambridge. *T:* Cambridge 4321.

Died 20 March 1944.

RADCLIFFE, Alexander Nelson; senior partner in the firm of Radcliffes and Co; *b* 30 Sept. 1856; 4th *s* of John Alexander Radcliffe of Ordsal, Cobham, Surrey; *m* 1884, Isabel Grace, *d* of Lt-Col Sir E. Y. W. Henderson, KCB, sometime Chief Commissioner of Metropolitan Police; two *s* (both killed in war) three *d. Educ:* Eton; Göttingen. Hon. Major, 18th Middlesex RV; for many years a member of the Committee of the Kennel Club, and a well-known judge of collies. *Address:* 45 Kensington Square, W8; Bag Park, Widecombe-in-the-Moor, Newton Abbot, S Devon. *T:* Western 6943.

Died 26 March 1944.

RADCLIFFE, Very Rev. Bennett Samuel, BD, Incumbent of Kells and Burnchurch, Co. Kilkenny, since 1936. *Educ:* Trinity College, Dublin. Curate of Carlow, 1897–1902; Diocesan Curate of Leighlin, 1902–05; of Moyliscar, 1905–07; Incumbent of Moynalty, 1907–11; of Killucan, 1911–32; Dean of Clonmacnoise, 1929–32. *Address:* Kells Priory, Thomastown, Co. Kilkenny.

Died Aug. 1943.

RADCLIFFE, Ven. Harry Sydney, MA; Archdeacon of Lynn, 1926–46; Emeritus since 1946; *b* 7 May 1867; 4th *s* of late Sir David Radcliffe; *m* 1904, Elspeth, *d* of late W. Tod; four *d. Educ:* Liverpool College, Exeter College, Oxford; Leeds Clergy School. Had five years' experience of commercial life in Liverpool; ordained, 1894; Curate in Charge, New Springs, 1896; Rector of Gaywood, 1906–46; Vicar of Mintlyn, 1937–46; Hon. Canon of Norwich Cathedral, 1924–26; Rural Dean of Lynn, 1918–26; Commandant BRCS, 1914–26. *Publications:* The Church Plate of the Rural Deanery of Lynn; The Church Plate of the old Deanery of Cranwich and part of the Deanery of Walsingham in Norfolk; The Church Plate of the Borough of King's Lynn and West Lynn; The Church Plate of the Deaneries of East and West Fincham, Lynn Marshland and Wisbech. *Recreation:* archæological research. *Address:* Ken Hill, Snettisham, King's Lynn, Norfolk.

Died 6 Oct. 1949.

RADCLIFFE, Sir Joseph (Edward), 4th Bt *cr* 1813; *b* 1 Aug. 1858; *e s* of 3rd Bt and Katharine Mary Elizabeth, *d* of Sir Edward Doughty Tichborne, 9th Bt; *S* father, 1908; *m* 1881, Mary Katherine (*d* 1943), *d* of J. R. Talbot of Rhode Hill, Devon; three *s* one *d. Educ:* Oscott. Late Capt. 3rd Batt. Yorkshire Regiment. *Heir: s* Everard Joseph, JP [*b* 27 Jan. 1884; *m* 1909, Daisy, 3rd *d* of Capt. Ashton Case of Beckford Hall, Gloucesters.; four *s.* Downside; Christ Church, Oxford (BA). Boodle's; Yorkshire, York]. *Address:* Rudding Park, Harrogate. *T:* 81350.

Died 29 Sept. 1949.

RADCLIFFE, Col Philip John Joseph, CMG 1918; late RE; *b* 1863; 3rd *s* of Sir J. E. Radcliffe, 3rd Bart; *m* 1893, Maud, *d* of late Sir F. A. Weld, GCMG; one *d.* Served European War, 1914–18 (CMG). *Address:* 70 Duke Street, Grosvenor Square, W1. *T:* Mayfair 2680. *Club:* Army and Navy.

Died 24 May 1943.

RADCLYFFE-HALL, Marguerite Antonia; *see* Hall, Miss Radclyffe.

RADFORD, Edmund Ashworth, FCA; MP (U) Rusholme Division of Manchester since 1933; MP (U) South Salford, 1924–29; chartered accountant; *b* Feb. 1881; *s* of late George Radford of Manchester and Church Stretton; *m* 1912, Beatrice, *d* of late William Hay of Cheadle Hulme; two *d. Educ:* Buxton College. Became a chartered accountant in 1902; senior partner of E. A. Radford, Edwards and Co., chartered accountants, of Royal Mail House, 76 Cross Street, Manchester. *Address:* White Gables, Wilmslow, Cheshire. *Clubs:* St Stephens, Royal Automobile, Constitutional; Engineers', Manchester.

Died 27 May 1944.

RADLEY, Brig. Hugh Poynton, CIE 1936; MC; *b* 14 Nov. 1891; *s* of Henry Radley and Frances Lyons; *m* 1922, Ilma de Poellnitz Healey; one *d*. *Educ*: Stonyhurst. European War, 1914–19; Mesopotamia, 1915–19; Waziristan Operations, 1922; Shanghai Defence Force, 1927; Bde Maj. Jhansi Bde; Mohmand Operations, 1933; Loe Agra Operations, 1935; retired, 1939, but serving again. *Address*: c/o Lloyds Bank, 6 Pall Mall, SW1. *Club:* Army and Navy.

Died 27 Aug. 1943.

RAE, Lt-Col Cecil, CBE 1937; JP; Managing Director Macphail & Co. (Ipoh) Ltd; Director of numerous Tin and Rubber Cos; *b* Melbourne, Australia, 1880; *s* of R. A. V. Rae; *m* 1912, Nancy (*d* 1940), *d* of Rev. William Wilson, Stirling, Scotland; no *c*. Served with Indian Army during European War; OC local Volunteer Forces for some years, at present Reserve of Officers; Senior Unofficial Member of Council FMS Legislature; Member Council of State, Perak. *Recreation:* motoring. *Address:* Ipoh, Perak, Federated Malay States. *TA:* Ipoh. *Clubs:* Junior Carlton; and various local. *[Interned Changi Camp.]*

Died 10 July 1945.

RAE, Cecil Douglas, CIE 1936; OBE 1927; India Posts and Telegraphs Service, retired; *b* 29 June 1882. Joined the Service 1899; Postmaster-General, United Provinces, 1930; Madras, 1932; Bombay, 1933; retired 1938.

Died 16 Jan. 1942.

RAEBURN, Henry Raeburn Macbeth-, RA 1933; ARA 1922; RE; artist and engraver; *b* 24 Sept. 1860; *s* of Norman Macbeth, RSA; *m* 1st, 1883, Isabel Elizabeth (*d* 1929); one *d*; 2nd, 1936, Marjorie May, *e d* of Arthur Bacon. *Educ:* Edinburgh Academy and University; Royal Scottish Academy; Julian's Studio, Paris. Started as portrait painter in London, 1884; became engraver, 1890; has been constant exhibitor at British and Continental Exhibitions since 1884. *Publication:* Engraved plates after all the well-known masters. *Recreations:* golf, fishing, sailing, and other outdoor sports. *Address:* 33 Southtown Road, Gt Yarmouth. *Clubs:* Arts, Northwood Golf.

Died 3 Dec. 1947.

RAEBURN, Sir William Norman, 2nd Bt *cr* 1923; CBE 1920; MA, LLB; KC 1919; *b* 1877; *e s* of Sir William H. Raeburn, 1st Bart, and Sarah Manifold; *S* father 1934; *m* 1912, Mary Irene (*d* 1927), *e d* of Fred. Lennard, Hove, Sussex; one *s* two *d*. *Educ:* Kelvinside Academy, Glasgow; Uppingham; Glasgow Univ. Called to Bar, 1903. *Publication:* 3rd edition of Blackburn on Sale. *Recreation:* golf. *Heir: s* Edward Alfred, *b* 18 May, 1919. *Address:* 5 Paper Buildings, Temple, EC4. *T:* Central 4763; The Mount, St John's, Woking. *T:* Woking 479. *Clubs:* Caledonian; Woking Golf.

Died 5 Feb. 1947.

RAFFETY, Frank Walter, OBE 1945; Barrister-at-law; Recorder of High Wycombe since 1905; *b* 1875; *s* of late Charles Walter Raffety, High Wycombe; *m* 1912, Jessie, *y d* of W. H. Brown, of Harts, Woodford Green; one *s*. Called to the Bar, Middle Temple, 1898; MP (L) Bath, 1923–24; contested West Lewisham by-election, Sept. 1921, and West Bristol, Nov. 1922; Bath, 1924; Cheltenham, 1929; East Dorset, 1935; Member LCC, West Islington, 1922–25; a Vice-Pres., Industrial Co-Partnership Association; Hon. Freeman of High Wycombe, 1943. *Publications:* joint editor, Burke's Works, 1906; Maxims and Reflections of Burke, 1908; Editor, Modern Business Practice, 1912; The Future of Party Politics, 1918; Our Part in the League of Nations, 1920; Partnership in Industry, 1928. *Address:* 4 Paper Buildings, Temple, EC4; Struan, Links Road, Bramley, Surrey. *Clubs:* Reform, National Liberal.

Died 8 Sept. 1946.

RAFFETY, Harold Vezey, CBE 1935; OBE 1917; *b* 1873; *s* of late Charles Walter Raffety, JP, Hon. Freeman of High Wycombe; *m* 1902, Etty, *d* of John Clayton; one *s* two *d*. Chartered Surveyor; Chief Land Commissioner, Ministry of Agriculture, 1921–37. *Address:* Walters Ash, Wood End Close, Farnham Common, Bucks. *T:* Farnham Common 519. *Club:* Beaconsfield Golf (Beaconsfield).

Died 12 Nov. 1948.

RAGG, Ven. Lonsdale, DD; Prebendary of Buckden in Lincoln Cathedral; Archdeacon of Gibraltar since 1934; *b* Wellington, Shropshire, 23 Oct. 1866; 5th *s* of Rev. Thomas Ragg, late Vicar of Lawley, Shropshire; *m* 1902, Laura, *d* of late Major Roberts, 31st Bengal Native Infantry; one *d*. *Educ:* Newport (Shropshire) School; Christ Church, Oxford; Cuddesdon Theological College. Curate of All Saints', Oxford, 1890; tutor and lecturer at Christ Church, 1891–95; Vice-Principal of Cuddesdon Theological College, 1895–98; Warden of the Bishop's Hostel, Lincoln, and Vice-Chancellor of Lincoln Cathedral, 1899–1903; Winter Chaplain at Bologna, 1904–05; British Chaplain at Venice, 1905–09; Rector of Tickencote, Rutland, 1909–12; Diocesan Inspector for the Archdeaconry of Northampton, 1912–15; Warden of Bangor and St Asaph Clerical Education Society, and Examining Chaplain to the Bishops of Bangor and St Asaph, 1917–22 Diocesan Missioner for the Diocese of Oxford, 1922–24; English Chaplain at Rome, 1924–30; English Chaplain at Valescure, 1930–31; at Bordighera, 1933–34 Public Preacher in diocese of Bath and Wells, 1941. Chaplain of Order of St John of Jerusalem 1943. *Publications:* Second Book of Samuel in The Books of the Bible Christian Evidences in Oxford Church Text Books; Aspects of the Atonement; Christ and our Ideals; Dante and his Italy; The Mohammedan Gospel of Barnabas (jointly with Mrs Ragg, authoress of The Women Artists of Bologna, of Things Seen in Venice, and of Crises in Venetian History); The Church of the Apostles; The Book of Books; Things Seen in Venice (with Mrs Ragg); Memoir of Edward Charles Wickham; Venice (with Mrs Ragg), 1916; Commentary on St Luke, 1922; Dante, Apostle of Freedom, 1922; Some of My Tree Friends, 1931; Trees I Have Met 1933; Tree Lore in the Bible, 1935; editor Tree Lover (Quarterly Magazine) from 1932; contributor to Macmillan's Encyclopædia for Teachers, 1932. *Address:* 5 St James Square, Bath. *Club:* Athenæum.

Died 31 July 1945.

RAGG, Rev. William Henry Murray; *b* Dec. 1861; *s* of Rev. Thomas Ragg, Vicar of Lawley, Salop; *m* 1894, Florence Stead, of Leamington; two *s* two *d*. *Educ:* St John's School, Leatherhead; Jesus College, Cambridge. Headmaster of Great Yarmouth Grammar School, 1888–98; of Hereford Cathedral School, 1898–1912; Prebendary of Hereford, 1911–38, Prebendary Emeritus since 1938; Vicar of Tenbury, 1912; Curate in charge of St Cynons Church, Fairbourne, N Wales, 1922–38. *Address:* Burford Rectory, Tenbury, Worcs.

Died 10 July 1944.

RAGHAVENDRA RAO, E. Civil Defence Member, Governor-General's Executive Council, India, since 1941. Member Governor's Executive Council, Central Provinces, India, 1931; acting Governor Central Provinces, May–Sept. 1936; Adviser to Secretary of State for India, 1939–41. *Address:* Governor-General's Executive Council, Delhi/Simla, India.

Died June 1942.

RAHIMTOOLA, Sir Ibrahim, GBE 1935; KCSI 1923; Kt 1911; CIE, 1908; was member Executive Council of the Governor of Bombay; *b* May 1862; *s* of Rahimtoola Kaderbhoy; *m* 1st, *d* of Khakibhoy Hemani; one *s* one *d*; 2nd, *d* of Cassambhoy Mahomed Mitha; three *s* three *d*. President, Bombay Legislative Council, 1923; President,

Indian Legislative Assembly, 1931–33. *Recreation:* President of the Islam Gymkhana. *Address:* Pedder Road, Cumballa Hill, Bombay. *TA:* Harmony. *T:* 41564 Bombay. *Clubs:* Orient, Bombay.

Died 1 June 1942.

RAIKES, Vice-Adm. Cecil Dacre Staveley, CBE 1922; *b* 1874; *s* of Rt Hon. H. C. Raikes of Llwynegrin, Mold, Flintshire; *m* 1924, Katherine Georgina Josephine, *o c* of Lt-Col Hon. Frank Weld-Forester of Decker Hill, Shifnal, Salop; one *s* one *d*. *Educ:* Stubbington House; HMS Britannia; RN Colleges. Served as Sub-Lt in HM Royal Yacht; Lieut on HMS Crescent under command of HM King George when Duke of York; commanded HMS Clio as SNO, Yangtse river, 1906–08; Liaison Officer to US Fleet for HM King George's Coronation ceremonies; Comdr RN College, Dartmouth, 1911–14; commanded St George in Patrol Flotillas, 1914–15; commanded HMS Raglan at Gallipoli and in Gulf of Smyrna and as Senior Naval Officer on right flank of Salonika Army, 1915–16; commanded HMS Minerva, and SNO on East Coast Africa, 1916–19, as SNO Aden Patrol and in support of King of Hedjas, 1916; Commodore and Chief of Staff to Com-in-Chief Western Approaches, 1919–21; commanded HMS Ramillies, Atlantic Fleet, 1921–22; Rear-Admiral, 1924; retired list, 1924; Admiralty Assessor to High Court of Appeal, 1926–32 and to Board of Trade, 1931–39; Vice-Admiral, retired, 1929; Commander of Portuguese Military Order of Avis. *Recreations:* hunting, fishing, shooting, golf. *Address:* Westfield, Wimborne Minster. *Clubs:* United Service; Hon. Member Royal Yacht Squadron, Cowes.

Died 15 Feb. 1947.

RAIKES, Maj.-Gen. George Leonard, CB 1926; DSC; late RM; *b* 18 April 1878; *s* of late Colonel George Whittington Raikes, late 6th (Mil.) Batt. KRRC, Woodville, Leamington Spa; *m* 1936, Christine Cycill, *d* of G. B. Collier, MA, Whinfield, South Brent, Devon. *Educ:* Army School, Stratford-on-Avon; RNC, Greenwich. 2nd Lieut RMA, 1896; Lieut, 1897; Capt., 1902; Maj., 1915; Lt-Col, 1921; Col, 1926; Col Commandant Plymouth Division Royal Marines, 1928–29; Brigadier, 1928; Major-Gen. 1929; served South African War with Naval Brigade, 1900 (Queen's medal and three clasps); Colonial Tour in HMS Ophir, 1901; served European War in France and Belgium, 1914–19, with RMA Howitzer Brigade (DSC 1915, despatches twice, three medals); ADC, 1928–29; retired list, 1930; Master of Dartmoor Otter Hounds, 1933–46. *Recreations:* hunting, motoring. *Address:* Millswood, S Brent, Devon. *T:* South Brent 2110. *Club:* Junior United Service.

Died 11 Oct. 1949.

RAIKES, Henry St John Digby, CBE 1920; KC 1921; JP; Recorder of King's Lynn since 1905; Chairman: Derbyshire Quarter Sessions, 1912; County Criminal Appeal Committee; County Rating Committee; County Probation Committee; formerly Chairman, Derbyshire War Savings Committee; Chairman, 2nd Div. Derbyshire Military Appeal Tribunal; Member of Coal Supplies Committee for the Midlands; *b* 23 Dec. 1863; *e s* of late Right Hon. Henry Cecil Raikes, MP, Postmaster-General, 1886–91, and Charlotte Blanche, *d* of C. B. Trevor-Roper of Plastêg, Flintshire; *m* Annie Lucinda (*d* 1936), *d* of late Gen. 'Dan' Mackinnon and *g d* of 4th Baron Dimsdale; one *s*. *Educ:* Charterhouse; Trinity College, Cambridge. Called to Bar, Inner Temple, 1887; contested (U) East Denbighshire, 1895; Mid-Derbyshire, 1900. *Publications:* Gleanings from Beaconsfield; Life in Him Yet; The Poems of Henry Cecil Raikes; The Life and Letters of Henry Cecil Raikes; Sesa; Saunders's Precedents of Indictments, 3rd edit., and various pamphlets and magazine articles. *Recreations:* shooting and fishing. *Address:* Makeney

Lodge, Derbyshire. *T:* Duffield 3144; 10 Eccleston Square, SW1. *T:* Vict. 3528; 4 Paper Buildings, Temple, EC4. *TA:* 55 Temple. *T:* Central 5476.

Died 1 May 1943.

RAILING, Max John, MIEE; Vice-Chairman and Joint Managing Director, The General Electric Co., Ltd; Vice-President, The British Electrical and Allied Manufacturers Association; also Radio Manufacturers Association; *b* 1868; *m* 1900, Amanda, *d* of H. Hirsch; two *d*. *Educ:* Munich. Has been associated with the General Electric Co., Ltd, for over 45 years; General Manager 1910; and a director of numerous other electrical companies; Member Board of Trade Advisory Council, 1935–37; Master Worshipful Company of Makers of Playing Cards, 1935–36. *Recreations:* golf, curling. *Address:* White-knights, Reading. *T:* Reading 81332. *Club:* Constitutional.

Died 14 Jan. 1942.

RAILTON, James, CBE 1918; *b* 1863; *s* of late James Railton, of Malpas, Mon; *m* 1902, Margery, *d* of Lewellen Wood, of Gardenhurst, Penarth, JP; three *d*. *Educ:* privately. *Address:* Fernbank House, Ascot. *Club:* Royal Automobile.

Died 3 May 1949.

RAILTON, Ven. Archdeacon Nathaniel Gerard; Archdeacon of Lindsey since 1941; Rector of Potter Hanworth since 1943; *b* 10 Feb. 1886; *s* of George Scott Railton and Marion Elen Porthyn Railton; *m* 1932, Inez Stuart (*née* Jackson), *widow* of Capt. A. L. Gresson, RN; one *s*. *Educ:* private tutors; Keble College, Oxford. Curate St John's, Fitzroy Square, London, 1912–13; Temp. CF, 1915–20; Rector of Toddington, Beds, 1916–20; Regular Commission Royal Army Chaplains Department, 1920; Chaplain 1st Cavalry Brigade, Aldershot, 1920–21; Chaplain Troops stationed at Chanock, 1921–23; Chaplain Guards Depôt, Caterham, 1923–26; Hon. Secretary Army Football Association, 1924–26; Senior Chaplain, York, 1926; Senior Chaplain, 13th Infty Bde Expeditionary Force, China, 1926–27; Chaplain to 2nd Cavalry Bde, Tidworth, 1927–30; Chaplain to now famous 2nd Cav. Bde Slum Boys Camps, Tidworth, 1927–30 and 1935; Senior Chaplain Royal Garrison Church, Aldershot, 1930–34; 2nd Cav. Bde Tidworth, 1934–35; Gibraltar Garrison, 1935–40; Hon. Sec. to Polo Club, Gibraltar, 1939–40; Acting Senior Chaplain RASC Yorkshire Area, 1941; Reserve of Officers, 1941; Rector of Bigby, Lincolnshire, 1941–43. *Recreations:* all games, hunting and polo and refereeing boxing, registered ABS referee. *Address:* Potter Hanworth Rectory, Lincs. *Club:* Junior Army and Navy.

Died 8 Sept. 1948.

RAINSFORD-HANNAY, Brig.-Gen. Frederick, CB 1911; CMG 1918; *b* 7 Sept. 1854; *s* of late Major F. Rainsford-Hannay, of Kirkdale, NB; *m* Emily Louisa, *d* of late D. E. Wilkie, of Rathobyres, Midlothian, and Melbourne, Australia; one *d*. *Educ:* Royal Military Academy, Woolwich. Entered Royal Engineers, 1873; has held the following appointments: Assistant Inspector-General of Fortifications, Chief Engineer in Ireland, Commandant School of Military Engineering, Director of Fortifications and Works, War Office; reappointed Commandant School of Military Engineering, 1914. *Address:* 21 De Vere Gardens, W8. *T:* Western 5760. *Club:* Naval and Military.

Died 23 Dec. 1950.

RAINY, Sir George, KCSI 1930; KCIE 1925; CSI 1921; CIE 1918; *b* 11 Feb. 1875; *s* of late Rev. Robert Rainy, DD, Principal of the New College, Edinburgh; unmarried. *Educ:* Edinburgh Academy; Merton College, Oxford. Appointed to the Indian Civil Service, 1899, and served as Assistant Magistrate and Collector; Under-Secretary to the Government of Bengal Financial Department 1904–06; Under-Secretary to the Govt of

India Commerce and Industry Department, 1906–09; Magistrate and Collector, Deputy Secretary to the Govt of India Finance Department, 1916–19; Chief Secretary to the Government of Behar and Orissa, 1919–23; President of the Indian Tariff Board, 1923–27; Member of the Governor-General's Executive Council in charge of the Commerce and Railway Departments, 1927–32; retired, 1934; Chairman of the Trustee Savings Banks Association, 1938. *Address:* 15 Comiston Drive, Edinburgh. *Clubs:* University, Edinburgh.

Died 27 Jan. 1946.

RAJWADE, Maj.-Gen. Ganpatrao Raghunath Raja, Mushir-i-Khas Bahadur, Shaukat-Jung, CBE, ADC; Army Minister Gwalior Government; ranks as a first-class Sardar in the Bombay Presidency, and is above Raja Bahadurs in the UP; *b* Jan. 1884; *m* Dr Laxmihai, MRCS, etc., *e d* of Sir M. V. Joshi, KCIE. *Educ:* Victoria College. *Address:* Gwalior, CI, India. *Clubs:* Elgin, Gwalior; Roshanara. Flying, Delhi; Royal Western India Turf, Willingdon, Bombay.

Died 1945.

RALSTON, Col Hon. James Layton, PC Canada, 1926; CMG 1918; DSO 1917; KC 1914; DCL (Acadia); LLD (Union, Dalhousie, Colgate, Toronto); Partner, Ralston, Kearney, Duquet & MacKay; MP (L) Prince division of PEI since 1940; Governor, Acadia University; Governor McMaster University; *b* Amherst, Nova Scotia, 27 Sept. 1881; *s* of Burnett William Ralston and Bessie Chipman Layton; *m* 1907, Nettie Winnifred, *d* of John McLeod, Amherst; one *s*. *Educ:* Amherst Academy; Dalhousie Law School. Called to Nova Scotia Bar, 1903; practised Amherst, 1903–12, Halifax, 1912–26, Montreal, 1930–39; elected to Nova Scotia Legislature for Cumberland, 1911 and 1916. Went overseas with 85th Canadian Infantry Battalion (Nova Scotia Highlanders), as Major, 1916; to France, Feb. 1917; served continuously until Armistice; commanded 85th Canadian Infantry Batt., April 1918, to demobilization (Lieut-Col 1918; CMG, DSO with bar, despatches twice); returned to Canada, 1919, and re-entered practice; Col 1924; was Chairman, Royal Commission Returned Soldiers' Pensions, Re-Establishment and Insurance, appointed by Federal Government; elected to House of Commons for Shelburne-Yarmouth, Nova Scotia, 1926 and 1930; Minister of National Defence, Canada, 1926–30; Minister of Finance, Canada, 1939–40; Minister of National Defence, 1940–44; Canadian Delegate to London Naval Conference, 1930; admitted to Quebec Bar, 1931; a Liberal; a Baptist. *Address:* Gleneagles Apartments, Montreal, Que. *Clubs:* Mount Royal, St James's, Forest and Stream, Reform, Montreal, Rotary (Montreal); Ridean Country (Ottawa).

Died 21 May 1948.

RAMSAY, Andrew Maitland, MD; LLD Glasgow; FRFPSG Glas.; FRS Edinburgh; retired; Consulting Ophthalmic Surgeon, Glasgow Royal Infirmary, etc.; Consultant in Diseases of the Eye; *b* Glasgow, 1859; *s* of Andrew Ramsay; *m* 1907, Elizabeth Margaret Pace, MD, London. *Educ:* Linlithgow Burgh Grammar School; University of Glasgow. Graduated MB, CM, 1882; MD, 1891; FRFPS Glas. 1892; FRSE 1938. Late House Surgeon Glasgow Western Infirmary and Glasgow Eye Infirmary; Demonstrator of Anatomy, Glasgow University; Lecturer on Diseases of the Eye, Glasgow Univ.; late Surgeon, Glasgow Eye Infirmary; late Surgeon, Ophthalmic Institution, Glasgow Royal Infirmary; late Ophthalmic Surgeon, Glasgow Western Infirmary; past President Ophthalmological Society of the United Kingdom, now Vice-Pres.; Past Vice-President Ophthalmological Section Royal Society of Medicine; Past President Ophthalmological Section of British Medical Association at Bradford; Past President Royal Medico-Chirurgical Society, Glasgow; Major, RAMC (TF), No. 3 Scottish General Hospital; late

Medical Referee for Ophthalmic cases under Workmen's Compensation Act for Lanarkshire, and Renfrew and Bute, Stirling, Clackmannan, Dumbarton and County of Ayr, First recipient William Mackenzie Memorial Medal, 1928. *Publications:* Atlas of External Diseases of the Eye, 1897; Eye Injuries and their Treatment, 1907; Diathesis and Ocular Diseases, 1909; Clinical Ophthalmology for the General Practitioner, 1920; The Eye in General Medicine, 1929; Three Cases of Blindness in which Sight was acquired in Adult Life; The Importance of General Therapeutics in Treatment of Ocular Diseases; numerous other papers. *Recreation:* golfing. *Address:* The Castle House, St Andrews. *T:* St Andrews 203. *Clubs:* Royal and Ancient, St Andrews; University, Edinburgh.

Died 20 March 1946.

RAMSAY, Adm. Sir Bertram Home, KCB 1940; KBE 1943; CB 1936; MVO 1918; Allied Naval Commander-in-Chief, Expeditionary Force, since 1944; *b* 1883; *y s* of late Brig.-Gen. W. A. Ramsay; *m* 1929, Helen Margaret, *o d* of late Col C. T. Menzies; two *s*. Entered Royal Navy, 1898; psc 1913; commanded Monitor 25 and HMS Broke in the Dover Patrol, 1915–19; accompanied Lord Jellicoe on his mission to India and the Dominions, 1919–20; commanded HM Ships Weymouth, 1924–25, and Danae, 1925–27; served on staff of RN War College, 1927–29; commanded HMS Kent and as Chief of the Staff, China Station, 1929–31; served on staff of Imperial Defence College, 1931–33; commanded HMS Royal Sovereign, 1933–36; Rear-Admiral and Chief of Staff, Home Fleet, 1935; retired list, 1938; Vice-Admiral, retired, 1938; Flag Officer Commanding Dover, 1939–42; Naval Commander, Eastern Task Force, Mediterranean, 1943; reinstated on active list 1944 and promoted to Admiral. *Address:* Bughtrig, Coldstream, Berwickshire. *Club:* United Service.

Died 2 Jan. 1945.

RAMSAY, Lt-Col Sir John, KCIE 1915; CSI 1911; CIE 1898; *b* 5 Dec. 1862; 2nd *s* of late Gen. the Hon. Sir Henry Ramsay and Laura, *d* of late Sir Henry Lushington, 3rd Bart; *m* 1889, Margaret, OBE, *e d* of late F. Henvey, Indian Civil Service; one *d*. *Educ:* private school, Wimbledon. Joined Cheshire Regt, 1882; Staff Corps; Assist Gov.-Gen.'s Agent in Central India, 1886; Political Agent, Sirdaipore, Central India, 1889; Assist Gov.-Gen.'s Agent in Central India, 1891; Political Agent, Bundelkhand, 1893; Political Agent and Deputy Commissioner, Quetta-Pishin and Revenue Commissioner, Baluchistan, 1898–1906; Political Resident in Turkish Arabia, 1907–10; Resident in Kashmir, 1910; Agent to the Governor-General in Baluchistan, 1911; retired, 5 Dec. 1917.

Died 2 March 1942.

RAMSAY, Sir John, Kt 1939; CBE 1924; MB; BS; MS; FRACS; Hon. Major AMC (retired); Consulting Surgeon to General Hospital, Launceston; *b* Scotland, 26 Dec. 1872; *s* of John Ramsay and Margaret Thomson; *m* Ella Elizabeth Pegus Dudley, London; three *s* two *d*. *Educ:* Melbourne University. Fourteen years Surgeon-Supt Launceston General Hospital; during European War was Surgeon to 12th AGH Tasmania; Past President British Medical Association (Tasmanian Branch); First President Rotary Club, Launceston; Certificate of Appreciation RS and SILA 1924. *Publications:* articles to Medical Journals. *Recreations:* cricket in early days, golf. *Address:* 159 St John Street, Launceston, Tasmania. *Clubs:* Launceston; Naval and Military, Hobart.

Died 6 Feb. 1944.

RAMSAY, Sir Malcolm Graham, KCB 1915; CB 1905; Hon. Member SAA; *b* 3 Feb. 1871; 2nd *s* of late George G. Ramsay, Professor of Humanity, Glasgow University, 1863–1906; *m* 1st, 1901, Edith Margaret (*d* 1926), *d* of Gilbert Wakefield, Machynlleth; no *c*; 2nd,

1928, Bessie (d 1945), d of John Clapperton, Greenock. *Educ:* Winchester (Scholar); New College, Oxford (Exhibitioner). Attaché in HM Diplomatic Service, 1896; transferred to Junior Clerkship in Foreign Office, 1896; 2nd Class Clerk in Treasury, 1897; Private Secretary to Earl of Balfour (First Lord of the Treasury and Prime Minister), 1902–05; Principal Clerk to 1914; Assistant Secretary, The Treasury, 1914–19; Controller of Establishments, Treasury, 1919–21; Chairman National Whitley Council for Civil Service, 1919–21; Comptroller and Auditor-General, 1921–31; retired, 1931. *Recreations:* shooting, fishing, golf. *Address:* Moine-Na-Vey, Ballater, Aberdeenshire. *T:* Ballater 59. *Clubs:* Oxford and Cambridge; Royal Northern, Aberdeen.

Died 22 March 1946.

RAMSAY-FAIRFAX, Lt-Col William George Astell, CMG 1919; DSO 1916; Commander RN (Emergency List); *b* 1876; 2nd *s* of Colonel Sir William Ramsay-Fairfax, 2nd Bt, of Maxton, Roxburghshire, and Mary Ann (d 1924), *o d* of William J. Pawson, of Shawdon, Northumberland; *m* 1909, Lilian, *d* of late Henry Rich, of Abbey Lodge, Malmesbury; two *s* one *d*. *Educ:* Cordwalles, Maidenhead; The Limes, Greenwich. HMS Britannia, 1890. Lieutenant RN; resigned, 1901; joined XXXth Regt Imperial Yeomanry, 1902; served in South Africa (with rank of Capt.) (medal and clasps); took part in late Sir William Northrup McMillan's Expedition for the Exploration of the Blue Nile, 1903; served with Abyssinian Army co-operating with British Somaliland Field Force, 1903–04 (medal and clasp); Served European War, at sea with the Royal Naval Division in Gallipoli and France, and with the Tank Corps in France (CMG, DSO, prom. temp. Brig.-Gen., despatches four times); holds the Bronze Medal of the Royal Humane Society; Founder of Divorce Law Reform Assoc., and joint founder of Divorce Law Reform Union. *Club:* Army and Navy.

Died 20 Nov. 1946.

RAMSDEN, John Watkinson; JP, High Sheriff of Lincolnshire, 1927; Master, Southwold Hounds, 1920–29; *b* 1880; *s* of John Taylor Ramsden, of Middleton Tower, King's Lynn, Norfolk; *m* 1906, Eleanor, *d* of late John Murgatroyd, JP, of Broadfold, Luddenden, Yorks. *Educ:* Harrow. *Recreations:* farming, hunting, and shooting. *Address:* Hareby House, Spilsby, Lincs. *T:* and *TA:* 2139 Spilsby. *Club:* Boodle's.

Died 15 June 1943.

RAMSDEN, Walter, MA, DM, late Johnston Professor of Bio-Chemistry, Liverpool University, now Professor Emeritus; Fellow of Pembroke College, Oxford; formerly Lecturer in Chemical Physiology, Oxford University; 4th *s* of W. H. F. Ramsden of Saddleworth, Physician, and of Catherine Kay. *Educ:* Oxford; Guy's Hospital; Zürich; Vienna; Radcliffe Travelling Fellow, 1893–96. Senior Proctor, 1909–10; Member of Physiological Society and Biochemical Society. *Publications:* on various Adsorption-Phenomena, and on Silk Fibroinogen. *Address:* Pembroke Coll., Oxford.

Died 26 March 1947.

RAMSON, Ven. John Luce, MA (Lond.); HCF; Archdeacon of Surrey, Jamaica, since 1933; Rector St George's Church 1907; Rural Dean of Kingston; Canon of St James' Cathedral, 1921; *b* 10 Oct. 1870; 3rd *s* of Ven. John Luce Ramson, Archdeacon of Cornwall, Jamaica; *m* 1897, Amabel, *d* of J. D. Ormsby, Lime Hall, Jamaica; two *s* two *d*. *Educ:* Potsdam School and University College, Jamaica. BA London, 1891; MA, 1893. Deacon, 1900; Priest, 1901; Second Master Wolmer's School, 1895–1907; Curate Kingston Parish Church, 1900–02; in charge, St Luke's, Cross Roads, 1902–07; Examining Chaplain to Archbishop of West Indies, 1915–16; to Bishop of Jamaica, 1916–17, and since 1927; Bishop's Commissary, 1929; Delegate from Jamaica to Pan-Latin Congress, Panama, 1916; Chaplain

to 6th Batt. British West India Regiment in Belgium, France, Italy, 1917–19; Member Board of Directors, St Peter's College, Shortwood College and Asylum; Vice-Chairman Board of Governors, Kingston Coll.; Member Diocesan Council and Diocesan Financial Board; Hon. Secretary Jamaica Home and Foreign Missionary Society; Member Advisory Council YMCA; Trustee, Verley Home, 1927; Chaplain (with rank of Major) Local Forces, Jamaica, 1928. *Publications:* Carry On; or, Pages from the Life of a West Indian Padre in the Field; Jaïrus' Daughter, a poem. *Recreations:* rifle shooting, billiards. *Address:* St George's Rectory, Kingston, Jamaica, WI.

Died 5 May 1944.

RAMUNNI MENON, Sir Konkoth, Kt 1933; Diwan Bahadur, 1927; LLD (Hon. Madras); MA (Cantab); *b* Trichur, 14 Sept. 1872; *m* V. K. Kalliani Amma, of Trichur; two *s* one *d*. *Educ:* Maharajah's College, Ernakulam; Presidency College, Madras; Christ's College, Cambridge (Scholar). Entered the Madras Education Dept, 1898; Professor of Zoology, 1910; retired, 1927; connected with the Madras University since 1912; Vice-Chancellor, 1928–34, Life Member of the Senate; nominated Member of the Madras Legislative Council on two occasions; represented the Madras University at the Congress of the Universities of the Empire at Edinburgh, 1931; Chairman, Inter-University Board, 1932–33; Member Council of State, India, 1934–36. *Recreations:* walking, chess. *Address:* Lakshmi Sadan, Vepery, Madras, India; Konkoth House, Trichur, Cochin State, South India. *Club:* Cosmopolitan (Madras).

Died 14 Jan. 1949.

RANDALL-MACIVER, David, FBA 1938; MA, DSc; archæologist, anthropologist, and author; *b* 1873; *s* of John MacIver, shipowner, and Eliza Mary Rutherford; stepson of Richard Randall, Barrister; *m* 1st, 1911, Joanna (d 1931), *d* of W. H. Davidge, New York, and Virginia Mason, Alexandria, Va; 2nd, 1936, Mabel Tuttle, *d* of late Edward S. Holden, St Louis, USA. *Educ:* Radley; Queen's College, Oxford. First Class in Lit. Hum., 1896; Laycock Student of Egyptology at Worcester College, Oxford, 1900–06. Director of the Eckley B. Coxe Jr Expedition of the Univ. of Philadelphia to Egypt and the Sudan, 1907–11; Librarian of American Geographical Society, New York, 1911–14. Served European War in France and Macedonia, 1914–19 (Captain Intelligence Staff); engaged in research work in Italy since 1921; Fellow of the Society of Antiquaries of London, the Society of Antiquaries of Scotland, and various other learned societies. *Publications:* Mediæval Rhodesia; Villanovans and Early Etruscans; The Iron Age in Italy; The Etruscans; Italy before the Romans; Greek Cities in Italy and Sicily; (part) Libyan Notes; El Amrah and Abydos; Ancient Races of the Thebaid; Areika; Karanog; Buhen. *Recreations:* golf, gardening. *Address:* c/o Brown Shipley & Co., 123 Pall Mall, SW1. *Club:* Royal Societies.

Died 30 April 1945.

RANDLES, Sir John (Scurrah), JP, Kt 1905; retired ironmaster; *b* Boston, Lincs, 25 Dec. 1857; *s* of Rev. Marshal Randles, DD; *m* 1883, Elizabeth Hartley, *d* of Robert Spencer. *Educ:* Lincoln; Woodhouse Grove School. MP (C) Cockermouth Division of Cumberland, 1900–06, and bye-election, Aug. 1906 till Dec. 1910; MP (U) North-West (now Exchange Division) Manchester, 1912–22; Director of Star Board (Eagle, Star and British Dominions Insurance Co. Ltd); Commander of the Order of the Crown of Belgium; Order of the Rising Sun (Japan), 2nd class. *Address:* Bristowe Hill, Keswick. *T:* Keswick 55. *Club:* Constitutional.

Died 11 Feb. 1945.

RANDOLPH, Mrs Evelyn St L.; *see* St Leger, E.

RANGNEKAR, Hon. Sir Saiba Shankar, Kt 1938; BA, LLB; Barrister-at-Law, Lincoln's Inn; Puisne Judge, High Court, Bombay, 1929–38; *b* 20 Dec. 1878; *m* 1900; one *s* one *d*. *Educ:* St Xavier's College, Bombay University. *Recreations:* tennis, bridge, and swimming. *Address:* c/o High Court, Bombay, India.
Died 21 Feb. 1949.

RANK, Joseph. Chairman of Joseph Rank, Ltd, Clarence Street, Hull, and Ranks Ltd. *Address:* Colley Corner, Reigate. *T:* Reigate 2138.
Died 13 Nov. 1943.

RANKEILLOUR, 1st Baron *cr* 1932, of Buxted; **James Fitzalan Hope;** PC 1922; JP Sussex; *b* 11 Dec. 1870; *s* of J. R. Hope-Scott, QC, of Abbotsford, and Lady Victoria Alexandrina Fitzalan-Howard, *d* of 14th Duke of Norfolk; *m* 1st, 1892, Mabel Ellen, OBE (*d* 1938), *d* of late Francis Riddell of Cheeseburn Grange, Northumberland; three *s* one *d*; 2nd, 1941, Lady Beatrice Kerr-Clark, *d* of 9th Earl of Drogheda and *widow* of Capt. S. R. Kerr-Clark. *Educ:* Oratory School; Christ Church, Oxford. MP (C) Brightside Division of Sheffield, 1900–06; MP (U) Central Sheffield, 1908–29; Treasurer of HM's Household, 1915–16; Lord of the Treasury, 1916–19; Financial Secretary, Ministry of Munitions, 1919–21; Chairman of Committees and Deputy-Speaker, 1921–Feb. 1924 and Dec. 1924–29. *Publications:* A History of the 1900 Parliament; Thoughts and Fancies. *Heir: s* Capt. Hon. Sir Arthur O. J. Hope, GCIE. *Address:* Heron's Ghyll, Uckfield. *T:* Nutley 8. *Club:* Carlton.
Died 14 Feb. 1949.

RANKEN, William Bruce Ellis, RI; ROI; *b* 11 April 1881; *s* of Robert Ranken, Writer to His Majesty's Signet, Edinburgh; unmarried. *Educ:* Eton; The Slade School. First exhibited in London at the New English Art Club; First One Man Show at Carfax Gallery, 1904; has since had shows of own work at Goupil Gallery and Royal Institute Galleries, and in Edinburgh, Glasgow, and Liverpool and America; has exhibited pictures at Royal Academy, the Salon des Beaux-Arts, Paris, New English Art Club, Royal Institute of Painters in Water Colours, Royal Society of Oil Painters, the National Portrait Society, Modern Society of Portrait Painters, and the Royal Portrait Society, also the Goupil, Carfax, and Fine Arts Galleries, the Royal Scottish Academy, and at the International both in London and in Venice; For many years Vice-President Royal Institute of Painters in Oil Colours; Member of the Royal Institute of Painters in Water Colour, the Pastel Society, the Royal Society of Portrait Painters, and the National Society of Portrait Painters; has exhibited portraits of The Queen, Queen Mary, Princess Christian, and interiors of Windsor Castle, Buckingham Palace, and the Royal Palace at Madrid; one of the four British painters who were given facilities to paint the coronation ceremony of King George VI in Westminster Abbey; Silver Medallist Salon des Artistes Français, 1928. *Recreation:* travelling. *Address:* Farley Hill Place, Arborfield, Reading. *T:* Eversley 2173. *Club:* Arts.
Died 31 March 1941.

RANKIN, Brig.-Gen. Charles Herbert, CB 1923; CMG 1916; DSO 1900; late 7th Hussars; *b* 26 May 1873; 2nd *s* of Sir James Rankin, 1st Bt; *m* 1908, Enid, (*d* 1938), *o d* of late Judge Williams; one *s* one *d*. Entered army, 1893; Captain, 1899; Major, 1911; served South Africa, 1896; South Africa, 1899–1902 (despatches, Queen's medal 8 clasps, King's medal 2 clasps, DSO); European War, 1914–18 (despatches twice, Bt Lieut-Col and Col, CMG); retired pay, 1927. *Club:* Cavalry.
Died 8 July 1946.

RANKIN, Rt Hon. Sir George Claus, PC 1935; Kt 1925; Member of Judicial Committee of the Privy Council, 1935–44; *b* 12 Aug. 1877; 2nd *s* of late Rev. Robert Rankin, BD, Minister of Lamington,

Lanarkshire; *m* 1910, Alice Maud Amy (*d* 1924), *o c* of late Geoffrey Sayer; two *d*. *Educ:* Edinburgh University; Trinity College, Cambridge. Barrister, Lincoln's Inn, 1904; Bencher, 1935; Northern Circuit; 2nd Lieut Royal Garrison Artillery, 1916; Lieut, 1917; Judge High Court, Calcutta, 1918–26; Chief Justice, 1926–34; Hon. LLD (Edin.), 1937. *Publications:* Studies in Indian Law, 1946; editor of 11th edition of Mulla's Mahomedan Law, 1938. *Address:* 51 George Square, Edinburgh 8. *Club:* Athenæum.
Died 8 April 1946.

RANKINE, Col Robert, DSO 1915; VD; Reserve of Officers, AMF; *b* 29 July 1868; *s* of late W. H. Rankine, JP, Falkirk; *m* Annie Christina Mildred, *d* of late Thomas Polden. Served in Dardanelles, European War, 1914–15 (DSO). *Address:* Dunmore, Avoca Avenue, St Kilda, Melbourne, Australia.
Died 6 June 1941.

RANSOM, Hon. Sir (Ethelbert) Alfred, KCMG 1935; MP for Pahiatua, Dannevirke, since 1922; *b* Lower Hutt, 1868; *s* of Robert John Ransom; *m* 1893, Antonette Katinka, *d* of A. E. Sondergaard, Ashhurst; one *s* one *d*. *Educ:* Lower Hutt, primary. Pominent in football and tennis; sheepfarmer; 1st President Dannevirke Chamber of Commerce; Mayor, 1910–19; Vice-President A and P Association, 1910–19; Chairman Fire Board, 1911–20; Member High School Board of Governors and Hospital Board; Chairman Efficiency Board of Trustees during War; Chairman H. B. War Relief Association, 1920–21; Chairman, Dannevirke Power Board; Lieut Ruahine MR Volunteers; Minister Public Works, 1928–30; Minister for Lands, and Commissioner of State Forests, NZ, 1930–35; acting Prime Minister, 1930 and 1935. *Address:* 35 Queen Street, Dannevirke, NZ.
Died 22 May 1943.

RANSOME, James, FIAA; *b* 1865; 4th *s* of late Allen Ransome, Newark-on-Trent; *m d* of late F. Marshall, KC; one *d*. *Educ:* Rugby. Professional training under C. H. Driver and Ernest George; practised in London, 1888–1902; in India as Consulting Architect to the Government, 1902–08; resumed practice in England, 1908; FRIBA, resigned, 1932. *Publications:* Professional Pitfalls; European Architecture in India; Some Designs for Indian Buildings, and Government of India Building Designs; Phenomena of Trade Unionism.
Died 19 Feb. 1944.

RAPER, Agnes Madeline; retired pottery-artist; *b* Murree, India; *y d* of late Maj.-Gen. John Fraser Raper, RA; unmarried. *Educ:* privately. Studied at The Camberwell School of Art. Founded The Glebe Pottery in Chelsea, 1924; first exhibited Glebe-Chelsea models at Chelsea Town Hall, 1924; specialised in models of historic buildings, town and country houses, cottages and gardens; amongst many others, Buckingham Palace, Flatford Mill, and Sulgrave Manor; retired, 1937. *Address:* Ennismore, Thornley Road, Felixstowe.
Died 22 Nov. 1948.

RAPER, Alfred Baldwin; *b* London, 8 May 1889; *y s* of late Walter and Maud Raper of Gerrard's Cross, Bucks; *m* 1st, 1922, Bessie Alice, Marchioness Conyngham (*d* 1933), *d* of late William Andrew Tobin, Australia; one *s*; 2nd, 1928, Renée Angèle Rosalie, *d* of late Hector Benoist, Lille, France; one *d*. *Educ:* Merchant Taylors' School; Brussels. Travelled widely in Europe, Asia Minor, United States, and near East; served as Pilot in Royal Air Force during War; received Order of St Stanislas from Russian Government in recognition of services to Russian Aviation Mission; prospective Unionist candidate for NE Bethnal Green, 1917–18; MP (Co. U) East Islington, 1918–22; undertook Special Mission to Finland, April 1918; White Rose of Finland, 1926, for services to Anglo-Finnish Commerce. *Publications:* articles in various newspapers and periodicals. *Recreations:* flying, motoring, and all outdoor sports. *Address:* Shell-Mex House, WC2. *T:* Temple Bar 2104; Bearwood, Gerrards Cross, Bucks. *T:* Gerrards Cross 2571. *Clubs:* Royal Air Force, City of London, Royal Thames Yacht.

Died 30 April 1941.

RAPHAEL, Francis Charles, MIEE, MConsE, FIES; consulting electrical engineer, specialising in legal work and in the electrical equipment of buildings. Before the 1914–18 War, Editor of Electrical Engineering; previously Editor of The Electrician for a number of years; an expert in electrical engineering matters, and author of some books on these subjects; consulting electrical engineer to various hospitals, and other institutions, public bodies and companies; during the 1914–18 War Lieut London Electrical Engineers, RE (T); afterwards a Departmental Manager with the Edison-Swan Electric Co., Ltd until 1922, and now devoting himself exclusively to consulting practice; *b* 1871; *m* 1919. *Educ:* Charterhouse; Central Technical College. *Address:* Napier House, 24–27 High Holborn, WC1; 2 Belgrave Gardens, Southgate, N14. *T:* Chancery 7961, Laburnum 4664.

Died 17 Nov. 1945.

RAPPOPORT, Angelo Solomon, PhD, BèsL; author, editor, and lecturer; *b* Little Russia, 1871; naturalised British subject, 1898; *s* of Anselm Rappoport and Haja Liflandsky; *m* Myriam Gourevitch, artist and writer; one *s. Educ:* Libau (Latvia); England; University of Paris and University of Basel. Sent on a mission to Falashas in Abyssinia by Alliance Israélite, 1900; lecturer on modern literature at Birkbeck College, London, 1902–05; revising editor of Historian's History of the World; on staff of Encyclopædia Britannica, 1906; editor of Twentieth Century Russia, 1915–16; editor of French Year Book for the Comité du Livre (under the auspices of the French Government), 1917–18; editor of the New Gresham Encyclopædia, 1918–24; editor of Illustrated Palestine, 1927–29; joint editor of the British Encyclopædia, 1933. Arrested in Dec. 1940 by the Gestapo and interned at Besançon; afterwards sent to the concentration camp at Drancy, on account of anti-Nazi propaganda (books and articles), and marked for deportation, contrary to conventions of Geneva; saved from a horrible fate thanks to Consular intervention (Swiss), and transferred to Vittel; liberated 4 Oct. 1944. *Publications:* Primer of Philosophy, 1903; Russian History, 1905; English Drama, 1906; History of Egypt (in 13 vols) with Maspéro, King and Hall, 1907; The Curse of the Romanovs, 1907; History of European Nations, 1912; Home Life in Russia, 1913; History of Poland, 1915; Labour, Social Reform, and Democracy, 1925; Dictionary of Socialism, 1926; Myths and Legends of Ancient Israel (3 vols), 1928; French History, 1929; History of Palestine, 1931; Mediæval Legends of Christ, 1934; The Psalms in Life, Legend and Literature, 1935; The Gauntlet against the Gospel, 1936; The Folklore of the Jews, 1937; numerous English translations of foreign works: Anti-Semitism throughout the Ages (Count Coudenhove), 1935; The Nation at War (Ludendorff), 1936; Fathers and Sons (Josué Yéhouda), 1938; contributor to English Reviews (Edinburgh, Fortnightly, National, etc.). *Address:* 45 Avenue de Paris, Versailles, France.

Died 2 June 1950.

RASHBROOK, Engr Rear-Adm. Henry Samuel, CBE 1919; Royal Navy; Retired; *b* 26 May 1856; *s* of late James Rashbrook; *m* 1881, Laurina Elizabeth, *d* of late Chas. Martin; two *s* one *d. Educ:* H. M. Dockyard, Devonport. Entered Royal Navy as Assistant Engineer, 1878; served in Egypt, 1881 (medal and star); Engineer, 1884; Chief Engineer, 1891; Engineer Commander, 1895; Engineer Captain, 1909; retired, 1912; served as Engineer Captain of Patrol Area XIV, 1916–19 (CBE and Promoted Engineer Rear-Admiral on Retired List

for War Service). *Address:* North Portland Cottage, 13 Portland Road, Stoke, Devonport, Devon. *T:* Devonport 663.

Died 6 Nov. 1942.

RASHLEIGH, Major Philip, DSO 1917; late Royal Artillery; *b* 7 Sept. 1881; *s* of Sir Colman Battie Rashleigh, 3rd Bt and Amy Young, *d* of James Young Jamieson. *Educ:* Newton College, South Devon. 2nd Lieut Cornwall and Devon Miners Artillery Militia, 1899; 2nd Lieut Royal Garrison Artillery, 1900; served throughout European war with Heavy Artillery, on staff 1917–19 (wounded, despatches, DSO); Retired on Pension, 1928. *Recreations:* shooting, fishing, tennis and golf. *Address:* Bellevue, Lostwithiel, Cornwall. *TA:* Lostwithiel. *T:* Lostwithiel 34. *Clubs:* Army and Navy, Royal Automobile; Royal Fowey Yacht; Cornish Riviera.

Died 21 Sept. 1949.

RASHLEIGH, Captain Vernon Stanhope, CBE 1919; RN; late Chief Inspector of HM Coastguard; *b* Stoke, Devon, 1879; *s* of late Paymaster-in-Chief G. V. Rashleigh, RN; *m* 1909, Dorothy Richenda, *d* of J. Cooper Wilkinson, Ashford, Kent; one *s* two *d. Educ:* Christ's Hospital. Naval Cadet, 1894; Midshipman, 1896; Sub-Lieutenant, 1899; Lieut 1900; Commander, 1913; Captain, 1924; Commander in DNE Department of Admiralty; Captain (acting) HMS Artois, Ocean Escort of Convoys (CBE, Order of El Nahda, 3rd cl.); retired on appointment as Inspector of Coastguard, 1923. *Address:* 20 Abbey Road, NW8. *Club:* Junior United Service.

Died 4 Jan. 1946.

RASTALL, Robert Heron; *b* 8 Nov. 1871; *e s* of Herbert Augustus Henry Rastall, JP, of Turnerdale Hall, Whitby, Yorks, and Isabel, *d* of William Frankland, of Bagdale, Whitby; unmarried. *Educ:* Christ's College, Cambridge. ScD Cantab, FGS. Member of Council of the Geological Society, 1915, and Mineralogical Society, 1918; Harkness Scholar, 1903; Fellow of Christ's College, 1906–13; re-elected, 1926; employed in War Office, 1915–19; has travelled in South Africa, Malaya, and elsewhere on geological work. Lord of the Manors of Eskdaleside and Ugglebarnby. *Publications:* Geology of the Metalliferous Deposits; Physico-Chemical Geology; (part) Textbook of Geology and Petrology of Sedimentary Rocks; numerous original papers on the geology of Cambs, Yorks, Cumberland, Malaya, and South Africa, and on ore-deposits, editor of the Geological Magazine. *Address:* The Red House, Ruswarp, Whitby, Yorks.

Died 3 Feb. 1950.

RATCLIFF, Robert Frederick, CMG 1916; JP Staffordshire; High Sheriff Derbyshire, 1929; *b* 1867; *s* of late Robert Ratcliff. *Educ:* Rossall; Jesus College, Cambridge (BA). Brevet Col 6th Batt. North Staffs Regiment; Ex-Director Bass, Ratcliff, and Gretton, brewers; served European War, 1914–16 (despatches, CMG); MP (LU) Burton Division of Staffs, 1900–18. *Address:* Newton Park, Burton-on-Trent. *Clubs:* Brooks's, Devonshire.

Died 19 Jan. 1943.

RATHBONE, Eleanor, MA; DCL Oxford; LLD Liverpool; MP (Ind) Combined English Universities since 1929; *d* of the late William Rathbone, Greenbank, Liverpool, MP Liverpool, 1868–80, North Carnarvonshire, 1881–96, and of Emily Rathbone, *d* of Acheson Lyle, the Oaks, Londonderry, ex-Lord-Lieut Londonderry. *Educ:* Kensington High School; Liverpool Univ.; Somerville College, Oxford. Liverpool City Council, 1909–34 (first woman member); JP Lancashire (retired); was responsible for organising the work of the Soldiers' and Sailors' Families Association in Liverpool throughout the last War; appointed President, in succession to Mrs Henry Fawcett, of the National Union for Equal Citizenship, 1919–29; Member of Executive Committee of League of Nations Union; Chairman, Family Endowment Society, Children's Nutrition Council and National Joint Committee for Spanish Relief; Hon. Sec. Parliamentary Committee on Refugees; Vice-Chairman National Committee for Rescue from Nazi Terror. *Publications:* Memoirs of William Rathbone, 1904; The Disinherited Family, a plea for Family Endowment, 1924; Child Marriage: the Indian Minotaur, 1934; War Can be Averted, 1938; The Case for Family Allowances, 1940; various reports, articles, etc. on Casual Labour, Woman's Work, and other Industrial, International, etc., problems. *Address:* 26 Hampstead Lane, Highgate, N6. *T:* Mountview 6000.

Died 2 Jan. 1946.

RATHBORNE, Air Cdre Charles Edward Harry, CB 1935; DSO 1919; RAF, retired; *m* 1919, Olive, *d* of H. H. B. Raines. Served European War, 1914–19 (despatches, DSO and Bar); Chief Staff Officer of the Inland Area, 1930–32; Air Officer commanding RAF, Mediterranean, 1932–35; retired list, 1935. *Address:* 7 Evelyn House, Hornton Street, Kensington, W8.

Died 21 Dec. 1943.

RATLAM, Maj.-Gen. HH Maharaja Sir Sajjan Singhji, GCIE 1931; KCSI 1909; KCVO 1922; Hon. ADC to the King since 1936; Ruler of Ratlam; *b* 13 Jan. 1880; *S* father (Sir Ranjit Singhji, KCIE), 1893; *m* 1st, 1902, *d* of H. H. Maharao of Kutch; 2nd, 1922, *d* of Soda Rajput family of Jamnagar; two *s* two *d*. The State is 693 square miles in extent, and has a population of 126,117. The Maharaja receives a salute of 15 guns (local) and a permanent salute of 13 guns. Recognised Head of the Rajputs in Malwa; Member of the Chamber of Princes; Member General Council of Daly College at Indore; Member General Council Mayo College at Ajmer; Vice-President Central India Rajput Hitkarini Sabha; the first Indian to be appointed as a Steward of the Indian Polo Association; granted hon. rank of Maj.-Gen. in His Majesty's army, 1936; served European War (France), 1915–18 (despatches, Croix d'officier de Légion d'Honneur); NW Frontier, 1919; placed personal services and resources of the State at the disposal of HM on declaration of War, 1939; contributed generously in men, money and material to the successful prosecution of the War; Col in CI Horse, 1946; enjoys plenary judicial powers. *Heir:* Maharaj Kumar Lokendra Singhji. *Address:* Ranjit Bilas Palace, Ratlam, Central India.

Died 3 Feb. 1947.

RATTRAY, Brig.-Gen. Charles, CB 1917; CSI 1919; Indian Army, retired; *b* 1868; *m* 1st, 1892, Adelaide, *d* of W. R. Balfour; one *d*; 2nd, 1921, Grace (*d* 1943), *d* of E. R. Colyer. Dongola Expedition, 1896 (medal); NW Frontier of India, 1897–98 (medal and clasp); European War (Mesopotamia), 1914–19 (despatches four times, Bt-Col, CB, CSI, St Stanislaus, crossed swords). *Club:* United Service.

Died 23 Sept. 1943.

RATTRAY, Col John Grant, CMG 1918; DSO 1916; Chairman Veterans' Assistance Commission; *b* near Aberlour, Banffshire, 15 Jan. 1867; *s* of Alexander Rattray and Jane, *d* of Wm Tennant, Aberlour; *m* 1895, Emily, *d* of Albert Wallace of Mt Forest, Ont, later of Carlyle, Saskatchewan; one *d*. *Educ:* High School, Park Hill, Ontario; Normal School, Ottawa, Ontario. Went to Canada, 1874; settled Middlesex County, Ontario; taught in a school, 1887–89; took 2nd class certificate with honours, 1890; went to Manitoba, 1890; taught in a school there until 1896; engaged in hardware business, 1896–1913; Inspector for Canada Life Assurance Company, Investment Department, 1912; joined 1st Canadian Contingent, Aug. 1914; organised 10th Canadian Infantry Battalion at Valcartier, Sept. 1914; served European War, 1914–18 (DSO, CMG); Lieut in

12th Manitoba Dragoons, 1906; organised and took command of 20th Border Horse, 1910; contested (L) for local Legislature the constituency of Virden, Manitoba, 1907. *Recreations:* golf, curling, general athletics. *Address:* Ottawa, Canada. *Clubs:* West Surrey Golf; Rivermead Golf, Ottawa; Rideau Curling; Chaudiere Golf.

Died 23 June 1944.

RATWATTE, Sir Jayatilaka Cudah, Kt 1939. Member State Council, Ceylon. *Address:* Colombo, Ceylon.

Died 15 March 1940.

RAU, Sir Raghavendra, Kt 1937; MA (Madras); Additional Secretary to Government of India Finance Department, since 1939; *b* 24 May 1889; *m* Satyabhama Rau. *Educ:* High School, Kundapur; Government College, Mangalore; Christian College, Madras. Entered Indian Audit and Accounts Service (competitive examination), 1912; after serving in various Accounts Offices, entered Government of India Secretariat Finance Dept, 1921; Under Secretary; Deputy Secretary; attached to Lee Commission as an Assistant Secretary on the financial side; joined Railway Dept, 1926; Director of Finance, 1928; Financial Commissioner of Railways, 1932–37; Accountant-General, Bombay, 1937–39. *Address:* Finance Dept, Government of India, New Delhi.

Died 23 Jan. 1942.

RAVEN-HILL, Leonard; artist; Punch cartoonist; *b* Bath, 10 March 1867; *m* 1st, Annie Rogers; 2nd, Marion Jean Lyon (*d* 1940). *Educ:* Bristol Grammar School; Devon County School. Studied at Lambeth, and later in Paris under MM Bougereau and Aimé Morot. Exhibited at Salon, 1886, and following years; Royal Academy, 1889, and following years; commenced drawing for Punch in 1896, retiring, through ill-health, 1935. *Address:* Mayfield, Queen's Road, Ryde, IW. *Club:* Savage.

Died 31 March 1942.

RAVENEL, Mazyck P., MD; Emeritus Professor; *b* South Carolina; *m* 1909, Adèle Petigru Van der Horst, Charleston, SC. *Educ:* private schools; Univ. of the South, Sewanee, Tennessee; Medical College of the State of South Carolina; Univ. of Pennsylvania; Pasteur Institute, Paris; Institute of Hygiene, University of Halle a/S. Member of numerous medical societies; Editor in Chief American Journal of Public Health; President, American Public Health Association, 1920; International Association against Tuberculosis; International Commission on Control of Bovine Tuberculosis; Member Sigma Xi Society; Phi Beta Kappa; 1st Lieutenant Medical Reserve Corps, USA, 1910–17; Major, Officers' Reserve Corps, Medical Section, USA, 1917–18; Lieut-Colonel Medical Corps, United States Army, 1918; Member of the National Advisory Health Council, 1914–33; Prof. of Bacteriology, Univ. of Wisconsin, 1907–14; Director, State Hygienic Laboratory of Wisconsin, 1908–14; Professor Preventive Medicine and Bacteriology, and Director Public Health Laboratory, University of Missouri, Columbia, Mo, 1914, retired. Returned to active duty as Professor of Medical Bacteriology and Preventive Medicine, 1942. *Publications:* A Half Century of Public Health; numerous papers on bacteriological subjects. *Address:* Columbia, Mo, USA.

Died 14 Jan. 1946.

RAVENSWORTH, 7th Baron *cr* 1821; **Robert Arthur Liddell;** Bt 1642; TD; DL; Major RA, TA, late Northumberland Hussars; *b* 2 Jan. 1902; *s* of 6th Baron and Isolda Blanche (*d* 1938), *d* of C. G. Prideaux-Brune; *S* father, 1932. *Educ:* Winchester; Christ Church, Oxford. DL Northumberland. *Recreations:* hunting, fishing, shooting, cricket, and golf. *Heir: cousin* Arthur Waller Liddell, *b* 25 July 1924. *Address:* Eslington Park, Whittingham, Alnwick, Northumberland. *T:*

Whittingham 239; Ravensworth Castle, Gateshead. *Clubs:* Brooks's, Bucks's; Northern Counties (Newcastle).

Died 4 Aug. 1950.

RAVILIOUS, Eric William; artist, painter and engraver; *b* 22 July 1903; *s* of Frank and Emma Ravilious; *m* 1930, Eileen Lucy, (Tirzah), Garwood; two *s* one *d. Educ:* Grammar School, Eastbourne; Eastbourne School of Art; Royal College of Art. Painted (with Edward Bawden) Morley College refreshment room 1929; engraved book illustrations since 1926 for various publishers; principal works—The Kynoch Press Note Book, the engravings in the first number of Signature, High Street, published by Country Life and the illustrations to Gilbert White's Selborne, published by the Nonesuch Press; painted three wall decorations; designed printed pottery, 1937–39 for Josiah Wedgwood, first production the Coronation Mug; two exhibitions of water-colours and drawings at the Zwemmer Gallery 1934 and 1937, and at Tooth's, 1939; Instructor of design at the Royal College of Art, 1929–38; Admiralty war artist, 1940. *Address:* Ironbridge Farm, Shalford, Braintree, Essex.

Died 2 Sept. 1942.

RAWLINGS, Justly John Gabriel, CBE 1926; late Managing Director of Anthony Hordern & Sons (Limited), of Brickfield Hill, Sydney; *b* 1868; *s* of late Joseph Rawlings, Salisbury, Eng.; *m* 1893, Julia Louisa, *d* of Arthur Marshall, West Dulwich, London; one *s* one *d. Educ:* Lloyd's Grammar School, Salisbury. Australian Commissioner British Empire Exhibition at Wembley, 1925 (CBE). *Recreations:* golf, gardening, industrial welfare. *Address:* Teffont, Bowral, NSW, Australia.

Died 20 April 1950.

RAWLINS, Lt-Col Arthur Kennedy, CIE 1916; CBE 1919; DSO 1898; late 24th Punjab Infantry; *b* Dharmasala, Punjab, 15 May 1868. *Educ:* Haileybury. Gazetted to East Surrey Regt; transferred to ISC 1892; served in NW Frontier disturbances, 1897–98 (despatches, DSO); served with China Field Force, 1900–01; with Somaliland Field Force, 1903–04 (despatches); served with Egyptian Expeditionary Force, 1914–19, as SSO Bikaner Camel Corps; retired 1921. *Address:* Lona, Weston-super-Mare.

Died 16 Nov. 1943.

RAWLINSON, Francis William, CBE 1922; *b* 1856; *e s* of Richard Rawlinson, Sunningdale, Berkshire; *m* 1886, Jean (*d* 1940), *e d* of late James Wylie, JP; one *s* two *d. Educ:* Edinburgh. Examiner in School Management and Method to Royal Educational Institute of Scotland, 1878–80; Private Secretary to Managers of Orient Line, 1882–88; Secretary of the Royal Merchant Navy School, 1888–1939; has been instrumental in the education, upbringing, and placing out in life of nearly three thousand British Merchant Seamen's orphans, of whom upward of seven hundred were commanding and officering merchant vessels during European War, while many others held commissions in the Royal Navy and the Army. *Publications:* Historical Outline of the Royal Merchant Navy School; Verses; Occasional papers. *Address:* Deepdene, Snaresbrook, Essex. *T:* Wanstead 705.

Died 23 March 1944.

RAWNSLEY, Col Claude, CMG 1917; CBE 1919; DSO 1902; late Army Service Corps; *b* Saltash, Cornwall, 4 Aug. 1862; *s* of late Lt-Col T. J. Rawnsley, Army Ordnance Department; *m* 1887, Lilian Maude (*d* 1939), *d* of late Captain Fred. Augustus Percy Wood, RMLI, and Receiver-General of the Gold Coast; one *d. Educ:* Cranbrook School; Royal Military Academy, Woolwich. Joined Royal Artillery 1882; transferred to Army Service Corps as Capt. 1889; served South African War, 1899–1902, first as DAAG and afterwards as AAG on the Headquarters Staff, Lines of Communication (despatches, Queen's medal 3 clasps, King's medal 2

clasps, DSO); European War, 1914–19 (despatches four times, 1914 Star, CMG, CBE). *Recreations:* formerly hunting, racquets, polo, golf. *Address:* c/o Lloyds Bank (G3), 6 Pall Mall, SW1.

Died 31 May 1944.

RAWNSLEY, Col Gerald Thomas, CB 1918; CMG 1916; late RAMC; Knight of Grace St John of Jerusalem; Order of Mercy; *b* 28 April 1865; *y s* of late Lieut-Col T. J. Rawnsley, AOD; *m* 1910, Margery (*d* 1929), *o c* of late George Somerville; one *d. Educ:* Cranbrook School; Guy's Hospital. MRCS Eng. 1886; LSA Lond. 1886. First Commission army, 1887; Late Adjutant VMSC London Companies; Senior Medical Officer Boer Prisoners of War Camps, Umballa and Kakool, India, 1901–02; DADMS East Lancs Division, 1911–15; served European War, 1914–18 (despatches four times, CB, CMG); ADMS 15th Division (with which served at battle and capture of Loos), 1915; ADMS 26th Division, 1915–16; DDMS 12th Corps, British Salonika Force, 1916–18; ADMS Grantham and North Midland District NC, 1918–19 (1914–15 Star, British War and Victory Medals); SMO Guernsey and Alderney District, 1920–30. *Recreations:* shooting, fishing, tennis. *Address:* Union Club, Malta.

Died 15 April 1942.

RAWSON, Sir Cooper, Kt 1926; *b* Whetstone Pastures, Leicester, 26 July 1876; *m* 1902, Elizabeth, *y d* of late J. Robson. MP (C) Brighton, Nov. 1922–44; Member of London County Council, 1913–22, and of Wandsworth Borough Council, 1911–22; Mayor of Wandsworth in 1918 and 1919; awarded Légion d'Honneur by French Government, 1927, in acknowledgment of services rendered to France through British League of Help; Sub-Lieut RND 1915; RNVR 1916–18; Hon. Captain RNVR 1940; Hon. British Govt Delegate at International Road Congress, Seville 1923, and Milan 1926; President of Institute of Quarrying, 1931–32; President Granite Guild, 1930; Hon. Fellow Inst. Highway Engineers. *Address:* 11 Upper Drive, Hove. *T:* Hove 5000. *Club:* Carlton.

Died 11 Jan. 1946.

RAY, Maharaja Rao Sir Jogendra Narayan, Kt 1938; CIE 1919; Zamindar, District, Murshidabad. Kaisar-i-Hind Medal, 1st Class, 1913. *Address:* Lalgola, Murshidabad, Bengal.

Died 18 Aug. 1946.

RAY, Matthew Burrow, DSO 1917; OBE 1945; Colonel, late Territorial Army; Physician to St Marylebone General Dispensary; Hon. Consulting Physician, The Arthur Stanley Institute of Middlesex Hospital; Fellow, Royal Society of Medicine; *s* of Richard Ray, Harrogate; *m* 1913, Edith Charlotte Frances, *d* of Lord Henry Cholmondeley and *widow* of Capt. R. E. Heaven; no *c. Educ:* Lancaster; Edinburgh University. MD, CM, MRCP. Has held among other appointments those of Assistant Medical Officer, West Riding Mental Hospital, and Hon. Surgeon to the Harrogate Infirmary; formerly ADMS 47th (2nd Lond.) Div. TA; a Past President of the Harrogate Medical Society; served with British Expeditionary Force as Lt-Col RAMC (TF), in command of No. 3 Casualty Clearing Station, 41 Stationary Hospital; acted as SMO Amiens (despatches, DSO). *Publications:* Rheumatic Diseases; On Prescribing Physical Treatment; Rheumatism in General Practice; various in medical journals. *Address:* 17 Upper Wimpole Street, W1. *T:* Welbeck 7848. *Club:* Athenæum.

Died 5 July 1950.

RAY, Sir Prafulla Chandra, Kt 1919; CIE 1912; DSc (Edin.); PhD (Cal.); late Senior Professor of Chemistry, University College of Science, Calcutta; *b* Bengal, 1861; unmarried. *Educ:* Calcutta; Edinburgh University. Graduated at Edinburgh, DSc; Hon. PhD Calcutta University, 1908; Hon. DSc Durham University, 1912.

Dean of the Faculty of Science, University of Calcutta, 1915; Professor Presidency College since the beginning of his career to 1916; Fellow of the Chemical Society, London, and of the Asiatic Society of Bengal; First President of the Indian Chemical Society, 1924–26; Founder-Director of the Bengal Chemical and Pharmaceutical Works. *Publications:* History of Hindu Chemistry, 2 vols; Makers of Modern Chemistry; Life and Experiences of a Bengali Chemist; contributions— Mercurous Nitrite and its numerous derivatives; Nitrites of the Alkylammonium Series; Nitrites of the Mercurialkyl and Mercurialky-larylammonium Series; Determination of Conductivity of Nitrites, and numerous other original papers on the allied subjects. *Recreations:* reading of works of Emerson, Shakespeare, and the novels of Dickens, George Eliot, and Thackeray; taking long walks in all kinds of weather. *Address:* College of Science, Calcutta.

Died 16 June 1944.

RAY-JONES, Raymond, RE; ARCA; painter and etcher; Fellow Royal Society of Painter-Etchers, 1926; Member Society of Graphic Art, 1920; Associate Royal College of Art, 1910; *b* Ashton-under-Lyne, 31 Aug. 1886; *m* 1926, Effie Irene, *e d* of J. W. E. Pearce, MA; two *s. Educ:* School of Art, Ashton-under-Lyne; Royal College of Art, South Kensington (Royal Exhibitioner and Lancashire County Scholar); Académie Julian, Paris. Studied under Prof. Gerald Moira and Sir Frank Short, RA, PRE; afterwards entered the studio of M. Jean Paul Laurens at the Académie Julian, Paris; awarded Prix and Medal for portrait painting; works acquired by British Museum; Victoria and Albert Museum, South Kensington; Trinity College, Cambridge; Contemporary Art Soc.; City Art Gallery, Manchester; Mappin Art Gallery, Sheffield, Ipswich Art Gallery, etc.; has exhibited at Royal Academy, Royal Society of Painter-Etchers, Society of Graphic Art, New English Art Club, Bristol, Liverpool, etc.; and at International and other exhibitions abroad—Paris, Venice, Hamburg, Dresden, Zürich, Geneva, Toronto, Sydney, Dunedin, etc. *Publication:* Portrait, Architectural and Landscape etchings. *Address:* Whealspeed, Chyangwheal, Carbis Bay, Cornwall; 6 and 8 Jubilee Place, SW3. *Club:* Chelsea Arts.

Died 26 Feb. 1942.

RAYLEIGH, 4th Baron *cr* 1821; **Robert John Strutt,** FRS 1905; JP, DL; MA, Hon. ScD Dublin; Hon. DSc Durham; Hon. LLD Edinburgh; President Royal Institution of Great Britain; Emeritus Professor of Physics, Imperial College of Science; *b* 28 Aug. 1875; *e s* of 3rd Baron Rayleigh and Evelyn Georgiana Mary (*d* 1934), *d* of James Maitland Balfour, Whittingehame, and Blanche, *d* of 2nd Marquis of Salisbury; *S* father, 1919; *m* 1st, 1905, Lady Hilda Clements (*d* 1919), 2nd *d* of 4th Earl of Leitrim; three *s* one *d*; 2nd, 1920, Kathleen Alice, *e d* of late John Coppin-Straker, Stagshaw House, Northumberland, and *widow* of Capt. James Harold Cuthbert, Scots Guards, Beaufront Castle, Northumberland; one *s. Educ:* Eton; Trinity College, Cambridge (Fellow, 1900). 1st Class Nat. Science Tripos parts I and II; Rumford Medallist of the Royal Society. Bakerian Lecturer, 1911 and 1919; Foreign Member of the Dutch Society of Sciences, Haarlem; Member of the Advisory Council of the Department of Scientific and Industrial Research, 1929–34; Chairman, Civil Research Committee on Radium Requirements, 1928; President, Section of Mathematics and Physics British Association, 1929; President of the British Association, Cambridge, 1938; Foreign Sec. of the Royal Society, 1929–34; Joint President, International Congress of Physics, London, 1934; President of the Physical Society, 1934–36; Trustee Beit Memorial Fellowships, 1928–46; President, Central Council of Milk recording Societies, 1939; Chairman of the Executive Committee, National Physical Laboratory, 1932–39; Chairman of Governing Body, Imperial College of Science, 1938–47. Fellow of

Eton College, 1935–45. Owns about 7000 acres. *Publications:* John William Strutt, Third Baron Rayleigh, OM, FRS, 1924; Life of Sir J. J. Thomson, 1942; numerous scientific papers in the Royal Society's Proceedings and elsewhere. *Heir: s* Hon. John Arthur Strutt. *Address:* Terling Place, Chelmsford, Essex. *Club:* Athenæum.

Died 13 Dec. 1947.

RAYMER, Rev. Robert Richmond, CMG 1919; DSO 1916; *b* 1 Nov. 1870; *e s* of late Captain Robert Raymer, Inspector of Army Schools; *m* 1905, Ethel, *d* of late Capt. E. G. Peyton, 106th Light Infantry; one *s. Educ:* Farnham Grammar School; Trinity College, Dublin (MA). Served with 1st Batt. Leicestershire Regt in S African War, 1901–02 (Queen's medal with five clasps); R. Jersey Militia, 1904–14; in command of OTC at Victoria College, Jersey, 1903–12, and at Clifton College, Bristol, 1912–14; Lt-Colonel 5th Bn South Staffordshire Regt, 1915–19; Colonel, May 1919; served European War, 1915–18 (despatches four times, wounded, DSO, CMG); DL, Gloucestershire, 1922; Chairman, Glos TA Association, 1924–27; ordained, 1920; Vicar of Abbots Leigh, 1923–27; Rector of Sheldon with Marston Green, near Birmingham, 1927–31; British Chaplain in Greece, 1931–41; OCF Greece, 1940–41 (1939–45, Star); Rector of West Wickham, Kent, 1942–43; Commander Royal Order of George I (Greek), 1944. *Address:* c/o Westminster Bank, Queen's Road, Clifton, Bristol.

Died 12 Jan. 1948.

RAYMOND, Col Francis, CIE 1912; FRCVS; *b* 5 June 1854. Entered Army Veterinary Dept, 1878; Capt. 1888; Major, 1898; Lt-Col 1905; Col 1908; retired, 1912; served S Africa, 1879; present at battle of Ulundi (medal with clasp); Suakim Expedition, 1885, on special embarkation duty (thanked by Govt of India); Chitral, 1895, forcing of the Malakand Pass (medal with clasp); European War, 1914–18; a Member of the Council of the Royal College of Veterinary Surgeons, 1891–94; President Southern Counties Veterinary Medical Association, 1892; Hon. Fellow Central Veterinary Medical Society of London; Vice-Chairman National Veterinary Medical Association and Senior Fitzwygram Examiner, 1892–95; Director Civil Veterinary Department of the Provinces of Bengal, Bihar, and Orissa 1896, and Principal Veterinary College of Calcutta, 1898; Founder and first Director of the Raymond (Govt) Research Laboratory, Calcutta, 1907–12; Membre Correspondant de la Société de Pathologie Exotique de France, 1908; Fellowship Examiner in Exotic Pathology at Royal College of Veterinary Surgeons, 1918. *Publications:* papers on educational and Pathological subjects including Rabies, Glanders, Cattle-plague, Fowl Cholera, Bacteriology, etc. *Club:* Constitutional.

Died 17 May 1945.

RAYNER, Frank, CBE 1943; DSO 1916; TD; Lieut-Colonel 7th Sherwood Foresters; Director and Consulting Engineer, Trent Navigation Company, since 1928; *b* 3 Oct. 1866; unmarried. *Educ:* University School and University College, Nottingham. Civil Engineer; associated with Trent Navigation Company as Engineer and General Manager until retirement in 1928; also generally engaged in Inland Waterway Transport policy. *Publications:* various papers. *Recreation:* cruising on rivers and at sea. *Address:* Gresley House, Sherwood Rise, Nottingham. *T:* Nottingham 64416. *Clubs:* Junior Army and Navy; Borough, Nottingham; Royal Yorkshire Yacht, Bridlington.

Died 8 Dec. 1945.

RAYNER, Mabel Mary Cheveley, DSc; sometime Head of Department of Botany, University College, Reading; now engaged in Forestry Research in collaboration with Research department of Forestry

Commission; *e d* of late Thomas Cheveley Rayner, AMICE, and Alicia Anne Rayner; *m* 1912, William Neilson Jones, MA. *Educ:* University College, London; University College, Reading. BSc London, 1908, 1st Class Honours Botany; DSc London, 1915. Has lectured extensively in many Universities and Research Stations throughout USA. *Publications:* Practical Plant Physiology (with Sir F. Keeble), 1911; A Text book of Plant Biology (with W. Neilson Jones), 1920; Mycorrhiza, 1927; Problems in Tree Nutrition, 1944; Trees and Toadstools, 1945; subsection Mycorrhiza in Encyclopaedia Britannica; numerous contributions to botanical and forestry journals. *Recreations:* rock climbing, riding, travel. *Address:* Bedford College, University of London, Regent's Park, NW1.

Died 17 Dec. 1948.

RAYNES, John Richard; journalist; *b* 5 Aug. 1881; *m* Margaret Annie Hunt; two *s* two *d*. Chairman of London District Institute of Journalists, 1935. *Publications:* Coal and Its Conflicts; Engines and Men, etc. *Address:* Malvern Lodge, 32 Ashburnham Road, Hastings.

Died 11 Aug. 1944.

RAZA ALI, Sir Syed, Kt 1935; CBE 1926; *b* Kundarki, district Moradabad, 29 April 1882; *o s* of late Syed Wahid Ali and Ashura Bano; *m* second *cousin* Saghir Fatima; one *s* one *d*. *Educ:* Government High School, Moradabad; Muhammadan College, Aligarh; 2nd class in BA, 1902, and 1st class in LLB, 1907, Allahabad University. Started practice at Bar in Moradabad, 1908; Member of the United Provinces Legislative Council, 1912–20; gave evidence before Islington Commission, 1913, and Southborough Committee, 1919; was one of those responsible for introducing separate Moslem representation in Municipal Boards in the United Provinces; took prominent part in negotiating the Congress-League Compact, 1916; same year removed to Allahabad to practise at High Court; took part in Swaraj and Khilafat movements, but strongly differing from non-co-operation movement, became independent in politics, 1920; Member of the Council of State, 1921–26; Member of the North-West Frontier Province Enquiry Committee, 1922; headed two deputations of non-official Moslem members of Indian Legislature to Viceroy in connection with Turkish question, 1922 and 1923; gave non-party evidence before Reforms Enquiry Committee, 1924; President of All-India Moslem League, Bombay Session, 1924; successfully moved Govt of India to adopt principle of safeguarding interests of minority communities in public services, March 1925; Member of Deputation sent by Government of India to South Africa in 1925 to negotiate a settlement of the Indian question with Union Government; laid foundation stone of an Indian School in Cape Town, Feb. 1926; Member Public Service Commission, 1926–31; Delegate, Government of India's Delegation to Assembly of League of Nations, Geneva, 1929; Agent General for India in Union of South Africa, 1935–38. *Publications:* Essays on Moslem Questions, 1912; My Impressions of Soviet Russia, 1930; political addresses. *Recreations:* walking and gardening. *Clubs:* Chelmsford (Delhi, and Simla).

Died 15 Aug. 1949.

REA, 1st Baron *cr* 1937, of Eskdale; **Walter Russell Rea;** 1st Bt *cr* 1935; Chairman, Rea Brothers, Ltd, Merchant Bankers; *b* Liverpool, 1873; *e s* of late Right Hon. Russell Rea; *m* 1st, 1896, Evelyn (*d* 1930), *d* of J. J. Muirhead; three *s* two *d*; 2nd, 1931, Jemima, *d* of Rev. Alex Ewing. *Educ:* University Coll. School; abroad. MP (L) Scarborough, 1906–18; Junior Lord of the Treasury, 1915–16 (unpaid); Liberal Whip, 1924; contested Oldham, Dec. 1918; Nelson and Colne, 1920; North Bradford, 1922 and 1924; Taunton, 1929; MP (L) North Bradford, 1923–24; Dewsbury, 1931–35; Comptroller of the Household, 1931–32; Chief Liberal Whip, 1931–35.

Heir: s Hon. Phillip Russell Rea, OBE. *Address:* 6 Barton Street, Westminster, SW1. *T:* Abbey 5553; Hollycombe, Liphook, Hants. *T:* Liphook 3233; Gatehouse, Eskdale, Cumberland. *T:* Eskdale 26. *Clubs:* Reform, National Liberal.

Died 26 May 1948.

READ, Alexander Llewellyn, CMG 1942; MVO 1934; ISO 1937; Under Secretary, Clerk of Executive Council, Secretary to Premier, Secretary, Minister of Health, Public Debt Commissioner, Commissioner of Charitable Funds, and Member of Classification and Efficiency Board, S Australia; *b* 27 Oct. 1877; *s* of Edward Read and Mary Tregonning; *m* 1901, Ellie Evelyn Weir; one *s* one *d*. *Educ:* Norwood Public School. Entered S Australia Civil Service, 1894; served in Cabinet Minister's Departments of Public Works, Treasury, and Chief Secretary; State Director for visit of Duke of Gloucester; Member Royal Society of St George; Fellow of Institute of Public Administration. *Recreation:* motoring. *Address:* 23 Knightsbridge Road, Seabrook, S Australia; Secretary's Department, Adelaide, S Australia.

Died 12 June 1942.

READ, Prof. Arthur Avery, TD; DMet (Sheffield); Hon. DSc (Wales); FIC, FCS; Emeritus Professor of Metallurgy, University College of South Wales and Monmouthshire, Cardiff; *b* 23 July 1868; *y s* of late Charles Read, Honiton, Devon. *Educ:* Exeter Grammar School; Owens College, Manchester; Sheffield University. Captain TA retired. *Address:* Broomfield, 9 Durley Chine Road, Bournemouth. *T:* Bournemouth 1794.

Died 24 Sept. 1943.

READ, Sir Herbert James, GCMG 1935 (KCMG 1918; CMG 1907); CB 1914; MA Oxon; FRAS; *b* 17 March 1863; *s* of Charles Read, Honiton, Devon; *m* 1905, Violet K., *y d* of late Major Duncan MacLachlan, 90th Regiment; one *d* (one *s* decd). *Educ:* Allhallows School, Honiton; Brasenose Coll. Oxford. Higher Division Clerk, War Office, 1887; 2nd class Clerk, Colonial Office, 1889; Asst Private Secretary to Mr Joseph Chamberlain, 1896–97; 1st class Clerk, 1898; Principal Clerk, 1905–16; Assistant Under-Secretary, Deputy Permanent Under-Secretary, Colonial Office, and Registrar of the Order of St Michael and St George, 1916–24; Governor of Mauritius, 1924–30; British Delegate African Liquor Conference, Brussels, 1895; and Plenipotentiary, 1906; Delegate on Commission on Anglo-German Frontier in East Africa, 1906; one of British Plenipotentiaries at Sleeping Sickness Conference, London, 1907–08, and at African Arms Traffic Conference, Brussels, 1908; Chairman of Colonial Survey Committee, 1905–24, of Colonial Advisory Medical and Sanitary Committee, 1909–24, and Bureau of Hygiene and Tropical Diseases, 1908–24; official visit to East Africa and Soudan, 1911–12; Senior Member of Colonial Office Delegacy at Paris Peace Conference, 1919; Chairman of Corona Club, 1930–46; Colonial Office representative on Governing Body of Imperial Coll. of Science S Kensington, 1930–41; Chm. of Executive Committee of Coll., 1931–38; Member of the Court of the London School of Hygiene and Tropical Medicine; Colonial Office representative on Governing Body of the Seamen's Hospital Society until 1946; also on Committee of Imperial Cancer Research Fund, 1900–43; a Crown Trustee of the London Parochial Charities, 1931–45; sometime Chairman of Executive of Christian Service Union (Wallingford Farm Training Colony, Lingfield Epileptic Colony). Hon. Fellow of the Royal Soc. of Tropical Medicine; and of Society for the Preservation of the Fauna of the Empire; an Hon. Vice-President of the Liverpool School of Tropical Medicine and of the Seamen's Hospital Society, Greenwich. Commander of the Belgian Order of the Crown, 1919. *Club:* Reform.

Died 16 Oct. 1949.

READ, Opie; *b* Nashville, Tennessee, USA, 22 Dec. 1852. *Educ:* privately, as was largely the custom in that part of the United States. *Publications:* A Kentucky Colonel; The Jucklins; My Young Master; Emmet Bonlore; The Waters of Caney Fork; An Arkansas Planter; Old Ebenezer; Son of the Swordmaker; The Starbucks; The Harkriders; Old Lem Jucklin; An American Cavalier; I Remember, 1932; etc. *Clubs:* Press, Chicago.

Died 2 Nov. 1939.

READE, Maj.-Gen. Raymond Northland Revell, CB 1908; CMG 1918; JP; Col King's Shropshire Light Infantry, 1921–31; *b* London, 16 Feb. 1861; *s* of John Page Reade, JP, DL, Crowe Hall, Suffolk, and Lady Mary Reade, *e d* of 2nd Earl of Ranfurly; *m* 1894, Mrs Chas. Greenway, *née* Spencer, *e d* of Col Almeric Spencer; one *d. Educ:* Eton; RMC, Sandhurst. Gazetted to 85th King's Light Infantry, 1880; served Afghan War, 1880 (medal); Ashanti Expedition, 1895 (star); Anam Expedition, Nigeria, 1898 (medal with clasp); South African War, 1899–1900, was present at actions of Belmont, Graspan, Modder River, Magersfontein, Rooidam, Zelikal's Nek, Leydenburg (despatches, promoted brevet Lt-Col, medal with 4 clasps); European War, 1914–19 (despatches, CMG, British War Medal, Victory Medal, Commander Greek Order of King George I, Greek Medal for Military Merit, 1st Class); served on the staff as DAAG in Egypt; ADC to GOC, Aldershot; DAAG Dublin; Special Service Officer and DAAG for Intelligence, South African War, 1899–1900; Commandant Royal Military College of Canada; Assistant Adjutant and Quartermaster-General at Malta; Brigadier-General in charge of Administration Northern Command; General Officer commanding troops in the Straits Settlements, 1914; commanded 59th and 68th Divisions, 1915–17; served as British Representative, Inter-Allied Military Mission, Greece, 1918; retired, 1920. *Address:* Stutton Manor, Ipswich. *Clubs:* Army and Navy; County, Ipswich.

Died 18 Oct. 1943.

READING, Sir Claude Hill, KCMG 1934; *b* Sydney, 10 May 1874; *s* of Edward Reading, Warwick, and Caroline Mary Burdett; *m* 1902, Mabel, *d* of J. R. Carey, Milson's Point, Sydney; one *s* one *d. Educ:* Sydney Grammar School. In Union Bank service for 6 years; Deputy Chairman of British Tobacco Co. (Aust.) Ltd 1928–34, and Director of British Australasian Tobacco Co. Pty Ltd, W. D. & H. O. Wills (Aust.) Ltd 1912–34, and the States Tobacco Co. Pty Ltd 1914–34; took degree in Accountancy 1909; Member of Council of Sydney Chamber of Commerce 1916; Hon. Treas. 1916–18; Deputy Chm. of Board of Business Administration Defence Dept 1918; member Commonwealth Board of Trade 1918; a Director of the Commonwealth Bank since 1927, Chairman since 1934; Director of Trustees Executors and Agency Co. Ltd (Chairman NSW Board); a Trustee of Sydney Grammar School, 1924–36; President of Boy Scouts Assoc. (NSW Branch) since 1940. *Recreations:* golf and tennis; President, Royal Sydney Golf Club, 1930–44. *Address:* Trelawney, Trelawney Street, Woollahra, Sydney, NSW. *T:* FM 5067. *Clubs:* Australian, Sydney; Melbourne, Melbourne.

Died 23 March 1946.

READING, Martin Luther; *b* Thame, Oxfordshire, 1869; 2nd *s* of William Reading, Leamington, England. Joined New Zealand Times, 1902, becoming later assistant editor; contributor to Manchester Guardian, Lone Hand Magazine, Sydney Bulletin; New Zealand correspondent for several years to Sydney Morning Herald; Editor of Lyttelton Times, 1914–24; Brisbane Evening Telegraph 1924–36; one of New Zealand members of delegation of oversea journalists to Britain and French war fronts as guests of the British

Government, 1918. *Recreations:* golfing and bowling. *Address:* Racecourse Road, Ascot, Brisbane, Queensland.

Died 31 Oct. 1943.

REAKES, Dr Charles John, CBE 1919; MRCVS, DVSc; *b* Littlebourne, Kent, 1865; *s* of George Reakes; *m* 1893, Charlotte, *d* of Capt. E. Bradbury, Kings's Dragoon Guards. Director of Veterinary Services and Remounts, New Zealand Forces, 1909–21; Director-General Department of Agriculture, New Zealand Government 1918–36; Chairman and Registrar of Veterinary Board, 1927–36; represented New Zealand at Imperial Agricultural Research Conference, London, 1927. *Address:* Lower Hutt, Wellington, New Zealand.

Died 3 Oct. 1943.

REARDON-SMITH, Sir Willie; *see* Smith.

REAVELL, Sir William, Kt 1938; MIMechE; MINA; Founder and Managing Director, Reavell and Co. Ltd, Ipswich; *b* 1866; *s* of George Reavell and Martha Rose Noble; *m* 1892, May, Louise Grieve; one *s. Educ:* Alnwick Grammar School; Armstrong College, Newcastle-upon-Tyne; City and Guilds College, Finsbury. Trained by Hawthorn Leslie & Co. Ltd, Newcastle-upon-Tyne; Marine Draughtsman with Maudslay Sons and Field, London; General Manager Marine Dept Babcock and Wilcox Ltd; General Manager Peter Brotherhood Ltd, London; Established the present business of Reavell and Co. Ltd 1898; Pres. IMechE, 1926–27; Pres. British Engineers' Association, 1930–36; British Standards Institution, Chairman of General Council 1936, Chairman Engineering Divisional Council 1931–44; Chairman Mechanical Industry Committee, 1929–44. *Publications:* papers and addresses Institutions of Civil Engineers, Mechanical Engineers, and Naval Architects, published in their transactions and the Technical Press. *Recreation:* fishing. *Address:* Broadwater, Ipswich. *TA:* Reavell Ipswich. *T:* Broadwater, 2840, Ipswich, Works 2124 Ipswich.

Died 25 April 1948.

RECKITT, Sir Philip Bealby, 3rd Bt *cr* 1894; OBE 1918; Director of Reckitt and Sons, Ltd, Hull and London; Director of Priestman Bros, Hull; *b* Hessle, near Hull, 1 Jan. 1873; 2nd *s* of Sir James Reckitt, 1st Bt of Swanland Manor, Hull; *S* brother 1930; *m* 1st, 1900; Hilda (*d* 1935), 2nd *d* of late F. Grotrian, of Ingmanthorpe Hall, Wetherby; two *d;* 2nd, 1939, Margarida, *widow* of Col Algernon Charles Bishop, Jericho Priory, Blackmore, Essex. *Educ:* privately; King's College, Cambridge. *Recreations:* shooting, travelling. *Heir:* none. *Address:* Little Green, Compton, Chichester, Sussex. *Club:* United University.

Died 17 Nov. 1944 (ext).

RECORD, Edgar W.; Editor of the Birmingham Post since 1933; *b* 1873. After serving articles on Leamington Chronicle held appointments in Birmingham, Sheffield, Manchester, and London; London Correspondent, Birmingham Post, 1924–33. *Address:* Sterling House, Hagley Road, Edgbaston. *Clubs:* Union, Birmingham.

Died 18 Feb. 1943.

REDDAWAY, William Fiddian, MA (Cambridge); Hon. PhD (Tartu); FRHistS; Corr. Member, Polish Academy of Sciences; Senior Fellow of King's College, Cambridge; President, C. U. Lacrosse Club, and C. U. Slavonic Society; *b* 2 Aug. 1872; *s* of Rev. J. C. Reddaway; *m* 1906, Kate Waterland Sills, MA; four *s* one *d. Educ:* Leys School and King's College, Cambridge. First Class Historical Tripos, 1894; Univ. (Whewell) scholar, 1895; Members' prize (Eng. essay), 1897. Lecturer at Fitzwilliam House, 1896–1907; Governor of Leys School; Censor of Fitzwilliam House, 1907–24; formerly University Lecturer in History and Director of Scandinavian Studies. *Publications:* The Monroe Doctrine; Frederick the Great; Chapters on

Russian and Scandinavian History, etc., in the Cambridge Modern History, the English Historical Review, Cambridge Historical Journal, Baltic Countries, History, the Encyclopædia Britannica, the History of the Nations, the Cambridge History of British Foreign Policy, Baltic and Caucasian States; Britain, 1852–1865; Modern European History (with T. F. Reddaway); Lord John Russell; Chapters in the Cambridge History of the British Empire; European Documents, 1492–1715; Documents of Catherine the Great; Eighteenth Century Europe; Marshal Pilsudski; Problems of the Baltic; Europe 1610–1715 and (3rd edn) 1715–1814; editor Cambridge History of Poland, etc. *Recreation:* golf. *Address:* 4 Adams Road, Cambridge. *T:* Cambridge 4041.

Died 31 Jan. 1949.

REDHEAD, Lt-Col Richard Henry M.; see Milne-Redhead.

REED, Col Sir Joseph, Kt 1922; late General Manager and part proprietor of Newcastle Chronicle publications; *b* 25 June 1867; *s* of late Richard Bagnall Reed, Forest Hall, Northumberland; *m* 1892, Annie, *e d* of late Frederick Robson, Newcastle-upon-Tyne; no *c. Educ:* Armstrong College, Newcastle-upon-Tyne. Succeeded his father as manager of the Chronicle, and afterwards became managing director of the Newcastle Chronicle, Ltd, severing his connection with the company in March 1925; became a member of the Committee of the Press Association, 1918; attended Imperial Press Conference, Melbourne, Australia, 1927; Chairman, 1921–23; an old Volunteer officer; took a leading part in raising the Tyneside Brigades for European War; given the rank of Honorary Colonel of the Tyneside Scottish; was a trustee of the Joseph Cowen Fund for financing the brigades, and was instrumental in establishing the Joseph and Jane Cowen Training School for disabled soldiers; Chairman of the Finance Committee of the Newcastle Royal Infirmary, and a Freeman of the City of London; President, Newcastle-upon-Tyne Aero Club; JP, Doctor of Civil Law (Durham); Hon. Treasurer of University of Durham. *Recreations:* shooting and flying. *Address:* Horton Grange, Seaton Burn, Northumberland. *T:* Ponteland 38; Rockcliffe, Dalbeattie. *T:* Rockcliffe Dalbeattie 238. *Clubs:* Junior Army and Navy, Livery, Royal Aero; Union, Newcastle-upon-Tyne.

Died 2 March 1942.

REED, William Henry, MVO; MusD Cantuar; FRAM, FRCM; conductor, violinist, and teacher; *b* Frome, 29 July 1877; *s* of Francis John Reed; *m* Eveline Dreyfus. *Educ:* privately. Royal Academy of Music under Emile Sauret and Professor Prout. Violin Prof. and Examiner Royal College of Music; Chairman of Directors and leader of the London Symphony Orchestra and late leader of Royal Philharmonic Orchestra; conductor of the Croydon Symphony Orchestra, Redhill Society of Instrumentalists, Bromley Orchestral Concerts, The Strolling Players Amateur Orchestral Soc., The Great Western Railway Music Society, and Tadworth Glee and Madrigal Society. *Compositions:* Suite Venitienne; Valse Brillante; Among the Mountains of Cambria; Scenes from the Ballet; Symphonic Poem, Caliban; Violin Concerto, The Lincoln Imp; Caprice, Will o' the Wisp; Orchestral Suite, Æsop's Fables; variations for string orchestra; Rhapsody for Viola and Orchestra; Orchestral Suite, Shockheaded Peter; A String Symphony; overture, Merry Andrew; chamber music, songs, violin, and piano music. *Publications:* Elgar as I knew him, 1936; Life of Elgar, 1938. *Recreation:* golf. *Address:* Froom, Chatsworth Road, Croydon. *T:* Croydon 0587.

Died 2 July 1942.

REES, Arthur J.; author; *b* St Kilda; *m. Educ:* Melbourne; England. *Publications:* Sussex novels: Cup of Silence; Simon of Hangeltree; Love Me Anise; Stories of Mystery and Suspense and Detective Tales: Greymarsh; The Threshold of Fear; Island of Destiny; The Moon Rock; The Hand in the Dark; The Pavilion by the Lake; The Shrieking Pit; Tragedy at Twelvetrees; Investigations of Colwin Grey; The River Mystery; Peak House; Aldringham's Last Chance; The Flying Argosy; Romance and Fantasy: The Brink; The Single Clue; The Sound of Wings; A Knight-Errant of Christmas Island (short stories); Belles Lettres: Maupassant; Old Sussex and Her Diarists; contributor of special articles and reviews to Sydney Daily Mirror and associated publications. *Recreations:* walking, languages. *Address:* Offington Hall, Worthing, Sussex. *Club:* PEN (Foundation member).

Died 22 Nov. 1942.

REES, Brig.-Gen. Hubert Conway, CMG 1918; DSO 1914; late 2nd Batt. the Welch Regiment; *b* 26 March 1882; *o s* of late Canon Henry Rees, The White Cottage, Shanklin; *m* 1914, Katharine Adelaide, *d* of late John Loring, The Cottage, Doddington, Nantwich; three *d. Educ:* Charterhouse. Entered army, 1903; Captain, 1912; Bt-Major, 1915; Temp. Brig.-Gen., 1916; served S Africa, 1901–02 (Queen's medal four clasps); European War, 1914–18 (despatches five times, DSO, CMG, Col); retired pay, 1922. *Address:* Kyrewood House, Tenbury, Worcs.

Died 3 Jan. 1948.

REES, Ven. Vaughan William Treharne, BA; Archdeacon of Newport, 1935–48; Vicar of Trevethin, Pontypool, since 1927; *b* 1879; *s* of John Rees, formerly Vicar of Tylorstown; *m* 1908, Margaret Elizabeth Hughes-Jones. *Educ:* Llandovery College; SDC Lampeter. Deacon, 1903; Priest, 1904; Curate of Mountain Ash, 1903–07; St John, Canton, Cardiff, 1907–11; St Andrew's Major, 1911–15; Vicar of Llanarth, 1915–27; Surrogate, 1916; Canon of Monmouth Cathedral, 1930; Chaplain Territorial Association. *Publications:* A History of Trevethin and its Churches, 1934; Handbook of Parish of Llanarth W Clytha, 1938. *Recreations:* walking, golf, etc. *Address:* Trevethin Vicarage, Pontypool, Mon. *T:* Pontypool 228.

Died 21 Aug. 1948.

REES-MOGG, Lt-Col Graham Beauchamp Coxeter, OBE 1919; FRCVS; JP Warwickshire; *b* 10 Sept. 1881; *s* of Rev. Henry James Rees-Mogg and Charlotte Elizabeth Sarah Newton; *m* 1922, Kathleen MCH (*d* 1949), *y d* of Sir Frederick Wills, Bt, Northmoor, Dulverton, and *widow* of Edward H. Douty, MD, FRCS, Cannes; no *c. Educ:* Haileybury College; Royal Veterinary College, London. MRCVS, 1906; FRCVS, 1914; joined Royal Army Veterinary Corps, 1907; transferred as Veterinary Officer to 1st Life Guards, 1912; to Royal Horse Guards, 1922; served European War, 1914–18 (despatches thrice); retired, 1936; High Sheriff of Warwickshire, 1941. Governor of Royal Veterinary College. *Recreation:* lawn tennis. *Address:* Clifford Manor, nr Stratford-upon-Avon. *T:* Stratford-upon-Avon 2616. *Club:* Guards'.

Died 4 May 1949.

REEVES, Edward Ayearst, FRAS, FRGS; Chevalier de l'Ordre de la Couronne (Belgium); Map Curator and Instructor in Practical Astronomy and Surveying to Royal Geographical Society, 1900, retired 1933; *b* Lewes, Sussex, 9 Feb. 1862; *s* of Abraham and Elizabeth Reeves; *m* 1888, Grace Eden Harley, London; one *s* one *d. Educ:* privately. Assistant in Map Dept of Royal Geographical Society, 1878; President of the Geographical Section of the British Association for the Advancement of Science, 1916; awarded Cullam Gold Medal of the American Geographical Society, New

York, for improvements in instruments and methods of geographical surveying, 1922; awarded Victoria Gold Medal of the Royal Geographical Society, 1928. *Publications:* Maps and Map Making; Trigonometry, Plane and Spherical; Recollections of a Geographer; Recent Psychic Experiences; Editor of the Royal Geographical Society's Hints to Travellers, 9th edition; numerous papers on surveying and geographical subjects in the Geographical Journal and other publications. *Address:* Green Ridges, Reigate, Surrey. *T:* Redhill, 2765.

Died 17 Oct. 1945.

REEVES-SMITH, Sir George, Kt 1938; Chevalier of the Legion of Honour, 1938; Knight Commander of the Order of the Crown of Italy, 1939; Vice-Chairman since 1916 and Managing Director since 1900 of the Savoy, Claridge's, and Berkeley Hotels, London, and since 1904 of Simpsons in the Strand; Chairman of Council of Hotels and Restaurants Association of Great Britain since 1931 and Chairman of the Executive Committee since 1910; Chairman of the Coronation Accommodation Committee, 1937; Hon. President, International Hotel Alliance and a member of the Executive Committee; Chairman of Advisory Committee, Ministry of Labour Hotel and Catering Trades Employment Exchange; Member of Executive and Finance Committees of The Travel and Industrial Development Association of Great Britain and Ireland; Director of Savoy Theatre Ltd; *s* of George Reeves-Smith; *m* Maud, *d* of Charles Hindle; one *d*. *Educ:* Brighton College. Instrumental in founding Preston Hall Treatment and Training Colony for Tuberculous Exservicemen at Aylesford, Kent; acted as Vice-President and Chairman of the Executive Committee and of the Sub-Committee of Management, 1919–25, when the undertaking and assets were transferred to the British Legion; instrumental in founding the British Sanatorium (Montana Hall), Montana-Vermala, Switzerland, for the reception of patients from the British Empire, the medical and nursing staff being all British. *Publication:* pamphlet, Stimulants and Narcotics. *Recreations:* fly-fishing, golf. *Address:* Claridge's Hotel, W1. *TA:* Claridge's Hotel, London. *T:* Mayfair 8860. *Club:* Garrick.

Died 29 May 1941.

REGAN, Charles Tate, MA (Camb.); Hon. DSc (Durham); Hon. Fellow Queens' College, Cambridge; FRS 1917; FZS; Foreign Member of the American Academy of Arts and Sciences and of the Royal Danish Academy; Honorary Member of the Yorkshire Philosophical Society, and of Soc. Cent. d'Aquiculture de France; Corresponding Member of Senckenbergische Gesellschaft, Frankfurt am-Main, and of the American Museum of Natural History, New York; Académico honorario, University of La Plata; *b* Sherborne, Dorset, 1878; *s* of C. J. Regan, ARAM; *m* 1904, Elsie, *e d* of late George Marlow of Arlington, Berks; two *s* two *d*. *Educ:* Derby School; Queens' College, Cambridge. Entered Museum, 1901; Deputy-Keeper of Zoology, 1919–21; Keeper, 1921–27; Director of the British Museum of Natural History, 1927–38; Member of Freshwater Fish Committee, 1917–20. Pres. of Section D, British Association, 1925; Geoffroy St Hilaire Medal for 1929, Soc. Nat. d'Acclimatation de France. *Publications:* British Freshwater Fishes; Biologia Centrali-Americana, Pisces, and Reptilia, Batrachia and Pisces in Introductory Volume; Monograph of the Loricariidae; Reports on Fishes of the Terra Nova and Scotia Antarctic Expeditions and the Stomiatoid and Ceratioid Fishes of the Dana Expeditions; numerous memoirs on structure and classification of fishes, and on geographical distribution and evolution. *Address:* 8 Carlton Avenue, Feltham, Middlesex.

Died 12 Jan. 1943.

REGAN, Col James Louis, CMG 1918; VD 1929; Departmental and Manufacturers' Agent; Adviser on Tariffs and Taxation; Customs Specialist, Ottawa; Representative the Government of the Province of Nova Scotia Purchasing Department; *b* 1888; *m* 1910, Hazel Rutherford Yould. Served European War, 1914–19 (CMG). *Address:* PO Box 14 and 596 Park Dale Av., Ottawa. *Clubs:* Canadian (Ottawa); United Services (Past Pres.) (Montreal).

Died Jan. 1948.

REGIS DE OLIVEIRA, Raul, GCVO 1937; GBE; Brazilian Ambassador in London, 1925–40; *m* D. Maria Georgina de Araujo Olinda; one *d*. *Educ:* Paris; São Paulo. Entered Diplomatic Service in 1902; Posts in Vienna, Rome, and the Hague; Minister in Cuba; Ambassador in Mexico; Under Secretary of State during European War. *Recreations:* riding, shooting. *Address:* c/o Brazilian Embassy, 19 Upper Brook Street, W1.

Died 9 July 1942.

REID, Col Alexander Kirkwood, CB 1933; CBE 1943; DSO 1919; MC; TD; DL County of City of Glasgow; Stockbroker; Col Territorial Army; Vice-Chairman Territorial, Army and Air Force Association, Glasgow; Military member Glasgow University Joint Recruiting Board; Hon. Area Organiser, Home Guard, Glasgow Area; *b* 18 July 1884; *s* of late James Reid, Glasgow; *m* 1917, Ina Doris, *d* of late William Law, shipowner, Glasgow; one *s* three *d*. *Educ:* Kelvinside Academy, Glasgow. 2nd Lieut 5th (Glasgow Highlanders), VB HLI, 1906; Captain, 9th (Glasgow Highlanders) HLI 1914; Major, 1916; Lt-Col 1923; Colonel TA 1927; commanded 9th (Glasgow Highlanders) HLI 1923–29; served with 9th (Glasgow Highlanders) HLI France and Flanders, 1914–16 and 1918 (DSO, MC, despatches twice); Chairman Glasgow Stock Exchange, 1936–37. *Address:* 5 Huntly Gardens, Glasgow, W2. *T:* Western 3658. *Clubs:* Western, New, Glasgow.

Died 21 March 1948.

REID, Prof. Edward Waymouth, BA, MB, ScD (Cantab), MRCS, LLD, FRS; late Professor of Physiology in University College, Dundee, St Andrews University; late Dean of the Medical Faculty of St Andrews University; *b* Canterbury, 11 Oct. 1862; 4th *s* of James Reid, FRCS. *Educ:* Sutton Valence Grammar School; (scholar) Cavendish Coll.; Cambridge: open classical scholarship, 1879; 1st class, with mark of distinction in Human Anatomy and Physiology in Natural Sciences Tripos, 1883; St Bartholomew's Hospital, London. Assistant Demonstrator of Human Anatomy, Cambridge, 1882–83; Proxime accessit in open science scholarship, St Bartholomew's Hospital, 1883; Assistant Electrician, St Bartholomew's Hospital, 1885; Demonstrator of Physiology to St Mary's Hospital, Medical School, 1885; Assistant Lecturer on Physiology, St Mary's, 1887; Professor of Physiology, University Coll. Dundee, 1889; research scholar to Grocers' Company of London, 1895–98; Fellow of Royal Society of London, 1898. *Recreation:* horticulture. *Address:* 53 Alnwickhill Road, Edinburgh.

Died 10 March 1948.

REID, Forrest, BA (Cantab); Hon. DLitt, Queen's University, Belfast, 1933; Member of the Irish Academy of Letters; novelist and critic; *b* Belfast, 24 June 1876. *Educ:* Royal Academical Institution, Belfast; Christ's College, Cambridge. *Publications:* The Bracknels, a Family Chronicle, 1911; Following Darkness, 1912; The Gentle Lover, 1913; At the Door of the Gate, 1915; W. B. Yeats, a Critical Study, 1915; The Spring Song, 1916; A Garden by the Sea, 1918; Pirates of the Spring, 1919; Pender among the Residents, 1922; Apostate, 1926; Demophon, 1927; Illustrators of the Sixties, 1928; Walter De la Mare, a Critical Study, 1929; Uncle Stephen, 1931; Brian Westby, 1934; The Retreat, 1936; Peter Waring, 1937; Private Road, 1940; Retrospective

Adventures, 1941; Notes and Impressions, 1942; Poems from the Greek Anthology, 1943; Young Tom, 1944 (James Tait Black Prize for 1944); The Milk of Paradise, 1946. *Recreation:* croquet. *Address:* 13 Ormiston Crescent, Belfast.

Died 4 Jan. 1947.

REID, George Agnew, RCA; artist; Principal Emeritus, Ontario College of Art, since 1929; *b* Wingham, Ontario, 1860; father and mother Scotch-Irish; *m* 1st, 1885, Mary Hiester, ARCA (*d* 1921); 2nd, 1923, Mary E. Wrinch, ARCA; no *c*. *Educ:* Ontario School of Art; Academy of Fine Arts, Philadelphia; Paris; Madrid. Exhibited paintings Toronto, Ottawa, Montreal, S Africa, Australia, USA, and London, England, 1883–89; exhibited Paris Salon, 1889–93; Medal, Chicago World's Fair, San Francisco Midwinter Exhibition, Ottawa Central Exhibition, 1889–93; exhibited again Salon 1896; Royal Academy, London, 1913; Mural Decorations, Toronto City Hall, 1900; Onteora Church, 1898–1911; Kingston University, 1905; Earlscourt Library, 1926; Jarvis Collegiate Institute, 1929; Royal Ontario Museum, 1934, 1938; various private houses; represented Art Gallery of Toronto, National Gallery, Ottawa, Saskatoon, Regina, Canada House, London; various private collections; President Ont Society of Artists, 1899–1903; Royal Canadian Academy, 1906–09; President Canadian Society of Painter Etchers, 1935–36; Principal Ontario College of Art, 1912–29; principal pictures painted: Flute Player, 1886; Drawing Lots, 1888; Logging, and Dreaming, 1889; The Story, and Mortgaging the Homestead, 1890; Family Prayer and Lullaby, 1891; A Modern Madonna and The Foreclosure of the Mortgage, 1893; The Clock Cleaner, 1894; Arrival of Champlain at Quebec, 1608, The Home Seekers and The Coming of the White Man, 1912. *Publications:* Art Education in United States, England, Scotland, France, Holland, 1924; various articles on art. *Recreation:* sketching. *Address:* 81 Wychwood Park, Toronto, Canada. *T:* Lakeside 9404. *Clubs:* Arts and Letters, Toronto.

Died 23 Aug. 1947.

REID, Lt-Col Harry Avery, OBE; FRCVS, DVH, FRSE 1913; Bacteriologist and Pathologist to the Department of Agriculture, New Zealand; *b* London, 1877; *s* of A. Reid, Walberton, Sussex; *m* Frieda, *d* of J. Martin, JP, Martinborough, New Zealand; one *s*. *Educ:* Oakfield School; University of Liverpool; Royal Veterinary College, London. Appointed to New Zealand Government Service, 1901; resigned, 1902; Egyptian Government Service, 1904; Senior Veterinarian in charge Serum Institute, Cairo; studied at Pasteur Institute, Paris, session 1904–05; re-entered New Zealand Government Service, 1907; Bacteriologist and Pathologist to Department of Agriculture, 1910; Assistant Director Veterinary Services, New Zealand Division, France; Lieut-Col New Zealand Military Forces; Assistant Director, Veterinary Services Wellington Military District. *Publications:* The Diseases of Farm Animals in New Zealand; contributions to various journals relating to veterinary Science. *Recreations:* golf, fishing.

Died 14 Sept. 1947.

REID, Rt Rev. Harry Seymour; *s* of D. Reid, shipowner, Glasgow; *m* Edith, *d* of late Professor P. G. Tait, University of Edinburgh; no *c*. *Educ:* Loretto School; University of Glasgow. Ordained 1894; Curate, St John the Evangelist, Edinburgh, 1894–1901; Senior Chaplain, St Mary's Cathedral, Edinburgh, 1901; Rector of St Mark's, Portobello, 1905; of St Paul's, York Place, Edinburgh, 1913; temporary Chaplain to the Forces in Gallipoli, Egypt, France, 1915–16; Dean of Edinburgh, 1919–29; Rector of St Cuthbert's Church, Colinton, Edinburgh, 1921–29; Bishop of Edinburgh, 1929–39; retired, 1939. *Address:* 3 Pilmour Place, St Andrews.

Died 18 Jan. 1943.

REID, Helen Richmond Young, CBE 1935; BA; LLD; Lady of Grace of St John of Jerusalem in England; Red Cross Gold medal of Italy; Médaille de Reconnaisance of France; holds many voluntary offices, locally, nationally, and internationally in educational, patriotic, and philanthropic work; *b* Montreal, Canada, 1869, of British parents; unmarried. *Educ:* Montreal High School; McGill University, Montreal (Gold Medallist); University of Geneva; Germany. One of first women to enter McGill University; Hon. Pres. and Co-Founder of the Montreal Charity Organisation Soc., 1900; offices held include: Vice-President Canadian Public Health Association; First Treasurer of Montreal Women's Canadian Club; several offices on local and National Victorian Order of Nurses; Vice-President Family Welfare Association of America; Convener of Montreal Branch of Canada's Great War Fund (Canadian Patriotic Fund) and on National Board of Management of Fund; Hon. LLD McGill and Queen's Universities; first woman appointed to Dominion Council of Health, also member of Canadian Repatriation Committee and of Advisory Council on Women's Immigration; Vice-President and Co-Founder of Canadian Welfare Council; President Montreal Council of Social Agencies and on Committee of Financial Federation Survey; President Child Welfare Association; Chairman Immigration Division of Canadian National Committee of Mental Hygiene; Director of Frontier College of Canada; Governors' Fellow McGill University; Chairman McGill School for Graduate Nurses; Trustee Montreal School of Social Work; Hon. Regent, Imperial Order Daughters of the Empire, etc.; Jubilee Medal, 1935; Coronation Medal, 1937. *Publications:* The Japanese Canadians (joint); magazine articles on Volunteer Service; Occasional Poems; The Citizen and Public Health; The Child in the Home; Hospital Social Service; Problem of Unemployed; Councils of Social Agencies; War Relief in Canada; Clinic Study of 1000 War Children; The School Child and Nutrition; Layman's Contribution to Nursing Service etc.; Translations of short stories from French and German; Editor of Racial Studies in Canada, published by Canadian Committee on Mental Hygiene. *Recreations:* gardening and country life, reading and conversation, theatre, concerts, bridge, and formerly tennis and golf. *Address:* 1452 Sherbrooke Street, W, Montreal, Canada. *T:* Plateau 1986. *Clubs:* University Women's, Women's Canadian, Montreal Women's, Montreal.

Died 8 June 1941.

REID, Lt-Col Herbert Cartwright, CB 1917; JP Fifeshire; MInstCE; RM; *b* 7 Nov. 1864; *s* of Thomas Reid, Hemel Hempstead; *m* 1891, Julia Lybina, *o d* of late Henry Miller; two *s* one *d*. *Educ:* Kirkby Lonsdale Grammar School. Trained as a civil engineer; Entered Admiralty service at Pembroke Dockyard as Assistant to Superintending Civil Engineer, 1889; on promotion served at Halifax, NS, and Esquimalt, BC, and subsequently at Chatham and London; Superintending Civil Engineer, 1903; carried out important Dock and Harbour Works at Malta; Superintending Civil Engineer HM Dockyard, Chatham, 1908–11; completed construction of HM Dockyard, Rosyth, 1911–17; Superintendent of Auxiliary Works, Admiralty, 1918; Lt-Col Royal Marine Engineers Belgian Ports Reconstruction, etc., 1918–19; acted as Consulting Engineer to Calcutta Port Trust in 1919; Deputy Civil Eng.-in-Chief, Admiralty, 1919–21; Eng.-in-Chief, Vizagapatam Harbour, India, 1921–28. *Recreation:* bridge. *Address:* Polperro, Pirbright Rd, Farnborough, Hants.

Died 16 July 1950.

REID, Ogden; Owner and Editor of the New York Herald Tribune; *b* New York City, 16 May 1882; *s* of Whitelaw and Elisabeth Mills Reid; *m* 1911, Helen Miles Rogers, Racine, Wisconsin; two *s*. *Educ:* Browning School, New York; University of Bonn; BA Yale 1904;

LLB, 1907. Worked in law office; admitted to NY Bar, 1908; began work on The Tribune as reporter, including copy desk, assistant to city editor, assistant night editor managing editor, spring of 1912, editor, 1913; President New York Tribune, Inc.; Vice-President Mills Estate, Inc.; director Mergenthaler Linotype Co.; Trustee, Trudeau Sanatorium; President, Tribune Fresh Air Fund. *Address:* 15 East 84th Street, New York City. *T:* Rhinelander 4–2285. *Clubs:* Knickerbocker, NY Yacht, Lotos, A pawamis, Union, Brook, Union League, Army and Navy, City, Pilgrims, Riding, Players, New York.

Died 4 Jan. 1947.

REID, Robert Payton, ARSA 1896; Society of Scottish Artists; *b* Edinburgh, 22 Oct. 1859; *m* 1916, Emily Esther Smith; one *d*. *Educ:* Edinburgh. Studied art at Royal Scottish Academy School and in Munich, Italy, and Paris. *Address:* 24 Dick Place, Edinburgh. *T:* Edinburgh 43245. *Clubs:* Scottish Arts, Edinburgh.

Died 17 Jan. 1945.

REID, Stephen; painter and illustrator; *b* Aberdeen, 1873; 5th *s* of John Reid, Aberdeen; *m* 1902, Kate, *e d* of William Cato; one *s* one *d*. *Educ:* Gordon's College, Aberdeen; Gray's School of Art, Aberdeen; Royal Scottish Academy Life School, Edinburgh. Exhibited RBA, RA, RSA, RI, and most provincial exhibitions. *Chief works:* Ophelia; Macbeth; four pictures in Reading Corporation Art Gallery: Heraclius, Thomas à Becket, Choosing a Mayor, and Parliament held at Reading Abbey, 1453; In Gloucester Guildhall—William the Conqueror ordering doomsday book, 1085, Twelfth Night; Jane Shore, The Call to Arms, in Boston, USA; General Booth, National Portrait Gallery. Aberdeen Art Gallery; The Landing of the First Settlers in Virginia, Norfolk Art Gallery, Va. USA; has illustrated many books of historical character. *Address:* Carlin, 13 Carlingford Road, NW3. *T:* Hampstead 7362.

Died 7 Dec. 1948.

REID, William Edwin Charles, CBE 1926; *b* 1870; *s* of William Reid; *m* 1892, Elizabeth (*d* 1919), *d* of John Pratt. Was Assistant Commissioner New Zealand Pavilion, British Empire Exhibition at Wembley, 1924–25 (CBE). *Address:* 10 Falcon Street, Roslyn, Dunedin, New Zealand.

Died 22 Feb. 1947.

REILLY, Sir Charles Herbert, Kt 1944; OBE 1920; MA; Hon. LLD; FRIBA; Hon. MTPI; Royal Gold Medallist for Architecture, 1943; Emeritus Professor of Architecture, University of Liverpool; Director, Liverpool School of Architecture, 1904–33; architect and writer; Past Vice-President, Royal Institute of British Architects; Hon. Corresponding Member, American Institute of Architects; Member, Faculty of Architecture, British School at Rome; Member of Comité Permanent International des Architects; Vice-President, Poetry Society; Vice-Chairman Liverpool Repertory Theatre, Ltd; *b* 1874; *s* of late Charles Reilly, FRIBA; *m* Dorothy, (*d* 1939), *d* of late J. Jerram Pratt; one *s* one *d*. *Educ:* Merchant Taylors' School, London; Queens' College, Camb. *Publications:* books on Modern Architecture; Scaffolding in the Sky, a semi-architectural Autobiography, 1938. *Address:* 1 South End House, Montpelier Row, Twickenham, Middlesex. *T:* Popesgrove 5119. *Clubs:* Athenæum; University Sandon (Liverpool).

Died 2 Feb. 1948.

REILLY, E. Albert, KC 1913; LLD; *b* Melrose, Westmorland County, NB, 1868. *Educ:* University of St Joseph's College (graduate in Arts). Admitted to Bar, 1896; twice Mayor of the City of Moncton; President of the Moncton Board of Trade for two years; President of the Moncton Canadian Club in 1913 and 1914; President of the Union of New Brunswick Municipalities, 1912; President of the Maritime Life; a Director of The Central Trust Company of Canada, and several other financial and industrial concerns; member of Provincial Legislature of the Province of New Brunswick to represent the city of Moncton, 1924–35; member of the Provincial Government, and Chairman New Brunswick Electric Power Commission, 1925–35; devotes his whole time to the practice of his profession. *Address:* Moncton, NB, Canada.

Died 22 Oct. 1943.

REILLY, Sir (Henry) D'Arcy (Cornelius), Kt 1938; *b* 15 Jan. 1876; 2nd *s* of Charles Reilly, FRIBA, and Annie Michael, *d* of Charles Mee; *m* 1903, Margaret Florence, *d* of Alfred Thomas Wilkinson; one *s*. *Educ:* Merchant Taylors' School, London; Corpus Christi College, Oxford. Indian Civil Service, Madras Presidency, 1899; Registrar of the High Court of Judicature at Madras, 1910; District Judge, 1916; officiating Judge of the High Court, 1924, 1925, 1926, 1927; Additional Judge of the High Court, 1927; Puisne Judge of the High Court, 1928–34; retired, 1934; Chief Justice of Mysore, 1934–43. *Address:* c/o The Standard Bank of South Africa, Durban. *Club:* Athenæum.

Died 12 June 1948.

REINHARDT, Prof. Max, Hon. DCL Oxford; Hon. Dr Goethe-Universität, Frankfurt/M; Hon. Dr Christian-Albrecht Universität Kiel; producer, stage manager; *b* 9 Sept. 1873; *s* of Wilhelm Goldmann and Rosa Wengraf; *m* (divorced); two *s*. *Educ:* Vienna. Studied for the stage with Emil Buerde, Vienna. First appearance in Salzburg, from where he was taken to Berlin by Otto Brahm; from actor, then producer at the Deutsche Theatre zu Berlin, 1895–1932, which he has owned since 1905; The Kammerspiele and the Grosse Schauspielhaus in Berlin were founded by him; the renewal of German classics, of the entire oeuvre of Shakespeare and of the most famous dramatic poets of the whole world is the résumé of his lifetime's work on the stage of the Deutsches Theatre and the other theatres he afterwards owned in Berlin; almost every modern German play of any value was always first produced by him during this period; he was first who offered collaboration to renowned painters and musicians; first to produce the early works of Richard Strauss, 1912; all these performances were taken on tour by him all over the world; in London he produced Sumurun, The Miracle (twice), Offenbach's Helen of Troy, and King Oedipus with English actors in Covent Garden Theatre; finally in Oxford, in an out-door production, A Midsummer Night's Dream, 1933; The Salzburg Festival owes its existence to his initiative idea; the old mystery play of Everyman (Jedermann) produced by him has been given there for 14 years running, ever since the Festivals first began, 1920; during all those years he was not only busy as a producer, but also as a teacher; The Reinhardt-Seminars in the Castle of Schoenbrunn in Vienna were founded by him as the first school in the world for producers; young actors and producers have the possibility of practical work there according to a unique method.

Died 31 Oct. 1943.

REISNER, George Andrew, PhD (Harvard); Professor of Egyptology at Harvard University; Curator of Egyptian Department of Boston Museum of Fine Arts since 1910; Director Harvard-Boston Egyptian Expedition; *b* Indianapolis, Indiana, USA, 5 Nov. 1867; *s* of George Andrew Reisner and Mary Elizabeth Mason; *m* 1892, Mary Putnam Bronson; one *d*. *Educ:* Indianapolis Classical High School; Harvard University (AB, AM, PhD). Travelling Fellow of Harvard University, 1893–96; Temporary Assistant, Berlin Museum, 1894–96; Instructor in Semitics, Harvard University, 1896–97; Member of International Catalogue Commission, Cairo Museum, 1897–99; Director of Hearst Egyptian Expedition of the University of California; Excavations at Dêr-el-Ballâs, Naga-'d-Dêr, and Giza Pyramids, 1899–1905; Director, Harvard-

Boston Egyptian Expedition, and Assistant Professor of Egyptology at Harvard University, 1905; Archæological Director of Nubian Archæological Survey by Egyptian Government, 1907–09; Corresponding Member Saxon Academy, 1929; Ordinary Member Archæological Institute of German State; Director of Harvard Excavations at Samaria (Palestine), 1909–10; Excavations at Giza Pyramids, Zawiyat-el-Aryan, etc., in Egypt Samaria, Nubian Survey, and in Sudan (Kerma, Gebel Barkal, Nuri, Ku'ruw, Begarawiyah, Semna). Important discoveries: History of Lower Nubia; The Pyramids of 68 sovereigns of Ethiopia; The Pyramids of five kings of Egypt (XXVth Dyn.); The Valley Temple of Mycerinus with 9 masterpieces of Egyptian sculpture; the tomb of the mother of Cheops. *Publications:* Sumerisch-Babylonische Hymnen; Tempel Urkunden aus Telloh; Amulets (Cairo Cat. Gen.); Models of Ships and Boats (Cairo Cat. Gen.); Hearst Medical Papyrus; Early Dynastic Cemeteries of Naga-'d-Dêr; Nubian Archæological Survey Report, 1907–1908; Harvard Excavations at Samaria, Kerma; Mycerinus; a Provincial Cemetery of the Pyramid Age; The Development of the Egyptian Tomb down to the Accession of Cheops; and many articles on the history of Ethiopia. *Address:* Harvard Camp, Pyramids PO, Cairo, Egypt. *TA:* Reisner, Menahouse, Egypt; Museum of Fine Arts, Boston, Mass, USA. *Clubs:* Harvard, Boston; Turf, Rotary, Cairo.

Died 6 June 1942.

REISS, Charles, CBE 1919; BA; *b* 1873; *s* of F. Reiss; *m* Esmé, *d* of late A. P. MacEwen; two *d. Educ:* Harrow; Christ Church, Oxford. Cross of the Officer of the Order of the Crown of Italy, 1922. *Address:* 14 Chester Street, SW1. *T:* Sloane 1911. *Club:* Oxford and Cambridge.

Died 7 March 1949.

REITZ, Col Deneys; High Commissioner for the Union of South Africa, London, since 1943; *b* Bloemfontein, 1882; *s* of Francis William Reitz, ex-President of the OFS; *m* 1919, *d* of Dr Claude Wright of Wynberg, CP. *Educ:* Bloemfontein. Attorney; Minister of Lands, 1933–35; Minister of Agriculture and Forests, 1935; Minister of Mines, 1938; Minister of Native Affairs and Deputy Prime Minister, 1939–43. *Publications:* Commando, 1929; Trekking On, 1933; No Outspan, 1943. *Address:* Bedwell End, Essendon, Herts. *Clubs:* Rand, Johannesburg Country, Johannesburg.

Died 19 Oct. 1944.

RELTON, Arthur John, CBE 1918; FCII; *b* 1856; *s* of late Francis Boyer Relton; *m* 1881, Geraldine Victoria (*d* 1943), *d* of Daniel Thomas Lyons Clanchy, of Charleville, Co. Cork; one *s* two *d. Educ:* Chatham House, Ramsgate; Germany. Westminster Fire Office, 1875; Guardian Assurance Coy, 1876; Manager Fire and other Departments, 1888–1915; a Member of the Government Aircraft Insurance Committee during the War. *Address:* 10 Eaton Gardens, Hove, Sussex. *T:* Hove 5391. *Club:* Hove.

Died 13 Feb. 1946.

REMER, John Rumney; *b* 2 July 1883; *m* 1913, Beatrice Humphrys (*d* 1921), *y d* of Henry Crummack, St Annes-on-Sea; one *d. Educ:* privately. MP (U) Macclesfield Division of Cheshire, Dec. 1918–39. Business career as Governing Director of The Remer Timber Co. Ltd, Manchester; Director of West African Mines and Estates Ltd; Chairman of Red Ray Company Ltd. *Recreation:* golf. *Address:* 3 Rutland Street, SW7. *Clubs:* Carlton; numerous golf.

Died 12 March 1948.

REMNANT, Ernest; Editor, English Review, 1923–31; *b* London, 1872. *Educ:* France; up country in Australia and Tasmania, 1888–91. Produce Exchange, London, 1892–97; Director, Electric Traction and Lighting undertakings; contributor to newspapers and reviews; led British Industrial Mission to Russia, 1929; Commander

of the Royal Order of The Phoenix (Greek). *Publication:* Security, 1925. *Recreation:* travel. *Address:* Ingoldsby, Birchington, Kent. *Club:* National.

Died 10 May 1941.

RENDALL, Athelstan; *b* 16 Nov. 1871; *s* of late Henry Rendall, JP, of Bridport; *m* 1st, 1897, Amy (*d* 1945) *d* of J. J. Young, JP, Northend, Portsmouth; one *d*; 2nd, 1946, Beatrice Sophia, *d* of Capt. A. W. Brooke Smith, RNR. *Educ:* London University College School. Commenced in journalism, but afterwards became a solicitor; candidate for Thornbury Division, 1903–04–1905; MP (L) Thornbury Division, Glos, 1906–22 and 1923–24; Member of House of Commons Select Committee on Debtors' Imprisonment, and drafted report of Committee; Member of Chairman's Panel, House of Commons; Introduced and passed bill enabling widow to marry deceased husband's brother. Member of Fabian Society since 1895; joined Labour Party, 1925. *Publications:* various magazine articles; Divorce Reform, etc. *Recreation:* politics. *Address:* Rowney House, Wimborne, Dorset. *T:* Wimborne 451. *Club:* Reform.

Died 12 July 1948.

RENDALL, Rev. Gerald Henry, BD, LittD, LLD; Hon. Canon of Chelmsford Cathedral, 1918–44, Canon Emeritus since 1944; *b* Harrow, 1851; *s* of Rev. F. Rendall, Assistant-master at Harrow; *m* 1887, Ellen (*d* 1938), *d* of John Rendall, Barrister-at-law. *Educ:* Cheam Preparatory School; Harrow; Trinity College, Cambridge. University Bell Scholar, 1871; Foundation Scholarship at Trinity College, 1872; graduated BA, 1874, 4th in Classical Tripos; Univ. Winchester Reading Prize; Univ. Lightfoot Scholar, 1875; Fellow of Trinity College; Hulsean Prize Essayist, 1876. Lecturer and Assistant Tutor at Trinity College, Cambridge, 1875–80; Principal of University College Liverpool; Gladstone Professor of Greek, 1880–97; Vice-Chancellor of Victoria University, 1890–92, 1892–94; Member of the Gresham University Commission, 1892–93; Headmaster Charterhouse School, 1897–1911. *Publications:* Text and Commentary to Epistle of Barnabas, ed. by Rev. W. Cunningham, 1877; Emperor Julian, Paganism and Christianity (Hulsean Essay), 1879; Introduction to Letters of Pliny, Book iii, ed. by Prof. Mayor, 1880; Cradle of the Aryans, 1889; M. Aur. Antoninus, Translation with Introduction, 1897; M. Aur. To Himself, in Golden Treasury, 1901; Epistles of St Paul to the Corinthians, 1909; Charterhouse Sermons, 1911; John Smith, of Harrow, 1913; Ep. James and Judaic Christianity, 1927; Shakespeare Sonnets and Edward de Vere, 1930; Shakespeare, Handwriting and Spelling, 1931; Personal Clues in Shakespeare Poems and Sonnets, 1934; Dedham in History, 1937; Dedham Described and Deciphered, 1937. *Address:* Dedham House, Dedham, Essex. *T:* 2173. *Club:* Alpine.

Died 4 Jan. 1945.

RENDALL, Montague John, CMG 1931; MA, LLD; JP; *b* Great Rollright, Oxon, 1862; 4th *s* of late Rev. Henry Rendall, Rector of Great Rollright. *Educ:* Elstree; Harrow; Trinity College, Cambridge. Foundation Scholar and Bell University Scholar, 1882; First Division of First Class, Classical Tripos, 1884; First Class, Second Pt, 1885; University Association Football Eleven, 1884 and 1885; also Corinthians. Assistant Master at Winchester, 1887; Second Master, 1899–1911; Headmaster, 1911–24; travelled round Empire for Rhodes Trustees, 1924–26; Vice-Pres. of BBC, 1927–33; Vice-President of Royal Empire Society; Chairman of Public School Empire Tours Committee; Vice-President of Overseas League; late Chairman of League of Empire; Member of Education Committee of East Suffolk County Council; Vice-Pres. of Framlingham College and Chairman of North Foreland Lodge; Trustee of Boyton Almshouses. Officer of Order of St John of Jerusalem. *Publications:* Sinai in Spring; The

Bells of Great Rollright; Editor of Freeman's Schools of Hellas. *Recreations:* walking, bicycling. *Address:* Butley Priory, Woodbridge, Suffolk. *T:* Orford 234. *Clubs:* Athenæum, Royal Empire Society, English-Speaking Union.

Died 5 Oct. 1950.

RENDELL, William Reginald, MA; Fellow of Trinity Hall, Cambridge; Barrister-at-law; JP Cornwall; *b* 10 Oct. 1868; *o s* of late Major Rendell; *m* 1906, Hon. Janet Marion, *d* of late Rt Hon. Lord Watson, Lord of Appeal; one *s* one *d. Educ:* Newton College; Jesus College, Cambridge. Barrister-at-law, Lincoln's Inn, 1893; MA, 1894; Fellow and Lecturer in Law, Trinity Hall, 1904; Bursar, 1912; Captain TF attached Gen. Staff, War Office, 1915–16; Gen. Manager Metropolitan Electric Supply Co., 1916–22; a Commissioner under Universities Act, 1923; JP Cornwall, 1927; Chairman of Rating Appeal Committee of Quarter Sessions, 1927–41; Vice-Chairman of Standing Joint Committee, 1940–46; High Sheriff of Cornwall, 1941. *Recreations:* shooting and fishing. *Address:* Lewarne, Two Waters Foot, Liskeard, Cornwall. *TA* and *T:* Dobwalls 217. *Club:* United University.

Died 6 Oct. 1948.

RENDLESHAM, 7th Baron *cr* 1806; **Percy Edward Thellusson;** *b* 30 Oct. 1874; 2nd *s* of 5th Baron Rendlesham and Lady Egidia Montgomery (*d* 1880), *d* of 13th Earl of Eglinton, KT; *S* brother, 1938; *m* 1922, Hon. Mrs Alfred Yorke (*d* 1933), *d* of Andrews Dunlop Best. *Educ:* Eton. Late Captain West Kent Yeomanry. *Heir: nephew* Charles Anthony Hugh Thellusson, *b* 15 March 1915. *Club:* White's.

Died 11 Dec. 1943.

RENNELL, 1st Baron *cr* 1933, of Rodd, Herefordshire; **James Rennell Rodd,** PC 1908; GCB 1920; GCMG 1915; GCVO 1905; KCMG 1899; CB 1897; *b* 9 Nov. 1858; *s* of the late Major James Rennell Rodd; *m* 1894, Lilias, *d* of the late J. A. Guthrie, Craigie, Forfar; three *s* two *d. Educ:* Haileybury; Balliol Coll. Oxford (BA); Newdigate Prize, 1880. Attaché Diplomatic Service, 1883; Berlin, 1884; Athens, 1888; 2nd Secretary, Rome, 1891; Paris, 1892; in charge of British Agency at Zanzibar throughout 1893; present at actions at Pumwani and Jongeni, 1893; received medal with 2nd Witu clasp; transferred to Cairo, 1894, acting Agent and Consul-General on various occasions; special envoy to King Menelik 1897, mission to Abyssinia; Secretary of Legation, Cairo, 1894–1901; Councillor of Embassy at Rome, 1901–04; HM's Envoy Extraordinary and Minister Plenipotentiary to Sweden, 1904–08; HM's Ambassador to the Court of Italy, 1908–19; MP (C) St Marylebone Division, 1928–32; accompanied Lord Milner's Mission to Egypt, 1920; Brit. Delegate to League of Nations, 1921 and 1923; President of Court of Conciliation between Austria and Switzerland, 1925; member of Permanent Commission of Conciliation between Italy and Chile, 1928; American non-national member of Permanent International Commission for Advancement of Peace between United States and Venezuela; Grand Cross of St Maurice and St Lazarus; Commander of the Osmanieh; Grand Cross of Polar Star; Grand Cross, Greek Order of Redeemer. *Publications:* prose—Frederick, Emperor and Crown Prince; Customs and Lore of Modern Greece; Sir Walter Raleigh; the Princes of Achaia and the Chronicles of Morea; Social and Diplomatic Memoirs, 1922; second series, 1894–1901, 1923; third series, 1926; Homer's Ithaka; Rome of the Renaissance and To-day, 1932; verse—Poems in Many Lands; Feda and other Poems; The Unknown Madonna; The Violet Crown; Ballads of the Fleet; Love, Worship, and Death; Trentaremi. *Recreations:* tastes catholic, but especially fencing. *Heir: s*

Hon. Francis J. R. Rodd. *Address:* 39 Bryanston Square, W1. *T:* Paddington 1020; Ardath, Shamley Green, Surrey. *Clubs:* Athenæum, Travellers'.

Died 26 July 1941.

RENNIE, Francis Pepys, CIE 1922; ICS retired; *b* 12 Oct. 1872; *s* of John Keith Rennie, JP, of Frensham Vale, Rowledge, Surrey, and Frances Maria, *d* of John Dick, of Pitkerrow House, Forfarshire; *m* 1908, Edith Augusta (*d* 1938), *d* of Rev. Charles Lyndhurst Vaughan, St Leonards; no *c. Educ:* Winchester College; Clare College, Cambridge. Passed into the Indian Civil Service, 1894; arrived in India 1895, and posted to Rawalpindi, Punjab, as Assistant Commissioner; Political Officer, Kurram Valley, 1900; Deputy-Commissioner Kohat, NWF Province, 1901, and Bannu, 1903; Divisional and Sessions Judge, Dera Ismail Khan, 1904; Assistant Resident, Mysore, 1906; Divisional and Sessions Judge, Dera Ismail Khan, 1908–09; Peshawar, 1912–18; Judicial Commissioner NWF Province, 1919; retired, 1923. *Recreations:* shooting, fishing. *Address:* Frensham Vale, Rowledge, Surrey. *T:* Farnham 54. *Club:* Reform.

Died 15 June 1946.

RENNIE, Lt-Col Horace Watt, CBE 1920; retired; *s* of J. Rennie; *m* 1899, Margaret, *d* of R. Dixon, Truro. *Address:* The Gable House, 42 Cartland Road, Kings Heath, Birmingham.

Died 2 March 1943.

RENNIE, Maj.-Gen. Robert, CB 1918; CMG 1917; DSO 1916; MVO 1910; Queen's Own Rifles, Canada; *b* 15 Dec. 1862; *m* 1891, Marion, *d* of late William Ross. Served European War, 1914–18 (DSO, CMG, CB). *Address:* 136 Adelaide Street East, Toronto.

Died 17 Dec. 1949.

RENNIE, Maj.-Gen. Tom Gordon, CB 1944; DSO 1942; MBE 1938; commanding 51st Highland Division since Sept. 1944; *b* 3 Jan. 1900; *s* of late Dr T. Rennie, Foochow, China, and Mrs Rennie, Radlett, Herts, and Torryburn, Kintore, Aberdeenshire; *m* 1932, HEC, *d* of H. Giles Walker, Over Rankeillour, Cupar, Fife; one *s* one *d. Educ:* Loretto; RMC, Sandhurst. Joined Black Watch, 1919; Adjutant 2nd Bn; Staff College, 1933–34; comd. 5th Black Watch, 1941–42; Bde of Highland Div. 1942–43; 3rd British Division, Dec. 1943–July 1944. Served El Alamein, 1942 (DSO); France, 1944 (CB). *Recreations:* shooting, fishing, golf. *Address:* c/o Lloyds Bank, Cox's & King's Branch, 6 Pall Mall, SW1. *Club:* Caledonian.

Died 24 March 1945.

RENTON, Major (Alexander) Leslie; late Major, Northants Yeomanry; JP; *b* 6 July 1868; *s* of late James Hall Renton; *m* 1895, Kathleen Elliot (*d* 1922), *d* of Charles Taylor of Horton Manor, Bucks; two *s* one *d. Educ:* Harrow; Royal Military College, Sandhurst. Joined Royal Scots Greys, 1888; served South African War (despatches, medal and three clasps); European War, 1914–18; travelled extensively in Africa and Central Asia; contested South Dorset, 1900; Reading, 1910; MP (LU) Gainsboro', 1906–10. *Recreations:* hunting, travelling, music. *Address:* Little Court, Wentworth, Surrey. *Clubs:* Broeks's, Cavalry.

Died 6 May 1947.

RENTOUL, Sir Gervais, Kt 1929; KC 1930; Metropolitan Magistrate for West London since 1934; *b* 1 Aug. 1884; *e s* of His Honour Judge Rentoul, KC, LLD (formerly MP for East Down); *m* 1912, Muriel, *o d* of Harold Alfred Smart, banker; one *d. Educ:* City of London School; Royal University, Ireland (Scholar); Christ Church, Oxford (MA 1907; First-class Honours in Jurisprudence; President of the Oxford Union Society, 1906). Barrister Gray's Inn, 1907; Legal Assistant, War Office 1915–17; Captain, Headquarters Staff, Eastern Command, 1917–20; Recorder of

Sandwich, 1929–34; MP (C) Lowestoft Division of Suffolk, 1922–34; Member of Select Committee on Betting Tax, 1923; on Capital Punishment, 1930; on Shop Assistants, 1930; Chairman, Conservative '1922' Committee, 1922–32; Parliamentary Private Secretary to the Attorney-General, 1925–29; Counsel for the Attorney-General in Legitimacy Cases and to the Inland Revenue in Licensing Matters, 1924–30; Master Guild of Freemen of City of London, 1924; President, United Wards Club, 1929, 1942–43; Member Kensington Borough Council since 1941; Member of Council, Imperial Soc. of Knights Bachelor; Liveryman, Fishmongers' Company. *Publications:* Sometimes I Think, 1940; Blockade and Contraband, 1942; This is My Case, 1944; numerous contributions to the Fortnightly, XIXth Century, Contemporary, Empire and other Reviews. *Recreations:* the theatre and motoring. *Address:* 101 Oakwood Court, W14. *T:* Western 7644. *Club:* Carlton.

Died 7 March 1946.

RENWICK, Sir John Robert, 2nd Bt *cr* 1921; *b* 13 Nov. 1877; *s* of 1st Bt and Mary Jane, *d* of late W. J. and Mary Thompson, Jubbulpore, India; *S* father, 1931; *m* 1902, Ethel, *d* of James Deuchar; two *s* one *d*. Heir: *s* Eustace Deuchar [*b* 1902; *m* 1934, Diana Mary, *e d* of Col Bernard Cruddas, DSO; one *s* one *d*]. *Address:* Rufflands, Cooden, Sussex.

Died 20 Nov. 1946.

REPPLIER, Agnes, LittD; American essayist; *b* Philadelphia, 1858; unmarried. *Educ:* Sacred Heart Convent, Torresdale, Pa. Lived several years in Europe; gold medal of the National Institute of Arts and Letters, 1935. *Publications:* Books and Men, 1888; Points of View, 1891; Essays in Idleness, 1893; Essays in Miniature, 1893; In the Dozy Hours, 1895; Book of Famous Verse, edited, 1892; Varia, 1897; Philadelphia: The Place and the People, 1898; The Fireside Sphinx, 1901; Compromises, 1904; In Our Convent Days, 1905; A Happy Half Century, 1908; Americans and Others, 1912; Counter-Currents, 1916; J. William White, MD, a biography, 1919; Points of Friction, 1920; Under Dispute, 1924; Père Marquette, 1929; Mère Marie of the Ursulines, 1931; Times and Tendencies, 1931; To Think of Tea, 1932; Junipero Serra, 1933; In Pursuit of Laughton, 1936. *Address:* 920 Clinton Street, Philadelphia, Pa, USA. *Clubs:* College, Acorn, Cosmopolitan (Philadelphia).

Died 15 Dec. 1950.

REWA, Bandhvesh Ex-Maharaja of, Sir Gulab Singh Bahadur, Maharajadhiraja, 1930; GCIE 1931; KCSI 1927; *b* 13 March 1903; *S,* 1918; attained Majority, 1922; invested with full ruling powers, Oct. 1922; *m* 1st, 1919, sister of H. H. the Maharaja of Jodhpur; 2nd, 1925, *d* of His late Highness Maharaja of Kishangarh; one *s* Shri Yuvraj Maharaj Kumar Martand Singhji, *b* March 1923. *Educ:* Daly College, Indore. Member of the Chamber of Princes and of the General Council of the Daly College, Indore; was invited to the 1st and 2nd Sessions of the Indian Round Table Conference; was a member of Federal Structure Sub-Committee of the Round Table Conference. *Address:* Rewa Central India.

Died 13 April 1950.

REYNARD, Helene, MA; *b* 1875. *Educ:* Bradford Girls' Grammar School; Girton College, Cambridge. Junior Bursar, Girton College, Cambridge, 1904–13; Director Bradford Wool Extracting Co., Ltd, 1914–22; Treasurer Somerville College, Oxford, 1922–25; Warden, King's College of Household and Social Science, 1925–45. *Publications:* Business Methods and Secretarial Work, 1912; Institutional Management and Accounts, 1934; What is a Balance Sheet? 1935; Book-Keeping by Easy Stages (with D. Hustler), 1937; Domestic Science as a

Career, 1947; articles and reviews in the Economic Journal and other periodicals. *Club:* University Women's.

Died 27 Dec. 1947.

REYNARD, Matthew Andrew; JP; Member of Assistance Board since 1934; *b* 28 April 1878; *s* of James and Marion Ballantyne Reynard; *m* 1908, Margaret Hamilton Bogle; two *d.* *Educ:* Allan Glen's School, Glasgow. Local Government Official; Clerk, Collector, and Inspector, District Board of Control and Parish Council of Glasgow, 1921–30; Director of Public Assistance, City of Glasgow, 1930–35. *Publications:* professional pamphlets and papers of various dates. *Recreations:* bowling, curling, gardening. *Address:* Sherbrooke, Sherbrooke Avenue, Glasgow, S1. *T:* Ibrox, Glasgow 1276. *Clubs:* Authors'; Town and County, Falkirk, Stirlingshire.

Died 9 June 1946.

REYNELL, Douglas, CIE 1936; Indian Educational Service, retired; *b* South Norwood, 23 Nov. 1877; *s* of late Henry Gibbs Reynell, London Stock Exchange; unmarried. *Educ:* Worcester College, Oxford (MA, BCL). Assistant Master, Queen's College Taunton, 1905–10; Professor of English and History, and Tutor, MAO College, Aligarh, India, 1910–19; Indian Educational Service, Inspector of Schools, 1919; Assistant Director of Public Instruction, Punjab, 1922–31; Secretary to Public Service Commission, India, 1931–36. *Address:* c/o Grindlay's Bank, Ltd, 54 Parliament Street, SW1. *Club:* Athenæum.

Died 27 June 1949.

REYNELL, Walter Rupert, MA, DM (Oxon); FRCP (London); Senior Physician, West End Hospital for Nervous Diseases; Physician and Neurologist to Royal Northern Hospital; *b* 1885; *s* of Walter Reynell, Reynella, South Australia; *m* 1916, Una Mary, *e d* of Rev. C. R. Shaw-Stewart; two *s* two *d.* *Educ:* St Peters College, Adelaide; Balliol College, Oxford (Rhodes Scholar); Guy's Hospital. Served European War, 1914–18, Capt. RAMC; Fellow of Medical Society of London and of Royal Society of Medicine; Member of Societies for the Study of Juvenile Delinquency, of Inebriety and of Epilepsy; Member of No. 1 Committee of National Council of Mental Hygiene. *Publications:* papers on neurological subjects and psychological medicine in scientific journals. *Recreations:* ski-ing, lawn tennis, golf. *Address:* 87 Harley Street, W1. *T:* Welbeck 4918, Welbeck 3240. *Club:* Athenæum.

Died 21 March 1948.

REYNOLDS, Edward, MA; *b* 6 Sept. 1874; *s* of Rev. Edward Reynolds and Clara Octavia Wilson; *m* 1910, Gladys Hawkins; one *s* two *d.* *Educ:* Oakham School; Queens' Coll., Cambridge (Scholar). Mathematical Master Ely Cathedral School, 1897–98; Senior Mathematical and Second Master Worcester, Royal Grammar School, 1899–1907; Headmaster Northampton School, 1907–21; HMI for Secondary Schools, 1921–22; Headmaster, Watford Grammar School, 1922–38; formerly Member of the Herts' County Council Education Committee; Chairman of Managers of Watford Elementary Schools. *Recreation:* gardening. *Address:* The White Cottage, Church Road, Watford.

Died 26 Feb. 1944.

REYNOLDS, Adm. Harry Campbell; (retired); *b* 1853; 2nd *s* of late Lawrence W. Reynolds, formerly 97th Reg. *Educ:* Switzerland. Joined Britannia, 1867; served in Ashantee War, 1873–74; expedition up the Niger, 1876; Lieutenant, Egyptian War, 1882; Capt. of Pique in China, 1900–03, during Boxer trouble; ADC to King Edward VII, 1906–07; Retired List, 1908; Admiral, 1915. *Address:* The Four Winds, St Nicholas Hill, Leatherhead. *Club:* United Service.

Died 7 Feb. 1949.

REYNOLDS, Captain Henry, VC 1917; MC 1917; late The Loyal Regt; Superintendent and Steward of Sir Frederick Milner Homes, Beckenham, since 1930; *b* 1881; 2nd *s* of late Thomas Henry Reynolds; *m* 1905, Gwendolen, *d* of William Jones; one *d*. Served European War, 1914–18 (MC, VC); retired, 1927. *Recreations:* fishing, shooting. *Address:* Frederick Milner House Leatherhead.

Died 26 March 1948.

REYNOLDS, Henry Osborne, CMG 1939; ICS, retired; *b* 11 Oct. 1883; *s* of Osborne Reynolds, MA, LLD, FRS, and Annie Charlotte Reynolds; *m* 1911, Theodora Madeleine Hardy; one *d*. *Educ:* Sedbergh School; Emmanuel College, Cambridge. Passed into ICS at open exam., 1906; Burma, 1907; successively Settlement Officer, Deputy Commissioner, Secretary to Government, and Commissioner; retired, 1942. *Publication:* Some Notes on Burmese Colloquial Syntax. *Address:* c/o High Commissioner for India, India House, Aldwych, WC2.

Died 29 July 1947.

REYNOLDS, John Henry; Ex-President of the RAS; *b* 27 June 1874; 2nd *s* of late Alderman A. J. Reynolds, Edgbaston, Birmingham; *m* 1907, Brenda Mary, *y d* of late W. H. Chalk, Redhill, Surrey; one *s* four *d*. *Educ:* King Edward's High School, Birmingham. Joined the firm of John Reynolds and Sons Ltd, now Managing Director; elected a Fellow of the RAS 1899; Assisted in the development of the Helwan Observatory, Egypt, by the presentation of a 30–in. Reflecting Telescope, 1906; Order of Osmanieh 3rd Class; Member of Council of RAS, 1920–46; Hon. Treas., 1929–35 and 1937–45; Member of Board of Visitors to Royal Observatory, Greenwich; for many years member of Council of Birmingham and Midland Institute, Vice-President 1917–18, Hon. Secretary since 1927; Life Governor of Birmingham University; Hon. MSc 1931; FInstP. *Publications:* many papers on astronomical subjects, principally on the Nebulæ in MNRAS Nature and other publications. *Recreations:* music and travel. *Address:* Low Wood, St Mary's Rd, Harborne. *Clubs:* Royal Societies; Clef (Birmingham).

Died 22 Nov. 1949.

REYNOLDS, Sir Leonard William, KCIE 1931; CSI 1928; CIE 1912; MC; *b* Feb. 1874; 4th *s* of late Thomas J. Reynolds of Totteridge House, Totteridge, Bucks; *m* 1919, Blanche Mortlock, *d* of late Rev. Chancellor Lias; one *s* two *d*. *Educ:* Bradfield College; Exeter College, Oxford (exhibitioner). Oxford University Association Football XI, 1896; Indian Civil Service, 1897; arrived in India, 1898; Assistant Magistrate, Allahabad, 1898; First Assistant to the Agent to Governor-General, Central India, 1905; Deputy Secretary Government of India Foreign Department, 1911–14; Kaisar-i-Hind Medal, 1st Class, 1905; served European War, 1914–16 (Military Cross, 1915); Commissioner of Ajmere-Merwara, 1916–18; Resident Western States of Rajputana, 1918–24; President of the Council of Regency, Jaipur State, Rajputana, 1924–27; Agent to the Governor-General in Rajputana, and Chief Commissioner Ajmere-Merwara, 1927–32; retired, 1933. *Recreations:* tennis, golf. *Address:* St Ann's, Fleet, Hants. *T:* Fleet 697. *Club:* East India and Sports.

Died 15 May 1946.

REYNOLDS, Louis George Stanley, CB 1943; CBE 1935; OBE 1919; Chevalier Légion d'Honneur, 1916; Secretary Standing Commission on Museums and Galleries, 1944; formerly Assistant Under-Secretary of State, Air Ministry; *s* of late Col E. Swatman Reynolds, Indian Staff Corps; *m* 1921, Mary Margaret, *d* of late J. H. Middleton, DCL, LLD; no *c*. *Educ:* Bradfield; Balliol College, Oxford (Maj. Exhibitioner). Entered Civil Service (General Post Office), 1906; War Office, 1909; Air Ministry, 1919; Private Secretary to Under-Secretary

of State for War, 1912; to Quartermaster-General, 1912–16; to Secretary of State for Air, 1930–33; retired, 1944. Military Service: Territorial Force, 1909–19; RFC and RAF (Flight Commander), 1917–19; Home Guard, 1940–41; Small Vessels Pool, RN, 1944. *Address:* Silton House, Silton, Nr Gillingham, Dorset. *T:* Bourton, 273. *Club:* Brooks's.

Died 29 June 1945.

REYNOLDS, Sidney Hugh, MA, ScD; FGS; *b* Brighton, 1867; *m*. *Educ:* Marlborough; Trinity College, Cambridge. Professor of Geology, Bristol University, 1910–33; Professor Emeritus, 1934; a Lyell Medal, Geological Society, 1928. *Publications:* on geological subjects. *Address:* 13 All Saints Road, Clifton, Bristol, 8. *T:* Bristol 35881.

Died 20 Aug. 1949.

REYNOLDS-STEPHENS, Sir William, Kt 1931; Chevalier of the Order of the Crown of Belgium; President of Royal Society of British Sculptors, 1921–33; awarded the RBS Gold Medal for distinguished services to Sculpture, 1928; Gold Medal for statuette, St George, Paris, 1939; FRBS, VPIAL; Hon. ARIBA; Hon. RI; *b* Detroit, 1862; of British parents; *s* of William Comben Stephens; assumed by deed poll, additional name of Reynolds, 1890; *m* Annie, *d* of late Thomas Ridpath. *Educ:* Blackheath; Germany; Royal Academy School, 1887 (prizeman in both sculpture and painting). Exhibited each year in Royal Academy since 1886, but exclusively as sculptor since 1894; Chief works, sculpture—Davidson Memorial, Lambeth Palace; The Scout in War; A Royal Game, Queen Elizabeth and Philip II purchased by trustees of Chantrey Fund for the National Collection; The Centenary Memorial to Charles Lamb outside Wren's Christ Church, Newgate Street; Love's Coronet; Castles in the Air; Guinevere's Redeeming; Sir Lancelot and the Nestling; Guinevere and the Nestling; and portrait statuettes in various materials; The Edward medal for Bravery in Mines, etc.; Painting—Summer; Love and Fate, etc.; has executed sculptural memorials of the European and South African Wars, also memorials to Sir Wm Q. Orchardson, RA (St Paul's Cathedral), Canon Brooke, Viscount Ridley, Bishop Sir Edwin Hoskyns (in Southwell Minster); Portrait busts: Archbishop of Canterbury, etc.; designed and executed the entire internal decoration, and such parts as choir and chapel screens, reredos, pulpit lectern, organ front, altar rail, etc., of Church of St Mary the Virgin, Great Warley, Brentwood; altar frontal for Holy Trinity, Sloane Street, and decorations in private houses; gold medals and other honours in Vienna, Paris, America, etc. *Recreations:* fishing and collecting. *Address:* 6 Mortimer Place, St John's Wood, NW6. *T:* Maida Vale 1022. *Club:* Burlington Fine Arts.

Died 23 Feb. 1943.

RHODES, Sir Campbell, KCIE 1935; Kt 1923; CBE 1920; Member, Council of India, 1925–35; Chairman, Hoare, Miller, Ltd, London; Chairman, 1930 Fund for District Nurses; Chairman Evelina Hospital for Children, Southwark; County Scout Commissioner for Berkshire; Rover Scout Leader, Wargrave-on-Thames; *b* 1874; *s* of Dr Francis Rhodes, Manchester; *m* 1905, Eleanor Wemyss (*d* 1921), *d* of late A. G. Reid, JP, Dublin; no *c*. *Educ:* Manchester Grammar School and Owens College. Joined Thomas Ashton & Sons, Manchester, 1891; Hoare, Miller & Co., Calcutta, 1896; First Chairman, Hoare, Miller & Co. Ltd, Calcutta; President Bengal Chamber of Commerce and President Associated Chambers of Commerce of India and Ceylon, 1922; Member of Indian Fiscal Commission and Bengal Retrenchment Committee; at times Member of Calcutta Corporation, Bengal Legislative Council, and Indian Legislative Assembly, representing European constituency, Bengal; sometime Governor of La Martinière School, Calcutta, Sumbhanath Pundit Hospital, etc.; World Economic Conference, 1927.

Publications: India To-morrow; Visions of Youth. *Recreations:* riding, scouting. *Address:* Kentons, Wargrave-on-Thames, Berks. *Clubs:* Oriental; Berkshire, Reading; Bengal, Calcutta.

Died 6 Feb. 1941.

RHODES, Charles Kenneth, CIE 1936; Joint Secretary, Home Department, Government of India; *b* 5 May 1889. *Educ:* Charterhouse, Brasenose College, Oxford. Entered Indian Civil Service, 1913; Joint Secretary, Reforms Office, Government of India, 1934; Officiating Chief Secretary, Government of Assam, 1937; Secretary to the Governor of Assam, 1938–39.

Died 6 Jan. 1941.

RHODES, Hon. Edgar Nelson, PC (Canada) 1921; KC; BA, LLB, LLD, DCL; Director Canadian Investment Fund, Ltd; Member Canadian Senate since 1935; *b* Amherst, NS, 5 Jan. 1877; *s* of late Nelson A. Rhodes and Sara D. C. Curry; *m* 1905, M. Grace (*d* 1934), 2nd *d* of late Hon. W. T. Pipes, KC, Premier of Nova Scotia; one *s* one *d*. *Educ:* Amherst Academy; Horton Collegiate Academy; Acadia University; Dalhousie University. House of Commons, 1908; Deputy Speaker, 1916; Speaker, 1917 and 1918; Premier, Provincial Secretary and Treasurer, Nova Scotia, 1925–30; Minister of Fisheries, Canada, 1930–32; Minister of Finance, Canada, 1932–35; Hon. DCL Acadia University, 1922; Hon. LLD Dalhousie University, 1929; elected to the Legislature of Nova Scotia, 1925; re-elected, 1928. *Address:* Ottawa, Canada. *T:* Queen 3971, Ottawa. *Clubs:* Rideau, Country, Royal Ottawa Golf, Chaudiere Golf, Ottawa; New York, New York; Halifax, Halifax; Mount Royal, Montreal.

Died 15 March 1942.

RHONDDA, Sybil, Viscountess, DBE 1920; *d* of George Augustus Haig, of Penithon, Radnorshire; *m* 1882, 1st Viscount Rhondda (*d* 1918); one *d*. *Address:* Llanwern, near Newport, Monmouthshire.

Died 11 March 1941.

RHYS, Ernest; author and editor; *b* London, 17 July 1859; *e s* of John Rhys, Newcastle and Carmarthen, and Emma, *d* of Robert Percival, Hockerell, Herts; *m* Grace (*d* 1929), *y d* of Bennett Little, JP, Co. Roscommon; one *s* two *d*. [Mrs Rhys published The Wooing of Sheila, The Diverted Village, Eleanor in the Loft, and other novels, also a vol. of essays, About many Things, 1920, a Celtic Anthology, 1927, and a Book of Grace, 1930]. Vice-President Hon. Society of Cymmrodorion; Member Council PEN Club. *Publications:* Camelot Series, 1886–1891; Dekker's Plays, 1888; The Lyric Poets, 1894–1899; A London Rose, 1894; The Fiddler of Carne, 1896; Welsh Ballads, 1898; The Whistling Maid, 1900; Lays of the Round Table, 1908; South Wales Coast, 1911; Lyric Poetry, 1913; Rabindranath Tagore, 1915; The Leaf Burners, 1918; Black Horse Pit, 1925; Everyman Remembers, 1931; Rhymes for Everyman, 1933; Letters from Limbo, 1936; Song of the Sun, 1937; Wales England Wed (autobiography), 1940; Editor Everyman's Library, 965 vol. 1940 (in progress). *Address:* Aldine House, 10 Bedford Street, WC2.

Died 25 May 1946.

RIACH, Col William, CMG 1916; MD Edin., DPH, late RAMC; *b* Edinburgh, 24 May 1873; *s* of late W. Riach of the Register of Sasines Office, and Helen Speeden; *m* 1922, May, *d* of late Captain William Turner, Washington, DC. *Educ:* Daniel Stewart's Coll., Edinburgh; the University, Edinburgh. Late House Physician, Royal Infirmary, Edinburgh; Resident Medical Officer, City Hospital, Edinburgh; Clinical Assist, R. Westminster Ophthalmic Hospital, London. Entered Army, 1900; Major, 1912; Lt-Col 1918; Bt Col 1919; served S African War, 1901–02 (Queen's medal 4 clasps); European War, 1914–18 (despatches, CMG);

retired pay, 1927. *Recreations:* golf, fishing. *Address:* Country Club Villas, Chula Vista, California, USA. *Club:* Caledonian.

Died 19 May 1942.

RIBBENTROP, Joachim von; Minister for Foreign Affairs, Germany, 1938–45; *b* 30 April 1893; *s* of Lt-Col Richard Ribbentrop and Sophie Hertwig; *m* 1920, Anna Elisabeth Henkell; two *s* two *d*. *Educ:* Kassel; Metz; Grenoble; London. Four years business in Canada; served European War, volunteer, 2nd and 1st Lieut western and eastern fronts (wounded, Iron Cross I and II); ADC to Plenipotentiary of German Ministry of War, Turkey, 1918; ADC to German peace delegation, 1919; left army, 1920; head of import and export firm in Berlin; helped at negotiations to form Hitler's Government, Chancellor's principal collaborator in questions of foreign policy, 1932–33; member of Reichstag, 1933; deputy of German government for disarmament questions, 1934; ambassador extraordinary and plenipotentiary of the Reich, 1935; leader of German delegation for naval talks in London; Anglo-German naval agreement, 1935; leader of German delegation in League of Nations' Council, 1936; SS-Gruppenführer, 1936; German Ambassador to Court of St James, 1936–38; Affiliation of Austria, March 1938; Affiliation of Sudeten Area, Oct. 1938; Protectorate of Bohemia and Moravia established, March 1939; return of the Memelland, March 1939. *Recreations:* sports and music. *Address:* Berlin.

Died 16 Oct. 1946.

RICARDO, Major Harry William Ralph, CVO 1939; *b* 12 July 1860; *y s* of late Harry Ricardo, Bath; unmarried. *Educ:* Eton. Soldier, 1883–1903; served in 17th Lancers; Sudan campaign, 1898; South African War, 1900–02, 2nd in command 17th Lancers; retired 1903 and appointed Adjutant Royal Hospital, Chelsea, till 1917; one of HM Bodyguard of the Hon. Corps Gentlemen-at-Arms, 1903–39 (CVO). *Recreations:* hunting, polo and golf. *Address:* Mayford, Woking, Surrey.

Died 10 Oct. 1945.

RICE, Mrs Alice Hegan; author; *d* of Samuel Hegan and Sarah Caldwell; *m* 1902, Cale Young Rice, LittD, poet. *Educ:* private schools; LittD Rollins College, 1928. LittD University of Louisville, 1937. With several others organized the Cabbage Patch Settlement in the factory district of Louisville, 1911; chief recreation is travel, having made several trips around the world and spent much time in Europe and the Orient. *Publications:* Mrs Wiggs of the Cabbage Patch; Lovey Mary; Sandy; Captain June; Mr Opp; A Romance of Billygoat Hill; The Honourable Percival; Calvary Alley; Miss Mink's Soldier; Quin; The Buffer; Mr Pete and Co.; The Lark Legacy; My Pillow Book; Our Ernie; The Inky Way, an autobiography (With Cale Young Rice); Turn About Tales; Winners and Losers; Passionate Follies; several of these books have been translated into German, French, Danish, Swedish, and Japanese; and three, Mrs Wiggs, The Romance of Billygoat Hill, and Mr Opp, have been put on the stage, and nearly all have been adapted to the cinema. *Address:* 1444 St James Court, Louisville, Kentucky, USA. *Clubs:* PEN; Woman's Arts, Louisville; Pen and Brush, New York.

Died 10 Feb. 1942.

RICE, Air Vice-Marshal Sir Edward Arthur Beckton, KBE 1946; CB 1944; CBE 1941; MC 1917; D. Director-General Civil Aviation, India; *b* 19 Dec. 1893; *s* of late Edward Rice, MD, Sutton Courtenay, Berks; *m* 1917, Dora Marguerite, *d* of F. L. Harman-Brown, OBE, Highweek, Devon; one *d*. *Educ:* private tutor. Transferred to RFC 1915 from Army; to RAF 1918 with rank of Squadron Leader; Wing Comdr 1928; Group Capt. 1938; Air Commodore, 1940; Air Vice-Marshal, 1943. Service abroad; France, 1914–18;

Germany, 1919; Iraq, 1920–22; Egypt, 1929–34; AOC West Africa, 1941–42; AOC No. 1 Group Bomber Command, 1942–45; retired, 1946. *Address:* Highweek, S Devon. *T:* Newton Abbot 665. *Club:* RAF.

Died 14 April 1948.

RICE, George S(amuel); Chief Mining Engineer, US Bureau of Mines, 1910–37, retired, also Chairman of its Mine Safety Board; Consulting Engineer from 1937; *b* Claremont, New Hamp., 8 Sept. 1866; *m* 1st, 1891, Julia Sessions (*d* 1934); one *s* one *d*; 2nd, 1935, Sarah Marie Benson. *Educ:* private and public schools; Columbia University. Mining Engineer, 1887; Hon. DSc Lafayette College, 1936; general mining practice, 1887–1908; US Geological Survey, 1908; specialized in investigations in prevention of coal dust explosions in mines and other kinds of accidents in metal as well as coal mines; research work in explosives and in underground military tunnelling methods, 1916–18; advisory on coal and iron resources in Europe to American Peace Commission in France, 1919; assisted in development and large scale tests of transverse system of ventilation of Holland Vehicular tunnel under Hudson River, New York; assisted in forming a mine safety research co-operation between the US Bureau of Mines and the Safety in Mines Research Board (British), 1923; Honorary member (British) Institution of Mining Engineers and recipient of its medal (1929), for all matters relating to safety in mines; Recipient of Columbia University Medal for achievements in mine safety methods, 1931; Hon. Member; La Société de L'Industrie Minérale, France; Can. Inst. Mining and Metallurgy; Am. Inst. Mining and Metallurgical Engineers; Fell. Am. Assoc. for Advancement of Science. Jos. A. Holmes Safety Assoc. Medal, 1946. *Publications:* many papers and bulletins on all phases of mining, such as mining methods, coal dust explosions, mine fires, mine rescue work, bumps and rock bursts, instantaneous outbursts of gas in mines in Canada, Europe and the United States, etc.; reports publ. by US Bureau of Mines and various agencies; last US Bureau of Mines Bulletin 414, Coal Mining in Europe, 1939. *Recreations:* at the University, shell rowing and tennis; in later years tennis, golf, and landscaping. *Address:* Wellington Villa, RFD1, Box 135, Alexandria, Va. *Clubs:* Cosmos, Torch (Washington).

Died 4 Jan. 1950.

RICE, Dame Margaret Ker P.; *see* Pryse-Rice.

RICE, Thomas Edmund, CMG 1921; Fellow of the Royal Society of Medicine; DPH (Honours) Royal College of Surgeons, Ireland. *Educ:* The Perse School, Cambridge; King's College and King's College Hospital, London. House Surgeon, King's College Hospital, London, 1895; Assistant Colonial Surgeon, Lagos, 1897; Senior Medical Officer, Southern Nigeria, 1903; Senior Sanitary Officer, Gold Coast, 1910; Principal Medical Officer, Sierra Leone, 1913; Principal Medical Officer, Gold Coast, 1916; Director of Medical and Sanitary Service, Nigeria, 1920–23; Chief medical Officer, Barbados, 1929–30; served with Lagos Hinterland and Southern Borghu Expedition, 1897 (medal and clasp); Kano expedition 1903 (medal and clasp). *Publication:* Evidence of the Endemicity of Yellow Fever in the Gold Coast Colony, Bull. Yellow Fever Bureau, 1913. *Clubs:* East India and Sports, Royal Automobile.

Died 9 June 1941.

RICE, Walter Francis, CSI 1910. *Educ:* Morrison's Academy, Crieff; Balliol College, Oxford. Entered ICS, 1890; Secretary to Government, 1897; Chief Secretary, Burma, 1907; Member of Lt-Governor's Council, 1909 and 1916; additional Member of the Imperial Legislative Council, India, 1913; Commissioner, 1918; retired, 1922. *Clubs:* Oriental, Union.

Died 21 March 1941.

RICE, Hon. and Rev. William Talbot; Vicar of St Paul's, Onslow Square, SW, 1919–35; Prebendary of St David's Cathedral, 1916–20; *b* 24 March 1861; *s* of 5th Baron Dynevor; *m* 1887, Marian Gurney; one *s* six *d*. *Educ:* Eton; Christ Church, Oxford (second class Theology). Curate of Old Portman Chapel, 1885–88; Vicar of All Saints', Plumstead, 1888–93; Rector of St Peter le Bailey, Oxford, 1893–1902; Vicar of Swansea, 1902–19. *Address:* 26 Nightingale Road, Guildford. *T:* Guildford 4439.

Died 13 Nov. 1945.

RICE-OXLEY, Sir Alfred James, Kt 1922; CBE 1919; MA, MD, MRCP; JP Co. London; late Physician in Ordinary to Princess Beatrice; Trustee Campden Charities (appointed by LCC); *b* 1856; 5th *s* of George Oxley and Mary Rice, Yorkshire; *m* 1883, Eva (*d* 1940), *d* of late CE Amos, CE; four *s*. *Educ:* Doncaster Grammar School; Balliol College, Oxford. Doncaster General Infirmary; London Hospital (Scholarships Human Anatomy and Clinical Medicine, Gold Medal Clinical Medicine); House Physician, London Hospital; House Physician, Radcliffe Infirmary, Oxford; late President, West London Medico-Chirurgical Society; was Mayor of Kensington for three years; late Hon. Medical Director and Acting Physician, Princess Beatrice Hospital for Wounded Officers, and Dorchester House Hospital for Wounded Officers (mentioned for valuable services); late Chairman, Society of Yorkshiremen in London; Vice-Chairman of Council, London Society; President, Kensington Council of Social Service; late Chairman, Grand Committee League of Nations (Kensington Branch); Chairman, Leighton House Society; late Vice-Chairman, Princess Beatrice Hospital; late Member of the Central Council British Medical Association; Member of Advisory Board, League of Remembrance; Member of the Order of Isabella the Catholic (Spain), 1907; Legion of Honour, 1927. *Publications:* Medical Men in English Literature; communications (various to The Lancet and British Medical Journal; Joint editor and translator Alimentation, par A. Gautier. *Recreations:* music, art, archæology. *Address:* Lingfield, 12 Priory Road, Chalfont St Peter, Bucks. *T:* Gerrards Cross 2315.

Died 10 Aug. 1941.

RICH, Sir Almeric Edmund Frederic, 5th Bt *cr* 1791; Lt-Col, retired pay; *b* 30 March 1859; *o s* of late Captain Frederic Dampier Rich, RN, 3rd *s* of 2nd Bt, and Jessie Catherine Hesketh, 3rd *d* of late Sir John Hesketh Lethbridge, Bt, of Sandhill Park, Taunton; *S* cousin, 1913; *m* 1st, 1894, Louise (*d* 1932), *d* of Hon. John Conness of Mattapan, Mass; one *s*; 2nd, 1932, Edith, Countess Dousmani, *widow* of Count Constantine Dousmani, Corfu. *Educ:* Wimbledon School; Royal Military College, Sandhurst. Joined 2nd Batt. 10th Foot, 1878; retired as Captain, 1892; recalled to Army, 1900; Major, Royal Garrison Regt 1902; retired pay, 1907; re-employed, Aug. 1914 to March 1919 (promoted Lt-Col). *Heir: s* Almeric Frederic Conness Rich. *Clubs:* Connaught: Royal London Yacht, West Cowes.

Died 2 July 1948.

RICHARDS, Albert Edwin George, CBE 1920; *b* 1856; *s* of George Richards; *m* Hannah Elizabeth Tucker. Was Assistant Director of Naval Construction, Admiralty. *Address:* Morlands, Rutford Road, SW16.

Died 19 Jan. 1942.

RICHARDS, Franklin Thomas Grant; publisher and author; *b* 21 Oct. 1872; *o s* of late Franklin Thomas Richards, Fellow and Tutor Trinity College, Oxford; *m* 2nd, 1915, Maria Magdalena de Csanády; two *s* two *d*. *Educ:* City of London School; 32 Paternoster Row; and the office of W. T. Stead. Left school at fifteen, and at seventeen joined W. T. Stead on Review of Reviews; started as publisher Jan. 1897. *Publications:* Occassional journalism; Novels; Caviare, 1912; Valentine, 1913;

Bittersweet, 1915; Double Life, 1920; Every Wife, 1924; Fair Exchange, 1927; Hasty Marriage, 1928; Vain Pursuit, 1931; The Amiable Charles, 1935; also guide-book to Riviera, The Coast of Pleasure, 1928; Memories of a Misspent Youth, 1932; Author Hunting, 1934; Housman: 1897–1936, 1941. *Recreations:* travelling, swimming, walking, motoring. *Address:* 46 Buckingham Court, W11. *T:* Park 7633.

Died 24 Feb. 1948.

RICHARDS, Miss Gertrude Mary, CBE 1919; RRC; Matron (retired), Queen Alexandra's Imperial Military Nursing Service. Served European War, 1914–19 (despatches twice, CBE, RRC, 1914 star, two medals). *Address:* The Croft, Edwalton, Notts.

Died 18 Sept. 1944.

RICHARDS, Lt-Col Harold Arthur David, CMG 1919; DSO 1917; late RASC; *b* 16 Feb. 1874; *s* of late Rev. A. J. Richards, Farlington, Havant, Hants; *m* 1899, Helen Dorothy, (*d* 1931), *d* of late R. L. Parker, Eastbourne; one *d. Educ:* Charterhouse. Joined the 3rd Batt. Gloucestershire Regt (Militia), 1893; 1st Batt Royal Sussex Regt 1896; ASC 1899; served South African War, 1899–1902 (despatches twice, Brevet Majority, King's and Queen's medals); European War (despatches four times, DSO, CMG, Belgian Croix de Guerre); retired pay, 1921. *Address:* The Corner House, Grosvenor Road, Godalming. *T:* Godalming 758. *Club:* Junior United Service.

Died 16 Jan. 1947.

RICHARDS, Harold Meredith; late Medical Officer, Ministry of Health; *b* Cardiff; *m* Mary Cecilia (decd), *d* of W. J. Todd; four *s. Educ:* University Coll., London (Fellow). MD Lond. Held various hospital and public health appointments; Deputy-Chairman, National Health Insurance Commission, Wales, 1911. *Publications:* numerous reports and contributions on Public Health, Health Insurance, and other medico-social problems. *Address:* 33 Norham Road, Oxford.

Died 25 Dec. 1942.

RICHARDS, Henry Caselli, DSc; Professor of Geology and Mineralogy, University of Queensland, since 1918; Deputy Chancellor since 1944; *b* Melton, Victoria, 16 Dec. 1884; 2nd *s* of Benjamin and Jane Richards; *m* 1911, Grace, 4th *d* of late Thos Christian, of Caulfield, Victoria; one *s* one *d. Educ:* Box Hill Grammar School: South Melbourne College; University of Melbourne Metallurgical experience at Broken Hill, 1907–08; Caroline Kay Research Scholar in Geology at University of Melbourne, 1908–09. Lecturer Technical College, Brisbane, 1910; Lecturer in Geology and Mineralogy, University of Queensland, 1911–18. *Publications:* numerous scientific publications, especially on the Great Barrier Reef of Australia, the Geology of Queensland, building stones and volcanic rocks, principally in the Proceedings of the Royal Societies of Victoria and Queensland. *Recreations:* golf, tennis. *Address:* University of Queensland, Brisbane, Australia. *Clubs:* Queensland, Brisbane.

Died 13 June 1947.

RICHARDS, Hugh Augustine, MA (Cantab); MRCS, LRCP, DA (RCP and S); Consulting Anæsthetist, King's College Hospital; Consulting Anæsthetist, City Road Lying-in-Hospital; *b* 1884; 3rd *s* of late R. S. Richards, Glascoed, Llangollen, N Wales. *Educ:* Rossall; Clare College, Cambridge; King's College Hospital. BA 1906. Surgeon HM troopships, 1914–16; RAMC 1916–20, Temp. Captain; late Resident Anæsthetist King's College Hospital; late Anæsthetist Hospital St John and St Elizabeth, West London Hospital and St Mark's Hospital for Diseases of the Rectum; Hon. Member and Past President of Anæsthetic Section, RSM. *Publication:* Anæsthetics in Obstetrics, Proceedings

Royal Society of Medicine. *Recreation:* golf. *Address:* 2 The Old Pines, Epsom. *T:* Epsom 9437. *Club:* Conservative.

Died 22 Jan. 1949.

RICHARDS, Engr Captain John Arthur, CBE 1919; RN (retired); Chevalier of Legion of Honour; Order of the Sacred Treasure, 3rd Class (Japan); Consultant Tubes Investments, Birmingham; *b* 1865; *s* of late Rev. John Richards, Rector of Shelton, Beds; *m* Marion Dorothy, *γ d* of late Henry Sparks of Woolston, Southampton. *Educ:* Royal Naval Engineering College, Keyham; HMS Marlborough; RN College, Greenwich. Served as Engineer Officer, RN, at sea and in HM Dockyards, 1886–1909; inspection of materials at boiler and tube works for all boilers of HM ships building by contract, 1909–14; controlled the iron and steel tube industry for war and other requirements for Admiralty, Ministry of Munitions, and all other departments, 1915–19; has written papers on tube-making, and lectured to Officers of the Fleet and learned Societies on the manufacture of steel tubes; MINA, MI and SI. *Address:* Hoe Cottage, Fishbourne, Chichester. *Clubs:* Army and Navy; Royal Naval (Portsmouth).

Died 16 Nov. 1949.

RICHARDS, Rev. Leyton, MA; *b* Sheffield, 12 March 1879; *s* of Charles Richards; *m* 1907, Edith, *d* of Rev. Samuel Pearson, Manchester; three *d. Educ:* Grand Rapids, USA; Reading; Glasgow Univ.; Mansfield College, Oxford. In late teens with Sutton & Sons, seedsmen, Reading. Student Pastor during College vacations for 3 successive years at Richmond, Maine, USA; after leaving College, Minister successively of Peterhead Congregational Church, Aberdeenshire; Collins Street Independent Church, Melbourne, Australia; Bowdon Downs Congregational Church, Manchester; and Carrs Lane Church, Birmingham; resigned Carrs Lane, 1941; from 1920 onwards, frequent visitor to USA and Canada as lecturer on international affairs. Warden of Woodbrooke Settlement, Birmingham, 1940–44. General Secretary of the Fellowship of Reconciliation, London, 1916–18, and fined £100 under the Defence of the Realm Act for refusing to mix Christianity and War. *Publications:* The Christian's Alternative to War; The Christian's Contribution to Peace; The Crisis and World Peace; Planning for Freedom (Swarthmore Lecture for 1943); Christian Pacifism after two world wars; and various pamphlets. *Address:* Woodview Mortimer Common, nr Reading.

Died 22 Aug. 1948.

RICHARDS, Owen, CMG 1918; DSO 1915; MD, MCh (Oxford); FRCS; *b* 30 Sept. 1873; *s* of Rev. H. W. P. Richards, Prebendary of St Paul's; *m* Catherine Cressall; one *d. Educ:* Eton (King's Scholar, 1887–92); New College, Oxford (Wykeham Prize Fellow, 1898–1905). Guy's Hospital; late temp. Col AMS and Consulting Surgeon to the BEF; served in S Africa (Queen's medal and 3 clasps); European War in France, 1914–18 (despatches thrice, DSO, CMG); Order of the Nile (2nd Class); Director, Egyptian Government School of Medicine, 1919–24. *Address:* Downes, Monkleigh, Bideford. *T:* Torrington 2244. *Clubs:* Travellers', Royal Cruising.

Died 18 April 1949.

RICHARDS, Reginald James, MA (NZ); Headmaster, Christ's College, Christchurch, NZ since 1932; 3rd *s* of late Rt Rev. Isaac Richards; *m* Joan Mary, *d* of F. L. Carter, Clifton College, Bristol; two *s* one *d. Educ:* Christ's College (NZ); Canterbury University College, NZ. NZ Rifle Brigade, European War; Assistant Master Clifton College, Bristol, 1919–31. *Recreations:* cricket, golf, tennis, fishing. *Address:* Christ's College, Christchurch, C1, NZ. *Clubs:* Christchurch, Rotary (Christchurch).

Died 16 July 1950.

RICHARDS, Rupert Peel, CBE 1920; JP Lancashire; a Director of the Vulcan Foundry, Ltd (Loco works), Newton-le-Willows, Lancs; *b* 1872; *s* of Rev. James Richards, MA, formerly Vicar of Newbold, Rochdale; *m* 1899, Helen, *d* of John Pilling, JP, of Duplish Hall, Rochdale; three *s*. *Educ:* privately. Pupil of the late F. W. Webb at Crewe Works, LNWR, 1888–94; afterwards an Inspector under the late Sir Alexander Rendle, KCIE; on leaving Sir Alex. Rendle's Staff joined the Vulcan Foundry, Ltd, Newton-le-Willows, as Assistant Manager, 1899; engaged in Locomotive Building, Manager, 1904–14; Assistant General Manager, 1914–17; General Manager, 1917–23. *Recreations:* yachting, fly-fishing. *Address:* Abergwynent Hall, Dolgelley, Wales.

Died 13 April 1941.

RICHARDS, Thomas Frederick; *b* Wednesbury, 25 March 1863; father, commercial traveller; *m* 1st, 1882, *d* of J. Mee; two *s* one *d*; 2nd, 1916, Miss M. J. Bell, Secretary of Leicester Women's Branch of the same Union. *Educ:* Church, then Board School. Started work at eleven years of age; appointed a permanent official of Leicester Branch of Boot and Shoe Operatives in 1893, and has held various positions since; Leicester Town Council, 1894–1903, and since 1929; MP (Lab) Wolverhampton, 1906–10; contested East Northants (Lab), 1910; General President of the National Union of Boot and Shoe Operatives, 1910–29; Leicester City Council, 1929–39; Member of the Management Committee of the Gen. Fed. Trades Unions, 1905–24; a Socialist since 1889. *Address:* 65 Hill Rise, Birstall, Leicester.

Died 4 Oct. 1942.

RICHARDSON, Sir Albion Henry Herbert, Kt 1919; CBE 1918; KC 1930. Recorder of Nottingham; A Master of the Bench of the Hon. Society of Gray's Inn; Member of the Standing Joint Committee of the Inns of Court on the duties and discipline of the Bar; Midland Circuit; appointed to Panel of Chairmen Grand Committees, House of Commons, 1919; a Chairman of the Appeal Tribunal for the County of London, 1916–18; appointed by the Prime Minister (with Rt Hon. Lord Justice Bankes (Chairman) and Rt Hon. James Craig, MP) to report to him upon the Employment of Aliens in Government Offices, 1917; Commissioner appointed by the Home Secretary to report upon the allegations made by Colonel Wedgwood, MP, against the Governor of Wandsworth Prison (Report presented to the House of Commons, 1918); Commissioner appointed by the Home Secretary on many occasions to enquire into and report upon allegations against the Police; Vice-Chairman Prisoners of War (House of Commons) Committee, 1916–18; MP (L) Peckham, 1910–18, (CL) 1918–22; Recorder of Warwick, 1931–36. *Recreations:* golf, tennis. *Address:* 12 King's Bench Walk, Temple, EC4. *T:* Central 4950. *Club:* Reform.

Died 7 July 1950.

RICHARDSON, Dr Arnold Edwin Victor, CMG 1938; MA (Adel.). DSc (Melb.), BSc (Agric.); *b* 12 Sept. 1883; *s* of George Edwin Richardson, Yorkshire, and Louise Mansfield, Devon; *m* Lilian M. Lucas; one *d*. *Educ:* University of Adelaide. Assistant, University Training College, Adelaide, 1908; Assistant Director of Agriculture, SA, 1908–10; Acting Director of Agriculture, SA, 1911; Superintendent of Agriculture, Victoria, 1911–24; Director Melbourne University School of Agriculture and Dean Faculty of Agriculture, 1919–24; Waite Professor of Agriculture and Director,

Waite Agricultural Research Institute, University of Adelaide, 1924–38; Deputy Chief Executive Officer, CSIR 1938–45; Chief Executive Officer of Commonwealth Council for Scientific and Industrial Research, 1946–49. Commissioned by Victorian Government to visit USA in 1918, and presented a report on Agricultural Education which led to the establishment in 1919 of the Melbourne University School of Agriculture; received DSc degree (Melb. University) for original research on Water requirements of Australian farm Crops and Wheat breeding investigations; appointed 1926 Member of Executive of Commonwealth Council for Scientific and Industrial Research; Commissioned by University of Adelaide, 1926, to visit Agricultural Research Institutes in S Africa, Europe, USA, Canada and Japan; appointed 1927 to represent Commonwealth of Australia as a delegate to the First Imperial Agricultural Research Conference, London; adviser on marketing problems to the Australian Delegation to the Imperial Conference at Ottawa, 1932; President Australian Institute of Agricultural Science, 1935–36; President, Aust. and NZ Association for the Advancement of Science, 1947–49. *Publications:* Agricultural Education in United States and Canada, 1919; Water Requirements of Farm Crops; Wheat and its Cultivation; numerous papers on Agricultural Science. *Recreation:* golf. *Address:* Cliveden Mansions, Melbourne, Australia. *Clubs:* Adelaide (Adelaide); Melbourne, Savage (Melbourne).

Died 5 Dec. 1949.

RICHARDSON, Lt-Col Edwin Hautonville, OBE; FZS; *b* Old Forge House, Co. Antrim, 25 Aug. 1863; *s* of J. P. Richardson and Charlotte Nicolson; *m* 1894, Blanche, *d* of late T. Riley Bannon; two *s*. *Educ:* Cheltenham; Sandhurst. Joined 45th Regt (Sherwood Foresters), 1882; West York Militia, 1895; took up study of dogs for military and police purposes, 1898; was attached with ambulance dogs to RAMC Volunteers; supplied Russian Army with ambulance dogs in Russo-Japanese War (thanks of Russian Red Cross Society, the war medal and a diamond watch from the Czar); took out an ambulance dog to Spanish Army in Morocco Campaign (personally thanked by King Alfonso and received cross); introduced dogs for duty with police into England, and supplied all leading towns and also inaugurated a service of dogs for the Admiralty; supplied the sentry dogs to the Abor Expedition in Northern India, 1911; and was present with the Italian Field Force in Tripoli same year; Balkan War, 1912–13; supplied sentry dog in Naga Hill Expedition, India, 1913; also dogs for Gibraltar; took out ambulance dogs to Belgium at commencement of war, and subsequently supplied a large number of sentry dogs to the army in France and the Dardanelles; Commandant War Dog Training School for the British Army, which he established (OBE) at request of War Office in 1917; received French Red Cross decoration, Belgian Red Cross decoration, etc. *Publications:* War, Police, and Watch Dogs, 1910; British War Dogs, 1920; Watchdogs: their Training and Management, 1923; Forty Years with Dogs, 1929. *Address:* Grasslands, Horsell Common, Woking. *T:* 678.

Died 4 Aug. 1948.

RICHARDSON, Foster; Operatic Bass Vocalist; *s* of Samuel Richardson, Mulberry Farm, Notts; *m* Gertrude Blanche Evans, Bishops Stortford, Herts; one *s* one *d*. *Educ:* Clough's Grammar School, Notts. Engineering; then winning open scholarship Royal Academy of Music; Principal Bass with Sir Thomas Beecham's Opera; toured the world giving recitals; lately singing for Choral Societies and the BBC; under contract with the Gramophone Co., Hayes, since 1915. *Publication:* The Magic Power of Song. *Recreation:* golf. *Address:* 284 Ealing Road, Alperton. *T:* Wembley 4551.

Died 29 Jan. 1942.

RICHARDSON, Harry Linley, RBA 1905; FRBA; FRSA; figure and landscape painter and black and white artist; Director of the Art Department, Palmerston North Technical School, since 1928; *b* London, 19 Oct. 1878; *s* of George Richardson and Mary Linley; *m* Constance, *d* of John Cooper; one *s* three *d. Educ:* Westminster School of Art; Julian's (Paris). Exhibitor RA, 1900–01 and 1936, oil painting, A Maori Chieftainess; has illustrated in various magazines, The Idler, and Phil May's Annual (1898), Designer of Georgian Issues, New Zealand Postage Stamps. Work in New Zealand National Art Gallery, Wellington; Auckland Art Gallery; Sarjent Art Gallery, Wanganui; Dominion Museum, Wellington; Christchurch Art Gallery, etc. *Publications:* has illustrated Goldsmith's Deserted Village, Book on Shooting (Haddon Hall Series), Samuel Lover's Plays, George Eliot's Works. *Recreation:* walking. *Address:* 148 Fitzherbert Avenue, Palmerston North, New Zealand.

Died 22 Jan. 1947.

RICHARDSON, Henry Handel; (pseudonym of Ethel Florence Lindesay Richardson); author; *b* Melbourne, Australia, 3 Jan. 1870; *er d* of late W. Lindesay Richardson, MD, Melbourne; *m* 1895, John George Robertson, FBA (*d* 1933). *Educ:* Melbourne; Germany. *Publications:* Maurice Guest, 1908; The Getting of Wisdom, 1910; The Fortunes of Richard Mahony (Australia Felix, 1917; The Way Home, 1925; Ultima Thule, 1929; in one volume, 1930); Two Studies, 1931; The End of a Childhood, 1934; The Young Cosima, 1939. *Address:* c/o Wm Heinemann, Ltd, 99 Great Russell Street, WC1.

Died 20 March 1946.

RICHARDSON, Col James Jardine, DSO 1916; bar to DSO 1918; Colonel of 13th/18th Royal Hussars (Queen Mary's Own) since 1938; *b* 26 Feb. 1873; *m* 1922, Rachael Edith, *o d* of late Lt-Col G. E. N. Booker, CBE; two *d.* Served NW Frontier of India, 1897–98 (medal with clasp); S Africa (Siege of Ladysmith, wounded), 1899–1902 (Queen's medal with clasp, King's medal with two clasps); European War, 1914–18 (despatches four times, DSO with bar, Croix de Guerre, wounded); retired pay, 1927. *Address:* Little Court, Littlebourne, near Canterbury. *Club:* Cavalry.

Died 14 April 1942.

RICHARDSON, Joseph Hall; author; Liveryman Spectacle Makers Co.; *b* 5 April 1857; *e s* of John Richardson, CC, Bishopsgate; *m* 1882, Harriet Eliza, *e d* of George G. Bussey. *Educ:* France; City of London Coll. In journalism since 1874; started Surrey Mirror, 1879; joined the Daily Telegraph as reporter, 1881; Assistant Editor, 1906; organised Great Shilling Funds, including South African Widows' and Orphans' Fund, Titanic Relief Fund, King George's Fund for Sailors, Boy Scouts' appeals; Member of the Mansion House Council of the National Disasters Fund until 1937; hon. Secretary Cavell Memorial Statue; General Manager of the Daily Telegraph, 1923; retired, 1928; acted as Special Correspondent in France, Belgium, Holland, Italy, Morocco, and Canada; an Estates Gov. of Dulwich College, 1925–29. *Publications:* Police!; The Rogues' Gallery, and other books on crime; Undercurrents of London Life; From the City to Fleet Street, 1927; Further Reminiscences, 1935–1936; Imperial Chiselhurst, 1939. *Recreations:* travel, photography and sketching. *Address:* 4 Stanley Road, Orpington.

Died 20 March 1945.

RICHARDSON, Maurice Robert, CIE 1935; BAI (Dublin University), Chief Engineer, United Provinces, India; *b* 12 Dec. 1884; *s* of Nicholas Gosselin Richardson, Tyaquin, Co. Galway; *m* 1st, 1916, Elsie (*d* 1922), *d* of W. H. Hutton; 2nd, 1926, Ruby May, *d* of

Lt-Col W. Dundas; one *s* one *d.* Entered Indian Service of Engineers, 1908; retired 1939. *Address:* Bramley, Acreman Street, Sherborne, Dorset. *T:* Sherborne 468.

Died 26 March 1950.

RICHARDSON, Robert; JP; miner; *b* 1 Feb. 1862; *m* 1886, Elizabeth Fletcher; one *s* three *d. Educ:* Ryhope National School. Alderman, Durham CC; Member County Education Committee; MP (Lab) Houghton-le-Spring Division of Durham, Dec. 1918–31; Parliamentary Charity Commissioner, 1924 and 1929–31; Miners Secretary Ryhope Lodge DMA, 1887–1919; Member of the Durham Miners Executive, 1897–1919; Durham County Council, 1901–25; Sunderland Rural District and Guardians, 1904–22; Chairman of the Durham County Education Authority. *Recreations:* billiards, chess, bowls.

Died 28 Dec. 1943.

RICHARDSON, Sir Thomas William, Kt 1922; Indian Civil Service (retired); *b* 16 Jan. 1865; *s* of T. W. Richardson, 27 Roland Gardens, SW; *m* 1894, Katherine, *d* of late John Roberton, Fallside Hill, near Kelso; one *s* three *d. Educ:* Brighton College; Cheltenham College; New College Oxford. Indian Civil Service, 1886–1924; Barrister-at-law, Inner Temple; Judge, High Court Calcutta, 1912–24. *Address:* 48 Queen's Gate Gardens, SW7. *T:* Western 0512. *Clubs:* Oriental; Bengal United Service, Royal Calcutta Turf, Calcutta.

Died 3 Jan. 1947.

RICHEY, Lt-Col George Henry Mills, CMG 1919; DSO 1900; late Royal Fusiliers; *b* 18 May 1867; *s* of late Captain W. M. Richey, RA, City Marshal of London. Served in Methuen's Horse, 12th R. Lancers, 2nd Dragoon Guards, BSA Police, and Cape Colonial Forces; was in Bechuanaland Expedition, 1884–85; Matabele War, 1896; Mashona rebellion, 1897–98; Boer War, 1899–1902; Adjt Kitchener's Horse; Staff Officer Doran's Column (wounded at Waterval Drift, 1900, and at Houtnek, 1900, recommended for VC, DSO, despatches three times); European War, 2nd in command 1st Sportsmans' Batt. Royal Fusiliers; Commanded 4th East Lancs Regt and 4th South Lancs Regt; Commandant VI Corps School; Commanded 1st Batt. Royal Fusiliers BEF; 25th Batt. The King's Regt, Palestine and Egypt EEF; temp. comd. a Brigade in France and Palestine (Bar-DSO, despatches thrice, wounded Ypres, 1917); assisted in organisation of Albanian Gendarmerie, 1925–29. *Recreations:* riding, shooting; winner of many prizes for skill-at-arms. *Address:* 68 Cadogan Square, SW1.

Died 26 Aug. 1949.

RICHMOND, Sir Daniel; *see* Richmond, Sir R. D.

RICHMOND, Adm. Sir Herbert W., KCB 1926; CB 1921; MA; DCL (Hon.) 1939; Master of Downing College, since 1936; Fellow, Royal Historical Society; Trustee, National Maritime Museum; Membre Associé, Académie de Marine, Paris; Fellow, British Academy; *b* 15 Sept. 1871; *s* of Sir William Richmond, RA, KCB, and Clara Jane Richards; *m* 1907, Florence Elsa, *d* of Sir Hugh Bell, 2nd Bt; one *s* four *d. Educ:* HMS Britannia. Lieut 1893; Commander, 1903; Captain, 1909; Commanded Dreadnought, Furious, Vindictive, 1909–12; Assistant Director of Operations; 1913–15; liaison officer with Italian Fleet, 1915; Commanded Commonwealth, Conqueror, and Erin in Grand Fleet; Director of Staff Duties and Training, 1918; Rear-Admiral, 1920; President of the RN War College, Greenwich, 1920–23; Commander-in-Chief, East Indies Squadron, 1924–25; Commandant of the Imperial Defence Coll., 1927–28; Adm. 1929; retired list, 1931; Pres. of the Internat. Conference on Safety of Life at Sea, 1929; Vere Harmsworth Prof. of Naval and Imperial History, Cambridge University, 1934–36. *Publications:* Papers relating to the Loss of Minorca; The Navy in the

War, 1739–1948 (Chesney Gold Medal of RUSI, 1926); The Spencer Papers, vols 3 and 4; Command and Discipline; National Policy and Naval Strength; Naval Warfare, 1930; The Navy in India, 1763–1783, 1931; Economy and Naval Security, 1931; Imperial Defence and Capture at Sea, 1932; Naval Training, 1933; Naval History and the Citizen, 1934; Sea Power in the Modern World, 1934; The Navy, 1938; Amphibious Warfare in British Strategy, 1941; British Strategy, 1941; The Invasion of Britain, 1941; Statesmen and Sea Power, 1946. *Address:* Downing College, Cambridge. *T:* Cambridge 5091.

Died 15 Dec. 1946.

RICHMOND, Herbert William, FRS; MA; LLD (Hon.) St Andrews; Pensioner Fellow of King's College, Cambridge; *b* 17 July 1863; *e s* of late Rev. W. H. Richmond. *Educ:* Merchant Taylors' School, London; King's College, Cambridge. Engaged on experimental Ballistics, 1916–22. *Publications:* papers in scientific journals. *Address:* King's College, Cambridge. *T:* Cambridge 4411. *Club:* Savile.

Died 22 April 1948.

RICHMOND, Sir (Robert) Daniel, Kt 1936; CIE 1932; *b* 29 Oct. 1878; *s* of J. Richmond, CMG, JP; *m* 1909, Monica, *d* of Sir James Davy, KCB; one *s. Educ:* Bedford Modern School; RIE Coll., Coopers Hill. Passed in to Indian Forest Service, 1898; after training in England and Germany joined the service in Madras, 1901; District Forest Officer, 1903; Principal, Madras Forest College, 1913; Assistant Inspector-General of Forests to the Government of India, 1919–22; Conservator of Forests, 1923; Member, Madras Legislative Council, 1923; Chief Conservator of Forests, Madras, 1927; retired from Indian Forest Service, 1932; appointed to Madras Public Service Commission, 1932, Chairman, 1935; retired, 1940. *Address:* Efford Mill House, Everton, Hants. *Club:* East India and Sports.

Died 1 May 1948.

RICKARD, Sir Arthur, KBE 1920; JP; *b* Currawang, NSW, 17 Nov. 1868; *m* 1902, Nellie Crudge, *d* of late Col Thomas Rowe, VD, Sydney; three *s* three *d.* President Millions Club of NSW; Chairman Dr Barnardo's Homes NSW Committee; Director of several public companies. *Recreation:* golf. *Address:* 55 York St, Sydney, NSW; 11 Lynwood Avenue, Killara, NSW. *Club:* Imperial Service (Sydney).

Died 13 April 1948.

RICKARDS, George William; MP (C) Skipton Division since 1933; *b* 1877; *s* of Charles Ayscough and Isabella Anne Rickards; *m* 1905, Katharine Rigby; three *s. Educ:* Sedbergh; Continent. Business in silk trade until the war; served in the Cheshire Regiment, 1915–20; County Councillor for the West Riding of Yorkshire, 1928–34. *Recreations:* hunting and shooting. *Address:* 6 Relton Mews, Cheval Place, SW7.

Died 27 Nov. 1943.

RIDDEL, Vice-Adm. Daniel MacNab, RN; late Naval Officer in charge, Jamaica, 1901; Commodore 2nd class; Captain HMS Renown, when Flagship on the North American and West Indies station, 1897. Entered service, 1861; Captain, 1892; Zulu medal, 1877–79; retired.

Died 31 Dec. 1941.

RIDDELL, Col Edward Vansittart Dick, CBE 1919; DSO 1915; late RA; *b* 30 March 1873; *s* of Col Robert Vansittart Riddell, *g g s* of 2nd Bt of Riddell, and Louisa Flora, *d* of Gen. A. Dick; *m* 1st, 1902, Edith Mary (*d* 1914), *d* of Maj.-Gen. E. P. Bingham-Turner; one *s;* 2nd, 1938, Vyvyan, *d* of Rev. J. J. Lewis, MA. *Educ:* Cheltenham College; RM Academy, Woolwich. Entered army, 1893; Captain, 1900; Brevet Major, 1902; Major, 1914; Brevet Lieutenant-Colonel, 1916; Lt-Col, 1918; Colonel, 1922; DAAG S Africa, 1900–02; Adjutant Militia, 1903–06; DAAG Jersey, 1911–14;

General Staff Officer, 2nd grade, 1914; DAA and QMG 1915; AA and QMG 1915–16; Chief Instructor and 2nd in Command RM Academy, Woolwich, 1917; AA and QMG 1918; DA and QMG (temp. Brig.-Gen.) 1918; Base Commandant, Italy, 1918–20; AA and QMG, SE Area, 1920–21; Commanding RA Portsmouth, 1921; Deputy Director of Artillery, Army Headquarters, India, 1923–28; retired pay, 1928; served South Africa, 1900–02 (Bt Major, Queen's medal 2 clasps, King's medal 2 clasps); European War, 1914–16 (despatch, Bt Lt-Col, DSO, CBE). *Address:* 1f Hyde Park Mansions, NW1. *Club:* Army and Navy.

Died 8 Sept. 1942.

RIDDELL, John Robertson; Printers' Consultant; formerly Principal of the London School of Printing and Kindred Trades; *b* Aberdeen, 1874; *s* of late John Riddell and Isobella Dunn; *m* 1900, Florence Ada Garland; two *s. Educ:* Rosemount School, Aberdeen. Apprenticed Taylor and Henderson, associated with A. B. Fleming and Co. Ltd, colour manufacturers, and Thomas Forman and Sons, Nottingham; First Principal of St Bride Foundation Printing School, City of London; transferred to the London School of Printing, 1922; acted as technical adviser to the training section of the Ministry of Labour in connection with the training of disabled men for the printing trades; Liveryman of the Worshipful Company of Stationers; Freeman of the City of London; Governor Stationers' Company's School; Member of Book Production Committee of the Royal Society of Arts; lecturer and writer on subjects appertaining to the printing crafts; technical adviser on printing matters; awarded the Stationers Company's Silver Medal; elected honorary member of the London Master Printers Association; The National Society of Operative Printers and Assistants, and International Printing Pressmans and Assistants' Union of North America in recognition of work done on behalf of the printing industry; Hon. Secretary, Printing Industry Technical Board; Member of Council The Printing Industry Research Association; and the Council of Hornsey Central Hospital; Organiser of craft lectures and exhibitions of printed work. *Publications:* Historical Notes on the Worshipful Company of Stationers; Colour Printing; Printing as a Vocation; The Training of the Printer; Apprenticeship in Printing Industry; articles on printing and kindred subjects in the Encyclopædia Britannica and printing trade publications. *Recreation:* motoring. *Club:* Press.

Died 28 March 1941.

RIDDELL, Hon. Mr Justice, (William Renwick Riddell); Justice of Appeal, Supreme Court of Ontario since 1923; *b* Hamilton Township, Upper Canada, 6 April 1852; *s* of Walter Riddell of Hamilton Tp., and Mary, *d* of Walter Renwick of Annan, Scotland; *m* 1884, Anna Hester Kirsop, *y d* of late James Crossen of Cedar Hedge, Cobourg, Ontario. *Educ:* Cobourg Collegiate Institute; Victoria University. BA (Mathematical and Nat. Science Prizeman); BSc; LLB; LHD (Hon.) Syracuse University; LLD (Hon.) Lafayette College, McMaster University, University of Toronto, North-western University, Rochester, Wesleyan, Boston, and Yale; JUD (Hon.) Trinity College, Hartford; DCL (Hon.) Colby College, Maine. Late Professor of Mathematics, Government Normal School, Ottawa; called to Bar, honours and gold medal, 1883; practised at Cobourg, 1883–92; Toronto, 1892–1906; Puisne Justice, King's Bench Division, High Court of Justice, 1906; Bencher, Law Society of Upper Canada, 1892; QC 1898; Special Counsel for City of Toronto in Civic Investigation, the Government of Ontario in Gamey Inquiry, etc.; President Canadian Social Hygiene Council and Health League of Canada; formerly Member of Senate and Board of Regents, Victoria Univ.; formerly Member of Senate, Univ. of Toronto; some years Examiner in Roman, Constitutional and International Law; Dodge Lecturer at Yale Univ.; Blumenthal Lecturer at Columbia Univ.; FRS Can.;

FRHistS; Fellow Academy of Medicine, Toronto. *Publications:* Constitution of Canada in its History and Practical Working (Dodge Lectures, Yale University); Old Province Tales; Travels of La Rochefoucauld in Canada, 1795; First Judge at Detroit and his Court; First Law Reporter in Upper Canada and his Reports; Magna Carta; The Legal Profession in Upper Canada in Early Times; The Life of Robert Fleming Gourlay; Life of John Richardson; Life of William Kirby; Upper Canada Sketches; The Early Courts of the Province; Life of Chief Justice William Dummer Powell; Life of Lieut-Governor John Graves Simcoe; British Courts in Michigan; Michigan under British Rule; The Courts of Ontario; The Bar of Ontario; The Works of Fracastorius on Morbus Gallicus; A Philadelphia Lawyer in Canada in 1810; Civics; The Constitution of Canada in Form and in Fact (Blumenthal Lectures, Columbia University); Editor Canadian Abridgement, 42 vols, etc.; and over seven hundred articles. *Address:* 109 St George Street, Toronto, Canada; Osgoode Hall, Toronto. *Clubs:* York, Ontario Jockey, London.

Died 18 Feb. 1945.

RIDDLE, Sir George, Kt 1942; CBE 1937; *b* 27 July 1875; *m* 1903, Ada Hannah Gedling; two *d. Educ:* The School, Kibblesworth, Co Durham. As a youth in mining industry; at 21 became a clerk in the service of the Birtly Co-operative Society Limited, County Durham; rose to position of Treasurer; Secretary to the Carlisle Southend Co-operative Society Ltd, Carlisle, 1912; held many executive offices with the movement; Director of the Co-operative Wholesale Society Ltd, Manchester, 1923–43; served 6 years on Dental Benefit Council; is on the Economic Advisory Council. *Publication:* Pamphlet on Collective Capital, Inaugural Address, Newcastle Co-operative Congress, 1936. *Recreations:* reading, music, and education. *Address:* 71 Fenham Hall Drive, Newcastle-upon-Tyne, Northumberland. *T:* 35131.

Died 12 Sept. 1944.

RIDDLE, John Wallace; *b* Philadelphia, 12 July 1864; *s* of John Wallace Riddle, and Rebecca Blair M'Clure; *m* 1916, Theodate Pope. *Educ:* Harvard University; École des Sciences Politiques, Paris. Sec. of Legation to Turkey, 1893–1900; Sec. of Embassy to Russia, 1901–03; Diplomatic Agent and Consul-General to Egypt, 1903; Minister to Roumania and Servia, 1905; US Ambassador to Russia, 1906–09; to the Argentine Republic, 1921–25. *Address:* Farmington, Connecticut, USA. *Clubs:* Brooks's; Union, New York.

Died Dec. 1941.

RIDDOCH, George, MD (Aberdeen); FRCP (London); late Brigadier, Consultant in Neurology to the Army; Hon. Consultant Adviser, EMS (Peripheral Nerve and Spinal Injuries); Hon. Consultant in Neurology, Ministry of Pensions; Physician, London Hospital, and Director, Department of Neurology and Psychiatry; Physician, National Hospital for Nervous Diseases, Queen Square; Consulting Neurologist, Claybury Mental Hospital; *b* 1888; *e s* of late George Riddoch of Tarryblake, Rothiemay, Banffshire; *m* 1916, Margaret, *d* of late John Ledingham, Aberdeen; two *s* one *d. Educ:* Gordon's College, Aberdeen; The University, Aberdeen. MB ChB (First Class honours), 1913; MD (Honours), 1917. Temp. Capt. RAMC and Medical Officer in charge of the Empire Hospital for Injuries of the Nervous System; External Examiner in Medicine, University of Aberdeen; Member of Association of Physicians of Great Britain and of Association of British Neurologists; Fellow of Royal Society of Medicine (late President Neurological Section) and of the Medical Society of London; Member of British Medical Association and late President of Section of Neurology and Psychological Medicine; Foreign Corresponding Member of the Neurological Society of Paris; Hon.

Member Neurological Society, Estonia. *Publications:* various papers on Diseases of the Nervous System in Brain and other journals. *Address:* 80 Harley Street, W1. *T:* Welbeck, 2017. *Club:* Athenæum.

Died 24 Oct. 1947.

RIDDOCH, William, TD, MA, LLD, JP; *b* Rothiemay, 1862; *s* of late John Riddoch, Rothiemay, Banffshire; *m* 1887, Effie, *d* of late Alexander McPherson, Aberdeen. *Educ:* Keith Grammar School; Aberdeen University. Senior Classical Master, Robert Gordon's College, Aberdeen, 1888; Rector of Mackie Academy, Stonehaven, 1893–1927; one of General Council's Assessors, Aberdeen University Court, 1931–37; was Captain in the 7th Battalion Gordon Highlanders when European War broke out; served in France, 1915 to date of Armistice (Croix de Guerre); resigned commission 1921, retaining the rank of Major. *Address:* The Briars, Bieldside, Aberdeenshire. *T:* Cults 256.

Died 16 March 1942.

RIDER, Engr Rear-Adm. Sydney, CMG 1919; retired; *m;* one *d.* Has Legion of Honour. *Address:* 130 Manor Way, Aldwick Bay Estate, Bognor Regis.

Died 21 March 1943.

RIDGEWAY, Brig. David Graeme, CB 1933; DSO 1925; Indian Army, retired; *b* 1879; *s* of Frederic Ridgeway, late Bishop of Salisbury; *m* 1st, 1916, Margaret Gladys Buchanan MacGeorge (who obtained a divorce, 1930); two *d;* 2nd, 1931, Jean Margaret Elizabeth Miller, *d* of late Philip Grierson Borrowman, MD. *Educ:* Haileybury; Sandhurst. Bedfordshire Regt, 1898; 3rd Gurkha Rifles, 1902; served European War, 1914–17 (wounded, despatches, Bt Lt-Colonel); NWF, India, 1919–21; NWF, India, 1923–24 (wounded, despatches, DSO); Commandant, 1/3rd QAO Gurkha Rifles, 1922–25; Director of Organisation, AHQ, India, 1928–31; Commander, Allahabad Brigade Area, India, 1931–35; retired 1935. *Recreations:* hunting, tennis, golf. *Address:* c/o National Provincial Bank, 69 Baker Street, W1. *Clubs:* Naval and Military, Junior Naval and Military.

Died 2 Feb. 1950.

RIDLEY, Lady Alice; 2nd *d* of late W. Bromley Davenport; *m* 1882, Rt Hon. Sir Edward Ridley (*d* 1928); two *s. Publications:* The Story of Aline, 1896; Anne Mainwaring, 1901; A Daughter of Jael; The Sparrow with One White Feather; Margery Fytton.

Died 6 June 1945.

RIDLEY, Wing-Comdr Claude Alward, DSO 1916; MC; late Royal Air Force; *b* Nov. 1896; *s* of Louis C. Ridley, *g s* of late Thomas Ridley, Barrister, Newcastle; *m* 1925, Lillias Elizabeth, *d* of Sir Robert McAlpine, 2nd Bt; one *s* two *d. Educ:* St Paul's, London; Sandhurst. Commission in Royal Fusiliers, 1915; took Royal Aero Club Certificate, June 1915; was decorated on the field by General Haig (DSO); despatches five times; MC for work during air raids, 1915–16, and in connection with the bringing down of Zepp. L15, 1916; retired list, 1928; recalled for service, 1939. *Address:* Bleak House, de Warrenne Road, Lewes. *T:* Lewes 736. *Club:* Royal Air Force.

Died 27 June 1942.

RIDLEY, George; Editor Railway Service Journal; MP (Lab) Clay Cross division of Derbyshire since 1936; *b* Holt, Norfolk, 29 Nov. 1886; *m* 1919, Ethel Winifred Sporne; one *s* one *d. Educ:* various Elementary Schools. Member Executive Committee Railway Clerks Association, 1909–20; permanent Secretarial Staff of Union since 1920; Auditor to Labour Party, 1934, 1935; Member Labour Party Executive since 1936 (Vice-Chairman, 1942). *Publications:* various articles Trade Union and Labour Journals. *Recreations:* reading, walking, talking. *Address:* House of Commons, SW1; Winscombe Crescent, W5. *T:* Welwyn Garden 3572, Perivale 3956. *Club:* Trade Union.

Died 4 Jan. 1944.

RIDLEY, Guy, CBE 1918; Assistant Master in Lunacy; *b* 21 June 1885; *s* of late Rt Hon. Sir Edward Ridley and of late Lady Ridley. *Educ:* Harrow; New College, Oxford. Barrister, Inner Temple, North-Eastern Circuit, 1911; Private Secretary to Sir Edward Ward, Bart, GBE, etc., Metropolitan Special Constabulary and Overseas Contingents, 1914; Staff Officer to Sir Edward Ward, 1915–18; Ministry of Labour, 1918–21; Secretary, Officers' Resettlement Committee, 1918–21; Solicitor, 1923. *Publication:* The Word of Teregor, 1913. *Address:* 55 Park Lane, W1. *Clubs:* Oxford and Cambridge, Burlington Fine Arts.

Died 15 Nov. 1947.

RIDLEY, Samuel Forde; JP; *b* 1864; *o s* of late S. E. Ridley, St Helens, Isle of Wight; *m* Muriel Paget (*d* 1928), *d* of Sir W. Paget Bowman, 2nd Bt of Joldwynds, near Dorking; one *s* two *d. Educ:* Clifton College. MP (C) SW Bethnal Green, 1900–06; Rochester, 1910. *Address:* The Pantiles, Budleigh Salterton, Devon. *T:* 383. *Club:* Carlton.

Died 17 Nov. 1944.

RIDOUT, Maj.-Gen. Sir Dudley Howard, KBE 1919; CB 1918; CMG 1915; Officer St John of Jerusalem; late RE; Borough Councillor, Richmond, Surrey; Governor and Committee of Management Star and Garter Home for Disabled Men; Vice-Chairman Royal Hospital Richmond, Holloway Sanatorium, Virginia Water; Chairman, South Middlesex and Richmond Joint Hospital Board; President Richmond Branch Soldiers and Sailors and Air Force Association, BP Scouts Group and Richmond Division St John Ambulance Brigade; Commissioner of Taxes, Surrey; Member Territorial Association, Surrey; *b* 15 Jan. 1866; *s* of late Lieut-Colonel Joseph Bramley Ridout, 80th Regiment and 90th LI; *m* 1904, Maud Elizabeth, *d* of C. H. Hutton of Middleburg, Cape Province; one *s* one *d. Educ:* Christ's Hospital; Kingston (Ont) Collegiate Institute; Royal Military College, Canada; gold medallist, diploma honours. Entered army, 1885; Capt. 1894; Major 1902; Lt-Col 1910; Col 1914; temp. Brig.-Gen. 1915; temp. Maj.-Gen. 1916; Maj.-Gen. 1921; commanding troops, Straits Settlements, 1915–21; Member Executive and Legislative Council, Straits Settlements, 1915–21; retired pay, 1924; served War Office, 1888–89, 1897–1900; South Africa, Intelligence Officer (Staff Captain) Cavalry Brigade, 1900–02 (despatches, Queen's medal 3 clasps, King's medal 2 clasps); European War, Singapore Command, 1914–18 (despatches, CB, KBE, CMG). *Address:* 22 Montague Road, Richmond, Surrey. *Club:* United Service.

Died 30 April 1941.

RIDPATH, Sir Henry, Kt 1943; FZS; General Trade Adviser, Ministry of Food; *b* Liverpool, 26 Aug. 1873; *m* 1899; two *d. Educ:* various elementary schools. Over 60 years' association with Food and Allied Trades. Managing Director, Ridpath Brothers, Ltd; Past Pres. Canadian Chamber of Commerce in London; Past President London Meat Trades and Drovers Benevolent Assoc.; Chairman New Zealand and Australian Agents Assoc.; Representative of Empire Countries on Bacon Supplies Consultative Committee; Member of Council of Imported Meat Trade Assoc.; Member of London and Liverpool Provision Exchanges. *Recreation:* golf. *Address:* Portman Court, Portman Square, W1. *TA:* Foodkeeper London. *T:* Welbeck 5500. *Clubs:* Royal Empire Society, Royal Automobile.

Died 3 May 1950.

RIESENFELD, Hugo; Violinist and Conductor in Imperial Opera house, Vienna; *b* 26 Jan. 1884; *s* of Leopold and Sophie Riesenfeld; *m*; one *d. Educ:* Conservatory of Music and University, Vienna. Concertmaster and conductor with Oscar Hammerstein opera house; Conductor and General Manager of Rialto and Rivoli Theatre, NY and General Manager of United Artists' Theatre Circuit; left United Artists, 1929; now freelancing. *Publications:* 2 Operettas, Songs, Suites, Overtures, Marches. *Address:* 937 North Sycamore Avenue, Hollywood, Calif, USA.

Died 10 Sept. 1939.

RIGBY, Col Sir Hugh (Mallinson), 1st Bt *cr* 1929; KCVO 1918; MS Lond.; FRCS Eng.; FRCSI (hon.); MCh, NUI (hon.), 1933; *b* Dublin, Ireland, May 1870; *s* of John Rigby, MA, late Superintendent RSA Factory, Enfield; *m* 1911, Flora, *d* of Norman Macbeth; two *s* two *d. Educ:* Dulwich College; University College and London Hospital. Late Sergeant-Surgeon to King George V, 1928–32; Consulting Surgeon to the London Hospital; Consulting Surgeon to the Poplar Hospital for Accidents; served European War (Bt Lt-Col, Col, despatches). *Publications:* various; papers in the medical and surgical publications. *Recreation:* golf. *Heir: s* Hugh John Macbeth, *b* 1914. *Address:* Long Durford, Petersfield. *T:* Liss 128.

Died 17 July 1944.

RIGG, John, CMG 1937; member of Representation Commissions; JP; *b* St Kilda, Melbourne, Victoria, 1858; Scotch parents; *m* Louise de Cleene; two *d. Educ:* private school, Port Chalmers; St Mary's Catholic School, Wellington; private tuition in French and Italian. Apprenticed as a compositor in the Government Printing Office, Wellington, 1872, and served 6 years; first representative position, member of Board of Management, Wellington Typographical Society, 1880; later, secy of same Union, and subsequently sole representative of New Zealand at the Intercolonial Typographical Conference held in Melbourne, Victoria, 1888; was representative on the Australasian Typographical Union from that date till 1890; founder of Wellington Trades Council; President of the Typographical Society of Wellington, and President of the Tailoresses' Union and Trades Council of the same city; Member of Legislative Council NZ, 1892–1914; Chairman of Committees and Acting Speaker of Legislative Council, 1904; first President Independent Political Labour League, 1905. *Publications:* A Cross of Gold: the Currency Question Explained, 1910; Elocution and Public Speaking (Lessons in), 1921; How to Conduct a Meeting, 1920; How to Take the Chair, 1925; Elocution for Schools, 1929; Platform Oratory and Debate, 1929. *Address:* 42 Wroxton Terrace, Fendalton, Christchurch, NW1, NZ.

Died 20 Oct. 1943.

RIGG, Major Richard, OBE 1918; JP; TD; FSA; Barr Inner Temple and King's Inns, Dublin; Mayor of the City of Westminster, 1939–40; Officer of the Order of St John of Jerusalem; *b* 1877; *m* 1904, Gertrude Anderson. *Educ:* Caius College, Cambridge (MA). Major (retd) 4th Border Regt; MP (R) North (Appleby) Division of Westmorland, 1900–05; High Sheriff of Westmorland, 1909–10; Past Grand Deacon of English Freemasons; Chairman of the Trained Nurses' Annuity Fund; President of the Chartered Institute of Secretaries, 1940; Governor of United Westminster Schools Foundation, Greycoat Hospital, and Northampton Polytechnic Institute and the John Cass Foundation; President of National Temperance Hospital, 1939; Member of the London Court of Arbitration; Member of the Council of the Metropolitan Hospital Sunday Fund; Chairman of Hospital Saturday Fund; Master of the Glovers' Company, 1939–40; Vice-Chairman Abbey Division of Westminster Constitutional Assoc. *Publications:* various articles on legal questions and social reform. *Recreation:*

rifle-shooting. *Address:* 157 Victoria Street, SW1. *T:* Victoria 4042. *Clubs:* United University; Union, Brighton.

Died 29 Aug. 1942.

RILEY, Athelstan, FSA; Seigneur de la Trinité; *b* London, 10 Aug. 1858; *o s* of John Riley, Mytholmroyd, Yorks; *m* 1887, Hon. Andalusia Louisa Charlotte Georgina Molesworth (*d* 1912), *e d* of 8th Viscount Molesworth; four *s* one *d. Educ:* Eton; Pembroke College, Oxford (MA, Hon. Fellow). Chairman of the Anglican and Eastern Church Association; Vice-President of the Alcuin Club; travelled in Persia, 1881; Turkey in Europe, 1883; Persia and Kurdistan, 1884, 1886, 1888; member of the House of Laymen of the Province of Canterbury to 1932; member London School Board, 1891–97; Vice-Pres. of the Church Union; Candidate for Oxford University at bye-election, 1919; Commander of the Order of King George I of Greece; Order of St Sava. *Publications:* Athos, or the Mountain of the Monks, 1887; The Religious Question in Education, 1911; various pamphlets and articles in the Nineteenth Century and other magazines on subjects connected with education, Eastern Christians, and foreign politics. *Address:* Manoir de la Trinité, Jersey. *Clubs:* Athenæum, United University.

Died 17 Nov. 1945.

RILEY, Ben; MP (Lab) for Dewsbury, Nov. 1922–23, 1924–31, and 1935–45; *b* Halifax, 1866; *s* of Samuel Riley, stonemason; *m* Lucy Rushworth, Halifax; one *s. Educ:* Public Elementary Schools. Apprenticed to the trade of bookbinding; worked as journeyman in Bath, Brighton, and London; employed by Land Restoration League as lecturer on the Land Question among agricultural labourers in Herefordshire, Warwickshire, Wiltshire, and other counties, 1892–96; commenced business as Library Bookbinder at Huddersfield, 1896; Labour Member to School Board, 1896; Labour Member Huddersfield Town Council, 1904; served for thirteen years on School Board and Education Committee, and seven years as a member of Town Council; contested Dewsbury as Labour candidate, 1918; one of the original members of the Independent Labour Party, and member of National Council of ILP; PPS to Lord Noel Buxton, 1929–30; has travelled extensively in the Balkans; visited Russia in 1935 and 1936, and described conditions in a series of articles to Yorkshire newspapers; made a tour of the West Indies in Feb. and March 1939, afterwards writing a series of articles on impressions. *Publications:* numerous articles in the Labour Leader and other Labour publications. *Address:* 28 Westfield Avenue, Huddersfield.

Died 6 Jan. 1946.

RILEY, Brig. Rupert (Farquhar), CMG 1917; DSO 1900; Yorks Light Infantry; *b* 1 Oct. 1873; *m* 1st, 1903, Violet Louise, *y d* of late Ernest St G. Cobbold; one *s;* 2nd, 1922, Hilda St Maur, *y d* of Cecil Willoughby, Wilford, Notts; one *s* one *d.* Entered army, 1896; served NW Frontier, India, 1898 (medal with clasp); served with Field Force South Africa, 1899–1902; commanded MI Company KO Yorkshire LI (despatches, medals with clasps), European War, 1914–16 (prom. Lt-Col); Col 1920; Deputy Director of the TF at War Office, 1920–24; retired pay, 1924.

Died 12 Oct. 1941.

RILOT, Charles Frederick, MRCS, LRCP, LDS Eng.; Vice-President British Dental Association; late Member and Joint Treasurer Dental Board of United Kingdom; late Member General Medical Council; *b* Nov. 1864; *s* of C. H. and Julia Rilot; *m* 1891, Annie Elizabeth Hammond; one *s. Educ:* Kings College School; Middlesex and Royal Dental Hospitals. Formerly Dental Surgeon, Royal Dental Hospital; President (1918) and Chairman of Rep. Board (1921–29) British Dental

Association; Member of Dental Benefit Council. *Address:* 84 St Andrew's Road, Worthing, Sussex. *T:* Worthing 3431.

Died 30 March 1942.

RIMINGTON, Maj.-Gen. Joseph Cameron, CB 1916; CSI 1918; RE; *b* 20 Sept. 1864; *m* 1st, Amy Gordon (*d* 1923), *d* of Maj.-Gen. H. G. Waterfield, CB, Indian Army; one *s* (and one killed in European War, 1915); two *d;* 2nd, 1932, Mrs Loetitia (Lettie) Scott (*née* Worthington) (*d* 1933). Entered army, RE, 1884; Captain, 1892; Major, 1901; Lieut-Col, 1908; Col, 1912; served Burma, 1886–87 (medal two clasps); European War, Engr-in-Chief (Mesopotamia), 1915–19 (prom. Maj.-Gen., despatches 7 times, CB, CSI); Director General Military Works, Army Headquarters, India, 1919–21; retired on Indian pension, 1921; Fellow: Royal Empire Society; Royal Society of St George; Nat. Soc. for Cancer Relief. *Address:* c/o Lloyds Bank, Ltd, 6 Pall Mall, SW1.

Died 30 April 1942.

RING, Rev. Timothy J.; Parish Priest and Rural Dean; Canon of Westminster Cathedral since 1918; Rector of St Mary and St Michael's Church, Commercial Road, E, since 1904; *b* Co. Cork, 1858. *Educ:* St Brendan's College, Killarney; Collège des Irlandais, Paris. Priest, 1884; first Rector of Catholic Church, Silvertown, 1887; organised Catholic Mission of Victoria Docks, 1895; built churches and schools for each of them and presbytery at Silvertown; on School Board of West Ham, 1895; Chairman of the West Ham School Board 1901, till the Local Authority took charge of Education; Co-opted on Essex Education Committee, 1903; Member of Catholic Education Council for England since 1900; Domestic Prelate to the Pope, 1937. *Address:* St Mary and St Michael's Church, Commercial Road, E1.

Died 8 Aug. 1941.

RIOS URRUTI, Fernando de los; *b* 8 Dec. 1879; *s* of Jose de los Rios Pinzon and Fernanda Urruti Rodriguez; *m* 1912, Gloria Giner; one *c. Educ:* Madrid University; Sorbonne de Paris; London School of Economics; University of Jena; University of Berlin; University of Marburg. Professor in Granada University, 1911–30; Prof. of Political Science in the University of Madrid 1930; Visiting Professor of Columbia University; Hon. Professor in Mexico University; Visiting Prof. in Porto-Rico University, Habana University; Membre de l'Institut International de Droit Public; Minister of Justice, Minister of Education and lately of Foreign Affairs, 1931–33; Spanish Ambassador to United States, 1936–39. *Publications:* Origenes del Socialismo Moderno, 1911; Génesis del Derecho Público Alemán, 1913; La Crisis de la Democracia, 1917; Mi viaje à la Rusia Sovietista, 1920; Instituciones políticas de Andorra, 1921; La Filosofia del Derecho en D. Francisco Giner y su relación con el pensamiento Contemporáneo, 1916; El Sentido Humanista del Socialismo, 1925; Religion y Estado en la España del Siglo XVI, 1927.

Died 1949.

RIPLEY, Sir Frederick Hugh, 2nd Bt *cr* 1897; late Capt. 3rd Batt. A. and S. Highlanders; late Lieut 2nd Life Guards; *b* 7 July 1878; *s* of 1st Bt and Kate, 2nd *d* of David Little, Bradford; *S* father, 1907; *m* 1902, Georgina Mary Shute, *y d* of Francis Adams, of Clifton and Llyfnant, Cheltenham. Served South Africa, 1900. *Heir:* *b* Geoffrey [Barrister Inner Temple, 1912; late Lieut 1st (Royal) Dragoons; *b* 4 Aug. 1883; *m* 1908, Sybil Augusta, *d* of T. N. F. Bardwell, JP, DL, Bolton Hall, Yorks. *Educ:* Eton; Oxford]. *Address:* Brinkley Hall, Newmarket.

Died 15 July 1945.

RIPMAN, Walter; *b* London, 2 Jan. 1869; *e s* of H. Rippmann, merchant; *m* 1905, Constance, *d* of Brockwill Grier Montreal; one *s* three *d. Educ:* Dulwich Caius College, Cambridge (Scholarship, 1887 Assistant

Lectureship in Modern Languages 1890); 2nd Class in Classical Tripos, Part I; 1st Class in Mediæval and Modern Languages Tripos; 2nd Class in Classical Tripos, Part II, 2nd Class in Indian Languages Tripos; Prize for German at Int. Arts and BA Exam (Lond.); 1st in MA (Modern Languages), 4th in MA (Classics) (Lond.). Retired 1943. *Publications:* Twenty Stories from Grimm, 1896; The Fairy Tales of Master Perrault, 1897; Eight Stories from Andersen, 1898; Grillparzer, Sappho, 1898; Dent's First and Second French Books, 1898; Hints on Teaching French, 1898; Dent's First German Book, 1898; Hints on Teaching German, 1898; Elements of Phonetics, 1899; German Reader, 1899; Hauff, der Scheik von Alessandria, 1900; Heine, Buch der Lieder, 1900; Andersen in German, 1902; Andersen's Bilderbuch ohne Bilder, 1903; Villinger, Der Töpfer von Kandern, 1904; A First English Book, 1904; The Sounds of Spoken English, 1906; French and German Picture Vocabularies, 1906; Der goldene Vogel, 1907; Specimens of English, 1908; Eisenhans, 1908; Sound Charts, 1908; German Poetry, 1909; German Grammar, 1909; English Picture Vocabulary (for Japanese Schools), 1909; German Free Composition, 1910; English Free Composition (for Japanese Schools), 1909; German Free Composition, 1910; English Free Composition (for Japanese Schools), and English Sounds, 1911; Der Silberne Schilling, 1912; A Second English Book, 1913; First Steps in French, 1915; Further Steps in French, 1916; Rapid French Course, 1917; Rapid Italian Course, 1919; Shorter French Course, 1919; Rapid German Course, 1921; French Dictation; Good Speech, 1922; Rapid Latin Course, 1923; Latin Reader, 1924; Heine, Harzreise, 1928; German Grammar, 1928; Passages of Standard Prose (with gramophone records), 1929; Handbook of The Latin Language, 1930; Hauff, Die Karavane, 1931; Stories from Andersen, 1931; Dictionary of English Rhymes, 1932; Easy French Course, 1934; Easy German Course, Elementary German Composition, English Course for Adult Foreigners, 1935; New Spelling, 1941; Dictionary of New Spelling, 1941. *Recreations:* idling, in the company of children if possible. *Address:* The Playhouse Flat, Amersham, Bucks. *T:* Amersham 81.

Died 5 Feb. 1947.

RITCHIE OF DUNDEE, 2nd Baron *cr* 1905; **Charles Ritchie;** one of HM's Lieuts for the City of London; Mayor of Winchelsea, 1924 and 1931; President, Poplar Hospital; *b* 18 Nov. 1866; *e s* of 1st Baron Ritchie and Margaret, *d* of Thomas Ower, Perth; *S* father, 1906; *m* 1898, Sarah Ruth, 4th *d* of late L. J. Jennings, MP; three *s* one *d*. *Educ:* Westminster; Trinity College, Oxford (BA 1888). Vice-Chairman of Port of London Authority, 1913–25, Chairman, 1925–41; President Dock and Harbour Authorities Assoc., 1939–41. *Heir: s* Capt. Hon. (John) Kenneth Ritchie, KRRC [*b* 22 Sept. 1902; *m* 1945, Joan Beatrice, *d* of late Rev. H. C. L. Tindall, Mill Field, Peasmarsh, Sussex]. *Address:* 40 Thurloe Square, SW; Playden, Rye, Sussex. *Club:* Carlton.

Died 19 July 1948.

RITCHIE, Charles John, CBE 1935; Lieutenant City of London, Knight of Grace St John of Jerusalem; JP County of London; *b* 12 Jan. 1871; *yr s* of late Sir James Thomson Ritchie, Bt; *m* 1897, Ethel Beatrice, *d* of late David Bruce, Broughty Ferry; one *s*. *Educ:* Westminster; Germany. Partner in firm of William Ritchie & Son; late Deputy Commandant-in-Chief Metropolitan Special Constabulary. *Recreations:* golf, fishing. *Address:* 31 Knightsbridge Court, Sloane Street, SW1. *Clubs:* Carlton, Royal Thames Yacht, Royal Mid-Surrey.

Died 6 July 1950.

RITCHIE, Hon. Sir George, KCMG 1935; Leader, Legislative Council, South Australia, 1933; Member of the Legislative Council, 1924–43; *b* Goolwa, Dec. 1864; *s* of late Captain James Ritchie, Cockenzie, Scotland; *m* Charlotte, *d* of William Knapman, Port Adelaide; two *s*

one *d*. *Educ:* Grammar School, Echuca., Victoria. Member House of Assembly, 1902–22; Commissioner Public Works and Minister Water Supply, Nov. 1914–April 1915; Commissioner Crown Lands and Minister of Agriculture, 1917; Commissioner of Public Works and Minister of Agriculture and Railways, 1919–20; Treasurer and Minister of Education, 1920–22; Minister of Afforestation, 1933–36; Chief Secretary, Minister of Health, and Minister of Mines, 1933–39; acting Premier, 1935 and 1937; Member Adelaide University Council, 1927–33; Deputy Chairman, State Centenary Executive Committee; Chairman Centenary Country Organisation Committee; which sponsored the Tree-Planting Scheme; Alderman Adelaide City Council, 1932–35; Chief Caledonian Society, 1936–38; Director, Broken Hill Proprietary By-Products Proprietary, Ltd. *Recreations:* motoring, swimming. *Address:* Port Seaton, Flinders Street, Kent Town, South Australia. *T:* F3827.

Died 8 Aug. 1944.

RITCHIE, Hugh, CMG 1929; OBE, ISO; *b* 19 Sept. 1864; *s* of John Ritchie, late of HM Customs; *m* 1891, Clara, *d* of Robert Blow, Grimsby; one *s*. *Educ:* Greenock Academy. Entered the Foreign Office, 1883; retired from the post of Technical Assistant in the Treaty Department of that Office, 1929. *Publications:* Revised 3rd edn of the late Sir E. Satow's Guide to Diplomatic Practice, 1932; The 'Navicert' system during the World War, 1938. *Recreations:* golf, music. *Address:* Twyford Abbey, Park Royal, NW10.

Died 10 May 1948.

RITCHIE, Sir John, Kt 1930. Chief Inspector of Customs and Excise, 1928; now retired. *Address:* Springvale, Shandon, Dumbartonshire.

Died 20 April 1947.

RITCHIE, William George Brookfield, CB 1931; *b* 1875; *s* of late William Irvine Ritchie; *m* 1st, 1905, Euphrosyne (*d* 1911), *d* of late William James Stillman; three *s*; 2nd, 1932, Hilda Mary, *d* of late Charles Edward Ryan, FRCSI. *Educ:* St Paul's School; Trinity College, Cambridge. Barrister-at-Law, Lincoln's Inn, 1901; entered Civil Service, 1905; Legal Adviser to the Board of Education, 1928–40. *Address:* 2 King's Garn, Arterberry Road, SW20. *T:* Wimbledon 6227. *Club:* Royal Societies.

Died 16 April 1949.

RITCHIE, William Thomas, OBE; LLD; MD (Edin.), MB, CM, FRCPE, FRSE; Emeritus Professor of Medicine and of Clinical Medicine, Edinburgh University; Consulting Physician, Royal Infirmary and Deaconess Hospital, Edinburgh; *b* 3 Nov. 1873; *s* of R. B. Ritchie and A. J. Scarth; *m* 1921, M. Tyrie; two *s* two *d*. *Educ:* Edinburgh; Vienna. MO 1/3rd Scottish Horse; Officer in Charge, Medical Division, No. 27 General Hospital; Examiner in Medicine, Universities of Aberdeen, St Andrews and Durham, etc. *Publications:* Auricular Flutter; Medical Diagnosis (with Graham Brown); Diseases of the Heart (with J. Cowan). *Address:* Penvalla, Barnshot Road, Edinburgh, 13. *T:* 87752.

Died 7 Feb. 1945.

RITSON, Col William Henry, CMG 1916; VD; Director of Newcastle and Gateshead Gas Co.; Chairman of Shotley Bridge and Consett District Gas Co; *b* 1867; *e s* of Utrick Alexander Ritson, DL, JP, Muggleswick Park, Co. Durham; *m* 1892, Alexina Cochrane, 3rd *d* of John Birnie Adam, Luddick, Newcastle-upon-Tyne; one *d*. *Educ:* Leys, Cambridge; abroad. Served with 3rd Vol. Batt. Northumberland Fusiliers, 1887–1908; Lt-Col commanding 6th Batt. Northumberland Fusiliers (TF), 1908–12; Hon. Col 1931; Lt-Col commanding 16th (S) Batt. Northumberland Fusiliers, 1914–16; served European

War, 1914–16; served European War, 1914–16 (CMG, despatches). *Address:* Hindley Hall, Stocksfield, Northumberland. *T:* Stocksfield 258.

Died 12 April 1942.

RIVARD, Adjutor, FRS Can., Judge of the Court of King's Bench, Province of Quebec; *b* 1868; *s* of L. L. Rivard, notary public, and Mrs P. Harper; *m* Mrs Josephine Hamel; one *s* one *d*. *Educ:* Laval University, Quebec. Admitted to the Bar, 1891; late Prof. of Elocution and International Law at Laval University; Chevalier de St Grégoire le Grand; Fellow of la Société des Chevaliers Pontificaux; Knight of Columbus. *Publications:* L'Art de dire; Manuel de la parole; Etudes sur les Parlers de France au Canada; Chez nous; De la Liberté de la Presse; articles in Mémoires de la Société Royale and in the Parler français, La Revue du Droit etc. *Address:* 107 Chemin Ste Foy Quebec.

Died 17 July 1945.

RIVERS, Very Rev. Arthur Richard, MA; Dean of Hobart, Tasmania, since 1920; *b* Teignmouth, Devon, 1857; *s* of Richard Rivers, merchant. *Educ:* the Athénée, Brussels, matriculated at St John's College, Oxford, 1878; BA 1881; MA 1884. Ordained by the Bishop of Gloucester and Bristol, 1882; Curate of Painswick; Precentor of Sydney Cathedral and Chaplain to the Primate of Australia, 1884; Archdeacon of the Wide Bay and Burnett, Queensland 1896. *Recreations:* rowed in the college eight, played football for the college. *Address:* The Deanery, Hobart, Tasmania.

Died 1 Nov. 1940.

RIVES, Amélie, (Princess Pierre Troubetskoy); novelist and playwright; *b* Richmond, Va, 1863; *d* of Alfred Landon Rives, Castle Hill, Virginia, and Sarah Catherine Macmurdo, Richmond, Virginia; *m* 1st, John Armstrong Chanler, New York, from whom she was divorced; 2nd, Prince Pierre Troubetzkoy. *Educ:* at home by Tutors and Governesses. *Publications:* The Quick or the Dead, 1888; A Brother to Dragons, 1888; Virginia of Virginia, 1888; Herod and Mariamne, 1888; Witness of the Sun, 1889; According to St John, 1891; Barbara Dering, 1892; Athelwold, 1893; Tanis, 1893; Selene, 1905; Augustine the Man, 1906; The Golden Rose, 1908; Pan's Mountain, 1910; Trix and Over the Moon, 1909; Hidden House, 1912; World's End, 1914; Shadows of Flames, 1915; a play called The Fear Market, produced at The Booth Theatre, New York, 1916; The Ghost Garden novel, 1918; a patriotic play, Allegiance, produced New York, Aug. 1918; a book of poems, As the Wind Blew, 1920; a play on Mark Twain's The Prince and the Pauper, 1920; a book of plays, The Sea-Woman's Cloak, 1923; Love-in-a-Mist, a Comedy written with Gilbert Emery; The Queerness of Celia, a novel, 1926; Firedamp, 1929; a series of sonnets in the Virginia Quarterly Review, The University, Virginia, 1931–1933; a poem: Great Britain, 1940; in the Western Independent of Plymouth, England. *Address:* Castle Hill, Cobham, Albermarle Co., Virginia, USA.

Died 15 June 1945.

RIVETT, Louis Carnac, MA, MC Cantab; FRCS Eng.; LRCP Lon.; FRCOG; Gynæcological and Obstetric Surgeon, Middlesex Hospital; Senior Surgeon, In-Patients Chelsea Hospital for Women; Consulting Obstetrical Surgeon, In-Patients Queen Charlotte's Hospital; Gynæcologist to Royal Masonic Hospital and Queen Victoria Memorial Hospital, Welwyn, Herts; Fellow Royal Society Medicine; Fellow Chelsea Clinical Society; Hunterian Society; *b* Stockport, 21 May 1888; 4th *s* of Louis Rivett, JP, High Sheriff of Carnarvon; *m* 1915, Mary Fredericka (*d* 1946), yr *d* of Arthur H. Rowan; one *d*. *Educ:* privately; Trinity College, Cambridge; Middlesex Hospital. *Publications:* The Queen Charlotte's Practice of Obstetrics (jointly), first edition, 1927, fifth edition, 1939; Sex Ethics: The Principles and Practice of Contraception, Abortion and

Sterilisation (jointly) Modern Operative Surgery Operations of Gynæcology 1943; Tumours of the Uterus (jointly) Cyclopædia of Medicine; A Simple Method of Putting up Fractures in the Region of the Elbow Joint in the Fully Flexed Position, British Medical Journal, 1916; The Toxæmias of Pregnancy, Clin. Journal, Vol. XLIV, 1923; A Calcified Tumour of the Recto-Vaginal Septum, Proc. Roy. Soc. Medicine, Vol. XVI, 1922–1923; A Ruptured Hæmatoma of the Ovary with Extensive Intraperitoneal Hæmorrhage, Proc. Roy. Soc. Med. Vol. XVI, 1922–1923; A new Volsellum Forceps and a New Tissue Forceps, Journal Obst. Gynæ. Brit. Emp. Vol. XXXII, 1925; Carcinoma of the Cervix; A Uterus and Vagina with Placenta in Situ, Proc. Roy. Soc. Med., Vol. XX, 1927; A Portable Operating Table, Journal Obst. Gynæ. Brit. Emp. Vol. XXXIV, 1927; Endometrioma, A Case for Diagnosis, Proc. Roy. Soc. Med. Vol. XXI, 1928; Prophylactic Treatment of Cases which have had Albuminuria in a Previous Pregnancy, Brit. Med. Jl, 1929. *Address:* 135 Harley Street, W1; 55 Harley House, NW1. *T:* Welbeck 7844. *Club:* Savage.

Died 5 Sept. 1947.

RIVIÈRE, A. Joseph, ScD, FICS; Docteur en Medicine de la Faculté de Paris; Officer d'Academie; Commandeur de la Légion d'Honneur; President Medical International Association for the Suppression of War; Director, Creator, and Proprietor of the Institut Physicothérapique de Paris; Chief Editor of Journal de Physicothérapie et Annales de Physicothérapie, réunis; *b* Mauritius, 20 Feb. 1859; *s* of Jules Rivière and Joséphine Pugin de Roche; unmarried. *Educ:* Paris. Was at first a general practitioner and surgeon; drew attention to the abortive and curative action of calomel, castor oil, heat, and water in the treatment of acute illnesses, British Medical Association, 1901; was the first to talk of the medical treatment of appendicitis by these means in different Medical Congresses; was the first to use the High Frequency Sparks and Effluvia in the Treatment of Malignant Tumours and to local Tuberculosis; the first to present cases of Lymphosarcoma, Sarcoma, and Epithelioma cured by X-rays. *Publications:* Electrotherapy; Physicotherapy, Indications, Advantages, 1903; Treatment of Fibroms, Tumours, Neoplasms by Physicotherapy, International Congress of Medicine at Madrid, 1903; Thermo-luminous Baths; Carbonic Acid Baths; The Hygienic Treatment of Obesity; Physicotherapy applied to the Cure of Cancer, National Academy of Medicine, Paris, 1903; Positivism in Medicine—Nervism; Three-fourths of Sick Infants die of Thirst; Esquisses cliniques de Physicothérapie, 4 vols. *Address:* 58 Rue des Mathurins, Opéra, Paris. *T:* Anjou 36·55. *Clubs:* Interallié, Union France Amérique, Paris.

Died 1946.

RIVINGTON, Albert Gibson; Master of the Supreme Court; *b* London, 14 Dec. 1883; *s* of late Walter Rivington, MB and MS (Lond.), Consulting Surgeon, London Hospital, E; *m* 1914, Elizabeth Waltham, o *d* of late Robert Allen of East Quantock's Head, Somerset; one *d*. *Educ:* Monkton Combe School, nr Bath. Admitted a solicitor, 1908. *Recreation:* golf. *Address:* 288 Royal Courts of Justice, Strand, WC: 26 Southlands, Littlehampton.

Died 8 April 1950.

RIX, Rt Rev. George Alexander, DD; Bishop of Caledonia, 1928–45; *b* Barrie, Ontario, Canada; father English and mother Scotch; *m* 1900, Sadie, *d* of Dr Donald Gillespie, Cannington, Ontario; one *s* one *d*. *Educ:* Wycliffe College, Toronto; Barrie Collegiate Institute. Incumbent of parish of Cannington and Beaverton; Assistant Minister of the Church of Redeemer, Toronto; Dean of Wycliffe College; Rector of Orangeville, Ontario; Rector of St Andrew's Cathedral, Prince Rupert, BC; Canon; Archdeacon of Prince Rupert; Administrator of the Diocese of Caledonia; interested in the Canadian Militia and holds the rank of Lt-Col and has the long service decorations (VD); King's Jubilee Medal, 1935. *Recreations:* fishing and boating. *Address:* Bishops Lodge, Prince Rupert, BC.

Died 12 April 1945.

ROACH, Alfred Thomas, LLB London; Town Clerk of the City of London since 1935; one of HM's Lieutenants for the City of London since 1935; *b* London, 1899; *m* 1928, May, *d* of Alfred Price. *Educ:* City of London School; University College, London. London Rifle Brigade and Machine Gun Corps, 1917–19; called to Bar, Gray's Inn, 1928. *Address:* 55–61 Moorgate, EC2. *T:* Clerkenwell 2011; Cutlers Close, Bledlow, Bucks. *T:* Princes Risborough 29.

Died 28 Nov. 1946.

ROBB, Maj.-Gen. Sir Frederick Spencer, KCB 1915; KCMG 1919; KCVO 1914; CB 1905, MVO 1902; *b* 8 Oct. 1858; *y s* of late Capt. J. Robb, RN, 46 Rutland Gate, SW, ADC to Queen Victoria, and Mary, *d* of late Mathew Robinson Boulton, Tew Park, Oxon; *m* 1897, Wilhelmine Rose, *y d* of late Charles William Stoughton, JP, DL, Grosvenor Place, SW, and Ballynoe, Co. Kerry; one *s*. *Educ:* Cheam; Harrow; Trinity Hall, Camb. (MA 1883); Sandhurst. Gazetted to 68th Light Infantry, 1880; Captain, 1889; Major, 1898; Lieut-Col 1898; Colonel, 1902; Maj.-Gen. 1909; Staff College, 1888–89; Adjutant, 1890–92; Brigade-Major, Aldershot, 1892–95; Staff-Captain (Intelligence Division) Army HQ, 1895–96; DAAG, Army HQ, 1896–1901; DAAG, Soudan 1898; AAG, Army HQ, 1902–04; commanding 11th Infantry Brigade and Colchester garrison, 1905–09; in charge of Administration, Aldershot, 1910–14; Assistant Chief of the Imperial General Star, 1914; Military Secretary to the Secretary of State for War, 1914–16; in charge of Administration, Eastern Command, 1916–19; served with Nile Expedition, 1898; battle of Khartoum (despatches, British medal and Khedive's medal with clasp, brevet of Lieut-Col); European War, 1914–15, as Inspector-General of Communications (despatches, KCB, KCMG); retired pay, 1920; Colonel of the Durham Light Infantry, 1923–28. *Address:* Hethe Cottage, Bicester. *Club:* Naval and Military.

Died 8 Feb. 1948.

ROBB, Hon. John Morrow, MD; *b* Township of Downie, Perth County, Ontario, 4 July 1876; *s* of late Samuel Robb and late Margaret Isabel Morrow, Stratford, Ontario; *m* 1909, Rebecca Olive, *d* of late John Kidd; two *s* one *d*. *Educ:* Public Schools and Collegiate Institute, Stratford, Ontario; University of Toronto. Taught School for three years in County of Middlesex attended University of Toronto Medical School and graduated in 1903; built and equipped own private hospital at Blind River; First elected to Legislature of Ontario for Constituency of Algoma, 1915; re-elected, 1926 and 1929; Minister of Health, Province of Ontario 1930–34 and Minister of Labour 1934. *Recreation:* farming. *Address:* 78 Roxboro Street, E Toronto, Ontario, Canada. *T:* Randolph 8581. *Clubs:* Albany, Blind River Gold and Country, Toronto.

Died 11 Dec. 1942.

ROBBERDS, Rt Rev. Walter John Forbes, DD Oxon and St Andrews, LLD Camb.; *b* Berhampore, Bengal, 6 Sept. 1863; *s* of Rev. Frederick Walter Robberds, BA, chaplain, Bengal Establishment, and Hon. Caroline Ann, sister of 17th Lord Sempill; *m* 1896, Mary Ethel Fox, *d* of late S. G. James, Lonach Lodge, Bath; four *d*. *Educ:* Trinity College, Glenalmond; Keble College, Oxford (graduated with Honours in Modern History); Cuddesdon Theol. College. Ordained Deacon, 1887; Priest, at Gloucester Cathedral, by Bishop of Gloucester and Bristol, 1888; Curate of St Mary Redcliffe, 1887–92; Chaplain of Cuddesdon Theological College, 1892–96;

Incumbent of St German's, Blackheath, SE; Sub-Warden of Bishop's College, 1896–97; Rector of St Mary's, Arbroath, NB, 1897–99; Vicar of St Mary Redcliffe, Bristol, 1899–1904; Rural Dean of Bedminster, Bristol, 1901–04; Bishop of Brechin, 1904–34; Primus of the Scottish Episcopal Church, 1908–34. *Address:* Milestones, Forest Road, Tunbridge Wells, Kent.

Died 16 Aug. 1944.

ROBBINS, Alfred Gordon; Chairman of Benn Brothers, Ltd; Deputy Chairman of Ernest Benn, Ltd; *b* London, 7 July 1883; *e s* of late Sir Alfred Robbins; *m* 1914, Josephine, *d* of R. L. Capell, Northampton; one *s* one *d*. *Educ:* City of London School. Engaged in journalism since 1902, and in publishing since 1927; joined the Yorkshire Daily Observer, 1902 (chief of Leeds staff, 1904–06); reporter on The Tribune, 1906–08; a member of the editorial staff of The Times, 1908–27 (Parliamentary Correspondent, 1914–20; Day Editor, 1920–27); Chairman of the Parliamentary Lobbyists, 1917–18; Vice-Pres. Institute of Journalists, Pres., 1942 and 1943, Fellow, 1920, a member of its Executive Committee, and Hon. Treasurer of its Orphan Fund; Treasurer and Vice-Pres. of Newspaper Press Fund, and member of its Council (Chairman, 1929–31); Almoner of the Alfred Robbins Lodge of Freemasons (Master, 1930–31); London Grand Rank. *Publication:* Fleet Street Blitzkrieg Diary, 1944. *Address:* Cherry Wood, Woldingham, Surrey. *T:* Woldingham 3186. *Club:* Reform.

Died 18 Aug. 1944.

ROBERTON, Rev. Ivor Johnstone; *b* Dunipace, Stirlingshire, 1865; *y c* of Rev. Thomas Roberton. *Educ:* Stirling High School; Edinburgh University (MA, 1st class honours in Philosophy); New College, Edinburgh. Ordained at Ratho, Midlothian, 1891; translated to Galashiels, 1898; Minister of Regent Square Presbyterian Church, London, 1907–25; Minister of St James' Presbyterian Church, Bristol, 1925–35; of Trinity Presbyterian Church, Whitby, 1935–41; visited USA and Canada, 1900 and 1929; India, 1902–03; Moderator of Presbyterian Church of England, 1922–23; Foreign Mission Convener Presbyterian Church of England, 1927–32; DD (Glas.), 1923. *Recreations:* travel and music. *Address:* 6 Well Close Terrace, Whitby, Yorks.

Died 16 June 1948.

ROBERTS, Countess (2nd in line) *cr* 1901; of Kandahar, Pretoria, and Waterford; **Aileen Mary Roberts,** DBE 1918; *b* 20 Sept. 1870; *d* of 1st Earl Roberts and Nora Henrietta (*d* 1920), *d* of Capt. Bews, 73rd Foot; *S* father, 1914; unmarried. *Heir: sister* Lady Ada Edwina Lewin [*b* 28 March 1875; *m* 1913, Brig.-Gen. Henry Frederick Elliott Lewin, CB, CMG (one *s*, Frederick Roberts Alexander, Lt Irish Guards, *b* 18 Jan. 1915, killed in action, May 1940)]. *Address:* The Camp, Ascot, Berks. *T:* Ascot 89.

Died 9 Oct. 1944.

ROBERTS, Aled Owen; *b* Liverpool, 1889; *e s* of late Robert Roberts, Liverpool; *m* Ione Ruth (*d* 1940), *y d* of late Henry Irwin, Stone, Staffs; two *s*. *Educ:* Liverpool College. Served European War, 1914–19; Overseas, 1916; Capt. RWF, 1915; Lt-Col Home Guard, 1941; Insurance Broker (Aled O. Roberts & Co.) and Underwriter, also manages Fire, Pensions and other insurance matters for Presbyterian Church of Wales; Director Morris & Jones Ltd; Provincial Insurance Co. Ltd; Monument Insurance Co. Ltd; Clarence Building Soc.; Member Merseyside and N Wales Electricity Board and Chm. of Area Consultative Council; MP Denbighshire, Wrexham, 1931–35; JP Liverpool; Chairman Licensing Cttee; member Liverpool City Council, 1936–; contested East Toxteth Division of Liverpool By- and General Election, 1929, and Kirkdale,

1945. *Recreation:* fishing. *Address:* Sutton Hall, Little Sutton, Cheshire. *T:* Hooton 3229; Fferam Bach, Ty Croes, Anglesey. *T:* Rhosneigr 260.

Died 25 Aug. 1949.

ROBERTS, Sir Arthur Cornelius, KBE 1917; FCA; senior partner in firm of A. C. Roberts, Wright & Co., Chartered Accountants, 9 and 10 Pancras Lane, Queen Street, EC4; *b* 15 Sept. 1869; *e s* of late Stephen Arthur Roberts, Clapham Park, SW; *m* 1st, 1905, Madeline Rose (*d* 1942), *e d* of late F. C. Brown and Mrs G. V. Macdona, Holton Rectory, Suffolk; two *s* two *d*; 2nd, 1943, Dorothy Isabella, *γ d* of late Thomas Bowden, Chartered Accountant, Newcastle-on-Tyne. *Educ:* Manor House School, Clapham; New College, Eastbourne. Commenced business career in Ocean Accident and Guarantee Corporation; articled to late Sidney F. Isitt, FCA, 1895; Middlesex Imperial Yeomanry, 1897–1906; with 8th Division in South Africa, 1900–01; has held following honorary appointments, Sept. 1916–Dec. 1918; Assistant Director-General, Royal Army Clothing Department; Chief Auditor of Works Accounts Finance Dept, Air Ministry; LCC Member for Streatham, 1919–25. *Address:* Courthope House, Church Road, Wimbledon. *T:* Wimbledon 3652 and 0045. *Club:* Constitutional.

Died 29 Aug. 1946.

ROBERTS, Arthur James Rooker, MA; Headmaster of Mill Hill School since 1940; *b* 4 March 1882; *s* of Rev. Edward Roberts, Braunton, N Devon; *m* 1906, P. Vincent; one *s* two *d*. *Educ:* Mill Hill School; Jesus College, Cambridge. Honours degree in History, 1903; Blue at Rugby football, 1902 and 1903. Assistant Master at Blundell's, 1905–12; Founded Belmont, Mill Hill School Junior School, 1912; Master of Belmont, 1912–37; recalled from retirement to Headship of Mill Hill. *Publication:* The Bird Book, 1902. *Recreations:* ornithology, rock gardens, water-colour painting (Exhibitor RI and RBA). *Address:* Mill Hill School, St Bees, Cumberland. *T:* St Bees 20. *Club:* Old Millhillians.

Died 8 Aug. 1943.

ROBERTS, Carl Eric Bechhofer; *b* London, 21 Nov. 1894. *Educ:* St Paul's School; Berlin University; Gray's Inn. Private in 9th Lancers, 1914; went to Russia same year and learned Russian; member Russian Government Committee (Board of Trade, London), 1917–19; attached British Military Mission in South Russia, 1919–20; correspondent to The Times, Morning Post, Economist, New York Tribune, New Age, Utro Rossii (Moscow), Lidovy Novini (Prague), Revue de Genève, etc. in Russia, Middle East, Far East and United States; interpreter throughout Europe to chairman of (Rockefeller) International Education Board, 1924; a Private Secretary to Lord Birkenhead, 1924–30; member of Daily Express staff, 1926–29; called to Bar and began practice, 1941. *Publications:* several books on Russia; The Literary Renaissance in America, 1923; Lord Birkenhead, 1926; Winston Churchill, 1927; This Side Idolatry (a novel about Charles Dickens), 1928; The Truth about Spiritualism, 1932; Bread and Butter (a novel about W. M. Thackeray), 1936; Stanley Baldwin, Man or Miracle? 1936; Paul Verlaine, 1937; Let's Begin Again, 1940; Sunrise in the West, 1945; numerous other novels and biographies; several novels in collaboration with George Goodchild; play produced, 1934 (with C. S. Forester) Nurse Cavell; pseudonym, Ephesian; editor of Old Bailey Trial Series, 1944–. *Address:* 3 Hare Court, Temple, EC4; Leylands Farm, Abinger Common, nr Dorking.

Died 14 Dec. 1949.

ROBERTS, Chalmers; *see* Roberts, H. C.

ROBERTS, Ven. Archdeacon Charles Frederic, MA, FSA; Archdeacon of St Asaph and Canon Residentiary since 1935; General Secretary of Cambrian Archæological Association, 1919–33, Chairman, 1933,

President, 1935–36; Member of the Royal Commission on Ancient Monuments in Wales and Monmouthshire, 1930; *γ* and *o surv. s* of Rev. David Roberts, MA, Rector of Llanelidan, Ruthin; *m* 1933, Maude, 2nd *d* of late J. C. Cadman, MICE, North Staffs, and *sister* of 1st Baron Cadman, GCMG, FRS. *Educ:* Ruthin School; Christ's Coll., Cambridge. Ordained, 1886; Assist Curate of Llanelidan, 1886; Keystone, Hunts, 1887–90; Llanfyllin, Montgs, 1890–94; Newtown, North Wales, 1894–95; Vicar Choral of St Asaph Cathedral and Vicar of St Asaph, 1895–97; Rector of Llanddulas, 1897–1933; Cursal Canon of St Asaph Cathedral, 1908–20; Residentiary, 1920–30; Chancellor of St Asaph Cathedral, and Canon Residentiary, 1930–35; Rural Dean of Rhos, 1919–35; Secretary of Diocesan Conference and Diocesan Board of Patronage, 1924–35; editor of St Asaph Diocesan Calendar and Clergy List, 1896–1923; Governor of Abergele County School, 1910–34; Chairman, 1916–20; Member of the Governing Body of the Church in Wales since 1920; Member of St Asaph Board of Guardians and Rural Dist Council, 1908–33; Chairman, Dist Councils Joint Hospital Board, 1912–33; Chairman of Housing and Sanitary Comn, 1920–30; Chairman Llandulas Parish Council, 1907–33. *Address:* Bryncliffe, Little Orme, Llandudno, North Wales. *T:* Penrhynside 39282.

Died 23 March 1942.

ROBERTS, Sir Charles George Douglas, Kt 1935; MA, LLD, DLitt; FRSC; Fellow of American National Institute of Arts and Letters; *b* Douglas, near Fredericton, NB, 10 Jan. 1860; *s* of Rev. G. Goodridge Roberts, LLD, Rector of Fredericton and Canon of Christ Church Cathedral, New Brunswick; *m* 1880; two *s* one *d*. *Educ:* Fredericton Collegiate School under Sir G. R. Parkin, KCMG, the Imperial Federationist orator, 1876; University of New Brunswick, 1876 (Douglas silver medal for Latin and Greek; alumni gold medal for Latin essay; classical scholarship; graduated with honours in metaphysics, ethics, and political economy, 1879). Headmaster Chatham Grammar School, 1879; editor of The Week, 1883–84; Professor of English and French Literature in King's College, Nova Scotia, 1885–87; of English and Economics, 1887–95; Associate-Editor Illustrated American, New York, 1897; Trooper in Legion of Frontiersmen, Southampton, Oct.–Nov. 1914; Lieut, 16th Battalion The King's Regiment, Liverpool, Dec. 1914; Captain, 1915; Major, OMFC, 1917. *Publications:* Verse—Orion and other Poems, 1880; In Divers Tones, 1887; Ave: An Ode for the Shelley Centenary, 1892; Songs of the Common Day, 1893; The Book of the Native, 1897; New York Nocturnes, 1898; Collected Poems, 1900; The Book of the Rose, 1903; New Poems, 1919; The Sweet o' the Year, 1926; The Vagrant of Time, 1927; The Iceberg and other Poems, 1934; Selected Poems, 1936; Twilight over Shaugamauk and Three other Poems, 1937; Canada Speaks of Britain and Other Poems of the War, 1941. Prose—The Canadians of Old (from the French of de Gaspé), 1889; Appleton's Canadian Guide, 1890; The Raid from Beauséjour, 1894; Reube Dare's Shad Boat, 1895; Around the Camp Fire, 1896; Earth's Enigams, 1896; A History of Canada, 1897; The Forge in the Forest, 1897; A Sister to Evangeline, 1898; By the Marshes of Minas, 1900; The Heart of the Ancient Wood, 1900; The Kindred of the Wild, 1902; Barbara Ladd, 1903; The Watchers of the Trails, 1904; The Prisoner of Mademoiselle, 1905; Red Fox, 1905; The Heart that Knows, 1906; Haunters of the Silences, 1907; The House in the Water, 1908; The Backwoodsmen, 1909; Kings in Exile, 1909; Neighbours Unknown, 1910; More Kindred of the Wild, 1911; The Feet of the Furtive, 1912; A Balkan Prince, 1913; Babes of the Wild, 1913; Hoof and Claw, 1913; The Secret Trails, 1916; Canada in Flanders, vol. iii; The Ledge on Bald Face, 1918; In the Morning of Time, 1919; Wisdom of the Wilderness, 1923; They that Walk in the Wild; Lovers in

Acadie, 1924; Eyes of the Wilderness, 1933; Editor-in-Chief of A Standard Dictionary of Canadian Biography, Vol. 1, 1934, Vol. 2, 1938; also Editor-in-Chief of the Canadian Who's Who, 1937. Editor of Flying Colours, an Anthology of War Poems, 1942. *Recreation:* canoeing. *Address:* 25 The Ernescliffe Apartments, Wellesley Street, Toronto, Canada. *Clubs:* Canadian Military Institute, PEN, Toronto; Writers'; Empire Club of Canada.

Died 27 Nov. 1943.

ROBERTS, Cyril, RBA 1904; Auditor, 1914–15; Member of Council, 1915–18; Secretary, 1918–31; Member of Pastel Society; Vice-President, Artists General Benevolent Institute; portrait painter; *b* 25 Sept. 1871; 4th *s* of late Charles Roberts, MRCS; *m* 1911, Winifred Theodora Debonnaire (*d* 1929), *d* of late Major Peploe of Garnstone Castle, Herefordshire. *Educ:* Haileybury. Studied art at S Kensington, Slade, and in Paris. Exhibitor at the Royal Academy, International, National Society of Portrait Painters, Paris Salon Liverpool, Manchester, Bradford, and many other Provincial Exhibitions; Hon. Secretary Chelsea Arts Club, 1933–34. *Address:* c/o Barclays Bank Ltd, 202 Fulham Road, SW10. *Clubs:* Garrick, Chelsea Arts.

Died 7 March 1949.

ROBERTS, Rt Hon. Frederick Owen; PC 1924; JP; Trade Union Representative; Member of Northampton Town Council; *b* East Haddon, Northants, 1876; *s* of late Thomas Andrew Roberts; *m* 1899, Celia Dorothea, *d* of late Francis Sexton, Northampton; one *s. Educ:* National School, East Haddon. MP (Lab) West Bromwich, Dec. 1918–31 and 1935–41; Minister of Pensions, 1924 and 1929–31; Hon. Life Vice-President Northampton Labour Party and of Northampton Trades Council; Member Executive Council Typographical Association; Member of Administrative Council Printing Trades Federation; Member Labour Party National Executive (Chairman, 1926–27); Chairman of the National Labour Club and Member of the General Committee of the National Trade Union Club; Member of Committee of Management Royal National Lifeboat Institution; Member Board of Trustees of Trustee Savings Bank (Northampton Branch). *Recreations:* bowls, music. *Address:* Sanbree, Broadway Corner, Northampton.

Died 23 Oct. 1941.

ROBERTS, Sir George, 1st Bt *cr* 1930; *b* 20 Oct. 1859; γ *s* of John and Minna Roberts; *m* 1886, Marthe Moutié (*d* 1932); two *d. Educ:* Lycée Charlemagne, Paris. Member of Council, King Edward's Hospital Fund for London; Governor, 1919, and Almoner, 1926–43, St Thomas's Hospital; Member of Council, Metropolitan Hospital Sunday Fund; President Bath and West Society, 1932–33; Officer of the Legion of Honour; Commander of the Order of St John of Jerusalem. *Heir:* none. *Address:* Monabri, Malvern Wells. *T:* Malvern 1220.

Died 27 Sept. 1950 (ext).

ROBERTS, George Quinlan, CBE; MA; *b* Hobart, Tasmania, Feb. 1860; *m* Mary Louise (*d* 1933), *d* of Henry Waters of Chisell Grange; two *s. Educ:* The Hutchins School, Hobart; Hertford College, Oxford. Rowed in the Oxford Eight, 1883; rowed in the Hertford College Eight to the Head of the River, 1881, and won many races, including the 'Varsity Sculls and the Steward's and Goblets at Henley; went to the London Hospital as Secretary, 1888; House Governor, 1891; Secretary and Receiver St Thomas's Hospital, 1903–28; Past-Master of the Worshipful Company of Pattenmakers; Officer of the Order of St John of Jerusalem. *Publications:* Short History of St Thomas's Hospital; several papers on the position of the Voluntary Hospitals. *Recreations:* golf and motoring. *Address:* Boar's Hill Hotel, Oxford. *Clubs:* Royal Automobile, Leander, Royal Empire Society.

Died 6 Sept. 1943.

ROBERTS, Gervase Henry, CBE 1918; *s* of late Alderman G. H. Roberts, JP, and Mayor of the City of Wakefield, Yorkshire. *Educ:* Stanley Hall, nr Wakefield. Engineering Education at Leeds University and practical workshop experience of some years in London and the north of England; ten years in the service of the Lancashire and Yorkshire Railway in various positions in the Locomotive, Carriage, and Wagon Depts; Assistant Mechanical Engineer at the Royal Arsenal; Superintendent of the Mechanical Engineering Dept of the Royal Arsenal four years, and Chief Mechanical Engineer, 1918–22; Superintendent, Royal Small Arms Factory, Enfield Lock, Middlesex, 1922–31; retired, 1931. *Publication:* short paper on Engineering Research and Co-ordination before the Cambridge Summer Meeting of the Institution of Mechanical Engineers. *Address:* Boathythe, Northam, N Devon.

Died 15 Feb. 1944.

ROBERTS, Very Rev. Griffith; Welsh Examining Chaplain to Bishop of Llandaff, 1897; *b* Ty'nycoed, Carnarvonshire, 27 June 1845; *m* 1870, Jane (*d* 1915), *d* of late David Jenkin, MA, Bottwnog, Carnarvonshire; two *s* three *d. Educ:* Bottwnog Grammar School; Trin. Coll., Dublin (MA). Ordained, 1870; Vicar of Llanegryn, 1873–80; Rector of Dowlais, 1880–89; Rector of Peterston-super-Ely, Cardiff, 1898; Diocesan Inspector of Schools, Estimaner, 1876–80; Warden of Llandaff Diocesan Deaconess Institution, 1899; Fellow of Woodard Society, 1910; Canon Residentiary of Llandaff and Diocesan Missioner for Diocese of Llandaff, 1889–1903; Dean of Bangor, 1903–34. *Publications:* The Marks of Christ's Body, 1891; Salvation Through Atonement, 1910; Why We Believe that Christ rose from the Dead, 1914; Holiadur Eglwysig, 1888; Guide to Bangor Cathedral, 1934; editor of The Llan, 1884–1886; translator into Welsh of Prebendary Sadler's Church Teacher's Manual. *Address:* Hafodunos, Bangor.

Died 11 Feb. 1943.

ROBERTS, Harold; MP (U) Handsworth Div. of Birmingham since 1945; *b* Bridgwater, Somerset, 23 Aug. 1884; *s* of William Henry and Ellen Roberts; *m* 1913, Ann, *d* of George Matts Pettifor, Anstey, Leicestershire; one *s. Educ:* privately. Solicitor, 1906; LLB London, 1907; City Council Birmingham, 1922; Chairman Public Health Committee, 1926–30; Chairman Salaries, Wages and Labour Committee, 1931–43; Chairman West Midland Joint Industrial Council for Non-Trading Services, 1943–45; Alderman, 1936; Lord Mayor Birmingham, 1936–37. *Recreation:* gardening. *Address:* The Cottage, Rose Hill, Rednal, Worcestershire. *T:* Rubery 70; 106 Colmore Row, Birmingham. *T:* Central 5410. *Clubs:* Constitutional, Royal Societies; Union, Cosmopolitan (Birmingham).

Died 28 Sept. 1950.

ROBERTS, Harry; *b* Bishop's-Lydeard, Somerset, 1871; *s* of Leonard Roberts and Jane Elizabeth, *d* of John Skinner, farmer; *m* 1890, Jessie Ellen Groves; one *s* one *d. Educ:* Miss Edney's School for Young Ladies, Bishop's-Lydeard; Berrington's Preparatory School, Taunton; Queen's College, Taunton; Univ. College, Bristol; St Mary's Hospital and Medical School, London. Prize-winner at all but the first school. Taught Science in Leek Grammar School, and lectured on Chemistry of Bleaching and Dyeing for the Staffs CC for six months. Afterwards practised medicine in Cornwall and Stepney. *Publications:* The Book of Old Fashioned Flowers; Chronicle of a Cornish Garden; The Beginner's Book of Gardening; Towards a National Policy; Constructive Conservatism; The Sayings of Jesus; The Tramp's Handbook; The Still Room; England, A National Policy for Labour; A National Health Policy; editor Whitman's Leaves of Grass; Vagabond's Library, Practitioners' Handbooks, Handbooks of Practical Gardening, Country Handbooks and Poets of the Renaissance; Thinking and Doing; Abortion; Everyman in Health and in Sickness; Euthanasia, and other Essays on Life and Death; Medical Modes and Morals; The Troubled Mind; The Art of Keeping Fit; The Miracle of the Human Body; (with Lord Horder) The Philosophy of Jesus (Joint Editor); numerous contributions to Nineteenth Century, Lancet, New Statesman, Times Literary Supplement, Saturday Review, Spectator, National Review, The Fortnightly, etc. *Recreations:* chatting with friends—old and new, reading, the avoidance of uncongenial society. *Address:* Oakshott Hanger, Hawkley, Hants. *T:* Hawkley 31.

Died 12 Nov. 1946.

ROBERTS, (Henry) Chalmers; Director of Heinemann Holdings Ltd; Managing Director of The World's Work (1913), Ltd; *b* Austin, Texas, USA; *s* of Maj.-Gen. A. S. Roberts and Fanny Chalmers; unmarried. *Educ:* private schools and universities in Virginia and Texas, including law course at latter. Second Secretary American Legation, Constantinople, 1893–97; went to Turco-Grecian war as correspondent of Daily News; to Spanish-American war as correspondent of Daily Mail; sent by Harpers to Egypt in 1899; joined staff of the World's Work of New York, 1900; later came to London and arranged for the publication of a sister magazine here, and edited The World To-day (World's Work) of London, 1906–32. Member of Council of Periodical Publishers Assoc., also of English Speaking Union; Member Pilgrims, also of Committee of American Society in London. *Address:* 25 Jermyn Street, SW1. *T:* Regent 3124. *Clubs:* White's, St James's.

Died 2 April 1949.

ROBERTS, Brig.-Gen. Hereward Llewelyn, CB 1917; MVO 1906; *b* 3 Oct. 1864; *m* 1895, Julie, *o d* of late Major-Gen. H. E. Waller; one *s. Educ:* Haileybury. Entered Army, 1883; Capt. ISC 1894; Major Indian Army, 1901; Lt-Col 1909; DAAG India, 1899–1904; Commandant 16th Cavalry, 1910–14; Brig.-General 1914; served Tirah, 1897 (medal and clasp); Mesopotamia, 1915–16, commanding 6th Cavalry Brigade; battle of Ctesiphon and subsequent retreat, battles of Shaikh Saad and Wadi River (despatches twice, CB); extra ADC to Prince of Wales in India, 1905–06; commanded 4th Cavalry Brigade; retired, 1920. *Address:* 11 Marlborough Buildings, Bath.

Died 30 Oct. 1947.

ROBERTS, Hugh Douglas, CBE 1932; *b* 1869; *s* of late T. H. K. Roberts; *m* Kathleen Cassels Brown (*d* 1939); no *c. Educ:* Oundle School. Called to Bar, Middle Temple; District Auditor under Local Govt Board and Ministry of Health; Inspector of Audit; retd, 1934. *Address:* 2 Albion Hill, Exmouth. *T:* Exmouth 2664.

Died 13 Sept. 1942.

ROBERTS, H(ugh) Leslie-, MD (Edin.); *b* Manchester, 1860; *s* of Alderman J. F. Roberts of Manchester; *m* Katie, *d* of Samuel Parker, Gosport, Hampshire; two *d. Educ:* Owens College, Manchester; University of Edinburgh; London; Hamburg; Vienna; Paris. Began practice in Liverpool, 1890; appointed to the Royal Infirmary, 1893; Lecturer, 1905; Consulting Physician to the Skin Department of Liverpool Royal Infirmary; late Lecturer on Diseases of the Skin, University of Liverpool; retired, 1941. *Publications:* Mould Fungi Parasitic on Man; various contributions to scientific journals. *Recreation:* landscape painting. *Address:* Hessle Moor, Heswall.

Died 8 Sept. 1949.

ROBERTS, James Alexander, CB 1917; MB, FACS, FRCS (Eng.); Colonel AMS; *b* Indianapolis, Indiana, USA, 14 Aug. 1876; *s* of Peter Roberts, Wales, and Helen, *d* of Alexander Gray, Stirling, Scotland; *m* 1905, Muriel Mildred Stewart, *niece* of Sir William Otter, KCB; three *s* one *d. Educ:* Ontario Public and High Schools; University of Toronto. Post graduate studies,

New York. Served with Canadian Contingent, South African War (despatches); OC No. IV Canadian General Hospital, CEF (University of Toronto); post graduate studies, Paris, Vienna, and Berlin; post graduate study, Surgery, London, MRCS, LRCP 1903; FRCS Eng. 1904; Fellow in Surgery, University of Toronto; Surgical Staff, Toronto General Hospital; taken active part in Canadian Militia continuously since 1894. *Publications:* professional articles, etc. *Recreation:* active in all sports. *Address:* 38 Charles Street East, Toronto, Canada. *T:* Kingsdale 2345, Toronto.

Died 23 July 1945.

ROBERTS, James Ernest Helme, OBE; MB, BS (Lond.); FRCS (Eng.); Consulting Surgeon, St Bartholomew's Hospital; Emeritus Surgeon, Brompton Hospital for Diseases of the Chest; Consulting Thoracic Surgeon, LCC Member (Past President), Tuberculosis Association; Fellow (Past President), Medical Society of London; FRSM; Fellow, Association of Surgeons of Great Britain and Ireland; Fellow (Past President), Society of Thoracic Surgeons of Great Britain and Ireland; Member, Société Internationale de Chirurgie; Hon. Fellow, American Association of Thoracic Surgeons and Polish Society of Surgeons, Warsaw; Hon. Assoc. Etranger de la Société Belge de Chirurgie; *s* of late James Roberts, West Bromwich, Staffs; *m* Coral, *d* of late Captain J. A. Elmslie, RNR. *Educ:* King Edward's School, Birmingham; St Bartholomew's Hospital. Served European War, 1914–19; Surgical Specialist No. 5 General Hospital and No. 41 Casualty Clearing Station; Major RAMC (despatches thrice); late Assistant Surgeon East London Hospital for Children; Surgeon, Queen Mary's Hospital, Roehampton, Surgical Registrar and Chief Assistant Orthopædic Department and Surgical Out-patients Department, St Bartholomew's Hospital, and Demonstrator Operative Surgery, St Bartholomew's Hospital Medical School. *Publications:* medical articles, mostly on Thoracic Surgery. *Recreation:* gardening. *Address:* The Croft, Ottershaw, Surrey. *T:* Ottershaw 104. *Club:* Athenæum.

Died 25 Aug. 1948.

ROBERTS, Lt-Col Sir James Reid, Kt 1913; CIE 1911; MB, MS, FRCS Eng.; late IMS; Member of Council Dewas State Service, Central India, 1932–39; *b* 24 Jan. 1861; *s* of William Hoskins Roberts of Colleonard, St Fillans, and Mary Wilson, *d* of late Lt-Col James Reid, 78th Highlanders; *m* 1907, Margaret Hariot, *d* of late Col W. P. Warburton, CSI; one *d. Educ:* Dollar; Lausanne; Middlesex Hospital, London; Durham College of Medicine. Entered IMS, 1888; Agency Surgeon, Gilgit, 1890; Residency Surgeon, Gwalior, 1900; Indore, 1901–12; Administrative Medical Officer for Central India, 1906–12; Surgeon to the Viceroy, 1912–16; served Chin Lushai Expedition, 1889–90; Hunza-Nagar Expedition, 1891 (despatches, medal two clasps); Mesopotamia, 1915; Member of Cabinet Jaipur State, Rajputana; Knight of Grace, Order of St John of Jerusalem; Kaisar-i-Hind Medal (gold), 1936. *Publication:* Treatment by Intrapulmonary Injections into the Lungs in Tuberculosis. *Address:* c/o Lloyds Bank, Bombay. *Club:* East India and Sports.

Died 30 May 1941.

ROBERTS, Captain John, CBE 1919; DSO 1917; RD; RNR; *b* 22 June 1867; *s* of John and Margaret Roberts; *m* Kathleen, *d* of Edwin Thomas Henry Eckford, Oxton, Cheshire; one *s* two *d. Educ:* Llangollen Schools. Apprenticed to the sea (Merchant Service) at 17, 1885; Extra Master in 1896, after serving 10½ years in sail; entered steamship service and Royal Naval Reserve, 1896; White Star Line, 1897; Second Officer of Troopship Britannic, South African War (Transport Medal); First Command in 1909; Command of Troopship Medic, 1912–15, at Suvla Bay, Gallipoli Campaign, Aug. 1915; Command of HM Yacht Amy, auxiliary North Sea Patrol, 1915–17; Commodore of

Mercantile Convoys, 1917–19, after which rejoined White Star Line; Command of Runic, followed by Canopic, Arabic, Celtic, Baltic, Homeric, Ceramic, latter ship, 1925–27; Captain RNR 1918; retired from White Star Line, 1927. *Address:* Chadmont, 16 Stocks Lane, Chester, Cheshire. *T:* Chester 2368.

Died 8 Oct. 1943.

ROBERTS, John Gwyndeg H.; *see* Hughes-Roberts.

ROBERTS, John Keith, FRS 1942; ScD Cambridge; Assistant Director of Research in Colloid Science, University of Cambridge; *b* 16 April 1897; *o s* of H. C. Roberts, Melbourne, Australia; *m* 1924, Margaret Sylvia, *er d* of Harold William Sanderson; two *d*. *Educ:* University, Melbourne and University, Cambridge. Demonstrator in Physics, University of Melbourne; Exhibition of 1851 Scholar; Assistant in Physics Dept, National Physical Laboratory; Moseley Student of Royal Society. *Publications:* Heat and Thermodynamics (3rd ed.), 1939; Some Problems in Adsorption, 1940; papers in scientific journals. *Address:* 27 Millington Road, Cambridge. *T:* Cambridge 2978. *Club:* United University.

Died 26 April 1944.

ROBERTS, Michael; author; Principal, College of St Mark and St John, Chelsea, SW10, since 1945; *b* 1902; *s* of Edward George and Henrietta Mary Roberts; *m* 1935, Janet Adam Smith; three *s* one *d*. *Educ:* Bournemouth School; King's College, London; Trinity College, Cambridge. Science Master, Royal Grammar School, Newcastle-upon-Tyne; European Service, BBC, 1941–45. *Publications:* Critique of Poetry, 1934; Newton and the Origin of Colours, 1934; Poems, 1936; The Modern Mind, 1937; T. E. Hulme, 1938; Orion Marches (poems), 1939; The Recovery of the West, 1941; also edited New Signatures, 1932; Elizabethan Prose, 1933; The Faber Book of Modern Verse, 1936; The Faber Book of Comic Verse, 1942. *Recreation:* mountaineering. *Club:* Alpine.

Died 13 Dec. 1948.

ROBERTS, Morley; novelist and journalist; *b* London, 29 Dec. 1857; *e s* of W. H. Roberts, late Superintending Inspector of Income Tax; *m* Alice, *d* of late Angiolo R. Selous. *Educ:* Bedford School; The Owens College, Manchester. Went to Australia, 1876, and worked on Victorian railroads and in the Bush of New South Wales, chiefly with sheep and cattle; was before the mast in the Essex, Corona, etc.; worked in QMG's Department, War Office, and IS Department, Indian Office, as writer; travelled and worked with sheep and cattle and on railroads and in sawmills in Texas, Missouri, Minnesota, Iowa, California, Oregon, Canada, Manitoba, and British Columbia, etc., 1884–86; more lately in South Seas, Sandwich Islands, Samoa, Cape Colony, Transvaal, Rhodesia, Grand Canary, Teneriffe, Corsica, and Central America. *Publications:* The Western Avernus, 1887; In Low Relief, 1890; Land-Travel, and Sea-Faring, 1891; Songs of Energy, 1891; King Billy of Ballarat, 1891; The Mate of the Vancouver, 1892; The Reputation of George Saxon, 1892; The Purification of Dolores Silva, 1894; Red Earth, 1894; The Master of the Silver Sea, 1895; The Degradation of Geoffrey Alwith, 1895; The Adventures of a Ship's Doctor, 1895; A Question of Instinct, 1895; The Earth-Mother, 1896; The Great Jester, 1896; The Circassian (in collaboration with Max Montesole), 1896; The Courage of Pauline, 1896; Maurice Quain, 1897; The Adventure of the Broad Arrow, 1897; Strong Men and True, 1897; The Keeper of the Waters, 1898; A Sea Comedy, 1899; The Colossus, 1899 The Plunderers, 1900; A Son of Empire, 1900; Shadow of Allah (in collaboration with Max Montesole), 1900; Lord Linlithgow, 1900; Taken by Assault, 1901; Immortal Youth, 1902; Rachel Marr, 1903; The Promotion of the Admiral, 1903; Bianca's Caprice, 1904; Lady Penelope, 1905; Captain Baalaam,

1905; The Idlers, 1905; The Prey of the Strongest, 1906; The Blue Peter, 1907; The Flying Cloud, 1907; Lady Anne, 1907; Captain Spink, 1908; David Bran, 1908; Midsummer Madness, 1909; Sea Dogs, 1910; The Wonderful Bishop, 1910; Thorpe's Way; Four Plays, 1911; The Man who Stroked Cats; The Private Life of Henry Maitland, 1912; Gloomy Fanny, 1913; Time and Thomas Waring; Sweet Herbs and Bitter, 1914; Hearts of Women, 1919; Warfare in the Human Body, 1920; Lyra Mutabilis, The Mirthful Nine, 1921; Followers of the Sea, 1923; W. H. Hudson, a Portrait; On the Earthquake Line, 1924; Malignancy and Evolution, 1926; On the Old Trail (British Columbia), 1927; The White Mamaloi, 1929; The Serpent's Fang, 1930; The Scent of Death, 1931; Women and Ships, 1931; A Humble Fisherman, 1932; Malignancy and Evolution, new edition, 1934; Bio-Politics, 1938; The Behaviour of Nations, 1941. *Recreations:* chess, fishing. *Address:* c/o Watt & Son, Hastings House, Norfolk Street, WC2.

Died 8 June 1942.

ROBERTS, Owen Glynne, CBE 1939; OBE 1925; *b* 15 Jan. 1880; *s* of late Owen Roberts, JP, Holyhead; *m* Ellen Roberta, *y d* of late Robert Owen, Holyhead; one *s*. Member of Council of University College of North Wales, Bangor; FCIS. Entered L & NW Railway service as Apprentice Clerk at Holyhead, 1896; served in various capacities in North Wales, Ireland, Manchester, and Euston; Chief Clerk to the General Manager, 1920; Assistant to General Manager, 1922; on amalgamation of Railways, Assistant to General Manager LM & S Railway, 1923; Assistant to the President of LMS Executive (late Lord Stamp) and Supt of Central Office, 1927; Secretary of LMS Railway Co. and Assistant to President, 1929, also Member and Secretary of LMS Executive Committee, Secretary of Dundalk, Newry, and Greenore Railway, West London Extension Railway, and a Director of Crosville Motor Services Ltd until retirement in 1941. *Address:* Menai Bridge, Anglesey.

Died 16 April 1947.

ROBERTS, Paul Ernest, MA; FRHistS; Fellow, Vice-Provost, of Worcester College, Oxford; Senior Tutor, 1920–45, Junior Bursar, 1919–36; Senior Bursar, 1941–46; Delegate of Local Examinations; Governor of Bromsgrove School; *b* 20 May 1873; *e s* of late Rev. P. Roberts of Southam House, Leamington Spa, and late Margaret Wright Alcock; unmarried. *Educ:* Bromsgrove School; Worcester College, Oxford. First-Class Classical Mods, 1894; First-Class Lit. Hum., 1896; Second-Class Mod. Hist., 1897. Private Secretary to late Sir William W. Hunter, KCSI, 1897–99; to late D. B. Monro, Vice-Chancellor of Oxford University, 1899–1901; engaged in private tuition, 1902–14; Classical Sixth Form and Senior History Master, Trinity College, Glenalmond, 1914–18. *Publications:* Historical Geography of India, Part I, 1916; Part II, 1920; History of British India under the Company and the Crown, 1921; India under Wellesley, 1929; contributions to Vols V, VI, and XII of the Cambridge Modern History, the Dictionary of National Biography, the Cambridge History of India, Vol. V, the Cambridge History of the British Empire, Vol. IV, and the Imperial Gazetteer of India, Nineteenth Century and other Reviews; completed and edited Vol II of Sir William W. Hunter's History of British India. *Address:* Worcester College, and Wood Croft, Boars Hill, Oxford. *Club:* Athenæum.

Died 4 June 1949.

ROBERTS, Very Rev. Richard, DD (University of Wales; Victoria University Toronto; Vermont University USA); DLitt (University of Syracuse, USA); *b* 31 May 1874; *s* of David Roberts and Margaret Jones; *m* 1902, Anne Catherine Thomas; three *d*. *Educ:* Liverpool Institute High School; University College of Wales, Aberystwyth; Bala Theological College. First Ministry in

South Wales Coalfield, 1896–98; Assistant and Secretary to Principal T. C. Edwards, Bala, 1899–1900; Minister, The Welsh Church, Willesden Green, NW 1900–03; St Paul's Presbyterian Church, Bayswater, 1903–10, and Crouch Hill Presbyterian Church, 1910–15; President of the Metropolitan Free Church Federation, 1911; Secretary, Fellowship of Reconciliation, 1915–16; Minister, The Church of the Pilgrims, Brooklyn, New York, USA, 1917–21, The American Presbyterian Church, Montreal, 1921–26, Sherbourne Church, Toronto, 1927–38; entered the United Church of Canada at the consummation of the union, 1925; Lecturer in Theology, Emmanuel College, Toronto, 1929–32; Moderator of the United Church of Canada, 1934–36. *Publications:* The Renascence of Faith, 1912; The Church in the Commonwealth, 1916; The Unfinished Programme of Democracy, 1919; The Untried Door, 1920; The Jesus of Poets and Prophets, 1919; The New Man and the Divine Society, 1923; The Gospel at Corinth, 1924; The Christian God, 1928; The Preacher as Man of Letters, 1930; The Strange Man on the Cross, 1934; The Contemporary Christ, 1938; and others. *Recreations:* walking, fishing. *Address:* c/o Rev. D. H. MacVicar, 701 River View, Verdun, PQ, Canada.

Died 10 April 1945.

ROBERTS, Richard Arthur; Hon. VPRHistS; a Royal Commissioner for Historical MSS since 1912; *b* Carmarthen, S Wales, 1851; *y s* of J. N. Roberts; *m* 1884, Agnes, *y d* of Samuel Hallam; one *s* three *d. Educ:* private schools. Entered the Public Record Office as a junior clerk, 1872, after open competitive examination, Class I; called to the Bar, Inner Temple, 1879; Secretary of the Royal Commission on Historical MSS, 1903–12; one of the Assistant Keepers of the Public Records, 1903, and Senior Assistant Keeper and Secretary, 1912–16; retired from the Public Record Office, 1916; Inspecting Officer (legal) under the Public Record Office Act 1887, 1900–19. *Publications:* Calendar of Home Office Papers of the Reign of George III, vols 3 and 4; editor of Calendar of Cecil MSS of the Reign of Elizabeth, vols 4 to 12; Introductions thereto; The Public Records relating to Wales; Ruthin Court Rolls, temp. King Edward I, in Cymmrodorion Record Series; Calendar of the Inner Temple Records, vols iv and v; etc. *Recreation:* reading. *Address:* 2 Hare Court, Temple, EC4; Smithy Cottage, Orford, Woodbridge. *T:* Oxford 218. *Club:* Athenæum.

Died 2 April 1943.

ROBERTS, Lt-Col Stephen Richard Harricks, DSO 1917; MBE 1937; VD, JP; Civil Service of Commonwealth of Australia, retired; *b* 15 Nov. 1874; *o s* of William and Susan Caroline Roberts, of Ararat, Victoria. *Educ:* Grammar School, Stawell, Victoria. Obtained Commission Goldfields Infantry Regiment, 1899; commanded Squadron Australian Light Horse South African War, 1902; served Egypt, 1914–15; landing Gallipoli, 1915; France, Belgium, 1916–18 (despatches twice, DSO); Deputy Director of Posts and Telegraphs for Western Australia, 1928–38. *Address:* 16 Chester Street, Subiaco, Western Australia.

Died 14 Sept. 1943.

ROBERTS, W. J., MA (Oxon). Fulton Professor of Political Economy, University College, Cardiff. *Address:* University College, Cardiff.

Died 18 July 1943.

ROBERTS-WRAY, Captain Thomas Henry; *see* Wray.

ROBERTSON, Hon. Lord; Thomas Graham Robertson; Senator of College of Justice in Scotland since 1936; *b* 23 Nov. 1881; *s* of late James Hinton Robertson, Writer, Glasgow; *m* 1911, Mary Snowdon, *d* of late James Robertson, Rangoon; two *s. Educ:* Glasgow Academy and Glasgow University (MA and LLB). Admitted member of Scottish bar, 1906; KC 1922;

Senior Legal Assessor for Edinburgh, 1924; Independent Chairman of General Conferences between the Shipbuilding Employers Federation, and Shipyard Trade Unions, 1930–36; FRSE, 1937. *Recreations:* fishing and golf. *Address:* 14 India Street, Edinburgh. *T:* Edinburgh 24063. *Clubs:* Caledonian; Northern, Edinburgh.

Died 10 March 1944.

ROBERTSON, Sir Charles Grant, Kt 1928; CVO 1914; MA; Hon. LLD (Edinburgh, Glasgow, Birmingham, and Bristol); Hon. DLitt, Sheffield; Fellow of All Souls, and Hon. Fellow of Hertford College, Oxford; Officer of the Order of St John of Jerusalem; Chairman of Executive Board, Birmingham Hospitals' Centre since 1925; President, Historical Association, 1938–42 and 1945; FRHistS; Acting Domestic Bursar All Souls College, 1939–45; *b* 1869; *s* of late J. G. Robertson, Bengal Civil Service; unmarried. *Educ:* Highgate School; Hertford College, Oxford (Scholar). First Class Lit. Hum. 1892; First Class Modern History, 1893; Stanhope Prize Essay, 1891. Tutor in History to Exeter College, 1895–99; Examiner in Honour School of Modern History, 1901–04 and 1918–19, Junior Proctor, 1905–06; Fellow since 1893, and Domestic Bursar, 1897–1920, of All Souls College; Senior Tutor in Modern History, 1905–20, Magdalen College, Oxford; Principal, 1920–38, and Vice-Chancellor, 1927–38, of Birmingham University; Creighton Lecturer, University of London, 1927; Beckley Lecturer, 1937. *Publications:* The Rise of the English Nation, 1895; A History of All Souls College, 1898, Select Statutes and Constitutional Documents, 1688–1832, 1904, 6th edition, 1935; (with J. G. Bartholomew) a Historical and Modern Atlas of the British Empire, 1905; England under the Hanoverians, 1911, new and revised edition (14th), 1939; A Historical Atlas of Modern Europe, 1915 (revised and enlarged, 1923); (with J. A. R. Marriott) The Evolution of Prussia (rev. ed., 1945); Bismarck, 1918; Chatham and the British Empire (Teach Yourself History Library), 1946; contributions to the Quarterly Review and other periodicals. *Recreations:* gardening and music. *Address:* The Shieling, Ringwood, Hants; All Souls College, Oxford. *T:* Ringwood 127. *Clubs:* Oxford and Cambridge; Union (Birmingham).

Died 28 Feb. 1948.

ROBERTSON, Adm. Charles Hope, CMG 1895; MVO 1905; *b* London, 19 May 1856; *e s* of G. Robertson, CE, of Hedderwick, Scotland; *m* 1st, 1879, Mabel Adelaide (*d* 1922), *d* of late J. Wiles; 2nd, 1924, Isabella, *d* of late R. Breckons. *Educ:* Edinburgh Academy. Entered Navy, 1869; Lieut 1879; Commander, 1894; Senior Naval Officer on Lake Nyasa, 1892–95 (African medal, two clasps); employed in Dongola Expeditionary Force; rendered great service getting gunboats and steamers over cataracts (despatches, Osmanieh 4th Class; Dongola medal with clasp); Admiral, retired 1917; served as Temp. Captain RNR in Aux. Patrol during 1915–17; retired, 1909. *Recreations:* various. *Address:* c/o Admiralty, Whitehall, SW1.

Died 16 Jan. 1942.

ROBERTSON, Lt-Col Charles Lonsdale, CMG 1903; late RE; *b* 13 Feb. 1867; *s* of late Charles Robertson, RWS; *m* 1st, Louise (*d* 1937), *d* of late Fleet Paymaster Singleton Hooper, RN; 2nd, 1938, Lilian May, *d* of late Arthur James Anderson. *Educ:* Charterhouse; Royal Military Academy, Woolwich. Entered Army, 1886; Captain, 1896; Major, 1905; Lieut-Col 1913; served Waziristan, 1894–95 (medal with clasp); NW Frontier, India, 1897–98 (despatches); Buner Field Force (despatches, medal with clasp); Mishmi Expedition, 1899–1900 (despatches); served on the Chile-Argentine Boundary Commission, 1902–03; Superintendent Survey of India, 1919; retired, 1921. *Address:* Fair-acre, Axminster, Devon. *T:* Axminster 2274. *Club:* Junior United Service.

Died 26 Sept. 1943.

ROBERTSON, Very Rev. Charles R., BA; Hon. Canon of Cathedral Church of St Andrew, Inverness, since 1946; Rector of Holy Trinity, Elgin, since 1932; *b* 28 Sept. 1873; *s* of Charles Robertson and Helen McLeish; *m* 1903, Jane Courtier-Dutton; no *c. Educ:* Durham School; University College, Durham. Curate St Mary's, Glasgow, 1896–99; Bamburgh (Northumberland) 1899–1900; St Augustine's, Dumbarton, 1900–01; Rector of St Augustine's, Dumbarton, 1901–12; of St Andrew's, Fort William, 1912–15; of St John's, Greenock, 1915–22; of St John's, Dumfries, 1922–32; Canon of St Mary's, Glasgow, 1922–32; Dean of Moray, Ross and Caithness, 1935–46. *Recreations:* fishing and golf. *Address:* Holy Trinity Rectory, Elgin, Morayshire. *TA:* Rectory Elgin. *T:* Elgin 2480.

Died 16 Dec. 1946.

ROBERTSON, David, DSc, MIEE, MIES; Professor of Electrical Engineering, Faculty of Engineering, University of Bristol since 1902; *b* 26 Dec. 1875; *s* of David Robertson and Jessie R. Campbell, of Glasgow; *g s* of the Naturalist of Cumbrae (David Robertson, LLD); *m* 1908, Gladys Mary Perkins of Bristol; one *s* two *d. Educ:* Hermitage School, Helensburgh. Trained at Glasgow Technical College (made Associate, with Pender gold medal, 1897) and Glasgow University (Walker prizeman, graduated BSc in Engineering, 1899, with special distinction in electrical subjects). Works training at James White, Ltd (now Kelvin, Bottomley & Baird, Ltd), Glasgow; lecturer in electrical engineering at the Bradford Technical College, 1900. *Publications:* Dust Figures of Electrostatic Lines of Force (Proc. RSE, 1898); On the Equilibrium of a Column of Air and the Atmospheric Temperature Gradient (Phil. Soc. of Glasgow, 1900); A General Formula for Regular Armature Windings; A Method of Studying Armature Windings by Means of Winding Diagrams (Jl Inst. EE, vol. 31, 1902); The Design of Transformers in a Treatise on Transformers by Bohle & Robertson, 1910; An Indicating Coil (Jl Inst. EE, vol. 48, 1912); Electrical Meters on Variable Loads (Jl Inst. EE, vol. 49, 1912); Stray Losses of C C Machines (Jl Inst. EE, vol. 53, 1915); Damped Oscillations (Jl Inst. EE, vol. 54, 1915); Mathematical Design of Transformers (*ibid.*); Chairman's Address on Scientific Research and our Future Supply of Energy (*ibid.* 1916); An Electrical Timing Device for Short Intervals (*ibid.* 1922); Experiments with the Slide-Wire Bridge, 1922; A Safety Brake for Boosters (Electrical Review, 1924); Some Electrical Laws and Definitions (Electrical Educator, 1926); Automatic Telephone Systems for Private Exchanges (World Power, 1926); The Clock and Striking Mechanisms for the Great Bell of the University of Bristol (Trans. Inst. of Engineers and Shipbuilders in Scotland, vol. 70, 1927); Theory of Pendulums and Escapements (Horological Journal, 1928–1931, serial); Vector Methods of Studying Mechanical Vibrations: The Engineer, vol. 151, 1931; The Vibrations of Revolving Shafts (Phil. Mag., 1932); Static Balance of a Shaft with Skew Stiffness (The Engineer, vol. 154, 1932); Whirling of a Shaft with Skew Stiffness (The Engineer, vol. 156, 1933); Whirling of a Journal in a Sleeve Bearing (Phil. Mag., 1933); The Whirling of Shafts (The Engineer, vol. 158, 1934); Harmonic Analysis (World Power, vol. 23, 1935); Transient Whirling of a Rotor (Phil. Mag., vol. 20, 1935); Hysteretic Influences on The Whirling of Rotors (Proc. Inst. of Mechanical Engineers, vol. 131, 1935); Subsidiary Whirling of Rotors due to Speed Oscillation (Phil. Mag., vol., 21, 1936); etc. *Address:* 19 Cotham Road, Bristol 6. *T:* 44202; The Merchant Venturers' Technical College, Bristol, 1. *T:* 23016.

Died 8 Jan. 1941.

ROBERTSON, George Scott, DSc, BSc (Agric.); FIC; Permanent Secretary, Ministry of Agriculture, Northern Ireland; President Agricultural Section British Association, 1948; Hon. LLD, Queen's University,

Belfast, 1948; *b* 22 June 1893; *e s* of William Robertson, late Editor North Eastern Daily Gazette, Middlesborough; *m* 1920; one *d. Educ:* Durham University (Armstrong College). Formerly Head of the Chemistry Dept Institute of Agriculture, Chelmsford; some time assist Lecturer Agricultural Chemistry at King's College; formerly Professor of Agricultural Chemistry and Dean of the Faculty of Agriculture, Queen's University, Belfast; Director of Agriculture, Food and Agriculture Organisation of the United Nations, 1947–48. *Publications:* Basic Slags and Rock Phosphates, 1922; also Scientific Publications appearing in various scientific journals. *Address:* Ministry of Agriculture, Belfast. *T:* Belfast 63210; The Large Park, Hillsborough, Co. Down. *T:* Hillsborough 210. *Club:* Constitutional.

Died 22 Dec. 1948.

ROBERTSON, Graham; *see* Robertson, W. G.

ROBERTSON, Sir Henry Beyer, Kt 1890; JP, DL; Chairman Merionethshire Quarter Sessions; *b* 4 May 1862; *m* 1890, Florence (*d* 1944), *d* of J. A. Keates; two *s* three *d. Educ:* Eton; Jesus College, Cambridge (BA 1884). High Sheriff, 1890; Chairman of Merioneth County Council, 1922–23. *Address:* Palé, Llandderfel, Merioneth. *Club:* Brooks's.

Died 2 June 1948.

ROBERTSON, Engr-Comdr Hugh, CMG 1917; CBE 1921; late Royal Indian Marine. Served Mesopotamia, 1915–17 (despatches twice, CMG), and 1920–21 (CBE).

Died 5 Aug. 1940.

ROBERTSON, Lt-Col James Archibald St George Fitzwarenne D.; *see* Despencer-Robertson.

ROBERTSON, Gp Captain James Leask, CBE 1942; retired; *b* 2 April 1882; *s* of Thomas Robertson, ISO; *m* 1913, Christina Lucia Ressich; one *d. Educ:* Edinburgh Academy. Actuary (Fellow of Faculty of Actuaries), 1904–14; served European War, 1914–18, 9th Royal Scots and Royal Air Force; Royal Air Force, 1918–42. *Recreations:* golf and tennis. *Address:* 8 Campbell Avenue, Edinburgh. *T:* Edinburgh 63470. *Clubs:* Royal Scots, Edinburgh.

Died 22 March 1945.

ROBERTSON, John Arthur Thomas; Sheriff-Substitute of Lothians and Peebles at Edinburgh since 1936; *b* Cheltenham, 1873. *Educ:* Dumfries Academy; Edinburgh University, MA, LLB. Called to Bar, 1896; Junior Counsel to the Inland Revenue, 1911; Sheriff-Substitute of Ayr at Kilmarnock, 1914–21; of Stirling, Dumbarton, and Clackmannan, 1921–36. *Address:* 2 Garscube Terrace, Edinburgh.

Died 13 May 1942.

ROBERTSON, Captain John Hercules, CBE 1919; RN, retired; *b* 1864. Served European War, 1914–19 (CBE). *Address:* c/o Lloyds Bank, Bath.

Died 11 Dec. 1943.

ROBERTSON, Laurence, CSI 1916; *s* of W. A. Robertson of Sandhills, Monkton, Ayrshire; *m* Marjorie Frances (*d* 1944), *d* of David Greig, Glasgow; two *s* three *d. Educ:* Glasgow Academy and Univ.; Balliol College, Oxford University. Passed ICS Exam. in 1892; served as Assistant Collector, Bombay; Colonization Officer, Jamrao Canal, 1898–1901; Under-Secretary, Government of India, 1903–07; Private Secretary to HE the Governor of Bombay, 1907–08; Secretary to Government of Bombay, 1908–11; Administrator, Junagarh State, Kathiawar, Bombay Presidency, 1911–13; Political Secretary, Bombay, 1913–18; Inspector-General, Police, 1919–21; retired, 1923. *Publication:* paper on Canal Colonies in India, read before

Society of Arts, 1907 (silver medal). *Recreations:* shooting, fishing, golf. *Address:* The Barn, Effingham, Surrey. *T:* Bookham 227. *Club:* East India and Sports.

Died 9 Jan. 1945.

ROBERTSON, Sir MacPherson, KBE 1935; Kt 1932; FRGS; Governing Director of MacRobertson, Confectionery Manufacturers, Melbourne; *b* Ballarat, 6 Sept. 1860; *s* of David and Margaret Robertson; *m* Elizabeth Robertson; two *s* one *d. Educ:* Ballarat; Leith, Scotland. Financed the British Australian and New Zealand Antarctic Expedition, 1929; also an exploring expedition by motor vehicles which made the circuit of Australia, 1928. Placed £100,000 at the disposal of the Victorian Government for use in connection with the Centenary Celebrations of the establishment of Melbourne, 1933. *Recreations:* croquet, and ball punching. *Address:* 217 Argyle Street, Fitzroy, Melbourne, N6, Australia. *TA:* Old Gold, Melbourne. *T:* J 3388.

Died 20 Aug. 1945.

ROBERTSON, Margaret Ethel; *b* 1861; 3rd *d* of late George S. Robertson; unmarried. *Educ:* home; Newnham College, Cambridge, Med. and Mod. Lang. Tripos, Class I, 1889; Ladies' College, Cheltenham (Training Department). Assistant Mistress Bedford High School, 1890–93; Head-Mistress Christ's Hospital (Girls' School), Hertford, 1893–1921; Acting Principal, St Hugh's College, Oxford, Trinity Term, 1924; President of the Association of Head Mistresses, 1913–15; Associate of Newnham College, Cambridge, 1896–1908. *Publication:* Contributor to Public Schools for Girls, 1910. *Recreation:* foreign travel. *Address:* 29 Leckford Road, Oxford. *Club:* University Women's.

Died 24 Jan. 1943.

ROBERTSON, Sir Robert, KBE 1918; FRS 1917; MA, DSc; LLD; Director of the Salters' Institute of Industrial Chemistry since 1937; *b* Cupar, 17 April 1869; *s* of late J. A. Robertson, DDS, Cupar; *m* 1903, Kathleen (*d* 1938), *e d* of late Hugh Stannus, FRIBA; one *s* one *d. Educ:* Madras Academy, Cupar; St Andrews University. Late chemist in charge of laboratory and sections of manufacture, Royal Gunpowder Factory, Waltham Abbey; Director of Explosives Research, Research Department, Royal Arsenal, Woolwich; Government Chemist, 1921–36; returned to Armament Research Dept, 1939–46; physical chemist, inventor of new explosives and processes; Pres., Faraday Society, 1923–24; Pres., Section B (Chemistry), British Assoc., 1924; Treasurer Royal Institution, 1929–46; Davy Medal, Royal Soc., 1944. *Publications:* articles on chemistry, on explosives, on absorption spectra in infra-red and on diamond, in Journals of Royal Society, Chemical Society, etc. *Recreations:* fishing, golf. *Address:* 51 Bedford Court Mansions, WC1. *T:* Museum 0942. *Club:* Athenæum.

Died 28 April 1949.

ROBERTSON, Tom; landscape painter; Hon. Member, Royal Institute of Oil Painters; Membre de l'Association des Artistes Peintres, Sculpteurs, Architectes, Graveurs, et Dessinateurs, Paris; *b* Glasgow, 25 June 1850; γ *s* of David Robertson, LLD, FLS, etc. *Educ:* Glasgow Academy. Studied art at Glasgow School of Art, and under Benjamin Constant in Paris; gold medal, Munich; hon. mention Paris Salon, 1904; gold medal, Nantes, 1910. Exhibitor at principal British and Continental galleries. Principal pictures: En Ecosse, exhibited at the Paris Salon, and purchased by the French Government for the Musée National du Luxembourg; Luna Sorgente, in the private collection of HM the King of Italy; The Morning Star, in the Musée des Beaux-Arts, Nantes; Nocturne, Venice, in the Dublin Art Gallery; The Silvery Sea, The Golden Moon, The Mystic Moon, The Haven under the Hill, pictures of Venice, Southern

Morocco, and the Atlas Mountains. *Publications:* magazine articles. *Recreation:* yachting. *Address:* Claremont, Denton Road, Eastbourne. *Club:* Savage.

Died 3 Feb. 1947.

ROBERTSON, (Walford) Graham, RP; RBA; ROI; artist; *b* 8 July 1866. *Educ:* Slough; Eton. Pupil of late Albert Moore. *Publications:* Author and illustrator of A Masque of May Morning; A Year of Songs for a Baby in a Garden; Gold, Frankincense, and Myrrh; The Baby's Day Book; illustrator and collector of Old English Songs and Dances, and Songs of Old Canada. *Plays:* Pinkie and the Fairies; The Slippers of Cinderella; Archibald; Alexander the Great; Old Chiddingfold, a Village Pageant Play; The Town of the Ford, a Pageant Play of Guildford; The Fountain of Youth (a comic opera); an adaption of Garrick's play, Miss in her Teens; and of George Colman's The Deuce is in Him; Time Was, a book of memories. *Address:* 9 Argyll Road, Kensington, W; Sandhills, Witley, Godalming, Surrey. *Club:* Garrick.

Died 4 Sept. 1948.

ROBERTSON, Walter James; Advocate; Sheriff-Substitute of Lanarkshire at Glasgow since 1925; *b* 1869; *s* of W. W. Robertson, HM Surveyor for Scotland, Office of Works, Edinburgh; *m* Mary McIver, *d* of Gilchrist Gray Pattison, of the firm of Pattison & McNair, stockbrokers, Edinburgh. *Educ:* Royal High School, Edinburgh; St Andrews University; Edinburgh University. Called to the Scots Bar, 1896; Sheriff-Substitute of the Sheriffdom of Ayr at Kilmarnock, 1922–25. *Address:* 13 Kew Terrace, Glasgow, W2.

Died 14 Dec. 1942.

ROBERTSON, Lt-Col William, VC 1899; CBE 1946 (OBE 1917); late Gordon Highlanders; Recruiting Staff Officer, Scottish Command, retd; *b* 27 Feb. 1865. Enlisted Gordon Highlanders, 1884; promoted Warrant Officer, RSM; commissioned, 1900; served European War, 1914–18; was promoted Lt-Col and granted OBE for war services, 1917; presented with freedom Royal Burgh of Dumfries, 1900; JP, City of Edinburgh, 1920; Chevalier Legion of Honour, 1935. Since retirement engaged in voluntary work for disabled ex-Service men; Vice-Pres. Lady Haig's Poppy Factory, Canongate, Edinburgh; Vice-Pres., British Legion (Scotland); Chairman, Lothians War Pensions Cttee; Exec. Member, Earl Haig Fund. *Address:* 3 East Brighton Crescent, Portobello, Midlothian.

Died 6 Dec. 1949.

ROBERTSON, William Albert, CBE 1939; MC; TD; Col, late RAMC, TA; Medical Practitioner; *b* 6 Sept. 1885; *s* of late John Robertson, manufacturer, Dundee and Mexico; *m* 1918, Elspeth Jessie, *yr d* of late Wm Lindsay, JP, Dundee and Broughty Ferry; two *s. Educ:* High School, Dundee; University College, Dundee; Edinburgh University. Certificate of Tropical Diseases and MB, ChB, Edinburgh Univ. 1907; MD (Edin.) 1926; Hon. Surgeon Hartlepools Hospital and Police Surgeon Hartlepool, 1913. Medical Officer Durham RGA 1914; BEF France, 50th (Northumbrian) Div., 1915–18 (despatches, MC); MO i/c North Scottish RGA, 1921; Officer Commanding 152nd (Highland) Field Ambulance, TA 1928–32; ADMS 51st (Highland) Div. TA, since 1935; served War of 1939–45 (prisoner); visiting MO, Dundee Convalescent Home, Barnhill; Hon. Consulting Surgeon and Physician, Royal Victoria Hospital, Dundee; Hon. MO Black Watch Memorial Home, Dunalistair; Medical Superintendent Armitstead Convalescent Home for Children and Infants. *Recreations:* British Rugby touring team, South Africa, 1910; golf, shooting, fishing. *Address:* Westbourne, Broughty Ferry, Dundee, Angus. *TA and T:* Broughty Ferry 7326. *Clubs:* Eastern, Dundee; Royal and Ancient Golf, St Andrews.

Died 26 March 1942.

ROBERTSON, William Haggerston A.; *see* Askew Robertson.

ROBERTSON, Rev. William Lewis, MA, DD; Minister Emeritus; *b* Kilmarnock, Ayrshire, 1860; *s* of Rev. Patrick W. Robertson, Portobello, Edinburgh, and Isobel Shaw; *m* Anne, *d* of James Glen, Greenock. *Educ:* Gilbertfield House, Hamilton; Collegiate School, Edinburgh; Edinburgh University; New College, Edinburgh. Minister of St Thomas' United Free Church, Greenock, 1888–1903; Minister of Windsor Place Presbyterian Church, Cardiff, 1903–18; Clerk of Synod, English Presbyterian Church, 1908–18; General Secretary of the Presbyterian Church of England, 1918–30; Secretary of the Federal Council of the Evangelical Free Churches of England, 1918–35; Moderator of General Assembly, 1930; Moderator of the Federal Council, 1932–34; Minister at Dulnain Bridge, Morayshire, 1935–39. *Address:* Corfe Cottage, Lossiemouth, Morayshire.

Died 4 Dec. 1947.

ROBINS, Ven. William Aubrey, MA; *b* 23 Sept. 1868; *s* of George A. Robins and H. C. Gott; *m* 1907; two *d*. *Educ:* Marlborough; Trinity College, Oxford; Wells Theological College. Curate, St Mary Redcliffe, Bristol; Missionary, British Columbia; Vicar, St Martin's, Bristol; Vicar, Cirencester; St Paul's, Bedford; Archdeacon of Bedford, 1935–45, Archdeacon Emeritus, 1946. *Recreation:* fishing. *Address:* Hatching Green House, Harpenden. *T:* 1088.

Died 22 Nov. 1949.

ROBINSON, Albert, CB 1938; LLB; *b* 5 Jan. 1878; *s* of John Robinson, Bandon, Cork, Ireland; *m* 1906, Florence Mary, *d* of Dr A. W. Higgs, Chelsea; three *s* one *d*. *Educ:* Bandon Grammar School, Co. Cork; Fermoy College, Co. Cork; London University. Solicitors' Final Examination (Honours), 1899. Entered Civil Service (Inland Revenue), 1899; LLB (Lond.), First in First Class Honours, University Law Scholar, 1902; Assistant Controller of Death Duties, 1932; Deputy Controller of Death Duties, 1933; Controller of Death Duties, 1935–38; retired, 1938; Registrar of Compensation (Defence) Tribunals, 1939. *Address:* Innisfree, Temple Sheen, SW14. *Club:* Devonshire.

Died 17 Nov. 1943.

ROBINSON, Rev. Canon Albert Gossage; Canon Residentiary of Winchester, 1908–33; Examining Chaplain to Bishop of Winchester, 1908–41, and to Bishop of Salisbury, 1939–46; Treasurer of Winchester Cathedral, 1909–32; Proctor in Convocation for Diocese of Winchester, 1924–33; Pro-Prolocutor, 1926–33; Cathedral Commissioner, 1931–33; *b* 12 Nov. 1863; *s* of late Joseph Henry Robinson, of Wellingborough, and Mary Anne, *d* of Thomas Gossage; *m* 1896, Edith (*d* 1941), *d* of late Rev. T. W. Sidebotham, Vicar of St Thomas-on-the-Bourne, Farnham; three *s* one *d*. *Educ:* Lord Williams' Grammar School, Thame; Christ's College, Cambridge (mathematical scholar, wrangler). Ordained, 1887; Curate of Darlington, 1887–89; Rownhams, Hants, 1889–90; Meole-Brace, 1890–95; Rector of Toft, 1895–98; Busbridge 1898–1905; Vicar of Ryde, 1905–08; Warden of the Winchester Diocesan Deaconess Home, Portsmouth, 1905–09; Archdeacon of Surrey, 1908–22; Editor of the Chronicle of Convocation, 1912–22; Select Preacher at Cambridge, 1917; Lady Margaret's Preacher at Cambridge, 1918 and 1929. *Address:* 30 The Close, Salisbury. *T:* 2392.

Died 13 Sept. 1948.

ROBINSON, Sir Alfred Theodore Vaughan, KBE 1939; CB 1936; CBE 1927; Regional Transport Commissioner, Bristol, since 1941; *b* 1879; *s* of Theodore and Ada Robinson; *m* 1908, Muriel, *d* of Dr J. R. Hill; two *s* one *d*. *Educ:* Merchant Taylors' School; St John's College, Oxford. Treasury Officer of Accounts,

1913; Controller of Cost Accounts, War Office, 1921; Deputy Secretary, Ministry of Transport, 1934–40. *Address:* 35 Julian Rd, Bristol 9. *Clubs:* National; Bristol.

Died 16 Dec. 1945.

ROBINSON, Arthur, MA, DCL; *b* 10 March 1864; 2nd *s* of David Metcalfe Robinson; *m* 1899, Edith Louise, *d* of Samuel Jones; two *d*. *Educ:* privately; Bishop Hatfield's Hall, Durham. Theol Scholar, 1887; Hebrew Prizeman, 1888–89; Theol Prize Exhibitioner, 1889; BA (Cl.-Hon.) 1891; Gabbett Essay Prizeman, 1892; MA, 1894; Fellow, 1895–99; BCL 1896; DCL 1900. Lecturer in Classics, 1899–1910; Junior Proctor, 1901–04, 1916–17; Senior Proctor, 1904–07, 1918–19; Censor of the Unattached Students, 1907–10; Secretary to the Council of the Durham Colleges, 1910–15; Bursar of Hatfield Hall, 1899–1919; Secretary of Examinations, 1919–22; Master of Hatfield College, Durham, 1923–40; Professor of Logic and Psychology, University of Durham, 1910–22, 1935–40; Vice-Chancellor of the University, 1922–23; Professor of Education and Psychology, and Head of the Department of Education (Durham Division), 1923–35; JP 1928. *Publications:* occasional contributions to philosophical reviews and societies. *Address:* 9 West Road, Cambridge.

Died 21 March 1948.

ROBINSON, Hon. Sir Arthur, KCMG 1923; CMG 1921; Member of Legislative Council of the State of Victoria, 1912–25; Solicitor-General and Attorney-General, and Minister in charge of Morwell Electricity Scheme, Victoria, 1918–24; *b* 23 April 1872; 4th *s* of Anthony Bennett and Harriet Robinson, of Melbourne; *m* 1st, Annie Summers (*d* 1937), 2nd *d* of W. S. Puckle, Melbourne, Banker; one *s* one *d*; 2nd, 1939, Beverley Nelson, *d* of B. L. Wood, Port Kembla, NSW; one *s*. *Educ:* Scotch College, Melbourne; Melbourne University. Admitted Solicitor, 1896; Hon. Sec., Law Institute of Victoria, 1902–18; Hon. Secretary, Council of Legal Education, 1904–18; MLA Victoria, 1900–02; member Federal House of Representatives, 1903–06; President Australian Natives Association, 1903; practising as a solicitor and notary in Melbourne. *Recreation:* golf. *Address:* 36 Walsh Street, South Yarra, SE1; Collins House, Collins Street, Melbourne, C1. *TA:* Mandamus, Melbourne. *Clubs:* Melbourne, Royal Melbourne Golf, Melbourne.

Died 17 May 1945.

ROBINSON, Prof. Arthur, LLD, MD, FRCS Eng. and Edin.; Emeritus Professor of Anatomy, The University, Edinburgh; Fellow King's College, London; *b* 1862; *m* 1888, Emily, 3rd *d* of John Baily. *Educ:* Edinburgh University (Gold medallist). Demonstrator of Anatomy, Edinburgh University; Demonstrator of Anatomy, Owens College, Manchester; Lecturer in the Victoria University; Lecturer on Anatomy, Middlesex Hospital; Professor of Anatomy, King's College, London; Hunterian Professor of Anatomy, Royal College of Surgeons; Professor of Anatomy, Birmingham University. *Publications:* Articles on Anatomy and Embryology in the Journal of Anatomy and the Quarterly Journal of Microscopical Science and the Transactions of the Royal Society of Edinburgh; editor of Cunningham's Manual of Practical Anatomy, 1910–1932; editor of Cunningham's Text-Book of Anatomy, 1913–1932. *Address:* Royal Bank of Scotland, Forrest Road Branch, Edinburgh.

Died 3 Dec. 1948.

ROBINSON, Sir Arthur; *see* Robinson, Sir W. A.

ROBINSON, Hon. Clifford William, BA, LLD; *b* Moncton, NB, 1 Sept. 1866; *s* of William J. Robinson and Margaret Trenholm, both Canadians; *m* 1st, 1890; no *c*; 2nd, 1933. *Educ:* common schools of Westmorland County; Mount Allison Male Academy; Univ. of Mount Allison Coll., Sackville, NB. Attorney-at-law, 1892; practised law at Moncton since that time; served as

Alderman and Mayor of Moncton; contested County of Westmorland as Liberal candidate, 1896; elected by acclamation Member of Provincial Parliament, 1897; re-elected 1899, 1903, and 1908; Speaker, 1903; Provincial Secretary, 1907; Prime Minister, 1907; Leader of Opposition in Provincial Parliament of New Brunswick, 1908–11; Member for Moncton City, 1917–24; called to the Senate, 1924; Member of Government of NB without portfolio; Minister of Lands and Mines, 1920. *Address:* Moncton, New Brunswick, Canada. *T:* 310.

Died 27 July 1944.

ROBINSON, Captain David Lubbock, DSO 1918; RMA retired; *b* 11 Aug. 1882; *s* of Very Rev. J. J. Robinson, Dean of St Ann's, Belfast, and Harriet, *d* of Sir John William Lubbock, 4th Bart, and *sister* of 1st Lord Avebury. *Educ:* St Columba's College, Rathfarnham; Trinity College, Dublin. Served European War (DSO, Croix de Guerre with palm, despatches); Senator, Eire. *Recreation:* shooting. *Address:* Glendalough House, Annamoe, Co. Wicklow. *Clubs:* Savile; St Stephen's Green, Dublin.

Died 21 Aug. 1943.

ROBINSON, Sir Douglas Innes, 6th Bt *cr* 1823; *b* 24 Sept. 1863; *s* of late Major-General John Innes Robinson; *S* brother, 1924; *m* 1st, 1903, *cousin* Violet (*d* 1931), *d* of late Charles Herbert Ames, HEICS; 2nd, 1932, Alice Diane, *d* of late Stephen de Maide Waller and *widow* of Arthur Cole Ellis. *Heir:* none. *Address:* 3 Station Villas, Winchcombe, near Cheltenham.

Died 7 Nov. 1944 (ext).

ROBINSON, Sir (Frederick) Percival, KCB 1944; CB 1941; Director (ex-officio) Anglo-Iranian Oil Co. since 1946; *b* 1887; *o s* of F. A. Robinson, The Tilt House, Cobham, Surrey; *m* 1st, Violet Mary Boileau Willock Pollen (*d* 1927); one *d*; 2nd, Marjorie Zuleika Thursfield. *Educ:* Winchester; Pembroke College, Cambridge (Wrangler 1909; Cl. 1, Hist. Tripos Pt II, 1910; Le Bas Prize 1911, MA). Entered Civil Service Class I, 1911; member of the Balfour Mission to USA, 1917; Private Secretary to the Shipping Controller, 1918; Principal HM Treasury, 1919; Assistant Financial Secretary, Sudan Government, 1926–30; Member of the (Indian) Federal Finance Committee, 1932; Assistant Secretary, HM Treasury, 1932, Financial Secretary to the King, 1937–41; Sec. to the War Damage Commission, 1941–43; Permanent Secretary Ministry of Works, 1943–46; Officer Légion d'Honneur, 1939; Hon. Mem. Phi Beta Kappa, 1917; Member of Court of Merchant Taylors Company. *Recreation:* fishing. *Address:* Hillands, Dedham, Essex. *Clubs:* Brooks's, Oxford and Cambridge.

Died 31 Aug. 1949.

ROBINSON, George Drummond, MD, BS (Lond.), FRCP; Consulting Surgeon for Diseases of Women, Westminster and West London Hospitals; late Examiner in Obstetric Medicine, University of Cambridge; late Examiner, Midwifery and Diseases of Women, University of London and Conjoint Board, Royal Colleges of Physicians and Surgeons; *b* Kingston, Jamaica, 1 Oct. 1864; *s* of Edward H. Robinson, MD; *m* 1906, Constance Evelyn, *d* of late Joseph Martin, JP; two *d*. *Educ:* Bedford School; St Bartholomew's Hospital; London University. Obstetric Resident and Tutor, St Bartholomew's Hospital; Assistant Obstetric Physician, West London Hospital, 1896; Westminster Hospital, 1900; Obstetric Physician, West London Hospital, 1909; Westminster Hospital, 1908; Examiner, Royal Colleges of Physicians and Surgeons, 1906–11; reappointed, 1912 and 1919; London University, 1910; Royal Colleges of Physicians and Surgeons, reappointed, 1919; University of Wales, 1920. *Publications:* Some Micro-organisms of Obstetrical and Gynæcological Interest, 1895; Progress of Gynæcology and Midwifery during the Queen's

reign, 1897; Vulval Discharges in Children, 1899; other medical papers. *Recreations:* cricket, Rugby football. *Address:* 296 The Hills' Road, Cambridge.

Died 19 Aug. 1950.

ROBINSON, Gerald Philip; *b* London, 1858; 3rd *s* of late Sir J. C. Robinson; *m* 1881, Rosa Adélé Macdonough; one *s* one *d*. *Educ:* Westminster; Germany; Slade School of Art. Appointed Mezzotinto Engraver to Queen Victoria, 1890; to the King, 1901; Founder and President of Society of Mezzotint Engravers; Hon. Member Académie des Beaux-Arts, Antwerp; medals, etc., for engraving, Paris Salon, 1880; also Berlin and Chicago; at present working on the eoliths of Somerset. *Principal Plates:* Henrietta Maria, after Vandyck; Burgomaster, after F. Hals; Princesses Mary and Sophia, after Hoppner; Parson's Daughter, after Romney; Passing of Arthur, after Dicksee; Perdita, after Gainsborough. *Publications:* Re-drafts of Copyright Bills; Encyclopædia articles. *Recreation:* art research. *Address:* Newton Cottage, Kelston, Bath.

Died 21 Nov. 1942.

ROBINSON, Prof. Gilbert Wooding, CBE 1948; FRS 1948; MA, ScD; Professor of Agricultural Chemistry, University College of North Wales, Bangor, since 1926; JP Caernarvonshire; *b* 7 Nov. 1888; *s* of John Fairs Robinson and Mary Emma Wooding; *m* 1st, 1913, Winifred Annie Rushforth (*d* 1945); one *s* three *d*; 2nd, 1949, Mary Isabel, *e d* of late Very Rev. H. L. James, DD, Dean of Bangor. *Educ:* Wolverhampton Grammar School; Gonville and Caius Coll., Cambridge (Scholar). Demonstrator School of Agriculture, Cambridge, 1911–12; Adviser in Agricultural Chemistry, University Coll., N Wales, Bangor, 1912–46; Independent lecturer in Agricultural Chemistry at UC NW Bangor, 1920; President of Commission I, International Society of Soil Science, since 1930; Director of Soil Surveys for England and Wales, 1939–46; Chm., Bangor Dio. Religious Education Committee, since 1939; Miembro de Honor, Instituto Español de Edafología, Ecología, y Fisiología Vegetal, Madrid. *Publications:* Survey of Soils and Agriculture of Shropshire, 1913; Soils, their Origin, Constitution, and Classification, An Introduction to Pedology, 1932, 1936 (2nd edn), 1949 (3rd edn), German Edition, 1939; Mother Earth, 1937, 1946 (2nd edn); Revised Edition of The Soil (by late Sir Daniel Hall), 1945; numerous papers. *Recreations:* golf, gardening. *Address:* Bodfair, Bangor, Caernarvonshire. *T:* Bangor 518.

Died 6 May 1950.

ROBINSON, Lt-Col Sir Heaton Forbes, Kt 1939; CMG 1930; MInstCE, ACGI; *b* 1873; 3rd *s* of Maj.-Gen. Wellesley G. W. Robinson, CB; *m* 1900, Jessie (*d* 1939), *y d* of D. Doddrell, Beechwood, Helensburgh. *Educ:* Westward Ho!; City and Guilds School of Engineering, South Kensington; Germany. Attached Staff of Sir John Wolfe Barry and Partners; travelled Africa, South America, Near East, etc.; Served European War, RASC France, Aug. 1914–19; promoted Major, 1915; commanding Outreau Depôt and Camp Commandant, 1916; promoted Lieut-Colonel, 1917; commanding No. 3 Base Supply Depôt, 1917–19 (despatches); Deputy Director of Works, Imperial War Graves Commission, 1920–25, Director of Works, 1926–38. *Address:* Fircones, RR1, Victoria, BC, Canada.

Died 13 July 1946.

ROBINSON, Maj.-Gen. Henry R.; *see* Rowan-Robinson.

ROBINSON, Rear-Adm. Sir Henry Russell, KCMG 1917; Director-General Ports and Lighthouses, Egypt, 1908–20; *b* 28 April 1856; *s* of late Rev. G. W. Robinson of Walmley, Warwickshire; *m* 1st, 1886, Ethel (*d* 1913), *d* of Hon. W. Eccles of Trinidad; two *d*; 2nd, 1917, Margaret, *widow* of late Judge Wakeman-Long. Entered Royal Navy, 1870; Commander, 1895;

Captain, 1900; retired Rear-Adm. 1909; when in command of HMS Tauranga rendered special assistant in establishing the Australasian Royal Naval Reserve, New Zealand Branch; second class orders of the Medjidie and the Nile; a Pasha of Egypt. *Address:* Brightwell Cottage, Burley, Ringwood, Hants.

Died 7 July 1942.

ROBINSON, Rev. Henry Wheeler, Hon. DD (Edin. and Man.); MA (Oxon and Edin.); Speaker's Lecturer in Biblical Studies and formerly Reader in Biblical Criticism in the University of Oxford; *b* 1872; *o c* of George Robinson, Northampton; *m* 1900, Alice Laura Ashford; one *s* two *d. Educ:* private schools; Regent's Park College; Edinburgh Univ.; Mansfield College, Oxford; University, Marburg and University, Strassburg; MA Edin. 1895; BA Oxford, 1898 (Class II, School of Oriental Studies, Hebrew and Arabic); Junior Kennicott Hebrew Scholar, 1898; Junior Hall-Houghton Septuagint Prizeman, 1899; Houghton Syriac Prizeman, 1900; Senior Septuagint Prizeman, 1901; Senior Kennicott Scholar, 1901. Minister of Pitlochry Baptist Church, 1900–03; Minister of St Michael's Baptist Church, Coventry, 1903–06; Professor of Church History and the Philosophy of Religion in Rawdon College, Leeds, 1906–20; Minister of South Parade Baptist Church, Leeds, 1917–20; Principal of Regent's Park College, (now) Oxford, 1920–42; Principal Emeritus, 1942–; Examiner in theology or Hebrew in the Universities of Oxford, London, Wales, Edinburgh, Birmingham, Bristol, Leeds, Liverpool, Manchester, 1915–42; Lecturer on Bible Study in the University of Leeds, 1914 and 1919; Pres. of the Baptist Historical Soc. since 1921; President of the Society for Old Testament Study, 1929; of the Oxford Society of Historical Theology, 1932; and of the London Society for the Study of Religion, 1932. Burkitt Medallist for Biblical Studies (British Academy), 1944. *Publications:* Deuteronomy and Joshua in the Century Bible, 1907; Hebrew Psychology in Relation to Pauline Anthropology (in) Mansfield College Essays, 1909; The Christian Doctrine of Man, 1911; Baptist Principles before the Rise of Baptist Churches (in) The Baptists of Yorkshire, 1912; The Religious Ideas of the Old Testament, 1913; The Cross of Job, 1916; Hebrew Psychology (in) The People and The Book, 1925; The Cross of Jeremiah, 1926; The Cross of the Servant, 1926; The Life and Faith of the Baptists, 1927; The Christian Experience of the Holy Spirit, 1928; The Veil of God, 1936; The Old Testament: its Making and Meaning, 1937; The History of Israel: its Facts and Factors, 1938; Suffering, Human and Divine, 1939; Redemption and Revelation, 1942; editor of Record and Revelation, 1938, and of The Bible in its Ancient and English Versions, 1940; contributor to the Ency. Britannica, the Ency. of Religion and Ethics, the Dict. of Apostolic Christianity, etc. *Recreation:* novel-reading. *Address:* 190 Iffley Road, Oxford.

Died 12 May 1945.

ROBINSON, Sir John Beverley Beverley, 5th Bt *cr* 1854; *b* 12 Feb. 1895; *s* of 4th Bt and Eleanor Biggar (*d* 1947), *d* of Charles H. Cooke, MD, FRCS (Edin.); *S* father, 1933; *m* 1934, Maud Eva, *d* of William Charles Coo, Toronto. *Heir: cousin* John Beverley, *b* 13 Jan. 1885. *Address:* 112 Moore Avenue, Toronto, Canada.

Died 6 Nov. 1948.

ROBINSON, John George, CBE 1920; MICE, MIME; *b* 1856; *s* of Matthew Robinson, Newburn Lodge, Knowle Road, Bristol; *m* 1884, Mary Ann (*d* 1938), 2nd *d* of late Richard Hildyard Dalton, Helston, Cornwall. *Educ:* privately. Past President of Association of Railway Locomotive Engineers and Carriage and Wagon Sups; Locomotive and Carriage and Wagon Sup., Waterford, Limerick and Western Railway of Ireland, 1888–1900; Chief Mechanical Engineer, Great Central Railway;

retired, 1924; inventor of the Robinson Superheater, the Intensifore Lubricator, and of Apparatus for burning Pulverised Coal, Oil, and Colloidal Mixtures. *Address:* Koyama, 44a West Cliff Road, Bournemouth.

Died 7 Dec. 1943.

ROBINSON, Maj.-Gen. Oliver Long, CB 1919, CMG 1916; MRCS, MRCP Lond.; DPH; late RAMC; Fellow Royal Society of Tropical Medicine and Hygiene; *b* 3 Jan. 1867; *m* 1st, Theodosia (*d* 1894), *d* of W. R. Crawford; 2nd, 1895, Rose Adela, *d* of late Sir Henry Leland Harrison, ICS; two *s* four *d. Educ:* Trinity College, Dublin. Late Secretary and Registrar R. Victoria Hospital, Netley; Acting Health Officer, Gibraltar; Professor of Tropical Medicine Royal Army Medical College; served European War 1914–18 (despatches, CMG, CB); Director of Medical Services in India, 1923–27; Hon. Physician to the King 1917; retired pay, 1927; Col Commandant RAMC, 1932–37. *Address:* Craigard, Burwood Park Road, Walton-on-Thames. *Club:* Naval and Military.

Died 21 May 1947.

ROBINSON, Most Rev. Mgr Paschal, OFM, Archbishop of Tyana since 1927; Papal Nuncio in Ireland since 1930; *b* Dublin, 1870. Associate editor of the North American Review, 1892–95; entered the Franciscan Order, 1896; ordained Priest in Rome, 1901; Lector Gen., 1902; after teaching theology in Washington for two years recalled to Europe to collaborate in historical research work at Quaracchi; subsequently explored and catalogued several archives in Italy hitherto inaccessible to students; went on an extended visitation of all the Franciscan Missions in the Near East, 1909; Prof. of Mediæval History at the Catholic University of America, 1913–19; lectured on this subject at other Universities, Catholic and non-Catholic, in America and elsewhere; attended Peace Conference at Paris March–July 1919 in connection with the question of the Holy Places, which took him to Palestine Sept.–Dec. 1919 and July 1920–April 1921; subsequently actively engaged in negotiating the settlement of different outstanding questions affecting Catholic rights and interests in the Near East, visited Greece, Palestine, and Egypt in regard to these questions, April–June 1925; Apostolic Visitor for Palestine, July 1925–July 1928; Apostolic Delegate to Malta, 1929; Consultor of the S Congregations of Religious, of the Propaganda, of Studies and of the Oriental Church. *Publications:* Seven volumes on Mediæval Religious Life and Literature; Contributor to Catholic Encyclopædia, Encyclopædia of Education, and to the Dublin, Historical, Ecclesiastical and other reviews. *Address:* Nunciature, Dublin.

Died 27 Aug. 1948.

ROBINSON, Sir Percival; *see* Robinson, Sir F. P.

ROBINSON, Percival James, CBE 1943; Ex-City Electrical Engineer and City Lighting Engineer, Corporation of Liverpool; retired 1944; *b* 8 Aug. 1879; *m* 1905; two *d. Educ:* Finsbury Technical College, London. Chief Asst in Test Rooms of British Insulated Wire Co., Prescot, 1900; Engineer and Manager, Garston & District Electric Supply & Tramways Co., 1901–02; joined Staff of Liverpool Corporation, 1902; in charge of every Dept before being made Deputy and finally Chief. Member, National Consultative Committee, Central Electricity Board, 1932. Hon. MEng Liverpool University, 1933; President IMEA, 1933–34; Council IEE, 1936; Chairman British Electrical Development Assoc., 1935–36. *Publication:* paper before IEE, etc. *Address:* Hycroft, Albert Drive, Deganwy, N Wales. *T:* Deganwy 83321. *Clubs:* Eccentric; Lyceum, Liverpool.

Died 23 Nov. 1944.

ROBINSON, Brig.-Gen. Percy Morris, CB 1919; CMG 1912; late The Queen's Own (Royal West Kent Regt); *b* Colchester, 20 Feb. 1873; 2nd *s* of Major Edgar John Robinson of the same regiment; *m* 1908, Ruth, *y d* of Major H. R. Worthington; one *s* one *d*. *Educ:* Cranleigh School; Sandhurst. Commissioned to 1st Batt. Royal Fusiliers, 1892; transferred to the Queen's Own (Royal West Kent Regt), 1893; served Indian Frontier, 1897; West Africa, 1903 (despatches twice); European War, 1914–18; commanded Brigade (despatches five times, Bt Lt-Col, CB); employed under the Colonial Office from 1903–06 and 1907–11; retired pay, 1925; DL Kent. *Address:* Florance House, Groombridge, Sussex. *T:* Groombridge 35.

Died 1 April 1949.

ROBINSON, Sir Sydney Maddock, Kt 1922; *b* 3 Dec. 1865; *e s* of Walter Allen Robinson and Gwenllian Rhys; *m* 1899, Mary Louisa, *e d* of Bayly Moore Collyns; one *d*. *Educ:* Hereford Cathedral School; Brasenose College, Oxford. Called to Bar, Middle Temple, 1888; practised at Lahore, Punjab, India; Public Prosecutor, Lahore, 1891, and then Junior Government Advocate; Government Advocate and Legal Remembrancer to the Punjab Government; Judge, 1920; Chief Court of Lower Burma, 1908; Chief Judge, 1920; Chief Justice High Court of Burma, 1922–25; retired, 1925. *Recreations:* ornithology and every sport. *Address:* Chesterfield House, 4 Camden Hill, Tunbridge Wells. *Clubs:* East India and Sports; Pegu (Rangoon).

Died 17 May 1948.

ROBINSON, Sir Sydney Walter, Kt 1934; JP, Essex; *b* Walthamstow, 1876; *s* of Alfred and Georgina Robinson, Walthamstow; *m* 1898, Gwendolene Edith King. *Educ:* Walthamstow; Metropolitan College, Chicago. Building contractor; farmer; MP (L) Chelmsford, 1923–24; Alderman of the Essex County Council 30 years; Chairman, Public Health Committee, etc. *Recreation:* breeding pedigree shorthorn dairy cows. *Address:* Woodside, The Drive, Snaresbrook, E18. *Club:* National Liberal.

Died 17 Nov. 1950.

ROBINSON, Sir Thomas William, Kt 1900; *b* 25 June 1864; *e s* of John Robinson, Clones, County Monaghan; *m* 1890, Lucie Florence (*d* 1929), *y d* of late Humphrey Smith, JP, Mountmellick; *m* 1930, Minnie, *d* of late Charles Kew, Liverpool. Chairman Kingstown Urban District Council, 1899–1900; JP Co. Dublin; Chairman; Hayes, Conyngham and Robinson, Limited, chemists; Metropole Hotels Co. (Ireland), Ltd; Director United Drug Co. Ltd, Nottingham; Millar and Beatty, Ltd, Dublin; Williams and Woods Ltd, Dublin. *Address:* 10 Herbert Park, Dublin. *Clubs:* Hibernian United Service, Dublin.

Died 8 Jan. 1946.

ROBINSON, William Albert; MP (Lab) St Helens, 1935–45. Chm. Nat. Labour Party, 1935; formerly; member, Liverpool City Council; political secretary, Nat. Union Distributive and Allied Workers. *Address:* York House, Walton Breck Road, Liverpool.

Died 31 Dec. 1949.

ROBINSON, Sir (William) Arthur, GCB 1929 (KCB 1919; CB 1915); GBE 1941 (CBE 1918); *b* 9 Sept. 1874; *s* of late William Robinson, Longmarton, Westmorland; *m* 1910, Jean Pasley, 2nd *d* of R. Mitchell; one *s*. *Educ:* Appleby School; Queen's College, Oxford (Classical Scholar). First Class Classical Moderations and Litterae Humaniores, 1893 and 1895. Entered Colonial Office, first place in Civil Service Examination, 1897; First Class Clerk, 1905; Assistant Secretary HM Office of Works, 1912–17; Permanent Secretary Air Ministry, 1917–20; Secretary to Ministry of Health, 1920–35; Assistant Secretary Imperial Conferences, 1907 and 1911; Secretary Dominions Royal Commission, 1911–12; Chairman of Supply Board, Committee of Imperial Defence, 1935; Secretary to the Ministry of Supply, 1939–40; Director Babcock & Wilcox Ltd, British Oxygen Co. Ltd, Super Oil Seals & Gaskets, Ltd, 1941–42. *Recreation:* golf. *Clubs:* Athenæum, Union.

Died 23 April 1950.

ROBINSON, William Heath; artist; *b* 31 May 1872; *s* of Thomas Robinson, artist and engraver, for many years principal artist on staff of Penny Illustrated Paper; *m* Josephine Constance, *d* of John Latey, for many years editor of Penny Illustrated Paper; four *s* one *d*. *Educ:* Islington; Royal Academy Schools. First published work issued by Mr Nutt; collaborated with brothers T. H. and Charles Robinson in illustrating Hans Andersen; illustrated Arabian Nights; Edgar Allan Poe's poems; Don Quixote; Rabelais; Twelfth Night and Rudyard Kipling's A Song of the English; Rudyard Kipling's Collected Verse, an original drawing from this series being bought by the Canadian National Gallery; A Midsummer Night's Dream; Hans Andersen's Fairy Tales; The Water Babies; Perrault's Tales, and Walter de la Mare's Peacock Pie; wrote and illustrated Uncle Lubin, 1902, and Bill the Minder, 1912; has contributed for many years large numbers of humorous drawings to The Sketch, The Bystander, The Graphic, Illustrated Sporting and Dramatic News, London Opinion, Strand Magazine, Puck, and other illustrated English and American periodicals; has designed comic scenery for stage productions at the Alhambra and Empire theatres, also decorations for the Knickerbocker Bar and Children's Room on the Empress of Britain. *Publications:* Absurdities, 1934; My Line of Life, autobiography, 1938; Heath Robinson at War, 1942. *Recreation:* walking. *Address:* 25 Southwood Avenue, Highgate, N6. *T:* Mountview 1282. *Clubs:* Savage, London Sketch.

Died 13 Sept. 1944.

ROBISON, Robert, FRS 1930; DSc (Lond.), PhD (Leipzig), FIC; Head of the Department of Biochemistry, Lister Institute of Preventive Medicine, London, since 1931; Professor of Biochemistry, London University; *b* Newark-on-Trent, 1883; *s* of Robert and Jessie Thomson Robison; *m* 1910, Ethel Ray, *d* of Samuel Walker, Newark; one *d*. *Educ:* Magnus Grammar School; University College, Nottingham; University of Leipzig. 1851 Exhibition Research Scholar. Lecturer and Demonstrator in Chemistry, University College, Galway, 1909, and in University College, Nottingham, 1910; Assistant Biochemist, Lister Institute, 1913; Captain RAMC (T); served with Mediterranean, Egyptian, and Italian Expeditionary Forces, 1915–19 (despatches); Herter Lecturer, New York University, 1931; Baly Medallist, Royal College of Physicians, 1933. *Publications:* The Significance of Phosphoric Esters in Metabolism, 1932; papers on chemical and bio-chemical subjects in the Biochemical Journal and other scientific journals. *Recreations:* gardening, photography. *Address:* 12 Genoa Avenue, Putney, SW15. *TA:* Bacteriology, Knights, London. *T:* Putney 7063.

Died 18 June 1941.

ROBSON, Lt-Col Henry William Cumine, CIE 1938; OBE 1929; Indian Army, retired; Indian Political Service; Resident for Eastern States, 1937–39; retired, 1941; *b* 8 Dec. 1886. *Address:* Two Birches, Shawford, Winchester.

Died 15 April 1942.

ROBSON, Hon. Hugh Amos; Chief Justice, Court of King's Bench, Manitoba, Winnipeg, since 1944; *b* Barrow-in-Furness, England, 9 Sept. 1871; *s* of Robert Robson and Jane Hay; *m* Fannie Laidlaw; two *s* four *d*. Formerly Judge, Court of Appeal, Manitoba, and Public Utility Commissioner, Manitoba; practising barrister at Regina, Saskatchewan, and Winnipeg, Manitoba. *Address:* The Law Courts, Winnipeg, Manitoba, Canada.

Died 9 July 1945.

ROBSON, John Henry Matthews, CBE; *b* 1870; *e s* of late Rev. Dr Robson, LLD; *m* 1921, Theodora (*d* 1937), *widow* of late Capt. Syers; no *c*. *Educ:* Christ College, Finchley; privately. Joined the Selangor Government Service, 1889; retired in 1896 to start the first daily paper published in the Federated Malay States; Member of the Federal Council, 1909–12 and 1921–27; Managing Director of the Malay Mail Press Co., Ltd, when residing in Malaya. *Publications:* Records and Recollections, 1889–1934; Bibliography of Malaya, 1941. *Address:* Kuala Lumpur, Federated Malay States. *[Interned Changi Camp, Singapore.]*

Died 20 July 1945.

ROBY, Arthur Godfrey, KC 1919; MA; *b* 1862; *s* of late Henry John Roby, LLD, Lancrigg, Grasmere; *m* 1890, Alice Keturah (*d* 1934), *d* of late Sir Evelyn Oakeley. *Educ:* St John's College, Cambridge (Exhibitioner). *Address:* 13 Phillimore Place, W8. *T:* Western 5351. *Club:* Oxford and Cambridge.

Died 15 April 1944.

ROCHDALE, 1st Baron *cr* 1913; **George Kemp,** CB 1937; Kt 1909; Lt-Col in Duke of Lancaster's Own (Yeomanry Cavalry); Hon. Col in army; Lord-Lieutenant of County of Middlesex since 1929; Chairman Kelsall and Kemp, Limited; *b* Rochdale, 9 June 1866; *o s* of late George Tawke Kemp, Beechwood, Rochdale, and Emily, *d* of Henry Kelsall, Butts House, Rochdale; *m* 1896, Lady Beatrice Egerton, 3rd *d* of 3rd Earl of Ellesmere; one *s* one *d*. *Educ:* Shrewsbury; Balliol College, Oxford; Trinity College, Cambridge (BA), Classical Tripos. Served South Africa, 1900, and 1901–02 (despatches); European War as Lt-Col in command of the 1/6th Batt. Lancs Fusiliers (TF), and temporarily as Brigadier of the 126th and 127th Brigades of the 42nd Division in Gallipoli; MP (LU) Heywood Division of Lancs, 1895–1906; MP (L) North-West Division, Manchester, 1910–12. *Recreations:* cricket, hunting, shooting, tennis, golf; Cambridge eleven, 1885–86, 1888; Lancashire eleven, 1885–93; Cambridge tennis, 1886. *Heir: s* Lt-Col (Temp. Col) Hon. John Durival Kemp, OBE 1945, RA, TA [*b* 5 June 1906; *m* 1931, Elinor Dorothea, *d* of late Ernest H. Pease]. *Address:* Old Hall, Highgate Village, N6. *T:* Mountview 3345; Lingholm, Keswick. *T:* Keswick 5. *Clubs:* Beefsteak, Carlton, White's.

Died 24 March 1945.

ROCHE, Col Henry John, CB 1915; Indian Army; *b* 12 Aug. 1864; *e surv. s* of Charles Philip Roche, of Ballyagran, Co. Limerick; *m* 1905, Gladys, *d* of Felix Drake, North Coker, Somerset; two *s* one *d*. *Educ:* Stonyhurst College. Entered army (Cheshire Regt), 1884; Captain ISC, 1895; Major Indian Army, 1902; Lt-Col 1910; Col 1915; served NW Frontier, India, 1897–98 (medal with clasp); China, 1900 (medal); European War, 1914–17 (despatches, CB, 1914 Star). *Recreations:* shooting, fishing, golf. *Address:* The Colony, Burnham-on-Sea, Somerset. *T:* Burnham 290.

Died 6 April 1944.

ROCHE, William, CIE 1927; *b* 20 Oct. 1880; *s* of John Roche, MD; *m* 1922, Florence Ruttledge. Entered PWD India, 1905; Assistant Engineer, United Provinces, 1907; Executive Engineer, 1915; Superintending Engineer, 1926; Lieutenant, United Provinces Horse (Indian Auxiliary Force); Chief Engineer, Bengal, 1931–35; retired, 1935.

Died 2 May 1942.

ROCKLEY, 1st Baron *cr* 1934, of Lytchett Heath; **Evelyn Cecil,** PC 1917; GBE 1922; Bailiff Grand Cross of the Order of St John of Jerusalem, 1932; is a Director of the Southern Railway; Deputy-Chairman Clerical, Medical, and General Life Assurance Society; President of East Dorset Hospital since 1931; *b* 30 May 1865; *e s* of late Lord Eustace Cecil; *m* 1898, Hon. Alicia-Margaret, CBE, MBE, *d* of 1st Baron Amherst of Hackney; one *s*

two *d*. *Educ:* Eton; New College, Oxford (MA). Barrister (Inner Temple), 1889, joined Western Circuit; assist private secretary to Prime Minister (Marquis of Salisbury), 1891–92, and 1895–1902; member of London School Board, 1894–99; MP (C) continuously for 31 years; East Herts, 1898–1900; Aston Manor, 1900–18; Aston Div. of Birmingham, 1918–29, when he retired; Chairman, Select Committee on Foreign Steamship Subsidies and their effect on British Trade, 1901–02; Chairman, Eastern Mail Service Committee, 1904; Member of the Permanent Commission, International Railway Congress, delegate at Washington, 1905, Berne, 1910, Rome, 1922, London, 1925, Madrid, 1930, Cairo, 1933, Paris, 1937; Member of the Committee on Public Retrenchment, 1915, and of Second Chamber Conference, 1918; Secretary-General of the Order of St John of Jerusalem, 1915–21 (GBE on retirement); Vice-Chairman Joint War Committee of British Red Cross Society and Order of St John till 1925; Member of the Interallied Parliamentary Committee, 1916–18; Chairman Select Committee on Telephone Service, 1921–22; Member of Royal Commission on Honours, 1922; Privy Council Honours Committee, 1923–24; Chairman of Home Office Committee on Young Offenders, 1925; Chairman, Unionist Parliamentary Committee on Empire Migration, 1926; called to NSW Bar at Sydney, as compliment, 1926; introduced Judicial Proceedings, Regulation of Reports (divorce, etc.) Bill, 1923–24–1925, passed 1926; Chairman, Board of Trade Committee on Deaths by Coal Gas Poisoning, 1930; introduced Life Peers Bill, House of Lords, passed 2nd reading, 1935; Chairman of Royal Commission on Safety and Health in Coal Mines, 1935–38; Chairman or Director of Foreign and Colonial and other Investment Trust Co.'s 1896–1940. *Publications:* Primogeniture, a Short History of its Development in various Countries and its Practical Effects, 1895; on the Eve of War, 1900. *Heir: s* Hon. Robert William Evelyn Cecil [*b* 28 Feb. 1901; *m* 1933, Anne Margaret, *d* of Adm. Hon. Sir Herbert Meade-Featherstonhaugh, GCVO, CB, DSO; two *s* one *d*]. *Address:* 2 Cadogan Sq., SW1. *T:* Sloane 7615; Lytchett Heath, Poole, Dorset. *Clubs:* Athenæum, Carlton.

Died 1 April 1941.

ROCKLEY, Dowager Baroness; (Alice-Margaret), CBE 1920; MBE 1918; Dame Grand Cross of the Order of St John of Jerusalem; Hon. Assistant Director of Horticulture, Food Production Department, Board of Agriculture, 1917–19; *d* of 1st Baron Amherst of Hackney; *m* 1898; Evelyn Cecil, afterwards 1st Baron Rockley, PC, GBE; one *s* two *d*. Received in 1896 the Freedom of the Worshipful Company of Gardeners, and afterwards the Freedom of the City of London; Vice-Chairman of Society for the Oversea Settlement of British Women for 20 years; on Board of Management Chelsea Physic Garden from its formation 1900 until 1941. Collected flowers for Kew. *Publications:* A History of Gardening in England, 1895, 1896; 3rd and enlarged edition, 1910; Children's Gardens, 1902; London Parks and Gardens, 1907; Wild Flowers of the Great Dominions of the British Empire, 1935; Some Canadian Wild Flowers, 1937; Historic Gardens of England, 1938. *Recreations:* gardening and sketching. *Address:* Lytchett Heath, Poole, Dorset. *T:* Lytchett-Minster 228.

Died 14 Sept. 1941.

RODGER, Adam Keir; JP; *b* Greenock, 1855; *s* of William Rodger, warehouseman; *m* 1888, Amy Lawton; two *s*. *Educ:* Glasgow High School. Founder, formerly Manager and now Ex-Chairman of Scottish Temperance and General Assurance Company; Ex-Chm., Great Northern Investment Trust, Ltd, and Home and Foreign Investment Trust, Ltd; Ex-Provost of the Royal Burgh of Rutherglen (four terms); Ex-Chm. Victoria Infirmary, Glasgow; MP (Co. L) Rutherglen Division of Lanarkshire, Dec. 1918–22; Freedom of Royal Burgh of Rutherglen, 1940; Ex-Vice-Chairman Income Tax

Commissioners of Lower Ward of Lanarkshire. *Address:* St Bernard's, Helensburgh. *T:* Helensburgh 533. *Clubs:* New, Glasgow.

Died 17 Feb. 1946.

RODGER, Sir Alexander, Kt 1930; OBE; *b* Greenock; *m* 1934, Pauline, *widow* of Major Brandon, 9th Gurkha Rifles. *Educ:* Blairlodge; Cooper's Hill. Indian Forest Service, Burma, 1898; Deputy Controller of Timber Supplies, Munition Board, Rangoon, 1916–20; in charge of Burma Pavilion, British Empire Exhibition, Wembley, 1923–24; President, Forest Research Institute and College, Dehra Dun, UP, India, 1925; Inspector-General of Forests to the Government of India, 1926–30; retired, 1930; Member of Forestry Commission, 1932–39; Home Guard, 1940–42; served under Somerset War Agricultural Executive Committee. *Publications:* Handbook of the Forest Products of Burma, 1920; List of Trees. Shrubs, etc., of Burma, 1922; other miscellaneous forest publications. *Recreations:* polo, shooting, fishing, tennis. *Address:* Tannachie, Findhorn, Forres, Morayshire. *T:* Findhorn 250. *Club:* East India and Sports.

Died 30 Sept. 1950.

RODGERS, Rt Rev. Harold Nickinson; Bishop Suffragan of Sherborne since 1936; Canon in Salisbury Cathedral since 1937; Archdeacon of Dorset since 1940; 2nd *s* of late John Jarvis Rodgers and Elizabeth Nickinson; *m* Elizabeth Harriet, 3rd *d* of Vice-Admiral W. Usborne Moore, RN. *Educ:* Corpus Christi College, Cambridge, MA. Was formerly Assistant Priest, St Jude's, Southsea; Domestic Chaplain to Bishop of Winchester (Bishop Talbot); Chaplain of Royal Military Academy, Woolwich; Rector of Havant, 1917–36; Rural Dean of Havant, 1922–27; Hon. Chaplain to the Bishop of Winchester (Bishop Woods), 1924–27; Archdeacon of Portsmouth and Examining Chaplain to Bishop of Portsmouth, 1927–36; Select Preacher before University of Cambridge, 1940. *Address:* The Church House, Salisbury. *T:* 3408. *Club:* Oxford and Cambridge.

Died 22 June 1947.

RODHAM, Rear-Adm. (S) Harold, CMG 1919; RN; *b* 1873; *s* of Fleet-Paymaster C. R. Rodham, RN; *m* 1899, Miriam, *d* of John Edward Boyd, Ottawa; one *s.* *Educ:* Plymouth Grammar School. Present at Battle of Heligoland, 28 Aug. 1914, Dogger Bank, 24 Jan. 1915, and Jutland, 31 May 1916, in HM Battle Cruiser Princess Royal (despatches, Croix de Guerre with Palms, CMG); served in HMS Delhi, Flagship of Admiral Sir Walter H. Cowan, in Baltic, 1919 (recommended for special promotion in Baltic despatches); retired list, 1928. *Address:* Frenchaye, Addlestone, Surrey. *T:* Weybridge 613.

Died 22 Dec. 1947.

ROE, Francis Reginald; *b* 5 Aug. 1869; *s* of late Sir Charles Roe. *Educ:* Winchester College; New College, Oxford. Joined Indian Civil Service, 1888; proceeded to India, 1890; held charge of various districts in Bengal and Behar as Magistrate and Collector, 1894–1902; a District and Sessions Judge, 1902; officiated as a Judge of the High Court at Calcutta, 1915 and 1916; Judge, High Court, Patna, 1916–19; retired 1919. *Address:* 15 Park Town, Oxford.

Died 5 March 1942.

ROE, Fred, RI; *γ s* of Robert Roe, miniature-painter and engraver, and Maria, *γ d* of Rev. W. Gordon Plees, MA, Vicar of Ashbocking, Suffolk; *m* 1890, Letitia Mabel (*d* 1940), *e d* of Sydney W. Lee, Dereham, Putney Hill; one *s. Educ:* Hon. FIBD. Historical and genre painter; exhibited at Royal Academy since 1887; Paris Salon and all Principal exhibitions in this country; represented at nearly 30 art galleries, etc. Works: Nelson leaving Portsmouth; The Night before Trafalgar (Dunedin); King Edward VII (King's Lynn); A City Banquet (Clothworkers' Hall); 4th Suffolks at Neuve Chapelle

(Ipswich); 1/5th Gloucesters at Hebuterne (Cheltenham); Colours of the Kensingtons (Kensington Town Hall); The Cardinal's Kitchen (Newport); 1st Monmouths at 2nd Battle of Ypres (Monmouth); King George VI at Coventry's ruined Cathedral, and others; Victory Thanks-giving Service at Kensington 1945 (Kensington Town Hall). *Publications:* Ancient Coffers and Cupboards; Old Oak Furniture; A History of Oak Furniture, 1920; Ancient Church Chests and Chairs round Greater London, 1929; Essex Survivals, 1929; Vanishing England (in collaboration), 1910. *Recreation:* study of antiquities. *Address:* Kingston Lodge, 24 Addison Road, W14. *T:* Western 5209. *Club:* Arts.

Died 16 Aug. 1947.

ROE, Humphrey Verdon; Pioneer in Aviation; Hon. Secretary Society for Constructive Birth Control and Racial Progress; *b* 18 April 1878; 3rd *s* of late Dr E. H. Roe; *m* 1918, Marie Carmichael Stopes, DSc; two *s.* As Lieut 1st Manchester Regiment, went through S African War, including Siege of Ladysmith; from 1909 onwards, when flying seemed a dream, his foresight and faith in its future led him to devote the whole of his capital and talents to helping his brother Sir Alliott Verdon-Roe, OBE, to establish the Avro biplane, they founded A. V. Roe and Co., Ltd; Managing Director until he retired from business, 1917, to join the RFC; wounded on active service in France, 1918; on 19 Oct. 1917, in order to reduce maternal and infantile mortality, he offered St Mary's Hospital, Manchester, a thousand pounds per annum for five years if they would agree to practise and carry out research in contraception; this offer was refused; jointly with Dr M. C. Stopes, DSc, founded in Holloway, N, first Clinic for Birth Control in British Empire, 1921; on Executive, etc., Committees of the National Industrial Alliance of Employers and Employed; Councillor, Leatherhead UDC 1921–27; Vice-Chairman Southern Counties Soaring Club, 1931; rejoined Royal Air Force, 1940–42. *Recreation:* travelling. *Address:* Norbury Park, Dorking, Surrey.

Died 25 July 1949.

ROERICH, Prof. Nicholas K.; Commander, Order of Imperial Russians of St Stanislas, St Anne and St Vladimir; Commander, First Class of Swedish Order of the Northern Star; French Legion of Honour; Yugoslavian St Sava I Class Grand Cross; Hon. President Roerich Museum, New York; President-Founder Master Institute of United Arts, New York; President-Founder International Art Centre of Roerich Museum, New York; Hon. President Union Internationale pour le Pacte Roerich, Bruges; Hon. Member of Bose Institute, Calcutta, and of Yugoslavian Academy of Art and Science; Vice-President of Archæological Institute of America; Academician of Russian Academy of Fine Arts; Member of Academy of Rheims, Sociétaire of Salon d'Automne, Paris, etc; Hon. Protector and President of 71 Roerich Societies in the world; *b* St Petersburg, 10 Oct. 1874; *s* of Konstantin Roerich and Marie V. Kalashnikoff; *m* 1901, Helena Ivanovna Shaposhnikov, St Petersburg; two *s. Educ:* School of Law, Univ. of St Petersburg; studied drawing and painting under Michail O. Mikeshine, also under Kuindjy at Acad. Fine Arts, St Petersburg, and under Cormon, in Paris. Professor at Imperial Archaeological Inst., St Petersburg; and Asst Editor of Art, 1898–1900; Dir, Sch. for Encouragement of Fine Arts in Russia, and Pres., Mus. of Russian Art, 1906–16; Archaeological Excavations of Kremlin of Novgorod; exhibition and lecture tours in Sweden, Finland, Denmark and England, 1916–19; came to United States, 1920; headed five years art exhibition in Central Asia, making 500 paintings and collecting data on Asiatic Culture and Philosophy, 1923–28; Roerich Mus., NY City, contained over 1000 of his paintings; 2000 other of his paintings in The Louvre, V&A Mus., Stockholm, Helsinki, Chicago Art Inst., Detroit Mus., Kansas City Mus., Omaha Mus., Tripoli Mus., etc; Pres.-Founder of Urusvati Himalayan Res. Inst., Naggar,

Punjab, India, etc; excavated prehistoric burials, Pondicherry, French India, 1930; headed US Dept of Agriculture's expedition into Central Asia in search for drought-resisting plants, 1934–35. *Publications:* Complete Works, 1914; Adamant, 1924, also published in Japanese; The Messenger, 1925; Paths of Blessing, 1925; Himalaya, 1926; Joys of Sikkim, 1928; Altai Himalaya, 1929; Heart of Asia, 1930 (also in Russian and Spanish); Flame in Chalice, 1930; Shambhala, 1930; Realm of LIght, 1931 (also in Russian); Fiery Stronghold, 1933 (also in Russian); Sacred Vigil, 1934; Gates into the Future, 1936 (in Russian). *Address:* Naggar, Kulu, Punjab, India.

Died 12 Dec. 1947.

ROGERS, Arthur William, ScD, FRS 1918; formerly Director of Geological Survey, South Africa; *b* 1872; *s* of George Rogers, Bishops-Hull. *Educ:* Clifton College; Christ's College, Cambridge. President XV International Geological Congress, South Africa, 1929; awarded Wollaston Medal of Geological Society of London, 1931; Hon. Fellow of Christ's College, 1935. *Publications:* on the Geology of South Africa. *Address:* 8 Rhodes Avenue, Mowbray, Cape Town, SA. *Clubs:* Athenæum; Civil Service, Cape Town.

Died 23 June 1946.

ROGERS, Rev. Clement Francis, MA; Lecturer on Pastoral Theology, King's College, University of London, 1907–19; Professor 1919–32, Emeritus Professor since 1932; *b* 1866; *s* of Professor James Edwin Thorold and Ann Susanna Charlotte Rogers; unmarried. *Educ:* St Peter's College, Westminster; Jesus College, Oxford. BA 1889; MA 1892. Deacon, 1890; Priest, 1891; worked in parishes in Yorkshire and London; took an active part in the work of the London Charity Organisation Society; and lectured on Christian Evidences on Sunday afternoons in Hyde Park. *Publications:* Baptism and Christian Archæology, 1903; Charitable Relief, 1904; Principles of Parish Work, 1905; Circumstances or Character? 1911; An Introduction to the Study of Pastoral Theology, 1912; Pastoral Theology and the Modern World, 1920; Question Time in Hyde Park, 1924; Lectures in Hyde Park, 1927; The Case for Christianity, 1928; Modes of Faith, 1934; Verify your References, 1938; The Fear of Hell, 1939; A Church genuinely Catholic, 1940; The Parson Preaching, 1947. *Address:* 89 Woodstock Road, Oxford.

Died 23 June 1949.

ROGERS, Rev. Frederick Arundel; *b* 3 Jan. 1876; *s* of Rev. W. M. Rogers, Chetnole, Bournemouth. *Educ:* Marlborough; Epsom; Keble College, Oxford; BA 1897, MA 1904; Cuddesdon College, 1900. Acting lay chaplain to the Forces in South Africa, 1899 (medal and clasp); deacon, 1901; priest, 1902; curate, St John the Divine, Kennington, 1901; assistant chaplain South African Church Railway Mission Diocese of Pretoria, 1905; Diocese of Bloemfontein, 1906; Diocese of N Rhodesia, 1908; Head of S African Church Railway Mission, 1911; Archdeacon of Pietersburg, 1914–21; Chief Sec. of SPG for Province of York, 1922; Assistant Secretary of Missionary Council of Church Assembly, 1925–28; Civil Chaplain, Baghdad, Iraq, 1928–29. *Recreation:* botany. *Address:* Chetnole, E Grinstead. *Club:* Golfers'.

Died 27 June 1944.

ROGERS, Herbert Lionel; *b* 23 Aug. 1871; *s* of John Robert Fydell Rogers (of Keen, Rogers & Co., solicitors, 59 Carter Lane) and Lucy Chapman, *d* of Rev. W. S. Meadows, Vicar of Chigwell, Essex; *m* 1910, Irene, 2nd *d* of Sir Henry James Hall, Kt, director of Stephen Smith & Co.; one *d. Educ:* St John's School, Leatherhead; classical scholar, Christ Church, Oxford; 1st class Classical Moderations; 2nd class Lit. Hum., MA. Sixth form master at Leatherhead, Lancing, and Radley successively; Headmaster King's College School,

1910–34. *Publications:* Articles on Higher Education of Boys in England, 1909; Roman Home Life and Religion, 1923; Vol. I Translation of Plautus (Broadway Translations), 1924; The Life of Rome, 1927. *Address:* 10b Rawlinson Road, Oxford.

Died 16 Feb. 1950.

ROGERS, John, CBE 1927; OBE 1918; retired; Director Globe Pneumatic Engineering Co. Ltd (temp. War address: 2a Coppice Avenue, Lower Willingdon, Sussex); one *s* one *d.* Late Deputy Director of Dockyards, after being Chief Constructor at Sheerness Dockyard and Manager Constructive Departments at Rosyth and Devonport Dockyards. *Address:* Stranraer, 47 Berriedale Avenue, Hove, Sussex. *T:* Hove 7401.

Died 23 Jan. 1945.

ROGERS, Lt-Col John Middleton, DSO 1900; late 1st Dragoons; JP, DL Kent; *b* 24 Aug. 1864; *e s* of late Capt John Thornton Rogers of Riverhill; *m* 1st, 1899, Muriel Blanche Gwendoline (decd), *d* of Sir Charles Morrison-Bell, 1st Bart of Otterburn Hall, Otterburn; two *s* two *d*; 2nd, 1921, Hilda, MBE, *o d* of Louis Rudd Stevenson, late 3rd Hussars, Birkenhead. Served South Africa, 1899–1901 (despatches 3 times, Queen's medal 7 clasps, DSO); European War, 1914–17; Sheriff of Kent, 1918–19. *Address:* Riverhill, Sevenoaks. *T:* Sevenoaks 2557. *Club:* Army and Navy.

Died 11 Aug. 1945.

ROGERS, Sir Percival Halse, KBE 1939; **Hon. Mr Justice Rogers;** Justice of Supreme Court of New South Wales since 1928; *b* Gunnedah, New South Wales, 1 Aug. 1883; *s* of Rev. William Halse Rogers; *m* 1911, Mabel Mary, *d* of Arthur Trevor Jones; two *d. Educ:* Newington College, Sydney; St Andrew's College, University of Sydney; Worcester College, Oxford (Rhodes Scholar). BA (Sydney), 1905; BCL Oxford, 1908. Called to New South Wales Bar, 1911; KC 1926; Fellow of Senate of University of Sydney, 1929; Deputy Chancellor, 1934–36; Chancellor, 1936–41. *Recreation:* golf. *Address:* Supreme Court, Sydney, NSW. *Clubs:* Oxford and Cambridge University; Union, University, Sydney.

Died 7 Oct. 1945.

ROHDE, Eleanour Sinclair; author; Ex-President of Society of Women Journalists; *o d* of late John Rohde (Travancore Civil Service) and Isabel Crawford. *Educ:* Cheltenham Ladies' College; St Hilda's Hall, Oxford. Horticultural Adviser to Heath and Heather, Ltd, Herb Specialists. *Publications:* A Garden of Herbs; The Old English Herbals; The Old English Gardening Books; Piedmont (with E. Canziani); The Old World Pleasaunce; Garden-craft in the Bible, and other essays; The Gardenlover's Days; The Star-lover's Days; Christmas; The Fairy-Lovers' Days; The Bird-Lovers' Days; The Scented Garden; Oxford's College Gardens; The Story of the Garden; Gardens of Delight; Preface to the Garden Book of Sir Thomas Hanmer; Shakespeare's Wild Flowers, Fairy Lore, Gardens, Herbs, Gatherers of Simples and Bee-Lore; My Garden Note-book; Herbs and Herb Gardening; (with Eric Parker) The Gardener's Week-End Book: Vegetable Cultivation and Cookery; The War-Time Vegetable Garden; Culinary and Salad Herbs; Uncommon Vegetables; How to grow and cook them; Your Own Herb Garden; numerous contributions to Encyclopædia of Gardening; occasional contributor to The Times, Spectator, Country Life, the Sphere, Journal of the Royal Horticultural Society, The Field, Good Housekeeping, Woman's Journal, Housewife, Health for All, Ideal Home Magazine, The Queen, My Garden, The Countryman, Britannia and Eve, etc. *Recreations:* reading and cottage gardening. *Address:* Cranham Lodge, Reigate, Surrey. *T:* Reigate 2355. *Club:* English-speaking Union.

Died 23 June 1950.

ROLFE, Captain Herbert Neville, Royal Navy (retired); DSO 1918; JP for County of Somerset, 1911; *b* 16 June 1854; 5th *s* of late Charles Fawcett Neville Rolfe of Heacham Hall, Norfolk; *m* 1896, Mabel, *o d* of late Canon H. T. Barff; one *s* two *d*. Entered Navy, 1868; Sub-Lieut in HMS Euryalus, Zulu War, 1887; as Lieutenant in Euryalus was employed on the Transport Staff at Suez, Egyptian War, 1882; as Captain (retired list) in command of HM yacht Jolaire on Patrol Service during the European War, 1916–19. *Address:* Barrow Cottage, Flax-Bourton, Somerset. *TA:* Flax-Bourton. *T:* Flax-Bourton 35.

Died 22 Feb. 1942.

ROLL, Grahame Winfield, BA, MB, BCh Cantab; FRCS Eng.; LRCP Lond.; Consulting Surgeon Royal Westminster Ophthalmic Hospital; Consulting Ophthalmic Surgeon, St Mary's Hospital for Women and Children, Plaistow. *Educ:* Bedford School; Christ's Coll., Cambridge; St Thomas' Hospital. Practising as an oculist; formerly Ophthalmic House Surgeon St Thomas' Hospital, and Surgeon, Royal Westminster Ophthalmic Hospital; Fellow of the Royal Empire Society.

Died 21 Feb. 1942.

ROLLAND, Romain; écrivain; *b* Clamecy, département de la Nièvre, France, 29 Jan. 1866. *Educ:* Collège de Clamecy. École Normale Supérieure, à Paris, 1886–89; membre de l'École française de Rome, 1889–91; agrégé d'histoire, docteur ès lettres; professeur d'histoire de l'art à l'École Normale Supérieure, puis à la Faculté des Lettres de Paris (Sorbonne), où il a introduit l'enseignement de l'histoire de la musique; reçut le Prix Nobel de littérature, 1916. *Publications: Théâtre:* Cycle de la Révolution (8 drames parus: Pâques Fleuries, le 14 Juillet, Les Loups, Le Triomphe de la Raison, Danton, Le Jeu de l'Amour et de la Mort, Robespierre, Les Léonides), St Louis, Aërt, Liluli, Le Temps viendra. *Romans:* Jean Christophe, 10 vol. (se divisant en trois séries: Jean-Christophe; Jean-Christophe à Paris; La Fin du Voyage); Colas Breugnon; Clerambault; Pierre et Luce; L'Ame Enchantée, 7 vol.; Annette et Sylvie; L'Eté; Mère et Fils; L'Annonciatrice; La Mort d'un Monde; L'Enfantement. *Histoire et Critique:* Vies des Hommes illustres. 3 vol. (i Beethoven; ii Michel-Ange; iii Tolstoy); Histoire de l'Opéra en Europe avant Lully et Scarlatti; Haendel; François Millet; Musiciens d'autrefois; Musiciens d'aujourd'hui; Voyage Musical au Pays du Passé; Beethoven: Les grandes époques créatrices, 3 vol.: De l'Héroique à l'Appassionata, Le Chant de la Résurrection, Goethe et Beethoven; Le Théâtre du Peuple; Compagnons de route (Essais littéraires); Empédocle d'Agrigente; Mahatma Gandhi; La Mystique et l'action dans l'Inde d'aujourd'hui, 3 vol. (i Ramakrishna; ii Vivekananda; iii L'Evangile Universel). *Écrits politiques:* Au dessus de la Mêlée; Les Précurseurs; Quinze ans de combat; Par la Révolution; la Paix; I will not rest.

Died 30 Dec. 1944.

ROLLER, Major George C., DCM, TD, JP; *b* 1856; *s* of late F. W. Roller; *m* 1st, 1884, Mary (*d* 1908), *d* of W. Halliday, of Thames, New Zealand; one *s*; 2nd, 1910, Emily, *d* of late H. Kirk Craig, of Crawley. *Educ:* Westminster School. Served with Imperial Yeomanry in Boer War, 1900 (despatches four times; recommended by Gen. Rundle for a VC; commission after Seneka Kopje, 25 May 1900; DCM); Major, Middlesex Yeomanry, 1903–11; commanded 3/3 County of London Yeomanry, 1914–16; seconded to Field Artillery, France; invalided out, 1918; Hon. Major in the Army; a Governor of St George's, St Thomas's, and Royal Berkshire Hospitals; considerable experience in Australia, California, Peru and Argentine; well known in many branches of art and sport; painter, writer;

gentleman rider under National Hunt Rules all through the 'eighties and 'nineties. *Address:* Tadley, Basingstoke. *T:* Heath End 258. *Club:* Arts.

Died 4 Jan. 1941.

ROLLESTON, Francis Joseph; Barrister and Solicitor, Timaru; *b* 11 May 1873; 4th *s* of late Hon. Wm Rolleston, Minister of Lands and Minister of Justice, NZ; *m* 1908, Mary Winifred, *d* of H. D. Blair, of Scarborough, Timaru, NZ; two *s* four *d*. *Educ:* Christ's College, Christchurch; Canterbury College (University of NZ), BA 1895, LLB 1897. Since 1900 engaged in practice as a barrister and solicitor in the firm of Tripp and Rolleston, Timaru; Member of Timaru Harbour Board, 1907–23; Chairman from 1912–23; Mayor of Timaru, 1921–23; elected to represent Timaru Electoral District in House of Representatives, 1922; re-elected 1925, defeated 1928; Attorney-General, Minister of Justice, Minister of Defence, New Zealand, 1926–28. *Recreations:* golf, tennis. *Address:* PO Box 27, Timaru, NZ. *T:* 263. *Club:* South Canterbury.

Died 8 Sept. 1946.

ROLLESTON, Sir Humphry (Davy), 1st Bt *cr* 1924; GCVO 1929; KCB 1918; CB 1916; MA, MD (Cantab), Hon. DSc Oxon, Penna, DCL Durham; LLD Glasgow, Edinburgh, Bristol, Birmingham, Nat. Univ. Ireland, and Jefferson; Doctor, hon. causa, Padua, Dublin, Bordeaux, Paris, FRCPI, FRFPS; FRCS Eng., FFR (Hon.); Officier de la Légion d'Honneur; Hon. Freeman Society of Apothecaries of London; Consultant, Army Medical Library, Washington, DC; Chairman British X-ray and Radium Protection Committee; Vice-President (Chairman Council, 1924–41) Imperial Cancer Research Funds; Member University Grants Committee, 1932; Vice-President and Emeritus Physician to St George's Hospital; Membre corr. étranger Acad. de Méd. de Paris; Accad. Onorario R. Accad. Med. di Roma; Miembra Corr. Col de Doctores, Madrid; Hon. Fellow New York Academy of Medicine; Hon. Member Assoc. Amer. Phys.; Vice-President, British Medical Association; Hon. Member (Past-Pres.) Röntgen Society; *b* Oxford, 21 June 1862; *e s* of late Prof. G. Rolleston, MD, FRS, of Oxford, and Grace Davy, *niece* of Sir Humphry Davy, Bt, PRS; *m* 1894, Lisette Eila, *d* of F. M. Ogilvy. *Educ:* Marlborough; St John's College, Cambridge (Fellow and Hon. Fellow). Physician-in-Ordinary 1923–32, and Physician Extraordinary to King George V 1932–36; Regius Professor of Physic, Univ. of Cambridge, 1925–32; Pres. of Royal College Physicians, 1922–26; the Royal Society of Medicine, 1918–20; Medical Society, London, 1926–27, Assoc. Physicians, Great Britain, 1925 and 1929, and British Institute of Radiology; Member of Royal Commissions on Lunacy and Mental Disorder, and on National Health Insurance; Consultant Physician (temp. Surgeon Rear-Admiral) to the Royal Navy, 1914–19; Member of Medical Consultative Board for the Navy, of Medical Administrative Committee, Royal Air Force; of Colonial Office Committee of Medical Services, and Chairman of the Ministry of Health's Committees on Vaccination and on Medical Records, and Home Office's Committee on Workmen's Compensation; Chairman Central Joint VAD Council, 1923–37; Consulting Physician to the Imperial Yeomanry Hospital, Pretoria, 1901 (medal); President Marlburian Club, London Cornish Association, Papworth Village Settlement, Eugenics Society, and Society Study Inebriety. *Publications:* Diseases of the Liver (3rd edition, 1929, with J. W. McNee); Some Medical Aspects of Old Age, 1922, 2nd edit. 1932; Memoir of Sir Clifford Allbutt, 1929; The Cambridge Medical School, 1932; The Endocrine Organs, 1936; Editor, British Encyclopaedia of Medical Practice; Joint Editor (with Sir Clifford Allbutt) of 2nd edition of A

System of Medicine in 11 vols. *Heir:* none. *Address:* Martins, Haslemere, Surrey. *T:* Haslemere 647. *Club:* Athenæum.

Died 23 Sept. 1944 (ext).

ROLLESTON, Mrs Iris Brenda, CBE 1919, MBE 1918; *b* New Zealand, 1880; *d* of late Rt Hon. Sir Francis Bell, GCMG; *m* 1903, late G. H. F. Rolleston, HM Trade Commissioner to NZ; one *s. Educ:* Roedean. Organised and was Matron of Taumara Military Hospital (NZ). *Club:* Forum.

Died 26 July 1948.

ROLLESTON, John Davy, MA, MD (Oxon), FRCP, FSA; formerly Medical Superintendent, Western Hospital; *b* 1873; *s* of Prof. G. Rolleston, Oxford; *m* 1917, Mary Edith, *d* of C. E. Waring, Cardiff; one *s* one *d. Educ:* Marlborough College (Classical Scholar); Brasenose Coll., Oxford (Classical Scholar); Charing Cross Hospital. Editor British Journal of Children's Diseases, 1910–44; FRSM (Hon. Librarian; Ex-Pres. Sections History of Medicine, Children, Epidemiology, and Clinical); Hon. Member Royal Roumanian Society History of Medicine; Mem. Soc. Franc. Hist. de Méd., Soc. de Péd. de Paris; General Secretary, International Congress History of Medicine, London, 1922; Vice-President of Honour, International Congress History of Med., Geneva, 1925; Member of Council, Soc. for Study of Inebriety and Folk-lore Soc.; Fitzpatrick Lecturer (RCP), 1935–36. *Publications:* Acute Infectious Diseases, 1925; 3rd ed. (with G. W. Ronaldson), 1940; History of the Acute Exanthemata, 1937; numerous contributions to medical journals, society transactions, and encyclopædias. *Recreation:* literature. *Address:* 91 Bedford Gardens, W8. *T:* Park 4595.

Died 13 March 1946.

ROLLESTON, Col Sir Lancelot, KCB 1911; DSO 1902; JP; DL; *b* 1847; *e surv. s* of late Col Lancelot Rolleston, MP, DL, and Eleanor Charlotte, *d* of late Robert Fraser of Torbeck; *m* 1882, Lady Charlotte Emma Maud Dalzell, CBE, *sister* of 14th Earl of Carnwath. *Educ:* Wellington; Christ Church, Oxford. High Sheriff, Notts, 1877. Served South Africa with Imperial Yeomanry (severely wounded, despatches, Queen's medal 4 clasps, DSO); Commanded South Notts Hussars Yeomanry, 1896–1906, and Notts and Derby Mounted Brigade, 1908–11; Chairman of Quarter Sessions for Nottinghamshire, 1912–32; Chairman Notts County Council, 1928–32; MFH South Notts, 1876–82; Rufford, 1889–1900. *Address:* Watnall Hall, Nottingham. *TA:* 3123 Kimberley, Notts. *Clubs:* Carlton; Royal Yacht Squadron, Cowes.

Died 26 March 1941.

ROLLESTON, Sir William Gustavus Stanhope, Kt 1929; DL, JP; Fellow, Surveyors' Institution; Past President, Land Agents' Society; formerly Chairman, Harborough Division, Conservative and Unionist Association; President, Leicester Central Conservative Association, 1925–36; late Major Leicestershire Yeomanry; *b* 1862; *s* of late Rev. W. L. Rolleston, Vicar of Scraptoft, and Mary Sophia, *d* of Sir Frederick Gustavus Fowke, Bt. *Address:* Glen Parva, Leicester. *Club:* Carlton.

Died 2 June 1944.

ROLLO, 11th Baron *cr* 1651; **William Charles Wordsworth Rollo;** Baron Dunning (UK), 1869, CB 1911; late Lt-Col 3rd Batt. Black Watch; Captain Royal Company of Archers; *b* 8 Jan. 1860; *s* of 10th Baron and Agnes (*d* 1906), *d* of late Colonel Trotter and Mary, *d* of 8th Baron; *S* father, 1916; *m* 1882, Mary Eleanor (*d* 1929), *d* of Beaumont Hotham; one *d.* Owns about 1250 acres. *Heir: nephew* Major John Eric Henry Rollo. *Address:* Duncrub Castle, Dunning, Perthshire. *T:* Dunning 202.

Died 3 March 1946.

ROLLO, 12th Baron *cr* 1651; **John Eric Henry Rollo;** Baron Dunning (UK), 1869; *b* 9 Jan. 1889; *s* of late Hon. Eric Rollo (2nd *s* of 10th Baron); *S* uncle 1946; *m* 1st, Helen Maud (*d* 1928), *o c* of Frederick Chetwynd Stapylton of Hatton Hill, Windlesham, Surrey; two *s* one *d*; 2nd, 1930, Phyllis Carina, *o d* of Bernard Sanderson; one *s*; 3rd, 1937, Mrs Lily Marie Cockshut, Hatch End, Middlesex; one *s. Educ:* Eton. Joined The Black Watch, 1910; served European War; Adjutant, Depot, 1919–22; Major, retired, 1930. *Recreations:* shooting, fishing, golf. *Heir: s* Master of Rollo. *Address:* Pitcairns, Dunning, Perthshire. *T:* Dunning 202.

Died 2 Sept. 1947.

ROLLO, Lt-Col George, CMG 1919; DSO 1917; late The King's Regt; Managing Director of Grayson, Rollo & Clover, Docks, Ltd, engineers and ship repairers; Director of R & J. Evans & Co. Ltd (Chairman), Jarvis Robinson Transport Ltd, Premier Electric Welding Co. (Mersey) Ltd; *b* 23 Dec. 1881; *s* of late George Rollo, JP, The Park, Waterloo, Lancs; *m* 1908, Winifred Russell Oliver; one *d. Educ:* Rugby. Served European War with the King's Liverpool Regiment, commanding 19th Batt., afterwards Brigadier-General 150th Infantry Brigade (wounded twice, despatches five times, DSO and Bar, CMG 1914–15 star, two medals). *Recreation:* coursing. *Address:* Inchcape, Hightown, Liverpool. *T:* Hightown 17. *Clubs:* Palatine, Liverpool.

Died 19 July 1944.

ROLLO, Rev. William, MA; late Professor of Divinity and Hebrew Lecturer, Trinity College, Toronto; retired, 1930; Licensed for occasional clerical duty by the Bishop of Glasgow and Galloway, 1930; Member of Glasgow University Oriental Society, 1902; *b* 25 March 1859; *s* of James and Mary Ann Rollo, Philorth, Fraserburgh; *m* 1882, Margaret Strachan Cruickshank, Cortes, Lonmay; one *s* five *d. Educ:* Aberdeen University. MA (Honours in Mathematics and Natural Philosophy), 1881; Edinburgh University Senior Hebrew Medallist, 1887; Theological College, Edinburgh, 1st Walker Bursar, Jamieson and Luscombe Scholar, 1st Class Preliminary Oxford and Cambridge Theological Examination, 1886–87. Glasgow University Additional Examiner in Arabic, 1904; Headmaster Public School, Monymusk, 1881–85; Rector of St James's, Glasgow, 1889–1913; Hebrew Lecturer at the Theological College of the Scottish Episcopal Church, Edinburgh, 1887–1913; Canon of St Mary's Cathedral, Glasgow, 1908–13; Diocesan Inspector of Church Schools, Glasgow and Galloway, 1891–1913; visiting Chaplain HM Prison, Barlinnie, 1889–1900; Sec. Glasgow Diocesan Sunday School Teachers' Association, 1892–1913. *Publication:* Appeal for a Christian Education in the National Schools, with Preface by Rev. Dr James Cooper, Regius Professor of Church History, Glasgow University. *Address:* Clydeholm, Roberton, Lanarkshire.

Died 24 Feb. 1949.

ROLO, Sir Robert, Kt 1938; CBE 1922; OBE 1919; a Director of the National Bank of Egypt, etc; *b* 1869; *s* of Simon Rolo; *m* 1896, Valentine Suares. *Educ:* Paris. *Address:* c/o National Bank of Egypt, Cairo, Egypt. *Clubs:* Mehemet Ali, Cairo; Travellers', Automobile, Paris.

Died 10 July 1944.

ROMER, Baron *cr* 1938 (Life Peer), of New Romney; **Mark Lemon Romer,** PC 1929; Kt 1922; a Lord of Appeal in Ordinary, 1938–44; *b* 1866; 2nd *s* of late Rt Hon. Sir Robert Romer, GCB; *m* 1893, Hon. Annie Wilmot, 4th *d* of 1st Baron Ritchie of Dundee, one *s. Educ:* Rugby; Trinity Hall, Cambridge (Hon. Fellow, 1922). Called to Bar, Lincoln's Inn, 1890; KC 1906; Counsel to Cambridge University, 1915; Counsel to Royal College of Physicians, 1914; Judge of Chancery

Division High Court, 1922–29; a Lord Justice of Appeal, 1929–38. *Address:* Pathways, The Avenue, Tadworth. *T:* Tadworth 2358. *Club:* Athenæum.

Died 19 Aug. 1944.

RONALDSON, Brig.-Gen. Robert William Hawthorn, CB 1915; late 1st Batt. Highland Light Infantry; *b* 7 Oct. 1864; *s* of late James Torrence Ronaldson; *m* 1st, 1896, Alice May (*d* 1908), *d* of late J. B. Summers, JP, of Rosemoor, Pembrokeshire; one *d*; 2nd, 1926, Mrs Gunter. Entered Army, 1886; Captain, 1893; Major, 1904; Lt-Col 1911; Col 1915; Adjutant, Militia, 1898; Volunteers, 1903; served NW Frontier, India, 1897–98 (medal with clasp); South Africa, 1901–02, in command of 22nd Mounted Infantry (Queen's medal 5 clasps); European War, 1914–15 (CB, despatches twice, very severely wounded); retired, 1920.

Died 11 March 1946.

RONALDSON, Thomas Martine, MA Oxon; painter; *b* Edinburgh, 1881; *s* of Thomas Rutherford Ronaldson, MB, FRCPE; *m* 1910, Dorothy, *d* of late Lt-Col Ferdinand Milner, RA; two *s* two *d*. *Educ:* Merchiston Castle School, Edinburgh; Trinity College, Oxford. Studied at School of Art, Edinburgh, Cope & Nicoll's, London Académie Julian, Paris, under J. P. Laurens. Captain, RGA, 1915–19; Exhibitor, RA, RSA, Paris (Silver Medal, 1926, Salon des Artistes Français); Portrait of Queen Elizabeth purchased by King George VI, 1937; pictures and drawings in the collections of Manchester, Plymouth, Falmouth, Eton College, Trinity College, Oxford, Trinity College, Cambridge and RE Mess, Chatham. *Publications:* Drawings of Trinity College, Oxford; Drawings of New College, Oxford. *Address:* 28 Aubrey Walk, Campden Hill, W8. *T:* Park 4685. *Clubs:* Arts, Garrick.

Died 12 March 1942.

ROOCROFT, Col William Mitchell, CMG 1918; VD; JP County of Lancaster; Army Medical Services (retired); Consulting Surgeon, Wigan Infirmary; *b* 1859; *s* of William Roocroft, JP, Wigan; *m* Helen Edith, *d* of Thomas Heald, Clerk of the Pence, Wigan; two *d*. *Educ:* Victoria University, Manchester; Middlesex Hospital. Hon. Surgeon, Wigan Infirmary, 1883–1917; Service: Volunteer and Territorial Force, 1884–1918; War Service: Army Medical Services, 1914–18; Assistant Director of Medical Services, 1914–18 (despatches thrice). *Publications:* various contributions to The Lancet. *Recreations:* hunting, tennis, golf. *Address:* 18 Rawlinson Road, Southport, Lancashire. *T:* 2087 Southport.

Died 20 Feb. 1943.

ROOKE, Charles Eustace, CMG 1943; MInstT; Colonial Govt Service (Retd), Company Director; Foreign Office (RD); *b* 22 May 1892; *s* of Lieut Charles Leonard Rooke, RN, and Frances Harcourt Rooke; *m* 1920, Irene Phyllis, *d* of Thomas Patterson, Littlebourne House; one *s*. *Educ:* Beachborough; Stowe. Indian Railways; IARO, 63rd PLI, 1914–17, BE Africa; Colonial Govt Railways, 1919. *Address:* Corbeaux, Puckle Lane, Canterbury. *T:* Canterbury 2068. *Clubs:* Royal Automobile; Royal Cinque Ports Yacht, Dover.

Died 21 July 1947.

ROOKE, Herbert K.; *b* Greenwich, 24 Dec. 1872; *s* of P. A. Rooke, and *nephew* of T. M. Rooke, RWS; unmarried. *Educ:* private school at Ealing; South Kensington and Slade School under Prof. Brown. Exhibited for first time at RBA 1894; Member, 1898–1912; at RA for first time, 1898. *Recreations:* model yacht sailing and building, cycling, and music. *Address:* 30 Park Road, Wimbledon, SW19.

Died 22 March 1944.

ROOKE, Thomas Matthews, RWS; Member Executive Committee National Trust; *b* 1842; *s* of Philip Rooke and Anne Kerr Matthews; *m* Leonora Jane Jones; one *s* one *d*. *Educ:* South Kensington and Royal Academy Schools. Works in Tate, Birmingham, Sheffield, and other public galleries. *Address:* 7 Queen Anne's Gardens, Bedford Park, W4.

Died 27 July 1942.

ROOME, Engr Rear-Adm. George W., CBE 1919; RN, retired; *b* 1865; *m* 1895, Catherine Anderson, *d* of William T. Stewart, Newburgh, Fife; two *s*. *Educ:* Aske's School, Hatcham; King's College, London; Royal Naval Engineering College, Keyham; Royal Naval College, Greenwich. *Address:* Bruach, Waterside Road, Paignton. *T:* Churston 81144. *Club:* Royal Torbay Yacht.

Died 21 March 1945.

ROOSEVELT, Franklin Delano; President of United States, since 1933; *b* Hyde Park, NY, 30 Jan. 1882; *s* of James Roosevelt and Sara Delano; *m* 1905, Anna Eleanor Roosevelt, New York; four *s* one *d*. *Educ:* Harvard Univ.; Columbia Univ. Law School. AB, Harvard, 1904; admitted to New York Bar, 1907; practised with Carter, Ledyard and Milburn, New York, 1907–10; member firm of Roosevelt and O'Connor, 1924–33; Member of Senate State of NY, 1910–13 (resigned); The Assistant Secretary of the Navy, 1913–20; in charge of inspections of US Naval Forces in European Waters, 1918, and of demobilisation in Europe, 1919; Governor of the State of New York, 1929–33; Nominated for Vice-President of US by Democratic Party, 1920; Dem. nominee for President of the US, 1932; Mem. Hudson Fulton Celebration Commn, 1909, Plattsburg, Centennial, 1913; mem. Nat. Commn, Panama PI Expn., 1915; overseer Harvard Univ., 1918–24; Pres. Am. Nat. Red Cross Ga. Warm Spring Foundation; Mem. Naval History Soc., NY Hist. Soc., Holland Soc. Alpha Delta Phi, Phi Beta Kappa. Mason. Episcopalian, sr. warden St James Church, Hyde Park. Congressional Medal Honor awarded posthumously, 1944. *Publications:* Whither Bound? 1926; The Happy Warrior—Alfred E. Smith, 1928; Government—Not Politics, 1932; Looking Forward, 1933; On Our Way, 1934; The Public Papers and Addresses of Franklin D. Roosevelt. *Address:* Hyde Park, Dutchess Co., NY; The White House, Washington, DC, USA.

Died 12 April 1945.

ROOSEVELT, Col Kermit; President, Roosevelt Steamship Company; Vice-President, US Lines and International Mercantile Marine Co.; *s* of Theodore Roosevelt and Edith Kermit Roosevelt of New York; *m* Belle Wyatt Willard of Richmond, Virginia; three *s* one *d*. *Educ:* Groton School; Harvard University. Spent 1909–10 with his father shooting in Africa; went to Brazil and spent three years engineering chiefly in the interior; went with his father on the exploration of the River of Doubt; spent two years banking in Argentina and Chile; commissioned in British Army and served in Mesopotamia as Captain in Motor Machine Guns (British Military Cross, Montenegrin War Cross, Order of Danilo); Transferred to American Army and served in France with the First Division, commanding a battery of 75's; Major, British Army, Sept. 1939 to March 1940, and June 1940–May 1941; Officer appointed to command British contingent International Volunteer Force to fight in Finland, 1940. *Publications:* War in the Garden of Eden; The Happy Hunting Grounds; Quentin Roosevelt: A Sketch, with Letters; East of the Sun and West of the Moon; Cleared for Strange Ports; American Backlogs; Trailing the Giant Panda. *Address:* 1 Broadway, New York. *Clubs:* Knickerbocker, New York.

Died 4 June 1943.

ROOSEVELT, Theodore, BA, MA, FRGS; Brigadier-General US Army; Vice-President, Boy Scouts of America; Trustee, Field Museum of Natural History, Chicago; National Chairman, United Council for Civilian Relief in China; *b* Oyster Bay, 1887; *e s* of Theodore Roosevelt (26th President of the United

States) and Edith Kermit Roosevelt; *m* 1910, Eleanor Butler Alexander, New York; three *s* one *d*. *Educ*: Groton School; Harvard University. Banker, 1912–17; Major, 1917; Lt-Col, 1918–19, 26th Infantry, First Division, AEF; commanded same regiment during latter part of war (wounded twice, Distinguished Service Medal, Distinguished Service Cross, Silver Star, Order of the Purple Heart (US), Legion of Honour, Croix de Guerre with three palms (France), Grand Croix de la Couronne, Croix de Guerre with palms (Belgium), Order of Brilliant Jade (China), War Cross, Order of Knights of Danilo (Montenegro)); an Organiser of American Legion, 1919; Member of New York State Assembly, 1919–20; Assistant Secretary of the Navy, 1921–24 (resigned); Chairman of International Committee of Naval Experts at Conference for Limitation of Armaments, Washington, 1921–22; Joint Head of Scientific Expeditions for Field Museum of Natural History, Chicago; Central Asia, 1925–26; China and Indo-China, 1928–29; Governor of Puerto Rico, 1929–32; Gov.-General of Philippine Islands, 1932–33; President, National Republican Club, 1934, 1935, 1936; Chairman of Board, American Express Company, 1934 and 1935; Vice-Pres. Doubleday Doran & Co. publishers, since 1935; Col, April 1941, commanding 26th Infantry, 1st Division; Brigadier-General, Dec. 1941, 2nd in command 1st Division; served in African campaign 1942–43, Sicilian campaign 1943 (Oak-leaf Cluster, to Silver Star, Croix de Guerre with palm). Chief liaison officer between American 5th Army and French Expeditionary Corps, Italy, until March 1944 (Officer Legion of Honor, palm for Croix de Guerre, American Legion of Merit); attached 4th (US) Infantry Division, led its first assault wave, Normandy, on D Day. *Publications*: Average Americans, 1919; East of the Sun and West of the Moon (with Kermit Roosevelt), 1926; Rank and File, 1927; All in the Family, 1928; Trailing the Giant Panda (with Kermit Roosevelt), 1929; Taps (Anthology of War verse, with Grantland Rice), 1932; The Three Kingdoms of Indo-China (with Harold J. Coolidge, Jr), 1933; Colonial Policies of the US, 1937; The Desk Drawer Anthology, 1937; Reader's Digest Reader, 1940. *Address*: Oyster Bay, New York. *Clubs*: Himalayan; Harvard, River, Explorers', New York.

Died 12 July 1944.

ROOTS, Rt Rev. Logan Herbert, DD; giving full time to the Oxford Group in the national morale building programme of Moral Rearmament; Bishop of Hankow, China, 1904–38; Chairman of the House of Bishops of the Chung Hua Sheng Kung Hui, 1926–31; Hon. Secretary, National Christian Council of China, 1924–29 and since 1931; *b* Tamaroa, Perry Co., Illinois, USA, 27 July 1870; *s* of P. K. Roots of Little Rock, Arkansas, and Frances Maria Blakeslee; *m* 1902, Eliza Lydia M'Cook, of Hartford, Conn; three *s* two *d*. *Educ*: Berkeley School, Boston, Mass; Harvard, AB 1891; Episcopal Theological School, Cambridge, Mass, 1893–96; BD. Graduate Secretary Harvard Christian Association, 1891–92; Travelling Sec. College Dept International Committee YMCAs, 1892–93; Deacon, Protestant Episcopal Church, 1896; Priest, 1898; went to China, 1896, and studied the language at Wuchang for two years; thence to Hankow; DD University of the South, 1906; Episcopal Theological School, Cambridge, Mass, 1922; Harvard, 1925. *Address*: 281 Fourth Avenue, New York; 3807 Ingomar Street, Washington, DC.

Died 23 Sept. 1945.

RORIE, Col David, DSO 1917; Chevalier de la Légion d' Honneur; late RAMC, TA (ret); TD; MD Edin. & CM, DPH Aber.; JP Cos. Fife and Aberdeen; Officer Order of the Hospital of St John of Jerusalem; Hon. Col RAMC units 51st (Highland) Division, 1930–35; *b* Edinburgh, 17 March 1867; 2nd *s* of late George Livingston Rorie; *m* Margaret Elizabeth, *d* of late J. W. Miller, MD, Dundee; one *s* one *d*. *Educ*: Aberdeen Collegiate School; University, Aberdeen and University,

Edinburgh. Part-time Medical Referee (National Health Insurance) to Department of Health for Scotland; Chairman Aberdeen Medical Board, Ministry of Labour and National Service; President, Aberdeen Branch BMA, 1932; Chairman, Aberdeen Division BMA, 1924–29; Chairman Aberdeenshire Panel Committee, 1912–33; Dr Alexander Black Lecturer RCP, Edinburgh, 1930; President Aberdeen Branch British Legion, 1922–45; Aberdeen Edinburgh University Association, 1925; Joint-Editor of Caledonian Med. Jl since 1912; Certifying Factory Surgeon, Cardenden, Fife, and MO Bowhill and other collieries, 1894–1905; practised at Cults, Aberdeenshire, 1905–33; mobilised as Capt. RAMC (TF) at outbreak of war; Major, Sept. 1914; temp. Lt-Col Jan. 1916; temp. Col AMS and ADMS 51st (Highland) Division in the Field, Dec. 1917 (despatches twice, Bt of Lt-Col, DSO, Chevalier de la Légion d'Honneur); TD. *Publications*: Folk-Lore of Mining Folk of Fife in Fifeshire Folk-Lore (Folk-Lore Society's County Series); numerous papers on Folk Lore and Folk-Medicine; The Auld Doctor (vol. of verse), 1920; A Medico's Luck in the War, 1929; The Lum Hat wantin' the Croon, and other poems, 1935. *Recreations*: reading, writing. *Address*: 17 Hazeldene Road, Aberdeen. *T*: Aberdeen 4471.

Died 18 Feb. 1946.

RORKE, Kate, (Mrs Douglas Cree); actress and teacher of elocution; *m* 1st, Edward Gardiner (*d* 1899); 2nd, Dr Douglas Cree (*d* 1932); one *d*. *Educ*: Convent of Notre Dame, Southwark. First appearance on stage as a child in 1878 in Olivia at Court Theatre; has played also at Haymarket, Criterion, Strand, Comedy, Vaudeville and Garrick Theatres; acted much with John Hare and in other first-class companies. *Address*: Meadow Cottage, Bury Green, Little Hadham, Herts. *T*: Bishop's Stortford 898.

Died 31 July 1945.

ROSBOTHAM, Sir Samuel Thomas, Kt 1933; JP; MP (Lab) Ormskirk Division of Lancs, 1929–31, (Nat. Lab) 1931–39; *b* 1864; *m* 1st, 1887, Jane (*d* 1945), *d* of John Heyes, of Bickerstaffe; four *s* one *d*; 2nd, 1946, Joan, *d* of late Rev. Dearden, Vicar of Waterfoot. *Address*: Teviotdale, Forest Road, Southport, Lancs. *T*: Southport 4337.

Died 12 March 1950.

ROSCOE, Frank, MA; Secretary Royal Society of Teachers (retired); *b* Bolton, 1870; *s* of late Alfred Roscoe, Bolton; *m* 1900, Margaret Elizabeth (*d* 1941), 2nd *d* of late W. Davies; two *s* one *d*. *Educ*: Borough Road Training College; Balliol College, Oxford. Lecturer Borough Road College, 1894–96; Head of Elementary Teachers' Training College in the University of Oxford, 1896–1900; Head of Training College for men, and Lecturer on Education in the University of Birmingham, 1900–13. *Publications*: Articles on Education in several journals; chapter on Teaching a Profession, in Cambridge Essays on Education; (with H. Ward) The Approach to Teaching. *Address*: 23 Shrublands Road, Berkhamsted, Herts.

Died 8 July 1942.

ROSE, Frederick Campbell, CSI 1920; Civil Engineer (retired); *b* 1865; *s* of William Rose and Alexa Anna Gordon Johnston, both of Elgin, Scotland; *m* 1893, Lucy Hamer, *d* of David Ireland Mack, JP, Ardrossan, Scotland, and Sarah Scott Clarkson, of Halbeath, Fifeshire; no *c*. *Educ*: Trinity College, Glenalmond; Royal Indian Engineering College, Coopers Hill. Joined the Public Works Department of the Govt of India, 1886; was attached to the Irrigation Branch of that Department in the Punjab; Secretary to Govt of India Public Works Department, 1916; Additional member of the Legislative Council Government of India, 1916–19; retired from active service in India, 1919; Chief Engineer to the Commission for the Improvement of the river system of the Chihli Province, North China, 1919–27. *Recreations:* golf, shooting, fishing, etc. *Address:* c/o Lloyds Bank Ltd, 6 Pall Mall, SW1. *Club:* East India and Sports.

Died 18 July 1946.

ROSE of Kilravock, Lt-Col Hugh, CMG 1916; late Commanding 42nd The Black Watch; *b* 1863; *s* of late Major James Rose, of Kilravock, IA, and Anna Maria, *d* of late Lt-Gen. George Twemlow, Bengal Artillery; *m* 1920, Ruth Antoinette, *e d* of late W. G. Guillemard, Malverleys, East Woodhay, Hants; two *d*. *Educ:* Wellington; Sandhurst. Served Nile Expedition, 1884–85 (medal 2 clasps, bronze star); S Africa, 1901–02 (Queen's medal 4 clasps) European War, 1914–18 (despatches four times, CMG). *Address:* Kilravock Castle, Gollanfield, Scotland.

Died 22 Feb. 1946.

ROSE, Hon. Hugh Edward; Chief Justice of the High Court (Ontario) since 1930; *b* Toronto, 16 Sept. 1869; *s* of late Hon. John Edward Rose, LLD, a Judge of the High Court of Justice (Ontario) and Kate Macdonald; unmarried. *Educ:* Toronto Collegiate Institute; University of Toronto, BA, 1891; LLB 1892. Called to Ontario Bar, 1894; KC, 1908; sometime examiner in Law, University of Toronto and Law Society of Upper Canada; practised profession in Toronto; Judge of the Supreme Court of Ontario and Member of the High Court Division, 1916; President High Court of Justice for Ontario, 1930; Comm. (Brother) of the Order of St John of Jerusalem, 1932; a Member of the Board of Governors of the University of Toronto (Hon. LLD 1944). *Recreations:* golf, riding. *Address:* 86 Roxborough Street East, Toronto 5, Canada. *Clubs:* Overseas; Toronto, Toronto Golf, Toronto.

Died 13 Oct. 1945.

ROSE, John Holland, LittD Cambridge University; Fellow of Christ's College, Cambridge; *b* Bedford, 1855; *m* 1880, Laura K. Haddon; one *s* two *d*. Exhibitioner of Bedford Modern School; winner of the Latin Prose Essay at Owens College, Manchester; Scholar of Christ's College, Cambridge; Reader in Modern History, Cambridge, 1911–19; Vere Harmsworth Professor of Naval History, Cambridge University, 1919–33; retired, 1933; Hon. Member of the Polish Academy of Arts and Sciences. *Publications:* The Revolutionary and Napoleonic Era; The Rise of Democracy, 1897; The Life of Napoleon I, 1902 (11th ed., 1935); an edition of Carlyle's French Revolution with critical and explanatory notes; chapters in the Cambridge Modern History (vols viii and ix), and the Cambridge History of British Foreign Policy (vol. i); Napoleonic Studies, 1904; Despatches relating to the Third Coalition, 1904; The Development of the European Nations, 1870–1921, 1923; (joint) Dumouriez and the Defence of England against Napoleon, 1908; Editor of the History of Malta (1798–1814); William Pitt and National Revival, 1911, William Pitt and the Great War, 1911; Pitt and Napoleon; Essays and Letters, 1912; The Personality of Napoleon, 1912, new edition, 1930; The Origins of the War, 1914; Nationality as a Factor in Modern History, 1916; Lord Hood and the Defence of Toulon, 1922; The Indecisiveness of Modern War, and other Essays, 1927; The Mediterranean in the Ancient World, 1933; Man and the Sea: Stages in Maritime and Human Progress, 1935; contributor to the Thinkers of the Revolutionary Era, 1930; Co-editor of and contributor to Cambridge History of the British Empire; articles in English Historical Review, Edinburgh, Nineteenth Century and After, Contemporary Review, Cambridge Historical Journal, etc. *Address:* Walsingham, Millington Road, Cambridge.

Died 3 March 1942.

ROSE, Col John Markham, DSO 1918; JP; retired pay; Member E Retford Rural District Council (Chairman 1939–40); *b* Markham, 22 March 1865; *m* 1888, Edith Mary, *d* of Inspector-General James Flanagan, RN. *Educ:* Cheltenham. Lieutenant Royal Marine Artillery, 1882; passed Staff College, 1893; Staff RM Academy, 1899–1903; Staff C-in-C, Mediterranean and Home Fleets, 1903–08; DAAG, Royal Marines, 1908–11; commanded Heavy Artillery, SW Africa, 1914–15 (DSO); raised and commanded S African Heavy Artillery for service in France, 1915–16; GSO (1) RNAS Aegean Wing, 1917–18; retired with rank of Colonel, 1919; Member of Council Union Jack Club and Hostel since 1908. *Publications:* many Essays on Military Subjects, Modern Tactics, contributed to Times History of War in S Africa; 1st Prize essay, RUSI 1903; contributor Universal Encyclopædia; Short History of Royal Marines, 7 editions. *Recreations:* keen Mason, passed Master and many Lodges and Chapters, Prov. Grand Rank, Hants and Notts; US Rugby half-back in the 'eighties, skating (NSA), cricket, golf, etc. *Address:* East Markham, Newark-on-Trent. *T:* Tuxford 221. *Club:* United Service.

Died 29 March 1942.

ROSE-INNES, Rt Hon. Sir James, PC 1914; KCMG 1901; KC; barrister and politician; *b* Grahamstown, 8 Jan. 1855; *s* of J. Rose-Innes, CMG, and nephew by marriage to Sir Gordon Sprigg, ex-Premier of Cape Colony; *m* 1881, Jessie, CBE, *y d* of late W. D. Pringle of Bedford. *Educ:* Bedford; Gill College, Somerset East; Cape University. Entered Cape Parliament 1884, as Member for Victoria East; returned for Cape Division, 1888; QC, 1889; Attorney-General in Rhodes Ministry, 1890; resigned, 1893; President of the Political Association; was retained by High Commissioner during trial of Reform prisoners in Transvaal to watch for British Government; Attorney-General Cape Colony, 1900–02; Chief Justice of Transvaal, 1902–10; Senior Puisne Judge Appellate Division Supreme Court of South Africa, 1910–14; Chief Justice of the Union of South Africa, 1914–27. *Address:* Kolara, Gibson Road, Kenilworth, Cape, S Africa.

Died 16 Jan. 1942.

ROSENTHAL, Moriz; pianist; *b* Lemberg, 1862. *Educ:* studied piano under Karl Mikuli in Lemberg, Raffael Joseffy in Vienna, and Franz Liszt in Weimar and Rome. At thirteen years old appeared in Vienna, Warsaw, and Bucharest; Court Pianist of Emperor of Austria and Queen of Roumania; studied philosophy and æsthetic of music at the University of Vienna; ten seasons in USA; compositions for piano (variations on an original theme, Romanza, Prelude, Papillons, Carnaval de Vienne, etc.).

Died 3 Sept. 1946.

ROSEVEARE, William Nicholas, MA; *b* Monmouth, 17 Feb. 1864; *m* 1893, *d* of late Rev. W. D. Bushell of Harrow; two *s* (also one *s* killed flying), two *d*. *Educ:* Fellow of St John's College, Cambridge, 1888. Assistant Master, Harrow School, 1889–1906; Professor of Mathematics, University College, University of South Africa, Natal; retired on pension, 1929. *Address:* North Parade, Monmouth. *T:* Monmouth 300.

Died 2 Feb. 1948.

ROSEWATER, Victor, AM, PhD; economist and writer; formerly editor of the Omaha Bee; *b* Omaha, 13 Feb. 1871; *s* of late Edward Rosewater; *m* 1904, Kate Katz of Baltimore; one *s* one *d*. *Educ:* Johns Hopkins University; Columbia University; University Fellow, 1892–93. Regent University of Nebraska, 1896–97; special lecturer on municipal finance University of Wisconsin, 1904; member Omaha Public Library Board, 1894–1905; delegate to National Conference on Conservation of Natural Resources, 1908; delegate-at-large for Nebraska to Republican National Convention, 1908; member Republican National Committee and as its chairman opened 1912 Chicago Convention; member Advisory Labour Committee, National Council of Defence, 1917–18; Administrator for Nebraska of Paper Section, War Industries Board, 1918; Chairman Nebraska Constitutional Convention Survey Committee, 1919; member American Jewish Committee, American Economic Association; Society of the US Military Telegraph Corps. *Publications:* Laissez-faire, in Palgrave's Dictionary of Political Economy; Special Assessments, a Study in Municipal Finance; Omaha, in Historic Towns of the West; The Liberty Bell, its History and Significance; History of Co-operative News-Gathering in the US; many magazine articles. *Address:* 1530 Locus Street, Philadelphia. *Clubs:* Omaha, Omaha.

Died 12 July 1940.

ROSLING, Sir Edward, Kt 1913; *b* 4 Dec. 1863; *s* of late Joseph Rosling, South Nutfield; *m* 1888, *d* of late Hugh White of Antrim; two *s* one *d*. *Educ:* Queenwood, Hampshire. For 10 years unofficial member of the Legislative Council of Ceylon representing the Planting Interests; planting in Ceylon 27 years; Chairman Anglo-Ceylon and General Estates Co., Ltd. *Address:* Aldersyde, Weybridge. *Clubs:* Oriental, City of London, Royal Automobile.

Died 19 Jan. 1946.

ROSS, Alexander Carnegie, CB 1900; MA; *b* 3 July 1859; *s* of late Major J. Ross of Tillycorthie; *m* 1st, 1888, Katherine Amelia (*d* 1894), *d* of late Robert Boyd Tytler of Palli Kelly, Ceylon; 2nd, 1897, Anne Emma, *d* of late Dr Watkin Williams, Birmingham; two *s* two *d*. *Educ:* Gymnasium and King's College, Aberdeen. British Consular Service; retired on a pension, 1921. *Address:* 57 Sunderland Road, Forest Hill, SE23. *T:* Forest Hill 2542.

Died 1 July 1940.

ROSS, Charles Griffith; Secretary to President of United States since 1945; *b* Independence, Mo, 9 Nov. 1885; *s* of James Bruce Ross and Ella Thomas; *m* 1913, Florence Griffin; two *s*. *Educ:* University of Missouri. AB 1905. Journalist, 1905–08; Member of Faculty, Univ. of Missouri School of Journalism, 1908–18; on sabbatical leave, Sub-editor Melbourne (Australia) Herald, 1916–17; successively, Washington Correspondent, Editor of editorial page, and Contributing Editor of St Louis Post-Dispatch, 1918–45. *Publications:* The Writing of News (textbook), 1911; The Country's Plight, 1932 (awarded Pulitzer prize for newspaper correspondence). *Recreation:* gardening. *Address:* The White House, Washington, DC. *T:* National 1414. *Clubs:* Gridiron, National Press, Overseas Writers (Washington, DC).

Died 5 Dec. 1950.

ROSS, Sir Charles (Henry Augustus Frederick Lockhart), 9th Bt *cr* 1672; DL; *b* 4 April 1872; *S* father, 1883; *m* 1st, 1893, Winifred, *d* of late A. A. Berens (marr. diss. 1897); 2nd, 1901, Patricia Burnley (who obtained a decree of divorce, 1928), *d* of Andrew Ellison, Louisville, USA. *Educ:* Eton; Trin. Coll. Camb. Rowed in University Eight, 1894. Lieut 3rd Batt. Seaforth Highlanders, retired 1894; served as Captain Boer War, 1899–1900; raised a corps and subsequently served on staff (medal, four clasps); Major in Lovat's Scouts; inventor of Canadian service rifle; Member of American Society Mechanical Engineers; consulting adviser on small arms, etc., to Canadian Government; Hon. Colonel. Owns about 356,600 acres. *Address:* Balnagowan Castle, Kildary, Rossshire. *Clubs:* White's, Marlborough, Royal Automobile, Royal Thames Yacht.

Died 28 June 1942 (ext).

ROSS, Edward Rowlandson; *b* 1868; *s* of Edward Ross, merchant, London; *m* 1903, Emily Florence Hand Foster; three *s* one *d*. *Educ:* Aldenham School. Madras Railways, 1893–1905; General Manager, Natal Government Railways, 1906–10; General Manager, Rhodesia Railways, 1911–19; Fellow Royal Empire Society. *Address:* Halkhed, Edgeborough Road, Guildford, Surrey. *T:* 2594.

Died 15 Feb. 1941.

ROSS, Rt Rev. Monsignor Canon Francis; Hon. Canon of Westminster Cathedral since 1919; *b* Harrow-on-the-Hill, 1873; *s* of Paul Ross, sculptor. *Educ:* St Edmund's College, Ware; St Mary's, Oscott. At St Edmund's College, Ware, teaching Classics, 1896–1904; Professor of Church History at Oscott College, 1904–10; Director of the English Branch of the Association for the Propagation of the Faith, 1910–31; Domestic Prelate to his Holiness Pope Pius XI, 1924. *Address:* 16 Roxborough Park, Harrow-on-the-Hill.

Died 12 Dec. 1945.

ROSS, Rear-Adm. George Parish, CB 1916; RN, retired; *b* 1875; *s* of late Horatio Senftenberg John Ross, BCS. Served Gambia Expedition, 1894 (medal with clasp); European War, 1914–17, including Jutland Bank (despatches, CB).

Died 1 Feb. 1942.

ROSS, Rev. Neil, CBE 1933, MA, DD, DLitt, JP, Minister of Laggan Parish, Inverness-shire; *b* 24 Sept. 1871; *s* of Kenneth Ross and Margaret Macleod; *m* 1907, Helen Annand Smith; two *s* one *d*. *Educ:* Glasgow High School; Edinburgh Univ. Parish Minister successively of St James, Kirkcaldy; Rosemount, Aberdeen; and Buccleuch, Edinburgh; served with Expeditionary Force in France; Ex-Pres. of An Comunn Gaidhealach; Ex-Editor of An Gaidheal, a monthly bilingual magazine; County Councillor. *Publication:* Heroic Poetry from The Book of the Dean of Lismore. *Recreation:* bagpipe music. *Address:* The Manse, Laggan, Inverness-shire. *Clubs:* Royal Scottish Pipers, Edinburgh.

Died 17 Dec. 1943.

ROSS, Philip Dansken; President and Editor of the Ottawa Journal; *b* 1 Jan. 1858; Scotch parentage; *m* 1891, Mary, *d* of Col W. A. Littlejohn of Plymouth, NC; no *c*. *Educ:* McGill University. Joined staff of Montreal Star, 1880; City Editor, Toronto Mail, 1882; Assistant Editor, Toronto News, 1883; Managing Editor, Montreal Star, 1885; founded Ottawa Journal, 1886; Member Ottawa City Council for several years; President Ottawa Board of Trade, 1902–03; LLD Queen's University, 1919, McGill University, 1936; President Canadian Daily Newspapers Association, 1920–21; appointed by Ontario Govt, in 1929, Chairman Royal Commission to investigate and report on the Hospitals, Reformatories, and other social welfare institutions of the Province. *Publication:* Retrospects of a Newspaper Person, 1931. *Recreations:* rowing and golf; stroke of amateur champion four-oared crews of Canada, 1883 (Toronto RC), and 1886 (Lachine RC); President, Royal Canadian Golf Association, 1909. *Address:* 17 Blackburn Avenue, Ottawa, Canada. *Clubs:* Rideau, University (Ottawa); Faculty (Montreal).

Died 5 July 1949.

ROSS, Brig.-Gen. Robert James, CB 1919; CMG 1917; *b* 1865; *s* of late Lt-Col R. H. Ross; *m* 1892, Frances Cecilia Caroline Knox, *d* of late Vesey Knox of Shimnah, Newcastle, Co. Down; two *s* one *d*. *Educ:* RMC, Sandhurst. Entered Army, 1886; Capt. 1895; served South African War, 1899–1901 (Queen's medal 4 clasps); Major 1904; Lt-Col 1914; Brevet Col 1915; Brig.-Gen. 1916; European War, 1914–18 (despatches, CB, CMG); retired pay, 1922; holds Legion of Honour. *Address:* Friar's Croft, Pilgrim's Way, Guildford.

Died 25 Dec. 1943.

ROSS, Roderick, CVO 1934; CBE 1920; MVO 1905; Chief Constable of Edinburgh; retired 1935; *b* 1863; *m* Elizabeth Esther, *d* of Henry Mills; four *s* five *d. Educ:* Helmsdale. Chief Constable, Ramsgate, 1895–97, Bradford, 1898–1900. *Address:* Lipton House, 28 Regent Terrace, Edinburgh.

Died 6 March 1943.

ROSS, Thomas Arthur, MD, FRCP; Specialist practice in Neuroses; *b* Edinburgh, 1875; *s* of Thomas Ross, LLD; *m* 1st, 1902, Emily, *d* of Baker Bridge; one *d*; 2nd, 1939, Mrs Norah Cecil Runge, OBE. *Educ:* Edinburgh Academy; Edinburgh University. Physician Royal National Hospital for Consumption, Ventnor, I of W, 1901–17; Medical Director of Cassel Hospital for Functional Nervous Disorders, Swaylands, Penshurst, Kent, 1919–34. *Publications:* The Common Neuroses; An Introduction to Analytical Psychotherapy; An Enquiry into Prognosis in the Neuroses. *Address:* St John's House, Smith Square, SW1. *T:* Abbey 1563.

Died 3 March 1941.

ROSS, Rev. Thomas Harry; Hon. Canon and late Hon. Canon Precentor of Leicester Cathedral; *b* 19 Nov. 1863; *o surv. s* of Edward and Esther Ross; *m* 1st, Minnie Reynolds, Springfield, Shawbury, Salop; 2nd, K. M. Freeman, *widow* of late C. F. Freeman, Solicitor, Cambridge; two *s. Educ:* Sidney Sussex College, Cambridge, MA. For seventeen years Master-in-Charge of The Grocers' Grammar School, Oundle; three years' war work at St John's College, Leatherhead; Patron and Rector of Church Langton, 1918–39; Director of Music for the Diocese of Leicester; Member of Advisory Committee of Music for Leicester and Rutland University College; Mus. Bac. Oxon; Mus. Bac. and Mus. Doc. Trinity College, Dublin; FRCO; Hon. Associate of Royal Institute of British Architects; Surrogate for the Diocese. *Works:* Evening Service in D.; Anthem, Shew us Thy mercy; Motet, Who would not then depart with gladness. Brochure on Langton and the Messiah. *Recreations:* cricket, croquet, golf, bowls. *Address:* Langthorpe, Ashfield Road, Leicester. *TA:* Langthorpe, Leicester. *T:* Leicester 7204.

Died 30 July 1943.

ROSS, Captain William Alston, CMG 1922; late Senior Resident S Provinces, Nigeria; *b* 1875; *s* of Rev. William Ross.

Died 8 Sept. 1944.

ROSS, Hon. William Donald; *b* Little Bras d'Or, NS, 20 June 1869; *s* of John Ross and Christina Isabel Mackay, both Scotch; *m* 1st, 1899, Susan, *d* of James D. McGregor, New Glasgow, NS; one *s* two *d*; 2nd, 1914, Isabel, *d* of George Forrest MacKay, New Glasgow, NS; one *s* one *d. Educ:* New Glasgow, NS, Public Schools. Entered the service of the Bank of Nova Scotia at New Glasgow, NS; General Manager of the Metropolitan Bank, Toronto, 1903–14; Lieut-Governor of the Province of Ontario, 1927–32; Director of Bank of Nova Scotia, General Electric Co., Limited, and of other important companies. *Address:* 330 Bay Street, Toronto, Ont. *Clubs:* York, Toronto, National, Toronto Hunt, Mississauga Golf (Toronto); St James' (Montreal); Halifax (Halifax).

Died 25 June 1947.

ROSS, William Henry, OBE; *b* 19 June 1862; *s* of John Ross and Euphemia Forrest; *m* 1888, Annie Gilmour Pollock Dalgleish; two *s* one *d. Educ:* George Watson's College, Edinburgh. Joined the Distillers Coy Ltd as junior clerk, 1878; Secretary, 1889; General Manager, 1897; Managing Director, 1900; Chairman, 1925; retired 1935; created W. H. Ross Foundation for the Study and Prevention of Blindness, Edinburgh, 1935. *Address:* Stanmore, Davidson's Mains, Edinburgh. *T:* Edinburgh 77031.

Died 22 Aug. 1944.

ROSS-FRAMES, Col Percival, CMG 1918; *b* 18 Dec. 1863; *s* of William Minett Frames; *m* 1891, Linda, *d* of late F. B. Brown. Served German South-West Africa, 1914–18 (despatches, CMG). *Address:* Kelston, Kenilworth, Cape Province, S Africa.

Died Nov. 1947.

ROSS-JOHNSON, Dennis, CBE 1920; VD; MInstT; retired; *b* 1860; *s* of H. C. Ross-Johnson, FRGS, Barrister-at-Law; *m* 1st, Edith, *d* of R. Restall, Uitenhage, Cape Colony; four *d*; 2nd, Evelyn Alice Fabling (*d* 1939), *d* of Com. General A. W. Downes, CB, JP. *Educ:* St Andrew's College, Grahamstown; University College School, London. Traffic Manager, Madras Railway, 1901–06; Secretary, Indian Railway Conference Association, 1906–11; General Manager and Secretary, Port of Bristol, 1911–28; Vice-Pres., Institute of Transport, 1935–38; Member of many Government Committees during the War. *Publications:* Modern Dock Operation; papers in Journal of Institute of Transport and Transport Journals, and article in Encyclopædia Britannica (14th edition). *Address:* 9 Harley Gardens, SW10. *T:* Kensington 6675. *Club:* Oriental.

Died 7 June 1941.

ROSSILLON, Rt Rev. Peter; RC Bishop of Vizagapatam since 1926; *b* 22 Sept. 1874. *Educ:* Lons-le-Saulnier, Jura, France. Consecrated, 1919; coadjutor to Rt Rev. J. M. Clerc, 1919. *Address:* Bishop's House, Maharanipeta PO (Vizagapatam), India.

Died 22 March 1947.

ROSTRON, Rev. Sydney N.; *see* Nowell-Rostron.

ROTHBAND, Sir Henry Lesser, 1st Bt *cr* 1923; *m* Ella, *e d* of late J. Mandleberg, Manchester; two *d*. Originator of the Scheme for the King's National Roll for finding Employment for disabled Sailors and Soldiers, 1915. *Publications:* four pamphlets in connection with the Rothband Employment Scheme. *Heir:* none.

Died 1 Nov. 1940 (ext).

ROTHENSTEIN, Sir William, Kt 1931; Hon. DLitt Oxon; MA Sheffield; Hon. ARCA; attached as unofficial artist to Royal Air Force since 1939; Principal, Royal College of Art, 1920–35; Trustee, Tate Gallery, 1927–33; Member of the Royal Fine Art Commission, 1931–38; an official artist to the British and afterwards to the Canadian Armies during European War; Professor of Civic Art, Sheffield University, 1917–26; Romanes Lecturer, Oxford University, 1934; a Governor of the Foundling Hospital since 1939; *b* Bradford, Yorks, 29 Jan. 1872; 2nd *s* of late M. Rothenstein and Bertha, *d* of late Wm Dux; *m* 1899, Alice Mary, *e c* of late Walter John Knewstub, of Chelsea; two *s* two *d. Educ:* Bradford Grammar School; Slade School, University College; Académie Julian, Paris. Paintings and Drawings: Tate Gallery; British Museum; Victoria and Albert Museum; St Stephen's Hall, Westminster; Fitzwilliam Museum, St John's College, Trinity Hall, Trinity College, and King's College, Cambridge; Magdalen College, Worcester College, and Ashmolean Museum, Oxford; Eton and Winchester Colleges, National Portrait Gallery and in many British, Dominion and American galleries. *Publications:* Oxford Characters, 1893–1896; Paul Verlaine, 1897; English Portraits, 1897–1898; The French Set: Rodin, Fantin-Latour, and Legros, 1898; Liber Juniorum, 1899; Manchester Portraits, 1900; a Life of Goya, 1900; Drawings by Hok'sai, 1910; six portraits of Sir Rabindranath Tagore, 1915; a Plea for a Wider Use of Artists and Craftsmen, 1917–1924 Portraits, 1920; 24 Portraits, 2nd series, 1923; (with K. de B. Codrington) Ancient India, 1926; Twelve Portraits, 1929; Men and Memories, vol. i, 1872–1900, 1931; vol. ii, 1900–1922, 1932; Since Fifty: Men and Memories, 1922–1938, 1939; Contemporaries, 24 portrait drawings,

1937; (with Lord David Cecil) Men of the RAF; 1942. *Address:* Far Oakridge, Stroud, Glos. *T:* Frampton Mansell 38. *Club:* Athenæum.

Died 14 Feb. 1945.

ROTHERHAM, 2nd Baron *cr* 1910; **Stuart Lund Holland;** Bt *cr* 1907; *b* 25 Oct. 1876; *o s* of 1st Baron and late Mary, *e d* of James Lund, DL, Malsis Hall, near Leeds; *S* father 1927; *m* 1909, Miriam Agnes, *d* of late Henry W. Wright. *Educ:* Harrow; Exeter College, Oxford. Was Captain 6th Inniskilling Dragoons; served South Africa, 1901–02 (Queen's medal 5 clasps); European War, France, 1914–16 and 1917–19 (1914–15 Star, Allied and Victory medals, despatches); Assistant Administrator Ministry of Munitions (Disposal Board), 1920–22; Inspector Ministry of Pensions, 1922–44. *Recreation:* golf. *Heir:* none. *Address:* 1 Bentley Road, Cambridge. *Club:* Naval and Military.

Died 24 Jan. 1950 (ext).

ROTHERHAM, Arthur, MA, MB, BC Cantab; 3rd *s* of Alexander Rotherham, of Coventry; *m* Winifred Kate, *d* of A. T. Dudgeon of Ewell, Surrey; two *s. Educ:* Uppingham School; Trinity College, Cambridge; St Thomas' Hospital. House Surgeon, St Thomas' Hospital; Assistant Medical Officer, London County Asylums, Cane Hill, Manor and Horton; Medical Superintendent, Darenth Industrial Colony, Dartford; Senior Commissioner of the Board of Control; a Lord Chancellor's Visitor in Lunacy, 1931–44; retired, 1944. *Recreations:* cricket, golf, Rugby football; represented England at Rugby football in 1898 and 1899 against Scotland twice, Wales twice, and Ireland once. *Address:* Hazards, Enton, Godalming. *T:* Godalming 373.

Died 3 March 1946.

ROTHERY, Guy Cadogan; *b* Havre, 1863; 2nd *s* of Robert Cadogan Rothery of Doctor's Commons and Suzanne Laure, *d* of Dr Muraour, Paris and Grasse. *Educ:* privately. Journalist and author; has contributed largely to the Daily Press and Magazines; edited several publications. Sectional Editor and Annotator, Standard Books; Joint Managing Editor Enciclopedia de la América del Sud. *Publications:* The Amazons in Antiquity and Modern Times; Symbols, Emblems, and Devices; Ceilings and their Decorations, Art and Archæology; Chimneypiece and Ingle Nooks; Staircases and Garden Steps; Armorial Insignia of the Princes of Wales; The ABC of Heraldry; The Occult in Heraldry; The Heraldry of Shakespeare; Chimneypieces and their Decoration: Examples in England; contributor to Hutchinson's Technical and Scientific Encyclopædia.

Died 2 May 1940.

ROTHSCHILD, Baron Henri de; Commandeur de la Légion d'Honneur; Docteur en Medecine et Homme de lettres; Fondateur de l'Hôpital Mathilde-Henri de Rothschild (clinique chirurgicale), 199 rue Marcadet; *b* Paris, 26 July 1872; *m* Mathilde Weisweiler (*d* 1926); two *s* one *d. Educ:* Lycées Louis le Grand et Janson. *Publications:* nombreuses études sur le lait et les maladies infantiles; œuvres dramatiques: La Rampe, 1909, Le Caducée, 1921, Le Moulin de la Galette, 1923, Héritage, 1924, La Vocation, 1926, Circé, 1929; Grand Patron, 1931; essais: Les autographes de Pierre Corneille, 1929, etc. *Address:* Castel Beau Cidre, Jouxtens près Lausanne, Suisse.

Died 10 Oct. 1947.

ROTHSCHILD, Lionel Nathan de, OBE 1917; partner in the firm of N. M. Rothschild & Sons; MP (U) Aylesbury Division, Bucks, 1910–23; *b* 25 Jan. 1882; *e s* of late Leopold de Rothschild; *m* 1912, Marie Louise, *y d* of late Edmond Beer; two *s* two *d. Educ:* Cambridge (MA). *Address:* 18 Kensington Palace Gardens, W8. *T:* Bayswater 2523; Exbury House, Exbury, Hants. *Clubs:* St James, Carlton; Royal Yacht Squadron, Cowes.

Died 28 Jan. 1942.

ROTHWELL, James Herbert, CBE 1920; *b* 7 July 1881; *s* of late John Rothwell, Southport; *m* 1914, Evelyn Mary, *o d* of late C. R. Johnson, Sheffield; three *d. Educ:* Southport Modern School. Articled to Town Clerk, Southport; admitted a Solicitor, 1906; Town Clerk and Clerk to Justices, Brighouse, Yorks, 1910–16; Town Clerk of Chesterfield, 1916–23; Town Clerk of Brighton; Clerk to the Brighton and Hove Intercepting Sewers Board; Clerk to the Public Assistance and Assessment Committees: Solicitor to the Brighton Hove and Worthing Airport; retired, 1938; Director and Deputy Assistant Secretary Rationing Division, Ministry of Food, 1917–19. *Recreations:* golf and tennis. *Address:* Berea House, Dyke Road Avenue, Brighton. *T:* Brighton (Preston) 2184. *Club:* Hove.

Died 6 Oct. 1944.

ROTTER, Rear-Adm. (S) Charles John Ehrhardt, CB 1915; *b* 5 April 1871; *s* of Charles G. Rotter, Croydon; *m* 1st, 1905, Constance Lillie Bartholomew (*d* 1919); four *d*; 2nd, 1924, Mary Chadwick (*d* 1925), *e d* of W. Dallas Ross, Alexandra Park, N; 3rd, 1930, Delena Caroline Ann, *d* of W. Parsons, Greenwich; one *s. Educ:* City of London School. Entered RN as Assistant Clerk, 1887; Paymaster Capt., 1921; Assistant-Paymaster of Centurion, 1900; landed with Naval Brigade for advance to Pekin (promoted); Naval Intelligence Dept, 1911–19; Director, Statistics Dept, Admiralty, 1919–32; retired with rank of Paymaster Rear-Admiral, 1923; Russian Order of St Vladimir, 4th Class, 1917. *Address:* 14 Beech House Road, Croydon, Surrey.

Died 31 Jan. 1948.

ROUND, Charles James; DL, JP, Essex; Farmer and Landowner; *b* 3 Sept. 1885; *s* of Rt Hon. James Round, PC, DL, and Sybilla Joanna Freeland; *m* 1910, Sylvia de Zoete; two *s* (and one killed in action, 1940), one *d. Educ:* Winchester College; Exeter College, Oxford. Captain, Essex Yeomanry; served in France; High Sheriff of Essex, 1913; Chairman of the Essex County Hospital since 1927; Secretary to the East Essex Hounds since 1918; President of the Hunt Club since 1918; Chairman of Essex Agricultural Society Council, 1936. *Recreations:* hunting, shooting, cricket. *Address:* Birch Hall, Colchester, Essex. *Club:* Bath.

Died 6 Oct. 1945.

ROUNDWAY, 2nd Baron *cr* 1916, of Devizes; **Edward Murray Colston,** CMG 1918; DSO 1916; MVO 1908; an Exon of the Yeomen of the Guard since 1932; *b* 31 Dec. 1880; *e s* of 1st Baron and Rosalind (*d* 1938), *d* of Col Gostling-Murray, Whitton Park, Hounslow, Middlesex; *S* father, 1925; *m* Blanche Gladys Duddell. Entered Grenadier Guards, 1900; Capt. 1908; Major, 1915; served South Africa, 1901–02 (wounded, Queen's medal three clasps); European War, 1914–18 (wounded, DSO, Bt Lieut-Col, CMG, despatches six times, Order of the Nile, Order of White Eagle of Serbia); temp. Brig.-Gen. Commanding 233 Infantry Brigade, EEF, 1917–19; Lieut-Col Grenadier Guards, 1920–24; Colonel, 1924; commanded 131st Surrey (Territorial) Infantry Brigade, 1927–31; retired pay with hon. rank of Brig.-Gen. 1932. *Heir:* none. *Address:* Hamilton House, Ashburn Place, SW7. *T:* Frobisher 7116; The Croft, Padworth, near Reading; Roundway Park, Devizes. *Clubs:* Guards', Queen's, Hurlingham, Kennel.

Died 29 March 1944 (ext).

ROUNTREE, Harry, Artist; Ex-President London Sketch Club; late Capt. RE; *b* Auckland, New Zealand, 1878; *s* of S. G. Rountree, banker, of NZ; *m* Estella Stewart of Auckland, NZ; one *s* one *d. Educ:* Queen's College, NZ Came to London, 1901. *Publications:* in Punch, Sketch, etc.; books of travel in colour; children's books, humorous animals, posters, golf illustrations. *Recreation:* fishing. *Address:* 5 Piazza Studios, St Ives, Cornwall. *Club:* Savage.

Died 26 Sept. 1950.

ROUSE, Col Hubert, CB 1916; DSO 1903; late RHA; *b* 22 Aug. 1864; *s* of H. J. Rouse, MICE, Sussex Place, NW; *m* 1893, Adeline Louisa (*d* 1939), *d* of N. C. Macnamara, FRCS, one *d*. Entered army, 1884; Capt. 1893; Maj. 1900; Lt-Col 1910; Col 1915; served NWF, India, 1897–98 (medal with clasp); South Africa, 1899–1900, and 1902 (despatches, Queen's medal 4 clasps, King's medal 2 clasps, DSO); European War, 1914–18 (despatches, CB); retired pay, 1919. *Address:* South Lodge, Dorchester. *Club:* Army and Navy.

Died 30 Nov. 1945.

ROUSE, William Henry Denham, LittD, MA, FRGS, MRAS; Lord of the Manor of Woodbridge, Suffolk; *b* Calcutta, 30 May 1863; *s* of Rev. G. H. Rouse, MA, LLB, and Lydia, 2nd *d* of Rev. W. H. R. Denham. *Educ:* Grammar School, Haverfordwest; Doveton College, Calcutta; Christ's College, Cambridge, Scholar, 1882–86; Fellow, 1888–94, Hon. Fellow, 1933. Classical Tripos, first class in each part. Bedford Grammar School, 1886–88; in residence at Cambridge, 1888–90; Cheltenham College, 1890–95; Worts Travelling Student, 1896, 1905. Master at Rugby School, 1896–1901; Headmaster Perse School, Cambridge, 1902–28; University Teacher of Sanskrit, 1903–39; Examiner in Latin to the Liverpool University, 1909–10; Acting Latin Professor at the Columbia Summer School, Teachers' College, New York, 1912; Pres. Folklore Soc., 1904–06. *Publications:* The Jataka, or Stories of the Buddha's former Births, translated from the Pali by various hands under editorship of Prof. Cowell, vol. ii (1895), iv (1901), vi (1907); The Giant Crab, and other Tales of Old India, retold by WHDR, 1897; Tales from the Isles of Greece, from the Mod. Greek of Eftaliotis, 1897; Atlas of Classical Portraits, 1898; A History of Rugby School, 1898; Demonstrations in Latin Elegiac Verse, 1899; Demonstrations in Greek Iambic Verse, 1899; The Talking Thrush, and other Indian Stories, collected by W. Crooke, and retold by WHDR, 1899; An Echo of Greek Song, 1899; edited in the Temple Classics North's Plutarch, Chapman's Iliad and Odyssey, Milton, Marcus Aurelius, Epictetus, Theophrastus, etc., 1896–1899; Greek Votive Offerings, 1902; Shakespeare's Ovid, a reprint of Golding's translation of the Metamorphoses, 1904; Jinacaritam, or Life of Buddha in Pali, edited from the MSS and translated, 1905; Sikshasamuccaya (Buddhist Scripture), 1919; Chanties in Latin and Greek, 1923; Latin on the Direct Method, 1925; Tom Noddy the Noodle, 1929; Stories of the Old Greeks, 1931; The Adventures of Ulysses, 1932; The Direct Method applied to Latin, 1932; Gods Heroes and Men of Greece, 1934; The Latin Struwwelpeter, 1934; Scenes from Sixth Form Life, 1935; The Story of Odysseus in plain English, 1937; The Story of Achilles in plain English, 1938; Homer, 1939; Achilles and the Great Quarrel at Troy, 1939; The Golden Ass, 1940; The Argonauts, 1940; The March up Country, 1947. *Address:* Meadowsweet, Hayling Island, Hants. *Club:* Athenæum.

Died 10 Feb. 1950.

ROUSE-BOUGHTON-KNIGHT, Charles Andrew; JP, Shropshire; DL, Herefordshire; Patron of Burrington-in-Aston; joint Patron of Downton; Lord of the Manor of Leintwardine; *b* 1859; *e s* of late Andrew Johnes Rouse-Boughton-Knight and Eliza, *y d* of late John Michael Severne, of Thenford, Northamptonshire, and of Wallop Hall, Shropshire; *m* 1902, Helen Dupré (*d* 1926), *e d* of late George Orr Wilson, of Dunardagh, Co. Dublin. *Educ:* Eton. High Sheriff, Herefordshire, 1926. *Address:* Downton Castle, Ludlow.

Died 21 Oct. 1947.

ROUTH, Vice-Adm. Henry Peter, MVO 1902; *b* 1851; *m* 1894, Ethel B., 3rd *d* of Lt-Col St J. Daubeny, of the Beacon, Kingswear, Devon; one *s*. Entered Navy, 1864; Commander, 1890; Captain, 1896; retired, 1906;

Rear-Adm. 1907; Vice-Admiral, 1910. *Address:* Farringdon, Alton, Hants. *T:* Tisted 226. *Club:* Naval and Military.

Died 8 Jan. 1944.

ROWAN, John, MBCM, FRFPSG; Honorary Consulting Ophthalmic Surgeon, Glasgow Royal Infirmary; Honorary Consulting Surgeon Ophthalmic Institution, Glasgow; Hon. Consulting Ophthalmic Surgeon, Royal Hospital for Sick Children, Glasgow; late Consulting Ophthalmic Surgeon, Glasgow Throat, Nose and Ear Hospital; Consulting Ophthalmic Surgeon to Glasgow Royal Mental Hospital and Deaf and Dumb Institution, Glasgow; Medical Referee for Ophthalmic Cases under Workmen's Compensation Act for Lanarkshire, Ayr, Renfrew, Bute, Stirling, Dumbarton, Clackmannan; *b* Greenock; *s* of late Thomas Ballantine Rowan, sugar refiner, Greenock, and of Redbrae, Maybole; unmarried. *Educ:* Glasgow University; studied at London, Dublin, Göttingen, Berlin, and Paris. Major RAMC (T) (retired) attached to the Clyde Division Royal Engineers Electrical Engineers; late Ophthalmic Surgeon, Glasgow Royal Infirmary; Surgeon, Ophthalmic Institution, Glasgow; Senior House Surgeon, Greenock Infirmary and Fever Hospital; Assist Royal London Ophthalmic Hospital, Moorfields; and Clinical Assistant, Royal Westminster Ophthalmic Hospital, London. *Publications:* numerous contributions on ophthalmic subjects to medical journals. *Recreations:* golf, shooting, and fishing. *Address:* Whitehaugh, Monkton, Ayrshire. *T:* Prestwick 7781. *Clubs:* Royal Automobile; Western, Royal Scottish Automobile (Glasgow); Prestwick Golf (Prestwick).

Died 17 March 1948.

ROWAN, Ven. Robert Philip, MA, TCD; *b* 10 Sept. 1870; *s* of Rev. Canon Rowan; *m* Sybil Mary, *d* of Rev. D. Moriarty; no *c*. *Educ:* Galway Grammar School; Trinity College, Dublin. Curate of Tralee, 1897–1901; Wexford, 1901–04; Acting Chaplain to Forces at Curragh and Shorncliffe, 1904–06; Senior Curate St John's Lowestott, 1906–07; Rector of Castle-island, 1907–14; of Kenmare, 1914–24; of Killarney, 1924–43. Dean of Ardfert and Chancellor of Limerick, 1923–37; Archdeacon of Ardfert and Aghadoe and Canon of Effin, 1938–43; retired, 1943. *Recreations:* cricket, tennis, fishing. *Address:* 98 The Rise, Mount Merrton Dublin.

Died 19 June 1946.

ROWAN-HAMILTON, Brig. (Hon.) Gawaine Basil, DSO 1917; MC; *b* 1884; *m* 1916, Phyllis Frances Agnes, *d* of late Lord Blackburn; three *s*. Served European War, 1914–18 (despatches, DSO, MC, Deferred Bt Lt-Col); psc 1919; Bt Maj. 1922; Lt-Col 1930; Col 1928; commanded 2nd Bn The Black Watch, 1930–33; commanded 153rd (Black Watch and Gordon) Infantry Bde, TA, 1936–40; ADC to the King, 1938–39; retired, 1945. *Address:* Bonkyl, Duns, Berwickshire. *T:* Cumledge 50. *Clubs:* United Service; New, Edinburgh.

Died 17 July 1947.

ROWAN-HAMILTON, His Hon. Sir Orme, Kt 1931; *b* Newtownards, Co. Down, 1877; *m* 1901, Vera, *d* of Major Barker of Frant; one *s*. *Educ:* Oxford Military College. Joined 3rd Batt. Royal Irish Rifles, 1894; gazetted West Indies Regt 1898; rejoined 2nd RI Rifles, 1900; served Boer War (Queen's medal and clasps); resigned in 1903; called to Bar, 1905; North-Eastern Circuit; Revising Barrister, Bradford and Keighley Divisions of Yorkshire, 1913; Puisne Judge, Leeward Islands, 1916; exchanged as Stipendiary Magistrate, Gibraltar; President, Land Court, Palestine, 1927; Chief Justice of Bermuda, 1927–39; Chairman Parliamentary Committee Great Britain, Canada, Bermuda, 1934; Chairman PEN Club, N Ireland, 1942–43. *Publications:* (plays) Mrs Ellison's Answer, 1905; The Sentence; The Anarchists, 1907; The Indiscretion of Mrs Carter, 1942; Novels and Poems: Burdens, 1922; Stray Thoughts,

1936; The Cry in the Night (trans. into French, Paris, 1946); (pen-name Rowan Orme): Dramatic Critic to Outlook, 1907–1908; and other articles; Trial of J. A. Dickman. *Recreations:* literature and fly-fishing. *Address:* 40 Sandycove Road, Dunlaoghaire, Co. Dublin. *Club:* Kildare Street (Dublin).

Died 4 Nov. 1949.

ROWAN-ROBINSON, Maj.-Gen. Henry, CB 1933; CMG 1918; DSO 1916; DL Hampshire, 1941–46; *b* 4 May 1873; *m* 1904, Evelyn Russell Bowlby; two *s*. *Educ:* King's School, Canterbury. Entered RA 1892; Military Governor of Libau, 1919; Inspector-General of Iraqi Army, 1930–34; Col Comdt Army Cadet Force, Hampshire, 1934–44; served S Africa, 1901–02; European War; operations Southern Kurdistan, 1930–31; operations North Kurdistan, 1932; received thanks of Army Council for services in preventing war between Poland and Lithuania; Batt. Comdr, Home Guard, 1940–43; Gold and Silver Medallist, RA Institution; Gold Medallist, Royal United Service Institution. *Publications:* mainly on Imperial Defence, Mechanization and the second global war. *Address:* Blyth House, Southwold. *T:* Southwold, 3200. *Club:* Army and Navy.

Died 23 Feb. 1947.

ROWATT, Thomas, OBE 1939; MM; *b* 7 Nov. 1879. Assistant in Technological Department of the Royal Scottish Museum, Edinburgh, 1902; Assistant Keeper 1909, Keeper 1921, Director 1934–44. *Address:* Spottiswoode, Colinton, Edinburgh. *T:* 87169.

Died 7 April 1950.

ROWBOTHAM, Sir (Samuel) Hanson, Kt 1935; JP, Warwickshire; *b* 1880; *s* of Thomas Rowbotham, JP, Gilbertstone, South Yardley; *m* 1904, Annie Maude, *d* of G. W. Merrett, Sheldon, Warwickshire. Sheriff of Warwickshire, 1937. *Address:* Brooke Hill, Brooke, Isle of Wight. *Clubs:* Carlton, Royal Automobile, Royal Thames Yacht; Birmingham Conservative.

Died 10 Oct. 1946.

ROWE, Charles Henry, MA. Fellow of Trinity College, Dublin; Erasmus Smith's Professor of Mathematics in the University of Dublin. *Address:* Trinity College, Dublin.

Died 3 Dec. 1943.

ROWE, Frederick Maurice, FRS 1945; FRIC; DSc (Leeds); Professor of Colour Chemistry and Dyeing, Leeds University, since 1926; *b* Stroud, 11 Feb. 1891; *s* of H. J. Rowe and Annie Ricketts; *m* 1916, Mary Nield, *d* of Sir George Cockburn, Leeds. *Educ:* Marling School, Stroud; University of Leeds; Technische Hochschule, Braunschweig. Leblanc Medallist, 1911; Clothworkers Research Scholar, 1911–12; Research Fellow, Leeds University, 1912–13. Research Chemist, Joseph Crosfield & Sons, Ltd, Warrington, 1913–16; Lecturer and Head of Dyestuffs Research Laboratory, Municipal College of Technology, University of Manchester, 1916–25; Reader in Tinctorial Chemistry, Municipal College of Technology, Univ. of Manchester, 1925–26; Medallist of the Company of Dyers, 1924–25, 1926–27, 1930–31, 1935–36, 1937–38; Liveryman of the Company of Dyers; Hon. Freeman of the Company of Clothworkers, 1944; Medallist of the Soc. of Dyers and Colourists, 1934, and Hon. Member, 1944; Editor Journal of the Society of Dyers and Colourists. *Publications:* Colour Index, 1924, and Supplement, 1928; Artificial Silk (with Reinthaler), 1928; numerous scientific and technical papers in Journal of the Chemical Society, the Journal of the Society of Chemical Industry, and the Journal of the Society of Dyers and Colourists. *Address:* Brentwood, Ashleigh Road, West Park, Leeds 6. *T:* Leeds 52489.

Died 8 Dec. 1946.

ROWE, John Clifford, CBE 1939; JP, FSS; Investment Adviser; Director of Companies; *b* 20 Jan. 1872; *s* of late Capt. Wm Rowe; *m* 1900, Gertrude Anne (*d* 1929), *d* of late Wm Howard, Canterbury. Trained in the Trust Company world; advises Companies, large Estates, Trustees and Corporate bodies; in European War was Inspector of Special Constabulary; Volunteer Recruiter under War Office; Capt. 3rd Vol. Bn The Queen's Own Royal West Kent Regt in charge of musketry; served on number of local war Committees in Sydenham district; Past Master worshipful Company of Barbers; first Chairman West Lewisham Conservative and Unionist Assoc. 1918–27; first President since 1927; President Invicta (Penge) Rifle Club. *Publications:* Foundations of Investment, 1929; many contributions to financial journals and weeklies on investment and statistical subjects. *Recreations:* politics, formerly walking, sailing, lawn tennis, golf. *Address:* Red Thorn, 5 Jews Walk, Sydenham, SE26. *T:* Sydenham 8640, London Wall 1435.

Died 21 March 1944.

ROWE, Rt Rev. Peter Trimble, DD, LLD; Bishop of the Missionary District, Alaska, since 1895; *b* Meadowville, Ontario, 20 Nov. 1856; *m* 1st, 1882 (wife *d* 1914); two *s*; 2nd, Rose Fullerton; three *s*. *Educ:* Canadian Public Schools; private tuition: Trinity College, Toronto. Graduated, 1878. Deacon, 1878; Priest, 1880; was Missionary among the Ojibway Indians, 1878–82; Missionary at Sault Ste Marie, Michigan, serving eleven missions for 14 years; acted as Commissioner of Schools for 5 years. *Publication:* Annual Missionary Reports to the Board of Missions, New York. *Address:* 418 Mutual Life Building, Seattle, USA. *T:* Main 1193.

Died 6 Jan. 1942.

ROWE, Sir Reginald P. P., Kt 1934; *γ s* of late Charles Rowe, Liverpool and London. *Educ:* Clifton College; Magdalen College, Oxford, MA. Rowed for Oxford v. Cambridge, 1889–92; Temp. Capt. R. W. Kent Regt, serving in France, 1915–16; Under Treasurer Hon. Society Lincoln's Inn, 1921–37; Chairman of the Improved Tenements Association since 1900; President and Chairman National Federation of Housing Societies; President Economic Reform Club and Institute; Chairman of: Housing Societies Investment Trust, Housing Centre Executive, Finance Committee of Oxford House, Music and Drama Committee National Association of Boys Clubs. Managing Governor of the Old Vic and Sadler's Wells; originated and organised the scheme for re-creating Sadler's Wells. *Publications:* The Badminton Volume on Rowing (with C. M. Pitman); Concise Chronicle of the Great War; two novels; Poems, 1928; The Root of all Evil, 1940; articles in The Times and Quarterly Review, etc. *Address:* 19 Old Buildings, Lincoln's Inn, WC2. *Clubs:* Athenæum, United University, Leander.

Died 21 Jan. 1945.

ROWE, William Hugh Cecil, CBE 1918; employed on Staff of British Broadcasting Corporation; *s* of late William Hugh Rowe, Asst Paymaster-General, Supreme Court. *Educ:* St Paul's School (scholar); Jesus College, Cambridge (exhibitioner). Inspector, Agricultural Bank of Egypt, 1906; temporary commission, RASC, 8 Aug. 1914; Captain, 1 Dec. 1914; Major, 17 May 1916; Lt-Col 18 April 1917; commanded Base Supply Depots, Dieppe, Abancourt, Havre, and Arquata (Italy) (despatches five times, CBE). *Recreations:* rugby football and rowing (at Cambridge), motoring, golf, archæology. *Address:* 1 Elvaston Mews, SW7. *T:* Western 8997. *Clubs:* Arts; Royal Mid-Surrey Golf.

Died Sept. 1939.

ROWELL, Hon. Newton Wesley, KC 1902; LLD; *b* Middlesex County, Ontario, 1 Nov. 1867; *s* of late Joseph Rowell and Nancy Green; *m* 1901, Nellie, *y d* of Rev. Alex. Langford, DD (Methodist); one *s* one *d*. *Educ:* Public Schools and Ontario Law Society. Called to Bar, 1891; Bencher Law Society of Upper Canada, 1911; Hon. Life Member American Bar Association, 1930; Hon. Bencher of Lincoln's Inn, 1932; President Canadian Bar Association, 1932–34; Treasurer Law Society, Upper Canada, 1935; Chief Justice of Ontario, 1936–38; Liberal Member, Ontario Legislative Assembly, North Oxford, 1911–17; Leader of Liberal Opposition in Ontario Legislature, 1911–17; Liberal Unionist Member Dominion Parliament, Durham, 1917–21; President of Council, 1917–20; Vice-Chairman War Committee of Cabinet, 1917–19; Acting Secretary State External Affairs, 1919–20; Member of Imperial War Cabinet and Imperial War Conference, 1918; represented Canada International Labour Conference, Washington (League of Nations), 1919; Canadian Delegate First Assembly League of Nations, Geneva, 1920; Vice-Chairman Institute of Pacific Relations, 1929–34; Hon. Chairman, Canadian Institute of International Affairs; Chairman, British Commonwealth Relations Conference (unofficial), 1933; Hon. Vice-Chairman, Canadian League of Nations Society; Fellow Royal Society of Canada, 1937. *Publications:* The British Empire and World Peace, 1922; Canada a Nation, 1923. *Address:* 134 Crescent Road, Toronto. *TA:* Rowell, Toronto. *T:* Randolph 2175. *Clubs:* Travellers', British Empire; National, Rosedale Golf, Toronto.

Died 22 Nov. 1941.

ROWLAND, Sir John, Kt 1938; CB 1922; CBE 1918; MVO 1911; late Chairman of Welsh Board of Health; *b* 1 June 1877; *s* of late John Rowland, Penbontfach, Tregaron; *m* Mair Lewis, Afan House, Aberystwyth; three *s*. *Educ:* Technical College, Cardiff; University College of Wales, Aberystwyth. Assistant Master Secondary School, Cardiff, 1902–05; Hon. Sec. to the Cardiff Cymmrodorion Society, 1904–06; Private Secretary to the President of the Board of Trade, 1905–08; Private Secretary to the Chancellor of the Exchequer, 1908–12; Administrative Adviser to the Corporation of Merthyr Tydfil, 1936–37; JP Cardiff. *Recreation:* walking. *Address:* 166 Cathedral Road, Cardiff; Penbontfach, Tregaron. *T:* Cardiff 2943.

Died 2 Jan. 1941.

ROWLAND, Col Michael Carmichael, CMG 1918; retired pay, Regular Army; *b* Limerick, 24 June 1862; *s* of P. J. Rowland, Croom; *m* Mary Anne Larkin, Tralee; one *s* one *d*; *m* 1903, Agnes Gertrude, *y d* of John Smith, Fox Hill, Pietermaritzburg, Natal; one *s* three *d*. *Educ:* privately. Joined Royal Munster Fusiliers, 1882; transferred to Royal Dublin Fusiliers, 1898; served Anglo-Boer War, 1899–1902 (promoted Captain, despatches, medals and 8 clasps); Natal Native Rebellion, 1906 (promoted Major, medal and clasp); European War, 1914–18; Quarter-Master-General, SA Defence Force; CMG for GS West Campaign; served GHQ, France and Italy, 1917–19 (despatches thrice, Commander of the Order of Christ, Portugal); retired, 1919. *Recreations:* music and welfare work. *Address:* 13 Kerry Road, Parkview, Johannesburg.

Died 11 April 1947.

ROWLAND, Sir William, Kt 1938; FSAA; JP County Borough of Southampton; *b* 1858; *s* of Edward Middleditch and Anne Mott; *m* 1881, Alice Thring; one *s* two *d*. *Educ:* Elementary School. Member of Southampton Borough Council, 1900–02; Chairman Finance Committee, 1900–02; Governor of Southampton University Coll., Trustee of Southampton Seamen's Orphanage for Boys. *Address:* 30 Westwood Road, Southampton.

Died 18 July 1945.

ROWLANDS, Sir Gwilym, Kt 1945; CBE 1929; JP; *b* 2 Dec. 1878; *s* of late Rowland Rowlands, Colliery Manager, Penygraig; *m* 1908; one *s*. *Educ:* Penygraig Board School; Heath School, Pontypridd. MP for Flint, 1935–45; President of the East Rhondda Conservative Association; Ex-Chairman of the Council of the National Union of Conservative Associations. *Address:* 19 Llanfair Road, Penygraig, Rhondda Valley.

Died 16 Jan. 1949.

ROWLANDS, John Wilfred; Solicitor; *b* Welshpool, Mongomeryshire, 1 March 1869; 2nd *s* of late Principal David Rowlands, BA (Dewi Mon) of the Congregational Memorial College, Brecon, S Wales; *m* 1902, Frances Mary, *o d* of Benjamin and Ellen Rees, London; one *s* one *d*. *Educ:* Christ College, Brecon, South Wales. Qualified as Solicitor 1897; in Australia 1885–88; practised at Maesteg, Glamorganshire, 1899–1903; Solicitor to Maesteg Branch of Miners Federation of England and Wales for several years; removed to London 1903; practised in Fleet Street for 30 years, as Solicitor; Member of Hornsey Borough Council since 1908, Alderman since 1930, Mayor 1931–33; Hon. Treasurer of Hornsey YMCA; Member Middlesex CC since 1934; JP Middlesex; Past Pres. Anglesey Society in London; Chairman Brecon and Radnor Society, London; High Sheriff of Breconshire 1939. *Address:* 25 Cholmeley Park, Highgate, N6. *T:* Mount View 3041.

Died 15 Jan. 1948.

ROWLATT, Sir Frederick Terry, KBE 1919; Fellow, Institute of Bankers, London; Grand Cordon of the Medjidieh, of the Nile and of Star of Ethiopia; *b* 10 Feb. 1865; *s* of late A. H. Rowlatt; *m* 1903, Edith May, 2nd *d* of J. E. Cornish, CMG; two *d*. *Educ:* Fettes College, Edinburgh. *Address:* National Bank of Egypt, Head Office, Cairo, Egypt. *TA:* National, Cairo.

Died 3 March 1950.

ROWLATT, Rt Hon. Sir Sidney Arthur Taylor, PC 1932; KCSI 1918; Kt 1912; *b* 20 July 1862; *s* of late A. H. Rowlatt of Alexandria; *m* 1890, Elizabeth Hemingway; four *s* two *d*. Sometime Fellow of King's College, Cambridge; Recorder of Windsor, 1905–06; Junior Counsel to the Treasury, 1905–12; Judge of High Court, King's Bench Division, 1912–32; Chairman Indian Sedition Committee, 1918; Chairman Royal Commission on Betting, 1932–33; Chairman General Claims Tribunal Compensation (Defence) Act, 1939. *Address:* Bagnor Manor, Newbury, Berks. *T:* Newbury 930. *Club:* Oxford and Cambridge.

Died 1 March 1945.

ROWLETTE, Robert James, MD (Dublin), FRCPI; Lt-Col late RAMC; a representative of Dublin University in the Senate of Ireland; King's Professor of Materia Medica and Pharmacy, Trinity College, Dublin; Physician to Mercer's Hospital, Dublin; Consulting Physician to the Royal Hospital for Incurables, Dublin; Consulting Visitor in Lunacy; Consulting Physician to Colonial Office; to Stillorgan Convalescent Home; and to Royal National Hospital, Newcastle, Co. Wicklow; Editor of Journal of The Irish Free State Medical Union; Member of the Medical Registration Council, and of the Dental Board, Irish Free State; Pres. of Irish Branch of Parliamentary Association; of RCP of Ireland; and of Royal Academy of Medicine of Ireland; a Trustee of National Health Insurance Society, Ireland, and Vice-Chairman of General Committee; Pres. of the Section of Pharmacology and Therapeutics, BMA, 1933; *b* 16 Oct. 1873; 2nd *s* of late Matthew Rowlette, Carn Cash, Sligo; *m* Gladys M., *d* of late R. Camper Day; one *s*. *Educ:* Sligo School; Trinity College, Dublin. Senior Moderator in Ethics and Logics, 1895; President of the University Philosophical Society, 1896–97; Vice-President and gold medallist in Oratory, College Historical Society; President of the Dublin University Biological

Association, 1907–08; President of the Irish Amateur Athletic Association, 1908–20; President of the Irish Medical Association, 1932–36; served in France, 1917–18 (despatches); Hon. Physician to British Olympic Team, Antwerp, 1920, and to the Irish Olympic Team, Paris, 1924, and Amsterdam, 1928; member of the Irish Public Health Council, 1919–25; Professor of Pharmacology, Royal College of Surgeons in Ireland, 1921–26; Member of Committee of Inquiry on National Health Insurance and the Public Medical Services; Member of Second House of the Oireachtas Commission, 1936; Representative of the University of Dublin in Dail Eireann, 1933–37; Vice-President Irish Free State Medical Union, 1936–37. *Publications:* Memoirs of Irish Physicians and Surgeons in Dictionary of National Biography; The Medical Press and Circular, 1839–1939; various articles on medical subjects. *Address:* 55 Fitzwilliam Square, Dublin. *T:* Dublin 62091. *Clubs:* University, Dublin.

Died 13 Oct. 1944.

ROWLEY, Brig.-Gen. Frank George Mathias, CB 1919; CMG 1915; DSO 1918; late the Duke of Cambridge's Own (Middlesex Regt); *b* 4 Jan. 1866; *m* 1st, 1894, Agnes Mary (*d* 1927), *d* of late Captain J. D. Travers, Leicester Regt, and *widow* of Captain Edgar Lonsdale, Royal Fusiliers; 2nd, 1930, Frances Helen Henderson, North Gate, Regent's Park. Entered army, 1886; Captain, 1895; Major, 1903; Brigade-Major, India, 1902–07; Brig.-Gen. 1916; served European War, 1914–18 (despatches six times, CB, CMG, DSO). *Address:* Waterfield, Chiddingfold, Surrey.

Died 28 July 1949.

ROWLEY, Hercules Douglas Edward; *b* 1 Aug. 1859; *e s* of late Col Hon. H. L. B. Rowley, DL, JP, of Marlay Grange, Rathfarnham, and Louisa Jane Campbell, sister of 1st Baron Blythswood, FRS; *heir pres.* to 7th Baron Langford; *m* 1884, Agnes Mary, *o d* of late Arthur Allen of Devizes; two *d*. *Educ:* Cheltenham College. Late Royal Meath Militia; DL and JP Co. Dublin, etc. *Address:* 10 Wilbraham Place, Sloane St, SW1. *T:* Sloane 4458; Marlay Grange, Rathfarnham, Co. Dublin. *Clubs:* Junior Carlton; Kildare Street, Dublin.

Died 15 Dec. 1945.

ROWLEY, Captain Howard Fiennes Julius, CBE 1919; Royal Navy (ret.); late Chief Inspector, Royal National Lifeboat Institution; *b* 14 Aug. 1868; 4th *s* of late Rev. Julius Henry Rowley, MA; *m* 1900, Alice Udall, 2nd *d* of late William Paterson Muir, Melbourne, Australia. *Educ:* Burney's Academy, Gosport. Entered Britannia, 1882; Lieutenant, 1892; Shadwell Prize, 1898, served in Royal Yacht Osborne, 1900–02; retired, 1902; Commander (retired), 1908; served European War, 1914–19, as Senior Naval Officer and Divisional Naval Transport Officer, Inverness; Acting Captain, Dec. 1914; confirmed, 1919; served in 6th Bn Dorset Home Guard, 1940–42, Corporal. Distinguished Service Medal, United States. *Address:* Myms Cottage, Wimborne Road, Kinson, Bournemouth. *T:* Northbourne 87.

Died 4 April 1948.

ROWNTREE, Arthur; Headmaster, Bootham School, 1899–1927; *b* 1861; *s* of John and Ann Rowntree; *m* Ellen, *d* of Dr W. F. Hurndall, formerly Headmaster of Mill Hill; two *d*. *Educ:* Bootham School; University Coll., London, BA; Flounders Training College; University of Heidelberg. Assistant Master as Bootham School and Oliver's Mount School; Private Tutor, sometime Examiner to the Teachers' Training Syndicate (Cambridge) in School Management and Method; Fellow of University College, London. *Publications:* (Editor) The History of Scarborough, 1931; Whittier, Crusader and Prophet, 1946; occasional essays in literature, history, education. *Recreations:* golf, fishing,

walking, Association football for Yorkshire in the good old days. *Address:* 26 Park Road, Southborough, Tunbridge Wells.

Died 11 May 1949.

ROWNTREE, Cecil, MB, BS, FRCS; Officier de l'Ordre de Léopold; Chevalier de la Légion d'Honneur; Consulting Surgeon to the Royal Cancer Hospital; Emeritus Surgeon to the Woolwich Memorial Hospital; Consulting Surgeon to the Caterham and East Grinstead Cottage Hospitals; Fellow of British Association of Surgeons; Brevet Major, RAMC, TF; Chairman, Westminster Division of BMA; President, Sub-Section of Proctology, RSM; Member of Grand Council, British Empire Cancer Campaign; Member of Executive Committee and Vice-President, Union Internationale Contre le Cancer; *s* of late Dr W. G. Rowntree; *m* 1908, Katharine Aylmer, *d* of late Henry Whitworth Jones; two *s* one *d*. *Educ:* University College, London. Late Surgeon to the Dreadnought Hospital; Surgical Registrar, Middlesex Hospital; Hunterian Professor of Surgery, Royal College of Surgeons of England. *Publications:* numerous papers on cancer and surgical subjects; contributor to English and Latham's System of Treatment. *Address:* 99 Harley Street, W1; Little Warren, East Grinstead.

Died 14 Oct. 1943.

ROWSELL, Philip Foale, CBE 1938; JP Devon and Exeter; FCS; FCII; *b* 1864; *s* of Benjamin Joseph Rowsell, Yeovil; *m* 1st, 1895, Florence Elizabeth Turner; one *s* one *d*; 2nd, Mrs F. I. M. Norton. *Educ:* Kingston School, Yeovil. Thrice Mayor of Exeter, 1921–24; Member of Central Profiteering Committee, 1920; Chairman Alkali Enquiry Committee, also of Glassware Enquiry; Vice-Chairman Committee on Trusts; President Pharmaceutical Society of Great Britain, 1926; Member of Trade Delegation to Virginia, 1927; Alderman and Chairman of Finance Committee of Devon CC; Vice-Pres. and Treasurer of Univ. Coll. of the South West; Founder and Chairman of Devon and Exeter Cancer Fund; President of Exeter and Western Counties Hospital Aid Society; Treasurer and Past President of National Association of Insurance Committees; Chairman Devon Insurance Committee, 1916–45; Director of South Western Board of Sun Insurance; Director North Devon and Cornwall Railway; Member of Central Advisory Committee for setting up National Health Insurance, 1911; contested (L) Totnes Division of Devon, 1929; during European War Chairman of Recruiting and War Savings Committees. *Address:* Nutbrook, Withycombe Raleigh, Exmouth. *TA:* Nutbrook, Exmouth. *T:* 2456 Exmouth; Ladybrook, Belstone, Okehampton. *Club:* National Liberal.

Died 1 May 1946.

ROXBURGH, Sir Thomas Laurence, Kt 1928; CMG 1910; *b* Jamaica, 29 March 1853; *s* of Thomas Francis Roxburgh and Catherine Gibson; *m* Anna (*d* 1937), *d* of John Edwards of Knockalva, Jamaica; three *s* one *d*. *Educ:* Durham; Edinburgh Univ. Clerk Petty Sessions, St Elizabeth, Jamaica, 1882; Clerk of Courts, 1888; First-class Clerk, Colonial Secretary's Office, Jamaica, 1890; Senior Clerk, 1899; Assistant Colonial Secretary, 1902; Administrator of St Christopher and Nevis, 1906; retired, 1915; was a Major in Jamaica Militia; hon. ADC to Governor, Sir A. Hemming, 1899–1904. *Recreations:* music, riding. *Address:* Annandale, Epworth, Jamaica, West Indies. *TA:* Claremont, Jamaica.

Died 13 July 1945.

ROXBY, Percy Maude, BA, FRGS, Chief Representative in China of the British Council since 1945; *b* 21 Nov. 1880; *y s* of late Rev. H. M. Roxby, Vicar of Buckden, Huntingdonshire; *m* 1941, Marjorie Peers, *d* of late John Stanley Howden, Liverpool. *Educ:* Bromsgrove School; Christ Church, Oxford (open

History Scholarship), Gladstone Memorial Prize, 1902, 1st Class Modern History, BA Oxon, 1903. Lecturer in Geography, University of Liverpool; Albert Khan Travelling Fellow, 1912–13; Professor of Geography, University of Liverpool, 1917–44; Member of China Education Commission, 1921–22; Visiting Professor, Egyptian University, Cairo, 1930; President Section E (Geography), British Association, 1930. *Publications:* Henry Grattan Gladstone Memorial Prize); The Far Eastern Question in its Geographical Setting (Geographical Association), 1920; Report to Albert Kahn Trustees; China (Oxford Pamphlets on World Affairs), 1942; contributions on China and other articles in Encyclopædia Britannica (14th edition); contributions to various Geographical journals and reviews. *Recreations:* games and walking. *Address:* Hardwick Dene, Buckden, Huntingdon. *Clubs:* University, Athenæum, Liverpool.
Died 17 Feb. 1947.

ROY, Camille; prêtre, protonotaire apostolique; licencié ès lettres, docteur en philosophie, docteur ès lettres; membre de la Société Royale du Canada; Professeur de Littérature Canadienne à l'Université Laval; Supérieur du Séminaire de Quebec et Recteur de l'Université Laval; *b* Berthier, Comté de Montmagny, Province de Québec, 22 Oct. 1870; 16e enfant de Benjamin Roy et de Desanges Gosselin; frère de Sa Grandeur Mgr. Paul-Eugène Roy, archevèque de Québec. *Educ:* Études au Petit Séminaire de Québec; à l'Université Laval, à L'Université Catholique de Paris, et en Sorbonne. Ordonné prêtre, 1894; Professeur de Philosophie au Séminaire de Québec, 1892–93; Professeur de Rhétorique au Séminaire de Québec, 1893–98 et 1901–18; Préfet des Études au Séminaire de Québec, 1918–23; séjour à Paris pour y étudier en Sorbonne et à l'Université Catholique, 1898–1901; licencié ès lettres en Sorbonne, 1900; retour à Québec, 1901; Membre fondateur de la Société du Parler français au Canada en 1902; président, 1906–08; Élu membre de la Société Royale du Canada en 1904; prédicateur du carême de Notre-Dame, à Montreal, en 1915. *Publications:* L'Université Laval et les fêtes du cinquantenaire, 1903; Essais sur la littérature canadienne, 1907; Nos Origines littéraires, 1909; Propos canadiens, 1912; Les Fêtes du troisième centenaire de Québec, 1911; Nouveaux Essais sur la littérature canadienne, 1914; Tableau de l'histoire de la littérature canadienne-française; Manuel de l'histoire de la littérature canadienne-française, 1918; La Critique littéraire au XIXe siècle, de Mme de Staël à Émile Faguet, 1918; Érables en fleurs, 1923; Monseigneur de Laval, 1923; A l'ombre des érables, 1924; Études et croquis, 1928; Les Leçons de notre histoire (discours), 1929; Histoire de la littérature canadienne, 1930; Regards sur les lettres, 1931; Poètes de chez nous, 1934; Historiens de chez nous, 1935; Romanciers de chez nous, 1935; Nos Problèmes d'enseignement, 1935; Pour conserver notre héritage français, 1937; Pour former des hommes nouveaux, 1941. *Address:* Séminaire de Québec, Canada.
Died June 1943.

ROY, Ferdinand; Judge of the Sessions of the Peace; Chief District Magistrate, Quebec; *b* Lorette, Quebec, 1 Sept. 1873; *s* of Anselme and Caroline R. Roy; *m* 1899, Mariette Le-Gendre; one *s* two *d. Educ:* Quebec Seminary and Laval University (LLD). Called to Bar, 1896; Professor of Civil Law and Dean of Law Faculty at Laval University, 1908; Batonnier General of the Bar of the Province of Quebec, 1920; out of politics. *Publications:* Le Droit de Plaider, a treatise on legal incapacity of women, minors, etc., 1902; The Appeal to Arms and the French-Canadian Response, 1917; contributions to newspapers or reviews; speeches; lectures. *Recreations:* camping, golf. *Address:* Quebec, Canada. *T:* 1690. *Clubs:* Garrison, Jacque Cartier Fishing and Hunting, Golf (Quebec).
Died 22 June 1948.

ROY, Sir Ganen, Kt 1926; Member of the Institute of Electrical Engineers; *b* 6 Feb. 1872; *s* of late Tarini Prosad Roy; *m* Martha Goodeve (*d* 1936), *y d* of late Dr Soorjo Comar Goodeve Chuckerbutty, MD (London), Surgeon-Major, IMS; two *d. Educ:* Royal Indian Engineering College, Coopers Hill. Assistant Superintendent Telegraphs, 1894; Superintendent, 1903; Director of Telegraphs, 1913; Postmaster-General, Bengal and Assam, 1920; Chief Engineer, Telegraphs, India, 1922; a Member of the Legislative Assembly of the Government of India, 1925; Director-General of Posts and Telegraphs, India, 1925–27; retired, 1927. *Address:* The Elms, 39 West End Avenue, Pinner, Middlesex.
Died 14 Jan. 1943.

ROY, Brig.-Gen. John William Gascoigne, CMG 1919; *b* 1863; *e s* of late Rev. R. C. Roy; *m* 1900, Agnes Maud, *d* of George D'Arcy Clark of Burnaston House, Etwall; two *d. Educ:* Rossall. Lieut Sherwood Foresters, 1884; served in Sikkim Expedition, 1888; S African War, 1900–02 (despatches, Queen's medal five clasps); European War, 1914–19 (despatches, CMG); Brevet Major, 1902; Brevet Lt-Col, 1911; Lt-Col Sherwood Foresters, 1911–13; DAAG War Office, 1906–10; AAG War Office, 1913–15; AQMG War Office, 1918–20; retired with hon. rank of Brig.-Gen., 1920. *Address:* Upton Lodge, Upper Hale, Farnham, Surrey.
Died 4 Dec. 1941.

ROYDEN, 1st Baron *cr* 1944, of Frankby in the Co. Palatine of Chester; **Thomas Royden;** 2nd Bt *cr* 1905, CH 1919; JP, DL Co. Chester; MP (CU) Bootle, 1918–22 (retired); *b* 22 May 1871; *e s* of Sir Thomas Royden, 1st Bt, and Alice Elizabeth, *d* of late Thomas Dowdall; *S* to father's baronetcy, 1917; *m* 1922, Quenelda Mary, *d* of H. Clegg, JP, DL, Plas Llanfair, Anglesey, and *sister* of Sir Rowland Clegg. *Educ:* Winchester; Magdalen College, Oxford. Director: Phœnix Assurance Corporation, Cunard Steamship Company, Midland Bank, Port Line, Brocklebank Line. Formerly: Chairman Liverpool Steamship Owners Assoc., and Pres. Chamber of Shipping of the UK; High Sheriff of Cheshire, 1917–18; has travelled extensively in the USA and Far East. Commandeur Légion d'Honneur; Comdr Order of St Maurice and St Lazarus. *Recreation:* shooting. *Heir:* (to Baronetcy only) *b* Ernest Bland [*b* 30 Jan. 1873; *m* 1901, Rachel Mary, *d* of Jerome Smith, of Frankby; two *s* four *d*]. *Address:* Brockwood Park, Alresford, Hants; Tillypronie, Tarland, Scotland. *Clubs:* Marlborough-Windham, Bath, Carlton; Royal Yacht Squadron (Cowes).
Died 6 Nov. 1950 (Barony ext).

ROYDS, Sir Edmund, Kt 1939; OBE, 1919; DL, Co. Lincoln; late Major in Lincolnshire Yeomanry, and Lieutenant-Colonel and County Commandant Lincolnshire Volunteer Force; *b* 6 July 1860; *s* of late Canon Francis Coulman Royds and Cornelia, *d* of Canon George Becher Blomfield of Mollington Hall, Cheshire; *m* 1889, Rachel Louisa (*d* 1943), *d* of Col Francis Fane of Fulbeck. *Educ:* Haileybury College. Senior partner in the firm of Royds, Rawstorne & Co., Solicitors, 46 Bedford Square, WC; Director of Life Association of Scotland; Chairman Lukwah Tea Co., Ltd; MP (C) Sleaford (now Grantham) Division of Lincolnshire, 1910–22; Sheriff of Lincs, 1931; Chm. Lincs Chamber of Agriculture; Pres. Noblemen and Gentlemen's Catch Club. *Recreations:* hunting, cricket, music. *Address:* Stubton Hall, Newark; 46 Bedford Square, WC. *TA:* Lingos, Westcent, London; Claypole. *T:* Museum 0306, Fenton-Claypole 32. *Club:* Carlton.
Died 31 March 1946.

ROYLE, Sir George, Kt 1920; CBE 1926; JP, FRGS; FCII; Barrister-at-law; *b* 3 Nov. 1861; *m* 1882, Rosetta (*d* 1945), *d* of W. Wilford, Northants; two *s* one *d.* Mayor of Bedford, 1903; Hon. Freeman of Bedford; Hon. Recruiting Officer for the counties of Bedford,

Hertford, and Huntingdon, 1914–18; Member National Savings Cttee, 1916–45; Chairman Beds National Health Insurance Cttee, 1912–48; President National Incorporated Beneficent Society and Counties Benevolent Association; Local Director of the Commercial Union Assurance Co., Ltd. *Recreations:* golf, motoring. *Address:* Rutland Road Bedford.

Died 17 Nov. 1949.

ROYSTON, Brig.-Gen. John Robinson, CMG 1902; DSO 1902; Imperial Light Horse; *b* 29 April 1860; *s* of William Royston, Bellair, Natal; *m* 1903, Lilian Earle, *d* of C. F. Heugh, Swaziland; one *s* one *d*; *m* 1937, Mildred, *d* of late John Wright Standley, Hampshire, England. Served South Africa, 1878–79 (medal, with clasp); S Africa, 1899–1902 (despatches thrice, Queen's medal 4 clasps, CMG, DSO); Zulu Rebellion, 1906; raised own Regt Royston's Horse; Hon. Col British Army, 1907; German SW Africa, 1914; raised own Regt Natal Light Horse, known as Royston's Horse; served in Palestine, 1915–16–1917; commanded 12th, 2nd and 3rd Australian Imperial Light Horse. *Address:* Mount Romain, Port Shepstone, Natal.

Died 25 April 1942.

RUBIE, Rev. Alfred Edward, DD; Hon. Canon of Peterborough, 1928; *b* 5 Dec. 1863; *m* 1895, Katherine, 2nd *d* of late W. J. Hodgson, MD. *Educ:* Bradfield College; Brasenose College, Oxford. Senior Hulmeian Exhibitioner; 1st class Mods 1884; 1st class Lit. Hum. and BA 1886; MA 1889; MA Durham, 1895; BD and DD 1904. Assistant Master, Bradfield Coll., 1888–90; ordained, 1889; Headmaster, Richmond School, Yorkshire, 1890–95; Headmaster of Eltham College, 1896–1909; Vicar of Goodshaw, Rawtenstall, 1909–12; Vicar of Holy Trinity, Burnley, 1912–15; Rector of Cottingham, Market Harborough, 1915–39; Rural Dean of Weldon (i) Deanery, 1917–39; Registrar of Lay Readers, Diocese of Peterborough, 1918–44. *Publications:* school editions of the Gospel according to St Mark, The Acts of the Apostles, and First Book of Kings. *Recreation:* hill-climbing (Member of Fell and Rock Climbing Club). *Address:* at Braunston Vicarage, Oakham, Rutland.

Died 27 Jan. 1948.

RUCKSTULL, Frederick Wellington; sculptor; *b* Alsace, 22 May 1853; *m* 1900, Adele Pohlman; one *s*. *Educ:* Public Schools of St Louis; Paris. Honourable mention, Paris Salon, 1888; awarded a Grand Medal, World's Columbian Exposition, 1893. Member of Fine Arts Jury, Atlanta International Exposition; Member Advisory Board of Charleston Exposition, 1902; Secretary of Committee National Sculpture Society, having in charge the sculpture decorations of Buffalo Exposition; Chief of Department of Sculpture, St Louis World's Fair, resigned; Organiser and first Secretary National Sculpture Society; second Vice-President NY Architectural League; second Vice-President Municipal Art Society, NY; Member National Inst. of Arts and Letters of America. *Works:* Evening (life-size female marble statue), Metrop. Mus., NY; Mercury Amusing Himself (bronze heroic group), Portland Place, St Louis; Victory (bronze heroic size), on Soldiers' and Sailors' Monument, Jamaica, LI; Solon (heroic bronze), Library of Congress, Washington; Franklin, Goethe, and Macaulay (colossal granite heads), Façade Library of Congress; equestrian statue of Brigadier-General John F. Hartranft, Harrisburg, Pa.; Wisdom and Force (colossal marble statues), Appellate Court House, NY; Gloria Victis (heroic bronze group), Baltimore Confederate Monument; Defence of the Flag, Confederate Monument, Little Rock, Ark; Phœnicia (colossal marble), Custom House, NY; equestrian statue of Lieutenant-General Wade Hampton, Columbia, SC; marble statue of John C. Calhoun, Capitol, Washington, DC; bronze statue of Colour Guard, Petersburg battlefield monument; Confederate Women's Monument, Columbia, SC; M'Iver Monument (bronze), Raleigh, NC; U. M. Rose (marble statue), Capitol, Washington, DC; Confederate Monument (bronze), Salisbury, NC; colossal bronze statue, Minerva, for Battle of Long Island Monument, Brooklyn, New York; America Remembers, heroic bronze for War Monument, Stafford Springs, Conn; marble statue of General Wade Hampton, also marble statue of U. M. Rose, Capitol, Washington, DC Lecturer and writer on Art; Editor, The Art World. *Publication:* Great Works of Art and what makes them Great, 1925. *Clubs:* National Arts, New York City.

Died 26 May 1942.

RUDD, Col Thomas William, CBE 1919; late RAVC; *b* 29 March 1869. Capt. RAVC, 1903; served NW Frontier of India, 1897–98 (medal); European War, 1914–19 (despatches, CBE); retired pay, 1924.

Died 11 May 1943.

RUDDELL, Ven. Joseph; *b* 9 Nov. 1866; *s* of John Ruddell and Louisa Wright; *m* 1905; two *s* one *d*. Archdeacon of Clogher, 1923–37; Rector of Augher, County Tyrone, 1934–36; of Donaghmoine, 1936–37. *Recreation:* golf.

Died 19 Aug. 1941.

RUDMOSE-BROWN, Thomas Brown; Friherre; Professor of French in the University of Dublin, since 1909; Lecturer in Provençal in the University of Dublin; Secretary of the University Council, University of Dublin; Extern Examiner in Italian to National University of Ireland; Additional Examiner in French, St Andrews University, 1938–39; Member of Dail Eireann Commission on Secondary Education, 1922; *b* London, 11 Jan. 1878; *e s* of late Robert Brown of Campster and late Friherreinde Kristiane Augusta Marie Eleonora Rudmose; *m* 1904, Anne Gordon (*d* 1936), *d* of late James Francis Gordon Shirrefs-Gordon of Craig Castle, Aberdeenshire; one *s* three *d*. *Educ:* Dulwich College; Woolwich; University College, London; Aberdeen University; Edinburgh University; Grenoble University. MA, Aberdeen, 1st Class Honours in French and German, 1901. Lecteur d'Anglais, University of Grenoble, France, 1902–03; Docteur de l'Université de Grenoble près la Faculté des Lettres, 1905; Lecturer in French and English, UFC Training College, Aberdeen, 1905–06; Assistant Lecturer in French Language and Romance Philology, Univ. of Leeds, 1906–09; Advising Examiner in French to the Intermediate Education Board for Ireland, 1912–16, 1922; Matriculation Examiner in French, London University, 1920–24; Extern Examiner in French, Queen's University of Belfast, 1922–24; Examiner in French for the Higher School Certificate, Cambridge University, 1929–38; Member of the Council of the Franco-Scottish Society, 1906–11, and 1923–27; Chairman of the Dublin University Co-operative Society, Limited, 1913–18; specially interested in Metrics (French, English, general Romance, and Teutonic), Mediæval Genealogy, Provençal; MA (Dublin), jure officii, 1921; LittD (Dublin), 1931; Sòci dóu Felibrige, 1932. *Publications:* Étude comparée de la versification française et de la versification anglaise, Grenoble, 1905; French Literary Studies, 1917; Walled Gardens (verse), 1918; critical editions of Racine's Andromaque, 1917, and Corneille's La Galerie du Palais, 1920; A Short History of French Literature, 1923; editions of School Texts; articles in Reviews. *Recreation:* gardening. *Address:* 35 Trinity College, Dublin; 94 Rathfarnham Road, Terenure, Dublin. *T:* Dublin 95688.

Died 13 May 1942.

RUDOLF, Robert Dawson, CBE 1918; MD (Edin.), FRCP (London), FRCP (C), FRGS; Expert Adviser *re* Proprietary and Patent Medicine Act; Emeritus Professor of Therapeutics, University of Toronto; Consulting Physician, Toronto General Hospital and Sick Children's

Hospital, Toronto; Colonel, CAMC (retired); late Consulting Physician to Canadian Forces in England; *b* Pictou, Nova Scotia, 1865; *s* of William Norman Rudolf; *m* 1894, Rosa Marguerite, *d* of late J. T. Danson of Grasmere; one *s* one *d*. *Educ*: Birkenhead School; Edinburgh University; Berlin and Paris. Emeritus Member Association American Physicians; Past-President and Fellow American Therapeutic Society; Life Member Ontario Medical Association; Senior Fellow Can. Medical Association; Hon. Fellow Toronto Academy of Medicine; Senior President Royal Medical Society, Edinburgh; Resident Physician, Royal Infirmary and Hospital for Sick Children, Edinburgh. After graduating at Edinburgh University, spent five years in India, and since then has resided in Toronto; was five years overseas with the Canadian Army. *Publications*: Medical Treatment (4th ed.); numerous scientific papers, and stories for children. *Recreations*: fishing, sailing, motoring. *Address*: 102 Blythwood Road, Toronto, Canada. *T*: Mo 3473; 511 Med. Arts Building, Toronto. *T*: Ki.5873. *Clubs*: York, Toronto Golf, Toronto.

Died 2 Nov. 1941.

RUEGG, His Honour Alfred Henry; KC 1902; JP Staffs, also Boroughs Stafford, Hanley, Stoke, and Newcastle-under-Lyme; 2nd *s* of late Edward James Ruegg, of Stroud, Glos. Bar, Middle Temple; QC 1895; elected a Bencher, 1903; C. C. Judge, Staffs, 1907–39, and Joint C. C. Judge, Birmingham; was one of the examiners for the Council of Legal Education; Editor of County Courts Annual Practice; was counsel for Mr O'Donnell, MP, in his action for libel against The Times, out of which arose the Parnell Commission. *Publications*: work on Employers' Liability and Workmen's Compensation, 9th ed.; The Law of Factories and Workshops; Ruegg and Mossop's Companies Act 1900; a Commentary on English Law for use in Schools; novels: John Clutterbuck; A Staffordshire Knot; Flash, 1928; David Betterton. *Recreation*: golf. *Address*: Highfields Hall, Uttoxeter, Staffs. *Club*: Union.

Died 22 April 1941.

RUGGLES-BRISE, Col Sir Edward Archibald, 1st Bt *cr* 1935; MC, TD, DL, JP; MP (C) Maldon Division of Essex, 1922–23, and since 1924; Chairman Agricultural Committee, House of Commons; Vice-Lieutenant, County of Essex; *b* 1882; *e s* of late Archibald Weyland Ruggles-Brise, JP, DL; *m* 1st, 1906, Agatha (*d* 1937), *e d* of J. H. Gurney, DL, JP, of Keswick Hall, Norfolk; two *s* two *d*; 2nd, 1939, Barbara Pym, *yr d* of late Bishop of Bombay. *Educ*: Eton; Trinity College, Cambridge. Lieutenant Eton College RV, 1900–01; joined Essex Yeomanry, 1903; Major, 1915; served European War, 1914–18; and Army of Occupation, 1918–19 (despatches); Lt-Col commanding 104th (Essex Yeomanry) Field Brigade RA (TA), 1927–34; Bt Col 1931; landowner, land agent, farmer, Fellow of Land Agents' Society. *Recreations*: hunting, shooting, fishing. *Heir*: *s* John Archibald, Major, 54th (City of London) AA Brig. RA (TA) [*b* 13 June 1908. *Educ*: Eton]. *Address*: Spains Hall, Finchingfield, Braintree, Essex. *TA*: Finchingfield. *T*: Gt Bardfield 66. *Clubs*: Carlton, Farmers'.

Died 12 May 1942.

RUGMAN, Sir Francis Dudley, KCMG 1942; CMG 1939; MC; *b* 31 May 1894; *s* of late Francis Rugman Iron Acton, Gloucestershire; *m* 1926, Cyrille Maud, *d* of late Edward G. Barclay, OBE, of Paris and Cupar, Fife; one *s*. *Educ*: privately and in France. Served European War, 1914–19, France, Italy and Belgium (MC and Bar, despatches); qualified as Chartered Accountant (not in practice), 1920; entered Sudan Civil Service as Inspector, Finance Dept, 1920; subsequently Director of Accounts, Assistant Financial Secretary and Deputy Financial Secretary; Financial Secretary, 1934–44; retired 1944; Member of Governor-General's Council, 1934; Order

of the Nile (Grand Officer), 1937. *Address*: 66 Harley House, NW1. *T*: Welbeck 1003. *Clubs*: Travellers', Junior Carlton.

Died 2 April 1946.

RUMBLE, Sir Bertram Thomas, Kt 1946; Hon. Treasurer Royal Air Force Benevolent Fund; Chairman Fullers' Earth Union Ltd; *b* 1 Nov. 1875; *s* of Thomas Rumble; *m* Florence Emily Pratt; two *s*. *Educ*: King's College, London. *Recreation*: yachting. *Address*: 8 Grand Avenue, Hove, Sussex. *Club*: Royal Thames Yacht.

Died 12 Jan. 1949.

RUMBOLD, Captain Charles E. A. L.; *b* 24 Aug. 1872; *s* of late C. J. A. Rumbold, MA, FRGS, and *g g s* of Sir Thomas Rumbold, Bart; *m* 1st, 1906, Anne Christian (*d* 1928). *d*, of Hon. Richard Nugent; one *s* one *d*; 2nd, 1938, Madame Yvonne Catherine Aurore Béatrice Garnon, *d* of Alphonse Marie Billot. *Educ*: Harrow. Formerly held a commission in the 2nd Dragoon Guards, Queen's Bays, and served in the South African War; and subsequently went to the General Reserve of Officers; served in France as a Capt. RE during European War; Chevalier de l'Ordre du Mérite Maritime. *Publications*: Yacht Cruising on Inland Waterways from the Baltic to the Mediterranean, 1935; many articles to the periodical press on hunting, yachting, marine motoring, and subjects connected with country life. *Recreations*: hunting, yachting and visiting ancient buildings. *Address*: Mas des Pins, Avenue Hector-Otto, Monaco. *Club*: Royal Southampton Yacht.

Died 9 April 1943.

RUMBOLD, Rt Hon. Sir Horace George Montagu, 9th Bt *cr* 1779; PC 1920; GCB 1934; GCMG 1923; KCMG 1917; MVO 1907; *b* 5 Feb. 1869; *e s* of Right Hon. Sir Horace Rumbold, 8th Bt, and Caroline (*d* 1872), *d* of George Harrington, United States Minister at Berne; *S* father, 1913; *m* 1905, Etheldred, CBE, 2nd *d* of late Sir Edmund Fane, KCMG; one *s* one *d*. *Educ*: Eton. Hon. Attaché, The Hague, 1888; Attaché, 1890; passed a competitive examination, 1891; appointed to Cairo, 1891; granted an allowance for knowledge of Arabic, 1892; for knowledge in Persian, 1896; for knowledge of Japanese, 1910; 3rd Secretary, 1893; passed an examination in Public Law, 1893; transferred to Athens, 1895 (did not proceed), to Teheran, 1895; 2nd Secretary, 1896; Vienna, 1897; Cairo, 1900; 1st Secretary, 1904; Madrid, 1906; Chargé d'Affaires at Munich, 1908; Councillor of Embassy, Tokio, 1909–13; Chargé d'Affaires at Tokio, 24 May to 28 Sept. 1909; 1 May to 31 July 1911; and 1 Nov. 1912 to 5 March 1913; Coronation Medal, 1911; Councillor of Embassy, Berlin, 1 Nov. 1913; Chargé d'Affaires at Berlin, 1 to 27 July 1914; left Berlin on declaration of war and was employed in the Foreign Office; British Minister Switzerland, 1916–19; Republic of Poland, 1919–20; British High Commissioner and Ambassador at Constantinople, 1920–24; British Ambassador, Madrid, 1924–28; British Ambassador at Berlin, 1928–33; retired, 1933; was second British Plenipotentiary at the Lausanne Conference, Nov. 1922–Feb. 1923, and Chief Delegate at the resumed Conference April–July 1923; signed the Lausanne Treaty on behalf of the British Empire, 24 July 1923; retired 1 Aug. 1933; British Representative at a Conference at Geneva to advise League Council on Refugees' question, Dec. 1935; Vice-Chairman of the Royal Commission on Palestine, 1936–37. *Publication*: The War Crisis in Berlin, July-August 1914, 1940. *Recreations*: golf, lawn tennis. *Heir*: *s* Horace Anthony Claude [third Secretary in HM Diplomatic Service; *b* 7 March 1911; *m* 1937, Felicity Ann, *yr d* of Lt-Col F. G. and Lady Janet Bailey; one *d*]. *Address*: 4 Grosvenor Crescent, SW1. *T*: Sloane 3827. *Clubs*: Turf, Travellers', Royal Automobile.

Died 24 May 1941.

RUMBOLD, Col William Edwin, CMG 1919; late RA; *b* St Petersburg, 22 Oct. 1870; *s* of late Right Hon. Sir Horace Rumbold, Bart, GCB, GCMG; *m* 1903, Elizabeth Gordon, *d* of late Rev. R. Cameron of Burntisland, Scotland; three *s* one *d*. *Educ:* Wellington College; RMA, Woolwich. 2nd Lt RA, 1891; Captain, 1899; Major, 1911; Lt-Colonel, 1917; Colonel, 1921; retired, 1921; Served East Africa, 1900, Nandi Expedition (medal with clasps); Suk Turkana Expedition 1901 (despatches); European War, 1914–18, France and Flanders, latterly on Staff of 18th Corps (despatches five times, French War Cross with palms, Belgian War Cross). *Recreations:* golf, shooting. *Address:* Invervar Lodge, North Berwick. *Clubs:* Naval and Military; New, North Berwick.

Died 25 Jan. 1947.

RUMNEY, Abraham Wren, MA; author; *b* 1863; *o c* of O. G. Rumney, MD, of Mellfell, Cumberland, and Julia, *o c* of Abraham Wren of Keswick; *m* 1907, Sarah, *y d* of Henry Tandy of Penrith; no *c*. *Educ:* Rugby; Trinity Hall, Cambridge (Law Tripos, 1885). Admitted Solicitor, 1889, but drifted into journalism, chiefly on cycling subjects, in numerous newspapers and magazines; for 12 years in charge of touring department of *Cycling*; editor of Cyclists' Touring Club Gazette, 1907–13; cycled to Damascus, Dead Sea, etc., 1906; has also cycled in France, Italy, Spain, Portugal, Corsica, Sicily, Algeria, Greece, and Switzerland. *Publications:* The Way About the English Lake District; Sprogues on the Fells; Cycle Touring, 1898; Cyclists' Guide to English Lakes, 1899; A Cyclists' Note Book, 1900; The Dalesman, 1911; From the Old South Sea House, 1914; Fifty Years a Cyclist, 1927; Uncle Peter, 1933; A Hank of Cycling Yarn, 1935; Tom Rumney, 1936. *Recreations:* cycling, mountaineering, swimming. *Address:* Skiddaw Cottage, Keswick; Skinburness, Silloth. *Club:* Cyclists' Touring.

Died 23 Feb. 1942.

RUNCIMAN OF DOXFORD, 1st Viscount *cr* 1937; **Walter Runciman;** Baron Runciman *cr* 1933, of Shoreston; Bart *cr* 1906, PC 1908; JP Co. Northumberland; Hon. DCL (Oxford); Hon. LLD (Manchester and Bristol); Elder Brother of Trinity House; *b* South Shields, 19 Nov. 1870; *o s* of 1st Baron Runciman and Ann Margaret, *e d* of late John Lawson, Blakemoor, Northumberland; *m* 1898; Hilda (Viscountess Runciman of Doxford, JP), 5th *d* of J. C. Stevenson, late MP for South Shields; two *s* two *d*. *Educ:* Trinity Coll., Camb. BA 1892; MA 1895; contested Gravesend, 1898; North Edinburgh, 1920. MP (L) Oldham, 1899–1900; Dewsbury, 1902–18; Swansea West, 1924–29; St Ives division of Cornwall, 1929–31, (LNat) 1931–37; Parliamentary Sec. to Local Government Board, 1905–07; Financial Secretary to Treasury, 1907–08; President Board of Education, 1908–11; of Agriculture, 1911–14; Commissioner HM's Woods, Forests, and Land Revenues, 1912–14; President of the Board of Trade, 1914–16 and 1931–37; Head of Mission to Czechoslovakia, 1938; Lord President of the Council, 1938–39; Pres. of Chamber of Shipping of United Kingdom, 1926–27; Deputy Chairman and Voting Trustee of Royal Mail Steam Packet Company and its associated companies, 1930–31; Chairman of United Kingdom Provident Institution, 1920–31. Heir: *s* Hon. (Walter) Leslie Runciman, OBE. *Address:* Doxford, Chathill, Northumberland; Isle of Eigg, Scotland. *Clubs:* Brooks's; Royal Yacht Squadron.

Died 14 Nov. 1949.

RUNDLE, Col George Richard Tyrrell, CB 1915; commanded 146th Brigade RFA, BEF; *b* 12 July 1860. Entered army, 1879; Lt-Col 1895; retired, 1910; served South Africa, 1899–1902 (despatches; Queen's medal 3 clasps, King's medal 2 clasps); European War, 1914–16 (CB).

Died 12 Dec. 1947.

RUSHBROOKE, Rev. James Henry, MA, DD; LLD; President, Baptist World Alliance; *b* 29 July 1870; *m* 1st, Kate (*d* 1922), *d* of James Partridge, Thorpe-le-Soken; 2nd, Dorothea Gertrud (*d* 1944), *d* of Professor Anton Weber, Berlin; one *d*. *Educ:* Midland and Univ. Colleges Nottingham; University, London; University, Berlin; University, Halle; MA Lond.; DD (Hon.), McMaster University, Canada; LLD (Hon.) Bates College, USA; DCL (Hon.) Acadia University, Nova Scotia. Minister of Churches in Derby and London, 1902–20; Baptist Commissioner for Europe, 1920–28; Eastern Secretary of Baptist World Alliance, 1925–28, and General Secretary, 1928–39; President of Baptist Union of Great Britain and Ireland, 1926–27; President of National Free Church Council, 1934–35; Chairman of Baptist Missionary Society, 1937–38; has travelled in North and South America, the West Indies, the Near and Far East, South Africa, Australia, New Zealand, and especially in Europe, including six visits to Soviet Russia; has administered extensive relief funds in Russia and other countries, and has devoted himself to the advocacy of full religious liberty in all lands, making personal representations to many heads of States, including King Carol of Rumania and President Kalinin of the USSR; organised and carried through the Baptist World Congresses in Toronto, 1928, Berlin, 1934, and Atlanta, Ga, USA, 1939; during the War visited USA and Canada, and in 1945–46 several European lands including Germany; Chairman of Special Committee for Baptist Reconstruction in Europe, and now organising Seventh Baptist World Congress to meet in Copenhagen in July 1947. *Publications:* The Baptist Movement in the Continent of Europe, 1915 (rewritten, 1923); Baptists in Europe (with Dr C. A. Brooks), 1920; Some Chapters of European Baptist History, 1929; a number of theological addresses delivered at World Congresses, etc., and especially Protestant of the Protestants, 1926; Baptists as Champions of Religious Freedom, 1938; Baptists in the USSR, 1943; The World Responsibility of Baptists, 1943; articles in Reviews, Dictionary of National Biography etc.; Editor, The Peacemaker, 1908–1914; Goodwill, 1915–1920; and other periodicals. *Address:* 4 Southampton Row, WC1. *TA:* Preacher, London. *T:* Holborn 2045.

Died 1 Feb. 1947.

RUSHCLIFFE, 1st Baron *cr* 1935, of Blackfordby; **Henry Bucknall Betterton;** PC 1931; 1st Bt *cr* 1929, GBE 1941 (CBE 1920; OBE 1918); *b* 1872; *e s* of late Henry Inman Betterton, JP, of Woodville, Leicestershire; *m* 1st, 1912, Violet (*d* 1947), *widow* of Capt. Hervey Greathed, 8th Hussars, and *y d* of late J. S. Gilliat, of Chorleywood Cedars, formerly MP for Clapham and Widnes, and Governor of the Bank of England; two *d*; 2nd, 1948, Inez Alfreda, *d* of late Alfred Lubbock. *Educ:* Rugby; Christ Church, Oxford. BA. Called to Bar, Inner Temple, 1896; JP Herts; MP (U) Rushcliffe Division Nottinghamshire, Dec. 1918–34; Parliamentary Sec., Min. of Labour, 1923–24, and Nov. 1924–29; Min. of Labour, 1931–34; Chm. of Assistance Board, 1934–41; Chairman National Service Hostels Corporation, 1941–46; Cust Lecturer Nottingham University, 1928; Member Palestine Commission, 1929; Member Political Honours Scrutiny Committee; Chairman Nurses' Salaries Committee; Chairman Midwives' Salaries Committee; Chairman Committee on Training of Nurses for the Colonies; Chairman of Advisory Committee on Welfare of the Blind; Chairman Committee on Legal Aid and Legal Advice, 1945. Vice-Chairman Borax Consolidated Ltd and Director Town Investments Ltd. *Address:* The Gables, Blatchington Hill, Seaford, Sx. *Clubs:* Carlton, Turf.

Died 18 Nov. 1949.

RUSHTON, George R., RI, RBA, RSBA, practising artist; *b* Birmingham; *s* of late George Rushton, Engineer; *m* Edith, *d* of late I. Ash, Bank Manager, Gateshead-on-Tyne; two *d*. *Educ:* Birmingham. Stain

Glass Artist 1st Period; 2nd period included the execution of large decorative paintings and smaller water-colour drawings; recently given full attention to the Art of Water Colour; frequent exhibitor at Royal Academy; many invitations to Provincial Galleries, also Canada; works in Public Art Galleries, including Auckland, NZ, Birmingham, Newcastle-on-Tyne, Ipswich, South Kensington Museum, Montreal, Canada, and Doncaster. *Address:* Upgrove, Belstead Road, Ipswich. *T:* Ipswich 4725.

Died 20 June 1948.

RUSSELL; *see* Hamilton-Russell.

RUSSELL OF KILLOWEN, Baron *cr* 1929 (Life Peer); **Frank Russell;** PC 1928; *b* 2 July 1867; 4th *s* of late Lord Russell of Killowen; *m* 1900, Hon. Mary Emily, 5th *d* of 1st Baron Ritchie of Dundee; one *s* two *d*. *Educ:* Beaumont College; Oriel College, Oxford. Called to Bar, Lincoln's Inn, 1893; KC 1908; a Judge of the High Court, 1919–28; a Lord Justice of Appeal, 1928–29; a Lord of Appeal in Ordinary, 1929–46. *Address:* Lane End, Walton on the Hill, Tadworth, Surrey. *T:* Tadworth 2253. *Club:* Garrick.

Died 20 Dec. 1946.

RUSSELL, Countess; (Elizabeth Mary); *d* of H. Herron Beauchamp; *m* 1st, Count Henning August Arnim (*d* 1910); one *s* three *d*; 2nd, 1916, 2nd Earl Russell (*d* 1931). *Publications:* Elizabeth and her German Garden, 1898; The Solitary Summer, 1899; The April Baby's Book of Tunes, 1900; The Benefactress, 1902; The Adventures of Elizabeth in Ruegen, 1904; The Princess Priscilla's Fortnight, 1906; Fräulein Schmidt and Mr Anstruther, 1907; The Caravaners, 1909; Priscilla Runs Away, 1910; The Pastor's Wife, 1914; Christopher and Columbus, 1919; In the Mountains, 1920; Vera, 1921; The Enchanted April, 1923; Love, 1925; Introduction to Sally, 1926; Expiation, 1929; Father, 1931; The Jasmine Farm, 1934; All the Dogs of my Life, 1936; Mr Skeffington, 1940. *Address:* Mas des Roses, Mougins, France, AM.

Died 9 Feb. 1941.

RUSSELL, Alexander, MA, DSc, LLD, FRS, Hon. MIEE; Advisory-Principal of Faraday House, London; *b* 1861; *s* of John Russell, of Glasgow; *m* 1890, Edith, *d* of H. B. Ince, QC, MP; one *s* one *d*. *Educ:* Glasgow University; Caius College, Cambridge. Assistant Lecturer, Caius College; Senior Mathematical Master, Oxford Military College; Past President and Faraday Medallist of the Institution of Electrical Engineers, of the Physical Society of London, and of the Junior Institution of Engineers; Past Vice-President of the Institute of Physics; appointed by the Electricity Commissioners as Electric Inspector to various towns; Examiner, Glasgow and London Universities. *Publications:* Alternating Currents; Theory of Cables; Life of Lord Kelvin; has translated Buchetti's Engine Tests; has written many papers on subjects connected with physics and engineering, some of which were communicated to the Royal Society, the Institution of Electrical Engineers, and the Physical Society. *Recreations:* boating, motoring. *Address:* 49 Welbeck Street, W1. *TA:* Standardizing London. *T:* Holborn 9001.

Died 14 Jan. 1943.

RUSSELL, Alfred Ernest, MD, BS (Lond.), FRCP; Consulting Physician, St Thomas's Hospital, London; *b* 1870; 2nd *s* of George Russell; *m* 1918, Dorothy, *y d* of late Lt-Col Northcote, Royal Marine Artillery, of Collingwood, Wallington, Surrey. *Educ:* Roan School, Greenwich; St Thomas's Hospital. Late Medical Referee, HM Treasury; House Physician, House Surgeon, Demonstrator of Physiology, Medical Registrar, Resident Assistant Physician, St Thomas's Hospital; Assistant Physician, West London Hospital; Examiner in Medicine and Materia Medica, Royal College of Physicians; Examiner in Medicine, Society of

Apothecaries; Goulstonian Lecturer on Disorders of the Cerebral Circulation and their Clinical Manifestations, Royal College of Physicians. *Publications:* Emergencies of General Practice (with Sir Percy Sargent); St Thomas's Hospital Medical Report, 1897–1898–1899; papers on medical subjects in medical journals. *Address:* Ridge End, Finchampstead, Berks. *T:* Eversley 2143.

Died 26 March 1944.

RUSSELL, Sir Alison, KCMG 1943; Kt 1928; KC; *b* 1875; *y s* of late George Russell, civil engineer; *m* 1916, Helen Cameron (author of The Sunwheel; Hindu Life and Customs, 1935), *y d* of late James Gordon. *Educ:* Rugby; Trinity, College, Cambridge; BA, LLB. Called to Bar, Inner Temple, 1900; practised at the Chancery Bar, 1900–06; Attorney General, Uganda, 1906–12; Acting Chief Secretary, Uganda, 1910–11; Attorney-General, Cyprus, 1912–24; Chief Justice, Tanganyika Territory, 1924; retired, 1929; Legal Adviser to Government of Malta, 1934; Chairman Committee of Enquiry into Disturbances in the Copperbelt, N Rhodesia, 1935; Chairman Appeal Committee, Motor Trade Association; Member Palestine Partition Committee, 1938; Ministry of Information (Commercial Relations), 1941; Chairman Commission of Enquiry, Bahamas, 1942; Assistant Legal Adviser, Colonial Office, 1943; Chairman Commission of Enquiry, Tafo, Gold Coast, 1945. Chairman or member of various Committees under the Colonial Office. *Publications:* contributor to Encyclopædia of Forms; Reprint of Statutes, Cyprus, 1914; Legislative Drafting and Forms (4th ed. 1938); Handbook for Magistrates (2nd ed. 1928); Reprint of Statutes, Tanganyika, 1931; Notes and Forms for Enquiries under the Colonial Regulations (3rd ed., 1948); The Magistrate: a handbook for Magistrates, 1945. *Recreations:* games, painting, and sailing; Fives Cup, Rugby, 1895; Manning Cup, Uganda team, winners, 1910; runner-up, Davos Bowl, 1911; Romola Cup, crew C. F. Duncan's Sirius, 1921; gold badge National Skating Association. *Address:* 9 King's Bench Walk, Temple, EC4. *T:* Central 2437. *Clubs:* Athenæum, Savile, Royal Cruising, Royal Skating.

Died 19 Sept. 1948.

RUSSELL, Frederick Vernon, CBE 1920; *b* Nunhead, Surrey, 7 May 1870; *s* of Henry Vernon Russell, RN, Warwick, and Annie Paul, Devonport; *m* Gladys Kathleen Sala, Inverness. *Educ:* Christ's Hospital; King's College. Apprentice to James Holden, GER Works, Stratford; Chief of Locomotive design, GER; Locomotive Running Superintendent, GER; Superintendent of Operation (Traffic and Locomotive) GER; Technical Assistant to Gen. Manager, LNER (Southern Division); special work for LNER, chiefly in connection with electrification of railway; retired, 1933. *Publication:* A Comparative Review of Heavy Suburban Passenger Train Operation by Steam and Electric Traction. *Recreation:* horticulture. *Address:* 17 Teesdale Road, Leytonstone, E11. *T:* Wanstead 0263.

Died 15 July 1942.

RUSSELL, Sir George Arthur Charles, 5th Bt *cr* 1812; *b* 28 June 1868; *e s* of 4th Bt and Constance, *g d* of 4th Duke of Richmond; *S* father, 1898. *Heir:* *b* Arthur Edward Ian Montagu [*b* 30 Nov. 1878; *m* 1st, 1904, Aileen Kerr (*d* 1920), *y d* of late Adm. M. R. Pechell; one *s* one *d*; 2nd, 1922, Cornéllie, *d* of Major Jacques de Bruijn, Amsterdam; one *s*; 3rd, 1933, Marjorie Elisabeth Josephine, *d* of Ernest Rudman, Foxhangers, Earley, Berks; one *s*]. *Address:* Swallowfield Park, Reading.

Died 14 Jan. 1944.

RUSSELL, Hamer; Managing Director, Hamer Russell, Ltd; Commander of the Order of St John of Jerusalem; *s* of late J. T. and Kate Russell, Hull; *m* 1904, Florence, *d* of John Marshall, Halifax; one *s*. *Educ:* Eton House School, Hull. Founder of Hamer Russell, Ltd, Timber and Building Material Merchants; was Chairman of the

Sheffield Liberal Federation; contested (L) Ecclesall Division; resigned from the Liberal and joined the Conservative party; contested (C) Brightside, 1930; MP (C) Brightside, 1931–35; during war held positions in Hospitals, and lectured to Troops on Field Ambulance work; Assistant Commissioner for East Surrey St John Ambulance Brigade; an expert on Ambulance work, particularly in regard to Transport, and the designer of modern equipment. *Publications:* Standard Regulations to be observed in Street Accidents; articles on the Standardisation of Motor Ambulance Bodies. *Address:* Brightside, Cookham Dene, Berkshire; 4 Warwick Square, SW1. *Clubs:* Constitutional, Devonshire.

Died 6 June 1941.

RUSSELL, Herbert John, CBE 1939; General Manager Newfoundland Railway since 1923; *b* 24 Dec. 1890; *m* 1918, Jean Campbell; four *s. Educ:* Commercial School, St John's. Joined Railway Co. at St John's, Newfoundland, 1906; various positions in Operating Dept; Train despatcher, Asst Supt, Supt, Asst Gen. Manager, Acting Gen. Manager. *Recreations:* fishing, shooting, curling. *Address:* 22 Leslie Street, St John's, Newfoundland. *TA:* Railway, St John's. *T:* 191.

Died 21 Feb. 1949.

RUSSELL, Sir Herbert (William Henry), KBE 1920; War Correspondent; *b* 28 March 1869; *e s* of W. Clark Russell, novelist; *m* 1st, Lucie Marion Meech (*d* 1931), one *s* two *d*; 2nd, 1932, Violet Reibey (*d* 1937), *widow of* Major John Straghan. *Educ:* Royal Grammar School, Newcastle-on-Tyne; private schools. Entered journalism under the ægis of the late Joseph Cowen, of the Newcastle Chronicle, 1893; joined the Daily Express when started by Sir Arthur Pearson; served as Reuter's War Correspondent during the Gallipoli Campaign and on the Western Front, June 1915–Nov. 1918 (Chevalier of the Legion of Honour); accompanied Prince of Wales throughout his tour of India and Japan. *Publications:* Novels: True Blue; The Longshoreman; My Atlantic Bride; With the Prince in the East, 1922; The Delectable West, 1932; Sea Warfare Today, 1940; Sea Shepherds, 1941; Ark Royal, 1942; frequent contributor to periodicals and press on naval matters. *Recreation:* yachting. *Address:* 54 Ormond Avenue, Hampton-on-Thames. *T:* Molesey 1122.

Died 23 March 1944.

RUSSELL, Maj.-Gen. John Joshua, CB 1916; MB, late AMS; *b* 26 Sept. 1862. Capt. RAMC 1886; Maj. 1898; Lt-Col 1906; Col AMS 1915; Assist-Director of Medical Services, 1914–16; Deputy Director, 1916; served S Africa, 1900–01 (Queen's medal 2 clasps); European War, 1914–17 (despatches twice, CB); retired pay, 1922.

Died 12 Jan. 1941.

RUSSELL, Mrs Lilian M.; Assisting Dr Albert Schweitzer at Lambarene and elsewhere since 1927; *b* May 1875; *d* of Major-General Christopher Palmer Rigby and Matilda Rigby; *m* 1909, Charles E. B. Russell (*d* 1917), HM Chief Inspector of Reformatory and Industrial Schools; no *c. Educ:* Queen's College. Inspector, Children's Department, Home Office, 1917–23. *Publications:* With Charles E. B. Russell: The Making of the Criminal, 1906; Working Lads' Clubs, 1908. Revised edition, Lads' Clubs, 1932; General Rigby, Zanzibar and the Slave Trade, 1935; My Monkey Friends, 1938; The Path to Reconstruction, 1941; Translator of Dr Albert Schweitzer's Indian Thought and its Development, 1936. From my African Notebook, 1938, Goethe, 1949. Working at leper colonies in SE Nigeria under Belra, 1937–1938 and 1946, and in Siam, 1939. *Address:* Ashburn, Strone, Argyll. *Club:* Overseas League.

Died 1 Oct. 1949.

RUSSELL, Maj.-Gen. Sir Michael (William), KCMG 1918; CB 1916; *b* 23 June 1860; *s of* late George Russell, Bawtry, Yorks; *m* 1892, Mary (*d* 1944), *d* of Col C. H. Plowden. Major RAMC 1897; Bt Lt-Col 1902; Col 1914; late Deputy Director-General, AMS, War Office; served Sudan, 1885–86 (medal, bronze star); Zhob Valley, 1890; South Africa, 1900–02 (Queen's medal 3 clasps, King's medal 2 clasps, despatches twice, Bt Lt-Col); European War, 1914–18 (CB, KCMG). *Address:* St Anthony's, Croft Road, Crowborough, Sussex.

Died 6 Dec. 1949.

RUSSELL, Col Reginald Edmund Maghlin, CVO 1931; CBE 1919; DSO 1915; one of HM's Body Guard of the Honourable Corps of Gentlemen at Arms since 1932; *b* 2 Sept. 1879; *s of* E. M. Russell, Milford House, Limerick; *m* 1918, Dorothy B., twin *d* of late Major E. B. Crake, Rifle Brigade; (one *s* killed in action 1943) one *d. Educ:* Cheltenham College; RMA, Woolwich. Second Lieut RE 1898; Bt Lt-Col 1918; Lt-Col 1924; Col 1927; Brigadier-Gen. (temp.) 1 March–2 Aug. 1917; Egyptian Army, 1905–15; served S African War, 1901–02 (Queen's medal 5 clasps, despatches); Anuak Expedition (Sudan), 1912 (1 medal, 1 clasp, 4th Class Mejidia); European War, Egyptian Expeditionary Force, 1914–18 (CBE, DSO, despatches six times, Cavalieri Italian Order of St Maurice and St Lazarus, 4th Class Order of Nile); GSO2 Force in Egypt; GSO1 Western Frontier Force and 52nd (Lowland) Div.; Chief Engineer (Brig.-Gen.) Desert Column; CRE Desert Mounted Corps (Lieut-Col); SO1 Air, Royal Air Force, SE Area; Training Battalion, Royal Engineers, Chatham; Military Attaché at Santiago, 1927–31; retired pay, 1931; re-employed 1939–44, Military Attaché Buenos Aires. *Recreations:* normal. *Address:* Hurst House, Church Crookham, Hants. *T:* Fleet 886. *Club:* Naval and Military.

Died 24 Nov. 1950.

RUSSELL, Reginald James Kingston; Editor-in-Chief and Managing Director of The Forum, which he founded in 1938; *b* Wells, Somerset, 12 March 1883; *e s* of James and Fanny Russell; *m* 1909, Elizabeth Tyrrell, 2nd *d* of E. R. Yerbury, Edinburgh. For several years on Editorial Staff Birmingham Post and London Daily News before the 1914–18 War; Assistant Editor Cape Times, 1920–26; Editor the Natal Mercury, 1926–36; delegate to Imperial Press Conference, London, 1930; served European War with Lothians and Border Horse (Capt. and Adjt) (despatches twice). *Publications:* (under pen-name Shaun Malory) Treasure of Tempest; The Quest of the Golden Spurs; Essays, etc. *Recreations:* golf, fishing, botany. *Clubs:* Civil Service, Capetown; Pretoria, Pretoria.

Died May 1943.

RUSSELL, Richard John; JP; MP (L) Eddisbury, March 1929–31, (LNat) since 1931; *b* 1872; *s* of R. J. Russell, Birkenhead; *m* Ellen (*d* 1942), *d* of William Atkinson, Skellgill, Wenslaydale, Yorks; two *d. Educ:* St Ann's, Birkenhead; Liverpool University; LDS, RCS (Eng.). Chairman many important committees on Merseyside, including with late Sir Archibald Salvidge, Merseyside Co-ordination Committee, Mersey Tunnel Joint Committee, etc.; contested Eddisbury, 1923 and 1924; for many years an Alderman of Birkenhead Town Council. *Address:* Blea Busk, Askrigg, Yorks. *T:* Bainbridge Yorks 233. *Club:* National Liberal.

Died 5 Feb. 1943.

RUSSELL, Captain Stuart Hugh Minto; Coldstream Guards; MP (U) Darwen Division of Lancaster since 1935; *b* 18 Jan. 1909; *er* and *o surv. s* of Sir (Charles) Lennox (Somerville) Russell. *Educ:* Rugby; Trinity College, Cambridge, BA (Honours). Parliamentary Private Secretary to Rt Hon. Sir Philip Sassoon, PC, when Under-Secretary of State for Air, Sept. 1936–June 1937; Parliamentary Private Secretary to Rt Hon. Sir

John Simon, Chancellor of the Exchequer, 1937–38. *Address:* Crooksbury, Hurst, near Farnham, Surrey. *T:* Runfold 88. *Clubs:* Carlton, Brooks's, Pratt's.

Died 30 Oct. 1943.

RUSSELL, Sir Walter Westley, Kt 1935; CVO 1931; RA 1926; ARA 1920; RWS 1930; *b* 31 May 1867; *m* 1900, Lydia (*d* 1944) *d* of late William Nelson Burton, Woburn Green, Bucks. Studied Westminster School of Art under Professor Frederick Brown; represented in Tate Gallery, London; Walker Art Gallery, Liverpool; National Gallery, Edinburgh; Oldham, Bradford, Birkenhead, Southport, Worthing, Cape Town, Johannesburg, Adelaide, Dublin, Cork, etc.; Served European War in France as Lieut RE, 1916–19 (despatches). *Address:* St Margarets, Bourne End, Bucks.

Died 16 April 1949.

RUSSELL, William; JP; MP (U) Bolton, 1922–23; Deputy Mayor, County Borough of Bolton; Councillor; Chairman of Bolton Incorporated Law Society; *b* 28 Aug. 1859; *s* of George Russell, *s* of John Russell of Bolton and Mary Jane, *d* of William Ferguson of Cockermouth; *m* Mary, *d* of Thomas Taylor of Bolton; three *s.* *Educ:* Booth's Academy; privately. Engaged in municipal and religious and social life of Bolton for many years, of which town he was Mayor, 1921–22; Solicitor for over 30 years, now retired. *Recreations:* fond of all outdoor sports, and taken part in many. *Club:* Bolton Constitutional.

Died 31 Oct. 1937.

RUSSELL, Col William Kelson, CMG 1919; DSO 1917; retired, late RE; *b* 1873; *s* of late Capt. Thos Russell, Bedfordshire Regt; *m* 1897, Emily Rose Cummins (*d* 1938); one *s.* *Educ:* private. Commissioned to RE 1893; served India, 1895–1914; France, 1914–19 (despatches, CMG, DSO); retired, 1924. *Address:* Beridth, Beaminster, Dorset. *T:* 271.

Died 14 Feb. 1949.

RUSSELL, Captain Wilmot Peregrine Maitland, MC, MA (Oxon); Captain retired (Regular Forces); *b* 1874; 3rd *s* of late Capt. T. Stuart Russell, DL; *m* 1932, Amy Moncrieff, *d* of late Scott Moncrieff Penney, Sheriff Substitute of Argyllshire; one *d.* *Educ:* Rugby; Exeter College, Oxford. Served in Foreign Office Service in China, 1898–1910; Peking Legations during siege 1900 (despatches), European War, 1914–18 (despatches); Gallipoli, Egypt, Belgium and France; Captain, Gordon Highlanders (MC); Acting 1st Secretary in HM's Diplomatic service at Helsingfors, 1920–21; Chargé d'Affaires at Helsingfors, 1921. *Publications:* various articles in the National Review, Contemporary Review, and other periodicals on military subjects, foreign affairs, travel, etc. *Recreations:* tennis, travel. *Address:* 24 Belgrave Crescent, Edinburgh. *T:* 25349. *Club:* New (Edinburgh).

Died 29 Nov. 1950.

RUST, William; Editor, Daily Worker; Member, Executive Committee of Communist Party; *b* 24 April 1903; *s* of Frederick George and Eliza Rust; *m* 1931, Tamara Kravetz; one *d.* *Educ:* Elementary School. Employed by Hulton Press; Secretary of Young Communist League, and Editor of Young Worker, 1924. Sent to prison for twelve months in 1925 on charge of incitement to mutiny. Appointed Editor of Daily Worker, on publication 1930. Correspondent with International Brigade in Spain, 1937–38; Communist Candidate Hackney South, 1945; at present Communist Candidate for Hackney North. *Publication:* Britons in Spain, 1939. *Recreations:* chess and swimming. *Address:* 45 Fitzroy Road, NW1. *T:* Primrose 4162.

Died 3 Feb. 1949.

RUTHERFORD, Hon. Alexander Cameron, BA, BCL, LLD, KC; Hon. LLD Universities of McGill, Toronto, McMaster and Alberta; Chancellor of University of Alberta since 1927; *b* 2 Feb. 1857; *s* of James and Elizabeth Rutherford; *m* 1888, M. Birkett, Ontario; one *s* one *d.* *Educ:* Public School, Ontario; Woodstock College and McGill University, Montreal; Osgoode Hall, Ontario. Studied Law; called to Bar, 1885; practised Law in Ottawa for 10 years; moved to Edmonton (South), 1895; Secretary-Treasurer and Solicitor for the town of Strathcona, 1899–1905; elected to the Legislature of the North-West Territories, 1902, 1905, and 1909; President of the Liberal Association of Alberta, 1905; first Premier of the Province of Alberta, 1905–10; Minister of Education and Provincial Treasurer. *Recreations:* travel, motoring, golf. *Address:* Edmonton (S), Alberta, Canada. *T:* 3237. *Clubs:* Canadian, Mayfair Golf and Country, Alberta.

Died 11 June 1941.

RUTHERFORD, Sir David Carter, Kt 1936; DL; JP; Director-General Accident Fire and Life Assur. Corporation and General Life Assurance Co; *b* 18 Oct. 1868; *s* of Peter Rutherford, Waltham Cross; *m* 1895, Charlotte Ann (*d* 1940), *d* of A. S. Morling Enfield; two *s.* *Educ:* privately. Merchant (retired); Herts County Council, 1904–13; re-elected 1925; Alderman 1931; Vice-Chairman, 1933; Chairman, 1939–46. *Recreations:* golf, motoring. *Address:* Powis Court, Bushey Heath, Herts. *TA:* Bushey-Heath. *Club:* City of London Constitutional.

Died 22 Aug. 1948.

RUTHERFORD, Sir John Hugo, 2nd Bt *cr* 1923; late (temp.) Capt. Liverpool Regt; *b* 1887; *o s* of 1st Bt and Elspeth Rose (*d* 1914), 2nd *d* of Captain Alexander Strachan, Great Crosby; *S* father, 1927; *m* 1913, Isabel, *d* of late J. T. Smith, Liverpool; three *d.* MP (U) Edge Hill Division, Liverpool, 1931–35. *Address:* Woodlands, Wood Lane, Gateacre, Liverpool.

Died 28 Dec. 1942 (ext).

RUTKOWSKI, Sir Miecislas de, KCMG 1916; Hon. Attaché of the Polish Embassy; *b* Poland (province of Novogrodek), of Polish nobility, 1853; *m* Kathleen Condon (*d* 1926); no *c.* *Educ:* Graduated at the Institute of Ways of Communication in St Petersburg, 1874. On the staff of Government inspectors of Railways in Russia, 1874; sent later by the Russian Government on various missions to Great Britain, France, Italy, Belgium and United States to study the railway systems of those countries; sent again by the Russian Government to Brazil, Paraguay, Uruguay, Argentine Republic, Chile, Peru and Bolivia, to study by what means could be extended the commerce between those countries and Russia, 1891–94; Financial Agent of Russia in United States, 1894, and transferred in the same capacity to Great Britain, 1903; during the war was Chairman of the Russian Government Purchasing Commission in London; after the Versailles Treaty appointed Financial Adviser to the Polish Government in London; retired from active service, 1924; Grand Commander Order of St Anne, and Russian Order of Stanislaus; Knight Commander Russian Order of St Vladimir; Commander of French Legion of Honour. *Publications:* many works on French, British and American Railways, and on Russian Finances and on the World's Financial Crisis, 1933. *Address:* 105 Lansdowne Road, Holland Park, W11. *T:* Park 6262. *Clubs:* St James's; Nouveau Cercle (Ancien Cercle de la Rue Royale), Paris; Chasseurs, Warsaw.

Died 28 March 1941.

RUTLAND, Charles; sculptor; *b* 27 April 1858. Exhibitor at Royal Academy of various works, Timid Nymph; Youth, Time and Immortality; Harp of Life; Morpheus, God of Dreams; Orpheus; Fair Luna, Goddess of the Milky Way; A relief, The Devotee, etc.;

also exhibited at the RA 1931 Exhibition, two marble head studies, The Wise Woman and Master John. *Address:* 168 Hartfield Road, Wimbledon; 20 Elm Park Gardens Mews, Chelsea, SW9.

Died Sept. 1943.

RUTLEDGE, Wiley; Associate Justice, Supreme Court of the United States since 1943; *b* 20 July 1894; *s* of Wiley Blount Rutledge and Mary Lou Wigginton; *m* 1917, Annabel Person; one *s* two *d. Educ:* Maryville College; University of Wisconsin; University of Indiana; and University of Colorado. Admitted to bar of Colorado 1922, of Iowa 1936. General practice, Boulder, Colorado, 1922–24; Associate Professor of Law, University of Colorado, 1924–26; Professor of Law, 1926–35, and Dean, 1930–35, Washington University, St Louis, Mo; Dean and Professor of Law, The State University of Iowa, 1935–39; Associate Justice. United States Court of Appeals for the District of Columbia, 1939–43. *Publications:* A Declaration of Legal Faith, 1947; articles in various legal and other periodicals. *Address:* Supreme Court of the United States, Washington, DC. *T:* Executive 1640.

Died 11 Sept. 1949.

RUTTER, Sir Frederick (William) Pascoe, Kt 1934; Governor of the London and Lancashire Insurance Company, Ltd, since 1921, Life-Governor, 1948, Chairman of the Board, 1921–47; Chairman British Fire Insurance Company; Director of the Law Union and Rock Insurance Company, Standard Marine Insurance Company, The Marine Insurance Company, Law Accident Insurance Society; *b* 28 June 1859; *s* of William Roger Pascoe Rutter; *m* 1st, 1893, Mary Agnes Robertson (*d* 1928), Peterhead; two *s*; 2nd, Lillian, *d* of David Hendrick, Washington, USA. *Educ:* Liverpool Coll. Apprenticed to the London and Lancashire Fire Insurance Company, 1873; Head of Foreign Department, 1885; Assistant Sec., 1890; Sub-Manager, 1891; General Manager and Secretary, 1899; President Insurance Inst. of Great Britain and Ireland, 1910–11; Fellow of Chartered Insurance Institute since 1912. *Publications:* A World in Travail, 1921; The Twinkle, 1937. *Recreations:* work, travel, and golf. *Address:* Coombe Ridge House, Kingston Hill. *TA:* c/o Londlanc, Estrand, London. *T:* Kingston 6683, Holborn 3733. *Clubs:* Carlton; Royal Liverpool Golf (Hoylake).

Died 24 June 1949.

RUTTER, Owen, FRGS; author, journalist, and lecturer; attached Press Division, Admiralty; *b* 7 Nov. 1889; *er s* of Engineer-Commander E. W. Rutter, RD, RNR; *m* 1919, Dorothy, *d* of James Younger, Mount Melville, St Andrews; one *d. Educ:* St Paul's School (Junior and Senior Scholarships). Five years in British North Borneo Civil Service as Magistrate and District Officer; served European War with the Wiltshire regiment in France and Macedonia (despatches); has travelled extensively in Europe, America and the Far East; editor of The Writer, 1922–24; Pres. of the Writer Circle; conducted publicity campaign for Soc. of Authors, 1927; part-proprietor of Golden Cockerel Press; duty in War Office and Postal and Telegraph Censorship, 1939–41. *Publications:* The Song of Tiadatha, 1919; The Travels of Tiadatha, 1922; Brit. N Borneo, 1922; Through Formosa, 1923; The Dragon of Kinabalu, 1923; General Sir John Cowans, 1924; The New Baltic States and their Future, 1925; Dog Days, 1926; Sepia, 1926; Chandu, 1927; Golden Rain, 1928; Ask me Another, 1928; The Pagans of North Borneo, 1929; Lucky Star, 1929 (filmed as Once in a New Moon); Cain's Birthday, 1930; The Pirate Wind, 1930; The Court Martial of the Bounty Mutineers, 1931; The Four Leaf Clover, 1931; One Family, 1931; White Rajah, 1931; The Monster of Mu, 1932; What, Where and Who; A Book of Questions for Children, 1933; If Crab No Walk; A Traveller in the West Indies, 1933; The Voyage of the Bounty's Launch, 1934; One Fair Daughter, 1934; Rajah Brooke and the

Baroness Burdett Coutts, 1935; The Journal of James Morrison, 1935; Mr Glasspoole and the Chinese Pirates, 1935; Clear Waters, 1936; The True Story of the Mutiny in the Bounty, 1936; Turbulent Journey; A Life of William Bligh, Vice-Admiral of the Blue, 1936; The Log of the Bounty, 1936; Bligh's Voyage in the Resource, 1937; The First Fleet, 1937; Good Bargain (play), 1937; Triumphant Pilgrimage, 1937; Anne Alone, 1938; Regent of Hungary: The Authorized Life of Admiral, Nicholas Horthy, 1939; Portrait of a Painter, the Authorized Life of Philip de Laszlo, 1939; John Fryer of the Bounty, 1939; The Scales of Karma, 1940; The Land of St Joan, 1940; Violation, 1941; Red Ensign: A History of Convoy, 1943; Ark Royal, the Admiralty account of her achievement, 1942; His Majesty's Mine-sweepers, 1943; The Fleet Air Arm, 1943; The Royal Marines, 1943; special articles to The Times and contributions to Times Literary Supplement and numerous reviews, annuals, and magazines. *Recreations:* temporarily suspended. *Address:* The Croft, Wargrave, Berks. *T:* Wargrave 152. *Club:* Athenæum.

Died 1 Aug. 1944.

RUVIGNY AND RAINEVAL, 10th Marquis of (France), 1651; **Charles Rupert Wriothesley Douglas Townsend Morris de La Caillemotte de Massue de Ruvigny;** Baron of Raineval before 1080; Baron of Ruvigny about 1524; Marquis of Raineval, 1621, Viscount of Ruvigny, 1637; Count of La Caillemotte, 1651; *b* Chertsey, Surrey, 22 April 1903; *s* of 9th Marquis and Rose Amalia (*d* 1915), *d* of late Poncrazio Gaminara of Tumaco; *S* father, 1921; *m* 1923, Violet Evelyn, *o d* of Alfred Pelly, 91 Inverness Terrace, W; one *s. Educ:* Harrow. *Heir: s* Michael Francis Wriothesley, *b* 11 Feb. 1927. *Address:* c/o National Bank of Australasia, 7 Lothbury, EC.

Died 10 May 1941.

RYAN, Sir Andrew, KBE 1925; CMG 1916; *b* 5 Nov. 1876; *s* of Edward Ryan of Ronayn's Court, Douglas, Cork; *m* Ruth Marguerite, *e d* of J. R. van Millingen of Leewood, Dunblane, Perthshire; four *s. Educ:* Christian Brothers College, Cork; Queen's College, Cork; Emmanuel College, Cambridge. Graduated BA Royal University of Ireland, 1896. Entered Levant Consular Service, 1897; Vice-Consul at Constantinople, 1903; 2nd Dragoman of HM's Embassy, Constantinople, 1907; acted as 1st Dragoman from June 1911 to July 1912, and from March 1914 until outbreak of war between Gt Britain and Turkey; employed in Contraband Dept of Foreign Office, 1915–18; 2nd Political Officer on Staff of British High Commissioner, Constantinople, on armistice with Turkey; Chief Dragoman, 1921, with rank of Counsellor; Member of British Delegation, Near East Peace Conference, Lausanne, 1922–23; Consul General at Rabat, Morocco, 1924–30; Minister at Jedda, 1930–36; in Albania, 1936–39. *Recreation:* walking. *Address:* Short Acre, East Bergholt, by Colchester.

Died 31 Dec. 1949.

RYAN, Adm. Frank Edward Cavendish, CBE 1919; (retired); *b* India, 6 Aug. 1865; *s* of Lieut-Colonel W. C. B. Ryan, Indian Army; *m* 1897, Eleanor Stuart (*d* 1935), *d* of C. H. Campbell, ICS; one *s* (and one killed, 1940). *Educ:* King Edward VI School, Bromsgrove; HMS Britannia. Mid. of Téméraire at bombardment of Alexandria and Egyptian war, 1882 (Egyptian Medal, Alexandria clasp, Khedive's bronze star); Lieut 1888; Commander, 1900; Capt. 1905; Naval Attaché at British Embassy, USA, 1905–07; commanded Astræa, in China, 1908–10; Mars, 1910–12; Cornwallis, Mediterranean, 1912–14; Chief of Staff to Vice-Admiral 2nd Fleet, 1914; Commodore at Portland, and in command of No. 13 Area, Feb. 1915–Oct. 1916; Rear-Admiral and Retired, 1916; commanded HM Yacht Jeannette in Mediterranean for patrol and convoy work as a temporary Captain RNR, Nov. 1916–Feb. 1919 (CBE,

Italian War Cross, 1914–15 Star and British and Allied Medals); Coronation Medal, 1911. *Recreation:* golf. *Clubs:* United Service; Royal Naval, Portsmouth.

Died 15 Feb. 1945.

RYAN, Sir Gerald Ellis, 2nd Bt *cr* 1919; MA Oxon; Barrister-at-law; *b* 17 Aug. 1888; *s* of Sir Gerald Hemmington Ryan, 1st Bt, and Ellen Amelia (*d* 1935), *d* of late Augustus Thomas Ellis; *S* father 1937; *m* 1914, Hylda Winifryde (*d* 1935), *d* of Major Spencer Herapath; one *s* one *d. Educ:* Harrow; New College, Oxford. Called to Bar, Inner Temple, 1912. *Heir: s* Derek Gerald, *b* 1922. *Address:* Chattisham Hall, Ipswich.

Died 1 Sept. 1947.

RYAN, Rt Rev. John A., DD, LLD, LittD; Director, Social Action Department, National Catholic Welfare Conference; *b* Minnesota, 25 May 1869; *s* of William Ryan and Mary, both born in Ireland. *Educ:* Christian Brothers, High School, Saint Thomas College and St Paul Seminary, St Paul, Minn. Priest 1898; took post-graduate course of four years at Catholic University; taught Moral Theology and Economics at St Paul Seminary, 1902–15; Political Science at Catholic University, 1915–16; Moral Theology, 1916–37, and Industrial Ethics at same Institution, 1916–39; Pioneer advocate of minimum wage legislation in US; written and lectured since 1903 on industrial questions; named a Domestic Prelate by Pope Pius XI with the title of Rt Rev. Monsignor, 1933; a Member of the Industrial Appeals Board of the NRA, 1934. *Publications:* A Living Wage, 1906; Socialism; Promise or Menace, 1914, being a debate with Morris Hillquit; Distributive Justice, 1916; The Church and Socialism, 1920; Social Reconstruction, 1920; The Church and Labour, 1922; The State and the Church, 1922; Declining Liberty and other papers, 1927; The Catholic Church and the Citizen, 1928; Questions of the Day, 1931; A Better Economic Order, 1935; Seven Troubled Years, 1937; Social Doctrine in Action: A Personal History, 1941; numerous pamphlets and articles in magazines and encyclopædias. *Address:* 1312 Massachusetts Avenue, NW, Washington, DC, USA.

Died 16 Sept. 1945.

RYAN, William Patrick, ('Liam P. O'Riain); Editorial Department, The Daily Herald, since 1912; *b* Co. Tipperary. Associated successively with Catholic Times, Sun and Weekly Sun (under T. P. O'Connor), Morning Leader, and Daily Chronicle; returned to Ireland to edit the Irish Peasant, 1905; conducted the Irish Nation, in Dublin, 1908–10. *Publications:* Starlight Through the Thatch, a story of Irish rural life; Sidheóga Ag Obair (new Irish fairy-tales; Oireachtas prize volume); Plays for the People (two in Irish, one in English); The Plough and the Cross (a novel based on the new Irish movements and ideas); Caoimhin O'Cearnaigh (a novel in Irish on similar ground): The Pope's Green Island; Inghean Mhanannáin (an Irish epic ballad); The Irish Labour Movement; Féile na n-Oglach (ballads and sonnets); Eden and Evolution; From Atlantis to Thames (an epic drama); The Song of the Salmon-God; Gaelachas i g-Céin, work of European scholars for Gaelic learning and literature; Poets in Paradise; King Arthur in Avalon; Feilm an Tobair Bheannuithe. *Address:* 15 Kempshott Road, SW16. *T:* Pollards 3080.

Died 31 Dec. 1942.

RYDER, Charles Foster; JP (West Riding); formerly MFH Newmarket and Thurlow; *e s* of Charles Ryder, Leeds; *m* 1st, 1888, Anna (*d* 1907), *d* of late William Potter, London; 2nd, Mabel, *d* of Mrs Sims, Oxford; five *s* four *d.* Lord of the Manors of Great and Little Thurlow and Withersfield. *Address:* The Hall, Thurlow, Suffolk; The Grange, Scarcroft, near Leeds. *Club:* Oriental.

Died 28 Feb. 1942.

RYDER, Col Charles Henry Dudley, CB 1922; CIE 1915; DSO 1905; late RE; late Surveyor-General of India; *b* 28 June 1868; 7th *s* of late Lt-Col Spencer Charles Dudley Ryder and Julia, *e d* of Rev. W. Money; *m* 1892, Ida Josephine, *e d* of late Lt-Col E. E. Grigg, of Orchard Court, Stevenage, Herts; two *s* (and one killed in action, 1940), three *d. Educ:* Cheltenham College. Served with China Field Force, 1901–02 (medal with clasp, despatches); Tibet Mission (medal with clasp, despatches) Mesopotamia Field Force, 1917–18 (despatches); retired, 1924; Patron's Gold Medal RGS, Silver Medal Scottish RGS, and Gold Medal French GS for explorations in China and Tibet.

Died 13 July 1945.

RYE, Frank Gibbs, CBE 1945; OBE 1937; Solicitor; *b* 12 Aug. 1874; *s* of late Walter and Georgina Eliza Rye; *m* 1901, Ethel Mary (*d* 1938), *e d* of E. M. Beloe, King's Lynn; three *s* one *d*; 1947, Nora, *widow* of Guy Gayford, Raynham, Norfolk. *Educ:* Fauconberg Grammar School, Beccles; St Paul's School. Admitted a Solicitor, 1901; Alderman Westminster City Council; Mayor of the City, 1922–23; Member of the Metropolitan Water Board and of the Thames Conservancy Board; Member LCC for Abbey Division of Westminster since 1937, Deputy Chairman, 1946–47; Master of the Company of Needlemakers, 1945–46; a Director of the County Fire Office, Limited; contested (C) Loughborough Division of Leicestershire, Dec. 1923, Oct. 1924, and May 1929; MP (C) Loughborough Division, 1924–29; Chairman National Conservative Association for Chertsey Division of Surrey; Chairman Westminster National Savings Committee; Pres. Thames Hare and Hounds Club. *Address:* Basing House, Thames Ditton, Surrey. *T:* Emberbrook 2071; Dorton Cottage, Selborne; 11 Golden Square, W1. *T:* Gerrard 1985. *Clubs:* Carlton, Union, Arts.

Died 18 Oct. 1948.

RYE, Reginald Arthur; Goldsmiths' Librarian of the University of London 1906–44; *b* 27 Sept. 1876; *s* of late Wm Brenchley Rye, formerly Keeper of Printed Books, British Museum; *m* 1915, Clare, *d* of Philip Hamill. *Educ:* Dulwich College; King's College, London; privately in France and Germany. Qualified as Marine Engineer; Librarian to Frederic David Mocatta, 1902–05; Assistant Librarian, University of London, 1905–06. *Publications:* Catalogue of the Mocatta Library, 1904 (destroyed by enemy action in 1940); The Libraries of London: a Guide for Students, 1908, 2nd edition 1910; 3rd edition enlarged, 1927; MSS. and Autograph Letters in London University Library, including 14th century MS. Life of the Black Prince, 1921, 1930; Catalogues of Proclamations and Broadsides in London University Library, 1928, 1930; Books on Archæology and Art in London University Library, 1937; The New University of London Library, 1937; Historical and Armorial Bookbindings (with MS Quinn), 1937; articles in journals and reviews. *Recreations:* Egyptology, carpentering, drawing, photography, book-collecting. *Address:* 50 Duke's Avenue, Chiswick, W.

Died 14 Sept. 1945.

RYLAND, Edward Charles, CIE 1918; JP; Indian Police (retired); *b* Serampore, Bengal, 26 Sept. 1864; *s* of late Wm H. Ryland, Provincial Service, Bengal, and late Mrs Ryland, Taunton, Somerset; *m* Alice Muriel, *d* of late Mr and Mrs John Wheeler of The Warren, Savernake, Wiltshire; one *s. Educ:* King's College School, London. Assistant Superintendent Indian Police, 1885; superintendent, 1895; officiated as Inspector-General in 1915 and 1916–17; served in Bengal, 1885–1906; Eastern Bengal and Assam, 1906–12; served Lushai Expedition, 1889–90; Delhi Coronation Durbar Medal, 1904; King's Police Medal, 1909; Delhi Coronation Durbar Medal, 1912. *Recreations:* football, School team and Calcutta FC Team, 1885–1900; cricket, Calcutta and Ballyganj CC; swimming, held the record for the Plunge, Calcutta SC 61° 4°, 1885–87; polo, member of the winning teams tournaments, Shillong, 1907, Dacca, 1910. *Address:* 6 Westgate Road, Beckenham, Kent. *T:* Beckenham 2732.

Died 24 Sept. 1941.

RYLANDS, Louis Gordon, BA, BSc (Lond.); Assistant Registrar, Manchester Tutorial College (Grime's); *b* 10 July 1862; *s* of Peter Rylands, Warrington and Caroline Wright Reynolds; *m* 1887, Katherine Edwards, Llangollen; one *d. Educ:* Charterhouse; University College, London. Secretary, Rylands Bros Ltd, Warrington, 1884–87; Science Master, Newcastle-on-Tyne Royal Grammar School, 1897–98; Private Tutor, 1898–1924; Hon. Secretary Proportional Representation Society Manchester Branch, 1911–18. *Publications:* Crime, its Causes and Remedy; Examples in Mechanics; A critical Analysis of the four chief Pauline Epistles; Did Jesus ever live?; The Christian Tradition; The Beginnings of Gnostic Christianity. *Recreation:* walking. *Address:* 62 Daisy Bank Road, Manchester 14. *T:* Rusholme 4301.

Died 20 Dec. 1942.

RYLANDS, Sir (William) Peter, 1st Bt *cr* 1939; Kt 1921; *b* 23 Oct. 1868; 3rd *s* of late Peter Rylands, MP, of Massey Hall, Thelwall, near Warrington; *m* 1894, Nora (*d* 1946), *d* of David De Angelis; no *c. Educ:* Charterhouse; Trinity College, Cambridge. Called to Bar, Inner Temple, 1894; Managing Director, Rylands Brothers, Ltd, 1898; President Iron, Steel Wire Manufacturers Association since 1900; President Federation of British Industries, 1919–21; President Iron and Steel Institute, 1926–27; President National Federation of Iron and Steel Manufacturers, 1930; JP Cheshire, 1906, Lancashire, 1905; High Sheriff of Cheshire, 1935–36; Commander of the Royal Order of Vasa. *Recreations:* shooting, fishing, golf, croquet. *Address:* Massey Hall, Thewall, near Warrington. *T:* Warrington, Lymm 16. *Clubs:* Oxford and Cambridge, Leander.

Died 22 Oct. 1948 (ext).

RYLE, John Alfred, MA (Oxon), MA, MD (Hon.) Camb., MD (Lond.), FRCP (Lond.); Hon. DSc (McGill); Professor of Social Medicine, Oxford University, 1943, resigned 1950; Physician Extraordinary to the King since 1936; Cons. Physician to Guy's Hospital; *b* 1889; *s* of late R. J. Ryle, MD, Brighton; *m* 1914, Miriam Power Scully; three *s* two *d. Educ:* Brighton College; Guy's Hospital. Gold Medal in Medicine, Guy's Hospital Medical School; Gold Medal in Medicine (London MD). Regius Professor of Physic, Cambridge University, 1935–43; late Fellow of Gonville and Caius College; Goulstonian Lecturer, RCP, 1925; Hunterian Professor RCS, 1932; Croonian Lecturer RCP, 1939; Maudsley Lecturer, 1947; formerly Astley Cooper Assistant to the Curator of the Gordon Museum (Guy's Hospital) and Lecturer in Medical Pathology; Physician to HM Household, 1932–36; Member Medical Research Council, 1935–39; Capt., RAMC (SR), 1914–19; Fellow of the Royal Society of Medicine; Member of Association of British Physicians; Consultant Adviser in Medicine to Minister of Health in Emergency Medical Service, 1941–43; Member Visiting Group to advise Health Survey and Development Committee of Govt of India, 1944; Member Asquith Commission on Higher Education in the Colonies, 1944–45. *Publications:* medical books, and contributions to medical journals. *Recreation:* natural history. *Address:* The Institute of Social Medicine, 10 Parks Road, Oxford. *T:* Oxford 47257.

Died 27 Feb. 1950.

S

SABATINI, Rafael; author and dramatist; *b* Jesi, Central Italy, 1875; *o s* of late Maestro Cav. Vincenzo Sabatini and Anna Trafford; *m* 1st, 1905, Ruth Goad Dixon; 2nd, 1935, Mrs Christine Dixon. *Educ:* Oporto, Zoug, and Coimbra. *Publications:* The Tavern Knight, 1904; Bardelys the Magnificent, 1906; The Trampling of the Lilies, 1906; Love-at-Arms, 1907; The Shame of Motley, 1908; St Martin's Summer, 1909; Anthony Wilding, 1910; The Lion's Skin, 1911; The Life of Cesare Borgia (a History), 1912; The Justice of the Duke, 1912; The Strolling Saint, 1913; Torquemada and the Spanish Inquisition (a History), 1913; The Gates of Doom, 1914; The Sea Hawk, 1915; The Banner of the Bull, 1915; The Snare, 1917; The Historical Nights' Entertainment, vol. i; 1918, vol. ii, 1919; vol. iii, 1938; Scaramouche, 1921; Captain Blood, 1922; Fortune's Fool, 1923; The Carolinian, 1925; Bellarion, 1926; The Nuptials of Corbal, 1927; The Hounds of God, 1928; The Romantic Prince, 1929; The Minion, 1930; The Chronicles of Captain Blood, 1931; Scaramouche The Kingmaker, 1931; The Black Swan, 1932; The Stalking Horse, 1933; Heroic Lives, 1934; Venetian Masque, 1934; Chivalry, 1935; The Fortunes of Captain Blood, 1936; The Lost King, 1937; The Sword of Islam, 1938; The Marquis of Carabas, 1940; Columbus, 1942; King in Prussia, 1944; Turbulent Tales, 1946; The Gamester, 1949; Plays: Bardelys the Magnificent (with Hy Hamilton); The Rattlesnake (with J. E. Harold Terry); In the Snare (with Leon M. Lion); Fugitives; Scaramouche; The Tyrant. *Recreation:* fishing. *Address:* Clock Mill, Clifford, Herefordshire. *Clubs:* Garrick, Savage, Authors'.

Died 13 Feb. 1950.

SADLER, Herbert Charles; Dean Emeritus; Professor of Naval Architecture and Marine Engineering in the University of Michigan, 1900–28; Dean of the College of Engineering, 1928–37, Dean Emeritus, 1940; Alexander Ziwet Professor of Engineering, 1937–39, University of Michigan; *b* London, 1872; *s* of Frederick Charles Sadler and Christina de Wilde Cater; *m* 1919, Margaret, *d* of late Prof. R. M. Wenley; one *s* three *d*. *Educ:* Dulwich College; University of Glasgow (BSc 1893, DSc 1902, Hon. LLD 1927). Practical shipbuilding on the Clyde, 1890–96; Assistant Professor of Naval Architecture in the University of Glasgow, 1896–1900; Consulting Naval Architect to various Steamship Lines and Shipbuilding Companies since 1900; designed and installed the experimental naval tank at the University of Michigan; Consulting Naval Architect to Board of US Army Engineers on Mississippi vessels, 1912–13; Naval Architect to US Shipping Board, 1918–19; Member Technical Committee American Bureau of Shipping; Member of the Institute of Naval Architects, London; Institute of Engineers and Shipbuilders, Scotland; Society of Naval Archit. and Marine Engineers, New York, Hon. Vice-Pres.; Soc. for the Promotion of Engineering Education. *Publications:* numerous papers in Transactions of various Insts of Naval Architects on questions relating to strength and resistance, etc., of ships. *Address:* 1510 Hill Street, Ann Arbor, Michigan, USA. *TA:* Ann Arbor, Mich. *Clubs:* Engineers (New York); Athletic (Detroit); Barton Hills (Ann Arbor).

Died 15 Dec. 1948.

SADLER, Sir Michael Ernest, KCSI 1919; CB 1911; Master of University College, Oxford, 1923–34; Hon. Student of Christ Church, Oxford; Hon. Fellow of University College, Oxford; Honorary Freeman of the Clothworkers' Company; *b* Barnsley, 3 July 1861; *e s* of late Michael Thomas Sadler, MD; *m* 1st, 1885, Mary (*d* 1931), *d* of Charles Harvey; one *s*; 2nd, 1934, Eva Margaret (*d* 1940), 2nd *d* of late Edmund Gilpin. *Educ:* Rugby; Trinity College, Oxford (Scholar, 1880–84). President of Oxford Union Society, 1882; secretary of the Oxford University Extension, 1885–95; steward of Christ Church, Oxford, 1886–95; student of Christ Church, Oxford, 1890–95; member of Royal Commission on Secondary Education, 1893–95; Director of special Inquiries and Reports in the Education Department, 1895–1903; Professor of the History and Administration of Education, Victoria University of Manchester, 1903–11; Vice-Chancellor, Leeds University, 1911–23; Chairman of the Teachers' Registration Council, 1915–22; President, Calcutta University Commission, 1917–19; Rede Lecturer, 1928; Sachs Lecturer of Teachers' College, Columbia University, New York, 1930; Hon. Freeman of the City of Oxford, 1931; Chairman International Institute Examinations Enquiry, 1932; Hon. LittD Manchester, Sheffield and Leeds Universities; Hon. LLD Columbia, Liverpool, Toronto, and Cambridge Universities; Officier de l'Instruction publique. *Publications:* edited, from the beginning of the series till 1903, the Special Reports on Educational Subjects issued by the Board of Education, himself contributing a number of papers (among which are Problems in Prussian Secondary Education; The Realschulen of Berlin; Higher Commercial Education at Antwerp, Leipzig, etc.; Unrest in Secondary Education in Germany, France, America, and elsewhere); Continuation Schools in England and elsewhere; Moral Instruction and Training; Reports on Secondary and Higher Education in Sheffield, Liverpool, Birkenhead, Derbyshire, Hampshire, Huddersfield, Exeter, and Newcastle-upon-Tyne; Our Public Elementary Schools, 1926; Liberal Education for Everybody (The Essex Hall Lecture), 1932; Arts of West Africa (editor), 1934. *Address:* The Rookery, Old Headington, Oxford. *T:* Oxford 6416. *Clubs:* Athenæum, Burlington Fine Arts.

Died 14 Oct. 1943.

SAHNI, Birbal, FRS 1936; MA, ScD (Cantab), DSc (Lond.); Professor of Botany, University of Lucknow, since 1921, and Hon. Professor, University of Benares, since 1936; Dean, Faculty of Science, Lucknow, since 1933; Founder and Hon. Director, Institute of Palæobotany, Lucknow; Member Scientific Manpower Committee, and Scientific Consultative Committee, Government of India; Professor of Botany, Benares, 1919–20; Lahore, 1920–21; *b* Bhera, Punjab, 14 Nov. 1891; *s* of late Ruchi Ram Sahni, MA, Emeritus Professor of Chemistry, Lahore, and of late Shrimati Ishwar Devi Anand, Bhera; *m* 1920, Savitri, *y d* of late Sundar Das Suri, MA, Inspector of Schools, Punjab. *Educ:* privately, Central Model School, Government College (scholar), Lahore; Emmanuel College, Cambridge (foundation scholar, exhibitioner, research student, Sudbury-Haryman research prize); Munich Univ. One of the founders and Pres., 1924, Indian Botanical Soc.; Pres. Lahore Philosophical Soc., 1921; Pres. Botanical Section, 1921, Geological Section, 1926, and Botany Section, 1938 (Jubilee Session), of Indian Science Congress; Pres., Nat. Acad. of Science, India, 1937–38, 1942–44; Vice-Pres. 1935, and Foreign Sec. 1936, Nat. Institute of Sciences, India; Vice-Pres. Palæobotanical Section, 5th Internat. Botanical Congress, Cambridge, 1930, and 6th Congress, Amsterdam, 1935; Barclay Medal, 1936, of Asiatic Soc. of Bengal; Special Univ. Lecturer, Lahore, 1932; extension lecturer, Lahore and Rohtak, 1936; Sukhraj Rai Reader in Natural Science, Patna University, 1937; Adharchandra Lecturer in Natural Science, Calcutta University, 1938; Gaekwad Lecturer, Baroda, 1944–45;

Pres. 27th Indian Science Congress, Madras, 1940; member Andhra Univ. Commission, 1932; non-official Member, Indian Delegation to Royal Society Scientific Conference, London, 1946. Hon. DSc Patna University, 1944, Allahabad Univ., 1947. Nelson Wright medal, Numismatic Society of India, 1945. Foreign Corr. Member, Botanical Soc. of America, 1947; Foreign Hon. Member, American Acad. of Arts and Sciences, Boston, 1948; Official deleg. from Govt of India to 18th Internat. Geological Congress, London, 1948. *Publications:* Text Book of Botany, Indian Ed. (with Lowson); original papers in scientific journals on a wide range of subjects, but chiefly on extinct plants, fossil floras and their geological bearings; quinquennial reports of research work done in Lucknow University dept of botany (1927; 1932, 1937); papers on Indian numismatics (technique of casting coins in Ancient India); editor Lucknow University Studies, Faculty of Science and Palæobotany in India, a Bulletin of Current Research. *Address:* The University, Lucknow, India. *T:* 815. *Club:* University.

Died 10 April 1949.

ST AUBYN, Sir Hugh M.; *see* Molesworth-St Aubyn.

ST CLAIR-MORFORD, Maj.-Gen. Albert Clarence, CBE 1941; MC; *b* 27 June 1893; *s* of Walter St Clair-Morford; *m* 1st, 1919, V. A. M. Kirkpatrick (*d* 1920); 2nd, 1925, V. M. Dean; one *s* three *d*. *Educ:* Elizabeth College, Guernsey. 2nd Lt Royal Guernsey Light Infantry, 1910; 2nd Lt Royal Marines, 1912; Capt. 1915; Maj.-Gen. 1943; served European War, 1914–18 (wounded four times, MC); seconded Royal Flying Corps, 1917; seconded Egyptian Government, 1921; commanded Royal Marine Brigade, 1940–41 (CBE); lent to Govt of India, 1942–43; ADC to the King, 1942–43; retired list, 1943. *Recreation:* most games. *Address:* Doe's Mead, Kemishford, Woking. *T:* Worplesdon 137. *Club:* Army and Navy.

Died 4 May 1945.

ST GEORGE, Sir Theophilus John, 6th Bt *cr* 1766; Master, Supreme Court, Natal; retired; *b* 25 Feb. 1856; 3rd *s* of Sir Theophilus John St George, 3rd Bart; *S* brother, 1938; *m* 1889, Florence Emma, *d* of late John Venderplank, Natal; three *s* five *d*. *Educ:* Stonyhurst College. *Heir: s* Robert Alan, *b* 20 March 1900. *Address:* 3 Burger Street, Pietermaritzburg, Natal. *T:* 3273. *Clubs:* Victoria, Pietermaritzburg.

Died 19 Aug. 1943.

ST GERMANS, 7th Earl of, *cr* 1815; **Granville John Eliot;** Baron Eliot, 1784; *b* 22 Sept. 1867; *s* of 6th *s* of 3rd Earl of St Germans and 4th *d* of Sir John Guest, 1st Bt; *S* cousin, 1922. *Educ:* Charterhouse. *Heir: b* Hon. Sir Montague Charles Eliot, KCVO. *Address:* Port Eliot, St Germans, Cornwall.

Died 20 Nov. 1942.

ST JOHN, Col Edmund Farquhar, CMG 1919; DSO 1917; late RA; *b* 27 Feb. 1879; *s* of late Hon. and Rev. E. T. St John, and late Hon. Mrs E. T. St John of Bletso, Aboyne, Aberdeenshire; *m* 1921, Henrietta Frances, *d* of late J. A. Dalmahoy, MVO, WS, and of Mrs Dalmahoy, 28 Royal Circus, Edin.; one *s* one *d*. *Educ:* Harrow School; RMA, Woolwich. Joined Royal Artillery, 1898; served in South Africa, 1899–1902 (despatches, King's and Queen's medals); European War (despatches 4 times, CMG, DSO and bar); AAG Egypt, 1929–33; retired pay, 1933. *Address:* Stonehouse, North Berwick.

Died 24 April 1945.

ST JOHN, Vice-Adm. Francis Gerald, CB 1917; MVO 1914; *b* 22 Dec. 1869; *s* of late Adm. H. Craven St John and Catherine Dora, *d* of J. Stratford Rodney; *m* 1st, 1898, Winifred Jessie (*d* 1898), *d* of G. H. Trollope of Fair Mile Hatch, Cobham; 2nd, 1902, Emily Frances Louise, *e d* of late Allan F. Turner, Bombay; one *s* three *d*. *Educ:* Dartmouth. Served Boer War (medal), Chinese War (medal), European War (despatches); ADC to the

King, 1920–21; Lieut 1891; Commander, 1904; Capt. 1910; Rear-Admiral, 1921; retired list, 1923. *Address:* Eddington Manor, St Helens, Isle of Wight. *T:* Bembridge, 148. *Club:* Junior Army and Navy.

Died 15 Feb. 1947.

ST JOHN, Hon. Rowland Tudor; Lt-Col, retired; Durham Light Infantry; *b* 1 May 1882; *s* of 16th Baron and *heir-pres.* to 19th Baron St John of Bletso; *m* 1912, Katherine Madge, *y d* of late Sir Frank Lockwood, QC, MP; two *s* one *d*. *Educ:* Winchester College; RMC, Sandhurst. Served European War, 1914–18 (despatches). *Address:* 29 Old Deer Park Gardens, Richmond, Surrey.

Died 17 Nov. 1948.

ST JOHN-MILDMAY; *see* Mildmay.

ST JOHNSTON, Sir Reginald, KCMG 1931 (CMG 1923); *b* Edgbaston, Warwickshire, 1881; *m* 1906, Alice (*d* 1948), *o d* of late Thomas Lethbridge, Babbacombe, Devonshire. *Educ:* Queen Elizabeth College, Guernsey; Cheltenham College. Barrister-at-law, Middle Temple; MRCS, LRCP, MSA Lond. 1905. Appointments under LGB 1906; joined Colonial Service, 1907; various judicial, medical and administrative appointments in Fiji, 1907–17 (latterly Comr of the Lau Islands); seconded for War service in France, and subsequently attached War Office for special duty (received thanks of Army Council, and promoted Bt Lt-Col); Acting Governor, Falkland Islands, Sept. 1919–April 1920; Colonial Secretary Leeward Islands, 1920–25; Acting Administrator of Dominica, 1925; Administrator of Antigua on various occasions; Administrator of St Kitts (St Christopher) and Nevis 1925–29; Governor and Commander-in-Chief of the Leeward Islands, 1929–36; retired 1936; returned to military duties in England, 1940; appointed to Ministry of Supply, 1942. *Publications:* Dream Faces, 1899; A History of Dancing, 1906; Anthology of English Verse (part), 1908; Lau Islands Folklore, 1918; The Falkland Islands, 1919; The Islanders of the Pacific, 1921; South Sea Reminiscences, 1922; The Pearl of Fortune, 1924; 'Neath Tropic Stars, 1925; A West Indian Pepper-pot, 1928, (also translated into Dutch and Danish); The Leeward Islands during the French Wars, 1932; From a Colonial Governor's Note-Book, 1936; Strange Places and Strange Peoples, 1936; Who has a Dog?, 1938; Dogs of Every Kind, 1949; Advisory Editor of the Story of the British Empire, 1939; various contributions to magazines, etc. *Recreations:* travel and literature. *Address:* c/o Barclays (DCO) Bank, 29 Gracechurch Street, EC3; Belsaye, Ratton Rd, Eastbourne.

Died 29 Aug. 1950.

ST JUST, 1st Baron *cr* 1935, of St Just in Penwith; **Edward Charles Grenfell;** Lieutenant of City of London; Director of firm of Morgan Grenfell & Co., Ltd; *b* 29 May 1870; *s* of Henry Riversdale Grenfell, MP, of Taplow, and Alethea Adeane of Babraham; *m* Florence, *e d* of late George W. Henderson; one *s*. *Educ:* Harrow; Trinity Coll., Camb. MP (C) City of London, 1922–35; Governor of Harrow School; Director, Bank of England, 1905–40, retired; Director, White Star Line and Shaw Savill & Co., 1928, retired. *Heir: s* Hon. Peter George Grenfell, *b* 22 July 1922. *Address:* Wilbury Park, Newton Tony, nr Salisbury; The Dunes, Sandwich Bay, Kent. *Clubs:* Brooks's, White's, Beefsteak.

Died 26 Nov. 1941.

ST LEGER, Evelyn; author; *d* of late Edward Bourchier Savile; *m* 1895, His Hon. J. R. Randolph (*d* 1936). *Publications:* Dapper, 1908; The Shape of the World, 1911; The Blackberry Pickers, 1912; The Tollhouse, 1914; edited Diaries of Three Women of the Last Century, 1907; contributor to Saturday Review, The Cornhill, XIXth Century, etc. *Address:* 10 Canterbury Road, Oxford. *T:* Oxford 2960. *Clubs:* Bath, Writers'.

Died June 1944.

ST VIGEANS, Lord, *cr* 1918; **David Anderson,** KC, LLD; *b* 26 Oct. 1862. Sheriff of Dumfries and Galloway, 1913–17; Sheriff of Renfrew and Bute, 1917–18; Chairman Scottish Land Court, 1918–35. *Address:* 15 Grosvenor Crescent, Edinburgh.

Died 1 June 1948.

ST VINCENT FERRERI, 7th Marquis of; **Daniel Testaferrata Bonici Ghâxaq;** 6th Baron of Qlejjgha; *b* 1880; *s* of Emanuele Testaferrata Bonici and Philomena, *d* of Carmelo de Marchesi de Piro Gourgion; *m* 1910, Agnes (*d* 1941), *yr d* of late Baroncino Nicholas Galea de San Marchiano; two *s* two *d. Educ:* St Ignatius' College, Malta; Mondragone College, Frascati, Italy. Hon. Treasurer of Committee of Privileges of Maltese Nobility; Knight of the holy Roman Empire; Patrician of Rome, Messina, and Citta di Castello. Senator in Maltese Parliament, 1927–30 and 1932–33. *Heir:* s Alno Maria, Marchesino di San Vincenzo Ferreri, Baroncino della Culeja, *b* 1911. *Address:* 29 Villegaignon Street, Mdina, Malta.

Died 25 March 1945.

SAIT, Edward M'Chesney, MA (Toronto), PhD (Columbia); author; Professor of Government, Pomona College; *b* Montreal, Canada, 1881; *m* 1910, Una Mirrielees, *d* of late Henry M. Bernard, FZS; two *s. Educ:* Upper Canada College; Trinity College, University of Toronto (Scholar and Prizeman in History); Columbia University (University Fellow in Political Science, Toppan Prize). Master, Upper Canada College, 1902; Lecturer in History, Trinity College, Toronto, 1903–06; Instructor, College of the City of New York, 1908; Assistant Professor of Politics, Columbia University, 1909–20; Professor of Political Science, University of California, 1920–26; Member Phi Beta Kappa, Skull and Keys; Social Science Research Conference, American Society of International Law, American Political Science Association. *Publications:* Clerical Control in Quebec, 1911; Government and Politics of France, 1920; British Politics in Transition, 1925; American Parties and Elections, 1927, 3rd ed. 1942; Democracy, 1929; Political Institutions, 1938; Editor of Houghton Mifflin Government Series. *Address:* 238 East 7th Street, Claremont, California, USA.

Died 25 Oct. 1943.

SALA, Antoni; international 'cellist; *b* Barcelona, 1 Nov. 1893; *s* of Salvador Sala, Professor of Piano in Barcelona; unmarried. *Educ:* Barcelona, École Municipale, where he finished the six years study in three years. Began playing at the age of seven; first public recital at the age of eleven, when he gave a classical programme at the Theatre Municipale, Barcelona; at age of fourteen went to Paris; has since often played by command to the King and Queen of Spain and has toured all Europe, the USA, and South America for some years past. *Recreations:* motoring; engineering; is interested in farming.

Died 14 Dec. 1945.

SALE, Charles Vincent; partner, Sale & Co; late Chairman Amalgamated Metal Corporation, Ltd; Director of Sun Life and Fire Offices; Chairman of the Japan Society, 1925–36; Member of the Orders of the Rising Sun and Sacred Treasure, Japan; Chevalier of the Legion of Honour; Officier de l'Ordre de la Couronne (Belgium); Knight of the Order of the Dannebrog, Denmark; *b* 18 Jan. 1868; *s* of George Sale and Marion Morley; *m* 1892, Mary Maud, *d* of W. A. Rose of Napanee, Ontario; three *s* one *d. Address:* 58 Eaton Place, SW1. *T:* Sloane 6731. *Club:* Brooks's.

Died 22 June 1943.

SALISBURY, 4th Marquess of, *cr* 1789; **James Edward Hubert Gascoyne-Cecil,** KG 1917; GCVO 1909; Baron Cecil, 1603; Viscount Cranborne, 1604; Earl of Salisbury, 1605; Hon. Maj.-Gen.; *b* London, 23 Oct. 1861; *co-heir* to Barony of Ogle; MA 1889; CB 1900; ADC to HM 1903; High Steward of Westminster; High Steward of Hertford; *e s* of 3rd Marquess of Salisbury and Georgina, *d* of Hon. Sir Edward Hall Alderson, a Baron of Exchequer; *S* father, 1903; *m* 1887, Lady Cicely Alice Gore, *d* of 5th Earl of Arran; two *s* two *d. Educ:* Eton; Univ. Coll., Oxford. Under-Secretary for Foreign Affairs, 1900–03; Lord Privy Seal, 1903–05; Lt-Col 4th Batt. Bedfordshire Regt in South Africa (despatches); MP (C) Darwen Division, 1885–92; Rochester, 1893–1903; Chairman of Church Parliamentary Committee to 1900; President Board of Trade, 1905; late Chairman of Hertford Quarter Sessions; Hon. Col Herts Volunteer Regt, 1918; Member of the National Assembly of the Church of England, 1921; Lord President of the Council, 1922–24; Chancellor of the Duchy of Lancaster, 1922–23; Lord Privy Seal, 1924–29; Leader of the House of Lords, 1925–29. *Heir:* s Viscount Cranborne, KG, PC. *Address:* Hatfield House, Hertfordshire. *T:* Hatfield 2702. *Clubs:* Athenæum, Carlton, Travellers'.

Died 4 April 1947.

SALISBURY, Lt-Col Alfred George (Grazier), CMG 1919; DSO 1917; *b* Brisbane, 1885; *m* 1916, Florence Ethel, *d* of M. L. Leonard, London, Eng.; one *s* one *d.* Served European War, 1915–19 (despatches, DSO with Bar, CMG, Chevalier of Legion of Honour); commanded 9th Bn, Gallipoli; commanded 50th Bn, 1916–19; 13th Bde (temp.), 1919; War of 1939–45, Col comdg AIF Training Depôts, N Command; comdg 1st Aust. Inf. Trng Bde, 1940–41. *Recreation:* yachting. *Address:* Koarlo, Kurrumbul, Queensland. *Club:* United Service (Brisbane).

Died 6 Jan. 1942.

SALMON, Sir Eric Cecil Heygate, Kt 1943; MC; DL; JP; Clerk of London County Council since 1939; Clerk to the Lieutenancy and Hon. Clerk of the Advisory Committee on the Selection of Justices of the Peace for the County of London; *b* 3 July 1896; *s* of late Herbert J. Salmon and Edith, *d* of late Frederick Lambert, Garratts Hall, Banstead; *m* 1929, Hilda Marion, *d* of late Rev. Canon Edward A. Welch; one *s* one *d. Educ:* Malvern; Corpus Christi College, Oxford (Classical Scholar). Served European War with 11th Bn (Queen's Own) Royal West Kent Regiment and as Divisional Observation Officer, 41st Division (MC); served also in the Army of Occupation as Education Officer 123rd Infantry Brigade. Entered Ministry of Health as Assistant Principal, 1919; Secretary to Departmental Committee on Smoke and Noxious Vapours Abatement, 1920; Departmental Committee on Rent Restriction, 1930; Housing (Rural Authorities) Committee, 1931; Departmental Committee on Housing (the Moyne Committee), 1933; Private Secretary to the Deputy Secretary, 1929–30; principal, 1930; Deputy Clerk of London County Council, 1934–39. *Recreations:* cricket, shooting, etc. *Address:* The Vale House, 115 Old Church St, SW3. *T:* Flaxman, 1867; The Cedar Cottage, Goring-on-Thames. *T:* Goring-on-Thames 261. *Clubs:* Oxford and Cambridge, MCC.

Died 9 July 1946.

SALMON, Harry; JP; Chairman of J. Lyons & Co. Ltd since 1941; Director of Alliance Assurance Co. Ltd; *b* 23 Aug. 1881; 5th *s* of Barnett Salmon; *m* 1903, Lena Gluckstein; two *s* one *d. Educ:* City of London School. Entered J. Lyons & Co. Ltd, 1896, and after an apprenticeship through the business, joined Board as Managing Director, 1909; relinquished appointment as Managing Director, 1949. *Recreations:* golf and bridge. *Address:* 3 Addison Road, W14; Grove House, Garlinge, nr Margate, Kent. *Club:* Union.

Died 13 Oct. 1950.

SALMON, Sir Isidore, Kt 1933; CBE 1920; DL; JP; MP (C) Harrow since 1924; Chairman and Managing Director of J. Lyons & Co., Ltd; *b* Feb. 1876; *s* of Barnet Salmon; *m* 1899, Kate Abrahams; two *s. Educ:* privately. Chairman of London War Pensions Committee,

1918–22; Member LCC 1907–25; Vice-Chairman, 1924–25; Chairman of Special Reorganisation Committee of LCC 1921; Member of Royal Commission on Transport, 1928–30; Chairman of Home Office Committee on Employment of Prisoners, 1932–34; of Inter-Departmental Committee to survey the Prices of Building Materials since 1932; of City of London Employment Exchange since 1922; Member of House of Commons Select Committee of Public Accounts since 1925; Estimates Committee since 1931; Chairman Estimates Committee since 1936; Chairman of Consultative Committee LCC Westminster Technical Inst. Hotel and Restaurant School; Chairman National Training College of Domestic Subjects; President of Decimal Association; Member of Governing Body of Regent Street Polytechnic; of the Central Housing Advisory Committee, Ministry of Health; of King Edward's Hospital Fund Outpatients Committee; Hon. Adviser on Catering to the British Army. *Recreation:* golf. *Address:* 51 Mount Street, W1. *T:* Grosvenor 2240. *Clubs:* Carlton, Junior Carlton.

Died 16 Sept. 1941.

SALMOND, Hubert George, CIE 1944; AMICE; ACGI; *b* 3 Jan. 1889; *e s* of late George Edward Salmond, MA (Oxon), and Cecily Mary Salmond, 31 St Michael's Road, Bedford; *m* 1915, Audrey Enid Doris, *d* and *co-heiress* of Walter Lane-Ryan, Indian Woods and Forests Dept, and Alice Lane-Ryan; one *d*. *Educ:* Bedford Grammar School; Central Technical College; City and Guilds. Joined Indian Public Works Dept 1911 and held various posts, including that of General Manager, Eastern Bengal Railway, and Chief Government Inspector of Railways, Posts, and Air Dept, Govt of India; retired, 1945. Served in European War, 1915–18, as Capt. RFC (wounded and prisoner). *Publication:* Technical Paper on Tube Railway Construction, 1925. *Recreations:* rowing, heraldry, and model engineering. *Address:* 71 Connaught Gardens, Muswell Hill, N10. *T:* Tudor 4737. *Club:* Junior Army and Navy.

Died 29 Oct. 1946.

SALMOND, Captain Hubert Mackenzie, CIE 1917; FRSA; Royal Indian Navy, retired; *b* 18 Dec. 1874; 2nd *s* of late Lt-Col Francis Mackenzie Salmond, Royal Scots Fusiliers and Isabel Clara, *d* of late Lt-Gen. H. G. Hart; *m* 1902, Emmie Juliet, 2nd *d* of Clarence Canute Hawkins, Southsea; one *d*. *Educ:* private schools. Served five years in Clipper Ships; Royal Indian Marine, 1896; retired 1926; served in suppression of Arms Traffic, Persian Gulf (Naval Medal); European War—Director of Sea Transport, Mesopotamia (Bar and Allied Medals, CIE, despatches three times); commanded ships for many years; Deputy Director Royal Indian Marine, 1922. Port Officer and Deputy Conservator, Karachi, 1923–26; received the thanks of Govt of India and Govt of Bombay for salving the SS Tannenfels; two Royal Humane Society's Medals and two Certificates; FRSA; co-inventor of the Graviner Automatic Fire Extinguisher and a director of the Graviner Manufacturing Co. *Address:* Briarwood, Fareham, Hants. *T:* Fareham 351. *Club:* Royal Societies.

Died 25 Dec. 1947.

SALTER, Alfred, MD, JP; MP (Lab) W Bermondsey, Nov. 1922–Dec. 1923, and Oct. 1924–45; Alderman, Bermondsey Borough Council; *b* Greenwich, 1873; *s* of W. H. Salter, Bromley, Kent; *m* 1900, Ada (*d* 1942), *d* of Samuel Brown of Thorpe House, Raunds; no *c*. *Educ:* Roan School, Greenwich: Guy's Hospital. Gold medal MD (Lond.), 1896; Gold medal, Medicine, and Triple First Class Honours in MB (Lond.), 1895; Golding-Bird Gold Medal and Scholarship in Public Health, 1897; Gull Research Scholarship in Pathology, 1897. House Physician and Resident Obstetric Physician, Guy's Hospital, 1896; Bacteriologist to the British Institute of Preventive Medicine, 1897–1900; Member of Bermondsey Borough Council and Board of Guardians;

Member of LCC, 1905–10. *Publications:* numerous articles on Bacteriological and Pathological subjects in English, French, and German scientific periodicals. *Recreations:* walking, archæology. *Address:* 75a Balham Park, SW12. *T:* Battersea 4649.

Died 24 Aug. 1945.

SALTMARSHE, Col Philip, late RA; JP E Yorks; County Councillor for E Yorks; *b* 9 June 1853; *s* of P. Saltmarshe of Saltmarshe and Blanche, *d* of Robert Denison of Kilnwick Percy, E Yorks; *m* 1883, Ethel Murray, *d* of C. Murray Adamson of North Jesmond, Newcastle-on-Tyne; one *s* three *d*. *Educ:* Eton; RMA, Woolwich. Received commission in R. Artillery, 1873; served in Afghanistan, 1878–79 (medal); S African War, 1899–1900 (medal and 3 clasps); retired, 1903; rejoined Oct. 1914, and commanded a Reserve Brigade of RFA till June 1916 (British War Medal); Chairman Howdenshire Bench of Magistrates, and of Board of Guardians and District Council; Chairman ER Education Committee and Higher Education Committee of E Riding County Council; President ER Antiquarian Society. *Publications:* History of the Hotham Family; History of the Saltmarshe Family (privately printed). *Recreations:* fishing, shooting, golf, and lawn tennis. *Address:* Saltmarshe, Howden, E Yorks. *Clubs:* Carlton, Yorkshire.

Died 15 March 1941.

SALTOUN, Master of; Hon. Alexander Simon Fraser, MC 1944; Lt Grenadier Guards; *b* 12 Dec. 1921; *o s* of 19th Baron Saltoun. *Educ:* Eton.

Died 9 Feb. 1944.

SALUSBURY-TRELAWNY, Sir John William; *see* Trelawny.

SALVAGE, Sir Samuel Agar, KBE 1942; industrialist; *b* London, 20 Nov. 1876; *s* of John Samuel Salvage and Margaret Smith; *m* 1908, Mary Katharine Richmond; three *d*. *Educ:* Queens College, Taunton. Went to USA, 1893; joined cotton yarn firm; obtained agency for British firms, including Courtaulds, Ltd, and set up own business. Consultant and Director, American Viscose Corp., etc. Member Amer. Assoc. Textile Technologists. *Address:* (home) Glen Head, LI, NY, USA; (office) 350 5th Ave, New York, NY.

Died 10 July 1946.

SALVESEN, Lord; Rt Hon. Edward Theodore Salvesen, PC 1922; KC; LLD (Edin.) 1926; Judge of Court of Session, Scotland, 1905–22; Member of the Judicial Committee of the Privy Council; *b* 20 July 1857; *s* of late Christian Salvesen, shipowner, Leith; *m* 1886, Isabelle (*d* 1939), *d* of late Lord Trayner; four *d*. *Educ:* Collegiate School and University (MA, LLB), Edinburgh. Scottish Bar, 1880; QC, 1899; contested (LU) Leith Burghs, 1900; Bute, 1905; Sheriff of Counties Roxburgh, Berwick and Selkirk, 1901–05; Solicitor-General for Scotland, 1905; Lord Rectors Assessor on the Courts of Edinburgh University, 1929–33; Commander of the Orders of the White Rose of Finland and of St Olaf of Norway; President of the Zoological Society of Scotland; Chairman The Royal Scots Association; Fellow of the Royal Society, Edinburgh; Chairman of the Association of Lowland Scots and of the Scottish Veterans' Garden City Association; President Royal Scottish Geographical Society, 1920–26; Chairman Departmental Committee on Puerperal Mortality, and of the Departmental Committee of Education and Industry in Scotland, 1927; Chairman Royal Scots Benevolent Fund; Chairman Scottish Public-House Reform League; President St George's School for Girls; Chairman of Melville College, and of the Edinburgh Crematorium; President of the Scottish Youths Hostel Association (Eastern Division); Chairman of the Scottish Modern Arts Association. *Recreations:* shooting, fishing, travelling. Honorary Fellow of the Zoological Society of London.

Address: Dean Park House, Edinburgh; Risobank, Norway. *Clubs:* Athenæum, Constitutional. Overseas; University, Edinburgh.

Died 23 Feb. 1942.

SALVIN, John Edmund Shorrock M.; *see* Moore-Salvin, J. E. S.

SALWEY, Rev. John, MA; Canon and Prebendary of Ferring in Chichester Cathedral, 1921; *b* 6 Aug. 1867; *s* of Rev. John Salwey, MA, Vicar of Broxbourne, Herts; *m* 1st, 1897, Hilda (*d* 1925), *d* of Compton Warner; one *s;* 2nd, 1932, Eva, *d* of F. Parris, Eastbourne. *Educ:* Westminster; Hertford College, Oxford; Wycliffe Hall Theological College, Oxon. Third Class. Mods. Ordained to curacy of All Saints', South Lambeth, 1890; Curate of St Jude's, South Kensington, 1895–96; first vicar of new parish of St Luke's, Hampstead, 1896–1906; Vicar of St John's, Meads, Eastbourne, 1906–32; Vicar of Westhampnett, 1932–38; Rural Dean of Eastbourne, 1930–32; Rural Dean of Chichester, 1935–37; Proctor in Convocation, 1921–35. *Recreation:* mountaineering. *Address:* Westmeads, Beech Avenue, Chichester. *T:* Chichester 2231.

Died 14 March 1943.

SAMBORNE-PALMER, Lt-Col Frederick Carey Stuckley, CBE 1920; Indian Army, retired; *b* 1868; *s* of late Rev. Richard Lane Stuckley Samborne-Palmer, JP Ashreigney, N Devon; *m* 1st, 1894, Constance Harriet (*d* 1901), *d* of Captain E. Anstey; 2nd, 1904, Caroline Mary (*d* 1940), *d* of late John Filmer Anstey; 3rd, 1946, Phoebe, *d* of late Rt Hon. Sir John Winfield-Bonser, PC, *widow* of Oliver Baring. *Educ:* Rossall School; RMC, Sandhurst. Served Chitral Relief Force, 1895 (medal with clasp); European War, 1915–16; Chitral, 1917–20. *Club:* Army and Navy.

Died 13 June 1950.

SAMPSON, George, retired Inspector of Schools (LCC); Hon. MA Camb. (St John's College); late Hon. General Secretary of the English Association; Member of the Departmental Committee on Teaching of English in England; Member of Cambridge Advisory Committee on Religious Instruction; Educationist and Man of Letters; *b* London, 6 April 1873. *Educ:* Southwark PT School; Winchester Training Coll. *Publications:* English for the English, 1921; Stopford Brooke's Primer of English Literature (continuation), 1924; Cambridge Lessons in English, 1926–1929; The Concise Cambridge History of English Literature, 1941; The Century of Divine Songs, 1943; Seven Essays, 1947; ed. of The Works of George Berkeley, 3 vols, 1897–1898; Burke's French Revolution, 1900; Newman's University Sketches, 1903; Newman's Select Essays, 1903; The Lyrical Ballads, 1903; More's Utopia and Roper's Life of More, 1903; Walton's Lives, 1904; The Golden Asse (of Apuleius), 1904; George Herbert's Poems, 1904; Keats, 2 vols, 1904; Works of Emerson, 5 vols, 1904; Selections from Lamb, Goldsmith, and Disraeli, 3 vols, 1908; Bagehot's Essays, 2 vols, 1911; Nineteenth Century Essays, 1912; Hazlitt's Essays, 1917; Cambridge Readings in Literature, 5 vols, 1918; Coleridge's Biographia Literaria and Wordsworth's Essays (with Quiller-Couch), 1920; Methuen's English Classics, 6 vols, 1922; Much Ado About Nothing, 1923; The Cambridge Book of Verse and Prose, 1924; Hamlet, 1924; Cambridge Readings in Literature (revised), 8 vols, 1932–1933; Romeo and Juliet, 1936. *Recreations:* music, travel, reading. *Address:* 33 Walsingham Road, Hove 3, Sussex. *T:* Hove 31439. *Club:* Reform.

Died 1 Feb. 1950.

SAMSON, Sir (Edward) Marlay, KBE 1920; CBE 1918; KC 1919; Barrister-at-law; Stipendiary Magistrate of Swansea since 1923, Recorder 1918–23; Esquire, Order of St John of Jerusalem, 1919; JP, DL Co. Pembroke; JP Co. of Glamorgan; *b* 27 March 1869; 2nd *s* of Louis Samson, JP, DL, Scotchwell, Haverfordwest.

Educ: Harrow; Trinity College, Oxford. 2nd Class Honours, School of Modern History. Called to Bar, 1892; S Wales and Chester Circuit; Chancellor, St David's Diocese, 1909; Swansea and Brecon Diocese, 1923–29; Chairman Quarter Sessions County of Pembroke, 1924–43; contested (U) County of Pembroke, Jan., Dec. 1910. *Recreation:* motoring. *Address:* 12 Richmond Road, Swansea; Scotchwell, Haverfordwest. *Club:* Carlton.

Died 3 April 1949.

SAMSON, Lt-Col Louis Lort Rhys, CMG 1913; CBE 1920; *b* 25 April 1866; *e s* of late Louis Samson, Scotchwell, Haverfordwest; *m* 1904, Gertrude Maud, *d* of Edwin Williams. *Educ:* Harrow; Sandhurst. Entered army (Lancashire Fusiliers), 1886; Captain, 1893; Major (King's Own Regiment), 1907; Bt Lt-Col 1916; served S Africa, 1900–02 (Queen's medal 2 clasps); Consul, Adrianople, 1907–14; served on staff in European War, 1914–18 (despatches); British Military Representative at Adrianople, Nov. 1918–20; retired pay, 1920; Officer of the Greek Order of the Redeemer; JP Pembrokeshire. *Recreations:* shooting, fishing. *Address:* Scotchwell, Haverfordwest. *Club:* Army and Navy.

Died 12 Jan. 1944.

SAMSON, Sir Marlay; *see* Samson, Sir E. M.

SAMUEL, Alexander L.; *see* Lyle-Samuel.

SAMUEL, Marcus; MP (Nat. C), Wandsworth, Putney, since 1934; *b* 1873; *s* of Joseph Samuel and Laura Victoria Davis; *m* 1903, Adelaide Esther Johnson; one *s*. *Educ:* University College School; abroad. Has always been associated with East India Trading; has been a free contributor to the Press in favour of Safeguarding and Protection, criticising Socialist fallacies; contested (C) N Southwark, 1929; stood down in 1931, in favour of National Liberal. *Publications:* Revolution by Miscalculation, against Oswald Mosley's Revolution by Reason; According to Bellamy; Socialism *verses* The Rest; The Five-Year Plan: Socialism in Theory and Practice in Russia; The Great Experiment. *Address:* 21 South Street, W. *T:* Grosvenor 2827. *Clubs:* Carlton, Constitutional.

Died 3 March 1942.

SAMUELS, His Honour Herbert David; KC 1933; Official Referee of the Supreme Court of Judicature since 1945; *b* 1880; *m* 1911, Beatrice Annie, *d* of Edward Smith, Nottingham; one *d*. Called to Bar, Lincoln's Inn, 1908, Bencher 1937; Recorder of Bournemouth, 1944–45. *Address:* 187 Queens Gate, SW7. *T:* Kensington 7862; Tower Barn, Farnham Common, Bucks. *Club:* Union.

Died 11 Dec. 1947.

SAMUELSON, Cecil Llewellyn, CBE 1944 (OBE 1920); *b* 7 June 1882; *e s* of Llewellyn Samuelson, London; *m* 1907, Norah, *d* of Henry Richardson, Kirklevington Hall, Yarm, Yorkshire; (son died on Active Service 24 Feb. 1945) one *d*. *Educ:* Cheltenham College. Served European War, France and N Russia, 1914–19 (OBE, despatches); JP Bucks, 1937; Home Guard, 1940 (CBE). High Sheriff of Buckinghamshire, 1948; DL Bucks, 1950. *Recreation:* fishing. *Address:* Rosehill, Burnham, Bucks. *T:* Burnham, Bucks, 129.

Died 16 Nov. 1950.

SAMUELSON, Sir Francis, 3rd Bt *cr* 1884; *b* Torquay, 26 Feb. 1861; 2nd *s* of late Sir Bernhard Samuelson, 1st Bt; *S* brother 1937; *m* Fanny Isabel (*d* 1897), *e d* of late William Merritt Wright of St John, New Brunswick, Canada; one *s* three *d*. *Educ:* Rugby; Balliol College, Oxford; BA 1885. High Sheriff of Yorkshire, 1917–18; President Iron and Steel Institute, 1922–24; Chairman Tees Conservancy Commission, 1931–42. *Heir: s* Francis Henry Bernhard [*b* 1890; *m* 1913, Margaret Kendall, *d* of late H. Kendall Barnes; three *s* two *d*]. *Address:* Breckenbrough Hall, Thirsk, Yorks. *TA:* and *T:* Thirsk 3137. *Clubs:* Yorkshire, York.

Died 3 Jan. 1946.

SAMUELSON, Godfrey (Blundell); *b* Banbury, 3 June 1863; 3rd *s* of Right Hon. Sir Bernhard Samuelson, 1st Bt; *m* 1st, 1887, Anne Jane (*d* 1920), *d* of late Rev. Weston Brocklesby Davis, Vicar of Ramsbury, Wilts; three *s*; 2nd, 1923, May, *widow* of John Parkin Sheffield. *Educ:* Rugby; Balliol College, Oxford. MP (L) 1887–92, Forest of Dean, Gloucestershire; contested in Liberal interest, 1885, Tewkesbury Division, Glos; 1886, Frome Division, Somerset; 1892, Tewkesbury Division, Glos; private secretary to late Rt Hon. A. J. Mundella, President Board of Trade. *Heir:* s Bernard Godfrey [*b* 17 Oct. 1888; *m* 1910, Hon. Evelyn Amy Akers-Douglas (*d* 1914), 4th *d* of 1st Viscount Chilston]. *Address:* Foxboro' Hills, Halstead, Essex.

Died 3 Nov. 1941.

SAND, Alec, FRS 1944; MSc (McGill), PhD (Cantab); Physiologist to Marine Biological Association since 1935; *b* Warsaw, 28 Dec. 1901; *o s* of late Elias and Bertha Zoond; *m* 1930, Edith, *e d* of late W. Herzfeld, Johannesburg; two *s*. *Educ:* Dame Alice Owen's School; Univ. of British Columbia; McGill Univ.; King's College, Cambridge. Assistant in Bacteriology, Macdonald College, McGill Univ., 1925–27; Lecturer in Zoology, Univ. of Cape Town, 1927–35; Lieut RNVR since 1940. *Publications:* papers on Comparative Physiology. *Address:* The Laboratory, Citadel Hill, Plymouth.

Died 11 July 1945.

SANDARS, Lt-Col Edward Carew, CMG 1918; late RA; *b* 1869; *s* of late Samuel Sandars, of Chalfont Grove, Bucks, and 7 de Vere Gardens; *m* 1906, Gertrude Annie (*d* 1934), *o d* of late Col R. W. Phipps, RA; two *d*. *Educ:* Harrow; RMA. Served S African War, 1900–02; retired pay, 1911; Assistant Director of Remounts, 1916–18; Bt Lt-Col 1916; Lt-Col Reserve of Officers, 1919–24; DL Oxon, 1936; Alderman Oxfordshire CC since 1934. *Address:* The Manor House, Little Tew, Oxon. *Club:* Army and Navy.

Died 21 March 1944.

SANDBACH, Emeritus Prof. Francis Edward, BA (Lond.), MA (Cantab), MA (Birmingham), PhD (Strassburg); temp. German Master at The Leys School, since 1941; *b* London, 24 Feb. 1874; *s* of Rev. F. B. Sandbach; *m* Ethel, *e d* of J. H. Bywater, Gomersal, nr Leeds; two *s*. *Educ:* Kingswood School, Bath; University College of Wales, Aberystwyth; University of Strassburg; Sorbonne, Paris; University of Cambridge. Assistant Lecturer, then Lecturer in German, in University of Birmingham, 1901–19; also Lecturer in German in Birmingham and Midland Institute, 1906–19; Prof. of German, Univ. of Birmingham, 1919–39; Dean of Faculty of Arts, 1934–37; Member of Education Committees: City of Coventry, 1905–08; West Bromwich, 1919–23; Sutton Coldfield, 1923–30; served in Naval Intelligence Department (Room 40) 1918; Chairman, Conference on Library Co-operation since 1925; President, Association of University Teachers, 1927; Chairman, Univ. Teachers of German, 1938–39; Examiner at various dates to Universities of Aberdeen, Belfast, Bristol, Cambridge, Leeds, London, Oxford Sheffield, Wales, and to other examining bodies. *Publications:* Handschriftliche Untersuchungen über Otto von Diemeringens deutsche Bearbeitung der Reisebeschreibungen Mandevilles, 1899; The Nibelungenlied and Gudrun in England and America, 1903; The Heroic Saga Cycle of Dietrich of Bern, 1906; A First German Course for Science Students, and A Second German Course for Science Students (with Professor H. G. Fiedler), 1906; Editions of Otto's German Conversation Grammar; Articles and reviews in the Modern Language Review, Publications of the English Goethe Society, Minerva-Zeitschrift, Monatshefte für deutsche Sprache und Pädogogik, The Universities Review, Library Association Record; Chapter in Germany, A Companion to German Studies (ed. J. Bithell); article in German Studies (volume presented to Prof. H. G. Fiedler). *Recreation:* golf. *Address:* The Leys School, Pitlochry, Perthshire.

Died 20 May 1946.

SANDBERG, Christer Peter, CBE 1920; MInstCE; *b* 1876; *s* of late Christer Peter Sandberg, MICE; *m* 1903, Alexandra, *d* of late Alexander Forbes. *Educ:* Dulwich College. Consulting Engineer to Chinese Government and other railways; Commander of Chinese Order of Chia Ho (3rd class), 1922 and Commander of Siamese Order of the White Elephant, 1925. *Address:* Crockham Hill, Kent; 40 Grosvenor Gardens, SW1. *T:* Sloane 6217.

Died 26 June 1941.

SANDBROOK, John Arthur; Editor-in-Chief Western Mail and Echo, Ltd, since 1931; *b* 3 May 1876. *Educ:* Swansea Grammar School. Entered journalism, 1892; Chief Assistant Editor, Western Mail, Cardiff, 1902–10; Editor of The Englishman, Calcutta, 1910–22; served in South African War (medal, 5 clasps); special correspondent, Mesopotamia, 1917; Western Front (with Indian Press delegation), 1918; Waziristan and North-West Frontier, 1921. *Recreation:* golf. *Address:* Fairwater Road, Llandaff. *T:* Llandaff 81. *Clubs:* Cardiff and County Cardiff; Bengal, Calcutta.

Died 13 Feb. 1942.

SANDERS, Sir Edgar (Christian), Kt 1918; *b* Skidby, Yorkshire, 17 Oct. 1871; 4th *s* of late Rev. Henry Martyn Sanders, Vicar of Sutton Forest, Yorks, and late Eliza Ann Fox; *m* 1898, Lilian, *d* of late Hill Motum, Town Clerk of Newcastle-upon-Tyne; one *s* one *d*. *Educ:* Rossall School; Durham University. Admitted Solicitor, 1898; Assistant Prosecuting Solicitor Liverpool, 1899–1902; Clerk to the Liverpool Justices and other appointments at Liverpool, 1902–16; three times President of Justices' Clerks' Society; Assessor to Central Control Board (Liquor Traffic), 1915; General Manager of Carlisle Undertaking of Central Control Board, 1916–21; Director of West African and several other Companies until 1932; now Director of The Brewers Society; a Vice-President of the Federation of British Industries, on Council of the Association of British Chambers of Commerce and on the Council and late Hon. Treas. of London Chamber of Commerce, and Chairman for three years of its West African Section; President of Institute of Trade mark Agents; Member of Council of Nigerian Chamber of Mines; Chairman of Jos Tin Area (Nigeria) Ltd. *Publication:* Text-book on Criminal Justice Administration Act, 1914. *Address:* Rignalls, Great Missenden, Bucks. *T:* 418. *Club:* Devonshire.

Died 28 March 1942.

SANDERS, Brig.-Gen. Gerard Arthur Fletcher, CB 1921; CMG 1919; late RE; *b* 1869; *s* of Rev. Henry Martyn Sanders; *m* 1898, Evelyn Bertha Kitchener; two *d*. *Educ:* Rossall School; RM Academy, Woolwich. Served Burma, 1892–93; Dongola Expedition, 1896; European War, 1914–19; Mesopotamia, 1920–21; retired, 1923. *Address:* The Grange, Ilmington, near Shipston-on-Stour, Warwickshire. *T:* Ilmington 49.

Died 8 March 1941.

SANDERS, Captain William Stephen, CBE 1918; *b* 2 Jan. 1871; *s* of Stephen Sanders, harnessmaker and saddler; *m* Beatrice Helen (*d* 1932), *d* of Leonard Martin; no *c*. *Educ:* Elementary School; Polytechnics; Evening Classes; Berlin University. Commenced work at eleven years of age; farmer's boy, then clerk; afterwards Lecturer under Hutchinson Trust Scheme; Secretary of Fabian Society, 1914–20; Member of Staff, International Labour Office, League of Nations, 1920–29 (Deputy Chief of

Administrative Section); joined Social Democratic Federation, 1888; Fabian Society, 1892; Alderman LCC, 1904–10; Member of LCC Education Committee, 1904–13; contested (Lab) Portsmouth, 1906 and 1910; MP (Lab) North Battersea, 1929–31 and 1935–40; Finan. Sec. to War Office, 1930–31; Member of National Executive Labour Party, 1913–15; served in Army during European War at home and abroad and was given rank of Captain. *Publications:* Political Reorganisation of the People; Early Socialist Days; numerous pamphlets, including Fabian Tracts on Social and Industrial Questions. *Recreation:* reading. *Address:* 3 Baskerville Road, SW18.

Died 6 Feb. 1941.

SANDERSON, Sir John, KBE 1937; *b* Victoria, Australia, 26 Dec. 1868; *s* of John Sanderson and Agnes Roberts; *m* 1908, Mary Stratford Hunt; one *s. Educ:* Harrow; Trinity College, Cambridge. Came to England, 1870; returned to Australia, 1893; Member of the firm of John Sanderson & Co., Melbourne and Sydney; during War was a member of the Federal Repatriation Commission; came back to London in 1920. *Address:* 7 Princes Gate, SW7. *Club:* Brooks's.

Died 5 Jan. 1945.

SANDERSON, Rt Hon. Sir Lancelot, PC 1926; Kt 1915; Chairman of the Quarter Sessions for the County of Lancashire holden at Lancaster, 1927; and of Westmorland Quarter Sessions since 1926; *b* 24 Oct. 1863; *e s* of late John Sanderson, JP, of Ward House, Ellel, near Lancs; *m* 1891, Edith Mabel (*d* 1926), *d* of Alfred Fletcher, DL, of Allerton, near Liverpool; one *s* one *d. Educ:* Elstree; Harrow; Trinity College, Cambridge (LLB 1885; MA 1895). Called to Bar at Inner Temple, 1886; KC 1903; contested (U) the City of Carlisle, 1905; MP (U) Appleby Division, Westmorland, 1910–15; Recorder of Wigan, 1901–15; Vice-Chancellor of the Calcutta University, 1918; Chief Justice of Bengal, 1915–26; Member of the Judicial Committee of the Privy Council since 1926. *Address:* Ward House, Ellel, Lancaster. *T:* Galgate 16. *Club:* Carlton.

Died 9 March 1944.

SANDERSON, Robert, CIE 1935; late Indian Educational Service; *b* 6 Jan. 1881; *m* 1910, Jean, *d* of John Barbour, South Shields. *Educ:* Shields High School; St John's College, Oxford. BA 1904; MA 1907. Entered Indian Educational Service, 1909; Director of Public Instruction, Punjab, 1931; retired, 1936. *Address:* Radcot House, Clanfield, Oxon.

Died 14 Feb. 1943.

SANDERSON, Col William Denziloe, CMG 1918; DSO 1916; late Royal Warwickshire and Loyal North Lancashire Regts; *b* 1868; *m* 1923, Lilian, *widow* of Lt-Cdr W. Crawfurd Harrison, RN. Served Nile Expedition, 1898 (medal and clasp); South African War, 1899–1901 (despatches, Queen's medal and six clasps); European War, 1914–18 (despatches, CMG, DSO); retired pay, 1918.

Died 11 Dec. 1941.

SANDERSON, William Waite, CBE 1921; Chartered Surveyor, Joint Consulting Valuer, Newcastle Rating Committee, and in private practice; *b* Newcastle-upon-Tyne, 19 April 1868; *s* of Thomas Barkas Sanderson; *m* 1905, Winifred Norah Young, Sutton, Surrey; four *d.* Deputy Chief Valuer, War Office, during European War; later Chief Valuer of Factories, Disposal Board, under Lord Inverforth; Past President Auctioneers' and Estate Agents' Institute; Past President of the Rating Surveyors' Association, and holding various other appointments in connection with his profession. *Address:* Underwood, Riding Mill, Northumberland. *T:* Riding Mill 7.

Died 31 Aug. 1944.

SANDFORD, Ven. Folliott George, MA; Archdeacon of Doncaster, 1913–41, Archdeacon emeritus since 1941; Canon of York; Commissary to the Archbishop of Melbourne, 1905; *b* 26 April 1861; *s* of late Rev. George Sandford, MA, Vicar of Ecclesall; *m* 1888, Rosamond Mary, *d* of Ralph Blakelock Smith of Bent's Green, Ecclesall, Sheffield; one *s* two *d. Educ:* Sheffield Collegiate School; Corpus Christi College, Cambridge; 2nd Class in Theological Tripos. Ordained Curate of Sheffield Parish Church, 1884; Rector Holy Trinity Goodramgate, with St John del Pyke, and St Maurice, Bedern, and part of Minster Yard, York, 1888; Vicar of St Andrew's Sharrow, Sheffield, 1893; Member of the Sheffield School Board, 1895; Chairman, 1897–1900, and 1900–03; Vicar and Rural Dean of Huddersfield, 1903; Vicar of Doncaster, 1905–28; Rural Dean of Doncaster, 1910–19 and 1929–34; Prebendary of Dunnington in York Minster, 1909–14; Proctor in Convocation for the Archdeaconry of Huddersfield; Official of the Archdeacon of Huddersfield, 1903; Chaplain to the Corporation of Doncaster; Chaplain to the 2nd Duke of Wellington's West Riding Regiment, 1903–05; Chaplain to the Queen's Own Yorkshire Dragoons, 1905; Hon. Canon Sheffield, 1914; Hon. Secretary of South Yorkshire Coalfields Church Extension Committee since 1909; Hon. Freedom of Doncaster. *Address:* Leahurst, Tickhill via Doncaster. *T:* Tickhill 207.

Died 14 July 1945.

SANDFORD, Sir George (Ritchie), KBE 1947 (OBE 1924), CMG 1938; Governor and Commander-in-Chief, Bahamas, since 1950; Administrator to the East Africa High Commission, 1948–49; Chief Secretary of East African Governors' Conf. 1946; *b* 9 Nov. 1892; *e s* of late Francis Berkeley Sandford, MA, Roselands, Ambleside, Westmorland; *m* 1928, Charis, *e d* of late D. W. Melhuish, Clevedon, Somerset; no *c. Educ:* Christ's Hospital; Queens' College, Cambridge. Barrister-at-law, Inner Temple; entered Colonial Service, 1915; Assistant District Commissioner, East African Protectorate, 1915; Clerk of Legislative Council, Kenya, 1926; Deputy Treasurer, Kenya, 1931; Treasurer, Tanganyika Territory, 1936; Financial Secretary, 1937; Financial Sec., Palestine, 1940–44; Chief Sec., Tanganyika Territory, 1944–46. *Recreation:* golf. *Address:* Government House, Nassau, Bahama Islands. *Club:* Lansdowne.

Died 17 Sept. 1950.

SANDHAM, E. Organized Committee for Consumptives, Chorley; MP (Lab) Kirkdale Division of Liverpool, 1929–31.

Died 7 May 1944.

SANDIFORD, Peter, MSc (Manc); MA, PhD (Columbia); Professor of Educational Psychology and Director of Educational Research, University of Toronto; *b* Little Hayfield, Derbyshire, 15 Jan. 1882; *o s* of John E. Sandiford, engineer; *m* 1912, Betti Primrose, *d* of Alfred Paterson; one *s* one *d. Educ:* New Mills Secondary School; University of Manchester; Columbia University, New York. Mackie Scholar, 1901–05; Derbyshire County Major Scholar, 1901–04; University Scholar, Manchester, 1905–06; Fellow of Teachers' College, Columbia University, 1908–09; Medal for Service, Columbia University, 1930; President, Manchester University Students' Union, 1907–08; Assistant Lecturer, Manchester University, 1906–08; Tutor, Teachers' College, Columbia Univesrity, 1909–10; Lecturer in Education, 1910–13, and Superintendent of the Fielden Demonstration Schools, Manchester University, 1911–13. *Publications:* Training of Teachers in England and Wales; Mental and Physical Life of School Children; Educational Psychology: an Objective Study, 1928; Foundations of Educational Psychology: Vol. I, Nature's Gifts to Man, 1938; Editor, Comparative Education; Studies of the Educational Systems of Six Modern Countries; editor Adult

Education in Canada; (with J. A. Long) Validation of Test Items; (with M. A. Cameron and others) Forecasting Teaching Ability; contributed to Sadler's Continuation Schools in England and elsewhere; Fielden Demonstration Schools Records, I and II; Monroe's Cyclopaedia of Education, etc. *Recreation:* travel. *Address:* University of Toronto, Canada. *Club:* Arts and Letters, Toronto.

Died 12 Oct. 1941.

SANDYS, 5th Baron *cr* 1802; **Michael Edwin Marcus Sandys;** *b* 31 Dec. 1855; *s* of 3rd Baron and Louisa, *d* of Joseph Blake, Gloucester Place, London; *S* brother, 1904; *m* 1886, Marjorie Clara Pentreath (*d* 1929), *d* of late John Morgan, Brighton. *Heir: cousin* Lt-Col A. F. S. Hill. *Address:* De Walden Court, W1. *T:* Langham 1529; Ombersley Court, Worcestershire. *Clubs:* Turf, Brooks's, Orleans.

Died 4 Aug. 1948.

SANDYS, Brig.-Gen. William Bain Richardson, CB 1918; CMG 1915; DL and JP West Riding; late RA; *b* 20 May 1868; *e s* of late Major Edwin William Sandys, RA, JP, Fulford House, and Frances Anne, *e d* of late Edwin Sandys Bain; *m* 1901, Joan (Officer of the Order of St John of Jerusalem), *d* of late Brig.-Gen. Andrew W. Proudfoot, late Indian Army; two *d. Educ:* Marlborough Coll.; RM Academy, Woolwich (Tombs Memorial Scholarship). Entered army, 1887; Lieut RHA 1892; Capt. 1897; Adjt RHA 1900–02; Major, 1902; Major, RHA 1908; Lt-Col 1914; Subst. Col 1918; served Tirah, 1897–98 (medal 2 clasps); European War, 1914–18 (wounded, despatches five times, CMG, CB, Bt Col 1917, temp. Brig.-Gen. 1915–19; CRA 14th (Light) Division, 1915–17; Commanding RA 19th Army Corps, 1917–19 (1914 Star with clasp, British War medal, Victory medal, French Croix de Guerre, Belgian Croix de Guerre); CRA 5th Division, 1920–22; retired pay, 1922; Commander of the Order of St John of Jerusalem; County Controller, West Riding Yorkshire VADs, 1927–44; Member of the West Riding Territorial Association, 1927; Member of the VAD Council, 1929–44. *Address:* Fulford House, Fulford, York. *T:* York 77214.

Died 18 Dec. 1946.

SANGER, William, CB 1918; *b* 6 Feb. 1873; *s* of late W. A. Sanger, The Grove, Neasden; *m* 1897, Agnes Hornby, *d* of Rev. H. T. Fountaine, Vicar of Sutton Bridge, Lincolnshire; two *s* one *d. Educ:* Woodcote House, Windlesham; Wellington College; Corpus Christi College, Oxford. Higher Division Clerk, Local Government Board, 1896; transferred Admiralty, 1897; Superintending Clerk, 1904; Assistant Accountant-General, 1914; Assistant Secretary Ministry of Pensions, 1917; Controller and Assistant Secretary, 1918; Director-General of Awards, 1919; Accountant-General, 1926; retired, 1934; rejoined Ministry of Pensions, Oct. 1939; member of Surbiton UDC and Borough Council since 1904; Commissioner of Chelsea Hospital, 1917–25; Member of Royal Patriotic Fund Corporation; Commander of the Order of the Christ of Portugal, 1919; JP London County, 1925–34; first Mayor and Alderman of the Borough of Surbiton, 1936, Hon. Freeman, 1944; Surrey County Council, 1937; Chairman of the Bermondsey Appeal Tribunal under the Unemployment Assistance Board, 1934; President Kingston and District YMCA; Surbiton Division of St John's Ambulance and Surbiton Branch of League of Nations Union. *Recreations:* tennis, swimming. *Address:* 55 The Avenue, Surbiton.

Died 14 Dec. 1948.

SANKEY, 1st Viscount *cr* 1932; of Moreton, Co. Gloucester; **John Sankey;** Baron *cr* 1929, PC 1928; GBE 1917; Kt 1914; DCL (Hon.) Oxford; LLD (Hon.), Universities of Wales, Cambridge and Bristol; *b* Moreton, 26 Oct. 1866; *s* of Thomas and Catalina Sankey; unmarried. *Educ:* Lancing College; Jesus College, Oxford (Scholar, Hon. Fellow, MA, BCL). Called of Bar, Middle Temple, 1892; KC 1909; Bencher, 1914; Chancellor of the Diocese of Llandaff, 1909–14; a Judge of the King's Bench Division, 1914–28; a Lord Justice of Appeal, 1928–29; Lord Chancellor 1929–35; a British member of the Permanent Court of Arbitration at the Hague, since 1930; Chairman of the Aliens Advisory Committee, 1915; Chm. of Coal Industry Commission, 1919; Knight of Grace of the Order of St John of Jerusalem; a Governor of Keble College and Pusey House, Oxford; Life Member of Governing Body and of the Representative Body of the Church in Wales; President of the British Institute of Adult Education; Chairman of the Inter-Imperial Relations Committee of the Imperial Conference, 1930; Chairman of the Federal Structure Committee of the Indian Round Table Conference, 1930; High Steward of Oxford University, 1930; a member of the Court of the University of Wales; Hon. Freeman of City of Cardiff, 1934; Vice-President of University College of South Wales and Monmouthshire, 1935; Treasurer of Middle Temple, 1935; Chairman of College Committee University College, University of London, 1936; of the Standing Committee of National Society, 1936–44; of Lancing College School Committee, 1936; Chairman Voluntary Hospitals Commission, 1937; Hon. Fellow, University College, University of London, 1938; Chairman of Building Societies Association, 1939–47; Chairman of Council of Magistrates' Association, 1941. *Recreations:* travelling and walking. *Address:* 13 Albert Place, Kensington, W8. *T:* Western 6060. *Club:* Oxford and Cambridge.

Died 6 Feb. 1948 (ext).

SANSOM, Col Charles Henry, CMG 1938; CBE 1942; *b* 14 Jan. 1886; *s* of Louis Sansom, JP, and Emily Skardon; *m* 1925, Sophia Godfrey; two *d. Educ:* Plymouth College. Appointed Federated Malay States Police, 1905; Adjutant, 1913–20; Commissioner of Police, Johore, 1921–24; Chief Police Officer, Singapore, 1925–31; acted Inspector-General, Straits Settlements; Inspector-General of Police, FMS 1931–39; ARP Chief Officer, Malta, 1939–42; also Director of Compulsory Service, Malta, 1941–42; Royal Observer Corps, 1943; attached to Colonial Office, 1944; Comr of Police, Hong Kong, 1945; retired, 1947. Barrister-at-Law, Middle Temple, 1923. *Recreations:* fishing, golf. *Address:* March House, Gillingham, Dorset. *T:* 265.

Died 29 Dec. 1949.

SANT, Maharana Shri Sir Jorawarsinhji Pratapsinhji, Raja of, KCIE 1943; *b* 24 March 1881; *S* 1896; *m;* one *s.* The State has an area of 527½ square miles and a population of 114,047, according to the last census of 1941. The State of Kadana has been absorbed into Sant State. The Raja's salute is 9 guns. *Heir:* Maharaj Kumar Shri Pravinsinhji. *Address:* Sant-Rampur, Gujarat States Agency, India.

Died 22 Dec. 1946.

SANT, Captain Mowbray Lees; DL, JP; *b* 18 Dec. 1863; *s* of late James Sant, CVO, RA; *m* Annie Marguerite, *d* of Chesborough Macdonald, late 22nd Regt; twin *d. Educ:* Charterhouse. Joined 1st Batt. Fifth Fusiliers, 1885; Capt. 1892; Adjt 3rd Batt. Northumberland Fusiliers, 1893–98; retired, 1899; Chief Constable of the County of Surrey, 1899–1930; King's Police Medal, 1925. *Recreations:* shooting, fishing, golf. *Address:* The Red House, Shalford, Surrey. *T:* Shalford 180.

Died 14 June 1943.

SANT-CASSIA, Francis Joseph Nicholas Paul Sant, 7th Count; *b* 8 Sept. 1889; *s* of 6th Count and Maria Anna Galia; *S* father, 1903; *m* 1910, Mary, *d* of 6th Count of Mont' Alto. *Address:* Palazzo Guerena Crendi, Malta.

Died 6 May 1947.

SANTI, Philip Robert William de, FRCS Eng. 1888; MRCS, LRCP, LSA, 1884; Consulting Surgeon, late Senior Surgeon Laryngologist and Aural Surgeon to Westminster Hospital; Lecturer on Diseases of the Throat, Nose, and Ear, Westminster Hospital Medical School; *s* of late Chevalier Charles de Santi, *g s* of late General Sir Henry Ferguson-Davie, 1st Bart, of Creedy Park, Crediton; *m* 1899, Violet, *o d* of late Ed. Leslie; one *s. Educ:* Victoria College, Jersey; Bath College, Bath; St Bartholomew's Hospital; Paris School of Medicine. Formerly House Surgeon, Gt Northern Hospital, London, and South Staffordshire General Hosp.; House Surgeon St Bart's, 1887; Senior Demonstrator of Anatomy, Durham University, 1890; Westm. Hospital Medical School, 1893; late Surgical Registrar and Senior Assistant Surgeon Westminster Hospital; late Surgeon Orient Steam Navigation Company; Fellow of the Royal Society of Medicine; late Senior Secretary Laryngological Society of London, and member of other learned societies. *Publications:* Malignant Disease of the Larynx, 1904; Golden Rules of Aural and Nasal Practice, 2nd ed.; various contributions in Surgery, Laryngology, and Otology to medical papers and societies and transactions. *Recreations:* yachting, shooting, fishing, photography. *Address:* c/o Westminster Bank, Hanover Square, W1.

Died 16 May 1942.

SAPRU, Rt Hon. Sir Tej Bahadur, PC 1934; KCSI 1923; LLD; Advocate, High Court of Judicature at Allahabad; widower; three *s* two *d. Educ:* Agra College, Agra. President of Indian Liberal Federation; at one time member of the All India Congress Committee; Member of the United Provinces Legislative Council, 1913–16; Member of the Imperial Legislative Council, 1916–20; Law Member of the Viceroy's Executive Council, 1920–23; represented Government of India at the Imperial Conference, London, 1923; Delegate at the Round Table Conferences in London, 1930, 1931 and 1932, and the Joint Parliamentary Committee, 1933; is a Zemindar (landlord). *Address:* Allahabad, UP, India.

Died 20 Jan. 1949.

SARAVANAMUTTU, Sir Ratnajoti; Kt, 1943; MB, CM; MRCS; LRCP.

Died 12 Sept. 1949.

SAREL, Rev. Prebendary Sydney Lancaster; *s* of Thomas Sarel; *m* 1939, Thora, *d* of late Col R. T. M. Lethbridge. *Educ:* Tonbridge; Keble College, Oxford. Science Master of Borlase School, Marlow, 1895; Resident at Oxford House, Bethnal Green, 1896–97; Student at Cuddesdon College, 1897–98; Deacon, 1898; Priest, 1899; Curate of St Saviour's, Hoxton, 1898–1908; Vicar of St Thomas's, Bethnal Green, 1908–16; Rector of St Matthew's, Bethnal Green, 1916–39; Vicar of St Philip's, Bethnal Green, 1933–39, in plurality; Rural Dean of Bethnal Green, 1916–43; Prebendary of St Paul's Cathedral, 1927. *Recreations:* cinder track walking and running, road walking, cross country running, lawn-tennis; represented the United Kingdom in the 3500 metres walking race in the Olympic Games, 1908; Vice-President London Athletic Club, President, 1928. *Address:* St Matthew's Vicarage, Oakley Crescent, City Road, EC1.

Died 23 Dec. 1950.

SARELL, Philip Charles; *b* Constantinople, 17 Feb. 1866; *s* of Richard Sarell, MD, FRCP, late of Constantinople; *m* Ethel Ida Rebecca, *d* of late John Alexander Dewar Campbell; two *s* one *d. Educ:* King Edward VI's School, East Retford; University College, London. Served in various capacities in Consular Service (Constantinople, Sulina, Dunkirk, Tunis, and Barcelona); employed at Foreign Office, 1897–98, and 1907–08; British Consul at Dunkirk throughout European War; received the thanks of the British, French and Italian Governments for services rendered (Chevalier de la Légion d'Honneur; Commander of the Crown of Italy). British Consul-General, Tunis, 1920–23; Barcelona, 1923–26; retired 1926. *Address:* Braeside, Ashurst Wood, East Grinstead, Sussex.

Died 5 Nov. 1942.

SARGANT, Rt Hon. Sir Charles Henry, PC 1923; Kt 1913; *b* 20 April 1856; 2nd *s* of late Henry Sargant of Lincoln's Inn, Barrister-at-law; *m* 1900, Amelia Julia (RRC, JP), *e d* of late Dion Gambardella, CE; one *s* two *d. Educ:* Rugby School; New College, Oxford. Called to Bar, Lincoln's Inn, 1882; Bencher, 1908; Junior Counsel to Treasury in Equity Matters, 1908; Judge of High Court (Chancery Division), 1913–23; Lord Justice of Appeal, 1923–28; retired, 1928. *Publications:* Urban Rating, 1890; The New Land Tax, 1931. *Recreations:* golf, fishing, billiards.

Died 23 July 1942.

SARGEANT, Sir Alfred Read, Kt 1921; BA; *b* 28 Aug. 1873; *s* of late Alfred Frank Sargeant, Hove; *m* 1910, Annie, *er d* of late Rev. Canon J. S. Flynn, MA, BD. *Educ:* Clifton College; Trinity College, Cambridge. Barrister; called to the Bar, Lincoln's Inn, 1901; Mayor of Hove, 1914–19; Chairman East Sussex County Council, 1925–28; JP County of Sussex, 1906. *Address:* Fairmount, Crowborough. *T:* Crowborough 314. *Clubs:* Royal Automobile; Hove (Hove).

Died 23 May 1949.

SARGENT, Arthur J., MA, Oxon; FRGS; Emeritus Professor of Commerce, University of London; *b* March 1871; *m* Margaret, *d* of W. Bax Branford, Dover: one *s* one *d. Educ:* King's College School; King's College, London; Brasenose College, Oxford. *Publications:* Economic Policy of Colbert; Anglo-Chinese Commerce and Diplomacy; The Sea Road to the East, Canada, Australasia, South Africa, in Visual Instruction Series; Seaways of Empire; Coal in International Trade; British Industries and Empire Markets; Seaports and Hinterlands. *Recreations:* rowing, sailing, lawn tennis, golf. *Address:* 3 The Crossways, Sutton. *T:* Vigilant 1306.

Died 16 Feb. 1947.

SARGENT, Rt Rev. Christopher Birdwood Roussel; Bishop in Fukien (China) since 1940; *b* 4 June 1906; *s* of late Rev. Douglas Harry Grose Sargent and Mary Josephine Thomson. *Educ:* St Paul's School, London (Scholar); St Catharine's College, Cambridge (Scholar). BA 1928; MA 1932. Assistant Master, Wellington College, Berks, 1928–32; Headmaster, Diocesan Boys School, Hong Kong, 1932–39; Assistant Bishop in Fukien, 1938–40; Deacon, 1934; Priest, 1935; Member of Board of Education, Hong Kong, 1934–38. *Recreations:* cricket, music. *Address:* Foochow, China.

Died 8 Aug. 1943.

SARGENT, Maj.-Gen. Harry Neptune, CB 1915; CBE 1919; DSO 1902; late RASC; retired from Army with hon. rank of Maj.-Gen., 16 Oct. 1919; *b* 6 April 1866; *s* of late Major-General E. W. Sargent; *m* 1st, 1897, Ethel (*d* 1915), *d* of late Daniel Twomey, of Kolor, Penshurst, Victoria, Australia; 2nd, 1918, Olive, *d* of Colonel N. Tufnell, Langleys, Great Waltham. *Educ:* Ireland. Commissioned to a lieutenancy in 2nd Devon Regiment from the Militia, 1886; joined Army Service Corps as Lieut 1890; Capt. 1892; Adjutant, 1895–97; Lt-Col 1906; Colonel, 1909. Nile Expedition, 1898; staff officer at Assouan; present at battle of Khartoum (despatches, brevet majority); South African War, 1899–1902; served as DAAG 1899–1902; present at the relief of Ladysmith, Tugela Heights, and Laing's Nek (Queen's medal with six clasps, King's medal with two, despatches three times, DSO); European War, 1914–18 (despatches 8 times, CB, CBE, Commandeur de la Légion d'Honneur, American Distinguished Service medal, 1914 Star, Victory and General Service medal); as AQMG 1st Corps., Aug.–Dec. 1914; Retreat from Mons, Battles of the Marne and Aisne, also first Battle of Ypres; DA and QMG 1st Corps, Dec. 1914–May 1916;

Battle of Loos, DA and QMG Reserve and Fifth Army, May 1916–Dec. 1917; Battle of the Somme, operations south of Arras, third Battle of Ypres; Chief of British Mission Headquarters Services of Supply, American EF, April 1918–July 1919. *Publications:* The Servant Nation, 1932; This Blind World, 1933; This Changing World, 1935; The Marvels of Bible Prophecy, 1938; The Modern World and its Delusions, 1944. *Club:* English-speaking Union.

Died 6 Feb. 1946.

SARGOOD, Mrs Lilian Mary, CBE 1918; *b* 1879; *d* of John Bassett Christian, Tudor Elizabeth Bay, Sydney, New South Wales; *m* 1st, 1902, Major E. A. Antill, Royal Australian Field Artillery (decd); 2nd, Mr Sargood. Organiser of War Chest Fund at Sydney during European War. *Address:* Waihemo, Bowral, New South Wales.

Died 23 May 1945.

SARL, Arthur J.; Larry Lynx, The People; *s* of Joseph Sarl and Jennie Maxwell Brown; *m* 1906, Frances Annie Rice; two *s* one *d*. *Educ:* privately, London. Actor in early days; came to Fleet Street as sub-editor, Echo, then Evening News, Daily Express, Daily Mail, and Daily Mirror; foreign editor Scripps-Macrae Press Association of America; editor Yes or No, Sketchy Bits, other periodicals; racing editor Sporting Budget; racing correspondent Sunday Dispatch; Vigilant and The Wizard, Sporting Times; author many short stories, serials. *Publications:* part author They're Off, 1934; Horses, Jockeys and Crooks, 1935; Gamblers of the Turf, 1938; Racing Ramp, 1939; Bitter Enemy, 1939. *Recreations:* gardening, golf and going racing. *Address:* 10 Woodbines Avenue, Kingston-upon-Thames. *T:* Kingston 2857.

Died 18 Sept. 1946.

SASSOON, Mrs Eugenie Louise Judith, CBE 1920; *b* 1854; *d* of late Achille Perugia, Trieste; *m* 1873, Arthur Abraham David Sassoon, CVO (*d* 1912). Was Head of Albert Gate Branch, Officers' Families Association. *Address:* 2 Albert Gate, SW1. *T:* Kensington 0608.

Died 14 Aug. 1943.

SASTRI, Rt Hon. V. S. Srinivasa, PC 1921; CH 1930; President Servants of India Society, 1915–27; Agent of the Government of India to South Africa, 1927–29; *b* 22 Sept. 1869; *s* of Valangiman Sankaranarayana Sastri, a Brahman; *m* (wife *d* 1934); one *s* one *d*. *Educ:* The Native High School, Kumbakonam; the Government College, Kumbakonam. School-master at various institutions till he became headmaster of one of the biggest high schools in the Presidency; resigned 1906 and joined the Servants of India Society, Poona; Madras Legislative Council, 1913; Fellow of the Madras University, 1909; Viceroy's Legislative Council, 1916–20; elected to the Council of State under the New Reforms Regime, 1920; member Reforms Committee under Lord Southborough; member Railway Committee under Sir William Acworth, 1921–22; visited England in 1919 as member of the Moderate Deputation, and again in 1921 as the Indian representative to the Imperial Conference; represented India at the League of Nations Assembly, 1921, and at the Conference on the Limitation of Armaments, Washington; made PC and presented with the Freedom of London; was deputed in 1922 by the Government of India to Australia, New Zealand, and Canada, to urge on those Governments the removal of disabilities of Indians lawfully domiciled there; visited England in 1923 as chairman of a deputation appointed by the unofficial members of the Indian Legislature to represent the case of Kenya Indians; and again in 1924 on behalf of the National Convention and the National Liberal Federation of India to press for further constitutional reforms in India; Vice-Chancellor, Annamalai Univ., 1935–40. *Publications:* three pamphlets: A Conscience Clause for Indians, Post-Puberty Marriage of Brahman Girls, Self-Government

for India under the British Flag; speeches and writings on Kenya. *Recreations:* swimming, tennis, and walking. *Address:* The Servants of India Society, Royapettah, Madras. *TA:* Servindia, Madras.

Died 17 April 1946.

SATOW, Captain Lawrence de W., CBE 1919; Royal Navy, retired; *b* 23 June 1865; 2nd *s* of David and Adah Satow, Blackheath; *m* 1907, Josephine M. E., *d* of J. Allen, Chislehurst; no *c*. *Educ:* Stubbington; HMS Britannia. Naval Cadet, 1878; retired Captain, 1911; called up for War Service, 1 Aug. 1914; Demobilised, March 1919. *Address:* 22 Salterton Road, Exmouth.

Died 23 Oct. 1948.

SAUL, Sir Ernest Wingate W.; *see* Wingate-Saul.

SAUMAREZ, Lt-Col Richard James, CMG 1918; RMLI; retired; *b* 1864; *o s* of late Admiral Thomas Saumarez, CB, formerly of the Firs, Jersey; *m* 1902, Elliot Mabel (*d* 1936), γ *d* of A. M. Ogston, DL, of Ardoe, Kincardineshire; one *s* one *d*. Joined Royal Marines, 1883; served European War, 1914–18 (CMG). *Club:* Army and Navy.

Died 26 Feb. 1943.

SAUNDERS, Edward Arthur, MA, MB, BCh Oxon; FRCP, MRCS, DPH Oxon; retired; *b* Reigate, 13 Aug. 1866; *s* of W. F. Saunders, FLS, and Anne, *d* of Sir Sydney Smith Saunders, CMG; unmarried. *Educ:* Merchant Taylors' School; St John's College, Oxford (Scholar); St Thomas's Hospital (Mead Medallist). House Physician, 1894; Senior and Junior Obstetric House Physician, 1895; Senior and Junior Ophthalmic House Surgeon, 1896; Clinical Assistant, Royal Ophthalmic Hospital, Moorfields, 1896; Clinical Assistant, Great Ormond Street Hospital for Children, 1897–1902; Assistant Superintendent, Emergency Fever Hospitals, Maidstone Typhoid Epidemic, 1898; Assistant Physician and Pathologist, West London Hospital, 1899; Consulting Physician West London Hospital; Consulting Physician to the Department for Medical Diseases of Children, West London Hospital; (late Lecturer on Medicine, and on Diseases of Children, Post Graduate College, West London Hospital); Consulting Physician to St John and St Elizabeth's Hospital, Lond.; Physician to St Luke's Hostel, Fitzroy Square; Consulting Physician, Eltham and Mottingham Cottage Hospital; Consult. Physician to the Fulham Babies' Hospital; Consulting Physician St Marylebone Almshouses; late Dean of Post-Graduate College, W Lond. Hospital; Fellow of the Roy. Society of Medicine; Member of the Association of Physicians. *Publications:* Medical Inspection of Children (Med. Officer, 1908); The Throat and Naso-pharynx in relation to General Medicine (Presidential Address, West London Medico-Chirurgical Association, 1916); The Baby (Public Health Series); contributions to medical papers. *Address:* The Lawn, Barcombe Mills, near Lewes, Sussex. *T:* Barcombe 23. *Club:* United University.

Died 8 Sept. 1947.

SAUNDERS, Sir George Rice P.; *see* Pryse-Saunders.

SAUNDERS, Margaret B.; *see* Baillie-Saunders.

SAUNDERS, Margaret Marshall, CBE 1934; MA; Author, Clubwoman, Lecturer, Magazine Writer, Broadcasts; *b* 13 April 1861; *d* of Edward Manning Saunders, DD, and Maria Kisborough Freeman. *Educ:* private schools, Nova Scotia, Edinburgh, Orléans. Hon. MA Acadia University. A member of the Authors' League of America; the English-speaking Union, New York; the Esperanto Club, Geneva; the Federated Humane Societies of America; the New Jersey Bird Soc.; a past honorary president of the Toronto Branch, Canadian Authors' Association; Member Institut Littéraire et Artistique de France; Friends of Italy, Toronto. *Publications:* 25 books and 5 booklets, including My Spanish Sailor (Her Sailor); Beautiful Joe; Daisy;

Charles and his Lamb; For the Other Boy's Sake; The House of Armour; The King of the Park; Rose à Charlitte; Deficient Saints; Tilda Jane; My Pets; The Wandering Dog; Bonnie Prince Fetlar; Jimmy Gold-Coast; Esther de Warren. *Recreations:* gardening, care of an aviary, travelling. *Club:* PEN.

Died 15 Feb. 1947.

SAUNDERS, Reginald George Francis, DSO 1916; Major, late Regular Reserve of Officers, RASC; Secretary of the East India and Sports Club; *b* 1882; *o s* of late Francis William Saunders, BA, journalist and war correspondent. *Educ:* St Paul's School. Served South African War with Paget's Horse, 1901–02 (Queen's medal with 5 clasps); European War, 1914–19 (despatches four times, DSO). *Recreations:* fishing and golf. *Address:* 16 St James's Sq., SW1. *Club:* Royal Bombay Yacht.

Died 23 Dec. 1947.

SAUNDERS, Rev. Canon Thomas Bekenn Avening; Canon Emeritus of Carlisle, 1932; *b* 29 Dec. 1870; *yr s* of late C. T. Saunders, of Ashley Grange, Moseley Wake Green, Birmingham; *m* 1st, 1897, Mary Theodora (*d* 1928), 2nd *d* of late James Slater of Bescot Hall, Walsall; one *s* one *d*; 2nd, 1936, Susan, *widow* of Gerald Wills. *Educ:* King Edward's School, Birmingham; University College, Oxford; 2nd Class Lit. Hum. MA 1896. Previously, between 1897 and 1921, Vicar of Thornthwaite and Rector of Greystoke in Cumberland, Sub-Dean and Rector of Newfoundland Cathedral, Rector of Brampton Ash (Northants), Vicar of St Agatha's, Birmingham, of Flamstead (Herts), and of St John's, Windermere; Canon Residentiary of Carlisle, 1920–32; Rector of Woolbeding, Sussex, 1932–35; Vicar of Easebourne, Sussex, 1935–36; Rector of Elsted w. Treyford and Didling, 1939–43; Rural Dean of Midhurst, 1934–46. *Address:* Lingy Acre, Portinscale, Keswick, Cumberland. *T:* Keswick 164.

Died 21 Jan. 1950.

SAUSMAREZ, Sir Havilland (Walter) de, 1st Bt *cr* 1928; Kt 1905; *b* 30 May 1861; 2nd *s* of Rev. Havilland de Sausmarez; *m* 1st, 1892, Dora Beatrice (*d* 1893), 2nd *d* of late Maj.-Gen. Gother Mann, CB; 2nd, 1896, Annie Elizabeth, GBE 1920, *y d* of late Rev. F. W. Mann, Rector of St Mary de Castro, Guernsey. *Educ:* Westminster; Trinity College, Cambridge. Ninth Senior Optime, 1883. Barr. Inner Temple, 1884; went the South-Eastern Circuit; after being in private practice in Lagos and acting as Attorney General, 1890–91, Assistant Judge in HM's Consular Court for Zanzibar, 1892–97; Assistant Judge Ottoman Dominions, 1897–1903; Judge Supreme Court, 1903–05; Judge of HBM's Supreme Court for China, 1905–21; when he retired; Bailiff of Guernsey, 1922–29; Hon. Doctor of Law, Caen University, 1927; President of La Société Guernesiaise, 1922–23 and 1931–32. *Publications:* The Earlier Charters of Guernsey, 1928; Guernsey and the Imperial Contribution, 1930; The Extentes of Guernsey, 1248 and 1331 and other documents, 1934; Captain Philip Saumarez: The Naval Uniform, 1936. *Address:* Sausmarez Manor, St Martin's, Guernsey. *Club:* Oxford and Cambridge.

Died 5 March 1941 (ext).

SAUVE, Hon. Arthur; journalist; *b* 1 Oct. 1875, of French-Canadian parents; *m* 1899, Marie-Louise, *d* of late Notary Lachaine, St Jérome; two *s* two *d*. *Educ:* Seminary of Ste Therese; University of Montreal. Sub-editor of La Patrie; Manager of Le Canadien; Mayor of St Benoit Municipality; director of Agriculture, Society of Two Mountains; a member of the Provincial House for the county of Two-Mountains, 1908–30; Chief of the Conservative Party, 1916–29; Member Laval Two-Mountains for the Federal House, 1930; Postmaster-General, Canada, 1930–35. *Address:* Outremont, PQ, Canada.

Died 6 Feb. 1944.

SAVAGE, Rev. Canon Edwin Sidney, MA; late Rector of St Bartholomew the Great, Smithfield; Hon. Chaplain to Butchers' Company; *b* 28 Feb. 1862; *m* Sibyl (*d* 1941), *d* of late Dean Farrar, DD, FRS. *Educ:* New College, Eastbourne; Magdalen College, Oxford. Curate of St James, Doncaster, 1885–87; St Margaret, Westminster, 1887–88; Vicar of St Mark, Barrow-in-Furness, 1889–94; Jesmond, 1894–97; Rector of Hexham and Mercers' Lecturer, 1898–1918; Hon. Canon of Newcastle Cathedral; restored Hexham Abbey; built the Abbey Institute; restored and conserved St Bartholomew the Great; Vicar of St Nicholas, Warwick, 1922–25; during the War travelled in War work, 8 times France, 5 times in Italy, 4 times Salonica and Ægean, borders of Palestine, and for Serbian Red Cross in United States and Canada; served on International Commission to report on Bulgarian Atrocities; travelled in Dalmatia, Herzegovina, Bosnia and Eastern Serbia; created Major in Royal Serbian Army by King Peter; Order of the Golden Cross and the Double Chain by Holy Orthodox Church; Order of Serbian Red Cross and S Sava; in America for Serbian Relief, 1919; travelled Serbia and South America, 1920; Round the World, 1921–22; Lecturer on Jugo Slavia; 1927 and 1929, Tours through Palestine; visit to New Zealand, 1936 and 1938; Round Africa, 1937. *Publications:* Record of Hexham Abbey; Rahere: Yesterday and To-day; magazine publications. *Address:* 18 London Road, Bexhill-on-Sea.

Died 26 Oct. 1947.

SAVARY, Ven. T. W., BA, DD, Rector of St Paul's Church, Halifax, since 1930; Archdeacon of Halifax since 1932; *b* 1878; *s* of A. W. Savary, MA, DCL (Judge) and Bessie C. Otty; *m* 1st, 1905, Annie Edna Neve; 2nd, 1915, Catherine Jean Chute; one *s* two *d*. *Educ:* University of Toronto; Wycliffe College, Toronto. Deacon, 1901; Priest, 1902; Curate of St James Church, Kingston, 1901–03; Rector of St Luke's, Winnipeg, 1903–09; Vicar of St James, Kingston, 1909–12; Rector, 1912–30; Canon of St George's Cathedral, Kingston, 1930; DD of Queen's University, 1929. *Address:* 354 Robie Street, Halifax, NS. *T:* B4320.

Died 3 June 1948.

SAVILE, Brig. Clare Ruxton Uvedale, DSO 1916; OBE 1919; *b* Bermuda, 1881; *s* of late Brig.-Gen. W. C. Savile, CB, DSO, and Helen Vernon Ruxton; *m* 1915, Katherine Gladys Ritchie. *Educ:* Wellington College; Sandhurst. Joined Royal Fusiliers, 1901; Nigeria Regt West African Frontier Force, 1905–10; operations Northern Nigeria, 1906 (medal and clasp); Brigade Major Nigeria Regt 1911–16; Cameroon Expedition, 1914–16 (DSO); Brigade Major 204th Infantry Brigade, 1916; Brigade Maj. 3rd Infantry Brigade, France, 1917; DAQMG Malta Command, 1918; AA and QMG 1918–19; Lt-Col, 2nd Batt. Hants Regt, 1927–30; GSO1, British Troops in China, 1930–32; Commander 2nd Infantry Brigade, 1932–35; retired pay, 1935. *Recreations:* hunting, fishing, shooting. *Address:* 46 Ashley Gardens, SW1. *Club:* Flyfishers'.

Died 28 Jan. 1949.

SAVILE, Robert Stewart; *b* 1863; *s* of Rev. F. A. S. Savile of Hollanden Park, Tonbridge, Kent; *m* 1892, Katharine Evelyn, *d* of Col Lumsden of Pitcaple Castle, Aberdeenshire; one *s* one *d*. *Educ:* Harrow; Cambridge. Lt Royal West Kent IY 1885–96; ADC to Earl of Onslow, Governor of New Zealand, 1889–90; Master of West Kent Foxhounds, 1893–95; JP Hants; appointed by the Admiralty to the command of the armed yacht Sea Fay for the winter 1914–15, in the North of Scotland; and then a Major in the Remount Service. *Recreations:* hunting, yachting, racing, shooting. *Address:* Oaklands, Bembridge, Isle of Wight. *TA:* Savile, Bembridge. *T:* Bembridge 11. *Clubs:* Windham; Royal Yacht Squadron, Cowes.

Died 24 Feb. 1945.

SAVILE, Lt-Col Robert Vesey, CBE 1919; b Clifton, 31 Dec. 1873; s of Col H. B. O. Savile, CB; m 1920, Evelyn Gertrude, d of R. L. Hunter of 17 Stratton Street, W1, and Lincoln's Inn. Educ: Clifton College; RMC, Sandhurst. 2nd Lt Sherwood Foresters, 1893; Lt 1896; Capt. 1900; joined Egyptian Army, 1899; served operations against the Khalifa, 1899 (Khedive's medal and clasp); joined the Sudan Civil Service, 1901; Assistant Civil Secretary, Sudan Government, 1907; Governor of Bahr el Ghazal Province, 1908; Governor Kordofan Province, Dec. 1908; retired from Army, 1909; promoted Major in the Reserve of Officers, 1915; Reconquest of Darfur Expedition, 1916 (Sultan's medal and clasp); Lt-Col Jan. 1917; Governor of Darfur Province, 1917–23; 3rd Class of the Order of the Medjedieh, 1905; 3rd Class of the Order of the Nile, 1916; 2nd Class of the Order of the Nile, 1923; OBE 1918; FRGS. Address: Itchen Lodge, Itchen Abbas, nr Winchester. Club: Army and Navy.

Died 13 Sept. 1947.

SAVILL, Lt-Col Alfred Cecil, DSO 1940; MC; RA; Commanding Worcestershire Yeomanry Anti-Tank Regt RA; b 22 Dec. 1897; 3rd s of Sir Edwin Savill; m 1921, Irene Cecilia Edith, e d of late Cecil Dawson, Brentwood, Essex; one s two d. Educ: Malvern College. Passed into Royal Military Academy, Woolwich, in Sept. 1914 and commissioned in Royal Field Artillery, 1915; served European War, 1915–18 (wounded); commanded a Battery in the Welsh Division and later in 57 West Lancs Division (MC and bar, 'promotion in the Field' to Brevet Major, despatches thrice); retired to Regular Army Reserve of Officers, 1919, and entered family business of Alfred Savill & Sons, Chartered Surveyors; holds appointment of Surveyor to Worshipful Company of Leathersellers; Liveryman of Worshipful Company of Inn-holders; recalled with Regular Reserve, July 1939; served France and Belgium, 1939–40; commanded Anti-Tank Battery in retreat back to Dunkirk (DSO); Lieut-Colonel, 1940. Recreations: hunting, fishing, shooting. Address: Sheepbell Farm, Stoke D'Abernon, Surrey. T: Oxshott 122. Clubs: Carlton, City of London.

Died 17 Sept. 1943.

SAVILL, Sir Edwin, Kt 1921; retired senior partner in the firm of Alfred Savill & Sons, Chartered Surveyors, of 51a Lincoln's Inn Fields, WC, and 18 Old Broad Street, EC; President of the Surveyors Institution, 1924–25; Member of the War Agricultural Committee, 1915–18; Vice-Chairman of the Land Union; b 4 Nov. 1868; 3rd s of Alfred Savill of Chigwell, Essex; m; two s one d. Educ: Uppingham. Address: The Home Field, Howe Green, Hertford.

Died 11 Sept. 1947.

SAWYER, Ethel V.; see Vaughan-Sawyer.

SAWYER, George Alexander, CBE 1920; MRI, etc.; Knight of Grace of St John, Knight of the Crown of Belgium, etc. Late Deputy Chairman of the British Empire Film Institute; late Hon. Treasurer of the National Liberal Council for London during Coalition Government; late Chairman of Westminster National Liberal Association (Abbey and St George's Divisions); a Life Governor and formerly an Hon. Treasurer of the Queen's Hospital for Children and Member of the Governing Board; organised many Art Exhibitions, amongst which were the First British Sculptors Exhibition, Medallic Art Exhibition, First Official War Photo Exhibition, British Women Artists Exhibition, Belgian Art at the Front Exhibition, Belgian Art at the Front Exhibition and Sculpture Exhibition, 1931; Hon. Secretary and Treasurer of the first British Industrial Art Exhibition, 1933; Hon. Organiser the first Contemporary Industrial Design Exhibition, 1935; Hon. Treasurer, Durham Distressed Area Committee; during European War organised and served with Voluntary Hospitals in France; member of board of London Child

Guidance Clinic, etc; m 1907, Doris Hunter (C St J); three s two d. Address: Southdown House, Eastbourne. T: Eastbourne 3882; 9 Hanover Square, W1. T: Mayfair 0371; Highclere, Gorran, Cornwall. T: Mevagissey 171.

Died 19 Feb. 1944.

SAXBY, Jessie Margaret Edmondston; JP 1920; b Halligarth, Shetland Isles, 30 June 1842; 9th c of Laurence Edmonston, MD, and Eliza Macbrair; m 1859, Henry Linckmyer Saxby, MD, author of The Birds of Shetland, etc. (d 1873). Educ: no education save that acquired by much reading and a close study of Nature, and the society of literary and scientific parents. Early literary ambition suppressed owing to necessity for maintaining five young sons left fatherless; contributed numerous articles to magazines and daily papers; gave opening address of Viking Club of London; was Hon. President of Edinburgh Orkney and Shetland Literary and Scientific Association; in politics a Liberal; took an active part in the Home Rule question and the Temperance Movement; visited Canada in the interests of Women's Emigration; author of more than 30 volumes of tales, poems, travels, the most popular of these being a series of Shetland adventure for boys; received an illuminated address and gift on her 90th birthday. Publications: Lichens from the Old Rock; The One Wee Lassie; Glamour from Argyllshire; Breakers Ahead; Lindeman Brothers; Dora Coyne; Sisters-in-Love; Sallie's Boy; The Lads of Lunda; The Earl's Yacht; Viking Boys; The Saga-Book of Lunda; Tom and his Crows; The Home of a Naturalist; West-nor'-West; Kate and Jean; Ben Hansen; Preston Tower; Milestones; Lucky Lines; A Camsterie Nacket; Wrecked on the Shetlands; Oil on the Troubled Waters; Hame-land and Hame-folk; Crumbs from the Children's Table; Dad Roy; Auld Lerwick; Birds of Omen; Daalamist; The Bonnie Earl; For Rank's Sake; Queen of the Isles; Revealed at Last; Constable A1; The Beauty of Brechin: Not False but Free; The Cradle of our Race; Joseph Bell, MD: an Appreciation; Leaves from the Psalmist's Life (poems); Traditional Lore of the Shetland Isles, 1932; Threads from a Tangled Skein (Poems and Ponderings), 1934. Recreations: the poetic study of plant and bird life; reading the Poets and trying to write in rhyme; whist, the only game worth playing. Address: Wullver's Hool, Baltasound, Unst, Shetland Isles.

Died 27 Dec. 1940.

SAXL, Fritz, FBA; PhD (Vienna); Director of the Warburg Institute, London, since 1933, and Professor of the History of the Classical Tradition in the University of London since 1945; b 8 Jan. 1890; s of Ignaz Saxl and Wilhemine Falk; m 1913, Elise Bienenfeld; one d. Educ: Vienna; University of Vienna and University of Berlin. Scholarship at Inst. f. oest. Gesch., Rome, 1912–13. Librarian, Warburg Institute, 1913–14; Director, Warburg Institute, Hamburg, 1929–33; Privat-dozent, Hamburg Univ.; Professor, Hamburg Univ., 1927–33; Member, Boards of Studies in Archæology, Germanic Languages and History, London Univ. Publications: Verzeichnis astrologischer und mythologischer ill. Handschriften des lat. Mittelalters, Vols I, II, 1916 and 1926; Frühes Christentum und spätes Heidentum in ihren künstlerischen Ausdrucksformen, Vienna, 1923; (with) Erwin Panofsky) Dürers Melencolia, 1. 1923; Antike Götter in der Spätrenaissance, 1927, Mithras, Typengeschichtliche Untersuchungen, 1931; (with Erwin Panofsky) Classical Mythology in mediæval art, in Metropolitan Museum Studies 4, 1933; La fede astrologica di Agostino Chigi, R. Accad, d'Italia, Rome, 1934; Costumes and Festivals of Milanese Society under Spanish Rule (Annual Italian Lecture of the British Academy 1936), 1938; Rembrandt's Sacrifice of Manoah, 1940; The Battle Scene without a Hero; The Classical Inscription in Renaissance Art and Politics; A Spiritual Encyclopædia of the Later Middle Ages; The Ruthwell Cross, in England and the Mediterranean Tradition, Oxford, 1945; other articles in Journal of the

Warburg and Courtauld Institutes. *Address:* 162 East Dulwich Grove, SE22. *T:* Gipsy Hill 1460. *Club:* Burlington Fine Arts.

Died 22 March 1948.

SAXON SNELL, Alfred Walter, FRIBA, FRSanI (Vice-President); architect; Hon. Surveyor and Member Committee, Brompton Hospital for Consumption; Trustee Rupture Society; *b* Brompton, 1 June 1860; 5th *s* of late Henry Saxon Snell; *m* 1884, Rosa (*d* 1947), 2nd *d* of late Edward Medwin Williams, HMEIS; two *d.* *Educ:* Private School, Maidenhead; University College, London. Articles to his father, 1877; succeeded to his practice in works mainly connected with hospitals, Poor Law buildings, public baths, etc. Principal works: St Helier's Hospital, Carshalton (Surrey County Council); Charing Cross Hospital; Middlesex Central Hospital, Park Royal; St Mary's Hospital, Plaistow; Whitehaven Hospital; Male Lock Hospital, Soho; Redhill Hospital (SCC); Brompton Hospital and Sanatorium additions; St Marylebone Workhouse. *Publications:* Papers in Journal Royal Institute of British Architects, viz. Modern Hospitals, Public Baths; also in Journal of Royal Sanitary Institute, viz. Hospitals, Notes on Fever Hospitals, A Hospital Ward, Isolated Homes for the Aged Poor versus the Workhouse, Public Baths, Physics of Air in relation to Ventilation, Sanitary Building Construction, Maternity and Children's Hospitals, Architects Journal, Modern Hospitals. *Recreations:* motoring, golf, etc. *Address:* 23 St Anne's Road, Caversham, Reading, Berks. *T:* Reading 2034; 9 Bentinck Street, W1. *T:* Welbeck 2827. *Club:* Royal Societies.

Died 8 June 1949.

SAYE AND SELE, 19th Baron *cr* 1447 and 1603; **Geoffrey Rupert Cecil Twisleton-Wykeham-Fiennes;** Major, late Queen's Own Oxfordshire Hussars; *b* 27 Dec. 1884; *e s* of 18th Baron and Marion Ruperta Murray (*d* 1946), *d* of Major Lawes; *S* father, 1937. *Educ:* Harrow; New College, Oxford; BA. Barrister, Inner Temple, 1911; contested Windsor, 1910; served European War, 1914–18. *Heir:* *b* Lt-Col Hon. Ivo Murray Twisleton-Wykeham-Fiennes, MC [*b* 1885; *m* 1919, Hersey Cecilia Hester, *d* of late Capt. Sir Thomas Dacres Butler, KCVO; three *s.* Served European War, 1914–18 (despatches, MC, French Croix de Guerre)]. *Address:* Broughton Castle, Banbury. *TA:* and *T:* Bloxham 224. *Club:* United University.

Died 18 Feb. 1949.

SAYER, Captain Humphrey, DSO 1919; MC; *b* 9 May 1889; *s* of late A. L. Sayer, Yew Tree House, Westfield, Sussex; *m* 1st, 1922, Ethel M., *d* of Colonel F. Hoply, Nairobi, Kenya Colony; one *s* one *d*; 2nd, 1930, Marjorie, *e d* of R. W. Stent, Pontrilas Court, Hereford. *Educ:* Haileybury College; Trinity College, Cambridge. Served European War, 1914–18, Gallipoli, Egypt and Palestine, France (DSO, MC); Sussex Yeomanry, Brigade Major. *Address:* East Johnstone, South Molton, Devon.

Died 21 April 1943.

SCAMMELL, Lt-Col Alfred George, DSO 1916; Managing Director Scammell Lorries, Ltd; engineer; *b* 1878; *m.* Served European War, 1914–17 (despatches, DSO). *Address:* Glyn Neath, Lemsford Road, St Albans, Herts. *Clubs:* Junior Army and Navy, Royal Automobile.

Died 4 Sept. 1941.

SCARBROUGH, 10th Earl of, *cr* 1690; **Aldred Frederick George Beresford Lumley,** KG 1929; GBE 1921; KCB 1911; CB 1904; Viscount Lumley in peerage of Ireland, 1628; Baron Lumley of Lumley Castle, Durham, 1681; Viscount Lumley, 1689; Earl of Scarbrough, 1690, all in peerage of Great Britain; Sub Prior Order of St John, 1923–43; Director-General Territorial and Volunteer Forces, 1917–21; Major-General (R), late ADC to the King; late Colonel

commanding Yorkshire Dragoons YC; *b* Tickhill Castle, 1857; *s* of 9th Earl and Frederica, *d* of late Andrew Robert Drummond; *S* father 1884; *m* 1899, Lucy Cecilia (*d* 1931), *widow* of Robert Ashton, and *e d* of Cecil Dunn Gardner; one *d.* Protestant. Conservative. *Educ:* Eton. Lieut 7th Hussars, 1876–83; Lord-Lieut West Riding of Yorkshire, 1892–1904; served in South Africa, 1900 (despatches). *Heir:* *nephew* Sir Lawrence Roger Lumley, GCSI, GCIE. *Address:* Sandbeck Park, Rotherham. *T:* Tickhill 210; Lumley Castle, Co. Durham. *Clubs:* Carlton, Army and Navy; Royal Yacht Squadron, Cowes.

Died 4 March 1945.

SCARLES, Sir Edward John, Kt 1936; OBE; *b* 30 April 1871; *s* of Edward Scarles, Norwich; *m* 1896, Kate Ramsbottom (*d* 1925), Norwich; one *s.* *Educ:* Norwich. In Customs and Excise Service since 1891; Assistant Collector of Customs, Liverpool, 1921; Collector at Cardiff, 1923; Collector, London Port, 1930; Chief Inspector, Board of Customs and Excise, 1931; retired, 1936; Mayor of Kingston-on-Thames, 1939–45. *Address:* 30 Lingfield Avenue, Kingston-on-Thames. *T:* Kingston 1395.

Died 25 Aug. 1947.

SCHILLER, Ferdinand Philip Maximilian; KC 1913; Recorder of Bristol since 1935; *b* Ealing, 28 July 1868; *y s* of Ferdinand Schiller, Calcutta. *Educ:* Clifton College; Magdalen College, Oxford (classical exhibitioner); 2nd class Classical Moderations, 2nd class Lit. Hum., 1890; MA. Called to Bar, 1893; Recorder of Southampton, 1928–35; Bencher of the Inner Temple, 1922; Treasurer of Inner Temple, 1942. *Recreations:* shooting, fishing, golf, mountaineering. *Address:* 1 Temple Gardens, Temple, EC4; Old House, Betchworth, Surrey. *TA:* Temple 70. *T:* Central 8558. *Clubs:* Windham, Garrick, Alpine.

Died 19 Jan. 1946.

SCHLESINGER, Frank, PhD, ScD; *b* New York City, 11 May 1871; *s* of William Joseph Schlesinger and Mary Wagner; *m* 1st, 1900, Eva (*d* 1928); one *s*; 2nd, 1929, Katharine Wilcox. *Educ:* College of the City of New York; Columbia University. Observor in charge of International Latitude Observatory at Ukiah, California, 1899–1903; Astronomer at Yerkes Observatory (under auspices of Carnegie Institution), 1903–05; Director, Allegheny Observatory, 1905–20; Director of Yale University Observatory, 1920–41; Pres., American Astronomical Society, 1919–22; Vice-President, International Astronomical Union, 1925–32; President, International Astronomical Union, 1932–35; Correspondant de l'Académie de Sciences, Paris; Gold Medal, Royal Astronomical Society, London, 1927; Darwin Lecturer before Royal Astronomical Society, 1927; Correspondent, French Bureau des Longitudes; Member, Swedish Academy of Sciences; Hon. Member Astronomical Societies in Great Britain, Italy, Canada, and Mexico; Valz Medal, Académie de Sciences, Paris, 1926; Bruce Medal of the Astronomical Society of the Pacific, 1929; AM Hon. Yale, 1920; ScD Hon. University of Pittsburgh, 1920; ScD Hon. Cambridge University, 1925; Officier, Légion d'Honneur. *Publication:* More than 200 monographs in astronomical journals and in Publications, Allegheny Observatory and Transactions, Yale University Observatory. *Recreations:* tennis, motoring, billiards. *Address:* Lyme, Connecticut, USA.

Died 10 July 1943.

SCHMIDT, Carl Friedrich, DPhil (Hon.); *b* 13 Nov. 1875; *s* of late Rev. F. A. Schmidt, Superintendent Berlin Mission, Cape Colony; *m* Annemarie, *d* of late Pastor G. Wagener, Lutheran Church, Long Street, Cape Town; one *s* one *d.* *Educ:* home; Riversdale, Cape. Entered Civil Service as clerk, Control and Audit Office, Cape Town, 1893; Secretary Education Dept, Bloemfontein, 1915; Director of Education, Orange

Free State, 1918; Secretary for the Interior, Union of SA, 1926; Controller and Auditor General, Union of South Africa, 1929; Chairman National Road Board, 1935; Rector, Pretoria University, Transvaal, 1935–40. *Address:* Die Branders, Strand, Cape Province. *T:* Strand 115.

Died 11 Oct. 1948.

SCHMIDT, Nathaniel, MA; DHL; Professor of Semitic Languages and Literatures and Oriental History in Cornell University, 1896–1932; Professor Emeritus since 1932; *b* Hudiksvall, Sweden, 22 May 1862; *s* of Lars Peter Anderson and Fredrika Wilhelmina Schmidt; *m* Ellen, *d* of Anders Alfvén and Charlotta Christina Axelson Puke; one *d*. *Educ:* Hudiksvall Gymnasium; Stockholm University; Hamilton Theological Seminary; Colgate University; University of Berlin. Professor of Semitic Languages and Literatures in Colgate University, 1888–96; Director of American School of Archæology in Jerusalem, 1904–05; Lecturer on Ancient and Oriental History in Columbia Univ., summer sessions, 1925–35; member of many American and foreign learned societies; Trustee of American Schools of Oriental Research since 1936. *Publications:* Biblical Criticism and Theological Belief, 1897; The Republic of Man, 1899; Ecclesiasticus, with Introduction and Notes, 1903; The Prophet of Nazareth, 1905; The Messages of the Poets, 1911; Ibn Khaldun, Historian, Sociologist, Philosopher, 1930; The Coming Religion, 1930; important articles in several encyclopædias; and contributions to theological journals and proceedings of learned societies. *Recreations:* walking, swimming. *Address:* Cornell University, Ithaca, NY, USA. *Clubs:* Cosmopolitan, Ithaca.

Died 29 June 1939.

SCHNEIDER, Charles Eugene; Membre de l'Institut de France; Past President of the Iron and Steel Institute; ironmaster; ex-member of the French Parliament; *b* Le Creusot, 29 Oct. 1868; *m* Mlle. de Saint-Sauveur. *Address:* 34 Cours Albert 1er, Paris. *T:* Elysées, 82–80; Château de la Verrerie, Le Creusot (Saône-et-Loire). *Clubs:* Automobile, Cercle Hoche, Polo, Cercle de l'Union, Yacht de France, Paris; Royal Victoria Yacht, Ryde.

Died 17 Nov. 1942.

SCHOFIELD, Lt-Col Frederick William, CMG 1918; TD; *b* 1856; *s* of late William Schofield; *m* 1st, 1891, Caroline Harriette Maude, *d* of late Rev. George Carpenter, MA Oxon, Chadlington; 2nd, 1914, Winifred Maud, *d* of late Thomas Usborne, of Writtle, Essex, DL, formerly MP for Mid Essex; one *d*. Served European War, 1914–17; commanded a battalion of the Oxfordshire and Buckinghamshire Light Infantry in France and Flanders, and afterwards on the Staff in France, 1915–17 (despatches, CMG); JP Oxon. *Address:* Langston House, Chadlington, Oxfordshire. *T:* Chadlington 36. *Clubs:* Junior Carlton; Oxford and County (Oxford).

Died 15 April 1949.

SCHOFIELD, J. W., RBA 1903; RI 1917; RBC 1924; portrait and landscape painter; *s* of Clayton Schofield; *m* 1891, Gussie, *d* of late Rev. J. Cunnick, Vicar of Aberdovey. *Educ:* Art under Professor Fred Brown at Westminster; under Bouguereau and Lefebvre in Paris. Exhibited in RA since 1888; Paris Salon. *Principal Works:* Spring Vapours; East and West; Shadowland and many moonlight pictures, etc.; portraits of Dean Kitchin, Major-Gen. Charley, Lady Flavia Giffard, Viscountess Tiverton. *Address:* 38 Marlborough Hill, NW8. *T:* Primrose Hill 2859. *Club:* Arts.

Died 23 Oct. 1944.

SCHOFIELD, W. Elmer, RBA 1907; ROI; Academician National Academy, New York; Member of American Institute of Arts and Letters; represented in the Musée de Luxembourg, Paris; *b* Philadelphia, Penn., 1867; *s* of Benj. Schofield and Mary Wolstencroft; *m*

Murielle, *d* of E. B. Redmayne, Southport, England; two *s*. *Educ:* Studied in Paris under Messrs Bouguereau, Ferrier, Aman-Jean; Fellow of Pennsylvania Academy Fine Arts, Philadelphia; represented in following permanent collections: National Collection of Uruguay; Corcoran Art Gallery, Washington; John Herron Art Gallery, Indianapolis; Art Museum, Cincinnati; Pennsylvania Academy Fine Arts; Carnegie Institute, Pittsburg; Sebright Art Gallery, Buffalo; Memorial Gallery, Rochester, NY, Art Institute of Chicago; Webb Prize, Society American Artists, 1900; Hon. Mention Exposition Universelle, Paris, 1900; Carnegie Institute, Pittsburg, 1900; First Hallgarten Prize, 1901, and 1st Altman Prize National Academy Designs, New York; Silver Medal, Pan-American Exhibition, Buffalo, 1901; Silver Medal, Universal Exhibition, St Louis, 1904; Gold Medal, Penn. Acad. Fine Arts, 1903; Gold Medal of First Class, Carnegie Institute, 1904; Member National Institute Arts and Letters, New York; The Inness Gold Medal, National Academy Design, New York; Gold Medal, International Exposition, Buenos Ayres; Gold Medal, National Arts Club, 1913; Temple Medal, Sesnan Gold Medal, Penna. Acad. Fine Arts, Philadelphia; Gold Medal, Chicago Art Institute. Served in 24th Batt. Royal Fusiliers (2nd Sportsman's); Captain RGA, BEF, France; Commander A/a Defences. *Address:* Godolphin Manor, Cornwall. *Clubs:* Arts; Lotos, Century, National Arts, New York; Art, Philadelphia.

Died 1 March 1944.

SCHOLEFIELD, Sir Joshua, Kt 1937; JP Surrey; KC 1922; Bencher of Middle Temple since 1929; Recorder of Middlesbrough, 1929–47; Chairman of Railway Assessment Authority since its foundation in 1930; 4th *s* of late John Scholefield of Hemsworth, near Wakefield; *m* 1893, Ethel Sylvia (*d* 1948), 7th *d* of late Henry Godfrey, Marlborough, NZ; one *d*. *Educ:* privately. Admitted a Solicitor, 1887; entered Middle Temple, 1900; Certificate of Honour from the Council of Legal Education, 1900; called to Bar, 1900; North-Eastern Circuit; Coalition candidate for Hemsworth Div., 1918; Conservative candidate for Pontefract Div., 1922; President London Passenger Transport Arbitration Tribunal, 1933–36. Treasurer Hon. Society of the Middle Temple, 1945. *Publications:* (Joint) Appeals from Justices of the Peace; Private Street Works Act, 1892; Joint-Editor of Lumley's Public Health, 7th, 8th, 9th, 10th and 11th eds; Editor of Encyclopædia of Local Government Law; Editor, Michael and Wills' Gas and Water, 6th ed. *Address:* Flat 42, 50 Sloane Street, SW1. *T:* Sloane 8171.

Died 11 March 1950.

SCHOLEY, Harry, CBE 1920; MIEE; *b* 1872; *e s* of late William Kay Scholey, Wakefield, Yorks; *m* 1893, Frances Edna, 2nd *d* of late Samuel Hallewell, Bradford. *Educ:* St John's, Wakefield; City and Guilds; private. Has been associated with electrical and chemical manufacturing for many years. *Publications:* Electric Tramways and Railways; has contributed extensively to engineering publications. *Recreations:* golf, fishing. *Address:* Glendower Hotel, South Kensington, SW7. *T:* Kensington 4472. *Club:* Constitutional.

Died 5 June 1945.

SCHRÖDER, Sir Walter, KBE 1923; *b* 9 June 1855; *s* of William Schröder; unmarried. Deputy-Coroner, Central Middlesex, 1894–1902; SW London and Surrey, 1895–99; Central London, 1899–1910; and City of London, 1914–18; Coroner, Central London, 1910–30; Hon. Treasurer, 1877–1902 of St Martin's League Houses of Rest and Holiday Home for postmen; Past President and Hon. Secretary, 1902–38, of Coroners' Society of England and Wales; Hon. Treasurer of Medico-Legal Society; Vice-President of Hampstead Scientific Society; member of London Council of Royal Society for preventing accidents; Life Governor, Royal

Free Hospital; Past Master Coachmakers' Company; Coronation Medal, 1937. *Address:* 3 Heath Mansions, NW3. *Club:* Reform.

Died 28 July 1942.

SCHRODER, Captain William Henry; late 9th Lancers and Remount Service; *b* 25 Oct. 1867; *e s* of late William Henry Schroder and Marie Carolina, *d* of Charles Horny; *m* 1896, Judith, *e d* of Edward Robert Gregge-Hopwood of Hopwood Hall, Lancashire; one *s* two *d*. *Educ:* Radley; Trinity College, Cambridge. Late Lieutenant 9th Lancers. *Address:* Wilherby, Sidmouth, Devon; Attadale, Strathcarron, Ross-shire. *Clubs:* Army and Navy; Royal Yacht Squadron Cowes; Royal Clyde Yacht, Glasgow.

Died 8 May 1945.

SCHURMAN, Jacob Gould; *b* Freetown, Prince Edward Island, 22 May 1854; 3rd *s* of late Robert Schurman; *m* 1884, Barbara Forrest, *e d* of late George Munro, New York; three *s* four *d*. *Educ:* Prince of Wales College, Charlottetown, Prince Edward Island; Acadia College, Nova Scotia; University College, London; Private Instruction, Paris; University of Edinburgh; University of Heidelberg; University of Berlin; University of Göttingen. Gilchrist Scholar for Canada, 1875–78; holder Hibbert Travelling Fellowship, 1878–80. Professor of English Literature and Philosophy, Acadia Coll., and Dalhousie Coll., Nova Scotia, 1880–86; Sage Prof. of Philosophy, Cornell University, 1886–92; President of Cornell University, 1892–1920; Member of the Prussian Academy of Science; Member of the German Academy (Munich); President of the US Commission to the Philippine Islands, 1899; US Minister to Greece and Montenegro, 1912–13; US Envoy Extraordinary and Minister Plenipotentiary to China, 1921–25; US Ambassador to Germany, 1925–30; Delegate at large and 1st Vice-Pres., NY State Constitutional Convention, spring and summer 1915; NY State Food Commission, 1917–18. BA MA Lond.; DSc Edin.; LLD Columbia, Yale, Edinburgh, Williams, Dartmouth, Harvard, Brown, Pennsylvania, and Missouri; Hon. PhD Marburg and Heidelberg. *Publications:* author Kantian Ethics and the Ethics of Evolution; The Ethical Import of Darwinism; Agnosticism and Religion; The Genesis of the Critical Philosophy; Report of the First Philippine Commission; Philippine Affairs, a Retrospect and Outlook; The Balkan Wars, 1912–1913; numerous articles and addresses. *Recreation:* walking. *Address:* Bedford Hills, Westchester County, New York. *Clubs:* University, Century, (New York); University (Washington); University (Shanghai); Peking, (Peking).

Died 12 Aug. 1942.

SCHÜTZE, Mrs Harrie; *see* Leslie, Henrietta.

SCHÜTZE, Harrie Leslie Hugo, MD; Bacteriologist, Lister Institute, London; *b* Melbourne, Australia, 1882; *yr s* of John and Caroline Schütze; *m* 1913, Gladys Henrietta (Henrietta Leslie) (*d* 1946), *o c* of Arthur and Mary Raphael. *Educ:* Brackley; Cumloden; University, Melbourne. MBBS. Assistant Bacteriologist, Melbourne University, 1905; MD Wurzburg, 1907; Assistant, Institute of Hygiene, Würzburg, 1908–12; Beit Fellow, 1912; Research Bacteriologist, Lister Institute of Preventive Medicine, 1913. *Publication:* publications in Pathological and Bacteriological Journals. *Recreation:* travelling. *Address:* Bronwen, Radlett, Herts. *T:* Radlett 6210.

Died 9 Aug. 1946.

SCHWABE, Randolph, RWS 1942; ARWS 1938; Slade Professor of Fine Art, University College, London, since 1930; Fellow of University College London, 1948; *b* Manchester, 1885; *s* of Lawrence Schwabe and Octavie Henriette Ermen; *m* Gwendolen, *d* of Herbert Jones, BA; one *d*. *Educ:* privately. Studied art at Slade School,

University College, and subsequently in Paris. Member of New English Art Club, and London Group. *Publications:* (with F. M. Kelly) Historic Costume, a Chronicle of Fashion in Western Europe, 1925; and A Short History of Costume and Armour, 1931; Occasional Notes and Reviews in the Burlington Magazine, Art-work, and the Print Collectors' Quarterly. *Address:* University College, WC1. *Club:* Athenæum.

Died 19 Sept. 1948.

SCIORTINO, Professor Anthony, Sculptor and Architect; Curator of the Arts in Malta; Hon. Director, British Academy of Fine Arts, Rome; Hon. CM, RIBA and FRSA; Membre, Syndicat des Journalistes et Ecrivains (Paris); *b* Malta, 1883. *Educ:* Royal Institute of Fine Arts, Rome. First success with bronze group, Les Gavroche, bought by Maltese Government, 1904; won prize offered by Russian Government for monument of Emperor Alexander II, 1911; won International Competition for the monument of the poet Chefchenko, Kieff, 1914; winner of the second prize in the International Competition for the equestrian monument of Bolivar in Paris, 1929. *Works:* Monument of Anton Chaikoff (in Rostoff sur Donn); Sir Adrian Dingle, Sir Edwin Egerton, Johannesburg Gallery; Field-Marshal Lord Grenfell; Monument, International Eucharistic Congress, Malta, 1917; Brown-Yung's grave, Campo Santo, Rome, 1918; Miss Court's grave, English Cemetery, Rome, 1918; Mlle du Chéne de Vère, Miss Lewis; Winifred Holt; Prof. Bajardi; Dewan Sir T. Vijayaraghavacharya; Prof. Sgambati; Baroness Hayashi; Princess Pignatelli; Ritmi di Vita, Marchesa Godi di Godio; The Queen Sophie of Greece; Monument of the Great Siege of 1565 in Malta, 1927; Monument to the Archbishop Mgr Pace in the Gozo Cathedral; other works on allegorical subjects. *Address:* The Museum, Valletta, Malta.

Died 31 Oct. 1947.

SCLATER, Mrs Charlotte Seymour, CBE 1917; RRC; late Hon. Secretary of Queen Alexandra's Fund; *b* 1858; *d* of late William Proctor Mellen; *m* 1896, William Lutley Sclater. *Address:* 10 Sloane Court, SW3. *T:* Sloane 1846.

Died 7 Jan. 1942.

SCLATER, Very Rev. John Robert Paterson, MA (Cantab), DD (St Andrews, Scotland, Queen's University, Kingston, Ont, and Victoria University, Toronto); LLD University of Toronto; Moderator of the United Church of Canada, 1942–44; Chairman, United Church Commission on Re-Union, since 1943; Minister of Old St Andrew's Church, Toronto, United Church of Canada, since 1943; *b* 9 April 1876; *s* of Rev. John Sclater and Ellen Gentle Paterson; *m* 1904, Nora Christian, 3rd *d* of Surgeon-Major-General P. S. Turnbull, KHS; two *s* one *d*. *Educ:* Hulme Grammar School, Manchester; Owen's Coll.; Emmanuel College, Cambridge; Westminster Theological College. Minister of Greenhill Presbyterian Church, Derby, 1902–07; New North Church, Edinburgh, 1907–23; Parkdale Church, Toronto, 1923–24; Warrack Lecturer, Scotland, 1921; Lyman Beecher Lecturer, Yale University, 1927; Dudleian Lecturer, Harvard University, 1937; various other lectureships in Canada and the USA; member of the Board of Preachers, Harvard Univ., 1930–32, 1934–35 and 1937–42; select preacher at Harvard, 1923–45. President, Cambridge Union, 1899; Chaplain, 9th Batt. (Hrs), Royal Scots (TF), 1909–23; war service, Forth Defences and France (1915–17, YMCA); two War Office mentions. *Publications:* The Sons of Strength, 1909; The Enterprise of Life, 1911; Impressions of Principal Cairns, 1914; The Eve of Battle, 1915; Modernist Fundamentalism, 1926; The Public Worship of God, 1928; and various pamphlets and articles: (with Dr Norman Maclean) God and the Soldier, 1917. *Recreations:* golf, travel. *Address:* 23 Elm Avenue, Toronto, Ontario, Canada. *T:* Randolph 4754. *Clubs:* Arts and Letters, York (Toronto).

Died 24 Aug. 1949.

SCLATER, William Lutley; zoologist; Hon. Secretary Royal Geographical Society; *b* 23 Sept. 1863; *e s* of late Philip Lutley Sclater, FRS, and Jane Anne Eliza, *y d* of Sir David Hunter Blair, 3rd Bart; *m* 1896, Charlotte Seymour Sclater, CBE, RRC (*d* 1942). *Educ:* Winchester; Keble Coll., Oxford (MA 1st Class Natural Science, 1885). Assistant Master Eton College, 1891–95; Director of the South African Museum at Cape Town, 1896–1906; President of the British Ornithologists' Union, 1928–33; Editor of the Ibis, 1913–30; Editor of the Zoological Record, 1921–38. *Publications:* many papers in scientific journals; also volumes on the Mammals and Birds of South Africa, the Birds of Colorado and the Systema Avium Aethiopicarum; The Birds of Kenya and Uganda (with late Sir F. Jackson). *Address:* 10 Sloane Court, SW3. *T:* Sloane 1846. *Club:* Athenæum.

Died July 1944.

SCOTT, Alexander, FRS; DSc Edin.; ScD Camb.; Director of Scientific Research at the British Museum, 1919–38; *b* Selkirk, 28 Dec. 1853; *e s* of late Alexander Scott, Rector of Selkirk Grammar School; *m* 1906, Agnes Mary, *d* of the late Dr W. J. Russell, FRS. *Educ:* Selkirk Grammar School; Edinburgh University; Trinity College, Cambridge. Senior Medallist in Chemistry Class, Edinburgh University, 1875. Assistant to Jacksonian Professor, Cambridge, 1875; Clothworkers Exhibitioner in Physical Science, 1876; Foundation Scholarship, Trinity College, 1878; 1st class in Natural Science Tripos, 1879; Science Master, Durham School, 1884; Demonstrator to Jacksonian Professor, 1891; Hon. Sec. of Chemical Society, 1899–1904, Treasurer, 1904–15; President, 1915–17; Vice-President, 1917–24; Superintendent of Davy-Faraday Research Laboratory of the Royal Institution, London, 1896–1911. *Publications:* Introduction to Chemical Theory, 1891; 2nd ed. 1910; articles in publications of Royal and Chemical Societies, etc. *Recreations:* photography, foreign travel. *Address:* 117 Hamilton Terrace, NW8. *T:* Maida Vale 4154. *Club:* Athenæum.

Died 10 March 1947.

SCOTT, Maj.-Gen. Sir Arthur (Binny), KCB 1918; CB 1914; DSO 1902; *b* 3 Jan. 1862; *m* Aimée Byng, *d* of General Charles H. Hall. *Educ:* Cheltenham College; RMA, Woolwich. Entered army, 1881; Capt. 1889; Major, 1899; Lt-Col 1906; Bt Col 1906; Col 1911; Maj.-Gen. 1916; Adjt 1894–98; AAG 1906–10; served S Africa, 1899–1902 (despatches twice, Bt Lt-Col, Queen's medal 4 clasps, King's medal 2 clasps, DSO); commanded 18th Battery, RFA; P Battery, RHA; and a mobile column; European War, 1914–18; GOC, RA, Meerut Division; Major-General, RA, 3rd Army, 1915; GOC 12th (Eastern) Division, 1915–18 (1914 Star, despatches five times, promoted Maj.-Gen., KCB, Commandeur Légion d'Honneur); commanded Lucknow Division, India, 1918–20; retired, 1920. *Address:* Red Leys, Chesham Bois, Bucks. *T:* Amersham 429.

Died 2 July 1944.

SCOTT, Rev. Charles Anderson, DD; *b* 1859; *e s* of Arch. D. Scott, Manchester; *m* 1892, Jane (*d* 1939), *d* of J. Muir Leitch, London; one *s* two *d*. *Educ:* Uppingham School under Rev. Edward Thring (Captain of the School, 1878); St John's College, Cambridge; New College, Edinburgh; University of Leipsic and University of Jena. Minor Scholar and Naden Divinity Student, St John's College, Cambridge; Classical Tripos, 1882; Class II Div. I Hulsean prize, 1884; MA 1896; Hon. DD Aberdeen, 1912; DD Cambridge, 1920. Moderator of the Presbyterian Church of England, 1923; Hulsean Lecturer, 1928–30. After Studying in Germany

became assistant to Rev. George Adam Smith, Queen's Cross Church, Aberdeen, 1887–89; minister in the Presbyterian Church of England at College Park, Willesden, 1892; St John's, Kensington, 1898–1907; Dunn Professor of New Testament, Theological College of Presbyterian Church of England, 1907–32; Examiner in Historical Theology, University of London, 1902–07; Tripos Examiner at Cambridge. *Publications:* Ulfilas, Apostle of the Goths, 1885; Evangelical Doctrine, Bible Truth, 1901; Revelation in Century Bible, 1902; Making of a Christian, 1903; The Book of the Revelation, 1905; No. XI in Cambridge Biblical Essays, 1909; Dominus Noster, 1918; Chap. IV in The Spirit, 1919; The Fellowship of the Spirit, 1921; Christianity according to St Paul, 1927; New Testament Ethics, 1930; Living Issues in the New Testament, 1933; Footnotes to St Paul, 1935; St Paul, The Man and the Teacher, 1936; Romanism and the Gospel, 1937; contributions to Encyclopædia Britannica, etc. *Address:* 165 Huntingdon Road, Cambridge. *T:* Cambridge 5168.

Died 23 July 1941.

SCOTT, Canon Charles Harold, MA; Priest-Vicar of Lincoln Cathedral since 1901; Rector of St Mary Magdalene, Lincoln, since 1926; *b* Wrexham, N Wales, 1 Dec. 1871; *o s* of Thomas and Harriet Scott, Ash Grove, Wrexham; *m* Emily, *y d* of Charles F. Radcliffe, Bottesford, Nottingham; two *s*. *Educ:* Grove Park School, Wrexham; Jesus College, Oxford. Assistant Master, Rockley House, Southport, 1893–94; Curate of Great Crosby, Liverpool, 1894–96; Stony Stratford, 1896–97; Chaplain All Saints' Orphanage, Lewisham, 1897–98; Curate of Ilford, 1898–1901; Priest-Vicar of Lincoln Cathedral, 1901; Chaplain HM Prison, Lincoln, 1901–26; Canon 1915, Succentor 1903, and Provost, 1913, of Lincoln Cathedral; Rural Dean of Christianity, 1931–35; has taken an active part in work of the Borstal Association and Societies for helping Discharged Prisoners; Grand Chaplain of England (United Grand Lodge of England), 1922. *Recreations:* cycling, music; has conducted many Choral and Orchestral Societies; Conductor of Lincoln Operatic Society for 16 years and Lincoln Orchestral Society for last 14 years, West Lindsey Musical Festival, etc. *Address:* Vicars' Court, Lincoln. *T:* Lincoln 1204.

Died 12 Aug. 1940.

SCOTT, Col Charles Inglis, CMG 1918; *b* 1866; *s* of James Scott (*d* 1884), of Kelly, Renfrewshire, DL; *m* Mary (*d* 1924), *d* of late Lt-Col W. Inglis, 5th Dragoon Guards. Served in 3rd Dragoon Guards; served S African War, 1899–1902 (despatches, Queen's medal and two clasps, King's medal and two clasps). *Address:* The House of Urrard and Druimuan, Killiecrankie, Perthshire. *Club:* Army and Navy.

Died 14 Oct. 1941.

SCOTT, Charles Paley; KC 1933; Barrister-at-law; Recorder of Leeds since 1943; Chancellor of the County Palatine of Durham, 1936; Chancellor of the Diocese of Bradford, 1946; *b* 17 June 1881; *s* of late H. V. Scott and Jane Dorothy Paley, of York; *m* 1912, Ruth, *d* of Canon Cooper Scott of Chester; two *s* (and eldest died in Malaya in War of 1939–45). *Educ:* St Peter's School, York; King's College, Cambridge. Called to Bar, Inner Temple, 1906, went NE Circuit; Bencher, 1930; Recorder of Doncaster, 1923–33; Recorder of Kingston-upon-Hull, 1933–43; joined the Army, 1917; Commissioned Feb. 1918; France, April 1918–Feb. 1919. *Address:* 19 Rotherwick Road, Golders Green, NW11. *T:* Speedwell 2971. *Club:* United University.

Died 30 Jan. 1950.

SCOTT, David Robert; KC 1934; Sheriff-Substitute of Ayrshire at Ayr since 1938; *s* of late James Mackenzie Illingworth Scott, Solicitor, Aberdeen, and late M. E. M. Wright; *m* Marguerite Leontine Boissonnet. *Educ:* Walker's Academy, Aberdeen; University of Edinburgh.

First prizeman in Scots Law and other law classes, Thow Scholar and bracketed Muirhead and Forensic Prizeman. Admitted as Solicitor, 1908 (aged 21); Advocate, 1914; Junior Counsel in Scotland to HM Postmaster-General, 1932–34; Hon. Sheriff-Substitute Lanarkshire and Ayrshire, 1937. *Publications:* numerous articles in Encyclopædia of the Laws of Scotland and other publications concerning Scots Law. *Address:* County Buildings, Ayr.

Died 28 Jan. 1943.

SCOTT, Duncan Campbell, CMG 1934; LittD; FRSL; FRSC; *b* 2 Aug. 1862; *s* of Rev. William Scott, Methodist Church; parents English and Scotch; *m* 1st, 1894, Belle W. Botsford (*d* 1929), American violinist, *d* of late Geo. W. Botsford, Boston, Mass; 2nd, Desirée Elise, *d* of Henry Aylen, KC, Ottawa. *Educ:* Canadian Common Schools; Stanstead College. Entered Canadian Civil Service, 1879; rapidly promoted through all grades; Deputy Superintendent General, Department of Indian Affairs, retired 1932; Hon. Secretary Royal Society of Canada, 1910–21; President, 1921. *Publications:* The Magic House (poems); Labor and the Angel (poems); In the Village of Viger (fiction); The Life of Simcoe (Makers of Canada); New World Lyrics and Ballads; Lundy's Lane, and other poems; Beauty and Life (a book of poems); The Witching of Elspie (short stories); Complete Poems, 1926; The Green Cloister, later poems, 1935; The Circle of Affection, A Miscellany of Prose and Verse, 1947; numerous short stories and poems in American and Canadian magazines; Joint-Editor with Pelham Edgar, PhD, of Makers of Canada, a series of historical biography. *Address:* 108 Lisgar Street, Ottawa. *Club:* Country (Ottawa).

Died 19 Dec. 1947.

SCOTT, Rev. Edward Anderson Seymour, MA; late Rector of Morecambe; late Hon. Canon of Blackburn; *b* 1865; *s* of David Wardlaw Scott and Sarah Emily Habershon; *m* 1896, Katharine Lillias Steuart; one *s* three *d*. *Educ:* Queens' College, Cambridge. *Publication:* What Happens after Death? *Address:* Hest Bank Lodge, Lancaster. *T:* Hest Bank 292. *Club:* Overseas.

Died 5 May 1941.

SCOTT, Major Finlay Forbes, CBE 1918. *Educ:* Ardingly College. Superintendent of the Line, London, Brighton and South Coast Railway, 1907–24; Major, Engineer and Railway Staff Corps. *Recreation:* golf. *Address:* Clydesdale, Altyre Road, Croydon. *T:* Croydon 1747.

Died 21 Feb. 1949.

SCOTT, Sir Francis Montagu Sibbald, 5th Bt *cr* 1806, of Dunninald, Forfarshire; late Lieutenant 3rd Royal Scots (Lothian Regt); *b* 23 July 1885; *s* of 4th Bt and Jane Catharine, *d* of late A. A. Pearson of Luce, Dumfriesshire; *S* father, 1906; *m* 1915, Gladys, *y d* of late Captain Rolt, Coldstream Guards, and *widow* of H. F. Taylor; one *d*. *Educ:* Clifton College. Tea-planting in Ceylon for seven years (Eastern Produce and Estates Co., Ltd). *Heir:* none. *Address:* The Oasthouse, Harrietsham, Kent.

Died 10 Aug. 1945 (ext).

SCOTT, Ven. Frederick George, CMG 1916; DSO 1918; MA, DD, LLD, DCL, FRSC; Rector of St Matthew's, Quebec, 1899; Canon of Quebec Cathedral, 1906; Archdeacon of Quebec, 1925–33; *b* Montreal, 1861; *s* of late William Edward Scott, MD, of Montreal, Professor of Anatomy, McGill University, for nearly forty years, and Elizabeth Sproston, both parents of English birth; *m* 1887, Amy, *d* of late George Brooks, Barnet, England; six *s* one *d*. *Educ:* Montreal High School; Proprietary School, McGill; Bishop's College, Lennoxville; King's College, London. Deacon, 1884; Master in St John's School, 1884; priest, 1886; curate of Coggeshall, Essex, 1886; rector of Drummondville, Quebec, 1887; curate of St Matthew's, Quebec, 1896;

FRSC, 1900; late Sen. Chaplain 1st Canadian Div. BEF (wounded, despatches four times, CMG, DSO); Sandford Gold Medal, Royal Canadian Humane Society, 1898. *Publications:* Soul's Quest, and other Poems, 1888; Elton Hazlewood, 1892; My Lattice, and other Poems, 1894; The Unnamed Lake, and other Poems, 1897; Poems Old and New, 1900; The Hymn of Empire and other Poems, 1906; The Key of Life, 1907; Poems, 1910; In the Battle Silences, and other Poems written at the Front, 1916; The Great War as I Saw It, 1922; In Sun and Shade: a book of Poems, 1926; New Poems, 1929; Selected Poems, 1933; Collected Poems, 1934; Poems, 1936; sundry short stories and pamphlets, etc. *Address:* Château St Louis, Quebec, Canada. *Clubs:* Canadian Military Institute, Toronto; Garrison, Quebec.

Died 19 Jan. 1944.

SCOTT, Lord George (William Montagu-Douglas-), OBE; late MFH Duke of Buccleuch's hounds; *b* 31 Aug. 1866; 3rd *s* of 6th Duke of Buccleuch; *m* 1903, Lady Elizabeth Manners (*d* 1924), *y d* of 7th Duke of Rutland; two *s* three *d*. *Educ:* Eton; Christ Church, Oxford. Entered 10th Hussars, 1889; Captain, 1897; served South Africa, 1899–1900; left the Army, 1902; O/C 2/1st Lothians and Border Horse until Jan. 1919, when gazetted out as Lt-Col. *Publications:* The Labrador dog, his home and history; Gronse Land, 1937; The Fleeting Opportunity, 1940. *Address:* Kirklands, Ancrum, Scotland. *Clubs:* Turf, Naval and Military; New Edinburgh.

Died 23 Feb. 1947.

SCOTT, Col Lord Henry (Francis Montagu-Douglas-); *b* 15 Jan. 1868; 4th *s* of 6th Duke of Buccleuch. *Educ:* Eton; Christ Church, Oxford, MA. Captain Royal Company of Archers, King's Body Guard for Scotland; served as Major in 3rd Battalion the Royal Scots during the South African War, 1900–02 (both medals); commanded the Battalion, 1905–12; Hon. Col of the Battalion since that date; served in European War, France, 1915–19, (despatches 5 times); contested (U) Roxburghshire, Jan. 1910; Chairman Life Association of Scotland; Deputy Governor Bank of Scotland. *Address:* Gledswood, Melrose, Scotland. *T:* St Boswells 27. *Clubs:* New, Edinburgh.

Died 19 April 1945.

SCOTT, Lord Herbert (Andrew Montagu-Douglas-), CMG 1916; DSO 1900; DL Co. of London, 1931; Hon. Air Commodore 949th Squadron RAF 1940; Lieut-Colonel Irish Guards, retired; Lt-Col TF, retired; *b* 30 Nov. 1872; 5th *s* of 6th Duke of Buccleuch; *m* 1905, Marie Josephine, *y d* of late James Edwards; one *s* two *d*. *Educ:* Eton; Trinity Hall, Cambridge. Entered Militia, 1890; 3rd Bn The Royal Scots; transferred to Irish Guards on formation, 1900; retired as Captain, 1907; ADC to Sir Arthur Havelock, Governor of Madras (India), 1896–98; ADC, Earl Roberts, KG (Commander-in-Chief, Ireland), 1899. ADC to General Sir Charles Mansfield Clarke, Governor and Commander-in-Chief, Malta, 1903–04; served South Africa as ADC to Field-Marshal Earl Roberts, KG, 1899–1901, and with the Guards Mounted Infantry, 1901–02 (despatches, Queen's South African medal with 8 clasps, DSO); European War, 1914–18 (CMG, despatches twice); Brevet Lt-Col R. of O. (Irish Guards) 1918; Commanded 23rd County of London Regt (Territorials) in France, 1915 (despatches); AMS in France and with Mediterranean Expeditionary Force, 1915–16 (despatches); DAMS, War Office, 1916–18; King George V Coronation Medal, 1910; Silver Jubilee Medal, 1935; Coronation Medal, 1937; Knight of Justice, St John of Jerusalem, 1914; Croix d'Officier, Légion d'Honneur, France, 1917; Member of the King's Bodyguard for Scotland (Royal Company of Archers), 1912; Member of HM's Bodyguard The Gentlemen-at-Arms, 1922–35; Member of Advisory Council Board of Trade, 1934–37; President the London Chamber of Commerce, 1928–31; Vice-Pres. the Assoc. Chambers of Commerce, since 1931; Chairman the London Chamber of Commerce Education Committee, 1934–43; President Federation of British Industries, 1934–35; President Royal Warrant Holders Association, 1936; Chairman of Rolls-Royce, Ltd; Director of Sun Life and Fire Offices, Tilbury Contracting and Dredging Company, and United Glass Bottle Manufacturers, Ltd; Continental Union Trust Co. Ltd Chairman Westinghouse Brakes and Signals, Ltd. *Address:* Shroner Wood, Martyr Worthy, Winchester, Hants. *T:* Winchester 2803. *Clubs:* White's, International Sportsmen's, MCC.

Died 17 June 1944.

SCOTT, James Cospatrick Hepburne-; Chamberlain to the Duke of Roxburghe; *b* 1882; *o surv. s* of late Hon. H. R. Scott and late Lady Ada Scott, 2nd *d* of 11th Earl of Home; *m* 1907, Lady Isobel Alice Adelaide Kerr, *y d* of 9th Marquess of Lothian; three *s*. *Address:* Broomlands, Kelso.

Died 20 July 1942.

SCOTT, Sir John, KBE 1932; CMG 1923; *b* 24 April 1878; *e s* of late Canon John Scott of Hull, Leeds, and Wanstead; *m* 1905, Mary Kathrine (*d* 1941), *d* of late Francis Adams of Greswold, Worcestershire; no *c*. *Educ:* Leeds Grammar School; Bath College; King's College, Cambridge. Ceylon Civil Service, 1901–21; Deputy Chief Secretary to the Government of Nigeria, 1921–24; Chief Secretary, Tanganyika Territory, 1924–29; Colonial Secretary Straits Settlements, 1929–33; retired. *Address:* The Manor House, Hartford, Huntingdon.

Died 19 Jan. 1946.

SCOTT, John Gordon Cameron, CIE 1933; Principal, Prince of Wales's Royal Indian Military College since 1921; *b* 14 March 1888; *s* of Rev. H. von E. Scott, South Lynn, Eastbourne, Sussex; *m* Audrey, *d* of Col J. Scully; one *d*. *Educ:* Marlborough; Pembroke College, Cambridge. Mediæval and Modern Languages Tripos, 1911. Assistant Master, Daly College, Indore, 1912. *Recreations:* cricket, golf, shooting, etc. *Address:* Prince of Wales's Royal Indian Military Coll., Dehra Dun, UP, India. *Clubs:* MCC. Free Foresters, etc.

Died 21 March 1946.

SCOTT, John Russell; Chairman and Governing Director of The Manchester Guardian and Evening News Ltd; *b* 12 July 1879; *s* of Charles Prestwich Scott and Rachel Susan Cook; *m* 1908, Olga, *y d* of late Archibald Briggs, Wakefield; two *s* two *d*. *Educ:* Rugby; Trinity College, Cambridge; Massachusetts Institute of Technology. *Address:* The Croft, Dean Row, Wilmslow, Manchester. *T:* Wilmslow 3327. *Clubs:* National Liberal, Press, Reform (Manchester).

Died 5 April 1949.

SCOTT, Lady (Kathleen); *see* Kennet, Lady.

SCOTT, Rt Hon. Sir Leslie (Frederic), PC 1927; Kt 1922; *b* 29 Oct. 1869; *e s* of late Sir John Scott, KCMG; *m* 1898, Ethel, *d* of late H. A. James, Cheltenham; no *c*. *Educ:* Rugby (Scholar); New College, Oxford (Exhibitioner; Hon. Fellow, 1939). Northern Circuit, 1894; Solicitor-General, 1922; a Lord Justice of Appeal, 1935–48; MP (C) Liverpool Exchange, 1910–29; Prés. d'Honneur of Comité Maritime Internat., 1947; represented HM's Government at International Conferences on Maritime Law, Brussels, 1909, 1910, 1922, and 1926; Chairman of the Agricultural Organisation Society, 1917–22; of the Acquisition of Land Committee, 1917–19, whose reports led to the Acquisition of Land (Compensation) Act 1919, the Mines (Working Facilities) Act, 1923, and the new Law of Property Acts, 1925; and (from 2 May 1931) of the Cttee on Ministers' Powers (reported March 1932); also of the Cttee, 1941–42, upon Land Utilisation in Rural Areas; Pres. Nat. Assoc. of Parish Councils and of Berks County Assoc.; Pres. and Chm. from start in 1914 of

Central Assoc. for Mental Welfare, till 1947 (when it was Nat. Assoc. for Mental Health); member Exec. CPRE, and Chm. Berks Branch; Grand Croix of Order of Leopold II of Belgium, 1926. *Publication:* The New Law of Property Acts (with Bertram Benas). *Recreations:* country life, painting. *Address:* The Red House, Sotwell, Wallingford, Berks. *T:* Wallingford 2229. *Clubs:* United University, Alpine.

Died 19 May 1950.

SCOTT, Mackay Hugh Baillie, FRIBA, MRAC; architect; *b* 1865; *m* Florence Kate Nash (*d* 1939); one *d*. *Educ:* privately; Royal Agricultural College, Cirencester. *Principal Works:* Houses in Germany, Poland, Russia, America, Switzerland, Roumania, etc., including furnishing and decorating palace at Darmstadt for Grand Duke of Hesse and Le Nid for Queen of Roumania; also houses at Windermere, Sunningdale, Gerrards Cross, Regent's Park, Cambridge, Hamble, Chilham, Limpsfield, Albrighton (Salop), Helensburgh, Dundee, Cardiff, Falmouth, Sidmouth, Sherborne, etc.; Village Halls at Iwerne Minster, Hardingham, etc.; Flats, Waterlow Court, Hampstead Garden Suburb, and Victoria Road, Kensington. *Publications:* Houses and Gardens, 1906; (with A. E. Beresford) Houses and Gardens, 1933; articles in the Studio and other periodicals; lectures at Carpenters' Hall and Royal Society of Arts. *Address:* Kensington Palace Mansions, De Vere Gardens, W8.

Died 10 Feb. 1945.

SCOTT, Rear-Adm. Malcolm Maxwell-, DSO 1917; RN; *b* 22 Oct. 1883; 3rd *s* of late Hon. J. C. and late Mrs Maxwell Scott of Abbotsford; *m* 1918, Fearga, *d* of late Sir Nicholas O'Conor; two *s* one *d*. *Educ:* Downside and Beaumont Colleges. Joined HMS Britannia, 1898; Lieut RN 1905; Lieut-Comdr 1913; Capt. 1925; Rear-Adm. 1936; served European War (despatches, DSO, prom. Comdr, Croix de Guerre); Capt.-Supt of Contract Built Ships, 1929–31; Capt. in Charge, HM Naval Base, Singapore, 1932–34; retired list, 1936. *Recreations:* shooting, fishing, games. *Club:* Naval and Military.

Died 23 Feb. 1943.

SCOTT, Maj.-Gen. Robert Kellock, CB 1919; CMG 1917; DSO 1902; *b* 29 Nov. 1871; 3rd *s* of Colonel Thomas Scott of Winnipeg, Canada; *m* 1899, Edith, 2nd *d* of G. Ferris W. Mortimer, Romsey; one *s*. *Educ:* RM College, Kingston, Canada. Entered army, 1891; Captain, RA 1899; Brevet Major, 1902; transferred to Army Ordnance Department, 1903; Lt-Col 1907; Maj.-Gen. 1924; served South Africa, 1899–1902 (despatches twice, brevet of Major, Queen's medal 3 clasps, King's medal 2 clasps, DSO); seconded for service with Canadian Militia, 1907; Principal Ordnance Officer, Canada, 1908; Chief Ordnance Officer, Bermuda, 1910–14; Assistant Director, Ordnance Department, War Office, 1914; European War in France and Flanders (CB); East African Force (CMG); Principal Ordnance Officer, 1924–27; retired pay, 1928. *Address:* Kingsburgh, L'Erée, Guernsey, CI.

Died 21 Feb. 1942.

SCOTT, Sir Samuel (Edward), 6th Bt *cr* 1821; DL; MP (C) West Marylebone, 1898; for the whole of Marylebone (East and West Marylebone now made one constituency), Dec. 1918–22; *b* 25 Oct. 1873; *s* of 5th Bart and Emilie (*d* 1922), *y d* of Lt-Col Henry Packe, Twyford Hall, Norfolk (she *m* 2nd, 1st Viscount Farquhar); *S* father, 1883; *m* 1896, Lady Sophie Beatrix Mary Cadogan, CBE 1917 (*d* 1937), *d* of 5th Earl Cadogan. *Educ:* Eton; Sandhurst. Lt Royal Horse Guards, 1894–96; served S Africa, 1899–1900; Major Royal West Kent Yeomanry to Feb. 1917, now Major Royal Horse Guards; served Gallipoli and Egypt. Owns about 2000 acres. *Heir: c* Robert Claude Scott [*b* 25 Oct. 1886; *m* 1920, Janet Foster, *y d* of late John Turner, Dalmelling, Ayr]. *Address:* Redenham House, Andover,

Hants. *T:* Weyhill 228; Amhuinnsuidh, North Harris, Scotland. *Clubs:* Turf, White's, Jockey; Royal Yacht Squadron, Cowes.

Died 21 Feb. 1943.

SCOTT, Sebastian Gilbert; Hon. Radiologist to British Red Cross Clinic for Treatment of Rheumatism, Peto Place and Charterhouse Rheumatism Clinic; Director of Nuffield Wide Field X-ray Research; Consulting Radiologist to the London Hospital and Queen Alexandra's Military Hospital; Member of Army X-ray Advisory Committee; late Radiologist to LCC Mental Hospitals; late President Royal Society of Medicine, Section of Electrotherapeutics; late Director of the Radiological Department at the London Hospital; *b* Hampstead, 1879; *s* of George Gilbert Scott, *g s* of Sir Gilbert Scott (Architects); *m* Alice O'Hara (Australia); two *s* two *d. Educ:* Beaumont College, Windsor. MRCS, LRCP Lond., 1904; DMRE (Camb.), 1921; Medical College; King's College Hospital. House Surgeon at King's College Hospital, 1905; House Physician Royal Free Hospital, 1906; Consulting Radiologist at National Hospital for Diseases of Heart. *Publications:* Charterhouse Rheumatism Clinic Original Papers, 1937; Radiological Atlas of Chronic Rheumatic Arthritis (The Hand), 1935; Radiology in Relation to Medical Jurisprudence, 1931; Case of X-ray Dermatitis with Fatal Termination, Archives of Röntgen Ray, 1911; Cervical Ribs seen Radiographically, BMJ, 1912; Dual Radiotherapy in Malignant Disease, BMJ, 1921; Present Day Value of the Opaque Meal Examination, Lancet, 1922; A Method for the Opaque Meal Examination of the Stomach, Archives of Radiology and Electrology, 1923; Method of Treating Asthma by Radiation, BMJ, 5 June 1926, and BMJ, 5 Jan. 1929; Diverticulum of Duodenum, BMJ, 28 Feb. 1931. *Recreations:* cricket, tennis. *Address:* 86 Brook Street, W1. *T:* Mayfair 5001; Brook House, Bourne End, Bucks. *T:* Bourne End 70.

Died 19 April 1941.

SCOTT, William Berryman, PhD, ScD, LLD; Blair Professor of Geology and Palæontology (now Emeritus) Princeton University, New Jersey, 1884–1930; *b* 1858; *s* of Rev. William M. Scott, DD; *m* 1883, Alice A. Post; four *d. Educ:* Princeton; Royal School of Mines, South Kensington; Cambridge Heidelberg (PhD). Assistant in Geology, Princeton University, 1880; Assistant Professor 1882; conducted several geological exploring expeditions in the western US; Past President American Philosophical Society, 1918–25; Member of National Academy of Sciences of US; Hon. Member Acad. Nat. Sci.; Philadelphia; NY Acad. Sci.; Past President Geological Society of America; Member Geological, Zoological, and Linnæan Societies of London; Hon. LLD University of Pennsylvania, 1906; Hon. ScD Harvard, 1909; Oxford, 1912; Princeton, 1930; E. K. Kane Medal, Geog. Soc., Philad., 1906; Wollaston Medal, Geological Society of London, 1910; Hayden Medal, Acad. Nat. Sci., 1926; Mary Clark Thompson Medal, National Academy of Sciences, 1930; Penrose Medal, Geolog. Soc., America, 1940; D. G. Elliot Medal, National Academy of Sciences; Walker Grand Prize, Boston Society of Natural History, 1934. *Publications:* An Introduction to Geology, 1897, 3rd ed. 1932; A History of Land Mammals in the Western Hemisphere, 1913, 2nd edn 1937; The Theory of Evolution, 1917; Physiography, 1922; Editor and Joint Author of Reports of the Princeton University Expeditions to Patagonia, 8 vols; some sixty monographs on Palæontological subjects; Monograph of White River Mammalia, Part I, Insectivora and Carnivora, 1935; Part II, Rodentia, 1937; Part IV, Artiodactyla, 1940; Part V, Perissodactyla, 1941 (with G. L. Jepsen and A. E. Wood); Some Memories of a Palæontologist, 1939; Mammalian Fauna of the Duchesne River Oligocene, 1943. *Recreations:* travel, gardening. *Address:* 7 Cleveland

Lane, Princeton, New Jersey, USA. *T:* 270; Cataumet, Mass. *T:* 485, Dodge Sedan. *Clubs:* Ivy, Nassau, Princeton; Princeton, Philadelphia.

Died 29 March 1947.

SCOTT-KERR, Brig.-Gen. Robert, CB 1914; CMG 1919; DSO 1900; MVO 1908; commanded 4th (Guards) Brigade at the beginning of the European War (severely wounded during the retreat from Mons); *b* 8 Nov. 1859; *e s* of late William Scott-Kerr of Sunlaws and Chatto, and 2nd wife, Frances Louisa, *d* of Robert Fennessy; *m* Isabel Margaret (*d* 1927). Entered army, 1879; Captain, 1890; Major, 1896; Col 1907; served Zulu War, 1879 (medal with clasp); Soudan Campaign, 1885 (medal with clasp, Khedive's star); S Africa, 1900–02 (despatches, Queen's medal 3 clasps, King's medal 2 clasps, DSO); European War, 1914–15 (despatches twice, Mons star, CMG). *Address:* Sunlaws, Kelso.

Died 25 Nov. 1942.

SCOTT O'CONNOR, Thomas Arthur Leslie, CIE 1929; late Indian Police Service; *b* 10 Jan. 1878. Joined Indian Police Service, 1901; Deputy Inspector-General of Police, United Provinces, 1925; retired 1932.

Died 6 April 1944.

SCOTT-OWEN, Col Arthur Lewis, CBE 1941; Mining Engineer and Officer commanding No. 3 Group Durham Home Guard and Sector Commander, Houghton le Spring Sector, Durham Area; *b* 1 June 1885; *m* 1917, Aileen Forster, Worcestershire; one *s. Educ:* Rugby School. Mining; Royal Engineers, European War, 1914–18. *Recreation:* all sports. *Address:* Eppleton Hall, Hetton le Hole, Co. Durham. *TA:* Hetton le Hole. *T:* Hetton le Hole 77. *Clubs:* Sunderland, Sunderland.

Died 2 Oct. 1944.

SCOTT-SMITH, Sir Henry, Kt 1924; *b* 6 May 1865; *s* of late Rev. F. Smith, Priest Chaplain, Holy Trinity, Stratford-on-Avon; *m* Aimée (*d* 1942), *d* of Dr Edward Smith of Londonderry; (one *s d* at Gallipoli, 1915), one *d. Educ:* Trinity Coll., Stratford-on-Avon; Keble College, Oxford. Entered ICS 1886; Judge Chief Court, Punjab, 1914; Judge, High Court, Punjab, 1919–25; Acting Chief Justice, June–July 1924; retired, May 1925. *Recreations:* golf and motoring. *Address:* The Holt, Camberley. *T:* Camberley 590.

Died 28 June 1950.

SCOVELL, Lt-Col George Julian Selwyn, CBE 1919; *e surv. s* of late Captain G. T. Scovell, 79th Highlanders; unmarried. *Educ:* Haileybury; Sandhurst. Joined QO Cameron Highlanders, 1900; served South African War, 1901–02, Adjutant 1st Batt. 1908–10; ADC to GOC 2nd Division, Aldershot, 1910–11; Private Secretary to Directors of British South African Company, 1911–14; General Staff, Northern Command, York, 1914–16; Assistant Adjutant-General, War Office, 1916–17; Deputy Director-General of Recruiting, Ministry of National Service, 1917–18; General Secretary National Liberal Party, 1919–22; contested Broxtowe Division, General Election, 1923; Chairman: Demolition and Construction Co., PCS Ltd; Rosterman Gold Mines Ltd; Swaziland and General Gold Mining Co. Ltd; Director, Alpine (Barberton) Gold Mine Ltd. *Address:* 26 Ashley Gardens, SW1. *Clubs:* Brooks's, Royal Automobile.

Died 16 April 1948.

SCRIMGEOUR, John Stuart, OBE 1924; KC 1945; *b* 3 Feb. 1887; *e s* of late William Douglas Scrimgeour, Dundee, and Margaret Susan Stewart; *m* 1914, Lilian Maud, *d* of late John Elias Bree, Fauvic, Jersey, CI; one *d. Educ:* Harris Academy, Dundee; University College, Dundee; Edinburgh University. Practised at Canadian Bar, 1911–16; Ministry of Munitions and Disposal and Liquidation Commission, 1917–22; called to Bar,

Middle Temple, 1922; practised since. *Recreation:* fishing. *Address:* 5 Paper Buildings, Temple, EC4. *T:* Central 1350; Aldermaston, Berks. *Club:* Oriental.

Died 30 Aug. 1950.

SCROPE, Henry Aloysius; *b* 3 Jan. 1862; *e surv. s* of late Simon Thomas Scrope and Emily Jane, 3rd *d* of late Robert Berkeley of Spetchley, Worcestershire; *m* 1899, Maria Mercedes, *y d* of Alexander de Laski and Joaquina, Marques de Souza Lisboa; four *s* two *d. Educ:* Stonyhurst College. *Heir: e s* of Richard (*m* 1934. Lady Jane Mary Egerton, 2nd *d* of 4th Earl of Ellesmere). *Address:* 147 Cranmer Court, Sloane Avenue, SW3. *T:* Kensington 7307.

Died 27 April 1950.

SCRYMGEOUR, Edwin; JP; Chaplain for East House and Maryfield Hospital, 1933; *b* Dundee, 28 July 1866; *s* of late James Scrymgeour, Pioneer of Scottish Temperance Movement, and Jeanette Calman, late co-operator in social service, Newport-on-Tay; *m* 1892, Margaret Croston, and has all along been ably and enthusiastically supported by her in the Prohibition Party Movement; no *c. Educ:* West End Academy, Dundee. Devoted earliest years of manhood largely to commercial career, but gradually accompanying same by service in the arena of public representation—Parish Council, Town Council, and latterly undergoing six Parliamentary contests in Dundee, specially with the view of advancing the Prohibition cause through inaugurating the Prohibition Party there in Nov. 1901; MP (Prohibition) Dundee, 1922–31; has devoted his whole time to the work for about 30 years. *Publications:* Pamphlets: Parish Council Experiences; The Unanswered Case for Prohibition; The Temperance Runaways, or Britain's Great Retreat; The Temperance Scotland Act: An Insult to Democracy and National Disgrace; Our National Wastage and its Stoppage. *Address:* 2 Errol Terrace, Dundee.

Died 1 Feb. 1947.

SCULLY, Major Vincent Joseph, DSO 1918; CF; Senior Chaplain (RC); *b* London, April 1876. *Educ:* College of Canons Regular of the Lateran. Priest, 1899; pastoral work in Dorsetshire and Cornwall; temporary commission as CF June 1915; 3rd class, Dec. 1916 (despatches twice, wounded, Nov. 1917, DSO); relinquished Commission, March 1919; Médaille du Roi Albert, 1920. *Publications:* Life of the Venerable Thomas à Kempis; A Medieval Mystic, B. John Ruysbroeck; Life of St Lyduine, Virgin; other translations from à Kempis, etc. *Recreation:* chess. *Address:* St Augustine's, Hoddesdon, Herts.

Died 12 Nov. 1941.

SCULLY, Lt-Col Vincent Marcus Barron, DSO 1918; OBE 1918; late Border Regiment; *b* 1881; *s* of late Vincent Scully, Mantlehill, Golden, Co. Tipperary, formerly DL, JP Co. Tipperary (High Sheriff, 1870); *m* 1st, 1924, Pleasance (marr. diss. 1938), *widow* of Lt-Col C. E. Johnston, DSO, MC; 2nd, Mrs Sybil de la Poer Cazenove, *née* Beresford. *Educ:* Oratory School. Served in South African Defence Forces, Permanent Forces (Staff Captain, 1912–13) resigned 1913; War of 1914–19, in Gallipoli, Serbia, Macedonia, Palestine, and France (wounded twice, despatches four times, torpedoed HMT Arcadian, 1917); Commanded 10th Bn Hampshire Regt in Macedonia and Serbia, 1915, and 5th Bn Cannaught Rangers in Macedonia, Palestine and France; White Eagle 4th Class (Serbia); invalided out of army as result of wounds, 1924; Assistant ARP Officer, Hants. *Address:* Clifton Lodge, Winchester. *Club:* Army and Navy.

Died 13 Dec. 1941.

SCURFIELD, Harold, MD, CM (Edin.), DPH; late Professor of Public Health, University of Sheffield; *b* 1863; *s* of George and Janetta Scurfield, Sunderland; *m* 1st, 1891, Charlotte Augusta, *d* of Maj.-Gen. G. F. C.

Bray; no *c*; 2nd, 1901, Mary Louisa, *d* of Henry Montague Bazeley, Bideford; four *s* four *d. Educ:* Birkenhead School; Edinburgh University. House Surgeon, Eccles and Patricroft, and Birkenhead Borough Hospitals; Medical Officer to the Post Office, and Surgeon and Agent to the Admiralty for Sunderland; Medical Officer of Health, County Borough and Port of Sunderland; Medical Officer of Health, City of Sheffield, 1904–21; Examiner Preventive Medicine and Public Health, University of Oxford, 1910–13; Reporter on Tuberculosis in the British Isles, International Tuberculosis Congress, Rome, 1912; Examiner in Public Health, University of Sheffield, 1933–35. *Publications:* Infant and Young Child Welfare, the English Public Health Series, 1919; Translated Prof. Nocard's Les Tuberculoses Animales; articles in British Medical Journal, etc. *Address:* 15 Turketel Road, Folkestone.

Died 8 Feb. 1941.

SEABROOK, William; author; *b* Westminster, Maryland, 22 Feb. 1886; *s* of Rev. William L. Seabrook and Myra Phelps; *m* 1st, 1912, Katherine Edmondson; 2nd, 1935, Marjorie Muir Worthington; 3rd, 1942, Constance Kuhr; one *s. Educ:* Mercersburg Academy; University of Geneva, Switzerland, PhB and AM. Journalist and Foreign Correspondent, 1898–1934; Explorer, Adventurer, and Author since 1934. Arabia, Kurdistan, Turkestan, Africa, including Sahara, Haiti, etc.; served European War with the French, 1915; gassed at Verdun in 1916 (Cited Croix de Guerre). *Publications:* Adventures in Arabia, 1927; The Magic Island, 1930; Jungle Ways, 1931; Air Adventure, 1933; The White Monk of Timbuctoo, 1934; Asylum, 1935; Foreign Americans, 1937; Theory of Witchcraft, 1939; Biography of a Scientist, 1940 (Biography of Robert Williams Wood, FRS); No Hiding Place (an autobiography), 1942; Negroes in America, 1944. *Recreations:* tennis, golf, chess, fishing, sailing, and the collection of African masks. *Address:* c/o George G. Harrap & Co., 182 High Holborn, WC2; Rhinebeck, NY. *TA:* Anwat NY.

Died 20 Sept. 1945.

SEABROOKE, Elliott; *b* Upton Park, Essex; *s* of Robert Elliott, late Superintendent of the King George V Docks, and Harriet Elizabeth Seabrooke; *m* 1930, Adolphine Christiana, *d* of Herbert Joosten, founder of the Concert Gebouw, Amsterdam. *Educ:* City of London School; Slade School. Early works painted in Epping Forest and the Lake District; later came visits to France, Italy and Holland; it is to the French School that he owes most of his influence, though his earlier enthusiasm was for the work of Constable, John Crome, and Richard Wilson; pictures in Tate Gallery, Dublin Art Gallery, Leeds University, Liverpool, and in many other provincial galleries; pictures and drawings have been bought by The Contemporary Art Society, and by Richard Sickert, Sir Edward Marsh, Earl of Sandwich, late Earl of Oxford, Sir Michael Sadler, Sir C. K. Butler, Lord Duveen, Laurence Housman, the late Havelock Ellis, and other private collectors. *Recreations:* kite-flying, coupled with study of cloud-forms. *Address:* 44 Baker St, W1. *T:* Welbeck 8062.

Died 6 March 1950.

SEAGER, Most Rev. Charles Allen, DD, LLD; Archbishop of Huron and Metropolitan of Ontario since 1944; *b* Goderich, Ont, Canada, 1872; *s* of Charles Seager; *m* Mary Lilian Paterson; one *s* three *d. Educ:* Trinity College, Toronto. Rector of St Cyprian's, Toronto, 1897–1911; Vernon, BC, 1911–12; Principal of St Mark's Divinity Hall, Vancouver, BC 1912–17; Rector of St Matthew's, Toronto, 1917–21; Provost and Vice-Chancellor, Univ. of Trinity College, Toronto, 1921–26; Prebendary and Chancellor of St Alban's Cathedral, Toronto; Bishop of Ontario, 1926–32;

Bishop of Huron, 1932–44. *Recreations:* fishing and motoring. *Address:* Bishopstowe, 150 St James Street, London, Ontario, Canada.

Died 9 Sept. 1948.

SEAGER, Sir William Henry, Kt 1918; DL, Glamorgan; JP Cardiff; *b* Cardiff, 1862; *s* of William Seager; *m* 1890, 2nd *d* of John Elliot, Woodfield, Newport Road, Cardiff; two *s* one *d.* Managing Director of W. H. Seager & Co., Ltd, 108–109–110 Bute Street, Cardiff, and Tempus Shipping Co.; Sir William Seager & Sons, Ltd; Director British Steamship Owners' Assoc. and North of England Protecting and Indemnity Association; Trustee of Cardiff Royal Infirmary; Past-President of the Chamber of Shipping of the United Kingdom; Governor Hamadryad Seamen's Hospital; late Chairman Cardiff Institute for the Blind; late President Cardiff and Bristol Channel Shipowners' Association; Past-Pres. Cardiff Chamber of Commerce (two years); Representative for the Cardiff Incorporated Chamber of Commerce on the Committee of Lloyd's Register of Shipping; High Sheriff, Monmouthshire, 1932–33; MP (CL) E Cardiff, Dec. 1918–22; Member of Executive Council of Shipping Federation; Chairman, Cardiff Pilotage Authority. *Address:* Lynwood, Newport Road, Cardiff. *TA:* Seager, Cardiff. *T:* Cardiff 3428 or 2720. *Club:* Cardiff Exchange.

Died 10 March 1941.

SEAMAN, Paymaster-Captain Tom, CMG 1918. RN; retired. *Address:* 9 Lansdowne Villas, Lansdowne Square, Rodwell, Weymouth.

Died 26 Feb. 1943.

SEARIGHT, Major Hugh fforde, DSO 1918; FRGS; *b* London, 9 June 1875; *m* 1918, Lilian Martinho; one *s.* *Educ:* Charterhouse; Royal Military College, Sandhurst. Joined 1st (King's) Dragoon Guards, 1895; served South African War, 1901–02 (Queen's medal with 5 clasps); Brigade-Major, Northern Nigeria, 1905–06; commanded Mounted Infantry N Nigeria, 1906–09 (despatches, medal and clasp); Reserve of Officers, 1910–14; acting Colonial Secretary, Falkland Islands, June–Sept. 1911 and Oct. 1912–March 1913; DAQMG Northern Command, 1915–16; 67th Division, 1916; 4th Division, France, 1917 (despatches, DSO, Allied and Victory medals); Ministry of National Service, i/c Administration Limerick Area. *Recreations:* hunting, shooting, cricket, football, and travel. *Clubs:* Army and Navy, MCC.

Died 5 Aug. 1942.

SEARLE, Col Frank, CBE 1919; DSO 1918; late Tank Corps; *m* Charlotte Louise (*d* 1944). Served European War, 1914–18 (despatches, CBE, DSO). *Address:* 6 Dunbar Road, Bournemouth.

Died 4 April 1948.

SEARS, John Edward, FRIBA; Editor, The Architect's Compendium; *b* 28 Nov. 1857; *s* of late Rev. Jas Sears, Baptist minister; *m* Selina Marianne, *d* of late Hugh Hansford Read; one *s.* *Educ:* private school; student of Royal Academy and University Coll. Member and Chairman of the Works Committee of the first Hendon School Board; late Member of the LCC for N Hackney and past Chairman of the Bridges and Housing Committees; MP (L) Cheltenham, 1906–10; has been identified with the work of the Free Churches and was one of the Members of the original Council of the Metropolitan Federation of Free Churches. *Recreation:* golf. *Address:* 11a Grosvenor Crescent, St Leonards-on-Sea. *T:* Hastings 3612.

Died 20 Jan. 1941.

SEDDON, Charles Norman, MA; *b* 18 Dec. 1870; *s* of Charles John Seddon, Liverpool, and Emily Washbourn, Gloucester; *m* Lucy Helena, *d* of J. F. M. Braga, Liverpool; one *s* two *d.* *Educ:* Liverpool College; Balliol College, Oxford. Joined the Indian Civil Service, 1891; held various appointments in the Bombay Presidency;

Settlement Commissioner, Bombay, 1913–15; Commissioner, Central Division, 1915–19; Reforms Commissioner, Bombay Presidency, 1920; temporary Executive Member of Council, Bombay, 1920; Member of the Council of State, India, Delhi, 1921; retired, 1921; on invitation of Maharaja Gaekwar became Revenue Minister, Baroda State, 1921–24; Lecturer in Persian and Marathi, Oxford University, 1924–37; Hon. MA Oxford University, 1926; MA by decree, 1928; President, Bombay Civil and Military Exam. Board, 1914–20; Hon. Secretary XVII International Congress of Orientalists, Oxford, 1928. *Publications:* An Elementary Marathi Grammar; A Chronicle of the Early Safawis; Miscellaneous Communications on Oriental subjects to Royal Asiatic Society. *Address:* 27 Northmoor Road, Oxford. *T:* Oxford 5651. *Clubs:* Union Society (Oxford); Western India (Poona).

Died 27 March 1950.

SEDDON, Harry Sterratt, CBE 1919; Director of Limited Companies; *b* Bolton, 1881; *s* of William Seddon; *m* 1930, Alice (*d* 1940), *d* of late William Flood, Batheaston, Somerset. *Educ:* Miles Platting Institute, Manchester. Entered Drapery Trade as a youth and later became head of several firms in this business; afterwards became interested in Tobacco Manufacturing; during the war was at Ministry of Munitions (Investigation of Accounts); Treasurer of Lancashire County War Comforts Association; and for several years Treasurer of Manchester Liberal Federation. *Recreations:* motoring, gardening. *Address:* 10 Hoxton Square, N1. *TA:* Trophy, London. *T:* Bishopsgate 1677. *Club:* National Liberal.

Died 6 Oct. 1944.

SEDGEFIELD, W. J., LittD; Emeritus Professor; *b* 1866. *Educ:* Christ's College, Cambridge. Smith Professor of English Language, Manchester University, 1913–31; retired, 1931.

Died 30 April 1945.

SEDGWICK, Rear-Adm. Cyril Gordon, CB 1942; retired; *b* 27 Nov. 1885; *s* of Rev. Gordon Sedgwick, Sherborne, Warwick; *m* 1909, Harriott Elsie, *d* of Capt. L. S. Dawson, RN. *Educ:* HMS Britannia. *Club:* United Service.

Died 28 June 1948.

SEDGWICK, Canon S. N., MA, RD; *b* 1 Sept. 1872; *s* of Richard and Emily Sedgwick; *m* 1896, Enid (*d* 1938); two *s.* *Educ:* King Edward's School, Birmingham; Emmanuel College, Cambridge. Curate, Holy Trinity, Stroud Green, 1895–97; Curate, Leatherhead, 1897–1905; Rector of Bishopstoke, 1905–22; Rector of Liss, 1922–34; Rector of Warnford, 1934–38; Hon. Canon of Portsmouth, 1935–41, Canon Emeritus since 1941; late Rural Dean of Petersfield; Member of Christian Cinema Council; Member of Religious Film Society; Composer and Producer of many musical comedies, and operas, produced by amateur Operatic Societies; Lecturer on Nature and literary subjects. Author of films, Barabbas, As we forgive, etc. *Publications:* British Nature Book; In Nature's Nursery; Dame Nature's Book; Ellice of Godbegot, etc. Plays: Barabbas; Judas which also—, what is your verdict, 1937; When Midnight passed, 1937; With Shakespeare's Fairies, etc. *Recreations:* music, photography, Nature study, dramatic production. *Address:* Beisan, Liss, Hants. *Club:* Whitefriars.

Died 16 Nov. 1941.

SEDGWICK, Rt Rev. William Walmsley, DD (hon.) 1918; *b* Fremantle, Hants, 1858; 2nd *s* of Rev. Abraham and Ellen Sedgwick; *m* 1887, 3rd *d* of Demetrius and Mercy Condi of Cazzambia, Corfu; one *d.* *Educ:* Christ's College, Cambridge. Ordained, 1882; Curate of Wateringbury, 1882–84; Chaplain, RN, 1884–86; served Souakin, 1884–85 (medal and clasp, Khedive's bronze star); Vicar of St Patrick, Hockley Heath,

1886–89; Vryburg, 1889–93; Rector of Bedford, Cape Colony, 1893–96; Curate of Evershott, Dorset, 1896–97; Chaplain to Earl of Home, 1897–1900; Vicar of Waikari, NZ, 1901–03; Akaroa, 1903–04; St Luke-Christchurch, 1904–14; Hon. Canon of Christ, Church Cathedral, 1911–14; Diocesan Missioner, Diocese of Christchurch, 1914; Bishop of Waiapu, 1914–29; Vicar of Detling, 1931–32. *Address:* c/o Bank of New Zealand, Queen St, Auckland, NZ.

Died 19 Feb. 1948.

SEEBOHM, Hugh Exton; JP; *b* 5 April 1867; *s* of Frederic Seebohm, Hon. LLD (Edin.), LittD (Camb.), DLitt (Oxford), and MA Exton; *m* 1st, 1904, Leslie Gribble (*d* 1913); three *s* one *d*; 2nd, 1933, Mrs Marjorie Lyall. *Educ:* Rugby; King's College, Cambridge. Partner in Sharples & Co., Bankers, Hitchin, 1892–96; Local Director Barclays Bank, Ltd, 1896; Director, 1906; Vice-Chairman, 1932; Deputy Chairman, 1944; Chairman, Barclays Bank (France) Ltd, 1934; Director of Yorkshire Penny Bank, Ltd, 1911; Friends Provident and Century Life Office, 1921 (Chairman, 1939–45); Chairman of Luton Water Co.; Chairman of Hitchin Guardians, 1911–13; Member of Herts Co. Council Education Committee; Chairman of Governors Hitchin Grammar Schools; Member of Council of Haileybury College (Treasurer). *Publication:* On the Structure of Greek Tribal Society, 1895. *Address:* Poynders End, Hitchin, Herts. *T:* Hitchin 136. *Club:* Athenæum.

Died 16 July 1946.

SEGRAVE, Captain Sir Thomas George, Kt 1923; CBE 1920; OBE 1918; Hon. Capt. RIM; Hon. Comdr RNR; late Shipping Surveyor and Adviser, Office of High Commissioner for India; RNR; *b* 1865; *s* of Captain T. G. Segrave, RM, of Cabra, Co. Dublin; *m* 1st, 1895, Hon. Harriet Rose Gertrude Daly (*d* 1930), *d* of 2nd Baron Dunsandle; 2nd, 1933, Violet Beatrice, MBE, *d* of late C. J. Fox. *Educ:* privately. Surveyor of Shipping and Adviser, India Office, 1903; Technical Adviser, Ministry of Shipping, 1914; Director of Shipping, India Office, 1919. *Address:* Ascotts, Felbridge, Sussex. *Club:* Union.

Died 11 Jan. 1941.

SEIGNOBOS, Charles; Professor in the Faculty of Letters, Paris; Commandeur of Legion of Honour; *b* 10 Sept. 1854. *Educ:* Lycée de Tournon; École Normale Supérieure. Was professor at Dijon and afterwards lecturer at the Sorbonne. *Publications:* Histoire de la civilisation, 1884–1886; Histoire politique de l'Europe contemporaine (English 1902) refondue et augmentée en 2 vol. 1924; Introduction aux études historiques, 1897; La Méthode historique appliquée aux sciences sociales, 1901; Histoire de France contemporaine, 3 vol. (de 1848 à 1914), 1924 sous le titre Lavisse, Histoire de France; Evolution of the French People, 1932; The Rise of European Civilization, 1939. *Address:* 38 rue des Écoles, Paris.

Died 24 April 1942.

SEKON, George Augustus; (pen-name of George Augustus Nokes); Editor of Transport and Travel Monthly, 1910–22; editor and founder of the Railway (later Transport) and Travel Monthly; one of the founders of the Railway Magazine and Railway Year Book; editor, 1897–1910; author and man of letters; *b* 5 Jan. 1867; *y s* of late Walter Nokes, of Crouch Hill, N, and Seaford, Sussex; *m* 1893, Annie Scott, *y d* of late Henry Ingle; two *s* two *d*. *Educ:* Hayes Grammar School and Hayes College. Articled to a Surveyor and Land Agent, 1885; at expiration of articles became a partner in the firm; retired; has made a life study of every branch of railroading; voluminous writer on all railway subjects; contributes to newspapers, magazines, and technical publications on railway matters; for several years contributed each week to the Railway Herald; originator of the Luggage in Advance system; Founder and President, Railway Control by Railway Stockholders

Association. *Publications:* History of the South-Eastern Railway, 1895; History of the London and South-Western Railway, 1896; History of the Great Western Railway, 1895; Evolution of the Steam Locomotive, 1899; Dictionary of Railway Words and Phrases, 1901; History of Great Northern Railway (pamphlet), 1904; From MSL to GCR (in Travels at Home), 1905; History of the LC and DR, 1920; article Railways in Nelson's Encyclopædia; About our Railways annually for many years in the British Almanac; wrote the historical sketches of 43 railways described in the pregrouping issues of Railway Year Book; Railway Control by Railway Stockholders—not by Railway Directors, 1929; Locomotion in Victorian London, 1937; Brief Survey of British Railways, 1830–1945. *Recreations:* unearthing the early history of railways, and collecting books on early railways. *Address:* Thurles, Hurstpierpoint, Sussex.

Died 19 Feb. 1948.

SELBIE, Rev. William Boothby, MA; Principal of Mansfield College, Oxford, 1909–32; *b* Chesterfield, 24 Dec. 1862; *e s* of late Rev. R. W. Selbie, BA, of Salford; *m* Mildred Mary, 2nd *d* of late Joseph Thompson, JP, LLD, of Wilmslow, Cheshire; two *s* one *d*. *Educ:* Manchester Grammar School; Brasenose and Mansfield Colleges, Oxford; incorporated MA at Trinity Hall, Cambridge, 1904; Hon. DD Glasgow, 1911 DD Oxford, 1921. Lecturer in Hebrew and Old Testament at Mansfield College, Oxford, 1889–90; Minister Highgate Congregational Church, London, 1890–1902; Emmanuel Congregational Church, Cambridge, 1902–09; Editor of the British Congregationalist, 1899–1909; Lecturer in Pastoral Theology at Cheshunt College, Cambridge, 1907–09; Chairman of Congregational Union, 1914–15; President of National Free Church Council, 1917; Wilde Lecturer in Natural and Comparative Religion, Oxford, 1921–24; Hon. Fellow of Brasenose College, 1926; retired 1932. *Publications:* The Life and Teaching of Jesus Christ; Aspects of Christ; The Servant of God; Nonconformity; Schleiermacher; Life of Dr Fairbairn; Nature and Message of the Bible; Belief and Life; Life of Sylvester Horne; The Psychology of Religion; Congregationalism; Theology and the Modern Man; Christian Ethics, Religion and Life; This Ministry; Faith and Life; The Fatherhood of God; Faith and Fact; The Christian Faith and the New Psychology; The Validity of Christian Belief; God and Ourselves. *Recreation:* gardening. *Address:* 174 Banbury Road, Oxford. *T:* Oxford 58080.

Died 28 April 1944.

SELBORNE, 2nd Earl of, *cr* 1882; **William Waldegrave Palmer,** KG 1909; PC 1900; GCMG 1905; JP; DCL, LLD, Viscount Wolmer, 1883; Baron Selborne, 1872; *b* 17 Oct. 1859; *s* of 1st Earl and Lady Laura Waldegrave, *d* of 8th Earl Waldegrave; *S* father, 1895; *m* 1883, Lady Beatrix Maud Cecil, *d* of 3rd Marquis of Salisbury, KG; two *s* one *d*. *Educ:* Winchester; University College, Oxford (1st Class History). Assistant Private Secretary to Secretary of State for War and Chancellor of Exchequer (Rt Hon. H. C. E. Childers), 1882–85; MP (L) E Hampshire, 1885–86; (LU) 1886–92; West Edinburgh, 1892–95; Under-Secretary for Colonies, 1895–1900; First Lord of the Admiralty, 1900–05; Governor of Transvaal and High Commissioner for South Africa, 1905–10; President of the Board of Agriculture, 1915–16; Elder Brother of Trinity House since 1904; a Director of Lloyds Bank. *Heir: s* Viscount Wolmer, PC. *Address:* Blackmoor, Liss, Hampshire; 14 Buckingham Palace Gardens, SW1. *Club:* Brooks's.

Died 26 Feb. 1942.

SELBY, Arthur Laidlaw, MA, FRAS; Professor of Physics, University College of South Wales and Monmouthshire, Cardiff, 1897–1926; Emeritus Professor, 1926; *b* 2 July 1861; *s* of Atherton Thomas Selby, of Atherton, Lancashire; *m* Dorothy, *d* of Ernest Beck of Great Amwell. *Educ:* Heversham Grammar

School; Queen's College, Oxford. Assistant Demonstrator in Physics at the Clarendon Laboratory, Oxford, 1884–90; Fellow of Merton College, 1886–93; Examiner in the Honour School of Natural Science, 1889–90 and 1900–01; Assistant Professor of Physics in University College, Cardiff, 1890–97. *Address:* Amwell, Llandaff, Cardiff.

Died 22 July 1942.

SELBY, Francis James, CBE, MA Cantab, BA Lond.; *b* 8 Aug. 1867; *s* of Edward Selby, Ravensbourne Park, Catford; *m* 1st, Mary Alice, *d* of Thomas Turner, Aldwarke, near Rotherham; 2nd, Mary Florence (*d* 1931), *d* of John Child, 10 Holland Villas Road, Kensington; one *d. Educ:* University College, London; Trinity College, Cambridge. Senior Mathematical Master, Bristol Grammar School, 1892–1901; on Staff of National Physical Laboratory, 1903–32; Secretary to Director, and Librarian, 1903–18; in charge Tide-Prediction, 1903–19; Optics, 1903–09; Secretary, Advisory Committee for Aeronautics, 1909–19; Secretary, National Physical Laboratory, 1918–32. *Address:* 30 Hampton Road, Teddington. *T:* Molesey 548.

Died 5 March 1942.

SELFRIDGE, (Harry) Gordon; *b* Ripon, Wis, USA, 11 Jan. 1858; *o s* of Robert O. and Lois F. Selfridge; *m* 1890, Rose Buckingham (*d* 1918), Chicago, USA; one *s* three *d. Educ:* public school, Jackson, Mich, USA. Was member of the firm of Marshall Field & Co. of Chicago, 1890–1903, in which year he retired from business, but re-entered same in 1909, when he became founder and head of the house of Selfridge & Co., which was established in London in 1909. *Publication:* The Romance of Commerce. *Recreations:* motoring, yachting, travel, reading. *Address:* Ross Court, Putney Heath. *T:* Putney 6463. *TA:* Selfridge London. *Clubs:* Pilgrims', American.

Died 8 May 1947.

SELINCOURT, Ernest de, MA, DLitt (Oxon); MA (Birm.); FBA; LLD (Edin.); Professor of English Language and Literature at the University of Birmingham, 1908–35; Vice-Principal, 1931–35; President of the English Association, 1935–36; *b* Streatham, 24 Sept. 1870; 3rd *s* of Charles Alexandre de Sélincourt and Theodora Bruce Bendall; *m* 1896, Ethel (*d* 1931), 3rd *d* of late William Tuer Shawcross, Rochdale; two *s* two *d. Educ:* Dulwich College; University College, Oxford. Lecturer in English Language and Literature, University College, Oxford, 1896–1909; Hon. Fellow, University College, 1930; Hon. Fellow Westfield College, London, 1937; Lecturer in Modern English Literature to the Univ. of Oxford, 1899–1909; Professor of Poetry, Oxford University, 1928–33; Clark Lecturer at Trinity College, Cambridge, 1934; Lecturer in the Fine Arts, Univ. of Belfast, 1937; Huxley Lecturer, Univ. of Birmingham, 1938; Dean of the Faculty of Arts, Birmingham University, 1919–30; Examiner in Honours School of English, Oxford Univ., 1904–06, 1927–28; University of Wales, 1904–07; Univ. of London, 1911–14; University of Durham, 1917–18; University of Edinburgh, 1918–21; University of Bristol, 1923–25; University of Leeds, 1934–36. *Publications:* Hyperion, a facsimile of Keats's autograph MS, edited with critical introduction and notes, 1905; The Poems of Keats, a critical edition, 1905; 5th edition revised, 1926; Poems of Keats (text), 1906; Wordsworth's Guide to the Lakes, critical edition, 1906; The Minor Poems of Spenser, with Introduction and textual notes, 1910; The Poems of Spenser, with biographical critical introduction, 1912; Introduction to Landor's Imaginary Conversations (World's Classics), 1915; English Poets and the National Ideal, 1915; Walt Whitman (World's Classics), 1919; Wordsworth's Prelude, edited from the MSS, 1926, 2nd ed. revised, 1928; Dorothy Wordsworth, 1933; Oxford Lectures on Poetry, 1934; Letters of William and Dorothy Wordsworth

(1787–1805), 1935, (1806–1820), 2 vols 1936, (1821–1850), 3 vols 1938; Wordsworth's Poetical Works edited from the MSS Vol. I, 1940; Journals of Dorothy Wordsworth, 2 vols 1941. *Address:* Ladywood, Grasmere. *T:* Grasmere 86. *Club:* Athenæum.

Died 22 May 1943.

SELWAY, Cornelius James, CVO 1941; CBE 1918; TD; Passenger Manager (retired) of London and North-Eastern Railway, Southern Area; *b* 28 July 1875; *s* of late James Selway, Pilton, Somerset; *m* 1904, Nellie Carr, 2nd *d* of late Edward Thomas, Oswestry; three *s* one *d. Educ:* Westminster City School. Superintendent of the Line, Great Northern Railway, 1914–23; Assistant Superintendent, 1910; Secretary of Railway Conciliation Boards, 1907; nominated by Railway Executive Committee to appear before Rates Advisory Committee on behalf of Railways of United Kingdom in inquiry into charges upon passenger train traffic, 1919; Chairman Fares and Services Committee under London Passenger Transport Act, 1933–38; Chairman of Superintendents Conference at Railway Clearing House, 1921, 1929, 1936–39; Chm. Railway Executive Cttee of Passenger Superintendents, 1939–42; late Chm. of Shropshire & Montgomeryshire Rly; Foundation Member and late Hon. Treasurer of Institute of Transport; Major Engineer and Railway Staff Corps (RE). *Address:* Three Ways, Frinton on Sea, Essex. *T:* Frinton 151. *Clubs:* Junior United Service, Royal Empire Society, Overseas League.

Died 24 Dec. 1948.

SEN, Jitendranath, MA Calcutta University; late Senior Professor of Physical Sciences, City College, and of Chemistry, National Medical College, Calcutta; *b* 1875; member of the Sen family of Calcutta; *s* of late Babu Satcowry Sen and late Srimutty Sarba Mongola Debi; *m* γ *d* (*d* 1925) of Rai Madhub Chandra Rai, Bahadur, late engineer, Calcutta; two *s* three *d. Educ:* Hindu School, Presidency College, City College and Science Association, Calcutta. Took up teaching as profession; passed with first-class honours in Physics and Chemistry, and secured the Woodrow Memorial Scholarship; taught physics, chemistry, logic, and mathematics up to the BA and BSc honours standard; was at Albert College, 1898–1900; at Central College, 1900–03; retired from City College, 1935. *Publications:* Urine Analysis; Notes on Milton's L'Allegro and Il Penseroso; on Trigonometry; on Deductive and Inductive Logic; on Mechanics; on Airy's Selections from The Spectator; edited with notes, Washington Irving's Rip Van Winkle, and Legend of the Sleepy Hollow; edited notes on Wordsworth's Selection by W. T. Webb. Edited Byron's Childe Harold, Cantos I and II, text only; Cowper's Task, Book IV, with notes; and Wave Theory of Light for Beginners; Elegy written in a Country Churchyard, by Thomas Gray, edited with notes and introduction; Geometrical optics (elementary); General Properties of Matter, 2 vols, 1932. *Recreations:* reading of books, and on rare occasions a game of chess, and travel into different parts of India. *Address:* 74/1/1 Amherst Street, Calcutta, India.

Died 12 Oct. 1945.

SEN, Susil C., CBE 1937; MSc, BL; Solicitor to Government of India in Bengal since 1937; *s* of Satish Chandra Sen, ex-member of Bengal Legislative Council and Imperial Legislative Assembly, Solicitor; *m* 1914, Mrs Ashalata Sen; three *s* three *d. Educ:* Presidency College; University Law College, Calcutta, MSc, BL (Gold Medalist). Belchamber Gold Medal of Incorporated Law Society. Practising as a Solicitor and Advocate of High Court of Calcutta since 1919; sometime lecturer in the University of Calcutta in the class for Advocates; Member of Corporation of Calcutta since 1929; appointed Officer on special duty by the Government of India to make recommendations as regards amendment of Indian Companies Act and Law of Insurance in British India; Assisted in piloting of Indian

Companies Act and Insurance Bill in Indian Legislative Assembly and in Council of State. *Publication:* Editor (with Hon. Sir N. N. Sircar, KCSI) Indian Companies Act. *Recreations:* tennis and bridge. *Address:* No. 6 Old Post Office St, Calcutta. *TA:* Okeel. *T:* Regent 82. *Clubs:* Calcutta; Chelmsford (New Delhi).

Died 23 Feb. 1946.

SENNETT, Sir Richard, Kt 1924; senior partner Sennett Brothers, Southwark; Knight St John of Jerusalem; *b* 1862; *s* of Richard Sennett, Southwark; *m* 1st, Amy Georgina (*d* 1927), *d* of William Hughes, Chelsea; two *s*; 2nd, 1928, Mrs Florence Jessie Nolan (Commander of the Order of St John). Father of the Loriners' Court; Past Master of Feltmakers' Company; Member Court of Basketmakers' and Liveryman of Clockmakers' Companies; Master of Guild of Freemen, 1929; a Sheriff of the City of London, 1923, 1924; has represented Farringdon Within on the Corporation of London; Member London Chamber of Commerce; Life Member of the Imperial Society of Knights Bachelor; President St John Ambulance Brigade, Wimbledon and Merton Division; Commander of the Crown of Italy; Commander of the Star of Roumania. Has a collection of blue and white Nankin china. *Address:* 45 Arthur Road, Wimbledon Park, SW19. *Clubs:* Royal Automobile, City Livery, London Tradesmen's (Pres. 1944), Ranelagh Sailing, Sandown Park; Wimbledon Park Conservative etc.

Died 19 Feb. 1947.

SENTER, George, DSc (Lond.); PhD (Leipzig); FIC; Principal of Birkbeck College, University of London, 1918–39; formerly Member of Senate, University of London, and Chairman of the University Extension and Tutorial Classes Council; Deputy Vice-Chancellor, 1933–34; Member of Government Tribunal for Conscientious Objectors, 1939; *b* Kildrummy, Aberdeenshire, 1874; *e s* of George Senter, farmer; unmarried. *Educ:* Kildrummy Public School; Pharmaceutical Society's School; University College, London; University of Leipzig and University of Göttingen. Bell Scholarship, Pharmaceutical Society, 1895; Pharmaceutical Chemist, Pereira Medallist, 1896; BSc Lond., 1st class Honours in Chemistry, 1900; 1851 Exhibition Research Scholarship (on nomination of University College, London), 1901–03. Head of Chemistry Department, Birkbeck College, 1914–32; Examiner in Chemistry, Royal Colleges of Physicians and Surgeons, 1906–10; External Examiner in Chemistry, University of Birmingham, 1913–15; Member of Senate and Reader in Chemistry, University of London, 1912–14; Honorary Secretary, Faculty of Science, 1911–17; Lecturer on Chemistry, St Mary's Hospital Medical School, 1904–13. *Publications:* Outlines of Physical Chemistry, 1909 (17th ed. 1933); Textbook of Inorganic Chemistry, 1911 (14th ed. 1934); papers on Physico-chemical and Bio-chemical Subjects in Proceedings of the Royal Society; Transactions of the Chemical Society and of the Faraday Society; Journal of Physical Chemistry; Zeitschrift für Physikalische Chemie; Zeitschrift für Physiologische Chemie, etc. *Recreations:* golf, motoring. *Address:* Tara, Moss Lane, Pinner, Middlesex. *T:* Pinner 545. *Club:* Athenæum.

Died 14 March 1942.

SEQUEIRA, James Harry, MD, FRCP, FRCS. Consulting Physician to Skin and Phototherapy Depts, London Hospital; late Consultant in Dermatology, etc., to East African Forces; Pres. Dermatological Section Royal Soc. of Medicine; Councillor, RCP; Corr. Member Société Française de Dermatologie et de Syphiligraphie, and of Dansk Dermatoloisk Selskab; Hon. Member Japanese Dermatological Assoc.; late President, Kenya Branch, British Medical Association; late Editor, British Journal of Dermatology and East African Medical Journal. *Publications:* Diseases of the Skin, 5th ed. (with Drs Ingram and Brain), 1947, Spanish trans., 1926; Tuberculosis of the Skin (Allbutt's System

of Medicine), 1911; Treatment of Cancer by X-rays and Radium; Carbon Arc Light Bath, in treatment of Lupus; and numerous articles on dermatology and syphilology; translated and edited Finsen's Photo-therapy, 1901. *Address:* PO N'Gong, Kenya. *T:* N'Gong, 267. *Clubs:* Authors'; Nairobi.

Died 5 Nov. 1948.

SERPELL, Henry Oberlin; DL, JP Surrey; *b* 30 April 1853; *y s* of late Robert Coad Serpell, JP, and former Mayor of Plymouth; *m* 1st, Louisa Jane (*d* 1939), 2nd *d* of William Butcher, Standish Moreton, Gloucestershire; one *s*; secured divorce, 1938; 2nd, 1938, Fanny *d* of late Edward R. Oliver, Park, Truro. *Educ:* private school. Past Master Wheelwrights' Company; Past Master Barbers' Company; High Sheriff of Surrey, 1924 and 1925; founder of H. O. Serpell & Co. Ltd, of Reading, who removed the biscuit factory from Plymouth, 1899; a Member of the Court of the Shipwrights' Company. *Recreations:* travelling, golf, riding, motoring. *Address:* West Croft Park, Chobham, Surrey. *TA:* Chobham. *T:* 2. *Club:* Reform.

Died 13 Sept. 1943.

SETALVAD, Sir Chimanlal Harilal, KCIE 1924; Kt 1919. Advocate, High Court, Bombay; Vice-Chancellor University of Bombay, 1917–29; late Member Executive Council, Bombay; late Member of the Royal Commission on the Superior Civil Services in India; late Member of Southborough Committees on Functions and Franchise under the Reforms in India; late Member of Hunter Committee regarding disorders in the Panjab. *Address:* Bombay.

Died 10 Dec. 1947.

SETON, Ernest Thompson; (nom de plume, Seton-Thompson); Naturalist to the Government of Manitoba; artist-naturalist; *b* 14 Aug. 1860; *m* 1st, 1896, Grace (marr. diss. 1935), *d* of Albert Gallatin, California (Sacramento); one *d*; 2nd, 1935, Julia M. Buttree (author of Rhythm of the Redman; Sing, Sing, What shall I Sing; Indian Arts and Crafts, Indian Costume Books, Pulse of the Pueblo, Trail and Campfire Stories, etc.); one *d*. *Educ:* Toronto, Canada; London Royal Academy. Descended direct from George Seton, last Earl of Winton; went to Canada at age of five, lived in the backwoods till 1870, then went to Toronto to be educated at the public schools and at the Collegiate Institute; went to London for art training, 1879–81; went to Manitoba to follow natural history; became Naturalist to the Government of that province; began lecturing on Wild Animals in 1899; started an Outdoor Life movement, called the Woodcraft Indians (The Woodcraft League), which now has some 80,000 followers in the United States, 1902; ARCA; Medallist Société d'Acclimation de France, 1918; John Burroughs Medal, 1928; Daniel Giraud Elliot Medal, 1930; Founder and President, College of Indian Wisdom (Seton Institute), Santa Fé. *Publications:* Wild Animals I have Known (10 edns), 1898; Art Anatomy of Animals; Birds of Manitoba; Mammals of Manitoba; Trail of the Sandhill Stag; Biography of a Grizzly; Lives of the Hunted, 1901; Two Little Savages; Pictures of Wild Animals; Monarch, the Big Bear; Woodmyth and Fable; Animal Heroes; Birch Bark Roll of the Woodcraft Indians; Natural History of the Ten Commandments; Biography of a Silver-fox, 1909; Life Histories of Northern Animals, 1910; Manual of Scouting, 1910; Rolf in the Woods, 1911; The Arctic Prairies, 1911; The Forester's Manual, 1911; The Book of Woodcraft and Indian Lore, 1912; Wild Animals at Home, 1913; Wild Animal Ways, 1916; The Preacher of Cedar Mountain, 1917; Sign Talk Dictionary, 1918; Woodland Tales, 1921; Bannertail, 1922; Lives of Game Animals, 1925; Birch Bark Roll of Woodcraft (29th edition), 1931; Lives of Game Animals, 4 vols, 1925–1927; Famous Animal Stories, 1932; Gospel of the Redman, 1936; Great Historic Animals, 1937; Biography of an Arctic Fox, 1937; Buffalo Wind, 1938; Trail of an Artist-

Naturalist, an autobiography, 1940; Santana, Hero Dog of France, 1945. *Recreations:* hunting big game with the camera; natural history and woodcraft. *Address:* Santa Fé, New Mexico.

Died 23 Oct. 1946.

SETON, Robert S., BSc. Emeritus Professor of Agriculture, Leeds, since 1932. *Address:* The University, Leeds.

Died 12 Jan. 1942.

SETON-THOMPSON; *see* Seton, E. T.

SEVESTRE, Robert, MA, MD, BC (Cantab), MRCS, LRCP; late Major, RAMC (T); retired; *b* 3 Feb. 1868; *m* 1922, Jane (decd), *y d* of late W. Irvine Ward; (son killed while on Military Duty in Dec. 1943). *Educ:* Rugby; Trinity College, Cambridge; St Bartholomew's Hospital. Consulting Physician, The Royal Infirmary, Leicester; JP City of Leicester. *Publications:* in various journals. *Recreation:* golf. *Address:* 38 Springfield Road, Leicester. *T:* 7450.

Died 13 Oct. 1949.

SEWARD, Sir Albert Charles, Kt 1936; ScD, ForSecRS; Hon. DSc Oxford; Hon. ScD (Dublin, Geneva, Manchester, Cape Town, Toronto); Hon. LLD Edinburgh, St Andrews, Glasgow and Birmingham; Professor of Botany, Cambridge, 1906–36; Vice-Chancellor of the University, 1924–26; Master of Downing College, 1915–36; Hon. Fellow of Emmanuel College, St John's College and Downing College; Member of Advisory Council to Committee of Privy Council for Scientific and Industrial Research since 1936; Member of Standing Commission of Museums and Galleries; Trustee of British Museum since 1938; Almoner, Christ's Hospital; member of Court of Reading University; *b* 9 Oct. 1863; *s* of A. Seward, Lancaster; *m* 1st, 1891, Marion (*d* 1924), *d* of R. Brewis, Darlington; four *d*; 2nd, 1927, Mary Adelia, *d* of late James H. Bogart, New York City. *Educ:* Lancaster Grammar School; St John's College, Cambridge. Fellow and Tutor of Emmanuel College, 1899–1906; University Lecturer in Botany, 1890–1906; Harkness Scholar, 1888; President Botanical Section, British Association, 1903, 1929; President British Association, 1939; President Yorkshire Naturalists Union, 1910; President, Geological Society of London, 1922–24; President Science Masters Association, 1929; President International Botanical Congress, 1930; President International Union of Biological Sciences, 1931; President Union of South Eastern Scientific Societies, 1935; Royal Medal, 1925; Darwin Medal, 1934 (R. Soc.); Murchison Medal, 1908; Wollaston Medal, 1930 (Geol. Soc.); Hon. Member American Academy of Arts and Science; R. Acad. Sci., Sweden; NZ Institute; Soc. R. Bot. Belg., Soc. géol. Belg.; Palæont. Soc. Russia; Geological Society, S Africa; Ind. Bot. Soc. Corr. Acad. Nat. Sci. Philad.; Assoc. R. Acad. Belg.; Corr. Deutsch. Bot. Ges.; Bot. Soc. America; Hon. Member Bot. Soc. Japan; Hon. Member Roy. Swedish Academy and Norwegian Academy; Hon. Member New York Acad. Sci.; Hon. Fellow Botanical Society, Edinburgh; Hon. Fellow Nat. Inst. Sci. India. *Publications:* Fossil Plants as Tests of Climate (Sedgwick Essay, 1892); The Wealden Flora, vols i and ii (British Museum Catalogues, 1894–1895); Fossil Plants for Students of Botany and Geology, vols i–iv (1898–1919); The Jurassic Flora, parts i and ii (British Museum Catalogue, 1900–1904); A Summer in Greenland, 1922; Plant Life through the Ages, 1931; Plants: What they are and What they do, 1932; joint-editor with Sir Francis Darwin of More Letters of Charles Darwin, 1903; edited Darwin and Modern Science, 1909; Science and the Nation, 1917; also various Botanical papers contributed to scientific journals. *Address:* 209 Cromwell Road, SW5. *T:* Frobisher 1926. *Club:* Athenæum.

Died 11 April 1941.

SEWELL, Rev. Canon Archibald Hankey, MA; Rector of Winterbourne, near Bristol, since 1932; Diocesan Chaplain to Bishop of Bristol since 1919; *b* 16 June 1874; *s* of Stephen Arthur Sewell, London Stock Exchange; *m* Christabel Hulbert, *d* of William Timmins, Ealing. *Educ:* St Paul's School (Scholar); St John's College, Oxford (Classical Scholar). BA 1897; MA 1900. Deacon, 1897; Priest, 1898; Curate of Ealing Parish Church, 1897–1900; St Paul's, Clifton, Bristol, 1900–11; Vicar of Bishopston, Bristol, 1911–17; Chaplain to Naval Brigade and Hospitals in Serbia, 1915; Senior Chaplain to British interned in Switzerland, 1917–18; Bristol Diocesan Missioner, 1919–32; Hon. CF, 1918; Hon. Canon of Bristol, 1921; President of Western Temperance League, 1922–32. *Publications:* articles on Church matters in various periodicals, and brochures on the temperance question. *Recreation:* travel. *Address:* Winterbourne Rectory, Bristol. *T:* Winterbourne 31. *Club:* Royal Automobile.

Died 15 Sept. 1943.

SEWELL, Rev. Henry, MA; Hon. LLD Bristol; Hon. Canon Gloucester Cathedral since 1899; *b* 21 Aug. 1847; *o s* of Henry Sewell, Claybury, Essex, and Charlotte, *d* of Rev. Dr Wood. *Educ:* Clare College, Cambridge. Curate of Leigh, Essex, 1870–73; Vicar of Aldsworth, Gloucester, 1873–81; Vicar of Wotton-under-Edge, 1881–1903; Vicar of Sandhurst S Laurence, 1903–37; Member of Education Authority for the county of Gloucester. *Address:* Abloads Court, Sandhurst, Gloucester. *T:* Twigworth 56.

Died 8 May 1943.

SEWELL, Brig.-Gen. Jonathan William Shirley, CB 1929; CMG 1918; late RE; *b* 1872; *s* of Rev. H. D. Sewell, MA, Quebec; *m* 1896, May, *d* of Vice-Admiral Orford Churchill; one *s*. Director of Engineering Stores, BEF; Brig.-General, 1918; Colonel, 1919; served South African War, 1899–1902 (Queen's medal and three clasps, King's medal and two clasps); European War, 1914–18 (despatches, CMG, Bt Lt-Col, Bt Col); retired pay, 1929. *Address:* Dunan, Aldeburgh, Suffolk. *T:* Aldeburgh 165. *Club:* United Service.

Died 10 Aug. 1941.

SEWELL, Sir Sidney (Valentine), Kt 1945; MD; ChB; FRCP; FRACP; *b* 14 Feb. 1880; *s* of Richard Blamire and Emma Sewell; *m* 1908, Alice Maud Cunning, MA; two *s* five *d*. *Educ:* Bendigo and Caulfield Grammar Schools; Melbourne University, Queens College. MB, BS with 1st cl. Hons in all subjects and Exhibitions in Medicine and Surgery, 1905. Senior RMO Royal Melb. Hosp., 1905–06; senior Demonstrator Melbourne University, 1907; Post-graduate work, England and Germany, 1908–09; MD Melb. Univ., Asst Physician Royal Melb. Hosp., Neurologist St Vincent's Hosp., 1910; Lt-Col in charge Neurological work AMF in State of Victoria, 1915–19; Senior Physician Royal Melb. Hosp., 1923–39; Member of Faculty Medicine, Melb. Univ.; Fellow Queens College, Melb. Univ.; Consulting Physician Royal Melb. Hosp., 1940, and resumed teaching work at the Hospital for war period; Member of Research Committee RAAF; Member Consultative Tuberculosis Council State of Victoria, 1944–45; President Australasian Assoc. of Physicians, 1936; President Australasian College of Physicians, 1940–42. Sole Examiner written work Univ. of New Zealand MD degree past 12 years. *Publications:* (with Sir Frederick Mott) section of Neuropathology in British General Pathology; numerous papers in medical journals. *Recreations:* breeding stud cattle and sheep. *Address:* 12 Collins St, Melbourne, Australia; Road's End, Berwick, Vic. *T:* JM 1938, Berwick 42. *Clubs:* Melbourne (Melbourne); Union (Sydney).

Died 13 March 1949.

SEXTON, Walter, CBE 1920; *b* 1877; *s* of late Alfred R. Sexton, JP, Dublin; *m* Emily Beatrice, *d* of Arthur Clews Russell, Bromsgrove, Worcestershire. An Officer of Order of St John of Jerusalem. *Clubs:* St Stephen's Green, Dublin.

Died 16 Sept. 1941.

SEYMOUR, Sir Albert Victor Francis, 2nd Bt *cr* 1869; late Bt Lancashire Fusiliers; *b* Kensington Palace, 1 Dec. 1879; *s* of Sir Francis Seymour, 1st Bt, and Agnes Austin (*d* 1915), *d* of Rev. Hill Dawe Wickham, Rector of Horsington, Somerset; *S* father, 1890. *Educ:* Harrow. Formerly Page of Honour to Queen Victoria; late Lieut 3rd Lancs Regt; served S Africa, 1899–1901 (Queen's medal 4 clasps). *Heir:* none. *Clubs:* Marlborough-Windham, Bachelors'.

Died 2 May 1949 (ext).

SEYMOUR, Vice-Adm. Claude, DSO 1916; retired; *b* 17 March 1876; 3rd *s* of late Alfred Seymour and Jessie Madeleine, *d* of Hon. William Macdougall, CB, Toronto; *m* 1919, Auriel Dorothy, *o d* of late Richard Quin, Falmouth. Served European War, 1914–18 (despatches twice, DSO); Commanding Signal School at Portsmouth, 1922–25; Commanding HMS Royal Oak, 1925–26; Rear-Adm. 1926; retired, 1926; Vice-Adm., retired, 1931. *Address:* Meadowland, Fareham, Hants. *T:* Titchfield 63. *Club:* United Service.

Died 2 Dec. 1941.

SEYMOUR, Major Sir Edward, KCVO 1934; CVO 1925; DSO 1917; MVO 1901; OBE 1919; Extra Equerry to HM since 1935; Grenadier Guards (retired, 1908); *b* 10 Feb. 1877; *m* 1905, Lady Blanche Frances Conyngham, *d* of 4th Marquis Conyngham; one *s* one *d*. Entered army, 1897; Captain, 1904; ADC to Commander-in-Chief, Ireland, 1904–08; Comptroller of the Household to late Duchess of Albany, 1908–22; Equerry to Queen Alexandra, 1923–25; Comptroller to Princess Victoria, 1926–35; served Nile Expedition, 1898; South Africa, 1900–02; European War, 1914–18 (despatches, DSO). *Address:* Upper Chilland House, Martyr Worthy, Winchester, Hants. *Clubs:* Brooks's, Guards'.

Died 28 Feb. 1948.

SHACKLE, Robert Jones, CMG 1941; Under-Secretary, Board of Trade, since 1947; *b* 27 March 1895; *e s* of George Harry Shackle, Cambridge; *m* 1942, Margaret Mary Gourlay Galloway; one *s* one *d*. *Educ:* Marlborough; Trinity College, Cambridge. Joined RASC (Temp. 2nd Lieut) 1915; Temp. Lieut, 1917; served in France, 1915–19; Assistant Principal, Board of Trade, 1920; Principal, 1929; Assistant Secretary, 1935; Principal Assist Sec., 1942–47. *Address:* Broomfield, Hooke Rd, East Horsley, Surrey.

Died 24 March 1950.

SHADI LAL, Rt Hon. Sir, PC 1934; Kt 1921; *b* Rewari (Panjab); May 1874; *m;* two *s* three *d*. *Educ:* Municipal Board School, Rewari; Forman Christian College and Government College, Lahore; Balliol College, Oxford; BA University Panjab, 1894 (Fuller's Exhibition, Government scholarship, Arnold Medal), MA in Physics, 1895; Govt of India Scholar, 1895; Balliol College, Oxford, 1895; Boden Sanscrit Scholar, 1896; BA (Honours in School of Jurisprudence) 1898, BCL (Honours) 1899; Honoursman of the Council of Legal Education, 1899; Special Prizeman of the Council of Legal Education, Constitutional Law, Constitutional History, and Legal History; Arden Law Scholar of Gray's Inn. Called to the Bar, 1899; joined Lahore Bar; Law Professor and subsequently Principal, Law College, Lahore; Fellow and Syndic, Panjab University, Dean, Law Faculty; elected to the Panjab Legislative Council by the Panjab University, 1909; re-elected, 1912 and 1913; officiated as Judge, Chief Court, Panjab, June–July 1913; reappointed March 1914; Judge, High Court, Lahore, 1919–20; Chief Justice High Court of Judicature, Lahore, 1920–34; Member of Judicial Committee of Privy Council, 1934–39; the first Indian to be appointed permanent Chief Justice of a High Court in India; a Member of the tribunal to deal with the disputes between England and India about military expenditure, 1932–33; Hon. LLD of the Panjab University, 1933; retired 1934; Hon. Bencher of Gray's Inn, 1935. *Publications:* lecture on Private International Law; Commentaries on Panjab Pre-emption Act; Commentaries on Panjab Alienation of Land Act. *Recreation:* tennis. *Address:* Queen Anne's Mansions, SW1. *Clubs:* Athenæum, National Liberal.

Died 27 March 1945.

SHAIRP, Lt-Col Alexander, CMG 1915; Indian Army, retired; *b* 1873; *s* of the late Norman William Shairp, JP; *m* 1st, 1907, Julia Margaret (*d* 1930), *d* of late Rear-Adm. John Crawford Wilson; one *s;* 2nd, 1933, Alice Jane Davidge, Lady Byrne. Served East Africa, 1902–04 (medal with clasp); European War, 1914–16 (CMG); retired, 1924. *Club:* Naval and Military.

Died 28 Jan. 1944.

SHAKERLEY, Sir George Herbert, 4th Bt *cr* 1838; JP; *b* 27 Sept. 1863; 2nd *s* of Sir Charles Watkin Shakerley, 2nd Bart, KCB (*d* 1898), and Georgiana Harriott (*d* 1907), *e d* of late George Holland Ackers of Moreton Hall; assumed additional surname of Ackers by Royal Licence, 1908; *S* brother 1943; abandoned by deed poll, 1943, the surname of Ackers; *m* 1891, Evelyn Mary, 2nd *d* of Col Charles Hosken France-Hayhurst of Bostock Hall, and Davenham Hall, Cheshire; one *s* three *d*. *Educ:* Harrow. Formerly Captain and Hon. Major 5th Vol. Batt. Cheshire Regt; and Lieut King's Royal Rifle Corps. *Heir: s* Cyril Holland [*b* 1897; *m* 1928, Elizabeth Averil, *d* of E. G. Eardley-Wilmot; two *s* one *d*]. *Address:* Duddleswell Manor, Uckfield, Sussex. *T:* Nutley 2.

Died 7 Aug. 1945.

SHAKERLEY, Sir Walter Geoffrey, 3rd Bt *cr* 1838; CBE 1919; Lt-Col commanded 2/7th Batt. Cheshire Regt 1914–16; *b* 26 Nov. 1859; *e s* of 2nd Bt and Georgiana Harriot, *e d* of G. H. Ackers of Moreton Hall, Cheshire; *S* father, 1898; *m* 1885, Hilda Mary (*d* 1927), CBE, *o d* of Henry Hodgson of Currarevagh, Co. Galway; four *d*. Late Lieut King's Royal Rifle Corps. *Heir: b* G. H. Shakerley-Ackers. *Address:* 1 Cavendish Place, Bournemouth.

Died 11 Jan. 1943.

SHAKESPEAR, Alexander Blake, CIE 1913; merchant; late partner in firm of Begg, Sutherland & Co; *b* 1873; *y s* of late Col Shakespear, ISC; *m* 1922, Clare, 2nd *d* of late Herbert O'Brien, Calcutta. *Educ:* Berkhampsted. Secretary Upper India Chamber of Commerce, 1905–12. *Address:* Cawnpore, India.

Died 24 April 1949.

SHAKESPEAR, Dame Ethel Mary Reader, DBE 1920; DSc, JP, FGS; *b* 1871; *d* of Rev. Henry Wood, of Biddenham, Beds; *m* 1906, Gilbert Arden, *s* of John Shakespear of Copston, Warwickshire; no *c. Educ:* Bedford High School; Newnham College, Cambridge. *Publications:* various original papers and memoirs on geology and palæontology, published in the Quarterly Journal of the Geological Society of London and the Proceedings of the Palæontographical Society. *Recreations:* music, gardening, farming. *Address:* Caldwell Hall, Upton Warren, Bromsgrove, Worcs.

Died 17 Jan. 1946.

SHAKESPEAR, Lt-Col John, CMG 1917; CIE 1896; DSO 1890; Indian Army; retired; *b* Indore, 1 Sept. 1861; *y s* of Col Sir R. C. Shakespear, CB, Bengal Artillery; *m* 1st, 1892, Charlotte Frances B. (*d* 1926), *d* of Arthur Disney Dunne; 2nd, 1926, Mary Katharine, *d* of late Rev. W. H. Grove. *Educ:* Wellington Coll.; RMC, Sandhurst. Gazetted 100th Regiment, 1881; Adjt 1886; Intelligence Officer, Lushai Ex. Force, 1888; do. Chin Lushai Ex. 1889 (medal); Assist Pol Officer, 1890; Supt

South Lushai Hills, 1891–96; Major, 1895; admitted to ISC 1896; assist Com. in Assam Commission, 1896; Deputy Commissioner, 1897; Pol Officer, North Lushai Hills, 1897; 1st Superintendent Lushai Hills, 1898; Political Agent, Manipur, 1905–14; Lt-Col 1907; retired, 1916; commanded 18th Northumberland Fusiliers, 1914–18. *Publications:* The Lushais and the Land they Live In (silver medal of Society of Arts), 1894; The Lushei Kuki Clans, 1912; Historical Records of 18th Northumberland Fusiliers, 1919; 34th Division from Ripon to the Rhine; A Record of the 17th and 32nd Battalions Northumberland Fusiliers, 1914–1919; John Shakespear of Shadwell and his descendants, 1619–1931 (published privately); George Nesbitt Thompson and Some of his Descendants (published privately). *Address:* 131 Hales Road, Cheltenham (for the duration); 1 Redburn Street, Chelsea, SW3.

Died 10 Feb. 1942.

SHAPCOTT, Louis Edward, CMG 1935; MVO, 1920; ISO 1927; *b* Kingston, Victoria, 7 June 1877; *m*; three *s* one *d*. *Educ:* Public Schools Kingston and Allendale, Victoria. Early life Mining and Station life Victoria; migrated to W Australia early 1897; two years' commercial and railway experience; Civil Service since 1899; Secretary to Minister for Mines, 1899–1914; Under-Secretary Premier's Dept, W Australia, 1914–41; Clerk of Executive Council, 1920–41; Director of Civil Defence in Western Australia, 1941; retired, 1941. President, Zoological and Acclimatisation Society; President, State Gardens Board; Officier d'Académie. *Recreations:* development of parks and gardens. *Address:* 68 The Av., Nedlands, W Australia.

Died 23 May 1950.

SHARP, Alphonse, CBE 1920; Principal of Alph Sharp, chemical manufacturers; *b* 1872; *s* of William Sharp, Norwood Green, Halifax; *m* 1897, Emily, *d* of John Whiteley, Rose Grove, Hipperholme; three *s*. Superintendent of HM Explosive Factory, Greetland, Ministry of Munitions and Chairman of Hipperholme Military Tribunal and War Savings Committee during European War; sometime Chairman Hipperholme Urban District Council. *Address:* Holmwood, Halifax. *TA:* Sharp CBE Halifax. *T:* 2555. *Clubs:* Albany, Halifax.

Died 28 March 1942.

SHARP, Rev. Canon John Herbert; Canon of St Paul's Cathedral, Valletta, Malta, since 1931; *b* Balmuir, Angus, 11 May 1887; *e s* of late John Sharp, Balmuir, near Dundee, and Dalnaglar, Perthshire, and Eleanor, *d* of late James Farquhar White, Balruddery, Angus; *m* 1915, Elsie, *d* of late Rear-Admiral H. J. May, CB; one *s* two *d*. *Educ:* Rugby; Balliol College, Oxford. Curate of St Farnborough, 1912–15; St James', Edinburgh, 1915; Rector, 1917; Chaplain at Naples, 1921; at Diano Marina, Italy, 1925; Hon. Organising Sec. Diocese of Gibraltar, 1926; Hon. Chaplain to the Bishop since 1928; Archdeacon in South-Eastern Europe (Diocese of Gibraltar), 1935–47. *Address:* Alderbourne Arches, Gerrards Cross, Bucks. *T:* Fulmer 242. *Club:* Athenæum.

Died 27 Jan. 1950.

SHARP, Sir Milton, 2nd Bt *cr* 1920; *b* 22 April 1880; *s* of 1st Bt and Annie, *d* of James Turner, Low Moor, Yorkshire; *S* father, 1924; *m* Gertrude (*d* 1940), *d* of late John Earl, of London; one *s*. *Educ:* Shrewsbury; Trinity Hall, Cambridge. *Heir:* *s* Milton Reginald, *b* 21 Nov. 1909. *Address:* Howtown, Penrith.

Died 17 Dec. 1941.

SHARP, Robert Farquharson, BA; *b* London, 31 Dec. 1864; 2nd *s* of late Thomas Sharp and Agnes, *d* of Robert Farquharson, of Breda and Allargue, Aberdeenshire; *m* 1904; one *s*. *Educ:* Haileybury; New College, Oxford. Assistant, Printed Books Department, British Museum, 1888; Assistant Keeper, 1914; Superintendent of Reading Room, 1914–19; Deputy-Keeper, 1920–24;

Keeper of Printed Books, 1924–29. *Publications:* edition of Lytton's Plays, 1890; Dictionary of English Authors, 1897; revised edition, 1904; Wagner's drama, Der Ring des Nibelungen, 1898; Translation of Victor Hugo's Hernani, 1898; Makers of Music, 1898, 4th ed. 1913; Architects of English Literature, 1900; Short History of the English Stage, 1909; Three Plays of Ibsen's, translated, 1910; second series, 1911; third series, 1913; fourth series, 1915; Three Plays of Björnson's, translated, 1912; second series, 1914; Ibsen's Peer Gynt, translated, 1921; Reader's Guide to Everyman's Library, 1932; Short Biographical Dictionary of Foreign Literature, 1933. *Recreations:* reading, music.

Died 3 Aug. 1945.

SHARP, W. H. Cartwright, KC 1934; MA, LLB; Recorder of Wolverhampton since 1938; Bencher of the Inner Temple; *b* 1883. *Educ:* King Edward's High School, Birmingham; St John's College, Cambridge. Called to Bar, 1907; Oxford Circuit; Recorder of Banbury, 1936–37. *Address:* 4 Paper Buildings, Temple, EC4. *T:* Central 8415; Chantries, Warwick's Bench, Guildford.

Died 20 Dec. 1950.

SHARPE, Ven. Ernest Newton, MA; Sub-Chaplain, St John of Jerusalem, 1937; Hon. Chaplain, St Dunstan's, Regent's Park; 3rd *s* of late Rev. Henry Sharpe, Vicar of Trinity Church, Hampstead; *m* Alice Eleanor (*d* 1931), *e d* of late Capt. Edward Carter, Bath; three *d*. *Educ:* Westminster School; Clare College, Cambridge; Ridley Hall, Cambridge. Ordained, 1890; Curate, Bath Abbey Church, 1890–94; Vicar of Emanuel Church, West Hampstead, 1894–1908; Rector of Kersal, Manchester, 1908–12; Rural Dean of Salford, 1910–12; Rector of Holy Trinity, St Marylebone, 1912–18; of St Mary, Woolnoth, with St Mary, Woolchurch, EC, 1918; Vicar of Paddington and Rural Dean, 1919–30; Prebendary of St Paul's Cathedral, 1920–30; Archdeacon of London and Canon of St Paul's, 1930–47; Proctor in Convocation, 1922–47. *Address:* St Margarets, Bishops Down, Tunbridge Wells. *Club:* Union.

Died 20 Jan. 1949.

SHARPE, Sir Montagu, Kt 1922; KC; DL, CA; Vice-Lieutenant Middlesex, 1926; *b* 28 Oct. 1856; *s* of Captain B. Sharpe, Royal Navy, JP, of Hanwell Park, Middlesex, and Marianne, *d* of Rev. G. Montagu, Rector of Pickenham; *m* 1st, 1888, Mary Annie (*d* 1929), *d* of Captain J. Parsons, RN; 2nd, Frances Eileen, *d* of Capt. J. R. Hobson, RFA. *Educ:* Felsted. Entered Civil Service; winner three years CS Mile Challenge Cup and other races; called to Bar, Gray's Inn, 1889; Bencher, 1909; Treasurer, 1920; Chairman Brentford Petty Sessions, 1897–1908; Deputy Chairman Middlesex Quarter Sessions, 1896; Chairman, 1908–34; Vice-Chairman and Chairman Middlesex County Council, 1889–1909; also Chairman of several Committees; Order of Mercy, 1904, Bar, 1922; Chairman Council Royal Society Protection of Birds since 1895; received the Gold Medal of the Society, 1927; has promoted several Acts of Parliament for Wild Birds' Preservation; late Member Home Office Advisory Committee on Wild Birds' Protection; Hon. Treasurer late Middlesex VA Organisation; Chairman Hanwell Con-Conservative Association, 1883–1922; President Society of Chairmen of Quarter Sessions, England and Wales, 1913–30; President Hanwell Hospital, 1900–32; Member Middlesex Territorial Force Association, 1908–29; also former Middlesex Appeal Tribunal; Hon. Colonel 4th Batt. Middlesex V. Regt; P. G. Deacon, Grand Lodge; Chairman Egyptian Delta Railways Co., Ltd and Tendring Hundred Water Co.; President London and Middlesex Archæological Society. *Publications:* Middlesex in British, Roman, and Saxon Times; The Domesday Land Measures in Middlesex; The Great Ford across the Lower Thames; Bygone Hanwell; Middlesex Parishes and their Antiquity; Middlesex in the 11th

Century. *Recreations:* shooting, boating, photography, workshop. *Address:* 1 Mount View, Ealing, W5. *T:* Perivale 4532; Middlesex Guildhall, Westminster, SW.

Died 23 Aug. 1942.

SHARPE, Phoebe Elizabeth, FRGS, FRSA, LLCM, FBEE, FRES, MRAS; Fellow American Geographical Society; Kaisar-i-Hind medallist; Hon. Head of Women's Education, Limbdi; Hon. Personal Secretary to the ruler; *b* 18 Feb. 1888; *d* of William Edward Dudley-Lavender. First European in India to be elected as Pres. of three Jain institutions; only European delegate, All India Jain Conference, Ajmere, 1933; First English woman to be President, Guru Nanak's Birthday Celebrations Anniversary, Bombay, 1935; Silver Jubilee Medal, 1935; Coronation Medal, 1937. *Publications:* Shri Krishna and Bhagavad Gita, 1924; Flame of God, 1929; Shiva, 1930; The Thakore Sahib of Limbdi, 1931; The Philosophy of Yoga, 1933; The Tantric Secret of the Immaculate Conception, 1933; The India that is India, 1934; The Kaula Circle, 1936; An Eight-Hundred-Year-Old Book of Indian Formulas, 1937; The Great Cremation Ground (Mahâsmasana), 1938; Tales from Old India, 1939; Recipes and Formulæ collected from Indian Ascetics, 1940; composer, Song of the River Bhramaputra, Adieu. *Recreations:* music, tennis, literature. *Address:* Shri Krishna Nivas, Limbdi, Kathiawar; Shri Krishna Nivas, Mt Abu, Rajputana. *T:* 33 Limbdi Exchange.

Died 8 Jan. 1941.

SHARPE, Major Robert William, CBE 1943; DL County of Berwick; JP; Joint Master Lauderdale Foxhounds; County Councillor for Berwickshire; Chairman West District Council; Chairman County Road Board; Director, Highland and Agricultural Society of Scotland; Chairman Science Committee; Chairman, Roxburgh District Mental Hospital; Hon. Vice-President British Legion (Scotland); ARP Controller for County of Berwick; Chairman County Agricultural Executive Committee for Berwickshire; Director, John Swan and Sons, Ltd; *b* 1886; *s* of late Robert Sharpe, Solicitor, and late Margaret Brown, Corberry House, Dumfries; *m* 1916, Gladys Robina, *yr d* of late James Stewart, Carpet Manufacturer, Eskbank; one *d*. *Educ:* Edinburgh University; East of Scotland College of Agriculture; abroad. Started training for Law and Banking; Member of Institute of Banking in Scotland; 2nd Lt 3rd VB, KOSB, 1905; Lt 5th KOSB, 1908; transferred 1911 to 4th KOSB; served European War, Gallipoli, Egypt, and Palestine, Captain; Brigade Machine Gun Officer, 155th Infantry Bde, 1914–16; Major and Commanded Bn short time, 1917 (twice wounded, right leg amputated); retired pay with rank of Major TA, 1919; Director Scottish Chamber of Agriculture and President, 1929; Landowner and farmer. *Recreations:* hunting and fishing. *Address:* The Park, Earlston, Berwickshire. *TA:* Earlston. *T:* 267 Earlston. *Clubs:* New, Scottish Conservative, Edinburgh.

Died 5 Dec. 1943.

SHARPLES, William Johnson, MA Cambridge; Headmaster of Parmiter's Foundation School, Victoria Park, NE, 1904–30; *b* 1865; *s* of James Sharples, of Prestwich, Lancashire; *m* 1st, Judith Penuel, *d* of A. F. A. Fairweather, MD, of Pocklington, Yorkshire; 2nd, Kate Emmeline, *d* of R. W. Pullen, of Manchester; one *s* one *d*. *Educ:* Manchester Gram. School (Foundation and Langworthy Scholar); Queens' College, Cambridge (Senior Foundation Scholar and Prizeman). Wrangler; Captain of College Boat Club; Senior Mathematical Master and Second Master of St Olave's Grammar School, Southwark, to 1904; Member of the Incorporated Association of Head Masters, 1904–30 (Chairman of London Division, 1910 and 1919; Secretary of London Division, 1911–18); Vice-Pres. of

the Society of Schoolmasters. *Recreations:* gardening and golf. *Address:* 48 York Hill, Loughton, Essex. *T:* Loughton 4178.

Died 13 April 1948.

SHASTRI, Prabhu Dutt, PhD (Kiel), BSc Litt Hum (Oxon), MA, BT, Hon. MOL (Punjab), MSG (Berlin), Mahamahādhyāpak' (Benares); Vidyāsagar' (Calcutta); Shāstravāchaspati' (Nadia) Indian Educational Service; Senior Professor of Mental and Moral Philosophy in Presidency College, Calcutta, since 1912; Principal, Government College, Hooghly, 1927; Principal, Rajshahi College, Rajshahi, 1933–35; *b* 20 June 1885; *e s* of Professor Ganesh Dutt Shastri; *m* 1904, Shrimati Taravati Devi Bhārati of Amritsar; three *s*. *Educ:* University of Lahore; University of Oxford (Christ Church); University of Kiel; University of Bonn; University of Paris. Obtained special grant from Boden Fund on results of research in Mental and Moral Science; Special Studentship in Philosophy and New Testament at Manchester College, Oxford; made a tour of study and research in Europe as Government of India Research Scholar, 1909–11; Delegate to and Sectional President at the Fourth International Congress of Philosophy held at Bologna in April 1911; Punjab University Reader, 1909; Lecturer in Methods of Teaching and Educational Psychology at the Lahore Central Training College, 1907–09; first Punjabi to be nominated a Government of India Sanskrit Scholar and first in the Punjab to be appointed to the Indian Educational Service; Calcutta University Lecturer in Philosophy and Sanskrit, 1913–41; Deputed as Private and Political Secretary to the Maharaja of Alwar, 1915–16. *Publications:* The Doctrine of Maya in the System of the Vedanta, 1910; The Elements of Deductive Logic; a Text-book of Inductive Logic, 1922; The Doctrine of Maya in Indian Philosophy; The Conception of Freedom in Hegel, Bergson and Indian Philosophy, 1913; Elementary Psychology, 1928; The Essentials of Eastern Philosophy; Toronto Lectures; several articles. *Recreations:* music, motoring, cricket, etc.

Deceased.

SHAW, Albert, LLD; journalist and historical author; *b* Shandon, Butler County, Ohio, 23 July 1857; *s* of Griffin M. Shaw, physician; *m* 1st, 1893, Elizabeth Leonard Bacon; two *s*; 2nd, 1933, Virginia McCall. *Educ:* Iowa (now Grinnell) College; Johns Hopkins University (PhD); LLD Univ. of Wisconsin, 1904, and Univ. of Missouri, 1908; Marietta Coll., 1910; Univ. of Cincinnati, 1913; Western Reserve University, 1917; Grinnell College, 1918; University of Porto Rico, 1921; LittD New York University, 1924; Hampden-Sidney College, 1928; Miami University, 1929. Formerly editor Grinnell Herald and Minneapolis Tribune; editor The National Revenues, 1888; founded the American Review of Reviews in 1891, continuing as editor and owner until 1937; Trustee Grinnell College (Iowa), and Anatolia College, Salonika, Greece. One of founders of American Historical Association; Senator, Phi Beta Kappa; Member various organizations relating to education and political and social reform; Fellow American Statistical Association, American Geographical Society; Member of Board of Arbitration in the matter of controversy between Locomotive Engineers and fifty-two railroads in Eastern section of United States, 1912; Member of first group of American Journalists who visited England and France as guests of the British Government during European War, 1918; Trustee New York Academy Political Science; Trustee of the Berry Schools, Georgia; Trustee of the Southern Education Foundation. *Publications:* Local Government in Illinois, 1883; Icaria, a Chapter in the History of Communism, 1884; Co-operation in the North-West, 1888; Municipal Government in Great Britain, 1895; Municipal Government in Continental Europe, 1895; The Outlook for the Average Man; Political Problems of American Development, 1907; A Cartoon History of

Roosevelt's Career, 1910; Abraham Lincoln, two volumes, 1929; Reminiscences of Life in Ohio, 1941; International Bearings of American Policy, 1943; Woodrow Wilson—Memories and Reflections, 1947; and numerous brochures and articles. *Recreation:* farming. *Address:* Hastings-on-Hudson, New York. *Clubs:* Century, City, Saint Andrew's Golf, Town Hall, New York; Cosmos, Washington; Sleepy Hollow Country, etc.

Died June 1947.

SHAW, Arthur Frederick Bernard, BA, MD, BCh, BAO (Dublin), FRCP (Ireland), DPH (Dublin); Commander of the Order of the Nile; Professor of Pathology, University of Durham, and Pathologist, Royal Victoria Infirmary, Newcastle-on-Tyne, since 1938; Adviser in Pathology to the Emergency Medical Service; *s* of late Arthur Wellington Bolton Shaw, Carraig-na-Chattan, Co. Dublin; *m* Gertrude Mary, *d* of late John Frimston, Liverpool; two *s. Educ:* Christ's College, Blackheath; Trinity College, University of Dublin (Senior Moderator in Natural Science); Johns Hopkins Univ., Baltimore, USA Rockefeller Fellow, Johns Hopkins Univ., Baltimore, USA. Demonstrator in Pathology, Univ. of Dublin, 1911–12; Senior Assistant, MOH, City and Port of Cardiff, 1912–19; Lieut RAMC (TF), 1913; Major RAMC (TF), 1918; served Gallipoli, Sinai, Palestine, 1915–19 (despatches); Pathologist, 69th General Hospital, Egyptian Expeditionary Force, 1917–18; Lecturer in Pathology, Univ. of Durham College of Medicine, 1919; Hon. Pathologist, Princess Mary Maternity Hosp., Newcastle-on-Tyne, 1926; Professor of Pathology, Egyptian Univ., Cairo, 1933–38; Member of Senate Univ. of Durham; Governor of Barnard Castle School; Member Pathological Society of Great Britain and Ireland; FRSM. *Publications:* various papers on Pathology and Haematology in Journal of Pathology and Bacteriology, Br. Med. Jl, Br. Jl of Surgery, etc. *Recreations:* literature, archæology, ornithology. *Address:* 36 Eslington Terrace, Newcastle-on-Tyne; Department of Pathology, Royal Victoria Infirmary, Newcastle-on-Tyne. *T:* Jesmond 2493, Newcastle 21151.

Died 3 June 1947.

SHAW, Arthur W.; *see* Winter-Shaw.

SHAW, Bernard; *see* Shaw, G. B.

SHAW, Mrs Clarice McNab. MP (Lab) Kilmarnock Division of Ayr and Bute since 1945; member Ayrshire County Council; former Chairman Scottish Labour Party. *Address:* 36 Titchfield Road, Troon, Ayrshire. *T:* 144.

Died 27 Oct. 1946.

SHAW, Captain (E) Cyril Arthur, CBE 1944; RN; Admiralty Engineer Overseer, London District; *b* 1 July 1894; 2nd *s* of A. B. Shaw, 37 Queens Park Avenue, Bournemouth; *m* 1925, Phyllis Adele Curtis, *o c* of late Paul Alfred Baumann, Kenmore, The Bishops Avenue, N2. *Educ:* Fairfield, Malvern; RN Colleges, Osborne and Dartmouth. Served in RN during European War, 1914–18, Engineer Officer in charge of Torpedo Range, Weymouth, and in HM Ships Devonshire and Glasgow. During War of 1939–45; Engineer Officer of HMS Furious, 1939–40; Captain (E), 1940; Squadron Engineer Officer (Destroyers) in Eastern Mediterranean, 1941–43; Engineer Officer in Charge, RNATE Newcastle-under-Lyme, 1944–45. *Address:* Kenmore, The Bishops Avenue, N2. *T:* Speedwell 3178.

Died 28 Sept. 1946.

SHAW, Lt-Gen. Rt Hon. Sir Frederick Charles, PC (Ireland) 1918; KCB 1917; CB 1913; *b* 31 July 1861; *s* of John Shaw, of Normanton, Derbyshire; *m* 1890, Florence Edith (*d* 1918), *d* of Rev. Canon Denton, of Ashby-de-la-Zouch, Leicestershire; one *d. Educ:* Repton. Joined the Sherwood Foresters (Derbyshire

Regt), 1882; commanded 2nd Bn 1907–11; served Egyptian War, 1882; served on Staff throughout SA War as Brigade-Major; DAAG and AAG (Bt Lt-Col, despatches twice); DAQMG 6th Div. 2nd Army Corps, 1903; General Staff Officer, 1st grade, Scottish Command, 1911–13; served European War, 1914–16 (prom. Maj.-Gen., despatches five times); commanded 9th Infantry Brigade, 1913–15; Divisional Commander, 1915; Director, Home Defence, War Office, 1915; Chief of Gen. Staff, Home Force, 1916–18; Commander-in-Chief, Ireland, 1918–20; Lieut-Gen. 3 June 1919; retired, 1920. *Club:* Army and Navy.

Died 6 Jan. 1942.

SHAW, Geoffrey Turton, BA, MusBac Cantab, MusDoc Cantuar; *b* 14 Nov. 1879; *s* of late James and Charlotte Shaw; *m* 1902, Mary Grace, *d* of late Charles and Ellen Putley; two *s* three *d. Educ:* St Paul's Choir School; Derby School; Gonville and Caius College, Cambridge. Director of Music, Gresham's School, Holt; Director of Music, St Mary, Primrose Hill; retired Inspector of Music, Board of Education; Chairman League of Arts; Conductor League of Arts Choir; Festival Adjudicator; Advisory Music Council BBC; Chairman School Music subcommittee BBC; Chairman Paddington Branch League of Nations Union. *Publications:* numerous, Choral, Orchestral, Vocal, Instrumental. *Recreations:* sailing, tennis, billiards, reading, patience. *Address:* The Cottage, Curridge, Newbury, Berks. *T:* Hermitage 251. *Club:* Oxford and Cambridge Musical.

Died 14 April 1943.

SHAW, (George) Bernard; *b* Dublin, 26 July 1856; *m* 1898, Charlotte Frances Payne-Townshend (*d* 1943). London, 1876; Fabian Society, 1884; Nobel Prize for Literature, 1925. *Publications:* Novels—Immaturity, The Irrational Knot, Love among the Artists, Cashel Byron's Profession, An Unsocial Socialist, 1880–1883; edited Fabian Essays, 1889; Fabianism and The Empire, 1900; Fabianism and the Fiscal Question, 1904; Sixty Years of Fabianism, 1947; various tracts on Socialism, published by the Fabian Society; The Quintessence of Ibsenism, 1891 and 1913, The Sanity of Art, 1895, and The Perfect Wagnerite, 1898 (collected 1931 as Major Critical Essays); The Common Sense of Municipal Trading, 1904; Socialism and Superior Brains, 1910; a Preface to three plays by Brieux, 1911; Common Sense about the War, 1914; How to Settle the Irish Question, 1917; Peace Conference Hints, 1919; What I Really Wrote about the War, 1931; A Preface to English Prisons under Local Government, by Sidney and Beatrice Webb, 1922; The Intelligent Woman's Guide to Socialism and Capitalism, 1928; Adventures of a Black Girl in Search of God, 1932; Pen Portraits and Reviews, 1932; weekly articles on Music in the Star signed 'Corno di Bassetto' (collected 1937 as London Music in 1888–1889), and in The World (collected 1931 as Music in London, 1890–1894, in three volumes); weekly articles on the Theatre in the Saturday Review, January 1895 to May 1898 (collected 1931 as Our Theatres in the Nineties, in three volumes); Doctors' Delusions, Sham Education and Crude Criminology, 1931; The Political Madhouse in America and Nearer Home, 1933; Preface to Dickens' Great Expectations and William Morris as I Knew Him, 1936; Everybody's Political What's What, 1944; Postscript to Back to Methuselah reprinted by the Oxford University Press as a World Classic, 1946; Sixteen Self-Sketches, 1948. Plays, Pleasant and Unpleasant (seven plays), 1898; Three Plays for Puritans, 1900; The Admirable Bashville, 1901; Man and Superman, 1903; John Bull's Other Island, 1904; How He Lied to Her Husband, 1904; Major Barbara, and Passion, Poison and Petrifaction (mock tragedy written for the Actors' Orphanage), 1905; The Doctor's Dilemma, 1906; Getting Married, 1908; The Shewing-up of Blanco Posnet, 1909; The Fascinating Foundling; The Glimpse of Reality, 1909; Press Cuttings, 1909; The

Dark Lady of The Sonnets, 1910; Misalliance 1910; Fanny's First Play, 1911; Androcles and the Lion, Pygmalion, and Overruled, 1912; Great Catherine, 1913; The Music Cure, 1914; O'Flaherty VC, The Inca of Perusalem, 1915; Augustus does His Bit, 1916; Heartbreak House, Annajanska, 1917; Back to Methuselah (cycle of five plays), 1921; Jitta's Atonement (translation of Fran Gitta's Sühne, by Siegfried Trebitsch), 1922; Saint Joan of Arc, 1923; The Apple Cart, 1929; Too True to be Good, 1932; Village Wooing and On the Rocks, 1933; The Six of Calais The Simpleton of the Unexpected Isles, 1934; The Millionairess, 1936; Cymbeline Refinished, 1936; Geneva, 1938; In Good King Charles's Golden Days, 1939; Buoyant Billions, 1947 (Malvern Festival, then London, 1949); Farfetched Fables, 1948; Shakes *versus* Shaw (posthumous). *Diet:* vegetarian. *Recreation:* being past ninety. *Address:* Ayot Saint Lawrence, Welwyn, Herts. *T:* Codicote 218. *Clubs:* Royal Automobile, Burlington Fine Arts. *Professional Association:* Society of Authors, Playwrights, and Composers.

Died 2 Nov. 1950.

SHAW, Rev. George William Hudson; *b* Bradford; *m* 1944, Agnes Maude Royden. *Educ:* Balliol College, Oxford (MA, Exhibitioner). President, Oxford Union, 1884; ordained, 1884; Curate of Horsham, 1884–86; St Margaret, Ilkley, 1887–89; Vicar of Thornthwaite, 1889–92; Fellow of Balliol College, 1890–99; Rector of South Luffenham, 1898–1907; Alderley, 1907–12; St Botolph's, Bishopsgate, 1912–35.

Died 30 Nov. 1944.

SHAW, Henry Selby H.; *see* Hele-Shaw.

SHAW, Herman, DSc; Director and Secretary, Science Museum, since 1945; *b* 14 Oct. 1891; *o s* of late G. H. Shaw, Huddersfield; *m* 1919, Constance, *e d* of F. Shaw, Harrow. *Educ:* Bradford Grammar School (Governor's Scholar); Imperial College of Science and Technology (Royal Scholar). Aeronautics Research Scholar, 1913–14; ARCS (Physics), 1913; Diploma Imperial College, 1914; BSc 1913; MSc 1922, DSc 1931. Lieut RNVR, 1915; Flight Lieut RNAS, 1916; transferred to RAF (Captain 1917); entered Science Museum, 1920; Deputy Keeper, 1931; Keeper, Department of Physics and Geophysics, 1935; Acting Director, 1940; a Governor of Imperial College of Science and Technology; a Member of the Delegacy of the City and Guilds Coll.; a Trustee of Imperial War Museum; Member of Board of Governors of Imperial Inst.; Pres. of the Museum Association; Hon. Treasurer of Phys. Soc.; Member of Board of Studies, Univ. of London, since 1937; Fellow of Inst. of Physics; Member of General Committee of British Assoc. for the Advancement of Science; Mem.: American Soc. of Exploration Geophysicists; American Inst. of Mining and Metallurgical Engineers. *Publications:* Text Book of Aeronautics, 1918; various official publications of the Science Museum; about twenty papers in scientific journals principally on applied geophysics; contributor to Encyclopedia Britannica. *Recreation:* motoring. *Address:* 12 Suffolk Road, SW13. *Club:* Athenæum.

Died 4 May 1950.

SHAW, Sir Napier; *see* Shaw, Sir W. N.

SHAW, Emeritus Prof. Philip Egerton, MA, DSc; retired from Chair of Physics, Nottingham University; *b* 5 Feb. 1866; *s* of Henry Shaw and Marion Hele; *m* 1901, Leonora Julia Truman. *Educ:* Bristol Grammar School; University College, Bristol; St John's College, Cambridge. Lecturer and later Professor at Nottingham; chief activity—experimental research in physics, notably in fine measuring machines, in gravitation, and in frictional electricity; Librarian, Church House and Thoroton Society, Nottingham. *Publications:* a succession of original papers, chiefly Proc. Roy. Soc., Phil. Mag.,

and Proc. Phys. Soc. *Recreations:* golf, gardening. *Address:* Holmegarth, Middleton Crescent, Beeston, Notts. *T:* Beeston Notts 54555.

Died 10 April 1949.

SHAW, Richard James Herbert, CBE 1920; Editoral Staff, The Times since 1919; *b* Dublin, 1885; *o s* of late James Herbert Shaw, Merrion, Parkstone, and Mary, *e surv. d* of R. O. Armstrong, Monkstown, County Dublin. *Educ:* Trinity College, Dublin; First Senior Moderator and Gold Medallist, BA. Called to Irish Bar, 1908; London Representative of Irish Unionist Alliance and Unionist Associations of Ireland, 1911–13; Secretary, Irish Unionist Alliance, 1913–14; Commission in 5th (Service) Bn The Connaught Rangers, 1914; Captain, 1915; served as Staff Captain, 29th Infantry Brigade Gallipoli, Macedonia and Serbia, 1915–16; Irish Rebellion, 1916; Assistant Press Censor, Ireland, 1916–18; Assistant Secretary, Irish Convention, 1917–18; Assistant Secretary to the Lord-Lieutenant of Ireland, 1918–19; Government service in Great Britain and USA, 1939–40; Director British Press Service, Washington, DC, 1941–42. *Address:* Printing House Square, EC4; 7 Royal Crescent, Bath. *Clubs:* Marlborough, Pratt's; Kildare Street, Dublin; Bath and County, Bath; Century, New York.

Died 12 July 1946.

SHAW, Sir (Theodore Frederick) Charles (Edward), 1st Bt *cr* 1908; *b* Wolverhampton, 11 Sept. 1859; *e s* of late Edward Dethick Shaw and Millicent Augusta, 2nd *d* of late R. D. Gough, both of Wolverhampton; *m* 1900, Emily White, *d* of late Henry Bursill, Hampstead; one *d*. *Educ:* Tettenhall College, Wolverhampton; Balliol College, Oxford. MP (L) Stafford, 1892–1911. *Publications:* newspaper articles, chiefly from abroad. *Recreations:* hunting, motoring, tennis. *Heir:* none. *Address:* Harewood, Sunninghill, Berks. *Clubs:* Reform, Bath.

Died 17 April 1942 (ext).

SHAW, William Arthur, FBA 1940; LittD; Editor of the Treasury Calendar, Public Record Office; *b* 19 April 1865; *y s* of late James Shaw of Stanley Mount, Ashton-under-Lyne; *m* 1st, Clara Edith (*d* 1919), Associate Royal Academy of Music, Associate Royal Philharmonic Society, *y d* of late Thomas W. Goldsbrough, MD, West Square, London; 2nd, Mabel Elizabeth, *d* of Angus Grant, Rothiemurchus, Co. Banff, and East Finchley; one *d*. *Educ:* Owens College, Manchester. MA 1886; LittD 1892; Cobden Club Prizeman; Shuttleworth Political Economy Scholar; Bradford History Scholar; Berkeley Fellow. *Publications:* The History of Currency, 1895; Writers on English Monetary History, 1896; History of the English Church under the Civil Wars and Commonwealth, 2 vols 1900; The Knights of England; a complete record of all the Orders of Chivalry and of Knights Bachelors of England, Scotland and Ireland, 2 vols, 1905; The Coming Reaction (under the Pseudonym of Legislator), 1905; Currency, Credit, and the Exchanges during the Great War, 1927; The Theory and Principles of Central Banking, 1931; The Principles of Currency, Credit and the Exchanges, 1934; Inventories of the Royal Collection of Pictures under Henry VIII and Edward VI 1937; The Catalogue of the Massie Tracts on trade, etc., 1937; has edited with a memoir the literary remains of R. C. Christie, and has also edited eleven different vols of historical material for the Record Soc., Chetham Soc., Huguenot Soc., and Royal Historical Society, and 45 vols of Calendar of Treasury Records for the Master of the Rolls and reports on the Sydney Papers for the Historical MSS Commission; a long series of essays and scattered papers in various reviews bearing on economics and 17th-century history, and especially on the native English school of portraiture of the 16th and 17th centuries. *Address:* Public Record Office, Chancery Lane, WC.

Died 15 April 1943.

SHAW, Sir (William) Napier, Kt 1915; MA, ScD; Hon. Fellow Emmanuel College, Cambridge; Hon. LLD (Aberdeen, Edinburgh); Hon. ScD (Athens, Dublin, Harvard, Manchester); Commander Order St Iago da Espada (Portugal); Hon. For. Mem. American Academy Arts and Science, Boston, Real, Accademia dei Lincei, Rome, Royal Swedish Academy, Norwegian Academy of Sciences, Oslo, American Geographical Society, New York, Russian Geographical Society, Austrian Meteorological Society, and German Meteorological Society; FRS 1891; Hon. FRSE; Hon. Fellow Royal Sanitary Institute, and Hon. Member Institution of Heating and Ventilating Engineers; Hon. Member of the International Meteorological Committee; Hon. President International Commission for the Exploration of the Upper Air, 1927; b 4 March 1854; 3rd s of late Charles Thomas Shaw, Birmingham; m 1885, Sarah Jane Dugdale (d 1923), 2nd d of late Thomas Harland, MD, Salford. Educ: King Edward's School, Birmingham; Emmanuel College Cambridge; University of Berlin. Fellow of Emmanuel College, 1877–1906; University Lecturer in Experimental Physics, Camb., 1887–99; Rede Lecturer, 1921; Senior Tutor of Emmanuel College, 1890–99; Member of Meteorological Council, 1897–1905, and Sec. 1900–05; Director of Meteorological Office, 1905–20; President Section A (Maths and Phys), British Association, 1908; Section L (Education), 1919; Guy Medallist, Royal Statistical Society, 1906; Symons Medallist, Royal Meteorological Society, 1910; President, 1918–19; Buijs-Ballot Medallist (Amsterdam), 1923; Royal Medal, Royal Society, 1923; Halley Lecturer, Oxford Univ., 1918; President International Meteorological Committee, 1907–23; Pres. International Conferences of Meteorologists, Paris, 1919, and Utrecht, 1923; Professor of Meteorology, Royal College of Science, 1920–24; President Meteorological Section of International Union of Geodesy and Geophysics, 1921–30. Publications: Text-book of Practical Physics (conjointly with Sir R. Glazebrook); Air Currents and the Laws of Ventilation, 1907; Forecasting Weather, 1911, 1923, and 1939; Manual of Meteorology, 1919–1931; The Air and its Ways, 1923; The Smoke Problem of Great Cities (with J. S. Owens), 1925; The Drama of Weather, 1933 and 1938; The Life-History of Surface Air Currents (with R. G. K. Lempfert), 1906; The Weather Map and Meteorological Glossary, 1916, and other official publications. Recreation: books. Address: 171 Old Brompton Road, SW5. T: 4065 Kensington.
Died 23 March 1945.

SHAW-STEWART, Sir (Michael) Hugh, 8th Bt cr 1667; KCB 1933; CB 1916; TD; LLD (Glasgow) 1936; Lord Lieutenant for Renfrewshire since 1922; b 11 July 1854; e s of Sir M. R. Shaw-Stewart, 7th Bt, and Lady Octavia Grosvenor, d of 2nd Marquis of Westminster; S father, 1903; m 1883, Lady Alice Emma Thynne, CBE (d 1942), d of 4th Marquis of Bath. Educ: Eton; Christ Church, Oxford. Formerly Capt. 4th Batt. Argyll and Sutherland Highlanders; Hon. Col 5/6th A and S Highlanders; Chairman Territorial Association and of County Council; MP (C) Renfrewshire, E, 1886–1906. Heir: nephew Bt Col Walter Guy, MC, b 10 Aug. 1892. Address: Ardgowan, Inverkip, Renfrewshire. TA: Inverkip. Club: Travellers'.
Died 29 June 1942.

SHAWE, Henry Benjamin, CMG 1923; ISO 1917; b 1864; s of Capt. Samuel Shawe, MLA; m 1890, Agnes Edith, d of late John Alfred Honeyborne. Entered Public Service, 1883; Assistant Under Colonial Secretary Union of S Africa, 1902; Acting Under-Secretary for Agriculture, 1907; Under-Secretary for Interior, 1910; Acting Secretary, 1914; Secretary, 1919.
Died 14 Sept. 1943.

SHEAD, Sir Samuel George, Kt 1917; b 1871; s of late William Shead; m 1st, 1892, Lucy (d 1928), d of late Charles Vidler; one d; 2nd, 1927, G. M., d of R. A. England, Yorkshire; one d. Member of London Stock Exchange; Lieut Army Service Corps, Knight Order of St Sava: Sheriff of London, 1915–16. Club: Royal Automobile.
Died 21 June 1948.

SHEARER, Cresswell, FRS; MA, DSc (Cantab), MD, CM (McGill), FZS; late University Lecturer in Embryology, Cambridge; b Montreal, 1874; y s of James Shearer; m Amy, y d of Col Hext of Trenarren, Cornwall. Educ: Montreal; Trinity College, Cambridge. Publications: Numerous papers on Animal Morphology and Embryology, Sex Determination and Experimental Zoology; The Renaissance of Architecture in Southern Italy, 1935. Recreations: golf and lawn tennis. Address: Clare College and 5 Grange Court, Pinehurst, Cambridge.
Died 7 Feb. 1941.

SHEARER, E., MA, BSc, FRSE; Emeritus-Professor of Agriculture and Rural Economy, Edinburgh University. Formerly Director-General Ministry of Agriculture, Egypt. Address: 11 George Square, Edinburgh.
Died 14 Sept. 1945.

SHEAT, Sir (William James) Oliver, Kt 1938; OBE 1920; JP Essex; b 1864; s of late James B. Sheat, San Francisco; m 1890, Susannah (d 1938), d of late John Back; two s. Address: 120 Cranbrook Road, Ilford. Club: City Livery.
Died 30 Aug. 1944.

SHEBBEARE, Rev. Charles John, DD (Oxon), Chaplain to the King since 1921; b 15 April 1865; e s of Rev. Charles Hooper Shebbeare, Vicar of Wykeham, York, and Lucy Marian, d of Rev. John Robert Inge, Vicar of Seamer, near Scarborough; m 1914, Evelyne, d of Rev. Conway Joyce, Vicar of Sydenham, Oxon; two s (and e s missing 18 July 1944, now presumed killed). Educ: St Peter's Coll., Westminster; Christ Church, Oxford. Rector of Swerford, Oxfordshire, 1898–1921; Rector of Stanhope, Co. Durham, 1921–42; Select Preacher University of Oxford, 1917–19; Wilde Lecturer in Natural and Comparative Religion, University of Oxford, 1924–26; Lecturer in Pastoral Theology, University of Cambridge, 1926; Select Preacher, University of Cambridge, 1927; former Member of Archbishops' Doctrinal Commission; Master of Wear Valley Beagles, 1930–42; President Society of Historical Theology, Oxford, 1937–38. Publications: The Greek Theory of the State, 1895; Religion in an Age of Doubt, 1914; The Challenge of the Universe, 1918; Problems of Providence, 1929; The Fioretti and the Gospels—a comparison and a moral, 1904; (with Joseph McCabe) The Argument from Design reconsidered (in USA under title Revelation of God in Nature), 1923; The Problem of the Future Life, 1939; Christianity and Other Religions, 1939; Articles in The Nineteenth Century, Hibbert Journal, Spectator, etc. Recreations: music, beagling, riding. Address: 5 St Cross Road, Holywell, Oxford.
Died 16 Oct. 1945.

SHEDDEN, Sir Lewis, Kt 1929; CBE 1920; JP 1905; Secretary Scottish Unionist Association (Western Divisional Council) and Glasgow Unionist Association; b 9 June 1870; s of late Lewis Shedden, Glasgow; m 1901, Marion Knox Burnett, d of late Robert Alan, Glasgow; one s. Educ: Glasgow. Secretary Glasgow Unionist Association, 1887; Secretary Scottish Association (Western Divisional Council) since 1909; Joint Honorary Secretary, West of Scotland Central Recruiting Committee, War Savings Committee, National Service Committee, War Aims Committee; Deputy Commissioner National Service (Agricultural Section), 1914–18; Ex-Deacon Incorporation of

Weavers; Governor of the Royal Samaritan Hospital for Women; Income Tax Commissioner for City of Glasgow; Director of the City of Glasgow Native Benevolent Association; Vice-President Royal National Lifeboat Institution, Glasgow Branch. *Address:* West Park, 14 Hamilton Avenue, Maxwell Park, Glasgow, S1. *T:* Ibrox 1612. *Clubs:* Conservative, Scottish Constitutional, Glasgow.

Died 22 Oct. 1941.

SHEEHAN, Sir Henry John, Kt 1937; CBE 1928; Governor of Commonwealth Bank of Australia since 1938; *b* St Kilda, Victoria, 26 Dec. 1883; *s* of late Arthur A. Sheehan, Blackburn, Victoria; *m* 1913, Mabel L., *d* of William Cust, Melbourne; one *s* two *d*. *Educ:* Victorian State Schools; South Melbourne College. Joined Commonwealth Treasury, 1903; Secretary to Australian Loan Council, 1923–32; Secretary to National Debt Commission, 1923–32; Assistant Secretary to Treasury, 1926–32; Secretary to the Treasury, 1932–38; Financial Adviser to Australian Delegation to World Economic Conference, 1933; Delegate to League of Nations, 1933; Director of Commonwealth Bank of Australia and Member of National Debt Commission since 1932; Member of Board of Trustees for National Insurance Funds, 1938. *Recreation:* golf. *Address:* Commonwealth Bank of Australia, Sydney, NSW, Australia. *Clubs:* Australian, Sydney, and Melbourne.

Died 26 March 1941.

SHEEHAN, Most Rev. Michael, DD, DPh (Bonn), MA; *b* Waterford, 1870. *Educ:* St John's College, Waterford; Maynooth; Universities of Oxford, Greifswald, Bonn. Priest, 1895; appointed Professor of Classics, Maynooth, 1897; Professor of Greek, 1905–22; Commissioner of Intermediate Education, 1906–22; Vice-President, 1919–22, St Patrick's College, Maynooth; Archbishop Coadjutor of Sydney, 1922–37; present title, Archbishop of Germia. *Publications:* Apologetics; Catholic Doctrine; A Child's Book of Religion; A Simple Course of Religion, and several works bearing on Irish studies. *Address:* c/o M. H. Gill, 50 O'Connell Street, Upper Dublin.

Died 1 March 1945.

SHEEHY, Sir John Francis, Kt 1943; CSI 1939; Assistant Financial Adviser (Executive) to the British Military Governor in Germany, since 1948; *b* 12 Oct. 1889. *Educ:* St Tarlath's College, Tuam; St Patrick's College, Maynooth; University College, Galway. Entered ICS 1914; Member Central Board of Revenue, Govt of India, from 1937, and Additional Secretary to Govt of India in Finance Department; Director of Public Revenue, CCG, 1947.

Died 11 May 1949.

SHEEN, Alfred William, CBE, 1918; DL, Co. Glamorgan; MS, MD (Lond.), FRCS (Eng.); Consulting Surgeon; Colonel (TA) retired; late RAMC (TA); County Controller Voluntary Aid, Glamorgan; Provost, Welsh National School of Medicine; Consulting Surgeon, Royal Infirmary, Cardiff, Seamen's Hospital, Cardiff, and other hospitals; *b* 30 April 1869; *s* of Alfred Sheen, MD, Cardiff, and Harriet Nell; *m* 1898, Christine (*d* 1939), 2nd *d* of J. P. Ingledew, JP, Cardiff; no *c*. *Educ:* University College, Cardiff (Scholar and Prizeman in Chemistry, Physics, and Biology); Guy's Hospital; London (*Proxime accessit*, entrance Scholarship, House Surgeon, and Obstetric Resident). Assistant Surgeon and Surgeon, Royal Infirmary, Cardiff; former Prof. of Surgery, Univ. of Wales; Past-President Hunterian Society, Surgical Section British Medical Assoc., Guy's Physical Society, Cardiff Medical Society, Cardiff Naturalists' Society; formerly OC 2nd Welch Field Ambulance and Welch RAMC School of Instruction; Surgeon, Imperial Yeomanry Field Hosp.; S African War (despatches); in European War, OC and Senior Surgeon, Welsh Hospital; OC No. 34 (Welsh) General Hospital, and Consultant Surgeon, War Hospitals, India (despatches, CBE); Fellow Royal Society of Medicine and Hunterian Society; formerly Visiting Surgeon, Special Surgical Hospital, Shepherd's Bush, and Orpington Hospital. *Publications:* Principles of Military Orthopædics, Indian Med. Gaz., 1918; Surgery of the Spleen (Hunterian Oration), Lancet, 1929; The Return to Work of the Injured Colliery Workman, British Medical Journal, 1938; and numerous other papers in professional journals. *Recreations:* fishing, golf. *Address:* 10 The Parade, Cardiff. *T:* Cardiff 3280; Blackgates, Llandaff, Cardiff. *T:* Llandaff 642. *Club:* Cardiff and County.

Died 28 March 1945.

SHEFFIELD, Sir Berkeley (Digby George), 6th Bt *cr* 1756; JP, DL; *b* 19 Jan. 1876; *o s* of 5th Bt and Priscilla Isabel Laura, *d* of Lt-Col and Lady Sophia Dumaresq; *S* father, 1886; *m* 1904, Baroness Julia, *e d* of Baron de Tuyll, OBE (a Lady of Grace, St John of Jerusalem, twice mentioned for distinguished services during the War); four *s* one *d*. *Educ:* Eton. Late Lieut Westmorland and Cumberland Yeomanry Cavalry; 2nd Lieut 4th Battalion Lincolnshire Regt, 1894–97; MP (U) Lincs (Brigg), 1907–10; MP (U) Brigg Division of Lindsey, 1922–29; Attaché French Embassy, Paris, 1897–1900; Capt. Lincolnshire Imperial Yeomanry, 1901–07, and since 1914; Member of Lindsey CC, 1902–06; High Sheriff Lincoln, 1905–06; Alderman, 1908–15; Chairman North Lindsey Light Railway; Director of the Great Central Railway, retired, owing to amalgamation, 1923; Charter Mayor for borough of Scunthorpe, 1936; DAQMG 62nd Div., 1915–16; ADC to Maj.-Gen. Hon. E. Stuart-Wortley, BEF, 1916; Acting Private Secretary to Viscount Milner with the Allied Missions to Petrograd, 1917 (Order of St Anne 3rd Class); Clerk in the Foreign Office, 1917; attached to the Supreme War Council, 1917–18. Owns about 40,000 acres. Patron of two livings. *Heir: s* Robert Arthur, *b* 18 Oct. 1905. *Address:* Normanby Park, Scunthorpe, Lincs; Meoble Forest, Lochailort, RSO, Inverness-shire. *Clubs:* Orleans, Turf, Travellers'; Jockey, Newmarket.

Died 26 Nov. 1946.

SHEILDS, Rt Rev. Wentworth Francis W.; *see* Wentworth-Sheilds.

SHELDON, Charles Monroe; Contributing Editor, Christian Herald, New York, since 1925; *b* Wellsville, New York, 1857; *s* of Stewart Sheldon and Sarah Ward; *m* 1891, Mary Abby Merriam; one *s*. *Educ:* Phillips Academy, Andover, Massachusetts; Brown University; Andover Theological Seminary. Ordained Congregational Ministry, 1886; Pastor, Congregational Church, Waterbury, Vt, 1886–89; edited the Topeka Capital once a week as a distinctively Christian daily, 1900; Pastor, Central Church, Topeka, 1889–1912, and since 1915; Minister at Large and Lecturer, 1912–15; Pastor Central Congregational Church, Topeka, Kansas, 1915–20; resigned pastorate, 1920; Forty Year Honour Man, Brown University, DD 1925; Member Flying Squadron (1914 and 1915) national organisation to secure national Prohibition. *Publications:* Richard Bruce, 1891; The Twentieth Door, 1893; The Crucifixion of Philip Strong, 1893; His Brother's Keeper, 1895; In His Steps, 1896; Malcolm Kirk, 1897; The Miracle at Markham, 1898; Born to Serve; Robert Hardy's Seven Days, 1892; John King's Question Class, 1894; The Redemption of Freetown, 1898; For Christ and the Church, 1899; Lend a Hand, 1897; One of the Two, 1898; Edward Blake, 1899; Who Killed Joe's Baby? 1901; The Wheels of the Machine; The Reformer; The Narrow Gate; The Christian Socialist, 1903; A Year Book, 1909; Paul Douglas, 1909; The High Calling, 1910; Brander Cushing, 1911; Jesus is Here, 1913; Of One Blood, 1915; Howard Chase, Red Hill, Kansas, 1917; All the World, 1918; In His Steps To-day, 1920; The Richest Man in Kansas; The Everyday Bible, 1924;

The Mere Man and his Problems, 1924; Charles M. Sheldon: his Life and Work, 1925; The Happiest Day of my Life, 1926; Let's Talk it Over, 1926; The 13th Resolution, 1926; Three Old Friends, 1926; Two Films, 1927; The Divine Dignity of Labor, 1928; Life's Treasure Book, 1930; What Did Jesus Really Teach, 1930; He Is Here, 1931; God's Finger Prints, 1941; The Golden Book of Bible Stories, 1941; Scrap Book, 1942; The Biggest Business in the World, 1944. *Address:* 1621 College Avenue, Topeka, Kansas, USA.

Died 24 Feb. 1946.

SHELDON, Norman Lindsay, CIE 1932; PhD, FRIC; *b* 1876; *s* of Edward Sheldon, Manchester; *m* 1912, Ruby E., *d* of Septimus Tristram Pruen, MD, Cheltenham (divorced 1929); one *d*; *m* 1940, Margaret Rhoda, *d* of Timothy Jones, Worcester. *Educ:* Victoria University, Manchester; Heidelberg. Chemical Engineer Cordite Factory, India, 1903; Manager Cordite Factory, 1915; Superintendent Acetone Factory, Nasik, 1919; Chief Inspector of Explosives, India, 1920; retired 1932. *Publications:* papers in chemical journals. *Recreations:* big game, tennis, golf. *Address:* The Farm House, Holmer Green, High Wycombe, Bucks.

Died 4 Oct. 1946.

SHELFORD, Frederic, BSc (Lond.), MICE; Barrister-at-law (Parliamentary Bar); Captain, late Royal Marine (Engineers); late Consulting Engineer for West African and other Government Railways; Vice-President Royal African Society; Chairman Chisambo Estates, Nyasaland Ltd; *b* 14 Nov. 1871; *s* of late Sir William Shelford, KCMG, MICE; *m* 1899, Mildred, *d* of Sir Montagu F. Ommanney, GCMG, KCB, ISO; two *s* one *d*. *Educ:* Westminster School; Dulwich College. Bachelor of Science, London University, 1892. Has been engaged in design and construction of various railways, waterworks, etc., at home; has visited, on behalf of Government and others, British Honduras, Sierra Leone, Gold Coast, Nigeria, Kenya, Nyasaland, Cape Province, Cyprus, Egypt, Holland, Belgium, France, Germany, Italy and Russia; formerly Unionist candidate Pudsey Division, Yorkshire. *Publications:* Pioneering; various pamphlets. *Recreations:* shooting, yachting, and lawn tennis. *Address:* Lingmoor, Parkstone, Dorset; Chisambo, Lujeri, Nyasaland. *Club:* Royal Naval Sailing.

Died 15 July 1943.

SHELL, Rita; Vice-President Society of Women Journalists, Hon. Treasurer 1932–36; Editor of The Lady, 1895–1925; *m* 1889, John Stewart; four *s* (one fell, 1916, European War). *Address:* Mrs Henrietta Stewart, Westminster Bank, 1 Kensington High Street, W8.

Died 8 Nov. 1950.

SHELLEY, Col Bertram Arthur Graham, CMG 1916; late RE; *b* 2 Aug. 1869; *γ s* of late Major-General T. M. Shelley, Indian Army; *m* 1901, Beryl Hubbard, *d* of late Major-General J. H. White, RE; one *s* one *d*. *Educ:* King's College, London; RM Academy, Woolwich. Served India, Malta, and S Africa; European War, 1914–18 (despatches, CMG); Col 1920; Chief Technical Examiner for Works Services, 1922–26; retired pay, 1926. *Address:* The Woodlands, Southwater, Horsham. *T:* Southwater 372.

Died 14 July 1947.

SHELMERDINE, Lt-Col Sir Francis Claude, Kt 1936; CIE 1931; OBE; FRAeS; FIAeS (New York); *b* Churchill, Chipping Norton, Oxon, 25 Oct. 1881; *γ s* of late Rev. Nathaniel and late Emma Shelmerdine of Great Comberton, Pershore, Worcestershire; *m* Lilian Sealey, *e d* of late James Haskins and late Eva Haskins, of Warmley Towers, Glos; no *c*. *Educ:* Rugby; Royal Military College, Sandhurst. Joined 2nd Batt. The Green Howards in India, 1901; served European War in France and Egypt; seconded to the Royal Flying Corps, 1915; Senior Assistant, Directorate of Civil Aviation, Air Ministry, 1919; Director of Civil Aviation in India,

1927–31; Director of Civil Aviation, Air Ministry 1931–34; Director General of Civil Aviation 1934–41. *Recreation:* golf. *Address:* 2 Cavendish Avenue, St John's Wood, NW8. *T:* Cunningham 2991. *Club:* Bath.

Died 9 July 1945.

SHENNAN, Theodore, MD, FRCSE; LLD (Aberdeen); *b* Bathgate, West Lothian; *s* of Rev. Alex. Shennan; *m* 1st, Minnie Green, LRCP and S Edin. and Glasgow, *d* of Alderman Green, Norwich; two *s*; 2nd, Ann Lindsay Thomson, MD, Aberdeen, *d* of Ben. Thomson, MA, LLD; one *d*. *Educ:* Royal High School and University, Edinburgh. MB, CM Edin. 1890; MD 1895; FRCSE 1898. Pathologist, Leith Hospital, 1896; Royal Edinburgh Hospital for Sick Children, 1900; Royal Infirmary, Edinburgh, 1902; Lecturer Pathology and Bacteriology, Surgeons' Hall, Edinburgh, 1899; Lecturer on Morbid Anatomy, University of Edinburgh, 1913; Professor of Pathology, University of Aberdeen, 1914–36. *Publications:* Post Mortems and Morbid Anatomy, 3rd edn 1935; Dissecting Aneurysm (Medical Research Council Special Reports Series No. 193); numerous papers in medical journals on pathological and bacteriological subjects. *Recreations:* fencing, golf and motoring. *Address:* 25 Fonthill Terrace, Aberdeen. *T:* Aberdeen 3376.

Died 21 Oct. 1948.

SHEPARD, Helen Gould; *b* New York, 20 June 1868; *d* of late Jay Gould and Helen Day Miller; *m* 1913, Finley J. Shepard. *Address:* Lyndhurst, Tarrytown, New York.

Died 21 Dec. 1938.

SHEPHARD, Firth; Producer and Presenter of Plays; *b* 27 April 1891; *s* of Richard Shephard and Elizabeth Oliver; *m* 1912, Constance Evans (*d* 1945); one *d*. *Educ:* London. Started business career (Insurance), and became an entertainer and author of musical plays; subsequently (in 1924) became a London manager; managerial partnership with Leslie Henson, 1928–34; has since produced independently, notably at the Gaiety (a series of continuously successful productions for five years), Strand, Princes, Savoy, and Saville Theatres and, from time to time, at almost all the West End of London theatres. Amongst numerous plays presented: It's a Boy; Counsel's Opinion; Night of the Garter; Seeing Stars; Swing Along; Going Greek; The Frog; Housemaster; Wild Oats; They Walk Alone; Shephard's Pie; Up and Doing; The Man Who Came to Dinner; Fine and Dandy; Arsenic and Old Lace; Junior Miss; The Last of Mrs Cheyney; Fifty-Fifty; Lady Frederick; Life with Father; Honour and Obey; Canaries Sometimes Sing (revival), A la carte, etc. Vice-Pres. Society of West End Theatre Managers. *Recreation:* golf. *Address:* 36 Curzon Street, W1. *Club:* Savage.

Died 3 Jan. 1949.

SHEPHERD, Arthur Edmond, CBE 1919; DSO 1918; VD; Consulting Surgeon, Adelaide Hospital; Medical Officer, Repatriation Department; Col AMC, CMF Retired List, 1927; *b* Adelaide, 19 Oct. 1867; Anglo-Australian Parentage; *s* of E. Shepherd; *m* 1896, Amanda Shepherd; four *s* two *d*. *Educ:* Norwood Grammar School; Prince Alfred College; Edinburgh. Held various Surgical and Public Health appointments, South Australia; joined AAMC Commonwealth Military Forces, 1900; retired Active List, 1922; on outbreak of war served as PMO and then as Director-General Medical services Australia till Dec. 1915, when embarked for active service; served Egypt, France, Belgium, in command 8th Aust. Field Ambulance; promoted Colonel ADMS 2nd Australia Division, 1917, and SMO Australian Corps, 1919; on arrival in Australia resumed PMO, which position was resigned to take up administrative medical position for Repatriation Department (despatches thrice, CBE, DSO, VD, Médaille de Reconnaissance Française). *Recreation:*

yachting. *Address:* 65 Northcote Terrace, Medindie, S Australia. *T:* M2603. *Clubs:* Returned Soldiers', Adelaide.

Died 27 April 1942.

SHEPHERD, F. H. S.; *s* of Rev. F. Shepherd, Stoke-under-Ham, Somerset; *m* 1930, Charlotte, *d* of G. H. Wollaston; no *c. Educ:* Rugby; Corpus Christi College, Oxford. Slade School of Art, 1898–1901. Member New English Art Club since 1912; Associé de la Société Nationale des Beaux-Arts, 1928; exhibited RA, etc. Chevalier of Belgian Order of the Crown, 1920. *Recreation:* Chamber music. *Address:* 19 Paultons Square, Chelsea, SW3. *T:* Flaxman 5831. *Club:* Chelsea Arts.

Died 23 May 1948.

SHEPHERD, Sir (Harry) Percy, Kt 1927. Sheriff of City of London, 1926–27. *Address:* 48 Porchester Terrace, W2. *T:* Paddington 7877.

Died 1 May 1946.

SHEPHERD, Very Rev. Henry Young, MBE 1935; *m* Amy Louise (*d* 1936). *Educ:* University of Durham, MA. Priest, 1882; Curate of St George, Antigua, 1881–82; St John, 1882–95; Rector of the Cathedral, 1895–1930; Dean of Antigua, 1906–30. *Address:* Avon Dassett, St John's, Antigua.

Died 18 March 1947.

SHEPHERD, James Affleck; artist; *b* London, 29 Nov. 1867; *o s* of William Shepherd, cigar importer; *m* 1897, Nellie Gertrude, 2nd *d* of G. L. Turner; two *s* one *d. Educ:* various small schools, assisted by private tutor. Studied under Alfred Bryan, the caricaturist, for three years. invented and illustrated 'Zig-Zags at the Zoo' for Strand Magazine; invented and illustrated 'The Arcadian Calendar' for same magazine; invited to join the staff of Punch, 1893; for some three years on the Staff of the Illustrated London News; awarded Gold Medal, International Exhibition of Humorous Art, Rivoli, Italy, 1911. *Publications:* Illustrated Uncle Remus, 1901; Wonders in Monsterland, 1901; Zig-Zag Fables, 1897; Nights with Uncle Remus, 1903; The Three Jovial Puppies, 1907; The Life of a Foxhound, 1910; The Story of Chanticleer, 1913; The Bodley Head Natural History, 1913; also illustrated Idlings in Arcadia. *Recreations:* hunting and interest in all animal life. *Address:* Woodmancote Manor, nr Cirencester, Glos. *Club:* Savage.

Died 11 May 1946.

SHEPHERD, Sir Percy; *see* Shepherd, Sir H. P.

SHEPHERD, William Kidd Ogilvy, DSO 1917; Major RA (TA); Solicitor and Notary Public; partner in firm of W. & J. Ogilvy Shepherd, Solicitors, Leven, Fife; *b* Edinburgh, 26 Dec. 1888; *e s* of late Major William Shepherd, TD, Brunton, Markinch, and Mrs Mary Shepherd, Netherton, Leven; *m* 1917, Norah, *yr d* of late T. G. M. Davidson, 7 Midmar Gardens, Edinburgh; one *s. Educ:* Edinburgh Academy; Edinburgh University. Commanded Fife Battery RFA (T), and No. 13 Mountain Battery, RGA, European War, France, 1915–16; Palestine, 1918–19 (despatches twice, DSO); Director Edinburgh Board of Royal Insurance Co.; Town Clerk and Treasurer Burgh of Markinch; Clerk River Leven Trust; Clerk Scoonie Heritors; Hon. Sec. Innerleven Golf Club; Clerk Fife Small Burghs Association. *Recreations:* tennis, badminton. *Address:* Drum Lodge, Largo, Fife. *TA:* Shepherd, Lower Largo. *T:* Lundin Links 22.

Died 10 Oct. 1941.

SHEPPARD, Alfred Tresidder; novelist; *b* 17 June 1871; *e s* of Alfred H. Sheppard and Harriet Winifred, *d* of Rev. James Sears; *m* 1930, Doreen, *e d* of Lieut-Col H. Moore. *Educ:* Bishop's Stortford. In North British and Mercantile Insurance Company for several years before devoting whole time to literature. *Publications:*

The Red Cravat, 1905; Running Horse Inn, 1906; The Rise of Ledgar Dunstan, 1916; The Quest of Ledgar Dunstan, 1917; A Son of the Manse, 1919; The Autobiography of Judas Iscariot, 1920; Brave Earth, 1925; Here Comes an Old Sailor, 1927; Queen Dick, 1928; The Art and Practice of Historical Fiction, and Tuck of Drum and other stories, 1930; The King's Goose, 1931; A Rose for Scotland (with Roderick MacLeod), 1933; The Making of Man and Other Poems, 1934; Rome's Gift, 1936; The Matins of Bruges, 1938; Editor of the Bible in Ireland, 1926; contributor of articles, reviews, short stories, and verse to many leading newspapers and magazines in Great Britain and the United States; Lectures on the Historical Novel, etc. *Recreations:* walking, reading. *Club:* Savage.

Died 9 May 1947.

SHEPPARD, Oliver, RHA, RBS, Professor of Sculpture; has executed many public memorials, and other works in sculpture; *b* Tyrone; *s* of Simpson Sheppard, sculptor; *m*; one *d. Educ:* RCA. *Recreation:* golf. *Address:* 30 Pembroke Road, Dublin.

Died 14 Sept. 1941.

SHEPPARD, Thomas, MSc, ALS; late Director Municipal Museum, Royal Institution, Museum of Fisheries and Shipping, Mortimer Museum of Archæology, Wilberforce House Museum, Hull, Museum of Transport and Commerce, Railway Museum, and the Folk-Lore Museum at Easington; *b* South Ferriby, Lincs, 2 Oct. 1876; *e s* of late Harvy Sheppard, FEIS; *m* 1901, Mary Isobel, *e d* of James Henry Osbourn; one *s. Educ:* Hull. Editor of Mortimer's Forty Years' Researches in the British and Anglo-Saxon Burial Mounds of East Yorkshire, 1905. *Publications:* Geological Rambles in East Yorkshire, 1903; Illustrated Catalogue of the Mortimer Museum, Driffield, 1900; The Making of East Yorkshire, 1905; The Evolution of Kingston-upon-Hull, 1911; Bacon is Alive! 1911; The Lost Towns of the Yorkshire Coast, 1912; Yorkshire Past and Present, 1913; Yorkshire by Pen and Picture, 1914; Yorkshire's Contribution to Science, 1915; Bibliography of Yorkshire Geology (1534–1914), 1915; William Smith: His Maps and Memoirs, 1916; The Correct Arms of Hull, 1917; Kingston-upon-Hull before, during, and after the War, 1919; Handbook to Hull and East Yorkshire, 1922; Money Scales and Weights, 1924; History of the Drama in Hull and District; Makers of History: William Wilberforce, 1937; The Fossils of the Yorkshire Lias, 1942; numerous Guides to the History and Commerce of Kingston-upon-Hull; Birthplace of Wilberforce; 230 Museum publications. *Recreations:* field geology and archæological investigations. *Address:* 46 Anlaby Park Road, Hull. *T:* Hull 11830.

Died 19 Feb. 1945.

SHEPPERSON, Sir Ernest Whittome, 1st Bt *cr* 1945; Kt 1929; MA, LLB; JP; Barrister-at-law; landowner and farmer; Deputy Chairman Isle of Ely Quarter Sessions; Isle of Ely CC; *b* 1874; *s* of Joseph Whitham Shepperson, JP, Keyworth House, Benwick, March, and Harriet Whittome; *m* 1916, Doris, *d* of Cole Ambrose, Stuntney Hall, Ely; two *d. Educ:* Christ's College, Cambridge. Called to Bar, Gray's Inn, 1908. Captain 3rd Bn Cambridge Regt (vols) 1915. Holds National Diploma in Agriculture and Diploma in Agriculture, Cambridge University; MP Herefordshire (Leominster), 1922–45; is deeply interested in the industry of agriculture, and has endeavoured to help that industry by the application of science. *Recreations:* yachting, shooting, skating; owner of yacht Blue Bird. *Address:* Upwood House, Hunts. *T:* Ramsey 58; Keyworth House, Benwick, March. *T:* Benwick 4; 6 Fig Tree Court, Temple, EC. *Clubs:* Carlton, 1900; Royal Norfolk and Suffolk Yacht.

Died 22 Aug. 1949 (ext).

SHERARD, Robert Harborough; author; Chevalier de la Légion d'Honneur; *b* London, 3 Dec. 1861; *s* of Rev. Bennet Sherard Kennedy, Stapleford Park, Melton Mowbray; *g g s* of William Wordsworth. Poet Laureate; *m* 1928, Alice Muriel Fiddian. *Educ:* Queen Elizabeth College, Guernsey; New College, Oxford; Bonn University. Special correspondent in various parts of the world for English, American, and Australian newspapers and reviews since 1884; founded the Vindex Publishing Co., Calvi, 1933. *Publications:* Whispers: Poems, 1882; Rogues; My First Voyage (with Daudet); Jacob Niemand; Emile Zola, 1893; Alphonse Daudet, 1894; The White Slaves of England, 1897; The Story of an Unhappy Friendship, 1902; Twenty Years in Paris, 1905; The Life of Oscar Wilde, 1906; After the Fault, 1907; The Real Oscar Wilde, 1912; Guy de Maupassant, 1926; Bernard Shaw, Frank Harris and Oscar Wilde, 1937; Why? (a novel), 1939; Romances of the Table, 1939; Ultima Verba (reply to Bernard Shaw), 1940; Memoirs of a Mug, 1941.

Died 30 Jan. 1943.

SHERBORNE, 6th Baron *cr* 1784; **James Huntly Dutton,** DSO 1915; late the Cameronians (Scottish Rifles); *b* 5 March 1873; *e s* of late Col Hon. Charles Dutton and May Arbuthnot, *d* of late George Noble Taylor; *S* uncle, 1919; *m* 1908, Ethel Mary, *e d* of late William Baird; two *s* two *d. Educ:* Wellington College; RMC, Sandhurst. Entered Army, 1893; retired, 1908; served S African War, 1899–1902; joined Royal Scots, 1914; European War, 1914–19 (despatches, DSO). Owns about 15,775 acres. *Heir: s* Hon. Charles Dutton [*b* 13 May 1911; *m* 1943, Mrs Anthony Jenkinson, *d* of Sir James Dunn, 1st Bt]. *Address:* Windrush Manor, Oxford; Sherborne Park, Glos. *TA:* Sherborne, Glos. *Clubs:* Marlborough-Windham, Flyfishers'.

Died 17 Sept. 1949.

SHERBROOKE, Col Nevile Hugh Cairns, CBE 1941; DSO 1917; *b* London, 8 April 1880; *s* of Rev. Henry Nevile Sherbrooke and Lady Lilias Sherbrooke, *e d* of 1st Earl Cairns; *m* 1906, Cicely (*d* 1938), *y d* of Rev. J. C. M. Mansel-Pleydell of Sturminster Newton, Dorset; one *s* two *d. Educ:* Eton College; Royal Military Academy, Woolwich. 2nd Lieut Royal Artillery, 1898; served South African War, 1900–02; served in RHA, India, 1902–04; Staff Captain Royal Artillery, Salisbury Plain, 1908–11; Staff College, Camberley, 1914; served on Western Front intermittently, 1914–19, as Brigade Major RA, Lieut-Col RHA, and GSO1; GSO1 Baltic Military Mission, 1919; GSO1 Mesopotamia (Arab Rising), 1920–21 (DSO, Bt Lt-Col, despatches six times); Commandant School of Artillery, India, 1927–29; Assistant Comdt, Royal Military Academy, Woolwich, 1929–32; Commander RA, 53rd (Welsh) Division TA, 1932–36; retired pay, 1936; commanded Woolwich Garrison, 1939–41. *Recreations:* fox-hunting, golf, lawn tennis. *Address:* Felden Croft, Boxmoor, Herts. *T:* Boxmoor 371. *Clubs:* United Service, MCC.

Died 6 March 1944.

SHERIDAN, Charles Cahill, CIE 1913. Joined the service, 1882; Deputy Postmaster-General and Inspector-General India Postal Department, 1910; Postmaster-General, Punjab, 1913; retired, 1915; served with Chitral Relief Force, 1895.

Died 10 March 1941.

SHERIDAN, Edward, FRCSI; MD, MDS, NUI, LRCPI, IDS, RCSI (Past Pres.); FDS, RCSE, 1948. Professor of Dental Surgery, NUI; Consulting Dental Surgeon, Mater Misericord Hospital; Surgeon Incorp. Dental Hospital, Ireland; late Chairman Dental Board of the UK; late Member of General Medical Council; MRIA. *Publication:* Perforation of Lr Molar by Mandib., N Brit. Dent. Jl, Dec. 1941. *Address:* 15 St Stephen's Green, Dublin. *T:* Dublin 61870.

Died 10 April 1949.

SHERIDAN, Sir Philip Cahill, Kt 1929; CMG 1919; *b* 1871; *s* of Philip Sheridan, late PMG Punjab, India; *m* 1906, Blanche, *d* of J. Robertson, QC, Dublin; one *d. Educ:* Beaumont College, Old Windsor. Joined East Indian Railway Company, 1894; Chief Superintendent, 1915; joined RE Corps as temporary Captain, 1917; served in France and Italy during European War; Assistant Director-General Transportation, 1917–20; Lt-Colonel, 1918; Colonel, 1919; retired from Army, 1920; Order SS Maurice and Lazarus, Italy, 1920; General Traffic Manager, East Indian Railway, 1920; Officiating General Manager, 1921; Member Indian Railway Board, 1923–29. *Address:* The Moorings, Heathfield Road, Woking, Surrey. *Club:* Oriental.

Died 2 Oct. 1949.

SHERLOCK, Sir Alfred Parker, Kt 1925; Chairman, Booker Bros, McConnel & Co. Ltd, Bookers Demerara Sugar Estates, Ltd; *b* 25 Sept. 1876; *s* of W. H. Sherlock and Emma Gregg; *m* 1909, Laura Decima Hill; three *s* one *d. Educ:* Rossall School. Joined staff of Curtis, Campbell & Co., Demerara, 1900; Assistant Secretary, Sprostons, Ltd, Demerara, 1906; Managing Director of Booker Bros, McConnell & Co. Ltd, Demerara Branch, 1909; Senior Member for Georgetown, Court of Policy, British Guiana, 1911–16; Member of Executive Council, British Guiana, 1914–26; Vice-Pres. West India Committee; British Guiana representative on Governing Body of Imperial College of Tropical Agriculture. *Recreation:* golf. *Address:* 37–41 Gracechurch Street, EC3. *Clubs:* Gresham, West Indian.

Died 24 Feb. 1946.

SHERREN, James, CBE 1919; FRCS Eng.; Col late Army Medical Service; Consulting Surgeon to London Hospital; Consulting Surgeon, Poplar Hospital for Accidents, and Stanmore Cottage Hospital; *b* Weymouth; *e s* of John A. Sherren, JP; *m* 1897, Madeleine, *e d* of George Thorne; three *s* two *d. Educ:* Weymouth College; London Hospital. Distinction in Anatomy and Physiology; Scholarships in Medicine and Obstetric Medicine. Late Consulting Surgeon attached to War Office; late Vice-President Royal College of Surgeons. Member of Council, Court of Examiners, Erasmus Wilson Lecturer (1906), Hunterian Professor (1920) and Bradshaw Lecturer (1925), Royal College of Surgeons; Examiner in Surgery and Member of Senate, Univ. of London; Surgeon King Edward VII Hospital for Officers, King George Military Hospital, and Yarrow Military Hospital, Broadstairs; Surgical Tutor and Demonstrator of Anatomy, London Hospital Medical Coll.; Examiner in Anatomy for the Primary FRCS. *Publications:* contributions to textbooks and medical journals on Abdominal Surgery and the Surgery of the Peripheral Nerves. *Recreations:* the sea, music. *Address:* White Barn, Broadstone, Dorset. *T:* Broadstone 1. *Club:* Union.

Died 29 Oct. 1945.

SHERSTON-BAKER, Lt-Col Sir Dodington George Richard, 5th Bt *cr* 1796; Indian Medical Service, retired; *b* 22 July 1877; *s* of 4th Bt; *S* father, 1923; *m* 1906, Irene Roper, *y d* of late Sir Roper Parkington; one *s* one *d.* Served European War on many fronts, including Egypt, Arabia, Persia, Transcaspia; formerly MO 7th Gurkha Rifles; OC Indian Station Hospital, Aden; retired, 1925. *Heir: s* Humphrey Dodington Benedict [*b* 1907; *m* 1938, Margaret Alice (Bobby), *o d* of H. W. Binns, 9 Campden Street, W, and Blythburgh, Suffolk; two *d.* Downside; Christ's College, Cambridge]. *Address:* 1 St Anthonys' Road, Bournemouth. *T:* 6397.

Died 18 Nov. 1944.

SHERWELL, Arthur; MP (L) Huddersfield, 1906–18; *b* London, 11 April 1863; *s* of late John Viney Sherwell, of Modbury, South Devon, and London; *m* 1909, Amy, *d* of late J. H. Whadcoat, JP, Bodiam, Sussex, and Harrogate. *Educ:* privately. Prior to entering Parliament was occupied in sociological and politico-economic studies and literary work; has travelled extensively; has been several times round the world; and has an intimate acquaintance with United States and the British Dominions and Colonies; has served on various Government Committees and Commissions. *Publications:* Life in West London; The Drink Peril in Scotland; The Russian Vodka Monopoly; State Purchase of the Liquor Trade; (Joint)—The Temperance Problem and Social Reform; The Taxation of the Liquor Trade; Public Control of the Liquor Trade; British Gothenburg Experiments; State Prohibition and Local Option, etc. *Recreations:* Bluebooks, gardening, and cricket. *Address:* Wychmont, Tunbridge Wells, Kent.

Died 13 Jan. 1942.

SHERWOOD, Rev. Edward Charles, MA; Tutor of St Andrew's Training House for Ordinands, Pampisford (formerly Whittlesford), Cambs, since 1946; *e s* of late Rev. Edward Purvis Sherwood, Kingsley, Kenilworth; *m* Naomi Claire (*d* 1937), *d* of late Rev. Dr W. H. Flecker, DCL; two *s* one *d*. *Educ:* Magdalen College School and Magdalen College, Oxford. Demy of Magdalen, 1891; BA 1896; Oxford and Cambridge Boat Race, 1896; Assistant Master, Magdalen College School, 1896–1900; Assistant Master, Westminster School, 1901–06; Deacon, 1903; priest, 1904; Hon. Curate at St Margaret's, Westminster, 1903–06; Headmaster of St Lawrence College, Ramsgate, 1906–18; Headmaster, Ipswich School, 1919–33; Vicar of Whittlesford, Cambs, 1933–43; Warden of St Andrew's, 1933–46. *Address:* St Andrew's, Pampisford. *TA:* Pampisford. *T:* Sawston 108.

Died 20 Feb. 1947.

SHERWOOD, Harry Leslie, CBE 1923; *b* 1863; *s* of late William Sherwood; *m* Adeline Myra, *d* of late Robert Taylor, Brighton; two *s*. *Educ:* privately. Served in Foreign Office, 1882–1915; Consul at Portland, Oregon, for Oregon, Washington, Idaho, Montana, and Alaska, 1915–19; Inspector-General of HM Consulates, with rank of Acting Counsellor of Embassy in HM Diplomatic Service, 1919–22; retired, 1922. *Publications:* for some years Joint Editor of Foreign Office List and British and Foreign State Papers; Joint Editor of 3rd ed. Map of Africa by Treaty. *Recreations:* philately, productive gardening. *Address:* The Old Place, Prinsted, near Emsworth. *T:* Emsworth 135.

Died 23 April 1946.

SHIEL, Matthew Phipps, BA Lond.; teacher, interpreter to the International Congress of Hygiene and Demography, journalist, author, inventor; placed on the Civil List, 1938, for Services to Literature; *b* 21 July 1865; *m* Carolina Garcia Gomez. *Publications:* The Rajah's Sapphire (with W. T. Stead); Shapes in the Fire; Prince Zaleski; The Yellow Danger; Contraband of War; Cold Steel; The Lord of the Sea; The Mantealers; The Purple Cloud (acquired by Paramount for motion-picture play); The Weird O't; The Pale Ape; The Evil that Men Do; The Yellow Wave; This Knot of Life; The Lost Viol; The Last Miracle; The Isle of Lies; Unto the Third Generation, 1903; The White Wedding, 1907; The Dragon, 1913; Children of the Wind, 1924; How the Old Woman got Home, 1927; Here Comes the Lady, 1928; Dr Krasinski's Secret, 1930; The Black Box, 1930; The Invisible Voices, 1936; Poems, 1936; The Young Men are Coming, 1937; Above all Else, 1943. *Recreations:* mountaineering, mathematics. *Address:* L'Abri, New Road Worthing Road, Horsham, Sussex.

Died 17 Feb. 1947.

SHIELDS, Hon. Tasman, CMG 1931; KC 1938; *b* 20 Nov. 1872; *s* of late George Shields, Launceston, Tasmania; *m* 1902, Maud Mary (*d* 1934), *d* of late Arthur Israel Allison, Tasmania; one *d*; *m* 1947, Hannah Doris, *d* of John Buckney, Manager, Launceston, Tasmania. *Educ:* Launceston Church Grammar School. Barrister of the

Supreme Court of Tasmania, 1894; Bachelor of Laws, University of Tasmania, 1906; Member for Launceston Legislative Council of Tasmania, 1915–36; Minister without Office, 1916–22. *Recreations:* golf, trout fishing. *Address:* 55 Paterson Street, Launceston, Tasmania. *Club:* Launceston.

Died 28 Aug. 1950.

SHIFFNER, Major Sir Henry Burrows, 7th Bt *cr* 1818; OBE 1941; RA; *b* 29 July 1902; *o surv. s* of 5th Bt and Elsie, *d* of Ogden Hoffman Burrows, of Rhode Island, USA; *S* brother, 1918; *m* 1929, Margaret Mary, *er d* of Sir Ernest Gowers, KCB, KBE; one *s*. *Educ:* Wellington; RMA, Woolwich. ADC to Governor of Uganda Protectorate, 1926–29. Served Middle East, 1941 (OBE). *Heir: s* Henry David, *b* 2 Feb. 1930. *Address:* Coombe Place, Lewes, Sussex.

Died 22 Nov. 1941.

SHILLAKER, James Frederick, MBE; *b* City of London, 28 Jan. 1870; father a policeman and freeman of the City; *m* 1891, Carrie J., *d* of Harry Heaton, variety artiste; one *s*. *Educ:* Taplow Grammar School; City of London College, under a 17th-century foundation for the education of children in St Sepulchre's parish, City of London. At sixteen obtained a rise of wages for City of London Police by writing a leaflet on cost of living basis which was distributed to Members of Common Council; one of the founders of the Fawcett Association for sorters in Post Office; at one time a member of the Association of Correctors of the Press; is now in the National Union of Journalists; was Editor Friends in Council, TP's Weekly for 14 years; Deputy Regional Director, Northern Region, Ministry of Pensions, 1919–23; MP (Lab) Acton Division of Middlesex, 1929–31; has been giving advice to other people for the last forty years. *Publications:* pamphlets, and Section on Pensions in the Book of the Labour Party. *Recreations:* politics and gardening. *Address:* 211 Powder Mill Lane, Twickenham, Middlesex.

Died 20 July 1943.

SHILLINGTON, Major Rt Hon. David Graham; PC Northern Ireland; DL, JP; *b* 10 Dec. 1872; *s* of Thomas Shillington, JP, Tavanagh House, Portadown, Co. Armagh; *m* 1895, Louisa S., *d* of John Collen, DL, JP, Killycomain House, Portadown; two *s* (*e s* killed in last War), three *d*. *Educ:* Methodist College, Belfast; Rydalmount, Colwyn Bay. MP Co. Armagh, 1921–29; Central Armagh, 1929–41; Parliament of Northern Ireland; Minister of Labour in Cabinet of Northern Ireland, 1937–38. *Address:* Melmore, Craigavad, Co. Down. *T:* Holywood 2383. *Clubs:* Ulster Reform, Belfast; County, Armagh.

Died 22 Jan. 1944.

SHILLITO, Rev. Edward, MA Victoria; BA Oxon; *b* 1872; *s* of late Rev. Francis Lomas Shillito; *m* 1901, Annie Elizabeth Brown; two *s* one *d*. *Educ:* Silcoates, Wakefield; Owens College (Victoria University); Mansfield College, Oxford. Held pastorates, Albion, Ashton-under-Lyne (Assistant), Tunbridge Wells, Brighton, Harlesden, Hampstead, Buckhurst Hill. *Publications:* Looking Inwards; The Hope and Mission of the Free Churches; Through the War to the Kingdom; The Omega and other Poems; Jesus of the Scars; The Christian Year in War-time; The New Days; The Return to God; François Coillard: A Wayfaring Man; Christian Citizenship: The Story and the Meaning of COPEC; Life and Work, 1926; Poetry and Prayer; Craftsmen All, 1932; Nationalism: Man's Other Religion, 1933; The Way of the Witnesses, 1936; You can find God, 1937; Christ and Everyman, Selection from Dom Bernard Clements' Broadcast Addresses. *Address:* Lyndhurst, Scotland Road, Buckhurst Hill, Essex. *T:* Buckhurst 1649.

Died 11 March 1948.

SHINN, Frederick George, Mus. Doc. (Dunelm), Hon. RAM, FRCM, FRCO; Professor at the Royal Academy of Music; Hon. Secretary, RCO, Pres. 1944–46; Treasurer, Incorporated Society of Musicians; Organist, St Bartholomew's Church, Sydenham; *b* London, 1867. *Educ:* Royal College of Music. *Publications:* a number of educational works upon Harmony, Aural Training, Musical Memory and related subjects. *Address:* 21 Lawrie Park Avenue Sydenham, SE26.

Died 8 Oct. 1950.

SHIRLEY, Herbert John, CMG 1901; MD, FRCS; TD; DL County of London; Consulting Anæsthetist, University College Hospital; late House Surgeon, House Physician, and Gynæcological Assistant, University College Hospital; late Clinical Assistant Out-Patient Hospital for Sick Children, Great Ormond Street; *b* 22 July 1868; *s* of late Dame Mary Scharlieb and of late William Scharlieb, barrister-at-law [name changed by deed poll, 1914]; *m* 1899, Edith Mabel (*d* 1938), *d* of Charles Tweedy, Redruth; one *s*. Served S Africa, with Langman's hospital, 1900 (despatches, CMG); Lt-Col 2/5 Lancashire Fusiliers BEF (despatches); exchanged RAMC and Consultant Anæsthetist Malta Command, 1917–18; SMO, RASC MT, R and T Area, 1918–19; Bt Col late commanding Artists' Rifles. *Publications:* The Action of Chloroform on the Heart and Blood-vessels (jointly with Prof. Sir E. Schäfer); article on Chloroform, The Practitioner's Encyclopædia of Medicine and Surgery. *Address:* Flat 1, 13 New Cavendish Street, W1. *T:* Welbeck 5859.

Died 14 May 1943.

SHIRLEY, Hon. Ralph; Director of William Rider & Son, Ltd, publishers, 1892–1925; *b* Oxford, 30 Dec. 1865; 2nd *s* of Rev. Walter Waddington Shirley, DD, Regius Professor of Ecclesiastical History in the University of Oxford; *brother* of 11th Earl Ferrers; *m* 1st, 1903, Florence Beatrice (*d* 1926), *d* of H. Wright, Didcot, Berks; 2nd, 1935, Lilian, *widow* of Major Venour Davidson, and *d* of Matthew Lisle Ingram, Feckenham, Worcestershire. *Educ:* Winchester; New College, Oxford. Founder, 1905 and Editor of the Occult Review, 1905–26. *Publications:* The New God, and other Essays, 1911; A Short Life of Abraham Lincoln, 1918; Occultists and Mystics of All Ages, 1920; The Problem of Rebirth, 1936; The Mystery of the Human Double, 1937. *Recreation:* boating. *Address:* Druim, Tithe Pit Shaw Lane, Warlingham, Surrey.

Died 29 Dec. 1946.

SHIRTCLIFFE, Sir George, KBE 1936; OBE; Company Director; *b* Worksop, England, 1862; *s* of John Shirtcliffe; *m* 1st, 1889, Jane Barbara, *d* of Wm Massey, Timaru; two *s* three *d*; 2nd, 1927, Margaret Elise, *d* of late William Priest, Timaru. *Educ:* Riccarton School; Christ's College. Accountant NM and A Co. Ltd, 1879–82; Accountant and Manager, Canterbury Farmers' Co-op. Association, Timaru, 1882–90; Manager and partner A. S. Paterson & Co., 1890–1912; Vice-Chairman and Managing Director, 1912–19 (ret.); Chairman, 1927; President Well. Chamber of Commerce, 1904–07; Member City Cl. about 1905–11; Harbour Board, 1906–08; Taxation Committee, 1922; Chairman of Committees, Anglican Synod; Taxation Committee, 1924; Chairman of Council of the Scientific and Industrial Research Dept, 1926–35; Chairman National Expenditure Commission, 1932. *Address:* 40 Tinakori Road, Wellington, N1, NZ.

Died 19 July 1941.

SHOOLBRED, Lt-Col Rupert, CMG 1915; late Commanding Queen's Westminster Rifles (TA); *b* 22 Aug. 1869; *e s* of John F. Wilkin [assumed, 1904, by Royal licence uncle's name of Shoolbred]. *Educ:* Haileybury. Served European War, 1914–17 (CMG). *Address:* 3 Down Street, W1; Rose Ash Barton, South Molton, N Devon.

Died 29 Sept. 1946.

SHORE, Lewis Erle, OBE 1919; MA, MD, BCh Camb.; late University Lecturer in Physiology and Fellow and Junior Bursar of St John's College; Neurologist to 1st Eastern Hospital, 1916–19; *b* 5 July 1863; 2nd *s* of late T. W. Shore, FGS, archæologist, of Southampton; *m* 1908, Agatha, *d* of R. Gresley Hall, DL, of Upton House, Bitton, Glos; one *s* one *d*. *Educ:* Grammar School and Hartley College, Southampton; St John's College, Cambridge; St Bartholomew's Hospital; Breslau University. *Publications:* Physiology for Beginners (with Sir M. Foster); papers in physiological and medical journals. *Recreations:* gardening, skating. *Address:* 8 Madingley Road, Cambridge. *T:* 4595.

Died 27 July 1944.

SHORE, Thomas William, OBE, MD, BSc; Emeritus Lecturer on Biology, St Bartholomew's Hospital Medical College; *b* 5 Nov. 1861; *m* 1st, Mary (*d* 1930), *e d* of H. E. Sargent, MD; two *s* two *d*; 2nd, 1931, Emily (Phyllis), (*d* 1935), *widow* of Dr Cann Sargent. *Educ:* Burnley Grammar School; Hartley College, Southampton; St Bartholomew's Hospital, London. House Physician, St Bartholomew's Hospital, 1883; Assist Demonstrator Physiology, 1884–87; Demonstrator Physiology, 1888; Lecturer Comparative Anatomy, 1886–1919; Lecturer Biology, 1892–1919; Warden of the College and Secretary to Medical School, 1891–98; Dean of the Medical College, 1906–30; Examiner Natural History, Univ. of Aberdeen, 1890–91; Examiner in Science for Naval Medical Service, 1890–1908; Examiner Natural History for Army and Indian Medical Services, 1892–97; Examiner in Biology, Royal College of Surgeons, 1892–95 and 1897–1901. *Publications:* Practical Biology, 1887; numerous articles in scientific journals. *Recreation:* golf. *Address:* Standerton, Seymour Road, Plymouth. *T:* Plymouth 3224.

Died 19 Feb. 1947.

SHORROCK, William Gordon; JP; Chairman Westmorland Emergency Committee and of Civil Defence Committee; *b* 1879; *s* of Christopher Shorrock, Darwen, Lancashire; *m* 1908, Ethel Hinemoa, *d* of M. J. Godby, Timaru, NZ; one *s* three *d*. *Educ:* Clifton College. Cotton Spinner, Manufacturer and Merchant, retired. Westmorland CC; Vice-Chairman Westmorland Education Committee; High Sheriff of Westmorland, 1942. *Recreation:* all country pursuits. *Address:* Morland, Westmorland, via Penrith. *TA and T:* 36 Morland.

Died 13 April 1944.

SHORT, Sir Frank, Kt 1911; RA 1911; ARA 1906; RI 1917; originally trained for an engineer; Assoc. MInstCE 1883; resigned, 1904; *b* 19 June 1857; *o s* of J. T. Short, Wollaston, Worcester; *m* 1889, Esther Rosamond (*d* 1925), *d* of B. Barker; one *d*. *Educ:* S Kensington; Westminster. Director of Engraving in the Royal College of Art, 1891; Professor, 1913; retired, 1924; holds gold medal, 1889, Paris, for engraving; also 1900, Paris, for engraving; President Royal Society of Painter-Etchers, 1910–38; Treasurer RA 1919–32; Past Master Art Workers' Guild. *Address:* 56 Brook Green, W6. *T:* Riverside 2572.

Died 22 April 1945.

SHORT, Vivian Augustus, CIE 1933; *b* 1 Oct. 1883; *s* of Augustus Panton Short and Edith Haughton; *m* 1911; one *s* two *d*. *Educ:* Connaught House, Weymouth; Cranleigh School. Joined Indian Police, 1904; Superintendent Police, 1913; District Officer, F. Constabulary, 1913; Officer in Charge, Intelligence Bureau NWFP 1924; Commandant, Frontier Constabulary NWFP, India, 1926–36; retired, 1936. *Address:* Fornham-All-Saints, Bury St Edmunds, Suffolk.

Died 21 July 1950.

SHORT, Wilfrid Maurice, CB 1920; *b* Kilnwick, Yorkshire, 22 June 1870; *e s* of Ellis A. and Lucy Short. *Educ:* City of London School. Clerk to Official Receiver in Bankruptcy, 1890–91; on staff of Royal Commission on Labour, 1891–94; Private Secretary to Rt Hon. A. J. Balfour (Earl of Balfour, KG, OM), 1894–1920; Political and Literary Secretary to Earl of Dunraven, KP, 1920–22. *Publications:* Arthur James Balfour as Philosopher and Thinker (selections from his non-political writings, speeches, and addresses, 1879–1912), 1912; revised and enlarged edition (American), 1918. *Recreations:* formerly cricket, lawn tennis, and golf. *Address:* Rayleigh, 56 Mount Ephraim Lane, Streatham, SW16. *T:* Streatham 4624.

Died 8 June 1947.

SHOVE, Gerald Frank, MA; Fellow and Lecturer of King's College, and Reader in Economics, Cambridge; *b* 1887; *s* of late Herbert Samuel Shove; *m* 1915, Fredegond, *d* of late Professor F. W. Maitland; no *c*. *Educ:* Uppingham; King's College, Cambridge. *Publications:* Papers on economics; articles on peace and war. *Address:* King's College, Cambridge. *Club:* Royal Societies.

Died 11 Aug. 1947.

SHOVE, Captain Herbert William, DSO 1917; OBE 1940; RN, retd; *b* 1886; *m* 1st, 1910, Guinevere (*d* 1920), *d* of J. A. E. Wren; four *d*; 2nd, 1920, Mary Myrtle, *d* of Col J. A. H. Reilly; three *s*. Served European War, 1914–19 (despatches, DSO). *Publications:* The Fairy Ring of Commerce; An Outline of Personalism, etc. *Address:* Halletts, Ditchling, Hassocks.

Died 5 Dec. 1943.

SHUTE, Lt-Col Cyril Aveling, CMG 1933; CBE 1919; Indian Army, retired; *b* 30 Jan. 1886; *s* of late Colonel G. E. Shute; *m* 1913, Florence Eugenie, *d* of late Francis Aylmer Lloyd. Served European War, 1914–19 (despatches thrice, CBE, Brevet-Major) Officer Commanding Trans-Jordan Frontier Force, 1928–33; retired 1933; served RAFVR War of 1939–43 (despatches twice); retired with rank Wing Comdr 1943. *Address:* Holme Farm, Ashbourne, Derbyshire. *T:* 69.

Died 2 Oct. 1950.

SHUTE, Col Sir John (Joseph), Kt 1935; CMG 1918; DSO 1916; TD; DL; JP; late commanding 5th Liverpool Regiment (TF); Member Imperial War Graves Commission; Chairman City of Liverpool Air Training Squadron; *b* Liverpool; 2nd *s* of John J. and Mary E. Shute of Ramona, Stoneycroft, Liverpool; unmarried. *Educ:* privately; Catholic Institute, Liverpool. Partner Reynolds and Gibson, cotton brokers, Liverpool, Manchester, and London; travelled all over United States, Egypt, Uganda, Tanganyika, Rhodesia, S Africa, and the Continent; much interested in philanthropic work, particularly that appertaining to child charity; Chairman Combined Egyptian Mills, Ltd; Trustee and Executive Empire Cotton Growing Corpn and Council British Cotton Growing Assoc.; Chairman United Trades' Assoc. Liverpool; Chairman Liverpool Youth Organisation Committee and of Liverpool Boys' Association; Chairman Playing Fields (Boys Association) Committee, Liverpool; Council Child Welfare Association, Liverpool; Chairman Liverpool Royal Infirmary and Liverpool Nurses Home; Chairman and Hon. Treasurer Liverpool Open-Air Hospital for Children, Leasowe; one of the original promoters and Chairman of Liverpool Repertory Theatre; Chairman, City of Liverpool Branch, British Legion; Pres. Liverpool Aero Club; Joint Hon. Treasurer Metropolitan Cathedral of Liverpool; went to France with 5th King's Liverpool Regt (TF), 2nd in Command, Feb. 1915; actions of Neuve Chapelle, Richebourg, Givenchy, and on the Somme, Ypres, La Bassee (DSO, CMG, despatches five times). MP (C) Exchange Division of Liverpool, 1933–45. *Recreations:* travelling, theatre, Territorial and numerous philanthropic works. *Address:* Rivacre, Hooton, Wirral, Cheshire. *T:* Hooton

2120; Ramona, Derwent Square, Stoneycroft, Liverpool. *Clubs:* Carlton, Travellers', Constitutional; Constitutional (Liverpool).

Died 13 Sept. 1948.

SHUTTLEWORTH, 3rd Baron *cr* 1902, of Gawthorpe; **Ronald Orlando Lawrence Kay-Shuttleworth;** Bt *cr* 1849, serving RA, Captain; *b* 7 Oct. 1917 (posthumous); 2nd *s* of Captain Hon. Lawrence Ughtred Kay-Shuttleworth, RFA (killed in action, 1917), and Selina Adine, *d* of Gen. Hon. Francis Bridgeman, and *g s* of 1st Baron Shuttleworth; *S* brother, 1941. *Educ:* Eton; Balliol College, Oxford. *Recreation:* shooting. *Heir: cousin* Major Charles Ughtred John Kay-Shuttleworth, MC, RA, *b* 1917. *Address:* 17 Kensington Court, W8. *T:* Western 7044; Gawthorpe Hall, Burnley, Lancs. *T:* Padiham 7.

Died 17 Nov. 1942.

SHUTTLEWORTH, Maj.-Gen. Sir Digby Inglis, KCIE 1937; CB 1925; CBE 1919; DSO 1919; *b* 23 Aug. 1876; *s* of late A. T. Shuttleworth, AM Imperial Forest Service, India; *m* 1926, Joan, *d* of late Sir G. B. Bowen, KBE; two *s. Educ:* Bedford School. Joined the 3rd Gurkha Rifles, 1898; passed Staff College, 1910–11; employed as Brigade-Major and General Staff Officer, 2nd Grade, India, 1912–16; General Staff Officer, 2nd Grade, 3rd Indian Army Corps, Mesopotamia; General Staff Officer, 1st Grade, 14th Indian Division; General Staff Officer, 1st Grade, NW Persian Force; BGGS 3rd Indian Army Corps; commanded 39th Infantry Brigade, Caucasus; 83rd Infantry Brigade Army of Black Sea, 1917–19; President Allied Commission of Control, Ottoman War Office, 1920; Brigade Commander, Allied Forces of Occupation, Constantinople; Commander 83rd Infantry Brigade, Chanak, Dardanelles, 1920–23 (Brev. Lieut-Col, Croix de Guerre, CB, CBE, DSO, despatches five times); Colonel Commandant, Jullundur Brigade, India, 1924–28; Maj.-Gen. 1929; DA and QMG, Northern Command, India, 1930–32; Commander Kohat District, 1932–36; retired 1936. *Recreations:* fishing and shooting. *Address:* Southey Green Farm, Sible Hedingham, Essex. *T:* Hedingham 5. *Club:* United Service.

Died 15 May 1948.

SHUTTLEWORTH, Edward Cheke Smalley, CIE 1920; *b* 1866; *s* of Edward Ingles Shuttleworth; *m* 1902, Evelyn Caroline, *d* of Charles Woodin Law, Barrister-at-Law; two *s* two *d*. Appointed to Burma Police, 1887; Burma medal with two clasps, 1890; Personal Assistant to Inspector-General, 1906; Deputy Inspector-General and Commissioner of Police, Rangoon, 1917; Inspector-General of Police, Burma, 1920; King's Police Medal; retired, 1923. *Address:* 39 Derek Avenue, West Hove, Sussex.

Died 11 Dec. 1943.

SIBBALD, Rev. Samuel James Ramsay, MVO 1911; DD; JP; Chaplain-in-Ordinary to HM; *b* Dumfriesshire, 23 Aug. 1869; *m* 1898, Elizabeth, *d* of Henry F. Begg, of Tillyfour, Aberdeenshire; two *s. Educ:* Wallace Hall Academy, Dumfriesshire; Edinburgh University. MA Edin. 1889; Jeffrey Scholar in Biblical Criticism (Edin.) 1892; BD Edin. 1892. Examiner in Divinity in the University of Edinburgh, 1905–08, University of Aberdeen, 1915–18, and University of Glasgow, 1931–34; Lecturer in New Testament Language and Literature, University of Glasgow, 1932–33; Assistant in St Giles' Cathedral, Edinburgh, 1892–97; Minister of Crathie, Aberdeenshire, 1897–1918; Minister of Pollokshields, 1918–40; travelled in S Africa, 1895. Chaplain-in-Ordinary to King Edward VII, 1907–10; to King George V, 1910–36; to King Edward VIII, 1936. *Publications:* articles in magazines and reviews. *Recreations:* walking, music, geology. *Address:* 73 Ravelston Dykes, Edinburgh 12. *T:* Edinburgh 62557.

Died 31 Aug. 1950.

SIBLEY, Walter Knowsley, MA, MD; BC Cambridge; MRCP London, MRCS England; Physician to St John's Hospital for Diseases of the Skin, London; Lecturer, London School of Dermatology; Deputy Chairman, Medical Sickness and Life Insurance Co., Ltd; Treasurer, London Dermatological Society; Fellow, Royal Society of Medicine; Member of the Dermatological and Electro-Therapeutical Sections; late Physician to North-West London Hospital; President, London Dermatological Society; Vice-President of the Metropolitan Counties Branch of the British Medical Association, and Chairman of the Westminster Division; Member of Council of the British Electro-Therapeutic Society; *b* 1862; *e s* of late S. W. Sibley, FRCS, and Clara, F., *d* of late Sir R. W. Carden, Bt, MP; *m* 1892, Georgina Marie, *d* of Captain G. Butlin; one *s* one *d*. *Educ:* University College School, London; Pembroke College, Cambridge; Middlesex Hospital, London; University of Paris; University of Strassburg; and University of Berlin. Double Honours in Natural Science, Cambridge. House Surgeon, House Physician, and Assistant in the Skin Department, Middlesex Hospital, Brompton Chest Hospital, and Chelsea Hospital for Women. *Publications:* The Treatment of Diseases of the Skin, 4th edition, 1933; numerous articles in medical and scientific journals in England, France, Germany, and America, especially on the treatment of diseases of the skin. *Address:* 5 Antrim Grove, NW3; Sans-Souci, Puys, Dieppe, France. *T:* Primrose 0581. *Club:* Bath.

Died 9 Aug. 1944.

SIBLY, Sir (Thomas) Franklin, KBE 1943; Kt 1938; DSc London and Bristol; Hon. LLD Wales, Liverpool and Bristol; Fellow of King's College, London; *b* Bristol, 25 Oct. 1883; *o s* of late Thomas Dix Sibly and late Virginia, *d* of Rev. Franklin Tonkin; *m* 1918, Maude Evelyn, 2nd *d* of late C. L. Barfoot, of Newport, Mon; one *s*. *Educ:* Wycliffe College, Stonehouse, Glos; University College, Bristol. BSc Lond. (1st class Hons in Experimental Physics), 1903; 1851 Exhibition Research Scholar, 1905–07; DSc Lond. (in Geology), 1908. Lecturer in Geology, King's College, London, 1908–13; Professor of Geology, University College, Cardiff, 1913–18; temporary Officer of HM Geological Survey (for investigation of mineral resources), 1917–18; Professor of Geology, Armstrong College, Newcastle upon Tyne (University of Durham), 1918; First Principal of University College, Swansea, 1920–26; Vice-Chancellor of the University of Wales, 1925–26; Principal Officer (1926–29), and Principal (1929) of the University of London; Vice-Chancellor of Reading Univ., 1929–46; Chairman of Executive Committee and Executive Council, Universities' Bureau of the British Empire, 1929–34; Member of Royal Commission on University of Durham, 1934; Statutory Commissioner under University of Durham Act, 1935; Member of Advisory Council, Department of Scientific and Industrial Research, 1932–37 and 1941–46; Chairman of Geological Survey Board, 1930–43; Chairman of Committee of Vice-Chancellors and Principals, 1938–43; Chm. of Governors of Reading School, 1932–46. *Publications:* various papers on Carboniferous Rocks in Quarterly Journal Geological Society and elsewhere; The Hæmatites of the Forest of Dean and South Wales (Mem. Geol Survey), 1919. *Address:* 21 Brooklyn Drive, Reading, Berks. *Clubs:* Athenæum; Berkshire (Reading).

Died 13 April 1948.

SICKERT, Walter Richard, RA 1934, resigned 1935; ARA 1924; Hon. LLD Manchester; Hon. DLitt Reading; painter and etcher; *b* 31 May 1860; *e s* of Oswald Sickert, painter; *m* 1st, 1885, Helen, *d* of Richard Cobdon; 2nd 1911, Christine, *d* of John Angus; 3rd, 1926, Thérèse Lessore, *d* of Jules Lessore. Works in British Museum, Tate Gallery, Bibliothèque Nationale, Luxembourg, Manchester, Johannesburg Art Galleries, Royal Gallery of Modern Art, Rome. *Address:* St George's Hill House, Bathampton, Bath, Somerset.

Died 22 Jan. 1942.

SIDGREAVES, Sir Arthur Frederick, Kt 1945; OBE 1918; *b* June 1882. *Educ:* Downside College. SF Edge, Ltd, Napier cars, and D. Napier & Sons, Ltd, 1902–16; RNVR, attached RNAS; on amalgamation of RNAS, and RFC became Major in RAF, and for some months prior to the end of European War, 1914–18, was in charge of production Department at the Ministry, dealing entirely with Rolls-Royce engines; rejoined Napiers early 1919; joined Rolls-Royce, July 1920, as Export Manager; General Sales Manager, 1926; Managing Director, 1929–46; retired. *Address:* Farsyde, Manor Road, Penn, Bucks. *Club:* Royal Aero.

Died 7 June 1948.

SIDGWICK, Alfred; *b* Skipton, Yorkshire, 1850; *e s* of R. H. Sidgwick; *m* Cecily (*d* 1934), *e c* of David and Wilhelmine Ullman. *Educ:* Rugby; Lincoln College, Oxford. *Publications:* Fallacies, 1883; Distinction and the Criticism of Belief, 1892; The Process of Argument, 1893; The Use of Words in Reasoning, 1901; The Application of Logic, 1910; Elementary Logic, 1914. *Address:* Trewoofe Orchard, St Buryan, Cornwall.

Died 22 Dec. 1943.

SIDNEY-HUMPHRIES, Sydney; *b* 7 Aug. 1862; *s* of John Humphries, late of Blakebrook House, Worcestershire; *m* Mary Elizabeth, *e d* of the late Robt Wm Rankine, JP, of Cunnoquhie, Fife, and 4 Ainslie Pl., Edinburgh. *Educ:* privately. Imperial Conservative Unionist. Life-member of the Worcestershire Historical and Archæological Societies. *Publications:* joint editor with William Mitchell, SSC, of The Edinburgh Parthenon, edition de luxe, 1907; Disjecta, privately printed, 1909; Declined with Thanks, privately printed, 1909; some Sonnets of Sir Philip Sydney, privately printed, 1910; Shakespeare's Hamlet, New Place edition, 1911; Milton's Areopagitica, 1911; A Calendar of Verse, privately printed, 1912; Bacon's Essays, Sydney Edition, 1912; Saxo's Amleth, Oliver Elton's translation, 1913; Imperialism, Patriotism, and The European Crisis, 1914; Agincourt 1415, Waterloo 1815, privately printed, 1915; Arma Virumque Cano, privately printed, 1915; Lamport Hall, Northamptonshire, privately printed, 1918; The Holy Order of the Four Leagues, privately printed, 1920; Imperial England and Imperial Unionism, privately printed, 1931; Sir Peter Peeve, Autobiographical Romance, privately printed, 1935. *Recreations:* interested in all sports; gave the Ranelagh Subalterns' Polo Gold Challenge Cup in 1912. *Address:* Thirlestaine Court, Cheltenham, Gloucestershire.

Died 16 Feb. 1941.

SIEVWRIGHT, J. D.; journalist, publicist; JP; *b* Kirriemuir, 1863; *m* 1890, *d* of A. M'Callum, of M'Callum and Co., Dunedin; two *s* three *d*. *Educ:* St Mary's, Kirriemuir. Began life in a lawyer's office, gravitated to the newspaper, served as journey-man at 'case'; became reporter on Southland Times; afterwards occupied important position on North Otago Times; sub-editor of New Zealand Times, 1899; day editor in 1903; editor of New Zealand Mail and Associate-Editor of New Zealand Times (now incorporated with The Dominion) for several years; formerly proprietor and editor of Northern Advocate; stood for Parliament, 1896; City Councillor since 1941; has lectured on a variety of subjects; is Liberal and Imperialistic in politics; Life Member of Navy League; member of Royal Society of St George. *Recreation:* golf. *Address:* Vailima, The Terrace, Wellington, New Zealand. *Clubs:* New Zealand, Savage, Automobile, National, Mornington.

Died 23 April 1947.

SIGGERS, Ven. William C.; *see* Curzon-Siggers.

SIKES, Alfred Walter, MD, DSc (Lond.), FRCS (Eng.), MRCP (Lond.); *b* Ballycogley Castle, Co. Wexford, 1869; *s* of Richard Cherry Sikes; *m* 1902, Mary Maitland, *e d* of late Thomas Townshend Somerville, Christiania; one *s. Educ:* privately; St Thomas's and St Bartholomew's Hospitals; Marburg University, Germany. Gold Medal (Intermed. MB), Gold Medal (MB), Treasurer's Gold Medal, Bristowe Medal, Mead Medal in Medicine, Entrance Scholarship, Tite Scholarship, Peacock Scholarship, St Thomas's Hosp. Late Divisional Medical Officer, Public Health Department, London County Council; Surgeon Ambulance Train, France, 1914–15; late Medical Registrar and Demonstrator of Practical Medicine to St Thomas's Hospital. *Address:* Moat House, Langley, Bucks. *T:* 18 Iver; Portscatho, Cornwall. *T:* Portscatho 35.

Died 25 May 1948.

SIKES, Francis Henry, MA; *b* 1862; 2nd *s* of Thomas Burr Sikes, Rector of Warbleton, Sussex; *m* Eleanor Sophia (*d* 1936), *d* of late Theobald Whitchurch; one *s* two *d. Educ:* Aldenham School; Pembroke College, Camb. (Scholar). Classical Honours 1st Div. 2nd Class 1884; Headmaster of Hawarden Grammar School, 1891–93; Sutton Preparatory School, 1894–1903; donor of the Sikes Collection of British Mollusca to the Natural History Museum, and of a Collection of his Icelandic paintings to Denmark; late member of Linnæan, Geographical, Conchological, and Malacological Societies; Keeper of Photographs, Imperial War Museum, 1918–19. *Publications:* Verse—or Worse; various writings on the subject of Natural History. *Recreation:* natural history. *Address:* 60 Hogarth Road, SW5.

Died 10 June 1943.

SIKES, Howard Lecky, CBE 1936; BA 1902; BE (Hons) 1903; MInstCE, FGS, FRGS; Senior Regional Technical Adviser, Ministry of Home Security; *b* 12 Dec. 1881; *γ s* of late Richard Cherry Sikes, The Grange, Co. Wexford, and Suzan Lecky Jacob; *m* 1919, Elsie Priscilla, *γ d* of late Edward Robson, Darlington; one *s* one *d. Educ:* Bootham School, York; Queen's College, Cork (late Royal Univ. of Ireland). Engineer, Water Works Construction, Northamptonshire, 1904–05; Engineer, Great Western Railway, 1905–07; Engineer, Public Works Department, East African Protectorate, 1907–13; Engineer, Magadi Water Works and Railway, 1913–15; Lieut EA Pioneers, 1915; Capt. 1916; Attached Royal Engineers as Asst Field Engineer, 1917, and Field Engineer, 1918; East African Campaign; Government Hydraulic Engineer, Colony and Protectorate of Kenya, 1919; Deputy Director Public Works, 1921; Director of Public Works, Colony and Protectorate of Kenya and Ex-officio Member of Legislative Council, 1923–36. *Publications:* Modern Water Legislation, 1922; The Underground Water Resources of Kenya Colony, 1934. *Recreation:* lawn tennis. *Address:* Lamwia, Conisboro Avenue, Caversham, Reading.

Died 23 May 1943.

SIKORSKI, Gen. Wladyslaw, GBE 1940; Prime Minister Polish Government and Commander-in-Chief Polish Army since 1939; *b* 1881; *m* 1912, Helena Zubczewska; one *d. Educ:* Univ. Technical Coll., Lwow. Graduated 1908. Chief Organiser of Pre-War Polish Military Organisations, 1909; Lt-Col Polish Legions during War; took prominent part in defences of Lwow and Przemysl against Ukrainians, 1919; Comdr 5th and 3rd Army Corps in War against Bolsheviks; Chief of General Staff, 1921–22; Prime Minister, 1922–23; Minister of Military Affairs, 1923–25; Comdr Lwow Army Region, 1926–28; on half-pay, 1928–39. Decorations: Polish Virtuti Militari 5th and 2nd div.; Military Cross with four bars; Grand Cross Polonia Restituta; Grand Cross Legion of Honour and many other decorations. *Publications:* La Campagne Polono-

Russe, 1928; Le Problème de la Paix, 1931; La Guerre Moderne, 1935; and various other military and political publications. *Address:* 18 Kensington Palace Gardens, W8.

Died 4 July 1943.

SILK, John Frederick William, MD (Lond.), MRCS, LSA; (retired); Consulting Anæsthetist, King's College Hospital; Fellow of King's College, London; referee on Anæsthetics, University of London; late Anæsthetist and Teacher of Anæsthetics, King's College Hospital; Teacher of Anæsthetics and Member of the Faculty of Medicine, University of London; Lt-Col RAMC; Consulting Anæsthetist, Malta, 1915–16; Home Commands, 1916–19; *b* Milton-next-Gravesend, 24 Jan. 1858; *s* of John Alexander Silk, solicitor; *m* 1884, Catherine Jane, *d* of late Captain Pettus Bachelor; three *s* two *d. Educ:* Cranbrook Grammar School, Kent; King's College, London. Matriculated at London University, 1875; Scholar, Prizeman, and Student, King's College and Hospital. Was Medical Officer at King's College Hospital and Leeds General Infirmary; President of Society of Anæsthetists, 1899–1900; Vice-President, 1903–04; has been anæsthetist to Guy's Hospital, the Royal Free, the National Epileptic, Great Northern Central, and National Dental Hospitals; Fellow Royal Society Medicine. *Publications:* Modern Anæsthetics, second edition; A Manual of Nitrous Oxide Anæsthesia; Chapters on Anæsthetics in Cheyne and Burghard's Surgical Treatment; many other articles, etc., on anæsthetics in the various professional publications. *Address:* Summerland, Dartmouth, S Devon. *T:* 225.

Died 18 Nov. 1943.

SILLEM, Maj.-Gen. Sir Arnold Frederick, KCMG 1919; CB 1916; *b* 3 June 1865; *s* of late Frederick Sillem, Esher; *m* 1903, Madge Estcourt (*d* 1942), *d* of Thomas Estcourt Rowles, King William's Town, South Africa; three *d. Educ:* Eastbourne College. Received first commission in Queen's Royal Regiment, 1887; employed with Egyptian Army, 1891–94; served as Adjutant 2nd Batt. Queen's, 1894–98; SA campaign, Oct. 1899 till conclusion hostilities (severely wounded, despatches twice, Bt Major, Queen's medal 5 clasps, King's medal 2 clasps); Graduate Staff College, 1907; Lt-Col to command a batt. Worcestershire Regt, 1910; on Staff BEF, 1915–19 (despatches 8 times); Bt Col and Temp. Brig.-Gen., 1915; Temp. Maj.-Gen. 1916; prom. Maj.-Gen., 1918, for service in the field; MGA Eastern Command, 1920–24; retired pay, 1924; Commandeur de la Légion d'honneur. *Clubs:* MCC, Free Foresters, I Zingari.

Died 27 Jan. 1949.

SILOTI, Alexander; Russian pianist and conductor; *b* South Russia, 10 Oct. 1863. *Educ:* pupil of Zvereff, Nicolas Rubinstein (piano), Tshaikovsky, S. Taneieff (theory), Moscow Conservatoire. First public appearance, Symphony Concert, Imperial Moscow Musical Society, Nov. 1880; studied under Liszt, 1883–86; Professor, Moscow Conservatoire, 1889–91; lived abroad, concert tours in Europe, 1891–1900; America, 1897; founded own concerts (symphony, choral, chamber music, popular, free) in Petrograd, 1903; 15 seasons till Russian Revolution; Manager State Opera, 1917 (Petrograd), till Bolsheviks in power; escaped from Russia, 1920—concert tours in Europe, 1920–22; in New York since, concert appearances and teaching Juilliard School of Music). *Publications:* numerous transcriptions and revisions, especially of Bach's works; Memories of Liszt (English translation, 1911). *Address:* Hotel Ansonia, New York City, USA.

Died 10 Dec. 1945.

SILVER, Vice-Adm. Mortimer L'E., CBE 1919; JP; retired; *b* 1869; *m* Kate Ethel, *d* of late General A. H. F. Barnes, RMLI. *Address:* White House, Bradenham, Bucks. *T:* Naphill 7.

Died 6 Dec. 1946.

SIMMONDS, Herbert John, CB, CBE; b 21 May 1867; s of John Simmonds, Barrister; m 1899, Zillah Gertrude, d of Rev. C. H. Andrews; two s one d. Educ: Repton; Christ's College, Cambridge. BA, 2nd Class Hist. Barrister, 1892; Charity Commission, 1895; Board of Education Junior Examiner, 1902; Assistant Secretary, 1911; Legal Adviser, 1925–28. Address: 14 Roxborough Avenue, Harrow. T: Byron 1469.

Died 29 Sept. 1950.

SIMONDS, John Hayes, CB 1939; Director, Barclays Bank Ltd, H. and G. Simonds, Ltd, Reading Building Society; b 16 April 1879; s of John Simonds, Newlands; m 1911, Aline Rhoda, d of Edward Murray Sturges, Barkham; one s two d. Educ: Wellington College; Magdalen College, Oxford. BA Oxon 1900. Partner in firm of J. and C. Simonds and Co., Reading Bank—acquired by Barclays Bank Ltd, 1913; Commissioned to 1st Vol. Batt. R. Berks Regt, 1900, subsequently 4th (T) Batt. R. Berks Regt; retired 1911; rejoined 2/4th Batt. 1914 as Major and served in France; Chairman Berks' Territorial Assoc., 1932–46; DL Berks; JP Reading. Recreations: hunting, shooting, fishing. Address: Newlands, Arborfield, Berks. T: Arborfield Cross 221. Club: Junior Carlton.

Died 5 Sept. 1946.

SIMOPOULOS, Charalambos John, LLD, Grand Cross of the Order of the Phœnix; His Hellenic Majesty's Ambassador Extraordinary and Plenipotentiary to the Court of St James's since 1942; b Athens, 12 July 1874; s of Professor John Simopoulos. Educ: Athens University (Degree of Doctor of Laws); studied in France and Germany. Entered Greek Diplomatic Service after a competitive examination, 1901; served in Egypt, Turkey, Bulgaria, Serbia, France; First Secretary and Counsellor to Greek Legation in Rome during European War; Chargé d'Affaires in London, 1917, Rome, 1919; Minister to Czechoslovakia, 1920, Hungary, 1921; High Commissioner for Greece in Constantinople, 1922; Minister to USA, 1924; Minister to Court of St James's, 1935; on arrival of Greek Govt in London, appointed also Under-Secretary of State for Foreign Affairs, a post he held until May 1942. Recreations: reading, music. Address: Royal Greek Embassy, 51 Upper Brook Street, W1. T: Mayfair 4519. Clubs: Royal Thames Yacht, Bath, Travellers'.

Died 24 Oct. 1942.

SIMPSON, Rev. Alan Haldane; Hon. Canon of S Michael's Cathedral, Coventry; b 1875; y s of late John Simpson, 59 Claverton Street, SW; m 1901, Florence Lætitia (d 1911), 6th d of R. J. Balston, Springfield, Maidstone, Kent; three s. Educ: Harrow; Trinity College, Cambridge. Curate of S Paul's, Maidstone, 1900–01; Chaplain to Bishop of Southwark, 1901–04; Chaplain to Bishop of Worcester, 1904–18; Chaplain to Bishop of Coventry, 1918–22; Member of S Saviour's College of Clergy, Southwark, 1901–04; Curate of S Peter's, S Wimbledon, 1905–06; Secretary, Bishop of Worcester's Church Extension Fund, 1906–11; Warden, Hartlebury College, 1910; Diocesan Missioner, Diocese of Coventry, 1911–28; Proctor in Convocation, 1921–29 and since 1936; Diocesan Missioner, Diocese of Oxford, 1929–36. Publications: Principles and Practice of Retreat; various articles. Recreations: ornithology, sand yachting. Address: S John's Vicarage, Leamington Spa. T: Leamington Spa 830. Club: Athenæum.

Died 9 June 1941.

SIMPSON, Rev. Albert Edward, BD; Canon Emeritus of Chester since 1943; b Dublin, 7 July 1868; s of James Simpson, Lieut Military Train; m Alice Maud, d of Andrew Goddard; two s. Educ: Corrig School, Kingstown; Trinity College, Dublin University. First Senior Moderator in Logics and Ethics, 1894; First Theological Exhibitioner, 1897; Ordained, 1897; held Curacies at St George's, Stockport, and Holy Trinity,

Birkenhead; Vicar of St Mary's, Liscard, Wallasey, 1908–29; Rural Dean of Wallasey, 1919–29; Rector of Narborough, Leicestershire, 1929–31; Residentiary Canon of Chester, 1931–43; Hon. Canon of Chester, 1925–29. Address: 49 Cambrian View, Chester. T: Chester 1791.

Died 3 Feb. 1947.

SIMPSON, Maj.-Gen. Charles Rudyerd, (retired); CB 1911; b 15 Nov. 1856; s of late Charles Turner Simpson; m 1st, 1884, Leonora (d 1927), d of late Charles F. Devas, Pickhurst Manor, Hayes, Kent; one s four d; 2nd, 1929, Mary Theresa (d 1932), d of late Rev. Thomas Cochrane. Educ: Marlborough College; privately. Entered the 10th Foot, 1875; Lieut-Col and commanded 4th Bn Duke of Cambridge's Own Middlesex Regt, 1900–04; ADC to Sir Arthur Borton, Governor and C-in-C Malta, 1881–84; psc 1886; Intelligence Division War Office, 1888–93; Professor Staff College, 1894–96; Colonel General Staff, Western Command, 1905–08; Brigade Commander, 5th Infantry Brigade, Aldershot, 1908–11; Major-General, 1911; Commanded Mauritius, 1912–16; Reserve Centre, 1916–18; Colonel The Lincolnshire Regiment, 1914–38; served Sudan Expedition, 1898; battles of the Atbara and Khartum (despatches twice, Brev. Lt-Col, British medal and Egyptian medal 2 clasps). Address: Artillery Mansions, SW1. Club: United Service.

Died 7 Dec. 1948.

SIMPSON, Rear-Adm. Cortland Herbert, CBE 1919; JP; retired; b 15 April 1856; e s of Vice-Admiral Cortland H. Simpson and Anna Maria Watson, Stoke-by-Nayland; m 1895, Edith Octavia, y d of Hon. W. Busby, Sydney, NSW; one s three d. Educ: RN School, Newcross; Britannia. Joined the Navy, 1869; served as cadet and midshipman in HMS Hercules, Channel Squadron, 1872–73; Midshipman of Charybdis, China Station, 1873–76; present at capture and destruction of piratical stockades on River Lingey, Malay Peninsula, in 1874 (India Medal, Perak clasp); Lieutenant, 1881 and joined Surveying branch of the Navy; Lieutenant of HMS Rambler employed in survey of Trinkitat Harbour, Red Sea during operations in Eastern Sudan in 1884 (Egyptian Medal); in command of Surveys in various parts of the world; Commander, 1897; Captain, 1903; retired, 1911; Rear-Admiral, 1913; at outbreak of war in 1914 appointed Rear-Admiral at Peterhead for formation and command of Patrol Base where remained until Dec. 1916; appointed Commodore RNR, 1917, for formation of Patrol Bases in West Indies, where continued until the close of war (despatches, CBE, medals). Recreations: fishing, painting. Address: Old Vicarage House, Stoke-by-Nayland, Suffolk. Club: United Service.

Died 18 May 1943.

SIMPSON, Col Sir Frank Robert, 1st Bt cr 1935; CB 1939; TD; JP, DL; mining engineer; b 12 April 1864; s of John Bell Simpson, DCL, JP, and Annie Elizabeth Thomlinson; m 1889, Alice Matilda, d of late James Finucane Draper; three s four d. Educ: Rugby School. Late Lt-Col Commanding and later Hon. Colonel 9th Bn The Durham Light Infantry (TA); High Sheriff for the County Palatine of Durham, 1935; President of Blaydon Conservative Association and a Kt of Grace of St John of Jerusalem; served European War, 1914–18, commanding 2/9th Bn The Durham Light Infantry, British Salonika Force, 1916–18 (despatches twice, two medals). Coal-owner until 1946; Member of Ryton Urban District Council, 1897, retired 1947; River Tyne Improvement Commission, 1921–47; Mem. Institution of Mining Engineers (President, 1939); Member of the North of England Institute of Mining and Mechanical Engineers (Pres., 1921 and 1935); Member of the Institute of Civil Engineers, 1935. Recreations: golf, tennis, shooting. Heir: s Basil Robert James Simpson, b

1898. *Address:* Bradley Hall, Wylam, Northumberland. *T:* Wylam 246. *Clubs:* Durham County, Union, Conservative (Newcastle upon Tyne).

Died 29 April 1949.

SIMPSON, Col Henry Charles, CMG 1919; DSO 1916; RA, retd; *b* 1879; *s* of Colonel R. H. Simpson; *m* 1906, Lydia Marion Hinton; two *d.* Served South African War, 1899–1902 (Queen's medal and three clasps, King's medal and two clasps); European War, 1914–18 (despatches, CMG, DSO, Order of Danilo, Croix de Guerre, Bt Lt-Col); commanded 27th (London) Air Defence Brigade, 1925–27; retired pay, 1927. *Address:* Kingsdene, Windlesham Road, Shoreham-by-Sea.

Died 24 Jan. 1943.

SIMPSON, Col Henry Cuthbert Conneli Dunlop, CMG 1900; *b* 7 June 1854; *s* of late Maj.-Gen. W. H. R. Simpson, RA; *m* 1884, Constance Mary, *y d* of late Col E. Oakes, IA. Entered army, RA, 1874; Capt. 1883; Major, 1891; Lt-Col 1901; Colonel, 1907; retired, 1908; served Burmah, 1886–87 (despatches, medal and clasp); served with International Field Force, Crete, during the disturbances, 1897; South Africa, 1899–1902 (despatches twice, Queen's medal with 4 clasps, King's medal 2 clasps, CMG); honourably mentioned for services in connection with European War. *Club:* United Service.

Died 19 Oct. 1942.

SIMPSON, Herbert Clayton; Professor of English Literature, Trinity College, Toronto, 1906, now Emeritus Professor; *b* Northampton, England, 26 Nov. 1872; *m* 1914, Nina Lawrence Rolph, Toronto; one *d.* *Educ:* Magdalen College School, Oxford. Magdalen College, Oxford (Exhibitioner in Natural Science), BA 1895. Fellow and Lecturer in Physics and Chemistry, Trinity College, Toronto, 1896–1900; MA Toronto, 1896; MA Harvard, 1912; Lecturer in English Literature, Trinity College, Toronto, 1900–06. *Publications:* magazine articles, literary and scientific. *Address:* 71 Bernard Avenue, Toronto.

Died 4 May 1947.

SIMPSON, Very Rev. James Gilliland, DD; Dean of Peterborough, 1928–42; *b* London, 16 Oct. 1865; *s* of late D. C. Simpson, a merchant in London and Liverpool, and Alison, *d* of late Walter Thorburn of Peebles; *m* 1st, Magdalen (*d* 1915), *d* of late Walter Shepherd, Dundee; two *s*; 2nd, Winifred, *d* of late Rev. Stuart Berkeley. *Educ:* City of London School; Trinity College, Oxford. 2nd class Moderations; 1st class Lit.Hum.; 1st class Theol. School. Ordained by Bishop of Ripon to curacy at Leeds Parish Church, 1889; Vice-Principal of the Scots Episcopal Theological College, 1893–95; Incumbent of St Paul's Episcopal Church, Dundee, 1895–1900; Principal of Leeds Clergy School, and Lecturer of Leeds Parish Church, 1900–10; Canon of Manchester, 1910–11; Canon of St Paul's, 1911–28. *Publications:* Fact and Faith, 1908; Christian Ideals, 1908; Christus Crucifixus, 1909; Preachers and Teachers, 1910; The Spirit and the Bride, 1911; Creative Revelation, 1912; Great Ideas of Religion, 1912; What is the Gospel? 1914; Liverpool Lectures, 1913, 1914, 1915; Catholic Evangelicalism, 1927. *Club:* National.

Died 10 Oct. 1948.

SIMPSON, Rt Rev. John Basil. Formerly Vicar of S Mary Magdalene's, Munster Square; Bishop of Kobe, 1925.

Died 28 April 1942.

SIMPSON, Lightly Stapleton, CBE 1919; DSO 1917; late RE; MICE. *Educ:* Charterhouse; Cambridge University, BA. Served European War, 1914–17 (despatches, DSO, CBE). *Address:* Dalbreck, Gullane, East Lothian. *T:* Gullane 2195. *Club:* United University.

Died 6 Sept. 1942.

SIMPSON, Rev. Patrick Carnegie, MA (Edin.); Hon. MA (Cambridge); DD (St Andrews); Emeritus Professor of Church History, Westminster (Theological) College, Cambridge; *b* 1865; *s* of Rev. Patrick Simpson, Horsham, Australia; *m* Agnes (*d* 1937), *d* of Hauptpastor Schmaltz, Copenhagen; one *d.* *Educ:* George Watson's School; University (first-class honours); New College, Edinburgh. Ordained at Wallington, Surrey, 1895; Minister of Renfield Church (United Free Church of Scotland), 1899–1911; Hon. Doctor of Divinity, 1910; chaplain to 8th Scottish Rifles (Cameronians), 1910–11; Minister of Egremont Church (Presbyterian Church of England), Cheshire, 1911–14; Professor, Westminster College, 1914–38; Moderator of the Federal Council of the Free Churches of England, 1926; re-elected, 1927; Moderator of the General Assembly of the Presbyterian Church of England, 1928. *Publications:* The Fact of Christ, 1900 (translated into several foreign languages); Love Never Faileth, 1902; The Site of Union, 1907; The Life of Principal Rainy, 1909; The Facts of Life, 1913; Church Principles, 1923; The Church and the State, 1929; Essentials, 1930. The Evangelical Church Catholic, 1934; Recollections—Mainly Ecclesiastical but sometimes Human, 1943. *Address:* Romsey House, Mill Road, Cambridge. *T:* Cambridge 87812.

Died 22 Dec. 1947.

SIMPSON, Rev. Percy John; Rector of Shobdon since 1919; *b* 1864; *m* Martha Olley, *d* of Richard Jones, sometime Colonial Treasurer, NSW. *Educ:* Wellington College; Christ Church, Oxford. Ordained, 1892; Curate of Lake Macquarie, 1892; St Peter, East Maitland, 1892–94; Incumbent of Merriwa, 1894–95; Precentor of Sydney Cathedral, and Principal Cathedral Choir School, 1895–1907; Chaplain Archbishop of Sydney, 1902; Rector of Cootamundra, 1907–14; Archdeacon of Wagga-Wagga, 1907–14; Vicar of Norton, Radnors, 1914–19. *Address:* The Rectory, Shobdon, Kingsland, Herefordshire.

Died 18 Jan. 1944.

SIMS, Ernest William Proctor-, CIE 1924; AMICE; Chartered Civil Engineer; *b* 1868; *s* of late Richard Proctor-Sims; *m* 1896, Ida Mary, *d* of T. A. Bulkley. *Address:* c/o The Imperial Bank of India, 25 Old Broad Street, EC2.

Died 15 March 1943.

SIMS, Francis John, CB 1922; MVO 1911; *b* 1856; late Principal Assistant Director of Public Prosecutions; *m* 1878, Mary Elizabeth, *d* of late Daniel Sims; three *s.* *Educ:* privately. *Address:* 6 Shandon Road, Worthing, Sussex.

Died 3 June 1950.

SIMSON, Harold F.; *see* Fraser-Simson.

SINBAD; *see* Dingle, A. E.

SINCLAIR, Rev. Hon. Charles Augustus; Hon. Canon of Gloucester since 1921; *b* 11 May 1865; *b* and *heir-pres.* of 18th Earl of Caithness, CBE; *m* 1899, Mary Ann (*d* 1933), 2nd *d* of late Rev. Edward Harman, Rector of Pickwell; one *s* [James Roderick, Lt-Col 1st Bn The Gordon Highlanders; *b* 1906; *m* 1933, Grizel Margaret, *d* of Sir George Miller-Cunningham, KBE, CB; three *d*] four *d.* *Educ:* Aberdeen Univ.; Trinity Coll., Oxford. Ordained Deacon, 1890; Priest, 1891; Curate of St Barnabas, Kensington, 1890–92; Hornsey, 1892–98; Rector of Hempsted, Gloucester, 1898–1941. *Address:* Roslin, Pirton Lane, Churchdown, Glos. *T:* Churchdown 247.

Died 9 March 1944.

SINCLAIR, Adm. Sir Edwyn Sinclair A.; *see* Alexander-Sinclair.

SINCLAIR, Mary Amelia St Clair, (May); b Rock Ferry, Cheshire, 24 Aug. 1863; d of William Sinclair, Liverpool. *Educ:* The Ladies' College, Cheltenham. Began by writing verses and philosophical criticism; first short story published in 1895; first novel in 1896; first successful novel, The Divine Fire, published in England and America, 1904; met with far greater success in America than in England; Fellow Royal Society of Literature, 1916. *Publications:* Nakiketas and Other Poems; Essays in Verse; Audrey Craven; Mr and Mrs Nevill Tyson; Two Sides of a Question; The Divine Fire; The Helpmate; The Judgment of Eve; Kitty Tailleur; The Creators; The Flaw in the Crystal; The Three Brontës; The Return of the Prodigal, and other stories; The Combined Maze; The Three Sisters, 1914; A Journal of Impressions in Belgium, 1915; Tasker Jevons, 1916; A Defence of Idealism, 1917; The Tree of Heaven, 1917; Mary Olivier; A Life, 1919; The Romantic, 1920; Mr Waddington of Wyck, 1921; The Life and Death of Harriet Frean, 1922; The New Idealism, 1922; Anne Severn and the Fieldings, 1922; Uncanny Stories, 1923; A Cure of Souls, 1923; The Dark Night, 1924; Arnold Waterlow, 1924; The Rector of Wyck, 1925; Far End, 1926; The Allinghams, 1927; History of Anthony Waring, 1927; Fame, 1929; Tales told by Simpson, 1930; The Intercessor and other Stories, 1931. *Address:* The Gables, Burcott Lane, Bierton, Aylesbury.

Died 14 Nov. 1946.

SINCLAIR, Col Thomas Charles, CBE 1934; b 18 May 1879; e s of late Rt Hon. Thomas Sinclair, DL, Hopefield House, Belfast, and late Mary, y d of late Chas. Duffin, Strandtown Lodge, Strandtown, Co. Down; m 1914, Iris Lucy, e d of late Captain Albert Lund; one s (y s killed in action in Italy, Feb. 1944, second s killed in Germany in Sept. 1944, while escaping as a Prisoner of War). *Educ:* Rugby; Corpus Christi College, Oxford. Sometime Commandant School of Anti-Aircraft Defence, Biggin Hill, Kent; retired, 1935. *Recreations:* golf, shooting, fishing. *Address:* High Wyck, Winchester. *T:* Winchester 4592. *Clubs:* United Service, Leander; Royal and Ancient (St Andrews).

Died 4 Dec. 1948.

SINCLAIR-MACLAGAN, Maj.-Gen. Ewen George, CB 1917; CMG 1919; DSO 1900; b 24 Dec. 1868; s of Robert Ewen Sinclair Maclagan, Glenquiech, Forfarshire, NB; m 1902, Kathleen (d 1928), d of late Maj.-Gen. Sir George A. French, KCMG; one d. Entered Army, 1889; Capt. 1898; Major, 1908; Adjutant 1st Border Regt, 1900–01; served with Commonwealth Military Forces of Australia as Adjutant Local Forces and DAAG New South Wales, 1901–04; Adjutant 2nd Border Regt, 1905–08; Director RM College, Australia, 1911–14; Commanded 3rd Infantry Brigade, 1914–17, and 4th Division, 1917–19 (both Australian Imperial Force); commanded 51st Highland Division and Area, 1919–23; Colonel of the Border Regiment, 1923–36; Waziristan Field Force, 1894–95 (medal with clasp); South Africa, 1899–1901 (severely wounded, despatches, Queen's medal 5 clasps, DSO); European War, Dardanelles, 1914–16, France and Flanders, 1916–19, prom. Maj.-General, 1919 (despatches five times, Brevet of Col 3rd Class White Eagle of Serbia, French Croix de Guerre, American Distinguished Service Medal); retired pay, 1925. *Address:* Glenquiech, by Forfar, Scotland.

Died 24 Nov. 1948.

SING, John Millington, MA; JP; b 1863; s of Joshua Sing, JP, of Liverpool; unmarried. *Educ:* Uppingham School; Christ's College, Cambridge. Assistant Master at St Edward's School, Oxford, 1886–1904; at Winchester Coll. 1914–19; Warden of St Edward's School, Oxford, 1904–13. *Publications:* Selections from Thucydides; Siege of Platæa; etc. *Address:* Malthouse, Iffley, Oxford. *T:* Oxford 7010. *Club:* National Liberal.

Died 13 July 1947.

SING, Rt Rev. Tsae-Seng, DD; President of Chinese CMS; Lecturer to the theological department, Trinity College; b 1861; father the first clergyman in Chekiang Province; m 1881 (d 1912); three s four d. *Educ:* Trinity College, Ningpo. Has been a master to a day school for 2 years, and headmaster to Trinity College for 29 years; Archdeacon in Chekiang, 1910–18; Pastor at Ningpo, 1911–16; Pastor at Hangchow, 1917–19; Assistant Bishop of Chekiang, 1918–31. *Address:* CMS, Ningpo, China.

Died 1940.

SINGH, Sir Ganesh Dutta, Kt 1928; Doctor of Law, 1933; Landlord; b 1868; s of Babu Deg Narain Singh of Chatiana, Patna; m 1879, Rukumini Kumari, d of Babu Jawhir Singh; two s one d. *Educ:* Patna Collegiate School; Patna College. Matriculated, 1891; BA, 1895; BL (Law), 1897. Joined District Court Bar, 1898; Calcutta High Court Bar, 1904; Patna High Court Bar, 1916; returned uncontested for East Patna, 1921; West Muzaffarpore, 1923; Gaya, 1926; Member of Assembly from Patna Division Landholders' Constituency, 1937–39; gave up practice at the Bar, 1922, to devote entire time to the Council work; was nominated member of all the important Committees of the Council; in 1921 moved a resolution that the salary of the Ministers should be Rs 1000 and not Rs 5000 a month, but it was not carried; Minister of Local Self-Government, Bihar and Orissa, 1923–37; after becoming Minister in 1923, took Rs 1000 as salary and gave the balance to charity; with the accumulated amount of the first term, an orphanage has been opened at Patna; at his instance in 1923 the salary of Ministers was reduced to Rs 4000; founded a High English School at Patna, called Patliputra High English School; Secretary of the Bihar Landholders' Association, 1917–19. *Address:* Krishan-Kunja (University Area), Bankipore PO, Patna, Bihar, India. *TA:* Krishan-Kunja, Bankipore, Patna. *T:* Patna 400.

Died 26 Sept. 1943.

SINGH, Kanwar Jasbir, CIE 1941; Barrister-at-Law; Secretary to Government, Information Department, United Provinces, India, since 1940; b 16 June 1889; m 1914, Mabel Goloknath; three s one d. *Educ:* Forman Christian College, Lahore, Punjab; Balliol College, Oxford. Joined UP Civil Service, 1913; Deputy Collector and Magistrate and Assistant Settlement Officer, 1913–20; Under-Secretary to Govt, United Provinces, 1921–22; Special Manager, Court of Wards, Balrampur Estate, 1922–32; Collector, Benares, in 1933 and 1934; Collector, Saharanpur, 1935–37; Deputy Commissioner, Lucknow, 1938–40. *Recreations:* football, hockey, cricket, tennis, golf, and wrestling. *Address:* 1 Secretaries Quarters, Lucknow. *T:* (Residence) 172. (Office) Council House 11. *Club:* United Service (Lucknow).

Died 15 Oct. 1942.

SINGH, Raja Sir Padam, KCIE 1945; CSI 1931; Raja of Bashahr since 1914; b 1873. *Address:* Bashahr, East Punjab, India.

Died 16 April 1947.

SINGTON, Gerald Henry Adolphus, CBE 1945; MIMechE; Director Platt Bros & Co. Ltd, Textile Machinery Makers, Ltd, Prince Smith & Stells, Ltd, etc.; Chairman Textile Machinery Industrial and Export Group; b Broughton, Manchester, 28 Dec. 1876; e s of late Joseph George Sington, Chapel-en-le-Frith, Derbyshire; m 1907, Eleanora, y d of late Thos Stevenson, Renfrew; one s one d. *Educ:* St Paul's School. Served European War, 1914–19, as Captain RE, TA (despatches). *Publications:* Novelties lately Introduced in Spinning Mills, 1931; Yet More Novelties in Cotton Spinning, 1938; The Past, Present and Future of Cotton Spinning Machinery, 1945. *Recreations:* travel, theatre, golf and bridge. *Address:* Abbot Brow, Alderley Edge, Cheshire. *T:* Alderley Edge 3266. *Clubs:* Bath; Clarendon, Manchester.

Died 22 Sept. 1946.

SINKER, Rev. Canon Edmund, MA; Hon. Canon of Southwark Cathedral, 1926; Proctor in Convocation, 1924–32; Surrogate, Diocese Southwark, 1927; *b* Cambridge, 26 Feb. 1872; 3rd *s* of late Rev. Robert Sinker, DD, and Mary Annette, *d* of late Rev. John Judge, Rector of Leighton; *m* 1898, Jane, *d* of late Rev. J. W. D'Evelyn, Rector of Armoy, Co. Antrim; one *d.* *Educ:* King's College Choir School, Cambridge; Fitzwilliam Hall, Cambridge University; Gibson Greek Testament Prize, 1891. Ordained, 1895; Curate of Whitechapel, 1895–97; Association Secretary Missions to Seamen for Metropolitan District, 1898–1902; Senior Chaplain, Missions to Seamen for Port of London, and Chaplain to Training Ship Arethusa, 1902–06; HMS President, 1903–06; Training Ship, Cornwall, 1905–06; Vicar of Bromley, 1906–10; Surrogate London Diocese; Vicar of Goole, Yorks, 1910–16; Surrogate, Dioceses York and Sheffield; Rector of Salwarpe, Worcs, 1916–21; Secretary of the Southwark Diocesan Board of Finance, and South London Church Fund, 1921–27; Rector of Charlton, SE7, 1927–39; Rural Dean of Woolwich, 1929–37. *Publications:* The Church in Bromley for 1000 Years, 1909; The Holy Communion, What Mean Ye by this Service? 1914; Are We Losing our Ideals? 1915; History of Salwarpe Parish, 1918; Six Facts of the After Life, 2nd ed., 1920. *Recreations:* golf and fishing.

Died March 1941.

SINNATT, Frank Sturdy, CB 1935; MBE, DSc, MSc (Tech.); FRS 1938; FIC; FInstP; Director of Fuel Research, Department of Scientific and Industrial Research, since 1931; *b* 1880; *s* of Francis Sinnatt; *m* Louie Midgley, *d* of Frank Badger. Lecturer in Fuels, Manchester Univ.; participated as Director of Research in formation of Lancashire and Cheshire Coal Research Association; directed Research on Chemical Aspects of Air Pollution for Advisory Board, Manchester; Assist Director of Fuel Research, 1924–31; Council Institution of Mining Engineers; Council of Institute of Fuel; Hon. Member Coke Oven Managers Association; Hon. Member Institution of Gas Engineers; Safety in Mines Research Board; Research Council British Iron and Steel Federation; Council British Colliery Owners Research Association; Council British Coal Utilisation Research Association; Royal Swedish Institute for Engineering Research; British National Committee and Executive Council World Power Congress; Territorial Force, 1908. *Publications:* Bulletins, Lancashire and Cheshire Coal Research Assoc.; Scientific and Technical papers on Coal; Constitution of Low-temperature Tar. *Recreation:* golf. *Address:* Fuel Research Station, Greenwich, SE10. *T:* Greenwich 1220. *Club:* Athenæum.

Died 27 Jan. 1943.

SINNOTT, John Joseph, CBE 1942; Assessor of Taxes, Newfoundland, since 1929; *b* 4 March 1882; *s* of Peter Sinnott and Ellen Dierney; *m* 1906, Margaret Cowan; three *s* two *d. Educ:* St Patrick's Hall School. Fire Insurance landed estates and Notary-average adjustments, 1898–1904; Clerical in General and Fishing trade of Newfoundland, 1905–19; Travelling Auditor in office of Assessor of Taxes, 1920–28. *Recreations:* motoring and fishing. *Address:* 12 Queen's Road, St John's, Newfoundland. *T:* 387.

Died 20 Dec. 1943.

SIRCAR, Sir Nilratan, Kt 1918, MA, MD (Cal.), DCL (Oxon), LLD (Edin.); consulting Physician; *b* 1 Oct. 1861; *s* of Nandalal Sircar and Thakomoni; *m* 1888, Nirmala Majumdar (Nee); one *s* five *d. Educ:* Calcutta University. Founder and Proprietor of National Soap Factory, and National Tannery Co.; one of the Founders

and President of the Carmichael Medical College and Hospitals and Medical Club, Calcutta; President Chittaranjan Seva Sadan, Jadavpur Tuberculosis Hospital, Chittaranjan Hospital and Post Graduate Department in Science of the Calcutta University; sometime Vice-Chancellor, Calcutta University; Member Legislative Council, Bengal. *Address:* 7 Short Street, Calcutta, India. *Clubs:* Medical, Calcutta.

Died May 1943.

SIRCAR, Sir Nripendra Nath, KCSI 1936; Kt 1931; MA, BL; Law Member of Executive Council of Governor-General of India, 1934–39; late Vice-President, Viceroy's Executive Council; Leader of Indian Legislative Assembly; *s* of Nagendra Nath Sircar, *g s* of Peary Churn Sircar, one of the pioneers of English Education in India; *m* Nabanalim Basu, *o d* of Durgadas Basu; eight *s. Educ:* Presidency College, Calcutta; Lincoln's Inn. Practised at Bhagalpore in Behar as pleader, 1897; Member of Subordinate Judicial Service, 1902–05; Advocate-General of Bengal, 1928–34; First Honoursman in Bar Final Michaelmas Term, 1907; Honours in Mathematics, Physics and Chemistry in BA; MA in Chemistry; Holder of Foundation Scholarship, Presidency College. *Recreation:* travelling. *Address:* 36/1 Elgin Road, Calcutta, India. *TA:* Enenes, Calcutta. *Club:* Calcutta.

Died Aug. 1945.

SIRE, Henry Alphonse, CBE 1920; retired Chief Commercial Manager Southern Railway; *b* 1864; *s* of late Alfred Sire, MVO; *m* 1899. *Address:* 41 Bassett Road, W10. *T:* Ladbroke 0383.

Died 16 Nov. 1947.

SIROHI, HH Maharajadhiraj, Maharao-Shri Sir Sarup Ram Singhji Bahadur, GCIE 1932; KCSI 1924; *b* 27 Sept. 1888; *m*; three *d. Educ:* English and Hindi. Worked as Masahib-i-ala for nine years, installed on *Gadi*, 1920. The State has an area of 1994 square miles, and a population of 233,879. *Address:* Sirohi, Rajputana, India.

Died 3 Feb. 1946.

SITWELL, Sir George Reresby, 4th Bt *cr* 1808; *b* London, 27 Jan. 1860; *o s* of 3rd Bt and Louisa, *d* of Col the Hon. H. Hely Hutchinson; *S* father, 1862; *m* 1886, Lady Ida Emily Augusta Denison (*d* 1937), *d* of 1st Earl of Londesborough; two *s* one *d. Educ:* Dr Chittenden's School, the Grange, Hoddesdon, Herts; Eton; Christ Church, Oxford. Contested Scarborough at two bye-elections in Nov. and Dec. 1884, 1886, 1895, and 1900; MP Scarborough, 1885–86, and 1892–95; captured a spirit at the headquarters of the Spiritualists, London, 1880; travelled a good deal, and was present at Moscow at coronation of Czar, 1883; formerly Captain Yorkshire Dragoons, Lieut-Col commanding 2nd Vol. Batt. PWO Yorkshire Regt, 1904–08; retired on disbandment of the Battalion with rank of Colonel; during the war, being unfit for service, farmed over 2000 acres, producing great quantities of wheat and potatoes. Owned about 6000 acres; Lord of the Manors of Eckington, Derbyshire; Whiston, South Yorkshire; and Long Itchington, Warwickshire. *Publications:* The First Whig; Country Life in the 17th Century; An Essay on the Making of Gardens; Tales of My Native Village, 1934; Idle Fancies in Prose and Verse, 1938, etc. *Recreations:* when younger, golf, cricket, hunting, cycling, lawn tennis. *Heir: s* Osbert. *Address:* Castle of Montegufoni, Montagnana, Val Di Pesa, Florence, Italy.

Died 8 July 1943.

SKELTON, Oscar Douglas, MA, PhD; LLD; Under-Secretary of State for External Affairs, Canada, since 1925; *b* Orangeville, Ontario, 1878; *s* of Jeremiah Skelton and Elizabeth Hall; *m* 1904, Isabel Murphy, MA; two *s* one *d. Educ:* Orangeville and Cornwall High Schools; Queen's University; University of Chicago. Newspaper and magazine work in Philadelphia,

1901–04; post-graduate work, University of Chicago, 1905–08; Lecturer in Political Science, Queen's University, 1907; Professor, 1908; Dean, Faculty of Arts, 1919; Counsellor, Department of External Affairs, Canada, 1924. *Publications:* Socialism, a Critical Analysis, 1910; Economic History of Canada since Confederation, 1913; The Railroad Builders, 1914; The Day of Sir Wilfrid Laurier, 1916; Life and Times of Sir A. T. Galt, 1919; The Canadian Dominion, 1919; Life and Letters of Sir Wilfrid Laurier, 1922; Our Generation: Its Gains and Losses, 1938; current magazine articles. *Address:* Edgehill, Rockcliffe Park, Ottawa, Canada. *Clubs:* Rideau, Country, Ottawa.

Died 28 Jan. 1941.

SKINNER, Rev. Albert James, BA London University; Headmaster, Sir William Borlase's School, Marlow, 1904–27; *b* 16 Nov. 1869; *m* Marie Isabella (*d* 1947), *d* of H. R. Roper-Curzon, *cousin* of late Lord Teynham. *Educ:* Oundle School. Second Master of King Edward VI Grammar School, Chelmsford; Headmaster of Worcester College for Blind Sons of Gentlemen; Senior Mathematical and House Master of Weymouth College; Headmaster of Hereford County College; House Master and Science Master at Reading School; Examiner in various schools. *Publications:* The Popular Fox Terrier, 1930; various school texts. *Recreations:* football, Rugby (Somerset County team); cricket, Worcester Club and Ground and Hereford Club and Ground; golf, fishing. *Address:* Borlase, West Hove, Sussex.

Died 9 Nov. 1949.

SKINNER, Sir Harry Ross, Kt 1917; MInstCE, MIMM; *b* Manse of Coull, Aberdeenshire, 14 July 1867; *y s* of Rev. William Skinner, MA, of Tarland and Migvie; *m* 1893, Annie Janet, *d* of late John Milne, Aberdeen; two *s* one *d*. *Educ:* privately. Served pupilage as Civil Engineer; Consulting Engineer, Durban Roodepoort Gold Mines, Transvaal, 1890–1917; Special Commissioner to China and the East for Transvaal Mining Industry to report on importation of unskilled labour for Witwatersrand mines, 1903; Technical Director and Consulting Engineer, East Rand Proprietary Mines, 1911–14; Director of the Central Mining and Investment Corporation, 1 London Wall Buildings, 1916–23; served South African War, Captain Rand Rifles (Mines Division), 1900–02 (Queen's medal); Major (2nd in command), Transvaal Scottish Volunteers, 1903–09; Member of various Government Commissions in South Africa; Ministry of Munitions (Volunteer); Director, High Explosives Supply under Lord Moulton, 1914–15; Deputy Director-General Munitions Inspection, 1916–17. *Address:* c/o National Bank of South Africa, Cape Town and London. *Clubs:* Caledonian, Windham's; Rand, Country, Johannesburg.

Died 18 Aug. 1943.

SKINNER, Robert Taylor, JP; MA, FRSE; FSAScot; House-Governor of Donaldson's Hospital, Edinburgh, 1899–1934; *b* Aberdeen, 22 May 1867; *s* of James Skinner, farmer, Bethelnie and Craibstone, and Jane, *d* of James Anderson, farmer, Hilton; unmarried. *Educ:* Old Aberdeen Grammar School; Aberdeen University. Taught at Folkestone and Sheffield, 1888–93; one of the masters in George Watson's College, Edinburgh, ultimately personal assistant to the Head Master, Dr George Ogilvie, 1893–99; Visitor and Examiner under the Dick Bequest Trust for 130 schools in the counties of Aberdeen, Banff, Moray, Inverness, 1916–29; has visited antiquities Carthage, Greece, Crete; has twice traversed the Cévennes Route of RLS; has delivered 751 lectures for churches, schools, charities. *Publications:* George Ogilvie and George Watson's College, 1899; The Oberammergan Play, 1900; Men of the North-East, 1920; The Royal Mile, 1920; enlarged edition, 1928; Twenty-five Years at Donaldson's Hospital, 1925; Cummy's Diary, 1926; In the Cévennes without a Donkey, 1926, second edition, 1929; A Notable Family

of Scots Printers, 1927; Yesterday and To-day, 1929; Figures and Figureheads, 1931; contributor to newspapers and journals. *Recreations:* antiquarian pursuits, swimming. *Address:* 35 Campbell Road, Edinburgh, 12. *T:* Edinburgh 63494.

Died 31 Aug. 1946.

SKINNER, Sidney, MA Cambridge; FInstP, MRI; Principal of the Chelsea Polytechnic, 1904–28; *b* 1863; *s* of late George Edward Skinner, civil servant, Royal Courts of Justice; *m* Marion Field (*d* 1942), *d* of Major Michaelis, PhD, US Army, *g d* of Major Francis Woodbridge, US Army; two *d*. *Educ:* Dulwich College (Exhibitioner); Christ's College, Cambridge (Scholar); BA 1886. Lecturer and Demonstrator in the Cavendish Laboratory, and Lecturer at Clare College. *Publications:* papers on physics and chemistry in Philosophical Magazine, Chemical Society's Journal, etc. *Address:* 17 Sollershott West, Letchworth, Herts. *T:* Letchworth 799.

Died 5 Nov. 1944.

SKINNER, Sir Sydney Martyn, Kt 1922; JP; Chairman of John Barker & Co., and other companies; *b* 21 July 1864; *m* 1902, Emelie Madeline, *d* of Samuel Belling, Bodmin, Cornwall. Past President Incorporated Association of Retail Distributors, of the Drapers Chamber of Trade, and of the Acton Hospital; has also done much municipal work, being Chairman of various Committees and Higher Education Committees. *Address:* Meadow Entry, Crofton Road, Ealing; West Watch, Chelwood Gate, Haywards Heath, Sussex.

Died 3 March 1941.

SKINNER, Waldo W., KC 1913; BCL; *b* St John, NB, 31 July 1878; *s* of Hon. Charles Nelson Skinner; *m* 1907, Marie Alice, *d* of Hon. L. J. Forget; no *c*. *Educ:* Davonport School; Upper Canada College; McGill University, Montreal. Called to Bar, 1901. *Address:* 1476 Sherbrooke Street West, Montreal. *TA:* Waldlaw Montreal. *Clubs:* Mount Royal, St James's, Senneville Golf, Montreal, Polo, Montreal; Rideau, Ottawa.

Died 13 Nov. 1943.

SKINNER, Rev. William, CIE 1919; DD; *b* 19 Sept. 1859; *s* of James Skinner, Inverurie; *m* 1892, Helen Rebecca Niven; one *s* two *d*. *Educ:* Gymnasium, Old Aberdeen; Aberdeen University; New College, Edinburgh. Professor of Madras Christian College, 1884; Principal, 1909; DD (Aberdeen), 1908; Kaisar-i-Hind Gold Medal, 1917; retired, 1921. *Address:* 22 Gladstone Place, Aberdeen.

Died 26 Aug. 1942.

SKIPTON, Rev. Horace Pitt Kennedy, FSA; FRHistSoc; Priest-in-charge S Philip's, Reigate, since 1927; *b* 1861; *s* of Daniel Pitt Skipton, MRCS, MRCP; *m* 1890, Jessie, *d* of W. H. Goodwin; one *d*. *Educ:* City of London School. India Police Service, 1883–99; has written for the press both in England and India; joint-editor of Electricity, 1898–1904; co-editor of The Churchwoman with G. M. Ireland Blackburne, 1899–1903; acting assistant editor of The Pilot, 1902; Editor of Church Bells, 1906; on Staff of Guardian, 1904–24; Secretary Indian Church Aid Association, and Editor Indian Church Magazine, 1907–24; Deacon, 1924; Priest, 1925. *Publications:* A Little Gallery of Hoppner, 1903; John Hoppner, 1905; A Song of the Celestial City, 1906; About Some Favourite Hymns, 1907; Nicholas Ferrar and his Times, 1907; Our Reproach in India, 1912; A Hundred Years of the Church in India, 1914; Underneath the Bough, A Book of Verses and Translations, 1934; The Pilgrims' Way and the Pilgrim's Progress, 1942; contributor to Nineteenth Century, The East and the West, Connoisseur, Church Quarterly Review, Theology, etc. *Recreations:* travel and sketching. *Address:* S Philip's Parsonage, Reigate, Surrey.

Died 16 Feb. 1943.

SKIPWITH, Sir Grey (Humberston d'Estoteville), 11th Bt *cr* 1622; JP Warwickshire and Worcestershire; Hon. Captain in the Army; *b* 4 Dec. 1884; *o s* of late 10th Bt and Alice Mary, *o d* of Maj.-Gen. Herrick (she *m* 2nd, Major J. H. Ward-Boughton-Leigh); *S* 1891; *m* 1st, 1910, Elsie Maude (who obtained a divorce, 1928), *y d* of late Major R. Allison-Browne; one *d*; 2nd, 1928, Cynthia Egerton, *d* of late Egerton Leigh, 20 Cadogan Place, SW; two *s*. *Educ:* Harrow; Trinity Coll., Cambridge. *Recreations:* shooting and fishing. *Heir: g s* Patrick Alexander d'Estoteville [*b* 1938; *s* of late Grey d'Estoteville Townsend Skipwith, Flying Officer RAFVR, and Sofka, *d* of late General Peter Dolgorouky]. *Address:* Upper Link House, St Mary Bourne, nr Andover, Hants. *T:* St Mary Bourne 264.

Died 3 Feb. 1950.

SKIRROW, Major Arthur George Walker, DSO 1919; retired; *b* 26 Sept. 1862; *s* of Walker Skirrow and Emily Rush; *m* 1891, Georgiana L. F. Banks; no *c*. *Educ:* Charterhouse. Joined 2nd Bn S Lancashire Regt, 1883; served in Zululand, Singapore, Gibraltar; Boer War, 1899, invalided with enteric fever; European War, 1914–19; Adjutant Regimental Depot, 1915; Adjutant 9th Division Base Depot at Étaples, commanded No. 25 Division Base Depot, 1915–16; DAAG on Staff, 1919 (DSO, despatches thrice); Secretary to King's Fund under Ministry of Pensions to Sept. 1919; Region Director of South West Region under Ministry of Pensions to Feb. 1923. *Recreations:* motoring, fishing. *Address:* Prospect House, Budleigh Salterton, Devon. *T:* Budleigh Salterton 205. *Club:* Naval and Military.

Died 26 March 1941.

SKUES, George Edward Mackenzie; retired Solicitor; *b* 13 Aug. 1858; *e s* of late William Mackenzie Skues, Brigade Surgeon, Army Medical Dept, and Margaret Ayre; unmarried. *Educ:* Winchester (Scholar). Articled to James Powell, solicitor, 1879; admitted Solicitor, 1884; Partner of Jas Powell, 1895, till his death in 1925; Senior Partner in firm of Powell, Skues & Graham Smith, till retirement, 1940 (address, through entire period, 34 Essex Street, Strand). *Publications:* Minor Tactics of the Chalk Stream, 1910 (2nd ed. 1914, 3rd, 1924); The Way of a Trout with a Fly, 1921 (2nd ed., 1923, 3rd, 1928); Side Lines, Side Lights and Reflections, 1932; Nymph Fishing for Chalk Stream Trout, 1939; Angling Letters of G. E. M. Skues (posthumous; ed. Walker), 1956; numerous articles in angling publications under pseudonyms. *Recreations:* trout fishing, trout fly dressing. *Club:* Flyfishers'.

Died 9 Aug. 1949.

SLADE, Cecil William Paulet, FRGS, FZS; *b* 22 Nov. 1863; *s* of Colonel William H. Slade, *s* of General Sir John Slade, Bt, and Cecilia Louisa, *d* of Sir Charles and Lady Cecilia Des Vœux. *Educ:* Royal Naval Academy, Gosport; privately. Served in British South Africa Company's Police in occupation of Rhodesia, 1890 (medal and clasp); formerly Captain 3rd Batt. Wiltshire Regiment; British South Africa Company's Police; Captain attached General Staff (Musketry), Aldershot Command, 1915–19. *Recreations:* shooting, yachting, travelling, motoring. *Address:* 3 Upper Belgrave Street, SW1. *T:* Sloane 1793. *Clubs:* Turf, Carlton; Royal Yacht Squadron, Cowes.

Died 5 Nov. 1943.

SLADE, George Penkivil; KC 1939; Acting Commander RNVR (Special Branch); *b* 30 June 1899; *s* of late George Slade, MA, Solicitor, and Edith Mary Beale; *m* 1923, Mary Albinia, *d* of Rev. Canon W. H. Carnegie; three *s* one *d*. *Educ:* Eton (scholar); Magdalen College, Oxford (Demy). Army, 1918–19; 1st Honour Mods (Classical); 2nd Law Final, BA Degree, 1922; called to Bar, 1923. *Recreations:* music, golf. *Address:* St Michaels, Painswick, Glos. *Club:* Oxford and Cambridge.

Died 13 Sept. 1942.

SLADE, Sir James Benjamin, Kt 1927; JP; Ex-Alderman of Essex County Council; *b* Hampstead, 12 Dec. 1861; *m* 1886, Emily Ellen Carter (*d* 1942), Eastbourne; one *s* two *d*. *Educ:* Hampstead. Auctioneer and surveyor; senior partner in the firm of Protheroe & Morris. For 48 years CC Essex. Royal Horticultural Society's Victoria Medal, 1943. *Address:* Protheroe & Morris, 14 Moorgate, EC2. *TA:* c/o Promptuary, Ave London. *T:* Monarch 8388/8389.

Died 15 April 1950.

SLADE, Wyndham Neave; *b* 17 Sept. 1867; *o s* of late Wyndham Slade of Montys Court, Taunton; *m* 1898, Evelyn Mary, *d* of William Clarence Watson of Colworth, Bedfordshire. *Educ:* Eton; Balliol College, Oxford (Honours in Moderations and Finals; became BA 1890, MA 1893). Called to Bar, Inner Temple, 1891; Recorder of Bridgwater, 1898–1936; Chairman of Taunton County Sessions; Chairman of Trade Boards; JP Co. Somerset. *Address:* Montys Court, Taunton. *T:* Bishops Lydeard 255. *Clubs:* Arthur's, Carlton, MCC; Somerset County, Taunton.

Died 11 Feb. 1941.

SLADEN, Arthur French, CMG 1911; CVO 1916; *b* 30 April 1866; *e s* of late Col Joseph Sladen; *m* 1891, Kathleen Hume (*d* 1936), 2nd *d* of late W. Powell of Edgewood, Ottawa; three *s*. *Educ:* Haileybury Coll.; Royal Naval Coll., Greenwich. Entered the Gov.-General's Office, Ottawa, 1890; Private Secretary to Lord Minto, 1899–1904; to Lord Grey, 1904–11; to the Duke of Connaught, 1911–16; to Duke of Devonshire, 1916–21; to Lord Byng of Vimy, 1921–26. *Recreation:* golf. *Address:* 102 Lewis Street, Ottawa, Canada. *Clubs:* Rideau, Country, Ottawa.

Died 7 March 1944.

SLADEN, Douglas (Brooke Wheelton), BA, LLB; *b* London, 5 Feb. 1856; *e s* of late Douglas Brooke Sladen and Mary, *d* of John Wheelton; *m* 1st, 1880, Margaret Isabel (*d* 1919), *d* of Robert Muirhead, The Grampians, Victoria, Australia; one *s*; 2nd, 1920, Christian Dorothea, *d* of late John Duthie, Cults House, Aberdeenshire. *Educ:* Temple Grove; Cheltenham College; Trinity College, Oxford (Scholar). 1st class in History at Oxford. First to hold the chair of History in Univ. of Sydney; travelled extensively; editor of Who's Who, 1897–99; The Green Book, 1910–11. He was instrumental in having a memorial bust of Adam Lindsay Gordon placed in the Poets Corner, Westminster Abbey. *Publications:* Frithjof and Ingebjorg, 1882; Australian Lyrics, 1882; a Poetry of Exiles, 1883; A Summer Christmas, 1884; In Cornwall and across the Sea, 1885; Edward the Black Prince, 1886; The Spanish Armada, 1888; Australian Ballads and Rhymes, 1888; A Century of Australian Song, 1888; Australian Poets, 1888; Lester the Loyalist, 1890; Younger American Poets, 1891; The Japs at Home, 1892; On the Cars and Off, 1895; A Japanese Marriage, 1895; Brittany for Britons, 1896; The Admiral, 1898; Trincolox, 1898; In Sicily, 1901; My Son Richard, 1901; Queer Things about Japan, 1903; Sicily the New Winter Resort, 1904; Playing the Game, 1904; A Sicilian Marriage, 1905; Carthage and Tunis, 1906; The Secrets of the Vatican, 1907; Egypt and the English, 1908; The Tragedy of the Pyramids, 1909; Queer Things about Egypt, 1910; Oriental Cairo, 1910; How to see Italy, 1911; edited A. L. Gordon's Poems, 1912; The Unholy Estate, 1912; The Curse of the Nile, 1913; Germany's Great Lie, 1914; Twenty Years of My Life, 1915; The Confessions of Frederick the Great, 1915; His German Wife, 1915; From Boundary. Rider to Prime Minister, 1916; The Douglas Romance, 1916; Grace Lorraine, 1917; In Ruhleben, 1917; Fair Inez, 1918; The Shadow of a Great Light, 1918; Paul's Wife or the Ostriches, 1919, The Crystal and the Sphinx, 1923; The Greek Slave, 1931; Eve, an Artist's Model, 1932; The Life and Poetry of Adam Lindsay Gordon, Westminster Abbey Memorial Volume, 1934; Meriel Brede, Secretary, 1935; My Long Life; Anecdotes and

Adventures, 1939; (with Norma Lorimer) Queer Things about Sicily, 1905; More Queer Things about Japan, 1904; (with Eustache de Lorey) Queer Things about Persia, 1907; The Moon at the Fourteenth Night, 1910; (with Miss E. M. Humphris) Adam Lindsay Gordon and his Friends, 1912; (with Miss O. M. Potter) Weeds, 1913. *Plays:* Paul's Wife; (with Peter Blundell) Mr Pootle. *Recreations:* rifle shooting, (winner of the Spencer Cup, 1874), golf, travel, architecture, curio collecting. *Address:* Palmeira Nursing Home, Hove 3, Sussex.

Died 12 Feb. 1947.

SLATER, Ernest, MIEE, MIME; (pseudonym Paul Gwynne). Trained as an engineer; editor of the Electrical Times, and author of numerous technical and semi-technical articles; spent many years on engineering schemes abroad, chiefly in Spain and Mexico, and under the above pseudonym has specialized in works of fiction with Spanish and French setting, generally Spanish. *Publications:* Novels—Marta; The Pagan at the Shrine; The Bandolero; Dr Pons; Nightshade; Peggie Gets the Sack; travel books; Pitman's Technical Dictionary in Seven Languages, 1929; Polyglot Index thereto, 1931. *Address:* Sardinia House, Kingsway, WC. *T:* Holborn 6016.

Died 1 April 1942.

SLATER, George, CBE 1920; herring merchant and exporter; a Director British Oil and Guano Co. Ltd. *Address:* 22 Louisville Avenue, Aberdeen.

Died 4 Dec. 1941.

SLAYTER, Col Edward Wheeler, CMG 1916; DSO 1918; late AMS; Resident in India; *b* 15 Jan. 1869; *y s* of late Dr W. B. Slayter, of Halifax, Nova Scotia; *m* Florence Mary, *o d* of late J. J. Richardson, Lammerburn, Merchiston, Edinburgh; two *s* two *d. Educ:* Germany; Dalhousie College, Nova Scotia; Edinburgh University (MB, CM 1891). Entered Army Medical Service, 1892; Captain, 1895; Major, 1904; Lt-Col 1914; Colonel, 1917; retired pay, 1921 served Tochi Valley Expeditionary Force, 1897 (medal and clasp); South African War, 1899 (Queen's medal with two clasps); European War, 1914–18 (despatches six times, CMG, DSO). *Recreations:* music, golf, etc. *Address:* Glyn, Mills & Co., Whitehall, SW1.

Died 22 Aug. 1946.

SLEATOR, James Sinton, RHA; portrait painter. *Educ:* Dublin, London, Florence. Exhibitor, London, Dublin, Glasgow. *Address:* Royal Hibernian Academy of Arts, 15 Ely Place, Dublin. *Club:* Chelsea Arts.

Died 19 Jan. 1950.

SLEE, Comdr John Ambrose, CBE 1919; late RN; late Manager Marconi Sounding Devices Co.; late Head of Wireless Telegraphy Board; *b* Cæsar's Camp, Wimbledon, 24 May 1878; *s* of late Arthur and Helen Slee. *Educ:* HMS Britannia. *Recreations:* lawn tennis, fishing, motoring, golf. *Club:* United Service.

Died 20 March 1944.

SLEIGH, Charles William, CBE 1939; Hon. LLD Aberdeen; MA; JP; Estate Agent; *b* 27 April 1863; *s* of John Sleigh, Estate Agent on Strichen and other Estates for 60 years, and Ann Gall; *m* 1895; three *s. Educ:* Grammar School, Aberdeen (Williamson Scholar and Gold Medallist); Aberdeen University (MA with 1st class Hons in Science). For 5 years in architects' and surveyors' offices; Estate Agent in Lanarkshire for 16½ years and in Aberdeenshire since 1911; Member of Aberdeen County Council, 1918–45, Vice-Convener, 1928–42 and Convener, 1942–45; Chairman of Education Committee for Aberdeenshire, 1919–42; Chairman of Aberdeen Provincial Committee for Training Teachers since 1922; Chairman of National Committee for Scotland and of the CEC for the Training of Teachers; Chairman of new Central Selection Board for Scotland, for obtaining extra teachers from HM Forces, Industry, etc.; founded Scottish Estate

Factors' Society and was Secretary and Editor of Scottish Estate Factors Magazine for 21 years. *Address:* Strichen, Aberdeenshire. *TA:* Sleigh, Strichen. *T:* Strichen 208. *Club:* Royal Northern (Aberdeen).

Died 8 Dec. 1949.

SLEIGH, Sir William Lowrie, Kt 1924; LLD Edinburgh University; *b* Lauder, Berwickshire, 26 Sept. 1865; *m* 1895, Jessie (*d* 1937), *d* of Charles Sime, merchant, Edinburgh; two *s. Educ:* Public School, Lauder. Founded the motor business of Rossleigh, Limited, Motor Engineers to the King, with headquarters at Edinburgh, and branches throughout Scotland; now Chairman and Director of the Company. Lord Provost of the City of Edinburgh, 1923–26. *Recreations:* golf and curling. *Address:* 6 Braid Avenue, Edinburgh. *TA:* Rossleigh, Edinburgh. *T:* Central 24043. *Clubs:* Scottish Conservative, Edinburgh; Royal Scottish Automobile, Glasgow.

Died 5 May 1945.

SLEIGHT, Major Sir Ernest, 2nd Bt *cr* 1920; OBE; TD; *b* 14 Oct. 1873; *e s* of 1st Bart and Rebecca, *d* of John Longden of Cleethorpes; *m* 1898, Margaret, *d* of C. F. Carter, JP, The Limes, Grimsby; one *s* one *d. Educ:* Overslade, Rugby; Rugby School. Director of steam-fishing and other companies; served in Flanders 46th (N Mid.) Division (OBE 1914–15 star); DL, Lincolnshire; JP Parts of Lindsey, Lincolnshire; Hon. Col 2nd Cadet Bn Lincolnshire Regt. *Heir: s* John Frederick Sleight [*b* 13 April 1909; *m* 1942, Jacqueline Margaret Mundell, *widow* of Ronald Mundell and *e d* of late Major H. R. Carter of Brisbane, Queensland]. *Address:* Stallingborough, Grimsby, Lincolnshire. *TA:* Sleight, Healing 2113. *T:* Healing 2113.

Died 16 July 1946.

SLIGO, 7th Marquess of, *cr* 1800; **Ulick de Burgh Browne,** MC; Baron Mount Eagle, 1760; Viscount Westport, 1768; Earl of Altamont, 1771; Earl of Clanricarde, 1800; Baron Monteagle (UK), 1806; *b* 30 March 1898; *o s* of 6th Marquess of Sligo and Agatha Stewart, *d* of late J. Stewart Hodgson; *S* father, 1935. *Educ:* Eton; Sandhurst. Captain 2nd Dragoons, Royal Scots Greys; retired, 1928; served European War, 1917–18 (MC). *Heir: uncle* Col Lord Arthur Browne, KBE, CB. *Address:* Westport House, Co. Mayo; 7 Upper Belgrave Street, SW1. *T:* Sloane 8640.

Died 7 Jan. 1941.

SLIWINSKI, Stanislaw; Artiste peintre; *b* Warsaw, 1893. *Educ:* Academy of Fine Arts, Cracow. At 17 entered enchanted world of the theatre in the room of St Jasinski at Grand Opera Theatre in Warsaw; here he worked for three years before joining Teatr Polski; returning to Warsaw in 1920, he volunteered for Russo-Polish war and afterwards continued his work at the Grand Opera and Teatr Polski, mostly carrying out the projects of Drabik and Frycz, until he began independent work and made considerable reputation with his settings for many Polish plays and The Merry Wives of Windsor, The Merchant of Venice, Midsummer Night's Dream, Danton, Man and Superman, Pygmalion, Too True to be Good, Queen Elizabeth of England, Samuel Zborowski, Peripherie, Caligula, etc. *Address:* 10 Obozna Street, Warsaw, Poland.

Died 30 Oct. 1940.

SLOAN, Alexander. MP (Lab) South Ayrshire since 1939; Secretary National Union of Scottish Mine Workers.

Died 16 Nov. 1945.

SLOAN, Maj.-Gen. John Macfarlane, CB 1927; CMG 1917; DSO 1902; MB, BCh; *b* 22 July 1872; *s* of Samuel Sloan, MD, Glasgow; *m* 1906, Alice Patricia, *d* of James Bridges, Dublin. *Educ:* Glasgow University. Entered Army, 1899; Capt. 1902; Maj. 1910; Bt Lt-Col 1915; Bt Col 1916; Col 1923; Maj.-Gen. 1926; served S Africa, 1899–1902 (despatches, DSO, Queen's medal 4 clasps, and King's medal 2 clasps); European War, 1914–18 (despatches six times, Bt Lt-Col and Col, CMG; 2nd Class St Anne of Russia); Assistant Director of Medical Services, 1916; DDMS, Mesopotamia, 1916–18; retired 1929.

Died 10 Sept. 1941.

SLOAN, Robert Patrick, CBE 1919; MIEE; Member Central Electricity Board since 1936; *b* Aberdeen, 1874; *s* of late Rev. John M. Sloan, MA; *m* 1st, India (*d* 1921), *e d* of late David Ellis, Santos, Brazil; one *s*; 2nd, 1933, Ethel Sophia, *widow* of William Hoar. *Educ:* Watson's College and Heriot-Watt College, Edinburgh; Finsbury College, London. Past President of British Electrical and Allied Industries Research Association; Past-Pres. Inc. Assoc. of Electric Power Companies; Past-Pres. of the British Electrical Development Association. *Address:* L'Ambassador, Nice, France.

Died 6 Dec. 1947.

SLOANE-STANLEY, Ronald Francis Assheton; late Acting Lt-Col Hants Yeomanry; JP County of Southampton; *b* 3 Nov. 1867; *s* of late Francis Sloane-Stanley, JP, DL of Leesthorpe, Melton Mowbray, and Bay House, Alverstoke, Hants; *m* 1st, 1898, Susan (*d* 1931), *y d* of William Johnstone, JP, of Claddens, Lenzie, Lanark; one *s*; 2nd, 1937, Mrs Audrey Alma Rivers, *d* of late Horace Humphreys. *Educ:* Eton. Served in 16th Lancers, 1887–1902; served South African War (severely wounded, despatches). *Recreations:* hunting, shooting, golf, yachting. *Address:* Hardwicke, Cowes, I of Wight. *T:* Cowes 640. *Clubs:* Army and Navy, Cavalry; Royal Yacht Squadron (Cowes).

Died 19 Aug. 1948.

SLOCOCK, Francis Samuel Alfred, CIE 1914. *Educ:* Marlborough; Trinity Coll., Oxford. Entered ICS 1889; served Madras as Assistant Collector and Magistrate; Central Provinces, 1898; Deputy Commissioner, 1900; Chief Secretary Chief Commissioner, 1906–08; Inspector-General of Police, 1908–14; on special duty Government of India Home Dept, 1914; Chief Secretary, CP, 1915–20; Commissioner, Jubbulpore, 1921–26; retired 1926. *Address:* Boldon, Minehead, Somerset.

Died 11 Nov. 1945.

SLOGGETT, Col Arthur John Henry, CBE 1949; DSO 1917; DL; *b* 4 May 1882; *o s* of late Lt-Gen. Sir Arthur Sloggett; *m* 1917, Gabrielle, *d* of late Monsieur de Lebois, Roubaix, France; two *d*. *Educ:* Harrow; RMC, Sandhurst. Entered Rifle Brigade, 1900, 1st Bn; served S African War, 1900–02. Assistant Provost Marshal, Guards Mounted Infantry (Medal, 5 clasps); Adjutant 4th Bn Rifle Bde European War, 1914–18 (GSO3); Bde Major and commanded a Bn Rifle Bde (1914 Star, despatches, DSO); retired pay, 1925; War of 1939–45; comd 10th Torbay Bn Devonshire Regt; Home Guard, 1940–44. County Comdt Devon Army Cadet Force, 1944–48. DL Devon, 1947. *Recreations:* formerly racquets (army champion; racquets singles, 1920; doubles racquets, 1922–23 (Regimental)). *Address:* Tremabyn, Paignton, S Devon. *Clubs:* Army and Navy, MCC; Green Jackets, I Zingari, Free Foresters.

Died 13 Dec. 1950.

SLOMAN, Brig.-Gen. Henry Stanhope, CMG 1918; DSO 1900; late East Surrey Regt and Staff; *b* 29 Aug. 1861; *s* of late Major J. Sloman, 61th Regt; *m* 1903, Mary Charlotte (*d* 1934), *d* of late Admiral Sir A. L. Douglas; one *s* one *d*. *Educ:* Sherborne. Entered army, 1882; served Soudan, 1885, with Mounted Inf. (medal with clasp, Khedive's star); Soudan, 1897–98, including Khartoum (despatches twice, British medal, 4th class Medjidie, Khedive's medal with three clasps); South Africa, 1900–02 (despatches, Queen's medal 4 clasps, King's medal 2 clasps, DSO); European War, 1914–18

(1914 Star, 2 medals, 2nd class Order of Sacred Treasure, CMG); retired, 1918. *Address:* Wick House, Wick, Bournemouth. *T:* Christchurch 186.

Died 29 Dec. 1945.

SMALL, Sir Alexander Sym, KBE 1939; CMG 1937; *b* 1887. *Educ:* Glasgow University, MA, BSc. Cadet, FMS, 1911; Treasurer, Straits Settlements, 1932; Colonial Secretary, Straits Settlements, 1935–40. *Address:* 42a View Street, Cottesloe, W Australia.

Died 13 Aug. 1944.

SMALLEY, Sir Herbert, Kt 1913; MD Durham; MRCS Eng.; LRCP Lond.; *b* 3 June 1851; 3rd *s* of Rev. Cornwall Smalley, MA; *m* 1885, Rose Christina Smalley, *d* of late G. F. Grammann. *Educ:* St Paul's School; King's College, London. Formerly Medical Officer at HM's Prisons, Dartmoor, Pentonville, and Parkhurst; Medical Inspector of Local Prisons and Superintending Officer of Convict Prisons, 1897–1914; a Prison Commissioner, 1914–17. *Address:* 72 Pembroke Crescent, Hove, Sussex.

Died 25 Jan. 1945.

SMALLMAN, Lt-Col Arthur Briton, CBE 1920; DSO 1916; MD; *b* 1 Dec. 1873; *e s* of Samuel Smallman and Sarah Jane Rowley; *m* 1916, Alice Florence, 2nd *d* of late Hon. R. G. Duncan; two *s*. *Educ:* Manchester Grammar School; Owens College, Manchester. Graduated MB, ChB (Hons) Victoria, 1897; MB London, 1903; DPH Cambridge, 1903; MD (commend) Victoria Univ. of Manchester, 1913. Civil Surgeon South African War, 1900–02 (Queen's medal three clasps, King's medal two clasps); entered RAMC 1902; Captain, 1906; Balkan War, 1912–13, with the Turkish Forces; Brevet Major, 1913; Major RAMC 1914; served European War, France, 1914–17, as DADMS 1st Div., DADMS, L of C, DADMS, GHQ, DADG, and ADG Army Medical Service, War Office, 1917–20; (despatches five times, CBE, DSO); retired pay, 1920; Medical Officer, Ministry of Health, 1920–38; Member, Radium Commission, 1929–35 and 1940–43. *Publications:* articles in Journal of the Royal Army Medical Corps on Typhoid Fever, Malaria, etc; Ministry of Health Report on Public Health and Medical Subjects, No. 79. *Address:* 2 Pilgrims Way, Guildford. *T:* 2458.

Died 4 March 1950.

SMALLWOOD, Henry Armstrong, CMG 1922; *b* 26 Feb. 1869; 2nd *s* of late Rev. W. J. Smallwood, MA; *m* 1896, Emily Louise Catherine Dartnell; two *s* one *d*. *Educ:* King's School, Canterbury; Fosters, Stubbington. Entered Royal Navy, 1886; on board HMS Victoria when sunk in collision with HMS Camperdown, June 1893; entered Colonial Service, 1894; served in Fiji, Cyprus, St Lucia (BWI), British East Africa (now Kenya), the Federated Malay States, Palestine, and Iraq; retired, 1924; temporarily re-employed on special duty in Bahamas, 1927–28; Chairman, Finance Commission, Greek Orthodox Patriarchate Jerusalem, 1928–37; Fellow, Royal Empire Society. *Recreation:* golf. *Address:* 12 Grange Road, Chiswick, W4. *T:* Chiswick 2959.

Died 3 Dec. 1942.

SMART, Borlase, ROI; RBC 1928; RWA; professional artist, painter, Etcher and Poster Designer; Hon. Treasurer, Society of Marine Artists; Pres. Hon. Secretary, St Ives Society of Artists, Cornwall; Member of the Cornish Gorsedd; *b* Kingsbridge, South Devon, 11 Feb. 1881; *o s* of late R. W. C. Smart, Schoolmaster; *m* 1917, Kathleen Irene, 2nd *d* of late G. Bird Godson; two *s*. *Educ:* Plymouth Public School. Joined St Ives Art Colony, 1919; Exhibitor at Royal Academy, Paris Salon (25 years) and principal galleries at home and abroad; Pictures in collections of Imperial War Museum, Nat. Maritime Museum, Leamington, Sheffield, Bristol, Plymouth, Truro Galleries, The Prince of Wales Museum, Bombay, and the Auckland Gallery, New

Zealand. *Publication:* The Technique of Seascape Painting. *Address:* Ty Bryn, St Ives, Cornwall. *TA:* Smart St Ives, C.

Died 3 Nov. 1947.

SMART, E. Hodgson; artist; *b* Alnwick; 2nd *s* of late George Stott Smart. *Educ:* Antwerp Academy, under Albert de Vriendt; Julian's, Paris, under Bougereau and Ferrier; with Sir Hubert von Herkomer, at Bushey. *Works:* King Edward and Queen Alexandra's Visit to Duke of Northumberland, which includes, besides their Majesties, portraits of the late Duke of Northumberland, Earl Carrington, and others; Dawn, exhibited in Paris Salon in 1909; Portrait of the Lady in Black, exhibited at the Royal Academy, 1906, also in the Paris Salon, 1908; Dr Annie Besant, exhibited in Royal Academy, 1934; My Mother, exhibited in the Royal Academy, 1906, and in Paris Salon, 1909; F. W. Ancott, exhibited in the Paris Salon, 1910; Marshal Foch, now in the Cleveland Museum of Art; President Harding, Prof. Wm H. Holmes and General Sir Geo. Owen Squier, in the National Gallery at Washington; Newton D. Baker, in the War Department, Washington; Francis L. Patton, LLD, in the House of Parliament, Washington; Admiral Sims; General Pershing; General Sir Arthur Currey; Sir Robert Borden, etc. *Recreations:* music, motoring, boating. *Address:* Thornbrae, Alnwick, Northumberland; Princess Hotel, Bermuda. *Clubs:* Chelsea Arts; Rowfant (Cleveland).

Died 14 Nov. 1942.

SMART, Sir Harold Nevil, Kt 1950; CMG 1917; OBE 1919; JP County of London; *b* 1883; *e s* of late Harold Alfred Smart, banker; *m* 1923, Janetta Neill, *o d* of late Sir Clement H. Newsum, Eastwood House, Lincoln; one *s* one *d*. *Educ:* Malvern College; Berlin University. Solicitor; President of the Law Society, 1949; Vice-Chairman Malvern College Council; served in North Sea Patrol, North Russia, and Ministry of Shipping, 1914–20; Acting Lieut-Commander RNVR; 1st Grade Transport Officer; holds Russian Order of St Anne, 3rd Class, 1916; Long Service Medal. *Address:* Wedderburn House, NW3. *T:* Hampstead 6996. *Club:* City of London.

Died 15 Dec. 1950.

SMART, William Wilkinson; ISO 1902; Superintending Veterinary Inspector (retired), Board of Agriculture; *s* of late Joseph Smart of Fulready and Coventry. *Educ:* private schools; Royal Veterinary College, London. Graduated Member of Royal College of Veterinary Surgeons, 1876. *Recreations:* field sports, horticulture. *Address:* Charlcombe Farm, Charlcombe, near Bath. *T:* Bath 2960.

Died 18 Jan. 1943.

SMEDLEY, Constance, (Mrs Maxwell Armfield); *d* of late W. T. Smedley and Annie Duckworth; *m* 1909, Maxwell Armfield, ARWS. *Educ:* Birmingham School of Art; King Edward VI High School. Founder of the International Association of Lyceum Clubs, The Cotswold Players, The Greenleaf Theatre, Grace Darling League. *Publications:* The April Princess; The Flower Book; Service, 1910; Mothers and Fathers, 1911; Commoners' Rights, 1912; Sylvia's Travels, 1912; New Wine and Old Bottles, 1913; Una and the Lions, 1914; On the Fighting Line, 1915; Redwing, 1916; The Armfield Animal Book, 1922; Tales of Timbuktu, 1923; The Unholy Experiment, 1924; Justice Walk, 1924; Crusaders (Reminiscences of Constance Smedley), 1929; Walls, 1929; The Woman in the Wilderness, 1930; The Magnolia Lady, 1932; Grace Darling and Her Times, 1932; Grace Darling and Her Islands, 1934; The Xmas Ship, 1940; Greenleaf Rhythmic Plays, First Series, 1922; Second Series, 1925, The Fortunate Shepherds; Acting Edition, Greenleaf Plays, 1930; Lectures on Community Drama, University of Columbia and of California, USA, 1918–1921; Greenleaf Elements: (1) Action, (2) Speech, 1925, (3) Production, 1926. *Plays:*

Miriam; The King's Progress, produced at the Greek Theatre, Berkeley, USA, 1920; The Curious Herbal; The Gilded Wreath, Belle and Beau, by Greenleaf Players, Arts League of Service, etc., 1915–1925; The Ladies of Edinburgh, 1938, Duchess Theatre; The King Decrees, and with Maxwell Armfield, The Seventh Devil, 1928, Kingsway; Pierrot's Welcome, Everyman, 1931. *Recreation:* music. *Club:* London Lyceum.

Died 9 March 1941.

SMILEY, Peter Kerr K.; *see* Kerr-Smiley.

SMITH, Albert, OBE 1919; *b* Cowling, Yorks, 15 June 1867; *s* of Leeming and Martha Smith; *m* 1890, Elizabeth Ann, *d* of John and Elizabeth Towler; one *d*. *Educ:* Colne Wesleyan School; evening schools. Commenced work in worsted mill as half-timer, 1875; was weaver and powerloom overlooker in cotton mill; Secretary to Nelson Overlookers' Association, 1898–1929; President, General Union of Powerloom Overlookers, Nelson and District Textile Trades Federation, and held various other offices connected with Trade Unions; for 25 years Chm. of Executive Comm., Nelson District Nursing Association; Mayor of Nelson, 1908–10; MP (Lab) Clitheroe Division of Lancashire, and Nelson and Colne Parliamentary Borough, 1910–20; served as an officer (Captain) in The King's Own Royal Lancaster Regiment, retired, 1928; JP County of Lancaster; DL County Palatine of Lancashire. *Address:* 70 Walton Lane, Nelson, Lancs.

Died 7 April 1942.

SMITH, Sir Albert, Kt 1938; JP; Governing director of Ashley and Dumville, Ltd; Vice-Chairman Samuel Marsden and Son, Ltd; *b* 1862; *m* 1884, Annie, *d* of T. Pilkington, Astley; one *s* three *d*. *Educ:* Astley Grammar School. *Address:* The Woodlands, Upper Chorlton Road, Whalley Range, Manchester.

Died 1 Jan. 1944.

SMITH, Alfred Emanuel; *b* New York City, 30 Dec. 1873; *s* of Alfred Emanuel Smith and Catherine Mulvehill; *m* 1900, Catherine A. Dunn, New York City; three *s* two *d*. Clerk in office of Commissioner of Jurors, New York City, 1895–1903; Member, New York Assembly, 1903–15; Democratic Leader in Assembly, 1911; Speaker of Assembly, 1913; Sheriff of New York County, 1915–17; President Board of Aldermen, 1917–18; Governor of New York, 1919–20, 1923–24, 1925–26, 1927–28. *Publication:* Up to Now: an Autobiography, 1929. *Recreations:* golf and swimming. *Address:* 25 Oliver Street, New York, USA.

Died 4 Oct. 1944.

SMITH, Sir Alfred van W. L.; *see* Lucie-Smith.

SMITH, Lt-Col Algernon Fox Eric, CB 1900; *b* 18 April 1857; *s* of Eric Carrington Smith of Ashfold, Sussex. Served in Vitu, 1890 (despatches); in British East Africa, under the Company and Foreign Office, 1890–99; South Africa with 10th Battalion Imperial Yeomanry, 1899–1901 (despatches, CB); in British and German E Africa, 1914–17 (despatches). *Address:* 59 Cadogan Square, SW1.

Died 25 Jan. 1942.

SMITH, Sir Allan (Macgregor), KBE 1918; MA, LLB; CIMechE; late Chairman of the Management Board of Engineering and Allied Employers' National Federation; Solicitor; *m* Isabella Clow (*d* 1933). MP (U) Croydon South, 1919–23. *Address:* 9 Greenaway Gardens, Hampstead, NW3. *T:* Hampstead 2646.

Died 21 Feb. 1941.

SMITH, Andrew Thomas; Director of Huth Coffee Sales, Ltd and Huth Produce Sales, Ltd; *b* 25 Jan. 1884; *s* of Andrew Cathie Smith and Anne Matilda Palmer; *m* 1909, Gladys Irene Margaret Power; two *s*. *Educ:* Alleyn's School, Dulwich; Frankfurt, Paris, and Salamanca. Entered Fredk Huth & Co., London, 1903;

served European War, 1915–19 (Chevalier Légion d'Honneur); Manager Fredk Huth & Co., 1922; Deputy Manager British Overseas Bank, 1932; Manager, 1933; Temp. service with Bank of England 1939–41. *Address:* Hillcrest, Downs Hill, Beckenham, Kent.

Died 2 Jan. 1943.

SMITH, Arthur C.; *see* Corbett-Smith.

SMITH, Arthur Hamilton, CB 1926; MA; Fellow of British Academy; Hon. ARIBA; *b* 2 Oct. 1860; *s* of late Archibald Smith, FRS, of Jordanhill, Renfrewshire; *m* 1897, Gertrude, *e d* of late Prebendary Blomfield Jackson, MA; one *d. Educ:* Winchester (Scholar); Trinity College, Cambridge; 1st class Classical Tripos, Pt ii 1883. Joined British Museum as Assistant, 1886; excavated in Cyprus for British Museum, 1893–94, 1896; Keeper of Greek and Roman Antiquities, British Museum, 1909–25; formerly Editor of Journal of Hellenic Studies; President of Hellenic Society, 1924–29; Vice-President of the Roman Society; Chairman of Faculty of Archæology, History, and Letters, British School at Rome, 1922–28; Director of British Sch. at Rome, 1928–30 and 1932; Member of German and Austrian Archaeological Insts; Hon. Member of the Art Workers' Guild and of the Yorkshire Philosophical Society. *Publications:* Guide to Department of Greek and Roman Antiquities, Brit. Mus.; Catalogue of Engraved Gems in Brit. Mus.; Catalogue of Sculpture in Brit. Mus.; The Sculptures of the Parthenon; Catalogues of Lansdowne, Yarborough, and Woburn Abbey Collections; Lord Elgin and his Collection; Corpus Vasorum (Great Britain), Fasc. 1, 2; White Athenian Vases in Brit. Mus., illustrated by the Cyclograph, a photographic apparatus of his own invention, awarded a gold medal at Berlin Photographic Exhibition, 1896. *Address:* 2 Balfour Road, Weybridge. *T:* Weybridge 861.

Died 28 Sept. 1941.

SMITH, Lt-Col Arthur M.; *see* Murray-Smith.

SMITH, Sir Aubrey; *see* Smith, Sir C. A.

SMITH, Col Bertram Abel, DSO 1918; MC; TD; ADC to the King, 1926; a Director of M. Samuel & Co. Ltd; Atlas Assurance Co. Ltd; the Shell Transport and Trading Co. Ltd; The Nineteen Twenty-eight Investment Trust Ltd; The Nineteen Twenty-nine Investment Trust Ltd; The Perham Investment Trust Ltd; The English and Dutch Investment Trust, Ltd; Bataafsche Petroleum Company; National Provincial Bank, Ltd; Chairman, Brown Harriman & Co. Ltd; *b* 1879; *s* of Robert Smith, Goldings, Hertford, and Isabel, *d* of Henry J. Adeane of Babraham, Cambridge; *m* 1st, 1905, Hon. Rhona Margaret Ada Hanbury Tracy (*d* 1926), *d* of 4th Baron Sudeley; two *s* one *d*; 2nd, 1932, Dorothy Maude Hall, *d* of late Fergus Fergusson. *Educ:* Eton; Trinity College, Cambridge. Formerly partner in banking firm of Samuel Smith & Co., Nottingham, and afterwards Director of the Union of London and Smith's Bank, Ltd; Major South Notts Hussar Yeomanry, Egypt, Gallipoli (MC), and Salonica; commanded 23rd Batt. Middlesex Regiment, 41st Division, in France (DSO); commanded 8th Batt. Sherwood Foresters, 1920–24; commanded the 139 Sherwood Forester Brigade, 46 Division TA, 1924–28; Hon. Colonel 8th Bn Sherwood Foresters; 1937–46. *Recreations:* hunting, shooting, fishing. *Address:* 44 Hans Place, SW1. *T:* Kensington 3283; Buriton House, Petersfield, Hants. *T:* Petersfield 248. *Clubs:* Brooks's, Turf.

Died 21 Sept. 1947.

SMITH, Captain Bertram Hornsby, CBE 1919; RN retired; *b* 1874; *s* of F. E. Smith; *m* 1913, Lucy Marion Wyatt; one *s* one *d. Educ:* Royal Naval School, New Cross. Entered Royal Navy, 1887; Lieutenant, 1894; Commander, 1905; Captain, 1912; commanded HMS Vengeance in Dardanelles, 1915; Naval Staff, Admiralty, 1915–19; Director of Mercantile Movements, 1919–20

(CBE); Officer Legion of Honour; Officer Crown of Belgium. *Recreation:* angling. *Address:* The Old Hall, Ruswarp, Yorks. *T:* Whitby 467. *Club:* Fly Fishers'.

Died 18 Nov. 1945.

SMITH, Lt-Col Bertram M.; *see* Metcalfe-Smith.

SMITH, Maj. Brooke H.; *see* Heckstall-Smith.

SMITH, Mrs Burnett, (Annie Shepherd Swan), CBE 1930; *b* Mountskip, Gorebridge, 8 July 1859; *d* of Edward Swan, farmer; *m* Dr James Burnett Smith (*d* 1927); one *s* one *d. Educ:* Ladies' College, Edinburgh; privately. Began contributing to local papers and writing children's books; first successful book Aldersyde; interested in the magazine The Women at Home. *Publications:* Aldersyde; Carlowrie; Gates of Eden; Maitland of Laurieston; A Lost Ideal; A Victory Won; Who Shall Serve; St Veda's A Divided House; Elizabeth Glen; The Curse of Cowden, 1897; The Ne'er-do-Weel, 1897; Sir Roderick's Will, and other stories, 1898; Not Yet, 1898; Prairie Fires, 1913; The Stepmother, 1915; The Pendulum, 1928; The Marching Feet, 1931; My Life, 1934. *Recreations:* walking, motoring, golfing. *Address:* Aldersyde, Gullane, East Lothian. *Clubs:* Empress; Scottish Women's, Edinburgh.

Died 17 June 1943.

SMITH, Carlton A., RI 1889; *b* London, 1853; father an engraver; *m* 1883, Martha (*d* 1935); two *d. Educ:* private school in London; Paris; studied art at West London School of Art, and at the Slade. After leaving school went to business for a short time only; becoming tired of it, took to lithography for some years for a living; painting in his spare time, ultimately taking to painting altogether; exhibited in Dudley Gallery and RBA; was member of the latter Society; Member Institute of Painters in Oil Colours, 1890; amongst his patrons are HM the King, the trustees of the National Gallery, Melbourne, Adelaide, etc.; several of his paintings have been published as photogravures and in other ways. *Recreation:* gardening. *Address:* Greenfield Hall, Laleham-on-Thames.

Died 3 Dec. 1946.

SMITH, Cecil Archibald, CIE 1911; MICE; *m* 1897, Frances (*d* 1943), *d* of H. M. Bazeley, Bideford; one *s* (and two killed in action, 1942 and 1943) three *d. Educ:* Cheltenham College; RIE College. Entered Madras Public Works Department, 1880; Executive Engineer, 1893; Superintending Engineer, 1905; Chief Engineer and Joint Secretary to Government, 1906; retired, 1913. *Address:* The Flagstaff, Northam, Devon.

Died 10 Dec. 1948.

SMITH, Sir Cecil Harcourt-, KCVO 1934; Kt 1909; CVO 1917; Adviser for the Royal Art Collections since 1925; Surveyor of the Royal Works of Art, 1928–36; JP Oxfordshire, 1926; *b* 11 Sept. 1859; *s* of William Smith, solicitor; *m* 1892, Alice Edith, *d* of H. W. Watson, Burnopfield, Co. Durham; two *s. Educ:* Brighton; Winchester College. Entered Department of Greek and Roman Antiquities, British Museum, 1879; Assistant Keeper, 1896; Keeper, 1904; attached to a diplomatic mission to Persia, 1887; Director of the British School at Athens, 1895–97; Director and Secretary of the Victoria and Albert Museum, 1909–24; Chairman of Commission appointed to consider rearrangement of Victoria and Albert Museum, 1908; Hon. LLD Aberdeen University, 1895; Hon. DLitt Oxford, 1928; Commander of the Order of the Saviour, 1903; Hon. Secretary of Dilettanti Society; Hon. FRIBA; Vice-Pres. of the Hellenic Society; formerly Pres., Society of Civil Servants, and Chairman, Civic Arts Association; formerly Chairman of Committee, Incorporated Church Building Society; formerly British representative on International Office of Museums; Vice-Chairman of British Institute of Industrial Art, of Central Society for Protection of Churches, and of Society of Master Glass Painters; Hon. Member of the Drama League; Order of

St Sava, 4th Class (Serbia), 1919; Officier de l'Ordre de la Couronne (Belgium), 1920; Officier of Légion d'Honneur, 1927; Grand Cross of Order of the Phœnix (Greece), 1932; Grand Officer of Order of the Three Stars (Latvia), 1939. *Publications:* The J. P. Morgan Antiquities; The Art Treasures of the Nation, 1929; The Society of Dilettanti, its Regalia and Pictures, 1932; various works on Archæology and official publications of the British and Victoria and Albert Museums; has been editor of the Classical Review and of the Annual of the British School at Athens. *Recreations:* golf, shooting, fencing. *Club:* Bath.

Died 27 March 1944.

SMITH, Sir (Charles) Aubrey, Kt 1944; CBE 1938; film actor; *b* 21 July 1863; *s* of Dr Charles John Smith and Sarah Ann Clode; *m* 1896; one *d. Educ:* Charterhouse; Cambridge. *Recreation:* cricket. *Address:* 629 N Rexfor Drive, Beverly Hills, California, USA. *TA:* Casmit, Los Angeles. *Clubs:* Garrick, Green Room; The Players (NY) The Masquers (Hollywood).

Died 20 Dec. 1948.

SMITH, Charles Bennett; Superintendent of Standards and Purchase for the State of New York since 1935; *b* Erie County, New York State, 14 Sept. 1870; *s* of James Smith, farmer, and Mary Barnes; *m* 1st, 1902, Frances G. Stanton (*d* 1931); 2nd, 1932, Frances E. Meyer. *Educ:* Arcade, New York Academy. Reporter, Buffalo Courier, 1889–91; Legislative Correspondent, Albany, 1892–94; editor, Buffalo Times, 1895–96; edited the Buffalo Courier and Buffalo Enquirer, 1897–1911; member, Board of Buffalo School Examiners, 1908–11; Chairman, 1910; re-elected to Congress, 1912, 1914, and 1916; Member of Committee on Foreign Affairs; Chairman, Committee on Patents; Representative in Congress, 41st District, New York, 1910–19; went into business after retiring from Congress in 1919. *Recreations:* hunting, fishing, photography, motoring, golf. *Address:* Lenox Hotel, Buffalo, NY; Wilmington, Essex County, New York.

Died 21 May 1939.

SMITH, Air Cdre Charles Gainer, CB 1946; CBE 1935; MIMechE; RAF (retd); *b* 22 Jan. 1880; *s* of Walter Edmund Smith; *m* 1917, Kathleen Mary Francis Wood (*d* 1946); one *s. Educ:* Combe Down School, Bath. *Recreations:* mechanics and gardening. *Address:* Buckland Cop, Buckland, Betchworth, Surrey.

Died 13 Oct. 1948.

SMITH, Hon. Sir Charles George, KCMG 1923; Chairman C. G. Smith & Co., Ltd, Sugar Estate Agents; *m* 1st, Matilda Filby (*d* 1933); 2nd, 1933, Frances Elizabeth Macgillivray. *Address:* Manor House, Ridge Road, Durban, Natal.

Died 24 April 1941.

SMITH, His Honour Charles H.; see Herbert-Smith.

SMITH, Sir (Charles) Herbert, Kt 1938; Senior partner in firms of C. Herbert Smith and Russell and Powell Jerome and Co., Chartered Accountants, Birmingham; *b* 1 May 1871; *s* of late Wallace Tyndall Smith, Birmingham; *m* 1907, Olive Annie, *d* of late Richard Owen Taylor, Perton Court, near Wolverhampton; one *d. Educ:* King Edward's School, Camp Hill. Fellow of Institute of Chartered Accountants in England and Wales. Member of Council of Institute of Chartered Accountants; Past President Birmingham and District Society of Chartered Accountants; Past President Birmingham Chartered Accountant Students' Society; Chairman of Radiation Ltd, H. P. Sauce Ltd, Lea and Perrins Ltd, James Booth and Co. (1915) Ltd, Midland Electric Manufacturing Co. Ltd, and Smith's Stamping Works (Coventry) Ltd; Deputy Chairman of Brown Brothers Ltd, and Director of W. and T. Avery Ltd and W. Canning and Co. Ltd; Honorary Secretary Birmingham Unionist Association; Life Governor University of Birmingham; A Governing Trustee of the Nuffield Provincial Hospitals Trust. *Address:* Eden Place Chambers, 71 Edmund Street, Birmingham. *T:* Central 6943; The Bracken, Barnt Green, nr Birmingham. *T:* Hillside, 1069. *Clubs:* Constitutional; Conservative, Union, Birmingham.

Died 22 June 1941.

SMITH, Charles Howard, CMG 1932; Minister at Reykjavik since 1940; *b* 17 May 1888; *yr s* of late Judge Howard Smith, The Ford House, Wolverhampton; *m* 1920, Sarah, 2nd *d* of late Augustus Thorne, 22 Great Cumberland Place, W; one *s* two *d. Educ:* Winchester; Brasenose College, Oxford. Entered Foreign Office, 1912; Private Secretary to Cecil Harmsworth, MP, Parliamentary Under Secretary for Foreign Affairs, 1920–22; Assistant Under-Secretary of State in Foreign Office, 1933–39; Minister at Copenhagen, Oct. 1939–April 1940. *Address:* British Legation, Reykjavik, Iceland; 5 Egerton Gardens, SW3. *T:* Kensington 7891. *Club:* Travellers'.

Died 23 July 1942.

SMITH, Charles Johnston, CBE 1935; OBE 1930; MB, FRCSE; Consulting Surgeon, Guernsey, CI; *b* 1880; *s* of late E. Johnston Smith, Edinburgh; *m* 1921, Kathleen, *d* of A. E. Scott, Manchester; two *d. Educ:* Royal High School, Edinburgh; Edinburgh University. MB, ChB, 1904; FRCS, 1909; LMS Singapore. Entered Malayan Medical Service, 1911; Medical Officer, Seremban, 1911–14; Professor Clinical Surgery, Singapore, 1914–18; Senior Surgeon and Senior Professor of Surgery, Singapore Medical School, 1918–35; retired from Malayan Medical Service, 1935; Surgeon Clare Hall, EMS Hospital, Middlesex, 1941–42. *Publications:* The Mechanical Etiology of Optic Neuritis, BMJ, 1911; Technique of Splenectomy, Edinburgh Medical Journal, 1915. *Recreations:* golf, billiards, bowls. *Address:* La Maison Blanche, Queens Road, Guernsey, CI. *T:* Guernsey 1611. *Clubs:* Grange, Royal Guernsey Golf, Guernsey.

Died 25 Jan. 1943.

SMITH, Sir Clarence, Kt 1895; late partner in Clarence and Gervase Smith & Co., stockbrokers; *b* 16 June 1849; *s* of Rev. Gervase Smith, DD; *m* 1875, Mary (*d* 1923), *d* of W. Webster, Highbury; three *s* four *d.* JP for Kent; DL City of London; Sheriff of London and Middlesex, 1883; Director Star Life Insurance Society, and Director Ocean Accident Insurance Corporation; MP E Hull, 1892–95; late Chairman of the Elham, Kent, Petty Sessions. *Address:* Wilmington Manor, Kent. *Club:* Reform.

Died 10 June 1941.

SMITH, Clifford P.; Editor of Bureau of History of Christian Science Mother Church; *b* Indiana, 1869; *s* of Joseph B. Smith and Amelia Pabody Smith; *m* 1899, Myrtle Holm; one *d. Educ:* Public Schools of Indiana; Vernon Academy; State University of Iowa. Practised law in Iowa, 1891–1901; Judge of District Court of Iowa, 1901–08; First Reader of Christian Science Mother Church, 1908–11; occupant of different positions for same Church since then; Lecturer on Law in Sioux City (Iowa) Law School, 1892–93. *Publications:* Historical Sketches, 1941; numerous articles on Christian Science in encyclopedias, periodicals and newspapers. *Address:* 196 Kent Road, Waban, Mass, USA.

Died 9 Aug. 1945.

SMITH, David Bonner-, FRHistS; late Admiralty Librarian; retired, 1950; *b* 19 May 1890; *m* Vlasta Eileen (*née* Done). *Publications:* Letters of Admiral of the Fleet the Earl of St Vincent, 1801–1804; The Barrington Papers; Captain Boteler's Recollections; and, in co-operation, The Russian War, 1854–1855. *Address:* Uplands, Lyth Hill Road, Bayston Hill, near Shrewsbury.

Died 10 Dec. 1950.

SMITH, Sir David Wadsworth, Kt 1945; JP (Yorks W Riding); FCIS, FBS; Director; Halifax Building Society; National Employers' Mutual General Insurance Association Ltd; Chairman: Halifax District Employment Committee; Halifax Council of Social Service; President: Halifax Property Owners' and Ratepayers' Association; Halifax and District Agricultural Society; West Yorkshire Branch of Chartered Institute of Secretaries; *b* 25 Aug. 1883; *s* of John Wadsworth Smith, Woollen Manufacturer, Greetland, nr Halifax; *m* 1907, Harriet Brodrick, Hull; two *d. Educ:* Heath Grammar School. Junior clerk with Halifax Permanent Building Society, 1900; became General Manager, 1938; retired, 1943. Chairman National Assoc. of Building Societies, 1940–42; member of Housing Advisory Committee, Ministry of Health; Chairman Greetland District Council, 1918–30; member West Riding Education Committee, 1908–24. *Recreations:* gardening, travel. *Address:* Rylston, Greenroyd, Halifax. *T:* Halifax 3465. *Clubs:* Halifax, (Halifax); Halifax (Bradley Hall) Golf.
Died 5 Dec. 1948.

SMITH, Sir Drummond Cunliffe, 4th Bt *cr* 1804; *b* 23 Feb. 1861; *s* of 3rd Bt and Agnes, *d* of Capel Cure, Blake Hall, Essex; *S* father, 1905. *Educ:* Eton; Trinity College, Cambridge. Late Essex Regiment; High Sheriff of Essex, 1915. Owns about 3000 acres. *Heir: cousin* Lt-Col Drummond Cospatric Spencer-Smith, OBE, late RH and RFA [*b* 4 Nov. 1876. United Service]. *Address:* Suttons, Romford, Essex.
Died 8 May 1947.

SMITH, Edmund Robinson, CBE 1919; VD; Colonel (retired list); Share Broker; parents British; *b* 26 July 1856; *m* Mary Catherine Pierpont Bowler; three *s* three *d. Educ:* Dunedin. *Recreations:* rifle shooting and gardening. *Address:* 139 London Street, Dunedin, NZ. *TA:* Quickly, Dunedin. *T:* 10114. *Clubs:* Otago, Otago Officers', Otago.
Died 20 March 1942.

SMITH, Edward B.; *see* Barclay-Smith.

SMITH, Col Edward Castleman C.; *see* Castleman-Smith.

SMITH, Lady Eleanor; *er d* of 1st Earl of Birkenhead. *Publications:* Red Wagon; Flamenco; Ballerina; Satan's Circus; Christmas Tree; Tzigane, 1935; Portrait of A Lady, 1936; The Spanish House, 1938; Life's a Circus, 1939; Lovers' Meeting, 1940; The Man in Grey, 1941; Magic Lantern, 1944.
Died 20 Oct. 1945.

SMITH, Captain Eric; *see* Smith, Captain E. C. E.

SMITH, Ernest, MA; schoolmaster; *b* Morley, Yorkshire, 19 Oct. 1869; *s* of late William Smith, Morley, editor of Old Yorkshire, etc; *m* 1895, Kathleen, *d* of Arthur Roope Hunt, Southwood, Torquay; one *s* one *d. Educ:* Clifton; University College, Oxford. Mathematical Scholar of above two colleges. Late Master at Elstree School; started preparatory school, 1900. *Recreations:* cricket, golf. *Address:* 1 Pearl Court, Eastbourne.
Died 9 April 1945.

SMITH, Hon. Ernest D'Israeli; Chairman of Board of E. D. Smith & Sons, Ltd, Winona, Ontario; *b* Winona, County of Wentworth, Ont, 8 Dec. 1853; *s* of Sylvester and D. I. M'Gee Smith; *m* Christina A., *d* of Elijah Armstrong of North York township, Ont; two *s* one *d. Educ:* Hamilton Collegiate Institute. Member of House of Commons for Wentworth, 1900–08. Senator in Dominion Parliament, 1913–46. *Recreation:* travelling. *Address:* Winona, Ont, Canada. *TA:* Helderleigh, Ont, Canada.
Died 15 Oct. 1948.

SMITH, Captain E(van) C(adogan) Eric; Chairman Rolls-Royce; Chairman National Provincial Bank; Director John Brown & Co. Ltd, Industrial & General Trust Ltd, Second Industrial Trust, National Mortgage & Agency of New Zealand, and other companies; *b* June 1894; *s* of Lindsay Eric Smith, Ashfold, Handcross, Sussex, and Helen Mary Collyer; *m* 1917, Beatrice Helen, *d* of A. H. Williams, Flinthouse, Langstone, Hants; three *s* one *d. Educ:* Eton; RMC, Sandhurst. 9th Lancers, 1913–19. Capt. (despatches twice, MC); invalided out of service. *Recreations:* hunting, fishing, shooting. *Address:* Lower Ashfold, Slaugham, Sussex. *T:* Handcross 214. *Clubs:* Brooks's, Cavalry.
Died 17 Oct. 1950.

SMITH, Sir Francis (Edward James), Kt 1938; a member of the firm of Lee & Pemberton, 46 Lincoln's Inn Fields, WC, solicitors, 1890–1948; *b* 23 Feb. 1863; 3rd *s* of late John Smith, Britwell House, Oxfordshire; *m* 1901, Adela Constance, 2nd *d* of late Col Ernest Villiers; one *s* two *d. Educ:* Winchester; New College, Oxford 2nd class Classical Moderations, 1884; 2nd class School of Literae Humaniores, 1886; admitted Solicitor, 1889; Knight of Grace of the Order of St John of Jerusalem. Director, and 1919–48, Chairman of the Clerical, Medical and General Life Assurance Society and Chairman of the General Reversionary and Investment Company; President of Council of Law Society, 1937–38. *Recreations:* reading and travelling. *Address:* 7 Orchard Court, Portman Square, W1; Ashdown House, Dane Hill, Sussex. *T:* Welbeck 2258, Chelwood Gate 11. *Club:* United University.
Died 27 Feb. 1950.

SMITH, Francis St George M.; *see* Manners-Smith.

SMITH, Frank Braybrook, CMG 1919; MA, FSI; Hon. Fellow of Downing College, Cambridge; *b* 1864; *s* of William Croxton Smith. *Educ:* privately; Downing College, Cambridge. Lecturer in Agriculture and Rural Economics at the South-Eastern Agricultural College, Wye, Kent, upon its foundation in 1894; Vice-Principal, 1895; agricultural adviser to Lord Milner, Governor of the Transvaal, 1902; in that capacity wrote a report advocating the formation of a Department of Agriculture for the Transvaal, and embodying a scheme for the same (see 1st Report of Transvaal Department of Agriculture), which was adopted; Director of Agriculture for the Transvaal, 1902–10; Acting Secretary of Agriculture Union of S Africa, 1910; prepared plans for the amalgamation of the Departments of Agriculture of the four colonies which formed the Union into a single Department, and also for the uniform administration of agricultural affairs throughout the Union; Secretary for Agriculture for the Union, 1910–20; Reader in Estate Management, University of Cambridge, 1920–28; Fellow and Bursar, Downing Coll., Cambridge, 1924–34; Member of Transvaal Legislative Council, 1903–05; made extensive tours in United States and Canada in order to investigate the system of agricultural education and administration in vogue in these countries, 1900 and 1908; in 1923 visited Australia and New Zealand as a member of the Delegation appointed by the Secretary of State for the Colonies to inquire into conditions affecting settlers from Great Britain in those Dominions; Member of Land Settlement Board, 1902–08, and of Transvaal Indigency Commission, 1906–08. *Publications:* Agriculture in the New World, and contributions to various agricultural papers and journals, and reports in Blue Books, etc. *Recreations:* hunting, shooting, and golf. *Address:* The Garden House Hotel, Folkestone. *Club:* Farmers'.
Died 11 Nov. 1950.

SMITH, Alderman Sir Frederick, Kt 1929; JP; Chairman and Managing Director of Frederick Smith, Ltd, Aston Model Brewery, Aston; *b* 12 June 1859; *m* 1st, Emily *d* of late W. F. Burley, Birmingham; 2nd, Sarah Louisa, *y d* of late Arthur Silk, of Nether Whitacre,

Warwickshire; two *s* two *d*. First Mayor of Aston, 1903. *Address:* Newstead, 75 Sutton Road, Erdington, Birmingham 23.

Died 30 Jan. 1945.

SMITH, Frederick A., OBE 1943; General Secretary AEU since'1933; *b* 23 Feb. 1887; *s* of Frederick Nicholas and Esther Smith; *m* 1912, C. F. Cox; one *s* one *d*. *Educ:* Bromley. Served apprenticeship as brass-finisher; joined late London United Metal Turners Society, 1907; became Branch Secretary and ultimately General Secretary of that Union until Amalgamated to what is now known as the Amalgamated Engineering Union, 1920; took office as Finance Officer; Assistant General Secretary, 1927. *Publication:* Editor of Amalgamated Engineering Union Monthly Journal. *Recreation:* work. *Address:* Pitsford Hall, Pitsford, nr Northampton.

Died 23 Jan. 1943.

SMITH, Very Rev. Sir George Adam, Kt 1916; MA, DD, LLD, LittD, FBA 1916; Chaplain to the King in Scotland since 1933; Chaplain 1st Class TF; Principal and Vice-Chancellor of Aberdeen University, 1909–35; *b* Calcutta, 19 Oct. 1856; *e s* of late George Smith, LLD, CIE, formerly editor of the Friend of India, and Janet Colquhoun, *d* of Robert Adam; *m* 1889, Lilian, *d* of Sir George Buchanan, FRS, late medical officer of the Local Government Board; one *s* (two killed in European War) three *d*. *Educ:* Royal High School, University, and New College, Edinburgh; University of Tübingen and University of Leipzig. After travelling in Egypt and Syria, became assistant to Rev. John Fraser, Free West Church, Brechin, 1880; Hebrew tutor, Free Church College, Aberdeen, 1880–82; minister of Queen's Cross Free Church, 1882–92; travelled in Syria and East of Jordan, 1891, 1901, 1904; Percy Turnbull Lect. on Hebrew Poetry, Johns Hopkins Univ., Baltimore, 1896; Lyman Beecher Lecturer, Yale Univ., 1899; Visiting Professor, Chicago University, and Earle Lecturer, Berkeley, California, 1909; Schweich Lecturer, British Academy, 1910; Jowett Lecturer, London, 1900; Professor of OT Lang. Liter and Theology, UF Church College, Glasgow, 1892; Chairman Scottish Council for Women's Trades; Moderator of the General Assembly United Free Church of Scotland, 1916–17; commissioned by British Foreign Office and American National Committee on the Moral Aims of the Allies to deliver addresses on this subject in the US, 1918; Baird Lecturer, Glasgow, 1922; President Sir Walter Scott Club, 1930. *Publications:* The Book of Isaiah (2 vols), 1888–1890; rev. edition, 1927; The Preaching of the Old Testament to the Age, 1893; Historical Geography of the Holy Land, 1894 (25th edit. 1931); The Twelve Prophets (2 vols), 1896–1897; rev. edition, 1928; The Life of Henry Drummond, 1898 (7th ed. 1902); Modern Criticism and the Preaching of the Old Testament, 1901; The Forgiveness of Sins, and other Sermons, 1904; Jerusalem; the Topography, Economics, and History, 1908; The Early Poetry of Israel (Schweich Lectures), 1912; Atlas of the Historical Geography of the Holy Land, with Dr J. G. Bartholomew, 1914; Syria and the Holy Land, 1918; Deuteronomy (The Cambridge Bible), 1918; Our Common Conscience, Addresses delivered in America during the Great War, 1918; The Teaching of the OT in Schools; Jeremiah, 1923, revised edition, 1929; (with John Buchan) The Kirk in Scotland, 1930. *Recreations:* Alpine Club, Scottish Mountaineering Club. *Address:* Sweethillocks, Balerno, Midlothian. *Clubs:* Athenæum; Royal Northern, Aberdeen.

Died 3 March 1942.

SMITH, George Douglas, CMG 1905; *b* 8 Feb. 1865; *s* of late Charles Adamson Smith, St Kitt's, West Indies, and Glasgow; *m* 1903, Helen Anna Barclay (*d* 1936), *d* of late James Leitch, Glasgow. *Educ:* Glasgow Academy. Services, Imperial British East Africa Company, 1890–94; Treasurer Uganda Protectorate, 1894–1918; East and Central African Medal with clasp, Uganda,

1897–98; Distribution Officer under Food Commissioner for Scotland, 1918–20; President, Uganda Society for Scotland, 1931–36. *Recreations:* gardening, bridge. *Address:* 7 Gladstone Place, Stirling.

Died 26 Jan. 1949.

SMITH, Brig.-Gen. George Edward, CMG 1909; DSO 1917; *b* 6 Aug. 1868; *s* of late Archibald Smith, FRS, Jordanhill. *Educ:* Winchester. Entered RE 1888; Captain, 1899; Major, 1907; Lt-Col, 1915; Brevet Colonel, 1919; Col, 1920; employed in East African Protectorate, Anglo-German Boundary, 1892–93; Sclater Road, Mombasa to Victoria Nyanza, 1895–97; Commissioner Anglo-German Boundary, 1904–06; Director of Surveys, East Africa Protectorate, 1906–10; served S Africa 1901–02 (Queen's medal five clasps); European War, 1914–18 (DSO, Croix d'Officier Légion d'Honneur, Commendatore of the Order of St Maurice and St Lazarus); retired pay, 1922. *Recreations:* fencing, sailing, golf, fishing, curling, etc., curled for England v Scotland five times (R. Caledonian Gold Medal, 1923). *Club:* United Service.

Died 7 Nov. 1944.

SMITH, Col George John, CBE 1918, TD; Chairman of Booth, Macdonald and Co. Ltd, Christchurch; *b* 1862; *s* of John Smith, Consett, Durham; *m* 1st, 1887, Eleanor (*d* 1917), *d* of Robert Dawson; two *s* one *d*; 2nd, 1924, Constance Margaret (*d* 1939), *widow* of Arthur A. Martin, MD, FRCS. Came to New Zealand, 1880; MHR Christchurch, 1893–99 and 1901–02; MLC 1907–14, and 1920–34; Member of Canterbury College Board of Governors, 1903–07, 1913–18 and 1920–32; Chairman, 1928–32; Fellow of the Senate of the University of New Zealand, 1932; Member of Lyttleton Harbour Board, 1903–07; Captain 1st Canterbury Regiment, 1898; Major, 1904; Lieut-Colonel, 1905; Colonel, 1914; Brigade Commander, 1914; Reserve of Officers, 1921; retired, 1924; served with NZEF, 1916–18; Hon. Colonel the Canterbury Regiment, 1923; President Canterbury (NZ) Officers' Club, 1911, 1918–21, 1924–26. *Address:* Riverlaw, Opawa, Christchurch, SE2, NZ.

Died 21 May 1946.

SMITH, Lt-Col George Maciver Campbell, CMG 1919; *b* 13 May 1869; *s* of Robert Smith, MD, Sedgefield, Co. Durham; *m* Mary Ovington (*d* 1945), *d* of J. O. Stephenson, Norton, Co. Durham; one *d*. *Educ:* Haileybury; Aberdeen University. MA, MB, CM Aber. 1891; MRCP Lond. 1907. Entered Indian Medical Service, 1892; Lt-Colonel, 1912; retired, 1921; served with Chitral Relief Force, 1895; Mohmand and Tirah Expeditionary Forces, 1897; Waziristan, 1901–02; Mesopotamia and Egyptian Expeditionary Forces, 1917–18 (despatches, CMG). *Address:* c/o Lloyds Bank Ltd, 6 Pall Mall, SW1.

Died 3 Dec. 1946.

SMITH, Sir George R.; *see* Reeves-Smith.

SMITH, George Stuart G.; *see* Graham-Smith.

SMITH, Major George Wilson, OBE 1919; late King's Own Scottish Borderers; *b* 24 May 1880; 2nd *s* of late Sir James B. Smith, of Clifford Park, Stirling; *m* 1908, Alice Oliphant (*d* 1927), *y d* of late Alexander Murray, CMG, RN; no *c*. *Educ:* Merchiston Castle School, Edinburgh. Joined KOSB 1900; served in India, Burma, Aden, 1900–06; Adjutant 3rd (Special Reserve) KOSB 1909–12; served European War (severely wounded, Oct. 1914, despatches, Chevalier Legion of Honour); Staff Officer Windward Islands, 1916–19; Adjutant 6th A and S Highlanders, 1920–22; Commandant Queen Victoria School, Dunblane, 1922–25. *Recreations:* golf, tennis, billiards. *Clubs:* New, Edinburgh.

Died 22 Aug. 1940.

SMITH, Gipsy Rodney, MBE; Evangelist; *b* 31 March 1860; *s* of Cornelius and Mary Smith; *m* 1st, 1879, Annie E. Pennock (*d* 1937); two *s* one *d*; 2nd, 1938, Mary Alice Shaw. *Educ:* self-taught. Associated with General Booth in the Christian Mission, and for five years worked with remarkable success; special missioner of the National Free Church Council, 1897–1912; spent three and a half years with the boys in France; actively engaged in evangelistic work throughout the world; has been twice round the world, South Africa, and thirty-five times to America; 1939–45 tour of America and Canada comprising sixty missions held for ministerial associations. *Publications:* Gipsy Smith, his Life and Work: an Autobiography; As Jesus Passed By; A Mission of Peace to South Africa; Real Religion; Evangelistic Talks; The Lost Christ; Your Boys; The Beauty of Jesus. *Recreations:* gardening and motoring. *Address:* c/o Manager, Lloyds Bank Ltd, Cambridge, England. *Club:* National Liberal.

Died 4 Aug. 1947.

SMITH, Ven. Godfrey Scott, MA; Vicar of Haverthwaite and Archdeacon of Furness since 1926; Hon. Canon of Carlisle since 1937; *b* 14 July 1878; 6th *s* of Francis Patrick Smith of Barnes Hall, Ecclesfield, Sheffield; *m* Katharine Isabella, *e d* of late Admiral Armand Temple Powlett of Frankton Manor, Rugby; three *s* three *d. Educ:* Charterhouse; Magdalen College, Oxford; Wells Theological College. Deacon, 1902; Priest, 1903; Curate of St George's, Barrow-in-Furness, 1902–06; Curate of Grange-over-Sands, 1906–07; Vicar of Walney Island, 1907–10; Vicar of Cartmel, 1910–19; Rural Dean of Cartmel, 1915–19; Vicar of Wentworth and Chaplain to Earl Fitzwilliam, 1919–26; Rural Dean of Wath, 1921–25. *Recreations:* cricket, fishing, manual labour. *Address:* Haverthwaite Vicarage, Ulverston.

Died 1 Aug. 1944.

SMITH, Guy Bellingham, MB, BS Lond., FRCS; Consulting Obstetric Surgeon, Guy's Hospital; Surgeon for Women's Diseases, N Herts and S Beds Hospitals; *b* 28 April 1865. *Educ:* St Paul's School; University College, London, and Guy's Hospital. *Address:* Yarrow, Felsted, Essex. *T:* Felsted 256. *Club:* Burlington Fine Arts.

Died 19 April 1945.

SMITH, Harold Hamel; Founder Tropical Life; Fellow Royal Empire Society; Member, WI Committee; *b* Croydon, 1867; *s* of Hamel Smith and Ellen, *d* of Dr Green; *m* Clara (*d* 1940), *d* of Josiah Purser; two *d. Educ:* Whitgift Grammar School. Visited West Indies and Venezuela, 1890–91 and 1895–98, and studied the production and export of the crops; started Tropical Life, 1905; suggested holding Exhibitions of Rubber and Tropical Products in London, etc. *Publications:* Some Notes on Cacao Planting in the West Indies, 1902; Bed-Time Fairy Tales, 1904; The Future of Cacao Planting, 1908; Notes on Soil and Plant Sanitation on Cacao and Rubber Estates, 1911; Aigrettes and Birdskins—the truth about the Millinery Plumage Trade; (with F. A. G. Pape) Coconuts—the Consols of the East, 1912; The Fermentation of Cacao, 1913; (with Joseph Froude Woodroffe) The Rubber Industry of the Amazon, 1915; The High Price of Sugar and How to Reduce it, 1917; How to Pay for the War, by developing our Resources within the Empire, with special sections on Russia and Latin America, 1918; Sisal, its Production and Preparation, 1929. *Address:* Bagatelle, 22 Chaldon Common Road, Upper Caterham, Surrey. *T:* Caterham 573. *Club:* Arts Theatre.

Died 14 Feb. 1944.

SMITH, Rev. Harry, MA, DD (Hon.); *b* Aberdeen, 14 Nov. 1865; *s* of late James Smith; *m* 1897, Jean, *d* of late John Frazer, Perth; two *d. Educ:* Grammar School, Old Aberdeen; Aberdeen University. Assistant Minister in St John's (East) Church, Perth, 1891–94; Minister of Tibbermore Parish, Perth, 1894–1916; Old Kilpatrick

Parish, 1916–28; Heriot Parish, 1928–36; Editor of Morning Rays (Children's Magazine of the Church of Scotland), 1899–1917; Editor of The Layman's Book of the General Assembly, 1912–21; Editor of Life and Work, the Church of Scotland Magazine, 1925–30. *Publications:* Odds and Ends in Prose and Verse, 1898; Bible Stories without Names, 1898 (2nd ed. n. d.); Talks on Favourite Texts (edited), 1902; More Bible Stories without Names, 1903; Our Heritage, 1916; Enduring Hardness, 1917; Not Against Flesh and Blood, 1923; included in Modern Scottish Poets, in A Book of Twentieth-Century Scots Verse, and in Oor Mither Tongue, Scots Anthology; contributions in prose and verse to newspapers and magazines. *Recreation:* trout fishing. *Address:* 4 Spence Street, Edinburgh. *TA:* Edinburgh. *T:* Edinburgh 43610.

Died 8 Aug. 1942.

SMITH, Sir Harry, KBE 1918; engineer; *b* 27 Sept. 1874; *s* of James and Martha Smith, Netherwood, Keighley; *m* 1901, Evangeline (*d* 1931), *d* of Pearson Atkinson, of Beachroyd, Keighley; one *s. Educ:* Keighley Grammar School; Pannal Coll., Harrogate. Commenced at the works, Dean Smith & Grace, Ltd, lathe manufacturers, Keighley, 1890; now joint managing director with his son James Pearson Smith; Chairman, HM National Shell Factories, Keighley, June 1915; Representative on Board of Management Representation Committee for No. 3 Area (Yorkshire), Oct. 1915, at the Ministry of Munitions, London; President, Keighley and District Chamber of Commerce, 1912; on Finance and Buildings Committees War Hospitals, Keighley, 1916–18; organised ambulances transport for war hospitals; Captain, WRASC (MT) V 1918. *Recreations:* motoring, shooting, and golf. *Address:* Yew Bank Keighley.

Died 3 Oct. 1949.

SMITH, Harry Worcester; inventor, financier, sportsman, and author; *b* Worcester, Mass, 5 Nov. 1865; *s* of Charles Worcester Smith and Josephine Lord; *m* 1892, Mildred, *d* of late George Crompton; one *s* one *d. Educ:* Worcester Polytechnic Institute; Boston Institute of Technology; Chemnitz Weaving School, Germany; Glasgow School of Design; Bradford Technical School. Inventor of the Standard Automatic Colour Loom and forty other patents on weaving machinery; six years one of the Park Commissioners of the City of Worcester. Won the two great classic Steeplechase events of America; the Champion in 1900, riding his own horse The Cad; ran first and second in the American Grand National, 1901; twice rode the winner of the Meadow brook Cup, and four times the winner of the Genessee Valley Point-to-Point; won, owner up, the Aiken and Camden, South Carolina; the Greenwich, Connecticut and the Middleburg, Virginia, Hunter Trials, 1929; bought, broke, trained and personally schooled Sobersides, winner of the Middleburg Point-to-Point, 1938, the Old Dominion Point-to-Point, 1939, and the Rokeby Cup presented by Paul Mellon, emblematic of victory in the Piedmont Point-to-Point, Virginia, 1938, his son Crompton Smith up; won the Grafton-Middlesex American-English Foxhound Match for $2000 a side and plate in Virginia in 1905; founded the Masters of Foxhounds Association of America in 1907. Judge at the leading horse and hound shows; founded the Frank Forester Society of America. *Publications:* A Sporting Tour through Ireland, England, Wales, and France, 1925; The True American Foxhound; Fox Hunting in America; The Cubbing Season; Amateur Sunday Games; The Pulse of the People; Life and Sport in Aiken and Those who Made It, 1935; A Sporting Family of the Old South, 1936; wrote for 14th Edition of the Encyclopædia Britannica the articles on Steeplechasing in the United States and Canada. *Recreations:* hunting, travelling, racing, and writing. *Address:* Worcester, Mass, USA.

Died 5 April 1945.

SMITH, Rt Hon. Hastings Bertrand L.; *see* Lees-Smith.

SMITH, Hely, RBA 1901; RBC 1927; FRSA 1928; artist, oil and water-colour, marine and figure; member and Hon. Treasurer of the Artists' Society and Langham Sketching Club; Hon. Treasurer Royal Society of British Artists since 1915; *b* Wambrook, Dorset, 15 Jan. 1862; *s* of late Rev. Hely Hutchinson Augustus Smith, MA Oxon, Vicar of Market Rasen, Lincolnshire; *m* 1905, Lucie E. (*d* 1909), *d* of Lt-Gen. W. H. Worthy Bennet. *Educ:* Loretto. Left school at the age of seventeen and went into Samuel Smith & Co.'s Bank at Derby for three years; then took up painting, studying at Lincoln School of Art and Antwerp Academy till 1888; first exhibited at the Royal Academy, 1890, The Fog Horn, purchased by the Canterbury Art Society, Christchurch, New Zealand, 1903; A Stormy Evening, bequeathed to Plymouth Corporation Art Gallery, and a Breezy Shore, to Victoria and Albert Museum, South Kensington; The Gulls of Blackfriars, purchased by late Queen Alexandra; de Laszlo Silver Medal, 1937; worked in Algeria, Egypt, etc. *Recreation:* making model ships. *Address:* Park Corner, 7 Ravenscourt Square, W6. *T:* Riverside 3741.
Died 21 Jan. 1941.

SMITH, Lt-Col Henry, CIE 1918; Indian Medical Service; retired; late Civil Surgeon, Amritsur, Punjab; *b* 16 Aug. 1862; *s* of Joseph Smith, Clogher, Co. Tyrone; *m* H. D., *d* of Rev. W. A. Russell; two *s. Educ:* Queen's College, Galway; Royal University of Ireland. *Publications:* many papers on ophthalmic and general surgery, and a monograph on the Treatment of Cataract. *Recreation:* the study of the things around. *Address:* Ashfield Park, Clogher, Co. Tyrone.
Died 28 Feb. 1948.

SMITH, Sir Henry S.; *see* Scott-Smith.

SMITH, Sir Henry W.; *see* White-Smith.

SMITH, Sir Herbert, 1st Bt *cr* 1920; *b* 22 June 1872; *m* 1892, Emily, *d* of George Pratt, Kidderminster; one *s* two *d.* Member of Board of Control of Wool and Textile Industries; Chairman of Carpet Trade Rationing Committee; Chairman of Man Power and Protection Committee. *Heir: s* Herbert [*b* 26 Sept. 1903; *m* 1929, Eileen, *yr d* of Bertram Norton, Sandford Hall, Claverley, Salop]. *Address:* Blakebrook House, Kidderminster; Witley Court, Worcestershire.
Died 14 July 1943.

SMITH, Sir Herbert; *see* Smith, Sir C. H.

SMITH, Col Herbert Austen, CIE 1918, Indian Medical Service, retired; late Inspector-General of Civil Hospitals, Behar and Orissa; Member of the Legislative Council; *b* 3 May 1866; *m* Harriet E., *d* of late Lt-Col Arthur Shewell; two *d. Educ:* Trinity College, Cambridge; Guy's Hospital, London; Honours, Natural Science Tripos, 1887; BA, MB, BC Cantab, MRCS Eng., LRCP London. Entered IMS 1892; Civil Surgeon and Principal Medical School, Agra; Civil Surgeon Mussoorie and Simla; Surgeon on the staff of the Viceroy of India, 1916–20; served NE Frontier of India, 1892–93, Lushai; Soudan, 1896 (medal, Khedive's medal), NW Frontier of India, 1897–98 medal with clasp); European War, 1914–18 (CIE); Hon. Surgeon to the King, 1922–24; retired 1923. *Publications:* contributed articles to the Indian Medical Gazette. *Address:* Springfield, Hawkhurst, Kent. *T:* Hawkhurst 77.
Died 30 Nov. 1949.

SMITH, Col Herbert Francis; *b* 10 May 1859; *s* of late Frederic Chatfield Smith and late Harriet Matilda, *d* of late Francis Pym; *m* 1894, Julia, *d* of late Major General Edmund M. Manningham Buller; one *s* one *d. Educ:* Eton; Christ Church, Oxford. Partner in Smith Payne

and Smiths; South Notts Hussars 1881–1906. Lt-Col 1900, Colonel, 1901; JP Notts and Norfolk; High Sheriff of Norfolk, 1918. *Recreations:* fishing, shooting, golf. *Address:* Didlington Hall, Norfolk. *TA:* Northwold. *T:* Mundford 213; Inholmes, Hartley Wintney, Hants. *Clubs:* Carlton, Royal Automobile.
Died 20 Dec. 1948.

SMITH, Rev. Herbert Maynard, DD; Canon Residentiary, Gloucester, 1921–40, Canon Emeritus, 1946; *b* 1869; *s* of John William Smith and Annie Gaimes. *Educ:* Wellington Coll., Trinity Coll., Oxford; Cuddesdon. Curate of Billesdon, Leicestershire, 1893–95; Gt Witley, Worcestershire, 1895–1900; Rector of Shelsley Beauchamp, Worcestershire, 1900–09; Vicar of Holy Trinity, Malvern, 1909–21; Proctor in Convocation, 1918–21, 1925–38; Examining Chaplain to the Bishop of Gloucester, 1923–45; Senior Chaplain to the Midland Province of the Woodard Schools. *Publications:* In Playtime, 1907; Playmates, 1908; John Evelyn in Naples, 1910; Lectures on the Epistle of St James, 1914; Church and Social Questions, 1917; Prayer, 1918; Early Life and Education of John Evelyn, 1920; Atonement, 1925; Frank, Bishop of Zanzibar, 1926; Pre-Reformation England, 1938; Editor of the Church Quarterly Review, 1926–1931; Henry VIII and the Reformation, 1948; The Seven Detective Stories of Inspector Frost. *Address:* Pontesbury Manor, Shrewsbury. *Clubs:* Athenæum; Shropshire (Shrewsbury).
Died 6 Jan. 1949.

SMITH, Sir Hubert Llewellyn, GCB 1919; KCB 1908; CB 1903; MA (Oxon), BSc London; Hon. Fellow of Corpus Christi College, Oxford, 1934; Chairman of Committee under Merchandise Marks Acts 1927; Member of Board of Trade Council for Art and Industry, 1934; Chief Economic Adviser to HM Government, 1919–27; Permanent Secretary to Board of Trade, 1907–19; *b* 1864; *y s* of Samuel Wyatt Smith of Bristol; *m* 1901, Edith, *e d* of G. M. Weekley of Hartlands, Cranford; four *s* two *d. Educ:* Bristol Grammar School; Corpus Christi College, Oxford. Mathematical scholar, 1883; 1st class Math. Mods 1884; 1st class Math. Finals, 1886; Cobden Prize (Oxford Univ.), 1886; BSc (Lond.), 1887. Lecturer on Political Economy to Oxford Univ. Extension and Toynbee Trust, 1887–88; Secretary of National Association for Promotion of Technical Education, 1888–92; Commissioner for Labour, Labour Department, Board of Trade, 1893; Member of the Royal Commission on Secondary Education, 1894–95; British Delegate for commercial treaty with Roumania, 1905; and with Japan, 1910. General Secretary Ministry of Munitions, 1915; President of Viceregal Committee on the Secretariat of the Government of India, 1919; British Representative on Anglo-Persian Tariff Committee, 1920; British Delegate at Barcelona Conference on Communications and Transit, 1921; Member of Economic Committee of League of Nations, 1920–27; Deputy Delegate to Assembly of League, 1923 and 1924; British Delegate to League Conferences on Customs Formalities, Maritime Ports, International Railways, etc., 1923; British Delegate to Hague Conference of Industrial Property Union, 1925; Chairman of British Institute of Industrial Art, 1920–35; Director of New Survey of London Life and Labour, 1928–35; Chairman of Council of National Association of Boys' Clubs, 1935–43. *Publications:* several monographs, and essays on Economic, Art and Educational subjects; The Economic Laws of Art Production, 1925; History of the Board of Trade, 1927; History of East London, 1939; joint author of Through the High Pyrenees, 1898; New Survey of London Life and Labour (1928–1935). *Address:* Greenhew, Upshire, Waltham Abbey. *T:* Waltham Cross 2773. *Club:* United University.
Died 19 Sept. 1945.

SMITH, James Alexander George; KC 1926; Barrister-at-law; Member of the Legislative Council for Clarendon, Jamaica, since 1916; *s* of late James and Letitia Smith; unmarried. *Educ:* Rusea's High School, Jamaica; private tuition, England. Called to Bar, Lincoln's Inn, 1910; Member of the North London Sessions Bar Mess; returned to Jamaica after nine months practice in England, 1910; President Jamaica Representative Govt Association; JP Parish of Clarendon; Chairman Jamaica Bar Council. *Recreations:* agriculture, tennis, reading. *Address:* Kingston, Jamaica. *Club:* West Indian.

Died 20 April 1942.

SMITH, Sir James Cowlishaw, Kt 1932; CIE 1921; *b* 14 April 1873; *m* 1905, Charlotte Dunne Forbes; one *s* four *d*. *Educ:* Derby; Caius Coll., Camb. BA, LLB. Entered ICS 1896; Joint Magistrate, 1905; Deputy-Commissioner, 1913; Magistrate and Collector 1914; Commissioner, 1924; Member Governor's Executive Council, UP, 1930 and 1931; retired, 1931. *Address:* 21 Pearl Court, Eastbourne, Sussex. *T:* Eastbourne 971.

Died 13 Oct. 1946.

SMITH, James Cruickshank, CBE 1918; LittD, LLD, MA; *b* Dun, Angus, Scotland, 28 Aug. 1867; *s* of James Smith; *m* 1896, Edith, *e d* of W. Philip, JP Dundee; four *d*. *Educ:* Edinburgh University; Trinity College, Oxford. Edinburgh University 1st class honours in Classics, Vans Dunlop Scholarship in English, Baxter Fellowship in Classics; Ferguson Scholarship in Classics; Oxford; Craven Scholarship, 1st class in Classical Moderations, 1st class in Litteræ Humaniores. Lecturer in Classics, Owens College, Manchester, 1892–95; Classical Examiner, Edin. Univ.; Rector of High School of Stirling, 1896–99; Classical Examiner, Glasgow University; HMI of Schools, 1899; HM Chief Inspector for Training of Teachers, 1911; Sen. Chief Inspector of Schools in Scotland 1927–32; Director of Wages, Ministry of Munitions, Vice-Chairman of Wages Tribunal, Chairman of Classification Committee, Ministry of Food, 1915–18; Hon. LittD (Toronto University), 1927; acting Prof. of English Lit. (Edinburgh Univ.) 1932–33; Hon. LLD (Edin. Univ.), 1933. *Publications:* Edited two vols of the Warwick Shakespeare; General Editor of Oxford University Press Select Plays of Shakespeare; Editor Spenser's Færie Queene, two vols and Spenser's Poems (1 vol.) with Prof. de Sélincourt; Organisation of Education in Carnarvonshire, 1911; A Study of Wordsworth, 1944; A Critical History of English Poetry (with Sir Herbert Grierson), 1944; Book of Verse for Boys and Girls; Clarendon Readers, and other anthologies. *Address:* 46 Murrayfield Avenue, Edinburgh. *T:* Edinburgh 61625. *Clubs:* Scottish Arts, Edinburgh.

Died 7 Nov. 1946.

SMITH, Hon. Sir (James) Joynton, KBE 1920; principal proprietor, Smith's Weekly; *b* 1855; *s* of James Smith, Hastings. Lord Mayor of Sydney, 1918; Member Legislative Council, NSW 1912–34. *Publication:* My Life Story, 1927. *Address:* Hastings, Baden Street, Randwick, Sydney, NSW.

Died 10 Oct. 1943.

SMITH, Surg. Rear-Adm. James Lawrence, CB 1918; MVO 1898; MB; *b* 1862; *s* of Alexander Emslie Smith, Advocate; *m* 1905, Maude, *d* of Inspector-Gen. Maxwell Rodgers, MD, RN; one *s*. Surgeon, 1884; Fleet Surgeon, 1900; Deputy Surgeon-General, 1912; Surgeon-General, 1916; served Suakim, 1884–85 (Egyptian medal, clasp, Khedive's bronze star); attended Prince Henry of Battenberg in his last illness (MVO); Officier Legion of Honour, 1917; retired, 1919; medal for General Service, European War. *Address:* Two Beeches, Wallis Road, Waterlooville, Hants.

Died 28 April 1945.

SMITH, Lt-Col John Grant, DSO 1916; TD; DL; late 6th Seaforth Highlanders; *b* Inverallan, Grantown-on-Spey; *m d* of late William Mackay, LLD, Inverness; two *s*. *Educ:* Watson's Coll., Edinburgh; Edinburgh University. Hon. Sheriff-Substitute, Inverness, Moray, and Nairn; JP and member of County Councils Inverness and Moray; served European War, 1915–18 (despatches twice, DSO); Lt-Col, 1915; factor for the Strathspey estates of the Seafield Trustees. *Address:* Inverallan, Grantown-on-Spey.

Died 7 Oct. 1942.

SMITH, John Keats C.; *see* Catterson-Smith.

SMITH, Sir Joseph (Benjamin George), Kt 1933; CIE 1927; Chief Engineer and Secretary to Government Punjab Irrigation PWD, retd; *b* Buxar, India, 14 Feb. 1878; *s* of Joseph Smith, Bristol; *m* Charlotte Edith Slane, Simla; two *s* one *d*. *Educ:* La Martinière College, Lucknow; Thomason College, Roorkee. Joined PWD Irrigation, Punjab, 1898; served continuously in that Province except for three months in Bengal as Member Irrigation Committee, 1930; Member Central Board of Irrigation, India, 1931–32. *Address:* 8 Keith Avenue, Remuera Auckland SE2, New Zealand.

Died 8 May 1950.

SMITH, Hon. Sir Joynton; *see* Smith, Hon. Sir James J.

SMITH, Kenneth Brooke Farley, DSO 1941; Wing Commander General Duties, RAF; *b* 9 Jan. 1913; *yr s* of Thomas Edward Smith, Whitemoor, Lyndhurst, Hants; *m* 1939, Esme Doris, *er d* of Capt. Cecil Sutton, Heathfield, Brockenhurst; one *s*. *Educ:* Charterhouse; Corpus Christi College, Oxford. 2nd Cl. Hons Jurisprudence, Oxford, 1935; Student of Inner Temple; joined RAF, 1936; trained at Cranwell. *Recreation:* sailing. *Address:* Heathfield House, Brockenhurst. *T:* Brockenhurst 45.

Died 11 April 1943.

SMITH, Brig.-Gen. Kenneth John K.; *see* Kincaid-Smith.

SMITH, Lancelot Grey Hugh, CBE 1917; late Lt Westminster Dragoons; a partner in Messrs Rowe & Pitman; *b* 4 Aug. 1870; *s* of late Hugh Colin Smith and Constance, *d* of Henry J. Adeane of Babraham, Cambridge, and Maud, *d* of 1st Baron Stanley of Alderley. *Educ:* Eton; Trinity College, Cambridge. Principal Delegate, British Mission to Sweden, 1915; Chairman of Tobacco Control Board. *Address:* Mount Clare, Roehampton. *T:* Prospect 1211; 9 Hill Street, Berkeley Square, W1; Old Hall, Garboldisham, Norfolk. *Clubs:* Brooks's, White's, Pratt's.

Died 23 March 1941.

SMITH, Launcelot Eustace, CBE 1918; Chairman (late Managing Director) Smith's Dock Co. Ltd, North Shields and South Bank-on-Tees; an Extraordinary Director of the Scottish Widows' Fund Life Assurance Society; *b* 1868; *m* 1898, Fanny Elizabeth Rosalie (*d* 1937), *d* of Major H. A. Doyne, RA. *Address:* Piper Close, Corbridge-on-Tyne. *T:* Corbridge 36. *Club:* Union (Newcastle-upon-Tyne).

Died 22 Aug. 1948.

SMITH, Col Leonard Kirke, CBE 1923; DSO 1900; late The Royal Scots; *b* 24 Jan. 1877; 5th *s* of F. P. Smith of Barnes Hall; *m* 1914, Vera, *d* of late Capt. C. H. Hicks; three *s*. *Educ:* Charterhouse. Entered Army, 1897; Capt. 1903; Maj. 1915; Lt-Col 1923; served S Africa, 1899–1902; relief Kimberley, Paardeberg, Driefontein, Bloemfontein, etc. (despatches twice, two medals six clasps, DSO); Egyptian Army, 1910–23; Adjutant-General, 1919–23 (1914 Star, Medal, Victory Medal, Sudan Medal, 2nd Class Order of the Nile); retired pay, 1926. *Address:* Twitchel Corner, Hooton Pagnell, Doncaster. *Club:* United Service.

Died 23 March 1941.

SMITH, Lewis, MD, FRCP, MRCS; retired; Consulting Physician to London Hospital; *b* Chelmsford, 8 May 1869; 3rd *s* of Joseph Alfred Smith of Chelmsford; *m* 1904, Ethel, *o d* of John Rigby, MA. *Educ:* Scarborough; London Hospital Medical College; MB London (Honours) 1897, MRCP Lond. 1900, MD Lond. (qualified for Gold Medal) 1901. Physician to Eastern Dispensary, 1900–02; Poplar Hospital, 1901–03; Physician to London Hospital, 1902–27; Examiner in Medicine to the Conjoint Board, 1923–26; Fellow Royal Society of Medicine. *Publications:* articles in Allchin's System of Medicine and Hutchison's Index of Treatment; papers in Medical Journals; Golden Rules of Medical Practice. *Recreations:* golf, fishing. *Address:* c/o Midland Bank, 129 New Bond Street, W1. *Club:* Flyfishers'.

Died 17 Sept. 1944.

SMITH, Brig.-Gen. Lionel A.; *see* Abel-Smith.

SMITH, Col Lionel Fergus, CMG 1917; late RAMC; *b* Co. Cork, 1869; *s* of late W. Smith; *m* Mabel Constance, *d* of late Major W. E. Hardy, RA; two *s*. *Educ:* Dublin University (Erasmus Smith Exhibitioner); Honoursman in Classics, Logics, Modern Literature, and Modern History. BA, MB, BCh, BAO Dublin, 1894; DPH Dublin, 1906. Entered RAMC 1895; Lt-Col 1915; served North-west Frontier of India, 1897–98 (medal and clasp); European War, 1914–17 (despatches thrice, CMG); Colonel, 1921; retd pay, 1925. *Recreations:* football, tennis, golf. *Address:* c/o Glyn, Mills & Co., Whitehall, SW1.

Died 8 Oct. 1945.

SMITH, Logan Pearsall; *b* 18 Oct. 1865; *s* of Robert Pearsall Smith and Hannah Whitall Smith, Philadelphia, USA; naturalised as British subject, 1913; unmarried. *Educ:* Haverford College; Harvard University; Balliol College, Oxford. BA, Oxford, 1893; MA, 1906. *Publications:* The Youth of Parnassus, 1895; Life and Letters of Sir Henry Wotton, 1907; Songs and Sonnets, 1909; The English Language, 1912; Trivia, 1918; More Trivia, 1921; Words and Idioms, 1925; On Reading Shakespeare, 1933; Reperusals and Re-collections, 1936; Unforgotten Years, 1938; Milton and his Modern Critics, 1940; The Golden Shakespeare, 1950 (posthumous). *Address:* 11 St Leonard's Terrace, SW3. *T:* Sloane 7705.

Died 2 March 1949.

SMITH, Marshall King, CBE 1932; *b* 22 June 1867; *y s* of late Michael Henry Smith; *m* 1917, Mary, *e d* of Robert Gray; no *c*. *Educ:* privately. Entered Trinity House Service, 1884; Secretary of Trinity House, 1919–32; retired 1932; FRGS. *Recreations:* mountaineering, boating. *Address:* 8 Victoria Mansions, West Hampstead, NW6. *T:* Hampstead 6991. *Clubs:* Alpine, Constitutional.

Died 29 Jan. 1946.

SMITH, Rt Rev. Martin Linton, DSO 1917; DD; *b* 4 July 1869; *s* of late Very Rev. James Allan Smith, DD, Dean of St David's, and Charlotte Isabella, *d* of Rev. Canon Linton; *m* 1897, Kathleen Dewe (*d* 1949), *d* of Thomas Mathews; one *s* one *d*. *Educ:* Repton; Hertford College, Oxford. Deacon, 1893; Priest, 1894; curacies in Whitechapel, Aston, Limpsfield, and Southwold; Rector of St Nicholas, Colchester, 1902; Vicar of St Saviour, Liverpool, 1903; St Nicholas, Blundellsands, 1906; Chaplain to the Forces, 1915–17; Hon. Canon of Liverpool, 1915–20; Rector of Winwick, Warrington, 1917–20; Suffragan Bishop of Warrington, 1918–20; Bishop of Hereford, 1920–30; Bishop of Rochester, 1930–39; Select Preacher, University of Oxford, 1928–29; Hon. Fellow of Hertford College, Oxford, 1930. *Recreation:* golf. *Address:* Tudor House Private Hotel, Cromer.

Died 7 Oct. 1950.

SMITH, Mrs Mary Isobel Barr, CBE 1918; *d* of Alexander Mitchell, Ayrshire; *m* Tom Elder Barr Smith. *Address:* Birksgate, Glen Osmond, S Australia.

Died 16 June 1941.

SMITH, Maj.-Gen. Merton B.; *see* Beckwith-Smith.

SMITH, Montague Bentley Talbot P.; *see* Paske-Smith.

SMITH, Percy John Delf, RDI; Draughtsman and Etcher, Practitioner and Consultant in lettering and book designing; *m* 1928, E. Marion Delf, DSc (Lond.), Head of Department of Botany, Westfield College, University of London. *Educ:* Camberwell School of Art, but chiefly in the school of life and books. Lecturer to Teachers, LCC 1934–38; Assistant Examiner in Lettering and Illuminating to Board of Education, 1939–; Cantor Lecturer, Royal Society of Arts, 1936. Active service, France, Royal Marine Artillery, 1915–17. Worked in USA 1927, Palestine, 1932. Master of the Art Workers' Guild, 1941. Master of the Faculty of Royal Designers in Industry, 1943–45. Principal work: Drawings, Etchings and Drypoints: official purchases include Contemporary Art Society, British Museum, Victoria and Albert Museum, Library of Congress, USA and various Provincial Galleries. Especially interested in Lettering which began largely from a desire to affirm importance of beauty in Industry and everyday life. Inscriptional work includes for Canadian National Memorial, Vimy Ridge; British Government and private memorials; RIBA Headquarters. Calligraphic work includes Elgin Roll of Honour in Ontario Cathedral. Book designing and wood engraving: official purchases include Victoria and Albert Museum, Contemporary Art Society. *Publications:* Quality in Life, 1919; The Dance of Death, 1914–1918 (7 etchings); Twelve Drypoints of the War, 1914–1918; Wuthering Heights (5 drypoints), 1923; 18 Drypoints and Etchings of the War, 1931; Lettering, a plea for its greater consideration, 1932; 21 Drawings and Etchings of Palestine, 1934; Lettering and its uses today (Cantor Lectures), 1936; Lettering: a handbook of Modern Alphabets, 1937; Civic and Memorial Lettering, 1946; contributions to professional journals. *Recreations:* variety of work, travelling. *Address:* 27 Rudall Crescent, Hampstead, NW3. *T:* Hampstead 4766. *Club:* Arts.

Died 30 Oct. 1948.

SMITH, Reginald Montagu B.; *see* Bosworth-Smith.

SMITH, Robert John, CBE; FSS; Chevalier of the Legion of Honour; chartered accountant practising in Glasgow; *b* Glasgow, 1866; *s* of Robert Burns Smith, FEIS, Pollokshields; *m* Kate Dinwoodie Linn; one *s*. *Educ:* Norland House; Pollokshields School; Anderson's College. Interested in the automobile movement since 1896; Founder Member of the Royal Automobile Club; Founder and Secretary of the Royal Scottish Automobile Club; has acted on numerous important Committees connected with automobilism and given evidence before various Royal and Parliamentary Commissions; during War of 1914–18 rendered various services to the Government; Member of War Committee and Chairman of Transport of Wounded Committee of Scottish Red Cross in last and present wars. *Address:* 2 Redlands Road, Kelvinside, Glasgow. *TA:* Calculus Glasgow. *T:* Western Glasgow, 1074. *Clubs:* Royal Automobile; Royal Scottish Automobile, Glasgow; Troon Golf.

Died 10 Sept. 1942.

SMITH, Robert Percy, MD, FRCP; Consulting Physician for Mental Disorders, St Thomas's Hospital; *s* of Robert Smith; *m* Alice Mary, *d* of Rev. W. B. Marriott. *Educ:* private school; St Thomas's Hospital and University of London. Formerly Resident Assistant Physician, St Thomas's Hospital; Resident Physician and Medical Superintendent, Bethlem Hospital, London; Examiner in Mental Diseases, University of London; Physician for Mental Disorders, Charing Cross Hospital;

Lecturer on Psychological Medicine, Charing Cross and St Thomas's Hospitals; President Medico-Psychological Association, and Sections of Neurology and Psychiatry, Royal Society of Medicine. *Publications:* (Joint) The Insane and the Law; articles on subjects connected with insanity in medical journals, etc. *Recreation:* golf. *Address:* 42 Albion Street, W2.

Died 4 June 1941.

SMITH, Samuel Walter Johnson, FRS; MA (Camb.), DSc (Lond.); late Professor of Physics, and Dean of the Faculty of Science, University of Birmingham, Emeritus Professor, 1937; *b* 1871; *s* of late Walter Mackersie Smith, inventor of many improvements in locomotive engines, and Margaret Black, both of Ferry-Port-on-Craig, Scotland; *m* 1900, Dorothy Muriel, *d* of Edward Blanshard Stamp of Hampstead; one *d. Educ:* West End Academy, Dundee; Tayport Public School; Rutherford College, Newcastle-on-Tyne. National Scholar. Royal College of Science, London, 1887–90; Major Scholar, Trinity College, Cambridge, 1891–96; Coutts-Trotter Student, 1894–96; 1st Class Natural Sciences Tripos, Pt I, 1892 and Pt II, 1894 (Physics and Chemistry). Late Assistant Professor of Physics, Imperial College, South Kensington; Vice-President, Physical Society of London, 1916–19; Hon. Sec. 1908–16. *Publications:* various papers, mainly of Electricity and Magnetism, published in the Philosophical Transactions of the Royal Society, Philosophical Magazine, Proceedings to the Physical Society, etc. *Address:* 130 Westfield Road, Edgbaston, Birmingham. *T:* Edgbaston 0050.

Died 20 Aug. 1948.

SMITH, Stephen Henry, CBE 1929; *b* Wollombi, NSW, 2 Aug. 1865; *s* of late S. S. Smith, Willesden, Killara. *Educ:* Grafton Superior Public School. Retired 1930, after fifty years' service in the Dept of Education, NSW; served in many capacities in that Dept, Director of Education and Under-Secretary 1920–30; founded (and edited for 16 years) the NSW School Magazine; founded the system of correspondence teaching for primary pupils in remote areas; represented Government of New South Wales at Imperial Education Conferences, London, 1911 and 1927, and Vancouver Education Conference, 1929; also at New Education Conference, Locarno, 1927; represented Federal Government of Australia at Pan-Pacific Education Conference, Honolulu, 1927. *Publications:* History of Education in Australia; William Timothy Cape and other pioneers of Secondary Education in Australia; Careers for Boys; The Law and the Teacher; A Commercial Geography of Australia; English History for senior pupils, 32 school books on history, geography, etc.; sometime editor of Official Education Gazette and of the School Magazine. *Address:* Box 3186 P, GPO, Sydney, Australia.

Died 20 Feb. 1943.

SMITH, Col Sydney Ernest, CBE 1919; OBE 1919; JP; MInstT, MIAE; Member Bristol Stock Exchange; Director West Gloucestershire Water Co., Bristol Aeroplane Co., Ltd; *b* 1881; *m* 1910, Ethel Mary, *d* of Robert J. Ball. Served European War, 1914–19 (despatches, OBE, CBE). *Address:* Stuckeridge, Oakford, Devon. *Club:* Royal Air Force.

Died 11 June 1943.

SMITH, Sydney Ure, OBE 1937; artist and publisher; Director, Empire-USA Art Trust; *b* Stoke Newington, London, Jan. 1887; *s* of John Ure Smith. *Educ:* Queen's College, Melbourne; Sydney Grammar School. Studied art under Julian Ashton. Founded Art in Australia, The Home, and other publications; resigned from editorship of Art in Australia and Home, 1938; founded Ure Smith Pty Limited, Publishing Firm, 1939; appointed Managing Director of same; edited and published Present Day Art in Australia series of books, and a series of *de luxe* publications which include The Art of William Dobell; Camellia Quest by Prof. E. G. Waterhouse; Max Dupain, Photographs; Houses of Australia; Adrian Feint;

Flower Paintings; The Art of Rupert Bunny. President of the Society of Artists, Sydney, for 26 years; resigned as Pres. and appointed Life Vice-Pres. 1948; is best known for his etchings and water-colour drawings, and has many prints and drawings in Australian Art galleries; Vice-Pres. of the Nat. Art Gallery of New South Wales; served as Trustee for 20 years, resigned 1947. Council Member, Australian Limited Editions Society; Editorial Representative for the Studio Publications in Australia. *Address:* Ure Smith Pty Limited, 166 Phillip Street, Sydney, New South Wales.

Died 11 Oct. 1949.

SMITH, Major Thomas Close; Royal Bucks Hussars, retired; *b* 1878; *s* of H. F. Smith; *m* 1909, Caroline Mary Elizabeth Grenville, *o d* of 8th Baroness Kinloss; three *s* one *d. Educ:* Winchester; Exeter Coll., Oxford (MA). Sheriff of Buckinghamshire, 1942. *Address:* Boycott Manor, Buckingham. *T:* Buckingham 32 7. *TA:* Manor, Dadford. *Club:* Cavalry.

Died 16 Nov. 1946.

SMITH, Thomas William, CVO 1921; CBE 1920; *b* 14 July 1878; *s* of late Walter Reeve Smith, N Tuddenham, Norfolk; *m* 1914, Mabel Foley, *d* of late Frank Alexander, Salisbury; two *c.* Assistant Director of Army Contracts, 1918–19; Principal Private Secretary to the Rt Hon. Lord Inverforth, PC, Minister of Munitions, 1919–20; Assistant Secretary and Principal Establishment Officer, Ministry of Munitions, and its successors Disposal and Liquidation Commission and Surplus Stores, etc., Liquidation Dept, Treasury, 1920–25; Assistant Army Auditor, Western Command, 1926–38. *Address:* Downton, Ormonde Road, Chester. *T:* Chester 3146. *Club:* National Liberal.

Died 11 March 1946.

SMITH, W. P. Haskett-, FSA; *e surv. s* of H. Haskett-Smith. *Educ:* Eton; Trinity College, Oxford (Scholar). Called to Bar (Lincoln's Inn), 1885; Prime Warden of the Fishmongers' Company, 1915–16. *Publications:* Climbing in the British Isles, 1894; Apprentices and Freemen of the Fishmongers' Co. (before 1650), 1916. *Clubs:* Climbers', Alpine.

Died 11 March 1946.

SMITH, Sir Walter B.; *see* Buchanan-Smith.

SMITH, Walter Robert; JP; *b* 7 May 1872; father, labourer; *m*; one *s* two *d. Educ:* Norwich. MP (Lab) Wellingborough Division of Northants, 1918–22; MP (Lab) Norwich, 1923–24, and 1929–31; Parliamentary Secretary, Ministry of Agriculture and Fisheries, 1924; Parliamentary Secretary, Board of Trade, 1929–31; Member of Forestry Commission; Member of Council of Agriculture (England). *Recreation:* gardening. *Address:* 9 West Parade, Norwich.

Died 25 Feb. 1942.

SMITH, Walter William Marriott, CBE 1919; retired Colonel Royal Artillery; *b* 1846; *s* of Rev. Canon Reginald Smith, Rector of West Stafford, Dorset; *m* Alice Mary (*d* 1932), *d* of J. H. Ley, of Trehill, Devon; one *s* four *d. Educ:* Marlborough; Woolwich. 1st Commission, 1867; Passed Staff College with honours, 1877; Brigade-Major, RA, Gibraltar, 1881; DAAG for Instruction, London, 1887; AQMG Plymouth, 1900; served Afghan War, 1878–79; Tirah, 1897–98; India with Territorial Brigade of RFA during European War, 1914–18; received reward for Distinguished and Meritorious Service, 1915. *Recreation:* forestry. *Address:* Downside, Winchester. *T:* Winchester 109.

Died 21 Dec. 1944.

SMITH, Maj.-Gen. Wilfrid Edward Bownas, CB 1917; CMG 1915; *b* 29 March 1867; *m* Florence, *d* of late W. R. Rigg of Turton Towers, Turton, Lancashire. Entered army (S Wales Borderers), 1888; Captain, 1896; Major, 1907; Lieut-Col Lincs Regt, 1914; Brigade-Maj.,

India, 1905–09; served Tibet, 1903–04 (medal); European War (despatches, CB, CMG). *Address:* Tor Royal, Princetown, Devon. *Club:* Army and Navy.

Died 5 May 1942.

SMITH, **William Benjamin**, AM, PhD, LLD; Professor Emeritus of Philosophy, Tulane University, since 1915; *b* Stanford, Kentucky, 26 Oct. 1850; *s* of Jeremiah Smith, Lawyer, and Angeline Kenley; *m* 1882, Katharyn Merrill (*d* 1899); two *s* one *d. Educ:* Kentucky University; Göttingen University AB 1870, AM 1871 (Ky Univ.). Taught in Kentucky Univ. Assistant, 1870–73; Acting Professor of Natural Science, 1873–74; Professor of Mathematics, St John's College, Prairie du Chien, Wisconsin, 1874–76; studied in Europe, 1876–79; received 2 prizes in Math.—Phys Seminary Göttingen, 1877–78; PhD Gött. 1879; taught in Bethel Military Academy Virginia, 1880–81; Professor of Mathematics, Central College, Missouri, 1881–85; Professor of Physics (1885–88) and Mathematics (1888–93), University of Missouri; Professor of Mathematics (1893–1906) and Philosophy (1906–15), Tulane University; United States Delegate to the First Pan-American Scientific Congress, Santiago, Chile, 1908–09; since 1915 writing three books: Who the Christ; What the Transfiguration?: A Study of the Folk-mind of Israel; also a line-for-line homometric translation of the Iliad; Mind the Maker. *Publications:* Coördinate Geometry, 1885; Clew to Trigonometry, 1889; Introductory Modern Geometry, 1893; Infinitesimal Analysis, I, 1898; Life of James Sidney Rollins, 1891; Tariff for Protection (1888), Tariff Reform (1892); various papers on the Silver question, 1896; The Color Line, 1905; The Merman and the Seraph, crowned in Poet Lore Competition, 1906; Der vorchristliche Jesus, 1906; Ecce Deus, 1911, 1912; Addresses as Push or Pull, Morsmortis, etc.; articles in monthly and quarterly journals, also in Encyclopædia Americana on Bible and New Testament, and in Encyclopædia Britannica on mathematical subjects. *Recreations:* walking, reading, music, art galleries, whist. *Address:* Tulane University, New Orleans, Louisiana; 9 Price Avenue, Columbia, Missouri. *T:* 3830, Columbia, Missouri.

Died 6 Aug. 1934.

SMITH, **William Brownhill**, MVO 1928; OBE 1917; DL, JP; *s* of William Smith, Glasgow; *m* Jessie Elizabeth, *y d* of Dr Monro, Arbroath. *Educ:* High School and Andersonian College, Glasgow. Councillor City of Glasgow, 1906–36; Magistrate, 1911–16; Chairman of Electricity Committee, 1912–15, and of Health Committee, 1924–27; originated the holding of Trade Fairs and Exhibitions, and the building of the Kelvin Hall; Member of Electric Power Supply Committee appointed by Board of Trade, 1917, and of the Departmental Committee on Smoke and Noxious Vapours Abatement appointed by the Ministry of Health, 1920; one of the founders of the Smoke Abatement League of Great Britain and Chairman of the Scottish Branch; Chairman of the Standing Conference of Co-operating Bodies, Investigation of Atmospheric Pollution, Department of Scientific and Industrial Research. *Publications:* lectures and articles on Air Pollution and Smoke Abatement. *Address:* Brownhill, 34 Newark Drive, Glasgow, S1.

Died 27 Dec. 1948.

SMITH, **Rev. William Hodson**; *b* Burntwood, Lichfield, 1856; *s* of William and Elizabeth Smith; *m* Eliza Ann Bamford (*d* 1930), Wardle, Rochdale; one *d. Educ:* private school, Lichfield. Entered Wesleyan Methodist ministry, 1880; for nine years with the Rev. Charles Garrett in the Liverpool Mission; Superintendent of North Cornwall Mission, 1900; Chairman of Cornwall District, 1908–12; Principal of the National Children's Home and Orphanage, 1912–33; retired, 1933; elected to Legal Hundred, 1907; deputation to Irish Conference, 1909; Alderman of the County of Cornwall, 1907 and 1913; Mem. of Educ.

Authority for County of Cornwall, and for eight years Chairman of Managers of Newquay and District Schools; Chairman of Governors, County School, Newquay, and Chairman of District Education Committee, 1910; a Representative to the Œcumenical Conference, Toronto, 1911; Representative from the British Conference to the Canadian Quadrennial Conference, Ottawa, 1914; President Wesleyan Methodist Conference, 1927; Delegate from the British Conference to the Australian General Conference, 1929; Order of St Sava. *Address:* Crossfield, Mount Wise, Newquay, Cornwall. *T:* Newquay 39.

Died 14 May 1943.

SMITH, **Captain W(illiam) Humphrey**, CBE 1938; retired auditor, Kenya; *b* 1879; *m* Ethel Margaret Coe; one *s* one *d. Educ:* Uppingham; Jesus College, Cambridge (Rustat Scholar, Abbot Univ. Scholar). BA 1st Class. Tripos. Audit Dept, 1903; on military service, 1914; Capt. KOYLI (wounded); relinquished commission owing to wounds, 1918; auditor, Uganda, 1923; Kenya, 1927. *Recreations:* fishing and shooting. *Address:* Ngong, Kenya. *T:* 230 Ngong.

Died 14 July 1942.

SMITH, **William Sydney**, CB 1922; OBE 1918; *b* Nottingham, 24 Feb. 1866; *s* of Samuel and Hannah Maria Smith; *m* 1st, 1895, Margaret Vernon Simpson, Nottingham; 2nd, 1907, Hilda Mary Tuke, Birkdale; three *d. Educ:* Nottingham High School; University College, Nottingham; London University, BSc; Victoria University, Manchester. Engineering apprentice, E. Reader & Sons, Nottingham; 2nd Whitworth Exhibitioner, 1889; assistant at Latimer, Clerk, Muirhead & Co. Ltd, Electrical Engineers, Westminster, and at Willans & Robinson, Ltd, Engineers, Thames Ditton; one of HM Inspectors of Factories, Home Office, 1895; served in the N Western Division till 1905; in charge of the Derbyshire district, 1905–08; HM Inspector for Dangerous Trades at the Home Office, 1908; Chief Superintendent of the Royal Aircraft Establishment, South Farnborough, 1918–28. *Recreation:* golf. *Address:* The Pines, Upper Park Road, Camberley, Surrey. *T:* Camberley 736.

Died 15 July 1945.

SMITH, **Sir Willie Reardon-**, 2nd Bt *cr* 1920; JP; shipowner and Director of numerous shipping companies; Director The London Assurance; *b* 26 May 1887; *e surv. s* of late Sir William Reardon Smith, DL, JP, 1st Bart, and Ellen (*d* 1939), *d* of Thomas Pickard Hamlyn; *S* father, 1935; *m* 1910, Elizabeth Ann, *d* of John and Mary Wakely; three *s* one *d*. High Sheriff for Glamorgan, 1946. Ex-Director The Ocean Coal and Wilsons Ltd. *Recreation:* golf. *Heir: s* Major William Reardon Reardon-, RA (TA) [*b* 12 March 1911; *m* 1935, Nesta, *d* of late Frederick J. Phillips; three *s* one *d*]. *Address:* Golding, Peterston-super-Ely, Glam. *TA:* Smithcraft, Cardiff. *T:* Cardiff and County.

Died 24 Nov. 1950.

SMITH-BINGHAM, **Brig.-Gen. Oswald Buckley Bingham**; *see* Bingham.

SMITH-MARRIOTT, **Rev. Sir Hugh Randolph Cavendish**, 9th Bt *cr* 1774; Rector of Horsmonden since 1922; *b* 4 Oct. 1868; *s* of late Rev. Hugh Forbes Smith-Marriott (3rd *s* of 4th Bt) and Frances Catherine Mary, *d* of late Hon. George Cavendish; *S* cousin 1943. *Educ:* Winchester; Magdalene College, Cambridge (BA 1890). *Heir: nephew* Ralph George Cavendish. *Address:* Horsmonden Rectory, Kent.

Died 21 March 1944.

SMITH-MARRIOTT, **Sir John Richard Wyldbore**, 7th Bt *cr* 1774; *b* 7 Dec. 1875; 2nd *s* of Sir W. H. Smith-Marriott, 5th Bt, and Eliza (*d* 1904), *d* of Hon. Richard Cavendish, Thornton Hall, Buckinghamshire; *S* brother, 1941; unmarried. *Educ:* Harrow. Land Agent, retired. *Recreations:* shooting, golf, cricket. *Heir: kinsman*

William, *b* 1865. *Address:* The Down House, Blandford, Dorsetshire; Broadford, Horsmonden. *Club:* Junior Carlton.

Died 5 Feb. 1942.

SMITH-MARRIOTT, Sir William, 8th Bt *cr* 1774; *b* 5 Aug. 1865; *s* of John Bosworth Smith-Marriott, 4th Dragoon Guards, and Frances Julia Radclyffe, Hyde, Dorset; *S* cousin, 1942; *m* 1st, 1887, Charlotte M. Austen (*d* 1910); one *d*; 2nd, 1911, Elinor L. Stronge (*d* 1910); one *d*. *Educ:* Marlborough; Christ Church, Oxford. Barrister. *Recreations:* hunting, shooting, fishing, lawn tennis. *Heir: cousin* Rev. Hugh Randolph Cavendish Smith-Marriott [Winchester; Magdalene Coll., Cambridge]. *Address:* Broad Ford House, Horsmonden, Kent.

Died 21 Dec. 1943.

SMITH-MARRIOTT, Sir William John, 6th Bt *cr* 1774; *b* 6 Nov. 1870; *s* of 5th Bt and Eliza (*d* 1904), *d* of Hon. Richard Cavendish, Thornton Hall, Buckinghamshire; *S* father, 1924. *Educ:* Harrow; Trinity Hall, Cambridge. Owns about 3900 acres. *Heir: b* John Richard Wyldbore, *b* 7 Dec. 1875. *Address:* The Down House, Blandford, Dorsetshire.

Died 24 May 1941.

SMITH-PEARSE, Rev. Thomas Northmore Hart, MA Oxon; *b* 9 June 1854; *e s* of Rev. W. Hart-Smith and Charlotte P., *d* of Northmore H. P. Lawrence, JP; *m* 1886, Edith Isabel (*d* 1933), JP, *d* of Rev. H. Wood, Vicar of Biddenham, nr Bedford; one *s* two *d*. *Educ:* Marlborough, 1868–73 (Scholar, left with Exhibition to Oxford). 1st Classical Mod. 1875; 2nd Classical Greats, 1877; Stapledon Scholar of Exeter Coll. Oxford. Study in Germany; matriculated at Bonn am Rhine, 1878. Assistant master, Repton, 1878; assistant master, Marlborough, 1879–89; ordained at Salisbury, 1881; house master, 1884–86; curator of school museum, and Pres. of Natural History Society, 1886–89; Headmaster of Epsom College, 1889–1914; licensed to preach in Diocese of Truro; edited various NHS reports, Marlborough and Epsom; written articles, etc.; Flora of Epsom, 1918. *Recreations:* natural history, croquet, fishing. *Address:* 9 Castle Street, Launceston, Cornwall. *Club:* Royal Societies.

Died 11 Jan. 1943.

SMITHWICK, Rear-Adm. Algernon Robert, DSO 1918; RN, retired; *b* 3 April 1887; 4th *s* of late Canon Standish Poole Smithwick of Monasterevan, and Chancellor of St Brigids Cathedral, Kildare; *m* 1915, Nora Kathleen, *d* of late Sir David Wilson, KCMG; (one *s* killed in action 1945) one *d*. *Educ:* Skelsmergh House School, Margate; Northwood Park, Winchester. Served European War, 1914–18 (despatches, DSO); commanded HMS Sandhurst, 1929–30; HMS Concord, 1931–32; Captain of the Dockyard, Chatham, 1932–35; Captain-in-charge, Simonstown, 1935–37; ADC to the King, 1938–39; Rear-Admiral, 1939; retired list, 1939; served with RAF Volunteer Reserve, 1939–41; rejoined RN, Captain of Dockyard, Devonport, Feb. 1941–Oct. 1943; Commodore of Convoys, Nov. 1943 till demobilisation. *Address:* The Manor Farm House, St James, Shaftesbury, Dorset. *T:* Shaftesbury 2343. *Club:* Junior Army and Navy.

Died 5 Nov. 1948.

SMOOT, Reed; *b* Salt Lake City, 10 Jan. 1862; *s* of Abraham O. Smoot; *m* 1884, Alpha M. Eldredge, of Salt Lake City. Senator of United States, 1903–33; one of the Presidency Utah State of the Church of Jesus Christ of Latter Day Saints, 1895; Apostle, 1900. *Address:* Salt Lake City, Utah, USA.

Died 9 Feb. 1941.

SMUTS, Field Marshal Rt Hon. Jan Christian, PC 1917; OM 1947; CH 1917; FRS 1930; KC 1906; Member, House of Assembly, for Pretoria East, since 1948; Chancellor, University of Capetown, since 1936; Chancellor, University of Cambridge, since 1948; *b* 24 May 1870; *s* of J. A. Smuts, MLA; *m* 1897, Sybella Margaretha, *d* of J. Krige, Stellenbosch; one *s* four *d* (and one *s* decd). *Educ:* Victoria College, Stellenbosch; Christ's College, Cambridge (Hon. Fellow); Double first Law Tripos. Bencher of the Middle Temple. Practised at Cape Town Bar; Johannesburg, 1896; State Attorney, S African Republic, 1898; served Boer War; given supreme command Republican Forces in Cape Colony, 1901; Colonial Secretary, Transvaal, 1907; commanded troops in British East Africa, 1916–17 (prom. hon. Lieut-Gen.); Minister of Interior and Minister of Mines, Union of South Africa, 1910–12; Minister of Defence, 1910–20; Minister of Finance, 1912–13; Prime Minister and Minister for Native Affairs, 1919–24; Minister of Justice, 1933–39; Prime Minister and Minister of External Affairs and Defence, 1939–48; Field Marshal, 1941; GOC Union Defence Forces in the Field, 1940–49. South African Representative Imperial War Cabinet, 1917 and 1918; Plenipotentiary (with General Botha) for South Africa at Peace Conference in Paris, 1919. Pres. British Assoc., 1925; Rhodes Memorial Lecturer, Oxford Univ., 1929–30; Rector of St Andrews Univ., 1931–34; Albert Gold Medal of RSA, 1943; Freeman of Cities of London, Manchester, Edinburgh, Glasgow, Bath, Cardiff, Newcastle-on-Tyne, Dundee, Bristol, York, Sheffield, Aberdeen, Malmesbury, Southampton, Athens, Ithaca, Johannesburg. Hon. degrees: LLD; Cape of Good Hope U, U of S Africa, 1915, Camb., Edin., Glas., Wales, Dublin, Manch., 1917, Cardiff, 1921, McGill, Toronto, Johns Hopkins, Columbia (NY), 1930, Sheffield, 1931, St Andrews, 1934, Utrecht, 1936, Leyden, 1946; DCL; Durham, 1918, Oxf., 1929; DLitt: Pretoria, 1930; DSc: Cape Town, London, 1931; PhD: Stellenbosch, 1931, Athens, Calif (Berkeley), 1945. Commander Legion of Honour, Croix de Guerre (France); Order of Merit (USA); Grand Cross Order of Leopold (Belgium), and many other honours. *Publications:* League of Nations—A Practical Plan, 1919; Wartime Speeches, 1919; Holism and Evolution, 1926; Africa and some World Problems, 1930; Plans for a Better World (Speeches), 1942. *Address:* Doornkloof, Irene, Transvaal, South Africa.

Died 11 Sept. 1950.

SMYLY, J. Gilbart, LittD 1915; Senior Fellow of Trinity College, Dublin; Regius Professor of Greek, Dublin University 1915–27; Professor of Latin, 1904–15; Librarian of Trinity College, Dublin, 1914; *b* 10 July 1867; 2nd *s* of late Sir Philip C. Smyly. *Educ:* Charterhouse; Trinity College, Dublin (Scholar, 1887; Fellow and Tutor, 1897). *Publications:* (with B. P. Grenfell and A. S. Hunt) Tebtunis Papyri, parts i and iii; (with Rev. J. P. Mahaffy) Flinders Petrie Papyri, part iii; Greek Papyri from Gurob; Urbanns Magnus Danielis Becclesiensis. *Address:* Trinity College, and The Turret, Cowper Gardens, Rathmines, Dublin.

Died 25 Dec. 1948.

SMYLY, Sir William Josiah, Kt 1905; MD, FRCPI and FRCSI; FRCOG (Hon.); *b* Dublin, 14 Nov. 1850; 3rd *s* of late Josiah Smyly and Ellen, *d* of Mathew Franks; *m* 1881, Eleanor Colpoys (*d* 1938), *y d* of Henry Tweedy, MD; one *s* three *d*. *Educ:* at home; Trinity College, Dublin; Vienna. Ex-President RCPI and British Gynæcological Society; Hon. Pres. Glasgow Obstetrical and Gynæcological Society; Master of Rotunda Hospital, Dublin, 1889–96; Hon. Fellow Obstet. and Gyn. Society, Leipsic and Edinburgh. *Publications:* various papers and reviews in medical journals, Allbutt's System of Medicine, etc. *Address:* Orton, Seapoint, Co. Dublin. *T:* Blackrock 517.

Died 19 March 1941.

SMYTH, Austin Edward Arthur Watt, CBE 1932; MA; *b* 28 May 1877; 3rd *s* of John Watt Smyth of Duneira, Larne, Co. Antrim, and Annabella Charlotte, *d* of Rev. Hon. Henry O'Brien. *Educ:* Winchester; Trinity College, Cambridge. Browne Medallist and Members'

Prizeman, 1897; Browne University Scholar, 1898; Craven Scholar, 1899; Fellow of Trinity Coll., Cambridge, 1902–08. A Clerk in the House of Commons, 1900; Assist Librarian, 1905; Librarian of the House of Commons, 1908–37. *Publication:* The Composition of the Iliad, 1914. *Address:* Red House, Hursley, Winchester. *Club:* Oxford and Cambridge.

Died 9 June 1949.

SMYTH, Dame Ethel Mary, DBE 1922; MusDoc; composer and writer; *b* 23 April 1858; *d* of late General J. H. Smyth, CB. *Educ:* (musical studies) taught by Heinrich von Herzogenberg, late Prof. of Composition at the Hochschule, Berlin, then Conductor of Bach Verein at Leipzig. Compositions performed, as follows: Chamber music at the Abonnement concerts, Leipzig; Sonata for Pianoforte and Violin at Leipzig Chamber Concerts; orchestral works at Mr Henschel's Symphony concerts and at Crystal Palace; Opera, Fantasio, brought out at Weimar and again at Carlsruhe by Mottl; Opera, Der Wald, at Berlin; The Wreckers, at Leipzig; Mass in D, Albert Hall, 1893. Was a militant suffragist, and composed, among other suffrage music, The March of the Women, the battle-song of the WSPU; Doctor of Music, Durham, 1910; Mus. Doc. Oxon, 1926; DLitt, St Andrews, 1928. *Compositions:* Symphonies; Overture to Anthony and Cleopatra; a Mass; The Prison. Operas: Fantasio; Der Wald; The Wreckers, 1906; Songs with chamber music accompaniment, 1907. Choruses: Hey Nonny No, and Sleepless Dreams, 1911; Dreamings (for Female Chorus), A Canticle of Spring, 1920; a string quartette, four orchestral songs, 1913; two books of songs, 1912; comic opera, The Boatswain's Mate, 1915; Fête Galante; A Dance Dream (one act opera), 1923; Entente Cordiale (comic opera in one act), 1925; Trio for Pf. Fl. and Ob.; Concerto for Vl. Horn and Orchestra, 1926 (arranged as Piano Trio); The Prison: Symphony for two solo Voices, Chorus, and Orchestra, 1931. *Publications:* 4 books of autobiography (Impressions that Remained, 2 vols 1919; As Time went on, 1935; What Happened Next, 1940); Streaks of Life, 1921; A Three-legged Tour in Greece, 1927; A Final Burning of Boats, 1928; Female Pipings in Eden, 1933; Beecham and Pharaoh, 1935; Inordinate (?) Affection (for dog lovers), 1936. *Address:* Coign, Woking. *TA:* Smyth, Woking 467.

Died 8 May 1944.

SMYTH, Lt-Col Henry, DSO 1918; *b* 1866; *s* of late General Henry Smyth, CB; *m* 1905, Alice Mary Caroline, *d* of Rev. A. J. Goodwin; one *s* one *d*. Served Chin Lushai Expedition, 1889–90 (medal and clasp); Tirah Expedition, 1897–98 (despatches, medal and two clasps); European War, 1914–18 (DSO, despatches, Greek medal for military merit, French and Greek Croix de Guerre); NW Persia (medal and clasp). *Address:* Brook Cottage, South Cerney, Cirencester.

Died 4 April 1943.

SMYTH, (Herbert) Warington, CMG 1919; MA, LLM, FGS, FRGS, MIMM; Lieut-Commander RNVR (SA), retired; *e s* of late Sir Warington Smyth, FRS; *m* 1900, Amabel, 3rd *d* of late Sir Henry Sutton; three *s* one *d*. *Educ:* Westminster; Trinity College, Cambridge (Capt. Third Trinity, Head of the River, 1889–90). Unpaid assistant to Mineral Adviser to the Office of Woods, 1890–91; Secretary Government Department of Mines, Siam, 1891–95; Director-General, 1895–97; Secretary Siamese Legation, 1898–1901; Commander of Order of the White Elephant of Siam, 1897; Murchison grant of RGS for journeys in Siam, 1898; called to the Bar, 1899; delegate for Siam to the Congrès Internationaux, Paris Exhibition, 1900; Hon. Secretary for London of National Committee for organisation of a Volunteer Naval Reserve, 1900–01; Secretary for Mines, Transvaal, 1901–10 (Queen's SA medal); President Transvaal Cornish Assoc., 1907–10; Secretary for Mines and Industries, South Africa, and Commissioner of Mines, Natal, 1910–27; Chief Inspector of Factories; retired, 1927; Member of Legislative and Executive Councils, Transvaal, 1906–07; JP and Advocate of the Supreme Court of the Transvaal; acting Sub-Lieut RNR, Nov. 1914; Assistant Naval Transport Officer, GSWA campaign, 1914–15 (despatches); Lieut RNVR and Acting Naval SO, Cape, 1915–16; Controller of Imports and Exports, Union of SA, 1917; South African Government Delegate to International Labour Conferences, Washington, 1919, and Geneva, 1922; Lieut RNVR, 1940. *Publications:* Journey on the Upper Me Kong, 1895; Five Years in Siam, 1898; Mast and Sail in Europe and Asia, 1906, 2nd edn 1929; Sea-Wake and Jungle Trail, 1925; Chase and Chance in Indo-China, 1934; a Naval Volunteer Force, etc. *Recreations:* rowing, yachting. *Address:* Calamansac, Falmouth. *T:* Constantine 202. *Clubs:* Royal Cruising; Royal Cornwall, Cambridge University and Bar Yacht.

Died 19 Dec. 1943.

SMYTH, Maj.-Gen. Sir Nevill Maskelyne, VC; KCB 1919; CB 1916; *b* 14 Aug. 1868; 2nd *s* of late Sir Warington Smyth, FRS, of Marazion, Cornwall; *m* 1918, Olwen, *d* of Sir A. Osmond Williams, 1st Bt; two *s* one *d*. *Educ:* Sandhurst (Honours). 2nd Lieut Queen's Bays, 1888; served Zhob Valley, 1890; Dongola Expedition, 1896; rode through the retreating dervishes with despatches to the Sirdar with flotilla at Debba (medal with 2 clasps, 4th class Medjidie, despatches); Soudan campaign, 1897 (bar); DAAG advanced posts on the Atbara; gun-boat bombardment of Metemmeh, 1st Jan. 1898; reconnaissance and battle of the Atbara (despatches, bar); battle of Khartoum (severe wound, VC, despatches, British medal); Sudan campaign, 1899; suppressed Khalifa Sherif's rising on Blue Nile; preliminary operations and final defeat and death of the two Khalifas at Gedid (4th class Osmanieh, 4 bars to Egyptian medal); assisted in the Sudan surveys; charted the Nile cataracts from Wadi Halfa to Abyssinia; established the fact of existence of S African horse sickness in the Sudan; Abyssinian Frontier Delimitation; South Africa, 1902 (medal 3 clasps, Brevet of Major); promoted Major to the Carabiniers, 1903; Colonel, 1912; Commandant Khartoum District, 1913; served European War; commanded 1st Australian Infantry Brigade in Dardanelles operations from 20 May 1915, including the assault of the Lone Pine Position, on 6 Aug. (despatches four times, CB); the Somme operations and capture of Pozières, 23 July 1916; 2nd Australian Div. operation near Bapaume and capture of Hindenburg Lines, 1917; Cross of Commander of Order of Leopold; 3rd Battle of Ypres, Sept. 1917; Belgian Croix de Guerre; promoted Maj.-Gen. 1918; operations E of Amiens, April 1918; led 59th Div. at Liberation of Lille, 17 Oct. 1918 (Officier, Légion d'Honneur, despatches five times, KCB); Colonel 3rd/6th Dragoon Guards, 1920–25; Hon. Colonel Natal Carbineers, 1920–25; Hon. Colonel, 37/39 Battalion, Australia, 1926; retired pay, 1924. *Recreations:* big game shooting, flying. *Address:* Kongbool, Balmoral, Victoria, Australia. *Club:* Cavalry.

Died 21 July 1941.

SMYTH, Brig.-Gen. Robert Napier, CBE 1919; DSO 1902; late 21st Lancers; *b* 26 June 1868; *o s* of late Gen. J. H. Smyth, CB, of Frimhurst. *Educ:* Wellington. Entered army, 1890; Captain, 1899; Major, 1905; Lt-Col 1910; Col 1914; served Soudan, 1898, including Khartoum (despatches, British medal, Khedive's medal with clasp); DAAG Intelligence, 1900–02; South Africa, 1899–1900, with 13th Hussars (despatches five times, Queen's medal 4 clasps, King's medal 2 clasps, Brevet Major, DSO); General Staff Officer, 2nd Grade, 1914–15; Brigade Commander, 1915; JP Beds. *Address:* Manor Farm, Houghton-Regis, Dunstable, Beds. *Club:* Naval and Military.

Died 14 Oct. 1947.

SMYTH, Lt-Col Robert Riversdale, CMG 1919; DSO 1917; retired; late Leinster Regt; *b* 1875; 3rd *s* of Percy Smyth of Headborough Tallow, Co. Waterford, and Monatrea, Youghal, Co. Cork. *Educ:* Charterhouse. Entered Army, 1900; served South African War (King's and Queen's medal 5 clasps); European War (despatches six times, DSO, CMG). *Address:* Headborough, Tallow, Co. Waterford. *Club:* Army and Navy.

Died 25 April 1946.

SMYTH, Warington; *see* Smyth, H. W.

SMYTH, William Bates; DL, JP Co. Tyrone; Chairman, District Hospital; Member of Tyrone Hospital Committee; *b* 27 Dec. 1874; *s* of Robert Smyth, JP, Strathfoyle, Strabane, and Annie, *d* of William Bates, Strabane; *m* 1919, Lillie Margaret, *d* of T. Coulter Dickie, Omagh, Sessional Crown Solicitor, Co. Tyrone; three *s*. *Educ:* Royal Academical Institution Belfast. Millowner; Lieutenant in North Irish Horse, 1915–19; Master of Strabane Harriers, 1920–40; High Sheriff of Co. Tyrone, 1926; Member of Tyrone County Council. *Recreations:* hunting, football, tennis, hockey, golf. *Address:* Strathfoyle, Strabane, Co. Tyrone, Ireland. *T:* Strabane 321. *Clubs:* Ulster, Belfast: Counties, Omagh: Northern Counties, Londonderry.

Died 28 Sept. 1946.

SMYTH, Rt Rev. William Edmund, MA, MB; *b* 13 April 1858; *s* of Rev. Christopher Smyth, Rector of Woodford, Northants, and Clementina Royds; unmarried. *Educ:* Eton; King's College, Cambridge (1st class Theol Tripos, 1882). Ordained, 1882; Curate St Mary the Less, Cambridge, 1882–86; St Peter's, London Docks, 1886–88; Chaplain to Bishop of Zululand, 1889; Missionary and Theol. Tutor at Isandhlwana, 1889–92; Bishop of Lebombo, 1893–1912; Rector of Woodstock, CP, 1915–20; Warden of the Anglican Hostel South African Native College, Fort Hare, 1921–33; retired, 1932. *Address:* Firwood, Chalford nr Stroud Glos.

Died 5 April 1950.

SMYTH-OSBOURNE, Brig.-Gen. George Nowell Thomas, CB 1920; CMG 1919; DSO 1915; DL, JP, Devonshire; *b* 6 Sept. 1877; *e surv. s* of late John Smyth Smyth-Osbourne of Ash, Co. Devon, and Wortley, Leeds, and Eliza Cotton, *d* of Col Prior of Sidney Place, Bath; *m* 1905, Gladys Marguerite, *o d* of late Sir Leslie Porter; two *s* two *d*. *Educ:* Eton; Sandhurst. Joined Devon Regt, 1898; served S African War, 1899–1902 (despatches); in India with Devon Regt, 1902–05; at Staff College, Camberley, 1907–08; DAA and QMG, Gibraltar, 1910–14; European War, 1914–19 (CB, CMG, DSO); with Devon Regt and on Staff of 4th Div. 4th Army and GHQ (CMG, DSO, Brevets of Maj. and Lt-Col); Expedition to N Russia, 1919 (CB); AA and QMG, 5th Division, 1929–33; retired pay, 1933. *Recreations:* hunting, fishing, shooting. *Address:* Ash, Iddesleigh, N Devon. *T:* Hatherleigh 25. *Club:* Junior United Service.

Died 13 Oct. 1942.

SMYTHE, Sir Edward Walter Joseph Patrick Herbert, 9th Bt *cr* 1660; *b* 20 March 1869; *s* of Sir Walter Smythe, 8th Bt and Marie Louise, 2nd *d* of William Herbert, Clytha Park, Monmouth; *S* father 1919. *Educ:* Downside. *Address:* Acton Burnell Park, Shrewsbury.

Died 9 March 1942.

SMYTHE, Francis Sydney; author; Lt-Col, General List (retd); *b* Ivythorne, Maidstone, 6 July 1900; *s* of late Algernon Sydney Smythe; *m* 1st, 1931, three *s*; 2nd, Nona Isobel Miller, Christchurch, NZ. *Educ:* Berkhamsted School. Electrical Engineer (Faraday House Engineering College), 1919–26; Royal Air Force, 1926–27 (invalided); International Kangchenjunga Expedition, 1930; Mount Kamet Expedition, 1931; Central Himalayas, 1937; Mount Everest Expeditions, 1933, 1936, and 1938, Canadian Rockies, 1946, 1947;

Lloyd George Range Expedition, 1947. *Publications:* Climbs and Ski Runs; The Kangchenjunga Adventure; Kamet Conquered, 1932; An Alpine Journey, 1934; The Spirit of the Hills, 1935; Over Tyrolese Hills, 1936; Camp Six; The Mountain Scene, 1937; The Valley of Flowers, 1938; Peaks and Valleys, 1938; A Camera in the Hills, 1939; Edward Whymper, 1940; Adventures of a Mountaineer, 1940; Mountaineering Holiday, 1940; My Alpine Album, 1940; The Mountain Vision, 1941; Over Welsh Hills, 1941; Secret Mission (a novel), 1942; Alpine Ways, 1942; Snow on the Hills, 1946; Rocky Mountains, 1948; Again Switzerland, 1948; (posthumous) Climbs in The Canadian Rockies, 1950. *Recreations:* gardening, mountaineering and ski-ing. *Address:* Yew Tree Cottage, Colgate, Sussex. *Clubs:* Alpine, Savage.

Died 27 June 1949.

SMYTHE, Lt-Col Rupert Cæsar, CMG 1919; DSO 1918; late Royal Inniskilling Fusiliers; *b* 1879; *s* of late Capt. R. A. Smythe, Court na Farraga, Killiney, Co. Dublin, and Frances, *d* of late Sir Alan Bellingham, 3rd Bart, Castle Bellingham, Co. Louth; *m* 1914, Cecile Isabel Caroline, *d* of late Major Frederick Munn, DSO; one *s*. Served South African War, 1900–02 (Queen's medal and four clasps, King's medal and two clasps); European War, 1914–18 (despatches, CMG, DSO); retired pay, 1930. *Address:* c/o Lloyds Bank, Ltd, 6 Pall Mall, SW1; Augher Castle, Augher, Co. Tyrone.

Died 2 Feb. 1943.

SNAGGE, Sir Harold (Edward), KBE 1920; Director of Barclays Bank, Ltd; Barclays Bank (Dominion, Colonial, and Overseas), Ltd; and other companies; a General Commissioner of Taxes for the City of London; JP Surrey; *b* 28 Dec. 1872; *s* of late Judge Sir Thomas William Snagge, KCMG, DL; *m* 1901, Inez Alfreda (marr. diss. 1943), *d* of Alfred Lubbock, Par, Cornwall; two *s* four *d*. *Educ:* Eton; New College, Oxford; MA. Director and Secretary (unpaid) to the Ministry of Information, 1918; Chairman of D. Napier & Son, Ltd, 1933–43; Fellow of Eton College, 1925–40. *Address:* 13 St Leonard's Terrace, SW3. *Clubs:* Beefsteak, Brooks's, Hurlingham (Chairman, 1922–30).

Died 19 March 1949.

SNEDDON, Rev. James; retired; *b* 2 July 1871; *s* of Richard Sneddon and Janet Govan; *m* Margaret Clark Taylor; no *c*. *Educ:* Glasgow University; Trinity College, Glasgow. Minister of Millerston United Free Church, Trinity Church, Newport, Fife, Wishaw Church, Lanarkshire and Rothesay Church; Treasurer Glasgow Presbytery; Clerk of Presbytery of Perth Fife and Angus; Clerk of Glasgow and District Presbytery; Moderator, United Free Church of Scotland, 1935–36. *Recreations:* golf and bowling. *Address:* 17 Millbrae Crescent, Glasgow, S2.

Died 29 March 1945.

SNELL, 1st Baron *cr* 1931, of Plumstead; **Henry Snell,** PC 1937; CH 1943; CBE 1930; LLD (Lon.), 1936; Captain of the Gentlemen-at-Arms since 1940; Deputy Leader of House of Lords since 1940; Member of Imperial Economic Committee, 1930; Vice-President of Royal Empire Society and Vice-Chairman Royal Institute of International Affairs, 1940–43; Joint-Treasurer of Empire Parliamentary Association; Vice-Chairman of the British Council; Pres. of National Council of Social Service, 1938; *b* 1 April 1865; parents agricultural labourers, Sutton-on-Trent, Newark, Notts; unmarried. *Educ:* Village School; Nottingham University College; London School of Economics; Heidelberg University. Began life as farm worker; was afterwards groom, ferryman, and potman; became clerk at the Nottingham Blind Institution, followed by nine years as Agent of the Woolwich and Nottingham Charity Organisation Societies; was a constant speaker on labour and religious topics; was Secretary to the first Director of the London School of Economics, and afterwards

Hutchinson Trust Lecturer to the Fabian Society; was appointed lecturer to the British Ethical Movement; Member of the London County Council, 1919–25; Chairman of LCC, 1934–38; contested Huddersfield twice in 1910, and again in 1918; MP (Lab) East Woolwich, 1922–31; Parliamentary Under-Secretary of State, India Office, 1931. *Publications:* Daily Life in Parliament; Men, Movements, and Myself, 1936; pamphlets on Co-operation, Alien Immigration, Secular Education, Sunday Games in the Parks, and on various aspects of the British and American Ethical Movement. *Recreations:* none. *Club:* Athenæum.

Died 21 April 1944.

SNELL, Alfred Walter S.; *see* Saxon Snell.

SNEYD, Ralph; DL, JP; *b* 10 Dec. 1863; *e s* of Rev. Walter Sneyd and Henrietta, *d* of Richard Malone Sneyd; *m* 1885, Mary Evelyn (*d* 1923), *e d* of late Maj.-Gen. Sir Arthur E. A. Ellis, GCVO; *m* 1926, Dorothy Charlotte, *er d* of late Dr Ralph S. Miller, of Edinburgh and Kobe, Japan. *Educ:* Radley; Magdalene College, Cambridge. High Sheriff, Stafford, 1892; Colonel Staffordshire Imperial Yeomanry; patron of two livings. *Address:* Keele Hall, Newcastle, Stoke-on-Trent; Bradwell Grange, Codford, Wilts. *Clubs:* White's; Royal Yacht Squadron (Cowes).

Died 25 Dec. 1949.

SNOWDEN, Arthur de Winton, CBE 1920; MA; MD; BCh (Camb.), MRCS LRCP; retired; *b* 12 Sept. 1872; *s* of late Preb. J. H. Snowden; *m* Elizabeth Cecil (*d* 1941), *d* of late Captain Cecil Drummond, of Enderby Hall, Leicester; one *s. Educ:* St Paul's School; Christ's College, Cambridge; St George's Hospital. RMO Grahamstown Hospital, Cape Colony, 1898–99. Civil Surgeon, South African War (Queen's medal with four bars); Hon. Major RAMC in charge of Medical Section of Red Cross Hospital, Netley; Sanatorium work from 1906 at Nordrach-upon-Mendip, Mundesley, and Linford. *Address:* 5 Grosvenor Road, Bournemouth W. *T:* Westbourne 61856.

Died 20 May 1950.

SNOWDEN, Keighley, (James Snowden); novelist and journalist; *b* Preston, Lancashire, 23 June 1860; *s* of late William Snowden of Keighley; *m* 1884, Agnes Wallace, *d* of Andrew Crawford, New Cumnock, Ayr; three *s* one *d. Educ:* School of Science and Art, Keighley. Formerly on the staffs of Yorkshire Observer, Birmingham Daily Post, Yorkshire Post, Daily Mail, Pall Mall Gazette, and Daily Citizen; War Editor, National Food Journal. *Publications:* Tales of the Yorkshire Wolds; The Weaver's Web; The Plunder Pit; Barbara West; Princess Joyce; The Sincler Story; Kate Bannister; Hate of Evil; The Life Class; The Forbidden Theatre; Verity Lads; The Free Marriage; Bright Shame; King Jack; Myth and Legend in the Bible; The Master Spinner: a Life of Sir Swire Smith, MP; Jack the Outlaw; Some Joys of Journalism; The Whip Hand (a play, with late Mrs S. A. P. Kitcat). *Recreations:* gardening and chess. *Address:* 15 Cavendish Road, Brondesbury, NW6. *T:* Willesden 7108. *Club:* Savage.

Died 17 Jan. 1947.

SNOWDEN, Councillor Tom, CBE 1949; JP; Head of Tom Snowden & Son, Ltd, Keighley; Member Keighley Borough Council; *b* Cowling, Yorks, 1875; *m* 1st, 1894, Alice Stephenson; 2nd, 1939, Dorothy E. Carlisle. *Educ:* Cowling Board School. Governor of the Giggleswick Grammar School; Chairman, Bingley Bench of Magistrates; Chairman, Bingley Grammar School Trust; contested Shipley Division, 1918; Skipton Division, 1922; Central Sheffield, 1923 and 1924; MP (Lab) Accrington, 1929–31; Chairman of Bingley UDC, 1921–22; Member of the West Riding County Council,

1913, 1919, and 1925–28; Mayor of Keighley, 1942–43. *Recreation:* golf. *Address:* Rosemount, Bramham Road, Bingley, Yorks.

Died 27 Nov. 1949.

SNOY, Baron Robert; (Belgian); President International Sleeping Car Co.; *b* 4 April 1879; *s* of Baron Maurice Snoy and Baroness H. de Woelmont; *m* 1919, Baroness Lucy de Tornaco; one *s. Educ:* Belgium. *Heir: s* Raoul. *Address:* 21 Boulevard Delessert, Paris. *T:* Trocadero 07250. *Clubs:* Jockey, Paris; Parc, Brussels.

Died 23 May 1946.

SOLOMON, Frank Oakley, FHAS; *b* 1867; *s* of Edwin Solomon; *m* 1896, Marion, *d* of Robert Wilkinson of Little Chilton, Co. Durham; one *s. Educ:* private schools; College of Agriculture, Downton. Received Diploma of membership of College of Agriculture, 1888; Diploma and Life Fellowship of Highland and Agricultural Society, 1892. Held appointments as farm steward in Wilts and Sussex, 1888–90; Agricultural Master in NE County School, Barnard Castle, 1890–93; Senior Lecturer in Agriculture, etc., in the Armstrong College, Newcastle-on-Tyne, and Lecturer in Agriculture to the County Councils of Durham and Northumberland, 1893–99; Headmaster, Dauntsey Agricultural School, Wilts, 1900–19. *Address:* Wimborne, Lansdown Road, Sidcup, Kent.

Died 22 Feb. 1941.

SOLTAU-SYMONS, Lt-Col George Algernon James; late KRR Corps; *b* 1867; *e s* of late G. W. C. Soltau-Symons and Hon. Adèle Isabella (*d* 1869), 2nd *d* of 3rd Lord Graves; *S* father, 1916; *m* 1898, Eleanor, *e d* of late Lt-Gen. Sir William Howley Goodenough, KCB; one *d. Educ:* Eton. Served European War, 1914–18. *Recreations:* shooting, fishing. *Address:* 4 Basil Mansions, Knightsbridge, SW3. *T:* Kensington 7565. *Club:* Naval and Military.

Died 17 Jan. 1947.

SOMBART, Werner, Dr phil., Dr rer. pol., Dr jur., Dr oec; Ordentl Professor der Staatswissenschaften an der Universität Berlin since 1917; *b* Ermsleben am Harz, 19 Jan. 1863; *s* of Anton Ludwig, Parlamentarier; *m* 1st, Felicitas, Tochter des Arztes Genzmer; 2nd, Corina, Tochter des Universitäts-Professor Leon in Jassy (Rumania); one *s* five *d. Educ:* Gymnasium, Berlin, and Schleusingen; University of Pisa and University of Berlin; Juristisches Staatsexamen, 1885; Syndikus der Handels-Kammer, Bremen, 1888; Ausserordentl. Professor, Universität Breslau, 1890; Professor, Handelshochschule, Berlin, 1906. *Publications:* Hauptschriften; Sozialismus und Soziale Bewegung, 1896, 10 Aufl. udT Proletarischer Sozialismus, 2 Bd. 1924; Der Moderne Kapitalismus, 1 Aufl. 1902; Neue Bearbeitung, 1917–1927, 3 Bde; Die Juden und das Wirtschaftsleben, 1911, 15 Tausend 1927; Der Bourgeois, 1913, 9 Tausend 1927; Die drei Nationalökonomien, 1930; Die Zukunft des Kapitalismus, 1932; Deutscher Sozialismus, 1934; Vom Menschen Versuch einer Geisteswissenschaftlichen Anthropologie, 1938. *Address:* Berlin Grünewald, Humboldtstrasse 35a, Germany. *T:* 97–6297.

Died 19 May 1941.

SOMERLEYTON, Phyllis, Baroness, CBE 1918; *y d* of General Sir Henry de Bathe, 4th Bt, KCB; *m* 1887, 1st Baron Somerleyton, PC, GCVO (*d* 1935); one *s* two *d. Educ:* home. *Address:* South View, Bury Road, Newmarket, Cambs. *T:* Newmarket 2788.

Died 22 Nov. 1948.

SOMERS, 6th Baron *cr* 1784; **Arthur Herbert Tennyson Somers Cocks;** Bt 1772, KCMG 1926; DSO 1918; MC; DL, JP Herefordshire, Lord Lieutenant, since 1933; Chief Scout for Great Britain since 1941; Chief Scout of the British Commonwealth since 1941; Red Cross Commission in the Middle East since 1940; *b* 20 March 1887; *s* of late Captain H. H. Somers Cocks,

Coldstream Guards, and Blanche Margaret Standish, d of Major Herbert Clogstoun, VC, RE; S great uncle, 1899; m 1921, Daisy Finola, yr d of late Capt. Bertram Meeking, and step d of Herbert Johnson, of Marsh Court, Stockbridge; one d. Educ: Mulgrave Castle; Charterhouse; New College, Oxford. Lt-Col, late 1st Life Guards; attached Tank Corps; served European War, 1914–18 (DSO, MC, Chevalier Légion d'honneur); retired, 1922; Joint MFH Ledbury, 1922–24; Governor of Victoria, 1926–31; acting Governor-General of Australia, 1930–31; Pres. MCC 1936–37. Publication: History of the 6th (Light) Tank Battalion. Heir: uncle Arthur Percy Somers Cocks, b 1864. Address: Eastnor Castle, Ledbury, Herefordshire. Club: Turf.

Died 14 July 1944.

SOMERSET, Henry Charles Somers Augustus; b 18 May 1874; s of late Rt Hon. Lord Henry Somerset, and Isabel (d 1921), e d and co-heiress of last Earl Somers; heir-pres. to 10th Duke of Beaufort, KG, PC, GCVO; m 1st, 1896, Katherine de Vere Beauclerk, 4th d of 10th Duke of St Albans (who divorced him, 1920, and m 2nd, 1921, Maj.-Gen. Hon. Sir W. Lambton); one s; 2nd, 1932, Brenda, Marchioness of Dufferin and Ava. Educ: Marlborough; Balliol College, Oxford; DL Herefordshire and Worcestershire; JP Surrey. Contested (L) Croydon, 1906; served S African War (Queen's medal); European War, 1914–18 (despatches twice, 1914 Star, Chevalier Legion of Honour, OBE). Address: Sheldon Manor, Chippenham, Wilts. Clubs: Brooks's, Turf, Beefsteak; Royal Yacht Squadron, Cowes.

Died 25 Nov. 1945.

SOMERSET, Sir Thomas, Kt 1944; DL, Managing Director, Thomas Somerset & Co. Ltd; Director, Commercial Insurance Co. of Ireland, Ltd; Thompsons (Belfast) Ltd, Belfast; Chairman Northern Counties Committee of the LMS Railway; b Belfast, 14 Dec. 1870; o s of James Somerset, engineer; m 1906, Ethel, y d of late Thomas Parker, Baguley House, Cheshire; one s one d. Educ: Largymore, Co. Down. Started in business for self, 1891, founding firm of Thos Somerset & Co. Ltd, with factories at Belfast, Greyabbey, and Portaferry, giving employment to about 1500. MP (U) North Belfast, 1929–45. Recreations: hunting and golf. Address: Malone, Belfast. TA: Somersault Belfast. T: Belfast 65070. Clubs: Carlton, Constitutional; Ulster Reform, Belfast; Royal Co. Down Golf.

Died 16 June 1947.

SOMERSET-THOMAS, William Edwin; Mus. Doc. Oxford; Professor of Music University College, Auckland, 1900–33; Conductor Auckland Choral Society and Royal Auckland Male Choir, 1900; Organist and Choirmaster, St Mary's Cathedral, since 1902; now Organist and Choirmaster St Paul's Church, Auckland; b Oxford, 1867; s of E. J. Thomas; m Agnes, d of Dr W. P. Somerset, Claydon, Bucks, and of Havering Manor, Wilts; two s two d. Educ: Christ Church Cathedral School; Oxford University. Organist, SS Mary and John, Cowley, Oxford; Organist and Director of Music, All Saints', Bloxham, Banbury; Organist and CM, St Clement's, Bournemouth; Mus. Bac. Oxford, 1888; Mus. Doc. Oxford, 1903; Examiner for NZ degrees, Matriculation Education Board of NZ; Founder University Glees Madrigal Society. Publications: Psalm 71; Cantata for solo voices and 8–part chorus, full orchestra; Cantata, The Nativity, solo, chorus, and full orchestra; Mass in C for male voices and full orchestra; Symphony in F full orchestra; numerous anthems, glees, part-songs, etc.; winner of three prizes for Madrigals in Elizabethan style. Recreations: riding, driving, cycling. Address: c/o University College, Auckland, NZ. Clubs: Pacific, Auckland.

Died 16 Aug. 1946.

SOMERVILLE, Sir Annesley Ashworth, KBE 1939; MA (Cantab); JP; VD; MP (C) Windsor Division of Berks since 1922; b 1858; e s of David A. Somerville, Ballincollig, Co. Cork; m Ethel Elizabeth, e d of late Dr William Orange, CB, Superintendent of Broadmoor (two s lost in war of 1914–18), three d. Educ: Queen's College, Cork; Trinity College, Cambridge (Mathematical Scholar), MA; 21st Wrangler Mathematical Tripos, 1880. Rowed in First Trinity Boat; lived in France, 1880–81; Assistant Master at Wellington College, 1882–84; Assistant Master and Head of the Army Class at Eton, 1885–1922; commanded Eton Volunteer Corps, 1902–06; Member of Eton Board of Guardians, 1892–1922; Chairman of Eton Urban District Council; Ruling Councillor of the Slough Habitation of the Primrose League; Commanded 1st Batt. Bucks Vol. Regt during the War; Hon. Sec. Eton Workingmen's Allotment Society since 1892; President of the Independent Schools Association since 1927; a Conservator of the River Thames. Publications: various educational works. Recreations: rowing, golf. Address: 4 Courthope Road, Wimbledon, SW19. T: Wimbledon 3164. Clubs: United University, 1900, Free Forester Cricket, MCC, Leander.

Died 15 May 1942.

SOMERVILLE, Arthur Fownes; JP; Recorder of Wells since 1916; b 23 April 1850; e s of J. C. Somerville, JP, DL, Dinder House, Wells, and Emily Periam, d of Sir Alexander Hood, 2nd Bt; m 1880, Ellen (d 1928), d of W. S. Sharland, Woodbridge, New Norfolk, Tasmania; two s one d. Educ: Marlborough College; Trinity Hall, Cambridge (LLB 1873). Bar, Middle Temple 1875; joined W Circuit; Lieut N Somerset Yeomanry, 1873–77; succeeded his father as owner of Dinder and Ham Estate, 1876; CC Somerset, 1892–1937; Deputy Chairman Quarter Sessions, 1910–31; Chairman Standing Joint Committee, 1917–32; High Sheriff, Somerset, 1909–10; Member of House of Laymen, 1905–25; Member, National Church Assembly, 1920–37; Fellow, Royal Colonial Institute, 1881; Member, Royal Sanitary Institute; Vice-President, Bath and West Society; President, Somerset Archæological Society, 1907 and 1933; represented Cambridge at the Inter-Varsity Athletic Sports, 1872–73, in the Three-Mile Race, and won four miles AAC Championship, 1873; during European War was Chairman of Somerset Appeal Tribunal sitting at Bath. Publications: articles in journals of Bath and West Agricultural Society, and papers read before Royal Sanitary Institute Conferences. Address: Dinder House, Wells, Somerset. TA: Dinder. T: Dinder 3. Club: Oxford and Cambridge.

Died 21 Nov. 1942.

SOMERVILLE, Edith Anna Œnone, Hon. LittD Trinity College, Dublin, 1932; b 2 May 1858; d of late Lt-Col Somerville, DL of Drishane, and Adelaide (d of Admiral Sir Josiah Coghill, 3rd Bt, and g d of Charles Kendal Bushe, Chief Justice of Ireland). Educ: home. Studied art at the studios of Colarossi and Délécluse in Paris; Royal Westminster School of Art, Lond., etc. Master of the West Carbery Foxhounds, 1903–08; re-established West Carbery Foxhounds, May 1912. MFH 1912–19; is a Founder Member of Irish Academy of Letters, 1933, awarded its Gregory Medal, 1941; Member, Union Internationale des Beaux-Arts et des lettres; has exhibited in London and Dublin (in oils), and has done a good deal of illustration in black and white and colours; One Man Shows, Goupil Galleries, Jan. 1920; Walkers' Galleries, Dec. 1923; Walkers Galleries, Dec. 1927; Aiken, New York, 1929; and New York, 1938; In collaboration with her cousin, the late 'Martin Ross' (Miss Violet Martin of Ross, Co. Galway), has written many books and magazine articles. Publications: Novels, etc., in collaboration with 'Martin Ross'—An Irish Cousin; Naboth's Vineyard Through Connemara in a Governess Cart; In the Vine Country; The Real Charlotte; The Silver Fox; Some Experiences of an Irish

RM; All on the Irish Shore; Some Irish Yester days; Further Experiences of an Irish RM; Dan Russel, the Fox; In Mr Knox's Country; Irish Memories; Mount Music; Strayaways; An Enthusiast; Wheel-Tracks; The Big House of Inver; French Leave; The States through Irish Eyes (illustrated by Author); An Incorruptible Irish man (Charles Kendal Bushe) The Smile and the Tear; The Sweet Cry of Hounds (illustrated by the Author); Sarah's Youth; Records of the Somerville family; Notions in Garrison; Happy Days; Essays of sorts (illustrated by the Author); Sporting Picture Books—A Patrick's Day Hunt; Slipper's ABC of Foxhunting. Children's Picture Book—The Discontented Little Elephant; an Edition de Luxe, entitled The Hitchcock Edition of the Sporting Works of E. Œ. Somerville and Martin Ross, 1927. *Recreations:* horses and dogs. *Address:* Tally Ho House, Castle Townshend, Co. Cork. *TA:* Castletownshend. *Clubs:* PEN; Cork County (Cork).

Died 8 Oct. 1949.

SOMERVILLE, Vice-Adm. Hugh Gaultier-Coghill, CB 1922; DSO 1918; *b* 1873; *s* of Lieut-Col T. H. Somerville, The Buffs, of Drishane, Skibbereen, Co. Cork; *m* Mary, *d* of E. Hancock, of Patras, Greece; one *s*. *Educ:* HMS Britannia. Served European War, 1914–19 (despatches, DSO Italian War Cross); retired list, 1924. *Address:* Malmaison, Castle Townshend, Co. Cork. *TA:* Castletownshend. *Club:* Cork County (Cork).

Died 16 Nov. 1950.

SOMERVILLE, Lt-Col James Aubrey Henry Bellingham, DSO 1919; *b* 1884; 2nd *s* of late B. A. Somerville, RIC; *m* 1927, Margaret Lucy, *y d* of Sir J. R. Starkey, 1st Bt. *Educ:* RMA, Woolwich. Served Royal Artillery, 1902–36; European War, 1914–19 (despatches, DSO) retired, 1936; RAFVR 1940–43; Squadron Leader RAFVR 1942; Lieut-Comdr RNVR 1944–45. *Address:* Twissells, Frampton Mansell, Glos. *Club:* Army and Navy.

Died 13 April 1950.

SOMERVILLE, Adm. of the Fleet Sir James Fownes, GCB 1944; GBE 1946; KCB 1939; KBE 1941; CB 1935; DSO 1916; Lord Lieutenant for the County of Somerset, since 1946; *b* 1882; *s* of late Arthur Fownes Somerville, Dinder House, Somerset; *m* 1913, Mary Kerr (*d* 1945), *d* of late Colonel T. Ryder Main, CB, CMG; one *s* one *d*. Entered Navy, 1898; Commander, 1915; Captain, 1921; Rear-Admiral, 1933; Vice-Admiral, 1937; served European War (Dardanelles), 1915–16 (despatches, DSO); Director of the Signal Department, Admiralty, 1925–27; Flag-Captain to Vice-Admiral John D. Kelly, 1927–29; Naval Instructor, Imperial Defence College, 1929–31; HMS Norfolk, 1931–32; Commodore of RN Barracks, Portsmouth, 1932–34; Director of Personal Services, Admiralty, 1934–36; Commanding Destroyer Flotillas, Mediterranean Fleet, 1936–38; Commander-in-Chief, East Indies, 1938–39; retired list, 1939; on special service at Admiralty, 1939; Officer commanding Force H, 1940–42; Admiral on retired list, 1942; Commander-in-Chief, Eastern Fleet, 1942–44; reinstated on active list, 1944; Head of British Admiralty Delegation, Washington, 1944–45; Admiral of the Fleet, 1945. *Address:* Dinder House, Somerset. *Clubs:* Junior United Service, Royal Cruising.

Died 19 March 1949.

SOMERVILLE, Comdr Philip, DSO 1939; DSC 1941; Bar to DSC 1942; Bar to DSO 1942; RN; *b* 5 Dec. 1906; *s* of Vice-Admiral H. G. C. Somerville, CB, DSO. *Educ:* RN Colleges, Osborne and Dartmouth. HMS Revenge, Naval Cadet, 1924; Lieutenant, RN and Pilot, Fleet Air Arm, 1929–31; Lieutenant HMS Keith, 1931–33; Ierissos Earthquake, 1932 (Officer of Order of the Phœnix of Greece); HMS Grimsby, 1933–36; Lt-Cmdr HMS Echo, 1937; in Command HMS Wren,

1938; in Command HMS Kingston, 1939; Commander, 1941. *Address:* Malmaison, Castletownshend, Co. Cork. *Club:* Naval and Military.

Died 4 April 1942.

SOMERVILLE, Col Thomas Cameron FitzGerald, MVO 1911; *b* 30 March 1860; *e s* of late Lt-Col Somerville, DL, of Drishane, and Adelaide, *d* of Admiral Sir Josiah Coghill, 3rd Bt, and *g d* of Charles Kendal Bushe, Chief Justice of Ireland; unmarried. *Educ:* Clifton College; Sandhurst. 2nd Lieut 1/4th The King's Own Royal Regt, 1879; ADC to GOC China and Straits Settlements, 1885–89; ADC to GOC S Africa, 1891–95; commanded 1/ The King's Own (Royal Lancaster Regt), 1906–10; Commandant Royal Military School of Music, Kneller Hall, June 1910–May 1919; selected to command the massed bands (1600 bandsmen drawn from 21 British and 25 Indian Army Bands) at the Delhi Coronation Durbar, 1911. *Recreation:* music. *Address:* Drishane, Skibbereen, Co. Cork, Ireland. *TA:* Castletownshend. *Clubs:* Overseas; Cork County.

Died 30 Jan. 1942.

SOMJEE, Mahomedbhoy Alladinbhoy; Puisne Judge Bombay High Court since 1937; *b* 19 Jan. 1889; 3rd *s* of late Alladibhoy Somjee, Bombay; *m* 1937, Jaloo, *o c* of late Nowroji Kaikobad Panthakey; no *c*. *Educ:* Elphinstone College, Bombay, MA, LLB (Bom.). Barrister-at-Law; Vakil of Bombay High Court, 1916–20; called to English Bar, Middle Temple, 1922; Advocate, High Court of Bombay, 1922–37; Professor of Law at Government Law College, Bombay for 3 years. *Recreation:* gardening. *Address:* Glenridge, Ridge Road, Malabar Hill, Bombay 6. *T:* 43368. *Club:* Bombay Bar Gymkhana.

Died 13 June 1942.

SOMMERVILLE, Norman; KC 1921; Chairman Central Council Canadian Red Cross Society since 1930; Vice-President, Sterling Trust Corporation; *b* Toronto, 24 Oct. 1878; *s* of Francis Sommerville and Margaret Kinnear; *m* 1907, Annabel Shipley; two *s* three *d*. *Educ:* Trinity University and Osgoode Hall, Toronto. Practised as Barrister since 1902; Member of Executive Canadian Red Cross since 1920; Chief Organizer Canada's Victory Loan Campaign, 1917, and many other patriotic campaigns; Parliamentary Counsel to House of Commons special Price Spreads Commission, 1934; Governor and Member Executive Committee, League of Red Cross Societies; Special Crown Counsel many important criminal trials including trial of the 8 governing members of the Communist Party and their conviction as members of an illegal association. *Recreations:* fishing, gardening, travel. *Address:* 1 St Edmunds Drive, Toronto, Canada. *TA:* Norsom. *T:* Hudson 2747. *Clubs:* National, Albany, Empire, Rotary, Toronto.

Died 4 July 1941.

SONDES, 3rd Earl *cr* 1880; **Lewis Arthur Milles;** Baron Sondes, 1760; Viscount Throwley, 1880; late Lt-Col 3rd Batt. Yorks Light Infantry (Militia); *b* 3 Oct. 1866; 3rd *s* of 1st Earl and Charlotte, *d* of Sir Henry Stracey, 5th Bt; *S* brother, 1907; *m* 1913, Beatrice (*d* 1935), *d* of late Percy Hale-Wallace, of Muckamore Abbey, Co. Antrim, and *widow* of James Meakin, Westwood Manor, Staffs. Formerly Capt. 16th Lancers; served with Imperial Yeomanry, S Africa, 1900 (Queen's medal three clasps). *Heir: nephew* George Henry Milles-Lade, *b* 8 Feb. 1914. *Address:* Lees Court, Faversham, Kent. *Club:* Cavalry.

Died 17 Jan. 1941.

SONG ONG SIANG, Sir, KBE 1936; CBE 1927; VD. Was an Unofficial Member of Legislative Council of Straits Settlements. *Address:* Singapore, SS.

Died 29 Sept. 1941.

SOPER, George, RE; artist; *b* 1870; *s* of George Robert Soper and Elizabeth Longman; *m*; two *d. Educ:* Ramsgate. *Publications:* various. *Recreation:* horticulture. *Address:* Harmer Green, Welwyn, Herts. *Club:* Print Collectors.

Died 13 Aug. 1942.

SOPWITH, Ven. Thomas Karl, MA; Archdeacon Emeritus of Canterbury since 1942, and Hon. Canon since 1943; *b* 28 May 1873; *e s* of late Arthur Sopwith, MInst.CE; *m* 1902, Esmé Marian, *o d* of late Frederick A. Hankey, MP, of Silverlands, Chertsey; two *d. Educ:* Emmanuel College (Cambridge) (Scholar and Thorpe Exhibitioner); Carus University Prizeman, 1895; BA 1895; MA 1899. Deacon, 1896; Priest, 1897; Curate of Walsall, 1896; of St Peter's Cranley Gardens, 1901; Vicar of Shoreham, Kent, 1903; St James-the-Less, Westminster, 1908; Aylesford, 1909; Ashford, Kent, 1915; Vicar of Maidstone, 1924–34; Rural Dean of Sutton, 1928–34; Hon. Canon of Canterbury, 1925–34; Examining Chaplain to Bishop of Lincoln, 1920–32; Canon of Canterbury, 1934–42; Archdeacon of Maidstone, 1934–39; Archdeacon of Canterbury, 1939–42; Proctor in Convocation, 1929–42. *Address:* Upway, St Martin's Hill, Canterbury. *T:* Canterbury 4537. *Club:* Union.

Died 14 Dec. 1945.

SORELL-CAMERON, Lt-Col George Cecil Minett; *see* Cameron.

SORSBIE, Brig.-Gen. Robert Fox, CB 1920; CSI 1919; CIE 1917; RE; *b* 19 March 1866; *s* of late Rev. R. Sorsbie; *m* Augusta Helen Craufurd, *d* of late Lt-Col J. B. Ridout, JP, CC; two *s. Educ:* Sutton Valence; Woolwich. Entered Army, Royal Engineers, 1885; Captain, 1894; Major, 1902; Lt-Col 1910; Col 1913; Chief Engineer, Northern Command, India, 1917–20; Deputy Director, Military Works, Southern Command, India, 1920–23; retired, 1923; Hon. Brig.-Gen.; served Upper Burma Field Force, 1887 (medal and two clasps), European War (Indian Frontier), 1917–18 (CIE, CSI); North-West Frontier Force (Afghan War), 1919 (CB). *Publication:* Geology for Engineers. *Address:* 61 Wimborne Road, Bournemouth. *T:* Bournemouth 2593. *Club:* Overseas League.

Died 29 April 1948.

SORSBY, Maurice, MD, FRCS; Hon. Assistant Surgeon, Metropolitan Ear, Nose and Throat Hospital; Hon. Ear, Nose and Throat Surgeon, London Jewish Hospital, and Plaistow Children's Hospital; Past President, Lond. Jewish Hospital Medical Society; late Editor Medical Forum; Joint Editor Pocket Monographs of Practical Medicine, and of Short Histories of Medicine; *b* 23 Nov. 1898; *s* of Jacob and Elka Sourasky; *m* 1933, Rose Goldfein; two *s. Educ:* Leeds, Edinburgh, London and Vienna. *Publications:* Cancer and Race, 1931; Beethoven's Deafness, Journal of Otolaryngology, 1930; Premedication in Tonsil Operations, Brit. Med. Jl, 1930; Deafness and its Prevention, Lancet, 1932; Tempero-Sphenoidal Abscess, Proc. Roy. Soc. of Medicine, 1936, etc. *Address:* 38 Creighton Avenue, N10.

Died 6 April 1949.

SOUTAR, Andrew; novelist; *b* 13 Dec. 1879. Travelled extensively Near and Far East, Spain, Portugal, America; served in Air Force during War and in North Russia during 1919. *Publications:* About fifty Novels, including The Chosen of the Gods, 1909; The Island of Test, 1910; Broken Ladders, 1912; Magpie House, 1913; Charity Corner, 1915 (published in New York under title The Honor of his House); The Green Orchard, 1916; The Road to Romance; Hornet's Nest; Neither do I Condemn Thee, 1924; Consider Your Verdict, 1928; Not Mentioned, 1930; Strange Bedfellows; Opportunity; Tomorrow Is Yesterday, 1933; Night of Horror, 1934; Cowards' Castle, 1934; Story of Peter Trussock, 1940; With Ironside in North Russia, 1940; play: If We But Knew: many film plays. *Recreation:* all sports. *Address:* c/o Hutchinson & Cc., 34 Paternoster Row, EC4.

Died 24 Nov. 1941.

SOUTAR, William, MA; *b* Perth, 28 April 1898; *s* of John Soutar, joiner and contractor, and Margaret Gow Smith. *Educ:* Southern District School, Perth. Perth Academy; Edinburgh University. Left school Dec. 1916, to join Navy; served on the lower deck in American waters, and with the Grand Fleet; experienced life aboard Q boat, light cruiser, battle-cruiser, and tramp; demob. Feb. 1919; entered Edinburgh University, Oct. 1919; published an anonymous book of verse, Feb. 1923; graduated MA (Hons in English), July 1923. *Publications:* Gleanings by An Undergraduate (anon.), 1923; Conflict, a selection of poems, 1931; Seeds in the Wind, verses in Scots for Children, 1933; The Solitary Way, poems, 1934; Brief Words (100 epigrams), 1935; Poems in Scots, 1935; A Handful of Earth, poems, 1936; Riddles in Scots, 1937; In the Time of Tyrants, poems privately printed, 1939; But the Earth Abideth, a verse-sequence, 1943; other work to be found in English, American and Continental periodicals, also anthologies. *Recreation:* reading. *Address:* Inglelowe, 27 Wilson Street, Craigie, Perth.

Died 15 Oct. 1943.

SOUTER, Prof. Alexander, DLitt (Aber.) 1905; MA (Oxon) 1908; BA (Cantab) 1896; MA (Cantab) 1930; DD (St Andrews) 1923; (Dublin) 1932, LLD (Aber.) 1938; FBA 1926 (Member of Council, 1938–47); Corresponding Fellow, Mediæval Academy of America, 1938; Active Member, New Society of Letters of Lund (Sweden) 1927; *b* Perth, 14 Aug. 1873; *e s* of Alexander Souter and Elsie Cruickshank; *m* 1899, Elizabeth Barr, *e d* of William Blair Anderson, Aberdeen, Scotland; three *d. Educ:* Sharp's Educational Institution, Perth; Robert Gordon's College and University, Aberdeen; Gonville and Caius College, Cambridge (Scholar); First Class in Classical Tripos, Part I, 1896, and Second Class in Part II, 1897; graduated MA, Aberdeen University, with First Class Honours Classics, and Jenkyns Prize in Classical Philology, 1893; Ferguson Scholar in Classics, 1893; Fullerton Scholar in Classics, 1894. Univ. Assistant in Humanity and Lecturer in Latin, 1897–1903; Lecturer in Mediæval Palæography, Aberdeen Univ., 1903, 1913–37; Vice-Chancellor, Aberdeen Univ., 1935–36; Yates Prof. of New Testament Greek and Exegesis, and Librarian Mansfield Coll., Oxford, 1903–11; Regius Professor of Humanity in the University of Aberdeen, 1911–37; Curator of Aberdeen Univ. Library, 1919–24; Stone Lecturer, Princeton Theological Seminary, 1924–25, 1927–28; Norton Lecturer, Southern Baptist Theological Seminary, Louisville, USA, 1924–25; Russell Lecturer, Auburn Theological Seminary, USA, 1932–33; awarded British Academy Medal for Biblical Studies, 1932; has served as external examiner in the Universities of Aberdeen, Birmingham, Cambridge, Edinburgh, Glasgow, London, Manchester, Oxford, Reading, St Andrews; formerly a Director of the London Missionary Society. *Publications:* edited Horæ Latinæ, by the late Robert Ogilvie, LLD, 1901; edited, with George Middleton, MA, Livy Book xxviii, 1902; De Codicibus Manuscriptis Augustini Quæstionum, 1905; A Study of Ambrosiaster, 1905; edited Pseudo-Augustini Quaestiones Veteris et Novi Testamenti cxxvii, 1908; Novum Testamentum Graece: textui a Retractatoribus Anglis adhibito brevem adparatum criticum subiecit, 1910, second edition, 1947; Text and Canon of the New Testament, 1913; a Pocket Lexicon to the Greek New Testament, 1916; Tertullian's Apology, Notes of the late Prof. John E. B. Mayor, 1917; Tertullian's Treatises translated (3 vols 1919, 1920, 1922); Pelagius's Expositions of Thirteen Epistles of St Paul—I Introduction, 1922; II Text, etc., 1926; III Appendix, 1931; part author of Novum Testamentum S. Irenaei by

Sanday, Turner, etc., 1923; editor of Tertulliani Apologeticus, 1926; The Earliest Latin Commentaries on the Epistles of St Paul, 1927; edited C. H. Turner's The Oldest Manuscript of the Vulgate Gospels, 1931; Glossary of the later Latin (ad 180–600), 1948; has written papers in various classical and theological journals. *Recreations:* walking, reading of French and Spanish literature, listening to orchestral music. *Address:* 3 Canterbury Road, Oxford.

Died 17 Jan. 1949.

SOUTER, Col (Brig.) Hugh Maurice Wellesley, CMG 1917; DSO 1916; *b* 1873; *s* of late Sir Frank Souter, KCSI, CIE. *Educ:* Clifton; RMC, Sandhurst. Joined Manchester Regt, 1892; 14th Bengal Lancers, 1897; commanded, 1916–20; served Tibet Expedition, 1903–04 (despatches, medal and clasp); operations, NW Frontier, 1911 (wounded, despatches); European War (France, Gallipoli, Egypt, and Mesopotamia), 1914–19 (despatches several times, CMG, DSO, Croix de Guerre avec palme); led the cavalry charge of the Dorset Yeomanry against the Senussis in Feb. 1916 (horse killed) and with an officer and trooper of the regt personally captured Ja'far Pasha-El Askari, the Turkish comdr of the force with all his staff; commanded column in Kurdistan, 1918–19 (horse killed, despatches); Commander Bareilly Brigade, also 1st and 2nd Cavalry Brigades in India, 1919–21; commanded 9th Infantry Brigade, Waziristan Field Force, 1921 (medal and clasp). *Clubs:* Cavalry; Turf, Cairo.

Died 6 Aug. 1941.

SOUTER, William Lochiel Berkeley, CIE 1910; King's Police Medal, 1909; *b* 27 Feb. 1865; *s* of Sir Frank Souter, KCSI. *Educ:* Cheltenham College. Joined Indian Police, 1885; Commissioner of Police, Bombay City, 1906; Deputy Director Criminal Intelligence under Govt of India, 1907; Deputy Inspector-General of Police, 1907–15; Inspector-General of Police, Bombay Presidency, 1915; retired, 1920. *Address:* c/o The National Bank of India, 26 Bishopsgate, EC2. *Clubs:* East India United Service, Roehampton; Byculla, Royal Bombay Yacht, Bombay; Sind, Karachi; Club of Western India, Western India, Turf, Poona.

Died 28 June 1945.

SOUTHALL, Joseph Edward, RWS 1931; ARWS 1925; artist and designer; Associé Société Nationale des Beaux Arts, Paris; Member of New English Art Club; *b* Nottingham, 1861; *m* 1903. *Educ:* Ackworth, York; Scarborough. After four years in architect's office, realized that all best art was architectural and that the architect must be an artist; accordingly studied drawing and carving; visited France and Italy to study ancient monuments of art; much influenced by Ruskin; became interested in Tempera Painting in Italy, 1883; practised this art with one interval till present time as being the most appropriate for decorative or monumental as opposed to portable art; has also painted in true fresco on wall of Art Gallery, Birmingham; and in public Reception Room, Council House, Birmingham; always a disciple of XIV and XV century Italians; received great help from Sir William Richmond, and later from Sir Edward Burne-Jones; designer of furniture and needlework and engraver on copper; member of Art Workers' Guild, Society of Painters in Tempera; Pres. Birmingham Royal Society of Artists. *Publications:* Illustrations to Blue Beard and Fables and Illustrations. *Address:* 13 Charlotte Road, Edgbaston, Birmingham.

Died 6 Nov. 1944.

SOUTHBOROUGH, 1st Baron *cr* 1917; **Francis John Stephens Hopwood,** PC 1912; GCB 1916; GCMG 1908; GCVO 1917; KCB 1901; KCSI 1920; KCMG 1906; CB 1895; CMG 1893; *b* 2 Dec. 1860; *s* of late James T. Hopwood, Barrister-at-law, Lincoln's Inn, and Anne Ellen, *d* of John Stone, DL, JP, of the Prebendal, Thame, Oxon, and Long Crendon, Bucks; *m* 1st, 1885,

Alice (*d* 1889), *sister* of Col Smith-Neill, Scots Guards, of Barnwell and Swindridge Muir, Ayrshire; one *s* one *d*; 2nd, 1892, Florence (*d* 1940), *d* of Lt-Gen. S. Black, CSI, CIE; one *s* one *d. Educ:* Louth. Admitted a Solicitor 1882; Assistant Solicitor to Board of Trade, 1885; Private Sec. to the President of the Board of Trade, 1892; Secretary to the Railway Department, 1893; employed upon several occasions on missions to Canada, Newfoundland, and the United States, 1887–93; founded the Hospital and Medical Service for the Canadian and Newfoundland fishermen; a British Delegate to the International Railway Congress in London, 1895, and in Paris, 1900; was member of Royal Commission on London Traffic, and member of Royal Commission on Shipping Rings, the Royal Commission on Electoral Reform; the Royal Commission on Canals; Secretary to the Chairman of the Select Committee on the Jameson Raid, and a member of the Commission to South Africa to advise on the Constitution for the Transvaal and Orange River Colonies; Permanent Secretary Board of Trade, 1901–07; Permanent Under-Secretary of State for Colonies, 1907–11; on staff of Prince of Wales during visit to Canada, 1908; Secretary of the Order of St Michael and St George, 1907–11; Vice-Chairman of the Development Commission, 1910; on staff of HRH the Duke of Connaught to open Union Parliament in South Africa, 1910; a Civil Lord of the Admiralty, 1912–17, and Chairman Grand Committee on War Trade during War; Hon. Secretary Irish Convention, 1917–18; President Commission to India on Reform, 1918–19; President China Association. *Heir: s* Hon. James Spencer Neill Hopwood. *Address:* 14 Campden Hill Square, W8. *Club:* Brooks's.

Died 17 Jan. 1947.

SOUTHESK, 10th Earl of, *cr* 1633; **Charles Noel Carnegie,** LLD (Hon. St Andrews); DL, JP; Baron Carnegie, 1616; Baron Balinhard (UK), 1869; Baronet of Nova Scotia, 1663; *b* 20 March 1854; *e s* of 9th Earl of Southesk and Lady Catherine Hamilton Noel, *d* of 1st Earl of Gainsborough; *S* father, 1905; *m* 1891, Ethel, *o c* of Sir Alexander Bannerman, 9th Bt of Elsick, three *s* two *d.* Col Comm. Forfar and Kincardine RGA (M). Conservative. Owns about 22,700 acres (the park within walls at Kinnaird, about 1300 acres, contains Japanese deer and fallow deer, and a herd of Highland cattle). Owns a large collection of pictures by old masters, Italian, Dutch and Flemish, French and German; also a number of family portraits by Jamesone, Lely, Alan Ramsay, Raeburn, etc.; among these the fine full-length portrait of Agnes, Lady Carnegie, by Raeburn, and the well-known portrait by Jamesone of the great Marquis of Montrose, æt. 17, when he married Lady Magdalene, *d* of 1st Earl of Southesk. He has also a cabinet of antique gems, chiefly intaglios, consisting of about 600, of many types, including 150 cylinders—Accadian, Babylonian, Assyrian, Persian, Hittite, etc. There is also at Kinnaird Castle a library comprising many valuable books, both ancient and modern; among these, especially, The Missal of Sarum, fol. 1497, and extremely fine copies of the 1632 and 1685 Shakespeare folios. *Heir: s* Lord Carnegie, KCVO. *Address:* Kinnaird Castle, Brechin, Scotland; Crimonmogate, Lonmay.

Died 10 Nov. 1941.

SOUTHWELL, 5th Viscount *cr* 1776; **Arthur Robert Pyers Southwell;** Bt 1662; Baron Southwell, 1717; Major late Shropshire Yeomanry; sometime Lt-Col Bn Machine Gun Corps; *b* Talacre, 16 Nov. 1872; *s* of 4th Viscount and Charlotte, *d* of Sir Pyers Mostyn, 8th Bt, Talacre, Flintshire; *S* father, 1878; *m* 1897, Dorothy Katharine, *d* of 1st Lord Waleran; three *s* two *d. Educ:* The Oratory School, Edgbaston. *Heir: s* Commander Hon. Robert A. W. J. Southwell, RN. *Address:* Bourne House, East Woodhay, Newbury. *T:* Highclere 109.

Died 5 Oct. 1944.

SOUTHWOOD, 1st Viscount *cr* 1946, of Fernhurst; **Julius Salter Elias;** 1st Baron *cr* 1937; Newspaper Proprietor and Publisher; Chairman and Managing Director of Odhams Press Limited, Odhams (Watford) Limited, Daily Herald (1929) Limited, Coming Fashions Limited, Dean and Son Limited, English Newspapers Limited, General Press Limited, Press Printers Limited, Victoria House Printing Co. Ltd, Wyman's London Printing Co. Ltd; Chairman of Illustrated Newspapers Ltd, Illustrated London News & Sketch Ltd, the Sporting & Dramatic Publishing Co. Ltd, Drapers' Record Ltd, Men's Wear Publishing Co. Ltd; Chairman and Managing Director of Odhams Properties Limited, Kinematograph Publications Limited, etc; *b* 5 Jan. 1873; *m* 1906, Alice Louise, *d* of late Charles Stone Collard. Chairman of the Red Cross Penny-a-Week Fund; Chairman of the Hospital for Sick Children; President of the Middlesex Voluntary Hospitals Association; Hon. Treasurer of British Wireless for the Blind Fund, Dec. 1943; Hon. Treasurer of Special Hospitals' Assoc.; Vice-Pres. of British Hospitals' Assoc. and of Nat. Assoc. of Boys' Clubs; Chairman Committee of Management, Institute of Child Health, University of London; Trustee (Festival President in 1931) of Newsvendors' Benevolent and Provident Institution; Trustee (Festival President in 1934) of Printers' Pension, Almshouse and Orphan Asylum Corporation; Trustee of Reuter's Trust; President Lloyd Memorial (Caxton) Seaside Home, Hornsey Central Hospital; President of Advisory Council of London School of Printing and Kindred Trades; President of Printing and Allied Trades Research Association; President Periodical, Trade Press and Weekly Newspaper Proprietors' Association; President Association of Teachers of Printing and Allied Subjects; Past President British Advertising Association, 1938. *Address:* Southwood Court, Highgate, N6; Tree Tops, Marley Heights, Fernhurst, near Haslemere. *Club:* Garrick.

Died 10 April 1946 (ext).

SOWARD, Sir Alfred (Walter), Kt 1919; CB 1912; a Com. of Inland Revenue 1916–18; Controller of Death Duties and Secretary of the Estate Duty Office, 1908–18; Assistant, 1904; *b* 28 Aug. 1856; *s* of late William James Soward; *m* 1891, Elizabeth, *e d* of late Joseph Wittleton; one *s* two *d. Educ:* Stationers' School; Birkbeck College. Member of the Royal Institution, and of the Society for Nautical Research; Past member of many scientific societies; President of the Cruising Association, 1924–26; awarded Romola Challenge Cup by the Royal Cruising Club, 1924. *Publications:* Law and Practice of the Estate Duty, 7 eds; Estate and other Death Duties, in Lord Halsbury's Laws of England; Taxation of Capital; To the Sands of the Riddle; A Summer Afloat; A North Sea Adventure; In the Waters of Seven Countries; Sea-Thrills; contributions to the Press. *Recreations:* cruising, motoring, scientific studies. *Address:* Wyvenhoe Cross, Essex. *T:* Wivenhoe 240. *Club:* Royal Cruising.

Died 23 Jan. 1949.

SOWDEN, Sir William John, Kt 1918; JP; part proprietor, 1899–1922, and editor of The Register, The Observer, and The Evening Journal newspapers; *b* Castlemaine, Victoria, 26 April 1858; *s* of late Thomas Sowden; *m* 1st, 1886, Letitia Grace Hampton (*d* 1928), *d* of late Joseph Adams, Melbourne; 2nd, 1929, Margaret Suttie, *d* of Mrs Suttie, Sydney. *Educ:* Castlemaine, Victoria. Entered the office of the Castlemaine Representative, and later that of The Mount Alexander Mail in Castlemaine; joined reporting staff South Australian Register, 1881; chief of reporting and Hansard staffs, 1882; accompanied parliamentary party to the Northern Territory, 1882; contributed to the Register special articles, Echoes from the Smoking Room, 1882–92; chief leader-writer, 1892; acting editor, 1897–99; editor in chief for 25 years; five years Chief President of SA Board of Directors of Australian Natives Association; Pres. Board of Governors National Library,

Museum, and Art Gallery, 1908–26; founder and first President Australian (Federal) Wattle League; State President of League; ex-President Royal Society of St George; ex-President and Acting Chief Scout, Boy Scouts Association (SA Branch) (recipient Silver Wolf) and Prisoners' Aid Association, of which he was a founder; President Forest League, Institutes Association of South Australia during many years, and also Adelaide Branch of Overseas League; Freemason, PM; a founder of four lodges and WM of three for over five years. *Publications:* The Northern Territory as it Is, 1882; Prison Reform; The Children of the Rising Sun; Chips from China; With the Nor'-West Mail; In Warm Waters and Elsewhere; An Australian Native's Standpoint—a Defence of Australia against Critics, etc.; as the sole representative of South Australia on a delegation of Australian editors, visited in 1918 the war fronts as a guest of the British Ministry of Information, and published illustrated volume, The Roving Editors, 1919; Another Australian Abroad (Travel Notes Egypt and Palestine), 1925. *Recreations:* world-travel, motoring, gardening, bowls, collecting curios; lecturing for charitable and educational purposes, also Municipal Councillor. *Address:* Castlemaine, Hindmarsh River, Victor Harbour 330. *Clubs:* British Empire; Adelaide; Commonwealth, Mt Osmond Country, Adelaide.

Died 10 Oct. 1943.

SPARKES, Henry, CBE 1927; Controller of Post Office, Stores Department, 1924–33; *b* 1871; *s* of Joseph Sparkes; *m* 1895, Louisa, *d* of Thomas Farndon. *Address:* 103 Sunny Gardens, NW4.

Died 8 April 1950.

SPEAIGHT, Frederick William; an Hon. 2nd Lt in HM Army; JP; Hon. Life Gov. Children's Hospital, Great Ormond Street; *b* 1869; *e surv. s* of late Charles William Speaight; *m* 1894, Emily Isabella, *d* of late Frederick Elliott; two *s. Educ:* Deal College. Founder and Hon. Director, Holborn Saturday League, 1886–93; a Founder of the Holborn Free Library, 1891; organised Roll of Ministering Children, 1897; Hon. designer Imperial Coronation Bazaar, 1902; originator of the Oxford Sweated Industries Exhibition, 1907; Hon. Designer of the Funeral Route of King Edward's Funeral; Hon. Director, Shakespeare Festivals, Angmering-on-Sea, 1923, 1924, 1925; Hon. Designer and Publicity Secretary, Hatfield Elizabethan Fête, 1924; for many years a member of the Hertfordshire County Council and Hon. Director of its Rural Industries Exhibitions, 1925–26, 1927–28–1929–30–1931; Hon. Director, Hertfordshire County Council Education Exhibition, 1926; Hon. Director Tudor Revels, Hatfield, and producer of the Pageant King Harry's Progress, 1927; Hon. Adviser Durban (Natal) Tudor Revels, 1927; designed Marble Arch Improvement Scheme, 1905; Improvement of the Horse Guards Parade, 1908; reconstructed (for Marquess of Salisbury) St Mary's Hospital, Ilford, 1927. *Publications:* The Work of the Hertfordshire County Council; An Architectural Example; The Marble Arch: A Suggested Improvement; The Marble Arch Improvement: Its Conception and Realisation; Hyde Park Corner: A Suggested Improvement; The Horse Guards Parade: A Suggested Improvement; Old Hertfordshire Prints; Tudor Revels. *Address:* 6 Maze Road, Kew, Surrey. *T:* Richmond 3757.

Died 15 Nov. 1942.

SPEAKMAN, Sir Harry, Kt 1936; on Retired List of Justices; retired Alderman Borough of Leigh; *b* 23 May 1865; *s* of John Speakman, Leigh; *m* 1889, Helen Frances, *d* of Peter McGregor, Larne, Co. Antrim; four *s.* Past President Lancashire and Cheshire Coal Association, 1911–12, 1919, 1920, and 1928; President, 1931–32, 1932–33, Manchester Geological and Mining Society; ex-Mayor and Hon. Freeman of Leigh.

Recreation: President and Ex-Captain Leigh Golf Club. *Address:* The Walmsleys, Leigh, Lancashire. *T:* Leigh 630.

Died 16 Feb. 1946.

SPEAKMAN, Lionel, MInstT; FRES; late Gen. Manager Dalgety & Co. Limited, 65–68 Leadenhall Street, EC; *y s* of late Thomas Speakman, Stanthorne Hill, Middlewich, Cheshire; *m* Kate, *y d* of late John Barton, Colton Hall, Staffordshire. *Educ:* Cheltenham College. For 22 years in service of London and North-Western Railway Company; Assistant District Goods Manager, Liverpool, 1902–11; District or Divisional Goods Officer at respectively Wolverhampton, Birmingham, and Manchester, 1911–18; General Manager Furness Railway, 1918–22. *Address:* Terrace House, Roehampton Vale. *T:* Putney 6483. *Clubs:* Oriental; Union (Sydney).

Died 5 July 1948.

SPEAR, Lt-Col Christopher Ronald, MVO 1937; MC; Military Attaché, British Embassy, China, 1938–39; *b* Kingstown, Ireland, 16 Dec. 1897; *s* of late C. S. Spear; *m* 1926, Geraldine Marian, *e d* of late Robert Lodge, Compton Wood, Eastbourne; no *c. Educ:* privately. Entered Indian Army, 1916; 2/Lt 58th Vaughan's Rifles, Frontier Force; Captain, 1920; Bt Major, 1937; Major, 1938; transferred to the Somerset Light Infantry (Prince Albert's), 1928; served European War, Palestine, 1917–18; Waziristan, 1919–21 and 1921–24; Shanghai Defence Force, 1927, Brigade Intelligence Officer Jhansi Brigade, attached Headquarters Staff Shanghai Defence Force (wounded, MC); Macgregor Memorial Medal, 1924, for travel in China and Thibet. *Recreations:* tennis, golf. *Address:* Valroy, Camberley, Surrey. *T:* Camberley 925. *Club:* United Service.

Died 10 May 1942.

SPEARMAN, Charles E., PhD (Leipzig); Hon. LLD (Wittenberg, USA); FRS; Hon. Member, Kaiserlich Deutsche Akademie der Naturforscher; Hon. Member, British Psychological Society; Foreign Associate, US National Academy Science; Associate Foreign Member, Société Française de Psychologie; Hon. Member, Deutsche Gesellschaft für Psychologie; Hon. Member, Kentucky Academy of Science; Hon. Member, Psychotech. Club, Prague; Professor of Psychology, University of London (University College), 1928–31; Emeritus Professor since 1931; Hon. Psychol. Adviser, Chesterfield; *b* London, 10 Sept. 1863; 2nd *s* of A. Y. Spearman and Louisa, *d* of G. P. Mainwaring; *m* 1901, Fanny, *d* of J. Aikman, Guernsey; (one *s*, Lieut RN, killed Crete, 1941) four *d. Educ:* Leamington College. Studied Experimental Psychology at University of Leipsic; University of Würzburg; and University of Göttingen. Experimental Reader in Psychology at University of London (University College), 1907; Grote Professor of Mind and Logic there, 1911; served Burmese War (medal and 2 clasps); during Boer War, DAAG at Guernsey; European War, General Staff, Tyne Defences; President British Psychological Society, 1923–26; President J Section British Association for the Advancement of Science, 1925; twice thanked by Admiralty for psychological services. *Publications:* numerous researches, including General Intelligence objectively determined and measured; Die Normaltäuschungen in der Lagewahrnehmung; An Economic Theory of Spatial Perception; The Method of Right and Wrong Cases without Gauss's Formulæ; Correlations of Sums or Differences; The Theory of Two Factors; The Principles of Cognition; The Abilities of Man, 1927; Creative Mind, 1931; Psychology down the Ages, 1937. *Address:* 67 Portland Court, W1.

Died 17 Sept. 1945.

SPEED, His Honour Sir Edwin Arney, Kt 1912; MA, LLB; JP; *b* 11 March 1869; 2nd *s* of R. H. Speed, solicitor, Nottingham; *m* 1901, Ada Frances, *d* of late Rev. William Ross, sometime Chaplain of the Black

Watch and Rector of Haddington; one *s. Educ:* Rugby; Trin. Coll., Camb. Called to Bar, Inner Temple, 1893; a District Commissioner of Gold Coast Colony, 1899; Attorney General of Lagos, 1900, and of Southern Nigeria, 1906; several times Acting Chief Justice, Colonial Secretary, and Deputy Governor of Lagos, and Acting Chief Justice of S Nigeria; Chief Justice of N Nigeria, 1908; Chief Justice of Nigeria, 1914; retired, 1918. *Address:* Remenham House, Henley-on-Thames. *T:* Henley 188. *Clubs:* Oxford and Cambridge, Royal Automobile.

Died 14 Dec. 1941.

SPEELMAN, Sir Cornelis Jacob, 7th Bt *cr* 1686; *b* 22 Sept. 1881; *s* of late Jacob Speelman, *brother* of 6th Bart; *S* uncle, 1907; *m* 1916, Maria Catharina Helena Castendijk; one *s. Heir: s* Cornelis Jacob Speelman, *b* 17 March 1917. *Address:* Zandvoort, Holland.

Died 3 Feb. 1949.

SPEER, Robert Elliott, BA (Princeton), MA (Yale), DD (Edinburgh), LLD (Rutgers, Wooster, Otterbein, Washington and Jefferson), LittD, (Juniata, Princeton); Secretary, Board of Foreign Missions, Presbyterian Church in the USA (Lay Secretary), 1891–1937, now retired; *b* Huntingdon, Pennsylvania, 10 Sept. 1867; *s* of Hon. Robert Milton Speer; *m* 1893, Emma Doll Bailey, Harrisburg, Penn.; one *s* two *d. Educ:* Princeton University. President of the Federal Council of the Churches of Christ in America, 1920–24; Moderator of the Presbyterian Church, USA, 1927–28. *Publications:* Missions and Modern History; Christianity and the Nations; Race and Race Relations; The Man Christ Jesus; Principles of Jesus: The Finality of Jesus Christ, and other books. *Address:* Lakeville, Conn, USA.

Died 23 Nov. 1947.

SPENCE, Sir Alexander, Kt 1927; OBE 1920; DL; JP; President Dundee Unionist Association; *b* 1866. Councillor and Magistrate for fourteen years, Lord Provost, City of Dundee, 1920–23. *Address:* Sunnylaw, Albany Terrace, Dundee. *T:* Dundee 2680.

Died 1 Sept. 1939.

SPENCE, John, CMG 1936; BA, LLB (Sydney, NSW); Chairman, Prince Henry Hospital Board, Trustee Australian Museum, and Director several Public Companies; *b* 6 Jan. 1878; *m* 1909, Ethel May, *d* of Bertram Cooke; three *d. Educ:* Sydney High School; Sydney University (Honours in French and Philosophy, Wigram Allen Scholar and Prizeman in Political Science). Admitted to Bar, Supreme Court of NSW, 1900; Business Manager, Building Construction Undertaking, Supervising Cost Accountant, Chief Accountant, Public Service Inspector, and Government Printer, 1912–22; Director of Finance and Permanent Head of Treasury, 1922–24; Member of Public Service Board, 1924–28; Auditor General for NSW, 1928–42; sometime Lecturer and Examiner for Public Examinations in Business Principles and Practice and Public Finance; Chairman, Government Insurance Board, and Member, Railway Superannuation Board, 1922–25; Chairman, NSW Budget Committee, 1928; Chairman, NSW Taxation Investigation Committee, 1933–36. *Recreations:* golf, bowls. *Address:* Union House, 247 George St, Sydney, NSW; 15 Springdale Road, Killara, Sydney, NSW. *Clubs:* New South Wales, University, Avondale Golf, Manly Surf (Sydney).

Died 26 June 1949.

SPENCER, Col Charles Louis, CBE 1919; DSO 1918; TD; retired; *b* 1870; *s* of John Spencer, Glasgow. *Educ:* Kelvinside Academy, Glasgow; College Chaptal, Paris. Served European War, 1914–18 (despatches thrice, DSO, CBE). *Publication:* Knots, Splices and Fancy Work. *Recreation:* yachting. *Address:* Warmanbie, by Annan, Dumfriesshire. *Clubs:* Junior United Service, Caledonian; Western, New (Glasgow).

Died 2 May 1948.

SPENCER, Frederic, MA (Cambridge), PhD (Leipzig); Officier de l'Instruction Publique; Chevalier de la Légion d'Honneur; late Staff Inspector of Secondary Schools; *b* Newbury, 29 Sept. 1861; 3rd *s* of Rev. Joseph Spencer; *m* 1887, Johanne Marie Helene (*d* 1941), 4th *d* of late August Soehlmann of Schloss Ricklingen, Hanover; one *s* two *d*. *Educ:* Kingswood School, Bath; École des Hautes Études, Paris; University of Camb.; BA Lond., 1882; BA Camb. (Medieval and Modern Languages Tripos), 1886. Frequently Examiner in the same Tripos between 1892 and 1904, and Chief Examiner in French to the University of London, 1899–1903; sometime Assistant Master in the Hull Grammar School and in Tonbridge School; Chief Master on the Modern side in the Leys School, Cambridge; Professor of French Language and Literature, University College of N Wales; Chairman of the Faculty of Arts in the University of Wales; Rector of the High School of Glasgow. *Publications:* editor of the 'Temple' Molière; Chapters on the Aims and Practice of Teaching; A Primer of French Verse; several minor Anglo-Norman texts; a Summary of the Song of Roland for English Readers (with A. S. Way); the stage version of Molière's Dépit amoureux; and an English verse rendering of the same (The Love-Tiff). *Address:* 12 Hove Manor, Hove, Sussex.

Died 26 April 1942.

SPENCER, Major Herbert Eames, CBE 1924; OBE 1919; *b* 6 May 1871; *s* of George and Emily Sarah Spencer; *m* Beatrice Mary Bull; three *d*. *Educ:* MCS Oxford. Joined 13th Hussars, 1893; Royal Wilts Yeomanry, 1898; served S African War, 1899–1902 (Queen's medal, King's medal, despatches); Military Member of Claims Commission and JP Orange River Colony, 1902–04; served European War, 1914–18, Expeditionary Force and later GSO 2nd grade in War Office (1914 Star, Victory and Allies Medal, Russian Order of St Anne, 3rd Class, Chevalier, Order of Leopold and Médaille du Roi Albert (Belgium), OBE, CBE); employed in Foreign Office, 1919–38. *Recreations:* fishing, shooting, golf. *Address:* The Cottage, West Byfleet, Surrey. *Club:* White's.

Died 8 Aug. 1945.

SPENCER, Herbert Ritchie, MD, BS, FRCP (London); Hon. LLD (Aberdeen); (retired); Consulting Obstetric Physician to University College Hospital; Emeritus Professor of Obstetric Medicine, University College, London; Obstetric Physician to University College Hospital, 1887–1925 (previously Obstetric Assistant, House Surgeon and House Physician); late President of Section of the History of Medicine and of Section of Obstetrics and Gynæcology, Royal Society of Medicine; late President Medical Society of London; late Examiner in Midwifery and Diseases of Women in Universities of Oxford, Cambridge, London, and Royal College of Physicians; Hon. Fellow American Gynæcological Society; membre honoraire de la Société d'Obstétrique et de Gynécologie de Paris; membre honoraire de la Société belge de gynécologie et d'obstétrique; Hon. Fellow Obstetrical Society of Edinburgh; Hon. Fellow Società Medica Chirurgica of Bologna; *b* Atherstone, 16 Jan. 1860; 2nd *s* of late Henry Spencer, Atherstone. *Educ:* Atherstone Grammar School; University College, London. *Publications:* (with T. W. P. Lawrence) Descriptive Catalogue of the specimens illustrating gynæcology and obstetrics in Museum of University College Hospital, 1911; Cæsarean Section, 1925; History of British Midwifery from 1650 to 1800, 1927; Medicine in the Days of Shakespeare, 1929; papers on Midwifery and Diseases of Women; Lettsomian Lectures (Med. Soc. Lond.), 1920; Harveian Oration, 1921; Lloyd Roberts Lecture, 1924. *Recreations:* shooting, ornithology, travelling. *Address:* 4f Bickenhall Mansions, W1. *T:* Welbeck 1171. *Club:* Oriental.

Died 28 Aug. 1941.

SPENCER, Prof. James Frederick, MA, PhD, DSc, FRIC; *b* 8 Feb. 1881; *e s* of Richard and Elizabeth Spencer, Walton, Liverpool; unmarried. *Educ:* University College, Liverpool; University of Breslau; University College, London. Leblanc medallist, 1901; 1851 Exhibition Scholar, 1903–06. Demonstrator, 1906; Assistant Lecturer, 1907, Lecturer, 1916, of Chemistry at Bedford College; Reader of Physical Chemistry, 1916–27; Head of Dept of Physical Chemistry, 1919; University Professor of Chemistry, Bedford College, University of London; Head of Department of Inorganic and Physical Chemistry and Director of the Chemical Laboratories; retired, 1946; Professor Emeritus, 1946. *Publications:* numerous chemical papers; an Experimental Course of Physical Chemistry, 1911; The Metals of the Rare Earths, 1919, translated into French, 1920; Elementary Practical Physical Chemistry, 1927. *Recreations:* reading, fishing. *Address:* Norwyn, 30 Eshe Road North, Blundellsands, Liverpool. *T:* Great Crosby 5687.

Died 31 Dec. 1950.

SPENCER, Col John H.; *see* Heatly-Spencer.

SPENDER, A. F., OBE; MA; founder of the British Institute, Florence, and first Director (Jan. 1918–May 1922); *s* of J. Kent and Mrs J. Kent Spender. *Educ:* Cambridge. Member of the Society of Leonardo da Vinci; Commendatore of the Corona d'Italia. *Address:* Palazzo Pisani, Venice. *Clubs:* Athenæum; Florence, Florence; Union, Venice.

Died 20 Nov. 1947.

SPENDER, (John) Alfred, CH 1937; *b* Bath, 1862; *e s* of late Dr and Mrs J. K. Spender (author of many novels); *m* May, *e d* of W. G. Rawlinson, Hill Lodge, Campden Hill, W. *Educ:* Bath College; Balliol College, Oxford (MA) (Classical Exhibition); 1st class Classical Moderations; 2nd class Final Classical School. Editor of Eastern Morning News, Hull, 1886–90; joined staff of Pall Mall Gazette, 1892; left it the same year on its transfer to Mr Astor; assistant editor of Westminster Gazette, 1893; Editor of the Westminster Gazette, Jan. 1896–1922; Member of Royal Commission on Divorce and Matrimonial Causes; Member of the Special Mission to Egypt, 1919–20; JP London; Member of County of London Territorial Association; DL County of London; Member of the Royal Commission on the Private Manufacture of Armaments, 1935; Charter President of the Institute of Journalists for its Jubilee year 1940. *Publications:* The State and Pensions in Old Age; The Comments of Bagshot; The Life of Sir Henry Campbell-Bannerman; The Public Life, 1925; The Changing East, 1926; Life, Journalism and Politics, 1927; The America of To-day, 1928; Weetman Pearson, First Viscount Cowdray, 1930; Sir Robert Hudson: a Memoir, 1930; The Life of Lord Oxford and Asquith (with the Hon. Cyril Asquith), 1932; Fifty Years of Europe, 1933; These Times, 1934; A Short History of Our Times, 1934; Great Britain, Empire and Commonwealth, 1886–1935, 1936; Men and Things, 1937; The Government of Mankind, 1938; New Lamps and Ancient Lights, 1940. *Address:* Warren End, Farnborough, Kent. *T:* Farnborough 147. *Clubs:* Athenæum, Reform, National Liberal.

Died 21 June 1942.

SPERRIN-JOHNSON, John Charles, MA, MSc, MB, BCh, BAO (National University of Ireland); LittD (University of New Zealand); FRGS; Professor of Botany, University College, Cork, since 1932; Life Member NZ Institute and Polynesian Society; Part founder and lately President Anthropological Section of NZ Institute, of NZ Avicultural Society and of Auckland Zoological Society; Captain, NZ Medical Corps, Territorial and Expeditionary Forces; *b* 2 Oct. 1885; *e s* of A. Johnson, Grenville House, Cork; unmarried. *Educ:* University College, Cork; St John's College, Cambridge. Medical Scholar (3 years); Senior Scholar in

Natural History and in Chemistry; Charles Medallist in Practical Physiology and Histology. Junior Demonstrator in Anatomy; Demonstrator in Physiology; Demonstrator in Biology, University College, Cork (3 years); BA (Hons), MA (Hons), MSc (by research); 1851 Research Scholar; Assistant-Demonstrator in Biology, Cambridge; Professor of Biology, University College, Auckland, NZ, 1914–31; Naturalist to the British School of Archæology in Egypt, 1931–32; late member of Senate and of Board of Studies and Examiner in University of New Zealand; Examiner to New Zealand Department of Education; short study and research periods in American Universities, 1920, etc.; attached to Instructional Staff, Awapuni Camp, Headquarters, NZ Medical Corps; MO and Bacteriologist, HMNZHS Maheno, 5th charter; OC No. 1 (Auckland) Field Ambulance, 1917–19; Lecturer on First Aid, Blackrock Local Security Force, Cork, 1940–41; Biological travels, especially in Pacific, East, Mediterranean, Palestine, North and South America. *Publications:* Scientific papers; essays. *Recreations:* music, travel. *Address:* Blackrock Castle, Cork, Ireland.

Died 19 May 1948.

SPICER, Gerald Sydney, CB 1917; *b* 21 May 1874; *m* 1906, Marion Ethel, *d* of Herbert Hardy, Danehurst, Uckfield. *Educ:* Eton. Clerk, Foreign Office, 1894; Acting 3rd Secretary Diplomatic Service, 1898; Private Secretary to Sir T. Sanderson; Permanent Secretary for Foreign Affairs, 1903–06; Assist Clerk, 1906; Gold Staff Officer at Coronation of King George V, 1911 (medal); Senior Clerk, 1912; resigned, 1922. *Address:* Great Dewes, Ardingly, Sussex.

Died 15 March 1942.

SPICER, Henry Gage; JP; Chairman of Spicers, Ltd, and Associated Companies; Chairman and Managing Director, 1923–39; *b* 1875; *yr s* of late Edward Spicer, JP, DL, and Susanna Gage Spicer; *m* Gertrude Maud, *d* of late G. E. Emms; one *s. Educ:* Harrow School; abroad. Entered the business of Spicer Brothers, Ltd, 1895, becoming Managing Director, 1912, and Chairman, 1920, which business in 1922 amalgamated with James Spicer & Sons, Ltd, under the title of Spicers, Ltd; High Sheriff of Cambs and Hunts, 1933. *Recreations:* squash rackets, motoring, shooting. *Address:* 20 Old Queen Street, Westminster, SW1. *TA:* Democracy, London. *T:* Whitehall 3000. *Clubs:* Conservative, Royal Automobile.

Died 11 March 1944.

SPICER, James Leonard; Chairman of Spicers Ltd; *b* 5 April 1873; *s* of James Spicer, Eltham; *m* 1901, Henrietta Lloyd Lloyd; one *s* two *d. Educ:* Leys School, Cambridge; Lausanne University, Switzerland. Started in the City of London, 1892, in the Shipping Trade. Entered firm of James Spicer & Sons, 1896; Partner, 1900; Director of James Spicer & Sons Ltd, and subsequently of Spicers Ltd Chairman of the Borough Road Polytechnic, 1906–20. *Recreations:* cricket, football, golf and riding. *Address:* 19 New Bridge Street, EC4. *Club:* Reform.

Died 4 Dec. 1949.

SPICER, Roy Godfrey Bullen, CMG 1934; MC; Col (GL) Allied Commission, CM Forces, 1943–45; *b* New Barnet, Herts, 12 Feb. 1889; *s* of Bullen and late Adele Spicer, formerly of North Molton, Devon; *m* 1926, Margaret Ina Frances, *e d* of late E. G. Money; one *s. Educ:* Colet Court; St Paul's (Scholar). Ceylon Police, 1909–25; served European War, 1915–18, The Carabiniers (wounded); Commissioner, the Kenya Police, 1925–31; Inspector-General of Police and Prisons, Palestine, 1931–38; Member Advisory Council (Palestine), 1931–38; Chief Constable of the Isle of Wight, 1938–45; President of the Automobile Club and Touring Association of Palestine; former President of the Amateur Boxing Association and the Football Association of East Africa; Master of the Errebodde Hunt (Ceylon), 1923–25 and Master of The Ramle Vale Hunt

(Palestine), 1932–37; King's Police Medal, Commander, Order of St John of Jerusalem. *Recreations:* hunting, shooting, cricket, fishing. *Address:* Woodend, Yarmouth, Isle of Wight. *T:* Yarmouth 343. *Club:* Brooks's.

Died 11 June 1946.

SPIELMANN, Marion Harry (Alexander), FSA, writer; Hon. ARIBA; Officer of the Order of the Crown of Belgium; Chevalier Order of Leopold; *b* London, 22 May 1858; *y s* of Adam Spielmann, banker, Lombard Street, and Hereford House, SW; *m* 1880, Mabel Henrietta (*d* 1938), *d* of Edwin L. Samuel and Clara Yates; one *s. Educ:* University Coll. School; University College; Lycée, France. Art writer Pall Mall Gazette, 1883–90, Westminster Gazette and other journals; contributor on literature, art, and art politics to leading papers, magazines, and reviews; for 17 years editor of the Magazine of Art; lecturer, Royal Institution, etc. *Publications:* Works of G. F. Watts, RA (Pall Mall Gazette Extra), 1886; Henriette Ronner, 1891; History of Punch, 1895; The Modern Poster (part-author), 1895; Millais and his Works, 1898; The Unidentified Contributions of Thackeray to Punch, 1899; John Ruskin, 1900 (London and Philadelphia); Notes on the Wallace Collection in Hertford House, 1900; The Portraits of Geoffrey Chaucer, 1900 (Chaucer Society, 1901); British Sculpture and Sculptors of To-day, 1901; Charles Keene, Etcher, 1903; The Portraits of Shakespeare (Stratford Town Edition of Shakespeare), 1907, 1924 and 1931; Kate Greenaway (with G. S. Layard), 1905; British Portrait Painting, 1910, 2 vols; The Angels appearing to the Shepherds, by Velazquez, 1913; The Title-Page of the First Folio (1623), 1924; Iconography of Andreas Vesalius, 1925; Hugh Thomson (with Walter Jerrold), 1931; editor 8th edition Unger's Belvidere Gallery; contributions to Bryan's Dictionary of Painters; Dictionary of National Biography; Shakespeare Book of Homage, 1916; editor (10th ed.), and contributor (also 11th and 14th editions) Art Section of Encyclopædia Britannica; Part-Editor of the New Art Library, 1910–1935; sole juror for England, Fine Art Section, Brussels International Exhibition; Member Fine Arts Committee, Royal Commission, Paris and Rome International Exhibitions and Franco-British Exhibition; Vice-President, Royal Society of Literature; Member of Council Royal Literary Fund, etc.; purchased and formed the collection for the State Art Gallery of Baroda at the desire of the Maharaja Gaekwar, 1911–1921. *Recreations:* books and friendships. *Address:* at 107 Banbury Road, Oxford; Uplands, Folkestone. *Clubs:* Athenæum, Arts; Radnor, Folkestone.

Died 2 Oct. 1948.

SPILLER, John Wyatt, CMG 1938; MInstCE; *b* 15 April 1878; *s* of late Henry J. Spiller, JP, Hatfield, Taunton; *m* 1905, Millicent (*d* 1943), *d* of late Robert Doughty, Alconbury one *s* one *d. Educ:* Wellington School (Som.). Engineering Dept Great Western Railway, 1896–1910; joined staff of Crown Agents for the Colonies, 1910; Ministry of Munitions, 1916–19; Acting General Manager and Chief Eng., Federated Malay States Railways, 1925–26; Chief Engineer, Crown Agents, 1922–25, 1926–41. *Address:* Riversdale, Maidenhead. *T:* Maidenhead 738.

Died 28 May 1949.

SPILSBURY, Sir Bernard Henry, Kt 1923; Hon. Pathologist, Home Office; Lecturer in Forensic Medicine, University College Hospital, London School of Medicine for Women, and St Thomas's Hospital; Fellow Royal Society of Medicine; *b* 1877. *Educ:* Magdalen College, Oxford; MA, MB, BCh, FRCP, London. *Address:* 20 Frognal, NW3.

Died 17 Dec. 1947.

SPINGARN, J. E., MA, PhD; *b* New York, 17 May 1875. *Educ:* Columbia; Harvard. Successively Tutor, Adjunct Professor, and Professor of Comparative Literature, Columbia University, 1899–1911. Contested

18th NY district as Republican candidate for Congress, 1908; founded movement for rural co-operative recreation, 1910–15; Chairman Board of Directors, National Association for the Advancement of Coloured People, 1913–19, Hon. Treasurer 1919–30, President since 1930; Delegate to the National Conventions of the Progressive Party, Chicago, 1912 and 1916; Major, Infantry, US Army, 1917–19 (AEF France, 1918–19); Lieutenant Colonel, ORC; Literary Adviser, Harcourt, Brace & Co., publishers, New York, 1919–32; Honorary Litt.D., University of Munich, 1924; Member Board of Managers, New York Botanical Gardens; a director of Horticultural Society of New York; awarded Jackson Dawson Memorial Medal by Massachusetts Horticultural Society, 1937. *Publications:* History of Literary Criticism in the Renaissance, 1899 (Italian translation, 1905, with Introduction by Benedetto Croce); Critical Essays of the Seventeenth Century, vols i, ii 1908, vol. iii 1909; The New Hesperides and other Poems, 1911; The New Criticism, 1911; The Galateo, a Renaissance Courtesy Book, 1914; Creative Criticism, 1917; Goethe's Literary Essays, 1921; Criticism in America, 1924; Poems, 1924; Poetry and Religion, 1924; Troutbeck Leaflets, 1924–1926; Creative Criticism and other Essays, 1931; edited European Library, 1920–1925; Contributor to Cambridge History of English Literature, Dictionary of American Biography, Civilization in the United States, Taylor's Garden Dictionary, etc. *Recreations:* gardening; writing about gardening. *Address:* Troutbeck, Amenia, Dutchess County, NY; 110 East 78th Street, New York. *TA:* (cable) Sirmio, New York. *Clubs:* Authors'; City, New York; Sharon Country.

Died 26 July 1939.

SPINNEY, George Wilbur, CMG 1943; DCL Acadia Univ. 1942; President, Bank of Montreal, since 1942; *b* 3 April 1889; *s* of George N. Spinney and Josephine Doty; *m* 1916, Martha Maud Ramsay; (one *s* died from injuries sustained on Active Service with RCN) two *d*. *Educ:* Yarmouth Public School; Yarmouth Academy. Entered Bank, Yarmouth, NS, 1906; later transferred to Edmundston, Quebec, Hamilton, and Montreal branches; Secretary to General Manager, Head Office, 1915; Asst to General Manager, 1922; Asst General Manager, 1928; General Manager, 1936; Vice-Pres. Canadian Bankers' Assoc., 1939–42; Chairman, Canada's First Victory Loan Organisation, 1941; Chairman, National War Finance Committee, 1941–43, Hon. Chairman since Aug. 1943. *Recreation:* golf. *Address:* 119 St James Street, Montreal, PQ. *Clubs:* Mount Royal, Saint James's (Montreal); Rideau (Ottawa); Toronto (Toronto).

Died 1 Feb. 1948.

SPOONER, Brig.-Gen. Arthur Hardwicke, CB 1935; CMG 1918; DSO 1915; *b* 27 May 1879; *s* of late Ven. G. H. Spooner; *m* 1st, 1907, Rosalie Augusta (*d* 1908), *d* of H. A. Pile, of Warleigh, Barbados; 2nd, 1912, Violet Hamilton, *d* of late Lieut-Col C. J. Robarts, Indian Army; one *s* four *d*. *Educ:* Haileybury. Entered army, 1900; Capt. 1910; Lt-Col 1924; Col 1928; served S African War, 1899–1901 (Queen's medal 3 clasps); European War, 1914–18 (despatches eight times, DSO and bar, Bt Lt-Col, Chevalier of Legion of Honour, CMG); Commander 4th (Quetta) Infantry Brig., 1931–35; Hon. Col 39th (Lancashire Fusiliers) Anti-Aircraft Bn; retired pay, 1935. *Address:* Little Waters End, Temple Ewell, Dover.

Died 16 Nov. 1945.

SPOONER, Rear-Adm. Ernest John, DSO 1919; RN; Rear-Admiral, Malaya, and in charge of Naval Establishments at Singapore since 1941; *b* 1887; *s* of J. D. Spooner; *m* 1926, Megan Foster; one *s*. Served European War (DSO); Deputy Director of Operations Division, Admiralty 1932–34; commanded Navigation School, Portsmouth, 1934–36; commanded HMS Vindictive,

1937–38; commanded HMS Repulse, 1938–41. *Recreations:* music, tennis, golf, racquets. *Club:* Naval and Military.

Died 15 April 1942.

SPOTTISWOODE, John Roderick Charles Herbert; *b* 1882; *e s* of late Capt. Charles Herbert and of 2nd wife, Helen, *o c* of late Col Andrew Spottiswoode; *S* great-aunt, Lady John Montagu-Douglas-Scott-Spottiswoode, 1900, and assumed additional surname of Spottiswoode; *m* 1st, 1906, Evelyn Anne Venables, *o c* of Richard Henry Venables Kyrke of Nantyffrith, Flintshire, and Anne Elizabeth, *d* of Peter Walker of Auchenflower, NB (marr. diss. 1915); 2nd, 1916, Hylda Marjorie (*d* 1931), *y d* of Col Arthur Venables Kyrke of Staplegrove, Somerset; one *s*. *Address:* Mincombe Posts, Sidbury, Devon.

Died 6 Jan. 1946.

SPRECKLEY, Herbert William, CBE 1920; *b* 1857. Chairman Spreckley Brothers, Ltd, Brewers, Worcester. Formerly Chairman Worcester Branch of Sailors' and Soldiers' Families Association. *Address:* Cove Cottage, Worcester.

Died 1 Sept. 1950.

SPRIGGS, Sir Edmund Ivens, KCVO 1935; MD (Lond.); FRCP (Lond.); JP Co. Denbigh; Consulting Physician Ruthin Castle Clinic and National Health Service in Wales; Member House Committee North Wales Sanatorium; *s* of late Joseph Spriggs of Foxton, Market Harborough; *m* 1st, Alice Mary (*d* 1932), *d* of late T. S. Watson of Foxton; two *s*; 2nd, 1936, Janet, *d* of Mrs MacIntosh, The Old Parsonage, Dunning, Perthshire, and the late William MacIntosh, MVO. *Educ:* Market Harborough Grammar School; Wycliffe College, Stonehouse; Firth College, Sheffield; Guy's Hospital (Scholar); University of Heidelberg. Formerly Physician, St George's Hospital, 1904–13, and Dean of the Medical School; also to Victoria Hospital for Children, and London Chest Hospital; Oliver-Sharpey Lecturer (1906), Croonian Lecturer (1933) and Harveian Orator (1944), Royal College of Physicians; President Liverpool Medical Institution, 1943; Examiner Royal College of Physicians and Universities of Aberdeen and Edinburgh; Demonstrator of Physiology, Guy's Hospital, 1898–1904; Capt. RAMC (Reserve); in 1913, after recovery from long illness, left London for Scotland, where he conducted Duff House, Banff, clinic till 1922, when it was removed to Ruthin, Senior Physician there till 1944; during European War acted as Hon. Medical Adviser to Ministry of Food, 1917–18; wrote the newspaper articles published by the Ministry entitled Food, and How to Save it, and sat on Departmental Committee on Rationing. High Sheriff for County of Denbigh, 1945–46. *Publications:* researches and articles on medical subjects; The Harveian Method in Literature (Harveian oration); Editor Duff House and Ruthin Castle Papers and Mahood's Guide to Banff and Neighbourhood. *Recreations:* shooting, fishing. *Address:* Cocd Marchan, Ruthin, N Wales. *T:* Ruthin 58. *Clubs:* Athenæum; University (Liverpool).

Died 4 Feb. 1949.

SPRINGFIELD, Lincoln; chief reporter of The Star for the first five years of its existence; editorial staff of Pall Mall Gazette throughout late H. C. Cust's editorship; news editor of Daily Mail for first five years of its existence; formed a company to purchase London Opinion, 1909, and edited it until 1924. *Publications:* Some Piquant People, 1924; The Girl Things Happened to, 1932. *Recreations:* golf, contract bridge. *Address:* 14 Grove Terrace, NW5. *Club:* Savage.

Died 18 Jan. 1950.

SPROT, Major Mark; of Riddell; proprietor of Riddell Estate, in the counties of Roxburgh and Selkirk; JP; DL; President, Scottish Agricultural Organisation Society; Member of Executive, Scottish Development Council;

President, Scottish Wool Growers, Ltd; Deputy-Chairman, Scottish Seaweed Research Association; Honorary President, Landowners Co-operative Forestry Society (Scotland); *b* 12 Nov. 1881; *e s* of late Lieut-General John Sprot of Riddell and 2nd wife Cecilia, *d* of Rev. William Blake Doveton, Vicar of Corston, near Bath; *m* 1909, Meliora, *e d* of late Sir John Adam Hay of Haystoun, Bart; two *s* two *d*. *Educ:* Sandhurst. Entered Royal Scots Greys, 1901; served South African War (medal and three clasps); Adjutant, Lothians and Border Horse, 1909–12 and 1915; Capt. in Special Reserve of Royal Scots Greys, 1912–22; 1914 Star, etc.; hon. rank of Major on demobilisation. County Councillor Roxburghshire, 1908–45, retd, 1945. Member of Committee on Scottish Agricultural Policy, 1925; Chm. of the Scottish Pig Industry Committee, 1926; Chairman of the Departmental Committee on Agricultural Co-operation in Scotland, 1929–30; Chairman of the Scottish Milk Marketing Committee, 1931–32; Chairman of Scottish Fat Stock Marketing Reorganisation Commission, 1932–34; Chairman of the Scottish Egg and Poultry Marketing Reorganisation Commission; Member of Great Britain Egg and Poultry Marketing Reorganisation Commission; Pres. Selkirkshire Branch National Farmers' Union of Scotland, 1927; Chm., County Road Board, Roxburghshire, 1930–39; Chairman, Roxburghshire Agricultural Executive Committee, 1939–46; landowner and farmer. *Address:* Riddell, by Melrose, Scotland. *TA:* Lilliesleaf. *T:* 3. *Clubs:* New, Edinburgh.

Died 31 Dec. 1946.

SPROTT, Sir Frederick Lawrence, Kt 1914; Chief Engineer Bombay PWD, retired; Chairman Bombay Port Trust, 1910–18; *b* 10 July 1863; *s* of James Sprott, solicitor, Shrewsbury, and Esther Sprott; *m* 1888, Amy (*d* 1938), *d* of Brig.-Surg. Henry William Graham; one *s*. *Educ:* Shrewsbury School; RIE College, Coopers Hill. Assistant Engineer, PWD, 1884; posted to Bombay Presidency, Oct. 1885; Assistant Engineer and Executive Engineer in several districts till 1899; Principal, College of Science, Poona, 1899–1903; Superintending Engineer, Indus River Commission, 1904–08; Sanitary Engineer to Government of Bombay, 1908–09; Dep. Chairman, Bombay Port Trust, 1909–10. *Address:* The Friary, Roydon, Diss, Norfolk.

Died 24 March 1943.

SPROTT, Rt Rev. Thomas Henry, OBE 1919; *m*; one *s*. *Educ:* Trinity College, Dublin (Hebrew Prizeman); BA 1878; Divinity Testimonium (1st class) and Church Formularies Prize, 1879; MA, 1882, BD and DD, 1911. Ordained, 1879; Curate of Holy Trinity, Kingston-on-Hull, 1879–82; St John the Evangelist, Waterloo Road, 1882–86; Minister of St Barnabas', Auckland, 1886–91; Examining Chaplain to Bishop of Auckland, 1888–91; Vicar of St Paul's Pro-Cathedral, Wellington, 1892–1911; Examining Chaplain to Bishop of Wellington, 1895–1911; Bishop of Wellington, 1911–36. *Publication:* Modern Study of the Old Testament and Inspiration, 1909. *Address:* 13 Washington Avenue, Brooklyn, Wellington, SW1, NZ.

Died 25 July 1942.

SPROULE, Hon. Robert, BA, LLB; *b* Omagh, Co. Tyrone; *s* of William Sproule; widower. *Educ:* Sydney University. Admitted as Barrister of Supreme Court of New South Wales, 1913; MLC, NSW, 1920–34; Solicitor General for New South Wales, 1920–22. *Address:* R. D. Meagher, Sproule and Co., Solicitors and Advocates, 63 Elizabeth Street, Sydney, NSW.

Died 16 July 1948.

SPURGEON, Caroline F. E., DLit Lond.; Doc Univ. Paris; Hon. LittD (Michigan); Emeritus Professor of English Literature in the University of London; Fellow of the Royal Society of Literature; *b* 1869; *d* of late Captain Christopher Spurgeon, 36th (Worcestershire) Regt, of Twyford, Norfolk. *Educ:* Cheltenham College;

Dresden; Paris; King's College and University College, London (Quain Essayist and Morley Medallist, 1898). First Class Final English Honours, Oxford, 1899; Docteur (Lettres) de l'Université de Paris, 1911; Research Fellowship, Federation of University Women, 1912. Assistant Lecturer in English, Bedford College, 1901–06; Lecturer in English Literature, 1906–13; Hildred Carlisle Professor of English Literature, University of London, 1913–29; Head of Department of English Literature, Bedford College for Women, London, 1913–29; Member of British Educational Mission to America, 1918; visited American Colleges on invitation of the Association of Collegiate Alumnæ, 1920, visiting Professor, Columbia University, New York, 1920–21; Member of the Departmental Committee to inquire into the position of English in the Educational System of England, 1920–21; President, International Federation of University Women, 1920–24. *Publications:* Editor of Richard Brathwait's Comments (Chaucer Society), 1902; The Castle of Otranto (King's Classics), 1908; Chaucer devant la critique en Angleterre et en France depuis son temps jusqu'à nos jours, 1911; Mysticism in English Literature (Cambridge Manuals), 1913; Five Hundred Years of Chaucer Criticism and Allusion (Chaucer Society), 1920–1925; reissued, with illustrations, 3 vols, 1925; Keats's Shakespeare, 1928; Annual Shakespeare Lecture, British Academy, 1931; Shakespeare's Imagery, and what it tells us, 1935; contributions to the Quarterly Review, Review of English Studies, Revue Germanique, Cambridge History of English Literature, etc. *Recreations:* reading detective stories, motoring, walking, gardening, sketching, tenniquoit. *Address:* c/o Dean Gildersleeve, Barnard College, New York City.

Died 24 Oct. 1942.

SPURR, Frederic Chambers; Baptist clergyman and Ex-President, National Free Church Council; *b* Sneinton, Nottingham, 4 May 1862; *s* of Frederic Spurr, merchant; *m* 1905, Ethel May, *e d* of Ald. F. M. Thompson, JP, Louth; two *s* one *d*. *Educ:* Nottingham; on Continent, privately. First charge, Cardiff, 1886–90; Special Missioner for Baptist Union, 1890–1904; Pastor Maze Pond Church, 1905–09; First Baptist Church, Melbourne, Australia, 1909–14; Regent's Park Chapel, 1914–22; Hamstead Road Church, Birmingham, 1922–36; occasional lecturer on social and travel subjects; travelled extensively on Continent, Africa, Syria, India and Australia. *Publications:* The Rights of God; The Holy Family; The Four Last Things; Christ or Cæsar; Knowing God for Certain; Authority in Religion; Religion and Family Life; Jesus Christ and the Social Question; Indifference in Religion; Certainty in Religion; Five Years under the Southern Cross; Our Social Disorders and Social Progress in the Light of Christ; The Master Key; Jesus Christ and the Modern Challenge; The New Psychology and the Christian Faith; Death and the Life Beyond (5 editions); A Liturgy for the Free Churches; The Christian use of Leisure; Sermon Substance; A Preachers' Notebook, 1933; The Man who holds the Keys; Christian Science; The Evangelism for our time; The Evangelist at Work, 1938; A Living Faith, 1939; Can God be Known, 1940; Editor Union Hymnal. *Recreations:* microscope, music, walking and climbing. *Address:* 61 Hove Park Road, Hove, Sussex. *T:* Preston (Brighton) 2926.

Died 6 Sept. 1942.

STABLER, Harold, RDI 1937; Designer, Craftsman, Silversmith; *b* 10 June 1872; *s* of George Stabler, Levens, Westmorland; *m* 1906, Phoebe Stabler, ARBS. *Educ:* Heversham, Westmorland. On Staff of Royal College of Art, 1912–26; Head of Art School of Sir John Cass Institute for 30 years prior to 1937; Member of Board of Trade Council for Art and Industry, 1937–40; one of Founders of Design and Industries Association; Works include: Collars of the Royal Victorian Order; Presentation enamelled casket from King George VI to the Shahinshan of Iran, 1938; Native Chief Chains for the Colonial Office; Presentation Pieces of Silver for City Livery Companies and Public and Ecclesiastical Bodies, including a Silver Cup presented to City of Paris by The Worshipful Company of Goldsmiths, 1937; a silver gilt rosewater Dish presented by the Goldsmiths Company to the Hon. Company of Master Mariners; a silver gilt rosewater dish commissioned by the Goldsmiths Company for their private collection as representative of modern silver work; also work for various Colleges and the Inns of Court, Posters and decorative work for the London Passenger Transport Board. *Recreations:* archæology and natural history. *Address:* 34 Upper Mall, Hammersmith, W6. *T:* Riverside 3301.

Died 11 April 1945.

STACK, Lt-Col Charles Spottiswoode, CMG; Indian Army retired; farming in Kenya; *b* 28 Sept. 1868; *s* of Colonel C. E. Stack, 3rd QO Bombay Light Cavalry; *g s* of Major-General Sir Maurice Stack, KCB, 3rd Bombay Light Cavalry; *m* Mary Nina, *d* of late Captain Frank Corbett, 33rd Foot; no *c*. *Educ:* Marlborough College; Sandhurst. Gazetted to 6th Dragoon Guards (Carabineers), 1888; appointed to Indian Staff Corps 33rd QVO Light Cavalry, in which he remained throughout his entire service and commanded the regiment during European War; served Miranzai Expedition, 1890; China Expeditionary Force, 1900; Mesopotamia, 1914–16; Afghanistan, 1918 (despatches four times, CMG, Servian Order of White Eagle, twice wounded). *Recreations:* farming, breeding polo ponies, polo and hunting. *Address:* Twin Peaks, Mau Summit, Kenya Colony.

Died 13 Jan. 1943.

STACPOOLE, Florence; author; Member of The Royal Institution of Great Britain, The British Astronomical Association, and The British Institute of Philosophical Studies; Member of The Modern Churchmen's Union; *d* of late Rev. W. Church Stacpoole, DD (TCD), Kingstown, Ireland; *g d* of late Capt. Charles Stacpoole, Ennis, Co. Clare. *Educ:* privately. *Publications:* various works on Hygiene, etc.; numerous pamphlets on medical subjects, published by the National Health Society; also serials and short stories. *Address:* The Hall, Gosport, Hants. *T:* Gosport 8071. *Club:* Lyceum.

Died 2 Dec. 1942.

STADDON, John Henry. JP Borough and County; Alderman Bedfordshire County Council; High Sheriff of Bedfordshire, 1938. *Address:* Withycombe, Ludlow Avenue, Luton. *T:* 60. *Club:* City Livery.

Died 2 June 1944.

STAFFORD, 13th Baron *cr* 1640, confirmed 1825; **Edward Stafford Fitzherbert,** KCB 1920; CB 1918; *b* 1864; 3rd *s* of Basil Thomas Fitzherbert of Swynnerton Park, Staffs, and Emily Charlotte, *d* of late Hon. Edward Stafford Jerningham; *S* brother 1932. *Educ:* Oscott College, Birmingham. Entered Navy, 1877; Lieut, 1886; Comdr, 1899; Captain, 1904; Rear-Admiral, 1915; Vice-Adm. 1920; served Egypt, 1882 (medal and Khedive's star); East Africa, 1888 (despatches); commanded Colossus, Grand Fleet, 1914–15; Admiral of Mine Sweepers, 1916; Director of Torpedoes and Mines, 1917; Commander-in-Chief Cape Station; ret. list, 1923; Admiral, retired, 1925; JP, DL. *Heir: nephew* Basil Francis Nicholas Fitzherbert [*b* 7 April 1926; *s* of late Hon. Thomas Charles Fitzherbert, and Beryl, *d* of John Waters and *widow* of Major Henry Brougham, RA]. *Address:* Swynnerton Park, Stone, Staffordshire. *TA* and *T:* Swynnerton 28. *Clubs:* Naval and Military; Royal Naval, Portsmouth; Royal Yacht Squadron, Cowes.

Died 28 Sept. 1941.

STAFFORD, James William, CMG 1941; OBE 1923; MBE 1918; Director, Passport and Permit Office since 1939; *b* 5 Oct. 1884; *s* of Ernest William Stafford, late of the Admiralty; *m* 1911, Lyndye Agnes Wakefield; one *s* one *d*. *Educ:* St Dunstan's College, Catford. Entered Civil Service, 1902; Foreign Office, 1905; Assistant Passport Officer, 1922; Chief Passport Officer, 1938. *Recreations:* swimming, gardening and outdoor pursuits. *Address:* Westfield, Oxshott, Surrey. *T:* Oxshott 2469.

Died 4 Nov. 1945.

STAFFORD, Rev. John T. Wardle, DD North Western University; DCL Durham; Methodist Minister; *b* Dudley, 30 Aug. 1861; *s* of late Rev. N. W. Stafford, Primitive Methodist minister; *m* Edith, 2nd *d* of late J. Hardcastle, York; one *s* one *d*. *Educ:* Elmfield College, York; London University. Master in Classics and English Literature at Grove Park School, Wrexham, 1880–83. Entered the Wesleyan Methodist Ministry, 1883; after three years at Headingley College, began his career at Spennymoor, Co. Durham; in 1909, while at Scarborough, he was elected Chairman of the York District; in 1911 to the Legal Hundred of the Wesleyan Conference; and in 1912 to the Chairmanship of the Newcastle District; President of the Wesleyan Methodist Conference, 1920; Chairman of the Chester and Warrington District, 1932; Minister of the Metropolitan Church, Toronto, 1923–26; Missioner of Pastoral Evangelism to the Free Churches of the United States and Canada, 1927–29; sent by the Methodist Conference of England as Fraternal Delegate to the General Conference of the Methodist Episcopal Church of America, 1912; appointed as Representative of Wesleyan Conference to the Inaugural Meetings of the United Church of Canada, 1925; Chaplain for six years to Lord Mayors of Newcastle. *Address:* 65 The Causeway, Potters Bar. *T:* Potters Bar 3607.

Died 31 Aug. 1944.

STAFFORD, Brig.-Gen. William Francis Howard, CB 1902; *b* 19 Dec. 1854; *e s* of late Maj.-Gen. W. J. F. Stafford, CB; *m* 1884, Edith Mary Culling Carr (*d* 1931), *d* of late F. C. Carr-Gomm; one *s* three *d*. Entered Army, 1873; Captain, 1885; Major, 1892; Lieut-Col 1900; served Afghan War, 1878–80 (medal); Mahsood Wuzeeree Expedition, 1881; South Africa, 1899–1902 (despatches, Queen's medal 3 clasps, King's medal 2 clasps, CB); retired, 1911. *Address:* Thornbury, Crowthorne, Berks.

Died 8 Aug. 1942.

STAIRS, Gilbert S., MC; KC 1920; Barrister and Solicitor in firm of Stairs, Dixon, Claxton, Senécal & Lynch-Staunton, Montreal; *b* Dartmouth, Nova Scotia, 11 Nov. 1882; *s* of John Fitz-William Stairs and Charlotte Fogo; *m* 1909, Amie Beatrice (*d* 1933), *d* of Angus Sinclair, CE, Toronto; two *s* three *d*. *Educ:* Halifax Academy; Dalhousie College, BA; Harvard Law School; New College, Oxford, MA, Rhodes Scholar. Practised law at Halifax, NS, 1909–11; removed to Montreal, 1911; served European War in 87th Canadian Infantry Bn (Canadian Grenadier Guards), France, Oct. 1917 till Armistice, as Captain and Major (MC Battle Canal du Nord, Sept.–Oct. 1918); Officer commanding Canadian Grenadier Guards (Canadian Militia), 1924–28, and 1935–39; Hon. Lt-Col, Canadian Grenadier Guards, 1939; Col commanding Brigade of Canadian Guards (R) CA, 1940; Secretary Quebec Rhodes Scholarship Selection Committee, 1920–33; President, Canadian Club of Montreal, 1943–44. *Recreations:* sailing, golf. *Address:* 3441 Peel Street, Montreal, Quebec, Canada. *Clubs:* University, St James's, United Services, Canadian, Royal Montreal Golf, Montreal; Halifax, Royal Nova Scotia Yacht Squadron, Halifax, NS.

Died 5 Aug. 1947.

STAIRS, Major Henry Bertram, DSO 1900; Major, retired, Canada; *b* 29 April 1871; *s* of late John Stairs, Halifax, NS; *m* 1903, Judith, *d* of late George Henderson. Barrister, Supreme Court, Nova Scotia, 1893; KC 1910. Served South Africa; present at Paardeberg, 18–27 Feb. 1900 (despatches, DSO, Brevet Majority), Driefontein, Hout Nek, Sand River, Johannesburg, etc. (Queen's medal 4 clasps). Colonial Auxiliary Forces Long Service Medal. *Address:* 33 Le Marchant Street, Halifax, Canada. *Club:* Halifax.
Died 16 Feb. 1940.

STALBRIDGE, 2nd Baron *cr* 1880; **Hugh Grosvenor;** formerly Lieut 14th Hussars; *b* 5 May 1880; *e s* of 1st Baron Stalbridge and Eleanor, *d* of late Robert Hamilton Stubber, Moyne, Queen's Co; *S* father, 1912; *m* 1903, Gladys Elizabeth, *γ d* of late Brinsley de Courcy Nixon. Served South Africa, 1899–1903 (despatches twice), European War (despatches twice, MC); Protestant, Liberal Unionist. *Heir:* none. *Address:* Pounds Farm, Newbury. *Clubs:* Royal Yacht Squadron, Cowes.
Died 24 Dec. 1949.

STALLARD, Lt-Col Sidney, CBE 1930 (OBE 1919); DSO 1918; late Divisional Road Engineer, Ministry of Transport; *b* 1870. Served S Africa, 1901–02 (despatches Queen's medal with five clasps, King's medal with two clasps), European War, 1914–19 (despatches, DSO, OBE, TD, Legion of Honour). *Address:* The Old Cottage, Shamley Green. *T:* Bramley 3253.
Died 10 Dec. 1949.

STALLYBRASS, William Teulon Swan, OBE 1918, DCL; of the Inner Temple, Barrister-at-law, Midland Circuit; Principal of Brasenose College, Oxford, since 1936; Hon. Master of the Bench of Inner Temple; Member of Lord Chancellors' Law Revision Committee; Vice-Chancellor of Oxford University, since 1947; Eldon Trustee; Member of Inter-University Council for Higher Education in the Colonies and of the Colonial Social Science Research Council; *b* 22 Nov. 1883; *o s* of late William Swan Stallybrass. *Educ:* St Peter's College, Westminster (Scholar); Christ Church, Oxford (Scholar); 1st Class Classical Moderations, 1904; 2nd Class Literae Humaniores, 1906; 1st Class and Certificate of Honour Inns of Court Examination, 1909. Called to Bar, 1909; Fellow of Brasenose, 1911; Vice-Principal, 1914–36; Pro-proctor, 1914–15; Senior Proctor, 1925–26; University Reader in Criminal Law and Evidence, 1923–39; Lecturer at Oriel College, 1914–36, at Lincoln College, 1914–22; Examiner to the Council of Legal Education, 1921–25; Badges Dept, Ministry of Munitions, 1915; Section Director, Priority Department, Ministry of Munitions, 1915–18; Examiner in Honour School of Jurisprudence, 1915, 1918–20, 1936–38; Examiner in BCL, 1926–27, 1934; Examiner in Cambridge Law Tripos, 1932–33; Hon. Sec., Oxford Branch of League of Nations Union, 1918–20; Director of French Hospital since 1909; Hon. Treasurer, Oxford University Cricket Club, 1914–46. Commander of the Legion of Honour. *Publications:* The Pocket Emerson, 1910; Pros and Cons, 1911 (edited and revised); The Society of States, 1918; edited Oxford Magazine, 1914–1919; edited Oxford, 1940–1946; Parallelo dei principii generali di Diritto penale inglese col Progetto definitivo del nuovo Codice penale italiano; Seventh, Eighth, Ninth and Tenth Edns of Salmond's Torts; contributions to Law Quarterly Review, Cambridge Law Journal, Harvard Law Review, Oxford, Annuario di Diritto Comparetto, Journal of Comparative Legislation, Britain Today, etc. *Recreations:* golf; ran cross-country for Oxford *versus* Cambridge, 1905. *Address:* Brasenose College, Oxford. *T:* Oxford 47328. *Clubs:* United University, Royal Automobile; Frilford Heath Golf (Abingdon); Tadmarton Heath Golf (Banbury).
Died 28 Oct. 1948.

STAMER, Arthur Cowie, CBE 1920; MIME; *b* 7 March 1869; 5th *s* of late Right Rev. Sir L. T. Stamer, Bart, DD, Suffragan Bishop of Shrewsbury; *m* 1900, Everilda Mary, *d* of late G. A. Thompson of Terrington Hall, Yorks; one *d. Educ:* Rugby. Engineering pupil with Beyer & Peacock, Manchester, for four years; joined the service of the North-Eastern Railway, 1891; Chief Assist Mechanical Engineer, 1910; President of Institution of Locomotive Engineers, 1923; Assistant Chief Mechanical Engineer, London and North-Eastern Railway, 1923–33. *Address:* Faverdale Hall, Darlington. *T:* 2461. *Club:* Royal Automobile.
Died 14 Feb. 1944.

STAMER, Sir Lovelace, 4th Bt *cr* 1809; *b* 4 April 1859; *s* of 3rd Bt and Ellen Isabel (*d* 1933), *d* of Joseph Dent, Ribston Hall, Yorkshire; *S* father, 1908; *m* 1909, Eva Mary, *e d* of R. C. Otter, Royston Manor, Clayworth, Notts; one *s* two *d. Educ:* Harrow; Trinity College, Cambridge. Formerly Major 16th Lancers; served Boer War with Reserve of Officers; with Imperial Yeomanry in European War; Lt-Col TFR; JP Staffs and Salop. *Heir:* *s* Lovelace Anthony, Officer RAF, *b* 28 Feb. 1917. *Address:* Ashmead House, Cam, Glos. *Clubs:* Naval and Military, Windham.
Died 1 Oct. 1941.

STAMFORD, Thomas William; MP (Lab) West Leeds, 1923–31 and since 1945; *b* Cambridge, 20 Dec. 1882; *m* 1910; one *s*. President Bradford Trades Council, 1921–24; Member Bradford City Council, 1912–22; Pres., City of Bradford Labour Party, 1936. *Address:* 108 Durham Road, Bradford.
Died 30 May 1949.

STAMP, 1st Baron *cr* 1938, of Shortlands; **Josiah Charles Stamp,** GCB 1935; GBE 1924; KBE 1920; CBE 1918; Knight of Grace, Order of St John of Jerusalem; Grand Cross with Star, Austrian Order of Merit, 1936; Hon. DSc Oxford; Hon. ScD Cambridge; Hon. LLD, St Andrews, Edinburgh, Leeds, Dublin, Sydney, McGill, Toronto, Western Ontario, MacMaster, Harvard, Columbia, California, North-western, Johns Hopkins, South-western, Syracuse, Duke, Washington and Lee; Hon. Dr of Economics, Lisbon; Hon. Dr of Law, Athens; DSc (Econ.) London; Hon. Associate College of Technology, Manchester University; Hon. Mem. Society Incorporated Accountants and Auditors; FBA 1926; Chairman of the London Midland and Scottish Railway, and President of the Executive; Director of the Bank of England; Member of the Economic Advisory Council; Adviser on Economic Co-ordination to Ministerial Committee since 1939; *b* 21 June 1880; *e s* of late Charles Stamp, Yomah, Bexley; *m* 1903, Olive (JP Kent; President Nat. Free Church Women's Council; Governor of University College, Aberystwyth), *d* of late Alfred Marsh, Grove Park; four *s. Educ:* London University (Faculty of Economics and Political Science). BSc First Class Hons 1911; Cobden Prizeman, 1912; DSc 1916; Hutchinson Research Medallist, 1916. Newmarch Lecturer in Statistics, 1919–21, 1923; Member of the Senate, 1924–26, and of Board of Studies in Economics and other University Committees; at various times Examiner (Economics, Political Science, Statistics, etc.) for Cambridge, London, Manchester, Edinburgh, and Glasgow Universities, and Society of Incorporated Accountants; Guy Medallist of Royal Statistical Society, 1919; Joint Secretary and Editor, 1920–30; President, 1930–32, now Hon. Vice-President; Treas. of International Statistical Institute; Hon. Member American Statistical Association; Hon. Member of Hungarian Statistical Society; First Beckly Lecturer on Social Service (York Wesleyan Conference, 1926); Fernley-Hartley Lecturer, 1936; Sidney Ball Lecturer, Oxford, 1926; Rede Lecturer, Cambridge, 1927; Mond Lecturer, Manchester, 1931; Rankin Lecturer Liverpool, 1938; Finlay Lecturer, Dublin 1938; Vice-President, Institute of Industrial Psychology; President Abbey Road Permanent Building Society;

President of the Institute of Transport, 1929–30; President, Geographical Assoc., 1936; President, Advertising Assoc., 1937; Pres. designate, Library Association; President, Institute of Public Administration; President National Institute of Economic and Social Research; Pres. Society of Genealogists; Chairman of London School of Economics, Governor of Birkbeck College, of University College, Aberystwyth; Chairman of the Leys School, and Chairman of Queenswood School; Chairman Rockefeller Social Science Advisory Committee; Pilgrim Trustee, Lieutenant of the City of London; Colonel Commanding (RE) Transport and Railway Corps; Hon. Col Transportation Unit, Royal Engineers, Supplementary Reserve; President of the British Association for the Advancement of Science, 1936 (Treasurer, 1929–35; President Sec. F Oxford, 1926); Hon. member American Philosophical Society and American Academy of Arts and Sciences; Member of Council of Duchy of Lancaster and Commissioner for Exhibition of 1851; Charter Mayor of Beckenham, 1935, and Freeman of the Borough, 1936; Freeman of Blackpool, 1937; Member, Royal Commission on Income Tax, 1919; Member, Northern Ireland Finance Arbitration Committee, 1923–24; Member, Committee on Taxation and National Debt, 1924; British representative on the Reparation Commission's (Dawes) Committee on German Currency and Finance, 1924, and upon (Young) Experts' Committee, 1929; Member Court of Inquiry, Coal Mining Industry Dispute, 1925; Statutory Commissioner under London University Act, 1926; Chairman Grain Futures Inquiry, Canada, 1931; Chairman, Lambert-Levita Case Enquiry, 1936; entered Civil Service, 1896; Inland Revenue Dept, 1896; Board of Trade (Marine Dept), 1898; Inland Revenue (Taxes), 1900; transferred to Secretariat, 1914; Assistant Secretary to the Board, 1916; resigned, March 1919; Sec. and Director Nobel Industries, Ltd, 1919–26; Director, Imperial Chemical Industries, 1927–28. *Publications:* British Incomes and Property; the Application of Official Statistics to Economic Problems, 1916 (3rd ed. 1922); Wealth and Income of the Chief Powers, 1919; The Fundamental Principles of Taxation in the light of Modern Developments, 1921 (2nd ed. 1923, revised ed. 1937), Italian trans, 1934; Wealth and Taxable Capacity, 1922 (2nd ed. 1923); Joint Report on Double Taxation (League of Nations), 1923; (with C. H. Nelson, Business Statistics and Financial Statements), 1924; Studies in Current Problems in Government and Finance, 1924; Report on Effect of Reparation Payments on Industry (International Chamber of Commerce), 1925; British edition of Rignano's Social Significance of Death Duties, 1925; The Christian Ethic as an Economic Factor, 1926; Articles in Ency. Brit., 13th and 14th eds; The National Income, 1924 (with Prof. Bowley), 1926; On Stimulus, 1927; Some Economic Factors in Modern Life, 1928; Criticism and Other Addresses, 1931; Internationalism, 1931; Papers on Gold and the Price Level, 1931; The Financial Aftermath of War, 1932; Taxation during the War, 1932; Ideals of a Student, 1933; Motive and Method in a Christian Order, 1936; The National Capital and other Statistical Studies, 1937; The Science of Social Adjustment, 1937; We Live and Learn, 1937; Christianity and Economics, 1939. *Heir: s* Hon. Wilfrid Carlyle Stamp, MA, ACA, *b* 1904. *Address:* Tantallon, Park Hill Road, Shortlands, Kent. *T:* Ravensbourne 2391. *Clubs:* Athenæum, Reform, University of London.

Died 16 April 1941.

STAMP, Ernest, ARE 1894; artist; *b* Sowerby, Yorks, 22 Feb. 1869; *s* of Edward Stamp and Charlotte Crook; *m* 1896, Lydia Soden; no *c. Educ:* private school. Studied Art under Professor Sir Hubert Herkomer, RA. Exhibited at Salon, Paris, Royal Academy, London, Franco-British Exhibition, London, St Louis Exhibition, USA, and other London and provincial Exhibitions; numerous paintings, mezzotints, and drawings are in the permanent collections of the Bibliothèque Nationale, Paris, British Museum, Victoria and Albert Museum, The City of London Guildhall, London Museum, LCC County Hall, Marylebone Town Hall, Hampstead Corporation a large number called the Ernest Stamp Collection, Brighton Corporation Art Gallery, Guildford Museum, Ashmolean Museum, Oxford, Fitzwilliam Museum, Cambridge, Birmingham City Art Gallery, Manchester City Art Gallery, Glasgow City Art Gallery, National Gallery of Scotland, Bankfield Museum, Halifax, etc. *Publications:* Principal Mezzotints engraved and published, Lord Russell of Killowen, Lord Chief Justice, Coventry Patmore, Sir Thomas Devitt, Bart, after John S. Sargent, RA, Duchess of Rutland, Lady Bamphilde, Lady Betty Delma, Mrs Musters, Lady Halliday, Miss Keppel, after Sir Joshua Reynolds, PRA, Countess of Warwick, after Carolus Duran, The Countess of Ossory, after Sir Peter Lely, The Hon. Mrs Graham, The Duchess of Devonshire, Lady Conyngham, Mrs Sheridan, after Thomas Gainsborough, The Farmer's Daughter, after Sir Wm Orchardson, RA, also mezzotints after Raeburn, Debucourt, Boucher, Meissonier, etc. *Recreation:* work. *Address:* 440 Upper Shoreham Road, Shoreham, Sussex.

Died Dec. 1942.

STAMPER, James William, RCA 1921, now Hon. retd academician; landscape painter; *b* Birmingham, 1873; *s* of late James Stamper, of the Potteries; *m* 1st, 1902, Ellen, *d* of late Benjamin Brierley, RN; 2nd, 1934, Winifred, *d* of Alfred Hutton, Amlwch. *Educ:* Central School, Technical School, and School of Art, Manchester. Entered the accountancy profession at the age of sixteen with Lonsdale Broderick, FCA; afterwards spent two years at the Manchester Technical School, resuming the profession of accountancy up to the year 1906; then went to reside at Conway, taking up landscape painting professionally; picture Wallflowers purchased by Manchester Corporation for permanent collection, 1926; exhibited pictures in London, Manchester, Liverpool, Birmingham, Oldham, Preston, Sheffield, Conway, Belfast, Cardiff, etc., many works reproduced. *Recreations:* walking, gardening. *Address:* Caban Hedd, Amlwch Port, Anglesey.

Died 14 Sept. 1947.

STANCOMB, William; *b* 17 March 1850; *s* of William Stancomb and Bridget Dowing Bowler Hare; *m* 1873, Frances Grace Milward (*d* 1939), Ledlade Manor; two *s* three *d. Educ:* Eton; Magdalen College, Oxford, MA. JP for County of Wilts since 1877; formerly Lieut in Royal Wiltshire Militia. *Recreations:* hunting and shooting, etc., and general country pursuits. *Address:* Blounts Court, Potterne, Wilts. *TA:* Potterne. *T:* 105 X1. *Club:* Constitutional.

Died 21 March 1941.

STANDEN, Sir Bertram Prior, KCIE 1925; CSI 1920; CIE 1901; *b* 1867; *s* of R. S. Standen, Lyndfield, Sussex; *m* 1890, Oona, OBE 1918 (*d* 1942), *d* of N. C. Macnamara. *Educ:* Uppingham; Trinity College, Cambridge. Entered ICS 1886; Registrar Judicial Comm. Court, Nagpur, 1891; Settlement Officer, 1894; Deputy Commissioner, 1897; Commissioner of Settlement, 1904; Director of Credit Societies, 1908; Chief Secretary to Chief Commissioner, 1908–11; Commissioner, Central Provinces, India, 1918; retired, 1926. *Address:* Ibthorpe Farm, Hurstbourne Tarrant, Andover, Hants.

Died 18 Oct. 1947.

STANISTREET, Maj.-Gen. Sir George Bradshaw, KBE 1919; CB 1918; CMG 1917; *b* 13 May 1866; *s* of late Richard Stanistreet, MD. *Educ:* Windermere College; Trinity College, Dublin; BA 1887; MB, BCh 1889. Entered Army, 1891; Major, 1903; Lt-Col 1913; Col 1917; Maj.-Gen. (temp.) 1918; Maj.-Gen. 1922; retired, 1922; served NW Frontier, India, 1897–98; European War, 1914–18 (despatches, KBE, CB, CMG).

Personal Assistant to PMO, Punjab Command, 1896–1901; Embarkation Medical Officer, Southampton, 1902; Staff Officer to PMO, Southern Command, 1906–10; Deputy Assistant Director-General, Army Medical Services, War Office, 1913–17; Assistant Director-General, Army Medical Services, 1917–18; Deputy-Director-General, Army Medical Services, 1918–22; Officer of Order of St John of Jerusalem, 1917; Commander of Order of Crown of Italy, 1919. *Publications:* Medical Arrangements on board Transports, Journal RAMC, July 1903. *Recreations:* yachting, lawn tennis. *Club:* Junior United Service.

Died 26 Jan. 1941.

STANLEY, Hon. Sir Arthur, GCVO 1944; GBE 1917; CB 1916; MVO 1905; LLD Leeds; Treasurer, St Thomas's Hospital, 1917–43, Vice-President since 1943; *b* 18 Nov. 1869; 3rd *s* of 16th Earl of Derby. *Educ:* Wellington. Attaché in Diplomatic Service; clerk in Foreign Office; Priv. Sec. to Mr Balfour (First Lord of Treasury, 1892); 3rd Sec. Diplomatic Service in Cairo; Hon. FRCP (Edinburgh); Commander Legion of Honour; Chairman Executive Committee of British Red Cross Society, 1914–43; Chairman, Joint Council British Red Cross Society and Order of St John; Chairman, Royal Automobile Club, 1905–07 and 1912–36; MP (C) Ormskirk division of SW Lancashire, 1898–1918; Chairman, Royal College of Nursing; DL, JP Lancashire. *Address:* Bolsover Court, Eastbourne, Sussex. *Club:* Royal Automobile.

Died 4 Nov. 1947.

STANLEY, Edward Arthur Vesey; JP Somerset; *b* 30 Aug. 1879; *o surv. s* of late E. J. Stanley of Cross Hall, Lancs, and late Hon. Mrs Stanley; *m* 1st, 1919, Sybil (from whom he obtained a divorce, 1932), *d* of late Maj. H. B. Dodgson, DSO; three *s*; 2nd, 1936, Marjorie Beatrice Booth; one *s*. *Educ:* Eton; Christ Church, Oxford. Master, Quantock Stag Hounds, 1900–07; Devon and Somerset Stag Hounds, 1907–09; Woodland Pytchley Fox Hounds, 1909–13; served European War in France with 21st Lancers; founded National Greyhound Racing Club. *Recreations:* hunt, shoot, race. *Address:* St Swithins, Maybury Hill, Woking, Surrey. *Clubs:* Bath, Orleans.

Died 11 June 1941.

STANLEY, Lt-Col Hon. Frederick William, DSO 1917; *b* 27 May 1878; *y s* of 16th Earl of Derby; *m* 1905, Lady Alexandra Louise Elizabeth Acheson, *e d* of 4th Earl of Gosford; one *s* two *d*. *Educ:* Wellington; Sandhurst. Bt Lt-Col Reserve of Officers; late Capt. 10th Hussars; served South Africa, 1899–1902 (severely wounded, Queen's medal six clasps, King's medal two clasps); European War, 1914–18 (DSO); extra ADC to Viceroy at Delhi Durbar, 1903. *Clubs:* Turf, Cavalry.

Died 9 Aug. 1942.

STANLEY, Col Geoffrey, CB 1900; late Army Service Corps; *b* 2 Dec. 1855; 2nd *s* of late Rev. Edmond Stanley, of Rhoscrowther, Pembrokeshire. Entered army, 1874; served Zulu War, 1879 (medal with clasp); Boer War, 1881; South Africa, 1899–1902 (despatches, Queen's and King's medals seven clasps, CB); retired, 1910. *Address:* 22 St Mary's Mansions, Paddington, W2. *Clubs:* Junior United Service, MCC.

Died 23 April 1943.

STANLEY, Harry Merridew; Senior partner of firm of St Quintin, Son and Stanley; *b* 12 May 1865; *e s* of late Henry Stanley; *m* 1894, Edith, 4th *d* of late John Bridges; one *s*. *Educ:* Felsted; Bury St Edmunds. Practising Surveyor, specialising in London property, particularly in City of London; After serving on principal Committees and for 7 years Chairman of Professional Practices Committee was elected President of Chartered

Surveyors Institution for 1935–36. *Recreations:* travelling and golf. *Address:* 43 Phillimore Gardens, Kensington, W8. *T:* Western 1760. *Clubs:* Conservative, Gresham.

Died 21 Jan. 1945.

STANLEY, Rt Hon. Oliver Frederick George; PC 1934; MP (C) Bristol West since 1945; Chancellor of Liverpool University since 1948; *b* 1896; *s* of 17th Earl of Derby, KG, PC, GCB, GCVO; *m* Lady Maureen Stewart (*d* 1942), *d* of 7th Marquess of Londonderry, KG, PC, MVO; one *s* one *d*. *Educ:* Eton. Major RFA; served European War, 1914–18 (MC, Croix de Guerre, despatches); called to Bar, 1919; contested (C) Edgehill Division of Liverpool, 1923; MP (C) Westmorland, 1924–45; Parliamentary Under-Secretary, Home Office, 1931–33; Minister of Transport, 1933–34; Minister of Labour, 1934–35; Pres. of Board of Education, 1935–37; President of Board of Trade, 1937–40; Secretary of State for War, 1940; Secretary of State for the Colonies, 1942–45. *Address:* Folly Farm, Sulhamstead, Reading, Berks. *T:* Theale 26. *Club:* Turf.

Died 10 Dec. 1950.

STANLEY, Ronald Francis Assheton S.; *see* Sloane-Stanley.

STANSBURY, Captain Hubert, CB 1918; RN; retired; *b* 1873; *m*; one *s* two *d*. Principal Naval Transport Officer at Southampton on the outbreak of war, 1914, organising the shipping of the Expeditionary Force to France during the first eight months of hostilities; Naval Assistant Director of Transport; and later Director of Technical Services at the Ministry of Shipping; Principal Sea Transport Officer at Southampton, 1919–33. *Address:* White Lodge, West Hill, Ottery St Mary, Devon.

Died 11 June 1949.

STANSFIELD, Alfred, DSc; FRSC; ARSM; Birks Professor of Metallurgy, and Head of Department of Metallurgy, McGill University, Montreal, 1901–36; now Emeritus Professor; *b* Bradford; *e s* of Frederic Stansfield; *m* 1905, Ethel Ernestine (*d* 1942), *d* of F. E. Grubb, of Cahir Abbey, County Tipperary; one *d*. *Educ:* Royal College of Science and Royal School of Mines, London. Carried out researches on alloys for Sir William Roberts-Austen, 1891–98; Doctor of Science of the London University, 1898; in charge of Metallurgical Laboratories of Royal School of Mines, 1898–1901; visited Sweden to report to Canadian Government on the electric smelting of iron ores, 1914; Member of Commission appointed by Canadian Minister of Militia and Defence to investigate the feasibility of producing refined copper and zinc in Canada, 1915; production of magnesium in Canada, 1915; experimental work on the electric smelting of zinc ores and of titaniferous ores of iron; Commissioner of the Pyx of the Ottawa Mint, 1911–31; Editor of Iron and Steel of Canada, 1918–19; report in 1918 to the Government of British Columbia on the possibility of smelting electrically the magnetite ores of that province; awarded Plummer medal by Engineering Institute of Canada, 1921; Vice-President of American Electrochemical Society, 1928. *Publications:* The Electric Furnace, its Construction, Operation, and Uses; 2nd ed. 1914; The Electric Furnace for Iron and Steel, 1923; papers on Pyrometry, Solution Theory of Carburized Iron, Constitution of Alloys, Burning of Steel, Smelting Titaniferous Ores of Iron, Electric Smelting, Graphical methods of teaching Thermochemistry, investigation of metallurgical reactions at high temperatures; Equilibria in the iron-carbon system, Canadian Electric Furnace Industry; Report to Dept of Mines, Ottawa, on the Electrothermic Smelting of Iron Ores in Sweden, 1915; Report to BC Minister of Mines on Electric Smelting of Iron Ores in BC. *Address:* McGill University, Montreal. *Clubs:* McGill Faculty, Montreal.

Died 5 Feb. 1944.

STANSFIELD, William, CMG 1918; DSO 1919; VD; Director of Remounts, 1st Military District, Australia, Sept. 1939; Liaison Officer, Civil and Military Defence, 1st Military District, 1941; *b* Todmorden, Yorks, 19 Nov. 1877; *s* of Mitchell and Margaret Stansfield of Todmorden; *m* 1897, Amy Louisa Rogers, Brisbane; three *s* two *d*. *Educ:* Kelvin Grove State School. Arrived Australia, 1884; joined Queensland Railway Service, 1898; enlisted CMF, 1901; AIF 18 Aug. 1914; Lieutenant, Supply Officer, 1st LH Brigade; Capt., Dec. 1914; Major, March 1916, and to command ASC, Anzac Mtd Division; Gallipoli, 12 May–29 Nov.; Lt-Col June 1917, and appointed ADST, Desert Mtd Corps (despatches, DSO, CMG, Colonial Forces medal); State Transport Officer to Royal Visits Prince of Wales, Duke and Duchess of York, Prince Henry. *Recreations:* golf, boating. *Address:* Le Geyt Street, Windsor, Brisbane, Queensland.

Died 19 May 1946.

STANTIALL, William, CIE 1923; *b* 1865; *s* of Alfred George Stantiall; *m* 1898, Alice Maude, 2nd *d* of G. W. Hammon; two *d*. *Educ:* City of London School. Entered India Office, 1882; Senior Clerk, 1903; Assistant Secretary Public Works Dept, 1911; Secretary, 1919–26; Railway Adviser at India Office and Government Director of Indian Railway Companies, 1926; retired, 1931. *Address:* Almora, 20 Brycedale Crescent, Southgate, N14. *T:* Palmers Green 3780.

Died 20 Nov. 1947.

STANTON, Charles Butt, CBE 1920; Vice-President British Workers' National League; Lecturer and Social Reformer; *b* Aberaman, S Wales, 1873; *m* 1893, Alice Maud Thomas, Aberdare; one *s*. *Educ:* Aberaman British Schools. Miner, Docker, Miners' Agent; fought election East Glam. Labour Candidate, 1912; MP (Ind Lab) Merthyr Tydfil, 1915–22; one of the miners' leaders during the National Coal Strike Rhondda Riots; Socialist Speaker National League; joined Liberal Party, 1928; was Governor of Cardiff and Aberystwyth Universities. *Publications:* Facts for Federationists; Maxims for Miners; Why we should Agitate, etc. *Recreations:* landscape painting in oils, violin music, etc.

Died 6 Dec. 1946.

STANTON, Col Edward Alexander, CMG 1916; *b* York, 15 Nov. 1867; *e s* of late General Sir E. Stanton; *m* 1900, Isabel, 2nd *d* of Capt. H. C. Willes, late Royal Welsh Fusiliers; (one *s* killed on active service). *Educ:* Marlborough; Sandhurst. Joined the Oxfordshire Light Infantry, 1887; Capt. 1894; Brevet Maj. 1898; served in Expedition to Dongola, 1896; Actions of Ferket and Hafir (despatches, medal and 2 clasps); served Nile Expedition, 1897 (despatches, clasp); Nile Expedition, 1898; battles of the Atbara and Omdurman (despatches twice, brevet of Major, 2 clasps, English medal); Nile Expedition, 1899 (clasp and 3rd class Medjidie); (Local) Lieut-Col, 1901; designed the Soudan Camel Stamp, 1897; Governor of Khartoum, 1900–08; retired, 1908; Secretary to Royal Patriotic Fund Corporation, 1909–14; Military, Secretary to Duke of Connaught in Canada, 1914–17; Assistant Secretary Pensions Ministry, 1917–18; Military Governor, Phœnicia district, Palestine, 1918–20; Acting Secretary Royal Patriotic Fund, 1939–42; created Pasha, awarded 2nd class Medjidie; Grand Officer of the Order of St Aziz, 3rd class Order of the Nile. *Address:* Thornsett, Budleigh Salterton, Devon. *T:* Budleigh Salterton 690. *Club:* Army and Navy.

Died 2 Dec. 1947.

STANTON, Maj.-Gen. Sir Henry Ernest, KCMG 1919; CB 1911; DSO 1887; *b* Yanworth, Gloucestershire, 10 Nov. 1861; *y s* of Rev. Canon W. H. Stanton, Hasleton, Gloucestershire; *m* 1899, Olive Talbot, *d* of General Sir R. Low, GCB; one *s* one *d*. *Educ:* Marlborough; RMA, Woolwich; Staff College. Joined RA, 1881; served with Upper Burma Field Force,

1885–87 and 1887–88 (despatches, medal 2 clasps, and DSO); Brigade-Major 1st Brigade Chitral Relief Force, 1895; actions Malakand Pass and Khar (despatches, medal and clasp); DAQMG, IB, Malakand and Buner Field Forces, 1897–98; actions Landakai. Nawagai Bedmany Pass; operations Mamund, Mohmand, Utmankhel; action Tanga Pass (despatches, brevet of Major clasp); DAAG Khyber Brigade, 1898; Asst Military Secretary, Bombay Command, 1899–1902; AAG India, 1902; Chief Staff Officer Somaliland Field Force, 1903–04 (action Jidablli, despatches, brevet of Lt-Col, medal and 2 clasps); ADC to the King and Bt Col, 1906; Gen. Staff, 1st grade (India), 1911; Dep. QMG (India), 1912; European War, 1914–19, AA & QMG Egypt and Commander (despatches, prom. Maj.-Gen. 1915, KCMG, 3 medals); retired, 1919. *Address:* Inschdene, Woodchester, Glos. *Club:* Naval and Military.

Died 13 Dec. 1943.

STAPLEDON, William Olaf, MA, PhD; *b* 10 May 1886; *s* of William Clibbett Stapledon; *m* 1919, Agnes Zena Miller; one *s* one *d*. *Educ:* Abbotsholme School; Balliol College, Oxford; Liverpool University. One year's teaching at the Manchester Grammar School, under J. Lewis Paton; Eighteen months in a shipping office (Alfred Holt and Co.), in Liverpool and in Port Said, Egypt; Extramural lecturing under the University of Liverpool, in English Literature, and Industrial History; served in France with the Friends' Ambulance Unit, 1915–19; Extramural lecturing under University of Liverpool, in psychology and philosophy. *Publications:* A Modern Theory of Ethics; Last and First Men; Last Men in London; Waking World; Odd John; Star Maker; Philosophy and Living; Saints and Revolutionaries; New Hope for Britain; Darkness and the Light; Beyond the 'Isms; Sirius: Youth and Tomorrow; Death into Life; The Flames; contributions in philosophical and other periodicals. *Recreations:* walking, swimming. *Address:* Simon's Field, Caldy, West Kirby, Wirral. *T:* Hoylake 1134. *Clubs:* Authors', PEN; University, Sandon (Liverpool).

Died 6 Sept. 1950.

STAPLES, Sir Robert Ponsonby, 12th Bt *cr* 1628; artist peintre; *b* 30 June 1853; 3rd *s* of late Sir Nathaniel A. Staples, 10th Bt; *S* brother, 1933; *m* 1883, Ada Louisa (*d* 1940), *d* of H. Stammers, London; one *s* three *d*. *Educ:* at home by his father; Louvain Academy of Fine Arts, 1865–70; under Portaels in Brussels, 1872–74; studied at Dresden, 1867. Visited Paris, 1869; first exhibited Royal Academy, Burlington House, 1875, and since more often than not; visited Australia, 1879–80; served as Art Master at the People's Palace, Mile-End Road, 1897; Member Union International des Beaux-Arts; The Belfast Art Society. *Publications and Works:* Guilty or Not Guilty, Queen's Annual Gifts to the Poor, Australia, England, 1887 (painted in conjunction with the late G. H. Barrable), now acquired by the MCC, Lords; The Emperor's Farewell: The Dying Emperor Wilhelm I, 1888; The Last Shot for the Queen's Prize—Wimbledon, 1887, acquired by Municipal Gallery, Worthing; Cardinal Manning's Last Reception (presented to Cardinal Vaughan by the Roman Catholics of England); Mr Gladstone introducing the Home Rule Bill, 13 February 1893; Mr Labouchere, Phil May bequest to the National Portrait Gallery, and J. McNeill Whistler, purchased by Trustees of National Portrait Gallery; besides recent bequest Charles Algernon Swinburne, executed: 1900; Earl Roberts, VC (purchased by King Edward); The Queen and King Edward VII; Dawn on the Matoppos; Lion guarding Cecil Rhodes' Grave; two Triptychs, illustrating Shipbuilding, for New City Hall, Belfast; Irish Political Cartoons; Lissan Waters, RA, 1923; Winter, Mid Derry and Tyrone, RA, 1926. *Recreations:* an argument, historical and metaphysical reading, plenty of fresh air, and early barefoot walking. *Heir:* *s* Robert George

Alexander [b 21 Sept. 1894; m 1922, Vera Lillian, d of John Jenkins, Iveresk, Dulwich Wood Park, SE; two d]. *Address:* Lissan House, Cookstown, Co. Tyrone, Ireland.

Died 18 Oct. 1943.

STARKEY, Thomas Albert; late Strathcona Prof. of Hygiene, McGill University, Montreal; *b* Cheshire, 1872; *s* of Thomas and Margaret Starkey of Hartford, Cheshire; *m* 1904, Mary Josephine, *d* of late Dr D. C. MacCallum of Montreal; one *s. Educ:* Witton School, Cheshire; Univ. Coll., London. MRCS (Eng.), LRCP (Lond.) 1894; MB (Lond. Univ.) 1895; DPH (Eng.) 1901; MD, CM (*ad eundem*), McGill Univ., Montreal, 1911; Fellow Royal Sanitary Institute, 1903. House Physician at University College Hospital and Brompton Hospital for Consumption; Medical Officer and Bacteriologist, North-Western Hospital, Metropolitan Asylums Board; Bacteriologist to Government Laboratory, Bombay under Haffkine; District Sanitary Officer, Satara and Poona, Bombay Presidency; Assistant to Dr Childs, University College, London. *Publications:* Practical or Applied Hygiene, 1914; Humidity in the Atmosphere (two publications, with Dr Howard Barnes); Transactions Royal Society, Canada; Sewage Purification; Montreal Medical Journal and Journal of Canadian Public Health Association; New Method of Isolation of Colon-Typhoid Bacilli, Journal American Medical Sciences; New Standard (Bacteriological) for Water Analyses, Journal Royal Sanitary Institute. *Recreation:* fishing. *Address:* 3591 University Street, Montreal. *T:* Marquette 3990 Montreal. *Clubs:* Facculty, Montreal.

Died 25 March 1939.

STARKIE, Rev. Prebendary Le Gendre George H.; *see* Horton-Starkie.

STARLING, Hubert John; Consulting Physician, Norfolk and Norwich Hospital and Norfolk Mental Hospital; *b* Bombay, 1874; *s* of late Mathew Henry Starling, Barrister-at-Law and Clerk of the Crown, Bombay; *m* Theodora Victoria E., *d* of late Dr Thomas Fairbank, Windsor; two *s. Educ:* St Paul's School; Guy's Hospital. Extraordinary member of Assoc. of Physicians and of Brit. Cardiac Society. *Publications:* various medical papers. *Recreations:* music, motoring. *Address:* 45 All Saints Green, Norwich. *T:* Norwich 20824.

Died 10 April 1950.

STARR, Col William Henderson, CB 1918; CMG 1917; CBE 1919; late AMS; *b* 1861; *s* of late Lt-Col E. H. Starr, RMA. *Educ:* St Bartholomew's Hospital. Served Waziristan Expedition, 1894–95 (medal and clasp); China, 1900 (medal); European War, France, 1914–15, Mesopotamia, 1916–19 (despatches, CB, CMG); retired pay, 1919. *Publication:* Medico-topographical Report on Weihai-Wei. *Address:* c/o Glyn Mills & Co. Whitehall, SW.

Died 19 May 1947.

STARTIN, Adm. Sir James, KCB 1917; CB 1914; *b* 20 May 1855; *s* of late William Startin, Leamington; *m* 1st, 1891, Alice (*d* 1923), 5th *d* of late Gilbert M'Micking of Miltonise, Wigtownshire; three *s* one *d*; 2nd, 1924, Ethel (*d* 1943), *widow* of Walter Edward Barratt of Linley Hall, Bishops Castle, Shropshire. *Educ:* Royal Naval School, New Cross. Entered Royal Navy, 1869; Sub-Lieut 1876; Lieut 1879; Commander, 1891; Capt. 1897; Rear-Adm. 1907; Lt-Com. RNR Sept. 1914; Commander RNR 1914; Capt. 1914; Commodore, 1915; Vice-Adm. 1911; retired, 1914; Admiral, retired, 1915; served European War in patrol vessels and Q boats; served Zulu War, 1878–79 (medal with clasp, despatches, prom.); Egyptian War, 1882, landed with Naval Brigade (medal with clasp, bronze star); Lieutenant in Royal Yacht Victoria and Albert, 1889–91; served Benin War, 1897 (medal with clasp, despatches, promoted); China War, 1900 (medal); ADC to the King, 1906–07; Rear-Admiral in Channel and Home Fleets, 1908–09; Royal

Humane Society's silver and bronze medals with two clasps; Officier de Légion d'Honneur; Albert medal, 1918. *Address:* Wyndlawn, Hayling Island, Hants. *TA:* Hayling Island. *T:* Hayling 77569. *Club:* United Service.

Died 25 Sept. 1948.

STATHAM, Hon. Sir Charles Ernest, Kt 1926; MLC since 1936; a Knight of Grace of the Order of St John of Jerusalem; *b* Dunedin, 10 May 1875; *e* and *o surv. s* of Rev. Canon Charles Hadfield Statham, Dunedin, NZ (Anglican); *m* 1905, Lilias Harata Hine te Aho, 2nd *d* of William Burnett, JP, Dunedin; one *d. Educ:* private schools; William Street School, Dunedin; Cathedral School, Christchurch; Otago Boys' High School, Dunedin. A Barrister and Solicitor of the Supreme Court of New Zealand; member of the Dunedin City Council, 1911–13 (retired); represented Dunedin Central in the House of Representatives, 1911–35 (retired); Speaker of the House of Representatives, New Zealand, 1923–36. *Recreations:* formerly rowing and Rugby football. *Address:* Parliament House, Wellington, NZ; 11 Park Street, Wellington, NZ.

Died 5 March 1946.

STATHAM, Sir Randulph Meverel, Kt 1942; CIE 1930; MA, IES; Director of Public Instruction, Madras, 1936; *b* 4 Sept. 1890; *s* of Rev. S. P. H. Statham, retired Chaplain Insp.-General of Prisons; *m* 1915, Marjorie Graham; two *s. Educ:* Dover College, Leatherhead; Peterhouse, Cambridge. Joined Indian Educational Service as additional Professor of History, Presidency College, Madras, 1913; Principal, Government College, Kumbakonam, 1914–19; Deputy Director of Public Instruction, Madras, 1920; special officer, Education, Health and Lands Dept, Government of India, 1927; Secretary, the Auxiliary Committee of the Indian Statutory Commission, 1928; Principal Presidency College, Madras, 1931; Chairman of the Travancore Education Reforms Committee, 1932; Director of Public Instruction, Travancore, 1933; Acting Educational Commissioner with the Government of India, 1935. *Clubs:* Madras, Madras.

Died 26 Dec. 1944.

STAVELEY-HILL, His Hon. Henry Staveley, JP, DL Staffordshire; JP Warwickshire and Northamptonshire; TD; *b* 22 May 1865; *o s* of late Alex. Staveley-Hill, PC; *m* 1901, Eileen de Grey, *d* of de Burgh d'Arcy; two *s* three *d. Educ:* Westminster; St John's College, Oxford. Barrister, Inner Temple, 1891; Oxford Circuit; Recorder of Banbury, 1903–22; County Court Judge, Circuit 23 (Coventry, Northampton, etc.), 1922–28; MP (C) Kingswinford Division of Staffordshire, 1905–18; County Councillor for Staffs; has travelled in the Colonies and throughout Europe; late Capt. Staffordshire Queen's Own Royal Regt Staffs Yeomanry; Major, 2/1 Staffs Yeomanry, 1914; Lt-Col, commanding 2/1 Staffs Yeomanry, 1915; Superintending Officer Labour Corps Scottish Command, 1917; assumed by Royal Licence the name of Staveley, 1906; appointed 1925 as Independent Chairman Eastern District Board under the National Agreement for Regulating Wages in the Coal Trade. *Recreations:* hunting, shooting, and fishing; rowed for College at Oxford. *Address:* Oxley, Longdon Hill, Evesham. *Clubs:* Garrick, Leander.

Died 25 March 1946.

STAVRIDI, Sir John, Kt 1919; solicitor; Chairman of Ionian Bank; Chairman of Hellenic and General Trust Ltd; *b* 27 April 1867; *s* of John Constantine Stavridi of Manchester; *m* 1894, Annina Olga, *d* of Octavius Valieri of London; one *s* three *d. Educ:* Geneva, Paris. Consul-General for Greece, 1903; resigned, 1916; sent by British Government on secret mission to Greece, Nov. 1915, after threat made by Greece to enforce strict neutrality by disarming and interning Allied Armies then retiring from Serbia; Jan. 1917 organised with a Committee of the Foreign Office and Board of Trade the chartering of the

Greek Mercantile Marine to England and the Allies; appointed Consul-General and Hon. Councillor of Diplomatic Agency of Salonica Government; Consul-General for Greece, 1917; resigned, 1920; Greek Delegate, Reparation Commission (Maritime Service), 1920, and International Parliamentary Commercial Conference, 1926. President of Honour of the National Association of Hellenes in Great Britain, 1942; Member Executive Committee Greek Red Cross. Commander Order of Redeemer of Greece. *Address:* 33 Lennox Gardens, SW1. *T:* Kensington 5601; Ferndale Cottage, The Holmwood, Surrey. *Club:* City of London.

Died 24 July 1948.

STAWELL, Mrs Rodolph; 2nd *d* of Admiral Rt Hon. Sir A. Cooper Key and Charlotte, *d* of Ed. McNeill of Cushendun; *m* 1900, Rodolph Stawell (*d* 1947), OBE, FRCS. *Publications:* Fairies and other Facts, 1902; Fairies I have Met, 1907; Motor Tours in Wales and the Border Counties, 1908; Motor Tours in Yorkshire, 1909; The Fairy of Old Spain, 1912; My Days with the Fairies (enlarged edition of Fairies I have Met), 1920; Motoring in the West Country, 1925; Motoring in Sussex and Kent, 1926; Meditations in Outline, 1936; The Well of Life, 1938. *Translations:* Flight of Marie Antoinette, 1906; Last Days of Marie Antoinette, 1907; Versailles and the Trianons, 1906; Return of Louis XVIII, 1909; A Gascon Royalist, 1910; Journal of the Comte d'Espinchal, 1912; Madame Royale, 1913; Memoirs of the Comte de Damas, 1913; The Innocents, 1918; The Question of Alsace Lorraine, 1918; Robespierre's Rise and Fall, 1927; The Guillotine and its Servants, 1929; The School of Jesus Christ, 1932; and compiler of Fabre's Book of Insects. *Address:* Agan Trigva Falmouth.

Died 27 March 1949.

STEACY, Hon. Col Rev. Richard Henry, CMG 1917; Rector of Westboro'; *b* 1869; *m* 1914, Elsie Mary, *d* of late Hon. Digby Denham; four *s* two *d.* Dir.-Gen. Canadian Chaplain Service, European War, 1914–17 (CMG, despatches). *Address:* The Rectory, Highland Park, Westboro', Ottawa, Canada.

Died 11 April 1950.

STEAD, Kingsley Willans, CBE 1933 (OBE 1928); *b* 1 Feb. 1883; *s* of late Geoffrey Stead, MD, and Emily Anderson; *m* 1906, Jessie, *d* of late Lewis Williams; one *s.* *Educ:* King Edward's School, Birmingham. Director of Customs, Excise and Trade, Palestine, 1924–38; retired from Colonial Service, 1938; Médaille de la Reconnaissance Française, 1922. *Address:* 20 Ingram House, Park Road, Hampton Wick, Middlesex.

Died 1 March 1950.

STEADMAN, Frank St J., DPH, MRCS, LRCP Lond.; LDSRCS Eng.; Hon. Senior Dental Surgeon Royal Dental Hospital and Consulting Dental Surgeon West London Hospital; recognised teacher in Dental Surgery London University; *b* 8 June 1880; *s* of Sidney Francis St J. Steadman, Solicitor, and Mary Louise Brinton; *m* 1907, Grace Hamilton; two *s* one *d.* *Educ:* Dulwich College; Royal Dental Hospital; Charing Cross Hospital. Examiner in Dental Surgery London University 1930–33 and in Orthodontics 1935–43, and Bristol University 1931–34; President of the Metropolitan Branch of the British Dental Association, 1932; Pres. of British Society for Study of Orthodontics, 1937; Vice-President, Royal Society of Medicine, 1939–40 (President Odontological Section, 1939–40); Member of the Representative Board of the British Dental Association; Secretary to the Board of Studies in Dentistry and Member of the Faculty of Medicine London University; Official Delegate for Great Britain, 8th International Congress, Paris, 1931; Lecturer in Oral Surgery, 1935–36; Lecturer on Dental Diseases in Children since 1919; Local Anæsthesia since 1922 and Bacteriology 1920–29, 1934, and 1939–43, Royal Dental Hospital Dental School; recognised teacher in Bacteriology London University 1926–29; Dental Board

Lecturer Technique of Local Anæsthesia 1928; Dental Surgeon National Dental Hospital 1911–14, The Belgrave Hospital for Children 1910–14, and the Metropolitan Hospital 1910–14; Major RAMC (TR); late DADMS XXth Corps. *Publications:* Pyorrhœa Alveolaris; Local Anæsthesia in Dental Surgery; Notes on Bacteriology. Papers: The Role of Oral Sepsis as an Aetiological Factor in the Production of Cancer in the Alimentary Canal; Technique of Various Surgical Operations about the Mouth and Their After-Treatment; Fractures with Special Reference to Treatment; A Note on the Pathology of Cancer of the Tongue. *Recreation:* chess. *Address:* 67 Wimpole Street, W1. *T:* Welbeck 4240; 4 Streatleigh Court, Streatham, SW16. *T:* Streatham 0367.

Died 11 April 1943.

STEBBING, (Lizzie) Susan; Professor of Philosophy in the University of London (Bedford College for Women) since 1933; *b* Dec. 1885; *d* of Alfred Charles Stebbing and Elizabeth Elstob; unmarried. *Educ:* Girton College, Cambridge. Historical Tripos Pt I, 1906, Part II, 1907; Moral Sciences Tripos Pt I, 1908 (Cantab); Master of Arts (Philosophy), University of London, 1912; DLit (Lond.), 1931. Visiting lecturer and subsequently Director in Moral Sciences Studies at Girton and Newnham Colleges, Cambridge, 1911–24; Lecturer in Philosophy at King's College, London, 1913–15; Visiting lecturer in Philosophy at Homerton Training College, 1914–21, and at Westfield College, London University, 1914–20; Lecturer in Philosophy at Bedford College, London University, 1920, and since 1924, Reader in Philosophy in the University of London; Research Fellow, Girton College, 1923–24; elected Fellow of the Royal Historical Society, 1916; Visiting Professor at Columbia University, 1931–32; President of the Aristotelian Society, 1933–34; President of the Mind Association, 1934–35. *Publications:* Pragmatism and French Voluntarism, 1914; A Modern Introduction to Logic, 1930; Logic in Practice, 1933; Logical Positivism and Analysis, the Annual Philosophical Lecture, British Academy (Henriette Hertz Foundation), 1933; Ideals and Illusions, 1941; papers and articles in Mind, Proc. Aristotelian Society, Journal of Philosophy, American Scholar (USA), Philosophy, Hibbert Journal, Science Progress (about 50 articles), art. on 'Logistic' in Encyclopædia Britannica 14th ed.; Some Ambiguities in Discussions concerning Time, Festschrift to Professor Cassirer, 1935; Philosophy and the Physicists, 1937; Thinking to Some Purpose, 1939; Men and Moral Principles (13th Hobhouse Memorial Lecture), 1943; Modern Elementary Logic, 1943. *Address:* Tremorrab, Tintagel, Cornwall. *T:* 40.

Died 11 Sept. 1943.

STEDMAN, Sir Leonard Foster, Kt 1937; DL and JP Co. of Monmouth; *b* Thurston Vicarage, Suffolk, 18 March 1871; *s* of Rev. Paul Methuen Stedman; *m* 1897, Mary Ellen, *d* of H. G. Lloyd, Pencarrig, Newport, Mon; one *d.* *Educ:* privately. Political Agent Southern Division of Monmouth, 1893–1913; Past President of Monmouthshire Chamber of Agriculture; Member of Council of Royal Agricultural Society and of Royal Welsh Agricultural Society; Member of Agricultural Advisory Board, University College, Cardiff; Chairman Mon. County War Agricultural Committee; Governor of Usk Agricultural College; Member of Monmouthshire County Council; Director of Royal Gwent Hospital, Newport, Mon; Chairman Committee of Management Cefn Mably Hospital. *Recreations:* cricket, tennis, shooting. *Address:* The Garth, Bassalleg, Newport, Mon. *TA:* Bassalleg. *T:* Rhiwderin 288. *Clubs:* MCC; County, Newport, Mon.

Died 2 June 1948.

STEEDS-BIRD, Elliott Beverley, DSO 1917; TD; LRCP and SI; FFR; Lt-Col RAMC (TA); retired; Hon. Radiologist, Royal Portsmouth Hospital, War Memorial Hospital, Gosport; Consultant Radiologist, Petersfield and Emsworth Cottage Hospitals; *b* 24 March 1881; *o s* of late George Beverley Bird, King's Own Yorkshire Light Infantry; *m* 1909, Hon. Gladys Rice, *e d* of 6th Baron Dynevor. *Educ:* Cheltenham College; Trinity College, Dublin. Served European War, 1914–19 (despatches four times, DSO, Brevet Lt-Col, Croix de Guerre Français). *Recreations:* gardening and mechanics. *Address:* 15 Clarence Parade, Southsea. *T:* Portsmouth 2163. *Clubs:* Royal Albert Yacht, Southsea; Royal Portsmouth Corinthian Yacht, Portsmouth.

Died 16 May 1945.

STEEL, Lt-Col Matthew Reginald, DSO 1918; MC; 4th Bn The Green Howards; *b* 8 May 1896; *s* of late William Steel; *m* Nancy Macfarlane; two *s* two *d*. Served European War, 1914–18 (DSO, MC and bar); War of 1939–40 (Bar to DSO). *Address:* Langbaurgh Cottage, Great Ayton SO, Yorkshire. *Club:* Farmers'.

Died 19 Aug. 1941.

STEELE, John Scott; journalist and broadcaster, retired; London and European Representative, Mutual Broadcasting System Inc.(1936–46); *b* Belfast, 15 Dec. 1870; *s* of late Frederick Macauley Steele; *m* 1st, 1894, Clare Krimont (*d* 1929); two *s*; 2nd, 1934, Winifred Herbert. *Educ:* privately, and in newspaper offices. Emigrated to United States and entered newspaper work on the New York Herald; served in almost every capacity on this and other American newspapers; Managing Editor, Edward Marshall Syndicate, London, 1917–19; London Correspondent and Chief of London Bureau of the Chicago Tribune, 1919–35. *Publications:* newspaper and magazine articles. *Recreations:* golf, reading, walking. *Address:* Underdowns, 134 Chaldon Way, Coulsdon, Surrey. *TA:* Underdowns, Coulsdon. *T:* Downland 176. *Clubs:* American, Savage; Silurians, New York.

Died 8 Jan. 1947.

STEELE, Robert, Hon. DLitt Durham; Corr. Fellow Mediæval Academy of America; *b* Kensington, 30 May 1860; Ulster parentage; *m* 1882, Caroline (*d* 1943), *d* of George Shury, mezzotint engraver; nine *c*. *Educ:* Cookstown Academy. Pupil teacher; elementary schoolmaster; Public School Science master; reviewer, student of mediæval literature; Civil List Pension, 1925. *Publications:* Lydgate and Burgh's Secrees, ed. prin.; Three prose translations of Secreta Secretorum; The Earliest English Arithmetics; Mediæval Lore; Story of Alexander; Huon of Bordeaux; Renaud of Montauban; Bibliography of English Music Printing to 1600; Tudor and Stuart Proclamations; Revival of Printing; Notes on English Books Printed Abroad; edited Chatterton, More's Utopia, Kingis Quair; Opera hactenus inedita Rogeri Bacon, 15 vols; Grosseteste's Compotus; Morris's Defence of Guinevere; Alexander de Villa Dei, Massa Compoti; Pierre d'Abernon, le Sécre de Secrez; Alchemical Works of Hermes and Rhases; English Poems of Charles d'Orleans; Vetus Metaphysica; Mum and the Sothsegger. *Address:* 7 Denny Crescent, SE11.

Died 27 March 1944.

STEELL, Graham, MD, FRCP; Emeritus Professor Victoria University of Manchester; Consulting Physician Manchester Royal Infirmary, Manchester and Salford Hospital for Diseases of the Skin, and Christie Hospital for Cancer; *b* 27 July 1851; *s* of Sir John Steell, Edinburgh; *m* 1886, Agnes Dunlop (*d* 1910), *e d* of Rev. Thomas M'Kie, Erskine. NB; one *s*. *Educ:* Edinburgh Academy and University. Was Professor of Clinical and of Systematic Medicine, Victoria University of Manchester; House Physician, Edinburgh Royal Infirmary; House Physician Fever House, Edinburgh Royal Infirmary; Resident Medical Officer Stirling Royal Infirmary, and Leeds Fever Hospital, and Manchester Royal Infirmary (5 years); Medical Registrar, London Fever Hospital. *Publications:* Text-Book on Diseases of the Heart, 1906; The Sphygmograph in Clinical Medicine, 1899; The Physical

Signs of Pulmonary Disease; 2nd ed. 1900; Bradshaw Lecture, Royal College of Physicians, 1911; various contributions to medical periodicals. *Address:* 64 Heybridge Avenue, Streatham Common, SW16.

Died 10 Jan. 1942.

STEER, George Lowther; author and editorial staff, Daily Telegraph; *b* Cambridge, East London, South Africa, 22 Nov. 1909; *s* of B. A. Steer; *m* 1st, 1936, Margarita Trinidad de Herrero y Hassett (*d* 1937); 2nd, 1939, Barbara Esmé, *y d* of Sir Sidney Barton, GBE, KCVO, CMG; one *s* one *d*. *Educ:* Winchester; Christ Church, Oxford (Classical schol). 1st cl. Hon. Mods 1930, Lit.Hum. 1932. Crime and baseball reporter, Argus, Capetown, 1932–33; Dramatic critic, Yorkshire Post, 1933–35; Special war correspondent, The Times, in Addis Ababa, 1935–36 and in Spain, 1936–37; Special Correspondent, Daily Telegraph, in Africa, 1938–39. *Publications:* Caesar in Abyssinia, 1936; The Tree of Gernika, 1938; Judgement on German Africa, 1939; A Date in the Desert, 1940; Sealed and Delivered, 1942. *Recreation:* archery. *Address:* c/o Daily Telegraph, Fleet Street, EC4. *Club:* avoided.

Died 25 Dec. 1944.

STEER, P. Wilson, OM 1931; artist; a member of the New English Art Club; *b* Birkenhead, 1860. *Educ:* The École des Beaux Arts, Paris; pupil of Cabanel. Honorary member of Liverpool Academy of Arts; represented in Uffizi Gallery, Florence, by auto-portrait; also in British Museum and Tate Gallery, London; Corporation Art Gallery, Bradford; Manchester City Art Gallery; Aberdeen Art Gallery; Johannesburg Art Gallery; The Metropolitan Museum, New York; The Municipal Gallery of Modern Art, Dublin; Welsh National Museum at Cardiff; The National Art Gallery of Victoria at Melbourne, and Gallery at Perth, Western Australia. *Address:* 109 Cheyne Walk, SW10. *T:* Flaxman 7652.

Died 21 March 1942.

STEER, Councillor William Bridgland; Proprietor of Oakcroft Press, Derby; Member of the Derby Borough Council; Chairman, Derby Education Committee; *b* East Grinstead, Sussex, 1867. *Educ:* East Grinstead Board School; Westminster Training Coll.; matriculated, London Univ. Assistant Master, Derby School Board, 1888, and Derby Municipal Secondary School, 1904–27; Pres. Derby Class Teachers' Association, 1906, 1917; President, Derby Teachers' Association, 1901 and 1925; Derbyshire Teachers' Association, 1904 and 1926; National Federation of Class Teachers, 1907; National Union of Teachers, 1914–16; Treasurer, NFCT, 1910–27; Member of Executive of National Union of Teachers, 1905–27; Member of Secondary School Burnham Committee, 1918–27; former Member of the Workers' National War Emergency Committee; contested Dudley and East Walthamstow Parliamentary Division as a Labour candidate. *Publications:* Senior History for Schools; A Book of Sonnets; Great Men and Women; Leaders of Men; The March of Time; Interesting Problems in Arithmetic; former editor of the Class Teacher and of the Teachers' World. *Address:* Oakcroft, Kedleston Road, Derby.

Died 26 March 1939.

STEIN, Sir Aurel, KCIE 1912; FBA; Correspondant de l'Institut de France; PhD; DLitt (Hon. Oxon); DSc (Hon. Camb.); DOL (Hon. Punjab); LLD (Hon. St Andrews); Officer on special duty, Indian Archæological Survey (retired 1929); *b* Budapest, 26 Nov. 1862; *s* of Nicholas and Anna Stein. *Educ:* Budapest and Dresden public schools; studied Oriental Languages and Antiquities at University of Vienna; University of Tübingen; Lahore, and in England. While Principal, Oriental College, Lahore, and Registrar of Punjab University, 1888–99, effected antiquarian researches in Kashmir and on Afghan frontier; appointed to Indian Educational Service as Principal of the Calcutta Madrasa, 1899; carried out archæological explorations for Indian

Government in Chinese Turkestan, 1900–01; after administrative work in Punjab and as Inspector-Gen. of Education, NW Frontier Province and Baluchistan, was engaged during 1906–08 on archæological and geographical explorations in Central Asia and W China (Royal Geographical Society's Gold Medal, 1909); transferred to Archæological Survey, 1910; carried out geographical and archæological explorations in Central Asia and Persia, 1913–16 (Gold Medals of Geographical Societies of France and Sweden); in Upper Swat, Baluchistan, and Makran, 1926–28; in S Persia, 1932–33; in W Iran, 1935–36; in Iraq and Trans-Jordan, 1938–39; in Rajputana and Bakawalpur, 1941; in Indus Kohistan, 1942; awarded Petrie Medal, 1928; Royal Asiatic Society's Gold Medal, 1932; Huxley Medal of Royal Anthropological Institute, 1934; Gold Medal of Society of Antiquaries, 1935. *Publications:* Chronicle of Kings of Kashmir (3 vols); Sand-buried Ruins of Khotan; Ancient Khotan (2 vols); Ruins of Desert Cathay (2 vols); Serindia (5 vols); The Thousand Buddhas; Maps of Chinese Turkestan and Kansu; Innermost Asia (4 vols); On Alexander's Track to the Indus, 1929; A Catalogue of Paintings Recovered from Tun-Huang, 1931, An Archæological Tour in Gedrosia, 1931; On Ancient Central-Asian Tracks, 1933; Archæological Reconnaisances in SE Iran, 1937; On Old Routes of Western Iran, 1940; numerous books and papers on Sanskrit literature, Indian and Central-Asian archæology, and geography. *Recreations:* climbing, riding, photography. *Address:* Srinagar, Kashmir. *Club:* East India and Sports.

Died 26 Oct. 1943.

STEIN, Gertrude; *b* 3 Feb. 1874; *d* of Daniel Stein and Emilia Keyser. *Educ:* Radcliffe College, annex of Harvard; Johns Hopkins Medical School. Specialised in brain anatomy; came to live permanently in Paris in 1904 and commenced her first book; interested in painting at once; met Matisse and Picasso; during war worked for French wounded; decorated at end of war by French government; lectured at Cambridge and at Oxford, 1925 and 1936; an opera, Four Saints In Three Acts, performed in Hartford, New York and Chicago, 1933 and 1934; Ballet, Wedding Bouquet (with Lord Berners), London, 1937. *Publications:* Three Lives, 1909; Making of Americans, 1925; Tender Buttons, 1915; Geography and Plays, 1922; Useful Knowledge, 1928; Composition as Explanation, 1926; Lucy Church Amiably, 1930; Before the Flowers of Friendship faded, 1931; How to Write, 1931; Operas and Plays, 1932; Matisse, Picasso and Gertrude Stein, 1933; Autobiography of Alice B. Toklas, 1933; Four Saints in Three Acts, 1934; Portraits and Prayers, 1934; Lectures in America, 1935; Narration, 1935; Everybodies Autobiography, 1937; Picasso, 1938; The World is Round, 1939; Paris France, 1940; Wars I Have Seen, 1945; Brewsie and Willie, 1946. *Recreations:* walking with white poodles, and driving a Ford car.

Died 27 July 1946.

STEINHARDT, Laurence A.; Lawyer, Economist, Diplomat; US Ambassador to Canada since 1948; *b* NY City, 6 Oct. 1892; *s* of Adolph M. Steinhardt (one of founders and exec. heads of National Enameling & Stamping Co.) and Addie Untermyer; *m* 1923, Dulcie Yates, *d* of Henry Hoffman, Banker; one *d*. *Educ:* Franklin School, NY City; Columbia University; Columbia University Law School. AB 1913, MA 1915, LLB 1915. Practised accountancy with Deloitte, Plender & Griffiths, British chartered accountants; Private in US Army, honourably discharged with rank of Sergeant, 1918; Counsel for Housing and Health Div. of War Dept, 1919; Member of law firm of Guggenheimer, Untermyer & Marshall, 1920–33. Minister from US to Sweden, 1933–37; US Ambassador to Peru, 1937–39; to USSR, 1939–41; to Turkey, 1942–45; to Czechoslovakia, 1945–48. Delegate of the US to Eighth Pan-American Conf. at Lima in 1948. Counsel to

Waslaw Nijinsky, dancer, in Metropolitan Opera affair, 1916; Counsel to Archduchess Marie Thérèse in recovery of Napoleon necklace; Nat. President of Pi Lambda Phi, 1915, permanent Treasurer Class of 1913, Columbia College, and Class of 1915 Columbia University Law School. Member of Pres. Roosevelt's preconvention campaign cttee, 1933; Member of Democratic National Finance Cttee and Executive Finance Cttee of the Democratic National Campaign Cttee Democrat. US Medal of Merit, 1946; US Typhus Commission Medal, 1945. *Publications:* Legal Status of the Trade Union; The Truth, The Whole Truth and Nothing But the Truth; series of articles on Medical Jurisprudence in Journal of American Medical Assoc., and articles on economic, financial and international affairs. *Recreations:* fishing and travel. *Address:* (office) 30 Pine Street, New York City, USA; (residence) American Embassy, Ottawa, Canada. *Clubs:* National Democratic, Bankers Club of New York, Columbia University, Atlantic Beach, American Bar Association, New York County Lawyers Assoc., Bar Assoc. of City of NY.

Died 28 March 1950.

STEMP, Major Charles Hubert, CBE 1920; OBE 1918; *b* 1871. Major, late Engineer and Railway Staff Corps. Formerly Superintendent London and North-Eastern Railway (South Scottish Area). *Address:* The Outlook, Anthony's Avenue, Lilliput, Parkstone, Dorset.

Died 18 March 1948.

STENNETT, Col Harry March, CBE 1924; DSO 1916; late Commandant Northern Rhodesia Police; *b* 2 Aug. 1877; *e s* of late H. J. Stennett, Nottingham; *m* 1912, Lydia Amy Dorothy, 2nd *d* of late John Robertson-Reid; one *s* one *d*. Served SA War (King's and Queen's medals 5 clasps); Chevalier of the Order of Leopold II, 1910; served in Campaign against German SW Africa and German East Africa (despatches, DSO). *Address:* Thornton, Penyffordd, Chester. *T:* Caergwrle 32.

Died 25 Feb. 1941.

STEPHEN, Campbell, MA, BD, BSc; MP (Lab) Camlachie, Glasgow, Nov. 1922–31 and since 1935; native of Bower parish, Caithness; *b* 1884; *m* 1946, Dorothy Jewson, BA. *Educ:* Townhead Public School, Allan Glen's School and Glasgow University. Barrister-at-law; resigned charge at Ardrossan, Ayrshire, 1918; contested Ayr Burghs, 1918; an ardent Socialist, especially interested in education, having been a teacher of science and mathematics for two and a half years before election to Parliament. *Recreation:* golf. *Address:* 45 Brougham Street, Greenock. *T:* Douglas 4209.

Died 25 Oct. 1947.

STEPHEN, Sir Harry Lushington, 3rd Bt *cr* 1891; Kt 1913; *b* 2 March 1860; 3rd *s* of late Sir James Fitzjames Stephen, 1st Bt; *S* brother, 1932; *m* 1904, Barbara, (author of Emily Davies and Girton College, 1927), *y d* of late W. Shore Nightingale of Embley, Romsey and Lea Hurst, Derbyshire; one *s*. *Educ:* Rugby; Trinity College, Cambridge (LLM). Called to Bar, 1885; practised on South Wales Circuit, 1886–1901; Judge of High Court, Calcutta, 1901–14; Alderman of the London County Council, 1916–28. *Heir: s* James Alexander, *b* 25 Feb. 1908. *Address:* Hale, Fordingbridge, Hants. *Clubs:* Athenæum, Savile.

Died 1 Nov. 1945.

STEPHEN, Norman Kenneth; *b* 1865; *s* of late Rev. Thomas Stephen of Kinloss, Morayshire; *m* 1893, Edith Laura (*d* 1912), *d* of late Rev. Edward Welldon, of Tonbridge; no *c*. *Educ:* Fettes College; Trinity College, Cambridge (Scholar). Porson Prizeman, 1885 and 1886; Powis Medallist, 1886 and 1887; Craven University Scholar, 1887; Chancellor's Classical Medallist, 1888; First Class Classical Tripos, Parts I and II. Assistant Master at Harrow School, 1888–1925. *Recreations:*

shooting, golf. *Address:* 42 Eton Avenue Hampstead, NW3. *T:* Primrose 0119. *Clubs:* Carlton, United University.

Died 4 July 1948.

STEPHEN, Brig.-Gen. Robert Campbell, CB 1916; *b* 26 Dec. 1867; *s* of late Septimus Alfred Stephen; *m* 1897, Mary (*d* 1925), *d* of late Henry Osborne; one *s* one *d.* *Educ:* Trinity College, Cambridge. Joined 14th Hussars, 1890; Capt. 1896; Adjutant, 1896–99; Major, 1904; Lt-Col 1911; Col 1914; Adjutant Warwickshire Imperial Yeomanry, 1899–1904; Commanded 4th Cavalry Brigade, Meerut, 1915; 6th Cavalry Brigade, Mesopotamia, 1916; served European War, 1914–17 (CB). *Address:* Enbridge, Newbury, Berks. *T:* Highclere 15.

Died 4 Dec. 1947.

STEPHENS, Berkeley John Byng, CIE 1915; Director The Cirencester Brewery, Ltd; *b* 22 July 1871; *s* of late Captain Frederick Stephens, late 2nd Life Guards, of Bentworth Lodge, Alton, Hants; *m* 1906, Gwendolen Elizabeth, *e d* of late E. William Cripps of Ampney Park, Cirencester; one *s.* *Educ:* Winchester College. Late Manager of the Bombay Burma Trading Corporation, Ltd; Member of the Legislative Council of the Lieutenant-Governor of Burma, 1913–14; Chairman of the Burma Chamber of Commerce, 1913–14; Vice-Chairman of the Commissioners for the Port of Rangoon, 1913–14. *Address:* Coxwell Street, Cirencester.

Died 5 May 1950.

STEPHENS, George Arbour, MD, BS, BSc (Lond.); Consulting Cardiologist, King Edward VII Welsh National Memorial Association and Carmarthenshire County Council; Senior Consulting Physician, Cardigan and District Hospital and Clydach-on-Tawe Cottage Hospital; Former President, Royal Institution of S Wales; Ex-Member of Council of National Library of Wales and of Welsh University Court; Saving Bank Trustees; *b* 19 Jan. 1870; *s* of late Marcus A. Stephens; *m* Prof. Mary Williams. *Educ:* Cromwellian Grammar School, Cardigan; University Colleges, Aberystwyth and London. Done much research work and industrial investigations; taken an interest in Industrial Welfare and Municipal Politics; pioneer of Mothercraft classes for schoolgirls; Originator milk for school children; co-founder of first Mothers' and Babies' Welfare in Wales; gave evidence before Royal Commission on University Education in Wales, and took active part in establishment of the University College at Swansea; original Member; Council University College, Swansea; National Museum; Ex-Alderman of Swansea Borough Council; Ex-Chairman Swansea Education Committee; Ex-Hon. Physician Royal Cambrian Institute for the Deaf; Certifying Factory Surgeon, Fellow Medical Society of London; formerly Major RAMC (T); formerly Chairman of Glamorgan Joint Poor Law Committee for Feeble-minded; Swansea Board of Guardians; late President Swansea Medical Society. *Publications:* Hospitals of Wales, 1912; Prevention and Relief on Heart Disease, 1920; Heart and Spleen in Health and Disease; articles dealing with heart-disease, lead-poisoning, chilblains, ulcers, Arthuriana. *Recreations:* golf, sociological work. *Address:* 61 Walter Road, Swansea. *T:* 2359. *Clubs:* PEN; Pennard Golf.

Died 1 Dec. 1945.

STEPHENS, George Washington; retired; *b* Montreal, Aug. 1866; *s* of George W. Stephens and Elizabeth McIntosh, both Scotch; *m* 1908, Rosalinda G. Bisacchi, Italian; no *c.* *Educ:* McGill University; University of Geneva and University of Hanover. MP Province Quebec; President Montreal Harbour Commission, 1907–12; Minister, Finance, Food, and Forests, Saar Governing Commission, 1923–26, Interior, Foreign Affairs, President, 1926–27; Member, International

Academy of Diplomacy. *Publications:* European Ports through Canadian Eyes, 1901; A Plea for the Readjustment of Marine Insurance Rates on the St Lawrence, 1909; The St Lawrence Waterway Project, 1929. *Recreations:* golf, fishing, travelling. *Address:* 470 St Alexis Street, Montreal, Canada. *TA:* Jonyde, Montreal. *Clubs:* Royal Automobile; St James, Montreal.

Died Feb. 1942.

STEPHENS, James. *Publications:* A Crock of Gold; Here are Ladies; The Charwoman's Daughter; Songs from the Clay; The Demi-Gods; Reincarnation, 1918; Deirdre, 1923; In the Land of Youth, 1924; A Poetry Recital, 1925; Collected Poems, 1926; Etched in Moonlight, 1928; Strict Joy: Poems, 1931; Kings and the Moon, 1938.

Died 26 Dec. 1950.

STEPHENS, John Edward Robert; *b* 9 Jan. 1869; *o s* of late Rev. J. E. Stephens, Vicar of Wilberfoss, York; *m* 1st, 1901, Euphemia Sarah (*d* 1938), *o d* of late Major Rutherford, 2nd West India Regt; one *d;* 2nd, 1938, Nellie, *d* of late Henry Marson. *Educ:* St Olave's School, York; Royal University of Ireland. Called to Bar, Middle Temple, 1894; joined Midland Circuit; formerly a Captain in the Donegal Artillery; retired with the rank of Hon. Captain in Regular Army, and with permission to wear the uniform, 1902; practised for 18 years at the Common Law Bar; a Magistrate of HBM's Court at Zanzibar, 1911, and of the Sultan of Zanzibar, 1912; a Judge of the Kingston Court Jamaica, BWI, 1922–25; Senior Puisne Judge of HM Supreme Court, Kenya Colony, and a Judge of the Appeal Court for Eastern Africa, 1925; retired 1931. Has taken part in various International Law Congresses on the Continent. *Publications:* Digest of Highway Cases; Digest of Public Health Cases-Demurrage; Freight; Charterparties; Bills of Lading; Editor-in-Chief of The Manual of Naval Law and Court-Martial Procedure, 1912 (4th edition); prepared a Collection of the Decisions of the Supreme Court, Jamaica, from 1774–1923; has contributed largely to publications in England and America; several articles to Encyclopædia of the Laws of England, and other Encyclopædias, and to Journal of Comparative Legislation. *Address:* c/o Barclays Bank Ltd, 19 Fleet Street, EC4.

Died 11 Feb. 1941.

STEPHENS, John William Watson, MD (Cantab), FRS 1920; Emeritus Professor of Tropical Medicine, Liverpool University, 1928; Consultant Physician for Tropical Diseases, Royal Infirmary, Liverpool, 1928; Lieut-Col RAMC 1917; Consultant in Malaria, Scottish, Northern and Western Commands; Alfred Jones Professor of Tropical Medicine, Liverpool University, 1913–28; Physician-in-Charge of Tropical Ward, Royal Infirmary, Liverpool; *b* Ferryside, Carmarthenshire, 1865; *s* of John Stephens, Barrister-at-law, and Martha, *d* of Capt. D. Davies, RM, Trawsmawr, Carmarthenshire; *m* 1901, Mary Sophie, *d* of Lieut-Col E. C. C. Sandys, Indian Army; two *s.* *Educ:* Dulwich College; Gonville and Caius College, Cambridge; St Bartholomew's Hospital. Sir Trevor Lawrence Research Studentship in Pathology and Bacteriology, 1895 and 1896. President Abernethian Society, 1896; John Lucas Walker Student in Pathology, University of Cambridge, 1897; Assistant Bacteriologist Government of India, 1897; Member Royal Society Malaria Commission in Africa and India, 1898–1902; Walter Myers Lecturer in Tropical Medicine, Liverpool School of Tropical Medicine, to 1913; BA, MB, BC, 1893; DPH (Camb.) 1894; MD (Cantab) 1898; Charles Kingsley medallist, 1918; Membre d'Honneur de la Société Belge de Médecine Tropicale, 1923; Membre d'Honneur de la Société de Pathologie Exotique, 1936; President Royal Society of of Tropical Medicine and Hygiene, 1927; Mary Kingsley medallist, 1929; Manson Medallist, 1935. *Publications:*

numerous papers on tropical diseases; a treatise on Blackwater Fever, 1937. *Recreations:* ornithology and archæology. *Address:* Holewm Ferryside, S Wales.

Died 17 May 1946.

STEPHENS, Rear-Adm. (S) Montague, CB 1916. Entered RN 1877; Paymaster Rear-Adm. (retired), 1920. Served European War, 1914–17 (CB). *Address:* 9 Warwick Road, Bexhill, Sussex.

Died 19 Dec. 1950.

STEPHENS, Sir William R.; *see* Reynolds-Stephens.

STEPHENSON, Lt-Col Arthur, CMG 1919; CBE 1939; DSO 1918; MC; Royal Scots; retired; *m* Olga M. F., *d* of Major D. B. Hook; two *s* one *d*. Served South African War (Queen's medal 3 clasps); European War, 1914–18 (despatches, CMG, DSO, MC); Commandant: Northern Rhodesia Rifles, 1919–25; Northern Rhodesia Police, 1925–30; Lt-Col, E African Forces, 1939–42; General Manager, Rhodesia Native Labour Supply Commission, 1947. *Address:* Box 1577, Salisbury, S Rhodesia. *Club:* Salisbury (S Rhodesia).

Died 21 March 1950.

STEPHENSON, Edward F., Fellow of the Royal College of Surgeons of Ireland, 1901; Diploma of Public Health, Royal College of Physicians and Royal College of Surgeons of Ireland, 1902; Fellow of the Royal College of Physicians of Ireland (Hon.), 1932; LRCPI and LRCSI, 1889; *b* 1868; *s* of Francis Stephenson, JP, and Kate O'Neill, Annsboro, Co. Kilkenny. *Educ:* Tullabeg College, Ireland; Carmichael School of Medicine and Royal College of Surgeons. Medical Officer of Health, Dunmore East, Co. Waterford; Medical Inspector (1914–18), and Medical Commissioner (1918–22), Local Government Board for Ireland; Chief Medical Officer, Dept of Public Health, Eire (1922–33); Member of the Irish Public Health Council, 1918–22; Member of Commissions on Health Insurance and Medical Services, 1924–26; Milk Standards, 1925, Cleanliness and Wholesomeness of Milk Supplies, 1926–28; Fellow of the Royal Institute of Public Health and of the Society of Medical Officers of Health; Hon. Member of the Society of Medical Officers of Health of Saorstat Eireann. *Address:* Strathearn, Monkstown, Co. Dublin. *TA:* Strathearn, Monkstown, Co. Dublin. *T:* Blackrock 82386. *Clubs:* Royal Societies; Royal Irish Yacht (Kingstown).

Died 16 June 1948.

STEPHENSON, Lt-Col Sir Henry Kenyon, 1st Bt *cr* 1936; DSO 1918; VD, DL, JP, W. R. Yorks, Derbyshire and City of Sheffield; LLD; Town Collector of Sheffield since 1932; Chairman Lord Chancellor's Advisory Committee for Sheffield, 1911–45; *b* 16 Aug. 1865; *e surv. s* of late Sir Henry Stephenson of The Glen, Sheffield; *m* 1894, Frances, *e d* of late Major W. G. Blake, DL, JP; four *s* four *d. Educ:* Rugby. Lt-Col Commanding 4th West Riding Brigade, RFA (TF), 1915; served European War in France and Belgium, 1915–18 (despatches thrice, DSO); Lord Mayor of Sheffield, 1908–09 and 1910–11; MP (Co. L) Park Division of Sheffield, 1918–23; Master Cutler, 1919–20; Pro-Chancellor University of Sheffield since 1910; High Sheriff, Derbyshire, 1931–32; Chairman of Stephenson, Blake & Co., Ltd, Thomas Turton & Sons, Ltd, Sheffield and District Gas Co.; Director, Sheepbridge Coal and Iron Co., Ltd; William Deacons Bank; Yorks Amalgamated Collieries, Ltd; Dinnington Main Coal Co., Ltd; Rossington Main Colliery Co., Ltd; Industrial Housing Association, Ltd; Lord of Manors, Calver, Rowland and Hassop (Derbyshire); received Hon. Freedom of City of Sheffield, Dec. 1929. *Recreations:* riding, shooting. *Heir: s* Lt-Col Henry Francis Blake, OBE [*b* 3 Dec. 1895; *m* 1925, Joan, *d* of Maj. John Herbert Upton (formerly Upton Cotterell-Dormer) JP; one *s* Lt-Col (QO) Yorks Dragoons; served European

War, BEF, 1915–18; JP City of Sheffield; Director of various companies]. *Address:* Hassop Hall, Hassop, Bakewell, Derbyshire. *T:* Great Longstone 10. *Clubs:* Reform, Windham, Royal Automobile, National Liberal; Derby County, Sheffield.

Died 20 Sept. 1947.

STEPHENSON, Sir Hugh Lansdown, GCIE 1936; KCSI 1927; KCIE 1924; CSI 1919; CIE 1913; *b* London, 8 April 1871; *s* of late Charles Stephenson, land surveyor; *m* 1905, Mary Daphne, *d* of late John M. Maidlow, barrister; one *s* one *d. Educ:* Westminster; Christ Church, Oxford. Entered Indian Civil Service, 1895; Under-Secretary to Government of Bengal, 1899–1902; Registrar Calcutta High Court, 1902; Acting Chief Secretary, 1902; Private Secretary to Lieutenant-Governor; Secretary to the Board of Revenue, Calcutta; Financial Secretary to the Government of Bengal, and additional Secretary; Member Southborough Reform Committee; Chief Secretary, 1920; member of Executive Council, Bengal, 1922–27; Acting Governor of Bengal, 1926 and 1930; Governor of Bihar and Orissa, 1927–32; Governor of Burma, 1932–36; Adviser to Secretary of State for Burma, 1937. *Recreations:* golf, riding. *Address:* 196 Ashley Gardens, SW1. *T:* Victoria 6780. *Clubs:* Oriental; Bengal, United Service, Calcutta.

Died 6 Sept. 1941.

STEPHENSON, Sir John Everard, KCMG 1942; CMG 1941; CVO 1937; OBE 1935; Deputy Under-Secretary of State, Commonwealth Relations Office; *b* 13 Jan. 1893; *s* of late Richard M. Stephenson, Barrister-at-law, and Gertrude Crosby; *m* 1924, Muriel, *d* of late H. Somerville Hope; two *s. Educ:* Winchester College; New College, Oxford (Scholar). 1st Class Classical Moderations, 1914. Served in India and Mesopotamia in 4th Bn Somerset LI, 1914–19 (Captain); entered Colonial Office, 1919; Assistant Private Secretary to Secretary of State for the Colonies, 1920–23; attached to Secretariat of Imperial Economic Conference, 1923 and Imperial Conference, 1926; Joint Secretary, Conference on Operation of Dominion Legislation, 1929; Administrative Assistant Secretary Imperial Conferences, 1930 and 1937. *Address:* 10 Holland Park Road, W14. *T:* Western 5671. *Club:* United University.

Died 31 May 1948.

STEPHENSON, Marjory, MBE 1918; FRS 1945; MA; ScD Cantab; Member Scientific Staff of Medical Research Council; Reader in Chemical Microbiology, Cambridge University; *b* 24 Jan. 1885; *d* of Robert Stephenson and Sarah Rogers. *Educ:* Berkhamsted School for Girls; Newnham College, Cambridge. Teaching and research, 1906–12; Beit Memorial Research Fellow for Medical Research (Dept of Biochemistry, University College, London), 1912; work for British Red Cross Soc. in France and Salonika, 1914–18; Research in Biochemical Dept, Cambridge, since 1919; Fellow and Associate of Newnham College, Cambridge. *Publications:* Bacterial Metabolism, 1930, 2nd Ed., 1939; numerous papers in Biochemical Journal and other scientific periodicals. *Address:* 16 Latham Road, Cambridge. *T:* Cambridge 3071. *Club:* University Women's.

Died 12 Dec. 1948.

STEPHENSON, Willie, RCA 1896; landscape painter. *Educ:* Huddersfield Technical College; S Kensington (medallist). Exhibited at RA, Royal Institute, Liverpool, etc. Works purchased by Liverpool Corporation (Morning Conway Harbour), Huddersfield Corporation (a Grey Morning), Still Waters, The Mill, Autumn Tints, Over the Hills. *Recreation:* music. *Address:* Arlunfa, Haden Park Road, Old Hill, Staffs.

Died 9 July 1938.

STEPTOE, Harry Nathaniel; Minister to El Salvador, Central America, since 1948; *b* Portsmouth, England, 11 March 1892; *o s* of Nathaniel and Louise Steptoe; *m* 1921, Jeannie, *e d* of late Dr Finlay Finlay Murchison; one *s* one *d. Educ:* privately. Served European War, 1914–18; Student Interpreter in China Consular Service, 1919; served at Chengtu, Chinkiang, Peking, Shanghai; one of HM Consuls in China, 1935; (prisoner in Japanese hands, 1941, exchanged 1942). Served in Lourenco Marques, Basra and Teheran. Consul-General for the Belgian Congo, etc., and Ruanda Urundi, and French Equatorial Africa and the Cameroons under French Mandate. *Recreations:* travel, reading. *Address:* British Legation, San Salvador, El Salvador, CA. *Clubs:* Travellers', Thatched House.

Died 14 March 1949.

STERNDALE-BENNETT, T. C., ARCM; composer and entertainer; *s* of late J. R. Sterndale-Bennett, MA; *g s* of Sir William Sterndale-Bennett; *m* 1st Christine (*d* 1931), *d* of late H. T. Bywater, Wolverhampton; one *d*; 2nd, 1934, Mary, *d* of late Nevil Maskelyne and *g d* of late J. N. Maskelyne. *Educ:* Derby School; Royal College of Music. Twice round the world with the Westminster Abbey Glee and Concert Party, 1904–06. *Publications:* over 300 songs and a Cantata. *Recreation:* golf. *Address:* Garden Flat, 181 Adelaide Road, NW3. *T:* Primrose 6593. *Club:* Savage.

Died 16 May 1944.

STETTINIUS, Edward R., (Jr); Rector University of Virginia since 1946; *b* Chicago, Ill, 22 Oct. 1900; *s* of Edward R. Stettinius, St Louis, Mo, and Judith Carrington, Richmond, Va; *m* 1926, Virginia Gordon Wallace, Richmond, Va.; three *s. Educ:* Pomfret School, Conn; University of Virginia. Began with Hyatt Roller Bearing Works, Harrison, New Jersey, becoming Employment Manager, 1924; asst to John L. Pratt, VP Gen. Motors Corp., 1926–30; asst to Alfred P. Sloan, jun., Pres. Gen. Motors, 1930; VP Gen. Motors in charge ind. and public relations, 1931; Vice-Chairman Finance Com. US Steel Corp. 1934; Director and Chairman Finance Com., 1936; Chairman Board Directors and Member Finance Com. 1938; resigned all positions and directorships with US Steel to accept Presidential appointment to membership Advisory Com. to Council Nat. Defense, 1940; Lend-Lease Administrator, USA, and Special Assistant to President, 1941–43; Under-Secretary of State, 1943–44; Secretary of State, USA, 1944–45; American Representative on the Security Council, and Chairman of US Delegation in General Assembly of United Nations, 1945–46. In charge National Share the Work Movement Second Fed. Reserve District, 1932; Liaison Officer between Nat. Indust. Recovery Adm. and Industrial Advisory Board, 1933; Chairman, 1939 Roll Call, New York Chapt. American Red Cross; Chairman War Resources Board, 1939; Chairman Priorities Board and Director Priorities Div. Office of Prod. Mgt, 1941; Advisory Board, Petroleum Administration for War; Chairman US Delegation to UN Conf. on Internat. Organization, 1945. Chairman of Board, The Liberia Company; Director: General Electric Co.; International General Electric Co.; World Commerce Corporation; Federal Reserve Bank, Richmond, Va.; Thomas Jefferson Memorial Foundation; Franklin D. Roosevelt Memorial Foundation; Trustee, Virginia Episcopal Theological Seminary; Chairman, The English-Speaking Union of the US; Member Delta Psi (Univ. of Va). Hon. Degrees: LLD Union College, Colgate College, Elmira College, American Univ., Rutgers Univ., New York Univ., Univ. of California, Columbia Univ., Lafayette Coll., Univ. of Chattanooga; Dr of Eng., Stevens Inst. of Technology; DCL Oxon; Dr of Humane Letters, Roanoke College. Medal for Merit; Commander, Legion of Honor. *Publications:* Lend-Lease: Weapon for Victory, 1944; Roosevelt and the Russians, 1949

(posthumous). *Address:* The Horseshoe, Rapidan, Culpeper County, Va, USA. *Clubs:* Union, Century, Manhattan (New York).

Died 31 Oct. 1949.

STEUART, Rev. Robert H. J., SJ; *b* Reigate, 13 April 1874; 3rd *s* of John Steuart, KSG, JP, DL, of Ballechin, Perthshire, and Caroline, *d* of Sir Albert de Hochepied-Larpent, Bt. *Educ:* Fort Augustus; RMA, Woolwich. Entered the Society of Jesus, 1893; Oxford (Campion Hall), 1896; Priest, 1907; Army Chaplain in France, 1916, attached 12th HLI in 15th and 35th Divisions (despatches); Army of Occupation, Cologne, 1919; Superior, St Aloysius, Oxford, 1921; Superior of Farm Street Church, Mayfair, 1926–35. *Publications:* The Book of Ruth; A Map of Prayer; The Inward Vision; March, Kind Comrade; Temples of Eternity; World Intangible; Diversity in Holiness; In Divers Manners; The Four First Things; articles in various periodicals. *Address:* 114 Mount Street, W1. *T:* Grosvenor 1608.

Died 9 July 1948.

STEUART-MENZIES, William George; JP, DL, of Culdares; Chief of Clan Menzies; *b* 28 Sept. 1858; *o s* of Ronald Steuart-Menzies and Marjory Alexandrina, *d* of William M'Dowall Grant of Arndilly; *m* 1883, Constance Anne Ellen (*d* 1939), *d* of Thomas Owen Wethered, MP, of Seymour Court, Marlow, Bucks; one *s* Ronald [*b* 8 April 1884; *m* 1st 1912, Olivia Anne, *d* of late Thomas Turner-Farley of Wartnaby Hall, Leicestershire; 2nd 1931, Sybil *d* of late Gerald Boulton, Hovingham, Yorkshire; one *s* two *d*] one *d. Educ:* Harrow. Thirteen years in 3rd Batt. Cameron Highlanders. *Recreations:* hunting, big-game shooting, fishing, racing. *Address:* Arndilly, Craigellachie, Scotland. *Clubs:* Carlton, Turf, Orleans.

Died 18 April 1941.

STEVENS, Col Charles Frederick, CMG 1915; late RA; *b* 28 Aug. 1866; *m* 1896; one *d*. Entered army, 1886; Captain, 1896; Major, 1901; Lt-Col 1914; Col 1918; served Burma, 1885–88 (medal 2 clasps); South African War, 1899–1901 (despatches; Queen's medal 7 clasps); European War, 1914–17 (despatches, CMG); retired pay, 1920. *Address:* Brampford Speke, Exeter.

Died 12 Aug. 1944.

STEVENS, Ernest Hamilton, BA (Lond.), PhD (Heidelberg); Officier de l'Instruction Publique; *b* Brighton, 17 Oct. 1864; *m* 1906, Elizabeth Hildersley. *Educ:* Brighton Grammar School (Head of School); University of London (Exhibitioner, 1883, BA 1885); University of Heidelberg (University Prize for Physics, University Gold Medal for Research, PhD summa cum laude, 1899). Assistant Master Brighton Grammar School and Brighton College; Head Master Westminster City School, 1906–29; Incorporated Association of Head Masters—twice Chairman of London Division, Chairman of Pensions, Press, and Parliamentary Committees, Hon. Treasurer Benevolent Fund, President 1925; Supervisor of Post-Graduate Students, Education Department, King's College, University of London, 1930–36; Associate Examiner in Education, University of London, 1931–41. *Publications:* Scientific Articles in Nature, Annalen der Physik, Verhandlungen der Deutschen Physikalischen Gesellschaft; Dr Paccard's Lost Narrative, Alpine Journal, 1929, 1930, 1934, 1936, 1937; The Grant-aided Secondary Schools of England and Wales, Year-Book of Education, 1932. *Recreations:* cricket (Gentlemen of Sussex), lawn tennis (Sussex County), football, lacrosse, mountaineering. *Address:* 1 Lion House, Exmouth. *Club:* Alpine.

Died 3 Sept. 1945.

STEVENS, Frederick Guy; Barrister-at-law, Inner Temple; *b* 24 Oct. 1878; *s* of Rev. M. O. Stevens; *m* 1913, Beatrice Aline (who obtained a divorce, 1941), *d* of late F. W. Storry, Stroud; two *s*; 1941, Mary Eileen Selina Bridge (*née* Birch). *Educ:* Winchester College;

New College, Oxford, 1st class Honours Mods, 1899; 2nd class Lit. Hum., 1901; BA 1901. SS Civil Service, 1902–07; called to Bar, 1908; Straits Settlements Bar, 1908–27; Judge, SS and FMS 1918; retired 1931; served in RA, 1916–19; acting Captain 352 Siege Battery, 1917; acting Major, 1918. *Publications:* The Registration of Deeds Ordnance (Straits Settlements), 1922; Maxims of La Rochefoucauld, 1939; A contribution to the early history of Prince of Wales' Island, Journal of RAS, Malayan Branch, 1929; Vauvenargues—Reflections and Maxims, 1940. *Recreations:* golf, bridge, chess. *Address:* 55 Upper Parliament Street, Liverpool 8. *Club:* Oxford and Cambridge.

Died 27 Aug. 1944.

STEVENS, Engr Captain John Greet, CBE 1919; RN (retd); *b* 1857; *o s* of late S. F. S. Stevens, South Devon; *m* 1890, Amy Florence, *d* of late Felix Foreman, RN; one *s.* Served Royal Navy, 1878–1909; Retired List, 1910; recalled to Active Service, 1914–19; served as Engr Captain at Naval Base, Invergordon, 1914–15, and at Southampton, Cowes and Poole for emergency repairs, 1915–19.

Died 30 May 1943.

STEVENS, Rt Rev. William Bertrand, PhD; DD; LLD; Bishop of Los Angeles since 1928; *b* Lewiston, Maine, 19 Nov. 1884; *s* of Albion Morse Stevens and Ada McKenzie Stevens; *m* 1911, Violet Bond, New York; four *d. Educ:* Bates College (BA); Columbia University (MA), New York University, (PhD), Cambridge Theological School, USA (BD); Hon. DD from Bates College; Hon. LLD from University of Southern California. Deacon, 1910; Priest, 1911; Curate, Holy Trinity Church, New York City, 1910–12; Rector, St Ann's Church, New York City, 1912–17; St Mark's Church, San Antonio, Texas, 1917–20; Bishop Coadjutor of Los Angeles, 1920; President, Harvard School, Bishop's School, Hospital of the Good Samaritan and other institutions; Trustee of Occidental College, Scripps College and School for Christian Service; Trustee, California College in China; Member Advisory Board, Yenching (China) University; Hon. Fellow in Philosophy, University of Southern California; Major, US Army Reserves; Chaplain, Society of Colonial Wars; Member Oxford Conference on Life and Work, 1937; Edinburgh Conference on Faith and Order, 1937. *Publications:* A Bishop Beloved, 1936; The Reconciling Christ, (collaborator) 1938; Reality in Fellowship, 1939; Editor's Quest, 1940; Christianity and the Contemporary Scene (collaborator), 1943; Victorious Mountaineer, 1943. *Recreations:* travel, music. *Address:* 615 South Figueroa Street, Los Angeles, California, USA. *Clubs:* University, Pasadena, Athletic, Jonathan, Los Angeles.

Died 22 Aug. 1947.

STEVENS, William Mitchell, MD (Lond.), FRCP (Lond.); Senior Physician to King Edward VII's Hospital, Cardiff; Lecturer in Pharmacology, University College, Cardiff; *b* St Ives, Cornwall, 20 March 1868; *s* of Vivian Stevens, St Ives; *m* 1900, Annie Jenkins, Cardiff; one *s* one *d. Educ:* University College, London. University scholar (London) in Medicine; University Exhibitioner and gold medallist in Anatomy, Physiology and Materia Medica; Fellow of University College, London. Consulting Physician to Royal Hamadryad Hospital, Cardiff, and to several other hospitals. *Publications:* Medical Diagnosis; numerous publications in various medical journals. *Recreations:* bowling, croquet.

Died 23 Aug. 1944.

STEVENSON, Allan, CBE 1942; MINA; Deputy Chairman David Rowan & Co. Ltd, Marine Engineers and Boilermakers, Glasgow, since 1948; *b* 7 Feb. 1878; *s* of James Stevenson, Balgray, Beith, Ayrshire; *m* 1902, Christian Kennedy Lawson; one *s* two *d. Educ:* Allan Glen's School, Glasgow; Royal Technical College,

Glasgow. Apprentice Engineer, A. W. Smith & Co., Glasgow; Chief Draughtsman and Estimator, David Rowan & Co., to 1917; Asst to Director Merchant Shipbuilding, 1917–19; Asst Director Merchant Shipbuilding and Repairs, Admiralty, 1939–40; Deputy Director Merchant Shipbuilding and Repairs, and Regional Director for Scotland and Northern Ireland for Merchant Shipbuilding and Repairs, Admiralty, 1940–42. Governor, Royal Technical College, Glasgow; Member of Committee of British Corporation Register of Shipping and Aircraft. President Institution of Engineers and Shipbuilders in Scotland, 1945–47. *Recreations:* golf, angling. *Address:* 1 Kingsborough Gardens, Glasgow, W2. *Club:* Royal Scottish Automobile (Glasgow).

Died 18 Oct. 1948.

STEVENSON, Sir Daniel Macaulay, 1st Bt *cr* 1914; LLD (Glasgow University); DL; Officier de la Légion d'Honneur; Grande Ufficiale della Corona d'Italia; Commander of the Order of the Crown of Belgium; Member of the Deutsche Akademie; Grand Order of Isabel la Catolica; Order of the German Eagle (First Class); Chancellor of Glasgow University since 1934; Lord Provost of Glasgow and Lord-Lieutenant of the County of the City of Glasgow, 1911–14; *b* Glasgow, 1 Aug. 1851; *s* of John Stevenson, engineer; unmarried. *Educ:* The Secular School and the Athenæum, Glasgow. Member of the Town Council of Glasgow, 1892–1914; and successively filled the offices of Magistrate, Honorary City Treasurer, and Convener of the Finance and other important committees; head of firm of D. M. Stevenson & Co. Ltd, coal exporters, Glasgow, Newcastle, Hull, Cardiff, Birmingham and London; was a Member of the Departmental Committee on Local and Imperial Taxation, and of the Advisory Committee under the National Insurance Act; was Chairman for eighteen years of the Scottish Coal Exporters' Association; was Chairman of the Central Executive Committee on Supply of Coal to France and Italy; a Member of Committee on Coal Trade after the War and of Coal-Controller's Advisory Committee; was Chairman of British Coal Exporters' Federation; Chairman of the Glasgow Workmen's Dwellings Co.; a Director of the Scottish National Housing Co.; Member of the War Pensions Committee; founded Chairs of Citizenship, Spanish, and Italian at Glasgow University, and International History at London University, and Interchange Scholarships between the Universities of Scotland and the Universities of France, Spain and Germany, also Directorship of International Affairs at Chatham House; a Founder and Hon. President of The Scottish National Academy of Music; President of the British Institute of Florence; was made a Freeman of the City of Glasgow in 1929. *Heir:* none. *Address:* 12 Waterloo Street, and 5 Cleveden Road, Glasgow, W2. *TA:* Stevenson, Glasgow. *T:* Western 2470. *Clubs:* National Liberal; Liberal, Automobile, Glasgow; Scottish Liberal, Edinburgh.

Died 11 July 1944 (ext).

STEVENSON, Edward Irenæus Prime-; author and (retired) critical editor, etc; Member of Bar of New Jersey (never practised); American-French origin; *b* Madison, State of New Jersey, USA, 1868; Italian and French descent; family in America since 1625. Many years staff-editor of The Independent, NYC, as music-critic, book-reviewer, and letter-writer; many years publisher's reader; contributor to periodicals, and member of editorial staff of Harper and Brothers; former speciality musical criticism (founder of Music Department of Harper's Weekly); lecturer on literature, music, and drama. *Publications:* White Cockades; A Matter of Temperament; Mrs Doe's Encore (You Will, Will You?); Left to Themselves (Philip and Gerald); The Square of Sevens; Her Enemy, Some Friends, and Other Personages; Long-Haired Iopas: Old Chapters from Twenty-Five Years of Music Criticism (1927–1928); A

Repertory of One Hundred Symphonic Programmes for Public Auditions of the Orthophonic Gramophone, 1932, etc. Under a pseudonym, several studies in a special branch of sexual psychiatrics. *Recreations:* work, social life, horticulture, linguistics—speaks, reads, and writes with idiomatic fluency seven languages; also the Orthophonic gramophone, as reproducing serious symphonic music; Conductor of the (private) Symphonic Auditions annually presented at Florence. *Address:* c/o The Fifth Avenue Bank, New York City.

Died 23 July 1942.

STEVENSON, Surg.-Gen. Henry Wickham, CSI 1912; JP; *b* 21 Dec. 1857; 4th *s* of late W. B. Stevenson, of Balladoole and Ballakeighan, Isle of Man; *m* 1890, Francis Clare (*d* 1943), *d* of Rev. Clermont Skrine, and *widow* of F. A. P. Knipe; one *s*. Major IMS 1893; Lt-Col 1901; Surgeon-General, 1909; Surg.-General with Government of Bombay, 1909–14; Additional Member Council of Bombay; retired, 1914. *Address:* Balladoole, nr Castletown, Isle of Man. *T:* Castletown 50.

Died 5 Dec. 1944.

STEVENSON, Lt-Col William David Henderson, CIE 1918; MA; MD, FRFPS (Glasgow); DPH (Royal Colleges), late Indian Medical Service; retired, 1927; Bacteriologist, Government Lymph Establishment, Ministry of Health; *s* of late Rev. W. Stevenson; *m* 1911, Mary Morris, *d* of late Archibald Walker; one *s* one *d.* *Educ:* Univ. of Glasgow. Entered Indian Medical Service, 1906; Assist Director-General IMS (Sanitary), 1919–22; Director Pasteur Institute of India, Kasauli, 1922–24; served North-West Frontier, 1915–16; European War, Mesopotamia, 1916–18 (despatches, CIE). *Address:* The Wych Elms, 5 Marsh Lane, Stanmore, Middlesex. *T:* Grimsdyke 331.

Died 3 Nov. 1945.

STEVENSON, Rt Rev. William Henry Webster, MA, Th. Soc; Bishop of Grafton, NSW, since 1938; *b* 9 June 1878; *s* of late Capt. James Barclay Stevenson and Annie Webster Stevenson; (both *b* Montrose, Scotland); *m* 1912, Katharine Saumarez Smith, *d* of Most Rev. Wm Saumarez Smith, formerly Archbishop of Sydney; two *s* (and one died on active service) one *d. Educ:* Sydney High School; Sydney Grammar School; Univ. of Sydney, BA 1903; MA 1910. Fellow Australian College of Theology, 1934. Deacon, 1904; Priest, 1905; Curate Castle Hill, NSW, 1904–07; Darlinghurst, 1907–09; Domestic Chaplain to Archbp of Sydney, 1909; Curate Randwick, 1909–11, Wimbledon, England, 1911–12; Vicar of Windsor, Queensland, 1920–26; Rector Fortitude Valley, 1916–18; Warden S John's College, Univ. of Queensland, 1920–26 and 1936–38; Examining Chaplain to Archbp of Brisbane, 1920–38; Editor Church Chronicle, Brisbane, 1924–28; Principal S Francis' Theol Coll., Brisbane, 1926–36; Residentiary Canon, Brisbane, 1926–38; Archdeacon of Brisbane, 1936–38. *Address:* Bishopsholme, Grafton, NSW.

Died 15 Aug. 1945.

STEVENSON-MOORE, Sir Charles James, KCIE 1920, CVO 1912; ICS; Member, Executive Council, Government of Bengal, 1920–21; Member of the Board of Revenue, Bengal, 1914–20; *b* 8 June 1866; *s* of late Rev. J. J. Stevenson-Moore, LLD, and Louisa Stewart; *m* 1896, Annie Hay, *d* of Henry Burrows of Doe Park, Woolton; one *d. Educ:* Felsted School, Essex; Emmanuel College, Cambridge. Joined the ICS 1885; Assistant Magistrate-Collector, 1887; Settlement Officer, 1896; Magistrate and Collector, 1898; Inspector-General Police, Bengal, 1904–07; Director of Criminal Intelligence, Simla, 1907–10; Chief Secretary Government of Bengal, 1910–14. *Recreations:* golf, riding, and climbing. *Clubs:* Oriental, Alpine, Alpine Ski.

Died 22 July 1947.

STEWARD, Maj.-Gen. Edward Merivale, CB, 1935; CSI, 1937; OBE; Indian Army, retired; *b* 5 Feb. 1881; *s* of Rev. Canon Edward Steward and Margaret Wilson; *m* 1907, Florence Mary Syme; three *s. Educ:* Haileybury College. Served South Africa, 1900–02; France, 1914; Mesopotamia, 1916; Afghanistan, 1919; retired 1937. *Address:* c/o Lloyds Bank Ltd, 6 Pall Mall, SW1.

Died 11 Jan. 1947.

STEWART, Alexander Carmichael, CIE 1922; MVO 1911; *b* 1 Aug. 1865; *s* of late Col W. J. Stewart, Bengal Staff Corps. *Educ:* privately. Assistant Superintendent, Indian Police, 1887; Superintendent, 1897; Deputy Inspector-General, 1911; Inspector-General Punjab Police, 1918; retired, 1921; was responsible for the organisation and control of the police traffic regulations and arrangement at the Coronation Durbar at Delhi, 1911. *Address:* Kasauli, Elmsleigh Park, Paignton. *Clubs:* East India and Sports; Punjab, Lahore.

Died 3 Dec. 1944.

STEWART, Alexander G.; *see* Graham-Stewart.

STEWART, Alfred Walter, DSc; *y s* of Professor William Stewart, DD, LLD, Dean of Faculties in Glasgow University; *m* 1916, Jessie Lily Coats; one *d. Educ:* University of Glasgow and University of Marburg; University College, London. Mackay-Smith Scholar, 1901; 1851 Exhibition Scholar, 1903–05; Carnegie Research Fellow, 1905–08; Lecturer on Organic Chemistry, Queen's University Belfast, 1909–14; Lecturer on Physical Chemistry and Radioactivity, Glasgow University, 1914–19; Professor of Chemistry in the Queen's University of Belfast, 1919–44. *Publications:* Stereochemistry; Recent Advances in Organic Chemistry; Chemistry and its Borderland; Some Physico-Chemical Themes, Recent Advances in Physical and Inorganic Chemistry; numerous papers in the Transactions of the Chemical Society, etc. *Address:* 83 Balmoral Avenue, Belfast.

Died 1 July 1947.

STEWART, Arthur, RBA 1899; *b* London, 1877; *s* of Alan Stewart of Christ Church, Oxford, and the Middle Temple, and Emily Louisa, *d* of late John James Sawyer of Halifax, Nova Scotia; *m* 1st, 1903, Geraldine Susan Louisa (*d* 1907), *d* of late Captain E. W. C. S. Lloyd; 2nd, 1910, Sharon Watson, *d* of late W. C. Helsby. *Educ:* Westminster School; studied art under Mr Loudan at Westminster School of Art. Elected Member of the Poster Academy, 1900; principal pictures, The Magic Mantle, Sir Galahad, Sir Bors, The Faerie Wood (Chaucer), The Departure of the Guards from Waterloo for South Africa, etc. *Recreation:* cycling.

Died 10 June 1941.

STEWART, Hon. Charles; Chairman Canadian Section of International Joint Commission since 1936; *b* Strabane, Ontario, 1868; *s* of Charles and Catherine Stewart; *m* 1891, Jane R. Sneath; three *s* four *d.* Elected to Alberta Legislature, 1909; re-elected, 1913, 1917, and 1921; Minister of Municipal Affairs, May–Nov. 1913; Minister of Public Works, Nov. 1913; Premier of Province of Alberta and Minister of Railways and Telephones, 1917–21; Minister of Interior, Minister of Mines, Supt-Gen. of Indian Affairs, Canada, 1921–26, and Sept. 1926–30; elected to Federal Government for Argenteuil (Quebec), 1922; Edmonton West, 1925–35. Liberal; Anglican. *Address:* Ottawa, Ontario, Canada.

Died 6 Dec. 1946.

STEWART, Brig.-Gen. Cosmo Gordon, CB 1921; CMG 1915; DSO 1895; late RA; *b* 21 Nov. 1869; 2nd *surv. s* of Sir J. M. Stewart, 3rd Bt; *m* 1911, Gladys Berry, *d* of late Dr J. H. Honeyman, of Auckland, NZ, and Lady Bruce-Porter, Little St Anne's, Englefield Green, Surrey; one *s*. Entered Army, 1888; Captain, 1898; Major, 1904; Bt Lt-Col 1914; Bt Col 1917; served Kurram Expedition, 1892; Relief of Chitral, 1895 (despatches, DSO, medal with clasp); Soudan, 1897

(British medal, Khedive's medal with clasp); Nile Expedition, 1898, including Khartoum (despatches, 4th class Medjidie, clasp); Nile Expedition, 1899 (clasp); Sudd Expedition, 1900; South Africa, 1902 (Queen's medal 4 clasps); European War, 1914–18, very severely wounded (despatches six times, CMG, Croix de Guerre, Bt Col); commanded Allahabad Brigade Area, 1921–25; retired, 1925; awarded pension for Distinguished Services. *Address:* Crossways, Shottermill, Haslemere, Surrey. *T:* Haslemere 549. *Club:* United Service.

Died 19 April 1948.

STEWART, David Macfarlane, CIE 1927; LLD (Glasgow, 1936); Indian Civil Service (retired); *b* 1878; *s* of John Smith Stewart; *m* 1916, Louisa Tolme, *d* of William Longmuir; one *d. Educ:* Hutchesons' Grammar School, Glasgow; Glasgow University; Magdalen College, Oxford. Settlement Officer, Gorakhpur, 1914–18 and Provincial Training Officer (Civil Service) at Moradabad, United Provinces, 1921–27; Hon. Secretary, Glasgow University Extra-mural Education Committee and West of Scotland Joint Committee on Adult Education, 1928–46. *Publication:* Survey of Adult Education in Scotland, 1938–1939 (jointly with C. Cochrane, MA, BSc), 1944. *Address:* Rosemount, Bearsden, Dumbartonshire. *T:* 0109.

Died 1 Nov. 1950.

STEWART, Lt-Col Douglas, DSO 1917; late RA; *b* 23 Nov. 1875; *m* 1st, 1907, Mabel Elizabeth Ponsonby (*d* 1913); two *d*; 2nd, 1919, Eileen Cecilia Ponsonby (*d* 1931); one *s*. Joined RA 1899; served in China, Straits Settlements, Northern and Southern Nigeria, Belgium, France, Egypt, and Asia Minor, European War, 1914–18 (DSO); retired pay, 1925. *Club:* United Service.

Died 30 Jan. 1943.

STEWART, Duncan George, CMG 1948; BA (Oxon); Governor and Commander-in-Chief, Sarawak, and High Commissioner Brunei, since 1949; *b* 22 Oct. 1904; *s* of late William Duncan Stewart of Achara, Duror, Argyll, and of Bertha Mary Steevens; *m* 1904, Patricia Iona Mary Carrick; one *s* two *d. Educ:* Horris Hill; Winchester; Oriel Coll., Oxford. Cadet, Colonial Administrative Service, 1928 (Nigeria); Assistant District Officer, 1931; District Officer, 1938; Sec. to West African Governors' Conf., 1939; Colonial Secretary, Bahamas, 1944–46; Financial Secretary, Palestine, 1947; in charge Palestine Accounts Clearance Office, Cyprus, 1948–49; temp. duty Colonial Office, 1949. *Recreations:* cricket, polo, shooting. *Address:* Astana, Kuching, Sarawak. *Club:* Union.

Died 10 Dec. 1949.

STEWART, Lt-Col Sir Edward, KBE 1917; MD, MRCP, MRCS, JP; DL Sussex; *b* 16 Feb. 1857; *m* 1888, Lady Philippa Fitzalan-Howard (*d* 1946), *sister* of 15th Duke of Norfolk; two *d. Educ:* Middlesex Hospital; University of Brussels (MD); Knight of Grace of the Order of St John of Jerusalem. Member of the Council of the BRCS; Medical Assessor to the Joint Commission Red Cross in France, 1914–18, with rank of Hon. Lt-Col RAMC (despatches); formerly Medical Officer of the Middlesex Yeomanry and the Sussex Yeomanry; Member of the Sussex Territorial Force Association; served as Civil Surgeon South African Field Force in Boer War (Queen's medal and three clasps); late Physician, St Marylebone General Dispensary; Assistant Physician Royal Chest Hospital. *Address:* Bullards, East Grinstead, Sussex. *Club:* Junior Carlton.

Died 4 Dec. 1948.

STEWART, Sir Edward Orde MacTaggart-, 2nd Bt of Southwick and Blairderry, 1892; DL, JP County of Wigtown; *b* 31 Jan. 1883; *s* of 1st Bart and Marianne Susanna (*d* 1914), *o d* of late John Orde Ommanney; *S* father, 1923; *m* 1917, Hon. Margaret, *e d* of 3rd Lord Donington; two *d. Educ:* Eton; Christ Church, Oxford BA, MA. Late Lieut 3rd Batt. Argyle and Sutherland

Highlanders; Capt., retired pay, Gren. Guards. The landed properties extend over 12,500 acres. *Heir:* none. *Address:* Ardwell Wigtownshire, Knockishee, Glenluce. *Clubs:* Carlton, Royal Automobile; New (Edinburgh).

Died 19 Oct. 1948.

STEWART, Mrs Ellen Frances, CBE 1920; *d* of Gen. W. S. Hatch, RA; *m* 1904, Athole Stewart, OBE, actor (*d* 1940). Commandant Women's Forage Corps RASC during European War. *Address:* Diblocks, Ivinghoe Aston, Leighton Buzzard. *T:* Cheddington 227.

Died 20 Dec. 1945.

STEWART OF COLL, Brig.-Gen. Ernest Moncrieff Paul, CB 1915; CBE 1919; FRGS; RE (retired); JP Argyll; *b* 2 Sept. 1864; *s* of H. M. Paul; *m* 1893, Katherine Harriette, *d* of late Wm Coldstream, ICS; three *s* one *d. Educ:* King's College School, London; Marlborough College; RIE College, Cooper's Hill; School of Military Engineering, Chatham. Lieut RE 1886; Capt. 1896; Major 1903; Lt-Col 1911; Colonel, 1915; Colonel, on the Staff, 1921; Brig.-Gen. 1915; in India, Military Works, 1888–93; Instructional Staff School of Military Engineering, Chatham, 1893–98, and 1904–08; Division Officer Harwich Defences, 1898–1900; Gibraltar and special duty, 1900–04; Major of Training Battalion, RE Chatham, 1908–10; OCT Bn, 1910; CRE Colchester, 1910–12; CRE Ceylon, 1912–15; Military interpreter Russian language; served European War, 1914–19, Ceylon, Gallipoli, Salonika, Egypt, Cyprus, Palestine (despatches four times, CB, CBE); Order of the Nile 2nd Class; Director of Works, Mediterranean, Egypt and Palestine Expeditionary Forces; Chief Engineer, Egypt, 1916–19; Chief Engineer Air Force, Egypt, 1916–19; acting Engineer in Chief, Palestine, 1917 and 1918; Staff War Office, 1919–21 and representative member Committee of Scientific and Industrial Research; retired pay, 1921; Lieut Home Guard, 1940–41; Executive Committee, Trustee and past Hon. Treasurer Palestine Exploration Fund; Trustee Royal Soldiers' Daughters' Home, Hampstead; Vice-Chairman Miss Sheppard's Annuitants' Homes; Life Governor, Marlborough College; Life Governor, London Orphan School, Watford; Royal Central Asian and Indian Empire Societies; Chairman British Trusts and Securities Corporation. *Publications:* Road Construction and Maintenance; various military Reports for War Office. *Recreation:* landed proprietor. *Address:* Flat 12, 5 Kensington Church Street, W8. *T:* Western 4080; Breachacha Castle, Isle of Coll, Argyllshire. *TA:* Stewart, Isle-of-Coll. *Club:* Army and Navy.

Died 11 April 1942.

STEWART, Col Sir Frederick (Charles), Kt 1944; DL, JP (Dunbartonshire); LLD; Chairman of Thermotank Ltd, Thermotank Engineering Co., Ltd, Glasgow, London, Liverpool and Newcastle, of Thermotank (SA) (Pty) Ltd Johannesburg, and of Thermotank (India) Ltd, also President of Thermotank (Canada) Ltd; Chairman: North British Locomotive Co., Ltd, Glasgow and London; North British Locomotive Co. (Africa) Ltd; Kelvin, Bottomley & Baird, Ltd, Glasgow, London and Basingstoke; Kelvin & Hughes, Ltd; Clyde Confections Ltd; Deputy Chairman; Brown Bros & Co., Ltd; Henry Hughes & Son, Ltd; Director: William Baird & Co., Ltd; The Clydesdale & North of Scotland Bank, Ltd; Eagle Star Insurance Co., Ltd; Scottish Industrial Estates Ltd; Hillington Industrial Estates Ltd; Bruas-Perak Rubber Estates Ltd; Caledonian Trust Co., Ltd, Second Caledonian Trust Co., Ltd, Third Caledonian Trust Co., Ltd; S. Smith & Sons (England) Ltd; Midland Bank Ltd; Midland Bank Executors & Trustee Co. Ltd; Western Reversion Trust Ltd; Consulting Ventilating Engineer to Ministry of Sea Transport; Past President, Institution of Engineers and Shipbuilders in Scotland, 1941–43 (now Hon. Member); Assessor to the Rector of Glasgow University; Hon. Vice-President: Glasgow County Scout Council; Royal Glasgow Institute of the Fine Arts; Glasgow Art Gallery and Museums Associations; Zoological Society of Glasgow; Vice-President Institute of Industrial Administration; Member of Council, Institution of Naval Architects; Governor, Royal Scottish Academy of Music; Member: Clyde Navigation Trust; Lloyds Register of Shipping (Glasgow Committee); Hon. Company of Master Mariners, London; Wardens' Court, The Worshipful Company of Shipwrights, London; Institute of British Engineers; Admiralty Aeronautical Research Advisory Panel; Railway Staff Tribunal; Executive Council (and of Scottish Committee) of Festival of Britain, 1951; etc; *s* of William and Isabella Sinclair Stewart, Blair Atholl, Perthshire; unmarried. *Educ:* High School, Glasgow. With his two brothers as partners he founded the first Thermotank Company. Served European War, 1914–18, with 9th Bn Argyll and Sutherland Highlanders, 1914–21, retiring in 1921 after commanding the 9th A. and SH Depot Chm., Dunbartonshire T. and AFA; Pres. Dunbartonshire Cadet Corps; Pres. ATC, Rosneath Peninsula, Dunbartonshire. *Address:* 8 Lancaster Cr., Glasgow, W. *T:* Western 2152; Craigrownie Castle, Cove, Dunbartonshire. *T:* Kilcreggan 2208. *Clubs:* Carlton, Junior Carlton, Royal Automobile, Caledonian; New, Western, Art, Royal Scottish Automobile, Royal Northern Yacht, Royal Clyde Yacht, Royal Western Yacht (Commodore), Cove and Kilcreggan Yacht.

Died 10 March 1950.

STEWART, Lt-Col Sir George Powell, 5th Bt *cr* 1803, of Athenry, Co. Tyrone; *b* 7 Oct. 1861; *s* of Sir John Marcus Stewart, 3rd Bt, and Annie Coote, *e d* and *co-heir* of George Powell Houghton of Kilmanock, Co. Wexford; *S* brother, 1942; *m* 1895, Florence Maria Georgina, *d* of late Col Sir James Godfray; one *s* (and one killed in action 1915 with Royal Inniskilling Fusiliers), one *d*. Formerly Major Royal Inniskilling Fusiliers; served in Burmah Campaign, and in South African War. Recalled from Reserve of Officers European War of 1914–18 and commanded Depot of his regt at Omagh, Co. Tyrone. *Heir: s* Major Hugh Charlie Godfray Stewart, formerly Major Royal Inniskilling Fusiliers, now serving in Natal, S Africa [*b* 1897; *m* 1929, Rosemary Elinor Dorothy, *d* of late Major George Peacocke; one *s* one *d*]. *Address:* c/o Guy Robin, Esq., Petit Menage, St Heliers, Jersey.

Died 16 July 1945.

STEWART, Haldane Campbell, MA, DMus, FRCO; *b* London, 28 Feb. 1868; *s* of late John Stewart, representative of Appin and Ardsheal; *m* Elinor Dorothy, *d* of late G. S. Hunt, Chislehurst; one *s* one *d*. *Educ:* Magdalen College School, and Magdalen College, Oxford (MA, DMus). Assistant Master at Lancing College, 1891–96; Wellington College, 1897–98; Director of Music, Tonbridge School, 1898–1919; Organist and Choirmaster, Magdalen College, Oxford, 1919–38. *Recreations:* cricket (Kent XI 1892–1902), golf, lawn tennis, etc. *Address:* Wayside, Hinksey Hill, nr Oxford.

Died 16 June 1942.

STEWART, Sir Harry Jocelyn Urquhart, 11th Bt *cr* 1623; *b* 1871; 2nd *s* of William Malloy Stewart and Ellen, *widow* of Francis Berkeley Drummond, BCS, and *d* of W. H. Urquhart; *S* brother 1894; *m* 1896, Isabel Mary, 2nd *d* of Col Mansfield, DL, Castle Wray, Co. Donegal; three *s* (and *e s* died of wounds in Normandy, 7 June 1944) four *d*. Major Donegal Artillery, 1895. Owns 14,000 acres. *Heir: s* Jocelyn Harry, *b* 1903. *Address:* Fort Stewart, Letterkenny, Co. Donegal.

Died 12 May 1945.

STEWART, Mrs Henrietta; *see* Shell, Rita.

STEWART, Rev. Hugh Fraser, DD; Emeritus Reader in French; Fellow of Trinity College, Cambridge; Fellow of Eton College; Chevalier de la Légion d'Honneur; *b* 1863; *s* of late Surgeon-General Ludovick

Stewart and Emma Ray; *m* 1902, Jessie Graham, *d* of William Graham Crum of Thornliebank; one *s* four *d*. *Educ:* Rugby, Trinity Coll., Camb. Assistant Master, Marlborough, 1889–95, Vice-Principal, Salisbury Theological College, 1895–99; Chaplain of Trinity College, Cambridge, 1899–1907; Fellow and Dean of St John's College, 1907–18; Fellow and Prælector in French, Trinity College, 1918; Senior Proctor, 1910; Hulsean Lecturer, 1914; Birkoeck Lecturer, 1930. *Publications:* Boethius: an Essay, 1891; Thirteen Homilies of St Augustine, 1900; Invocation of Saints, 1907; Memoir of J. E. B. Mayor, 1911; Romantic Movement in French Literature, 1910; French Romanticists, 1914; The Holiness of Pascal, 1915; Translation of Boethius, 1918; Edition of Les Provinciales, 1920; Classical Movement in French Literature; French Patriotism in XIXth Century, 1923; Memoir of F. Jenkinson, 1926; The Secret of Pascal, 1941; The Apology of Pascal, 1942; The Heart of Pascal, 1945. *Address:* Girton Gate, Cambridge. *Club:* Savile.

Died 23 Jan. 1948.

STEWART, Brig.-Gen. Sir Hugh Houghton, 4th Bt of Athenry, Co. Tyrone, 1803; JP, DL; *b* 15 Sept. 1858; *e s* of 3rd Bt and Annie Coote, *e d* and *co-heir* of George Powell Houghton of Kilmanock, Co. Wexford; *S* father, 1905; *m* 1st, 1915, Amy (*d* 1924), *widow* of F. C. Caldwell, *d* of late W. E. Greenwell; 2nd, 1925, Agatha Mary, *d* of late Robert Rutherford Morton, Halstead, Essex. Com. 4th Royal Inniskilling Fusiliers; High Sheriff of Tyrone, 1903; Commanded 22nd Batt. Imperial Yeomanry (Roughriders), S Africa, 1901–02, and 3rd Batt. Essex Regt 1902 (Queen's medal 5 clasps); served in European War, 1914–15; commanded 77th Infantry Brigade. *Heir: b* Col George Powell Stewart [*b* 7 Oct. 1861; *m* 1895, Florence Maria Georgina, *d* of late Col Sir James Godfray; one *s* one *d*. Formerly Major Royal Inniskilling Fusiliers].

Died 18 Jan. 1942.

STEWART, Brig.-Gen. Ian, CMG 1919; DSO 1915; late Scottish Rifles; *b* 2 Nov. 1874; 3rd *s* of late James Stewart, Garvocks, Renfrew; *m* Myra, *d* of James Kennedy of Doonholm, Ayr. one *s* two *d*. Entered Army, 1895; Captain, 1900; Major, 1915; Staff College, 1908–09; General Staff Officer, 3rd Grade S Africa, 1911–12; 2nd Grade, 1912–14; served South Africa, 1899–1902 (despatches, twice Bt Maj.; Queen's medal 2 clasps, King's medal 2 clasps); European War, 1914–18; GSO 2nd Grade, 1914; 1st Grade, 1915; Brig.-Gen. General Staff, 1916 (despatches seven times, Bt Lt-Col and Col CMG, DSO); retired with rank of Brig.-Gen. 1921. *Address:* Eyton Hall, Leominster, Herefordshire. *T:* Leominster 120. *Club:* Army and Navy.

Died 6 May 1941.

STEWART, James, MVO 1927; OBE, DL; *b* Glasgow, 26 May 1867; *s* of Archibald Stewart, Glasgow; *m* 1896; one *s* three *d*. *Educ:* St Stephen's Parish School, High School, and Allen Glen's School, Glasgow. Ex-Member of Town Council; JP for County of City of Glasgow; served three years as Convener Cleansing Committee; served three years as Convener Watching and Lighting Committee; Past Deacon of Incorporation of Tailors; served as Magistrate of City; Ex-Treasurer of the City of Glasgow and Convener of General Finance Committee; Deputy Chairman of Corporation, 1930–31 and 1931–32. *Recreations:* golf, bowling and fishing. *Address:* 99 Millbrae Road, Langside, Glasgow, S2. *Clubs:* Royal Scottish Automobile, Glasgow.

Died 21 Jan. 1943.

STEWART, Brig.-Gen. James Campbell, CMG 1919; DSO 1917; VD; *b* 19 Jan. 1884; *m* 1925. Chairman of Farmers' Relief Board, Victoria, 1933; Member of Closer Settlement Board, Victoria, 1932–33; late Chief Inspector of Land Settlement, Victoria Served

European War, 1914–19 (despatches, DSO with bar, CMG). *Address:* 22 Queen's Road, Melbourne, Australia.

Died 2 June 1947.

STEWART, Maj.-Gen. Sir James Marshall, KCB 1924; KCMG 1919; CB 1911; Indian Army, 5th (Royal) Gurkhas, FF (retired); *b* 9 Aug. 1861; *s* of Hon. Alexander Stewart; *m* 1897, Barbara Marion, *y c* of Major Hon. L. A. Addington, RA; one *d. Educ:* Clifton; Malvern; Royal Military College, Sandhurst. Entered Army, Gloucestershire Regiment, 1881; Indian Army, 1883; Captain, 1892; Brevet-Major, 1900; Major, 1901; Lt-Col 1905; Bt-Col 1905; Col 1908; Brig.-Gen. 1914; ADC to King, 1908–15; served Takht-i-Suleiman Expedition, 1883; Hazara Expedition, 1888 (medal with clasp); Burma, 1889; Chin-Lushai Expedition, 1889–90 (despatches, clasp); Hazara Expedition, 1891 (clasp); Miranzai 2nd Expedition (clasp); was on special duty in Gilgit and the Pamirs, 1891; Isazai Expedition, 1892; Waziristan Expedition, 1894–95 (despatches, clasp); Chitral, 1895; China, 1900 (despatches, medal, brevet Major); Tibet, 1903–04 (despatches, medal); NW Frontier, India, 1907–08 (despatches, medal with clasp, ADC to the King); European War, East Africa (specially promoted Major-General); Aden Field Force (KCMG, Commander of the Legion of Honour); Somaliland, 1920 (despatches); retired, 1920; Distinguished Service Pension, 1922; Chief Commissioner, British Red Cross Society, in Greece and the Near East, 1923 (received thanks of Greek Government); Colonel 5th (Royal) Gurkhas FF, 1927–31. *Recreations:* formerly cricket, polo, hunting. *Address:* Home Down, Whitchurch, Devon. *Clubs:* United Service, MCC.

Died 20 July 1943.

STEWART, Sir James Purves-, KCMG 1918; CB 1916; MA, MD Edin. 1894, FRCP Lond.; KJStJ; Companion Order of St Sava (Serbia); Hon. Col in Army; Consulting Physician Westminster Hospital; and to West End Hospital for Nervous Diseases; Physician to Royal National Orthopædic Hospital; Consulting Physician to King Edward VII Hospital for Officers, Osborne; Member of Lloyds; Freeman of City of London; late Consulting Physician to HM Forces in Mediterranean; *b* 20 Nov. 1869; *s* of John Stewart, JP and master tailor, Edin; *m* 1st, 1910, Elizabeth Phipps (*d* 1944), *d* of Wm Franks, Liverpool; 2nd, 1948, José, *widow* of Arthur Reiss. *Educ:* Royal High School of Edinburgh; University of Edinburgh and University of Jena. Vans Dunlop Scholar, 1891; Univ. Medallist in Chemistry, Pathology, Anatomy, Surgery, and Medicine; Ettles Scholar as most distinguished graduate of year, 1894. FRSM (Ex-Pres. Neurological Section); late Assist to Professor of Physiology, and afterwards to Professor of Medicine, University of Edinburgh; Physician to Imperial Yeomanry Field Hospital during South African campaign, 1900–01 (despatches, medal and 4 clasps); served in Mediterranean during European War, 1914–18, Malta, Gallipoli, Salonika, Egypt (despatches thrice); Examiner in Medicine, Universities of Aberdeen and Wales; also to Royal College of Physicians, Conjoint Board. Joint Commissioner Scottish Survey of neuro-psychiatric institutions. *Publications:* Diagnosis of Nervous Diseases, 10th ed. 1948, translated in French, Spanish, German, and Arabic; A Physician's Tour in Soviet Russia, 1932; Intracranial Tumours, 1927, translated in Russian edition; Healing of Nerves (with late Sir C. Ballance); Diseases of Peripheral Nerves, in Allchin's System of Medicine; Nerve Injuries and their Treatment (with Arthur Evans), 2nd ed. 1919; Robert Burns, a Medical Aspect, 1935; Sands of Time (autobiography), 1939; Over Military Age, 1942; editor of Neurological Volume of Oxford Medicine; various articles in Encyclopædia Medica, Medical Annual, Index

of Treatment, and other medical and scientific journals. *Recreations:* golf, travel, languages. *Address:* 45 Edwardes Square, W8. *T:* Westerrn 7892. *Club:* Reform.

Died 14 June 1949.

STEWART, Sir John, Kt 1937; *b* Perth, Scotland, 1867; *m* 1887, Mary Cameron; two *s* one *d. Educ:* Glasgow. Political Member Independent Labour Party since its inception; 7 years Member Parish Council; 26 years Glasgow Town Council; Lord Provost and Lord Lieutenant of City of Glasgow, 1935–38; in business as Brush Manufacturer since 1885. *Recreations:* various, golf, swimming, football. *Address:* Allandale, Park Road, Giffnock. *T:* Giffnock 1522.

Died 29 May 1947.

STEWART, John Alexander, CIE 1934, MC, MA, LLD (Aberdeen); Professor of Burmese, School of Oriental and African Studies (University of London); *b* 19 Jan. 1882; *s* of John Stewart and Margaret Robertson; *m* 1915, Kin Le, *d* of U An, KSM, Extra Assistant Commissioner, Bassein, Burma; one *s* (and two killed in action, 1943 and 1944) one *d. Educ:* Strichen School; Aberdeen Grammar School; Aberdeen University; Christ Church, Oxford. Passed into the ICS 1904. Arrived Burma, 1905; Subdivisional Officer, Assistant Settlement Officer, Forest Settlement Officer till 1915; served with Burma Sappers and Miners in Burma, Mesopotamia (mentioned in despatches), and NW Frontier, 1915–19; Settlement Officer, Deputy Commissioner, 1919–27; Commissioner, 1927–33; took leave preparatory to retirement, 1933. *Publications:* Contributions to Journal of the Burma Research Soc., Aberdeen Univ. Review, Journal of the Royal Asiatic Society and School of Oriental and African Studies Bulletin; An Introduction to Colloquial Burmese; A Burmese-English Dictionary (with C. W. Dunn) appearing in parts. *Recreation:* golf. *Address:* 17 Avenue Road, Bishop's Stortford, Herts. *T:* Bishop's Stortford 503.

Died 1 May 1948.

STEWART, Louisa Mary, CBE 1919; RRC; retired; *b* Aug. 1861; *e d* of late Major-General R. C. Stewart, CB. *Educ:* Miss Clarke's, Warrington Crescent, Maida Vale, London; University College Hospital, WC, 1886–89. Army Nursing Service, 1889; Matron, Queen Alexandra's Military Nursing Service to 1919; served South Africa, 1900–02 (despatches, Queen's and King's medals, RRC); European War, 1914–19 (CBE). *Address:* Carmel, Warden Road, Minehead, Somerset. *T:* 372.

Died 23 July 1943.

STEWART, Sir Michael Hugh S.; *see* Shaw-Stewart.

STEWART, Robert Bruce; Chief of Clan Stewart of Appin; *b* 23 April 1863; *e surv. s* of John Stewart, Barrister-at-law, Chief of Clan; *m* 1932, Nora Peek, 2nd *d* of late Arthur William Ballance, The Manor House, Herringswell, Suffolk. *Educ:* Magdalen College, Oxford, BA. Formerly partner in Markby, Stewart & Co., of 57 Coleman Street, EC, Solicitors. *Recreations:* shooting, fishing, cricket, golf, skating, etc. *Address:* The Homestead, Bladon, Oxfordshire. *T:* Woodstock 16. *Clubs:* Union, MCC; St George's, Sandwich.

Died 1 Jan. 1948.

STEWART, Hon. William Downie, LLB; Director National Insurance Co. of NZ, Westport Coal Co., Provident Life Co., Perpetual Trustees Co.; Pro-Chancellor Otago University; *b* 29 July 1878; *s* of Hon. Wm Downie Stewart, MLC Dunedin, New Zealand, unmarried. *Educ:* Otago Boys' High School; Otago University. Mayor of Dunedin, 1913; served in European War in Egypt and France, 1916, as 2nd Lieut Otago Regt; invalided home, Dec. 1916; MP for Dunedin West, 1914–35; Minister of Customs, 1921–28; Minister of Internal Affairs, 1921–24; Minister of Industries and Commerce, 1923–26; Attorney-General, 1926; Minister Finance, 1926–28, 1931–33;

Acting Prime Minister, 1926; Represented New Zealand at Ottawa Conference (with Rt Hon. J. G. Coates), 1932; resigned from Ministry Jan. 1933; delegate to British Commonwealth Relations Conference, Toronto, 1933, Sydney, 1938; Institute Pacific Relations Conference, Banff, 1933. *Publications:* (with Prof. J. E. Le Rossignol) State Socialism in New Zealand, 1910; Life and Times of Rt Hon. Sir Francis Bell, PC, GCMG, 1936; Life of Wm Rolleston, 1940; Portrait of a Judge, 1946; Mr Justice Richmond and the Taranaki War of 1860, 1947 (reprinted, 1948); also introduction to English translation of Democracy in New Zealand by Dr Siegfried, 1914; edited the Journal of George Hepburn in 1850, 1934. *Address:* 11 Heriot Row, Dunedin, C2, NZ. *Club:* Dunedin (Dunedin).

Died 29 Sept. 1949.

STEWART, William John; *b* Belfast; *s* of John Stewart and Sarah Dickson Rodgers; *m* Caroline Margaret, *d* of Jason Law, Enniskillen; four *d*. *Educ:* private tuition; Queen's College, Belfast. Governing Director of Stewart and Partners, Ltd, Public Works Contractors, 105 Baker Street, W1, and Belfast. MP (C). South Belfast, 1929–45. *Address:* 2 Temple wood Avenue, Hampstead, NW3; Crawfordsburn, Co. Down, Northern Ireland. *Clubs:* Devonshire, Royal Automobile; Ulster Reform, Belfast.

Died 14 May 1946.

STEWART, Lt-Col William Murray, CMG 1919; DSO 1918, late QO Cameron Highlanders; *b* 1875; *s* of J. R. Stewart, MA; *m* Frances Alice Debnam, *d* of late Maj.-Gen. Collis, CB; Colonel 21st Punjabis; two *s* one *d*. *Educ:* Charterhouse. Served Soudan, 1898 (Queen's medal and Khedive's medal with clasp); S African War, 1900–02 (despatches, Queen's medal and three clasps, King's medal and two clasps); European War, 1914–18 (despatches four times, Bt Lt-Col, CMG, DSO); retd pay, 1924. *Address:* 5 Rectory Road, Burnham-on-Sea, Somerset.

Died 24 Dec. 1948.

STEWART, Hon. William Snodgrass; KC 1894; Judge of Queens, Prince Edward Island, 1914; Admiralty Judge since 1917; late Member of the Prince Edward Island Government and for the City of Charlottetown in the Prince Edward Island Legislature; *b* Marshfield, Prince Edward Island Island, 13 Feb. 1855; *s* of Alexander and Flora Stewart; *m* 1892, Annie Augusta, *d* of Hon. Lieut-Col Henry Beer, formerly Mayor of Charlottetown and Speaker of the Prince Edward Island Legislature. *Educ:* Prince of Wales College, Charlottetown; McGill College, Montreal. BA degree and 1st class honours in Classics, and the Chapman Gold Medal for Classics. Admitted to the Prince Edward Island Bar, 1882; became a partner in the law firm of Peters, Peters & Stewart; retired from this firm, 1885, and began the practice of law in Charlottetown, which he has carried on ever since; has been leading counsel in many of the most important civil and criminal cases litigated in the province during the past 22 years; contested (C) West Queens, 1900. *Recreation:* golf. *Address:* Charlottetown, Prince Edward Island. *T:* 265 and 113. *Club:* Charlottetown.

Died 11 Feb. 1938.

STEWART-WILSON, Sir Charles, KCIE 1911; BA; Barrister-at-law; *b* 27 Sept. 1864; *e s* of Rev. J. Stewart-Wilson, DD; *m* Blanche, *γ d* of Very Rev. Principal Tulloch, DD, St Andrews University; one *d*. *Educ:* Royal High School, Edinburgh; Edinburgh University; London University. Joined Indian Civil Service, 1885; served as Under-Secretary to Government NW Provinces, and as Private Secretary to Lieut-Governor; appointed to Post Office in 1892; Director-General of the Post Office of India, 1906; member of the Viceroy's Legislative Council, 1910; Director-General of Posts and Telegraphs, 1912; retired, 1913; Member of Committee on the organisation of the British Telegraph service, 1914; Assistant Secretary, Ministry of Munitions,

1915–21; Inter-Allied Commission, Bulgaria, 1921; Officier of the Legion of Honour, 1921. *Address:* Gomm's Wood, Knotty Green, near Beaconsfield, Bucks. *T:* Beaconsfield 122. *Club:* Travellers'.

Died 20 July 1950.

STIBBE, Edward Philip, FRCS; Professor of Anatomy, University of London, King's College, since 1938; Hunterian Professor, Royal College of Surgeons; Examiner in Anatomy, RCS, Society of Apothecaries, and Universities of Durham and Liverpool; *b* 1884; *s* of late Godfrey Stibbe and Sophie Dennis; *m* 1st, 1909, Celia Evelyn Rail; two *s* one *d*; 2nd, 1924, Florence Kate Roy. *Educ:* Allan Glen's School, Glasgow; Wyggeston School, Leicester; Charing Cross Hospital, London. Govt Medical Officer, Fiji, 1909; District M/O and JP, Vosburg, Cape, 1912; M/O 1st Northern General Hospital, 1915–18; Professor of Anatomy, Univ. of S Africa, 1919; Demonstrator of Anatomy, successively, in Universities of Durham, Liverpool, London (University College), and London Hospital; Reader in Anatomy, University of London, 1935. *Publications:* Textbook of Physical Anthropology, 1930, 2nd Ed. 1938; Editor Six Teachers' Anatomy, 1932, Anatomy for Dental Students, 1934; Aids to Anatomy, 1940; papers on medical, anatomical and neurological subjects in S African medical journal, Journal of Anatomy, British Journal of Surgery, Lancet. *Address:* Hardby, Gerrards Cross, Bucks; King's College, Strand, WC2. *T:* Gerrards Cross 3226, Temple Bar 5651. *Clubs:* Athenæum, Stadium; Gerrards Cross Golf.

Died 23 July 1943.

STIEBEL, Sir Arthur, Kt 1943; *b* 27 Feb. 1875; *e s* of D. C. Stiebel, merchant, and Ada, *d* of George Lousada; *m* 1906, Frances E. Lucas; one *d*. *Educ:* Clifton; University College, Oxford. Called to Bar, Lincoln's Inn, 1899; served European War, 1914–18, Lieutenant Royal West Kent Regiment (wounded); Registrar in Companies (Winding up) and in Bankruptcy of the High Court of Justice, 1920–47; Senior and Chief Registrar, 1936–47; retired, 1947; member of Company Law Amendment Committee, appointed by the President of the Board of Trade, 1925; President of the Jewish Board of Guardians, 1920–30. *Publications:* Stiebel Company Law and Precedents, 3rd edition, 1929; Australian and New Zealand Company Law. *Recreation:* reading. *Address:* Bangor Lodge, Ascot. *T:* Ascot 134. *Club:* Reform.

Died 15 Feb. 1949.

STIEBEL, Herbert Cecil, CMG 1932; OBE; FRGS; *b* Kent, 1876; *s* of L. Stiebel, Merchant, London; *m* 1903, Helen Mary Hocking; two *s*. *Educ:* privately in Kent; St Aidan's College, Grahamstown. Left England with parents, 1888; Mining, E Transvaal, 1895–99; served Boer War, Capt. Scottish Horse, 1899–1902 (King's and Queen's medals); Transvaal Civil Service, 1902–15; served European War, E Africa, 1916, Political Officer (Major); entered administration German E Africa under British, 1916; Senior Commissioner, 1920; Provincial Commissioner, 1926–32; retired 1932. *Recreations:* hunting, golf. *Address:* c/o Standard Bank of S Africa, West End Branch, 9 Northumberland Avenue, WC2.

Died 9 Nov. 1941.

STILES, Charles Wardell, PhD; LLD; Hon. Associate, Smithsonian Institution, 1931; Medical Director, 1930 (retired, 1931), and Professor of Zoology, US Public Health Service, Washington, 1902–30; Assistant Surgeon General (Research), 1919–30; *b* Spring Valley, New York, 15 May 1867; *s* of Rev. S. M. Stiles; *m* 1897, Virginia, *d* of Hon. Lewis Baker; two *d*. *Educ:* Wesleyan Univ., Middletown, Conn; Paris, Berlin, and Leipzig. AM, PhD, Leipzig; MS, Φ BK and DSc, Wesleyan; LLD, University NC; MD, University College of Medicine, Richmond; DSc, Yale. Zoologist, US Department of Agriculture, 1891–1902; Prof. of Medical Zoology at Georgetown University, Washington; Special Lecturer on Med. Zool. at Johns Hopkins

University, Baltimore, and Navy Medical School; Scientific Attaché, US Embassy, Berlin, 1898–1900; Sec. Internat. Commission Zool Nomenclature 1897–1937; Vice-President International Zoological Congress, 1910, 1913, 1927; and Scientific Sec., Rockefeller Sanitary Commission, 1910–14; Chairman, Board on Excreta Disposal, 1918–25; Prof. of Zoology Rollins Coll., Winter Park, Fla, 1932–37; Member French Academy of Medicine, and of numerous American and foreign medical and scientific societies; Medallist, National Academy, 1921; Liverpool School of Tropical Medicine, 1920. *Publications:* numerous publications on zoology in its relation to medicine and public hygiene, as: Notes on Parasites, 1–62; Inspection of Meats for Animal Parasites; Emergency Report on Surra; Report upon the Prevalence and Geographic Distribution of Hookworm Disease (Uncinariasis or Anchylostomiasis) in the United States; Index-Catalogue of Medical and Veterinary Zoology; Experimental Pollution of Wells via Ground Water; The Nomenclature for Man, The Chimpanzee, The Orang-utan, and the Barbary Ape; Key-catalogue to Parasites; What Constitutes Publication; Early History (in part esoteric) of the hookworm campaign in our Southern United States, 1939, etc. *Recreations:* motoring, music. *Address:* Smithsonian Institution, Washington, DC; Winter Park, Fla, USA. *Clubs:* Cosmos, Washington; University, Winter Park, Fla; Beach, Bradley Beach, NJ.

Died 12 Jan. 1941.

STILES, Lt-Col Sir Harold Jalland, KBE 1919; Kt 1918, FRS (Edin.), MB, CM, FRCS (Edin.); Hon. LLD (St Andrews and Edinburgh); Hon. DSc (Leeds); Bt Col RAMC; FACS (Hon.); Hon. FRCSI; Consulting Surgeon, Edinburgh Royal Infirmary, Royal Edinburgh Hospital for Sick Children, and Chalmers' Hospital; Emeritus Regius Professor of Clinical Surgery, 1919–25; Ex-President Royal College of Surgeons of Edinburgh; Ex-President of the Association of Surgeons of Great Britain and Ireland; *b* Spalding, 21 March 1863; *s* of Henry T. Stiles, MD, JP; *m* 1st, 1889, Cecilia Norton (*d* 1930), *d* of David Law, Glasgow; one *d*; 2nd, 1931, Jean Morrison, *y d* of late J. B. Thorburn, Edinburgh. *Educ:* Totteridge Park; Edinburgh; Freiburg and Berne. First class honours, Ettles Scholar and Beaney Prizeman, Edin., 1885; Walker Prizeman RCS Eng., 1891–95, for work done in advancing knowledge of Pathology and Therapeutics of Cancer. Member of General Committee, Cancer Research Fund; Hon. Member American Medical Association; Hon. Member British Orthopaedic Association; Hon. Fellow American Surgical Association; formerly examiner in Surgery, University of Oxford and Victoria University of Manchester; Hon. Member Royal Academy of Medicine, Rome; Hon. Extra Surgeon to King George V in Scotland. *Publications:* Kocher's Operative Surgery (translated); papers in various medical journals and publications. *Recreations:* geology and botany. *Address:* Pinchbeck, Gullane, East Lothian. *T:* Gullane 2247. *Clubs:* University, Edinburgh.

Died 19 April 1946.

STILGOE, Henry Edward, CBE 1932; MInstCE; FSA; *s* of late Z. W. and A. B. Stilgoe, Adderbury, Oxfordshire; *m* Henrietta Stitt, *d* of late Archibald Cleland Tweedie, sometime City Treasurer of Liverpool; one *s* two *d*. *Educ:* Christ's College, Finchley; Crystal Palace Engineering School. Has been engaged upon Railway, Sea Defence, Tramway, Municipal, and Water Engineering Works; for 13 years was City Engineer of Birmingham; Chief Engineer of the Metropolitan Water Board, 1919–33; gave the engineering evidence before the Select Committees of the Houses of Lords and Commons and the Local Government Board in connection with the Greater Birmingham Scheme; prepared Town Planning Schemes for 25,000 acres in Birmingham and the Great Arterial Road Scheme for that city; prepared the Scheme of

Future Supplies of Water to the Metropolis, which received the sanction of Parliament in the Metropolitan Water Board's (Various Powers) Act of 1921; has been responsible for the work of constructing the Queen Mary Reservoir (6750 million gallons capacity), the river intake and pumping station at Littleton, Middlesex; also pumping stations and pumping machinery at several of the Board's works, and for the construction of eight service reservoirs; a past President of the Institution of Water Engineers; Past President of the Institution of Municipal and County Engineers; past President of the Town Planning Institute; Fellow of the Royal Sanitary Institute and a Fellow of the Society of Antiquaries of London; was a member of the Royal Commission on Fire Brigades and Fire Prevention; a member of the War Office Road Stone Control Committee during the war and of other Ministerial Committees. *Publications:* several papers on Water supply; Arterial Roads, Town Planning and Municipal Engineering. *Recreations:* shooting and antiquarian pursuits. *Address:* Braemar, Kersfield Road, Putney, SW15. *T:* Putney 1877.

Died 12 March 1943.

STILL, Dame Alicia Frances Jane Lloyd, DBE 1934; CBE 1917; RRC; Lady of Grace of Order of Hospital of St John of Jerusalem in England; Member of Queen Alexandra's Army Nursing Board and Imperial Nursing Service Committee; President Association of Hospital Matrons, 1919–37; President International Council of Nurses, 1933–37; President Florence Nightingale International Memorial Foundation and Chairman of Committee of Management, 1934–39; Vice-President National Florence Nightingale Memorial Committee and member of Executive Committee; International Florence Nightingale Medal, 1933, of the League of Red Cross Societies; *d* of late Henry Lloyd Still, Ceylon Civil Service, of Walton by Clevedon, Somerset. *Educ:* at home. Trained at the Nightingale Training School, St Thomas's Hospital; Sister St Thomas's Hospital; Matron Brompton Hospital; Matron Middlesex Hospital; Matron St Thomas's Hospital and Superintendent Nightingale Training School, St Thomas's Hospital, 1913–37. *Address:* Wiltown Place, Curry Rivel, Taunton.

Died 23 July 1944.

STILL, Sir George Frederic, KCVO 1937; MA, MD, Cantab, FRCP London; Hon. LLD Edin.; Fellow and Member of Council of King's College, London; Physician Extraordinary to the King since 1937; Consulting Physician for Diseases of Children, King's College Hospital; Consulting Physician to Hospital for Sick Children, Great Ormond Street, WC, to Infants' Hospital, Vincent Square, to Dr Barnardo's Homes and Society for Waifs and Strays; Emeritus Professor of Diseases of Children, King's College, London; *b* Holloway, London, Feb. 1868; *s* of George Still, Surveyor of HM Customs. *Educ:* Merchant Taylors' School; Caius College, Camb.; Guy's Hospital; Winchester Prizeman of Univ. of Cambridge; Murchison Scholar of the Royal College of Physicians, 1894. Goulstonian Lecturer, 1902; Lumleian Lecturer, 1918; Fitzpatrick Lecturer, 1928; Ingleby Lecturer (Univ. Birmingham), 1927; Physician-in-Ordinary to Duke and Duchess of York, 1936; first President of the British Pædiatric Association; President of the International Pædiatric Congress, 1933; Chairman, National Association for Prevention of Infant Mortality, 1917–37; Hon. FRSM, 1936; Hon. Member of American Pædiatric Society, 1903, and of Canadian Society Study Diseases of Children, 1923; Hon. Fellow of the Societa Medica Chirurgica of Bologna, 1934; Mem. Corr. de la Société de Pédiatrie, Paris, 1935; Dawson Williams Memorial Prize (for work for sick children), 1934. *Publications:* Common Disorders and Diseases of Childhood; History of Pædiatrics; Common Happenings in Childhood; Concerning Children and other things; (with Sir James Goodhart) A Textbook on

Diseases of Children; articles on diseases of children in many text-books and journals; contributor to Ency. Brit. and Dict. Nat. Biogr. *Address:* 28 Queen Anne Street, W1. *T:* Langham 1050; Harnham Croft, Salisbury.

Died 28 June 1941.

STILWELL, Gen. Joseph W., DSC 1943; on War Department Equipment Board, since Nov. 1945; *b* State of Florida, 1883; *m;* two *s* three *d. Educ:* United States Military Academy, West Point (graduate 1904). Served with US Infantry in the Philippines; Instructor in French and Spanish at West Point; served European War, 1917–18; went to China as a foreign language student attached to the US Army; studied at North China Language School, Peking, 1920–23; headquarters at Tientsin, 1926–29, served with 15th Infantry; then Chief of Staff of American Forces in China, 1929–33; Ft. Benning, Head of Dept of Tactics, 1933–35; organised Reserve Duty at San Diego, Calif, 1935–39; Military Attaché, Peking, 1939–40; with 2nd Division, 1940–41; Formed 7th Div., 1941; CG, 3rd Corps, 1942–44; Commander of United States Forces in China, Burma, and India; one of Generalissimo Chiang Kai-Shek's chiefs of staff, 1942–44, and also commanding Chinese Army in India in second Burma Campaign (Commanded 5th and 6th Chinese Armies in Burma Campaign in 1942); Comdr US Army ground forces, 1945; left in June to command 10th Army.

Died 12 Oct. 1946.

STIMSON, Henry Lewis; Member Inter-American Panel on Good Offices since 1938; *b* NY City, 21 Sept. 1867; *s* of Lewis Atterbury Stimson and Candace Wheeler; *m* 1893, Mabel Wellington White, New Haven. AB Yale, 1888; AM Harvard, 1889; Harvard Law School, 1889, 1890. Admitted to Bar, 1891; member of firm of Root & Clarke, 1893; Root, Howard, Winthrop & Stimson, 1897; Winthrop & Stimson, 1901–29; US Attorney Southern District NY, 1906–09; Republican candidate for Governor of New York, 1910; Secretary of War in Cabinet of President Taft, 1911–13; Delegate at large, New York Constitutional Convention, 1915; Commd Maj. judge advocate US Res. Mar 1917; Lt-Col 305th FA, Aug. 1917; Col 31st FA, Aug. 1918; with AEF in France, Dec. 1917–Aug. 1918; Special Envoy President Coolidge to settle revolution in Nicaragua, April–May 1927; Governor-General of the Philippine Islands, 1928–29; Secretary of State, United States, 1929–33; Chairman, American Delegation to Naval Armaments Conference at London, 1930; Delegate to Seven Power Conference, London, 1931; Member of Panel Permanent Court of Arbitration. The Hague, 1938–48, resigned; President Commission of Conciliation between Switzerland and Italy, 1937–47, resigned; Secretary of War, USA, 1940–45; Republican: Presbyterian; Mem. Bd of Trustees, Internat. House; American City and State Bar Assns; Psi Upsilon; Skull and Bones (Yale). *Publications:* American Policy in Nicaragua, 1927; Democracy and Nationalism in Europe, 1934; The Far Eastern Crisis, 1936; On Active Service in Peace and War, 1948. *Address:* Huntington, New York, USA. *Clubs:* Century University, Republican, Down Town (New York); Metropolitan (Washington).

Died 21 Oct. 1950.

STIRLING, Edward; *b* Birmingham, 26 May 1891; *s* of William Stirling; of Scottish descent; *m* 1912, Margaret Vaughan, actress; two *d. Educ:* King Edward VI School, Birmingham. Studied for stage under late William Mollison. Debut in Wolverhampton, 1909, in The Merchant of Venice; during next five years toured widely in England; first London appearance, Scala Theatre, 1914, in Anna Karenina; enlisted in 1914 but was discharged through ill health; in partnership with late Sir Phillip Ben Greet, 1921–23; Actor Manager and Director of The English Players, the only permanent English Theatrical Company on the Continent of Europe, South America, etc., 1922–40; producing plays

in London and broadcasting in European Section of BBC, 1941–44; Drama Adviser to the Forces in the London Region; Director Drama French Institute; Gen. Manager ENSA Allied Entertainments, Paris, 1944–45; playing in French, and attached to Radiodiffusion Française, 1946; broadcasting: Films: Colomba and L'Aigle a Deux Têtes, 1947; in his Paris Theatre has presented works of nearly every celebrated English dramatist; has performed in 37 countries; Chevalier de la Couronne de la Belgique. *Publications:* Plays: Captain Swing (with Francis Brett Young), 1919; The Mayflower (with Alfred Hayes), 1920; Crepe de Chine (Novel), 1922; The New Will, 1938; autobiography, Something to Declare, 1942. *Recreations:* flying, ski-ing. *Address:* 117 rue D'Asnieres, Courbevoie, Paris. *Club:* Green Room.

Died 12 Jan. 1948.

STIRLING, Col Sir George Murray Home, 5th Bt *cr* 1666; CBE 1919; DSO 1900; Retired List; JP; Lord Lieutenant for Stirlingshire since 1936; DL Dumbartonshire; *b* 4 Sept. 1869; *e s* of 8th Bart and Anne Georgina, *e d* of James Murray; *S* father, 1910; *m* 1904, Mabel Elizabeth, CBE 1946 (author of Barbara Mary and other novels), 2nd *d* of late Sir Alexander Sprot, 1st Bt; (*s* Capt. G. A. Mungo Stirling, MC, died of wounds 14 Dec. 1941) three *d. Educ:* Eton; Sandhurst. Joined 2nd Essex Regiment (56th Foot, the Pompadours), 1889; Captain, 1900; Major, 1912; served in Chitral Campaign, 1895 (medal and clasp); Tirah Campaign, 1897–98 (two clasps); South Africa, 1900–02 (wounded at Zandfontein, despatches, DSO, South African medal and 4 clasps, King's medal and 2 clasps); Special Service Officer, Somaliland, 1903–04 (medal and clasp); European War, 1914–18 (despatches four times, 3 medals, CBE, Brevet Lieutenant-Colonel, wounded); DAAG, Mhow Division, 1911–14; Assistant Provost Marshal, 5th Army Corps in France, Jan. to Oct. 1915; Commanded 2nd Batt. Essex Regiment 15 Nov. till wounded 1 July 1916, afterwards 1st Essex till April 1918; Brigadier of the King's Bodyguard for Scotland; Commanded 9th Batt. Argyll and Sutherland Highlanders (TF), 1924–28; appointed Keeper of Dumbarton Castle by King George, 1927. *Address:* Glorat, Milton of Campsie, Stirlingshire. *T:* Lennoxtown 214. *Clubs:* Army and Navy; New (Edinburgh); Stirling County (Stirling). *[Baronetcy in abeyance.]*

Died 1 May 1949.

STIRLING, Brig.-Gen. William, CMG 1919; DSO 1917; *b* 15 March 1876; 2nd *s* of late General Sir William Stirling, KCB, Colonel Commandant RA; *m* 1915, Kathleen Henrietta, *er d* of late Lt-Col J. A. T. Garratt, Grenadier Guards, of Bishop's Court, Exeter; no *c. Educ:* Wellington College; RMA, Woolwich. Served European War, 1914–18 (despatches, DSO, CMG); Brigadier-General commanding RA 50th Division, 1918–19; Instructor, Senior Officers' School, Belgaum, 1920–22; Commandant of the School of Artillery, 1922–26; half-pay, 1926–28; Commander RA 2nd Division, Aldershot, 1928–32; retired pay, 1932. *Address:* Urgashay, Bridgehampton, Yeovil, Som. *Club:* Army and Navy.

Died 31 Oct. 1949.

STIRLING-HAMILTON, Sir William; *see* Hamilton.

STIRTON, Rev. John, CVO, 1936; MVO 1927; DD (St Andrews) 1926; FSA (Scot.); senior minister of Crathie; Chaplain in Ordinary to the King since 1936; Chaplain to the Duke of Kent when Lord High Commissioner to General Assembly of the Church of Scotland, 1935; *b* Perth, 3 Sept. 1871; *s* of John Stirton, merchant, Perth, and Stewart Maria Lawson; *m* 1917, Edith Georgina Katherine, *o d* of George Dickson of Monybuie, Kirkcudbrightshire, advocate, Sheriff-Substitute of Dumfries and Galloway. *Educ:* University of St Andrews and University of Glasgow. MA

(Glasgow) 1894; BD (St Andrews) 1897; Tulloch Memorial Scholarship, 1897. Assistant in St Giles' Cathedral, Edinburgh, 1897–1902; Hon. Chaplain, St Giles' Cathedral, 1902; Minister of Corsock, Kirkcudbrightshire, 1902–04; Minister of Glamis, Forfarshire, 1904–19; Volunteer and Territorial Chaplain from 1904; served with Lowland Division during European War of 1914–18; Hon. Chaplain, 2nd class, Royal Army Chaplain Department; Domestic Chaplain to the King, 1919–36; Librarian at Balmoral Castle, 1919–36. *Publications:* Historical Account of Glamis, 1904; An Old Scottish Divine, 1911; Glamis, a Parish History, 1913; A Day that is Dead, 1913, 2nd Edition, 1929; Pastime Papers, 1917; History of Family of De Maria, 1920; History of Family of Stirton, 1920, 2nd Edition 1935; Papers in Proceedings of Society of Antiquaries, Scotland, 1910, 1920; Balmoral in Former Times, 1921; Mirrors of Memory; The Celtic Church and the Influence of the East, 1923; Crathie and Braemar, a History of the Parish, 1925; The Red House, and other Papers, 1926; Notes on the Chapel Royal of Scotland and the Order of the Thistle, 1927; My Manuscript Portfolio, 1929; Links with Lady Nairne and the Oliphants of Gask, 1930; Three Periods of English Poetry, 1670–1824, 1930; St Fergus, the Saint of Glamis, 1930; Erasmus: a character study, 1930; Incident in the life of HM Queen Elizabeth, 1931; The Very Rev. James Cameron Lees, DD, KCVO, an appreciation, 1931; A Royal Letter, 1931; Crathie Parish Church, An Historical Survey, 1932, seventh edition, 1938; The Spanish Match, 1933; Funeral Expenses of King William III, with Introduction and Notes, 1934; Notes on Some Manuscripts and Early Printed Works, 1934; The Chantry Chapel at Glamis, 1936; The Inneses of Balnacraig and Ballogie—A Family History; Glamis Castle: Its Origin and History, 1938; Balmoral Castle: Its Past and Present History, 1940. *Recreations:* walking tours, curling, music. *Address:* Delvine, Dreghorn Loan, Colinton, Edinburgh, 13. *T:* Edinburgh 87753. *Clubs:* University, Edinburgh.

Died 8 Oct. 1944.

STITT, Rear-Adm. Edward Rhodes; *b* Charlotte, North Carolina, USA, 22 July 1867; *m* 1st, 1892, Emma W. Scott; one *s* two *d*; 2nd, 1935, Laura Armistead Carter; 3rd, 1937, Helen B. Newton. *Educ:* University of South Carolina (AB); University of Pennsylvania (MD). Entered US Navy (Medical Corps), 1889; Rear-Admiral, Medical Corps, 1917; Surgeon General, US Navy, 1920–28; placed on retired list, 1931; ScD Jefferson College and University of Pennsylvania; LLD University of South Carolina and University of Michigan. *Publications:* Practical Bacteriology and Animal Parasitology, 9th edition; Diagnostics and Treatment of Tropical Diseases, 6th edition. *Recreation:* music. *Address:* Navy Department, Washington, DC, USA. *Clubs:* Cosmos, Army-Navy (Washington); NY Yacht (New York City).

Died 13 Nov. 1948.

STOBART, Col George Herbert, CBE 1919; DSO 1915; late RA; Hon. Col 6th Battalion The Durham Light Infantry; *b* 18 Feb. 1873; *s* of William Culley Stobart and Frances Dorothea, *d* of Rev. George P. Wilkinson; *m* 1900, Mary, *d* of late Rev. H. G. Kinnear, one *s* two *d*. Entered Army, 1894; Major, 1911; Bt Col 1924; Col 1925; retired, 1911; served S Africa, 1899–1900 (Queen's medal with clasp); European War, 1914–18 (despatches, DSO, Bt Lt-Col); Commanded 151st Infantry Brigade (TA), 1925–29; DL, JP Co. Durham; High Sheriff, 1925; Chairman Durham County Territorial Association, 1926–36; additional ADC to the King, 1930–40. *Address:* Helme Park, Tow Law, Co. Durham. *TA:* and *T:* Tow Law 41. *Club:* Army and Navy.

Died 25 May 1943.

STOBIE, Harry, FRCS, LRCP Lond. 1911; FDSRCS Eng. 1947; Professor, Dental Surgery and Pathology, University of London, Dean and Director of Studies, Royal Dental Hospital of London, School of Dental Surgery; Examiner in Dental Surgery, Universities of Leeds and Durham; Consulting Dental Surgeon, King Edward VII Memorial Hospital, Ealing; President, Odontological Section, RSM; Vice-President and Member of Council, and Member Advisory and Legal Committee, Medical Protection Society; FRSM; *b* Liverpool, 23 Sept. 1882; *s* of George Stobie; *m* 1912, Emmeline Mary, *d* of F. M. Guanziroli, Paris and London; two *s*. *Educ:* Royal Dental Hospital, Charing Cross, and St Thomas' Hospitals. Demonstrator, 1911–15, Clinical Assist 1919–20, and Lecturer Operative Dental Surgery, 1919–20, Lecturer in Dental Surgery and Pathology, 1933–39; Hon. Dental Surgeon, 1915, 1939; Roy. Dental Hosp.; Consulting Dental Surgeon to the Army at Home, Brigadier 1940–44; Late External Examiner in Dental Surgery-Univs of London, Birmingham and Bristol; Mem. of Board of Examiners in Dental Surgery, Royal College of Surgeons, England; late Hon. Dental Surgeon Sutton Cottage Hospital; Clinical Assistant Dental Department St Thomas' Hospital, 1910; served European War as temp. Captain RAMC; Surgeon Specialist Injuries of Jaws, 1915–19; National representative at 2nd International Stomatological Congress (Bologna) 1935. *Publications:* Case of Osteomyelitis of Mandible; Problem of Apical Infection; the Diagnosis and Surgical Principles underlying the Treatment of Cysts and other Common Tumours of Jaws: The Lower Third Molar. *Address:* Royal Dental Hospital of London, School of Dental Surgery, 32 Leicester Square, WC2; Trevena, Mulgrave Road, Sutton, Surrey. *T:* Whitehall 6427, Vigilant 1066.

Died 27 April 1948.

STOCKDALE, Sir Frank Arthur, GCMG 1945; KCMG 1937; CMG 1932; CBE 1925; Vice-Chairman, Colonial Development Corp., since 1948; *b* 24 June 1883; *s* of late George Edmund Stockdale; *m* 1908, Annie Dora Packer (*d* 1948); two *s*. *Educ:* Wisbech; Magdalene Coll., Cambridge, MA. Mycologist and Lecturer in Agricultural Science, Imperial Department of Agriculture for the West Indies, 1905; Assistant Director, Department of Science and Agriculture, and Government Botanist, British Guiana, 1908; Director of Agriculture, Mauritius, 1912; Registrar, Co-operative Credit Societies, 1913; Official member of the Council of Government, 1913–16; Director of Agriculture and Registrar of Co-Operative Societies, Ceylon, 1916–29; MLC Ceylon, 1921–29; Agricultural Adviser to the Secretary of State for the Colonies, 1929–40; Comptroller for Development and Welfare in the West Indies, 1940–45; Vice-Chairman Colonial Advisory Council of Agriculture and Animal Health, 1929–40; Chairman of East African Agricultural Conference, 1931; Chairman Colonial Directors of Agriculture Conferences, 1931 and 1937; Vice-Chairman West Indian Fruit and Vegetable Conference, 1933; Chairman Imperial Institute Advisory Council on Plant and Animal Products, 1935–40; Co-Chm. of Anglo-American Caribbean Commission, 1942–45; Adviser on Development Planning, Colonial Office, 1945–48. Travelled extensively. *Publications:* reports and articles relating to Tropical Agriculture and Co-operation; Editor of the Tropical Agriculturist, 1916–1928. *Address:* 42 Marsham Court, SW1. *Club:* Athenæum.

Died 3 Aug. 1949.

STOCKINGS, Major Arthur Perry, CBE 1920; *b* Norwich, 3 Jan. 1880; *s* of late George Stockings, Boscombe, Hants; *m* 1913, Dorothy, *d* of Richard England, Rumney Court, Cardiff; one *d*. *Educ:* privately; Marburg University. Chief Engineer and General Manager of several important British companies in S America, principally in Bolivia; earlier work of a similar nature in S Africa; Hon. Secretary to the Joint War

Committee of the Order of St John and British Red Cross, 1914; granted a commission in the 2/2 London Regt Royal Fusiliers (T), and fought in the Dardanelles after service in Malta and Egypt; placed on light duty; appointed Director of Supply Section in the Trench Warfare Dept, Ministry of Munitions; appointed Sub-Commissioner of the British Red Cross for Italy; after the Armistice appointed BRC Commissioner for Italy to carry out Demobilisation (despatches, Italian Military Cross, Chevalier Order of St Maurice and St Lazarus). *Recreations:* golf and gardening. *Address:* White Gables, Radlett, Herts.

Died 29 Jan. 1943.

STOCKLEY, Brig.-Gen. Ernest Norman, DSO 1917; RE, retd; *b* 25 Sept. 1872; *s* of Col George Watts Stockley, Royal Engineers; *m* 1898, Elsie Shewell, *d* of late Col H. F. Cooper, Royal Marines; three *s* one *d*. *Educ:* Wellington College; Royal Military Academy, Woolwich. 2nd Lieut Royal Engineers, 1891; Captain, 1902; Major, 1911; Lt-Col 1918; Bt Col 1919; served with Tochi Field Force, 1897 (Indian Frontier medal with clasp); European War, 1914–18; served in France and Flanders (despatches five times, DSO and bar, Légion d'honneur, Croix de Guerre, Bt Lt-Col, Bt Col); retired with hon. rank of Brig.-Gen., 1929. *Address:* c/o Lloyds Bank, 6 Pall Mall, SW1.

Died 6 Oct. 1946.

STOCKLEY, Rev. Joseph John Gabbett, MA; Canon Residentiary of Lichfield and Chancellor of the Cathedral, 1928–44, Canon Emeritus, 1944; *b* Kilkee, Co. Clare, 12 May 1862; *s* of John Surtees and Alicia Catherine Diana Stockley; *m* Sarah, *d* of Thomas Gibson Cant, Croft House, Penrith; one *s* one *d*. *Educ:* Rathmines School, Dublin; Trinity Coll., Dublin. Ordained, 1886; Curate of Penrith, Cumberland, 1886–88; S Peter's Streatham, 1888–94; Thurgarton, Notts, 1894–97; Vicar of Lowdham, Notts, 1897–1900; S George's Nottingham, 1900–01; S Paul's, Burton-on-Trent, 1901–19; Rector of Wolverhampton (S Peter's Collegiate Church), 1919–28; Rural Dean of Wolverhampton, 1919; Prebendary of Lichfield, 1923; Lecturer in Pastoral Theology, Lichfield Theological College, 1916–20; Member of the Mission of Help to India, 1922–23; President of the Johnson Society of Lichfield, 1936. *Address:* The Close, Lichfield. *T:* Lichfield 2218.

Died 17 Aug. 1949.

STOCKLEY, William F. P., MA, DLitt; Emeritus Professor of English, University College, Cork (National University of Ireland); *b* Templeogue, Co. Dublin, 1859; *s* of John Surtees Stockley, RHA, and Alicia, *d* of Joseph Gabbett, Co. Limerick; *m* 1st, 1892, Violet (*d* 1893), *d* of William Osborne, RHA; one *d*; 2nd, 1908, Marie Germaine, *d* of Kgl. Hofrat Max Kolb, Royal Botanic Gardens, Munich; one *d*. *Educ:* Rathmines School; Trinity College, Dublin (Senior Moderator in Modern Literature). Professor in the University of New Brunswick, 1886–1902, and in the University of Ottawa, 1902–03; Headmaster of St Mary's College, Halifax, 1903–05; Alderman, 1920–25; MP for the National University, 1921–23. *Publications:* How to read a Shakespeare Play; Commentary on Newman's Dream of Gerontius; Henry the Fifth's Poet Historical (Shakespeare and his Fighting King); English Visitors from Ralegh to Newman; Shakespeare Papers; Studies in Irish Biography; Newman, Education and Ireland. *Address:* Arundel Cork Ireland.

Died 22 July 1943.

STOCKMAN, Ralph, MD, LLD; FRCPE, FRFPSG, FRSE; *b* Leith, 3 Aug. 1861; 2nd *s* of W. J. Stockman, merchant. *Educ:* High School and University, Edinburgh; University of Vienna and University of Strassburg. Assistant in the University of Edinburgh for six years, and afterwards Lecturer on Materia Medica in the School of Medicine; practised medicine there, and

held several hospital appointments; Professor of Materia Medica and Therapeutics, Univ. of Glasgow, 1897–1936. *Publications:* Rheumatism and Arthritis, 1920; numerous contributions to medical journals. *Address:* White Lodge, Barnton Avenue, Edinburgh, 4. *T:* 77115.

Died 27 Feb. 1946.

STODDART, Jane T.; on staff of British Weekly, 1890–1937; *b* Kelso, Scotland. *Educ:* Edinburgh and Hanover. *Publications:* Translation of Richard Rothe's Stille Stunden, 1888, and Maeterlinck's Ruysbroeck and the Mystics, 1895; The Earl of Rosebery, an Illustrated Biography, 1900; An Editor's Life-Story; Dr W. Robertson Nicoll, 1903; The Life of the Empress Eugénie, 1906; The Girlhood of Mary Queen of Scots, 1908; The New Socialism; An Impartial Inquiry, 1909; The Old Testament in Life and Literature, 1913; The New Testament in Life and Literature, 1914; The Christian Year in Human Story, 1919; The Case against Spiritualism, 1919; Private Prayer in Christian Story, 1927; Great Lives Divinely Planned, 1930; A Book of the Golden Rule, 1933; My Harvest of the Years, 1938; The Psalms for Every Day, 1939. *Address:* at 20 Colinton Road, Edinburgh.

Died 15 Dec. 1944.

STODDART, William Henry Butter, MD Lond.; FRCP Lond.; late Physician Superintendent of Bethlem Royal Hospital; late Lecturer on Mental Disease, St Thomas's Hospital; late Examiner at the University of London. *Educ:* City of London School. *Publications:* Mind and its Disorders, 5th ed., 1926; The New Psychiatry, 1915, etc. *Address:* 217 Bickenhall Mansions, W1. *T:* Welbeck 6060.

Died 5 April 1950.

STOKER, William Henry; KC Barbados, 1903; *s* of William Coates Stoker, solicitor, London; *widower*; one *s* two *d*. *Educ:* University College School, London. Called to Bar, Middle Temple, 1895; North-Eastern Circuit; Privy Council and Parliamentary Committees; Chairman of the Appeal Court for Flour Milling Industry; Arbitrator and Chairman for Ministry of Labour in industrial disputes since 1916; Chm. of the Civil Engineering and Construction Conciliation Board; is on the Panel of Arbitrators under the Electricity (Supply) Act, 1926, and is Independent Chm. of the Joint District Board for North Wales under the Coal Mines (Minimum Wages) Act, 1912; was British member of the Haytian Claims Commission, 1926; Leading Counsel for the Arab Executive before the Parliamentary Palestine Commission of Enquiry, 1929; British Commissioner on Anglo-Mexican Special Claims Commission, 1931; was a Chairman of General Munitions Tribunals under Munitions of War Acts, of the London Appeal Tribunal under the Military Service Act, and of the interim Court of Arbitration; Attorney-General, Leeward Islands, 1898; Barbados, 1902; President West Indian Quarantine Conference of 1904; Puisne Judge, Southern Nigeria, 1907–14. *Publications:* joint author of The Military Service Tribunals Practice; The Industrial Courts Act, 1919, and Conciliation and Arbitration in Industrial Disputes; articles in monthlies and weeklies. *Address:* 6 New Square, Lincoln's Inn, WC2. *T:* Holborn 5604. *Club:* Athenæum.

Died 16 June 1944.

STOKES, Col Claude Bayfield, CIE 1917; DSO 1919; OBE 1919; late 3rd Skinner's Horse; *b* 27 Oct. 1875; *m* 1921, Olga, *d* of Lt-Gen. Peter Postovsky; one *d*. *Educ:* St John's School, Leatherhead; RMC, Sandhurst. Joined East Kent Regiment, 1895; Lieut Indian Army, 1897; Captain 1904; Major, 1913; Lieut-Col 1917; Colonel 1922; served North-West Frontier, India, 1897–98 (medal with clasp); European War, 1914–18 (CIE, DSO, OBE); Military Attaché, Tehran, 1907–11; Political Officer at Baku, 1919; Chief British Commissioner in

Trans-Caucasia, 1920–21; retired, 1922; British Vice-Consul, Nice, 1931–40. *Address:* c/o Grindlay's Bank, Ltd, 54 Parliament Street, SW1.

Died 7 Dec. 1948.

STOKES, Col Harold William Puzey, CBE 1923; DSO 1918; *b* All Saints' Vicarage, New Town Park, Co. Dublin, 15 Jan. 1878; third *s* of late Canon G. T. Stokes, DD; *m* 1914, Miriam, *o d* of W. Alexander; one *d. Educ:* Trinity College, Dublin, BA Studied law; commissioned as a university candidate in Army. Service Corps, 1900; served SA Campaign, 1901–02; European War, 1914–18 (despatches four times, DSO, Chevalier of Legion of Honour); retired pay, 1934. Re-employed in rank of Lt-Col Sept. 1939–Nov. 1941; enrolled 25th Hamps Bn Home Guard, 1941–44. *Recreations:* hunting and golf. *Address:* c/o Lloyds Bank, Fleet, Hants.

Died 13 March 1949.

STOLL, Sir Oswald, Kt 1919; Chairman and Managing Director, Coliseum Syndicate, Ltd; Stoll Picture Theatre (Kingsway), Ltd; Manchester Hippodrome and Ardwick Empire, Ltd; Hackney and Shepherd's Bush Empire Palaces, Ltd; Leicester Palace, Ltd; Chatham Empire, Ltd; Chiswick Empire, Ltd; Stoll Picture Productions, Ltd; St Augustine's Parade Hippodrome (Bristol), Ltd; Stoll Theatres Corporation, Ltd; *b* Melbourne, Australia, 20 Jan. 1866; *m* 1st, 1892, Harriet Lewis (*d* 1902); one *d*; 2nd, 1903, Millicent Shaw; three *s. Educ:* Liverpool. *Publications:* The Grand Survival; A Theory of Immortality by Natural Law; The People's Credit, 1916; Freedom in Finance, 1918; Broadsheets on National Finance, 1920; National Productive Credit, 1933; initiated the Sir Oswald Stoll Foundation. *Recreations:* reading and theatres. *Address:* Carlton House, Putney Hill, SW15. *T:* Putney 1764. *Clubs:* Junior Constitutional, Royal Automobile.

Died 9 Jan. 1942.

STONE, Rev. Darwell, MA, DD; Hon. Canon of Christ Church, 1919; *b* 1859; *s* of Rev. G. L. Stone, Vicar of Rossett, Denbighshire; unmarried. *Educ:* Merton College, Oxford. 2nd class Classical Mods 1880; 2nd class Lit. Hum. 1882. Curate of Ashbourne, 1883–85; Vice-Principal of Dorchester Missionary College, 1885–88; Principal of Dorchester Missionary College, 1888–1903; Pusey Librarian, 1903–09; Principal of Pusey House 1909–34; Examiner in Theological Honour School. University of Oxford, 1912–14. *Publications:* Holy Baptism, in the Oxford Library of Practical Theology, 1899; Outlines of Christian Dogma, 1900; Christ and Human Life, 1901; Outlines of Meditations for use in Retreat, 1902; The Church, its Ministry and Authority, 1902; The Invocation of Saints, 1903; The Holy Communion (Oxford Library of Practical Theology), 1904; The Discipline of Faith, 1904; The Christian Church, 1905; A History of the Doctrine of the Holy Eucharist, 1909; The Notes of the Church, 1910; Episcopacy and Valid Orders, 1910; Divorce and Re-marriage, 1913; The Reserved Sacrament, 1917; The Eucharistic Sacrifice, 1920; The Faith of an English Catholic, 1926; The Prayer Book Measure and the Deposited Book, 1928; joint-author, with Canon Newbolt, of The Church of England; An Appeal to Facts and Principles, 1903; (with Rev. F. W. Puller) Who are Members of the Church?, 1922; Contributor to the Church Quarterly Review and the Journal of Theological Studies; Editor of the Lexicon of Patristic Greek now in preparation. *Address:* 14 St Margaret's Road, Oxford. *T:* Oxford 3009.

Died 10 Feb. 1941.

STONE, Harlan F.; Chief Justice of the United States, Washington, DC, since 1941; *b* Chesterfield, New Hampshire, 11 Oct. 1872; *s* of Frederick L. Stone and Anne Sophia Butler; *m* 1899, Agnes Harvey, Chesterfield, New Hampshire; two *s. Educ:* Amherst College, BS 1894; MA 1897; Columbia Univ. Law School, LLB 1898; (Hon. LLD of numerous universities

and colleges); Hon. DCL Syracuse Univ., 1928. Member International Academy of Comparative Law since 1923; FAAS, 1933; Hon. Bencher, Lincoln's Inn, London; Trustee of Amherst College and of Folger Shakespeare Library, 1933; Chairman, National Gallery of Art; Chancellor, Smithsonian Institution; Admitted to New York Bar, 1899; Member of law firm of Wilmer and Canfield, and later of its successor Satterlee, Canfield and Stone; lectured on law in Columbia Law School, 1899–1902, 1910–23; Adjunct Professor of Law, 1903; devoted himself exclusively to practice, 1905–10; Kent Professor of Law and Dean of Columbia Law School, 1910–23; Member of law firm of Sullivan and Cromwell, New York City, 1923; Attorney-General of United States, 1924–25; Associate Justice of Supreme Court, 1925–41. *Publications:* contributions to legal periodicals. *Recreations:* travel and fishing. *Address:* 2340 Wyoming Avenue, NW, Washington, DC, USA. *T:* Decatur 0210. *Clubs:* Athenæum (hon. member); Century, Lawyers, New York City; Univ., Washington; Chevy Chase Country, Chevy Chase, Maryland.

Died 22 April 1946.

STONE, Sir Joseph Henry, Kt 1919; CIE 1913; MA; DLitt (Madras); *b* 9 June 1858; *m* 1889, *y d* of J. W. Brassington of Madras; one *s. Educ:* King's Coll., Cambridge. Entered Madras Educational Service, 1886; Prof. of History, Presidency Coll., 1887; Principal, Kumbakonam College, 1895; Inspector of European and Training Schools, 1903; Mem. Leg. Council of Madras, 1908; Principal and Professor, English Literature, Presidency College, Madras, 1907–12; Special Deputy-Director of Public Instruction, 1912; Director of Public Instruction, 1914–19; retired, 1919. *Address:* Poneys Close, Bracknell, Berks.

Died 9 Oct. 1941.

STONE, Col Lionel George Tempest, CMG 1918; CBE 1926; *b* 1874; *s* of late Edward Coutts Tempest Stone, Lieut Royal Welch Fusiliers; *m* 1906, Alice Campbell Walker; two *s. Educ:* St Paul's School; Wren's; Royal Military College, Sandhurst. Gazetted Royal Fusiliers, 1895; served Tibet Expedition, 1904–05 (medal); retired as Major, 1911; Organising Officer, City of London Police Reserve, 1913; commanded South Belfast Regt Ulster Volunteer Force, 1914; appointed to Embarkation Staff Aug. 1914; Assistant Director of Railway Transport and Assistant Embarkation Commandant, Southampton; Lt-Col 1916; Col 1919; mentioned for Very Valuable Services 1918; orders of St Maurice and St Lazarus of Italy, and White Eagle of Serbia; Area Transport Commissioner Ministry of Transport, 1920–21; Controller of Transport and Ground, British Empire Exhibition, 1921–25. *Address:* 20 Argyll Mansions, W14. *T:* Fulham 7443. *Clubs:* Army and Navy, Naval and Military.

Died 27 April 1946.

STONEHAVEN, 1st Viscount *cr* 1938, of Ury; **John Lawrence Baird;** 1st Baron (*cr* 1925); 2nd Bt *cr* 1897, PC 1922; GCMG 1925; CMG 1904; DSO 1915; JP, DL; LLD Aberdeen and Sydney Universities, 1930; *b* 27 April 1874; *e s* of 1st Bart and late Hon. Annette Palk, *d* of 1st Baron Haldon; *S* father, 1920; *m* 1905, Lady Ethel Keith-Falconer, *e d* of 10th Earl of Kintore; two *s* three *d. Educ:* Eton; Christ Church, Oxford. Late Diplomatic Service; Vienna, 1896; Cairo, 1898; Abyssinia, 1899; Private Secretary to Sir Wm Garstin, Under-Secretary for Public Works in Egypt, 1900–02; Acting Agent and Consul-General in Abyssinia, 1902; Political Officer, British East Africa and Abyssinia Frontier Survey, 1902–03; Political Officer with Abyssinian Army in Somaliland, 1903–04 (medal and clasp, despatches, CMG); 2nd Secretary, Paris, 1904–06; Buenos Aires, 1906–08; served as Intelligence Officer, European War, 1914–15 (despatches, DSO); Parliamentary Member of the Air Board, 1916–18; Parliamentary Under Secretary of State for the Royal Air Force, 1918; MP (Co. U) Rugby Division, Warwickshire, Jan. 1910–22, and Ayr

Burghs, 1922–25; Parliamentary Under-Sec. of State, Home Office, 1919–22; Minister of Transport and First Commissioner of Works, 1922–24; Governor-General and Commander-in-Chief, Commonwealth of Australia, 1925–30; Chairman of the Conservative Party Organization, 1931–36. *Heir: e s* Hon. James Ian Baird. *Address:* 37 Bryanston Square, W1. *T:* Paddington 4141; Ury, Stonehaven, Kincardineshire. *Clubs:* Turf, Carlton, Royal Yacht Squadron, Cowes; New, Edinburgh.

Died 20 Aug. 1941.

STONES, Sir Frederick, Kt 1941; OBE; MLC; JP; Director, E. D. Sassoon & Co., Ltd, Bombay, since 1920; *b* 4 Oct. 1886; *s* of John Thomas Stones and Mary Mason, 16 Tennyson Road, Fleetwood, Lancs; *m* 1913, Sarah Danson; two *d. Educ:* Culcheth; Central Secondary School and College of Technology, Manchester. Served apprenticeship with J. Howarth & Sons, Manufacturers, Meadow Mills, Failsworth; Manager's Asst Wilton Mfg Co., Middleton, England, 1903–04; Weaving Master, Bengal Cotton Mills, Calcutta, India, 1904–08; Weaving Master, Swan Mills, Ltd, Bombay, 1908–09; Mill Superintendent, Bombay Dyeing & Mfg. Co., Bombay, 1909–20; Technical Director, E. D. Sassoon & Co., Ltd, Bombay, since 1920. *Recreation:* breeding of throughbred race horses. *Address:* Bombay Club, Bombay, India. *TA:* c/o Spindles, Bombay. *T:* Bombay 26511. *Clubs:* National Liberal; Royal Bombay Yacht, Willingdon Sports, Bombay Gym khana, Royal Western India Turf (Bombay)-Aero (Delhi).

Died 12 July 1947.

STONEY, George Gerald, MAI (Dublin), DSc (Durham); FRS; MInstCE, MInstEE; MInstME; Consulting Engineer; *b* Dublin, 28 Nov. 1863; *e s* of late G. Johnstone Stoney, ScD, FRS; *m* Isabella Mary (*d* 1930), 2nd *d* of late Michael Lowes, Corbridge-on-Tyne; no *c. Educ:* private; Trinity Coll., Dublin. Second Senr Moderator and Gold Medallist in Experimental Science. Was with the late Bindon B. Stoney, FRS, at the Port and Docks Board, Dublin, and, 1888–1912, with C. A. Parsons & Co., Newcastle-on-Tyne, being intimately associated with the development of the steam turbine, both land and marine, and the other manufactures of that firm; Joint-Secretary of the Tyneside Irish Battalions of the Northumberland Fusiliers, 1914–17; Prof. of Mechanical Engineering in the College of Technology and in the Victoria University, Manchester, 1917–26; Director of Research at C. A. Parsons and Co., Newcastle-on-Tyne, 1926–30. *Publications:* Cantor Lectures on The Steam Turbine, The Tension of Metallic Films deposited by Electrolysis, in the Proceedings of the Royal Society, and various papers in the Proceedings of the Royal Dublin Society, Institution of Civil Engineers, Institution of Electrical Engineers, etc., on Steam Turbines and other subjects. *Recreations:* cycling, motoring, and experimental mechanics. *Address:* Oakley, 250 Heaton Road, Newcastle-on-Tyne 6. *T:* 55670. *Clubs:* Union, Newcastle-on-Tyne.

Died 15 May 1942.

STOPFORD, Maj.-Gen. Sir Lionel Arthur Montagu, KCVO 1919; CB 1916; *b* 10 May 1860; *s* of late Admiral Sir Montagu Stopford, *s* of 3rd Earl of Courtown, and 2nd wife, Lucy, *d* of John Cay; *m* 1891, Mabel Georgina Emily, *o c* of late George Alexander Mackenzie of Applecross, Ross-shire; two *s.* Served Egypt, 1882 (medal, bronze star); Sikkim Expedition, 1888 (medal with clasp); European War, 1914–16 (despatches, CB). *Address:* Summercourt, Wrotham, Kent. *T:* Borough Green 8. *Club:* United Service.

Died 13 Sept. 1942.

STOPPANI, Rt Rev. Antonio; *b* Lecco, Lake of Como, 6 Jan. 1873; *s* of Ferdinando Stoppani and maria Pecoroni. *Educ:* Monza. Priest, 1895; joined Mission Society, 1905; came to Egypt, 1899; Khartoum, 1902; Wau (Bahr-el-Ghazal), 1911; Prefect Apostolic of the new Prefecture Apostolic of the Bahr-el-Ghazal, 1913; Bishop of the Vicariate of Bahr-el-Ghazal, 1917–33. *Address:* Italian Catholic Mission, Bahr-el-Ghazal, Post Office, Wau, Sudan, AE. *TA:* Stoppani, Wau.

Died 11 Aug. 1940.

STOREY, Major Charles Ernest, DSO 1917; *b* 1877; *m* Violet, *widow* of George Henry Knapp; one *d. Educ:* Cranleigh. Served S Africa, Imperial Light Horse, 1900–02; European War, 18th Royal Fusiliers and Royal Tank Corps, 1914–19 (despatches, DSO). *Address:* Linkside, Hindhead, Surrey.

Died 27 July 1943.

STORKE, Arthur Ditchfield, CMG 1947; President Climax Molybdenum Co., New York; *b* 21 May 1894; *s* of Frederic Elliott and Kathleen Storke; *m* 1921, Mary Rice. *Educ:* Leland Stanford University. *Recreation:* skiing. *Address:* Climax Molybdenum Co. of Europe, Ltd, 2 and 3 Crosby Square, EC2; 500 Fifth Avenue, New York, USA. *Club:* Metropolitan (New York).

Died 9 Sept. 1949.

STORR, Lt-Col Lancelot, CB 1919; Chevalier of the Legion of Honour, 1917; late Assistant Secretary to the Cabinet; *b* 18 Jan. 1874; *s* of late Rev. Charles Storr of Matfield; *m* 1905, Josephine Mary (*d* 1936), *d* of Edward Harriman Dickinson. *Educ:* Harrow (classical scholar); RMC, Sandhurst (Honours); Graduate, Indian Staff College, 1907; took Course of Economics and Political Science, London, 1912. Attached Dorsetshire Regt, 1893; 20th MI 1894; 54th Sikhs (Frontier Force), 1895; served Tirah Campaign, 1898–99 (medal with two clasps); China, 1900–01 (medal); ADC to Commander-in-Chief, India, 1902; Brigade Major, Jullundur, 1908–10; and Sirhind Brigade, 1911–12; Assistant Military Secretary to Commander-in-Chief, India, 1912; European War, 1914–18; DAAG, War Office, 1914–16, while also attached to Personal Staff of Lord Kitchener; Asst Sec., Committee of Imperial Defence, 1916–21; Asst Sec., War Cabinet, Dec. 1916; Asst Sec., Imperial War Cabinet, at sessions held in 1917–18; was the first Secretary of the British Section, Supreme War Council, Nov. 1917 to May 1918; General Staff Officer, first grade; retired from the Army, 1921; Secretary to the Shadow Cabinet of the Unionist Party, 1924; Ecclesiastical Secretary to the Lord Chancellor, 1924–28; Personal Assistant to the Chairman of the Unionist Party Organisation, 1929–30. *Publications:* contributed leading and other articles, and verse, to various Indian newspapers, etc. *Recreations:* racquets, cricket, travelling. *Club:* Union.

Died 7 Aug. 1944.

STOUT, George Frederick; *b* South Shields, 6 Jan. 1860; *e s* of late George Stout; *m* 1899, Ella (*d* 1935), *d* of the late Rev. W. T. Ker, Free Church minister; one *s. Educ:* private school; St John's College, Cambridge (MA). First Class Classical Tripos, part i 1881; First Class with mark of special distinction in Ancient Philosophy, Classical Tripos, part ii 1882; First Class with mark of special distinction in Metaphysics, Moral Sciences Tripos, 1883. University Lecturer in the Moral Sciences at Cambridge, 1894; Fellow of St John's College, Cambridge, 1884; Anderson Lecturer in Comparative Psychology in Aberdeen University, 1896–98; Wilde Reader in Mental Philosophy in the University of Oxford, 1898; Professor of Logic and Metaphysics, St Andrews, 1903–36, retired; Examiner, University of London, 1899; editor of Mind, 1891–1920; Member of British Academy, 1903; Gifford Lecturer in Edinburgh, 1919–21; Hon. LLD Aberdeen, 1899; Hon. DLitt Durham, 1923; Hon. LLD, St Andrews, 1937; Hon. Fellow St John's College, Cambridge, 1927. *Publications:* many articles in Mind and in Proceedings of the Aristotelian Society; Analytic Psychology, 1896; Manual of Psychology, 1st Ed. 1898, 5th Ed. 1938; Groundwork of Psychology, 1903; Studies in Philosophy and

Psychology, 1930; Mind and Matter (Gifford Lectures) 1931, etc. *Recreations:* chess, walking. *Address:* 560 Pacific Highway, Killara, Sydney, NSW.

Died 18 Aug. 1944.

STOW, Robert Frederic Philipson-; *b* 8 March 1878; 2nd *s* of Sir Frederic Philipson-Stow, 1st Bt, Blackdown House, Fernhurst, Sussex; *m* 1st, 1906, Fernande (*d* 1920), *d* of late Marc Dieuset of Paris, and Paris Plage; 2nd, 1922, Hélène Marguerite Dieuset. *Educ:* Harrow; Balliol College, Oxford; Leyden. Barrister-at-law, Inner Temple; Advocate of the Supreme Court, Cape of Good Hope; served with the Imperial Yeomanry in the South African War, 1900–02; Lt 1901 (King's and Queen's medals 5 clasps); Editor South African News, Cape Town, 1908–10; Delegate for Cape Town to the Imperial Press Conference, London, 1909. *Address:* The Manor House, Little Comberton, Worcs.

Died 3 June 1949.

STOWELL, Lt-Col Arthur Terence, CIE 1928; VD; *b* 1873; *s* of late John Alexander and Caroline Amelia Stowell. Late Lieut-Colonel NW Railway Regiment, Auxiliary Force, India; entered Indian State Railway Service, 1895; Assistant Secretary Railway Board, 1914; Deputy Controller of Traffic, 1918; Deputy Director Railway Transport, Afghan War, 1919; Chief Operating Superintendent NW Railway, 1924; Agent, 1927; Manager Indian Railways Bureau, London, 1928; retired, 1932. FR Empire Soc. *Address:* 18 South Park Court, Park Road, Peckenham.

Died 28 Aug. 1945.

STRACEY, Sir Edward Paulet, 7th Bt *cr* 1818; *b* 5 July 1871; *e s* of 6th Bt and Mary Gertrude, *d* of Sir Charles Des Vœux, 2nd Bt; *S* father, 1888; *m* 1st, 1902, Mary Elizabeth Brinsley, *e d* of late Algernon Sheridan, Frampton Court, Dorchester; one *s* one *d*; 2nd, 1935, Kathleen Emily, *d* of late Robert Alexander Robertson, Old Castle, Collooney, Co. Sligo; one *d*. Major, Reserve Regt 2nd Life Guards, 1916–18; Major, 2nd City of London Yeomanry, 1914–16; Lieut, 2nd Life Guards, 1894–1900; Lieut, 3rd Batt. Norfolk Regiment, 1890–94. Owns 3000 acres. *Heir:* *s* Michael George Motley, *b* 1911. *Address:* Rackheath Park, Norwich; 13 Devonshire Place, W1; Fermoyle Lodge, Costelloe, Co. Galway. *Clubs:* Guards', Cavalry.

Died 23 Aug. 1949.

STRACHAN, Douglas, LLD (Aber.); Hon. RSA 1920; *b* Aberdeen, 1875; *m* Elsie Isobel, *d* of John Cromar, Aberdeen; two *d*. *Educ:* Robert Gordon's College, Aberdeen. Studied in RSA Life Schools; thereafter in France, Italy, and Spain. Practised first as portrait and figure painter; commissioned to execute the stained glass windows which constituted Great Britain's gift to the Palace of Peace, The Hague; has since worked almost exclusively in that medium; complete series of windows; Scottish National War Memorial, Edinburgh; Winchelsea Church, Sussex, Goldsmiths' Window in St Paul's Cathedral (destroyed by enemy action); Whittington Window, Guildhall, London; Univ. of Aberdeen and Glasgow. *Address:* Pittendriech, Lasswade, Midlothian.

Died 20 Nov. 1950.

STRACHEY, Sir Charles, KCMG 1926; CB 1920; *b* 1862; 3rd *s* of late Sir John Strachey, GCSI; *m* 1893, Ada Margaret (*d* 1925), *d* of late Rev. Alexander Raleigh, DD, and *sister* of late Sir Walter Raleigh; one *s*. *Educ:* King's College, Cambridge. Was in Foreign Office, 1885–99; travelled in West Africa, 1913–14; represented Colonial Office at Peace Conference, 1919; Assistant Under-Secretary of State for Colonies, 1924–27; Member of Gypsy Lore, and Essex Archæological Societies. *Address:* 61 Clifton Hill, NW8. *Club:* Union.

Died 15 March 1942.

STRADBROKE, 3rd Earl of, *cr* 1821; **George Edward John Mowbray Rous,** KCMG 1920; CB 1904; CVO 1906; CBE 1919; JP; VD, TD, MA; Bart, 1660; Baron Rous, 1796; Viscount Dunwich, 1821; Lord-Lieutenant for the County of Suffolk, since 1935; Vice-Admiral of Suffolk, since 1890; Knight of Grace of St John; for 32 years Councillor, Alderman, for 12 years Chairman East Suffolk County Council, and Chairman County of Suffolk Territorial Army Association; formerly ADC to King Edward VII (1902–11) and to King George V (1911–29) and President, National Sea Fisheries Protection Association; President of the Council, National Artillery Association; *b* 19 Nov. 1862; *s* of 2nd Earl and Augusta, *d* of Rev. Sir Christopher John Musgrave, 9th Bt, *widow* of Colonel Bonham, 10th Hussars; *S* father, 1886; *m* 1898, Helena Violet Alice (DBE 1927), Lady of Grace of St John, *d* of Gen. Keith Fraser; four *s* three *d*. *Educ:* Harrow; Cambridge (MA). Col 1st Norfolk RGA Volunteers, 1888–1908; Col 3rd (Howitzer) Brig., E Anglian Division, RFA, 1908–17; Col 272nd Brigade RFA, Jan.–Nov. 1917; 64th DA, Nov. 1917–July 1918; 321st Brigade RFA, July 1918–March 1919; 172nd Brigade RFA, April–June 1919; 191st Brigade RFA, June–Oct. 1919; Kantara Area to July 1920; serving in France, Egypt and Palestine during European War; Governor of Victoria, 1920–26; Parliamentary Secretary Ministry of Agriculture, 1928–29; Grand Master, United Grand Lodge of Victoria, Australia, 1922–26; Provincial GM of Suffolk Freemasons and of East Anglian Mark Masons; Grand Master of M. Masons of England from 1943; Past Grand Warden. Owns about 10,000 acres. *Heir:* *s* Comdr Viscount Dunwich, RN, retired. *Address:* Henham Hall, Wangford, Beccles, Suffolk. *T:* Wangford 214; Inverlael, Lochbroom, Ross-shire. *T:* Lochbroom 12. *Clubs:* Carlton; Suffolk County; Norfolk County (Norwich); Royal Yacht Squadron (Cowes); Royal Norfolk and Suffolk Yacht (Lowestoft).

Died 20 Dec. 1947.

STRAIGHT, Major Douglas Marshall, CIE 1916; formerly Inspector-General of the Police Force, United Provinces of Agra and Oudh; *b* 1869; *o s* of late Sir Douglas Straight. Joined the service, 1887; District Superintendent, 1890; Inspector-General, 1911; retired, 1916; King's police medal, 1913; gazetted Captain RASC, 1916; Commandant German Prisoners of War Camp, Spalding, 1918, and in similar capacity at Bromley; retired, 1920, with rank of Major. *Address:* 48 Clifton Hill, NW8. *Club:* Peefsteak.

Died 28 Aug. 1949.

STRAKER, William, CBE 1930; JP; General Secretary, Northumberland Miners' Association, 1905–35; *b* Snitter, near Rothbury, Northumberland, 13 July 1855; father, agricultural labourer; *m* 1881, Margaret Ann Sinclair; two *s* five *d*. *Educ:* various Elementary Educational Schools. Commenced to work on a farm for 6d per day, 1866; continued for 4 to 5 years working during summer and going to school during winter; engaged at various general labouring jobs until 1872, when he commenced to work in and about coal mines; for 18 consecutive years member of the National Committee of the Miners' Federation of Great Britain; for 32 years a member of the Northumberland Education Committee; 27 years member of the Royal Infirmary House Committee, Newcastle; 28 years a Director of the Co-operative Printing Society; Social and religious work in various ways too numerous to mention; Land Tax Commissioner; Member of Investigation Committee, Northumberland, Mines Act, 1930. *Publications:* Contributor to Quarterly Circular to Miners dealing with social, trades' union and political questions; newspaper articles and poems on many subjects. *Recreations:* gardening and walking, studying the works of nature, especially botany. *Address:* 16 Brackenfield Road, Gosforth, Newcastle-on-Tyne. *T:* Gosforth 51357.

Died 31 Dec. 1941.

STRAKOSCH, Sir Henry, GBE 1927; KBE 1924; Kt 1921; Hon. LLD (Manchester); Hon. Financial Consultant to Secretary of State for India since 1942; Chairman Union Corporation, Ltd; Director of several S African and other companies; *b* 9 May 1871; *s* of Edward Strakosch; *m* 1941, Mrs Mabel Elizabeth Vincent Temperley. Entered upon a banking career in City of London, 1891; since 1895 has been closely connected with South African industrial development, especially the gold mining industry; author of South African Currency and Banking Act 1920; represented South Africa at International Financial Conference at Brussels, 1920, and acted as financial adviser of the South African Government at League of Nations Assemblies, the Genoa Conference, and Imperial Conference, 1923, and as delegate for South Africa at the Assemblies of the League, 1923 and 1924; Member of Council of India, 1930, until its dissolution, 1937; Adviser to Secretary of State for India, 1937–42; Member of Financial Committee, League of Nations, 1920–37; Member of Royal Commission on Indian Currency and Finance, 1925–26; Member of Channel Tunnel Committee, 1929–30; Delegate of India, Imperial Economic Conference, Ottawa, 1932; Delegate of India, Monetary and Economic Conference, 1933. *Publications:* The South African Currency and Exchange Problem; Monetary Stability and the Gold Standard; The Economic Consequences of Changes in the Value of Gold; The Crisis; The Road to Recovery. *Recreation:* golf. *Address:* Heatherside, Walton-on-the-Hill, Surrey. *T:* Tadworth 2350. *Clubs:* Athenæum, St James's.

Died 30 Oct. 1943.

STRALIA, Elsa, (Mrs A. T. Christensen); *b* Adelaide; *d* of Hugo Fischer, baritone; *m* 1st, William Mountfort Moses (from whom she obtained a decree *nisi*, 1935); 2nd, 1935, Adolph Theodore Christensen, Patea, New Zealand. *Educ:* Marshall Hall Conservatoire, Melbourne (Scholar). Made her début on the concert platform under the name of Elsa Fischer; came to Europe 1910, studying in Milan, and later to London to study with Mme Falchi; made first appearance in Grand Opera at Covent Garden as Donna Elvira, 1913. *Address:* c/o Thomas Cook & Son, Tourist Agents, Collins Street, Melbourne, Australia.

Died 31 Aug. 1945.

STRANGE, Brig.-Gen. Robert George, CIE 1918; RA; retired; *b* 1861; *s* of late Major C. J. Strange, RA; *m* Frances Mary Fitzherbert (*d* 1934), *d* of Capt. S. J. Nicholls. Served Egypt, 1882 (medal, bronze star); NW Frontier of India, 1897–98 (medal and three clasps), and 1908 (despatches, medal and clasp); European War, 1914–19 (despatches, CIE); Reward for Distinguished Service. *Address:* c/o Lloyds Bank, 6 Pall Mall, SW1.

Died 2 March 1949.

STRANGWAYS, Arthur Henry Fox; *b* Norwich, 14 Sept. 1859; *e s* of Col Fox Strangways, RA. *Educ:* Wellington College; Balliol College, Oxford. Assistant Master, Wellington College, 1887–1910; Music Critic on The Times, 1911–25 and of Observer, 1925–39. *Publications:* Music of Hindostan; Life of Cecil Sharp; Music Observed, 1936. *Address:* The Hut, Bovey Tracey, Devon. *T:* Bovey 21.

Died 2 May 1948.

STRANGWAYS, Madame Mary, FGSM; Professor of Singing, Guildhall School of Music, since 1918; *d* of late Rev. Canon M. B. Hogg, MA, TCD; *m* 1910; one *s*. *Educ:* Strand House School, Londonderry; Royal College of Music and Guildhall School of Music. Professional engagements as an Oratorio and lieder singer Queen's Hall, Albert Hall, etc. *Publications:* articles on voice culture, etc. *Recreations:* travel and swimming. *Address:* 3 Eaton Rise, Ealing, W5; The Weekes Studios, Hanover Street, W1.

Died Oct. 1945.

STRATHEARN, Sir John Calderwood, Kt 1936; CBE 1928 (OBE 1918); Lieut-Colonel RAMC (TF), Ret.; MD, ChB, FRCS (Edin.); KGStJ; Member Faculty of Ophthalmologists; formerly Hon. Consulting Ophthalmic Surgeon, Government of Palestine, etc; *b* 1878; *m* Edith Amy Josephine, *d* of John Cyster, Gate Court, Northiam, Sussex. *Educ:* High School, Glasgow; University of Glasgow and University of Edinburgh. House Surgeon, Glasgow Royal Infirmary; House Physician, Glasgow Western Infirmary; House Surgeon, Hospital for Skin Diseases; House Surgeon, Glasgow Eye Infirmary, etc.; Ophthalmic Surgeon to the Dundee School Board, and to the Educational Authority, County of Fife; Assistant Surgeon to the British Ophthalmic Hospital, Jerusalem; Warden and Chief Surgeon of the St John Ophthalmic Hospital, Jerusalem. *Publication:* The Problem of Blindness in Palestine (Folia Ophthalmologica Orientalia, 1933). *Address:* The Manor House Verwood, Wimborne Minster, Dorset.

Died 14 Aug. 1950.

STRATHMORE AND KINGHORNE, 14th Earl of, *cr* 1677; Earl (UK) *cr* 1937; **Claud George Bowes-Lyon,** KG 1937; KT 1928; GCVO 1923; TD, LLD, DL, JP; Baron Glamis, (Scotland), 1445; Earl of Kinghorne, Lord Lyon, Baron Glamis, 1606; Earl of Strathmore and Kinghorne, Viscount Lyon, Lord Glamis Tannadyce, Sydlaw, and Strathdichtie, 1677; Baron Bowes, (UK), 1887; *b* 14 March 1855; *e s* of 13th Earl of Strathmore and Frances, *d* of Oswald Smith, Blendon Hall, Kent; *S* father, 1904; *m* 1881, Cecilia (GCVO 1937) (*d* 1938), *d* of late Rev. Charles W. Cavendish Bentinck; three *s* three *d*. Lieut 2nd Life Guards, 1882; Lord-Lieut of Forfarshire, 1904–36. Owns about 24,700 acres. *Heir: s* Lord Glamis, *b* 22 Sept. 1884. *Address:* Glamis Castle, Angus.

Died 7 Nov. 1944.

STRATHMORE AND KINGHORNE, 15th Earl of, *cr* 1677; Earl (UK) *cr* 1937; **Patrick Bowes-Lyon;** Baron Glamis (Scotland), 1445; Earl of Kinghorne, Lord Lyon, Baron Glamis, 1606; Earl of Strathmore and Kinghorne, Viscount Lyon, Lord Glamis, Tannadyce, Sydlaw, and Strathdichtie, 1677; Baron Bowes, (UK), 1887; *b* 22 Sept. 1884; *e s* of 14th Earl and Cecilia (GCVO 1937) (*d* 1938), *d* of late Rev. Charles W. Cavendish Bentinck; *S* father 1944; *m* 1908, Lady Dorothy Osborne (*d* 1946), 3rd *d* of 10th Duke of Leeds; one *s* one *d*. Entered Army, 1904; Reserve of Officers, 1909; served European War, 1914–15; Chairman, John Bowes and Partners, Ltd, and Marley Hill Chemical Co., Ltd, both of Newcastle-on-Tyne; Deputy Governor, Royal Bank of Scotland. DL Angus; JP, Co. Durham. *Heir: s* Lord Glamis. *Address:* Shovelstrode Manor, East Grinstead; Glamis Castle, Angus.

Died 25 May 1949.

STRATHSPEY, 4th Baron *cr* 1884; **Trevor Ogilvie-Grant of Grant;** Bt of Nova Scotia *cr* 1625; 31st Chief of Grant; *b* Oamaru, NZ, 2 March 1879; 2nd *s* of 10th Earl of Seafield (*d* 1888); *S* brother (11th Earl of Seafield), 1915; *m* 1st, 1905, Alice Louisa (*d* 1945), *d* of T. M. Hardy-Johnston MICE London, of Christchurch, NZ; one *s* one *d*; 2nd, 1947, Mrs Cloete Capron, *widow* of Lt-Col Capron, late York and Lancaster Regt, and 3rd *d* of late Gordon Cloete, JP, Cape Colony. *Educ:* Waitaki High School; St John's College, New Zealand. New Zealand Civil Service, 1906–13; Gas Officer, 1917–18; Member Putney Hospital Board, 1919; Putney Member of Wandsworth Borough Council, 1919–22. *Publication:* The Case of Colonial Representation in an Imperial Parliament. *Recreations:* all outdoor sports and travelling. *Heir: s* Major Hon. (Donald) Patrick Trevor Ogilvie-Grant of Grant [*b* 18 March 1912; *m* 1938, Alice, *o c* of late Francis Bowe; one *s* (*b* 9 Sept. 1943) two *d*]. *Address:* Rose Cottage, Southwick, near Fareham, Hants.

Died 11 Nov. 1948.

STRATTON, Lt-Col Wallace Christopher Ramsay, IA; CIE 1911; retired; *b* 19 Aug. 1862; *s* of late Brig.-Surg. John Proudfoot Stratton; *m* Barbara Jegon, *d* of late E. Killingworth Johnson, RWS, of Bakers, Sible Hedingham, Essex; one *s* two *d*. *Educ:* United Services College; RM Academy, Woolwich. Entered Royal Artillery, 1881; Indian Army, 1883; Government of India Political Department, 1885; reverted to Military employ, 1917; retired, 1919. *Address:* 11 St Alban's Grove, W8. *T:* Western 0270.

Died 27 Aug. 1942.

STRAUS, Ralph, BA; novelist and biographer; *b* Manchester, 15 Sept. 1882; *s* of late Sidney R. Straus; unmarried. *Educ:* Harrow; Pembroke Coll., Cambridge (Foundation Scholar in Biology). *Publications:* The Man Apart, 1906; John Baskerville, a Memoir (with R. K. Dent), 1907; The Dust which is God, 1907; The Little God's Drum, 1908; The Scandalous Mr Waldo, 1909; Robert Dodsley, Poet, Publisher, and Playwright, 1910; 5000 ad, 1911; The Prison without a Wall, 1912; Carriages and Coaches, 1912; The Orley Tradition, 1914; Mrs Holmes, Commandant (with Miss A. Barnett), 1918; Pengard Awake, 1920; Volcano, 1922; The Unseemly Adventure, 1924; The Transactions of Oliver Prince, 1924; An Odd Bibliography, 1925; Married Alive, 1925; Our Wiser Sons, 1926; The Unspeakable Curll, 1927; Dickens: a Portrait in Pencil, 1928; A Whip for the Woman, 1931; Five Men go to Prison, 1935; Dickens, the Man and the Book, 1936; Lloyd's: a Historical Sketch, 1937; Sala: the Portrait of an Eminent Victorian, 1942; articles and privately printed books from his own press. *Recreation:* real tennis. *Address:* 64a Eccleston Square, SW1. *T:* Victoria 0570. *Club:* Savile.

Died 5 June 1950.

STRAUSS, Adm. Joseph, Hon. KCMG 1918; *b* Livingston Co., New York, 16 Nov. 1861; *m* 1901, Mary, *d* of late General Sweitzer, US Army; one *s* one *d*. *Educ:* US Naval Academy. Entered US Navy, 1887; Lieutenant 1899; Lieutenant-Comdr 1904; Comdr 1908; Capt. 1912; engaged in hydrographic surveys on east and west coast of US and in Alaska, 1887–90; Ordnance Dept 1893–96; invented superposed turret system of mounting guns on battleships, 1895; served blockade of Cuban Coast, 1898; Commanding Naval Proving Ground Indian Head, 1901–03 and 1906–08; Inspector of Ordnance Naval Proving Ground, 1906–08; Commanded cruiser Montgomery in experimental work on torpedoes, 1909–10; battleship Ohio, 1910–13; Chief of Bureau of Ordnance, with rank of Rear-Admiral, 1913–16; in command of the battleship Nevada at outbreak of war; REar-Admiral and in command of the Mine Force, US Atlantic Fleet, 1918; Member General Board Navy Dept, 1920; C-in-C Asiatic Fleet, 1921–22; Member of General Board, 1922–25; retired, 1925; promoted to Admiral on the retired list by Act of Congress, 1930. *Address:* 2208 Mass Ave, NW, Washington, DC.

Died 30 Dec. 1948.

STRAUSS, Richard, Hon. DMus Oxon; *b* Munich, 11 June 1864; *m* 1894, Pauline de Ahna; one *s*. Conductor at Meiningen, 1885; Hofcapelmeister at Weimar and Munich; Director Vienna State Opera, 1919–24; Chevalier Legion of Honour, 1907; Officer, 1914. *Works:* Guntram, Feuersnot, Salome. Operas; Tod und Verklärung; Don Juan; Macbeth; Till Eulenspiegel; Don Quixote; Ein Heldenleben; Elektra; Also Sprach Zarathustra; Sinfonia domestica; Taillefer; Bardengesang. Songs: Le Bourgeois Gentilhomme, 1911; Ariadne auf Naxos, 1912; Deutsche Motette, 1913; La Légende de Joseph, 1914; The Woman without a Shadow, 1916; Schlagobers, Ballet, 1924; Intermezzo, 1924; Parergon zur Sinfonia Domestica, 1925; Die Aegyptische Helena, 1928; Arabella, 1933; Die Schweigsame Frau, 1935; Friedenstag, 1937; Daphne, 1938; Capriccio, 1941; Die Liebe der Danae, 1943; Metamorphosen, 1945; Oboe Concerto, 1945. *Address:* Garmisch-Partenkirchen, Bavaria.

Died 8 Sept. 1949.

STREATFEILD, Mrs Granville, (Lucy Anne Evelyn), CBE 1918; JP Kent; *d* of late Col Bonar Deane and Hon. Lucy Boscawen, sister of Viscount Falmouth; *m* 1911, Granville Edward Stewart Streatfeild, DSO, OBE (*d* 1947). HM Senior Inspector of Factories; Mem. War Office Commission of Enquiry to Concentration Camps during Boer War; Mem. Roy. Commission on Civil Service; First Woman Organising Officer, Nat. Health Insurance Commission, London; appointed Member of various Trades Boards under the Trade Boards Act; Commission of Enquiry into the Conditions of the WAAC in France; Member Kent Executive Committee of Women's Land Army; Vice-Chairman Kent Council of Social Service. *Address:* Westerham, Kent. *T:* Westerham 23. *Club:* University Womens'.

Died 3 July 1950.

STREATFEILD, Henry Cuthbert, CIE 1913; Indian Civil Service, retired; *b* Howick, Northumberland, 24 Oct. 1866; *s* of late Rev. William Champion Streatfeild; *m* 1st, 1893, Marion Elsie (*d* 1924), *d* of Augustus Morand of Germantown, USA; one *s* one *d*; 2nd, 1933, Cecilia, *widow* of W. M. Stevenson, CBE. *Educ:* Marlborough; Pembroke College, Camb. Joined Indian Civil Service, 1887; appointed to Bengal; Under-Secretary to the Bengal Government, 1890–93; District Officer of Darbhanga, 1894–95; Palamau, 1895–96, and 1910–11; Ranchi, 1896–1901; Backerganj, 1903–05; Rangpur, 1905–06; Manbhum, 1906; Secretary to the Bengal Government, 1907–08; officiated as Commissioner of Dacca, 1904; Bhagalpur, 1910; Commissioner of Tirhut, 1911–12; retired, 1913; Temporarily employed War Office, 1914–18; Home Office, 1918–19. *Address:* Beauchamp, Ventnor, IW.

Died 8 Aug. 1950.

STREET, Lt-Col Ashton, MB, FRCS, IMS (retired); late Principal, and Professor of Surgery, Grant Medical College, Bombay; *b* 1864; *m* Clare, OBE (*d* 1944), *d* of Herbert Davies, MD, Senior Physician, London Hospital; two *d*. *Educ:* Downing Coll., Cambridge. *Club:* East India and Sports.

Died 8 Sept. 1946.

STREETON, Sir Arthur, Kt 1937; *b* Victoria, Australia, 8 April 1867; *s* of C. H. Streeton and Mary Johnstone; *m* 1908, Esther Leonora Clench (*d* 1938), violinist; one *s*. *Educ:* Public schools, Australia. Awarded hon. mention, also gold medal, Paris Salon, 1892, and gold medal, Paris Salon, 1909; diplomas from International Exhibition, Pittsburgh, US. Has exhibited in all leading International Exhibitions, and important Exhibitions in Great Britain; some of his more important works are in the state collections of Australia; enlisted in RAMC as a private, April 1915; invalid out after two years' service; commissioned as Lieutenant to France as official war artist for Australia, May 1918. *Address:* 17 Grange Road, Toorak, Melbourne, SE2, Australia.

Died 1 Sept. 1943.

STREICHER, Most Rev. Henry, CBE (Hon.) 1934; Archbishop of Brysis since 1933; *b* Haguenau, Alsace, 1863. *Educ:* St Cyr College, Nevers, France. Entered the Noviciate of Society of Missionaries of Africa (White Fathers), 1884; Holy Priesthood, Carthage, Tunisia, 1887; Professor of Theology at Jerusalem, 1887; Professor of Theology at Carthage, Tunisia, 1889; sent as missionary to the Uganda Protectorate, 1890; Administrator of the White Fathers' Mission, 1896; Bishop of Tabarka and Vicar Apostolic of Uganda, 1897. *Address:* Mbarara, PO Uganda.

Died Feb. 1944.

STRETTON, Lt-Col Arthur John, MVO; Senior Director of Music, Kneller Hall, Royal Military School of Music, 1896–1921; retired pay, 1921; *b* 1863; *m* Mrs A. M. Ray, Dollis Hill. *Educ:* Studied music, both practical and theoretical, under late Dr Warwick Jordan, J. T. Carrodus, Battison Haynes, etc. *Address:* 14 Hamilton Road, NW10.

Died 27 Feb. 1947.

STRINGER, Hon. Sir (Thomas) Walter, Kt 1928; KC 1907; *b* 4 Nov. 1855; *s* of Wm Stringer, of Christchurch, New Zealand; *m* 1882, Ada Davies (*d* 1932), Dunedin, NZ; two *s*. *Educ:* High School, Christchurch; Canterbury College. Admitted Barrister of Supreme Court of NZ, 1879; Crown Prosecutor for Canterbury Judicial District, 1890–1913; Judge of the Supreme Court of New Zealand, 1913–27; Judge of Arbitration Court, 1913–20; Chairman of New Zealand Prisons Board, 1926–27; Chairman of New Zealand War Pensions Appeal Board, 1927–40. *Recreations:* tennis, golf, angling. *Address:* Northern Club, Auckland, New Zealand. *Clubs:* Canterbury; Northern, Dunedin.

Died 8 Dec. 1944.

STRONG, Rev. Charles, DD; founded Australian Church at Melbourne, 1885; *b* the Manse, Dailly, Ayrshire, 26 Sept. 1844; *s* of Rev. David Strong, Parish Minister, and Margaret, *d* of Rev. J. Roxburgh, Parish Minister of Kilmaurs, Ayrshire; *m* 1872, *d* of Archibald Denniston, WS, Greenock; five *s* two *d*. *Educ:* Ayr Academy; Glasgow Academy and University. Formerly Minister of the Old West Parish Church, Greenock; Anderston Church, Glasgow; Scots Church, Melbourne, 1875–83; resigned, 1883, and returned to Scotland; revisited Melbourne, 1884, and formed a free unsectarian church, the Australian Church; Editor Australian Herald, now The Commonweal, including Peacewords, organ of the Peace Society and WIL for Peace and Freedom, also the Howard Leaflet; President of Melbourne Branch of London Peace Society, and of Melbourne Branch of the Howard League; President of Anti-Sweating League. *Publications:* Christianity Re-interpreted; Some Recent Protestant Theology; A Primer of Religion for Families and Schools; compiler and part composer of Church Worship, being Hymns, Psalms, and Prayers used in the Australian Church. *Address:* The Australian Church, Melbourne.

Died 12 Feb. 1942.

STRONG, Eugénie, CBE 1927; *b* 25 March 1860; *d* of Frederick William Sellers; *m* 1897, late S. Arthur Strong, Librarian to the House of Lords. *Educ:* in France at the Convent of St Paul; Girton College, Camb. (Honours class Tripos); Hon. LLD St Andrews, 1897; LittD Dublin, 1907; first Life Fellow of Girton College, 1910; Hon. LittD, Manchester, 1923. Lectured on Greek Art and Archæology at the British and S Kensington Museums, and subsequently in Rome; delivered the Hermione Lectures at the Alexandra College, Dublin, 1904, the Norton lectures for the Archæological Institute of America, 1913, and the Rhind lectures for the Society of Antiquaries for Scotland, 1920; Member of Council of the Hellenic Society since 1892 (Vice-President, 1922); Vice-President of Society for Promotion of Roman Studies, 1929; Member of Committee of the National Art Collections Fund, 1906–13; organised the Exhibition of Greek Art at the Burlington Fine Arts Club, 1903; Hon. Member of the Archæological Society of Athens and of the Archæological Institute of America; succeeded her husband as Librarian to the Duke of Devonshire at Chatsworth, 1904–09; Assistant Director of the British School of Archæology in Rome, 1909–25; elected Fellow of the Society of Antiquaries, 1920; member of the Reale Accademia Ponteficia (Rome), of the Reale Accademia dei Lincei, 1928; of the Reale Accademia di San Luca, 1932; Hon. Member of the Virtuosi del Pantheon; member of the Societa Italiana di Storia Patria, 1924; Member of the Arcadian Academy (1924), of the German Archæological Institute (1925), and of the Assoc. Artistica fra cultori di Architettura. *Publications:* Roman Sculpture from Augustus to Constantine, 1907 (new ed. in Italian, 1923); Apotheosis and After Life, 1915; La Chiesa Nuova (in Italian, with Piero Misciattelli) 1923; Art in Ancient Rome for the Ars Una Series, 1929; English editor of G. Schuchardt's 'Schliemann's Excavations, of Furtwängler's 'Masterpieces of Greek Sculpture,' and of F. Wickhoff's 'Roman Art'; has brought out the Latin text, with notes and historical introduction, of Books 34–36 of Pliny's Natural History (joint translator, Miss K. Jex-Blake of Girton College, Cambridge); Chapters on Roman Art for the Cambridge Ancient History; article Greek and Roman portraiture for the Enciclopedia Italiana, 1935; awarded the Serena gold medal for Italian studies by British Academy, 1938; Gold medal of the City of Rome, 1938. *Address:* 35 Via Balbo, Rome. *Club:* Albemarle.

Died 16 Sept. 1943.

STRONG, Lt-Col Henry Stuart, CIE 1929; *b* 1873. Entered Indian Army, 1894; Acting Agent to Gov.-Gen. in States of W India; 1928; retired, 1928.

Died 12 Nov. 1949.

STRONG, John, CBE 1918; MA (Lond.); Hon. LLD St Andrews University, 1918; FRSE; FEIS; *b* Barrow-in-Furness, 15 Jan. 1868; *m* Ethel May, *y d* of late A. Knapton Dobson, Newton Lodge, Leeds; one *s* three *d*. *Educ:* Westminster Training Coll.; Yorkshire College (Leeds Univ.). Senior Master in the Central High School, Leeds, 1897–1900; Rector of Montrose Academy, 1900–14; of the Royal High School, Edinburgh, 1914–19; Professor of Education in the University of Leeds 1919–33, now Emeritus Professor; Pro-Vice-Chancellor in the University of Leeds, 1931–33; Member of St Andrew Provincial Committee, 1906–14; Pres. of Secondary Education Association of Scotland, 1916–17; First President of the Reconstituted Educational Institute of Scotland, 1917–18; Member of Departmental Committee on Remuneration of Teachers in Scotland, 1917; President of the Association of University Teachers, 1920–22; Chairman of Council of Yorkshire Union of Institutes and Yorkshire Village Library, 1921–25; Chairman of the Educational Handwork Association, 1922–35; Chm. of Advisory Committee on Craft Teaching, 1934–37; Educational Adviser to HM Prisons at Leeds and Wakefield, 1923–26. *Publications:* The Higher Training of Teachers in America, 1908; A History of Secondary Education in Scotland, 1910; Education (Scot.) Act 1918 (edited); articles on educational topics in various encyclopædias, journals and reviews. *Recreations:* golf and climbing. *Address:* The Colt, Ashburnham Road, Eastbourne.

Died 7 Oct. 1945.

STRONG, Dr Richard Pearson, CB 1919 (Hon.); Professor of Tropical Medicine, Harvard University Medical School, 1913–38; Professor Emeritus, 1938; Trustee Carnegie Institution; Consultant Secretary of War, and Director of Tropical Medicine, Army Medical School, Washington; Colonel, MCAHQ, 1942–December 1945 (Legion of Merit 1946); General Medical Director, League of Red Cross Societies, Geneva, 1919–20; *b* Fortress Monroe, Va, 18 March 1872; *s* of Col Richard P. Strong and Marion Burfort Smith; *m* 1936, Grace Nichols (*d* 1944), Boston, Mass. *Educ:* Yale University, PhB, 1893; ScD, 1914 (Hon.); Johns Hopkins University, MD 1897; Harvard University, SD, 1916 (Hon.). 1st Lt and Asst Surgeon. US Army, 1898–1902. Established and directed Army Pathological Laboratory, Manila, PI; Director, Govt Biological Laboratory, Manila, 1901–13; Prof. of Tropical Medicine, Univ. of Philippines, 1907–13; Chief of Medical Dept, General Hospital, 1910–13; Editor of Medical Section Philippine Journal of Science, Manila, 1906–13; Director of American Red Cross and International Sanitary Commissions, Serbia, 1915; Member, Medical Board Council of National Defence,

Washington, 1917; Member, Committee of National Research Council to Great Britain and France, 1917; Major, Lt-Col, Col, US Army, 1917–19; Col Medical Section, ORC, 1920 (Distinguished Service Medal, AEF, Officer of the Legion of Honour, France, Striped Tiger, China, Grand Officer Cross of St Sava, Serbia, etc.); Member of Inter-Allied Sanitary Commission, 1917–19; Member, Mass Public Health Council, 1921–43; Past Pres. of numerous tropical medicine societies, etc.; also Hon. Fellow of similar societies. Awarded Theobald Smith Medal Am. Acad. Tropical Medicine, 1939; Medal of Am. Foundation for Tropical Medicine, 1944. *Publications:* Report of Harvard Expedition to South America, 1915; Trench Fever Report, 1918; Harvard Expedition to the Amazon, 1926; The African Republic of Liberia and the Belgian Congo, 1930; Onchocerciasis, 1934; Diagnosis, Prevention, and Treatment of Tropical Diseases (joint), 1942 and 1944; also numerous scientific publications and monographs upon tropical diseases. *Address:* 107 Chestnut Street, Boston, Mass; Riddle Rocks, Newport, RI: Harvard Medical School, Boston Mass, USA. *Clubs:* Authors', Boodle's; Country (Brookline); Army and Navy, Metropolitan, Chevy Chase (Washington); Harvard, Somerset, Travellers', Tavern, Yale (Boston); Harvard, River (New York); Newport Casino, Clambake, Reading Room (Newport, RI).

Died 4 July 1948.

STRONG, Rt Rev. Thomas Banks, GBE 1918; DD; Hon. DD, Durham, 1913; Hon. DMus Oxford, 1917; Hon. DLitt Leeds, 1922; Clerk of the Closet to the King, 1925–37; *b* 24 Oct. 1861. *Educ:* Westminster, Christ Church, Oxford (Junior Student). Ordained Deacon, 1885; Priest, 1886; Bampton Lecturer, 1895; Dean of Christ Church, Oxford, 1901–20; Vice-Chancellor, 1913–17; Bishop of Ripon, 1920–25; Bishop of Oxford, 1925–37. *Publications:* A Manual of Theology, 1892; Christian Ethics (Bampton Lectures), 1896; Doctrine of the Real Presence, 1899; (Editor) Lectures on the Method of Science, 1906; Religion, Philosophy, and History, 1923. *Address:* 5 Collingham Gardens, SW5. *Club:* Athenæum.

Died 8 June 1944.

STROYAN, John; JP, DL; *b* 1856; *e s* of late John Stroyan of Kirkchrist; *m* 1889, Edith, *d* of late T. E. Dean, Aliwal North, SA. MP (U) West Perthshire, 1900–06; Hon. Pres. of the Scottish Chamber of Agriculture, 1904–05. Owns the estates of Lanrick and Kirkchrist. Heir: *s* Capt. John R. A. Stroyan [*m* Margaret (*d* 1927), *er d* of Sir John H. Ropner, 2nd Bt]. *Address:* Lanrick Castle, Doune, Perthshire; Kirkchrist, Kirkcowan, Wigtownshire. *Clubs:* Carlton, Caledonian; Stirling County, Stirling.

Died 5 Dec. 1941.

STRUTT, Lt-Col Edward Lisle, CBE 1919; DSO 1917; *b* 1874; *e s* of late Hon. Arthur Strutt, 2nd *s* of 1st Lord Belper; *m* 1905, Florence Nina, *d* of John Hollond, of Wonham, Bampton, Devon. *Educ:* Beaumont Coll., Windsor; Innsbruck University; Christ Church, Oxford. Served Royal Scots, South African War, 1900–02 (despatches, Queen's medal and four clasps, King's medal and two clasps), European War, 1914–19 (wounded, CBE, DSO, despatches four times, Croix de Guerre with four palms, Chevalier and Officer of Legion of Honour, Chevalier of Order of Leopold, Belgian Croix de Guerre and Palm, Officer of Star of Roumania, 1914 Star and clasp); High Commissioner, Danzig, 1920; second in command Mount Everest Expedition, 1922. *Recreations:* mountaineering, cricket, shooting, fishing. *Address:* 9 Ann Street, Edinburgh 4. *Clubs:* Turf, Alpine; New (Edinburgh).

Died 7 July 1948.

STRZYGOWSKI, Josef, Dr phil; University Professor; *b* 7 March 1862; *s* of Josef Strzygowski and Josefine Edle von Friedenfeldt; *m* 1st, 1895, Frieda Hofmann; 2nd, 1925, Herta Strzygowski; one *s* four *d*. *Educ:* Jena; Brunn, Vienna; Berlin; Munich. Privatdocent Wien; professor in Graz, 1892; Vienna, 1909; Professor in Abo, 1921–25; first time in England 1883, then nearly every year; lectures in London, Oxford and Edinburgh. *Publications:* Origin of Christian Church Art, 1923; Early Church Art in Northern Europa, with special reference to timber construction and decoration, 1928; Old Christian and Mediaeval Art in Marvin and Clutton-Brock's Art and Civilisation (The Unity series VIII). Asiens bildende Kunst, 1930; Der Norden in der bildenden Kunst Westeuropas, 1930; L'ancien Art chrétien de Syrie, 1935; Spuren indogermanischen Glaubens, 1936; Durer und der nordische Schicksalshain, 1937; Auf gang des Nordens, 1937; Geistige Umkehr, 1938; Nordischer Heilbringer und Bildende Kunst, 1939; Die deutsche Nordseele, 1940; (posthumous) Europas Machtkunst im Rahmen des Erdkreises, 1943. *Address:* Wien (Vienna) XIII Würzburggasse 29.

Died 2 Jan. 1941.

STUART, Viscount; David Andrew Noel Stuart; 2nd Lt RAC; *b* 7 Oct. 1921; *e s* of 7th Earl Castle Stewart.

Died 10 Nov. 1942.

STUART, Viscount; Robert John Ochiltree Stuart; *b* 1923; *s* of 7th Earl Castle Stewart.

Died 17 Sept. 1944.

STUART, Arthur Constable M.; *see* Maxwell Stuart.

STUART, Lt-Col Charles Kennedy-Craufurd-, CVO 1922; CBE 1920; DSO 1915; late 127th Queen Mary's Own Baluch Light Infantry; *e s* of late Robert Stuart of Rye, Sussex, and Margaret Elizabeth, *d* of Clifford Craufurd of Ardmillan. *Educ:* Merchant Taylors' School, London. Entered 1st Battalion Manchester Regiment from South Lancs Militia, 1900; transferred to 1st Punjab Cavalry, 1903; exchanged to 127th Baluchis, 1913; served in Burma Military Police, 1908–14; South African War, 1900–02 (2 medals, 5 clasps); Royal Naval Brigade in Gallipoli as Lt-Col Commanding Hood Batt. (severely wounded, despatches, DSO, 1914–15 Star; Fourth Class of Royal Order of George I of Greece); Sudan on Special Service, Feb. 1916–Oct. 1917 (received thanks of Sudan Government for successful action against Chief Ashwol in Bahr-el-Ghazel Province); in United States as Private Secretary to the Earl of Reading, High Commissioner and Ambassador, Jan. 1918–May 1919; Private Secretary to Viscount Grey of Falloden, 1919–20; Military Secretary to Viceroy of India, April 1921–Oct. 1923; retired from Indian Army, 1927; Member of the Royal Company of Archers. *Publications:* two songs: At Gloaming Tide, Make-Believe Land. *Recreations:* polo, golf, music, photography, exhibited at London Salon of Photography; Fellow of the Zoological Society; Fellow Royal Horticultural Society. *Clubs:* Carlton; New, Edinburgh; Bengal, Calcutta.

Died 21 Aug. 1942.

STUART, Brig.-Gen. Donald MacKenzie, CBE 1919; DL; JP Lanarkshire; retired; Member Royal Company of Archers (King's Bodyguard for Scotland); *b* 1864; *s* of Gen. J. Ramsay Stuart, CB; *m* 1907, Margaret Isabella, *d* of Major T. D. Milburne, 7 Evelyn Gardens, SW; one *s*. *Educ:* Dulwich Coll.; RMC, Sandhurst. 2nd Lt 1883; served in Royal Scots Fusiliers; commanded 2/RSF, 1910–14; commanded 7/RSF, 1914–15; served NW Frontier, India, 1897 (medal and two clasps); European War, 1914–18 (despatches, CBE). *Recreations:* shooting, tennis, etc. *Address:* Carwood, Biggar, Lanarkshire. *T:* Biggar 45. *Clubs:* Army and Navy; New, Edinburgh.

Died 9 Sept. 1946.

STUART, John Matthew Blackwood, CIE, MInstCE; Consulting Engineer, Rendel, Palmer & Tritton, 55 Broadway, SW1; *b* 14 March 1882; *s* of Andrew Stuart and Mary Blackwood; *m* 1923, Joan Daria Elliot Taylor; one *s* two *d*. *Educ:* Portora Royal School; Trinity College, Dublin. Served South African War, Private in North Irish Imperial Yeomanry, 1900–01; appointed to Indian Service of Engineers and posted to Burma Irrigation Department as Assistant Engineer, 1905; Executive Engineer, 1914; served European War with Queen Victoria's Own Sappers and Miners, 1914–19; Captain, 1916; Major, 1919; Assistant to Chief Engineer and Under Secretary to Govt of Burma, 1920; Superintending Engineer, Irrigation Branh, 1923; Chief Engineer PWD Irrigation Branch, 1930; Retired from PWD 1935. *Publications:* Old Burmese Irrigation Works; The Sittang River and its Vagaries. *Recreations:* golf and shooting. *Address:* Brooklands, Paddockhall Road, Haywards Heath. *T:* Haywards Heath 562. *Club:* East India and Sports.

Died 31 Oct. 1942.

STUART, Lt.-Gen. Kenneth, CB 1943; DSO 1919; MC 1917; *b* 9 Sept. 1891; *s* of Rev. H. C. Stuart, MA, and Annie M. Colston; *m* 1916, Marguerite Dorothy Bauld; one *s* one *d*. *Educ:* Bishops College School, Lennoxville, PQ; RMC of Canada. Lieut Royal Canadian Engineers, 1911; attended School of Military Engineering, 1911–13; served European War, RCE, France and Belgium, 1916–19 (wounded); psc 1927; Asst Director of Military Intelligence, 1929–33; GSO1, RMC of Canada, 1934–37; Prof. of Tactics, RMC, 1937–38; Director of Military Operations and Intelligence, National Defence HQ, 1938–39; Comdt, RMC of Canada, 1939–40; Deputy Chief of Gen. Staff (Canada), 1940–41; Vice-Chief of Gen. Staff, March–Dec. 1941; Chief of General Staff, 1941–43. Capt. 1915; Maj. 1917; Lt-Col 1932; Brig. 1939; Maj.-Gen. 1941; Lt-Gen. 1941; Chief of Staff at Canadian Military HQ, London, 1944. *Clubs:* Rideau, Country, Ottawa.

Died 3 Nov. 1945.

STUART, Sir Louis, Kt 1926; CIE 1919; *b* 12 March 1870; *s* of Dr Kenneth Bruce Stuart, MD, and Sara Matilda, *d* of William Wotherspoon, SSC, Edinburgh; *m* 1896, Mary Curzon Molison (*d* 1948), *d* of Dr Robert Smith, MD, of Sedgefield, Durham County; one *s* one *d*. *Educ:* Charterhouse; Balliol College, Oxford. Entered Indian Civil Service, 1891; Judicial Secretary to Government, 1910–12; First Additional Judicial Commissioner, Oudh, 1914; Judicial Commissioner, Oudh, 1921; Puisne Judge, High Court, Allahabad, 1922–25; Chief Judge of Oudh Chief Court, 1925–30; retired, 1930; Hon. Secretary Indian Empire Society; Editor, Indian Empire Review, 1932. *Address:* 57 Bassett Road, W10. *T:* Ladbroke 1865.

Died 26 Dec. 1949.

STUART, Maj.-Gen. Sir Robert Charles Ochiltree, KCSI 1917; CSI 1915; *b* 22 Aug. 1861; *s* of Lt-Col Robert A. W. C. Stuart, 17th Madras Infantry, and Louisa Frances, *d* of E. S. Burton; *m* 1885, Edith Jane (*d* 1936), *d* of late Herbert M. Birdwood, CIS; no *c*. *Educ:* Royal Military Academy, Woolwich. Entered Royal Artillery, 1880; Indian Ordnance Department, 1889; Ordnance Consulting Officer for India, 1906–11; Director-General of Ordnance, India, 1911–17; Member Indian Munitions Board, 1917–19; served Burma Campaign, 1885–87. *Address:* 18 Tivoli Road, Cheltenham.

Died 14 Oct. 1948.

STUART-WORTLEY, Lt.-Gen. Hon. Sir (Alan) Richard Montagu-, KCB 1924; KCMG 1918; CB 1915; DSO 1900; *b* 20 Jan. 1868; *brother* of 2nd Earl of Wharncliffe; *m* 1900, Hon. Maud Julia Mary Winn (*d* 1938), *d* of 1st Baron St Oswald; one *s* one *d*. *Educ:* Wellington. Joined King's Royal Rifles, 1887; Capt., 1895; Major, 1904; Lieut-Col, 1910; Col, 1914; Maj.-

Gen. 1917; Lt-Gen. 1924; served Chitral Relief Force, 1895 (medal with clasp); South Africa, 1899–1900 (severely wounded, despatches, Queen's medal 3 clasps, DSO); European War, 1914–17; Assistant-Director of Movements, War Office, 1914–Jan. 1915; Director, Jan. 1915–Jan. 1917 (CB, specially promoted Major-Gen.); commanded 68th Infantry Brigade and 19th and 32nd Divisions; DQMG Mesopotamia, 1917–19 (despatches, KCMG); General Staff Officer at the War Office, 1904–08; passed Staff College; in charge of Administration, Southern Command, 1919–23; QMG in India, 1924–27; retired pay, 1927; Hon. Col of Engineer and Railway Staff Corps, RE (TA), 1924–48; and Col Commandant, 1st Batt. K. R. Rifle Corps, 1925–38; Commander of the Legion of Honour and the Ordre de la Couronne of Belgium and the Crown of Italy. *Recreations:* shooting, golf. *Address:* Home Close, Highclere, Newbury, Berks. *T:* Highclere 9. *Club:* Army and Navy.

Died 23 Sept. 1949.

STUART-WORTLEY, Hon. Clare Euphemia; art historian; *b* London, 1889; *d* of 1st Baron Stuart of Wortley (*d* 1926), and 2nd wife, Alice (*d* 1936), *d* of Sir John Everett Millais, PRA; *m* 1909, *d* of Sir John Everett Millais, PRA. War work at QMNG Headquarters, 1914–16, and as Red Cross VAD, 1916–18. *Publications:* Art as we Endure It, 1926; articles in various periodicals, Old Master Drawings, 1931–1937, Print Collector's Quarterly; etc. *Address:* Turret House, 35 Park Street, Windsor, Berks.

Died 15 Jan. 1945.

STUBBS, Rev. Arthur James; Ordained to Parish of All Saints, Chatham, 1931; Holy Trinity, Selhurst, 1935; *b* 1861; *m*; two *s* four *d*. Received a training in architecture in the firm of Habershon and Pite; entered the Post Office, 1880; Superintending Engineer of Metropolitan (North) District of Postal Telegraphs, 1902; an Assistant Engineer-in-Chief, 1907–21; MInstCE, MIEE. *Publications:* The Manual of Telephony (with late Sir W. H. Preece); technical papers. *Address:* 173 Coombe Road, Croydon. *T:* Croydon 1843.

Died 8 Dec. 1945.

STUBBS, Sir (Reginald) Edward, GCMG 1928; KCMG 1919; CMG 1914; *b* 13 Oct. 1876; *y* *s* of late Rt Rev. William Stubbs, DD, Bishop of Oxford; *m* 1909, Marjory, CBE 1919, *d* of F. Womack, MB; two *s* one *d*. *Educ:* Radley, Corpus Christi College, Oxford (exhibitioner). 1st Class Classical Moderations, 1897; 1st Lit.Hum. 1899; BA 1899; MA 1920; Hon. Fellow Corpus Christi College, 1926; Hon. LLD Hong-Kong, 1926. Second-Class Clerk, Colonial Office, 1900; Acting First-Class Clerk, 1907; 1st Class Clerk, 1910; sent on special mission to Malay Peninsula and Hong-Kong, 1910–11; Member of West African Lands Committee, 1912; Colonial Secretary of Ceylon, 1913–19; Administered Government, Ceylon, on several occasions; Governor of Hong-Kong, 1919–25; Captain-General and Governor-in-Chief of Jamaica, 1926–32; Governor and C-in-C of Cyprus, 1932–33; of Ceylon, 1933–37; retired, 1937; Vice-Chairman, Royal Commission on the West Indies, 1938; Chairman Northern Division Appellate Tribunal for Conscientious Objectors, 1941–47; JP for Kent; FZS. *Address:* Commonwood, Bearsted, Maidstone. *Club:* Athenæum.

Died 7 Dec. 1947.

STUCKEY, Reginald Robert, CMG 1932; AIA; Chairman of Board of State Bank of SA; President SA Superannuation Fund Board; *b* Adelaide, SA, 25 Feb. 1881; 3rd *s* of Joseph James Stuckey, MA, AIA, solicitor; *m* 1911, Jessie Bridgman (*d* 1942), Adelaide; one *s* two *d*; 1946, Mary Hazel Kenney, Toorak Gardens. *Educ:* St Peter's Coll. Adelaide. Passed Senior Public Examination of Adelaide University in 1896 with credit; awarded scholarship to attend University but relinquished this to enter Commerce; spent 17 years with Australian Mutual

Provident Society; passed examinations for Associate of Institute of Actuaries (London) and also internal examinations of AMP Society; Public Actuary of South Australia, 1914–23; Under-Treasurer of South Australia and Chairman Public Debt Commission of SA, 1923–46; services specially requisitioned by Commonwealth Government in connection with Australian Conversion Loan converting whole of internal debt of Australia; Chairman of Committee appointed to prepare case for South Australia on disabilities sustained under Federation; Member of Advisory Committee on Finance and other Committees. *Publications:* papers to Actuarial Society of Australasia and to Economic Society of Australia and New Zealand. *Address:* 178 Fullarton Road, Highgate, South Australia.

Died 5 July 1948.

STUDD, Brig.-Gen. Herbert William, CB 1918; CMG 1917; DSO 1900; *b* 20 Dec. 1870; *s* of late Edward Studd, of Tidworth House and 2 Hyde Park Gardens, W; *m* 1st, 1894, Mary (*d* 1930), *d* of late Major Horace de Vere of Curragh Chase, Co. Limerick, and of late Mrs Maxwell of Issercleran, County Galway; *widow* of Major W. U. Cole, 3rd Dragoon Guards; two *d*; 2nd, 1930, Alice Maude, *y d* of late David Tullis, Glencairn, Rutherglen. *Educ:* Eton Trinity College, Cambridge. Joined Coldstream Guards, 1891; Captain, 1900; Major, 1908; Lt-Col 1916; Bt Col 1917; Passed Staff Coll., 1905; served South Africa, 1899–1902 (despatches, Queen's medal 6 clasps, King's medal 2 clasps, DSO); European War, 1914–18 (despatches, dangerously wounded, CMG, Bt Col, CB); GSO2 1st Corps; commanded 1st Bn Coldstream Guards; commanded 180th Brigade, 1915–16; General Staff Officer, 1905–09; General Staff War Office, 1912–14; Brig.-Gen. General Staff, XI Corps, 1916–17; Chief of Staff British Section Supreme War Council, 1917–19; Commanded Coldstream Guards, 1919; retired pay, 1923; Commander Légion d'Honneur (France); Commander Order of Crown of Italy; Commander Order of Aviz (Portugal); Officer Order of Leopold (Belgium); Italian Croix de Guerre; Distinguished Service Medal (USA). *Clubs:* Guards', Travellers'.

Died 8 Aug. 1947.

STUDD, Sir (John Edward) Kynaston, 1st Bt *cr* 1929; Kt 1923; OBE; MA, LLD (Cantab); President and Chairman (Hon.) of The Polytechnic, 307–311 Regent Street, W, since 1903; *b* 26 July 1858; *s* of late Edward Studd of Tidworth House, Wilts, and 2 Hyde Park Gardens, W; *m* 1st, Hilda (*d* 1921), *d* of Sir Thomas Beauchamp, 4th Bart, and Caroline, *d* of 2nd Lord Radstock; three *s* one *d*; 2nd, 1924, Princess Alexandra Lieven, *d* of late Prince Paul Lieven, Grand Master of Ceremonies at the Russian Imperial Court. *Educ:* Eton; Trinity College, Cambridge. Eton XI, 1876–77; Cambridge XI, 1881–84; Captain, 1884; Hon. Secretary The Polytechnic, 1885; Member of the General Purposes Committee of Territorial Force Association of the County of London; Deputy Commandant of the Cadet Force in the County of London; Hon. Colonel Polytechnic Schools Cadet Corps; Major and commanded 21st Batt. (St Marylebone) County of London Volunteer Regiment; Senior Grand Deacon of English Freemasons, 1910; Junior Grand Warden, 1929; President of Board of Benevolence, 1929; Provincial Grand Master for Cambridgeshire, 1934; Senior Sheriff of London, 1922–23; Alderman of the City of London for the Ward of Farringdon Without, 1923–42, Bridge Without since 1942; Lord Mayor of London, 1928–29; President of Old Etonian Association, 1929–30; President of MCC 1930, Trustee, 1939. *Heir: s* Eric. *Address:* 67 Harley Street, W1. *TA:* Polytechnic, London. *T:* Langham 1404. *Club:* Royal Automobile.

Died 14 Jan. 1944.

STURGE, Arthur Lloyd; *b* Moseley, 1868; *s* of late Wilson Sturge; *m* 1896, Jessie Katharine, *d* of late Theodore Howard; two *s* three *d*. *Educ:* Trinity College School. Underwriter at Lloyd's since 1894; Chairman of Lloyd's, 1922 and 1923. *Address:* Shepherd's Green, Chislehurst; Ashmore, near Salisbury. *T:* Chislehurst, 41.

Died 4 Dec. 1942.

STURGIS, Sir Mark Beresford Russell G.; *see* Grant-Sturgis.

STURROCK, John Leng; *b* Newport, Fife, 1878; *m* 1925, Winifred Mary, *o d* of William Anning; one *s* one *d*. *Educ:* High School and University College, Dundee. Formerly Managing Director of John Leng & Co. Ltd, newspaper publishers; MP (L) Montrose Burghs, Dec. 1918–Oct. 1924; Secretary, Coalition Liberals in House of Commons, 1920–22; Constitutional candidate Tottenham N, 1924. *Address:* 2 Oban Road, Talbot Avenue, Bournemouth. *Clubs:* Reform, Royal Automobile; Eastern, Dundee.

Died 22 July 1943.

STURROCK, William Duncan, DSO 1918; MA; MD; Hon. Assistant Obstetric Physician to Radcliffe Infirmary, Oxford; *b* 16 May 1880; *s* of John Sturrock and Mary Dobbie; *m* 1909, Mary Macpherson; one *s*. *Educ:* Charterhouse; Magdalen College, Oxford; King's College Hospital, 1st Class Final Honour Schools Oxford (Physiology), 1903. Practised medicine at Oxford since 1908; Medical Officer to Radley College since 1927; served European War 1914–19 in Flanders, Macedonia and, after Armistice, in Transcaucasia (despatches twice, DSO); was Lt-Col in command of 82nd Field Ambulance. *Publications:* First Principles of Hygiene, 1913; Articles in BM Journal. *Recreations:* golf, fishing, bridge. *Address:* 32 Holywell, Oxford. *T:* 2629. *Clubs:* Savile; Royal North Devon Golf.

Died 29 June 1942.

STUTTAFORD, Hon. Richard; *b* 13 June 1870; English; *m* 1903, Ada Steel; two *s* two *d*. Chairman of Directors, Stuttaford and Co. Ltd; Director Cape Times Ltd; late Minister without Portfolio, Union of South Africa, 1933; Minister of the Interior and Public Health, 1936; Minister of Commerce and Industries, 1939–43. *Address:* Stellenrust, Stellenbosch, Union of South Africa.

Died 19 Oct. 1945.

STYLE, Sir William Frederick, 11th Bt *cr* 1627; *b* 11 July 1887; *s* of 10th Bt and Caroline (*d* 1933), *er d* of late Frederick Schultz; *S* father, 1930; *m* 1st, 1911, Florence (*d* 1918), *d* of J. Timm; one *s* one *d*; 2nd, 1923, Genevieve, *d* of Peter L'Estrange; one *d*. Owns about 20,000 acres. *Heir: s* William Montague, *b* 1916. *Address:* 5806 Washington Boulevard, Milwaukee, Wis, USA.

Died 27 June 1943.

SUART, Evelyn (Lady Harcourt); pianist, retired except for occasional appearances; *b* India; *d* of late Brig.-Gen. Suart, CMG; early childhood spent between India and England and Gibraltar; *m* 1st, 1910, Gerard Gould (*d* 1916); one *s* two *d*; 2nd, 1920, Adm. Sir Cecil Harcourt, KCB. *Educ:* Brussels (Storck); Paris (Pugno); Vienna (Leschetizky). Début made in Vienna; English début, with Sir Henry J. Wood at Queen's Hall; has since played at leading concerts in British Isles; made six tours; played with Warsaw Philharmonic, Berlin Philharmonic, Vienna Symphony Concerts, 1910, and in Brussels; Balfour Gardiner Orchestral Concerts, 1913, etc.; also before late King and Queen Alexandra; several times with Dr Hans Richter and Eugène Ysaye, made record at Saturday and Monday Pops. Pioneer of modern music; Pres. of the Society of Women Musicians, 1930–32. *Recreations:* making music and reading. *Address:* Mulberry House, Chelsea, SW3.

Died 24 Oct. 1950.

SUCKLING, Rev. Charles William B.; see Baron-Suckling.

SUDELEY, 6th Baron cr 1838; **Richard Algernon Frederick Hanbury-Tracy;** Major, Royal Horse Guards; b 20 April 1911; o s of late Major Hon. A. H. C. Hanbury-Tracy, Royal Horse Guards; S uncle 1932; m 1940, Elizabeth Mary, d of Rear-Adm. Sir Arthur Bromley, KCMG, CVO. Educ: Stowe. Heir: cousin Merlyn Charles Sainthill Hanbury-Tracy [b 1939; s of late Capt. Michael David Charles Hanbury-Tracy, Scots Guards, and Colline Ammabel, d of late Lieutenant-Colonel C. G. H. St Hill and widow of Lieutenant-Colonel Frank King, DSO, OBE].

Died 26 Aug. 1941.

SUFFIELD, 7th Baron cr 1786; **Victor Alexander Charles Harbord;** Bt 1745; Capt. late Royal Norfolk Regt; late Scots Guards; retired, 1924; Page of Honour to King George, 1910–15; b 12 Sept. 1897; e s of 6th Baron and Evelyn Wilson-Patten, d of Marchioness of Headfort; S father, 1924; m 1925, Hon. Olwen Philipps (from whom he obtained a divorce, 1937), 2nd d of 1st Baron Kylsant. Heir: b Hon. John Harbord, b 1 July 1907. Address: Gunton Park, Norwich. Club: Guards'.

Died 10 June 1943.

SUFFIELD, 8th Baron cr 1786; **John Harbord;** Bt cr 1745; b 1 July 1907; 2nd s of 6th Baron and Evelyn Wilson-Patten, d of Marchioness of Headfort; S brother, 1943; unmarried. Educ: Gresham's School, Holt. Heir: kinsman Geoffrey Walter Harbord, b 12 Nov. 1861. Address: Gunton Park, Norwich. Clubs: Pratt's, Royal Automobile.

Died 23 June 1945.

SUFFIELD, 9th Baron cr 1786; **Geoffrey Walter Harbord;** Bt cr 1745; b 12 Nov. 1861; s of late Hon. William Harbord, 4th s of 3rd Baron; S kinsman, 1945; m 1902, Eliza Jane (d 1933) widow of A. R. Beaumont. Heir: cousin Admiral Richard Morden Harbord-Hamond.

Died 23 May 1946.

SUFFOLK, 20th Earl of, cr 1603, **AND BERKSHIRE,** 13th Earl of, cr 1626; **Charles Henry George Howard,** GC 1941; FRSE 1936; BSc, First Class Honours in Pharmacology, 1937; Viscount Andover and Baron Howard, 1622; Scientist; b 2 March 1906; e s of 19th Earl and Margaret Hyde, y d of late Levi Z. Leiter; S father, 1917; m 1934, Mimi, yr d of late A. G. Forde Pigott; three s. Sailed round world before mast of sailing ship; sometime 2nd Lt of Scots Guards; ranched in Australia. Owns 10,000 acres; celebrated picture-gallery and well-known collection of Old Masters. Heir: s Viscount Andover. Address: Charlton Park, Malmesbury. Club: Carlton.

Died 12 May 1941.

SUGDEN, Samuel, FRS 1934, DSc Lond., ARCSc Lond.; University Professor of Chemistry, University College, London, since 1937; b Leeds, 1892; e s of late Samuel Sugden; m 1926, Eleanor, d of late Thomas Dunlop, Glasgow; no c. Educ: Batley Grammar School; Royal College of Science, London. BEF France, 1915–16; Research Chemist, Royal Arsenal, Woolwich, 1916–19; Lecturer in Chemistry, Birkbeck College, 1919–28; Reader in Physical Chemistry, Birkbeck College, 1928–32; Professor of Physical Chemistry, Birkbeck College, 1932–37. Publications: The Structure of Atoms, 1923; A Class Book of Physical Chemistry (with late Professor TM Lowry, FRS), 1929; The Parachor and Valency, 1929; Scientific papers mostly in the Journal of the Chemical Society. Address: 34 West Hill Avenue, Epsom, Surrey. Club: Athenæum.

Died 20 Oct. 1950.

SUGGIA, Guilhermina; 'cellist; b Oporto, 27 June 1888; of Italian descent; m 1927, Dr Jose Carteado Mena (d 1949). Educ: Studied under her father and under Klengel at Leipzig. Debut at Gewandhaus concerts, Leipzig, 1905; has toured in the principal European countries; Order of San Tiago da Espada of Portugal, 1923. Owner of two precious 'cellos, Stradivarius and Montagnana. Recreations: house decorating; great friend of dogs. Address: Rue da Algeria, 665, Oporto, Portugal. T: Porto 552.

Died 31 July 1950.

SUHRAWARDY, Lt-Col Sir Hassan, Kt 1932; OBE 1927; JP; LLD (Hon. Lond.), DSc, MD, FRCS, DPH; b Dacca, 1884; s of Maulana Obaidullah Elobaidy Suhrawardy, Midnapore, Bengal, and Makbulanessa Begum, d of Maulvi Muhammad Mukkaram; m Shahar Banu Begum, d of Nawab Syed Muhammad, Dacca; one d. Educ: Dacca Madrasah; Dacca College; Calcutta Medical College; Post-grad. Dublin, Edinburgh and London. Adviser to Secretary of State for India, London, 1939–44; Member Public Service Commission, Bengal, 1937–39; Vice-Chancellor, Calcutta University, 1930–34; Chief Medical and Health Officer (Indian State Railways), 1928–37; Hon. Surgeon to Viceroy, 1935–39; Vice-Pres. Medical Council of India, 1933–36; Member Bengal Legislative Council, 1921–25; Deputy President, 1923–25; Member Bengal Industrial Unrest Committee, 1921; Dean, Faculty of Medicine, 1930–33; Chairman Calcutta Branch BMA, 1933; Professor Public Health and Hygiene, Calcutta University (Hon.), since 1931, and of Islamic History and Culture, 1945; Leader Indian Delegation, British Empire University Congress, 1931; Member Governing Body London School of Oriental Studies; Member Council Asiatic Society of Great Britain; President and Founder The Servants of Humanity Society; represented the ITF Medical Branch with Indian Coronation Contingent in London, 1937; Kaisar-i-Hind Medal (Gold) 1st Class; CStJ; Founder EI Railway Ambulance and Nursing Divisions. Has travelled extensively in Europe, Asia, Africa, the USA and Canada. Has been on pilgrimage to Mecca, Medina, Jerusalem, Najaf, Karbla, Meshad and other places of sanctity in the Islamic countries. Has been on a welfare mission to the Indian troops in the Middle Eastern countries during the War 1939–45. Publications: Truth about Muhammad and Muhammadanism; Mother and Infant Welfare for India; Manual of Post-Operative Treatment; Manual of First Aid for India, and many others. Address: Kashana, 3 Suhrawardy Avenue, Calcutta. Clubs: Athenæum; Calcutta, Calcutta.

Died 18 Sept. 1946.

SUHRAWARDY, Sir Zahhadur Rahim Zahid, Kt 1927; MA, BL; Barrister-at-law; President Railway Rates Advisory Committee since 1933; b Midnapur, Bengal, 27 Nov. 1870; s of Maulvi Mubarak Ali Suhrawardy, Subordinate Judge; m Khujasta Akhtar Banu, d of Hazrat Maulana Obeidulla-el-Obeidi Suhrawardy; two s. Educ: Dacca College; Ripon Law College, Calcutta; Lincoln's Inn, London. First Class First BA (Hon.); First Class First MA (Persian); First Class BL. Certificate of Honour, Bar Council; Advocate High Court Calcutta, 1912; Judge, Presidency Small Cause Court, 1916; Judge, Calcutta High Court, 1921; retired, 1931; Member Bengal Legislative Council, 1916 and 1921. Address: 21 Theatre Road, Calcutta, India. T: Regent 696. Club: Calcutta.

Died 2 Jan. 1949.

SULAIMAN, Sir Shah Muhammad, Kt 1929; MA, LLD, DSc; **Hon. Mr Justice Sulaiman;** Puisne Judge, Federal Court of India, since 1937; b 3 Feb. 1886; s of Moulvi Muhammad Usman, Vakil; m; three s one d. Educ: Muir Central College, Allahabad; Christ's College, Cambridge; Trinity College, Dublin. Came out first in the first division at the BA examination of the Allahabad University and won the Government of India Scholarship, 1906; Mathematical Tripos, Part II,

Cambridge, 1909; Law Tripos, 1910. Called to Bar, Middle Temple, 1910; Doctor of Laws, Dublin, 1911, Aligarh, 1935; DSc, Allahabad, 1937; joined the Allahabad High Court, 1912; Acting Judge of the Allahabad High Court at the age of 34, 1920; Officiating Judge, 1921 and 1922; Puisne Judge, 1923–32; Acting Chief Justice, 1928, 1929, and 1931; Permanent Chief Justice, 1932–37; Vice-Chancellor, Muslim University, Aligarh, 1929, 1930 and 1938; President National Academy of Sciences, India; President, Anglo-Arabic College, Delhi. *Address:* Federal Court, Delhi, India.

Died 13 March 1941.

SULLIVAN, Rev. Canon Arnold Moon, MA, Hon. CF; *b* 30 Aug. 1878; *e s* of Rev. Michael Sullivan, late Vicar of Brackenfield, Derbyshire; *m e d* of late Sir Walter Kent, CBE; three *s* one *d. Educ:* St Peter's School, York; Christ's College, Cambridge. Master St Andrew's School, Eastbourne, 1900–06; Curate at St John's, Meads, Eastbourne, 1903–06; Senior Curate, Clerk in orders, Precentor of Leeds Parish Church, 1906–14; Vicar of Chapel Allerton, Leeds, 1914–27; Rector of Richmond, and Vicar of Holy Trinity, Richmond, Yorkshire, 1927–40; Rural Dean of Richmond West, 1930–40; Hon. Canon of Ripon, 1930, Canon Emeritus, 1940. *Publications:* Choristers' Manual; Story of Richmond Parish Church. *Address:* 3 St Peter's Court, Chesterfield Road, Eastbourne. *T:* Eastbourne 1699.

Died 27 June 1943.

SULLIVAN, Basil Martin, CIE 1937; OBE 1924; FRIBA; AMTPI; Partner in firm of L. Sylvester Sullivan and Basil M. Sullivan; Chairman, RIBA, Board of Architectural Education; Member, Architectural Education Committee, University of London; Member of Council, Chairman of Board of Architectural Education and Member of Discipline Committee of Architects Registration Council of the UK; *b* 30 Aug. 1882; 7th *s* of late Michael Sullivan, ARCA; unmarried. Chief Assistant to Lanchester and Rickards and other architects in London, and in private practice, 1904–13; appointed to serve in India, 1914; retired as Superintending Architect and Town Planner to Punjab Govt, 1938. *Official works include:* Civic Centre and Punjab Legislative Council Chamber, Lahore; Chemical Laboratory and other buildings for Punjab Univ.; New Courts for Punjab High Court; additions to Government House, Lahore. *Private works include:* British Legation at Kabul; Legislative Council Chamber, Peshawar. *Recreations:* tennis, golf, travel, sketching. *Address:* 1 South Square, Gray's Inn, WC1. *T:* Chancery 6919. *Club:* Athenæum.

Died 30 March 1946.

SULLIVAN, Hon. Daniel Giles; JP; MP for Avon, Christchurch, since 1919; Minister of Industries and Commerce, Scientific and Industrial Research of New Zealand, since 1935; *b* Christchurch, NZ, 1882; *s* of Flurence Sullivan and Mary Dow; *m* 1905, Daisy Ethel Webster; one *s* one *d. Educ:* at Marist Brothers and St Mary's Schools, Christchurch. Apprentice to W. Bates & Son, Furniture Manufacturers, Christchurch, 1895; journalist, Christchurch Times, 1912, and Christchurch Sun, 1915–20. Member Christchurch City Council for many years; Mayor of Christchurch, 1931–35. Minister of Railways, 1935–41; Minister of Supply and Munitions, 1939; Acting Prime Minister parts of 1942 and 1944. Was Secretary, President Organiser and National President of Furniture Trades Union; former President Canterbury Trades and Labour Council, Federation of Labour, and Political Labour League of New Zealand; President New Zealand Centennial Exhibition Co. 1939–40. Led NZ Delegation to International Civil Aviation Conference at Chicago, USA, 1944; visited Canada, United Kingdom, Egypt and NZ Forces in Italy, 1944. *Publications:* Post War

Reconstruction, 1916; Dan Sullivan's Magazine, 1919. *Address:* 111 Sullivan Avenue, Woolston, Christchurch, NZ; Parliament Buildings, Wellington, NZ.

Died 8 April 1947.

SULLIVAN, Brig.-Gen. Edward Langford, CB 1918, CMG 1915; *b* 8 Jan. 1865; *s* of late T. K. Sullivan, Bandon; *m* 1901, Winifred, *d* of late Adam Burns Halifax, Nova Scotia; one *s* (and *s* killed in action, 1940) one *d.* Entered Army (Leicestershire Regiment), 1885; Captain, Indian Army, 1896; Major, 1903; Lieut-Col 1910; Colonel, 1915; retired, 1920; served Burma, 1888–89 (medal with clasp); Dongola, 1896 (Egyptian medal; medal); Tirah, 1897–98 (severely wounded; medal, 2 clasps); Waziristan, 1901–02 (despatches, clasp); European War, 1914–18 (despatches thrice, CB, CMG). *Address:* 55 Rouge Bouillon, St Helier, Jersey, CI; Glanmire House, Co. Cork. *Club:* Naval and Military.

Died 7 July 1949.

SULLIVAN, Timothy, hon. LLD (TCD); *b* 1874; *s* of late Timothy Daniel Sullivan, MP, Dublin; *m* 1913, Maey, 2nd *d* of late T. M. Healy. *Educ:* Belvedere College, Dublin. Barrister, King's Inns, 1895; KC 1918; Bencher of King's Inns, 1921; President of the High Court of Justice, Irish Free State, 1924–36; President of Supreme Court and Chief Justice of Irish Free State, 1936–37, and of Eire, 1937–46. *Address:* Shamrock Hill, Stillorgan Road, Dublin.

Died 29 March 1949.

SUMMERHAYES, Lt-Col John Orlando, DSO 1917; MRCS, LRCP; Medical Officer, Newhaven Infirmary; Police Surgeon; SMO, Newhaven Area; late RAMC, TF; Reserve of Officers; *b* 1869; *s* of William Summerhayes, MD; *m* 1895, Lucy Alexa Heathcote, *d* of late Robert George Currie. *Educ:* Yarmouth Grammar School. Served as Lt-Col 1/1 South Midland Field Ambulance, European War, 1914–18 (despatches, DSO); Chairman Brighton Division BMA, 1933–34; Chairman East Sussex Insurance Committee in 1934; Medical Inspector, Factories, Newhaven. *Address:* Saxonholme, Newhaven, Sussex. *T:* Newhaven 27.

Died 28 Oct. 1942.

SUMMERS, Rev. Alphonsus Joseph-Mary Augustus Montague, MA, FRSL; *b* 10 April 1880; *y s* of late Augustus William Summers, JP. *Educ:* Clifton College; Trinity College, Oxford. Has lived largely abroad, particularly in Italy; founded The Phœnix, a Society for the Production of Old Plays, 1919; superintended the production of eighteen plays, as well as of a complete Congreve cycle, and many other revivals in London. *Publications:* St Catherine of Siena, 1903; Lourdes, 1904; Poems, 1907; A Great Mistress of Romance, 1917; Jane Austen, An Appreciation, 1919; St Antonio-Maria Zaccaria, 1921; The History of Witchcraft, 1926; The Geography of Witchcraft, 1927; Horrid Mysteries, 1927; The Necromancer of the Black Forest, 1927; Zofloya, 1927; Roscius Anglicanus, 1928; Discovery of Witchcraft, 1928; Essays in Petto, 1928; The Vampire, His Kith and Kin, 1928; The Vampire in Europe, 1929; Architecture and the Gothic Novel, 1931; Joseph Sheridan Le Fanu and his Houses, 1932; J. K. Huysmans and Chartres, 1932; The Werewolf, 1933; The Restoration Theatre, 1 vol., 1934; Bibliography of the Restoration Drama, 1935; The Playhouse of Pepys, 1935; The Grimoire and other Ghostly Tales, 1936; A Popular History of Witchcraft, 1937; Six Ghost Stories, 1937; The Gothic Quest, a study of romantic fiction, 1938; The Gothic Achievement, 1939; William Henry, a play, 1939; Edward II, a play, 1940; A Bibliography of the Gothic Novel, 1940; Witchcraft and Black Magic, 1946; The Physical Phenomena of Mysticism, 1947; The Sins of the Fathers, Supernatural Tales, 1947; edited Nonesuch Congreve, 1923, Wycherley, 1924, Dryden, 1931–1932 and many editions of Restoration and other plays, and edited and translated works on witchcraft, etc.; contributor to The Times Literary Supplement, etc.

Recreations: travel; staying in unknown monasteries and villages in Italy; pilgrimages to famous shrines; the investigation of occult phenomena; ghost stories; talking to intelligent dogs, that is, all dogs; research in hagiology, liturgies, mysticism, the older English drama; late Latin literature. *Address:* c/o 17 The Green, Richmond, Surrey.

Died 10 Aug. 1948.

SUMMERS, Thomas, CIE 1914; DSc, MICE; *m* 1911, Anne Honora, *d* of late Major F. C. Ward; three *s. Educ:* Melville College; Edinburgh Univ.; RIE College. Joined Bombay Public Works Dept, 1877; Executive Engineer, 1886; Superintending Engineer and Secretary, Indus River Commission, 1902; Chief Engineer, 1910; retired, 1911. *Publications:* Development of Cotton in India, 1914; The Sukkur Barrage and Empire Cotton, 1921. *Recreations:* walking, gardening. *Address:* 17 Blacket Place, Edinburgh. *T:* 41989. *Clubs:* Caledonian United Service, Edinburgh.

Died 26 July 1944.

SUMNER, Captain Berkeley H.; *see* Holme-Sumner.

SUNDAR SINGH MAJITHIA, Dr Sirdar Sir, Kt 1926; CIE 1920; DOL 1933; Sirdar Bahadur; landlord and house owner; *b* 17 Feb. 1872; *s* of Raja Surat Singh, CSI; *m* 1st, 1887, *cousin* of HH Raja Bikram Singh (*d* 1887), of Faridkot State; 2nd, 1889, *g d* of Sirdar Sir Attar Singh, KCIE, of Bahadaur, Patiala State; three *s* one *d. Educ:* Aitchison Chief's College, Lahore; Government College, Lahore. Settled in Amritsar, 1893; served the Khalsa College, Amritsar, as Honorary Secretary of the College Council and Managing Committee, 1902–12; served in the Imperial Council, first in Lord Minto's time in 1909, for three months; was a Member of the Reformed Council for five years before the Montague Chelmsford reforms; Member of the Punjab Executive Council as Revenue Member, 1921–26; Honorary Secretary of the Chief Khalsa Diwan, 1902–20; President of the Khalsa College Council since 1921. *Address:* Majitha House, Albert Road, Amritsar, Punjab, India; Saraya Estate, PO Sandarnagar District, Gorakhpur, UP of Agra and Oudh, India.

Died June 1941.

SUNDERLAND, Septimus Philip, MD, MRCP, Chevalier de la Legion d'Honneur, Palmes en Or de l'Ordre de la Couronne de Belgique; Consulting Obstetric Physician to the French Hospital; Consulting Physician Royal Waterloo Hospital for Children and Women; late Physician, Royal Maternity Charity of London; FRSM (ex-Pres. Balneological and Climatological Section); late Editor of Journal of Balneology and Climatology; *s* of late William Sunderland, Edgbaston. *Educ:* Collège Chaptal, Paris; Edgbaston Proprietary School, Queen's College and General Hospital, Birmingham; Charing Cross Hospital. *Publications:* Old London's Spas, Baths and Wells, 1915; contributions to A System of Treatment and to various medical journals on gynæcological and other subjects. *Clubs:* Arts, Royal Automobile.

Died 7 Oct. 1950.

SUTCLIFFE, Bt Col Richard Douglas, DSO 1918; OBE 1939; RA. Served European War, 1914–18 (despatches, DSO). *Address:* 97 Prince of Wales' Mansions, SW11. *T:* Macaulay 3027.

Died 16 April 1941.

SUTCLIFFE, Very Rev. Canon William Ormond, MA; *b* 24 Oct. 1856; *s* of Joseph Sutcliffe and Mary Ellen Furness of Halifax. *Educ:* Shrewsbury; St John's College, Cambridge; First Class in Classical Tripos, 1880. Received into Catholic Church, 1881; Priest, 1888; Assistant Diocesan Inspector in the diocese of Westminster to 1897; Head of St Edmund's House, Cambridge, to 1904; Canon of Westminster Cathedral,

1909; Chief Diocesan Inspector, 1906–35. *Recreation:* reading. *Address:* 23 Magdalen Road, St Leonard's-on-Sea. *T:* Hastings 3483.

Died 16 Nov. 1944.

SUTHER, Brig. Percival, CMG 1918; DSO 1916; *b* 5 Nov. 1873; *s* of late General C. C. Suther, Royal Marine Artillery; *m* 1st, 1904, Margaret Russell (*d* 1929), *e d* of H. B. Hunter, Spetisbury, Dorset; one *s*; 2nd, 1931, Wilhelmina Buchanan Hunter (*d* 1940). *Educ:* Royal Naval School; Royal Military Academy, Woolwich. 2nd Lt RA 1893; Colonel, 1921; Chief Instructor, School of Artillery, 1920–24; Brigadier Royal Artillery, Southern Command, 1927–30; retired pay, 1930; served European War, 1914–18; France and Flanders. *Address:* c/o Lloyds Bank, Ltd, 6 Pall Mall, SW1.

Died 3 Nov. 1945.

SUTHERLAND, Lt-Col Hon. Donald Matheson, PC Canada; DSO 1919; *b* 1879; *s* of Fitzgerald Sutherland. Served European War, 1914–19 (twice wounded, despatches, DSO, 1914–15 Star, two medals). Member of Canadian House of Commons, 1925–26, and 1930–35; Minister of National Defence, Canada, 1930–34; Minister of Health and Pensions, 1934–35. *Address:* Embro, Ontario, Canada.

Died 1 Jan. 1949.

SUTHERLAND, Joan; author; *y d* of late Henry Collings, journalist, Bishop Stortford; *m* 1914, Richard Kelly; three *s* two *d. Educ:* Collegiate School, Leicester; Paris. Written since childhood; studied singing under Jacques Bouhy in Paris; spent some time in Canada, the United States, and the East. *Publications:* Cavanagh of Kultann; The Dawn; Beyond the Shadow; Hidden Road; The Locust; Wynnegate Sahib; Cophetua's Son; Desborough of the NW Frontier; Adrian Grey; Beauty for Ashes; novel of Cyril Harcourt's play, In the Night; The Garland of Olive; The Enchanted Country; The Circle of the Stars; Novel of the play by Dorothy Brandon, The Outsider; Challenge; Unquenchable Fire; Onslaught; The Golden Altar, a novel of French politics; Secret Places; Undertow; The Idle Wind; Cheat; In the Midst of the Years; One Man's Journey; Silver Mist; Shining River; Thirsty Land; Dust Before the Wind; Wide Horizon, 1941; Hazard, 1944. *Recreations:* swimming, riding, tennis, etc. *Address:* 3b Dean's Yard, SW1; The Gote, Street, Sussex.

Died 6 June 1947.

SUTHERLAND, Rt Hon. Sir William, PC 1922, KCB 1919; Commander of the Order of Leopold; MP (L) Argyllshire, Dec. 1918–Oct. 1924; *b* Glasgow, 4 March 1880; *m* 1921, Annie Christine Fountain, CBE (*d* 1949). *Educ:* Glasgow Univ.; MA. Secretary to the Cabinet Cttee on Supply of Munitions, 1915; Private Secretary to Mr Lloyd George as Minister of Munitions, 1915–16, Secretary of State for War, June to Dec. 1916, and Prime Minister, Dec. 1916–18; Parliamentary Secretary to the Prime Minister, 1918–20; Lord of the Treasury, 1920–22; Chancellor of the Duchy of Lancaster, 1922. *Address:* Birthwaite Hall, nr Barnsley, Yorks. *T:* Darton 20.

Died 19 Sept. 1949.

SUTHERLAND, William, CSI 1924; VD 1913; Colonel (retired) Auxiliary Force (India); *s* of Mackay Forbes Sutherland and Elizabeth, *d* of Capt. William Campbell, 46th Regt; *m* Nannie McQuisten, *yr d* of late Rev. John Jackson; one *s. Educ:* Blairlodge School, Polmont; RIEC, Coopers Hill. Appointed Indian Telegraph Dept 1891; Director, Telegraph Construction; Postmaster-General, Burma; Deputy Director-General, Telegraph Traffic; Postmaster-General, United Provinces, Central Provinces; Chief Engineer, Posts and Telegraphs Dept; retired Indian Posts and Telegraphs Dept 1925; Assistant to the Director-in-Chief, Indo-European Telegraph Department, India Office, 1925–31; six months' service in France (Victory and GS medals). *Recreations:* fishing, motoring, golf. *Address:* c/o Lloyds Bank, Cox's and King's Branch, G 3 Section, 6 Pall Mall, SW1.

Died 18 Jan. 1945.

SUTTIE, Sir George Grant-, 7th Bt *cr* 1702; *b* 2 Sept. 1870; *e s* of 6th Bt and Lady Susan Harriet Innes-Ker, *e d* of 6th Duke of Roxburghe; *S* father, 1878. *Educ:* Eton; New College, Oxford. Owns about 11,100 acres. *Heir: cousin* George Philip, *b* 1938. *Address:* Cobbles, Sutton-Scotney, Hants.

Died 19 May 1947.

SUTTON, Maj.-Gen. Alexander Arthur, CB 1917; DSO 1900; LRCP Edin.; late AMS; *b* 30 Nov. 1861; *m* 1st, 1887, Annie, *e d* of late Gen. H. F. Dunsford, CB; two *s* two *d*; 2nd, 1917, Mary Wilson, RRC (with bar). Entered Army, 1885; Major, 1897; served Sierra Leone Protectorate Expedition, 1898–99 (severely wounded, medal and clasp); South Africa, 1899–1902 (despatches, Queen's medal 4 clasps, King's medal 2 clasps, DSO); European War, Salonika Force (Order of St Sava, Serbia, 3rd Class); retired pay, 1920. *Address:* 38 Court Road, Tunbridge Wells. *T:* Tunbridge Wells 1205. *Club:* Junior United Service.

Died 12 May 1941.

SUTTON, Sir Arthur, 7th Bt *cr* 1772; *b* 24 Sept. 1857; *S* nephew, 1918; *m* 1885, Cecile Blanche, *d* of W. D. Dumbleton, Cape Colony; one *s* one *d*. *Heir: s* Robert Lexington, *b* 18 Jan. 1897. *Address:* Shanks, Wincanton, Somerset.

Died 4 Feb. 1948.

SUTTON, Air Marshal Sir Bertine Entwisle, KBE 1942; CB 1939; DSO 1917; OBE 1919; MC; *b* 1886; *o s* of late Rev. Alfred Sutton; *m* 1928, Margaret Griselda, *o d* of late Alexander Wedderburn, CBE, KC, and *widow* of Stuart de la Rue; two *s*. *Educ:* Eton; University College, Oxford. Served European War, 1914–19 (despatches, MC, DSO, OBE); operations against Upper Mohmands, 1933 (despatches); Instructor at Imperial Defence College, 1929–32; Commanded No. 1 Indian Group, RAF, Péshawar, 1932–34; Senior Air Staff Officer, RAF, India, 1934–36; AOC No. 22 Group, 1936–39; 23 Group, 1939–40; No. 24 Group, 1940; Commandant RAF Staff College, 1941; Air Member for Personnel, 1942–45; retired list, 1945. *Address:* Little Park Farm, Crookham, Newbury. *Clubs:* Army and Navy, Royal Air Force.

Died 28 Sept. 1946.

SUTTON, Maj.-Gen. F. A., MC; AMICE; engaged in business in Hong Kong; *b* 14 Feb. 1884; *s* of Francis Richard Sutton and *d* of Arthur Pryor, Hylands, Chelmsford; *m* 1910, Carina Descon Chester, Bedford; two *d*. *Educ:* Eton; University College, London. Went to Argentine, 1904; engaged in railway construction and contracting until 1909; with Lord Cowdray on engineering work on the Mexican Oil Fields, 1909–10; Contracting Engineer, railway and bridge work in Argentina, 1910–14; with the Royal Engineers, 1914–19 (lost right hand in Gallipoli); was sent to America by the British Government to supervise and instruct in the use of Trench Mortars, etc., 1917; went to Siberia and transported and erected the first modern Gold Dredge in the Amur Province, 1919; went into the Province of Szchwen, on the Upper Yangtze, and constructed an arsenal for Gen. Yang-sen, 1921–22; joined Marshal Chang-tso-lin at Mukden, becoming Director-General of his arsenal in Mukden, reorganising his artillery and enabling him to defeat Wu-pei-fu and occupy Pekin, Shanghai, etc., 1922–27; Vancouver, BC, interested in development of the Peace River Country, 1927–31; returned to China to re-engage in mining, 1932; mining in Korea, 1933–38. *Publication:* One Arm Sutton, 1933.

Recreations: shooting, fishing, golf. *Address:* Hongkong and Shanghai Bank, Hongkong. *Clubs:* Peking, Peking; Tienisin, Tientsin.

Died Oct. 1944.

SUTTON, Sir George Augustus, 1st Bt *cr* 1919; Director Daily Man and General Trust Ltd, Anglo-Newfoundland Development Co. Ltd; *b* 21 Sept. 1869; *m* 1893, Elizabeth, *d* of Joseph Adams; no *c*. Director of Publicity, National War Bonds Campaign, 1917–19; Chairman, Amalgamated Press, Ltd, 1915–26; Managing Director Associated Newspapers, Ltd, 1927; Vice-Chairman, 1934–37. Member of Lord Chancellor's Committee on the Law of Defamation, 1939. *Heir:* none. *Address:* Folkington Manor, Polegate, Sussex. *Club:* Carlton.

Died 7 Nov. 1947 (ext).

SUTTON, John Edward; JP; late Agent for Lancashire and Cheshire Miners' Federation; *b* 1862. Worked in mills and coal mine; MP (Lab) East Manchester, 1910–18; Clayton Div. of Manchester, 1922, and 1923–31; late Secretary to a branch of Miners Federation; late Senior Member Manchester City Council. *Address:* 115 Egerton Road South, Chorlton-Cum-Hardy, Manchester.

Died 29 Nov. 1945.

SUTTON, Sir John Smale, KBE 1941; CB 1936. Deputy Chairman Board of Customs and Excise since 1938. *Address:* Board of Customs and Excise, City Gate House, Finsbury Square, EC2.

Died 30 Aug. 1942.

SUTTON, Brig. William Moxhay, DSO 1919; MC; *b* 1885; *s* of late Rev. E. Sutton, Melton, Suffolk; *m* 1918, Barbara Marie Corballis; two *s* one *d*. *Educ:* Haileybury. Served European War, 1914–19 (despatches, MC, DSO, Order of Agricultural Merit of France); Shanghai Defence Force, 1927; Staff Officer to Inspector-General, King's African Rifles, 1929–32; commander Royal Tank Corps, Northern Command, India, 1932–35; Commandant Royal Tanks Corps Centre, and AFV School, Bovington Camp, 1935–39; retired pay, 1939; re-employed HQ Aldershot District, 1940–45; reverted to retired pay, 1945. *Address:* Parkleigh, Park Gardens, Bath. *T:* Bath 7466.

Died 2 Nov. 1949.

SWABY, Ven. J. A. R.; *s* of Rev. Frederick B. and Mary Swaby; *m* 1906, Caroline, *y d* of the late Thomas Toovey. *Educ:* The College, Spanish Town, Jamaica. Second Master of the Grammar School, Mannings, Sar-la-Mar, Jamaica; Headmaster, Diocesan School, Belize, British Honduras; Deacon, 1890; Priest, 1891; Curate of St John's, Belize, British Honduras; Registrar of Diocese of Honduras, 1894; Examining Chaplain to Bishop of Honduras, 1895; Archdeacon British Honduras, 1898–1910; Bishop's Commissary for Central America; Rector of St Mark's Church, Port Limon, Costa Rica; Canon of St John's Cathedral, Belize, 1898–1910; Rector of Lytchett Matravers, 1917–39. *Address:* Pigeon Plotte, Lytchett Matravers, Poole, Dorset.

Died 3 Aug. 1944.

SWAIN, Rt Rev. Edgar Priestley; Bishop Sufragan of Burnley since 1931; Rector and Rural Dean of Burnley since 1931; Hon. Canon of Blackburn, 1932; Proctor in Convocation, 1934; *b* 1881; *er s* of Harry Edwin Swain, of Sorrento, Bournemouth West, and Elizabeth, *d* of Henry Milsted; *m* 1919, Gwendolyn, *o d* of Rev. J. T. Jones, Sigglestherne Rectory, E Yorks; two *d*. *Educ:* St John's College, Oxford; Cuddesdon College. BA (Theol Hons) 1909; MA 1913; Oxford House, Bethnal Green, 1902–06; President Oxford Union Society, 1909; Deacon, 1910; Priest, 1911; Curate Holy Trinity with All Souls, Birchfield, 1910–14; Vicar, 1914–23; Chaplain to Bishop of Birmingham, 1915–24; Member of Mission of Help to India, 1922–23; Vicar of Putney (St Mary, St John and All Saints), 1923–31; Hon. Clerical Secretary

Southwark Diocesan Conference, 1927–31; Commissary for Bishop of Colombo, 1924–31; Rural Dean of Richmond and Barnes, 1930–31; Chairman of Bishop of Southwark's Commission on Sunday Religious Education, 1931. *Publications:* Editor and Contributor India and the Church, 1923; Bishop Seaton of Wakefield, 1939; various theological and sociological articles and reviews. *Recreations:* walking, bridge. *Address:* Palace House, Burnley. *T:* Burnley 3564.

Died 25 July 1949.

SWAIN, Walter, CIE 1922; *b* 17 Jan. 1876; *s* of R. H. Swain of Wrangle Manor and Ellen, *d* of George Saul of Wrangle Hall; *m* 1900, Annie Mathilde, *d* of Charles Fox, of Kuttea, Behar, India, and Edinburgh; two *s* one *d*. *Educ:* Boston Grammar School. Assistant Superintendent of Police, 1895; Principal Police Training College and Commandant Military Police, 1900; Superintendent of Police, 1905; Deputy Inspector-General of Police, 1919; Inspector-General of Police, Behar and Orissa, India, 1920–31; Delhi Durbar Medal, 1912; Volunteer Long Service Medal; King's Police Medal, 1918; MLC Behar and Orissa. *Publications:* Manual of Instructions for Constables (English, Bengali, and Kaithi); The Construction of Police Buildings. *Address:* Kitale, Trans Nzoia, Kenya Colony.

Died 19 Dec. 1945.

SWAN, Sir Alexander Brown, Kt 1935; Lord Provost of the City of Glasgow, 1932–35; Deputy Lieutenant of the County of the City of Glasgow; *b* 18 Sept. 1869; *s* of Richard Swan; *m* 1st, 1895, Marion Scott Scotland (*d* 1911); 2nd, 1913, Jean Thomson; one *s* three *d*. *Educ:* Bellshill and Hutchesons' Grammar School, Glasgow. Head of the Manufacturing Firm of Munro and Co. (Glasgow) Ltd; Chairman of Director of many prominent industrial undertakings; entered Glasgow Town Council, 1923; Convener, Municipal Buildings Committee, 1927–29; Sub-Convener, Housing Committee, 1929–31; Convener, Housing Committee, 1931–32; Magistrate, 1927–30. *Recreations:* bowling, curling, fishing. *Address:* Hazelwood, 157 Camphill Avenue, Glasgow, S1. *T:* Langside 1509.

Died 3 Sept. 1941.

SWAN, Annie Shepherd; *see* Smith, Mrs Burnett.

SWAN, Col Charles Arthur, CMG 1902; JP; Hon. Col 3rd Batt. Lincolns Regiment; *b* 1854; *s* of late Rev. C. T. Swan and Grace, *d* of Rev. S. Martin; *m* 1885, Ethel (*d* 1916), *o d* of Lieut-Col Conway Gordon of Lynwode Manor, Co. Lincoln; one *s* two *d*. *Educ:* Eton; Magdalen College, Oxford. MA 1881. High Sheriff, Lincoln, 1895; served S Africa, 1902 (Queen's medal 2 clasps, CMG); Chairman of the Spilsby Bench of Magistrates, 1919–36; Jubilee medal, 1935; Coronation Medal, 1937. *Address:* Sausthorpe Hall, Spilsby. *T:* Spilsby 3232.

Died 9 Jan. 1941.

SWAN, Sir Charles Sheriton, Kt 1944; Chairman, Swan, Hunter & Wigham Richardson Ltd, Shipbuilders, Wallsend-on-Tyne, since 1938; *b* 6 May 1870; *s* of Charles Sheriton Swan, Newcastle-on-Tyne; *m* 1901, Gertrude Mary Clements, *d* of late George Clements Hassell; one *s* three *d*. *Educ:* Giggleswick. Apprenticed to engineering with Wallsend Slipway & Engineering Co. Ltd, also to shipbuilding with Swan & Hunter; became Director on the Amalgamation with Wigham Richardson Ltd forming Swan, Hunter & Wigham Richardson Ltd. *Address:* Broomley Grange, Stocksfield, Northumberland. *T:* Stocksfield 3271.

Died 30 Dec. 1944.

SWAN, Ernest William, OBE 1928; VD; DL Northumberland; Captain, RNVR (Retd); *b* 9 May 1883; 2nd *s* of Col H. F. Swan, CB, VD; *m* 1915, May Evelyn, *d* of Major H. Harward, Royal Warwickshire Regt; two *s* one *d*. *Educ:* Harrow School. Articled pupil Sir W. G. Armstrong-Whitworth & Co., Elswick Works, 1902; Outside Manager, in charge of installation

of all Naval gun-mountings and guns, 1910–28; joined Tyne Division RNVR 1906; Mobilised Aug. 1914, and served in European War; Commanding Officer, 1929–39; ADC to King George V, 1933, and to King Edward VIII, 1936; retired from RNVR, 1939; rejoined for service, Sept. 1939; demobilized Nov. 1945. AMINA; FRGS; Member Committee of Management, RNLI. *Address:* Newbrough Park, Fourstones, Northumberland. *T:* Newbrough 25. *Clubs:* Constitutional; Northern Counties (Newcastle).

Died 6 April 1948.

SWAN, Russell Henry Jocelyn, OBE 1919; MS, MB Lond., FRCS Eng.; Consulting Surgeon, Royal Cancer Hospital, Fulham Road, SW; Director, Surgical Division at Park Prewett Hospital, Basingstoke, in Emergency Medical Service of Ministry of Health; Consulting Surgeon to St Paul's Hospital for Genito-urinary Diseases; Consulting Surgeon, Walton-on-Thames Hospital, and to the Peace Memorial Hospital, Watford; late temporary Major RAMC (despatches); Surgical Specialist and Senior Operating Surgeon to the Royal Herbert Hospital, Woolwich; Consulting Surgeon to Woolwich District, Eastern Command; Surgeon RAF Hospital and the American Red Cross Hospital for Officers; *b* 20 July 1876; *s* of Richard Jocelyn Swan, MRCS, etc; *m* 1st, 1908, Una Gladys (*d* 1924), *d* of Alfred Waterlow; one *s* three *d*; 2nd, 1927, Joyce Hazel, *yr d* of late H. M. Thornton, JP, The Old House, Purley. *Educ:* Wilson's School; Guy's Hospital. Qualified MB (1st Class Honours in Medicine); BS, London Univ., 1898; MS Lond. and FRCS Eng., 1902; Fellow of Royal Society of Medicine. Late President of the Urological Section, Fellow and late Member of Council of the Medical Society of London; Fellow of the Association of Surgeons of Great Britain and Ireland; Member of Grand Council of British Empire Cancer Campaign; Member of Soc. International d'Urologie; late Demonstrator of Anatomy and Biology, House Surgeon and Resident Obstetric Officer, Guy's Hospital; House Surgeon, St Peter's Hospital for Stone; Surgical Registrar and Assistant Surgeon, Surgeon and Emeritus Surgeon, Royal Cancer Hospital, Fulham Road. *Publications:* Primary Unilateral Renal Tuberculosis; Estimation of Renal Functional Activity; Value of Cystoscope in Diagnosis of Urinary Disease; Sarcoma of the Tongue; Carcinoma of the Breast; Tumours of the Kidney; Tumours of the Urinary Bladder; articles in Index of Differential Diagnosis (French) and several articles on Military Surgery. *Recreations:* golf and travel. *Address:* 75 Wimpole Street, W1; Ingram's Copse, Farnham Common, Bucks. *T:* Welbeck 3323 and Farnham Common 41. *Club:* Stoke Poges.

Died 2 March 1943.

SWAN, Maj.-Gen. William Travers, CB 1915; MB, late AMS; *b* 28 Sept. 1861; *s* of E. L. Swan of Allworth, Abbeyleix; *m* 1903, Muriel, *d* of late Lt-Col Dominick Downes McCausland, 98th Regt; two *d*. *Educ:* Trinity Coll., Dublin (MB and BCh 1884). Major, 1897; Lt-Col 1905; Col 1914; served Chitral, 1895 (medal with clasp); NW Frontier, India, 1897–98 (clasp); S Africa, 1900–02 (Queen's medal 3 clasps, King's medal 2 clasps); European War, 1914–18 (despatches four times, 1914 Star, CB); retired pay, 1919; Hon. MD Dublin University. *Address:* 9 Park Close, Eastbourne Sussex.

Died 15 Jan. 1949.

SWANN, Rev. Ernest Henry, MA; *b* Hempstead Essex, 23 Oct. 1869; *s* of Rev. Johnson Fowell and Sarah Swann; *m* 1st, 1900, Constance Stead (*d* 1926); 2nd, 1928, Helen Margaret Young, ARCM. *Educ:* St John's School, Leatherhead; Corpus Christi College, Cambridge (Organ Scholar and Exhibitioner), BA (Junior Optime). Assistant Master, Gt Yarmouth Grammar School, 1891–99; Deacon, 1897; Priest, 1898; Curate of Gorleston, 1897–99; Succentor of Ripon Cathedral, 1899–1905; Minor Canon of Ripon Cathedral and Vicar of Ripon, 1905–17; Warden of St

Michael's College, Tenbury, and Vicar of St Michael and All Angels, Tenbury, 1917–36; Vicar of Bridstow, 1936–41; Surrogate for Diocese of Ripon, 1906–17; Precentor of Ripon Cathedral, 1908–17; Chaplain of St John's Hospital, Ripon, 1908–17; Chairman of Hereford Diocesan Church Music Cttee, 1928–36; Rural Dean of Burford, 1931–36; Fellow of St Michael's College, Tenbury, 1936. *Publications:* The Ripon Psalter, 1908; The Hereford Psalter, 1929. *Recreations:* Association football, cricket, lawn tennis, golf. *Address:* Stratton Corner, Cirencester.

Died 12 Nov. 1948.

SWANN, Louis Herbert H.; *see* Hartland-Swann.

SWANN, Air Vice-Marshal Sir Oliver, KCB 1924; CBE 1919; *b* 1878; *s* of T. F. Swann, JP, Wimbledon, London SW19; *m* 1913, Elizabeth Laidlaw-Purves; one *s* two *d*. Royal Navy, 1891; Admiralty, 1912; Port Captain, 1914; commanded HMS Campania, Fleet aircraft carrier, 1915–17; transferred to RAF, 1919; Air Member for Personnel, Air Ministry, 1922; AOC Middle East, 1924; retired, 1926; AOC Halton, 1939; Air Liaison Officer, North Midland Region, 1940–43. *Address:* Orange Grove, Littleton, Guildford.

Died 7 March 1948.

SWANN, Rev. Sidney, MA, Vicar of Lindfield, 1929–37; *b* 30 Sept. 1862; *s* of John Bellingham Swann, RN; *m* 1st; two *s* one *d*; 2nd, 1920, Lady Bagot (*d* 1940). *Educ:* Marlborough; Trinity Hall, Cambridge. Rowed in the Oxford and Cambridge boat race, 1883, 1884, and 1885 (Swann junior stroked Cambridge, 1912); won Cambridge sculls and pairs, also Grand Challenge, 1886 and 1887, and Stewards', 1885 and 1887, in record times; in Japan won most things started for on land and sea; rowing, hurdling, cycling, running, pole-jumping, weight and hammer; first to cycle round Syria; rode Land's End to John o' Groats; Carlisle to London in a day; rowed home-made boat from Crosby Vicarage down the rapids of the Eden to the sea, and cut the record from England to France, 1911, rowing the Channel in 3 hours 50 minutes, faster time than any one had ever gone between England and France by muscular power; built several flying machines, and drove motor ambulance in Belgium (1914 medal, 1915 medal, Roi de Belge order). In 1917, when 55 years old, cycled, walked, ran, paddled, rowed, and swam 6 consecutive half-miles in 26 min. 20 secs, in competition with Lieut Muller of the Danish army; President of the National Amateur Rowing Association since 1934. *Recreations:* rowing, tennis, cycling, motoring. *Address:* Lindfield, Haywards Heath, Sussex.

Died 3 Aug. 1942.

SWANN-MASON, Rev. Richard Swann, OBE; MA; Vicar, Christ Church, Albany Street, NW; Chaplain Royal Horse Guards, Regent's Park Barracks; Chaplain to the Earl of Yarborough; Chaplain West End Hospital and King Edward VII Hospital for Officers (Sister Agnes); Acting Chaplain of the Royal Chapel of St Katharine's, Regent's Park; *b* Cambridge; *s* of M. Mason, merchant; *m* Margarita, *d* of Sir Archibald Milman, KCB, Clerk to House of Commons; one *d. Educ:* Perse School; St Catharine's College, Cambridge (Exhibitioner). Assistant and House Master, Perse School, Cambridge; Boston Grammar School; Hymers College, Hull; Aysgarth School, Yorks; Chaplain and Tutor, S Wales College, Carmarthen; Voluntary Inspector of Religious Knowledge in Diocese of London; Curate, Kirk Ella, Hull; Patrick Brompton, Yorks; Chaplain Egerton House, New-market, 1906; Councillor St Pancras Borough Council, 1931; Christ Church, Mayfair; Secretary of St John's School, Leatherhead; Public Preacher Diocese of St David's and Ely; Chaplain Royal Navy, 1914–19; served in North Sea, Suez Canal (Turkish attack), Dardanelles (Chaplain of HMS Ocean, sunk in action); rescued victims of Lusitania and buried them at Queenstown, 1915; sent on

Political Mission in Persian Gulf; raised funds and built St Nicholas Church for sailors at Immingham Dock, 1917; lectured for Admiralty at East Coast Ports; Provincial Grand Chaplain Cambridgeshire (Freemasons), 1936. *Publications:* Straight Talks to Stable Lads, 1909; Plain Talks to Sailor Men, 1919; Articles in Saturday Review on Church Matters. *Recreations:* cricket (has made 75 centuries), shooting, fishing, and all field sports. *Address:* 3 Chester Place, Regent's Park, NW. *T:* Welbeck 3255. *Clubs:* MCC, Constitutional.

Died 21 Feb. 1942.

SWANZY, Canon Thomas Erskine; Vicar of All Saints, Lincoln, 1919–47; Canon and Prebendary of Leighton Beaudesert in Lincoln Cathedral, 1926–47, emeritus since 1947; *b* Newry, Co. Down, 25 Nov. 1869; *e s* of Thomas Biddall Swanzy (Vicar of Newry, 1876–84) and Elizabeth Anne, *d* of Henry Swanzy, Rector of Kilshannig and Canon of Cloyne; unmarried. *Educ:* Newry Intermediate School; St Lawrence College, Ramsgate; Trinity College, Dublin (Stewart Literary Scholar, 1890, and Senior Moderator in Modern Literature, 1891). BA, 1891; St John's College, Oxford (Second Class Honours School of Theology), BA, 1893; MA, 1897. Curate of St Swithin's, Lincoln, 1894–1904; Vicar of Hibaldstow, Lincolnshire, 1904–09; Curate of All Saints, Lincoln, 1909–19; Proctor in Convocation for Lincoln Diocese, 1932–45. *Recreation:* novel reading. *Address:* The Vicarage, Newry, Co. Down, N Ireland.

Died 29 April 1950.

SWAYNE, Rt Rev. William Shuckburgh, MA; DD; *b* 1862; *s* of William John Swayne, formerly Vicar of Heytesbury, Wilts, and Diana, *d* of William Coles Shuckburgh, of The Moot, Downton; *m* 1st, Emma Louise des Réaux (*d* 1916), of St Mary's Manor, Jersey; one *s* one *d*; 2nd, 1917, Madeline Angelique, *y d* of late W. W. Farquharson, Edinburgh. *Educ:* St Paul's, Stony Stratford; New Coll., Oxford (Open Scholar). Took a 2nd Class in the Final School of Literæ Humaniores, and a 1st Class in the Final School of Theology. Deacon, 1885; held curacies at Emery Down, Hants, and Stalbridge, Dorset; Diocesan Lecturer in the Diocese of Lichfield, 1890–92; Vicar of Walsall, 1892; Vicar of St Peter's, Cranley Gardens, SW, 1901–18; Prebendary of St Paul's, 1916; Dean of Manchester, 1918–20; Bishop of Lincoln, 1920–32; served as Chaplain to the Forces during South African War, 1900; Examining Chaplain to the Bishop of Salisbury, 1911. *Publications:* Our Lord's Knowledge as Man; The Psalm of the Saints; The Beatitudes; St Paul and his Gospel; Personal Union with Christ; Parsons Pleasure, 1934. *Address:* 69 Great King Street, Edinburgh. *Club:* New (Edinburgh).

Died 30 June 1941.

SWEENEY, James Augustine, CIE 1931; *b* 25 May 1883; *m* 1939, Una Greene. *Educ:* French College, Blackrock; RUI and Dublin University. Entered Indian Civil Service, 1907; Dist and Sess. Judge Bihar and Orissa, Legal Remembrancer and Sec. to Govt Judicial Dept; retired, 1934. *Address:* Ard Na Chree, Foxrock, Co. Dublin. *Clubs:* Stephen's Green, Dublin.

Died 6 Nov. 1945.

SWEET-ESCOTT, Sir (Ernest) Bickham, KCMG 1904; CMG 1895; FRCI since 1883; *b* Bath, 20 Aug. 1857; *y s* of late Rev. Hay Sweet-Escott, MA, Balliol College, Oxford, Rector of Kilve, Bridgwater; *m* 1881, Mary (*d* 1935), *d* of Thomas Wingfield Hunt, HEICS; one *s. Educ:* Somersetshire College, Bath; Bromsgrove School; Balliol Coll., Oxford. 2nd class, Classical Moderations, 1878; 3rd class, Modern History (finals), 1880; BA 1880; MA 1911. Entered Colonial Service 1881 as Classical Professor, Royal College, Mauritius; Assistant Colonial Secretary, Mauritius, 1886; Acting Colonial Secretary, Mauritius, 1889; Colonial Secretary, British Honduras, 1893; administered the government of that colony, 1893, 1895 and 1897; acted as Senior Clerk, Colonial Office, in 1898–99; Administrator of Seychelles

Islands, 1899–1903; First Governor and Commander-in-Chief, Seychelles, 1903–04; Governor and Commander-in-Chief of British Honduras, 1904–06; Leeward Islands, 1906–12; received Coronation Medal, 1911, and Silver Jubilee Medal, 1935; Governor of Fiji and High Commissioner and Consul-General for Western Pacific, 1912–18; retired at own request, July 1918; Representative of Fiji at British Empire Exhibition, 1924, and received thanks of the Colonial Government and of the Secretary of State for services; Fellow of the Royal Empire Society since 1883; President Pedestrians' Association, Worthing. *Address:* Willett, Chaucer Road, Worthing. *T:* Worthing 1593.

Died 10 April 1941.

SWEETMAN, Sir Henry, Kt 1935; JP; *b* 31 March 1858; *s* of Edward Sweetman and Elizabeth Sheppard; *m* 1st, Ellen Mary Drysdale (*d* 1880); one *s*; 2nd, Nellie Edith Fenner (*d* 1887); one *d*; 3rd, Eliza Mary Harris (*d* 1934); two *d*. *Educ:* Hanover House School, Ryde. 15 years' service, 1884–99, Isle of Wight (Princess Beatrice's) Rifles (Volunteers); Member of Ryde Town Council, 1884–1920; Senior Alderman on retirement; JP, Borough of Ryde, since 1898; Chairman, Isle of Wight Conservative and Unionist Association; Chairman, Isle of Wight County Press Newspaper and Printing and Publishing Co. Ltd; Past President (1933) Royal Isle of Wight Agricultural Soc. *Address:* Eversley, Queen's Road, Ryde, Isle of Wight. *T:* Ryde 2336.

Died 8 June 1944.

SWETTENHAM, Sir Frank Athelstane, GCMG 1909; KCMG 1897; CH 1917; *b* 1850; *y s* of late James Oldham Swettenham, Belper Lodge, Belper, Derbyshire. Deputy Commissioner with Perak Expedition (despatches, medal and clasp), 1875–76; British Resident, Selangor, 1882; British Resident, Perak, 1889–95; Resident-General, Federated Malay States, 1896–1901; Governor and Commander-in-Chief. Straits Settlements, 1901–04; King of Arms, Order of St Michael and St George, 1925–38; Chairman of Royal Commission to enquire into the affairs of Mauritius, 1909; Joint Director of the Official Press Bureau, 1915–19; Officier d'Académie, 1887. *Publications:* Malay-English Vocabulary, 1880; Malay Sketches, 1895; Unaddressed Letters, 1898; The Real Malay, 1899; British Malaya, 1906, Also and Perhaps, 1912; Arabella in Africa, 1925; Footprints in Malaya, 1942. *Address:* 22 Mount Street, W1. *T:* Mayfair 1916. *Clubs:* MCC, Bath.

Died 11 June 1946.

SWETTENHAM, Lt-Col William Alexander Whybault, CBE 1919; late RA; *b* 16 Dec. 1870; *s* of William Norman Swettenham, Belper; *m* 1922, Helen Constance, *d* of George Marriott Barber, 42 Clapham Road, Bedford. *Educ:* Shrewsbury School; Bedford Grammar School. Served China, 1900 (medal); European War, 1914–19 (despatches, CBE); retired pay, 1922. *Address:* Orkney House, Clapham Road, Bedford.

Died 31 Jan. 1947.

SWIFT, Brig.-Gen. Albert Edward, DSO 1916; late Canadian Army; Mine Owner; President Anglo-Swift Gold Mines; Northern Ontario, Canada; *b* Quebec, 1870; *s* of Henry and Henrietta Swift; *m* 1905, Jessie Guthrie (*d* 1916), *d* of late Lt-Col E. G. Scott; one *s* one *d*. *Educ:* Richmond Grammar School, Richmond, Quebec. Permanent Force Officer; served Boer War, South Africa, 1899–1902 (Queen's medal with five clasps, King's medal with two clasps); European war, 1914–18 (despatches, DSO); Siberia, 1918–19; Commandant Canadian Musketry School, Ottawa, 1919–21; President Canadian Legion BES League Kirkland Lake Branch, Ont. *Recreations:* golf, curling, polo, hunting, fishing, yachting; in younger days hockey, snowshoe racing, lacrosse, football, skating, all athletic

sports. *Address:* Dane, Ont, and Quebec City, Canada. *TA:* Swastika, Ont. *T:* 388 Kirkland Lake. *Club:* Garrison (Quebec).

Died 20 April 1948.

SWINDELL, Rev. Canon Frederic Smith, MA Oxon; Canon of Cathedral, Birmingham, 1921; *s* of Rev. Thomas Swindell, Norwich; *m* Allas Hindle, *d* of Francis Pearse, Lowestoft; no *c*. *Educ:* Exeter College, Oxford. Formerly Curate of Holy Trinity, Heigham, Norwich; LDHM in charge of the Seven Dials, London; Vicar of Erdington, Birmingham, 1887–1936; retired; Hon. Chap. to Bishop (Russell Wakefield) of Birmingham and Rural Dean of Aston-juxta-Birmingham. *Recreations:* curios, horticulture, etc. *Address:* 9 Church Road, Erdington, Birmingham.

Died 2 July 1941.

SWINTON, John Edulf Blagrave; *b* 6 Aug. 1864; *o s* of John Edulf Swinton (*d* 1871) and Frances Jane (*d* 1895), *o d* of late Daniel Ainslie, of The Gart, Perthshire; *m* 1910, Frances Harriet, *o d* of late Sir W. J. G. Baird, 8th Bt. Lieut Lothians and Border Horse Yeo. *Clubs:* Arthur's; New, Edinburgh.

Died 25 March 1941.

SWINY, Brig.-Gen. William Frederick, CMG 1919; DSO 1917; *b* 25 June 1873; 2nd *s* of Col G. A. Sweny, Royal Fusiliers, Rohallion, St George Street, Toronto; *m* 1st, 1910, Gladys Cole (*d* 1913), *d* of late R. H. Metge, Athlumney, Co. Meath; one *s* (and one *s* killed on duty in India, 1933); 2nd, 1918, Kathleen Prudence Eirene, *widow* of Capt. W. Blackett of Arbigland, and *d* of B. F. Bagenal of Benekerry House, Carlow. *Educ:* Wellington College; Trinity College School; RMC, Kingston, Canada. Joined Royal Fusiliers, 1893; served Egyptian Army, 1902–06; commanded the Arab Batt.; Senior Inspector Bahr el Ghazel during 1906 incident; commanded 2nd MI, S Africa, 1911–13; attached Canadian Militia, 1914; was AAG first Canadian Contingent at Valcartier; commanded 2nd S Lancashire Regt, 2nd E Yorks Regt, 4th Roy. Fusiliers and 61st, 72nd, and 41st Infantry Brigades, France (despatches seven times, Bt Lt-Col, CMG, DSO, Officier Légion d'Honneur, three times wounded); retired, 1920. *Address:* 31 Trevor Square, SW7. *Clubs:* Bath, Hurlingham.

Died 16 Aug. 1950.

SWIRE, William, CBE 1918; DL, JP; *b* 1862; *s* of late William Hudson Swire; *m* Edith Jessie Lindsay, *e d* of late George Jardine Kidston, DL, of Finlaystone, Renfrewshire; one *s* two *d*. *Educ:* Charterhouse. Sheriff, 1915. *Address:* Longden Manor, Shrewsbury. *TA:* Longden. *T:* Hanwood 14. *Club:* Conservative.

Died 24 March 1942.

SYDENHAM, Engr Rear-Adm. Frederick William, CB 1928; OBE 1919; retired list; *b* 13 May 1871; *e s* of late L. J. Sydenham, Plymouth; *m* 1897, Millie, *d* of late Edward Gard, Plymouth; no *c*. *Educ:* Park Grammar School, Plymouth; RNE College, Keyham. Assistant Engineer, 1892; Engineer, 1898; Eng.-Lieut 1902; Eng.-Com. 1910; Charge of machinery of HMTBD Ghurka, 1906–10; HMS Yarmouth, 1910–11; HMS Valiant, 1914–19; served European War, present at Battle of Jutland (OBE); Chief Engineer HM Dockyard, Cape of Good Hope, 1919–23; Engineer Manager, HM Dockyard, Malta, 1924–27; retired at own request, 1928. *Recreations:* motoring, golf, reading. *Address:* National Provincial Bank, Ltd, Southsea. *Clubs:* Union, Malta.

Died 8 Feb. 1946.

SYED SIRDAR ALI KHAN, Nawab; created Nawab Sirdar Nawaz Jung Bahadur, 1921; *b* 26 March 1879; *e surv. s* of late Nawab Sirdar Diler Jung, Sirdar Diler-ud-dowla, Sirdar Diler-ul-mulk Bahadur, CIE, sometime Home Secretary at Hyderabad; *g s* of the Nawab of Karnalla; *m* 1896, six *s* two *d*. *Educ:* privately. Entered the Nizam's service, 1911; held several responsible positions, including the Commissionership of Gulburga Province; Postmaster-General of HEH the Nizam's Dominions, 1922–29; retired; Life Member Anjuman-e-Islam, Bombay, since 1904; Member All-India Moslem Deputation to the Viceroy, 1906; FRGS 1909, FRSA 1936; Member, East India Association, London, 1937. *Publications:* Lord Curzon's Administration of India, 1905; Unrest in India, 1907; India of To-day, 1908; Historical Furniture, 1908; Life of Lord Morley, 1923; The Earl of Reading, 1924; British India, 1926; The Indian Moslems, 1928; contributions to the English and Indian Press with regard to the Indian political situation and Palestine. *Recreation:* motoring. *Address:* Hyderabad, Deccan, India.

Died 8 Nov. 1942.

SYKES, Sir Alan John, 1st Bt *cr* 1917; MA; JP; DL; VD; MP (Co. U) Knutsford Division of Cheshire, 1910–22; *b* 11 April 1868; 2nd *s* of late Thos Hardcastle Sykes, JP; DL; and Mary, *d* of late John Platt, MP, Oldham; unmarried. *Educ:* Rugby; Oriel College, Oxford. Chairman, Bleachers' Association, Ltd; Lt-Col comdg 6th Cheshire Regiment, 1911–14, Mayor of Stockport, 1910–11; Group Commandant (A Group) and Hon. Secretary, Cheshire Volunteer Regt, 1916–20. *Recreations:* automobilism, and travel. *Heir:* none. *Address:* South View, Cheadle, Cheshire. *T:* Gatley 2834. *TA:* Sykesie Cheadle, Cheshire. *Clubs:* Carlton, Royal Automobile; Union (Manchester).

Died 21 May 1950 (ext).

SYKES, Sir Charles, 1st Bt *cr* 1921; KBE 1918; JP; *b* 31 Dec. 1867; *s* of late Benjamin Sykes; *m* 1892, Mary (*d* 1944), *y d* of late Benjamin Newsome; three *s* one *d.* Director of Wool Textile Production and Chairman of Board of Control of the Worsted and Woollen Trades during European War; MP (Co. L) Borough of Huddersfield, Dec. 1918–22. *Heir: s* Benjamin Hugh Sykes, [*b* 8 June, 1893; *m* 1935, Audrey Winifred, *o d* of F. C. Thompson]. *Address:* Little Ridge, Hockering Gdns, Woking, Sv.

Died 16 Nov. 1950.

SYKES, Brig.-Gen. Sir Percy (Molesworth), KCIE 1915; CB 1919; CMG 1902; CIE 1911; *b* 28 Feb. 1867; *m* 1902, Evelyn, *e d* of late Colonel Bruce Seton, RE; four *s* two *d. Educ:* Rugby; Sandhurst. Gazetted 16th Lancers, 1888; transferred 2nd Dragoon Guards, 1888; founded Consulate for Kermán and Persian Baluchistán, 1894; Assist Commissioner, Perso-Baluch Boundary Commission, 1896; mission to the Kárun Valley, 1896; in charge of HE the Násir-ul-Mulk, special ambassador to the Court of St James's, 1897; founded Consulate in Sistán, 1899; served in South Africa in Intelligence Department, and also in command of Montgomery Imperial Yeomanry under Lord Methuen, 1901 (wounded, despatches, South African War Medal with three clasps); Consul-General for Khorasan, 1905–13; City Comdt Southampton, Aug.–Sept. 1914; in charge of Interpreters of the Lahore Division in France (Mons Star and two medals); Consul-General (temp.) Chinese Turkestan, 1915; appointed to raise South Persia Rifles with title of Inspector-General, 1916; GOC Southern Persia until Dec. 1918; retired, Sept. 1920, awarded special South Persian medal; awarded Silver Medal by the Royal Society of Arts, 1897; Back Grant, 1899, and Gold Medal, 1902, by the Royal Geographical Society; special gold Macgregor Memorial medal, 1910; gold medal of the Royal Empire Society, 1934; delivered Lowell Lectures, Boston, USA, in 1923; lectured in Canada under the auspices of the National Council of Education of Canada, 1934; Hon. Secretary Royal Central Asian Society since 1932. *Publications:* Ten Thousand Miles in Persia, 1902; The Glory of the Shia World, 1910; History of Persia, 1915, 3rd edition 1930; (with Ella Sykes) Through Deserts and Oases of Central Asia, 1920; Sir Mortimer Durand, a Biography, 1926; A History of Exploration, 1934; The Quest for Cathay,

1936; A History of Afghanistan, 1940. *Address:* Edgeley Fold, Sunningdale, Berks. *T:* Ascot 540. *Club:* Athenæum.

Died 11 June 1945.

SYKES, Rev. Simon Joseph; Canon Emeritus of Liverpool; *b* Inyati, Bulawayo, 1867; *s* of Rev. W. Sykes, pioneer missionary; *m* Alice Maud (*d* 1941). *Educ:* University of London; BA. Ordained, 1891; Curate of Lower Mitton, 1891–93; St Luke's, Leicester, 1895–96; St Andrew's, Worcester, 1896–98; Vicar of St Mary's, Waterloo, 1898–1939. *Publications:* Penitence, Opportunity and Power; Our Homeward Way; The Cathedral Church of Christ. *Recreation:* bowling. *Address:* Ainsdale, Southport.

Died 12 Dec. 1941.

SYME, Sir Geoffrey, KBE 1941; managing editor and part proprietor of the Age, Melbourne; *b* Melbourne, 1873; 4th *s* of late David Syme; *m* 1902, Violet Addison, *e d* of Tom Garnett, Clitheroe, Lancs; four *d. Educ:* Kew High School; University of Melbourne. *Address:* The Age, Melbourne.

Died 30 July 1942.

SYMON, Lt-Col Walter Conover, CMG 1917; late RA; *b* 26 April 1874; *m* 1906, Dorothy Norah Harriette, *d* of late Maj.-Gen. Sir Edward O. F. Hamilton, KCB; one *s.* Entered Army, 1893; Major, 1910; retired, 1912; served S Africa, 1900–02 (despatches, Queen's medal 6 clasps, King's medal 2 clasps); European War, 1914–18 (CMG; Brevet Lt-Col; Légion d'Honneur (Officier); Crown of Belgium (Officier); St Vladimir (3rd Class); retired pay. *Address:* 21 Draycott Place, SW3. *T:* Kensington 5080.

Died 15 Feb. 1949.

SYMONS, Albert James Alroy; author; Director of the First Edition Club; Secretary of the Wine and Food Society; *b* London, 16 Aug. 1900; *né* Alphonse James Albert Symonds; *e surv. s* of Maurice Albert Symons; *m* 1924, Victoria Emily Weeks, Tenterden, Kent; no *c. Educ:* privately. Founded First Edition Club, 1922; Book-Collector's Quarterly, 1930; associated with Andrè L. Simon and others in foundation of the Saintsbury Club, 1931, Wine and Food Society, 1933; Organised selection of the Fifty Books of the Year since 1926; is an authority upon the literature and bibliography of the eighteen-nineties, and on book-collecting in general; now engaged in writing Life of Oscar Wilde and editing definitive edition of his works; has made an extensive study of Victoriana in general, particularly musical boxes, of which he possesses many fine examples. *Publications:* Frederick Baron Corvo, 1926; Emin, Governor of Equatoria, 1928; An Anthology of Nineties Verse, 1930; HM Stanley, 1933; The Quest for Corvo, 1934; The Nonesuch Century, 1936. *Recreations:* walking, talking, and searching for musical boxes and lost manuscripts of Baron Corvo. *Address:* Brick House, Finching-field, Essex. *T:* Holborn 9606, Great Bardfield 52. *Clubs:* Savile, Saintsbury, First Edition, Sette of Odd Volumes.

Died 25 Aug. 1941.

SYMONS, Arthur; writer of verse and prose; *b* Wales, 28 Feb. 1865; of Cornish parentage; *m* 1901, Rhoda (*d* 1936), 3rd *d* of J. E. Bowser. *Educ:* various private schools. *Publications:* An Introduction to the Study of Browning, 1886; Days and Nights, 1889; Silhouettes, 1892; London Nights, 1895; Amoris Victima, 1897; Studies in Two Literatures, 1897; The Symbolist Movement in Literature, 1899; Images of Good and Evil, 1900; Collected Poems, 1901; Plays, Acting, and Music, 1908; Cities, 1903; Studies in Prose and Verse 1904; Spiritual Adventures, 1905; A Book of Twenty Songs, 1905; The Fool of the World, and other poems, 1906; Studies in Seven Arts, 1906; William Blake, 1907; Cities of Italy, 1907; The Romantic Movement in English Poetry, 1909; Knave of Hearts, 1913; Figures of

Several Centuries, 1915; Tragedies, 1916; Tristan and Iseult, 1917; Cities and Sea Coasts and Islands, 1918; Colour Studies in Paris, 1918; The Toy Cart, 1919; Studies in Elizabethan Drama, 1920; Charles Baudelaire, 1921; Translations from Baudelaire, 1925; Dramatis Personæ, 1926; A Study of Thomas Hardy, 1927; Translation of Baudelaire's Letters to His Mother, 1928; Studies in Strange Souls, 1929; Confessions, 1930; Translation of the Adventures of Giuseppe Pignata, 1930; Wanderings, 1931; Jexebel Mort and other Poems, 1931. *Recreations:* hearing and playing music, seeing dancing. *Address:* Island Cottage, Wittersham.

Died 22 Jan. 1945.

SYMONS, Col Charles Bertie Owen, CMG 1919; DSO 1915; late RE; *b* 29 Nov. 1874; *e s* of late Col C. E. H. Symons, Colombo; *m* 1st, 1918, Sylvia (*d* 1931), 2nd *d* of late Charles Lenox-Simpson, Sen. Commissioner in China; 2nd, 1934, Mabel, *widow* of H. A. Fife-Cookson. Entered Army, 1894; Captain, 1904; Major, 1914; Lt-Col 1921; Col 1925; Prof. RMC, Canada, 1899–1904; Survey Duty, Gold Coast, 1905–07; served European War, 1914–18 (despatches, DSO, CMG, wounded); Chief Eng. under Air Ministry, Iraq, 1923–25; retired pay, 1926. *Address:* 704 Grenville House, Dolphin Square, SW1.

Died 8 May 1948.

SYMONS, Rev. Charles Douglas, CB 1942; MC; MA, DD 1939; Chaplain, Order of St John of Jerusalem, since 1941; *b* 13 Oct. 1885; *s* of late Mark Symons, Bridge House, Wadebridge, and Jane Lankelly Tresawson, *y d* of Henry Harris, MD, Trengweath, Redruth; *m* 1919, Amy Mary Downing; one *d*. *Educ:* Kelly College, Tavistock; Trinity College, Cambridge (Prizeman, 2nd Class Theological Tripos). Ordained 1908; served in ranks of RAMC, 1915–16; Chaplain to the Forces, 1916, 57th Division; Personal Staff of Deputy Chaplain-General, BEF, 1918; 2nd Assistant to Deputy Chaplain-General GHQ, BEF, 1919; SCF C/E Headquarters BT in France and Flanders, 1919–20; Tower of London, 1920–23; Rhine Army, 1923–24; Hounslow and Kneller Hall, 1924–28; 3rd Class CF, 1927; Catterick, 1928–29; Alexandria, 1929–30; Sudan, 1930–31; 2nd Class CF, 1931; SCF C/E Plymouth, 1932; Chaplain to the Brigade of Guards and SCF C/E Chatham, 1934–37; CF 1st Class and Assistant Chaplain-General in Egypt, 1937–38; Assistant Chaplain-General, Aldershot, 1938–39; Chaplain-General to the Forces, 1939–44; Hon. Chaplain to the King, 1939–44; retired pay, 1944. *Recreation:* golf. *Address:* c/o Lloyds Bank, Wadebridge, Cornwall. *Club:* Athenæum.

Died 15 Oct. 1949.

SYMONS, Lt-Col George Algernon James S.; *see* Soltau-Symons.

SYMONS, Maj.-Gen. Sir (Thomas) Henry, KBE 1929; CSI 1925; OBE 1917; late IMS; *b* 17 May 1872; *s* of Edward Symons, Falmouth; *m* 1918, Mary Laugharne, *d* of late Frederick Laugharne-Humphreys, Monte

Video. *Educ:* privately; Charing Cross Hospital. Joined Indian Medical Service, 1896; served on military side until 1901; went to Madras General Hospital; filled various appointments until European War; in command of Hospital Ship Madras, 1915–18; Surgeon-Gen., Madras, 1923–26; Director-General, Indian Medical Service, 1926; retired, 1930. *Address:* The Cottage, Church Crookham, Hants.

Died 3 July 1948.

SYNGE, Sir Robert Millington, 7th Bt *cr* 1801; *b* 17 Nov. 1877; *s* of 6th Bt and Frances (*d* 1911), *d* of Robert Evans, Rock Ferry, Cheshire; *S* father, 1924. *Heir: b* Neale Hutchinson, *b* 22 Oct. 1880. *Address:* Syngefield, Birr, King's Co.

Died 21 Dec. 1942.

SYNNOT, Brig.-Gen. Arthur Henry Seton H.; *see* Hart-Synnot.

SYNNOTT, Bt Lt-Col Wilfrid Thomas, DSO 1917; retired pay; late RGA; *b* 1877; *s* of Thomas Synnott of Innismore, Co. Dublin; *m* 1907, Gwendoline Hermione, *d* of Capt. Keown-Boyd. *Educ:* Stonyhurst. Entered RA 1898; Major, RFA 1915; served S African War; European War (despatches thrice, DSO).

Died 18 Jan. 1941.

SYRETT, Netta; novelist. *Educ:* The North London Collegiate School for Girls. *Publications:* Novels—Nobody's Fault; The Tree of Life; Rosanne; The Day's Journey; The Child of Promise; Anne Page; A Castle of Dreams; Olivia L. Carew; Drender's Daughter; Three Women; Barbara of the Thorn; The Jam Queen, 1914; The Victorians, 1915; Rose Cottingham Married, 1916; Troublers of the Peace, 1917; The Wife of a Hero, 1918; The God of Chance, 1920; One of Three, 1921; Lady Jem, 1922; The House in Garden Square, 1924; The Path to the Sun, 1924; As the Stars Come Out. 1925; The Mystery of Jenifer; Julian Carroll; The Shuttles of Eternity, 1928; Portrait of a Rebel; Strange Marriage, 1930; The Manor House, 1932; Sketches of European History, 1932; Aunt Elizabeth, 1933; Linda, 1935; The Farm on the Downs, 1936; Angel Unawares, 1937; Fulfilment, 1938; The Sheltering Tree (Autobiography), 1939; The House that Was; For Children—Six Fairy Plays; Godmother's Garden; Toby and the Odd Beasts; Seven Wonders; Magic London.

Died 15 Dec. 1943.

SZARVASY, Frederick Alexander. Chairman Amalgamated Anthracite Colleries Ltd, British Anthracite Sales Ltd, Gresham Mutual Indemnity Ltd and Anglo-Federal Banking Corporation Ltd; Director Daily Mail and General Trust Ltd, Martin's Bank Ltd (London Board), Guardian Assurance Co. Ltd, Dunlop Cotton Mills Ltd, Dunlop Rubber Co. Ltd, Hellenic and General Trust Ltd, and Nineteen Twenty-Eight Investment Trust Ltd. *Address:* 74 Portland Place, W1.

Died 3 July 1948.

T

TADEMA, Anna A.; see Alma-Tadema.

TAGORE, Hon. Maharaja Bahadur Sir Prodyot Coomar, KCIE 1936; Kt 1906; b 17 Sept. 1873; o s of late Maharaja Bahadur Sir Jotindra Mohun Tagore, KCSI, Calcutta; m 1892, Sooraja Bala, d of Nirode Nath Mookerjee, Sheriff of Calcutta, 1909. Hon. Sec. British Indian Association, 1899–1911; Trustee and Chairman, Indian Museum; Hon. Presidency Magistrate, Calcutta; Fellow Royal Photographic Society of Great Britain; Member of Asiatic Society of Bengal; served for six years as a Commissioner of the Corporation of Calcutta; Governor, Mayo Hospital; Member, Government Fisheries Board; formerly Member Bengal Legislative Council; Hon. Sec. Imperial Reception Committee, 1911–12; represented the City of Calcutta at the Coronation of King Edward VII; President Calcutta Silver Jubilee Celebration Committee. *Recreations:* music, photography, and motoring. *Address:* Tagore Castle, Calcutta; The Prasad, Calcutta; Emerald Bower, Calcutta; Haradham Palace, Benares; Tagore Cot, Madhupur, India. *Clubs:* Calcutta, Calcutta.

Died 28 Aug. 1942.

TAGORE, Sir Rabindranath, Kt 1915; DLit (Calcutta Univ., Hindu Univ., Benares, Dacca Univ., Dacca and Osmania Univ., Hyderabad); DLitt Oxford; b 6 May 1861; s of Maharshi Debendra Nath Tagore; g s of Prince Dwarkanath Tagore; m 1883; one s one d. *Educ:* privately. Lived at Calcutta first; went to the country at the age of 24 to take charge of his father's estates; there he wrote many of his works; he founded (1901) a school at Santiniketan, Bolpur, Bengal, which later developed into an International Institution, called Visva-Bharati; this has been his life-work ever since; visited England, 1912, and translated some of his Bengali works into English; visited Europe several times; Japan, Soviet Russia, China, USA, S America, Persia, Canada; writes regularly in the Visvabharati Quarterly; Nobel Prize for Literature, 1913; delivered the Hibbert Lectures at Oxford, 1930; took to painting at age of 68; pictures exhibited in Moscow, Berlin, Munich, Paris, Birmingham and New York. *Publications:* about 60 poetical works and numerous prose works, including novels, short stories, essays, sermons, dramas, etc.; is also a musical composer, having written and set to music over 3000 songs. In English—Gitanjali, 1912; The Gardener, The Crescent Moon, Chitra, 1913; The King of the Dark Chamber; The Post Office, a Play; Sādhanā, 1914; Kabir's Poems, 1915; Fruit-Gathering; Stray Birds; Hungry Stones, 1916; Sacrifice, and other plays; Cycle of Spring; Reminiscences; Personality; Nationalism, 1917; Lover's Gift; Mashi, and other stories; Parrot's Training; Stories from Tagore, 1918; The Home and the World, 1919; The Wreck, 1921; Glimpses of Bengal; Thought Relics, 1921; The Fugitive, 1921; Creative Unity, 1922; Greater India, 1923; Gora, a novel; Letters from Abroad; Eye Sore; Red Oleander, a Play, 1924; Broken Ties (Stories), 1925; Fire-Flies, 1928; Letters to a Friend, 1928; The Religion of Man, 1931. *Address:* Santiniketan, Bengal, India.

Died 7 Aug. 1941.

TAIT, Rev. Arthur James, DD; Canon Residentiary of Peterborough since 1924; b 8 Nov. 1872; s of late George Martin Tait (of HM Customs, London) and Alice Maberby; m 1898, Jane Dumerque (d 1943), e d of Rt Rev. T. W. Drury, DD; two s two d. *Educ:* St Lawrence College, Ramsgate; Merchant Taylors' School, London; St John's College and Ridley Hall, Cambridge (2nd class Classical Tripos; 1st class Theological Tripos). Foundation Scholar and Naden Divinity Student of St John's College, Cambridge; Tutor CMS College, Islington, 1896–98. Assistant Curate of Holy Trinity Church, Eastbourne, under Rev. W. A. Bathurst, MA, 1893–1901; Principal, St Aidan's Theological College, Birkenhead, 1901–07; Principal, Ridley Hall, Cambridge, 1907–27. *Publications:* Christ and the Nations; Lecture Outlines on the Articles; The Heavenly Session of Our Lord; Christus Redemptor; The Prophecy of Micah: The Nature and Functions of the Sacraments; At the King's Table; Sacrament and Presence; Charles Simeon and his Trust. *Address:* Minster Precincts, Peterborough.

Died 3 April 1944.

TAIT, Adm. Sir Campbell; see Tait, Adm. Sir W. E. C.

TAIT, George Hope, FSA (Scot.); Town Magistrate, Galashiels; JP; decorative artist and designer; b 1861; m 1897, K. Riach, Edin.; five d. *Educ:* Innerleithen; Edinburgh Art School. Decorative art painting, journalism; author of many articles on Historic Border Lore; won British Competition for a Fresco painting, Interchange of the Nations, 1901; articles and lectures on the literature of Burns and Scott; discovered the famous lines of the Scott Clarion in the Bee, 1916; proposed and carried through the presentation of a Pennon to FM Earl Haig of Bemersyde, 1920; founder and literary correspondent of the Abbotsford Scott Fellowship; promoter of historic wayside records and memorials in the Border country; carried through International Memorial at Mercat Cross of Galashiels, commemorating marriage of James IV of Scotland with Margaret Tudor of England, which led to Union of the Crowns in 1603. *Publications:* Rab and his Maister; A Highland Arcadia; The Gala Raid, 1545; author of many martial poems and songs, including The Gates of the Borderland, The Roman Charioteer, The Blinded Warrior, Poems of the Borderland, 1941. *Recreations:* hill walking, golf. *Address:* Quair House, Galashiels. *T:* Gala 2107. *Clubs:* Unionist, Galashiels.

Died 24 Jan. 1943.

TAIT, James; b Manchester, 19 June 1863; 2nd s of Robert Tait. *Educ:* private school; Owens College (Scholar, MA Vict. 1886; LittD Manchester 1920); Balliol College, Oxford (Exhibitioner, MA 1891, Hon. DLitt 1933). Fellow of Pembroke College, Oxford, 1890; Hon. Fellow, 1933. Examiner in Honours School of Modern History, 1897–99; Assistant Lecturer in History and English Literature, Owens College, 1887; Lecturer in Ancient History, 1896; Warburton Lecturer, 1900; Professor of Ancient and Mediæval Hist. 1902–19; Honorary Professor, 1920; FBA 1921–44; Pres. Chetham Society, 1915–25; President of the English Place-Name Soc., 1923–32; Chairman of the Manchester Univ. Press, 1925–35; Governor of John Rylands Library, 1929–32. *Publications:* Mediæval Manchester and the Beginnings of Lancashire, 1904; History of Mediæval Lancashire (Victoria County Histories), 1908; Chronica Johannis de Reading et Anonymi Cantuariensis, 1346–1367, 1914; Domesday Survey of Cheshire, 1916, Lancashire Quarter Sessions Records, Vol. I, 1918, Chartulary of Chester Abbey, 1920–1923. Taxation in Salford Hundred 1524–1802, 1924 (Chetham Society); The Study of Early Municipal History in England (British Academy), 1922; (with the late A. Ballard) British Borough Charters, 1216–1307, 1923; The Medieval English Borough, 1936; (with Mrs Varley) A Middlewich Chartulary, Part II (Chetham Soc.), 1944; numerous contributions to the Dictionary of National Biography, etc. *Recreation:* walking. *Address:* 28 Hawthorn Lane, Wilmslow, Manchester. *T:* Wilmslow 3592.

Died 4 July 1944.

TAIT, John, MD (Edin.), DSc (Edin.); Emeritus Professor of Physiology, McGill University, Montreal, since 1939; *b* Orkney, 1878; *e s* of Jas Tait, Merchant, Kirkwall; *m* Jean Carlisle, *y d* of Robert Bowie, Edinburgh; one *s* three *d*. *Educ:* Edinburgh; Göttingen; Berlin, Milner Fothergill Medal (Therapeutics), MD Gold Medal Thesis; Neill Medal, Royal Society, Edinburgh. *Publications:* numerous papers on physiological journals and Equilibrial Labyrinth, in Nelson Loose-leaf Medicine of the Ear. *Address:* Lower Midgarth, Stronsay, Kirkwall, Scotland.

Died 21 Oct. 1944.

TAIT, Sir Thomas, Kt 1911; LLD 1928; Knight of Grace of the Order of St John of Jerusalem in England; President of Montreal Citizens' Recruiting Association and Director-General of National Service, Canada, in 1915 and 1916; *b* Melbourne, Province of Quebec, 24 July 1864; *s* of Sir Melbourne Tait, late Chief Justice of Superior Court, and Monica Holmes; *m* 1890, Emily St Aubert, *d* of late George R. R. Cockburn, Toronto, and Mary Zane, Louisville. *Educ:* High School and McGill University, Montreal. Entered Railway Service, 1880; filled various positions with Grand Trunk and Canadian Pacific Railway Companies, becoming Assistant General Manager (all lines), Manager of Eastern lines, and Manager of Transportation (all lines) with latter Company; Chairman of the Commissioner of the Victorian (Australia) State Railways, 1903–10; Hon. President Montreal Branch, Royal Empire Society, 1930–31. *Address:* 762 Sherbrooke Street West, Montreal; Links Crest, St Andrews By-the-Sea, New Brunswick, Canada. *Clubs:* Mount Royal, Montreal.

Died 25 July 1940.

TAIT, Adm. Sir (William Eric) Campbell, KCB 1943; CB 1940; MVO 1917; retired; Governor of Southern Rhodesia since 1945; *b* 1886; *s* of late Deputy Surgeon-General William Tait, MB, RN (retired), of Kirknewton, Alverstoke, Hants; *m* 1919, Katie Cynthia, *d* of late Captain H. H. Grenfell, RN; two *d*. Served European War; Royal Yacht Victoria and Albert, 1919–21; Commander HMS Hawkins, flagship China Station, 1921–23; Captain, HMS Dragon, Mediterranean Station, 1928; HMS Capetown and HMS Delhi, America and West Indies Station, 1929–31; Deputy Director of Naval Intelligence, Admiralty, 1932–33; on staff of Commander-in-Chief, China, 1933–34; commanded HMS Shropshire, 1934–37; Commodore, 2nd Class, in charge of RN Barracks, Portsmouth, 1937–39; ADC to the King, 1938; Rear-Admiral, 1938; Vice-Admiral, 1941; Admiral, 1945; Director of Personal Services, 1941; C-in-C, South Atlantic Station, 1942–44. *Address:* Government House Salisbury, S Rhodesia. *Club:* United Service.

Died 17 July 1946.

TAITE, Charles Davis; *b* 30 Dec. 1872; *s* of William Alfred Taite and Susan Little; *m* 1908, Eleanor Kathleen Corneille; one *s* one *d*. *Educ:* Norwich Grammar School; Technical Training, Faraday House. Apprenticeship, Ronald A. Scott, Acton. Staff of Ferranti Ltd, 1893–95; Electrical Engineer to Corporation of Southport, 1895–1900; Salford, 1901–06; Served European War in 8th Lancashire Fusiliers as Capt. on retirement; Past Pres. of the Incorporated Association of Electric Power Coys; Member of the Lancashire Industrial Development Council; retired, 1947. *Publications:* technical papers and articles in the technical and daily press. *Recreation:* golf. *Address:* Fairlie, Catherine Road, Bowdon, Cheshire. *Club:* Devonshire.

Died 1 Feb. 1948.

TAITT, Rt Rev. Francis Marion, STD, LLD, LittD; Bishop of Pennsylvania since 1931; *b* 3 Jan. 1862; *s* of James Monroe Taitt and Elizabeth Ward Conway; unmarried. *Educ:* Central High, Philadelphia Divinity School; extra work at University of Pennsylvania. Assistant at St Peter's, Philadelphia, 1883–87; Rector of Trinity Church, Southwark, Philadelphia, 1887–93; St Paul's, Chester, Pennsylvania, 1893–1929; Bishop Coadjutor of Pennsylvania, 1929–31; STD University of Pennsylvania, 1930; STD Philadelphia Divinity School, 1930; LLD Temple University, 1932; LittD Hahnemann, 1937. *Address:* 202 S 19th Street, Philadelphia, Pa, USA. *T:* Spruce 6650.

Died 17 July 1943.

TALBOT DE MALAHIDE, 6th Baron *cr* 1831; **James Boswell Talbot**; Baron Talbot of Malahide, Baron Malahide of Malahide, 1831; Baron Talbot de Malahide (UK), 1856; Hereditary Lord Admiral of Malahide and adjacent seas (15 Edward IV); *b* 18 May 1874; *s* of 5th Baron and Emily (*d* 1898), *d* of Sir James Boswell, last Bt; *S* father, 1921; *m* 1924, Joyce Gunning, *er d* of late Frederick Kerr. Owns 300 acres. *Heir: cousin* Milo John Reginald Talbot, *b* 1 Dec. 1912. *Address:* Malahide Castle, Co. Dublin; Mountshannon House, Co. Clare. *Clubs:* Kildare Street, Dublin.

Died 22 Aug. 1948.

TALBOT, Benjamin; JP; Chairman and Managing Director of the Cargo Fleet Iron Company, Limited, and South Durham Steel and Iron Company, Limited, and is interested in many other important iron and steel and colliery undertakings on the north-east coast; *b* 1864; 2nd *s* of Benjamin Talbot, Wellington, Salop; *m* Frances, *d* of J. P. Chapman, Siddington, Cheshire; one *s* two *d*. *Educ:* Fulneck School, nr Leeds. Inventor of the continuous process of steel manufacture which bears his name, also of a mechanical gas producer and of the Talbot hydrocarbon lining; awarded the Elliott Cressen Gold Medal and John Scott Medal of the Franklin Institute of Philadelphia, and the Bessemer Medal of the Iron and Steel Institute, 1908; President of the Iron and Steel Institute and of the National Federation of Iron and Steel Manufacturers, 1928; during War of 1914–18 acted in expert advisory capacity to Ministry of Munitions, and also as a Member of the Departmental Committee of the Board of Trade (1917) to consider the position of the iron and steel trades after the War; Member of the Coal Conservation Committee. *Publications:* papers to the Iron and Steel Institute. *Address:* Solberge, Northallerton. *TA:* Talbot Solberge Northallerton. *T:* Northallerton 40.

Died 16 Dec. 1947.

TALBOT, Rev. Edward Keble, MC; *b* 31 Dec. 1877; *s* of late Rt Rev. Edward Stuart Talbot and Hon. Lavinia Lyttelton; unmarried. *Educ:* Winchester; Christ Church, Oxford, 2nd class Lit.Hum. Ordained, 1904; Curate of S Mary's, Woolwich, 1904–06; joined the Community of the Resurrection, 1906; TCF, 1914–19 (MC); Superior of the Community of the Resurrection, 1922–40; late Chaplain to the King. *Address:* House of the Resurrection, Mirfield Yorkshire. *T:* Mirfield 3318.

Died 21 Oct. 1949.

TALBOT, Lt-Col George James Francis, DSO 1917; late RFA; *b* 1857; *s* of late Capt. George Talbot, CB, Knockmullen, Co. Wexford, and Mary, *e d* of Francis O'Beirne, of Jamestown, Co. Leitrim; *m* 1890, Mary Frederica, *e d* of Henry Schlesinger, 5 Kensington Park Gardens, W; one *s*. *Educ:* Oratory School, Edgbaston; RM Academy, Woolwich. Lieut 1877; served in RFA, RHA, and RGA; retired as Major, 1905; re-employed Oct. 1914 from retired list as Major; formed and trained a Battery of RFA of 14th Div.; temp. Lieut-Col to command a Divisional Ammunition Column; formed and trained same, and commanded it on Active Service overseas, Sept. 1915–May 1918; served South Africa, 1890 (despatches, medal 2 claps); European War (despatches thrice, DSO). *Recreation:* yachting. *Address:* The Oaks, Balcombe, Haywards Heath, Sussex. *TA:* Balcombe. *T:* Balcombe 14. *Club:* Royal Thames Yacht.

Died 15 Feb. 1941.

TALBOT, Sir Gerald Francis, KCVO 1922; CMG 1920; OBE 1919; RNVR; *b* 21 Aug. 1881; *γ s* of late Lt-Col G. F. Talbot and Henrietta Clarissa Noyes, *e d* of Henry M. Bradhurst, New York; *m* 1920, Helène, *widow* of Capt. C. Labouchere, French Army; one *d*. *Educ:* Cheltenham College; Caius College, Cambridge. HBM Naval Attaché at Athens, 1917–20. *Recreations:* shooting, fishing. *Address:* Burnley Hall, East Somerton, Norfolk. *TA:* Winterton. *T:* Winterton 31; 50 Avenue du President Wilson, Paris. *T:* Passy 21.31. *Clubs:* Carlton, Junior Carlton, Royal Automobile.

Died 17 April 1945.

TALBOT, Rt Rev. Neville Stuart, MC, DD; Vicar of St Mary, Nottingham, and Rural Dean of Nottingham, 1933–43; Assistant Bishop of Southwell since 1934; *s* of late Rt Rev. E. S. Talbot; *m* 1918, Cecil Mary (*d* 1921), *o d* of Wm Seymour Eastwood, West Stoke House, Chichester; one *s* one *d*. *Educ:* Haileybury College; Christ Church, Oxford, MA; Cuddesdon College, Oxford. Served in Rifle Brigade, 1899–1903; Deacon, 1908; Priest, 1909; Curate of St Bartholomew, Armley, 1908–09; Examining Chaplain to Archbishop of York, 1909–10; Fellow, Tutor, and Chaplain of Balliol College, Oxford, 1909–14; served as Chaplain (First Class) in France, 1914–19 (MC); Bishop of Pretoria, 1920–33. *Publications:* The Mind of the Disciples, 1914; Thoughts on Religion at the Front, 1917; Thoughts on Unity; Religion behind the Front and after the War; The Returning Tide of Faith; A Biblical Thoroughfare; The Riddle of Life; Great Issues.

Died 3 April 1943.

TALBOT, Percy Amaury, MA, DSc (Oxon); *b* 26 June 1877; *m* 1st, 1903, (*d* 1916); no *c*; 2nd, 1919. *Educ:* University College, Oxford. Assistant Commissioner, Anglo-Liberian Boundary Commission, 1902–03; with Alexander-Gosling Expedition to Lake Chad, 1904–05; Assistant District Commissioner, Southern Nigeria, 1905; Expedition to North Cameroons and French Central Africa, 1910–11; District Commissioner, Southern Nigeria, 1911; Resident, Nigeria, 1921; Seconded as Census Commissioner, 1921; retired from Nigerian Service, 1931; made Natural History and Ethnographical collections, presented to British and other museums, including over 300 flowers new to science; Catalogue of Talbot's Nigerian Plants, published by British Museum, 1913; Silver Medal of the African Society, the first awarded, 1923; all work done in collaboration with wife. *Publications:* Surveying chapters in Boyd Alexander's From the Niger to the Nile, 1907; In the Shadow of the Bush, a study of the Ekoi of Southern Nigeria, 1912; Life in Southern Nigeria. The Magic, Beliefs and Customs of the Ibibio Tribe of Southern Nigeria, 1923; The Peoples of Southern Nigeria (vol. i History; vols ii and iii Ethnology; vol. iv Statistics and Linguistics), 1926; Some Nigerian Fertility Cults, 1927; Tribes of the Niger Delta, 1932. *Address:* c/o Barclays Bank, 19 Fleet Street, EC4.

Died 28 Dec. 1945.

TALBOT, Sir William J., Kt 1935; JP; Chairman, Talbot-Stead Tube Co., Walsall; Chairman, Chesterfield Tube Co. Ltd, Chesterfield; *b* 24 April 1872; *s* of John Farrow Talbot and Ellen Palmer; *m* 1896; one *s* one *d*. *Educ:* George Dixon School, Birmingham; Mason College, Birmingham. Trained as engineer at Bellis and Morcom, Birmingham, after which was awarded Whit. Exhibition; Works' Manager at Perfecta Tube Co., Birmingham, afterwards John Russell and Co. Ltd, Walsall; started Talbot-Stead Tube Co., 1906; President of Walsall Conservative and Unionist Party; Pres. Walsall Chamber of Commerce; Trustee, Walsall National Savings Bank; Walsall General Hospital, etc. High Sheriff

of Staffordshire, 1947–48. *Publications:* various technical papers. *Recreations:* sport, literature. *Address:* Highcroft, Birmingham Road, Walsall. *T:* Walsall 2530. *Clubs:* Constitutional, Junior Carlton; Walsall Unionist (Walsall).

Died 10 Dec. 1947.

TALLIS, Sir George, Kt 1922; Director, late Managing Director, J. C. Williamson, Ltd, theatrical managers; *b* 1869; *s* of John Tallis, Callan, Co. Kilkenny; *m* Millie Young (*d* 1933); three *s* one *d*. Connected with several commercial and industrial enterprises of Australia. *Address:* Beleura, Mornington, Victoria, Australia. *Clubs:* Athenæum, Melbourne.

Died 14 Aug. 1948.

TALVANDE, Countess de M.; *see* Mauny-Talvande.

TANCOCK, Col Osborne Kendall, CMG 1916; RA; retired; *b* Sherborne, 30 Oct. 1866; *e s* of late Rev. Osborne William Tancock, MA; *m* 1894, Theodosia Louisa Hartnell (*d* 1938); one *s* one *d*. *Educ:* Sherborne School; King Edward VI School, Norwich; Royal Military Academy, Woolwich. First Commission, RA, 1886; Lt-Col RGA, 1914; served Chitral, 1895; NW Frontier, India, 1902; East Africa, 1914–16 (despatches, CMG); Palestine, 1917–19. *Address:* 54 Goldington Avenue, Bedford.

Died 12 Nov. 1946.

TANCRED, Vice-Adm. James Charles; retired; *b* 17 Sept. 1864; 2nd *s* of George Tancred, of Weens and Arden; *m* 1901, Cécile Margaret Macmillan-Scott; one *d*. Served Egyptian war, 1882; Naval Superintendent North Sea Fisheries, 1900–03; King's Harbour Master, Malta, 1908–10; Senior Officer Persian Gulf Suppression of Gun-running, 1911–13; European War, 1914–18; retired, 1919. *Address:* Wayside, Exmouth.

Died 9 Dec. 1943.

TANCRED, Maj.-Gen. Thomas Angus, CB 1917; CMG 1915; DSO 1918; late RA; *b* 16 Sept. 1867; 3rd *s* of G. Tancred of Weens, Hawick, Roxburghshire. *Educ:* Harrow. Entered Army, 1886; Capt., 1896; Major, 1904; Lieut-Colonel, 1914; Major-General, 1921; with Bechuanaland Border Police, 1893–96; served Matabeleland, 1893–94; China, 1900 (medal); European War, 1914–17 (despatches six times, CMG, CB, DSO, Bt Col, 1914 Star, Comm. Legion of Honour); retired pay, 1914. *Address:* Murdan, Bieldside, Aberdeen. *T:* Cults 36.

Died 8 July 1944.

TANCRED, Maj. Sir Thomas Selby L.; *see* Lawson-Tancred.

TANDY, Brig. Sir Edward Aldborough, Kt 1929; late RE; *b* 26 Dec. 1871; *e s* of late Col E. O. Tandy, IMS, and Gertrude O'Connor; *m* 1909, Mary, *d* of late George Eaglesome; one *s*. *Educ:* Tonbridge School; RMA, Woolwich. Commissioned Royal Engineers, 1891; India, 1893–1928; Survey of India, 1898–1928; Surveyor-General of India, 1924–28; served Tirah Campaign, 1897–98; Mesopotamia (Works), 1916–17; largely responsible for improvements in organisation of Survey of India. *Publications:* Survey of India publications on scientific and administrative questions; India's Opportunity, 1918; and other papers on the administrative organisation of the Indian Empire; The Circulation of the Earth's Crust (Geographical Journal, May 1921). *Recreations:* most games and forms of sport in the past; Art, Literature and Science. *Address:* 240 Iffley Road, Oxford.

Died 30 Nov. 1950.

TANDY, Col Maurice O'Connor, DSO 1918; OBE 1919 late RE; MA (Oxon); *b* 17 Nov. 1873; 2nd *s* of late Col E. O. Tandy, IMS; *m* 1911, Mabel, *er d* of late James Dillon, of Kingstown, Co. Dublin; two *s* two *d*. *Educ:* Tonbridge School; RMA, Woolwich. Commissioned in

Royal Engineers, 1893; served Chatham, 1893–95; Gibraltar, 1895–98; India, 1898–1928; Lt-Col 1921; Col 1925; served operations in Aden Hinterland, 1902–04; European War in France and Mesopotamia, 1914–18 (despatches, DSO, OBE); Afghan War, 1919 (despatches); Director, Survey of India, 1926; retired from Army, 1928; Instructor in Surveying, Oxford University, 1927–40. *Recreations:* cricket, golf. *Address:* c/o Lloyds Bank, 6 Pall Mall, SW1. *Club:* United Service.

Died 18 April 1942.

TANGYE, Lt-Col Richard Trevithick Gilbertstone, OBE 1917; BA, LLB, DL, JP (Cornwall); Joint Chairman Cornwall Quarter Sessions, 1930 (Chairman since 1941); Assistant Commandant, Cornwall Special Constabulary; *b* 26 June 1875; 3rd *s* of late Sir Richard Tangye and *uncle* of Sir Basil Tangye, Bt; *m* 1903, Sophie Elizabeth Frieda, *d* of James Kidman, Liverpool; three *s*. *Educ:* Bromsgrove; Heidelberg; Trinity College, Cambridge. Called to Bar, Inner Temple, 1899; practised until 1914; served continuously overseas 1914–27 in France and on General Staff, British Army of the Rhine (despatches twice, OBE, 1914 Star, Croix de Guerre avec Palme, Ordre de Léopold); Chairman of Tangyes Ltd, 1930–34; Deputy Licensing Authority for Metropolitan and South-Eastern Traffic Areas, 1934–40. *Recreations:* travel, golf. *Address:* Glendorgal, St Columb Minor, Cornwall. *T:* Newquay 2949; 29 Thackeray Court, Elystan Place, SW3. *T:* Kensington 5891. *Club:* United University.

Died 12 June 1944.

TANNER, Charles Elliott; KC 1895; *b* Pictou, NS, 7 Oct. 1857; father Irish, mother Scotch; *m* 1886, Alicia May McDonald, Pictou; one *s*. *Educ:* Pictou Academy. Studied Law in Pictou. Admitted Bar of NS, 1878; now retired from practice, Member, Legislature of Nova Scotia, 1894; House leader of Conservative Opposition; 1911; called to Senate of Canada, 1917. *Recreation:* interested and participant in current games and sports. *Address:* Pictou, NS.

Died 13 Jan. 1946.

TANNER, Henry, FRIBA; Architect; Member of Court of Common Council, City Corporation; *b* 26 June 1876; *s* of late Sir Henry Tanner; *m* 1938, Lucy Jacks. *Educ:* Merchant Taylors; Royal Academy Schools (Travelling Studentship); Matriculated London University. Past Pres. of Architectural Assoc., London; carried out with his firm many large buildings in London; Past Master of Worshipful Company of Glaziers. *Publications:* English Interior Woodwork; Some works of Inigo Jones (with H. I. Triggs); English Doorways (with G. Davie). *Recreation:* golf. *Address:* 134 Fenchurch Street, EC3. *T:* Mansion House 9463. *Clubs:* Conservative; Royal St Georges, Sandwich.

Died 22 Jan. 1947.

TANNER, Maj.-Gen. William Ernest Collins, CB 1919; CMG 1916; DSO 1918; *b* Fort Jackson, 16 Nov. 1875; *m* 1909, Isobel Erskine; two *s*. *Educ:* Hilton College, Natal; Pietermaritzburg Coll. Lt in Natal Carabineers and Scottish Horse. Staff Officer, Permanent Staff of Natal Militia, 1903; student at Royal Staff College, 1909–10; at Union of South African Colonies, appointed District Staff Officer No. 4 District, Natal; Permanent Force Staff, commanded 2nd S African Infantry, 8th Infantry Brigade, and 1st SA Infantry Brigade; served South African War (King's and Queen's medal, Siege of Ladysmith); Zululand Rebellion, 1906; German South-West Campaign, Egypt, France, and Flanders 1914–18; Adjutant-General, Union Defence Forces. *Address:* Glen Erskine, Elgin, Cape, S Africa.

Died 29 Sept. 1943.

TANQUEREY, F. J.; B ès Sc. (Rennes), D ès L (Paris). University Professor of French Language and Literature at Birkbeck College since 1925; Officier d'Académie; Lauréat de l'Institut; Assistant Lecturer, Victoria University, Manchester, 1906–09; Lecturer in French Language and Literature, University of St Andrews, 1909–25. *Publications:* L'évolution du Verbe en Anglo-français; Recueil de Lettres Anglo-françaises (1265–1399); Les Plaintes de la Vierge; Le Roman des Romans, etc. *Address:* Birkbeck College, Bream's Buildings, EC.

Died 24 March 1942.

TARBOLTON, Harold Ogle, RSA 1934; firm of H. O. Tarbolton and Sir Matthew M. Ochterlony, Bt, FFRIBA; *s* of Marriott Ogle Tarbolton, CE, Nottingham, and E. M. Stanfield, Wakefield, Yorks; *m* 1897, Beatrice Dudgeon (*d* 1943), 2nd *d* of Charles Gulland of Falkland, Fife; no *c*. *Educ:* Chigwell, Essex; RA School of Architecture. Articled to Geo. T. Hine, FRIBA, Nottingham and London; works in recent years include the completion of Bermuda Cathedral; Church of St Theresa and other buildings in that Colony; Pattishall House, Northamptonshire; Elsie Inglis Memorial Hospital, Edinburgh; Blackhouse, Ayr; Church of Our Lady, Bangour; St Bride's Church, Glasgow; Member Royal Fine Art Commission for Scotland since 1938; Advisory Architect to the North of Scotland Hydro-Electric Board; Consulting Architect to the Deans and Chapters of St Ninian's Cathedral, Perth, and Oban Cathedral, Argyllshire. *Publications:* various papers on Architectural and Building Subjects. *Recreations:* fishing and golf. *Address:* (office) 4 St Colme Street, Edinburgh. *T:* 27442. *Clubs:* Caledonian United Service, Edinburgh; Scottish Automobile, Glasgow.

Died 31 July 1947.

TARDIEU, André Pierre Gabriel Amedée; Officer Legion of Honour; War Cross; *b* Paris, 22 Sept. 1876. *Educ:* Lycée Condorcet; Ecole Normale Supérieure. Attaché at Berlin, 1897; to the Minister of Foreign Affairs, 1898; Secretary Council of Ministers, 1899–1902; Member of the French Chamber of Deputies, 1914–36; High Commissioner of France to the US (1917–19); Secretary of Franco-American War Co-operation; Minister of Liberated Regions, 1919–20; French Plenipotentiary at the Peace Conference, 1919–20; Minister of Public Works, 1926–28; Minister of Interior, 1928–30, and 1930; Prime Minister, 1929–30, and 1930; Minister of Agriculture, 1931–32; Minister of War, 1932; Prime Minister and Minister for Foreign Affairs, 1932; Minister without portfolio, 1934. *Publications:* Questions diplomatiques de l'année 1904; La Conference d'Algésiras; Notes sur les Etats-Unis, 1908; France and the Alliances, 1909; Le Prince de Bülow, 1909; Le Mystère d'Agadir, 1912; L'Amerique en Armes, 1918; The Truth about the Treaty, 1921; France and America, 1927; L'épreuve du pouvoir, 1931; Devant le pays, 1932; L'heure de la décision, 1934; La réforme de l'Etat, 1934; Sur la pente, 1935; Le Souverain captif, 1936; La Profession parlementaire 1937; L'Année de Munich, 1939. *Address:* Menton, Alpes Maritimes.

Died 15 Sept. 1945.

TARKINGTON, Booth, LHD, LittD; *b* Indianapolis, 29 July 1869; *s* of John S. Tarkington and Elizabeth Booth; *m* 1912; one *d*. *Educ:* Exeter Academy; Princeton University. Member American Academy and National Institute Arts and Letters; Medal of the Institute for Fiction, 1933; the Pulitzer Prize, 1918 and 1921; Theo. Roosevelt Memorial Medal for Lit. Distinction, 1943; Acad. Medal for Fiction, 1945; Member Authors' League; Member Indiana Legislature, 1903. *Publications:* The Gentleman from Indiana, 1899; Monsieur Beaucaire, 1900; The Two Van Revels, 1902; Cherry, 1903; In the Arena, 1905; The Conquest of Canaan, 1905; The Beautiful Lady, 1905; His Own People, 1907; The Guest of Quesnay, 1908; Beasley's Christmas Party,

1909; Beauty and the Jacobin, 1912; The Flirt, 1913; Penrod, 1914; The Turmoil, 1915; Seventeen, 1916; The Magnificent Ambersons, 1918; Alice Adams, 1921; Gentle Julia, 1922; The Midlander, 1924; Women, 1926; The Plutocrat, 1927; Claire Ambler, 1928; The World does Move, 1929; Young Mrs Greeley, 1929; Mirthful Haven, 1930; Mary's Neck, 1931; Wanton Mally, 1933; Presenting Lily Mars, 1934; Little Orvie, 1935; The Lorenzo Bunch, 1936; Mr White, The Red Barn, Hell, and Bridewater, 1937; Rumbin Galleries, 1937; Some Old Portraits, 1938; The Heritage of Hatcher Ide, 1939; The Fighting Littles, 1941; Kate Fennigate, 1942; Image of Josephine, 1945. *Plays:* Monsieur Beaucaire, 1902; The Man from Home, 1907; Cameo Kirby, 1908; Springtime, 1909; Getting a Polish, 1910 (all with Harry Leon Wilson); The Man on Horseback, 1912; Your Humble Servant, 1909; Mister Antonio, 1915; The Country Cousin (with Julian Street), 1916; Up from Nowhere, 1919; Clarence, 1919; Poldekin, 1920; The Gibson Upright, 1920; Magnolia, 1922; Tweedles, 1923; The Wren, 1923; The Intimate Strangers, 1923; Rose Briar, 1924; Colonel Satan, 1930. *Address:* 4270 N Meridian Street, Indianapolis, USA.

Died 19 May 1946.

TARRANT, William Charles, CBE 1936; OBE 1919; Master, Merchant Navy, Royal Mail Lines Ltd; *b* 25 June 1881; *s* of William Charles and Sophia Amelia Tarrant; *m* 1910; one *s* two *d*. *Educ:* High School, Simonstown. Went to sea in 1897 as an apprentice in sail; midshipman RNR, 1899; after 6 years in sailing ships went into steamers; joined Royal Mail Steam Packet Co., 1906; served in Royal Navy, 1914–19 (despatches twice, OBE); Captain RNR 1930; RNR, ADC of King George V and Edward VIII. *Address:* Field House, Castle Avenue, Havant, Hants. *T:* Havant 355. *Club:* Master Mariners'.

Died 30 April 1941.

TARVER, Maj.-Gen. Alexander Leigh, CB 1922; CIE 1920; DSO 1908; Indian Army, retired; late 124th Duchess of Connaught's Own Baluchistan Infantry; *b* 30 Aug. 1871; *m* 1897, Anna Beatrice Fanny Wadeson. Joined Royal Welsh Fusiliers, 1890; Captain, Indian Army, 1901; Major, 1908; Major-Gen., 1923; served East Africa, 1895–96 (medal); Tirah, 1897–98 (medal with two clasps); Zakka Khel and Mohmand expeditions, 1908 (medal with clasp, DSO); European War, 1915–16 (prom. Brevet Lt-Col); Afghan War, 1919 (CIE); ADC to the King and Bt Col 1918; GOC 14th Indian Infantry Brigade, 1921–24; 22nd Indian Infantry Brigade, 1924–26; Commanded Madras District, 1926–30; retired, 1930. *Address:* Easton Maudit, Forest Road, Bournemouth.

Died 10 Dec. 1941.

TATE, Maj.-Gen. Godfrey, CIE 1930; IMS (retd); *b* 5 March 1873; 4th *s* of John Tate, Downpatrick, Co. Down; *m* 1907, Dorothy, 2nd *d* of late Edmund Beeton; three *d*. *Educ:* RAI Belfast; Trinity College, Dublin. Entered IMS 1898; MO 22nd Sam Browne's Cavalry FF; Surgeon to C in C India, 1913–16; Civil Surgeon Simla East, 1914–19; Professor Medical College, Lahore, 1920; Administrative appointments: Chief Medical Officer NWFP and IGCH Punjab (acting); IGCH, UP and Surgeon General with the Government of Bengal; Field Service, China, 1900–01, Mohmand and Zakka Khel Expeditionary Forces, 1908; VHS 1926; KHS 1928; Governor and Medical Superintendent King Edward VII Convalescent Home, Osborne, 1931–35. *Recreations:* hunting, shooting, golf. *Address:* Knowle Cottage, Beaminster, Dorset. *T:* Beaminster 280. *Clubs:* Overseas; Royal Calcutta Turf, Calcutta.

Died 29 July 1944.

TATE, Mavis Constance; *d* of late Guy Weir Hogg; *m* 1st, Captain Gerald Ewart Gott; 2nd, Henry Burton Tate (from whom she obtained a divorce, 1944). *Educ:* privately; St Paul's Girls' School. Contested Islington in the LCC Election, March 1931; JP MP (National) West Willesden, 1931–35; MP (Nat. C) Frome division of Somerset, 1935–45. *Recreations:* gardening, reading and travelling. *Address:* 6 Bloomfield Terrace, SW1.

Died 5 June 1947.

TATTERSALL, John Lincoln; Chairman, NCT League and L and C Band of Hope; *b* 16 April 1865. MP (L) Stalybridge, 1923–24. *Address:* Woodeaves, Prestbury, Cheshire.

Died 6 June 1942.

TATTERSALL, Rev. Thomas Newell, DSO 1917; Baptist minister; Pastor of Marshall Street Church, Edinburgh, since 1937; *b* Rishton, 12 July 1879; *s* of Thomas Tattersall; *m* 1906, Harriet Jane Brook, Nelson, Lancs; one *s* two *d*. *Educ:* Brighton Grove College, Manchester. Began ministry at Maryport, 1905; Fulham, London, 1909; Fuller Kettering, 1913; Chaplain to the Forces, 1914–17 (despatches thrice, DSO); Adelaide Place, Glasgow, 1921; Mount Pleasant, Swansea, 1924–29; St Clair Avenue, Toronto, 1930. *Publications:* The Man who Refused a Kingdom; Spiritual Life and Social Service. *Recreation:* golf. *Address:* Marshall Street Baptist Church, Edinburgh.

Died 1 March 1943.

TATTERSALL, William Boothman; Chairman, W. B. Tattersall Ltd; R. E. Taylor & Son, Ltd; National Publicity Co. Ltd; *b* Accrington, 1873; *m* 1896; one *s* one *d*. *Educ:* Blackburn. Founded and developed a series of trade and technical publications; Vice-Chairman, Fancy Goods Section, London Chamber of Commerce. *Publications:* The Sports Trader; The Toy Trader; The Fancy Goods Trader; Leather Goods, and others. *Recreations:* motor-boat racing; winner of Trophy de Paris and many other speed-boat contests and trophies. *Address:* 43/44 Shoe Lane, EC4. *TA:* Unitrader London. *T:* Central 7871. *Clubs:* Constitutional, British Motor Boat; Alexandra Yacht; Westcliff Yacht; Benfleet Yacht.

Died 8 July 1943.

TAUBER, Richard; Kammersanger; singer, composer, conductor; *b* Linz on Danube, Austria, 16 May 1891; *s* of late A. Richard Tauber, Generalintendant; became a British subject, 1940; *m* Diana Napier. *Educ:* Conservatoire, Frankfurt am Main (conductor); Freiburg (Baden) with Prof. Carl Beines (singer). Debut in Chemnitz, later State Operas, Dresden, Wien, Berlin; Concerts and Guest performances in all Europe, America, Australia and Africa. *Principal parts:* Octavio, Tamino, Belmonte; Rudolf, Pinkerton, Kalaf, Cavaradossi; Alfred, Richard; Almaviva, Faust, Hoffman, Don José, Canio, Turiddo, Pedro, Hans, Mathias; Operetta; Eisenstein, Barinkay and numerous Lehar Operettas; composer of Der Singende Traum (first produced 1934 in Vienna, Theater an der Wien), and Old Chelsea (17 Feb. 1943 Princes Theatre, London), symphonic music and Lieder; conducted leading orchestras in Europe, America, Australia and Africa. English Films: Blossom Time, Heart's Desire, Land Without Music, Pagliacci; Kt cross 1st class of Austrian Order of Merit; Royal Swedish Wasa Order, 1st Class; Kt of French Légion d'honneur; Hon. Chamberlain of St Loretto House. *Recreations:* motoring, cine-camera. *Address:* Grosvenor House, W1.

Died 8 Jan. 1948.

TAUBMAN, Frank Mowbray; *b* London, 1868; *e s* of late Robert Taubman, Ballaugh, Isle of Man; unmarried. *Educ:* privately; Univ. Coll. School, Gower Street. Studied chemistry under Redwood, Attfield, and Wyndham Dunstan; attended evening classes at Lambeth, sculpture under W. S. Frith; went to Paris 1893, Julian's Atelier, under Puèch, and Jardin des Plantes (animals), under Frémiet. After six months went to Brussels to study under Charles Vander Stappen at Académie des Beaux Arts et École des Arts Décoratifs, Ville de Bruxelles; double gold medallist, année scolaire,

1893–94; proxime accessit in Grand Concours, 1894–95; returned London, 1897; represented at RA 30 times since 1894. 6 months' visit to Canada, 1906; Statue of Canada (RA 1907) to University College School unveiled there. Memorials in Scotland, Dublin, Bristol, Calcutta, Salisbury S Rhodesia, London, etc.; exhibited ROI, RSPP, London, Birmingham, Cheltenham, Edinburgh, Glasgow, Winnipeg, Rome, Venice, New York Vienna (Cartoons). Left London Nov. 1933; since then exhibited chiefly with Cotswold Art Club, Cheltenham Art Gallery. One Man Exhibition there of Sculpture, 1940. Three Equestrian Groups: The Greek Captive, or the Revenge of Semiramis, RA, 1924; Elaphebolia—The Deer Hunting, RA, 1926; Helios, RA, 1930; Monument, Samson, RA, 1932; The Dance, RA, 1935. St George, Coronation 1937, and about 40 other medals designed since War of 1914–18. Served LDV 1940, until formation of HG (retired on age), ARP Warden. *Publications:* occasional verse (privately). *Recreations:* caricaturing brother artists, trying to play cricket (Artists' CC and Old Gowers CC), and most other games when younger. *Address:* Brook Side, Kemerton, Tewkesbury, Gloucester.

Died 9 Dec. 1946.

TAUNTON, Agnes, CBE 1935; JP; Social Worker at Birmingham Citizens' Society; *b* 1877; *d* of Frederick Hill, Merchant, Birmingham; *m* 1897, Richard Cromwell Taunton. *Educ:* Church of England College; Weimar, Germany. Social Worker for Birmingham Citizens' Society; Hon. Sec. for Cases' Committee at their Offices since 1916; Vice-President Birmingham Girl Guides Committee; Vice-President Society for Prevention of Nervous Diseases; Member of Sutton War Pensions Committee; also Birth Control Committee; Chairman Women's Advisory Committee of Birmingham Board for Occupational Work. *Publications:* Short stories in various magazines; Translations from German and French. *Recreation:* bridge.

Died 25 April 1941.

TAUSSIG, Francis William, PhD, LLB, LittD, LLD; Professor of Economics Harvard University, 1892; Emeritus, 1935; *b* 28 Dec. 1859. *Educ:* Harvard. Successively instructor, assistant professor, and professor in Harvard Univ.; editor of Quarterly Journal of Economics, 1897–1937; President of American Economic Association, 1903–05; Chairman of the United States Tariff Commission, 1917–19; Foreign Member of British Academy and of the Italian Accademia dei Lincei. *Publications:* The Tariff History of the United States, 1st ed. 1888, 9th ed. 1930; The Silver Situation in the United States, 1st ed. 1890, 3rd ed. 1896; Wages and Capital, 1896; Principles of Economics, 1911, 4th ed., 1939; Inventors and Money-makers, 1915; Some Aspects of the Tariff Question, 3rd edition, 1930; Free Trade, Reciprocity and the Tariff, 1920; International Trade, 1927; American Business Leaders, 1932. *Address:* Harvard University, Cambridge, Mass, USA.

Died 11 Nov. 1940.

TAYLOR, Alfred Edward, MA (Oxon); DLitt (St Andrews); LittD (Manchester); LLD (Aber.); LLD (St Andrews); FBA; Professor of Moral Philosophy in Edinburgh University, 1924–41, Professor Emeritus since 1941; Hon. Fellow of New College, Oxford; *b* 22 Dec. 1869; *s* of Rev. A. Taylor; *m* 1900, Lydia Jutsum (*d* 1938), 2nd *d* of Edmund Passmore; one *s. Educ:* Kingswood School, Bath; New College, Oxford (Scholar). Fellow of Merton College, Oxford, 1891–98, re-elected, 1901; Green Moral Philosophy Prizeman, University of Oxford, 1899. Assistant Lecturer, Greek and Philosophy, Owens College, Manchester, 1896–1903; Frothingham Professor of Philosophy in McGill University, Montreal, 1903–08; Professor of Moral Philosophy in St Andrews University, 1908–24; Examiner in Philosophy to University of Manchester,

1911–13, to University of Birmingham, 1913, to University of Wales and Queen's University of Belfast, 1914; Gifford Lecturer in the University of St Andrews, 1926–28. *Publications:* The Problem of Conduct, 1901; Elements of Metaphysics, 1903; Aristotle on his Predecessors, 1906; Plato and Thomas Hobbes in Philosophies Ancient and Modern, 1908; Epicurus in Philosophies Ancient and Modern, 1911; Varia Socratica, First Series, 1911; Aristotle in The People's Books, 1912; St Thomas Aquinas as a Philosopher, 1924; De Morgan Formal Logic (edited), 1926; Plato, the Man and his Work, 1927; Francis Bacon (Annual Master-Mind Lecture), 1926; David Hume and the Miraculous (Leslie Stephen Lecture), 1927; A Commentary on Plato's Timæus, 1928; Plato and the Authorship of the Epinomis, 1930; The Faith of a Moralist, 1930; Socrates, 1933; Philosophical Studies, 1934; Ancient and Mediaeval Philosophy, European Civilization, vol. iii, 1935; Modern Philosophy, European Civilization, vol. vi 1937; The Christian Hope of Immortality, 1938; The Problem of Evil, 1929; articles in Encyclopædias, etc.; various translations of Plato. *Address:* The University, Edinburgh.

Died 31 Oct. 1945.

TAYLOR, Col Bertie Harry Waters, CB 1932; CBE 1919; late Prince of Wales's Volunteers; *e s* of late Colonel H. Taylor and Agnes Dorothea Waters, Sarnau, Carmarthenshire; *m* Marjorie Alexander (*d* 1929), *d* of late A. de Lande Long, Crosby Cote, Northallerton, and Mrs A. de Lande Long, Thorpe Hall, Castle Barnard. S Africa, 1893–1902; served in Cape Mounted Riflemen; Annexation of Pondo Land, Griqua Rebellion, S African War; Commission in Royal Berkshire Regt for service in the field; served on staff (Queen's medal 4 clasps, King's medal 2 clasps, despatches); N Territories of Gold Coast in WAFF; Commissioner Salaga and Black Volta Province; transferred to South Staffordshire Regt; Nigeria, 1909–10 (WAGS medal, clasp); European War Australian and New Zealand Forces in 1915; Staff Delta and Western Force, EEF, and Force in Egypt, 1916–17; AA and QMG, 54th Division, 1918; occupied Enemy Territory Administration South; acted as Military Governor, Jerusalem; Military Governor, Galilee; Colonel General Staff (OET), GHQ; Chief of Staff, OETAS (despatches, six times Bt Lt-Col, CBE, Officier Légion d'Honneur, Order of the Nile 3rd Class, Order of the African Society and Royal Central Asian Nahda, 2nd Class, Order of La Solidaridad 2nd Class), retired pay, 1931. *Recreations:* travelling and golf. *Clubs:* Travellers'; Royal and Ancient, St Andrews; Turf, Cairo.

Died 16 June 1946.

TAYLOR, Lt-Col Charles Newton, CBE 1919; VD; *b* 1866; *s* of late Rev. Robert Taylor, Easter Logie, Blairgowrie, Perthshire; *m* 1895, Helena Jessie, *d* of late John Taylor, The Rocks, Marshfield, Gloucestershire; one *s* (killed on active service, 1940) one *d.* Served European War, 1914–19 (despatches, CBE). *Address:* Lower Holcombe, Uplyme, Lyme Regis. *T:* Lyme Regis 241.

Died 11 May 1949.

TAYLOR, Very Rev. Charles William Gray, CBE 1950; DD; Hon. Chaplain to Forces, 1919; Minister of St George's Parish Church, Edinburgh, since 1918; *b* 1879; *s* of Alexander Taylor and Jane Davidson; *m* 1907, Catharine Beatrice, *d* of James Hawkins Sayer and Ann Eliza Day. *Educ:* Daniel Stewart's College, Edinburgh; University of Edinburgh (MA 1900, DD 1933). Travelling Secretary, 1900–01, London Secretary, 1904–06, Student Christian Movement; First Warden Edinburgh University Settlement, 1906–07; Minister of Glencairn Parish, 1907; Uddingston Parish, 1914; CF in France in European War; Church of Scotland Editor Sunday School Teachers' Magazine, 1921–25; Convener Pastoral Institutes Board, 1925–29; Convener Foreign Mission Committee, 1928–36, 1941–44. Visited India on behalf of Church of Scotland Foreign Mission Committee, 1930–31. Hon. Secretary, Inter-Church Relations Committee; Moderator of General Assembly of Church of Scotland, 1942; Chairman Scottish Advisory Council on treatment and rehabilitation of offenders since 1944. Commissioned by the General Assembly to visit HM Forces in SEAC and CMF, 1945–46. *Publications:* In Search of Scotsmen, notes of a visit to the troops in SEAC and CMF, 1946; pamphlets and magazine articles. *Recreations:* golf, curling, swimming, chess. *Address:* 17 Wester Coates Terrace, Edinburgh. *T:* 63700. *Club:* University (Edinburgh).

Died 21 Sept. 1950.

TAYLOR, Dorothy Daisy C.; *see* Cottington-Taylor.

TAYLOR, Col Ernest Fitzwilliam, CB 1915; late RASC; *b* 16 Nov. 1867; *s* of Rev. Fitzwilliam Taylor, Rector of Ogwell, Newton Abbot, Devon; *m* 1901, Eileen Josephine Mary Bridget, *y d* of late Walter Hussey Walsh, Cranagh and Mulhussey, Co. Roscommon; two *s. Educ:* Newton College, Devon; RMC, Sandhurst. Entered Army (Worcester Regt), 1888; Captain ASC 1896; Major, 1903; Lt-Col 1911; Col 1917; Deputy Assistant Director of Supplies and Transport, Southern Command, 1905–06; served S African War, 1899–1901 (Queen's medal 4 clasps); European War, AA and QMG 15th Division, 1914–18 (despatches, CB); Assistant Director of Military Transport, Woolwich Arsenal, 1919–22; retired pay, 1922.

Died 11 May 1944.

TAYLOR, Fanny Isabel, CBE 1946; OBE 1937; BSc; HM Deputy Inspector of Factories, Home Office, since 1933; 3rd *d* of late William Robert Taylor and Mary Gardner King. *Educ:* Sutton High School, London School of Economics. One of HM Inspectors of Factories; 1909; Superintending Inspector of Factories, 1930; Member of Departmental Committee on the Hours of Employment of Young Persons in certain unregulated occupations, 1937; Technical Adviser to British Government Delegates to nineteenth, twentieth and twenty-eighth sessions of International Labour Conference, Geneva and Paris; Member Institute of International Affairs. *Address:* 48 Coleherne Court, Old Brompton Road, SW5. *T:* Frobisher 0260. *Club:* University Women's.

Died 4 May 1947.

TAYLOR, Lt-Col Hon. Fawcett Gowler, DSO 1917; VD; Judge of His Majesty's Court of King's Bench for Manitoba, since 1933; *b* Meadow Lea, Manitoba, 29 April 1878; *s* of William Taylor and Marietta Jane Plummer; *m* 1901, Mabel Agnes, *d* of Albert and Agnes Melissa Dykeman; no *c. Educ:* Public Schools and Collegiate Institute, Winnipeg. Barrister, 1900; KC 1913; Alderman City of Portage la Prairie three years; Mayor three years; resigned in 1915 to enlist in CEF; Captain in 99th Manitoba Rangers, 1910; Major, 1915; Major 45th Batt. CEF Feb. 1915; served in France with 1st CMR's Batt. BEF, Aug. 1916–Oct. 1918 (DSO, despatches); Pres. Army and Navy Veterans in Canada, 1920–21; Member Legislative Assembly, 1920–33; leader of the Conservative Party in Manitoba, 1922–33; appointed an ad hoc Judge of the Pension Appeal Court in 1933; Acting Chairman for one year of the Canadian Pension Commission in 1934 and again 1935. *Recreations:* walking and reading. *Address:* 108 Law Courts, Winnipeg, Man, Canada. *Clubs:* Manitoba, Winnipeg.

Died 1 Jan. 1940.

TAYLOR, Sir Frederick W.; *see* Williams-Taylor.

TAYLOR, George Simon Arthur W.; *see* Watson-Taylor.

TAYLOR, Brig.-Gen. Gerald Kyffin-, CBE 1918; VD; DL; Solicitor, 1884; *b* Liverpool, 9 March 1863; 3rd *s* of late Archdeacon Taylor of Liverpool; *m* 1st, 1892, Bessie (*d* 1922), 3rd *d* of late Thomas Cope, JP, of Huyton; 2nd, 1927, Olive, *d* of William Hamilton, Belfast, and *widow* of Rev. W. J. Adams, Vicar of St Augustine's, Liverpool. *Educ:* Liverpool College. Partner in Snowball, Kyffin-Taylor & Pruddah, Liverpool; late commanding 2nd line West Lancashire Divisional Artillery, TF; Hon. Brig.-Gen. Aug. 1917; Director of National Service, NW Region, 1918; Housing Commissioner for Lancs and Cheshire, 1919–22; MP (U) Kirkdale Division, Liverpool, 1910–15; Life Governor of Liverpool College; represented Everton Ward in Liverpool City Council, 1904–19; Chairman of Housing Committee, 1907–19. *Address:* 23 Ashville Road, Birkenhead.

Died 11 Dec. 1949.

TAYLOR, Dame Gladys, DBE 1949 (CBE 1946); RRC 1938; retd; *b* 23 July 1890; *d* of Alfred Taylor, Tunbridge Wells; unmarried. *Educ:* Tunbridge Wells High School; Seaford Ladies' College, Seaford, Sussex. Trained as a nurse, Queen's Hospital for Children, Hackney Road, London, E, 1910–13; University College Hospital, Gower St, London, WC, 1914–18; Princess Mary's Royal Air Force Nursing Service, 1918–48, Matron-in-Chief, 1943–48. Officer (Sister) Order of St John of Jerusalem, 1945. *Address:* 11 Hayes Road, Bromley, Kent. *T:* Ravensbourne 6861. *Club:* Cowdray.

Died 11 Jan. 1950.

TAYLOR, Rev. Henry James; Methodist Minister; *e s* of late Charles Taylor, Curragh Camp, Ireland, and South Staffs; *m d* of Rev. J. W. Chisholm; one *s* three *d. Educ:* Sunderland Institute; Hartley College; New College, London. Ministered in East London; Superintendent South East London Mission; Pastorates in Hull, Southport, and Liverpool; Financial Missionary Secretary of the Denomination, Deputation to the Mission Stations in South and South Central Africa and the Chartered Company of Rhodesia; President of the Christian Endeavour Union of Great Britain and Ireland; Hartley Lecturer; President of the Primitive Methodist Conference, 1922–23; Pres. Federation of the Free Church Councils of Liverpool and District, 1926–27; National Pres. of Sunday School Union, 1927–28; Governor Methodist Residential Colleges; Chairman Woking and District Education Committee; one time Examiner in Psychology and Political Economy and Lecturer on Social, Political and Ecclesiastical subjects. *Publications:* The Challenge of Freedom; Capetown to Kafue; Endeavour Handbooks, etc. *Recreations:* lecturing, golf, Freemasonry. *Address:* 6 York Road, Woking, Surrey. *T:* Woking 1994.

Died 16 Jan. 1945.

TAYLOR, Henry Osborn, LittD, LHD; *b* New York City, 5 Dec. 1856; *s* of Henry Augustus and Catharine Osborn Taylor; *m* 1905, Julia Isham, New York City; no *c. Educ:* Harvard College; Columbia Law School; Leipsic University. Admitted to the Bar in New York City, 1881; practised a very little and soon retired to devote himself to study and writing; has never been a professor, but has lectured at various Universities, also Lowell Lecturer (Boston), 1917; West Lecturer, Leland Stanford, 1920; corresponding member Massachusetts Historical Society; Member American Philosophical Society, National Institute of Arts and Letters; President Harvard Chapter Phi Beta Kappa, 1917–18; President American Historical Association, 1927; Associate Member of the Royal Academy of Belgium. *Publications:* A Treatise on the Law of Private Corporations (5th ed. 1902); Ancient Ideals: A Study of Intellectual and Spiritual Growth from Early Times to the Establishment of Christianity, 2 vols (2nd edit. 1913); The Classical Heritage of the Middle Ages (4th edit. 1925); The

Mediæval Mind, 2 vols (4th edit. 1925); Deliverance: the Freeing of the Spirit in the Ancient World, 1915; Thought and Expression in the Sixteenth Century, 2 vols (2nd edit. 1930); Greek Biology and Medicine, 1922) Freedom of the Mind in History (2nd edit. 1924); Human Values and Verities, 1928; Fact, the Romance of Mind, 1932; A Layman's View of History, 1935; A Historian's Creed, 1939. *Recreation:* nature. *Address:* 135 East 66th Street, New York, USA. *Clubs:* Century, New York; Harvard, Boston.

Died 13 April 1941.

TAYLOR, Captain Herbert Bardsley, CMG 1942; Royal Navy (retired); *b* 30 March 1884; *s* of James Taylor; *m* Renée le Clerc, *y d* of Surgeon-General John J. Faught; no *c. Educ:* HMS Britannia; Dartmouth. Entered Royal Navy, 1900; served HMS Queen Elizabeth, 1914–19; Instructor RN Staff College, 1919–20; retired, 1929; services rendered to the Foreign Office (CMG). *Club:* United Service.

Died 29 April 1947.

TAYLOR, Sir Herbert John, Kt 1924; late Chief Native Commissioner Southern Rhodesia; retired, 1928; *b* 1865; *s* of late Rev. Thomas Taylor, Greytower, Natal; *m* 1901, *d* of late Professor Haben, PhD.

Died 15 Aug. 1943.

TAYLOR, Hobart Chatfield C.; *see* Chatfield-Taylor.

TAYLOR, James, CBE 1920; MA, MD Edin.; FRCP London; Consulting Physician to National Hospital for Nervous Diseases; to Moorfields Eye Hospital, and to Queen's Hospital for Children; Hon. Physician Royal Scottish Corp.; late Medical Referee Pensions Commutation Board; late Deputy Medical Referee to the Treasury; late Consultant, Osborne Home for Officers; late Chief Physician, Guardian Assurance Co; *b* Forres, Morayshire, 1859; *s* of Peter Taylor; *m* 1905, Elizabeth Marian, *d* of Chas. E. Cooke, UP House, Weasenham, Norfolk; one *d. Educ:* Forres Academy; Edinburgh University; Germany and London. MA degree with honours in Natural Science; MB Edin. 1886; MD, 1890. House Physician in Roy. Infirmary, Edinburgh, and in Sick Children's Hospital; House Physician and subsequently Pathologist, National Hospital, Queen's Square, FRSM; Member of various Medical Societies. *Publications:* Paralysis and other Nervous Diseases of Childhood and Early Life, 1905; co-editor with Sir Wm Gowers of Gowers' Manual of Diseases of the Nervous System; Hughlings Jackson's Neurological Fragments, 1925; Editor of selected writings of John Hughlings Jackson, 1931; various articles on medical subjects. *Recreations:* golf and trout fishing. *Address:* 41 Hanover House, St John's Wood, NW8. *Club:* Arts.

Died 6 June 1946.

TAYLOR, James, CBE 1933; FCA (Aust.); Chevalier Légion d'Honneur; Chartered Accountant; Director of Companies; Member, International Olympic Committee; President, Australian Olympic Federation and Swimming Union; *b* 1 Dec. 1871; *s* of Edmund Taylor and Mary Poole; *m* 1901; one *d. Educ:* Balmain School; Sydney University. Independent of his professional and business career has been associated with the development of amateur recreation (starting with the schools) for over 40 years; directly controlling the Olympic movement in Australia since 1902. *Recreations:* were swimming, cricket, football, rowing and tennis. *Address:* Kelton, Brae, Wahroonga, Sydney, NSW. *TA:* Yatlor. *T:* Wahroonga 615. *Clubs:* NSW Amateur Sports, Sydney; Athenæum, Melbourne; Newcastle, Newcastle.

Died 27 June 1944.

TAYLOR, James Benjamin; *b* 20 Dec. 1860; *s* of J. R. Taylor; *m* Mary, *d* of Charles Gordon, Maritzburg, Natal; two *s* two *d. Educ:* Hermansburg College, Natal. Early life spent mining, exploring, and hunting; joined the firm of Wernher, Beit & Co., 1886; retired, 1893; was first president of National Bank of South Africa, and connected largely with the mines on the Rand. *Publication:* A Pioneer Looks Back, 1939. *Recreations:* fishing, shooting, and hunting. *Clubs:* Boodle's, Hurlingham.

Died 24 Dec. 1944.

TAYLOR, Sir James Braid, KCIE 1939; Kt 1935; CIE 1933; Governor of Reserve Bank of India since 1937; *b* 21 April 1891; *s* of James Taylor, MA, FRSE, and Amelia Sutherland; *m* 1926, Betty, *d* of H. E. Coles, Indian Police; one *s. Educ:* Edinburgh Academy and University. MA 1st Class Honours Classics and History. Barrister-at-law, Lincoln's Inn; ICS 1914–35; Deputy Governor, Reserve Bank of India, 1935–37; served TF Reserve (1st/4th The Buffs), 1915–19. *Address:* Reserve Bank of India, Mint Road, Bombay. *Clubs:* Bengal, Calcutta; United Service, Simla; Royal Bombay Yacht.

Died 17 Feb. 1943.

TAYLOR, John, CBE 1920; OBE 1918; Vice-Chairman of Mather & Platt (Limited), Manchester; *b* 1861; *m* 1883, *d* of J. Roberts, Bolton-le-Moors. Was Chairman Lancashire Anti-Submarine Committee and a Member of Federation of British Industries and a Vice-Chairman of British Electrical and Allied Manufactures Assoc. *Address:* 1 Westbourne Road, Southport; Helmside, Giasmere, Westmorland.

Died 13 Dec. 1945.

TAYLOR, John Gray; British Vice-Consul, Cannes, 1921; owner of John Taylor and Son, estate agents, Cannes and Nice; administrator of Anglo-American Hospital, Cannes; *b* 25 June 1890; *e s* of Walter John Taylor and Ellen Fish, of Cannes; *m* Evelyn, *y d* of late Admiral Sir Charles Fane, KCB; one *d. Educ:* Trent College. Served European War in Royal Horse Artillery, 1915–18; Hon. Lieut RFA (despatches). *Recreation:* agriculture. *Address:* Mott's Farm, St Lawrence Bay, Steeple, Essex; St Michel, La Croisette, Cannes. *Clubs:* Boodle's; Traveller's, Paris.

Died 24 Nov. 1944.

TAYLOR, Sir John James, KCB 1919; CB 1905; ISO 1903; *b* 1859; *s* of late James B. Taylor, Liverpool; *m* 1884, Mary, *d* of late Robert Keely of New York, USA; two *d.* Clerk of the Privy Council (Ireland) and Deputy Keeper of the Privy Seal, 1918–20; Private Sec. to Under-Secretary for Ireland, 1892–93; Assistant Private Secretary to Chief Sec., 1903–05; Private Sec. to Chief Sec. (Rt Hon. W. H. Long), 1905; Principal Clerk in Chief Sec.'s Office, Dublin Castle, 1911–18; Assistant Under-Secretary to Lord Lieutenant of Ireland, 1918–20. *Address:* c/o The National Bank Ltd, 15 Whitehall, SW1.

Died 14 Jan. 1945.

TAYLOR, John Norman, CIE 1916; OBE; *b* Kehmare, Co. Kerry; *s* of Frederick William Taylor; *m*; three *s.* Joined Service, 1891; Executive Engineer, 1905; Under-Secretary to Govt Punjab Irrigation Branch, 1910–13; served Miranzai Expedition (medal and clasp); served on famine work in the Punjab (Kaiser-i-Hind medal); served European War as a RE in France, India and Persia (despatches, OBE); demobilised in July 1919 and permitted to retain the rank of Lt-Col; Chief Engineer and Secretary of the Local Administration, Assam, 1922–24; retired, 1924. *Address:* Lisnalurg, Shankill, Co. Dublin.

Died 26 Jan. 1945.

TAYLOR, Sir John W.; *see* Wilson Taylor.

TAYLOR, Mark Ronald, MRCS Eng., LRCP Lond.; late Regional Medical Officer, Ministry of Health; s of Thomas Taylor, MRCSE, Bocking, Essex; m 1st, Florence, d of T. H. Bodilly, Penzance; one s; 2nd, Elizabeth, d of E. G. Baker, Lowestoft. *Educ:* Eaton House, Aldeburgh; Rossall; St Bartholomew's Hospital. Late Lieut 2nd VB Somerset LI. *Publications:* articles in BMJ, St Bart's Gazette and Folklore. *Recreations:* shooting, fishing and folklore. *Address:* 4 Wicks Lane, Formby, Lancashire. *T:* Formby 759.

Died 22 July 1942.

TAYLOR, Brig.-Gen. Reginald O'Bryen, CMG 1918; CIE 1912; b 6 Feb. 1872; m 1924, Gladys (d 1947), widow of Charles Dunning Hunt. Served S African War, 1900 (Queen's medal and 4 clasps); European War (CMG); Afghan War, 1919; retired, 1921.

Died 31 Oct. 1949.

TAYLOR, Brig.-Gen. Reynell Hamilton Baylay, CB 1918; Royal Army Ordnance Corps (retired); b Drhumsala, E Indies, 24 Nov. 1858; 2nd s of late General Reynell Taylor, CB, CSI, of Newton Abbot, South Devon, and Anne, d of A. B. E. Holdsworth, of Widdicombe, S Devon; m 1891, Gertrude, 2nd d of Rev. W. Houghton, MA, FLS, Rector of Preston-in-Wealds-Moors, Salop. *Educ:* Cheltenham; Sandhurst. Obtained Commission in 82nd Foot, 1879; transferred to 25th King's Own Borderers, and joined that regiment in India, 1880; served Afghan War, 1880 (medal); joined Royal Army Ordnance Corps, 1888; served as chief ordnance officer, Sierra Leone, to troops operating in Sierra Leone Protectorate Expeditions, during the Hut Tax Rebellion (medal with clasp); served in the Royal Arsenal in the Royal Army Ordnance Corps during European War (CB). *Recreations:* cricket, fishing, tennis. *Address:* Rosebank, Ryde, IW.

Died 23 March 1942.

TAYLOR, Very Rev. Robert Oswald Patrick, MA; Vicar of Ringwood, Hants, since 1926; Lecturer in Pastoral Theology and Select Preacher in the University of Cambridge for 1933–34; b 1873; s of Joseph Taylor and Eleanor Violet Taylor, latterly of Whitley Bay; m 1907, Frances Noel Richards of Heaton, Newcastle; one s two d. *Educ:* St John's College, Cambridge. Curate of St Mary's, Blyth, 1899–1902; St Gabriel's, Heaton, Newcastle, 1903; in charge of Cowpen, 1904–09; All Saints, Edinburgh (Priest-Organist), 1909–15; Vicar of Prestwold, Loughborough, 1915–17; Vice-Provost and Canon of Cumbrae, 1917; Provost of Cumbrae, 1918–25. *Publications:* The Athanasian Creed in the 20th Century, 1911; Communion and Fellowship, 1924; How Can I Pray? 1926; How you Know God, 1928; The Meeting of the Roads, 1931; Does Science leave Room for God? 1933. *Recreation:* music. *Address:* The Vicarage, Ringwood, Hants. *T:* Ringwood 219.

Died 14 Dec. 1944.

TAYLOR, Sir Thomas, Kt 1925; proprietor of Thomas Taylor & Co., 55 Brown Street, Manchester, silk merchants and shippers; Director of Kemil, Ltd, Manchester; Vice-President of Silk Association of Great Britain and Ireland; b 7 March 1876; o s of late Richard Taylor of Hollins, Whitefield; m 1903, Lydia Barlow, e d of late John Slingsby, JP of Radcliffe and Lytham; one s one d. *Educ:* Bury Grammar School; privately for Civil Service. Established the above-named business, 1903. *Recreations:* golf, motoring, and gardening. *Address:* The Beeches, Upton, Macclesfield. *T:* Macclesfield 2708, Deansgate 5171 Manchester. *Clubs:* Constitutional; Constitutional, Manchester.

Died 8 April 1941.

TAYLOR, Sir Thomas Marris, Kt 1928; CBE 1917; b 21 Aug. 1871; s of late George Marris Taylor; m 1898, Mary Dorothea, 4th d of late Walter Wren, MA, 7 Powis Square, W. *Educ:* Gonville and Caius College, Cambridge. Senior Chancellor's Medallist for Classics,

1894; Fellow of College, 1895–1901. Principal of Wren's, Powis Square, 1898–1915; entered the Ministry of Munitions to organise Training of Munition Workers, 1915; Director of Labour Supply Dept, 1917; Asst Controller-General, Demobilisation Department, Ministry of Labour, 1918; Sec. of the Lord Kitchener National Memorial Fund, 1919–28; Member of the Hants County Council, 1922; Alderman, 1928; Chairman of Hampshire Education Committee, 1926–29; Vice-Chairman of the Special Grants Committee, Ministry of Pensions, 1926–28; Member of Consultative Committee, Board of Education, 1926–28; Vice-Chairman, Hants County Council, 1930–33; Chairman of Finance Committee, 1932–33; JP County of Southampton, 1922. *Publication:* Constitutional and Political History of Rome. *Recreation:* all country pursuits. *Address:* Whitedale, Hambledon, Hants. *T:* Hambledon 2. *Club:* Hampshire County.

Died 5 Nov. 1941.

TAYLOR, Gen. Sir Walter William P.; see Pitt-Taylor.

TEBBITT, Sir Alfred St Valery, Kt 1936; Royal Victorian Order; Officier de la Légion d'Honneur; s of Charles Tebbitt and Emily Houston; m 1904, Gladys Pendrell Smith; two s one d. *Educ:* Paris and England. Managing Director, Kirby, Beard and Co., Paris; Chairman of the Hertford British Hospital, Paris; Trustee, British Charitable Fund, Paris; Director British Chamber of Commerce, Paris; Chairman of Paris Board of Yorkshire Insurance Company. *Address:* 134 Rue de Courcelles, Paris. *T:* Wag. 21 65. *Clubs:* Interallié, Paris.

Died 30 March 1941.

TEELING, Luke Alexander; b 1856; s of late Charles George Teeling; m 1898, Margaret Mary (d 1917), o c of William Joseph Burke, JP, of Ower, County Galway; one s. *Educ:* Trinity College, Dublin. BA 1877. Called Irish Bar, 1881; Accountant-General, Supreme Court of Judicature, Ireland, 1898–1921; JP Counties Galway and Mayo, 1898; member of Council of the Queen's Institute of District Nursing, 1920–32; Hon. Treasurer Irish War Hospital Supply Depot, 1917–19. *Address:* Spa Hotel, Tunbridge Wells. *Clubs:* University, Dublin.

Died 2 Nov. 1943.

TEGART, Sir Charles Augustus, KCIE 1937; Kt 1926; CSI 1931; CIE 1917; MVO 1912; late Indian Police; Ministry of Food, Portman Square, London, since 1942; b 5 Oct. 1881; s of late Rev. J. P. Tegart Dunboyne, Co. Meath; m Kathleen Frances, d of Rev. J. L. Herbert of Disserth, Llandrindod Wells. *Educ:* Portora Royal School, Enniskillen; Trinity College, Dublin. Joined Indian Police, 1901; retired 1931; Member of Council of India, 1932–36; went to Palestine, 1937, to advise Government on police organization; King's Police Medal, 1911; served European War, France, with RFA, 1918–19; Hon. LLD (Dublin), 1933. *Club:* East India and Sports.

Died 6 April 1946.

TEICHMAN, Sir Eric, GCMG 1944; KCMG 1933; CMG 1927; CIE 1919; b 16 Jan. 1884; s of E. Teichman, Chislehurst, Kent; m 1921, Ellen Cecilia, widow of Major D. S. Niven, OBE, IA, d of M. J. Teesdale, Walton-on-the-Hill, Surrey. *Educ:* Charterhouse; Caius College, Cambridge. Entered HM Consular Services in China, 1907; attached to the Legation at Peking, 1907–17; on special service, 1917–19; assistant Chinese Secretary to HM Legation at Peking, 1919–20; employed in Foreign Office, 1921–22; Chinese Secretary at HM Legation, Peking, from 1922; Counsellor of Embassy from 1927; retired, 1936; re-employed as Counsellor of Embassy, 1942–44; awarded Murchison Grant Royal Geographical Society, 1925. *Publications:* Travels of a Consular Officer in North-West China, 1921; Travels of a Consular Officer in Eastern Tibet, 1922; Journey to

Turkistan, 1937; Affairs of China, 1938. *Recreation:* shooting. *Address:* Honingham Hall, Norfolk. *Clubs:* United University; Norfolk, Norwich.

Died 3 Dec. 1944.

TEMPEST, Dame Mary Susan, DBE 1937; *b* London, 15 July 1866; *e d* of Edwin and Sarah Etherington; *m* 2nd, 1898, Cosmo Charles Gordon-Lennox (*d* 1921); 3rd, 1921, W. Graham Browne (*d* 1937). *Educ:* Convent des Ursulines, Thildonck, Belgium. Received medals— bronze for light singing, silver for Italian singing, gold for declamatory English singing. Began career on stage in Bocaccio, followed by Fay of Five, Fiametta, Ermine, Dorothy, Doris, The Red Hussar; first tour in America; Fencing Master, Mignon, Manon and Carmen; in London; Artist's Model, Geisha, Greek Slave and San Toy; left musical comedy and created Nell Gwyn in English Nell, 1900; Becky Sharp, 1901, etc.; produced The Marriage of Kitty; joined Chas. Frohman as star, playing The Truth, Mrs Dot, Penelope, etc.; toured in America and returned to England to go into management in 1911, since when she has produced The Honeymoon, by Arnold Bennett, and At the Barn, by Anthony Wharton; Art and Opportunity, by Harold Chapin; a Triple Bill, including An Imaginary Conversation, by Norreys Connell; The Dumb and the Blind, by Harold Chapin; The Malingerer, by P. L. Ransom; Esther Castways, by Jerome K. Jerome; The Handful, by Gordon Edwards; Mary Goes First, by Hy Arthur Jones; The Marriage of Columbine, by Harold Chapin; Thank your Lordship, by Norreys Connell; The Wynmartons, by Richard Powell; The Duke of Killiecrankie, by Robert Marshall; in 1914 began a World Tour which embraced New York, Melbourne, The Victoria Falls, Pekin, Manilla; returned London, 1922; produced Good Gracious Annabelle, Alice Sit by the Fire, Far Above Rubies, Midsummer Madness; The Torchbearers; Hay Fever, by Noel Coward; The Cat's Cradle, by Aimée and Philip Stewart; Masque of Venice, by George Gribble; Her Shop, by Aimée Stewart; The First Mrs Frazer, by St John Ervine; Five Farthings; Marry at Leisure; Little Catherine; So far and no Father; The Vinegar Tree; When Ladies Meet; Old Folks at Home, Theatre Royal; on May 28 1935, played acts from The Marriage of Kitty and Little Catherine at a matinee at Drury Lane in honour of her 50th year on the stage; Mrs Leigh in Short Story, 1936; first talking film with Paderewski, 1936.

Died 14 Oct. 1942.

TEMPEST, Brig.-Gen. Roger Stephen, CMG 1918; DSO 1917; *b* 1876; *o s* of late Major A. C. Tempest of Broughton Hall, Skipton; *m* 1912, Valerie Arthur, *e d* of late A. L. Glover, Ryarsh, Kent; two *s* one *d*. *Educ:* Oratory School; Stonyhurst College. Joined the 3rd Batt. 19th Yorkshire Regt (Militia), 1894; Scots Guards, 1908; served S African War, 1900–02 (King's medal and Queen's medal, despatches twice); Adjt 3rd Batt. Scots Guards, 1904–07; Regt Adjt 1914; served European War 1914–18; Brigade-Major, 40th London Inf. Brig. and 3rd Guards Brigade, present at action of Festubert, Loos, Somme; wounded on the Somme, 15 Sept.; commanded 43rd Infantry Brigade, 1917–18 (despatches six times, Croix de Guerre, Bt Lt-Col, Bt Col 1919, DSO, CMG); retired, 1921, DL JP. *Address:* Broughton Hall, Skipton. *T:* Gargrave 204. *Club:* Guards'.

Died 12 Feb. 1948.

TEMPLE, Most Rev. and Rt Hon. William, PC 1929; MA; DLitt; Hon. DD, Hon. LLD; Hon. DCL; Archbishop of Canterbury since 1942; *b* The Palace, Exeter, 15 Oct. 1881; *s* of late Most Rev. and Rt Hon. Frederick Temple, PC, DD, 93rd Lord Archbishop of Canterbury; *m* 1916, Frances Gertrude Acland, *y d* of late F. H. Anson, 72 St George's Square, SW. *Educ:* Rugby (Scholar); Balliol College, Oxford (Exhibitioner). 1st class Classical Mods., 1902; 1st class Lit. Hum., 1904; President Oxford Union, 1904; Fellow and Lecturer in

Philosophy, Queen's College, Oxford, 1904–10. Deacon, 1908; Priest, 1909; Chaplain to Archbishop of Canterbury, 1910–21; Headmaster, Repton School, 1910–14; Rector of St James, Piccadilly, 1914–18; Hon. Chaplain to the King, 1915–21; Editor of The Challenge, 1915–18; Canon of Westminster, 1919–21; Bishop of Manchester, 1921–29; Archbishop of York, 1929–42; President of the Workers Educational Association, 1908–24; editor of The Pilgrim, 1920–27. *Publications:* The Faith and Modern Thought (Six Lectures); The Nature of Personality; The Kingdom of God; Repton School Sermons; two essays in Foundations; articles in Mind; Studies in the Spirit and Truth of Christianity; Church and Nation, 1915; Plato and Christianity, 1916; Mens Creatrix: an Essay, 1917; Issues of Faith, 1918; Fellowship with God, 1920; The Universality of Christ, 1921; Life of Bishop Percival, 1921; Christus Veritas, 1924; Christ in His Church, 1925; Personal Religion and the Life of Fellowship, 1926; Essays in Christian Politics, 1927; Christianity and the State, 1928; Christian Faith and Life; Thoughts on Some Problems of the Day, 1931; Nature, Man and God, 1934; Readings in St John's Gospel, 1939; Christianity and Social Order, 1942. *Address:* Lambeth Palace, SE1. *T:* Waterloo 4366; Old Palace, Canterbury. *T:* Canterbury 3003.

Died 26 Oct. 1944.

TEMPLER, Brig.-Gen. Cyril Frank, CMG 1916; CIE 1918; Indian Army, retired; *b* 1869; *m* 1909, Harriet Mary Currie; one *s* two *d*. First Commission Royal Field Artillery, 1889; transferred to 1st DCO Bombay Lancers, 1894; Bt Col 1919; Director General Remount Dept, Indian Army, 1915–20; served Dongola Expedition, 1896 (two medals); European War, 1914–16 (despatches, CMG, CIE); retired, 1920. *Recreations:* shooting, sailing, hunting. *Address:* Chapelton House, Forres. *Club:* United Service.

Died 28 Jan. 1947.

TEMPLER, Lt-Col Walter Francis, CBE 1919; DL; *b* 1865; 2nd *s* of R. B. Templer, Armagh; *m* 1895, Mabel Eileen Johnston; one *s*. *Educ:* Charterhouse; Pembroke College, Cambridge, BA; RM College, Sandhurst. Served in Army in The Royal Irish Fusiliers and RAPC, 1888–1921. *Address:* The Manor House, Loughgall, Co. Armagh, N Ireland.

Died 18 Dec. 1942.

TENNANT, Francis John; *b* 20 Oct. 1861; 2nd *surv. s* of Sir Charles Tennant, 1st Bt; *m* 1886, Annie Geraldine, *d* of late John Marriner Redmayne of South Dene, Co. Durham; one *s* two *d*. *Address:* Hyndford House, North Berwick; Innes House, Morayshire. *Club:* Brooks's.

Died 4 Sept. 1942.

TENNANT, Lt-Col John Edward, DSO 1918; MC; JP; Scots Guards Reserve of Officers; Acting Group Capt. RAFVR; *b* 12 Oct. 1890; *e s* of Francis John Tennant; *m* 1st, 1918, Georgina Helen (who obtained a divorce, 1925), *d* of General Sir George Kirkpatrick, KCB, KCSI; one *s*; 2nd, Victoria Maud Vericona, *d* of late Sir Robin Duff, Bart, Life Guards (killed in action, 1914), and Lady Juliet Duff, *d* of 4th Earl of Lonsdale; two *s* two *d*. *Educ:* RN Colleges, Osborne and Dartmouth. Midshipman, 1908–10; 2nd Lieutenant Scots Guards, 1910; seconded to Royal Flying Corps, Sept. 1914; served in France, 1914–16, and as OC RFC and RAF in Mesopotamia, 1916–18 (despatches five times, MC, Bt Major in Army, DSO, Chevalier de la Légion d'Honneur); was shot down and captured while in Mesopotamia, but rescued four days later by armoured cars; Director of Aeronautics in India, 1918–19; senior partner firm of Hohler & Co., banking agents, 33 Cornhill, EC3; Director, C. Tennant, Sons, & Co. Ltd, 9 Mincing Lane, EC3; Caledonian Associated Cinemas; Wing-Commander RAFVR, 1939; Intelligence Staff, Air Ministry; Personal Air Secretary to Chief of Air Staff, Sir Charles Portal, 1940–41; Commandant for Scotland,

Air Training Corps, 1941. Contested (L) Moray and Nairn, General Election, 1929. *Publication:* In the Clouds above Bagdad, 1920. *Recreations:* Yachting (BOT Master's Certificate), golf, shooting, hunting, has carried out Shikar expeditions up the White Nile, in India, and the Sinai Peninsula; Member, Oxford University Arctic Expedition to North East Land, 1924. *Address:* Innes House, Elgin, Morayshire. *TA:* Elgin; 10a Lansdowne House, Berkeley Square, W1. *Clubs:* Brooks's, Guards', City of London; Royal Yacht Squadron, Cowes; New, Edinburgh.

Died 7 Aug. 1941.

TENNANT, Mrs May, CH 1917; JP; Central Consultative Council of Voluntary Organisations; National Association for Prevention of Tuberculosis; Governor of Bedford College; Chairman of Maternal Health Committee; Director of the Gardener's Chronicle; Director of the Mysore and Champion Reef Gold Mines; *b* 1869; *d* of late George Whitley Abraham, of Rathgar, Co. Dublin; *m* 1896, as his second wife, the Rt Hon. Harold John Tennant (*d* 1935); three *s* one *d*. Has been Asst Commissioner Royal Labour Commission; HM Superintending Inspector of Factories; Member of Dangerous Trades Committee; Member of Royal Commission on Divorce; Director of Women's Department National Service; Chief Adviser Women's Welfare, Ministry of Munitions; Member of the Health of Munition Workers and other War Committees. *Publication:* The Law Relating to Factories and Workshops. *Recreations:* gardening, fishing, lawn tennis. *Address:* 12 Victoria Square, SW1. *T:* Victoria 9191; Great Maytham, Rolvenden, Cranbrook, Kent. *T:* Rolvenden 302; Edinglassie, Strathdon, Alford, Aberdeenshire. *T:* Strathdon 3. *Clubs:* Ladies' Empire, Guards', VAD Ladies.

Died 11 July 1946.

TENNEY, John, CBE 1920; ISO; *b* 1856; *s* of late John Tenney of Treninnow, Maker, Cornwall; *m* 1917, Mary King, *widow* of R. D. Roberts, DSc. Entered Exchequer and Audit Department, 1875; served in S Africa, 1904–07; retired, 1919. *Club:* National Liberal.

Died 3 Sept. 1944.

TERNAN, Brig.-Gen. Trevor Patrick Breffney, CB 1917; CMG 1900; DSO 1889; *b* Bath, 1 April 1860; 5th *s* of General A. H. Ternan, ISC; *m* 1906, Dorothy, *d* of G. Alsop, Teignmouth and South Africa; one *s* two *d*. *Educ:* Bromsgrove School; Sandhurst. Joined 63rd Foot, 1879; served Afghan War, 1880–81 (medal); Egyptian War, 1882 (medal and Khedive's star); joined Egyptian army, 1884; with 9th Soudanese Batt. in Nile Expedition, 1884 (clasp); present at action of Ginnis, 1885; DAAG with Nile Frontier Force, 1886–87, 1888–89 (4th class Osmanieh, despatches, clasp, DSO); present at battle of Toski (horse shot); AAG War Office, Cairo, 1890–91; commanded 1st Battalion Egyptian army, 1892–93; joined Uganda Rifles, 1894; served in expedition in Unyoro, 1895 (despatches, medal); Commandant Uganda Rifles, 1896; acted as Commissioner and Consul-General Uganda Protectorate, 1897; commanded operations against King Mwanga, 1897 (promoted Major in Royal Warwickshire Regt and Brevet Lieut-Col); commanded troops in Uganda against mutineers and rebels, Oct. 1898–99 (wounded, medal and clasp); promoted Brevet Col; acted as Comr and Consul-Gen. Uganda Protectorate, 1899 (CMG); acted as Commissioner and Consul-General, British East Africa, 1900; commanded punitive expedition against Ogaden Somalis, 1900–01 (medal and clasp); served in South African War, 1901–02 (medal and 4 clasps); AAG Southern District, Portsmouth, 1903; AAG South Africa, 1903–05; Brig.-General Commanding Standerton District, Transvaal, 1906–07; retired 1907; rejoined, 4 Aug. 1914, as AAG and Quartermaster-General, Northumbrian Division (T); Brig.-General 102nd Tyneside Scottish Brigade (20th,

21st, 22nd, 23rd Northumberland Fusiliers), 28 Dec. 1914 to 23 April 1917 (despatches thrice, CB); present at battles of the Somme, 1916, and Arras, 1917. *Publications:* The Story of the Tyneside Scottish; Some Experiences of an Old Bromsgrovian. *Address:* Abbey Lodge, Storrington, Sussex.

Died 14 Nov. 1949.

TERRELL, His Honour Judge Henry; KC 1897; *b* 1856; *s* of late Judge Terrell. Called to Bar, Middle Temple, 1882; Bencher, 1904; MP (U) Gloucester, 1910–18; County Court Judge of the Exeter and Plymouth Courts, 1920–22; on Circuit 49, East Kent, 1923–29; retired 1929; 2nd in command 11th Battalion Gloucestershire Regiment, 1915. *Address:* 32 Brunswick Square, Hove 2, Sussex.

Died 9 Sept. 1944.

TERROT, Brig. Charles Russell, DSO 1917; Légion d'honneur; late V-VI Dragoons; *s* of Lieut-Colonel Charles Ellison Terrot and Alice, *d* of J. Hartley, of Tong Castle, Shifnal, Shropshire; *m* E. M. S., *d* of Sir F. Ripley, 1st Bt, Acacia, Yorkshire; one *s* two *d*. *Educ:* Harrow. 2nd Lieut Shropshire Light Infantry (Militia), 1897; 2nd Lieut Inniskilling Dragoons, 1899; Temporary Command of 5th Dragoon Guards, 1918; Temporary Command Inniskilling Dragoons, 1918; Command Inniskilling Dragoons, 1921; Command Amalgamated Regiments 5th Dragoons and Inniskilling Dragoons, 1922; Commandant Iraq Levies, 1926–27; Commanded 2nd Indian Cavalry Brigade, Sialkot, 1928–32; served South African War, 1899–1902 (despatches); European War, 1914–18 (wounded twice, despatches thrice, DSO and bar, Brevet Lieut-Colonel); retired pay, 1933. *Recreations:* hunting, polo, golf. *Clubs:* Cavalry, MCC.

Died 1 May 1944.

TERRY, Lt-Col Claude Henry Maxwell I.; *see* Imbert-Terry.

TERRY, George Percy Warner, OBE 1937; ARICS; FACCA; barrister-at-Law; *b* 2 June 1867; *e s* of George Terry, formerly of Putney; *m* 1904, Annie Elizabeth Ruth Clark; two *d*. *Educ:* Westminster United City Schools; Polytechnic; King's College, London. Junior Clerk, Westminster Vestry and Board of Works, 1884; Vestry Clerk and Assistant Overseer, St Margaret's Westminster; Assistant Sec. Lambeth Water Co. 1903, Statistical Officer, Metropolitan Water Board, 1905; Deputy Clerk to the Board, superannuated 1932, Sec. British Waterworks Assoc., 1915–40; retired 1940; Parliamentary Sec. to Sir Dickson-Poynder, MP (Lord Islington), and Sir Edmund Barnard, MP Joint Hon. Sec. Advisory Committee on Water of Ministry of Health; of Conjoint Conference of Public Utility Associations; and of Central Council for Rivers Protection; Hon. Sec. Public Health Services Congress and Exhibition. *Publications:* Knight's Overseers' Manual, 4th and 5th editions; Textbook on London Government Act, 1899; Representation of the People Acts, 1918–1928, three editions; Rating and Valuation Acts, 1925–1932, three editions; The Story of Greater Westminster; for some 30 years legal and literary contributor to local government journals; originator and first editor, British Waterworks Directory; also of BWA Official Circular. *Recreations:* London History and Topography, particularly Westminster; Municipal law, history and heraldry; invented the Arms of the Westminster City Council and the Metropolitan Water Board. *Address:* 7 Alleyn Road, West Dulwich, SE21. *T:* Gipsy Hill 2779. *Club:* National Liberal.

Died 1 April 1949.

TESCHEMACHER, Edward; lyric writer; *b* London, 1876. *Songs:* Because; I Know a Lovely Garden; O Lovely Night; Little Irish Girl; Until; Tommy Lad, etc. *Recreation:* gardening.

Died 15 May 1940.

TESLA, Nikola; electrician and inventor; *b* Smiljau, Servia, 1857; *s* of a priest of Greek Church. *Educ:* Realschuler, Karlstadt; Polytechnic School, Gratz; Prague; Buda-Pesth. Served Government Telegraph Engineering Dept; employed by large electric lighting companies, Paris, 1881; went to America, 1882; employed for some time in establishment of T. A. Edison; Grand Cross of the Serbian Order of St Sava, 1926; Hon. Doctor Universities of Belgrade and Zagreb, 1926. *Address:* Wardenclyffe, Long Island, New York.

Died 7 Jan. 1943.

TEW, Lt-Col Harold Stuart, CMG 1916; late E Surrey Regt; *b* 1869; *s* of late Edward Tew, JP of Gunfield, Dartmouth; *m* Katherine Mary, *d* of late Richard Yeo of Drayton House, Ealing; one *s* two *d. Educ:* Clifton College. Served South African War, 1899–1902 (despatches thrice, Bt Major, Queen's medal 5 clasps, King's medal 2 clasps); European War, 1914–18 (despatches 4 times, CMG, Bt Lt-Col); retired pay, 1919. *Address:* Hardwick House, 158 Sandgate Road, Folkestone.

Died 1 March 1945.

TEWSLEY, Dr Cyril Hocken, CMG 1918; MD, FRCS, FRCP (Edin.); FRACP; Col NZ Medical Corps; formerly ADMS Northern Military District, NZ; late Hon. Physician Auckland Hospital; *b* 1878; *s* of late Henry Tewsley, Dunedin; *m* 1917, Marjorie Douglas, *d* of late Dr P. A. Lindsay. *Educ:* University, New Zealand and University, Edinburgh. Served European War, 1914–18 (CMG). *Address:* 5 O'Rorke Street, Auckland, CI, NZ.

Died 2 Dec. 1950.

TEYEN, Charles St Leger, CIE 1933; OBE 1930; ISO; Member of Legislative Council, UP, India; *b* 1877; *m* 1901, Grace Florence, *d* of Felix Fernandez, Bhopal; one *s* five *d. Educ:* Victoria College, Jersey; North Point College, Darjeeling. Secretary Government of UP Finance Department, 1931–33; retired. *Address:* Naini Tal, UP, India.

Died 8 May 1947.

THACKER, Maj.-Gen. Percival Edward, CB 1917; CMG 1916; retired; *b* 1873; *s* of late Major-Gen. John Thacker, Bombay Staff Corps; *m* 1st, 1912, Gladys Howland (*d* 1919), Toronto; 2nd, 1920, Hon. Mabel Louise (Maid of Honour to Queen Mary, 1911–20), 2nd *d* of late Captain Herbert F. Gye, MVO, RN, and Hon. Mrs Gye, 5 Westbourne Gardens, Folkestone. *Educ:* Upper Canada Coll.; RMC, Kingston; passed Staff College, Camberley, 1908. AAG Ottawa, 1909–10; Director of Military Training, 1911–12; on Imperial General Staff, War Office, 1912–14; Adjutant-General Canadian Overseas Forces, 1917–19. Served Yukon Field Force, 1898–1900; South Africa, 1901–02 (Queen's medal 3 clasps); European War, 1914–19 (CMG, CB). *Club:* East India and Sports.

Died 23 July 1945.

THAINE, Robert Niemann, CMG; *b* 1 Jan. 1875; *s* of Philip Thaine; *m* 1902, Helen, *d* of Ashley Walker; no *c. Educ:* Eastbourne College; St John's College, Cambridge. Entered Ceylon Civil Service, 1898; Government Agent Western Province, Colombo, and President Local Government Board, 1923–31; retired 1931. *Recreation:* golf. *Address:* Alfriston, Elvetham Road, Fleet, Hants.

Died 11 July 1943.

THANKERTON, Baron *cr* 1929 (Life Peer), of Thankerton; **William Watson;** PC 1922; KC 1914; a Lord of Appeal in Ordinary since 1929; *b* 8 Dec. 1873; 2nd *surv. s* of Rt Hon. William Watson, Baron Watson of Thankerton, Lord of Appeal in Ordinary; *m* 1902, Sophia Mariorie, *d* of J. J. Cowan, Bavelaw Castle, Balerno, Midlothian; two *s* one *d. Educ:* Winchester; Jesus College, Cambridge. Advocate, 1899; MP (U)

South Lanarkshire, 1913–18; Carlisle, 1924–29 Advocate Depute, 1919; Procurator of the Church of Scotland, 1918–22; Solicitor-General for Scotland, 1922; Lord Advocate, 1922–24 and 1924–29; Hon. Bencher, Gray's Inn, 1928; Hon. LLD (Edin.) 1929; Hon. Fellow, Jesus College (Camb.), 1929; Member of Royal Company of Archers (King's Bodyguard for Scotland). *Recreations:* shooting, fishing, golfing. *Address:* 132 Oakwood Court, W14. *T:* Western 4403. *Club:* Carlton.

Died 13 June 1948.

THATCHER, J. Wells; Rochester Diocesan lay reader (retired); *b* Marylebone, 17 Feb. 1856; *s* of James and Elizabeth Thatcher; *m* 1st, Jane, *d* of Alexander Anderson, Lismore Ireland; three *s* one *d*; 2nd, Ethel Schaeffer, (*d* 1933), *d* of George Edwin Swithinbank, LLD; one *s* one *d. Educ:* privately. Young manhood spent in charitable undertakings; took deep practical interest in the Feminist movement; was permitted to give free legal advice to poor people in the East End in their general and marital difficulties; Barrister-at-law SE Circuit, London and Surrey Sessions CCC; Financial Adviser, Given-Wilson Institute, Plaistow. *Publications:* Called to the Bar; Poems and Miscellaneous Verse; certain modest Legal Text Books. *Recreations:* all the Roman prose writers and poets of the Augustan Age, trees and flowers of the countryside. *Address:* Phillips Nursing Home, 48 London Lane, Bromley, Kent.

Died 2 Aug. 1946.

THAVENOT, Alexander Frank Noel, CBE 1939; President of High Court of Ethiopia since 1944; *b* 21 Dec. 1883; *e s* of late A. V. M. Thavenot; *m* 1st, 1913, Maude Moncaster Hilbery (*d* 1930); 2nd, 1932, Louise Ponthier Newman; one *s. Educ:* privately. Called to Bar, Gray's Inn, 1905; Probationary Legal Adviser, Siam, 1909; Asst Legal Adviser, 1911; Legal Adviser, 1922; Judge of Court of Appeal, 1932; Judicial Adviser to the Siamese Ministry of Justice, and Judge of the Supreme Court of Appeal, 1936; retired from Siam, 1941; Thai Editor, BBC; retired from BBC 1943. Grand Cross of the Crown of Siam; Second Class of the White Elephant of Siam. *Recreation:* bridge. *Address:* Addis Ababa, Ethiopia. *Club:* Junior Carlton.

Died 21 April 1947.

THEODORE, Hon. Edward Granville; Chairman of Directors of Consolidated Press Limited, Sydney, which publishes the Daily Telegraph, Sunday Telegraph, and the Australian Women's Weekly; *b* Port Adelaide, South Australia, 1884; 2nd *s* of Basil Theodore, Aldgate, South Australia; *m* 1909, Esther, *d* of Patrick Mahoney, Toowoomba, Queensland; two *s* two *d. Educ:* Le Fevre's Peninsular Public School, South Australia. Member Legislative Assembly, Queensland, 1909–25; State Treasurer and Minister for Public Works, 1915; Leader of Labour Party and Premier of the State, 1919–25; Member Federal Parlt for Dalley Div., Sydney, 1927–31; Commonwealth Treasurer, 1929–30 and 1931; Deputy Leader Parliamentary Labour Party, 1928–30 and 1931; on being defeated at the General Elections in 1931 retired from political life. Director-General of Allied Works Council, 1942–44. *Address:* 168 Castlereagh Street, Sydney, Australia.

Died 9 Feb. 1950.

THEW, Sir Edgar William, Kt 1939; Chief Inspector HM Customs and Excise; *b* 18 July 1879. *Address:* City Gate House, Finsbury Square, EC2.

Died 8 Feb. 1942.

THICKNESSE, Ven. Francis Norman; Archdeacon Emeritus, 1933; *b* 9 Aug. 1858; *s* of late Rt Rev. Francis Henry Thicknesse, Bishop of Leicester; *m* Mary Sibylla (*d* 1940), *d* of Rev. J. Walker, Vice-Principal of BNC, Oxford; one *s* one *d. Educ:* Winchester; BNC, Oxford. Rector of Limehouse, E, 1887–94; All Saints', Northampton, 1899–1904; Rector and Rural Dean of Hornsey, 1904–11; Rector of St George's, Hanover

Square, 1911–33; Rural Dean of Westminster, 1912–27; Archdeacon of Middlesex, 1930–33; Secretary of Church Congress, 1902. *Address:* at The Deanery, St Albans.

Died 13 April 1946.

THIN, Robert, MA, MB, CM, FRCP, LLD (Edin.); medical practitioner; *b* 1861; *s* of James Thin and Catherine Traquair; *m* 1894, May Glover, *d* of John Wright, merchant, Leith; one *s* two *d*. *Educ:* Royal High School, Edinburgh; University of Edinburgh and University of Marburg. Graduated MB CM, 1887. Resident Surgeon and Resident Physician, Royal Infirmary, Edinburgh, and Resident Physician Royal Hospital for Sick Children, Edinburgh; did post graduate work Vienna and Prague; Assistant Surgeon, Forth Bridge Works; in practice since 1890; Hon. Librarian, Royal College of Physicians, Edinburgh, 1923–31; Vice-President, 1928–30; President, 1931–33; Governor, George Heriot's Trust. *Publications:* various articles in medical journals, mostly on medical history. *Recreations:* golf, travelling. *Address:* 25 Abercromby Place, Edinburgh. *T:* 21129.

Died 18 Sept. 1941.

THOM, Lt-Col Sir John Gibb, Kt 1937; DSO 1917; MC; Chief Justice, High Court, Allahabad, since 1937; *b* 1891; *s* of late John Thom, Solicitor, Linlithgow; *m* 1932, Anna Elizabeth Taylor, *d* of Robert Brown, Edinburgh. *Educ:* Edinburgh University. Graduated MA, LLB. Called to Scottish Bar, 1919; Advocate-Depute, 1931–32; MP (C) Dumbartonshire, 1926–29, and 1931–32; Puisne Judge, High Court, Allahabad, 1932–37; served in Lothians and Border Horse, 1908–11; commanded 8/10th and 6th Batts Gordon Highlanders, European War, 1914–18 (DSO, MC, Bt Lt-Col, despatches four times). *Recreations:* shooting, fishing, golf. *Address:* 31 Thornhill Road, Allahabad, UP, India. *Clubs:* Constitutional; Caledonian United Service, Edinburgh.

Died 19 Feb. 1941.

THOMAS, Sir (Alfred) Brumwell, Kt 1906; FRIBA; *b* 1868. Architect in private practice; Member of Council of the Royal British Colonial Society of Artists. His principal works are the Belfast City Hall, the Town Halls of Woolwich, Stockport, Clacton, and the Skefko Works, Luton; Dunkirk War Memorial, Belfast War Memorial. *Address:* F3 Albany, Piccadilly, W1. *Club:* Arts.

Died 22 Jan. 1948.

THOMAS, Bertram Sidney, CMG 1949; OBE 1920; PhD Cantab; DLitt (Hon.) Bristol; DSc (Hon.) Acadia, NS; Grand Cordon Order of Al Said Muscat Oman, 1928; Arabian Explorer and Orientalist: Adviser to Shell Group in Middle East, 1948–49; Warden and Dir ME Centre for Arab Studies, Palestine, 1944–46; Lebanon, 1947–48; *b* 13 June 1892; *s* of late W. H. Thomas, Easton-in-Gordano, nr Bristol; *m* 1933, Bessie Mary, *d* of late Brigade Surgeon Lt-Col Edmond Hoile, 17th Lancers, and of Mrs Frank Ford; one *d*. *Educ:* privately; Trinity College, Cambridge, Fellow Commoner. Civil Service, 1908–14; North Somerset Yeomanry in Belgium (ranks), 1914–15; Somerset Light Infantry, Mesopotamia, 1916–18; Mesopotamian Insurrection, Captain (despatches), 1920; War of 1939; General List, Lieut-Colonel; Public Relations Officer in the Persian Gulf, 1942–43; Col 1944–46. Asst Political Officer, Mesopotamia, 1918–22; Assist British Representative, Trans-Jordan, 1922–24; Wazir and Finance Minister, Muscat and Oman, 1925–30; 1926–31 made many camel-journeys into unknown South Arabia and first mapping; first European to cross Rub' al Khali Desert; gold medallist of Royal Geographical Societies of England, Belgium and Scotland, of Geographical Society of New York and Burton Memorial medallist of Royal Asiatic Society; delivered Lowell Lectures, Boston, USA, 1934. *Publications:* Alarms and Excursions in Arabia;

Arabia Felix; The Arabs; Four Strange Tongues from South Arabia—the Hadara group. *Address:* British Post Office POB 60, Tangier, Morocco. *Club:* Athenæum.

Died 27 Dec. 1950.

THOMAS, Sir Brumwell; *see* Thomas, Sir A. B.

THOMAS, Carmichael; Chairman of the Graphic, Daily Graphic, and Bystander from 1900 until his retirement in 1917 after forty-three years' active service as Art Editor, General Manager, etc; Past President of the Newspaper Society; Member of Council or Chairman of the Central London Throat and Ear Hospital, 1899–1938; Chairman of the Piccadilly Art Galleries Co. Ltd, 1900–29; Chairman of Council of the London Society, retired, 1934; Member of Council, Vice-President, or Treasurer of the Royal Society of Arts, 1900–41; *b* June 1856; *m* Rose Eugenie (*d* 1925), *d* of Thomas Oliver, FRIBA, Newcastle-on-Tyne; two *s* two *d*. *Recreation:* gardening. *Address:* Mount Cottage, Borough Green, Kent. *Club:* Athenæum.

Died 13 May 1942.

THOMAS, Lt-Col Sir Charles John Howell, KCB 1928; KCMG 1934; Kt 1927; CMG 1925; TD, Hon. LLD (Wales); Chairman of Tithe Redemption Commission since 1936; Hon. Fellow, Queen's College, Cambridge, 1935; Chairman of Samaritan Free Hospital for Women; Member Council of Management, Henry Ford Institute of Agricultural Engineering; Deputy-President Red Cross Agriculture Fund; Member Board of Governors, College of Estate Management; Chairman of Board of Studies in Estate Management, London University; Member of Court of Governors of London School of Economics; *b* 1874; *o surv. s* of late John Howell Thomas; unmarried. Served European War, 1914–18, France, Egypt, and India; Lieut-Col RFA Chief Valuer, Board of Inland Revenue, 1925; Permanent Secretary of Ministry of Agriculture and Fisheries, 1927–36; Member of Council Surveyors Institution, 1923–27; Member of Treasury Committee on Post Office Buildings, 1911; British Member of International Valuation Board Reparation Commission, Paris, set up under Treaty of Versailles; British Member of International Committee on Ceded Property, Paris, under Treaties of Trianon, Neuilly, and St Germain, 1922; British Member of Compensation (Ireland) Commission, 1922–25; Member of United Kingdom Delegations, Imperial Economic Conference, Ottawa, 1932, and World Monetary and Economic Conference, London, 1934; Chairman, 1934–36, and United Kingdom Representative on Executive Council of the Imperial Agricultural Bureaux, 1928–37; Chairman and principal UK Delegate, British Commonwealth Scientific Conference, London, 1936; Chairman, Stores Committee, BRC and St John War Organisation, 1939–41. *Address:* Lancaster Cottage, Gregories Road, Beaconsfield, Bucks. *T:* Beaconsfield 1214. *Clubs:* Athenæum, Union.

Died 26 Nov. 1943.

THOMAS, Ethel Nancy Miles, DSc, FLS; Fellow of University College, London; Examiner for University of London; formerly Head of the Department of Botany, University College, Leicester; Reader in University of London; in charge Botanical Department, University of S Wales and Monmouthshire, and National Museum of Wales; *d* of Mary Emily Davies and David Miles Thomas; *m* Hugh Henry Francis Hyndman, Barrister-at-Law. *Educ:* home; Mayo High School; Royal College of Science and University College. Gold Medal at University College; President of Women's Union; Prize of Apothecaries Society. Member of Council of Linnæan Society for five years; Member of Executive Committee for Imperial Botanical Conference; Vice-President, formerly Recorder, of Botany Section of British Association; Member of General and Sectional and Research Committees; Hon. Director Botanical Research Trust Laboratory. War work: Pathological work for War Office and for Medical Research Committee; President of Leicester Branch of British Federation of University Women, Delegate to International Council, etc.; formerly President of Association of University Land Workers; temporary Inspector Board of Agriculture. *Publications:* Anatomy of Acrosticum aureum; New Phytologist; The Plant as Healer; Agricultural Section of Labour and Finance: War and Reconstruction; Morphology and Anatomy of the Young Pineapple; papers to botanical journals, reviews, etc. *Recreations:* travelling, etc.

Died 28 Aug. 1944.

THOMAS, Col Francis Herbert Sullivan, CB 1916; *b* 2 Oct. 1862. Entered Army, 1882; Capt. ISC 1893; Major Indian Army, 1901; Lt-Col 1908; Col 1912; served Burma, 1886–88 (medal 2 clasps); Chinlushai Expedition, 1889–90 (despatches, clasp); Manipur, 1891 (despatches, clasp); retired, 1919. *Address:* Culmcott, Uffculme, Devon.

Died 8 June 1944.

THOMAS, Lt-Col Frank S.; *see* Williams-Thomas.

THOMAS, George Arthur, CIE 1925; *b* Coaley, Gloucestershire, 4 May 1877; *m* Gwenllian Dorothy, *d* of Very Rev. David Howell, Dean of St Davids; two *s*. *Educ:* Clifton College; Emmanuel College, Cambridge (Senior Scholar and Stewart of Rannock Scholar). First Class Classical Tripos, 1899. Appointed to the ICS, 1900; served in the Bombay Presidency, Revenue Department; Secretary to the Government of Bombay in the Revenue and General Depts, 1916–26; Chief Secretary, 1926; Member of the Council of State, 1927; Commissioner in Sind, 1929–31; Member of Exec. Council of Governor of Bombay, 1931; retd, 1935. *Address:* Red Tiles, Bray, Berks.

Died 5 Feb. 1950.

THOMAS, Brig.-Gen. Gwyn G.; *see* Gwyn-Thomas.

THOMAS, Herbert J., FRAeS; Director Bristol Aeroplane Co. Ltd; Member of Council Society of British Aircraft Constructors (Chairman, 1933–35); *b* 1892; *s* of late Samuel Herbert and Victoria Thomas; *m* 1920, Vera, *d* of Stephen Codrington; two *s*. *Educ:* London; Clifton College. In France on various balloon and aeroplane experimental work, 1909 and 1910; started in foundation of Bristol Aeroplane Co., 1910; Pilot-Aviators certificate No. 51. Sheriff of Bristol, 1946–47. *Address:* Home Farm, Old Sodbury, near Bristol. *T:* Chipping Sodbury 2264. *Clubs:* Royal Aero, Royal Automobile; Royal Aero of Belgium; Aero de France.

Died 20 May 1947.

THOMAS, Sir Illtyd, Kt 1925; DL, JP Cardiff; Senior Alderman, Cardiff; Hon. Treasurer of National Museum of Wales, 1917–25; Hon. Freeman of City of Cardiff; *b* 6 June 1864; *γ s* of late George Thomas of Ely, Cardiff; *m* 1st, 1885; two *d*; 2nd, 1927, Henrietta (*d* 1929), *widow* of Charles M. Morgan, Cardiff. *Educ:* Bedford; Cardiff. Is a mining and civil engineer, chartered surveyor, and auctioneer; Councillor of Cardiff, 1895; Alderman, 1905; Lord Mayor, 1907–08; Chairman of National Economy, Food Control, and War Savings Committees during War of 1914–18; suggested to Chancellor of Exchequer the Thrift or Savings (War) Stamps; originator of idea of abolition of Immature Spirits Act and of the No Treating Order; one of the original Members of Council and Court of Governors of the National Museum of Wales, and as such collected over £40,000 for its Building Fund; ex-Chairman of South Wales Branch of Surveyors' Institution and of Auctioneers' Inst.; Founder and first Pres. S Wales Agricultural Valuers' Association and Pres., 1939–40; Ex-Pres. Central Association of Agricultural Valuers; Member of Court of Governors of University College of South Wales and Monmouthshire (Chairman

Agricultural Advisory Board); Chm. (1928–34) of Lord Chancellor's Magisterial Advisory Committee for Cardiff; Member of the South Wales Institute of Engineers; certificated Colliery Manager (First Class); Referee under Rating and Valuation Act 1925; Member of Council of Institute of Arbitrators. *Recreations:* agricultural pursuits, public work. *Address:* The Mead, Llandaff, Cardiff. *T:* Cardiff 490, Llandaff 47. *Clubs:* Farmers'; Cardiff Conservatives, Cardiff and County, Cardiff.

Died 22 June 1943.

THOMAS, Ivor Cradock, MVO 1911; OBE 1919; MIEE; *b* Llanelly, S Wales, 4 April 1861; *s* of late Benjamin Thomas, FRCS (Eng.); *m* 1903, Laura Mulgrave, *d* of late Maj.-Gen. Campbell Hardy, RA; one *s* one *d*. *Educ:* Cowbridge College; Epsom College; RIE College, Coopers Hill. Appointed to Telegraph Department of Government of India, 1881; served Black Mountain Expedition (India Frontier Medal, Hazara Clasp, despatches), 1891; Coronation Durbar, Delhi, 1903; International Telegraph Conference, London, 1903; in charge telegraph arrangements Coronation Durbar, Delhi, 1911; Director of Traffic, Indian Telegraph Dept, 1912–14; Chief Engineer, Telegraphs, India, 1914–16; retired 4 April 1916; Ministry of Munitions, Priority Department, Nov. 1916–June 1919. *Address:* Alverstone, Wych Hill Lane, Woking, Surrey. *T:* Woking 928. *Club:* East India and Sports.

Died 23 Feb. 1942.

THOMAS, Rt Hon. James Henry; PC 1917; *b* Newport, 3 Oct. 1874; labouring parents; *m* 1898, Agnes Hill Newport, Mon; two *s* two *d*. *Educ:* Council schools. Commenced work at nine years of age as an errand boy; from that to engine-cleaner, and stage to stage as fireman and engine-driver (GWR); General Secretary, National Union of Railwaymen, 1918–24, and 1925–31; MP (Lab) Derby, 1910–31 (Nat. Lab) 1931–36; Secretary of State for Colonies, 1924 and 1931; Lord Privy Seal and Minister of Employment, 1929–30; Secretary of State for the Dominions 1930–35; for the Colonies 1935–36; elected Town Councillor of Swindon, Wilts, Chairman Finance Committee and Electricity and Tramways Committee; President ASRS, 1910; Hon. LLD Cambridge, 1920; Hon. DCL Oxford, 1926; Vice-Chairman of Parliamentary Labour Party, 1921; JP Kent; President of International Federation of Trade Unions, 1920–24; President and Chairman of Parliamentary Committee of TUC, 1920–21; was a Governor of Dulwich College. *Publications:* When Labour Rules, 1920; My Story, 1937. *Recreation:* interested in all outdoor sports.

Died 21 Jan. 1949.

THOMAS, Col Lionel B.; *see* Beaumont-Thomas.

THOMAS, Llewelyn E.; *see* Evan-Thomas.

THOMAS, Captain Mervyn Somerset, DSO 1940; Royal Navy; commanding HMS Boscawen and as Captain-in-Charge, HM Naval Base, Portland, Dorset; *b* 30 Aug. 1900; *s* of late William Edwin Somerset-Thomas and Agnes Somerset; *m* 1923, Gabrielle Iolanthe, *d* of Ernest Bentley Shaw-Yates, Banwell Castle, Somerset; one *d*. *Educ:* Royal Naval Colleges, Osborne and Dartmouth. Joined RN 1914; HMS Queen Elizabeth, 1917 (Flagship Admiral Beatty); HMS New Zealand, 1919–20 as Sub-Lieut (Flag of Admiral of the Fleet Earl Jellicoe for world cruise); lent to NZ Division of Royal Navy, 1923–26; HMS Thracian as Executive Officer, 1926–29 (China Station); Commanded HMS Tetrach in 1930 and many destroyers before and after 1936 (when promoted Commander) and during War of 1939–45 Grafton, Dainty, Auckland, Faulkner (Dainty and Auckland sunk off Tobruk, 1941); then served on staffs of Admiral Sir Henry Pridham-Wippell, Vice-Adm. Sir Bernard Rawlings and Vice-Adm. Sir William Tennant, at Alexandria, 1941–45 and

RNAS Yeovilton (HMS Heron), 1942–43. War Cross, Greek. *Address:* Chatterpark, Courtlands Lane, Lympstone, S Devon.

Died 21 Aug. 1947.

THOMAS, Rev. Canon Richard Albert, OBE 1919; MA; FSA; Hon. Canon of Chester Cathedral, 1921; Canon-Emeritus, 1935; Hon. CF, 1919; *b* Bagillt, Flints, 7 Oct. 1873; 3rd and *γ s* of late Owen and Ellen Thomas; *m* 1909, Mabel Annie (Headmistress of Newport, IOW, County Secondary School, 1903–09), (*d* 1939), *e d* of late Joseph John and Fanny Hinton, Sturminster Marshall, Dorset; one *s. Educ:* King's School, Chester; Trinity Hall, Cambridge (Senior Scholar, College Prizeman in Maths, First Cressingham English Essay Prize). BA Mathl Tripos (Fifth Sen. Opt.), 1895; Nat. Sci. Tripos, 1896; Prox. Acc. Maitland Univ. Essay Prize, 1898. Deacon, 1897; Priest, 1898; Lecturer in Maths and Science at Chester Diocesan Training College, 1896–1905; Assistant Chaplain, 1897–1905; Vice-Principal, 1898–1905; Vice-Principal and Assistant Chaplain at Winchester Training College, 1906–10; Principal and Chaplain of Chester Diocesan Training College, 1910–35; Vicar of Gazeley and Rector of Kentford, 1935–36; Vicar of Gazeley and Rector of Dalham, 1936–38; Temp. CF on service in France, 1916–19; Assistant to ACG, HQ, Fifth Army (CF Third Class), 1918–19; Acting ACG at HQ, Fifth Army and later Acting ACG at HQ Fourth Army, during the March Retreat, 1918 (OBE, despatches). *Recreations:* archæology and monastic history. *Address:* (temp. for the duration: Rock Close, Kington, Herefordshire); The Rookery, Waterbeach, Cambridge. *T:* Waterbeach 237.

Died 31 July 1943.

THOMAS, Ven. Richard Rice; Archdeacon of St David's since 1937; Vicar of Lamphey with Hodgeston since 1941. *Educ:* Keble College, Oxford; Cuddesdon College. BA 1895; MA 1898. Deacon, 1896; priest, 1897; Curate of Wantage, Berks, 1896–1908; Vicar of Haroldston West with Lambston, 1908–23; Vicar of Llanstadwell, 1923–41; TCF, 1916–17; Hon. CF, 1918. *Address:* Lamphey Vicarage, Pembroke.

Died 17 May 1942.

THOMAS, Brig. Robert Henry, CSI 1934; DSO 1919; Surveyor-General of India, 1928–33; *b* 23 April 1877. *Educ:* St Edmund's College; St Paul's School. Served European War, 1914–19 (despatches, DSO, French Croix de Guerre); retired, 1933. *Club:* Army and Navy.

Died 17 Oct. 1946.

THOMAS, Salusbury Vaughan; *b* 20 Nov. 1856; *s* of late Rev. J. W. Thomas of Tapton Manor, Derbyshire, and Stansted Vicarage, Hertford; *m* 1888, *o c* of J. Hunter, 9 New Square, Lincoln's Inn, Tregenna, Exmouth, and The Avenue, Worcester Park. *Educ:* privately. *Recreations:* hunting, Master of the Dove Valley Harriers, Master of the Foxhounds 28 years, Harriers 12 years, and Salmon Fishing 50 years; largest salmon killed with fly on the Erne in Ireland, 43 lbs, in 1904. *Club:* East India and Sports.

Died 7 Dec. 1943.

THOMAS, William Edwin S.; *see* Somerset-Thomas.

THOMAS, Sir William Henry, Kt 1921; MBE; Solicitor, Deputy Alderman of the City of London; Chief Commoner, 1913; *b* 24 Dec. 1859; *s* of Richard Thomas; *m* 1891, Mary Davidson (*d* 1943), *er d* of J. Grant Shepherd, JP, Bournemouth; one *s* two *d. Educ:* Commercial School, Bournemouth. Head of the firm of Parker, Thomas & Co., Solicitors 20–21 Lawrence Lane, EC; an Arbitrator of the London Court of Arbitration; one of HM Lieutenants for the City of London, Governor St Thomas's Hospital; Governor City and Guilds Institute; late Hon. Treasurer City of London

Conservative and Unionist Association; Chevalier de la Légion d'Honneur. *Address:* Talbot, Overbury Avenue, Beckenham, Kent. *T:* Beckenham 1936.

Died 1 Oct. 1947.

THOMAS, Sir William James, 1st Bt *cr* 1919; Kt 1914; JP; *b* 10 March 1867; *m* 1917, Maud Mary, *d* of late Alderman George Cooper, Bexhill. Equipped the Welsh University Medical School at King Edward VII Hospital, Cardiff; Sheriff of Glamorgan, 1936. *Heir: s* William James Cooper, *b* 7 May 1919. *Address:* Birchwood Grange, Penylan, Cardiff.

Died 3 Jan. 1945.

THOMASSON, Lt-Col Franklin; late 5th North Lancashire Regiment; *s* of John Pennington Thomasson, formerly MP for Bolton, and Katherine Lucas Thomasson, *niece* of John Bright; *m* 1st, Elizabeth Lawton (*d* 1927), *d* of late Caleb Coffin of New York; one *s* two *d*; 2nd, 1929, Gertrude Margaret Prescott-Smith; one *s* two *d. Educ:* private schools. Cotton-spinner retired; contested Westhoughton, 1900; Stretford, 1901; MP (L) Leicester, 1906–10. *Address:* Parkhill, Lyndhurst, Hants. *Clubs:* Queen's, All England Lawn Tennis.

Died 29 Oct. 1941.

THOMLINSON, Lt-Col Sir William, Kt 1936; DL, JP; *b* 1854; *m* 1882, Hannah (*d* 1926), *d* of Thomas Kirk, Eaglescliffe, Co. Durham; one *s* two *d. Address:* The Green, Seaton Carew, West Hartlepool. *T:* 217.

Died 15 May 1943.

THOMPSON, Alexander M.; *b* Carlsruhe, Baden, 9 March 1861; parents English; *m* 1st, Fanny Veail; 2nd, Louisa Helen Robinson; one *s. Educ:* Lycée St Louis, Paris; London. Clerk, then writer, on Manchester Examiner; contributor of Echoes of the Day to Sporting Chronicle; dramatic critic, Sunday Chronicle; founded Clarion with Blatchford, 1891; part proprietor and acting editor; contributor to Sunday Chronicle, John Bull, Daily Mail, etc. *Publications:* Haunts of Old Cockaigne; Dangle's Mixture; Dangle's Rough-Cut; Dangle's Guide to Paris; a book on Japan; Here I Lie (autobiography); political pamphlets; musical plays. *Recreation:* work. *Address:* 22 York Mansions, Battersea Park, SW11. *T:* Macaulay 1248.

Died 25 March 1948.

THOMPSON, Rev. Austin Henry, MA; Vicar of St Peter's, Eaton Square, SW1; Rural Dean of Westminster; Prebendary of St Paul's Cathedral; *b* 29 April 1870; *s* of late Lt-Col John Baylis and Gertrude Tottenham Thompson; *m* 1909, Anstace Mary Mylne; one *s* two *d. Educ:* King's School, Canterbury; St Edmund Hall, Oxford (2nd Class Classical Moderations, 3rd Class Litterae Humaniores). Curate, St Paul's, Truro, 1894–97; St John's, Norwood, 1897–1900; All Hallows, Barking-by-the-Tower, 1900–06; Tait Missioner, Diocese of Canterbury and Six Preacher in Canterbury Cathedral, 1906–09; Vicar of St Peter's, Ealing W, 1909–16. *Address:* St Peter's Vicarage, 24 Chester Square, SW. *T:* Sloane 7790.

Died April 1941.

THOMPSON, Charles Henry, MA; Fellow since 1897 of Queen's College, Oxford; *b* 18 Jan. 1865; *e s* of Henry Lynn Thompson and Elizabeth Sarah Hudston; *m* 1904, Emily, *e d* of G. F. Hornsby, Huddersfield; one *s. Educ:* Ripon Grammar School; Hoddesdon School; Queen's College, Oxford (Scholar). Senior University Mathematical Scholar, 1889; Student of Christ Church, 1890–97; Lecturer at St David's College, Lampeter, 1889–90; Lecturer at the Durham College of Science (now King's College), 1891–93; Praelector in Mathematics at Queen's College, Oxford, 1893–1936; Tutor (subsequently Senior Tutor) 1908–36. *Publication:*

Paper in the Quarterly Journal of Mathematics. *Recreations:* climbing and cycling. *Address:* Brookfield House, Greystoke Avenue, Brooklands, Cheshire.

Died 4 Dec. 1948.

THOMPSON, Charles John S., MBE, PhD; Commander of the Order of the Hospital of St John of Jerusalem; Member of the Royal Society of Medicine; Associate, Royal Academy of Medicine (Turin); Associate, Royal Academy of Agriculture (Turin); Hon. Curator of Historical Collection of the Museum of Royal College of Surgeons of England; *b* Liverpool; *s* of J. Thompson, Sheffield; *m* 1893, Ethel May, *d* of Rev. W. H. Tindall; two *s* two *d. Educ:* Liverpool Institute; Liverpool University. Late Curator, Historical Medical Museum, London, from its foundation; founder and officer-in-charge, Holmleigh Auxiliary Military Hospital, 1914–19. *Publications:* Mystery and Romance of Alchemy and Pharmacy; Poison Mysteries in History, Romance, and Crime; Compendium of Pharmacopœias; Mystery and Lure of Perfume; Mysteries and Secrets of Magic; Public Hygiene in the Early Civilisations; Mysteries of History; The Quacks of Old London; The Mystery and Art of the Apothecary; The Mystery and Romance of Astrology; The Mystery and Lore of Apparitions; The Mystery and Lore of Monsters; Poisons and Poisoners; The Lure and Romance of Alchemy; Zorastro'; Guide to the Surgical Instruments and Objects in the Historical Series of Museum, Royal College of Surgeons of England, with their History and Development; The Hand of Destiny; The Witchery of Jane Shore, 1933; Lord Lister; The Mystic Mandrake in lore and legend, 1934; Fair Rosamond, the romance of a royal mistress; Love, Matrimony and Romance in Old London, 1936; Poison Mysteries Unsolved: By person or persons unknown, 1937; Mysteries of Sex, 1938; Dancing: an historical sketch, 1939; The Evolution and Development of Surgical Instruments, 1941; Magic and Healing. *Address:* Old Place, Cuddington, Bucks. *T:* Haddenham 48.

Died 14 July 1943.

THOMPSON, Sir D'Arcy Wentworth, Kt 1937; CB 1898; FRS; DLitt (Cambridge); Hon. DCL (Oxford); DSc (Dublin, Witwatersrand, Delhi); LLD (Aberdeen, Edinburgh); Professor of Natural History, St Andrews University, in Dundee, 1884–1917, in St Andrews, since 1917; Past President, Classical Association, 1929, Scottish Classical Association, 1935, Royal Phys. Soc. Edin. and Royal Soc. Edin. 1934–39; R. Sc. Geog. Soc. 1942–46; Foreign, Corr. or Hon. Member of Nat. Acad. Sci., USA; Amer. Philos. Soc. (Philadelphia); Amer. Acad. Arts and Sci. (Boston); Polish Acad. (Cracow); Schweiz. Naturf. Ges.; Friends of NH (Moscow); Boston Soc. NH; Soc. Biol. Paris; Soc. Zool. France; Zool. Soc. London; Malacological Soc.; Edin. Mathem. Soc.; Linnean medallist, 1938; David Giraud Elliot medallist, 1942; Darwin Medallist, Royal Soc., 1946; scientific member of Fishery Board for Scotland, 1898–1939; *b* 1860; *s* of D'Arcy Wentworth Thompson, Prof. of Greek, Queen's College, Galway; *m* 1901, Maureen, *d* of William Drury; three *d.* British Delegate Behring Sea Fisheries Conference, 1897; North Sea Conferences, Stockholm, 1899; Christiania, 1901, etc.; Herbert Spencer Lecturer, Oxford, 1913; Huxley Lecturer, Birmingham, 1917; Lowell Lecturer, Boston, Mass, 1936, etc. *Publications:* Science and the Classics, 1939; A Glossary of Greek Birds, 1895, new ed., 1936; A Glossary of Greek Fishes, 1947; Aristotle's Historia Animalium, 1910; On Growth and Form, 1917, new ed. 1942, etc. *Address:* 44 South Street, St Andrews. *Clubs:* Athenæum; University (Edinburgh).

Died 21 June 1948.

THOMPSON, Edward (John), MC; MA (Oxon); PhD (Lond.); Fellow of Oriel College, Oxford; Moncure Conway Memorial Lecturer, 1942; *b* 9 April 1886; *e s* of J. M. Thompson; *m* Theodosia, *e d* of Dr William Jessup,

USA; two *s. Educ:* Kingswood School, Bath. Educational missionary, Bankura College, Bengal, 1910–22; Campaigns of Mesopotamia, 1916–17 (MC and despatches), and Palestine, 1918. *Publications:* The Knight Mystic, 1907; John in Prison, 1912; Atonement, 1924; Tagore, Poet and Dramatist, 1926; An Indian Day, 1927; These Men Thy Friends, 1927; The Thracian Stranger, 1928; Crusader's Coast, 1928; In Araby Orion, 1930; Collected Poems, 1930; A Farewell to India, 1931; Lament for Adonis, 1932; Rise and Fulfilment of British Rule in India, 1934; Last Voyage; Sir Walter Ralegh; Introducing the Arnisons, 1935; Burmese Silver, 1937; Lord Metcalfe, 1937; The Youngest Disciple, 1938; An End of the Hours, 1938; John Arnison, 1939; New Recessional, 1942; Essex and Elizabeth, 1943; The Making of the Indian Princes, 1943; One Hundred Poems, 1944; Robert Bridges, 1944. Play, The King's Pirate, St Martin's Theatre, 1937. *Address:* Bledlow, Bucks.

Died 28 April 1946.

THOMPSON, Sir Ernest, Kt 1929; Company Director; JP County of Chester; *b* 2 April 1865; *s* of William Thompson, Rock Ferry, Cheshire; *m* Elisabeth Alice, *d* of Arthur Goodwin of Peterchurch, Herefordshire; one *s* one *d. Address:* Delveron House, Mottram St Andrew, Prestbury, Cheshire.

Died 12 July 1941.

THOMPSON, Ernest Claude M.; see Meysey-Thompson.

THOMPSON, Fred; dramatic author since 1913; *b* London, 24 Jan. 1884; *o s* of Frederick Edwin Thompson and Grace Margaret Trery Sinclair; *m* Clarice Eileen Rudge; no *c. Educ:* Newton Abbot; Slade School of Art. Was articled pupil to an architect for four years; afterwards became a theatrical and sporting caricaturist; served in RNVR 1914–16. In the year 1919 was author or part-author of six musical plays running concurrently at West End theatres in London. *Productions:* Many musical plays and revues; including To-Night's the Night, The Boy (founded on Sir Arthur Pinero's farce, The Magistrate), The Bing Boys Are Here (with George Grossmith), Alice Up-to-Date, part author of Mr Manhattan, Pell Mell, 8d. a Mile, The Bing Boys on Broadway, author of Who's Hooper? (founded on Sir Arthur Pinero's farce In Chancery), 1919; The Kiss Call, 1919; part author of Afgar, Baby Bunting, Maggie, and The Eclipse, 1919; The Golden Moth (with P. G. Wodehouse), 1921; Phi-Phi, 1922; The Cousin from Nowhere, 1923; Stop Flirting! 1923; Lady Be Good! 1924; Tell Me More, 1925; Tip-Toes, 1926; Rio Rita and Five O'Clock Girl, 1927–28; Funny Face, 1929; Sons o' Guns, 1930; The Song of the Drum, 1931; Out of the Bottle, 1932; author of several talking pictures, 1933–35; This'll Make You Whistle, 1935; Seeing Stars, 1935; Swing Along, 1936; Going Places, 1936; Going Greek; Hide and Seek, 1937; The Fleet's Lit Up, 1938; Magyar Melody (with Eric Maschwitz and Guy Boltor), 1939; Present Arms, 1940; Follow the Girls, 1944. *Clubs:* Buck's; Lotos (New York).

Died 10 April 1949.

THOMPSON, Brig.-Gen. Frederick Hacket-, CB 1902; CBE 1919; *b* 1 July 1858. Entered army, 1879; Capt., 1884; Major, 1894; Lieut-Col, 1901; served as Transport Officer, Egyptian War, 1882 (medal with clasp, Khedive's star); Soudan, 1885–86 (wounded); Soudan, 1898 (despatches, 4th class Osmanieh, British medal, Khedive's medal with two clasps); South Africa, 1900–02 (Queen's medal 4 clasps, despatches, CB); commanded 1st Battalion Cameron Highlanders; commanded No. 7 District, 1911–14; commanded troops in Ceylon, 1915–18. *Club:* Naval and Military.

Died 15 Feb. 1944.

THOMPSON, Rev. George; *m*; one *s* one *d*. *Educ:* Corpus Christi Coll. Camb. MA. Ordained 1881; Curate of Holy Trinity, South Shields, 1881–82; Chaplain of Mission to Seamen, Hartlepool, 1883–87; Vicar of Harley Wood, 1887–97; Diocesan Chaplain, and General Secretary of Wakefield Diocesan Societies, 1897–1908; Hon. Canon, Wakefield, 1902–08; editor Wakefield Diocesan Calendar, 1909–20; Missioner, Canon Assistant Wakefield Cathedral, 1908–20; Rector, Penticton, BC, Canada, 1921–28; Vicar, Arrow Lakes, BC, 1928–35; retired 1935. *Address:* Okanagan Mission, BC, Canada.

Died 16 Nov. 1941.

THOMPSON, Gustav Weber, CBE; General Medical Practitioner; *b* Formby, Lancs, 8 Dec. 1878; *s* of John Robinson Thompson; *m* 1919, Marie Antoinette Stringer, *née* Bannwart; three *s*. *Educ:* Trinity College, Dublin. *Recreation:* bridge. *Address:* The Villa, Wellington, Salop. *T:* Wellington 72.

Died 14 May 1944.

THOMPSON, Sir (Henry Francis) Herbert, 2nd Bt *cr* 1899; FBA 1933; Hon. DLitt (Oxon); Fellow of University College, London; *b* 2 April 1859; *s* of Sir Henry Thompson, FRCS; *S* father, 1904; unmarried. *Educ:* Marlborough; Trinity College, Cambridge. Barrister-at-Law. *Heir:* none. *Address:* 17 Macaulay Buildings, Bath. *Club:* Athenæum.

Died 26 May 1944.

THOMPSON, Rt Rev. Henry Gregory, OSB; *b* 27 March 1871; *y s* of Edward Thompson, JP, of Plas Annie, Mold, Flintshire, banker and coal-master, for many years Director of N and S Wales Bank and Ocean Coal Co., and Anna Maria Griffiths. *Educ:* St Mary's, Oscott; St Augustine's, Ramsgate; St Anselm's Benedictine College, Rome. Professed a monk of the Benedictine Order, 1896; studied for the Priesthood in Rome, 1896–1903; Priest, 1902; returned to England and worked, chiefly in the school at St Augustine's, Ramsgate, till 1910; Catholic Bishop of Gibraltar, 1910–27. *Address:* St Augustine's Abbey, Ramsgate.

Died 27 Oct. 1942.

THOMPSON, Herbert; *b* Hunslet, Leeds, 11 Aug. 1856; *s* of John Thompson, bank manager, and Jane, *d* of William Thurnam; *m* 1897, Edith Mary, *d* of F. R. Spark, JP. *Educ:* Wiesbaden; St John's College, Cambridge MA, LLM LittD (hon. causa) Leeds University, 1924. Barrister-at-law, Inner Temple, 1879; Music and Art Critic to the Yorkshire Post 1886–1936. *Publication:* Wagner and Wagenseil, 1926. *Recreation:* sketching from Nature. *Address:* 11 Oak Bank, Headingley, Leeds, 6.

Died 6 May 1945.

THOMPSON, Sir Herbert; *see* Thompson, Sir H. F. H.

THOMPSON, Herbert, CSI 1911; late Indian Civil Service; *b* 2 Oct. 1870; *s* of John Thompson of Balne, Yorkshire; *m* 1900, Margaret, *d* of late John Hutchinson. *Educ:* St Peter's School, York; Trinity College, Cambridge. Appointed to ICS 1889; posted to Burma, 1891; held appointments as Assistant and Deputy Commissioner, Commissioner of Excise and Revenue, Chief Secretary to Government of Burma, and Financial Commissioner, Burma; retired 1920. *Recreations:* boating, golf, tennis, etc. *Club:* East India and Sports.

Died 3 Sept. 1949.

THOMPSON, Herbert Marshall; KC 1920; Recorder of Belfast and County Court Judge of Antrim, 1921–41; *b* Belfast; 4th *s* of Rev. William Thompson, MA, Rector of Layde, Co. Antrim; *m* Mary Stuart, *d* of Robert Harrison, Dromore, Co. Down. *Educ:* Coleraine Academical Institution; Trinity College, Dublin. Victoria Prizeman and Medallist in Oratory and Legal subjects, Kings' Inns, Dublin; Medallist in Oratory and

Composition, College Historical Society, TCD. Called to Irish Bar, 1902. *Recreations:* music, golf. *Address:* Kilnadore, Windsor Avenue, Belfast. *T:* Belfast 66790. *Clubs:* Union, Ulster, Belfast.

Died 11 Feb. 1945.

THOMPSON, John Baird, CBE 1929; *b* Ballymena, Ireland, 20 Dec. 1868; *s* of late Geo. L. Thompson, Saintfield, Ireland; *m* 1st, 1895, Kathleen L. (decd), *d* of Jas Edmiston; three *s*; 2nd, 1935, Ethel, *d* of late Thomas Wyatt, Southampton. *Educ:* private and public schools. Entered as Civil Engineer and Surveyor and served articles; entered service Lands and Survey Department, NZ as Assistant Surveyor, 1891; District Surveyor, 1907; Land Drainage Engineer, 1910; Chief Drainage Engineer NZ, 1921; visited Canada and US in connection with business of NZ Govt, 1920; Under-Secretary for Lands and Permanent Head Lands and Survey Dept NZ, 1922–31; Controller of Land Purchase and Chairmanship of several official Boards; retired, 1931. *Address:* 16 Litchfield Street, Parnell, Auckland, NZ.

Died 30 Aug. 1948.

THOMPSON, Sir Luke, Kt 1934; MP (U) Sunderland, 1922–29, and 1931–35; Director of John Thompson & Sons (Sunderland), Ltd, coal merchants; *b* 18 July 1867; *s* of John and Catherine Thompson; *m* 1895, Ann Trobe, *d* of Cuthbert Potts, Sunderland; two *d*. *Educ:* Grange School. *Recreation:* keen horseman. *Address:* Thornhill, Beresford Park, Sunderland; Fell End, Slaggyford, Northumberland. *T:* Sunderland 4235. *Club:* Overseas.

Died 15 Jan. 1941.

THOMPSON, Adm. Percival Henry H.; *see* Hall-Thompson.

THOMPSON, Sir Percy, KBE 1920; CB 1916; *b* 18 Dec. 1872; *s* of Richard Thompson, JP, Whalley, Lancashire; *m* 1903, Eugénie Elaine, *d* of Leicester Edwards, RN; two *s* four *d*. *Educ:* Rugby; Brasenose College, Oxford. Assistant Secretary, Board of Inland Revenue, 1909; Secretary, 1913–19; Commissioner, 1916–19; Deputy Chairman Board of Inland Revenue, 1919–35. *Recreations:* golf, fishing, shooting. *Club:* Union.

Died 12 July 1946.

THOMPSON, Reginald Campbell, MA, DLitt, FBA, FSA; Shillito Reader in Assyriology; Fellow of Merton College (Sub-Warden 1933–35) Oxford; Editor of Iraq; *b* 21 Aug. 1876; *s* of Reginald Edward Thompson, MD and Annie Isabella De Morgan; *m* 1911, Barbara Brodrick, *d* of late Sir Richard Atkinson Robinson; one *s* one *d*. *Educ:* St Paul's School; Caius College, Cambridge. Exhibitioner Caius College, 1895; Open Stewart of Rannoch Scholarship (Hebrew); First Class Oriental (Semitic) Tripos, 1898. Assistant, Egyptian and Assyrian Dept, British Museum, 1899–1905; Sudan Survey Dept, 1906; Assistant Professor, Semitic Languages, Chicago University, 1907–09; Conducted excavations on behalf of the British Museum, at Nineveh, 1904, 1927, 1929, 1930, 1931; at Carchemish, 1911; at Abu Shahrain, 1918; on behalf of the Byzantine Fund, at Wadi Sarga, 1913; with L. W. King collated the rock-inscription of Darius at Behistun, 1904; Captain of St Paul's School and Cambridge University Shooting Eights; Territorial Efficiency Medal; Captain, SSO, GHQ, Intelligence, Mesopotamia, Feb. 1915–March 1918 (four times in despatches) and subsequently until May 1918 attached Political; Home Guard, 1940; travelled in Tripoli, Sinai, Sudan, Asia Minor, Mesopotamia, Persia. *Publications:* Reports of the Magicians and Astrologers of Nineveh and Babylon, 2 vols, 1900; The Devils and Evil Spirits of Babylonia, 2 vols, 1903–1904; Late Babylonian Letters, 1906; (with L. W. King) The Inscription of Darius the Great at Behistun, 1907; Semitic Magic, 1908; A Pilgrim's Scrip, 1915; A Small Hdbk to the History and Antiquities of Mesopotamia, 1918; Assyrian Medical Texts, 1923; The

Assyrian Herbal, 1924; and On the Chemistry of the Ancient Assyrians, 1925 (both originally communicated as papers to the Royal Society); A Catalogue of Late Babylonian Tablets, 1927; The Epic of Gilgamish (translation), 1928; (text) 1930; (With R. W. Hutchinson) A Century of Exploration at Nineveh, 1929; The Prisms of Esarhaddon and of Ashurbanipal, 1931; A Dictionary of Assyrian Chemistry and Geology, 1936; 500 plates of cuneiform texts in Cuneiform Texts from Babylonian Tablets, 1900–1906; Two novels under a pseudonym; The Seatonian Prize Poem, Ignatius, 1933; Digger's Fancy, 1938; Contributed to the Cambridge Ancient History, and Hastings' Dict. of Rel. and Ethics; various articles to Scientific Journals (on Assyrian medical texts, etc.; on excavations at Abu Shahrain, Archæologia, 1918; at Nineveh, with Messrs Hutchinson, Hamilton and Mallowan, Arch., 1929, and Liv. Annals, 1931, 1932, 1933; at Wadi Sarga, in Coptica, 1922; A New Decipherment of Hittite Hieroglyphs, Arch., 1912). *Recreations:* sailing, swimming, diving, fishing and shooting, and formerly gymnastics. *Address:* Trackways, Boars Hill, Oxford. *T:* Oxford 85114.

Died 23 May 1941.

THOMPSON, Lt-Col Richard James Campbell, CMG 1917; DSO 1916; MD; late RAMC; Secretary, St Thomas' Hospital Medical School, 1928–46; *b* 1 Aug. 1880; *s* of Richard Phillips Thompson, of Stamford, and Caroline Gwatkin; *m* 1916, Juliette, *e d* of late Commandant Cottin de Melville, Chevalier de la Légion d'Honneur; (one *s* killed on Active Service, 1940, Flying Officer RAFVR). *Educ:* Marlborough; St Thomas's Hospital. Joined RAMC 1905; Captain, 1908; Major, 1915; seconded to Egyptian Army, 1910–13 (Sudan Sleeping Sickness Commission); served European War, 1914–18 (despatches, DSO, CMG); retired pay, 1922. Master of the Salters' Company, 1941–43. *Address:* 68 Courtfield Gardens, SW5. *Clubs:* Athenæum, Junior Carlton.

Died 2 Oct. 1946.

THOMPSON, Viginti Tertius; *b* 1862; 4th *s* of Alderman Robert Thompson, JP, of West Hall, Whitburn, Co. Durham; *m* 1st, 1888, Violet, 4th *d* of late Col W. H. Allison of Whitburn; one *d*; 2nd, 1908, Euphemia, *o d* of late Charles Barnes of Plymouth; one *s* one *d*. *Educ:* Highgate School. High-Sheriff of Hants, 1924–25; JP for Counties Durham and Hampshire, retired. *Address:* Norton Manor, Sutton Scotney, Hants. *T:* Sutton Scotney 8.

Died 16 March 1946.

THOMPSON, Brig.-Gen. William George Hemsley, CMG 1919; DSO 1917; late Royal Artillery; *b* Stamford, 13 April 1871; *s* of William Thompson and Julia Ann Hunt; *m* 1912, Annette Wilhelmina, *d* of late Theodore Bryant of Juniper Hill, Dorking, and Gt Cumberland Place, W; two *d*. *Educ:* Marlborough. Haddington Artillery Militia, 1890–92; Royal Artillery, 1893; RHA 1898; served Tirah, NW Frontier, India, 1897–98 (medal and 3 clasps); S Africa 1899–1900 (wounded, despatches, Queen's medal and 2 clasps); European War, France, 1914–18 (despatches, CMG, DSO, Russian Order of St Anne); retired pay, 1920. *Address:* Woodman Mead, Warminster, Wilts.

Died 29 Nov. 1944.

THOMPSON, William Harding, MC, FRIBA, MTPI; *b* 1887; *s* of late William Cooper Thompson, Lancaster; *m* 1914, Anne, *d* of late R. A. Mitchel, Glasgow. *Educ:* Giggleswick School; University of London. Holt Travelling Scholar and Lever Prizeman, Liverpool University School of Architecture; London University Diploma in Town Planning and Civic Architecture; Student at the British School at Rome, 1913; Society of Architects' Post-Graduate American Scholarship, 1924. Served 1914–19 with the Honourable Artillery

Company and Royal Field Artillery; Adjutant 79th Bde, RFA, 1916–18; in command of a battery 79th Bde, 1918–19; Architect for Enham Village Centre (Hants) for Disabled Ex-service Men, 1920–27; in private practice as a Chartered Architect and Town Planning Consultant, 1920–40; Pres., Town Planning Institute, 1939–40; Technical Consultant to Regional Planning Committees in Hertfordshire, Oxfordshire and Dorset. Served in RAFVR, 1941–43. *Publications:* Cornwall, Coast, Moors, and Valleys; Devon, Coast, Moors and Rivers; Somerset Regional Survey; The County Landscape Series: Devon, Dorset, Surrey, Sussex, and Lakeland (with Geoffrey Clark); Contributions to various technical journals. *Address:* 8 Blackhall Road, Oxford. *T:* Oxford 2802.

Died 3 Nov. 1946.

THOMSON, Col Alexander M.; *see* Milne-Thomson.

THOMSON, Vice-Adm. Evelyn Claude Ogilvie, CB 1938; DSO 1917; *b* 13 April 1884; *s* of late Andrew Thomson, 21 Chester Street, Edinburgh; *m* 1918, Agnes Motherwell, *d* of Sir John Wilson, 1st Bt; two *s*. Served European War, 1914–18 (despatches, DSO); commanded Third Destroyer Flotilla, 1926–28; Captain-in-Charge at Singapore, 1929–31; commanded HMS St Vincent boys' training establishment, Gosport, 1932–34; Commodore 2nd class, commanding Home Fleet Destroyer Flotillas 1935–36; ADC to the King, 1935–36; Rear-Admiral, 1936; Comdg Officer, Coast of Scotland, 1937–39; Vice-Admiral, 1939; retired list, 1939. *Club:* United Service.

Died 21 Dec. 1941.

THOMSON, Lt-Col George Ritchie, CMG 1919; MB; FRSE, LLD; retired Consulting Surgeon. *Educ:* Edinburgh University. Served South African War, 1900–02; European War, 1915–19 (despatches twice, CMG); Professor of Surgery, University of Witwatersrand, 1920–30. *Address:* Ulva Cottage, Tobermory, Isle of Mull, Argyll, Scotland. *Clubs:* Keyhaven Yacht; Western Isles Yacht, Tobermory.

Died 14 March 1946.

THOMSON, George Walker; Editor, The Draughtsman; President of National Federation of Professional Workers since 1937; Member of General Council TUC since 1935; *b* 19 Jan. 1883; *s* of George Thomson, marine engineer, and Janet Riddell; *m* 1910, Isabel Buchanan; one *s*. *Educ:* Allan Glen's School; Glasgow School of Art; Glasgow and West of Scotland Technical College. Modeller and Designer for 4 years; Engineer and Designer 20 years; journalist 20 years; part founder Guildsman, 1916; founder Draughtsman, 1918; Arbiter Hull Trawler Dispute, 1935; PO Advisory Committee, 1935; WEA Executive, 1936; Royal Commission on Location of Industry, 1937; Unemployment Insurance Statutory Committee, 1938; Export Credits Guarantee Committee, 1939; National Youth Committee (Board of Education), 1939; National Joint Advisory Council, 1939; Synthetic Comm. (Ministry of Mines), 1939; Tank Board (Ministry of Supply), 1940; Chairman, London Regional Board of Production Executive, 1940; Clyde Dock Enquiry, 1940; Joint Advisory Council to Production Executive, 1941; Consultative Panel on Reconstruction; Member Catering Wages Commission; Commission on the Companies Act, 1929; Committee on Higher Appointments. *Publications:* Short Course of Industrial History, 1923; Grammar of Power, 1924; Mirrors of Modernity, 1933. *Recreations:* reading and walking. *Address:* 96 St George's Square, SW1. *T:* Victoria 0747.

Died 7 July 1949.

THOMSON, Harry Torrance, MD (Edin.); *b* 22 June 1868; 4th *s* of H. Torrance Thomson, Edinburgh; *m* Helen, *d* of late Rev. George Style, Headmaster Giggleswick School; one *s* two *d*. *Educ:* Leys School, Cambridge; Edinburgh University. House Surgeon

Royal Infirmary, Edinburgh; House Physician, Leith Hospital; after engaging for a few years in general practice, became specialist in anæsthesia; temporary Captain RAMC during European War; Member (late President) Scottish Society of Anæsthetists; Member British Psychological Society, British Psycho-Analytical Society; late Anæsthetist Royal Infirmary, Edinburgh; late Anæsthetist Leith Hospital and Royal Hospital for Sick Children, Edinburgh. *Publications:* various scientific papers in Edinburgh Medical Journal. *Recreations:* golf, walking. *Address:* 79a Longfleet Road, Poole, Dorset.

Died 18 Dec. 1944.

THOMSON, Henry Wagstaffe, CMG 1927; Order of Crown of Siam, 4th Class, 1905; *b* 22 Feb. 1874; *o s* of late Henry John Phipps Thomson; *m* 1907, Yvonne Mary, *o d* of late Dr A. Winn, Southsea. *Educ:* King's College, Taunton; Winchester College; Trinity College, Oxford; BA, 1907. Entered Malayan Civil Service, 1896; served in Selangor and Pahang, 1896–1902; seconded for service in Kelantan under Siamese Government, 1903; resigned and joined Siamese Service, 1906; rejoined Malayan Civil Service, 1909; served in Selangor and Perak, 1910–19; British Adviser, Kelantan, 1919; British Resident, Pahang, 1921 but did not assume duties until 1922; British Resident, Selangor, 1925; British Resident, Perak, 1926–29. *Recreations:* walking, shooting. *Address:* 33 Nettlecombe Avenue, Southsea, Hants.

Died 22 April 1941.

THOMSON, James Park, CBE 1920; LLD (Queen's University, Canada); JP; Hon. Corr. Member, New York Academy of Science, National Academy of Sciences, Alzate, Mexico, Royal Scottish Geographical Society, Commercial Geographical Society, Paris, and Geographical Societies of Lisbon, Marseilles, Halle, and Manchester; Life Member, National Geographic Society; *b* Shetland, 20 June 1854; *m* 1887, Ada, *o d* of late J. T. Gannon, MP, Goulburn, NSW; three *s* one *d.* Government Surveyor, Fiji, 1880–84; observed Transit of Venus, 1882; founded Royal Geographical Society of Australasia, Queensland, 1885; Pres. of Society, 1894–97; awarded Thomson Foundation Gold Medal (established by the Society in his honour) for Eminent Services to Geographical Science, 1901; received engraved piece of plate at Jubilee Celebrations, 1935; Hon. General Secretary and Treasurer of Society and Editor of Queensland Geographical Journal; successfully observed Transit of Mercury at Brisbane, Feb. 1894; Hon. Vice-President Sixth International Geographical Congress, London, 1895; Sec. Section A Australasian Association for the Advancement of Science, 1895; originated the Zone System of Time Reckoning in Australia; Representative Member of Council, Queensland University; Peek award of the Royal Geographical Society, London, 1902; Medal Société de Géographie, Paris, 1935; went on Round the World Scientific Mission, 1903; examined and reported on NSW Govt Water Conservation and Irrigation Schemes, 1906; undertook a successful journey to the Gulf of Carpentaria to identify and astronomically determine the position of the ill-fated Victorian Explorers', Burke and Wills, most northerly camp on the Bynoe River, 1909; assisted to observe Total Solar Eclipse Goondiwindi, Queensland, 1922; Delegate representing New York Academy of Sciences and Roy. Geographical Soc. of Australasia, Queensland, to Pan-Pacific Science Congress, Sydney and Melbourne, 1923; represented Royal Geographical Society of Australasia, New York Academy of Sciences, Royal Scottish Geographical Society and Manchester Geographical Society at official opening of Sydney Harbour Bridge, March 1932; donated ethnological, concological and economical mineralogical collection to Queen's University, Canada. *Publications:* British New Guinea; Physical Geography of Australia; Round the World; over 250 papers on Geography and allied subjects in scientific periodicals.

Recreations: scientific investigations; walking. *Address:* Turbot Street, Brisbane, Queensland, Australia. *T:* B 7638.

Died 10 May 1941.

THOMSON, Sir StClair, Kt 1912; MD, FRCP Lond.; FRCS England; LLD Manitoba; Swiss Federal Diploma; Ex-President of Royal Society of Medicine (Hon. Fellow) and of Medical Society; Fellow of King's College; Emeritus Professor of Laryngology and Consulting Surgeon for Diseases of the Throat and Nose in King's College Hospital; Consulting Throat Surgeon to the Italian Hospital and the Throat and Ear Hospital, Maidstone; Physician for the Throat to King Edward Sanatorium, Midhurst; late Professor of Laryngology and Otology, RAM College; Surgeon for Throat and Ear, Seamen's Hospital, Greenwich; Physician to the Throat Hospital, Golden Square, to the Royal Italian Opera, and Surgeon to the Royal Ear Hospital; *b* 28 July 1859; *s* of J. Gibson Thomson of Ardrishaig, Argyllshire, and *g s* of John Sinclair of Lochaline House, Sound of Mull; *m* 1901, Isabel (*d* 1905), *widow* of late Henry Vignoles. *Educ:* King's College, London; Paris; Vienna; Lausanne (MD 1891). Officier de la Légion d'Honneur; Commander, with Crossed Swords, Order of Leopold; Médaille de la Reconnaissance Française; Commendatore della Corona d'Italia; Corresponding Member of the Académie de Médecine, the Società Italiana di Laringologia, the Wiener Laryngologische Gesellschaft, the Berliner Laryngologische Gesellschaft, the American Laryngological Association, the American Medical Association, the Swedish Medical Society, the Danish Medical Soc., the Société Belge d'Oto-laryngologie, the Checko-Slovak Society, the Rumanian Society, and the Société Française de Laryngologie. *Publications:* various bacteriological, physiological and clinical papers on the throat and nose; Diseases of the Nose and Throat (4th ed.); Tuberculosis of the Larynx; Cancer of the Larynx; Atlas of Nasal Anatomy; the Cerebrospinal Fluid; Shakespeare and Medicine; A House-Surgeon's Memories of Lord Lister; European editor of The Laryngoscope. *Address:* Westminster Bank, Hanover Square, W1. *Club:* Royal Automobile.

Died 29 Jan. 1943.

THOMSON, Sir William, Kt 1922; FRSE; *b* 31 Dec. 1856; *m* 1884, Annie C., *d* of F. J. Van der Riet, Resident Magistrate of Simonstown; two *d. Educ:* Perth Academy; University of Edinburgh, MA, BSc, LLD (Hon.). Assistant to the Professor of Mathematics, University of Edinburgh, 1878–83; Professor of Mathematics, Victoria College, Stellenbosch, 1883–95; Member of Council, University of the Cape of Good Hope, 1883–95; Registrar, University of the Cape of Good Hope, 1895, 1918; Registrar, University of South Africa, 1918–22; Principal, University of the Witwatersrand, Johannesburg, 1924–28; Mathematical Examiner, Univ. of Edinburgh, 1886–87; Chm. Higher Education Commission, 1911; Member of the SA Universities Statutes Commission, 1917. *Publications:* Introduction to Determinants, 1882; Algebra for Schools, 1886; Chambers's Algebra for Schools, 1898. *Address:* Dunedin, Glencairn, Simonstown, S Africa.

Died 6 Aug. 1947.

THOMSON, Col William David, CMG 1918; Indian Army; *b* 1858; *s* of Major-Gen. W. B. Thomson; *m* Adeliza, *d* of W. Davis, of Well Close, near Gloucester; one *s* two *d. Educ:* Clifton College; Royal Military College, Sandhurst. Served in 1st Lancers, Indian Army, and was Judge Advocate-General in India; Manipur Expedition, 1891 (medal and clasp); European War, 1914–18 (CMG, two medals). *Address:* Longview, Coopers Hill, Brockworth, near Gloucester; Baidland, St Andrews, Fife. *Clubs:* Royal and Ancient, St Andrews.

Died 4 Dec. 1941.

THOMSON, Sir William Johnston, Kt 1934; KStJ; DL; *b* 1881; *s* of Thomas Thomson and Esther Mackay; *m* 1908; two *d*. *Educ:* Glasgow. Entered Town Council, 1921; Magistrate, 1926; Lord Provost of Edinburgh, 1932–35; Chairman and Managing Director of Scottish Motor Traction Ltd and subsidiary companies; President Scottish Amicable Building Society; Director United Automobile Services, and Gilmerton Colliery Co.; DL County of the City of Edinburgh and also of the County of Peebles-shire; JP; MIMechE, MIAE, MInsT, LLD, Edinburgh Univ. *Recreations:* golf, curling, fishing, shooting. *Address:* 11 Learmonth Terrace, Edinburgh; Blythbank, Blythbridge, West Linton. *Clubs:* Royal Automobile; Scottish Conservative (Edinburgh); Royal Scottish Automobile (Glasgow).

Died 18 Sept. 1949.

THOMSON, Sir William Willis Dalziel, Kt 1950; Professor of Medicine, QUB, since 1923; Physician, Royal Victoria Hospital Belfast, since 1919; Representative of Queen's University of Belfast on General Medical Council; DL County of the City of Belfast; *s* of late William Thomson, MD, JP, Anahilt House, Hillsborough, Co. Down; *m* Josephine, *y d* of Humphrey Barron, JP, of Walton, Fortwilliam Park, Belfast. *Educ:* Campbell College, Belfast; Queen's University, Belfast; Dublin; London; Buda-Pest; Paris. Henry Hutchinson Stewart Scholarship, Royal University of Ireland, 1906; Dunville Studentship, Queen's College, Belfast, 1907; Senior Scholarship in Chemistry, Queen's College, Belfast, 1907; BA, First Class honours, Royal University of Ireland, 1907. President of the Students' Representative Society and Member of the Senate, Queen's University, 1908; MB, BCh, BAO, First Class honours, 1910, Queen's University; Resident Medical Officer Purdysburn Fever Hospital, 1910–11; Demonstrator of Physiology, Queen's University, 1911–12; DPH 1912; Demonstrator of Pathology, Queen's University, 1912–16; BSc, First Class honours, 1912; Physician Mater Infirmorum Hospital, 1912–19; MD, Gold Medal, 1916; Captain RAMC, 1916–18; attached to Research Laboratory, BEF; Examiner in Medicine, National University of Ireland, 1925–27; FRCP London, 1928; President, North of Ireland Branch of BMA, 1932–33; Examiner in Medicine, TCD, 1935–38; President, Irish Medical Schools and Graduates Association, 1936–37; Pres. Section of Medicine BMA, 1937; President, Ulster Medical Society, 1937–38; Lumleian Lecturer, RCP, London, 1939; Pres. Assoc. of Physicians of Great Britain and Ireland, 1949–50. *Publications:* papers on medical subjects in leading medical journals. *Recreations:* golf and gardening. *Address:* 25 University Square, Belfast. *T:* Belfast 25056; Seven Tides, Donaghadee, Co. Down. *T:* Donaghadee 107.

Died 26 Nov. 1950.

THORNE, Rt Hon. Will, PC 1945; CBE 1930; MP (Lab) West Ham, 1906–45; *b* Birmingham, 8 Oct. 1857; *m* 4th, 1930, Beatrice, *d* of Charles Collins; two *s* six *d*. Commenced working life at age six in a barber's shop; founded with others the National Union of General and Municipal Workers in 1889, and General Secretary, 1889–1934; Member of Parliamentary Committee of Trades Union Congress, 1894–1934; first delegate sent by organised labour of England to Canadian Trade Union Congress, 1913; Member of West Ham Town Council since 1890; Deputy Mayor, 1898; Mayor, 1917–18; Freeman of West Ham, 1930. *Publications:* My Life's Battles, 1925; numerous short articles to newspapers and magazines on subjects important to work-people. *Address:* 1 Lawrence Road, Upton Manor, E13. *T:* Grangewood 3131.

Died 2 Jan. 1946.

THORNELY, Thomas, MA, LLM; late Fellow of Trinity Hall, Cambridge, and University Lecturer in History; Barrister-at-law, Inner Temple; *b* 1855; *e s* of late James Thornely of Baycliff, Woolton, Lancs; *m* 1885, Mabel M., *d* of late Thos Bolton Ogden of Kirkby Stephen. *Educ:* Uppingham School; Trinity Hall, Cambridge. *Publications:* Cambridge Memories; Whims and Moods; Aganella and other poems; Provocative Verse and Libellous Limericks, 1936; Collected Verse, 1939. *Address:* Sunnyside, Mount Pleasant, Cambridge.

Died 6 Jan. 1949.

THORNEYCROFT, Major George Edward Mervyn, DSO 1918; *b* 4 Oct. 1883; *s* of late George Thorneycroft of Dunston; *m* 1st, 1908, Dorothy Hope (*d* 1929), *d* of Sir W. Franklyn, KCB; one *s* one *d*; 2nd, 1938, Gertrude, *er d* of William Harpham, Leamington Spa. *Educ:* Clifton; RMA, Woolwich. Joined RA, 1902; served European War, 1914–18 (despatches, DSO); retired, 1923. *Address:* Dunston, Stafford. *Club:* Naval and Military.

Died 15 June 1943.

THORNHILL, Sir Anthony John Compton-, 2nd Bt *cr* 1885; JP; late Capt. and Hon. Major Reserve of Officers, late PWO, Norfolk RFA; JP Suffolk, 1891; *b* 2 Aug. 1868; *s* of 1st Bt and Edith, *o d* and *heiress* of Richard Hodgson Huntley, Carham Hall, Northumberland; *S* father, 1900; *m* 1891, Ethel Margaret, *d* of late Lt-Col Miller of Shotover, Oxon; (one *s*, Lieut Scots Guards, killed in action, Sept. 1914). *Educ:* Eton. Assumed by Royal Licence additional name and arms of Compton, 1902; served with RGA 1914–17. *Heir:* none. *Address:* Barham Hall, Ipswich. *T:* Claydon 315. *Club:* St James's.

Died 17 March 1949 (ext).

THORNHILL, Lt-Col Sir Henry Beaufoy, KCIE 1911; CMG 1918; CIE 1903; Indian Army, retired; *b* 7 Jan. 1854; *s* of late C. B. Thornhill, CSI; *m* 1st, 1882, Margaret Massy (*d* 1917), *d* of late Lt-Gen. George Wheeler, Indian Army; two *s* one *d*; 2nd, 1925, Ethel May, *o d* of late William Jobson. Entered Army, 1873; Capt. 1885; Maj. 1893; Lt-Col 1899; served Afghan War, 1878–79 (medal). *Address:* La Vedette, Montreux, Switzerland.

Died 26 April 1942.

THORNLEY, Reginald Ernest, CBE 1920; MBE 1919; Assistant Secretary, Ministry of Finance, N Ireland; *b* 1872; *s* of late Joseph Thornley, JP; *m* Madge, *d* of F. G. Moss. Was Principal Establishment Officer, Ministry of Food, during European War. *Address:* Redroofs, Knockmore Park, Bangor, Co. Down.

Died 24 Jan. 1942.

THORNLEY, Major Samuel Kerr; Director of Thornley and Knight, Ltd; *b* 11 Oct. 1871; *e s* of Samuel Thornley, Gilbertstone, Warwickshire; *m* 1905, Edith Mary Pullen, Chilcomb, Winchester; two *s* two *d*. *Educ:* St Edward's School, Oxford. Member Advisory Council to Committee of Privy Council for Scientific and Industrial Research, 1937–42; President Research Association of British Paint Colour and Varnish Manufacturers, 1926–45; Member Sugar Commission appointed under Sugar Industries (Reorganisation) Act since 1936. *Recreations:* golf, shooting, motoring. *Address:* Highmeade, Copt Heath, Knowle, Warwickshire. *T:* Knowle 2469.

Died 18 April 1947.

THORNTON, Lt-Col Charles Edward, CMG 1917; late 16th Bengal Cavalry, Indian Army; *b* 10 Nov. 1867; *er s* of late Maj.-Gen. C. J. M. Thornton, RA; *m* 1921, Frances Emily, *d* of late Frank J. Bright, Rochdale. *Educ:* Bath College; Royal Military College, Sandhurst. 2nd Lieut N Lancs Regt 1887; Capt. Indian Army, 1898; Maj., 1905; Lieut-Col 1913; served China, 1900 (medal); Thibet, 1903–04 (medal); European War

(Mesopotamia) 1914 in command of 16th Cavalry Indian Army in the 6th Cavalry Brigade (very severely wounded, despatches twice, CMG, 1915 Star, general service medal, victory medal); retired owing to ill-health, Sept. 1919. *Address:* c/o Coutts & Co. Ltd, 440 Strand, WC2. *Club:* Bath.

Died 21 Jan. 1946.

THORNTON, Brig. Sir Edward Newbury, KBE 1919; CBE 1918; VD; MRCS England; LRCP London; DPH Camb.; SAMC; Director-General of Medical Services, Union Defence Forces; Chairman Central Housing Board; Chairman Public Hospitals Advisory Council for the Transvaal; late Secretary for Public Health and Chief Health Officer for the Union of South Africa; *b* 10 June 1878; 6th *s* of Thomas Thornton, Woolferton House, Sporle, nr Swaffham, Norfolk; *m* 1905, Maud Annie, *e d* of Lt-Col W. F. Gregory, VD, DEOR of Cape Town, S Africa; two *d. Educ:* Cheltenham College; London Hospital. Served as Asst MO with the Imperial Yeomanry Hospitals, Dealfontein and Maitland, during Boer War, 1900–01; Plague Medical Officer in the Punjab, India, 1902–03; Additional MO in Cape Colony, 1903–10; Medical Adviser to the Cape Provincial Administration, Medical Inspector of Hospitals and Charitable Institutions, 1910; Officer Commanding S African Military Hospital, Richmond Park, Surrey, 1915–20; inaugurated a scheme for the vocational training of disabled soldiers in hospital, and was Chairman of the Executive Committee on Vocational Training in Military Hospitals in the London district; visited Nigeria at request of the Government of that territory to advise of plague, 1926; similarly visited the Uganda Protectorate, 1930; KGStJ. *Publications:* Government Reports (Blue Books); State-aided Hospitals and Charitable Institutions; scientific articles in various medical journals; The Training of the Disabled South African Soldier and its Lesson; contributed to the Interallied Conference on Disablement Problems arising out of the War held in London in May 1918. *Recreations:* cricket, tennis. *Address:* Department of Public Health, Pretoria, SA. *TA:* Health Pretoria.

Died 26 Oct. 1946.

THORNTON, Maxwell Ruthven; *b* Bengeo, Herts, 11 July 1878; *s* of late George Ruthven Thornton, MA, Vicar of St Barnabas, Addison Road, Kensington, and Teresa, *d* of John Labouchere; *m* 1909, Katherine, *d* of Edward Yates; one *d. Educ:* St Paul's School. A Solicitor, 1901; Advocate and Solicitor Straits Settlements, 1903; Acting Member, Legislative Council of the Straits Settlements, April to Oct. 1908; MP (Lib.) Tavistock, 1922–24. *Recreations:* travelling, golf, etc. *Address:* 11 Brunswick Square, Hove 2, Sussex.

Died 30 Aug. 1950.

THORNTON, Major Robert Lawrence, CBE 1920; late Deputy Chairman, E Sussex Quarter Sessions; Chairman, E Sussex Standing Joint Committee, 1914–46; DL and JP Sussex; Chairman Uckfield Bench, 1913–44; MA Cantab; Ex-President Sussex County Cricket Club; *b* 17 Sept. 1865; *o s* of Robert Thornton, DL, JP, of High Cross, Framfield and Thornton in Lonsdale, Yorks; *m* 1890, Charlotte (JP Sussex), *d* of Rev. W. Raynes; one *s* (elder son killed June 1915). *Educ:* Eton. Trinity College, Cambridge. E Sussex County Council, 1895–1946; Vice-Chairman, 1910–13; Chairman, 1913–16; Alderman, 1910–46; 3rd Bn Royal Sussex Regt, 1883–1900 (retired as Major); High Sheriff of Sussex, 1900–01; Barrister-at-law, Inner Temple; formerly First Chairman (3 years) Sussex Agricultural Wages Board, First Chairman (7 years), Brighton Employment Committee; Chairman East Sussex Education Committee, Roads Committee, and Public Health Committee; late Chairman, Chichester Diocesan Board of Finance; during the 1914–18 War Chairman County Appeal Tribunal; Chairman County Emergency Committee, Road Transport Committee, etc.;

Provincial Grand Master of Sussex Freemasons. *Publication:* a brochure on Education as applied to Rural Areas. *Recreations:* shooting; formerly cricket, Association football, lawn tennis, and fives. *Address:* High Cross, Framfield, Sussex. *T:* Halland 202.

Died 19 March 1947.

THORNTON, William Mundell, OBE 1920; DSc; DEng; Professor of Electrical Engineering, Armstrong College, Newcastle-upon-Tyne, 1906–37, Emeritus Professor since 1937; *b* 16 Feb. 1870. *Educ:* The Liverpool Institute. In works, 1884–92; University College, Liverpool, Hons Schools Physics and Engineering (Victoria); University Scholar in Physics, 1895. Senior Lecturer in Engineering, University College, Bristol, 1896–98; Lecturer and Professor in Electrical Engineering, Durham College of Science, now King's College, 1898; Chairman Newcastle Section IEE, 1905–06, 1921–22; President Association of Mining Electrical Engineers, 1920–21; Pres. IEE, 1934–35; Greenwell Gold Medal of the North of England Institute Mining and Mechanical Engineers for Researches on Safety in Mines, 1925. *Publications:* papers, chiefly electrical. *Address:* King's College, Newcastle-on-Tyne.

Died 2 May 1944.

THORNYCROFT, Lt-Col Charles Mytton, CBE 1919; DSO 1916; late 3rd (SR) Batt. Manchester Regiment; *b* 6 Aug. 1879; *e s* of late C. E. Thornycroft, JP, of Thornycroft Hall, Cheshire, and Courtlands, Lympstone, S Devon, and Edith Frances Cresswell; *m* Vida Maude, 2nd *d* of late G. W. Deakin, Blawith, Grange-over-Sands; two *s* one *d. Educ:* Eton; Sandhurst. Entered Army, 1899; Capt. 1903; Maj. (Special Reserve), 1915; served S African War, 1900–02, on Staff (despatches); European War, 1914–18 (despatches thrice, CBE, DSO). *Recreations:* Boy Scouts, shooting, and cricket. *Address:* Wycliffe House, Breinton, Hereford. *T:* Hereford 3437.

Died 25 Oct. 1948.

THORP, Linton Theodore; KC 1932; Recorder, Saffron Walden and Maldon, since 1932; Chairman of Essex Quarter Sessions since 1946; Chancellor of diocese of Chelmsford since 1948; a Governor of Felsted Charities; *b* 21 Feb. 1884; 3rd *s* of F. W. T. Thorp, solicitor; *m* Stella, *er d* of late Dr J. F. W. Silk; one *d. Educ:* Manchester Grammar School; University College, LLB University of London (Honours in Common Law and Equity), 1905; Special Prize Bar Final Exam. and Certificate of Honour, 1905. Barrister-at-law, Lincoln's Inn, 1906; Bencher, 1936; Deputy Chairman, Essex Quarter Sessions, 1936, Chairman, 1946; practises London and SE Circuit; served European War, 1914–19 (wounded); Major, RA (Res. of O); 1st Class Judge, Native Courts, Egypt, 1919; Acting Judge, HBM Supreme Court, Egypt, and HBM Prize Court Egypt and Special Court for Germans and Austrians, 1919–20; appointed thereto, 1921; British Delegate, Provisional Mixed Judicial Commission, Constantinople, 1921–22; last British Judge of HBM Supreme Court, Constantinople, 1921–24; contested (C) Nelson and Colne, 1929 and 1935, Farnham (Surrey), 1937; MP (C) Nelson and Colne, 1931–35. Governor of Felsted School, 1946. *Publications:* joint author of Boundaries and Fences in Halsbury's Laws of England; The Law of Moneylending; Quarter Sessions Handbook. *Recreations:* sport, sailing and outdoor games. *Address:* 3 Hare Court, Temple, EC4. *T:* Central 7742; Wisby, Chalfont St Giles. *T:* Little Chalfont 2160. *Club:* Carlton (Rear Commodore) Bar Yacht.

Died 6 July 1950.

THORP, William Henry, FRIBA; architect (retired); *b* 15 May 1852; *s* of John Hall Thorp, Headingley, Leeds; *m* 1879, Catharine Sarah Dymond; two *s* four *d. Educ:* Ackworth School; Bootham, York. Articled to Alfred M. Fowler, CE, Borough Surveyor of Leeds; afterwards with Edward Birchall, FRIBA, for three years; then

Head Assistant Architects' Dept for Leeds School Board; commenced practice, 1876; retired, 1923; Member of the Leeds City Art Gallery Committee for 35 years; Chairman of the Leeds City School of Art for 15 years; Director of the Leeds Institute. *Principal Works:* Leeds Fine Art Gallery; Leeds University School of Medicine; Leeds YMCA Buildings; City Library, Chapel Allerton; Selby Town Hall; various residences, warehouse and shop property, schools, etc. *Publications:* An Architect's Sketch Book at Home and Abroad; John N. Rhodes, a Yorkshire Painter; An Old Court Quarter in Paris; Villas and Gardens of Italy; Sculpture of the Early Italian Renaissance. *Recreations:* foreign travel, literature, watercolour work, and etching. *Address:* Prospect House, Clifton Hill, Bristol. *T:* Bristol 33298.

Died 16 Jan. 1944.

THORPE, Brig.-Gen. Edward Ivan de Sausmarez, CMG 1919; DSO 1917; *b* 1871; *s* of late Captain Thomas Edward Thorpe, Madras Infantry, of Choisi, Guernsey; *m* 1896, Mary Elizabeth, *d* of Randolph Charles Want, Sydney, NSW; one *d*. Served Niger Expedition, 1897 (despatches, medal with clasp); European War, 1914–19 (despatches, DSO, Brevet Lieut-Col, CMG); served in Bedfordshire Regt from 1892; Col 1922; retired 1922. *Club:* Junior United Service.

Died 16 Jan. 1942.

THORPE, James; illustrator and writer; *b* 13 March 1876; *s* of George Langwith Thorpe and Mary Ann Wood; unmarried. *Educ:* Bancroft's School. Schoolmaster (very indifferent) King's College, London, 1894–1902; did many drawings for advertising and for illustrated weekly papers and Windsor Magazine; first drawing in Punch, 1909; contributed fairly regularly until 1938; served European War, 1915–19, in Artists Rifles and RFC. *Publications:* A Cricket Bag, 1929; Phil May, 1932; Jane Hollybrand (edited and illustrated), 1932; Happy Days, 1933; English Illustration, The Nineties, 1935; Come for a Walk, 1940; Edmund J. Sullivan, 1948. Illustrated: Izaak Walton's Compleat Angler, 1911; Hugh de Sélincourt's Over, 1932, Moreover, 1934, The Saturday Match, 1937; A. Clitheroe's Silly Point, 1939. *Recreations:* cricket (until 1930; once bowled A. C. Maclaren first ball, 1916), fives (until 1939), now walking, collecting and remembering. *Address:* Dean Prior, Buckfastleigh, S Devon. *TA:* Thorpe, Dean, Buckfastleigh. *Club:* Chelsea Arts.

Died 22 Feb. 1949.

THORPE, John Henry, OBE 1919; KC 1935; JP 1925; Recorder of Blackburn since 1925; Deputy Chairman Middlesex Quarter Sessions, 1941; Chairman Appeal Tribunal (Architect's Registration Act 1931), 1940; a Bencher of Hon. Society of Inner Temple, 1941; Barrister-at-law; Chairman Central Price Regulation Committee since 1942; Capt. (TF); *b* Cork, 7 Aug. 1887; *s* of late Ven. J. H. Thorpe; *m* 1922, Ursula, *er d* of late Sir John Norton-Griffiths, 1st Bart; one *s* two *d*. *Educ:* Leatherhead; Trinity College, Oxford. Served European War (despatches, OBE); MP (U) Rusholme Division of Manchester, 1919–23. *Address:* Little Heath House, Limpsfield, Surrey; Farrars' Building, Temple, EC4. *T:* Limpsfield Chart 2229, Central 4113. *Club:* Carlton.

Died 31 Oct. 1944.

THORPE, Surg. Rear-Adm. Vidal Gunson, CBE 1919; retired; MRCS Eng.; LSA Lond.; *b* 24 Feb. 1864; *s* of Rev. R. O. T. Thorpe, MA, Rector of Anstey, Herts; *m* Maude, *d* of Fleet Paymaster C. R. Rodham, RN; three *s*. *Educ:* Merchant Taylors' School; King's College Hospital. Joined Royal Navy, 1886; retired, 1919. Served in European War, 1914–19 as Surgeon Captain i/c Surgical Section RN Hospital, Plymouth, 1916–19. *Address:* 37 Priory Avenue, Bedford Park, W4. *T:* Chiswick 2445.

Died 23 June 1948.

THREIPLAND, Col William M.; *see* Murray-Threipland.

THRESHER, Lt-Col James Henville, CMG 1919; MVO 1917; late Rifle Brigade; *b* 1870; *s* of late Rev. J. H. Thresher, Winchester; *m* 1904, Dorothy Margaret, *d* of late Richard Ramsden, of Chadwick Manor, Knowle, Warwick; one *s* two *d*. *Educ:* Winchester. Served European War, 1914–19 (despatches, MVO, Croix de Guerre, CMG, Officer of Legion of Honour and of Crown of Belgium, Order of Agricole Mérite of France). *Address:* Rowners, Fleet, Hants.

Died 16 Feb. 1943.

THRIFT, William Edward, ScD; Provost, Trinity College, Dublin; Commissioner of Charitable Donations and Bequests, 1933; Member of Second House of Oireachtas Commission, 1936; *b* 1870; *s* of Henry George Thrift, Inland Revenue; *m d* of C. H. Robinson, MD; two *s* three *d*. *Educ:* High School, Dublin. *Publication:* edited 4th ed. Preston's Theory of Light. *Address:* Provost's House, Trinity College, Dublin. *T:* 43888.

Died 23 April 1942.

THRING, George Herbert; solicitor; *b* Uppingham, 28 Nov. 1859; 2nd *s* of Edward Thring, late headmaster of Uppingham School; *m* 1886, Katharine Ida Sybil, *d* of late Col Emilio Linati. *Educ:* Uppingham; Hertford College, Oxford (BA). On leaving college was in an office on the Stock Exchange for two years; gained considerable business experience; articled to a solicitor in the City, and then practised on his own account; Secretary of the Authors' Club, 1891–1906 and 1935–37; Secretary of the Incorporated Soc. of Authors, Playwrights, and Composers, 1892; superannuated 1930; during his tenure of office the Society increased from 800 to about 4000 members, with a proportionate increase in its income; visited Ottawa at request of Canadian Government, 1898, and other Canadian centres as delegate of the Society with regard to Canadian Copyright, 1898 and 1920; visited Canada (Montreal, Ottawa, Winnipeg, Toronto), as guest of the Canadian Authors' Association, 1931; visited the United States as delegate of the Society in the matter of US Copyright, 1920; and in 1931 on behalf of British Dramatists to discuss the Minimum Basic Agreement; on the two first occasions he visited Canada with the object of placing the Society's views before the Canadian Government; was present in Rome in 1928 (as delegate of the Society) on the occasion of the meeting of the International Copyright Conference; Delegate of Society at the Meeting of International Dramatic Unions at Paris 1923 and Buda Pesth 1939; Chairman on behalf of the Society of the Organising Committee to arrange the meeting of the Confederation of International Dramatic Unions that took place in London, 1931; Legal Representative in England of La Société des gens de Lettres, Paris. *Publication:* The Marketing of Literary Property, 1933. *Recreation:* walking. *Club:* Authors'.

Died 23 Nov. 1941.

THRING, Captain Walter Hugh Charles Samuel, CBE 1920; RN, retired; *b* 1873; *s* of Rev. John Charles Thring; *m* 1st, Dorothy Wooldridge; one *s* two *d*; 2nd, 1927, Mrs Syria E. Pearson. *Educ:* HMS Britannia. Served in Royal Australian Navy during War; Director of Australian Naval War Staff (CBE, Order of the Rising Sun of Japan). *Recreation:* fishing. *Address:* The Elms, Bishop Sutton, Somerset.

Died 17 Jan. 1949.

THROSSELL, Arthur Graham, MA (Melbourne), BA (Oxon); Motor Correspondent of the Daily Telegraph, since 1929; *b* Melbourne, 31 Jan. 1881; *m* 1920, Alice Mary, 2nd *d* of late William Russell, Ardnagale, Downpatrick; one *s*. Journalist and writer (motoring and bridge); editor The Sportsman, 1911–13; War Service, 1914–19 (twice wounded). *Address:* Sorrett, Milllane, Chalfont St Giles, Bucks.

Died 18 March 1942.

THUBRON, John Brown Sydney, CIE 1918; *b* 26 Aug. 1879. *Educ:* RIEC Coopers Hill. Entered Public Works Dept, India, 1901; Chief Engineer, Bombay, 1928; Chairman, Aden Port Trust, 1912–19; Chairman, Karachi Port Trust, 1919–31; retired 1933.

Died 29 Sept. 1949.

THUILLIER, Brig.-Gen. Willoughby, CBE 1919; *b* 1860. Served NW Frontier of India, 1897–98 (medal with clasp); European War, 1914–19 (despatches, CBE).

Died 24 Oct. 1941.

THUNDER, Lt-Col Stuart Harman Joseph, CMG 1919; DSO 1917; MC; *b* Kilcairne, Co. Meath, 23 March 1879; *s* of M. H. D. Thunder, late 58th Foot, of Seneschalstown, Co. Meath, and Mary, *e d* of late Sir Stuart Knill, Bart, of the Crosslets, Blackheath; *m* 1910, Ethel, *e d* of David Tidmarsh of Lota, Limerick; two *s.* *Educ:* Fort Augustus, Inverness-shire. Joined Northamptonshire Regt from Militia, 1900; served with 1st Batt. in India; with 1st Chinese Regt at Wei-hai-Wei, 1904–06; Adjutant, 1st Batt. Northamptonshire Regt; 4th (TF) Batt. Northamptonshire Regt till Nov. 1914; joined 1st Batt. in France, Nov. 1914; service on Staff in France, Dec. 1914–18 (despatches seven times, CMG, DSO, MC, Brevet Lieut-Col 1918); commanded 1st Batt. Northamptonshire Regiment, 1926–30; retired pay, 1931. *Address:* The Grange, Shalbourne, Marlborough.

Died 6 March 1948.

THUREAU-DANGIN, François; Conservateur honoraire des Musées Nationaux; Membre de l'Institut de France; *b* 3 Janvier 1872; *s* of Paul Thureau-Dangin and Louise Henriquel; *m* 1899, Marguerite Daire; one *s* two *d.* *Educ:* Collège Stanislas, Paris. Attaché au Département des Antiquités Orientales au Musée du Louvre, 1902; Conservateur-adjoint, 1908; Conservateur, 1925; Démissionnaire, 1928; élu à l'Académie des Inscriptions et Belles Lettres, 1917; Doctor of Letters, honoris causa, de l'Université d'Oxford, 1925; Honorary Fellow of Queen's College, Oxford, 1925; Corresponding Fellow of the British Academy, 1938; Codirecteur (avec le Père V. Scheil), depuis 1910, de la Revue d'Assyriologie; a dirigé des fouilles en Mésopotamie, à Arslan-Tash (printemps et automne, 1928) et à Tell-Ahmar (1929, 1930 et 1931). *Publications:* Les Inscriptions de Sumer et d'Akkad, 1905; Une Relation de la huitième Campagne de Sargon 1912; Rituels Accadiens, 1921; Tablettes d'Uruk, 1922; Arslan-Tash (en collaboration avec A. Barrois, G. Dossin et M. Dunand), 1931; Esquisse d'une histoire du Système Sexagésimal, 1932; Til Barsib (avec M. Dunand), 1936; Textes Mathématiques Babyloniens, 1938. *Address:* 11 rue Garancière, Paris VI. *T:* Danton 33.55.

Died 24 Jan. 1944.

THURNHEER, Walter; *b* Baden Aargau, 1884; *s* of Kaspar Thurnheer and Emma Rohn; *m* Greta de Toll; no *c.* *Educ:* College Switzerland; Baden and Aarau; University, Zürich; University, Leipzig; University, Lausanne Law). Attaché Foreign Office, Berne; Legation Berlin, 1915–16; Foreign Office, Berne, First Secretary and later Assistant Head of the Division Foreign Affairs, 1917–21; Secretary, Paris, 1921–23; Counsellor, Washington, 1923–25; afterwards Consul-General in Canada; Swiss Minister, Japan, 1934; Swiss Minister in London, 1940–44. *Recreations:* fishing, golf, shooting. *Address:* Zürich, Switzerland. *Clubs:* St James's, Travellers; Grande Société, Berne.

Died 6 Aug. 1945.

THURSBY, Sir George James, 3rd Bt *cr* 1887; JP; *b* 17 Nov. 1869; *s* of 1st Bt; *S* half-brother, 1920; *m* 1894, Mary Augusta, *e d* of Thomas Hardcastle of Bradshaw Hall, Bolton-le-Moors. *Educ:* Radley. Leading Amateur Jockey for many years, and rode 2nd twice in the Derby and twice in two Thousand Guineas. *Recreation:* fond of shooting. *Heir:* none. *Address:* Fountain Court, Brook, Lyndhurst. *TA:* Thursby, Bramshaw. *T:* Cadnam 2213. *Clubs:* White's, Orleans.

Died 8 June 1941 (ext).

THURSBY-PELHAM, James; *b* 1869; *s* of Walter Thursby-Pelham of Cound Hall, Shropshire, and Emily, *d* of Hon. James Butler, *s* of 23rd Lord Dunboyne; *m* 1890, Alice (*d* 1947), *d* of Admiral Sir Arthur Farquhar, KCB, of Dumnagesk, NB; two *d.* *Educ:* Magdalene College, Cambridge, late JP and DL, Salop. Late High Sheriff. *Recreations:* shooting, hunting, golf. *Address:* 55 Cadogan Gardens, SW3. *T:* Kensington 7113. *Clubs:* Carlton, Hurlingham.

Died 24 March 1947.

THURSFIELD, Hugh, MD (Oxon); FRCP (London); (retired); Consulting Physician to St Bartholomew's Hospital and Hospital for Sick Children, Great Ormond Street; *s* of late T. W. Thursfield, MD, FRCP; unmarried. *Educ:* Leamington College; Trinity College, Oxford (Classical Exhibitioner); Medical School of St Bartholomew's Hospital. 1st Class Hons Mods; 2nd Class Lit. Hum. Has held various posts in the Medical School and Hospital of St Bartholomew's. *Publications:* papers in the Medical Journals, etc.; joint-author of a handbook of Medical Morbid Anatomy; co-editor of Diseases of Children, 1913, 1928 and 1935. *Address:* Beechwood, Cliddesden Road, Basingstoke. *Club:* Athenæum.

Died 20 June 1944.

THURSTAN, Edward William Paget, CMG 1917; *b* 23 Sept. 1880; *e s* of late E. P. Thurstan, BA, MD; *m* 1921, Christina (*d* 1944), *d* of late J. H. Boyd Thomson, Reston Hall, Westmorland; one *s.* *Educ:* Bradfield. Vice-Consul, New Orleans, 1905; First Vice-Consul New York, 1906; Vice-Consul, Kasai District, Belgian Congo, 1909; seconded for service under Zanzibar Govt 1911; Secretary to First Minister of the Sultan and as Director of Public Education (3rd Class Order of Brilliant Star); employed in Colonial Office in connection with transfer of Zanzibar to that Dept 1913; Consul, Calais, 1913; Mexico City, 1914; Consul-General for Republic of Mexico, 1915; in charge of HM Legation, 1915 and 1916; HM Chargé d'Affaires, Mexico, 1917 and 1918; Acting Consul-General, Algiers, 1919 and 1920; Consul-General at Cologne, 1920; at Rotterdam, 1924; at Genoa, 1927–35; at Milan, 1935–37; retired, 1937. *Address:* Lansdowne, Budleigh Salterson, S Devon. *T:* Budleigh Salterton 210. *Club:* East India and Sports.

Died 26 March 1947.

THURSTON, Sir George; *see* Thurston, Sir T. G. O.

THURSTON, Col Hugh Stanley, CB 1917; CMG 1915; CBE 1919; late AMS; FRGS; *b* 21 May 1869; *s* of Hugh K. Thurston. *Educ:* St Bartholomew's Hospital. Captain, 1895; Major, 1904; served NW Frontier, India, 1897–98 (medal with clasp); South Africa, 1902 (despatches, Queen's medal 3 clasps); European War, 1914–18 (despatches eight times, 1914 Star, CMG, CB, CBE, Commander of Order of Aviz of Portugal); retired pay, 1922. *Address:* 23 Queen's Gate Gardens, SW7. *T:* Western 3287. *Club:* Army and Navy.

Died 18 Nov. 1945.

THURSTON, Sir (T.) George (O.), KBE 1920; Consulting Naval Architect, Engineer, and Mixed Fuel Specialist; *m* 1901, Ada King (*d* 1946); six *s* one *d.* *Educ:* Liverpool. Responsible for the design and construction of war vessels, including battleships and cruisers, destroyers, submarines, troopships, etc., for most of the navies of the world. For many years Confidential Adviser of late Sir Basil Zaharoff and Naval Director of Vickers Ltd MINA, MICE; Order of Naval Merit, Spain; Order of Rising Sun, Japan. *Publications:* many on Naval Vessels. *Address:* 2 Caxton Street, SW1.

Died 22 Jan. 1950.

THWAITES, Gen. Sir William, KCB 1927; KCMG 1919; CB 1917; psc; *b* 9 June 1868; *s* of William Thwaites and Jeanette Threlfall; *m* 1892, Mabel Cubitt; no *c. Educ:* Wellington; Woolwich. 2nd Lieut RA, 1887; Lieut 1890; Capt. 1898; Major, 1902; Lt-Col 1914; Bt-Col 1916; Major-Gen. 1918; Lt-Gen. 1926; Gen. 1931; Adjutant 33rd Brigade, RFA 1900–02; Staff College, 1903–04; Military Operations, War Office, as Staff Captain, 1905–06; and GSO2, 1906–10; GSO2, 2nd London Div. TF 1912–14; GSO1, 47th (2nd London) Div. TF 1914–15; temp. Brig.-General, 141st Inf. Brigade, 1915–16; Commanded 46th Division, 1916–18; Director of Military Intelligence War Office, Sept. 1918–April 1922; Director Military Operations and Intelligence, April–Sept. 1922; GOC 47th (2nd London) Division, TA, 1923–26; GOC-in-Chief, British Army of the Rhine, 1927–29; Director-General of Territorial Army, 1931–33; ADC General to the King, 1931–35; Colonel Commandant RA, 1929–38; served South African War, 1899–1900 (Queen's medal with clasp, Defence of Ladysmith, despatches); European War, France and Flanders, 1915–18 (despatches six times, Bt-Col, CB, prom. Maj.-Gen., KCMG; Commander Order of Leopold, Commander Legion of Honour, 2nd Class Order of White Eagle, 2nd Class Order of Rising Sun, American DSM, Croix de Guerre (twice), Belgian Croix de Guerre); retired pay, 1933; Divisional Officer Special Constabulary, Berks, 1940. *Address:* The Halfway House, Kintbury, Berks. *Club:* Junior United Service.

Died 22 June 1947.

TIBBITS, Vice-Adm. Charles, CBE 1919; MVO 1904; *b* 19 June 1872; *m* Elsie (*d* 1930), *d* of late T. Eastman, Northwood Park, near Winchester; one *s.* Entered Navy, 1885; Comdr 1905; Capt. 1914; in charge of repair work carried out by HMS Cyclops (CBE); Captain of the Dockyard and Deputy-Superintendent and King's Harbour Master at Portsmouth, 1920; Rear-Admiral, 1924 (retired); Vice-Admiral (retired), 1929. *Address:* Titchfield Abbey Cottage, near Fareham. *T:* Titchfield 31.

Died 13 Oct. 1947.

TICKELL, Lt-Col Edward James, DSO 1899; JP Co. Kildare; 14th Hussars; retired, 1914; in command 13th Cavalry Reserve, 1915; *b* 9 Feb. 1861; *e s* of late T. Tickell, Commander RN, of The Lypiatts, Cheltenham; *m* 1902, Eliza, *e d* of Lt-Col T. Maxwell, Resident Magistrate, Pomeroy, Natal, South Africa. *Educ:* Trinity Coll., Cambridge. Entered West India Regt 1885; 14th Hussars, 1888; Adjutant, 1892–96; Major, 1899; served Uganda and Equatorial Provinces, 1898–1900 (despatches, medal and clasp, DSO); South Africa, 1900–01 (despatches, medal and 4 clasps); Cavaliere Ufficiale della Corona d'Italia. Owns 3175 acres in County Kildare. *Recreations:* field sports, big-game shooting, fencing, revolver shooting. *Address:* 33a Brunswick Square, Hove 2, Sussex. *T:* Hove 6864; Villa Pace, San Remo, Italy. *Clubs:* Naval and Military, Cavalry; Kildare Street, Dublin.

Died 4 Jan. 1942.

TICKELL, Richard Hugh, CIE 1914; MICE; *s* of late Col James Tickell and Sophia Victoria, *d* of Gen. G. Moseley, CB; *m* 1916, Marion Louise (*d* 1943), *y d* of late W. T. Lewis, MD, Loughton, Essex. *Educ:* RIE College. Entered India Public Works Dept; served in Central India and Kotah State, 1894–1902; rest of service in the Punjab and NWF Province Irrigation; decorated for services in surveying and constructing the Upper Swat Canal in the NWFP; Superintending Engineer, 1906; Chief Engineer, Punjab and Central Provinces,

1913–15; Member CP Legislative Council; retired, 1915. *Recreation:* all sports. *Address:* 90 Richmond Park Avenue, Bournemouth. *Clubs:* Junior Carlton, East India and Sports.

Died 10 Feb. 1948.

TICKLE, Ernest William; editor Timber and Plywood; *b* Bootle, Liverpool, 23 June 1882; *s* of late Gilbert Young Tickle, JP, and late Alice Killip; *m* 1910, Matilda Kate, *d* of late Charles Aldridge, London; one *s* one *d. Educ:* Bootle College; Merchant Taylors' School, Great Crosby. Nine years Banking with Parrs Bank Ltd; joined the family business of Tickle, Bell and Co., Timber Agents, Liverpool, 1906; partner with father, 1911; served with RGA as a gunner in France, 1917–18, discharged owing to ill-health Oct. 1918, and resumed timber trade until appointed to present editorship, 1930. *Address:* 37 Green Hill, Hampstead, NW3. *T:* Hampstead 1496.

Died 25 March 1947.

TIGHE, Henry, (Harry); author; *b* Waratah, NSW, 7 Feb. 1877; *s* of Atkinson Alfred Patrick Tighe, MP; *m* 1943, Doris Edith, *d* of late Charles Stanger-Leathes, Sydney. *Educ:* Sydney Grammar School; private tutor; Peterhouse, Cambridge. Took up writing after leaving Cambridge; travelled extensively; connected with movements for social welfare. *Publications:* Emily Reed; With the Tide; Life's Antagonisms; Women of the Hills; Silent Room; Sheep Path; The Model in Green; Calore Girl; Queen of Unrest; Intellectual Marie; The Four Candles; As I saw It, 1937; By the Wayside, 1939; Remorse, and other essays, etc.; contributor to magazines on Art and the Theatre and Travel. *Plays:* Open Spaces, 1927; Old Mrs Wiley; The Atonement (with Cecil Rose); Insult (with J. E. Harold Terry), 1930; Bush Fire; Intrigue, produced Sydney 1941. *Recreations:* travelling, the theatre. *Address:* c/o Bank of New South Wales, 47 Berkeley Square, W1. *Clubs:* Royal Sydney Golf, PEN, Sydney.

Died 16 June 1946.

TILBY, A. Wyatt; author and journalist; *b* Addiscombe, Surrey, 1880; *m* 1909, Kathleen Norah, *d* of late George Brewer, Harrogate; one *s* two *d. Educ:* privately; abroad. Editorial Staff Globe, 1905–12; Saturday Review, 1913–15; Editor Evening Standard, 1915–16; Outlook, 1924–28; Saturday Review, 1930–32. *Publications:* The English People Overseas, 6 vols, 1908–1914; The Evolution of Consciousness, 1922; The Quest of Reality, 1927; Lord John Russell, 1930; Right, 1933. *Address:* 5 Princes Court, Pilgrims Lane, NW3. *T:* Hampstead 2937. *Club:* Constitutional.

Died 1 Sept. 1948.

TILLETT, Benjamin; Secretary, Dock, Wharf, Riverside, and General Workers' Union of Great Britain and Ireland from its inception in 1887 to its amalgamation with the Transport and General Workers' Union in 1922; now associated with that Union; Chairman of General Council, TUC, 1928–29; *b* Bristol, 1860. Worked in a brickyard at 8; was a 'Risley' boy for two years; served six months on a fishing smack at 12; apprenticed to a boot-maker; joined Royal Navy (invalided); after several voyages in merchant ships settled at the Docks and organised Dockers' Union; contested West Bradford, 1892 and 1895; Eccles, 1906; Swansea, 1910; MP (Lab) N Salford, 1917–24 and 1929–31; alderman, LCC, 1892–98; was imprisoned at and ejected from Antwerp and Hamburg, where he had gone to help the strikers; one of the pioneer organisers of General Federation of Trade Unions, National Transport Workers' Federation, National Federation of General Workers, International Transport Workers Federation; Labour Party; a Socialist; visited the English, French and Belgian battle-fronts; several times took strong line and delivered thousands of lectures on the War, emphasising the need for an ample supply of munitions; two Empire Lecturing Tours; several Tours in America and USSR.

Publications: pamphlets—Character and Environment, Collectivism, Socialism and Trade Unionism; books—A Brief History of the Dockers' Union, commemorating the 1889 Dockers' Strike; History of the London Transport Workers' Strike, 1911, and has issued a lengthy statement based on personal investigation of the position in the Ruhr and Russia; Memories and Reflections, 1931; lectures—State and Individualism, Christ and Labour, etc. *Address:* Transport House, SW1. *T:* Victoria 7617. *Clubs:* Royal Automobile, National Trade Union.

Died 27 Jan. 1943.

TILLEY, Arthur Augustus, Fellow of King's College, Cambridge; Hon. LittD Manchester; *b* 1 Dec. 1851; *e s* of Sir John Tilley, KCB, Secretary to the General Post Office; *m* Margaret, *d* of J. A. Clutton-Brock; three *d.* *Educ:* Eton; King's College, Cambridge. *Publications:* The Literature of the French Renaissance; François Rabelais; From Montaigne to Molière; The Dawn of the French Renaissance; Cambridge Readings in French Literature; Molière; Studies in the French Renaissance; The Decline of the Age of Louis XIV; Three French Dramatists; Madame de Sévigné; Editor of Medieval France, and of Modern France. *Address:* 2 Selwyn Gardens, Cambridge. *T:* Cambridge 4167.

Died 4 Dec. 1942.

TILLEY, Sir George, Kt 1936; FCII; Knight of Order of Crown, Belgium, 1938; Life President and Chairman, Pearl Assurance Company, Ltd; Chairman People's Land Building & Dwellings Co.; Vice-Pres., L'Ancre Belge Société Anonyme, Antwerp; Vice-Pres., National Amalgamated Approved Society; Director, City and International Trust, London Border and General Trust; Life Governor of Masonic and other hospitals; *b* 26 June 1866; *s* of late Charles and Sarah Tilley; *m* 1896, Amy, *d* of late Martin Gray, Watford; one *s* three *d.* *Educ:* Cheltenham Private School (Barwells). *Recreations:* yachting, music. *Address:* Primrose House, Clarence Lane, Roehampton, SW15. *T:* Prospect 3672. *Clubs:* Carlton, Roehampton, Royal Motor Yacht.

Died 2 May 1948.

TILLEY, Herbert, BS (Lond.); FRCS (Eng.); Consulting Surgeon, Ear, Nose, and Throat Department (Royal Ear Hospital), University College Hospital; Laryngologist to the Radium Institute; University of London Lecturer (Laryngology), 1934; Ex-President of Laryngological and Otological Sections, Royal Society of Medicine; President Medical Society of London, 1931–22; Hon. Fellow American and Belgian Laryngological Society; Hon. Member, American Academy, Otol Laryngol and Ophthalmology; Fellow of University College, London; Consulting Aural Surgeon, Ministry of Pensions; Ex-Examiner (Laryngol and Otol) Royal College Physicians and Surgeons; *b* Shepton Mallet, Somerset. *Educ:* Queen's College, Taunton; University College Hospital, London. Exhibition London University in Zoology and Comparative Anatomy; Entrance Medical Exhibition, Filliter Exhibition; Achison Medical Scholar, University College Hospital. Formerly Surgeon, Golden Square Throat Hospital; President, Section Laryngology, British Medical Association, 1910. *Publications:* Diseases Nose and Throat, 1919; Diseases of Nasal Sinuses, Allbutt's System of Medicine; Articles on Diseases of the Nose and Throat, Encyclopædia of Medicine; Semon Lecturer, 1934, Chronic Pyogenic Inflammation of the Maxillary Antrum and other accessory Sinuses; Acute Streptococcus Laryngitis, British Med. Jl 1935; various publications on Diseases of the Ear, Nose, and Throat in Medical Journals, and the Proceedings of Medical Societies. *Address:* 72 Harley Street, W1. *T:* Langham 2475.

Died 6 Jan. 1941.

TILLEY, Leonard Percy De Wolfe, KC 1914; LLD (Toronto University, 1933, University of New Brunswick, 1933; Bowdoin University, Brunswick, Maine, USA, 1933); *b* 21 May 1870; *s* of Sir Samuel Leonard Tilley, KCMG, CB; *m* 1903, Laura Tremaine, *d* of Archdeacon Richardson; one *s* two *d.* *Educ:* Ottawa Model School; Fredericton Collegiate; University of New Brunswick; Dalhousie University. Attorney, 1893; called to Bar of New Brunswick, 1894; NB Legislature for Saint John, 1912–21 and 1925–35; District Judge in Admiralty, 1935–45; Judge of Kings and Albert County Courts, 1935–45; retd, 1945; Pres. Executive Council, New Brunswick, 1925–31; Minister Lands and Mines, 1931–35; Premier, 1933–35. *Recreations:* golf, fishing, shooting, bridge. *Address:* Carleton House, Rothesay, New Brunswick, Canada. *Club:* Union (Saint John).

Died 26 Dec. 1947.

TILLY, Maj.-Gen. Justice Crosland, DSO 1919; MC; a Comdr since 1940; *b* 1888; *s* of late Lt-Col J. C. Tilly, Biddenham, Bedford; *m* Mary Lucy, *d* of late Capt. James Lee Stewart, The Manor House, Aylesbury; one *d.* Served East Africa, 1913–14 (medal with clasp); European War, 1914–19 (DSO, MC and bar, two medals, despatches); NW Frontier of India, 1924 (medal and clasp); Chief Instructor, Royal Tank Corps; Central School, Bovington Camp, 1935–37; Chief Instructor, Gunnery Wing, Army Armoured Fighting Vehicles School, 1937–38; Commander 1st Tank Brigade, 1938. *Address:* c/o Lloyds Bank, 6 Pall Mall, SW1. *Club:* Junior Army and Navy.

Died 16 Jan. 1941.

TILNEY, Lt-Col Norman Eccles, CBE 1919; DSO 1916; late Royal Artillery; *b* 2 March 1872; *s* of late G. A. Tilney, JP, Somerset; *m* 1904, Cicely Sara (*d* 1928), *d* of late C. H. Alston; two *s* one *d.* *Educ:* Clifton College; RMA, Woolwich. Served China, 1900 (Medal); European War, 1914–19 (despatches 4 times, severely wounded, DSO, CBE, 1914 Star, King's Medal, Victory Medal). *Recreations:* usual country recreations, and occasionally training and running a spaniel at Field Trials. *Address:* Clonyard, Colvend, Dalbeattie, Scotland. *TA:* Clonyard, Kippford. *T:* Kippford 3. *Club:* Army and Navy.

Died 27 June 1950.

TIMINS, Rev. Francis Charles, DSO 1917; Rector of Westonbirt with Lasborough, Glos, since 1920; *b* Brighton, 1866; *e s* of Capt. O. F. Timins, HM 82nd Regt; *m* Emily, *d* of John Kynaston Cross, MP, Under-Secretary for India; one *s* three *d.* *Educ:* Tonbridge School; Clare College, Cambridge. Curate of Warrington, 1889–93; Rector of Brattleby, Lincs, 1893–96; Hastingleigh with Elmsted, Kent, 1896–1904; Rector of Smeeth, Kent, 1904–20; served with 4th Cavalry Brigade, as CF in France, 1915–19 (despatches twice, DSO); TD 1923. *Recreations:* riding, hunting, polo. *Address:* Westonbirt Rectory, Tetbury, Glos. *T:* Westonbirt 2.

Died 18 May 1941.

TIMS, Ven. John William, DD St John's College, Winnipeg, Manitoba, 1905; *b* Oxford, England, 1857; *s* of late John Tims, boat-builder, Staines; *m* 1890, Violet Winifred, *d* of late Rev. J. G. Wood, naturalist; two *s* one *d.* *Educ:* Church Missionary College, Islington, 2nd cl. Prelim. Exam. for Holy Orders, 1883. Ordained, 1883, for the Colonies; appointed as first missionary to the Blackfoot Indians by CMS, 1883; removed to Sarcee Indian Mission, 1895; Chaplain to Bishop of Calgary, 1888; Incumbent of St Paul's, Fish Creek, and St Peter's, Glenmore, 1916; member of Provincial Synod of Rupert's Land, 1887–1939, and of the General Synod of the Church of England in Canada, 1902–34; Archdeacon of Macleod, 1895–1927; Archdeacon of Calgary, 1927–43. *Publications:* Grammar and Dictionary of Blackfoot Language; Readings from Holy Scripture in Blackfoot; Gospel of St Matthew in Blackfoot; Manual of Instruction for use in Schools amongst Blackfeet. *Address:* 1616 Eleventh Avenue West, Calgary, Alberta, Canada.

Died Oct. 1945.

TINAYRE, (Marguerite Suzanne) Marcelle; femme de lettres; Prix Montyon, 1900; prix Vitet, 1907; grand-prix Barthou de l'Académie française, 1938; *b* Tulle, Corrèze; *née* Chasteau; *m* Julien Tinayre, peintre graveur (decd); one *s* two *d. Publications:* Avant l'amour, 1897: la Rançon, 1898; Hellé, 1899; l'Oiseau d'orage, 1900; la Maison du péché, 1902; la Vie amoureuse de François Barbazanges, 1904; la Rebelle, 1906; la Consolatrice, 1908; Hellé, 1913; la douceur de vivre; Madeleine au miroir, 1913; L'Ombre de l'amour, 1916; Le Départ, 1915; Perséphone, 1920; Les Lampes Voilées, 1921; Le Bouclier d'Alexandre, 1922; Priscilla Severac, 1923; Madame de Pompadour: a Study in Temperament, 1925; Figures dans la nuit, 1926; Une Provinciale en 1830, 1927; Terres étrangères, 1928; L'Ennemie intime, 1931; Château en Limousin, L'Affaire Lafarge, 1935; La Porte rouge, 1936; Le Rendez-vous du Soir, 1938; Collaboration au Temps, à la Revue de Paris, à l'Illustration à la Revue des Deux-Mondes, etc. *Address:* 19 rue de Lille, Paris; La Clairière, Gros-Rouvre, Seine-et-Oise.

Died 23 Aug. 1948.

TINDAL-CARILL-WORSLEY, Philip Ernest, JP Norfolk; BA; *b* 21 Oct. 1881; 2nd *s* of Ernest Frank, Pendleton nr Manchester; *m* 1907, Clementia, *o d* of Nicolas Tindal-Carill-Worsley, Platt Hall, nr Manchester: whose name and arms he adopted by Royal Licence; two *s* one *d. Educ:* Eton College; Magdalen College, Oxford. BA Oxon 1904. Called to Bar, Inner Temple, 1905; Commandant Norfolk County Special Constabulary, 1941-45. Shropshire Yeomanry, 1912-15; seconded to RE Signals (Staff); Major RE (SS), 1920; Diploma in Forestry; Ex-chairman and now Trustee, Norfolk and Norwich Hospital; High Sheriff of Norfolk, 1937; Landowner. *Recreations:* hunting, shooting, ski-ing, stalking, fishing. *Address:* The Dower House, East Carleton, Mulbarton, Norwich. *T:* Mulbarton 9. *Clubs:* Royal Automobile, Lansdowne; Norfolk Norwich.

Died 18 March 1946.

TINSLEY, Captain Richard Bolton, CBE 1919; RD; RNR, retired; *b* Nov. 1875. *Club:* Constitutional.

Died 12 March 1944.

TIPPET, Captain Arthur Grendon, DSO, RN retd; recalled to Active Service, 1940; Principal of St Piran's-on-the-Hill School, Maidenhead, since 1926; *b* 14 June 1885; 3rd *s* of Henry Grendon Tippet and Edith Harriette Jackson; *m* 1911, Dorothy Denyer Lowther, *d* of Col A. Froom, VIth Inniskilling Dragoons; one *s* two *d. Educ:* HMS Britannia; Dartmouth. Served European War, Grand Fleet; commanded HMS Ariel at Battle of Jutland (despatches); commanded HMS Oracle at destruction of German Submarine U 44 (DSO); commanded HMS Windsor at surrender of German High Sea Fleet; Commander, 1919; Chairman R/T Committee; Baltic Expeditions, 1919-20; Chief of Staff, Riga, 1919; Plans Division, Admiralty, 1921-22; Member Royal United Service Institution; Member Royal Society of Teachers. *Recreation:* country pursuits. *Address:* St Piran's-on-the-Hill, Maidenhead. *TA:* Tippet, Maidenhead. *T:* 316. *Club:* United Service.

Died 8 Feb. 1943.

TIPPETTS, Sydney Atterbury; *b* London, 18 Sept. 1878; 2nd *s* of late W. J. B. Tippetts; *m* 1919, Marion Fairrie (*d* 1941), *d* of late John Clarke, Chanonry, Old Aberdeen. *Educ:* St Paul's School; Merton Coll., Oxford. Called to Bar, Inner Temple, 1902; joined Sudan Political Service, 1902; Deputy Governor Sennar Province, 1911-14; Deputy Governor Red Sea Province, 1914-16; Governor Halfa Province, 1916-22;

Governor Red Sea Province, 1922-27; retired, 1927; employed as Political Officer Red Sea Naval Patrol, 1915, and as Liaison Officer to the Idrisi Yemen, 1917 (despatches twice, 4th Class Osmanie, 3rd Class Order of the Nile); Bursar, Bradfield College, 1929-33 and Shrewsbury School, 1933-37; Berkshire CC, 1938. *Recreations:* ran for Oxford Univ. Mile, 1900 and 1901; golf. *Address:* 3 Bath Road, Reading. *Club:* United University.

Died 26 Feb. 1946.

TITO, Pittore Ettore; Chevalier de la Légion d'Honneur; *b* Castellamare di Statia, 1860; *m* Lucia Velluti. *Educ:* Venezia, Studio all'Accademia di Venezia; viaggio in Francia, Inghilterra, Germania per perfezionarti nell' arte; medaglia d'oro d'1er classe Parigi Universale, Monaco, Bavaria, Vienna, Roma, Venezia; Quadri nei musei Lutternburgo Parigi, Budapest museo Nazionale, Venezia museo d'arte moderna, Trieste museo d'arte moderna, Roma museo d'arte moderna. Professore Istituto Belle Arti, Venezia. *Address:* c/o Istituto elle Arti, Venezia.

Died 26 June 1941.

TITTERINGTON, Meredith Farrar; MP (Co-op. and Lab) Bradford South since 1945; JP; *b* Bradford, 1886; *s* of George and Ann Titterington; C of E; British; *m* Phyllis, *d* of Thomas Midgley; one *d. Educ:* Bradford Education Authority (day); Evening Institutes and Technical College; Ruskin College and Labour College, Oxford. Studied Languages, Textiles, etc. Employment and apprenticeship in Wool Textile and Dyeing and Finishing Industry. Social Studies, 1909-10-1911. District Sec., National Society, Dyers, Bleachers and Textile Workers; Representative on Wool Control Cttees and Joint Industrial Council, etc.; Acting Secretary, 1919, of National Assoc. of Unions in the Textile Trade, and President, 1930-36; Member of the Board of Trade Advisory Council, 1930-33; Member of the Bradford City Council, 1919-45; Alderman; Chairman of Labour Group; Chairman, Technical Education Cttee; Lord Mayor, 1939-40. Chairman, Ministry of Information Comm.; Chairman, Civil Defence Emergency Comm. Member of the Co-operative and Labour Parties since foundation; former Director of City of Bradford Co-operative Soc., etc. National Advisory Council on Education for Industry and Commerce. *Address:* 38 Homestead, Menston in Wharfedale, Yorkshire. *T:* Menston 235.

Died 28 Oct. 1949.

TITULESCO, Nicolas; *b* Craiova, Roumania, 1883; *s* of Jean Titulesco, President of the Court of Appeal; *m* 1910, Caterina, *d* of George Burca, MP. *Educ:* College King Carol I, Craiova; specialised in Law, Diplomacy and Economics; passed first in Faculté de Droit examination, Paris; Docteur en Droit and twice Laureate Paris University. Professor of Civil Rights in University of Jassy, 1905; transferred to University of Bucarest, 1909; elected Deputy to Roumanian Parliament, 1912; Minister of Finance, 1917; Delegate to the Peace Conference and one of the signers of the Treaty of Trianon; Minister of Finance, 1920-22; introduced Income Tax in Roumania, 1921, and made other sweeping changes in taxation system; Envoy Extraordinary and Minister Plenipotentiary of the King of Roumania to the Court of St James, 1922-26 and 1928-32; Minister for Foreign Affairs, Roumania, 1927 and 1932-36; late Roumanian Permanent Delegate to the League of Nations; Grande Croix de la Couronne de Roumanie; Grand-Croix de l'Etoile de Roumania; Grand Cross of the Victorian Order; Grand Cross of the Order of the White Lion of Czechoslovakia; Grand Cross Pologna Restituta. *Publications:* numerous treatises on law and finance, —La théorie des droits éventuels, La Distribution du Patrimone; L'Impôt sur le Capital, etc. *Recreations:* reading, motoring. *Address:* Monaco.

Died 18 March 1941.

TIVEY, Maj.-Gen. Edwin, CB 1917; CMG 1919; DSO 1901; VD; Retired List; commanded 2nd Australian Cavalry Division, 1921–26; *b* 1866; *m* 1906, Annie Bird (decd), *d* of John Robb, Toorak, Victoria; (only *s* died 26 March 1943 of wounds received at El Alamein) one *d*. Served South Africa, 1900–02 (despatches twice, Queen's medal and four clasps, DSO for prompt action and brave defence at Philipstown, Cape Colony); European War, 1915–19, commanded 8th Australian Infantry Brigade and 5th Australian Division (CB, CMG, despatches six times). *Address:* Nauroy, Kooyong Road, Toorak, SE2, Victoria, Australia. *Clubs:* Australian, Naval, Army and Air Force, Melbourne.

Died 25 May 1947.

TOCHER, James Fowler, DSc, LLD; FIC; Lecturer in Statistics, University of Aberdeen, 1911–41; Analyst and Official Agricultural Analyst for Aberdeen and other northern Scottish Counties; Consulting Chemist to the Highland and Agricultural Society of Scotland since 1912; *b* 1864. *Educ:* Mason College, Birmingham; University College, London; Univ. of Aberdeen. Late Member of Consultative Council (Medical and Allied Services) Scottish Department of Health; Examiner in Statistics, University of London, 1916–19; Examiner in Statistics, University of Leeds, 1929–31; Examiner for National Diplomas (Agriculture and Dairying); late member of various Interdepartmental Committees. *Publications:* Many papers on chemical, statistical, and allied subjects in various scientific journals; What is Probable Error; The Book of Buchan; Departmental and other Reports: A Study of the Variations in the Composition of Milk; Anthropometric Survey of Inmates of Asylums in Scotland; A Study of the Chief Physical Characters of Soldiers of Scottish Nationality; Pigmentation Survey of School Children in Scotland; Modern Milk Problems; The Scottish People; An Anthropological Study of the Scots and Germans. *Address:* 17 Carden Place, Aberdeen. *T:* 1739, 2729. *Club:* Athenæum.

Died 8 Nov. 1945.

TOD, James Niebuhr, CBE 1920; JP; woollen manufacturer; *b* 1876; *s* of late J. Tod, St Albans; *m* 1905, May, *d* of late Comdr Keppel Garnier, RN; three *s* one *d*. *Educ:* privately; Heriot-Watt College, Edinburgh. Sometime Assistant Director, Wool Textile Production. *Address:* The Lawn, Nailsworth, Gloucestershire.

Died 12 May 1947.

TOD, Col John Kelso, CMG 1919; FRGS; retired; Col of 18th KE VII O Cavalry, 1931–45; *s* of Lt-Col Alexander Tod, Madras Staff Corps; *m* 1899, Lilian, *d* of James Henry; two *s* two *d*. *Educ:* Clifton College; RMC Sandhurst. Commission RI Fusiliers, 1884; Indian Army, 1885, 7th Bengal Cavalry, afterwards 7th Hariana Lancers; served Burma Campaign, 1886–88, ADC to Sir Geo White (medal, despatches); Staff College, Camberley, 1895–96; NWF Campaign, 1897–98; Burma-China Boundary Commission, 1898–99; Aden Hinterland Boundary Commission, 1901–03; War Office London, 1905–09; Army Headquarters Staff India, 1913; Staff in India, 1915–17; European War, 1914–18; Campaign in Trans-Caspia 1918–19 (despatches, CMG); Afghanistan, 1919; Comd. Force in NE Persia; retired, 1920. *Address:* Round Windows, Headley Down, Hants. *TA:* Headley Down. *T:* Headley Down 3233. *Club:* United Service.

Died 4 Aug. 1946.

TODD, Frederick, MRCS Eng; LDS Eng.; late Dental Surgeon to Bethlehem Royal Hospital, King Edward School; late Dental Surgeon to the Royal Free Hospital; late Assist Dental Surgeon, St Thomas's Hospital; *y s* of late William Todd of 23 Gresham Street, EC; *m* 1895, Miss A. Deckers, Senior Optime, Mathematics, Newnham College, Cambridge. *Educ:* private school. *Address:* The Lodge, Dawlish, S Devon.

Died 5 Dec. 1940.

TODD, Frederick Augustus, BA (Sydney); PhD (Jena); Professor of Latin, University of Sydney, since 1922; *b* Sydney, 14 March 1880; *s* of William Alexander Todd; *m* 1919, Florence Helen Grahame, *d* of Rev. James Glover; two *s* three *d*. *Educ:* University of Sydney; University of Leipzig; University of Jena. BA, Classical Medallist, University of Sydney, 1901; Woolley Travelling Scholar, 1901–03; PhD Jena, 1903. Lecturer in Latin at University of Sydney, 1903–13; Assistant Professor, 1914–21; twice President of the Union; Secretary of University Extension Board, 1912–21; Dean of the Faculty of Arts 1930–37. *Publications:* De Musis, 1903; Australasian Students' Song Book (founder and chief editor), 1911; University Company Song Book (chief editor), 1918; Selections from Martial, 1922; Campanarum Canticum, 1928; Some Ancient Novels, 1940; numerous contributions to periodicals. *Address:* 70 Murdoch Street, Cremorne, NSW. *T:* XM 1275.

Died 13 June 1944.

TODD, George William, MA (Cantab); MSc (Dunelm); DSc (Birm.); FInstP; Fellow of Physical Society, London; Member of Faraday Society, London; Professor of Experimental Physics, King's College (University of Durham), Newcastle-upon-Tyne, since 1919; *b* 1886; *e s* of H. Todd, Birmingham; *m* 1913, Margaret Ellen, *d* of E. H. Wallace, Somerset; one *d*. *Educ:* University of Birmingham; Emmanuel College, Cambridge (Exhibition Scholar); 1851 Exhibition Scholar of University of Birmingham. Original research under Prof. J. H. Poynting, FRS, at Birmingham, and under Sir J. J. Thomason, OM, FRS, at Cavendish Laboratory; Head of Physics Section Munitions Inventions Department Laboratories, London, 1915–18; Dean of the Faculty of Science (University of Durham), 1939–41. *Publications:* papers contributed to various learned societies on original scientific research; compiler of Physical and Chemical Data of Nitrogen Fixation, 1919; revised 14th ed. of Properties of Matter by Poynting and Thomson, 1947; Editor of Proceedings of University of Durham Philosophical Society. *Recreations:* gardening, sketching. *Address:* Kenilworth, Darras Road, Ponteland, Northumberland.

Died 24 Feb. 1950.

TODD, James Eadie, MA Oxon; FRHistSoc. Emeritus Professor of Modern History, The Queen's University of Belfast. *Address:* 31 Colinton Road, Edinburgh.

Died 21 Oct. 1949.

TODD, John L., BA, MD, MRCS Eng., Hon. DSc Liverpool; retired; *b* 1876; *m* 1912, Marjory Clouston (*d* 1945), *o c* of Sir Edward Clouston, 1st Bt; three *d*. *Educ:* Upper Canada College, Toronto; McGill Univ., Montreal. Expeditions for the Liverpool School of Tropical Medicine to Senegambia and the Congo Free State, 1902–05, 1911; Director of Runcorn Research Laboratories same school, 1905–07; Associate Prof. of Parasitology, McGill Univ., Montreal, 1907–26; Commander Order of Leopold II (Belgium); Mary Kingsley Medal, Liverpool School, 1910; Chevalier of the Order of Polonia Restituta, 1922; Major CAMC, 1914–16; Canadian Pension Commissioner, 1916–19; Typhus Research Commission, League of Red Cross Societies, to Poland, 1920. *Publications:* on medical subjects. *Address:* c/o Royal Trust Co., Montreal, Canada. *Club:* Mount Royal (Montreal).

Died 26 Aug. 1949.

TODD, Sir William Alexander Forster, Kt 1918; Lord Mayor of York, 1915–19, and 1931. Was Chairman of Food Control Committee, War Savings Committee, and Local Tribunal; Past Master of the Feltmakers' Company. *Address:* The Limes, Heworth, York.

Died 15 April 1946.

TODD, (William James) Walker, ARSA; FRIBA; Senior partner, Dick Peddie, Todd and Jamieson, Architects, Edinburgh; *b* Glasgow, 6 Feb. 1884; *s* of Ruthven C. Todd, CA; *m* 1913, Christian, *d* of James Craik, WS; five *s* five *d*. *Educ:* Fettes College, Edinburgh. Articled to late T. P. Marwick, ARIBA; Edinburgh College of Art, 1902–07; commenced private practice, 1909; served European War, 1915–19, France, 8th Batt. the Royal Scots, Captain; entered partnership with late J. M. Dick Peddie, 1920; President Edinburgh Architectural Association, 1936–38. *Buildings:* Merchiston Castle School, Colinton; County Buildings for East Lothian County, Peeblesshire and West Lothian County; Royal Bank of Scotland Buildings in Edinburgh, Kilmarnock, etc.; British Linen Bank Buildings in Edinburgh, Oban, etc., and other works, domestic and ecclesiastical. *Address:* 34 Inverleith Terrace, Edinburgh. *T:* 22311. *Clubs:* Public Schools; Scottish Arts, Edinburgh.

Died 29 April 1944.

TODHUNTER, Sir Charles George, KCSI 1921; CSI; OStJ; FRHistS; *b* 16 Feb. 1869; *s* of late Charles Franklin Todhunter, Christchurch, NZ; *m* 1901, Alice, OBE, K-i-H (*d* 1945), *d* of late Captain Charles Losack, 93rd Highlanders; no *c*. *Educ:* Aldenham; Kings' College, Cambridge. Passed into ICS 1888; Members' Prizeman, Cambridge University, 1889. Served in Madras as Assistant Collector, Registrar High Court, Deputy Commissioner Salt, Abkari and Customs and Secretary Board of Revenue, 1890–1900; on special duty in connection with reorganisation of customs and excise arrangements in Kashmir, the Central Provinces, and the Central India States; Secretary Indian Excise Committee; Collector of Customs and Inspector-General of Excise and Salt to the Government of India, 1900–10; returned to Madras and served as Collector, Secretary to Government, Member Board of Revenue, Chief Secretary, and Member of Council, 1910–24; President Indian Taxation Enquiry Committee, 1924–26; Private Secretary to Maharaja of Mysore, 1926–42; Economic and Industrial Adviser to Govt of Bikaner, 1942–44. *Address:* Grouville Hall Hotel, Jersey. *Club:* East India and Sports.

Died 1 March 1949.

TOFT, Albert, Hon. FRBS, Hon. ARCA; *b* Birmingham, 1862. *Educ:* Birmingham; Schools of Art, Hanley and Newcastle-under-Lyme; Royal College of Art, London, under Professor Lanteri. Apprenticed to the firm of Josiah Wedgwood & Sons at Etruria, as a modeller for pottery; gained a National Scholarship from the Newcastle-under-Lyme School of Art at age 17; this brought him to study at the Roy. Coll. of Art, South Kensington, for two years. *Works:* Lilith, 1889; Fate-Led, 1892 (Walker Art Gallery, Liverpool); The Sere and Yellow Leaf, 1892; The Oracle, 1894; The Goblet of Life, 1894; Spring (Birmingham Art Gallery); The Vision, 1897; Hagar, 1899; Victory, 1900; The Spirit of Contemplation, 1901 (Newcastle Art Gallery); Mother and Child, 1899 (Preston Art Gallery); The Bather, 1914 (Chantrey Bequest); Iron, 1916; W. E. Gladstone; G. J. Holyoake Memorial; Marble Statue of HH Rajah Sudhal Deb Bahadur KCIE, of Bamra, 1901. Statues, Queen Victoria, for Leamington, Nottingham, and South Shields; King Edward VII for Birmingham and for Warwick; numerous war memorials including: The Royal Fusiliers at Holborn Bars, The Oldham, Royal Leamington, National Welsh at Cardiff, The Warwickshire and The East Suffolk. Memorial bust in marble of late King George V for Eastbourne; Statuette Prince Dhairyashilrao, Gaekwar of Baroda; Bust of late Sir Alfred Gilbert, RA; Bronze bust of Sir Frank Brangwyn, RA, Brangwyn Hall, Swansea. *Publication:* Modelling and Sculpture. *Recreation:* shooting. *Address:* 30a Abbey Road, NW8. *Club:* Savage.

Died 18 Dec. 1949.

TOLER, Otway Scarlett Graham; *b* 1886; *c* and heir-pres. to 4th Earl of Norbury; *m* 1923, Mona Marian, *y d* of Lt-Col John Maxwell Low of Sunvale, Co. Limerick. *Educ:* Wellington College. High Sheriff of King's County, 1911; DL 1923. *Recreations:* shooting, farming, and horse breeding. *Address:* Durrow Abbey, King's County. *Club:* Bath.

Died 18 Nov. 1941.

TOLLEMACHE, Lt-Col Hon. Denis Plantagenet; late 7th Hussars; *b* 12 Jan. 1884; *b* and heir-pres. to 3rd Baron Tollemache. *Educ:* Winchester; Sandhurst. Entered army, 1902; Capt. 1911; General Staff Officer, 3rd Grade, 1914; Brigade-Major in France, 1914; Bt-Major, 1916; Acting Lt-Col, Northamptonshire Regt, 1916; Lt-Col 7th Hussars, 1923; served European War, 1914–19 (wounded, prisoner, DSO); retired pay, 1928; Sheriff of Rutland, 1933. *Recreations:* hunting, shooting. *Address:* 40 Moore Street, SW3. *T:* Kensington 5523; Manton House, nr Oakham. *Clubs:* Cavalry, Pratt's.

Died 1 May 1942.

TOLLEMACHE, Hon. Douglas Alfred; JP Suffolk; *b* 27 June 1862; *s* of 1st Lord Tollemache; *m* 1887, Alice Mary, *d* of late John Head; one *s* two *d*. *Educ:* Eton College; Cambridge University, BA 1884. Managing Director of Tollemache's Breweries, Ltd. *Address:* The Moat, Ipswich. *T:* Ipswich 3110. *Club:* Carlton.

Died 31 Dec. 1944.

TOLLEMACHE, Maj.-Gen. Edward Devereux Hamilton, DSO 1919, MC; retd; *b* 1 June 1885; heir-pres. to 3rd Baron Tollemache; late Coldstream Guards; *er s* of late Hon. Hamilton James Tollemache and Mabel, 2nd *d* of Robert Culling Hanbury, MP, of Bedwell Park, Herts; *m* 1909, Violet Aline, *o c* of late Rt Hon. Sir West Ridgeway, GCB, GCMG; one *s*. *Educ:* Eton; Royal Military College; passed Staff College, 1920. Served European War, 1914–19 (wounded, despatches, brevet majority, DSO, MC); order of the White Eagle of Serbia with swords; commanded 1st Bn Coldstream Guards, 1925–28; Asst Commandant RMC, Sandhurst, 1929–32; General Staff Officer, 1st Grade, 1st Div., 1932–36; Commander 128th (Hampshire) Infantry Brigade, TA, 1936–39; Commanded Southampton Garrison, 1939; Commander Portsmouth Area, 1940; ADC to the King 1937–40; retired 1940. *Publications:* British Army at War; The Turning Tide; Mirage; Green Wounds. *Address:* Devenish House, Sunningdale, Berks. *T:* Ascot 311. *Club:* Guards' Turf.

Died 27 Aug. 1947.

TOLLEMACHE, Hon. Mortimer Granville; *b* 12 April 1872; *y s* of 1st Baron Tollemache; *m* 1894, Margaret, *d* of Arthur Gorst; one *d*. Late Lieut Suffolk Imperial Yeomanry.

Died 27 March 1950.

TOLLER, Brig. Hamlet Bush, CB 1931; CMG 1918; *b* 1871; *s* of Captain J. E. Toller, RE; *m* 1899, Rose Eva, *d* of John Redington of Galway; one *s* one *d*. *Educ:* Oxford Military College. Served South African War, 1901–02 (Queen's medal and five clasps); Chief Paymaster, War Office, and Officer in Charge of Records, Royal Army Pay Corps, 1927–30; retired pay 1930.

Died 25 July 1950.

TOLLIT, Percy Kitto, MA; *b* Oxford, 6 Aug. 1863; *s* of H. J. Tollit of Oxford; *m* Mildred, *e d* of C. Steer of Stoke Prior; four *s* two *d*. *Educ:* Magdalen College School; Magdalen College, Oxford. Demy, 1881; 1st Class Mathematical Moderations, 1883, and honourable mention for the Junior Math. University Scholarship; 1st Class Mathematical Final School, 1885; 1st Class Natural Science Final School, 1886; BA 1886; MA 1888. Assistant Master at Bromsgrove School, 1887–98; Headmaster of Derby School, 1898–1906; Head of

Mathematical Side, Brighton College, 1906–27. *Recreations:* music, botany, golf. *Address:* Mallards, Moulsford, Berks.

Died 27 Dec. 1942.

TOLMIE, Hon. James; *b* at sea, 25 July 1862; of Scottish parents; unmarried. *Educ:* Queensland State schools. After leaving school trained as a teacher; subsequently took to journalism, and became part proprietor of Darling Downs Gazette, daily newspaper, published in Toowoomba; Member for Drayton and Toowoomba, 1901, 1902, 1904, and 1909; Toowoomba, 1912; Minister for Agriculture, 1911–12; Secretary for Public Lands, Queensland, 1912–15. *Recreations:* walking and gardening. *Address:* Kinbeachie, Hill Street, Toowoomba, Queensland, Australia. *T:* 195 Toowoomba. *Clubs:* Downs (Toowoomba); Johnsonian (Brisbane).

Died 5 April 1939.

TOMB, John Walker, OBE 1919; Director Endemic Diseases Section, Public Health Department, Egypt; *b* 18 Sept. 1882; *e s* of James Tomb, JP Co. Derry; *m* 1912, Mary Frances, *d* of W. Healy, Co. Tipperary. *Educ:* Academical Institution, Coleraine; Trinity College, Dublin; London School Tropical Medicine. MA, MD, BCh, DPH; Honorman in English Literature, Physics and Surgery, Dublin University; LM Rotunda Hospital, Dublin. Organised the Asansol Mines Board of Health; has made original researches into the bacteriology and epidemiology of cholera; originator of the 'essential oils' treatment of cholera. *Publications:* papers to British and Indian medical and psychological journals. *Recreations:* tennis, swimming, shooting, travelling. *Address:* Public Health Dept, Cairo; c/o Standard Bank of South Africa, Cape Town SA. *Clubs:* Sporting, Turf, Cairo.

Died 22 Feb. 1948.

TOMKINS, Stanley Charles, CMG 1900; MBE 1919; *m* 1910, Vera Louisa, *d* of late Edward Masterman, of Hook, Hants. Appointed by Foreign Office to Administrative Service, Uganda Protectorate, 1896, as Asst Political Officer; Chief Officer, Uganda Rifles, 1897; served through Nandi Expedition, 1897, and during Mutiny in Uganda, 1897–98 (despatches, medal, 2 clasps); Political Officer in charge of Kavirondo, 1897; took over charge of Kingdom of Uganda, 1900; Judicial Officer, Uganda Protectorate, 1900; in charge of Western Province, Uganda Protectorate, 1902; Sessions Judge, Uganda Protectorate, 1903; Sub-Commissioner, 1904; Acting Deputy-Commissioner, 1906–07; Chief Secretary to the Government, 1908; Acting Governor and C-in-C, Uganda Protectorate, April 1909 and 1910–11; retired, 1911; special duty under War Office, 1915–17; transferred to Air Ministry, 1917; retired, 1918. *Address:* Milestone Corner, Golf Drive, Camberley.

Died 17 Dec. 1946.

TOMLIN, Vice-Adm. George Napier, Pacha (in Egypt), CMG 1919; MVO 1912; *b* 25 July 1875; *s* of late Captain George James Tomlin, RN; *m* 1912, Violet Seymour Osborne; one *s* two *d*. *Educ:* private tutor; HMS Britannia. Entered Royal Navy, 1888; Midshipman in HMS Raleigh, Cape Station, 1894; landed during operations Gambia Expedition (West African Medal); Sub-Lieutenant in Philomel, 1894, landed during operations Benin River Expedition (Benin River Clasp); Lieutenant, 1896; Commander, 1908; Captain, 1915; Rear-Admiral, 1925; Vice-Admiral, retired, 1930; Navigating Officer of HMS Medina during visit of their Majesties King George V and Queen Mary to India, 1911–12 (Durbar Medal); Commander in HM Yacht Victoria and Albert prior to European War; served European War, 1914–18 (promoted Captain, despatches); lent to Government of Chile as President of Chilean Naval War College, 1922–24; Chilean decoration Al Merito; ADC to the

King, 1925; retired on promotion, 1925; Director-General of Egyptian Ports and Lights Administration, 1927–32; Secretary Prince's Club, London, 1934–39; Hon. Flight Lieut RAFVR 1939; Home Guard (Lieut), 1910; Grand Officier Order of Leopold II of Belgium; Grand Officer Crown of Italy; Order of Nile II Class. *Recreations:* out-door sports and games. *Address:* Nash Hill Cottage, Whitestaunton, Somerset. *Clubs:* Somerset County, Taunton.

Died 7 May 1947.

TOMLINSON, Robert Parkinson; JP Poulton-le-Fylde; Vice-Chairman, Fylde Water Board; Chairman, Preston, Garstang and Fylde Joint Hospital Board; Member, County Licensing Committee; Member, Quarter Sessions Appeals Committee; Vice-Chairman, Advisory Committee Assistance Board; Member, Lancashire Agricultural Wages Board; *b* Poulton-le-Fylde; *s* of William and Agnes Ormond Tomlinson; unmarried. *Educ:* Poulton-le-Fylde Grammar School; Claremont Coll., Blackpool. Went into business, Parkinson & Tomlinson, corn and oatmeal millers and seed merchants in the Fylde district; early took interest in public affairs; when 24 years of age elected to Poulton-le-Fylde UDC and has been a member ever since; on six occasions Chairman of the Council; for 30 years Chairman of Finance Committee and representative on many other committees; MP (L) Lancaster, 1928–29; President Methodist Local Preachers Mutual Aid Association; late Vice-President of Methodist Conference. *Address:* Poulton-le-Fylde. *TA:* Tomlinson Poulton-le-Fylde. *T:* Poulton-le-Fylde 17. *Club:* National Liberal.

Died 3 June 1943.

TONER, Rt Rev. John, DD; Bishop of Dunkeld, (RC), 1914–49; *b* Glasgow, 14 March 1857. *Educ:* Blairs College, Aberdeen; Scots College, Valladolid. Priest, 1882; Assistant Priest in St Lawrence, Greenock, 1882–87; Professor in Diocesan College, Glasgow, 1887–90; in charge of the Mission of St Michael, Glasgow, 1890–97; Administrator of St Patrick's, Glasgow, 1897–1901; Missionary Rector of St Columbkille's, Rutherglen, 1901–14; Canon Glasgow Chapter, 1902–14. *Address:* Bishop's House, Dundee.

Died 31 May 1949.

TONGE, Col William Corrie, DSO 1902; *b* 14 April 1862; *s* of William John Tonge of Morants Court, Sevenoaks, Kent; *m* 1898, Caroline Annie (*d* 1939), *d* of Thos Oliver of Horsham, Sussex; one *s*. *Educ:* Brighton; Tonbridge School; Cheltenham Coll. Entered RM Coll., Sandhurst, 1881; Lt Norfolk Regt, 1882; Captain, 1889; Major, 1902; Lieut-Col 3rd Batt. 1910; served in South Africa with Sir Charles Warren's Expedition to Bechuanaland, 1884–85; South African War, 1900–02 (despatches twice, Queen's medal 3 clasps, King's medal 2 clasps, DSO); European War (Bt-Col, despatches twice). *Recreations:* cricket, racquets, golf, shooting. *Clubs:* MCC; Radnor, Folkestone.

Died 2 May 1943.

TONK, HH Said-ud-Daulah Wazir-ul-Mulk Nawab Hafiz Sir Mohammed Saadat Ali Khan Bahadur Sowlat-i-Jung, GCIE 1934; *b* 1879; *S* 1930. The State has an area of 2553 sq. miles and a population of 357,933. *Address:* Tonk, Rajputana.

Died 31 May 1947.

TOOLE, Joseph; JP; Alderman for Openshaw Ward, Manchester; *b* Salford, 1887; *m* 1908, Margaret Dearden; one *s* two *d*. *Educ:* Mount Carmel RC School, Salford. Commenced life as newsboy, and then worked as labourer in iron foundry and electrical shops; contested Everton Division, Liverpool, 1923; MP (Lab) for Salford (South Division), 1923–24 and 1929–31; Lord Mayor of Manchester, 1936–37. *Publications:* Fighting through

Life, 1935; My Year as Lord Mayor, 1937; Serial, Her Name was Mary, 1940. *Address:* 57 Princess Street, Manchester 2. *T:* Central 5757.

Died 4 June 1945.

TOOLEY, Mrs Sarah A.; literary and journalistic; *d* of late Thomas Southall of Brierley Hill, Staffs; *m* late Rev. George Walter Tooley, formerly of Dumfries. *Educ:* Greenhill House, Stourbridge; studied literature under late Prof. Henry Morley, University College, London. Discovered the birthplace and birth certificate of Mrs Gaskell; Member Council, a Vice-Pres. and Vice-Chm. Society of Women Journalists; Corporation Royal Literary Fund; Gilbert White Fellowship. *Publications:* Lives Great and Simple; Life of Harriet Beecher Stowe; The Personal Life of Queen Victoria; The Life of Queen Alexandra; Royal Palaces and their Memories; The Life of Florence Nightingale; The History of Nursing in the British Empire; The Royal Family by Pen and Camera; Introductory Chapter on Nursing, Past and Present, in the Science and Art of Nursing; contributed various subjects Every Woman's Encyclopædia; Lantern Lectures on The Story of the Red Cross and The Red Cross in the Great War; The Story of the May-flower; Stories of the Palaces; Psychic Phenomena in the Old Testament; Our Village in Wartime; The Women's Land Fête in our Village; a constant contributor to leading magazines and periodicals. *Recreations:* country walking, exploring interesting districts, and studying people. *Address:* 99 Addison Road, Kensington, W. *Club:* English-Speaking Union.

Died 24 Dec. 1946.

TOOP, Engr Rear-Adm. William, CB 1918; *m* Alice Edith (*d* 1947); two *s.* Served European War, 1914–19 (CB), Retired List, 1923.

Died 9 May 1950.

TOPLEY, William Whiteman Carlton, FRS 1930; MA, MD, BC Cantab; MSc Manch., FRCP; Hon. Physician to the King since 1941; Hon. Fellow, St John's College, Cambridge; Secretary of Agricultural Research Council since 1941; Member of War Cabinet Scientific Advisory Committee, and of Colonial Research Advisory Committee; *b* 1886; *s* of late Ebenezer Topley; *m* 1912, Kate, *d* of late Frederick W. Amsden, Sevenoaks, Kent; two *d. Educ:* City of London School; University of Cambridge; St Thomas' Hospital. Assistant Director of Pathologocal Laboratory, St Thomas Hospital, 1910; Director of Pathological Department, Charing Cross Hospital, 1911–22; Professor of Bacteriology, University of Manchester, 1922–27; Professor of Bacteriology and Immunology, University of London, and Director of Division of Bacteriology and Immunology, London School of Hygiene and Tropical Medicine, 1927–41; Member of Medical Research Council, 1938–41; Goulstonian Lecturer, RCP 1919; Milroy Lecturer, RCP, 1926; Harben Lecturer, R Inst. Pub. Health, 1926; Linacre Lecturer, St John's College, Cambridge, 1940; Croonian Lecturer, Royal Society, 1941; Royal Medal of Royal Society, 1942; Captain, RAMC, and Bacteriologist to British San. Mission to Serbia, 1915 (Order of St Sava). *Publications:* various papers on Bacteriology and allied subjects; The Principles of Bacteriology and Immunity (conjointly). *Address:* Agricultural Research Council, 6a Dean's Yard, WC1; The Court Lodge, East Malling, Kent. *Club:* Oxford and Cambridge.

Died 21 Jan. 1944.

TORRINGTON, 9th Viscount *cr* 1721; **George Master Byng;** Bt 1715; Baron Byng, 1721; *b* 10 Sept. 1886; *s* of 8th Viscount and 2nd wife, Emmeline St Maur, *d* of Rev. Henry Seymour, Rector of Holme Pierrepont, Nottinghamshire; *S* father, 1889; *m* 1st, 1910, Eleanor (who obtained a divorce, 1921; she died 1931), *e d* of Edwin Souray of Long Ditton, Surrey; 2nd, 1923, Norah Elizabeth Ursula, *d* of late Capt. Robert Wood-Pottle, 5th Lancers and formerly wife of late Harold Ferens.

Educ: Eton; Sandhurst. Page of Honour to Queen Victoria, 1899–1901; to King Edward VII, 1901–02; late Lieut Rifle Brigade; enlisted as trooper in 19th Hussars, 1914; given Commission in RNVR; Flight Observer, Royal Naval Air Service; Capt. RAF; taken prisoner 2 Dec. 1916 whilst flying; was a prisoner at Philippopolis, Bulgaria; now demobilised. *Religion:* Roman Catholic; received into the Church, 1931. *Recreations:* hunting, shooting, racing. *Heir: cousin* Lt-Col A. S. Byng. *Address:* Lisheen, Buckfast, S Devon. *T:* Buckfastleigh 3109.

Died 24 May 1944.

TORY, Henry Marshall, MA, DSc, LLD, DCL, FRS Can., FRHS; *b* 11 Jan. 1864; *s* of Robert K. Tory and Anorah Ferguson; *m* 1893, Annie Gertrude Frost; no *c. Educ:* Guysboro, Nova Scotia; McGill University, Montreal; Cambridge, England. Graduated McGill University, 1890; gold medallist in Mathematics and Physics; MA 1896; DSc, 1903; LLD St Francis Xavier College, 1905, McGill, 1908, Univ. of Toronto, 1927, of Sask, 1928, of Alberta, 1928, of McMaster, 1932, Western Ontario, 1932. Queen's, 1938; DCL Acadia, 1935. Lecturer Mathematics, McGill, 1891; Associate Professor, 1903; Governors' Fellow, McGill Univ., 1905–08; Non-Resident Fellow, 1908–15; Member Executive Committee Universities Bureau British Empire, 1912–26; Member the Royal Conservation Commission for Canada; was Member of American Commission for the Study of Agricultural Credit in Europe, 1913; Col Director of Educational Services Canadian Overseas Force, 1917–19; Member Imperial Educ. Committee; Pres. Univ. of Alberta, 1908–28; Pres. National Research Council of Canada, 1923–35, and Director National Research Laboratories 1927–35; Commissioner on Agricultural Credits for Canadian Gov., 1923–24; Special Commissioner for Canadian Gov., to Pan Pacific Science Congress Japan, 1926; Chairman of Committee on Taxation, Province of Alberta, 1926–28; Pres. League of Nations Society in Canada, 1928–33; Chairman of Royal Commission to Study the Fruit Industry in Nova Scotia, 1930; Royal Commissioner, Government of Canada on Importation and Distribution of Anthracite Coal in Canada, 1936; President Pacific Science Congress, 1929–33; President Royal Society of Canada, 1938–39; Director Technical Branch Vol. Serv. Bureau, 1939–41; President and Chairman Board of Governors, Carlton College, Ottawa, 1942. *Publications:* Manual, Laboratory Physics; various papers in scientific journals on Pyrometry and Education; Reports on Agricultural Credit and Taxation; Editor, History of Science in Canada, 1939. *Recreations:* golf, curling. *Address:* Rockcliffe Park, Ottawa, Canada. *Clubs:* University, Rideau, Royal Ottawa Golf, Ottawa.

Died 6 Feb. 1947.

TORY, Hon. James Cranswick, LLD; *b* Guysboro' County, Nova Scotia; *s* of Robert Kirk Tory and Anorah Ferguson; *m* Caroline Emma, *d* of Abraham N. Whitman, Canso, Nova Scotia; no *c. Educ:* Guysboro' Academy; Wesleyan Theological College, and McGill Univ., Montreal. With A. J. O. Maguire & Co., Guysboro', Nova Scotia, and A. N. Whitman & Son, Canso, Nova Scotia, 1885–91; Special Representative, Sun Life Assurance Co. of Canada, West Indies, 1891; Superintendent of Agencies, WI, 1892; Manager for Michigan, Detroit, 1895; Superintendent of Agencies, Montreal, 1897; General Manager, Western Foreign Dept, 1901; General Manager of Agencies Montreal, 1915–25; elected to Nova Scotia Legislature for Guysboro' County, 1911; re-elected 1916 and 1920; Minister without Portfolio, 1921; re-appointed, 1923; Lieutenant-Governor of Nova Scotia, 1925–30; Liberal; United Church of Canada. *Address:* 6 Young Avenue, Halifax, Nova Scotia; Belmont Farm, Guysboro', Nova Scotia. *Clubs:* Halifax, Gorsebrook Golf, Canadian, Halifax, NS.

Died 26 June 1944.

TOTTENHAM, Sir Alexander Robert Loftus, Kt 1931; CIE 1925; Administrator Pudukkottai State, 1934–44, Diwan, 1944; late ICS; Member Central Board of Revenue, and Joint Secretary, Finance Department, Government of India, 1923–32; *b* 31 July 1873; *s* of late Commander John Francis Tottenham, RN, JP (*s* of late Lord Robert Tottenham, Bishop of Clogher); unmarried. *Educ:* Clifton College; Queen's College, Oxford (Scholar). 1st Class Classical Mods; 1st Cl. Lit. Hum.; BA 1896; MA 1906. Joined ICS, Madras, 1897; served in Madras Presidency (except for a few months) up to 1923; retired, 1933. *Address:* Pudukkottai State, S India; c/o Grindlay & Co. Ltd, Westminster, SW1. *Clubs:* East India and Sports, Royal Automobile.

Died 13 Dec. 1946.

TOTTENHAM, Adm. Henry Loftus, CB 1914; *b* 1860; *e surv. s* of late Commander J. F. Tottenham, RN, of Lofthouse, Torquay; *m* 1897, Florence Elizabeth, *d* of late Thomas Coles, of Titchmarsh, Northamptonshire; one *s. Educ:* Royal Naval Academy, Gosport. Entered Royal Navy, 1873; as Sub-Lieut in 1882 was at battle of Tel-el-Kebir with Naval Brigade; as Lieutenant in command of HM Gunboat Thrush took part in the Brass River Expedition, 1895; Naval ADC to King Edward VII, 1908–10; Rear-Admiral, 1910; Rear-Admiral 3rd Division Home Fleet, 1912–13; from outbreak of war was employed afloat in several commands, including 7th Cruiser Squadron, Grand Fleet, until promoted to Vice-Admiral, Oct. 1915; Admiral retired, Oct. 1918.

Died 24 Feb. 1950.

TOURS, Berthold George, CMG 1914; late HM Consul-General in China; *b* London, 24 Jan. 1871; *e s* of late Berthold Tours; *m* 1897, Ada Theophila, *d* of late Samuel Harwood, and *g d* of late Edward Harwood, JP, of Almondesbury, Glos; two *s* one *d. Educ:* Godolphin School; King's College, London, Matriculated London University, 1887; Inter. Arts, 1889. Student Interpreter in China, 1893; received the China medal and clasp for defence of the Legations at Peking, 1900; HM Vice-Consul, 1906; HM Consul, 1908; HM Consul at Nanking in 1913; Special Opium Commissioner, 1914; HM Consul-General, 1922; FRGS, FZS; Barrister-at-Law, of the Middle Temple. *Recreation:* music. *Address:* At Holmer Park, Hereford. *Clubs:* Shanghai, Shanghai Country.

Died 24 Sept. 1944.

TOUT, Sir Frederick Henry, Kt 1935. President Bank of NSW; Dep. Chm. Dirs, Australian Mutual Provident Soc.; Director: Associated Newspapers Ltd; Goldsbrough, Mort & Co. Ltd; McGarvie Smith Institute; Grazcos Co-op. Ltd; Late Pres. Graziers Assoc. *Address:* Wambanumba, Young, NSW.

Died 4 July 1950.

TOUT, W. J.; Secretary, Todmorden Weavers' Association; *b* 1870. MP (Lab) Oldham, 1922–24; Sowerby Div. of Yorks, WR 1929–31. *Address:* 18 Hare Hill Street, Todmorden.

Died 24 Feb. 1946.

TOVEY, Lt-Col George Strangways, CMG 1918; DSO 1916; late RA; *b* 1875; *s* of late Col Hamilton Tovey, RE; *m* 1910, Lilian Mary (*d* 1939), *d* of Rev. A. Conder; one *s* one *d.* Entered RA 1896; Capt. 1902; Maj. 1913; Bt Lt-Col 1916; Lt-Col Feb. 1917; served S African War (despatches, Queen's medal with 3 clasps, King's medal with 2 clasps); European War, 1914–18 (DSO, CMG); retired pay, 1921.

Died 13 Jan. 1943.

TOWER, Comdr Francis FitzPatrick; late RNVR; *b* June 1859; *s* of Thomas Tower, 2nd *s* of Christopher Tower, of Weald Hall, Essex; *m* 1884, Laura, *d* of Thomas Butler, late Royal Fusiliers; two *s* three *d. Educ:* Wellington College; Trinity College, Cambridge. Served European War, Lieut Commander RNR,

1914–15; Commander RNVR 1915–19 (OBE Mil. 1919; Italian bronze medal, 1918). *Address:* Upper Holmwood, Cowes. *Clubs:* Royal Yacht Squadron, Cowes.

Died 28 March 1944.

TOWER, Rev. Henry, CVO 1935; MA; *b* 15 July 1862; *s* of late Rev. F. E. Tower, Rector of Holy Trinity, Guildford; *m* Kate Theresa (*d* 1940), *widow* of S. F. Gedge, of Horton Lodge, Slough, and *e d* of late Rt Hon. Harry Escombe, Premier of Natal; two *d. Educ:* Lancing College; Hertford College, Oxford. Curate St Andrew's, Leicester, 1886–92; Vicar Weedon Beck, and Chaplain to Troops, 1892–99; St Andrew's, Leicester, and Chaplain to Gaol, 1899–1900; Rector of Holy Trinity, Windsor, and Acting Chaplain to Household Troops, 1900–45; Surrogate for Archdeaconry of Berks, 1907; Hon. Canon of Christ Church, Oxford, 1938–46; retired, 1946; Chairman of Berkshire War Pensions Executive Committee, 1918–23. *Recreations:* gardening, photography. *Address:* Monkton House, Montague Road, Datchet, Bucks.

Died 3 Feb. 1948.

TOWERS, Samuel, RCA; *b* 1863. *Address:* Firbank, Harvington, nr Evesham.

Died 27 June 1943.

TOWLE, Arthur Edward, CBE 1919; Member of the Food Council and of the Consumers' Committee for England; *b* 22 Aug. 1878; *s* of late Sir Wm Towle; *m* Margery Lawrence, writer. *Educ:* Marlborough. Assistant Manager Midland Hotels, 1898; Joint Manager, 1913; Manager, 1920; reported to South African Government on re-organisation of Railway Catering, 1902; Director Ministry of Food, 1917; Assistant Secretary Ministry of Food, 1919; Controller of Hotels for Peace Conference in Paris, 1919–20; Controller of the LMS Hotel Services, 1925–44; reported on Catering at the Universities to the Royal Commission on Oxford and Cambridge, 1921. *Recreation:* golf. *Address:* 25 Princess Court, Bryanston Place, W1. *Club:* Royal Automobile.

Died 26 Aug. 1948.

TOWNEND, Harry, MA; *b* Bradford, 1872; *s* of William Townend; *m* 1905, Kate Walker. *Educ:* Bradford. Assistant Curator, Bradford Art Gallery, 1891; Librarian, Bradford Reference Library, 1897; Curator and Librarian, Bury Art Gallery and Library, 1904; Director and Curator, Aberdeen Art Gallery, 1914–39; Lecturer in Painting, Aberdeen University; Examiner in Art and Archæology, Edinburgh University, 1924–28. *Publications:* Life of J. M. W. Turner, RA, 1924; numerous catalogues, articles, and reviews. *Recreation:* music. *Address:* Eccleshill, Bieldside, Aberdeenshire. *T:* Aberdeen 47231.

Died 12 Feb. 1949.

TOWNEND, Herbert Patrick Victor, CIE 1936; *b* 11 March 1887; *s* of Rev. Alfred John Townend; *m* 1913, Lettice Joan, *d* of Timothy Bevington; one *s* two *d. Educ:* King's School, Canterbury; St John's College, Oxford. Entered ICS 1911; Under Secretary Finance Dept Govt of Bengal, 1917; Director of Civil Supplies, Govt of Bengal, 1918; Officiating Director General Commercial Intelligence, Jan.–Nov. 1920; Collector Bakarganj, 1922; Dy Sec. Finance Dept Govt of Bengal, 1923; Sec. Indian Coal Committee, 1924–25; Dy Commissioner Jalpaiguri, 1926; Land Acquisition Collector, Calcutta, 1929; Sec. Agricultural and Industry Dept Govt of Bengal, 1930; Sec. Local Self Govt Dept Govt of Bengal, 1932; Rural Development Commissioner, Bengal, 1934–37; Commissioner, Burdwan Division, 1938–40; Commissioner Presidency Division, 1941–42; retired, Dec. 1944. *Address:* Field House, Jack Straw's Lane, Headington Hill, Oxford.

Died 23 Dec. 1950.

TOWNLEY, Rev. Charles Gale, MA; Hon. Canon of Carlisle, 1920; Rural Dean of Cartmel, 1929; *b* 14 Jan. 1848; 3rd *s* of Rev. Edmund Townley, of Townhead; *m* 1887, Mary Sophia, *e d* of Rev. William Alderson of Heath, nr Wakefield; no *c. Educ:* Rossall; Wadham College, Oxford. Ordained, 1872; Curate of Claverdon with Norton Lindsey, Warwick; Curate of Buckland St Mary, Somerset, 1874–88; Vicar of Troutbeck, Windermere, 1882–93; Vicar of Egton with Newland, Ulverston, 1893–1900; succeeded to the Townhead estate on the death of Edmund James Townley, of Brasenose College, Oxford, and Lincoln's Inn, Barrister-at-Law. *Publications:* Dedications of Five Churches in the Lake Country, 1893; History of the Church and Schools of Egton, 1898; An Account of the Parish of Staveley-in-Cartmel, 1933. *Recreations:* rowed bow and stroke of Wadham Eight, 1870–72; held College Sculls, 1869–70; present member of Coniston Fox Hunt. *Address:* Townhead, Newby Bridge, Ulverston, Lancashire. *T:* Newby Bridge 321.

Died 9 Aug. 1942.

TOWNLEY, Maximilian Gowran; JP Cambs; *b* 22 June 1864; 5th *s* of late Charles Watson Townley, of Fulbourn Manor, Cambridge; *m* 1902, Hon. Ellen Sydney St John, *e d* of 15th Baron St John, of Bletsoe. *Educ:* Eton; Trinity College, Cambridge. MP (CU) Mid Beds, Dec. 1918–22. *Address:* Monadh Liadh, Aviemore, Invernesshire.

Died 12 Dec. 1942.

TOWNLEY, Sir Walter Beaupre, KCMG 1911; *b* Fulbourn Manor, Cambridge, 8 Jan. 1863; *s* of Charles Watson Townley, of Fulbourn, Camb., late Lord Lieut Camb., and Georgiana, *d* of Max Dalison, of Hamptons, Kent; *m* 1896, Lady Susan Mary Keppel, *d* of 7th Earl of Albemarle. *Educ:* Eton. Nominated an Attaché, 1885; passed a competitive examination, 1885; appointed to Paris 1886; passed an exam. in Public Law, 1886; 3rd Secretary, 1887; transferred to Teheran, 1889; granted an allowance for knowledge of Persian, 1890; transferred to Paris, 1892; 2nd Secretary, 1892; transferred to Bucharest, 1894, where he acted as Chargé d'Affaires, 20 March to 9 Dec. 1894, and to Paris, 12 Nov. 1894, where he acted as Chargé d'Affaires, 22 to 27 Oct. 1896; transferred to Lisbon, 1897; Berlin, 1898; Rome, 1900; Secretary of Legation, Peking, 1901; acted Chargé d'Affaires, 1902–03; Councillor of Embassy, 1903; transferred to Constantinople, 1903; acted Chargé d'Affaires, 1905; transferred to Washington, 1905; acted Chargé d'Affaires, 1906; Envoy Extraordinary and Minister Plenipotentiary to Argentine Republic and Republic of Paraguay, 1906–10; to Roumania, 1910–12; Persia, 1912–15; employed Foreign Office, 1916; Envoy Extraordinary and Minister Plenipotentiary to the Queen of the Netherlands, 1917–Aug. 1919, when he retired from the Diplomatic Service.

Died 5 April 1945.

TOWNSEND, Adm. Cyril Samuel, CB 1918; *b* 1875; *y s* of late Vice-Admiral S. P. Townsend of Fareham, Hants; *m* 1905, Mary Elizabeth, *d* of late Captain W. H. Moseley of Leaton Hall, Staffs; two *s* three *d. Educ:* Stubbington House, Fareham. Commander of HMS Duncan, 1908–10; Order of Commander of Crown of Italy for services rendered after Messina earthquake; Captain, Dec. 1913; Rear-Adm., 1924; Vice-Adm. 1929; Beachmaster at W Beach, Gallipoli, at original landing (despatches); commanded HMS Constance, 4th LCS in North Sea, at Jutland, 1916–19 (CB); Captain of Gunnery School, Chatham, 1919–21; Captain, HMS Resolution, 1921–22; Commodore RN Barracks, Portsmouth, 1922–24; Head of the British Naval Mission to Greece, 1925–26; Rear-Admiral in Charge, Gibraltar, 1927–29; retired list, 1929; Adm. retired, 1933. *Address:* The Old Rectory, Bishopstoke, Hants.

Died 31 March 1949.

TOWNSHEND, James, RBA 1903. *Educ:* Paris, under Carolus Duran and Professor Bouguereau (silver and three bronze medals); many years Royal Academy, New Gallery, and all the leading exhibitions. *Works:* Between two Fires; Pots and Pans, Kettles and Cans, Oh, Village Flirts; Once Bit, Twice Shy; Xmas Eve in Shakespeare's Country, now in the possession of the King. *Address:* Royal British Artists, Suffolk Street, Pall Mall, SW1.

Died 27 Dec. 1949.

TOWNSHEND, William Tower; JP Co. Cork; *b* 1855; *m* 1901, Hon. Geraline Emily Curzon (*d* 1940), *d* of Lord Scarsdale, and *sister* of Marquess Curzon, Viceroy of India, 1899–1905; three *d. Educ:* Haileybury; Brackenbury's Army School; on the Continent. Late Capt. in Queen's Own Royal West Kent Regiment; High Sheriff for County Cork, 1913. *Address:* Bodiam Manor, Sussex; Myross Wood, Leap, County Cork. *TA:* Townshend, Bodiam, Ewhurst, Sussex. *T:* Staple Cross, Sussex, 35.

Died 6 Feb. 1943.

TOWSE, Captain Sir (Ernest) Beachcroft (Beckwith), VC; KCVO 1927; CBE 1920; Gordon Highlanders, retired; Sergeant-at-Arms in Ordinary to His Majesty, 1900, Gentleman-at-Arms 1903, retired 1939; *b* 23 April 1864; *m* 1892, Gertrude (*d* 1935), *d* of late John Christie. *Educ:* Stubbington; Wellington College. 3rd Seaforth Highlanders, 1883; entered army, 1885; Captain, 1896; served Chitral Relief Force, 1895, including Malakand (medal with clasp); NW Frontier of India and Tirah, 1897–98 (two clasps); South Africa, 1899–1900 (VC, with 2 dates 1900 and 1901, despatches twice, Queen's medal 3 clasps, dangerously wounded); European War in France, 1914–18, as Honorary Staff Captain for Base Hospitals without pay and allowances (despatches); KGStJ; ex-Pres. National Institute for the Blind; National Vice-Pres. of British Legion. *Address:* Long Meadow, Goring, Oxfordshire. *TA:* Towse Goring. *T:* Goring 84. *Clubs:* Naval and Military, Flyfishers; Caledonian United Service (Edinburgh).

Died 21 June 1948.

TOWSEY, Brig.-Gen. Francis William, CMG 1917; CBE 1919; DSO 1918; retired; *s* of Captain G. W. Towsey, RN, of Linden House, Lymington, Hants; *m* 1898, Florence Harriet, *d* of Lieut-Gen. Fisher, Royal Artillery; one *s. Educ:* Rugby School. Joined 4th Batt. PWO West Yorkshire Regt 1883; 2nd Batt. 1885; served Lushai Expedition, 1892 (medal); Ashanti Expedition, 1896 (Ashanti Star); European War, 1914–18 (CMG, CBE, DSO); JP. *Address:* Tollgate House, Shrub End, Colchester.

Died 31 May 1948.

TOYE, Major Edward Geoffrey, Hon. ARCM; Member of Lloyd's; American Liaison and Censorship Department, BBC, since 1940; *b* 17 Feb. 1889; 2nd *s* of late A. J. Toye, Housemaster of Winchester College; *m* 1st, 1915, Doris Lytton Partington; no *c*; 2nd, Dorothy Fleitman; one *s. Educ:* Horris Hill; Winchester; Royal College of Music (Exhibitioner and Scholar); abroad. Conducted Blue Bird at Haymarket Theatre, and Opera for Miss Marie Brema at the Savoy; also Ellis Concerts of Modern Music at Queen's Hall, 1914; enlisted in DCL Infantry, 1 Sept. 1914, afterwards obtained commission in that regiment; transferred to RFC on account of ill-health, 1915; entered the Photographic Section; conducted Opera for Sir Thomas Beecham, Aldwych Theatre, and Philharmonic Concerts, Season, 1918–19; Liverpool Philharmonic Concerts, Gilbert and Sullivan Opera Seasons; Lloyds' Choir; Elizabethan Madrigal Choir; Governor of the Old Vic, 1925; Governor Sadler's Wells, 1931; Joint Manager of Opera at these theatres, 1932–34; composed and produced Ballets, Douanes, 1932, Haunted Ballroom, 1934; Conductor Royal Choral Society, 1932–33; Managing Director Royal Opera, Covent Garden, 1934–36; Producer and

Artistic Director of Mikado Film, 1938. *Publications:* various. *Recreation:* golf. *Clubs:* Bath; New Zealand, Byfleet.

Died 11 June 1942.

TOYNBEE, Brig. Guy Elliston, CMG 1918; CBE 1919, Indian Army, rtd; late Royal Army Service Corps; *b* 1884; *s* of late George Toynbee, Indian Civil Service; *m* 1912, Winifred Mary, *y d* of late Alfred Harris, MB; two *d*. *Educ:* Charterhouse (Verites), Sandhurst. 2nd Lieut Unattached List Indian Army, 1905; served in India with the 1st Batt. Lincolnshire Regt until end of 1906; transferred to Royal Army Service Corps; Capt. 4 Aug. 1914; Major, 1925; Indian Army, 1927; Lt-Col 1931; Col 1936; temp. Brig. 1938; served European War (despatches 4 times, Brevet majority, CMG, CBE, 4th Class Serbian White Eagle (with swords), 1914 Star, Officier de la Couronne Belgium); Waziristan, 1923 (IGS Medal); retired 1940; Jubilee Medal; Coronation Medal. *Address:* c/o Grindlay & Co., 54 Parliament Street, SW1.

Died 12 Feb. 1947.

TOZER, Basil; *b* 1896; *y s* of late J. H. Tozer, Teignmouth, and Mary Herbert, Llanarth Court, Mon; *m* Beatrice Langley, violinist; two *s*. *Educ:* Beaumont Coll.; Crystal Palace Engineering School. Articled Tozer, Whidborne & Tozer, solicitors; Editor Daily Messenger, Paris; travelled extensively; special correspondent in Canada to inquire into emigration question; staff of Daily Mail, Daily Express, etc.; Press Manager Thomas Beecham Opera Company; Sir Joseph Beecham's Opera Company; Imperial International Exhibition, etc.; regular writer for principal monthly reviews and magazines, weekly and daily papers; Temp. Officer RASC, 1914–21. *Publications:* Freelance Journalism and how to make it Pay; Hints on Shooting; Hints on Riding to Hounds; The Horse in History; Round the World with a Millionaire; The Irony of Marriage; A Daughter of Belial; Vengeance; How to Buy a Gun; Recollections of a Rolling Stone; A Dealer in Antiques; The Story of a Terrible Life; Confidence Crooks and Blackmailers; The Riddle of the Forest; Life's Lighter Side; Secret Traffic. The Elusive Lord Bagtor; etc. *Recreations:* mostly reading and writing; formerly riding to hounds, shooting, steeple-chasing (retired from all clubs during war). *Address:* Reed Lodge, Teignmouth, S Devon. *T:* Teignmouth 712.

Died 7 Dec. 1949.

TRAILL, Lt-Col John Charles Merriman, DSO 1917; MC; Wool Representative at Warracknabeal on staff of the New Zealand Loan and Mercantile Agency Co., Ltd, Melbourne; *b* 24 Jan. 1881; *s* of George William and Phebe Marshall Traill; *m* 1928, Mollie Helen Roche; two *s*. *Educ:* George Watson's College and University, Edinburgh. Sub-Manager Argentine Southern Land Coy, Patagonia; served South African War; European war with AIF, Egypt, Gallipoli, France, 1914–18 (despatches 3 times, wounded twice, DSO, MC); Grazier, Victoria, Australia. *Recreation:* golf. *Address:* Inchmarlo, Warracknabeal, Victoria, Australia. *T:* Warracknabeal 347. *Clubs:* Naval and Military of Victoria, Melbourne.

Died 4 June 1942.

TRAIN, Arthur; author and playwright; President of National Institute of Arts and Letters; *b* Boston, 6 Sept. 1875; *s* of Charles Russell Train and Sarah M. Cheney; *m* 1st, 1897, Ethel (*d* 1923), *d* of Benjamin P. Kissam; one *s* three *d*; 2nd, 1926, Mrs Helen Coster Gerard, NY. *Educ:* Harvard Univ., AB, 1896; LLB, 1899. *Publications:* McAllister and his Double, 1905; The Prisoner at the Bar, 1906; True Stories of Crime, 1908; The Butler's Story, 1909; Mortmain, 1909; Confessions of Artemus Quibble, 1909; CQ: or, in the Wireless House, 1910; Courts, Criminals and the Camorra, 1911; The Goldfish, 1914; (with Robert Williams Wood) The Man who Rocked the Earth, 1915; The World and Thomas Kelly,

1917; The Earthquake, 1918; Tutt and Mr Tutt, 1920; By Advice of Counsel, 1921; The Hermit of Turkey Hollow, 1921; As it Was in the Beginning, 1921; Tut, Tut, Mr Tutt 1923; His Children's Children, 1923; The Needle's Eye, 1924; On the Trail of the Bad Men, 1925; The Lost Gospel, 1925; Blind Goddess, 1926; High Winds, When Tutt meets Tutt, 1927; Ambition, 1928; The Horns of Ramadan, 1928; Illusion, 1929; Mr Tutt's Case Book, 1936; My Day in Court, 1936; From the District Attorney's Office, 1939; Old Man Tutt, 1938; Tassels on Her Boots, 1940; Mr Tutt Comes Home, 1941; Yankee Lawyer, the Autobiography of Ephraim Tutt, 1943. Mr Tutt (play), 1944. *Address:* 113 E 73rd Street, New York, NY. *Clubs:* Century, University, Harvard, New York.

Died 22 Dec. 1945.

TRAIN, Sir John, Kt 1936; DL, JP; MP (C) Cathcart Division, Glasgow, since 1929; *b* Cambusnethan, Lanarkshire, 8 May 1873; *s* of James Train; *m* 1898, Sarah, *d* of late Charles Wark; two *s* three *d*. *Educ:* Glasgow Technical College. Managing Director of John Train & Co., Ltd, Building Contractors, 30 George Square, Glasgow; Chairman of Rutherglen Parish Council, 1912–18; Member of Lanark County Council, 1916–30; Vice-Convener, 1923–30; served on the Board of the Clyde Navigation Trustees; Deacon Convener of The Trades House of Glasgow, 1927–29; Member of the Corporation of Glasgow, 1927–29; on Boards of Glasgow Royal Infirmary and similar institutions; various Government Committees, including Committee of Inquiry into High Cost of Working Class Dwellings in Scotland, 1921, Committee of Schemes of Assistance to Necessitous Areas, 1926, and Housing (Rural Authorities) Committee, 1931; Chairman of Advisory Committee to Board of Health on Housing during its existence; Chairman of the National Wages Board for Scotland for the Building Trade during its existence. *Recreation:* golf. *Address:* Cathkin, Rutherglen, Lanarkshire. *TA:* Trainard, Glasgow. *T:* Rutherglen 476. *Clubs:* Carlton, Royal Automobile, Constitutional; Royal Scottish Automobile, Conservative, Glasgow; Conservative, Edinburgh.

Died 18 March 1942.

TRAPNELL, John Graham; KC 1931; Barrister-at-Law; an Official Referee of the Supreme Court since 1943; *s* of Caleb Trapnell, Stoke Bishop, Bristol; *m* Ethel, *d* of Thomas Chappel Gardiner; two *s*. *Educ:* Harrogate College; King's College, Cambridge. Called to Bar, 1903; joined the Western Circuit; Recorder of Plymouth, 1932–43; Judge Advocate of the Fleet, 1933–43; Naval Service, European War, RNVR. *Address:* 1 Hare Court, EC4. *T:* Central 8557; Keepers, Heath Common, Pulborough. *T:* Storrington 226. *Club:* RAF.

Died 3 Nov. 1949.

TRAVERS, Lt-Col George Alfred, CMG 1919; Retired Royal Engineers; *b* 21 May 1867; *s* of Capt. Augustus Travers of Timoleague, Co. Cork. *Educ:* Wellington College. Joined RE, 1885; served North West Frontier India (Samana), 1891; Waziristan, 1894–95 (despatches); South African War, 1899–1902 (despatches, Brevet Major); European War, 1914–19 (Brevet Lt-Colonel, CMG). *Recreations:* shooting, golf. *Address:* 5 Davies Street, W1. *T:* Mayfair 2832. *Clubs:* Army and Navy, Hurlingham.

Died 19 Feb. 1950.

TRAVIS-CLEGG, Sir James Travis, Kt 1933; JP, DL; Constable of Lancaster Castle; *b* Crompton, Lancashire, Jan. 1874; *s* of John Travis-Clegg, JP, West Hall, Crompton; *m* 1895, Ada Chisholm, *d* of William Roy, MD, JP, Crompton, Lancashire and Perth; one *s*. *Educ:* Eton. Took up public work soon after leaving school; contested Stalybridge (C.) by-election, 1905 and 1906; County Councillor, 1898; Alderman, 1911; Chairman,

1931–37, retired 1937. *Recreation:* reading. *Address:* Bailrigg, near Lancaster. *T:* Galgate 33. *Clubs:* County, Lancaster.

Died 13 Oct. 1942.

TREADGOLD, Gp Captain Henry A., CBE 1936; MD; FRCP; RAF retired; *b* Bolton, Lancs, 1883; *s* of F. C. A. Treadgold, BA, MD and Mary Louisa, *d* of Charles Sumner; *m* 1909, Evelyn Diana Landor; one *s* one *d. Educ:* Fettes; Cambridge. BA Cantab 1906; MRCS, LRCP 1909; MB, BS London, 1910; MD 1911; MRCP 1932; FRCP 1937. House Physician Royal Free Hospital, 1909; Sambrooke Medical Registrar, King's College Hospital, 1910–12; served European War, 1914–18, Belgium and Iraq (despatches); RAF 1918–36; Consultant in Medicine RAF 1926–36; Member of Association of Physicians Great Britain and Ireland. *Publications:* Albumen re-action in Sputum—its significance and causation (with P. B. Ridge), Lancet 1913; Arneths re-action in pulmonary tuberculosis, ibid. 1919; Aerial Transport of Service Casualties, RAMC Journal, 1925; Cardiac Functional Efficiency in the Young Male Adult, Royal Society of Medicine, 1930; The size of the healthy heart and its measurement (with D. E. Bedford), Lancet 1931; Relationship of heart size and body build to Cardio-vascular efficiency (with H. L. Burton), Lancet 1932; Blood pressure in the young male adult, ibid. 1933; Body build and physical efficiency, ibid., 1934. *Recreations:* salmon and sea fishing, gardening. *Address:* Hither Deacons, Elstree Herts. *T:* Elstree 1523. *Club:* Royal Societies.

Died 15 Sept. 1941.

TREDEGAR, 2nd Viscount *cr* 1926; **Evan Frederic Morgan;** Baron *cr* 1859; 6th Bt *cr* 1792, FRSA, FRSL, FRHortS, FZS, FIL, FAGS; founder of Tredegar Memorial Lecture Royal Society of Literature; formerly Lieut Welsh Guards; DL, JP County of Monmouth; *b* 13 July 1893; *o c* of 1st Viscount and Lady Katherine Agnes Blanche Carnegie, *d* of 9th Earl of Southesk; *S* father, 1934; *m* 1st, 1928, Hon. Lois Sturt (*d* 1937), *yr d* of 2nd Baron Allington; 2nd, 1939, Princess Olga, *d* of Prince Serge Dolgorouky; annulled, 1943. *Educ:* Eton; Christ Church, Oxford. Private Sec. (unpaid) to Parliamentary Sec. Ministry of Labour, 1917; in Foreign Press Bureau, Allied Peace Conference, 1919; Hon. Col 17th London Regt TA; 38th (Welsh) Div. RE; Military County Social Welfare Officer for Mon, 1939–42; Bn Comdr 3rd (Mon) Bn Home Guard, 1940–42; Major Royal Corps of Signals, attached War Office for Special Duties, 1942–43; British Legion Liaison Officer for Wales; Vice-Pres. Wales Area; President Mon County Committee; KJStJ (Almoner for Wales); Knight Grand Cross of Order of Holy Sepulchre; late Knight of Sovereign Order of Malta; Privy Chamberlain of Sword and Cape to Popes Benedict XV and Pius XI; President Royal Gwent Hospital; Trustee Brecon War Memorial Hospital; Hon. Treas. Prince of Wales' Orthopaedic Hosp.; Hon. Treas. People's Dispensary for Sick Animals of the Poor; Governor Royal Agric. Soc. of England and Royal Welsh Agric. Soc.; Founder Vice-Pres., Oxford University Celtic Society; President Newport Branch Navy League; contested (C) Limehouse Division of Stepney, 1929; President Wales and Mon Conservative and Unionist Council. *Address:* Tredegar Park, Newport, Mon. *T:* Newport 2875; Honeywood House, Oakwood Hill, Dorking. *T:* Oakwood Hill 389.

Died 27 April 1949 (ext).

TREDENNICK, Rev. George Nesbitt Haydon, MA; Vicar of Sparkbrook, 1889–1940; Hon. Canon of Birmingham; *b* Guildford, Surrey, 5 April 1860; *e s* of Lt-Col J. G. Tredennick of Camlin, Co. Donegal, *g s* of Archbishop Magee, and Emily Dodsworth, *d* of Joseph Haydon, late Mayor of Guildford; *m* 1889, Alice Jane, *e d* of Archdeacon Phair of Rupert's Land; two *s. Educ:* Windermere College; Trinity Coll., Cambridge. Formerly Curate Emmanuel Church, Hastings; Section

Leader E Division Special Constabulary, Birmingham, 1917–19; Chaplain and Sub-Commander, 1926; now in Reserve. *Publications:* article on spiritual and permanent value of Old Testament; article on the Confessional; Booklets: Why should I go to the Lord's Table?; A Right Judgement in all Things; How not to Fast; The Glorious Reformation. *Address:* Emmanuel Vicarage, Southport.

Died 16 Nov. 1942.

TREFFRY, Col Edward, CMG 1915; OBE 1919; TD; Hon. Colonel 4/5 DCLI, 1927; Hon. Captain in army; DL, JP Cornwall and Vice-Lieutenant since 1936; Joint Chairman Cornwall Quarter Sessions since 1923; *b* 1 March 1869; *e s* of late Charles Ebenezer Treffry; *m* 1913, Anne, *o d* of Rev. Reginald Heber Treffry, Rector of St Endellion; two *s* two *d. Educ:* Eton. Served South Africa, 1900–01 (Queen's medal 5 clasps); served Uganda Protectorate as Assistant District Commissioner, 1905–09; European War, 1914–18 (despatches, CMG, OBE); Commanded Honourable Artillery Company (Infantry), 1910–24; 4/5th Duke of Cornwall's Light Infantry, 1924–25; Commanded 130th (Devon and Cornwall) Infantry Brigade, TA, 1925–28; High Sheriff of Cornwall, 1928; ADC to King George V, 1927–36. *Address:* Place, Fowey, Cornwall. *T:* Fowey 10. *Clubs:* Arthur's; Royal Yacht Squadron, Cowes; Royal Western Yacht.

Died 7 Jan. 1942.

TREFFRY, Mary Beatrice, CBE; *b* 1865; *yr d* of Rev. Robert Henry Poole, Rector of Rainton, Durham; *m* 1899, John de Cressy Treffry, Penarwyn, Cornwall. *Educ:* Ladies' College, Cheltenham. *Address:* Castle Ruins, Fowey, Cornwall.

Died 13 Nov. 1942.

TREFUSIS, Hon. Henry Walter Hepburn-Stuart-Forbes; Deputy Warden of the Stanneries; *b* 8 Dec. 1864; *m* 1905, Lady Mary (*d* 1927), *d* of 6th Earl Beauchamp; one *s. Educ:* Eton. Entered Army, 1886; ADC to Maj.-Gen. W. J. Gascoigne, KCMG, Commanding Troops, Hong Kong, 1898–1903; Major, 1902; retired (Scots Guards), 1907; Lieut-Col 4th Batt. Duke of Cornwall's LI 1909–14; 9th Batt. DCLI 1914–16; rejoined Scots Guards, employed London District, 1917–19; Lt-Col Reserve of Officers, 1919; JP, DL Cornwall; High Sheriff of Cornwall, 1923; a Vice-President Cornwall British Legion. *Address:* Trefusis, Falmouth. *T:* Flushing 35.

Died 2 June 1948.

TRELAWNY, Sir John William Salusbury-, 11th Bt *cr* 1628; late Lieut 3rd Batt. Welsh Regt; *b* 6 May 1869; *s* of 10th Bt and Jessy, *o d* of Sir John Murray, 6th Bt (*d* 1871); *m* 1st, 1891, Agnes Hedewig Helga (who divorced him), *e d* of W. B. Braddick; one *d*; 2nd, 1905, Catherine Penelope (Mrs W. C. Howard), (*d* 1930), *d* of late A. S. Cave-Browne-Cave; one *s*; 3rd, 1936, Andrée Alexandra Alles (*d* 1944). *Heir: s* John William Robin Maurice, Ft-Lt, RAFVR [*b* 16 Jan. 1908; *m* 1st, 1932; one *s*; 2nd, 1937, Rosamund Helen, *d* of late Arthur Reed Ropes; one *s* one *d*. Sunnyside, Henfield, Sussex]. *Address:* La Louveterie, Puyvert, Vaucluse, France.

Died 7 Feb. 1944.

TRENCH, Col Frederic John Arthur, CVO 1906; DSO 1902; late RA; *b* 2 Feb. 1857; *s* of late Rev. J. E. Trench, MA; *m* 1900, Anne Somerville, *d* of John N. Craddock, of Tuscaloosa, USA. *Educ:* Geneva Univ.; RMA and Staff College. Served Zulu War, 1879 (despatches for 'conduct especially deserving of commendation' at battle of Ulundi, medal and clasp); Boer War, 1900–02 (despatches DSO, medal and 5 clasps); Adjt RHA 1883–84, 1891–92; Dist Gunnery Instructor, 1889; DAAG at Headquarters, Ireland, 1895–98; Brigade Major RA Western District, 1899–1901; DAAG Army Headquarters, South Africa, 1901–02; attached to German Headquarters during operations in German South-west Africa, 1905–06 (despatches, Commander of Red Eagle, with Swords and Diamonds, medal with 3 clasps); returned all German decorations as protest against their barbarities to women and wounded, 1914; Military Attaché, Berlin, 1906–10; retired in 1910 to work for Boy Scouts and National Service, and warn against the German Peril. *Publication:* Manœuvre Ordres.

Died 20 March 1942.

TRENCH, Lt-Col Frederick Amelius Le P.; *see* Le Poer Trench.

TRENCH, Hon. William Cosby; *b* 1869; 2nd *s* of late Hon. F. S. C. Trench and Lady Anne, *e d* of 3rd Earl Clancarty, and *g s* of 2nd Lord Ashtown; *m* 1893, Frances, *o d* of Walter Taylor Newton Mure-Taylor of Castle Taylor. High Sheriff, Co. Limerick, 1895.

Died 12 March 1944.

TRENCH, William Launcelot Crosbie, CIE 1936; MInstCE; *s* of late George Frederic Trench, JP, Ardfert, Co. Kerry, Ireland and late Charlotte Frances Talbot-Crosbie, Ardfert; *m* 1st, 1910, Margaret Zephanie Huddleston (*d* 1934); two *s*; 2nd, 1935, Eileen Beatrice Cecil Marsh. *Educ:* The Leys School, Cambridge; Trinity College, Dublin. BA, BAI, 1904; PWD, Bombay, 1905. Deputy Secretary, Govt of Bombay, 1928–29; Chief Engineer, Sind, 1934–36; Secretary, Government of Sind, 1936; retired, 1936–. *Recreations:* golf, sailing. *Address:* Ashfield, Yateley, Camberley, Surrey.

Died 2 June 1949.

TREVOR, 3rd Baron *cr* 1880; **Charles Edward Hill-Trevor;** *b* 22 Dec. 1863; *s* of 1st Baron and 2nd wife, Hon. Mary Catherine Curzon; *S* half-brother, 1923; *m* 1927, Phyllis May, 2nd *d* of J. A. Sims, Ings House, Kirton-in-Lindsey, Lincs; two *s*. Served European War, 1917–18, as ambulance driver with British Red Cross St John of Jerusalem attached French Army (Croix de Guerre with Silver Star). *Heir: s* Hon. Charles Edwin Hill-Trevor, *b* 13 Aug. 1928. *Address:* Brynkinalt, Chirk, Wrexham. *T:* Chirk 3125.

Died 22 Dec. 1950.

TREVOR, Lady Rosamond; Rosamond Catherine, MBE 1918; *b* 25 Aug. 1857; *o d* of late Hon. Edmund George Petre, 5th *s* of 11th Baron Petre; *m* 1st, 1886, 4th Earl of Bantry (*d* 1891); 2nd, 1897, 2nd Baron Trevor (*d* 1923). *Address:* The Rest House, Jarvis Brook, Sussex.

Died 5 Feb. 1942.

TRIMBLE, Charles Joseph, CB 1918; CMG 1902; VD, TD; LRCPEd; *b* 16 March 1856; *s* of late John Trimble, MD, Castle-Bellingham Ireland; *m* 1882, Bessie, *d* of late Robert Oram of Bury, Lancs; two *d*. *Educ:* Queen's Univ., Ireland. Hon. Colonel (formerly comdg) 88th Field Regiment RA (West Lancashire); Hon. Representative Royal Humane Society; Alderman Lancashire County Council; DL, JP Lancs; Bailiff Grand Cross, Order of St John of Jerusalem; Inspecting Officer, No. 4 District, St John Ambulance Brigade; Lt-Col RAMC, late o/c St John Ambulance Brigade Hospital, France (CB, despatches thrice). *Address:* Broadoak, Penwortham, near Preston. *TA:* Trimble, Penwortham, Preston. *T:* Preston 83285.

Died 8 Oct. 1944.

TRIMBLE, S. Delmege, OBE; Prop. and Editor of the Armagh Guardian; *b* 9 Sept. 1857; *y s* of William and Anne Trimble, Enniskillen; *m* 1st, Margaret (Madge), *e d* of Charles and Isa Hersée, Seaton House, Acton, W3; two *s* four *d*; 2nd; Susan E., *e d* of William and Susan Weir, Upper Baggot Street, Dublin. *Educ:* Enniskillen Royal School. On father's newspaper. The Impartial Reporter; then on Dublin Press; founded the Donegal Independent, Ballyshannon, and in 1893 sold it and purchased the Armagh Guardian; ran Comfort Funds for Royal Irish Fusiliers during S African War, also during European War, and cared for Irish Fusilier prisoners of war in Germany and Bulgaria; made an hon. Old

Comrade by the Royal Irish Fusiliers OC Association, and OBE (five presentations by regimental battalions); in charge Comforts Fund and Comforts for Prisoners of War, War of 1939–45. *Recreation:* gardening. *Address:* 4 Beresford Row, The Mall, Armagh.

Died 1 April 1947.

TRIMBLE, William Copeland, JP; FJI; *b* 1851; *s* of Wm Trimble, Enniskillen; *m* 1st, Le, *d* of John Weir; 2nd, Lily, *d* of Henry Reilly; three *s* three *d*. *Educ:* Ennis. Royal School, Portora. Proprietor and Editor of the Impartial Reporter; Founder and Commander of the Enniskillen Horse; at the outbreak of the war in 1915 raised the Service Squadron of the Inniskilling Dragoons; a Governor of the Royal School; First President of the Irish Newspaper Owners' Association, 1917; re-elected, 1918–20; made a round the world tour of English-speaking nations, delivering addresses by request to Clubs, Colleges, etc., Australia, Canada, and the United States, 1921; Revisited Canada and the States to study Local Option, Prohibition, and Government Control of Liquor Traffic, 1929. *Publications:* Historical Records of the 27th Inniskilling Regiment; the History of Enniskillen (three vols); writer on local History and Archæology. *Address:* Century House, Enniskillen. *TA:* Trimble, Enniskillen. *T:* 60.

Died 24 Nov. 1941.

TRIPP, Bernard Edward Howard, CBE 1923; MBE 1920; JP; FRGS; former Member, NZ Red Cross Council, and of New Zealand Council of Agriculture; Member, Timaru Agricultural and Pastoral Society (President, 1919); *b* Orari Gorge Station, Canterbury, NZ, 1868; *s* of late C. G. Tripp, Barrister, London, afterwards sheep farmer, New Zealand, and *d* of late Bishop Harper, first Primate of New Zealand; *m* 1901, Cecilia Maud Fletcher, of Melbourne; no *c*. *Educ:* Christ's College, New Zealand. Life Member of the Royal Colonial Institute and of the Royal Geographical Society; Chm. Mt Peel Road Board 1914–16; President Canterbury Sheepowners' Union, 1908–09; Director Lincoln Agricultural College, 1914–21; Member for Otipua Timaru Harbour Board, 1914–23; Member of Taxation Commission, 1922; Member of Producers' Committee, 1921; Director of Pyne Gould and Guinness, Atlas Milling Co. and Timaru Woollen Mills; Part owner in: Orari Gorge, Glenary, Glengary, Sheep Stations, NZ; also was part owner in Richmond Downs and Chudleigh Park Cattle Stations, Queensland, Australia; during European War was the first New Zealand Red Cross representative to go to Egypt and England to organise committees and depôts for receiving Red Cross goods for New Zealand soldiers; a Delegate to represent New Zealand at the Geneva International Red Cross Conference, 1920; NZ delegate Red Cross Conference held in Paris, 1924; NZ Delegate, representing Sheepowners' Union and Farmers' Union, Empire Wool Conference at Melbourne, 1932 and 1937; Member NZ Wool Publicity and Research Committee, Wellington; Delegate for New Zealand at Empire Red Cross Conference, London, 1930; Commander of the Order of St John's. *Recreations:* shooting, motoring, farming and fishing. *Address:* Orielton, Gleniti, Timaru, New Zealand. *TA:* Timaru. *Clubs:* Bath, British Empire; Christchurch; Dunedin; South Canterbury.

Died 20 Dec. 1940.

TRIPURA, Col HH Maharaja Manikya Sir Bir Bikram Kishore Deb Barman Bahadur, Maharaja and Ruler of, GBE 1946; KCSI 1935; *b* 19 Aug. 1908. Is one of the Ruling Princes of India; Commander-in-Chief, Tripura State Forces; Hon. Lieut-Col in the Army; Hon. Col 5th (Bengal Presidency) Urban Infantry Territorial Army, India; FRGS, FRSL and MRCAS (Lond.), MRAS (Bengal). *Address:* Agartala, Tripura State, India.

Died 17 May 1947.

TRISTRAM, Henry Barrington; *b* 1861; *s* of late Canon Tristram, DD, FRS; *m* 1903, Emmeline, *d* of late Robert Worrall; one *d. Educ:* Winchester; Loretto; Hertford College, Oxford (Scholar). Senior Classical Master, Newton Coll., S Devon, 1886–87; Master at Loretto, 1887; Viceregent, 1891; Headmaster of Loretto School, 1903–08; resigned owing to ill-health; House Master at St Paul's School, 1909–12; temporary House Master at Victoria College, Jersey, for the war, 1915. Played Rugby football for England, 1883–87. *Publications:* Loretto School Past and Present; stray articles on Physical Education in various magazines. *Address:* 11 Ralegh Avenue, Jersey.

Died 1 Oct. 1946.

TRISTRAM, Katharine Alice Salvin, BA, London; Vice-President Church Missionary Society; Japan Blue Ribbon Distinguished Service Medal; Principal Emeritus of Poole Girls' School, Osaka; Hon. Fellow of Westfield College; *b* Castle Eden, Co. Durham, 29 April 1858; *d* of Rev. H. B. Tristram, Canon of Durham, FRS, DCL. *Educ:* Cheltenham Ladies' College; Westfield College, London University (BA). Lecturer at Westfield College; went to Japan in connection with Church Missionary Society, 1888; Principal of Poole Girls' School, Osaka, 1890; resigned Principalship, 1927; returned to England, 1938. *Address:* 11 South Bailey, Durham.

Died 24 Aug. 1948.

TRITTON, Sir William Ashbee, Kt 1917; JP; member of Tritton, Foster & Co., Lincoln; *b* 1876. Sometime at Ministry of Munitions; took a share in development of Tanks; JP Kesteven. *Address:* c/o Tritton, Foster & Co., Lincoln.

Died 24 Sept. 1946.

TROFIMOV, M. V., MA; Sir William Mather Professor of Russian, Manchester University, from 1919. *Educ:* University of Petrograd (Honours). Assistant Lecturer in Russian, Liverpool University, 1910–14; University Reader in Russian, King's College, London, 1914–19. *Address:* The University Manchester.

Died 24 Oct. 1948.

TROTTER, Alexander Pelham; consulting engineer; *b* Woodford, Essex, 1857; *s* of Alexander Trotter and Isabella, *d* of Sir Thomas Strange; *m* 1886, Alys Fane, *d* of Maurice Keatinge, Registrar of Court of Probate, Dublin; one *d. Educ:* Harrow; Trinity College, Cambridge. Natural Science Tripos. Apprenticed to Easton and Anderson, Erith; Patents for prismatic glassware, 1881–83; partner in Goolden and Trotter, dynamo manufacturers, Halifax, 1883–87; Editor of The Electrician, 1890–95; Government electrician, Cape of Good Hope, 1896–99; Electrical Adviser to Board of Trade, 1899–1917; MICE and MIEE; FPhysS; member and Past Pres. of The Illuminating Engineering Soc. and member of other scientific societies. *Publications:* Illumination: its Distribution and Measurement, 1911; The Elements of Illuminating Engineering, 1929; numerous papers. *Recreation:* remembering that he is no longer a Government official. *Address:* Greystones, Teffont, Salisbury, Wilts.

Died 23 July 1947.

TROTTER, Col (Hon. Brig.-Gen.) Gerald Frederic, CB 1917; CMG 1916; CVO 1926; CBE 1919; DSO 1900; MVO 1906; *b* 21 July 1871; 2nd *s* of late Maj.-Gen. Sir H. Trotter, GCVO and Hon. Eva Gifford. *Educ:* HMS Britannia. Entered army, 3rd Batt. Royal Scots, 1885; joined Grenadier Guards, 1892; served South Africa, 1899–1902 (despatches, Queen's and King's medals 6 clasps, DSO); European War, 1914–17 (despatches, Bt Lt-Col, CMG, CB); commanded British Military Mission (Instructional) to USA, 1917–18; Gentleman Usher to King George V, 1919–36; Groom-in-Waiting to Prince of Wales; 1921–36. *Address:* 37 Clanricarde Gardens, W2. *T:* Bayswater 1644. *Club:* Turf.

Died 14 June 1945.

TROTTER, Henry Alexander; late Director Alliance Assurance Co., Ltd; *b* 1 Sept. 1869; *y s* of late William Trotter of King's Beeches, Ascot; *m* 1914, Madeline Dorothy, *o d* of Maj. J. Herbert How. Called to Bar, Inner Temple, 1894; late Director of Bank of England. *Address:* 2 Culford Gardens, SW3.

Died 21 Oct. 1949.

TROTTER, Rev. John Crawford; *b* Holywood, Belfast, 18 May 1848; *s* of John C. Trotter, Belfast merchant, and Anne Tucker; *m* 1876, Fanny Rebie Torrens (*d* 1940), of Glenleary, Ramelton; four *s* (two sons killed in war), seven *d. Educ:* Bell's Academy and Methodist College, Belfast. Was for some years in the Methodist ministry in Ireland; ordained deacon of Church of Ireland, 1889; priest, 1890; curate-in-charge of Ardrahan parish, 1889; Rector of Ardrahan, Diocese of Kilmacduagh, Co. Galway, 1891–1926; Canon of Clonfert and Kilmacduagh, 1921–26; has conducted several parochial missions in England and Ireland. *Publications:* abbreviated Life of Robert Murray McCheyne; contributes to various magazines and religious newspapers articles on theology; historic, biographic, and social sketches; poetry, short stories and tales for children; has published several tracts, and for many years reviewed books for the late Dublin Daily Express and other newspapers. *Recreations:* gardening, music, and chess. *Address:* Glenleary, Ramelton, Co. Donegal, IFS.

Died 29 Nov. 1942.

TROTTER, Thomas, KC 1933; BL, DL JP Caithness; Advocate; Sheriff-Substitute of Caithness, Orkney and Shetland at Wick, 1911–32, Hon. Sheriff-Substitute, 1932–40, reappointed salaried Sheriff-Substitute, 1940; *b* Leith, 1 Oct. 1868; *e surv. s* of late Robert Trotter, RN. *Educ:* George Watson's College and University, Edinburgh. Graduated in law at Edinburgh University, 1891. Called to Scottish Bar, 1893; appointed Counsel to the Crown as Ultimus Hæres in Scotland, 1909; Lecturer on Commercial Law at Leith Technical College, 1909 and 1910; acted as Interim Sheriff-Substitute of Inverness, Elgin and Nairn at Portree, 1910; is an Honorary Sheriff-Substitute of Inverness, Elgin and Nairn. *Publications:* The Law of Summary Criminal Jurisdiction; The Law as to Children and Young Persons; Treatise on the Representation of the People Act 1918, as applicable to Scotland; Commentary on the Hire-Purchase and Small Debt (Scotland) Act, 1932; various contributions to legal journals. *Address:* Bruan Lodge, Mid Clyth, Caithness. *Club:* Scottish Liberal. Edinburgh.

Died 20 Sept. 1944.

TROTTER, William Finlayson, KC 1919; MA, LLD; Emeritus Professor of Law at Sheffield University; *b* Leith, 1871; 4th *s* of late Robert Trotter, RN; *m* 1898, Agnes Elizabeth, *d* of late John Davidson, Lochans, Wigtownshire. *Educ:* University of Edinburgh; University of Cambridge; and University of Aberdeen. First Gray Essay Prizeman, Rhind Philosophical Scholar, and MA (with Honours in Philosophy), Edinburgh University; Major Scholar of Trinity Coll. Camb., and First Class in both parts of the Moral Sciences Tripos, and Senior in Part I; MA, LLD (Cantab). Advocates Society Prizeman in Scots Law and Society of Solicitors' Prizeman in Conveyancing in the University of Aberdeen; called to Scottish Bar, 1898; English Bar, 1903; Holder of Certificate of Honour from the Council of Legal Education and Lincoln's Inn Prizeman; lately Examiner in Law Universities of Birmingham, Cambridge, Leeds, Liverpool, and Wales; formerly Examiner in Philosophy in Glasgow University; Dean of the Faculty of Law, and Professor of Law in the University of Sheffield, 1908–36. *Publications:* Pascal's

Thoughts translated and edited, 1904, since reprinted with an Introduction by T. S. Eliot; The Government of Greater Britain, 1905; The Citizen and his Duties, 1907; The Law of Contract in Scotland, 1913; The Law of Contract during and after War (4th ed.), 1940. *Address:* 37 Buckingham Terrace, Edinburgh.

Died 8 Feb. 1945.

TROUBETSKOY, Princess Pierre; *see* Rives, Amélie.

TROUBRIDGE, Lady Laura; *widow* of Sir Thomas Troubridge, 4th Bt. *Publications:* Memories and Reflections, 1925; Dangerous Bonds, 1926; The Dusty Angel, 1927; The Purse Strings, 1929; Exit Marriage, 1929; The Story of Leonora, 1930; Life of the late Lord Montagu of Beaulieu (with Archibald Marshall), 1930; The Property of a Gentleman, 1931; The Marriages of Georgia, 1932; The Brighthavens at Home, 1934, etc.; a constant contributor to the leading magazines. *Address:* Old Ways, Beaulieu, Hants.

Died 8 July 1946.

TROUBRIDGE, Vice-Adm. Sir Thomas Hope, KCB 1945; CB 1945; DSO 1942; *b* 1 Feb. 1895; *s* of Adm. Sir Ernest Troubridge and Edith, *d* of Wm Duffus, Halifax, NS; cousin and *heir-pres.* to Sir St V. Troubridge, 5th Bt; *m* 1925, Lilly, *d* of H. G. Kleinwort; three *s* one *d. Educ:* RNC, Osborne and Dartmouth. Served European War, 1914–18, Mediterranean Grand Fleet, Dover; Lt, 1916; Cdr., 1930; Capt., 1935; Naval Attaché, Berlin, 1936–39; War of 1939–45; served Atlantic, East Indies, Mediterranean; 5th Sea Lord (Air), 1945–46; Flag Officer Air (Home), 1946–47; Rear-Adm. 1943 (DSO and Bar, CB, KCB, American DSM); Vice-Adm. 1947; Flag Officer (Air) and Second in Command, Mediterranean Station, 1948. Legion of Honour (France). *Address:* Middle Oakshott, Hawkley, Hants. *T:* Hawkley 28. *Clubs:* Travellers', Beefsteak, White's.

Died 29 Sept. 1949.

TROUNCER, Harold Moltke, MA, FIA; Director of London Life Association Limited, and of Associated Offices; Chairman Dorking District Hospital; Vice-President Surbiton Hospital; Chairman Eastbourne College Council; *b* 20 Feb. 1871; *s* of J. H. Trouncer, MD, Lond.; *m* 1905, Alice Beatrice, *d* of Frederick Cornes of Hampton Wick; two *s* three *d. Educ:* Cranbrook School; Eastbourne College (scholar); University College, Oxford (scholar). 2nd Class Final Honour School in Mathematics. Actuary and Manager of London Life Association, Ltd, 1911–33; Fellow of Institute of Actuaries, 1899; Vice-President, 1923–25, President, 1930–32; Chairman, Life Offices Association, 1925–26; Chairman, British Insurance Association, 1929–31; Member of Board of Trade Departmental Committee for amending the Assurance Companies Act, 1909; Member Royal Commission on Unemployment Insurance, 1930–32. *Recreations:* formerly rowing; stroke of University College Eight, 1892 and 1894; stroke of Kingston Eight, 1896–98; golf, lawn tennis, and music conductor Genesta ADC orchestra, 1910–30. *Address:* Henfold, Beare Green, Dorking. *T:* Newdigate 258.

Died 23 June 1948.

TROUP, Sir (Charles) Edward, KCB 1909; KCVO 1918; Hon. LLD Aberdeen, 1912; *b* Huntly, Aberdeenshire, 27 March 1857; *e s* of Rev. Robert Troup, MA; *m* 1897, Winifred Louisa, *y d* of late George Macdonald, LLD, of Bordighera, Italy. *Educ:* Aberdeen University, MA; Balliol College, Oxford, BA; Cobden Prize (Oxford University), 1883. Barr. Middle Temple, 1888. Entered Home Office, 1880; Chairman of Committee on Identification of Habitual Criminals, 1893; editor of Judicial Statistics of England and Wales, 1894–1903; Chairman of Committee on Cremation, 1902; Assistant Under-Secretary of State, 1903–08; Permanent Under-Secretary of State in the Home Office, 1908–22; Chairman of RIC Tribunal, 1922–23;

Chairman of the Safety in Mines Research Board, 1923–39; and Chairman Health Advisory Committee (Mines Department); Chairman of Special Grants Committee (Ministry of Pensions), 1929–38; Treasurer, 1922–39, and Fellow of University of London King's College. *Publications:* Future of Free Trade, 1884; edited Place Names of West Aberdeenshire for the Sven Spalding Club, 1900; The Home Office, in Whitehall Series, 1925. *Address:* 13 Addison Road, Kensington, W14. *T:* Park 4974. *Club:* Athenæum.

Died 8 July 1941.

TROUP, Francis William, FSA, FRIBA; architect; *b* Huntly, Aberdeenshire, 11 June 1859; *s* of Rev. Robert Troup, MA; unmarried. *Educ:* Huntly; Gymnasium, Old Aberdeen; Student, Royal Academy Schools. Master Art Workers' Guild for 1923; Architect for Mansfield House University Settlement E; Rampton Criminal Lunatic Asylum, Notts; St Luke's Printing Works, Record Office, Works Department, etc.; for the Bank of England and the Restaurant for the Bank of England, Tokenhouse Yard, EC; Engineering College, Cambridge University; Low Temperature Research Station and University Press, Cambridge; Blackfriars House, New Bridge St, EC4; Sandhouse, Witley; Thistlegate, Dorset; Nethergate House, Norfolk, and other works of domestic and civil architecture; Consulting Architect to the Receiver of the Metropolitan Police and to King's College, Strand, WC. *Publications:* lectures in The Arts connected with Building, various articles and papers on leadwork and on other subjects in professional journals. *Address:* 14 Gray's Inn Square, WC1. *T:* Chancery 7539; 17 Addison Gardens, W14. *Club:* Arts.

Died 2 April 1941.

TROUP, Sir George Alexander, Kt 1937; CMG 1931; FRIBA; *b* London, 1863; *s* of George Troup, Aberdeen; *m d* of James Sloan; one *s* three *d. Educ:* Gordon's College, Aberdeen. Arrived NZ, 1884; joined Govt Survey Party, Otago; Chief Draftsman, Railway Dept, 1890; Officer in Charge of Architectural Branch, 1919–24; retired 1924; Mayor of Wellington, New Zealand, 1927–31. *Address:* 5 Cluny Avenue, Kelburn, Wellington, W1 NZ.

Died 4 Oct. 1941.

TROWER, Col Courtney Vor, CMG 1917; retired pay; *b* 17 Dec. 1856; *s* of late Capt. Frederic Courtney Trower, 9th Lancers; *m* Bessie (*d* 1932), *y d* of late Judge Owen of Withybush, Pembrokeshire. Entered Army, 1876; Lieut-Col, 1901; retired, 1906; served So. Africa, 1877–79 (medal with clasp), 1899–1901 (Queen's medal 3 clasps); commanded 1st Batt. South Wales Borderers, 1901–05, and 5th Service Battalion, 1914–18, in France and Belgium (despatches, officer Legion of Honour, S Anne of Russia, 1914 Star, Victory and Allied Medals). *Address:* Ty Gwyn, Maidenhead. *Club:* United Service.

Died 29 Nov. 1947.

TROYTE-BULLOCK, Lt-Col Edward George, CMG 1916; TD 1918; JP, DL; Commanded 1st Dorset Yeomanry, 1914–17 (retired); *b* 1862; *e s* of late George Troyte-Chafyn-Grove and 2nd wife, Alice, 3rd *d* of Sir Glynne Earle Welby Gregory, 3rd Bt; *m* 1898, Grace Amy Margaret, *e d* of Lt-Col John Mount Batten, CB; one *s* three *d. Educ:* Eton. Late Capt. 1st Royal Dragoons; High Sheriff of Dorsetshire, 1930; Patron of two livings. Served European War, 1914–17 (CMG). *Address:* Zeals House, Wilts. *TA:* Mere, Wilts. *T:* Mere 264. *Clubs:* Dorset County, Dorchester.

Died 29 Aug. 1942.

TRUBSHAW, Wilfred, CBE 1931; *b* 1870; *s* of late Alfred Trubshaw, MRCS, Mold, Flints; *m* Bessie Andre, *d* of late Walter Edward Perkins, JP, Astwood Bank, Worcs and Bodegroes, Pwllheli, Carnarvonshire. *Educ:* Epsom College. Admitted Solicitor, 1893; Assistant prosecuting Solicitor for Liverpool, 1902–04; Assistant

Solicitor Lancashire County Council, 1904–14; Assistant Chief Constable of Lancashire, 1914–27; Chief Constable of Lancashire, 1927–35; Order of St John of Jerusalem; Order Astaur 3 (Afghanistan); King's Jubilee Medal, 1935. *Address:* Clogwyn Isa, Portmadoc, N Wales. *T:* Portmadoc 2132.

Died 21 Dec. 1944.

TRUEMAN, George Johnstone, MA, PhD, DCL, LLD; President Mount Allison University, 1923–45, now President Emeritus; *b* 30 Jan. 1872; *s* of Howard Trueman, English Canadian, and Jean Main Trueman, Scottish Canadian; *m* 1897, Agnes, *d* of W. W. Fawcett, Upper Sackville, NB. *Educ:* Mount Allison University, Sackville, NB; University of Berlin; Heidelberg University; Columbia University, New York. Taught school in the Province of New Brunswick for eleven years; Principal of Stanstead College, Stanstead, Quebec, for twelve years; Secretary, Board of Education, Methodist Church in Canada, for three years; President Mental Hygiene Council of New Brunswick; Chairman, Common Examining Board Maritime Provinces and Newfoundland. *Publications:* Dykelands of the Bay of Fundy, 1894; School Funds in the Province of Quebec, 1920. *Recreations:* golf, swimming, rowing. *Address:* Mount Allison University, Sackville, NB, Canada. *TA:* Mount Allison, Sackville. *T:* 145. *Clubs:* Rotary, Sackville Country (Sackville); Columbia Chapter, Phi Delta Kappa (Columbia).

Died 18 Feb. 1949.

TRUMP, John, ISO 1914; MInstCE; *b* 1858; *m*; one *s* two *d*. Entered Public Works Dept, Ceylon, 1878; State Engineer, Perak, 1901; Director of Public Works, Federated Malay States, 1908; retired, 1914. *Address:* The Nore, Sarlesdown Road, Exmouth, Devon.

Died 1 Feb. 1941.

TRUSCOTT, Sir George (Wyatt), 1st Bt *cr* 1909; Kt 1902; *b* 9 Oct. 1857; *e surv. s* of late Alderman Sir; Francis Wyatt Truscott, Lord Mayor of London, 1879–80, and Eliza, *d* of late James Freeman; *m* Jessie (*d* 1921), Lady of Grace of the Order of St John of Jerusalem, *e d* of late Geo. Gordon Stanham, architect; one *s* (*er s* killed in War) two *d*. *Educ:* private schools; Paris. Common Councilman, City of London, 1882–95; elected Alderman of Dowgate Ward, City of London, in succession to his late father, 1895; Lord Mayor, London, 1908–09; Sheriff of London, 1902–03; on Commission of Lieutenancy for City of London; Received Hon. Freedom of City of London, 1937; Officer of the Orders of the Legion of Honour of France and Leopold of Belgium; Knight Commander of the Orders of Wasa of Sweden, and Rising Sun of Japan, and Grand Cross of Russian Order of Stanislas; Chairman of Visiting Committee of the City of London Mental Hospital; Governor of St Bartholomew's, St Thomas's, Christ's and Bethlehem Hospitals, and of Queen Ann's Bounty. *Heir: s* Eric Homewood Stanham, MA [*b* 16 Feb. 1898; *m* 1924, Mary Dorcas, *d* of late Rev. Canon T. H. Irving; one *s* (*b* 24 Oct. 1929) one *d*. *Education:* Rugby; Trinity College, Cambridge]. *Address:* Suffolk Lane, Cannon Street, EC; 30 Albert Hall Mansions, SW7. *T:* Kensington 7864. *Clubs:* Carlton, City Carlton.

Died 16 April 1941.

TRUSCOTT, Prof. Samuel John, DSc; Professor of Mining, Imperial College of Science and Technology (Royal School of Mines), 1919–36; Emeritus Professor since 1936; Hon. Fellow Imperial College; *b* Fowey, Cornwall, 6 Aug. 1870; *s* of John Truscott, of HM Customs; *m* 1894, Mary Earle, *d* of James Vaughan, of Liverpool; three *s* three *d*. *Educ:* Taunton's School; Hartley College, Southampton; Royal School of Mines, London. Gold and tin mining in the Federated Malay States, 1889–92; visited Aschio Copper Mines, Japan, 1892; Lisbon Berlyn Mining Co., Lydenburg, Transvaal, 1893; Witwatersrand Goldfields, 1894–97; visited the Ural Goldfields, 1898; Exploration Work in Borneo,

1899–1900; Gold Mining in the Celebes, 1900–01; Exploration in West Africa, 1902; Gold Mining in Sumatra, 1902–08; Consulting Engineer in London, 1909–13; Assistant Professor of Mining at the Royal School of Mines, 1913–19; Pres. 1928–29, Hon. Mem. and Medallist, Inst. MM; Hon. Life Mem., Chemical Metallurgical and Mining Soc. S Africa; a Senior Mem., Geological Soc., London. *Publications:* The Witwatersrand Goldfields, 1898; Translation of Ore Deposits, by Beyschlag, Vogt and Krusch, 1916; Ore-Dressing, 1920; Mine Economics, 1935, 1947. *Address:* 10 Dunrobin Court, NW3. *T:* Hampstead 4183.

Died 26 Sept. 1950.

TRUTER, Sir Theodore Gustaff, KBE 1924; CMG 1918; *b* George, Cape Province, 13 Oct. 1873; *m* 1902, Henrietta Maria Wagner; three *c*. *Educ:* Normal College, Cape Town; Diocesan College, Rondebosch. Commissioner of Police, South Africa, 1910–28; Chief Control Officer, Union of S Africa, 1939. *Address:* 152 Pine St, Pretoria. *Club:* Pretoria (Pretoria).

Died 11 April 1949.

TUBBS, Sir Stanley William, 1st Bt *cr* 1929; JP; *b* Finchley, 22 March 1871; *s* of Henry Thomas Tubbs, JP, of Nether Court, Finchley, and Littlestone-on-Sea, Kent; *m* 1st, 1901, Ellen Emma (*d* 1918), *d* of Compton Prescott; 2nd, Evelyn Sherbrooke, *d* of C. A. Crane, of The Reddings House, Cheltenham. *Educ:* Highgate School; privately. Has travelled extensively in United States, Canada, Japan, and on the Continent; is Governing Director of Tubbs, Lewis & Co., Ltd; CC Gloucestershire, 1905–09; Chairman of Mid-Gloucestershire Conservative and Unionist Association; MP (C) Stroud Division of Gloucestershire, Nov. 1922–Dec. 1923; Member of Executive Committee of National Union of Conservative and Unionist Association, 1925–30; Member of Executive Committee of Midland Union; High Sheriff County of Gloucestershire, 1931; Pres. Gloucestershire County Cricket Club; Chairman Gloucestershire Playing Fields Assoc.; Joint-Master Berkeley Hounds, 1931–33. *Recreations:* hunting, golf, lawn tennis. *Address:* Ellerncroft, Wotton-under-Edge, Gloucestershire. *T:* Wotton-under-Edge 82. *Club:* Carlton.

Died 11 Dec. 1941 (ext).

TUCK, Gustave; *b* 7 Nov. 1857; 3rd *s* of late Raphael Tuck; *m* 1884, Esther Lyon (*d* 1930); three *d*. *Educ:* privately in London. Chairman and Managing Director of Raphael Tuck & Sons, Ltd, art and book publishers, 1926–37, Vice-Chairman, 1900–37; President Raphael Tuck & Sons, Ltd, New York; President of the Jewish Historical Society of England, 1929–34, and Treasurer since 1904; reconstructed, equipped and presented to the University of London for University College, Gower Street, in memory of Esther Tuck, the Mocatta Library and Museum, and the Gustave Tuck Theatre, Dec. 1932; a Member of the Board of Deputies of British Jews; one of the Founders of the Stoke Newington Synagogue, 1904; Warden of St John's Wood Synagogue since 1916; late President and Treasurer of the Soup Kitchen for the Jewish Poor; a Vice-President of The Jewish Lads' Brigade; a Manager of the Jews' Infant Schools; Member of Committee of the Home and Hospital for Jewish Incurables. *Recreations:* golf, billiards. *Address:* 119 Hamilton Terrace, NW8. *T:* Maida Vale 7141. *Clubs:* Sandy Lodge Golf; Hartsbourne Golf.

Died 9 Jan. 1942.

TUCKER, Alexander Lauzun Pendock, CIE 1901; Indian Civil Service, retired; *b* 2 Nov. 1861; *s* of late H. P. St G. Tucker, ICS; *m* 1908, Eva Beatrice, *y d* of Thomas Egerton Tatton of Wythenshawe Hall, Cheshire. *Educ:* Winchester; Balliol College, Oxford. Acting Resident in Mysore, 1904; Agent of Governor-General in Baluchistan, 1905–07; Consul-General and Resident in the Persian Gulf, 1907–08 (*in absentia*); Revenue and Judicial Commissioner of the North-West

Frontier Province, 1909–12; Agent, Governor-General in Central India, 1913; retired, 1913; JP Flintshire 1929. *Publication*: Life of Sir Robert Sandeman, Pioneer Series Empire Builders, 1921. *Address*: The Lodge, Overton, Ellesmere, Shropshire. *TA*: Overton, Flintshire. *T*: Overton 13.

Died 30 Nov. 1941.

TUCKER, Alfred Brook; writer on Overseas topics; *b* 19 June 1861; *e s* of late Alfred Tucker (Scholar Magdalene College, Cambridge, Indian Civil Servant, afterwards Tutor, and latterly on staff of the Times) and late Eliza Penkivil, *d* of Rev. William Brook; *m* Fanny (*d* 1936), *d* of late Captain Robert Howard (91st Foot); one *s* one *d*. *Educ*: Blackheath School. Matriculated London University (Honours Division), 1879. Joined the Times staff; joined the Graphic staff in 1895; Editor of the Graphic, 1906–08; Editor of the Empire Illustrated, 1910–12, and of the Canadian Mail, 1911–13; toured in Canada as Special Commissioner for Canadian Mail, 1912; Member West India Committee. *Publications*: The Romance of the King's Army, 1907; A Book of Anniversaries, 1909; Canada and the War (Oxford Univ. pamphlet), 1915; The Battle Glory of Canada, 1915; articles on military and Colonial subjects. *Address*: Worsted Cottage, Babraham, Cambs.

Died 25 Jan. 1945.

TUCKER, Thomas George, CMG 1920; LittD Camb.; Hon. LittD Dublin; Emeritus Professor of Classical Philology, University of Melbourne; *b* Burnham, Bucks, 29 March 1859; *s* of Charles Tucker; *m* 1st, Annie Mary, *d* of T. Muckalt, Forton Bank, Lancashire; one *s* two *d*; 2nd, Anne Sophie Henrietta (*d* 1941), *widow* of Mr Justice Weigall of the Supreme Court of Victoria, and *d* of Sir Robert Hamilton, KCB. *Educ*: Royal Grammar School, Lancaster; St John's College, Cambridge. Craven Scholar, Brown's Medallist; Sen. Classic and Chancellor's Medallist, 1882; Fellow of St John's College, 1882. Professor of Classics and English, University College, Auckland, and Member of Education Board of the Province, 1883; Professor of Classical Philology, Melbourne University, 1885–1919; Dean of Faculty of Arts; ex-Trustee of Public Library and National Gallery of Victoria. *Publications*: Æschylus, Supplices, Septem, and Choephori; Plato, Proem to Ideal Commonwealth; Thucydides, Bk. viii.; Aristotle, Poetica; Aristophanes, Frogs; Life in Ancient Athens; Life in the Roman World of Nero and St Paul; Introduction to the Natural History of Language; The Sonnets of Shakespeare; Etymological Dictionary of Latin; The Judgement and Appreciation of Literature. *Recreations*: motoring, billiards. *Address*: University, Melbourne, N3, Victoria.

Died 24 Jan. 1946.

TUCKER, William Kidger, CMG 1902; Government Land Surveyor; *b* Cradock, Cape Colony, 1 April 1857; *m* 1881, Agnes, *d* of late George Bottomley, Griqualand West; five *s* three *d*. *Educ*: Lesseyton College; Grey College, Bloemfontein; Diocesan College, Rondebosch. Entered Johannesburg Town Council, 1903; Mayor, 1906–07; Senator, Parliament of the Union of S Africa, 1910–29; served South African War (CMG); MLA for Roodepoort in late Transvaal Parliament. *Address*: 38 St Patrick Road, Houghton Estate, Johannesburg.

Died 1 Jan. 1944.

TUCKEY, Rev. Canon James Grove White, CBE 1919; BD; MA; KHC; Canon Residentiary of Ripon, 1923–45, Canon Emeritus 1945; *b* 5 June 1864; 2nd *s* of late Dr Charles Caufeild Tuckey of Charleville, Kew; *m* 1896, Emily Louise (*d* 1938), *y d* of late George Mason, Manchester; one *s* one *d*. *Educ*: King's School, Canterbury; Trinity College, Oxford; (Ford Student), 1st Class Hon. Classical Moderations, 3rd Class Lit. Hum.; Heidelberg University. Lecturer Durham University, 1889–95; Deacon, 1893; Priest, 1894; Chaplain University College, Durham, 1893–95; Acting

Chaplain to the Forces, 1895–97; Chaplain to the Forces, 1897; served in South African War, 1889–1902, including Defence of Ladysmith (despatches, specially promoted; Queen's medal six clasps, King's medal two clasps); European War with BEF 1914–16 (despatches thrice, 1914 star with bar, British war medal, Victory medal with oakleaf); Senior Chaplain 4th Division, 3rd Army Corps, and 2nd Army; ACG, Rouen Area; Home Service, 1916–23, as Assistant Chaplain-General, Southern Command (mentioned in Home List for services); retired pay, 1923; Hon. Chaplain to the King, 1918; Hon. Chaplain to the Bishop of Salisbury, 1922–24; Rural Dean of Ripon, 1927–30; Representative of the Church of England on the Interdenominational Advisory Committee at the War Office, 1925; Jubilee Medal, 1935: Coronation Medal, 1937. *Publication*: Translator Hatschek's Amphioxus. *Club*: Oxford and Cambridge.

Died 25 Oct. 1947.

TUDOR, Adm. Sir Frederick (Charles Tudor), KCB 1921; KCMG 1918; CB 1913; DL (Surrey); *b* 29 March 1863; *s* of H. R. Jones and H. A. Tudor; assumed surname of Tudor, 1891; *m* 1913, Netta, *widow* of Admiral R. Craigie. Passed 1st into HMS Britannia, 1876; served on Mediterranean, Australian, and China Stations; Commanded HM Ships Prometheus, Challenger, Superb, and Gunnery School Excellent at Whale Island, 1910–12; Director of Naval Ordnance and Torpedoes, 1912–14; Third Sea Lord, 1914–17; Commander-in-Chief, China Station, 1917–19; Admiral, 1921; President of the Royal Naval College, Greenwich, 1920–22; Retired List, 1922; Orders 1st Class Sacred Treasure and Rising Sun 2nd class, Japan; St Anne, 1st class, Russia; 1st Class Striped Tiger, China. *Address*: Dennistoun, Camberley. *T*: Camberley 431. *Club*: United Service.

Died 14 April 1946.

TUDOR-CRAIG, Major Sir Algernon Tudor, KBE 1918; CBE 1918; FSA; *b* 3 Jan. 1873; 2nd *s* of late Rev. Allen Tudor Craig, MA, Marbœuf Church, Paris; *m* 1st, 1898, Emily Mary, CBE 1920 (*d* 1939), *d* of late Rev. James Lukin, Felbrigg Lodge, Romsey; one *s*; 2nd, 1940, Grace, Commander Order of St John of Jerusalem, *d* of late Thomas William Jennings, Highgate, Middlesex. Major, late 4th Royal Irish Rifles, 1902; Secretary, Inc. Soldiers' and Sailors' Help Society, 1903–21, and Veterans' Relief Fund, 1908–21; Director, Admiralty Convalescent Homes, 1914–20; DAAG 1914–20; Acting Assistant Provost Marshal, London District, 1915–20; Comptroller, The Lord Roberts Memorial Fund and Workshops, 1915–21; Librarian and Curator, United Grand Lodge of England, 1935; Knight of Justice of Order of St John of Jerusalem; Chevalier Order Crown of Belgium. *Publications*: (jointly with Sir Frank Benson) The Book of the Army Pageant, 1910; Armorial Porcelain of the Eighteenth Century, 1925; Melusine and the Lukin Family, 1932; The Catalogues of the United Grand Lodge of England, 3 vols, 1938. *Address*: 17 Wildcroft Manor, Putney Heath, SW15. *T*: Putney 1320. *Club*: Royal Automobile.

Died 10 April 1943.

TUDSBERY, Col Henry Tudsbery, OBE 1928, MC, TD; MInstCE; Divisional Road Engineer, Southern Division, Ministry of Transport, Exeter, since 1935; *b* Yokohama, 1886; *s* of late J. H. T. Tudsbery; *m* 1915, Winnie Davis, *y d* of late Sir James B. Smith and Lady Smith, of Clifford Park, Stirling; one *s* two *d*. *Educ*: Marlborough College; King's College, London University; Millar Prizeman, James Forrest Medallist and Manby Premium of the Institution of Civil Engineers. Trained in the Locomotive Works and Civil Engineers' Department of the L. and SW Railway; Assistant Engineer on Southampton Dock Works; Resident Engineer on Kingston-upon-Thames Bridge Reconstruction and Southwark Bridge Reconstruction;

commissioned in Corps of Royal Engineers and served with the British Army in France, 1915–19 (MC, Officier de l'Ordre de la Couronne de Belgique, despatches); held office of Assistant Director of Roads to the 4th British Army, with rank of Lt-Col RE, 1918–19; Commander Royal Engineers, Essex Group AAS/L Companies RE from its creation 1924–32; substantive Colonel, 1928; Hon. Colonel Essex Group AAS/L Coys RE, 1933–38; joined the staff of the Roads Department, Ministry of Transport, as Director of Engineering, 1919; transferred to Birmingham as Divisional Road Engineer, Midland Division, Ministry of Transport, 1929; served for a number of years on various Committees of the British Engineering Standards Association. *Publications:* various professional papers, Inventions. *Recreations:* fishing, ski-mountaineering. *Address:* Southtown, Lympstone, Devonshire. *T:* Exmouth 3122; Ministry of War Transport, Northernhay Gate, Exeter. *Clubs:* Junior Carlton, Royal Automobile; Devon and Exeter, Exeter.

Died 19 Feb. 1946.

TUDWAY, Brig.-Gen. Robert John, CB 1909; CMG 1916; DSO 1902; Essex Regt; *b* 19 Nov. 1859; *s* of Rev. Henry Tudway of Walton-in-Gordano, Somerset; *m* 1906, Olive Winifred, *d* of E. W. Browne. Entered 56th Regt, 1879; Capt. Essex Regt, 1886; Bt Maj. 1896; Bt Lt-Col 1898; served with Mounted Infantry Nile Expedition, 1884–85 (despatches, medal with two clasps, bronze star); Egyptian Frontier, 1886–87; Suakin, 1888 (despatches, clasp, 4th class Medjidie); in command of Camel Corps, 1894; Dongola Expedition, 1896, action of Firket; Nile Expedition, 1897–98, action of Omdurman; relief of Gedaref, 1899 (despatches 3 times, Egyptian medal, five clasps); South African War, 1899–1902 (severely wounded at Paardeberg, despatches twice, Queen's and King's medals 3 clasps, DSO); DAAG Harrismith District, 1900; DAAG South-East District, 1903; commanded Essex Regt (Pompadours), 1906; commanded a District, 1911; served European War (Dardanelles), 1915 (CMG, Officer of the Legion of Honour), France, 1916. *Address:* Meon Lea, Droxford, Hants. *T:* Droxford 19. *Club:* Army and Navy.

Died 3 Sept. 1944.

TUFFILL, Comdr (S) Harold Birch, CBE 1921; RD, RNR (retired); *b* Clapham, SW, 5 April 1870; *s* of Daniel Fensham Tuffill, banker, and Eliza M. C. Birch; *m* 1911, Margaret Emily, *d* of Canon Charles H. Bowly, MA, Toppesfield Rectory, Essex; one *s* (*yr s* a midshipman, RN, killed in action, 12 Aug. 1942) one *d*. *Educ:* Merchant Taylors' School. War service, 1914–18, Accountant Officer and Secretary, RNR; Secretary, Port and Transit Executive Committee, 1917–20; Master of the Worshipful Company of Vintners. *Recreations:* motoring, fishing, antiquarian and statistical research. *Address:* Toppesfield, Garden Road, Bromley, Kent. *T:* Ravensbourne 1311.

Died 30 Oct. 1950.

TUFNELL, Brig.-Gen. Lionel Charles Gostling, CB 1916; DL Essex; *b* 24 Sept. 1865; 2nd *s* of late Colonel W. N. Tufnell, JP, DL, of Langleys, Chelmsford, Essex, and Eleanor Francis, *d* of late Major-Gen. Charles Gostling, RA; *m* Grace Margery, *y d* of late Thomas Hughes Earle, of Enham, Hants; one *s* four *d*. *Educ:* Marlborough; Oxford Military College, Cowley. Served in 4th Essex Regiment (Militia), 1883–85; 2nd East Surrey Regiment, 1886–1908; Adjutant 3rd and 5th Worcestershire Regiment, and Recruiting Officer, Worcestershire Area, 1896–1901; Chief Ordnance Officer, Natal, Transvaal, Tidworth, Colchester, 1903–10; officer i/c Records and commanding Army Ordnance Corps, 1911–16; Deputy Director Army Ordnance Services, Lines of Communications (North) in France, and with the Third Army, 1916–19; Assistant Director Aldershot Command, 1919–21 and Gibraltar, 1921–22; served South African War, 1901–02 (Queen's medal and five clasps); European War, 1914–19

(despatches thrice, Hon. Brig. Gen., two medals, CB); retired pay, 1922. *Recreations:* cricket, tennis, golf. *Address:* Byways, Weeley, Essex. *T:* Weeley 239.

Died 29 May 1941.

TUFTS, James Hayden; retired; *b* Monson, Massachusetts, 9 July 1862; *s* of Rev. James and Mary E. Warren Tufts; *m* 1st, 1891, Cynthia Hobart Whitaker (*d* 1920); 2nd, 1923, Matilde Castro; one *s* one *d*. *Educ:* Amherst College, AB, 1884; Yale University, BD, 1889; University of Berlin, 1891; University of Freiburg, PhD, 1892; Amherst, LLD, 1904; California, LLD, 1937. Instructor in Mathematics, Amherst, 1885–87; Instructor, Philosophy, University of Michigan, 1889–91; Assistant Professor of Philosophy, 1892–94; Associate Professor, 1894–1900; Professor, 1900–30; Emeritus, 1930; Head of Department, 1905–29; Dean, Senior College, 1899–1904 and 1907–08; Dean of Faculties, 1923–26; Vice-President, the University of Chicago, 1924–26; Chairman, Board of Arbitration, Men's Clothing Industry, Chicago, 1919–20; Visiting Professor, Columbia University, NY, 1920–21; Lecturer in Philosophy, University of California at Los Angeles 1931–33; Member, American Philosophical Association (President, 1914); Member, Western Philosophical Association (President, 1906, 1914); AAAS; NEA. *Publications:* Our Democracy, 1917; The Real Business of Living, 1918; Ethics of Co-operation, 1918; Education and Training for Social Work, 1923; America's Social Morality, 1934; various monographs; Editor, The School Review, 1906–1909; International Journal of Ethics, 1914–1930; Translator, Windelband's History of Philosophy, 1893; contributor to Baldwin's Dictionary of Philosophy and Psychology, 1901; Co-editor: Studies in Philosophy and Psychology, 1906; Letters, Lectures and Addresses of Charles Edward Garman, 1909; joint-author, Ethics, 1908, revised 1932. *Address:* c/o County National Bank, Santa Barbara, California, USA. *Clubs:* Beta Theta Pi Fraternity, Quadrangle, Chicago.

Died 5 Aug. 1942.

TUITE, Sir Morgan Harry Paulet, 11th Bt *cr* 1622; late Lieut 9th Batt. Rifle Brigade; *b* Woolwich, 27 Oct. 1861; *e s* of Gen. Hugh Manley Tuite, RA; *S uncle* 1898. *Educ:* Woolwich. *Recreations:* music, geology. *Heir:* *nephew* Brian Hugh Morgan [*b* 1 May 1897; *s* of late Capt. Hugh G. S. Tuite and Eva Geraldine, *d* of Peter Valentine Hatton. Late Lieut London Regiment; served European War, 1914–18 (wounded)].

Died 16 Nov. 1946.

TUKE, Lt-Col George Francis Stratford, DSO 1917; RA (retired); *b* 1876; *e s* of late Capt. Stratford Tuke, RN; *m* 1900, May, *d* of F. Hevey-Langan of Mount Hevey, Co. Meath; one *s*. Royal Artillery, 1899; served South African War, 1899–1902 (despatches twice); European War, 1914–18; in command 8th Brigade RGA France and Belgium, Aug. 1917–June 1919 (DSO, despatches twice); retired pay, 1926. *Club:* Junior United Service.

Died 11 Oct. 1948.

TUKE, Captain Godfrey, CBE 1919; RN; JP Devon; *b* Borden, Kent, 21 Feb. 1871; *y s* of late Rev. Francis Edward Tuke, MA (Oxon), of Borden, Kent, and of Highfield, Maidstone, and Sarah Helen, *e d* of Major John Osborne Burridge, 16th Lancers and 10th Hussars, of Lillesden Park, Hawkhurst, Kent, and Barton Fields, Canterbury; *m* 1899, Margaret Edith, *d* of late Edmund H. Chapman and Mrs Chapman, Combe Manor, Dulverton, Somerset. Passed into the Royal Navy, 1884; HMS Britannia, 1884–85; Lieut 1893; Commander, 1905; Acting Captain and Senior Naval Officer, Channel Isles, 1914–19; served on the staffs of late Admiral of the Fleet Sir Arthur Wilson, Bt, VC, and Admiral Lord Charles Beresford, as Intelligence Officer and Confidential Agent at the Admiralty, 1905–08; retired Captain, 1920; served in HM Sultan as Naval Cadet during International Blockade of Greece, 1886, and European War, 1914–19 (despatches twice, CBE). *Recreation:* field sports. *Address:* Langdon, Tamerton Foliott, nr Plymouth, Devon. *T:* Plymouth 71815. *TA:* Tamerton Foliott, Devon. *Clubs:* Royal Yacht Squadron, Cowes (Naval Member).

Died 23 Feb. 1944.

TUKE, Dame Margaret Janson, DBE 1932; MA; late Principal of Bedford College for Women, London; *b* 1862; *d* of late James Hack Tuke of Hitchin, Herts, HM Commissioner on Congested Districts Board, Ireland. *Educ:* St John's, Withdean, Brighton; Newnham College, Cambridge. Mediæval and Modern Languages Tripos, Cambridge, June 1888. Staff Lecturer in Modern Languages at Newnham College, Cambridge, 1890–1905; MA Trinity College, Dublin, 1905; MA Cantab, 1931; Tutor to Women Students and Lecturer in French, University College, Bristol, 1905–07; Fellow of Newnham College, 1905–36; Fellow of Bedford College, 1930; Member of the Senate of the Univ. of London, 1911–29; DLitt (Reading), 1937. *Publication:* A History of Bedford College, 1939. *Recreation:* reading. *Address:* The Old Hall, Pirton, nr Hitchin. *Club:* University Women's.

Died 21 Feb. 1947.

TULLOCH, Brig.-Gen. James Bruce Gregorie, CB 1919, CMG 1916; late King's Own Yorks LI; *s* of late Maj.-Gen. Sir Alexander Bruce Tulloch, KCB; *m* 1900, Agnes Alison, *d* of late Henry Charles Smith, estate owner; one *d.* Served NW Frontier, India, 1897–98 (medal with clasp); S Africa, 1901–02 (Queen's medal 3 clasps); European War, 1914–18 (despatches, CMG, CB, Bt Lt-Col and Col); retired pay, 1927; JP, DL Monmouthshire. *Address:* Hill Abergsvenny. *T:* 261.

Died 25 Jan. 1946.

TULLOCH, Brig.-Gen. John Arthur Stamford, CB 1915, CMG 1917; late RE; *b* 3 Dec. 1865; *m*; one *s* two *d.* Entered Army, 1884; Captain, 1893; Major, 1901; Lt-Col 1910; Col 1913; served Burma, 1887–89 (medal with 2 clasps); China, 1900 (despatches, medal with clasp); European War, 1914–17 (CB despatches five times, Legion of Honour, 4th class, CMG); retired pay, 1921. *Address:* Ways de Salisbury Rd, Farnborough, Hants. *T:* 323.

Died 22 Dec. 1946.

TUNBRIDGE, Brig.-Gen. Walter Howard, CB 1900; CMG 1918; CBE 1919; Queensland Mounted Infantry; *b* 2 Nov. 1856; *s* of John N. Tunbridge; *m* 1902, Leila Emily, *e d* of Hon. Villiers Brown, MLC, Queensland; one *s* two *d. Educ:* privately. Served South Africa, 1900–01 (despatches twice, Queen's medal 4 clasps, CB); European War, 1914–18 (CMG); ADC to Governor-General. *Address:* 36 Berkeley Street, Hawthorn, E2, Melbourne, Australia.

Died 11 Oct. 1943.

TUNNECLIFFE, Hon. Thomas, JP; MLA; *b* Ascot, near Ballarat, Victoria, 13 July 1869; *s* of John Tunnecliffe, Derby and Sarah Thomson, Dublin; *m* 1st, 1907, Bertha Bishop; 2nd, 1913, Bertha L. Gross; one *s* one *d. Educ:* State School; Working Men's College, Victoria. Chief Secretary in Prendergast Labour Govt, July 1924–Nov. 1924; Delegate to First International Socialist Congress, Sydney, 1888; Editor Stead's Review, 1925–27; Minister for Railways and Minister in Charge of Electrical Undertakings, Victoria, 1927–28; Chief Secretary, Victoria, 1929–32; Leader State Labour Party, 1932–37; Speaker of Legislative Assembly, Victoria, 1937–40; Secretary Public Service Association; Editor Public Service Journal, 1921–24; Editor State Clerical, 1920–21. *Publications:* Socialism: its Aims and Objects; Solution of Unemployment Problem: Successful Socialism; Women Suffrage; Problem of Poverty; The Great Land Robbery; Public *versus* Private Enterprise; The Fallacy of Price Fixing; etc. *Recreations:*

reading, walking, journalism. *Address:* Neangar, 28 North Terrace, Clifton Hill, Victoria, Australia. *T:* JW 2572.

Died 2 Feb. 1948.

TUPPER, Adm. Sir Reginald Godfrey Otway, GBE 1923; KCB 1917; CB 1916; CVO 1910; *b* 16 Oct. 1859; *s* of Capt. C. W. Tupper, 7th Fusiliers, and Letitia Frances, *d* of Sir J. Wheeler-Cuffe, Bart, of Leyrath, Kilkenny; *m* 1st, 1888, Emily Charlotte (*d* 1929), *d* of late Lt-Gen. H. H. Greer, CB; two *d*; 2nd, 1933, Caroline Maud, *d* of Colonel Fanshawe Gostling, and *widow* of Major-General H. R. Abadie, 9th Queen's Royal Lancers. Entered Navy, 1873; Commander, 1894; Captain 1901; Rear-Admiral, 1910; Vice-Admiral, 1916; Admiral 1919; served E Africa, 1890 (despatches, medal, clasp); Deputy Commissioner Western Pacific, 1898–1901; Asst DNO; Admiralty, 1901–03; Capt. of Excellent, 1907–10; member Naval Intelligence Department, 1898; Rear-Adm. Home Fleet, 1912–13; served European War, 1915–18, as Rear-Admiral West Coast Scotland and Hebrides, as Vice-Admiral Atlantic Blockade, and as Admiral Northern Patrol; C in C Western Approaches, Queenstown, 1919–21; retired list, 1921; Commander, Legion of Honour, France; Chevalier Naval Order of Merit, Spain. *Publication:* Reminiscences, 1929. *Address:* 22 Draycott Place, SW3. *Clubs:* United Service; Royal Yacht Squadron (Hon.), Cowes.

Died 5 March 1945.

TUPPER, William Johnston; KC 1914; Lieutenant Governor of Manitoba since 1934; Barrister-at-law; *b* 29 June 1862; 3rd *s* of Rt Hon. Sir Charles Tupper, 1st Bt; *m* 1887, Margaret, *d* of late Hon. James M'Donald of Blink Bonnie, Chief Justice of Nova Scotia; two *s* three *d. Address:* Elmhurst, Winnipeg, Canada.

Died Dec. 1947.

TUPPER-CAREY, Rev. Albert Darell; SPG Chaplain at Monte Carlo, 1930; Chaplain to the King since 1938; *b* 1866; *s* of Rev. Tupper-Carey, RD of Chalke; *m* 1st, Helen Mary (*d* 1938), *d* of Rev. H. E. Chapman, Rector of Donhead, St Andrew; two *s* three *d*; 2nd, 1942, Ruth (née Barran), widow of Frank Donner. *Educ:* Eton; Christ Church, Oxford (BA, 2nd Class Hist., 2nd Class Theol.); Cuddesdon College. Deacon, 1890; Priest, 1892; Curate at Leeds Parish Church, 1890–98; Head of Christ Church Oxford Mission, Poplar, E, 1898–1901; Rector of Lowestoft, 1902–10; Canon Residentiary of York, 1910–17; Proctor in Convocation, 1923; Vicar of Huddersfield, 1917–24; Hon. Canon of Wakefield, 1917–24 and 1927–30, Canon Emeritus since 1931; Chaplain at St Raphael, France, 1925–27; SPG Secretary, Dioceses of Ripon, Wakefield, and Bradford, 1927–30. *Club:* Alpine.

Died 21 Sept. 1943.

TURBERVILLE, Arthur Stanley, MC, MA, BLitt; Professor of Modern History, University of Leeds, since 1929; *b* 15 April 1888; *s* of late Rev. A. C. Turberville, Vicar of Stansted, Essex; *m* 1917, Kate, 3rd *d* of late R. Drummond, Glasgow, and niece of late A. M. Brown, Gryffe Castle, Rentrewshire. *Educ:* Cheltenham College; New Coll., Oxford (Scholar); 1st Class Honours Modern History, 1909. Engaged in research work and teaching in Oxford till 1913; Lecturer in Modern History, University of Liverpool, 1913–14; Lecturer in Modern History, University College of North Wales, Bangor, 1914–26; Commission in 14th Batt. KRRC, 1915; served with 20th Bn KRRC in France, Belgium, and Germany, 1916–19 (Captain, MC, despatches); Senior Lecturer in History, University of Manchester, 1926–27; Reader in History in the University of Leeds, 1927–29; Pres. of the Historical Assoc. Pres. of the Thoresby Society; a Governor of Giggleswick School; Chairman, Northern Universities Joint Matriculation Board; Member of National Council, Society of Individualists. *Publications:* The House of Lords in the Reign of William

III, 1913; The Making of Blaise, 1914; Kenneth Dugdale, 1919; Mediæval Hersey and the Inquisition, 1920; Great Britain in the Latest Age (with F. A. Howe), 1921; A History of the 20th KRRC, 1923; English Men and Manners in the 18th Century, 1926, 2nd ed. 1929; The House of Lords in the 18th Century, 1927; Commonwealth and Restoration, 1928, 2nd ed. 1936; Charles Talbot, Duke of Shrewsbury (with T. C. Nicholson), 1930; The Spanish Inquisition, 1932; Welbeck Abbey and its Owners, vol. i, 1938, vol. ii, 1939; To Perish Never, 1941. Editor of Johnson's England, 1933; contributions to Cambridge Medieval History, vol. vi, English Historical Review, etc. *Address:* 94 Potternewton Lane, Leeds; Duncreggan, Blairmore, Argyll.

Died 9 May 1945.

TURING, Harvey Doria; angling editor of The Field from 1931 to outbreak of War; organising secretary of the Salmon and Trout Association, 1925–33; Editor of The Salmon and Trout Magazine since 1933; *b* Edwinstowe, Notts, 1877; *s* of late Rev. J. R. Turing, Vicar of Edwinstowe; *m* 1918, Violet Ethel, *d* of late Rev. H. A. Sheringham; one *d. Educ:* Christ's Hospital; Hurstpierpoint College. *Publications:* Trout Fishing (The Sportsman's Library), 1935; Modern Coarse Fishing, 1937; Trout Problems, 1948; Pollution Survey of the Rivers of England and Scotland for the British Field Sports Society—Reports I, II, III (England), IV (Scotland), 1947–1949; Editor, 1931–1940, of Where to Fish; numerous articles in newspapers and magazines. *Recreations:* fishing, gardening. *Address:* The Mount, Aston Clinton, Bucks. *T:* Aston Clinton 239.

Died 7 Sept. 1950.

TURNBULL, Sir (Reginald) March (Kesterson), Kt 1941; Adviser on Foreign Shipping, Ministry of War Transport; *b* 23 Nov. 1878; *s* of Reginald March Turnbull, Shipowner; *m* 1902, Addy Gertrude Clarkson; one *s. Educ:* Highgate. Shipowner. *Address:* Flowergate, Rowley Green, Barnet, Herts. *Clubs:* Bath, Royal Automobile.

Died 11 Oct. 1943.

TURNER, Sir Ben, Kt 1931; CBE 1930; OBE 1917; JP; Alderman; *b* 1863; *m* 1884; five *d. Educ:* National School. Half-timer; weaver; Member School Board, 1892; Town Councillor, 1893; Freeman of the Borough of Batley; Mayor, 1913–16 and 1934–35; Chairman Labour Party, 1911; Delegate to America for Trades Congress, 1910; Chairman, Trades Union Congress, 1928; Member of Labour Party, EC, for 18 years; Chairman TUC General Council, 1927–28; MP (Lab) Batley and Morley, 1922–24, and 1929–31; Secretary for Mines, 1929–30; late General President, National Union of Textile Workers; Joint-Chairman Industrial Council for the Woollen Trade. *Publications:* Dialect verses and sketches; two histories of Textile Unions in Yorkshire; A Biographical Book, About Myself, 1930; Volumes of Verse, 1909 and 1934. *Recreation:* reading. *Address:* Carlton Avenue, Batley. *T:* Batley 221.

Died 30 Sept. 1942.

TURNER, Maj.-Gen. Ernest Vere, CB 1925; CMG; DSO; late RE; 2nd *s* of Edward John Turner, late Assistant Master, Winchester College, and Celia Budgett; unmarried. *Educ:* Winchester; RMA, Woolwich. 2nd Lieutenant RE, 1892; employed with West African Frontier Force, Lagos hinterland, 1897–98 (despatches, Brevet of Major); served South African War, 1899–1902 (despatches); Captain, 1903; Brevet-Major, 1903; employed with GPO Telegraphs, 1902–04; with Egyptian Army as Director of Posts and Telegraphs, Sudan Government, 1904–12 (3rd Class Medjidieh); Major, 1912; Superintending Engineer, GPO Telegraphs, Ireland, 1912–14; served France and Belgium, 1914–18 (Brevets of Lieut-Col and Col, CMG, DSO, despatches 6 times, Military Order of

Savoy, 5th Class); Chief Signal Officer, Egypt, 1920–24; GSO1, War Office, 1925–29; Maj.-Gen. 1929; retired pay, 1929. *Recreations:* lawn tennis, golf. *Address:* 122 St James' Court, Buckingham Gate, SW1. *Clubs:* United Service, Hurlingham.

Died 28 Feb. 1949.

TURNER, Lt-Col Francis Charles, CMG 1916; late Northumberland Fusiliers; *b* 1866; *e s* of late Sir Alfred E. Turner; *m* 1893, Gertrude Elizabeth, *d* of late Thomas Diggles. Served S Africa, 1899–1901 (despatches, Bt Major, Queen's medal 5 clasps); European War, 1914–17 (despatches, CMG). *Address:* 1 West Halkin Street, Belgrave Square, SW1. *T:* Sloane 4211. *Clubs:* Arthur's, Roehampton.

Died 31 May 1942.

TURNER, Frederick Charles, CIE 1925; *b* 22 Aug. 1872. *Educ:* Christ's Hospital; University College, Oxford, BA. Entered ICS 1894; served in Central Provinces as Assistant Commissioner; Deputy Commissioner, 1908; Commissioner, 1923; retired 1931. *Address:* The Little Place, Lyme Regis, Dorset. *T:* Lyme Regis 355.

Died 19 Jan. 1950.

TURNER, Col George Frederick Brown, DSO 1919; *b* 30 March 1876. Served European War, 1914–19 (despatches, DSO, two medals); Deputy Chief Superintendent, Research Department, Royal Arsenal, 1928–30; Superintendent, Design Department, Royal Arsenal, 1930–33; retired pay, 1933. *Address:* 6 Morden Road, SE3. *T:* Lee Green 3552.

Died 30 Jan. 1941.

TURNER, George James, MA Camb., FBA 1932; 2nd and (since 1878) *e surv. s* of late Anselm and Catharine Turner. Called to Bar, Lincoln's Inn, 1893; Fellow of Society of Antiquaries, 1900; Member of Council of British Academy, 1937; Assisted late F. W. Maitland in his editions of the Year Books of Edw. II; Special lecturer for Society of Public Teachers of Law, 1928; Ford's Lecturer, Oxford, 1937; Joint Literary Director of Selden Society Publications, 1937; is interested in Ancient and Mediæval History (legal and institutional). (Is now blind.). *Publications:* Editions of Mediæval Law Reports; various contributions to historical publications and works of reference. *Address:* South Lodge, Surbiton Hill, Surrey; Armidale, Salcombe, South Devon. *Club:* Athenæum.

Died 14 June 1946.

TURNER, Sir George Robertson, KBE 1919; CB 1917; FRCS Eng., LRCP Lond.; Consulting Surgeon St George's Hospital; Consulting Surgeon Railway Passengers' Assurance Company; late Surgeon Rear-Admiral Royal Navy; Lt-Col RAMC (TA); *b* 22 Oct. 1855; *s* of late George Turner of 9 Sussex Gardens, Hyde Park; *m* 1882, Isabel Beatrice (*d* 1926), *d* of late F. A. Du Croz of Courtlands, East Grinstead; one *s* (and one killed European War, 1917) three *d. Educ:* Uppingham School. Surgeon to the Dreadnought Seamen's Hospital, 1881–98; late Lecturer on Anatomy, St George's Hospital; and Examiner in Anatomy, Conjoint Board; RCP and RCS. *Publications:* Clinical Lectures on Appendicitis; Radical Cure of Hernia; Gastric Ulcer; various articles in Heath's Dictionary of Surgery; The Treatment of Hernia, Latham and English's System of Treatment; Papers read before the Royal Medical and Chirurgical, the Clinical and Medical Societies; articles in medical papers and journals; Unorthodox Reminiscences, 1931; Mary Stuart Forgotten Forgeries, 1933 2nd ed. 1935. *Recreations:* motoring, and sport generally; played Rugby football for England v. Scotland, 1876. *Address:* 37 Adelaide Crescent, Hove, Sussex. *T:* Hove 3913. *Clubs:* Union, Brighton.

Died 7 April 1941.

TURNER, Maj.-Gen. James Gibbon, CB 1911; *b* 24 Aug. 1859; *s* of Gen. Sir Frank Turner, KCB, RA; *m* 1887, Blanche, *d* of Col T. T. Boileau; one *d. Educ:* Wellington College. Entered RA 1878; Capt. ISC 1890; Major Indian Army, 1896; Lt-Col 1904; Colonel, 1907; ADC to Commander-in-Chief, East Indies, 1885–86; Commanded Viceroy's Bodyguard, 4th Cavalry and Risalpur Cavalry Brigade; served Kandahar, 1881; Chitral, 1895 (despatches, Brevet Major, medal with clasp); Tirah, 1897–98 (clasp); China, 1900 (despatches, medal); S Africa, 1902 (Queen's medal two clasps); Col 2nd Royal Lancers (Gardner's Horse), 1917–38; DL Warwickshire, 1924. *Address:* c/o Grindlay's Bank Ltd, 54 Parliament Street, SW1.

Died 20 Oct. 1950.

TURNER, Joseph Harling, CBE, 1918; JP; Commissioner and Land Agent for the Duke of Portland's Scotch estates; Honorary Sheriff-Substitute for the County of Ayr; Ex-Convener of the County of Ayr; Chairman of the West of Scotland Agricultural College; *b* 1859; *m* 1883, Mary (*d* 1932), *d* of late John Adam, Closeburn; one *s* four *d. Educ:* Dollar Academy. *Address:* Cessnock Castle, Galston, Ayrshire. *Clubs:* Conservative; County, Ayr; Western, Glasgow.

Died 9 Jan. 1942.

TURNER, Brig.-Gen. Martin Newman, CB 1915; CMG 1918; CBE 1920; late Duke of Cornwall's LI and 15th Infantry Brigade, BEF; *b* 24 June 1865; *e s* of late C. W. Turner of Blackheath; *m* 1897, Ethel Mary Marshall (*d* 1934), *d* of late J. S. Hannagan; one *s.* 2nd Lieut Duke of Cornwall's LI 1890; Lt-Col 1912; Col 1916; Brig.-Gen. 1915; Adjutant Upper Burma Volunteer Rifles, 1897–1902; served Burma, 1892–93, 1895–96 (medal with clasp); European War, 1914–18 (wounded, despatches four times, CB, CMG); N Russia, 1918–19 (despatches, CBE); Colonel, The Duke of Cornwall's Light Infantry, 1932–35; Order of Danilo (Montenegro) 2nd class, 1917; Order of St Vladimir 3rd class, 1919. *Address:* Westbrook, Staines.

Died 23 May 1944.

TURNER, Walter James (Redfern); Literary Editor, The Spectator; *b* 13 Oct. 1889; *e s* of late W. J. Turner, organist, St Paul's Pro-Cathedral, Melbourne; *g s* of late William Redfern Watson, Liverpool and Ballarat. *Educ:* Scotch College, Melbourne. Travelled S Africa, Germany, Austria, Italy, 1910–14; RGA 1916–18; CIR 1918–19; musical critic, New Statesman, 1916–40; dramatic critic, London Mercury, 1919–23; literary editor, Daily Herald, 1920–23. *Publications:* The Hunter, and other Poems, 1916; The Dark Fire, 1918; Paris and Helen, 1921; In Time like Glass, 1921; Music and Life, 1921; The Man who Ate the Popomack, 1922; Landscape of Cytherea, 1923; Variations on the Theme of Music, 1924; Smaragda's Lover, 1924; The Seven Days of the Sun, 1925; Orpheus, or The Music of the Future, 1926; Marigold, an Idyll of the Sea, 1926; Beethoven, 1927; The Aesthetes, 1927; New Poems, 1928; Miss America, 1930; Pursuit of Psyche, 1931; Music: a Short History, 1932; Wagner, 1933; Facing the Music, 1933; Jack and Jill, 1934; Berlioz, 1934; Blow for Balloons, 1935; Henry Airbubble, 1936; Songs and Incantations, 1936; Mozart, 1938; Selected Poems, 1939; The Duchess of Popocatapetl, 1939; Plo's, Parables and Fables, 1944; Fossils of a Future Time?, 1946. *Recreation:* music. *Club:* Savile.

Died 18 Nov. 1946.

TURNER, William, MS, FRCS; Consulting Surgeon and Vice-President, late Senior Surgeon and Lecturer in Clinical Surgery, Westminster Hospital; Examiner, London University; Major RAMC (T) 4th London General Hospital; Consulting Surgeon, King Edward's Memorial Hospital, Ealing; Dreadnought Hospital, Greenwich; Royal Hospital for Diseases of the Chest, City Road, EC; American Red Cross Hospital No. 22, and Mrs Mitchison's Hospital, Clock House, Chelsea; Earl of Beaconsfield Hospital, High Wycombe, Ilford, and Bexley Cottage Hospital; *s* of late Frederic Turner of Nizels, Sevenoaks, Kent; *m* 1904, Lily, *o d* of J. Kerr Hamilton, Tavistock, Devon; one *s. Educ:* King's College School, London; King's College Hospital; London University. Late Consulting Surgeon LB and SC Railway; Surgeon Imperial Yeomanry Base Hospital, Deelfontein, 1900; Medical Officer in charge Imperial Yeomanry Branch Hospital, M'Kenzie's Farm, South Africa, 1900–01; Surgeon King George Hospital; House Physician, House Surgeon, Tutor in Surgery, King's College Hospital. *Publication:* Treatment after Operation (with E. Rock Carling). *Recreations:* motoring, croquet, golf. *Address:* 104 Harley Street, W1. *T:* Welbeck 2101.

Died 30 April 1944.

TURNER, William Aldren, CB 1917; MD (Edin.); FRCP (Lond.); Consulting Physician and Senior Neurologist to King's College Hospital and the National Hospital, Queen's Square, WC; *b* 5 May 1864; *s* of late Sir William Turner, KCB; *m* 1909; Helen Mary Mackenzie, 3rd *d* of Dr J. A. MacDougall; three *s. Educ:* Fettes College, Edinburgh; University of Edinburgh (Gold Medal). Fellow of Royal Society of Medicine (President Neurological and Psychiatric Sections). Examiner in Medicine, Conjoint Board, 1921–25; and other professional societies; Morison Lecturer, College of Physicians of Edinburgh, 1909; Bradshaw Lecturer, College of Physicians, London, 1918. Temporary Col AMS for special duty with nervous and mental shock cases in France, 1914–15; consulting neurologist with the Forces at home, 1915–19. Member of Army Nursing Board, Member War Office Committee on Shell Shock, 1920–21; Neurologist, War Office Medical Board, 1919–40, and Consultant Adviser, Ministry of Pensions, 1930–45. *Publications:* A Text Book of Nervous Diseases (with Dr Grainger Stewart), 1910; Epilepsy, 1907; papers to Trans. Roy. Soc., etc. *Address:* 27 Evelyn Gardens, SW7. *T:* Kensington 1086. *Club:* Athenæum.

Died 29 July 1945.

TURPIN, George Sherbrooke, MA, DSc; *m* 1923, Gertrude Caroline Waite Johnson, of Lenton House, The Park, Nottingham. Late Headmaster the High School, Nottingham. *Address:* Combe Hill House, Monkton Combe, near Bath.

Died 28 Dec. 1948.

TURRELL, Walter John, MA, MD, BCh Oxon; Consulting Physician, specialising in Electro-Therapeutics; Major RAMC (TF) 3rd Southern General Hospital, Oxford; late Hon. Consulting Physician to Department of Physical Medicine, Radcliffe Infirmary, Oxford; late Examiner DMRE University, Cambridge; *b* Oxford, 9 April 1865; *s* of Rev. H. J. Turrell, Master of Turrell's Hall, Oxford; *m* Margaret Sybil, *d* of E. Lywood, Clatford, Andover. *Educ:* Turrell's Hall and Exeter College, Oxford; Radcliffe Infirmary, Oxford; London Hospital. Formerly House Surgeon, Radcliffe Infirmary, Oxford; Fellow Royal Society of Medicine; Fellow American Electro-Therapeutic Society; Ex-President Electro-Therapeutic Section, Royal Society of Medicine; Golden Key for research in Electrotherapy, American Congress of Physiotherapy, 1933. *Publications:* The Principles of Electro-Therapy; Electro-Therapy at a Base Hospital; The Electrical Treatment of Frost-bite; Operative Treatment of Bronchocele; Importance of a Pure Milk Supply, and various other papers to Medical Journals; John Wesley: Physician and Electrotherapist, 1938; Ancient Angling Authors; Angling in Oxfordshire (Victorian History of Oxfordshire); Art. Electrotherapy: Ency. Brit. *Recreations:* angling, sailing, cycling, skating. *Address:* Cherwell Lodge, Oxford. *TA:* Dr Turrell, Oxford. *T:* Oxford 2319.

Died 27 Jan. 1943.

TURVILLE-PETRE, Lt-Col Oswald Henry Philip, DL, TD, JP; Kt of Malta; late Warwick Yeomanry; Lord of the Manor of Husbands Bosworth, Leicestershire, and of Samlesbury, Lancs; *b* 1862; *s* of late E. H. Petre, and late Lady Gwendeline Petre; *m* 1899, Margaret, *d* of late Laurence Cave, of Ditcham Park, Hants; two *s* three *d*. *Educ:* Christ Church, Oxford, BA. High Sheriff of Leicestershire, 1912; joined the Northants Yeomanry as Major and Hon. Lt-Col (temp.) Feb. 1915. *Address:* Bosworth Hall, Rugby. *TA:* Husbands, Bosworth. *Club:* Travellers'.

Died 16 June 1941.

TUSSAUD, John Theodore, FRSA; director of and artist to Madame Tussaud and Sons' Exhibition, since 1886; *b* Kensington, 2 May 1858; *s* of Joseph Randall Tussaud, and *g g s* of the foundress of the Exhibition; *m* 1889, Ruth Helena, 2nd *d* of late Thos Grew; seven *s* three *d*. *Educ:* Cardinal Manning's Coll., Bayswater; Benedictine Monastery, Ramsgate; began to study modelling and sculpture under his father at the age of 14, his first important portrait model being that of Milan, at that time king of Servia, modelled 1873; succeeded his father as artist of the Exhibition on the latter's retirement. Has contributed to the Exhibition over a thousand portrait models of the most eminent personages of the period; has also made a specially of models grouped into dramatic tableaux illustrating both historical and contemporary scenes; exhibitor at the Royal Academy; has made many contributions to current literature, mostly dealing with the French Revolutionary and Napoleonic wars. *Publications:* The Romance of Madame Tussauds, 1919; The Chosen Four, 1928. *Recreations:* gardening, riding, driving. *Address:* Croxley Green, Rickmansworth. *T:* Rickmansworth 2114.

Died 13 Oct. 1943.

TUTE, Sir Richard Clifford, Kt 1937; *b* 1874; *s* of Arthur Clifford Tute. Indian Civil Service; *m* 1910, Katherine, *d* of Samuel Torrington, of Anlaby Hall, Anlaby, Yorks. *Educ:* Royal School of St Peter, York; London University. Barrister-at-law, Inner Temple, Honours Bar Final, 1926; passed Indian Civil Service, 1898; posted to United Provinces; thanked by Government 1907 for service to Co-operative credit movement; retired from ICS, 1913; served European War, 1914–19, retiring with rank of Major RGA: District Judge, Galilee District, Palestine, 1919; President, Land Court, Samaria, 1921; President, Land Court, Jerusalem, 1925; Chief Justice of the Bahamas 1932–39; inventor of the Tute ranging protractor for artillery. *Publications:* Commentary on the Ottoman Land Code; After Materialism:—What? (New York); Joint author of a metrical translation of Omar Khayyám. *Recreations:* fishing, shooting, golf. *Club:* Flyfishers'.

Died 27 Feb. 1950.

TUXFORD, Brig.-Gen. George Stuart, CB 1917; CMG 1916; DSO 1918; *b* 7 Feb. 1870; *s* of James George Tuxford, of West Kirby; one *s*. *Educ:* Wellingboro' Grammar School, Northants. Went to Canada, 1888; served European War, 1914–19 (despatches eight times, CB, CMG, DSO and bar); late Commanding 5th Canadian Infantry Overseas Battalion, which he organised; commanded 3rd Canadian Infantry Brigade, 1st Canadian Division, 1916–19; Legion of Honour, CMG, CB, DSO and bar, despatches eight times); occupied bridge-heads across Rhine; Brigadier-General, 1916; Efficiency Decoration, Canadian, 1934; King George VI Medal, 1937. *Recreations:* all athletics and open air. *Address:* Victoria, BC, Canada. *Clubs:* Canadian, Kiwanis United Services, Moose Jaw.

Died 4 Feb. 1943.

TWEEDALE, Rev. Charles L.; Vicar of Weston since 1901; *s* of Thomas Tweedale, MD, of Stainland and Crawshawbooth, and Mary, *d* of Charles Coates, engineer, of Crawshawbooth; *m* 1899, Margaret Eleanor, *d* of Francis Burnett; one *s* three *d*. *Educ:*

Giggleswick; Durham University. Curate of Hyson Green; of Ormskirk and of Bilton, Harrogate; patentee of processes and inventions. *Publications:* Man's Survival after Death (4th ed., Italian, Norwegian, Dutch, Greek, Swedish, and other foreign editions); News from the Next World, 2nd ed., 1940; Present Day Spirit Phenomena and the Churches (43rd ed.); Death and the Grave Defeated (3rd ed.); Reflecting Telescope Construction, Experiences with Comets, The Daylight Comet of 1910, The Total Solar Eclipse of 1927, and the life of With and Calver; The Vindication of William Hope (2nd ed.); many articles. *Recreations:* natural sciences and the arts; astronomy (independently discovered comet *f*, 1886); violin construction; psychical research. *Address:* Weston Vicarage, nr Otley, Yorks. *TA:* Tweedale, Weston, Otley.

Died 29 June 1944.

TWEEDIE, Lt-Col David Keltie, DSO 1915; late RA; *b* 29 Nov. 1878; *s* of late David Tweedie. *Educ:* Trinity College, Glenalmond. Entered army, 1900; Captain, 1911; Adjutant, TF, 1908–11; served European War, 1914–18 (despatches six times, DSO). *Address:* La Trelade, St Martin's, Guernsey. *Club:* United Service.

Died 5 Dec. 1941.

TWEEDY, Ernest Hastings, FRCPI; MD (Hon.) Dublin University; Hon. FRCOG 1944; Hon. Fellow Royal Academy, Ireland; Consulting Gynæcologist to Dr Steevens Hospital; retired, 1923; late Professor of Obstetrics and Gynæcology, Royal College of Surgeons in Ireland; Consulting Gynæcologist Rotunda Hospital (former Master, 1903–10); *b* Sept. 1862; *s* of John J. Tweedy, solicitor, Dublin, and Emily Griffin, Wexford; *m* 1900, Margaret, *o d* of late Sir Stewart Woodhouse; one *s* one *d*. Former President, Obstetric Section, Royal Academy of Medicine, Ireland, and Obstetrical Section, BMA, Exeter meeting. *Publications:* Tweedy and Wrench's Practical Obstetrics; several Clinical Reports of Rotunda Hospital; many original papers to Trans. RSM, etc. *Address:* 10 Wellington Road, Dublin. *T:* Ballsbridge 64867. *Clubs:* Friendly Brothers, Dublin.

Died 22 Jan. 1945.

TWIDALE, Lt-Col (William) Cecil (Erasmus), CMG 1918; DSO 1917, late RA; *b* 1877; *s* of late R. E. Twidale, Calcutta; *m* 1923, Winifred, *d* of late Robert Butler and late Mrs Butler, Lyncombe House, Tetbury, Glos. *Educ:* Marlborough College; Royal Military Academy, Woolwich. Served S African War, 1899–1902 (despatches, Queen's medal and five clasps, King's medal and two clasps); European War, 1914–18 (despatches, CMG, DSO). *Address:* Pinecote, King's Ave, Parkstone, Dorset.

Died 28 Oct. 1949.

TWISLETON-WYKEHAM-FIENNES, Lt-Col Sir Ranulph; see Fiennes.

TWISS, Brig.-Gen. John Henry, CB 1915; CBE 1919; late RE; *b* 12 June 1867; *s* of Godfrey Twiss, Lt-Col RA; *m* Evelyn, *d* of Major-General A. T. Searle; one *d*. Entered Army, 1885; Captain, 1895; Major, 1903; Lt-Col 1911; Assistant-Director of Railways, South Africa, 1899–1902; Director of Railway Transport, 1914; served South Africa, 1899–1902 (despatches, Bt Major; Queen's medal 3 clasps, King's medal 2 clasps); European War, 1914–16 (CB, CBE); Commander Legion of Honour; Officer Order of Leopold; retired pay, 1921. *Address:* Brevent, London Road, Camberley. *Clubs:* MCC, Free Foresters.

Died 29 July 1941.

TWITCHELL, Rt Rev. Thomas Clayton, DD; *b* 1864; *s* of late J. B. Twitchell; unmarried. *Educ:* private; Cambridge; King's College, London. Worked at St George's, Barrow-in-Furness, 1889–93; at St Peter's, Cranley Gardens, 1893–1903; Vicar of All Hallows, East India Docks, 1903–08; Bishop of Polynesia, 1908–21;

Rector of St Margaret's, Buxted, 1921–25; of Selsey, Chichester, 1925–34; Fellow of King's College, London. *Recreation:* golf. *Address:* Ightham, Sevenoaks, Kent. *Club:* Golfers'.

Died 9 Oct. 1947.

TWITCHETT, Ven. Cyril Frederick; Archdeacon of Liverpool since 1934; Chaplain to the King since 1939; Commissary to the Bishop of Waiapu, NZ since 1948; General Diocesan Secretary and Secretary of the Liverpool Diocesan Board of Finance, 1925; Editor Liverpool Diocesan Calendar, 1927; Hon. MA, Liverpool University, 1941; Dio. Canon of Liverpool Cathedral, 1941; Vice-Chairman Central Board of Finance, 1948; Treasurer Council of the Church Training Colleges, 1940; *b* Sudbury, Suffolk, 1890; *e s* of Freeland Oakley Twitchett; *m* 1916, Blanche Nettleship, *y d* of John Hanchett; one *d*. *Educ:* King's College, London. AKC 1912; FKC 1935; FCIS 1937. Ordained, 1913; Curate of St Benet Fink, Tottenham, 1913; Thurnscoe, Yorks, with charge of St Hilda's, 1916; St Paul's, Sheffield, 1919; Clerical Secretary of the Life and Liberty Movement, 1920–24; Bishop's Messenger, Liverpool Cathedral, 1925–31; Chaplain to the Warrington Training College, 1930–34; Hon. Canon of Liverpool, 1928–31; Residentiary Canon of Liverpool Cathedral, 1931–33; Archdeacon of Warrington, 1933–34; Examining Chaplain to Bishop of Liverpool, 1935–44. *Recreations:* music, work. *Address:* 3 Devonshire Road, Princes Park, Liverpool 8; Church House, Liverpool 2. *T:* Lark Lane, 1440 (office) Central 6541. *Club:* Authors'.

Died 3 Sept. 1950.

TWORT, Frederick William, FRS 1929; MRCS; LRCP; Bacteriologist, late Supt of the Brown Institution (1909 until its destruction by bombing), and Professor of Bacteriology in the Faculties of Medicine and Science, University of London; *b* Camberley, 22 Oct. 1877; *e s* of late Dr William Henry Twort and late Elizabeth Crampton, *o c* of Joseph Crampton Webster; *m* 1919, Dorothy Nony, *e d* of late Frederick J. Banister, ARIBA, and Annie Reta Barrow, *g d* of Sir John Barrow, Bt, Secretary to the Admiralty; one *s* three *d*. *Educ:* St Thomas' Hospital Medical School. Roger's prize (University of London) jointly, 1908. Assistant Superintendent Clinical Laboratory, St Thomas' Hospital, 1901–02; Assistant Bacteriologist, London Hospital, 1902–09; Captain, RAMC, and Officer in charge of Base Laboratory, Salonika, 1916. *Publications:* Monograph on Johne's Disease; numerous contributions to scientific literature, including discovery of first vitamin (K) for growing leprosy bacillus, etc., Proc. Roy. Soc., 1910, and discovery of the Bacteriophage, Lancet, 1915. *Recreations:* various. *Address:* The Wilderness, Camberley, Surrey. *T:* Camberley 524.

Died 20 March 1950.

TWYSDEN, Sir Anthony Roger Duncan, 11th Bt *cr* 1611; Lt Royal Irish Fusiliers; *b* 11 March 1918; *s* of Sir Roger Twysden, 10th Bt, and Mary Duff Stirling, *e d* of late B. W. Smurthwaite; *S* father 1934; *m* 1945, Mary, *d* of late Rear-Adm. H. E. C. Blagrove. *Educ:* West Downs, Winchester; Eton. Served War of 1939–45 (prisoner). *Heir: uncle* William Adam Duncan, *b* 1897. *Address:* Downton Lodge, Hordle, Hants.

Died 10 Oct. 1946.

TYLDEN, Brig.-Gen. William; DL; *s* of Rev. W. Tylden of Stanford, Kent, and Dersingham, Norfolk, and Eleanor, 2nd *d* of Rev. J. W. Bellamy, Rector of Sellinge, Kent; *m* 1st, Alice Constance (*d* 1916), *d* of Deputy Surgeon-General B. Tydd, CB; one *d*; 2nd, Evelyn Margaret (*d* 1937), *d* of D. A. Reid, MD, JP. *Educ:* Uppingham School; RM Academy, Woolwich. Joined Royal Artillery, 1873; served S African War,

1899–1900 (despatches); commanded RA 4th Division, 1906–09; retired, 1910. *Recreation:* shooting. *Address:* Brockhill, Hythe, Kent.

Died 5 July 1942.

TYLER, Brig.-Gen. Arthur Malcolm, CMG 1919; DSO 1917; *b* 1866; *s* of late Sir Henry Whatley Tyler; *m* 1892, Caroline (*d* 1938), *d* of late R. L. Bowles. Served European War, 1914–19 (despatches, DSO, CMG). *Address:* Ticklerton Court, Church Stretton, Shropshire.

Died 31 July 1950.

TYLER, Brig.-Gen. James Arbuthnot, CB 1919; CMG 1916; late RA; *b* 15 Oct. 1867. Served S Africa, 1899–1902 (despatches, Bt-Major, Queen's medal 5 clasps, King's medal 2 clasps); European War, 1914–18 (despatches, CB, CMG, Bt Col); retired pay, 1921.

Died 6 Feb. 1945.

TYNDALE, Henry Edmund Guise, MBE 1919; Assistant Master, since 1911, and Housemaster, 1923–46, Winchester College; *b* Headington, Oxon, 10 Dec. 1887; *s* of Rev. E. F. G. Tyndale and Marcia Louisa Edersheim; *m* 1st, 1917, Katharine Seely Leach (*d* 1921); 2nd, 1923, Ruth Isabel Walcott Radcliffe; one *s* three *d*. *Educ:* Winchester College; New College, Oxford (Scholar). 1st Class Honour Moderations, 1908; 1st Class Literae Humaniores, 1910. Served with 8th (Service) Battalion, King's Royal Rifle Corps, 1914–15; War Office, 1916–18; Editor of Alpine Journal since 1938. *Publications:* Edited: Adventures of an Alpine Guide; Whymper's Scrambles amongst the Alps; trans various German mountaineering books. *Recreation:* mountaineering. *Address:* 23 Kingsgate Street, Winchester. *T:* Winchester 4306. *Clubs:* Athenæum, Alpine.

Died 3 Aug. 1948.

TYNDALE, Walter, RI; RBC; *b* Bruges, Aug. 1855; of English parents; *m* Evelyn Dorothea (*d* 1933), *d* of Rev. Thomas Barnard; three *s*. *Educ:* Belgium. Artist; was a student at the Antwerp Academy and in the studio of M. Bonnat; his first exhibits were in oil, but later he confined himself to water colours; held several exhibitions in London; appointed to the Censor staff at Havre, 1914; Head Censor, Boulogne (despatches). *Publications:* Below the Cataracts; An Artist in Egypt; An Artist in Italy; An Artist in the Riviera; Japan and the Japanese; illustrations in colour for The New Forest, Wessex, Japanese Gardens, The Dalmatian Coast, 1925. *Address:* 29 Brunswick Gardens, W8. *T:* Bayswater 5039. *Club:* Arts.

Died 16 Dec. 1943.

TYNDALE-BISCOE, Rev. Cecil Earle, MA; late Principal of CMS Schools, Kashmir, N India; retired, 1940; Hon. Canon Lahore Cathedral, 1932; Canon Emeritus, 1942; *b* Holton, Oxon, 9 Feb. 1863; *s* of William Earle Biscoe, JP, DL, Holton Park, Oxon; *m* 1901, Blanche Violet (*d* 1947), *d* of Rev. Richard Burges; three *s* one *d*. *Educ:* Park Hall, nr Evesham; Bradfield College; Jesus College, Cambridge. Coxed the Cambridge boat 1884 defeated Oxford, and the Jesus College boat head of the river for three years and won the Grand Challenge at Henley, 1886; deacon, 1887; priest, 1890; curate at Bradfield, Berks, 1887; at St Mary's, Whitechapel, 1888–90; arrived Kashmir, N India, Church Missionary Society, 1890; Hon. Fellow Jesus College, Cambridge, 1945. Kaisar-i-Hind Gold Medal 1st Class, 1912, and Bar, 1929. *Publications:* Character Building; Kashmir in Sunlight and Shade. *Recreations:* boating, swimming. *Address:* Chartered Bank of South Africa, Salisbury, S Rhodesia, S Africa.

Died 1 Aug. 1949.

TYNDALL, Lt-Col Henry Stuart, DSO 1917; *b* 1875; *s* of late Maj.-Gen. Henry Tyndall, CB; *m* 1903, Audrey, *d* of Rev. Alfred Herbert Hildesley, Rector of Wyton, near Huntingdon. *Educ:* Wellington College; RMC,

Sandhurst. Served NW Frontier of India, 1897–98 (medal with two clasps); France, 1915; E Africa, 1916–17 (DSO, Croix de Guerre, despatches); Afghan War, 1919 (medal and clasp). *Address:* Greenhurst, Storrington, Sussex.

Died 2 Feb. 1942.

TYRER, William Henry, CBE 1937; OBE 1920; Hon. LLM Liverpool Univ. 1938; Town Clerk of Wigan, 1911–July 1946, and Clerk of the Peace, 1940–46, when retired; *b* 1876; *e surv. s* of late Stephen Tyrer, Wigan; *m* 1912, Ellen, *o c* of late George James Bridge, Wigan; one *s. Educ:* Wigan Grammar School; Liverpool University. Common Law, Conveyancing and Parliamentary Assistant to Town Clerk of Salford, 1902–10; Assistant Solicitor, Salford Corporation, 1910–11; Medaille Roi Albert, 1920, for war services; Honorary Freeman of Wigan, 1933. *Recreations:* church architecture, walking and motoring. *Address:* Garth, Wigan. *T:* 3306. *Clubs:* University, Liverpool.

Died 27 March 1947.

TYRRELL, 1st Baron *cr* 1929, of Avon; **William George Tyrrell,** PC 1928; GCB 1934; GCMG 1925; KCB 1927; KCMG 1913; KCVO 1919; CB 1909; President of British Board of Film Censors since 1935; *b* 17 Aug. 1866; *s* of late Hon. William Tyrrell, Judge of the High Court of Judicature, NW Provinces of India, and Julia, *d* of late Col Wakefield; *m* 1891, Margaret Ann (*d* 1939), *d* of late David Urquhart, MP; one *d. Educ:* Balliol College, Oxford. Entered Foreign Office, 1889; Private Secretary to Lord Sanderson, Under-Secretary of State for Foreign Affairs, 1896–1903; Secretary to the Imperial Defence Committee, 1903–04; Acting 2nd Secretary of Embassy at Rome, 1904; Senior Clerk in the Foreign Office, 1907–15, and Private Secretary to Right Hon. Sir E. Grey, Bart, MP, Secretary of State for Foreign Affairs, 1907–15; Assistant Under-Secretary, 1919–25; Permanent Under-Secretary of State at Foreign Office, 1925–28; British Ambassador in Paris, 1928–34; received the Coronation medals, 1902 and 1911; Grand Cordon Legion of Honour, 1934. *Address:* Chesham House, Chesham Place, SW1. *T:* Sloane 2053. *Clubs:* Turf, Garrick.

Died 14 March 1947 (ext).

TYRRELL, Col John Frederick, CBE 1920; Royal Artillery; retired, 1926; *b* Secunderabad, 14 Dec. 1872; *s* of late Lt-Gen. F. H. Tyrrell, Madras Army; *m* 1899, Annie Macleod, *d* of late Major-General H. Wylie, CSI; no *c. Educ:* Stubbington House, Fareham; RMA, Woolwich. First Commission, 1893; served in RGA in Mauritius, The Cape and Quetta, 1893–99; Indian Ordnance Department since 1899; served Mesopotamia, 1914–16 (despatches thrice); Afghan War, 1919 (despatches, CBE). *Address:* Corwen, Farnham, Surrey.

Died 28 Dec. 1944.

U

ULLSWATER, 1st Viscount *cr* 1921, of Campsea Ashe, Suffolk; **James William Lowther,** PC, 1898; GCB 1921; JP, LLM, DL; DCL (Oxford); LLD (Camb.); DCL (Leeds); *b* 1 April 1855; *s* of late Hon. William Lowther, 25 years MP for Westmorland, and Alice, 3rd *d* of Baron Wensleydale; *m* 1886, Mary Frances (*d* 1944), *y d* of late Rt Hon. A. J. B. Beresford Hope, Bedgebury, Kent; one *s* one *d. Educ:* Eton; King's Coll., London; Trin. Coll., Camb. Honours in Classical and Law Tripos, Camb. Barr. 1879; Bencher Inner Temple, 1906; MP Rutland, 1883; contested Mid-Cumberland, 1885; 4th Charity Commissioner, 1887; Under-Secretary for Foreign Affairs, 1891; MP (C) Penrith Division of Cumberland, 1886–1921; Speaker of House of Commons, 1905–21; represented Great Britain at International Conference at Venice, 1892, and at the International Conference on Emigration at Rome, 1924; Chairman of Quarter Sessions for Cumberland, 1900; Chairman of Committee of Ways and Means and Deputy Speaker, 1895–1905, of the Speakers' Electoral Reform Conference, 1916–17, of the Boundary Commissions (Great Britain and Ireland), 1917, of the Royal Commission on Proportional Representation, 1918, Devolution Conference, 1919, of the Royal Commission on London Government, 1921–22; of Review Committee Political Honours, 1923–24, and Statutory Commission on Cambridge Univ., 1923; of Agricultural Wages Board, 1930–40; Lords and Commons Committee on Electoral Reform, 1929–30; and of BBC Enquiry Committee, 1935; Trustee British Museum, 1922–31; Trustee National Portrait Gallery, 1925. *Publication:* A Speaker's Commentaries, 1925. *Heir: g g s* Nicholas James Christopher Lowther, *b* 9 Jan. 1942. *Address:* Campsea Ashe, Woodbridge, Suffolk.

Died 27 March 1949.

UNDERHILL, Evelyn, (Mrs Stuart Moore), Fellow of King's College, London, 1927; Hon. DD (Aberdeen) 1939; *b* 1875; *o c* of late Sir Arthur Underhill, Barrister-at-law; *m* 1907, Hubert Stuart Moore, FSA, Barrister-at-law. *Educ:* privately; King's College for Women, London (Hon. Fellow, 1913). Upton Lecturer on Religion, Manchester College, Oxford, 1921–22. *Publications:* A Barlamb's Ballad Book; The Grey World; The Miracles of our Lady St Mary; The Lost Word; The Column of Dust; Mysticism, a study in the Nature and Development of Man's Spiritual Consciousness (13th ed., 1940); Immanence, a Book of Verses (3rd ed.); The Mystic Way (3rd ed.); Practical Mysticism; Ruysbrœck; Theophanies; Jacopone da Todi; The Essentials of Mysticism; The Life of the Spirit and the Life of To-day (7th ed.); The Mystics of the Church; Concerning the Inner Life (5th ed.); Man and The Supernatural; The House of the Soul, 2nd ed.; The Golden Sequence (3rd ed.); Mixed Pasture; The School of Charity; Worship (Library of Constructive Theology), 1936, 2nd ed.; The Mystery of Sacrifice, 1938; Abba, 1940; Editor of The Cloud of Unknowing; One Hundred Poems of Kabir (with Sir Rabindranath Tagore); John of Ruysbrœck; Hilton's Scale of Perfection; Eucharistic Prayers from Ancient Liturgies. *Recreations:* reading, gardening, walking, talking to cats. *Address:* 50 Campden Hill Square, W8.

Died 15 June 1941.

UNDERHILL, Rt Rev. Francis, DD, Lambeth, 1932; Bishop of Bath and Wells since 1937; *b* 16 May 1878; *s* of Francis William Underhill, FRCS and Ellen Julia Underhill; unmarried. *Educ:* Shrewsbury School; Exeter College, Oxford, BA, 2nd cl. Mod. Hist., 1900; MA 1903, and Cuddesdon Theological College. Curate of St Paul's Swindon, 1901–03; St Thomas the Martyr, Oxford, 1903–11; Vicar of St Alban's Birmingham, 1911–23; SS Mary and John, Oxford, 1923–25; Select Preacher in the University of Oxford, 1929–31; Cambridge, 1934; Canon Theologian of Liverpool Cathedral, 1931–32; Warden of Liddon House, and Priest in charge of Grosvenor Chapel, Mayfair, 1925–32; Dean of Rochester, 1932–37; Member Council of Keble College, Oxford; Visitor of Wadham College, Oxford; Hon. Canon of Birmingham Cathedral, 1921–23. *Publications:* The Catholic Faith in Practice, 1918; The Life of Prayer in the World, 1923; Can We Enjoy Religion? 1926; The Young Englishman, a Study, 1926; Prayer in Modern Life, 1928; My Duty towards my Neighbour, 1929; Editor of Feed My Sheep, Essays in Pastoral Theology, 1928; Christian Life in the Modern World, 1934; The Building of Character, 1935; St Peter, etc. *Recreations:* motoring and foreign travel. *Address:* The Palace, Wells, Somerset.

Died 24 Jan. 1943.

UNDERWOOD, Rev. Alfred Clair, MA, BLitt (Oxon), DD (Lond.), Principal of Rawdon College, Leeds, since 1926 and Professor of Church History and the History of Religion since 1920: Governor of the John Rylands Library, Manchester, since 1927; *b* Leicester, 16 Feb. 1885; *e s* of late Alfred Henry Underwood; *m* 1913, Nellie, 2nd *d* of Joseph and Elizabeth Rawson, Nottingham; one *s* one *d. Educ:* Alderman Newton's School, Leicester; Midland Baptist and University Colleges, Nottingham; Oxford University; Second Class Final Honour School of Theology, 1911; in London University, BD 1910; a First Class in the BD Honours Examination, 1918; DD, 1924. Professor of Church History in Serampore College, Bengal, 1911–19; Carey Professor of New Testament Interpretation, 1919–20; Bursar, 1916–20; Examiner in the Universities of Calcutta, London, Manchester and Bristol; Pres. of the Yorkshire Association of Baptist Churches, 1932. *Publications:* The Story of Serampore and its College, 1918 (with Principal Howells); Conversion: Christian and Non-Christian, 1925; The Continental Reformation, 1928; Contemporary Thought in India, 1930; Shintoism 1934; Contributor to the Ministry and the Sacraments, 1937; A History of the English Baptists, 1947. *Recreation:* golf. *Address:* Rawdon College, Leeds. *T:* Rawdon 120.

Died 19 April 1948.

UNDSET, Fru Sigrid; author; *b* Kallundborg, Denmark, 20 May 1882; *d* of Dr Ingvald M. Undset, archaeologist, Kristiania, and Charlotte Gyth; *m* 1912, A. C. Svarstad, painter; marriage annulled, 1925; two *s* one *d. Educ:* private day-school; commercial academy. Commercial secretary, 1898–1909; published first novel, 1907; later many books; Nobel prize, 1928. *Publications:* Fru Marta Oulie, 1907; later several novels and novelettes; of which Jenny, Kristin Lavransdatter I–III, and Olav Audunsson, I–II have been translated into English; In the Wilderness, 1929; The Son Avenger, 1930; The Wild Orchid, 1931; The Burning Bush, 1932; Ida Elisabeth, 1933; Saga of Saints, 1934; Gunnar's Daughter, 1936; The Faithful Wife, 1937; Images in a Mirror, 1938; Men, Women, and Places, 1939; Madam Dorthea, 1941. *Address:* Lillehammer, Norway.

Died 10 June 1949.

UNGER, Gladys Buchanan; dramatist; *b* San Francisco; *d* of Frank L. and Minnie Buchanan Unger; *m* 1920, Kai Kushrou Ardaschir. *Educ:* London and Paris. Educated to be an artist; studied at Julian's under Benjamin Constant; obtained Honourable Mention, Paris Salon, 1900. Made début as dramatist at the Vaudeville Theatre in 1904 with Edmund Kean, one act original play; since then has had over 20 plays, including adaptations, produced in London; among these were Mr Sheridan (original, 4 acts), 1907; Henry of Lancaster (original, 4 acts), produced in provinces by Ellen Terry, 1908; Inconstant George (adapted), 1910; Marionettes (adapted), 1911; The Son and Heir (original), 1913; Marriage Market, Betty, Toto; Our Mr Hepplewhite, original comedy, 1919; and, in collaboration, London Pride, 1916–17; Sunshine of the World, etc. *Publications:* The Son and Heir; Our Mr Hepplewhite. *Recreation:* going to the theatre.

Died 25 May 1940.

UNWIN, Captain Edward, VC 1915; CB 1919; CMG 1916; DL, RN, retired; *b* 17 March 1864; *s* of Edward Wilberforce Unwin, MA, JP, Forest Lodge, Fawley, Hants; *m* 1897, Evelyn Agnes Carew (*d* 1948), *d* of Maj.-Gen. W. Dobree Carey; two *s* two *d*. Served in punitive naval expedition to Benin, 1897 (medal and clasp); Dardanelles (despatches, VC); retired with rank of Captain, RN, 1920. *Recreations:* yachting, holds cup for 3 successive years best cruise; in motor yacht club, also croquet and tennis. *Address:* Ling Cottage, Hindhead, Surrey. *Club:* Army and Navy.

Died 19 April 1950.

UPDIKE, Daniel Berkeley; Senior Partner, D. B. Updike, The Merrymount Press; *b* Providence, RI, 1860; *s* of Hon. C. A. Updike and Elisabeth Bigelow Adams. *Educ:* private schools in Providence, RI. Work done under name of D. B. Updike, The Merrymount Press, Boston, founded in 1893, has been one of chief factors in the improvement of typography in the United States; Lecturer on printing, Post-Graduate Business School, Harvard, 1910–17; Lecturer Department of Printing and Graphic Arts, Harvard Univ., 1940; Lecturer, California Institute of Technology and Henry E. Huntington Library, Pasadena, California, 1940; Member board of managers John Carter Brown Library, Providence; trustee Boston Athenæum; hon. MA, Brown University, 1910; hon. MA, Harvard University, 1929; Member Antiquarian Society, Worcester, Massachusetts Historical Society, hon. member American Library Assoc., Phi Beta Kappa (Harvard and Brown), hon. member and Gold Medallist American Inst. of Graphic Arts, New York, Society of Arts and Crafts, Boston. *Publications:* (with Harold Brown) On the Dedication of American Churches, 1892; Printing Types, Their History, Forms and Use, 1921; In the Day's Work, 1924; Notes on the Merrymount Press, 1934; Richard Smith, First English Settler of the Narragansett Country, Rhode Island, 1937; Some Aspects of Printing, Old and New, 1941; Editor: More's Dissertation on English Typographical Founders and Foundries, 1924. *Address:* 712 Beacon Street, Boston, Mass, USA. *TA:* Updike, Boston. *T:* Commonwealth 4110. *Clubs:* Double Crown (hon.); Somerset, Odd Volumes, Boston; Elizabethan, New Haven (hon.); Grolier, New York (hon.).

Died 28 Dec. 1941.

UPJOHN, William Henry; KC; *b* Aug. 1853; *m* 1881, Lucy, *d* of late Rees Williams, of Cefn Pennar, Aberdare; two *s* two *d*. *Educ:* King's College School, London. LLB London University (University Law Exhibitioner and Scholar). Called to Bar, 1881; QC 1897; retired, 1936. *Address:* Annesley Bank, Lyndhurst, Hants. *T:* Lyndhurst 4.

Died 16 July 1941.

UPTON, Captain Edward James Gott, DSO 1902; *s* of late Major R. D. Upton, 9th Lancers; *m* 1914, Joanna Mary, 2nd *d* of Vice-Adm. William Wilson, Clyffe Manor, Swindon. Served South Africa with Imperial Yeomanry, 1900–02 (despatches, Queen's medal 3 clasps, King's medal 2 clasps, DSO); served with Brand's

Horse as Lieutenant in suppression of Boer Rebellion, 1914; European War, 1915, in German South-West Africa, Otzimbingue and Otavifontein. *Address:* Waschbank, Jammerdrift, OFS, South Africa.

Died 4 Feb. 1943.

UPWARD, Herbert; Editor, 1911, and Director, 1915, Church Family Newspaper (title changed, 1923, to Church of England Newspaper); retired 1942; *y s* of late William Upward, Blandford, Dorset; *m y d* of M. Inge, Northborne, Deal; two *s*. *Educ:* National School; privately; King's Coll., London. Started journalistic career on Warrington Guardian, subsequently Manchester and Northampton; drifted to London; acted as lay secretary of a church society for five years; returned to first love—sub-editor Church Family Newspaper, 1906; Member of National Church Assembly for St Albans. *Publications:* articles Social, Religious and Literary, journals. *Address:* Ty Mawr, Marshals Drive, St Albans. *T:* St Albans 812.

Died 1 Dec. 1944.

URE, Percy Neville; Emeritus Professor of Classics, The University, Reading; *b* Stoke Newington, 1879; *e s* of E. A. and L. A. Ure; *m* 1918, Annie Dunman Hunt, BA; one *s* one *d*. *Educ:* City of London School; Caius College, Cambridge. Scholar, 1st Class Classical Tripos, Part I 1901, Part II (Archæology) 1902. Assistant Lecturer in Greek, University College, Cardiff, 1903–07; Assistant Lecturer in Classics, University of Leeds, 1908–11; Professor of Classics, Reading Univ., 1911–36. *Publications:* various articles on Greek history and archæology in Cambridge Ancient History, etc.; Black Glaze Pottery from Rhitsona 1913; The Greek Renaissance, 1921; The Origin of Tyranny, 1922; Sixth and Fifth Century Pottery from Rhitsona, 1927; Bœotian Pottery of the Geometric and Archaic Styles (Union Académique Internationale, Classification des Céramiques Antiques), 1927; Aryballoi and Figurines from Rhitsona, 1934; Justinian and his Age, 1949. *Address:* 1 Upper Redlands Road, Reading. *T:* Reading 62128.

Died 3 April 1950.

URICH, John; composer; *b* Trinidad, West Indies, 1849; British. *Educ:* Paris, Pupil of Gounod. Founded in Paris, Figaro Musical; Operas performed: The Storm, in Brussels; Flora Macdonald, at Bologna and other Italian stages; The Pilot at Monte Carlo, in France, at Berlin, and various German and Swiss stages; Hermann and Dorothea, at Berlin; The Carillon, at Berlin Royal Opera House; The Cicada, Savoy Theatre, London, matinée performances; Tama, opera ballet, at the Royal Opera of Antwerp; Disarm! Opera in one act and four sceneries; The Maid of Athens, opera comique in 3 acts; The Dawn of Peace, Aria for Soprano, Chorus, and Orchestra. *Publication:* The Pilot and Carillon. *Address:* 28 Dorset Street, W1. *T:* Welbeck 3433.

Died 14 Dec. 1939.

URQUHART, Alexander; Editor of Dundee Advertiser since 1910; and joint editor and leader writer of Courier and Advertiser since their amalgamation; *b* Nairn, 1867; *m* 1st, Catherine Macdonald; two *d*; 2nd, Barbara Abercrombie Lamont. *Educ:* Nairn. Began journalism on the Nairnshire Telegraph; served in the Press Gallery as sketch writer for Scottish Leader, and for a time as an assistant editor of that paper; subsequently joined Dundee Advertiser as leader writer. *Publication:* a volume of nature papers entitled Odd Hours with Nature. *Recreations:* motoring, nature studies, and sketching. *Address:* Cedarlea, 324 Blackness Road, Dundee.

Died 29 July 1942.

URWICK, Edward Johns; Professor Emeritus of Political Economy, University of Toronto; *b* 1867; *m* 1905, Ethel Alexandra, *d* of Lt-Col Wynch; two *s*. *Educ:* Uppingham; Oxford. 1st Class Lit. Hum., 1890. Sub-Warden of Toynbee Hall, 1899–1902, late Prof. of

Social Philosophy, Univ. of London; President of Morley Memorial College. *Publications:* Studies of Boy Life; Luxury and Waste; A Philosophy of Social Progress; The Message of Plato; The Social Good, 1927. *Recreation:* farming. *Address:* The University, Toronto, Canada.

Died 18 Feb. 1945.

USHER, Rev. Philip Charles Alexander; Squadron Leader RAFVR; Warden of Liddon House and Priest-in-charge of Grosvenor Chapel, South Audley St, W1, since 1937; Ministry of Information since 1939; Editor Church Quarterly Review since 1930; *b* 18 March 1899; *o s* of Thomas Charles Usher, Seend, and Constance Emma, *d* of late Alexander Bell; unmarried. *Educ:* Westminster School; Christ Church, Oxford (Scholar). 2nd Lt RGA (British Salonica Force), 1918–19; BA, 1922; MA, 1925; Deacon and Priest, 1923; Domestic Chaplain to Bishop of Gloucester, 1923–24 and 1930–37; Assistant Chaplain of St George's Collegiate Church, Jerusalem, 1924–25; Chaplain of HM Legation, Athens, 1926–30; Assistant Secretary, Church of England Council on Foreign Relations, 1933–39; Select Preacher, Cambridge 1936; Commander of the Order of the Star of Rumania, 1935. *Recreations:* travelling and motoring. *Address:* 24 South Audley Street, W1. *T:* Grosvenor 1684; Seend Green House, Wilts. *T:* Seend 4. *Club:* Athenæum.

Died 6 June 1941.

USSHER, Col Allan Vesey, CMG 1917; *b* 13 Sept. 1860; 4th *s* of late Major-Gen. J. T. Ussher; *m* Florence, *o d* of late Bernard Critchley-Salmonson. *Educ:* Stubbington House, Fareham. Joined 26 Cameronians, 1881; commanded 2nd Battalion, Cameronians (Scottish Rifles), 1907–11; served in the Expedition against the Jebus, Lagos, W Africa, 1892 (medal with clasp, despatches); South African War, 1902 (Queen's medal 2 clasps); European War, 1914–18 (despatches thrice, CMG, Bt-Col). *Address:* 21 Ashburham Gardens, Eastbourne. *Club:* Army and Navy.

Died 23 Oct. 1941.

USSISHKIN, Menahem; President Board of Directors of the Keren Kayemeth Leisrael (Jewish National Fund) Ltd; President, Zionist General Council; Member, Board of Directors and Executive Council, Hebrew University; Director of Anglo-Palestine Bank; *b* Dubrovna, Russia, 1863; *m* Esther Paley of Ekaterinoslav, Russia; one *s* one *d. Educ:* High Technical School, Moscow. *Publications:* various articles on Jewish problems. *Address:* Ussishkin Street, Rehavia, Jerusalem. *T:* 56.

Died 2 Oct. 1941.

UTHWATT, Baron *cr* 1946 (Life Peer), of Lathbury; **Augustus Andrewes Uthwatt,** PC 1946; Kt 1941; a Lord of Appeal in Ordinary since 1946; Hon. Fellow of Balliol College; *b* 1879; *s* of Thomas Andrewes Uthwatt and Annie Hazlitt; *m* 1927, Mary Baxter Bonhote; no *c. Educ:* Ballarat College, Victoria; Balliol College, Oxford. BCL Vinerian Scholar, 1904. Called to Bar, Gray's Inn, 1904; Legal Adviser to the Ministry of Food, 1915–18; Bencher, Gray's Inn, 1927; Member of the Council of Legal Education, 1929; Junior Counsel (on the Chancery side) to the Treasury and the Board of Trade and Junior Counsel to the Attorney General in Charity Matters, 1934; Judge of Chancery Div. of High Court of Justice, 1941–46; Treasurer of Gray's Inn, 1939 and 1940; Vice-Treasurer of Gray's Inn, 1941; Chm. of Committee on Responsibility for Repair of Premises Damaged by Hostilities (1939), on Liability for War Damage to the subject matter of Contracts (1939), and on Principles of Assessment of War Damage to Property (1940); Chairman of Expert Committee on Compensation and Betterment, 1941; Chairman of the Leasehold Cttee, 1948. *Recreations:* golf, lawn tennis. *Address:* 11a de Vere Cottages, W8; White Friars, Sandwich, Kent. *Clubs:* Athenæum, Reform, Beefsteak, Garrick.

Died 24 April 1949.

V

VACARESCO, Helen; authoress and poet; Maid of Honour to the Queen of Roumania, and with her has visited almost all the Courts of Europe; Roumanian delegate to the League of Nations; *b* Bucharest; *d* of John Vacaresco, Ex-Minister Plenipotentiary, and Euphrosnie. *Educ:* Paris and Bucharest. Prix Archon Desperouses for poems; holds a very brilliant literary and social position in Paris; Officier de l'Instruction Publique, Legion d'Honneur, and the Order in brilliants of the Queen of Roumania; Grand Officier de la Couronne de Roumanie. *Publications:* Chants d'Aurore, crowned by the French Academy; L'Ame Sereine, Roumanian Ballads (French Academy prize Jules Favre); Lueurs et Flammes; Kings and Queens I have known; The King's Wife; The Queen's Friend; has especially devoted herself to giving form to the weird romantic legends of her native land; has also written numerous articles in English. *Recreations:* conversation, travelling. *Clubs:* Interalliée, Lyceum, Paris.

Died Feb. 1947.

VALENTIA, (de jure) 12th Viscount *cr* 1621, (Viscountcy dormant, 1844–1958, when succession proved); **Caryl Arthur James Annesley,** CVO 1924; Bt 1620; Baron Mountnorris, 1628; Baron Annesley (UK) *cr* 1917; Premier Baronet of Ireland; Captain Special Reserve 1st Dragoons; JP, DL Oxon; *b* 3 July 1883; *o surv. s* of 11th Viscount and Laura Sarah (*d* 1933), *y d* of Daniel Hale Webb, Wykham Park, Oxfordshire, and *widow* of Sir Algernon William Peyton, 4th Bt; *S* father, 1927. *Educ:* Eton; RMC. Late Lieutenant Oxfords Light Infantry. Owns about 2000 acres. *Heir:* (to Irish Viscountcy only) Rev. William Monckton Annesley, *b* 1875. *Address:* 112 Oakwood Court, W14. *Clubs:* Turf, White's.

Died 6 Oct. 1949.

VALENTINE, George Donald, BA, MA, LLB; Sheriff-Substitute, retired; *b* Girvan, Ayrshire, 7 Feb. 1877; *e s* of Dr Valentine and Margaret Warden; *m* 1916, Edith Jane Mitchell. *Educ:* Glasgow Univ.; Trinity College, Cambridge. Advocate, 1903; Interim Sheriff-Substitute at Ayr, 1913; thereafter at Elgin and Airdrie; Commissioner Military Service (Civil Liabilities) Department at Glasgow and thereafter at Dundee, 1917–18; Sheriff-Substitute of Inverness, Elgin and Nairn at Portree, 1920; of Dumfries and Galloway at Newton-Stewart, 1925–26; of Perthshire at Perth, 1926–46. *Publications:* The Heart of Bruce, by George Henderland, 1912; Reasons of State, 1922; Saul, 1924; Dawn, by George Henderland, 1929; Olaf's Son, privately printed, 1936; The Air a Realm of Law (Juridical Review), 1910; Doubts regarding the Foundations of Jurisprudence (Juridical Review), 1925. *Recreations:* mountaineering, fishing. *Address:* Craigellachie, Edzell, Angus.

Died 27 Nov. 1946.

VALENTINE, Wing-Comdr George Engebret, DSO 1940; RAF; *b* 23 Dec. 1909; *s* of James Valentine, MA, Dovercourt, Essex, and Ragna Amundsen, Oslo; *m* 1933, Kathleen Gwendoline Parry; no *c*. *Educ:* Bishops Stortford College; St Catharine's College, Cambridge. Commissioned, 1932; Flight-Lieutenant, 1936; Squadron Leader, 1938; Wing-Commander, 1940; served in 13 and 26 Army Co-operation squadrons, 1933–36; studied Russian in Tallinn, 1937; from 1938 to outbreak of war, was on staff of No. 11 Group, Uxbridge. *Recreations:* Rugby football (Cambridge Univ., 1931, Eastern Counties, English Final Trial,

1933), cricket, gardening. *Address:* Silver Farm, Lawshall, Bury St Edmunds. *T:* Cockfield Green 227. *Club:* Lansdowne.

Died 3 Sept. 1941.

VALÉRY, Paul, Member of the French Academy since 1925; Hon. DLitt (Oxon); President of Committee of Letters and Arts of League of Nations; Administrateur du Centre Méditerranéen de Nice; Professeur de Poétique au Collège de France; poet and philosopher; *b* 1871. *Publications:* Introduction to the Methods of Leonardo da Vinci, 1895; La Soirée avec Monsieur Teste; La Jeune Parque, 1917; Album de Vers Anciens, 1920; Charmes, 1922; Fragments du Narcisse, 1922; Poésies, 1923; Variété, 1924; Eupalinos ou l'Architecte; L'Ame et la Danse, 1923; Regards sur le Monde Actuel; Variété III; Pièces sur l'Art; Introducteur a la poétique; two Melodramas: Amphion and Semiramis; Variété IV, 1939. *Address:* 40 rue de Villeiust, Paris XVIᵉ.

Died 20 July 1945.

VALINTINE, Thomas Harcourt Ambrose, CBE 1919; FRSI, DPH, MRCS, LRCP; *b* 1865; *s* of late Captain T. B. Valintine; *m* 1st, 1891, Margaret, *d* of Francis Ellis McTaggart; 2nd, Barbara, *d* of E. Vickers. *Educ:* Marlborough. Inspector-General of Hospitals for New Zealand, 1908; Chief Health Officer, 1909; Director of Military Hospitals, 1915, and Director-General of Health, 1920–30.

Died 30 Aug. 1945.

VAN NOTTEN POLE, Sir Cecil Pery P.; *see* Pole.

VAN ANROOY, A., RI; artist painter; *b* Holland, 11 Jan. 1870; *s* of Dr P. G. van Anrooy; *m* 1912, Rachel Keith. *Educ:* Delft College. Graduated Civil Engineer (State Diploma, 1891); Academy of Art, The Hague. Settled in England, 1896; contributed to weekly and monthly illustrated magazines; exhibitor at leading exhibitions; represented by works in British Museum, South Kensington Museum, Amsterdam Municipal Museum, Canadian National Gallery, and many provincial galleries; Foundation Member and active Collaborator Thames Barrage Association; naturalised British subject; Knight of the Order of Orange Nassau. *Address:* 106 Randolph Avenue, W9. *T:* Cunningham 5648. *Club:* Dutch.

Died 13 Feb. 1949.

VANBRUGH, Dame Irene, DBE 1941; actress; President The Theatrical Ladies Guild of Charity, 50 Great Russell Street, WC1; President, RADA, Gower Street, WC; *b* Heavitree, Exeter, 2 Dec. 1872; *y d* of late Rev. R. H. Barnes, Vicar of Heavitree and Prebendary of Exeter Cathedral; *m* 1901, Dion Boucicault (*d* 1929). *Educ:* Exeter High School; schools in Paris. Acted with Miss Sarah Thorne at Margate; joined J. L. Toole in autumn of 1889; Beerbohm Tree, 1892; George Alexander 1893; A. Bourchier 1895; creating part in Chili Widow, Kitty Clive; created Lady Rosamund in The Liars, 1897; Rose Trelawny in Trelawny of the Wells, 1898; Stella in His Excellency the Governor; Mrs Millin Dale in When a Man's in Love; joined Mr John Hare, 1899, to create the part of Sophy Fullgarney in The Gay Lord Quex; created Lady Mary Lazenby in Admirable Crichton, 1902; title rôle in Letty, 1903; Amy Grey in Alice-sit-by-the-Fire, 1905; Nina in His House in Order, 1906; Jeanne de Briante in The Great Conspiracy, 1907; Marise in The Thief, Zöe Blundell in Mid-Channel, 1909; title rôle in Grace, 1910; Margaret Summers in Passers By, 1911; Kate in The £12 Look, 1911; in Rosalind, 1912; Cynthia Herrick in Open

Windows, 1913; Lady Lilian Garson in Half an Hour, 1913; Nora Marsh in The Land of Promise, 1914; The Spirit of Culture in Sir James Barrie's Der Tag, and Lady Falkland in The Right to Kill, 1915; Caroline in Caroline, 1916, and Mrs Lytton in The Riddle, 1916; Emily Ladew in Her Husband's Wife, 1916; Leonora in Seven Women, by J. M. Barrie, 1917; Belinda, 1918; Mr Pim Passes By, 1920; Miss Nell O'New Orleans, 1921; The Truth About Blaydes, 1921; Eileen, 1922; Mid Channel, 1923; South Africa, Australia and New Zealand, 1923–25; reappeared in All the King's Horses; in a revival of Caroline, and in Miss Marlow at Play; return visit to Australia and New Zealand, playing a variety of parts, 1927–29; Art and Mrs Bottle; The Swan, 1930; Queen in Hamlet, 1931; Revival on Tour Mid-Channel, 1932, and production Price of Wisdom, by Lionel Brown; Millicent Jordan in Dinner at Eight, 1933; Duchess of Marlborough in Viceroy Sarah, 1935; Our Own Lives, 1935; Tour, in The Old Maid, 1936; Tour, Viceroy Sarah, 1937; Countess of Messiter, Operette, 1938; Lady Shuflepenny in The Jealous God, 1939; Lady Villiers in Only Yesterday, 1939; in All the King's Horses, 1939; Malvern Festival: Dowager Lady Farnleigh in Dead Heat, and Catherine of Braganza in In Good King Charles's Golden Days, 1939; Tour of In Good King Charles's Golden Days, 1940; Forty-Eight Hours Leave, Apollo Theatre, 1941; in revival of What Every Woman Knows, Lyric Theatre, 1943; Lady Markby in An Ideal Husband, 1944; Mrs Catchpole in film I Live in Grosvenor Square, 1944–45; Tour, Appointment with Fear, 1945; Fit for Heroes, Embassy Theatre Tour and Whitehall Theatre, 1945; Tour, King Maker, then St James' Theatre, 1946; Tour, Solitary Lover, then Winter Gardens Theatre, 1948. *Publication:* To Tell My Story, 1948. *Recreations:* embroidery, and being read to. *Address:* 6 Stourcliffe Close, Stourcliffe Street, W1. *T:* Paddington 2988.

Died 30 Nov. 1949.

VANBRUGH, Violet, (Mrs Arthur Bourchier); actress; *b* Exeter, 11 June 1867; *née* Violet Augusta Mary Barnes; *e d* of late Rev. R. H. Barnes; *m* 1894, Arthur Bourchier (marr. diss. 1917; he *d* 1927); one *d. Educ:* High School, Exeter; France and Germany. First went on the stage under Miss Sarah Thorne; appeared first in London with Mr Toole in The Butler; joined the Kendals for season in London, playing in The Weaker Sex; then went with them on their first visit to America; joined Mr Irving to play Anne Bullen in Henry VIII; joined Mr Daly to play Countess Olivia in Twelfth Night; joined Mr Bourchier's company, playing The Chili Widow, Jacinta in M. de Paris, and Lady Crofton in The Queen's Proctor; created Lady Beauvedere in The Ambassador, Lady Winifred Crosby in Hearts are Trumps, and Kate Ommaney in The Wedding Guest; played in The Undercurrent, 1901; 1902, The Duchess in The Bishop's Move; Mrs Bramley Burville in My Lady Virtue; 1903, the title rôle in Whitewashing Julia and in The Golden Silence, Yanetta in The Arm of the Law; Lady Angela Wealdstone in The Fairy's Dilemma; Lady Anne Kellard in The Chevalier; Lady Alethea in Walls of Jericho; Portia to her husband's Shylock; Clarice in The Fascinating Mrs Vanderveldt; The Duchess in the English version of Le Duel, 1907; Lady Macbeth, 1907; Gladys in Simple Simon, and Muriel Glayde in John Glayde's Honour, 1908; Anne Marie in Samson, 1909; Claire Forster in The Woman in the Case, 1909 and 1910; Monica Carteret in Glasshouses, and Katharine of Aragon in Henry VIII; Mrs Ford in The Merry Wives of Windsor; Lady Macbeth, 1911; Martha in The Firescreen, and Annie Jeffreys in Find the Woman, 1912; Katharine Parr in Bluff King Hal, and Roncha in The Double Mystery, 1914; Mrs Pomeroy's Reputation, 1916; toured in 1918 with Trimmed in Scarlet; played in the Laughing Lady by Alfred Sutro; toured in an adaptation of La Flamme, and played in it in

1923; toured in The Letter of the Law with Prudence Vanbrugh; produced a play by Herr Trebitsch adapted by George Bernard Shaw in 1925; toured during 1926–27 in the Duchess Decides; played in a revival of the Woman in the Case, 1928; played with Madame Alice Délysia in Her Past, 1929; played with her daughter Prudence in Aldous Huxley's Play, This Way to Paradise, 1930; played The Sleep Walking Scene in the Festival in memory of Ellen Terry, 1931; toured the Provinces with her daughter, Prudence Vanbrugh, in After All, by John Van Druten, 1931; played the Princess Stephanie Rabnitz in Edward Knoblock and Beverley Nichols play Evensong; played Mrs Ford in the Merry Wives of Windsor, 1934; Lady Madehurst in Family Affairs, 1935; four months in Australia; Merry Wives of Windsor, Newcastle and Open Air Theatre, 1937; Strand Theatre, London, and on tour; Mistress Ford in Merry Wives of Windsor with Donald Wolfit and Irene Vanbrugh, 1940 and 1941. Collected £2000 from the 'V.'s' of Great Britain towards a Spitfire for Russia. *Recreations:* reading, sitting in the open air. *Address:* 10 Stourcliffe Close, George Street, W1.

Died 11 Nov. 1942.

VAN DEN BERGH, Donald Stanley, Lt-Col, retired; DL County of London; Hon. Colonel 453rd (City of London) Anti-Aircraft Regiment RA, TA; Co-opted Member County of Sussex T. & AFA; *b* London, 1888; *e s* of late Henry Van den Bergh; *m* 1913, Norah, *d* of late Gilbert and Dame Louise Samuel, DBE; one *d. Educ:* Clifton College. Served in European War, 1914–18 (despatches). War of 1939–45 (despatches); takes an active interest in philanthropic work; Member Board of Governors, St George's Hosp.; Chairman House Cttee, Princess Beatrice Hosp.; Chairman House Cttee Crawley and District Hosp.; President Netherlands Benevolent Society; JP, County of London; Chairman Ifield and Crawley Conservative Assoc. *Publications:* regular contributor to various pages on questions of public interest. *Recreations:* farming and stock breeding, collecting of prints. *Address:* The Mount Farm, Ifield, Sussex. *T:* Rusper 369. *Club:* Carlton.

Died 3 Nov. 1949.

VAN DER BIJL, Hendrik Johannes, PhD, Hon. DSc Stellenbosch, Hon. LLD Capetown, MAmIEE, FIRE, FRS 1944; FRSSA etc.; Chairman, Electricity Supply Commission, since 1923; Chairman, SA Iron and Steel Industrial Corporation, Ltd, since 1928; Chairman and Managing Director, African Metals Corporation, Ltd, since 1937; Chairman, Industrial Development Corporation of SA Ltd, 1940–44; Director of SA Board, Barclays Bank, since 1939; Director-General of Supplies, 1943–46; Chancellor, University of Pretoria, since 1934; Hon. Colonel SA Tank Corps, 1942; Chairman, Vanderbijl Engineering Corporation Ltd since 1945; Chairman, Vanderbijl Park Estate Company since 1945; *b* Pretoria, South Africa, 23 Nov. 1887; *s* of Pieter G. van der Bijl and Hester Groenewald; *m* 1942, Ethel Buxton; one *d. Educ:* Stellenbosch Univ. (BSc); Leipzig University (PhD). Instructor in Physics at Royal School of Technology, Dresden, 1912–13; Research Physicist, Am. Telephone and Telegraph Co. and Western Electric Co., New York, 1913–20; Technical Adviser on industrial development to the Dept of Mines and Industries of the Union of S Africa, 1920–22; Director-General of War Supplies, 1939–42; Foreign Associate of National Academy of Science, USA, 1943; Erelid Koninklyk Instituut van Inginieurs (Holland), 1937. *Publications:* on Pure and Applied Physics; Conduction of Electricity through Liquids, Gases and High Vacuum; Thermionics; Thermionic Vacuum Tube, etc. *Recreation:* golf. *Address:* Escom House, Rissik Street, Johannesburg. *Clubs:* Rand, Country (Johannesburg); Pretoria (Pretoria).

Died 2 Dec. 1948.

VANDERBILT, Brig.-Gen. Cornelius; b New York, 1873; s of Cornelius Vanderbilt and Alice Claypoole Gwynne; m 1896, Grace Graham, d of Richard T. Wilson. *Educ:* Yale. AB 1895; PhB 1898; ME 1899. Director of many companies. *Address:* 640 Fifth Avenue, New York.

Died 1 March 1942.

VAN DER KISTE, Lt-Col Freegift William, DSO 1917; late Royal Artillery; b Limerick, 11 May 1875; s of late Capt. W. Van der Kiste (84th Regt) and S. M. Harding; m 1900, Evelyn Grace (d 1939) d of late Gen. R. Y. Shipley, CB, Royal Fusiliers; four s; 1943, Anne Parker, d of John Parker Norfolk, Harewood. *Educ:* Trinity College School, Stratford-on-Avon; RMA, Woolwich. Commission, RA 1894; Capt. 1900; Major, 1914; Acting Lt-Col 1918; Lt-Col 1921; chiefly served in India; European War, 1914–19; France and Salonica (despatches twice, 1914 Star, DSO); retired, 1925; Major, Home Guard, 1939. *Address:* Lloyds Bank, Weymouth.

Died 17 April 1948.

VANDERLYN, Nathan; b Coventry, 1872; m 1912, M. A. Todd (d 1942); one s one d. *Educ:* Coventry Grammar School. National Scholarship, Royal College of Art. Black and White artist, craftsman, water colour painter; Exhibitor, Salon. Academy, Royal Institute and London Group; One-man show at Brook Street Art Gallery, 1937. *Recreation:* gardening. *Address:* 38 Palace Road, Streatham, SW2. *T:* Tulse Hill 4976.

Died 23 April 1946.

VAN DE WEYER, Major William John Bates, MVO 1900; late Captain 3rd Batt. Royal Berks Regiment; Hon. Capt. in Army; b 29 Dec. 1870; e s of late V. W. B. and late Lady Emily Van de Weyer; m 1908, Hon. Olive Elizabeth Wingfield, e d of 7th Viscount Powerscourt; one s three d. *Educ:* Eton. ADC and Acting Military Secretary to Lord Lieutenant of Ireland, 1895–1902; High Sheriff of Dorset, 1942. *Recreations:* shooting, hunting, gardening. *Address:* Clyffe, Dorchester, Dorset. *T:* Puddletown 217.

Died 1 April 1946.

VANE, Harry Tempest, CBE 1917; s of James and Martha Vane; m 1st, 1897, Florence Emma Maud Burley (d 1936); three s two d; 2nd, 1942, Aenny Adriana, *widow* of Baron Willy von Liebermann. *Educ:* Holborn Estate Grammar School. London Manager, Dunlop Tyre Co. six years, to 1904; Secretary and General Manager of S. F. Edge, Ltd, 1904–12; Managing Director of D. Napier & Son, Ltd, Acton, 1913–31; Chm. and Managing Director, April 1931–March 1932. *Recreations:* motoring, golf, etc. *Address:* Orchardleigh, Beaconsfield. *T:* Beaconsfield 65. *Clubs:* Royal Automobile; Beaconsfield Golf.

Died 9 Oct. 1943.

VAN LOON, Hendrik Willem, PhD; historian; s of Hendrik Willem van Loon and Johanna Hanken, both born in Rotterdam; m 1907, Eliza Bowditch; two s. *Educ:* private schools in Holland; Cornell University, Harvard University, University of Munich. Went to United States at age of 21; after graduation entered service of the Associated Press; worked in Russia during 1906 revolution, Moscow, Petersburg, and Warsaw; then Munich; then taught history until beginning of European War when reentered Service, beginning with siege of Antwerp; accident obliged his return to America, 1917; entered business, but since 1921 has devoted himself entirely to writing. *Publications:* The Fall of the Dutch Republic, 1913; The Rise of the Dutch Kingdom, 1915; The Golden Book of the Dutch Navigators, 1916; A Short History of Discovery, 1917; Ancient Man, 1920; The Story of Mankind, 1921; The Story of the Bible, 1923; The Story of Wilbur the Hat, 1925; Tolerance, 1925; America, 1927; Adriaen Block, 1928; Life and Times of Pieter Stuyvesant, 1928; Man

the Miracle Maker, 1928; Rembrandt van Rijn, 1930; Van Loon's Geography, 1932; An Elephant up a Tree, 1933; An Indiscreet Itinerary, 1933; Ships, 1935; Around the World with the Alphabet, 1935; Air-Storming, 1935; The Songs we Sing, 1936; The Arts, 1937; Christmas Carols, 1937; Folksongs of many Lands, 1938; Our Battle, 1939; The Last of the Troubadours, 1939; The Songs America Sings, 1939; The Pacific, 1940; Invasion, 1940; Life and Times of Johann Sebastian Bach, 1940; Good Tidings, 1941; Intro. to Praise of Folly, 1942; Lives, 1942; Christmas Songs, 1942; Message of the Bells, 1942; Thomas Jefferson, 1943; Simón Bolivar, 1943; and translations of these different books. *Recreations:* violin playing and etching. *Address:* Old Greenwich, Connecticut, USA. *Clubs:* Harvard, Players', New York.

Died 10 March 1944.

VANS AGNEW, Lt-Col John, of Barnbarroch and Sheuchan, OBE; DL, JP, FRGS; b 23 Aug. 1859; m 1879, Ada Sybil (d 1941), d of R. Bates. S Lancs Regt 28th Light Cavalry, Indian Army; Scottish Horse, 25 Aug. 1914; served Burmese War; S African War (three medals, eight clasps, despatches); commanded 2/2 Scottish Horse, Yeomanry, Aug. 1914–Nov. 1917, France, Feb. 1916 (War medal, Victory medal, OBE). *Recreations:* science, travel, shooting, fishing, golf. *Address:* Barnbarroch, Wigtownshire. *Club:* Cavalry.

Died 7 Oct. 1943.

VAN SOMEREN, William Taylor, CIE 1898; Consulting Administrative Officer, King Edward Memorial Hospital, Ealing, W13; b 1855; s of Surgeon-General W. J. Van Someren, IMS; m Alice Beatrice, d of Leonard Bean, Public Works Dept, Punjab; two s three d. Served Afghan War, 1878–79 (medal); Hazara, 1888; Hazara, 1901; Waziristan, 1894–95 (frontier medal with 3 clasps, despatches); Tochi, 1897; Samana and Tirah, 1897–98 (new frontier medal 3 clasps, despatches); China Expeditionary Force, 1900–01 (medal and clasp, despatches); retired as Officiating Postmaster-General, Bombay Presidency, 1910; La Médaille de Roi Albert (Roi des Belges), 1920. *Address:* 31 Colebrooke Avenue, W13. *T:* Perivale 2748.

Died 22 Aug. 1944.

VAN STRAUBENZEE, Brig.-Gen. Casimir Henry Claude, CB 1916; CBE 1919; Retired List; b 30 Jan. 1864; s of Lt-Col Frederick van Straubenzee, 13th Somerset LI; m Evelyn, d of Robert Bell. *Educ:* Sherborne School. Served European War, 1914–17 (despatches, CB). *Address:* 18 Basil Mansions, Knightsbridge, SW. *T:* Kens. 6869. *Club:* Army and Navy.

Died 23 Feb. 1943.

VARLEY-HAIGH, Ernest; *see* Haigh.

VARRIER-JONES, Sir Pendrill Charles, Kt 1931; MA (Cantab), FRCP (Lond.); Founder and Director, Papworth Village Settlement, Cambridge; Hon. Consulting Tuberculosis Officer, County of Cambridge; Hon. Medical Director, Enham Village Centre for Disabled ex-Service Men, Andover, 1927, Director since 1934; Member of Medical Council, People's League of Health; Fellow, Royal Society of Medicine; Member, Central Council for the Care of Cripples; President Wycliffe College; Chairman of Rehabilitation Committee, International Union against Tuberculosis; Member of Council, Colonie Franco-Britanniques de Sillery; b 24 Feb. 1883; o s of Dr Charles Morgan Jones and Margaret, d of late William Jenkins. *Educ:* Epsom College; Wycliffe College, Stonehouse; St John's College, Cambridge (Foundation Scholar and Prizeman, 1st Class Natural Science Tripos); BA, 1905, MA 1909; St Bartholomew's Hospital. House Physician and Wix Prizeman St Bartholomew's Hospital. Engaged in Research at Cambridge University Medical Schools; Acting Tuberculosis Officer, County of Cambridge;

founded, with Sir German Sims-Woodhead and Sir T. Clifford-Allbutt, the Cambridgeshire Tuberculosis Colony, at Bourn, 1915; Hon. Medical Director, 1915; Medical Director, Papworth Village Settlement, 1918, Member of Tuberculin Committee, Medical Research Council, 1921; Hon. Medical Director, British Legion Village, 1925–27, during re-organisation, and Peamount Village Settlement, Dublin, 1930–35; Mitchell Lecturer, RCP Lond., 1927; MRCP, 1929; FRCP, 1934; Parkes-Weber Prize, 1939. *Publications:* Tuberculosis and the Working Man, 1916; Investigations on Clinical Thermometry (Lancet) with Sir German Sims-Woodhead, 1916; Industrial Colonies and Village Settlements for the Consumptive (with Sir German Sims-Woodhead), 1920; The Cellular Content of Milk (Lancet), 1924; An Investigation of the Treatment of Pulmonary Tuberculosis by Dreyers Diaplyte Vaccine (with L. B. Stott, MB), 1924; Papworth-Administrative and Economic Problems in Tuberculosis (with Sir T. Clifford-Allbutt, KCB, etc. and Sir German Sims-Woodhead), in 1925; The Significance of Temperature Variations in Tuberculous Disease, 1927; occasional contributions to Medical Press. *Address:* Papworth Hall, Cambridge; Bryntirion, Hereford. *T:* Caxton 271, Hereford 2510. *Clubs:* Athenæum, Royal Automobile.

Died 30 Jan. 1941.

VASEY, Maj.-Gen. George Alan, CB 1943; CBE 1941; DSO 1918; Australian Staff Corps; Comd 7 Aust. Div.; *b* 1895; 3rd *s* of late G. B. Vasey, Barrister-at-law, Melbourne; *m* 1921, Jessie, *e d* of J. Halbert, Melbourne; two *s. Educ:* Wesley College, Melbourne; Royal Military College of Australia. Served European War, 1915–18 (DSO, despatches twice); War of 1939–45 (CBE, Bar to DSO, CB). *Address:* Mountain Highway, Wantirna, Vic., Australia. *Clubs:* Australian, Army, Navy, and Air Force, Melbourne.

Died 5 March 1945.

VASSAR-SMITH, Sir John George Lawley, 2nd Bt *cr* 1917; *b* 10 Dec. 1868; *s* of 1st Bt and Mary, *d* of John Partridge, Malvern; *S* father, 1922. *Educ:* Cheltenham College; Trinity College, Cambridge, BA. Served Boer War; European War with 2nd Canadian Division. *Recreation:* reading. *Heir: nephew* Richard Rathborne [*b* 24 Nov. 1909; *m* Mary-Dawn Woods; one *s*]. *Address:* Keynsham Villa, Cheltenham.

Died 2 May 1942.

VAUGHAN, Col Charles Jerome, OBE; FZS; late 7th Dragoon Guards, now retd Major R. Monmouthshire RE; Hon. Col R. Monmouth RE (SR) since 1938; *b* 30 Sept. 1873; *s* of late Col F. B. Vaughan and Caroline Ruth, *d* of Charles Alexander Pope, of St Louis, USA, *nephew* of late Cardinal Vaughan; *m* 1908, Florence, 3rd *d* of Sir Cecil Lister-Kaye, 4th Bt; one *s. Educ:* Oratory School, Edgbaston. Private Chamberlain to Pius X, Benedict XV, Pius XI and Pius XII. Served S African War (dangerously wounded); European War on Staff (despatches thrice, OBE); Adjutant to 4 regts of Cavalry: Royals, Greys, Bays and 7th DG's for Coronation of King Edward VII; Gold Staff Officer for Coronations of Kings George V and VI; Member Order of St Maurice and St Lazarus (Italy): DL Monmouthshire; High Sheriff of Herefordshire, 1933; JP Monmouthshire and Herefordshire; Lord of the Manors of Ruardean and Welsh Bicknor. *Recreations:* shooting, fishing, racing (formerly hunting). *Address:* Courtfield, Ross, Herefordshire. *Clubs:* Cavalry, MCC, English-Speaking Union.

Died 30 Jan. 1948.

VAUGHAN, Hon. Crawford; Hon. Secretary British-American Co-operation, 1936–38; *b* Adelaide, South Australia, 1874; *s* of Alfred Vaughan, retired Civil Servant; *m* 1st, Evelyn Maria (*d* 1927), *d* of late Thomas Goode; one *d*; 2nd, 1934, Millicent Preston-Stanley, *d* of late Francis Stanley and Fannie Preston-Stanley. *Educ:* State schools; Prince Alfred College. Member (Lab) for District Torrens, House of Assembly, South Australia, 1905; Whip, 1909; Treasurer and Commissioner, Crown Lands, 1910–12; Leader of State Opposition and Labour Party, 1913; Premier, Treasurer, Minister of Education, 1915–17; Member for District of Sturt, 1915–18; Member of British War Mission to USA under late Lord Reading 1917–18; honorary representative Commonwealth of Australia in USA 1918; Managing Director British Cotton-Growing Association, Ltd, 1921–24; delivered Lowell lecturers, Boston, 1920, on Australian Industrial Legislation.

Died Dec. 1947.

VAUGHAN, Herbert Millingchamp, JP, FSA; *b* 1870; *e s* of late John Vaughan, JP, of Llangoedmore, Cardiganshire. *Educ:* Clifton College; Keble College, Oxford, MA. High Sheriff, Cardiganshire, 1916; corr. member various learned societies; Member of Advisory Board of Ancient Monuments (Wales). *Publications:* Last of the Royal Stuarts, 1906; The Naples Rivera, 1907; The Medici Popes, 1908; Essays on the Welsh Church, 1908; The Last Stuart Queen, 1910; Florence and her Treasures, 1911; An Australasian Wander-Year, 1914; Meleager: a Fantasy, 1916; The Dial of Ahaz, 1917; Sonnets of Italy and other Poems, 1919; Welsh Book-Plates, 1920; a contributor to the Encyclopædia Britannica (1911 and 1929 editions); The South Wales Squires, 1926; Nephelococcygia: or Letters from Paradise, 1929; Studies in the Italian Renaissance, 1930; From Anne to Victoria, 1931; Catalogue of Aneurin Williams Book Plates, 1938. *Recreations:* reading, travel, and bridge. *Address:* 32 Victoria Street, Tenby. *Club:* Marlborough-Windham.

Died 31 July 1948.

VAUGHAN, Col Herbert Radclyffe, CBE 1919; *b* 1864; 2nd *s* of late Capt. Herbert Vaughan, 68th Regt, Brynog, Felinfach, Cardiganshire; *m* 1902, Amy (*d* 1942), *e d* of late Rev. W. G. Boyce, Dublin. Served NW Frontier, India, 1908; European War, 1914–19 (despatches, CBE). *Recreation:* golf. *Address:* Elkaduwa, Berwick Road, Bournemouth. *T:* Bournemouth 3782. *Club:* Army and Navy.

Died 8 Dec. 1947.

VAUGHAN, Lt-Gen. Sir Louis (Ridley), KCB 1928; KBE 1922; CB 1918; DSO 1915; psc Indian Army, retired; *b* 7 Aug. 1875; 2nd *s* of late Cedric Vaughan, JP, Leyfield House, Millom, Cumberland; *m* 1913, Emilie Kate Desmond Deane. *Educ:* Uppingham; RMC, Sandhurst; Staff College, Cmaberley. Entered army, 1895; Captain, Indian Army, 1904; Major, 1913; General Staff Officer, India, 1910–12; 3rd grade, War Office, 1912–14; 2nd grade, 1914; 1st grade, 1915; Brig.-Gen. 1916; Maj.-Gen. 1917; Lt-Gen. 1926; served European War, 1914–18 (CB, DSO, Bt Lt-Col and Col, Maj.-Gen. 1918, despatches nine times, 1914 Star); served third Afghan War in command 4th War Division, July–Sept. 1919 (despatches, medal and clasp); Commandant of the Staff College, Quetta, 1919–22; commanded Central Provinces District, 1923–24; Rawalpindi District, 1925–26; retired, 1928; Officier of the Légion d'Honneur. *Address:* Broadmead, Folkestone. *T:* Cheriton 85455.

Died 7 Dec. 1942.

VAUGHAN, Sir Robert, KBE 1937; *b* 18 Sept. 1866; *s* of John and Eleanor Anne Vaughan, Nannau, Dolgelly; *m* 1904, Patricia Steuart, *d* of Sir Frederic Goldsmid, KCSI, CB; no *c. Educ:* Eton; Downton Agricultural College. Life-long farming; ten years County Branch NFU Delegate to Head Quarters; Alderman Merioneth County Council; Vice-Chairman Merioneth Quarter Sessions; JP, DL; Supervising Recruiting Officers

Merioneth and Montgomery during first part of War, etc. *Recreation:* general country sports. *Address:* Garthmaelan, Dolgelly.

Died 16 Jan. 1941.

VAUGHAN, Maj.-Gen. Robert Edward, CB 1918, Indian Army, retired; *b* 12 Aug. 1866; *s* of T. H. Vaughan, Felhampton, Craven Arms, Salop; *m* 1890, Amy Woodward, *d* of W. P. Woodward; one *s* one *d.* *Educ:* Woodbridge; Clifton; Sandhurst. 2nd Lieut Norfolk Regt 1887; joined Bengal Staff Corps, 11th Rajputs; transferred to Supply and Transport Corps; Assist QMG for Transport and Deputy Director of Transport in India; AA and QMG Indian Cavalry Corps, and DA and QMG Indian Cavalry Corps, 1914–16; DA and QMG 7th Corps BEF 1916; Director Supplies and Transport in Mesopotamia, July–Sept. 1916; Director of Supplies and Transport in India, Oct. 1916; retired 1920; served in China, 1900–01 (medal and clasp, Bt-Maj.); European War (despatches, Bt Col, CB, 1914 Star); Maj.-Gen. 1920; Col Commandant Indian AS Corps. *Publication:* (joint author) Dairy Manual, India. *Address:* c/o Holt & Co., Kirkland House, Whitehall, SW1.

Died 4 May 1946.

VAUGHAN-SAWYER, Ethel, MD, BS Lond.; Honours in Surgery and Medicine; Gynæcologist; Consulting Gynæcologist, Royal Free Hospital; retired on account of blindness; *b* 6 July 1868; *d* of Cedric Vaughan, JP, Millom, Cumberland; *m* Captain Henry Vaughan-Sawyer (*d* 1914), IA, *s* of Col George Sawyer, IA. *Educ:* Lausanne; Univ. College, London; London School of Medicine for Women. Assistant Medical Officer, Camberwell Infirmary, 1897–98; Pathologist Royal Free Hospital, 1899–1902; Assistant Physician, Diseases of Women, and Assistant Obstetrician Royal Free Hospital, 1902–08; Senior Gynæcologist and Obstetrician, 1908–28; London University Lecturer in Gynæcology, 1902–29; FRSM. *Address:* Bolney Court, Bolney, near Haywards Heath, Sussex.

Died 9 March 1949.

VAUX, Sir Richard Augustus, Kt 1937; *b* 19 Sept. 1869; *o surv. s* of late William Sandys Wright Vaux, FRS, and Louisa, *d* of late Francis Rivington; unmarried. *Educ:* Lancing College; Lincoln College, Oxford. BA 1892; MA 1899. Called to Bar, Lincolns Inn, 1896; Law Degree, Paris University, 1902; entered service of Egyptian Government, 1903; Judge in Native Tribunals, 1905; Judge in Mixed Tribunal of Alexandria, 1909; promoted to Mixed Court of Appeal, 1920; Pres. Mixed Court of Appeal, Alexandria, Egypt, 1932–39; Grand Cordon of the Order of the Nile, 1938. *Address:* (temp.): at Thornbury, Frant, Sussex. *Club:* Oxford and Cambridge.

Died 11 Nov. 1946.

VEIDT, Conrad; *b* Berlin, 22 Jan. 1893; *m*; one *s. Educ:* Berlin High School. Pupil of Max Reinhardt. *Films* include: Caligari, Student of Prague, The Beloved Rogue, The Man Who Laughs, Jerusalem, A Man's Past, Eric The Great, Black Hussar, FPI, NJU, Hands of Orlac, The Last Company, Congress Dances, Rome Expres, Cape Forlorn, I was a Spy, The Wandering Jew, Jew Suss, The Passing of the Third Floor Back, Dark Journey, Spy in Black, Thief of Bagdad, The Conjurer.

Died 3 April 1943.

VEITCH, George Stead, MA, LittD; Andrew Geddes and John Rankin Professor of Modern History, University of Liverpool, since 1923; *b* Rochdale, 22 Nov. 1885; *e s* of late Rev. R. Veitch, MA; *m* 1919, Janet Inches (BA Liverpool, MA 1927, PhD 1932). *Educ:* Liverpool Institute High School; University of Liverpool; Sorbonne, Paris; First Class Honours, School of History, 1906; Charles Beard Research Fellow, 1906–07; University Fellow, 1907–08. Assistant Lecturer in Modern History, 1909; Lecturer, 1915; Senior Lecturer, 1919; in charge of the Dept of Modern

History, 1913–14 and 1915–19; External Examiner in History, University Birmingham, 1918, 1920–22, Reading, 1934–36, London, 1934–37; Examiner in the Final Honour School of Modern History, Oxford, 1926–28; Secretary to the University Extension Board, Univ. of Liverpool, 1920–23. *Publications:* The Genesis of Parliamentary Reform, 1913; Empire and Democracy (1837–1913), 1914; History of the British People (1815–1914), 1925; Huskisson and Liverpool, 1929; The Struggle for the Liverpool and Manchester Railway, 1930; articles and reviews. *Address:* 8 Brompton Avenue, Liverpool 17. *Clubs:* University, Athenæum, Liverpool.

Died 23 June 1943.

VENABLES, Harry Archbutt, CBE 1920; ISO 1916; *b* 23 July 1858; *s* of late John Venables of Kinderton, Cheshire; *m* 1886, Florence, *d* of late Charles Baretti of Ashford, Kent; two *s* three *d. Educ:* privately. Served for a short period in the Civil Service Commission and the Admiralty; joined the War Office, 1877; became Assistant Principal (Acting) of the Pension Branch; transferred to the Ministry of Pensions as a Principal, 1917; Deputy Director-General of Finance (Acting), 1918; was in charge of the Widows' and Dependants' Branch from the first day of European War until Armistice Day; retired on pension, 1920; OBE 1918. *Address:* 3 Marine Parade, Bognor Regis Sussex.

Died 13 Nov. 1944.

VENKATA REDDI NAIDU, Sir Kurma, Rai Bahadur, KCIE 1937; Kt 1923; Vice-Chancellor, Annamalai University, Annamalainagar; Member of Madras Legislative Council since 1937; *b* 1875; *m* 1896, R. Laxmi Kantamma; three *s* two *d. Educ:* Arts College, Rajahmundry; The Madras Christian College; Madras Law College, BA Madras University, 1895; BL 1900. Professor of Physics in the Arts College, Rajahmundry, 1895; joined the Madras Bar, 1900; Member and Vice-President, Polavarum Taluk Board, 1901–04; Member District Board, Godavery, 1901–04; Member Municipal Council, Rajahmundry, 1901–04; Chairman Municipal Council, Rajahmundry, 1903; Member Municipal Council, Ellore, 1906–15; President Ellore Taluk Board, 1912–20; Member Krishna District Board, 1912–20; led the Non-Brahmin deputation before the Joint Parliamentary Committee on Indian Constitutional Reforms, 1919; Member of the Imperial Legislative Council, 1920; Minister for Agriculture and Industries in the Madras Government, 1920–23; Member of the Madras Legislative Council, 1920–26; Member of the Senate of the Madras University, 1924–26; Member of the Syndicate of the Andhra University, 1924–26; Chairman Board of Visitors, Indian Institute of Science, Bangalore, 1924–28; Special Lecturer on Indian Constitutional Law, Madras Law College, 1927–28; Agent of Government of India in South Africa, 1929–32; Member of Council of State, 1933–34; Member of Governor's Executive Council, Madras, 1934–37; Acting Governor of Madras, June–Oct. 1936; Prime Minister, Government of Madras, April–July 1937; Indian Delegate to the Assembly of the League of Nations, Geneva, 1928. *Address:* Kurma House, Thyagarayanagar, Madras, S India. *Clubs:* Cosmopolitan, Madras; Ootacamund, Ootacamund; Orient, Durban.

Died Sept. 1942.

VERITY, Rev. Heron Beresford; retired. Ordained, 1903; Rector of St Peter's, Orange Walk, British Honduras, 1903–06; Christ Church, Guatemala, 1907–09; Christ Church, Stann Creek, 1909–10; Rector of St Paul, Corozal, 1906–07 and 1910–18; Canon, British Honduras Cathedral, 1909–18; Rector of St Thomas-ye-Vale Parish Church and of Holy Trinity, Linstead, 1918–22; Rector St Saviour's, Chichester, Jamaica, 1922–25. *Address:* Ivah, Mandeville, Jamaica, BW1.

Died 25 Jan. 1940.

VERNEY, Sir Harry Lloyd, GCVO 1936 (KCVO 1927; CVO, 1917; MVO 1909); Extra Groom in Waiting to King George VI since 1936; *b* 23 Jan. 1872; *s* of late Col Lloyd-Verney and Mrs Lloyd-Verney of Clochfaen, and *g s* of late Rt Hon. Sir Harry Verney, 2nd Bart; *m* 1899, Lady Joan E. M. Cuffe, an Extra Woman of the Bedchamber to Queen Mary, *e d* of 5th Earl of Desart, KP, PC, KCB and Lady Margaret, *d* of 4th Earl of Harewood; three *s. Educ:* Eton. Hon. Attaché in Diplomatic Service; Assistant Private Secretary to Marquess of Lansdowne, Secretary of State for Foreign Affairs; a Gentleman Usher to the King, 1905–07; Deputy Master of HM Household, 1907–11; Groom in Waiting to King George V, 1911–31, an Extra Groom in Waiting, 1931–35, and to King Edward VIII; Private Secretary to the Queen, 1919–35, and Treasurer, 1932–35; Private Home Guard, 1940 and 1941; Legion of Honour and other Foreign Decorations. *Address:* 33 Hyde Park Gate, SW7. *T:* Western 1890. *Clubs:* St James', Turf.

Died 28 Feb. 1950.

VERNON, Harold Anselm Bellamy, CSI 1930; CIE 1929; ICS retired; *b* 12 Sept. 1874; *s* of late Rev. Prebendary I. R. Vernon; *m* Rhona Warre (*d* 1938), *d* of Admiral Sir Edmond Warre Slade; two *s. Educ:* Clifton College; St John's College, Oxford. Entered ICS, 1898; Private Secretary to Governor of Madras, 1911; Secretary, Indian Marine Committee, 1912; Collector and District Magistrate, 1914–21; Member of Legislative Assembly, 1924; Resident of South Indian States, 1925; Member of Council of State, 1927; Member of Board of Revenue, Madras, 1928–32; retired 1932. *Publication:* Notes on Salt Manufacture, translated from Italian. *Recreations:* fishing, hunting, shooting, weaving. *Clubs:* Royal Automobile; County, Taunton.

Died 8 Dec. 1945.

VERNON, Brig.-Gen. Henry Albemarle, DSO 1916; JP; *b* 5 Dec. 1879; *e s* of H. C. E. Vernon, ICE; *m* 1916, Maud Valerie, *o c* of Maj.-Gen. J. G. Turner, CB; one *s* one *d. Educ:* Wellington College; Sandhurst. Joined KR Rifles, 1900; 2nd Batt. South Africa, May 1900 (Queen's medal and clasp); Capt. 1910; Maj. 1915; temp. Lt-Col Jan. 1916; Lt-Col 1920; Col 1922; ADC to C-in-C in India, 1914; France, Oct. 1914, OC Signal Squadron, Indian Cavalry Corps; 2nd in command 1st KRR, Dec. 1915; commanded Sportsman's Bn, 23rd RF, 1916–17; commanded 158th Infantry Brigade in Palestine, 1917, to end of campaign (Chevalier Légion d'honneur, DSO, despatches twice, Bt Lt-Col, Order of the Nile, 3rd Class); transferred to Royal Corps of Signals, 1920; retired with hon. rank of Brigadier-General, 1933. *Address:* Eyhorne Cottage, Hollingbourne, Kent. *T:* Hollingbourne 12.

Died 27 Oct. 1943.

VERNON, Roland Venables, CB 1924; 3rd *s* of G. V. Vernon, Osborne Place, Old Trafford, Manchester; *m* 1913, Marjorie, *d* of A. L. Leon, Stoatley Rough, Haslemere; one *d. Educ:* Clifton; Balliol College, Oxford (Scholar and Jenkyns Exhibitioner); Craven University Scholar, proxime accessit Hertford Scholarship, 1897; 1st class literæ humaniores, 1899. Colonial Office, 1900; on special service West Indies, 1903; South African Union medal, 1910; Private Secretary to Lord Denman, Governor-General of Australia, 1911–13; on special service British Solomon Islands, 1912; member of Anglo-French Commission on New Hebrides, 1914; transferred to Treasury, 1914; Assistant General Secretary, Ministry of Munitions, 1915–18; on special service, France and Belgium, 1917; Assistant Secretary, Irish National Convention, 1917–18; Deputy Accountant-General, Board of Education, 1920–21; returned to Colonial Office, 1921; on special service, Egypt and Palestine, 1921–22; at Lausanne for Turkish Treaty negotiations, 1922–23; British Agent for case before Permanent Court of International Justice at the

Hague, Feb. 1925; appointed on financial mission to Iraq for British and Iraq Governments, 1925; represented British and Iraq Governments in Ottoman Public Debt negotiations, Paris, 1925; Financial Adviser to Government of Iraq, 1925–28; Member of British Delegation, International Labour Conference, Geneva, 1929, 1930, 1935, and 1936; retired from Colonial Office, 1937; Chairman Advisory Committee for East London of Assistance Board, 1938; member of Governing Body of Imperial College of Science and Technology, 1941. *Address:* Lawn House, Hampstead Square, NW3. *Clubs:* Alpine, Reform.

Died 4 Nov. 1942.

VERNON-WENTWORTH, Captain Frederick Charles Ulick, CB 1919; RN; JP, DL; a Director of Mann, Egerton & Co. Ltd; *b* 1866; *s* of late Thomas F. C. Vernon-Wentworth, of Wentworth Castle, near Barnsley; *m* 1899, Mary Emily, *d* of late Lt-Gen. John Christopher Guise, VC, CB. High Sheriff, Suffolk, 1912; served Egyptian War, 1882; European War, 1914–19 (despatches, CB). *Address:* Blackheath, Saxmundham, Suffolk.

Died 21 Sept. 1947.

VERULAM, 4th Earl of; James Walter Grimston; Baronet, 1628; Baron Forrester, (Scotland), 1633; Baron Dunboyne, and Viscount Grimston (Ireland), 1719; Baron Verulam, (Great Britain), 1790; Viscount Grimston and Earl of Verulam (United Kingdom), 1815; electrical engineer; Chairman Enfield Cables, Ltd; *b* 17 April 1880; *e s* of 3rd Earl and Margaret Frances, *d* of Sir Frederic Ulric Graham, 3rd Bt, and Hermione, *d* of 12th Duke of Somerset; S father, 1924; *m* 1909, Lady Violet Brabazon (*d* 1936), *y d* of 12th Earl of Meath; two *s* (and two killed in action). *Educ:* Eton; Christ Church, Oxford. Rowed in Eton Eight, 1898 and 1899; Oxford Eight, 1900. *Heir: e s* Lord Forrester. *Address:* Gorhambury, St Albans, Herts. *Clubs:* St James', Bath.

Died 29 Nov. 1949.

VESEY, Col Hon. Thomas Eustace; late Irish Guards; *b* 21 Dec. 1885; *s* of Captain Hon. Eustace Vesey and Constance, *d* of 3rd Baron Wenlock; *m* 1911, Lady Cecily Browne, 2nd *d* of 5th Earl of Kenmare; one *s* two *d.* Formerly Commanded Irish Guards. *Address:* Parkhill, Englefield Green, Surrey. *T:* Egham 139. *Club:* Turf.

Died 1 Feb. 1946.

VIAL, Rev. Frank Gifford, MA, BD; DCL; *b* Quebec, 1872, of Huguenot ancestry; *s* of Rev. W. S. Vial; *m* Susan Isabel Ready, *d* of late Lieut-Col Ready, of 71st Highland Light Infantry. *Educ:* Quebec High School; QHS Silver Medallist; University of Bishop's College, Lennoxville (BA 1st Class Classical Honours), 1892; Mackie Essay Prizeman, 1895; MA 1901; BD 1905; DCL 1925. Ordained, 1897; Priest, 1898; Curate of Stanstead, 1897; Sherbrooke, 1898–1901; Incumbent of Fitch Bay and Georgeville, 1901–06; Windsor Mills, 1906–07; Lecturer in Classics, University of Bishop's College, Lennoxville, Canada, 1907–10, Professor of Pastoral Theology and Warden of the Divinity House, 1910–35. *Publications:* Three Measures of Meal: A Study in Religion, 1923; articles on theological and literary subjects. *Recreations:* golf, chess.

Died 20 Oct. 1948.

VICARS, Edward Robert Eckersall, CBE 1918; *b* Rugby, 6 March 1869; *m* 1898, Evelyn, *d* of Edward A. Scott of The Lawn, Rugby. *Educ:* Rugby. Clerk in the Foreign Office, 1889; Acting 3rd Secretary at HM Legation at Athens in 1895, 1897, 1898, and 1901–05; Acting 2nd Secretary at HM Embassy at Constantinople, 1896; Secretary to British Delegates at Hydrographical Conference at Stockholm, June–July 1899, and at Conference at Brussels on Protection of Industrial Property, 1900; Assistant Clerk in the Foreign Office, 1903; HM Consul at Madeira, 1905; Lyons, 1907; Coronation Medal, 1911; Consul-General, Lyons, 1916;

Consul-General at Marseilles, 1919; retired on a pension, 1923. *Address:* Villa Carraia, 21 Via San Leonardo, Florence.

Died 9 Aug. 1949.

VICTOR, Rt Rev. Dennis; *b* 4 Jan. 1882; *s* of Henry Ernest and Edith Caroline Victor; unmarried. *Educ:* St Chad's College, Denstone; Hatfield College, Durham. Deacon, 1905; Priest, 1906; at Church of the Ascension, Victoria Docks (Felsted School Mission) 1905–08; joined Universities Mission to Central Africa, 1908, Diocese of Nyasaland; Principal of Teachers Training College, 1912–25; Canon of Likoma Cathedral, 1922; Archdeacon of Shire, 1932; Bishop of Lebombo, 1936–47. *Address:* 31 Castle St, Hereford.

Died 7 Jan. 1949.

VIENER, Rev. Harry Dan Leigh, CBE 1919; Licensed to officiate in the Dioceses of Chichester, Winchester, Portsmouth, and Guildford; *b* Blackpool, 26 Dec. 1868; *s* of Adolph Moritz and Kate Urquhart Viener; *m* 1925, Violet Margaret, 2nd *d* of P. E. F. Keatch of Twickenham and India. *Educ:* Malvern Coll.; St John's Coll., Oxford. Casberd Exhibitioner, BA 1892, MA 1907; Schoolmaster and Private Tutor, 1892–99; Deacon, 1899; Priest, 1900; Curate St Peter's, Walsall, 1899–1901; Chaplain RN 1901; served in numerous ships; lent to RAF, May 1918, to organise their Chaplaincy Service; Permanent Commission as Chap.-in-Chief, Oct. 1918; Chaplain-in-Chief, 1918–26; Hon. Chaplain to the King, 1924; Retired List, 1926; Messina medal and Order of Crown of Italy for services at Earthquake at Messina, 1908; served European War in HMS Prince of Wales in Channel and Mediterranean (Dardanelles); Rector of Chawton, Hants, 1927–34. *Recreations:* tennis, shooting, motoring, yachting, etc. *Address:* 16 Alinora Avenue, Goring by Sea, Sussex. *T:* Goring 41126.

Died 7 May 1947.

VIGORS, Edward Cliffe, CB 1936; JP; High Sheriff, Co. Carlow, 1916; Member of Representative Church Body and of Board of Widows and Orphans Fund of Church of Ireland; Governor and Hon. Secretary of Inc. Society of Schools in Ireland; *e s* of late T. M. C. Vigors of Burgage, Co. Carlow, and Mary Louisa Handcock; *m* 1914, Mary Selina, *d* of late Lieut-Gen. Henry Ellenborough Dyneley. *Educ:* Charterhouse (scholar); Christ Church, Oxford (Holford Exhibitioner). Late Examiner of Standing Orders, House of Lords and House of Commons, Principal Clerk of Committees, House of Lords, and Secretary to the Ecclesiastical Committee. *Address:* Burgage, Co. Carlow. *Clubs:* Kildare Street, Dublin.

Died 6 March 1945.

VILLARD, Oswald Garrison; journalist; Editor, the New York Nation, 1918–33, owner, 1918–35; *b* 13 March 1872; *s* of Henry Villard and Fanny Garrison; *g s* of William Lloyd Garrison, the Abolitionist; *m* 1903, Julia Breckinridge Sandford, of Covington, Ky; two *s* one *d. Educ:* Harvard University; AB, 1893; AM, 1896; LittD Washington and Lee University, 1906; LLD Lafayette College, Pennsylvania, 1915, Howard University, 1933, University of Oregon, 1935. Assistant in US History, Harvard, 1894–96; Reporter Philadelphia Press, 1896–97; Editorial Writer, Owner and President, New York Evening Post, 1897–1918; sold the property, 1918; Founder of Yachting; Proprietor Nautical Gazette, 1918–36. *Publications:* John Brown; A Biography Fifty Years After, 1910; Germany Embattled, 1915; Newspapers and Newspaper Men, 1923, 2nd edition 1926; Prophets, True and False, 1928; Russia from a Car Window, 1930; The German Phœnix, 1933; Fighting Years, Memoirs of a Liberal Editor, 1939; Our Military Chaos, 1939; Inside Germany, 1939; The Disappearing Daily, 1944; Free Trade—Free World, 1947; and numerous articles in American magazines. *Recreations:*

travel, motoring. *Address:* 79 East 79 Street, New York City 21, USA. *Clubs:* Harvard, Century (New York); Cosmos (Washington).

Died 1 Oct. 1949.

VILLASANTE, Prof. Julian Martinez-Villasante y Navarro, LLD, Madrid; *b* Madrid, 1876; *m* 1899, Mary Murphy; one *s* two *d. Educ:* College of the Escolapios, Madrid; University of Santiago and University of Madrid. Teacher of the Spanish language and literature, Cambridge University, 1909–17; Senior Lecturer, Dept of Spanish Studies, King's College, University of London, 1913–36; retired, 1936; European War, Press Bureau Propaganda work, etc.; Examiner London University; Civil Service Commission, Royal Society of Arts, University of Reading, The London County Council, The London Chamber of Commerce, The Institution of Civil Engineers; The Incorporated Secretaries Association, etc. *Publications:* contributions to South America, Spanish literary reviews and others. *Recreations:* motoring, gardening. *Address:* Northcote, East Lane, West Horsley, Surrey. *T:* East Horsley 304.

Died 20 Dec. 1945.

VILLENEUVE, Son Éminence le Cardinal J. M. Rodrigue, OMI, DD, DDC, DPh, Archevêque de Québec since 1931, Cardinal since 1933; *b* Sacré-Cœur de Montréal, PQ, 2 Nov. 1883; *s* of Rodrigue Villeneuve, cordonnier, et Marie-Louise Lalonde. *Educ:* Mont-Saint-Louis and Plessis, Montréal; Scolasticat des Pères Oblats, Ottawa, Ont; Oblat de Marie Immaculée, 1903. Prêtre 1907; Professeur de Philosophie, 1907–13; Professeur de Théologie, 1913–20; Docteur en Philosophie, 1919, Supérieur du Scolasticat, 1928; Docteur en Théologie, 1922, Docteur en Droit Canonique, 1930, Université d'Ottawa; Hon. Docteur en Philosophie, Université Laval, 1930; Hon. Docteur en Droit, Université McGill, 1933, Toronto, 1934, Edmonton, 1936; Queen's, Kingston, 1942; premier Évêque de Gravelbourg en Saskatchewan, 1930. *Publications:* L'Un des vôtres, 1927; Le Mariage, 1936; Entretiens liturgiques, 1937; La Messe, 1938; Quelques pierres de doctrine, 1938; Le Saint Baptême, 1940; Le Sacrement de la Confirmation, 1941; La Pénitence, 1942; La Divine Eucharistie, 1942; nombreux articles de philosophie religieuse dans les revues et journaux; lettres pastorales et circulaires. *Address:* Palais Cardinalice, Quebec, Canada.

Died 17 Jan. 1947.

VILLIERS, Lt-Col Charles Hyde, CVO 1941; *e s* of late Rev. Charles Villiers, Croft, Darlington; *m* 1901, Lady Victoria Alexandrina Innes Ker, *d* of 7th Duke of Roxburghe; two *s* four *d. Educ:* Marlborough; Oxford (Honours in History School); Sandhurst. Roy. Horse Guards, 1887–1903; 1st City of London Imperial Yeomanry, 1903–15; Egypt, 1889; German Manœuvres, Hanover, 1889; exploring-surveying expedition in Somaliland, 1891; served as ADC to late Sir Gerald Portal during mission to Uganda, 1893; Mahommedan rebellion, 1893; raised the Uganda Rifles; Unyoro Campaign, 1893–94 (despatches, medal, Zanzibar Star); Matabeleland, 1895; raised the Rhodesia Horse; Jameson Riad, 1896; S Africa, 1899–1900 (raised South African Light Horse, despatches, medal and 3 clasps); contested (LU) South Wolverhampton, 1906; one of HM Body-guard of Hon. Corps of Gentlemen-at-Arms, 1907–39; King George V's Coronation Medal; King George V's Jubilee Medal; King George VI's Coronation Medal; Lt-Colonel, 1907; Commanded the City of London Yeomanry, Mediterranean Expeditionary Force, 1914–15; Commanded 2/1 Suffolk Yeomanry (Southern Army), 1916 (despatches, 1915 Star, two medals and territorial Officer decoration); commanded 7th Yeomanry Cyclist Regt 1917; Director of the Royal Insurance Company, North Rhodesia Company, Rhodesia Copper Company, the Fanti Consolidated Company, East Africa Land and Development

Company. *Address:* Folly Court, Wokingham, Berks. *T:* Wokingham, 41. *Clubs:* Marlborough, Guards', City of London.

Died 23 May 1947.

VINCENT, Frank Arthur Money, CIE 1919; CBE 1926; MVO 1911; CIMechE 1943; Indian Police, retired; *b* 23 Oct. 1875; *s* of late Robert W. E. Hampe-Vincent, CIE; *m* 1st, 1901, Helen (*d* 1930), *d* of late G. E. Trevor-Roper; 2nd, 1930, Elizabeth Ashfield, *d* of late Thomas Gooch Appleton. *Educ:* Dulwich College; City and Guilds Technical College. Joined Indian Police Dept 1895; Superintendent of Police, 1901; held post of Assistant Inspector-General of Police CID Principal Police Training School, 1906–08; Deputy Commissioner of Police CID, Bombay, 1909; Deputy Director Criminal Intelligence, Simla, 1913–16; Commissioner of Police, Bombay, 1916–19; Organising Secretary Indian Section British Empire Exhibition, 1924 (CBE); King's Police Medal, 1910; Controller Indian Section British Empire Exhibition; Administrator Indian Commercial Section Philadelphia International Exposition, 1926; Joint Social Secretary, Indian Round Table Conference, 1930–31; Secretary, Indian Delegation Bureau, 1932–33; Regional Controller, E and W Ridings, Ministry of Aircraft Production, 1940–46. *Address:* Flat 4, Moor Park Club, Rickmansworth, Herts. *T:* 4546. *Club:* Moor Park (Rickmansworth).

Died 21 Oct. 1950.

VINCENT, George Edgar; *b* Rockford, Illinois, 21 March 1864; *s* of John Heyl Vincent, Bishop of the Methodist Episcopal Church, and Elizabeth Dusenbury; *m* 1890, Louise Palmer of Wilkes-Barre, Pa; one *s* two *d*. *Educ:* Yale University, AB 1885; University of Chicago, PhD 1896; LLD Chicago, Yale, 1911, Michigan, 1913, and Minnesota, 1931. Editorial work, 1885–86; in Europe and Orient, 1886–87; Literary editor Chautauqua Press, 1886; Vice-Principal Chautauqua System, 1888–98; Principal of Instruction, 1898; President, Chautauqua Institution, 1907–15, and honorary President since 1915; Fellow in Sociology, 1892–94; Assistant, 1894–95; Instructor, 1895–96; Assistant Professor, 1896–1900; Associate Professor, 1900–04; Professor, 1904–11; Dean Junior Colleges, 1900–07; Dean Faculties of Arts, Literature and Science, University of Chicago, 1907–11; President University of Minnesota, 1911–17 (resigned); President of the Rockefeller Foundation, New York, 1917–29 (retired); Chairman, Hospital Survey Committee of United Hospital Fund, New York City, 1935–36. *Address:* Greenwich, Conn, USA. *Clubs:* Century, Yale, New York; University, Chicago.

Died 1 Feb. 1941.

VINCENT, Brig.-Gen. Henry Osman, CB 1916; CMG 1917; RA; *b* 10 Oct. 1863; *s* of late Rev. R. Vincent, Vicar of Crockham Hill, Kent; *m* Violet Amy (*d* 1939), *d* of late Col H. A. Barker, RA; one *s* one *d*. *Educ:* Haileybury; RMA, Woolwich. Entered Army, 1882; Captain, 1891; Major, 1900; Lt-Col 1911; served European War, 1915–18 (CB, CMG, despatches 4 times); retired pay, 1920. *Club:* United Service.

Died 13 Jan. 1945.

VINCENT, Sir Percy, 1st Bt *cr* 1936; Kt 1927; JP; *b* 1868; *m* 1901, Christine Emily, *d* of George Horatio Board. Sheriff of City of London, 1926–27; Alderman, 1929–42; Lord Mayor, 1935–36. *Address:* Norfolk House, Promenade de Verdun, Purley, Surrey. *T:* Uplands 5577. *Club:* Constitutional.

Died 22 Jan. 1943.

VINCENT, Sir William Henry Hoare, GCIE 1922; KCSI 1918; Kt 1913; LLD (Wales), 1937; *b* 1866; *s* of Rev. James Crawley Vincent, sometime Vicar of Carnarvon; *m* 1889, Grace Minna, *d* of late W. H. Trotter; two *d*. *Educ:* Christ College, Brecon; Trinity College, Dublin. Entered Indian Civil Service, 1887; served in Bengal in various capacities in Executive and Judicial branches; officiated as Judge, Calcutta High Court, 1909 and 1910; Secretary in the Legislative Department, Government of India, 1911–15; Member Executive Council Lt-Gov. of Bihar and Orissa, 1915–17; Member of Mesopotamian Medical Commission, 1916; Member of Governor-General's Council of India, 1917; Vice-President of Council, 1921; Member of Council of India, 1923–31; High Sheriff of Anglesey, 1931; Member of Council of University of Wales, 1937. *Address:* Treborth, Uchaf, Bangor. *Club:* East India and Sports.

Died 17 April 1941.

VIPAN, Alfred, CIE 1938; *b* 9 Nov. 1884; *s* of late Arthur Vipan; *m* 1913, Eulalie May Lushington; one *s* one *d*. *Educ:* Wyggeston School. Joined Public Works Department, India, as Assistant Engineer, 1907; Chief Engineer and Secretary to Government, PWD, Orissa, India, 1936; retired. *Address:* 137 Park West, W2.

Died 24 Jan. 1947.

VISCHER, Sir Hanns, Kt 1941; CMG 1934; CBE 1919; Secretary General (hon.) International Institute of African Languages, London, since 1926; *b* Basel, Switzerland, 14 Sept. 1876; *s* of A. E. Vischer, and R. Sarasin; *m* 1911, Isabelle, *d* of G. de Tscharner, and S. de Watteville; four *s*. *Educ:* Switzerland; Emmanuel College, Cambridge. Church Missionary Society Hausa Mission, 1900–01; Political Service, N Nigeria, 1903–08; Director of Education, 1908–18; Secretary and Member of the Secretary of State's Education Advisory Committee, Colonial Office, 1923–39; African General Service Medal, 1904; crossed Sahara from Tripoli to Lake Chad, 1906; Back Grant, Royal Geog. Society, 1910; Seconded War Office, 1915–18 (Commander Etoile Noire, Légion d'Honneur, Crown of Belgium, Crown of Italy, CBE); demobilised with rank of Major, 1918; represented Colonial Office Phelps-Stokes Education Commission East Africa, 1924; Member, Gordon College Commission of Inspection, 1929; member various learned foreign societies. *Publication:* Across the Sahara, 1910. *Recreations:* rowing, riding, golf. *Address:* Tykeford Lodge, Newport Pagnell, Bucks. *Clubs:* Royal Societies, St James'; Travellers', Paris.

Died 19 Feb. 1945.

VISSANJI, Sir Mathuradas, Kt 1943; DLitt; JP; FRSA 1948; Merchant; *b* 11 April 1881; *s* of late Rao Bahadur Vissanji Khimji; one *s* one *d*. *Educ:* Elphinstone High School, Bombay. Entered business at age of 18 and was trained under his father; The Brokerage and Muccadumage of Bombay Company and Wallace & Co., and the management of Wallace Flour Mills form the centre of his business activities; was chairman and director of various commercial and industrial concerns and was the director, founder, and first president of East India Cotton Assoc.; ex-pres. of Indian Merchants' Chamber, and pres. of many educational and charitable institutions and trustee in numerous others; was a member of Indian Legislative Assembly; has travelled extensively; acknowledged leader of the Hindus in Bombay. *Recreations:* formerly cricket and billiards. *Address:* 9 Wallace Street, Fort, Bombay. *TA:* Filter. *T:* 26281. *Club:* Orient (Bombay).

Died 22 Dec. 1949.

VIVIAN, Lt-Col Valentine, CMG 1918; DSO 1916; MVO 1905; late Grenadier Guards; Clerk of the Cheque and Adjutant, His Majesty's Bodyguard of the Hon. Corps of Gentlemen-at-Arms; *b* 1880; *e s* of late William Vivian, 185 Queen's Gate, SW; *m* 1904, Lady Aline Mary Seymour Dawson-Damer, MBE 1945, *e d* of 5th Earl of Portarlington; two *d*. Served South Africa, 1899–1902 (Queen's medal 3 clasps, King's medal 2 clasps); European War, 1914–18 (despatches, DSO, Bt Lt-Col, CMG); Assistant Military Attaché at Paris,

1920–22; retired pay, 1922. Officer of the Legion of Honour, Croix de Guerre. *Address:* 71 Park Street, W1. *Club:* Brooks's.

Died 1 Feb. 1948.

VIZARD, Brig.-Gen. Robert Davenport, CBE 1919; *b* 19 April 1861; *s* of Henry Brougham Vizard, Blandford, Dorset; *m* 1892, *d* of late T. W. Parker, Blackheath. Served Egyptian Expedition, 1882 (medal, bronze star); South Africa, 1899–1902 (despatches, Queen's medal with three clasps, King's medal with two clasps, Bt Lt-Col); retired pay, 1910; European War, 1914–19 (CBE). *Address:* 2 Donyatt, Mount Street, Taunton, Somerset.

Died 1 Sept. 1941.

VLIELAND, Alice Edith, CBE 1927; *d* of William Millen, Syndale Valley, Faversham, Kent; *m* Charles James Vlieland, MD, JP (*d* 1942); one *s* one *d*. *Educ:* Burleigh House, Margate. President Maternity and Child Welfare Committee and Blanket Society, Exeter Lying-in Charity; Governor Royal Devon and Exeter Hospital, and Girls' Modern School, Exeter; Chairman Conservative and Unionist Association, Exeter, Women's Branch; Vice-President Devon Conservative and Unionist Association. *Address:* 2 Fitzwilliam House, The Green, Richmond, Surrey.

Died 13 July 1944.

VOELCKER, Arthur Francis, MD, FRCP; Consulting Physician, Middlesex Hospital; late Lecturer on Medicine, Middlesex Hospital Medical School; Consulting Physician, Hospital for Sick Children, Great Ormond Street; Hon. Physician, St Luke's Hostel; Consulting Physician, Halwill Cottage Hospital, St Columba Hospital, Home for Working Girls in London, St Saviour's Hospital, Surgical Aid Society and London City Mission; late Maj. RAMC (T); late Hon. Librarian (late President), Medical Society of London; late Examiner in Medicine, Conjoint Board, University of Aberdeen, Society of Apothecaries and University of Birmingham; late President, Section of Medicine, Royal Society of Medicine; *b* 1861; 4th *s* of Dr Aug. Voelcker, FRS; *m* Katharine Isabel English (*d* 1932). *Educ:* University College School and Hospital, London; Berlin; Vienna; Paris. *Recreations:* fishing and shooting. *Address:* Langford Hill, Marhamchurch, Bude, Cornwall. *T:* Widemouth 235. *Clubs:* Fly-fishers', London Athletic.

Died 9 June 1946.

VOGEL, Harry Benjamin; late Chairman of V. V. & V. Ltd, proprietors of John Browning, Spectroscope Makers and Opticians, established 1765; *b* Dunedin, New Zealand, 1868; *e s* of late Hon. Sir Julius Vogel, KCMG, Prime Minister of New Zealand; *m* 1900, Elsa Jessie Geraldine, *e d* of late W. H. Levin, Wellington, NZ; two *s* (eldest killed in action 14 Nov. 1942). *Educ:* Charterhouse. Barrister of Supreme Court of NZ; came to England in 1894; entered into journalism, and until appointment to The People, was the acting editor of the Royal Magazine; editor of The People to 1900; Managing Director Kingswinford Forge Ltd, Steel Sheet Rolling Mills, etc., 1913–23; during War of 1914–18 rolled helmet steel sheet, reducing press-waste from 11% to 0.75%. *Publications:* A Maori Maid; My Dear Sir!; Gentleman Garnet; The Tragedy of a Flirtation; Two Millons; A Village Millionaire (as Richard Kinver); also contributes largely to various magazines. *Recreations:* writing; won the Spencer Cup for Charterhouse in 1885 at Wimbledon.

Died 30 Sept. 1947.

VOGT, Alfred; Professor of Ophthalmology, The University, Zürich, since 1923; *b* Aargau, 31 Oct. 1879; *m* 1906; two *d*. *Educ:* Aarau Oberarzt, Aarau, 1909; Hauptarbeitsgebiet Altersstarforschung (Herausgeber des Hdb. Graefe-Saemisch, Pathologie des Linsensystems); Verfeinerung der Spaltlampenmikroskopie, 1919; Einführung des optischen Schnittes; Lehrbuch und Atl der Spaltlampenmikroskopie des lebenden Auges (Springer 1921 und 1930–31); Einführung des rotfreien Lichts in die Ophthalmoskopie zur Feinuntersuchung der Netzhaut; Experimentelle Untersuchungen über Strahlenwirkungen auf das Auge (Nachweis des Glasmacher-Schmiede und Giesserstars als Ulstrarotstar); Arbeiten über Heilung der Netzhautablösung, Entdeckung des Linsenkapselglaukoms, verschiedener neuer Starformen usw. *Address:* Universitäts-Augenklinik, Zürich, Switzerland.

Died Dec. 1943.

VOGT, Paul Benjamin, GCVO; Hon. LLD, St Andrews; *b* Christiansand, Norway, 1863; *s* of late Cabinet Minister N. Vogt; *m* Daisy, *d* of Colonel Heyerdahl; three *s* six *d*. *Educ:* University of Oslo. Barrister of the Supreme Court of Norway; Cabinet Minister, 1903–05; one of the delegates of Norway at the negotiations with Sweden at Karlstad, 1905; Envoy Extraordinary and Minister Plenipotentiary at Stockholm, 1906–10; Norwegian Envoy Extraordinary and Minister Plenipotentiary to the Court of St James, 1910–34; Member of the Norwegian-American Court of Arbitration at the Hague, 1922; Member of the Danish-Finnish and of the Dutch-Norwegian Commissions of Conciliation; Judge ad hoc at the Permanent Court of International Justice, 1932–33. *Publications:* Indtil 1910, 1940; Elter 1910, 1945. *Address:* Vinderen pr. Oslo.

Died 1 Jan. 1947.

VON DONOP, Maj.-Gen. Sir Stanley (Brenton), KCB 1914; KCMG 1916; CB 1913; Col Commandant Royal Artillery since 1925; *b* 22 Feb. 1860; *s* of Vice-Admiral E. P. B. von Donop; *m* 1888, Alice (*d* 1934), *d* of Rev. Thomas Cox; no *c*. *Educ:* Somersetshire College, Bath; Wimbledon School. Received commission in Royal Artillery, 1880; Captain, 1888; Major, 1897; Bt Lieut-Col 1902; Col 1906; Major-Gen. 1914; served South African War, 1900–02 (despatches, Queen's medal and King's medal, Bt Lt-Col); held the appointments of Professor of Artillery, RM Academy, Woolwich; Superintendent of Experiments, Shoeburyness; Secretary, Ordnance Committee; Chief Instructor, School of Gunnery; Director of Artillery, War Office, 1911–13; Master-General of the Ordnance and 4th Military Member of Army Council, 1913–16; Commander Humber Garrison, 1917–20; Commander of the Order of Leopold (Belgium); Commander of the Legion of Honour, 1917; Order of the Rising Sun (Japan). *Address:* 40 St James' Square, Bath. *T:* Bath 3906. *Clubs:* United Service, MCC; Bath and County, Bath.

Died 17 Oct. 1941.

VON SAUER, Emil; pianist and composer; Leader of the Masterschool for Piano at the Academy in Vienna; *b* Hamburg, 8 Oct. 1862. *Educ:* Pupil of Rubinstein and Liszt. *Compositions:* Suite Moderne, Concertos in E minor, C minor; Sonatas in D and E flat major; 33 Concert-studies for Piano; works for Pianoforte; Songs. *Autobiography:* Meine Welt. *Address:* Vienna IV, Starhemberggasse 4, Austria.

Died 27 April 1942.

VORA, Sir Manmohandas Ramji, Kt 1927; Member of Council of State, 1925–30; *b* 19 Aug. 1857; *s* of Ramji Purshottam Vora; *m* 1872; three *s* three *d*. *Educ:* Bombay High School. Founder of the Indian Merchants' Chamber, Bombay; President, 1907–13, 1924 and 1933; Member of the Committee of the Chamber, 1907–28; Pres. of the Bombay Native Piece Goods Merchants' Assoc. for more than thirty years; Member of the Board of Trustees of the Victoria Jubilee Technical Institute; Member Advisory Committee BB and CI Railway; Member old Bombay Legislative Council representing Indian commercial community, 1910–20; Member Indian Legislative Assembly representing Indian

Merchants' Chamber, Bombay, 1921–23; Member of the Bombay Municipal Corporation for eighteen years, and President, 1912–13; Member Advisory Committee to the Director of Industries. *Recreation:* reading. *Address:* The Ridge, Ridge Road, Malabar Hill, Bombay, India. *TA:* Ghorupdeo, Bombay. *T:* 20181.

Died 13 Aug. 1934.

VOS, Philip; KC 1937; *b* 1891; 2nd *s* of Jack Vos; *m* 1925, Esther, *y d* of late David Bloom; one *s* one *d*. *Educ:* Owen's School; London School of Economics; Caius College, Cambridge. Scholar and Research Student in Economics, Caius College, Cambridge, 1909–14. Served European War, Lieut Norfolk Regiment (Croix de Guerre, avec palme); Assistant Director of Priority, War Office, 1917–18; Barrister-at-law, Inner Temple, 1921. *Publications:* The Necessity for Capitalism, 1929; The Betrayal of the Nation, 1931; Various articles on economic and political subjects. *Recreations:* golf, gardening. *Address:* H5 and 6, Albany, W1; The Dipperays, East Dean, Sussex; 2 Hare Court, Temple, EC4.

Died 6 Jan. 1948.

VOSPER, Sydney Curnow, RWS 1914; *b* Stonehouse, Devon, 1866; *y s* of late S. Vosper, Brewer; *m* 1902, Constance (*d* 1910), *y d* of late Frank James of Merthyr Tydfil, solicitor; two *s*. *Educ:* King's Coll., Taunton; Plymouth Coll. After leaving school, worked for three years in architect's office as articled pupil; gave up architecture; studied art in Paris for three years under Raphael Collin and G. Courtois; worked in London for some years illustrating for various publications; exhibited water-colours at RA, RI, Paris Salon, Liverpool, Manchester, and other provincial Art Galleries; Represented by works in Victoria and Albert Museum, National Museum of Wales, Cardiff (Breton Saints), Municipal Galleries of Merthyr Tydfil, Plymouth, Exeter, Bournemouth, and Important Private Collections; worked in Southern Brittany and North Wales; ARWS, 1906. *Recreations:* cycling, swimming. *Address:* 77 Bedford Gardens, W8. *T:* Park 5812. *Club:* Chelsea Arts.

Died 10 July 1942.

VOULES, Sir Francis Minchin, Kt 1921; CBE 1920; FRHortS; *b* 9 May 1867; *e s* of late Sir Gordon Blennerhassett Voules; *m* 1st, 1893, Isabel Janet (*d* 1934), *g d* of Dr B. H. Kennedy, Shrewsbury; one *d*; 2nd, 1934, Louise Renée, *d* of Jean Rol, Dorzenac, Corrèze, France. *Educ:* Dulwich; abroad. Entered City life, 1885; Solicitor, 1890; retired, 1918; Chairman Ethelburga Agency Ltd, Gordon (Malaya) Rubber Estates, Limited, Kepong (Malay) Rubber Estates, Kuala Muda Rubber Estates, Ltd, Para Telephone Co. Ltd, etc.; Commissioner for Holland, British Red Cross Society, 1917–19; did extensive work for British and Russian prisoners; KGStJ. *Recreations:* motoring, golf, bridge, travel. *Address:* Fieldgate, Worth, Sussex. *T:* Pound Hill 2105; 3 Gracechurch Street, EC3. *Clubs:* Reform, City of London, MCC.

Died 12 Sept. 1947.

VOYSEY, Charles Francis Annesley, FRIBA; RDI; *b* May 1857; *e s* of late Rev. C. Voysey; *m* 1885; two *s* one *d*. *Educ:* Dulwich Coll.; privately. Master of Art Workers Guild for 1924; articled for 5 years to J. P. Seddon; Civil list pensioner; Royal Academy of Arts pensioner; Royal Institute of British Architects pensioner; Royal Gold Medalist for Architecture, 1940. *Publications:* Reason as a Basis of Art; Individuality; Lectures on Art; designs for houses, furniture, wallpapers, and fabrics, etc. *Address:* 73 St James's Street, SW1. *Club:* Arts.

Died 12 Feb. 1941.

VOYSEY, Violet Mary Annesley, CBE 1920; *b* 1880; *d* of Annesley W. Voysey. President, War Work Fund, and Local War Pensions Committee, Queenstown. *Address:* 72 Arlington House, St James's, SW1.

Died 19 Nov. 1943.

VROOM, Ven. Fenwick Williams, MA, DD; Hon. DCL Lennoxville; Hon. LLD Dalhousie, 1937; Dean of Divinity (Emeritus) at King's College, Halifax, NS; *b* St Stephen, NB, 25 July 1856; *s* of William Vroom and Frances Eliza Foster; *m* 1885, Agnes Jessie, *d* of Hon. Colin Campbell, of Weymouth, NS; one *d*. *Educ:* King's Coll., Windsor, NS (DD). Deacon, 1881; Priest, 1882; Curate, Petitcodiac, NB, 1881; Rector, Richmond, NB, 1883; Shediac, NB, 1885; Prof. of Divinity, King's College, Windsor, 1888; retired 1936; Canon, 1895; Archdeacon of Nova Scotia, 1919–39; Member of General Synod of the Church of England in Canada; President of the Alumni of King's College, 1923–33; Clerical Secretary of Provincial Synod of Canada, 1924; Commissioner of Legislative Library, 1930. *Publications:* Prayer Book Revision in Canada, 1914; The First Six Centuries, 1923; An Introduction to the Prayer Book, 1930; King's College, A Chronicle, 1789–1939. *Address:* 1 Payzant Avenue, Halifax, NS. *T:* B 5766.

Died 8 Jan. 1944.

VYVYAN, Col Sir Courtenay (Bourchier), 10th Bt *cr* 1644; CB 1906; CMG 1915; late The Buffs (Royal East Kent Regt); DL, JP Cornwall; *b* 5 June 1858; *e s* of Rev. Sir V. D. Vyvyan, 9th Bt, and Mary Frederica Louisa Bourchier (*d* 1907); *S* father, 1917; *m* 1st, 1887, Eva Catharine Forestier (*d* 1928), *e d* of late Major-General George Edmond L. Walker, RE; 2nd, 1929, Clara Coltman (author of Cornish Silhouettes, Gwendra Cove, etc., Bird Symphony, 1933), 2nd *d* of late Edward Powys Rogers. *Educ:* Westminster School; RMC, Sandhurst. Entered army, 1878; Captain, 1886; Major, 1897; Lt-Col 1902; Bt Col 1904; Brig. Major, Gibraltar, 1895–98; AAG, South Africa, 1902; served South Africa, 1879 (medal with clasp), 1896 (despatches, medal, Bt Major); 1899–1902 (despatches twice, Bt Lt-Col, Queen's medal with clasp, King's medal with two clasps); European War, 1914–18 (despatches thrice, CMG); retired pay. *Heir:* nephew Richard Philip Vyvyan, *b* 21 Nov. 1891. *Address:* Trelowarren, Mawgan, Helston, Cornwall.

Died 15 Nov. 1941.

W

WADDEL, William, CBE 1931; JP; Member of State Fire Insurance Board, Disabled Servicemen's Re-Establishment League, Wellington Branch, and of Executive of the Great War Funds Administrative Committee of the Order of St John and the New Zealand Red Cross Society; *b* 22 May 1868; 3rd *s* of James Waddel, JP, Southland, NZ, a native of Sunderland; *m* 1893, Hannah Emily, *e d* of John Tayler, Port Chalmers, NZ, formerly of Mitcham; two *s* two *d*. *Educ:* State School and Southland Boys' High School. Followed mercantile pursuits; joined the State Advances Department when it was inaugurated, 1895; Officer-in-charge, 1897; Deputy-Superintendent, 1907–22; Superintendent, State Advances Department, 1922–31; Member of the Public Trust Office Investment Board, The Government Insurance Investment Board, The Dominion Land Purchase Board and The Public Service Superannuation Board; Member of the Rural Intermediate Credit Board, and The Hawkes Bay Rehabilitation Committee. *Recreations:* bowls, etc. *Address:* 10 Kelburn Parade, Wellington, W1, New Zealand. *T:* 42.608. *Clubs:* Racing, Bowling, Wellington.

Died 17 Oct. 1946.

WADDELL, John J.; *see* Jeffrey-Waddell.

WADDELL, William Gillan, MA (Glasgow), MA (with distinction), London; formerly Professor of Classics in Fuad el Awal University, Cairo; *b* Neilston, Renfrewshire, 1884; *s* of late R. G. Waddell, Railway Manager; *m* Margaret, *d* of late Rev. George Blair, minister of Quarter Parish Church, Lanarkshire; one *d*. *Educ:* The Grammar School, Uddingston; Glasgow University (Prizeman in Latin and in Greek). Principal teacher of Classics in the Grammar School, Uddingston, 1906–19; lecturer in Classics, Armstrong College, Newcastle-upon-Tyne (in the University of Durham) 1919–28; Professor of Classics in Fuad e Awal University, Cairo, 1929–32, 1937–44; lecturer in Classics, Armstrong College, 1932–36; examiner in Latin for the Scottish Education Department, 1920–24, and for the Joint Matriculation Board, 1922–27, 1933–35. *Publications:* Selections from Menander, 1927; The Lighter Side of the Greek Papyri, 1932; assisted Professor G. Milligan, DD, with The Vocabulary of the Greek Testament, 1930; has contributed to classical journals, etc., and to Mélanges Maspero, 1934; collaborator in P. Fouad I, 1939; school-text (with notes) of Herodotus II, 1939; text and translation of Manetho (Loeb Classical Library), 1940. *Recreation:* music. *Address:* 56 Great George Street, Glasgow, W2.

Died 25 Jan. 1945.

WADDINGTON, Charles Willoughby, CIE 1904; MVO 1911; MA; *b* 29 Dec. 1865; *e s* of late Maj.-Gen. Thomas Waddington, JP, ISC, of The Chestnuts, Pangbourne, Berks and of Emilie, *d* of Gen. Michael Willoughby, ISC; *m* 1903, Ethel Caroline, *y d* of Alonzo H. Stocker, of Craigweil House, Aldwick, Sussex; two *s* one *d*. *Educ:* Charterhouse (Scholar); Oriel College, Oxford (scholar; 1st class Classical Moderations, 2nd class Literis Humanioribus); Old Carthusian Football XI, 1884–88; 'Blue' for Association Football, Oxford University, 1887–88. Principal, Gujarat College, Ahmedabad, 1889–92; Principal, Rajkumar College, Rajkot, 1892–1903; Principal, Mayo College, Ajmer, 1903–16; Indian Army Remount Dept, 1916–18; Secretary, Food Control Board, Simla, 1918–19; Guardian to HH the Maharaja of Jodhpur, 1919–23; Guardian to Maharaj Kumar of Jodhpur, 1933–37.

Publications: Indian Ink (Poems), 1909; Indian India, 1933. *Address:* 156 Sloane Street, SW3. *T:* Sloane 7355. *Clubs:* Travellers', Beefsteak.

Died 19 July 1946.

WADDINGTON, Sir Robert, Kt 1937; *b* 13 Dec. 1868; *s* of William and Elizabeth Waddington of Rawtenstall, Lancashire; *m* 1896, Pollie *d* of James Rothwell, Stonefold, Haslingden; one *s* one *d*. *Educ:* St Mary's School, Rawtenstall. Cotton spinner and manufacturer; MP (U) Rossendale Division of Lancs, Dec. 1918–22 and 1923–29; Chairman Dyestuffs Advisory Licensing Committee; Chairman Dyestuffs Development Committee; Controller of Dyestuffs since 1939; Member of Council of Empire Cotton Growing Corporation; Member of Chelmsford Committee on British Industries Fair, 1930; Member of United Kingdom Economic Mission to South Africa, 1930; formerly member of Lancashire County Council and Haslingden Town Council; first Chairman of Governors Haslingden Grammar School; former Chairman of Bury and District Joint Water Board Finance Committee. *Recreation:* walking. *Address:* Clifton Hall, Clifton, near Preston. *T:* Freckleton 280. *Club:* Constitutional.

Died 25 June 1941.

WADE, Arthur Shepherd; journalist; Statistical Consultant to a Stock Exchange firm; late Financial Editor of the Evening Standard; formerly City Editor of the Daily News and The Star; *b* Preston, Lancashire; *s* of John Alexander and Catherine Wade; *m* 1906, Eva, *d* of William and Mary Walmsley; two *d*. *Educ:* St James's School and the Harris Institute, Preston; College of Technology, Manchester (evening classes). Began business as newsboy at ten years of age, earning money for evening class fees; afterwards was private secretary to business men, bookkeeper, general secretary to a social reform organisation, bookseller, excursion party guide; at twenty-two became a reporter for the Preston Herald, and afterwards for the Lancashire Daily Post and the Hulton papers in Manchester. *Publications:* Cotton Spinning, 1921; Modern Finance and Industry, 1926, second edition 1927; The Plain Man and his Money, 1928; various articles in newspapers and weekly and monthly periodicals. *Recreations:* tennis, ping-pong, billiards, walking. *Address:* Windrush, Clarendon Way, Chislehurst, Kent. *T:* Orpington 3615.

Died 23 Jan. 1941.

WADE, Rev. George Woosung, DD (Oxon); Hon. DD (Wales); formerly Professor of Latin, and Senior Tutor at St David's College, Lampeter; Canon Emeritus of St Asaph; *b* 1858; *s* of J. H. Wade; *m* Rachel Elinor, *d* of Rev. F. H. Joyce. *Educ:* Monmouth Grammar School; Oriel College, Oxford (Scholar). First Class Classical Moderations, 1879; Second Class Lit. Hum., 1882. Ordained 1885; Curate of Basing, Hants, 1885–88. *Publications:* Elementary chapters in Comparative Philology, 1887; The Book of Genesis, with Introduction, Critical Analysis, and Notes, 1896; Old Testament History, 1901, 12th ed. 1934; The Book of the Prophet Isaiah (Westminster Commentaries), 1911, 2nd ed. 1929; New Testament History, 1922; 2nd ed. 1932; The Books of Micah, Obadiah, Joel, and Jonah (Westminster Commentaries), 1925; The Documents of the New Testament, translated and historically arranged with critical introductions, 1934; (with Rev. J. H. Wade) Little Guides to Somerset, 1907, 9th ed. 1933; Monmouthshire, 1909, 2nd ed. 1930; South Wales, 1913, 2nd ed. 1930; and Herefordshire, 1917, 3rd ed. 1930; 2 Samuel, 1918; (with the late Rev. G. G. V.

Stonehouse) The Books of Zephaniah, Nahum and Habakkuk (Westminster Commentaries), 1929. *Address:* Kingscot, North Parade, Monmouth.

Died 15 Oct. 1941.

WADE, Col Henry Oswald, DSO 1917; TD; W Yorks Regt; *b* 1869; *s* of John Henry Wade; *m* 1st, 1901, Alice Lilian (*d* 1905), *d* of John Robert Vaizey of Attwoods, Halstead; two *s* one *d*; 2nd, 1916, Eileen Lucy, *d* of John William Rawson-Ackroyd of Dean Grange, Bedfordshire; two *s*. *Educ:* Bradford; Trinity College, Camb. (LLB). Served European War, 1914–19 (despatches twice, DSO); JP, Beds. *Address:* Dean Grange, Upper Dean, Huntingdon.

Died 24 Nov. 1941.

WADIA, Sir Bomanji Jamsetji, Kt 1945; MA, LLB; Barrister-at-Law; *b* 4 Aug. 1881; *m* 1st, Ruttonbai Hormusji Wadya; two *s*; 2nd, Perin Nowroji Chinoy, Secunderabad; one *s* one *d*. *Educ:* St Xavier's College, Bombay; Inner Temple. Principal, Government Law College, Bombay, 1919–25; Acting Puisne Judge of Bombay High Court, 1928, 1929, and 1930; Additional Judge, 1930–31; Judge of the High Court of Bombay, 1931–41; Vice-Chancellor, University of Bombay, 1942–47; President Bombay Branch Royal Asiatic Society, 1942–47. *Address:* 162 Queen's Road, Bombay, India. *Club:* (Vice-President) Ripon (Bombay).

Died 17 Aug. 1947.

WADIA, Sir Cusrow, Kt 1932; CIE; retired; late Chairman, Indian Cables and Radio Telegraph Co., Ltd; Chairman Century Manufacturing Co., Ltd, Bombay; *b* 1869; *s* of late Hon. N. N. Wadia, CIE, Bombay; *m* Madeleine, *d* of late J. Landquist, Stockholm, Sweden. *Educ:* King's College, London. Started business in Bombay. *Recreations:* racing, gardening. *Address:* Neville House, Bombay.

Died 3 Oct. 1950.

WADLEY, Lt-Col Edward John, CBE 1919; DSO 1916; late Royal Army Veterinary Corps; *b* 5 Jan. 1880; *s* of Thomas Wadley, Penarth; *m* 1927, Winifred, *widow* of Thomas Cuthbertson, Barrister-at-law, Inner Temple; one *s*. Served S African War, 1901–02 (Queen's medal 5 clasps); European War, 1914–18 (despatches, CBE, DSO, Bt Lt-Col); retired pay, 1921. *Address:* Caerleon, PO Parklands, Johannesburg.

Died 1 April 1950.

WADSWORTH, Edward Alexander, ARA 1943; artist; *b* Cleckheaton, Oct. 1889; *s* of Fred Wadsworth; *m* 1912, Fanny Eveleigh; one *d*. *Educ:* Fettes College; Munich; Slade School; and the Home Guard. Formerly member London Group, X Group, New English Art Club, and Unit One; has exhibited chiefly in London, Paris, and USA; public decorations executed for Canadian War Museum, RMS Queen Mary, and De la Warr Pavilion, Bexhill; designed set of Initial Letters used by Col T. E. Lawrence in Seven Pillars of Wisdom. Paintings and drawings acquired by the Tate Gallery, British Museum, Stedlijk Museum, Amsterdam, many provincial museums, and for private collections in Great Britain, USA, Siam, etc.; Member of Recommending Committee of Chantrey Bequest, 1945 and 1946; served European War, RNVR, 1915–18. *Publications:* The Black Country (drawings, with text by Arnold Bennett), 1920; Sailing Ships and Barges of the Western Mediterranean and Adriatic Sea (copper engravings), 1926; Selection, Cahier XIII; Antwerp, 1933; The Aesthetic Aspect of Civil Engineering Design, Inst. of CEs, 1945. *Address:* Dairy House, Maresfield, nr Uckfield, Sussex. *Club:* Royal Automobile.

Died 21 June 1949.

WAIT, Col Hugh Godfrey Killigrew, CBE 1919; DSO 1916; late Royal Engineers; *b* 8 Feb. 1871; *γ s* of late W. K. Wait, St Vincent's Hall, Clifton; *m* 1905, Helen Mary Lothian (*d* 1946), *γ d* of Gen. Sir Lothian Nicholson, KCB. 2nd Lieut 1889; Capt. 1900; Major, 1909; Chief Instructor School of Military Engineering, 1912; Assistant Director of Works, 1916; ADFW War Office, 1919–22; President of the Royal Engineer Board, 1923–27; served European War, 1914–18 (despatches, DSO, CBE); retired pay, 1927. *Address:* The Knapp, Sutton Veny, Wilts. *Club:* Junior United Service.

Died 28 Jan. 1948.

WAITE, Arthur Edward, LittD; the exponent in poetical and prose writings of sacramental religion and the higher mysticism, understood in its absolute separation from psychic and occult phenomena; *b* Brooklyn, New York, 2 Oct. 1857, of an English mother and brought in infancy to England; *m* 1st, Ada Lakeman, of Devonshire family and Greek extraction; one *d*; 2nd, Mary Broadbent Schofield, formerly of Clarksfield, Oldham and Southport. *Publications:* Shadows of Life and Thought in the Form of Memoirs, A Retrospective Review, 1938; The Secret Tradition in Freemasonry, enlarged and transformed, 1937; A Mystagogical Quintology, 1935; Seventh issue of an Encyclopædia of Freemasonry, 2 vols, 1934; The Holy Grail, its Legends and Symbolism, 1933; The Holy Kabbalah, 1929; The Book of Life in the Rose, 1928; The Quest of the Golden Stairs, 1927; The Secret Tradition in Alchemy, 1926; Emblematic Freemasonry and the Evolution of its Deeper Issues, 1925; The Brotherhood of the Rosy Cross, 1924; Lamps of Western Mysticism, 1923; Transcendental Magic of Éliphas Lévi (2nd ed.), revised, annotated, and enlarged, 1923, fourth issue, 1938; Louis Claude de Saint-Martin, the French Mystic, and the Story of Modern Martinism, new issue, 1939; Raymund Lully, Illuminated Doctor, Alchemist, and Christian Mystic, new issue, 1939; History of Magic, translated from the French of Éliphas Lévi, third issue, 1939; Pictorial Key to the Tarot, new issue, 1922; Book of the Holy Grail, a mystical poem, 1921; Encyclopædia of Freemasonry, 1921; The Works of Thomas Vaughan, 1919; The Way of Divine Union, 1915; Collected Poems, 2 vols, 1914; The Secret Doctrine in Israel, 1913; Lopukhin's Characteristics of the Interior Church, 1912; The Secret Tradition in Freemasonry, 1911; The Book of Ceremonial Magic, 1911; Thomas Vaughan's Lumen de Lumine, 1910; Eckartshausen's Cloud upon the Sanctuary, 1909; The Hidden Church of the Holy Grail, 1908; Mulford's Gift of Understanding, 1907; Strange Houses of Sleep, Studies in Mysticism, Steps to the Crown, 1906; The House of the Hidden Light, 1904; De Senancour's Obermann, 1903; Book of Mystery and Vision, 1902; Doctrine and Literature of the Kabbalah, 1902; The Unknown Philosopher, 1900; Braid on Hypnotism, 1899; Book of Black Magic, 1898; Mulford's Gift of the Spirit, 1898; Devil Worship in France, 1896; Hermetic and Alchemical Writings of Paracelsus, 2 vols, 1894; Belle and the Dragon, 1894; New Pearl of Great Price, 1894; Hermetic Museum, 2 vols, 1893; Collectanea Alchemica, 1893; Golden and Blessed Casket of Nature's Marvels, 1893; Alchemical Writings of Edward Kelley, 1893; Basil Valentine's Triumphal Chariot, 1893; Azoth, or The Star in the East, 1893; The Occult Sciences, 1891; Lucasta; Parables and Poems, 1891; Prince Starbeam, 1890; Lives of Alchemystical Philosophers, 1888; Magical Writings of Thomas Vaughan, 1888; Songs and Poems of Fairyland: An Anthology, 1888; Elfin Music, 1888; A Soul's Comedy, 1887; Real History of the Rosicrucians, 1887; Mysteries of Magic, 1886; Israfel: Letters, Visions, and Poems, 1886. *Address:* Gordon House, Bridge, Canterbury.

Died 19 May 1942.

WAKE, Lt-Col Edward St Aubyn, CMG 1919; JP; Indian Army; retired; *b* 20 July 1862; 2nd *s* of Admiral Charles Wake and Emma, *e d* of Sir Edward St Aubyn; *m* Vera Cecilia, *γ d* of Francis Johnston, of Westerham, Kent; one *s*. *Educ:* Felsted; Charterhouse; Christ Church, Oxford; Sandhurst. Entered army, King's Regiment, 1884; served Burmah Campaign, 1885–86 (medal and clasp); transferred 10th Bengal Lancers; Waziristan Field Force, 1893; Samana, 1897 (despatches, medal and two clasps); Tirah (despatches and clasp); Cantonment Magistrate Dept (Kaiser-i-Hind gold medal for services in plague, 1903; clasp for service as Special Relief Commissioner in Haidarabad Flood, 1909); tutor and guardian to Maharaj Kumar, of Bikanir, 1910–13; Red Cross Commissioner in France, 1914; raised and commanded 21st Service Bn Middlesex Regt, 1915; Military Intelligence Depart, GSO, War Office, 1916–19 (despatches, 1914 Star, 2 medals, CMG). *Publication:* Daily Review of the Foreign Press, 1916–1919. *Recreation:* shooting. *Address:* 14 Embankment Gardens, Chelsea, SW3. *T:* Flaxman 4255. *Club:* United Service.

Died 20 Oct. 1944.

WAKE-WALKER, Adm. Sir William Frederic, KCB 1943; CB 1940; CBE 1941; OBE 1919; 3rd Sea Lord Controller since 1942; *b* 24 March 1888; *s* of G. F. A. Wake-Walker; *m* 1916, Muriel, *d* of Sir Collingwood Hughes, 10th Bt; two *s* two *d.* Capt., 1927; Rear-Adm., 1939; Vice-Adm., 1942; Adm., 1945; served European War, 1914–18; War of 1939–45 (CB). *Address:* East Bergholt Lodge, Suffolk. *T:* East Bergholt 78. *Club:* United Service.

Died 24 Sept. 1945.

WAKEFIELD, 1st Viscount *cr* 1934, of Hythe; **Charles Cheers Wakefield;** 1st Baron *cr* 1930; 1st Bt *cr* 1917, GCVO 1936; Kt 1908; CBE 1919; Hon. FBA 1938; LLD Hon., Colgate Univ.; TD; Alderman of the City of London; Order of the Legion of Honour; Order of the Crown (Belgium); Grand Cross Order of Leopold (Belgium); Knight of Justice of St John of Jerusalem; Order of St Sava, Serbia; White Lion (Czechoslovakia); Order of the Sacred Treasure Japan); Hon. Col 9th (2nd City of London) Batt. (Royal Fusiliers); a Lieut for the City; a JP City of London; Pres. Royal Hospitals of Bridewell and Bethlem; President, Mental Aftercare Association; Hon. Treasurer, National Children's Home and Orphanage, 1901–35; Chairman, Royal Masonic Hospital; President, Tower Hill Improvement; Hon. Fellow of King's College, London Univ.; President, College of Aeronautical Engineering, Chelsea; Past Master Cordwainers, Gardeners, Haberdashers, and Spectacle-Makers Companies; President, City of London Branch, League of Mercy; Headed civic deputation to Festival of Freedom, Czechoslovakia, 1920; Headed British Sulgrave Delegation and presented statues of Burke, Pitt and Bryce to Washington, Pittsburgh and New York, 1922; Hon. Fellow Royal Aeronautical Society; Hon. Member Oxford Society; Vice-President, Royal Aero Club; Life Patron or Vice-President numerous flying clubs, including Toronto, NS Wales, Delhi, Singapore, East Africa, Nyassaland, Marlborough (NZ), Johannesburgh, RAF Cambridge Univ., Northern Rhodesia; associated with Sir Alan Cobham's Flight to Australia and back, 1926, and the Flight of Survey round Africa, 1927–28; purchased (1929) and endowed (1932) Talbot House, Poperinghe, birthplace of Toc H Movement; purchased at Christies, May 1931, and presented to the nation, the Howard Grace Cup, known also as the Thomas à Becket Cup, also (1935) The Armada Jewel (now at Victoria and Albert Museum, South Kensington); also (1936) Papers of Sir Isaac Newton: The Mint Collection (now at the Royal Mint); presented (1928) panelling and architectural re-decoration, Balfour Room, British Academy, Burlington House, and also portrait of Lord Balfour (President), by Sir William Orpen; donor, Wakefield Gold Trophy for maximum speed on land; owner of motor speed boats, Miss England I, II and III, with which successive and successful attacks were made upon the World's Water Speed Record; made a special gift of £25,000 in aid of the Empire research work of the Imperial Institute, 1932; presented 'Lord Wakefield' Research Block and the 'Lady Wakefield' Chapel to the new Bethlem Hospital at Monks Orchard, 1931; presented Swimming Baths and Gymnasium, King Edward's School (Witley), Bridewell Royal Hospital, 1936; Presented Lifeboat, The Viscountess Wakefield and Lifeboat House to Hythe, Kent, 1936; presented Whittington Window, designed by Dr Douglas Strachan, to the Guildhall, 1932; donor 1932 to St Mildred's Church, Bread Street, of National Historical Memorial to Adm. Arthur Phillip, RN, Founder and First Governor of Australia; presented to National Portrait Gallery collection of portraits of British and Empire soldiers and statesmen of the Great War by Orpen and Sargent, 1933; also presented the Orpen Portrait of M. Paul Hymans to the Belgian Nation; purchased and presented to the Prime Minister for the British Museum, Nelson's personal Log-Book with entries carried to the eve of Trafalgar; also previously presented to the Guildhall Nelson's Sword of Honour given him with the Freedom of the City; presented early English manuscript, Great Chronicle of London to the Guildhall Library, together with a limited edition of a reprint thereof, 1934; Trustee, The Sir John Soane's Museum; President Dickens Fellowship, 1927–29; twice President Motor and Cycle Trades Benevolent Fund; Chairman, Royal Air Force Benevolent Fund; President Aldwych Club, 1925–27; PGW in English Freemasonry; Sheriff of the City of London, 1907–08; *b* 1859; *s* of John Wakefield, of HM Customs, and Mary Cheers; *m* 1888, Sarah Frances Graham, Dame of Grace of St John of Jerusalem. *Educ:* Liverpool Institute. Governing Director of C. C. Wakefield & Co. Ltd, oil manufacturers, etc., Wakefield House, Cheapside, London EC2; Chairman North British and Mercantile Insurance Co.; President, British Aviation Insurance Co. Ltd; Lord Mayor of London, 1915–16; Hon. Freeman of the City of London, 1935; Hon. Freeman of Hythe, Kent; Honorary Life Member of Australasian Pioneers' Club and Women's Pioneer Society of Australasia; Member of the Royal Australian Historical Society. *Publications:* Future Trade in the Far East; America To-day and To-morrow; On Leaving School and the Choice of a Career; numerous contributions to the press and to commercial text-books. *Address:* Wakefield House, Cheapside, EC2; Hythe, Kent. *T:* City 4411. *TA:* Cheery Cent, London. *Club:* Carlton.

Died 15 Jan. 1941 (ext).

WAKEFIELD, George Edward Campbell, CIE 1928; OBE 1918; Managing Director Northern India Farms; *b* 16 April 1873; *s* of late George Edward Wakefield, Punjab Commission; *m* 1902, Minnie Caroline, 3rd *d* of late E. J. Keelan, MICE; three *s* one *d.* Assistant Engineer, Punjab Irrigation, 1892; Special Duty Rajputana great famine, 1899–1900; Superintendent Land Revenue and Irrigation, Tonk State, Rajputana, 1900; Silver Kaiser-i-Hind Medal, 1901; service of HH the Maharana Udaipur State Rajputana as Boundary Settlement Officer; Superintending Engineer Irrigation; Tutor to the Heir-Apparent and confidential Secretary to the Maharana, 1903–09; Gold Kaiser-i-Hind Medal, 1909; Service of HE Highness the Nizam Hyderabad Deccan, as Irrigation Settlement Officer, Deputy Director-General of Revenue, Director-General of Revenue, Director-General of Commerce and Industries, 1909–21; Chief Secretary to General Raja Sir Hari-singh of Jammu and Kashmir, 1921; State Secretary to the Maharaja of Jammu and Kashmir, and Director of his private domains, 1925; Minister-in-charge of Police and Public Works, Jammu and Kashmir State, 1926; Minister for Development, Jammu and Kashmir State, 1928; Cabinet Minister, Jammu and Kashmir State, 1928; Foreign and Political and Development Minister, 1929; Army and Political Minister, 1931; retired. *Address:* Rawalpindi, Punjab, India.

Died March 1944.

WAKELY, His Hon. Judge John; KC, DL, JP; Judge of the Counties of Roscommon and Sligo County Courts, 1904–24; Judge of Midland Circuit Court, Irish Free State, 1924–30; *b* 30 Sept. 1861; *e s* of late John Wakely,

DL, and Mary Catherine, *d* of Rev. Richard George of Kentstown, Co. Meath; *m* 1888, Raby Low Montserrat (*d* 1923), *d* of Rev. Morgan Woodward Jellett, Canon of Christ Church Cathedral, and Rector of St Peter's Church, Dublin; three *d*. *Educ*: Kingstown School; Trinity College, Dublin (MA). Called to Irish Bar, 1888; QC 1899; Lord of the Manor of Ballyburly; Bencher of Hon. Society of King's Inns, Dublin, 1902. *Publications*: (with R. R. Cherry, KC): The Irish Land Law and Land Purchase Acts; Articles on the Land Purchase (Ireland) Act 1903. *Recreations*: fishing, shooting. *Clubs*: University, Dublin.

Died 15 July 1942.

WALBROOK, Henry Mackinnon; *e s* of Mary and Mackinnon Walbrook of Rathmines, nr Dublin; *m* Ruth, *y d* of late Rev. Augustus Moore, MA, Vicar of St John Baptist, Spalding. *Educ*: Battersea Grammar School; King's College; and in his father's library. Art Critic of The Man of the World, 1888–89; Editor of Brighton Guardian, 1890–1904; joined the staff of the Pall Mall Gazette, 1904, dramatic critic, 1906–15; Army Education Scheme Lecturer, 1919–20; President, the Critics' Circle, 1933. *Publications*: Murders and Murder-trials; A Playgoer's Wanderings; Gilbert and Sullivan Opera; J. M. Barrie and the Theatre; Hove and the Great War; Nights at the Play; Life of Adam Lindsay Gordon; John Drayton, Millionaire; The Visitor; The Knock at the Door; The Touch of Truth; The Jug of Wine; and other books and plays; articles or Poetry in Nineteenth Century, Fortnightly Review, English Review, London Mercury, Observer, Saturday Review, Times, Manchester Guardian, Birmingham Post, Truth, Pall Mall Magazine, Sussex County Magazine, etc. *Recreations*: reading and music. *Club*: Authors'.

Died 10 Feb. 1941.

WALCOT, William, FRIBA, RE; architect, painter and etcher; *b* Russia, 1874; *g g s* of John Walcot of Worcester, solicitor; *m*; one *s* three *d*. *Educ*: Paris; Imperial Academy of Art, St Petersburg. Associate of British School of Rome; First Exhibition in London, 1908. *Publications*: Roman Compositions; Architectural Water-Colours and Etchings; Book Illustration; Salammbo, Gustave Flaubert, 1926; Herodias, 1928; The Ludlow Pageant Folio (with F. Brangwyn), 1934. *Recreations*: archæological research, travel. *Address*: 5 Grafton Street, W1. *Club*: Arts.

Died June 1943.

WALDER, Alderman Hon. Sir Samuel (Robert), Kt 1933; MLC, NS Wales since 1932; general merchant (S. Walder, Ltd), 340 Pitt Street, Sydney, NSW; *b* 8 Oct. 1879; *s* of late Samuel Walder and late Mary Amelia Hatton; *m* 1915, Elsie, *d* of late William Blunt, Millthorpe, NSW; one *s* one *d*. *Educ*: Cleveland Street School and Christ Church School, Sydney. At an early age entered father's business, that of canvas manufacturer, established 1856; took over the business at the age of 18 years, and developed it into that of general merchant; Lord Mayor of Sydney, 1932. *Recreation*: golf. *Address*: Deauville, Longworth Avenue, Point Piper, Sydney, NSW. *T*: FM 3297. *Clubs*: Royal Empire Society; Millions, Australian Golf, NSW, National, Rotary of NSW, Sydney.

Died 24 Nov. 1946.

WALDRAM, Percy John, FRICS; LRIBA, MRI; Senior Partner in firm of Jno. Waldram and Son, Civil Engineers and Surveyors; Specialist in Natural Illumination; *b* 27 April 1869; *e surv. s* of late John Waldram, CE, and Louisa Malyon; *m* 1st, 1900, Georgiana (*d* 1931), *d* of W. Sangwin, St Feock, Cornwall; two *s*; 2nd, 1935, Jessie, also *d* of W. Sangwin. *Educ*: Latymers School, Edmonton. Private practice and lecturing on structural work, 1890–1915; Designing and testing aeroplanes, 1915–16; Aircraft, Ministry of Munitions and Air Ministry, 1916–18; Land Reclamation and Land Settlement, Ministry of Agriculture and Fisheries, 1918–20; Special Surveys HM Office of Works, 1920–22; Private practice, 1922–49; Advisory Committee on Illumination, Dept of Scientific and Industrial Research; International Commission on Illumination; Member of Council, RIBA, 1926–32 and 1933–38; Science Standing Committee RIBA, 1925–31 and 1932–38; Examiner RIBA, 1919–26; Chartered Surveyors Institution, 1927–44; Chairman Joint Committee on Orientation of Buildings; Chairman Joint Committee on Lighting of Schools. *Publications*: A Standard of Daylight Illumination of Interiors, 1909; Principles of Structural Mechanics, 1911; Steel Frame Buildings, 1915; Window Design and the Predetermination of Daylight Illumination (with J. M. Waldram), 1923; Report on the Penetration of Daylight and Sunlight into Buildings, Dept of Scientific and Industrial Research, 1927 and 1932; The Use of Photographs in Town Planning and Design, 1934; Possibilities of Securing Standards of Adequacy in the Natural Lighting of Dwellings by Regulations under Town and Country Planning Act, 1938; The Photogrammetric Analysis of Photographs of Buildings, 1941; The Natural Illumination of Factories and Workshops, 1943; also reprinted papers and articles. *Recreation*: work. *Address*: Robins Croft, 113 Whitchurch Gardens, Edgware. *T*: Edgware 0068.

Died 8 Nov. 1949.

WALES, Hubert; (pen name of William Pigott); novelist; *b* Brigg, Lincolnshire, 10 Aug. 1870; *m* 1st, 1895, Beatrice (*d* 1923), *y d* of John Rowcroft Macfarlane; one *d*; 2nd, 1932, Dora *o c* of John Albert Drinan, Co. Cork and Nice. *Educ*: Oundle; Harrow. Studied law. Admitted a solicitor in 1894; subsequently relinquished the legal profession and devoted himself to literary work, particularly the writing of fiction; Member of the Society for Psychical Research. *Publications*: In Royal Purple, 1899; Mr and Mrs Villiers, 1906; The Yoke, 1907; Cynthia in the Wilderness, 1907; The Old Allegiance (In Royal Purple, revised), 1908; Hilary Thornton, 1909; The Wife of Colonel Hughes, 1910; The Spinster, 1912; The Purpose; Reflections and Digressions, 1914; The Thirty Days, 1915; The Rationalist, 1917; Blue Flame, 1918; A Report on a Series of Cases of Apparent Thought Transference without Conscious Agency (Proceedings Society for Psychical Research), 1920. *Recreations*: golf, correspondence. *Address*: Homewood Heath, Hindhead, Surrey.

Died 5 July 1943.

WALKER, Maj. Alan Richard H.; *see* Hill-Walker.

WALKER, Sir Alexander, KBE 1920; *b* 1869; *s* of late A. Walker of Piersland, Troon, Ayrshire; *m* 1895, Rosaline (*d* 1948), *d* of late A. S. Josling of Arkley, Herts; two *s* two *d*. Former Chairman, John Walker & Sons, Whisky Distillers, Kilmarnock. Freeman of Troon. *Address*: Piersland, Troon, Ayrshire.

Died 13 May 1950.

WALKER, Alexander, CBE 1918; DL, JP County of City of Glasgow; Solicitor; was Assessor under the Lands Valuation Acts; Registration Officer under the Representation of the People Acts; and Surveyor of Local Rates under the Glasgow Corporation Acts—all for the City of Glasgow, 1908–35; for 24 years previously he was in the Town Clerk's Department, Glasgow, and for some years acted as Depute Town Clerk; *b* Glasgow, 28 March 1866; *s* of late Andrew Walker, Glasgow; *m* 1896, Jessie, *d* of late John Winchester, JP, Loanhead, Portessie; one *s* two *d*. *Educ*: Wilson Sch.; Glasgow Univ. Investigated systems of Rating and Municipal Administration in USA and Canada, 1914; Belgian Refugee Committee work, also Housing Director on behalf of Admiralty in housing shipyard workers and others, 1914–18; Commander Order of the Crown, Belgium, 1919; Member, Order of St Sava, Serbia, 1919; an enthusiastic Freemason; ex-President for Scotland of National Association of Local

Government Officers; Ex-Deacon of the Incorporation of Cordiners, Glasgow. *Publications:* several in connection with Municipal Administration and questions of Rating and Registration. *Address:* 98 Dowanhill Street, Glasgow, W2. *Clubs:* St Andrew's; Royal Scottish Automobile, Glasgow.

Died 20 Nov. 1945.

WALKER, Archibald, MA Oxon; FIC; DL County of Ayr; Director of The Clydesdale Bank, Ltd, 1911–41, Deputy Chairman, 1923–40; Vice-Chairman, Royal Maternity and Women's Hospital, Glasgow, Chairman, 1924–36, Director since 1886; Vice-Chairman, Ayrshire Territorial Army Association, 1922–38; *b* 1858; *s* of Archibald Walker, Glasgow; *m* 1903, Adelaide Orr (*d* 1924), *d* of James M. Thomson, Glasgow; one *s* one *d*. *Educ:* Loretto; Trinity College, Oxford, MA; First Class Honours in Natural Science. Distiller; developed Yeast Industry; amalgamated with Distillers Company, Ltd, 1902–34; Director of Glasgow and South-Western Railway Company, 1917–23; Director of the Glasgow Merchants House, 1898–1910; Governor of Victoria Infirmary, Glasgow, 1899–1917; Hon. Lt-Col 1st VBRSF, 1917; Member of Royal Company of Archers, The King's Bodyguard for Scotland; JP, Ayrshire. *Recreations:* played football for Oxford University Rugby Union Fifteen; for Scotland 1881, 1882, 1883; rowed in College Eight. *Address:* Newark Castle, Ayr. *T:* Alloway, Ayr, 204. *Clubs:* Oxford and Cambridge; Western, Glasgow; County, Ayr.

Died 10 June 1945.

WALKER, Rear-Adm. Arthur Horace, OBE 1918; *b* 17 Aug. 1881; 5th *s* of late Thomas James Walker, MD, FRCS, JP, Peterborough, Northants; *m* 1910, Madeline Edith Margaret, *e d* of late Brig.-Gen. A. J. A. Wright, CB; one *d*. *Educ:* Haileybury College; HMS Britannia. Entered RN as Naval Cadet, 1896; gained five Firsts in examinations for Lieut; Commander 1914; served European War, 1914–18 (despatches, OBE); Captain, 1920; Commodore, 1930–32; ADC to the King, 1932; Rear-Admiral, 1932. Served as Commodore 2nd cl., RNR, 1939–40; and as Captain RN with British Admiralty Technical Mission, in Canada, 1940–46. *Address:* c/o National Provincial Bank, Bournemouth.

Died 3 July 1947.

WALKER, Bertram James, CMG 1919; DSO 1918; Proprietor of Rolcut; *b* 1880; *m* 1909, Josepha Margaret (who obtained a divorce 1926), *d* of late Sir George Donaldson; one *s*. Served European War, 1914–19 (despatches, CMG, DSO). *Address:* Water End House, Wheathampstead Herts.

Died 8 March 1947.

WALKER, Rev. Edward Mewburn, Chaplain to the King from 1920; Hon. LLD University of Michigan; Hon. DD University of Glasgow; Hon. LittD, University of Sheffield, 1933; Hon. DLitt Oxford, 1936; Hon. Fellow of Queen's College, Oxford, 1934; Hon. Fellow of Trinity College, Dublin, 1931; *b* Hampstead, 29 Nov. 1857; *s* of Thomas Walker, solicitor of Furnival's Inn; *m* 1st, 1890, Gertrude May (*d* 1930), *d* of Rev. Alfred Hamilton, DD, Rector of Taney and Canon of Christ Church, Dublin, and *widow* of E. R. Wilmot-Chetwode, of Woodbrook, Queen's Co., Ireland; one *s* one *d*; 2nd, 1933, Dorothy Alice, *e d* of George Cunningham, Cape Town. *Educ:* Blackheath Proprietary School; Queen's College, Oxford. 1st class in Classical Moderations; 1st class in final classical school. Public examiner in final classical school; senior proctor, 1898–99; Fellow of Queen's College, Oxford, 1881–1930; Pro-Provost, 1922–30; Provost, 1930–33; Member of the Hebdomadal Council, 1902–26, and of the Visitatorial Board; Select Preacher to the University of Oxford, 1911–12; Oxford representative on British Universities Mission to the USA, 1918. *Publications:* Signs of the Times, 1912; Hellenica Oxyrhynchia, its Authorship and Authority, 1913; Greek History, its

Problems and its Meaning, 1921; articles on Greek History in the Encyclopædia Britannica, and of chapters in the Cambridge Ancient History. *Address:* Queen's College, Oxford.

Died 25 July 1941.

WALKER, Ernest, MA, DMus; composer, author, pianist; Hon. Fellow, 1926, and late Director of Music, Balliol College, Oxford; *b* 15 July 1870; *s* of Edward and Caroline Walker. *Educ:* privately. On Balliol Staff continuously since taking of BA degree (in Literæ Humaniores), 1891–1925. *Publications:* Compositions of various kinds; A History of Music in England; Beethoven; Free Thought and the Musician, and other essays; articles in Dictionaries and Periodicals, Programme Analyses, etc. *Address:* Balliol College, Oxford. *Club:* Oxford Union (Oxford).

Died 21 Feb. 1949.

WALKER, Maj.-Gen. Sir Ernest Alexander, KCIE 1938; CB 1934; MB, ChB, FRCSE, IMS, retired; *b* 20 Oct. 1880; *s* of Rev. A. Walker, Senior Chaplain Church of Scotland and Mary Mowbray Esdaile; *m* 1906, Juanita Mary, *d* of Surgeon-Major R. Power, IMS; one *s*. *Educ:* Forfar Academy; University of Edinburgh. Hon. Surgeon to Viceroy, 1930; DADMS (Mob.) 1920–21; DDMS and Director HO 1929–31; DDMS Army Hdqrs, 1932; DDMS Eastern Command, India, 1932–33; Hon. Surgeon to the King, 1932–37; Director of Medical Services in India, 1933–37; retired, 1937; served European War, 1914–21, Iraq, 1915–16; Siege of Kut-al-amara (Prisoner of War, 1916–18, despatches twice). *Publications:* various technical. *Recreations:* shooting, fishing. *Address:* Duncan, Vancouver, Island BC, Canada.

Died 5 Sept. 1944.

WALKER, Lt-Col Francis Spring, CBE 1919; FRCS; late RAMC; *b* 1876; *s* of A. F. Walker; *m* 1903, Rosamond, *d* of Capt. R. Chute, late Cameronians; one *d*. Served S Africa, 1900 (Queen's medal with two clasps); European War, 1914–19 (despatches, CBE). *Address:* Woodquest, Crosshaven, Co. Cork. *Club:* County of Cork.

Died 24 June 1941.

WALKER, Captain Frederic John, CB 1943; DSO 1942; RN; commanding one of HM Ships; *b* 3 June 1896; *s* of late Capt. F. M. Walker, RN; *m* 1919, Jessica Eilleen Ryder Stobart; one *s* one *d*. *Educ:* RN College, Dartmouth. Continuous service in RN since 1914. Served War of 1939–45 (despatches for Dunkirk, DSO and two Bars, CB). *Address:* White House, Grassendale Park, Liverpool 19. *T:* Garston 1124.

Died 9 July 1944.

WALKER, Col George Kemp, CIE 1913; OBE 1918; VD 1923; DL; Fellow and Member of Council Royal College of Veterinary Surgeons; C. C. Berks; *b* 20 March 1872; *o s* of late William Alfred Walker; *m* 1899, Ethel Maria, *y d* of late William Herbert Wall; one *s* two *d*. *Educ:* Warwick School; Royal Veterinary College, London. Commission, Army Veterinary Department, 1894; transferred to Indian Veterinary Service, 1897; Major, 1909; Lt-Col 1917; Col 1922; retired pay, 1927. Held various civil appointments, including Assistant Bacteriologist to the Government of India; Civil Veterinary Department, Punjab; Professor, Punjab Veterinary College; Superintendent, Civil Veterinary Department, Bombay; Principal, Punjab Veterinary College; Fellow, Punjab University; commanding Poona Volunteer Rifles, 1916; commanding 35th Poona Battalion, IDF, 1917–19 (despatches, Commander-in-Chief, India) (' D' Expeditionary Force); commanding Punjab Light Horse, AFI, 1920–24; commanding Lahore Contingent, AFI, 1924–25; Honorary ADC to Commander-in-Chief, India, 1919–25. Freemasonry, Past Grand Deacon (Eng.), etc. *Publications:* contributions to professional papers and scientific bodies in veterinary science and education; *Some Diseases of Cattle in India; Diseases of Animals in Tropical Countries* (Edmonds and Walker). *Address:* Norman House, Abingdon-on-Thames. *T:* Abingdon 207. *Clubs:* United Service, Simla.

Died 21 April 1942.

WALKER, Sir Herbert Ashcombe, Kt 1915; KCB 1917; *b* 16 May 1868; *s* of Dr Walker of Hove, Sussex; *m* 1st, 1895, Ethel (*d* 1909), *d* of J. R. Griffith, solicitor, Llanrwst, N Wales; 2nd, 1910, Lorina, *widow* of A. Shields of the Stock Exchange. *Educ:* North London Collegiate School; St Francis Xavier's College, Bruges. Entered the service of the L & NW Rly, 1885; Assistant to General Manager, 1911; General Manager LSW, 1912; General Manager Southern Railway, 1923–37; Colonel Engineer and Railway Staff Corps (retired); Lieut of the City of London; KGStJ; Grand Officer Legion of Honour. *Address:* White Walls, Arundel Dr, Saltdean, Sussex. *T:* Rottingdean 9406. *Clubs:* Devonshire, Eccentric.

Died 29 Sept. 1949.

WALKER, James; MP (Lab) Motherwell division of Lanarkshire since 1935; Member of the British Council; *b* Glasgow. *Educ:* Ruskin College, Oxford. Organiser for Iron and Steel Trades Association since 1908; MP (Lab) Newport, 1929–31; was Chairman of Scottish TUC; Member of Glasgow City Council 17 years; Magistrate of Glasgow 7 years; Chairman of British Labour Party, 1940–41. *Address:* 324 Gray's Inn Road, WC1.

Died 5 Jan. 1945.

WALKER, Brig.-Gen. James Workman, CMG 1919; DSO 1918; TD; DL; JP; Hon. Col 79th Regt Artillery; Hon. Col RE 52nd Div.; *b* 1873; *m* 1907, Janie, *d* of Hugh Stevenson, Glasgow; two *s* one *d. Educ:* Glasgow University. Brig.-Gen. RA 53rd Div., GOC 53rd Div.; European War, 1914–19, Palestine (despatches, CMG, DSO). Order of the Nile. *Address:* Redburn, Irvine, Ayrshire; The Garth, Troon, Ayrshire.

Died 15 Sept. 1945.

WALKER, John Crampton; ARHA 1930; *b* 22 Sept. 1890; *e s* of late Garrett William Walker, KC; *m* 1928, May, *d* of late James Savage, Belfast. *Educ:* St Stephen's Green School, Dublin; Trinity College, Dublin; Metropolitan School of Art, Dublin. Landscape and flower painter; Art Critic and Organiser of many Exhibitions in London and provinces; FRSA; Hon. Secretary, Exhibition of Irish Art, Brussels, 1930. *Recreations:* shooting and croquet. *Address:* 18 Fitzwilliam Square, Dublin. *Clubs:* Croquet and Lawn tennis, Carrickmines.

Died 9 June 1942.

WALKER, Kenneth; *b* 1874; *o surv. s* of late James Douglas Walker, KC, Blairton, Aberdeenshire; *m* 1909, Ida, *d* of late John Taylor Gordon, Nethermuir, Aberdeenshire, and *widow* of Capt. W. Leetham, 5th Dragoon Gds. *Educ:* Rugby; Trinity College, Cambridge, MA. Served European War, 1914–19, Capt. Remount Service; JP, CC Pembrokeshire; High Sheriff, 1928; MFH Pembrokeshire Hounds, 1940–46, except 1945. Vice-Chairman Wells and Winch Brewery, Biggleswade. *Recreations:* hunting, fishing, and shooting. *Address:* Boulston Manor, Haverfordwest, Pembrokeshire. *TA:* and *T:* Haverfordwest 195. *Club:* Orleans.

Died 5 July 1947.

WALKER, Miles, FRS 1931; DSc (Eng.) London, 1918; MA (Cantab), MIEE; Professor of Electrical Engineering in the Faculty of Technology, University of Manchester, 1912–32, Professor Emeritus since 1932; *b* Carlisle; *e s* of Dr Robert Walker; *m* 1st, 1903, Eveline Sargent; 2nd, 1935, Valeria D. Ellis. *Educ:* Finsbury Technical College; St John's College, Cambridge (Scholar), took first-class honours in the Natural Science Tripos, 1898, and in the Mechanical Science Tripos, 1899. First educated for the

law; passed final law examination with honours, 1890, and practised in London till 1894. The British Westinghouse Company sent him to America with other British engineers, to get an insight into American manufacturing methods; stayed 3½ years in the States, studying design and manufacture in the Company's works at Pittsburg; designer of alternating-current machinery to the British Westinghouse Company, 1903; in that capacity designed the line of high-speed engine-type alternators, and developed the cylindrical type of field-magnet for turbo-generators, as made by the Westinghouse Company; invented the Walker self-regulating alternator and an electric harmonic analyser; is the patentee of a number of improvements in electrical machinery; Special Lecturer in turbo machinery and rotary converter design in the Imperial College of Science, 1911; acts as Consulting Designer to the Metropolitan-Vickers Electrical Co., Ltd, and other firms in heavy electrical engineering. *Publications:* The Specification and Design of Dynamo-Electric Machinery; The Diagnosing of Troubles in Dynamo-Electric Machinery; The Control of Speed and Power Factor of Induction Motors; Conjugate Functions for Engineers; What Everybody ought to know about Electricity; various papers in the Journal of the Institution of Electrical Engineers. *Recreation:* walking. *Address:* Dunkirk House, Amberley, Glos. *TA:* Walker, Dunkirk House, Nailsworth. *T:* Amberley 131.

Died 22 Jan. 1941.

WALKER, Sir Norman, Kt 1923; MD, FRCP (Edin.); Hon. LLD (St Andrews, Edin. and Bristol); MD Dublin; Hon. Fellow Royal Society of Medicine; Direct Representative for Scotland, General Medical Council, 1906–41; Hon. Member of the American, and Corresponding Member of the New York, French and Danish Dermatological Societies; former Member of Court and a Curator of Patronage of Edinburgh University; *b* Dysart, Fife, 2 Aug. 1862; *o s* of Rev. Dr Norman L. Walker, for many years editor of the Magazine of the Free Church of Scotland; *m* 1887, Annie, *o d* of Edward Trimble of Green Lane, Dalston, Cumberland; three *s* one *d. Educ:* Edinburgh Academy; University of Edinburgh; University of Vienna; and University of Prague. Graduated, 1884. Resident Physician, Royal Infirmary, 1885; in general practice in Cumberland, 1885–90; President, Carlisle Medical Society, 1890; President Fife Med. Association, 1906; President RCP Ed., 1929–31; formerly editor Scottish Medical and Surgical Journal and Edinburgh Medical Journal, and Convener Scottish Medical Service Emergency Committee, 1914–20. *Publications:* An Introduction to Dermatology, 10th Edit., 1939; Translator of Unna's Histopathology of the Skin, and of Hansen's Leprosy. *Address:* Greensyke, Balerno, Midlothian. *T:* 2234.

Died 7 Nov. 1942.

WALKER, Samuel, CIE 1930; AMICE; *b* 16 Oct. 1875; 2nd *s* of Robert Walker, Architect, Cork; *m* 1906, Helen, 2nd *d* of William Ross, Leeholme, Cork; one *s* four *d. Educ:* privately; completed articles in Architecture, 1895; Bachelor of Engineering RUI, 1899. Joined Indian Service of Engineers, 1901; Under Secretary to Govt Punjab Irrigation Branch, 1921; Administrative rank, 1922; Secretary to Govt NWFP, 1925–27; Chief Engineer and Secretary to Govt NWFP, 1927–30; retired, 1931. *Address:* c/o Lloyds Bank, 6 Pall Mall, SW1; Birik, Avenue Road, Fleet, Hants. *T:* Fleet 753.

Died 1 Feb. 1945.

WALKER, Thomas Hollis, CMG 1935; KC 1910; Chairman of Lindsey Quarter Sessions, 1932–38; *b* 22 Oct. 1860; 3rd *s* of late John West Walker, JP, Hundleby House, Spilsby, Lincs; *m* 1895, Margaret (*d* 1928), *y d* of late W. A. Stuckey, 14 The Drive, Hove; no *c. Educ:* Epsom College; Christ Church, Oxford (Junior Student, 1880; BA 1883). Called to Bar, Inner Temple, 1886;

Recorder of Derby, 1918–38; JP Lincolnshire (parts of Lindsey), and Buckinghamshire; Commissioner of Assize, 1924, 1931, 1932 and 1933; Bencher Inner Temple, 1920; Treasurer, 1941. *Address:* The Barn, Burke's Road, Beaconsfield. *T:* Beaconsfield 224. *Club:* Oxford and Cambridge.

Died 12 Oct. 1945.

WALKER, Thomas Leonard, MA, PhD; FGS; Professor Emeritus, University of Toronto; Professor of Mineralogy, University of Toronto, 1901–37; Director of Royal Ontario Museum of Mineralogy since 1912; *b* County of Peel, Province of Ontario, Canada, 30 Dec. 1867; married. *Educ:* Queen's University, Kingston; University of Leipzig, Germany. MA (Queen's University), with honours in Chemistry and Mineralogy, 1890. Granted a Scholarship of £150 per year by HM Commissioners for the Exhibition of 1851, 1895; studied in Leipzig (Ph. D), 1896; Assist Superint Geol. Survey of India, 1897–1902; while in India made a scientific expedition across the high passes of the Himalayas into Thibet. *Publications:* numerous papers from 1894 onward, in scientific publications. *Address:* East 20 Avondale Avenue, Toronto, Canada.

Died 6 Aug. 1942.

WALKER, Col William Eric, CBE 1935; TD 1930; MSc Manchester; Engine Works Department Vickers-Armstrongs Ltd, Vickers House, Broadway, SW1; *b* Lawrencetown, Co. Down, 28 June 1885; *s* of late William James Dickson Walker, CB; *m* 1915, Dorothy Edith d'Insula, 2nd *d* of late Robert Norman Redmayne; one *s* two *d. Educ:* Edinburgh Academy; Manchester University. Woolwich Arsenal, 1905–09; on staff of Sir W. G. Armstrong Whitworth & Co., Ltd, 1909–14 and 1916–27; Manager, Shell Dept, Vickers-Armstrongs, Elswick Works, 1928–39; Director of Ammunition Production (Shell), Ministry of Supply, 1940–44; Principal Director of Gun Ammunition Production, Ministry of Supply, 1944–45; joined 1st Northumbrian Brigade, RFA, Territorial Army, 1911; served in European War, 1914–18; seconded from active service at request of Ministry of Munitions to manage Cartridge Case Factories at Elswick, Scotswood, and Birtley; commanded 72nd Field Brigade, RA; Territorial Army, 1929–35; Bt Col 1933; Col 1936. *Recreations:* fishing, golf, squash racquets. *Address:* Vickers House, Broadway, SW1. *T:* Abbey 7777, Extn 161.

Died 14 April 1949.

WALKER, Adm. Sir William Frederic W.; *see* Wake-Walker.

WALL, Rt Rev. Francis Joseph; Consecrated Titular Bishop of Thasos and Auxiliary to the Archbishop of Dublin by the Nuncio Apostolic, 1931; Parish Priest of St Mary's Haddington Road, Dublin, and Vicar General since 1925; *b* Dublin, 16 Oct. 1866; *s* of John Wall and Alicia Connolly. *Educ:* Christian Brothers, N Richmond Street, Dublin; Belvedere College, SJ, Dublin; Holy Cross College, Clonliffe, Dublin; College of the Propaganda, Rome; A graduate of the RU of Ireland (now National University of Ireland). Priest, 1889; on return from Rome in 1890, appointed Assistant Religious Examiner of Schools; then Senior Examiner till 1898; Curate at St Mary's, Haddington Road, 1898–1922; Parish Priest of St Columba's, Iona Road, Dublin, 1922; Chaplain Conventual Knights of Malta (Irish Association); Assistant at the Pontifical Throne, 1941. *Address:* St Mary's, Haddington Road, Dublin.

Died May 1947.

WALL, Col Frank, CMG 1915; KHS 1924; CMZS; FLS; FAS Bengal; HCZS India; IMS, retired; *b* 21 April 1868; *s* of late George Wall, FRAS, FLS, Colombo; *m* 1st, 1903, Margaret Georgina, *d* of late John Stagg Cusse; one *s*; 2nd, 1924, Mildred Constance, *d* of late Captain R. W. Evans, RN. *Educ:* Middlesex Hospital. Captain, 1898; Major, 1904; Lt-Col 1914; Col 1921; retired,

1925; served European War, 1914–18 (despatches twice, CMG, Bt Lt-Col). *Publications:* The Poisonous Terrestrial Snakes of our British Indian Dominions; Ophidia Taprobanica, or the Snakes of Ceylon; How to Identify the Snakes of India. *Address:* c/o Lloyds Bank Ltd, 6 Pall Mall, SW1.

Died 19 May 1950.

WALL, Sir Frederick (Joseph), Kt 1930; FCIS; *b* 14 April 1858; *y s* of late William Wall and Elizabeth Mansfield, Wormley, Hertfordshire. *Educ:* St Mark's College, Chelsea. Elected Member of the Council of the London Football Association, 1881; Vice-President, 1892; elected a Member of the Council of the Middlesex County Association, 1888; Hon. Secretary and Treasurer, 1890; represented the Middlesex County Association on the Council of the Football Association, 1891–95; Secretary, The Football Association, 1895–1934. *Publication:* Fifty Years of Football, 1935. *Recreations:* rowing, cricket, football. *Address:* Weetwood, 35 Langley Park Road, Sutton, Surrey. *T:* Vigilant 2820.

Died 25 March 1944.

WALL, Engr Rear-Adm. Henry, CMG 1918; *b* 1867; *s* of Charles Wall; *m* 1901. Retired List, 1925. *Address:* Firlands, Glenferness Avenue, Bournemouth.

Died 30 July 1950.

WALL, Reginald Cecil Bligh, MA, DM Oxon; FRCP; Consulting Physician, London Hospital and Brompton Hospital for Diseases of Chest; Archivist and Past Master of the Society of Apothecaries; Fitzpatrick Lecturer, RCP, 1944–45; Thomas Vicary Lecturer, RCS 1935; *b* 1869; *s* of late Reginald Bligh Wall of Bayswater and Irene, *d* of late James Luke, PRCS, FRS; *m* Dorothy, *d* of H. Innes Fripp; one *s* two *d. Educ:* Bradfield College, Queen's College, Oxford; London Hospital. *Publications:* The Surgeon's Company, 1745–1800, 1937; contributions to medical journals. *Address:* 14 Regents Park Terrace, NW1. *T:* Gulliver 1844.

Died 19 June 1947.

WALLACE, Maj.-Gen. Charles John, CB 1941; DSO 1918; OBE 1919; MC; Commander East Central District, Dunstable; *b* 1890. *Educ:* Charterhouse. Served European War, 1914–19 (DSO, OBE, MC, despatches); AA and QMG 1st Division at Aldershot, 1935–38; Commander 3rd (Jhelum) Infantry Brigade, India, 1939; ADC to the King, 1938–40.

Died 20 Dec. 1943.

WALLACE, Charles Redwood Vachell, CBE 1938; Assistant Director of Public Prosecutions; *b* 3 April 1877; *e s* of Thomas Wallace, MD and Jane Vachell; *m* 1921, Elaine Gladys Jenkins; no *c. Educ:* Rugby; Exeter College, Oxford. Articled in Cardiff, 1899–1902; admitted Solicitor, 1903; entered Department of Director of Public Prosecutions, 1903; enlisted Royal Fusiliers 1914 (wounded); discharged unfit, 1917. *Recreation:* walking. *Address:* 190 Rivermead Court, Hurlingham, SW6. *Club:* Public Schools.

Died 25 March 1944.

WALLACE, Sir Cuthbert Sidney, 1st Bt *cr* 1937; KCMG 1919; CB 1918; CMG 1916; MB, BS Lond.; Hon. DSc Oxford; Hon. DCL Durham; Hon. LLD Birmingham; FRCS Eng.; JP, London County; Member, Army Advisory Medical Council; Director of Medical Services, Mount Vernon Hospital; Consultant Adviser, EMS Ministry of Health; late President, Royal College of Surgeons, England; late Surgeon to St Thomas's Hospital; late Surgeon, East London Hospital for Children; late Lecturer on Surgery, St Thomas's Hospital; late Member of Court of Examiners; late Member Medical Research Council; late Member of Radium Commission; *b* 20 June 1867; 3rd *s* of Rev. John Wallace; *m* 1912, Florence Mildred, *y d* of Herbert Jackson, 4 Sussex Place, Regent's Park. *Educ:* Haileybury College; St Thomas's Hospital. Served in South Africa as

Surgeon to Portland Hospital, 1900; European War, 1914–18; Major-General AMS; Consulting Surgeon, 1st Army, BEF, France (despatches, CB, CMG, KCMG, DSM America); Officer of Legion of Honour. *Publications:* various works on surgical subjects. *Address:* 5 Cambridge Terrace, Regent's Park, NW. *T:* Welbeck 9493. *Clubs:* Athenæum, Savile.

Died 24 May 1944 (ext).

WALLACE, Captain Rt Hon. (David) Euan, PC 1936; MC; MP (U) Rugby Division of Warwickshire, 1922–23, Hornsey since 1924; Senior Regional Commissioner for Civil Defence in London, 1940; *b* 1892; *s* of late John Wallace of Glassingall, Dunblane; *m* 1st, 1913, Lady Idina Sackville (whom he divorced 1919); two *s*; 2nd, 1920, Barbara, *e d* of Sir Edwin Lutyens, RA; three *s. Educ:* Harrow; RMC, Sandhurst. Joined 2nd Life Guards, 1911; Adjutant, 1915–18; now Capt., Reserve of Officers; served France, 1914–18 (wounded, despatches 4 times, MC); Assistant Military Attaché at Washington, 1919; ADC Governor-General of Canada, 1920; Parliamentary Private Secretary (unpaid) to First Lord of the Admiralty, 1922–23, and to the Secretary of State for the Colonies, 1924–28; an Asst Govt Whip 1928–29; Lord of the Treasury, 1929 and 1931; Civil Lord of the Admiralty, 1931–35; Under-Secretary of State for Home Affairs, 1935; Secretary, Dept of Overseas Trade, 1935–37; Parliamentary Secretary, Board of Trade, 1937–38; Financial Secretary to the Treasury, 1938–39; Ministry of Transport, 1939–40. *Recreations:* shooting and golf. *Address:* 19 Hill Street, W1. *T:* Mayfair 6212; Lavington Park, Petworth. *T:* Graffham 45. *Clubs:* Carlton, Turf, Beefsteak, Buck's.

Died 9 Feb. 1941.

WALLACE, Sir Edward Hamilton, Kt 1931; *b* 13 May 1873; *s* of late Rev. George Wallace, UF Church, Scotland, and Elizabeth Smith, Sunderland; *m* 1901, Anna Richmond Miller, *d* of late John Loudon, Ayr; two *s. Educ:* Hamilton Academy; Glasgow High School and University; Balliol College, Oxford, MA (Glas.); BA (Oxon); ICS, passed 1895. Joined at Madras, 1896; served as Assistant Collector, Sub-Collector and District Judge; services lent to Mysore State as Puisne Judge, Chief Court, Mysore, 1912–14; Puisne Judge, High Court, Madras, 1924–33; retired, 1933. *Recreations:* sketching, music, golf. *Address:* Whinnyknowe, Elgin, Scotland. *T:* Elgin 2384.

Died 31 Aug. 1943.

WALLACE, Edward Wilson, MA, DD; Chancellor and President, Victoria University, University of Toronto, since 1930; *b* Metuchen, NJ, 2 Nov. 1880; *s* of late Rev. Prof. Francis Huston Wallace, DD, Toronto, and Joy, *d* of Bishop Edward Wilson, Metuchen, NJ; *m* 1st, 1912, Rose N. Cullen (*d* 1924); 2nd, 1929, Velma M. Hamill; one *s. Educ:* Harbord Collegiate Institute, Toronto; Victoria College, University of Toronto; Columbia University. Appointed by the Methodist Church of Canada, to its West China Mission as an educational missionary, 1906; professor of Educational Administration in West China Union University, and general secretary of the West China Christian Educational Union, 1912, serving all missions in West China through the development of a modern curriculum for primary and secondary schools, the training of teachers, and the inspection of schools throughout the province of Szechwan; a member of the China Educational Commission, sent to survey all Christian educational institutions throughout China, 1921–22; called to Shanghai to become general secretary of the China Christian Educational Association, and editor of the Educational Review, 1923; one of the six missionary representatives from China at the Jerusalem Conference, 1928. *Publications:* The Heart of Szchuan, 1904; The New Life in China, 1914; Editor, Educational Review, Shanghai, 1923–1928. *Address:* Victoria University, Toronto, Canada.

Died 20 June 1941.

WALLACE, Captain Rt Hon. Euan; *see* Wallace, D. E.

WALLACE, Sir John, Kt 1935; Director of Michael Nairn & Co., Ltd; *b* 1 July 1868; *s* of John Wallace and Catherine Oswald; *m* 1913, Mary M'Adam Bryce, *d* of J. G. Temple; one *s. Educ:* Kirkcaldy Public School. MP (CL) Dunfermline Burghs, Dec. 1918–22, and (Nat.), 1931–35. *Recreation:* golf. *Address:* St Oswald's, Stormont Road, Highgate, N6. *T:* Mountview 1269.

Died 12 April 1949.

WALLACE, Sir Lawrence Aubrey, KBE 1918; CMG 1910; *b* 2 Feb. 1857; *s* of late John Henry Wallace; *m* 1907, Marguerite-Marie, CBE, *e d* of Professor Henry Duboc of Le Havre, France; one *s* one *d.* Civil engineer; on railway construction in S Africa and S America till 1894; travel and sport in Central Africa, 1895–1902; joined NE Rhodesia Administration as chief surveyor, 1902; Administrator North-Eastern Rhodesia, 1907; Acting Administrator North-Western Rhodesia, 1909; Administrator Northern Rhodesia, 1911; retired, 1921. *Publications:* papers on NE Rhodesia in Royal Geographical Journal. *Address:* Magali, Avenue de la Mer, Cabourg, Calvados, France.

Died 26 Jan. 1942.

WALLACE, O. C. S., DD; LLD; LittD; Pastor Eutaw Place Baptist Church, Baltimore, 1921–35, now Pastor Emeritus; *b* Canaan, County of King's, Nova Scotia, 1856; *e s* of William John and Rachel Witter Wallace; *m* 1st, 1885, Leonette Crosby (*d* 1902), 2nd *d* of Harris Harding Crosby, of Hebron, NS; 2nd, 1904, Frances B. Moule Wells (*d* 1917), *y d* of late John Moule of London, Ontario, and *widow* of Prof. J. E. Wells, LLD; 3rd, 1919, Helen, *d* of late Rev. John Wright Moore, of Folkestone, England; one *s* one *d. Educ:* Horton Academy, Wolfville, NS; Worcester Academy; Acadia University, BA 1883, MA 1888, DD 1897, LittD 1926; Newton Theological Institution. A country schoolmaster in Nova Scotia at 15; a home missionary preacher at 17; student-pastor at Chelmsford, Mass, USA, at 18; ordained as pastor of the First Baptist Church, Lawrence, Mass, USA, 1885–91; pastor Bloor Street Baptist Church, Toronto, Canada, 1891–95; Chancellor McMaster University, Toronto, 1895–1905; Principal, *ex officio,* of the McMaster University Faculty and Professor of Homiletics; Pastor, 1st Baptist Church, Lowell, Mass, 1905–08; 1st Baptist Church, Baltimore, Md, 1908–13; Westmount Baptist Church, Montreal, 1913–21; President Baptist Convention of Ontario and Quebec, 1918; President, Baptist Convention of Maryland, USA, 1922–25; LLD Mercer Univ. 1897, Queen's Univ. 1903, McMaster Univ. 1909. *Publications:* Life of Jesus; Teachings of Jesus; Labours and Letters of the Apostles; What Baptists Believe; From Montreal to Vimy Ridge and Beyond; Looking Towards the Heights; Clover, Brier, and Tansy; As Thorns Thrust Forth; Pastor and People; Newspaper Correspondent. *Recreations:* Rugby football player when a student; tennis also; later, an enthusiastic wheelman; then golf and curling, expert checker-player when a lad. *Address:* 2223 Sulgrave Avenue, Mount Washington, Baltimore 9, USA. *Clubs:* Eclectic, Baltimore.

Died 29 Aug. 1947.

WALLACE, Percy Maxwell, MA; Secretary to the Senate of the University of London, 1901–23; *b* Loughborough, 20 Jan. 1863; *e s* of late Rev. James Wallace, MA, Headmaster of Loughborough Grammar School, and Fanny, *o d* of Charles Gore; *m* 1906, Helen Margaret, *d* of late John Philip Duigan, MD. *Educ:* Bradfield; Malvern; Lincoln Coll., Oxford (classical scholar). BA 1885; MA 1889. Professor of English Literature at the Mohammedan Anglo-Oriental College, Aligarh, NWP, India, 1887–90; Examiner in Univ. of Allahabad, 1889–90; Assistant Secretary to the London Society for the Extension of University Teaching, 1891–1901; has examined for Civil Service Commission, University of London, London County Council, etc.

Publications: Editor of Tennyson's Princess, 1891; has contributed articles to Nineteenth Century, Dictionary of National Biography, Lancet, etc., and stories to Temple Bar, etc. *Address:* 39 Coleherne Court, SW5. *T:* Frobisher 2056.

Died 26 Feb. 1943.

WALLAS, Katharine Talbot, CBE 1933; MA; *b* 11 April 1864; *d* of late Rev. Gilbert Innes Wallas and late Frances Talbot Peacock. *Educ:* Girton College, Cambridge. Co-opted Member, London County Council Education Committee, 1910–13 and 1934–37; Alderman, LCC 1913–34. *Address:* 34 Princes House, Kensington Park Road, W11.

Died 14 April 1944.

WALLER, Vice-Adm. Arthur Craig, CB 1916; RN; late President Ordnance Committee; *b* 18 June 1872; *s* of late Very Rev. Dean Craig of Clonmacnois; *m* 1910, Ella Mary, *d* of A. F. Beaufort; two *s*. Served European War, 1914–19; Commanding HMS Albermarle, Barham, 1915–18 (battle of Jutland); and Renown, 1918–19 (CB, despatches, St Anne, Rising Sun, Legion of Honour); retired list, 1922; DL Co. Meath. *Address:* Chargate Lodge, Burwood Park, Walton-on-Thames. *T:* 1806. *Club:* United Service.

Died 21 Feb. 1943.

WALLER, Rev. Charles Cameron, MA, DD; Professor of Hebrew, University of Western Ontario, London, Canada; *b* 1869; 2nd *s* of Rev. Chas. Henry Waller, DD, of St John's Hall, Highbury; *m* 1st, Susanna Jane Gertrude (*d* 1923), *d* of late Archibald Jerdon, younger of Bonjedward; one *d*; 2nd, 1924, Louisa Frances, *y d* of late Alexander Johnson, LLD, Vice-Principal of McGill Univ., Montreal; one *s*. *Educ:* Highgate Grammar School; St John's College and Ridley Hall, Cambridge; McGill University, Montreal. Classical Tutor and Librarian Diocesan College, Montreal, 1890–97; Deacon, 1892; Priest, 1893; Curate Church of Advent, 1892–94; St Jude's, Montreal, 1894–96; Christ Church Cathedral, Montreal, 1896–97; Tutor St John's Hall, Highbury, London, England, 1897–1900; Assistant Curate St Mary's, Stoke Newington; Chaplain Homburg, 1900–02; Principal and Divinity Professor, Huron College, London, Canada, 1902–41, Principal Emeritus, 1942; Lecturer in St Paul's Cathedral, London, since 1902; Member of Provincial Synod of Ontario, 1913; of General Synod, 1915; Delegate to Congress of Universities of British Empire, 1926, 1931, 1936; to World Conference on Faith and Order, Edinburgh, 1937; Assistant Grand Chaplain Grand Lodge of Ontario, 1940–41. *Publications:* Date of Epistle to Galatians; Song, Canada Land for Me. *Recreations:* carpenter and builder, boating, fishing, sketching. *Address:* 551 St George Street, London, Canada; Gregory, Muskoka, Ontario. *TA:* London, Canada. *T:* Metcalf 1536.

Died 11 Dec. 1944.

WALLER, Sir David Grierson, Kt 1932; *b* 4 July 1872; *s* of late Lt-Col W. F. F. Waller, VC, Bombay Staff Corps; *m* Eileen Nevill, *d* of Rev. W. N. Leeson; one *d*. *Educ:* Bath College; Trinity College, Oxford. MCS, 1896. Puisne Judge, High Court, Madras, 1924–32; retired, 1932. *Address:* Greenacre, Fleet, Hants.

Died 20 Nov. 1949.

WALLER, Rt Rev. Edward Harry Mansfield, MA (Cantab); DD Western University of Canada; DD Trinity College, Toronto; *b* 8 Dec. 1871; *s* of late Rev. Dr Waller, Principal, St John's Hall, Highbury; *m* Irene Juliana Louisa Doudney (*d* 1933). *Educ:* Highgate School; Corpus Christi Coll., Cambridge (Scholar, 2nd class Classical Tripos). Ordained deacon, 1894; priest, 1895; tutor, St John's Hall, 1893; Assistant Chaplain, 1894; Vice-Principal, St Paul's Divinity School, Allahabad, 1897; Principal, 1903; Principal, Jay Narayan's School, Benares, 1907; Secretary CMS, United Provinces, India, 1909; Secretary of the Church

Missionary Society (Indian Group), 1913; Canon of Lucknow, 1910–15; Bishop of Tinnevelly, 1915–22; Bishop of Madras, 1923–41. *Publications:* Commentary Revelation in Bishops' Commentaries for Indian Church; The Divinity of Jesus Christ. *Recreations:* sculling, rowing (winner of Colquhoun Sculls, 1892; Cambridge University Boat, 1893), etc.

Died 16 May 1942.

WALLER, Sir Wathen Arthur, 5th Bt *cr* 1815; *b* 6 Oct. 1881; *s* of 3rd Bt and Beatrice Katharine Frances, 5th *d* of Christopher and Lady Sophia Tower; *S* brother, 1914; *m* 1904, Viola, *d* of Henry Le Sueur, ISO, Cape Town. *Educ:* Harrow School; RMC, Sandhurst. Late Northumberland Fusiliers; JP, DL, Warwickshire. *Heir:* cousin Edmund Waller, *b* 1871. *Address:* Woodcote, Warwick. *T:* Kenilworth 58. *Club:* Army and Navy.

Died 26 April 1947.

WALLER, Sir William Edgar, 7th Bt *cr* 1780; *b* 22 Nov. 1863; *S* 1912; *m* 1890, Mary Augusta Meyers; two *s* two *d*. *Heir:* *s* Roland Edgar, *b* 11 Jan. 1892. *Address:* 112 West Newell Avenue, Rutherford, New Jersey, USA.

Died 16 April 1943.

WALLING, Robert Alfred John; Director Whitfield and Newman, Ltd; Editor, Western Independent, Plymouth; Chairman of Justices, Plymouth; *b* Exeter, 11 Jan. 1869; *s* of late R. H. Walling, journalist; *m* 1894, Florence Victoria (*d* 1948), *d* of late Commander Joseph Greet, RN; two *s* one *d*. Reporter. Western Daily Mercury; Editor, Bicycling News; Editor, Western Evening Herald; Managing Editor, Western Daily Mercury, Plymouth. *Publications:* Flaunting Moll, 1898, etc.; Borrow in Cornwall; Sir John Hawkins; A Book of Plymouth; A Sea Dog of Devon; George Borrow; The Man and His Work; On the British Front; Adventures of a Rubberneck; The Diaries of John Bright; The Charm of Brittany; The West Country; Green Hills of England. Mystery Stories: The Strong Room; That Dinner at Bardolph's; Murder at the Keyhole; The Man with the Squeaky Voice; The Stroke of One; The Fatal Five Minutes; Behind the Yellow Blind; Follow the Blue Car; The Tolliver Case; Eight to Nine; The Five Suspects; The Cat and the Corpse; The Corpse in the Crimson Slippers; The Mystery of Mr Mock; Bury Him Deeper; The Coroner Doubts; More than One Serpent; Dust in the Vault; They Liked Entwhistle; Why did Trethewy Die?; Castle-Dinas; The Doodled Asterisk; The Corpse without a Clue; The Late Unlamented. *Recreation:* the piano. *Address:* Crofton, Merafield Rd, Plympton, S Devon. *T:* Plympton 3261. *Club:* National Liberal.

Died 4 Sept. 1949.

WALLIS, Major Charles Braithwaite, MA, MLitt, LLB, Cambridge; FGS, FRGS; HM Envoy Extraordinary, Minister Plenipotentiary and Consul-General, Diplomatic Service (retd); late The Cameronians; of the Middle Temple, Barrister-at-law; *e s* of late Charles W. Wallis, MA, Middle Temple, Barrister, and Gertrude, 3rd *d* of late E. Edmonds, DL, JP, of Berryfield, and Belcombe Court, Bradford, Wilts; *m* 1913, Bessie Agnes, *o d* of late George Laird, Birkenhead. *Educ:* Oxford Military College. Joined 4th Manchester Regiment 1894; Capt. 1898; seconded and appointed to Sierra Leone Frontier Force, 1898; Sherbro and Protectorate Expeditions, 1898–99 (despatches, West African medal and clasp); transferred to The Cameronians (Scottish Rifles), 1899; Maj. 1918; served in India, 1899–1901; Assistant Commissioner in Sierra Leone, 1901; Commissioner, 1905; entered Middle Temple, 1905; served under Foreign Office as acting British Consul for Liberia, 1905; operations in Liberian hinterland (African General Service Medal and clasp); Consul for Liberia, 1906; Consul-General for Liberia to reside at Monrovia, 1908; HM Consul-General at Dakar for French Western Africa and the Sudan, 1909–20; HM Consul-General, New Orleans, USA, 1920–23; in charge of Spanish interests at Dakar, 1912–13;

Coronation medal, 1911; called to Bar, Middle Temple, 1917; Member of St John's College, Cambridge; European War, 1915–19; Bronze Star, British War and Victory medals; JP Sierra Leone; HM's Minister and Consul-General to Panama and the Canal Zone and Costa Rica, 1923–31; negotiated Treaty of Friendship and Commerce with Panama and Commercial Agreement with Costa Rica, 1928; Civil Defence Service, 1939–40; Home Guard, 1940–44; Member Price Regulation Cttee, Eastern Region, at Cambridge, 1944. *Publications:* The Advance of our West African Empire; West African Warfare; papers in the Journals of the African and Royal Geographical Societies; various official reports. *Clubs:* United Service, Royal Societies.

Died 4 Aug. 1945.

WALLIS, Frederick Samuel; *b* Macclesfield, South Australia, 22 Nov. 1857; *s* of Richard Wallis, formerly of London, and Annie Gamble, formerly of Leicester. *Educ:* public and private schools, Adelaide and Norwood. President (three years) and Secretary (twenty-two years) SA Typographical Society; Secretary Trades and Labour Council of SA twelve years; Member Legislative Council (Central District), 1907–21; Chief Secretary and Minister of Industry, 1909; Chief Secretary, 1910–12; Parliamentary Representative on Council of University of Adelaide, 1915–21; Chairman Relief Committee South Australian Soldiers' Fund 1915–36; Foundation member (1885) SA Branch Royal Geographical Society. *Recreation:* gardening.

Died 13 Nov. 1939.

WALLIS, Henry Richard, CMG 1911; CBE 1918; Commander of the Crown of Belgium, 1924; *b* 28 May 1866; *s* of late S. Wallis, jun., of Darlington, England; *m* Jane Robina, *d* of late Robert Wallace of Rhynd, Fifeshire, Scotland; one *s* one *d*. *Educ:* privately. Entered Colonial Service, 1889; Vice-Consul, Fort Johnston, British Central Africa, 1897; Assistant Deputy-Governor, Nyasaland Protectorate, 1904; acted as Commissioner and Commander-in-Chief, 1905, and as Governor and Commander-in-Chief, 1910; Acting Governor, Uganda, during 1912, 1913, 1914, 1917–18; Chief Secretary to the Government, Uganda Protectorate, 1911; retired, Sept. 1918; 1914 Star, War and Victory Medals. *Publication:* The Handbook of Uganda, 1914. *Address:* 1 Lypiatt Lawn, Cheltenham. *Clubs:* New, Cheltenham.

Died 6 March 1946.

WALLIS, Rt Hon. Sir John Edward Power, PC 1926; Kt 1912; MA; Member of Judicial Committee of Privy Council since 1926; *b* Nov. 1861; *s* of late John E. Wallis, Inner Temple, Judge in the Mixed Tribunals of Egypt; *m* 1903, Dorothea Margaret (*d* 1930), *d* of late W. R. Fowke. Called to Bar, Middle Temple, 1886; Inns of Court Reader in Constitutional Law, circa, 1892–97; Advocate-General, Madras, 1900–07; Vice-Chancellor Madras University, 1908–16; Puisne Judge, 1907–14; Chief Justice, 1914–21; edited vols iv to viii of State Trials, new series, for the State Trials Committee. *Club:* Athenæum.

Died 8 June 1946.

WALLS, Tom; owner, trainer and actor; *b* Kingsthorpe, Northamptonshire, 18 Feb. 1883; *s* of John Wm Walls and Ellen Brewer; *m* Hilda Edwardes; one *s*. *Educ:* Northampton County School. First appearance on stage, Glasgow, 1905; toured in America and Canada, 1906–07; first London appearance, the Empire, 1907; in musical comedies at the Empire and on tour, 1908–10; toured in Australia, 1910–11; at Daly's, the Adelphi, the Empire, the Gaiety, London Hippodrome, etc. 1912–22; in management with Leslie Henson at the Shaftesbury, 1922, with Tons of Money, which ran for two years; at the Aldwych produced and played in A Cuckoo in the Nest 1925, Rookery Nook 1926, Thark 1927, Plunder 1928, A Cup of Kindness 1929, A Night Like This 1930, Marry the Girl 1930, Turkey Time 1931; manager of

Fortune Theatre, where he produced On Approval 1927, Mischief 1928, Aren't We All 1929; The Last Enemy, 1929; Cape Forlorn, 1930; The High Road at Shaftesbury Theatre, 1927. Entered films 1929 and has directed and acted in, among others, Rookery Nook, On Approval, Canaries Sometimes Sing, A Cuckoo in the Nest, Foreign Affaires, Me and Marlborough, Just Smith, For Valour, Second Best Bed, Crackerjack, Strange Boarders, Dishonour Bright, Undercover, They Met in the Dark, Halfway House, Love Story, Johnny Frenchman, He Belongs to Me, The Crowthers of Bankdam, While I Live, Spring in Park Lane. Maytime in Mayfair, Interrupted Journey. Owned and trained April the Fifth, winner of the Derby 1932. Trained the winners of many races including the Victory Steeplechase, Grand Military Gold Cup, Brighton Cup, Liverpool Cup, and Epsom Derby. *Address:* The Looe, Ewell, Epsom. *T:* Ewell 1419.

Died 27 Nov. 1949.

WALLS, William, RSA, 1914; RSW; *b* Dunfermline, 1860; *m* Elizabeth, *d* of Henry Maclellan, Castle-Douglas; one *s* one *d*. *Educ:* High School, Dunfermline. Studied at School of Design and RSA Life School, Edinburgh, and at Antwerp Academy. Painted principally in Antwerp and London Zoos, the Fen country, and latterly in the Highlands; exhibits in RA, RSA, Munich, Vienna, and Venice; principal pictures— High Noon in the Fens, property of representatives of the late Sir Henry Campbell-Bannerman; Peace after War, property of Sir John Gilmour, Montrave; The Twa Dugs, and The Falls of Shin, property of Andrew Carnegie; The Snow Leopard's Toilet, property of The Scottish Modern Arts Association; Cave Dwellers at Play, property of Scottish Modern Arts Association; Out of Reach, property of Dundee Art Gallery; In the Arena, purchased by Thorburn Ross Bequest; Suspicion, Glasgow Corporation; Snow Leopards, Paisley; Lioness and Cubs, Dunfermline Carnegie Trust. *Recreations:* angling, gardening, painting. *Address:* Studio, Kaimes Road, Corstorphine, Midlothian. *T:* Corstorphine 86361.

Died 2 June 1942.

WALMSLEY, Sir Hugh, Kt 1923; JP, MA, ICS; *b* 1871; *m* 1905, Marion (*d* 1929), *y d* of Richard Lea Early; three *d*. *Educ:* Merton College, Oxford. Entered ICS 1893; Magistrate and Collector, 1906; Judge of High Court, Calcutta, 1915–26. *Address:* Park Farm, Knockholt, Kent.

Died 11 May 1950.

WALPOLE, Sir Hugh Seymour, Kt 1937; CBE 1918; novelist; *b* 1884; *s* of late Rt Rev. G. H. S. Walpole, Bishop of Edinburgh; unmarried. *Educ:* King's School, Canterbury; Emmanuel College, Cambridge. Served with Russian Red Cross in European War, 1914–16 (Georgian medal). *Publications:* The Wooden Horse, 1909; Maradick at Forty, 1910; Mr Perrin and Mr Traill, 1911; The Prelude to Adventure, 1912; Fortitude, 1913; The Duchess of Wrexe, 1914; The Golden Scarecrow, 1915; The Dark Forest, 1916; Joseph Conrad, 1916; The Green Mirror, 1918; The Secret City, 1919 (awarded James Tait Black Prize); Jeremy, 1919; The Captives, 1920; The Thirteen Travellers, 1921; The Young Enchanted, 1922; The Cathedral, 1922 (dramatised 1932); Jeremy and Hamlet, 1923; The Old Ladies, 1924; Portrait of a Man with Red Hair, 1925; The English Novel (Rede Lecture); Harmer John, 1926; These Diversions: Reading, 1926; Jeremy at Crale, 1927; Wintersmoon, 1928; The Silver Thorn, 1928; Anthony Trollope (English Men of Letters), 1928; (with J. B. Priestley) Farthing Hall, 1929; Hans Frost, 1929; Rogue Herries, 1930; Above the Dark Circus, 1931; Judith Paris, 1931; The Fortress, 1932; The Waverley Pageant, 1932; All Souls' Night, 1933; Vanessa, 1933; The Apple Trees: Four Reminiscences, 1933; Captain Nicholas, 1934; The Inquisitor, 1935; A Prayer for My Son, 1936; John Cornelius, 1937; Head in Green Bronze, 1938; The

Joyful Delaneys, 1938; The Sea Tower, 1939; Roman Fountain, 1940; The Bright Pavilions, 1940; The Blind Man's House, 1941; The Killer and the Slain, 1942; The Herries Chronicle, 1942; Katherine Christian, 1944; plays produced, The Cathedral; The Young Huntress, 1933; The Haxtons, 1939. *Recreations:* walking, talking. *Address:* c/o Macmillan and Co. Ltd, St Martin's Street, WC2. *Clubs:* Athenæum, Garrick, Beefsteak.

Died 1 June 1941.

WALROND, Arthur Melville Hood; *b* 17 March 1861; *s* of Sir John Walrond, 1st Bt, Bradfield, Cullompton, Devon; *m* 1st, 1888, Marion, *d* of W. R. Coleridge, Salston, Ottery St Mary; (one *s* killed Arras, 1917) one *d*; 2nd, 1928, Elizabeth Naomi, *widow* of Major Dominick Browne. *Educ:* HMS Britannia, Dartmouth. Was in the Navy, 1875–81; then farming and ranching in Canada until 1888; joined Exeter Bank, Exeter, as a partner; became a Director of Prescott's Bank, 1902, and Union of London and Smith's Bank, 1903–19; served European War, Lt-Col Remount Services. Egypt and Italy (despatches) and on Staff Admiral Dover Patrol. *Club:* Naval and Military.

Died 24 June 1946.

WALSH, Sir Cecil, Kt 1926; KC; *b* 26 March 1869; 3rd *s* of Percival Walsh, solicitor, Stanton Harcourt, Oxon; *m* 1st, Gertrude (*d* 1906), *d* of Rev. Prebendary Whittington; two *s* one *d*; 2nd, 1915, Isabel Hellmund (*d* 1932), *widow*, *d* of Madame de la Sota, Paris; 3rd, 1933, Phyllis, *y d* of late Oswald Cole, Chief Constable of the City of Oxford. *Educ:* Honiton Grammar School; St John's College, Oxford; BA History, 1890; MA 1910. Barr Gray's Inn, 1895; Oxford Circuit; Mayor of Wimbledon, 1909; King's Counsel, 1913; Puisne Judge, India, 1915–28; Bencher of Gray's Inn, 1916; Treasurer, 1931; acting Chief Justice, March–Aug. 1924, July 1926–Feb. 1927. *Publications:* (India) The Advocate, Revision, Usurious Loans Act, Indian Village Tragedies; (Joint) Pleadings in India; (England) The Agra Double Murder; Indian Village Crimes, 1929; Crime in India, 1930. *Recreations:* gardening, music, writing. *Address:* North Seat, Sea View, Isle of Wight. *T:* Seaview 3130. *Club:* Union.

Died 24 Nov. 1946.

WALSH, Sir Charles Arthur, KBE 1922; *b* 1869; *s* of Richard Walsh, LRCP, Clogheen; *m* 1898, Isabel, *d* of Robert Malcolmson, solicitor, Carlow; one *s* four *d*. *Educ:* Royal University of Ireland, BA. *Address:* Ivanhoe, 53 Sidney Parade Avenue, Dublin.

Died 9 Nov. 1949.

WALSH, Geoffrey, CMG 1943; CBE 1930; Food Controller, Palestine, 1942; Economic and Financial Adviser to the GOC Palestine, Transjordan, and Syria, and to the Spears Mission (Syria) with rank of Brigadier, 1941; Economic Adviser to the High Commissioner for Palestine; Chairman of the Standing Committee for Commerce and Industry, Member of the Advisory Council, Palestine, 1938; *b* 1884; *s* of late John Walsh, Shirley, Southampton; *m* 1921, Gladys Mary, *widow* of Leonard Atkins, *o d* of Arthur Griffith; one *d*. *Educ:* King Edward's School, Southampton. Imperial Customs service, April 1906; Collector of Customs, Mombasa, 1913; seconded to occupied territory of German East Africa to organise customs service, with rank of Capt., 1916–17; in charge of Customs Dept, civil area of German East Africa, Jan.–July 1917; Deputy Commissioner of Customs, Kenya and Uganda, 1920; Chairman of the Kenya Harbour Advisory Board, 1927–33; Commissioner of Customs, Kenya and Uganda, 1923–34; Treasurer of Kenya Colony, Member of Executive, Legislative and Railway Advisory Councils, Currency Officer, 1934–38; retired, 1938. *Address:* PO Box 1248, Jerusalem, Palestine. *Club:* East India and Sports.

Died 22 July 1946.

WALSH, James J., BA, AM, MD, PhD, ScD, LittD, LLDEdD; KCStG; KM; Trustee Catholic Summer School of America; Carnegie Church Peace Union; *b* 12 April 1865; *s* of Martin J. Walsh and Bridget Golden; *m* 1915, Julia Huelat Freed; one *s* one *d*. *Educ:* St John's College, Fordham University; University of Pennsylvania; Paris, Vienna, Berlin. Instructor in Medicine NY Polyclinic Medical School, 1900; Adjunct Professor, 1904; Dean and Professor of Nervous Diseases and The History of Medicine, Fordham University School of Medicine, 1907–13; late Professor of Physiological Psychology at Cathedral College, NYC; held several other important teaching positions; popular lecturer for Open Forums and occasional lecturer on historical and social subjects for many colleges and universities. *Publications:* The Thirteenth, Greatest of Centuries; Popes and Science; Catholic Churchmen in Science (3 vols); Pastoral Medicine; Makers of Modern Medicine, Old Time Makers of Medicine; Education How Old the New; Makers of Electricity (with Brother Potamian); Modern Progress and History; Health Through Will Power; History of Medicine in New York State, 5 vols; Medieval Medicine; Success in a New Era; Religion and Health; Psychotherapy; Cures; What Civilization Owes to Italy; The World's Debt to the Catholic Church; Century of Columbus; Safeguarding Children's Nerves (with Dr John Foote); Spiritualism a Fake (with Hereward Carrington's Spiritualism a Fact); Our American Cardinals; The World's Debt to the Irish; These Splendid Sisters; These Splendid Priests; Laughter and Health; The Church and Healing; Priests and Long Life; The History of Nursing; Life of Mother Alphonsa (Rose Hawthorne Lathrop); A Catholic Looks at Life; A Golden Treasury of Medieval Literature; Sex Instruction; American Jesuits; Education of the Founding Fathers of the Republic; High Points of Medieval Culture. *Recreation:* walking. *Address:* 344 West 72nd Street, New York City, NY. *T:* Trafalgar 7–7440. *Club:* National Arts.

Died 28 Feb. 1942.

WALSH, James Joseph; Irish Free State Minister for Posts and Telegraphs, 1922–27; Member Dail Eireann for Cork City, 1918–27; Director Tailteann Games; Alderman Cork City, 1918–26; *b* 20 Jan. 1880; *s* of James J. and Mary Walsh, Rathroon House, Bandon; *m* 1921, Jennie J. Turner, of Turner's Hotel, Cork. no *c*. *Educ:* Cork Christian Brothers; King's College, London. Manufacturer; President, Federation of Irish Industries. *Recreation:* participated in all Gaelic pastimes. *Address:* Ailesbury House, Ailesbury Road, Dublin.

Died 3 Feb. 1948.

WALSH, Hon. Patrick Joseph Stanislaus, KC 1910; PhD; *b* 1872. Formerly President District Courts, Cyprus; Chief Justice Seychelles, 1931–35.

Died 19 May 1943.

WALSHE, Lt-Col Henry Ernest, CMG 1915; late South Staffs Regt; *b* 10 April 1866; *m* 1930, Christine Margared, *d* of H. R. Charley Richards; one *s*. *Educ:* Trinity College, Dublin. Entered Army, 1889; Captain, 1896; Maj. 1907; Lt-Col 1915; temp. Brig.-Gen. 1915; served South Africa, 1899–1902 (Queen's medal 4 clasps, King's medal 2 clasps); European War, 1914 (despatches, CMG). *Address:* Carra Cottage, West Clandon, Guildford. *T:* Clandon 234. *Club:* Army and Navy.

Died 4 March 1947.

WALTER, William; ex-Agent-General, British Columbia; *b* Bristol, 1852; *m*; three *s* three *d*. *Educ:* Grammar School, Bristol. 14 years in China, Hankow, and Shanghai; in British Columbia, and connected therewith subsequently 15 years. *Address:* Uplands, St Peter Port, Guernsey. *T:* Guernsey 158.

Died 8 Feb. 1942.

WALTERS, Arthur Melmoth, MA; Senior Partner of Walters and Company, Solicitors, New Square, Lincoln's Inn, WC; Director of London Guarantee and Accident Co., Phœnix Assurance Co. Ltd; *b* 26 Jan. 1865; *s* of late William Melmoth Walters, ex-President of Council of Incorporated Law Society; *m* 1892, Amy Constance, *d* of late George William Parbury, Melbourne; five *s* four *d*. *Educ:* Charterhouse; Trinity College, Cambridge (Honours Degree in Mathematics). Admitted a Solicitor in 1889; Registrar of Charterhouse, 1911–38. *Recreations:* shooting, fishing; played Association Football for Cambridge against Oxford in 1884, 1885, 1886, and 1887; played for England on many occasions. *Address:* Minnick Wood, Holmwood, Surrey.

Died 2 May 1941.

WALTERS, Henry Beauchamp, OBE 1920; MA; *b* 6 April 1867; *s* of Ven. Wm Walters, Archdeacon of Worcester; *m* 1898, Margaret, *e d* of F. E. Thompson, Marlborough; one *s*. *Educ:* Eton; King's College, Cambridge; Bell Scholar, 1887; Chancellor's Class. Medal, 1890; 1st class Classical Trip. 1889, 1890. Entered British Museum, 1890; Keeper of Greek and Roman Antiquities, British Museum, 1925–32; retired, 1932; attached to Commission Internationale de Ravitaillement, 1916–19; Member of Central Council for Protection of Ancient Churches. *Publications:* Little Book on Greek Art, 1903; History of Ancient Pottery, 2 vols 1905; The Art of the Greeks, 1906; Church Bells, 1908; The Art of the Romans, 1911; Church Bells of England, 1912; Catalogue of Engraved Gems, 1926; The English Antiquaries, 1934; London Churches at the Reformation, 1938; articles in Hellenic Journal and other periodicals. *Address:* 128 High Street, Marlborough, Wilts.

Died 24 April 1944.

WALTON, Allan, RDI 1940; FSIA 1945; Member, Special Committee on Technical Education, Advisory Council on Education in Scotland, 1944; Director of Allan Walton Textiles; Member of the London Group; Member Council of Industrial Design, 1944, and of Scottish Committee of the Council, 1944; *b* 20 Oct. 1891; *y s* of Allan Walton, Cheadle Hulme, Cheshire. *Educ:* Harrow School. Studied Architecture in London, then painting at the Académie de la Grande Chaumière in Paris and Westminster School of Art under Mr Sickert. Exhibited pictures at many London Galleries; has carried out many schemes for interior decoration, designed gardens, etc.; founded in conjunction with his brother the firm of Allan Walton Textiles. Director of Glasgow School of Art, 1943–45. *Recreations:* gardening, swimming, sailing. *Address:* Hill House, Shotley, Suffolk. *T:* Shotley 234. *Clubs:* Arts: Art, Glasgow.

Died 12 Sept. 1948.

WALTON, Hon. Sir Edgar (Harris), KCMG 1911; Member, House of Assembly, 1910–21; *b* 25 July 1856; *s* of Rev. John Walton, MA; *m* 1st, Elizabeth Anne (*d* 1919), 2nd *d* of W. A. Richards, late of Cape Town; two *s* three *d*; 2nd, 1920, Marguerite Isobel McIntyre, of Port Elizabeth; two *s*. *Educ:* private schools. Went to Colony, 1879; became editor and proprietor of Eastern Province Herald, of Port Elizabeth, Cape Colony; entered Parliament, 1898; Treasurer of the Colony of the Cape of Good Hope, 1904–08; Member of the National Union Convention, 1908–09; Public Debt Commissioner, 1911–14; High Commissioner in London for the Union of S Africa, 1920–24. *Publication:* Inner History of the S African Convention. *Recreations:* golf, shooting, fishing. *Address:* Port Elizabeth. *Clubs:* Reform; Port Elizabeth.

Died 8 April 1942.

WALTON, Frederick Parker, MA, LLD; KC (Quebec); *b* 1858; *s* of I. Walton, Buxton; *m* Mary (*d* 1932), *d* of Rev. D. Taylor. *Educ:* Lincoln College, Oxford, (Hon. Fellow, 1933), first class Cl. Moderations;

second class Lit. Hum.; BA 1883; Edinburgh, LLB 1886; Marburg; hon. LLD Aberdeen, 1906; McGill, 1915; 2nd class of Order of the Nile. Member International Academy of Comparative Law; Hon. Member American Bar Association; Scottish Bar, 1886; Quebec Bar, 1906; Lecturer in Roman Law, Glasgow University; Legal Secretary to Lord Advocate (Right Hon. J. B. Balfour), 1894; Dean of the Faculty of Law, and Professor of Roman Law, McGill University, Montreal, 1897–1914; Director of Royal School of Law, Cairo, 1915–23; Editor, Journal of Comparative Legislation, 1927–32. *Publications:* Handbook of Law of Husband and Wife in Scotland; Scotch Marriages, Regular and Irregular; Historical Introduction to the Roman Law, 4th ed. 1917; Scope and Interpretation of Civil Code of Lower Canada; Workmen's Compensation Act of Quebec, with Commentary; Egyptian Law of Obligations; Assistant Editor of Burge's Commentaries on Colonial and Foreign Laws; (with Sir M. Amos) Introduction to French Law; edited for Stair Society Lord Hermand's Consistorial Decisions, 1940; and contributions to legal journals. *Recreation:* travel. *Address:* 6 Great King Street, Edinburgh. *T:* 31414. *Club:* University (Edinburgh).

Died 21 March 1948.

WALTON, Sir George O'Donnell, Kt 1925; *b* Montreal, Canada, 1871; *s* of Dr G. O'Donnell Walton, Barbados, and Sarah Louisa, *d* of H. B. Gall; *m* 1901, Emily Clarice, *d* of J. W. C. Catford, King's Solicitor of Barbados; two *d*. Called to Bar, Middle Temple, 1893; entered the Colonial Civil Service, 1902; held successively the posts of Magistrate, Barbados; Magistrate, St Kitts; Attorney-General of St Lucia; Attorney General of British Honduras; Chief Justice of Grenada, 1921–26; First Puisne Judge, Trinidad and Tobago, 1926–31; retired, 1933; Member of Barbados House of Assembly, 1932–36; of Legislative Council, Barbados, 1936–45. *Address:* Barbados, British West Indies.

Died 19 Oct. 1950.

WALTON, Norman Burdett, CBE 1944; Executive Vice-President, Canadian National Railways, Montreal, since 1943; *b* Palmerston, Ontario, 27 July 1884; *s* of Henry Walton and Elizabeth Rowan; *m* 1911, Eva Tait; one *s* one *d*. *Educ:* Public and High School and Business College, Stratford, Ontario. Clerk and Stenographer, Grand Trunk Railway, Toronto, 1900; Sec. to Supt 1902; Telegraph Operator and Sec. to Vice-Pres. at Montreal, 1903; Assistant Trainmaster at Palmerston, 1906; Sec. to Vice-Pres. Great Northern Railway at St Paul, Minn, 1907; Inspector of Transportation, 1907; Claims Agent (personal injuries) Grand Trunk Railway, Toronto, 1908; Sec. to General Supt Grand Trunk Pacific Railway, Winnipeg, 1908; Trainmaster at Wainwright, 1910; Asst to General Supt 1911; Supt, Edmonton, 1911; Asst General Supt, Prince Rupert, Canadian National Railways, 1920; General Supt, Winnipeg, 1924; General Supt, Transportation, Western Region, 1930; Chief of Transportation, Montreal, 1936; Vice-Pres. Operation, Construction and Maintenance of Way, Montreal, 1938. *Address:* 360 McGill St, Montreal, Quebec, Canada; The Towers, Côte St Luc Road, Montreal, Quebec. *Clubs:* St James, Canadian (Montreal); Manitoba (Winnipeg).

Died 21 Jan. 1950.

WANKLYN, Lt-Comdr Malcolm David, VC 1941; DSO 1941; RN; *b* 28 June 1911; 3rd *s* of late William L. Wanklyn and of Mrs Wanklyn, Flat, 159, Chatsworth Court, W8; *m* 1938, Elspeth, 2nd *d* of James Kinloch; one *s*. *Educ:* RNC, Dartmouth. Served War of 1939–45 (VC, DSO and two Bars). *Address:* c/o Ellangowan, Meigle, Perthshire. *T:* Meigle 238.

Died 18 April 1942.

WANLESS-O'GOWAN, Maj.-Gen. Robert, CB 1915; CMG 1919; *b* 5 Sept. 1864; *m* 1887, Alice Phillis (*d* 1940), *d* of F. C. Bland of Derryquin Castle, Co. Kerry; one *s* one *d*. Entered Army, 1886; Captain, 1896; Major, 1903; Lieut-Col 1909; Col 1913; Railway Staff Officer, S Africa, 1900–01; District Inspector of Musketry, Southern District, 1901–03; DAAG, NE District, 1903–05; AQMG 1914; AAG 1914; AA and QMG 6th Division, 1914; temp. Brig.-Gen. commanding 13th Brigade, 5th Division, 1915, 31st Division, 1915–18; a Reserve Centre, 1918–20; Temp. Major-Gen. 1915; served South Africa, 1899–1901 (severely wounded, despatches twice, Bt Major; Queen's medal 5 clasps); European War, 1914–18 (despatches six times, CB, CMG, 4th Class Order of Vladimir with swords, French Croix de Guerre avec Palme, Commander Belgian Ordre de la Couronne). *Address:* Islanmore, Tilford, Surrey. *T:* Frensham 199. *Club:* Army and Navy.

Died 15 Dec. 1947.

WANLISS, Col David Sydney, CMG 1915; VD; late 5th Batt. (Victoria) Australian Imperial Force; *b* 1864. Barrister Inner Temple, 1888. Served European War, 1914–17 (despatches, CMG); Military Commandant in Tasmania; retired list, 1924; Chief Justice of Mandated Territory of New Guinea, 1921–38. *Clubs:* Naval and Military, Melbourne.

Died 25 Sept. 1943.

WANSBROUGH, Hon. Lt-Col Thomas Percival, CBE 1919; late Agency Manager, Eagle Star Insurance Co., Ltd; *b* 4 June 1875; *s* of late Rev. Charles E. Wansbrough. *Educ:* Kingswood School, Bath. Served European War, RASC, 1915–19 (despatches twice, CBE). *Address:* Littledene, Guildown, Guildford.

Died 25 Oct. 1943.

WARD; *see* Barrington-Ward.

WARD, Ven. Algernon, MA; FRSL, FRGS, FSA Scot.; Officer and Sub-Chaplain of the Order of St John of Jerusalem, 1946; *b* 1869; *s* of Rev. R. Ward, BA, Vicar of Ashby Puerorum, Horncastle; *m* 1896, Elizabeth Mary (*d* 1938), *e d* of David Waters, Coventry. *Educ:* Horncastle Grammar School; private study; Corpus Christi Coll., Cambridge (Scholar, Theological Prizeman, Sub-Librarian); Cambridge Clergy School. BA 1890; MA 1894; MATCD and Durham. Deacon, 1892; Priest, 1893; Curate, St Michael's, Coventry, 1892–94; Senior Curate and Mission Priest, St Augustine's, Edgbaston, 1894–1902; Divinity Lecturer of Queen's Coll., Birmingham, 1897; Tutor and Sub-Warden, 1898–1902; Chaplain of St Mark's, Alexandria, Egypt, 1902–15; Vicar of Sturminster Newton, Dorset, 1915–22; Member of Archbishop's Eastern Churches Committee, 1921; Vicar of Stowe, Salop, 1922–26; Rector of Church Lawford and Vicar of Newnham Regis, 1926–36; Archdeacon of Warwick, 1936–45; Rector of Hampton Lucy, Warwick, 1936–45; Rural Dean of Rugby, 1929–36; Hon. Canon of Coventry Cathedral, 1932; Warden of Coventry Diocesan Lay Readers, 1937; Hon. Canon of St George's Coll. Church, Jerusalem, 1904; Archdeacon of the Church of England in Egypt, 1907; Bishop's Commissary in Egypt, 1908; Delegate to Pan-Anglican Congress, 1908; Editor of the Jerusalem Bishopric Kalendar; CF 1914–15; Surrogate in the Diocese of Salisbury, 1916; Rural Dean, 1917; Fellow of Incorporated Guild of Church Musicians, 1916; Commissary to Bishop in Jerusalem and the East, 1915–43; medals, 1914–15, Bronze Star, British War medal, Victory medal. *Publications:* A Guide to the Study of the Book of Common Prayer; Psalmi Poenitentiales; Palestinian Memoirs, Trees and Shrubs of the Bible, and the Holy Land; The Seven Deadly Sins; The Coptic Church; The Cardinal Virtues; The Ascension; The Transfiguration of Christ; The Fellowship of the Holy Spirit, 1931; The Seven Words from the Cross, 1930; etc.; Editor of Bible Lands, 1915–1930. *Recreations:* shooting, fishing, tennis. *Address:* c/o Lloyds Bank, Paignton, S Devon.

Died 9 July 1947.

WARD, Arnold Sandwith; *b* 8 Nov. 1876; *o s* of late T. Humphry Ward. *Educ:* Eton; Balliol College, Oxford (Scholar); Newcastle Scholar; Craven Scholar; Craven Scholar; Chancellor's Prizeman; two firsts in schools. Acted as special correspondent of The Times in Egypt, the Sudan, and India, 1899–1902; called to bar, 1903; contested Cricklade Division, Wiltshire, 1906; MP (U) West Herts, 1910–18; is Lieutenant in Herts Yeomanry; served with that force in Egypt, 1914–15; later served in Cyprus. *Recreations:* cricket, Eton XI, 1895, shooting, golf. *Clubs:* Carlton, St James', Athenæum.

Died 1 Jan. 1950.

WARD, Lt-Col Arthur Blackwood, CBE 1919; DSO 1917; SAMC (retired); late Director of Emergency Medical Services, Ministry of Health; *b* Wandsworth, Surrey, 2 July 1870; *e s* of John Hext Ward, HM Inland Revenue Department, Somerset House; *m* 1902, Angela Susan Dorothea, *d* of late H. Finch, JP, Redheath, Herts; two *s* one *d*. *Educ:* Christ's Hospital; Selwyn College, Cambridge (Classical Scholar); St Bartholomew's Hospital. BA Cantab (Nat. Sci. Tripos Honours), 1892; MB, BC Cantab 1896; MRCS Eng., LRCP Lond. 1896. Ophthalmic House Surgeon, St Bartholomew's Hospital, 1896; Medical Officer, Grey College, Bloemfontein, S Africa, 1902–14; Member, 1905, and President, 1908, Medical and Pharmacy Council OFS, S Africa; OC Medical Division and OC No. 1 General Hospital, Wynberg, S Africa, 1914–15 (GSW African Campaign) (despatches); S African Expeditionary Force, 1915–19. OC No. 1 S African General Hospital, France, and DDMS S African Expeditionary Force (temporary Colonel) (despatches DSO, CBE); Deputy Director-General of Medical Services, Ministry of Pensions; Medical Superintendent Queen Mary's Hospital, Roehampton; retired, 1936. Member BMA. *Publication:* Nephritis, South African Medical Record, 1912. *Address:* Westfield Court, Surbiton, Surrey. *T:* Kingston 5852. *Club:* Royal Empire Society.

Died 11 March 1950.

WARD, Rev. Canon Arthur Evelyn; Canon Residentiary of Rochester Cathedral since 1940; *b* 13 Sept. 1877; *s* of Lt-Col Arthur Clitheroe Ward, RE, and Evelyn Mary, *d* of Canon T. D. Bernard, High Hall, Wimborne, Dorset; *m* 1909, Eileen, *d* of T. C. Vigors, JP, Burgage, Co. Carlow; three *s* two *d*. *Educ:* Sherborne School; Balliol College, Oxford (Exhibitioner); Bishop's Hostel, Farnham. First Class Modern History, 1900. Curate of Hatfield, Herts, 1902–04; Vicar of Lemsford, Herts, 1904–20; Exam. Chaplain to Bishop of Exeter, 1918; Vicar of Holy Trinity, Twickenham, 1920–22; Vicar of Ilsham (S Matthias, Torquay), 1922–40; Prebendary of Exeter Cathedral, 1934–40. *Address:* Priors Gate House, Rochester.

Died 23 Dec. 1944.

WARD, Ebenezer Thomas, CBE 1935; OBE 1925; *b* 1879; *s* of late Ebenezer Ward, Reading; *m* 1908, Annie Augusta Meayers, Leyton, Essex; one *s*. *Educ:* Reading School; University College, London. Asst Engr London and India Docks Company, 1901; Asst Engr to European Commission of the Danube, 1908; Resident Engineer, 1919; Engineer-in-Chief, 1922; resigned, 1935; was Production Officer, Aircraft Supply Dept, Ministry of Munitions, 1917–19. *Address:* 3 Downs Road, Seaford, Sussex.

Died 22 July 1942.

WARD, Frederick Josiah, CBE 1920; *b* 1861; *m* 1894, Rose Brooks (*d* 1923). Superintendent of Torpedo Stores and Deputy Director Armament Supply, Admiralty, during European War, retired, 1922. *Address:* Fairlight, 3 Elm Bank Gardens, Barnes, SW.

Died 5 Feb. 1941.

WARD, Ven. George Herbert; Rector of Hilgay, Norfolk, since 1914; *b* 1862; *s* of late Rev. George Sturton Ward, Fellow and Tutor of Hertford College, Oxford; *m* 1889, Mary Sophia, *d* of William Scroggs of Kidlington, Oxon; two *d. Educ:* Malvern College; Hertford College, Oxford (1st Class Math. Mod., 1882); BA (1st Class Math.), 1884; MA 1888. Deacon, 1893; Priest, 1894; Assistant Master at S Paul's School, London, 1887–98; Curate of S Matthias, Earl's Court, 1893–98; Headmaster of All Saints' School, Bloxham, 1898–1914; Proctor in Convocation for the Diocese of Ely, 1922–35; Archdeacon of Wisbech, 1924–45. *Address:* Hilgay Rectory Downham, Norfolk.

Died 1 May 1946.

WARD, Maj.-Gen. Henry Dudley Ossulston, CB 1918; CMG 1916; RA; *b* 23 May 1872; *m* 1919, Mary, *d* of late Right Hon. C. G. Milnes Gaskell; one *s.* Served S Africa, 1899–1900 (despatches, Queen's medal five clasps); European War, 1914–18 (despatches seven times, CMG, Bt Col, CB); Chevalier Légion d'Honneur; OStJ; Commanded Presidency and Assam District 1926–30; retired pay, 1930. *Address:* Linley Hall, Broseley, Shropshire. *T:* Iron Bridge 3151.

Died 7 Dec. 1947.

WARD, Ida Caroline, CBE 1948; DLit; BLitt; Adviser in African Studies, School of Oriental and African Studies, University of London, since 1948; Professor Emeritus since 1949; *b* 4 Oct. 1880; *d* of Samson Ward. *Educ:* Bradford; Darlington Training College; Durham University. Secondary School Teaching, 1902–19; Lecturer in Phonetics, Univ. Coll., London, 1919–32; Lecturer, Reader, Prof. West African Langs, School of Oriental and African Studies, Univ. of London, 1932–48. *Publications:* Speech Defects and their Cure, 1923; (with L. E. Armstrong) Handbook of English Intonation, 1929; Phonetics of English, 1930; (with Prof. D. Westermann) Practical Phonetics for students of African Languages, 1933; Phonetic and Tonal Structure of Efik, 1933; Introduction to the Ibo Language, 1936; Practical Suggestions for Learning an African Language in the Field, 1937; Introduction to the Yoruda Language, 1949; pamphlets and articles. *Address:* Coneyhurst Cottage, Peaslake, nr Guildford. *T:* Abinger 166. *Club:* Royal Empire Society.

Died 10 Oct. 1949.

WARD, Col Sir John Chappell, KBE 1937; CMG 1933; CIE 1919; DSO 1917; MBE 1918; Port Director and Director-General of Navigation, Basrah, Iraq; *b* 28 Dec. 1877; 3rd *s* of late Almond James Ward; *m* 1910, Bessie Matilda, *d* of Horace Boileau Goad, Simla; one *s* one *d. Educ:* School of Science and Art; Royal Naval College, Greenwich. Sub-Lieut Royal Indian Marine (now Royal Indian Navy), 1899; Lieutenant, 1903; Commander, 1917; Captain, 1925; Seconded to Bengal Government, 1913–15; Deputy Port Officer and Deputy Shipping Master, Calcutta; served Somaliland, 1902–04 (Medal and Clasp); Persian Gulf Gunrunning operation, 1909–14 (Medal and Clasp); Royal Humane Society's Medal and Certificate, 1910; European War, 1914–18; Chief Examination Officer, Orissa and Behar Coasts (despatches twice); transferred to Indian Expeditionary Force, 1915; Marine Transport Officer and Controller of Native Craft Base, Basrah, 1916; Director of River Transport, 1916; transferred to Royal Engineers with relative rank of Major and appointed Assistant Director, Inland Water Transport, 1916; T. Lieut-Col and Deputy Director, Inland Water Transport, 1917; T. Colonel, 1917; officiating Director, Inland Water Transport, 1918;

served during Iraq Rebellion, 1920; Mesopotamia (DSO, CIE, despatches six times, Bronze Star, 1914–15, British and Victory Medals, Iraq Medal and Clasp, 2nd Class Order of Rafidian in recognition of services during disturbances, Middle Euphrates, 1935); Port Director to develop and commercialise the Military Port of Basrah, 1919; Director-General of Navigation, Iraq, 1921; reverted to Royal Indian Marine and seconded to Iraq Government, 1922; retired from Royal Indian Marine, 1927; as Director-General of Dredging Operations successfully carried out the Dredging Operations across Shatt-al-Arab Bar, 1925–30; undertook, on behalf of Indian Government, with consent of Iraq Government, administration Persian Gulf Lights; Member of Institute of Transport, 1927; Director-General of Iraq State Railways, 1936–39. *Recreations:* swimming, tennis, golf, badminton. *Clubs:* Junior Naval and Military, Junior United Service.

Died 10 Oct. 1942.

WARD, Richard Percyvale, CIE 1943; MC; DFC; Civil Liaison Officer for Orissa at Eastern Army Headquarters; *b* 28 Aug. 1894. *Educ:* Trinity College, Dublin. Entered Indian Civil Service, 1921. *Address:* c/o Secretariat, Govt of Orissa, Cuttack, Orissa, India.

Died 17 Oct. 1945.

WARD, Hon. Robert Arthur; late Captain in the Army, and Lieut Worcestershire Yeomanry Cavalry; *b* 23 Feb. 1871; 3rd *s* of 1st Earl of Dudley and Georgiana, *d* of Sir Thomas Moncrieffe, 7th Bt; *m* 1906, Lady Mary Acheson, *d* of 4th Earl of Gosford; one *s* one *d. Educ:* Eton; Trin. Hall, Camb. MP (C) Crewe Div. Cheshire, 1895–1900; served Matabeleland, 1896 (medal); South Africa, 1901–02 (Queen's medal five clasps); European War, 1914–19, on Staff (despatches twice; OBE (Mil.), Legion of Honour). *Address:* 33 Sussex Gardens, Hyde Park, W2. *T:* Paddington 3136.

Died 14 June 1942.

WARD, Brig.-Gen. Thomas, CMG 1916; formerly Queen's Bays; *b* 1861; 2nd *s* of Joseph Ward, JP, of St Peter's, Kent; *m* 1st, 1892, Jeannette Octavia (*d* 1913), *d* of Wm Cliff, JP, of West Derby, Lancs; three *d*; 2nd, 1919, Lady Kathleen Lowry-Corry, *y d* of 4th Earl of Belmore; (one son killed in action, 1944) one *d.* Served South Africa, 1901–02 (dangerously wounded, despatches, Queen's medal 5 clasps); European War, 1914–18 (CMG, despatches, Officer Legion of Honour). *Address:* Brynhir, Criccieth, Carnarvonshire.

Died 16 Jan. 1949.

WARD, Sir Thomas Robert John, Kt 1920; CIE 1906; MVO 1911; *b* 1863; *s* of late Capt. Walter Ward, JP, Kimberley. *Educ:* St Cyprians, Kimberley, SA; Framlingham School; RIE College, Coopers Hill. Entered India Public Works Dept 1883; on deputation with Seistan Boundary Commission, 1902–06; Member Colonies Committee, Punjab, 1908; Engineer Officer for irrigation and drainage, Delhi Coronation Durbar, 1911; Engineer Officer to the Home Department, Government, India, for the selection of a site for the new capital, Delhi, 1912; Engineer in Delhi Province for training River Jamna at Delhi, 1913; services lent for 18 months to King of Siam to inaugurate irrigation works in Valley of Menam Chao Phraya; Chief Engineer and Secretary to Government, Punjab, PWD, 1915; Member Punjab Legislative Council, 1915; Inspector General of Irrigation in India, 1917; services placed at disposal of Commander-in-Chief in India, to report on agricultural irrigational development in Mesopotamia, 1918; Member Council Institution Civil Engineers, London, 1919–20; Consulting Engineer for Norton, Griffiths & Co., Ltd, Administrators to the Brazilian Government for Irrigation Dams in the State of Ceara, NE Brazil, 1922; advised on Irrigation Development in the Argentine, Iraq, and Bulgaria. Fellow Royal Empire

Society; FRGS, MICE; MAmCE; Honorary Life Member Institution Engineers (India). *Address:* c/o Barclays Bank, 135 Finchley Road, NW3. *Club:* Savile.

Died 27 Jan. 1944.

WARD, Col Walter, CBE 1922; 2nd *s* of Richard Blanchard Ward, Kilpin, Howden, Yorkshire; *m* 1st, Lily (*d* 1931), *d* of Alfred Wood, CB, RN; 2nd, 1934, Frances Margaret *o d* of late Major John Frazer Vans Agnew RA, Barnbarroch, Co. Wigton; two *s*. *Address:* c/o The Manager, Imperial Bank of India, 25 Old Broad Street, EC2; 9 Burrow Villas, Seaton, Devon.

Died 10 Jan. 1948.

WARD, Rt Hon. William Dudley; PC 1922; Barrister; *b* 1877; *e s* of late William Humble Dudley Ward and Hon. Eugenie Violet Adele Brett, *d* of 1st Viscount Esher; *m* 1913, Winifred (who obtained a divorce, 1931), *d* of late Col Charles Birkin, Lamcote, Radcliffe-on-Trent; two *d*. *Educ:* Eton; Trinity College, Cambridge. Called to Bar, 1904; MP (Co. L) Southampton 1906–22; Treasurer of HM's Household, 1909–12; Vice-Chamberlain, 1917–22; rowed three years in Cambridge Eight. *Recreations:* yachting, rowing, fishing. *Clubs:* Windham, Beefsteak; Royal Yacht Squadron, Cowes.

Died 11 Nov. 1946.

WARDALE, Edith Elizabeth, MA Oxon; PhD Zürich; Hon. Fellow of St Hugh's College; *b* 6 March 1863; *d* of Rev. John Wardale. *Educ:* Miss Bidwell's School, Devizes; Lady Margaret Hall and St Hugh's College, Oxford. Vice-Principal (for a few years) of St Hugh's College; formerly Tutor in English to the Asson. Educ. of Women and to St Hugh's College, Lecturer in English to Lady Margaret Hall and St Hilda's College, all in Oxford; Lecturer in English, Royal Holloway College. *Publications:* An Old English Grammar, 1922; Chapters on Old English Literature, 1935; An Introduction to Middle English, 1937. *Address:* 12 St Margarets Road, Oxford. *T:* Oxford 3453. *Club:* University Women's.

Died 27 Feb. 1943.

WARDEN, Archibald A., MA, MD; Physician in Cannes; late visiting Physician to the Hertford British Hospital, Paris, and Consulting Physician to the American Hospital of Paris; Medical Examiner of the Equitable Life Assurance Society of the United States (Paris and vicinity); *b* 11 May 1869; *y s* of William Warden of Edinburgh, Glasgow and New York; *m* 1900, Rachel, *e d* of late Professor J. G. M'Kendrick, FRS; two *s* two *d*. *Educ:* Kelvinside Academy; Rossall School; University of Glasgow and University of Paris. MA Glasgow, 1889; MD 1893. Docteur en Médecine de la Faculté de Paris, 1899; held several hospital appointments before settling in medical practice in Paris; retired to South of France, 1925. *Publications:* English Handbook to the Paris Medical School; numerous papers in the Lancet, British Medical Journal, etc.; Results of Radium-therapy in Malignant Disease, 1912; Common-sense Patriotism, 1915. *Recreations:* lawn tennis (won French Doubles Championship with W. S. M. Vines, 1896), cycling, automobiling, walking and climbing. *Address:* Villa Serpolette, Cannes, France.

Died 7 Oct. 1943.

WARDEN, Herbert Lawton, CBE 1924; DSO 1918; DL, JP; Solicitor Supreme Courts, Edinburgh; Director of Pensions for Scotland, 1919–25; *b* Edinburgh, 31 May 1877; *m* 1904, Jessie Knight, *d* of James Watt; two *d*. Inaugurated Edinburgh Military Training Association, Aug. 1914, and appointed first President; Second-in-Command 16th Batt. the Royal Scots, 1914–16; Commanded 27th Batt. Northumberland Fusiliers and 13th Batt. East Surrey Regiment; served in France during European War (despatches thrice, CBE, DSO and bar). *Recreations:* golf, motoring. *Address:* 42 Melville Street, Edinburgh; 54 Great King Street, Edinburgh. *Clubs:* Royal Societies, Overseas; Scottish Conservative, Royal Scots, Edinburgh; Royal Scottish Automobile, Glasgow.

Died 8 Aug. 1946.

WARDEN, William Luck; *er s* of J. H. Warden, for forty years owner of the Hendon Times, of which he is still the principal shareholder and Managing Director; *m* Alice Grace Wauthier, of Metz and London; two *d*. *Educ:* France; Germany. Has now retired after editing Galignani's Messenger (Paris), New York Herald, European edition (Editor-in-charge), Continental Daily Mail and Daily Mail, London; A Director of Associated Newspapers London until 1939; Officer of the Legion of Honour; has written much on travel. *Address:* 71 Church Road, Hendon, NW4.

Died 30 Jan. 1942.

WARDINGTON, 1st Baron *cr* 1936, of Alnmouth in the County of Northumberland; **John William Beaumont Pease;** Chairman Lloyds Bank, Ltd, 1922–45, and Bank of London and South America, 1922–48; alternate Chairman of Lloyds and National Provincial Foreign Bank, Ltd; Director Alliance Assurance Co. Ltd; *b* 4 July 1869; *s* of late John William Pease, JP, DL, of Pendower, Newcastle-upon-Tyne and Nether Grange, Alnmouth; *m* 1923, Hon. Mrs Dorothy Charlotte Lubbock, *widow* of Hon. Harold Lubbock, and *er d* of 1st Baron Forster, two *s*. *Educ:* Marlborough; New College, Oxford. On Leaving Oxford entered into the private banking partnership of Hodgkin, Barnett, Pease, Spence & Co. in Northumberland; on the amalgamation of the Bank with Lloyds Bank he was elected a Director of Lloyds Bank, and subsequently became Deputy Chairman; Master of the Percy Foxhounds, 1906–10. *Recreations:* hunting, golf, shooting, and lawn tennis; represented Oxford University at golf and lawn tennis, and England at golf. *Heir: s* Capt. Hon. Christopher Pease, Scots Guards, *b* 22 Jan. 1924. *Address:* 16 St James's Street, SW1. *T:* Abbey 6605; Wardington Manor, Banbury. *Club:* Turf.

Died 7 Aug. 1950.

WARDLE, Arthur, RI, RBC; painter, Member Pastel Society; *b* London, 1864; *m* 1892; one *s*. *Educ:* private school. First exhibited at Royal Academy at age of seventeen; has works in public galleries—Chantrey Bequest Collection, National Gallery of British Art; City Art Gallery, Leeds; Municipal Art Gallery, Durban; M'Kelvie Gallery, Auckland, New Zealand; Perth, Western Australia; Canterbury Art Society, New Zealand Bronze and Silver Medal, Crystal Palace; Victoria and Albert Museum. *Recreation:* music. *Address:* 203 Goldhawk Road, W12. *Club:* Arts.

Died 16 July 1949.

WARDLE, George James, Companion of Honour, 1917; FJI; JP, Hove 1928; *b* Newhall, 15 May 1865; *s* of George Wardle, railway carman; *m* 1889, Atla Matilda Terry of Keighley; one *s* one *d*. *Educ:* private school, Wisbech; Wesleyan Day School, Keighley, Yorks. Was in service Midland Railway from 15 years of age to March 1898; Editor of Railway Review, 1898–1919 edited Keighley Labour Journal, 1893–97; Parliamentary Secretary Board of Trade, 1917–18; Acting Chairman Labour Party, 1916–17; Parliamentary Secretary Ministry of Labour, 1919–20; MP (Labour), Stockport, 1906–20; retired on account of ill-health, 1920; Co-operator, Trade Unionist, Socialist. *Publications:* Problems of the Age, and other Poems, 1897; The Principles of Association, Pamphlet, 1904; A Railway Garland (Poems), edited and arranged, 1904; Railway Nationalisation, 1908. *Recreations:* bowls, reading, and music. *Address:* Whin Knowle, Shirley Drive, Hove Sussex.

Died 18 June 1947.

WARDLE, Vice-Adm. Thomas Erskine, CB 1926; DSO 1916; *b* 1877; *s* of late Henry Wardle, MP, DL, of Highfield, Burton-on-Trent. Entered HMS Britannia, 1890; Midshipman, 1892; Sub-Lieut 1896; Lieut 1897; Commander, 1908; Captain, 1915; in command of HMS Alcantara action with SMS Greif (DSO); Chief of Staff, British Naval Mission to Greece, 1921–23; Senior Officer Nore Reserve Fleet, 1923–24; Naval ADC to the King, 1925; Commodore, 1st Class, in Command of Royal Australian Fleet, 1924–26; Rear-Admiral, 1926; retired list, 1926; Vice-Admiral, retired, 1931. *Address:* Coniston, Caledon Road, Beaconsfield. *T:* Beaconsfield 547.

Died 9 May 1944.

WARDLE, Rev. William Lansdell, MA, DD, Hon. CF; *b* 21 Jan. 1877; *s* of Rev. A. T. Wardle, Primitive Methodist Minister; *m* 1906; Maud Emma, *d* of T. B. E. Barker, Cambridge; one *s*. *Educ:* Perse Grammar School, Cambridge; Gonville and Caius College, Cambridge; Hartley College, Manchester. Entered Primitive Methodist Ministry, 1901; Tutor, Hartley College, 1903–28; Principal Hartley Victoria College, Manchester, 1928–43; Lecturer in Hebrew, Manchester University, 1910–16; Chaplain to the Forces, 1916–18; Lecturer in Old Testament, Manchester University, 1919–30; Reader in Old Testament, Manchester University, 1930–45; Dean of Faculty of Theology, 1937–38; President of Methodist Church, 1938–39; Past President of Society for Old Testament Study; Editor of Holborn Review, 1929–31. *Publications:* Commentaries on Deutero-Isaiah and Joel in Peake's Commentary, 1920; Israel and Babylon, 1925; Commentary on Ezekiel, in The Abingdon Bible Commentary, 1929; History and Religion of Israel, 1936; Old Testament articles in the Encyclopædia Britannica. *Recreation:* golf. *Address:* 10 Douns Cote View, Westbury-on-Trym, Bristol. *T:* Bristol 66762. *Club:* Authors'.

Died 31 Aug. 1946.

WARDLEY, Donald Joule, CMG 1946; MC 1917; Deputy Master and Comptroller of the Royal Mint and ex-officio Engraver of the King's Seals; *b* 23 Oct. 1893; *s* of J. W. Wardley, Buxton, Derbyshire; *m* 1923, Joan, *d* of A. H. Blundell; one *s* one *d*. *Educ:* St Bees School; Selwyn College, Cambridge. Served in France and Flanders, 1915–19 (MC and Bar); Adjutant 23rd Bn London Regt, 1916–18; Staff Captain 64th Infantry Brigade, 1918; Treasury, 1919; served with Empire Marketing Board, 1927–28; Private Secretary to Sir Oswald Mosley as Chancellor of the Duchy of Lancaster, 1929–30; to Lord Parmoor as Leader of the House of Lords, 1930–31; to Lord Peel as Lord Privy Seal, 1931; to Mr Walter Elliot as Financial Secretary to the Treasury, 1931–32; Controller, Clearing Offices, 1938–41; Principal Officer to SW Regional Commissioner, 1941–44; Deputy Secretary, Minister Resident, Cairo, and British Middle East Office, 1944–46. *Recreations:* the practice of music, and the enjoyment of all the arts. *Address:* Wern, Mortimer, Berkshire. *T:* Mortimer 101. *Clubs:* St James', Queen's, Royal Tennis Court.

Died 10 Sept. 1950.

WARDROP, Sir (John) Oliver, KBE 1922; CMG 1917; retired Consul-General; *b* London, 10 Oct. 1864; *e s* of Thomas Caldwell Wardrop and Marjory Cameron Scott; *m* 1912, Margrethe Collett; two *s* one *d*. *Educ:* Balliol Coll., Oxford. Held a Commission in 19th Middlesex RV Corps, 1890–94; Army Interpreter for Russian; Private Sec. in St Petersburg to Sir R. Morier, 1892–93; Vice-Consul at Kertch, 1895–1902; Sevastopol, 1899; Acting Consul-General in Poland, 1900; Rumania, 1901; Tunis, 1901; Hayti, 1902–03; Consul, St Petersburg, 1903–06; Rumania, 1906–10; retired, 1910; Educational Adviser to the City of London College, Feb. 1914; Consul (and then Consul-General)

at Bergen, Nov. 1914; Consul-General at Moscow, Nov. 1917; employed in the Foreign Office (Political Intelligence Dept) from Jan. 1919; Chief British Commissioner in Georgia, Armenia, and Azerbaijan, 1919–20; employed in Foreign Office (Dept of Overseas Trade) till Nov. 1920; a British Delegate on Inter-Allied (afterwards International) Commission for Relief of Russia at Paris and Brussels, 1921; Consul-General at Strasbourg, 1920–27; Member of Council, Royal Asiatic Society, 1928, and Vice-President, 1944; a Governor of London School of Oriental and African Studies, 1935–45. *Publications:* The Kingdom of Georgia, 1888; The Book of Wisdom and Lies, 1894; translation (with Dr F. C. Conybeare) of Georgian version of Liturgy of St James; Visramiani, 1914; Catalogue of Georgian MSS in British Museum. *Address:* 49 Downshire Hill, NW3.

Died 19 Oct. 1948.

WARDROPE, William Hugh; KC; *b* Ottawa, 13 Aug. 1860; *s* of late Thomas Wardrope, DD, Ex-Moderator of the General Assembly of the Presbyterian Church in Canada, and Sarah, *d* of late Thomas Masson of Kingston, Ontario; *m* Elizabeth Stewart, *d* of John Duff Macdonald, RN, late of Hamilton, Ontario; three *s* one *d*. *Educ:* Guelph Collegiate institute; private tuition; Osgoode Hall, Toronto. Practised law in Guelph for some years and since 1892 in Hamilton; PGM, AF, and AM of Canada. *Recreation:* active interest in Freemasonry. *Address:* 35 Glentern Ave, Hamilton, Ontario.

Died 27 June 1947.

WARE, Maj.-Gen. Sir Fabian (Arthur Goulstone), KCVO 1922; KBE 1920; CB 1919; CMG 1917; LLD (Aberdeen 1929; Hon. ARIBA 1928; a Director-General, War Office, 1939–44; Hon. Adviser to War Office on Graves Registration and Enquiries since 1944. Founder Imperial War Graves Commission, Vice-Chairman, 1917–48; European War, 1914–19; (Temp. Major 1915; Temp. Lt-Col 1916; Temp. Brig.-Gen. 1916; Temp. Major-Gen. 1918; despatches twice); *b* Clifton, Bristol, 1869; *s* of Charles and Amy Carew Ware; *m* 1895, Anna Margaret (Medaille de la Reine Elisabeth, Belgium), *d* of E. W. Phibbs; one *s* one *d*. *Educ:* private tutors; University of London and University of Paris; Bachelier-ès-Sciences, 1894. Ten years assistant master in secondary schools (Bradford, 1895–99); Assistant Director of Education, Transvaal, 1901; Acting Director of Education for the Transvaal and Orange River Colony, Jan. to June 1903; Member of the Transvaal Legislative Council, 1903–05; Director of Education, Transvaal, 1903–05; Editor of The Morning Post, 1905–11; Special Commissioner to the Board of the Rio Tinto Company, 1912, Commanded Mobile Unit, British Red Cross Society, with French Army, 1914–15 (Chevalier of Legion of Honour, Croix de Guerre, Commander Crown of Belgium); Commander Legion of Honour, 1932, Grand Officer, 1938; Member of Imperial Committee on Economic Consultation and Co-operation, 1933; Chairman of Executive, Parents' National Educational Union (Pres. 1945); President, Gloucestershire Rural Community Council; Chairman, Gloucestershire Branch of Council for the Preservation of Rural England; Chairman of Ladies' Empire Club. *Publications:* Contributions to the Special Reports of the Board of Education; Translation of Père Hyacinthe's Mon Testament, 1898; Educational Reform—The Task of the Board of Education, 1900; Educational Foundations of Trade and Industry, 1901; The Worker and his Country, 1912; The Immortal Heritage, The Work of the Imperial War Graves Commission, 1937; Articles on Imperial Questions in The Nineteenth Century, etc. *Recreations:* gardening, golf. *Address:* The Dial Cottage, Amberley, Gloucestershire. *Club:* Athenæum.

Died 28 April 1949.

WARE, Lt-Col George William Webb, DSO 1918; late RAMC; *m* 1919, Marie, *o c* of late Eloi Lambert, Liége; one *s*. Served European War, 1914–18 (despatches, DSO, Order of St Maurice and St Lazarus of Italy, Legion of Honour); retired pay, 1934.

Died 29 March 1943.

WAREING, Alfred; Founder of League of Audiences and Repertory Theatre pioneer; *b* Greenwich, 26 Oct. 1876; *e s* of Alfred Hooton Wareing, of Weedon, Northants, and Henrietta Helena Weil; *m* Gertrude, *grandniece* of Rev. Stephen Hawker of Morwenstow; two *d*. *Educ*: Roan Grammar School; Birkbeck Institute; Toynbee Hall. Began life as bookseller's assistant, 1891; joined Sir Frank Benson's Company, 1900; has been his manager, and also to Sir Herbert Tree and Oscar Asche; founded the Glasgow Repertory Theatre, the first Citizens' Theatre in an English-speaking country, 1909; Director, Theatre Royal, Huddersfield, 1918–31; has produced plays and managed many Repertory seasons; was literary assistant to William Ernest Henley. *Publications:* articles on Shakespeare and the Theatre; organised the collected edition of Leonard Merrick's works. *Recreations:* reading and travel. *Address:* The Old Manse, Payton Street, Stratford-on-Avon. *T:* 2493. *Club:* Savage.

Died 11 April 1942.

WARING, Col Anthony Henry, DSO 1917; *b* 1871; *s* of late Henry R. Waring, Palma-de-Mallorca, Spain; *m* 1904, Isabel, *d* of late Colonel F. M. Salmond; 1926, Evaline, *d* of late J. W. W. Willis; four *s*. *Educ*: University College, London. MRCS (Eng.) and LRCP (Lond.), 1895. Entered Army Medical Service, 1896; retired with rank of Colonel, 1921; served European War, 1914–19 (despatches twice, DSO, Commander Military Order of Aviz of Portugal). *Address:* Whitegates, Maresfield, Sussex. *T:* Uckfield 301.

Died 9 Aug. 1941.

WARK, Lord; John Lean Wark; one of the Senators of the College of Justice in Scotland since 1933; *b* 1877; *s* of late John Wark, Writer, Glasgow; *m* 1907, Mary, *d* of late Thomas Wright, Glasgow; three *s*. *Educ*: High School, Glasgow; University, Glasgow and University, Berlin. MA, LLB (Glas.); LLD (Aber.). Called to Scottish Bar, 1901; Advocate Depute, 1919–20; KC 1920; Sheriff of Argyll, 1920–33; General Editor, Encyclopædia of the Laws of Scotland. *Address:* Norwood, 54 Fountainhall Road, Edinburgh. *Clubs:* Northern, Edinburgh.

Died 17 Dec. 1943.

WARK, Anna Elisa, CBE 1927; *b* 1867; *d* of James Wark, Myroe, Londonderry. *Educ*: Strand House School; Magee College, Londonderry; Royal University of Ireland, BA. Was Chief Woman Inspector, Board of Education. *Address:* Stoke Court, Stoke Poges, Bucks.

Died 20 July 1944.

WARK, Lt-Col Blair Anderson, VC, DSO 1918; Quantity Surveyor, 3 Spring Street, Sydney; Director of National Roads and Motorists' Association, NSW; Director Australian Morotists' Petrol Co. Ltd, NRMA Insurance Ltd, Car Credits (NSW) Ltd, Car Repairs Ltd; *b* 27 July 1894; *s* of late Alexander Wark of Bathurst, NSW, and Mrs Wark of Sydney, NSW; *m* Catherine Davis; one *s* two *d*. *Educ*: All Saints College, Bathurst, NSW. Served European War, 1915–18 (despatches, DSO, VC). *Recreations:* fishing, golf. *Address:* Pentecost, Highway, Pymble, NSW. *T:* B3711 and JX 2230. *Clubs:* Tattersalls, Imperial Service, Sydney.

Died 13 June 1941.

WARNER, Brodrick Ashton, CMG 1939; retired; *b* 23 Dec. 1888; *s* of F. Ashton Warner, FRCS (Ed.) and Sydney Anne Grove; unmarried. *Educ*: Winchester College. Entered Colonial Administrative Service, 1912, as Asst Dist Comr, Uganda Protectorate; Provincial

Commissioner, 1933; retired, 1939; Captain (Retd) LRB (TF). *Recreation:* fishing. *Address:* The Old Rectory, West Knoyle, Mere, Wilts. *T:* East Knoyle 94.

Died 25 March 1942.

WARNER, Rev. Canon Charles Edward; Canon and Precentor of Hereford Cathedral since 1936; *b* 3 May 1868; *s* of Charles Warner, Birmingham; *m* 1898, Charlotte Elizabeth, *d* of George Turner, Birkdale; one *s* one *d*. *Educ*: King Edward's School Birmingham; Selwyn College, Cambridge (Scholar). BA (Classical Tripos), 1890; MA 1894. Curate of St Helens, Lancs, 1891–98; Vicar of Bishop's Castle, 1909–20; Vicar of Lugwardine, 1920–28; Rector of Cradley (Malvern), 1928–36; Rural Dean of Ledbury, 1929–36; Prebendary of Hereford, 1920. *Recreation:* croquet. *Address:* Cathedral Close, Hereford. *T:* Hereford 2873.

Died 24 Feb. 1945.

WARNER, Robert Stewart Aucher; KC; *b* The Hall, Port of Spain, 9 May 1859; *s* of Charles William Warner, CB; *m* 1886; Maud Isabel, *d* of Sir William Robinson, GCMG; four *d*. *Educ*: Queen's Royal College, Trinidad; Oriel College, Oxford. BA 1882. Called to the Bar, Inner Temple, 1882; practised Trinidad Bar; unofficial member Legislative Council, 1900; Attorney-General, 1918; retired 1922; Member of Executive of West India Committee, 1923. *Publication:* Sir Thomas Warner.

Died 1 Dec. 1944.

WARNER, Rev. Canon Stephen Mortimer, MA; Prebendary of Chichester Cathedral since 1930; Vicar of Holy Trinity, Eastbourne; *b* 17 Jan. 1873; *s* of late Alfred Warner; *m* Marion Gower (*d* 1934), *d* of late Frederick Tooth, Sevenoaks, and Sydney, NSW; three *s* one *d*. *Educ*: University College, Durham; St John's Hall, Highbury. Curate at St Simon's, Southsea, two years; Vicar of Savernake, Wilts; St Paul, Poole; All Saints, Shooter's Hill; Sandown, Isle of Wight; St Paul's, Upper Norwood; during War of 1914–18 was R. Naval Chaplain; Hon. Chaplain RN, 1917; before that War one of the Mission of Help to Canada; Proctor for Diocese, 1931; Officiating Chaplain RAF 1942; OCF 1942. *Recreation:* motoring. *Address:* Holy Trinity Vicarage, Eastbourne. *T:* Eastbourne 954. *Club:* Junior Carlton.

Died 29 Dec. 1947.

WARNER, Brig.-Gen. (retired) William Ward, CMG 1918; *b* 1867; *s* of late Capt. George Augustus Alves Warner, Indian Staff Corps; *m* Hon. Clarice May Borwick, *d* of 1st Baron Borwick of Hawkshead, three *d*. *Educ*: privately. Joined 1st Batt Royal Warwickshire Regt, 1887; transferred to the Indian Army, 1888; served with 3rd Lancers, Hyderabad contingent, and 30th Lancers, Indian Army; Inspecting Officer, Imperial Service Troops, Hyderabad and Mysore, 1904–07 retired as Major, 1907; Assistant Adjutant-General Royal Flying Corps, April 1915; Brevet Lieut-Colonel; Director Air Personal Service of the Royal Air Force, Feb. 1918, with temporary rank of Brigadier-General (special mention three times, CMG, Russian Order St Stanislaus and St Anne); retired, 1918; served on LCC as Member for Fulham, 1919–22; Chairman Parks and Open Spaces of London, 1921–22; MP (C) Mid Beds, 1924–29; Chairman General Hydraulic Company. *Recreations:* polo and hunting in old days; now golf. *Address:* 2 Weymouth Street, W1. *T:* Langham 6778. *Clubs:* Carlton, Cavalry.

Died 21 March 1950.

WARNOCK, John, CMG 1917; MD, BSc (Public Health), Edinburgh University; 2nd Class, Order of the Nile; 3rd Class, Order of the Osmanieh; late Director Lunacy Division, Ministry of Interior, Cairo, Egypt; *b* Maldon, Victoria, Australia, 23 May 1864; *s* of late Samuel Warnock; *m* Ethel Marion, *d* of late S. Sidley, RBA; two *s*. *Educ*: Horton College, Tasmania;

Edinburgh University. Tasmanian Scholar, 1881. *Address:* 234 Kew Road, Richmond, Surrey. *T:* Richmond 4525.

Died 4 June 1942.

WARR, Sir George Godfrey, Kt 1939; MA (Oxon); JP; Solicitor; Lieutenant of the City of London; *b* 9 June 1882; *o s* of late Augustus Frederick Warr, Liverpool (for many years MP East Toxteth Division of Liverpool) and Henrietta Georgina Barnes; *m* 1912, Hannah Mary Reynolds, *d* of Hugh Reynolds Rathbone, Liverpool, JP, LLD; one *s*. *Educ:* Winchester College; Christ Church, Oxford. Partner in firm of Godfrey Warr & Co., Solicitors; Past Master of Worshipful Company of Drapers; Sheriff of the City of London, 1938–39; Alderman, Vintry Ward, 1936–42. *Address:* 21 Cottesmore Court, W8. *Club:* Oxford and Cambridge.

Died 18 Dec. 1943.

WARREN, Ernest, DSc (Lond.); late Director Natal Museum, Pietermaritzburg, Natal; *b* England, 1871; *m* 1901. *Educ:* University College, London. Assistant Professor of Zoology, University College, London, 1900. *Publications:* Variability of Human Skeleton (Trans. Roy. Soc. London, 1897); and many other papers. *Address:* 1 Ethelbert Road, Canterbury, Kent.

Died 29 Jan. 1946.

WARREN, Major George Ernest, DSO 1915; late The Border Regiment; *b* 18 Jan. 1871; *s* of late George K. Warren, formerly of British Guiana and Fairlawn, Market Harborough; *m* 1902, Norah Ingate, *widow* of H. G. T. Ingate Warren, and *d* of late W. J. Roche of Belfast; one *s*. *Educ:* St John's College, Cambridge; RMC, Sandhurst. Entered Army, 1892; Captain, 1902; Major, 1914; retired, 1920; served S African War, 1899–1902 (Queen's medal 5 clasps, King's medal 2 clasps); European War, 1914–19 (despatches, DSO). *Club:* United Service.

Died 4 May 1942.

WARREN, Rev. Henry George; *b* Oct. 1851; *m. Educ:* Trinity College, Dublin (MA). Ordained 1874; Curate of Desertmartin, 1875–76; Incumbent of Castledawson, 1877–86; Vicar of Dungiven, 1886–1930; Canon of Derry, 1901–30. *Address:* Lisbigny, Seapark, Portstewart, Co. Derry.

Died 20 Feb. 1942.

WARREN, Low, FJI; Formerly Managing Editor Kinematograph Weekly; *s* of late Capt. A. R. Warren, JP, Warrenfield, Emsworth; *m* 1908; Dorothy Mary, *y d* of late George Ellis, Worth. *Educ:* Worthing; Winchester. For three years literary assistant to one of The Times editors. Food Controller (Ministry of Food) Skegness, 1939–41. *Publications:* Sussex Tokens, 1888; Sidelights on Sussex History, 1892; Journalism and Journalists, 1893; Chichester Past and Present, 1895; Gentlemen Gyps, 1899 (2nd edit.); Last Addresses, 1901; History of Chichester (two editions), 1901; The Story of St Agatha's, 1901; Short Stories, 1902; Chasing the Sun, 1902; Chats with Celebrities, 1905; Story of King Charles, 1913; The Showman's Advertising Book, 1914; edited How I Filmed the War, 1920; Journalism, 1922; New and Revised Editions, 1931 and 1935; Shakespeare Country, 1936; The Film Game, 1937; part author pantomimes Robinson Crusoe and Cinderella, 1905–1906; author drama, Revenge, produced Brighton, 1906; film plays; King Charles, Old St Paul's, etc.; Gold Medallist (Press Section) Internat. Kinematograph Exhibition, Olympia, 1913; arranged and managed first Royal Film Command performance at Buckingham Palace (Tom Brown's Schooldays), Feb. 24, 1917. *Recreation:* gardening. *Address:* Seacroft, Skegness.

Died 24 Dec. 1941.

WARREN, Sir Norcot (Hastings Yeeles), KCIE 1922, Kt 1917; Managing Governor, Imperial Bank of India, 1921–27; *b* 1864; *m* 1893, Mabel, *d* of Col Edward Peters, RE; two *s* one *d*.

Died 23 April 1947.

WARRENDER, Lady Maud; *b* 16 Dec. 1870; 5th *d* of 8th Earl of Shaftesbury; *m* 1894, Sir George Warrender, 7th Bart; two *s* one *d*. *Publications:* My first Sixty Years, 1933; My Medley, 1941. *Address:* 2 Holland Park, W11. *T:* Park 6203.

Died 3 Sept. 1945.

WARTON, Rear-Adm. John Fenwick, CMG 1918; CBE 1919; RN, retired; *b* 1877. Served European War, 1914–19; present at Battle of Jutland; with Mission to N Russia and in White Sea (CMG, CBE); Rear-Adm. 1928. *Address:* 30 Twynham Rd, Southbourne, Bournemouth, Hants.

Died 1 May 1950.

WARWICK, Marjorie, Countess of; (Elfrida Marjorie); *b* 1887; *d* of Sir William Eden, 7th and 5th Bart, and Sybil Frances, *d* of late Sir William Grey, KCSI; *m* 1909, Leopold Guy Francis Maynard Greville (6th Earl of Warwick, CMG, MVO) (*d* 1928); three *s*. Lady of Grace, St John of Jerusalem; served in RAMC, British Expeditionary Force, 1914; Mayor of Warwick, 1929–31; JP for Borough of Warwick; President, Warwick Conservative Association; President, Toc H. Builders Fund, Warwickshire. *Address:* Warwick Castle, Warwick; Villa Grevillea, St Jean, Cap Ferrat, AM, France. *Clubs:* Bath, International Sportsmen's.

Died 10 Feb. 1943.

WARWICK, William Turner, MA, MB, BCh (Cantab); FRCS; Senior Surgeon Middlesex Hospital (with charge of Rectal Clinic); Senior Surgeon, Middlesex Sector, EMS: Consulting Surgeon, Peterborough War Memorial Hospital; Director Bournemouth Cancer Clinic; Consulting Surgeon, LCC: Hunterian Professor, 1942; *b* 1 March 1888; *s* of W. G. Warwick, Hatfield, Yorks; *m* 1921, Joan, *d* of Theodore Harris, Limpsfield; three *s* one *d*. *Educ:* Doncaster Grammar School; Emmanuel College, Cambridge (Sizar); Entrance and Broderip Scholar, Middlesex Hospital. Temp. Lieut RAMC 1916; Resident Surgical Officer, St Mark's Hospital for Diseases of the Rectum, 1919; Resident Surgical Officer, Leeds General Infirmary, 1920; Pathological Registrar (Surgical), Middlesex Hospital, 1921; Assistant Surgeon, Middlesex Hospital, 1922; Examiner in Surgery London Univ. FRSM (Member Council of Section of Surgery, Vice-President, late Secretary Proctological section). *Publications:* The rational treatment of Varicose Veins and Varicocele; numerous contributions to leading medical journals. *Recreations:* member of Cambridge athletic team, 1907, golf. *Address:* Fitzroy Farm Cottage, N6. *T:* Mountview 6700.

Died 21 Aug. 1949.

WASON, Rear-Adm. Cathcart Romer, CIE 1919; CMG 1916; late RN; *b* 1874; 2nd *s* of late Rt Hon. Eugene Wason; *m* 1st, 1905, Helen Muriel (*d* 1916), *d* of late Allen D. Graham, of Cossington and Stawell; one *s*; 2nd, 1918, Agnes, *d* of late J. C. Edwards, Trevor Hall, Llangollen, and *widow* of Walter Richardson. *Educ:* Stubbington. Commander, 1908; Capt. 1916; War Staff Officer, 1913; served Persian Gulf, 1914; Mesopotamia, 1915–17 (despatches, CMG); Retired List, 1922; Rear-Adm. retired, 1927. *Address:* Cossington, Bridgwater. *Club:* Army and Navy.

Died 12 Dec. 1941.

WATERFIELD, Bt-Col Arthur Charles Mallison, MVO 1902; late 11th King Edward's Own Lancers, Indian Army; passed Staff College; *b* 4 July 1866. Entered Army, 1887; Lt ISC 1888; Capt. Indian Army, 1898; Brev.-Maj., 1900; served Hazara Expedition, 1888 (medal clasp); Hazara, 1891 (clasp); Chitral, 1895 (medal with clasp); NW Frontier, India, 1897–98 (two clasps); S African War, 1899–1901 (despatches, Brevet-Major, Queen's medal six clasps); Prof. Indian Staff College, 1906; retired, 1919. *Address:* c/o India Office, Army Dept, Whitehall, SW1.

Died 23 Oct. 1943.

WATERHOUSE, Osborn, MA; Professor of English and Philosophy, Natal University College, 1910–43; Acting Registrar, 1925; *b* Bradford, Yorks, 1881; *s* of Samuel Gray Waterhouse; *m* Edith F., *d* of Myers Murgatroyd; no *c*. *Educ:* Bradford Grammar School; University of Leeds and University of Berlin. University Scholar and John Bright Fellow in English Literature, Victoria University of Manchester; University Fellow in Arts, Leeds University. English Lektor, Koenigliche Akademie, Posen, 1906; Head of Department of English, University College, Exeter, 1907. *Publications:* Contributions to Anglia, The State, Encyclopædia of Education, etc.; The Non-Cycle Mystery Plays, Early English Text Society. *Recreations:* music, golf. *Address:* c/o Standard Bank, Durban.

Died 29 Oct. 1945.

WATERHOUSE, Lt-Col Sir Ronald, KCB 1923; CB 1921; CMG 1919; CVO 1922; late 6th Dragoon Guards; one of HM's Lieutenants for the City of London; *b* 28 Dec. 1878; *m* 1st, 1904, Violet (*d* 1928), *y d* of late John Dalrymple Goldingham, ICS; no *c*; 2nd, 1928, Nourah (author of Private and Official, 1942), *o d* of late Harry Athelstan Chard, Clevedon, Somerset. *Educ:* Marlborough; Oxford University. Served Mashonaland, 1896–97 (Matabele Medal); entered Militia, 1898; 1st Commission, Lincolnshire Regiment, 1899; subsequently transferred to 6th Dragoon Guards, Carabiniers; South African War, 1899–1902 (despatches, Queen's medal four clasps, King's medal two clasps); Bangalore, India, 1903–04; retired pay, 1910, on account of wounds and wound pension; European War, 1914–18 (despatches, Mons Star, British War Medal, Victory Medal); War Office, Intelligence Department, June 1915; Major and General Staff Officer 3rd Grade Oct. 1915; 2nd Grade, 1917; Lieut-Colonel and Staff Officer 1st Grade, 1918; Private Secretary to Chief of Air Staff, Air Ministry, 1918; to Controller-General of Civil Aviation, 1919; to Lord Privy Seal and Leader of the House of Commons (Mr Bonar Law, Mr Austen Chamberlain), 1920–21; Private Secretary and Equerry to the Duke of York, 1921; Principal Private Secretary to the Prime Minister, 1922–28 (Mr Bonar Law, Mr Stanley Baldwin, Mr J. Ramsay MacDonald, and Mr Stanley Baldwin); Member of Air Section and British Delegation to Peace Conference, Paris; Pilot Officer, RAFVR 1929; Flight Lieutenant and Staff Officer, 1940; Fellow of the Royal Geographical Society; Order of St John of Jerusalem; Queen's Jubilee Medal, 1897; GO White Eagle, Serbia; St Maurice and St Lazarus, Italy; GC Crown of Roumania and Lion and Sun of Persia; has also Order of Leopold I of Belgium, and Sacred Treasure of Japan. *Clubs:* Naval and Military, Royal Thames Yacht, Beefsteak.

Died 28 Nov. 1942.

WATERLOW, Col James Francis, DSO 1900; TD; Colonel, TA, retired; late 5th Queen's Royal Regt and 4th Border Regt, TA; Hon. Capt. in the Army; *b* 25 April 1869; *s* of late James Jameson Waterlow and Kate Frances, *d* of Rev. J. Lawson Sisson; *m* 1916, Rosalie Marie, *d* of Alphonse Lorenz, of Monthey, Canton du Valais, Switzerland. *Educ:* Charterhouse. Served South Africa, 1900 (despatches, Queen's medal 6 clasps, DSO); European War (despatches). *Address:* 5 Marlow Court, Pinner Road, Harrow, Middlesex.

Died 19 Nov. 1942.

WATERLOW, Sir Sydney Philip, KCMG 1935; CBE 1920; MA; JP; *b* 22 Oct. 1878; *e s* of late G. S. Waterlow; *m* Margery, *d* of G. Eckhard, Didsbury; one *s* two *d*. *Educ:* Eton College; Trinity College, Cambridge

(Scholar). Entered Diplomatic Service, 1900; appointed to Washington, 1901; resigned, 1905; employed at the Peace Conference at Paris, 1919; re-appointed to the Foreign Office, 1920; Director of the Foreign Division of the Department of Overseas Trade, 1922–24; Counsellor, Foreign Office, 1924–26; British Minister at Bangkok, 1926–28; at Addis Ababa, 1928–29; at Sofia 1929–33; at Athens, 1933–39; Chev. of Legion of Honour. *Publications:* Translation of the Medea and Hippolytus of Euripides (Temple Classics, 1906); A Cambridge Anthology 1909; Shelley (People's Books Series), 1912. *Recreations:* gardening, chess. *Address:* Oare, Wilts. *Club:* Carlton.

Died 4 Dec. 1944.

WATERPARK, 6th Baron *cr* 1792; **Henry Sheppard Hart Cavendish;** Bt 1755; traveller and explorer; *b* 18 May 1876; *e s* of late William Thomas Cavendish; *S* cousin, 1932; *m* 1st, 1902, Isabel Emelie (marr. diss. 1906), *d* of John Wimburn Jay, of Savoy Theatre and Daly's Theatre; one *d*; (she *m* 2nd, 1910, Frank Curzon and *d* 1927); 2nd, 1906, May, *d* of W. E. Burbidge (who divorced him 1912); two *d*; 3rd, Elise, *d* of E. A. Herran. Formerly Lieut 4th Batt. Royal Warwickshire Regiment. Winner of silver medal for non-skidding mechanical device in Automobile Club non-skidding tests, 1904. *Heir: nephew* Frederick Caryll Phillip Cavendish, *b* 6 Oct. 1926. *Address:* Route de St Ouger, Bergerac, Dordogne, France.

Died 26 Nov. 1948.

WATERS, Sir Harry G., Kt 1924; VD; JP; Capt. Med. Officer Stroud Coy Home Guard, Glos, 7th Bn; Knight of St John of Jerusalem; Hon. Pathologist to the Stroud General Hospital; Chairman of the Unemployment Exchange; Chief Med. Officer East Indian Railway, retired; DPH; DTM and H Cantab; Hon. Col EI Ry Regt; Hon. Col AFMC; *b* Rathmullen, Co. Donegal, 1868; *s* of Alfred Waters, Inspector MRN; *m* 1900, Winifred Pierce, MB, CM Edin.; two *s*. *Educ:* RN School, New Cross; St Thomas's Hospital. Hon. Magistrate and Hon. Medical Officer, Tundla Dist, UP; Hon. Magistrate and Hon. Plague Officer, Jamalpore, Bengal; President Conference of Chief Medical Officers Ry, 1918–23; Examiner Hygiene, Calcutta University; Member Bengal Sanitary Board; started St John Ambulance First Aid Classes on the EI Ry, 1897. *Address:* Upper Grange, Stroud, Glos. *TA* and *T:* Stroud 37. *Clubs:* Allahabad; Bengal.

Died 19 Dec. 1946.

WATERS, Brig.-Gen. Wallscourt Hely-Hutchinson, CMG 1904; CVO 1901; MVO 1896; *b* 6 Nov. 1855; *s* of late Edward Waters, MD, of Chester and Sarnau, Co. Carmarthen, and Georgina, *d* of Hon. L. Hely-Hutchinson; *m* 1898, Edith M. (*d* 1932) *d* of G. Oakley of Lawrence End, Herts. *Educ:* Lycée, Versailles; Gymnasium, Berlin. Entered RA 1876; Col, 1901; Military Attaché, St Petersburg, 1893–98; Berlin, 1900–03; served South Africa, 1899–1900 (Queen's medal with clasp); attached to Russian army in Manchuria, 1904–05; commanded troops in North China, 1906–10; retired, 1911; Chief of British Military Mission, Imperial Russian GHQ 1916; Jubilee and Coronation medals; Order of St Stanislas, 1st Class. *Publications:* Secret and Confidential, the Experiences of a Military Attaché, 1926; Private and Personal, 1928; Russia Then and Now, 1935. *Address:* Ottery St Mary, Devon. *Club:* Army and Navy.

Died 14 June 1945.

WATERSON, David, MA, MD, FRCSE, FRSE, etc; Bute Professor of Anatomy, St Andrews University since 1914; Hon. Consultant James MacKenzie Institute; Town Councillor; *s* of Rev. R. Waterston; *m* Isabel Amy, *d* of R. Simson, HMBCS; three *s*. *Educ:* Edinburgh University, etc. Late Demonstrator of Anatomy, University of Edinburgh; Professor of

Anatomy, London University, 1909–14; and Dean of the Faculty of Science (Medical), King's College, WC; Arris and Gale lecturer, Royal College of Surgeons; Struthers Memorial lecturer Royal College of Surgeons of Edinburgh, 1927; represented St Andrews University on General Medical Council. *Publications:* Anatomy in the Living Model; Editor of the Edinburgh Stereoscopic Atlas of Anatomy; numerous contributions on anthropology, embryology, and comparative anatomy in the scientific journals and publications of scientific societies. *Recreations:* golf, tennis, fishing. *Address:* St Andrews University, Scotland. *T:* St Andrews 67. *Clubs:* Athenæum; Royal and Ancient, St Andrews.

Died 4 Sept. 1942.

WATKINS, Col Fredric Mostyn, CBE 1919; *b* 26 Feb. 1873; *s* of Rev. Chas. Watkins, Vicar of Hinton-Charterhouse, Bath; *m.* *Educ:* Leamington College. Joined the 18th Royal Irish Regt, 1893; transferred to the RAPD 1899; Major, 1909; Lieut-Col 1914; temp. Col and Chief Paymaster, 1918; Substantive Colonel and Chief Paymaster, 1921; served NW Frontier, 1897 (medal and two clasps); European War (CBE); Iraq, 1919–21 (despatches, Subs. Colonel, medal and clasp, Iraq); retired pay, 1933. *Address:* West Grove, Hersham, Surrey.

Died 23 April 1946.

WATKINS, Rear-Adm. Geoffrey Robert Sladen, DSO 1917; *b* 1885; *s* of Robert Arundel Watkins and Mary Etheldred Sladen; *m* 1909, Phillis Mabel, *d* of Mortimer Rooke, The Ivy, Chippenham, Wilts; one *s* three *d*. *Educ:* HMS Britannia. Captain, 1928; served for 19 years in the Submarine Service; served in submarines during European War, for the greater part in submarine minelayers (despatches, DSO and bar); possesses air pilotage certificate; Younger Brother of Trinity House; obtained bar to DSO when in command of HMS/M E45 by torpedoing German Submarine UC 62; attached to the Air Ministry, 1927–29; commanded HMS Champion, 1930–31; Fifth Destroyer Flotilla, Atlantic Fleet, 1931–33; HMS Centurion, 1934; commanded 2nd Submarine Flotilla, Home Fleet, 1934–36; Senior Officer the Reserve Fleet, the Nore, 1936–38; ADC to the King, 1938; Chief Staff Officer to Rear-Admiral in Charge, Gibraltar, 1938–40; Rear-Admiral, 1940; British Naval Liaison Officer to French Naval C-in-C Mediterranean, 1940–41; commanded the Base at Harwich, 1941–42; North Africa, 1943–44; West Coast of Scotland, 1945–46. *Recreation:* gardening. *Address:* Five Thorns, Brockenhurst, Hants. *T:* Brockenhurst 2364. *Clubs:* United Service, Seven Seas.

Died 30 July 1950.

WATKINS, Sir Metford, Kt 1947; Chairman of the Council, Royal College of Art; Deputy Chairman John Lewis & Co. Ltd, and Suburban & Provincial Stores Ltd; *b* 22 April 1900; *s* of William Watkins, Wootton Bassett, Wiltshire; *m* 1928, Elizabeth, *d* of Colonel H. K. Umfreville, DSO; two *d*. *Educ:* Swindon; Cambridge. MA (Camb.) 1925. Mathematics Master, Westminster School, 1922–26; John Lewis & Co., Ltd, 1926–, Dep. Chm. 1935–; Member of Industrial and Export Council, Board of Trade, 1940; Director-Gen. of Civilian Clothing, 1941; Chm. Gen. Purposes Cttee of Retail Distributors Association, 1938–40 and 1942–47. *Recreations:* painting, fishing, riding. *Address:* 38 South Audley St, W1; Longstock Grange, Stockbridge, Hants. *Club:* Savile.

Died 27 Nov. 1950.

WATKINS, Michael John, CBE 1943; General Manager and Secretary, Belfast Harbour Commissioners, since 1922; *b* 12 July 1875; *s* of Capt. John and Catherine Watkins, Liverpool and Old Colwyn; *m* 1904, Mary Elizabeth, *d* of J. Tysilio Jones, MBE, JP, Wrexham; one *s* two *d*. *Educ:* Granby Street; Liverpool Institute; Liverpool University. Entered service of Mersey Docks and Harbour Board as an apprentice, 1892; Asst

Secretary to Humber Conservancy Board, Hull, 1911. *Publication:* Developments in Belfast Harbour, 1920–1933, 1934. *Address:* Kenmuir, 12 Deramore Park South, Belfast. *TA:* Harboard, Belfast. *T:* Belfast 65438. *Clubs:* Ulster Reform, Belfast.

Died 15 Aug. 1945.

WATKINS, Lt-Col Oscar Ferris, CMG 1933; CBE 1918; DSO 1916; MA Oxon; *b* Allahabad, 23 Dec. 1877; *e s* of late Ven. O. D. Watkins; *m* 1917, Olga Florence, *o d* of late W. A. Baillie-Grohman; three *d*. *Educ:* Marlborough; Oxford. Served South African War, 1900–01; in SA Constabulary, 1902–04; Transvaal Civil Service, 1904–07; BEA Protectorate Service, 1908; District Commissioner, 1914; during European War Director of Military Labour in operations against German East Africa (despatches four times, CBE, DSO) Acting Chief Native Commissioner, 1920–21; Deputy Chief Native Commissioner, 1921–27; MLC at various times; retired from Kenya CS, 1933; Editor of Baraza (Swahili Weekly) since 1939; FRAI. *Address:* Wispers Farm, Nairobi, Kenya Colony. *Club:* Royal Societies.

Died 27 Dec. 1943.

WATKINS, Sir Percy E., Kt 1930; *b* Dec. 1871; *s* of Evan Watkins (*d* 1906), of Llanfyllin, North Wales, and Mary, *d* of late Richard Mills, Llanidloes; *m* 1898, Mollie (*d* 1939), *d* of late Rev. Richard Jones, CM minister, N Wales; one *s*; 1941, Lil, *d* of late Augustus Lewis, Swansea, and *widow* of F. F. Bush, Wakefield. *Educ:* The High School, Oswestry. Clerk to Llanfyllin School Board, etc., 1892–96; Clerk to the Central Welsh Board for Intermediate Education, 1896–1903; Chief Clerk, Education Dept of West Riding County Council, 1904–11; Registrar, University College of South Wales and Monmouthshire, Cardiff, 1911–13; Asst Secretary Welsh Insurance Commissioners, 1913–20; Secretary, Welsh Board of Health, 1920–25; Permanent Secretary, Welsh Dept Board of Education, 1925–33; Secretary, Welsh Dept, National Council of Social Service, Cardiff, 1933–38; Chairman, Wales Division of Appellate Tribunal for Conscientious Objectors since 1941. *Address:* 14 Charlotte Square, Rhiwbina, Cardiff.

Died 5 May 1946.

WATLINGTON, Sir Henry William, Kt 1933; OBE 1923; Senior Partner Watlington and Conyers, Agents Furness-Bermuda Line, since 1908; Member Bermuda Colonial Parliament for Devonshire since 1906; Chairman Bermuda Board of Education since 1924; President Watlington Water Works; Treasurer Synod of the Church of England in Bermuda since 1916; President Bermudiana Hotel Co.; Chairman Bermuda Development Co.; Mayor, City of Hamilton, 1933–37; *b* 8 June 1866; *s* of Henry Joseph Watlington and Anna Maria Peniston; *m* 1891, Lucy Trott; one *s* four *d*. *Educ:* Pembroke Grammar School; Ontario Business College, Canada. Entered as clerk, Trott & Cox, Steamship Agents, 1885; Member Executive Council, Bermuda 1923–32; Chairman King Edward VII Memorial Hospital, Bermuda, 1925–31; leader in Legislative Franchise to the Bermuda Railway, 1924; Establisher and Financier of the Watlington Water Works, 1932. *Recreation:* chess. *Address:* Woodside, Devonshire, Bermuda. *TA:* Watlington, Bermuda. *T:* Hamilton 1362. *Clubs:* Royal Bermuda Yacht, Hamilton Dinghey.

Died 14 Dec. 1942.

WATSON, Andrew Gordon, MD; Spa Physician, Consulting Surgeon Victoria Hospital; Honorary Physician, Royal Mineral Water Hospital Bath, and Consulting Physician Physiotherapy Department, Royal United Hospital, Bath; *s* of late Hugh Watson, Torsonce, Scotland, and *d* of General Liddell, CB; *m* 1907, Clementina, *d* of late Andrew Macdonald, Inverness; one *s* one *d*. *Educ:* Cargilfield; privately; Edinburgh University; Paris and Vienna. Civil Surgeon, S African War, 1900–02 (medal and clasps); European War, 1914–17. *Publications:* numerous articles on Rheumatic diseases and Gout. *Recreations:* fishing, shooting and yachting. *Address:* 21 The Circus, Bath. *TA and T:* Bath 2309. *Club:* Bath and County (Bath).

Died 15 Oct. 1949.

WATSON, Archibald, MD, FRCS; Professor of Anatomy, Adelaide University, 1885; retired with the title of Emeritus Professor, 1920; *b* 1849. Late Demonstrator of Anatomy, Charing Cross Medical School; served Boer War; as Surgeon European War. *Club:* Adelaide.

Died Aug. 1940.

WATSON, Arthur Kenelm, MA; *b* Harrow, 23 March 1867; *e s* of late A. G. Watson of Uplands, Wadhurst, Sussex; *m* 1897, Carolino Margaret, *y d* of late Charles Warrack, Sheriff Clerk Depute for Aberdeenshire; one *s* two *d.* *Educ:* Harrow; Balliol College, Oxford. Assistant Master at Rugby, 1891–1906; Headmaster Queen Elizabeth's School, Ipswich, 1906–18; Principal of Darululum School, Panchgani, Bombay Presidency, 1920–21. *Address:* 5 Roxborough Park, Harrow-on-the-Hill. *T:* Byron 1606; Dyke End, Upton, Acle, Norfolk.

Died 2 Jan. 1947.

WATSON, Basil Bernard, KC 1923; Metropolitan Police Magistrate, North London Police Court, since 1926; Old Street, EC, 1923–26. Barrister, Inner Temple. *Address:* 2 Ryder Street, SW1.

Died 20 Jan. 1941.

WATSON, Sir Bertrand, Kt 1942; Chief Metropolitan Magistrate, Bow Street, since 1941; *b* Stockton-on-Tees, 16 May 1878; *s* of late John Wilson Watson, JP, timber merchant, Woodlands, Stockton; *m* 1909, Ethelwynne Gladys *d* of Ralph Jameson, West Bank, Stockton; one *s* two *d.* *Educ:* Harrogate College. Admitted Solicitor (Hons), 1900; Deputy-Coroner for the County of Durham, 1902–11; MP (Coal.) Stockton-on-Tees, 1917–23; Mayor of Stockton, 1915–16; Member of Durham County Council, 1912–19; Barrister-at-law of Gray's Inn and North-Eastern Circuit; Bencher of Gray's Inn, 1942; Parliamentary Private Secretary to Rt Hon. Edward Shortt, KC, MP, Home Secretary, 1919; Metropolitan Police Magistrate (North London), 1928; Clerkenwell, 1931–36; retired, 1936; reinstated, 1938; Metropolitan Magistrate, Lambeth, 1938–41. *Recreations:* golf, and motoring. *Address:* 26 Harley House, NW1. *T:* Welbeck 1835. *Clubs:* Reform, Garrick.

Died 16 Feb. 1948.

WATSON, Chalmers, MD, FRCPE; retired; Consulting Physician, Royal Infirmary, Edinburgh; Alvarenga Prizeman, College of Physicians, Philadelphia; *b* Midcalder, Midlothian, 1870; *s* of late Walter Watson, MD, Midcalder; *m* 1st, 1898, Alexandra Mary Chalmers Watson (CBE 1917) (*d* 1936); two *s*; 2nd, 1938, Lily Brayton (Mrs Oscar Asche), Marlow. *Educ:* Edinburgh Univ. (Wightman Prizeman in Clinical Medicine); Marburg. Editor of the Ency. Medica. *Publications:* Food and Feeding in Health and Disease; The Book of Diet; Lectures on Clinical Medicine; numerous papers on Gout, Rheumatism, Intestinal Disorders, Diet, and articles on various agricultural subjects, 1936–1945. *Address:* Fenton Barns, Drem, East Lothian. *T:* Dirleton 63. *Club:* Caledonian United Service Edinburgh.

Died 6 April 1946.

WATSON, Brig.-Gen. Charles Frederic, CMG 1916; DSO 1900; *b* 29 June 1877; *s* of late Col Fred. Watson; *m* 1906, Winifred, *e d* of W. H. Woodruff; two *s.* *Educ:* Wellington College. Entered The Queen's Royal Regiment, 1898; Captain, 1903; Brevet Major, 1914; Lieutenant-Colonel, 1917; Colonel, 1919; served South Africa, 1899–1902 (despatches twice, Queen's medal 6 clasps, King's medal 2 clasps, DSO); European War, 1914–18 (despatches four times, CMG, Bt Colonel, 1914 Star, British War Medal, Victory Medal, Légion d'honneur, Croix d'officier); Lieut-Col Royal

Warwickshire Regt, 1922; Commanded Rangoon Brigade, 1927–31; retired pay, 1931. *Club:* United Service.

Died 8 July 1948.

WATSON, Maj.-Gen. Sir Charles Gordon G.; *see* Gordon-Watson.

WATSON, Sir David M.; *see* Milne-Watson.

WATSON, Edmund Henry Lacon; author; *b* Sharnford, Leicestershire, 15 Aug. 1865; *o s* late Canon Henry Lacon Watson, Rector of Sharnford; *m* 1896, Ruth, *d* of Rev. J. G. Darling, Rector of Eyke, Suffolk. *Educ:* Winchester (Scholar); Caius College, Camb. (2nd Class Classical Tripos, 1887). Schoolmaster for seven years; Admiralty, 1914; in Postal Censorship, 1915–17 (DAC and Travelling Censor); Reuter's Special Correspondent on Italian Front, 1917–18; on French Front and on Rhine, 1918–19. *Publications:* The Unconscious Humorist, 1896; Verses Suggested and Original; An Attic in Bohemia, 1897; Benedictine, 1898; Christopher Deane, 1901; Hints to Young Authors, 1902; The Templars, 1903; The Making of a Man, 1904; Reflections of a Householder, 1905; The Barony of Brendon, 1907; The Happy Elopement, 1909; Barker's, 1910; The Family Living, 1912; Cloudesley Tempest; A Conversational Tour in America, 1914; Phyllis and a Philosopher, 1922; Devenish, Wave Lengths, 1923; Lectures to Living Authors, 1925; The Strange Family, 1926; Rudolf Strange, Lectures on Dead Authors, 1927; The Last of the Stranges, 1928 Tommy Picton and Certain Women, 1930; Notes and Memories of a Sports Reporter, Contemporary Comments, 1931; In the Days of His Youth, 1935; I Look Back Seventy Years, 1938; Diana goes Hunting, 1943; Perdita finds Herself, 1944; Anne, 1946. *Recreations:* formerly golf and billiards, now chiefly bridge. *Address:* 19 Scarsdale Villas, W8. *T:* 3366 Western. *Club:* Authors'.

Died 9 March 1948.

WATSON, Sir Francis, Kt 1919, JP City of Bradford; senior partner of firm of Watson, Son & Smith, Solicitors, Bradford; *b* 1864; *e s* of Thomas Adam Watson, JP, of Thorn Garth, Thackley; *m* 1892; Maude, *er d* of William Glossop of Endsleigh, Hull; one *s* one *d.* *Educ:* Bradford Grammar School; France. MP (U) Pudsey and Otley Division of West Riding, Yorkshire, 1923–29; Chairman of Bradford Conservative, etc., Association, 1919, 1924; Member of the Bradford City Council, 1899–1907; Chairman of Bradford Distress Committee under Unemployed Workmen's Act since 1905; Military Representative of Bradford under the Military Service Act; Member of the Council of the Bradford Chamber of Commerce. *Address:* Rawdon Cragg, nr Leeds. *T:* Rawdon 212. *Clubs:* Carlton; Union, Bradford.

Died 27 Aug. 1947.

WATSON, Sir Frank Pears, KCMG 1933; OBE 1918; *b* 13 Sept. 1878; *s* of late Major-General James Kiero Watson, 60th Rifles, and Alice, *d* of Col Pears; *m* 1913, Audrey Florence, *d* of late David Reid; one *d.* *Educ:* Winchester. Entered Egyptian Ministry of Public Works, 1899; Financial Secretary to the Ministry of Public Works, 1920; Financial Adviser to the Egyptian Government, 1927–37; Medjidieh 4th Class, 1904; Nile 3rd Class, 1918; Grand Cordon of the Nile, 1936. *Address:* Zamalik, Cairo, Egypt. *Club:* Travellers'.

Died 13 Feb. 1941.

WATSON, Frederick, CMG 1937; OBE 1923; *b* Starston, 19 May 1880; *s* of late Rev. Frederick Watson, DD, Hon. Canon of Ely; *m* 1910, late Mary Carlyon Vavasor, *d* of late Rev. John Durell, Fulbourne Rectory, Cambridge; one *s* one *d.* *Educ:* King's School, Canterbury; Queens' College, Cambridge. Vice-Consul in Consular Service, 1906; served at Valparaiso, 1907; at Soulina, 1909, at Odessa 1911, at Taranto, 1913, at San Francisco, 1918; Consul at New York, 1919; Consul

General at Philadelphia, 1923–40. *Address:* The Ashwood, Overbrook Avenue, Philadelphia. *Clubs:* University, Philadelphia.

Died 14 Sept. 1947.

WATSON, Gilbert; *b* 12 Nov. 1864. *Publications:* Three Rolling Stones in Japan, 1903; Sunshine and Sentiment in Portugal, 1908; The Voice of the South, 1905; Skipper, 1906; Forbidden Ground, 1910; Toddie, 1911; The Amazing Guest, 1924. *Address:* The End House, St Andrews.

Died 8 Feb. 1941.

WATSON, Lt-Col Harold Farnell, CMG 1917; DSO 1900; late Sherwood Foresters and 4th Batt. Lancashire Fusiliers; *b* 25 July 1876; *s* of W. Farnell Watson; *m* 1st, 1901, Georgina Barbara (*d* 1930), *d* of George Allan; 2nd, 1938, Marie Kostukevitch. Entered Army, 1897; served North-West Frontier, India, 1897–98 (medal with clasp); served South Africa, first as Adjt 9th MI, then as Adjt 22nd MI (despatches, Queen's medal with three clasps, King's medal two clasps, DSO); promoted Capt. into Lancashire Fusiliers, 1902; resigned commission, 1903; joined 4th Batt. Lancashire Fusiliers as Captain, 1903; Major, 1910; temp. Lt-Col 11th Batt. Sherwood Foresters, 1915; Maj., Sherwood Foresters, 1917; retired pay, 1923. *Address:* PR Salisbury, S Rhodesia. *Club:* Junior United Service.

Died 18 April 1941.

WATSON, Harrison; ISO 1935; *b* 13 June 1864; *o s* of Charles S. Watson, JP, of Montreal, Canada; *m* 1890, Ruth Appleton, *o d* of William Blake. *Educ:* Canada, England, France, and Germany. Engaged in business in Canada; appointed in 1892 to take charge of the commercial and emigration work of the Canadian Section of the Imperial Institute, and afterwards acted as a commercial agent of the Canadian Government; Canadian Government Trade Commissioner in London, 1913; Chief Canadian Government Trade Commissioner in the United Kingdom 1916–34; Hon. Agent-General for Prince Edward Island, 1902–17; Canadian representative on the Imperial Economic Committee, 1927–34. *Address:* Catsfield Place, Battle, Sussex. *Club:* St James's (Montreal).

Died 22 Jan. 1948.

WATSON, Maj.-Gen. Sir Harry Davis, KBE 1919; CB 1918; CMG 1915; CIE 1906; MVO 1911; 9th Gurkha Rifles; Extra Equerry to HM the King; *b* 18 July 1866; *y s* of late Gen. Sir John Watson, GCB, VC; *m* 1895, Ada May, *d* of W. H. Reynolds; one *s* two *d*. Entered Dorset Regt 1885; Captain, Indian Army, 1896; Major, 1903; Lt-Col 1910; Col 1914; Maj.-Gen. 1918; served Sikkim Expedition, 1888 (medal with clasp); Chin Lushai Expedition, 1899–1902 (clasp); China, 1900–01 (medal); European War, 1914–18 (KBE, CMG, CB); retired, 1924; Order of the Nile, 3rd Class, 1916; Légion d'Honneur, officier. *Address:* Longwater, Finchampstead, Berks.

Died 7 May 1945.

WATSON, Captain Horace Cyril, CBE 1919; RN, retired; *b* The Grange, W Cowes, Isle of Wight, 9 Oct. 1876; 5th *s* of Rev. Arthur Watson, MA; *m* Marjorie Ruth, 2nd *d* of Ernest Edmonds, FCA, Portsmouth. *Educ:* The Grange, Cowes; HMS Britannia. Midshipman, 1892; Sub-Lieutenant, 1896; Lieutenant, 1898; Commander, 1911; Captain, 1917; joined the Surveying Service as Sub.-Lieut; subsequently transferred to Navigating Dept as Lieutenant; Navigating Officer of Perseus, Nymphe, Thames, Blake, Goliath, Terpsichore for War Staff Duties; 1st Lieut and Navigating Officer of Carnarvon and Agamemnon; served in Collingwood and Resolution in Grand Fleet, European War; Captain of Hildebrand in 10th Cruiser Squadron and on Convoy Service (CBE); Captain of Bacchante after war; Captain Attendant and King's Harbour Master, Malta, 1919–21; Captain of Dockyard, Deputy Superintendent, and King's Harbour Master, Devonport, 1922–23; retired list, 1923. *Recreation:* gardening. *Address:* Barton House, Meonstoke, Hants. *T:* Droxford 80.

Died 18 April 1949.

WATSON, Hubert Digby, CIE 1919; CBE 1932; MA; *b* 31 Dec. 1869; *y s* of A. G. Watson, DCL, late of Uplands, Wadhurst, Sussex; *m* 1912, Florence Dorothy, *y d* of late Thomas Usborne, Bradfield, Berks; one *s* three *d*. *Educ:* Harrow School: Balliol College, Oxford. Indian Civil Service; in the Punjab Commission; served as Assistant-Commissioner, Political Officer on the Frontier, Settlement Officer, and Deputy Commissioner; retired, 1919. *Publications:* Gazetteer of Hazara, NWF Province, 1908; The Hunting of the Snark in Latin Elegiacs, 1936; Jabberwocky, 1937, etc. *Address:* Windrush, Inkpen, Newbury. *T:* Inkpen 211. *Clubs:* Athenæum, MCC.

Died 9 Oct. 1947.

WATSON, Lt-Col James Kiero, CMG 1901; CVO 1912; CBE 1919; DSO 1896; late King's Royal Rifles; *b* 19 June 1865; *s* of late Maj.-Gen. James Kiero Watson (late 60th Rifles); *m* 1902, Katharine Emelia, *d* of H. C. Nisbet, of The Old House, Wimbledon; one *s*. *Educ:* Clifton College; Sandhurst. Joined King's Royal Rifles, 1885; served in Chin Hills, Burma (medal and clasp); attached Egyptian Army, 1894–99, and served as ADC to the Sirdar during Dongola and Khartoum expeditions (despatches, DSO, Brevet Majority, 4th Class Medjidieh and 3rd Class Osmanieh); served S Africa as ADC to Lord Kitchener, 1899–1901 (despatches, CMG); returned to Egyptian Army, 1901; retired, 1905; 1st ADC to the Khedive, 1905–14; served European War, 1914–16 (despatches, Legion of Honour); Military Attaché, Egypt, 1916–19; Equerry to Duke of Connaught, 1939; Commander Crown of Rumania; 2nd Class Order Nile; Commander Order of Leopold II. *Address:* c/o Lloyds Bank Ltd, 6 Pall Mall, SW1; Gorse Cottage, Firwood Drive, Camberley, Surrey. *T:* Camberley 1336.

Died 13 Jan. 1942.

WATSON, Sir John Charles, Kt 1931; MBE; KC 1929; Sheriff of Caithness, Orkney, and Zetland since 1931; *b* 9 July 1883; *e s* of late Henry Currie Watson, Journalist; *m* 1915, Dr Olive Robertson; one *s*. *Educ:* John Neilson Institution, Paisley; University, Glasgow and University, Edinburgh, MA (Hons) LLB. Called Scots Bar, 1909; Solicitor-General for Scotland, 1929–31; Served European War 1915 to end, Infantry 15th Royal Fusiliers, RFC and RAF, Captain Flying and Captain SO3 RAF; Service MEF, EEF also in Arabia. *Recreations:* fishing, shooting, golf. *Address:* 10 Forres Street, Edinburgh. *T:* Edinburgh 23565; Drummore, Wigtownshire. *Clubs:* RAF; Northern, Royal Scots, Edinburgh; Royal Burgess Golfing Society, Barnton.

Died 8 Feb. 1944.

WATSON, Hon. John Christian; *b* Valparaiso, 9 April 1867; *m* 1st, 1889, Ada Jane Low; 2nd, 1925, Antonia, *d* of late M. Lane, Western Australia. *Educ:* Public School, Oamaru, New Zealand. Was President of the Sydney Trades and Labour Council; began life as a compositor; MLA for Young, NSW, 1894–1901; Member of the Commonwealth House of Representatives, 1901–10; Prime Minister and Treasurer of Australia, 1904. *Address:* Anderson Street, Double Bay, Sydney, NSW, Australia.

Died 18 Nov. 1941.

WATSON, John Duncan; Consulting Engineer, Westminster; *b* 7 March 1860; *s* of late D. M. Watson, Lincoln; *m* 1888, Margaret (*d* 1936), *d* of Alexander Clark, Montrose; one *s* one *d*. *Educ:* High School, Dundee. Apprenticed to late James Watson, MInstCE of Bradford; Borough Surveyor, Arbroath, 1884–90 County Engineer Aberdeen, 1890–99; Engineer to the Birmingham Tame and Rea Drainage Board, 1899–1923; Consulting Engineer on Water Supply,

Sewerage, and Sewage purification to various towns in United States, Canada, India, S Africa, Straits Settlements, Iran, Palestine, and many towns in British Isles; Past President Inst. of Civil Engineers; Vice-Pres. Royal Sanitary Institute; Past Pres. Assoc. of Consulting Engineers, Inst. of Sanitary Engineers, and Inst. of Sewage Purification. *Recreation:* formerly golf. *Address:* Northfield, Birmingham; 18 Queen Anne's Gate, Westminster, SW1. *Clubs:* National Liberal; Union, Birmingham.

Died 23 Nov. 1946.

WATSON, John Harry, MB, BS (Lond.), FRCS (Eng.); Consulting Surgeon, Burnley; Hon. Surgeon to Victoria Hospital; Consulting Surgeon to Municipal Hospital Burnley, Reedyford Hospital, Nelson and Hartley Hospital, Colne; Director of Radium Clinic, Burnley; *b* 1875; *s* of Thomas Watson, Atherton, Lancs; *m* Margaret Winifred, *d* of John Humphreys, MA, FSA, Birmingham; no *c*. *Educ:* Rivington Grammar School; University College, Liverpool; King's College, London; London Hospital. Holt Fellow in Physiology, Liverpool University, 1899. Demonstrator of Anatomy, London Hospital; Lecturer on Anatomy, University of Birmingham; Arris and Gale Lecturer, RCS 1906; Surgical Specialist with Salonika Force attached to Serbian Army (Order of St Sava); FRSM (Surgical Section). *Publications:* Fundamentals of the Art of Surgery, 1926; Translation of Professor Jeanneney's Cancer; numerous articles. *Recreations:* tennis and golf. *Address:* 66 Bank Parade, Burnley. *T:* Burnley 3760; Green Gables, Nelson. *T:* Nelson 366. *Club:* Pendle Forest Golf.

Died 27 Nov. 1944.

WATSON, Sir John Mathewson, Kt 1932; JP; *b* Crossford, Lanarkshire; *m* 1904, Margaret Boyd Baillie, Motherwell; no *c*. *Educ:* Glasgow University. Became Political Secretary to MP; Alderman of City of Manchester; Magistrate for 17 years; Chairman of Henshaws' Institution for the Blind; Chairman for the White Heather Fund; Life Governor of the Manchester Royal Infirmary and Jewish Hospital; Vice-President of National Institute for the Blind; has been Chairman, Hon. Secretary or Treasurer of different organisations since 1911, in Manchester, and raised funds of over a million pounds for charitable purposes; Member of the Board of Med. Charities; Member of the Board of the YMCA; Chairman of the White Heather Home for Blind Children at Old Colwyn; retired from business, 1937. *Recreation:* golf. *Address:* 39 Park Range, Victoria Park, Manchester, 14. *T:* Rusholme 1970; 90 Deansgate, Manchester. *T:* Blackfriars 7287. *Club:* Reform.

Died 14 Feb. 1942.

WATSON, Engr Rear-Adm. Lewis Jones, CB 1925; OBE 1919; *b* 1871; 3rd *s* of late Rev. Edward Collis Watson, Vicar of Meltham, Yorkshire, and Mrs Watson, Charmouth, Dorset; *m* 1904, 3rd *d* of William Hardy Charlesworth, Tandridge Hall, Surrey; one *d*. *Educ:* Magdalen College School, Oxford; St James' School, Almondbury. Entered Navy, 1887; at RNE College to 1892; RN College, Greenwich, 1892–95; HMS Immortalité, China, 1895–99; RN College, Greenwich, as Instructor of Applied Mechanics, 1900–04; HMS Doris, HMS Magnificent, HMS Venerable, and various appointments in Naval Yards, 1905–15; HMS Lord Nelson, Mediterranean, 1916–18; Engineer Captain, 1919; Engineer Rear-Admiral, 1924; Assistant Engineer-in-Chief, Admiralty, 1922–27; Retired List, 1927. *Club:* Naval and Military.

Died 1 Jan. 1942.

WATSON, Robert, FRGS; novelist, historian, poet, and editor; film writer; *b* Glasgow, 28 May 1882; *m* 1911, Anna McNaught Johnstone. *Educ:* Pollok and Shawlands Academies. *Publications:* My Brave and Gallant

Gentleman, 1918; The Girl of OK Valley, 1919; Stronger than his Sea, 1920; The Mad Minstrel (ballads and poems), 1921; The Spoilers of the Valley, 1923; Gordon of the Lost Lagoon, 1925; Canada's Fur Bearers (Children's Poems), 1925; Me—and Peter, 1926; High Hazard, 1927; Lower Fort Garry, 1928; Famous Forts of Manitoba, 1929; A Boy of the Great North-West, 1930; The Indians of Manitoba, 1931; Dreams of Fort Garry, 1931; The Native Returns, 1932; When Christmas Came to Fort Garry, 1935; Babes in Babylon, 1937; many Hollywood Screen Assignments; contributor to leading journals of short stories and on Canadian historical matters, Motion Pictures, Sports, etc. *Address:* Anita Street, Laguna Beach, California, USA.

Died 31 Jan. 1948.

WATSON, Lt-Col Stancliffe Wallace, CMG 1919; DSO 1917; stockbroker; *b* Montreal, 17 Nov. 1889; *s* of late William Wallace Watson and Florence Stancliffe, Macclesfield; *m* 1921, May Fair Wilson, *d* of late James Wilson, Montreal. *Educ:* Loretto School, Musselburgh. Sept. 1914 joined 5th Royal Highlanders of Canada; Oct. 1914 transferred to 24th Battalion (VRC); May 1915 proceeded overseas as Lieutenant; Sept. 1915 appointed MG Officer, 5th Canadian Infantry Brigade; Jan. 1916 promoted Captain and assumed command of Canadian MG Company; Sept. 1916 promoted Major; July 1917 appointed Divisional MG Officer, 1st Canadian Division; Feb. 1918 promoted Lieutenant-Colonel and assumed command 1st Canadian MG Battalion (CMG, DSO). *Address:* 1625 Sherbrooke Street West, Montreal, Quebec, Canada. *Clubs:* Royal Montreal Golf, St James', Racket, Automobile, Forest and Stream, Montreal.

Died 28 April 1947.

WATSON, Sir Thomas Aubrey, 4th Bt *cr* 1866; *b* 7 Nov. 1911; *s* of 3rd Bt and Evelyn (*d* 1937), *d* of late Aubrey Cartwright, of Edgcote; *S* father, 1922; *m* 1935, Ella Marguerite, *y d* of late Sir George Farrar, 1st Bt; one *s*. *Educ:* Eton. *Heir:* *s* James Andrew, *b* 30 Dec. 1937. *Address:* Kineton Glebe, Kineton, Warwickshire.

Died 10 Jan. 1941.

WATSON, Major William, DSO 1915; late Border Regt; *b* 19 Jan. 1885; *m* 1916, Theodora, 2nd *d* of A. R. Norrington and *widow* of Capt. W. T. Stackhouse, Sherwood Foresters. Entered Army, 1906; Captain, 1914; Major, 1923; served with W African Frontier Force, 1912–13; European War, 1914–18 (despatches twice, DSO); retired pay, 1930. *Club:* Army and Navy.

Died 2 March 1942.

WATSON, Maj.-Gen. William Arthur, CB 1914; CMG 1917; CIE 1906; psc; *b* Delhi, 25 Sept. 1860; *e s* of late Gen. Sir John Watson, GCB, VC, Finchampstead; *m* 1897, Marguerite Audrey, *d* of late Lieut-Col Alfred Stowell Jones, VC. *Educ:* Charterhouse. Second Lieutenant, 29th Foot, 1880; joined Central India Horse, 1882; served Suakin Campaign as Adjutant of Camel Corps, 1885 (despatches); ADC to Sir Fred. Roberts, 1888; Staff College, 1892 and 1893; ADC to Sir George White, 1894–95; ADC to Sir W. Galbraith, Quetta, 1895–96; DAAG for Instruction, Dalhousie, 1896–1900; served China Campaign, 1900–01, as Orderly Officer to Gen. O'Moore Creagh, VC, and Commissioner of International Police, Shanghai (despatches); First Commandant, Imperial Cadet Corps, 1901–06; Commandant 39th KGO Central India Horse, 1906–11; Deputy Quartermaster-General in India, 1911–12; Commandant, Cavalry School, Saugor, 1912; European War, Egypt, 1914–17 (despatches four times); Maj.-Gen. 1916; Order of the Nile, 2nd Class, 1916; Hon. Col 39th KGO Central India Horse, 1918. *Publication:* King George's Own Central India Horse, 1930. *Address:* North Corner, Lewes. *Club:* Army and Navy.

Died 27 June 1944.

WATSON, William John, MA, LLD; DLitt Celt., FSA Scot.; Hon. FEIS; *b* 17 Feb. 1865; *s* of Hugh Watson, Kindeace, Ross-shire; *m* 1st, 1895, Isabella Christina, *d* of George Munro, Lonroidge, Alness, Ross-shire; 2nd, 1906, Elizabeth Catherine, *d* of Alexander Carmichael, LLD, Edinburgh; three *s* (two killed on Active Service). *Educ:* Boath Public School, Alness; Grammar School, Old Aberdeen; Aberdeen University (1st Class Hons in Classics; Seafield Latin Medal; Blackie Prize); Merton College, Oxford (1st Class Classical Moderations, 1889; 1st Class Lit. Hum. 1891). Assist to Prof. of Humanity, Aberdeen, 1887–88; Assist Master, Kelvinside Academy, Glasgow, 1891–94; Rector of Inverness Royal Academy, 1894–1909; Rector of Royal High School, Edinburgh, 1909–14; Professor of Celtic Languages, Literature, History and Antiquities, Edinburgh University, 1914–38. *Publications:* Place Names of Ross and Cromarty, 1904; Prints of the Past around Inverness, 2nd edition, 1925; Specimens of Gaelic Prose, 1915; 2nd edition, 1929; Specimens of Gaelic Poetry, 1918; 2nd edition, 1932; Geography of Ross and Cromarty, 1924; Celtic Place-Names of Scotland, 1926; Scottish Poetry from the Book of the Dean of Lismore, 1937; Notes on the Study of Gaelic; articles on Celtic topology, etc. *Recreations:* walking, golf; Oxford Blue for Hammer and Weight. *Address:* 17 Merchiston Avenue, Edinburgh. *T:* 54882.

Died 9 March 1948.

WATSON, William Trevor; KC 1930; Bencher of Gray's Inn; Member General Council of the Bar; *b* Llansannor, South Wales, 30 June 1886; *s* of Reverend Wm Watson; *m* Clare, *d* of John Watson, Wilmslow, Eltham Park; no *c. Educ:* Kingsbridge Grammar School, Devon; Merton College, Oxford (Senior Mathematical Postmaster). Called to Bar, Gray's Inn, 1911; Captain RAF 1918; specialises in patent and scientific cases; Member Incorporated Council of Law Reporters, 1935–42; Member Commission on Trade Mark Law, 1936–37. *Recreations:* golf, theatre. *Address:* 83 Neville Court, St John's Wood, NW3; Tighna Mara, Kingsgate, Thanet; 1 Grays Inn Square, Grays Inn, WC1. *Club:* Garrick.

Died 24 March 1943.

WATSON-TAYLOR, George Simon Arthur; JP Wilts; *b* 1850; *e s* of late Simon Watson-Taylor and Lady Hannah Charlotte, 2nd *d* of 8th Marquis of Tweeddale; *m* 1st, 1895, Evelyn Matilda (*d* 1931), *y d* of late Henry Fitzroy of Salcey Lawn, Northamptonshire; 2nd, 1931, Mary Edith, *o d* of late Lieut-Col Delves Broughton, Delverne, Farnham, Surrey. *Educ:* Eton; Trinity College, Cambridge (MA). Late Capt. R. Wilts Yeomanry; Sheriff of Wiltshire, 1914. *Address:* Stert, Devizes.

Died 4 Oct. 1942.

WATT, Alexander Strahan, CBE 1918; senior partner of A. P. Watt & Son, literary agents; 2nd *s* of late A. P. Watt, who created the profession of literary agent; *m* Lesley Gordon, *d* of late John Anderson; one *s. Educ:* privately in London and New York. *Recreations:* picture exhibitions; motoring. *Address:* 82 Finchley Road, NW8. *Club:* Reform.

Died 30 Dec. 1948.

WATT, Brig.-Gen. Donald Munro, CIE 1921; DSO 1915; *b* 18 June 1871; *m* 1925, Dorothy King. *Educ:* Fettes; RMC Sandhurst. 2nd Lieut 1891; psc 1907; Col 1920; Retired 1920; Served in Gordon Highlanders, and 2nd Gurkhas, on Staff, and Command 145 Infantry Brigade, War Service; Chitral, 1895; Tirah and NWF, 1897–98; Somaliland, 1904; European War, 1914–18, France, Belgium and Italy; Third Afghan War, 1919; Waziristan, 1920; Despatches 8 times, Brevet Lt-Col CIE, DSO and bar. *Address:* c/o Holt, Kirkland House, Whitehall, SW1.

Died 12 Oct. 1942.

WATT, James, WS, FFA; Hon. LLD (Edin.); senior partner of Davidson & Syme, WS, Edinburgh; Treasurer WS Society, 1925–35; Treasurer RSE 1926–37, Vice-Pres., 1937–40 and 1941–44; Acting Pres. University of Edinburgh Graduates' Association; *b* 21 March 1863; *m* Menie, *er d* of late Rev. W. C. E. Jamieson; four *s* one *d. Educ:* Royal High School, Edinburgh; Edinburgh University. *Address:* 23 Charlotte Square, Edinburgh. *Clubs:* Reform, Athenæum, Chemical; Northern, Edinburgh; Western, Glasgow.

Died 3 Dec. 1945.

WATT, James, CMG 1924; *b* 1870; *s* of late James Watt; *m* Lilian Verelst (*d* 1938), *d* of late Rev. T. J. Hodgson, Charterhouse, Godalming; one *s* one *d. Educ:* Dumfries Academy; Edinburgh University, MA; Balliol College, Oxford, BA. Assistant District Commissioner, S Nigeria, 1899; District Commissioner, 1902; Senior Resident; retired, 1923. *Address:* Whiteleaf, Montague Road, Berkhamsted, Herts.

Died 5 April 1945.

WATT, James Cromar, LLD Aberdeen, 1931; architect and enameller; *b* Aberdeen, 1862; unmarried. *Educ:* Aberdeen Grammar School. Trained as Architect; entered Architectural School of the Royal Academy, London, 1888; studied Architecture in France, Spain, Italy, and Greece; RIBA Tite prizeman, 1890; ARIBA, 1892; subsequently relinquished practising architecture for decorative craft work, especially enamelling; further study-travel in Turkey, Greece, and Egypt. *Publication:* Examples of Greek and Pompeian Decorative Work, 1897. *Recreations:* travel; horticulture (FRHS; made botanical expedition to Sikkim, 1925); the collecting of Chinese works of art (Collection permanently on exhibition in Aberdeen Art Gallery). *Address:* 71 Dee Street, Aberdeen.

Died 19 Nov. 1940.

WATT, Captain Samuel Alexander; *b* 1876; *e s* of Andrew Alexander Watt, DL, Thorn Hill, Londonderry, Ireland; *m* 1901, Blanche Moore-Munn; two *d. Educ:* Winchester. Director Inglis and Coy. Ltd; Captain South Irish Horse (Cavalry Reserve); served in France during European War; High Sheriff of Rutland, 1937–38; Represented Ireland International Polo team 4 years. *Recreations:* hunting, shooting, polo. *Address:* Belton House, Belton, Uppingham, Rutland. *Clubs:* Cavalry; Kildare Street (Dublin); Ulster (Belfast).

Died 1 Feb. 1950.

WATT, Theodore, MA, LLD, JP; Managing Director, The Aberdeen University Press, Ltd; *b* Aberdeen, 5 Feb. 1884; 3rd *s* of William Watt, joint editor and proprietor Aberdeen Free Press, and Marjorie M. W. Robertson; *m* 1911, Mabel Florence, *yr d* of George Murray, JP Aberdeen; three *s* one *d. Educ:* Aberdeen Grammar School; Aberdeen University (MA 1904, Hon. LLD 1938). Entered service of Rosemount Press, Aberdeen, 1904, becoming Manager in 1914; Governing Director, Rosemount Press, Ltd 1927; Joint Managing Director, Aberdeen University Press, Ltd, 1932 (on amalgamation of Rosemount Press with University Press); Pres. Scottish Alliance of Master Printers, 1930–32 (thereafter an Hon. Pres.); Pres. British Federation of Master Printers, 1937–38; headed British delegation to International Master Printers' Congress, Budapest, 1937; Editor of Alma Master (Aberdeen University Magazine) 1904–06; VP Aberdeen University Alumnus Association, 1939; an Assessor of General Council of Aberdeen University on the University Court, 1942. *Publications:* Compiled Record of Celebration of Tercentenary of Introduction of Art of Printing into Aberdeen by Edward Raban in the year 1622, 1922; Aberdeen Grammar School Roll of Pupils, 1795–1919, annotated from 1863, 1923; Roll of the Graduates of the University of Aberdeen, 1901–1925, with Supplement

1860–1900, 1935. *Address:* Culter House, Milltimber, Aberdeenshire. *T:* Culter 184; (Temporary War: 18 Rubislaw Den North, Aberdeen. *T:* Aberdeen 4953).

Died 5 July 1946.

WATT, Hon. Sir Thomas, KCMG 1912; CMG 1906; MP South Africa, 1910–29; *b* Glasgow, 20 Jan. 1857; *m* 1st, 1886, May Lindup (*d* 1923); 2nd, Adéle, *widow* of Chas. J. Mudie. *Educ:* private schools; Glasgow University. Served articles with firm of Glasgow Solicitors; went to Natal, 1883; practised as an Attorney and Advocate since 1885; represented Newcastle in Natal Parliament, 1901–10, and Dundee in Union Parliament; held Portfolios of Justice and Education, in Natal, 1903–06; held several portfolios, 1912–19 and 1919–24; was a delegate from Natal to South African National Convention for drafting Act of Union; served Boer War, 1899–1902 (despatches). *Address:* Newcastle, Natal.

Died 11 Sept. 1947.

WATT, Rt Hon. William Alex; PC 1920; *b* Kyneton, 23 Nov. 1871; *s* of James Michie Watt, late of Aberdeen, Scotland; *m* 1st, 1894; 2nd, 1907; two *s* three *d*. *Educ:* Melbourne State School. Entered Legislative Assembly, 1897; appointed Minister of Crown, 1899; MP Victoria; Postmaster-General of Colony, 1899–1900; resigned 1900; Premier, 1912–14, and Treasurer of Victoria, 1909–14; resigned Premiership, 1914, and entered Commonwealth Parliament as Member for Balaclava, 1914–29; Minister for Commonwealth Works and Railways, 1917–18; Commonwealth Treasurer, 1918–20; Acting Prime Minister, 1918–19; Speaker, House of Representatives, 1923–26; has held prominent positions in Australian Natives' Association; Commander Legion of Honour; Chairman of Directors of Dunlop Rubber (Australia) Ltd, Taranaki Oilfields, Bankers and Traders Insurance Co., Victoria, and other companies. *Recreations:* motoring, golf, cricket, etc. *Address:* 220 Orrong Road, Toorak, Melbourne, SE2. *T:* U1934. *Clubs:* Yorick, Athenæum, Melbourne.

Died 13 Sept. 1946.

WATT, William Robert, CBE 1941; Deputy Managing Director and Vice-Chairman of Directors, British India Corporation Ltd; Hon. Adviser to Government of India, Woollen Industry, 1939–46; *b* Knockando, Morayshire, 29 April 1888; *s* of Charles Watt, MA, and Mary Anne Watt; *m* 1916, Marion Isabel Lothian; one *s*. *Educ:* Knockando Public School; Mackie Academy, Stonehaven; University of Aberdeen; Royal College of Science, London, MA 1910, BSc 1911, Aberdeen; 1st class hons in Mathematics, Natural Philosophy, and Geology; DIC, FGS, 1913. Joined staff of Cawnpore Woollen Mills Co. Ltd, Nov. 1913; Pres. Upper India Chamber of Commerce, 1925; Chairman Federation of Woollen Manufacturers in India, 1947. *Publication:* Geology of Environs of Huntly, Aberdeenshire, QJGS, 1914. *Recreation:* execrable golf. *Address:* Park House, Civil Lines, Cawnpore, India. *Club:* Caledonian.

Died 11 Sept. 1949.

WATTIE, James MacPherson, Hon. LLD Aberdeen; Senior Chief Inspector of Schools (retired); *b* Wales Street, Aberdeen, 17 Nov. 1862; *s* of Alexander Wattie; *m* 1892, Katherine Carney Diack; four *d*. *Educ:* Old Aberdeen Grammar School; Aberdeen University; Pembroke College, Oxford (Henney Scholar); MA Aberdeen 1883, 1st cl. hon. in classics and mathematics; 1st cl. classical moderations, Oxford, 1885; 1st cl. math. mods, 1885; 1st cl. Lit.Hum., 1887. Master in Edinburgh Watson's College, 1887–93; Lecturer Aberdeen Church of Scotland Training College, 1893–97; HM Inspector of Schools, 1897–1910; Chief Inspector, 1910–27. *Publications:* Contributions to the Year Book of Education, 1932; English Association's Essays and

Studies; Transactions of Glasgow Philosophical Society. *Recreation:* walking. *Address:* 24 Burnbank Gardens, Glasgow, NW. *T:* Douglas 262.

Died 6 Jan. 1943.

WATTS, Charles Albert; Editor of the Literary Guide since 1885, and of the Rationalist Annual, 1883–1943; Vice-Chairman and a Director of the Rationalist Press Association, Ltd, since 1889; *b* 1858; *m* 1st, 1885; 2nd, 1916; one *s* one *d*. *Educ:* National Schools; evening colleges. Apprenticed to the printing and publishing business of Austin Holyoake (brother of G. J. Holyoake), 1870; started the firm of Watts & Co., 1892, now C. A. Watts & Co. Ltd; founded the Rationalist Press Association, Ltd, 1889. *Recreations:* mainly reading and writing. *Address:* 5 and 6 Johnson's Court, Fleet Street, EC4. *TA:* Ratiopres, Fleet, London. *T:* Central 8812.

Died 15 May 1946.

WATTS, Maj.-Gen. Charles Donald Raynsford, CB 1919; CMG 1915; Royal Army Ordnance Corps; *b* 4 Feb. 1871; *e s* of late Charles William Paxton Watts, Bengal Civil Service; *m* Amy, *d* of late John Miller Grant; two *d*. *Educ:* Marlborough College. Entered Army (RA), 1890; Captain, 1899; Major, AOD, 1905; Lt-Col 1913; Bt Colonel; Colonel, 1921; Major-General 1928; served South African War, 1899–1902 (despatches, Queen's medal 5 clasps, King's medal 2 clasps); European War, 1914–18 (despatches, CB, CMG; Order of Leopold 1st and Belgium Croix de Guerre); HQ Staff War Office, 1918–26; Director of Ordnance Services, War Office, 1928–31; retired pay, 1932; Colonel Commandant RAOC, 1932–41. *Address:* Tregenna, Fleet, Hants.

Died 19 May 1943.

WATTS, William Walter, FSA; late Keeper of the Department of Metalwork, Victoria and Albert Museum; retired after forty-four years service, 1923; *b* 13 July 1862; unmarried. *Educ:* Fulham Church School; City of London School. Citizen of London, and Liveryman of the Company of Goldsmiths, 1929; on Sub-Committee of National Art-Collections Fund; VP of Church Crafts League; Member of the Central Council for the care of Churches, and has served on six Diocesan Advisory Boards; has lectured for London County Council, Courtauld Institute of Art, etc. *Publications:* Old English Silver, 1924; Catalogue of Loan Exhibition of Silver Plate belonging to the Colleges of the University of Oxford, 1928; Catalogues of private collections of silver including those of Viscount Lee of Fareham (1936) and Baron Bruno Schröder; for the Victoria and Albert Museum, Catalogue of English Silversmiths' Work, Chalices and other Communion Vessels, Pastoral Staves, Revision of Handbooks on Ironwork, Parts II and III; Catalogue of an Exhibition of Works of Art belonging to the Livery Companies of the City of London, 1926; articles on Metalwork in Encyclopædia Britannica, and Numerous art publications. *Address:* 64 East Sheen Avenue, SW14. *T:* Prospect 4391.

Died 25 Dec. 1948.

WATTS, William Whitehead, MA, ScD (Camb.); MSc (Birm.); Hon. LLD (St Andrews, Edin.), FRS 1904; Hon. FRSC 1925; Hon. FRSE 1934; Emeritus Professor of Geology and hon. Fellow Imperial College of Science and Technology, South Kensington and of London University; President British Association, 1935; *b* 1860; *e s* of Isaac Watts, of Broseley, Shropshire; *m* 1st, 1889, L. A. Atchison (*d* 1891); one *d*; 2nd, 1894, R. Atchison (*née* Rogers) (*d* 1940); one *d*. *Educ:* Denstone College; Sidney Sussex Coll., Cambridge (Hon. Fellow). Cambridge University-Extension Lecturer, 1882–91; HM Geological Survey, 1891–97; Fellow of Sidney Sussex College, 1888–94; Deputy-Professor of Geology, Oxford, 1888; Assist-Professor of Geology, and Professor of Geography, Birmingham Univ., 1897–1906; Professor of Geology, Imperial College, 1906–30; Secretary of Geological Society, 1898–1909; President,

1910–12; Wollaston Medallist, 1927; President of Geologists' Association, 1908–10 and 1930–32; Pres. of Section C British Association, 1903 and 1924; President of Mineralogical Society, 1924–27; Dean of Faculty of Science, London University, 1913–17; Secretary of Conjoint Board of Scientific Societies, 1917–23. *Publications:* Description of Rocks and Fossils in Collection of Geological Survey of Ireland; Geology for Beginners; Shropshire, the Geography of the County; editor of British Geological Photographs; numerous geological papers and memoirs. *Address:* 39 Langley Park, Sutton, Surrey. *Clubs:* Athenæum, Royal Automobile.

Died 30 July 1947.

WAUCHOPE, Gen. Sir Arthur Grenfell, GCB 1938; GCMG 1933; KCB 1931; CB 1923; CMG 1917; CIE 1919; DSO 1900; *b* 1 March 1874; *s* of David Baird Wauchope, Edinburgh. *Educ:* St Ninian's, Moffat; Repton. 2nd Lieut 4th A & SH 1893; 2nd Batt. The Black Watch, 1896; Capt., 1901; Maj., 1914; Col 1922; Maj.-Gen. 1923; Lt-Gen. 1931; Gen. 1936; served on the staff of the late Major-General Wauchope commanding Highland Brigade in South Africa (severely wounded at Magersfontein, despatches, Queen's medal with clasp, King's medal with 2 clasps, DSO); European War, 1914–18; commanded 2nd Battalion Black Watch in France and Mesopotamia, 34th Brigade, and temporarily 7th Division Indian Corps (despatches, wounded, CMG, Bt Lt-Col and Col); ADC to C-in-C, Cape of Good Hope, 1902–03; Military Member of Overseas Settlement Delegation to Australia and New Zealand, 1923; Chief of British Section, Military Inter-Allied Commission of Control, Berlin, 1924–27; GOC 44th Home Counties Division TA, 1927–29; GOC Northern Ireland District, 1929–31; High Commissioner and Commander-in-Chief, Palestine and Trans-Jordania, 1931–38; retired pay, 1936; Col Black Watch, 1940–46; KGStJ; Officer, Legion of Honour. *Address:* Lythanger, Empshott, Liss, Hants. *Clubs:* Naval and Military; New, Edinburgh; Royal and Ancient, St Andrews.

Died 14 Sept. 1947.

WAUCHOPE, Mrs Jean, CBE; of Niddrie; *d* of late Sir William Muir, KCSI; *m* 1893, late General Andrew Gilbert Wauchope, CB, CMG, of Niddrie, who was killed in the South African War, 1899, when commanding the Highland Brigade. *Address:* Niddrie Marischal, Craigmillar, Midlothian; The Hall, Yetholm, Roxburgh.

Died 13 Aug. 1942.

WAUGH, Sir (Alexander) Telford, KCMG 1930 (CMG 1919); *b* London, 22 Oct. 1865; *s* of Alex. Waugh of 177 Regent Street, and Leatherhead; *m* 1925, Gwendda Kate, *d* of late Arthur Cecil Hugh-Jones, PWD. *Educ:* St John's School, Leatherhead; Forest School; Germany. Appointed Student Interpreter in HM's Consular Service in the Levant, 1885; Vice-Consul, 1890; Consul, 1903; placed at disposal of American Ambassador at Constantinople to assist in protection of British interests in Turkey on departure of the British Embassy, 1 Nov. 1914; employed in Foreign Office, Feb.–June 1915; Commercial Attaché to HM's Legation in Athens, June 1915; organised the Commercial Contraband Department of the Legation for the control of Greek trade during the War; attached to British High Commission, Constantinople, 1918–20; Consul-General at Constantinople, 1920–29; acting Commercial Secretary at Constantinople, 1920–21; retired on a pension, 1930. *Publication:* Turkey Yesterday, To-day and To-morrow, 1930. *Address:* Lytton Hall Hotel, Lytton Grove, Putney, SW15.

Died 7 Jan. 1950.

WAUGH, Arthur; Chairman of Chapman & Hall. Ltd; *b* 24 Aug. 1866; *e s* of Alexander Waugh, MD, of Midsomer Norton, Somerset; *m* 1893, Catherine, 2nd *d* of H. C. B. C. Raban, BCS; two *s*. *Educ:* Sherborne;

New College, Oxford. Newdigate English Verse, 1888; BA 1889. Came to London, 1890; London correspondent to the New York Critic, 1893–97; sub-edited the New Review, 1894, under Archibald Grove, MP; literary adviser to Kegan Paul & Co. Ltd 1895–1902; Managing Director, Chapman and Hall Ltd, 1902–30; Chm. 1926–36 and 1940. *Publications:* Gordon in Africa, 1888; Schoolroom Theatricals, 1890; Alfred, Lord Tennyson, a Study of his Life and Work, 1892; edited Johnson's Lives of the Poets (6 vols), 1896; edited the Pamphlet Library, 1897; Legends of the Wheel, 1898; Rhymes to Nicholson's Square Book of Animals, 1899; Robert Browning in Westminster Biographies, 1900; edited Biographical Edition of Dickens (19 vols), 1902–1903; edited Milton and Tennyson in English Poets, 1903; edited Tennyson, Arnold, and Lamb., 1905; edited George Herbert in the World's Classics, 1907; Reticence in Literature, 1915; Tradition and Change, 1919; A Hundred Years of Publishing: Messrs. Chapman & Hall, 1930; One Man's Road, 1931. *Address:* 14a Hampstead Lane, Highgate, N6. *T:* Mountview 2022.

Died 26 June 1943.

WAUGH, Sir Telford; *see* Waugh, Sir A. T.

WAVELL, 1st Earl *cr* 1947; **Field Marshal Archibald Percival Wavell,** PC 1943; GCB 1941 (KCB 1939; CB 1935); GCSI 1943; GCIE 1943; CMG 1919; MC; Viscount Wavell of Cyrenaica and of Winchester, 1943; Viscount Keren of Eritrea and Winchester, 1947; High Steward of Colchester since 1947; Chancellor Aberdeen University since 1945; Colonel The Black Watch (RHR), 1946; Constable of the Tower of London since 1948; Lord Lieutenant of County of London, 1949; a Governor of Shakespeare Memorial Theatre, Stratford-on-Avon, since 1949; *b* May 1883; *s* of late Maj.-Gen. A. G. Wavell, CB; *m* 1915, Eugenie Marie, CI 1943, *o c* of late Col Owen Quirk, CB, DSO; one *s* three *d*. *Educ:* Winchester Coll.; RMC, Sandhurst; Staff Coll. Appointed The Black Watch, 1901; served S African War (medal with 4 clasps); Indian Frontier, 1908 (medal with clasp); European War, 1914–18; served in France, 1914–16 (wounded, MC) as Military Attaché with Russian Army in Caucasus, Oct. 1916–June 1917 (Orders of St Vladimir and St Stanislas), and with Egyptian Expeditionary Force, 1917–20; BGGS XX Corps, 1918–19, BGGS, EEF 1919–20; Brevet Lieut-Colonel, 1917; Colonel, 1921; Maj.-Gen., 1933; Lt-Gen., 1938; General, 1940; Field-Marshal, 1943; Commander, 6th Infantry Brigade, Aldershot, 1930–34; ADC to the King, 1932–33; Commander, 2nd Division, Aldershot, 1935–37; commanded Troops in Palestine and Transjordan, 1937–38; GOC-in-C, Southern Command, 1938–39; Commander-in-Chief, Middle East, 1939–41; Commander-in-Chief, India, 1941–43; Supreme Commander, SW Pacific, Jan.–March 1942; ADC General to the King, 1941–43; Viceroy and Governor-General of India, 1943–47. LLD (St Andrews); DCL (Oxford); LLD (Cambridge, Aberdeen and London); Commander Legion of Honour, Order of the Nile, Order of El Nahda, Order of George (Greece), Virtuti Militari (Poland) Greek Military Cross, Seal of Solomon (Ethiopia), Military Cross, Czechoslovakia, Order of Orange-Nassau (Holland), ChC Legion of Merit (USA), Star of Nepal, Cloud and Banner (China). *Publications:* The Palestine Campaigns, 1928; Allenby, 1940; Generals and Generalship, 1941; Allenby in Egypt, 1943; Other Men's Flowers (Anthology), 1944; Speaking Generally, 1946; The Good Soldier, 1947. *Recreations:* golf, shooting. *Heir:* *s* Viscount Keren, MC. *Address:* 23 Kingston House South, SW7. *T:* Kensington 9893. *Clubs:* Athenæum, United Service, MCC; Royal and Ancient (St Andrews).

Died 24 May 1950.

WAY, Rev. Charles Parry, MA; *b* 10 Jan. 1870; *γ s* of late Canon John Hugh Way, Vicar of Henbury, Glos; *m* Ethel Mary Danks; one *s* one *d*. *Educ:* Repton School; St John's College, Cambridge; Wells Theological College.

Curate of St Peter's Collegiate Church, Wolverhampton; Priest St Mark, Basford, Stoke-on-Trent; Vicar of Henbury, 1906–28; Vicar of Chesterton, North Staffs, 1928–30; Hon. Canon of Bristol Cathedral, 1926–29; Rector of St Chad's, Lichfield, Staffs, 1930–33; Vicar of Eccleshall, and Rural Dean of Eccleshall, 1933–39; Rector of Denham, Bucks, 1939–46; retired, 1946; Prebendary of Bobenhull in Lichfield Cathedral, 1939–40, Preb. Emeritus since 1940. *Recreations:* exploring and gardening. *Address:* Denham Lodge, Eccleshall, Stafford. *T:* Eccleshall 327.

Died 30 Nov. 1949.

WAYLAND, Lt-Col Sir William Abraham, Kt 1920; JP, FCS, FSA; Chairman of the Empire Day Movement, 1927–48; *b* Sept. 1869; *s* of W. R. Wayland of Civil Service. *Educ:* Marlowes College. Raised 39th Division RFA 137th Heavy Battery, 16th Batt. County London Vol. Regt; MP (C) Canterbury Division, 1927–45; Mayor of Deptford, 1914–20. *Publications:* essays on Fermentation and articles on agriculture. *Recreation:* farming. *Address:* Hempton Lodge, Monks-Horton, Kent. *T:* Lyminge 87283. *Clubs:* Carlton, Authors', Royal Automobile, Farmers'.

Died 15 July 1950.

WEAR, Col Algernon Edward Luke, CMG 1915; MD, AMS, retired; late Chief Medical Officer, Leeds Education Committee; *b* 20 June 1866; *s* of late Geo. Claridge Wear, Newcastle-on-Tyne; *m* Emily, *o d* of late Rev. F. Peel, Vicar of Heslington, York; two *s* two *d*. *Educ:* Royal Grammar School, Newcastle-on-Tyne; Durham University; University College, London. Served European War 1914–19 (despatches, CMG); commanded No. 7 Cas. Clearing Station, BEF. *Address:* 20 Woodside, Harrogate.

Died 30 Nov. 1941.

WEATHERALL, John Henry, MA Oxon; *b* Liverpool, 1868; *m* 1st, 1897, Florence (*d* 1915), *d* of George Atkins, Leicester; 2nd, 1917, Mary (*d* 1945), *d* of Rudolph Neele, London; one *s* one *d*. *Educ:* Liverpool; Owens College, Manchester; Unitarian College, Manchester; Exeter College and Manchester College, Oxford. Unitarian Minister, Darlington, 1896–98; Professor of Hebrew and Hellenistic Greek in the Presbyterian College, Carmarthen, 1898–1904; Minister of Bank Street Chapel, Bolton, 1904–14; Minister of Essex Church, London, 1915–30; Principal of Manchester College, Oxford, 1931–38; London University Extension Lecturer in European Literature, 1917–29; Preacher to American Unitarian Association, Boston, 1921; and at Centenary Service of the British and Foreign Unitarian Association, London, 1925; Preacher to Czecho-Slovakian Church, Vinorhady, Prague, 1934. *Publications:* The Books of the Old Testament, 1902; Twelve Sermons, 1907; Recollections of an Oxford Student at Manchester College, 1929; The significance of the Unitarians, Essex Hall Lecture, 1938; various contributions in The Inquirer, Manchester Guardian, Hibbert Journal. *Recreations:* chess (Oxford University Chess Team v Cambridge, 1894) and walking. *Address:* 26 Llanedeyrn Road, Cardiff.

Died 15 Jan. 1950.

WEATHERHEAD, Very Rev. James, DD, Minister of St Paul's Church, Dundee, since 1906; Moderator of General Assembly of United Free Church, 1927–28; *b* Whitsome, Berwickshire, 1863; *m* 1895, Margaret McDougall Kilpatrick, Glasgow; four *s* two *d*. *Educ:* Moffat Academy; Glasgow University; Glasgow Free Church Theological Hall; MA 1885; BD 1889. Ordained Minister of North Woodside Free Church, 1891; inducted first Minister of Giffnock United Free Church, 1900; degree of DD conferred by Glasgow University, 1924. *Publications:* articles in magazines.

Recreations: boating, fishing, bowling. *Address:* 13 Bradbury Street, Downfield, Dundee. *T:* Dundee 85198. *Clubs:* Scottish Liberal, Edinburgh.

Died 13 March 1944.

WEATHERILL, Charles, CBE 1932; *b* 6 April 1874; *m* 1904, Ellen Maud Fowles (*d* 1922); two *s* one *d*. Entered Civil Service by open competition (Second Division), 1892; passed as Associate of Institute of Actuaries, 1902; served in War Office (Chelsea Hospital), 1892; Fishery Board for Scotland, 1892–93; Scottish Office, 1893–1912 (Head of Accounts Branch, 1908); transferred to Board of Agriculture (Scotland) as Accountant on creation of that Office, 1912; Assistant Secretary, 1913; promoted Secretary, 1918; on reorganisation of Board as Department in 1929, promoted Assistant Secretary and Deputy Secretary to the Department; retired, 1939; Chairman, Fishery Board for Scotland (temp.), 1939; Member of Scottish Agricultural Wages Board, 1940; Chairman of Herring Industry Board, 1942–44. *Address:* 193 Bruntsfield Place, Edinburgh. *Clubs:* Caledonian United Service, Edinburgh; Mortonhall (Edin.) and Moray Golf; Scarborough Cricket.

Died 9 Dec. 1944.

WEATHERILL, Henry, CBE 1928; OBE 1918; FIA, late Assistant Comptroller and Actuary to the Commissioners for the Reduction of the National Debt; *b* 21 Sept. 1868; *s* of Henry Weatherill; *m* 1903, Emily Frances, *d* of late John Wm Turner, Ash Lea, Driffield, E Yorks; three *s*. *Educ:* privately. Entered National Debt Office, 1888; Fellow of Institute of Actuaries, 1904; Actuary to National Debt Commissioners, 1911; Principal Clerk, 1916; Assistant Comptroller, 1924; retired, 1933; Member of St Albans Diocesan Conference and Diocesan Board of Finance; Treasurer of the Local Conservative Association. *Recreations:* golf and walking. *Address:* Bayston, Cross Oak Road, Berkhamsted, Herts. *T:* Berkhamsted 382.

Died 9 June 1943.

WEAVER, Herbert Parsons, RBA, RWA, RCA, FSAM; late Principal, Shrewsbury School of Art; *b* 26 May 1872; *m* 1904, Alice E. Parker; one *s* one *d*. *Educ:* Worcester Grammar School. Studied in the Worcester School of Art and the Royal College of Art (gold and silver medallist); studied Art abroad for several years, Normandy, Brittany, Holland, France, etc. Exhibitor at Royal Academy and Paris Salon. *Recreations:* golf, fishing, and motoring. *Address:* Hillside House, Lyth Hill, Shrewsbury.

Died 8 June 1945.

WEAVER, Percy William, CBE 1939; *b* 6 Nov. 1882; *yr s* of late Henry Weaver, MBE; *m* 1926, Daisy Olive, *o c* of J. Cartmail, Chester. Trained Great Western Railway; Joined Egyptian Civil Service, 1906; Assistant Goods Manager, 1919; Goods Manager, 1924–30; Traffic Manager, 1930–38; Grand Officer of the Order of the Crown of Italy: 3rd Class Order of the Nile; 4th Class Order of Mohammed Aly. *Address:* Carriden House, Slade Oak Lane, Gerrards Cross, Bucks. *T:* Denham 2453. *Clubs:* Constitutional; Turf, Gezira Sporting, Cairo.

Died 21 May 1943.

WEBB, Lt-Col Andrew Henry, CMG 1919; DSO 1916; late RGA; *b* 1873; *s* of Captain H. J. Webb, late 11th Regt; *m* 1906, Evelyn Dorothea, *d* of Henry Brady, Deputy-Accountant-General, RN; one *s* three *d*. *Educ:* privately; RMA, Woolwich. Served South African War, 1899–1900 (Queen's medal with 3 clasps); European War (CMG, DSO); retired pay, 1922. *Address:* Blakenhall Seal, Sevenoaks, Kent.

Died 18 Oct. 1949.

WEBB, Col Sir (Arthur) Lisle (Ambrose), KBE 1920; CB 1919; CMG 1915; DPH Camb.; DTM; MRCS, LRCP; late RAMC; *b* 19 July 1871; *m* Hilda Caroline (*d* 1945), *d* of late T. P. Priestley. Lt RAMC 1899; Capt., 1902; Major, 1911; Lt-Col 1914; served S Africa, 1899–1902 (Queen's medal 5 clasps, King's medal 2 clasps); European War, 1914–18 (despatches, CMG, Bt Col); retired pay, 1922; Director-General of Medical Services, Ministry of Pensions, 1919–33; Secretary and Treasurer of Queen Mary's (Roehampton) Hospital, 1933–42; KGStJ; Hon. Fellow University College Hospital. *Address:* High Coombe, Balcombe, Sussex. *T:* Balcombe 224.

Died 7 Oct. 1945.

WEBB, Francis Gilbert; music critic, organist; Vice-President, Musical Association; Lancelot of The Referee, 1900–32; London correspondent of The Yorkshire Post since 1898; *b* Isleworth, 25 Jan. 1853; father, Chancery Barrister; Scotch mother; *m* 1st, 1888, Florence Courtenay Whitmarsh (*d* 1916); no *c*; 2nd, 1932, Ada Eliza Petter (*d* 1936). *Educ:* London University; private tutors. On staff of The Standard, daily, 1897; principal music critic, 1901–05; on the Morning Post, 1898–1901; on staff of The Daily Telegraph, 1905; wrote for many years on the Musical World, the Observer, the Sunday Times, the Musical Times since 1898; one of the founders of the Musical News and The Folk-song Society; inventor of Pianola devices (patented); authority on vocal production; staunch upholder of British composers and artists. *Publications:* several volumes of Analyses of Musical Works. *Recreations:* cycling and tennis. *Address:* 19 Cathcart Road, South Kensington, SW10.

Died 11 April 1941.

WEBB, Lt-Col George Ambrose Congreve, DSO 1917; *b* 1869; 2nd *s* of Rev. Ambrose Congreve Webb, MA, of Dysartgallen, Queen's Co; *m* 1902, Hilda Dynely, *d* of Lt-Col Schreiber; two *s*. *Educ:* Chard; Royal Military College, Sandhurst. Entered Army, 1890; joined 1st Batt. Royal Munster Fusiliers; Adjutant for three and a half years until joined Egyptian Army, 1898; served Nile Expedition (medal, clasp, and 4th Class Medjidieh); S African War, commanded Rimington's Guides, later Damant's Horse (dangerously wounded, 1901; Queen's medal, 5 clasps, Bt Major, despatches); Commandant Royal Hospital, Dublin, 1906; rejoined from Reserve of Officers on outbreak of European War, Aug. 1914–18 (DSO, despatches thrice, Bt Lt-Col). *Club:* Army and Navy.

Died 13 May 1942.

WEBB, Brig. George Clifford, CBE 1943; DSO 1944; MBE 1940; General Staff since 1942; *b* 27 Aug. 1905; *s* of John Webb and Clara Annie Frost; *m* 1932, Barbara Stammer Fowle; one *d*. *Educ:* Central Foundation School; RMC, Sandhurst. Served War of 1939–45 (despatches twice, MBE, CBE, DSO). Commanded 1 Royal Tank Regt June 1942. *Recreations:* International and Army and County Athletics and Cross-country running; County and Army hockey; fencing. *Address:* HQ 30 Corps, BLA; Wooda Bay, Marlborough Road, Gillingham, Kent. *T:* Gillingham 5365. *Club:* Army and Navy.

Died April 1945.

WEBB, John Curtis, MA (Camb. Hons); MB, BCh (Camb.); MRCS, LRCP; late Major RAMC; *b* Tenby, Oct. 1868; *s* of late Commander A. H. Webb. *Educ:* Cheltenham; Clare College, Cambridge; Edinburgh; King's College Hospital; Berlin. Associate of King's College; Order of Merit Cruz Vermehla, Portugal. Practised in Liverpool, 1896–98; London, 1898–1914; served in France, 1914–19 as specialist in Radiology and Electro Therapy (despatches); since the war has practised as specialist in Radiology and Electro-Therapy in Cheltenham; Hon. Consulting Radiologist, Gloucester Royal Infirmary and Eye Institution, Cheltenham General and Eye Hospitals and Cheltenham Hospital for Children; Hon. Corr. Mem. Sect. of Radiology, RSM; retired. *Publications:* Electrotherapy; various articles in the Medical Press. *Recreations:* carpentering, travel and croquet. *Address:* 4 Clarendon Villas, Pittville Gates, Cheltenham. *T:* 2801. *Club:* New (Cheltenham).

Died 23 May 1949.

WEBB, Col Sir Lisle; *see* Webb, Col Sir A. L. A.

WEBB, Maurice, CIE 1930; MA; *b* 23 April 1880; *e s* of late John Cother Webb; *m* 1914, Alice Clare (*d* 1944), *d* of John Walter Tyas, Registrar of Adelaide Univ.; three *d*. *Educ:* St Paul's School; Corpus Christi College, Oxford. ICS Bombay, 1904–30; Secretary to the Senate, University of London, 1930–45. *Address:* 135 Haverstock Hill, NW3. *T:* Primrose 5270. *Club:* Athenæum.

Died 3 July 1946.

WEBB, Adm. Sir Richard, KCMG 1920; CB 1915; *b* 1870; *y s* of late Richard C. Webb, Avening, Glos; *m* 1918, Agnes E., *o d* of late Robert J. Foster of Stockeld Park, Wetherby, Yorkshire, and of late Hon. Mrs Robert Foster; one *d*. *Educ:* Fonthill, Wilts; HMS Britannia. Midshipman, 1885; obtained four First-Class Certificates; Lieut 1891; Comdr 1902; Capt. 1907; Rear-Adm. 1918; Vice-Adm. 1924; Admiral, 1928; commanded Amethyst on east coast of South America, 1909–11; RN War College, 1911–13; Illustrious, 1913; Director of Trade Division, Admiralty War Staff, 1914–17; commanded New Zealand in Grand Fleet, 1917–18; Assist High Commissioner to Turkey, 1918–20; Rear-Admiral in the Fourth Battle Squadron, Mediterranean Fleet, 1920–22; Naval ADC to the King, 1917–18; Head of Naval Mission to Greece, 1924–25; President RN College, Greenwich, and Admiral Commanding RN War College, 1926–29; retired list, 1929; Bronze medal, Royal Humane Society, and Lloyd's Silver medal, for saving life at sea, 1898; Order of the Swords, Sweden; Order of St Anne, Russia; Knight Commander of the Order of the Redeemer, Greece; Commander of the Legion of Honour; Younger Brother of Trinity House. *Address:* 9 Alexander Square, SW3. *T:* Kensington 9164. *Clubs:* United Service, Lansdowne.

Died 20 Jan. 1950.

WEBB, Mrs Sidney, (Beatrice Potter), Hon. DLitt (Manchester); Hon. LLD (Edinburgh); Hon. D in Political Econ. (Munich); FBA; JP London, 1919–27; *b* 22 Jan. 1858; 8th *d* of Richard Potter, at one time Chairman of the Great Western Railway of England, and President of the Grand Trunk Railway of Canada; *m* 1892, Sidney James Webb (1st Baron Passfield, PC, OM). *Educ:* privately. Personally investigated social and industrial conditions; contributed to Charles Booth's Life and Labour of the People; Member of Royal Commission on Poor Law and Unemployment, 1905–09, and joint-author of the Minority Report; Member of Government Committee upon Grants in Aid of Distress in London, 1914–15; of Statutory War Pensions Committee, 1916–17; of Reconstruction Committee, 1917–18; of Committee on National Registration, 1917–18; of Committee on the Machinery of Government, 1918–19; of War Cabinet Committee on Women in Industry, 1918–19; and of Lord Chancellor's Advisory Committee for Women Justices, 1919–20. *Publications:* The Co-operative Movement in Great Britain, 1891; Men's and Women's Wages: Should they be Equal? 1919; My Apprenticeship, 1926; editor of The Case for the Factory Acts, 1901; and The Case for the National Minimum, 1913; contributed to Living Philosophies (New York); and (jointly with her husband) of History of Trade Unionism, Industrial Democracy; Problems of Modern Industry; The State and the Doctor; English Local Government (7 vols), The Prevention of Destitution, A Constitution for the Socialist Commonwealth of Great Britain, The Consumers' Co-operative Movement; Decay of

Capitalist Civilisation; English Poor Law History (3 vols); Methods of Social Study; Soviet Communism—a New Civilisation? third edition, 1941; and other works; in 1940 contributed one of the 23 Living Philosophies to I Believe. *Address:* Passfield Corner, Liphook, Hants. *TA:* Passfield. *T:* Passfield 6. *Club:* Fabian Society.
Died 30 April 1943.

WEBBE, Alexander Josiah; President Middlesex County Cricket Club; late Captain of the Middlesex Eleven; *b* 16 Jan. 1855; *m* 1893, Peroline Maud, *e d* of late Edward Cutler, KC; four *d*. *Educ:* Harrow; Trinity College, Oxford. *Recreations:* cricket, played for Harrow, 1872–74; Oxford, 1875–78; Middlesex, 1875–98; racquets. *Address:* 9 Vale Avenue, Chelsea, SW3. *T:* Flaxman 8448. *Clubs:* Conservative, MCC.
Died 19 Feb. 1941.

WEBBER, Brig.-Gen. Adrian Beare I.; *see* Incledon-Webber.

WEBBER, Brig.-Gen. Norman William, CMG 1918; DSO 1916; *b* 22 Feb. 1881; *e s* of late Henry Webber of Horley, Surrey; *m* 1905, Maud, *d* of late Godfrey Critchley-Salmonson, Rosenan, Torquay; one *s* one *d*. *Educ:* Bradfield; Woolwich. Joined Royal Engineers, 1899; Captain, 1908; passed Staff College, 1914; Major, 1915; Colonel, 1920; retired pay, 1921; served S African War, 1901–02 (Queen's medal 4 clasps); European War, with Royal Engineers and General Staff, 1914–18 (despatches 9 times, CMG, DSO, Chevalier Legion of Honour, Croix de Guerre, Bt Maj., Bt Lt-Col, Bt Col); Hon. Treasurer Br Empire Service League. *Address:* The Old Mill, Battle, Sussex. *T:* Battle 231.
Died 19 April 1950.

WEBSTER, Benjamin; actor; *b* London, 2 June 1864; *s* of W. S. Webster, and *g s* of Ben. Webster, actor; *m* 1892, May Whitty (Dame May Webster); one *d*. *Educ:* Stationers' School; King's Coll., London. Barr Inner Temple, Nov. 1885; practised as a barrister till March 1887; joined Hare and Kendal management at St James's Theatre. *Recreations:* golf, rowing, punting. *Address:* Hampshire House, 8431 De Longpre Avenue, Hollywood 46, California. *T:* Hempstead 5434.
Died 26 Feb. 1947.

WEBSTER, Sir Hugh Calthrop, Kt 1939; Official Arbitrator (Acquisition of Land Assessment of Compensation Act 1919) since 1926; *b* 6 Aug. 1869; *s* of late Rev. Thomas Calthrop Webster, Rettendon Rectory, Essex; *m* 1900, Doris Dalton; one *s* three *d*. Chartered Surveyor; Fellow of Chartered Surveyors' Institution. *Address:* Old Manor, Little Berkhamsted, Hertford. *TA:* Little Berkhamsted. *T:* Essendon 262. *Club:* Union.
Died 14 April 1941.

WEBSTER, John, CMG 1934; Soldiers' Nominee Repatriation Commission, 1935–45, Acting Chairman, 1941–45, Deputy Chairman since 1945; *b* 1 Oct. 1891; *s* of John Webster; *m* 1st, 1926, Margaret (decd), *d* of late A. C. Douglas, Launceston, Tasmania; 2nd, 1937, Winifred, *d* of C. V. Hunt; two *d*. *Educ:* Church of Eng. Grammar School, Launceston. Served with 12th Bn AIF 1915–18 (wounded twice, French Croix de Guerre with palm, rank Lieutenant promoted in field); invalided from service 1918; Secretary Launceston Branch RSSAILA 1921; Gen. Sec. RSSAILA, 1929–35. *Address:* Clarendon, Fitzgibbon Crescent, Caulfield, Victoria, Australia. *Clubs:* Navy, Army and Air Force, Melbourne.
Died 25 May 1947.

WEBSTER, John Clarence, CMG 1935; *b* Shediac, NB, Canada, 21 Oct. 1863; *s* of James Webster; *m* 1899, Alice Lusk, *d* of late Dr Wm Lusk, New York. *Educ:* Mount Allison College, New Brunswick; University of Edinburgh; University of Leipsic; University of Berlin. BA, MD (Edin.), Hon. DSc, LLD, FRCPE, FRSE,

FRSC, FACS. Officier de l'Instruction Publique, France; Commander of Order of St Maurice and St Lazarus, Italy; FRSL; Chairman, Historic Sites and Monuments Board of Canada; Hon. President, New Brunswick Museum; formerly First Assistant in the Dept of Midwifery and Gynecology, University of Edinburgh, 1890–96; Lecturer in Gynecology, McGill University, Montreal, Canada, 1897–99; Assistant Gynecologist, Royal Victoria Hospital, Montreal, 1897–99; Professor of Obstetrics and Gynecology. Rush Medical College (affil. with University of Chicago); Obstetrician and Gynecologist to Presbyterian Hospital, Chicago. *Publications:* Researches in Female Pelvic Anatomy, 1892; Tubo-peritoneal Ectopic Gestation, 1892; Ectopic Gestation, 1895; Text-book of Obstetrics, 1903; Text-book of Diseases of Women, 1907; and other papers; Collector of Canadiana. *Address:* Shediac, NB, Canada. *Clubs:* University (Montreal); Union (Saint John, NB).
Died 16 March 1950.

WEBSTER, John Edward, CSI 1922; CIE 1916; ICS; retired, 1927; *b* Ranchi, 3 Sept. 1870; *s* of G. K. Webster, ICS (retired); *m* 1900, Mabel Helen, *d* of H. W. Steel, ICS (retired); two *s*. *Educ:* Charterhouse; Trinity Hall, Cambridge. Entered ICS 1891; attached to Eastern Bengal and Assam Commission, and after 1911 to Assam; Magistrate and Collector, 1903; Deputy Commissioner, 1905–19; Commissioner, Assam, 1919. *Address:* Handley Cross, Cheltenham. *T:* Cheltenham 4401.
Died 7 May 1943.

WEBSTER, Lorne C.; Dominion Senator since 1920; President Holt, Renfrew & Co.; Financial Trust Co.; Canadian Chairman Union Insurance Society of Canton; Director Sun Life Assurance Co. of Canada; Canadian General Insurance Co.; Canadian Car and Foundry Co., Ltd; Quebec Power Co.; Dominion Steel and Coal Co., Ltd; Canadian Liquid Air Co., Ltd; Canadian Tube and Steel Products, Ltd; Canada Steamships Lines; Canadian General Investment Trusts, Limited; Canadian Fur Auction Co. Limited; Dealer's Finance Corporation; *b* Quebec, 30 Sept. 1871; *s* of A. D. Webster and Jean MacLerie; *m* Muriel Warren Taylor (decd); five *s* one *d*. *Educ:* Quebec High School; Montmagny College. Identified with Finance, Coal, and Business of Canada; has always taken an interest in charitable institutions. *Recreations:* travelling, outdoor sports. *Address:* 7 Edgehill Road, Westmount, PQ, Canada. *TA:* Canimpco, Montreal, Canada. *Clubs:* Garrison, Quebec; Canada, Montreal, Seigniory, Royal Montreal Golf, Mount Bruno Golf, Kanawaki Golf, Montreal; Rideau, Ottawa; Lake Placid, New York.
Died Sept. 1941.

WEBSTER, Dame May, DBE 1918; Vice-President, British War Relief, Los Angeles; Chairman, British Actors' Orphanage, Hollywood; actress (professional name Dame May Whitty); *b* 19 June 1865; *m* 1892, Benjamin Webster (*d* 1947); one *d*. Chm. Theatrical Ladies' Guild. *Address:* 8431 De Longpre Ave, Hollywood 46, California. *Clubs:* Three Arts, Arts Theatre.
Died 29 May 1948.

WEDD, Major Aubrey Pattisson Wallman, CBE 1942; OBE 1919; JP, DL; RE retd; ARP Controller Essex; Chairman, ARP Committee Essex CC; Alderman Essex CC; *b* 22 Feb. 1885; *s* of E. A. Wedd, Fowlmere, Cambridgeshire, and Great Wakering, Essex, and Katherine May, Maldon, Essex; *m* 1914, Charlotte Isobel Cook; no *c*. *Educ:* Stubbington, Hants; Cheltenham College. Commissioned RE 1904; European War, 1914–18 (Bt Major, OBE, officer Star of Roumania); retired, 1924. *Recreations:* yachting, shooting, fishing. *Address:* Hazelwood, Southminster, Essex. *T:* Southminster 273.
Died 23 Jan. 1945.

WEDDERBURN, Prof. Joseph Henry Maclagan, FRS, DSc; Professor Emeritus of Mathematics, Princeton University since 1945; *b* 26 Feb. 1882; *s* of Alexander S. Maclagan Wedderburn and Anne Ogilvie; unmarried. *Educ:* George Watson's College, Edinburgh; Edinburgh University. Assistant in Mathematics, Edinburgh University, 1905–09; Assistant Professor, Princeton Univ., 1909–21; Associate Professor, 1921–28; Professor, 1928–45. *Publications:* Lectures on Matrices, 1934; contributions to various mathematical journals. *Address:* Fine Hall, Princeton, New Jersey, USA.

Died 9 Oct. 1948.

WEDGWOOD, 1st Baron *cr* 1942, of Barlaston; **Josiah Clement Wedgwood,** PC 1924; DSO 1915; late Commander RNAS; Colonel (GS); DL, JP (Staffs); *b* 16 March 1872; 2nd *s* of C. F. Wedgwood of Barlaston and Etruria (Staffs) and Emily C. Rendel; *m* 1st, Hon. Ethel Kate Bowen, *d* of Charles, Lord Bowen; two *s* five *d*; 2nd, Florence Ethel, *d* of Guy Willett. *Educ:* Clifton College; Royal Naval College, Greenwich (Scholar, 1892). Asst Constructor, Portsmouth Dockyard, 1895–96; Naval Architect, Elswick Shipyard, 1896–1900; Captain, Elswick Battery, S Africa, 1900–01 (medal and 3 clasps); Resident Magistrate, Ermelo, Transvaal, 1902–04; formerly Hon. Sec. Wm Salt Archæological Society and President of the English League for the Taxation of Land Values; served European War, 1914–16, Antwerp, France, Dardanelles, East Africa (wounded, DSO, despatches twice); on Mesopotamia Commission, July 1916; Asst Director, Trench Warfare, 1917; on Mission to Siberia, with temporary rank as Colonel, 1918; MP (Lab, prev. L), Newcastle-under-Lyme, 1906–42; Chancellor of the Duchy of Lancaster, 1924. Chairman Committee on House of Commons Records, appointed 1929; one of the trustees for the History of Parliament; CC (Staffs), 1910–19; Vice-Chairman of Labour Party, 1921–24; Mayor of Newcastle-under-Lyme, 1930–32. *Publications:* Staffordshire Pottery and its History, 1913; Staffordshire Parliamentary History, 1258–1919; Indo-British Commonwealth, 1922; Essays and Adventures of a Labour MP, 1924; The Seventh Dominion, 1927; Local Taxation in the Empire, 1928; History of Parliament, 1439–1509; Memoirs of a Fighting Life, 1940; Forever Freedom (an Anthology with Prof. Nevins), 1941; Testament to Democracy, 1942. *Recreation:* writing. *Heir:* *s* Hon. Charles Bowen Wedgwood. *Address:* 903 Howard House, Dolphin Square, SW1.

Died 26 July 1943.

WEEKES, Ven. Christian William Hampton; Archdeacon of the Isle of Wight since 1937; Canon of Portsmouth; Vicar of Brading since 1913; Rector of Yaverland since 1920; Officiating Chaplain to the Forces; *b* 3 Sept. 1880; *s* of Charles Hampton Weekes and Laura Smith. *Educ:* Charterhouse; Trinity College, Cambridge. Deacon, 1906; Priest, 1907; Curate of Hale, Surrey, 1906–09; Rector of Yaverland, 1909–13. Rural Dean of East Wight, 1934–37. *Recreation:* walking. *Address:* The Vicarage, Brading. *T:* Brading 57.

Died 31 Aug. 1948.

WEEKES, Col Henry Wilson, DSO 1916; OBE 1919; late RE; *b* 1870; *s* of late Rev. W. J. Weekes, at one time precentor of Rochester Cathedral; *m* 1894, Katherine, *d* of late Rev. Chancellor Harman, Cork Diocese; one *d*. *Educ:* King's School, Rochester; RMA, Woolwich. Joined RE 1888; served in MWD and Sappers and Miners, India, 1891–97; took part in expedition for relief of Chitral (medal with clasp); Adjutant RE, Chatham, 1900–04; South Africa, 1905–06; Staff-Captain WO, 1906–10; Brigade Major and Secretary, SME, Chatham, 1910–15; served European War in France with 1st Division, and as CRE 51st Division (despatches twice, DSO, OBE); commanded Training Batt. RE, 1918–21;

Assistant Director WO, 1921–25; retired, Jan. 1925. *Recreations:* usual. *Address:* c/o Lloyds Bank, Shepton Mallet, Somerset.

Died 29 Dec. 1943.

WEEKES, Rev. William Haye; Dean of Bloemfontein, 1922–40, Canon Emeritus, 1940; *b* Cambridge, 5 March 1867; *e s* of late Arthur Weekes, MA Cantab; *m* 1907, May, *d* of J. W. Miles of Beaconsfield; one *s* one *d*. *Educ:* Bristol Grammar School; Sidney Sussex Coll., Camb. Mathematical Scholarship, 1886; BA, Junior Optime, 1889; MA 1896. Clergy Training School, Cambridge, 1899–1900. Deacon, 1890; Priest, 1891; Assistant-Curate St Sidwell's, Exeter, 1890; Priest-Vicar, Bloemfontein Cathedral, 1894; Rector of Mafeking, 1896 (including siege); Chaplain Bechuanaland Rifles, 1898; Chaplain to Mafeking Garrison during the siege; Archdeacon of Kimberley; Rector of Beaconsfield, Cape Colony, 1901–12; Rector of Kroonstad, 1912–17; Archdeacon of Bloemfontein and Vicar of the Cathedral Parish, 1917–40; Chaplain Order of St John of Jerusalem, 1931. *Recreations:* rowing, cricket. *Address:* 23 Leighwoods, Kenilworth, CP, South Africa.

Died 2 Aug. 1945.

WEIGALL, Julian William Wellesley; Barrister-at-law, Recorder of Gravesend since 1922; *b* 30 Dec. 1868; 2nd *s* of late Henry Weigall, JP, DL, and late Lady Rose Weigall, *d* of 11th Earl of Westmorland; unmarried. *Educ:* Wellington College (Scholar); University College, Oxford; 2nd Class Hon. Mods, 3rd Class Hon. Lit. Hum., BA. Called to Bar Inner Temple, 1894; contested (L) Isle of Thanet, Jan. 1910; member of First British Red Cross Unit in Serbia, 1915; Admiralty Intelligence, unpaid; Recruiting Staff of War Office, 1914 etc.; Legal Adviser Ministry of National Service (British and Victory War Medals, Order of White Eagle 4th Class, and Serbian Red Cross First Class). *Address:* 91 Onslow Gardens, SW7; 6 Pump Court, Temple, EC. *T:* Central 6579. *Club:* Athenæum.

Died 17 July 1945.

WEIGHTMAN, Sir Hugh, Kt 1947; CSI 1946; CIE 1941; Kaisar-i-Hind Medal (Gold), 1936; *b* 29 Nov. 1898; *m* 1924, Margaret Elizabeth Agnes, *d* of R. Storry Deans. *Educ:* Hymer's College; Corpus Christi College, Cambridge, BA Lieut RFC and RAF, 1917–18. Entered Indian Civil Service, 1922. Transferred to Indian Political Service, 1929; served in Assam, Central India, Baluchistan, Persian Gulf and Delhi; Sec. to Gov. of India, External Affairs Dept. Retired, 1947. *Recreations:* shooting and fishing. *Clubs:* RAF, Flyfishers'.

Died 28 Oct. 1949.

WEINGARTNER, Felix; composer and author; *b* Zara, Dalmatia, 2 June 1863; *s* of Guido Weingartner and Caroline Strobl; *m* Carmen Studer. *Educ:* Graz and Leipzig (pupil of F. Liszt). Conductor in Königsberg, Danzig, Hamburg, Mannheim, Berlin, Munich, Vienna; Director of the Conservatory and the Allgemeine Musikgesellschaft, Basel, 1927–34; musical director of Vienna Opera, 1935–36. *Publications:* Operas: Genesius, Orestes, Kain und Abel, Madame Kobold, Dorfschule (The Village School), Master Andrea; six symphonies, four string quartets, two violin sonates, one string quintuor, one sextet for strings and piano, one quintuor for clarinet, strings and piano, one octuor for clarinet, horn, fagott, strings and piano; King Lear, a symphonic poem; Das Gefilde der Seligen (The Field of Heaven), a symphonic poem; Frühling (The Spring) a symphonic poem; La Burla (Orchestral Burlesques); songs, chorus works, music to Faust, music to The Tempest; Der Weg, cycle of 15 songs; Die Symphonie nach Beethoven, 4th edition; Über das Dirigieren, 5th edition; Ratschläge für Aufführungen klassischer Symphonieen, I Beethoven, 3rd ed.; II Schubert, 2nd ed., und Schumann; III Mozart; Akkorde, gesammelte Aufsätze; Carl Spitteler, ein künstlerisches Erlebnis, 2nd edition; eine Künstlerfahrt nach Südamerika; Lebenserinnerungen, two volumes,

2nd edition, English edition, Buffets and Rewards; Bô Yin Râ, 2nd edition; Terra, ein Symbol: Prolog, drei Spiele, Epilog; Unwirkliches und Wirkliches, Essays. *Address:* Lausanne (Switzerland), Avenue de la gare, 17.

Died 7 May 1942.

WEIR, George Moir, MA; Dr of Education; Minister of Education, British Columbia, 1945–47, resigned; *b* 10 May 1885; *s* of Richard Weir and Margaret Moir; *m* 1926, Marie E. Smith; two *d. Educ:* McGill; Saskatchewan; Queen's; Chicago. Normal School Principal and Inspector of Schools in Saskatchewan; Grand Master AF and AM Saskatchewan; Head of the Department of Education, University of British Columbia; Provincial Secretary and Minister of Education, Government of BC, 1933–41; re-elected BC Legislature, 1945, retired, 1949; Liberal. *Publications:* Separate School Law in the Prairie Provinces; Survey of the School System of British Columbia (joint author); Survey of Nursing Education in Canada; The Separate School Question in Canada. *Club:* Rotary.

Died 5 Dec. 1949.

WEIR, Lt-Col James Leslie Rose, CIE 1933; Indian Political Service (retired); *b* 29 Jan. 1883; *e s* of late Colonel Patrick A. Weir, IMS, and Alice Mary Reid; *m* Thyra, *d* of Christian Sommers, Christchurch, New Zealand; two *d. Educ:* Wellingborough; Jena; RMA, Woolwich. Joined Royal Artillery, 1900; transferred to Indian Army, 5th Cavalry, 1904; joined Political Dept, 1908; Asst Resdt Gwalior, 1908; British Trade Agent Gyantse-Tibet, 1909–12; Baluchistan, 1912–14; on active service NW Frontier and Mesopotamia, 1914–18; Consul in Kermanshah, 1918–20; Consul in Shiraz, 1920; Deputy Comm. Hazara, 1922; Political Agent Baghelkhand, 1923; Sec. to AGG Baluchistan, 1924; Political Agent Quetta, 1925; Kashmir, 1926–28; Political Officer in Sikkim, 1928–33, during which time was deputed on two missions to Lhasa; Resident for Baroda and Gujarat States, 1933–38; Indian Red Cross Comr, MEF Cairo, 1943–45. *Recreations:* shooting, golf. *Address:* Barclays Bank Ltd, Nairobi, Kenya. *Club:* United Service.

Died 7 Dec. 1950.

WEIR, Brig.-Gen. Stanley Price, DSO 1917; VD; JP; Secretary, Adelaide Benevolent Society, Adelaide; Conciliation Comr for Matrimonial Cases, S Australia; Col 10th Regiment Australian Military Forces since 1925; *b* 23 April 1866; *s* of Alfred Weir of Aberdeen; *m* 1st, 1890, Rosa (*d* 1923), *e d* of James Wadham; one *s* one *d*; 2nd, 1926, Lydia, *d* of late Alfred Schrapel. *Educ:* Norwood Public School. Entered Surveyor-General's Dept, 1879; enlisted in Militia Force, 1885; 1st Commission, 1890; Capt 1893; Major, 1904; Lt-Col 1908; Col 1913; Brig.-Gen. 1921; commanded 19th Infantry Brigade, 1912; 10th AIF 1914; commanded Batt. at landing at Gallipoli, 1915; and in France, 1916 (despatches, DSO, Russian Order of St Anne); Hon. Colonel 10th Batt. AMF 1925. *Recreation:* bowls. *Address:* 64 Second Avenue, St Peters, South Australia. *T:* 1795. *Clubs:* Commercial Travellers', Adelaide.

Died 14 Nov. 1944.

WELCH, Rev. Prof. Adam C., MA, DD; Professor of Hebrew and Old Testament Exegesis, New College, Edinburgh, 1913–34; now Emeritus; *b* Goshen Manse, Jamaica, 14 May 1864; *s* of Rev. John Welch, Missionary, Jamaica; *m* 1903, Grace, *y d* of Thomas Steven, Ardlui House, Helensburgh; two *d. Educ:* Galashiels Academy; George Watson's School, Edinburgh; Edinburgh University; United Presbyterian Theological College; Erlangen University. Ordained Minister in Waterbeck, Dumfriesshire, 1887; St Columba's, Helensburgh, 1892; Claremont Church, Glasgow, 1902. *Publications:* Code of Deuteronomy; Deuteronomy, The Framework to the Code; Post-Exilic

Judaism; Prophet and Priest in Old Israel; The Work of the Chronicler, Schweich Lecture. *Address:* 54 Murrayfield Gardens, Edinburgh.

Died 19 Feb. 1943.

WELCH, Surg. Rear-Adm. Sir George, KCMG 1919; CB 1917; *b* 13 Sept. 1858; *m* 1893, Rosa (*d* 1933), *e d* of Rev. W. Tuckwell. *Educ:* University College, and University College Hospital, London. Entered RN 1884; Surg. of Royalist, Niger Expedition, 1886; Staff-Surg. of Tyne during Cretan troubles, 1896–97; specially promoted Fleet-Surg. 1899; Assist to Medical Director-Gen. 1899–1906; Instructor in Naval Hygiene to Surgeons on entry at Haslar, 1906–10 Deputy Surgeon-General, 1910; member of commission to inquire into tuberculosis in Navy, 1911; Deputy Director-General, Medical Dept, RN, 1912–16; PMO, RN Hospital, Haslar, 1916–18; member of Committee on Vision of Naval Officers, 1911–13. *Address:* 8 Crescent Road, Alverstoke, Hants. *T:* Gosport 8460. *Club:* Army and Navy.

Died 26 Oct. 1947.

WELCH, John Joseph, DSc; MInstCE; MINA; Professor of Naval Architecture, Armstrong, now King's, College (University of Durham), Newcastle on Tyne 1907–28; Emeritus Professor, since 1928; *b* Chatham, 9 Nov. 1861; *m* 1886, Jessie S. (*d* 1943), *o d* of John Little of Sheffield; one *s* one *d. Educ:* Public Schools, Sheffield and New Brompton; Dockyard School, Chatham; Royal Naval College, Greenwich. Served apprenticeship in Chatham Dockyard; took first place in scholarship competition, open to all apprentices, for entry into the Royal Naval College, Greenwich, 1881; Assistant Constructor at Chatham Dockyard, 1884; Junior Instructor in Naval Architecture at RN College, 1886; Senior Lecturer, 1890; joined staff of Director of Naval Construction at Admiralty, 1890; Inspector of Contract Work, 1895; manager of Shipbuilding Department of Laird Bros, now Cammell Laird and Co., 1899–1907; served upon Admiralty and Board of Trade Committees and Inquiries, and the several Bulkhead Committees concerned with the Safety of Life at Sea; Hon. Vice-President of the Institution of Naval Architects; is on the Livery of the Worshipful Company of Shipwrights; Dean of Faculty of Science, Durham University, Sessions 1925–26 and 1926–27; was Member of original Advisory Committee for the William Froude Laboratory, National Physical Laboratory; Examiner in Naval Architecture to Board of Education for many years. *Publications:* Text-Book of Naval Architecture for the Use of Officers of the Royal Navy; also contributor of papers to professional Institutions, etc. *Recreations:* golf, bowls. *Address:* Dunoon, 11 Beechwood Av., Boscombe, Bournemouth. *T:* Boscombe 182.

Died 28 Feb. 1950.

WELCH, Brig.-Gen. Malcolm Hammond Edward, CB 1919; CMG 1916; late Royal Irish Regiment; *b* 1 Sept. 1872; *e s* of late Colonel F. G. T. Welch, Indian Army; *m* 1904, Irene, 2nd *d* of late Sir Howard Elphinstone, VC, KCB, CMG; one *s* two *d. Educ:* privately. Joined Royal Irish Regt 1893; served S African War, 1899–1900 (severely wounded); employed with Mounted Infantry; served European War (despatches four times, Bt Lt-Col and Col CB, CMG); retired pay, 1928. Chairman Midhurst RDC; JP. *Recreations:* fishing and shooting. *Address:* Stedham Mill, Midhurst, Sussex. *T:* Midhurst 201.

Died 31 Dec. 1946.

WELDON, Lt-Col Ernest Steuart, CBE 1921; DSO 1919; late Dorset Regt; *b* 1877; *s* of Col F. Weldon, IA, of Erlimount, Earley; *m* 1916, Helen Cecilia, *d* of late Alfred Greaves of Haversham, Bucks; two *s. Educ:* Wellington College. Served South African War, 1899–1902 (Queen's medal four clasps, King's medal two clasps); European War, 1914–19 (despatches, DSO);

Malabar Rebellion, 1921 (Indian GS medal, despatches, CBE); Lt-Col 1927. *Address:* The Hollies, Burghfield, Berks.

Died 12 Jan. 1946.

WELLER, Major (Brevet Lt-Col) Bernard George, CB 1918; DSC; late RMLI; *b* 2 Dec. 1881; *s* of late Rev. F. Weller, North Pickenham Rectory, Swaffham, Norfolk; *m* 1927, Lilian Margaret, *d* of late J. D. FitzSimons, JP, of Somerton, Wexford, Ireland. 2nd Lieut RMLI 1900; Lieut 1903; Captain, 1911; Major, 1917; served European War, Gallipoli, 1915 (DSC, despatches twice); Zeebrugge, 1918 (CB, French Croix de Guerre, promoted to Brevet Lt-Col); Retired List, 1922. *Address:* Musgrave House, Henlade, Taunton. *T:* Henlade 226.

Died 6 June 1941.

WELLER, Bernard Williams; critic and author; *b* 19 July 1870; 2nd *s* of late John Weller, merchant. *Educ:* educated for Civil Service. Entered journalism at an early age and specialised chiefly in theatrical criticism; editor and leader writer of The Stage, in which he has written largely on theatrical conditions and questions of reform; has acted as dramatic critic for various daily papers; an authority on theatrical law and on copyright; author of Stage Copyright: At Home and Abroad, 1912; How to Protect a Play, and other treatises thereon; London Chairman, Institute of Journalists, 1923; Vice-President, Institute of Journalists, 1923–24/1928; Editor, Art Trade Journal, 1923–24; Vice-President, Critics' Circle, 1925; President, Critics' Circle, 1926–27; Treasurer since 1913; Chairman, Economic Section Institute of Journalists and also Central Economic Board and its Executive. *Recreation:* picture collecting. *Address:* 44 Abbey Road, NW8. *T:* Maida Vale 3981, Temple Bar 5213. *Club:* Savage.

Died 23 Aug. 1943.

WELLINGTON, 5th Duke of, *cr* 1814; **Arthur Charles Wellesley;** Baron Mornington, 1746; Earl of Mornington; Viscount Wellesley, 1760; Viscount Wellington of Talavera and Wellington, Somersetshire; Baron Douro, 1809; Earl of Wellington, Feb. 1812; Marquess of Wellington, Oct. 1812; Marquess Douro, 1814; Conde do Vimeiro, 1811; Marquez de Torres Vedras and Duque da Victoria, 1812, Portugal; Duque de Ciudad Rodrigo and a Grandee of 1st Class, 1812, Spain; Prince of Waterloo, 1815, Netherlands; *b* 9 June 1876; *e s* of 4th Duke and Kathleen Emily Bulkeley (*d* 1927), *d* of Captain Robert Williams, ADC; *S* father, 1934; *m* 1909, Hon. (Lilian) Maud Glen Coats, *yr d* of 1st Baron Glentanar; one *s* one *d*. *Educ:* Eton; Trinity Hall, Cambridge. Late Lieut, Grenadier Guards; served South Africa, 1900. *Heir: s* Earl of Mornington. *Address:* Strathfieldsaye House, Mortimer, Berks; Apsley House, Piccadilly, W1.

Died 11 Dec. 1941.

WELLINGTON, 6th Duke of, *cr* 1814; **Henry Valerian George Wellesley;** Baron Mornington, 1746; Earl of Mornington; Viscount Wellesley, 1760; Viscount Wellington of Talavera and Wellington, Somersetshire; Baron Douro, 1809; Earl of Wellington, Feb. 1812; Marquess of Wellington, Oct. 1812; Marquess Douro, 1814; Conde do Vimeiro, 1811; Marquez de Torres Vedras and Duque da Victoria, 1812, Portugal; Duque de Ciudad Rodrigo and a Grandee of 1st Class, 1812, Spain; Prince of Waterloo, 1815, Netherlands; Lieut Duke of Wellington's Regiment, at present in Commando, rank Temp. Captain; *b* 14 July 1912; *o s* of 5th Duke and Hon. (Lilian) Maud Glen Coats, *yr d* of 1st Baron Glentanar; *S* father, 1941. *Educ:* Stowe School. Served 1st Bn Duke of Wellington's Regt, 1935–39; East Africa, King's African Rifles, 1939–42. *Heir: uncle* Major Lord Gerald Wellesley. *Address:* Strathfieldsaye House, Mortimer, Berks; Apsley House, Piccadilly, W1.

Died 16 Sept. 1943.

WELLISH, Edward Montague, BA (Cantab), MA (Sydney); Emeritus Professor of Mathematics, University of Sydney, 1946; Associate Professor of Applied Mathematics 1926–46; *b* Sydney, 14 April 1882; *m* 1925, Margaret A. Buxton. *Educ:* Sydney University; Cambridge University. Clerk Maxwell Scholar in Experimental Physics, University of Cambridge, 1909; Assistant Professor of Physics, Yale University, 1911–15; lecturer in Applied Mathematics, University of Sydney, 1916–25. *Publications:* various papers on Experimental Physics and Mathematics in Proc. Roy. Soc. etc. *Address:* Belgium Avenue, Roseville, Sydney, Australia.

Died 22 July 1948.

WELLS, Vice-Adm. Sir Gerard Aylmer, KBE 1937; Director General Ports and Lighthouses Administration of Egypt (with rank of Lewa and Pasha) since 1932; 2nd *s* of Admiral Sir Richard Wells, KCB; *m* 1910, Jocelyn Mary Mort, Sydney, New South Wales; one *s* two *d*. *Educ:* Summerfields, Oxford; HMS Britannia. Joined HMS Britannia, 1893; went to sea in HMS Blenheim, 1895; Sub-Lieut and Lieut in HMS Ophir in tour of the Duke and Duchess of York to British Dominions, 1901; HMS Good Hope with Mr Joseph Chamberlain to South Africa, 1903; Commander in British Naval Mission to Greece, 1913; Commander HMS Centurion, Grand Fleet, 1916; British Naval Attaché, Holland, Poland, and South America, 1922–25; Commanded HMS Royal Sovereign, 1927–29; Rear-Admiral, 1929; retired, 1930; Vice-Admiral, 1934. *Publication:* Naval Customs and Traditions. *Recreations:* golf, tennis, sailing. *Address:* Port House, Alexandria, Egypt. *TA:* Fanarat, Alexandria. *Clubs:* United Service, Royal Yacht Club of Egypt (Commodore).

Died 2 Aug. 1943.

WELLS, Herbert George, DSc Lond.; Hon. DLit Lond.; Hon. Fellow of Imperial College of Science and Technology; *b* Bromley, Kent, 21 Sept. 1866; *s* of Joseph Wells, professional cricketer; *m* Amy Catherine Robbins (*d* 1927); two *s*. *Educ:* private school, Bromley, Kent; Midhurst Grammar School; Royal College of Science. *Publications:* Select Conversations with an Uncle, 1895; The Time Machine, 1895; The Wonderful Visit, 1895; The Island of Doctor Moreau, 1896; The Wheels of Chance, 1896; Certain Personal Matters (essays), 1897; The Invisible Man, 1897; The War of the Worlds, 1898; When the Sleeper awakes, 1899; revised, 1911; Love and Mr Lewisham, 1900; The First Men in the Moon, 1901; Anticipations, 1901; The Sea Lady, 1902; Mankind in the Making, 1903; Twelve Stories and a Dream, 1903; The Food of the Gods, 1904; A Modern Utopia, 1905; Kipps, 1905; In the Days of the Comet, 1906; The Future of America, 1906; The War in the Air, 1908; Tono Bungay, 1909; Ann Veronica, 1909; The History of Mr Polly, 1910; The New Machiavelli, 1911; Floor Games for Children, 1911; Marriage, 1912; Little Wars, a floor game book, 1913; The Passionate Friends, 1913; The Wife of Sir Isaac Harman, 1914; The World Set Free, 1914; Boon (under pseudonym Reginald Bliss), 1915; Bealby, 1915; The Research Magnificent, 1915; Mr Britling Sees it Through, 1916; God, the Invisible King; The Soul of a Bishop, 1917; Joan and Peter, 1918; The Undying Fire, 1919; The Outline of History, 1920; The Secret Places of the Heart; A Short History of the World, 1922; Men like Gods, 1923; The Story of a Great Schoolmaster (F. W. Sanderson); The Dream, 1924; Christina Alberta's Father, 1925; The World of William Clissold, 1926; Meanwhile, 1927; The Book of Catherine Wells, 1928; Mr Blettsworthy on Rampole Island, 1928; Common Sense of World Peace (Address in Reichstag), 1929; The Science of Life (with Julian Huxley and G. P. Wells), a companion to the Outline of History, 1929; The Autocracy of Mr Parham, 1930; The Work, Wealth and Happiness of Mankind, 1932; The Bulpington of Blup, 1933; The Shape of Things to Come, 1933; Experiment in Autobiography, 1934; The Croquet Player, 1936; Star Begotten, 1937; Brynhild,

1937; The Brothers, 1937; The Camford Visitation, 1937; World Brain, 1938; Apropos of Dolores, 1938; The Holy Terror, 1939; Babes in the Darkling Wood, 1940; You can't be too Careful, 1941; The Conquest of Time; Phoenix, 1942; Crux Ansata, an Indictment of the Roman Catholic Church, 1943; '42–'44, 1944; The Happy Turning, 1944; Mind at the End of its Tether, 1945; has written numerous short stories, political pamphlets, newspaper articles, film synopses, etc. *Address:* 13 Hanover Terrace, Regent's Park, NW1. *T:* Paddington 6204. *Club:* Savile.

Died 13 Aug. 1946.

WELLS, Major John Stuart Kerr, CBE 1918; *b* 1873; *s* of late Captain John Wells, Monaghan, Ireland; *m* 1905, Mary Florence, 3rd *d* of late Major Brenan, Lifford; two *s* one *d*. Transferred to permanent staff as Senior Commissioner; served as Political Officer in German East Africa; District Resident Nyasaland Protectorate; retired on pension, 1923. *Address:* Musekera Estate, Tukuyu, Rungwe District, Tanganyika Territory.

Died 26 Jan. 1937.

WELLS, Thomas Bucklin; *b* USA, 5 April 1875; *m*. *Educ:* Yale University. Editor of Harper's Magazine, 1920–31; a member (late Chairman) of the Board of Harper and Brothers, Publishers, New York and London. *Address:* c/o The Guaranty Trust Company, 4 Place de la Concorde, Paris. *Clubs:* Century, Coffee House, New York; Union Interalliée, Paris.

Died 2 Aug. 1944.

WELLS, Thomas Grantham; Headmaster of Bancroft's School, Woodford Green, Essex, since 1931; *b* 21 Oct. 1901; *s* of William Daniel Wells and Elizabeth Mary Hodgkins; *m* 1934, Winifred Harding (*d* 1943); two *s* one *d*. *Educ:* St Bartholomew's Grammar School, Newbury; St John's College, Oxford (Open Classical Scholar); 1st class Hons Honour Moderations, 1st class Hons Litterae Humaniores. Assistant Master, Cheltenham College, 1924–31; Pres., Essex Public and Secondary Schools Athletic Assoc. *Publication:* The Shorter Caesar. *Recreations:* cabinet-making, beekeeping. *Address:* Bancroft's School, Woodford Green, Essex. *T:* Buckhurst 2495.

Died 12 Sept. 1943.

WELLSTOOD, Frederick Christian, MA, FSA, FLA; Secretary and Librarian to the Trustees and Guardians of Shakespeare's Birthplace, and Deputy-keeper Records of the Corporation of Stratford-upon-Avon since 1910; a Governor, Member of Council and Hon. Librarian Shakespeare Memorial Theatre; *b* 28 March 1884; *γ s* of late Charles James Wellstood, Oxford; *m* 1st, 1910, Mildred Violet (*d* 1927), *e d* of late Walter Cowling Fynn, Cambridge; one *s*; 2nd, 1930, Constance Winifred, *e d* of James L. Langley, Bridgetown, Stratford-upon-Avon; one *s* two *d*. *Educ:* New Coll. School; Oxford University. Joined staff of the Bodleian Library, Oxford, 1899; a senior assistant, 1902; first Superintendent of the new reading room, 1908; served on the Consultative Committee for the Shakespeare Exhibition held in the Bodleian Library in commemoration of the tercentenary of the death of Shakespeare, 1916; Hon. Secretary of the Shakespeare Club, Stratford-upon-Avon, 1916–25; a member of the Bishop's Advisory Committee for the Diocese of Coventry since 1923; founded the Dugdale Society for the publication of historical records of Warwickshire, 1920; is a local sec. for Warwickshire of Society of Antiquaries; Member Foreign Advisory Council Theatre Libraries Assoc. of America; carried out excavation of late Saxon cemetery at Milcote, 1915; assisted in excavation of pagan Saxon cemetery at Bidford-on-Avon, 1922–23; discovered extensive Romano-British site at Tiddington, near Stratford-on-Avon, 1925; excavated pagan Saxon cemetery at Stratford-on-Avon, 1934–37; Chairman Stratford-on-Avon Amateur Operatic and Dramatic Society, 1920–34. *Publications:*

Reports on the records in the possession of the Corporation of Stratford-upon-Avon and of the Trustees of Shakespeare's Birthplace, presented to the Royal Commission on Public Records, 1915; Catalogue of an exhibition of original documents of the 16th and 17th centuries preserved in Stratford-upon-Avon, illustrating Shakespeare's life in the town, 1916; Records of the Manor of Henley-in-Arden, Warwickshire, 1919; Catalogue of the books, manuscripts, works of art, antiquities and relics exhibited in Shakespeare's birthplace, 1925, new ed., 1937; Stratford-upon-Avon, illustrated by Joseph Pike, 1929; (with Thomas May) A Romano-British Industrial Settlement near Tiddington, Stratford-upon-Avon, 1931; An Inventory of the civic insignia and other antiquities belonging to the Corporation of Stratford-upon-Avon, 1940; edited the Publications of the Dugdale Society since 1920; edited E. I. Fripp's Shakespeare, man and artist, 1938; Literary and Archæological contributions to leading newspapers and publications of various societies. *Recreations:* archæological excavation; fishing, motoring. *Address:* The Old Vicarage, Loxley, Warwick. *T:* Wellesbourne 254.

Died 7 Aug. 1942.

WELSH, David Arthur, MA, BSc, MD, FRCP Edin.; Professor of Pathology, University of Sydney, 1902–35; Professor Emeritus 1936; Dean of the Faculty of Medicine, 1927–29; late Pathologist, Resident Physician and University Clinical Tutor, Royal Infirmary, Edinburgh. Lecturer on Pathological Bacteriology, and Senior Assistant to Professor of Pathology, University of Edinburgh; Pathologist, Royal Hospital for Sick Children and Royal Infirmary, Edinburgh. *Publications:* scientific papers on the parathyroid glands, precipitin reactions, cancer hydatid disease, hæmogregarines in marsupials, etc. *Address:* University, Sydney.

Died 13 May 1948.

WELSH, John, CBE 1944; Chief Manager, Bank of London & South America Ltd for Uruguay, Argentina, and Paraguay, retd, 1947; Director of Banco Central de la República Argentina, 1936–38, 1940–41, 1943–45 and member of the official body Comisión de Valores de Bolsa; Director of numerous companies; *b* 16 May 1887; *s* of John Welsh and Marion Skeoch; *m* Catalina Acuña Chaparteguy; two *s* one *d*. *Educ:* Greenhead Grammar School. Royal Bank of Scotland, Glasgow, and London, 1902; Bank of London & South America Ltd 1908; first in Uruguay then, in 1934, in Buenos Aires. Appointed by Uruguayan Govt in 1932 to the committee to investigate Anglo-Uruguayan trade relations; Member of Board of Directors of the Gold Bond Bureau of Uruguay, 1933–34. *Recreations:* yachting, fishing, and shooting. *Address:* José E. Uriburu 1540, Buenos Aires. *T:* 41/0869. *Clubs:* Argentine; Jockey, Strangers', English, Nautico San Fernando, Nautico San Isidro, Golf Club Argentino (Buenos Aires).

Died 27 Oct. 1950.

WELTON, James; formerly Professor of Education, Leeds University; *b* Great Yarmouth, 17 Aug. 1854; unmarried. *Educ:* St Mark's College, Chelsea; Caius College, Cambridge (MA). Moral Sciences Tripos, 1st Class; DLit London. For some years a teacher in elementary schools; then Scholar of Caius College, Cambridge; in 1891 took charge of department for training teachers at the Yorkshire College, Leeds. *Publications:* A Manual of Logic; Logical Bases of Education; Forms for Criticism Lessons; Article on Education in Encyclopædia Britannica (11th ed.); The Principles of Teaching, 1906; The Principles of Moral Training, 1909; The Psychology of Education, 1911; What do we Mean by Education?, 1914; Ground-work of Logic, 1918; Groundwork of Ethics, 1922. *Recreations:* walking, travel. *Address:* 21 Holland Road, Hove.

Died 10 June 1942.

WENLOCK, Lady; Dame Annie Allen, GBE 1917; *d* of Sir Edward Cunard, 2nd Bt; *m* 1885, Hon. Arthur Lawley (6th Baron Wenlock, GCSI, GCIE, KCMG) (*d* 1932); two *d*. Hon. Secretary Queen Mary's Needlework Guild; DGStJ. *Address:* Tyntesfield, Bristol.
Died 29 April 1944.

WENSINCK, Arent Jan; Doctor Litt; Professor of Arabic in the University of Leiden, since 1927; *b* 7 Aug. 1882; *s* of Johan Herman Wensinck and Anna Vermeer; *m* Maria Elizabeth Daubanton; two *s* two *d*. *Educ:* Utrecht; Berlin; Leiden. Secretary to the Redaction of the Encyclopædia of Islam, 1908; Professor of Hebrew in Leiden University, 1912; Member of the Royal Academy of Sciences at Amsterdam, 1917; editor of the Encyclopædia of Islam, 1924; honorary member of Royal Asiatic Society of Great Britain and Ireland, 1936; hon. Doctor of the University of Algier, 1938; Sir William Jones Medal of Royal Asiatic Society of Bengal, 1938. *Publications:* The Navel of the Earth, 1916; The Ocean in the Literature of the Western Semites, 1918; Tree and Bird, 1921; Rites of Mourning, 1917; Bar Hebræus's Book of the Dove, translated, 1919; A Handbook of Early Mohammedan Tradition, 1927; The Muslim Creed, 1932; Concordance et Indices de la Tradition Musulmane, 1933; La Pensée de Ghazzali, 1938. *Address:* 21 Witte Singel, Leiden, Holland.
Died 19 Sept. 1939.

WENTWORTH, Captain Frederick Charles Ulick V.; *see* Vernon-Wentworth.

WENTWORTH-SHEILDS, Rt Rev. Wentworth Francis; Assistant Bishop to Archbishop of Wales since 1935; *b* London, 1867; *s* of late F. Wentworth-Sheilds, MInstCE; *m* 1902, Annie (*d* 1927), 4th *d* of late Rt Rev. W. Boyd-Carpenter; two *s*. *Educ:* St Paul's School (Junior and Senior Scholarships); Univ. of London (MA). Ordained, 1898; Curate of St John Baptist, Plumstead, 1898–1900; St George's, Bloomsbury, 1900–02; Precentor of St Saviour's Cathedral, Goulburn, 1904–05; Archdeacon of Wagga-Wagga, 1905–16; Warden of Bishop's College, Goulburn, 1906–16; in charge of All Saints, St Kilda, Melbourne, 1910; Rector of St James', Sydney, 1910–16; Bishop of Armidale, 1916–29; Warden of St Deiniol's Library, Hawarden, Chester, 1930–39. *Address:* Branxton, Elmsleigh Gardens, Bassett, Southampton.
Died 12 Sept. 1944.

WENYON, Charles Morley, CMG 1918; CBE 1919; FRS; MB; BS, BSc (Lond.); temp. Col AMS; Consultant in Tropical Medicine to the Wellcome Foundation; Director-in-Chief, Wellcome Research Institution, until 1944; *s* of Charles Wenyon, MD, pioneer Medical Missionary in China. *Educ:* Kingswood School, Bath; Victoria University, Leeds; University College, London; Guy's Hospital. Formerly Protozoologist to the London School of Tropical Medicine. *Publications:* Protozoology: a Manual for the use of Medical Men, Veterinarians and Zoologists; numerous papers dealing with the Protozoa. *Address:* Welcome Research Institution, Euston Road, NW1.
Died 24 Oct. 1948.

WENYON, Herbert John, DSO 1917; Managing Director, Moussec Ltd, since 1932; Springwell Ltd since 1919; *b* 18 April 1888; *s* of Charles Wenyon, MD, and Eliza Morley Gittins; *m* 1916, Jessie C. Forrester; one *s* three *d*. *Educ:* Kingswood School, Bath. Fellow of Institute of Actuaries. Served European War, Lt-Colonel commanding 8th Royal West Kent Regiment, 1917–18 (DSO and bar, Ordre de la Couronne (Belgium), Croix de Guerre (Belgium), despatches thrice). *Publication:* History of 8th Royal West Kent Regiment. *Recreations:* cricket, Middlesex County XI, 1921–23. *Address:* The Hawthorns, Chester Road, Northwood, Millddlesex. *Clubs:* MCC, East India and Sports.
Died 19 Aug. 1944.

WERFEL, Franz; Freier Schriftsteller; *b* Prag, 10 Sept. 1890; *s* of Fabrikant Rudolf Werfel; *m* Alma Maria Mahler-Werfel, die Witwe Gustav Mahlers. *Educ:* Volksschule, Gymnasium und Universität, Prag. Lektor des Kurt Wolff Verlages in Leipzig, 1912–14; im Feld, 1915–17; in Wien und Venedig, 1917–37; in Paris und Sanary, 1938–40; von 1940 in New York and Los Angeles. *Publications:* Gedichte; Der Weltfreund, 1911; Wir sind, 1913; Einander, 1915; Der Gerichstag, 1918; Beschwörungen, 1922; Hymnarium neuer Gedichte, 1934; Schlaf und Erwachen, 1935; Dramatische Dichtungen: Die Troerinnen, Tragödie, 1913; Die Mittagsgöttin, Zauberspiel, 1919; Spiegelmensch; Bocksgesang Schweiger; Juarez und Maximilian; Paulus unter den Juden; Das Reich Gottes in Böhmen; Der Weg der Verheissung, ein Bibelspiel, 1934. Drama: In einer Nacht, 1937. Romane: Nicht der Mörder, der Ermordete ist schuldig; Verdi; Barbara; Die Geschwister von Neapel; Die vierzig Tage des Mùsa Dagh, Roman des Armenischen Volks, 1933; Höret die Stimme, der Roman eines biblischen Propheten, 1937. Novellen: Spielhof; Der Abituriententag; Geheimnis eines Menschen; Der Tod des Kleinbürgers; Kleine Verhältnisse; The Twilight of a World, 1937. Essays: Realismus und Innerlichkeit; Können wir ohne Gottesglauben Leben?; Von der reinsten Glückseligkeit der Menschen, 1938; April in Oct., 1940; Embezzled Heaven, 1941; The Song of Bernadette, 1942; Die wahre Geschichte vom wiederhergestellten Kreuz, 1942; Jacobowsky and the Colonel, 1943; Between Above and Below (Philosophical Essays), 1944; Ein Reiseroman, 1945; Star of the Unborn, novel, 1945. *Address:* c/o Viking Press, 18 East 48th Street, New York City.
Died 26 Aug. 1945.

WERNHER, Sir Derrick Julius, 2nd Bt *cr* 1905; *b* 7 June 1889; *s* of 1st Bt and Alice S. Mankiewicz (afterwards Lady Ludlow); *S* father, 1912; *m* 1922, Theodora Anna Romanov; one *d*. *Heir: b* Sir Harold Augustus Wernher, KCVO. *Address:* Deal, NJ, USA.
Died 6 March 1948.

WERTH, Albertus Johannes, BA; MP for George, Union House of Assembly; *b* Malmesbury, Cape Province, 6 March 1888; German Parentage; *m* A. E. Klerck; one *s* two *d*. *Educ:* Victoria College, Stellenbosch (graduated in Arts and Literature). Started life as a schoolmaster, and was for nearly ten years on staff of Grey College, Bloemfontein; member of the Union House of Assembly for the constituency of Kroonstad in Orange Free State, 1920–26; Administrator of South-West Africa 1926–33. *Recreations:* represented the Orange Free State Province in tennis and hockey, in inter-provincial sport, and also against visiting teams from England. *Address:* Caledon Street, George, Cape Province.
Died 4 March 1948.

WEST, Andrew F.; Professor of Latin, 1883–1928, and first Dean of the Graduate School, 1901–28, Princeton University; *b* Alleghany (now Pittsburg), Pennsylvania, 17 May 1853; *s* of Rev. Nathaniel and Mary Fleming West; *m* 1889, Lucy Marshall Fitz-Randolph; one *s*. *Educ:* private schools; Princeton Univ. Classical Fellow, 1874. Instructor in Classics in schools, 1874–83; AB Princeton, 1874; PhD 1882; LLD 1897; Hon. DLitt (Oxon), 1902; President American Philological Association, 1902; Chairman American School of Classical Studies in Rome, 1901–13; Vice-President Archæological Institute of America since 1914; Trustee American Academy in Rome; planned and put in operation the Graduate College of Princeton University; President American Classical League, 1919–26; a Vice-President of the Classical Association of Great Britain since 1925. *Publications:* An edition of the plays of Terence, 1888; Philobiblon of Richard de Bury, 1889; Alcuin, 1892; A Latin Grammar for Schools, 1902; American Liberal Education, 1907; The Graduate College of Princeton, 1913; edited Value of the Classics,

1917; Education and the War, 1919; Presentations, 1929; Stray Verses, 1931; American General Education, 1932. *Address:* Princeton University, USA. *Clubs:* Century, Grolier, New York.

Died 27 Dec. 1943.

WEST, Sir Glynn (Hamilton), Kt 1916; MInstCE; *b* 24 Sept. 1877; 4th *s* of late Alfred Thomas West; *m* 1st, 1903, Katrine Mary (who obtained a divorce, 1940), *d* of John Mather, Newcastle on Tyne; one *s* one *d*; 2nd, 1940, Winifred Stevenson, JP, *d* of late Sir William High, Dundee. *Educ:* Sedbergh School. Deputy Director-General of Munitions Supply, 1915–16; Controller of Shell Manufacture, 1916–17; Director-General of Shell Manufacture, 1917; Director-General of Shell and Gun Manufacture, 1917; Member of Munitions Council, 1917–18; was Chairman, Sir W. G. Armstrong, Whitworth & Co. Ltd, Chairman of the Armstrong Siddeley Motors Ltd, etc, until retirement in 1926; now Chairman of Marb-L-Cote Manufacturing Co. Ltd and Director of McMichael Radio, Ltd; holder of Order of St Stanislas, 2nd Class, and Commander of the Order of Crown of Italy. *Recreation:* golf. *Address:* The White Cottage, Stevenage, Herts. *Club:* Carlton.

Died 6 Nov. 1945.

WEST, Maj.-Gen. John Weir, CB 1935; CMG 1919; CBE 1932; *b* 1875; *s* of Rev. T. West, BA, DD, Ex-Moderator, Irish Presbyterian Church; *m* 1905, Dora Isabel, *d* of Surgeon-Major Andrew Knox Rickards; one *d*. *Educ:* Royal Academical Institution, Belfast; Queen's College, Belfast. MB, BCh Royal University of Ireland, 1899; LLD Queen's University, Belfast, 1937. House Surgeon, Royal Victoria Hospital, Belfast, 1899–1900; joined the Royal Army Medical Corps as Lieutenant, 1900; proceeded to South Africa, 1901, and took part in operations in Cape Colony and the Orange River Colony (Queen's SA medal with four clasps); Captain, 1903; Major, 1911; Lieutenant-Colonel, 1917; Brevet Colonel, 1922; Colonel, 1927; Major-General, 1932; proceeded to France with the original Expeditionary Force in command of 3rd Cavalry Field Ambulance; later was Officer in command Surgical Division of 13 Gen. Hospital; then took command of 11 General Hospital and proceeded to Italy, and later commanded 62 General Hospital in Italy (1914 Star, Chevalier Legion of Honour, CMG); Order della Salute Publico, Italy; Master of Surgery, 1917; Honorary Surgeon to the King, April 1922, and promoted to Bt Col; Promoted Col 1927; Consulting Surgeon to the British Army, 1924–27; ADMS, Burma District, 1927–31 (despatches, CBE); Professor of Military Surgery, Royal Army Medical College, and Consulting Surgeon to the Army, 1932–35; retired pay, 1935, House Governor and Medical Superintendent, King Edward VII's Convalescent Home for Officers, Isle of Wight, 1935–39; Commandant BRC Hospital for Officers, Jan.–June 1940; Deputy Med. Supt Botleys Park War Hospital, 1940–44. Col Comdt RAMC, 1942–45. *Recreation:* golf. *Address:* Weir Cottage, Fleet, Hants.

Died 6 March 1949.

WEST, Sir Leonard Henry, Kt 1933; OBE; LLD, JP, DL; *b* 27 March 1864; *s* of Edward Henry West of Glenrock Brough, East Yorkshire; *m* 1922, Meriel, *d* of S. P. Crosland, Huddersfield. *Educ:* private; London University. Solicitor; Tutor to the Law Society; retired, 1906; Chairman and subsequently President of the Mid Bucks Conservative Association, 1916–32 and 1934–38; Chm. of the Buckinghamshire Count; Council 1921–47; Chm. Wessex Division Nat. Union, 1929–31; Chairman of the Aylesbury Division of the Bucks County Bench since 1928; Chairman of the Bucks Discharged Prisoners' Aid Society; late Member of the Thames Conservancy Board; Chairman Bucks Water Board; Chairman of County Civil Defence Committee; President Bucks County Federation of Young Farmers' Clubs.

Publications: History of Wendover; edited several legal books. *Recreations:* gardening, motoring. *Address:* Long Hazard, Ellesborough, nr Aylesbury, Bucks.

Died 1 Jan. 1950.

WESTBURY, Lt-Col Frederic Newell, CB 1937; OBE 1919; *b* 1877; *s* of W. F. Westbury, London; *m* 1908, Ethel, *d* of Thomas Greenstreet, Elgin, two *s* two *d*. *Educ:* King's College, London. Entered Post Office, Accountant-General's Department 1896; Assistant Surveyor, Class II 1905, Class I 1919; Ministry of Transport, 1919; returned to Post Office, 1921; Postmaster-Surveyor, Sheffield 1921 and Glasgow, 1926; Regional Director, Scottish Region, General Post Office, 1935–39; and member of Post Office Board; retired, 1939, Principal Assistant to Civil Commissioner Western District of Scotland, Nov. 1939; served European War with RE Posta Service, 1914–19 (OBE); Lieut-Col 1918; Hon. Col, GHQ Signals (SR), since 1938. *Address:* 116 Braid Road, Edinburgh, 10. *T:* 53695.

Died 26 Aug. 1946.

WESTCOTT, Rt Rev. Foss; *b* 23 Oct. 1863; *s* of Rt Rev. B. F. Westcott (late Bishop of Durham) and S. L. M. Westcott. *Educ:* Cheltenham College; Peterhouse, Cambridge (Hon. Fellow), DD Cambridge and Oxford, 1920. Deacon, 1886; priest, 1887; curate of St Peter's Church, Bishopwearmouth; joined the SPG Mission, Cawnpore, 1889; Bishop of Chota Nagpore, 1905–19; Bishop of Calcutta and Metropolitan of India, Burma and Ceylon, 1919–45. *Recreations:* formerly took an active part in cricket, football, and tennis. *Address:* SPG Mission, Siramtoli, Ranchi, BN Railway, Bihar, India.

Died 19 Oct. 1949.

WESTELL, William Percival, FLS, FRSA, FSA Scot; author, lecturer and museum curator; *b* 21 Dec. 1874; *e c* of late W. T. Westell, St Albans, Herts; *m* 1896, Alice, *y d* of late David Moules, Stevenage, Herts; one *s*. *Educ:* St Albans Grammar School. One of modern school of litterateurs whose special theme is Nature; author of a great many books on Natural History; has lectured for past thirty-five years before Literary and Lecture Societies, Public Schools and Institutions; Bronze Medallist Botany and Entomology (1909) of the Société Nationale d'Acclimatation de France; Exhibitioner of the Royal Society, 1905; Curator of Letchworth Museum since its opening in 1914; late Lecturer in Nature Study to Cambridgeshire County Council, etc. *Publications:* The All-Round Nature Books; The Gates of the Forest; The Boys' Own Nature book; Every Boy's Book of Geology; The Songs of a Nature Lover; Poems of Bonnie Scotland; Fifty-Two Nature Rambles; The Book of Nature; The Circling Year; My Life as a Naturalist; Historic Hertfordshire; How to Know the Country; Yesterdays, An Autobiography; Look and Find Out Nature Books; Let's Watch the Birds; and others; Archæological Papers, etc. *Recreations:* watching cricket and football, gardening, reading, excavating, wandering. *Address:* The Museum, Letchworth, Herts. *TA:* Westell, Museum, Letchworth. *T:* Letchworth 459.

Died 1 Nov. 1943.

WESTERN, Lt-Col Bertram Charles Maximilian, DSO 1916; late E Lancs Regt; *b* 25 June 1886; *o s* of late Rev. W. T. Western; *m* 1926, Dorothy, *d* of Robert Wilson, Stirlingshire; two *d*. *Educ:* Haileybury; Sandhurst. Served European War, 1914–18 (despatches, DSO and bar, Bt Maj.). *Address:* Southbroom Hotel, South Coast, Natal. *Club:* Bath.

Died 21 April 1942.

WESTERN, George Trench, MA, MD Camb.; Physician in charge of Inoculation Department, London Hospital, 1905–38; *b* 1877; *s* of late G. A. Western, Shortlands; *m* 1907, Augusta Sophia, *d* of W. H. Carter; one *s* two *d*. *Educ:* Monkton Combe; Pembroke College, Cambridge; London Hospital. *Publications:*

various papers on medical subjects. *Recreations:* rowing (spare man for Cambridge Eight, 1901), climbing. *Address:* The Corderries, Chalford, Gols. *Clubs:* London Rowing, Alpine.

Died 5 Oct. 1948.

WESTMACOTT, Brig.-Gen. Claude Berners, CBE 1919; *b* 1865; *s* of late Percy G. B. Westmacott, Rosemount, Ascot; *m* 1898, Lily (*d* 1947), *d* of late Col Henry Taylor, Shorne, Kent. Served European War, 1914–19 (despatches, CBE). *Address:* Wall House, Lichfield.

Died 15 March 1948.

WESTMORLAND, 14th Earl of, *cr* 1624; **Vere Anthony Francis St Clair Fane;** Baron Burghersh, 1624; *b* 15 March 1893; *e s* of 13th Earl and Lady Sybil Mary St Clair Erskine (*d* 1910), *d* of 4th Earl of Rosslyn; *S* father, 1922; *m* 1923, Hon. Mrs Arthur Capel, *y d* of 4th Baron Ribblesdale; two *s* one *d*. Lt RN 1916; retired, 1919; Lt-Comdr, retired, 1924. *Heir: s* Lord Burghersh. *Address:* Lyegrove, Badminton, Glos. *Clubs:* Turf, Bath.

Died 12 May 1948.

WESTON, Col Claude Horace, DSO 1918; VD; KC 1934; LLB New Zealand University; NZ Infantry; Barrister-at-law, Wellington, New Zealand; *b* 29 Dec. 1879; *s* of late Thomas Shailer Weston, Barrister, Christchurch, NZ; *m*; one *s* one *d*. *Educ:* Christ's College Grammar School; Canterbury College. Practised in New Plymouth, Auckland, Wellington, NZ, since 1902; served European War, 1915–17 (DSO, despatches); Judge Advocate-General, 1935; Commandant NZ Legion of Frontiersmen, 1926–31; Knight of Order of Orange Nassau (Netherlands), 1939. *Publications:* Three Years with the New Zealanders, 1919; Contractors and Workmen's Liens, 1933; (Joint) Handbook NZ Military Law, 1937. *Recreations:* farming and stock raising. *Address:* 33 Johnston Street, Wellington, C1, New Zealand. *Clubs:* Taranaki, New Plymouth; Northern, Auckland; Wellington, Wellington.

Died 10 Nov. 1946.

WESTON, Lt-Gen. Eric Culpeper, CB 1942; *b* 5 June 1888. 2nd Lt Royal Marines, 1906; Lt, RMA, 1907; Capt. 1917; Major, 1928; Bt Lt-Col 1933; Lt-Col 1934; Col 2nd Commandant, 1937; Col Commandant, 1939; Maj.-Gen. 1942; Lt-Gen. 1943; retired list, 1943. ADC to the King, 1940–43. Served European War, 1914–18; War of 1939–45 (CB, Greek Military Cross, 1st class). *Address:* Moor Edge, Liss, Hants.

Died 19 Feb. 1950.

WESTON, Lt-Col Reginald Salter, CMG 1915; late Manchester Regiment; *b* 10 Aug. 1867. *Educ:* Marlborough; RMC, Sandhurst. Entered Army, 1888; Captain, 1897; Adjutant, 1901–03; Major, 1903; served NW Frontier, India, 1897–98 (medal with clasp); European War, 1914–15 (despatches, wounded twice, CMG); retired pay, 1919. *Recreation:* shooting. *Address:* Steeple Ashton, Trowbridge, Wilts. *Club:* Naval and Military.

Died 5 Jan. 1944.

WESTPHAL, Augustus, BD; Bishop of the Moravian Church in Jamaica, since 1903, and Missionary at Fairfield, Jamaica, since 1896; *b* Germany, 2 July 1864; *s* of Jacob and Rosalie Westphal; *m* 1892, Georgine W., *d* of Bishop Benjamin Romig; one *s* one *d*. *Educ:* Moravian College and Theological Seminary, Bethlehem, Pa, USA. Deacon of Moravian Church, 1888; Moravian Minister in Milwaukee, Wisconsin; removal to Jamaica, 1890, subsequently joining the Missionary Staff of the Moravian Church in Jamaica; Missionary at Salem, Jamaica, 1890–96; a member of the Government Board, 1896; President of the Mandeville Convention; Chairman of the School Board of Manchester, Jamaica; Member of the Board of Education; President of

Moravian Executive Board, Jamaica; Delegate of the Moravian Church in Jamaica to the General Synod held in Herrnhut, Saxony, 1931. *Recreation:* horticulture. *Address:* Fairfield, Lincoln PO, Jamaica, West Indies.

Died 25 Nov. 1939.

WESTROPP, Col George O'C.; *see* O'Callaghan-Westropp.

WESTWOOD, Rt Hon. Joseph; PC 1943; JP; MP (Lab) Stirling and Falkirk since 1935; Member National Advisory Council for Physical Training and Recreation and Committee for Consolidation of Scottish Local Government Law; *b* 11 Feb. 1884; *s* of S. Westwood and H. Sidaway; *m* Frances, *d* of James Scarlett and Frances Harvey; three *s* five *d*. *Educ:* Buckhaven Higher Grade School. Left school at 13 years of age; started work as draper's apprentice, then message boy, and on attaining 14 years of age entered the mines, and was a miner until 1916; appointed Fife Miners' Industrial Organiser; MP (Lab) Peebles and South Midlothian, 1922–31; Political Organiser Scottish Miners, 1918–29; Parliamentary Under-Secretary of State for Scotland, 1931 and 1940–45; Secretary of State for Scotland, 1945–47; Member of Educational Endowments (Scotland) Commission; National Committee on Scottish Health Services, Departmental (Scotland) Committee on Vagrancy, Chairman Scottish Housing Advisory Committee, and a Magistrate of Kirkcaldy; also numerous local activities. *Recreation:* cycling. *Address:* 50 Viewforth Street Kirkcaldy, Fifeshire. *T:* Dysart 5362.

Died 17 July 1948.

WETHERED, Col Joseph Robert, CMG 1919; DSO 1916; late Gloucester Regiment; *b* 26 Nov. 1873; *s* of late Rev. F. T. Wethered, Vicar of Hurley; *m* 1913, Dorothy, *d* of late Brig.-Gen. H. S. FitzGerald, CB; one *s* one *d*. *Educ:* Radley. Joined Gloucestershire Regiment, 1893; served throughout South African War (Queen's medal 4 clasps, King's medal 2 clasps); European War, 1914–18 (despatches six times, DSO, CMG); Bt Lieut-Col 1918; Lt-Col 1921; Colonel, 1925; AAG War Office, 1925–26; retired, 1926. *Club:* Leander.

Died 8 March 1942.

WHAITE, Col Thomas du Bédat, CB 1919; CMG 1917; AMS (retired, 1919); *b* 7 July 1862; *s* of late Major John Edmund Whaite, 10th Foot (Lincs Regt), and Adjt 3rd Batt. Connaught Rangers, and Isabella, *d* of late Peter L. du Bédat, Sec. Bank of Ireland; *m* Nora Mary (*d* 1937), *d* of late Thomas Manifold Craig, Rockmount, Dundrum, Co. Dublin; one *d*. *Educ:* Diocesan School, Tuam; Galway Grammar School; Trinity College, Dublin (BA, MB, BCh). Entered Army Medical Service, 1886; Major RAMC 1898; Lt-Col 1906; Col Army Medical Service, 1915; served S Africa, 1899–1902 (Queen's medal 4 clasps, King's medal 2 clasps, severely wounded at Driefontein, 10 March 1900); European War with Lahore Division in India and France, 1914, and afterwards on staff as ADMS 3rd Division and DDMS XIV Army Corps in France and Italy (despatches, CB, CMG, and Croix de Guerre, France). *Recreations:* motoring, carpentry, gardening, sketching, music. *Address:* c/o Glyn Mills & Co., Ltd, Holts Branch, Kirkland House, Whitehall, SW1.

Died 15 Dec. 1943.

WHALE, George Harold Lawson, MD Cant., FRCS Eng.; Surgeon for Diseases of the Ear, Throat and Nose; *b* Woolwich, 1876; *s* of George and Matilda Whale; *m* 1928; no *c*. *Educ:* Bradfield; Jesus College, Cambridge; St Bartholomew's Hospital. Surgeon to the Hampstead General Hospital, and to the National Temperance Hospital; Capt. RAMC (TF); 1914 Star; Order of St John of Jerusalem. *Publications:* Injuries to the Head and Neck, 1919; Modern Treatment of Diseases of Ear, Throat and Nose, 1930; several medical publications.

Recreations: golf, bridge. *Address:* 84 Wimpole Street, W1. *T:* Welbeck 1646. *Clubs:* Royal Thames Yacht; Moor Park Golf.

Died 17 June 1943.

WHALE, Philip Barrett, BSc (Econ.), MCom; Brunner Professor of Economic Science, University of Liverpool, since 1947; *b* 23 March 1898; *s* of Philip Howard Whale and Katherine Maud Marie Harries; *m* 1929, Winefride Jane Hunt; no *c*. *Educ:* private schools; University College, Cardiff. Lecturer in Economics, Univ. of Birmingham, 1919–26; Sir E. Cassel Lecturer in Economics, London School of Economics, University of London, 1926–30; Reader in Economics (with special reference to Money and Banking), London School of Economics, 1930–45; Chaddock Professor of Economics, University of Liverpool, 1945–47; appointed member of Agricultural Wages Board for England and Wales since 1942; Member of Advisory Committee on the Provincial Agricultural Economics Service. *Publications:* Joint Stock Banking in Germany, 1930; International Trade (Home University Library), 1932; articles and papers, chiefly in Economica. *Address:* Hope Lodge, Poplar Road, Oxton, Birkenhead. *T:* Birkenhead 1706.

Died 16 March 1950.

WHALE, Winifred Stephens; writer on French history and literature; editor of the Book of France, 1915; the Soul of Russia, 1916; formerly Hon. Secretary, Femina Vie Heureuse and Heinemann Prize Committees; *b* Naunton, Glos; *d* of late Catherine and Rev. John Mortimer Stephens; *m* 1923, George Whale (*d* 1925). *Educ:* in France and at Tudor Hall School. *Publications:* French Novelists of To-day, 1st series 1908; 2nd series 1915; Margaret of France, 1912; From the Crusades to the French Revolution, 1914; Madame Adam, La Grande Française, 1917; The France I Know, 1918; Women of the French Revolution, 1922; articles in various literary journals; L'Europe Nouvelle, etc.; translations from the French of Anatole France—(La vie de Jeanne d'Arc (2 vols), and other works); Marcelle Tinayre; Jacques de Lacretelle; Pierre Champion; André Malraux and others. *Address:* Porch House, Blockley, Moreton-in-Marsh, Glos.

Died 8 Sept. 1944.

WHALLEY, Philip Guy Rothay, CBE 1945; MA, LLB; Joint Managing Director Lewis's Investment Trust Ltd; Director Westpool Investment Trust; Joint Managing Director of Lewis's, Ltd, and Associated Companies; *b* 6 April 1901; *o s* of Harold G. W. Whalley and Ada Mary McNay, Liverpool; *m* 1929, Norah Helen Mawdsley; two *s*. *Educ:* Aldenham School; Gonville and Caius College, Cambridge. Tancred Scholar, Lincoln's Inn, 1921; called to Bar, 1924; joined Lewis's, Ltd, 1929; Ministry of Food, 1940–45, Deputy Secretary. Member Council of Industrial Design, 1944; Vice-President Royal Society of Arts, 1949. *Recreations:* golf and walking. *Address:* Lane Farm, Bovingdon, Herts. *T:* Bovingdon 2211. *Club:* Savile.

Died 1 March 1950.

WHALLEY, Major Richard Cyril Rae, CBE 1935; RARO, RE; attached British Legation, Addis Ababa, since 1943; *b* 1896; *s* of late Frederick Herbert Whalley, MIME; *m* Barbara (from whom he obtained a divorce, 1933), *d* of late Lt-Col G. Tyacke, RA; one *s* one *d*. *Educ:* abroad; London University. Served European War, 1914–19, in Gallipoli with 29th Division, later in Egypt with Desert Column and Desert Mounted Corps (wounded, 1914–15 star, two medals); in charge survey party Kenya and Uganda Railways, Nakuru-Eldoret, 1920–22; Assistant Resident Engineer Construction Mile 30–60, 1922–23; District Engineer in charge Railway Survey, Sudan Government Railways, Rahad-Talodi, 1927; Sudan Political Service as District Commissioner Opari-Kajo Kaji District, Mongalla Province, 1927–30; HM Consul Maji, SW Ethiopia,

1930–38; Frontier Agent, Sudan Govt, Boma Plateau, 1938–41; SPO Maji-Kaffa Area, 1941–42, after patriot activity in SW Ethiopia. *Publications:* few articles in Sudan Notes and Records. *Recreations:* all games, fishing, shooting, sailing, photography, motoring, surveying. *Address:* care British Legation, Addis Ababa, Ethiopia. *Clubs:* East India and Sports; Muthaiga, Nairobi; Sudan, Khartoum.

Died 11 June 1944.

WHARHIRST, Sir Robert William, Kt 1946; CB 1944; CBE 1938; OBE 1927; *b* 1885. Entered Civil Service 1904; Director of the Armament Supply Department, Admiralty, 1937–47. Grand Officer, Order of Orange-Nassau, 1947. *Address:* Uppingham, 22 Marlborough Rd, Bournemouth.

Died 26 Aug. 1949.

WHARTON, Anthony, (Alister McAllister), BA; *b* Dublin, 1877; *s* of P. F. McAllister. Served European War, 1915–18, Machine Gun Corps, Intelligence, etc. *Publications: Plays:* Irene Wycherley, 1907; Nocturne, 1908; At the Barn, 1911; 13 Simon St, 1912; The Riddle, 1912; Benvenuto Cellini, 1925; Needles and Pins, 1929; The O'Cuddy, 1942. *Novels:* Joan of Over Barrow, 1922; The Man on the Hill, 1923; Be Good, Sweet Maid, 1924; Evil Communications, 1925; The Two of Diamonds, 1926. *Short Stories:* Saturday Evening Post, Pictorial Review, Empire Review, Nash's, etc. Also under pseudonym Lynn Brock: The Deductions of Colonel Gore, 1924; Colonel Gore's Second Case, 1926; The Kink (Colonel Gore's Third Case), 1927; The Slip-Carriage (Colonel Gore's Fourth Case), 1928; The Dagwort Coombe Murder, 1929; The Mendip Mystery (Colonel Gore's Fifth Case), 1929; QED (Colonel Gore's Sixth Case), 1930; Nightmare, 1932; The Silver Sickle Case, 1937; Fourfingers, 1938; The Riddle of the Roost, 1939; The Stoat, 1940. *Address:* c/o Collins, Sons and Co. Ltd, 48 Pall Mall, SW1.

Died 6 April 1943.

WHATELY, Ven. Herbert Edward; Archdeacon of Ludlow since 1939; Rector of Church Stretton, Salop, since 1937; Prebendary de Hampton, Hereford Cathedral, 1940; OCF; *b* 10 Aug. 1876; 3rd *s* of late Ven. E. W. Whately, Archdeacon of Glendalough and Chancellor of St Patrick's Cathedral, Dublin; *m* 1911, Emily Grace, *d* of late Canon F. B. Plummer, Rector of Halewood, Liverpool; two *s* one *d*. *Educ:* Blackheath School; Trinity College and Wycliffe Hall, Oxford. Ordained, 1900; Rector of St Mary's, Wavertree, 1904–16; Vicar of St Michael and All Angels, Blackheath, 1916–30; Vicar of St Augustine's, Honor Oak Park, 1930–37. *Address:* The Rectory, Church Stretton, Salop. *TA:* and *T:* Church Stretton 185.

Died 7 Dec. 1947.

WHEATLEY, Major Cyril Moreton, DSO 1917; *b* London, 1 Aug. 1870; 2nd *s* of late Colonel M. J. Wheatley, CB, RE, and *g s* of Thomas Randall Wheatley of Gwersyllt Park, Denbighshire; *m* 1923, Alethea Fort, of The Coppice House, Spleen, 2nd *d* of late Rev. Richard Fort, Alderbury House, Wilts. *Educ:* Marlborough. Joined 3rd Essex Regt 1900; served South African War, 1900–02 (Queen's medal 3 clasps); retired, 1913; joined Essex Regt 1914, as Major (despatches, DSO). *Address:* Hinderton, Boughton Aluph, Ashford, Kent. *T:* Wye 28. *Club:* Windham.

Died 3 Aug. 1942.

WHEATLEY, Sir Zachariah, Kt 1920; JP; *b* Coventry, 28 March 1865; 3rd *s* of Zachariah Wheatley, Coventry; *m* 1890, Martha (*d* 1948), *γ d* of John Laviers, Maesteg, Glam.; one *s* one *d*. Mayor of Abergavenny, 1914–19; elected Member of First Town Council, 1899; Alderman, 1908; Member of the First School Board in Abergavenny; served in Volunteers a number of years; formed and in command of First Cycle Corps, 4th VB, SWB; Quartermaster and Hon. Lt 38th Div. RE (unpaid), Welsh Army Corps (Gold Palms of the Belgian Order of the Crown); created a Welsh Bard at the Royal National Eisteddfod of Wales at Corwen with the title of Maer Hedd Y Fenni, Peace Mayor of Abergavenny. *Recreation:* athletics in general. *Heir: s* John Wheatley. *Address:* Maindiff, Ribblesdale Place, Barrowford, Lancs. *TA:* and *T:* Nelson 1391.

Died 6 June 1950.

WHEELER, Rev. Alfred, MA; Canon Emeritus of St Paul's Cathedral, Melbourne, 1937; *b* London; *s* of Elijah Wheeler and Harriet Priest; *m* 1893, Fanny Cynthia Polhill; one *d. Educ:* City of London School; St John's College, Cambridge. Deacon, 1890; Priest, 1892; formerly Curate of St James, West Hartlepool, 1890–91; SE Mission, Diocese of Adelaide, 1891–92; Narracoorte, etc., 1891–95; Incumbent of Christ Church, Strathalbyn, 1895–99; Minor Canon and Precentor of St Paul's Cathedral, Melbourne, 1899–1908; Chaplain of Homœopathic Hospital, 1904–08; Lecturer of St John's College, 1908; Vicar of All Saints, Geelong, 1909–37; Canon of St Paul's, Melbourne, 1914; retired, 1937; Chaplain of Geelong Hospital, Victoria, 1937; Director of the Australasian Performing Right Association, 1939. *Publications:* mostly musical; Anthems, Part Songs, Children's Cantatas, Piano Pieces, Musical Arrangements, etc. *Recreations:* reading and walking. *Address:* 10 Stephen Street, Geelong, Victoria, Australia. *Club:* Savage (Melbourne).

Died 11 Oct. 1949.

WHEELER, Sir Arthur, 1st Bt *cr* 1920; DL, JP Leicestershire; *b* 18 Sept. 1860; *yr s* of late Benjamin Wheeler; *m* 1896, Mary (*d* 1938), *e d* of late Frederick Pullman; two *s* two *d. Heir: s* Arthur Frederick Pullman [*b* 10 Dec. 1900; *m* 1938, Alice Webster Stones]. *Address:* Holme next Sea, Norfolk. *T:* Holme 233.

Died 20 May 1943.

WHEELER, Edwin Paul, FRIBA; formerly Architect to London County Council and Superintending Architect of Metropolitan Buildings; retired 1939; Member of Council, RIBA; *b* 1874; *m* 1912, Madeline Mary, *e d* of Dr C. Sanders; two *d.* Articled in London; studied Architectural Association; served in France with HM Forces (Captain) and in Eastern Command. *Address:* 10 St Martin's Avenue, Epsom, Surrey. *Club:* Reform.

Died 1 March 1944.

WHEELER, Sir Henry, KCSI 1921 (CSI 1914); KCIE 1917 (CIE 1910); *b* 2 June 1870; *s* of late Dr Henry Wheeler; *m* 1909, Marjory, *d* of late Sir Harold Stuart, GCMG; one *d. Educ:* Christ's College, Camb. Entered Indian Civil Service, 1891; served in various capacities up country; Under-Secretary, Government of Bengal, 1897–98; Junior Secretary, Board of Revenue, 1901–03; Secretary, Salt Committee, 1903–04; Deputy Secretary, Government of India, in the Finance Department, 1907–08; Secretary, Royal Commission on Decentralisation, 1908–09; Financial Secretary, Government of Bengal, 1909–12; Home Secretary, Government of India, 1912–16; Member of Executive Council, Bengal, 1917–22; Governor of Bihar and Orissa, 1922–April 1927; Member of Council of India, 1927–37; Second Delegate for India on Disarmament Commission, Geneva, 1932–33–1934; went to India 1935 as Chairman of Committee to examine procedure of Govt of India's Secretariat under the new Constitution. *Address:* 77 Ashley Gardens, Westminster, SW1. *Club:* Oriental.

Died 2 June 1950.

WHEELER, Rev. Hugh Trevor; *b* Belfast, 27 Sept. 1874; *m* Kathleen Russell, *d* of D. R. Gunning Bath; one *s. Educ:* Trinity College, Dublin. Curate of Tullyish, Dromore; Curate of Simla, 1900–02; Chaplain to Govt of India, 1902–30; Temp. Chaplain to Forces, Mediterranean Expeditionary Force, 1915–16; Hon.

Canon of Lahore Cathedral, 1918; Archdeacon of Lahore, 1919–29; Rector of Broughton Astley, 1930–35. *Address:* Ashleigh, Shottermill, Haslemere.

Died 11 Feb. 1949.

WHEELER, Sir William Ireland de Courcy, Kt 1919; MD, BCh, BAO, FRCSI, FACS (Hon.); MCh (Hon.) University of Egypt; Surgeon Rear-Adm. (Consulting) RN, 1939; Past President, Royal College of Surgeons, Ireland; Consulting Surgeon to New Southend-on-Sea Hospital and Senior Surgeon All Saints Hospital, London; ex-President and Hon. Member Post Grad. Assembly of North America; late Surgeon-in-Ordinary to Lord-Lieutenant; late Chairman, City of Dublin Nursing Institute; Donor and Surgeon, Dublin Hospital for Wounded Officers; Consulting General Surgeon, Metropolitan Hospital, London; late Consulting Surgeon, Ministry of Pensions, Ireland and to Kilkenny, Arklow and Newcastle Hospitals and Sunshine Home for Children and Rotunda Hospital; late Consulting Surgeon, LMS Railway and Consulting Surgeon to Orient Steam Navigation Co. Ltd; Consulting Surgeon and late Visiting Surgeon to Mercer's Hospital, Ministry of Pensions Hospital, and National Children's Hospital, Dublin; Hon. Fellow American College of Surgeons; President and Medallist, Dublin University Biological Association; Demonstrator and Assistant to Professor of Anatomy, TCD; *b* Dublin, 8 May 1879; *s* of late William Ireland de Courcy Wheeler, Past Pres. Royal College of Surgeons; *m* 1909, Hon. Elsie, *e d* of 1st Baron Craigmyle; one *s* one *d. Educ:* Trinity College, Dublin; Berne. BA, TCD Moderator and Medallist; Honours and prizes in Natural Science, Experimental Science, and Anatomy. Lt-Col, RAMC, and Member of War Office Council of Consultants, 1917; Member, Advisory Council, Ministry of Pensions, on Artificial Limbs; Member of War Office Tetanus Committee; served European War (despatches twice); late Hon. Surgeon to the Forces in Ireland; Lecturer in Surgery, Post Graduates, Univ. of Dublin; ex-Pres. British Medical Association (Leinster branch) and late Member of Ethical Committee and General Council; ex-Chairman of Council and Pres. Metropolitan Counties Branch BMA (1938); ex-Pres. Surgical Section Royal Acad. of Medicine; ex-Pres., and Arnott Gold Medal Irish Medical Schools and Graduates Assoc.; Vice-Pres. Four Provinces of Ireland Club, Extern. Exam. in Surgery, National University and Queen's Univ. (Belfast), Edinburgh, and Glasgow Universities; Visitor King Edward's Hospital Fund for London; Inspector of Exams. Medical Registration Council, Ireland; President Orthopædic Section, BMA, 1933; Vice-President, Surgical Section, BMA (Winnipeg), 1930; Member of Departmental Com. to report on Compensation Acts (Ireland); Surgical Specialist Military Hospital, Blackrock, and Medical Referee under Workmen's Compensation Acts; ex-Chancery Visitor in Lunacy; late Member of Editorial Committee, British Journal of Surgery, and formerly Consulting Editorial Staff, American Journal Surgery, Gynæcology, and Obstetrics, and British Journal of Urology; Member of American Editors Association. *Publications:* Murphy Oration USA 1932; Operative Surgery, 4th edit. 1924; Injuries and Diseases of Bone, 1928; General Surgery in Medical Annual, 1916–1936; contributions on general surgical subjects to British Medical Journal, Lancet, Medical Press, Practitioner, and numerous monographs. *Recreations:* shooting, fishing, and motoring. *Address:* c/o Admiralty, 64 St James's Street, SW. *Club:* Royal Irish Yacht.

Died 11 Sept. 1943.

WHEELOCK, Frank E.; *b* Brooklyn, Nova Scotia, 7 June 1877; *s* of Samuel M. Wheelock and Mary E. Prince; *m* 1911, Cora Blenkhorn Canning, NS; two *s. Educ:* Acadia University, Wolfville, NS; Yale University (PhD). Taught in Nova Scotia High Schools for four years before entering College; after graduating from

Acadia in 1905, taught for one year in The Macdonald Consolidated School, Middleton, NS; entered Yale University in fall of 1906 to study Physics; Instructor in Physics, University of Missouri, 1910–12; Professor of Physics, Mount Allison University, 1912–17; Dean M'Clelan School of Applied Science of Mount Allison University, 1914–17; Professor of Physics, Acadia University, since 1917; Dean Faculty Applied Science, 1917–23; Provost since 1923; Provost and Registrar since 1939. *Publication:* A Study of the Properties of the α-rays from Polonium. *Recreation:* golf. *Address:* Acadia University, Wolfville, NS.

Died 10 Jan. 1941.

WHETHAM, Rear-Adm. Edye Kington B.; *see* Boddam-Whetham.

WHIBLEY, Leonard, MA; Fellow of Pembroke College, Cambridge; University Lecturer in Ancient History, 1899–1910; *b* 20 April 1863; *m* 1920, Rhita, *d* of General W. B. Barwell and late Countess Leiningen. *Publications:* Political Parties at Athens in the Peloponnesian War; Greek Oligarchies; Editor of A Companion to Greek Studies; The Correspondence of Richard Hurd and William Mason, 1932; The Poems of Thomas Gray, 1939, in the World's Classics; Joint Editor, The Correspondence of Thomas Gray, 1935. *Address:* Pembroke College, Cambridge; The Dial House, Frensham, Farnham, Surrey.

Died 8 Nov. 1941.

WHICHCOTE, Sir George, 9th Bt *cr* 1660; JP, DL; *b* 3 Sept. 1870; *e s* of 8th Bart and Louisa Day, 3rd *d* of T. W. Claggett, of Fetcham, Surrey; *S* father, 1893. Capt. 3rd and 4th Batts Northamptonshire Regt (retired); High Sheriff for Lincolnshire, 1900. Heir: *b* Hugh [*b* 18 April 1874; *m* 1909, Flora Lilian, *d* of late Rev. C. S. Sundius; three *d*]. *Address:* Aswarby Park, Sleaford, Lincolnshire. *T:* Culverthorpe 47.

Died 5 Dec. 1946.

WHICHCOTE, Sir Hugh Christopher, 10th Bt *cr* 1660; *b* 18 April 1874; *s* of 8th Bt and Louisa Day, 3rd *d* of T. W. Claggett, of Fetcham, Surrey; *S* brother 1946; *m* 1909, Flora Lilian, *d* of late Rev. C. S. Sundius; three *d*. *Recreation:* shooting. Heir: none. *Address:* Aswarby Park, Sleaford, Lincolnshire. *TA:* Aswarby. *T:* Culverthorpe 47. *Club:* Junior Carlton.

Died 7 May 1949 (ext).

WHIGHAM, Gen. Sir Robert Dundas, GCB 1931 (KCB 1917; CB 1915); KCMG 1919; DSO 1902; *b* 5 Aug. 1865; *s* of late David Dundas Whigham, Prestwick, Ayrshire, and Ellen Murray, *y d* of late James Campbell of Craigie, Ayrshire; *m* 1899, Isabel Adeline, *y d* of late F. A. Muntz of Rossmore, Leamington; (one *s* killed in action, 1941) one *d*. *Educ:* Fettes College, Edinburgh; RMC, Sandhurst. Joined 1st Batt. Royal Warwickshire Regiment, 1885; served Nile Expedition, 1898, with the 13th Soudanese Battalion of the Egyptian army, including the battles of Atbara and Khartoum; served South African Campaign, 1899–1902; European War, 1914–18; Deputy Chief Imperial General Staff, 1916–18; commanded 62nd West Riding Division (France), 1918; Adjutant-General to the Forces, 1923–27; GOC-in-C Eastern Command, 1927–31; ADC General to HM 1930–31; retired pay, 1931; Commissioner of The Duke of York's Royal Military School, 1932–46; Commander, Legion of Honour, Croix de Guerre, Commander Order of Leopold (Belgium), Rising Sun, 2nd Class (Japan). *Address:* Belmont, St Andrews. *Club:* Royal and Ancient (St Andrews).

Died 23 June 1950.

WHIGHAM, Walter Kennedy, OBE; Banker; Deputy Chairman, London and N-E Railway until 1948; Member Central Electricity Board; *b* 1878; 5th *s* of late D. Dundas Whigham of Prestwick, Ayrshire; *m* 1st, 1917, Jacqueline (*d* 1940), 2nd *d* of Baron Henri de

Salignac Fénelon of Hermaville, France; three *s*; 2nd, 1943, Patience Mary, *d* of late Capt. J. McBain Ronald, and of Mrs Ronald, Patrixbourne, Kent; one *s* one *d*. Served European War, Aug. 1914–Jan. 1919, first in North Staffordshire Regt and afterwards on Staffs of 51st (Highland) Division and 4th Corps (despatches three times). High Sheriff, County of London, 1923–24, of Kent, 1935 and 1947. *Address:* 14 Hyde Park Gardens, W2; Highland Court, Brigade, nr Canterbury. *T:* Paddington 5563, Bridge 305. *Clubs:* Prestwick Golf (Prestwick); Royal St George's Golf (Sandwich).

Died 14 Aug. 1948.

WHIPHAM, Thomas Rowland Charles, MA, MD, BCh (Oxon); MRCP (Lond.), MRCS (Eng.); Ex-President and Consulting Physician Exeter Dispensary; Consulting Physician Children's Convalescent Home, Exmouth; FRIPHH; Liveryman of the Goldsmith's Company; late Physician Evelina Hospital for Children; Assistant Physician and Physician in charge of the Children's Department the Prince of Wales' Hospital; Physician to the Legal and General Life Assurance Society; Lecturer at NE London Post-Graduate Medical College; Assistant Physician to the Royal Devon and Exeter Hospital; *b* 1871; *s* of late Thomas Tillyer Whipham, MD; *m* Urania F. J. Trevor (*d* 1940), *d* of late Major Richard Meade. *Educ:* Rugby School; New College, Oxford (Honours in Final School, Nat. Sci.); St George's Hospital (Prizeman). Formerly Physician to St George's, Hanover Square Dispensary, Demonstrator in Materia Medica, Assistant Curator of the Museum and Medical Registrar at St George's Hospital. *Publications:* The Medical Diseases of Children; contributions to various medical journals. *Address:* Newlands, St Thomas's Exeter. *Club:* MCC.

Died 20 Jan. 1945.

WHIPPLE, Francis John Welsh, ScD, FInstP; *b* 17 March 1876; *s* of late George Mathews Whipple, Superintendent of Kew Observatory, 1878–93, and late Elizabeth Martha Beckley; *m* 1911, Violet Mary Josephine (*d* 1926), *d* of Sir Thomas J. Pittar, KCB, CMG; one *s*. *Educ:* Merchant Taylors' School; Trinity College, Cambridge; Mathematical Tripos Part I, 1897, Second Wrangler; Part 2, 1898, Cl. 1, Div. 1; BA 1897; MA 1901; ScD 1929. Assistant Master Merchant Taylors' School, 1899–1912; Meteorological Office, 1912; Assistant-Director Meteorological Office and Superintendent of Kew Observatory, 1925–39; retd 1939; Pres. R. Meteorological Soc., 1936–38. *Address:* 6 Addison Road, Chiswick, W4. *T:* Chiswick 2160.

Died 25 Sept. 1943.

WHITAKER, Col Sir Albert Edward, 1st Bt *cr* 1936; Kt 1928; CBE 1919; TD; DL, JP; Lord High Steward of East Retford; Chairman Retford Hospital; *b* 1860; *m* 1896, Eileen, MBE, *d* of Col J. Croker; one *s*. *Educ:* Harrow. Served Afghan War, 1879–80; Egypt, 1915–16. *Recreations:* shooting, fishing, hunting, polo, cricket. Heir: *s* Maj.-Gen. John Albert Charles Whitaker, CB, CBE. *Address:* Babworth Hall, Retford, Notts. *T:* Retford 54; Auchnafree Lodge, Dunkeld, Scotland. *Clubs:* Carlton, Naval and Military.

Died 11 June 1945.

WHITAKER, Sir Cuthbert Wilfrid, Kt 1946; FSA; Editor of Whitaker's Almanack; *b* 26 May 1873; *y s* of J. Whitaker, FSA, White Lodge, Enfield; *m* 1909, Ella, *d* of late Charles Dinham, Broadhurst Gardens, Hampstead; three *d*. *Educ:* Lancing; University College, Oxford. Common Councilman, City of London, 1905; Member of Lieutenancy since 1921; Chief Commoner, 1924; Chairman of Special Committee since 1930, and of City of London Food Control Committee, since 1940. Lieut-Col late 3rd Bn King's Regt (Liverpool); served in France and North Russia. *Address:* 13 Bedford Square, WC1. *Clubs:* Athenæum, Junior United Service.

Died 4 April 1950.

WHITAKER, James; JP; *b* 1863; *e s* of late John Whitaker of Broadclough and Winsley, and 1st wife Elizabeth Ann, *d* of Robert Munn; *m* 1905, Hon. Mary Isabella Sophia Louisa Weld Forester, *y d* of 5th Lord Forester; one *d.* *Educ:* Rugby. Major late Montgomeryshire Imperial Yeomanry; was Captain 20th Hussars; Lord of the Manor of Westbury; High Sheriff of Shropshire, 1921. *Address:* Winsley, near Shrewsbury. *T:* Minsterley 6. *Club:* Cavalry.

Died 18 March 1946.

WHITBREAD, Francis Pelham; *b* 16 Oct. 1867; 3rd *s* of late Samuel Whitbread and Lady Isabella Charlotte, *d* of 3rd Earl of Chichester; *m* 1894, Hon. Ida Madeleine Agnes, 2nd *d* of 4th Baron Sudeley; one *s* one *d.* *Educ:* Eton; Trinity College, Cambridge. Barrister (Inner Temple), 1891; Managing Director, Whitbread & Co. Ltd, since 1892; Chairman Brewers' Society, 1905–07; Chairman and Treasurer National Trade Defence Association since 1907; Master Brewers Company, 1907–08; Chairman of Governing Body of Aldenham School since 1912; President, Institute of Brewing, 1913–15; Vice-Chairman, National Society for the Prevention of Cruelty to Children, since 1911; Governor since 1910, and Treasurer since 1924, of Guy's Hospital; Chairman, Royal Society for the Assistance of Discharged Prisoners, since 1916; President, Central Discharged Prisoners' Aid Society, since 1921. *Recreations:* fishing, shooting. *Address:* 36 Hans Place, SW1. *T:* Kensington 2537. *Clubs:* Brooks's, Arthur's, Beefsteak.

Died 29 Oct. 1941.

WHITBREAD, Samuel Howard, CB 1917; Chairman, Messrs Whitbread & Co., Ltd; Alderman Bedfordshire County Council; *b* 8 Jan. 1858; *e s* of late Samuel Whitbread and Lady Isabella Charlotte, *d* of 3rd Earl of Chichester; *m* 1904, Madeleine, *d* of Maj. Hon. Edward Bourke; two *s.* *Educ:* Eton; Trinity College, Cambridge. MP (L) Luton Division, Bedfordshire, 1892–95; Huntingdon Div., Hunts, 1906–; late HM Lieut; late President Bedfordshire TA Association; late Chairman, Quarter Sessions, Bedfordshire. *Address:* Southill, Biggleswade; 9 Montagu Square, W1. *T:* Welbeck 2049.

Died 29 July 1944.

WHITE, Adam Seaton, BSc; FSAM; Principal, Cheltenham School of Art, and Director of Art for County of Gloucester; *s* of late Prof. Philip J. White, MB, FRSE, FZS; *m* 1930, Gwendolen M. Jones, ARCA *d* of late Alderman A. E. Jones. *Educ:* University College of North Wales; Slade School of Art, University of London. Staff Officer for Reconnaissance, Royal Artillery 9th Corps; Prix de Rome (Sculpture) finalist, 1923; Sculptural designs executed for Royal Institute of British Architects Building, New University Library, Cambridge, Union of Home Students, Oxford, New Bodleian Library, Oxford, Electricity Building, Bristol, etc.; Vice-Pres. Cheltenham Group of Artists; Ex-Pres. National Society of Art Masters. *Address:* 2 Queensholme, Pittville Circus Road, Cheltenham. *T:* Cheltenham 4369.

Died 30 Jan. 1950.

WHITE, Alfred George Hastings, CBE 1937; Consulting Librarian to the Royal Society; *b* 1859; *s* of Dr Henry White, MA; *m* 1929, Beatrice Lewis; no *c.* *Publication:* Stukeley's Memoirs of Sir Isaac Newton, 1936. *Address:* 57 Princes Avenue, W3. *T:* Acorn 3686.

Died 8 July 1945.

WHITE, Sir Archibald Woollaston, 4th Bt *cr* 1802; *b* 14 Oct. 1877; *s* of late W. K. H. R. White, 2nd *s* of 2nd Bt, and Edith Laura, *d* of late Rev. Archibald Paris; *S* uncle, 1907; *m* 1903, Gladys Becher, *d* of Rev. E. A. B. Pitman; three *s.* *Educ:* Wellington College; Trinity College, Cambridge. *Heir: s* Thomas Astley Woollaston,

[*b* 13 May 1904; *m* 1935, Daphne Margaret, *er d* of Lt-Col F. R. I. Athill, CMG]. *Address:* Torhouse Muir, Wigtownshire. *T:* Wigtown 38.

Died 16 Dec. 1945.

WHITE, Lt-Col Arthur Denham-, CIE 1944; MB, BS Lond.; FRCS Ed.; IMS retd; Hon. Visiting MO to Presidency General Hospital, Calcutta, from 1940; Hon. Physician to Governor of Bengal from 1939; *b* 26 Feb. 1879; English parentage; *m* 1921, Evelyn, *widow* of F. G. Geary, ICS; one *d.* *Educ:* Malvern College; St Bartholomew's Hospital. Army Gold Medallist. Entered IMS 1905; served European War in Mesopotamia; officiated as Professor of Surgery in Medical College, Calcutta, 1924; Civil Surgeon, Darjeeling, 1919–22; retired, 1934 and continued consulting practice in Calcutta. *Recreation:* fishing. *Address:* c/o Lloyds Bank Ltd, Bond St, W1; 4 Asoka Road, Calcutta. *Clubs:* Oriental, East India and Sports.

Died 19 Aug. 1950.

WHITE, Maj.-Gen. Arthur Thomas, CMG 1918; VD; (retired) AAMC; *b* Torquay, 27 Oct. 1860; 2nd *s* of John William White, London; *m* 1896, May Sophia, *d* of Dr C. H. Elliott; three *s.* *Educ:* Torquay; Dublin. Qualified LRCP and SE 1884. Arrived in Australia, 1888; Medical Officer to local forces with rank of Captain, 1896; Major, 1904; Lt-Col 1907; enlisted for active service, Aug. 1914; CO No. 2 Australian Stationary Hospital which left Australia for Overseas, 1914; ADMS at Tel-el-Kebir, 1916; ADMS of 3rd Australian Division with rank of Colonel, 1916; served with the Division in France until March 1918; also served Gallipoli and Egypt (CMG, despatches). *Recreations:* boating and riding. *Clubs:* Naval and Military, Perth.

Died 13 June 1947.

WHITE, Sir Ernest, Kt 1932; JP; Director, Norvic Shoe Co. Ltd Shoe Manufacturers; *b* Norwich, 6 Feb. 1867; *s* of Sir George White, Kt, Norwich, and Anne Ransome; *m* 1897, Frances Evelyn Copeland; one *s.* *Educ:* King Edward VI Grammar School, Norwich. Joined firm of Howlett and White, 1885; Elected to City Council, 1915; Sheriff for City of Norwich, 1916–17; Lord Mayor of Norwich, 1931; Chairman of the Arbitration Board for Boot and Shoe Industry for Norwich and District, 1912–47. *Recreations:* golf, gardening, and horticulture. *Address:* Eaton House, Norwich. *T:* Eaton 15 Norwich. *Club:* National Liberal.

Died 26 Jan. 1949.

WHITE, Col Frank Augustin Kinder, CMG 1919; DSO 1918; RE (retired); *b* 1873; *s* of Capt. C. A. White; *m* Winifred, *d* of Spencer Harrison, Wolverton House, Bucks. Served European War, 1914–19 (despatches, DSO, CMG). *Address:* Benham Grange, Newbury Berks. *Club:* United Service.

Died 17 March 1948.

WHITE, Col Hon. Gerald Verner, CBE 1918; VD; Member of the Senate of Canada since 1919; *b* Pembroke, Ontario, 6 July 1879; *s* of late Hon. Peter White, PC, MP, and Janet Reid Thomson; *m* 1906, Mary Elizabeth Trites, Petitcodiac, NB; one *d.* *Educ:* McGill University, Montreal, BSc. Spent three years in British Columbia and in Nova Scotia, mining; engaged in lumbering, 1904–21; MP North Renfrew, 1906 (bye-election); re-elected, 1908–11; served Overseas as Director of timber operations Canadian Forestry Corps, 1916–19, with rank of Colonel; Hon. Lieut-Col of Lanark and Renfrew Scottish Regiment; Director of several companies; Fellow Royal Colonial Institute. *Recreations:* tennis, golf. *Address:* Pembroke, Ontario, Canada. *Clubs:* Rideau, Royal Ottawa Golf, Ottawa; University, United Services, Montreal.

Died 24 Oct. 1948.

WHITE, Ven. Graham, OBE 1941; MA; Hon. CF; Archdeacon of Singapore and Chaplain-in-charge St Andrew's Cathedral since 1931; *b* Winchester, 1884; 4th *s* of late Henry White, Solicitor; *m* 1919, Georgina, *d* of George Miller, Leicester. *Educ:* Winchester College; University College, Oxford. Deacon, 1907; Priest, 1908; Vicar of Dawdon, Co. Durham, 1920–25; Ipoh, FMS, 1925; Commissary to the Bishop of Singapore, 1934 and 1937–38; to the Archbishop of Canterbury, 1941. *Recreations:* visiting and travel. *Address:* Cathedral House, Cavenagh Road, Singapore, SS. *T:* Singapore 6187. *Club:* Church Imperial.

Died 8 May 1945.

WHITE, Rt Rev. Harry Vere; *b* 1853; *s* of Rev. H. Vere White, Dublin; *m* 1879, Alice, *d* of G. T. Meredith; two *s* one *d.* *Educ:* Academic Institute and Trinity College, Dublin. Ordained for Curacy of Ardbraccan, 1878; accepted work in New Zealand, 1879; returned thence in 1885 to Ireland, where he has resided since; Rector of Almoritia, 1885–88; Killesk, 1888–94; Secretary of SPG, 1894–1901; Secretary of Incorporated Society, 1901–05; Treasurer of St Patrick's Cathedral, Dublin, 1902–11; Chancellor of St Patrick's Cathedral, Dublin, 1911–18; Chaplain to the Lord-Lieutenant, 1900–18; Hon. Chaplain to Archbishop of Dublin, 1915–18; Vicar of St Bartholomew's, 1905–18; Archdeacon of Dublin, 1917–18; Dean of Christ Church Cathedral, 1918–21; Bishop of Limerick, 1921–33; Hon. Secretary of the General Synod, 1918–21; Select Preacher before University of Dublin, 1904, 1915, 1920, and 1924; retired, 1933. *Publications:* Children of St Columba: a History of the SPG in Ireland; Bishop Jebb of Limerick; Pamphlets on the Temperance question, on lives of Bishop Inglis and Bishop Berkeley, and various sermons. *Address:* 4 Ailesbury Road, Dublin. *T:* Ballsbridge, Dublin 805.

Died 20 Jan. 1941.

WHITE, Sir Herbert Edward, KCMG 1917; CMG 1905; *b* 30 Oct. 1855; *s* of Horace P. White, late HM Consul at Tangier; *m* 1887, Helen, *d* of late Roderick Hugonin, JP, of Kinmvlies House, Inverness; one *s* one *d.* *Educ:* Uppingham; St John's College, Cambridge (MA; honours in Historical Tripos). Clerk to Legation at Tangier, 1882; Consul, 1885–1907; HBM Consul-General for Morocco, 1908, with local rank of 2nd Secretary in Diplomatic Service, 1895, and of 1st Secretary in Diplomatic Service, 1906; HBM Agent for Morocco, 1914; retired, 1921; Jubilee medal, 1887; British Representative at the Conference at Madrid for the Internationalisation of Tangier, 1912 and 1913; Coronation medal, 1911; Commander of the Legion of d'Honneur. *Address:* Villa Tingitana, Saint Jean-de-Luz, Basses Pyrénées, France. *Club:* Travellers'.

Died 7 June 1947.

WHITE, John, RI 1884; ROI; *b* Edinburgh, 18 Sept. 1851; *m* 1876, Emma Homewood Sanders; six *s* two *d.* *Educ:* Dr Brunton's School, Melbourne, Australia. Winner of Keith prize at Royal Scottish Academy for design, 1875. Parents emigrated to Australia, 1856; entered schools of Royal Scottish Academy, Edinburgh, 1871; migrated south, 1877; has since been painting and exhibiting regularly at Royal Academy and at Royal Institute of Painters in Water Colours. *Recreations:* amateur carpentry, and an occasional game at cricket or golf. *Address:* 21 Park Road, Beer E Devon.

Died 21 Dec. 1933.

WHITE, Maj.-Gen. John Burton, CBE 1943; DSO; ED; Vice-Pres., Canadian International Paper Co., Montreal, since 1925; also Director, etc., of other companies; *b* 1 Jan. 1874; *s* of Henry White and Amelia Kelly; *m* 1906, Margaret Jane Ferguson; two *s.* *Educ:* High School and Business College, Ottawa. Hull Lumber Co., Ottawa, 1896–1904; Woods Manager, G. H. Perley & Co., Ottawa and Calumet, Quebec, 1904–09; Director and Manager, Woods and Sawmills,

Riordon Pulp & Paper Co., Ltd, Montreal, 1909–24. Served European War, 1915–18 (despatches, DSO); in command overseas of Canadian Forestry Corps, 1940–43; Past Pres. Canadian Pulp & Paper Assoc., Canadian Lumbermen's Assoc., Canadian Forestry Assoc., and Quebec Forest Industries Assoc. *Recreations:* golf and fishing. *Address:* 630 Carlton Avenue, Westmount, Quebec. *Clubs:* St James's, Royal Montreal Golf, Montreal; Rideau, Ottawa, etc.

Died 31 May 1945.

WHITE, Lt-Col John Henry, CMG 1917; VD; MICE; *b* 1868; *s* of late Nicholas White; *m* 1903, Louisa Winifred (*d* 1936), *d* of J. H. Gartrell; four *s.* *Educ:* Coopers Hill. Entered PWD, India, 1891; retired, 1923; Director of Railways, Mesopotamia, 1916–17 (despatches CMG); was Chief Engineer, Indian State Railways, and Agent, E Bengal Railway. *Address:* Le Bocage, Springfield, Jersey Channel Islands. *Club:* East India and Sports.

Died 27 Aug. 1942.

WHITE, P. Bruce, FRS 1941; member of scientific staff, National Institute for Medical Research, Hampstead. *Address:* National Institute for Medical Research, Mount Vernon, NW3.

Died 19 March 1949.

WHITE, Col Reginald Strelley Moresby, CBE 1942; OBE 1931; *b* 22 Feb. 1893; *s* of Lt-Col R. F. Moresby White, OBE, VD, Grantham; unmarried. *Educ:* Malvern College; Brasenose College, Oxford (Exhibitioner, BA). 2nd Lt Leicestershire Regt, Sept. 1914; psc; Brevet Major, 1931; served Kurdistan, 1931; Lt-Col, 1939; Commandant (local Colonel), Ceylon Defence Force, 1939; retired 1946, with Hon. rank of Col. *Recreations:* Past: Association football, Harlequin and Army, cricket, squash racquets. Present: golf. *Clubs:* United Service, MCC, I Zingari, Corinthians.

Died 3 March 1947.

WHITE, Col Richard Stephen Murray-, CBE 1926; DSO 1917; *b* 1876; *s* of late Capt. S. Murray-White; *m* 1906, Gwendolen (*d* 1941), *y d* of late J. Latimer, Southampton; one *s* three *d.* Served Bechuanaland, 1896 (medal with clasp); S African War, 1899–1902 (despatches twice, two medals with seven clasps); European War, 1914–18 (despatches, DSO); commanded 156th West Scottish Infantry Brigade, Territorial Army, 1923–27. *Address:* Ivy Lodge, Hounslow.

Died 21 Feb. 1942.

WHITE, Wilbert Webster, DD, PhD; Director, Columbiona-on-Lake George, Silver Bay, New York; *b* 16 Jan. 1863; *s* of John M. White and Martha Ann Campbell; *m* 1885, Ella Henderson, St Clairsville, O; one *s* one *d.* *Educ:* College of Wooster, Ohio, AB 1881; AM 1884; Xenia Theological Seminary graduated 1885; Yale University, PhD 1891. Ordained United Presbyterian Ministry 1885; Pastor, United Presbyterian Church, Peotone, Ill, 1885–86; Prof. of Hebrew and Old Testament Literature, Xenia Theological Seminary, 1890–95; Associate Director, Moody Bible Institute, 1895–97; Bible work (teaching) India and England, 1897–1900; Bible work (teaching) in China, Japan and Korea, summers, 1910, 1911, 1912; Founder, The Biblical Seminary in New York, and President, 1900–40; Hon. President since 1940; President and Founder, Columbiona-on-Lake George, 1925. *Publications:* Thirty Studies in the Gospel by John, 1895; Thirty Studies in the Revelation, 1897; Inductive Studies in the Minor Prophets, 1894; Thirty Studies in Jeremiah, 1895; Studies in Old Testament Characters, 1900; Thirty Studies in the Gospel by Matthew, 1903; The Resurrection Body, 1923; Numerous pamphlets, etc. *Address:* Columbiona-on-Lake George, Silver Bay, NY, USA.

Died 12 Aug. 1944.

WHITE, Rt Rev. William Charles, DD, DCL; *b* Trinity, Newfoundland, 31 Aug. 1865; *s* of Dr Robert White; *m* 1891, Frederica Thorne Bayly; two *s* two *d*. *Educ:* Church of England Academy, St John's, Newfoundland; St Augustine's College, Canterbury. Deacon, 1888, and Curate to late Rev. Æ C. Bayly, Rural Dean at Bonavista; Priest, 1890; Vicar of Fogo, 1890–1900; Rector of Heart's Content, 1900–08; Rector of the Cathedral Parish, and Canon and sub-Dean, 1908; Bishop of Newfoundland, 1918–42. *Address:* Church Hill, St John's, Newfoundland.
Died 14 June 1943.

WHITE, Sir William H.; *see* Hale-White.

WHITE, Rev. Wilson Woodhouse, MA; Rector of Gunton and Vicar of Hanworth; *b* 28 April 1864; *s* of Henry White, late Rector of Brockdish, and Catherine Sowdon; *m* 1894, late Edith Isabella, 2nd *d* of late Rev. E. H. Morton; one *s* (killed in the war). *Educ:* St Paul's College, Stony Stratford; Norwich School; Selwyn College, Cambridge. Curate of Tooting, Graveney, 1887–93; Chaplain to Duke of Buccleuch at Langholm, 1893–1903; Curate of Brockdish, 1903–05; Rector of Brockdish, 1906–27; Rural Dean of Redenhall, 1915–27; Honorary Canon of Norwich Cathedral, 1934. *Recreations:* cricket, golf, tennis. *Address:* Gunton with Hanworth Rectory, Norwich, Norfolk. *TA:* Hanworth Norfolk.
Died 3 Jan. 1941.

WHITE-JERVIS; *see* Jervis.

WHITE-SMITH, Sir Henry, Kt 1921; CBE 1918; Chevalier Légion d'Honneur; *b* 6 July 1878; *s* of late W. G. Smith; *m*; three *s* two *d*. *Educ:* privately. First Chairman the Society of British Aircraft Constructors, Ltd; Member of first Govt Advisory Committee on Civil Aviation; was Commercial Delegate representing the British Aircraft Industry on the International Air Convention of the Peace Conference, occupying position of Vice-Chairman to Legal and Commercial Sub-Commission; was Member of Government Civil Aerial Transport Committee. *Recreations:* golf, fishing. *Address:* 17 Ennismore Gardens, SW7. *T:* Kensington 7266; Court Lodge, Hooe, near Battle. *T:* Cooden 256. *Clubs:* Royal Aero, Conservative.
Died 26 Dec. 1943.

WHITEHEAD, Alfred North, OM 1945; FRS 1903; FBA 1931; ScD; Hon. DSc (Manchester University); Hon. LLD St Andrews and University of Wisconsin; Hon. ScD Harvard, Yale and Montreal; Professor Emeritus, Harvard University, Professor of Philosophy, 1924–37; Fellow, late Senior Mathematical Lecturer, Trinity College, Cambridge; Professor Emeritus of Imperial College, London; Council of Royal Society, 1914–15; Governor of Borough Polytechnic, Southwark; sometime Senator of University of London and Dean of Faculty of Science; Chairman of the Academic Council, Chairman of the Delegacy Administering Goldsmith's College; President of the Mathematical Association, 1915–16; President of Section A, British Association, 1916; Tarner Lecturer Trinity College, 1919; Gifford Lecturer, Edinburgh University, 1927–28; 1st recipient James Scott Prize, Royal Society, Edin., 1922; Sylvester Medal, Royal Society, London, 1925; Butler Medal, Columbia University, New York, 1930; *b* 15 Feb. 1861; *s* of Canon Whitehead, Vicar of St Peter's, Isle of Thanet; *m* Evelyn, *d* of late Capt. A. Wade, Seaforth Highlanders; one *s* one *d*. *Educ:* Sherborne School; Trinity Coll. Camb. Lecturer, Applied Mathematics and Mechanics, and later, Reader in Geometry, University College, London, 1911–14; Professor of Applied Mathematics, Imperial College of Science, 1914–24. *Publications:* A Treatise on Universal Algebra, 1898; Science and the Modern World, 1926; The Aims of Education, 1929; Process and Reality, An Essay in Cosmology, 1929; Adventures of Ideas, 1933;

Nature and Life, 1934; Modes of Thought, 1938; Religion in the Making, 1926; Symbolism; The Function of Reason; Memoirs on Algebra Symbolic Logic in American Journal of Mathematics vols XXIII–XXV; Mathematical Concepts of the Material World, Phil. Trans. RS, 1906; articles Mathematics, Axioms of Geometry, and Non-Euclidean Geometry in new edition of Ency. Brit., and other scientific memoirs; Introduction to Mathematics; The Organisation of Thought; Principles of Natural Knowledge, 1919; The Concept of Nature, 1920; The Principle of Relativity; The Rhythm of Education; and with Earl Russell, Principia Mathematica. *Address:* Harvard University and 1737 Cambridge Street, Cambridge, Mass, USA. *Club:* Athenæum.
Died 30 Dec. 1947.

WHITEHEAD, Rt Rev. Henry, DD; *b* 19 Dec. 1853; *m* 1903, Isabel, CBE, *d* of Canon Duncan; one *s*. *Educ:* Sherborne; Trinity College, Oxford (Fellow; Lecturer, 1878–83). Ordained 1879; Principal of Bishop's College, Calcutta, 1883–99; Superior of the Oxford Mission, Calcutta, 1890–99; Bishop of Madras, 1899–1922; Hon. Fellow, Trinity Coll., Oxford, 1920. Ordained 1879; Principal of Bishop's College, Calcutta, 1883–99; Superior of the Oxford Mission, Calcutta, 1890–99; Bishop of Madras, 1899–1922; Hon. Fellow, Trinity Coll., Oxford, 1920. *Publications:* The Village Gods of South India, 1916, Indian Problems in Religion, Education, Politics, 1924; Christ in the Indian Villages, 1930; Christian Education in India, 1932. *Address:* Pincent's Hill, Calcot, Reading.
Died 14 April 1947.

WHITEHEAD, Sir Rowland Edward, 3rd Bt *cr* 1889; KC 1910; *b* 1 Sept. 1863; 2nd *s* of Sir James Whitehead, 1st Bart; *S* brother, 1931; *m* 1893, Ethel M. L., *d* of late Philip H. Rathbone; two *s* two *d*. *Educ:* Clifton College; University College, Oxon, Second Class Classical Moderations; First Class Final History; MA. One of HM's Lieutenants for the City of London; late Chairman of Council of Clifton College; Member of Committee on Work of National Importance, 1916–19; Lieut 2nd Vol. Bn City of London Regt; Bencher of Lincoln's Inn; MP (L) SE Essex, 1906–10; Private Secretary (unpaid) to Right Hon. Herbert Samuel, MP, 1906–09; Parliamentary Secretary (unpaid) to the Attorney-General, 1909–10; JP Berks; formerly Berks County Council. *Heir:* *s* Major Philip Henry Rathbone, *b* 24 July 1897. *Address:* White Cross, Wallingford.
Died 9 Oct. 1942.

WHITEHOUSE, Arthur Wildman, MA; Principal, Glasgow Veterinary College since 1922; Member of Council RCVS since 1926. Vice-President, 1939–41, President, 1941–42; *b* 25 Sept. 1865; *s* of Edward Orange Wildman Whitehouse and Hannah Statham; *m* 1892, Sara (*d* 1939), *d* of Samuel Shreve, New York; no *c*. *Educ:* Winchester College; Oriel Coll., Oxford; Ontario Veterinary Coll., Toronto. Veterinary Department State Agricultural College, Colorado, USA; Veterinary Department University of Liverpool. Owned and conducted horse and cattle ranches in Wyoming and Colorado, USA; engaged in general veterinary practice in Laramie, Wyoming, Walden and Boulder, Colorado, USA; taught Veterinary Anatomy at Veterinary Department State Agricultural College, Fort Collins, Colorado, USA, and at Glasgow Veterinary College; Captain US Army Veterinary Corps, France; VS Ontario Veterinary College; DVS State Ag. Coll. Colo USA (Doctor), MRCVS. *Recreation:* anything to do with horses. *Address:* Glasgow Veterinary College. *T:* Douglas 0419. *Clubs:* Conservative, Glasgow.
Died 23 May 1944.

WHITEHOUSE, Sir Harold Beckwith, Kt 1937; Professor of Midwifery and Diseases of Women, University of Birmingham, and Hon. Gynæcological Surgeon to General and Queen Elizabeth Hospitals,

Birmingham; Hon. Surgeon to Maternity Hospital, Birmingham; Consulting Obstetric Physician to the Lucy Baldwin Maternity Hospital, and the Worcestershire County Council; Consulting Obstetric Physician to Hammerwich Cottage Hospital; Consulting Gynæcological Surgeon to the Smallwood Hospital, Redditch, the General Hospital, Nuneaton, and the Sutton Cottage Hospital; sometime Examiner in Midwifery and Diseases of Women to Royal College of Surgeons (England), Universities of Sheffield, Bristol and Wales, Central Midwives Board, etc; *b* Ocker Hill, Staffs, 26 Oct. 1882; *s* of late Michael J. Whitehouse of Montrose, Portman Crescent, Bournemouth and Mary A. Whitehouse; *m* 1909, Madge Rae, *d* of late Walter Griffith of the Friary, Handsworth Wood; two *s* one *d*. *Educ:* Malvern College; St Thomas's Hospital, London (First Entrance Science Scholarship); William Tite Scholarship, 1902; Bachelor of Medicine and Bachelor of Surgery of University of London, 1906; Sutton Sams Memorial Prize for work in Obstetric Medicine and Diseases of Women, 1906; MS, London, 1908; qualified for Gold Medal in Surgery, FRCS Eng. President British Medical Assoc.; Hon. Member Canadian Medical Assoc., 1937; Hon. FACS 1933; Hunterian Professor, Royal College of Surgeons of England, 1913–14; Ingleby Lecturer, University of Birmingham, 1920; at the outbreak of war, 1914; received a temporary commission in the RAMC, and proceeded to France with the British Expeditionary Force on 20 Aug. 1914; served in France as Officer in charge of the Surgical Division, and Surgical Specialist to No. 8 General Hospital, Rouen, and to No. 56 General Hospital, Etaples, 1917; Member of Radium Commission of Great Britain, 1933–37. *Publications:* various scientific papers to the Lancet, British Medical Journal, Proceedings of the Royal Society of Medicine and Medical Annual, etc.; editor, fourth edition Eden and Lockyer's Gynæcology, 1935. *Recreations:* botany, entomology, shooting. *Address:* 62 Hagley Road, Edgbaston, Birmingham. *T:* Birmingham, Edgbaston 0852; Grey Friars, Edgbaston, Birmingham; High Glanau, Trellech, Mon. *Club:* Athenæum.

Died 28 July 1943.

WHITEHOUSE, Sir Julian Osborn, Kt 1942; JP Staffs; Chairman of the Staffordshire County Council since 1941; *b* 1876; *m* 1900, Florence, *e d* of late W. H. Gallatley, JP; three *s*. Chairman Staffordshire Education Committee, 1928–41. *Address:* Woodstock, Cannock, Staffs. *T:* Cannock 3331.

Died 24 Nov. 1942.

WHITELAW, William; *b* 15 March 1868; 3rd *s* of late Alex. Whitelaw of Gartshore, Dumbartonshire; *m* 1890, Gertrude, *d* of late T. C. Thompson, Milton Hall, Cumberland; two *d*. *Educ:* Harrow; Trinity College, Cambridge (BA). MP (C) Perth City, 1892–95; Director, Bank of Scotland; Director, Forth Bridge Railway Company. *Address:* Hatton House, Kirknewton, Midlothian. *Club:* Conservative.

Died 19 Jan. 1946.

WHITELEY, Cecil; KC 1921; JP, DL; Common Serjeant of City of London since 1934; a Governor of Dulwich College; Bencher Middle Temple; *b* 10 May 1875; 2nd *s* of late George Crispe Whiteley, MA, of The Chestnuts, Dulwich Common, SE. *Educ:* Dulwich College; King's College, Cambridge; BA 1897; MA 1898. Called to Bar, Middle Temple, 1900; Recorder of Sandwich, 1920–29; West Ham, 1929–30; Southend-on-Sea, 1930; Chairman of the London Quarter Sessions, 1931–32; Judge of Mayor's and City of London Court, 1932–34; late Chairman of Surrey Quarter Sessions; Referee under Safeguarding of Industries and Finance Acts, 1928; Commissioner of Assize, 1930; Junior Counsel to the Treasury at Central Criminal

Court, 1912–21. *Publications:* Whiteley's Licensing Laws; Brief Life, 1942. *Address:* Park Lane Hotel, W1. *T:* Grosvenor 6321. *Clubs:* Brooks's, Beefsteak.

Died 15 Oct. 1942.

WHITELEY, Brig. John Percival, OBE 1940; TD; MP (Nat. U.) Buckingham Division since 1937; *s* of Frank Whiteley, CMG, JP, Ilkley, Yorkshire; *m* 1925, Amy Beatrice, *d* of H. G. Tetley, Alderbrook, Surrey; three *s*. *Educ:* Shrewsbury School; R. Military Acad., Woolwich. Entered R. Artillery, 1916; Transferred to Life Guards, 1926; Retired, 1928; JP (Bucks), 1930. *Recreations:* hunting, shooting, fishing, cricket. *Address:* The Grange, Bletchley; 49 Hallam Street, W1. *T:* Bletchley 4, Langham 2759. *Clubs:* Carlton, Cavalry, Naval and Military.

Died 4 July 1943.

WHITESIDE, Borras Noel Hamilton; local West End Director of London and Scottish Assurance Co. Ltd; Director of Hunting Aerosurveys Ltd, and of Percival Aircraft; *b* 1903; *s* of late Captain and Hon. Mrs Borras Whiteside; *g s* of 9th Lord Belhaven and Stenton; *m* 1935, Dorothy Mai, *o d* of late John Farrington, Resident Rotuman; one *d*. *Educ:* Wellington College; University Coll., London. MP (U) South Leeds, 1931–35; Asst Hon. Sec. Parliamentary Air Committee, 1934–35; Assist London Divisional Food Officer, Sept. 1939; Principal at Board of Trade, 1941; Dep. to Principal Director, Salvage and Recovery, Ministry of Supply, 1942. *Recreations:* flying, swimming, squash. *Address:* 87 Cadogan Gardens, SW3. *T:* Kensington 6401. *Clubs:* Carlton, United, Royal Aero.

Died 13 June 1948.

WHITESIDE, Surg. Rear-Adm. Henry Cadman, CB 1929; retired; late Medical Superintendent Mount Vernon War Emergency Hospital; *s* of late Robert Whiteside, Isle of Man; *m* Ellen Muriel, *d* of late H. Jackson, 4 Sussex Place, NW; no *c*. *Educ:* King William's College, IOM; Middle sex Hospital. Joined Navy Medical Service, 1898; Surgeon Captain, 1923; Surgeon Rear-Admiral, 1927; served South African War, 1899–1902; General Service, Persian Gulf, 1910–12; European War, 1914–18; in charge Royal Naval Hospital, Haslar, 1929–32; Danish Order of Dannebrog, 1922. *Address:* 20 Festing Road, Southsea, Hants.

Died 19 May 1949.

WHITFIELD, Arthur, MD (Lond.), FRCP, MRCS; Emeritus Professor of Dermatology, King's College, London; Consulting Physician to Skin Department of King's College Hospital and to Queen Alexandra's Military Hospital; *s* of late George Whitfield, of 28 Nottingham Place, W; *m* Margaret, *e d* of late Charles Tuttle, Rochester, NY; one *s* two *d*. *Educ:* King's College School and College (Fellow). Lumleian Lecturer, Royal College of Physicians, 1921. *Publications:* A Handbook of Skin Diseases; articles on various skin diseases, Encyclopædia Medica; and to Allbutt's System of Medicine; and numerous papers on Skin Diseases in medical journals. *Recreation:* golf. *Address:* (temp.): Walk Wood, Burke's Road, Beaconsfield, Bucks.

Died 31 Jan. 1947.

WHITHAM, Air Cdre (Temp. Air Vice-Marshal) Robert Parker Musgrave, CB 1942; OBE 1934; MC; RAF; Director of War Organization, Air Ministry; *b* 1895; *s* of late Robert Musgrave, Craven Lodge, Burnley; *m* 1939, Margaret, *d* of Abraham Nutter, Burnley; one *d*. *Educ:* Burnley Grammar School; Manchester University. Served European War, 1914–18, Northumberland Fusiliers and RFC (MC); transferred to RAF, 1919 (mention); Commendation, 1941.

Died 22 March 1943.

WHITING, Arthur John, MD, MRCP; Consulting Physician to the Prince of Wales's General Hospital, London, N; Consulting Physician to King Edward Memorial Cottage Hospital, Hendon, NW; Physician to the City Dispensary; Vice-President, late Hon. Secretary, Fellowship of Medicine and Post-Graduate Medical Association, London. *Educ:* privately; University of Edinburgh; Middlesex Hospital. Resident Physician, Royal Edinburgh Infirmary; Assistant Professor of Physiology and of Clinical Medicine in the University of Edinburgh; House Physician and Medical Registrar to the National Hospital for the Paralysed and Epileptic, London; Physician to the Mount Vernon Hospital for Consumption and other Diseases of the Chest, London; sometime President, Dean and Lecturer in the NE London Post-Graduate College; gold medallist for the MD degree, Murchison Memorial scholar, Goodsir prizeman. *Publications:* Book on Medical Diagnosis (5th ed., 1939); scientific and medical papers in the Transactions of the Royal Society of Edinburgh, Proceedings Royal Society of Medicine, Brain, the Lancet, British Medical Journal, Post-Graduate Medical Journal, and other English and foreign medical publications. *Recreations:* walking, reading, water-colour sketching, etc. *Address:* 14 Welbeck Street, W1. *T:* Welbeck 9441.

Died 9 Feb. 1941.

WHITING, William Robert Gerald, MBE 1918; MA; MInstCE; Royal Corps of Naval Constructors (temp.); Warship Production Superintendent, East Coast of Scotland; *b* London, 15 May 1884; *e s* of late W. H. Whiting, CB; *m* 1911, Irene Helena, *e d* of late Emeritus Professor Henry Stroud; two *s* one *d*. *Educ:* Mill Hill; Queens' College, Cambridge, 2nd Class Mechanical Sciences Tripos, 1906; Order of Sa. Sava 3rd Class, 1928, for services to Kingdom of Serbs, Croats, and Slovenes. Member of Council Inst. Naval Architects; General Manager, Sir W. G. Armstrong-Whitworth & Co. (Shipbuilders), Ltd, Newcastle on Tyne, 1928–34. *Publications:* The Newcastle Galley of 1295, Arch. Ael., 1936; Professional papers in Transactions of above Societies and Engineering Press. *Address:* 30 Victoria Square, Newcastle-on-Tyne. *T:* Jesmond 2663.

Died 5 Sept. 1947.

WHITLEY, William Thomas, MA, LLM (Cambridge), LLD (Melbourne); FRHistS; Council, Baptist Union; Committee, Northern Baptist Education Society; President, Baptist Historical Society; *b* 16 May 1861; *s* of Thomas Whitley, London merchant; *m* 1st, 1889, A. E. Goodman of Belvedere; 2nd, 1897, Sarah, *d* of Alderman John Walker, Melbourne, Australia; two *s* three *d*. *Educ:* Univ. College School; King's College, Cambridge; Rawdon College, Leeds. Principal, Baptist College of Victoria, 1891–1902, and Lecturer, Queen's College, University of Melbourne; Minister at Preston, 1902; Droitwich, 1917–28; winter visiting Indian Missions, whence Hon. Sec. Victorian Baptist Foreign Missions, 1896–1902; nine visits to study education in Canada and USA. *Publications:* Works of John Smyth, 1594–1612; Baptist Bibliography, 1526–1837; Minutes of the General Assembly, 1654–1811; History of British Baptists; Baptists of North-West England; Church, Ministry and Sacraments in the New Testament; Missionary Achievement; Roman Catholic and Protestant Bibles; The Story of Droitwich; Studies in Modern Christendom; Baptists of London; The Work of a Minister; Calvinism and Evangelism; Congregational Hymn-Singing; Handbook to the Baptist Church Hymnal; The English Bible under the Tudor Sovereigns. *Recreation:* archæology. *Address:* 18 London Road, Chelmsford.

Died 18 Dec. 1947.

WHITLEY, William Thomas; writer on the history of art in England; *b* London, 27 Jan. 1858; *s* of William Whitley, Kensington, and Mary Gilder; *m* 1888, Mary Alford (*d* 1931); one *s*. *Educ:* private schools. Painted when younger, and exhibited landscapes and figure pictures at the Royal Academy, the Royal Glasgow Institute of Fine Arts, the Dudley Gallery, the Royal Birmingham Society of Artists, the Royal Institute of Oil Painters, the Royal Society of British Artists, etc.; has since contributed articles to Art Journal, Magazine of Art, Studio, Burlington Magazine, Connoisseur, and the annual publication of the Walpole Society; and has for many years written records of contemporary art history for the Annual Register and Whitaker's Almanack; was the original representative and principal writer, under Mr Nicol Dunn's editorship, of the bi-weekly, non-critical articles, Art and Artists, which for some years were a feature of the Morning Post. *Publications:* Thomas Gainsborough; Artists and their Friends in England, 1700–1799; Art in England, 1800–1820; Art in England, 1821–1837; Life of Gilbert Stuart (published in America by Harvard University) and Thomas Heaphy. *Recreation:* sleeping. *Address:* 3r Grove End House, NW8.

Died 17 Nov. 1942.

WHITNALL, S. E., MA, MD, BCh (Oxon), MRCS, LRCP (London); FRS (C); late Capt. RAMC (TF); *b* 1876; *s* of A. W. Whitnall, of Flixton, Lancashire; *m* Zoë, *d* of late C. C. Wyllie; two *s* one *d*. *Educ:* Owens College, Manchester Radley College, Berks; Magdalen College, Oxford; St Thomas's Hospital, London; Welch Memorial Prize, 1902. Formerly University Demonstrator in Human Anatomy, Oxford; Professor of Anatomy at McGill University, Montreal, 1919–34; Professor of Anatomy, University of Bristol, 1935–41; Radcliffe Prize, 1913; Nettleship Prize, 1923. MO Oxford Hussars, France, 1916. *Publications:* Anatomy of the Human Orbit, 1921; The Study of Anatomy, 1923; papers on Ophthalmological Anatomy and anatomical sections in text books. *Address:* Barclays Bank, High Street Oxford.

Died 19 Feb. 1950.

WHITSON, Sir Thomas Barnby, Kt 1931; DL, JP, LLD, CA, FRSE; *b* 10 March 1869; *e s* of late Thomas Whitson, CA, Edinburgh; *m* 1st, Wilhelmina Jamieson, 2nd *d* of W. J. Adie, Voe, Shetland; two *s* one *d*; 2nd, Mabel Christian, *d* of late George Edward Forbes, Edinburgh. *Educ:* George Watson's College; Loretto School; Edinburgh University. Member of the Society of Accountants in Edinburgh, 1892; one of the founders of the Scottish Zoological Park, 1912; Member of the Town Council of Edinburgh, 1916–32; Lord Provost of Edinburgh, 1929–32; Chairman of the Board of Management, Royal Infirmary, Edinburgh, 1932–37; Chairman Scottish Departmental Committee on Housing, 1933; Chairman Herring Industry Board, 1935–38; Vice-Chairman Edinburgh College of Art, 1938–44; Pres. Society of Accountants, Edinburgh, 1937–38; Director Scottish Union and National Insurance Co., Ltd; Governor Loretto School; Member of Council of British Hospitals Association; A Warden of King George Jubilee Trust; Member of the Finance Committee of National Trust for Scotland; Member of Scottish Central Probation Council. *Publication:* The Lord Provosts of Edinburgh, 1296–1932. *Address:* 27 Eglinton Crescent, Edinburgh. *T:* Edinburgh 62155. *Clubs:* New, Edinburgh.

Died 1 Oct. 1948.

WHITTAKER, William Gillies, MA (Glas.); DMus (Edin. et Dunelm); Officier d'Académie; Hon. RAM; FRCM; Hon. LTSC; FRCO; *b* Newcastle on Tyne, 1876; *s* of John Whittaker, Cumberland, and Mary Jane Gillies, Hexham-on-Tyne; *m* 1908, Clara Watkins, Gateshead-on-Tyne; two *d*. *Educ:* Clarence St Wesleyan Day School; School of Science and Art, and Armstrong College, Newcastle on Tyne. Intended for teacher of science, but abandoned it for music; studied locally, with numerous holiday courses in London; Organist of Presbyterian Churches for 15 years; joined Armstrong College staff, 1899; resigned, 1929; Gardiner Professor of Music, Glasgow Univ. and Principal, Scottish National Academy of Music, 1930–41; ENSA Musical Adviser, Scottish Region, 1942; founded Newcastle Bach Choir, 1915; and Conductor till 1930; conducted three days' Bach Festival in London, 1922; visited Australia for

Associated Board of RAM and RCM 1923–24; Alsop lecturer, Liverpool University, Oct.–Nov., 1927 and 1929; Lecturer, Cornell University, Summer, 1928; 3 Lectures, Royal Institution, 1928; Member Scottish Advisory BBC Committee; President of Incorporated Soc. of Musicians, 1934. *Publications and Compositions:* Two Carnegie awards, Piano quintet, Among the Northumbrian Hills; A Lyke-Wake Dirge for chorus and orchestra (first perf. London Bach Choir, March 1925); The Coelestial Sphaere (chorus and orchestra); Psalm CXXXIX (unaccompanied choir); A Festal Psalm (male choir and orchestra); Odes from The Choephorei (female chorus and orchestra); Piano Concerto, Chamber Music, Songs, Piano and Violin pieces, Part Songs, Anthems, many choral arrangements of North Country Folk Songs; editor, 2 volumes North Countrie Ballads, Songs, and Pipes Tunes; Oxford Choral Songs; Oxford Church Music, Oxford Orchestral Music; Oxford series of arias of Handel and Bach, Bach Sinfonias, Cantatas and Motets, Extended Chorales, William Young's Works, etc.; editor String Sonatas of Purcell and Blow. *Books:* Fugitive Notes on certain Cantatas and the Motets of J. S. Bach; Collected Essays; Class Singing. *Recreations:* reading, motoring. *Address:* 60 Cleveden Drive, Glasgow, W2.

Died 5 July 1944.

WHITTALL, Lt-Col Percival Frederick, DSO 1917; formerly Provincial Commissioner Northern Territories of the Gold Coast; retired, 1932; *b* 15 July 1877; *y s* of late Fleet Paymaster J. Whittall, RN; *m* 1921, Mary Gwendolen Dalzell, *o d* of Mr Justice Green of Nigeria. *Educ:* Felsted. Joined RE, in ranks, 1896; served S African War, 1899–1900 (Queen's medal three clasps); Commissioned Lincolnshire Regiment, 1902; posted to Political Service, Gold Coast, 1912; seconded from Political Service to organise Transport, 1920–22; received thanks of Secretary of State for services in yellow fever outbreak at Sekondi, 1910; served European War with RE, 1915–19 (despatches four times, 1914–15 Star, DSO and bar, French Croix de Guerre). *Address:* The Firs, Lympstone, Exmouth, Devon. *T:* Exmouth 3638. *Club:* Army and Navy.

Died 8 Feb. 1943.

WHITTEN, Wilfred; (pseudonym, John o'London). Assistant Editor of The Academy, 1896–1902; Acting Editor of TP's Weekly from its foundation in 1902 to 1911; on staff of The Daily Mail, 1916–19; Editor of John o' London's Weekly, 1919–36; Consulting Editor since 1936. *Publications:* Daniel Defoe (Westminster Biographies); London in Song; Between the Cupolas; annotated edition of John Thomas Smith's Book for a Rainy Day; edited London Stories, 1911; A Londoner's London, 1913; J. T. Smith's Nollekens and his Times.

Died 19 Dec. 1942.

WHITTEN-BROWN, Sir Arthur, KBE 1919; late RAF; MIEE, MSAIE; DL Glamorgan; *b* 1886; *s* of A. G. Brown, Manchester; *m* 1919, Marguerite Kathleen, *d* of Major D. H. Kennedy, Penn, Bucks. Decorated for first crossing the Atlantic in an aeroplane, Newfoundland to Clifden, Ireland, 4.28 pm, 14 June–8.40 am 15 June, 1919. *Address:* Belgrave Court, Uplands, Swansea. *Club:* Royal Air Force.

Died 4 Oct. 1948.

WHITTINGHAM, Rev. George Gustavus Napier, DD (Hon.) Nashotah Theological Seminary, 1936; Vicar of St Matthias, Earl's Court, since 1934; *b* 18 Nov. 1866; 2nd *s* of late Major-General Fernando Santiago Nicolas Whittingham, CB, and Charlotte Anne Reid, Runnymede, Old Windsor; *m* 1891, Maud Marion, *d* of late Bartholomew Arcedeckne Duncan, MD, 29 Wimpole Street, W1; one *s*. *Educ:* Haileybury College; École Alsacienne, Paris; Worcester College, Oxford. Deacon, 1890; Priest, 1891; curacies, 1890–92; Rector of Duntisbourne Abbots, Glos, 1892–95; Vicar of

Evesham, 1895–1900; Priest-in-charge of Good Shepherd Mission, Birmingham, 1901–04; Hon. Assistant Chaplain, Chapel Royal, Savoy, 1894–1907; travelled or lived on continent, 1905–07; Priest-in-charge of St Silas Mission, Kentish Town, 1907–12; built the church and formed the new parish of St Silas-the-Martyr, Kentish Town, 1912; Vicar of that church, 1912–30; Chap. of St Mark's Anglican Church, Florence, 1930–32; of St Paul's, Cannes, 1933; preached missions in Brooklyn and New York City, Lent, 1914 and 1916; founded the Anglo-Catholic Pilgrimage Association to revive Pilgrimages to Palestine, 1924; Hon. Sec. of the Association, 1924; Kt Commander of the Order of the Holy Sepulchre, 1925; Russian Archpriest's Cross, 1926; Co-founder and Chairman of the Russian Church Aid Fund, 1923; Chairman of the Bishop of London's Housing Committee, 1928. *Publications:* Who is to Blame?, 1916; The Home of Fadeless Splendour, or Palestine of To-day, 1921; second ed., 1928, third ed., 1931. *Recreations:* boating, cycling, travelling. *Address:* 81a Philbeach Gardens, Earl's Court, SW5. *T:* Frobisher 1326. *Club:* Junior Constitutional.

Died 11 Jan. 1941.

WHITTINGHAM, Rt Rev. Walter Godfrey, DD; *e s* of late Walter Basden Whittingham of Walthamstow; *m* Edith Mary Gordon, 3rd *d* of late William Thomas Bensly, LLD, FSA, Norwich; three *s* one *d*. *Educ:* St Peter's College, Cambridge. Ordained, 1886; Curate of St Margaret, Leicester, 1886–91; S Wigston, 1891–93; Vicar, 1893–99; Vicar of Weedon, 1899–1904; of Knighton, Leicester, 1904–17; Rector of Glaston, Rutland, 1917–23; Rural Dean, 1901–04; of Leicester, 1915–17; of Rutland III, 1918–19; Archdeacon of Oakham, 1918–23; Hon. Canon of Peterborough, 1915–16; Residentiary Canon of Peterborough, 1922–23; Bishop of St Edmundsbury, 1923–40. *Address:* The Mill House, Horstead, Norwich.

Died 17 June 1941.

WHITTINGSTALL, Francis Herbert F.; *see* Fearnley-Whittingstall.

WHITTY, Sir John Tarlton, Kt 1935; CSI 1932; CIE 1916; OBE 1946; *b* 1 Feb. 1876; *s* of H. T. Whitty of Dewhurst Lodge, Wadhurst, Sussex; *m* 1904, Grace Newland; four *s*. *Educ:* Clifton Coll.; New Coll., Oxford; Univ. College, London. Entered ICS 1898; Magistrate and Collector, Bihar and Orissa, 1912; Commissioner, 1928; Member Board of Revenue, 1930; Member of Executive Council, 1931–35; acting Governor of Bihar and Orissa, 1934; retired 1935; Chief ARP Warden of Westminster, 1939–42. Member Clifton College Council, Westminster City Council; Director Peel River Land and Mineral Co. Ltd. *Recreation:* golf. *Club:* East India and Sports.

Died 8 May 1948.

WHITTY, Dame May; *see* Webster, Dame M.

WHITWELL, William Fry; Chairman and Managing Director The Horden Collieries Ltd, Darlington; JP North Riding of Yorkshire; Sheriff of Yorkshire, 1919; Alderman and Chairman of the North Riding of Yorkshire County Council; Mayor of Thornaby-on-Tees, 1913–19; *b* 1867; *e s* of William Whitwell, JP, DL, Saltburn-by-the-sea, Yorkshire, and Henrietta, *d* of Joseph Fry, Bristol. *Educ:* Uppingham; Abroad. *Recreations:* formerly hunting, shooting, and cricket. *Address:* Clockwood House, Yarm, Yorkshire. *Clubs:* Conservative, Royal Automobile, MCC.

Died 12 April 1942.

WHYMPER, Charles, RI; JP Hunts; *b* London, 31 Aug. 1853; *s* of late J. W. Whymper, RI. For 25 years illustrated books on travel, sport, and natural history. *Publications:* Egyptian Birds; several papers on The Peasantry of England; Bird Life, etc., besides many etchings of shooting and fishing from his oil pictures and water-colour drawings. *Address:* Houghton, Huntingdonshire. *Club:* Arts.

Died 25 April 1941.

WHYTE, Frederic; author and journalist; *b* 1867; *s* of late Henry F. Whyte, CE; *m* 1916, Karin, *d* of Carl Ewald Lilja of Jönköping, Sweden; one *s. Educ:* Stonyhurst and elsewhere. On the editorial staff of Cassell & Co., publishers, 1889–1904; one of Methuen & Co.'s literary advisers, 1907–09; contributor to Encyclopædia Britannica, Fortnightly Review, Contemporary Review, Cornhill, Bookman, etc. *Publications:* Actors of the Century, 1898; Life of W. T. Stead, 1925; A Wayfarer in Sweden, 1926; William Heinemann, a Memoir, 1928; A Bachelor's London, 1931; Translations: A. Filon's The English Stage, 1897; C. G. Schillings's With Flashlight and Rifle, 1905; Flaubert's Trois Contes, 1910; Count von Waldersee's A Field Marshal's Memoirs, 1924; Jules Lemaître's Theatrical Impressions (a selection), 1925; Count F. Cronstedt's Grip and I, 1925; Margherita Sarfatti's Life of Mussolini, 1926; and other French, German, Swedish, and Italian books. *Address:* c/o The National Provincial Bank, 2 Princes Street, EC2.

Died 29 April 1941.

WHYTE, Sir William, Kt 1943; DL, JP. Late Cashier and General Manager, Royal Bank of Scotland, Edinburgh; Director of Glyn, Mills & Co., Scottish Agricultural Securities Corporation, Ltd, Railway Passengers Assurance Co., Scottish Widows' Fund and Life Assurance Society. *Address:* Royal Bank of Scotland, Edinburgh.

Died 21 April 1945.

WHYTE, Sir William Edward, Kt 1930; OBE; FRSE; solicitor; *s* of William Whyte and Margaret Steel; *m* 1909, Jessie Brown, *d* of Major James Fraser; three *s* one *d. Educ:* Normal School, Glasgow; Glasgow University. Member of Coal Mines Re-organisation Commission; Chairman, Scottish Advisory Cttee, Housing (Rural Authorities) Act, 1931: Hon. Pres., Scottish National Housing and Town Planning Council; Sec. Clyde Valley Regional Planning Cttee; Chm. Scottish Housing Advisory Committee (Urban Committee); Chairman Consultative Council Department of Health for Scotland; Member of Unemployment of Health for Scotland; Member of Unemployment Grants Committee; JP County of Lanark; Chairman Scottish Advisory Committee on Rivers Pollution Prevention; Member of Royal Commission on Licensing (Scotland); Member of Royal Commission on the Location of Industry; lately Member of War Damage Commission. *Publications:* Local Government in Scotland; The Law of Housing and Town Planning in Scotland; The Local Government (Scotland) Act, 1929, Town and Country Planning in Scotland, etc. *Address:* Balgay, Uddingston, Lanarkshire. *T:* Uddingston 132. *Club:* (Chairman) Royal Scottish Automobile (Glasgow).

Died 1 April 1950.

WICKHAM-BOYNTON, Captain Thomas Lamplugh; JP, VL; Alderman of the E Riding County Council; Master of East Middleton Foxhounds; *b* 24 Oct. 1869; *e s* of late William Wickham, of Chestnut Grove, Boston Spa; *m* 1899, Cycely Mabel, *o c* of Sir H. S. Boynton, 11th Bart of Burton Agnes, E Yorks, and assumed additional name of Boynton; two *s. Educ:* Eton. *Address:* Burton Agnes Hall, Driffield, Yorks. *Clubs:* Boodle's; Yorkshire, York.

Died 19 Nov. 1942.

WICKLOW, 7th Earl of, *cr* 1793; **Ralph Francis Howard;** Baron of Clonmore; Irish Representative Peer; Senator Irish Free State, 1922–28; Lt-Col late South Irish Horse; late Captain 2nd Life Guards; *b* Southsea, 24 Dec. 1877; *s* of 6th Earl of Wicklow, and Francesca, *d* of Thomas Chamberlayne, Cranbury Park, Hants; *S* father, 1891; *m* 1st, 1902, Lady Gladys Mary

Hamilton (*d* 1917), *y d* of 2nd Duke of Abercorn; one *s*; 2nd, 1942, Lady Beatrix Wilkinson, *widow* of Sir Nevile R. Wilkinson, KCVO, Ulster King of Arms, *e d* of 14th Earl of Pembroke. *Educ:* Eton; Sandhurst. Served S African War. Protestant. *Heir: s* Lord Clonmore. *Address:* Shelton Abbey, Arklow, Co. Wicklow, Ireland. *Clubs:* Carlton, Marlborough, MCC; Kildare Street, Dublin.

Died 11 Oct. 1946.

WICKREMESINGHE, Cyril Leonard, CMG 1944; *b* 17 Aug. 1890; 4th *s* of late James and Mary Wickremesinghe; *m* 1919, Esme Goonewardene; three *s* one *d. Educ:* Richmond and Royal Colleges, Ceylon. Served over 31 years in Ceylon Civil Service; Principal Appointments: Asst Govt Agent, Mannar, 1922; District Judge, Nuwara Eliya, 1925; Asst Govt Agent, Puttalam, 1926; Kalutara, 1928; Govt Agent, Province of Sabaragamuwa, 1930, North-Central Province, 1931; Commissioner of Lands, Ceylon, 1934; retired, 1944. *Address:* Lakmahal, Seventh Lane, Colombo, Ceylon. *T:* Colombo 8556.

Died 24 June 1945.

WIDDOWS, Archibald Edwards, CB 1912; Chevalier Legion of Honour, 1920; *b* 27 Jan. 1878; *m* 1917, Margharita Defries; two *s. Educ:* Dulwich College; Brasenose College, Oxford. Appointed to the War Office, 1901; Private Secretary to the Secretary of State for War (Viscount Haldane), 1905–12; Assistant Under-Secretary of State, War Office, 1926–38. Temp. Administrative Officer, Air Ministry since 1939; Hon. Treasurer Royal Military Benevolent Fund. *Address:* 6 Campden Hill Square, W8.

Died 11 Oct. 1942.

WIDDRINGTON, Brig.-Gen. Bertram FitzHerbert, CMG 1918; DSO 1916; KRRC; *b* 14 Sept. 1873; 2nd *s* of late Shallcross FitzHerbert Widdrington; *m* 1912, Clothilde Enid, *d* of late E. Onslow Ford, RA; two *s. Educ:* Winchester; Sandhurst. Entered army, 1894; Capt. 1901; Major, 1912; Bt Lt-Col 1917; commanded 4th Batt. 60th Rifles, 1914–16; Infantry Brigade, 1916–19; served S Africa, 1900 (Queen's medal 4 clasps); European War, 1914–18 (despatches, CMG, DSO); retired, 1919; Order of Holy Redeemer, 3rd Class; JP, Bucks; DL, Northumberland; High Sheriff, Northumberland, 1925–26. *Address:* Newton Hall, Felton Morpeth, Northumberland. *T:* Shilbottle 25; Maids Moreton House, Buckingham. *T:* Buckingham 3155.

Died 30 Jan. 1942.

WIDENER, Joseph E.; financier, sportsman and art collector; *m* Ella H. Pancoast (*d* 1929), Philadelphia, Pa. *Educ:* University of Penna. Interested in horse racing; maintains stud near Lexington, Ky, and Chantilly, France; principal owner, Belmont Park and Hialeah Park Race-tracks; owner of art collection, some 300 paintings, including 16 Rembrandts, Titians, Raphaels, Gainsboroughs, Van Dycks, Holbeins, Millets. *Address:* Land Title Building, Philadelphia, Pa, USA.

Died 26 Oct. 1943.

WIENER, Prof. Leo; Professor Emeritus of Slavic Languages, Harvard University; *b* 27 July 1862; father German, mother Russian; *m* 1893; two *s* two *d. Educ:* Gymnasia of Minsk and Warsaw; University of Warsaw; Polytechnic of Berlin. As a Russian student went from Russia to Germany to study engineering. Having become a vegetarian, formed a plan for a vegetarian colony in British Belize; went to New Orleans; there worked in cotton factory; later worked on railroad, and sold fruit in Kansas City; attracted attention of the superintendent of public schools; got a post as teacher in Odessa (US), Missouri, later in Kansas City, and afterwards professor in University of Missouri. *Publications:* History of Yiddish Literature in the Nineteenth Century; Anthology of Russian Literature; Slavic Anthology, in Universal Anthology; An

Interpretation of the Russian People; Commentary to the Germanic Laws and Mediæval Documents; Contributions Toward a History of Arabico-Gothic Culture; Africa and the Discovery of America; The Contemporary Drama of Russia; Mayan and Mexican Origins; translation of Tolstoy's complete works (24 vols); edited Songs from the Ghetto. *Recreations:* long tramps, mushrooming, travels. *Address:* Belmont, Mass, USA.

Died 12 Dec. 1939.

WIGGINS, William Martin; *b* Burnham, Somersetshire, 4 Aug. 1870; *s* of Rev. William Wiggins; *m* 1st, 1896, Flora Isabel, *d* of George Alfred Coleman of Oldham; 2nd, 1917, Elizabeth, *d* of Stephen Hayhurst of Hellifield. *Educ:* privately. MP (L) Oldham, 1925–29; JP for Borough of Middleton, Lancs, 1906; Hon. Freeman of the Borough of Middleton, 1919; Mayor of Middleton, 1914–19; Past Pres., Federation of Master Cotton Spinners Assoc. Ltd; President International Federation of Cotton Spinners and Manufacturers. *Address:* Midland Hotel, Manchester. *Club:* Reform (Manchester).

Died 4 Oct. 1950.

WIGHTMAN, Sir Owen William, Kt 1936; CBE 1920; JP; brewer; *b* 29 Dec. 1869; *s* of Rev. William Arnett Wightman, Vicar of Stillingfleet, Yorks; *m* 1895, Ethel Maria (*d* 1938), *d* of Hy Hall, of the Manor House, Alton, Hants. *Educ:* Radley; Exeter College, Oxford. *Recreations:* shooting, fishing. *Address:* The Garden House, Bengeo, Hertford, Herts. *TA:* Bengeo, Hertford. *Clubs:* Conservative, Leander.

Died 9 Nov. 1948.

WIGMORE, John Henry; Emeritus Dean of the Faculty of Law, North-Western University; *b* San Francisco, 4 March 1863; *s* of John Wigmore, Youghal, Co. Cork, and Harriet Joyner, Henley-in-Arden; *m* 1889, Emma Hunt Vogl, Cambridge Mass. *Educ:* Harvard University; AM, LLB; LLD (Hon.) Wisconsin Univ. 1908, Harvard Univ., 1909, Louvain Univ., 1927, North-western Univ., 1936, Lyon Univ., 1938. Admitted to Massachusetts Bar, 1887; Professor of Law, Keio Univ., Tokyo, 1889–92; North-western Univ., Chicago, 1893; Member of Illinois Commission on Uniform State Laws, 1910–25, and since 1933; President American Institute of Criminal Law and Criminology, 1909; President Association of American University Professors, 1915; Member of Inter-American High Commission, 1915–20; Colonel, Judge Advocate, US Army, 1916–19 (DS Medal); Honorary Member of Asiatic Society of Japan, 1912, and Society of Public Teachers of Law, 1917; Chevalier of the Legion of Honour, 1919; International Academy of Comparative Law, 1932; American Bar Assoc. gold medal, 1932; corr. mem. Comité de Leg. Etrangère, Paris, 1933, Assoc. Belgian Royal Academy, 1936; Order of the Sacred Treasure, 1936 (Japan). *Publications:* Australian Ballot System, 1888; Private Law in Old Japan, 1892; System of Evidence at Common Law, 1905; 2nd ed. 1923–1933; 3rd ed. 1940; Principles of Judicial Proof, 1913, 1931, 1937; Code of Evidence, 1909, 1935; Cases on Torts, 1913; Problems of Law, Past, Present, and Future, 1920; Panorama of the World's Legal Systems, 3 vols, 1928, 1 vol. 1936; Students Text-book of the Law of Evidence, 1935; Kaleidoscope of Justice, 1941; Guide to American International Law, 1942; Anglo-American Legal History Series (ed.), 1907 Science and Learning in France (ed.), 1917; Modern Criminal Science Series (ed.), 1907–1916; Modern Legal Philosophy Series (ed.), 1912; Continental Legal History Series (ed.), 1910. *Recreations:* detective stories, and travelling in Europe. *Address:* 850 Lake Shore Drive, Chicago, Illinois, USA. *T:* Superior 4500. *Clubs:* Army and Navy, University, Evanston, Chicago; Cosmos, Washington.

Died 20 April 1943.

WIGNALL, Joshua Jennings, CMG 1936; JP; *b* Lymington, Tasmania, 2 Nov. 1859; *s* of Benjamin Wignall, Bradford, Yorkshire; *m* 1st, 1882, Henrietta D., Mrs L. Poulston; 2nd, 1913, Mary Jane, MBE 1939, *d* of late Emily Smith; one *s*. *Educ:* Collegiate School, Hobart. Apprenticed as a Basket-maker and was engaged in this trade for some years; Master Butcher, 1887; retired, 1915; Councillor, Municipal Council, New Town, 1918; Alderman City of Hobart since 1921; Mayor, 1927–29, and 1932–34; Lord Mayor of Hobart, 1934–38; Officer of the Order of St John of Jerusalem. *Recreation:* gardening. *Address:* 40 Pedder Street, New Town, Hobart. *TA:* Wignall Hobart. *T:* W. 1044.

Died 2 Nov. 1941.

WIGRAM, Vice-Adm. Ernest, CMG 1918; DSO 1916; *b* 1877; *brother* of 1st Baron Wigram, PC, GCB. Served European War (Falkland Islands, Dardanelles, Belgian Coast), 1914–18 (despatches, CMG, DSO); Retired List, 1926; Vice-Adm., retired, 1931. *Club:* United Service.

Died 29 Oct. 1944.

WIGRAM, Gen. Sir Kenneth, GCB 1935 (KCB 1930, CB 1918); CSI 1921; CBE 1919; DSO 1917; *b* 5 Dec. 1875; *s* of late Herbert Wigram, Indian Civil Service; unmarried. *Educ:* Winchester Sandhurst. Served NW Frontier, 1897–98 (medal with clasp); Tirah, 1897–98 (clasp); NW Frontier (Waziristan), 1901–02 (clasp); Thibet (march to Lhasa), 1903–04 (medal with clasp). European War, 1914–18 (despatches, CB, CBE, DSO); DSD, AHQ, India, 1919–21; Commanded Delhi Brigade Area, 1922–24; DA and QMG Northern Command, India, 1924–26; Commanded Waziristan District, India, 1926–29; Lt-Gen., 1929; Chief of General Staff, India, 1931–34; General, 1932; General Officer Commanding-in-Chief Northern Command, India, 1934–36; ADC General to the King, 1933–36; retired, 1936. *Club:* United Service.

Died 11 July 1949.

WILBERFORCE, Col Harold Hartley, DSO 1918, TD, MA, LLB (Cantab), Solicitor, Chairman Transport and Supply Committee West Riding of Yorkshire, Territorial Association; *b* 12 Aug. 1881; *s* of William Wilkinson Wilberforce, JP; *m* 1922, Lydia Tessa Cosmo Trevor. *Educ:* Aysgarth School; Malvern College; Corpus Christi College, Cambridge. Admitted Solicitor, 1907; granted Commission in Territorial Army, 1909; served European War with 49th (WR) Divisional Train RASC (1914–15) and in command of 62nd (WR) Divisional Train RASC 1915–19 (DSO, TD, despatches, Croix de Guerre); Hon. Treasurer Bootham Park, Yorks, Yorkshire School for the Blind and York Dispensary; Hon. Treasurer and Secretary York and District Animals Hospital and York Home for Stray Dogs. *Recreation:* Delwood Kennels of Show Collies. *Address:* Delwood Croft, Fulford, York. *T:* Fulford 26.

Died 11 July 1943.

WILBERFORCE, Sir Herbert William Wrangham, Kt 1931; *b* 1864; 2nd *s* of late Edward Wilberforce, Master of the Supreme Court, and *g g s* of the Emancipator, William Wilberforce; *m* 1892, Florence (*d* 1937), *d* of late C. J. Monk, sometime MP for Gloucester; two *d*. *Educ:* London International College; University College, London; Downing College, Cambridge (Exhibitioner and Scholar); Law Exhibitioner, London University; 1st Class Law Tripos, 1885; BA and LLB; represented Cambridge at lawn tennis against Oxford, 1883–86; winner of University Singles and Doubles; Northern LT champion, 1883; and four-handed champion (with Hon. P. Bowes Lyon), 1887. Called to Bar, Inner Temple, 1888; contested North Hackney, 1900; LCC for N St Pancras, 1901–04; Chairman Local Government Committee; Vice-Chairman Parliamentary Committee; has been Church Warden, Chairman of Parish Council, and member of various education authorities; Stipendiary Magistrate for Bradford, 1908–14; Metropolitan Police Magistrate, Old

Street, 1914–23; Marylebone, 1923; Bow Street, 1925–26; Deputy Chairman County of London Sessions, 1926–38. *Publications:* Private Bill Procedure (with the late Judge Dodd, KC); Lawn Tennis, All England Series; various articles on Lawn Tennis in Badminton Library and elsewhere. *Recreations:* reading and talking. *Address:* 2 York House, Kensington Church Street, W8. *T:* Western 2358. *Club:* Bath.

Died 28 March 1941.

WILBERFORCE, Lionel Robert, MA; Professor of Physics in the University of Liverpool, 1900, Professor Emeritus since 1935; *b* Munich, 18 April 1861; *e s* of Edward Wilberforce, Master of the Supreme Court; *m* 1891, Margaret (*d* 1929), 2nd *d* of Rev. W. Raynes. *Educ:* London International College, Isleworth; Trinity Coll., Cambridge. Assistant Demonstrator at the Cavendish Laboratory, Cambridge, 1887; Demonstrator, 1890; University Lecturer in Physics, 1900. *Publications:* various papers in the Philosophical Magazine and elsewhere. *Recreations:* skating, climbing. *Address:* 5 Ashfield Road, Aigburth, Liverpool, 17. *T:* 3213 Lark Lane, Liverpool. *Club:* Alpine.

Died 1 April 1944.

WILBRAHAM, Lt-Col Bernard Hugh, DSO 1916; late RE; *s* of late Hugh Wilbraham of Oldhead, Westport, Co. Mayo, and late Lady Marian Browne, *d* of 2nd Marquess of Sligo; *m* 1910, Bernice, *d* of James Segrave, Tasmania, and *widow* of Arthur R. Browne; one *d*. *Educ:* Marlborough, RMA, Woolwich. Commission in RE 1899; Captain, 1908; Maj. 1916; Lt-Col 1925; in Egyptian Army, 1908–10; served in South African War, 1901–02; European War, 1914–18 (DSO); retired pay, 1929. *Recreations:* motoring, photography. *Club:* Naval and Military.

Died 2 May 1942.

WILBY, Col (Arthur William) Roger, CBE 1919; Agent Marine Department, Federal Government of Canada, Victoria, BC; *b* 27 March 1875; *o s* of late Lieut A. E. Wilby, 61st Regiment, and Mrs Wilby, Knebworth; *m* 1919, Eva Mary (*d* 1934), *y d* of late Arthur P. Blathwayt; three *s*. *Educ:* Royal Military College of Canada. Served South African War; European War, 1915–19 (despatches, CBE). *Address:* 1065 Moss Street, Victoria, BC.

Died 2 April 1942.

WILD, F. Percy, RBA; 2nd *s* of Thomas and Mary Ann Wild, late of Bramley Grange, Thorner, near Leeds; *m* 1893, Beatrice Emily, 3rd *d* of Alfred Chilcott; one *s* one *d*. *Educ:* Leeds Gram. School; Yorkshire Coll.; France and Germany. Gained the Grand Médaille d'Argent at the Académie Royale des Beaux Arts, Antwerp, 1888. Educated as an engineer; took up art in 1884, and studied at Antwerp for four years. Worked in Spain and at Julien's studio, Paris; best known for portraits, miniatures on ivory, and for pictures illustrating subjects of life on the Thames. *Pictures:* Happy Days with Old Father Thames; The Morning Swim; A Lesson in Punting; A Race; In Sight, etc. *Recreations:* golf, punting, tennis, motoring. *Address:* Gossmore, Marlow, Bucks. *Clubs:* Chelsea Arts; Temple Golf.

Died 14 April 1950.

WILD, Robert Briggs, MD (Lond.), FRCP (Lond.), MSc (Victoria), MRCS; Emeritus Professor of Materia Medica and Therapeutics in the University of Manchester; Physician to Manchester Hospital for Skin Diseases and to Christie Hospital for Cancer; Major (retired) RAMC (TF); *b* 1862; *s* of Robert Wild, of Holcombe; *m* Florence (*d* 1941), *d* of Lt-Col Hillkirk, of Withington; two *d*. *Educ:* Owens College. BSc (Victoria) with Honours in Physiology, 1883; Exhibition and Gold Medal in Physiology, University of London, 1883; Parkin Prizeman, Royal College of Physicians, Edinburgh, 1896. Pathologist, Manchester Royal

Infirmary, and Assistant Lecturer in Pathology (Owens Coll.), 1888–91; late Pro-Vice-Chancellor and ex-Chm. of Convocation, Victoria University; Ex-Dean of Faculty of Medicine, and Member of General Medical Council; Fellow of the Royal Society of Medicine; Member of Manchester Literary and Philosophical Society, ex-President Manchester Medical Society, and ex-President Manchester Pathological Society. *Publications:* articles on Pathology, Pharmacology, Dermatology, Life Insurance, and University Education. *Recreations:* literary and scientific, travelling. *Address:* 180 Horninglow Street, Burton-on-Trent, Staffordshire.

Died 7 Oct. 1941.

WILE, Frederic William; American journalist, author and political columnist; Chief of Frederic William Wile News Syndicate, Washington; member editorial staff, Washington Star, since 1923; Berlin correspondent of The Daily Mail, New York Times, Chicago Daily News, Observer, etc. (1902–14); edited Germany Day by Day in Daily Mail during European War; *b* La Porte, Indiana, USA, 30 Nov. 1873; *s* of Jacob Wile, JP, banker; *m* 1901, Ada Shakman; one *s* one *d*. *Educ:* University of Notre Dame, Indiana (Hon. LLD 1924); Hon. LLD Ursinus College, 1929. Special service on headquarters staff of American Expeditionary Forces, 1917–19; Lieutenant-Colonel Organised Reserve Corps, United States Army; 1923–38, analyses of The Political Situation in Washington weekly throughout the United States and Canada over the wireless network of the Columbia Broadcasting System; First transatlantic broadcaster of a great news event—the London Naval Conference of 1930. *Publications:* Men Around the Kaiser, 1913; The German-American Plot, 1915; The Assault, 1916; Explaining the Britishers, 1918; Life of Emile Berliner, Maker of the Microphone, 1926; A Century of Industrial Progress (Editor), 1928; News Is Where You Find It (autobiography), 1939. *Recreation:* golfing. *Address:* 3313 Sixteenth Street, Washington, DC. *Clubs:* Garrick; National Press, Cosmos, Overseas Writers, Washington.

Died 7 April 1941.

WILGAR, Lt-Col William Percy, DSO 1917; Professor of Civil Engineering, Queen's University, Kingston, Canada; *b* Coburg, Ont, 9 March 1877; *s* of James Wilgar and Maria Sykes; *m* 1st, 1906, Emilie Stewart Low, *d* of Edward Low, Ottawa; one *s*; 2nd, 1916, Gertrude Ross Low. *Educ:* Queen's University, Kingston. Engaged in railway engineering since 1899; as Resident Engineer, B of Q Railway, Central Ontario Railway, Kingston and Pembroke Railway; in charge of locating party on Transcontinental Railway, 1904; Division Engineer, Transcontinental Railway, 1907; Assistant District Engineer, 1909; joined Expeditionary Force for European War, 1915; Commanded 10th Field Co. CE, and 10th Batt. CE; Hon. ADC to Governor General of Canada, 1933. *Recreations:* outdoor sports, fishing, hunting, etc. *Address:* Queen's University, Kingston, Ont, Canada. *Clubs:* Cataraqui Golf and Country, Kingston; Canadian Military Institute, Toronto.

Died 3 Aug. 1940.

WILKIN, Sir Albert (Scholick), Kt 1939; JP; Chairman and Managing Director A. S. Wilkin, Ltd; *b* 22 April 1883; *s* of William Wilkin; *m* 1924, Mina Fraser; three *s*. *Educ:* Barton Grammar School. Member Executive and Grand Council Federation British Industries; appointed Member Sugar Confectionery and Food Preserving Trade Board of Great Britain; Hon. Freeman of City of London; Liveryman of Worshipful Company of Feltmakers; Member of Council of Commerce, King's College, University of Durham. *Address:* The Grove, Gosforth, Northumberland.

Died 19 Sept. 1943.

WILKINS, Roland Field, CB 1912; *b* 3 Jan. 1872; *s* of A. S. Wilkins, Professor of Latin, Victoria University, Manchester; *m* 1907, Louisa, OBE (*d* 1929), *d* of late Arthur Trevor Jebb, The Lyth, Ellesmere, Salop; two *d*. *Educ:* Sedbergh; Owens College, Manchester; Balliol College, Oxford. Scholarships at Owens College, Victoria Univ., and London Univ.; Major Exhibition, Balliol College, Oxford, 1890; 1st class Moderations, 1892; hon. mention Craven and Ireland Scholarships Examination, 1892; Craven Scholarship, 1893; 2nd class, Lit. Hum., 1894; 1st place Civil Service (Class I) Examination, 1895. Private Sec. to: Mr Hanbury, 1899–1900, to Sir Austen Chamberlain, 1900–02, and Mr Hayes Fisher (Lord Downham), 1902–03; when Financial Secretary to the Treasury. Principal Clerk, 1908; Treasury Officer of Accounts, 1913–19; Assistant Comptroller and Auditor, 1920, held that post until its abolition by Statute, when he returned to service in the Treasury, 1922; Assistant Paymaster-General 1924–35; retired 1935. *Recreations:* ski-ing, skating, fishing. *Club:* Savile.

Died 1 May 1950.

WILKINSON, Col Arthur Clement, CMG 1918; DSO 1915; late RA; *b* 1870; *e s* of late Clement Wilkinson; *m* 1909, Florence Camilla, *d* of Arthur Ellershaw; two *s*. *Educ:* RMA, Woolwich. Commission in Artillery, 1890; served at Bermuda, Halifax, and Mountain Artillery in India (India medal and clasp, 1897–98); commanded 35th Heavy Battery, RGA, British Expeditionary Force, Aug. 1914; served in France, 1914–18 (DSO, CMG, Mons Star, Belgian Croix de Guerre), retired pay, 1922. *Address:* Crofton, Collington Avenue, Bexhill-on-Sea. *Club:* Junior United Service.

Died 21 Oct. 1950.

WILKINSON, Edward Sheldon, CBE 1938; Chartered Accountant, Shanghai; Secretary of The Lester Trust; *b* 29 Sept. 1883; *s* of Edward Robert Wilkinson, MIME, Darlington; *m* 1914, Minnie, *d* of Alexander Law; one *d*. *Educ:* Queen Elizabeth's Grammar School; Stationers' Co. School. ACA, 1906. Entered Shanghai Municipal Council service, 1909; senior partner of Thomson and Co. Chartered Accountants, Shanghai, 1919–38; concurrently Secretary of the Lester Trust; Military service: Honourable Artillery Co. and Shanghai Volunteer Corps. Was interned at Lungnwa Civil Assembly Centre, Kiangsu, China. *Publications:* Shanghai Birds, 1929; Shanghai Country Walks, 1932; Shanghai Bird Year, 1935; Country Diary, North China Daily News, current. *Recreations:* ornithology, zoology, etc. *Address:* 193 Route Gve. de Boissezon, Shanghai. *TA:* Scrutiny, Shanghai. *Clubs:* Thatched House: Shanghai, Shanghai Country, etc.

Died 17 Jan. 1950.

WILKINSON, Rt Hon. Ellen Cicely, PC 1915; MA; MP (Lab) Jarrow division of Durham, since 1935; Minister of Education, since 1945; *b* 1891; *d* of late Richard and Ellen Wilkinson. *Educ:* Ardwick Higher Elementary School; Stretford Road Secondary School; Manchester Univ. MP (Lab) Middlesbrough E, 1924–31; Parliamentary Secretary, Ministry of Pensions, 1940; Parly Sec. Ministry of Home Security, 1940–45; National Organiser, National Union of Distributive and Allied Workers, since 1915; Manchester City Council, 1923–26. *Publications:* Clash, 1929; Peeps at Politicians, 1930; Division Bell Mystery, 1932; Why War, 1934; Why Fascism (with Dr E. Conze), 1934; The Town that was Murdered, 1939, articles various. *Recreations:* chess, reading. *Address:* Ministry of Education, 14 Belgrave Sq., SW1.; Twixtlands, Penn, Bucks. *T:* Penn 3224. *Club:* National Trade Union.

Died 6 Feb. 1947.

WILKINSON, Frederick Edgar, CMG 1912; *b* 15 May 1871; *s* of late Richard Wilkinson, HBM Consul at Salonica, etc.; widower; two *s* two *d*. *Educ:* Sherborne School; Germany. Entered HBM Consular Service,

China, 1893; Vice-Consul, Shanghai, 1906; Consul, Kiungchow and Pakhoi, 1908; Nanking, 1911–14; Foochow, 1914–20; HBM Consul-General, Mukden, China, 1921–28; retd, 1928. *Address:* Woodruff Corner, Dyke Rd, Hove.

Died 11 Feb. 1950.

WILKINSON, Col George Alexander Eason, CBE 1919; DSO 1900; *b* 1860; *e s* of late Mathew Eason-Wilkinson, Middlethorpe and Greenheys, Manchester, and 2nd wife Louisa, *o c* of George Henry Walker of Longford, Philadelphia, USA; *m* 1886, Hon. Caroline Catherine (*d* 1929), *e d* of 3rd Baron Decies. *Educ:* Charterhouse. JP West Riding and East Riding, Yorks. Served South Africa with 4th Batt. Sherwood Foresters, 1899–1900 (despatches, Queen's medal 3 clasps, DSO); European War (CBE). *Address:* Dringhouses Manor, York. *TA:* Dringhouses. *T:* York 6272. *Clubs:* Yorkshire, York.

Died 13 Jan. 1941.

WILKINSON, Lt-Col Henry Benfield Des Voeux, CBE 1919; DSO 1917; *b* 18 Oct. 1870; *e s* of late Major H. C. Wilkinson, Oswald House, nr Durham; *m* 1908, Bridget, *y d* of late Col J. Blencowe Cookson, CB, of Meldon Park, Morpeth. *Educ:* Cheam School; Wellington College; Royal Military College, Sandhurst; psc; qs. Joined the Durham Light Infantry, 1892; ADC to GOC Poona Division; ADC to Commander-in-Chief, India; ADC to Governor of Bombay; ADC to Viceroy in India; served S African War as staff officer of column (Queen's medal and 5 clasps, despatches); Brigade Major, 1904; Attaché Army Headquarters, Simla, 1910; GSO 2nd grade Peshawar Division, 1911; served European War in France, 1914; as Assistant Provost Marshal, Indian Corps; as DAQMG Lahore Division; as AA and QMG 33rd Division; AA and QMG 23rd Division: AA and QMG 68th Division; Assistant Military Secretary Western Command (CBE, DSO, Bt Lt-Col, Chevalier de l'Ordre de la Couronne, despatches 7 times). *Address:* 20 Cliveden Place, Eaton Square, SW1.

Died 15 Feb. 1943.

WILKINSON, Brig.-Gen. Lewis Frederic G.; see Green-Wilkinson.

WILKINSON, Brig. Maurice Lean, CBE 1926; (retired), JP Bucks; *b* 22 June 1873; *e s* of late T. L. Wilkinson, Barrister-at-law; *m* 1st, 1900, Margaret Constance (*d* 1938), *y d* of late R. L. Knight, of Bobbing, Kent; one *s* (*yr s* reported shot escaping from Japanese 1943); 2nd, 1944, Violet widow of R. A. Buckmaster. *Educ:* Oxford Military Coll.; Royal Military Academy, Woolwich. Entered RA 1892; Lieut 1895, Capt. 1900, Major, 1912; Bt Lt-Col 1917; Lt-Col 1917; Col 1921; temp. Brigadier, 1927; retired, 1930; pac 1907; served Gibraltar, Malta, Hong-Kong; Instructor, School of Gunnery, 1902–05; Instructor, and Chief Instructor, Ordnance College, 1908–12 and 1914; Assistant Superintendent, Ordnance Factories, 1914–18; Deputy Superintendent, 1918–21; Supt of Design, Woolwich Arsenal, 1921–24; Comdt Art. Coll. 1924–27; Mil. Coll. of Science, 1927–28; Vice-Pres. Ordnance Committee, 1928–30. *Address:* Oxford Cottage, Marlow, Bucks. *T:* Marlow 18. *Club:* United Service.

Died 23 Feb. 1946.

WILKINSON, Brig.-Gen. Montagu Grant, CB 1916; CMG 1919; CVO 1927; MVO 1909; *b* 13 March 1857; *s* of Montagu C. Wilkinson, DL, 52 Gloucester Terrace, W2; *m* 1st, 1885, Georgina (*d* 1908), *o c* of Col William Johnston, DL, JP, of Castle Lyons, Co. Cork; 2nd, 1916, Lina Florence, *e d* of late Captain Lennard Dick, RN; one *d*. *Educ:* Harrow; Sandhurst. Joined King's Own Scottish Borderers 1878; served Nile Expedition, 1884–85 (medal and clasp, Khedive's star); Soudan Expedition, 1888 (clasp, despatches); South African War, 1899–1902 (Queen's medal 5 clasps, King's medal); held several staff appointments; Colonel, 1907; Commanded 44th Highland Brigade, Sept. 1914, and at battle of Loos in Sept. 1915 (despatches four times, CB, CMG, Bronze Star, 2 medals); Gentleman Usher to King George V, 1919–27; Extra Gentleman Usher, 1927–36, to King Edward VIII, 1936, and to King George VI since 1937. *Recreations:* hunting, shooting, cricket, racquets, etc. *Address:* Westways, Bracknell, Berks. *Club:* Naval and Military.

Died 28 Nov. 1943.

WILKINSON, Richard James, CMG 1912; *b* 1867; *e s* of late R. Wilkinson, HBM Consul, Salonica; *m* 1912, Edith Sinclair, *d* of late James Baird, Glasgow. *Educ:* Trinity College, Cambridge (Exhibitioner). Cadet, Straits Settlements, 1889; District Officer Dindings, 1902; Inspector of Schools, Federated Malay States, 1903; Resident of Negri Sembilan, 1911; Colonial Secretary, Straits Settlements, 1911–16; Governor and Commander-in-Chief of Sierra Leone, 1916–22; retired, 1922.

Died 5 Dec. 1941.

WILKINSON, Walter Sutherland, CBE 1938; *b* 26 June 1875; *s* of Walter L. Wilkinson; *m* 1st, 1904, Annette (*d* 1925), *d* of Sir John Esmonde, 10th Bart; one *s*; 2nd, 1929, Christine, *d* of A. Macfarlane. *Educ:* Beaumont College, Old Windsor, Berks. Civil Service; Chief Inspector of Audit, Ministry of Health; retired, 1938; called to Bar, Middle Temple, 1899.

Died 8 July 1943.

WILKINSON, William, OBE; FTI; Head of College, Municipal Technical College, Blackburn, since 1925; *b* 18 Feb. 1882; *s* of Elisha and Emma Wilkinson; *m* 1908, Ethel Annie Folley; two *s. Educ:* Technical Schools, Clitheroe and Manchester. Cotton Weaver, Overlooker, Designer and Cotton Mill Manager; Head of Weaving Classes, Clitheroe Technical School, 1908–12; Weaving Master Accrington Technical School, 1911–12; Head of Textile Department Nelson Technical School, 1912–18; Head of Textile Department Blackburn Technical College, 1918–25. *Publications:* Practical Weaving, 1915; Students Lecture Notes; Weaving Problems, etc. *Recreations:* keen sportsman, football, mainly interested in textile problems and research. *Address:* Shandon, 50 Lammack Road, Blackburn. *T:* Blackburn 44080.

Died 16 Sept. 1944.

WILLANS, Sir Frederic Jeune, KCVO 1933; CVO 1925; MVO 1923; Surgeon-Apothecary to HM Household at Sandringham since 1924, and late Surgeon-Apothecary to Queen Alexandra; *e s* of late Dr W. Blundell Willans, Much Hadham, Herts; *m* Wynefred, *o d* of late Sir Alan Manby, KCVO. *Educ:* Framlingham; Durham University; London Hospital, MRCS, LRCP 1910. *Recreations:* lawn tennis, golf. *Address:* West Newton House, Sandringham, Norfolk. *TA:* Sandringham. *T:* King's Lynn 2675.

Died 27 Jan. 1949.

WILLANS, Maj.-Gen. Harry, CB 1943; CBE 1939; DSO 1918; MC; TD; late The Bedfordshire Regt; Director-General, Welfare and Education, War Office, since 1940; *b* 1892; *o s* of late James Tetley Willans; *m* 1917; two *d. Educ:* Aldenham. Served European War; France, 1914–18; Italy, 1917 (DSO, MC, despatches twice, 1914 Star, wounded); commanded the Artists Rifles, 1933–38; Commander, 2nd (London) Infantry Brigade, TA, 1938–39; Commander Territorial Army Division, 1939–40. *Club:* United Service.

Died 5 Feb. 1943.

WILLCOX, Lt-Col Walter Temple, CMG 1916; 3rd (King's Own) Hussars, retd; *b* 23 Dec. 1869; *s* of Temple Willcox; *m* 1938, Cecily, *o d* of Cecil Haig, The Chase, Monnington-on-Wye, Hereford; one *s*. Promoted 2nd Lieutenant 5th Royal Irish Lancers from 18th Hussars, 1894; Major, 3rd King's Own Hussars, 1906; Lt-Colonel commanding 3rd Hussars, 1915–21; Adjutant 5th

Lancers, and also of the Imperial Light Horse and South African Constabulary upon their formation; served throughout South African War, and was wounded in defence of Ladysmith (Queen's medal 4 clasps, King's medal 2 clasps); served with 3rd Hussars throughout European War, and present with the British Cavalry Division at Mons, The Retreat, The Marne, The Aisne, both battles of Ypres, etc., Army of the Rhine (despatches, CMG, Croix de Guerre avec Palme, France); retired pay, 1921. *Publications:* History of the 5th Lancers; The 3rd (King's Own) Hussars, 1914–1919, 1926. *Address:* Down Manor, Bromyard Down, Herefordshire. *Club:* Cavalry.

Died 16 May 1943.

WILLCOX, Col (Hon.) Sir William Henry, KCIE 1921; CB 1917; CMG 1916; MD, BSc (London University), DPH, FRCP (Lond.), FIC; Knight of Grace, Order of St John of Jerusalem; Consulting Physician to St Mary's Hospital, London, W; Senior Physician, London Fever Hospital and St Luke's Hostel for the Clergy; Visitor for Privy Council to the Examinations of the Pharmaceutical Society of Great Britain; *b* 18 Jan. 1870; *s* of late William Willcox, Melton Mowbray, Leicestershire; *m* Mildred, *e d* of late W. Griffin of Clapton, Northamptonshire; three *s* one *d*. *Educ:* Wymondham Grammar School, Oakham; The Wyggeston School, Leicester; University College, London; St Mary's Hospital Medical School, London (Senior Science Scholar). Gold Medallist at London University in Anatomy, Organic Chemistry, Materia Medica, and Therapeutics, and Forensic Medicine (MB examinations); Cheadle Gold Medal, St Mary's Hospital, for. Research Work in Clinical Medicine; Medical Registrar, St Mary's Hospital, 1904–06; Lecturer on Chemical Pathology, St Mary's Hospital, 1900–30; Lecturer on Forensic Medicine, St Mary's Hospital, 1906–35; President of West London Medico-Chirurgical Society, 1923; President Medico-Legal Society, 1928, 1929; Past President of Harveian Society of London, 1922; President Medical Society of London, 1936–37; Master of Society of Apothecaries, 1935–36; Medical Adviser to Home Office since 1919; Examiner in Pharmacology and Therapeutics at University of Cambridge, 1928–34; Fellow of the Royal Society of Medicine; (Pres. Section of Pharmacology and Therapeutics, 1940–41); served European War, 1915–18 (CMG, CB); temp. Lt-Colonel, 1915; temp. Colonel, 1916 (despatches four times). *Publications:* numerous original papers in the medical journals on Medicine, Forensic Medicine and Chemical Pathology; publications in The Lancet, British Medical Journal, Practitioner, Transactions of the Medical Society of London, the Pathological Society of London, St Mary's Hospital Gazette, and the Transactions of the Medico-Legal Society of London. *Recreations:* cycling, riding. *Address:* 40 Welbeck Street, Cavendish Square, W1. *T:* Langham 4030. *Club:* Athenæum.

Died 8 July 1941.

WILLEY, Arthur, FRS 1902; MA, DSc; Strathcona Emeritus Professor of Zoology, McGill University, Montreal; *b* Scarborough, 1867; *s* of Rev. William Willey; *m* 1902. *Educ:* Kingswood School, Bath; University College, London (Fellow). Balfour Student of the University of Cambridge, 1894–99. Lecturer in Biology, Guy's Hospital, 1899–1901; Director of Colombo Museum, and editor of Spolia Zeylanica, 1902–10; Corresponding Member of the Zoological Society of London, 1924. *Publications:* Amphioxus and the Ancestry of the Vertebrates, 1894; Convergence in Evolution, 1911; edited Zoological Results, 1898–1902; Lectures on Darwinism, 1930; articles in scientific journals; studies in bionomical variation (in progress). *Address:* Mille Isles, Que., Canada. *Clubs:* Faculty, Montreal.

Died 26 Dec. 1942.

WILLIAMS, Col Alfred Ernest, DSO 1917; *b* 1871; *e s* of late Rev. A. H. Williams, Chaplain in Ordinary to Queen Victoria and King Edward; *m* 1896, May (*d* 1926), *d* of late Gen. F. Roome, CB; two *s* three *d*. *Educ:* Charterhouse. Formerly Lt-Col Royal Warwickshire Regt; served South Africa, 1900–01; European War, 1914–18 (despatches five times, DSO); retired, 1928; ADC to the King, 1919–38. *Club:* Thatched House.

Died 27 Sept. 1941.

WILLIAMS, Alyn, PRMS, RCA; Founder and President Royal Society of Miniature Painters, Sculptors, and Gravers; Vice-President of the Royal Colonial Society of Artists and Imperial Arts League; 3rd *s* of late William Mattieu Williams, FRAS, FCS, author of The Fuel of the Sun, Through Norway with a Knapsack, etc; *m* 2nd, 1913, Anna Vernon Dorsey of Maryland, USA. *Educ:* under father's supervision. Studied art first at the Slade School and under Prof. F. Brown at Westminster; afterwards at Julien's Academy, Paris. Had special sittings from the late King Edward and Queen Alexandra for miniature portraits; Pope Pius XI and Premier Mussolini, 1926; exhibited miniature portraits in Royal Academy, New Gallery, Paris Salon, and all leading exhibitions for many years; first miniature exhibited in Royal Academy, 1890. *Publications:* various articles upon miniature painting in the Artist and elsewhere; How to paint Portrait Miniatures. *Recreations:* motoring, swimming, yachting. *Address:* Cambridge Studio, W Cowes, IW. *T:* Cowes 533. *Club:* Arts.

Died 25 July 1941.

WILLIAMS, (Arthur Frederic) Basil, OBE 1919; FBA; Professor Emeritus (Edin.); *b* London, 4 April 1867; *s* of F. G. A. Williams, Barrister-at-law; *m* 1905, Dorothy (*d* 1948), *d* of Francis W. Caulfeild; two *s*. *Educ:* Marlborough; New Coll., Oxford (Scholar), 1st Class Classical Mods, 2nd Class Lit Hum. Clerk in House of Commons, 1892–1901; served in HAC Battery of CIV in South Africa; Secretary Transvaal Education Dept, 1903–04; special correspondent to The Times at S African Convention, 1908–09; Vice-Chairman, Borough Polytechnic Institute, 1921; Liberal candidate for Mid-Sussex, Jan. 1910; Rugby Division, Dec. 1910; organised reception of Belgian Refugees at Folkestone for LGB, 1914 (Med. du Roi Albert); Captain RFA (T), July 1915; Major on General Staff 1918–19; Ford Lecturer at Oxford, 1921; Professor of History at McGill University, 1921–25; Associate Member of All Souls, 1924–25; Professor of History at Edinburgh, 1925–37; took History 6th form, Harrow, summer 1944. *Publications:* Foreign Policy of Walpole (Eng. Hist Rev., 1900–1901); Times History of South African War, vol. iv; The Life of William Pitt, Earl of Chatham, 1913; Cecil Rhodes, 1921; The British Empire (Home University Library), 1928; Stanhope, 1932; The Whig Supremacy, 1714–1760 (Vol. XI of Oxford History of England) 1939; Carteret and Newcastle, 1943; articles in Dictionary National Biography and Ency. Brit.; Editor of Makers of the 19th Century: Botha, Smuts and South Africa, 1946. *Address:* 5 Fernshaw Mansions, SW10. *Club:* Athenæum.

Died 5 Jan. 1950.

WILLIAMS, Brig.-Gen. Sir Arthur John A.; *see* Allen-Williams.

WILLIAMS, Rev. Arthur Lukyn, DD; Hon. Canon of Ely; *b* Dummer House, Hants, 4 Jan. 1853; *s* of Rev. James Augustus Williams; *m* 1878, Caroline Marian Isabella Bessie (*d* 1919), *d* of John Parry; one *s* one *d*. *Educ:* Haileybury; Jesus College, Cambridge. Principal of Moore Theological College, Sydney, NSW, 1878–84; Rector of Ampton, Suffolk, 1885–91; Head of the London Mission of the London Jews' Society, 1891–95; Examining Chaplain to the Bishop of Durham, 1901–13; Warburton Lecturer at Lincoln's Inn, 1911–15; Vicar of Guilden Morden, 1895–1919; Warden of the Central Society of Sacred Study in Diocese of Ely, 1914–28.

Publications: St Matthew i–xiv in the Pulpit Commentary, 1894; Galatians, 1910, Colossians and Philemon, 1907, in the Cambridge Greek Testament; Galatians in the Cambridge Bible, 1911; A Manual of Christian Evidences for Jewish People, vol. i, 1911, vol. ii, 1919; The Hebrew-Christian Messiah (Warburton Lectures), 1916; Minor Prophets Unfolded, 1917, 1918, 1919, 1920, Mishna, Berakoth, 1921; Ecclesiastes in the Cambridge Bible, 1922; Justin Martyr's Dialogue with Trypho, 1930; Talmudic Judaism and Christianity, 1933; The Foundation of the Christian Faith, 1935; Adversus Judæos, a bird's-eye view of Christian Apologiæ until the Renaissance, 1935; The Doctrines of Modern Judaism Considered, 1939. *Address:* 99 Grantchester Meadows, Cambridge.

Died 6 Oct. 1943.

WILLIAMS, Brig. Augustus John, DSO 1918; FRCVS; Royal Army Veterinary Corps (retd); *b* Usk, Monmouthshire, 7 Nov. 1876; *e s* of late John Williams, MRCVS, Pontypool, Monmouthshire; *m* Florence Edith Elizabeth, *d* of late Edward Waters, Usk, Monmouthshire; one *d*. *Educ:* Usk Grammar School; Royal (Dick) Veterinary College, Edinburgh; MRCVS 1898; FRCVS 1906. Joined Army Veterinary Service, 1898; Captain, 1903; Major, 1913; Lieut-Colonel, 1921; Colonel, 1926; Brigadier, 1928; served S African war, 1899–1902 (Queen's medal, 4 clasps, King's medal, 2 clasps); Tibet Expedition, 1904 (medal); with Egyptian Army, 1907–09; Nvima Expedition (Egyptian medal and clasp); European War, Mesopotamia, 1917–19 (DSO, British war medal, Victory medal, despatches twice); Senior VO 6th Div. S African war; Veterinary Inspector L of C Tibet Expedition; officiating PVO Egyptian Army and Soudan Civil Vet. Dept, Inspecting VO Southern Circle; ADVS Eastern Command, and DDVS Northern Command, India; DADVS 15th Div.; Officiating DDVS, GHQ; ADVS, GHQ, Mesopotamia; Assistant Director General AVS War Office, 1921–23; Commandant Royal Army Veterinary School, Aldershot, 1923–24; Director of Veterinary Services in India, 1928–32; retired pay 1932. *Address:* c/o Glyn, Mills & Co., Kirkland House, Whitehall, SW1.

Died 19 Jan. 1945.

WILLIAMS, Basil; *see* Williams, A. F. B.

WILLIAMS, Brig. Cecil James, CBE 1943; OBE 1941; MC 1918; *b* 15 Oct. 1898; *s* of C. Williams, Bedford; *m* 1922, Anna, *y d* of late Rev. Professor James Dick, MA, DD, Belfast; no *c*. *Educ:* Aldershot and Sandhurst. Regular Army (RASC), 1916–48; Col 1945; retired 1948. *Address:* c/o Lloyds Bank, Ltd, Aldershot, Hampshire. *Club:* Junior United Service.

Died 29 Oct. 1948.

WILLIAMS, Charles Walter Stansby, Hon. MA (Oxon); *b* 20 Sept. 1886; *o s* of R. W. Stansby Williams; *m* 1917, Florence, *y d* of James Warrell Conway; one *s*. *Educ:* St Albans School; Univ. Coll., London. *Publications: Poetry:* The Silver Stair, 1912; Poems of Conformity, 1917; Divorce, 1920; Windows of Night, 1925; Stabat mater trans., and other words for music; A Myth of Shakespeare, 1929; Heroes and Kings, 1930; Three Plays, 1931; Thomas Cranmer of Canterbury (the Canterbury play, 1936); Taliessin through Logres, 1938; Judgement at Chelmsford; The Region of the Summer Stars, 1944. *Prose:* Victorian Narrative Verse (a selection with intro.), 1927; Poetry at Present, 1930; War in Heaven, 1930; Introduction to Gerard Hopkins's Poems (2nd edition) 1930; Many Dimensions, 1931; The Place of the Lion, 1931; The Greater Trumps, 1932; The English Poetic Mind, 1932; Shadows of Ecstasy, 1933; Bacon (a Biography), 1933; Reason and Beauty in the Poetic Mind, 1933; James I, 1934; Rochester, 1935; Elizabeth 1936; New Book of English Verse, 1935; Descent into Hell, 1937; Henry VII, 1937; He came down from Heaven, 1937; Descent of the Dove, 1939; Witchcraft, 1941; The Forgiveness of Sins, 1942; The

Figure of Beatrice, 1943; All Hallows' Eve, 1944. *Address:* Oxford University Press, Amen House, Warwick Sq., EC4.

Died 15 May 1945.

WILLIAMS, Christopher A.; *see* Addams Williams.

WILLIAMS, Daniel, CBE 1934; JP, Caernarvonshire; *b* Portmadoc, N Wales, 23 March 1876; *s* of late Daniel Williams, Perthi, Beddgelert; *m* 1903, Blodwen Anne, *o d* of Edward Williams, JP, Dolgelley; one *s* one *d. Educ:* Portmadoc School; Llandovery College. Solicitor, 1898; Assistant Official Receiver in Bankruptcy, Chester, North Wales, and Liverpool, 1902–07; High Court of Justice, 1907–18; Official Receiver High Court, 1919–29; Controller of the Clearing Office (Enemy Debts), and Custodian and Administrator of ex-enemy property, Director of Russian Claims Dept, Custodian for China, Egypt and the Sudan, 1929–35; Inspector-General in Bankruptcy, 1932–41. *Recreations:* golf, Captain of Royal St David's Golf Club, Harlech, N Wales, 1929–30. *Address:* Talarfor, Morfa Nevin, N Wales. *Club:* Sandy Lodge Golf.

Died 20 Oct. 1944.

WILLIAMS, David; Chairman of Swansea Co-operative Society from its inception, Sept. 1900; Alderman of the Borough; President of Swansea and District Co-operative Society; boilermaker; JP; *b* 8 Sept. 1865; 2nd *s* of David and Mary Williams; father a copper worker; *m* 1889, Elizabeth, *d* of George and Hannah Colwill; four *s* one *d. Educ:* Kilvey Copper Works School. Was page boy with Grenfell family, 1877–79; apprenticed boilermaker and attended evening school 4 years; MP (Lab) East Swansea, 1922–40; entered Swansea County Borough Council as first Labour member, 1898 (first Labour Mayor, 1912–13); has been Chairman of the Swansea Health Committee and a Member of Swansea Harbour Trust; Hon. Freedom of the Borough for valuable services, 1924. *Address:* 25 Windmill Terrace, Swansea.

Died 22 Jan. 1941.

WILLIAMS, Dr David L.; *see* Llewellyn-Williams.

WILLIAMS, Brig.-Gen. Edward George, CMG 1915; late the Devonshire Regiment; *b* 2 Sept. 1867. Entered Army, 1886; Captain, 1895; Major, 1906; Lt-Col 1914; served European War, 1914–17 (despatches thrice, CMG); retired, 1920. *Club:* Army and Navy.

Died 6 Nov. 1941.

WILLIAMS, Rt Hon. Sir Ellis H.; *see* Hume-Williams.

WILLIAMS, Ethel Mary Nucella, MD, Lond., DPH Camb.; JP; Physician and Surgeon retired; late President, British Federation of Medical Women; late President, NE Federation of University Women; *b* Cromer, 8 July 1863; *d* of Charles and Mary Elizabeth Williams of the White House, Thwaite All Saints, Norfolk. *Educ:* Norwich High School; Newnham College, Cambridge; London School of Medicine for Women. General Practice for between 30 and 40 years mainly at Newcastle on Tyne; was Chairman of the North Eastern Federation of the National Union of Women's Suffrage Societies; was instrumental in starting various women's societies; served on the Newcastle School Board and later on the Education Committee. Ex-Member of Senate of Durham Univ. *Publications:* papers in medical journals. *Recreations:* gardening, walking. *Address:* Low Bridges, Stocksfield.

Died 29 Jan. 1948.

WILLIAMS, Evan James, FRS 1939; Professor of Physics at University College of Wales, Aberystwyth, since 1938; *b* 8 June 1903. *Educ:* Llandyssul County School; University of Wales. BSc (Wales) 1st Class Hons Physics, 1923; PhD (Manchester) 1926; PhD (Cambridge) 1929; DSc (Wales) 1930. Engaged on Research (mainly in Atomic Physics) at Univ. of Manchester, 1924–27, Univ. of Cambridge, 1927–29, Univ. of Copenhagen, 1933–34; Teaching and Research at Univ. of Manchester, 1929–33, 1934–36; Univ. of Liverpool, 1936–38; 1851 Exhibition Senior Research Student, 1927–29; F Inst. P; attended many foreign conferences on Physics; Lectured at Ann Arbor University, USA, Summer, 1939; engaged on war work, 1939–45. Principal Scientific Officer at Royal Aircraft Establishment, Farnborough, 1939–41; Director of Operational Research at RAF Coastal Command, 1941–42; Scientific Adviser on Anti-U-boat warfare at Admiralty, 1943–45; Asst Director of Naval Operational Research, 1944–45. *Publications:* papers on Atomic Physics in various British and foreign scientific journals, 1924–1939. *Recreations:* lawn tennis, motoring. *Address:* Brynawel, Llanybyther, Cardiganshire.

Died 29 Sept. 1945.

WILLIAMS, Frederick Sims, KC 1913; LLB; Commissioner, Board of Trade (retired); *b* 18 Jan. 1855; *y s* of late F. Sims Williams of Penryhn, Pembrokeshire; *m* 1889, Alice Temple (*d* 1939), *d* of W. Boyd Buckle, Bengal CS, Queen's Representative at the Palace of Moorshedabad; four *s* three *d. Educ:* Trinity Hall, Cambridge; London University. Called to Inner Temple, 1879; Commercial and Insurance Cases; Hon. Treasurer, Scripture Gift Mission. *Recreation:* played Rugby football for Surrey Co. and Richmond. *Address:* Temple Grove, Windlesham, Surrey. *T:* Bagshot 109; 5 Crown Office Row, Temple, EC; Murvagh, Ballintra, Co. Donegal. *Club:* New University.

Died 27 Dec. 1941.

WILLIAMS, Brig.-Gen. G. Coventry, CB 1915; *b* 23 Nov. 1860; *y s* of late B. B. Williams of Buscot, Berks, and Clara, *d* of T. Darby Coventry of Greenlands, Bucks; *m* 1889, Alice Maude, *y d* of John Scollick. *Educ:* Eton. Entered Army, 1880; Captain, 1886; Adjutant 13th Hussars, 1896–97; Major, 1897; Lt-Col 1903, to command Royal Scots Greys; Col 1907; ADC to Maj.-Gen. Cavalry Brigade, Aldershot, 1890–94; AAG S Africa, 1902; served South Africa, 1899–1902 (despatches twice; Bt Lt-Col; Queen's medal 5 clasps, King's medal 2 clasps); European War, 1914–18 (CB); retired; has Russian Order of St Anne. *Address:* Buscot, York Avenue, Hove. *T:* Hove 4730.

Died 2 May 1947.

WILLIAMS, Comdr George Davies, CMG 1939; DSO 1919; RD 1922; RNR (retd); Naval Control Service Officer, Sydney, 1942–46; Hon. Controller of Shipping, Commonwealth of Australia, 1939–40; President Maritime Services Board, NSW, 1937–42; *b* St Dogmaels, Pembrokeshire, 17 Sept. 1879; *y s* of Capt. J. Williams; *m* 1921, Helen Isabel, *d* of F. J. Sheppard, Mooren Station, NSW. *Educ:* St Dogmaels Council School; Cardigan Collegiate. Entered Merchant Service, 1896; Chief Officer, White Star Line Training Ship Mersey, 1908–11; Sub-Lieut, RNR, 1909; Capt. Supt Victorian Training Ship John Murray, 1911–14; Lieut, RNR, 1913; Lieut, HMAS Australia, 1914–15; HMAS Sydney, 1916–17; 1st Lieut HMS Patia, 1917; 1st Lieut, HMS Hindustan; Zeebrugge operations, 1918 in command HMS Marguerite and HMS Tuberose, Mediterranean, 1918; Senior Officer, Paddle Mine-Sweeping Division (HMS Minerva II), Ægean and Black Seas, 1919 (DSO); Chairman, Naval War Gratuity Board, Melbourne, 1920; Deputy Director of Navigation, Commonwealth Navigation Service, 1920; Member Maritime Services, Co-Ordination Board, NSW, 1933; Royal Humane Society Diploma for life-saving; King's Jubilee Medal, 1935; Coronation Medal, 1937. *Address:* 44 Bridge Street, Sydney, NSW. *Clubs:* Royal Sydney Golf, Imperial Service, Sydney.

Died 29 Aug. 1947.

WILLIAMS, Brig.-Gen. George Mostyn, CB 1925; CMG 1918; retired; *b* 1868; *m* 1922. Served NW Frontier of India, 1897–98 (clasp); South African War, 1899–1902 (despatches, Queen's medal and three clasps, King's medal and two clasps); European War, 1914–18 (despatches, CMG). *Address:* Ardaghowen, Fleet, Hants. *Club:* Naval and Military.

Died 15 Aug. 1943.

WILLIAMS, Henry Owen, OBE 1918; ISO 1903; late Director of Contracts, Ministry of Munitions; *b* 1855; *s* of late John Williams of North Littleton, Worcestershire, and formerly of Luton and Dunstable, Bedfordshire; *m* 1882, Annie (*d* 1904), *d* of late Henry Dugard, of Edgbaston, Birmingham; two *d.* Served at Sir John Lawes' Laboratory, Harpenden, for two years before entering War Office after competitive examination, 1875, Staff Clerk, 1896; Chief Examiner, 1902; Visiting Inspector, 1908; Assistant Principal, 1914; lent to new Munitions Department, 1915; Assistant Director, 1915; Director, 1917; retired, 1917; a member of the Harpenden School Board, 1894–1900; now on the Committee of the National Children's Home and Orphanage. *Recreations:* chess, bowls. *Address:* Branscombe, 4 Kirkdale Road, Harpenden.

Died 19 Aug. 1943.

WILLIAMS, Maj.-Gen. Sir Hugh Bruce Bruce-, KCB 1919; CB 1915; DSO 1901; RE; *b* 24 July 1865; *o s* of late Gen. Sir E. C. S. Williams, KCIE; *m* 1889, Mabel, *o d* of late Stephen Heward of Toronto; one *s* one *d.* *Educ:* Winchester; Royal Military Academy. Entered Army, 1885; Capt. 1894; Brevet Major, 1900; Major, 1902; specially promoted to a half-pay Lt-Colonelcy, 1908; Colonel, 1912; passed Staff College, 1899; served South Africa, 1899–1902 (despatches four times, brevet of major, Queen's medal and 3 clasps, King's medal and 2 clasps, DSO); European War, France and Flanders, 1914–18 (despatches, KCB, CB); retired pay, 1923; Col Comdt RE, 1930–35. *Club:* Naval and Military.

Died 14 Dec. 1942.

WILLIAMS, Sir (I.) Thomas, Kt 1919; Director of the London, Midland and Scottish Railway; West London Extension, Dundalk; Newry and Greenore Railways and Baldwins, Ltd; Chairman Birmingham Canals Navigation; *b* 1853; *m* 1877, Annie (*d* 1928), *d* of John Lewis; one *s.* Late General Manager of the London and North-Western Railway Company; Lieut-Col Engineer and Railway Staff Corps, RETF; selected by the Railway Executive Committee to give evidence on railways and canals before the Select Committee on Transport. *Address:* Oakdene, St Margarets, Middlesex. *T:* Popesgrove 2083.

Died 19 May 1941.

WILLIAMS, J. H.; Wayfarer of Northern Despatch; *b* Newport, Oct. 1855. *Educ:* Dosworks School. Worked as journalist in Tewkesbury, South Norwood, SE, Liverpool, Hereford, Bishop Auckland, Middlesborough, and Darlington; editor of the North Star, 1899–1913. *Recreations:* reading, music, gardening, cycling, boating. *Address:* Menevia, South Terrace, Darlington.

Died 13 Oct. 1942.

WILLIAMS, Prof. J. Lloyd, DSc; MusDoc (Hon.) 1936; Professor of Botany, Aberystwyth, retired Sept. 1926; Editor of the Welsh Folk Song Journal, Bangor; Lecturer on the History of Welsh Music; President, Section K, British Association, 1925. Editor of Y Cerddor (the Welsh musical monthly). *Publications:* Studies in the Dictyotaceae and the Laminariaceae, Byd y Blodau, Byd y Blodau, Eng. Ed.; History of Welsh Music; Atgofion Vol. I, II, III, IV; Composer of several Welsh musical plays and volumes of settings of Welsh melodies. *Address:* Ashgrove Villa, Peasedown, Bath.

Died 15 Nov. 1945.

WILLIAMS, James Leslie, CMG 1915; MBE 1919; Barrister-at-law; retired 1933; *b* Parramatta, NSW, 10 March 1870; *s* of James Williams; *m* 1911; one *d.* *Educ:* Sydney University (BA). Called to the Bar, NSW, 1903; entered Public Service, NSW, 1884; Under-Secretary of Justice, NSW, 1904–19; Member (1919), and Chairman (1925–33) Public Service Board, NSW; served with AIF, 1916–19; Lieut (temp. Capt.). *Clubs:* Australian (Sydney, NSW).

Died 14 Nov. 1949.

WILLIAMS, Lt-Col John, CBE 1918; VD; *b* 1874. Served European War, 1914–19 (CBE).

Died 31 March 1942.

WILLIAMS, Sir John Fischer, Kt 1923; CBE 1917; KC 1921; British Member of Permanent Court of Arbitration at the Hague since 1936; *b* 26 Feb. 1870; *o s* of John Williams, 5 Elvaston Place, SW; *m* 1st, 1896, Florence Keown-Boyd; 2nd, 1911, Marjorie, *e d* of late Evelyn Hay Murray, Hascombe, Godalming; five *d.* *Educ:* Harrow; New College, Oxford. First Classes in Moderation and Lit. Hum. Fellow, New College, 1892–99; Arnold Essay Prize, 1893. Called to Bar, Lincoln's Inn, 1894; practised until the War at the Chancery Bar; Liberal Candidate for Oxford City, Dec. 1910; Assistant Legal Adviser, Home Office, 1918–20; British Legal Representative on the Reparation Commission under the Treaty of Versailles, 1920–30; Chairman Royal Commission on Tithe Rent Charge, 1934; Governor of the Fisheries Organisation Society; Member of the Institute of International Law and of Belgian Royal Academy. *Publications:* Chapters on Current International Law; Proportional Representation and British Politics, 1914; Life Insurance and the Poor; Some Aspects of the Covenant of the League of Nations, 1934; International Change and Peace, Aspects of Modern International Law; occasional articles, etc. *Address:* Lamledra, Gorran Haven, Cornwall. *Club:* Athenæum.

Died 17 May 1947.

WILLIAMS, Maj.-Gen. Sir John H.; *see* Hanbury-Williams.

WILLIAMS, Sir (John Lloyd Vaughan) Seymour, KBE 1925; TD; Lt-Col (retired) RE (TA); a member of firm of Lawrence, Williams & Co., Solicitors, Bristol; and of Seymour, Williams & Co., Parliamentary Agents, Westminster; *b* 1868; *s* of late John Rees Williams, Brecon; *m* 1897, Edna Beatrice, *d* of Joseph Tippett Howes, Kingswood, near Bristol; three *s* two *d.* *Educ:* King Edward VI School, Bath. Admitted a Solicitor, 1890; a Member of Royal Commission on Local Govt, of Committee under Ministry of Transport dealing with Licensing of Hackney Carriages, of Roads Advisory Committee, Ministry of Transport and Transport Advisory Committee; Chairman Sub-Committee on Accidents to Cyclists, 1937–38; Member Council of Coroners Society, President, 1937–38; one of British Representatives at International Road Congresses, Seville, 1924, Milan, 1927, Washington, 1930, Munich, 1934, The Hague, 1938; Member Standing Committee for England of Union Internationale des Villes, of Consultative Committee of Ministry of Health, and of Rents Tribunal under Housing Act, Member of Advisory Committee under the Rural Housing Act, 1931; Member of Central Housing Advisory Committee, 1935; and of Rural Housing Committee, 1936; Member of Local Government Law Consolidation Committee and of Local Government Economy Committee; Member Highway Law Consolidation Committee, 1937–38; and Coroner for Lower Division of Gloucestershire; Member of SW Regional Committee, Ministry of Information, and of SW Regional Fire Consultative Committee, 1942; Clerk to the Rural District Council of Warmley since 1897; Clerk Kingswood Assessment Committee; Chairman of Executive, Rural District Councils Association for

England and Wales, 1902–39; Clerk ARP Committee Area 11, Glos; Member of Gloucestershire CC, 1901–06; CRE, 61st and 71st and 48th Divisions, 1914–22; Hon. Colonel S Midland RE, 1933. *Address:* The Lodge, Warmley, near Bristol. *T:* 73486 Kingswood, Bristol. *Clubs:* National Liberal; Bristol.

Died 24 Feb. 1945.

WILLIAMS, Mary Atkinson, MA London, BA Queensland; *b* Belfast; *d* of Valentine Atkinson Williams of Belfast. *Educ:* Private School, Clifton, Bristol; Southlands College; attended lectures at various Colleges of University of London. Successively Lecturer in English, Southlands College. Lecturer in Education, University Extension Lecturer, and Examiner for Teacher's Diploma, University of Melbourne; Headmistress Brisbane Girls' Grammar School; Principal Southlands College, Battersea; Prin. Sanieh Training College, Cairo, 1918; Organising Inspector Leeds Education Committee; Diploma in Pedagogy (University of London); Gilchrist Travelling Scholarship, University of London; studied the Teaching of English in US America, and published Report on the Teaching of English in USA; retired 1931. *Publications:* various articles on Education in Journal of Education and various Australian papers. *Recreation:* travel. *Address:* 14 The Paragon, Clifton, Bristol, 8. *T:* Bristol 36655. *Club:* Crosby Hall.

Died 22 Sept. 1949.

WILLIAMS, Rev. Norman Powell, MA, DD; Lady Margaret Professor of Divinity in the University of Oxford, and Canon of Christ Church since 1927; Treasurer of Christ Church Cathedral, Oxford, since 1936; Subdean, 1939; Proctor in Convocation of Canterbury for the University of Oxford, 1936; *b* Durham, 5 Sept. 1883; *e s* of Rev. T. P. Williams, Vicar of St Mary's, South Shields; *m* 1927, Muriel de Lérisson, *o d* of late Arthur Philip Cazenove; two *s* two *d*. *Educ:* Durham School; Christ Church, Oxford (Scholar); 1st Class Class. Mods 1904; BA (1st Class Lit. Hum.), 1906; Fellow of Magdalen College, Oxford, 1906–09; Cuddesdon College, 1907; studied at University of Strasburg and University of Berlin, 1907–08; Ellerton Theological Essay Prize, 1908. Deacon, 1908; Priest, 1909; Chaplain Fellow of Exeter College, Oxford, 1909–27; Librarian, 1909–16; Examining Chaplain to the Bishop of Newcastle, 1916–27; temp. Assistant Master at Eton Coll., 1916–17; in Military Intelligence Department, War Office, 1917–18; temporary Chaplain RN, and Chaplain of HMS Pomone (additional) for duty at Royal Naval College, Dartmouth, 1918; Examiner in the Final Honour School of Theology at Oxford, 1921–23, and 1938–40; Chm. of Board of Theological Faculty, Oxford, 1934–37; Select Preacher at Oxford, 1922–24, and at Cambridge, 1932; Bampton Lecturer, 1924. *Publications:* contributed to Oxford Studies in the Synoptic Problem, ed. Dr Sanday, 1911; Miracles (Modern Oxford Tracts), 1914; joint author, with Dr Sanday, of Form and Content in the Christian Tradition, 1916; Our Case as against Rome, 1918; contributed to The Place of the Laity in the Church, 1918; The First Easter Morning, 1919; article Tradition in Hastings' Encyclopædia of Religion and Ethics, 1921; contributed to Essays Catholic and Critical, 1926; The Ideas of the Fall and of Original Sin (Bampton Lectures), 1927; The Epistle to the Romans, in The SPCK New Commentary, 1928; The Grace of God, 1930; joint editor (with Dr C. Harris) Northern Catholicism (Essays on the Oxford and Parallel Movements), 1933; contributed to The Study of Theology, 1939; The Epistle to the Romans (Westminster Commentary), 1943; articles and reviews in Expository Times, Church Quarterly Review, Journal of Theological Studies. *Address:* The Priory House, Christ Church, Oxford. *Club:* Athenæum.

Died 11 May 1943.

WILLIAMS, Penry; MP (L) Middlesbrough, 1910–18; East Division, 1918–22 and 1923–24; *b* 5 Sept. 1866; *s* of late Edward Williams, JP, Middlesbrough; *m* 1st, Alexandra Octavia, *d* of William Jenkins, Consett Hall, Co. Durham; one *d*; 2nd, Edith Martha, *d* of William Petherick, London. *Educ:* privately at Surbiton. JP North Riding of Yorkshire and for Middlesbrough; late Officer Commanding 1st North Riding of York Volunteer Artillery. *Recreation:* shooting. *Address:* Pinchinthorpe Hall, Guisborough, Yorks. *TA:* Williams, Guisborough 12. *T:* Guisborough 12. *Club:* Reform.

Died 26 June 1945.

WILLIAMS, Sir Richard John, Kt 1921; *b* 26 Feb. 1853; *m* 1889, Mary Emily, *d* of Hugh Pritchard, Liverpool; one *s* three *d*. Mayor of Bangor, 1913–20; Alderman of Carnarvonshire County Council and JP, DL for County; Alderman of Bangor City Council; Chairman of North-West Wales War Pension Committee; Director of Morris & Jones, Ltd, Liverpool; Governor and Vice-President of the Council of the University College of North Wales. *Address:* Cynfal, Bangor. *T:* Bangor 119. *Club:* Royal Welsh Yacht.

Died 25 Jan. 1941.

WILLIAMS, Col Sir Robert, 1st Bt *cr* 1915; VD, TD; JP, DL Dorset, and a Commissioner of Lieutenancy for the City of London; Director Williams Deacon's Bank, Ltd; late Hon. Col 4th Batt. Dorset Regiment; *b* 15 June 1848; *s* of Robert Williams and Mary Anne, *d* of Rev. J. W. Cunningham, Harrow; *m* 1869, Rosa Walker (*d* 1916), *y d* of late N. P. Simes of Strood Park, Horsham; one *s* three *d*. *Educ:* Eton; Christ Church, Oxford. Owns about 3000 acres. MP (C) West Dorset, 1895–1922. *Heir: s* Philip Francis Cunningham Williams [*b* 1884; *m* Margaret, *d* of late Sir Cuthbert and Hon. Lady Peek; three *s* seven *d*]. *Address:* Bridehead, Dorchester, Dorset. *Club:* National.

Died 15 April 1943.

WILLIAMS, Maj.-Gen. Robert Ernest, CMG 1917; VD; retired teacher; journalist; *b* Ballarat, 13 Aug. 1855; *m* 1884, Annie Clare Hylton; one *s* one *d*. *Educ:* Public schools. CMG for services in connection with the European War, 1915–17; despatches; retired, 1919; JP; acting Commandant, 3rd Military District, 1915–18. *Address:* 65 Toorak Road, South Camberwell, E6, Victoria, Australia. *T:* WF 7506. *Clubs:* Royal Automobile of Victoria, Melbourne.

Died 7 July 1943.

WILLIAMS, Roland Edmund Lomax Vaughan; KC 1913; Recorder of Cardiff, 1930–45; formerly of Carmarthen and of Swansea; *b* 1866; *e* and *o surv. s* of late Right Hon. Sir Roland L. Vaughan Williams; *m* 1911, Grace Agnes, *y d* of 1st Baron Phillimore of Shiplake. *Educ:* Merton College, Oxford. Called to Bar, Lincoln's Inn, 1893; Bencher, 1918; joined Middle Temple and South Wales Circuit; British Member of Anglo-German Mixed Arbitral Tribunal under Treaty of Versailles, 1920–28; Chairman of Aliens Deportation Advisory Committee; Vice-Chairman of Bar Council, 1935; contested Houghton-le-Spring Div. of Durham; South Shields; West Cornwall. *Recreations:* foreign travel, riding. *Address:* 2 Garden Court, Temple, EC4. *TA:* Williams, 84 Temple, London. *T:* Central 1456; Tanhurst, Leith Hill, Dorking, Surrey. *T:* Dorking 73159.

Died 22 Jan. 1949.

WILLIAMS, Romer; DL; JP for Co. Merioneth; late Chairman now Director of the Legal and General Life Assurance Society; late Chairman now Director of the Law Fire Assurance Society; Chairman of the Law Accident Assurance Society; Chairman of Hurst Park Race-course; *b* 24 Sept. 1850; *s* of Charles Reynolds Williams of Dolmelynllyn and Margaret Marshall Romer; *m* Dora Louisa (*d* 1933), *d* of late David Williams, MP for Merionethshire; one *s* one *d*. *Educ:*

Rugby. Late Pres. of Hunters Improvement Society; one of the Ruling Council of Roy. Vet. Coll.; High Sheriff, Merionethshire, 1902. *Recreations:* all sports; well known as judge at all important horse shows. *Address:* Newnham Hall, Daventry. *TA:* 30 Daventry. *Club:* Orleans.

Died 6 Feb. 1942.

WILLIAMS, Captain Rupert Stanley G.; *see* Gwatkin-Williams.

WILLIAMS, Sir Seymour; *see* Williams, Sir J. L. V. S.

WILLIAMS, Brig.-Gen. Sydney Frederick, CMG 1916; *b* 29 Dec. 1866; *s* of Rev. S. F. Williams, Rector of Cold Norton, Essex; *m* 1896, Mary Grant (*d* 1940), *d* of late Cecil Gwyer. *Educ:* Haileybury College. Passed direct into Royal Engineers, 1886; served in Malta, 1889–94; Ordnance Survey of Scotland, 1895–1904; Horse Guards, 1906–12; on Lord Kitchener's Coronation Staff, 1911 (Coronation medal); joined 12th Division as Commanding RE, Oct. 1914; proceeded to France with 12th Division, May 1915 (despatches four times, CMG); retired pay, 1919. *Publication:* Drill or Education (National Review July, 1940). *Recreations:* tennis, lawn tennis, croquet. *Address:* c/o Lloyds Bank, 6 Pall Mall, SW1. *Club:* United Service.

Died 12 May 1942.

WILLIAMS, Sir Thomas; *see* Williams, Sir I. T.

WILLIAMS, Very Rev. Thomas Alfred; Dean of Bangor, since 1940; *b* 16 June 1870; *s* of D. Williams, Llansawel, Carmarthenshire; *m* 1906, Martha Grace, *d* of Rev. E. A. Davies, Vicar of Cwmamman, Carmarthenshire; one *s* one *d*. *Educ:* St David's College, Lampeter. Curate of Llanfaelog, Anglesey, 1894–95; Llanfair PG and Menai Bridge, 1895–1900; Portmadoc, 1900–06; Vicar of Bryncoedifor, Dolgelly, 1906–13; Rector of Festiniog and Maentwrog, 1913–40; Rural Dean of Ardudwy, 1930–31; Archdeacon of Merioneth, 1931–40. *Address:* The Deanery, Bangor, Caernarvonshire.

Died 27 July 1941.

WILLIAMS, Most Rev. Thomas Leighton; Archbishop of Birmingham (RC) since 1929; *b* 20 March 1877; *s* of James Anthony Williams and Emma Mary Leighton. *Educ:* Cotton College, North Staffs; Oscott College, Birmingham; Christ's College, Cambridge. BA 1903, Second class, Historical Tripos, MA, 1909. Priest, 1900; Master of St Edmund's House, Cambridge, 1909–18; Chaplain to the Forces, 1916–20; Principal, St Charles's House, Oxford, 1920–22; Rector of Cotton College, North Staffs, 1922–29. *Publication:* Co-editor with Canon Burton of Volumes I and II of the Douay Diaries, published 1911 by Catholic Record Society. *Recreations:* golf, tennis. *Address:* Archbishop's House, 6 Norfolk Road, Edgbaston, Birmingham, 15. *T:* Edgbaston 0564.

Died 1 April 1946.

WILLIAMS, Rev. Thomas Rhondda, DD; *b* Cowbridge, Glamorgan, 1860; *s* of Rev. T. Williams, Calvinistic Methodist minister; *m* 1882; two *s* four *d*. *Educ:* Grammar School, Cardiff; Presbyterian College, Carmarthen. Began public preaching at 13½ years of age; entered Carmarthen College with a Dr Williams Scholarship, 1877; ordained at Dowlais at age of 20, 1880; ministered at Neath, 1884–88; Bradford, 1888–1909; Congregational Minister, Union Church, Brighton, 1909–31; Chairman, Congregational Union of England and Wales, 1929. *Publications:* Belief and Life; God's Open Doors; Shall We Understand the Bible?; Does Science Destroy Religion?; The Social Gospel; The Evangel of the New Theology; Sermons to Children and Young People; The New Theology; The Workingfaith of a Liberal Theologian; Old Testament Stories in Modern Light; Faith Without Fear, 1933; How I found my Faith: a Religious Pilgrimage, 1938;

Articles in various papers in England and America. *Recreation:* walking. *Address:* Avalon, Hove Park Road, Hove, Sussex. *T:* Preston 2578.

Died 21 Nov. 1945.

WILLIAMS, Maj.-Gen. Thomas Rhys, CMG 1919; DSO 1917; Deputy Controller Imperial War Graves Commission, Eastern District, 1943; *b* 10 April 1884; *s* of late Thomas Williams; *m* 1914. Served European War, 1915–19 (despatches four times, DSO, Belgian Croix de Guerre, CMG); Bt-Col, 1934; Maj.-Gen., 1939; Master-General of the Ordnance, AHQ, Australia, 1939–40; Chief Military Adviser to Dept of Munitions, Australia, 1941. *Address:* Army HQ, Melbourne, SC1.

Died 23 Oct. 1950.

WILLIAMS, Valentine, MC; Chevalier of the Order of the Crown of Belgium; author; *b* 20 Oct. 1883; *e s* of late G. Douglas Williams, Chief Editor of Reuter's, and *g s* of late W. J. Skerrett, DL, of Finavara, Co. Clare; *m* Alice, *d* of G. Hunter Crawford, of Bendigo, Victoria, Australia. *Educ:* Downside School; privately in Germany. Joined Reuter's Agency as sub-editor, 1902; Berlin correspondent of Reuter's, 1904–09; Paris correspondent of the Daily Mail, 1909–13; Special correspondent of the Daily Mail in the Portuguese Revolution, 1910, Spain, Austria and the Balkans; war correspondent of the Daily Mail in the Balkan War, 1913; first accredited correspondent at British GHQ March 1915; 2nd Lieut Irish Guards, Dec. 1915 (MC, twice wounded); attached Staff London District, 1918; Captain attached Staff Guards Div. Aug. 1918; demobilised Feb. 1919; in charge of the Daily Mail Staff at the Versailles Peace Conference; fulfilled various journalistic missions to Egypt (Tutankhamen's Tomb), Morocco, Tunisia, and United States; wrote and acted in four radio plays for the National Broadcasting Co. of America (with Alice Crawford) and has broadcast extensively in Great Britain and US; served in a Dept of Foreign Office, 1939–41; attached to British Embassy, Washington, 1941–42; screen play writer for 20th Century Fox and Metro-Goldwyn-Mayer, 1942–45. *Publications:* With Our Army in Flanders; Adventures of an Ensign; The Man with the Clubfoot; The Secret Hand; The Yellow Streak; The Return of Clubfoot; The Orange Divan; The Three of Clubs; The Red Mass; Mr Ramosi; The Pigeon House; The Eye in Attendance; The Crouching Beast; The Knife Behind the Curtain; Mannequin; Death Answers the Bell, The Gold Comfit Box, 1932; The Clock Ticks On, 1933; Fog, 1933; The Portcullis Room; Masks Off at Midnight, 1934; The Clue of the Rising Moon, 1935; Dead Man Manor, 1935; The Spider's Touch, 1936; Mr Treadgold Cuts In, 1937; The World of Action, 1938; The Fox Prowls, 1939; Courier to Marrakesh, 1945; Skeleton Out of The Cupboard, 1946. *Recreations:* tennis, lawn tennis, squash, swimming, ice skating. *Address:* c/o A. M. Heath & Co., Princes House, Jermyn Street, SW1. *Clubs:* Guards', Pratt's.

Died 20 Nov. 1946.

WILLIAMS, Rt Rev. Watkin Herbert, MA; *b* 22 Aug. 1845; *m* 1879, Alice (*d* 1937), *d* of late Gen. Monckton. *Educ:* Westminster; Christ Church, Oxford. Vicar of Bodelwyddan, Flints, 1872–92; Chaplain to Bishop of St Asaph, 1889; Archdeacon of St Asaph, 1889–92; Dean of St Asaph, 1892–98; Bishop of Bangor, 1899–1924. *Publication:* The Duties of Church-wardens, 1890. *Address:* Pant Eidal, Aberdovey. *Clubs:* Athenæum, Oxford and Cambridge.

Died 19 Nov. 1944.

WILLIAMS, Rev. Watkin (Wynn), MA, FRHistS; Membre du Comité des Annales de Bourgogne; Member of the Mediæval Academy of America; Membre de la Société pour l'Histoire du Droit de Bourgogne; *b* 25 Sept. 1859; *e s* of late Watkin Wynn Williams, London; *m* 1905, Charlotte Philippa Stephana, *y d* of late Gen. Sir Charles Warren, GCMG, KCB,

FRS; one s one d. *Educ:* Radley; Christ Church, Oxford. With Dr Vaughan, 1882–83; ordained, 1883; Priest, 1884; Curate of St Peter, Battersea, 1883–86; Holy Trinity, Upper Chelsea, 1886–88; Vice-Principal, Dorchester Missionary College, 1888–91; Fellow and Tutor, St Augustine's College, Canterbury, 1891–1904; Vicar of Monkton, Thanet, 1904–15; Hon. Fellow, St Augustine's College, Canterbury, 1907–16; Rector of Drayton St Leonard, 1915–28; Founder and First President, South Oxon Labour Party, 1924 (Resigned, 1927); Official Delegate of University of Oxford at the Congress of the Association Bourguignonne des Sociétés Savantes, Dijon, 1927; Active Member of the International Congress of Historical Sciences, Warsaw, 1933. *Publications:* Resources and Responsibilities, 1899; Letters of Savonarola, 1907; Maxims of the Mystics, 1909; The Moral Theology of the Sacrament of Penance, 3rd ed., 1931; Advent Sermons of Bourdaloue, 1919; Considerations for Confessors, 1919; St Bernard Concerning Grace and Free Will, 1920; Studies in St Bernard of Clairvaux, 1927; Thoughts of St Bernard of Clairvaux for every day in the year, 1928; L'Aspect Ethique du Mysticisme de Saint Bernard (in Saint Bernard et son temps, 1929); The Mysticism of St Bernard of Clairvaux, 2nd edn 1939; The Life of St Bernard of Clairvaux, 1935; St Bernard, Of Conversion, the text of the Anchin MS with Translation and Notes, 1938; Monastic Studies, 1938; The Individualism of St Bernard of Clairvaux, 1939; St Bernard, the Man and His Message, 1943; articles in various periodicals. (Joint) Author: An Introduction to the Articles of the Church of England (with late Rev. Dr G. F. Maclear), 3rd edition, 1909; Select Treatises of St Bernard (with late Rev. Barton Mills), 1926. *Recreations:* travel and reading. *Address:* Wentworth House, Great Malvern. *T:* Malvern 341.

Died 22 June 1944.

WILLIAMS, William Henry, MA; Professor of Classics and English Literature in the University of Tasmania, 1893; retired, 1925; Emeritus Professor, 1926; *b* Birmingham, 7 Nov. 1852; *s* of William and Amelia Burley Williams; *m* 1st, 1883, Ethel (*d* 1926), *d* of late Martin Swindells of Bollington, Cheshire; two *s*; 2nd, 1931, Ruth Mary, *d* of William Newbery, Sydney, NSW. *Educ:* Newark Magnus School; Trinity College, Cambridge (Scholar and Prizeman). First Class in the Classical Tripos, 1876. Assistant Master at Leys School, Cambridge, 1876–84; Headmaster of Newington College, Sydney, 1884–93. *Publications:* Edited Dryden, The Hind and the Panther; Ralph Roister Doister in the Temple Dramatists; Selections from Skelton; Specimens of the Elizabethan Drama; Preface to Dryden's Fables; Jacke Jugeler; Shakespeare—The Tempest (Australasian) Shakespeare; Gay, Trivia; Selection from Thackeray's Roundabout Papers, 1927; Matthew Green's The Spleen, 1935. *Address:* Kelham, Wellesley Street, Hobart, Tasmania.

Died 12 Sept. 1941.

WILLIAMS-BULKELEY, Sir Richard Henry; see Bulkeley.

WILLIAMS-TAYLOR, Sir Frederick, Kt 1913; Director Bank of Montreal since 1929; *b* Monckton, New Brunswick, 23 Oct. 1863; *s* of Ezekiel Moore Taylor and Rosalind Beatty; *m* 1888, Jane Fayrer, *o d* of Joshua Henshaw, Montreal; one *d*. *Educ:* privately by his father. Entered Bank of Montreal, 1878; Assistant Inspector at Head Office, 1897; Joint Manager, Chicago, 1903; Manager, London, 1905; General Manager, 1913–29; Chairman, London Advisory Committee, Royal Trust Company; Director, Royal Trust Company, Montreal; Dominion Textile Company, Ltd; Montreal, London and General Investors, Ltd; an Hon. President of Canadian Bankers' Assoc.; awarded the Silver Medal of the Royal Society of Arts for his paper on Canada and Canadian Banking, 1911; Knight Commander of the Order of St Olaf of Norway; Knight

Commander of the Order of St Sava of Serbia; Hon. LLD New Brunswick Univ., 1915; Officer Legion of Honour, 1927; Hon. Colonel New Brunswick Tank Corps, 1940. *Recreations:* golf, billiards. *Address:* Claridge's Hotel, W1. *Cables:* Montcalm, London; Ritz Carlton, Montreal; Star Acres, Nassau, Bahamas. *Cables:* Hermit. *Clubs:* Marlborough, Carlton, Bath, Travellers'; Mount Royal, St James's, Montreal.

Died 2 Aug. 1945.

WILLIAMS-THOMAS, Lt-Col Frank S., DSO 1919; TD; Resident, Nigeria Administrative Service; retired, 1930; *b* 1879; *er s* of late J. S. Williams-Thomas, OBE, Parkfield, Stourbridge, Worcestershire. *Educ:* Shrewsbury; Trinity College, Camb. Barrister-at-Law Middle Temple; in the QO Worcestershire Hussars, 1907–27; served European War, 1914–19, Gallipoli and Egypt with Worcestershire Hussars, and in North Russia with Relief Force, 1919. *Address:* Hingham, Norfolk. *Club:* Cavalry.

Died 1 July 1942.

WILLIAMS-WYNN, Col Sir Herbert Lloyd Watkin, 7th Bt *cr* 1688; CB 1902; BA, JP, DL; Lord-Lieutenant of Montgomeryshire, since 1891; Director of the Great Western Railway; *b* Wales, 6 June 1860; *s* of late Lieut-Col Herbert W. Williams Wynn and Anna, *d* and *heiress* of Edward Lloyd, Cefn, Co. Denbigh; *S* uncle, 1885; *m* 1884, *cousin*, Louise Alexandra, *d* of 6th Bt (whom he divorced 1898); *d* 1911; one *s* two *d*. *Educ:* Wellington; Trin. Coll., Camb. (BA). MP Denbighshire, 1885; High Sheriff, 1890; late commanding Montgomeryshire Yeomanry Cavalry; retired, 1906; Chairman Denbighshire Quarter Sessions, 1905. Owns about 100,000 acres. *Recreations:* hunting, shooting; owns and hunts a pack of foxhounds (Wynnstay); is very fond of engineering work and building; takes great interest in estate improvements. *Heir: s* Watkin [*b* 25 Jan. 1891; *m* 1920, Daisy, *yr d* of late J. Johnson Houghton, Westwood, Neston, Cheshire; one *s* three *d*]. *Address:* Wynnstay, Ruabon. *TA:* Ruabon. *T:* Ruabon 13.

Died 24 May 1944.

WILLIAMS-WYNN, Sir Watkin, 8th Bt *cr* 1688; High Sheriff of Denbighshire, 1948–49; *b* 25 Jan. 1891; *s* of Sir Watkin Williams-Wynn, 7th Bt, and Louise Alexandra, *d* of 6th Bt; *S* father, 1944; *m* 1920, Daisy, *yr d* of late J. Johnson Houghton, Westwood, Neston, Cheshire; three *d*. *Educ:* Eton; Trin. Coll. Camb. (BA). *Heir: uncle* Sir R. W. H. W. Williams-Wynn, KCB. *Address:* Wynnstay, Ruabon; Llangedwyn Hall, nr Oswestry.

Died 9 May 1949.

WILLIAMSON, Rev. Charles David Robertson; a Catholic priest; *b* 1853; *s* of late Col D. R. Williamson and Hon. Selina Maria Morgan, *d* of 1st Lord Tredegar. *Educ:* Eton; University College, Oxford. *Address:* Tomperran, Comrie, Perthshire.

Died 20 Jan. 1943.

WILLIAMSON, Sir Charles Hedworth, 10th Bt *cr* 1642; *b* 6 Sept. 1903; *s* of late Frederick Charles Williamson (3rd *s* of 8th Bt) and Phyllis, *d* of late Lt-Col C. E. Hunter; *S* uncle, 1942. *Educ:* Oundle; Christ Church, Oxford. *Heir: nephew* Nicholas Frederick Hedworth, *b* 1937. *Address:* Whitburn Hall, Whitburn, Co. Durham. *Clubs:* Brooks's, Bath.

Died 8 April 1946.

WILLIAMSON, George Charles, LittD; Fellow Royal Society of Literature, and Zoological Society; Chevalier Legion of Honour; JP (County of London and Borough of Guildford); Hon. Remembrancer of Guildford since 1933; *b* Guildford, 1858; *m* 1883, Louisa Mary Lethbridge; two *s* one *d*. *Educ:* privately; London University. As an author, commenced with newspaper articles on local archæological matters, and issued a small book on local coins; was the author of a large book on Traders' Tokens and a small one on Coins of the Bible, and then commenced to write on Art, and has done so steadily ever since; has been for many years art editor to George Bell & Sons; has travelled largely, visiting the picture galleries of Europe, both public and private. *Publications:* Life of John Russell, RA; Richard Cosway, RA; George J. Pinwell; Portrait Miniatures; Luini; Perugino; Francia; George Engleheart; Velazquez; Fra Angelico; Holman Hunt; Lord Leighton; Murillo; Raphael; The Cities of Northern Italy; Andrew and Nathaniel Plimer; The History of Portrait Miniatures; The Anonimo Morelliano; How to Identify Portrait Miniatures; Life of George Morland; Life of Milton; Guildford in the Olden Time; Portrait Drawings; John Downman, ARA; Catalogue of the Pierpont Morgan Collection of Miniatures, 4 vols, and Pierpont Morgan Collection of Jewels, 1 vol., and Pierpont Morgan Collection of Watches, 1 vol.; The Imperial Wedgwood Dinner Service; Miniatures, English and Foreign (Studio); Catalogue of the Portraits of Milton; Ye Roll of ye Sette of Odd Volumes, 1913, and second Volume, 1920; The Keats Letters, Papers, and other Relics at Hampstead, full transcriptions and notes; Who was Lady Anne?; Ozias Humphry, RA, 1918; Murray Marks and His Friends, 1919; Lodowick Muggleton, 1919; George, Third Earl of Cumberland: His Life and Voyages, 1920; John Zoffany, RA, 1920; Lady Anne Clifford, Behind my Library Door, The Miniature Collector, Daniel Gardner, 1921; Curious Survivals, 1923; Everybody's Book on Collecting, 1923; Angelica Kauffmann, RA, 1924; Famille Rose Porcelain, 1925; Stories of an Expert, 1925; Guildford Castle, 1926; Guildford Guildhall, 1927; Guildford Grammar School, 1928; St Edward's Church, Sutton Park, 1929; Guildford Caverns, 1930; Guildford Charities, 1930; English Conversation Pictures, 1932; The Book of Amber, 1932; The Book of Ivory, 1938; Memoirs in Miniature, 1933; edited the Keats Memorial Volume, 1921, etc.; The Art of the Miniature Painter, 1926; edited new edition of Bryan's Dictionary of Painters and Engravers, 5 vols. *Recreation:* the collection of miniatures and portrait drawings in pencil. *Address:* Mount Manor House, Mount Street, Guildford, Surrey. *T:* Guildford 1053. *Clubs:* Burlington Fine Arts, First Edition (Chairman); County, Guildford.

Died 4 July 1942.

WILLIAMSON, Sir Hedworth, 9th Bt *cr* 1642; *b* 23 May 1867; *s* of 8th Bt and Lady Elizabeth Jane Hay Liddell, *d* of 1st Earl of Ravensworth. *Educ:* Eton; Christ Church, Oxford. *Heir: nephew* Charles Hedworth Williamson, *b* 1903. *Address:* Appley Hall, Ryde, I of W.

Died 27 Oct. 1942.

WILLIAMSON, Oliver Key, MA, MD, BChir (Cantab); FRCP (Lond.); MRCS (Eng.); Consulting Physician City of London Hospital for Diseases of the Heart and Lungs; Hon. Consulting Physician Buchanan Hospital, St Leonards; Consulting Physician Johannesburg Hospital, formerly Professor of Medicine, University of the Witwatersrand, Johannesburg; and Examiner in Medicine, University of Cape Town; Hon. Life Member, Cape Town Section Mountain Club of South Africa; *s* of late Alexander William Williamson, FRS, Professor of Chemistry at University College, London, and Emma Catherine Williamson; *m* 1912, Edith Gertrude (*d* 1937), *d* of late John Adolphus Edington and Mrs Edington of Golcar, Yorks. *Educ:* University College School; University College and Hospital, London; Trinity College, Cambridge. Honours Natural Science Tripos, Cambridge. House Physician, University College Hospital; Junior Resident Medical Officer and Registrar, Evelina Hospital for Children; House Physician and Pathologist, Victoria Park Hospital, and Medical Registrar, Middlesex Hospital; Orator Hunterian Society; Vice-President Hunterian Society; Assistant Physician, Westminster Hospital; joint lecturer in Medicine, Westminster Hospital Medical School; and Physician, East London Children's Hospital, Shadwell; Vice-President Section of

Medicine Centenary Meeting, BMA. *Publications:* articles on Blood Pressure and Arterial Disease in Dictionary of Medicine, edited by Malcolm Morris, Langmead, and Holmes; The Prevention of the Common Cold; various papers in Transactions of Medical Societies and Medical Journals, chiefly on Blood Pressure and Diseases of the Chest; papers on Mountaineering in Alpine Journal; is interested in Arterial and Chest Diseases. *Recreations:* mountaineering, photography. *Address:* c/o Standard Bank of South Africa, Ltd, 10 Clements Lane, EC4. *Club:* Alpine.

Died 17 Oct. 1941.

WILLIAMSON, Richard Harcourt, CIE 1931; Indian Civil Service (retired); *b* 1879; *s* of Lt-Col F. H. Williamson; unmarried. *Educ:* St Paul's School; Exeter College, Oxford. Entered Indian Civil Service, 1903; Magistrate and Collector, 1915–31; Commissioner Rohilkhund Division 1933–37; served in Mesopotamia in Civil Administration, 1918–19. *Recreations:* golf, fishing. *Address:* Ramslade, Bracknell, Berks. *Club:* East India and Sports.

Died 20 May 1941.

WILLIAMSON, Samuel; *m* Jennie (*d* 1936). Late Secretary and General Manager, Cambrian Railways Company: retired on the amalgamation of that company with the Great Western Company under the provisions of the Railways Act 1921; Lt-Col in the Engineer and Railway Staff Corps, RE (TA); Chairman of Gregynog Estates Co.; Deputy Chairman of the Welsh Housing and Town-Planning Trust; Director of Wrexham Tenants Company; Goitre Brickworks, Ltd; Maclaurin Carbonisation, Ltd; Member of Board of Management of Railway Benevolent Institution. *Address:* The Old House, Maisemore, Glos.

Died 13 March 1950.

WILLINGDON, 1st Marquis of, *cr* 1936; **Freeman Freeman-Thomas;** 1st Earl of *cr* 1931; Viscount Ratendone of Willingdon *cr* 1931; 1st Viscount *cr* 1924; 1st Baron, of Ratton *cr* 1910, PC 1931; GCSI 1918; GCMG 1926; GCIE 1913; GBE 1917; Lord Warden of Cinque Ports since 1936; Chairman Briggs Motor Bodies Ltd, Director of London and Lancashire Insurance Co., and of Westminster Bank Ltd; Chancellor of Order of St Michael and St George since 1936; *b* 12 Sept. 1866; *s* of Frederick Freeman Thomas and Mabel, *d* of 1st Viscount Hampden; *m* 1892, Lady Marie Adelaide (CI; GBE 1924), *d* of 1st Earl Brassey; one *s*. ADC to Lord Brassey when Gov. of Victoria, 1895; MP (L) Hastings, 1900–06; Bodmin Div. of Cornwall, 1906–10; Jun. Lord of Treasury, 1905–12; JP; Governor of Bombay, 1913–19; of Madras, 1919–24; was present as Delegate for India at the Assembly of the League of Nations, 1924; Governor-General of Canada, 1926–31; Viceroy and Gov.-Gen. of India, 1931–36; Chairman of the Delegation from the Boxer Indemnity Committee which visited China, Jan.–July 1926; Major Sussex Imperial Yeomanry; Lord-in-Waiting to HM, 1911–13; Hon. LLD Cambridge, Edinburgh, and St Andrews. *Recreation:* was in Eton and Cambridge elevens. *Heir: s* Viscount Ratendone. *Address:* 5 Lygon Place, Grosvenor Gardens, SW; Walmer Castle, Kent. *T:* Deal 115. *Club:* Brooks's.

Died 12 Aug. 1941.

WILLIS, Alderman Sir Edward William, Kt 1933; JP; Chairman Chatham Conservative Association for 31 years; *b* 1849; *s* of Edward Willis, Rochester; *m* Helen, *d* of late Charles French Gilbert, Maidstone; one *s* two *d*. *Educ:* Dr Burns, Rochester. Chairman Chatham and District Water Company, Rochester Printing Company; Councillor Rochester Corporation, 1880; Mayor, 1893–94; Alderman, 1910; received the Honorary Freedom of the City, 1927. *Address:* 4 King Edward Road, Rochester.

Died 13 Feb. 1941.

WILLIS, Sir Frederick James, KBE 1920; CB 1914; JP Surrey; *b* 16 March 1863; *m* 1896, Agnes Maud, 3rd *d* of late H. J. Infield, JP, Brighton; two *s*. *Educ:* Merchant Venturers' School, Bristol; University College, Clifton. Called to Bar, Middle Temple, 1900; Chairman, Board of Control, 1921–28. Has served on various Departmental Committees and Royal Commissions; Commander Order of Leopold. *Address:* Farleys, Bramley, Guildford. *T:* Bramley 3297. *Club:* Reform.

Died 17 June 1946.

WILLIS, Hon. Henry; grazier; *b* Port Adelaide, SA, 6 April 1860; *s* of John Willis, of Leamington, England, and Jane Emerson, of London; *m* 1889, Annie Louisa, 2nd *d* of Edward Lomas Moore, of Badgally, Campbelltown, NSW, squatter; one *s* two *d* (and two *s* decd). *Educ:* Adelaide. Councillor, Municipal Council, Hindmarsh, Adelaide, Mayor and Alderman, Cabramatta and Cauley Vale, NSW; Alderman, Municipal Council, Camden, NSW; Alderman, Municipal Council, Randwick, Sydney, NSW; elected to First Commonwealth Parliament as Member of House of Representatives; sat in three successive Parliaments 1901–10; elected to Legislative Assem. of NSW; Speaker, 1911–13. *Address:* Innisfallen, Middle Harbour, via Chatswood, Sydney.

Died 23 Feb. 1950.

WILLIS, Samuel William Ward, RBS; *b* Paddington, London, 1870; *s* of Samuel James Willis, Paddington; *m* Phoebe Helen, *d* of James Hampton, architect, London; one *d*. *Educ:* St Augustine's Grammar School, Kilburn. Studied Art, West London School of Art, and Royal Academy Schools, where obtained silver medal, etc. Exhibits at Royal Academy, Edinburgh, Liverpool; amongst ideal works exhibited at the Royal Academy: The Outrage, 1918; Right Triumphant, 1919; The Past, 1921; Fear, 1923; Memorials to late Earl of Warwick, Lieut R. D. Sandford, VC, RN, Yorkshire, Blackmore Centenary Memorial, Teddington; Memorial to the Barristers at the Old Bailey, and Chartered Bank of India Memorial, European War; Statue of Robert Burns, Brisbane; Memorial to the Boy Scouts erected at Oxshott, Surrey, 1929; 1930, The Father Wainright Memorial erected at St Peter's, London Docks; exhibited various Equestrian portraits of famous people at the Royal Academy, 1928–35; William John Mills Memorial, Carharrack, Cornwall, 1934; Model of the Acropolis, Athens, restored, 1936; Bronze Portrait of Exhibitionist, winner of the Oaks, 1937. *Recreations:* boating, cricket. *Address:* Charlton, Woodside Road, Parkstone, Dorset.

Died 1 March 1948.

WILLISON, Herbert; MP (L) Nuneaton Division of Warwickshire,   1923–24;   *b*   Cosgrove, Northamptonshire; *m* Frances Mary Birmingham, *d* of George Pearson; two *d*. *Educ:* Northamptonshire; Birmingham. Solicitor, practising in Birmingham; well known as an Advocate throughout the Midlands; his firm (Philip Baker & Co.) are solicitors to many large societies. *Recreation:* golf. *Address:* The Homestead, Chessets Wood, Knowle, Warwickshire. *T:* Lapworth 72. *TA:* Advocatus, Birmingham *T:* Central Birmingham 2245. *Clubs:* National Liberal; Birmingham Liberal.

Died 30 Nov. 1943.

WILLKIE, Wendell Lewis; Lawyer, Willkie, Owen, Otis, Farr and Gallagher, 15 Broad Street, NY, NY, USA; *b* Elwood, Ind, 18 Feb. 1892; *s* of Herman F. and Henrietta Wilkie; *m* 1918; one *s*. *Educ:* Indiana University. Lawyer, Elwood, Ind, 1916–17; Field Artillery, war of 1917–19; Lawyer, Akron, Ohio, 1919–29; Lawyer, New York City, 1929–33; President Commonwealth and Southern Corp., 1933–40; Republican Candidate for President of US, 1940. *Publications:* One World, 1943; various magazine articles for USA Magazines. *Address:* 15 Broad Street, also 1010 Fifth Avenue, New York, USA. *T:* Rhinelander 4–3290.

Died 8 Oct. 1944.

WILLOUGHBY,   Brig.-Gen.   Hon.   Charles Strathavon Heathcote-Drummond-, CB 1918; CMG 1916; late Scots Guards; *b* 18 May 1870; 2nd *s* of 1st Earl of Ancaster; *m* 1903, Lady Muriel Agnes Stuart Erskine, *d* of 14th Earl of Buchan; one *s* one *d*. Entered Scots Guards, 1890; Captain, 1899; Major, 1902; served South African War, 1900–02 (despatches twice, Brevet Major, Queen's medal 3 clasps, King's medal 2 clasps); European War, 1914–18 (CMG, CB). *Address:* 65 Avenue Road, NW8.

Died 15 Dec. 1949.

WILLOUGHBY, Lt-Col Hon. Claud Heathcote-Drummond; MP (U) Stamford Division, Lincolnshire, 1910; Rutland and Stamford Division, 1918–22; late Coldstream Guards; *b* 15 Oct. 1872; 3rd *s* of 1st Earl of Ancaster; *m* 1905, Lady Florence Astley, (*d* 1946), *d* of 3rd Marquess Conyngham and *widow* of Bertram F. Frankland Russell Astley. Entered Coldstream Guards, 1891; Capt., 1900; Major, 1908; served S Africa, 1899–1902 (Queen's medal 5 clasps, King's medal 2 clasps); retired pay. *Address:* Empingham, Oakham, Rutland. *T:* Empingham 203.

Died 24 Feb. 1950.

WILLOUGHBY, Col Douglas Vere, CBE 1928; DSO 1917; Chevalier Legion of Honour; Indian Army, retired; *b* 1882; *s* of late Lt-Col R. F. Willoughby, R. Scots Fus; *m* 1933, Mrs Esther Ray Logan (*d* 1947); one *s*. *Educ:* Haileybury. Served European War, 1915–18 (despatches, DSO, Bt Lt-Col). *Address:* The Court, S Lopham, nr Diss, Norfolk. *Club:* Junior Army and Navy.

Died 16 July 1949.

WILLS, Arthur Walters, BA, LLB; Barrister-at-law; *b* 1868; *s* of late George Wills of 3 Hyde Park Gate, SW, and Pepperdon, Moretonhampstead, Devon; *m* 1908, Margery, *o d* of W. Eyre-Walker of Byfleet, Surrey; two *s* two *d*. *Educ:* Harrow; Trinity College, Cambridge. Took honours in law, 1890. Called to Bar, 1894; joined Western Circuit; MP (L) North Dorset, 1905–10. *Recreations:* fishing, fencing, shooting, golf, etc. *Address:* Highbridge End, Bambridge, nr Eastleigh, Hants.

Died 17 Nov. 1948.

WILLS, Sir (George) Peter (Vernon), 3rd Bt *cr* 1923; Lt Coldstream Guards; *b* 8 Jan. 1922; *er s* of Sir G. Vernon P. Wills, 2nd Bt, and Nellie Jeannie, *y d* of late J. T. Rutherford, Abergavenny; *S* father, 1931. *Educ:* Eton; Trinity College, Cambridge. *Heir:* *b* John Vernon Wills, *b* 3 July 1928. *Address:* Coombe Lodge, Blagdon, nr Bristol. *Clubs:* Carlton, Boodle's.

Died 19 April 1945.

WILLSHIRE, Sir Gerard (Arthur) Maxwell-, 3rd Bt *cr* 1841; *b* 21 Aug. 1892; *s* of 2nd Bt and Frederica (*d* 1912), *d* of late Sir Sanford Freeling, KCMG; *S* father, 1919; *m* 1923, Vera, *d* of late John Gainford, Sydney, Australia; one *d*. *Educ:* RN Colleges Osborne and Dartmouth; RMC Sandhurst. Served with Hon. Artillery Company, 1914–18 (despatches). *Heir:* none. *Address:* 83 Palace Court, W2.

Died 1 April 1947 (ext).

WILLSON, Beckles; author; *b* Montreal, 26 Aug. 1869; *e s* of Henry Willson, Colborne, Ontario (*d* 1878); *m* 1st, 1899, Ethel Grace (*d* 1922), *d* of A. W. Dudley, Colborne; two *s* one *d*; 2nd, 1924, Ida, *er d* of late J. A. Parkes, MA (Oxon), of Sheffield, and Paris. *Educ:* Kingston. Journalism in America; came to England, 1892; Staff of Daily Mail, 1896–98; special writer on colonial subjects and contributor to reviews and magazines; founded Wolfe Society; organised General Wolfe Memorial, 1908; organised Charles Dickens Centenary Fund, 1911–12; served in Canadian

Expeditionary Force; Town Major of Ypres; Lt-Col, 1918; Inspector of War Trophies, BEF, 1917; Inspector of War Trophies, Palestine and Mesopotamia, 1918; founded the Ypres League, 1920; British Colonial Service, West Africa, 1920–21; Founded the Anti-Noise League, 1933. *Publications:* Harold; An Experiment, 1891; Poems, 1893; Newfoundland, the Tenth Island, 1897; The Hudson's Bay Company, 1899; The East India Company; The New America; The Romance of Canada; George the Third, 1907; Occultism and Common Sense, 1908; Life and Letters of James Wolfe, 1909; Nova Scotia, 1911; Quebec: The Laurentian Province, 1913; The Life of Lord Strathcona, 1915; In the Ypres Salient, 1916; Ypres: The Holy Ground of British Arms, 1919; A British Empire Primer, 1922; England: by an Overseas Englishman, 1922; Redemption, 1924; The Paris Embassy, 1927; America's Ambassadors to France, 1928; America's Ambassadors to England, 1929; From Quebec to Piccadilly, 1929; If I had Fifty Millions, 1931; John Slidell; and the Confederates in Paris, 1932; Friendly Relations: The British Embassy at Washington, 1934; Monetary Essays, 1935; The Purple Cloud, 1936; Heartache in Canaan, 1938; Youth be Damned, 1938; Life of Edward Tuck, 1941. *Recreations:* reading, golf, and travel. *Address:* 6 Avenue Jeanne d'Arc, Beaulieu, France A/M.

Died 18 Sept. 1942.

WILLSON, Rt Rev. St J. Basil Wynne, DD; *b* 28 Aug. 1868; *s* of late Rev. W. Wynne Willson, Fellow of St John's College, Oxford; *m* 1919, Lilian, 2nd *d* of late Sir George A. Wills, 1st Bt. *Educ:* Cheltenham Coll.; St John's Coll., Cambridge. First class Classical Tripos; Browne University Medallist. Master at The Leys School, 1891–98; at Rugby School, 1898–1905; Master of Haileybury College, 1905–11; of Marlborough College, 1911–16; Dean of Bristol, 1916–21; TCF 1917–18; Bishop of Bath and Wells, 1921–37; Examining Chaplain to Bishop of Durham, 1906–11; to Bishop of Salisbury, 1912; Select Preacher, Cambridge, 1908 and 1916; Hon. LLD Bristol, 1925. *Publications:* editions of Æschylus Prometheus Vinctus; Cæsar De Bello Gallico, Books IV and V; Virgil's Æneid, V and VI; Lucian's Wonderland. *Address:* Titan Barrow, Bathford, Bath.

Died 15 Oct. 1946.

WILMOT, Captain (Temp. Major) Sir Arthur Ralph, 7th Bt *cr* 1759; The Black Watch; *b* 2 Feb. 1909; *s* of 6th Bt and Lady Ada Marian Maitland, *d* of 13th Earl of Lauderdale (she *m* 2nd, 1921, Arnold Nield); *S* father, 1918; *m* 1936, Pamela Vera, twin *d* of Major Garrard, Welton Place, Daventry; one *s* one *d*. *Educ:* Wellington; RMC Sandhurst. *Heir:* *s*, *b* 8 Oct. 1939. *Address:* Alresford Grange, Colchester, Essex. *T:* Wivenhoe 331; Glenfarg House, Abernethy, Perthshire. *T:* Abernethy 41. *Clubs:* Army and Navy, Orleans.

Died 3 Oct. 1942.

WILMOTT, Alfred James, MA (Camb.), FLS, FRGS; Deputy Keeper of Botany, British Museum (Natural History), since 1931; *b* Tottenham, Middx, 1888; *s* of Alfred John Wilmott, MA (Camb.); *m* 1914, Jessie Eveline, *d* of late Daniel Bell; one *s*. *Educ:* County High School, Cambridge; St John's College, Cambridge. Frank Smart Prizeman and Hutchinson Research Student, 1910. Entered Museum, 1911. *Publications:* Edited last edition of Babington's Manual of British Botany; articles in Botanical Journals (European and British Floras, especially origin of British Flora). *Recreations:* table tennis (English International), cricket, photography, botanical collecting. *Address:* British Museum (Natural History), SW7; Fourwents, Melrose Road, Merton Park, SW19.

Died 27 Jan. 1950.

WILMSHURST, Thomas Percival, MBE; Electricity Commissioner, 1926–35; *b* Retford, Notts; *s* of Edwin Wilmshurst; *m* Henrietta Louise Reynolds (*d* 1941), Taunton, Somerset; three *s* (one killed in the War). *Educ:* King Edward VI School, Retford. Pupil of late Sir Charles Bright; late Chief Engineer, Exeter Electric Light Co.; late Borough Electrical Engineer, Halifax; late Borough Electrical Engineer, Derby; Chartered Member of Institution of Electrical Engineers; Past President of Incorporated Municipal Electrical Association. *Address:* Otterhaven, Budleigh Salterton, Devon.

Died 27 Oct. 1950.

WILSHIRE, Frederick Allan; Barrister-at-Law; Recorder of Bridgwater; *b* 8 July 1868; *s* of Reuben Wilshire; *m* 1897, Minnie Creech; two *d*. *Educ:* Samuel White Wesleyan School, Hanham, Bristol. Professional musician before reading for the Bar; called to Bar, Middle Temple, 1914; Western Circuit; President Bristol and District Brotherhood Federation; President Bristol and Clifton Dickens Society; President Bristol Monday Musical Club. *Publication:* (joint author) Mentality and the Criminal Law. *Recreations:* music, theatre, archæology walking. *Address:* Albion Chambers, Bristol; 1 Hare Court, Temple, EC4. *TA:* Wilshire 35470 Bristol. *T:* 24721. *Club:* Bristol.

Died 19 March 1944.

WILSON, Captain Alexander Guy Berners, DSO 1919; MVO 1934; RN; *b* 18 Nov. 1890; *yr s* of Alexander Wilson, FRCS; *m* 1926, Mary Savill, *d* of late Major C. F. Marriott, 6th Dragoon Guards. Served European War, 1914–19 (despatches, DSO); Senior Naval Officer, West Coast of Africa, 1931; Captain, 1933; served in HM Yacht Victoria and Albert, 1932–34; Superintendent of Commonwealth Dockyard at Garden Island, Sydney, 1936–38; Assistant Director of Senior Officers' Tactical School, 1939; retired list, 1942. *Address:* Newlands, Headley Down, Bordon, Hants. *Club:* Naval and Military.

Died 11 April 1942.

WILSON, Rt Rev. Cecil, DD; *b* 1860; *γ s* of late Alex. Wilson of Beckenham; *m* 1899, Ethel, *d* of late Most Rev. Churchill Julius; three *s* four *d*. *Educ:* Tonbridge School; Jesus Coll., Camb. BA 1883; MA 1886; DD 1908. Curate Portsea, 1886–91; Vicar of Moordown, Hants, 1891–94; Bishop of Melanesia, 1894–1911; Rector of Walkerville, South Australia, and Archdeacon of Adelaide, 1911–17; Bishop of Bunbury, 1917–37. *Publication:* The Wake of the Southern Cross, 1932. *Recreation:* captain, school and college cricket elevens, played in county eleven. *Address:* 8 Hensman Street, South Perth, West Australia. *TA:* Bishop Wilson, South Perth, WA. *T:* South Perth 637.

Died 20 Jan. 1941.

WILSON, Cecil Henry; JP; *b* Mansfield, Notts, 8 Sept. 1862; *s* of Henry Joseph Wilson, for 27 years MP for the Holmfirth Div. of Yorkshire, and Charlotte, *d* of Charles Cowan, MP for Edinburgh, and President of Women's Total Abstinence Union (both parents actively associated with the work of Josephine Butler); *m* 1st, 1890, Sarah Catherine (*d* 1909), *d* of E. L. Turner, Sheffield; 2nd, 1912, Grace, *d* of Rev. W. Satchwell, Nuneaton; one *s*. *Educ:* Friends' School, Kendal; Wesley Coll., Sheffield; Victoria University, Manchester. For 37 years a Director of the Sheffield Smelting Co. Ltd; City Councillor for Darnall Ward, Sheffield, 1903–23; Leader of Labour group in City Council, 1919–23; MP (Soc.) Attercliffe Div. Sheffield, 1922–31 and 1935–44; Christian Socialist; Freeman of City of Sheffield, 1929; Chairman Executive National Anti-Gambling League and Convener, Political Pacifist Group. *Address:* House of Commons, SW1.

Died 7 Nov. 1945.

WILSON, Charles Ashley C.; *see* Carus-Wilson.

WILSON, Prof. Charles Edward, BA, PhD, DLit (Lond.); for fourteen years Professor of Persian at University College, London; Gilchrist Scholar in Turkish, University of London, 1913; *b* 1848; *s* of John Wilson; married. *Educ:* Swiss schools; private tuition. Began the study of Persian in early youth; first assisted by Jules Mohl, and afterwards by N. de Khanikoff, S. Guyard, and Professor Palmer; from natives of Persia acquired a knowledge of the colloquial; afterwards read Arabic with Drs Percy Badger, Sabunjie, Tien, and natives of Syria, from whom he also acquired the colloquial Syrian Arabic. Travelled in Egypt and Morocco; he has also made a considerable study of Turkish, and some study of Hindustani; he has served on the Council of the Royal Asiatic Society, and was for five years University Teacher of Persian at Cambridge; graduated at the University of London, passing in Arabic in one of the examinations, 1887. *Publications:* for many years contributor to and reviewer of Persian and Turkish works in the Academy and the Athenæum, etc.; The Masnavi of Rumi, Book ii, Translation and Commentary; Nizami's Haft Paikar, Translation and Commentary; Persian Wit and Humour, from Jami's Baharistan; The Wall of Alexander against Gog and Magog; aids to reading Persian MSS in view of editorial work; among his unpublished works are Texts and Translations of Attar's Ilahi-nama; the whole of Jami's Baharistan; and Arabic-English Dialogues. *Recreations:* riding, swimming, and skating. *Address:* The Datcha, Limpsfield Chart, Surrey.

Died 28 Feb. 1938.

WILSON, Sir Charles S.; *see* Stewart-Wilson.

WILSON, Rev. Charles William Goodall, MA; Canon and Prebendary of Chichester; *b* 1860; *s* of Rev. John P. Wilson, DD, Vicar of Moxley, Staffs; *m* Eliza Winifree T., *o c* of Frederick Trueman of Brighton; one *s* three *d.* *Educ:* Pembroke College, Oxford. Vicar of Mountfield, Sussex, 1898–1909; Rector and Vicar of Selsey, Sussex, 1909–15; Vicar of Cuckfield, 1915–36; Diocesan Inspector of Schools, 1906–09; Rural Dean of Cuckfield, 1919–33. *Address:* Fardells, Lindfield, Sussex. *T:* Lindfield 182.

Died 5 Nov. 1948.

WILSON, Sir Courthope; *see* Wilson, Sir W. C. T.

WILSON, D. Forrester, RSA; *m* 1906, Jessie Ann Eglinton; three *s. Educ:* Glasgow. Pictures in permanent collections in Glasgow, Paisley, Birkenhead, Edinburgh, etc.; also decorative panel in Banqueting Hall, City Chambers, Glasgow. *Recreations:* gardening and fishing. *Address:* Abbotsford, Bruichalddich, Islay; 15 Woodside Terrace, Glasgow, C3. *Club:* Glasgow Art.

Died 9 Jan. 1950.

WILSON, Sir Duncan (Randolph), Kt 1938; CVO 1935; CBE 1928; JP Kent; *b* 1875; *s* of late George Wilson, Banner Cross Hall, Sheffield; *m* 1915, Freda Noel, *y d* of late James Lee, Warwick Gardens, SW. *Educ:* Eton College; Magdalen College, Oxford. First Class Honours Natural Science, 1898; MA 1901. Lecturer, Magdalen College, Oxford, 1898–1903; HM Inspector of Factories, Home Office, 1904; a Deputy Chief Inspector of Factories, 1930–32; HM Chief Inspector of Factories, 1932–40; Secretary to Home Office Committees on Humidity in Cotton-Weaving Sheds, 1907–11; Member of Home Office Committees on Lighting of Factories, 1913–23; Investigator in Foreign Trade Department, 1915–16; Commissioner for London and SE Counties, National Service Dept, 1916–17; Deputy Assistant Secretary, Ministry of Food, 1917–18; Member of Illumination Research Committee (DS&IR), 1924, and of Home Office Committee on Humidity in Cotton Cloth Factories, 1924–27; Secretary to the Industrial Health Research Board, 1918–30; Chairman, Home Office Committee on Factory Lighting, 1940; Chairman, National Industrial Electric Lighting Service, 1940; Chairman, London Building Trades Employment Committee, 1941; Chairman, Regional Advisory Council, Min. of Information, 1941. *Publications:* various Technical Reports and Papers. *Recreations:* music, travelling. *Address:* Catt's Cottage, Underriver, Kent. *T:* Hildenborough 2186. *Clubs:* United University, Oxford and Cambridge Musical.

Died 1 March 1945.

WILSON, Brig. Sir Eric Edward Boketon H.; *see* Holt-Wilson.

WILSON, Forsyth James, DSc (Edin.), PhD (Leipzig); FIC; Freeland Professor of Chemistry, The Royal Technical College, Glasgow; *b* Moffat, Dumfriesshire, June 1880; *s* of John Wilson and Isabella K. Smith; unmarried. *Educ:* University of Edinburgh (Hope Prize Scholar); University of Leipzig; and University of Leeds. Lecturer in Chemistry, Royal Technical College, Glasgow, 1906; Professor of Inorganic and Analytical Chemistry, 1919; Professor of Organic Chemistry, 1920–35; Army service (France and Italy), 1914–18, latterly as a Corps Chemical Adviser. *Publications:* has contributed a number of papers chiefly to the Journal of the Chemical Society; part author with Professor Heilbron of Chemical Theory and Calculations. *Recreations:* walking, swimming, and reading. *Address:* 13 Hillhead Street, Glasgow, W2. *T:* Western 2335. *Clubs:* Chemical; Literary, Glasgow.

Died 18 Oct. 1944.

WILSON, George, CB 1899; *b* 1862; *m* 1900, Clarissa Adelina, *d* of late Col J. Charlton Humphreys. 1st Class Assistant, Uganda, 1894; HM Deputy Commissioner in the Protectorate of Uganda, 1902–09; Acting Commissioner and Consul-General, 1897–98; Acting Commissioners and Commander-in-Chief, 1904–05 and 1905–06; retired, 1909. *Address:* 74 London Road, Tunbridge Wells, Kent. *T:* Tunbridge Wells 2406.

Died 12 Dec. 1943.

WILSON, George Maryon Maryon-; JP; *b* 10 Oct. 1861; 2nd *s* of Sir Spencer Maryon Maryon-Wilson, 10th Bart; *m* 1886, Hon. Stephanie Allanson-Winn (*d* 1940), sister of 5th Baron Headley; one *s* two *d.* Barrister-at-law. *Address:* Searles, Fletching, Sussex. *Club:* Junior Carlton.

Died 26 July 1941.

WILSON, Col Hon. Guy Greville, CMG 1919; DSO 1902; DL East Riding, Yorks; *b* 19 May 1877; *brother of* 2nd Baron Nunburnholme; *m* 1st, 1904, Lady Isabel Innes-Ker (*d* 1905), 3rd *d* of 7th Duke of Roxburghe; 2nd, 1911, Avery, 3rd *d* of late Geoffrey F. Buxton, CB; one *s* three *d. Educ:* Eton. Entered Army (11th Hussars), 1898; served South Africa (Damant's Horse), 1901–02 (despatches twice, Queen's medal 5 clasps, DSO); left the Army, 1903; served European War in East Riding Yeomanry, 1914–18, in Egypt and Palestine (despatches three times, CMG); MP (L) West Hull, 1907–18. *Recreations:* shooting, golf. *Address:* Tixover Grange, Stamford. *Club:* Turf.

Died 1 Feb. 1943.

WILSON, Col Harold René, DSO 1918; TD 1924; Territorial Army; DL Essex; *b* 1890; *s* of Capt. A. Needham Wilson, ARIBA; *m* 1914, Alice Isabella, *d* of late Col W. S. Duff, TD, DL; one *s* one *d.* Commissioned in TA 1909; served European War, 1914–19 in Flanders and Palestine in RA (TA) as Capt., Battery Commander, and Brigade Commander (despatches, DSO); Commanded 85th Field Bde RA (TA), 1921–32; Hon. Colonel 85th Field Brigade RA (TA), 1932–36; Colonel, TA, 1932. *Recreation:* cricket. *Address:* Buckhurst Hill, Essex. *T:* Buckhurst 0501.

Died 28 Jan. 1941.

WILSON, Rear-Adm. (S) Harry George, CBE 1928; RN (retd); *b* 1874; *s* of late George Lambert Wilson. Served Benin River, 1894; China, 1900; European War, 1914–19; Port Accountant Officer on Staff of Commander-in-Chief, Plymouth, 1927–29. *Club:* Junior Army and Navy.

Died 16 July 1947.

WILSON, Lt-Gen. Sir Henry Fuller Maitland, KCB 1915; KCMG 1918; CB 1910; *b* 18 Feb. 1859; *s* of Col Fuller Maitland Wilson of Stowlangtoft Hall, Suffolk; *m* 1884, Charlotte Elise, *d* of late Gen. Sir Hugh Gough, GCB, VC; one *s* one *d. Educ:* Eton. Joined Rifle Brigade, 1878; Capt. 1884; Major, 1895; Lt-Col 1900; Col 1904; ADC to Maj.-General, Bengal, 1887–89; Adjutant, Militia, 1892–97; AAG and General Staff, India, 1907–11; served Afghanistan, 1878–79 (medal with clasp); Mahsud Waziri Expedition, 1881; S Africa, 1899–1900, and 1902 (despatches thrice, brevet Lt-Col, Queen's medal six clasps); European War, 1914–18 (despatches twice, promoted Maj.-Gen. and Lt-Gen. distinguished service, KCB, KCMG); retired pay, 1921. *Club:* Naval and Military.

Died 16 Nov. 1941.

WILSON, His Honour Sir Herbert W. L.; *see* Lush-Wilson.

WILSON, Hubert Wilberforce, CMG 1930; CBE 1923 (OBE 1918); *b* 1867; *e s* of Wilberforce Wilson, sometime Surveyor General, Hong Kong; *m* 1st, 1905, Willie E. Tomlinson, of USA (divorced 1912); 2nd, Mary Ellen McDonnell (*d* 1936); one *s. Educ:* University School, Hastings; Boulogne S/M. Vice-Consul at San Luis, Potosi, Mexico, 1904; Consul, 1907; Consul at Tampico during the revolution, 1913–14; at Guayaquil, Ecuador, 1915; in charge of the Legation at Quito and Acting Consul-General, 1917–18; Consul-General, 1919; HM's Consul-General at Buenos Aires, 1921–30; motored from Punta Arenas through Patagonia on Consular tour of inspection, 1922; retired, 1930. *Recreations:* motoring, rowing, etc. *Address:* c/o Bank of Montreal, Victoria, BC. *Clubs:* Union (Victoria, BC).

Died 6 April 1949.

WILSON, Sir Isaac Henry, Kt 1939; JP. *Address:* Birches, Lower Green, Mitcham. *T:* Mitcham 2496.

Died 26 Sept. 1944.

WILSON, James, MA, BSc; late Professor of Agriculture, Royal College of Science, Dublin; *b* Cluny, Aberdeenshire, 1861; *s* of late James Wilson, Westmains, Dolphinton, Lanarkshire. *Educ:* Forfar Academy; Edinburgh University. Lecturer in Agriculture, University College of Wales, Aberystwyth, 1891–95; Fordyce Lecturer in Agriculture, Aberdeen University, 1895–1902. *Publications:* The Evolution of British Cattle; The Principles of Stock-breeding; A Manual of Mendelism; Principles of Stock-feeding, etc. *Recreation:* golf.

Died 9 Dec. 1941.

WILSON, James; JP; Railwayman; *b* 24 Aug. 1879; British parents; *m* 1899; three *s* one *d. Educ:* Elementary School, Oldmeldrum, Aberdeenshire. Commenced as agricultural labourer at thirteen years of age; joined Railway Service, 1902; Member Executive NUR, 1916–19; MP (Lab) Dudley, 1921–22; MP (Lab) Oldham, 1929–31. *Recreations:* football, cricket, and general sports. *Address:* 61 Dunholme Road, Newcastle on Tyne.

Died 15 Aug. 1943.

WILSON, Sir James Arthur, Kt 1946; CBE 1939 (OBE 1924; MBE 1918); Barrister-at-law; *b* 27 Feb. 1877; *s* of William and Elizabeth Wilson, Bramley, Leeds; *m* 1900, Annie Elizabeth, *d* of William W. Lloyd, Penarth; two *s* one *d. Educ:* Bramley Nat. Sch.; Central Higher Grade

Sch., Leeds; Cardiff University. Served West Yorks Regt, 1st Bn Coldstream Guards; Barnsley Boro' Police; Glamorgan Constabulary; Chief Constable, Merthyr, 1908–20; Chief Constable, Cardiff, 1920–46, retd 1946. Called to Bar, Gray's Inn, 1939. *Address:* Ael-y-Bryn, Cefn Coed Road, Cardiff. *TA:* Sir James Wilson Cardiff.

Died 17 Dec. 1950.

WILSON, James Thomas, FRS 1909; FZS; MA Cantab; MB; ChM; Hon. LLD Edin.; Emeritus Professor of Anatomy, University of Cambridge; Fellow of St John's College, Cambridge, since 1920; *b* Moniaive, Dumfriesshire, 14 April 1861; *s* of Thomas Wilson and Helen Brown; *m* 1st, 1890, Jane Elizabeth Smith; 2nd, 1898, Mabel M. M. Salomons (*d* 1944); three *s* four *d. Educ:* Edinburgh University, graduated 1883. Demonstrator of Anatomy in University of Edinburgh, 1885–87, and in the University of Sydney, 1887–90; Challis Professor of Anatomy, University of Sydney, 1890–1920; Professor of Anatomy, Univ. of Cambridge, 1920–34; Member of Council, Royal Society, 1922–23; President Anatomical Society Great Britain and Ireland, 1924–25; Hon. Member Royal Society, NSW; Hon. FRS of South Australia; represented Australian Universities on Executive Council of Universities' Bureau of British Empire, 1921–38. *Publications:* numerous papers on human and comparative Anatomy and Embryology in Proc. Roy. Soc., etc. *Address:* 24 Millington Road, Cambridge. *T:* 4330.

Died 2 Sept. 1945.

WILSON, Rev. John Kenneth, CB 1947; CBE 1945; MA; Chaplain Blatchington Court, Seaford, since 1948; *b* 15 Oct. 1890; *s* of William Wilson, MB, and Grace Mary Wilson; *m* 1918, Gwendoline May Bousfield; one *s* one *d. Educ:* Colet Court; St Paul's School; Corpus Christi Coll., Cambridge; Clergy Training School, Cambridge. Curate of St Michael at Bowes, London, 1913–17; TCF 1917–20; Curate of Newton Nottage, 1920–26; of St James, Portsmouth (in charge of St Patrick's Mission), 1926–28; Chaplain RN HMS Egmont II, 1928–30; HMS Warspite, 1930–32; Depot RM Deal, 1932–34; HMS Kent, 1934–37; RN Barracks, Devonport, 1937–40; RM Barracks, Eastney, 1940–43; Chaplain of the Fleet, 1943–47; Archdeacon for the Royal Navy, 1943–47; retired list, 1947; KHC, 1944–47. *Address:* 28 Kedale Rd, Seaford, Sussex.

Died 17 Aug. 1949.

WILSON, Hon. Joseph Marcellin; Senator, since 1911; retired from business, 1921; *b* 26 Dec. 1859; *m* 1887, Alexina Geoffrion, Terrebonne, PQ; six *d.* Interested in many financial and industrial corporations; Chairman of the Board of the Banque Canadienne Nationale; President, Trust Général du Canada; Director Montreal Light, Heat and Power Consolidated, Montreal Island Power Company and Canadian Pacific Railway Company. *Address:* 3501 Ontario Avenue, Montreal, Canada.

Died 10 Sept. 1940.

WILSON, Brig.-Gen. Lachlan Chisholm, CB 1919; CMG 1916; DSO 1919; VD; Solicitor and Notary Public, Brisbane; *b* 11 July 1871; *m*; one *s* one *d. Educ:* Brisbane Grammar School. Served S Africa, 1900–01 (Queen's medal 5 clasps); European War, 1914–19 Commander 3rd Light Horse Brigade, AIF (CB, CMG, DSO, despatches five times, Croix de Guerre); commanded 1st Cavalry Brigade, 1929–31; First Corps Commander (Queensland) VDC, 1941–42; Chairman Queensland Recruiting Drive Comm. RAAF ADC to Gov.-General of Australia, 1923–27. *Address:* Tully & Wilson, Solicitors, London Bank Chambers, Brisbane, Queensland. *Clubs:* Queensland, United Service, Brisbane.

Died 7 April 1947.

WILSON, Col Lancelot Machell, CMG 1919; DSO 1915; late RFA; *b* 23 July 1873; *s* of Canon Wilson, JP Bolton, Yorkshire; *m* 1st, Lilian Stewart (*d* 1917), *y d* of late Colonel J. Richardson, KHP, IMS; 2nd, 1920, *widow* of Capt. St John ffrench Blake, 21st Lancers, and *d* of A. J. Tweedie; one *s*. *Educ:* Sedbergh; RMA, Woolwich. Entered Army, 1893; Captain, 1900; Major, 1910; Lieut-Colonel, 1915; Instructor, 1st class, School of Gunnery, 1912; DD of A, War Office, 1918–20; served Tirah, 1897–98 (medal 2 clasps); Relief of Peking, 1900 (medal with clasp); S African War, 1902 (Queen's medal 2 clasps); European War, 1914–18 (despatches thrice, CMG, DSO, Bt Col); retired pay, 1920. *Address:* Lower Lease, Saunton, N Devon. *Club:* Army and Navy.

Died 28 Feb. 1950.

WILSON, Morris W., CMG 1944; President Royal Bank of Canada, Montreal, since 1934; Vice-President of Montreal Trust Company; Director of: British Columbia Power Corporation, Ltd, Canada Cement Company Ltd, Canadian Pacific Railway Company, Dominion Bridge Co. Ltd, Montreal Light, Heat & Power Consolidated, Ogilvie Flour Mills, Ltd, Shawinigan Water and Power Company, Sun Life Assurance Company of Canada; ex-Chairman, British Supply Council in North America; *b* Lunenburg, Nova Scotia, 1 March 1883; *m* Clara Leone Mason. *Educ:* High School, Lunenburg. *Address:* The Royal Bank of Canada, Montreal, Canada.

Died 14 May 1946.

WILSON, Lt-Col Sir Murrough John, KBE 1927; *b* 14 Sept. 1875; *s* of Colonel John Gerald Wilson, CB, of Cliffe Hall, Darlington; *m* 1st, 1904, Sybil May (*d* 1930), *d* of Sir Powlett Milbank, 2nd Bart; one *s* three *d*; 2nd, 1934, Gladys Rhoda, *widow* of Hon. Alec. P. Henderson. *Educ:* Marlborough. Served with North-Eastern Railway Co., 1893–1902; Director, 1912; Deputy Chairman since 1934; served with Yorkshire Regt, 1914–18; MP (U) Richmond Division of Yorkshire, 1918–29; JP Yorks, NR; DL, Yorkshire. *Recreations:* shooting, golf. *Address:* Cliffe Hall, Darlington. *TA:* Piercebridge. *T:* Piercebridge 22. *Club:* Carlton.

Died 30 April 1946.

WILSON, Lt-Col Nathaniel, CMG 1917; DSO 1900; late RE; Cape Pioneer Railway Regt; *m*; two *d*. Late of Johannesburg; served South Africa, 1899–1900 (despatches, Queen's medal 4 clasps, DSO). *Address:* Lanrick, Berkhamsted, Herts.

Died 8 May 1944.

WILSON, Captain Neville Frederick Jarvis, CMG 1917; CBE 1918; *b* 1865; *s* of late Maj. Gen. Charles Watson Wilson, RA; *m* Helena Dorothy (*d* 1917), *d* of late Brig. Surg. Hunter Alexander Coghlan, Army Medical Dept. *Educ:* St John's College and Royal Academy, Gosport. Formerly Captain, Royal Indian Marine; retired, 1920; served Suakin; European War, 1914–17 (despatches, CMG); Assistant Port Officer, Bombay, 1904–07; Port Officer, Karachi, 1909–14; Deputy Director, Royal Indian Marine, 1916; Director, 1917; Principal Naval Transport Officer, E Indies with rank of Capt. RN, 1920. *Address:* c/o Lloyds Bank, King's Branch, 6 Pall Mall, SW1.

Died 20 June 1947.

WILSON, Maj.-Gen. Nigel Maitland, CB 1938; DSO 1916; OBE 1924; Indian Army, retired; *b* 1884; *s* of Arthur Maitland Wilson, OBE; *m* 1909, Lady Violet Freddie FitzRoy, *d* of late Lord Charles Edward FitzRoy and Hon. Ismay Mary Helen Augusta, *d* of 3rd Baron Southampton, Hawstead Lodge, Bury St Edmunds; one *d*. *Educ:* Eton College. Entered Army, 1904; served European War, 1914–16 (despatches, DSO); Waziristan, 1922–23 (OBE); AA & QMG, Rawalpindi District, 1933–35; Colonel, 1933; Brigadier, 1935; Commander Sind Independent Brigade Area, 1935–36; Director of Personal Services AHQ, India, 1936–38; Maj.-Gen.,

1938; Deputy Adjutant-General and Director of Organization, Army Headquarters, India, 1938–40; retired, 1941. Colonel Royal Welch Fusiliers, 1942–46; Secretary to The Lord Great Chamberlain, 1945–48. *Address:* 121 Queens Road, Bury St Edmunds, Suffolk.

Died 24 Feb. 1950.

WILSON, Reginald Page, CBE 1918; MInstCE; *γ s* of Charles Herbert Ball Wilson, late of Calcutta; *m* 1st, 1896, Ada Sarah Behrend (*d* 1930); one *d*; 2nd, 1933, Marjorie Elizabeth, *yr d* of late S. J. Fraser Macleod, KC. *Educ:* privately. Consulting Engineer; Director, National Telephone Co. till 1887; Grosvenor Gallery Electric Light Co. till 1892; has since that date practised as consulting engineer, and in that capacity has designed and carried out electric lighting power of tram way undertakings at Greenwich, Beckenham, Dudley, Aston Manor, Pontypridd, etc.; he also carried out (in partnership with Messrs Merz and McLellan) the electrification of the Melbourne Suburban Railways and the Perth power station, etc.; joined RN as AB 1915; received commission, 1916; became Director of Aircraft Supply under the Air Ministry (CBE). *Address:* 26 York House, Kensington, W8. *T:* Western 8308.

Died 20 March 1950.

WILSON, Richard Henry George, CBE 1923; Lt-Col late The Lincolnshire Regiment; *b* Woolwich, 9 March 1874; *s* of Captain G. F. Wilson, Royal Artillery; *m* 1900, Helen Macgregor Finlay; two *s*. *Educ:* Sherborne; Royal Military College, Sandhurst. Served Nile Expedition, South African War, European War (wounded, despatches, Brevet Lieut-Col); Ireland, 1919–23. *Address:* Petley Lodge, Whatlington, nr Battle, Sussex.

Died 20 July 1944.

WILSON, Sir Robert, Kt 1921; Chairman of John Horn, Ltd, printers, Glasgow, and Managing Director John Horn (England) Ltd, London; last Chairman Education Authority of Glasgow; *b* 20 Dec. 1865; *s* of Robert Wilson and Elizabeth Brown; *m* 1896, Helen Cram (*d* 1937), *d* of late John Horn; one *d*. *Educ:* Glasgow. Provost of Pollokshaws, 1903; DL County of the City of Glasgow; JP County of the City of Glasgow and Renfrew; LLD Glasgow University, 1930. President of the Glasgow Eye Infirmary. *Recreations:* Ex-Captain Cowglen Golf Club; Ex-President Kingston Bowling Club. *Address:* Dalsalloch, 18 Aytoun Road, Pollokshields, Glasgow. *T:* Pollok 0914. *Clubs:* Liberal, Arts, Glasgow.

Died 18 Aug. 1943.

WILSON, Robert John; JP; retired; *b* Gateshead, 1865; *m* 1888, Catherine Soulsby of Blyth; one *s* two *d*. *Educ:* privately at Durham City. Originally Drapery Manager; later entered upon literary pursuits; Member of Sunderland Town Council, 1907–23; MP (Labour) Jarrow Division, 1922–31; Parliamentary Private Secretary to the Under-Secretary of State for Air (unpaid), 1924. *Publications:* Apprenticeship; Salesmanship; Organisation and Management; magazine articles and book reviews. *Recreations:* gardening, golfing, motor cycling. *Address:* 105 Side Cliff Road, Sunderland. *Club:* Labour.

Died 5 Nov. 1946.

WILSON, Sir (Roderick) Roy, Kt 1929; *b* Alton, Hants, 10 Aug. 1876; *s* of late Dr Thomas Wilson; *m* 1908, Florence Emily, *e d* of late George Garratt, Runcorn, Cheshire; three *s*. *Educ:* privately. In the service of Bank of British West Africa, Ltd, 1895–1924; Manager at Liverpool, 1909–20; Asst General Manager, Head Office, London, 1920–24; Director, 1929; Vice-Chairman, 1937; Contested (C) Lichfield Division (Staffordshire), General Election 1923; MP (U) Lichfield Division of Staffordshire, 1924–29; Chairman British Guiana Parliamentary Commission, 1926; Chairman, Select Committee on Transport in Western Highlands and Islands of Scotland, 1928; Member, West African Currency Board; Director Standard Bank of South Africa, Ltd; travelled in West Africa, Morocco, Egypt. *Address:* Wood End, Pyrford, Woking, Surrey. *T:* Byfleet 27.

Died 27 Aug. 1942.

WILSON, Lt-Col Roger Parker, CIE 1925; FRCS Eng.; DPH Cantab; Indian Medical Service; retired, 1926; *b* 13 May 1870; 3rd *s* of late Wm Wilson, Walton Priory, Liverpool; *m* 1904, Elsie Dora, *y d* of late Walter Twiss, Withington, Manchester; no *c. Educ:* Liverpool College; University College, Liverpool; St Bart's Hospital, London; MRCS, LRCP Lond., 1893. Entered Indian Medical Service, 1896; served with troops in military employ until 1903; appointed to Civil duties under Govt of Bengal, 1903; Civil Surgeon of various districts and Superintendent of District and Central Jails, 1903–13; Superintendent, Campbell Medical School, Calcutta, 1913–18; Professor, Clinical Surgery, 1918–20; Professor of Surgery, Calcutta Medical College, and Surgeon to the Medical College Hospitals, 1920–25; Examiner in Anatomy and Surgery to the Calcutta University and the Bengal State Medical Faculty, 1914–25; President, Bengal State Medical Faculty and Bengal Council of Medical Regtn, 1922 and 1925; acted as Surgeon-General to the Govt of Bengal, and Bengal MLC, 1922 and 1925; VHS, 1920. *Recreations:* football, golf, racing. *Address:* c/o Grindlay & Co., 54 Parliament St, SW1.

Died 12 Dec. 1943.

WILSON, Sir Roy; *see* Wilson, Sir Roderick R.

WILSON, Brig.-Gen. Sir Samuel Herbert, GCMG 1929; (KCMG 1922; CMG 1914); KCB 1927; (CB 1918); KBE 1921; *b* 31 Oct. 1873; *s* of James Wilson, LLD, Dublin; *m* 1902, Ida, *d* of F. T. Gervers; (one son killed on active service, 1943) one *d. Educ:* private school; Royal Military Academy, Woolwich. Entered Army, RE 1893; Captain, 1904; Major, 1913; Bt Lt-Col 1916; Bt Colonel 1917; General Staff War Office, 1906–10; Gen. Staff, RM College, Sandhurst, 1911; Assistant Secretary Committee of Imperial Defence and Sec. Oversea Defence Committee, 1911–14; Gen. Staff, 27th Division, and 1st Army, Western Front, 1914–16; Brig.-Gen., Gen. Staff, II Army Corps, Western Front, 1916–18; Principal Assistant Sec., Committee of Imperial Defence; Secretary to Oversea Defence Committee, Home Ports Defence Committee, and Imperial Communication Com., 1918–21; Governor and Commander-in-Chief, Trinidad and Tobago, 1921–24; Captain-General and Governor-in-Chief of Jamaica, 1924–25; retired pay, 1923; Permanent Under-Secretary of State for the Colonies, 1925–33; served SA 1899–1900 (Queen's medal two clasps); European War, 1914–18 (Bt Col, CB, and despatches seven times); Officer Légion d'Honneur; French Croix de Guerre avec palme; Commandeur de la Couronne and Belgian Croix de Guerre avec palme. *Address:* 12 Whitelands House, SW3. *T:* Sloane 4051. *Clubs:* Army and Navy; Wentworth (Virginia Water).

Died 5 Aug. 1950.

WILSON, Sir Spencer Pocklington Maryon Maryon-, 11th Bt of East Borne, 1661; DL, JP for London; Chairman, West End Board of Royal Insurance Co.; Hon. Treasurer Standing Council of the Baronetage; Lord of the Manor of Hampstead; *b* 19 July 1859; *e s* of 10th Bt and Rose Emily, *d* of Rev. H. S. Pocklington; *S* father, 1897; *m* 1887, Minnie Elizabeth, *o c* of late General A. R. Thornhill, MSC; one *d.* Formerly Captain West Kent Yeomanry Cavalry. Owns about 1200 acres. *Heir:* nephew Rev. George Percy Maryon Maryon-Wilson. *Clubs:* Carlton, Cavalry.

Died 12 May 1944.

WILSON, T. Henry, MA, TCD, FRCPI; Ex-President, Royal College of Physicians, Ireland; King's Professor of Midwifery, Trinity College, University of Dublin; *er s* of late Capt. John Wilson, XIV Regt; *m* 1922, Gladys Mary, *er d* of late Col W. Lyster Smythe, Barbavilla, Co. Westmeath. Gynæcologist to Sir Patrick Dun's Hospital; late Extern University Examiner in Midwifery, Durham; Extern Examiner in Midwifery, Queen's University, Belfast. *Address:* 81 Merrion Square, Dublin. *T:* Dublin 61037.

Died 20 Nov. 1941.

WILSON, Theodora Wilson; author; *b* Kendal; *e d* of Isaac Whitwell Wilson, JP, and Anne Bagster. *Educ:* Stramongate School, Kendal; Croydon High School, and abroad. A writer of North Country novels, short stories, plays, and books for children; interested in social and religious work. *Publications:* T'Bacca Queen; Bess of Hardendale; Ursula Raven; Moll o' the Toll-Bar; The Islanders; Five of Them; Jim's Children; The Last Weapon Unsheathed; The Wrestlers; Jack O'Peterloo; The Explorer's Son; Adventures of Billy; The Laughing Band; Those Strange Years; Plays; Champion North; Bess of Hardendale; Through the Bible; The Grants and Jane; The Disappearing Twins, etc. *Address:* 16 Townsend Drive, St Albans.

Died 8 Nov. 1941.

WILSON, Theodore Stacey, MD, BSc (Edin.); FRCP (Lond.); MRCS (Eng.); FGS; Hon. Consulting Physician, Birmingham United Hospital; *b* Edgbaston, 1861; *s* of late J. E. Wilson, Wyddrington, Edgbaston; *m* 1st, 1903, Ada (*d* 1914), *d* of late Henry de Pothonier, London; one *d*; 2nd, 1917, Winifred Adams (*d* 1927), *d* of late Ernest Pattison, Leicester. *Educ:* Grove House School, Tottenham; Edinburgh University; Vienna. House Physician, Edinburgh Royal Infirmary, 1883; Resident Medical Officer to Birmingham General Hospital, 1885; Assistant Physician, 1889; Hon. Physician, 1892–1917. *Publications:* Early Diagnosis of Heart Failure and other Essays on the Heart and Circulation; Thought Transference; Speculations upon Psychology and Religion; Tonic Hardening of the Colon; The Spiritual Life viewed from a Scientific Standpoint; many contributions to the medical press. *Recreations:* field geology, entomology, fishing, etc. *Address:* 76 Farquhar Road, Edgbaston. *T:* Birmingham, Edg. 0422. *Club:* Union (Birmingham).

Died 30 July 1949.

WILSON, Prof. William; Advocate; Regius Professor of Public Law in the University of Edinburgh since 1922; *b* 1884; *y s* of late William Wilson, Dalhousie Chesters, Midlothian; *m* 1927, Sophia Latta, MA (*d* 1940). *Educ:* George Watson's College, Edinburgh; Univ. of Edinburgh. MA 1906; LLB with distinction, 1909; Thow Scholar in Scots Law and in Conveyancing; Muirhead Prizeman in Roman Law; Medallist in Forensic Medicine; awarded the Grierson Bursary in successive years. Called to the Scottish Bar, 1910; External Examiner for Law Degrees in the University of Glasgow, 1912–16, and in the University of Aberdeen, 1925–29; Commissioned Territorial Force Reserve General List, 1916–19; Secretary to the University of Edinburgh, 1919–25; Dean of Faculty of Law, 1938–43; Member of University Court, 1935–43; JP for the County of the City of Edinburgh; FRSE; a Representative of the University on the Board of Managers of the Royal Infirmary of Edinburgh, 1925–29; an Associate Member of All Souls College, Oxford, 1929. *Address:* The University, Edinburgh.

Died 22 Nov. 1944.

WILSON, Sir (William) Courthope (Townshend), Kt 1930; *b* 1865; *e s* of late Richard Duff Wilson, Liverpool; *m* 1892, Catherine (*d* 1940), *yr d* of late Rev. James Alexander Macdonald; three *s* two *d. Educ:* Birkenhead College; Liverpool Institute (High School). Barrister,

Gray's Inn, 1900; KC, 1919; Bencher, 1920; Treasurer, 1932; Vice-Chancellor of the County Palatine of Lancaster, 1925–36. *Address:* 68 Chandos Avenue, N20.

Died 5 Jan. 1944.

WILSON, Sir William Tweedley, Kt 1941; Director-General of Equipment and Stores, Ministry of Supply, since 1940; *b* 9 Nov. 1882; *s* of late John Wilson; *m* 1909, Louisa Emily Sefton, *d* of William Smith. *Educ:* London. In service of London County Council, 1905–40; appointed Chief Officer of Supplies, 1935; Member of Food Council. *Address:* St Margarets, Hayes Lane, Kenley, Surrey. *T:* Uplands 1368.

Died 2 May 1942.

WILSON-JOHNSTON, Maj.-Gen. Walter Edward; *see* Johnston.

WILSON TAYLOR, Sir John, Kt 1934; FCIS; late Secretary of The Bath Club; Hon. Secretary and Treasurer of the Pilgrims of Great Britain; Founder and Hon. Secretary of the Inter-Club Golf Tournament; Hon. Secretary of the Inter-Club Squash Racquets Tournament; Steward Amateur Squash Racquets Championship Meeting; Organiser of the Public Schools annual Swimming Contests at the Bath Club; Life Governor of the Royal Life Saving Society. During the War, Sub-Lieut RNVR (anti-aircraft corps) in charge of Foreign Office Gun Station; one of the Founders and Chairman of the House Committee of the American Officers' Club in Lord Leconfield's house; Vice-Chairman of the American Officers' Inn, Cavendish Square; Committee of Disabled Officers' Home, Westbourne Terrace; Committee of King George and Queen Mary Club for Overseas Soldiers; gave assistance to other Clubs formed for hospitality to Canadian, American and Colonial Officers; appointed Grand Deacon of United Grand Lodge of Freemasons when the American Freemasons paid official visit to England; Hon. Secretary of the Sports Club in connection with first Olympic Games. *Recreation:* golf. *Address:* 34 Dover Street, W1. *T:* Regent 7200. *Clubs:* Royal Societies, Queen's; Addington Golf.

Died 13 May 1943.

WILTON, Captain Sir James M., Kt 1937; MC; President Council of Education Authorities of Northern Ireland; Chairman, Northern Ireland War Pensions Committee. *Educ:* Foyle College; Magee University College, Londonderry; Queen's University, Belfast. Mayor of Londonderry, 1935–40; Alderman; JP. *Address:* 21 Marlborough Avenue, Londonderry. *T:* Londonderry 2164. *Clubs:* Northern Counties, Londonderry.

Died 8 Feb. 1946.

WILTON, John Raymond, ScD (Cantab), DSc (Adelaide), Elder Professor of Mathematics in the University of Adelaide since 1920; *b* 2 May 1884; *s* of late Charles Richard Wilton, Adelaide; *m* 1st, 1910, Annie Martha (*d* 1932), *d* of late James Nairn Gladstone, Forest Hill, London; 2nd, 1936, Winifred Aimée, *d* of Edward Welbourn, North Adelaide; one *s* one *d*. *Educ:* Prince Alfred College, Adelaide; Adelaide University; Trinity College, Cambridge. Lecturer in Mathematics Sheffield Univ., 1909–19; Manchester, 1919. *Address:* The University, Adelaide, South Australia.

Died 12 April 1944.

WILTSHIRE, Sir Frank H. C., Kt 1938; MC; Judge of Alderney, Channel Is, since Nov. 1947; *b* 27 Nov. 1881; *s* of Charles H. Wiltshire, Bradwell House, Suffolk; *m* 1909, Daisy Culver, *d* of John F. Rogers, Manor House, Little Easton, Essex; one *d*. *Educ:* Felsted School, Essex. Admitted Solicitor, 1908; Assistant Solicitor to Southampton, Gt Yarmouth and Birmingham, 1908–18; Solicitor to Birmingham Tame and Rea District Drainage Board, 1919–46; Town Clerk, Birmingham Oct. 1919–Nov. 1946 and Clerk of the Peace, 1937–46, Birmingham; Hon. Freeman City of Birmingham. Vice-

Pres. Institute of Public Administration. *Address:* White Place, Cranleigh, Surrey. *T:* Cranleigh 319; St Catherine's, Alderney. *Club:* Union (Birmingham).

Died 19 March 1949.

WIMBERLEY, Col Charles Neil Campbell, CMG 1917; MB, IMS, retired; *b* 1867; *s* of late Capt. Douglas Wimberley, JP, Inverness, Cameron Highlanders; *m* 1893, Lesmoir (*d* 1944), *d* of Col R. J. Wimberley; one *s*. *Educ:* Inverness Coll., Edinburgh University. Served Chitral Relief Force, 1895 (medal and clasp); N-W Frontier of India, 1897–98 (3 clasps); Tibet Expedition, 1903–04 (despatches, medal and clasp); European War, 1915–18 (despatches, CMG); retired, 1920. *Address:* 53 Fountainhall Road, Edinburgh.

Died 26 May 1949.

WINANT, Hon. John Gilbert, OM 1946; Ambassador of the United States to Court of St James, 1941–46; American Representative on European Advisory Commission, 1943–47; *b* 23 Feb. 1889; *s* of Frederick Winant and Jeannette L. Gilbert; *m* 1919, Constance Rivington Russell; two *s* one *d*. *Educ:* St Paul's School, Concord, New Hampshire; Princeton University, MA; Dartmouth College, MA, LLD; University of New Hampshire; University of Princeton; University of Bristol; University of Edinburgh; University of Leeds; University of Aberdeen; University of Manchester; University of Liverpool; University of Oxford; University of Cambridge; Knox College and Oberlin College. Member New Hampshire Legislature, 1917, 1923; New Hampshire State Senate, 1921; Governor of New Hampshire, 1925–27, 1931–33, 1933–35; Chairman of Federal Textile Inquiry Board, 1934; Chairman of Social Security Board, 1935–37; Assistant Director of International Labor Office, 1935 and 1937–38, Director 1938–41; Chairman World Textile Conference, Washington, 1937; American Expeditionary Force, 1917–19; Vice-President National Recreation Association; President Nat. Municipal League; Director National Tuberculosis Assoc.; Trustee International YMCA; Trustee Brookings Institution: member New England Council Boy Scouts of America; Member Social Science Research Council. *Publications:* A Letter from Grosvenor Square, 1947; Our Greatest Harvest (war-time speeches) (posthumous), 1950. *Address:* Concord, New Hampshire, USA. *Clubs:* Athenaeum; Century, Racquet, NY.

Died 3 Nov. 1947.

WINCHILSEA, 15th Earl of, *cr* 1628, **and NOTTINGHAM,** 10th Earl of *cr* 1675; **Christopher Guy Heneage Finch-Hatton;** Bart 1611; Viscount Maidstone, 1623; Bart English, 1660; Baron Finch, 1674; Hereditary Lord of Royal Manor of Wye; Lieutenant RNVR; *b* 2 Aug. 1911; *o s* of 14th Earl; *S* father 1939; *m* 1935, Countess Gladys Széchényi (who obtained a divorce, 1946), 3rd *d* of Count László Széchényi; two *s*; *m* 1946, Agnes Mary, 3rd *d* of late P. J. Conroy, JP, Malvern House, Wigan, Lancashire. *Educ:* Eton. *Heir:* *s* Viscount Maidstone. *Address:* Rag's Corner, Nether Wallop, Hants.

Died 7 March 1950.

WINDER, Maj. William John C.; *see* Corbett-Winder.

WINDHAM, Lt-Col Charles Joseph, CIE 1915; *b* 1867; *e s* of Major George Smijth-Windham, Rifle Brigade, and Clarissa, *d* of Lord Charles Russell, MP, *s* of 6th Duke of Bedford, KG; *m* Mildred, *d* of late John Bayntun Starky of Spye Park, Wilts.; one *s*. Entered Army, 1886; Indian Political Service, 1893; First Assistant to Governor-General's Agent in Rajputana and in Central India; First Assistant Resident in Kashmir; Political Officer with the Ex-Amir Yakub Khan of Kabul; Resident in Jodhpur and Bikaner, 1910–18; Political Agent in Kotah and Jhalawar, 1919; Resident in Baroda, 1920; Resident in Kashmir, 1921–23; retired, 1923; Vice-President of the Council, Jodhpur State,

India, 1927–32; Guardian to the Heir-Apparent, Kashmir State, India, 1935–37. *Recreations:* polo, fishing, shooting. *Address:* c/o Lloyds Bank Ltd, Cox and King's Branch, 6 Pall Mall, SW1. *Clubs:* United Service, Royal Automobile.

Died 28 Dec. 1941.

WINDHAM, Comdr Sir Walter George, Kt 1923; late RN; RIM, RNR, RNLI; *b* 1868; *s* of Major George Smijth Windham, Rifle Brigade, and *d* of Lord Charles James Fox Russell, MP, *s* of 6th Duke of Bedford, KG; *m* Helene, *d* of late Spencer Chapman and *widow* of Capt. Glen Kidston, 3rd Black Watch. Served on first plague commission for erection and maintenance of hospitals, Bombay, 1897; Queen's Messenger, 1900; King's Foreign Service Messenger, 1901–09; founder of the Aeroplane Club, 1908; took part in first motor drive to Brighton; owner of cars since 1897; Controller of the 1st Aerial Meeting (England) at Doncaster; entered a monoplane, also a biplane at Bournemouth meeting, 1910, which won a prize, both constructed by himself; sent a letter by Latham from France to England, described in the press as probably the first letter ever carried by air, 10 Aug. 1909; founded the first Aerial Post in India, Feb. 1911, and in the British Isles, Sept. 1911, both under Government supervision; imported the first aeroplanes into India for educational purposes to the Government, Oct. 1910, and made the first passenger flight in Asia, Dec. 1910; holds the silver and bronze medals of Royal Humane Society; Lloyd's silver medal for life-saving; also King's Coronation and Mons 1914 Star and Allies medals; was twice recommended for the Albert medal; sailed round the world four times under sail, 1884–88; collected by the Aerial Post £930 for King Edward's Hospital, Windsor, to endow a bed for aviators, 1911; offered in 1908 a gold cup to the first aviator who flew the Channel, won by Bleriot in 1909; mentioned in Government despatches, 1897, for connecting RIMS Warren Hastings with a rope to the shore, over which 1200 troops were landed; made an hon. member for life of the mess of the 1st Batt. King's RR for saving life and property from the wreck of the troopship Warren Hastings; carried Anglo-Russian pre-war treaty from Petersburg to London; crashed in aeroplane, Brooklands, 16 July 1910; drove the first car into Whitehall Court, 12 Nov. 1902, carrying foreign despatches; exhibited aeroplane, Olympia, 1909; stood as prospective (C) candidate for Willinghall, Central Hackney, and Great Yarmouth; contested Lewisham constituency; a Freeman of the City of London, 1933. *Address:* Tyrcelyn, Builth Wells. *T:* Erwood 8.

Died 5 July 1942.

WINDSOR, Walter; MP (Lab) Central division, Kingston-upon-Hull, since 1935; Secretary Bethnal Green National Union of General Workers; President of NE Bethnal Green Labour Party; Member of LCC for Greenwich, 1934–37; *s* of dock labourer. *Educ:* Cranbrook Street LCC Schools, Bethnal Green. Secretary, Bethnal Green SDF for many years; MP (Lab) NE Bethnal Green, 1923–29; fought Board of Guardians, 1907; served on Bethnal Green Borough Council for three years; was Chairman, Work and Stores Committee; Chairman of Libraries Committee; Secretary of Bethnal Green Trades Council 8 years; trade labourer furnishing trades. *Recreation:* politics.

Died 29 June 1945.

WINFREY, Sir Richard, Kt 1914; JP; *b* Lincs, 5 Aug. 1858; *s* of late R. F. Winfrey, of Long Sutton, Lincs; *m* 1897, Annie Lucy, *d* of William Pattinson, Ruskington, Lincs. Town Councillor; MP (Co. L) SW Norfolk, 1906–23, Gainsborough Division, 1923–24; Parliamentary Secretary to Earl Carrington, 1906–10; Parliamentary Secretary to Board of Agriculture, 1916–18; Chairman Lincolnshire Norfolk Small

Holdings Association, Ltd; contested SW Norfolk, 1895 and 1900. *Address:* Castor House, near Peterborough. *Clubs:* Reform, National Liberal.

Died 18 April 1944.

WINGATE, Temp. Maj.-Gen. Orde Charles, DSO; RA; Commander of Special Force, India Command; *b* 26 Feb. 1903; *s* of late Col G. Wingate, CIE and Mary Ethel Stanley, *d* of Capt. C. Orde Browne, RA; *m* 1935, Lorna Elizabeth Margaret, *o d* of Walter Moncrieff Paterson. *Educ:* private; Hillside; Charterhouse; RMA; self. 2nd Lt RA 1923; Capt. 1936; Major 1940; Temp. Lt-Col 1941. Attached to Sudan Defence Force, 1928–33; Adjt TA, 1935–36; Special appointment Palestine and Trans-Jordan, 1936–39 (despatches, DSO); War of 1939–45 (despatches, two bars to DSO); Lawrence of Arabia Memorial Medal from Royal Central Asian Society, 1943. Languages: Hebrew and Arabic. *Publication:* In Search of Zerzura (RGS Magazine, April 1934). *Recreations:* walking and talking. *Address:* 49 Hill St, SW1. *T:* Grosvenor 3895. *Club:* Army and Navy.

Died 24 March 1944.

WINGATE-SAUL, Sir Ernest Wingate, Kt 1933; KC 1919; Umpire under Unemployment Insurance Act since 1928; and Umpire under Reinstatement in Civil Employment Act since 1944; *b* 25 March 1873; *e s* of late William Wingate Wingate-Saul; *m* 1st, 1902, Violet (*d* 1935), 2nd *d* of Thomas Edmondson Stedman Satterthwaite, Castle Park, Lancaster; three *s* two *d*; 2nd, 1938, Dorothy, 3rd *d* of late Edmund Sharpe, Halton Hall, Lancaster. *Educ:* Rugby; Christ Church, Oxford. Barrister, Inner Temple, 1897; Bencher, 1925; Recorder of Preston and Judge and Assessor of Borough Court of Pleas, 1921–28; Judge of Appeal in the Isle of Man, 1925–28. *Club:* Oxford and Cambridge.

Died 13 Dec. 1944.

WINLOCK, Herbert Eustis; Director Emeritus, Metropolitan Museum of Art, New York City; *b* Washington, DC, 1 Feb. 1884; *s* of William Crawford Winlock and Alice Broom; *m* 1912, Helen Chandler, Boston, Massachusetts; one *d*. *Educ:* Harvard University, AB, 1906. Engaged in Archæological excavations, 1906–31, at Lisht, Oasis of Khargeh, and Luxor, Egypt, for the Metropolitan Museum of Art; director Egyptian Expedition, 1928–32; curator Egyptian Department, 1929–39; Director of the Museum, 1932–39; served as Captain, later Major, CAC USA, European War, 1917–18; Chevalier of Orders of Leopold and of the Crown (Belgium), and of Legion of Honour (France); LittD (hon.), Yale, Princeton, Michigan; Art. D (hon.), Harvard. *Publications:* (with A. C. Mace) The Tomb of Senebtisi, 1916; Bas-reliefs from the Temple of Rameses I at Abydos, 1921; (with W. E. Crum) The Monastery of Epiphanius, 1926; The Tomb of Meryet-Amun, 1932; The Treasure of Lahun, 1934; Ed Dakhleh Oasis, 1936; The Temple of Rameses I at Abydos, 1937; The Temple of Hibis in el Khargeh Oasis, 1941; Materials used in the Embalming of Tũtánkh-Amũn, 1941; Excavations at Deir el Bahri, 1942; Slain Soldiers of Neb-hepet-Rē' Mentu-hotpe, 1945; The Rise and Fall of the Middle Kingdom in Thebes, 1947; The Treasure of the Three Princesses, 1948; contributions to various journals. *Address:* North Haven, Maine, USA. *Clubs:* Century, Round Table (New York).

Died 27 Jan. 1950.

WINNICOTT, Sir (John) Frederick, Kt 1924; JP; *b* 1855; *m* 1887, Elizabeth Martha (*d* 1925), *d* of William Woods. Mayor of Plymouth, 1906–07 and 1921–22; Ex-Chairman, Chamber of Commerce; a Manager SD of EC Hospital; Trustee Plymouth and South Devon Savings Bank; presented Freeman, City of Plymouth, 1934. *Address:* Rockville, Mannamead, Plymouth.

Died 31 Dec. 1948.

WINNING, Theodore Norman; Barrister-at-law; Recorder of Grantham (Lincs) since 1943; Chairman of County of Derby Quarter Sessions, 1943; *b* 8 Aug. 1884; *s* of late Rev. William Winning, Vicar of Glaisdale, N Yorks; *m* 1913, Florence Marshall, *d* of late George Bonner, Darley Dale, Derbyshire; three *s* (and one killed in action 1941) one *d*. *Educ:* Pocklington School, E Yorks. Joined 5th Bn The Sherwood Foresters in 1905; Capt. 1912; Brigade Signalling Officer, 1908–12; Divisional Signalling Officer, 1912–13; served in France and at War Office during European War; called to Bar, Gray's Inn, 1919; Legal Chairman of Coal Investigation Committee for Staffordshire and Worcestershire Coal Fields, 1937–39. *Recreations:* fishing and shooting. *Address:* 4 Brick Court, EC4; 71 Temple Row, Birmingham. *T:* Birmingham Midland 3487. *Clubs:* Reform; Union, Birmingham; County, Derby.

Died 19 Aug. 1946.

WINSTANLEY, Denys Arthur; Vice-Master of Trinity College, Cambridge; *b* 5 Dec. 1877; *s* of Howard Winstanley. *Educ:* Merchant Taylors' School; Trinity College, Cambridge (scholar); 1st class Historical Tripos, 1899 and 1900, Lightfoot Scholar, 1901. Junior Inspector of Board of Education, 1903–06; Fellow and Lecturer of Trinity College, 1906; Tutor of Trinity College, 1919–31; Senior Tutor, 1925–31. *Publications:* Personal and Party Government, 1910; Lord Chatham and the Whig Opposition, 1912; The University of Cambridge in the Eighteenth Century, 1922; Unreformed Cambridge, 1935; Early Victorian Cambridge, 1940; Later Victorian Cambridge, 1946. *Address:* Trinity College, Cambridge.

Died 20 March 1947.

WINTER-SHAW, Arthur, HRI. Honorary retired member of Royal Institute of Painters in Water-Colours. *Address:* Rose Cottage, 58 London Road, Cowplain, nr Portsmouth.

Died 30 Jan. 1948.

WINTERBOTHAM, Brig. Harold St John Loyd, CB 1935; CMG 1918; DSO 1916; *b* 5 Feb. 1878; 2nd *s* of Canon R. Winterbotham; *m* 1909, Daisy, *d* of G. Stocking; one *s* two *d*. *Educ:* Fettes College, Edinburgh; RMA, Woolwich. Received Commission in Royal Engineers, 1897; served South African War, 1899–1900 (Queen's medal 3 clasps); St Helena, 1902–06; Colonial Survey Section, Orange Free State, 1908–11; Ordnance Survey, Southampton, 1911–14; served European War, 1914–18; to France, Oct. 1914, as OC Ranging Section, RE; Maps, 3rd Army, 1915–17; attached General Staff, GHQ 1917 to end of war (despatches thrice, DSO, CMG, Bt Lt-Col); Geographical Section, General Staff, 1922–29; employed to inspect Colonial Survey Departments, 1929–30; Director-General of Ordnance Survey, 1930–35; ADC to the King, 1931–35; retired pay, 1935; General Secretary International Geodetic and Geophysical Union, 1930–45. Officer French Legion of Honour; Grand Officer of the Order of St Sava (Yugoslavia); American DSM; Victoria Medal RGS, 1929; Hon. DSc George Washington University, 1939. *Publications:* Ordnance Survey: the National Plans, 1934; A Key to Maps, 1936. *Recreations:* golf and garden. *Address:* River Cottage, Sutton Courtenay, Berks.

Died 10 Dec. 1946.

WINTERBOTTOM, Lt-Col Archibald Dickson, DSO 1918; 5th Dragoon Guards, retired; *b* 11 May 1885; *e s* of late Lt-Col W. D. Winterbottom of Aston Hall, Derby, and late Clara Fletcher of Hope Avenue, Eccles, Manchester; *m* 1st, 1910, Gladys Hughes Appleton; one *s*; 2nd, 1929, Dorothy Gwendolen, widow of Charles E. Coleman, RFA and *d* of late Charles Wright Petchell, Durban, SA; two *d*. *Educ:* Eton. 2nd Lt Derbyshire Yeomanry 1904; 2nd Lt 5th (PCW) Dragoon Guards, 1908; Lt 1911; Capt. 1915; served European War, 1914–April 1919, France and Army of Occupation, Germany (DSO, Officier de la Couronne

Belge, Croix de Guerre Belge, despatches twice); retired as Captain, July 1919; Lt-Col 14th Sussex (Hove) Home Guard. *Recreations:* hunting, polo, golf, lawn tennis. *Address:* Tudor House, Dyke Road Avenue, Brighton 5. *T:* Preston 3575.

Died 29 April 1942.

WINTERTON, George Ernest; lecturer and journalist; *b* 17 May 1873; *m* 1902; two *s* one *d*. *Educ:* Charnwood Street Elementary School, Leicester; Borough Road College, Isleworth. Trained as schoolmaster; First Secretary of West Ham Teachers' Association; became Secretary and Organiser for the Temperance Movement at Leicester and Manchester, and afterwards Secretary of the Strength of Britain Movement to secure War Time Prohibition; associated with late John Kempster, JP, in securing One Day's Rest in Seven for the Police, and became organiser of the Adult Suffrage Movement; joined the ILP, 1911; formed the Richmond Labour Party, 1917, and became Chairman of the East Surrey Labour Party, 1921; Official Lecturer to the Daily Herald, 1920–29; contested Loughborough Division 1923, 1924, 1929, 1931 and 1935; MP (Lab), Loughborough Division of Leicestershire, 1929–31; Introduced First Bill for Holidays with Pay and secured Second Reading on 15th Nov. 1929; Assist Secretary and organiser in connection with Peace Ballot, 1935. *Publications:* editor The White Ribbon, organ National British Women's Total Abstinence Union; contributor religious and secular press; various pamphlets and handbooks dealing with Temperance, Peace, the Press, etc. *Recreation:* gardening. *Address:* Sonoma, Oak Avenue, Chichester, Sussex.

Died May 1942.

WINTOUR, Maj.-Gen. Fitzgerald, CB 1910; CBE 1919; *b* 30 Dec. 1860; *m* 1st, 1899, Cicely Winifred (*d* 1904), *d* of late Sir W. Spencer Stanhope, KCB, Cannon Hall, Barnsley; 2nd, 1912, Alice Jane Blanche, *d* of late Major J. F. Foster, 13th Hussars, of Glyde Court, Louth, Ireland; one *s* one *d*. Entered Army, 1880; Capt. R. West Kent, 1887; Major, 1900; Lt-Col Norfolk Regt 1904; Col 1908; served Egypt, 1882 (medal, bronze star); Soudan, 1884–85 (despatches, clasp, brevet Major); Soudan, 1885–86; NW Frontier, India 1897 (despatches, medal with clasp); South Africa, 1899–1901 (despatches, brevet Lt-Col, Queen's medal and two clasps); commanded a Brigade in France, 1914–15; DA and QMG Headquarters, 2nd Army, 1915 (despatches); retired, 31 March 1918.

Died 18 June 1949.

WINTOUR, Ulick Fitzgerald, CB 1916; CMG 1914; *b* 20 April 1877; *s* of Thomas Fitzgerald Wintour, of High Hoyland, Barnsley; *m* 1st, 1901, Hylda Frances Catherine, *d* of Capt. F. H. Garnett; two *s*; 2nd, 1923, Sybille Isabelle Alice d'Anjou. *Educ:* Winchester; Wrens. Chinese Customs Service, 1898–1904; appointed to Board of Trade, 1904; Director, Exhibitions Branch, Board of Trade, 1908; British Commissioner-General, Brussels Exhibition, 1910; Turin, 1911; Ghent, 1913; Director of Army Contracts, 1914–17; First Secretary Ministry of Food, 1917–18; Controller Stationery Office, 1918–19; Officer Legion of Honour; Commander Order of Leopold; Order of St Sava, Serbia (2nd Class). *Address:* Villa Margaritta, Chemin des Mougins, Cap d'Antibes, Alpes Maritimes, France.

Died 5 Aug. 1947.

WINTRINGHAM, Thomas Henry; *b* 15 May 1898; 2nd *s* of John Fildes Wintringham, solicitor, and Eliza Mapson Wintringham, Grimsby, Lincs. *Educ:* Gresham's School, Holt, Norfolk; Balliol Coll., Oxford. Served RFC and RAF, France, 1916–18; commanded British battalion International Brigade, near Madrid, Feb. 1937; helped to found Osterley Park Training School for Home Guard, 1940. *Publications:* English Captain, 1939; New Ways of War (Penguin), 1940; Armies of Freemen, 1940; Politics of Victory, 1941; People's War (Penguin),

1942; Weapons and Tactics, 1943; Your MP, 1945. *Address:* 19 Laverockbank Rd, Edinburgh 5. *T:* Edinburgh 83167.

Died 16 Aug. 1949.

WISDOM, Brig.-Gen.Evan Alexander, CB 1917; CMG 1919; DSO 1916; VD; *b* Inverness, 1869; *s* of Francis William Wisdom and Mary Cameron; *m* 1895, Agnes Bell (*d* 1931), *d* of Francis Bell Jackson, Edinburgh. *Educ:* Inverness; Edinburgh. Went to West Australia, 1891; engaged in gold-mining and other business until 1895; joined Commonwealth Military Forces, 1901; later, Adjutant 18th Regt Light Horse, and then a Staff-Officer; Brigade Major, Mixed Brigade, West Australia, 1908; Mayor of Cottesloe, WA, 1908–12; Member Legislative Assembly, WA, Claremont Constituency, 1911–17; Assistant General Staff-Officer, WA, on outbreak of war; later, Camp Commandant for WA; Brigade Major 5th Aus. Brigade (NSW), 1915; served Gallipoli, Aug. 20 to evacuation, 1915; Sinai Peninsula, Feb. 1916; France, 1916 to end of War (despatches six times, CMG, DSO, CB); Administrator of former German territory in New Guinea, 1921–32; Order of Danilo, 3rd Class, 1917. *Recreations:* yachting, motoring. *Clubs:* Australian, Sydney; Melbourne, Melbourne; Perth, Perth.

Died 7 Dec. 1945.

WISE, Hon. George Henry; *b* Melbourne, Australia, 1 July 1853; *e s* of James and Mary B. Wise; *m* 1880, Mary Thornton Smith (*d* 1939); one *s* three *d*. *Educ:* Scotch Coll., Melbourne. Admitted to Supreme Court of Victoria as a Solicitor, 1874; Member of Borough Council of Sale, Victoria, 1880–1904; Mayor of the Borough six times; Member of Board of Directors of the Australian Natives Assoc., Victoria, 1887; retired 1946; Chief President of that body, 1891; member of the House of Representatives for Gippsland, Victoria, in the Commonwealth Parliament, 1906, 1910, 1914, 1917, and 1919; Assistant Minister of Defence, 1918–19; PMG, 1920–21. *Address:* Sale, Victoria, Australia. *T:* Sale 1 and 2.

Died 31 July 1950.

WISE, Lt-Col Henry Edward Disbrowe Disbrowe-, CBE 1919; *b* 1868; *s* of late Henry Christopher Wise, MP, Woodcote, Warwick; *m* 1896, Katharine Mary, *d* of Thomas Levett Prinsep, of Croxall Hall, Derbyshire. Served European War, 1914–19 (despatches, CBE); assumed by deed poll the additional surname of Disbrowe, 1919. *Address:* Walton Hall, Burton-on-Trent.

Died 9 Sept. 1948.

WISE, Rabbi Stephen S.; Founder 1907 and Rabbi 1907 of the Free Synagogue, NY, now its Senior Rabbi; Founder 1922 and Pres. since 1922 of the Jewish Institute of Religion; *b* 17 March 1874; *s* of Rabbi Dr Aaron Wise and Sabine de Fischer Farkashasy; *m* 1900; one *s* one *d*. *Educ:* City Coll., NY; Columbia Univ.; European Univs. Rabbi Cong. B'nai Jeshurun, 1893–1900; Temple Beth Israel, Portland, O, 1900–06; President at different times, Zionist Organization of America; a Founder and President American Jewish Congress; Founder and President World Jewish Congress; Editor, Opinion. Officer Legion of Honour. Hon. Degrees: Temple Univ., Syracuse Univ., Bates Univ., Roanoke Univ., Oregon Univ., Hebrew Union College, Cincinnati. *Publications:* Ibn Gabirol and the Moral Qualities, 1901; How to Face Life; Child vs Parent; As I See It. *Address:* 40 W 68th Street, New York. *TA:* Worldgress. *T:* Trafalgar 7–4050.

Died 19 April 1949.

WISEMAN, Arthur Maurice, CMG 1941; MC; HM Senior Trade Commissioner for the United Kingdom in Canada since 1938; *b* 5 Oct. 1893; *s* of late Rev. A. R. Wiseman, Guildford; unmarried. *Educ:* Charterhouse; New College, Oxford. Left University to serve in war of

1914–18, first as Private 19th Royal Fusiliers, then as 2nd Lieut 13th Rifle Brigade (severely wounded, 1916, discharged from army, 1918, MC); joined Dept of Overseas Trade, 1918; Asst to HM Senior Trade Commissioner in Canada, Montreal, 1920; Deputy Trade Commissioner, Winnipeg, 1923; Trade Commissioner, Toronto, 1928; idc 1935. *Address:* 56 Sparks Street, Ottawa, Ontario, Canada. *TA:* Sencom Ottawa. *T:* 38814. *Clubs:* United University; Rideau (Ottawa); University (Montreal).

Died 6 April 1948.

WISEMAN, Rev. Frederick Luke, BA (Lond.), LittD (Hon. Leeds); Minister of Wesley's Chapel, London, since 1940; Deputy Treasurer of the Home Mission Department, Methodist Church; *b* 29 Jan. 1858; *s* of Rev. Luke H. Wiseman, MA (President, Wesleyan Conference, 1872); *m* Lois Elsie Daniel (*d* 1917), of Biggleswade; two *s* one *d*. *Educ:* Sutherland House, Highgate; Didsbury Theological College. Assistant Tutor (Hebrew, etc.) at Didsbury Theological College, 1881–87; Superintendent of the Birmingham Central Mission and Minister of the Central Hall, Corporation Street, Birmingham, 1887–1913; Secretary of Home Mission Department, Methodist Church 1913–39; President of the Wesleyan Conference, 1912–13; President of the National Council of Evangelical Free Churches, 1914; President Methodist Conference, 1933–34. *Publications:* Charles Wesley, evangelist and poet; Songs of the Twelve Hours; other musical compositions (sacred). *Address:* 33 Routh Road, SW18. *T:* Battersea 4058. *Clubs:* National Liberal; Reform, Manchester.

Died 16 Jan. 1944.

WISEMAN, Air-Cdre Percy John, CBE 1943; *b* 30 July 1888; *s* of P. F. Wiseman; *m* 1913, G. M., *d* of Comdr J. W. J. Savage; two *s* three *d*. *Educ:* Buckingham Academy. Served in RNAS and Supreme Headquarters Allied Expeditionary Force. Chairman of Council, Philosophical Society of Great Britain; President, The Crusaders Union; Vice-Chairman, Officers' Christian Union. *Publications:* Babylon in the Days of Hammurabi and Nebuchadnezzar, 1926; New Discoveries in Babylonia, 1937; Modern Archæology and The Bible, 1947. *Recreations:* golf, tennis, etc. *Address:* Hamberlins, Berkhamsted. *TA:* Wiseman, Hamberlins, Berkhamsted. *T:* Berkhamsted 793.

Died 16 Oct. 1948.

WISHART, Captain Robert, DSO 1903; retired; *b* 1875; *s* of late Andrew and late Alena Wishart; *m;* two *s* one *d*. Served S Africa with Bethune's Mounted Infantry and Johannesburg Mounted Rifles, 1900–02 (despatches, King's medal 2 clasps, Queen's medal 4 clasps, DSO); Coronation medal. *Address:* Austral Estates, Holmdene, Transvaal, South Africa. *T:* Holmdene 820. *Clubs:* South African, Johannesburg.

Died 3 Nov. 1938.

WITHERBY, Harry Forbes, MBE, FZS, FRGS, MBOU; publisher; *b* 7 Oct. 1873; 2nd *surv. s* of late Henry Forbes Witherby, RBA; *m* 1904, Lilian, *d* of late Rev. S. Gillson, Itchen Abbas, Hants; two *s* three *d*. Made journeys chiefly in pursuit of ornithology to Spain, Russian Lapland, White Nile, South-west Persia, Algeria, etc.; since an early age has devoted all spare time to the study of ornithology, specialising in recent years on British and Spanish birds, and especially their distribution, migrations, and plumages; founded in 1907 the magazine of British Birds, and has edited it since in conjunction with others; Hon. Secretary and Treasurer (1904–14), and Chairman (1924–27) British Ornithologists' Club; President British Ornithologists' Union, 1933–38; Godman-Salvin gold medal, 1938; Hon. Fellow American Ornithologists' Union, 1928; Lt RNVR 1917–18 (despatches, MBE). *Publications:* Bird-hunting on the White Nile; (joint) A Handlist of British Birds; (editor and joint-author) Practical Handbook of

British Birds and the Handbook of British Birds; many papers in various natural history journals. *Recreations:* ornithology, gardening. *Address:* Gracious Pond Farm, Chobham, Surrey. *T:* Longcross 332.

Died 11 Dec. 1943.

WITHERS, Hartley; Director Allied Investers' Trusts; *b* 15 July 1867; *m* 1921, Alice, *y d* of J. R. Elliott; one *d. Educ:* Westminster; Christ Church, Oxford; MA Cantab 1938. Asst Master Clifton Coll., 1890; Stock Exchange clerk, 1891–93; City Office of Times, 1894; City Editor of Times, 1905–10; City Editor of Morning Post, 1910–11; entered employment of Seligman Brothers, 1911; Director of Financial Enquiries in the Treasury, 1915–16; Editor of the Economist, 1916–21; of Financial Supplement of Saturday Review, 1921–23. *Publications:* The Meaning of Money, 1909; Stocks and Shares, 1910; Money-Changing, 1913; Poverty and Waste, 1914; War and Lombard Street, 1915; International Finance, 1916; Our Money and the State, 1917; The Business of Finance, 1918; War-Time Financial Problems, 1919; The Case for Capitalism, 1920; Bankers and Credit, 1924; Hints about Investments, 1926; Money, 1927; Quicksands of the City, and a Way Through for Investors, 1930; Everybody's Business, 1931; Money in the Melting Pot, 1932; National Provincial Bank, 1833 to 1933, 1933; Investing Simplified, 1934; The Way to Wealth, 1935; The Defeat of Poverty, 1939; Archiepiscopal Economics, 1942. *Address:* Copford Place, Colchester.

Died 21 March 1950.

WITHERS, Lt-Col Henry Hastings Cavendish, DSO 1940; RE; *b* 11 Oct. 1904; *s* of late Lt-Col S. H. Withers, CMG, and Kathleen Cavendish; *m* 1st, 1931, Deirdre G. H. MacLeod (*d* 1934); no *c*; 2nd, 1937, Ethel Geddes Williamson; no *c*; 3rd, 1944, Sara N. E. Raymond; one *s* one *d. Educ:* Cheltenham College; RMA, Woolwich. Commissioned in RE 1924; served War of 1939–45 (DSO, wounded). *Recreations:* Rugby football (Irish International, 1931–32), ski-ing. *Address:* Panthill, Barcombe, Sussex.

Died 6 Sept. 1948.

WITHERS, Percy; *b* 1867; 4th *s* of late John Withers, Sale, Cheshire; *m* 1896, Mary Woolley, *d* of late John Summers, Staleybridge; one *s* two *d. Educ:* Manchester Grammar School; Owens College, Univ. of Manchester. Late House-Surgeon Manchester Royal Infirmary; English Poem Prize; late Lecturer in English Literature, Oxford University Extension. On Executive of Nat. Trust 32 years. *Publications:* Egypt of Yesterday and To-day, 1909; The Garland of Childhood, 1910; In a Cumberland Dale, 1914; Friends in Solitude, 1923; A Buried Life: Personal Recollections of A. E. Housman, 1940. *Recreations:* friendships, books, pictures, and Church architecture. *Address:* Epwell Mill, Banbury. *T:* Swalcliffe 20.

Died 19 June 1945.

WITHERS, Lt-Col Samuel Henry, CMG 1917; MB, BCh and BAO, RUI; late RAMC. *Educ:* Queen's College, Belfast. Served NW Frontier, India, 1897–98 (medal 2 clasps); S Africa, 1899–1902 (Queen's medal 3 clasps, King's medal 2 clasps); European War, 1914–18 (CMG). *Address:* Maumbury Lodge, Monmouth Road, Dorchester, Dorset.

Died 10 Feb. 1942.

WITTS, Brig. Frank Hole, DSO 1919; MC; Commander 8th Infantry Brigade; *b* 22 Feb. 1887; 4th *s* of late Rev. Canon F. E. Broome Witts, of Upper Slaughter, Gloucester; *m* 1919, Ruth Leonide, 2nd *d* of late Harold Brocklebank of Grizedale Hall, Lancs. *Educ:* Radley; Trinity College, Oxford. Joined the Irish Guards, Aug. 1914; served in France with 1st and 2nd Battalions and afterwards on the Staff during the European War (DSO, MC, despatches twice); PSC 1924; Major, 1926; Bt Lt-Col 1928; Lt-Col 1933; Col

1935. Commanded 1st Bn King's Own Royal Regt (Lancaster) 1933–35; AQMG Aldershot Command, 1935–37. *Recreations:* golf, shooting. *Address:* Fort House, Crown Hill, Plymouth. *Club:* Guards'.

Died 9 May 1941.

WODEHOUSE, Vice-Adm. Norman Atherton, CB 1939; *b* 18 May 1887; *s* of Rev. F. A. Wodehouse; *m* Theodosia, *d* of late Captain E. L. D. Boyle, CMG, RN (retired) and *widow* of Douglas William Swire, Captain Shropshire Yeomanry; two *s. Educ:* Royal Naval School, Lee-on-the-Solent; HMS Britannia. Lieut 1907; Commander, 1919; Captain, 1926; Rear-Adm., 1937; Rear-Admiral-in-Charge, Gibraltar, and Admiral Superintendent HM Dockyard, Gibraltar, 1939; Vice-Adm., retired, 1940; retired list, 1940; Order of Striped Tiger of China, 1919; Royal Humane Society Silver Medal, 1915. *Recreations:* golf, tennis, yachting, sketching. *Club:* United Service.

Died 4 July 1941.

WOLF, Abraham, MA, DLit; sometime Fellow of St John's College, Cambridge; Fellow of University College, London; Professor Emeritus of Logic and Scientific Method in the University of London (Head of the Department of the History and Method of Science at University College, London, and of the Department of Logic and Philosophy at the London School of Economics and Political Science), retd 1941; Co-Editor of the Encyclopædia Britannica (14th ed.); Member of Senate and of the Academic and External Councils of the University of London till 1944; Dean of the Faculty of Economics and Political Science, 1938–41; Governor of Haberdashers' Aske's Schools, 1935–41; Examiner in Philosophy in the University of London, 1915, in the University of Oxford, 1922; sometime Member Executive Committee Aristotelian Society; Member Executive Committee International Congress of Philosophy, London, 1915, and President elect of the Section on Logic and Scientific Method; *b* 1876; *m* 1901; one *s* three *d. Educ:* University College, London; St John's College, Cambridge. *Publications:* Studies in Logic, 1905; Spinoza, his Life and Treatise on God and Man, 1910; The Philosophy of Nietzsche, 1915 (new ed. 1923); Exercises in Logic and Scientific Method, 1919 (4th ed. 1942); Essentials of Scientific Method, 1925 (new ed. 1928); Key to Exercises in Logic and Scientific Method, 1926; Essentials of Logic, 1926; The Oldest Biography of Spinoza, 1927; The Correspondence of Spinoza, 1928; Text-book of Logic, 1930 (3rd ed. 1943); History of Science, Technology, and Philosophy in the 16th and 17th Centuries, 1935; History of Science, Technology, and Philosophy in the 18th Century, 1938; Higher Education in Nazi Germany, 1944; Higher Education in German Occupied Countries, 1945. Editor of the History of Science Library. *Recreations:* walking, gardening, chess, etc. *Address:* 13 Battlefield Road, St Albans, Herts. *T:* St Albans 5195.

Died 19 May 1948.

WOLF-FERRARI, Ermanno; composer; *b* Italy, 12 Jan. 1876; *s* of August Wolff, painter. *Educ:* Munich. *Works:* Suzanna's Secret; Il Quatro Rusteghi; The Jewels of the Madonna; Donne Curiose; Sly; The Crafty Widow; Il Campiello; La Niña Boba. *Address:* Planegg bei Munich, Germany.

Died 21 Jan. 1948.

WOLFE, George; *b* 1859; *o surv. s* of late Theobald George Wolfe and late Elizabeth Henrietta Ball; *m* Emily Maud Mary, *widow* of J. J. Leeman, MP, York (*d* 1910), and *o c* of late R. Smethurst, DL, JP; one *d. Educ:* Trinity College, Dublin; Sandhurst. Served in 1st Batt. Royal Irish Fusiliers, 1882–85; 8th Hussars, 1885–90; present at battle of Tel-el-Kebir (medal with clasp and Khedive's star); High Sheriff, Co. Kildare, 1900; Ranger of the Curragh, 1910; Peace Commissioner, Co. Kildare; CC 1899–1920; Vice-Chairman, 1911–20; TD for Kildare in Dail Eireann, 1923–32; JP Co. Kildare. *Address:*

Forenaughts, Naas, Co. Kildare. *T:* 17X1 Naas. *Clubs:* Army and Navy; St Stephen's Green, Irish Automobile, Dublin.

Died 1 Dec. 1941.

WOLFF, Lt-Col Arnold Johnston, DSO 1916; late RE; FRGS; *b* Whalley Range, 1 Sept. 1873; *s* of Arnold Holford, Wolff, merchant, and Jean Johnston Crawford; *m* 1905, Nora Gladys, *d* of Dr Platt, St James' Lodge, Hampstead; no *c. Educ:* Merchiston; Royal Military Academy, Woolwich. 2nd Lieut RE 1893; served South African War, 1899–1902 (King's and Queen's medals with 5 clasps); on Ordnance Survey, 1902–09; on Staff of Royal Military College, Kingston, Canada, 1910–14; served European War with 13th Div. in France, Gallipoli, Egypt, Mesopotamia (despatches thrice, DSO); on Ordnance Survey, 1918–25; retired pay, 1926. *Address:* Sandihayes, Bitterne Park, Southampton. *T:* Southampton 74424.

Died 23 May 1941.

WOLFF, Ernest Charteris Holford, CMG 1928; JP Hants; *b* 3 July 1875; *y s* of late Arnold Holford Wolff of Whalley Range, Manchester; *m* 1911, Mary Lilias, 3rd *d* of late Rev. John Alison, DD; two *d. Educ:* Merchiston Castle School, Edinburgh; Trinity College Oxford; BA 1897. Entered Malayan Civil Service, 1897; Assistant Colonial Secretary SS, 1915; Director of Education SS and FMS, 1921; British Resident, Negri Sembilan, Federated Malay States, 1924; Acting Colonial Secretary SS, 1927; President, Rivers Commission, FMS, 1927; retired, 1928; Hants County Council, 1934; Count Aldermany, 1945; Winchester Rural District Council; Chairman, Hants and I of W Agricultural Wages Committee. *Address:* Cheniston, Compton, Winchester. *T:* Twyford 2178. *Club:* East India and Sports.

Died 23 April 1946.

WOLFF, Johannes; violinist; *b* 1862. Won travelling scholarship of the King of Holland when 12 years of age; studied in Rotterdam under Professor Wirth; at Dresden and Paris; obtained first prize at Paris Conservatoire; has played all over Europe and America; decorated by the Czar of Russia, King of Holland, King of Portugal; is Officier d'Instruction publique in France; received the Ludwig Order from Grand Duke of Hesse; Jubilee Medal from Queen Victoria; the Order of Orange and Nassau from the Queen of Holland; the medal of Art and Science from Anhalt; Chevalier of the Legion of Honour. *Recreations:* bicycling, fishing. *Address:* 39 rue Jouvenet, Paris, xvi^e.

Deceased.

WOLFFLIN, Heinrich; Professor a. d. Universität Zürich since 1924; *b* 21 June 1864; *s* of Eduard Wölfflin and Bertha Troll. *Educ:* München. Professor in Basel, 1893; in Berlin, 1901; in München, 1912. *Publications:* Renaissance und Barock; Klassische Kunst; Kunst Albrecht Dürer's; Kunstgeschichtliche Grundbegriffe; Italien und das deutsche Formgefühl; Gedanken zur Kunstgeschichte. *Address:* Zürich, Talacker 39, Switzerland. *T:* 31076.

Died 19 July 1945.

WOLLEY-DOD, Brig.-Gen. Owen Cadogan, CB 1915; DSO 1900; *b* 2 May 1863; 6th *s* of late Rev. C. Wolley-Dod, of Edge Hall, Malpas, Cheshire. *Educ:* Eton; Sandhurst. Graduate of Staff College. Joined Lancashire Fusiliers, 1883; Captain, 1892; Major, 1901; transferred to Sherwood Foresters, 1904; Lieut-Col 1908; Colonel 1911; Brig.-Gen. 1915; Brigade-Major 4th Inf. Brigade, Aldershot, 1902–04; Assistant Commandant RMC, Sandhurst, 1912; GSO1, 5th Division, 1914; War Office, 1914; 29th Division, 1915; Commanded 86th Infantry Brigade, 1915; Inspector of Infantry, 1915; Commanding Lucknow Brigade, 1917; Bangalore Brigade, 1918; served in Soudan campaign, 1898 (despatches); South African war, 1899–1900 (despatches, Queen's medal 2 clasps, DSO); in the

occupation of Crete, 1898; in European War, 1914–18 (despatches thrice, CB). *Recreation:* bowls. *Address:* 80 North Walls, Winchester. *Club:* Army and Navy.

Died 1 Feb. 1942.

WOLMER, Viscount; William Matthew Palmer; Hampshire Regt (TA); *b* 27 May 1912; *s* of 3rd Earl of Selborne; *m* 1936, Priscilla, *d* of late Capt. John Egerton-Warburton, Arley Hall, Cheshire; two *s* one *d. Educ:* Winchester; Balliol College, Oxford. *Address:* Bradshott Hall, Blackmoor, Liss, Hants. *T:* Blackmoor 278. *Club:* Travellers'.

Died 2 Oct. 1942.

WOLSELEY, Rev. Sir William Augustus, 11th Bt *cr* 1744; *b* Demerara, British Guiana, 19 April 1865; *s* of Charles Wolseley and Margaret FitzGerald; *S* cousin, 1933; *m* 1932, Sarah Helen, *d* of late William Cotton Grummitt; lived most of early life in Ireland. *Educ:* Trinity College, Dublin (Hebrew Prizeman, Greek Testament Prizeman, Downes and Butcher Exhibitioner, Wall Heb. Scholar). 1st of 1st Theology Exhibitioner, 1st Class Divinity Testimonium; Prizeman in Literature and History, BA. In Ireland 1889–1906, Curate, Tarbert, and thence to Bunbury, W Australia, as Rector of Ravensthorpe, 1906–10, and of Denmark, 1910–20; Senior Curate, Christ Church, Felling; St James', Burnopfield did locum tenens duty several years, all in Diocese of Durham; Vicar of Alnham, 1932; retired, 1942; a keen student of Biblical Greek; ardent Imperialist. *Heir: cousin* Garnet, *b* 27 May 1915. *Address:* 6 Coquet Vale, Felton, Morpeth. *T:* Felton 266.

Died 19 Feb. 1950.

WOLVERHAMPTON, 2nd Viscount *cr* 1908; **Henry Ernest Fowler;** *b* 4 April 1870; *o s* of 1st Viscount Wolverhampton and Ellen C. I. (*d* 1911), *d* of late G. B. Thorneycroft, of Chapel House, Wolverhampton, and Hadley Park, Salop; *S* father, 1911; *m* 1910, Hon. Evelyn Henrietta Wrottesley, *o d* of 3rd Baron Wrottesley. *Educ:* Charterhouse; Christ Church, Oxford. *Recreation:* photography. *Heir:* none. *Address:* Carrwood House, Overstrand, Norfolk. *T:* Overstrand 224. *TA:* Overstrand.

Died 9 March 1943 (ext).

WOLVIN, Roy Mitchell; President, Kingston Shipbuilding Co. Ltd, The Collingwood Shipyards Ltd, Port Arthur Shipbuilding Co. Ltd, Midland Shipyards Ltd; Ex-President Dominion Steel Corporation; *b* St Clair, Mich, 21 Jan. 1880; *s* of George A. and Mary Wolvin; *m* 1916, Geraldine Faro, Chicago; two *s. Educ:* Public Schools, St Clair, Mich. *Address:* Montreal, Canada. *Clubs:* St James', Montreal, Montreal.

Died 7 April 1945.

WONHAM, Rear-Adm. (S) Charles Scrivener, CBE 1917; *b* 7 April 1870; *s* of Captain A. R. Wonham, RN; *m* Claire Marie Le Marchand; two *s. Educ:* Christ's Hospital. Entered Royal Navy, 1886; retired 1925 with rank of Paymaster Rear-Admiral; served European War in HMS Marlborough; commended for services in action (Jutland, 1916); served in France, 1917–20 (Army despatches for special services with Naval Transport Department); Russian Order of St Stanislaus (with swords), 1916; 1914 Star and other war medals; Councillor, Borough of Wandsworth, 1925. *Recreations:* fishing, motoring. *Address:* Petersham Cottage, Byfleet, Surrey. *T:* Byfleet 151.

Died 15 Feb. 1946.

WOOD, Alexander, MA (Cantab), DSc (Glasgow); Fellow of Emmanuel College and formerly University Lecturer in Experimental Physics, Cambridge; *b* 3 May 1879; *s* of late Sir Alexander Wood, Partick; *m* 1907, Eleanor Annie, *d* of Charles Mann; four *d. Educ:* Hamilton Crescent Public School, Partick; Glasgow University; Cambridge University. DSc Glasgow, 1907, MA, Cambridge, 1909 Fellow of Emmanuel College, 1907. Tutor 1910–40; University Lecturer, 1920–44;

Borough Councillor, 1926; Alderman, 1945; Chairman Cambridge Univ. Labour Party, 1927–39; Labour Candidate for the Univ., 1929; Chm. Cambridge Regional Planning Cttee, 1930; Labour Candidate Borough of Cambridge, 1931, 1934 and 1935; President Cambridge Trustee Savings Bank; Parliamentary Commissioner for University of Durham, 1935; Chairman, Peace Pledge Union, 1940–46; Chairman, Cambridgeshire Joint Planning Committee, 1945–48; Chm. of Executive, Nat. Peace Council, 1948. *Publications:* Physical Basis of Music; Joule and the Study of Energy; In Pursuit of Truth; Sound Waves and their Uses; Planning for Good Acoustics; Text-book of Acoustics; Physics of Music; History of the Cavendish Laboratory; various scientific papers. *Recreation:* sailing. *Address:* Emmanuel College, Cambridge. *T:* Cambridge 4025.

Died 1 April 1950.

WOOD, Brooks Crompton, CBE 1920; JP; *s* of late Charles Manby Wood of Sketty, nr Swansea; *m* 1900, Mary Elizabeth Margaret, *d* of late Sir Alfred Billson, MP; one *s* two *d*. *Educ:* Birkenhead School; Liverpool University. Served during War as Chairman of the Board of Trade Egyptian Cotton Control Committee, and raw cotton adviser to the War Office; MP Bridgwater Division of Somerset, 1924–29. Master of the Exmoor Foxhounds, 1921–24. *Recreations:* hunting, etc. *Address:* Bruern Abbey, Churchill, Oxfordshire. *T:* Shipton-under-Wychwood 27. *Club:* Carlton.

Died 29 July 1946.

WOOD, Sir (Charles) Edgar, Kt 1931; *b* 1877; *s* of Arthur J. H. Wood, late of Bellwood, Ripon, Yorks; *m* 1919, Janet Mary, *d* of Sir Alexander Cardew, KCSI, ICS; one *s* one *d*. *Educ:* Ripon School. Director of various companies; lately a governor, Imperial Bank of India, Chairman Madras Chamber of Commerce and Sheriff of Madras; served (vol.) Ministry of Munitions, London, 1917–18; Member, Madras Legislative Council, 1920–30; Member, Indian Legislative Assembly, 1932; Delegate to Indian Round Table Conference, 1930–31. *Club:* Oriental.

Died 8 March 1941.

WOOD, Edmund Walter Hanbury; JP County of London; Member LCC for St George's Division, Westminster, 1932–46; Chairman London Municipal Society; *b* 16 Nov. 1898; 2nd *s* of Sir John Wood, 1st Bart, MP; *m* 1920, Margaret Coles-Walton; one *d*. *Educ:* Eton College; Sandhurst. Served in 2nd Life Guards, 1917–20; MP (U) Stalybridge and Hyde Division, 1924–29. *Recreations:* golf, tennis, and shooting. *Address:* 59 Cadogan Square, SW1; The Lodge, Hengrave, Bury St Edmunds. *Clubs:* Carlton, Cavalry.

Died 12 Dec. 1947.

WOOD, Edward Stephen, CB 1943; Director of Naval Stores, Admiralty; *b* 1 June 1890; *s* of late John Wood, of Hampstead and Harrow. *Educ:* Westminster (King's Scholar). Entered Civil Service, Intermediate Examination, 1910, taking 2nd place; served as Asst Naval Store Officer at Devonport, Portland, Hong-Kong, and Mudros (with rank of Lt RNVR); subsequently served as Deputy Naval Store Officer and Naval Store Officer, Admiralty, Malta and Chatham; Asst Director of Stores, 1936; Deputy Director, 1939; Director, 1940. *Address:* 33 Cholmeley Lodge, Highgate Hill, N6. *T:* Mountview 8975.

Died 11 Dec. 1948.

WOOD, Hon. Col Evelyn Fitzgerald Michell, CB 1937; DSO 1900; OBE 1918; Secretary of the City of London Territorial Association, 1915–37; one of HM Lieutenants for the City of London; a Deputy Lieutenant for County of Essex; late Major the Royal Dragoons, Lieut-Col London Heavy Brigade, RA; *b* 16 Nov. 1869; *e s* of late FM Sir E. Wood, VC; *m* 1st, 1893, Lilian (*d*

1910), *d* of late C. E. Hutton, 63 Porchester Terrace; three *d*; 2nd, 1915, Alla, *d* of R. Morton and *widow* of Hatherley Page Wood; one *s* one *d*. *Educ:* Beaumont College; Wellington College; RMC Sandhurst. Joined Devonshire Regiment, 1889; Captain, 1898; served Ashanti, 1895 (star); South Africa, 1899–1901, on special service, including Belmont, Graspan, Modder River, Magersfontein (medal with three clasps, DSO), and as AMS and ADC to Sir F. Forestier Walker; DAAG Dublin District Staff; Welsh and Midland Command; psc 1901; Gen. Staff Officer, 2nd Grade, 1st Div., 1909–14; retired, 1914; European War, 1914–18 (Hon. Col). *Address:* Norwood Lodge, Weeley Heath, Essex. *Club:* Army and Navy.

Died 1 Dec. 1943.

WOOD, Henry Ernest; JP County of London; *b* Camberwell, 9 Jan. 1868; *o s* of Henry Wood, JP, FSI, and Elizabeth Mary, *er d* of Abraham Madge of Gittisham, Devon; *m* 1902, Eliza Stephen, *y d* of Rev. Robert Howie, MA, DD of Glasgow, Moderator of United Free Church of Scotland; two *s* two *d*. *Educ:* privately; King's College, London. Landed interests and Director of Companies; Lord of the Manor of Hutton; Member Standing Joint Committee of County of London, 1917–44 (Vice-Chairman, 1929–32); Member LCC, 1919–22; Essex CC, 1927–37; President of Baptist Union of Great Britain and Ireland, 1935–36; Chairman Baptist Missionary Society, 1928–29; President London Baptist Association, 1925–26; Vice-Chairman National Temperance Hospital, 1920–30; Chairman Shaftesbury Society and RSU, 1912 and 1933. *Publication:* Presidential Address Baptist Union of Great Britain and Ireland, 1935. *Recreations:* motoring, golf, lay preaching, politics. *Address:* The Homestead, Hutton Mount Brentwood, Essex. *T:* Brentwood 384; Bowhay, Musbury, Devon. *T:* Colyton 60. *Club:* National Liberal.

Died 2 Aug. 1946.

WOOD, Sir Henry Joseph, Kt 1911; CH 1944; FRAM 1920; FRCM 1923; Hon. MusDoc, Manchester University, 1923; Oxford University, 1926; Cambridge University, 1935; musician; *b* 3 March 1869; *m* 1st, 1898, Princess Olga Ourousoff (*d* 1909) of Podolia (Russia); 2nd, 1911, Muriel, *d* of Major Greatrex; two *d*. Dep. organist, St Mary's, Aldermanbury, 1879; gave organ recitals at Fisheries, Inventions, and other Exhibitions, 1883–89. Conductor Rousbey Opera Company, 1889; Marie Roze Concert Tour, 1890; Carl Rosa Opera Company, 1891; Leslie Crotty and Georgina Burns Opera Company, 1892; Signor Lago's Italian Opera Season, 1893; Farewell Concert Tour of Marie Roze, 1894; Avenue Theatre, The Lady Slavey, 1894; Queen's Hall Promenade Concerts, 1895; Queen's Hall Symphony Concerts, 1897; Queen's Hall Choral Society Concerts, 1897; Queen's Hall Choral Society Concerts, 1897; Queen's Hall Sunday Orchestral Concerts, 1897; founded Wagner Festival Concerts, Albert Hall, 1901; Queen's Hall Saturday Symphony Concerts, Crystal Palace, 1901–02; Provincial Tours, 1904–05; Conductor Queen's Hall Orchestra, 1905; Royal Albert Hall Sunday Afternoon Orchestral Concerts, 1906; London Philharmonic Concerts, 1908; Shakespeare's England, Earl's Court, Historical Concerts, 1912; Parsifal Tableaux, London Coliseum, 1913; Philharmonic Gold Medal, 1921; Trainer of the Orchestra RAM and Conductor of its Orchestral Concerts, Queen's Hall, 1924; visited America, July 1925 and July 1926, directing on each occasion eight Symphony Concerts with the Los Angeles Philharmonic Orchestra; Handel Festival, Crystal Palace, June 1925; BBC, Wednesday Symphony Concerts, Queen's Hall; Zürich International Musical Festival, 1932; Capetown Orchestral Concerts, 1931; Boston, New York, Augusteo, Rome, Copenhagen, Oslo, 1934; Jubilee Celebrations Royal Albert Hall Concert, 5 Oct. 1938, through which nine beds in London Hospitals were endowed for use of Orchestral Musicians and a Fund started to aid dependents of Orchestral Musicians; Reopening Alexandra Palace, Muswell Hill, Handel Festival, 1939; after destruction of Queen's Hall through enemy action, Queen's Hall Promenade Concerts opened 47th consecutive year at Royal Albert Hall, 1941; has conducted many musical festivals and concerts in the provinces. Officer of the Legion of Honour, 1926; Order of Crown of Belgium. *Publications:* The Gentle Art of Singing, in four volumes; My Life of Music, 1938; About Conducting, 1945. *Recreations:* drawing, painting, science. *Address:* 63 Harley House, Regent's Park, NW1.

Died 19 Aug. 1944.

WOOD, Herbert; *b* 18 Sept. 1893; *s* of Thomas H. Wood, JP, and Mary E. Hoyle, Glenthorne, Brighouse, Yorks; *m* 1916, Gladys Cheetham, Oaklands, Brighouse; one *d*. *Educ:* Hipperholme School, Yorkshire. High Sheriff of Caernarvonshire, 1937–38. *Recreations:* cricket, golf. *Address:* Greenroyd, Brighouse; The Cottage, Llandudno; 72 Troy Court, W8. *T:* Brighouse 162, Western 8645. *Clubs:* National Liberal, Royal Automobile; Huddersfield.

Died 27 March 1950.

WOOD, Rev. Hugh Singleton, MA 1885, DD Oxford (hon. causa), 1906; Vicar of Milland, Sussex, since 1920; Chaplain-in-Ordinary to King George VI since 1937; *b* 1859; *s* of late Rev. L. C. Wood, Vicar of Singleton, Lancashire; *m* 1904, Lilian Marion, *d* of Rev. D. C. Mackenzie, Laird of Glack, Aberdeen; one *d*. *Educ:* Queen's Coll. Ox. (Exhibitioner). Curate of Holy Trinity, Haverstock Hill, 1883–86; Chaplain in HM Navy, 1886; served in HMS Hector Northampton, and Impérieuse, Southampton Water, 1886; Dreadnought, Mediterranean, 1886–90; Defiance, Devonport, 1890–91; Blake, N America, 1892–95; Royal Sovereign and Majestic, Channel Squadron, 1895–96; Revenge and Ramillies, Mediterranean, 1896–1900; Howe, Queenstown, 1900–01; Ophir, Special Tour with Prince and Princess of Wales, 1901; St Vincent, Portsmouth, 1901–04; Greenwich Hospital and Royal Hospital School, 1904–06; Archdeacon for RN; Chaplain of the Fleet and Chaplain of the Royal Hospital, Greenwich, 1906–17; Hon. Chaplain to King Edward VII, 1909; Chaplain-in-Ordinary to King George V, 1910–36; to King Edward VIII, 1936; Coronation Medal, 1911; General Service Medal, European War, 1918; King George V Jubilee Medal, 1935; Coronation Medal, 1937. *Recreations:* cricket, rowing, tennis, shooting, fishing. Represented Oxford in the Inter-Varsity Sports, 1880 and 1882. *Address:* Milland Vicarage, Liphook, Hants. *T:* Milland 215.

Died 8 Oct. 1941.

WOOD, Captain Sir Ian Lindsay, 3rd Bt *cr* 1897; 13th/18th Royal Hussars (QMO); *b* 14 March 1909; *s* of late Capt. Collingwood Lindsay Wood; *S* uncle 1939; *m* 1936, Dorothy Elizabeth Emory, *d* of Emory Chubb, Marchmount, Chorley Wood. *Educ:* Harrow; RMC, Sandhurst. *Recreations:* hunting, shooting, polo. *Heir:* none. *Clubs:* Cavalry, Royal Automobile.

Died 28 Nov. 1946 (ext).

WOOD, Lt-Col Sir James L.; *see* Leigh-Wood.

WOOD, Sir James Lockwood, Kt 1938; JP. *Address:* Oaks Villa, Allerton, Bradford.

Died 7 April 1941.

WOOD, Rt Hon. Sir Kingsley, PC 1928; Kt 1918; Chancellor of the Exchequer since May 1940; MP (U) Woolwich West since Dec. 1918; introduced Early Closing Bill, 1920, Summer Time Bill and Allotments Bill, 1924; Member of the Departmental Committee on Tuberculosis amongst Discharged Soldiers and Sailors; *b* 1881; *s* of late Rev. Arthur Wood, Wesleyan Minister; *m* Agnes, *d* of Henry Fawcett. Parliamentary Private Secretary to the Minister of Health, 1919–22; Parliamentary Sec. Ministry of Health, Nov. 1924–June

1929; Parliamentary Secretary, Board of Education, 1931; Postmaster-General, 1931–35; Minister of Health, 1935–38; Secretary of State for Air, 1938–40; Lord Privy Seal April–May 1940; Member of LCC for Woolwich, 1911–19; Chairman of Building Acts Committee, 1913 and 1914; Chairman of London Old Age Pension Authority, 1915; Chairman of London Insurance Committee, 1917–18; Vice-Chairman, 1914–19, of Special London Committee administering separation allowances; promoted in 1917 Memorial to Food Controller that all bread should be sold by weight; also in 1918 National Memorial to Prime Minister urging immediate establishment of a Ministry of Health; Chairman of Faculty of Insurance, 1916–19; President, 1920, 1922 and 1923; Member of National Insurance Advisory Committee, 1911–19; Treasurer, Wesley's Chapel, City Road; Master of the Worshipful Company of Wheelwrights, 1924; Civil Commissioner Northern Division, General Strike; Chairman of Executive Committee of National Conservative and Unionist Association, 1930–32; JP for County Borough of Brighton; Solicitor (Honours-man and John Mackrell Prizeman), 1903; senior partner of Kingsley Wood, Williams & Co., Solicitors, of Walbrook, EC, and Euston Square, NW. *Publications:* (joint) Law of National Insurance; Law and Practice relating to Housing in England and Wales, 1921; Daily Mail Rent Act Guide; Dental Registration—Law and Practice; National Health Insurance Manual; Relief for the Ratepayer. *Address:* Broomhill Bank, Tunbridge Wells. *Clubs:* Carlton, Constitutional, Athenæum.

Died 21 Sept. 1943.

WOOD, Leslie Stuart; chartered land agent (retired); *b* Banstead, Sx, 29 Jan. 1873; 4th *s* of John Wood and Fanny, *d* of John Braby of Wimblehurst, Horsham, Sx; *m* 1910, Constance Ethel (*d* 1948), 6th *d* of Edward Cooke of Beverley, Enfield; no *c*. *Educ:* University College School, Fellow and Prizeman of the Royal Institution of Chartered Surveyors. Past President of the Land Agents' Society; Chm. English Consultative Committee of Forestry Commission, 1928–45; Past President, Hon. Member and Hon. Treas., 1907–47 of Royal Forestry Soc. of England and Wales; Carpenters' Company's Forestry Prize, 1901. Editor of the Journal of the Land Agents' Society, 1907–33; Member of Council of Land Union; an examiner for Estate Management Degree of University of London; delegate to World's Forestry Congress, Rome, 1926; served in the Royal Engineers in 1st European War (2 service medals; retired with rank of Major). *Publications:* Principles and Practice of Farm Valuations, 1901; several papers and essays. *Recreation:* travelling. *Address:* Woodlands, College Lane, East Grinstead, Sussex. *TA:* 110 East Grinstead.

Died 13 Oct. 1948.

WOOD, Metcalfe; 2nd *s* of late Rev. William Wood, MA, Rector of Thorpe, Notts. *Educ:* Bath College, Bromsgrove; Clare College, Cambridge (BA). University coach for some years; then joined Miss Sarah Thorne's company; afterwards played in England and America with Mr Arthur Bourchier, Mr Seymour Hicks, Mr and Mrs Kendal and other managements. *Publications:* journalism and magazine articles. Translations: Perfumed Tigers, Confucius in a Tail Coat, A Frenchman in Japan, etc. by Maurice Dekobra; Corsican Brothers, by Dumas, Last Days of a Condemned Man, by V. Hugo, etc. Plays: The Elder Miss Blossom, The Poverty of Riches, and The Housekeeper (in collaboration); O Mats' San, Dombey and Son, Two Peeps at Pickwick, Micawber Aubrey Explains, etc. *Recreation:* sport of all kinds. *Address:* 3 Creddocks Avenue, Ashtead Surrey.

Died 1944.

WOOD, Major Sir Murdoch McKenzie, Kt 1932; OBE 1919; *b* 1881; 2nd *s* of late James Wood, Cullen, Banffshire; *m* 1924, Muriel, *d* of late Moss Davis, 30 Norfolk Street, W1. *Educ:* Edinburgh University. Called to Bar (Gray's Inn), 1910; was on Editorial Staff of Daily

Mail: served European War in Gordon Highlanders (severely wounded); served Administrative Staff, Royal Air Force; contested Ayr Burghs, 1918; MP (Lib.) Central Aberdeenshire, April 1919–Oct. 1924, Banffshire 1929–35; Assistant Government Whip (unpaid) 1931–32; Liberal Whip, 1923–24 and 1932–34. DL for Banffshire. *Address:* 51 South Street Mayfair, W1. *T:* Grosvenor 1337. *Clubs:* Reform National Liberal; Scottish Liberal (Edinburgh).

Died 11 Oct. 1949.

WOOD, Percival Arthur Gilbert, JP Surrey, FJI; late Chairman of Gilbert Wood and Co. Ltd, Proprietors of the Architect and Building News, and the English and Amateur Mechanics; retired, 1936; Visiting Justice, Brixton Prison; Past President Norwood Athenæum; *b* 26 June 1866; *e surv. s* of Gilbert Wood, FRGS, late of Shawfield Park, Bickley, Kent; *m* Evelyn Mary Louisa (*d* 1936), *o c* of William B. Stuttard, of Wood Street and Tottenham; one *d.* Chairman Institute of Journalists, 1914 and 1915, Member of Council 6 years; Freeman City of London. *Address:* Oakhurst, New Milton, Hants. *T:* New Milton 707.

Died 1 April 1945.

WOOD, Brig.-Gen. Philip Richard, CB 1917; CMG 1915; late 2nd Batt. Royal Irish Fusiliers; *b* 4 Feb. 1868; *m.* Entered Army, 1887; Captain, 1897; Major, 1906; Lt-Col 1913; Bt Col 1916; Col 1917; with Egyptian army, 1899–1906; served Nile Expedition, 1899; Bahr-el-Ghazal, 1901 (Egyptian medal with two clasps); European War, 1914–17 (despatches six times, CMG, CB, Brevet of Colonel); retired pay, 1919. *Address:* Heath House, Ganghill, Guildford.

Died 10 Oct. 1945.

WOOD, Maj. Sir Samuel Hill H.; *see* Hill-Wood.

WOOD, Starr; caricaturist, known as The Snark; *b* London, 1 Feb. 1870; *e s* of late Starr Tidd Wood, HM Customs; *m* 1904, Winifred, *e d* of Wm Humpherson of Clifford's Mesne, Glos; one *s. Educ:* privately. Entered office of a chartered accountant, 1887; left, 1890; drawn professionally since; one of the founders and first art editor of The Windmill, quarterly. *Publications:* The Snark's Annuals, summer and winter; Rhymes of the Regiments, 1896; Cocktail Time, 1933; caricatures and sketches in the Humorous Press. *Recreations:* none. *Address:* 33 Mount View, Rickmansworth, Herts. *T:* Rickmansworth 3495. *Club:* Savage.

Died 2 Sept. 1944.

WOOD, Thomas, MA, DMus (Oxon); Hon. RAM; Hon. ARCM; composer; Hon. Fellow of Exeter College, Oxford; Member Executive Committee and Chairman Music Panel, Arts Council of Great Britain, since 1949; *b* 28 Nov. 1892; *o c* of Thomas Wood, RNR, Master Mariner, and Hannah Lee; *m* 1924, St Osyth Mahala Eustace Smith, OBE, *o c* of Thomas Eustace Smith, JP, CC, and Katherine St Osyth Howard. *Educ:* The Grammar School, Barrow-in-Furness; Exeter College, Oxford; Royal College of Music. Volunteered for active service, Aug. 1914; was rejected and served in Admiralty; Director of Music, Tonbridge School, 1919–24; Lecturer and Precentor, Exeter College, Oxford, 1924–29; and quondam Examiner for Degrees in Music, Oxford; travelled extensively in Australasia, Ceylon, and the East, 1930–32, and in Canada, including the NWT, 1937; OC Bures Home Guard, 1940; principal war work in England, 1939–44, broadcasting; went again to Australia by invitation of HM Govt to tell of Gt Britain in wartime, and visited the fronts in New Guinea and Burma, 1944–45. Member since 1921 (Chm. 1946–48) Royal Philharmonic Soc.; member of BBC Central Music Advisory Cttee, 1947–50; liveryman Worshipful Company of Musicians, 1947; FRGS. *Publications: music:* Men's Voices and Brass Band: The Rainbow, 1951 (commissioned for Festival of Britain); Chorus and Soloists (unaccompanied), Chanticleer,

1947; Over the Hills and Far Away, 1949; Dogwatch, 1950; Chorus and Orchestra: Forty Singing Seamen, 1925; Master Mariners, 1927; The Ballad of Hampstead Heath, 1927; Merchantmen (words and music), 1934; Daniel and the Lions, 1938; Norwich Fair, 1951 (commissioned for Norwich Triennial Festival); Orchestra: St George's Day, 1949. Theatre: Incidental music to Clemence Dane's Will Shakespeare, 1921; over sixty smaller works for voices, piano, organ, military band, brass band; *books:* Music and Boyhood, 1925; The Oxford Song Book, Vol. II, 1928; The Tonbridge School Song Book, 1928; Cobbers, 1934; True Thomas, 1936; Cobbers Campaigning (all proceeds being given to Australian Red Cross), 1940. *Recreations:* travel, photography, ships, books, growing trees; making and keeping friends. *Address:* Parsonage Hall, Bures, Suffolk. *T:* Bures 225. *Clubs:* Athenæum, Savile, Chelsea Arts (hon.).

Died 19 Nov. 1950.

WOOD, Thomas Alfred, CMG 1922; MBE 1918; Company Director; Nairobi; *b* Sheffield, 1867; *m* 1904, Emilie, *d* of late Booth Waddington JP Wingerworth, Chesterfield; two *s.* Pioneering Transvaal Goldfields, 1886; Barberton and Lydenburg District, Kenya (British East Africa), since 1900, including periods of Service on Legislative and Executive Councils as unofficial member. *Recreation:* change of work. *Address:* PO Box 10, Nairobi, Kenya Colony.

Died 19 April 1944.

WOOD, Brig.-Gen. Thomas Birchall, CMG 1916; psc; late RA; *b* 26 July 1865; *m* Lissa, *d* of late Wm Hilliard, JP, Cahirslee, Tralee; one *d.* Served Burma, 1887–89 (medal with clasp); S Africa, 1900–01 (Queen's medal 3 clasps); European War, 1914–18 (despatches thrice, Bt-Col, CMG). *Address:* Ross, Belton Road, Camberley, Surrey.

Died 27 March 1944.

WOOD, Walter Gunnell, CSI 1914; AMICE; *b* 19 Oct. 1861; *s* of J. R. Wood, Melton Hall, Woodbridge, Suffolk; *m* Mary, *d* of Col O. Woodhouse, IA; two *s* one *d. Educ:* Wellington College; RIE College. Entered India Public Works Department, 1882; Executive Engineer, 1894; Superintending Engineer, 1905; Chief Engineer and Secretary to Govt UP, 1912–16; Principal, Thomason Civil Engineering College, Roorkee, 1916; retired, 1920. *Address:* c/o Lloyds Bank, 6 Pall Mall, SW1.

Died 25 Nov. 1942.

WOOD, Wilfrid Burton, MA, MD; BCh, DPH (Cantab), MRCP (Lond.), FRCP (hon.); Physician; *b* Southport, Lancashire, 28 Dec. 1883; 2nd *s* of late Peter Frederick Wood, Camden Lodge, Chislehurst, Kent; *m* 1929, Lucy Heald, *d* of John Boston, Birkdale, Lancs; one *s* two *d. Educ:* Leys School, Cambridge; Jesus College, Cambridge; St Bartholomew's Hospital. RAMC 1914–19, Lieut-Major, War Service in Gallipoli, Mesopotamia, and North-West Frontier of India (despatches); Physician to the London Chest Hospital; Consulting Physician for diseases of the Chest, to the Essex County Council. *Publications:* Lipiodol in the Diagnosis of Thoracic Diseases (Oxford Medical Publications); contributions to the Medical Press on Diseases of the Chest. *Recreations:* tennis, swimming. *Address:* 24 Upper Wimpole Street, W1. *T:* Welbeck 6533; Garretts, Panfield, Essex. *Club:* Authors'.

Died 3 Nov. 1943.

WOOD, Lt-Col Wyndham Madden Pierpoint, CIE 1918; *s* of Rev. James Russell Wood, Woodbridge; *m* Dorothy Margaret, *d* of H. Byers, Sunderland; one *s* (and one *s*, RN, killed Dunkirk, 1940). *Educ:* Woodbridge Grammar School. Lancashire Militia, 1889; Leinster Regiment, 1892; Indian Army, 1894; Bombay Political Dept, 1899; retired from post of Agent to the Governor in Kathiawa, 1925; Chevalier Legion of Honour. *Address:* Bugley House, Gillingham, Dorset. *T:* Gillingham 141.

Died 10 March 1950.

WOODBRIDGE, 1st Baron *cr* 1932, of Ipswich, Suffolk; **Arthur Charles Churchman;** 1st, Bt *cr* 1917; formerly a Vice-Chairman, British-American Tobacco Co., Ltd; *b* 7 Sept. 1867; *s* of late Henry C. Churchman, Paget House, Ipswich; *m* 1891, Edith, *d* of late J. A. Harvey, London; one *d. Educ:* Ipswich School. Lieut-Col commanding 2/6 Batt. Suffolk Regiment until 1917; Hon. Colonel RA since 1948; was Controller Mineral Oil Department, Ministry of Munitions; MP (U) Woodbridge Div. of Suffolk, 1920–29; High Steward of Ipswich; JP, DL Suffolk; High Sheriff, 1931–32; Mayor of Ipswich, 1901–02. *Heir:* none. *Address:* Abbey Oaks, Sproughton, nr Ipswich; 20 Kingston House, Prince's Gate, SW7. *T:* Ipswich 81262, *T:* Kensington 4322. *Clubs:* Carlton, Junior Carlton, Royal Automobile.

Died 3 Feb. 1949 (ext).

WOODBURN, Rev. George, MA, LLD, (QUB, Dublin, hc); Professor of Philosophy in Magee University College, Londonderry, and President of the College; formerly Fellow of the Royal University of Ireland (by examination); *b* 1867; *s* of Rev. Matthew Woodburn, Ballywillan; *m* Elizabeth Kerr, Grillagh, Maghera; one *s* two *d. Address:* Magee College, Londonderry.

Died 23 June 1947.

WOODCOCK, Col Herbert Charles, TD; JP, DL Co. Gloucester and City and County of Bristol; Member of Bristol Stock Exchange since 1898; Freeman of City of London; *b* 2 June 1871; *e s* of Alderman Charles Woodcock, JP, of Smethwick, Staffs (thrice Mayor), and Annie, *d* of John Robertson of Bristol. Alderman for City of Bristol; served on most of the important City Council Committees and acted as Chairman of several; Director of several public companies; FCIS; commanded 6th Batt. Gloucestershire Regt from 1911 and mobilised unit in Aug. 1914 at full strength; served on active service throughout European War, and commanded a Brigade during part of time; First President Bristol and Wessex Aeroplane Club; MP (U) Thornbury Division of Gloucestershire, 1922–23; Liverpool (Everton Division), 1924–29; Member of Parliamentary Select Committee on Estimates; Member of Parliamentary Commercial Committee; visited W1, Canada, and US as representative of the Inter-Parliamentary Conference at Washington and Ottawa; visited SA and Rhodesia as representative of Federation of Chambers of Commerce of British Empire; Master of Court of Worshipful Company of Wheelwrights; Chevalier de la Légion d'Honneur; CStJ; Vice-President Royal Life Savine Society (Gold Medal) and President Bristol. Branch. *Publications:* papers on various financial subjects. *Recreations:* golf, swimming. *Address:* St Nicholas Street, Bristol. *TA:* Woodcock, Bristol. *T:* Bristol 20411. *Clubs:* Carlton, Royal Automobile, 1900.

Died 18 Jan. 1950.

WOODGATE, Sir Alfred, Kt 1921; CBE 1918; *b* 20 May 1860. Appointed to Board of Education, 1879; transferred to National Health Insurance Commission (Engd.) 1911; seconded to the Admiralty, 1916; Assistant Secretary Ministry of Shipping, 1917–19; Director of Establishments, Ministry of Health, 1919–24; Chairman West Ham Appointed Board of Guardians, 1926–29; Mayor of Kingston-on-Thames, 1932–33, 1933–34, and 1934–35. *Address:* Tudor House, Queen's Road, Kingston Hill, Surrey. *T:* Kingston 2768.

Died 24 Jan. 1943.

WOODHEAD, Ernest, MA, JP; Chairman of Directors Huddersfield Daily Examiner and Huddersfield Weekly Examiner; *b* Woodland Mount, Huddersfield, 10 Feb. 1857; *s* of late Joseph Woodhead, MP, Spen Valley Division of Yorkshire; *m* 1892, Lilian, 3rd *d* of Joah Moorhouse, Woodthorpe, Huddersfield. *Educ:* Huddersfield College; Edinburgh University. Six years member Huddersfield School Board; thirty years Councillor and Alderman Huddersfield County Borough Council; retired, 1923; Chairman, Huddersfield Education Committee, 1917–20; Mayor of Huddersfield, 1901–02; Chairman Governors Huddersfield Technical College, 1920–23; Ex-Chairman Municipal Mutual Insurance; Ex-Chairman Congregational Insurance Co.; Freeman of Huddersfield County Borough; JP West Riding of County of York and Huddersfield County Borough. *Publications:* Student Recollections of Professor Hodgson; Light Operas—Robin Hood's Wedding; Chu Chih (Peerless Pearl); The Golden Rook; Princess Chantusa, etc.; several newspaper serials. *Recreations:* English International Rugby Football, 1880; golf, landscape painting. *Address:* Langdale, Huddersfield.

Died 10 June 1944.

WOODHOUSE, Albert Cyril, CIE 1937; Collector, Madras Civil Service; *b* 5 Nov. 1887; *m* 1914, Ethel Mabel Gertrude Edwards; one *d. Educ:* in India. Entered Madras Civil Service, 1912. *Address:* c/o Barclays Bank, Station Parade, Eastbourne.

Died 27 Dec. 1940.

WOODIFIELD, Col Anthony Hudson, CB 1923; CMG 1919; OBE; late RAO Corps; *b* Cape Town, 26 June 1867; *s* of Matthew Woodifield, Durham; *m* Nellie, *d* of late Rev. Albert Willan; one *s. Educ:* Cheltenham College; RM Academy, Woolwich. Obtained Commission in Royal Artillery, 1886; Adjutant of the 2nd Cinque Ports Artillery Volunteers, 1893–98; attached to the Army Ordnance Department, 1900; transferred permanently to this Department, 1907; has served abroad in India, Malta, West Africa and Egypt; on active service in Egypt, Aug. 1914–16 (despatches); retired pay, 1924; Recruiting Office, Hastings, 1939–40; Assistant Recruiting Office, Brighton, 1940–41. *Address:* 62 West Hill, St Leonards-on-Sea. *T:* Hastings 1497.

Died 27 Jan. 1946.

WOODS, Albert, ARCA; artist; *b* Preston, Lancashire; *m*; one *s* one *d. Educ:* private school. Studied at St Ives, Cornwall, with Julius Olsoon, Algernon Talmage and others. Exhibited at Royal Academy, Royal Glasgow Institute, Walker Art Gallery, and others; numerous works purchased by the Corporation of Preston since 1910; also by Corporations of Blackpool and Oldham; Miniature painted by invitation for the Queen's Doll's House. *Recreations:* cycling, motoring, sketching, etc. *Address:* 3 Farringdon Lane, Ribbleton, Preston.

Died 13 May 1944.

WOODS, Alice, MA; *b* Walthamstow, 1849; *d* of Samuel Woods, of Quaker origin, and of Emma Woods. *Educ:* home; Girton College, Cambridge. Assistant Mistress at Chelsea High School under Miss Mary Woods, 1875–77; at Girton College, took Moral Science Tripos (2nd class Honours), 1877–80; Assistant Mistress at St Andrews Girls' School under Miss Lumsden, 1880–82; Head of Junior Department Girls' High School, Clifton, under Miss Mary Woods, 1882–84; Headmistress of Co-education School, Bedford Park, Chiswick, 1884–92; Principal of the Maria Grey Training College, Brondesbury, NW, 1892–1913; co-opted on Middlesex CC Education Committee, 1902–12. *Publications:* Educational Experiments in England, 1920; George Meredith as champion of women and of Progressive Education, 1937; a pamphlet on some of George Meredith's poems, 1908; edited and contributed to Co-education, 1903; and Advance in Co-education, 1919; an article on co-education in the Quarterly Review, Oct. 1935; various articles in different educational papers and magazines. *Recreations:* reading, chess, sketching. *Address:* Radlett, Herts. *TA:* Radlett. *T:* Radlett 6117. *Club:* Penn.

Died 7 Jan. 1941.

WOODS, Sir James (Edward), Kt 1922; *b* 1850; *m* 1885, Mary Heron (*d* 1939), *d* of late C. M. Adamson of North Jesmond, Newcastle-on-Tyne; one *s* two *d*. *Educ:* Trinity Hall, Cambridge, MA. High Sheriff for the County of Northumberland, 1908; formerly Treasurer of the Royal Victoria Infirmary; formerly Treasurer and President of the Newcastle on Tyne Conservative Association. *Address:* 30 Thurloe Square, SW7. *T:* Kensington 6445. *Club:* Carlton.

Died 30 Oct. 1944.

WOODS, Hon. Lt-Col James Hossack, CMG 1935; LLD 1940; Pres. Calgary Herald; *b* 12 July 1867; *s* of Alexander Woods and Elizabeth Banfield; *m* 1900, Leonora C. Eby; one *d*. *Educ:* Quebec High School; McGill University; Manitoba University. Reporter Mail and Empire, Toronto, 1893; later News Editor of Montreal Herald; City Editor Mail and Empire; Business Manager, Toronto News; founder Woods-Norris Advt Agency; came to Calgary as Editor and Managing Director, Calgary Daily Herald, 1907; was one of those responsible for the founding of the Western Associated Press; President Canadian Press, 1917 and 1925–28; Chairman Canadian Overseas Press Party, 1918; Chevalier of the Order of Leopold II, Belgium; Hon. Lt-Col 1st Bn Calgary Highlanders, 1922; Chairman Canadian Delegation to Imperial Press Conference in Australia, 1925, and in Great Britain, 1930; Chairman Canadian Section Empire Press Union since 1928; President Canadian Chamber of Commerce, 1929–31; Director Southam Co. Ltd, Montreal; Member Advisory Board Royal Trust Co.; Director Dominion Agricultural Credit Company; Provincial Commissioner of the Boy Scouts Association since 1932; Chairman Can. Delegation League of Nations Con., Geneva, 1935; Order Silver Wolf, Boy Scouts, 1939; Member Dom. Ex. Council, Red Cross, 1939. *Publications:* contributions to magazines, technical and otherwise, and editorial work on various newspapers. *Recreations:* golf, motoring, etc. *Address:* The Gables, Elbow Park, Calgary, Alberta, Canada. *TA:* Woods, Calgary. *T:* S0534, M 89. *Clubs:* Royal Thames Yacht, British Empire; Mount Royal, Montreal; Ranchmen's, Calgary Golf and Country, Calgary.

Died 20 May 1941.

WOODS, Sir James William, KBE 1919. Director of Purchases, British War Mission to USA during World War.

Died 25 April 1941.

WOODS, Joseph Ainsworth, MDS (Univ. of L'pool); LDSRCS Eng.; Consulting Dental Surgeon, Liverpool Dental Hospital; Member of Court of University of L'pool; Editor of the Dental Record (London); *b* 18 June 1870; *s* of William and Jane Woods; *m* 1899, Margaret Isabel Benington; no *c*. *Educ:* Wallasey Grammar School; University of Liverpool. Now retired from private practice as Dental Surgeon; was Demonstrator and later Lecturer in Dental Anatomy and Histology, University of Liverpool; External Examiner Universities of Manchester, Birmingham and Bristol; Hon. Dental Surgeon to British Prisoners of War Interned in Switzerland, 1916–18; Chairman of Convocation, University of Liverpool (3 Years); late Member of Dental Board of United Kingdom and Additional Member of General Medical Council. *Publications:* various papers in dental journals; contributed to Bennett's Science and Practice of Dental Surgery. *Recreations:* tramping and travelling. *Address:* Briarwood, Carnatic Road, Mossley Hill, Liverpool, 18. *TA:* and *T:* Allerton 2036. *Clubs:* English-Speaking Union; Athenæum, University, Liverpool.

Died 14 Aug. 1947.

WOODS, Margaret Louisa; Member of the Council of the Royal Society of Literature; *b* Rugby, 1856; 2nd *d* of late George Granville Bradley, DD, Dean of Westminster; *m* 1879, Rev. H. G. Woods, President Trinity College, Oxford, 1887–97, Master of the Temple, 1904–15 (*d* 1915); two *s*. *Educ:* at home; Miss Gawthrop's school, Leamington. *Publications:* A Village Tragedy, 1887; Lyrics and Ballads, 1889; Esther Vanhomrigh, 1891; The Vagabonds, 1894; Wild Justice, 1896; Aeromancy, 1896; Weeping Ferry, and other Stories, 1898; Sons of the Sword, 1901; The Princess of Hanover, 1902; The King's Revoke, 1905; The Invader, 1907; Poems New and Old, 1907; Pastels under the Southern Cross, 1911; Collected Poems, 1913; Come unto these Yellow Sands, 1914; The Return, and other Poems, 1921; A Poet's Youth, 1923; The Spanish Lady, 1927. *Address:* Vine Cottage, Thursley, Godalming. *Club:* Forum.

Died 1 Dec. 1945.

WOODS, Sir Raymond Wybrow, Kt 1930; CBE 1918; Solicitor to the Post Office since 1921; *b* 28 Aug. 1882; *s* of James Chapman Woods, Swansea; *m* 1909, Maud, *d* of Walter R. Collins, Langland Bay, Glam.; four *d*. *Educ:* Cathedral School, Hereford. Chief Clerk, Treasury, Solicitors Dept; Secretary HM Procurator-General, Prize Department, Treasury, SW, 1917. *Address:* 76 Campden Hill Court, W8. *T:* Western 0371; Quarryfield, Seaview, Isle of Wight. *Club:* Garrick.

Died 12 Sept. 1943.

WOODS, Sir Wilfrid Wentworth, KCMG 1935; KBE 1943; Kt 1930; CMG 1926; *b* 11 Nov. 1876; *s* of William Woods; *m* 1905, Ethel Maud (*d* 1942), *d* of late Captain John Palmer, RN; one *s*. *Educ:* St John's, Leatherhead; BA (Oxon). Colonial Civil Service (West Africa), 1901; Assistant Colonial Auditor, Ceylon, 1908; Colonial Auditor, Ceylon, 1915; Colonial Treasurer of Ceylon, 1922; Financial Secretary to the Government of Ceylon, Member of Board of Ministers and Member of the State Council, 1931; retired, 1935; Chairman of Mui Tsai Commission (Hong-Kong and Malaya), 1936; Member of Commission of Govt of Newfoundland, 1937–44. Financial Inquiry, Malta, 1945; Fiscal Survey, East Africa, 1946. *Address:* c/o The National Provincial Bank, Ltd, 250 Regent Street, W1.

Died 6 Jan. 1947.

WOODS, William Forster, CBE 1939; late Chairman of Stock Exchange of Melbourne; *b* 1865; *s* of late Edward Woods; *m* 1888, Claire Josephine, *d* of late Hon. James Service. *Educ:* Queen's College, St Kilda, Melbourne. Entered office of Davey, Cole and Flack, Public Accountants; from there to South British Insurance Company for five years; then started business on own account in 1887; joined Stock Exchange of Melbourne, 1895. *Address:* 15 Kensington Road, South Yarra, Melbourne, Australia.

Died 3 Dec. 1942.

WOODWARD, Sir Arthur Smith, Kt 1924; FRS 1901; Hon. LLD Glasgow, 1900; St Andrews, 1911; Hon. PhD Tartu, 1932; Hon. DSc Athens, 1937; *b* Macclesfield, 23 May 1864; *m* Maud L. I., *d* of the late Professor H. G. Seeley; one *d*. *Educ:* Macclesfield Grammar School; Owens College, Manchester. Entered British Museum, 1882; assistant-keeper of geology, 1892; Keeper of Geological Department, British Museum (Cromwell Road), 1901–24; occupied with researches in extinct vertebrata, especially fishes; has travelled extensively, and since journeys to South America in 1896 and 1907, has devoted much attention to the extinct vertebrata of that continent; made excavations in Greece in 1901 for the trustees of the British Museum, and obtained a collection of fossil bones from Pikermi, near Athens; co-operated with Mr Charles Dawson in the discovery and interpretation of the Piltdown skull, 1912–14; received Wollaston grant, 1889, Lyell Medal, 1896, and Wollaston Medal 1924 from the Geological Society of London; the Clarke Medal from the Royal Society of New South Wales, 1914; the Bolitho Medal from the Royal Geological Society of Cornwall, 1916; a Royal Medal from the Royal Society of London, 1917; Prix Cuvier from the French Academy, 1918; Linnean Medal from Linnean Society of London, 1940; Hayden Medal from Philadelphia Academy of Natural Sciences, 1940; Thompson Medal from US National Academy of Sciences, 1942; foreign member of the Geological Societies of Russia, China, America, Belgium, and Sweden; hon. or corr. member of various academies of science in Europe and USA; Associate of the Belgian Royal Academy; Secretary, Palæontographical Society, 1900–34; President Geologists' Association, 1904–06; Pres. Section C, British Association, Winnipeg, 1909, and Section H. Norwich, 1935; Pres. Geological Society, 1914–16, Linnean Society, 1919–23, Palæontographical Society, Fishes in the British Museum (4 vols), 1889–1901; Outlines of Vertebrate Palæontology, 1898; Fossil Fishes of the English Chalk (Palæont. Soc., 1902–11); Memoirs for the Geological Surveys of New South Wales and India, and the La Plata Museum; numerous papers. *Address:* Hill Place, Haywards Heath, Sussex. *T:* Haywards Heath 80.

Died 2 Sept. 1944.

WOODWARD, Edward Gilbert; Metropolitan Magistrate since 1948; *b* 11 June 1900; *o s* of Edward Robert and Catherine Woodward, Norwich; *m* 1931, Violet Stephanie, *yr d* of late Dr Edwin Morton and of Mrs Morton, Oxford; one *s* two *d. Educ:* Shrewsbury School; Balliol College, Oxford. MA, BCL. Barrister-at-Law, Middle Temple, and Northern Circuit, 1923. Territorial Army 1922–29, Active List; TARO, 1930–39. Liveryman Painters Company and Freeman of City of London, 1921. *Publications:* Archbolds Poor Law, 16th ed., 1930; Road Traffic Acts and Orders, 1934; and other books on road traffic law; Water Act, 1945–1946. *Recreations:* fishing; model making and joinery. *Address:* 15 Vicarage Gardens, Kensington, W8. *T:* Bayswater 6984. *Club:* United University.

Died 11 March 1950.

WOODWARD, Maj.-Gen. Sir Edward (Mabbott), KCMG 1917; CB 1915; FRGS; *b* 29 July 1861; *s* of late Lionel Mabbott Woodward, Hadlow Down, Sussex; *m* 1888, Edith Trenchard, *e d* of Richard Edmund Elkins Davies, formerly of Daresbury, Great Malvern; one *s. Educ:* Harrow; RMC, Sandhurst. Entered army, Leicestershire Regt, 1882; Capt., 1892; Maj., 1902; Lt-Col 1907; Col 1911; DAAG Malta, 1893–96; Brigade Major, Curragh, 1899; Staff Captain Intelligence Division, 1900–03; DAAG, Ireland, 1899–1900; DAQMG Headquarters, War Office, 1904–05; DAAG Headquarters, 1906–11; AAG Southern Command, 1912–13; Director of Mobilisation, War Office, 1913–14; Director of Organisation, 1916–17; served Uganda, 1897–98 (despatches, Bt Major, medal 2 clasps); East Africa, 1903–04 (despatches, medal with clasp); European War, with Mediterranean Expeditionary Force, 1915–16 (despatches four times, CB, prom. Maj.-Gen.); Col Leics Regt 1916. *Recreations:* shooting, tennis, croquet. *Address:* 3 Spencer Road, S Croydon. *Club:* Army and Navy.

Died 21 March 1943.

WOODWARD, William Harrison; *b* 1855; *m* 1880, K. Mary Ross, *g d* of John Sterling; three *s* one *d. Educ:* Christ Church, Oxford (1st Class Hons History). Lecturer in Education, 1892–99; City of Liverpool Professor of Education, University of Liverpool 1899–1907. *Publications:* Vittorino da Feltre, 1897; History of the Expansion of the British Empire (6th ed.), 1930; Erasmus concerning Education, 1904; Studies in Education during the Age of the Renaissance, 1400–1600, 1907; Cesare Borgia, a Biography, 1913; contributor to the Cambridge History of English

Literature, 1909; to the American Encyclopædia of Education, 1912; Elena, an Italian Romance, 1929; The Night-Jaw, a play, 1929; Utterthorpe, a Chronicle, 1935; The Sterlings of Stirlingshire, Ireland and London, 1935; translations from the Italian, etc. *Address:* 22 Causewayside, Cambridge. *Club:* Athenæum.

Died 30 Nov. 1941.

WOODWARK, Sir (Arthur) Stanley, Kt 1932; CMG 1918; CBE 1919; JP, DL, County of London; Col AMS, MD, BS (Lond.), FRCP, MRCS (Eng.); Officer Order of St John of Jerusalem; Hon. Life Member British Red Cross Soc.; Physician, Lecturer on Medicine, and late Dean of the Medical School, Westminster Hospital; Physician to the Royal Waterloo Hospital for Women and Children and South-Eastern General Hospital; Hon. Consulting Physician to Ministry of Pensions; Examiner in Medicine, Conjoint Board, Society of Apothecaries and Red Cross Society; State Examiner Medicine, General Nursing Council; Freeman of City of London; Pres. Royal Institute of Public Health and Hygiene; Vice-Pres. Medical Defence Union; Master of Soc. of Apothecaries, 1941–44, and Past Master of Worshipful Company of Barber Surgeons, 1942; Master of Worshipful Company of Turners, 1943; Chadwick Trust representative on Chelsea Physic Garden; Governor of the Foundling and Westminster Hospitals; FZS, FRSM, etc; *m* 1912, Hilda Mary, *d* of late Sir Richard A. Robinson; two *s* one *d. Educ:* Felsted; London University (Hons in Medicine and Surgery); St Bartholomew's Hospital. Late Consulting Physician and Deputy Assistant Director-General, War Office; Deputy Asst Director Medical Services, London, and Consulting Physician, Queen Alexandra Military Hospital, London; Medical Tutor to King's College Hospital and Westminster Hospital; Extramural Lecturer to the Dreadnought Hospital; Consulting Physician to the Throat Hospital, Golden Square; Physician to the Casualty Dept, St Bartholomew's Hospital; Senior Resident Medical Officer, Royal Free Hospital. *Publications:* A Manual of Medicine (4th edition, 1934); Medical Nursing; numerous medical papers. *Recreations:* none. *Address:* 15 Buckingham Palace Mansions, SW1. *T:* Sloane 3806; Furnace Mill, Cowden, Kent. *T:* Cowden 2136. *Clubs:* Athenæum, Savage, City Livery, Knights of the Round Table.

Died 11 May 1945.

WOODWRIGHT, Surg. Rear-Adm. Charles Sharman, CBE 1919; RN (retd); *b* 1870; *s* of late Col Charles Woodwright, 18th Royal Irish Regt; *m* 1893, *o d* of late Col G. G. Stewart, 1st Royal Scots. LRCP and LRCS Ireland; served Blockade of Crete, 1896; European War, 1914–19 (despatches, CBE).

Died 2 May 1949.

WOOF, Rowsby; Professor of the Violin at the Royal Academy of Music since 1909; *b* 18 Jan. 1883; *m* 1911, Victoria Fox; no *c. Educ:* privately. Studied various branches of music since childhood; entered the RAM as a student, 1903; Fellow, 1916. Before settling as a teacher appeared at numerous concerts in London and provinces as a violinist. *Publications:* Violin Playing and Teaching; numerous instrumental pieces (chiefly for violin). *Recreations:* walking, gardening. *Address:* 52 Chatsworth Road, NW2.

Died 31 Dec. 1943.

WOOLCOCK, William James Uglow, CMG 1933; CBE 1920; *b* 1878; *s* of Rev. James Woolcock, Nonconformist minister; *m* 1903, Katherine Maud, *d* of J. T. Homer; two *s.* Parliamentary Private Secretary to the Ministry of Munitions, 1919–21; Secretary of Pharmaceutical Society and Registrar, Pharmacy Acts, 1913–18; Parliamentary Private Secretary to Postmaster General, 1921; MP (CL) Central Hackney, Dec. 1918–22; President, Society of Chemical Industry, 1924–26; General Manager of the Association of British

Chemical Manufacturers, 1918–28. *Recreation:* golf. *Address:* 18 Elmwood, Welwyn Garden City. *Club:* Savage.

Died 13 Nov. 1947.

WOOLF, Mrs Virginia; writer and publisher; *b* 25 Jan. 1882; *y d* of late Sir Leslie Stephen, KCB; *m* 1912, Leonard Sidney Woolf. *Educ:* at home. *Publications:* The Voyage Out, 1915; Night and Day, 1919; Monday or Tuesday, 1921; Jacob's Room, 1922; The Common Reader, 1925; Mrs Dalloway, 1925; To the Lighthouse, 1927; Orlando; A Room of One's Own, 1929; The Waves, 1931; The Common Reader, Second Series, 1932; Flush, 1933; The Years, 1937; Three Guineas, 1938; Reviewing, 1939; Roger Fry, A Biography, 1940; Between the Acts, 1941; (posthumous), The Death of the Moth, 1942; (posthumous) The Captain's Death Bed, 1950. *Recreation:* printing. *Address:* 52 Tavistock Square, WC1. *T:* Museum 2621.

Died 31 March 1941.

WOOLLCOMBE, Rt Rev. Henry St John Stirling, DD; *b* 27 Dec. 1869; *s* of late Rev. George Woollcombe; *m* Florence Hilda, *d* of late Canon Argles; four *d*. *Educ:* Clifton College; Keble College, Oxford. Curate of Stepney, 1895–1901; Head of Oxford House University Settlement, Bethnal Green, 1901–09; Travelling Secretary Church of England Men's Society, 1909–11 (Australia, New Zealand, S Africa, and India); Hon. Chaplain to the Archbishop of York; Proctor in Convocation, 1923–24; Domestic Chaplain to Archbishop of York, 1912–13; Vicar of St Bartholomew's Armley, 1913–22; Rector of Bolton Percy, York, 1923–40; Bishop suffragan of Whitby, 1923–39; Bishop suffragan of Selby, 1939–40; formerly Sub-Dean, Canon and Vicar of St Michael's Cathedral Church, Coventry. *Publication:* Beneath the Southern Cross. *Recreations:* shooting and fishing. *Address:* The White House, Bishopthorpe, York.

Died 1 Dec. 1941.

WOOLLCOTT, Alexander; journalist without portfolio; *b* 19 Jan. 1887; 4th *s* of Walter and Frances Bucklin Woollcott. *Educ:* public schools; Hamilton College. Twenty years of newspaper work in New York, including thirteen seasons as dramatic critic on the New York Times and other New York papers; intermittent broadcasting since 1929, including one series from America to England and one series from London for the BBC in 1941. *Publications:* While Rome Burns, 1934; The Woollcott Reader, 1935; Woollcott's Second Reader, 1937. *Address:* Bomoseen, Vermont, USA.

Died 23 Jan. 1943.

WOOLLEY-HART, Arthur; Coalowner; *b* Dec. 1859; *m* 1st, 1884, Elsie (*d* 1923), *d* of Henry Hill, banker, Australia; one *s*; 2nd, 1928, Marguerite Vivienne, Countess Bernstorff. *Educ:* King's College; privately. Chairman of British Tar Products Ltd; John Delaney Ltd and Associated Companies; Glass Houghton and Castleford Collieries Ltd; Pontefract Collieries Ltd; The Yorkshire Coking and Chemical Co. Ltd; Breedon and Cloud Hill Lime Works Ltd; Chairman of first Kent Colliery Owners' Association, and Joint Board; late Member of the Executive Committee of the Mining Association of Great Britain; Member of Executive Board, Export Committee, and Central Sale Committee of Midland (Amalgamated) District (Coal Mines) Scheme 1930. *Recreations:* golf, skating, shooting, dancing. *Clubs:* Carlton, International Sportsmen's; Sandown Park, etc.

Died 26 Nov. 1941.

WOOTTON, Hubert Arthur; *b* Nottingham, 1 Feb. 1884; *m* 1917, Eileen Mary Masaroon; two *d*. *Educ:* Nottingham High School; Clare College, Cambridge (Scholar) 1st class Part I of the National Science Tripos, in Chemistry, Physics, Geology, and Mineralogy; 1st class Part II in Chemistry. Thirteen years Chief Science

Master, Westminster School; Headmaster Kingswood School, Bath, 1919–28; Headmaster Perse School, Cambridge, 1928–45; during War Captain Special List. Commandant Young Officers Training School, Sub-Section Technical Director of Shell Filling, Ministry of Munitions (despatches). *Publications:* Text Book of Chemistry (Wootton and Hooker); Heat for Schools; Journal of the Chemical Society. *Recreation:* gardening. *Address:* 2 Erskine Hill, NW11.

Died 12 March 1947.

WORDSWORTH, William Christopher, CIE 1942; Assistant Editor and Director Statesman, Calcutta; late Officiating Director of Public Instruction, Bengal; *b* 1878. *Educ:* University Coll., Aberystwyth; Jesus College, Oxford. Lecturer St John's College, Battersea, 1905–07; joined Indian Educational Service, 1907; Professor of Political Economy, Presidency College, Calcutta; Assistant Director of Public Instruction for Bengal; Principal, Presidency College, 1915; Director of Public Instruction, 1917; Bengal MLA; Fellow, Univ. of Calcutta. *Address:* Statesman Office, Calcutta.

Died 12 Dec. 1950.

WORGAN, Col Sydney Drummond, CBE 1919; *b* 1872; *s* of late John Berney Worgan, ICS; *m* 1899, Evelyn Elizabeth Lester, *d* of late Comm. G. P. Heath, RN; one *s* one *d*. *Educ:* Clifton College. Officer in Royal Sussex Regt, 1892–98; joined Army Pay Dept; retired with rank of Colonel; served Tirah Campaign, 1897–98; S Africa, 1901–02; European War, 1914–19 (despatches, CBE). *Address:* 18 Westbourne Park Rd, Bournemouth, Hants. *T:* Westbourne 63625.

Died 14 Dec. 1950.

WORKMAN, Charles Rufus Marshall, CBE 1927; JP. *Educ:* Christ Church, Oxford, MA. Called to Bar, Inner Temple, 1900; Administrator, Nauru, 1914; Resident Commissioner, Solomon Islands, 1917; Colonial Secretary, The Gambia, 1921–31. *Recreation:* sailing. *Address:* Owmby, Grasby, Lincoln. *Club:* Bath.

Died 28 June 1942.

WORMS, Percy George de; Barrister-at-law; *b* 3 Nov. 1873; 2nd *s* of 2nd Baron de Worms; *m* 1900, Nora, *o d* of late Rt Hon. Sir Harry Simon Samuel; one *s* one *d*. *Address:* 2 Weymouth Street, W1. *Club:* Carlton.

Died 2 April 1941.

WORSLEY, Comdr Frank Arthur, DSO 1917; OBE; RD; Comdr RNR at RN College, Greenwich, since June 1942; *b* Akaroa, New Zealand, 1872; *s* of Henry Theophilus Worsley; *m* 1926, Margaret Jane Cumming. Captain of SY Endurance in Shackleton's South Pole Expedition; navigated Shackleton's boat from Elephant Island to South Georgia; served European War, 1916–19 (despatches, DSO and bar, OBE, RD, Order of St Stanislaus, Russia); lent to War Office for Director of Arctic Equipment and Transport, Archangel Front, N Russia; commanded two mystery ships, one gunboat, HMS Cricket, one Monitor, No. 24, in War; Sailing Master and Hydrographer in the Quest, 1921; Joint Leader of the British Arctic Expedition, 1925; lectured to RAF in France, Jan. 1940; went to Norway and back on Red Cross duties, May–July 1940; CO of Red Cross Motor Ambulance Training Station at Balham, July–Dec. 1940; in command of SS Dalriada blowing up wrecks and clearing Channel on East Coast, April–Dec. 1941; Comdr RNR of RN Training Establishment at Hove, April–June 1942. *Publications:* Shackleton's Boat Journey and Crossing South Georgia, 1924; Under Sail in the Frozen North, 1926; Endurance, 1931; First Voyage, 1938. *Recreation:* chess. *Address:* c/o High Commissioner for New Zealand, 415 Strand, WC2. *Clubs:* Antarctic, Arctic, Little Ship, Master Mariners.

Died 1 Feb. 1943.

WORSLEY, Philip Ernest Tindal-C.; *see* Tindal-Carill-Worsley.

WORTHINGTON, Col Edward Bruen, CMG 1919; Notary Public; *b* Sherbrooke, PQ, 1 Dec. 1860; *e s* of Edward Dagge Worthington, MD, FRCS Edin., and Frances Louisa, *d* of Hon. Hollis Smith, MLC; *m* 1890, Mabel Isabel, 6th *d* of Captain J. Dinham Molson, HM's 99th Regt; one *d*. *Educ:* Sherbrooke Academy; Bishop's College School, Lennoxville; Bishop's College University, Lennoxville; LLB 1883. Alderman 1889 and Mayor 1901, City of Sherbrooke; Lieut-Col Sherbrooke Regiment, for three periods; Brigadier Infantry Brigade for two periods; organised 11th Hussars, Canada; Brigadier, Eastern Townships Mounted Rifles; enlisted in Canadian Expeditionary Force, Headquarters Staff, Sept. 1914; served in France and Belgium nearly 4 years as Officer Commanding Canadian Base Depot; now Hon. Colonel, Sherbrooke Regiment; CMG, 1914 Star, Victory Medal, King's Medal for War, Médaille d'honneur en Vermeil avec glaives, despatches; Auxiliary Officers' long service medal. *Recreations:* shooting, fishing, canoeing and snow-shoeing. *Address:* 20 Montreal Street, Sherbrooke, Quebec, Canada. *Club:* Sherbrooke Snowshoe.

Died 20 Oct. 1945.

WORTLEY; *see* Stuart-Wortley.

WORTLEY, Edward Jocelyn, CMG 1935; OBE 1926; Director of Agriculture, Trinidad, 1930; *b* 1884; *s* of late Rev. Canon Wortley; *m* 1907, Annie Marjory Rose, *d* of late W. Peploe Forwood. *Educ:* Jamaica College. Director of Agriculture, Bermuda, 1913–20; Director of Agriculture, Nyasaland, 1920. *Publication:* Companion to Blackie's Tropical Readers.

Died 27 April 1942.

WORTLEY, Harry Almond Saville, MA; DL, JP Nottingham and Notts; Principal of University College, Nottingham, since 1935; *b* 24 Dec. 1885; *s* of late Harry Saville Wortley, Cambridge; *m* 1915, Grace, *d* of late William Pritchard, Liverpool; one *d*. *Educ:* County School, Cambridge; Downing College, Cambridge. Natural Sciences Tripos; Moral Sciences; Geographical Diploma and Teachers' Certificate, Cambridge, 1904–09. Lecturer in Education, University College, Bangor, 1909–14; Head of the Teachers' Training Department in University College, Exeter, 1919–23; Professor of Education and Head of the Teachers Training Department in University College, Nottingham, 1923–35; Examiner in Education to several Joint Boards, 1929–35; Member of Central Council for School Broadcasting; Chm. of the Geography Sub-Committee since 1932; served European War, 11 Aug. 1914 to Sept. 1919; Captain, RGA (despatches twice). Deputy Regional Commissioner, North-Midland Region Civil Defence Scheme, 1939–45. *Publications:* educational articles on Teaching or Geography, etc. *Recreation:* golf. *Address:* Highfield House, University Park, Nottingham. *T:* Nottingham 54504. *Clubs:* University of London; County, Reform, Borough, Nottingham.

Died 21 Feb. 1947.

WRAIGHT, Ernest Alfred, CIE 1936; *b* 5 March 1879; *s* of late Alfred James Wraight; *m* 1907, Henrietta, *d* of Henry Merrett, Wallington; twin *s*. *Educ:* St Olave's, Southwark; Royal School of Mines, ARSM; Royal Indian Engineering College, Cooper's Hill. Demonstrator, Royal School of Mines, 1902; Temp. Assist Assayer Royal Mint, 1903; Senior Demonstrator and Lecturer Royal School of Mines, 1903–14; during War, 1914–16, Paymaster to RE Chatham and subsequently Supervising Paymaster, RDC; transferred to Aeronautical Inspection Directorate with rank of Lieut RAF 1916; Captain RAF, 1918; Resigned, 1920; Metallurgical Inspector, 1925–37, and Collector of Excise, 1934–37, Govt of India; retired, 1937; MInst MM, 1909; Member of Iron and Steel Institute, 1906; FRIC, 1924; Carnegie Scholar Iron and Steel Inst., 1904–05–1906; Matthey Prizeman (RSM) for Original

Research, 1903; Founding Fellow National Inst. of Sciences (India). *Publications:* numerous scientific works; many papers. *Recreations:* swimming, tennis, golf. *Address:* Moda, Higher Drive, Banstead, Surrey. *T:* Ewell 2523.

Died 25 Aug. 1946.

WRANGHAM, Rev. Francis, MA; Rector of Burton Agnes with Harpham, Yorks, since 1926; *o s* of Rev. Digby Strangeways Wrangham, MA, Vicar of Darrington, Yorks (*d* 1892). *Educ:* Shrewsbury School; Selwyn College and Clergy Training School, Cambridge. Ordained, 1895; Curate of Darrington, 1895–1901; Rector of Long Newnton, 1901–17; Proctor in Convocation, 1919–22 and 1924; Rector of Hardenhuish; Rural Dean of Chippenham; Vicar of Highworth, 1920–26; Rural Dean of Cricklade, 1920; Hon. Canon of Bristol Cathedral, 1918–36, Canon Emeritus since 1936. *Address:* Burton Agnes Rectory, Driffield, Yorks. *TA:* Burton Agnes. *T:* Burton Agnes 29.

Died 14 Jan. 1941.

WRAY, Brig.-Gen. Cecil; *see* Wray, Brig.-Gen. J. C.

WRAY, Rev. Canon Frederick William, CMG 1916; CBE 1919; VD; *b* Taradale, Victoria, 29 Sept. 1864; *s* of Robert Mackie Wray, of Leeds, England; *m* 1902, Olive, *d* of Rev. Henry Catford; two *s* three *d*. *Educ:* Castlemaine; Trinity College, Melbourne University. Served as Chaplain, South Africa, 1900–01 (Queen's medal 6 clasps); European War, 1914–19, Gallipoli, France, Belgium (despatches twice, CMG, CBE); Rector and Canon of Holy Trinity Cathedral, Wangaratta, 1919–34; retired 1934 as Canon Emeritus. *Recreations:* football, rifle shooting. *Address:* 70 Victoria Street, Sandringham, Victoria, Australia.

Died 18 Nov. 1943.

WRAY, Brig.-Gen. (John) Cecil, CB 1918; CMG 1916; CVO 1927; MVO 1903; TD 1919; *b* 31 July 1864; *o c* of late Col Copley Wray; *m* Mary Caroline, *d* of Richard Hoare of Marden Hill, Hertford, and North Lodge, Cromer; two *d*. *Educ:* Harrow. Served Frontier Field Force, Soudan, 1886–87; Adjt Hon. Artillery Cos., 1894–99; and of Royal Horse Artillery, 1st Cavalry Brigade, South African War, 1900; Major, 1900; retired and rejoined Hon. Artillery Cos., 1902; served European War, as CRA 47 and 57 Divisions BEF, 1914–18 (despatches 4 times, CMG, CB); Equerry to Prince and Princess Christian, 1902–23; Extra Equerry to the Duke of Connaught, 1933; OSt John; Exon of the King's Bodyguard of the Yeomen of the Guard, 1908, and Clerk of the Cheque and Adjutant, 1925–37. *Address:* Corner Cottage, St Margaret-at-Cliffe, Kent. *T:* St Margaret's Bay 3168. *Clubs:* Leander, MCC, United Service.

Died 23 Jan. 1947.

WRAY, Leonard, ISO 1903; MIEE, CMPS, MRPS; Hon. Radiographer, Haslemere Hospital; 2nd *s* of the late Leonard Hume Wray; unmarried. *Educ:* private schools. Invented a Telephone and exhibited it at Society of Telegraph Engineers, 1876, and Royal Society, 1877; entered Perak Civil Service as Superintendent Government Hill Garden, 1881; Curator State Museum, Perak, 1883; State Geologist, 1890; Director of Museums, Federated Malay States, 1904–08; collected and prepared Perak exhibits for Colonial and Indian Exhibition of 1886 and the Imperial Institute. Has done much exploring and collecting, and added largely to the known flora and fauna of the Malay Peninsula; Commissioner for Straits Settlements and Federated Malay States at the London International Rubber Exhibition, 1908, and Delegate at that of 1911; Commissioner for British Malaya at the International Rubber Exposition in New York, 1912; and at those of 1914 and 1921 in London; Acting Deputy Agent Malay States Information Agency; during European War did the X-ray work for four Auxiliary Military Hospitals. *Publications:* Alluvial Tin Prospecting; various scientific papers in Kew Bulletin, Journal of Royal Asiatic Society, Journal Anthropological Institute, Perak Museum Notes, Pharmaceutical Journal, Journal of Society of Arts, etc. *Address:* The Laurels, Grayshott.

Died 14 March 1942.

WRAY, Captain Thomas Henry Roberts-, CB 1923; OBE 1918; VD; RNVR; AMIEE; Past Master the Worshipful Company of Plumbers; *m* 1895, Florence Anne Grace, *e d* of Thomas Vincent. Assisted to organise RND, 1914. *Address:* Kenwood, Hampstead Lane, NW3. *T:* Mountview 2664. *Club:* Junior Army and Navy.

Died 14 Jan. 1943.

WREN, Percival Christopher, JP; MA (Oxon); *b* 1 Nov. 1875. *Publications:* Dew and Mildew, 1912; Father Gregory, 1913; Snake and Sword, 1914; Driftwood Spars, 1915; The Wages of Virtue, 1916; The Young Stagers, 1917; Stepsons of France, 1917; Beau Geste, 1924; Beau Sabreur, 1926; Beau Ideal, 1928; Good Gestes; Soldiers of Misfortune, 1929; The Mammon of Righteousness; Mysterious Waye, 1930; Sowing Glory, 1931; Valiant Dust; Flawed Blades, 1932; Action and Passion, 1933; Port o' Missing Men; Beggars' Horses, 1934; Sinbad the Soldier; Explosion; Spanish Maine, 1935; Bubble Reputation; The Fort in the Jungle, 1936; The Man of a Ghost; Worth Wile, 1937; Rough Shooting; Cardboard Castle, 1938; Paper Prison, 1939; The Disappearance of General Jason, 1940; Two Fleet from Heaven, 1940; Odd—But Even So, 1941. *Address:* 50 Albemarle Street, W1.

Died 22 Nov. 1941.

WRENCH, Sir Charles Arthur, Kt 1935; Director Stevenson and Howell Ltd, 95a Southwark Street, SE1; President London Federation of Boys' Clubs, 222 Blackfriars Road, SE1; *b* 20 Jan. 1875; *s* of Arthur Charles Wrench and Marion Emily Howell; unmarried. *Educ:* Repton. *Address:* Whitehall Court, SW1. *Clubs:* National Liberal; Royal St George's Golf (Sandwich).

Died 21 Sept. 1948.

WREY, Rev. Sir Albany Bourchier Sherard, 13th Bt *cr* 1628; Rector of Tawstock with Harracott since 1893; *b* 4 Jan. 1861; *s* of Sir H. B. T. Wrey, 10th Bt, and Hon. Marianne Sherard, *d* of Philip Castel, 9th Baron Sherard; *S* brother, 1936; *m* 1896, Isabel Frances Sophia, *e d* of Thomas Horn Fleet, JP, DL, Darenth Grange, near Dartford, Kent. *Educ:* Hertford College, Oxford, MA; Wells Theological College. Deacon, 1888; priest, 1889; RD of Barnstaple, 1911–16; Chairman of Barnstaple RDC since 1916; JP Devon, and CC Devon. *Heir:* nephew Castel Richard Bourchier, Temp. Lt RNVR, *b* 1903. *Address:* Tawstock Rectory, Barnstaple.

Died 10 April 1948.

WRIGHT, Comdr Alexander Galloway, CBE 1919; RN, retired; *b* 1 July 1874; *s* of Major Boydell-Wright and Mrs N. E. Pollard; *m* 1914, Mrs Ethel M. Lepper, Laurel Lodge, Bangor, Co. Down. *Educ:* Collier's Academy, Southsea; HMS Conway, Rock Ferry, Liverpool. Entered RN through Conway, 1890; awarded HM Queen Victoria's Prize; specialised as Navigating Officer; Lieut, 1897; Commander, 1910; as Navigating Officer of HMS Algerine (1897–1900), carried out extensive survey of the Min River, China; in HMS Brilliant, 1903; surveyed Beirout Harbour; served on China Station, Mediterranean, SW Coast, Africa, and Home Stations; Commands HMS Bacchante, HMS Pactolus; served in Majestic during operations in the Dardanelles; sunk by enemy submarine, 27 May 1915, while flying the Flag of Rear-Admiral Nicholson; commanded Pactolus and appointed Senior Naval Officer at Ardrossan in charge of the defences of the Clyde tidal waters (promoted to Actg Captain, despatches, CBE); retired, 1921; as Navigating Officer in

HMS Lancaster, Capt. Sir George Warrander, carried out extensive experiments with extempore fitted boom, on the methods of obtaining soundings from forward when ship travelling at high speed. *Recreations:* formerly Rugby football; motoring. *Address:* Farlington House, Farlington, Hants. *TA:* Farlington Hants. *T:* Cosham 11. *Club:* Junior Naval and Military.

Died 19 May 1943.

WRIGHT, Sir Almroth (Edward), Kt 1906; KBE 1918; CB 1915; FRS 1906; MD; Corresponding Member of the Institute of France; Officier de la Couronne, Belgium; 1st Class Order of St Sava, Serbia; Hon. FRCSI; Hon. Fellow Trinity College, Dublin; Hon. FRCP, Ireland; Hon. ScD (Dublin and Leeds); Doctor (Hon.) University of Paris; Hon. LLD Edinburgh and Belfast; Forthergillian Gold Medal, Medical Society of London, 1908; Hungarian Prize, International Medical Congress, London, 1913; Leconte Prize, Académie des Sciences, 1915; Gold Medallist Royal Society of Medicine, 1920; Hon. Burgess of the City of Belfast; Principal of the Institute of Pathology and Research, St Mary's Hospital, Paddington, W; Professor of Experimental Pathology, University of London; *b* 1861; 2nd *s* of late Rev. Charles H. H. Wright, DD; *m* Jane Georgina (*d* 1926), *e d* of R. M. Wilson, JP, Coolcarrigan, Co. Kildare; one *s* one *d*. *Educ:* Dublin University (BA; 1st Gold Medallist in Modern Literature; MB, BCh, Medical Travelling Prize); Studentship at Inns of Court in Jurisprudence and Roman and International Law; Universities of Leipzic, Strasburg, and Marburg. Demonstrator of Pathology, Cambridge University, 1887; of Physiology, Sydney University, 1889; Professor of Pathology, Army Medical School, Netley, 1892–1902; Member of the Indian Plague Commission, 1898–1900; Originator of the System of Anti-Typhoid Inoculation, the System of Therapeutic Inoculation for Bacterial Infections (Vaccinotherapy), and of methods for measuring the protective substances in human blood; served as Consultant Physician in France, European War, 1914–19 (despatches, CB, KBE). *Publications:* System of Anti-Typhoid Inoculation; Principles of Microscopy; Studies in Immunisation; Technique of the Teat and Capillary Glass Tube, 2nd Edition, 1921; The Unexpurgated Case against Woman Suffrage, 1913; Prolegomena to the Logic that searches for Truth, 1941; Treatment of War Wounds, 1942; numerous contributions to scientific literature. *Address:* Southernwood, Farnham Common, Bucks. *T:* Farnham Common 63.

Died 30 April 1947.

WRIGHT, Brig.-Gen. Archibald John Arnott, CB 1900; *b* 19 Jan. 1851; *s* of Surgeon-General Alexander Wright, Bombay Army; *m* 1882, Emily Morton (*d* 1930), *d* of Colonel Young, Bengal Army. *Educ:* Glasgow Academy; private schools; Sandhurst. Ensign, 30th Regiment, 1870; Captain, 1880; Major, 1890; Lieut-Col, 1899; Adjutant, 1879–80; DAAG (Musketry) Bengal, 1883–88; Adjutant 3rd East Lancashire Regiment, 1890–95; served with Chitral Relief Force, 1895 (medal with clasp); South Africa, 1900–02 (despatches twice, Queen's medal 3 clasps, King's medal 2 clasps; CB); late commanding 15th Regimental District, and in charge of Infantry Records; commanded West Riding Territorial Division, 1908–10; Brig.-General commanding No. 5 Regimental District; retired, 1910; recalled to service Nov. 1914 as Brig.-General commanding 90th Inf. Brigade; served European War, 1914–18. *Address:* Keverstone Court Hotel, Bournemouth.

Died 18 Jan. 1943.

WRIGHT, Arnold; author; *b* Ipswich; *s* of the late Herbert Wright; *m* 1881, Fanny Elizabeth Cockman (*d* 1939). *Educ:* Christ's Hospital, Ipswich. Trained as a journalist under his father; proceeded to India to take up appointment on Times of India, 1879; served till 1887, acting frequently as special correspondent at important functions in various parts of India; proceeded to Australia, 1887; was there engaged as private secretary by the first Lady Brassey; was on board the Sunbeam when Lady Brassey died; subsequently, at Lady Brassey's dying request, assisted in the production of The Last Voyage, her post-humous work; returned to England in the Sunbeam; London editor of the Yorkshire Post, 1888–1900; founded the London Argus, 1897; proceeded Ceylon, 1906, to complete Twentieth Century Impressions of Ceylon; granted a pension from the Civil List, 1933. *Publications:* Baboo English as 'tis Writ; Parliament, Past and Present (joint author); Great Orations; Histories of British Malaya, Hong-Kong, Shanghai, and other Treaty Ports; Siam, Egypt, Netherlands, India, Argentina, Uruguay, and Brazil (20th Century Impressions series); The Malay Peninsula (with T. H. Reid); Disturbed Dublin; The Story of the Great Strike; Early English Adventurers in the East; Annesley of Surat and his Times; Sterne's Eliza (with W. L. Sclater); The Romance of Colonisation. *Recreation:* gardening. *Address:* 32 Bramham Gardens, Earl's Court, SW5.

Died 9 Feb. 1941.

WRIGHT, Mrs Cecily Gertrude, CBE 1920; *d* of late Henry Cartwright; *m* William Frederick Wright. *Educ:* privately. Hon. Organiser and Director Sutton War Hospital Supply Depot in connection with Queen Mary's Needlework Guild, during European War. *Address:* Lismore, Langley Park, Sutton, Surrey. *T:* Vigilant 0364.

Died 4 June 1942.

WRIGHT, Col Sir Charles; *see* Wright, Col Sir W. C.

WRIGHT, Charles Edward, MSc London; Professor of Gunnery and Mathematics at Military College of Science; *s* of Walter Wright, Diss; *m* Lily, 2nd *d* of Alfred Miller, Newmarket; one *s* two *d. Educ:* King Edward VI School, Norwich; King's College, London; East London College. Tutor, University Correspondence College, Cambridge, since 1908. *Address:* 89 Brampton Road, Bexley Heath, Kent.

Died 30 Oct. 1945.

WRIGHT, Charles Henry, FRMS, ALS; *b* Oxford, 5 June 1864. *Educ:* New College School, Oxford; Birkbeck College. Assistant in Herbarium, Royal Botanic Gardens, Kew, 1884; Assistant Keeper, 1908–29; Lecturer in Systematic Botany, 1905–29; Assistant Examiner in Botany, Science, and Art Department, South Kensington, 1899–1901; Captain, Church Lads' Brigade, 1905; Cadet Captain (Surrey), 1914. *Publications:* monographs of various natural orders in the Flora of Tropical Africa, Flora Capensis, Index Florae Sinensis and Flora of Devon, 1939; also papers in various botanical journals. *Address:* Kew Cottage, Townsend, Seaton, Devon.

Died 21 June 1941.

WRIGHT, Dudley, PhilD, FSP, FZS; formerly Editor Masonic News; Editor The Freemason; English Editor The Master Mason (USA); lecturer and author, London Correspondent to several American Australian, and Canadian magazines; *b* Chelsea, 19 Feb. 1868. *Educ:* Ware; King's and University Colleges. Tutor, Journalist, Nonconformist Minister before appointed to present position. *Publications:* The Fourth Dimension, 1906; Was Jesus an Essene? 1908; Spiritualism in Relation to the Doctrine of Immortality, 1910; The Rationale of Spiritualism, 1910; Prayer, 1912; A Manual of Buddhism 1912; Vampires and Vampirism, 1914 (new edition, 1924); Robert Burns and Freemasonry, 1917 (new edition, 1925); The Epworth Phenomena, 1917; The Eleusinian Mysteries and Rites, 1919; Studies in Islam and Christianity, 1919, revised ed. 1946; Masonic Legends and Traditions, 1920; Woman and Freemasonry, 1922; Roman Catholicism and Freemasonry, 1923; Druidism: an Ancient Faith, 1924; England's Masonic Pioneers, 1925; Chips from a Mason's Quarry, 1925; Select Bibliography of the Works of Israel Abrahams, 1927; History of Henry Muggridge Lodge (1679), 1927; History of Home County Lodge (3451), 1931; The Jew and Freemasonry, 1931; Robert Burns and His Masonic Circle, 1929; The Talmud, 1932; The Holy Year, 1933; The Catholic Church and the Jews, 1935; Jesus, Judas and Pilate, 1937; The Five Pillars of Islam, 1946; History of Naturism (as Patrick McNulty), 1937; editor, The Masonic Who's Who, 1926; editor R. F. Gould's History of Freemasonry (5 vols), 1930; translator of Dr Paul Joire's Psychical and Supernormal Phenomena, 1910, and Dr Emile Boirac's Psychology of the Unknown, 1912. *Recreations:* reading, feeding museum sparrows and pigeons. *Address:* 128 Candon Street, NW1.

Died 7 March 1949.

WRIGHT, Dudley d'Auvergne, FRCS; Chevalier of the Legion of Honour, 1921; Consulting Surgeon to London Homœopathie Hospital; late Senior Surgeon to the Manor House Orthopædic Hospital, Hampstead; *b* Colombo, 11 Feb. 1867; *s* of late William Dumaresq Wright, Treasurer of Ceylon CCS; *m* Ethel, *d* of A. Morse of Appuldurcombe, Isle of Wight; one *s* one *d. Educ:* Haileybury College; University College Hospital; Vienna. Appointed by the French Government Chief Surgeon to the Hôpital de l'Alliance at Dieppe, 1914, and Médecin Chef to the Allies Military Hospital at Yvetot, Seine-Inférieure, 1915, Retired from practice. *Publications:* Contributions to various Medical Journals; Man and Nature; The Evolution of the Human Consciousness. *Recreations:* horticulture, motoring. *Address:* Summers, Bembridge, IOW. *T:* 268 Bembridge; Lotus Cottage, Wynberg Park, Cape Town. *Club:* Royal Automobile.

Died 22 Jan. 1948.

WRIGHT, Frederick Adam; late Professor of Classics, University of London; *b* Gorleston, Suffolk, 16 Feb. 1869; 2nd *s* of Adam John Wright; *m* 1895, Ada, *d* of Donoghue Dee, Tralee; three *s* two *d. Educ:* Gt Yarmouth Grammar School; Magdalene College, Cambridge. 1st class Classical Tripos, 1889. VIth form master at Brighton College and Mill Hill School, 1893–1913; Head of Classical Department Birkbeck College 1913–35. *Publications:* Arts in Greece, Feminism in Greek Literature, Girdle of Aphrodite, Letters of Alciphron, 1923; Ovid Lover's Handbook, Heliodorus Aethiopica, Meleager of Gadara, Plautus Rudens, 1924; The Poets of the Greek Anthology, Martial's Epigrams, Ovid Mirror of Venus, Greek Athletics, Greek Social Life, 1925; Catullus, 1926; Juvenal Sixth Satire, 1927; A book of Latin prose and verse, Fathers of the Church, 1928; Liudprand of Cremona, 1929; Love Poems of Joannes Secundus; History of later Latin Literature, 1930; History of Later Greek Literature, 1931; Life in the Ancient World, 1932; St Jerome's Letters, 1933; Alexander the Great, 1934; Marcus Agrippa, 1937; Three Roman Poets, 1938; Lemprière's Dictionary, a revised Edition, with memoir of Lemprière, 1946. *Address:* c/o Barclays Bank, Falmouth.

Died 2 Aug. 1946.

WRIGHT, Col George, CBE 1919; DSO 1900; late Royal Artillery; *b* 18 July 1860. Entered Army, 1879; Captain, 1887; Major, 1897; served South Africa, 1899–1900 and 1902 (despatches, Queen's medal 4 clasps, King's medal 2 clasps, DSO); Bt Col 1907, Col 1909; retired, 1910. *Address:* c/o Glyn, Mills & Co., Whitehall, SW1. *Club:* United Service.

Died 18 Jan. 1942.

WRIGHT, Lt-Col Guy Jefferys H.; *see* Hornsby-Wright.

WRIGHT, Harold Bell; author; *b* Rome, Oneida County, New York, 4 May 1872; *s* of William A. Wright and Alma T. Watson; *m* 1st, 1899, Frances E. Long, Buffalo, New York; 2nd, 1920, Mrs Winifred Mary Potter Duncan, Los Angeles, California; two *s. Educ:* District School. Painter and Decorator, 1887–93; Landscape Painter, 1892–97; Pastor, Christian (Disciples) Church, Pierce City, Missouri, 1897–98; Pittsburg, Kansas, 1898–1903; Kansas City, Mo, 1903–05; Lebanon, Missouri, 1905–07; Redlands, California, 1907–08; retired from Ministry, 1908; Member, Sons of the Revolution. *Publications:* That Printer of Udell's, 1903; The Shepherd of the Hills, 1907; The Calling of Dan Matthews, 1909; The Uncrowned King, 1910; The Winning of Barbara Worth, 1911; Their Yesterdays, 1912; The Eyes of the World, 1914; When a Man's a Man, 1916; The Re-Creation of Brian Kent, 1919; Helen of the Old House, 1921; The Mine with the Iron Door, 1923; A Son of his Father, 1925; God and the Groceryman, 1927; Long Ago Told, 1929; Exit, 1930; Ma Cinderella, 1932; To My Sons, 1934. *Recreations:* riding, fishing. *Address:* Escondido, California, USA.

Died 24 May 1944.

WRIGHT, Harold Edward; Chief Metallurgist Dorman Long & Co. Ltd since 1918; *b* Dudley, Worcs, 25 Sept. 1868; 2nd *s* of James Wright, Engineer and Works Manager; *m* 1894, M. A. H. Farnworth; four *s* five *d. Educ:* Bridge Trust Grammar School, Birmingham; private Grammar school, Stockton-on-Tees. Apprentice chemist North Eastern Steel Co., Middlesbrough, 1883–88; Chief Assistant Chemist with that firm and the Acklam Iron Co. then co-opted, 1888–98; Chief Chemist to Sir B. Samuelson & Co. Ltd, Middlesbrough, Collieries, Mines, Coke Ovens by-products and Blast Furnaces, 1898–1908; Coke Oven manager, Blast furnace manager and chief chemist to that firm, 1908–18; President Cleveland Engineers, 1927–29; President Cleveland Technical Institute, 1931–32; Bessemer Gold Medallist Iron and Steel Inst., 1945; Member of Iron and Steel Federation Advisory Research Council and of various other bodies. *Publications:* various papers and lectures before Society of Chemical Industry, Cleveland Institute of Engineers, Cleveland Technical Institute, Iron and Steel Institute, etc. *Recreations:* chess—played in N *versus* S matches, 1893–94, won Yorks correspondence championship, played in matches N of England *versus* Scotland, Yorks *versus* Lancs, etc.; cricket; golf, past Captain and President, now hon. life member Tees Side Golf Club. *Address:* Herdholt, 65 The Avenue, Middlesbrough.

Died 28 March 1946.

WRIGHT, Lt-Col Harry, CMG 1916; DSO 1900; retired; late commanding 2nd Batt. Gordon Highlanders; *b* 5 Dec. 1856; *m* 1884, Nys Roberta M. Aitken (*d* 1940); one *s.* Entered Army, 1876; Capt., 1886; Major, 1895; Lieut-Col 1903; served Afghan War, 1879–80 (medal with 3 clasps; bronze decoration); Boer War, 1881 (despatches twice); South Africa, 1899–1902 (severely wounded, despatches, Queen's medal 4 clasps, King's medal 2 clasps, DSO); European War, 1914–16 (CMG, despatches, severely wounded); Palestine, 1917–18 (despatches). *Address:* Auch-na-Cloich, Clynder, Dumbartonshire. *TA:* Garelochhead. *Club:* Bath.

Died 4 March 1942.

WRIGHT, Hedley Duncan; Professor of Bacteriology, University of Liverpool and City Bacteriologist, Liverpool Corporation; *b* Ulverstone, Tasmania, 3 March 1891; *s* of Robert Stuart Wright; *m* 1917, Matilda B. Spittal (*d* 1942); three *s. Educ:* Univ. of Tasmania; Univ. of Edinburgh. BA Tasmania, 1910, MB, ChB, Edin. 1916, MD Edin. 1925, DSc Edin. 1927, MRCP Edinburgh 1921. Served as dresser in Serbian Army, 1912; served in RAMC in France, India, and Persia, 1916–20; Lecturer in Bacteriology, Edinburgh University; 1920; Assistant Superintendent, Research Laboratory, Royal College of Physicians, Edinburgh,

1921–22; Lecturer and Reader in the University of London at University College Hospital, 1923–30; Professor of Bacteriology, University of Sydney, 1930–34. *Publications:* articles on bacteriological subjects in journals. *Address:* Hazelhurst, Elmsley Road, Mossley Hill, Liverpool. *T:* Allerton 2752.

Died 9 Sept. 1942.

WRIGHT, Maj.-Gen. Henry Brooke Hagstromer, CB 1917; CMG 1915; *b* 1 Feb. 1864; 4th *s* of late Rev. C. H. H. Wright, DD; *m* Helen, *d* of late Sir John Kirk, GCMG; two *d.* Entered Army, 1884; Captain, 1892; Major, 1901; Lt-Col 1908; Col 1912; Maj.-Gen. 1919; retired, 1920; served Burma, 1886–89 (despatches, medal 2 clasps); Chin-Lushai Expedition, 1889–90 (clasp); NW Frontier India, 1897–98 (medal 2 clasps); Tirah, 1897–98 (despatches, clasp); South Africa, 1899–1902 (despatches; Queen's medal 3 clasps, King's medal 2 clasps); European War, 1914–17 (despatches, CMG, CB). *Address:* Seaton Down House, Seaton, Devon.

Died 21 Sept. 1948.

WRIGHT, Henry FitzHerbert; *b* 9 Oct. 1870; *e s* of late FitzHerbert Wright of The Hayes, Swanwick, Derbyshire, and Louisa Charlotte Rudolphine, *d* of Pastor von Beckmann, of Holzendorf, Mecklenburg Schwerin; *m* 1894, Muriel Harriet, *d* of late Col H. C. Fletcher, CMG, and late Lady Harriet Fletcher; two *s* five *d. Educ:* Eton; Trinity College, Cambridge, BA (Honours). Called to Bar, Inner Temple, 1895; JP Derbyshire; High Sheriff County Derbyshire, 1927; formerly Alderman, Vice-Chairman of Derbyshire CC and Chairman River Trent Catchment Board and Governor of Repton School; Captain 1st Derbyshire (Howitzer) Battery, RFA, 1908–11, and 1914–17; MP (U) Leominster Division of Hereford, 1912–18; Chairman, The Butterley Co. Ltd, 1938–44. *Address:* Yeldersley Hall, Derby. *T:* Ashbourne 65.

Died 23 Feb. 1947.

WRIGHT, Huntley; *b* London, 7 Aug. 1869; *s* of late Frederick Wright; *m* Mary Fraser. Enlisted Sept. 1914; 2nd Lieut Dec. 1914; Lieut Nov. 1916; Captain, 1917; demobilised, 1919. *Address:* Brae Cottage, 74 Brent Street, Hendon, NW4. *T:* Hendon 1440. *Clubs:* Green Room, Stage Golfing Society.

Died 10 July 1941.

WRIGHT, James, RSW 1920; *b* Ayr; *m* 1910, Isobelle Miller, Dunfermline. *Educ:* Ayr Academy; Glasgow School of Art. *Address:* Tigh Bhan, Garelochhead, Dumbartonshire. *Club:* Glasgow Art.

Died 20 Oct. 1947.

WRIGHT, John Graham, CBE; retired shipowner and timber broker; late senior partner of Wright, Graham & Co., Glasgow; *b* 1873; *s* of William G. Wright, Irvine, Ayrshire; *m* Elizabeth Macfarlan (*d* 1932), *d* of late John Young, Cross Lynne, New Kilpatrick; no *c*; 1945, Lily, *d* of late Sir Thomas Mason, Craigie Hall, Glasgow. *Educ:* Blairlodge, Stirlingshire. Rendered voluntary service to Ministry of Shipping; Assistant Director of Overseas Ship Purchase Department, 1917–19. *Address:* Westermillig, Helensburgh, Dumbartonshire. *Club:* New (Glasgow).

Died 15 Oct. 1949.

WRIGHT, Louise; fashion artist; *b* Leeds, of a Yorkshire family. *Educ:* private school in Leeds. At one time principal artist on The Queen and other fashion papers. *Address:* Redland, 627 Upper Richmond Road, Richmond, Surrey. *T:* Prospect 5275.

Died 7 Feb. 1944.

WRIGHT, Mark Robinson, MBE 1918; MA; Emeritus Professor of Education in Durham University, King's College, Newcastle; Professor, 1895–1920; JP Northumberland; *b* 1854; *y s* of late John Wright; *m* Ellen Phœbe, *d* of late James Franklyn Cooper. *Educ:* Borough Road College. Tutor in Borough Road College; Headmaster of schools in Birmingham and

Sheffield; opened Higher Grade School, Gateshead, 1884; Principal of Day Training College, Newcastle upon Tyne, 1890. *Publications:* Sound, Light, and Heat; Elementary Physics; Advanced Heat; many contributions to educational literature. *Recreations:* gardening, music, foreign travel. *Address:* Monkseaton, Northumberland. *T:* Whitley Bay 47. *Clubs:* National Liberal; Pen and Palette, Newcastle upon Tyne.

Died 10 Oct. 1944.

WRIGHT, Orville; aviator; *b* Dayton, Ohio, 19 Aug. 1871; *s* of Milton Wright and Susan Catharine Koerner; unmarried. *Educ:* Earlham College, Ind; Oberlin College, Ohio; LLD. With his late brother, Wilbur Wright, was the first to fly with a heavier-than-air machine, 17 Dec. 1903; and with his brother Wilbur the inventor of the system of control used in all flying machines of to-day; has made numerous flights in US and abroad, awarded gold medal by French Academy of Sciences, 1909; Member National Advisory Committee for Aeronautics; Member Aero Club of America; Major Aviation Corps, USA, May 1917; Cross of Chevalier of Legion of Honour, 1909; Doctor of Technical Science, Royal Technical College, Munich, 1909; Master of Science, Earlham College, Indiana, 1909; Doctor of Science, Trinity College, Connecticut, 1915; Doctor of Science, University of Cincinnati, Ohio, 1917; Master of Arts, Yale University, 1919. *Address:* Harmon and Park Avenues, Dayton, Ohio, USA.

Died 30 Jan. 1948.

WRIGHT, Wilfrid Thomas Mermoud, CIE 1924; *b* 19 Dec. 1882; *s* of late J. G. Wright, Streatham Park, London; *m* Vera, *d* of late J. M. Wright, ICS, CIE; one *s*. *Educ:* Dulwich College; Wadham College Oxford. Indian Civil Service, 1906; District and Sessions Judge, United Provinces, 1916–18; Deputy Secretary, Legislative Dept, Govt of India, 1919–20; Joint Secretary and Draftsman, Legislative Department, Government of India, 1921; retired, 1932; Chairman, Bexhill Hospital, 1940. *Recreations:* golf, motoring, bridge (Winner BBL National Individual Championship, 1938). *Address:* Thalassa Cooden Beach, Sussex. *T:* Cooden 214.

Died 22 Sept. 1946.

WRIGHT, Col Sir (William) Charles, 2nd Bt *cr* 1920; GBE 1943 (KBE 1920); CB 1918; lately Chairman of Baldwins (Holdings), Ltd, and lately Director of Guest Keen Baldwins Iron & Steel Co. Ltd and Richard Thomas and Baldwins Ltd; Director 'Shell' Transport and Trading Co. Ltd, and other Companies; *b* 12 Jan. 1876; *o s* of Colonel Sir J. R. Wright, 1st Bt, and Jane Eliza, *d* of Charles Wilson, Birmingham; *S* father, 1926; *m* 1898, Maud, *d* of late Isaac Butler, JP, of Panteg, Monmouthshire. Hon. Capt. in the Army, 1900; Lt-Col Comdg (Hon. Col, 1909) Glamorgan RF Res. Artillery, 1907–09; General Reserve of Officers, 1909–31; Controller of Iron and Steel Production, Ministry of Munitions of War, 1917–19; President of Iron & Steel Institute, 1931–33; President of British Iron & Steel Federation, 1937–38; Controller of Iron and Steel Production, Ministry of Supply, 1940–43; Officier Legion d'Honneur; Knight Commander Crown of Italy; Sheriff, Glamorganshire, 1912. *Address:* Englemere Hill, Ascot, Berkshire. *T:* Ascot 1277. *Club:* Carlton.

Died 14 Aug. 1950 (ext).

WRIGHTSON, Sir Thomas Garmondsway, (Sir Guy), 2nd Bt *cr* 1900; *b* 21 Aug. 1871; *s* of 1st Bt and Elizabeth, *d* of Samuel Wise of Ripon; *S* father, 1921; *m* 1909, Gwendolin Cotterill, *d* of G. Harding Neame; four *s*. *Educ:* Trinity College, Cambridge (MA). *Heir: s* John Garmondsway, Major [*b* 18 June 1911; *m* 1939, Hon. Rosemary Dawson, *y d* of 1st Viscount Dawson, PC, GCVO, KCB, KCMG; three *d*]. *Address:* Neasham Hall, Darlington. *Club:* Oxford and Cambridge.

Died 7 Jan. 1950.

WRONG, George Mackinnon, MA; Emeritus Professor of History in the University of Toronto; *b* Canada, 25 June 1860; *m* 1st, 1886, Sophia Hume, *o surv. d* of Hon. Edward Blake, KC; one *s* two *d*; 2nd, 1933, Elizabeth Burgwynne. *Educ:* University College and Wycliffe College, Toronto; and sojourn, at different times, for private study in Germany, Oxford; FRSC; MA, LLD, Univ. of Toronto; LLD McGill University. Took orders in the Church of England, 1883, but engaged continuously in academical work, succeeding in 1894 the late Sir Daniel Wilson as Professor of History in the University of Toronto; retired, 1927. *Publications:* The British Nation: a History, 1903; The Earl of Elgin, 1905; A Canadian Manor and its Seigneurs, 1908; The Fall of Canada, 1914; The Conquest of New France, 1918; Washington and his Comrades in Arms, 1920; The Rise and Fall of New France, 1928; Canada and the American Revolution, 1935; The Canadians, the story of a people, 1938. *Recreations:* golf, walking. *Address:* 73 Walmer Road, Toronto, Canada. *T:* Kingsdale 0988. *Clubs:* York, Toronto Golf (Toronto).

Died 29 June 1948.

WROTTESLEY, Rt Hon. Sir Frederic John, Kt 1937; PC 1947; **Rt Hon. Lord Justice Wrottesley;** *b* 20 March 1880; *s* of late Rev. Francis Wrottesley, Vicar of Denstone, Staffs; *m* 1915, Marion Cecil, *d* of late Lt-Col W. Patterson, DCLI. *Educ:* Tonbridge School; Lincoln Coll., Oxford (Scholar). Called to Bar, Inner Temple, 1907; KC 1926; Recorder of Wolverhampton, 1930–37; Judge of High Court of Justice, King's Bench Div., 1937–47; a Lord Justice of Appeal, 1947–48. Major, late 3rd N Mid. Brig. RFA (46th Division); served European War, France, 1915–16 (despatches). *Publications:* The Examination of Witnesses, 1910; Criminal Appeal, 1912; Letters to a Young Barrister, 1930. *Address:* Manor Farm, Newnham, Basingstoke. *Clubs:* United University, Carlton.

Died 14 Nov. 1948.

WYARD, Stanley, MD, FRCP; Physician to Princess Beatrice, The Royal Cancer Hospitals, and the Victoria Hospital for Children; *b* 23 Dec. 1887; *s* of Rev. G. L. Wyard, Canford Cliffs, Bournemouth; *m* Constance Enid, *d* of late Rev. W. R. Lloyd, Llandarog, Carmarthen; one *d*. *Educ:* private; University College, Cardiff and University College Hospital, London. After several resident hospital appointments was appointed Research Assistant in Pathology in the University of Leeds; later returned to London as Pathologist to the Victoria Hospital for Children and others; granted a commission in the RAMC Sept. 1914, and served in France; resumed practice as consulting Physician, 1919; for some time has been a member of Departmental Committee on Cancer at the Ministry of Health. *Publications:* Handbook of Diseases of the Stomach, 1927; Clinical Atlas of Blood Diseases (with A. Piney), (6th edition), 1945; a number of papers and articles. *Recreations:* golf, motoring. *Address:* 48 Harley Street, W1. *Club:* Walton Heath Golf.

Died 29 Sept. 1946.

WYCHE, Rev. Canon Cyrill John; *b* 2 April 1867; *e s* of late Rev. Cyrill H. E. Wyche; *m* 1896, Kate Harriet (*d* 1929), *o d* of R. J. Dick; two *s* one *d*. *Educ:* Merchant Taylors' School; St Augustine's College, Canterbury; Hon. Fellow 1925. Worked in a railway accounting office; then took Holy Orders; Missionary amongst Amaxosa; Director of Native Missions in Diocese of Grahamstown, 1910–17; Secretary and Treasurer of the Diocese of Grahamstown, 1913–38; Archdeacon of Cradock, South Africa, 1937–41; Bursar of St Matthew's College, St Matthew's Mission, CP, 1942–43; Canon of the Cathedral of St Michael and St George, 1911; Chancellor of the Cathedral, 1922; Vicar-General, 1928, 1934; Member of Provincial Synod of Church of South Africa since 1909; of the Provincial Standing Committee of Church of S Africa since 1911; Member of Provincial Pensions Board, Church of South Africa, since 1915;

District Grand Master, Mark Master Masons, South Africa, ED 1925–32. *Publication:* joint compiler Xosa Hymn Book. *Recreation:* Studies in Xosa Vernacular. *Address:* St Philip's Mission, Grahamstown S Africa.

Died 24 Jan. 1945.

WYFOLD, 2nd Baron *cr* 1919, of Accrington; **Roland Hermon Hermon-Hodge,** DSO 1917; MVO 1910; Officer of the Order of St John; 2nd Bt *cr* 1902; Lieutenant-Colonel, late Grenadier Guards; *b* 10 July 1880; *e s* of 1st Baron and Frances Caroline (*d* 1929), *o d* of Edward Hermon, formerly MP for Preston; *S* father 1937; *m* 1906, Dorothy, *e d* of late Robert Fleming, Joyce Grove, Oxford; one *s* four *d. Educ:* Winchester. Served S Africa, 1900–02; European War, 1914–19, Brig.-Maj., DAQMG Guards Div., DAAG War Office (DSO, Brevet, despatches twice); DL, JP Oxfordshire. *Heir: s* Hon. Hermon Robert Fleming Hermon-Hodge, *b* 26 June 1915. *Address:* Sarsden House, Churchill, Oxfordshire; Glen Kinglass Lodge, Tavnuilt, Argyll. *T:* Chipping-Norton 51. *Clubs:* Turf, White's; New, Edinburgh.

Died 14 Oct. 1942.

WYLD, Henry Cecil Kennedy, BLitt, MA Oxon; Hon. PhD, Upsala; Merton Professor of English Language and Literature, University of Oxford, and Fellow of Merton, since 1920; *b* 27 March 1870; *s* of late Henry Wyld, Commander HEICS (5th *s* of James Wyld, DL, of Gilston, Fife), and Louise, *d* of Benjamin Kennedy; *m* 1890, Grace Muriel, *d* of late John Proctor of Ballina, Co. Mayo; two *s* two *d. Educ:* Charterhouse (1883–85); private tutor in Lausanne (1885–88); Universities of Bonn, Heidelberg, Oxford (Corpus Christi Coll.). Lecturer in the English Language at University College, Liverpool, 1899; Special Inspector of the Teaching of Phonetics in the Training Colleges of Scotland 1902–10; Baines Prof. of English Language and Philology, Liverpool Univ., 1904–20; awarded the Biennial Prize for contributions to the study of the English Language and Literature by the British Academy, 1932. *Publications:* Contributions to the History of the Guttural Sounds in English, 1899; Initial Palatal Sounds in the Dialects of Middle and Modern English 1902; The Study of Living Popular Dialects and its Place in the Modern Science of Language, 1904; The Historical Study of the Mother Tongue, 1906; The Place of the Mother Tongue in National Education, 1906; The Growth of English, 1907; The Teaching of Reading in Training Colleges, 1908; Elementary Lessons in English Grammar, 1909; The Place Names of Lancashire (with Dr T. O. Hirst), 1911; edited Collected Papers of Henry Sweet, 1913; A Short History of English, 1914 (third, enlarged edition, 1927); History of Modern Colloquial English, 1920 (third edition, with additions 1936); Studies in English Rhymes, 1923 Editor of The Universal Dictionary of the English Language, 1932; Some Aspects of the Diction of English Poetry, 1933; numerous other articles and monographs in English American, Dutch, and German periodicals on philological subjects. *Recreations:* when young—swimming, riding, driving, fishing, billiards; now—gardening and conversation; always—English literature, especially poetry and fiction. *Address:* Merton College, Oxford; Alvescot, Oxon.

Died 26 Jan. 1945.

WYLDE, Col Charles Fenwick, CB 1919; MD; *b* 1867. Served European War 1914–19 (despatches, CB). *Address:* 1461 Crescent Street, Montreal, Canada.

Died 24 Nov. 1946.

WYLDE, Rev. John; Canon Emeritus of Ripon; *b* 13 April 1841; *s* of Rev. John Wylde, Belbroughton, Worcestershire, and Jane Philpott; unmarried. *Educ:* Bromsgrove School; Magdalen College, Oxford (Demy); Cuddesdon Theological College; Second class Lit. Hum. 1863; BA 1863; MA 1865. Deacon, 1866; Priest, 1868; Curate of West Bromwich, 1866–77; Vicar of St Saviour's, Leeds, 1877–1929; Hon. Canon of Ripon, 1918–29; a Governor of Pusey House, Oxford. *Recreations:* music, travel. *Address:* 3 Oakhill Road, Beckenham, Kent.

Died 26 Dec. 1941.

WYLIE, James, CBE 1919; OBE 1917; Barrister-at-law; *b* 15 June 1875; *e s* of James Hamilton Wylie, MA, DLitt, and Agnes Wylie. *Educ:* Manchester Grammar School; Wadham College, Oxford. Called to Bar, 1901; Legal Assistant in Department of HM Treasury Solicitor, 1914–19. *Publications:* Legal text-books; Dramatic criticism in Westminster Gazette, Illustrated Sporting and Dramatic News, and other papers, 1901–1920. *Recreation:* golf. *Address:* 1 South Square, Gray's Inn, WC; 5 Paper Buildings, Temple, EC4. *T:* Chancery 7242, Central 4840.

Died 9 Feb. 1941.

WYLLARDE, Dolf, FRGS. *Educ:* King's College, London. Trained as a journalist, and still works for the press occasionally. *Publications:* A Lonely Little Lady; The Guardians of Pansy; The Story of Eden; Uriah the Hittite; Captain Amyas; As ve have Sown; Mafoota; The Pathway of the Pioneer; Rose-white Youth; Tropical Tales; The Riding Master; The Unofficial Honeymoon; The Career of Beauty Darling; Youth will be Served; Verses; Things, 1915; Exile, 1916; There was a Crooked Man, 1916; The Pathetic Snobs 1918; The Holiday Husband, 1919; Temperament, and Magdalene and other Verses 1920; Wandering Fires, 1921; The Lavender Lady, 1922; Our Earth Here, 1923; The Water Diviner, 1924; The Second Establishment, 1925; The Week-end Wife 1929; Take Your Choice, 1926; The Undesigning Widow, 1927; Felise, 1928; Miss Pretty in the Wood, 1929; Stories of Strange Happenings; The Nuntial Night, 1931; The Miserable Sinner, 1932; Experiment, 1934; Twin-born, 1935; Almost Meadows, 1936; The Girl Groom, 1937; The Peace of Zirmi, 1938; Claimed under Heriot 1930.

Died 10 May 1950.

WYNCOLL, Col Charles Edward, CB 1916; retired pay; *b* 26 Oct. 1857; *s* of late Rev. Charles Wyncoll, sometime Rector of Yelvertoft, Northants; *m* Mary Johanna, *d* of Hon. I. E. Fowler of St Helena; three *s* one *d. Educ:* King's School, Canterbury. Served with 88th Connaught Rangers; Kaffir War, 1877–78; Zulu War, 1879; on staff as AAG, S African War, 1899–1902; Assistant Director Supplies and Transport, Eastern Command, 1914–18. *Publication:* The Wyncolls of Suffolk and Essex. *Address:* c/o Cox & Co., 6 Pall Mall, SW1.

Died 4 Jan. 1943.

WYNDHAM, Col Guy Percy, CB 1913; MVO 1908; *b* 19 Jan. 1865; 2nd *s* of late Hon. Percy Scawen Wyndham; *m* 1st, 1892, Edwina Virginia, *d* of Rev. Frederick Fitzpatrick, of Warren Hall, Broughton, Cheshire, and *widow* of John Monck Brooke; one *s* one *d*; 2nd, 1923, Violet L., *d* of late Ernest Leverson; two *s. Educ:* Eton; Sandhurst. Lieut 11th Hussars, 1884; Capt. 16th Lancers, 1898; Major, 1900; Lt-Col 1904; Col 1908; served S Africa, 1899–1902 (despatches thrice, Drevet Lt-Col, Queen's medal 5 clasps, King's medal 2 clasps); Military Attaché, Petrograd, 1907–13. *Publication:* Life and Letters of George Wyndham, 1924. *Address:* Parliament Piece, Ramsbury, Wilts. *Club:* Cavalry.

Died 17 April 1941.

WYNDHAM, Major Guy Richard Charles, MC; late KRBC and RA, TA; artist and author; *b* 1896; *s* of late Colonel Guy Percy Wyndham, CB; *S* cousin, 1914; *m* 1st, 1920, Iris Winifred Youell Bennett (who obtained a divorce, 1924); one *d*; 2nd, 1930, Marguereta Wulfsberg (who obtained a divorce 1941); one *d. Educ:* Wellington College. Works purchased Manchester Art Gallery, Contemporary Art Society, Hull Art Gallery and Belfast Art Gallery; Exhibited New English, Venice

International, Leicester Gallery, etc. *Publications:* A Book of Towers: The Gentle Savage; Painters Progress; South Eastern Survey. *Address:* Tickerage Mill, Uckfield. *Clubs:* White's, Chelsea Arts.

Died 19 May 1948.

WYNDHAM, Percy, CIE 1909; CBE 1918; FRGS; *b* 13 Dec. 1867; *s* of Horace Robert Wyndham of Cockermouth, Cumberland; unmarried. *Educ:* Giggleswick School; Queen's College, Oxford, MA. Joined Indian Civil Service, 1889; posted to Fyzabad as Assist Commissioner; Deputy Superintendent, Benares Family Domains, 1894; Deputy Commissioner of Rai Bareli District, Oudh, 1897; Magistrate and Collector of Mirzapur, 1900; Commissioner, Kumaon, 1914; retired, 1924; MLC, Tanganyika Territory, 1930–35. *Recreation:* fishing. *Address:* Moorland Close, Cockermouth, Cumberland; Kericho, Kenya Colony. *Clubs:* East India and Sports, Oriental.

Died 7 Sept. 1947.

WYNDHAM, Sir Percy, KCMG 1919; *b* 23 Sept. 1864; *e s* of late Sir Hugh Wyndham, KCMG, CB. *Educ:* Eton; New College, Oxford. Entered the Diplomatic Service, 1890; served at Berlin, Teheran, Constantinople, Madrid, Washington, Caracas, Brussels, and Rome; Councillor, 1908; Envoy Extraordinary and Minister Plenipotentiary to the Republic of Colombia, 1911–18; British Commissioner to Poland, 1919; resigned, 1920; JP West Sussex. *Address:* Rogate Lodge, Rogate, Sussex.

Died 6 Oct. 1943.

WYNDHAM, Col Walter George Crole, CB 1898; *b* Chiddingstone, Kent, 9 Aug. 1857; *s* of Sir George Barker, KCB, RA, and Mary Anne, *d* of Walter Stewart; *m* 1891, Evelyn Mary, *d* of late Capt. Stewart. *Educ:* Eton College. Joined 21st Hussars, 1875; passed Staff Coll., 1886; Zulu War, 1879 (medal and clasp, Nile Expedition, 1884–85 (medal and clasp; bronze star); Soudan, 1898; Khartoum (despatches, medal, Khedive's medal and clasp, CB). *Recreation:* shooting. *Address:* Gorse Cottage, Firwood Drive, Camberley, Surrey. *Club:* Naval and Military.

Died 7 Dec. 1948.

WYNFORD, 7th Baron *cr* 1829; **Samuel John Best;** *b* 24 June 1874; *s* of 5th Baron and Edith Anne, *d* of Matthew Henry Marsh of Ramridge, Andover, Hants; *S* brother, 1940; *m* 1st, 1914, Evelyn (*d* 1929), *d* of late Major-Gen. Sir Edward S. May, KCB, CMG; three *s* one *d*; 2nd, 1930, Marguerite, *d* of Charles Pratt. *Educ:* Wellington. *Heir:* *s* Major Hon. Robert Samuel Best, Royal Welch Fusiliers [*b* 5 Jan. 1917; *m* 1941, Anne Daphne Mametz, *d* of Major-Gen. J. R. Minshull Ford, CB; one *d*]. *Address:* Wynford House, Maidon Newton, Dorset; 14 Wildcroft Manor, Putney Hill, SW15. *Club:* Oriental.

Died 29 Aug. 1943.

WYNN; *see* Williams-Wynn.

WYNNE, Frederick Horton, CBE 1932; BSc; *b* 20 Sept. 1877; *s* of Richard Horton Wynne and Sarah Ann Walford; *m*; one *d*. *Educ:* High School, Newcastle-under-Lyme; Armstrong College, Newcastle upon Tyne. Mining pupil under late J. C. Cadman, Silverdale Collieries, North Staffs, 1895–1902; Assistant in consulting practice, 1902–04; HM Chief Inspector of Mines, 1904; HM Chief Inspector of Mines, 1938–42. *Address:* 26 Lingfield Avenue, Kingston-on-Thames. *T:* Kingston 3951.

Died 20 May 1943.

WYNNE, Rt Hon. Sir Henry (Arthur), PC Ireland, 1922; Kt 1919; LLD; Barrister, Gray's Inn, 1929; *b* 14 June 1867; *s* of Robert Wynne, Solicitor, Cork; *m* 1899, Georgie Elden (*d* 1928), *d* of Dwight C. Golder of Portland, Maine, USA. *Educ:* Queen's College, Cork (Scholar in Arts and Law Faculties); Royal University of Ireland. BA 1888; LLB 1891; LLD 1892. Admitted a Solicitor, 1889; Crown Solicitor for Cork City and Cork County (WR) and Sessional Crown Solicitor for Cork City, 1905–16; senior member of firm of Wynne & Wynne, solicitors, of Cork, where he practised in partnership with his brother, Frederick William Wynne, 1896–1916; Chief Crown Solicitor for Ireland, 1916–22. *Address:* 15 Lichfield Road, Kew Gardens. *T:* Richmond 2859.

Died 21 Aug. 1943.

WYNNE, May; *see* Knowles, M. W.

WYNNE, Sir Trevredyn Rashleigh, KCSI 1911; KCIE 1909; CIE 1903; VD; Member of Railway Board of India, 1905–14; President, 1908–14; Member of the Imperial Legislative Council of India, 1908–14; Government Director of Indian Railway Companies at the India Office, London, 1914–15; Managing Director of Bengal Nagpur Railway Company, London, 1915; Chairman, 1930; a Director of the Anglo-Persian Oil Co., Burma Corporation; Knight of Grace of the Order of St John of Jerusalem; *b* 1853; *s* of Llewelyn Wynne, of Mold, Flints; *m* 1896, Winifred, *d* of Henry Conduitt; one *s*. *Educ:* Brighton College; RIE College, Coopers Hill. Member of the Institution of Civil Engineers. Has for many years been largely interested in the construction and management of Indian railways; in China, reorganising a commercial and mining company, 1902–04. *Address:* Yew Tree House, Leatherhead, Surrey.

Died 28 June 1942.

WYNNE, William Palmer, FRS, DSc (Lond.); Hon. MA (Cantab); Hon. DSc (Sheff.); ARCS; FRIC; Hon. Fellow of Imperial College; *b* 1861; *s* of late Wm Palmer Wynne, Stafford; *m* 1st, Margaret Emma, *d* of late Henry Curtis, Brighton; 2nd, Alice Julia, *d* of late Henry Seelenmever, Melbourne, Australia; one *d*. *Educ:* King Edward VI Grammar School, Birmingham; Royal College of Science, London. Lecturer on Chemistry at City and Guilds of London Institute's Central Technical College, 1888–90; Assistant Professor of Chemistry, Royal College of Science, London, 1890–1902; Professor of Chemistry, Pharmaceutical Society's School of Pharmacy, 1902–04; Professor of Chemistry, University of Sheffield, 1904–31; Examiner in Chemistry, Universities of London and Birmingham, Board of Education and Institute of Chemistry; Editor of the Journal of the Chemical Society, 1900–03; Hon. Secretary of the Chemical Society, 1898–99 and 1903–05; Vice-President, 1905–08 and 1918–21, and President, 1923–25; President, Section B. British Association, Birmingham, 1913; Member of University Grants Committee, 1934–43; hon. member of high table at Sidney Sussex College, 1934–46; representative of Sheffield diocese on National Assembly of Church of England, 1925–35. *Publications:* numerous papers in Journal and Proceedings of Chemical Society; Naphthalene and other articles in Thorpe's Dictionary of Applied Chemistry. *Recreations:* walking, golf, dancing. *Address:* 50 Westbourne Road, Urmston, Manchester.

Died 16 Feb. 1950.

WYNNE-EDWARDS, Rev. John Rosindale; *b* 1864; *s* of late J. C. Wynne-Edwards, solicitor, Denbigh; *m* Lilian Agnes, *d* of late Rev. C. W. Streatfield, Emsdale, Lillington, Leamington; four *s* one *d*. *Educ:* Giggleswick School; Christ Church, Oxford (1st class honours). Assistant Master at Giggleswick School, 1887–91; Cheltenham College, 1891–1902; Headmaster of Leeds Grammar School, 1902–22; Rector of Kirklington 1922–37; Hon. Canon of Ripon, 1922–37; Canon Emeritus, 1937; Rural Dean of Bedale, 1932–37; Examining Chaplain to Bishop of Ripon, 1923–40; Added Member North Riding Education Committee, 1925–42. *Publication:* Short Commentaries on the Synoptic Gospels and The Acts. *Address:* Huntley House, Austwick, Lancaster.

Died 13 Feb. 1943.

WYNTER, Brig.-Gen. Francis Arthur, CMG 1918; DSO 1898; RA, retired; *b* 19 July 1870. Entered Army, 1890; Capt., 1899; Major, 1910; served NW Frontier India, 1897 (wounded twice, despatches twice, DSO, medal with two clasps); Mahsud Blockade (clasp); Waziristan, 1901–02; European War; Dardanelles, Egypt, 1915–16; France, 1916–18 (wounded, despatches four times, CMG, Bt Lt-Col, Bt Col); retired, 1919. *Address:* c/o Midland Bank, Lewes, Sussex. *Club:* Army and Navy.

Died 27 Jan. 1942.

WYNTER, Maj.-Gen. (temp. Lt-Gen.) Henry Douglas, CB 1942; CMG 1919; DSO 1918; idc, psc; Lt-Gen. in charge of Administration, Army Headquarters, Melbourne, since 1942; *b* Winterton, Burnett River, Queensland, 5 June 1886; *s* of late Henry Philip Walker Wynter and Maria Louisa Maunsell, Ballybrood, Limerick, Ireland; *m* Ethel May, *y d* of late John Hawkshaw White, Bundaberg, Queensland; two *s*. *Educ:* Maryborough Grammar School, Queensland. Appointed to commission in Wide Bay Infantry Regiment, Queensland, 26 Feb. 1907, and to Permanent Staff Australian Military Forces, 1911; transferred to Australian Staff Corps, 1920; served European War, 1914–18 (despatches 5 times, DSO, CMG, Bt Lieut-Colonel); GOC, Northern Command Australia, 1939–40; GOC, AIF in United Kingdom, 1940; Major-General, General Staff and later GOC, Eastern Command, Australia, 1941. *Address:* Army HQ, Melbourne, Australia.

Died Feb. 1945.

WYNTER, Walter Essex, MD; BS Lond.; FRCP, FRCS; retired; *b* 1860; *e s* of Andrew Wynter, MD; *m* Ada Margaret (*d* 1937), *d* of Samuel Wills, JP, Bristol. *Educ:* Epsom Coll.; Middlesex and St Bartholomew's Hospitals; Freiburg; London University. Physician and Lecturer on Medicine, Middlesex Hospital; Major RAMC (T) attached 3rd London General Hospital, 2nd London Division. *Publications:* Manual of Clinical and Practical Pathology, 1890; Minor Medicine, Middlesex Hospital Medical Reports, 1889–1891; various contributions to journals. *Recreations:* travelling, fishing, four-handed chess. *Address:* Bartholomew Manor, Newbury, Berks. *T:* 89.

Died 4 Jan. 1945.

WYTHES, Ernest James, CBE 1920; *b* 1868; *γ s* of late George Edward Wythes and 1st wife, Catherine Sarah, *d* of late C. E. Jemmett; *m* 1894, Aline, *e d* of Sir John Henry Thorold, 12th Bt; three *d*. *Educ:* Eton; Christ Church, Oxford. Patron of three livings. High Sheriff of Essex, 1901. *Address:* The Wood House, Epping. *T:* Epping 2048. *Clubs:* Carlton; Royal Yacht Squadron (Cowes).

Died 13 Dec. 1949.

Y

YAKUB, Moulvi Sir Mohammad, Kt 1931; Reforms Adviser to the Nizam's Government, since 1941; Pleader, Moradabad; *b* Moradabad, 27 Aug. 1879; *m* twice (both wives dead); no *c. Educ:* MAO College, Aligarh. Member and First Non-official Chairman, Moradabad Municipal Board; Member and Senior Vice-Chairman, Moradabad District Board; Trustee, MAO Coll., Aligarh; Member, Court Muslim University, Aligarh; Presided over the UP Muslim League Session, 1926; the Annual Session of the All-India Muslim League, Calcutta, 1927; Member of the Age of Consent Committee, 1928–29; the All-India Palestine Conference, Bombay, 1929; and the Bundehlkhand Muslim Political Conference at Banda, 1928; Member, Legislative Assembly, 1924–38; Deputy-President, 1927–30; President, 1930; Hon.-Secretary, All-India Muslim League, 1930–35; Member of the Indian Franchise Committee, 1932; Member of the Statutory Railway Board Committee in London, 1938; officiated as Commerce and Industries Member Government of India, Jan.–March and June and July 1938; Member of the Council of State, 1938–42. *Address:* Moradabad, UP, India; Hyderabad, Deccan, India.

Died 23 Nov. 1942.

YARBOROUGH, 5th Earl of, *cr* 1837; **Sackville George Pelham;** Baron Fauconberg *cr* 1295; Baron Conyers *cr* 1509; Baron Yarborough, Baron Worsley, 1794; late Capt. 11th Hussars; Lieut-Col commanding Nottinghamshire Yeomanry, 1936–40; *b* 17 Dec. 1888; *e surv. s* of 4th Earl and Marcia (*d* 1926), *e d* of 12th Lord Conyers, Baroness Conyers, 1892, and Baroness Fauconberg, 1903, in her own right; *S* mother, 1926, and father, 1936; *m* 1919, Nancye, *y d* of late Alfred Brocklehurst; two *d. Educ:* Eton; Trinity College, Cambridge. Served European War, 1914–18 (despatches, MC). *Heir:* (to Earldom) *b* Hon. Marcus Pelham; (to Baronies of Conyers and Fauconberg): *d* Lady Diana Mary Pelham, *b* 1920, and *d* Lady June Wendy Pelham, *b* 1924. *Address:* Brocklesby Park, Lincolnshire.

Died 7 Feb. 1948.

YARBOROUGH, Rev. John James Cooke-, MA; *b* 7 Oct. 1855; *m* 1890, Emily, *d* of Richard Foster, Chislehurst; five *d. Educ:* Keble College, Oxford. Ordained, 1880; Zanzibar, UMCA, 1880; St Luke, Stepney, 1881–83; Hemsworth, 1883–84; Organising Secretary, Universities Mission to Central Africa, 1884–87; Curate of Chislehurst, 1887–92; Vicar of Romsey, 1892–1910; Vicar of Christchurch, 1910–15; Hon. Canon of Winchester, 1909; Rector of Puttenham, 1918–25. *Address:* 2 Sumner Place, SW7. *T:* Kensington 7427.

Died 16 Feb. 1941.

YATES, Walter Baldwyn, CBE 1924; DL, JP; Deputy Chairman Quarter Sessions, Flintshire; Chancellor of Diocese of Bangor since 1942; *s* of J. St J. Yates, County Court Judge; *m* Rose Caroline, *widow* of Walter Buddicom of Penbedw, Flints, and *d* of J. S. Bankes, Soughton Hall, Northop; three *d. Educ:* Shrewsbury; Trinity College, Cambridge. Barrister, Inner Temple; N Wales Circuit; member of LCC and subsequently Alderman; first Chairman of Trade Boards, 1910; Umpire (Crown) Unemployment Insurance, 1912; during European War Chairman of Government Committee to compensate sailors for loss of personal effects by hostile operations at sea; Chairman Midland and SW Munitions Tribunals; Appointed member Central Agricultural Wages Board. *Publication:* (joint) Law of Ejectment. *Address:* Cilcen Hall, Mold, Flintshire.

Died 27 April 1947.

YATMAN, Col Arthur Hamilton, DSO 1919; DL Somerset; *b* 1874; *s* of Rev. John Augustus Yatman, of Winscombe, Somerset. Served South Africa, 1899–1902 (Queen's medal with five clasps, King's medal with two clasps); European War, 1914–19 (despatches four times, DSO, 1914 Star, two medals); Sheriff of Somersetshire, 1940. *Address:* The Hall Winscombe Somerset. *Club:* Army and Navy.

Died 17 Dec. 1947.

YEATS-BROWN, Francis, DFC; author; *b* Genoa, 15 Aug. 1886; 3rd *s* of late Montagu Yeats-Brown, CMG, HBM's Consul-General in Genoa, and Agnes Matilda Bellingham; *m* 1938, Olga, *widow* of Denzil Phillips, late RAF and *d* of Col Apollon Zoueff. *Educ:* Harrow-on-the-Hill; Sandhurst. Attached as 2nd Lieut to King's Royal Rifle Corps at Bareilly, India, 1906; posted 17th Cavalry, Indian Army, 1907; Adjutant, 1913; served in France with 5th Lancers and in Mesopotamia with Royal Flying Corps (despatches twice, DFC); prisoner in Turkey, Nov. 1915; escaped, 1918; retired on pension, 1925; Assistant Editor of the Spectator, 1926–28. *Publications:* Bengal Lancer, 1930; Golden Horn, 1932; Dogs of War! 1934; Lancer at Large, 1936; Yoga Explained, 1937; European Jungle, 1939; Indian Pageant, 1942; (posthumous) Martial India, 1945; numerous articles. *Recreation:* travel. *Club:* Bath.

Died 19 Dec. 1944.

YEATTS, Maurice William Walter Murray, CSI 1946; CIE 1938; Secretary, Government of India, Industries Department, since 1945; *b* 1894; *yr s* of late Murray Yeatts, Edinburgh; unmarried. *Educ:* Edinburgh University. MA (Hons Mathematics). Served European War, Royal Artillery, France and Flanders; entered ICS 1920; Under Secretary, Govt of Madras, 1926; Superintendent of Census, Madras, 1930; Deputy and Joint Secretary Govt of India, 1932–39; Census Commissioner for India, March 1939. *Publications:* Madras Census Report and Tables, 1932; All-India Report and Tables, 1942. *Recreations:* golf, swimming, travel, music. *Clubs:* Caledonian, East India and Sports.

Died 4 Aug. 1950.

YENCKEN, Arthur F., CMG 1941; Minister Plenipotentiary (local rank), British Embassy, Madrid, since 1940; *b* 1 April 1894; 2nd *s* of Edward L. Yencken, Toorak, Melbourne, Australia; *m* 1926, Joyce, *d* of late George Russell, Langiwilli, Vic., Australia, and Mrs G. R. Blackwood; two *s* one *d. Educ:* C of E Grammar School, Melbourne; Corpus Christi College, Cambridge (BA Hist. Tripos, Lawn Tennis Blue and International). Trooper Inns of Court Cavalry, Aug. 1914; 2nd Lt RFA 47th London Div. T; Regular Commission, 1916 (wounded and gassed, MC, despatches twice); gazetted RHA; retired 1919 with substantive rank of Major and entered Diplomatic Service; served in Washington, Foreign Office, Copenhagen, Berlin (Chargé d'affaires, 1929, 1930), Egypt (where Acting High Commissioner, 1933, 1934, 1935, 1936), Rome and Madrid. *Publications:* Imperial Federation, 1914; 1919—The Danger of Imperial Federation; A Scheme for Imperial Liaison; Studies in Dominion Constitutional Developments. *Recreations:* lawn tennis, golf, ski-ing, shooting, sailing. *Address:* c/o Foreign Office, SW1. *Clubs:* Bath, Travellers', All England Lawn Tennis, Hurlingham.

Died 18 May 1944.

YOLLAND, John Horatio, CBE 1918; MRCS (Eng.), LSA (Lond.); Hon. Col North Kent Engineer Cadet Corps; Lieut-Colonel RAMC(V), Officer in Charge (K)RAMC(V), Officer, Order St John of Jerusalem; *b* 18 Dec. 1863; *e s* of late Rev. John Yolland, MA Oxon; *m*; two *s*. *Educ:* King William's College, Isle of Man; University College Hospital, London. Been in practice in Bromley since 1889; Hon. Consulting Medical Officer, Bromley Cottage Hospital; Chief Staff Officer, Kent VAD, TF; Kent County Council Examiner in First Aid, Nursing, Elementary Physiology and Hygiene; Lecturer and Examiner St John AA; Chief Staff Officer Kent VAD; Hon. Secretary and Treasurer Kent County War Fund; A Vice-President, late County Director, Kent BRCS; Hon. Life Member BRCS; Hon. Life Member St John AA; County Administrator Kent Emergency Help Fund. *Recreation:* croquet. *Address:* 125 Bromley Common, Kent. *TA:* Bromley, Kent. *T:* Ravensbourne 0381.

Died 24 Jan. 1944.

YORK, Ven. George William; *b* Nelson, NZ; *m* 1900, Lillian, ALCM, *d* of Joseph Petrie, Mayor of Greymouth. *Educ:* Bishopdale College, Nelson; LTh, NZ. Ordained, 1885; Curate of Brunnerton and the Grey Valley, 1885–89; Curate of St Paul's Pro-Cathedral, Dunedin, 1890–92; Incumbent of Holy Trinity, Greymouth, 1893–1918; Vicar of Blenheim, 1919–29; Archdeacon of Mawhera, 1903–19; Archdeacon of Marlborough, 1919–30; travelled round the world twice. *Recreations:* motor cycling and motor car driving. *Address:* c/o S Peter's Vicarage, Riccarton, Christchurch, NZ.

Died 13 Oct. 1944.

YORKE, Miss Dorothy, CVO 1937; Extra Lady in Waiting to the Princess Royal; *b* 1879; *d* of late John Reginald Yorke, Forthampton Court, Gloucester. Former Lady in Waiting to the late Duchess of Connaught, Princess Patricia of Connaught and the Princess Royal. *Address:* 5 Spanish Place, W1. *T:* Welbeck 8831.

Died 20 Nov. 1946.

YORKE, Warrington, FRS 1932; MD, FRCP; Alfred Jones Professor of Tropical Medicine in the University of Liverpool and Liverpool School of Tropical Medicine since 1929; formerly Professor of Parasitology; *b* Lancaster, 1883; *s* of Rev. H. Lefroy Yorke, MA, BD; *m* Elsie Greening; one *s* one *d*. *Educ:* University of Liverpool; Strassburg; etc. Holt Fellow in Physiology, University of Liverpool, 1906. Member of Blackwater Fever Expedition of the Liverpool School of Tropical Medicine to Nyasaland, 1907–09; Director of the Runcorn Research Laboratory, 1909–13; member of the British S Africa Sleeping Sickness Commission to N Rhodesia, 1911–12; Sleeping Sickness Commission to Sierra Leone, 1914–15; Chemotherapy Committee of Medical Research Council, 1927; Malaria Commission of League of Nations, 1935; Tropical Medical Research Committee of Medical Research Council, 1936; Chalmers Memorial Gold Medal, 1925, Royal Society of Tropical Medicine and Hygiene. *Publications:* The Mechanism of Production of Blackwater, Annals of Tropical Medicine, 1909; Estimation of the Total Volume of Blood in the Living Animal, Roy. Soc. Proc., 1909; Reports of the British South Africa Sleeping Sickness Commission, 1912–1913; Relation of Big Game to the Spread of Sleeping Sickness, Proc. Zool. Soc., 1913; The Nematode Parasites of Vertebrates, 1926; various papers dealing with Chemotherapy, 1928–1940. *Address:* Tropical School, University of

Liverpool; 4 Bryanston Road, Prenton, Birkenhead. *TA:* Malaria, Liverpool. *T:* Royal 611, Mountwood 1025. *Clubs:* Royal Societies; University, Liverpool.

Died 24 April 1943.

YOUNG, Sir Alban; *see* Young, Sir C. A.

YOUNG, Sir Alfred Karney, Kt 1923; *b* 1865; *s* of late W. A. G. Young, CMG, Governor of Gold Coast Colony; *m* 1930, Frances M. Buckley, widow of St John Buckley. *Educ:* Magdalen College, Oxford (BA). Called to Bar, Inner Temple, 1889; joined Colonial Service, British Honduras, 1890; served in various capacities in Seychelles, Nyasaland, Trinidad; administered the Government of Seychelles, 1911; Chief Justice of Seychelles, 1909–14; Chief Justice of the Leeward Islands, WI, 1921–22; Attorney-General, Fiji, 1914–21; Ch. Justice Fiji and Ch. Judicial Commissioner Western Pacific, 1923–29; retired, 1929; played cricket for Kent County on several occasions before going abroad. *Publications:* compiler of various Colonial Laws. *Recreation:* all outdoor sports. *Club:* United University.

Died 5 Jan. 1942.

YOUNG, Andrew; JP; Bailie of City of Edinburgh; Curator of Patronage of University of Edinburgh; Governor of Heriot Trust; Member of Edinburgh Educational Endowments Trust; Member of Scottish Central After-Care Council and Earl Haig Unity Relief Fund; *b* Edinburgh, 1858. *Educ:* Church of Scotland Training College; Heriot-Watt College, and University, Edinburgh. MP (Lab) Partick Division of Glasgow, 1923–24. *Address:* 13 Gayfield Square, Edinburgh.

Died 9 Feb. 1943.

YOUNG, Sir Arthur Stewart Leslie, 1st Bt *cr* 1945; MP (C) for Partick 1935–50, Scotstoun Division of Glasgow since 1950; *b* 10 Oct. 1889; *s* of late D. H. L. Young and E. Alice Templeton; *m* 1913, Dorothy Spencer; two *s* two *d*. *Educ:* Fettes College; abroad. Served European War, 1914–18, Major, Scottish Rifles; Parliamentary Private Secretary to Under-Secretary of State for Scotland, 1937, and to Secretary of State for Scotland, 1939; Scottish Unionist Whip, 1941; a Lord Commissioner of the Treasury, 1942–44; Vice-Chamberlain of HM Household, 1944–45. *Recreation:* yachting. *Address:* 1 The Grove, Highgate, N6. *Clubs:* Carlton, Caledonian; Western (Glasgow); Royal Yacht Squadron (Cowes).

Died 14 Aug. 1950.

YOUNG, Rev. Augustus Blayney Russell; *b* 17 Sept. 1845; *s* of Andrew Knight Young, MD, FRCSI, JP; *m* 1st, Annie Louise, widow of J. C. Brady, Newry, and *d* of John Johnston, Monaghan; 2nd, Ellen Grace, *d* of late Hamilton Price, QC; three *s* two *d*. *Educ:* Ennis College; Trinity College, Dublin; Erasmus Smyth Scholar, 1864–69; BA, 1869; MA 1873. Curate of Currin, Diocese of Clogher, 1869–72; Curate in charge of Tullycorbet, 1885; Member of County Committee of Agriculture and Technical Instruction; Member of Board of Co. Infirmary; Chaplain St George's Church, Santa Cruz de Tenerife, 1913 and 1914; Chairman Co. Monaghan War Pensions Committee; Chairman Old Age Pensions Committee; Rector of Ballybay, 1872–1920; Canon of Devenish in St Macartan's Cathedral, Clogher, 1906; Precentor, 1913; Member of Diocesan Council; Representative to General Synod; HE the Lord-Lieutenant's Inspector of Schools; retired on super-annuation, 1920. *Publications:* Reminiscences of an Irish Priest, 1848–1920; A true Irish ghost story. *Address:* 5 Victoria Place, Grosvenor, Bath.

Died 23 Jan. 1941.

YOUNG, Sir (Charles) Alban, 9th Bt *cr* 1769; KCMG 1918; MVO 1906; *b* 18 Nov. 1865; 2nd *s* of Sir Charles Lawrence Young, 7th Bt; *S* brother, 1921; *m* 1908, Frances Clara, 2nd *d* of late Sir Francis Edmund Hugh Elliot, GCMG, GCVO; two *d*. Attaché, 1890; Constantinople, 1892; 3rd Secretary, 1893; 2nd

Secretary, Buenos Ayres, 1896; employed in Foreign Office, 1896–98 and 1905; 2nd Secretary, Rome, 1898; Teheran, 1900; Constantinople, 1902; 1st Secretary, 1904; 1st Secretary at Athens, 1905 and 1910; Councillor of Embassy, 1909; Councillor at Teheran, 1910–13; Minister to Republics of Guatemala, Honduras, Nicaragua, and Salvador, 1913–19; Envoy Extraordinary and Minister Plenipotentiary to the Serbs, Croats and Slovenes, 1919–25; retired, 1925. *Heir: g s* William Niel [*b* 22 Jan. 1941; *s* of Capt. William Elliot Young, RAMC (killed in action, 27 May 1942), and Mary, *d* of late Rev. John Macdonald]. *Address:* 6 Canterbury Road, Oxford. *T:* 3027. *Club:* Travellers'.

Died 2 March 1944.

YOUNG, Col Charles Augustus, CB 1919; CMG 1916; Army Medical Service (retired); *b* 15 Nov. 1863; *s* of late Colonel Wm Young, 49th and 14th Regiments; *m* Rosa (*d* 1943), *e d* of James Young, of Harristown, Co. Roscommon; one *s* one *d*. *Educ:* privately. Entered Army Medical Service, 1887; Major, 1899; Lieut-Col 1911; Col 1915; retired, 1919; served Burmese Campaign, 1890–92 (medal with clasp); European War, 1914–19 (despatches, CMG, CB). *Address:* 6 Crescent Road, Wokingham. *T:* Wokingham 339.

Died 7 April 1944.

YOUNG, Clyde, FRIBA, architect; *b* 1871; *s* of late William Young; *m* 1898, Grace Emilie, *d* of Horatio Brandon. *Educ:* private school; University College; Lille. Student, Art Training College, S Kensington; studied in France, Belgium, and Italy; Associate, RIBA 1900; Fellow, 1910. *Works:* War Office, Whitehall; The Indian Hall, Elveden; University College, Southampton (with H. S. East); Class Room Block additions to Chapel; War Memorial New Entrance Gateway, King Edward's Horse Hall, Kipling Memorial Buildings, at the Imperial Service College, Windsor; Restorations to Lamb Buildings, Pump Court, The Cloisters and other buildings in the Middle Temple; War Damage to the Middle Temple; Bayham Church; Additions, etc. *Publications:* 1900–1946; (with Bernard Engel) Dilapidation Assessments; Editor, Spons' Architect and Builders' Price Book; Coleman's Approximate Estimates. *Recreations:* motoring, travelling. *Address:* 8 New Square, Lincoln's Inn, WC. *T:* Holborn 1772. *Club:* Royal Societies.

Died 4 May 1948.

YOUNG, Sir Douglas; *see* Young, Sir W. D.

YOUNG, E(mily) H(ilda); novelist; *b* 21 March 1880; *d* of William Michael and Frances Jane Young; *m* J. A. H. Daniell. *Publications: novels:* Yonder, Moor Fires, The Misses Mallett, William, The Vicar's Daughter, Miss Mole (James Tait Black Memorial Book Prize), Jenny Wren, The Curate's Wife, Celia, Chatterton Square; *books for children:* Caravan Island, River Holiday. *Address:* Prior's Close, Bradford-on-Avon, Wiltshire.

Died 8 Aug. 1949.

YOUNG, F. E. Mills; author. *Educ:* England, Paris, South Africa. *Publications:* A Mistaken Marriage, 1908; Chip, 1909; Atonement, 1910; Sam's Kid, 1911; Grit Lawless, 1912; Myles Calthorpe, IDB, 1913; The Purple Mists, 1914; Valley of a Thousand Hills, 1914; The Great Unrest, 1915; The Bywonner, 1916; The Bigamist, 1916; Coelebs, 1917; Laws of Chance, 1918; Beatrice Ashleigh, 1918; The Shadow of the Past, 1919; The Dominant Race, 1919; Almonds of Life, 1920; Imprudence, 1920; Foreshadowed, 1921; The Pace of the Ox, 1921; The Stronger Influence, 1922; Dawn at Sundays River, 1922; Selwyn Brothers, 1923; The Long Path, 1923; The Art of Michael Haslett, 1924; The Wine Farm, 1924; The Jealous Keys, 1925; The Future, 1925; Ailsa, 1926; The Broken Silence, 1926; The White Locust, 1927; The Romantic Tragedy, 1927; The Inheritance, 1928; The Immovable Flame, 1928; The Barrier, 1929; Four Seasons, 1929; Penny Rose, 1930;

Wife of Hess, 1930; The Unlicensed Prospector, 1931; Brief Youth, 1932; The Rich Cargo, 1932; Missing, 1933; Sunshine Lane, 1934; In Command, 1935; His Brother's Keeper, 1935; Old Man's Money, 1936; Unlucky Farm, 1937; Dreamlight, 1938; Hoax Millions, 1939; The Lamp, 1939; The Bitter Philosopher, 1940; Hidden Passage, 1941; Two Streams, 1945. *Recreations:* gardening, croquet, and billiards. *Address:* c/o Watcombe Priors, Watcombe, Torquay, Devon.

Died 7 Nov. 1945.

YOUNG, Francis Watson, CBE 1925; FRSE, FCS; HM Inspector of Schools in Scotland (retired); *b* 1851; *s* of Captain David Young, Dundee; *m* 1877, Alice, *d* of George H. Rose, Southampton; three *s* two *d*. *Educ:* West End Academy and High School, Dundee; Royal College of Science, South Kensington. Science Master, High School of Dundee, and Lecturer in Chemistry and Director of Studies in the Technical Institute, Dundee; HM Inspector of Science and Art Schools and Classes in the Western Division of Scotland, 1900; Principal Education Officer, 1919, under the Scheme of the Scottish Education Department for the Training of Ex-Service Officers and Men in Universities and Colleges and Schools of Art in Scotland; since retirement has travelled in Canada, New Zealand, Australia, and Ceylon. *Publications:* Education Reports in Blue Books of Scottish Education Department. *Recreations:* walking and mountaineering. *Address:* Panera, Shortheath Road, Farnham, Surrey. *Clubs:* Angus, Edinburgh.

Died 10 Jan. 1941.

YOUNG, Frederick, CIE 1924; CBE 1944; *b* 16 May 1890; *s* of John Young; unmarried. *Educ:* George Watson's College, Edinburgh; Edinburgh University. Assistant Superintendent Police United Provinces, 1909; on special duty, operations against Dacoits, Nepalese Border, 1913; King's Police Medal, 1914; Supdt Police Hardoi, 1916; bar to King's Police Medal, 1921; Supdt Police, Saharanpur, 1921; detailed, 1922, formation Special Dacoity Police, UP, which captured and broke up numerous Dacoit Gangs, 1923–30; Inspector-General of Police, Jaipur State, India, 1931; in charge operations Sikar Rebellion, 1938; Deputy Inspector General of Police, United Provinces, India, 1939. *Recreations:* shooting, golf. *Clubs:* Caledonian, East India and Sports; Caledonian United Service (Edinburgh); Nainital.

Died 21 Dec. 1948.

YOUNG, Sir Frederick (William), Kt 1918; LLB; *b* 5 Jan. 1876; *s* of late John Young of Mount Templeton, S Australia; *m* 1904, Florence (*d* 1947), *d* of late John Darling of Adelaide, South Australia; one *s*. *Educ:* Prince Alfred College and University, Adelaide. Commandeur de l'Ordre de la Couronne, Belgium; Member of the South Australian Bar, and of the Commonwealth Bar; Member of House of Assembly of the South Australian Parliament for eight years; Member of the Peake Ministry as Commissioner of Crown Lands and Immigration for three years; Agent-General for South Australia, 1915–18; MP (U) Swindon Div. of Wiltshire, 1918–22; Chm. of the English, Scottish, and Australian Bank, Ltd; Chairman of The Australian Estates Co. Ltd. *Address:* 22 St James' Court, SW1. *T:* Victoria 2360.

Died 26 Aug. 1948.

YOUNG, Grace Chisholm; *b* 1868; *d* of late H. W. Chisholm, Warden of the Standards; *m* 1896, Professor W. H. Young, FRS (*d* 1942). *Educ:* private; Girton College, Cambridge (Sir Francis Goldsmid scholar). 23rd Wrangler; 1st class Final Mathematical Schools, Oxford, 1892; studied in Göttingen, 1893–95; took there the degree of Doctor of Philosophy, magna cum laude, 1895, in Mathematics, Physics and Astronomy, being the first woman allowed a degree in Prussia; has since studied medicine at Göttingen and Geneva; Gamble Prize (Girton), 1915. *Publications:* Bimbo; Bimbo and the Frogs; (with her husband) The Theory of Sets of Points and The First Book of Geometry; articles in Nature;

poems; various mathematical and astronomical papers. *Recreations:* music, vine-culture, domestic occupations, literature and languages, history (especially 16th century), philosophy, chess, etc., and formerly tennis, croquet, billiards. *Address:* 98 Park Lane, Croydon. *T:* Croydon 6477.

Died 29 March 1944.

YOUNG, Lt-Col Harry Norman, CIE 1919; Indian Army, retired; *b* 1874; *e s* of late Colonel T. H. B. Young, Indian Army; *m* 1904, Eleanora Anne (*d* 1941), *d* of late Major W. P. Terry, Norfolk Regt. Served China, 1900–02; Relief of Peking (medal and clasp); European War, 1914–18 (despatches, CIE). *Address:* c/o Lloyds Bank, 6 Pall Mall, SW1.

Died 28 Jan. 1944.

YOUNG, Brig.-Gen. Henry Alfred, CIE 1917; CBE 1919; late RA; Director of Sheffield Steel Products, Ltd, and of Fisher & Ludlow, Ltd; Liveryman of the Worshipful Company of Fishmongers; *b* 5 Dec. 1867; *m* 1894, Ellen Maud (*d* 1926), *d* of Major C. Hills. Joined RA 1888; Captain, 1898; Major 1906; Bt Lieut-Col, 1914; Col, 1918; Director of Ordnance Inspection, India, 1915–17; Director of Ordnance Factories, India, 1917–21 (despatches); retired, 1921. *Publications:* The East India Company's Arsenals and Manufactories, 1937; also various articles on Economy in Military Administration, and on Indian Industry. *Address:* Devoncourt Hotel, Exmouth. *T:* Exmouth 2277. *Clubs:* Union, East India and Sports.

Died 21 Nov. 1941.

YOUNG, Henry Alfred; KC 1919; Puisne Judge, Sierra Leone, since 1930; *s* of late Rt Hon. George Young, Senator of the College of Justice; *m*; two *d. Educ:* Edinburgh University. Assistant Crown Advocate, British East Africa, 1906–09; Assistant Attorney-General, 1909–17; Senior Magistrate, Kenya, 1917–22; Police Magistrate, Nigeria, 1922–30. *Recreation:* golf. *Clubs:* University, Edinburgh.

Died 11 Dec. 1942.

YOUNG, Major Sir Hubert Winthrop, KCMG 1934 (CMG 1923); Kt 1932; DSO 1919; late Indian Army; Chairman, Royal Free Hospital and West Wilts Hospital Management Committee; Chairman Consultative Council, Southern Electricity Area; *b* 1885; 2nd *s* of late Sir W. Mackworth Young, KCSI; *m* 1924, Margaret Rose Mary, *d* of late Col F. R. Reynolds, RE; three *s. Educ:* Eton (King's Scholar); RMA, Woolwich. RGA 1904; 116th Mahrattas, Indian Army, 1908; served NW Frontier of India, 1915 (1914–15 Star); Assistant Political Officer, Mesopotamia, 1915–17; Deputy Director Local Resources, 1917–18 (despatches); General Staff Officer, 2nd grade, Hejaz operations, 1918 (despatches, DSO, Order of Nahda, 3rd class); President, Local Resources Board, Damascus, 1918; Foreign Office, 1919–21; Assistant Secretary, Middle East Department; Colonial Office, 1921–27; Colonial Secretary, Gibraltar, 1927–29; Counsellor to High Commissioner for Iraq, 1929–32; Envoy Extraordinary and Minister Plenipotentiary at Baghdad, Oct.–Nov. 1932; Governor and Commander-in-Chief of Nyasaland, 1932–34; of Northern Rhodesia, 1934–38, and of Trinidad and Tobago, 1938–42; Assistant Secretary, Relief Department, 1943–44; European Regional Office, UNRRA, 1944–45; contested (L) Harrow West, 1945; Edge Hill, 1947. *Publications:* The Independent Arab, 1933; article in T. E. Lawrence by his Friends, and other articles and reviews in various journals. *Recreations:* music, chess, languages. *Address:* South Wraxall Lodge, Bradford-on-Avon, Wilts. *T:* Bradford-on-Avon 3202. *Clubs:* Travellers', Lansdowne.

Died 20 April 1950.

YOUNG, Hugh Hampton, BA, MA, MD, FACS, FRCSI; DSM; DSc (Queen's University); Professor of Urology, Johns Hopkins University; Director, Brady Urological Institute, Johns Hopkins Hospital, Baltimore, Md, USA; Visiting Urologist, Johns Hopkins Hospital, Baltimore, USA; Editor of Journal of Urology since its foundation in 1917; President, Société Internationale d'Urologie, American Association of Genito-Urinary Surgeons, and American Urological Association; Royal Society of Medicine; Chairman, State Aviation Commission of Maryland; Chairman State Lunacy Commission of Maryland; President Gibson Island Club; Civilian Aide (3rd Corps Area) to Secretary of War; *b* San Antonio, Texas, 18 Sept. 1870; *s* of General William Hugh Young and Frances Michie Kemper; *m* 1901; one *s* three *d. Educ:* University of Virginia; Johns Hopkins University. Assistant Resident Surgeon, Johns Hopkins Hospital, 1895; in charge of Department of Urology, Johns Hopkins Hospital, since 1898; Senior Consultant in Urology in AEF during European War; remained in France two years, discharged with rank of Col, MRC; Edward L. Keyes medal for advances in Urology. *Publications:* Young's Practice of Urology; Urological Roentgenology; Genital Abnormalities, Hermaphroditism and Related Adrenal Diseases; Hugh Young: A Surgeon's Autobiography, Chapter on Surgery of the Prostate, Nelson's Loose Leaf Surgery, and Lewis' System of Surgery; over 350 articles on surgical and urological subjects. *Recreations:* music, hunting, fishing, travel. *Address:* 100 West Cold Spring Lane, Baltimore, Md, USA. *TA:* Johns Hopkins Hospital. *T:* (Office) Wolfe 5500, (Home) University 3520, University 9763. *Clubs:* Gibson Island; Maryland; Elkridge Kennels.

Died 23 Aug. 1945.

YOUNG, Karl; Professor of English in Yale University since 1923; *b* 2 Nov. 1879; *s* of George Billings Young and Frances Eliza Hinman; *m* 1911, Frances Campbell Berkeley; two *s. Educ:* University of Michigan (BA); Harvard University MA, PhD. Professor of English, United States Naval Academy, 1903–05; Parker Fellow, Harvard University, 1907–08; Professor of English, University of Wisconsin, 1908–23; LittD, University of Wisconsin, 1934; LLD, University of Michigan, 1937; FRSL, FAAS; Pres., Modern Language Assoc. of America, 1940; Gollancz Memorial Prize, British Academy, 1941. *Publications:* Origin and Development of the Story of Troilus and Crisayde, Chaucer Society, London, 1908; Ordo Rachelis, 1919; Dramatic Association of the Easter Sepulchre, 1920; The Drama of the Medieval Church, 2 vols, 1933; Studies in literary and philological periodicals. *Recreation:* tennis. *Address:* 195 Everit Street, New Haven, Connecticut, USA. *T:* New Haven 5–6511. *Clubs:* Graduates, Elizabethan, New Haven.

Died 17 Nov. 1943.

YOUNG, M'Gregor, KC; MA; Official Guardian, Supreme Court of Ontario, since 1928; late Lecturer, Law School of Ontario; *b* Hillier, Ontario, Canada, 6 June 1864; *m* 1906, Alice Maude, *d* of late William Williams, Winnipeg; one *s* two *d. Educ:* Pictou; University of Toronto. Professor of Constitutional Law and History and International Law, University of Toronto, 1900–13. *Clubs:* Toronto, Toronto Hunt, Toronto.

Died 1 April 1942.

YOUNG, Morris Yudlevitz, CIE 1917; MB, ChB Glas.; Medical Adviser to Anglo-Iranian Oil Co. (late Chief MO). *Educ:* Glasgow Univ. MB, ChB 1906. Donat of Order of St John of Jerusalem. *Address:* Ahwaz, Persian Gulf; 5 Palace Mansions, Kensington Court, W8; Britannic House, Finsbury Circus, EC2.

Died 18 May 1950.

YOUNG, Norwood; *b* 1860; *e s* of Major-General R. Young, RE, JP; *m* Ada, *d* of George Meakin, of Cresswell Hall, Stafford, JP; one *s. Educ:* Clifton College. *Publications:* The Story of Rome, tenth edition, 1926; The Growth of Napoleon, 1911; Napoleon in Exile at Elba, 1914; at St Helena, two vols, 1915; The Life of Frederick the Great, 1919; Carlyle, his Rise and Fall, 1927; Fortuna, or Chance and Design (To-day and To-morrow Series), 1928; George Washington, 1932. *Address:* Lloyds Bank, St James's Street, SW1.

Died 22 April 1943.

YOUNG, Thomas Moffat, CB 1938; retired Civil Servant; *b* Ballyeaston, Northern Ireland, 1873; *e s* of Rev. W. Young and Sarah, *d* of Alex. Bell Filson, MD, Portaferry; *m* 1900, Agnes, *d* of R. P. Hewit, Manchester; two *d. Educ:* Manchester Grammar School (Classical Side). Editorial Staff of Manchester Guardian, 1896-1913; Special Correspondent in America, Ireland and France; Commercial and Financial Editor, leader writer, and reviewer; entered Civil Service (Public Trustee Dept) to organise and control the Northern branch of the Dept at Manchester, 1913; Deputy Public Trustee, 1914-38; Comdt of Auxiliary Fire Service, Manchester, 1938-39. *Publications:* The American Cotton Industry, 1902; Other People's Money, by a Trustee, 1921; contributions to principal London daily and weekly newspapers. *Recreations:* gardening, fishing, reading. *Address:* Brampton Lodge, Withington, Manchester. *T:* Didsbury 3547. *Clubs:* Savile; Reform, Manchester.

Died 13 June 1946.

YOUNG, William; MP (L) East Perth, 1910-18; Perth Division, Dec. 1918-22; merchant; formerly Director of Wm Young & Co., foreign merchants and bankers, London and Mexico City; *b* 5 Feb. 1863; *s* of James Young, Braickley Farm, Glenmuick, Aberdeenshire; *m. Educ:* Ballater Public School. Started business career at 16 years of age; 7 years with Messrs. Matheson & Co., London, merchants and bankers; has lived abroad for some years and travelled considerably. *Recreations:* motoring, golf, etc. *Address:* 3 Albemarle Street, W1. *T:* Regent 2857. *Clubs:* Reform, Royal Automobile.

Died 7 June 1942.

YOUNG, Sir (William) Douglas, KBE 1919; CMG 1907; *b* 27 Jan. 1859; *e s* of late W. Alexander George Young, CMG, Governor of Gold Coast Colony. *Educ:* Charterhouse. Entered Colonial Service, 1877; Chief Clerk, Government Secretary Office, British Guiana, 1889; Assistant Colonial Secretary, Mauritius, 1895; Acting Colonial Secretary, 2½ years; Commissioner, Turks and Caicos Islands, 1901; Administrator Dominica, 1906-13; acted Governor and Commander-in-Chief, Leeward Islands, 1909; Administrator and Colonial Secretary, St Lucia, 1913-14; acting Governor and Commander-in-Chief of Windward Islands, May to Dec. 1914; Governor and Commander-in-Chief, Falkland Islands and its Dependencies, 1914-20; retired, 1920. *Address:* The Wilderness, Hackington, Canterbury.

Died 7 March 1943.

YOUNG, William Henry, MA, ScD (Camb.); Hon. Dr ès Sc. Math. (Genève); Hon. DSc (Calcutta); FRS; Hon. Dr University of Strasbourg; President of London Mathematical Society, 1922-24; sometime Vice-President of the British Section of the New Commonwealth; President de l'Union Internationale de Mathématiciens, 1929-36; Member of the Executive Committee of the International Research Council, and Foreign Secretary of the National Committee on Mathematics; Hon. Member of the Bureau of the Société Mathématique de France; Corr. Member of the Institute of Coimbra; on Livery of the Fishmongers' Company; *b* London, 20 Oct. 1863; *m* 1896, Grace, *d* of late H. W. Chisholm; two *s* three *d. Educ:* City of London School; Peterhouse, Cambridge (Fellow 1868-92). Lecturer at Girton College for many years; Chief Examiner to Central Welsh Board, 1902-05; Exam. to Universities of Cambridge, London, and Wales at various times; resident for many years at German, Swiss, and Italian universities; has been twice round the world, and recently all round South America, 1936-37; has visited most of the chief universities or other educational institutions not only of Europe, but also, and for the most part in an official capacity, of the USA, Canada, Japan, Korea, Manchuria, China, India, Ceylon, the Sahara, and British South Africa; first Hardinge Professor of Mathematics at the University of Calcutta, 1913-16; Professor of the Philosophy and History of Mathematics, Liverpool University, 1913-19; Sylvester Medallist of the Royal Society, 1928; De Morgan Medallist, London Mathematical Society, 1917; Professor of Pure Mathematics in the University of Wales, 1919-23; nominated Hon. Professor by University of Lausanne, 1924. *Publications:* The Fundamental Theorems of the Differential Calculus, 1910; nearly 200 mathematical papers, as well as articles dealing with educational and academic topics; joint-author with his wife of The Theory of Sets of Points, 1906, and The First Book of Geometry, 1905, translated into German under title Der kleine Geometer, 1908, into Italian, 1910, into Swedish, 1920, and into Magyar, 1925. *Recreations:* running, rowing, chess, tennis, history, philosophy, economics, political science, comparative law and modern languages (French, German, Italian, Danish, Dutch, Swedish, Spanish, Portuguese, Yougoslavian, Polish). *Address:* Collonge, La Conversion, Vaud, Switzerland. *TA:* and *T:* Lausanne 29694. *Club:* Athenæum.

Died 7 July 1942.

YOUNG, William John, DSc (London and Melbourne); MSc (Manchester); Professor of Biochemistry, the University of Melbourne; *b* Manchester, 1878; *s* of William John Bristow Young; *m* Janet Taylor; one *d. Educ:* The Hulme Grammar School, Manchester; the University of Manchester. Assistant Biochemist to the Lister Institute of Preventive Medicine, London, 1902-12; Biochemist to the Australian Institute of Tropical Medicine, Townsville, Queensland, 1912-19. *Publications:* (joint) Elementary Practical Biochemistry; author of numerous papers in the scientific journals. *Recreations:* carpentering and walking. *Address:* University, Melbourne, N3, Australia.

Died 14 May 1942.

YOUNG, Sir William Muston Need, 3rd Bt *cr* 1821; JP; Superintendent of Telegraphs in India (retired, 1897); *b* 20 Jan. 1847; *s* of Thomas Young, 2nd *s* of 1st Bt and Mary J. Duncan, *d* of William Pitt Muston; *S* uncle Lord Lisgar in baronetcy, 1876; *m* 1st, 1870, Isabella, *d* of John Leach, Exeter, and Black Torrington, Devon; one *s* one *d*; 2nd, 1932, Sarah, *d* of late James Hallinan. Served Afghan War, 1878-79; commanded F Company Rangoon Volunteer Battalion, 1882-84; served in Upper Burmah Campaign, 1885-89 (medal and two clasps). *Recreations:* polo, lawn tennis, billiards, whist, skating, hunting, yachting, shooting, and cycling. *Heir: s* Cyril Roe Muston, *b* 21 Aug. 1881.

Died 31 March 1934.

YOUNGER OF LECKIE, 2nd Viscount *cr* 1923, of Alloa, Clackmannanshire; **James Younger,** DSO 1919; 2nd Bart of Leckie *cr* 1911; Hon. Colonel, Fife and Forfar Yeomanry; Vice-Lieutenant of County of Clackmannan, 1930; Chairman; George Younger and Son Ltd; Director National Bank of Scotland; Director North British and Mercantile Insurance Co. and others; *b* 19 May 1880; *o surv. s* of 1st Viscount and Lucy (*d* 1921), *d* of Edward Smith, MD, FRS, Med. Officer to Local Govt Board; *S* father 1929; *m* 1906, Maud, *e d* of Sir John Gilmour, 1st Bt; two *s* two *d. Educ:* Winchester; New College, Oxford (BA). Served European War, 1914-19 (wounded, despatches, DSO); Ensign, King's Bodyguard for Scotland (Royal Company of Archers);

2nd in command 1st Stirlingshire Bn Home Guard. *Heir: s* Hon. Edward George Younger, OBE. *Address:* Leckie, Gargunnock; Stirlingshire. *T:* Kippen 211. *Clubs:* Carlton; New, Edinburgh.

Died 4 Dec. 1946.

YOUNGHUSBAND, Sir Francis (Edward), KCSI 1917; KCIE 1904; CIE 1891; Gold Medal Royal Geographical Society, 1891; Kaiser-i-Hind medal, 1901; LLD (Hon.) Edin.; DSc (Hon.) Cambridge; Rede Lecturer, Cambridge, 1905; LLD (Hon.) Bristol; *b* Murree, 31 May 1863; 2nd *s* of late Major-General John Wm Younghusband, CSI; *m* 1897, Helen Augusta, *e d* of late Chas. Magniac, MP, of Colworth, Beds, and 16 Charles Street, Berkeley Square, and 3 Lombard Street, London, and late Hon. Augusta Fitzpatrick, *d* of Lord Castletown of Upper Ossory and *widow* of Colonel Hon. T. Vesey Dawson, Coldstream Guards; one *d. Educ:* Clifton; Sandhurst. Joined 1st Dragoon Guards, 1882; Captain, 1889; transferred to Indian Political Department, 1890; Explorations in and Government of India Missions to Manchuria, 1886; from Peking to India *via* Chinese Turkestan, 1887; on the Pamirs and in Hunza, 1889; on the Pamirs, 1890–91; Political Officer, Hunza, 1892; Political Agent, Chitral, 1893–94; Special Correspondent of The Times in Chitral Expedition, 1895; Transvaal and Rhodesia, 1896–97; Political Agent, Haraoti and Tonk, 1898; Resident, Indore, Central India, 1902–03; British Commissioner to Tibet, 1902–04; Resident, Kashmir, 1906–09; President Royal Geographical Society, 1919. *Publications:* Heart of a Continent; Relief of Chitral; South Africa of To-day, 1898; Kashmir, 1909; India and Tibet; Within, 1912; The Heart of Nature, 1921; The Gleam, 1923; Wonders of the Himalaya, 1924; But in Our Lives, 1926; The Epic of Everest; The Light of Experience, 1927; Life in the Stars, 1927; The Coming Country, 1928; Dawn in India, 1930; The Living Universe, 1933; Modern Mystics, 1935; Everest: The Challenge, 1936; A Venture of Faith, 1937; The Sum of Things, 1939; Vital Religion. *Club:* Travellers'.

Died 31 July 1942.

YOUNGHUSBAND, Maj.-Gen. Sir George John, KCMG 1915; KCIE 1913; CB 1900; Keeper of the Jewel House, Tower of London, since 1917; late Colonel Queen Victoria's Own Corps of Guides; *b* 9 July 1859; *e s* of late Maj.-Gen. John William Younghusband, CSI; *m* 1891, Madeline, *d* of late Edward Wood of Culmington Manor, Shropshire; one *s. Educ:* Clifton Coll.; RMC Sandhurst. Entered Army, 1878; Capt. 1889; Maj. 1896; Lt-Col 1900; Maj.-Gen. 1911; passed Staff College, 1891; served Afghan War, 1878–80 (medal with clasp); Soudan, 1885 (medal with two clasps, Khedive's star); NW Frontier of India, 1886 (despatches); Burmah War, 1886–87 (medal with clasp); Chitral Relief Force, 1895 (despatches, brevet of Major, medal with clasps); Spanish-American War, Campaign in the Philippines, 1898 (medal); S Africa, 1899–1902 (severely wounded, despatches, brevet of Lieut-Col, CB, Queen's medal and three clasps, King's medal and two clasps); Mohmand Expedition, NWF India (medal and clasp); European War, 1914–19 (despatches, 1914–15 Star, British Medal, Victory Medal, KCMG). *Publications:* The Story of the Guides; The Tower of London; The Crown Jewels of England; The Jewel House; Forty Years a Soldier, 1923; etc. *Address:* Tower of London, EC3. *T:* Royal 2136. *Clubs:* United Service, Hurlingham.

Died 30 Sept. 1944.

YULE, Lady Annie Henrietta; *o d* of late Andrew Yule, Calcutta; *m* 1900, Sir David Yule, 1st Bt (*d* 1928); one *d. Address:* Hanstead House, Bricket Wood, St Albans. *T:* Garston 2343.

Died 14 July 1950.

Z

ZAFAR ALI, Sir, Khan Bahadur, Mirza, Kt 1931; BA; *b* 20 Feb. 1870. Joined Punjab Judicial Dept 1893; District and Sessions Judge, 1918; Judge, Punjab High Court, 1926; retired 1930. *Address:* c/o High Court, Lahore, Punjab.

Died 20 Sept. 1942.

ZAMORA Y TORRES, Exema Senor Don Niceto Alcalá; *b* 6 July 1877; *s* of Manuel Alcalá Zamora and Francisca Torres; *m* Doña Purificación Castillo (*d* 1939); three *s* three *d*. *Educ:* Universities of Granada and Madrid. Doctor in Law; President of the Spanish Republic, 1931–36. *Publications:* La Concesión administrativa como contrato y como Derecho Real; La Jurisprudencia y la vida del Derecho; La potestad jurídica sobre el más allá de la vida; La idea jurídica de Manzoni en los novios; Los derroteros de la expropiación forzosa; Los intentos del pacifismo contemporáneo; La condena en costas (with his son Niceto Alcalá Zamora, Doctor in Law).

Died 18 Feb. 1949.

ZANGWILL, Edith Ayrton; *d* of William Edward Ayrton, FRS, and Matilda Chaplin Ayrton, MD; *widow* of Israel Zangwill; two *s* one *d*. *Educ:* Bedford Coll., London. *Publications:* Barbarous Babes 1904; The First Mrs Molivar, 1905, Teresa, 1909; The Rise of a Star, 1918; The Call, 1924; The House, 1928. *Recreations:* bicycling and reading. *Address:* Far End, East Preston, Littlehampton, Sussex. *TA:* Zangwill, East Preston. *T:* Rustington 325.

Died 5 May 1945.

ZAVERTAL, Hon. Captain Ladislao Joseph Philip Paul, MVO 1901; Lieutenant and Conductor Royal Artillery Band, 1881–1906; *b* Milan, 29 Sept. 1849; *s* of late V. H. Zavertal; *m* 1874, E. Charlotte, *d* of S. Wulf Dunallen, Glasgow; one *d*. Conductor of Sunday Orchestral Concerts, Royal Albert Hall, 1895–1906; Member of S Cecilia in Rome; Knight Companion Royal Servian Order of Takova, Saxe-Coburg Ernestine Order for Art and Science, Jubilee Medal, Orders of Crown of Italy, Redeemer of Greece, Commander's Star of Osmanieh, 3rd Class; naturalised British subject. *Compositions:* Operas: Adriana; A Night in Florence; Mirra; Symphonies; Chamber Music; Songs, etc. *Address:* Griante, Cadenabbia, Lake of Como, Italy.

Died 29 Jan. 1942.

ZELIE, Rev. John Sheridan, DD, DLitt; LHD; Presbyterian minister; *b* Princeton, Mass, 3 May 1866; *m* 1891, Henrietta Campbell; one *s* one *d*. *Educ:* Williams College; Yale Divinity School. Pastor of Congregational and Presbyterian Churches, 1890–1927; College Preacher; Chaplain with the American Army in France, 1918–19; on Staff of American Relief Administration, Russia, 1922; American Interchange Preacher in Great Britain, 1929. *Publications:* (with Carrol Perry) Life of Bill Pratt, the Saw-Back Philosopher; The Book of the Kindly Light; (with E. L. Adams) Joseph Conrad; The Man; many religious essays and occasional articles in the Atlantic Monthly. *Recreation:* motoring. *Address:* (winter) Seabreeze, Daytona Beach, Florida; (summer) Cherryfield, Maine.

Died 9 Nov. 1942.

ZIELINSKI, Thaddeus, DrPhil (Leipsic and Dorpat); DrPhil Hon. (Athens, Brünn, Brussels, Cracow, Groningen, Leopol, Lyon, Milan, Paris, Poznan, Riga, Vilno and Warsaw); LLD Hon. (Oxford); Professor of Classics, Warsaw University, since 1920; *b* Kiev, Russia, 14 Sept. 1859; *s* of late Francis and Ludvica Zielinski; *m* Louisa Elizabet (*d* 1923); one *s* three *d*. *Educ:* St Petersburg. Lecturer, 1884; Professor of Classics in St Petersburg University, 1887; Fellow of numerous foreign academies. Hon. Freeman of Delphi. *Publications:* More than 1000 writings, the greater number in Polish or Russian; in English: Our Debt to Antiquity, 1909; Religion of Ancient Greece, 1926; in French: La Sibylle, 1925; Histoire de la Civilisation Antique, 1930; Horace et la Société Romaine du temps d'Auguste, 1938; in German: Die letzten Jahre des zweiten punischen Krieges, 1880; die Gliederung der altattischen Komoedie, 1885; die Märchenkomoedie in Athen, 1885; Cicero im Wandel der Jahrhunderte, 1897, 4th ed. 1929; das Clauselgesetz in Ciceros Reden, 1904; der constructive Rhythmus in Ciceros Reden, 1913; in Latin: Quaestiones comicae, 1887; Tragodumenon 1. III, 1925; Iresione, 2 vols, 1930 and 1937. *Recreation:* travelling. *Address:* University, Warsaw, Poland. *T:* 204–30.

Died 8 May 1944.

ZIGOMALA, Hilda, CBE 1926; *b* 1869; *d* of Charles North of Rougham Hall, Norfolk; *m* 1889, Major P. J. Zigomala (*d* 1933), 19th Hussars; one *s* killed European War. Given the CBE for work at Lord Roberts' Memorial Workshops. *Address:* 3 Sloane Gate Mansions, SW1; Gate Cottage, Cookham Dean, Berks.

Died 16 June 1946.

ZIWER, Ahmad Pasha, GCMG 1925; late Prime Minister of Egypt, and Minister of Interior and Foreign Affairs; *b* Alexandria, 14 Nov. 1864; *s* of late Ziwer Bey, High Official during the reign of HH Said Pasha, Viceroy of Egypt; *m* Fatanat Hanoum, *d* of Ibrahim bey Adham Daghestany; three *c*. *Educ:* College of Lazarists, Alexandria; University of St Joseph (Jesuit Fathers), Beirout (Syria); Graduate in Law from the Faculty of Law at Aix-en-Provence. All his career was achieved in Native Courts of Justice till 1913; held the office of Supreme Judge at the Court of Appeal, Cairo, 1899–1913; Governor of Alexandria, 1913–17; Minister of Wakfs; Minister of Education, and Minister of Communications; Minister Plenipotentiary at Rome and President of the Senate, 1918–24; Commandeur du Medjidieh; Grand Officier de la Couronne d'Itale; Grand Officer de Wasa; Grand Cordon du Nil; Grand Cordon de d'uammed Ali; Grand Cordon de La Légion d'Honneur; Grand Cordon de la Couronne de Belgique; Grande Croix des Stes. Maurice et Lazare; Grande Croix du Saint Sauveur. *Address:* 62 rue Fouad, Alexandria, Egypt. *Clubs:* Mohammed Aly, Sultan Hussein, Alexandria; Mohammed Aly, Cairo.

Died 21 Aug. 1945.

ZULOAGA, Ignacio; peintre; *b* 26 Juillet 1870; *m* Valentine Dethomas; one *s* one *d*. *Educ:* Paris; et l'Espagne. *Works:* Daniel Zuloaga and his daughters, 1899 (Luxembourg); Promenade after the Bull Fight; Spanish Dancers; Segovians Drinking; El Coriano; The Penitents, etc. *Publications:* Beaucoup, entre autres, le Figaro Illustré, le Studio; Die Jugend, l'Art Ancien et Moderne; Art et Decoration, Le Paris Illustré, etc.

Died 31 Oct. 1945.

ZWAR, Bernard T., CMG 1941; MD; MS; FRACS; President and Consulting Surgeon Royal Melbourne Hospital; Member of Medical Board of Victoria; *b* 20 June 1876; *s* of John and Anne Zwar; *m* 1916, Essy Craig; one *s*. *Educ:* Prince Alfred College, Adelaide; Universities of Adelaide and Melbourne. Senior Resident Surgeon, Melbourne Hospital, 1900–01; Medical Superintendent, Austin Hospital, 1901–04;

Hon. Surgeon, St Vincents Hospital, 1908–11; Hon. Surgeon, Melbourne Hospital, 1912–35; Major AAMC (2nd Aust. Stationary Hospital and 2nd Aust. General Hospital), European War, 1914–18; Stewart Lecturer in Surgery, University of Melbourne, 1924–35; Deputy Chancellor University of Melbourne, 1943–44; one of Founders RACS, 1927; President Victorian Branch, BMA, 1929; Vice-Pres. Section of Surgery, 4th and 5th Australasian Medical Congress. *Publications:* various, on subjects of Surgical Interest in Medical Journals. *Recreations:* tennis, golf, gardening, walking. *Address:* 2 Hamilton Road, Malvern, Victoria. *Clubs:* Melbourne, Melbourne.

Died 16 Jan. 1947.

ZWEIG, Stefan, MA. *Educ:* Vienna, Austria. Naturalised, 1940. *Publications:* (in English Translation), Amok; Conflicts; Letter of an unknown woman; Kaleidoscope (short novels); Volpone (comedy); Marie Antoinette; Fouché; Romain Rolland; The Queen of Scots (biography); Three Masters (essays); Mental Healers (essays); Adepts in Self Portraiture (essays); Jeremiah (tragedy); Erasmus (essay); The Right to Heresy; The Buried Candelabrum; Conqueror of the Seas (the story of Magellan); Beware of Pity (novel), 1939; The Tide of Fortune (Historic Miniatures), 1940; Brazil: Land of the Future, 1941; Amerigo, 1942; (posthumous) Balzac, 1947. *Address:* Petropolis, Brazil; Rosemount, Lyncombe Hill, Bath.

Died 23 Feb. 1942.